S0-AGY-032

THE LINCOLN LIBRARY OF ESSENTIAL INFORMATION

AN UP-TO-DATE MANUAL
FOR DAILY REFERENCE, FOR SELF-INSTRUCTION,
AND FOR GENERAL CULTURE
NAMED IN APPRECIATIVE REMEMBRANCE OF
ABRAHAM LINCOLN
THE FOREMOST AMERICAN EXEMPLAR
OF SELF-EDUCATION

Thoroughly Revised at Each New Printing

THE FRONTIER PRESS COMPANY
BUFFALO, NEW YORK
1949

First Edition, 1924
Eighteenth Edition, 1949

PREFACE

THE Lincoln Library of Essential Information has been prepared with two controlling ideas constantly in view. One has been to embody in a single volume the largest amount of helpful information for the average reader that has ever been placed between two covers. The other aim has been to select, condense, arrange, and verify this material with a degree of thoroughness and accuracy much greater than has ever been attained in any work of similar scope. In our judgment, confirmed by years of publishing experience, the accomplishment of these aims insures the production of a book that stands in a class by itself.

NAME. The title of this work, The Lincoln Library of Essential Information, expresses the fact that the volume contains the essentials of a library of informational material. The name signifies also that this essential information has been carefully adapted to the needs of those who, following in the steps of Abraham Lincoln, will eagerly welcome every available means of self-education.

SCOPE. This work is far more than a mere source book of information and presents a range of knowledge much greater than even experienced users of books would at first imagine possible. It offers first a vast array of practical information on subjects which are fundamental. These embrace English, History, Geography, and Mathematics. In the extensive sections devoted to their treatment, the essentials of each are set forth with unusual completeness. Science is introduced, and a separate treatment is accorded to each of its chief divisions—physiography, geology, mineralogy, astronomy, physics, chemistry, physiology, psychology, psychiatry, zoology, and botany. Following Science is an extensive Department of Economics and Useful Arts, after which will be found a remarkably complete exposition of the subject of Government and Politics.

The cultural divisions of the work embrace large departments on Literature and on the Fine Arts, including an especially full exposition of Music, and a valuable Department of Education. The interesting field of human achievement is covered in Biography, the largest separate division of the work, which contains sketches of over 3600 of the world's most noted men and women. A large amount of valuable information not directly referable to the foregoing divisions has been grouped under Miscellany. The whole body of information is made available by the comprehensive Index.

METHOD AND PLAN. The plan of presenting the subject matter of The Lincoln Library is unique. It is in no sense an experiment, however, but is a development based on more than 30 years' experience. During this period, the needs and desires of many million purchasers and users of books containing helpful information have been carefully and systematically studied. This study has settled beyond question many significant points, one of the most important of which is that, for practically all readers, the most satisfactory source of general information is a *comprehensive single volume.*

The careful planning by means of which this whole library has been published in a single volume obviates several of the chief obstacles to the average reader's use of the best reference works. Practically all such works are in many volumes, and the price is consequently prohibitive to the great majority of people. Moreover, in the libraries of those who have purchased such works, the individual volumes, after being used, are frequently returned to the shelves in the wrong order, thereby causing vexatious delay when they are next needed. Further loss of time is occasioned by cross references, which, in works of many volumes, usually involve the consulting of a second and sometimes a third volume. Such discouraging delays are virtually eliminated in using a one-volume work like The Lincoln Library.

Our study has shown also that the rigid alphabetical arrangement of subjects followed in the encyclopedias is not suitable for a single volume designed to contain the most information possible. When totally unrelated subjects are ranked next to each other in a uniform A-to-Z arrangement, a vast amount of information is unavoidably repeated or duplicated. This means a great loss of space, which, under the group plan, is utilized for additional information.

On the other hand, it has appeared desirable to avoid the methods of the coldly formal treatise, which often involve the inclusion of relatively unimportant matter. The elaborate refinements, also, which are seen in highly specialized textbooks, have been excluded. Without being a fact book, this work contains a much larger number of carefully selected facts than any fact book in print. It is not a dictionary, but it embraces the best features found in a dictionary. In short, adaptations of many widely used methods have been worked out under the guidance of knowledge gained by long experience, and, in some instances, entirely new arrangements have been devised. In all cases, these methods have been designed to meet the fundamental requirement of placing the greatest amount of useful information in the least possible space.

ACCURACY. While realizing that absolute perfection is unattainable, nevertheless, in conformity with our fixed policy of maintaining the highest standards, we have taken the utmost care that the material in every section of this volume should be as nearly accurate as is humanly possible. The services of many eminent scholars and specialists have been enlisted in preparing the different sections, and all material has been subjected to an intensive system of verification. As a result, the work will be found more generally free from error than many more extensive and costly reference works that are widely accepted as authoritative.

UP-TO-DATENESS. Perhaps in no age have the rapid advances in knowledge and in mechanical inventions so quickly rendered obsolete much information that was accurate at the time it was published. Whole new fields have been added to human knowledge within the very recent past. In this work, it has been made a matter of especial care that such subjects should be adequately treated and that the most recent positive contributions to human knowledge should be duly recorded.

Social and political changes, largely caused by the impact of new inventions on society, have made the 20th century a period of flux. National boundaries and governmental forms ebb and flow, rendering much of the older books of reference quickly obsolete. The Lincoln Library meets this problem partly by reason of the fact that it is one of the most recently planned of all reference works and partly by its policy of thorough revision with each new printing.

Before each new edition goes to press, the contents have been systematically tested and extensively revised. Not merely the individual facts, but the perspective of the work has been kept abreast of a world constantly changing in aspect, interests, and viewpoint. While this procedure has necessarily been expensive, nothing less would satisfy the exacting standards of usefulness on which we have at all times insisted. On the whole, this work will be found to surpass the large encyclopedias in up-to-dateness just as it excels all other single volumes in completeness.

In the case of statistics regarding populations and other factors that vary continually, the most recent authentic figures are given rather than still later estimates, which, at best, are only glorified guesses. In other words, it has appeared more desirable to present the most authoritative information rather than that which is merely recent but lacks the essential of all statements of alleged facts—reliability.

MASS OF CONTENTS. By means of utilizing every available square inch of space, the mass of contents in this single volume has been made to exceed that of many well-known works consisting of from six to twenty volumes. The Department of Science alone, for example, greatly exceeds in actual contents the whole four volumes of the widely known work entitled *The Outline of Science*. Similar comparisons may be made with reference to other and more costly works. This disparity in mass of contents, however, is only part of the difference between The Lincoln Library and the average work of several volumes. Not only does it excel in the amount of material presented, but the material itself is in a much more concise and highly condensed form. Consequently, this one volume contains from twice to many times as much information as the average work of many volumes.

By reason of this fact, The Lincoln Library occupies a unique place in the world of books. The elaborate work of many volumes has had a recognized place ever since the 18th century, when Diderot and his associates in France produced, by 21 years of labor, their monumental *Encyclopédie*. Such extensive works provide a digest of all human knowledge and are intended for the use of specialists and others having means and a certain amount of leisure. On the other hand, the one-volume reference work containing from 800 to 1000 pages has met the needs of a wider public, whose purposes are best served by a reference work of smaller cost containing the *minimum* essentials of knowledge. This type of reference book also has a well established place and has been used for a number of decades. The Lincoln Library occupies a position intermediate between these two recognized types. It combines the advantages of comparatively low cost and ease in consultation with a completeness in essential information which closely approaches that attained by the larger works.

Legibility and Compactness. In spite of the great amount of material that has been presented in this one volume, the utmost care has been exercised that the text should be legible and attractive. Apart from certain sections intended to be used as dictionaries, the type is of the same size as that employed in practically all newspapers. Nevertheless, by reason of its superior face, or design, and because of the quality of paper on which it is printed, the type is actually much more readable than that in the average newspaper. Moreover, frequent and careful paragraphing, combined with the division of the page into two columns, insures an openness of appearance that makes each page a delight to the eye.

The surprisingly small bulk of The Lincoln Library is due in large part to the choice of a superior quality of thin paper. This paper has the added advantage of a firmness that makes it easily handled. Thus, both by reason of the paper and type employed and of the openness and pleasing arrangement of the printed text, The Lincoln Library is, in a very real sense, a triumph of the bookmaker's art.

Introductions. Preceding the treatment of each major subject, such as The English Language, History, Science, or Government, there is a valuable explanatory section setting forth the scope of the subject, its importance, and its usefulness. In addition, many subdivisions, as, for example, Synonyms and Antonyms, have instructive introductory sections. These introductions give the user a clear idea of the value of the subject itself and they lead to accurate knowledge of branches with which he has not previously been acquainted. For purposes of self-education, the importance of this feature cannot be overestimated.

Dictionaries. In practically every department there is at least one dictionary, or group of specially selected topics arranged in alphabetical order. These dictionaries supplement, in a most effective manner, the other material in the department. Following the instructive discussions on government, there is a valuable Dictionary of Political Terms and Institutions. The Department of Science is especially well provided with dictionaries, which include alphabetically arranged articles on plants, animals, minerals, electrical terms, and many other groups of subjects on which it is often important to obtain the most reliable information with a minimum expenditure of time and labor.

TABULATIONS. As a storehouse of condensed information, there is no superior to a well constructed tabulation. This work has utilized carefully planned tables to an extent never before carried out in a single volume and has thus, to a quite exceptional degree, been able to display condensed information in an attractive and readily accessible form. There are in all some hundreds of these helpful tables. Many of them, if expanded into descriptive text, would each provide material for a substantial volume. In numerous instances, single pages among these tables represent the labor of weeks or even of months. Several are of unique value. Among these are the table of Modern Literature, the table of the Growth of the United States, the numerous tables on agriculture, and especially the table of Vice Presidents of the United States, which involved extensive research at the Congressional library.

ILLUSTRATIONS. Each department is introduced by an appropriate full page illustration in color. The larger departments contain numerous color pages and half tones illustrating in all nearly 800 subjects. Many of these are exceedingly beautiful, and all are interesting and instructive. Under History, Geography, Science, and Fine Arts, there is a wealth of educational and artistic illustration which renders these important departments doubly valuable. In the section on Animals, there are full page illustrations from original paintings made for this work by Louis Agassiz Fuertes. The section on Plants contains a number of full page color studies of American wild flowers by Miss Mary E. Eaton. The Department of Biography is notable for its array of portraits of the world's great men and women.

MAPS. Recently prepared maps of the world, of the different continents, and particularly of the United States and Canada complete the extensive descriptive material in the highly useful Department of Geography.

PRONUNCIATION. Throughout the volume the pronunciation of unfamiliar words, especially names of persons and places, has been carefully indicated. Moreover, the section on Correct Pronunciation contains a dictionary of more than 1600 words which are frequently mispronounced.

BIBLIOGRAPHIES. The user who may desire to extend his knowledge of some special subject beyond the generous array of information afforded by this volume will find, at the end of each of the several departments, a classified list of authoritative works. From these suggestive bibliographies, which have been carefully prepared for his aid, he will be able to select books in which he may pursue a favorite subject at greater length.

TEST QUESTIONS. At the end of each department will be found carefully selected questions covering essentials of the subjects treated. In all, there are approximately 10,000 such questions, the answers to which, in themselves, constitute the foundations of a liberal education. Yet this great number forms only a small fraction of the questions which the volume will answer. This special feature will be found a stimulating means of self-improvement for students, teachers, parents, club women, debaters, and all others who desire to be widely informed.

INDEX. The comprehensive Index enables the reader to obtain information with great speed and precision. While necessarily of generous size because of the extensive contents of the volume, this index is so simple and compact that the utmost ease will be experienced in the use of it. The Index and the twelve departments of The Lincoln Library may be quickly located by means of convenient thumb notches.

THE BUILDERS

This unique and comprehensive volume owes its origin, development, and completion to the constructive foresight and the untiring energy of Mr. M. J. Kinsella, the founder and first president of The Frontier Press Company. Under his vigorous and able management, this organization grew until it now stands in the foremost rank of American educational publishing houses.

By academic training and especially by practical and successful experience, Mr. Kinsella was unusually well qualified for the colossal task of building this volume. While the book itself is the best evidence of the intelligent manner in which it was planned and constructed, a few words concerning the training and experience of its chief builder may not be out of place.

Having had the usual preparatory training, Mr. Kinsella entered the Buffalo state normal school, where he completed a four-year classical course. Later he entered Cornell university, at which institution he was graduated in 1900. Incidentally, he devoted three years to teaching, an experience which subsequently proved of great value to him in that it made him familiar with the needs of the average pupil. Finally, Mr. Kinsella was always a diligent student of *instructive* books.

Publishing Experience. But by far the more significant part of the training enjoyed by the projector of this volume was that obtained in the course of his experience as a publisher of single-volume reference works of an educational nature. For many years prior to the preparation of this volume, he was engaged in the publication and distribution of one-volume reference works, and his labors were rewarded with an enviable degree of success. This wide experience brought him into intimate touch with all classes of people through the personal contact of an enormous force of educational salesmen and peculiarly fitted him for the great task of building The Lincoln Library.

Constructive Ideas. The completion of The Lincoln Library was the culmination of efforts directed by certain ideas which Mr. Kinsella entertained with strong conviction for many years. These ideas may be briefly stated as follows: that the typical one-volume reference book of from 800 to 1000 pages should be greatly expanded if it was completely to fulfill its mission; that the many-volume sets of encyclopedias are so costly that too small a percentage of the general public is able to purchase them; that extensive sets built on the A-to-Z plan are more difficult to use than a highly comprehensive one-volume work in which related subjects are brought together; that the material which is usually found in textbooks and special treatises can be greatly *condensed* and the real substance of it can be placed in an exceedingly small space; that, consequently, a single volume of sufficient size to contain the essentials of a liberal education is the ideal publication for general use.

With these ideas in mind, plans for the building of this volume were made, a corps of editors was engaged, and certain standards of accuracy, quality, and comprehensiveness were set up by the builder in chief. From the original plan to the finished product, Mr. Kinsella made it a cardinal point that quality should be the first and paramount consideration.

CONTRIBUTORS AND EDITORS

The following pages contain a list of 60 men and women, occupying various positions of importance in the United States, Canada, and Australia, who have collaborated extensively in building The Lincoln Library. After each name in this list is given the person's scholastic degree. Next is indicated the present or former position occupied by each collaborator, following which, in many cases, appears a list of some of the typical publications of which he is the author. Finally, there is a statement indicating in each instance exactly what task was performed.

In case a department, section, or article was prepared *in toto* by one of these collaborators, it is stated that he *contributed* it.

In case a section, prepared by the office editorial staff or by an outside contributor, was edited, revised, expanded, or approved by one of these collaborators, the exact service performed is specifically defined.

For several years, a corps of office contributors and editors with numerous assistants was continuously engaged on the work of building this volume. The task of preliminary selection and the original preparation of considerable portions of the material necessarily devolved mainly upon this group. The names of the principal editors in this group, with their academic degrees, will be found separately listed.

REVISIONS

One of the most serious problems facing the publishers of a modern reference book is that of keeping it abreast of the times. The policy adopted in that regard for The Lincoln Library is in keeping with the high standards established during its preparation. At each new printing, those portions which are affected by the passage of events are thoroughly revised.

In some cases, the original contributor of a section or Department has made the necessary revisions. In other cases, the services of different outside editors have been secured, the list of editors being revised accordingly. A large part of this revision work, however, has necessarily been carried out by the editorial staff, which is engaged continually in surveying the progress of the world in order to select and report the most significant developments. In all such revisions, the original character of the articles has been left unaltered except insofar as necessary in order to present each topic in the perspective of the present time.

The policy of thorough revision at each new printing was established by Mr. M. J. Kinsella, who continued in direction of the work to which he had devoted the major part of his life until his untimely death in 1928.

From that time on, his brother Mr. Burt S. Kinsella, who had long been associated with him in the publication and distribution of reference books, took charge of the work. Under his directorship, the same policy was followed in respect to revisions and the same high standards of accuracy were insisted on, with the result that the Lincoln Library's leadership in its field has continued without serious challenge.

CONTRIBUTORS AND EDITORS

ABBOTT, FRANK FROST, PH. D.

Late Kennedy Professor of Latin Language and Literature, Princeton University. Author: *A Short History of Rome; Society and Politics in Ancient Rome.*

Contributed the articles on Roman History and Latin Literature.

ALEXANDER, WILLIAM P., PH. D.

Late Director of Extension Work, Buffalo Society of Natural Sciences; formerly, Department of Entomology, Cornell University.

Contributed the articles on the Ant and the Honeybee; also reviewed and revised the material on Plants for the section on Botany.

ATWOOD, WALLACE WALTER, PH. D.

Former President, and Professor of Physical and Regional Geography, Clark University, Worcester, Mass. Author: *Interpretation of Topographic Maps; New Geography, Book II.*

Revised and expanded the section devoted to Physiography.

BARROWS, DAVID PRESCOTT, PH. D., LL. D.

Former President, and Professor of Political Science, University of California, 1919–23. Author: *A History of the Philippines; A Decade of American Government in the Philippines.*

Contributed the Department of Government and Politics for the first edition.

BOTHNE, GISLE C., M. A.

Professor of Scandinavian Languages and Literatures, and Head of the Department of Scandinavian Languages, University of Minnesota.

Contributed the articles on Norwegian, Danish, Swedish, and Icelandic Literatures; also on Norwegian, Danish, and Swedish History.

BOURNE, HENRY ELDRIDGE, A. B., B. D., L. H. D.

Professor Emeritus of History, Graduate School of Western Reserve University. Author: *Mediæval and Modern History.*

Revised and materially extended the article on French History; also 47 items on French History for the Dictionary of World History.

BROCK, REGINALD WALTER, M. A., LL. D., F. G. S., F. R. S. C.

Dean of the Faculty of Applied Science and Head of the Department of Geology and Geography, University of British Columbia.

Revised and expanded the section devoted to Canadian Geography.

CASE, ERMINE COWLES, PH. D.

Professor of Historical Geology and Paleontology, and Curator of the Paleontological Collection, University of Michigan. Author: *Geology and Physical Geography of Wisconsin.*

Contributed the section on Geology and Paleontology.

CHURCHILL, GEORGE MORTON, PH. D.

Professor Emeritus of English History, The George Washington University.

Extensively revised the Department of Government for the eleventh edition and History and other departments for later editions.

COHEN, PAUL P., B. A., LL. B.

Formerly Lecturer in Government, University of Buffalo; Lecturer in Banking, American Institute of Banking.

Contributed the section devoted to Business, Banking, and Legal Terms; also numerous dictionary articles embodied chiefly in the Dictionary of American History.

DEWING, HENRY BRONSON, PH. D.

President of Athens College, Athens, Greece.

Contributed the articles on Greek History and Greek Literature.

FARMA, WILLIAM J., PH. D.

New York University, Department of Education.

Reviewed and revised the Department of English for the seventeenth edition.

FINEGAN, THOMAS EDWARD, M. A., PH. D., LL. D., LITT. D.

Superintendent of Education for State of Pennsylvania, 1919–23. Author: *Judicial Decisions in Education.*

Reviewed, revised, and approved sections on Introduction to the English Language, Word Building, and Forms of Literary Composition.

FRANKLIN, EDWARD CURTIS, B. S., M. S., PH. D.

Late Professor of Organic Chemistry, Stanford University.

Reviewed, revised, and approved the section devoted to Chemistry for the first edition.

FRYER, CHARLES EDMUND, M. A., PH. D.

Professor of History, McGill University, Montreal, Canada.

Contributed the articles on the History of Canada and the British Commonwealth of Nations; also tabulations relating to the history and development of Canada; revised and extensively expanded the section on English history.

GAUSS, CHRISTIAN, A. M., LITT. D.

Dean Emeritus of the College and Dean of the Alumni, Princeton University; Critic of Modern European History and Literature. Author: *The German Emperor; Through College on Nothing a Year.*

Contributed the Introduction to Literature and the table showing the Development of Modern Literature.

GIBBONS, OLIPHANT, A. B.

Head of Department of English, Bennett High School, Buffalo, New York; also lecturer in English, University of Buffalo.

Reviewed, revised, and expanded the section on Synonyms and Antonyms.

HALL, CALVIN SPRINGER, A. B., PH. D.

Chairman, Division of Psychology, Western Reserve University.

Contributed the section on Psychology.

HARPER, EDWARD O., A. B., M. D.

Assistant Professor of Psychiatry, School of Medicine, Western Reserve University; Associate Physician, University Hospitals, Cleveland, Ohio; Diplomat of American Board of Psychology and Neurology.

Contributed the Section on Psychiatry.

HAWORTH, PAUL LELAND, PH. D.

Professor of History, Butler College; formerly Lecturer in History, Columbia University and Bryn Mawr College. Author: *United States in Our Own Times, 1865–1920.*

Contributed the section on World War I.

HOEING, CHARLES, PH. D.

Trevor Professor of Latin, and Dean of Graduate Studies, University of Rochester.

Reviewed and revised the section on English Words Derived from the Latin; also revised and expanded the section on Latin Words and Phrases.

HOWARD, JOHN TASKER, A. M.

Musician, Composer, Author.

Revised the Department of Music for the seventeenth edition.

HUEBNER, SOLOMON S., B. S., M. S., PH. D.

Professor of Insurance and Commerce, Wharton School of Finance and Commerce, University of Pennsylvania. Author: *Life Insurance; Property Insurance; Marine Insurance.*

Contributed the article on Insurance.

HUTCHINSON, MILDRED, A. B.

Instructor of Spanish, McKinley Technical High School, Washington, D. C.

Contributed the table on Vice Presidents of the United States; also contributed one hundred of the more lengthy biographical sketches.

IVEY, PAUL W., PH. D.

Professor of Merchandising, University of Southern California. Author: *Elements of Retail Salesmanship; Salesmanship Applied.*

Reviewed and revised the article on Salesmanship.

JOHNSON, EMORY RICHARD, B. L., M. L., PH. D. (SC. D.)

Professor of Transportation and Commerce, and formerly Dean of the Wharton School of Finance and Commerce, University of Pennsylvania. Author: *American Railway Transportation; Ocean and Inland Water Transportation.*

Contributed the section on Transportation.

JOHNSON, ROSSITER, A. M., (HON. PH. D., LL. D.)

Author: *A History of the French War Ending in the Conquest of Canada; A History of the War of 1812 between the United States and Great Britain; A History of the War of Secession; The Alphabet of Rhetoric.* Editor of The Universal Cyclopædia; Cyclopædia of Notable Americans.

Contributed the section on Meanings of Place Names; Reviewed and revised some of the History articles; also reviewed original material on Biography.

JORDAN, DAVID FRANCIS, B. C. S.

Late of the Department of Finance, New York University. Author: *Business Forecasting; Jordan on Investments.*

Contributed the original sections on Investments and Money and Banking.

JUDD, CHARLES HUBBARD, PH. D., LL. D.

Late Professor and Director of the School of Education; also Chairman of the Department of Psychology, University of Chicago. Director of National Youth Administration. Author: *Introduction to the Scientific Study of Education; The Evolution of a Democratic School System.*

Contributed the entire Department of Education for the first edition.

LEARY, DANIEL BELL, M. A., PH. D.

Late Professor of Psychology and instructor in Russian, University of Buffalo. Author: *Education and Autocracy in Russia, from the Origins to the Bolsheviki;* report on Russian education to the Peace Conference; translator of several books and pamphlets from the Russian; Lecturer on Russian History and Literature.

Reviewed and revised Russian Literature and Russian History.

LEIGHTON, FREDERICK, B. S.

Late Superintendent of Schools, Oswego, New York. Author: *Students' Hand Book of Parliamentary Law.*

Contributed the section on Parliamentary Law.

LEWIS, CALVIN LESLIE, A. B., A. M.

Late Upson Professor of Rhetoric and Oratory, Hamilton College, Clinton, New York. Author: *American Speech.*

Reviewed and revised the section on Speaking and Writing in the first edition.

LINK, JOSEPH F., JR., PH. B., B. S., A. M., D. ED.

Associate Professor of Economics and Head, Dept. of Commerce, Xavier University, Cincinnati, Ohio. Edited European Editions *Stars and Stripes,* U. S. Army Newspaper.

Revised Department of Economics for the eighteenth edition.

LÓPEZ, MANUEL LEÓN, A. B., A. M.

Department of Romance Languages, University of Oregon.

Reviewed and revised Spanish Literature and Spanish History; also Latin American Literature.

MACCRACKEN, HENRY NOBLE, PH. D., LL. D., L. H. D.

Former President of Vassar College. Author: *First Year English; Manual of Good English* (part author); *English Composition in Theory and Practice* (part author).

Reviewed, with constructive suggestions, the original manuscript on Sentence Building, Prepositions, and Conjunctions; also reviewed and approved the final proofs.

MCCREA, ROSWELL CHENEY, PH. D.

Dean Emeritus of the School of Business, and executive officer of the Department of Economics, Columbia University. Author: *The Humane Movement.*

Reviewed and revised the sections on Inventions and How Things Are Made.

MACIVER, ROBERT MORRISON, B. A., M. A., D. PHIL., F. R. S. C.

Professor of Political Philosophy and Sociology, Columbia University. Author: *Community, A Sociological Study; Labor in the Changing World.*

Contributed the Introduction to Economics and Useful Arts and the section on Business Crises; also reviewed and revised the section on Engineering and Building.

MOODIE, ROY LEE, PH. D.

Professor of Paleodontology, College of Dentistry, University of Southern California. Author: *Paleopathology; Antiquity of Disease.*

Reviewed, revised, and materially extended the section devoted to Mineralogy.

MORGAN, BAYARD QUINCY, PH. D.

Professor and Chairman of German Department, Stanford University.

Revised and materially expanded the articles on German Literature and German History.

MORGENSTERN, JULIAN, PH. D.

President Emeritus of The Hebrew Union College, Cincinnati, Ohio. Author: *A Jewish Interpretation of the Book of Genesis.*

Contributed the article on Jewish History; also the articles on Hebrew, Syriac, and Ethiopic Literatures; revised and largely rewrote the articles on Arabic and Assyro-Babylonian Literatures.

Moulton, Forest Ray, Ph. D., Sc. D.
Formerly Professor of Astronomy, University of Chicago
Author: *Introduction to Astronomy; Descriptive Astronomy.*

Contributed the section on Astronomy.

Needham, James George, Litt. D., Ph. D.
Former Professor of Entomology and Limnology, Cornell University. Author: *Outdoor Studies; General Biology.*

Revised and materially expanded the section on Zoology.

Nye, Herbert Arnold, B. A., M. A., Ph. D.
Associate Professor of Physics, University of Buffalo.

Assisted in preparing Department of Physics.

Park, Julian, Ph. D.
Professor and Head of Department of History, University of Buffalo; also Dean of the College of Arts and Sciences. Author: *Philatelic Rambles; Cuba in the Seven Years' War.*

Reviewed and Revised the Dictionary of World History; also the World History Tables for the first edition.

Phillips, Lyle W., B. S., M. A., Ph. D.
Professor and Head of Department of Physics, University of Buffalo.

Contributed the Department of Physics.

Reeder, Ward Glen, A. B., A. M., Ph. D.
Professor of Education, Ohio State University.

Reviewed and revised Department of Education for the seventeenth edition.

Rhodenizer, Vernon Blair, Ph. D.
Professor of English Language and Literature, Acadia University, Wolfville, N. S.

Contributed the article on Canadian Literature.

Ross, Wilbert Davidson, A. B., A. M.
Professor and Head of Department of History and Government, Kansas State Normal School, Emporia, Kansas. Formerly State Superintendent of Public Instruction, Kansas.

Reviewed and revised the historical articles on the countries of Central America and South America.

Sargent, Irene, Litt. D.
Late Professor of History of Fine Arts and of Italian Literature, Syracuse University.

Contributed the Introduction to Fine Arts; also the sections devoted to Painting, Architecture, and Sculpture; revised and expanded the Dictionary of Art Terms.

Schwendeman, Joseph R., M. A., Ph. D.
Head of Department of Geography, University of Kentucky. Contributor to *World Political Geography.*

Reviewed and revised the articles on Asia, Africa, and Australia in the Department of Geography for the eighteenth edition.

Scott, Ernest
Professor in the Department of History in the University of Melbourne, Australia.

Contributed the article on Australian History.

Seaborg, Glenn Theodore, A. B., Ph. D.
Professor of Chemistry, University of California.

Revised the Department of Chemistry for the seventeenth edition.

Snow, Royall H., S. B., B. A., B. Litt.
Professor of English, Ohio State University.

Reviewed and revised American and English Literature and Literary Plots for the seventeenth edition.

Suzzallo, Henry, Ph. D., LL. D.
Late President, Carnegie Foundation for Advancement of Teaching; formerly President, University of Washington; National Umpire, U. S. War Labor Board.

Contributed original manuscript for section on Labor Relations.

Vizetelly, Frank Horace, Litt. D., LL. D.
Late Managing Editor of New Standard Dictionary of the English Language. Author: *Essentials of English Speech and Literature; Words We Misspell in Business.*

Reviewed, revised, and extensively expanded the section devoted to Good Usage.

Weston, George Benson, A. M.
Associate Professor of Romance Languages, Harvard University.

Contributed the article on Italian Literature; also reviewed and revised the article on Italian History and the section on Modern Phrases.

Williams, Edward Thomas, M. A., LL. D.
Agassiz Professor of Oriental Languages and Literature, University of California, 1918–27. Author: *Recent Chinese Legislation; A Short History of China.*

Contributed the articles on Chinese Literature and History, Japanese Literature and History.

Wilson, G. Lloyd, M. A., Ph. D., M. B. A.
Professor of Commerce and Transportation, Wharton School of Finance and Commerce, University of Pennsylvania. Author: *Traffic Management; Transit Services; Traffic Geography.*

Reviewed and revised the section on Transportation for the second edition.

Zenkert, Charles Anthony, B. A.
Research Associate in Botany, Buffalo Museum of Science.

Reviewed and revised the section on Botany for the sixteenth edition.

OFFICE EDITORIAL STAFF

Corrigan, T. D'Arcy, Ph. D., Litt. D.

Dawson, Charles Addison, M. A., Ph. D.

Johnson, Frank William, M. A.

Park, Clyde W., A. B., A. M.

Taylor, John Wilson, M. A., Ph. D.

Webster, Paul Fred, B. A.

Tarbell, Ruth H., chief editorial assistant

CONTENTS

VI. MATHEMATICS

VII. ECONOMICS AND USEFUL ARTS

VIII. GOVERNMENT AND POLITICS

IX. FINE ARTS

X. EDUCATION

XI. BIOGRAPHY

XII. MISCELLANY

INDEX

LIST OF ILLUSTRATIONS

KEY TO PRONUNCIATION

ä, as in farm, father; *ȧ*, as in ask, fast; *ă*, as in at, fat; *ā*, as in day, fate; *â*, as in care, fare. *ĕ*, as in met, set; *ē*, as in me, see; *ẽ*, as in her, perform. *ĭ*, as in pin, ill; *ī*, as in pine, ice. *ŏ*, as in hot, got; *ō*, as in note, old; *ô*, as in for, fought; *o͝o*, as in cook, look; *o͞o*, as in moon, spoon. *ŭ*, as in cup, duck; *ū*, as in use, amuse; *û*, as in fur, urge. *ou*, as in out, about. *oi*, as in oil, boil.

â, ê, ô, û represent the sounds *ā, ē, ō, ū*; they are of shorter quantity but do not lose the quality of the "long" vowel, as in senâte, event, ôbey, lectûre.

TH indicates the sound of th in thee, though. In foreign words this symbol indicates a more distinct d sound than in English words, as in the Irish word *Dail.* *zh* stands for the sound of z in azure.

ü cannot be exactly represented in English. The English sound of u as in *luke* and *duke* resembles the original sound of *ü*. *ö* cannot be exactly represented in English. The English sound of u in *burn* and *burnt* is perhaps the nearest equivalent to ö, or œ. K represents ch in German *ich, ach.* N represents the nasal tone (as in French) of the preceding vowel, as in *encore* (*äN′kōr′*). H represents the guttural g or j in Spanish words, as in *jefe.*

The principal accent is indicated by a heavy mark,′, and the secondary accent by a lighter mark,′, placed at the end of the syllable.

SPECIAL MARKS AND THEIR USES

PUNCTUATION: For use see pages 85 and 86.

- , Comma
- ; Semicolon
- : Colon
- . Period
- — Dash
- ? Interrogation point, question mark
- ! Exclamation point
- ( ) Parentheses
- [ ] Brackets
- ’ Apostrophe
- \- Hyphen

FOOTNOTE INDICATORS: Used when number of footnotes is small, otherwise numbers or letters are employed, or special indicator marks may be used double.

- * Asterisk
- † Dagger
- ‡ Double Dagger
- § Also used to mean section or clause
- ‖ Also used to mean "is parallel to"
- ¶ or ¶ Also used to indicate paragraph

PRONUNCIATION INDICATORS: More common signs used, in English and some foreign languages, usually to show the value or quality of a vowel. Letters are supplied below to show how sign is applied.

- ĕ Breve. Pronounce vowel short
- ā Macron. Pronounce vowel long
- aë Diaeresis. Pronounce vowels as separate sounds
- é Acute accent (French)
- è Grave accent (French)
- ê or â Circumflex accent (French)
- ä Umlaut (German). Alters quality of vowels a, o, or u
- ç Cedilla (French). Converts hard c to soft c
- ñ Tilde (Spanish). Gives effect of a following y

WORD SUBSTITUTES: Many signs are used as a species of shorthand. Some of the more commonly used follow. Where the sign has a name, the name precedes the meaning.

- ‸ Caret. Insert
- { or } Brace. Lines belong together
- = Is equal to
- ☞ Index. See
- @ At or to
- % Per cent
- ° Degree
- ′ Minute (subdivision of degree) or foot (feet)
- *** or . . . Ellipsis. Words are omitted.
- ″ Second or inch (inches)
- π Pi. The number 3.14159
- + Plus. Add
- − Minus. Subtract
- × Multiply
- ÷ Divide
- > Is greater than
- < Is less than
- ∴ Therefore
- ∵ Since
- : Is to (term used in expressing proportion)
- :: As (term used in expressing proportion)
- √‾ Radical. Square root of
- ℞ Take (used at beginning of prescriptions for drugs)

PROOFREADER'S MARKS: These are the more common signs used by publication and printing proofreaders.

- ₰ Delete letters or words. Take ~~it~~ out.
- \# Insert space where‸indicated.
- 9 Turn inverted letter marked.
- tr Transpose letters or words indicated.
- ⁀ Close up let ters or words.
- = Straighten alignment of type.
- [or] Move right or left to point indicated.
- ⊓ or ⊔ Raise or lower to point indicated.
- eq# Equalize spacing of words.
- wf Wrong font. Incorrect size, weight or style of letter
- X Broken letter or poor type.
- stet Let it stand. Disregard marks made.
- cap replace letter marked with a capital.
- lc Replace With a lower case (small) letter.
- bf Reset words in **bold face** type.
- ital Reset words in *italic* type.
- rom Reset words in roman (regular) type.
- ⊙ Insert period where marked
- ‸ Insert comma where marked.
- ∨ Insert apostrophe per proofreaders mark.

SUGGESTIONS FOR THE USER

The usefulness of this volume is so manifest and the information which it contains is so readily accessible that, in a certain sense, there is little need for this section. Nevertheless, since The Lincoln Library contains far more than the conventional books of reference and is intended for so many different classes of readers, it has seemed desirable to set forth certain suggestions that will enable every reader to derive from the work the greatest possible advantage.

Although this work, like all books of reference, is designed particularly to furnish general information of a wide range, nevertheless it is specially adapted also for the guidance of home students and as an aid to pupils and teachers in the preparation of supplementary school work. It will be found no less valuable for parents wishing to keep abreast of their children's education and for busy men and women in commercial life who are desirous of improving their business efficiency. In a like degree, this work will prove helpful to persons interested in civic improvement and better citizenship, to literary and other club workers, and to all who aspire to a higher degree of culture through self-improvement.

FOR GENERAL REFERENCE

Experience has shown that the information contained in The Lincoln Library will furnish satisfactory answers to innumerable questions that arise in the average person's daily life and affairs. These include questions that come up through contact with associates at work, in business, or at clubs; questions suggested through the reading of newspapers, magazines, and books; questions asked by children in connection with school work; and also questions growing out of political and various other discussions.

It should be remembered, on the other hand, that this volume will not furnish information on trivial matters or on matters of purely local or temporary interest. That such items have no part in this volume is made clear by its title. No attempt, for example, is made to include mention of the innumerable athletic contests which are a part of normal physical activity everywhere. Nevertheless, an athletic event of historic and international interest, such as the Olympic games, receives a treatment befitting its importance.

Strictly technical subjects, also, such as those connected with the practice of law or of medicine, will not be found treated in this volume. The work is not designed to assist a specialist in the practice of his speciality. It does not undertake to tell the farmer how to grow wheat, the miller how to grind it into flour, or the baker how to make it into bread. It will, however, enable the farmer, the miller, or the baker to become thoroughly informed in the whole range of things that tend to make him a more helpful parent, a more intelligent citizen, and a more effective business man. For such purposes, this volume will be of inestimable service.

The true value of The Lincoln Library, however, can be realized only by constant use. USE is the key which will unlock every door in this treasure house of knowledge. The familiar adage regarding the value of a "little farm well tilled" has application to The Lincoln Library, the use of which, if cultivated assiduously, will yield abundant harvests in personal achievement.

It should be borne in mind also that even the fortunate possessor of Aladdin's wonderful lamp could not have called to his assistance its magical powers unless he had kept it where he could rub it with his own hands. So it is with The Lincoln Library. It will be of no more practical value than a mummy in a museum if it is stored on a high shelf, hidden in a closet, or locked behind glass doors. It should have its place on the family reading table, the child's study table, or the office desk, where it will always be within easy reach.

The Table of Contents gives the names of the twelve departments under which all the material in the work is grouped. Facing the first page of each department there is a frontispiece in color, on the back of which will be found an explanatory outline of the contents of the department which follows. Taken in connection with the Table of Contents, these outlines at the beginning of the different departments reveal quickly what the volume as a whole covers.

The arrangement of the material in each department, wherever it lends itself to such a system, has been ordered with a view to bringing into especial prominence the subjects likely to prove useful most frequently. Thus, in the Department of Geography, the United States and Canada are described first, and Antarctica is dealt with last. In other divisions of the work, the most convenient arrangement of the minor topics is plainly alphabetic, and this system has been followed in all such cases.

The device of greatest utility in obtaining information from any book is a good index. To the busy user, in particular, even a good book with a poor index is of little or no value. The Index of The Lincoln Library has been made so comprehensive that every passage of importance bearing upon any subject may be found with the least possible expenditure of time. The immense number of subjects treated in the work makes it inevitable that the Index should be large, particularly as the subjects are carefully cross-indexed and subindexed. Nevertheless the preparation of this important part of the volume has been carried through with such care and judgment that the use of it will be found surprisingly simple.

With a view to its greater usefulness, the Index has been kept free of several classes of entries which would add bulk with little corresponding advantage and which, in some cases, might amount to positive hindrances.

In the first place, every single occurrence of a word or subject is not recorded in the Index. To do so would cause the reader a waste of time instead of enabling him to save it. Thus, to enter in the Index all the cities in the United States which are given in the table on pages 741–746 would serve no real purpose. All cities which are treated topically are separately indexed; for all others, the reader is referred to this table. These and similar features of the Index are made clear in a number of explanatory paragraphs preceding the Index.

Another class of reference excluded is that which some works list in order to be able to claim completeness but which do not lead to any helpful information. Thus, under *Switzerland* will be found references to separate articles treating its history, its geography, and its government as well as to tables containing facts regarding the country. No reference will be found, however, to many other passages where Switzerland is mentioned but in which little or no light is thrown on the country as such. Thus, in Biography, it is stated that Rousseau resided in Switzerland, but to refer to this passage under *Switzerland* would serve merely to detract from the usefulness of the Index.

No attempt is made to incorporate in the Index such supplementary material as, with more careful editing, would be placed in other parts of the work. In other words, the Index is rigorously restricted to the fulfillment of its proper purposes.

FOR SELF-EDUCATION

In years gone by, thousands of promising young men and women abandoned the hope of becoming educated simply because they could not attend high school or college. With this humiliating acceptance of failure, they relinquished the honors, the usefulness, and the happiness which only education can bring.

In recent years, however, it has become much more generally recognized that it is not positively essential to attend college in order to become educated. Moreover, this changing point of view is not confined to the young. Mature men and women who left the day schools years ago are now enrolled by thousands in the night classes of universities, colleges, and vocational schools. Still greater numbers, who cannot arrange for classroom attendance, are devoting their spare moments to systematic study and self-improvement.

The Lincoln Library is, in a special sense, dedicated to the task of meeting the needs of these people, and the work has been planned throughout with this end in view. It represents a determined effort to bring to every conscientious user of this book the advantages formerly supposed to be open only to those who could actually attend advanced institutions of learning. The accomplishment of this purpose involved enlisting the co-operation of a large number of professors of the outstanding universities of the United States, Canada, and Australia, and, in numerous sections throughout the work, may be seen the cream of the material which these teachers and scholars present before their classes in the universities.

Every department of this work is adapted for study by the careful student, but among those with which especial pains have been taken in order to make the subject easily intelligible is the Department of Mathematics. On account of the difficulty ordinarily experienced by learners in this field, the material has been explained with a care that is probably unexampled among the printed textbooks on mathematics.

Another feature of The Lincoln Library which makes it of exceptional value for self-education is the inclusion of Test Questions in each department. In no way can the mind be so sharply focused on a subject as by first becoming conscious of not knowing various aspects of the subject and then having such active inquiry satisfied as a result of search. It will, therefore, be found extremely helpful to read from the Test Questions first and then to obtain the answers to them by referring to the text.

FOR THE STUDY OF SPECIAL SUBJECTS

The Lincoln Library contains in brief and convenient form all the essentials for a detailed study of a large number of the most important departments of knowledge. Among the numerous subjects for the study of which it affords exceptional facilities are American history, arithmetic, astronomy, British history, chemistry, foreign government, geology, history of education, how things are made, invention, letter writing, mineralogy, physics, physiography, physiology, psychology, science of education, transportation, United States government, and zoology. The material on the different subjects necessarily varies in length and in manner of treatment; consequently the best method of mastering the different branches of knowledge covered in this work will differ somewhat in detail. In practically all cases, however, the following suggested procedure will be found helpful to one who is undertaking the systematic study of a special subject.

SUGGESTIVE METHOD

1. Consult the Index, locate the subject to be studied, and turn to the beginning of the section in which it is treated.
2. Read with especial care the introductory material.
3. Study the important divisions of the subject indicated in the introduction. These divisions may be located partly by means of the conspicuous headings and, in other cases, may be located best by a reference to the Index. Follow up all cross references to related topics.
4. Study the various minor topics mentioned in each of the chief divisions of the subject.
5. Consult the list of illustrations and turn to those which are related to any feature of the subject under study.
6. Whenever the text mentions unfamiliar persons or places, look them up in the Index and read the descriptions of such as are topically treated. The location of places mentioned should be fixed in the mind by a reference to the maps in the Department of Geography. The Index should be consulted also in regard to every term or subject that you do not fully understand.
7. By using the Test Questions, confirm the knowledge gained in this study. These questions will be found at the end of the department in which the subject is treated.
8. For more extensive study and for supplementary reading, consult the Bibliography, which either immediately precedes or follows the Test Questions. Here will be found a select list chosen from the best books on the subject.

Suppose, for example, that you desire to improve your knowledge of astronomy. Following the foregoing outline, turn to the section Astronomy, which, as the Index shows, begins on page 911. Read the introduction, which, in brief compass, gives the history, the value, and the scope of the subject. Under Scope, you learn that astronomy treats of the earth, sun, moon, planets, planetoids, meteors, comets, stars, and nebulæ. You are informed also that these subjects have received additional treatment in separate articles.

Turning to the article on the earth, page 915, you learn the important astronomical facts concerning it. The closing paragraph states its relation to the sun and, in addition, gives cross references to the moon and planets. Taking next the article on the sun, you learn its size, heat, composition, and other characteristics. Following up the cross references from the earth, you then study the moon, page 918. For additional information, you are referred to the satellites, page 920, where you learn about other moons than ours, and to tides, page 883, where their cause and effect are explained.

Following up the cross reference to the planets from the article on the earth, you discover a general article, page 919, with references to a separate article on each of the major planets. When these articles, with their references, have been studied, you can extend your knowledge of the solar system by reading the articles on the planetoids, comets, and meteors, and then more fully complete it by mastering the articles on time, day, length of days, year, calendar, equinoxes, solstice, eclipse, aphelion, perihelion, sun spots, and other subjects in the list of alphabetically arranged topics in this section.

Next, following the cross reference from the article on the sun, you study the article on the stars. From this you are referred to articles on the constellations, Sirius, Betelgeuse, and the Pole Star. Then read the explanation of nebulæ, including the references, and finish your study by a very careful consideration of the articles on the Milky Way, light year, and cosmogony.

By consulting the list of illustrations, you will be directed to instructive pictures of heavenly bodies and also of astronomical observatories, whose powerful instruments are described in the article on telescopes.

After completing this study, examine yourself by means of the Test Questions on page 1125. By following this procedure, you will have learned the fundamentals of the fascinating science of astronomy. Should you desire to carry your study still further, you will find some of the best books for the purpose listed in the Bibliography at the end of the Department of Science.

FOR SUPPLEMENTING SCHOOL WORK

The busy teacher in need of reference material in fields outside the regular textbooks will find this volume an invaluable aid. Timely selections made from the immense store of knowledge which it contains, particularly in the subjects of history, civics, and geography, will add greatly to the interest and effectiveness of her work in the classroom. Much suggestive material for supplemental reading will also be found, and excellent outlines for review may be prepared by reference to the work. The Department of Mathematics will afford valuable hints for a clear and forceful presentation of many points in this difficult subject.

In the classroom, it is inevitable that questions should arise which no teacher could answer authoritatively at a moment's notice. This volume will furnish the answers to a large percentage of them. Therefore, it should always have a place in the classroom for ready reference. Time will thereby be saved, and a valuable educational advantage will be gained.

The Test Questions are useful for purposes of review. They will serve also as model questions and will thus be of value to many teachers, particularly to those who, through lack of experience, find the art of questioning a difficult one. The character of the questions asked by teachers is often an index of their improvement and an important factor in their advancement.

For any pupil who is sufficiently mature to use an index, this volume is a veritable treasure house. While it makes no attempt to write advanced subjects down to the mental level of the child learning to read, nevertheless it is surprising how early young pupils who can read will learn to use it with great profit and interest. This interest finds encouragement in the simplicity of language with which the essentials of each topic are stated.

From an educational standpoint, the importance of having children discover that they can look up information for themselves can scarcely be overestimated. Nothing gives a child a greater degree of pleasure or of confidence in his own powers than to be able to find things out for himself. It is scarcely less important that parents should encourage the natural curiosity of still younger children by being able to provide their eager minds with correct answers to the many questions which they ask. To perform this pleasurable duty aright, it is positively necessary to have at hand such a comprehensive and easily consulted work as The Lincoln Library.

For pupils of grammar, intermediate, and high school grade, this volume provides not only the essentials of nearly all subjects studied but furnishes also supplementary material covering thousands of points connected with daily work in school. No other volume contains so much useful information for pupils of these grades. The subjects in which the material will be of unusual helpfulness, however, are arithmetic, English, geography, and history—the great fundamental branches which underlie education for any walk in life. In these and other subjects, the material can be used by the pupil for purposes of review, and the Test Questions will greatly assist him in preparing for examinations.

The student who, by the use of this work, widens the scope of his knowledge as attained at school will find himself enjoying a distinct advantage over those who neglect to make use of such a help. The "home work," which is so embarrassing to pupils not provided with satisfactory sources of information, will then become a source of pleasure and will be multiplied many times in value.

High school pupils, particularly, will be greatly assisted by the material on literature, ancient and modern history, physiology, zoology, botany, and other sciences, and especially by the valuable section on Algebra and other branches of mathematics studied in high school.

The usefulness of The Lincoln Library extends also to the student in college. It will be found helpful particularly in the newest fields of knowledge, in regard to which most of the large encyclopedias are deficient. Equally valuable are the lists of carefully selected books given under the heading of Bibliography. By means of these lists, the student is directed to more exhaustive treatments of special phases of the different subjects.

FOR PARENT-TEACHER ASSOCIATIONS

In the Department of Education, there is a special section devoted to parent-teacher associations, in which their function is described with examples of their methods and their work. There is also ample discussion of the curriculum and purposes of the modern school. The various intelligence tests and educational measurements are clearly explained with their application to children as well as to adults. Moreover, there is a discussion of the methods and results of school surveys together with a concrete example of the results of co-operative community action in substituting an efficient centralized school for several inefficient district schools.

Among other helpful features for both the parent and the teacher is the treatment of the problem of the junior high school, the vocational school, and the junior college. Throughout the text there are valuable condensed tables which show what the modern schools are doing. In addition, there are charts showing how greatly the curriculum in the elementary schools has been changed in recent years. Another feature of value, particularly for those who desire to be well informed on school matters, is a discussion of the national associations now studying educational problems. This section indicates also what sources of information on educational progress are now available.

Not only are the foregoing special features of great interest, but the entire section on the Science of Education will be found exceedingly helpful. Familiarity with these essentials will enable parents and teachers to co-operate more effectively in improving the work of the schools.

FOR LITERARY AND OTHER CLUB WORK

For aid in the preparation of literary club programs, courses of study, reviews, essays, or other papers, this volume offers an inexhaustible supply of valuable material. Every important literature, ancient or modern, is clearly outlined, and the most important authors and their works are mentioned. The wide field of English literature is treated in sections devoted to American, English, Canadian, Australian, and Irish writers. The whole is supplemented by the comprehensive Outline of Modern Literature; by the interesting section on Literary Plots, Characters, and Allusions; and by the section on Mythological Persons, Places, and Stories.

Moreover, the Department of Biography contains sketches of all the great writers and of a large number of minor authors, and includes mention of their most noteworthy works. When this biographical material is used in connection with the information to be found in the Department of Literature, it affords the opportunity of studying an author in a threefold way. He may be studied (1) in connection with the literature of his country or period, (2) through the characters which he has created, and (3) individually and personally, as in a biography.

Other departments of The Lincoln Library likewise furnish a wealth of material for the literary club worker. The extensive Department of Geography and Travel, with its instructive illustrations and maps, can be unfailingly drawn upon with profit. Similarly, the Department of Fine Arts, especially the section on Music and the dictionary of terms and subjects in architecture, painting, and sculpture, will contribute hundreds of interesting points.

But literature considers the works of nature as well as the works of man. Consequently, such sections as Astronomy, Physiography, Mineralogy, Plants, and Animals will make plain innumerable points that constantly arise in the study of great works of literature. Allusions to still other subjects will be frequently found in almost any important author. In following up all such allusions, every department in this volume will be found helpful. The student of literature should therefore make frequent use of the Index.

For members of all organizations having for their object better citizenship, civic improvement, or any form of cultural advancement, the information furnished by The Lincoln Library will be found indispensable. A member of a good citizenship league will derive great assistance from the section on the United States Government and from the Dictionary of Political Terms and Institutions. A member of a civic improvement association will gain much help from the section on Architecture, from the Dictionary of Art Terms and Subjects, and also from the Dictionary of American Geography, especially the articles on great cities, wherein important streets, parks, buildings, and other civic improvements are especially noted.

FOR IMPROVEMENT IN BUSINESS EFFICIENCY

At no time perhaps in the world's history has it been so necessary for the successful business man to be well informed, not only in his special department of activity, but also in regard to the wider questions affecting this activity. This need is due partly to the greater complexity of conditions affecting his business, and it is due partly to the higher level of education which prevails in modern communities. A business man who betrays conspicuous ignorance on matters of general information is likely to find that, for no other reason, people will distrust his knowledge of his own business. Such factors play a much larger part in business than many people suppose.

The Lincoln Library has many features which make it especially valuable for the business man. The Department of Economics and Useful Arts, for example, contains in convenient form the latest authoritative material on commerce, transportation, finance, insurance, crop production, animal industry, mineral production, and manufactures. This information is not available in any other single work of reference. It would, in fact, require a substantial library of carefully selected authoritative works to furnish the information which has been condensed and carefully arranged for the business man's use in this unique section.

Again, a careful study of the articles on Money and Banking, Investments, Insurance, Labor Relations, Advertising, and Salesmanship will be amply rewarded by the results. A thorough knowledge of these and other subjects of basic importance for business will contribute greatly to the efficiency of the business man and will be of value alike to the proprietor of a crossroads grocery and to the manager of a great department store.

As in the other divisions of this volume, the Test Questions at the end will prove stimulating to those who wish to test and extend their knowledge of economic and commercial subjects.

FOR TRAINING IN GOOD CITIZENSHIP

The growing complexity of government in modern society places an increasing weight of responsibility on the citizens of a democratic country. Good citizenship demands that one should at least have available such information as is necessary for arriving at an intelligent judgment regarding the various political questions that arise. To meet this need, the extensive Department of Government and Politics was prepared. The value of the information which it presents for those who desire to become more intelligent citizens is not easily exaggerated.

Following the outline for the study of special subjects, the user may pursue an exceedingly profitable course in civics. Because of the importance of acquiring this knowledge, a few special suggestions are offered. First, the introductory material is of unusual value; it should be studied carefully so as to grasp with the utmost clearness the purpose of government in our own country and in foreign countries, the relation of politics to history, and the importance of social ideas in politics. Next, the reader should note that the whole subject is treated in two main divisions—the United States Government and Foreign Governments. The knowledge embraced in the first section will be found of the highest value to the American citizen who wishes authentic information concerning the political institutions of his own country, and the contents of the second section will enable him to become well informed regarding other countries. Moreover, the discussions in each are supplemented by a very great amount of helpful information condensed in tabular form. The whole treatment is rendered still more complete by a Dictionary of Political Terms and Institutions.

The Department of Geography also contains a large amount of up-to-date material which every student of foreign countries will be pleased to find available. The recently prepared maps in this department will be of great service in definitely fixing in the mind the location of countries mentioned in the text.

Features of the department of Government which will appeal strongly to thoughtful persons are its freshness, up-to-dateness, and thoroughness. Under the United States, for example, not only are the older Civil Service Commission, Interstate Commerce Commission, and Smithsonian Institution explained, but there are explanations also of important newer bodies, such as the Federal Reserve Board, the Federal Trade Commission, the Veterans' Administration, Federal Security Agency, and the Federal Loan Agency. Similarly, under Foreign Governments, the changes resulting from the ferment since the World War are seen in articles on Germany, Russia, and Eire.

FOR GENERAL CULTURE AND SELF-IMPROVEMENT

Because of its range and its freshness of treatment, this volume is a most timely and effective handbook of self-improvement for persons of all ages and of all degrees of education. It is designed to serve all classes and to be of benefit alike to the farmer, the carpenter, the schoolteacher, and the university president.

In order to make a wide appeal, it is necessary that a book should be scrupulously nonpartisan in character. For this reason, the greatest care has been taken that The Lincoln Library should have no material exhibiting a partisan point of view. It contains no secret propaganda and seeks to serve no factions.

Although The Lincoln Library is extraordinarily rich in the number of authoritative statements of fact which it contains, it has avoided the dullness that often characterizes a mere fact book. The material in it has been so arranged and indexed that the user will not only find readily what he is looking for but, in doing so, will unexpectedly encounter related information of an interesting character. His search will thus become doubly valuable, and, by stimulating him to consult the work frequently, it will lead him to acquire one of the most essential elements in all culture—the habit of effectively seeking to become better informed.

Educated people may usually be recognized as such by their familiarity with the achievements of great men and women both in past ages and in the present generation. An intimate knowledge of the lives of the famous may be not only an inspiration to greater accomplishment but also a means of broadening one's experience and widening the horizon of one's life.

It is an interesting and enlightening experience to open at any passage in the Department of Biography and to read at random the biographical sketches. Glimpses may thus be obtained into different ages and different types of society. By leafing casually through the letter A, for example, one may see Saint Anthony the Great tormented in the desert by visions of sinful delights; Archimedes deeply pondering over his mathematical discoveries and mechanical inventions; George Arliss, the celebrated impersonator of "The Devil" on the modern stage; and Arrhenius, a Swedish chemist whose researches were crowned by the award of a Nobel prize.

Among the many other fields in which reference to The Lincoln Library will be found profitable are those of literature, music, painting, sculpture, and architecture. In the divisions on Literature and on Music and the other arts, the careful user will find a surprisingly large storehouse of information. If one desires to learn the titles of an author's most important books, the names and locations of the masterpieces painted by a noted artist, the features of a city which one should see when traveling, or information on any one of hundreds of similar subjects, a brief search in this volume will furnish it.

I

The English Language

SUBJECT GUIDE

LINCOLN LIBRARY INDEXES

Keystone View Company

IN THE SHAKSPERE COUNTRY

Shakspere's Birthplace

Ann Hathaway's Cottage

Trinity Church, Stratford-on-Avon

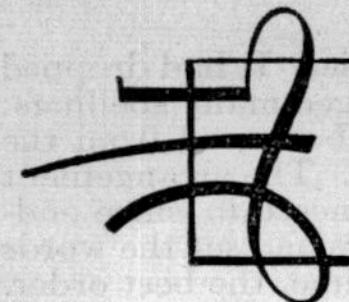

THE ENGLISH LANGUAGE

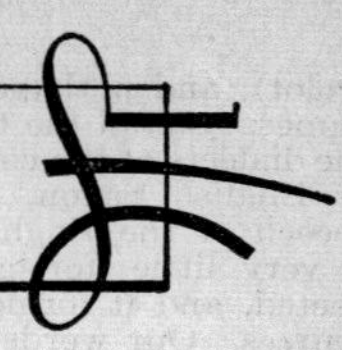

INTRODUCTORY

LANGUAGE, spoken and written, is mankind's most valuable asset. How language first arose has long been a matter of debate, but it is certain that it was originally much simpler than at present and that it developed from a group of bodily movements and from sounds with which certain meanings were arbitrarily associated. As men's experience became more varied and complex, such gestures and sounds were elaborated and multiplied until there arose what might be called spoken language. Written language followed, when an ingenious man thought of making marks to represent spoken words. By writing a symbol for each sound, an alphabet was devised and written speech was simplified. Thus communications could be sent long distances and thoughts could be recorded and preserved for the use of later times. Each generation was thereby enabled to instruct the next, and rapid progress in knowledge and in skill became possible.

Our English Tongue. To no people has there fallen a richer inheritance of language or a more splendid opportunity to further enrich and perfect that heritage than belongs to the English-speaking nations. The English language has grown to its present excellence through the development of one of the world's great literatures. This fact means that the work of scholars, poets, story-tellers, orators, and scientists has been contributing, through a thousand years, to enlarge, strengthen, and refine the English vocabulary and grammar. Moreover, the nations that speak this tongue have been modern pioneers in free, democratic government, with all that this implies in popular education, in free discussion of political questions, and in wide circulation of books, magazines, and newspapers.

The English and the Americans have been adventurous, trading, and colonizing people, sailing all the seas, exploring every continent, trading with, civilizing, and governing, peoples of every race. Whenever, for unaccustomed things, strange ways, or novel ideas, new words have been needed, these men of English speech have unhesitatingly adopted the foreign words that met the need. During a thousand years they have been borrowing words and phrases from all the peoples of the world and have been assimilating them to the forms of English speech. Thus the language has gained an unparalleled variety of synonyms and turns of speech, and it is fitted better than any other to be the language of a nation made up, as are the Americans, of a people sprung from many races.

In the European theater of World War II, men from America, England, Canada, Australia, and South Africa met upon the ground of a common language. Allowing for minor differences of dialect, colloquialisms, and slang, they understood and misunderstood each other in the English tongue. Nowadays, also, newspapers and books, whether published in London, New York, Melbourne, or Montreal, in South Africa or in New Zealand, circulate freely throughout the large territories represented by these men.

English and Related Tongues. In connection with this world-wide use of the English language, it is important to observe its relationship to other tongues. A person of native English speech who begins the study of any western European language, such as French or German, finds at once certain striking resemblances to English in forms of words and in grammar. The student of Latin and Greek observes similar likenesses among their evident dissimilarities. If he pursues his studies into the Slavic languages of Eastern Europe, such as Russian and Polish, he finds that they also resemble English in notable particulars. Further, similar phenomena appear to the student of certain ancient Asiatic languages, notably Zend and Sanskrit, the former spoken by the ancient Iranians or Persians, and deciphered only in the 19th century through its resemblance to Sanskrit, once the language of the Hindus.

Careful study of such facts has led scholars to the conclusion that all these languages are to be regarded as belonging to a great family of languages, sprung from a single tongue spoken by an ancient people of central Asia, to whom the term Aryan is sometimes applied. Properly, Aryan designates this ancient language, but it is used also to include all the ancient and modern languages which developed from it. This family is also called Indo-European, because its members are the great languages of India and Europe.

The outstanding characteristics of these Indo-European languages, which mark their relationship to each other and distinguish them from all others, are three: (1) They possess in common a number of words not found in other languages. (2) They indicate grammatical relations by means of endings added to words. (3) They are similar in the sounds they employ and in the general laws of their syntax. Other characteristics, also, such as uniform consonant changes, serve to distinguish groups and branches of languages within the general family. In the course of centuries, among different groups of people, the original consonant sounds in words have passed into other closely related sounds.

The close resemblance between the languages of Europe and those of India and Persia is shown clearly in the following table:

English	*German*	*Latin*	*Greek*	*Zend*	*Tokhar*	*Sanskrit*
mother	mutter	mater	mētēr	matar	macar	mātā
father	vater	pater	patēr	pitar	pacar	pitā
brother	bruder	frater	phratēr	brata	pracar	bhrātā

The Story of Old English. The beginnings of the English language, spoken today by more people than speak any one other tongue, are to be found in the dialects of the Saxons, Angles, and Jutes. At the invitation of British chieftains, these tribes came to Britain in the early part of the 5th century from the low-lying shores and islands of what are now the Dutch, German, and Danish North Sea coasts, bringing with them other adventurers from the Scandinavian countries. Having aided the Britons to drive back their foes, the Picts, these settlers turned upon the Britons themselves, forcing them back to the west and to the north. The Jutes settled in Kent, in the Southeast of England; the Angles, in the North, the East, and the Midlands; and the Saxons, in the South and the Southwest. The language of these tribes belonged to the West Germanic group of the Teutonic languages, and was more closely related to the Dutch than to the modern German.

From the old tongue of the conquered Britons a few words, such as *druid, bannock, down* (hill), *dun* (color), and perhaps *lawn* (land), with a few place names, entered the new language. The mingling of the dialects of the conquerors produced Anglo-Saxon or English Saxon, virtually a new language, the speech of the English Kin. This language had in it very little foreign element; it was highly inflected, and it formed new words from its own resources. Our words of common life, such as *while, nevertheless, man, god, loaf,* and *town,* indicate that Anglo-Saxon is still the bone and sinew of the English language.

Probably the tribes brought a few words of Latin origin, such as *mint* (money), *pound, mile, street,* and *church* (of Greek derivation), from the continent; for Roman and Greek merchants as well as Roman armies had penetrated to the lands along the North Sea. However, though the Romans had ruled Britain for 400 years and Latin had been spoken in the towns, the new conquerors seem to have found but few words they wished to adopt. The Latin *castra* (camp) survives in the name *Chester* and in other place names ending in *caster* and *cester.* The name *London,* of British origin, remains from this early time. But, with the coming of Christianity in the 6th century, numerous Latin words, such as *creed, verse, clerk, rose, lily,* and *turtle* (dove), were introduced. This number increased to perhaps 300 by the end of the 10th century.

In the 9th century the Danish or Scandinavian pirates overran the northeast districts of England,—Northumbria and Anglia; in the 10th century there were in this territory probably as many Danes as there were English; a Danish king ruled England in the early part of the 11th century. The conquest by the Danes was marked by pillage and cruelty, so that culture and literature were practically destroyed in the territory they ruled. For this reason, they left little trace of their language in the Anglo-Saxon of the time, though many words were preserved in local dialects and appeared in written English 200 years later. Curiously enough, these people gave to the English the word *law,* perhaps by way of the Dane law, as the district was called to which the West Saxon king Alfred at one time confined them. We owe to the Danes also such words as *call, care, fellow, husband, sister, die, same, thrive, take,* such place name endings as *-by, -thorpe, -thwaite,* and many surnames ending in *-son.*

While the Danes were harrying England, another body of Scandinavian rovers had settled in northern France. Normandy perpetuates the memory of these Northmen. Like their fellows in England, they adopted the tongue of their subjects, so producing the Norman French. Between these Normans and the Englishmen, intercourse grew in the 11th century. Edward the Confessor was educated in Normandy and to his court brought Normans, who made Norman French the language of the court society.

The Middle English Period. When William the Norman won the battle of Hastings in 1066, Anglo-Saxon fell to the position of the tongue of a conquered race, a people excluded from the court and from public office by decrees of the conqueror as well as by their own pride. Yet, though shut out from literary, courtly, and school use, the vitality of the language remained unimpaired. Not only did it maintain itself, but, when the struggle against royal tyranny in the 12th and the 13th century had wrung from King John a great charter written in Latin, and had brought Norman nobles and Saxon commons together in a common cause, English emerged as the language of the English Kin and their conquerors. We are told that about 1350 John Cornwall, a "master of grammar," changed instruction in his grammar school from French into English. In 1368 English was declared the language of the law courts. The poetry of Chaucer and the prose of the Wiclif-Purvey Bible raised the Midland dialect to the level of a literary language.

The language of this period, now called by scholars Middle English, was, however, very different from the Anglo-Saxon of 300 years earlier. It had dropped inflectional endings and had changed many spellings; it had lost some words and had borrowed from the French and the Latin many more. The arrangement of the words in a sentence was uncertain, since endings had been dropped and writers had set the words in what seemed to them, at the time, the best order. It was not until the 16th century that rules for word order were again reasonably well settled. A most important fact, however, is that in the 13th and the 14th century, through borrowing and Anglicizing, there began that generous enrichment of the language which has ever since characterized English speech.

The Anglo-Saxon Chronicle, which closed in 1154, contained a very few French words, such as *rent, treasure, countess,* and *castle;* but the immediate predecessors of Chaucer in the 14th century drew lavishly upon the French for synonyms and for words having no equivalent in the English. Already many Latin words had come in through the language of religion and the law. The new learning brought more, and, since most of the borrowed French words were of Latin origin, the total Latin element in English became very large. In everyday speech, however, the French is now the most striking part of our borrowed vocabulary.

From the 14th century to the 16th, with the Midland dialect, or London English, as a nucleus, the processes of forming the language on its new scale of greatness went on. Inflections were dropped, word order was fixed, spellings were changed, and new words were borrowed—some to be retained and others to be finally rejected. Thus the beginnings of modern English were prepared in the 16th century.

Making the Modern English. The 16th century translations of the Bible and the writings of Shakspere and of other great Elizabethans contain many old forms of words and of grammar unfamiliar to us. But these works mark the beginning of modern English. Their wide circulation by means of the printing press has helped to stabilize the language, and, during the last three centuries, to make slower its rate of change in respect to spelling and grammar. However, as long as the language is living, changes will occur; some words will be dropped, new ones will be made or borrowed, and new meanings will be given to old words. In this modern period, the extension of commerce and the development of science have brought about the introduction of thousands of new words, science especially drawing very largely from the Greek.

A comparison of English synonyms tells vividly the story of this borrowing. For example, the word *royal* is from the French, *regal* is directly from the Latin, while *kingly* is the Anglo-Saxon word. These words, side by side, have taken on important distinctions of meaning. *Acute* is Latin, *keen* is Anglo-Saxon, *shrewd* appears in Middle English and probably is Anglo-Saxon. Similarly, *admit* is Latin; *receive* comes from the Latin through the French.

Another group of words, applying to manners and conduct, is illustrated by *brave,* which comes from either French or Italian. *Gallant* is directly from the French or Italian, though perhaps it was originally a German word. *Business* is of Anglo-Saxon or Danish origin, *trade* is Anglo-Saxon, while *profession* and *art* come from the Latin through the French. *Copy* comes from the French, *model* from the French or Italian, *pattern* from the French, *specimen* from the Latin. The business terms, *cost, expense, price, charge,* were very early taken into the language from the Old French.

The sources of the following synonyms, relating either to law or to religion, are interesting: *crime* comes from the Latin through the French, *vice* is from the same source, and *sin* is from the Anglo-Saxon; *holiness* is Anglo-Saxon, while *sanctity* comes directly from the Latin. The common word *draw* is Anglo-Saxon; its synonym, *haul,* is of French origin, perhaps originally from the German or

Scandinavian; while *pull* is Anglo-Saxon and *tug* is probably Scandinavian.

The following list of words of French origin will show to what degree the French element has been worked into our language of daily use: *age, air, aunt, beauty, boil, boot, broil, cape, card, chair, cloak, coat, cousin, cry, dainty, debt, dine, ease, engine, face, fame, fork, grace, hasty, jolly, justice, napkin, nephew, niece, peace, plate, river, roast, soil, supper, table, uncle, virtue.*

Another group will illustrate well the picturesque interest that may be found in English synonyms· *breeze* is French or Spanish; *gale* may be Danish; *blast* and *storm* are certainly Anglo-Saxon; *gust* finds a likely source in Icelandic; *tempest*, so common a colloquial word in New England, is from the Old French; while *hurricane* is a Carib word which has entered the English through the Spanish.

The Dutch were the sailors and traders of the 17th century, and they gave us such terms as *boom, skipper, sloop,* besides some common words like *spool* and *wagon.* From the Portuguese come the words *binnacle, caste,* and *junta.* From the Arabic, we get the words *alkali, algebra,* and *tariff.* Hebrew contributions to English are chiefly religious words: *cherub, seraph, hallelujah, Messiah, Satan, Jehovah. Cabal* is of this origin as is also *cinnamon,* itself borrowed by the Hebrew from some other source. *Pilgrim,* the earliest Italian word in English, is recorded in the 12th century. This was in the time of the Crusades. Since the 14th century, we have taken from the Italian many musical and art terms, such as *opera, fresco, prima donna, sonnet, cartoon, cameo.* Other words of Italian origin, some borrowed through the French, are *fiasco, alarm, piazza, balcony, caprice.*

American Words. America has added to our stock of words in several interesting ways. Exploration in the 16th and the 17th century brought us, through the Spanish, such words as *potato, tobacco, cargo,* and *banana.* The contact of Americans and Spaniards in the West has given us such words as *pueblo, burro, broncho, coyote, loco, adobe, mesa, cinch, tornado, ranch, canyon, arroyo,* and *stampede,* besides some slang words like *vamoose,* and, in the Southwest, hundreds of plant and place names, such as *chaparral, mesquite, madroña, manzanita,* and *tule, Sierra, Santa Fe,* and *Colorado.* At the present time, because of increasingly close relations with the South American countries, we are constantly getting words of Spanish origin, such as *peon* and *hacienda.* From the French in America we have taken over *depot, levee* (dike), *bayou,* and *crevasse,* also place names like *Butte, Boise, Saint Louis,* and *Terre Haute.* The Dutch in New York are responsible for the words *patroon* and *stoop* (porch or steps).

Out of our political life in America have come the words *congressional, presidential, federalist, nullification, gerrymander.* We have coined the word *mileage,* the word *eagle* means a coin, *corduroy* is American English for a kind of road, and we speak of *locating* land. *Outsider* and *creek* (stream) are Americanisms, while several old or dialect English words, such as *fall* (autumn), *rare* (underdone), *slump, spry, lam,* have been preserved in America. At Baltimore the word *clipper* was first applied to sharp-prowed, fast-sailing ships; and at Gloucester the first *schooner* was christened.

No less interesting are the words taken from the American Indians: *squaw, wigwam, pemmican, tepee, papoose, cayuse, hominy, moccasin, chinquapin, opossum, skunk, succotash, toboggan,* and very many place names like *Canandaigua, Spokane, Chautauqua, Chattahoochee,* and *Willamette.* Some of these Indian words, such as *tepee,* and place names, like *Willamette,* have been affected in form by the analogy of French, others by the Spanish, as *potato, tobacco.*

These illustrations will suggest that, in addition to the practical value to be realized from the study of words and the acquisition of skill in the use of them, there is the further worth of such study as an approach to the history of the race. Words are the symbols of ideas, and ideas have made history.

Word Building. Many words, as they were needed to express ideas, have been built from simple forms by the process called "composition." The simplest sounds or groups of sounds that had, in the beginnings of language, a separate existence and meaning are called roots. Examples are *duc,* meaning "lead," *ag,* meaning "drive," *ed,* meaning "eat," *cad,* meaning "fall." By the addition of other so-called nominal roots, as *i* which appears now in the pronoun "it," we reach the stage of stems. So from *agri,* meaning "of a field," and *colere,* meaning "to cultivate," the Latin formed the word *agricola,* meaning "a cultivator of a field," or "a farmer."

Some simple words have had very little change from the earliest stems, except alteration of the vowel sound. Frequently this change has resulted from altering the position of the accent. The following will illustrate this development:

The word *arm* is from a root *ar,* meaning a "joint." This word is to be distinguished from the word *arms* or *arm,* meaning "weapons," which comes from the Latin, although the Latin word may be from the same source. The word *book* comes from the stem *boc,* meaning "beech," probably because in early times, in northern Europe, letters were carved upon blocks of beechwood or upon beech trees themselves.

Birth was not used in Old English but probably was taken later from the Old Norse. It is derived from an ancient Aryan stem allied to the Sanskrit *bhrti,* which meant "bearing." Bread was in Anglo-Saxon *brēad* and in Old Saxon *brôd,* having the meaning originally of "piece" or "fragment." The Anglo-Saxon rarely used this word to mean *bread,* employing instead the word *hláf* in the sense both of "bread" and of "loaf." However, before the beginning of the 13th century, *bread* came to mean the substance, and *hláf* assumed the limited meaning it still retains in loaf. *Comb* is from an ancient Teutonic root, related apparently to the Sanskrit *gambha,* meaning "jaw" or "teeth." *Deep* is from a very ancient root *dhup,* meaning originally "hollow." *God* seems to come from a root *g'heu,* meaning "to invoke." *Hand,* a common Teutonic word, is thought by some to be derived from a Gothic word *hinthan,* meaning "catch" or "take."

Language and History. In the vocabulary of the English tongue we find embodied the power men possess of readily and happily imaging or ideally representing the mysterious world in which we live. In our words are recorded their inventions as well as their ideals and schemes for the establishment of religion, society, and education. Here are mirrored the growth and the decay of ideas and ideals, the rise of the new and the displacement of the old. The lofty and the low in human thought and imagination are reflected in our language.

Our word *guest,* for example, is from the same root as is the Latin word *hostis* meaning "enemy," the original meaning of the root being "stranger." *Cheat* is from the old word *escheator,* the name of an officer whose duty it was to look after estates which, on the death of the owner, reverted to the state, a sense still retained in the legal term *escheat.* The real or suspected corruption of the *escheators* in the 15th or 16th century probably brought about the degradation of the word.

History finds still further illustration in such words as *cabal,* which comes from the Hebrew through the Latin and the French and meant originally "tradition." In the middle ages it came to mean "secret scheming," and in English this meaning was re-enforced by the fact that the initials of the names of five members of the Foreign Affairs Council of Charles II spelled this word *cabal.* In similar fashion, the words *earl* and *alderman* in their changing meanings represent much of English and American local government history.

The word *cross* suggests Christianity; but we should see in it also the early faith and learning of the great Irish schools of the 5th and the 6th century, from which the Norsemen of Northumbria took the word and passed it on to the Anglo-Saxons. Our word *world* also carries in its form the thinking of our pagan ancestors, who made it from *wer* meaning "man" and *old* meaning "age." It thus carries the sense of the "age of man or mankind," hence the "dwelling place of man."

In the early 13th century the foreign words in common use in English made up probably 12 per cent of the entire vocabulary. In Shakspere's works the foreign element is estimated at 40 per cent. Today in our writing it is probably 60 per cent. It is estimated that in the dictionaries of today about 20 per cent of the words are of Anglo-Saxon origin, about 35 per cent are from the French, about 15 per cent from the Latin directly, about 12 per cent from the Greek. But the proportion of Anglo-Saxon words in our everyday speech is much greater than these figures show, because our grammar is English and our connective words, such as *or, and, but,* are Anglo-Saxon. The English language has borrowed vocabulary, but not syntax, and it has Anglicized foreign words. Therefore, in spite of great differences of spelling, pronunciation, and accent, we may include in the term *English* the Anglo-Saxon of the 7th century, the Middle English of the 14th century, and the tongue of today.

The making of dictionaries has maintained a record of words and usage which presents a vivid picture of the growth of the language in the last 300 years. Samuel Johnson's dictionary of 1755 contained about 15,000 words. The latest dictionaries record more than 400,000. It is estimated that the average person without special education may know and use from 5000 to 10,000 words, while the educated man may use and be familiar with the meanings of from 20,000 to 50,000.

The Study of English. Language grows by adding new words, by giving new meanings to old words, and by developing the figurative or poetic senses of many words. All these processes depend upon increase of knowledge, upon invention and discovery, and upon the cultivation of art and poetry.

Words are, after all, only means to right understanding and true feeling; but many accurate, fine words are necessary to much good thinking. There is always a *best* word to express thought accurately and clearly. The student who would better his command of language will first direct his attention to those things which can be felt and seen, so that he may have something definite and concrete about which to talk or to write. He will next consult the dictionary for the meanings and the history of words; he will examine closely synonyms and antonyms for their accurate distinctions in meaning; nor will he fail to attend to the poetic suggestiveness of those words which give especial beauty both to the spoken and to the written phrase. He will, in a word, be always on his guard to avoid and to correct the errors and improprieties of usage which are likely to creep into his conversation.

Order of Study. English is treated in the following pages in a form to be referred to readily, to be used easily for help in speaking or writing, and to serve as a guide for systematic study. The various parts of the subject are arranged in the general order in which the boy or girl meets them in studying this most important of all school subjects. This arrangement would appear to be also the most convenient for older people.

Usage.—The correct and appropriate uses of words are given first place. During the early years of the child's life, before he knows much about sentences, he learns many words. Afterward, the value of his ability to use the correct and appropriate word, "to say the right thing in the right way," can never be overestimated. Therefore Usage, or approved uses of common words, is treated first.

Word Building and Spelling.—Again, the child's first words are naturally simple; most of them have but one syllable. In the beginning these are all nouns, for he does not yet know the use of the pronoun. By degrees, as the infant mind develops, the child finds the need of other words to express his thoughts and ideas. Soon he discovers that, by adding little syllables to the words with which he is already familiar, he can make himself understood. Thus unknowingly does the child arrive at the art of word building.

It will at once be seen that a knowledge of word building is of great value to the student of English as an aid in enlarging his vocabulary. For this reason, the section on Word Building follows Usage. It precedes the important subject of Spelling, because a knowledge of the structure of many English words helps equally both in grasping their meanings and in learning their component parts.

Pronunciation.—The guide of everyday usefulness has directed the making of the spelling and pronunciation lists. These are arranged to help the child with troublesome school words and also to give ready aid in the use of common words in business, in the household, and in social life. Correct spelling and correct pronunciation are essential to a perfect command of the English language.

Sentence Building, Capitals, and Punctuation.—Following Word Building or etymology comes syntax or Sentence Building, which is the next important stage in the study of language. The essential rules and principles of grammar are given in this section. Rules for the use of capital letters and for the use of punctuation marks logically follow the treatment of the sentence.

Speaking and Writing.—The section which presents helps in writing papers and essays and in making talks and speeches appropriately follows the study of words and sentences. To the student who desires advanced work in oral and in written language, this section is invaluable.

Forms of Literary Composition.—Having made an exhaustive study of words, sentences, and practical composition, the student is next introduced to the various forms of literature. In this section the principal divisions and subdivisions of prose and poetry are described and illustrated.

Letter Writing.—Because of its importance, Letter Writing follows Speaking and Writing in a separate section. The writing of an interesting letter may be counted as one of the finest accomplishments. In writing letters, we must apply the principles given in all the preceding sections on words, sentences, and composition.

Reading.—The language a person uses is influenced largely by the kind of books and papers he reads. Therefore a condensed guide to the best types and examples of English reading is here given. The lists of books direct the reader to the masterpieces of English literature. They are arranged in groups suited to the various school grades. In each group are the books that teachers, librarians, and parents have found to interest most readily boys and girls of the corresponding grade or age. A lifetime might be spent in becoming acquainted with the books in these lists. Reading will reenforce all that can be learned from the preceding sections.

Synonyms and Antonyms.—The value of knowing the correct and appropriate word is pointed out above. We should now add to this the knowledge of how to choose with a nicety from among several appropriate words. It is this interest which leads to the study of the rich store of English Synonyms and Antonyms.

Foreign Words and Phrases.—Two dictionaries close this department: first, a dictionary of Latin phrases which are frequently found in English books; second, a similar dictionary made up of phrases from Modern Languages. These complete the material for the study of English.

GOOD USAGE

When a language has ceased to be spoken, as is true of Latin and ancient Greek, we refer to it as a "dead language." Its rules are fixed. They must be rigidly observed by those who may sometimes use such a language as a medium of expression.

It is otherwise with a living language. The rules and the principles governing it cannot be permanently established. For the grammar and the rhetoric of a language are but a compilation of the rules that govern it. These rules, however, are not the invention of the grammarian, nor are they dependent upon his authority for their validity.

Province of the Grammarian. It is not the duty of the grammarian to make the laws of language, but to teach it agreeably to the best usage. It is obvious, then, that the ultimate principle by which he must be governed is that species of custom which critics call "good use." This principle is the only proper standard of grammatical purity.

Essentials of Good Usage. The usage which gives law to language must be *reputable*. Such usage is to be found in the writings of those whose works are esteemed by the discriminating public and who, therefore, may be called authors of good repute. In the second place, this usage must be *national*; that is, it must not be confined to any particular state or province. Thirdly, it must be *present*; that is, it must be the usage of the most careful speakers and writers of the present time.

In general, words and forms of speech which have long been in disuse should not be employed. On the other hand, the usage of the present day is not, in all cases, implicitly to be adopted. To embrace every new-fangled upstart at its birth would argue a fondness for singularity and novelty. Whatever receives the sanction of reputable usage must be acknowledged.

The Canons of Good Usage. We must not forget that the language is growing. What was thought to be correct and elegant English in the time of Shakspere and Milton contains many expressions now regarded as solecisms. Even at the present time, there are many unsettled questions as to the correctness of certain forms of speech. Good usage is not always uniform in its decisions, and, in unquestionable authorities, there are found varying modes of expression. In such cases the student of usage may be guided by the following canons:

1. When usage is divided between any two words or phrases, if one of the expressions is susceptible of a meaning different from the one in question, while the other is not, the latter should be employed; for example, to express *consequently*, the two phrases *by consequence* and *of consequence* are used. The former is preferable because the expression *of consequence* may also mean *of moment, of importance*.
2. In doubtful cases, the *analogy* of the language should be regarded. By this means do we trace the similarity of relationship between words; as, Learning *enlightens* the mind, because it is to the mind what *light* is to the eye—enabling it to discover things hidden.
3. Among several different forms of expression, in other respects equal, that which is most *agreeable to the ear* should be preferred. Thus *amiableness* and *amiability* are correct words, but the latter, being more harmonious, should have preference.
4. When none of the preceding rules solves the problem, regard should be given to *simplicity*.

Province of the Critic. The province of criticism is not only to remonstrate against the introduction of any word or phraseology which may be either unnecessary or contrary to analogy, but also to eliminate whatever is reprehensible, though in general use. It is in this way that languages are gradually refined and improved. At the same time, criticism may not presume to condemn instantly any phraseology which it may deem objectionable, though it may by repeated remonstrances eventually effect its expulsion.

Principles Governing Criticism. The decisions of criticism should be directed by the following rules:

1. All harsh and unnecessary words and phrases should be dismissed.
2. When etymology plainly points to a different signification from that which a word bears, simplicity requires the elimination of such a word.
3. Words which are obsolete should be repudiated as serving only to obscurity in style.
4. All words and phrases which include a solecism should be dismissed.
5. All expressions, which according to established rules involve a contradiction or seem to convey a meaning different from that intended, should be rejected.

Definitions. From the foregoing it is evident that forms of speech may be disapproved for one or more of several reasons. In the criticism of usage, the following terms are frequently used:

Colloquialisms are forms of speech acceptable in daily conversation but not always approved in formal writing; as, *aren't, isn't*.

Idioms are properly expressions which are peculiar to a language and which distinguish it from others. They do not fall readily under regular grammatical rules, and they are difficult to translate literally into another tongue; as, *How do you do? Monday week*, etc.

Provincialisms are forms of speech current in certain districts of a country.

Dialect, as generally understood, is a provincial form of speech so different from the literary language as almost to form a language by itself; for instance, the Scotch, Lancashire, and Cornish dialects.

Slang, originally the cant of thieves, gypsies, and underworld elements, is now a language used in all classes of society. The term designates a large department of specially colored English, usually vulgar or low colloquial, and is heard in the speech of young people, seeking lively modes of expression, and in the language of people who have smart, flippant, or sporting moments. To use it effectively requires acute linguistic discrimination. With most speakers it is merely a bad habit.

Barbarisms are offenses against purity of diction, especially the employment of foreign expressions; as, *You do me proud, politesse, fraicheur*.

Solecisms (*sŏl'ĕ-sĭz'mz*) are wrong grammatical forms; as, "*Every one*, except those who handle coins most, *are pleased* (correct, *is pleased*) with them." "*Each one* of them received *their* (correct, *his*) wages."

Vulgarisms are expressions which are common but not in good use; as, *to get into a scrape*.

Neologisms (*nê-ŏl'ô-jĭz'mz*) are new words whose meanings or forms are not yet well established or sanctioned by good usage.

Cant is the language belonging particularly to a craft, trade, or profession. It is applied also to the speech peculiar to a society or a group of people; as, the *cant* of fashion or of the stage.

Redundancy, or *over-flowing-ness*, is the fault of using too many words, often words of similar or nearly identical meaning (*tautology*). Economy in the use of words is a mark of good style in speech and writing.

Obsolete words, phrases, or meanings are those that have passed out of good usage. Words are said to be *archaic* or *antiquated* when they have gone out of common use although found in poetry and in the Scriptures; as, *doth* for "does," *ye* for "you."

CORRECT USE OF SOME COMMON WORDS AND PHRASES

A. General usage in America approves the use of the article *a* before consonants, before initial *h* when sounded, before long *u*, and before the words *one* and *once: a house, a hospital, a historical society; a university; such a one.*

Colloquially, when two objects are thought of as belonging together or as used together, *a* need not be repeated: *a coat and hat; a cup and saucer; a sword and belt.* But, "She bought *a coat and a hat,*" meaning two purchases, is correct.

The expression "*a black and white dress*" means but one, while "*a black and a white dress*" means two dresses—one black and one white. This second expression is awkward, and the form "*a black dress and a white one*" or "*a black dress and a white*" may be substituted. "They elected *a secretary and a treasurer*" implies two persons; but "*a secretary and treasurer*" implies one person.

Absolutely. This word, so frequently used instead of *indeed, assuredly, of course,* or *certainly,* should be discarded in favor of the accurate and appropriate word: "*Certainly* (not *absolutely*), I shall go." However, "It is *absolutely* certain that he will come" is correct when one intends to express positive assurance.

Accept, Except. *Accept* means "take when offered"; *except* means "leave out," "exclude": "I *accept* the gift." "We will *except* him from our requirements."

Accept of. Never use the preposition after this transitive verb: We *accept* invitations, presents, hospitality, and the like.

Accord. The primary meaning of *accord* is "agree" or "harmonize": "What you say *accords* well with my own opinion." It may mean, also, "award": "High praise was *accorded* him." It should not be used as a synonym for *give* or *furnish.* Say, "The information he desired was *furnished* (not *accorded*) him."

Acoustics. Although of plural form, this word is used as a singular. We say correctly: "*Acoustics is* a science"; "The *acoustics* of the hall *is* faulty."

Acquire. This word should be distinguished from *obtain* and *procure.* We *acquire* that which we retain more or less permanently, but we *obtain* or *procure* anything which we enjoy temporarily. Thus, we *acquire* wealth, *obtain* a loan, *procure* supplies.

Across. "To get something *across,*" "to put a thing *across,*" "to come *across,*" are slang phrases. The first means usually "to make something understood," as an actor is said "to get it *across* (or *over*) to the audience." The second phrase implies *succeeding*; the third, *acceding,* as to a request or demand.

Adage. As this word describes a proverb, or old saying, one should never speak of an *old adage.*

Addict. This word, formed from the adjective *addicted,* has come into wide newspaper use. It means "one who has the habit of using" something generally harmful; as, "a drug *addict.*" It is widely used in medical works but has not yet come into general use. The term is a useful addition to our vocabulary. *Addicted* usually implies evil.

Addition. Number of verb. We say correctly, "Two and three *are* five," not "Two and three *is* five."

Administer. Do not say, "The man died from blows *administered* by the policeman." Oaths, medicine, affairs of state, are *administered.* Blows are *dealt.*

Admittance, Admission. In some uses these words are likely to be confused. *Admittance* refers to entrance to a place. "No *admittance*" means "entrance forbidden": "No *admittance* before 8 o'clock." *Admission* refers to entrance into a society or an audience, or into certain privileges: "*Admission* to the club depended upon scholarship." *Admission* may mean also the price or fee of entertainment: "*Admission* One Dollar."

Adore. This word means "worship," "venerate," or "hold in high respect or admiration." It is not appropriate to express a liking for chocolates.

Advert, Allude, Refer. The meanings of these words are sometimes confused. We *advert* to that to which we turn the attention or the mind; we *allude* to a matter that we touch upon playfully, lightly, or incidentally; we *refer* to a subject which we desire to bring back to notice.

Aesthetic. This adjective preferably refers to abstract ideas, not to persons or objects. Do not speak of "an *aesthetic* person" or "an *aesthetic* decoration," but of "*aesthetic* standards" or "*aesthetic* considerations."

Affect. See *Effect.*

Agendum, Agenda. The first (singular) indicates an item, as of business, to be considered; the second (plural), the list of all items for consideration or a program of business to be done.

Aggravate. Often inaccurately used when the speaker means *provoke, irritate,* or *anger.* The word means "increase" or "intensify." The following are correct uses: "His misery was *aggravated.*" "He is *irritated* by continually dealing with small matters." "She is easily *provoked* to jealousy."

Ago, Since. We say correctly, "a long time *ago*" and "some time *since,*" or "many years *ago*" and "a few days *since.*" *Ago* means before a certain time. If no point of time is specified, the word means before the present: "a year *ago* last Tuesday"; or, if we count back from the present, "a year *ago.*" *Since* means after a certain time and up to the present: "We have not met *since* 1910."

Agree. Do not use *agree* for *admit.* We *admit* a fact but *agree* in doing or thinking something. We may *admit* that a wall is not attractive but we *agree* in refusing to spend any more money to improve its appearance.

Agriculturist. Prefer this form to *agriculturalist.*

Aim. The not infrequent colloquial use of this word as a verb instead of *intend* or *plan,* as, "I *aim* to treat all customers fairly," is not approved by careful speakers, though formerly it was good English. As a noun, meaning "purpose," it is an excellent figurative word: "Young man, have an *aim* in life."

Ain't. The word is not an acceptable contraction today. Formerly, used as a substitute for "*Am not,*" it had wide vogue, but in present usage it is vulgar. Say, "I *am not,*" "He *is not,*" etc.

Alike. This word should not be preceded by *both,* nor by *both just,* as in "These hats are *both alike*" or "*both just alike.*" Say, "These hats are *alike* (or *just alike*)." *Both* is superfluous in these phrases. See *Both* and *Just.*

All, All of. In spite of critics, popular usage has sanctioned the employment of *all of it, all of them,* like *some of them.* The idioms may be regarded as established. One may say either, "I have *all of it*" or "I have *it all.*" From the viewpoint of economy, *it all* is preferable.

Similarly, the phrase *all over* has established itself, as in the sentence, "We have searched *all over* the place."

Do not say, "This is *all* the *farther* I have read." The use is vulgar. Say, "This is as far as I have read" or "I have read no farther." See *Farther, Further.*

Allege. Do not use this word as a synonym for *say* or *tell*, as in "He *alleges* that the engine ran sixty miles an hour." Instead, "He *says* or *tells* us that, etc." The word has a legal sense, and with this meaning it is used in news writing. To say "The reasons *alleged* for the nomination are, etc." is to imply doubt as to the truth of what is *alleged* or to disclaim responsibility for the statement. See *Assert*.

Allow. This word is frequently used in some parts of the United States to mean "think," "think likely," "intend," or "say": "He *allowed* you would buy that horse." Such use is not approved today, although formerly it was correct. The word properly means "refrain from preventing": "He always *allowed* us to pick apples in his orchard." It is used correctly and frequently as in the following sentence: "The purchaser failed to *allow* for depreciation of the car." *Allow* here means "take into account."

All right. The phrase should never be written *alright*, though formerly this usage was correct.

All together, Altogether. *All together* means "all in the same place at the same time" or "all acting at once": "We are *all together* in the business" or "Let us pull *all together*" or "Now, *all together*, boys." *Altogether* means "entirely"; as, "The time was *altogether* too short."

Almost, Nearly. These two adverbs should not be used indiscriminately. *Almost* suggests the ending of an act; *nearly*, its beginning. A man who receives an injury so severe that he barely comes off with his life *almost* loses it; a man who just escapes what would have killed him is *nearly* killed, or, as we say, "comes *very near* to being killed." These words are correctly used in "I have *almost* finished my work" and "I *nearly* ran over the child."

Almost never. Because *almost* means "nearly," "well-nigh," "for the greatest part," it should not be used with the emphatic word *never*, which means "not ever." Do not say, "I *almost never* go there." Use *very seldom* or *hardly ever* instead.

Alone, Only. To avoid ambiguity, observe the following distinction between these words: That is *alone* which is unaccompanied; that is *only* of which there is no other. "*Only* virtue makes us happy" means that nothing else can do it. "Virtue *alone* makes us happy" means that virtue unaided makes us happy. "This means of locomotion is used by man *only*." See *Only*.

Already, All ready. Discriminate carefully between these terms. *Already* means "beforehand" or "so soon"; *all ready*, "everything prepared" or "prepared in every way."

Also. Like *only*, this particle is often misplaced, as in "If he is satisfied, I am satisfied *also*." Write instead, "If he is satisfied, I *also* am satisfied." Place the word as close as possible to and usually following the word to which it applies.

Alternative. Do not use this word when more than two things are referred to. You may have the choice of three courses, not of three *alternatives*.

Alumni, Alumnæ. An *alumnus* is a graduate of a college, a university, or a school. *Alumni* (pronounced *ȧ-lŭm′nī*) is the masculine plural, but is used of men or women graduates. The feminine is *alumna*; plural, *alumnæ*, correctly pronounced *ȧ-lŭm′nē*: "Association of Collegiate *Alumnæ*."

Always. Often used redundantly. Say, "Whenever I see her, I think of mother," not "I *always* think of mother."

Amateur, Novice. *Amateur* means properly "one who pursues an art or plays a game *for the love of it*." The *amateur* may be highly skilled. The *novice* is a beginner; therefore, presumably unskilled.

Ameliorated. This word means "bettered," "improved." "Her troubles are greatly *lessened* (not *ameliorated*)." We say correctly, "Conditions in the famine district have been *ameliorated*."

Among. "He was there *among* the rest" should read "with the rest," because *rest* contradicts the idea of "mingling or including in a group" which is implied in *among*. "He was there *among* the first" is correct. *With* denotes simply accompaniment. Similarly, avoid such expressions as "*among one another, each other*." "*One another*" and "*each other*" imply individuals by themselves so that when they are used with *among* the resulting expression is self-contradictory. Say, "*among themselves*," "*with each other*," "*with one another*"; as "They exchanged hats *with each other*."

Amount. Used only of substances or material: "Only a small *amount* of grain could be purchased." Do not say, "a large *amount* of perfection" or "a large *amount* of people." *Degree of perfection* and *number of people* are correct.

Ample. This word should not be used, as it frequently is, to mean simply "sufficient." *Sufficient* means "enough to supply a need." *Ample* is a larger word and carries the sense of enough, as of space, time, supplies, with a wide margin for comfort or unforeseen demands.

An. Use this form of the article before words beginning with a vowel or a silent *h*; as, *an* inkpot, *an* oil well, *an* heir, *an* honor, *an* hour, *an* honest man.

And. See *Conjunctions*.

Answer, Reply. We *answer* a question, but we *reply* to a statement. *Reply* implies a more definitely planned expression than *answer*.

Answer to, for. We speak properly of the *answer to* a problem, but of the *solution of* or *for* it. But we also say, "I may *answer for* his truthfulness" and "That will *answer*," meaning that the matter referred to is suitable for a purpose.

Ante-, Anti-. These prefixes are frequently confused. *Ante-* means "before"; *anti-* means "against" or "contrary to": "In *ante*-suffrage days the *anti*-suffragists were active." Pronounce the latter *ăn′tĭ*, not *ăn′tī*.

Antecedents. The use of this word to mean the ancestry and the past life of a person has good authority, though the use is of recent origin and the need for it infrequent. We may say of a person whose life history we wish to know, "What can you tell me of his *antecedents*?"

Anticipate. A stronger word than *expect* or *foresee*, and in some senses not synonymous with either. It means "take beforehand" (from Latin *ante*, "before," and *capere*, "to take"), "forestall," "get ahead of": "The committee was *anticipated* by the senator in introducing the water power bill." The second meaning of the word is "look forward to," usually implying approval or enjoyment: "Only a few politicians *anticipated* his election" or "We *anticipated* a delightful vacation." One should say, "His death is daily *expected* (not *anticipated*)."

Antiquated, Ancient, Antique, Old. These words are frequently confused. *Old* is the opposite of *new, young, fresh; ancient* applies to what existed long ago, as *ancient states; antiquated* is a disparaging term for that which is old and in disuse or out of date, as "*antiquated* methods of business"; *antique* may be applied to something that has come down from olden times, as a vase or a piece of furniture, or to an imitation of the "real *antique*." See *Synonyms*.

Any. Sometimes used erroneously as an adverb to modify a verb; as, "Did you fish *any*?" Say rather, "Did you do *any* fishing?" *Any* should not be used for *all* in comparisons. Not, "That is the most beautiful car of *any* in the show," but "most beautiful car in the show." *Any* may modify adjectives; as, "*any* longer."

Anyhow, Anyway. Although sometimes disapproved as unscholarly, these are idiomatic expressions, meaning "in any event," "At any rate," or "be that as it may." Avoid *anyways* as vulgar.

Any place, Some place. These phrases should not be used for *anywhere* and *somewhere.* One should say, "I cannot find my umbrella *anywhere,*" not "*any place.*" One says properly, " I want to go *somewhere*"; but the expression "I want to go *some place*" is vulgar. The fault lies in needlessly using a noun in place of an adverb which accurately expresses the idea.

Anywheres. A vulgarism for *anywhere.* Similar vulgarisms are *somewheres* and *nowheres.*

A one. In such a sentence as "All who promised to come arrived, but not *a one* was on time," *a* is superfluous.

Appear, Seem. *Appear* refers usually to what is evident to the senses: "The fruit *appears* to be well ripened." Every object may *appear,* but nothing *seems* except that which the mind admits to *appear* in a given form. Thus, *seems* is used to imply a result of thought or reflection: "He *seems* to be an honorable man."

Approach. Sometimes improperly used in the sense of *address, petition, appeal to*; as, "The committee has *approached* the council in some matters that concern the interests of the neighborhood." In popular use, *approach* conveys the impression of "feeling one's way" so as to learn the sentiments of the one *approached* before appealing to him. Because *approach* in this sense suggests an unusual and indirect or perhaps underhanded method of proceeding, it is in disfavor: "When he *approached* me on the subject, I refused to entertain the idea." The word is frequently used as a noun, as, "I repelled his *approaches* with indignation," especially when advances of financial assistance are implied or suggested.

Apt. Often misused for *likely,* and sometimes for *liable.* The following are examples of correct usage: "What is he *likely* to be doing?" "Where shall I be *likely* to find him?" *Liable* properly introduces some unhappy or disagreeable possibility: "If you go there, you are *liable* to incur his displeasure." *Apt* implies natural *fitness* or *tendency*: "Experienced men are *apt* to give good advice."

Arise, Arouse. The first form belongs to archaic, literary contexts: "I will *arise* and go to my father." In everyday use, *rise* is preferred: "We *rise* at six o'clock." *Arouse* refers to feelings: "This act *aroused* our anger." *Rouse* is used, transitively, in a literal sense: "We *roused* him from his slumbers."

As—as, So—as. Either combination may be used in negative statements involving comparison, but care should be taken to apply them appropriately. "James is not *as* tall *as* Tom" is a direct statement concerning the height of the two *without* implication that the speaker considers either of the persons spoken of as *tall.* But, if *so* be used instead of the first *as,* then it is understood that the second person referred to is notably tall in comparison with the first. Likewise, when age is spoken of, if one says, "My daughter is not *as* young *as* yours," the idea conveyed is that they may be nearly of the same age; but, by substituting *so* for the first *as,* one changes the sense and emphasizes the youth of the younger child and a marked difference between the two ages: "My daughter is not *so* young *as* yours."

As—as, only, may be used in affirmative declarative statements; as, "He is *as* good a man *as* anyone can find." *So—as,* however, is appropriate in some affirmative interrogative sentences when comparison is involved: "Is his estate *so* large *as* that?" Here an estate of great size is implied.

As for *that* is a vulgarism in such a sentence as "I do not know *as* I like him." Say, "*that* I like him." In such an erroneous expression as "Not *as* I am aware of," substitute *that* for *as.*

As, Than. One thing is *as* good *as* another, but better *than* another. "Better *as*" is illiterate.

As a matter of fact. Trite phrase, overused by many speakers and writers. If emphasis is wanted, use a phrase specifically suited, such as: "Scientists agree that . ." or "It is universally understood that . .".

Aspiration, Ambition. *Aspiration* is exalted desire and properly implies striving for something high and ennobling; as, "To the *aspiration* of the poet we owe Milton's *Paradise Regained.*" *Ambition* may imply worthy eagerness to achieve some great purpose, but it also connotes persistent, often overweening or inordinate, desire for personal advancement: "An *ambitious* man may *aspire* to greatness"; but it is used in the bad sense by Shakspere in "*Ambition* should be made of sterner stuff." It is not properly used for *energy* or *fitness* for work, as in "He shows no *ambition* since his illness"; but it is correctly employed in "Repeated reverses curbed his *ambition.*"

Assert, Allege. Two words often erroneously applied. Properly, one *asserts* that which one is ready to prove if called upon to do so, as a claim to property; one *alleges* that which is open to doubt or to question, as the existence of a will or the commission of a crime. See *Allege.*

As though. Often used for *as if.* This use has been condemned; but it is accepted as idiomatic English, notwithstanding the claim that it expresses a condition of remoteness approaching to impossibility; "We were received *as though* (or *as if*) there had been no war between our countries." *As if* is generally followed by a clause containing (1) a past subjunctive or (2) an infinitive expressing purpose or destination: (1) "Treating history *as if* it were a panorama intended to please the eye." "*As if* the dead the living should exceed." (2) "Buying agate and aluminum ware *as if* to set up housekeeping."

At. Redundant in the expressions "Where are we *at*?" "Where does he live *at*?"

At, In. *At* is a less definite word than *in.* Distinctions between them are not clearly drawn. The following examples, however, represent authoritative usage. We may say, "*in* the South," "*in* Chicago," also "The meeting was held *at* (or *in*) Baltimore." Of small towns or villages we say correctly, "They live *at* Walden"; but of larger cities, "His home is *in* Boston." To distinguish between points in a journey and the final destination, it is correct to say, "The ship calls *at* Halifax but docks *in* New York." A similar distinction is appropriate with the verb *arrive.* Either "We arrived *at* Denver," in which case the city is considered as one of the points to be reached in the journey, or "We arrived *in* Denver," which then is considered as the final stopping place. But, if the final destination is a small place, *at* is the correct word.

At all. An intensive colloquial phrase condemned by some critics, but entitled to standing as emphatic idiomatic English. There is a difference of emphasis between "I do not know him" and "I do not know him *at all*"; for, while the former denies acquaintance, it does not dispose of the possibility of acquaintance as emphatically as does the latter and more decided statement.

At best, At worst, At last. These are well-established idioms and are preferable to *at the best,* etc. They arose from an early joining of the preposition and the article into the form *atte,* whence *at.* See *Prepositions.*

At fault, In fault. Both phrases are correctly used for *in the wrong, in error, blameworthy. At fault* is the more common American usage.

Athletics. The word, when restricted to mean a system of physical exercises and training, should take a verb in the singular. But, when it is understood to mean the games and sports of a school, a verb in the plural is frequently used and is not incorrect. Similar use is current for *gymnastics* and *tactics.* Avoid the common error of saying *atheletics,* for the word is one of three syllables, *ath-let'ics.*

At last, At length. Two phrases having meanings that are akin in that they imply waiting. But while *at last* connotes finality, *at length* suggests that something more may follow: "We have been expecting you for a long time; *at last* you have come." "We have repeatedly invited him, and *at length* (that is, *after a long period*) he has consented to come."

At one fell swoop. A trite expression, unpleasant to those hearers who appreciate its literary power in Shakspere's *Macbeth.*

At that. This colloquialism used as an intensified ending is usually redundant and as such is better omitted: "The new car has arrived, and is a beauty *at that.*" This construction has been traced to the use of the phrase in matters in which the cost of an article is considered; as, "Here is a good umbrella for $8.00 and cheap *at that* (price, understood)."

Audience. Often inaccurately used in place of spectators: The *audience* hears; the *spectators* see. Say: "the *spectators* at the ball game," not "the *audience*"; "the *audience* at the concert," not "the *spectators.*"

Aught, Naught, Ought. *Aught* means "anything"; *naught* means "not anything," "nothing," or "cipher, 0." *Ought* is a verb, implying duty: "I *ought* to go." *Aught* or *ought* should never be used in the sense of *nothing* or a *cipher.*

Auspicious, Propitious. The word *auspicious* is applied to an occasion, the beginning of an important undertaking, or the like, and indicates that such occasions are favored by the conditions and by the circumstances. *Propitious* is applied to the conditions themselves and indicates that they are favorable. The word was originally applicable to a person or to a god and was later transferred to the signs which showed favor. A picnic has an *auspicious* beginning when the weather is *propitious.*

Avenge, Revenge. To *avenge* is to punish on behalf of another; to *revenge* is to punish on one's own behalf. We *avenge* a wrong to satisfy justice; but we may take *revenge* merely to satisfy our own angry resentment.

Averse, Aversion. *Averse to* is the accepted usage instead of *averse from:* "He was not *averse to* discussing his failure." Also *aversion to:* "His *aversion to* hard work is well known."

Avoid. This word means "to free oneself from" or "keep away from," but is often inaccurately used for *prevent* or *hinder*; as, "Nothing shall be lost if I can *avoid* it." Here *prevent* is the correct word to use: "if I can *prevent* it." But, "I shall not go if I can *avoid* it" is correct, for *avoid* here means "to free oneself from."

Awful, Awfully. Too frequently used as intensives. Avoid such phrases as "an *awful* shame," "*awfully* glad to see you." *Awful* is correctly used of that which fills with dread or inspires fear: "an *awful* catastrophe." Both of these words are colloquialisms that border on vulgarity when they are used in the sense of *extraordinary, highly remarkable,* or *excessively.*

Bad. Such phrases as *bad* cold, *bad* break, *bad* case are in wide colloquial use. Careful speakers try to use a more accurate and appropriate word, such as *serious, severe, troublesome.*

Badly, Bad. Discriminating people will try to avoid too general use of these words. When *feel* is used intransitively, like *seem,* the adjective *bad* (a predicate adjective) is grammatically correct: "She feels *bad* about the failure." In such a sentence as "I shall miss you *badly,*" *very much* is to be preferred.

Balance. In bookkeeping, the sum to be added to the less or to be deducted from the greater of two amounts, as receipts and expenditures, so that the two "balance." It is incorrect to speak of the *balance* of a meal, the *balance* of an edition, etc. Here *rest* or *remainder* is correct. One may speak of the *balance* of an account.

Bank on. A slang phrase, meaning "depend upon," as in "Can I *bank on* him?"

Be back, Been to. Such expressions as "I will *be back* soon" and "I have *been to* town" are widely current. The first is approved, if *be back* signifies state or condition, not movement. For "I have *been to* town," one would better substitute "I have *been in* town." *In,* not *to,* is appropriate to the state or condition implied in *have been.*

Beastly. The word *beastly* when applied to weather or conditions, as, "It's a *beastly* nuisance," is English slang, and, in America, English affectation. The word should be avoided altogether in such application.

Because. The word is a contraction of *by cause* and means "for the reason that." Therefore it is redundant in such constructions as "The reason we go is *because* we have been summoned." The correct form is "The *reason* we go is that we have been summoned" or, preferably, "We go *because* we have been summoned." The use of *why* after *because,* in "*because why,*" is a vulgarism in which *why* is redundant.

Begin, Commence. Although, historically, these words are precisely alike in meaning, *begin,* the Anglo-Saxon word, is preferred by careful speakers for general use. *Commence* has more formal associations and implies a beginning which involves a certain procedure and completion: One *begins* the practice of law, but one *commences* a lawsuit. We *begin* a day's work, but we *commence* a ceremony.

Behalf (on, in). A distinction worth noting is that *on behalf of* means "in the name of," while *in behalf of* means "in the interest of": "*On behalf of* the school, we thank you." "I make this appeal *in behalf of* the prisoner."

Beside, Besides. *Beside,* in present day usage, is a preposition and means "by the side of," as in "She stood *beside* the chair." *Besides* is either adverb or preposition and means "moreover," "beyond what has been said," or "in addition to": "*Besides,* they knew the road better"; "*Besides* wealth, he desired culture."

Better. This word is correctly used in the idiomatic form, *had better,* as in "We *had better* go."

Between. In its literal sense, this word applies to only two objects: "The candy was to be divided *between* the two boys, or *among* the four children." When used of more than two objects, it brings them severally and individually into the relation expressed: "a treaty *between* three powers." One may say, "The steamers ply *between* San Francisco, Honolulu, and Yokohama."

"*Between* each desk there is a wide space." This is a frequent error. Say, "There is a wide space *between* each two desks" or "Wide spaces are left *between* desks."

Between may express contrast: "The two boys are brothers, but there is a great difference *between* them."

Biscuit. *Biscuits* is the correct plural. Although "Please pass the *biscuit*" is frequently heard, no one says, "Please pass the *cracker*." There is a tendency to use *biscuit* as a collective singular by analogy with *bread*, but no one would say "Please pass the *roll*" of a number of rolls served at table.

Blame it on. A vulgarism used in place of *accuse* or *suspect*: "He *blames it on* his brother" should be "He *suspects* or *accuses* his brother" or "He *blames* his brother for it." In such an idiomatic phrase as "She is to *blame*" the passive meaning, "She is to be *blamed*," is intended.

Borrow. This word should not be confused with *lend*: We *borrow* from others that which we need and *lend* to them that which we own.

Both. Regarded as superfluous in the sentence "They are *both* alike." In "They *both* ran away from school," *both* has an intensive force. *Both*, as adjective or pronoun, may be applied to two objects or persons only. In "*Both* women spoke," *both* is an adjective; in "The general invited the colonel and the major and *both* went," *both* is a pronoun.

In the sentence, "They *both* met at the station," *both* is superfluous. "*Both* were alike good," meaning "*Both* were equally good," while approved usage, is not to be preferred to the latter sentence which is rhythmically perfect and linguistically sound.

As a conjunction, *both* may be used in connection with more than two things: "They lost all their property, *both* houses, barns, and crops."

Both of. Frequently condemned as colloquial; but the phrase has the support of literary usage, as in "*Both of* these arguments are sound."

Bother. Critics condemn this word when used as an imprecation or expression of impatience; as, "Oh, *bother* it all!" It is excellent English if used in the sense of *take trouble*, as in the sentence "You need not *bother* to return the paper."

Boughten. Although it has long been used, this word is a provincialism for *bought* and as such is disapproved by careful speakers and writers.

Bound. In colloquial use to mean "determined" or "resolved," but challenged by the critics. *Bound* implies *compulsion* or *legal obligation*; as, "He is *bound* to pay it." "He is *bound* to do it" is correct if the person referred to is under obligation or promise, but not when the act depends on the resolution of the individual. Then say, "He is *certain, resolved*, or *determined* to do it." "He is *bound* to fail" should be "He is *sure* to fail." But we may say, "He is *bound* for destruction," meaning "He is *on the way* to destruction."

Brainy. A colloquialism meaning "mentally alert," "of quick understanding," or "of vigorous intellect"; as, a *brainy* man.

Broadcast. The past tense of this word is usually given as *broadcast*. In its new sense, however, of transmitting speech or programs by radio, the form *broadcasted* is so widely employed as to be regarded by many as standard usage.

Bursted. A vulgarism sometimes rendered *busted*. Both are forms that cannot be too severely condemned, for the past participle and the past tense of the verb are the same as the infinitive, *burst*.

But. Frequently redundant before *that*, although sometimes required to make sense. When *but* is a preposition and *that* is a pronoun, there is no danger of error, for the meaning is "except that," as in "Nothing would please him *but that*." It is when both words are used as conjunctions that care must be exercised. In such a construction as "You need have no fear *that* she will go," the sense is clear that "she *will not* go"; but, in "You need have no fear *but that* she will go," the intention is clearly to express the feeling that "she is *sure* to go."

Best usage would eliminate *but* from "I have no doubt *but that* he will go," when the intention is to convey the feeling of certainty of his going. The form *but that* preceded by a negative becomes a positive—but it is more emphatic and less involved to say "I have no doubt *that* he will go."

"I cannot think (believe) *that* they will come" means that I believe strongly that they *will not* come; "I cannot think (believe) *but that* they will come" means that I must believe that they *will come*. "I can *but* believe him" means that, notwithstanding my own doubts, there is no other course open to me than to believe him; "I cannot *but* believe him" means that I am compelled to believe him—even against my will I am convinced. *But what* when used for *but that* is regarded as a vulgarism. These examples of the use of *but* illustrate what is meant by "English idiom."

By, With. *By* generally introduces the agent or doer; *with*, the instrument or means: "The window was broken *by* a boy *with* a ball." "The electricity is generated *by* water power." "The manager filled the theater *with* children." But, "The theater was crowded *by* the patrons of the opera."

By the name of. This phrase should not be confused with *of the name of*: "The business is owned by a man *of the name of* Brown." *Of the name* implies the real name; *by the name* suggests an assumed name; as, "Charles Farrar Browne was better known *by the name of* Artemus Ward than by his own name." It is well to substitute "a man *named* Brown" for "a man *of the name of* Brown."

By way of. We say correctly, "*by way of* illustration," meaning "*as* an illustration," or "*by way of* Cleveland" for "*through* Cleveland." In "He was *by way of* learning the country," *by way of* is an English colloquialism meaning "making progress in" or "occupied in."

Calamity. The word means, in an abstract sense, "source of misery or of loss," rather than the "loss" itself, for which it is often misused. *Calamities* are causes, of which *losses* may be the results. Any disaster produced by natural causes, as a hurricane, a cyclone, or a volcanic eruption, and attended by widespread destruction, is a *calamity* whether or not it be attended by loss of life.

Calculate. In the sense of *surmise, think, guess*, or *judge at random*, this word is a provincialism and is to be avoided: "I *think* (not *calculate*) tomorrow will be a fine day" but "His next move was *calculated* (that is, *designed*) to discourage his opponents."

Caliber. Often misused for *order*, as in "His work is of a higher *caliber* than hers." *Caliber* in its figurative sense applies to mental endowments. Thus, we may speak of a woman possessing great intellectual ability as being a person of *high caliber*, and of her work as being of high order, or excellent.

Can but, Cannot but. See *But*.

Can, May. Frequently confused. *Can* expresses power or ability; in most cases *may* expresses permission. Avoid "*Can* I speak to you a moment?" When you know that you *can speak* but wish merely for permission to do so, then substitute *may* for *can*. But, "*Can* you go?" is correct when the inquirer senses the possibility of obstacles that might prevent going; "*May* you go?" is also correct if permission to do so is involved.

Can not. Commonly and correctly written *cannot*. The origin of this form is in the shortened colloquial pronunciation of the two words.

Can't hardly. As *hardly* means "*not* easily" or "*not* quite," it must never be used with another negative as in this phrase. Substitute *can hardly*: "I *can hardly* believe the story."

Can't seem. Such an expression as "I *can't seem* to understand this problem" is to be avoided. Say, "I *seem unable* to understand." The inability is not in the *seeming* but in the *understanding*.

Capable, Susceptible. *Capable* is said of one's ability to do things, and in general it applies to the individual as having the capacity or intelligence to do; *susceptible* connotes action upon or sensitiveness to. Plans are *susceptible* of alteration; we are all *susceptible* to pain, that is, *capable* of being acted upon by it. One man may be *capable* of judging the fitness of another to fill a vacancy, yet he may not be *susceptible* to the blandishments of the applicant.

Capacity, Ability. These words are frequently confused. *Capacity* is the power of receiving or containing, and is used of the ability of the mind to accept ideas; it is the receptive mental faculty. *Ability* is power, either bodily or mental, and the word is sometimes used to describe mental endowments, or talents, of a superior kind. Some men possess the *ability* to help others although they have not the *capacity* to better their own conditions.

Carry. Provincial in the sense of *take, bring*, as in a carriage; as, "Father *carried* us all home with him." The word is archaic in the sense of *escort*: "He *carried* us to the party." Prefer "He *escorted* (*accompanied*) us."

Carry on. The phrase is in rather common colloquial use to mean "playing or behaving boisterously or indiscreetly." The World War gave us an intensified form of an old colloquial meaning, "maintain spirit and courage" or "keep work going in spite of difficulties."

Casuality, Causality, Casualty. *Casuality* is an obsolete word meaning the "condition or quality of being casual (accidental)"; *causality* is an agency that causes, or is the relation of cause and effect; a *casualty* is an accident.

Chairman. Correct usage sanctions *Mr. Chairman* and *Madam Chairman* as forms in which to address a presiding officer.

Claim. This word, as a verb, means "ask for" or "demand" by virtue of some authority or right, as in "We *claim* our share of the estate." It should not be used loosely for *say, assert, declare*, or *maintain*, as in "They *claim* that the water of the lake is warm."

Cleave. There are in English two verbs of this spelling but they are of different origins. The first, *cleave*, derived from the Anglo-Saxon *clifian*, means "adhere" or "unite": "The skin *cleaves* to the bones." The second, *cleave*, derived from the Anglo-Saxon *clēofan*, means "split" or "hew": "We can *cleave* our way through the rocks." *Cleave* is sometimes wrongly used with *from*, in the intransitive sense of *separate* or *peel*.

Clever. As used in the sense of *good-natured* or *kindly*, this word is dialectal: "She is a *clever* woman." The commonly accepted sense today is *skillful, dexterous*, or *quick*. The word is used of mental alertness or mechanical ability. See *Synonyms*.

Clipped Endings. The practice of "*clipping*" the ending *-ing* is a vulgar error, as in *talkin', walkin', comin'*.

Close. This word is in colloquial use as meaning "stingy." *Near* and *nigh* are dialectal or provincial in a similar sense.

Coke Fiend. This is a vulgarism for an unfortunate individual addicted to cocaine or morphine. The recently introduced *addict* is the correct word to use. *Coke fiend* is in the same class as *rum hound* or *booze fighter*.

Commandeer. This word originated in South Africa during the Boer war. Its military meaning is "to compel to perform military service or to take for military purposes." As meaning "to take arbitrarily" it is in colloquial use only, the word *levy* or *requisition* being preferred by some as the literary term.

Company. The word is disapproved when used to mean "guests." Some writers look upon it as less formal, and therefore preferable, but no better word than *friends* need be used to express the intimacy of informal occasions. "The *company* has come" is decidedly provincial. "Our *friends* are here" and "The *guests* have arrived" serve to mark different degrees of formality.

Company, Corporation, Firm. With *company* or *firm*, either a singular or a plural verb is permissible; the word *corporation* takes a singular verb. A *corporation* is considered only as a unity, while one may think of a *company* or a *firm* either as a unit or as a number of partners.

Compared to, with. We may *compare* one thing *with* another in discussing the relative merits of both, but we *compare* one thing *to* another to point out some likeness: "*Compare* dead happiness *with* living woe." "*Compare* my life *with* his." "Life is *compared to* a voyage."

Comparison. In the *superlative degree*, comparison implies the inclusion of the things compared in a single group; in the *comparative degree* the things compared are thought of as in separate groups: *best of all; better than others*. See *Any, As, Else, Of*.

Complected. This is a dialectal word to be avoided. Say, "She is *dark-* (or *fair-*) *complexioned* (not *complected*)." Better still is the form, "She is of a dark (or fair) complexion." Frequently the simple "She is fair (or dark)" will serve.

Compliment, Complement. These words, so nearly alike and of the same origin, should not be confused. We say correctly, "They paid me the *compliment* of close attention" and "The ship had her *complement* (full number) of officers."

Comprised, Composed. These words are frequently confused. *Comprised* means "included"; *composed* means "made up" or "put together." We say correctly, "The ship's company *comprised* men of many nationalities," but "The bricks are *composed* of sand and clay."

Condign. This word seems to be commonly mistaken for *severe*, whereas it really means "well worthy," that is, "merited," "suitable," "deserved," or "fitting." In "They should receive *condign* punishment," the intention is to say that the punishment should adequately meet the offense; for "*condign* punishment" may be lenient or severe.

Condone. The word should not be used for *compensate* or *atone*: "The abolition of the income tax would more than *compensate* (not *condone*) for the turmoil of an election." *Condone* means "forgive tacitly" or "overlook": "For the sake of tranquillity we *condone* many public faults."

Conferring. We speak correctly of the *conferring* of a degree or other honor, not using *conference* for this meaning. The form *conferment* is possible but unusual.

Conscious, Aware. *Conscious* applies to the workings of one's mind and to what it may produce; *aware* refers to things outside. One is *conscious* of joy or of pain, of a thought or of reminiscence, of a sensation, of cold, or of hunger; but one is *aware* of, that is, "sensible of," danger or of an approaching object.

Consequence. Etymologically, "a following together" and, from its original sense, "that which follows as a result of something that has preceded it." By an inversion, it has come to be used to signify importance or prominence acquired, as through the exercise of an office or through the ownership of land. Though some critics condemn this use of the word, it is authoritatively recognized and is logically sound: "He was a man of some *consequence* in his district."

Consider. The correct meaning of this word is "meditate," "deliberate," "reflect," "revolve in the mind." It should not be made to do service for *think, suppose,* and *believe*; as, "I *consider* that I have a bargain." This use, though frequent, is inappropriate.

Considerable. Frequently misused. Its association is with abstract rather than with concrete terms. A rich man may be one of *considerable* wealth, but we should not describe him as having *considerable* money. "We have had *considerable* rain" should be avoided. Prefer "an *abundance* of rain" or, more succinctly, "*plentiful* rain."

Co-operate together. A tautological phrase, for *co-* connotes *together*, or *with*, and *co-operate* means "operate with" or "work together."

Couple. The use of *couple* to mean merely "two" or "several" is vulgar or dialectal. The word correctly means "two like things or two persons acting in concert or so joined as to act together or to be considered together," as two mechanical parts or two partners in a dance.

Credible, Creditable. The latter word should not be used instead of *credible,* "believable." Say, "two *credible* (not *creditable*) witnesses." Say, "I am *credibly* (not *creditably*) informed." Formerly, *creditable* meant "credible," but this use is obsolete. It now means "commendable."

Curious. This word does not always mean "inquisitive," but frequently signifies "wrought with such care as to excite surprise" or "fashioned in such a way as to evoke surprise." The use of *curious* to mean "interesting," "unusual," or "novel" is sometimes condemned, but it is in good taste: "The museum possesses a collection of *curious* ornaments."

Dangerous. This word is misused in the sentence "He is *dangerous,*" when we mean "He is sick." Say, "He is not in *danger*" or "He is not *dangerously* ill."

Dare not. If a contraction must be made, prefer *daren't* to *daresn't* or the vulgar *dassent.* The general preference for *dare not* rather than *dares not* is for the sake of euphony, though a feeling for the subjunctive sense of *dare* may have an influence in the matter, prompting the use of the subjunctive form; as, "I think he *dare not* go." See *Subjunctive Mode.*

Data, Memoranda, Strata. These words are the plural forms of *datum, memorandum,* and *stratum,* but are sometimes construed erroneously as singulars: "The *datum* (singular) is here"; "The *data* (plural) are all here"; "This *memorandum* is clear"; "These *memoranda* are correct." To form the plural, an *s* has sometimes been added to the words *stratum, memorandum,* but never to *datum. Stratum,* being a technical word, should be more carefully used and its plural be written *strata.*

Deceiving. This should not be used in place of *trying to deceive.* When we suspect deception but are not *deceived,* we should say, not "He is *deceiving* me," but "He is *trying to deceive* me."

Demand. A transitive verb which always requires an object. We *demand* the payment of a debt. Do not say, "He *demanded* me to do it." Say, "He *demanded* that I should do it." "It" stands for the thing or act required. "They *demanded* their pay" is correct. The direct object of *demand* must be other than the person *of,* or *upon,* whom the demand is made.

Demean. While this word, in the sense of *debase* or *humble,* is in wide literary as well as colloquial use, especially in England, it is disapproved by American critics as "lacking in distinction."

Deprecate, Depreciate. These words should not be confused. *Deprecate* means "regret," "express disapproval of": "His friends *deprecated* his hasty action." *Depreciate* means to "undervalue" or "decrease in value": "They *depreciated* the value of freedom"; "That stock has *depreciated* very greatly."

Desperately. The word should not be used to mean merely "seriously." It means "violently," "recklessly," "in a desperate manner." "He was *desperately* wounded" means wounded so seriously that he was beyond apparent hope of recovery.

Despite. This word may be preceded by *in* and followed by *of,* although *despite* has good standing as a preposition. Say, "*despite* all our efforts" or "*in spite of* all our efforts." *Notwithstanding* is a more dignified expression and has the same meaning.

Differ, Different. Persons or things *differ from* each other in appearance, size, etc. Persons may *differ with* each other in opinion. *Different from* is approved American usage, not *different to* or *different than,* both of which are accepted idioms in England, having substantial literary support, as of Goldsmith, John Henry Newman, and Thackeray. Shakspere used *different from.*

Direct, Call. *To direct* some one's attention to a thing is more accurate and specific than *to call* his attention to a thing.

Directly, Immediately. The use of *directly* as a synonym for *immediately* is sanctioned by good usage, though some critics pronounce it colloquial. One may say, "We will proceed *immediately* the train arrives" or "*immediately* after the train arrives." American usage prefers *immediately.* English usage favors *directly.*

Dirty. Refinement in speech prompts the use of the word *soiled* for ordinarily grimy and stained objects, saving the stronger word for really *dirty* or foul occasions. Although *dirty* is sometimes used correctly to characterize a base, mean, or despicable act, and we shall always hear of "*dirty* tricks," persons of refined instincts should encourage the use of *base* or *mean* instead. Avoid "washing their *dirty* linen in public" as coarse.

Disapproval. Say, "He expressed *disapproval of* (not *with*) the dance."

Dissent. This word should be followed by *from*: "They *dissent from* our judgment." "They *dissent from* us." Compare *Differ.*

Dive. The past tense of this verb is *dived.* The form *dove* in colloquial use is a dialectal form occasionally met in formal writing, and is based on faulty analogy with *drive, drove; thrive, throve.*

Do. This word has many idiomatic uses, which should be studied with the aid of a dictionary. Careful speakers select the most appropriate terms. "I am *done* with the book" should be "I have *done* (that is, *finished*) with the book" or, colloquially, "I am through with it."

Dock, Wharf. A *wharf* is a landing stage or pier; a *dock* is a body of water beside a *wharf* or between *wharves.* In American practice, *dock* is misused for *wharf.* Originally, *wharf* meant "bank" or "shore," and *dock* meant "ditch," "pit," or "pool." The distinction is more clearly apparent when one refers to the different forms of *dock* as *dry* or *graving dock, floating* and *wet dock.*

Don't, Doesn't. The first is a colloquial contraction for *do not*; the second, for *does not.* They should be used with care. Avoid "He *don't* want it." Say: "They *don't,*" or "He *doesn't* want it."

Don't hardly. The expression "I *don't hardly* think they will go" is tautological, for *hardly* means "not quite" or "not easily." Say, "I *don't think* they will go," or "I *hardly think* they will go."

Don't think. "I *don't think* it will rain" is an established idiom, as are other similar expressions in use.

Dope. A word to be avoided. *Addict* is preferable to *dope fiend.* In a slang use *dope* means "material" or "information": "I gave him the *dope* for that article." Avoid also "I *doped* it out," meaning "thought" or "mapped," as vulgar.

Double Possessive. This construction is accepted as idiomatic English. Such phrases as "that house *of Brown's*" and "that car *of mine*" show the double possessive and may be used if required, but "*Brown's* house" and "*my* car" will usually express the thought more economically.

Dozen, Dozens. After indications of price, *a dozen* or *the dozen* is correct. In American usage *a dozen* is preferred: "fifty cents *a dozen.*" The phrases, "a pair," "a gross," "a tale," are used in like manner. Correctly we say, "several (or many) *dozens*"; but, when linked with definite numbers or used with *pairs, dozen* is the approved form, as, "four *dozen* pairs." See *Pair.*

Drowned. Avoid *drownded* as illiterate. The correct forms of the verb are *drown, drowned, drowning, drowned.*

Due to. That which may be attributed to a cause is *due to* it, but, to express *cause* or *reason, due to* should be used *only when modifying a noun or standing as complement*: "His failure was *due to* unusual conditions" or "Failure *due to* the unusual conditions was not expected." Do not say, "He failed *due to* unusual conditions," but "His failure was *due to*, etc." or "He failed *because of* or *owing to* unusual conditions."

Each other. Properly applied to two only; *one another* must be used when the number referred to exceeds two. We say, "Great authors address themselves to *one another*," unless we refer to only two authors.

Eat, Ate, Eaten. These are the correct parts of the verb. Say, "He *ate* rapidly"; "I have *eaten* my dinner."

Effect, Affect. *Effect* means "bring about"; *affect* means "influence": "A man may *effect* a reform." "His ideas will *affect* the character of the reform." *Affect* may mean "pretend": "They *affect* an interest in the matter."

Egoism, Egotism. One may be an *egoist*, that is, may habitually advocate the doctrine of *egoism*, or the pursuit of self-interest, as the supreme aim of human effort, and yet he may not be an *egotist. Egotism* is offensive conceit.

Either, Each, Both. Note the following correct expressions: "You may enter by *either* door (meaning *one* or the *other*)." "A bench is placed at *each* side of the doorway (that is, one on *one* side, one on the *other*)." "There were windows on *both* sides (or *each* side) of the doorway." Formerly, *either* was widely used in the sense of *each*, but this use is rare today.

Elicit, Illicit. *Elicit* is a verb, meaning "draw out," "discover": "By questioning him we *elicited* the information." *Illicit*, an adjective, means "*illegal*" and "not allowed": "They operated an *illicit* still."

Else, Else's. Such an expression as "Do not take *anyone else's* place" is good form and to be preferred to "Do not take *anyone's else* place," which has some defenders but is not accepted as sterling.

Else but. Avoid the use of *else* before *but* in the expression "I have no one *else but* you."

Emigrant, Immigrant. *Emigrants* are persons *going out* of a country, and *immigrants* are persons *coming into* it. *Emigrate* is derived from the Latin *e*, "out," and *migrare*, "to go from the land"; *immigrate*, from the Latin *im* for *in*, "into," and *migrare.*

Eminent, Imminent. Two words of similar sound but of widely different meanings. *Eminent* signifies "distinguished" or "well known": "He has become *eminent* in his profession." *Imminent* means "about to happen" or "threatening": "The defeat of the army was *imminent.*"

Enclose, Inclose. The history of these words as well as general English usage favors *enclose* rather than *inclose.* But most recent dictionaries give *inclose* the preference. Either is correct.

Endorse, Indorse. Either form is correct, but, while *endorse* is used in literature, *indorse* finds favor in law and commerce. Do not say, "I *endorse* the movement." Say, "I *approve* it." Do not say, "*Indorse* the check *on the back.*" Omit the last three words. *Indorse* means to write one's name *on the back* of commercial paper or documents.

Enjoyed the advantage. Trite phrase, elaborate and cumbersome substitute for "had."

Enthuse. The use of this word as meaning "inspire" or "give or gain inspiration or enthusiasm" is generally disapproved.

Equally as well. An incorrect phrase. *As well* and *equally well* are correct forms.

Everlastingly. The word means "in a manner lasting forever," "perpetually," "eternally," and should not be used when *repeatedly* is meant. Do not say, "The horse was *everlastingly* running away."

Ever so, Never so. *Ever so* is correctly used to mean "exceedingly." Both phrases are used to mean "however" or "no matter how," as in "were he *ever so* (or *never so*) rich." Modern usage prefers *ever so* in all such cases.

Except. Formerly, this word was used as a conjunction for *unless*; as, "I will not go *except* you go with me." This is no longer good usage.

Excuse, Pardon. While *pardon* is the more formal official word in respect to offenses, and *excuse* the more familiar in respect to minor matters, a further distinction is to be noted. For instance, when interrupting a conversation, one says, "*Pardon* the interruption," and, when leaving a guest, "*Excuse* me."

Exemption, Immunity. One claims *exemption* from taxes or from duty; one acquires *immunity* from disease, as by inoculation, or is granted *immunity* from punishment.

Exercise, Exorcise. Do not use these words interchangeably. *Exercise* means "put into use, action, or practice"; *exorcise* means "cast or drive out" (as evil spirits), by religious or magical formulas or ceremonies.

Expect. As this word means "look forward to as a contingency," it should never be used of any retrogression, for one cannot *expect* baskwards. Not, "I *expect* you thought I would come yesterday," but "I *suppose*, etc." "I *expect* you know all about it" should be "*imagine*," "*think*," or "*suspect* you know." But "We *expect* that they will come" or "We *expect* them" is correct. Compare *Anticipate.*

Extempore, Impromptu. An *extempore* address is one delivered without manuscript and without memorization, though previous preparation may have been made by thought upon the subject treated. An *impromptu* speech is given on the moment, without previous preparation.

Extend. "They *showed* me every kindness" is better than "They *extended* every kindness to me." But, in such phrases as *extend sympathy* and *extend hospitality,* meaning "bestow" or "impart," that is, "show by words or deeds," the word is in good use.

Farther, Further. Careful speakers and writers use *farther* for distances in space and *further* for continuity of other kinds: "We walked *farther* today than yesterday"; "The chairman said *further* (that is, *in addition*) that all dues must be paid promptly." *Further,* then, is used for expressions of continuity, as of thought or action: "I had no *further* dealings with him"; "a *further* rise in temperature."

Fascinating. As that which *fascinates* operates on its object as by some irresistible power, *fascinating* should not be used when *charming* or *attractive* is meant. Properly, that is *fascinating* or *bewitching* which possesses the art to please beyond the power of resistance; as, "Her *fascinating* manner and words disarmed suspicion."

Faulty Comparisons. Avoid double comparatives and superlatives. Say, "*worse,*" not "*worser*"; "*abler,*" not "*more abler.*" Avoid impossible comparisons. Say, "*more nearly perpendicular, more nearly universal,*" not "*more perpendicular, more universal.*" Use the comparative degree for two objects, the superlative for more than two.

Fearful. A much overworked word. The meanings of the nouns from which such words as *dreadful, terrible,* and *fearful* are derived should always be borne in mind when the adjectives are used. The colloquial use of these words to express intense feeling or annoyance easily passes into extravagant hyperbole. Do not describe the falling of a horse as a *terrible* but rather as a *serious* accident. "He was *fearful* for our safety," that is, "He *feared* that we were in danger" is correct.

Felicitate, Facilitate. We *felicitate* or *congratulate* people on success; we *facilitate* or *make easier* their progress toward their destination.

Female. In polite speech this word is restricted to sex or to animals. When applied to women it is derogatory, and it should not be used in such expressions as "What is more delightful than the blush of a beautiful young *female*!"

Fewer, Less. *Fewer* refers to number; *less,* to quantity. Instead of "There were not *less* than ten chapters in the book," we should say, "There were not *fewer* than ten chapters in the book." But say, "The box weighed not *less* than ten pounds."

Fine. An adjective which should not be used as an adverb. Do not say, "She sang that *fine,*" when you mean "well." "I like that *fine*" and "He is doing *fine*" are incorrect. Say, "I like that *well* or *very much*" and "He is doing *well* or *very well.*"

First. When used in conjunction with other numerals, *first* should always precede not follow them: "Take the *first two* plates off the rack," not "the *two first.*" There is but one *first.*

First-rate. Do not use this adjective as an adverb. "She plays *first-rate*" is a vulgarism. *First-rate* means "of the highest excellence or quality." "He is a man of *first-rate* ability" is correct.

Fix. Often misused colloquially for *arrange* or *repair*: "I must *fix* the books." "Who *fixed* the dishes on the shelves?" "He had the clock *fixed.*" It is vulgarly used thus: "I will *fix* him"; "The jury was *fixed*"; "You must *fix* up, if you go"; "Your affairs are in a bad *fix.*" *Fix* means "fasten," "make firm," or "settle": "The hooks are *fixed* in the wall." "Their income is a *fixed* amount."

Folk, Folks. Often incorrectly used interchangeably. Both words are construed as plurals, but the first refers to *people* or *peoples* generally, as "folk tales" or "fairy folk." In colloquial usage, *folks* has displaced *folk.* In "My *folks* have gone South," *folks* signifies "relatives." In "the *folks* next door," the word means "neighbors."

Forceful, Forcible. We speak of a "*forceful* style" or a "*forceful* personality," but of *forcible* ejection or *forcible* action of any kind. In usage, *forcible* is the more common word, and *forceful* the more special one.

Former—Latter. These words should be used only when they really economize space and save the reader's time. By repeating the antecedents (nouns or phrases), one avoids sending the reader back to see which is *former* and which is *latter.* Sometimes, however, a disagreeable repetition is avoided by using "the *former*—the *latter.*"

Funny. A word too frequently used when humor or amusement is not meant. Of something unusual, use *strange, odd, peculiar,* or a similar accurate word instead of *funny*: "It was a *peculiar* situation," not "*funny*" unless it is laughable.

Get, Got, Have. *Get,* like *do,* has many different meanings and is carelessly used. Avoid *get* for *be* and especially such expressions as "She will *get* laughed at for her pains." Say rather, "She will *be* laughed at, etc." If a man has inherited a fortune and has not dissipated it, we say correctly, "He *has* money"; if he obtains money through his own effort, we say correctly, "He *has gotten* money."

"*Get* a move on" is a forceful but inelegant Americanism for "Be quick about it."

Do not say, "*Get* up a show" when you mean plan or prepare. Colloquially, a *get-up* is an equipment consisting of dress and accessories and is very frequently correctly used, as in "a clever *get-up*" or "a stylish *get-up.*" Avoid "Do you *get* me?" as the height of vulgarity.

"He *has got* to do it" is a common colloquialism. "He *has got* it to do" shows the wasteful character of the phrase. "He *has* it to do," "He *must* do it," or "He *has* to do it" is correct. We may, however, say correctly, "The cat *has got* the mouse," but "*caught* the mouse" is preferable.

Both *got* and *gotten* are correct forms of *get,* but careful writers tend to avoid *gotten.* As William Lyon Phelps said, "*Gotten* has *got* to go."

Get, meaning "become," is colloquial: "He will *get* well"; "as we *get* older."

Goes. In the phrase "anything *goes*" we have slang; in "the machine *goes*" we have idiomatic English. "That *goes* without saying" is a literal translation of a French idiom, in colloquial use.

Going to. "We are *going to* do it" is correct idiom. Do not say "*gonta.*" Avoid "Where are you *going to*?" in which the *to* is redundant.

Good. The use of the adjective *good* for the adverb *well* is vulgar. Avoid "I feel *good*" and "He is working *good.*" Say rather: "I feel *well*"; "He is working *well.*"

Grand. That which is *grand* is "magnificent," "noble," or "splendid," yet there is strong tendency to misapply the word. Today anything from a bit of chewing gum to Mt. Shasta is described as *grand.* The word should be used only of that which possesses grandeur.

Great. The indiscriminate use of this word is evidence of a poverty-stricken vocabulary: "We had a *great* time" is a colloquialism; "I like it *great*" is a vulgarism.

Had. "*Had* I thought of that, I should have come." This sentence is correct; but the common practice of inserting *have* after the pronoun is reprehensible. Shun "*Had* I have known," "*Had* I've known," "If I *had've,*" "If I *had of* (*uv*)," if you wish to avoid being classed as illiterate.

Had better, as in "He *had better* look out," is excellent English idiom.

Had ought is a solecism for *should have. Ought* is not a participle. Say, "We *should have* or we *ought,*" not "We *had ought.*"

Hanged, Hung. Criminals are *hanged,* clothes are *hung.* This is an old distinction, still in force.

Hardly. This adverb is correctly followed by *when,* not *than,* as in "We had *hardly* taken our seats *when* the boat began to leak." The use of hardly with a negative, as in "I *can't hardly* tell," is a solecism. "I *can hardly* tell" is correct.

Hate. A word that signifies "having a great aversion for," but used colloquially for *dislike:* "I *hate* to do that kind of work." *Hate* is too strong a word for such use. Say, "I *dislike* to do that kind of work" or "I *detest* that kind of work."

Haven't but. A solecism, for it contradicts itself. "I have *but* a dollar" means "I have *only* a dollar," which is what is intended when one says, "I *haven't but* a dollar." *Haven't but* means "have not only."

Have to have. Avoid this useless repetition. Not, "I *have to have* my work done by three o'clock," but "I *must have* my work, etc." Do not say, "I have *got to get*" when "I *have to get*" is what you should say.

Healthful, Healthy. Note the distinction in meaning between these words. *Healthful* is applied to conditions or environments: "Children should be reared in *healthful* surroundings." *Healthy* describes a good physical condition, without disease. "A *healthy* mind in a *healthy* body is desirable."

Hear to it. We "*hear of*" an incident or "will not *hear of*" a course being pursued, but *hear to it* is archaic. *Hear* signifies "listen to"; formerly, "He will not *hear to* reason" was accepted as idiomatic, but it is now rendered "He will not *listen to* reason."

Hearty. "He ate a *hearty* breakfast" is good English idiom. *Hearty* means "strengthening" and "satisfying."

Hectic. A word which specifically means "habitual," "constitutional," being derived from the Greek *hexis,* "habit of body"; but it has come to mean "flushed" as with fever, or affected with such fever as accompanies tuberculosis. It is often misapplied, as in "*hectic* haste," in the sense of *feverish* or *excited.*

Heighth. A corrupt form due to confusion with *width, length,* and *breadth.* The correct word is *height.*

Hence, Thence, Whence. These words connote *removal from;* therefore, they should not be used with *from. Hence* is superfluous in such a sentence as "It will be many years *hence,* we apprehend, before he returns."

Hisself. A vulgar substitute for *himself.* Similarly, *theirselves* is an error for *themselves:* "He went *himself*"; "They wanted it for *themselves.*" See *Pronouns.*

Home. We say correctly, "*go home,*" but the phrases *stay home* and *be home* are not approved. *Stay at home* and *be at home* are better. One should never be *to home. Be home* in the sense of *return* is, however, an allowable colloquialism: "He will *be home* soon."

How. "I have heard *how,* in Italy, one is beset on all sides by beggars" should read "I have heard *that,* in Italy, etc." But "He told me *how* he worked his passage" is correct, since the reference is not to the fact, as in the first sentence, but to the manner of action.

How that and *as how,* as in "He told *how that* he would never return" or "He said *as how* he would go," are most objectionable colloquialisms.

However. Frequently misused for *how,* in such a sentence as "*However* could you tell such a story!" One should say, "*How* could you *ever* tell such a story!" *However* means "no matter what the extent of." "*However* careful you may be, you will make mistakes" is correct.

Hustle. Properly this word means "shove," "push," or "jostle roughly." Although frequently used colloquially for *hurry,* as in "*Hustle* that order along," it is not properly a synonym for *hurry.*

I, Me. These forms of the personal pronoun of the first person are frequently confused. *Me* is the form to use with a preposition. Say "between you and *me,*" not "between you and *I.*" Similarly, "with her (him) and *me,*" not "with she (he) and *I.*"

If. *Whether* in place of *if* is preferred by most authorities in sentences like these: "I do not know *if* (*whether*) the book will suit you"; "I wonder *if* (*whether*) he has come." The use of *if* for *whether* is colloquial or poetic.

Ill, Sick. English usage confines the word *sick* chiefly to the meaning "nausea," as, *a sick headache;* but in America *ill* and *sick* are generally synonymous. However, we say: "He is a *sick* man," never "He is an *ill* man"; but, either "He is *ill*" or "He is *sick.*"

In, Into. *In* is sometimes an adverb and sometimes a preposition, but its employment as an adverb is really an elliptical use of the preposition. As an adverb, *in* is correctly used in these sentences: "Come *in,*" for here *in* means "into the house, room, etc."; and likewise, "Go *in,*" meaning "Go into the room, house, etc." As a preposition, *in* may be used with verbs of rest or of motion and *into* with verbs of motion only: "He sat *in* his chair"; "The child runs *in* the yard"; "He walked *into* the house."

Inaugurate. A word that connotes solemn induction with appropriate ceremonies. It should not be used for *begin* or *institute,* properly applied to the simple things of daily life. It is a noble word suited only to high office.

In back of. The expression "They sat *in back of* us," meaning "behind," though analogous to "They sat *in front of* us," is disapproved. *Behind* accurately expresses the thought. As to *in front of,* we have no corresponding preposition, since *before* may convey the idea of *facing* and thus may produce ambiguity.

Incite, Insight. *Incite* means "to rouse to a particular action": "The mob was *incited* to riot." *Insight* is a noun and means "the power or faculty of immediate and acute perception or understanding": "The best *insight* we obtain into nature is that which we gain through careful first-hand observation."

Indict, Indite. Though pronounced alike, these words are very different in meaning. *Indict* means "charge formally with crime": "The jury *indicted* him for murder." *Indite* means "write" or "compose." See *Word Building.*

Individual. The word is jocosely or contemptuously used for *person.* It is used correctly in "Changes both in *individuals* and in communities are often produced by trifles"; contemptuously in "That *individual* left here several hours ago."

Indulge. This word means "give oneself up to (something)"; "yield to one's longings or passions unrestrainedly"; "give free course to one's habits"; "humor to excess, as children." Thus, one *indulges* in idleness, or one *indulges* children's whims or wishes. While one may *indulge* a thirst for fame, one should avoid "I never *indulge*" as objectionable in declining an offer of refreshment.

Infer, Imply. These words are frequently confused. One *infers* or *reasons* or *draws a conclusion* from something heard or read. One may *imply* (*suggest*) in what one writes or says, for example "One *infers* from what Jefferson wrote that the Declaration of Independence *implies* belief in democracy."

-ing. See *Clipped Endings*.

Ingenious, Ingenuous. *Ingenious* means "skillful," "inventive": "The boy is *ingenious* and loves machinery." *Ingenuous* means "candid," "frank," "open," "innocent," "guileless": "He made an *ingenuous* reply."

Innumerable number. The phrase is tautological. Therefore it should not be used. Say, "a *countless number*," that is, a number incapable of computation. Avoid "an *innumerable number* of times"; say instead, "*innumerable* times" or "*numberless* times."

In our midst. Condemned by most critics as a substitute for *in the midst of* (*us*). The purist prefers *among us*.

In so far as. A phrase formed on the analogy of *in as much as*, but *so far as* expresses the thought and *far* is itself an adverb; therefore *in* is superfluous. "*In so far as* I know" should be "*so far as* I know." In "in as much as," *much* is a noun and requires a preposition to give the phrase adverbial force.

Intend. See *Mean*.

Interesting. This is a word to beware of, for it is frequently used equivocally or ironically. When something is said that is *not at all interesting* to the hearer, he may take refuge behind "How *interesting*!" or "That is *very interesting*."

In or **Under the circumstances.** Both phrases are in good use. *Circumstances* may imply merely attendant conditions not thought of as seriously modifying action. *In* is then the proper preposition; as, "*In the circumstances* he hesitated." But when *action* is thought of as determined by the circumstances, as, "*Under the circumstances* prosecution of the case could not be avoided," *under* is the approved word.

Irrelevant. The word means "unconnected with" or "not related to": "His remarks were *irrelevant* to the discussion." Do not pronounce it *irrevelant*.

Is that so? Courtesy will prompt a thoughtful person to be careful *how* and *when* he uses this and the similar phrase, "You don't say so," for they imply doubt or disbelief as well as express surprise. As subject to equivocal interpretation they should be avoided. "I want to know," used in a similar sense, is vulgar.

Junk. Colloquial or slang when used as a verb for *discard*, or "throw away as useless."

Just. This adverb is correctly used for *precisely, only, merely*, or *by a slight margin*; it is colloquial when the meaning is "quite," "very," "altogether," or "simply." Say, "I *just* missed the car," but not "The hostess was *just* lovely, but the food was *just* awful." Such a statement is ambiguous.

Just going to. Instead of "I was *just going to* go," one may better say, "*just about to* go" and so avoid repetition of the word *go*. Such expressions as "I was *just going to* make the same remark" and "We are *just going to* visit our friends" are good idiomatic English, although they border on the colloquial.

Killing. *Perfectly killing*, like *perfectly dear*, belongs to the class of extravagant slang.

Kind. The word is singular. One should say, "this *kind*," not "these *kind*." But "those *kinds*," not "those *kind*," is correct.

Kind of. Avoid the use of *a* as a modifier before a noun when preceded by *kind of*. "What *kind of* man is he?" is correct. "What *kind of a* man is he?" is incorrect.

Kind of tired, amusing, etc., are slovenly speech. *Somewhat tired, rather amusing*, are preferred.

Lady. Address a woman who is a stranger to you as *Madam*, and not as *Lady*. Persons of culture do not say, "She is a fine *lady*," "a clever *lady*"; they use *woman* instead. Ladies say, "The *women* of America," "*women's* interests." In like manner use *man* or *men* instead of *gentleman* or *gentlemen*.

Last, Latest. We speak of an author's *latest* book, but hardly of his *last* book until he is dead. But we say properly, "Have you read the *last* number of this magazine?" Here *last* means "latest in a series."

Last two. This phrase is preferred by most authorities to *two last*: "They bought the *last two* copies."

Laundered. The clothes were *laundered*, not *laundried*.

Lay, Lie (verbs). *Lay* is transitive and denotes an *action* on an object; *lie* is intransitive and designates a *state* or a *condition*: "I *lay* the rug on the floor, and it *lies* there." "They *laid* him with his fathers." "He *lies* with his fathers." The following expressions are idiomatic: "A thing *lies* by us until we bring it into use"; "We *lay* it by for some future purpose."

The confusion arises probably from the fact that *lay* appears in both verbs. The words are correctly used in the following sentences:

I *lay* the book on the table today.
I *laid* it there yesterday.
I have *laid* it there every day.
I am *laying* it there now.
I *lie* on my bed today.
I *lay* there yesterday.
I have *lain* there every day.
I am *lying* there now.

Lay, Lie (nouns). Both of these words are in good use to signify the manner in which land *lies* in its relation to the surrounding country. "The *lay* of the land" is in popular favor; "the *lie* of the land" has the support of the scientists. The latter is the older English usage.

Learn, Teach. Formerly, *learn* and *teach* were used interchangeably, but now to confuse them is a mark of illiteracy. We *learn* things for ourselves; we try to *teach* others.

Leave, Let. One takes one's *leave*, after a call or visit. We ask *leave* or *permission*. One is *on leave*, that is, enjoying a permitted absence from his usual place of duty. Do not say "*Leave* him do it," but "*Let* him do it." Properly, one *leaves* (goes away from) a place, but he *lets* a person or thing alone, that is, does not meddle or interfere. Still, one correctly asks to be "*left* to himself," that is, asks others to "*leave*" or "go away from" him.

Lend, Loan. The verb *lend* is the general word to use when we supply something to another with the understanding that it is to be returned. Say, "*Lend* (not *loan*) me the books or money." The use of *loan* as a synonym for *lend*, although of English origin, has been condemned as an Americanism; but it has fallen into disuse except in financial circles. One says correctly, "He tried to get a *loan* from the bank," where *loan* is used as a noun. "The company *loans* money on good security"; here the word is used as a verb.

Less. See *Fewer*.

Let alone. A vulgarism when used to mean "excluding," "not to mention." Avoid such expressions as "The inconvenience was bad enough, *let alone* the expense."

Like, As. *Like* is not used for *as* in the New England States; the use is common in the South and the West. The phrase *like of that* should be avoided in "We spend our days fishing, canoeing, and the *like of that* (or *like that*)," for it is a vulgarism. Do not say: "Do *like* I do"; "I felt *like* I would faint"; "My feet were heavy *like*"; or "He had *liked* to have been killed," meaning "came near to being killed." Say: "Do *as* I do"; "I felt *as if*"; "My feet *seemed* heavy." But one may say, "She walks *like* a queen," meaning "in the manner of." To use the tautological phrase *like as if* is to display one's ignorance.

Like, Likely. The first is frequently erroneously used in conversation instead of the second. *Like* means "similar," "corresponding," "equal," and "resembling." *Likely*, as an adjective, means "probable," "suitable," "adaptable," or, adverbially, "to be reasonably expected." Avoid "He is *like* to call today" as illiterate. The following is correct: "In *like* circumstances, a repetition of the occurrence is *likely*."

Like, Love. See *Love*.

Listen! A word very much abused and overused in trying to arrest attention or to obtain a hearing on the telephone.

Loan. See *Lend*.

Locate. Colloquial for *settle* or *establish*. Prefer "He *settled* in Colorado"; "They *established* their business in Birmingham."

Lot, Lots. These words are in colloquial use for *much, many*; as, "a *lot* of money," "*lots* of people." Prefer "a *great deal* of money," "*much* money," "*many* people."

Love, Like. *Love* is a much abused English word. In modern practice *like* is used where taste is concerned and where no strong emotion is involved. One who delights in sweets is appropriately said to *like* candy. Of course one may *like* a person without *loving* him—that is, enjoy his companionship. We *love* wives, husbands, sweethearts, children, friends, truth, country.

Lunch, Luncheon. *Luncheon* is the more formal of these words. The first is a colloquial contraction of the second, and the second is the equivalent of the early English *noonshun*, spelled also *nunchion*, in which *nunch* means "a piece" or "morsel" of food; hence, "a bite."

Luxurious, Luxuriant. Do not confuse these words. The first describes that which is "gratifying to the senses"; the second means "growing in abundance." Correctly we speak of *luxurious* furnishings and of *luxuriant* foliage or vegetation.

Mad. When used to signify "very angry," this word is a careless colloquialism. *Mad* properly means "crazy."

Make a visit. The phrase is a provincialism. The correct word to use is *pay*: "One *pays* a visit to an acquaintance."

Manner, Manor. The correct phrase is *to the manner born*, not *to the manor born*. The phrase means "familiar with from birth."

Materialize. When used to mean "take shape" or "happen," the word is colloquial. Improperly used in the general sense of *appear*.

Mathematics. When considered as embracing the science of mathematics in its entirety as a concrete term, this word is construed with a verb in the singular; as, "*Mathematics is* the science that treats of quantities, their properties and relations, especially by the use of symbols"; "*Mathematics is* a subject in the course of study." But, when used distributively, to convey the idea of its different branches or divisions, the word is construed with a verb in the plural; as, "*Mathematics are* mere evolutions of necessary ideas." It should be borne in mind that mathematics are classified as *pure* or *abstract, applied* or *mixed*, and *qualitative*, as projective geometry.

Mean. Do not use *mean* as an adjective for *sick, unpleasant*, or *ashamed*. Say, "He felt *ashamed* of it," not "He felt *mean* about it."

Mean, Intend, Purpose. Best usage may be illustrated as follows: "By this statement I *mean*, etc."; "We *intend* to go"; "He *purposes* a thorough test of the machine." *Purpose* is a stronger word than *intend* and implies more careful thought.

Meet. To say, "*Meet* Mr. A.," when introducing a friend, is bad form. But we say correctly, "Have you ever *met* Mrs. B.?" meaning "been introduced to." Prefer "I want you to *meet* Mrs. A." or "May I introduce Mr. A.?"

Middling. This word is an adjective, meaning "moderate," and should not be used as an adverb; therefore, we should not say that a thing is *middling* good, or that a thing is *middling* well done. "He resided in a town of *middling* size" is correct, but "of *moderate* size" is preferable.

Mighty. When used instead of *exceedingly, very*, or *extremely*, this word is a colloquial intensive. Correctly used, *mighty* is a strong word indicating power of unusual force or quality; as, a *mighty* flood, a *mighty* monarch. It may connote uncommon size; as, *mighty* mountains.

Mind. Often misused for *obey*. To *mind* is to pay attention to and, colloquially, to attend to a thing so that it shall not be forgotten: "Will you *obey* me?" not "Will you *mind* me?" But, "*Mind* what I say"; "Never *mind* the difference, we'll balance accounts later."

Mistaken. The expression "If I am not *mistaken*," though sometimes condemned as incorrect, is idiomatic and has been in use for several centuries with the sense "If I am not making a *mistake*." "If I *mistake* not" is more formal, but it is thought by some to be stilted.

More than. Although its form implies plurality, this phrase is correctly construed as a singular: "*More than* one *is* there" or "There *is more than* one there."

Most. As a contraction of *almost*, this word is a provincialism: "The dress is *almost* (not *most*) finished." The use of *most* in the phrases *most perfect, most complete*, is sanctioned by good usage, on the ground that things are at best but relatively perfect or complete. Avoid the misuse of *most* in such colloquial forms as *most anybody* or *most anything*.

Move you. In submitting a motion for formal consideration by a deliberative body, "I *move* that, etc." is correct. It is not considered necessary to say, "I *move you* that, etc."

Muskrat. Do not say *mushrat*.

Mutual, Common. Recent writers do not insist so strongly upon the distinction between these two words. "We have *common* friends" or "We have *mutual* friends." *Mutual*, strictly, means "reciprocal," "existing between two parties"; but, because the meaning "ordinary" may be implied by the word *common*, many people prefer to say, "*mutual* friends," in spite of critics. There is, however, a clear and worth while distinction between the two words. *Common* means "belonging to all" as well as "ordinary." When we speak of a *mutual* friend we mean "one who reciprocates our friendship," and, when we refer to a *common* friend, we mean "one whose friendship we share in common with other friends of his." The sentence "We have many friends in *common*" illustrates the point clearly, and is a good substitute for "We have many *common* friends." Persons interested in the same things have *common* interests. When they are interested in each other, their interest is *mutual*.

Myself. This pronoun is an emphatic or reflexive form for the first person and should be used only where emphasis is required, as in "Who did it? I *myself*," that is, "I alone did it." It is incorrect to say, "Mary and *myself* were satisfied" or "Two friends and *myself* went." Say, "Two friends and I went" or "I went with two friends." Do not say, "*Myself*, I do not like it."

Near. When used to mean "almost," as in *near* beer, *near* great, the word takes on a rather forceful colloquial sense, but it is not in good literary use. It is a comment upon an era of "substitutes."

Never expect. In the sentence "I *never expect* to see them again," the position of *never* is incorrect. Here *never* modifies *see*. Say, "I expect *never* to see them again." But one may say, "The man is ill-bred; I *never expect* courtesy from him."

New. Distinguish between *new* and *novel*. That which is *new* may be *novel*, but that which is *novel* need not be *new*. Anything striking or *different* from things with which we are familiar may be called *novel*. To say "*new* beginner" seems to argue utter indifference to the sense of words. To be a beginner is quite sufficient.

Nice. This word means "exact" or "discriminating," not "pleasant" or "good." A *nice* distinction is one resulting from discriminating reasoning; one who is *nice* in regard to matters of food is fastidious and hard to please; *nice* food is inviting, dainty food. Anything that is done or made with scrupulous exactness, precision, or accuracy is termed *nice*; as, a *nice* balance, that is, an exact balance; *nice* workmanship, that is, the result of skilled labor.

Nicely. This word is frequently misused in the attempt to make it do service for *well*, in this wise: "How will this pen do?" "*Nicely*." "How are you?" "*Nicely*." Use *well* or *very well*, for *nicely* means "accurately," "becomingly," "exactly."

None. A word that may be used with a verb in either the singular or the plural, depending on the intention of the person who uses it; as, "*None* of *these* things *move* me"; "*None* but the brave *deserves* the fair."

Nor, Not. Use *nor* and not *or* after *no* when the definite exclusion of two distinct persons or things is intended; as, "He has *no* father *nor* mother." But we use *or* when the following word merely explains the preceding: "The boy has *no* father *or* guardian." After *not*, when the single negation applies to both objects, use *or:* "They do *not* see *or* hear." But say, "They do *not* come, *nor* do they intend to come," where two separate negations are implied. Here *nor* is, logically, the equivalent of *and not*. For logic, watch the position of *not*. Do not say, for example, "All Democrats are *not* Free Traders," but "*Not* all Democrats are Free Traders."

Notorious. The word is not to be confused with *notable* or *noted*, as it frequently is, for *notorious* implies discredit and has an unfavorable sense. It should not be used for *well known*.

No use. "It is *no use* to do that" should be "It is *of no use* to do that" or, preferably, "It is *useless* to do that."

Novice. See *Amateur*.

Nowhere. Do not say, "*nowhere* (or *nowheres*) near so much," because *nowhere* means "not in any place or anywhere" or, by extension, "at no time." "Not nearly so much" is correct.

Number. A word that can be correctly construed with a verb in the singular or the plural, depending on the idea to be expressed or the word on which emphasis is placed. We say correctly, when thinking of the individuals of a group, "A large *number were* (not *was*) there." Similarly, "There *are* a large *number* of people" or "There *are* many." But, if we intend to convey the idea of a unit, we say "The *number* of women present *was* small." When any phrase that has qualifying force seems to contradict in number the noun or verb with which it is used, an adjective should be substituted, so that the sentence shall correspond in form with the idea it is intended to convey. For example, "A *number* of changes *was* made," or "A *number* of changes *were* made." Better,—"*Numerous changes were* made."

Oblige. It is old fashioned to end a letter with the expression, "and *oblige*, Yours very truly." The expression is replaced now with "I am."

Observance, Observation. *Observe* the following distinction: "Close *observation* of our customs shows too little *observance* of Sunday and of patriotic anniversaries." *Observation* means "the act of looking at or examining," or the result of such action. *Observance* implies recognition, as with service or ceremony.

Of, Off. See *Prepositions*. The two words are from the same source and are subject to confusion in common speech.

When *of* follows a superlative, the thing referred to as best, largest, etc., is to be thought of as included in a whole group; hence the rule requiring *of all* in the following: "She was the loveliest *of all* (not *any*)." "He was the least observed *of all* (not *all others*)." *Any* and *others* imply separation of groups for comparison, and are used appropriately only with the comparative degree: "He was less observed than *any* of the others (who were observed—understood)." *Any* requires *other(s)* or *one else* or a similar expression to follow it.

Off of, Off from. *Of* or *from*, in these phrases, should be omitted from such a sentence as the following: "The pears fell *off* (*of*) (*from*) the tree." *Off* expresses the idea of separation. *Of* and *from* are superfluous.

O. K. This commercial expression is used as noun, adjective, and verb: "Give this your *O. K.* (approval)"; "His work is *O. K.* (all right, correct)"; "He refused to *O. K.* (approve) the order." Since *O. K.* as an adjective means "all right," do not say "all O. K.": "The requisition is *O. K.* (not *all O. K.*)."

Old Adage. See *Adage*.

One—One's. While purists insist that *one*, as in the sentence "*One* meets *one's* friends in the city," should be followed by *one's* and never by *her* or *his*, usage sanctions either form where no ambiguity would result. But after *anyone, every one, no one*, etc., use *he* (*his*) or *she* (*hers*): "*No one* knows where *he* will meet an acquaintance." Never use *they* (*their*) with *one* in such a sentence as "*Every one* makes *his* own choice," for *one* is singular. Do not say, "When *one* travels, *you* want pleasant companions," for *one* is a pronoun of the third person, and any following pronoun used in its place should be of the same person. Generally, avoid the use of *one* when a repetition of the word would be required.

Ones. Instead of saying, "I do not like the other *ones*," say, "I do not like the *others*." *Ones* is in good use only in such phrases as "big *ones*" and "little *ones*": "Here are big stones and little *ones*."

One time, Then. Such expressions as her *one time* guardian and the *then* bishop of New York are convenient, clear, and economical, and they are approved by good authority.

Only. This word is probably more often misplaced than any other word in the language. "He *only* sang for us." "He sang *only* for us." The first sentence means that he *sang*, but did not *play* for us; the second means that he sang for *us* and not for *anyone else. Only* is regularly placed before the word it modifies: "*Only* he (or *only* John) sang for us. That is, no one else sang.

Onto, On to. The use of *onto* in such expressions as "He got *onto* the platform with difficulty" is justified by good authority. This use follows the analogy of *upon, into,* and others implying motion. Some authorities do not yet allow *onto,* although they approve *on to,* but the two forms have quite distinct uses. One should not say, "He walked *onto* the next town," but "He walked *on to* the next town."

Oral, Verbal. *Verbal* means "in words," either *spoken* or *written*; *oral* means "uttered by the mouth," "spoken."

Other. This word should not be omitted from sentences like the following: "He said that his wife was dressed better than any *other* woman there." The omission of *other* makes the statement include the person spoken of in the group with which she is compared. In stating a comparison avoid comparing a thing with itself.

Ought, Should. *Ought* is the stronger term. What we *ought* to do, we are morally bound to do: We *ought* to be truthful and honest, and we *should* be respectful to our elders.

Over, Across. There is a nice distinction between these words: A dog walks *across* the street, but he leaps *over* an obstruction. *Across* suggests merely passage from one limit to another; *over* also implies elevation. See *Prepositions.*

Overlook, Oversee. *Overlook* means, usually, "miss seeing," "not notice": "He *overlooked* the important point." *Oversee* means "supervise." *Look over* may mean "examine."

Overly. The word is not in good use. Where it has been used, *over* may usually be substituted: "He is *overbold.*"

Over with. In this phrase, *with* is superfluous. Say simply, "I am glad that ordeal is *over.*"

Own. The use of *own* to mean "admit to be true" or "concede" is supported by good usage; as, "He *owned* to his fault." Colloquially, *own* has come to mean "confess" or "clear one's mind of a matter," as in the sentence "He was accused and finally *owned* up."

Pair. With numbers, as "three *pairs,*" best usage favors the plural, the use of the singular, as "three *pair,*" being confined to trade cant. See *Dozen.*

Parcel post. This form is correct, not *parcels post.*

Partake. The word means, literally, "take part," "share." In this sense, several persons may *partake,* or one may *partake* with others. But the word is also in good use to mean "take" or "appropriate," without reference to sharing; as, "He *partook* of the food."

Party. The word should not be used generally for *person.* Not "the *party* that I saw," but "the *person* that I saw." We speak correctly, however, of the *parties* to a contract or an agreement.

Passive Progressive. Modern practice prefers "The church *is being built*" or "Cattle *are being sold* at fifty dollars a head" to the former usage "The church *is building*" or "Cattle *are selling,* etc." Say, "The boy *is being taught,*" not "The boy *is teaching,*" when the intention is to express the idea that the lad is receiving instruction.

Peeved, Peevish. Words used to signify "fretfulness" and familiarly applied to a whimpering child. The terms *irritated* and *vexed* are often preferable in a serious style.

Pep. Expressive slang for *energy, vigor,* but as yet it seems usually to need an apology.

Per. *Per* day, *per* man, *per* pound, etc. are better expressed by the plain English *a* day, *a* man, *a* pound, etc. *Ten dollars per* is the slang for ten dollars a week, a month, apiece, etc.

Perform. Say, "She *plays* the piano beautifully," not "She *performs* beautifully on the piano." This sentence would be improved by using *well* or *admirably* in place of *beautifully.*

Peruse. This word is not merely a synonym for *read.* "He *perused* the article" implies an attentive and careful reading.

Place (verb). *Place* means "lay in position." Some authorities think one should say, "*place* a thing *into* a box"; but there is hardly enough of the idea of motion in the word *place* to justify *into. Place in* is more appropriate.

Plan on. "Do you *plan on* going?" A provincialism better expressed by "Do you *plan* going?"

Plebiscite. A word introduced into English from the French more than fifty years ago. Its recent revival is one of the results of the World War. The word means "a referendum, or vote of the people, in a district or state."

Plenty, Plentiful. One may say, "There will be *plenty* of fruit this fall"; but good usage calls for "Fruit will be *plentiful* (not *plenty*)."

Plurality, Majority. "The president received a *plurality* of the votes cast for all candidates throughout the country" means that he received more than any other candidate. "The election of an officer requires a *majority*" means that election requires one vote or more in excess of half the total number of votes.

Point of view. Frequently expressed by *standpoint* or *viewpoint* in common usage. Most authorities frown upon *viewpoint* and prefer *point of view. Standpoint* is well established. Some would even use *angle* as a synonym. This last word is still colloquial, but there is a tendency to accept it.

Polite. This word should not be used for *kind* before the word *invitation.*

Politics. American usage approves *politics is*; English usage approves *politics are.*

Possessive with Verbal Noun. "We did not know of *his* going." "The idea of *our* doing such a thing." "The fact of the *team's* playing at home interested him." These sentences represent approved usage. Occasionally, in the use of nouns, the possessive seems awkward or sounds harsh, and is omitted as unnecessary.

Post, Mail. The distinction in the use of these words is merely national. We *mail* letters in the United States and *post* them in Great Britain.

Posted. The use of this word for *informed,* in such expressions as "The man *posted* me" and "If I had been better *posted,*" should be discouraged in favor of *informed.*

Powerful. Avoid the provincial use of this word to mean "great" or "large," as in "That is a *powerful* sum of money." "A *powerful* sight of corn" is also provincial usage.

Practical, Practicable. *Practical* means "not theoretical" or "concerned with doing rather than with reasoning." *Practicable* means "capable of being done under given conditions": "A *practical* man will suggest *practicable* plans."

Practically, Virtually. These words are both used to mean "essentially" or "in reality": "The battle was *practically* over"; "He is *virtually* bankrupt." *Virtually* is preferred as expressing actuality in referring to conditions that exist but are not self-evident; for example, "Fighting continued *practically* all night, but the issue of the battle had already been *virtually* decided."

Prefer. "For making bread, do you *prefer* wheaten flour or corn flour?" "I *prefer* wheat *to* corn." Do not say, "I *prefer* wheat *rather than* corn." The *pre-* in *prefer* supplies the sense of *rather* or *before*.

Prejudice. This word connotes a bias or unfavorable attitude toward a person or thing and should not be used to indicate approbation, as in "The man is *prejudiced* in his favor." We should say, "He is *predisposed* (or *prepossessed*) in his favor."

Prepositions at Ends of Sentences. Sentences that end with prepositions are frequently more terse, always quite as idiomatic, and invariably simpler than they might be if differently constructed: "the man I gave it *to*" or "the man *to* whom I gave it"; "the verb it belongs *to*" or "the verb *to* which it belongs."

Pressure. This word in the sense of *influence* frequently carries a sinister meaning, but when it signifies *urgency* it is in good use; as, "the *pressure* of affairs or of business."

Pretty. Correctly used as an adverb, in such expressions as *pretty soon* or *pretty well*, meaning "rather," "somewhat." However, its repeated use tends to restrict one's vocabulary, to the exclusion of more appropriate words.

Preventive. This is to be preferred to the form *preventative*.

Previous to, Previously to. Both are in good use, but *previously* is necessary when the idea is adverbial: "*Previously to* our coming the affair had been settled." But we say correctly, "That event was *previous to* our coming." The same principle applies to *subsequent, relative*, etc.

Price. When used as a verb to mean "set a price on" or "ask the cost of," the word is colloquial: "The butter was *priced* at sixty cents"; "She *priced* everything before buying." *Price* with the meaning "suffer the consequences of" is current: "He will pay the *price* of his follies."

Principal, Principle. *Principal*, usually an adjective ("The *principal* advantage"), is also used as a noun: "The *principal* of a school," "*principal* and interest." *Principle* is always a noun: "Both machines operate on this *principle*."

Proceeds. Use the plural verb with this word: "The *proceeds were* (not *was*) applied."

Procure. Usually, Anglo-Saxon *get* is preferable to Latin *procure*; e.g., "Where did you *get* it?", not "Where did you *procure* it?" *Procure* suggests provision for the future, as in the *procurement* of military supplies.

Prodigy. This word is frequently misspelled and mispronounced. The correct form is *prodigy*, meaning "wonder": "He was a *prodigy* (not *progidy*) of learning."

Profiteer. One who takes undue profits in business. A product of war times, formed after good English analogy. This is a neologism.

Promise. Often misused for *assure*, as in "I *promise* you I was agreeably surprised," which should be "I *assure* you, etc." The word *promise* refers to the future: "We *promise* to do our best."

Propose, Purpose. These words are not exact synonyms, as the following sentence shows: "I *propose* to build a house and *purpose* to live in it when it is ready." *Propose* implies a definite, specific plan; *purpose*, a more general intention.

Proposition. Commercial cant for *proposal, task*, or *undertaking*, all of which are preferable.

Prove. In the past tense and the past participle, *proved*, not *proven*, is correct, except in legal papers.

Providing. This should not be used for *provided*: "He offered to furnish a car, *provided* (not *providing*) the company would pay for gasoline and repairs."

Punch. Slang for *energy, effectiveness*.

Put. Like *do, put* has many meanings that are not in good literary use: *put*, meaning "go" or "get out"; *put up with* (*endure*); *put out* (*displease*); *put past*, as in "I should not *put* it *past* him," meaning "I suspect him to be capable of it"; *put up*, as in "He *put up* at the hotel (*stayed at*)."

Quite. The word means "entirely," "completely," "altogether": "The building is *quite* complete." It means, in addition, "to a considerable extent or degree," "noticeably"; as, "The water is *quite* cold"; "The day was *quite* warm." The word is not properly used to mean "very" or "rather," as in "The book is *quite* interesting" or "She is *quite* ill." Such a colloquial phrase as *quite a bit* is questionable. *Quite some* is vulgar.

Raise. This word is applied in America to the bringing up of children, although formerly its use was common in this sense in England also. Modern usage applies the word to the breeding and rearing of animals and to the propagation and nurture of plants. Thus one may raise children, animals, and plants. Children and animals may be reared.

Re, In re. A piece of old law Latin transferred to business letters and not an abbreviation of *regarding*, as it is frequently taken to be. It means "matter," "in the matter of," or "on the subject of." The English phrase *referring to* is preferable and is, in fact, very generally used.

Real. Avoid the misuse of this word as an adverb in the sense of *very*. Say, "The house is *very* (not *real*) pleasant." The adverb *really* means "actually," as in "The story is *really* true."

Recipe, Receipt. The confusion of these two words is very old. Both words formerly meant a "medical formula," for which today we use the word prescription. While both are still applied to *cookery directions* there is a strong tendency in the best modern usage to reserve this sense for the word *recipe, receipt* being employed for commercial and other use in the sense of *receiving* or in *acknowledgment of receiving*. Say, "He paid the bill and was given a *receipt*"; "She has an excellent *recipe* for making clam chowder."

Recollect, Remember. *Recollect* refers to the recalling of events or facts, while *remember* refers to what may be in the mind continually: "He *remembers* very well his early youth." "I *recollect* now my first visit to the circus."

Regard. The plural of this word is sometimes erroneously used in the phrase *in regards to*, meaning "relating to," "concerning," or "about." It is correctly used in "He spoke *in regard to* bonuses."

Relations, Relatives. The following sentence illustrates the preferred use of these words: "One's *relations* with one's *relatives* may be pleasant or unpleasant." *Kin* or *kinsfolk* implies blood relationship.

Respectively, Respectfully. Do not confuse these words: "They were called *respectively* (that is, *in the order named*) Jim, Sam, and Al"; but "They were *respectfully* called (that is, *in a respectful manner*) James, Samuel, and Albert." See *Letter Writing: Complimentary Close*, page 124.

Risqué. Sometimes written *risky.* The words are not properly used as synonyms. That which is *risqué* is broadly suggestive to the point of obscenity; it borders on the obscene or questionable in art or writing: "a *risqué* story." In English usage, *risky* means "bold," "audacious," "daring," but lacks the equivocal force of the French word.

Same. Disapproved as a substitute for *it, they,* etc.: "We have sent the goods by express, and we hope you will receive *them* (not *same*) promptly." Legal usage allows *the same* for *it*: "If said tenant defaces *the same,* etc."

Say. Avoid this word in addressing another, as in "*Say,* Brown, when do you leave town?" as a vulgarism. *Listen,* similarly used, can well be spared from conversation.

"Says I." A vulgarism.

Scared. Do not use *scared of* when you mean *scared by.* Many people use this phrase carelessly. Prefer *afraid of* or *fearful of.*

Scrap. This is commercial cant, meaning, as a verb, "discard" as out-of-date or unprofitable: "The ships and the plant will be *scrapped.*"

Secondhand. Say, "We bought the car *secondhand,* not *secondhanded.*"

See. The frequent interrogatory "*See?*," with which some persons sprinkle their conversation in their anxiety to secure attention, is most objectionable from the point of view either of manners or of language.

Seen. Not to be used for *saw,* which is the correct past tense of *see.* Avoid "I *seen* him last week" or "He *seen* that," as the height of vulgarity.

Seldom or ever. This is a common error for *seldom if ever.* Say, "He *seldom if ever* interferes."

Sell. Formerly, "to *sell* a person" meant "to play a joke upon him." Now the same phrase is commercial cant, meaning "to *sell* something to him."

Sequel. *Sequel* means "something that follows," as a continuation or consequence. It is used frequently of events or stories related in books: "The *Gay-Dombeys* may be called a *sequel* to *Dombey and Son*"; "The *sequel* of their marriage was a divorce."

Set, Sit. These verbs, like *lay* and *lie,* have long been subject to confusion. In modern usage, *set* is transitive; *sit* is intransitive. I *set* the hen, but she *sits* on her eggs. Incorrectly we speak of a *setting* hen, instead of a *sitting* hen. In Matthew, it was prophesied that Christ should come "*sitting* upon an ass," and his disciples took a colt and "*set* him thereon." The verbs are correctly used in these sentences: "My coat *sits* well"; "We will *sit* up," that is, "will not go to bed"; "Congress *sits.*" "We *set* down figures"; but "We *sit* down on the ground." But a very old intransitive use of *set* persists in the expressions, "the sun *sets,*" "*sunset,*" "*setting* sun," which are accepted as correct.

Sat.—This is both past tense and past participle of *sit.* I *have sat* is correct.

Sewage, Sewerage. *Sewerage* is the system of pipes and tunnels for carrying away the *sewage,* or waste matter, from buildings.

Shall, Will. These are auxiliary (helping) verbs, used to determine various modes and tenses of the action involved in a principal verb. In respect to these words, there are four important groups of idiomatic uses: (1) in declarative statements; (2) in questions; (3) in subordinate clauses; (4) in expressions of future requirement (veiled command).

1. *Declarative Statements.*—The following are the correct uses of *shall* and *will* with the personal pronouns, to express simple future action, declaratively and interrogatively:

Declarative	Interrogative
I shall	Shall I?
You will	Shall you?
He will	Will he?
We shall	Shall we?
You will	Shall you?
They will	Will they?

For the expression of the speaker's determination or command, *shall* and *will* exchange places in the foregoing table. For example: "I *shall*" becomes "I *will*"; "He *will*" becomes "He *shall.*"

In the sense of *willing, determining, commanding,* or *requiring,* neither *shall* nor *will* has anything to do with "time," except as any command must be executed "after" it is given. This is clear in certain cases, where expression and action may well come together: "*Will* you sit here?" "Yes; I *will,*" where the action is suited to the word, or, "*Wilt* thou have this woman to be thy wedded wife?" "I *will.*"

2. *Questions.*—In questions, one uses the word expected in the answer: "*Shall* you speak?" expecting "I *shall* speak"; but "*Will* you speak?" expecting "I *will* speak."

But notice that "*Shall* you be glad to go?" is appropriate, while "*Will* you be glad to go?" is not, since gladness is not a matter of will. Only rarely may *will* be used interrogatively in the first person, because, as long as there is question in the mind, there is no will. Such a formal sentence as "We *will* ratify this treaty, *will* we not?" is approved; and we not infrequently exclaim, somewhat ironically, "Will I?" as if to say, "I *will* not" or "I certainly *will.*"

3. *Subordinate Clauses.*—In subordinate clauses introduced by *that,* after such expressions as "It is said" or "Some one has said" or "It has been commanded," use the auxiliary that would be used in the original principal statement. For example: when the original statement or command was "He (or You) *shall* do the work," the clause of indirect quotation becomes "He has said that he (or you or I) *shall* do the work"; similarly, "He (or You) *will* do the work" becomes "He has said that he (or you or I) *will* do the work." In the former case *shall* retains its ancient force of obligation; in the latter, *will* retains its essential meaning of willingness or readiness. The following sentence further illustrates the use of *shall* to express determination: "We have decided that the contract *shall* be let to you, and that you *shall* follow specifications." If the subordinate clause follows such a verb as *suppose, think, believe,* or *know,* then the usage for *shall* and *will* in the subordinate clause is the same as for an independent declarative statement.

In subordinate clauses introduced by such conjunctions as *if, when, whether,* or *although, shall* expresses simple future action in every person, while *will,* in every person, expresses willingness or determination. Examples: "If you *will* remember the rule, I *shall* be greatly obliged." "Although I *shall* see him, I *will* not speak." "If he *will* not meet me, I *will* not seek him."

Such use of *shall* is usually avoided by some other expression. Examples: "If I *see* him, I *will* speak"; "If he *does not meet* me, I *shall* not need to speak."

4. *Requirements and Commands.*—*Will* has a peculiar use to express a verbal command or a courteous request: "You *will* report back to headquarters on Sunday morning," that is, "You are required to report"; "You *will* please say no more about the matter" means that it is my wish, entreaty, or pleasure that you say no more about it.

Should, Would. Although, in origin, these are past tenses of *shall* and *will,* they are now properly to be thought of as independent of the latter verbs. Their uses are highly idiomatic.

In affirmative principal clauses, *should* may express obligation in all persons: "I (You or He) *should* (*ought to*) attend the lecture." *Would*, in affirmative principal clauses and in all persons, may express willingness or determination dependent upon circumstances: "We (You, They) *would* come, if an invitation were given."

1. In the first person, *should*, and, in other persons, *would*, may express simply action dependent upon circumstances: "I *should* (They *would*) come, were it convenient."

2. In simple questions, the word expected in the answer is used: "*Should* he go?" "He *should*"; "*Would* you consider it?" "I *would*."

3. In *if* clauses, *should* expresses a condition involving action merely, *would* expresses a condition involving will: "If I *should* correct the error, the work would be approved"; "If you *would* permit me, I would correct the error."

4. *Would* may express intense desire: "I *would* that we might see them again." It expresses also, in reference to past time, habitual action: "He *would* walk up and down."

5. It should be observed that *would* is rarely used interrogatively in the first person except in such a half-ironical expression as "*Would* I?" implying "I certainly *would*" or "I certainly *would* not."

6. Many of the shades of meaning attached to *should* and *would* can be expressed only by changes in the tone of the voice. A fair-sized volume might be written about them.

Should seem, Would seem. These are useless locutions when plain *seem* or *seems* would express the meaning. They are appropriate, however, to suggest doubt, hesitation, or modesty in expressing a judgment.

Show me. Slang for *prove to me.*

Sick, Ill. See *Ill.*

Signature. Present day usage prefers *under my* (*his*) *signature* to *over my* (*his*) *signature.* Compare "under my hand and seal."

Since when. This phrase, in which *when* is employed as a substantive, is used correctly in a relative clause: "We moved out West, *since when* (or *since which time*) we have not moved again." How ever, it is not approved in interrogative constructions; as, "*Since when* have you known that?" "How long have you known that?" is correct.

Sit up. We say to a child, "*Sit up*," meaning "sit erectly." We *sit up*, that is, *remain out of bed* until a late hour. Compare the expressive slang, "Make one *sit up* and take notice." These phrases are not in good literary use.

Size up. Slang for *estimate, judge, classify. Up* is very frequent in careless colloquial speech and slang; as, *eat up, all up* (*with*), *stay up*, etc.

Slow, Slowly. Many adjectives in English need no change of form for adverbial use. *Fast* and *slow* are examples of these. Space economy on signs probably helps to maintain this form *slow* in such expressions as "Go *slow*," though it has a long history in the language.

Smart. One should carefully observe the various meanings of this word. It is in good use for *bright, intelligent, brisk*, and *lively*. But in "He is a *smart* boy," the word may have the sense commonly attributed to it formerly, "sharp and impertinent," or that implied by bright and intelligent. After the English manner, one hears of *smart* clothes. The phrase *right smart*, meaning "much," "a good deal of," is provincial.

Smell of. We *smell* the rose, not *smell of* it. But we say properly, "The jar *smells of* rose leaves." The verb is transitive and intransitive.

Some, Somewhat. *Some*, properly an indefinite adjective denoting number or quantity, is often used erroneously for *somewhat*, an adverb of degree, even by educated men and women. Such use appears frequently in the newspapers; but it is condemned as dialectal or provincial by all authorities, and it has no support in literary usage. Say, "I am *somewhat* tired," never "I am *some* tired"; "His estimate is *somewhat* greater," not "*some* greater." The colloquial use of *some*, to suggest exceptional quality or importance, as in "He is *some* manager," is equally to be disapproved.

Sort of. See *Kind.*

Sparrowgrass. A very old dialectal corruption of the correct form *asparagus.*

Spend, Pass. Although *spend the holidays* is sometimes condemned, it is idiomatic English, and is just as good as *pass the summer.*

Split Infinitive. A great deal of ink has been wasted upon this subject. The fact is that English infinitives have been used with discrimination, either *whole* or *split*, for several hundred years. Insistence on *never* putting a word between *to* and the verb is a super-refinement. The following sentence illustrates good usage: "Probably one ought *to come promptly*, if he wants *to thoroughly enjoy* the play." The position of the adverb is a matter of the writer's judgment. Usually, however, good expression will not require a *split infinitive.*

Stand. Colloquial for *endure* in such an expression as "They can't *stand* it."

Stand a chance. Colloquial for *be likely.* "Does he *stand a chance* of election?" means "*Is* he *likely* to be elected?"

Stand for. Colloquial for *endure* or *allow*; as, "We will not *stand for* such conduct."

Standpoint. See *Point of view.*

State. We may say, "He *stated* his reasons in writing." *State* is a formal word and should not be used, as it frequently is in newspapers, to mean simply "say" or "tell."

Station, Depot. A *depot* is properly a place where goods or stores of any kind are kept; the places at which the trains of a railroad stop for passengers and the points they start from or arrive at are properly the *stations*. But, as a *depot* is a place of storage, so a *terminal* of a railroad line, where the rolling stock is kept to make up trains, may be spoken of correctly as a *depot.*

Stop, Stay. The colloquial phrases, *stop off, stop in, stop over*, are frowned on by critics. The first means to "step off" or "alight and stay at" some place; the second means "step in and call" or merely "call"; the last has gained position in railway cant, as in "*stop-over* privileges."

To stop is to arrest motion; *to stay* is to remain where motion is arrested. We may *stop* at a hotel; but how long we *stay* depends upon circumstances.

Storm. A violent commotion of the atmosphere is a *storm*. Avoid the word when referring to *rains* or *snows*, unless *rainstorms* or *snowstorms* are involved.

Street. Many careful speakers regard the expression "They live *in* John *street*" as better and more accurate than "They live *on* John *street.*" General American usage seems to approve *on the street*. Colloquially, we say, "play *in the street*," one's house being thought of as bordering *on* the real *street*. "He has offices *in* Wall *street*" is a form of speech frequently heard. This implies the idea of the *street* as a financial center, including the buildings on it. The whole question turns upon our idea of what the word *street* includes.

Stricken. This form of the past participle of *strike* is used when misfortune or disability is implied: "He was *stricken* with fever"; "They were panic-*stricken*." *Struck* is the usual form for other meanings: "He was *struck* by a stone."

Studying. Avoid the use of such expressions as "He is *studying* for a doctor," when you mean "*studying* medicine" or "preparing to be a doctor." The phrase is school cant. See *Taking.*

Such. "I have never seen *such a small* man" should be "I have never seen *so small a* man," as may be seen by transposing the words of the first sentence, which then becomes "I have never seen a man *such small.*" Similarly, *such a pretty, lovely,* etc., should be *so pretty a, lovely a.* However, in the sentence "It was *such a large* package as could not be carried in the car," *such a* is regarded as correct, meaning "a *large package* like this one."

Suffixes. See *Word Building.* Several suffixes are sources of common error, because of indiscriminate use:

-ette. This syllable is a French feminine diminutive, the masculine being *-et.* A *kitchenette,* then, is a little kitchen, feminine because of associations, probably. But *leatherette* is imitation leather. So we pass to the half-humorous, half-contemptuous *farmerette* and *suffragette.*

-let. This is another French ending, meaning "little." One should not say, "little *booklet,*" the *little* being superfluous.

Sure. "He will *surely* be here," not "He will be here *sure.*" "*Sure,* I'll do it" is slang. *Surely* is the adverb; *sure,* the adjective.

Suspicion. *Suspicion* is not in good use as a verb; prefer *suspect.*

Take. A verb, either transitive or intransitive. Combined with various prepositions and adverbs, it forms many idiomatic phrases and also many colloquial and slang phrases: "One *takes* leave," that is, assumes or receives permission to leave a place or a company; "One *takes to* a person," that is, *likes him.* Some uses, however, are to be avoided as vulgarisms: "She *took on* (*scolded, raged, cried*) dreadfully"; "School *takes up* at 8:30." Compare "*lets out* at 4:00," which is school cant.

Taking. Such phrases as *taking music, taking lessons,* are school cant, probably often in the interest of truth, when *studying,* while more dignified diction, would hardly represent the facts.

Tasty. This word is an objectionable colloquialism for *tasteful,* when applied to persons, dress, furniture, etc. It is allowable in application to food. The following distinction is correct: Pie may be *tasty,* but the decorations of a room should be *tasteful.*

Teach. See *Learn.*

Terrible, Frightful. These belong to the class of extravagant adjectives. *Terribly* and *frightfully* are similarly misused for *very* or *very much* or *extraordinarily,* when "terror" and "fright" are not involved. Save strong words for occasions that demand them.

Than. See *Any, Else, Of.*

That, So. *That* is not in good use as an adverb in such phrases as the following: "*that* good," "*that* worthy." "She was *so* worthy that they could not turn her away" is correct. Do not say, "She was *that* worthy, etc." *That,* however, is approved as a demonstrative adverb with expressions of measure or degree: "We could not stay *that* long"; "You will be *that* much farther on your way."

The. As in the case of the indefinite article, the repetition of the definite article *the* in such a series as "*the* bear, *the* deer, and *the* panther" serves to emphasize the individual separateness of the things named. Such repetition is necessary in expressions like the following, to avoid ambiguity: "*the* secretary and *the* treasurer (two persons)," "*the* finished and *the* unfinished manuscript (two manuscripts)." "*The* secretary and treasurer" means one person only.

If used before the first adjective, *the* should be used before each of a series of adjectives applied to one substantive, but distinguishing different objects; as, "*the* expensive, *the* cheap, and *the* medium-priced goods." See *A, An.*

Them, Those. Do not confuse these words. *Them* is the objective case of the plural third personal pronoun; *those* is a plural demonstrative adjective. Say "*those* facts," never "*them* facts."

Then. Used in such a phrase as "the *then* Chief Justice," this word is approved. The use has a long and honorable history. The phrase *then some* for *some more* is slang.

Thence. The preposition *from* with *thence* is superfluous. "He came *thence*" is correct.

Think for. Such a word as *suppose* or *suspect* should be substituted for the phrase *think for* in a barbarous sentence like "He hears more than you *think for.*"

Those kind. "*That kind* of shoe is good," not "*those kind.*" *Those* is plural; *kind* is singular. Care should be taken to preserve the number in the sentence. See *Kind.*

Through. *To be through* is an American colloquialism, meaning "to have finished," "to have done": "How soon will you *be through* with the work?" The phrase is frequently used and may be classed among our idioms.

To. Never say, "She was *to* my house yesterday." Use *at* in place of *to.* We say, colloquially, "I have been *to* town," and some critics allow the phrase as idiomatic. See *Be back.*

Together. In *meet together* or *converse together, together* is superfluous.

Tomorrow. One may say, "*Tomorrow is* or *will be* Monday." But one should say, "*Tomorrow will be* a memorable day."

Too funny for words. A trite phrase, an easy evasion of the difficulty of telling just how a thing is funny.

Touch. Slang in the phrase "*touch* one for money." The phrases, "get into *touch* with" and "keep in *touch* with," where *touch* means "communication," are business cant.

Transparent, Translucent. *Transparent* means "clear," allowing light to pass so that objects may be seen through the substance. *Translucent* means "partially transparent," allowing light to pass but not permitting vision.

Transpire. Do not use this word to mean *happen.* We may say, "No information or news has *transpired,*" meaning "None has become public."

Treat. A book *treats of* (not *treats on*) the subject of its contents.

Try. We *make* experiments, not *try* them, say some critics. Others point out that *try* experiments is laboratory usage; but *perform* is the more generally approved verb in this sense. "*Do* experiments" is school cant.

Try and. It is better to avoid the use of the phrase *try and do.* Use *try to do* instead. The use of this phrase is not quite like that of the phrase *come and see,* which is in good use.

Under the circumstances. See *In the circumstances.*

Unique. This adjective is not to be compared. One should not say *very unique,* though he may say *quite* or *altogether unique.*

United States. Whether to use *is* or *are* after these words may be a political as well as a linguistic question. General usage approves *is,* though in government official usage there is warrant for *are.*

Universally, All. Do not say, "He was *universally* praised by *all* who heard him." The two words are so similar in meaning that the use of both is redundant. Say, "He was *universally* praised" or "He was praised by *all* who heard him."

Unkempt. Literally, the word means "uncombed," or, figuratively, "rough," "unpolished." It is not to be used generally to mean "disordered," as in *unkempt* rooms. A person may be *unkempt,* a room never.

Up. Superfluously added to many verbs, as in *add up, open up,* etc. *Up* should be used with verbs only when it contributes definitely to the meaning or is in good colloquial use.

Use of Infinitive. The present infinitive is used after all tenses unless it refers to action occurring before the time implied in the assertion of the principal verb. Say, "He intended *to do* it," never "He intended *to have done* it." But "He is said *to have been* present" is correct, since his "being present" preceded the saying. *Ought,* being a defective verb, is followed by the present infinitive to express present or future duty, and by the perfect infinitive to express duty in past time: "They ought *to speak*"; "They ought *to have spoken.*"

Use to. *Use to,* in the past tense, should be *used to.* "We *used to* live there" is correct.

Verbs, Agreement of. The verb in a sentence must agree with the substantive of the subject in person and number. But there are several puzzling cases which give rise to frequent error.

(1) The subject includes substantives of different numbers: Either the master or his servants *are* at fault. Usage approves a verb agreeing with the nearest substantive. Usually it is better to recast such a sentence and avoid this construction: "The fault lies either with the master or his servants."

(2) Subject collective or distributive: "There *are* (*is*) six dollars in the drawer." If the thought is of the total amount of money, use the singular verb; if the idea of several pieces of money is uppermost, use the plural verb.

Verdict. A word loosely used for *opinion. Verdict* should be reserved for official decisions, as of a jury, or for opinion publicly and formally expressed: "That he is unreliable is the *opinion* (not the *verdict*) of all who know him."

Very. Most critics insist that *very* should not immediately precede a past participle used as an adjective. Not, "He was *very* pleased," but "He was *very much* pleased." *Very* may directly precede an adjective: "That is a *very* good article." Where the participle has chiefly an adjective sense, *very* is authoritatively used: "She is a *very* charming person."

View of, to. "He worked with a *view to* the establishment of a business." "We talked with a *view of* discovering each other's opinions." These sentences represent approved usage.

Viewpoint. *Point of view* is preferable. It has more character when used in a sentence in written English and in spoken English.

Vocation, Avocation. A person's *vocation* is his profession, his calling, his business; his *avocations* are the things that occupy him incidentally; "Mr. Wharton's *vocation* is banking; his *avocation* is photography."

Want, Need. *Need* refers to the actual fact of lack; *want* implies a personal sense or view of the situation. A man may *want* an automobile, when he does not *need* it for his business. Avoid using *want* and *need* loosely in the sense of *lack.*

Was, Is. When, in a subordinate clause, an unchanging truth or a present fact is to be stated, use *is,* not *was,* no matter what the tense of the principal verb: "He knew that ice *is* formed at 32°." The same rule applies to the use of the present tense of any verb: "They should have realized that war *settles* no disputes."

Ways. Wrongly used for *way.* "The house is a long *ways* off" should be "The house is a long *way* off."

Well, Why. The use of these words as exclamations of surprise or dismay may be defended, but too frequently they are simply drawling noises at the beginning of a sentence.

Welsh Rabbit. This excellent product of culinary art has always been just a *rabbit.* The spelling *rarebit* is an error.

Went, Gone. These forms of the verb *go* are frequently confused. *Went* is the past tense; *gone* is the past participle. Say, "They *have gone* (not *have went*)."

Wharf. See *Dock.*

What. "He would not believe *but what* I said it" should be "He would not believe *but that* I said it." See *But.*

Whence. "*Whence* came ye?" not "*From whence* came ye?" *Whence* means "from what place, source, or cause."

Whereabouts. In "His *whereabouts* is unknown," observe the correct singular verb.

Who, Whom. Avoid the common error of misusing *who* for *whom.* Say, "*Whom* are you thinking of?" not "*Who* are you thinking of?" "*Whom* did they mention?" not "*Who* did they mention?" *Whom* is the form to use as the object of a verb or preposition.

Whoever. One should write, "I will give it to *whoever* can use it," but, "I will give it to *whomever* you designate." The syntax of the pronoun in the subordinate clause determines the case.

Whole lot. As a substitute for *much* or *a great deal, whole lot* is only in vulgar use; as, "I don't care a *whole lot* for the theater."

Whose, Of which. Some critics object to the use of *whose* in referring to things, but there is precedent for the usage. Sometimes *of which* would bring in an awkward manner of speech. In such cases *whose* should be used: "This is the latest of those political changes *whose* causes we can easily find."

Widow woman. The word *woman* is superfluous here.

Without. This word is a preposition and should not take the place of the conjunction *unless*: "I shall not go *without* my father consents" should read "*unless* my father consents," or the expression might be changed to "*without* my father's consent," where *without* is a preposition.

Worst kind. A vulgarism frequently used in the sense of *very much*; as, "I want to go the *worst kind.*"

Yes. Avoid the various vulgar and provincial varieties of this important little word: *yeh, ya, yep, eh-uh.*

You-all. When used to mean simply "you," and applied to more than one person, this is a provincialism of the southern United States. It is not properly used to mean one person only.

Z. The letter is *zee* or *zed,* the former being the common American name, the latter the British.

WORD BUILDING

To be skilled in language, one must know words and their right uses. The elements of spoken language are articulate sounds; those of written language are characters or letters which *represent* those sounds. From these elements, which are known as roots or stems, prefixes and suffixes, words are formed.

Roots. The *root* is the primitive form of any word and existed before the addition of prefix, suffix, or inflectional ending. The syllable preceding it is called the *prefix*; that which comes after it is named the *suffix*. For instance, the root of the word *prefix* is *fig* or *fix* from the Latin *figere*, "to attach"; the syllable *pre* signifies "before." Thus we get the meaning "to attach before." Similarly, the word *suffix*, from *sub* or *suf* meaning "under" or "after" and *figere* "to attach," means "to attach after." Since prefixes are attached before words or roots and suffixes are added at the end, prefixes or suffixes are called *affixes*, from *ad* or *af* meaning "to" and *figere* "to attach." Therefore, an *affix* is one or more letters or syllables added at the beginning or at the end of a word.

Stems. The *stem* is that part of a word to which the case endings or personal endings and tense signs are affixed; sometimes the *stem* is identical with the *root*, though generally it is derived from it with some formative suffix. Stems are so called because inflections were added to parts of words found in other languages, as branches are grafted to the stem or trunk of a tree. They have gradually been transplanted into the English language and may now be studied as constituent parts of our everyday speech. For example, in the Latin word *crucifigere*, "to crucify," we have the root *crux*, "a cross," changed into *cruci*, "to a cross," by the stem ending, *ci*; combining *cruci* and *figere*, which signifies "to attach," we get a word meaning "to attach to a cross."

By learning words from their etymology, we not only remember the meaning of the particular words thus studied, but we also immediately recognize all other words that are similarly formed.

Structure and Relations of Words. We know things best when we can relate them to other things and make comparisons. Besides, to understand a thing thoroughly we must know its parts; for instance, we know a house when we are familiar with its different rooms and the parts of its construction. Many words are built very much as houses are built; they have foundations, and to these are added various parts which are distinguished one from the other, thus making each word useful for definite purposes. We shall, therefore, learn words more intelligently if we are able to recognize the elements out of which they are built.

English has borrowed from Latin and Greek not only entire words, but also the elements of words; that is, stems, suffixes, and prefixes, out of which to make new combinations. By combining these elements, large groups of words have been built up, the words of each group being related through having the same stem.

An Aid to Memory. The meanings of words seldom used are easily forgotten. Recalling them is like groping in the dark. If, however, we know the elements of which these words are made, the difficulty largely disappears. Few people have time to learn Latin or Greek to get the meanings of these word elements; but the essential matters can be selected and grouped for ready reference and study. A little *grouping* of syllables will do away with much *groping* for word meanings. Learn the common meanings of the stems, prefixes, and suffixes given in this section. Master them, a few at a time. This study will largely increase your ability to remember and understand thousands of unfamiliar words. It will also enable you to make much better use of the English dictionary.

Native and Foreign Words. The English language may be regarded as made up, for the most part, of the following groups of words:

1. Simple words retaining exactly or nearly their original Anglo-Saxon form and meaning; as, *man, will, and.*
2. Simple words borrowed from other languages, which words retain their original sense or become somewhat modified in meaning; as, *grand* (French), *pedal* (Latin).
3. Compound words made up of Anglo-Saxon, Latin, Greek, or other elements; as, *roadway* (Anglo-Saxon), *camshaft* (Dutch or French and Anglo-Saxon), *phonograph* (Greek).
4. Anglo-Saxon words formed of a stem and a prefix or suffix; as, *willful, undo, lengthen.*
5. Words made up of stems and prefixes or suffixes from other languages; as, *excise* (Latin), *engage* (French).

Short and Long Words. The English language, like every other cultivated tongue, comprises both short and long words, or, to express it better, "popular" and "learned" words. The former belong to the people in common—are limited to no particular class; the latter are words which may be used by educated speakers in ordinary conversation and are to be met with in general literature.

The short or popular words are those we have known from childhood—they are sufficient to express our immature thoughts and ideas. Later, the mind develops, and, through reading good literature, we become acquainted with a more formal and distinctive style of phraseology. It is thus unconsciously, yet naturally, that we pass from the use of simple words of Anglo-Saxon origin to those so-called learned words derived from the French, the Latin, or the Greek.

The following examples will illustrate methods of building up words to express more or less complicated ideas:

Cablegram, cable-gram (writing) means a writing or message sent by cable or wire.

Centrifugal, centri (center) -fug (fleeing) -al (adj.) means fleeing, or tending to go, from a center.

Comprehensive, com (together) -prehens (grasping) -ive (adj.) means having the quality of seizing or grasping (much) together.

Cosmopolitan, cosmo (world) -polit (citizen) -an (adj.) means having the character or quality of a world citizen.

Impervious, im (not) -per (through) -vi (way) -ous (adj.) means having no way or passage through.

Paraffine, par (um) (too little) -affine (relation) means a substance having little relation, or tendency to unite, with other substances.

Periscope, peri (around) -scope (looker) means literally a looker around, or an instrument to look around with.

Prefixes and Suffixes. In the following lists are grouped the principal prefixes and suffixes and the most commonly used Latin stems of the English language. Their uses are illustrated by the analysis of about 350 common words. The principles illustrated in these lists may be applied generally, and the student will find his grasp of English meanings and spelling greatly improved by careful study of the significations, forms, and uses of the various word elements.

Prefixes commonly *alter the meaning* of the stem in some manner, while *suffixes convert the stem* into various parts of speech, usually without changing the meaning.

In English the same word is freely used as various parts of speech. Consequently, words here given as adjectives may often be met with as nouns, and nouns as adjectives or verbs.

WORD FORMATIONS

Throughout the following lists of words compounded under *Prefixes*, the prefixes are printed in **boldface**, the rest of each word is printed in *italics*; thus, **ob**-*stinate*. Similarly, under *Suffixes*, the suffixes are in **boldface**, other syllables in *italics*; as, *verd*-**ant.** In the list of *Stems*, the stems are in **boldface**, other syllables in *italics*; as, *in*-**clus**-*ive*. Meanings of foreign language syllables not defined at the head of each group are given in parentheses; as, *pro* (forth) **-duce.** The word (noun), (adj.), (verb), (adv.), following a suffix, indicates that the suffix gives to the word of which it is a part the force of a noun, a verb, an adjective, or an adverb.

Anglo-Saxon Prefixes

A-, meaning *on* or *in*.
 A- *live* means *on* or *in* life.
 A- *board* means *on* board.
 A- *sleep* means *in* sleep.

Be-, meaning *affecting with* or *by*, or merely emphatic.
 Be- *witched* means *affected by* witchcraft.
 Be- *dewed* means wet as *with* dew.
 Be- *spattered* means spattered or spotted *all over*, as with mud.

For-, meaning *away* or *not*.
 For- *bid* means bid or command *not*, or refuse.
 For- *get* means *not* to hold, lose hold of.
 For- *give* means give or let go *away*.
 For- *bear* means keep *away* or *from*.

Fore-, meaning *in front, beforehand*, or *ahead of*.
 Fore- *arm* means the arm from elbow to hand.
 Fore- *tell* means tell *ahead of* time.
 Fore- *stall* means stop *beforehand*.
 Fore- *shadow* means to shadow or typify *beforehand*.

Half- and **No-**, as in half-done. nowhere.

Out-, meaning *excelling*.
 Out- *shine* means surpass (another) in brightness.
 Out- *play* means defeat at play.

To-, meaning *this* or *the*.
 To- *morrow* means *the* morrow or morning.
 To- *day* means *this* day.

Un-, a negative prefix.
 Un- *aware* means *not* heeding or noticing.
 Un- *kind* means *not* kind.
 Un- *fasten* means loosen bonds or fastenings.
 Un- *fair* means *not* fair.

Latin Prefixes

Ab-, meaning *from, not*.
 Ab- *duct* (lead) means lead *away*.
 Ab- *norm* (rule) *-al* (adj.) means *away* from the rule (norm).
 Ab- *sent* (being) means being *away* from, not present.
 Ab- *sorb* (suck in) means suck in *from*, as a blotter.

A-, Ad-, Ac-, Ag-, meaning *to*.
 A- *scribe* (write) means write *to* or give *to*, grant.
 Ad- *here* (stick) means stick *to*.
 Ac- *cede* (yield) means yield *to*.
 Ag- *gression* (stepping) means a stepping *to* or *forward*, crowding.
 Ag- *grav* (weight) *-ate* (verb) means add weight *to*, increase.

Ante-, meaning *before*.
 Ante- *cedent* (going) means going *before*.
 Ante- *date* means date *before* or *ahead of* time.

Bi-, Bis-, meaning *two*.
 Bi- *weekly* means every *two* weeks.
 Bis- *cuit* (cooked) means *twice* cooked (dry and hard).
 Bi- *sect* (cut) means cut in *two*.

Circum-, meaning *around*.
 Circum- *stance* (standing) means that which stands *around*, or accompanies.
 Circum- *scribe* (write) means write or draw *around*.
 Circum- *spect* (looking) means looking *around*, hence careful.

Com-, Con-, Co-, meaning *with, together*, or *completely*.
 Com- *pose* (place) means place *together*, to make.
 Con- *ceive* (take) means take to one's self *completely*, understand.
 Con- *dole* (sorrow) means sorrow *with*.
 Co- *oper* (work) *-ate* (verb) means work *together*.

Contra-, Contro-, meaning *against*.
 Contra- *dict* (speak) means speak *against*.
 Contro- *versy* (turning) means a turning *against*.

De-, meaning *down, out of, from, completely*.
 De- *scend* (climb) means climb *down*.
 De- *pend* (hang) means hang *down from*.
 De- *ment* (mind) *-ed* (adj.) means *out of* one's mind, insane.
 De- *port* (carry) means carry *from* or *away*.
 De- *nude* (bare) means make *completely* bare.

Dis-, Dif-, meaning *apart from, from*.
 Dis- *sect* (cut) means cut *apart*.
 Dis- *perse* (strew) means strew *apart*, scatter.
 Dis- *tend* (stretch) means stretch *apart*.
 Dis- *sent* (think) means think *apart* or *differently from*.
 Dif- *ferent* (bearing) means bearing *away from*, *not like*.

E-, Ef-, Ex-, meaning *from, out of*.
 E- *vade* (walk, go) means walk *away from*.
 Ef- *fect* (doing) means a doing *from*, something made *from* another.
 Ex- *claim* (cry) means cry *out*.
 Ex- *tort* (wrench) means wrench or force *from* or *out of*.
 Ex- *tradition* (giving over) means surrender *from*, as a prisoner is given over *from* one authority to another.

Extra-, meaning *outside*.
 Extra- *ordinary* (common) means *out of* the common.
 Extra- *territorial* means *out of* the territory.

In-, Il-, meaning *not* or *contrary*.
 In- *ept* (apt) means *not* apt or fit.
 In- *sensible* (feeling) means *not* feeling.
 In- *nocuous* (harmful) means *not* harmful.
 Il- *legal* (lawful) means *not* lawful.

In-, Im-, Il-, meaning *in, on*, or *upon*.
 In- *hale* (breathe) means breathe *in*.
 In- *voke* (call) means call *on* or *upon*.
 Im- *press* means press *upon*.
 Il- *lustr* (light) *-ate* (verb) means throw light *upon*.

Inter-, meaning *between*.
 Inter- *urban* (city) means *between* cities.
 Inter- *national* means *between* nations.

Intra-, Intro-, meaning *between, among*, or *within*.
 Intra- *mural* (wall) means *between* or *within* the walls.
 Intro- *duce* (lead) means lead *within* or *into* (knowledge).

Non-, meaning *not*.
 Non- *partisan* means *not* related to a party.
 Non- *entity* (something) means *not* anything.

Ob-, Op-, meaning *against, to, upon*.
 Ob- *stinate* (standing) means standing *against*.
 Ob- *ligate* (bind) means bind *to*, as *to* a promise.
 Op- *posite* (placed) means placed *against*.
 Op- *press* means press *upon*, crush; hence burden, tyrannize over.

Per-, meaning *through, completely, very.*
Per- *ceive* (take) means take *through* (thoroughly) therefore, learn.
Per- *manent* (staying) means staying *through*, continuing.
Per- *forate* (bore) means bore *through*.
Per- *verse* (turned) means turned *around*.

Post-, meaning *after*.
Post- *pone* (place) means place *after*, put off, or defer.
Post- *mortem* (death) means *after* death.
Post- *lude* (play) means (music) played *after*.

Pre-, meaning *before* (in time, place, rank, or degree).
Pre- *lude* (play) means play *before*, hence, music played *before*. Compare *Postlude*.
Pre- *face* (say or speak) means something said or spoken *before*.
Pre- *eminence* (elevation) means an elevation *before*, i.e., *above* others.
Pre- *vail* (strength) means be strong *before* or *in excess of*, hence to be master of.

Pro-, meaning *forth, forward.*
Pro- *pel* (drive) means drive *forward*.
Pro- *ceed* (go) means go *forward* or *forth*.
Pro- *ject* (throw) means throw or extend *forward*.
Pro- *mote* (move) means move *forward*.

Re-, meaning *again* or *back*.
Re- *form* (shape) means change *back*, or into a new shape or form.
Re- *pel* (drive) means drive *back*.
Re- *claim* (call) means call (for) *again*, hence get *back*.
Re- *view* (look at) means look at *again*.

Retro-, meaning *backward*.
Retro- *spect* (looking) means a looking *backward*.
Retro- *gression* (going) means a going *backward*.

Se-, meaning *from, away.*
Se- *cede* (go) means go *away* or *from*, withdraw,
Se- *duce* (lead) means lead *away*.
Se- *cure* (care) means *free from* care or anxiety.

Semi-, meaning *half*.
Semi- *annual* (yearly) means every six months or *half*-yearly.

Sub-, Sup-, Sus-, meaning *under*.
Sub- *marine* (sea) means *under* the sea.
Sub- *soil* means the layer of material *under* or *below* the surface soil.
Sup- *port* (carry) means carry *under*, that is, carry by being *under*.
Sus- *pend* (hang) means hang *under*.

Super-, Sur-, meaning *above, upon.*
Super- *structure* (building) means the building *above* the foundation.
Sur- *pass* means pass *over* or *above*, hence excel.
Sur- *tax* means a tax *above* another.

Trans-, Tra-, meaning *across*.
Trans- *fer* (carry) means carry *across*.
Tra- *verse* (turn, go) means turn or go *across*.

Greek Prefixes

A-, An-, meaning *without, not.*
A- *byss* (bottom) means *without* bottom.
A- *chromat* (color) *-ic* (adj.) means *not* colored.
An- *archy* (government) means *no* government.

Amphi-, meaning *around*.
Amphi- *theater*, means a theater *around* an open space.

Ana-, An-, meaning *up, according to, backward.*
Ana- *tom* (cut) *-y* (noun) means cutting *up*.
Ana- *gram* (writing) means a writing *backwards*, opposed to the usual order.
Ana- *logy* (ratio or proportion) means *up* to the proportion; hence, a resemblance, a likeness.

Anti-, meaning *against*.
Anti- *christian* means *opposed* to Christianity.
Anti- *pathy* (suffering) means a suffering *against*, hence opposition of feeling.

Cata-, Cath-, meaning *down, according to, in respect to.*
Cata- *lepsy* (falling) means a falling *down*.
Cata- *log* (name) means *according to* the name, a list so arranged.
Cath- *olic* (whole) means *in respect to* or *having to do with* the whole; hence, universal.

Dia-, meaning *through, across.*
Dia- *meter* (measure) means a measure or distance *through*.
Dia- *gonal* (angle) means *through* the angle or corner.
Dia- *gram* (writing) means a writing *through*, a plan or drawing.
Dia- *dem* (bind) means something that binds *across*, as a band or fillet across the head.

Hyper-, meaning *over, above.*
Hyper- *critical* means *over*-critical.

Hypo-, meaning *below* or *under*.
Hypo- *dermic* (skin) means *under* the skin.
Hypo- *thesis* (placed) means something placed *under*, as a foundation for reasoning.

Meta-, most often denoting change.
Meta- *phor* (carrying) means a carrying *over* (to another meaning).
Meta- *morphosis* (form) means a *change of* form.

Syl-, Sym-, Syn-, meaning *with, together.*
Syl- *lable* (taken) means taken *together*.
Sym- *pathy* (suffering) means suffering *with*. Compare *Condole*.
Syn- *opsis* (view) means a view *together*, hence a general view or exhibit.
Syn- *thetic* (put) means put *together*.

Anglo-Saxon Suffixes

The following are the principal Anglo-Saxon suffixes. Like the prefixes, these are used with either Anglo-Saxon or foreign stems in their appropriate meanings.

-dom, noun suffix, meaning state or authority of, as in *kingdom*.

-ed, or **-d,** suffix for the past tense and the past participle of verb, as in *load, loaded*; *hear, heard*.

-en, a verb suffix, meaning to make or cause, as n *deepen, lengthen*.

-er, noun suffix, meaning the agent, as in *leader* or *doer*.

-ful, noun or adjective suffix, meaning full or, sometimes, inclined to, as in *armful, handful, playful*.

-hood, noun suffix of state or quality, as in *manhood* or *hardihood*.

-ing, verbal noun or participial ending, conveying the idea of process, continuance, art, etc., as in *homing, speaking, painting*.

-ish, an adjective ending, with the meaning of resembling, somewhat like or inclined toward, as *bookish, childish*.

-le, a verb suffix often with frequentative and diminutive force, as in *handle, kindle, joggle, nestle, sprinkle*.

-less, adjective suffix, meaning lacking, deprived of, as in *armless, godless, homeless*.

-let, noun suffix, meaning little, as in *booklet, streamlet*.

-like, an adjective suffix, meaning resembling, as in *godlike*.

-ly, an adjective suffix, meaning resembling or having the quality of, as in *godly, homely*; also an adverbial suffix, as in *deeply, warmly*.

-ness, noun suffix, signifying quality, as in *lightness.*

-ship, noun suffix, signifying state, condition, office, or quality, as in *lordship, marksmanship.*

-some, an adjective suffix denoting considerable degree or quality, as in *handsome, wholesome, gladsome, winsome.*

-ty, meaning "ten times," as in *fifty.*

-wise, an adjective or adverbial suffix, signifying manner, as in *lengthwise, otherwise.*

-y, an adjective suffix, meaning like or pertaining to, as in *handy, windy*; or noun suffix, often equal to Latin *-ia* or French *-ie,* as in *history, villainy.*

Suffixes from the Latin, Greek, and French

-able, -ible, adjective suffix.
Vis (see) **-ible** means *possible to see.*
Sal (sell) **-able** means *possible to sell.*
Peace (peace) **-able** means *tending to peace.*
Terr (fright) **-ible** means *tending to create terror.*

-acious, -icious, adjective suffix.
Avar (greed) **-icious** means *given to greed, greedy.*
Aud (dare) **-acious** means *abounding in daring.*
Ten (hold) **-acious** means *given to holding.*

-acity, -icity, noun suffix, often equals *-ness.*
Cap (take) **-acity** means *power of holding* or *taking in.*
Authent (original) **-icity** means the *quality of genuineness.*
Loqu (talk) **-acity** means the *habit of excessive talking, talkativeness.*
Pugn (fight) **-acity** means *fighting quality.*

-acy, noun suffix.
Liter (letter) **-acy** means the *quality of knowing letters.*
Candid (white) **-acy** means *condition of whiteness* (Roman candidates for office were so called because clothed in white.).
Prim (first) **-acy** means the *state of being first or chief.*

-al, adjective or noun suffix.
Leg (law) **-al** means *according,* or *pertaining, to law.*
Plur (many) **-al** means *pertaining to more than one.*
Fin (end) **-al** means *pertaining to the end.*
Gener (class) **-al** means *pertaining to a whole class or body.*

-an, adjective suffix.
Hum (man) **-an** means *pertaining to mankind.*
Urb (city) **-an** means *pertaining to the city.*

-ant, -ent, adjective (-ing) or noun suffix.
Expect (await) **-ant** means *awaiting.*
Verd (green) **-ant** means *of green* or *like green.*
Ard (burn) **-ent** means *burning.*
Pot (power) **-ent** means *powerful.*
Visit **-ant** means *one who visits.*

-ary, adjective or noun suffix, signifying *like* or *connected with.*
Exempl (pattern) **-ary** means *fitted to be a model.*
Liter (letter) **-ary** means *having to do with letters.*
Plen (full) **-ary** means *having fullness* (as of power).

-ate, verb or adjective suffix.
Ex- (out) *cav* (hollow) **-ate** means *to make hollow, hollow out.*
Hibern (winter) **-ate** means *to winter, sleep through winter.*
Dis (out of) *-loc* (place) **-ate** means *to put out of place.*
Plac (please) **-ate** means *to please.*
Aspir (breath) **-ate** means *like breath, breathy.*
De (lacking) *-sper* (hope) **-ate** means *without hope.*

-ation, noun suffix.
Cre (make) **-ation** means *that which is made,* or *making.*
Ex (out of) *-clam* (cry) **-ation** means *that which is cried out,* or *a crying out.*
E (out of) *-limin* (bound) **-ation** means *putting out of bounds, getting rid of.*
Found (basis) **-ation** means that on which anything *stands* or *is founded.*

-ative, adjective suffix.
Authorit **-ative** means *serving for authority.*
Talk **-ative** means *inclined to talk.*
Tent (try) **-ative** means *serving for a trial* or *test.*

-fy, verb suffix.
Ampli (large) **-fy** means *make large.*
Veri (true) **-fy** means *make* or *establish as true.*
Testi (witness) **-fy** means *bear witness.*

-ic, adjective suffix.
Hero **-ic** means *like a hero.*
Poet **-ic** means *like poetry.*
Ascet (exercise, discipline) **-ic** means *pertaining to* or *characterized by self-denial.*

-ile, adjective suffix.
Ag (do, act) **-ile** means *capable of (easy) action.*
Fac (do) **-ile** means *fit for doing, easy.*
Duct (draw) **-ile** means *capable of being drawn,* as *metal into wire.*
Puer (child) **-ile** means *suited to,* or *like, a child.*

-ine (-in), adjective suffix.
Alkal (lye) **-ine** means *like an alkali* or *lye.*
Femin (woman) **-ine** means *pertaining to a woman.*
Sal (salt) **-ine** means *like salt.*

-ion, noun suffix, equals *-ing.*
Act (do) **-ion** means the *process of doing.*
Re (back) *-tent* (hold) **-ion** means the *act of holding back.*
Solut (loosen) **-ion** means the *process of loosening* or *clearing up.*

-ism, noun suffix.
American **-ism** means a *characteristic of,* or the *spirit of, America.*
Despot **-ism** means the *power of a despot.*
Buddh **-ism** means the *system of religion founded by Buddha.*

-ist, noun suffix.
Flor **-ist** means *seller of flowers.*
Pian **-ist** means *one who plays the piano.*

-ive, adjective suffix.
Primit (first) **-ive** means *like first things* or *beginnings.*
Ef (out) *-fus* (pour) **-ive** means *pouring out* or *like a pouring out.*

-ize, verb suffix.
Real **-ize** means *make real* or *think of as real.*
Civil **-ize** means *make civil* or *refined.*
Agon (struggle) **-ize** means *make,* or *go through, a struggle.*
Critic (judge) **-ize** means *judge* or *cause to pass under judgment.*

-or, noun suffix, equals *-er.*
Fact (do) **-or** means a *doer,* hence something that affects a result.
Con-duct (lead) **-or** means *one who leads (with).*
In-struct (build) **-or** means *one who builds* or *prepares (teaches).*

-ous, adjective suffix, often equals Anglo-Saxon *-y.*
Aque (water) **-ous** means *watery.*
Courage (boldness) **-ous** means *possessed of boldness.*
Lumin (light) **-ous** means *having* or *giving light.*
Por (hole) **-ous** means *full of minute holes* or *pores.*

-tude, noun suffix, often equals *-ness.*
Ampli (full) **-tude** means *fullness* or *large size.*
Soli (alone) **-tude** means *condition of being alone.*

-ure, noun suffix, often equals *-ing.*
Press **-ure** means a *pressing upon.*
En-clos (shut) **-ure** means a *shutting in.*

Latin Stems

Ag, Act, meaning *do.*
Act *-or* (noun) means *doer.*
Ag *-ent* (noun) means *doer,* especially for another, (derived through the French).
In (not) **-act** *-ive* (adj.) means not *doing* or *acting.*
Re (back) **-act** *-ion -ary* (adj.) means given to *acting back,* or acting according to former habits.

Anim, meaning *life.*
Anim *-al* (adj.) (having quality of) *-cule* (little) means a little thing *having life.*
Anim *-ated* (adj.) (having) means *lively.*
In (not) **-anim** *-ate* (adj.) means not *having life.*

Cap, Capt, Cept, Cip, meaning *take, get.*
Ac (to) **-cept** *-ance* (noun) (the act of) means the act of *taking* to one's self.
Cap *-able* (adj.) means able to *take.*
Cap *-acity* (noun) means power of *taking in* or *holding.*
Capt *-iv* (like) *-ate* (verb) means cause to be like one *taken.*
Con (together) **-cept** *-ion* (noun) (result) means the result of *taking* together or completely, e.g., an idea.
Per (through) **-cept** *-ion* (noun) means a *taking* thoroughly, seeing clearly.
Re (back) **-cept** *-ive* (adj.) (inclined to) means inclined to *take,* or *receive.*

Ced, Cess, meaning *move, go, yield.*
Ac (to) **-cede** means *yield* to.
Ac (to) **-cess** *-ible* (adj.) (possible) means possible to *go* to, or get at.
De (away) **-ced** *-ent* (noun) (one who) means one who *has gone* away, died.
Ex (from, beyond) **-ceed** means *go* beyond.
Pro (forward) **-ceed** means *go* forward.
Pro (forth) **-cess** *-ion -al* (noun) means something related to a *going* forth.
Re (back) **-cess** *-ion -al* (noun) means something related to a *going* back.
(These last two words are used of the music accompanying the entrance and the exit of a choir.)
Se (apart) **-cede** means *go* apart from.
Un (not) *-suc* (under) **-cess** *-ful -ly* (adverb) means not *going* or *following* under, that is, not attaining or succeeding.

Clud, Clus, meaning *close, shut.*
Con (completely) **-clude** means *shut* finally.
In (not) *-con* **-clus** *-ive* (adj.) *-ly* (adv.) means not *closing* completely.
In (in) **-clus** *-ive* (adj.) means *shutting* in or including.
Pre (before) **-clude** means *shut before,* hence put up a barrier against.
Se (away) **-clude** means *shut* away, withdraw.
Re (away) **-cluse** means one who is *shut away,* one who lives apart from society.

Dic, Dict, meaning *speak, tell, declare.*
Ab (away) **-dic** *-ate* (verb) means *speak* or *declare* away, as a position, a throne, give up.
De (apart) **-dic** *-ation* (noun) (an act) means an act of *speaking,* or *declaring* (a thing) apart; hence, setting apart, as a church.
Dict *-at* (the act) *-or* (noun) (agent) *-ial* (adj.) means characterized by the act or manner of a *speaker* or commander—like a dictator.
In (against) **-dict** *-ment* (noun) means a *declaration* against (a person), an accusation.

Domin, meaning *power* or *rule.*
Domin *-ant* (adj.) means *ruling, controlling,* or *principal.*
Domin *-ation* (noun) (state of) means the state or act of *ruling.*
Pre (above) **-domin** *-ate* (verb) means *rule* above or as superior to.

Duc, Duct, meaning *lead, draw, bring.*
Ad (to) **-duce** means *lead* or bring to, as proof to a statement.
Con (with) **-duc** *-ive* (adj.) (tending to) means tending to lead, or suitable to be led with, that is, helpful.
De (from) **-duce** means *draw* from, as a conclusion from a statement.
De (from) **-duct** *-ion* (noun) (act of) means a *taking* away from.
In (into) **-duct** *-ion* (noun) (act of) means a *leading* into, as an electric current is led into one coil from another.
Pro (forth) **-duce** means *bring* forth.
Pro (forth) **-duct** *-iv* (having power of) *-ity* (state of) means the state of having power of *bringing* forth.

Fac, Fact, Fect, Fict, meaning *make* or *do.*
Af (to) **-fect** means *do* to, as one thing does something to another.
Af (to) **-fect** *-ion* (noun) (-ing) means *making* toward, aspiring to, hence love.
Fac *-simile* (likeness) means a *made* likeness.
Fact *-ory* (noun) (place for) means a place for *making.*
Per (thoroughly) **-fect** means *made* completely.

Fer, Lat, meaning *bear, carry, move.*
Dif (apart) **-fer** *-ent* (adj.) means *bearing* apart.
E (from) **-lated** means *carried* from or out of, as out of one's usual self.
Ob (to) **-lat** *-ion* (noun) means something *borne* to or offered.
Re (back) **-late** means *bear* or *carry* back, that is, to some one or to something else, connect.
Super (above) **-lat** *-ive* (adj.) means *borne* over or above, the highest.
Un (not) *-trans* (across) **-lat** *-able* means not possible to *carry* across, as from one language to another.

Fid, meaning *belief, trust, faith.*
Con (with) **-fide** means share *trust* with.
Dif (apart) **-fid** *-ent* (adj.) means lacking *trust* or *faith,* especially in oneself.
In (not) **-fid** *-el* (noun) (one who) means one who lacks *faith,* unbeliever.

Fin, meaning *end* or *limit.*
De (from) **-fin** *-ition* (noun) (that which) means something that marks off or *limits* one thing from another.
In (not) **-fin** *-ite* (adj.) means not *limited.*
Un (not) *-con* (together) **-fin** *-ed* (Anglo-Saxon participle ending) means not *bounded* or shut in.
Fin *-ish* (verb) means make an *end.*

Flect, meaning *bend.*
De (from) **-flect** means *bend* from or aside.
Re (back) **-flect** *-ion* (-ing) means a *bending* back.

Flict, meaning *strike.*
Af (to, at) **-flict** means *strike* at.
In (on) **-flict** means *strike* on.

Frang, Frag, Fract, meaning *break.*
Frang *-ible* (adj.) means possible to *break.*
Frag *-ile* (adj.) means fitted, or likely, to *break.*
Frag *-ment* (noun) means that which is *broken.*
Fract *-ure* (noun) means a break or a result of *breaking.*

Grad, Gred, Gress, meaning *step, go.*
Con (together) **-gress** means that which *goes* together, hence, an official gathering or body.
De (down) **-grade** means cause to *step* down.

In (in) **-gred** *-i -ent* (noun) means that which *goes* into, as a part of a mixture.
Retro (backward) **-grade** (adj.) means *going* backward.
Un (not) *-pro* (forward) **-gress** *-ive* (adj.) means not *going* forward.

Leg, Lig, Lect, meaning *choose, pick, read.*
E (from) **-lect** *-or* (noun) means one who *chooses* from, as from a number of candidates.
In (not) *-e* (out) **-lig** *-ible* (adj.) means not possible to be *chosen.*
Intel (between) **-lig** *-ent* (adj.) means fitted to *select* between, or choose.
Leg *-ibil -ity* (noun) means *readableness.*
Se (from) **-lect** *-ive* (adj.) means fitted to *choose* from, or concerned with choosing.

Mand, Mend, probably from *manus* (hand) and *dare* (to give).
The stems imply authority.
Com (emphatic) **-mand** (verb) means exercise *authority.*
Com (emphatic) **-mend** *-at -ion* (noun) means an *authoritative* approval.
De (from) **-mand** (verb) means ask from with *authority.*

Mitt, Miss, meaning *send, let go.*
Ad (to) **-miss** *-ion* (noun) means a *sending* or letting in.
Com (with) **-mit** means *send* with.
Re (back) **-mit** means *send back,* hence *restore* or *forgive.*
Miss *-ive* (noun) means that which is *sent.*
Inter (between) **-miss** *-ion* (noun) means a *sending between,* hence an interruption or recess.
Per (through) **-miss** *-ion* (noun) means *letting go* altogether, allowing.

Mov, Mot, Mob, meaning *move.*
Auto (self) **-mob** *-ile* (adj.) means able to *move* itself. Used as noun.
Com (emphatic) **-mot** *-ion* (noun) means a disturbed, violent *moving.*
Mot *-or* (noun) means that which *moves.*
Pro (forward) **-mot** *-er* (noun) means one who *moves* (things) forward.
Re (back) **-move** means *move* back or away.

Pend, Pens, meaning *hang.*
Ap (to) **-pend** means *hang* to.
De (from) **-pend** *-ent* (noun) means one who *hangs* from.
Sus (under) **-pense** means a *hanging* under.

Pon, Pos, meaning *place, put.*
Com (together) **-pos** *-ite* (adj.) means *put* together.
Im (on) **-pos** *-it -ion* (noun) means something *put* upon, a burden.
Ex (forth, out) **-pon** *-ent* (noun) means *that which puts forth, sets out,* or *explains.*
Op (against) **-pon** *-ent* (noun) means one *placed* against.
Pro (forth) **-pose** means *put* forth or forward.

Port, meaning *carry.*
Ex (out) **-port** means *carry* out.
Im (in) **-port** means *carry* in.
Im (in) **-port** *-ant* (adj.) means *carrying* in, as if something weighty or of worth.
Re (back) **-port** means *carry* back.

Prob, meaning *proof, esteem.*
Prob *-at -ion* (noun) means a state or process of *proving.*
Re (back) **-prov** *-ing -ly* (adv.) means in a manner indicating withdrawal of *esteem.*

Reg, Rect, meaning *rule, lead, straight.*
Cor (with) **-rect** means *straight* with, as with some standard.
Di (apart, asunder, i.e., distinctly) **-rect** means distinctly *straight.*
E (out) **-rect** means *straight* out, or up, from.
Reg *-ul -ar* (adj.) means according to *rule.*
Reg *-ul -ate* (verb) means bring under *rule.*

Rupt, meaning *break, burst.*
Ab (off) **-rupt** means *broken off,* hence sudden or hasty.
Cor (together, altogether) **-rupt** means *break,* destroy completely.
Inter (between) **-rupt** means *break* in between.

Scrib, Script, meaning *write.*
De (down) **-scribe** means *write* down.
In (in or on) **-scribe** means *write* in or on.
Pre (before) **-script** *-ion* (noun) means something *written* before to be followed.
Sub (under) **-scribe** means *write* under, as one's name.

Sent, Sens, meaning *feel, think.*
Sense *-less* (adj.) means lacking *thought* or *feeling.*
Sent *-i -ment* (noun) means that which is *felt.*
Con (with) **-sent** means *feeling with,* hence agreement.

Sequ, Secut, meaning *follow.*
Con (with) **-sequ** *-ence* (noun) means that which *follows* with.
Per (through, thoroughly) **-secut** *-ion* (noun) means a *following* through to the end.

Sta, Sist, Stin, meaning *stand.*
As (to) **-sist** *-ance* (noun) means that which *stands* to or by.
Con (with) **-sist** *-ent* (adj.) means *standing,* or agreeing, with.
Per (through) **-sist** means *stand* through, hence remain unmoved, continue steadfastly.
De (apart) **-stine** means cause to *stand* apart, or to make fast for a particular end.
Un (not) **-sta** *-ble* (adj.) means not able to *stand.*

Tend, Tent, Tens, meaning *stretch.*
At (to) **-tend** means *stretch* to or toward.
Ex (out) **-tend** means *stretch* out.
Ex (out) **-tens** *-ive* (adj.) means *stretched* out.
In (to) **-tent** *-ion* (noun) means a *stretching* to or toward, as of the mind toward an object.

Tent, Tin, meaning *hold.*
Dis (apart) *-con* (together) **-tin** *-u -ous* (adj.) means not *holding* together, but apart.
Re (back) **-tent** *-ive* (adj.) means fitted with or able to *hold* back, or keep.

Tract, meaning *draw, lead.*
Con (together) **-tract** *-ion* (noun) means *drawing* together.
Re (back) **-tract** means *take* back.
Tract *-able* (adj.) means possible to be *led.*

Ven, meaning *come.*
Ad (to) **-vent** *-ure* (noun) means something that is *come* to or met, a happening.
Con (together) **-vent** *-ion* (noun) means a *coming* together.
Inter (between) **-vene** means *come* between.
Pre (before) **-vent** means *come* before.

Vert, Vers, meaning *turn.*
A (from) **-vert** means *turn* from.
Ir (not) *-re* (back) **-vers** *-ible* (adj.) means not possible to be *turned* back.
Sub (under) **-vert** means *turn* under or destroy.

Vid, Vis, meaning *see, look.*
In (not) **-vis** *-ible* (adj.) means not possible to be *seen.*
Pro (forward) **-vis** *-ion* (noun) means a *looking* forward, getting ready.
Re (again) **-vise** means *look at again,* hence examine again and alter.

Viv, Vit, meaning *live, life.*
Re (again) **-vive** means *live,* or cause to *live,* again.
Vit *-al* (adj.) means like or connected with *life.*
Viv *-ac -ious* (adj.), characterized by *life, lively.*

Voc, meaning *call.*
E (out) **-voke** means *call* out.
In (on) **-voc** *-ation* (noun) means a *calling* on.
Ir (not) *-re* (back) **-voc** *-able* (adj.) means not possible to be *called* back.

DERIVATION OF ENGLISH WORDS FROM THE LATIN

The foregoing list of prefixes, suffixes, and stems will aid in the study of the derivation of words. Moreover, it serves as a key to the means by which words are deduced from others known as primitives. Since more than half the words in the English language come directly or indirectly from the Latin, a study of the derivation of these words will be found of inestimable value.

While it is true that the study of one language may help one to learn another language, and that the study of Latin in particular makes one know English better, it does not follow that it is necessary to have studied Latin in order to understand words of Latin origin.

In the following groups of derivatives will be found first the Latin word with its English equivalent. That the structure of the English words built on the Latin may stand out as clearly as possible, the nominative and genitive (possessive) cases of the nouns have been given, while each verb is shown in the first person singular present indicative, together with the perfect participle.

No attempt has been made to give a list of all words derived from each root. With the aid of the dictionary, it will be found both interesting and instructive to see how many more words from the same root or stem may be added to the different groups. Always compare carefully each English word with the Latin word placed at the head of each group. Note how much or how little of the Latin word enters into the formation of the English word derived from it. The analysis of a few words taken from the list will serve as an excellent guide:

Capio is a Latin word meaning *I take.* It is formed from the verb stem *cap.* By attaching to the verb stem *cap* the Latin adjective suffix *a-ble* (able), meaning *tending* or *possible to,* we get the word *capable,* meaning *possible to take,* hence *having ability.*

The Latin word *duco, I lead,* is formed from the verb stem *duc.* The perfect participle of *duco* is *ductus.* The Latin stem, known as the supine stem, is *duct.* By affixing *intro,* a Latin prefix meaning *within* or *into,* and affixing the Latin noun suffix *ion,* meaning *the act of,* we get the word *introduction,* meaning the *act of leading into.*

Labor is a Latin word meaning *work.* The genitive singular, corresponding to the English possessive, is *laboris.* The stem is *labor.* By adding to the stem the Anglo-Saxon noun suffix *er,* meaning *one who does,* we get the word *laborer,* a workman.

Dens is a Latin word meaning *tooth.* The genitive singular is *dentis.* The stem is *dent.* By affixing to the stem the Greek noun suffix *ist,* meaning *one who is skilled in,* we get the word *dentist,* a tooth doctor. By adding to the stem *dent* the Latin prefix *tri,* meaning *three,* we get the word *trident,* meaning three toothed, hence a three-pronged fork or spear.

AL'TUS, high.

al'tar, a raised place for sacrifice.
al-tis'o-nant, high-sounding, lofty.
al'ti-tude, height, extent upward.
al'to, high, a term in music.
ex-alt', to raise, to extol, to elevate.
ex-al-ta'tion, a lifting up.

AN'GU-LUS, a corner. AN'GU-LI, of a corner.

an'gle, a corner.
an'gu-lar, having angles or corners.
e'qui-an-gu-lar, having equal angles.
quad'ran-gle, a figure having four angles, a square.
rec'tan-gle, a figure having right angles.
tri'an-gle, a three-angled figure.

AN'I-MA, life, breath. AN'I-MÆ, of life, breath.

an'i-mal, a living creature.
an-i-mal'cule, a small animal.
an'i-mate, to impart life to.
an-i-ma'tion, state of possessing life.
in-an'i-mate, without life.
re-an'i-mate, to bring back to life.

AN'NUS, a year. AN'NI, of a year.

an-ni-ver'sa-ry, a yearly festival.
an'nu-al, yearly.
an-nu'i-tant, one who receives a yearly allowance.
an-nu'i-ty, an amount payable yearly.
bi-en'ni-al, occurring every two years.
cen-ten'ni-al, once in a hundred years.
per-en'ni-al, lasting for years.
su-per-an'nu-at-ed, disqualified by age.
su-per-an-nu-a'tion, a retiring allowance.
tri-en'ni-al, occurring every three years.

A'QUA, water. A'QUÆ, of water.

a-qua-for'tis, (literally, powerful water) nitric acid.
a-qua'ri-um, an artificial pond for aquatic plants or animals.
a-qua'ri-us, the water bearer, a constellation.
a-quat'ic, adapted to water.
aq'ue-duct, a conduit for water.
a'que-ous, watery.
a'qui-form, in the form of water.
sub-a'que-ous, being under water.
ter-ra'que-ous, consisting of land and water.

AR'MA, arms, weapons. AR-MO'RUM, of arms, weapons.

arm, a weapon, a limb.
ar'ma-ment, an armed force.
ar'mor-er, a maker of arms.
ar'mor-y, a place for arms, an arsenal.
ar'my, a body of soldiers.
dis-arm', to deprive of arms.
un-armed', without arms or weapons.

BE'NE, well, kindly.

ben-e-fac'tion, a doing good, a gift.
ben-e-fac'tor, one who benefits others.
ben-e-fi'cial, useful, advantageous.
ben'e-fit, aid, an act of kindness.
be-nev'o-lence, good will.
be-nev'o-lent, kind, charitable.
be-nign', gentle, mild.
be-nig'ni-ty, mildness, kindness.

CA'DO, I fall. CA'SUS, fallen.

ac'ci-dent, that which comes or falls by chance.
ca'dence, a fall of the voice.
case, condition, state.
cas'u-al, accidental, unexpected.
cas'u-al-ty, that which occurs by chance.
cas'u-ist, one who settles cases of conscience.
de-ca'dence, a falling away, a deterioration.
de-cay', to fall away, to decline.

CAL'CU-LUS, a pebble. CAL'CU-LI, of a pebble.

cal'cu-la-ble, that may be reckoned or depended on.
cal'cu-la-ry, pertaining to counting.
cal'cu-late, to count, to estimate, to plan.
cal-cu-la'tion, the process of counting.
cal'cu-la-tor, a ready reckoner, one who calculates.
cal'cu-li-form, shaped like a pebble.
cal'cu-lus, a stony concretion in the body, a disease; also a branch of mathematics.

CAP'I-O, I take. CAP'TUS, taken.

ac-cept', to take when offered.
ca'pa-ble, having ability, mental or physical.
ca-pa'cious, able to take on a large scale, spacious.
cap'tious, peevish, faultfinding.
cap'ti-vate, to capture, to take by charm.
cap'tive, one who is taken prisoner.
cap-tiv'i-ty, imprisonment, bondage.
cap'tor, one who takes or holds captive.
cap'ture, a seizure, a prize.

CA'PUT, the head. CAP'I-TIS, of the head.

cape, a headland.
cap'i-tal, standing at the head, chief.
cap-i-ta'tion, counting by heads.
pre-cip-i-ta'tion, headlong or rash haste.
re-ca-pit'u-late, to sum up or enumerate by heads.

CA'RO, flesh. CAR'NIS, of flesh.

car'nage, slain flesh, slaughter.
car'nal, fleshy, not spiritual.
car-na'tion, flesh color; a flower.
car-niv'o-rous, devouring flesh.
in-car'nate, clothed with flesh.
in-car-na'tion, state of being clothed with flesh.

CA'VE-O, I take care. CAU'TUS, avoided.

cau'tion, care, prudence.
cau'tion-a-ry, warning or caution.
cau'tious, careful, prudent.
ca've-at, a warning, a legal caution.
in-cau'tious, heedless, careless, rash.
pre-cau'tion, care beforehand.

CE'DO, I go, I yield, I give up. CES'SUS, given up.

cede, to give up, to grant, to surrender.
ces'sion, a yielding or a giving up.
con-cede', to yield, to grant, to admit to be true.
con-ces'sion, a conceding or yielding.
ex-ceed', to go beyond.
ex-cess', more than is necessary.
pre-cede', to go before.
pre-ced'ence, priority of place or rank.
pre-ced'ent, going before, previous.
prec'e-dent, an authoritative example.
pred-e-ces'sor, one who goes before.
pro-ceed', to go forward, to advance.

CEN'TRUM, the middle. CEN'TRI, of the middle.

cen'ter, the middle.
cen'tral, relating to the center.
cen-trif'u-gal, proceeding or flying away from the center.
cen-trip'e-tal, tending toward the center.
con'cen-trate, to bring to a common center.
con-cen'tric, having a common center.
ec-cen'tric, out of the center.
ec-cen-tric'i-ty, oddity.

CEN'TUM, a hundred.

cent, the hundredth part of a dollar.
cen'te-na-ry, a period of one hundred years.
cen-ten'ni-al, completing a hundred years.
cen'ti-pede, an insect with a hundred feet.
cen-tu'ri-on, the captain of a hundred soldiers.
cen'tu-ple, a hundredfold.
cen'tu-ry, one hundred consecutive years.

CIR'CU-LUS, dim. of CIR'CUS, a circle. CIR'CU-LI, of a circle.

cir'cle, a ring, a circumference.
cir'cled, surrounded.
cir'clet, a little circle.
cir'cuit, distance round any space or area.
cir-cu'i-tous, roundabout, indirect.
cir'cu-lar, in the form of a circle.
cir'cu-late, to move round.
cir'cus, an open space for sports.
en-cir'cle, to enclose in a circle, to surround.
sem-i-cir'cle, half of a circle.

CI'VIS, a citizen. CI'VIS, of a citizen.

civ'ic, pertaining to a city or a citizen.
civ'il, polite; pertaining to the rights of a citizen.
ci-vil'ian, a citizen, not a soldier.
ci-vil'i-ty, politeness; a state of civilization.
civ'i-lize, reclaim from savagery.
in-ci-vil'i-ty, neglect of courtesy.

CRE'DO, I believe. CRED'I-TUS, believed.

cre'dence, belief, credit.
cre-den'da, things to be believed.
cre-den'tial, that which gives a title to belief.
cred'i-ble, worthy of belief.
cred'it, belief, trust.
cred'i-ta-ble, worthy of belief.
cred'i-tor, one who believes, trusts, or credits.
cre-du'li-ty, belief, or readiness of belief.
cred'u-lous, believing too readily.
creed, that which is believed, doctrine.
dis-cred'it, to disbelieve.
in-cre-du'li-ty, unbelief.

CRE'O, I create. CRE-A'TUS, created.

cre-ate', to make, to form.
cre-a'tion, the act of creating.
cre-a'tive, having the power to create.
cre-a'tor, one who creates.
crea'ture, that which has been created.
re-cre-a'tion, making or forming anew.
rec-re-a'tion, refreshment after toil.

DENS, a tooth. DEN'TIS, of a tooth.

dent, a slight depression.
den'tal, pertaining to the teeth.
den'ti-frice, tooth powder, paste, or wash.
den'tist, a tooth doctor.
in-dent', to make a toothlike cut into.
tri'dent, a three-pronged fork or spear.

DEX'TER, (on) the right hand (adj.).

am-bi-dex'trous, using both hands equally.
dex'ter, pertaining to the right hand (heraldry).
dex-ter'i-ty, skill in using the hands.
dex'ter-ous, clever, handy.
dex'ter-ous-ly, skillfully.
dex-tral'i-ty, state of being more efficient with the right hand.

DE'US, God. DE'I, of God. DI-VI'NUS, from DI'VUS, pertaining to God.

de'i-fy, to make a god of.
de'ist, one who believes in God, but denies supernatural revelation.
de'i-ty, divinity, godhead.
di-vine', holy, sacred.
div-i-na'tion, a foretelling of future events, the act of divining.
di-vin'i-ty, theology, the Deity.

DI'CO, I appoint, DI-CA'TUS, appointed.

ab'di-cate, to give up or relinquish.
ded'i-cate, to devote to a special use.
in'di-cate, to point out, to show.
in-di-ca'tion, a pointing out, a hint or suggestion.
in-dic'a-tive, pointing out.
pred'i-cate, to proclaim, declare, affirm.

DI'CO, I say. DIC'TUS, said.

ben-e-dic'tion, a blessing.
con-tra-dict', to say against.
dic'tate, to say to, to declare with authority.
dic-ta'tor, one who has power to command.
dic'tion, a mode of speech.
dic'tion-a-ry, a wordbook.
dic'tum, an authoritative statement.
in'ter-dict, to forbid, to prohibit.
mal-e-dic'tion, evil speaking.
pre-dict', to say beforehand.
val-e-dic'tion, a farewell.
ver'dict, opinion pronounced.

DI'ES, a day. DI-E'I, of a day.

an-te-me-rid'i-an, before noon.
di'al, a plate marked with the hours of the day.
di'a-ry, a daily record.
di-ur'nal, daily.
me-rid'i-an, mid-day, or noon.
post-me-rid'i-an, after noon.
quo-tid'i-an, recurring daily.
si'ne di'e, without day.

DI'GE-RO, I dissolve, separate. DI-GES'TUS, dissolved, separated.

di-gest' (verb), to dissolve (as of food).
di'gest (noun), a compilation, a compendium.
di-gest'i-ble, capable of being dissolved.
di-ges'tion, the process of dissolving food.
di-ges'tive, that which aids digestion.
in-di-gest'ed, not digested, without order.
in-di-gest'i-ble, not easily dissolved.
in-di-ges'tion, lack of digestion, dyspepsia.

DI'VI-DO, I divide. DI-VI'SUS, divided.

di-vide', to sever, to separate.
div'i-dend, the number to be divided.
di-vis'i-ble, capable of being divided.
di-vi'sion, the process of dividing.
di-vi'sor, the number that divides.
in-di-vis'i-ble, not separable into parts.

DOM'I-NUS, a lord or master. DOM'I-NI, of a lord or master.

dom'i-nant, ruling, governing, prevailing.
dom'i-nate, to exercise control over.
dom-in-eer', to rule with insolence.
do-min'i-cal, belonging to the Lord's day.
do-min'ion, supreme authority, the power of ruling.
don, a Spanish title.
pre-dom'i-nance, superiority, ascendancy.
pre-dom'i-nate, to prevail, to rule.

DU'CO, I lead. DUC'TUS, led.

con-duct', to lead, to guide.
de-duc'tion, a withdrawing, an inference.
duc'at, a ducal coin.
duc'tile, capable of being drawn out.
duke, a leader, a chief.
ed'u-cate, to lead forth, to instruct.
in-duct', to lead in, to install.
in-tro-duc'tion, a leading into.
pro-duce', to bring forward, to lead forth.
pro-duc'tive, having the power to produce, fertile.
re-duc'tion, act of reducing, bringing down.
tra-duce', to slander, to defame.

DU'RUS, hard, solid, lasting.

du'ra-ble, able to endure, lasting.
dur'ance, personal restraint, imprisonment.
du-ra'tion, continuance in time.
dur'ing, throughout.
en-dur'ance, ability to bear, sufferance, patience.
en-dure', to last, to withstand, to suffer.

ER'RO, I wander. ER-RA'TUS, wandered.

err, to mistake, to wander from truth.
er'rant, roving, wandering.
er-rat'ic, wandering, moving.
er-ra'tum, an error or mistake in writing or printing.
er'ror, a wandering from the truth.

E-RUM'PO, I burst forth, break out. E-RUP'TUS, burst, broken out.

dis-rupt', to break asunder forcibly.
dis-rup'tion, bursting of rocks (in an earthquake).
e-rum'pent, bursting out (as of buds).
e-rupt', to burst forth (as a volcano).
e-rup'tion, a breaking out.
e-rup'tive, inclined to break out.
rup'ture, a breaking of tissues, or of a blood vessel.
rup'tured, having a hernia.

FAL'LO, I deceive. FAL'SUS, deceived.

fal-la'cious, misleading, deceptive.
fal'la-cy, a deception.
fal'li-ble, liable to err.
false, not true.
fal-set'to, a feigned voice.
fal'si-fy, to make false.
fal'si-ty, an untruth.
in-fal'li-ble, not liable to err.

FE'RO, I carry, bring. LA'TUS, carried, brought.

con-fer', to consult together.
de-fer', to put off, to delay, to withhold.
fer'tile, capable of bearing, carrying.
pre-fer', to carry before or regard as better.
re-late', to bring into relation, to connect (as of facts).
rel'a-tive, that which can be brought close together, compared, connected.
trans-fer', to carry over.
trans-late', to carry across, to render into another language.

FI'DES, faith, trust. FI-DE'I, of faith, trust.

af-fi-da'vit, pledging one's faith, a declaration made on oath.
bo'na fi'de, in good faith.
con-fide', to trust in.
con'fi-dence, a firm trust.
dif'fi-dence, want of faith.
fi-del'i-ty, faithfulness.
fi-du'ci-a-ry, one who holds in trust.
in-fi-del'i-ty, unfaithfulness, unbelief.
per'fi-dy, a breach of faith.

FI-GU'RA, a shape. FI-GU'RÆ, of a shape.

con-fig'ure, to give form or shape to.
dis-fig'ure, to deform, to deface.
ef'fi-gy, an image, a likeness.
fig'ur-a-tive, not literal.
fig'ure, a shape, a digit.
pre-fig'ure, to shape beforehand, to foreshadow.

FI'NIS, the end or limit. FI'NIS, of the end or limit.

con-fine', to keep within limits.
con'fines, boundaries, limits.
de-fine', to mark limits.
def'i-nite, clearly defined.
fi'nal, at an end.
fin'ish, to bring to an end.
fi'nite, having an end.
in'fi-nite, without end.

FIR'MUS, strong, durable.

af-firm', to declare or assert positively.
con-firm', to make strong, to corroborate.
firm, fixed, strong, durable.
in-firm', weak, not strong.
in-fir'ma-ry, a place for the sick.
in-fir'mi-ty, weakness, feebleness.

FLAM'MA, a flame. FLAM'MÆ, of a flame.

flam'beau (*through Fr.*), a flaming torch.
flame, a stream of fire.
in-flame', to kindle, to excite.
in-flam'ma-ble, capable of being easily set on fire.
in-flam-ma'tion, a heated swelling, an excitement.
in-flam'ma-to-ry, tending to inflame, kindle.

FO'LI-UM, a leaf. FO'LI-I, of a leaf.

cinque'foil (*through Fr.*), a five-leaved clover.
foil, a leaf or thin sheet of metal.
fo-li-a'ceous, having the texture of leaves.
fo'li-age, a cluster of leaves, flowers, and branches.
fo'li-ate, to beat into leaves.
fo'li-o, a four-paged sheet.
port-fo'li-o, case for loose leaves.
tre'foil (*through Fr.*), a three-leaved clover.

FOR'MA, form, appearance. FOR'MÆ, of form, of appearance.

form, shape, figure.
for'mal, according to form.
for-mal'i-ty, state of being formal, ceremony.
for-ma'tion, the act of forming.
in-for'mal, without ceremony.
mul'ti-form, having many shapes.
ref-or-ma'tion, a reforming or changing for the better.
re-for-ma'tion, forming anew.
trans-form', to change form.
u'ni-form, alike in form.

FOR'TIS, strong, valiant.

com'fort, to give strength, to cheer.
ef'fort, to put forth strength.
en-force', to put in force.
fort, a stronghold.
for-ti-fi-ca'tion, a strong place.
for'ti-fy, to make strong.
for-tis'si-mo (*It.*), in music, a direction to sing with the utmost strength.
for'ti-tude, strength or firmness of mind.
for'tress, a fortified place.
re-en-force', to strengthen.

FRA'TER, a brother. FRA'TRIS, of a brother.

con-fra-ter'ni-ty, a society, a brotherhood.
fra-ter'nal, brotherly.
fra-ter'ni-ty, brotherhood.
frat'er-nize, to join as brothers.
frat'ri-cide, killing a brother.
fri'ar (*through Fr.*), a monk.

FU'GI-O, I flee. FU'GI-TUS, fled.

cen-trif'u-gal, flying away from the center.
fu-ga'cious, fleeing away.
fu'gi-tive, a runaway.
ref'uge, a place of shelter.
ref-u-gee', one who flees for refuge.
sub'ter-fuge, a fleeing under, or an artful evasion.

GRA'DI-OR, I step. GRES'SUS, stepped.

deg-ra-da'tion, a lowering in degree.
di-gress', to step aside, to diverge.
e'gress, a stepping out of.
gra-da'tion, an advance step by step.
grade, step, rank, or degree.
grad'u-al, step by step.
grad'u-ate, to grade.
in'gress, a stepping into.
prog'ress, a stepping forward.
ret'ro-grade, stepping backward.

GRA'TUS, thankful, acceptable.

grate'ful, thankful, agreeable.
grat'i-fy, to delight, to please.
gra'tis, free, without recompense.
grat'i-tude, thankfulness.
gra-tu'i-tous, free, uncalled for.
gra-tu'i-ty, a free gift.

GREX, a flock. GRE'GIS, of a flock.

ag'gre-gate, to collect or unite into a mass.
con'gre-gate, to collect or assemble as a flock.
con-gre-ga'tion, a gathering, an assembly.
e-gre'gious, away from the flock, hence remarkably bad.
gre-ga'ri-ous, moving in flocks.
seg're-gate, to set apart, to separate.

HA'BE-O, I have. HAB'I-TUS, had, or held.

ex-hib'it, to hold forth to view.
hab'it, custom, use.
hab-i-ta'tion, a place held as an abode.
ha-bit'u-al, customary, commonly done.
in-hab'it, to dwell or live in.
pro-hib'it, to hold away, to prevent, to forbid.

HÆ'RE-O, I stick, or adhere. HÆ'SUS, adhered.

ad-here', to stick to.
ad-he'sion, a sticking to.
ad-he'sive, sticky.
co-her'ent, sticking together, cleaving.
in-co-her'ent, loose, unconnected.
in-her'ent, inseparable by nature.

HOS'PES, a host. HOS'PIT-IS, of a host (*through hostis*, a stranger, an enemy).

hos'pi-ta-ble, kind to guests.
hos'pi-tal, a place for the sick.
hos-pi-tal'i-ty, generosity, liberality toward guests.
host'ess, a female host, a landlady.
hos'tler, originally master of an inn, one who takes care of horses.

HU'MUS, the ground. HU'MI, of the ground.

ex-hu-ma'tion, the act of taking up from a grave.
ex-hume', to take up from the ground, to disinter.
hu-mil'i-ate, to reduce to a low condition.
hu-mil'i-ty, lowness of spirit (as on the ground).
in-hu-ma'tion, putting into the grave.
in-hume', to bury.

JU'DEX, a judge. JU'DI-CIS, of a judge.

ad-judge', to order or decree.
ad-ju'di-cate, to give sentence.
judge, one who decides.
judg'ment, decision, sentence.
ju-di'cial, pertaining to justice.
ju-di'cious, prudent, wise.
pre-judge', to decide before hearing.
prej'u-dice, judgment beforehand.
prej-u-di'cial, hurtful, injurious.
un-prej'u-diced, free from bias.

JUN'GO, I join. JUNC'TUS, joined.

ad'junct, something joined, but not essential.
con-join', to unite, to combine.
con-junc'tion, a connecting word.
en-join', to command, to order.
join, to unite.
junc'tion, a joining, a union.
junc'ture, a joint, or union.
sub-junc'tive, binding together, connecting.

JU'RO, I swear an oath. JU-RA'TUS, sworn on oath.

ab-ju-ra'tion, the act of forswearing.
ab-jure', to deny or renounce upon oath.
con-ju-ra'tion, solemn entreaty.
con-jure', to put under oath.
con'jure, to practice magic, to conspire.
con'jur-er, a juggler.
ju'ror, one of a jury.
ju'ry, a body of sworn men.

LA'BOR, work. LA-BO'RIS, of work.

e-lab'o-rate, to work out with care.
la'bor, hard work, toil.
lab'o-ra-to-ry, a scientist's workroom.
la'bor-er, a workman.
la-bo'ri-ous, toilsome, involving much labor.

LEV'O, I lift up. LE-VA'TUS, lifted up.

al-le'vi-ate, to lighten sorrow.
el'e-vate, to raise, to lift up.
el-e-va'tion, a lifting up.
le'ver, a bar for lifting.
lev'i-ty, lightness of manner.
lev'y, to raise money or soldiers.

LEX, a law. LE'GIS, of a law.

al-le'giance, loyalty.
il-le'gal, unlawful.
le'gal, according to law.
le'gal-ize, to make lawful.
leg'is-late, to make laws.
leg'is-la-ture, the parliament or power that makes laws.
le-git'i-mate, lawful.

LO'CO, I place. LO-CA'TUS, placed.

a-lo-ca'tion, a placing for a set purpose.
dis'lo-cate, to displace, to disjoint.
lo'cal, belonging to a place.
lo-cal'i-ty, a place or situation.
lo'cate, to place.
lo-co-mo'tion, the act or power of changing place.

MAG'NUS, great. MA'JOR, greater.

mag-nif'i-cence, grandeur, spectacular beauty.
mag'ni-fy, to make great.
mag-nil'o-quence, pompous discourse.
mag'ni-tude, size, greatness.
ma'jor, greater, a military officer above a captain.
ma-jor'i-ty, the number greater than half; the age of 21 years.

MAN'DO, I command, MAN-DA'TUS, commanded.

com-mand', to give orders to.
com-mand'er, one who commands.
com-mand'ment, a precept.
coun-ter-mand', to revoke a command.
de-mand', to claim as a right.
man-da'mus, a legal order.
man'date, a command.
re-mand', to order or send back.

MA'NUS, a hand. MA'NUS, of a hand.

a-man-u-en'sis, one who writes what another dictates, a copyist.
e-man'ci-pate, to set free, to liberate.
man'a-cles, handcuffs.
ma-nip'u-late, to handle.
man'u-al, done by hand, a handbook.
man-u-fac'ture, made by hand or by machinery.
man-u-mit', to release from slavery, to set free.
man'u-script, literally, written by hand.
quad-ru'ma-nous, having four hands.

MAR'E, the sea. MAR'IS, of the sea.

ma-rine', pertaining to the sea.
mar'i-ner, a seaman, a sailor.
mar'i-time, near the sea.
mer'maid (*through Fr.*), a sea monster.
sub-ma-rine', under the sea.
trans-ma-rine', across the sea.
ul-tra-ma-rine', a beautiful blue color (beyond the sea in color).

MI'GRO, I go from the land. MI-GRA'TUS, gone from the land.

em'i-grant, one who leaves his own country.
em'i-grate, to leave one's country.
im'mi-grate, to settle in another country.
mi'grate, to remove to another country.
mi'gra-to-ry, roving, wandering.
trans-mi-gra'tion, removal from one place to another.

MI'NOR, MI'NUS, less (comparative of PAR'VUS, small, little).

di-min'ish, to lessen.
dim-i-nu'tion, a reduction in size, a lessening.
di-min'u-tive, small in size.
min'i-a-ture, a small likeness.
min'i-mum, smallest amount.
mi'nor, less, inferior.
mi-nor'i-ty, the smaller of two numbers (or parties) making up a whole; the state of being under age.
min'ute, a brief time, a moment.
mi-nute', very small, little.

MORS, death. MOR'TIS, of death.

im-mor'tal, not subject to death.
im-mor'tal-ize, to cause to live forever.
mor'tal, subject to death.
mor-tal'i-ty, death.
mor-ti-fi-ca'tion, the death of a part of the body; vexation.
mor'ti-fy, to cause death; to humiliate.

MO'VE-O, I move. MO'TUS, moved.

com-mo'tion, excited movement.
e-mo'tion, a movement of the mind.
mo'tion, a movement.
mo'tive, the moving power.
move, to put in motion.
move'ment, change of place or position.
pro-mote', to advance, to forward.
pro-mo'tion, a moving forward.
re-mov'al, a change of place.
re-move', to move from its place.

MUL'TUS, much, or many.

mul-ti-fa'ri-ous, having much diversity.
mul'ti-form, of many forms.
mul-ti-lat'er-al, having many sides.
mul'ti-plex, manifold.
mul'ti-ply, to increase in number.
mul'ti-tude, a great number.

NA'VIS, a ship. NA'VIS, of a ship. NAU'TA, a sailor. NAU'TÆ, of a sailor.

cir-cum-nav-i-ga'tion, sailing round the globe.
nau'ti-cal, seafaring.
nau'ti-lus, a shellfish that sails.
na'val, pertaining to ships.
nav-i-ga'tion, the art of sailing.
nav'i-ga-tor, a sailor.
na'vy, a fleet of ships.

NO'MEN, a name. NO'MIN-IS, of a name.

de-nom-i-na'tion, a distinguishing name.
mis-no'mer (*through Fr.*), a wrong name.
no'men-cla-ture, a list of names in any art or science.
nom'i-nal, in name only.
nom'i-nate, to name.
nom'i-na-tive, the case denoting the subject of a finite verb.
nom-i-nee', a person named.

NO'VUS, new.

in-no-va'tion, introduction of something new.
nov'el, new.
nov'el-ty, newness.
nov'ice, a beginner.
no-vi'ti-ate, state of being a novice.
ren'o-vate, to make new, to renew.

NU'TRI-O, I nourish. NU-TRI'TUS, nourished.

nour'ish (*through Fr.*), to cherish, to feed.
nour'ish-ing (*through Fr.*), promoting growth.
nour'ish-ment (*through Fr.*), act of nourishing.
nurse (*through Fr.*), one who nourishes.
nurs'er-y (*through Fr.*), apartment, in a house, appropriated to the care of children.
nur'ture (*through Fr.*), to feed, to foster.
nu'tri-ent, a nourishing substance.
nu'tri-ment, sustaining food.
nu-tri'tious, health giving.

OP'ER-A, work, labor. OP'ER-Æ, of work, labor.

co-op'er-ate, to work together.
in-op'er-a-tive, not at work.
op'er-a, a musical play.
op'er-ate, to work, to act.
op-er-a'tion, action.
op'er-a-tor, one who performs.

OS, a bone. OS'SIS, of a bone.

os'se-ous, bony.
os-sif'er-ous, containing or yielding bones.
os-si-fi-ca'tion, the process of changing into bone.
os'si-frage, the sea-eagle, or bone-breaker.
os'si-fy, to change into bone.
os-siv'o-rous, feeding on bones.

PA'TER, a father. PA'TRIS, of a father. PA'TRI-A, fatherland. PA'TRI-Æ, of the fatherland.

com-pa'tri-ot, a fellow countryman.
pa-ter'nal, fatherly.
pa-ter'ni-ty, fatherhood.
pa'tri-arch, a father and ruler.
pa'tri-ot, a lover of his country.
pa'tri-ot-ism, a love of country.

PEN'DE-O, I hang. PEN'SUS, hung. PEN'DO, I weigh, or value. PEN'SUS, weighed or valued.

de-pend', to hang from, to rely upon.
ex-pend', to lay out, to use up.
ex-pense', money, time, etc. laid out.
im-pend'ing, hanging over, threatening.
pend'ant, (n.) something hanging.
pend'ent, (a.) something hanging, awaiting decision.
sus-pend', to hang, to delay.
sus-pen'sion, a temporary withholding, a hanging up.

PES, a foot. PE'DIS, of a foot.

bi'ped, a two-footed animal.
cen'ti-pede, having a hundred feet.
ex-pe'di-ent, apt or suitable.
ex'pe-dite, to hasten, to facilitate.
ex-pe-di'tion, haste, speed.
im-ped'i-ment, something which impedes or hinders.
ped'al, pertaining to the foot.
ped'es-tal, the base or foot of a pillar, vase, or lamp, etc.
pe-des'tri-an, one who goes on foot.
ped'i-cle, a little foot, hence the stalk, or stem of a flower.
quad'ru-ped, having four feet.

PE'TO, I seek. PE-TI'TUS, sought.

ap'pe-tite, desire, longing.
cen-trip'e-tal, directed toward the center.
com-pete', to strive with another.
com-pe-ti'tion, common strife for the same object.
im'pe-tus, the force with which a body is driven forward.
pe-ti'tion, a request, a seeking after something.
re-peat', to say again, to recite.

PO'NO, I put, or place. POS'I-TUS, put, or placed.

com-pose', to put together.
com-pos'i-tor, one who sets up printing type.
dis-pose', to put in place, to arrange.
ex-pose', to place out, to lay open.
ex-pos'i-tor, one who explains.
op-pose', to set against.
op'po-site, placed against.
po-si'tion, place, situation.
post, a place or station.
pos'ture, the mode in which anything is placed, an attitude.
sup-pose', to put under, or imagine.

POR'TO, I carry. POR-TA'TUS, carried.

ex-port', to carry out.
im-port', to carry in.
port, carriage, bearing, demeanor.
port'a-ble, capable of being carried.
por'ter, a carrier.
port'ly, of noble carriage, stately.
re-port', to carry back or give an account of.
sup-port', to sustain, to carry, to hold up.

PRI'MUS, first.

pri'ma fa'ci-e, at first view.
pri'ma-ry, first in order of time.
pri'mate, an archbishop, ranking first among others.
prime, of the first rank.
prim'er, a first book.
pri-me'val, belonging to the first ages.
prim'i-tive, original, pertaining to early times.
pri-mo-gen'i-ture, the right which belongs to the first-born.
pri-mor'di-al, first in order.

QUÆ'RO, I seek, I inquire. QUÆ-SI'TUS, sought.

ex'qui-site, sought out with care, hence, matchless, perfect.
in'quest, an inquiry into the cause of death.
in-quire', to seek into.
in-qui-si'tion, a searching into.
in-quis'i-tive, prying, curious.
que'ry, a question.
quest, search, inquiry.
re-quest', to ask, to solicit.
re-quire', to demand, to ask.

RA'DO, I scrape, I shave. RA'SUS, scraped.

a-brade', to scrape off.
ab-ra'sion, a rubbing off.
e-rase', to scratch or rub out.
e-ra'sure, a scratching out.
raze, to level with the ground.
ra'zor, a shaving knife.

RID'E-O, I laugh at. RI'SUS, laughed at.

de-ride', to laugh at.
de-ri'sion, scorn, mockery.
rid'i-cule, to expose to laughter.
ri-dic'u-lous, laughable, silly.
ris-i-bil'i-ty, proneness to laugh.
ris'i-ble, exciting laughter.

RO'GO, I ask, I demand. RO-GA'TUS, asked, demanded.

ar'ro-gance, pride, making undue claims to self-importance.
in-ter'ro-gate, to ask questions
in-ter-ro-ga'tion, inquiry.
in-ter-rog'a-tive, a word used in asking questions; as, *Who? What?*
su-per-er-o-ga'tion, doing more than is asked.

SANC'TUS, holy, sacred.

sanc'ti-fy, to make holy.
sanc-ti-mo'ni-ous, having the appearance of holiness.
sanc'ti-ty, holiness.
sanc'tu-a-ry, a consecrated place.
sanc'tum sanc-to'rum, the most holy place.

SA'NUS, sound, healthful.

in-sane', of unsound mind.
in-san'i-ty, madness, lunacy.
san'a-tive, curative, tending to heal.
sane, sound, healthy.
san'i-ta-ry, pertaining to health.
san'i-ty, soundness of mind.

SCI'O, I know. SCI'ENS (pres. part.), knowing.

con'science, inward conviction or acknowledgment.
con'scious, aware of, knowing.
om-nis'cience, knowing all things.
pre'sci-ence, foreknowledge.
sci'ence, precise knowledge.
sci-en-tif'ic, according to science.
sci'o-list, a pretender to science, one who knows little.

SE'CO, I cut. SEC'TUS, cut.

bi-sect', to cut in two.
dis-sect', to cut in pieces.
dis-sec'tion, the art of cutting up, anatomy.
in'sect, a small animal that appears to be cut into or divided.
in'ter-sect, to cut between.
sec-ta'ri-an, belonging to a sect.
sec'tion, a cutting, a division.
seg'ment, a piece cut off.
tri-sect', to cut in three.

SER'VO, I preserve, I keep. SER-VA'TUS, preserved.

con-serv'a-tive, wishing to preserve.
con-serv'a-to-ry, a place where choice plants are preserved.
con-serve', to preserve from loss.
ob-serve', to notice, to keep in view.
res-er-va'tion, a keeping back.
re-serve', to keep back.
un-re-served', not kept back.

STRIN'GO, I bind, I hold fast. STRIC'TUS, bound or held.

as-trin'gent, binding, contracting.
con-strict', to draw together, to bind.
con-stric'tor, that which draws together; a class of serpents that crush their prey.
re-stric'tion, a holding back.
strict, held close, bound.
stric'ture, a contraction; a critical remark.
strin'gent, binding strongly.

TEN'DO, I stretch out. TEN'TUS or TEN'SUS, stretched out.

dis-ten'sion, a stretching asunder.
ex-tend', to spread out.
ex-ten'sion, a stretching out.
in-tense', strained, excessive.
pre-tend', to allege falsely.
pre-ten'sion, a claim, true or false.
su-per-in-tend', to overlook, to direct.
tend, to stretch towards.
tend'en-cy, direction, course.
ten'der, to offer, to stretch out the arm.
ten'don, a hard cord by which a muscle is attached to a bone.
tense, stretched to stiffness, rigid.
ten'sion, the state of being stretched.

TEN'E-O, I hold. TEN'TUS, held.

ab-stain', to hold back from.
ab'sti-nence, forbearance.
con-tain', to hold within limits.
con-tin'ue, to hold on.
de-tain', to hold from, to keep back.
de-ten'tion, a withholding.
main-tain', to uphold.
re-tain', to hold back, to keep.
ten'a-ble, capable of being held.
ten'ant, one who holds property of another.
ten'e-ment, that which is held by a tenant.
ten'et, a doctrine held.
ten'or, a state of holding on in a continuous course.
ten'ure, the manner of holding an estate.

TER'RA, the earth. TER'RÆ, of the earth.

dis-in-ter', to take out of the grave.
in-ter', to cover with earth, to bury.
in-ter'ment, burial, funeral.
sub-ter-ra'ne-an, underground.
ter'race, a raised level walk or platform of earth.
ter'ra cot'ta (*through It.*), cooked clay, potter's clay, of which statues and vases are made.
ter-ra'que-ous, consisting of land and water.
ter-res'tri-al, pertaining to the earth.

TEST'IS, a witness. TEST'IS, of a witness.

at-test', to bear witness.
pro-test', to declare, to witness against.
prot'es-tant, a Christian who rejects the tenets of the Roman Church.
test, a trial, a proof.
tes'ta-ment, a last will, a covenant.
tes'ti-fy, to bear witness to.
tes-ti-mo'ni-al, a writing which bears witness to one's character.

U'NUS, one. U-NI'US, of one.

u'ni-corn, a one-horned beast.
u'ni-form, of one appearance.
un'ion, concord, agreement.
u'ni-son, of one sound.
u'nit, a single thing.
u-nit'ed, joined, made one.
u'ni-ty, oneness, agreement.
u-niv'o-cal, of one meaning.

VE'RUS, true.

ve-ra'cious, observant of truth.
ve-rac'i-ty, truthfulness.
ver-i-fi-ca'tion, a proof of truth.
ver'i-fy, to prove true.
ver'i-ly, truly, indeed.
ver'i-ty, truth.

VI'A, a way, a road. VI'Æ, of a way, a road.

de'vi-ate, to go out of the way.
de-vi-a'tion, a wandering.
ob'vi-ate, to clear the way of.
ob'vi-ous, easily discovered, plain, clear.
per'vi-ous, capable of being penetrated.
pre'vi-ous, going before.
vi'a, by the way of.
vi'a-duct, a large bridge built to carry a road.

VI'VO, I live. VIC'TUS, lived. VI'TA, life. VI'TÆ, of life.

re-vive', to live again, to arouse.
sur-vive', to live longer than, to outlive.
vi'tal, necessary to life.
vi-va'cious, full of life.
viv'id, lively, bright.
viv-i-sec'tion, anatomy practiced on living animals.

VO'LO, I wish, I am willing.

be-nev'o-lent, well-wishing, desirous of doing good.
in-vol'un-ta-ry, not having will or the power of choice.
ma-lev'o-lent, wishing evil.
vo-li'tion, the act of willing; the act of forming a purpose.
vol'un-ta-ry, of free will.
vol-un-teer', one who serves of free will.

CORRECT SPELLING

To be able to spell correctly is an accomplishment greatly to be desired. Two important elements enter into the habit of correct spelling: (1) to *observe* words correctly; (2) to *hear* words correctly. Errors often arise from a lack of *thoughtful attention* when studying spelling. In this way the impression made upon the mind by the word as a whole is *incorrect*, or the impression of the correct word has been so dimly made as to be easily forgotten. Difficult words are often more easily spelled because of the added attention they receive and, conversely, the short simple words are misspelled because of undirected attention to them.

It is well to be able to spell all words correctly, but especially should one be able to spell words in common use. Your stock of everyday words may number 2000 or 2500. These are the words of first importance in learning to spell.

The habit of consulting the dictionary is invaluable. The use of diacritical marks and the divisions of words into syllables are an aid to correct pronunciation; but it is only by practice and by a conscientious and frequent reference to the dictionary that proficiency in correct spelling can be acquired.

The meaning of words should be learned along with their spelling. This is particularly important in the case of homonyms, like *there* and *their*, which are pronounced the same but spelled differently. If the spelling and the meaning are learned together, no confusion arises in the use of these words.

How to Improve Your Spelling. With the hope of helping to overcome the poor spelling of the present day, the following suggestions are offered:

Pronounce words correctly and distinctly; clear enunciation is of great value.

Learn the analysis of words, that is, learn to recognize the syllables, prefixes, suffixes, and their values; for the analysis of words makes one's spelling more reliable.

With the analysis and meanings of words, associate their uses. This will lead to a mastery of words and tends to better power in spelling.

Make a special study of those words which by reason of a peculiar combination of letters present some difficulty; for example, *believe, receive, precede, proceed.*

Observe particularly silent letters, obscure vowels, or variations in vowel sounds which appear in certain words, as in *homage, heir, subtle, benefit, separate.*

A most troublesome factor in the spelling problem is the repetition of common errors. The habit of repeatedly misspelling the same words may be overcome by any method of study which directs special attention to them.

There is no better way to master the art of spelling than by repeated oral and written practice; for it is the *repetition* which forms the habit.

Because they lack special aptitude for spelling, or because of some difficulty not easily overcome, some persons believe they can never learn to spell. This is an error. Any person of average intelligence can learn to spell if he fully determines to do so, and then diligently strives toward the accomplishment of that end.

Spelling Lists. The following lists are prepared to give ever present help in spelling. They will be found useful for reference, for study, and for review. The first list contains one hundred "spelling demons" first published in *A Concrete Investigation of the Materials of English Spelling*, issued from the University of South Dakota. A comparison of these words with the spelling scale prepared by L. P. Ayres for the Russell Sage Foundation indicates that eighth grade pupils should earn marks of 90 to 100 on groups of 20 words each, selected from the list. However, a large number of these words are among those found to be most frequently misspelled in the College Entrance Board examinations. The other lists have been prepared after a careful study of frequent spelling errors and everyday vocabularies, such as *The Child and His Spelling* by W. A. Cook and M. V. O'Shea and *The Spelling Vocabularies of Personal and Business Letters* by L. P. Ayres.

Rules for Spelling

1. If a termination beginning with *e, i,* or *y* is added to a word ending in *c*, when *c* is not to be pronounced as *s*, *k* is inserted after *c*: *picnic, picnicking*; *traffic, trafficker.*

2. If a word of one syllable or a word accented on the last syllable ends in a single consonant preceded by a single vowel, the final consonant is doubled before a termination beginning with a vowel: *fit, fitting*; *clan, clannish*; *prefer, preferring*; *permit, permitted.*

3. When a digraph, that is, two coupled vowels, precedes the final consonant, or when the accent is not on the last syllable, or when it goes to a preceding syllable in the new word, the final consonant is not doubled before a termination beginning with a vowel: *sail, sailing*; *travel, traveler*; *benefit, benefited*; *prefer, preferable.* Exceptions are: *handicapped, humbugged.*

4. When a word ends in silent *e*, unless *e* is preceded by another vowel, the *e* is usually retained before a termination beginning with a consonant and omitted before a termination beginning with a vowel: *hide, hiding*; *come, coming*; *late, lateness*; *race, racial*; *provoke, provoking*; *fine, fineness*; *spite, spiteful, spiting*; *use, usable.* Exceptions: *judgment, acknowledgment, abridgment, duly, truly,* and *awful.*

5. Words ending in *ce* or *ge* do not drop the *e* before *able* or *ous.* Retaining *e* in this case preserves the soft sound of *g* and the *s* sound of *c*: *notice, noticeable*; *change, changeable.*

6. Words ending in *y* preceded by a consonant usually change *y* into *i* before an additional letter or syllable: *spy, spies*; *cry, crier*; *gratify, gratifies.* But *y* is not changed before *-ing*: *deny, denying*; *reply, replying.*

Words ending in *y* preceded by a vowel usually retain the *y* unchanged, as in *boy, boys, boyish, boyhood. Laid, paid, said,* are exceptions.

7. The spelling of many words in *ie* and *ei* may be determined by the following rule: If the coupled vowels follow *c*, the *e* comes first; if they follow *l* or *r*, the *i* comes first: *receive, believe, grief.* Some exceptions are: *financier, leisure, sleigh.*

8. In the singular number, the possessive of nouns is formed by adding to the noun an apostrophe and *s*: *Burns's, Jones's, St. James's, St. Giles's, Dickens's, Douglas's.*

The *s* is omitted in the singular when too many hissing sounds would come together: for *Jesus'* sake; for *conscience'* sake; for *goodness'* sake; *Damocles'* sword. When the word consists of more than two syllables, the apostrophe only is added: *Achilles'* sword; *Socrates'* wife; *Euripides'* dramas; *Demosthenes'* orations.

9. Derivatives formed from the Latin stem *ced* are usually spelled *cede*; the exceptions are *exceed, proceed, succeed.*

10. Generally spell in full rather than use abbreviations or numerals for the following: Titles of business, honor, or respect, preceding proper names; Christian names; numbers of fewer than three digits, unless the number is followed by a word of measure; all numbers beginning a sentence; the time of day, except when the number is used with A. M. or P. M.; numbers of centuries, sessions of congress, and the words "United States."

11. *Plurals.* Most nouns form the plural number by adding *s* or *es* to the singular: *state, states*; *inch, inches.*

The plural of numerals and of unusual or artificial word formations is formed by adding an apostrophe and *s*: *7's, 9's,* the *1900's, t's, y's.*

Plurals of proper names are generally formed by adding *s* or *es*: *Brown, Browns*; *James, Jameses.*

COMMON WORDS FREQUENTLY MISSPELLED

One Hundred Spelling Demons

ache
again
always
among
answer
any
been
beginning
believe
blue
break
built
business
busy
buy
can't
choose
color
coming
cough
could
country
dear
doctor
does
done
don't
early
easy
enough
every
February
forty
friend
grammar
guess
half
having
hear
heard
here
hoarse
hour
instead
just
knew
laid
loose
lose
making
many
meant
minute
much
none
often
once
piece
quiet
raise
read
ready
said
says
seems
separate
shoes
since
some
straight
sugar
sure
tear
their
there
they
though
through
tired
to-night
too
trouble
truly
Tuesday
two
used
very
wear
Wednesday
week
where
whether
which
whole
women
won't
would
write
writing
wrote

School Words

abbreviate
absence
absolutely
academy
accessory
accident
accidentally
accomplice
accomplish
accurate
accustom
acid
across
addition
adjoin
adjourn
affairs
affect
aggravate
algebraic
all right
almost
alphabet
already
ambition
ammonia
analogous
analysis
ancient
anecdote
angle
aniline (-in)
antarctic
antecedent
anthracite
Apollo
apostrophe
apparatus
apparent
appearance
appliance
appositive
architecture
arctic
argument
arithmetic
artificially
arouse
assembly
assignment
athletic
atmosphere
attempt
attendance
autobiography
auxiliary
avalanche
average
avoidance
awkward
barrier
battalion
benefit
biography
biology
blizzard
buoyant
cafeteria
candidate
canyon
caterpillar
chalk
changeable
chautauqua
chemistry
chosen
circuit
circumference
circumstance
citizenship
civilization
clever
climate
coherence
college
colloquial
combination
comedy
commencement
commission
communication
comparison
compulsory
concede
conceivable
conceive
conception
conscientious
consequence
conspicuous
contemplate
continent
continually
control
courageous
crater
criminally
criticism
crucifixion
crucify
curriculum
customary
cyclone
cylinder
daily
decide
decimal
declension
definitely
demonstrable
demonstrative
demonstrator
denominator
descend
description
descriptive
desirable
despair
desperately
develop
diagonal
dialogue (-log)
diameter
dictionary
difference
diligence
diphthong
disappear
discipline
disinfect
dismissal
dissatisfied
dissipated
distribute
division
dynasty
eclipse
e'er
effect
eighth
elegy
embarrass
emphasis
encouragement
encyclopedia
enemy
enmity
enthusiasm
envious
equation
equator
equipped
eraser
ere
erroneous
essential
exaggerate
examination
exceed
excel
excellent
exemption
exercise
exhibition
existence
expensive
explain
explanation
exposition
expression
extension
extremely
factoring
fascinate
felonious
figure
foreign
foresee
formally
formerly
frigid
gasoline
gauge (gage)
generally
genius
genuine
geology
geometry
glacier
granite
guard
gymnastics
happiness
height
hemisphere
hexagon
history
horizontal
humorous
hygiene
hypocrisy
hysterics
iambic
idiom
ignominious
ignominy
ignorance
illustrate
imagination
imperative
improvable
inborn
incident
incitement
incriminate
indefinitely
independence
independent
indictment
indispensable
infinite
infinitesimal
infinitive
influential
influentially
instigation
instigator
institute
intelligence
intelligible
intention
interrogative
intransitive
irregular
irresistible
island
isosceles
isthmus
its
it's
kindergarten
laboratory
later
latitude
latter
lead
lead pencil
learn
lecture
led
legend
lightning
literary
literature
livelihood
longitude
loyalty
Macaulay
machinist
malefactor
malign
malignant
malignity
maneuver
manual
marriage
martyr
martyrdom
mathematics
mechanic
mechanical
mechanism
mediocre
mediocrity
mercury
meridian
metaphor
metonymy
microscope
mirage
misspell
modifies
modifying
monosyllable
mountain
multiplication
municipal
muscular
naphtha
narration
nativity
neuter
nineteen
ninety
nominative
noticeable
numerator
obedience
occasion
occur
occurred
occurrence
o'clock
offense
omitted
opportunity
ostensible
ostentatious
oxygen
pageant
paragraph
parallel
paraphernalia
parliament
participial
participle
particularly
passed
passion
passionate
past
peaceful
peninsula
perfect
perfectly
perform
permanent
permission
perpendicular
perpetration
perpetrator
phenomenon
Philip
phrase
physics
physiology
picturesque
planet
plateau
poetry
polygon
polysyllable
positively
possess
possessive
possibility
practicable
practically
practice
prairie
precede
precinct
predicate
prejudice
preparation
principal
principle
prism
privilege
proceed
professor
progressive
pronounce
pronunciation
prophecy
prophesy
propitious
proportion
prove
psychology
punctuation
pyramid
quiet
quite
rabbit
rarefaction
rarefy
rareness
rarity
ravine
readiness
realize
reasonable
recess
recital
recognize
recollect
recommend
remember
remembrance
repellent
repetition
representative
review
rhetoric
rhythm
rhythmic
ridicule
rime (rhyme)
sacrifice
sacrificial
sacrilege
sacrilegious
satire
satyr
saucy
scholarship
seize
semicircle
seminary
senate
sentence
separately
session
severely
shepherd
siege
signature
simile
socialist
soliloquies
soliloquy
solution
sometimes
sophomore
specific
specimen
speech
squirrel
statement
strait
strengthen
strenuous
studying
subordinate
subtraction
succeed

sufficiently
suit
suite
summary
superintendent
surely
susceptibility
susceptible
syllable
sympathize
synonym
syntax
synthesis
systematic
talented
tariff
technical
temperature
temptation
tendency
therefore
thermometer
tournament
tragedy
traveler
tropical
turpentine
twelfth
typical
unanimous
uncomfortable
undoubtedly
university
until
usually
vacation
valuable
vertical
villain
vocabulary
volume
wealthily
weird
whimper
wholly
zoology

Social and Personal Words

accept
accompany
acquaintance
aeronaut
aeroplane
affectionately
afford
agreeable
airplane
aisle
almanac
altar
amateur
angel
angry
animal
anniversary
announcement
annual
anxiety
apartment
apologize
appetite
appreciate
appreciative
arrangement
arrival
assistance
association
asylum
audience
automobile
bachelor
baggage
banquet
baptize
baseball
bazaar
bicycle
billiards
borrow
breakfast
burglar
campaign
candidate
canoe
captain
career
carriage
catechism
cathedral
celebration
cemetery
ceremony
chapel
chaperon
character
chauffeur
chivalry
circus
citizen
cologne
colonel
committee
complement
complexion
compliment
conductor
congregation
contribution
convenient
coquette
cordially
cousin
croquet
crowd
daughter
delegate
delicate
dentist
dependent
dietitian
din
diner
dining
dinner
disappoint
economical
elaborate
embarrassment
emergency
engagement
environment
etiquette
euchre
excursion
fashionable
fatigue
fellowship
fiancé
fiancée
funeral
garage
golf
grief
guest
hammock
harassment
heathen
heavy
heresy
hospitable
hungry
icicle
idol
innuendo
invitation
kodak
laugh
league
liquor
luncheon
magazine
majority
matron
mischief
missionary
mosquitoes
motor
mucilage
neighbor
niece
nuisance
occupy
oculist
optician
orchestra
organization
pamphlet
parade
parasol
passenger
pennant
phonograph
photographer
pianist
picnic
picnicking
plaguy
playwright
pleasure
priest
prodigal
prohibition
promenade
protégé
providence
psalm
quarrel
quoits
rehearse
relative
religious
rendezvous
repentance
restaurant
revival
scene
sight-seeing
sincerely
sleigh
souvenir
spectacles
suffrage
surprise
synagogue
tabernacle
taxicab
temperance
tenant
tenement
testament
theater
thief
tobacco
tournament
umbrella
umpire
unfortunate
valise
vaudeville
vilify
village
waltz
wasteful
wealth
whistle
wholesome
yacht

Business Words

acceptance
accommodate
accountant
accrued
acknowledge
acquire
acre
address
administration
advertise
affidavit
agency
agreement
allege
annuity
application
approximately
arbitration
article
assets
assignment
assure
attorney
auction
auditor
balance
bankrupt
bankruptcy
bargain
bookkeeper
brief
calculation
calendar
capacity
capital
cashier
catalogue (-log)
certificate
check
clerical
collateral
collectable (-ible)
commercial
commodity
competent
competition
compromise
comptroller
confidential
consideration
consignment
convenient
conveyance
corporation
correspondent
counterfeit
credentials
credit
creditor
criminal
customer
debt
debtor
decision
defer
deficit
delivery
depositor
diary
difficulty
discount
discussion
dividends
draft
due
economical
efficient
elevator
embezzle
employee
enterprise
especially
estimate
evidence
expenditure
expense
experience
factory
finally
finance
financial
financier
fiscal
foreclosure
foreign
forfeit
forgery
franchise
fraudulent
freight
government
guarantee
heir
hundred
immediate
indorsement
information
insolvency
installment
insurance
interest
inventory
investment
invoice
issue
itemized
items
janitor
journal
judgment
judicial
lease
ledger
legacy
legislature
liability
license
lucrative
machinery
manager
manufacture
material
maturity
mercantile
merchandise
millionaire
mortgage
mortgagee
mortgagor
municipal
necessary
notary
oblige
operator
parcel
particular
position
preferred
preliminary
president
probably
proceeds
profitable
profits
promissory
proprietor
purchase
receipt
recommend
reference
referring
register
regular
remittance
renewal
request
requisite
resources
respectfully
responsible
résumé
retail
revenue
salary
salesman
schedule
secretary
securities
sincerely
situation
speculate
stationery
statistics
stenographer
stockholder
storage
substantial
success
suggest
surplus
syndicate
taxes
telegraph
telephone
testimony
treasurer
typewriter
unique
usury
value
warehouse
warrant
weight
wholesale

Household Words

abscess
ague
alcohol
almond
ambulance
anesthetic
anoint
antitoxine
appendix
apron
artery
asbestos
asparagus
asthma
automatic
banana
bandage
baste
bilious
biscuit
blouse
bread
breathe
bronchitis
bruise
buffet
bungalow
bureau
butcher
button
cabbage
calico
cambric
camphor
cancer
cantaloupe
capsule
caramel
carpenter
cashmere
casserole
cataract
catarrh
ceiling
celery
cellar
cereal
chamois
chandelier
chiffonier
chloroform
chocolate
cholera
cinder
cinnamon
cloth
clothes
coat
cocoa
coffee
collar
contagious
convalescent
corduroy
cough
cretonne
crochet
croquette
crystal
cucumber
culinary
currant
curtain
dairy
desiccate
dessert
diamond
diarrhea
diary
digestion
diphtheria
disease
doily
dye
electricity
embroidery
enamel
epidemic
ether
faucet
feather
flannel
flour
forehead
fragile
frieze

furnace
furniture
gasoline (-ene)
gelatine
gingham
glycerine
grease
grippe (grip)
groceries
handkerchief
hearth
hemorrhage
herbs
hoarse
homeopathic
hosiery
hospital
inoculate
invalid
iodine (-in)
ironing
jewelry
kernel
kerosene
khaki
kimono
knead
knee
knife
knob
knot
knuckle
larynx
lattice
lemon
lemonade
lettuce
library
licorice
ligament
liniment
macaroni
mackerel
mackintosh
mahogany
mantelpiece
mattress
measles
measure
medicine
melon
meringue
milliner
mirror
molasses
muscle
mustard
nainsook
nausea
nervous
neuralgia
odor
omelet
organdie (-y)
ostrich
oyster
palate
paneling
paraffine
paralysis
pattern
peach
pear
peritonitis
perspiration
physically
physician
picture
pillow
pitcher
plaid
plaited
plumber
pneumonia
poached
porcelain
porch
portière
portrait
potatoes
poultice
poultry
prescription
ptomaine (-in)
pumpkin
quinine
radiator
raisin
raspberry
recipe
refrigerator
relief
remedy
reservoir
rheumatism
rhubarb
roast
salad
sandwich
sanitary
sateen
satin
saucer
sausage
scissors
settee
sieve
sirloin
skein
sleeve
specialist
spigot
spinach
steak
stomach
sugar
sulphur (-fur)
surgeon
syringe
taffeta
tailor
threshold
tissue
tomato
tongue
trousers
trousseau
tuberculosis
turkeys
turnip
typhoid
unbleached
utensil
vaccinate
vacuum
vanilla
vaseline (-in)
vegetable
veil
ventilate
ventilation
veranda
vinegar
waist
woolen
worsted
yolk
zephyr

Irregular Plurals

Singular	Plural
beef	beeves
calf	calves
elf	elves
half	halves
knife	knives
leaf	leaves
life	lives
loaf	loaves
self	selves
sheaf	sheaves
shelf	shelves
thief	thieves
wife	wives
wolf	wolves
ally	allies
city	cities
daisy	daisies
fairy	fairies
fancy	fancies
lady	ladies
lily	lilies
mystery	mysteries
gentleman	gentlemen
goose	geese
man	men
mouse	mice
tooth	teeth
woman	women
deer	deer
gross	gross
grouse	grouse
hose	hose
mackerel	mackerel
salmon	salmon
series	series
sheep	sheep
species	species
trout	trout
swine	swine
attorney at law	attorneys at law
commander in chief	commanders in chief
court-martial	courts-martial
editor in chief	editors in chief
father-in-law	fathers-in-law
governor-general	governors-general
maid of honor	maids of honor
man-of-war	men-of-war
son-in-law	sons-in-law
knight templar	knights templars
man-child	men-children
manservant	menservants
woman servant	women servants
alumna (feminine)	alumnæ
alumnus (masculine)	alumni
analysis	analyses
animalcule	animalcules
antithesis	antitheses
apparatus	apparatuses apparatus
appendix	appendices appendixes
axis	axes
bacillus	bacilli
bacterium	bacteria
bandit	banditti bandits
basis	bases
beau	beaux beaus
brother	brothers (relatives) brethren (of the same society)
candelabrum	candelabra
cannon	cannons (individuals) cannon (collectively)
cherub	cherubim (collectively) cherubs
crisis	crises
cumulus	cumuli
curriculum	curricula curriculums
datum	data
die	dies (for stamping) dice (for gaming)
ellipsis	ellipses
erratum	errata
fish	fishes (individually) fish (collectively)
foot	feet (parts of the body) foot (infantry)
formula	formulæ formulas
genius	geniuses (men of genius) genii (spirits)
genus	genera
gymnasium	gymnasia gymnasiums
head	heads (parts of bodies) head (of cattle)
heathen	heathens (individuals) heathen (collectively)
hippopotamus	hippopotami hippopotamuses
horse	horses (animals) horse (cavalry)
hypothesis	hypotheses
index	indexes (tables of reference) indices (signs in algebra)
larva	larvæ
memorandum	memoranda memorandums
nebula	nebulæ
oasis	oases
parenthesis	parentheses
penny	pennies (single coins) pence (quantity in value)
phenomenon	phenomena
radius	radii
sail	sails (pieces of canvas) sail (vessels)
seraph	seraphim (collectively) seraphs
shot	shots (number of times fired) shot (number of balls)
stratum	strata
synopsis	synopses
tableau	tableaux
terminus	termini
thesis	theses
trousseau	trousseaux
vertebra	vertebræ

HOMONYMS

Words pronounced the same but differing in spelling and in meaning.

air, that which we breathe.
ere, before.
e'er, ever.
heir, one that is to inherit.

aloud, audibly.
allowed, permitted.

altar, a place for worship.
alter, to change.

arc, part of a circle.
ark, as Noah's ark; a chest.

ascent, going up; an upward slope.
assent, to agree to.

ate, past tense of eat.
eight, twice four.

aught, anything.
ought, is (are) bound in duty.

bad, ill or wicked.
bade, past tense of bid.

bale, a bundle.
bail, surety for some one; a handle.

ball, a sphere; a dance
bawl, to shout; to cry out.

band, that which binds; a narrow strip.
banned, forbidden.

bard, a poet.
barred, hindered; shut out.

bare, naked.
bear, to carry; a wild beast.

base, the lowest part; mean.
bass, the lowest part in harmonized music.

beech, a kind of tree.
beach, shore.

beer, a drink.
bier, anything on which the dead are carried to burial.

beet, a vegetable.
beat, to strike.

bell, a hollow metal body that rings or tolls.
belle, a beautiful or admired young woman.

berry, a small fruit.
bury, to inter; to conceal.

birth, being born; descent.
berth, a sleeping place.

bold, daring; courageous.
bowled, rolled, as in a game of bowling.

bole, the trunk of a tree.
boll, seed vessel of cotton plant.
bowl, a circular vessel.

bow, a weapon for shooting arrows; a kind of knot.
beau, a man of dress; a lover.

brake, a thicket.
break, to split.

bred, reared.
bread, baked flour.

breech, the lower or hinder part of a thing.
breach, a gap or opening.

brews, ferments; plots.
bruise, to crush; a contusion.

broach, a spit; to pierce.
brooch, an ornament for the breast.

brows, plur., the forehead.
browse, to eat the tender leaves of shrubs, as "sheep browse."

burrow, hole in ground made by an animal.
borough, a corporate town.
burro, a donkey.

by, a preposition and a prefix.
buy, to purchase.
bye, as in good-bye; a goal.
bi-, two, as in biweekly.

call, cry out; a visit.
caul, a membrane.

canon, a law; a rule.
cannon, a large gun.

canvas, a coarse cloth.
canvass, to solicit.

cast, to throw; a form.
caste, a tribe; a class.

cede, to give up.
seed, the embryo of a future plant.

ceiling, cover of a room.
sealing, tight closing, as with wax.

cell, a small cavity; a room.
sell, to exchange for a price.

cellar, an excavation in the ground.
seller, one who sells.

cent, a hundred.
sent, past tense of send.
scent, perfume; to smell.

cereal, pertaining to grain; food made of grain.
serial, pertaining to successive parts, as in a series.

cession, a giving up.
session, a sitting; a meeting.

chews, grinds with the teeth.
choose, to select.

choir, a company of singers.
quire, a set of sheets of paper.

cite, to summon; to quote.
site, place; position.
sight, the power of seeing; a look.

clause, part of a sentence.
claws, sharp nails or toes of animal or bird.

clime, a region; a country.
climb, to mount; to ascend.

core, an innermost part; a center.
corps, an organized company, as of soldiers.

course, a place for running; career.
coarse, not fine.

coward, one wanting in courage.
cowered, crouched through fear.

creek, a small stream.
creak, to make a harsh, grating noise.

crews, bodies of seamen for ships.
cruise, to sail from place to place on the ocean.
cruse, a small cup; a small bottle.

currents, streams.
currants, small fruit.

dew, moisture condensed and deposited from the air.
due, owing.

discreet, prudent; cautious.
discrete, distinct; disjoined.

doe, female of deer.
do, a musical sound name.
dough, unbaked bread.

done, performed.
dun, a color; to demand payment of debt.

dying, ceasing to live.
dyeing, shading or coloring.

faint, very fatigued; to swoon.
feint, a pretense.

fane, a temple.
fain, anxious; desirous.
feign, to pretend.

fare, money paid for a journey; food.
fair, beautiful; right; a market.

faun, a sylvan deity.
fawn, a young deer; to flatter meanly.

find, to discover.
fined, subject to a money penalty.

flour, fine part of meal.
flower, blossom of a plant.

fore, in front.
four, a number.

forth, forward; out.
fourth, the ordinal of four.

freeze, to congeal.
frieze, a coarse woolen fabric; an ornamented band on a wall.

gate, entrance; a door.
gait, one's way of walking.

gild, to overlay and adorn with gold.
guild, a society or corporation.

gilt, overlaid with gold.
guilt, responsibility for crime.

great, large.
grate, a fireplace; to rub against.

grieves, laments; causes grief.
greaves, armor for the legs.

guessed, estimated at random.
guest, one who is entertained.

hair, as of the head.
hare, an animal.

hale, strong in health; to drag.
hail, rain frozen in coming from the clouds; to greet.

hall, a large room.
haul, to drag; to pull.

heel, the hind part of the foot.
heal, to cure; to grow sound.
he'll, contraction for "he will."

herd, a collection of cattle.
heard, past tense of hear.

hoard, to lay up in secret.
horde, a wandering tribe; a savage band.

hoes, uses a hoe.
hose, stockings; socks.
hose, rubber pipe.

I, a pronoun.
aye or **ay**, yes.
eye, organ of sight.

indite, to compose and write.
indict, to charge or accuse formally.

isle, a contraction for island.
aisle, passage in an auditorium.
I'll, contraction for "I will."

kernel, the central part.
colonel, chief officer of a regiment.

lane, a narrow passage.
lain, past participle of lie, to rest lengthwise on or against.

leaf, as of a book, a tree, etc.
lief, willingly.

least, little; beyond all others.
leased, held on lease.

led, past tense and participle of led.
lead, a metal.

liar, one who tells lies.
lyre, a musical instrument.

lone, solitary; alone.
loan, a temporary grant.

male, opposite of female.
mail, armor; letters.

mane, the long hair on the neck of an animal.
main, the sea; principal; chief.

manner, method or way.
manor, an estate; a domain.

mantle, a cloak; a cover.
mantel, the slab or shelf above a fireplace.

marshal, a military or police officer.
martial, warlike.

maze, an intricate place.
maize, Indian corn.

mean, shabby; low; to intend.
mien, manner of look or appearance.

meet, fit; to assemble.
mete, to measure.
meat, food; flesh.

mind, the understanding.
mined, excavated.

miner, a worker in mines.
minor, one under age.

mite, something very small.
might, power; strength.

moan, to lament.
mown, cut down.

mussel, a shellfish.
muscle, the fleshy parts of an animal body.

mustard, a kind of plant.
mustered, assembled.

nave, hub of a wheel; main portion of a cathedral.
knave, a rogue.

nay, no.
neigh, cry of a horse.

need, want; poverty.
knead, to work the materials into dough.

new, not old.
knew, past tense of know.
gnu, a wild ox.

night, opposite of day.
knight, a title of honor.

no, opposite of yes.
know, to understand.

nose, the organ of smell.
noes, plural of no.
knows, has knowledge; understands.

oar, implement for rowing a boat.
ore, metal as it comes from the earth.
o'er, contraction for over.

ode, a short poem.
owed, indebted to; past tense of owe.

our, a pronoun.
hour, sixty minutes.

pain, soreness.
pane, a piece of glass.

pair, two; a couple.
pare, to slice thinly.
pear, a kind of fruit.

passed, gone through; gone.
past, not present or future.

pause, a stop.
paws, feet of a beast.

peace, a state of quiet.
piece, a part.

pedal, a foot lever; to operate such a lever.
peddle, to sell from house to house.

peel, skin; outside.
peal, sound of bells.

peer, to look intently; an equal.
pier, a wharf.

plane, a perfectly flat or level surface; a kind of tree.
plain, level, flat country.

plate, a flat piece of metal; a shallow dish.
plait, to fold; to braid.

please, to delight or gratify.
pleas, pleadings in law; excuses.

plum, a fruit.
plumb, perpendicular; an instrument to determine whether a wall is perpendicular.

pray, to entreat.
prey, plunder.

prays, supplicates.
praise, approbation; to approve.
preys, attacks, as a wild beast.

principal, invested funds; chief.
principle, a fundamental rule or law.

quarts, measures of two pints each.
quartz, a variety of rock crystal.

rain, water from clouds.
rein, part of a harness; to check.
reign, to rule as a king.

rap, to strike sharply.
wrap, to wind or roll together; to fold.

rapped, struck.
rapt, transported; ravished.
wrapped, folded; enclosed.

rays, beams of light.
raise, to exalt; to lift up.
raze, to destroy utterly.

read, as a book; to study.
reed, a hollow cane.

recks, cares or takes account of.
wrecks, destroys or shatters.

red, a color.
read, past tense of read.

rest, peace; quiet.
wrest, to twist; to wrench.

right, just; correct.
rite, a ceremony.
write, to trace letters or characters.
wright, a workman.

road, a path; a way.
rode, past tense of ride.
rowed, propelled with oars.

rôle, a part in acting a play.
roll, a round thing; a register.

rood, fourth part of an acre.
rude, uncultivated; rough.
rued, grieved for.

root, as of a plant; origin.
route, direction; road.

ruff, an article of dress.
rough, unpolished; rugged.

rung, sounded, as a bell.
wrung, twisted.

rye, a sort of grain.
wry, crooked.

sac, a membranous receptacle.
sack, a large, strong bag.

sail, to navigate.
sale, act of selling.

scene, a sight; part of a play.
seen, observed.

sea, a wide expanse of water.
see, to perceive.

sees, looks at.
seize, to take hold of.

skull, the whole bone of the head.
scull, a small boat; a light, short oar.

soared, mounted on the wing.
sword, a weapon of war.

sold, given for a price.
soled, furnished with a sole.

sore, painful.
soar, to mount by flight.

soul, the spirit.
sole, only; bottom of the foot; a fish.

sow, to scatter seed.
sew, to fasten, as with a needle.
so, in this manner.

staid, steady; grave.
stayed, supported with ropes, as a mast.

stair, flight of steps.
stare, to look at.

stake, a pointed piece of wood.
steak, a slice of meat.

straight, direct; not curved.
strait, narrow; confined.

style, manner of dress or action.
stile, steps over a wall.

sucker, a young shoot of a tree.
succor, help; to relieve.

sum, the amount of anything; to add up.
some, more or less of a quantity.

sutler, one who follows a camp to sell provisions, etc.
subtler, more cunning; more acute.

sweet, pleasant; delightful.
suite, attendants; a set of rooms.

tale, a story.
tail, an appendage; hinder part.

tare, a weed; allowance for weight.
tear, a rent; to rend.

tear, water from the eye.
tier, a row; a series.

teem, to produce in abundance.
team, a pair of horses or oxen, working together.

their, possessive of they.
there, adv., in that place.

threw, past tense of throw.
through, from side to side, or from end to end.

throw, to cast; to fling.
throe, extreme pain.

time, fit season.
thyme, a garden plant.

told, expressed in words.
tolled, rung, as a bell.

tract, a quantity of land.
tracked, followed by the marks left.

two, a pair; twice one.
too, adv., also; excess, as too much.
to, preposition.

use, to apply or handle for some purpose.
ewes, female sheep.
yews, evergreen trees.

vale, a valley.
veil, a curtain, a covering.

vice, a fault.
vise, a tool.

wade, to walk through water.
weighed, past tense of weigh.

wait, to remain; to stay.
weight, heaviness; importance.

ware, sing. of wares; goods.
wear, to last; to endure.

waste, to squander.
waist, the middle part, as of the body.

wave, a moving ridge; to undulate.
waive, to defer; to abandon.

way, a road; manner.
weigh, to determine heaviness; to ponder.

wood, a forest; timber.
would, verb of wish or determination.

HETERONYMS

Words spelled the same but differing in sound and in meaning. Strictly, heteronyms, from the very etymology of the word, have no alliance between them except the accidental one of the same orthography. They are derived from different roots and their meanings are so distinct that their separate origin is at once indicated by such meanings. Mere change of accent, moreover, does not constitute a heteronym.

bass (*bās*), a term in music.
bass (*băs*), a fish.

bow (*bou*), the forward part of a vessel.
bow (*bō*), an archer's weapon; an implement for playing the violin; a knot.

chap (*chăp*), a fellow.
chap (*chŏp*), fleshy covering of a jaw.

dives (*dīvz*), goes under water.
Dives (*dī'vēz*), the rich man.

does (*dōz*), female deer.
does (*dŭz*), from the verb *do*.

gill (*jĭl*), quarter of a pint.
gill (*gĭl*), the organ of respiration of a fish.

glower (*glou'ẽr*), to stare.
glower (*glō'ẽr*), something that glows.

hinder (*hĭn'dẽr*), to prevent.
hinder (*hīn'dẽr*), back part.

job (*jŏb*), petty work.
Job (*jōb*), a man's name.

lead (*lĕd*), a metal.
lead (*lēd*), to conduct.

lower (*lō'ẽr*), to descend.
lower (*lou'ẽr*), to frown.

manes (*mānz*), the hair on the neck of animals.
manes (*mā'nēz*), departed spirits.

mate (*māt*), a companion.
mate (*mä'tā*), a beverage.

mow (*mō*), to cut down.
mow (*mou*), a heap of grain; a compartment for storing grain.

mowing (*mō'ĭng*), the act of cutting.
mowing (*mou'ĭng*), to store away.

polish (*pŏl'ĭsh*), to shine.
Polish (*pōl'ĭsh*), adjective derived from *Pole*—pertaining to Poland.

poll (*pŏl*), a degree without honors.
poll (*pōl*), the head; a tax.

put (*po͝ot*), to move; to push.
put (*pŭt*), a rustic; a clown.

repent (*rē'pĕnt*), creeping; prostrate; reptant.
repent (*rė-pĕnt'*), to feel penitence, contrition, or regret, for what one has done or has omitted to do.

row (*rō*), a rank or file; to propel with oars.
row (*rou*), a tumult.

sake (*sāk*), purpose, end, cause.
sake (*sä'kĕ*), liquor made from rice.

sewer (*sū'ẽr*), a ditch or a drain.
sewer (*sō'ẽr*), one who sews.

shower (*shō'ẽr*), one that exhibits.
shower (*shou'ẽr*), a light rain.

singer (*sĭn'jẽr*), one that singes.
singer (*sĭng'ẽr*), one that sings.

slough (*slou, slo͞o*), a hole full of mire; a marshy place.
slough (*slŭf*), cast-off skin of a serpent.

sow (*sō*), to scatter seeds.
sow (*sou*), female pig.

stingy (*stĭn'jĭ*), penurious.
stingy (*stĭng'ĭ*), piercing.

swinger (*swĭng'ẽr*), one that swings.
swinger (*swĭn'jẽr*), one that beats or chastises.

tarry (*tär'ĭ*), covered with, or like, tar.
tarry (*tăr'ĭ*), to abide at or in a place; to stay; to loiter; to delay.

tear (*târ*), to divide or separate on being pulled.
tear (*tēr*), a drop of limpid saline fluid secreted by the lachrymal gland.

tower (*tou'ẽr*), a high edifice; a citadel.
tower (*tō'ẽr*), that which tows.

wind (*wĭnd*), air in motion.
wind (*wīnd*), to twist.

wound (*wo͞ond*), an injury.
wound (*wound*), twisted.

SENTENCE BUILDING

English Grammar is both a science and an art. As a science, it investigates the principles in general on which the English language is based; as an art, it teaches the method of applying these principles in speaking and in writing the English language correctly.

In the whole range of school subjects there is none of greater importance than that of language. To facilitate the study of the English language, therefore, the true principles of grammar have been outlined in the following pages in a convenient form, expressed in a simple manner, and illustrated by appropriate examples.

The English Sentence

Word Groups. We express our thoughts in groups of words,—sentences, clauses, phrases.

A *sentence* is a group of words used to express a complete thought.

The complete sentence must always contain a subject and a predicate. The subject is the thing named; the predicate is the assertion about the thing named: "*Autumn* (subj.) *lingers* (pred.)."

In an imperative sentence, like "Go to him," the subject "you" is not usually expressed. This is an instance of *ellipsis*, or the omission of words otherwise necessary to grammatical completeness, when their meaning is well understood by the reader or hearer: "The knife belongs to Tom; the pencil (belongs) to William."

A *clause* is a group of words containing, like the sentence, a subject and a predicate, but used only as part of a complete sentence: "The motor, | *which was new,* | suddenly failed to work."

A clause may be either *independent* (principal) or *dependent* (subordinate): "*He commanded,* | *who had never commanded before.*" The first words, *he commanded,* form an independent clause. The other words form a dependent clause; for, as they stand, they do not make a sentence. See *Complex Sentence.*

A *phrase* is a group of words so closely related as to express a single idea. The phrase is used as a part of speech: "*To become rich* (noun) was his ambition." "It was a matter *of importance* (adjective)." "Come *at your convenience* (adverb)."

Parts of Speech. In building sentences, we use name-words, action-words, modifiers, and connectives of various kinds. According to their use in sentences, these words are classified as *parts of speech,* of which there are eight:

1. A *noun* is a word used to name a person, a place, or a thing: *boy, city, foot, air, size.*

2. A *pronoun* is a word used in place of a noun: *it, her, none, who.*

Note.—Nouns, pronouns, and phrases or clauses used as nouns are called *substantives.*

3. A *verb* is a word used to say, or assert, something about a person, a place, or a thing: *walk, soften, drive, is.*

4. An *adjective* is a word used to modify, that is, describe or limit, a noun or pronoun: "*bright* sunshine," "*few* people," "I *alone.*"

5. An *adverb* is a word used to modify the meaning of a verb, an adjective, or another adverb: "speak *well,*" "walk *swiftly,*" "run *homeward,*" "*very* pretty," "*so* quickly."

6. A *conjunction* is a word used to connect words, phrases, clauses, or sentences: *and, but, if, unless.*

7. A *preposition* is a word used to show the relation of some particular word, called its object, to another word: "flocks *of* birds (obj.)"; "strength *through* exercise (obj.)"; "peace *with* honor (obj.)."

8. An *interjection* is a word of exclamation used to express any emotion or feeling, as surprise, joy, grief, etc.: *ah! alas!*

Note.—Some words may be used as *several different parts of speech:*

Noun: "The *storm* was soon over."
Adjective: "The station displayed *storm* signals."
Verb: "The troops will *storm* the outworks."

Noun: "The *inside* of the house is pleasing."
Adjective: "He has *inside* information."
Adverb: "Will you step *inside?*"
Preposition: "*Inside* the door stood a clock."

Preposition: "I have been waiting *since* noon."
Conjunction: "*Since* I saw you, much has happened."

Adjective: "*Which* hat have you?"
Pronoun: "The hat *which* you see is mine."

Adjective: "*That* hat is mine."
Pronoun: "I want *that.*"
Conjunction: "He said *that* he would go."

Parts of the Sentence

The Subject. The subject of a sentence is that about which the predicate says something: "*The weather* is cold." "*Health* counts for more than wealth."

Simple Subject.—The essential part of the *subject* is a substantive, that is, a noun, a pronoun, or a phrase or clause used as a noun. Noun means "name." The substantive is called the *essential,* or *simple, subject,* or the *subject substantive:* "A great *city* (noun substantive) is interesting"; "*She* (pro. substantive) is my friend"; "*To read well* (subst. phrase) requires much practice"; "*What he saw* (subst. clause) startled him."

Complete Subject.—The substantive with its modifiers is called the *complete subject:* "*His deposit* (subst.) *in the bank* (adj. phrase) | was large"; "*The nature* (subst.) *of his occupation* (adj. phrase) *in the city* (adj. phrase) | was never revealed"; "*The evil* (subst.) *that men do* (adj. clause) lives after them."

These modifiers of the substantive may be adjectives, possessive nouns or pronouns, nouns in apposition, clauses or phrases used as adjectives or nouns.

The Predicate. The word *predicate* means "something said." The predicate of a sentence is that which is said about the subject: "Roses *were blooming.*"

The essential part of a predicate is a *verb.* We call the verb in the predicate the *essential,* or *simple, predicate,* or the *predicate verb.* "The car *ran* (pred. verb) *against the curb.*" *Ran* is the simple predicate; *ran against the curb* is the complete predicate.

The *complete predicate* includes the verb with its modifiers and complements,—adverbs, predicate nouns or pronouns, predicate adjectives, object nouns or pronouns, phrases or clauses used as adverbs or nouns: "He *ran* (pred. verb) *fast* (adv.)." "George *is* (pred. verb) *king* (pred. noun)." "It *is* (pred. verb) *he* (pred. pro.)." "The air *turned* (pred. verb) *cold* (pred. adj.)." "All *love* (pred. verb) *truth* (object)." "He *writes* (pred. verb) *with a pen* (adverb phrase)." "The sun *had set* (pred. verb) *when we started* (adverb. clause)." "Children *like* (pred. verb) *to play* (noun phrase)." "I *heard* (pred. verb) *what you said* (noun clause)."

For compound subject and compound predicate, see *Simple Sentence.*

Classification of Sentences

Kinds of Sentences. In respect to their *meaning,* sentences may be classified as declarative, interrogative, imperative, and exclamatory.

The *declarative sentence* makes a statement: "*John is not here.*"

The *interrogative sentence* asks a question: "*Where is my hat?*"

The *imperative sentence* gives a command; "*Answer his question.*"

The *exclamatory sentence* expresses a strong feeling, as of surprise, joy, etc.: "*How free are the pleasures of youth!*"

Note.—The foregoing is the common grouping of sentences. A more logical classification is the following: (1) *affirmative* and *negative*; (2) *declarative* and *interrogative*; (3) *exclamatory* and *nonexclamatory*.

Forms of Sentences. In respect to their *grammatical form*, sentences are simple, compound, or complex.

The *simple sentence* is a sentence of one clause, that is, a sentence having but one subject and one predicate. The simple sentence may be very short: "*Birds* | *sing.*" It may be longer, when the subject and the predicate are modified by several words and phrases: "*Those furs in the window* | *have been gathered from many different countries and climates.*"

A simple sentence may have a *compound subject*; as, "*The house and the grounds* | are beautiful." It may have a *compound predicate*; as, "They | *sat and listened* to the music." Both subject and predicate may be compound; as, "*Mary and Elizabeth* | *lived and reigned* in England." These are important distinctions. Do not confuse the *long* sentence with the *complex* sentence.

The *compound sentence* is formed of two or more independent, or co-ordinate, clauses, which may or may not be joined by co-ordinating conjunctions, such as *and, but, for*: "*A man approached,* | *and* | *we asked him about the road*"; "*Some men are born great;*| *others achieve greatness.*"

The *complex sentence* is formed of a principal, or independent, clause and of one or more subordinate, or dependent, clauses. These subordinate clauses are introduced by subordinate conjunctions, such as *if, unless, because,* by relative pronouns, *who, which, what, that,* and by conjunctive adverbs, such as *when, where, while*: "I shall go *if it stops raining*"; "The child *that is happy* makes friends"; "Make hay *while the sun shines.*"

The Parts of Speech

Grammatical Relations. The relations of a word, a phrase, or a clause to other words in a sentence are called its *syntax* or *construction.* Either of these words means "placing or bringing together."

Inflection, in grammar, is the changing of the forms of words to indicate grammatical relation and change of meaning. Inflection of verbs is called *conjugation.* Inflection of nouns and pronouns is called *declension.* Inflection of adjectives and adverbs is called *comparison.*

In the English sentence, the grammatical relations of words are indicated by their position and by the use of connectives. The English language has dropped so many of the endings formerly attached to nouns and verbs that inflection in English grammar is of slight importance. So-called declension becomes in English the systematic arrangement in tables of the various forms of nouns and pronouns used for different cases and numbers. Conjugation consists in arranging in tables the various verb forms and verb phrases used for different modes and tenses.

Kinds of Substantives: Nouns and Pronouns

A *substantive* is a word, phrase, or clause used as a noun.

KINDS OF NOUNS

Proper Nouns. A *proper noun* is the name of a particular person, place, or thing. It is always written with a capital letter; as, *John, Paris, England, Europe.*

Common Nouns. A *common noun* is the name of any one of a class of persons, places, or things; as, *table, book, rabbit, boy, weather.*

Abstract Nouns. An *abstract noun* is the name of an idea; as, *honesty, hope, truth, system.*

Collective Nouns. A *collective noun* is the name of a group or collection of single things, considered as one; as, *crowd, army, jury, family, committee.*

Verbal Nouns. A *verbal noun,* or *gerund,* is the name of an action; as, *walking, skating, working.*

An *appositive* is a noun used after another noun or pronoun to describe or explain the meaning of that noun or pronoun. An appositive is said to be *in apposition to* the noun or pronoun it defines or explains: "Milton, the *poet,* became blind."

A *predicate noun* or *pronoun* is a noun or a pronoun that completes the predicate verb and refers to the subject: "Lincoln was *president.*" "It is *I.*"

KINDS OF PRONOUNS

Pronouns are classified as *personal, interrogative, demonstrative, relative* or *conjunctive,* and *indefinite.*

Personal Pronouns. The following are the forms of personal pronouns:

Singular

	First Person	Second Person	Third Person Mas.	Third Person Fem.	Third Person Neut.
Nominative	I	you	he	she	it
Possessive	my, mine	your, yours	his	her, hers	its
Objective	me	you	him	her	it

Plural

	First Person	Second Person	Third Person
Nominative	we	you	they
Possessive	our, ours	your, yours	their, theirs
Objective	us	you	them

The possessive forms given in the table are sometimes called *possessive pronouns.* They are pronouns in origin, but in use they are *possessive adjectives.*

Special Uses. *Ye* and *thou, thy, thine, thee,* are old forms, now seldom used except in poetry or in the language of religion.

The masculine pronouns, *he, his,* and *him,* are used also as of common gender: "Let every child use *his* own book."

You, whether referring to one person or more, always takes the plural verb.

It often stands as the *impersonal subject* of a verb: "*It* rains"; "*It* is cold"; "*It* grew dark."

It may be used as the *impersonal object* of a verb: "He footed *it* all the way"; "They are roughing *it* in the woods."

It is sometimes used as an introductory word, the real subject following the verb: "*It* is well to think before you speak." See *There.*

Compound Personal Pronouns. The word *self* added to *my, thy, your, him, her, it,* and the plural *selves* to *our, your, them,* form *compound personal pronouns,* often called *reflexive pronouns.* They are used chiefly (1) to express emphasis, with or without the simple pronoun: "I *myself* am positive"; "She talks of no one but *herself.*" (2) as reflexive object of a verb, the object and the subject of the verb being the same person or thing: "He dressed *himself*"; "You will hurt *yourself.*"

These pronouns have the same form for *nominative* and *objective* cases. They are not used in the *possessive.*

The simple personal pronoun is sometimes used reflexively in poetry: "I lay *me* down."

Interrogative Pronouns. Pronouns used in asking questions are *interrogative pronouns*: *who, which, what.* "*Who* is here?" "*Which* do you like?" "*What* did you say?"

Singular and Plural	
Nominative	who
Possessive	whose
Objective	whom

The interrogatives *which* and *what* have no declension or change of form, however used. *Who* and *whom* refer to persons only; the other forms, to persons or things.

Which, what, and *whose* are used also as *interrogative adjectives*: "*Which* train did he take?" "*What* number is that?" "*Whose* book is this?"

Demonstrative Pronouns. *This, that,* and the plurals, *these* and *those,* are called *demonstratives,* because they point out definitely the persons or things to which they refer. Latin *demonstrare* means "to point out": "*That* is the question"; "*Those* are the bills"; "The reasons are *these.*"

When used with nouns, like adjectives, the demonstratives are often called *demonstrative adjectives*: "*this* farm"; "*those* cattle."

Relative Pronouns. A relative pronoun is both pronoun and conjunction. As a *pronoun,* the word is used like a noun; as a *conjunction,* it joins clauses. Hence relative pronouns are sometimes called *conjunctive pronouns.* The relative pronouns are *who, which, what, that.* *As* and *but* may be used as relative pronouns.

	Singular and Plural	
Nominative	who	which
Possessive	whose	whose
Objective	whom	which

What and *that* have no change of form for the *nominative* and the *objective* and are not used in the *possessive.*

Who and *whom* refer to persons only.

Whose is used of both persons and things.

Which, as a relative, refers to things only.

That refers to both persons and things.

What may be called a *double relative,* being equivalent to *that which,* the demonstrative pronoun *that* and the relative pronoun *which*: "We know *what* (*that which*) he wants."

As is used as *relative pronoun*: "I want such *as* (*those which*) are desirable."

But is used as *relative pronoun*: "There is no fireside *but* (*that not*) has one vacant chair."

Which and *what* are used also as *relative adjectives*: "I know *which* (*that which*) book you mean"; "I see *what* (*that which*) reward she will receive."

Compound Relative Pronouns. *Who, which,* and *what* are combined with *ever* and *soever* to form *compound relative pronouns*: *whoever. whosoever, whichever, whichsoever, whatever, whatsoever.* The forms with *so* are rarely used.

Indefinite Pronouns. Indefinite pronouns do not point out definitely, but they refer in a general manner to persons or objects. Those commonly used are *each, every, either, neither, some, all, any, few, many, one, none, other, another, both.* Many of these words are used as indefinite adjectives:

(pro.) "*Some* dislike animals."

(adj.) "*Some* people dislike animals."

The only indefinite pronouns which have plural forms are *one* and *other*: "Give me a small *one* (sing.)"; "Give me small *ones* (plur.)"; "I want the *other* (sing.)"; "I want the *others* (plur.)."

Adjective Pronouns. The *demonstrative* and *indefinite pronouns* are also called *adjective pronouns,* because they are used both as adjectives and as nouns.

Grammatical Relations of Nouns and Pronouns

For nouns and pronouns, grammatical relations are said to be relations of *case, number, person,* and *gender.*

CASE

Nominative Case. The following are said to be in the *nominative* (naming) *case*:

1. A noun or pronoun used as subject: "The *boy* plays." "*He* came home."

2. A noun in apposition to a noun or pronoun in the nominative case: "John, my *brother,* is here." "She, the *woman* in black, wept bitterly."

3. A predicate noun or pronoun: "The man was *master.*" "It is *he* whom you want."

4. A noun or pronoun used in direct address: "*Citizens,* remember your duties"; "O *thou* that rollest above! whence are thy beams?"

5. A noun or pronoun used absolutely with a participle: "The *storm* abating, the air grew colder."

6. A noun or pronoun used in exclamation: "A *horse*! A *horse*! My kingdom for a horse." "*He,* lost!"

Objective Case. The following are said to be in the *objective case* (*objective* meaning "thrown, or directed, toward," as the action of a verb is directed toward a noun):

1. A noun, a pronoun, a phrase or a clause used as the object of a transitive verb (*transitive* meaning "going across," as the action of a verb goes across to the object): "James studies *spelling.*" "I like *her.*" "I tried *to learn a foreign language.*" "He said, '*I shall go.*'" "She knew *that all was well.*"

2. Indirect object: "He wrote (to) his *brother* (indirect object) a *letter* (direct object)."

One may recognize the indirect object by the possibility of using *to* before it without changing the meaning of the sentence.

3. The object of a preposition: "He went into the *store.*"

4. A word in apposition to a noun or pronoun in the objective case: "He found the house, a large stone *building.*"

5. Objective of exclamation: "Oh, happy *me*!"

6. A noun of time, distance, or quantity used adverbially. This is called an *adverbial objective*: "I slept four *hours*"; "He walked three *miles.*"

7. An objective complement (called also *predicate objective* and *adjunct accusative*): "They made him *chairman*"; "She called Mary *queen.*"

8. The secondary object: "They allowed each speaker an *hour.*" When such sentences are changed to the passive construction, the *secondary object* is retained as an object: "Each speaker was allowed an *hour.*"

9. A subject of an infinitive: "I know *him* to be truthful."

10. A predicate of an infinitive: "I know it to be *her.*"

Note.—Many recent authorities prefer the term *accusative case* for the foregoing constructions, except that of indirect object, for which they use the term *dative.*

Possessive Case. 1. A word expressing ownership or possession is in the *possessive case*: "*John's* books"; "*their* work."

2. When two nouns in the possessive case are in apposition, the second alone takes the possessive sign: "Webster the *statesman's* speeches"; "Jack the *giant-killer's* exploits."

3. The possessive form is used also to limit or define and does not necessarily indicate ownership: "six *days'* journey"; "*man's* duty"; "the *river's* brink."

Note.—Many authorities prefer the name *genitive* for the so-called possessive case.

Inflection.—English nouns have no inflection, or change of form, to denote cases, except the adding of the apostrophe and *s* for the possessive. See *Spelling.* Certain pronouns are inflected to denote cases. See *Kinds of Pronouns.*

Note.—Recent works on English grammar recommend the following classification of case forms and uses:

Forms,—*common* and *genitive.*

Uses,—*nominative, genitive, dative, accusative.*

Special Uses

Compound names and groups of words add the possessive sign to the last word: "*William the Conqueror's* throne"; "the *king of England's* palace"; "my *father-in-law's* house."

Joint Possession. If two or more possessive nouns imply joint possession of the same thing, and are connected by *and*, the possessive sign is used with the last noun only: "*Mary* and *John's* mother" implies common possession —one mother.

"*Mason* and *Hamlin's* organs."

"*Wheeler* and *Wilson's* store."

Separate Possession. If separate possession is implied, or if the nouns are connected by *or* or *nor*, each one takes the possessive sign:

"*Mary's* and *John's* mother" implies separate possession —two mothers.

"*Taft's* and *Wilson's* administration."

"Is that a *girl's* or a *boy's* voice?"

"He accepted neither the *skeptic's* nor the *clergyman's* view."

The possessive (genitive) case may be denoted by the objective case following the preposition *of*; "*Job's* patience," or "the patience *of Job*"; "*Somebody else's* work," or "the work *of somebody else*."

NUMBER

Nouns and pronouns denoting one person or thing are *singular*: *farm, wife*. Nouns and pronouns denoting more than one are *plural*: *farms, wives*. See *Spelling*.

Inflection.—English nouns regularly add *s* or *es* to form the plural. See *Spelling*. For pronoun plurals, see *Kinds of Pronouns*.

PERSON

The speaker or writer is the first person, *I, we*; the one addressed is the second person, *thou, you*; the person or thing spoken of is the third person, *he, it, they*.

Inflection.—English nouns are not inflected to distinguish person. See *Personal Pronouns*.

GENDER

In English, a noun or pronoun naming a male is *masculine*: *stag*. One naming a female, *feminine*: *girl*. One naming an object without sex, *neuter* (a Latin word, meaning "neither"): *tree*. Words which may be applied to either males or females are said to be of *common* gender: *animal*.

Inflection.—Nouns and pronouns are not inflected to distinguish gender. Personal pronouns have different forms to distinguish gender.

Antecedent. The substantive—word, phrase, or clause—for which a pronoun stands, and to which it refers, is called its *antecedent*, a Latin word, meaning "something going before":

"The man who planned the building made it his masterpiece." *Man* is the antecedent of *who* and of *his*.

"To sleep well, which is a blessing, is to repair and renew the body." *To sleep well* is a phrase, the antecedent of *which*.

Agreement. The pronoun is said to agree with its antecedent in *gender, person,* and *number*, but its *case* depends upon its use in the sentence:

"The book which you found is mine." The antecedent of *which* is *book*. *Book* is in the *nominative case*, the subject of *is*: *which* is in the *objective case*, the object of *found*.

"He is one of those who prefer winter." The antecedent of *who* is *those*, not *one*. Hence *who* is plural and requires a plural verb.

Verbs

KINDS OF VERBS

According to use, verbs are either *transitive* or *intransitive*.

Transitive Verbs. A transitive verb is one which requires an object to complete its meaning. The object, sometimes called *object complement*, names the receiver of the action of the verb: "The man *built* (verb) the *house* (object)."

Intransitive Verbs. An intransitive verb is one which does not require an object to complete its meaning. Some intransitives, however, need to be completed by a predicate noun or adjective, often called *attribute complement*, which refers to or modifies the subject: "That village *is* (verb) *Millville* (attribute complement)"; "The action *seems* (verb) *right* (attribute complement)."

GRAMMATICAL RELATIONS OF VERBS

The syntax of verbs involves relations of *voice, mode, tense, person,* and *number*. For the forms to express these, see *Table of Specimen Verb Forms*.

VOICE

Meaning of the Voices. *Voice* is often defined as that property of verbs which indicates whether the subject acts or is acted upon.

Active Voice.—If the subject is acting, the verb is in the *active*, or "doing," *voice*: "The man *broke* his cane."

Passive Voice.—If the subject is being acted upon, or receiving an action, the verb is in the *passive*, or "suffering," *voice*: "The cane *was broken*."

Forms to Denote Voice. The terms "active voice" and "passive voice" are applied also to the forms of the verb.

That form of the verb which shows that the subject is acting is called *active voice*: "Mary *broke* the dish."

That form of the verb which shows that the subject is acted upon is called *passive voice*: "The dish *was broken* by Mary." Some part of the verb *be* is joined to the past participle of a transitive verb to make the *passive voice*: *is sold, were made*.

Any transitive verb may be used in the passive voice, its object in the active becoming its subject in the passive: "The boy *lights* (active) the lamps"; "The lamps *are lighted* (passive) by the boy."

Intransitive verbs ordinarily are active, but some verbs are used either as intransitive or transitive: "He *spoke* (intrans.) truthfully"; "He *spoke* (trans.) the truth." When used transitively, such verbs may become passive: "The truth *was spoken* by him."

Some intransitive verbs, used with a following preposition, have a transitive meaning; as, *laugh at, look over, wonder at*: "He *laughed at* me"; "She *looked over* the work"; "They *wondered at* his skill." Such phrases are transitive in the fullest sense as tested by the passive construction: "I *was laughed at* by him"; "The work *was looked over* by her"; "His skill *was wondered at* by them."

MODE

Meaning of the Modes. *Mode* (or *mood*) may be defined as that property of verbs which shows the manner in which the action or state is conceived.

If the action or state expressed is thought of simply as a fact, the mode is *indicative*; if it is regarded as doubtful or merely as desired, the mode is *subjunctive*; if it is viewed as a command, the mode is *imperative*.

Forms to Denote Modes. The term "modes" is applied also to the several series of verb forms. In this use, *mode* is the form of the verb which shows the manner of expressing an action or a state.

The indicative mode states a fact or asks a simple question; as, "The sun shines"; "Has the rain been heavy?"

The indicative forms, however, are commonly used to express subjunctive and imperative ideas: "The dam will break if the river *rises* (condition)"; "You *will report* at seven (command)."

The imperative mode expresses a command or an entreaty; as, "*Come* here"; "*Have* mercy upon me."

The subjunctive mode makes a doubtful or conditional assertion; as, "Though he *slay* me, yet will I trust him."

For the so-called *potential mode*, see *Modal Auxiliaries*.

TENSE

Meaning of Tenses. The *tense* of a verb indicates the time of the action or state.

As applied to verb forms, *tense* is the form the verb takes to indicate time.

According to the time expressed and the completeness or incompleteness of the action, state, or condition, the verb varies in tense.

Simple Tenses.—The simple (or incomplete) tenses, *present, past, future,* signify action or condition as continuing in present, past, or future time: "I *go*"; "I *went*"; "I *shall go.*"

Perfect Tenses.—The perfect (or complete) tenses imply the completion of an act in present time (*present perfect*), in past time (*past perfect*), or in future time (*future perfect*): "I *have gone*"; "I *had gone*"; "I *shall have gone.*" See *Table of Specimen Verb Forms.*

Other Tenses.—Some authorities distinguish a *past future* tense, as, "We thought he *would go,*" and a *past future perfect* tense, as, "We thought he *would have gone.*"

PERSON AND NUMBER

A verb must agree with its subject in person and in number: "I *do* not"; "He *does* not"; "You *do* not"; "They *do* not."

VERB FORMS

Inflection of Verbs, or Conjugation. In conjugation, English verbs change form to show voice, mode, tense, person, and number. The usually inflected forms are the third person singular of the present active indicative; the past active indicative; the present and past participles: *has, had, having, had.* For exceptions, see *Table of Specimen Verb Forms*: the verb *be*; *Subjunctive Mode.* See also *Thou Forms.*

Verb Phrases. All other mode, tense, and voice meanings are expressed by the simple verb or by verb phrases. A *verb phrase* is a group of verbs used as a single verb. A verb phrase is formed by prefixing an auxiliary (helping) verb to some infinitive or participle form of a principal verb: "Wars *shall cease*"; "It *may rain*"; "Fashions *have been changing.*"

Principal Parts. In order to conjugate any verb throughout its various modes and tenses, it is necessary to know only the *infinitive*, the *past tense*, and the *past participle.* These three, therefore, are called the *principal parts*: *find, found, found*; *go, went, gone.*

Regular Verbs. A regular (or weak) verb, in English, forms its past tense and past participle by adding *d* or *ed* to the present: *load, loaded*; *love, loved*; *wash, washed*; *persuade, persuaded.*

Irregular Verbs. An irregular (or strong) verb forms its past tense and past participle by a vowel change, frequently adding a change of ending: *hide, hid, hidden*; *drink, drank, drunk*; *eat, ate, eaten.*

A Defective Verb is one that lacks some of its principal parts; as, *ought, may, can.*

A Redundant Verb is one that has both a regular and an irregular form; as, *bereave, bereaved* or *bereft, bereaved* or *bereft.*

A Copulative Verb is an intransitive verb which connects the subject with a predicate noun or pronoun or with a predicate adjective. Such a verb is called a *linking* verb. Among intransitive verbs thus used are *be, become, seem, appear, feel, grow, remain, sit, stand*: "Mary *became* queen"; "He *grows* tall"; "She *feels* better."

A Reflexive Verb is a transitive verb, the subject and the object of which are the same individual: "I *wash* myself"; "He *contradicted* himself."

An Impersonal Verb is one used only in the third person singular with no definite personal subject: "It *rains*"; "It *snows.*"

Auxiliary Verbs. Auxiliary comes from the Latin *auxilium,* meaning "help"; hence, auxiliary verbs are verbs that help in the conjugation of other verbs. They are of two classes:

1. *Auxiliaries of tense and voice: will, shall, have, be, do, did.*

The forms of the auxiliary *be* used with a past participle make the passive voice; as, *are told, was told, shall have been told.*

Have and *had* are auxiliaries used with the past participle to form the present perfect and the past perfect tense, hence *have* and *had* are called "signs" of the perfect and past perfect tenses respectively:

Present Perfect.—I *have* told
Past Perfect.—I *had* told

Do and *did* are either emphatic or interrogative auxiliaries used with the present infinitive of another verb to form the present and past tenses respectively.

Present.—I *do* tell; *do* I tell?
Past.—I *did* tell; *did* I tell?

2. *Modal auxiliaries: may, might, can, could, would, should, must,* (in some cases *shall, will,* and *have*). For the uses of *shall, will, should, would,* see *Good Usage.*

The modal auxiliaries may be prefixed to the present infinitive or to the perfect infinitive of any verb in order to express various modes. They suggest doubt, permission, wish, ability, or duty: "I *may* tell, *may* have told"; "He *can* go"; "You *should* read."

May and *might* express permission, possibility, or doubt. *Might* was formerly used in the past tense, and it now expresses more doubt or dependence upon conditions than *may.* The time of the verb phrase formed with these auxiliaries is determined by the verb form following the auxiliary: "It *may* (*might*) have happened (past)."

Can and *could* express ability. *Can* signifies either present or future time: "We *can* go." *Could* may express past time: "Yesterday, I *could* do nothing." *Could* usually implies an uncertain condition: "They *could* have gone (if something had not interfered)."

Potential Mode.—The phrases formed with *may, might, can,* and *could* are called *potential verb phrases,* because these verbs imply power (potential from Latin *potentia* meaning "power"). They are often classified in tables as *potential* forms.

Must, followed by the present infinitive, usually expresses obligation or necessity: "You *must* hear him." Otherwise, it may express the speaker's certainty in respect to something in spite of contrary appearances: "His story *must* be true"; "They *must* have started."

Have is often used to express duty or necessity. For this meaning, it is prefixed to the present infinitive (with *to*): "We *have* (*had*) to listen to his tale."

Ought is sometimes called a *modal auxiliary.* It is used to express duty or obligation: "He *ought* to go"; "You *ought* to have spoken."

Participles. The participle, meaning "sharer," is the verb form that *shares* or *partakes* of the nature of an adjective. While modifying a noun, like an adjective, it may take an object or, like a verb, have adverbial modifiers: "Let *sleeping* dogs lie"; "The *burnt* child fears the fire"; "*Having found* his *mother* (obj.), the child was quiet"; "They found him *weeping bitterly* (adv.)."

A verb has three participles:

Present participle—*speaking* (action is in progress): "He stood *speaking.*"

Past participle—*spoken* (action is completed): "A little word in kindness *spoken.*"

Perfect participle—*having spoken* (action is completed before the time implied in the principal verb): "*Having spoken* the word, he departed." See *Table of Specimen Verb Forms.*

Gerund or **Verbal Noun.** Verb forms ending in *-ing* are used also as nouns. They may be modified by adverbs, since they are verbal, or by adjectives, since they are used as nouns: "*Fishing constantly* (adv.) makes one taciturn"; "He found *good* (adj.) *fishing*." A gerund may also take an object: "*Writing* the *letter* (obj.) was difficult."

When the gerund is preceded by an article, *a*, *an*, or *the*, or by an adjective, it requires a following phrase with *of*, signifying the *object* of its action: "The *building of* the ship took many days"; "Success depends upon careful *planning of* work."

The Subjunctive. With the exception of the forms given under the conjugation of *be*, English has no regularly inflected subjunctive forms. *Have* is used occasionally for *has* in the third person singular, and in other verbs the indicative singular third personal ending *s* is dropped, to make a subjunctive form: "If he *tell*."

The ideas of *doubt, uncertainty, condition,* and *desire,* usually called *subjunctive,* are commonly expressed by the indicative or by various verb phrases. See *Good Usage: Should, Would.*

The past subjunctive *were* or *had* is often used in past conditional sentences when *if* is omitted. In such cases the verb precedes the subject: "*Were* I *going*, I should take supplies"; "*Had* we *thought* of it, we would have called on him."

The Infinitive. The *infinitive,* meaning "unlimited," is a form of the verb which partakes of the nature of a noun. It expresses action without person or number. The *present infinitive* represents incomplete action, *to go*; the *perfect infinitive* represents completed action, *to have gone.* Verb phrases are formed with the auxiliaries *be* and *have* to serve as present and perfect passive infinitives: *to be seen, to have been seen.* See *Table of Verb Forms.*

The English infinitive is usually preceded by the word *to*, which is a relic of an early stage of the language and no essential part of the infinitive. Most verbs, when they take a following infinitive, require the form with *to*: "I *want* him *to go*." The following verbs generally take the infinitive without *to*: *bid, dare, feel, hear, let, make, need, see,* and all auxiliaries; as, "*See* him *go*," "They *may return.*"

The infinitive may be used as a *noun*, as an *adjective*, or as an *adverb*; but it takes only an adverbial modifier, and, if transitive, may take an object: "*To tell* the *facts* (obj.) *accurately* (adv.) is difficult."

In the sentence "I want you to buy some oranges," some authorities regard *you to buy some oranges* as an *infinitive clause*, the object of the verb *want*; *you* is the subject and *oranges* is the object of *to buy*. Others call the *infinitive phrase, to buy some oranges*, the objective complement, and *you* the object complement, of the verb *want*.

Thou Forms. An old form of the second person singular in present and past tenses, now found only in poetical or religious use, is made by adding *st* or *est* to the first person singular: "*Thou tellest*"; "*Thou toldst*"; "*Thou hast*"; "*Thou hadst*"; "*Thou lovest*"; "*Thou lovedst.*" The verb *be* has the following forms: "*Thou art*"; "*Thou wast.*"

Adjectives

Kinds of Adjectives according to Meaning. Adjectives are classified, according to meaning, as *limiting* and *descriptive*. An adjective modifies a noun or pronoun either by *limiting*, that is, setting it apart definitely from others, or by *describing*, that is, naming a quality of the thing for which the noun or pronoun stands. To say "a *third* report" is merely to set apart, or limit, the report as belonging to one class; to say "a *complete* report" is to describe it by a certain quality.

Such words as *three, five, eleven, second,* are limiting adjectives. They are called *numerals*. Those which merely give a number, as *two, four,* are called *cardinals*; those which designate an order in a series, as *seventh*, are called *ordinals*.

The, a, an, are limiting adjectives. *The* is called the *definite article*; *a* and *an* are called *indefinite articles*. *A* is used before consonant sounds, *an* before vowels. See *Good Usage.*

Kinds of Adjectives according to Use. Adjectives are commonly classified, according to their use in the sentence, as *attributive* and *predicate*.

Attributive Adjectives.—An adjective used in close connection with a noun is called an *attributive adjective*, although some prefer the term *adherent adjective*. Regularly the attributive adjective precedes its noun: "*pretty* flowers." For emphasis, it may sometimes be placed after the noun: "the city *beautiful*."

Predicate Adjectives.—An adjective which modifies the noun of the subject but is placed in the predicate, usually following the verb, is called a *predicate adjective*: "The book is *large*." For *demonstrative, interrogative, relative,* and *indefinite* adjectives, see *Kinds of Pronouns.*

Appositive Adjectives.—Some authorities distinguish a third type of adjective, the *appositive*; as, "The boy, *careless* and *indifferent*, paid no attention." Such adjectives do not limit their nouns but describe them. They usually follow the nouns.

Other adjectives regularly follow their nouns, some of them only as predicate adjectives,—*alone, awake, aware, asleep, alive*: "Man *alive*!" "The child is *asleep*"; "One star *alone*."

Grammatical Relations. The use of English adjectives is very simple, because, except *this* and *that*, they are not inflected to distinguish gender, person, number, or case. The only inflection used is that employed to distinguish the degrees of comparison.

Comparison.—Most English adjectives are compared by adding to the simple form, or positive degree, of the adjective, *r* or *er*, to form the comparative degree, and *st* or *est*, to form the superlative: *high, higher, highest*; *fine, finer, finest*. The comparative degree expresses a greater or lesser degree of the quality named by the adjective; the superlative expresses the greatest or least degree of that quality.

For spelling changes with added syllables, see *Spelling.*

Many adjectives, especially those of more than two syllables, are compared by prefixing *more* or *less* for the comparative, *most* or *least* for the superlative: "*more* merciful"; "*least* troublesome." Some adjectives admit of both forms of comparison: *able, abler* (*more able*), *ablest* (*most able*). A few adjectives are compared irregularly: *bad, worse, worst*; *good, better, best.*

Adverbs

Meaning of Adverbs. Adverbs modify the meaning of verbs, adjectives, and other adverbs, in respect to some one of the following ideas:

1. Place,—there, nowhere, yonder.
2. Time,—now, afterwards, soon.
3. Manner,—well, badly, thoroughly.
4. Cause,—therefore, consequently.
5. Number,—first, secondly, rarely.
6. Degree,—somewhat, more, highly.

They are classified, therefore, as adverbs of *place, time, manner, cause, number,* and *degree.*

Interrogative Adverbs. The adverbs *how, whence, wherefore, why,* and a few others are used to introduce questions, either direct or indirect: "*How* shall you go?" "They wanted to know *why* he did that."

Relative Adverbs. *As, how, now, since, so, thence, when, whence, whenever, where, wherever, whither, why,* and a few others are used to introduce *subordinate clauses.*

Forms. Most English adverbs end in *-ly*. Many of these are formed from adjectives: *quick* (adj.), *quickly* (adv.); *easy* (adj.), *easily* (adv.). Some adverbs have the same form as the corresponding adjectives: *early, hard, long, loud, deep.*

Caution.—*Goodly, lovely, manly, lonely,* and *homely* are adjectives.

Comparison.—Most adverbs are compared by prefixing to the simple form or positive degree *more* or *less* to form the comparative and *most* or *least* to form the superlative: easily, *more* easily, *most* easily; truly, *more* truly, *most* truly, *less* truly, *least* truly.

Some adverbs having the same form as the corresponding adjectives are compared by adding *er* and *est* to the simple form: *early, earlier, earliest; deep, deeper, deepest.*

A few adverbs are compared irregularly: *well, better, best; badly, worse, worst; much, more, most.*

There.—The adverb *there* is sometimes used to introduce a sentence, with no idea of place. When so used, *there* is called an *expletive,* because it "fills up" and is unnecessary to the sense: "*There* are many ways of doing good." See *It* under *Pronouns: Special Uses.*

The.—The definite article *the* is sometimes used as an adverb before comparatives: "*the* more, *the* merrier; *the* sooner, *the* better."

First.—The word *first* may be an adjective or an adverb: "The *first* (adj.) boy is my brother"; "He came *first* (adv.)." See *Good Usage.*

Position of Adverbs. Because great liberty is allowed as to the position of English adverbs, care should be taken so to place an adverb that its grammatical relation shall be clear.

Prepositions

Position of Prepositions. The word preposition comes from the Latin *pre,* before, and *ponere,* to place. Hence prepositions commonly stand before the words they govern ("Give the pencil *to him.*"); but they may come after them. In English this inversion occurs most frequently when the preposition governs a *relative* or an *interrogative word*: "They are people *whom* we know nothing *about*"; "*What* are you looking *for*?" See *Good Usage.*

Prepositional Phrases. The preposition and its object, with the modifiers of the object, form a phrase, which may be used as an adjective or an adverb: "The picture *on the screen* (adj.)"; "He ran *at top speed* (adv.)"; "Home *at last* (adv.)." Some prepositions form such close combinations with certain verbs that these expressions have the force of single words: *look over, laugh at, carry off.* See *Verbs, Prepositions.*

Subordinate Clauses

According to use, subordinate clauses are *substantive, adjective,* and *adverbial.*

A *substantive clause* is a clause that performs the function of a noun: "*That he came* (subj. of verb) is true"; "I know *that he came* (obj. of verb)"; "He was anxious for *what had been promised him* (obj. of prep.)"; "He is *what he seems* (attribute complement)"; "The fact *that he did it* (appositive) is wonderful."

An *adjective clause* is a clause that modifies a noun or a pronoun. It may be introduced by a relative pronoun: "He *whom thou lovest* is sick"; "This is the tree *that we planted.*" It may be introduced by a conjunctive adverb: "The town *where* (in which) *she lived*"; "The time *when* (at which) *Rome was built.*"

An adjective clause may be *restrictive*: "I took the peach *that was ripe.*" It was a particular peach. *That was ripe* restricts or limits *peach,* telling which one was taken.

An adjective clause may be *non-restrictive*: "I read 'Marmion,' *which was written by Scott.*" *Marmion* defines what book was read. *Which was written by Scott* is a *non-restrictive* clause, merely adding another thought to the one already expressed. A comma is used after *Marmion* to separate the non-restrictive clause from the rest of the sentence.

Relative Clause.—A clause introduced by a relative pronoun is sometimes called a *relative clause*: "This tree, *which has stood for years,* bears no fruit."

An *adverbial clause* is a clause that modifies the meaning of a verb, an adjective, or another adverb.

Adverbial clauses are introduced by subordinate conjunctions or by conjunctive adverbs:

Time—"*When duty calls,* I obey."
Place—"*Where I go,* ye cannot come."
Degree—"It is better *than I expected.*"
Manner—"The child does *as he pleases.*"
Purpose—"He came *that he might learn.*"
Result—"She was so weak *that she fainted.*"
Cause—"The snow melted *because it rained.*"
Condition—"*If you do right,* you will win."
Concession—"*Though I failed,* I shall try again."

Conjunctions. See special section devoted to this subject.

Parsing

To parse a word is to classify it as a part of speech, explain its form, and show its relation to other words in the sentence.

In the sentence "He bought a car," *car* is a common noun, of neuter gender, in the third person, singular number, and in the objective case because it is the object of the verb *bought.*

Bought is an irregular, transitive verb. The principal parts are *buy, bought, bought.* It is active voice indicative mode, past tense; third person, singular number, to agree with its subject *he.*

He is a personal pronoun. Its declension is singular, nom. *he,* poss. *his,* obj. *him*; plural, nom. *they,* poss. *their* or *theirs,* obj. *them.* Third person, singular number; nominative case, the subject of the verb *bought.*

Sentence Analysis

To analyze a sentence, first classify the sentence according to *form* and *use.* Then point out the simple subject; the complete subject. Classify the modifiers of the simple subject, analyzing phrases and clauses. Point out the simple predicate; the complete predicate. Classify the modifiers of the simple predicate, analyzing phrases and clauses. If the sentence is complex or compound, also name and classify the clauses and the connectives which join them.

Simple Sentence. "Truth, crushed to earth, shall rise again" is a *simple, declarative* sentence. *Truth* is the *simple* subject; *truth, crushed to earth* is the *complete* subject; *crushed* is a participle formed from the verb *crush* and modifies the noun *truth*; *to earth* is an adverbial phrase, modifying *crushed*; *shall rise* is the *simple* predicate; *shall rise again* is the *complete* predicate; *shall rise* is the predicate verb, which is modified by the adverb *again.*

Complex Sentence. "Blessed is he who has found his work" is a *complex, declarative* sentence, composed of one independent clause, *blessed is he,* and one dependent clause, *who has found his work.* The subject of the independent clause is *he*; the predicate is *is blessed.* The predicate consists of the copulative verb *is* and the predicate adjective *blessed,* which modifies the subject *he.* The dependent clause, *who has found his work,* is an adjective clause modifying the pronoun *he.* The subject of the clause is the relative pronoun *who*; the complete predicate is *has found his work*; *has found* is the predicate verb, the direct object of which is *work*; *his* is a possessive pronoun modifying *work.* The relative pronoun *who* joins the two clauses; its antecedent is *he.*

TABLE OF SPECIMEN VERB FORMS

The Verb, **tell.** Principal Parts: *tell, told, told*

INDICATIVE MODE

ACTIVE VOICE		PASSIVE VOICE	
	Present Tense		
	Ordinary Form		
SINGULAR	PLURAL	SINGULAR	PLURAL
I tell	We tell	I am told	We are told
You tell	You tell	You are told	You are told
He tells	They tell	He is told	They are told
	Progressive Form		
I am telling	We are telling	I am being told	We are being told
You are telling	You are telling	You are being told	You are being told
He is telling	They are telling	He is being told	They are being told
	Emphatic Form		
I do tell	We do tell	No corresponding forms in the passive voice.	
You do tell	You do tell		
He does tell	They do tell		
	Negative Form		
I do not tell	We do not tell	I am not told	We are not told
You do not tell	You do not tell	You are not told	You are not told
He does not tell	They do not tell	He is not told	They are not told
	Negative Progressive Form		
I am not telling	We are not telling	I am not being told	We are not being told
You are not telling	You are not telling	You are not being told	You are not being told
He is not telling	They are not telling	He is not being told	They are not being told
	Present Perfect Tense		
I have told	We have told	I have been told	We have been told
You have told	You have told	You have been told	You have been told
He has told	They have told	He has been told	They have been told
	Past Tense		
	Ordinary Form		
I told	We told	I was told	We were told
You told	You told	You were told	You were told
He told	They told	He was told	They were told
	Progressive Form		
I was telling	We were telling	I was being told	We were being told
You were telling	You were telling	You were being told	You were being told
He was telling	They were telling	He was being told	They were being told
	Emphatic Form		
I did tell	We did tell	No corresponding forms in the passive voice.	
You did tell	You did tell		
He did tell	They did tell		
	Negative Form		
I did not tell	We did not tell	I was not told	We were not told
You did not tell	You did not tell	You were not told	You were not told
He did not tell	They did not tell	He was not told	They were not told
	Negative Progressive Form		
I was not telling	We were not telling	I was not being told	We were not being told
You were not telling	You were not telling	You were not being told	You were not being told
He was not telling	They were not telling	He was not being told	They were not being told
	Past Perfect, or Pluperfect, Tense		
I had told	We had told	I had been told	We had been told
You had told	You had told	You had been told	You had been told
He had told	They had told	He had been told	They had been told
	Future Tense		
I shall tell	We shall tell	I shall be told	We shall be told
You will tell	You will tell	You will be told	You will be told
He will tell	They will tell	He will be told	They will be told
	Future Perfect Tense		
I shall have told	We shall have told	I shall have been told	We shall have been told
You will have told	You will have told	You will have been told	You will have been told
He will have told	They will have told	He will have been told	They will have been told

Infinitive Forms

Active	Passive
Present.—(to) tell	Present.—(to) be told
Perfect.—(to) have told	Perfect.—(to) have been told

Participle Forms

Active	Passive
Present.—telling	Present.—being told
Perfect.—having told	Past.—told
	Perfect.—having been told

Imperative Forms

Tell (Negative) Do not tell *or* Tell not — Be told (Negative) Do not be told *or* Be not told

The Verb **be.** Principal Parts: *am, was, been*

Present Tense		**Past Tense**	
SINGULAR	PLURAL	SINGULAR	PLURAL
I am	We are	I was	We were
You are	You are	You were	You were
He is	They are	He was	They were

The Verb **have.** Principal Parts: *have, had, had*

I have	We have	I had	We had
You have	You have	You had	You had
He has	They have	He had	They had

PREPOSITIONS

Through the study of prepositions, one gains a command of many idiomatic phrases found in every civilized language. Especially is this true of English, because English prepositions united with other words often take the place of corresponding inflected word forms in other languages.

From the following list of the more important English prepositions, the reader will learn the distinctive meanings attached to each according to the varied purposes for which it is used.

About. In its usual meanings of *around, close to, because of, concerning, not far from, over*, etc., this preposition is employed to express: (1) indefinite position, "The idlers hung *about* the saloon"; (2) in attendance on, "The king had his bodyguard *about* him"; (3) close at hand, on one's person, "He had no money *about* him"; (4) attention to, "We sent him *about* (*to attend to*) his business"; (5) abstract connection in the sense of concerning, "to see, ask, hear, write, think, dream *about* a thing"; (6) approximation in weight, measure, time, or scale, "He is *about* my size."

Above. Commonly this word means *over, higher than, superior to*: "The colonel ranks *above* the major." "The airplane rose rapidly *above* the city." "Clouds seem to float just *above* the trees." "The man's record is *above* suspicion." "The president does not stand *above* the law." "Mr. Utterson could hear the footsteps *above* the hum of the city." "*Above* all, avoid the appearance of suspicion."

After. This word usually means *behind, following, as a result of, in spite of, for*, and *according to*. It may be used with the verb *be* and with any verb of motion, also after *seek, ask, hunt*, although, with these, modern usage generally prefers *for*. The following are examples of common usage: "The troops passed first and the supply train came *after* (*behind*) them." "It was *after* (*later than*) twelve when our friends left." "*After* (*as a result of*) careful examination the board approved the plans." "The picture is fashioned *after* (*according to*) an antique model." "Book *after* book was read." "Time *after* time Mr. Blank inquired *after* (*for*) you." "*After* (*in spite of*) all, they have failed." "*After* a while they grew tired."

Against. Common meanings: *opposite to* (in this sense expressed by *over against*), *opposed to, pressing upon, contrary, from*. Examples: "The mast stood out clearly *against* (*contrasting with*) the sky." "The governor had long held his ground *against* suffrage." "The machine was leaning *against* (*pressing upon*) the wall." "Such action seems *against* (*contrary to*) nature." "*Defend us against* (*from*) our enemies."

Along. Implies *motion* or *extension upon, at* or *near the side of*. In such connections it may mean *near, beside, following the line of*: "We wandered *along* (*beside*) the river bank." "Rare plants grow *along* (*by the side of*) that embankment." "Trees are planted *along* (*the whole length of*) the roadway." "The car proceeded *along* (*following the line of*) the Boston road."

Amid, Amidst. The two words do not differ essentially in meaning. Their first sense is that of *among, surrounded by*, used generally with plural *substantives*: "She dwelt *amid* (*surrounded by*) the ruins of her former glory." In an extended sense, the words apply to circumstances and conditions: "He was bewildered *amid* (*among*) the perplexities and temptations of his position." In poetry, *amid* is used with a singular noun to indicate *in the middle of*, or *surrounded by* some extended object: "*amid* the billowy deep"; "She strayed *amid* the corn."

Around, Round. Used interchangeably to signify motion or position *about, encircling, on all sides of, in all directions from, at random through*: "They made a journey *around* (*encircling*) the world." "*Around* (*on all sides of*) the mansion were gardens." "The beams of light radiate *around* (*in all directions from*) the central mass." "We spent the day riding *around* (*at random through*) the city." "They gathered *round* (*about*) the hearth."

At. This word primarily expresses the relation of *presence*, of *contact in place or time*, or of *direction towards*. (1) It designates more or less indefinitely the point or place where a thing is: "*at* the center," "*at* home," "*at* hand." (2) Sometimes it emphasizes contact with a place better than *in* or *by*: "*at* school," "*at* the helm." (3) It denotes presence at an event: "*at* the wedding," "*at* the ball"; also location of a feeling or quality: "sick *at* heart," "out *at* elbow." (4) It is likewise used to signify the end or object of directed effort: "look *at* it," "aim *at* the bull's eye"; similarly, with the verbs *strike, shout, wink, mock, laugh, be angry*, etc. (5) It implies action, occupation with, or employment: "*at* work," "*at* meals," "to pull *at* an oar."

Athwart. A word used of position or motion in space, meaning *across, from side to side of*: "The shadow fell *athwart* (*across*) his path." "*Athwart* (*from side to side of*) the darkness a flash of light appeared." Figuratively, *athwart* is used to suggest opposition: "The suspicions of his rivals were thrown *athwart* (*in hindrance of*) his plans."

Before. Usual meanings: *ahead of, preceding, face to face with, rather than, higher than*. Examples: "The visitors came *before* (*ahead of*) the appointed time." "The customer just *before* (*preceding*) you bought the last pound." "The culprit was brought *before* (*face to face with*) the judge." "The question is now *before* (*claiming the attention of*) (*subject to disposition by*) the house." "The ship drove *before* the wind." "Shakspere comes *before* (*higher than*) Chaucer in rank though not in time."

Behind. Common meanings: *in the rear, at the back, toward the rear, not up with, supporting, backing*. Examples: "The garden was planted *behind* the house." "*Behind* (*in the rear of*) the army came the stragglers." "His shadow betrayed his presence *behind* (*at the back of*) the screen." "Many, worn out by the march, fell *behind* (*to the rear of*) their comrades." "His ideas are *behind* (*not up with*) the times." "The contractor did not have sufficient capital *behind* (*supporting*) him." "The train was *behind* time."

Below. Used literally of position or direction, signifying *lower than, under*: "The shot struck *below* (*lower than*) the water line." "The signature is placed on the line *below* (*under*) the complimentary close." "Three miles *below* (*farther down than*) the town, on the bank of the stream, stands the fort." Figuratively, *below* is used to express an inferior degree of rank, dignity, and excellence: "The corporal ranks *below* the sergeant." "They are as inferior as the fields are *below* the stars."

Beneath. This preposition is used generally of lower position. It suggests also influence or control and unworthiness. The following examples illustrate accurate uses of the word: "The plank roadway echoed *beneath* their tread." "Loch Katrine lay *beneath* him." "The trees were bent *beneath* their burden of fruit." "His knees shook *beneath* him." "The people were held *beneath* the yoke of the conqueror." "She thought her neighbors *beneath* her notice."

Beside. In its literal sense, used to mean *by the side of, near*: "The guard rode *beside* the carriage." Figuratively, *beside* is used to suggest comparison: "*Beside* (*in comparison with*) his son's achievement, his own seemed petty." *Beside* has the force of *outside of* in "*beside* himself" and "*beside* the question."

Besides. Formerly used interchangeably with *beside*, this word now signifies *over and above, in addition to, as well as*, and also *apart from*: "The house had many rooms *besides* (*in addition to*) those." "*Besides* (*as well as*) his income, he had other resources." "They are interested in nothing *besides* (*apart from*) their art."

Between. Used of position or movement in space separating two objects: "The courthouse was built *between* the rival towns." "He walks *between* his house and his office." *Between* is used also of intermediate qualities and conditions: "something intermediate *between* vice and virtue"; "a shade *between* orange and red." It may denote joint or reciprocal action either in agreement or opposition: "A struggle ensued *between* (*opposition*) the champions." "A compact was made *between* (*agreement*) the families." "*Between* them (*together*) they brought the game into camp." *Between* is likewise used to express confinement or restriction: "He took the bit *between* his teeth." It is employed particularly to signify privacy in conversation: "*between* ourselves," "*between* you and me."

Beyond. Used of an object in regard to both space and time, and signifying *farther on than, past, later than*: "They traveled *beyond* (*farther on than*) the mountains." "*Beyond* (*past*) the Alps lies Rome." "We were detained *beyond* (*past*) the usual hour of closing." Figuratively, the word is used in various senses of *exceeding* or *surpassing*: "The thing is *beyond* (*exceeds*) his power." "A scene lovely *beyond* (*surpassing*) expression was disclosed to view."

But. With the force of a preposition, *but* signifies *except, leaving out*: "The collector took all *but* (*except*) three." "There was no course open *but* (*except*) to submit." Some authorities treat these uses as conjunctive.

By. This word usually means *near, next to, in the course of, through the agency of, through the use of, according to* (*a specified unit of measure*). Examples: "The factory stands *by* (*near to*) the river." "Flight *by* (*in the course of the*) night was very dangerous." "No honest official is injured *by* (*through the agency of*) publicity." "*By* (*according to*) all physicians' rules he should have died." "More freight should be shipped *by* (*by way of*) water." "*By* whatever name it may be called, the tree is known *by* (*through the use of*) its fruit." "He works only *by* the day (work reckoned *according to* a day as a unit)." It may indicate a succession of units: "two *by* two"; "piece *by* piece"; "The timbers were dragged up the mountain one *by* one." The following are idiomatic expressions: "to take *by* and large" (to consider generally), "*by* seven o'clock," "to take *by* the hand," "two *by* the clock," "come *by*" (get), "do well *by* a person," "judge *by* appearance," "learn *by* experience," "take *by* surprise," "*by* the way," "*by* the pound," "*by* the book," "*by* hook and *by* crook," "*by* means of," "*by* dint of," "near *by*," "stand *by*" (help or support).

Down. Used literally of place and time and figuratively in various phrases, in the general sense of *descending direction*: "The machine sped easily *down* the incline." "A strange tradition comes *down* the years." The expression "*down* town" has the meaning of *into*, as denoting motion from a more elevated locality *down into* a lower one.

During. This word is used exclusively with reference to time, meaning *in the course of* or *throughout*: "We were repeatedly interrupted *during* (*in the course of*) the discussion." "*During* (*throughout*) this period a high temperature prevailed."

Except, Excepting. The two words are used interchangeably, in the sense of *exclusion* or *omission*: "Everybody was gay *except* the Major." "*Excepting* the last two articles, they adopted the agreement."

For. This preposition is a word of widely varied uses in reference to extent of space or of time, amounts of money, cause or occasion, purpose, seeking or reaching. It may mean *during, toward, in the interest of, in proportion to, in place of, in return, seeming, in relation to, in spite of*. Examples: "The road was torn up *for* (*throughout*) a distance of half a mile." "The firm's note is good *for* (*to the extent of*) that amount." "The mayor was censured *for* (*because of his*) permitting the meeting." "The farmers gave them ball *for* (*in return for*) ball." "*For* (*in proportion to*) one who sees anything, ten people look." "*For* (*in spite of*) all his bluster, the man was a coward." The following phrases are idiomatic: "leave *for* a destination," "atone *for*," "argue *for*," "account *for*," "allow *for*," "apologize *for*," "pay *for*," "call *for*," "care *for*," "go *for*," "write *for*," "look *for*," "name *for*" (*after*), "to be well *for*," "*for* thirty dollars," "*for* once," "*for* a while," "indebted *for*," "a time *for* anything," "a taste *for* luxuries," "a longing *for* home," "*for* the asking," "the train *for* (*going to*) Philadelphia."

From. This word denotes primarily separation in space; but it is used also of a starting point in time, and it may express distinction of ideas and the relation of cause or source. Examples: "The house was placed about three hundred feet *from* the barn." "*From* boyhood he was interested in flowers and trees." "Men pass quickly *from* youth to age." "Skill arises *from* constant practice." "Deliver us *from* (*out of the power of*) evil."

In. This word may mean "*within* a place, a group of people or a society, or a period of time." It may denote also the end of a period of time or the object of a motion or a feeling. It may further be used in respect to manner, method, material, cause or occasion, and of duty or measure. *In* should be carefully distinguished from *into*, which implies motion or change only. Examples: "The family lives *in* Jamestown." "*In* the 19th century there were many wars." "The note is due *in* three months." "*In* whom can one put confidence?" "He took great delight *in* his friends." "*In* my judgment, the man is guilty." "The picture was done *in* oils." "Undoubtedly you spoke *in* haste." We may say, "Come *in*"; but we must say, "Come *into* the house." The following are idiomatic expressions: "*in* the name of the law," "*in* time," "*in* wrath," "*in* health," "*in* doubt," "*in* error," "*in* scorn," "*in* fact," "*in* truth," "*in* love," "one *in* a thousand," "call *in* question," "hope *in*," "believe *in*," "trustworthy *in* word and deed," "originate *in*," "steeped *in*," "persist *in*."

Into. A preposition implying direction or motion, used regularly after the verbs *go, come, bring, put, send*, etc., also in referring to state or condition: "They went *into* the house." "He thrust the money *into* his purse." "The work extended well *into* the next month." "Their fathers had gone *into* business together." "The child burst *into* tears."

Notwithstanding. This word belongs to the class of participial prepositions. It means *in spite of* or *in the face of*: "The plan succeeded, *notwithstanding* strong opposition."

Of. This is the most commonly used English preposition. It may refer to position or location, distance, possession, extent of time, separation, source, material or character, relief. The following expressions will illustrate these meanings: "North *of* Boston," "the mountains *of* California," "a shore line *of* forty miles," "a creature *of* (*living only*) a day," "deprived *of* liberty," "the shadow *of* the glen," "a man *of* honor," "a form *of* great beauty," "cured *of* a cold," "a bridge *of* stone and iron." The following are idiomatic expressions: "fond *of*," "tired *of*," "best *of* all," "warned *of* danger," "hear *of*," "talk *of*," "beware *of*," "conscious *of*," "convicted *of*," "accounted *of*," "think well *of*," "afraid *of*," "big *of* heart," "*of* a cruel temper," "built *of*," "born *of*."

Off. This word means *from*, and is used chiefly to denote separation. It is employed idiomatically in various ways implying former dependence: "*off* one's hands," "*off* one's head." It sometimes indicates source or material with such verbs as *dine, eat*; as, "He dined *off* roast beef." It also signifies deduction or rebate; as, "They took it *off* the bill."

On, Upon. *On* and *upon* are generally identical in meaning. *On* is used to indicate: (1) support or contact from elsewhere than beneath: "a fly *on* the wall"; (2) nearness: "a house situated *on* the river"; (3) employment or activity with or in respect to: "*on* the committee," "*on* duty," "*on* the run." It indicates the ground or basis of action: "stated *on* authority," "He bet *on* the red"; also position and boundary: "The town lay *on* the east." It likewise denotes state or condition: "*on* fire," "*on* sale," "*on* tap." Where simple contact or proximity to the surface is implied, *upon* is used interchangeably with *on*. The following are idiomatic uses: "The gifts arrived *on* time (*at the time set*)." "They bought the goods *on* time (*payment being deferred*)." "They lived *on* vegetables." To talk *on* or *upon* a subject implies more careful treatment of the theme than to talk *about* it.

Out. As a preposition, *out* is now obsolete or colloquial. *Out of* is used in its place. Examples: "He came *out of* (*from*) his retirement." "We frequently see things *out of* (*not according to*) their true proportion." "The bells were *out of* tune and harsh." The following are idiomatic phrases: "made *out of*," "*out of* order," "*out of* doors," "*out of* supplies," "*out of* season," "*out of* sight," "*out of* mind."

Over. In the sense of *above*, this preposition is used to imply superiority, power, dignity, value, and preference; as, "to triumph *over* difficulties." It signifies *beyond*, in degree: "It cost *over* four dollars"; a whole surface: "to wander *over* the earth"; duration of time: "He let it soak *over* night." It has also the meanings of *across, from side to side*; as, "The dog leaped *over* the stream." *Over* is used idiomatically in such expressions as "*over* one's signature," "*over* head and ears in debt," etc.

Past. Used literally of space, time, and age, signifying *beyond, farther on than, later than*: "He walked *past* (*farther on than*) the house." "They were just *past* (*beyond*) the boundary." "It is now ten minutes *past* (*later than*) twelve." "The old lady was *past* (*beyond the age of*) seventy." *Past* denotes also *beyond the power of*: "The man was troubled *past* endurance."

Round. See *Around*.

Save. Used in the sense of *except* or *excepting*: "There was no sign of human life *save* the chimney smoke."

Since. With the force of a preposition, this word is used altogether of time, signifying *from a time, within a following time*, and *duration*: "*Since* (*from*) that day we have not heard from him." "Where have you been *since* (*within the time after*) yesterday?" "It is a fortnight *since* he embarked."

Through. Used of space and time and in various other connections. It signifies *from one limit to another of, into every part of, passing within* in the sense of penetrating or transmitting, *during the period of, by means of, on account of*: "The hall runs *through* (*from end to end of*) the house." "The visitors were shown *through* (*into every part of*) the town." "A light shone *through* (*penetrating*) the woods." "The noise continued *through* (*during*) the night." "*Through* (*by means of*) his own perseverance, he held the position." "We were detained *through* (*on account of*) his blundering."

Throughout. The preposition *through*, reenforced by *out*, signifying *the whole of, every part of, space, region, period of time*, or *course of action*: "*throughout* the length and breadth of the land"; "*throughout* the night."

Till, Until. These words are used interchangeably in reference to time, signifying *to, up to*: "They can wait *till* (*up to*) next week." "He will not reply to the letter *until* (*up to*) the end of the month."

To. Used primarily to denote relation of approach and arrival. It indicates that toward which there is movement—a terminal point: "He went *to* law about it." "She stretched her arms *to* heaven." Idiomatic uses: "The remarks were addressed *to* the audience." "Let us keep this *to* ourselves." "It was sweet *to* the taste." "We were bored *to* death." "The hall rang *to* the tramp of armed men." "The drawing was made *to* scale." "It was John *to* the very life."

Touching. Used with the force of a preposition in the sense of *concerning, with regard to*: "*Touching* the life of the interior villages, we have no authentic information."

Toward, Towards. Used interchangeably in the sense of *facing* or *looking in the direction of, approaching, aiming at, in respect to*: "The door was open *toward* (*facing*) the east." "A procession came *toward* (*approaching*) the village." "*Toward* (*approaching*) night the sky became overcast." "A strong trend *toward* (*aiming at*) independence was evident." "She maintained a critical attitude *towards* (*in respect to*) her family."

Under. The primary meaning of this word is *below, lower than*; as, "*under* a tree," "a cellar *under* the house." Hence, analogously it may have the meaning of *being weighed upon, oppressed*, or *controlled by* affliction, subjection, government, authority, and the like: "to travel *under* a heavy burden"; "to be brave *under* trials"; "*Under* (*during the government of*) the Tudors, England made great political progress."

Underneath. Used in the sense of *directly below*: "*Underneath* the desk, papers were piled."

Up. With respect to motion or position, this word signifies *from a lower to a higher place on or along, at a higher place upon, toward, near, at the top of*: "The party tramped *up* (*from a lower place*) the slope." "His farm lies *up* (*at a higher point upon*) the river." It may also denote movement from the coast to the interior; as, "to journey *up* the country." It may indicate direction from the mouth to the source of the river; as, "He sailed *up* the Hudson."

With. Denotes relation of contact or association. After the verbs *fight, contend, vie*, and the like, it has the meaning of *against*; as, "The Greeks fought *with* the Persians." "They are *with* (*in the employ of*) the telephone company." It may signify association in the sense of attribute; as, "a man *with* (*characterized by*) a clean record"; also the instrument or means; as, "He slew him *with* a sword." It may denote an accessory, as of contents, material, etc.; as, "to fill the stable *with* straw," "to line the hat *with* silk." *With* is used idiomatically in such phrases as "*with* all one's heart," "*with* tooth and nail," "to bear *with*," "to put up *with*," and the like.

Within. Used of place, signifying *inside of*: "*Within* the building were many curious objects." Used of time, signifying *inside the limits of*: "The train will arrive *within* an hour." The word is used of various other relations: "It is not *within* (*in the limits of*) his power to forbid the transfer." "Such an act does not come *within* (*in the scope of*) the court's jurisdiction." *Within* also implies limitation as to quantity: "He lived *within* his income."

Without. This word in the sense of *outside of* or *excluded from* is now seldom used and may be regarded as almost obsolete: "The poor folk dwelt *without* the walls." "She was *without* the pale of society." Its present meaning denotes *lack of, absence of, deprivation*: "The association was *without* (*lacked*) funds." "He was buried *without* (*deprived of*) the usual rites."

Special Prepositions

The following is a list of certain nouns, adjectives, and verbs, which require *special prepositions*:

Abhorrence *of* evil.

Abhorrent *to* his strict principles.

Abide *in* a place, *for* a while, *with* a company, *by* a promise.

Abound *in* vigor and courage, *with* theaters and churches.

Absolve *from* debt or allegiance or a charge of guilt.

A plant **absorbs** moisture *from* the air; one becomes absorbed *in* thought; nutriment may be absorbed *into* the system *through* the skin.

An **accessory** *to* the crime, *before* or *after* the fact; the accessories *of* an automobile.

The **accident** *of* family; an accident *to* the car.

Accommodate *to* circumstances, *with* money, material, etc.

Accompanied *by* several friends, *with* a suggestion.

Accord *with* (agree) looks or profession.

Accuse *of* a crime or fault.

Acquaint *with* the facts.

Acquaintance *with* a subject, *of* one person *with* another, *between* persons.

Acquit a person *of* a charge.

Active *in* temperament, *in* business, *for* an object or purpose, *with* instruments, *about* something.

Adapted *to* a use or situation, *for* a purpose, *from* a source, as *from* Shakspere.

Adequate *to* a demand, *for* a purpose.

Admit *to* membership, *into* a house, *of* exceptions.

Admonish *of* error or duty, *against* a proposed act.

Advantage *of* education, *of* some one as "to get the advantage *of* us," *over* an opponent.

Advocate *of* free speech, *for* another person.

Affinity *between* colors and sounds, *of* one chemical element *for* another.

We **agree** *in* opinion *with* the speaker, *to* a proposition; persons agree *on* or *upon* a statement of principles, a contract, etc.; men should agree *among* themselves.

Alarm was felt *in* the village, *among* the women, *at* the sound.

Aliens *to* our national customs and thought; aliens *in* a country, *among* a people.

Alive *in* every fiber; alive *to* every good suggestion; alive *with* fervor, hope, resolve.

Allegiance *of* the citizen *to* the government; the government has a right to allegiance *from* the citizen.

Alliance *with* a state or people, *against* the common enemy, *for* offense and defense; alliance *of*, *between*, or *among* nations.

Allied. Wit allied *to* madness, a state allied *with* another.

Alter *from* one form *to* another.

Amazement *at* such reckless driving.

Ambitious *of* power.

Amused *with* toys, *at* a remark or a situation.

The **analogy** *between* a society and the plant body; the analogy *of* sound *to* light.

Anger *at* the insult prompted a retort in kind; anger *toward* an offender exaggerates the offense; angry *with* a person.

An **answer** *to* the question, *in* writing, *by* post, or *by* word of mouth.

Antipathy *to* (sometimes *for* or *against*) a person or thing; antipathy *between* two persons.

Anxious *for* a decision, *about* or *concerning* a persons, safety.

An **apology** *to* a person *for* an error is fitting.

Appeal *to* an authority, *from* a decision, *for* help.

Appear *at* the theater, *among* the first, *on* or *upon* the surface, *to* the eye, *in* evidence, *in* print, *from* reports, *near* the place, *before* the audience, *through* the mist; appear *for in behalf of*, or *against* one in court.

Apportion *to* each a fair share; apportion the property *among* the creditors, *between* two claimants; apportion *according to* rank, etc.

Apprehensive *of* danger, *for* one's safety.

Approximation *to* the correct solution.

Arraign *at* the bar, *before* the court, *of* or *for* a crime, *on* or *upon* an indictment.

Arrested *for* crime, *on* suspicion, *by* the officer, *on*, *upon*, or *by virtue of* a warrant.

Ask *for* a thing; ask a thing *of* or *from* a person; ask *after* or *about* one's health, welfare, friends, etc.

Astonished *at* a situation or a person's attitude, *by* an event.

Attend *to* (listen) instructions, *on* or *upon* (wait) an official or dignitary.

Attended *by* a train of servants, *with* difficulties, advantages, etc.

Behavior *of* a person *to* or *toward* people, *on* or *upon* the streets, *before* the multitude, or *in* a place, *with* companions.

Benevolence *of* or *from* a person, *to* or *toward* others.

Break *to* pieces or *in* pieces, *into* several pieces (when the object is thought of as divided rather than shattered), *with* a friend, *away from* a habit; break *into* a house, *out of* prison; break *across* one's knee; break *through* a barrier.

Burn *in* fire; burn *with* fire; burn *to* the ground; burn *to* ashes; burn *through* the skin or the roof; burn *into* the conscience, etc.

Call *on* or *upon* a person (to visit him), *after* (by the name of), *in* question, *at* a house.

Care *of* a property, *for* the future, *about* a matter.

Carry *to* a place; carry *from* or *out of* a place; carry qualities *into* conduct; carry *across* the street, *over* the bridge; carry a cable *under* the sea.

Catch *at* a straw; catch a person *by* the collar; catch a ball *with* the hand; catch a disease *from* a patient; catch one *in* the act, a bird *in* a snare.

Cause *of* disaster; cause *for* interference.

Change a house gown *for* a street dress; change *from* a caterpillar *to* or *into* a butterfly.

Cheat one *of* his desires, *out of* a right.

Choose *from* or *from among* a number; choose *out of* the army; choose *between* two, *among* many; choose *for* a purpose.

Commit *to* a person *for* safe-keeping; commit *to* prison *for* trial.

Complain *of* a thing *to* a person, *of* one person *to* another, *of* or *against* a person *for* an act, *to* an officer, *before* the court, *about* a thing.

Concerned *with* a person, *in* a result, *in* a proceeding, *about* a matter, *for* a person's health, etc.

Concur *with* a person, *in* an opinion.

Confirm *by* testimony; confirm *in* a belief.

Conformity *with* an opinion, *to* an order, custom, etc.

Considerate *of* a person's feelings.

Contend *with* a person, difficulties, trials, temptations, etc., *for* a principle, a truth, *against* an obstacle, *for* an object.

Contrast two things, one *with* another.

Controversy *with* a person, *between* two or more, *about* or *over* a subject.

Conversant *with* a subject or the facts in a case.

Conversation *with* people, *between* or *among* persons, *about* a matter.

Convey *to* a friend, a purchaser, etc.; convey *from* one place *to* another; convey *by* express, *by* hand, etc.

Copy *after* a person, a model, an example, *from* life, nature, *from* or *out of* a work.

Correspond *with* a person, *to* ideas, models, etc.

Deliver *from* temptation, *out of* difficulty, trouble, etc., *of* an opinion.

Die *of* fever, *by* violence; die *for* one's country; die *at* sea, *in* one's bed, *in* agony; die *to* the world.

Differ *among* themselves, *from* one another, *from* or *with* another in judgment, opinion, etc., *about*, *concerning* a question, subject, etc.

Discriminate *between* two or more things, one thing *from* another, *against* a person.

Disgusted *with* a person, *at*, *by*, *with* a thing.

Divide *between* two, *among* two or more, *in* or *into* parts, something *with* another person, a thing *from* another, *upon* a question.

Draw water *from* or *out of* a well; draw one *into* an argument; draw *with* cords or ropes; the truck is drawn *by* a tractor *along* the road, *across* the lots, *over* the bridge, *through* the streets, *to* the station.

Employ *in*, *on*, *upon*, or *about* a work, business, etc., *for* a purpose, *at* a certain rate of salary or wage.

Entrance *into* a place, *on* or *upon* a work or course of action, *into* or *upon* office, *into* a contest, *by* or *through* a door, *within* the gates, *into* or *among* the company.

Envious *of* (formerly *at* or *against*) a person; envious *of* another's wealth or power.

Faint *with* hunger; faint *in* color.

Fall *under* censure, observation, etc., *from* a high place, *into* water, a hole, bad habits, etc., *on* or *upon* a foe, *among* thieves, *to* or *on* the ground.

Friendship *of* one person *for* or *toward* another, or friendship *between* persons.

Good *at* a business or task, *for* some purpose, *to* another person.

Gratified *at* an action or course of conduct.

Grief *at* a loss, *for* a friend.

Hanker *after* or *for* amusement, dainties, luxury, etc.

A result **happy** *for* a person; happy *at* a reply; happy *in* his home, *with* his friends, *among* his children; happy *at* a discovery, *over* a success.

Help *in* business or emergency, *with* money; help *to* success, *against* opposition.

Impatient *with* a person, *at* conduct, delay, etc., *for* something expected, *under* grief, misfortune, etc.

Injury *of* a cause; injury *to* a structure; injury *by* fire, *by* or *from* collision, interference, etc.

Inquisitive *about, concerning, in regard to, regarding* matters.

Join *to* something more numerous or greater, *with* something equal.

A **journey** *from* Naples *to* Rome, *through* Mexico, *across* the continent, *over* the sea; a journey *into* Asia, *among* savages, *by* land, *by* rail, *for* health, *on* foot, *on* the cars, etc.

We **listen** *for* what we expect or desire to hear; we listen *to* what we actually do hear.

Love *of* country, *for* humanity; love *to* or *toward* God and man.

Made *of, out of* or *from* certain materials, *into* a certain form, *for* a certain purpose or person; made *with* hands, *by* hand.

Martyr *for* or *to* a cause, *to* disease, disappointment, sorrow, etc.

Mastery *of* a subject or a task, *over* an enemy or opponent.

Mourn *for* a loss, *over* misfortune or trouble.

Necessary *to* a purpose, *for* or *to* a result or a person; unity is necessary *to* completeness; decision is necessary *for* command, *for* or *in* a commander.

Offended *at* a remark or course of action, *by* a word or act, *with* a person.

Opinion *on* a question, *about* a subject or a person.

Opportunity *of* doing something, *for* service, thought, etc.

Pardon *for* the offenders, *for* all offenses; pardon *of* offenders or offenses.

Patient *of* toil, *with* a person, *toward* learners, *under* difficulty.

Plead *with* the tyrant, *for* the captive; plead *against* injustice; plead *to* the indictment, *at* the bar, *before* the court.

Pleasant *to, with* or *toward* persons, *about* a matter.

Present *to* a person, a person *with* something.

Prevail *on, upon,* or *with* (to persuade), *over* or *against* (to overcome).

Profit *of* labor, *on* capital, *in* business.

Provide *with* supplies, *for* the future, *against* misfortune.

Purchase *at* a price, *at* a public sale, *of* or *from* a person, *for* cash, *with* money, *on* time.

Rejoice *at* an occurrence or an event, *in* personal qualities or possessions.

Relieve *from* pain, trouble, *of* duty or responsibility.

Reproach a person *for* acts.

Rise *from* slumber; rise *to* an occasion or responsibility; *at* a summons; rise *with* the dawn.

Security *for* the payment *of* a debt; security *to* the state, *for* the prisoner, *in* a specified sum; security *from* attack, *against* loss.

Send *from* the hand *to* or *toward* a mark; send *to* a friend *by* a messenger or *by* mail; send a person *into* danger.

Shelter *under* a roof *from* a storm, *in* a stronghold, *behind* or *within* walls.

Skillful *at* or *in* a task, *with* tools.

Strive *with* or *against* a person opposed or a thing in opposition, *for* something to be obtained.

Suffer *from* a disease, *by* some one's act or conduct, *with* another (sympathy).

Taste *of* food, etc., *for* painting, music.

Versed *in* a subject.

CONJUNCTIONS

The correct use of conjunctions is necessary to well constructed, intelligible sentences. No matter how accurate a writer's use of other words may be, if he does not indicate appropriately the relations between words or clauses, his sentences cannot be clear.

Conjunctions are divided into two general classes, *co-ordinate* and *subordinate.*

A *co-ordinate* conjunction connects words, phrases, or clauses of the same rank; as, *and, but, or, nor, either, neither*: "Sun *and* moon are heavenly bodies." "To be *or* not to be, that is the question." "Be not overcome of evil, *but* overcome evil with good."

A *subordinate* conjunction connects clauses of different rank; as, *since, unless, because, for, if, though, although*: "*Unless* it rains, the crops will fail."

Conjunctions include adverbs used as conjunctions and known as *conjunctive adverbs,* such as *when, where, whence, whereby, while, why*: "*While* we sleep, the body is rebuilt."

Correlative conjunctions are those which are used in pairs; as, *both—and, either—or, neither—nor, whether—or, though—yet*: "He *neither* ate *nor* slept." "*Though* all men deny Thee, *yet* will I not."

The following list of the more important English conjunctions shows varied shades of meaning that these parts of speech may assume, according to the demands of the different sentences in which they are used.

Although and **Though.** These words do not differ in meaning. They introduce concessive ideas: "We must be content with this, *though* we had hoped for more." "*Although* clear writing is difficult to produce, it is worth earnest endeavor." Equivalent phrases are: *in spite of the fact that*; *granted that*; *albeit. Even though* is more emphatic, as *although* was formerly more emphatic than *though.*

And. The most nearly universal connective. It is the original Saxon word used to join sentence elements that are grammatically alike and is the typical copulative of narration. It has, besides, a variety of effective uses as follows: (1) to intensify a statement,—"He talked on for hours *and* hours"; "They worked, *and* worked hard, to get results"; (2) as almost equivalent to *but,*—"It is one thing to plan *and* quite another to carry out plans"; (3) in such expressions as "There are boys *and* boys," indicating differences of condition, class, or character; (4) to express result,—"After long search he found the lode *and* became very wealthy." *And* may be used to begin a sentence, especially where some feeling or thought of surprise or reproach is implied: "*And* did you once see Shelley plain?" "*And* do you mean to tell me such a story?"

As. Used where comparisons of quality, close likeness, or proportion are implied: "He was as happy *as* only a man with a clear conscience can be"; "*As* we approached the rapids, the roar became deafening." *As* may denote cause or reason: "*As* the ship was unseaworthy, it was abandoned."

Because. Originally a phrase consisting of preposition and substantive, *by cause.* The word signifies *for the reason that* or *in consequence of.* See *For.*

Both. This conjunction is used regularly to precede the first of two co-ordinate words or phrases, and is followed by *and* before the second. It signifies *alike, as well as, too, also*: "a masterpiece for *both* argument and style." It may follow the coordinate words; as, "Malice mars logic and charity *both* (*alike, too, also*)."

But. Used in a great variety of ways, the primary sense being that of contrast or opposition: "His progress was slow *but* sure"; "We cannot *but* believe." Sometimes *but* implies a concession:

"Lincoln is dead, *but* the government at Washington still lives." *But* may mean "that—not": "There is no rose *but* bears its thorn."

Either. A disjunctive connective used before two co-ordinated alternatives and followed by the correlative *or*: "*Either* the light is distant *or* it is dim." "We must *either* stay where we are *or* risk being carried away by the flood."

Ere. A conjunction used mostly in poetry, thus differing from its synonym, *before*: "We shall meet *ere* set of sun." *Ere* must be distinguished carefully from *e'er*, which is a poetic contraction of *ever*.

Except. The use of *unless* instead of *except* is preferred by modern writers: "I will not be satisfied *unless* (*except*) you come." After *except* or *unless*, the phrases *it be, it were*, etc. are frequently used instead of repeating the principal verb: "He never goes to church *except it be* (he goes) to hear the music." "He seldom laughed *except it were* (he laughed) at his own jokes."

For. As a conjunction, *for* introduces only clauses or sentences of cause or reason. It should be distinguished carefully from *as, since, because. Because* is now used to introduce a real cause; as, "The water boils *because* it is heated." But one may say, "The water must be hot, *for* I saw John light the gas." In the latter case, *for* introduces a reason for a belief. *As* and *since* introduce causes or reasons that may be taken for granted: "*Since* (*as*) the hat was mine, I took it."

If. Used to introduce a clause of condition with the *subjunctive* signifying *doubt*, and with the *indicative* implying *suspended opinion* in regard to a statement: "*If* that be true, this is false." "He shall not secure the property *if* we can prevent it." *If* also introduces a concession, as equivalent to *although*: "*If* (*although*) he is competent, he sometimes makes mistakes."

Lest. Used to introduce a negative intention or purpose, equivalent to *that—not* or *for fear that*: "We hastened to return *lest* our friends should be alarmed."

Neither. The negative of *either*, used to introduce the first of two or more co-ordinate words or clauses, and followed by *nor*: "They had *neither* food *nor* clothing." "Quarter was *neither* given *nor* asked."

Nevertheless. In meaning, this compound is equivalent to *yet, notwithstanding*, or *in spite of that*: "Although entrance is forbidden, *nevertheless* they will use the house."

Nor. See *Neither*.

Notwithstanding. Equivalent in meaning to *although* or *in spite of the fact that*: "John was a stranger to most of the villagers, *notwithstanding* he had lived in Oakfield for thirty years."

Or. See *Either*.

Save. Used with the force of a conjunction, this word is equivalent to *except* or *unless*: "The night was still, *save* that the distant cataract rumbled steadily." "'Tis said there were no thought of hell, *save* (*unless*) hell were taught."

Since. This word denotes either sequence or duration in time or a logical relation. As applied to time, it signifies *from* a time or *subsequent to* or *during* a time: "Many years have passed *since* they met." "It is a fortnight *since* he embarked." Logically, *since* means *because* or *inasmuch as*: "*Since* she has inquired, you may give her the facts."

So. In its conjunctive use, this particle has the sense of *provided that, on condition that*; as, "They will be satisfied, *so* their children receive an education." It is used also to introduce a clause of result; as, "The car had disappeared, *so* the entire party walked home."

Than. Formerly this word was thought of both as conjunction and as preposition, and such expressions as "older *than* me," "taller *than* him" were allowable. Now, however, *than* is recognized only as a conjunction; hence one must say "older *than* I," "taller *than* he." The expression *than whom* is an exception to the rule given; as, "Roosevelt, *than whom* no American has been better loved or more sincerely hated." This construction is now universally approved.

That. A few common uses of *that* should be noticed. Besides being generally used to introduce an objective or adjective clause, *that* is likewise employed to denote time, definitely or indefinitely: "It is time *that* we should be going home." "We left the day *that* he arrived." It may also denote the relation of purpose or result: "He was given leave *that* he might go to Paris." Both in speaking and in writing we often omit *that* when the connection may readily be supplied: "We believe (*that*) the work can be done in a week."

Therefore. A conjunction of formal sense, used to introduce a conclusion or consequence. Its meanings may be expressed by *in consequence, for this reason, on that ground, consequently*: "We have completed our examination of the case; *therefore* we should make our report."

Till, Until. These two words are used as conjunctions without any difference in meaning. Their general sense is that of expectancy or continuance, expressed by *(up) to the time when*: "They could not vote *until* the polls were opened." "It was his custom to remain in the house *till* darkness had fallen."

Unless. A word compounded of *on* and *less*, and meaning literally *in less* or *on less*, that is, *on any less grounds or condition than*, the conditions being stated in a following clause. Other equivalent phrases are *if—not, in the event that—not, supposing that—not*. The following are typical uses of the word: "How shall they learn *unless* they are willing to hear?" "*Unless* the government's plans miscarry, the ships will be built." "I cannot explain his conduct, *unless* he has not been warned."

Whereas. A conjunction of two principal uses: (1) In formal documents and arguments, expressing the idea of *since, considering*, it introduces a preamble or a reason upon which a conclusion or a resolution is based: "*Whereas*, The society has accepted the plan of the committee, therefore, be it Resolved, etc." (2) Like *although*, it may imply a contradiction between the clause it introduces and a preceding statement: "They claimed a victory, *whereas* they had really lost the contest."

Whether. As a conjunction, this word introduces an implied question. (1) It may introduce alternatives, followed by *or* before the second alternative: "He was uncertain *whether* he should reply *or* be silent." When the second alternative is a negative of the first, it is frequently expressed by *not* or *no* following *or*: "They will move, *whether* the order arrives *or not*." (2) It may introduce a single indirect question, with an alternative omitted but implied: "We do not know *whether* he has read that book (*or* not) (*or* some other)."

While. Used of time, in the sense of *as long as* or *during the time that*: "*While* I was musing, the fire burned." It may also have the sense of *although*, implying some contradiction: "*While* the cloth is very heavy, it is not firm in texture."

Yet. As a conjunction, meaning *however, nevertheless, yet* implies usually some opposition, or unlikeness: "The board approved the plan, *yet* was not ready to act." "The tools are similar in form, *yet* very different in use." It may be used in the sense of *although*, signifying a concession: "They were determined, *yet* courteous."

CAPITAL LETTERS

In early forms of writing, capital letters were exclusively employed. Gradually small letters appeared and initial letters were used at the beginnings of sections and paragraphs only. Later the first word of a sentence was capitalized to call attention to its importance. Finally words within the sentence were treated in the same manner. It became the custom to begin every noun with a capital. This custom, however, conducing to no useful end, has long since been laid aside.

Modern capitalization is determined somewhat by the thought to be conveyed. The chief uses of capitals are (1) to show the beginning of a unit of thought; (2) to give particular prominence to certain words, as names of countries, cities, persons, etc.; (3) to relieve the uniformity of the page.

Certain rules for capitalization are fixed. However, a slight variation in some instances may result from the individual usage of competent writers.

In the sciences, such as botany and geology, as well as in other departments of knowledge, certain customs of capitalization have become well established. Many of these special rules are to be found in the "stylebooks" issued by various publishers.

The following list contains the most generally approved rules and customs of capitalization in present day writing:

Rules for Capitals

1. The first word of every sentence should begin with a capital.

We receive good by doing good.
Always speak the truth.

2. The first word of every line of poetry should begin with a capital.

Like to a coin, passing from hand to hand,
Are common memories, and day by day
The sharpness of their impress wears away.

3. The first word of every direct quotation should begin with a capital.

Coleridge said, "Friendship is a sheltering tree."

4. The first word of every direct question should begin with a capital.

Ask yourself this question: Are you making the best use of your time?

5. The pronoun I and the interjection O should be capitalized.

Guide me, O thou great Jehovah.

6. Every proper noun should begin with a capital letter.

Europe, America, Chicago, James.

7. Words derived from proper nouns should begin with capitals unless, by long usage, they have lost all association with the nouns from which they are derived.

American, Americanize, Christian, Christianize, Roman, Hebrew, Elizabethan, etc.

But china dishes, india ink, prussian blue, turkey red, majolica ware, delft, castile soap, oriental rugs, galvanize, pasteurize, romance.

Capitalize all abbreviations of proper names.

Eng. (England), Sun. (Sunday), N. J. (New Jersey).

8. Names of geographical sections of the world, when used as proper nouns, should be capitalized.

The Far North, the Orient, the Near East, the Riviera, in the West.

9. The words North, South, East, and West and their compounds should begin with capitals whenever they refer to parts of the country, and not simply to points of the compass.

I have a friend in the South.
The river flows southwest.
Gold is found in the great Northwest.

10. The names of the days of the week, of the months of the year, and of feasts, fasts, festivals, and holidays, both religious and civic, should begin with capitals.

Tuesday, June, Arbor Day, Easter.

The names of the seasons are not capitalized except when personified.

The New England autumn is a delightful season.
Thou breath of Autumn's being.

11. Names of personified objects should be capitalized.

O Death! where is thy sting?
Then Memory disclosed her face divine.

12. All names and expressions which may be regarded as titles of the Deity should be capitalized.

Lord, God, Father, Son, Son of Man, Heavenly Father.
But write King of kings, Father of mercies, Prince of peace, where the phrase is merely descriptive and not an essential part of the name.

As a rule, a personal pronoun referring to Deity should be capitalized when the meaning might otherwise be mistaken.

Be true thyself, and follow Me!

In general, do not capitalize a relative pronoun referring to Deity, because its antecedent is usually given.

Follow Him, whose truth shall deliver you.

13. The names of versions and of books and divisions of the Bible, names of sacred books of all religions, and titles of psalms and of parables should be capitalized.

Exodus, Psalms, New Testament, Epistle to the Romans, Sermon on the Mount, the Pentateuch, the Koran, Parable of the Vineyard.

14. The words street, river, gulf, sea, canal, coast, etc., may begin with capital letters when they are used in connection with proper names.

Bryant Street, Hudson River, Persian Gulf, North Sea, Erie Canal, Pacific Coast.

15. Names of political parties and of religious organizations, and generally the first word and all other important words in the names of societies and corporations, should be capitalized.

Conservative, Liberal, Republican, Democrat, Presbyterians, The Society for the Prevention of Cruelty to Animals.

16. Capitalize the first word and all other words, except articles, prepositions, and conjunctions, in titles of books, poems, essays, periodicals, plays, and pictures.

Gray's Elegy in a Country Churchyard.
Hawthorne's The Great Stone Face.
The Inside of the Cup.

Some publishers and the American Library Association capitalize only the first word and proper nouns and proper adjectives in titles.

A history of English local government.

17. Titles of honor, of respect, and of relationship, when used before the names of persons, should be capitalized; but, when used after the name, such titles are not capitalized.

King George, President Harding, Sir James, Uncle John, Aunt Edith.

Warren G. Harding, president of the United States; Honorable Joseph G. Cannon, representative from Illinois; George V, king of Great Britain.

Abbreviated titles of honor or respect should be capitalized.

James Bryce, D.C.L.; Dr. S. Weir Mitchell; Henry Brown, D.D., LL.D.

18. Names of important historical events and movements are capitalized.

The Revolution, the World War, the Reformation, the Colonial Period, the Renaissance.

19. In formal resolutions, capitalize the words Whereas and Resolved and the word immediately following each.

Whereas, This society, etc.; therefore, be it Resolved, That the office of secretary, etc.

PUNCTUATION

Punctuation is the art of separating composition or discourse into sentences, and members of a sentence, by means of certain marks or points (1) to make clear the author's meaning and (2) to show grammatical relations between words.

In spoken language, these relations are indicated by the pauses and by the inflections of the voice; but in written language there are no such aids, and it is necessary to supply the deficiency with definite marks.

As a means of conveying thought, punctuation does not generally receive the attention its importance demands. An omission, an insertion, or a transposition of points may completely alter the meaning of a sentence. To illustrate: An English statesman, having charged a government officer with dishonesty, was required publicly to retract the accusation in the House of Commons. The statesman read the following recantation: "I said he was dishonest, it is true; and I am sorry for it." The following day the papers printed the retraction thus: "I said he was dishonest; it is true, and I am sorry for it." By a simple transposition of the comma and the semicolon, the printed statement not only failed to carry an apology, but it also reiterated the original charge of dishonesty.

To a limited extent it is true that usage varies. But it is equally true that, as an art, punctuation is founded upon certain definite principles; and, while some latitude is allowed in their application, whatever directly violates these principles is incorrect and inadmissible.

Punctuation is, therefore, an essential part of good writing. A clear idea of what one wishes to say, a knowledge of the structure of sentences, and intelligent care in the application of definite rules will do much to perfect one in the use of this important art.

The generally accepted rules for punctuation are as follows:

Rules for Punctuation

The Period

1. A period should be placed at the close of every declarative or imperative sentence.

Washington is a beautiful city.
Think before you speak.

2. Place a period after all abbreviations, but not after chemical symbols, Roman numerals, per cent, or 8vo, 4to, 2d, 9th, etc. When an abbreviation ends a sentence, use only one period.

I know John Jones, M.D., LL.D.

When omission of letters is indicated by an apostrophe, a period is not used after the contraction: m'f'g for manufacturing; ass'n for association.

3. A period is not necessary after titles, headings, etc., on a page; but subheads and paragraph topics, not in separate lines, should be followed by a period.

The Exclamation Point

1. Place an exclamation point after every exclamatory sentence and after interjections and other expressions of emotion.

How welcome is the rain!
Alas! He died on the battlefield.
God forbid! May I never see it again!

In some cases, when an interjection is very closely connected with other words, the exclamation point is not placed between them, but is reserved for the close of the expression.

Oh, never may sun that morrow see!

2. The exclamation point is often used to express contempt or sarcasm.

And he is a writer!

The Interrogation Point

1. Place an interrogation point at the end of every direct question.

Is he telling the truth?
She asked, "When does school begin?"

The Colon

1. Place a colon between the great divisions of sentences, when minor subdivisions occur that are separated by semicolons.

We perceive the shadow to have moved along the dial, but did not see it moving; we observe that the grass has grown, though it was impossible to see it grow: so the advances we make in knowledge, consisting of minute and gradual steps, are perceivable only after intervals of time.

2. The colon separates a clause from the following clause or group of clauses illustrating or amplifying its meaning.

There is a singular and perpetual charm in a letter of yours: it never grows old; it never loses its novelty.

3. A colon precedes a formal enumeration of particulars.

Man consists of three parts: first, the body, with its sensual appetites; second, the mind, with its thirst for knowledge and other noble aspirations; third, the soul, with its undying principle.

4. A colon should be used before a long direct quotation.

Lord Bacon said: "Reading maketh a full man; conference, a ready man; writing, an exact man."

5. A colon follows *thus, as follows, this, these,* and similar expressions, introducing a statement or a series of clauses.

His credentials are as follows: he has studied economics; he has employed men; he has succeeded in business.

6. A colon usually follows the salutation in a letter.

My dear Mary: Sirs:

In short, informal letters, a comma may be used.

My dear Friend,

The Semicolon

1. A semicolon should be used to separate the parts of a compound sentence, when one or both members contain commas.

Mirth should be the embroidery of conversation, not the web; and wit the ornament of the mind, not the furniture.

2. When two clauses are joined by *for, but, and,* or an equivalent word, the one clause perfect in itself, and the other added as a matter of inference, contrast, or explanation, they are separated by a semicolon.

Economy is no disgrace; for it is better to live on a little than to outlive a great deal.

3. When the parts of a compound sentence, even though they are short, are not closely connected in thought, they should be separated by a semicolon.

Man proposes; God disposes.

4. If a series of expressions depends on a commencing or concluding portion of the sentence, the expressions should be separated by semicolons.

If we think of glory in the field; of wisdom in the cabinet; of the purest patriotism; of the highest integrity, public and private; of morals * * *.—the august figure of Washington presents itself as the personification of all these ideas.

5. A semicolon is commonly used before and a comma after *as, viz., to wit, namely, for example, i.e.,* or *that is,* when they precede examples or illustrations.

We have three great bulwarks of liberty; viz., schools, colleges, and universities.

The Comma

1. All nouns of direct address should be set off by commas.

Mary, shut the door.
I say, John, it is not true.

2. Parenthetical expressions or additional expressions that break the directness of the statement should be set off by commas.

Industry, as well as genius, is essential to the production of great works.
It is mind, after all, that does the work of the world.

3. Words or expressions used in apposition should be set off from the rest of the sentence by commas.

Milton, the blind poet, wrote *Paradise Lost.*
We, the people of the United States, do ordain and establish this constitution.

4. A comma is used to mark the omission of words grammatically essential.

To err is human; to forgive, divine.
Go today if you can; if not, tomorrow.

5. A comma is used before a short direct quotation or question.

He said, "Time will tell."
Jane shouted, "Are you going?"

6. A nominative absolute construction or an expression used independently should be separated from the rest of the sentence by a comma.

To tell the truth, I do not know.
Rome having fallen, the world relapsed into barbarism.

7. A series of words in the same construction should be separated by commas.

Ulysses was wise, eloquent, cautious, and intrepid.
Men, women, and children filled the building.

8. When the subject consists of a series of words not joined by a conjunction, use a comma before the predicate.

Men, women, children, filled the building.

9. As a rule, when a clause is used as the subject of a verb, it should not, even though long, be followed by a comma, unless it ends with a verb.

That he is a man well qualified to fill the position must be admitted.
Whatever is, is right.

A comma is sometimes needed to prevent ambiguity.

He who teaches, often learns himself.

10. Use a comma between words in the same construction when they are modified in different ways.

They saw fields, and hills covered with trees.

11. When the separation of sentence elements is desirable and is slightly marked, a comma is used between co-ordinate clauses.

I heard him speak, but I made no reply.
Jane frowned, and her friend turned away.

12. Words used in pairs take a comma after each pair.

The dying man cares not for pomp or luxury, palace or estate, silver or gold.

13. A phrase or a clause out of its natural order should be separated from the rest of the sentence by a comma. If the sentence is short, the comma may be omitted.

Of the five races, the Caucasian is the most enlightened.
To those who labor, sleep is doubly pleasant.
With this I am satisfied.

14. In a complex sentence, if the dependent clause comes first, it should be followed by a comma.

Where I go, ye cannot come.

15. When two or more antecedent portions of a sentence have a common connection with some succeeding clause or word, a comma should be placed after each.

She is as tall, though not as handsome, as her sister.

16. A comma should be placed before a relative clause, when it is explanatory of the antecedent, or presents an additional thought.

Why ask John, who knows nothing about it?

A comma should not be placed between a restrictive adjunct or clause and that which it restricts.

Bring me the book that lies on the table.
Who can respect a man that is not governed by good principles?

Quotation Marks

1. Every direct quotation should be enclosed in double quotation marks.

Franklin said, "One today is worth two tomorrows."

2. A quotation within a quotation should be enclosed in single quotation marks.

Said he, "I quoted Burns's line, 'A man's a man for a' that.'"

3. Words or phrases of unusual, technical, or ironical meaning, or to which particular attention is directed, may be enclosed in single or double quotation marks.

Ann was made "master of ceremonies."
The phrase "producer to consumer" is popular.
He always talks about 'contacts and aerials.'

4. When a quotation consists of more than one paragraph, quotation marks should be placed at the *beginning* of *each* paragraph, but at the *end* of the *last* paragraph only.

The period and the comma are always placed inside the quotation marks. If at the close of a quotation any grammatical point other than the period or comma is required, it should be placed before the quotation marks if it is applicable to the quotation alone, but after them if it belongs to the sentence or member as a whole.

I read Tennyson's "In Memoriam."
He answered briefly, "Am I a knave that you should suspect me of this?"
Are our lots indeed cast "in the brazen age"?

The Parenthesis

1. Marks of parenthesis are used to enclose words loosely connected with the rest of the sentence in thought and structure.

Every star (and this great truth is inferred from indisputable facts) is the center of a planetary system.

Words within parenthesis should be punctuated as they would be in any other position, except before the last parenthetical mark. There, if the subject matter is complete in itself as regards both construction and sense, a period, an interrogation point, or an exclamation point should be used, according to the character of the sentence. If the parenthesis is incomplete in sense, there should be no point before the last mark.

Men are born equal (can you doubt it?); it is circumstances only that cast their lot in different stations.
Jane (such was her name) smiled sweetly.

The Dash

1. The dash is used to denote a sudden change in thought or in construction.

Closely following came—What do you suppose?

2. A dash is used after other points when a greater pause than they usually denote is required.

A traitor!—Yes.

3. A dash is used to set off parenthetical expressions which have a closer connection with the rest of the sentence than parenthesis marks would show.

You have a whole day—two days, if needful—to finish your work.

4. A dash is frequently used to set off an appositive or a supplementary word or phrase added for emphasis or for explanation.

He wrote an excellent article on chemistry—a subject to which he has devoted the greater part of his life.

Her features were plain but not repulsive—at least not so when you heard her speak.

The Hyphen

1. A hyphen should be used between syllables at the end of a line when a part of a word must be continued on the next line.

2. The hyphen is used in forming compound words which are not permanent compounds. Such words rightly united by a hyphen are of two kinds:

(1) Those used conventionally or for a certain occasion only.

A well-known man; fresh-water fish; open-hearth furnace.
After-deliberation showed they were wrong.

(2) Those which are attributively used as a phrase to transfer to an object a certain meaning that the literal sense of the words would not otherwise indicate.

A forget-me-not; Jack-in-the-pulpit; love-lies-bleeding.

DICTIONARY OF ABBREVIATIONS

A. Alto.
A1. First class.
A., *a.*, *adj.* Adjective.
A., *ans.* Answer.
a., *@.* (Lat. *ad*), To; At.
A. A. A. Agricultural Adjustment Administration; American Automobile Association.
A. A. A. & L. American Academy of Arts and Letters.
A. A. A. S. American Association for the Advancement of Science.
A. A. G. Assistant Adjutant General.
A. A. O. N. M. S. Ancient Arabic Order of the Nobles of the Mystic Shrine.
a. a. r. Against all risks.
A. & A. S. R. Ancient and Accepted Scottish Rite.
A. A. S. S. (Lat. *Academiæ Antiquarinæ Societatis Socius*), Member of the American Antiquarian Society.
A. A. U. Amateur Athletic Union.
A. A. U. P. American Association of University Professors.
A. A. U. W. American Association of University Women.
A. b. Able Bodied (seaman).
A. B. (Lat. *artium baccalaureus*), Bachelor of Arts.
Abbr., *Abbrev.* Abbreviated, abbreviation.
Abp. Archbishop.
A. B. S. American Bible Society.
A. C. (Lat. *ante Christum*), Before Christ; Analytical Chemist; Alternating Current.
A. C. A. American Congregational Association.
Acc., *Acct.* Account.
A. D. (Lat. *anno Domini*), In the year of our Lord.
Ad., *advt.* Advertisement. Plur. *ads.*
Ad. inf. To infinity.
Adjt. Adjutant.
Adjt. Gen. Adjutant General.
Ad lib., *Ad libit.* (Lat. *ad libitum*), At pleasure.
Adm. Admiral.
Admr. Administrator.
Admx. Administratrix.
Adv. Advertising; Advocate; Adverb.
Æ., *Æt.* (Lat. *ætatis*), Of age, aged.
A.E.F. American Expeditionary Force.
A. F. L., *A. F. of L.* American Federation of Labor.
Agr., *Agric.* Agriculture, agricultural.
Agt. Agent.
A. H. (Lat. *anno Hegiræ*), In the year of the Hegira, or flight of Mohammed.
A. H. C. American Hospital Corps.
A. H. M. S. American Home Missionary Society.
A. H. S. (Lat. *anno humanæ salutis*), In the year of human salvation.
A. L. American Legion.
A. L. A. American Library Association.
Ala. Alabama.
Ald. Alderman.
A. L. of H. American Legion of Honor.
Alta. Alberta.
A. M. (Lat. *anno mundi*), In the year of the world.
A. M. (Lat. *ante meridiem*), Before noon.
A. M. (Lat. *artium magister*), Master of Arts.
Am., *Amer.* America, American.
A. M. D. Army Medical Department.
Amer. Phil. Soc. American Philosophical Society.
Amp. Ampere; amperage.
Amt. Amount.
A. N. Anglo-Norman.
an. (Lat. *anno*), In the year.
Anat. Anatomy, anatomical.
Anc. Ancient.
Anon. Anonymous.
A. N. S. Army Nursing Service.
A. N. S. S. Associate of the Normal School of Science.
Ant., *Antiq.* Antiquities, antiquarian.
A. O. H. Ancient Order of Hibernians.
A. O. U. American Ornithologists' Union.
A. O. U. W. Ancient Order of United Workmen.
Ap., *App.* Apostle, apostles; Appendix.
A. P. A. American Protestant Association; American Protective Association.
Apl., *Apr.* April.
Apoc. Apocalypse; Apocrypha.
Apog. Apogee.
approx. Approximate, -ly.
A. P. S. Associate of the Pharmaceutical Society.
Aq. (Lat. *aqua*), Water.
A. Q. M. Assistant Quartermaster.
A. Q. M. G. Assistant Quartermaster-General.
Ar., *Arab.* Arabic, Arabian.
Ar., *Arr.* Arrives, arrived, arrival.
A. R. A. Associate of the Royal Academy.
Aram. Aramaic.
Arch. Architecture.
Archæol. Archæology.
Archd. Archdeacon; Archduke.
Ariz. Arizona.
Ark. Arkansas.
Arm. Armorican; Armenian.
Art. Article; Artificial; Artillery.
A. S., *A.-S.* Anglo-Saxon.
Assoc., *Assn.* Association.
Asst. Assistant.
A. S. S. U. American Sunday School Union.
Astrol. Astrology.
Astron. Astronomy, astronomical.
A. T. S. American Tract Society; Army Transport Service.
Atty. Attorney.
A. U. A. American Unitarian Association.
A. U. C. (Lat. *anno urbis conditæ*), In the year of the building of the city (Rome).
Aug. Augustus; August.
A. V. Authorized Version.
A. V. C. American Veterans Committee.
Avoir. Avoirdupois.
A. w. o. l. Absent without leave.

B. Bass; Book.
b. Born.
B., *Brit.* British.
B. A. Bachelor of Arts.
Bal. Balance.
Balt., *Balto.* Baltimore.
Bap., *Bapt.* Baptist.
Bar. Barrel; Barometer.
Bart., *Bt.* Baronet.
Bat., *Batt.* Battalion, battery.
B.B.C. British Broadcasting Corporation.
bbl. Barrel. Plur. *bbls.*
B. C. Before Christ; British Columbia.
B. Ch. (Lat. *baccalaureus chirurgiæ*), Bachelor of Surgery.
B. C. L. (Lat. *baccalaureus civilis legis*), Bachelor of Civil Law.
B. C. S. Bachelor of Commercial Science.
B. D. (Lat. *baccalaureus divinitatis*), Bachelor of Divinity.
Bd. Bound; Bond; Board; Band.
Bdls. Bundles.
Bds. Bound in boards.
B. E. Bachelor of Engineering; Bachelor of Elocution.
b. e. Bill of exchange.
Belg. Belgic, Belgian.
Ben., *Benj.* Benjamin.
Berks. Berkshire (England).
Bib. Bible, biblical.
Biog. Biography, biographical.
Biol. Biology, biological.
B. L., *B.LL.* (Lat. *baccalaureus legum*), Bachelor of Laws.
bldg. Building.
bls. Bales.
B. M. (Lat. *baccalaureus medicinæ*), Bachelor of Medicine.
B. M., *B. Mus.* (Lat. *baccalaureus musicæ*), Bachelor of Music.
B. O. Branch Office; Board of Ordnance; Bachelor of Oratory.
Bot. Botany, botanical.
Bp. Bishop.
B. P. O. E. Benevolent and Protective Order of Elks.
Br., *Bro.* Brother.
Brig. Brigade, brigadier.
Brig. Gen. Brigadier General.
B. S. Bachelor of Surgery; Bachelor of Science.
B. Sc. (Lat. *baccalaureus scientiæ*), Bachelor of Science.
B. S. L. Botanical Society, London.
bu., *bush.* Bushel.
B. V. Blessed Virgin.
B. V. M. Blessed Virgin Mary.

C. Cent, cents; Centigrade; Consul; Centime, centimes; Hundred.
C., *Cap.* (Lat. *caput*), Chapter.
C. A. Chartered Accountant.
C. A. A. Civil Aeronautics Administration.
C. A. B. Civil Aeronautics Board.
Cal. Calendar.
Cal., *Calif.* California.
Cam., *Camb.* Cambridge.
Cant. Canticle; Canterbury.
Cantab. (Lat. *Cantabrigiensis*), Of Cambridge.
Cap. (Lat. *caput*), Capital; Chapter.
Caps. Capitals.
Capt. Captain.
car., *k.* Carat.
Card. Cardinal.
Cath. Catharine; Catholic; Cathedral.
C. B. Companion of the Bath.
C. B. I. China Burma India (World War II theater of operations).
C. C. Catholic Clergyman, Catholic Curate.
C. C. C. Civilian Conservation Corps.
C. D. S. Companion of the Distinguished Service Order.
C. D. V. or *c. d. v.* Carte-de-Visite.
C. E. Civil Engineer.
Celt. Celtic.
Cent. (Lat. *centum*), Hundred; Centigrade.
Cert., *Certif.* Certify, certificate.
Cf. (Lat. *confer*), Compare.
c. f. i. Cost, freight, and insurance.
c. ft. Cubic feet.
C. G. Coast guard; Commissary General; Consul General.
C. G. S. Centimeter-Gram-Second.
C. H. Court House.
Ch. Church; Chapter.
Chal., *Chald.* Chaldee.
Chanc. Chancellor, chancery.
Chap. Chapter; Chaplain.
Chas. Charles.
Chem. Chemistry, chemical.
Ch. Hist. Church History.
Chin. Chinese.
Chr. Christ; Christian.
Chron. Chronology, chronological.
C. I. Order of the Crown of India.
C. I. O. Congress of Industrial Organizations.
Cit. Citation; Citizen.
Civ. Civil.
C. J. Chief Justice.
Cl. Clergyman.
Class. Classical.
Clk. Clerk.
cm. Centimeter.
C. M. Common meter.
C. M. (Lat. *chirurgiæ magister*), Master in Surgery.
cml. Commercial.
C. M. T. C. Citizens Military Training Camp.
C. M. Z. S. Corresponding Member of the Zoological Society.
Co. Company; County.
C. O. D. Cash on Delivery; Collect (payment) on delivery.
C. of C. Chamber of Commerce.
Col. Colonel; Colossians: Column.
Coll. College; Collection.

Colloq. Colloquial, colloquialism.
Colo. Colorado.
Com. Commander; Commerce; Commissioner; Committee; Commodore.
Comm. Commentary; Commerce.
Comp. Compare, comparative; Compound, compounded.
Compar. Comparative.
Com. Ver. Common Version.
Con. (Lat. *contra*), Against.
Cong. Congregation, Congregational, Congregationalist; Congress.
Conj. Conjunction.
Conn., Ct. Connecticut.
Cont. Contents; Continued.
Contr. Contracted, contraction.
Coop. Cooperative.
Cop., Copt. Coptic.
Cor. Corinthians.
Corn. Cornwall, Cornish.
Corrup. Corruption, corrupted.
Cor. Sec. Corresponding Secretary.
C. P. Clerk of the Peace; Common Pleas; Chemically Pure.
C. P. A. Certified Public Accountant; Civilian Production Administration.
C. Q. D. Come quick—danger.
Cr. Credit, creditor.
Cres. Crescendo.
Crim. con. Criminal conversation, or adultery.
cryst., crystal. Crystallography.
C. S. A. Confederate States of America.
Csks. Casks.
Ct. (Lat. *centum*), A hundred.
Ct. Court.
C. T. A. U. Catholic Total Abstinence Union.
ctge. Cartage.
Cu., Cub. Cubic.
Cu. ft. Cubic foot.
Cur., Curt. Current—this month.
Cwt. A hundredweight, hundredweights.
C. Y. M. A. Catholic Young Men's Association.

D. Deputy; Democrat; Dutch.
d. (Lat. *denarius, denarii*), Penny, pence.
d. Died; Daughter.
Dan. Daniel; Danish.
D. A. R. Daughter(s) of the American Revolution.
Dat. Dative.
D. C. Doctor of Chiropractic.
D. C. (Ital. *da capo*), From the beginning; Direct Current.
D. C., Dist. Col. District of Columbia.
D. C. L. Doctor of Civil (or Canon) Law.
D. D. (Lat. *divinitatis doctor*), Doctor of Divinity.
D-Day. Day designated for military operation against enemy.
D. D. S. Doctor of Dental Surgery.
D. E. Dynamic Engineer.
Dec. December.
decim. Decimeter.
Def. Definition; Defendant.
Deg. Degree, degrees.
Del. Delaware.
Del. (Lat. *delineavit*), He (or she) drew.
D. Eng. Doctor of Engineering.
Dep., Dept. Department; Deputy; Deposit.
Der. Derived, derivation.
Deut. Deuteronomy.
D. F. Dean of the Faculty; Defender of the Faith.
dft. Draft; Defendant.
D. G. (Lat. *Dei gratia*), By the grace of God.
Dict. Dictionary.
Dim., Dimin. Diminutive.
Dis., Disct. Discount.
Dist. District.
Dist. Atty. District Attorney.
Div. Divide, dividend, division, divisor.
D. Lit., D. Litt. Doctor of Literature.
D. L. O. Dead Letter Office.
D. M., D. Mus. Doctor of Music.
D. M. D. Doctor of Dental Medicine.
D. O. Doctor of Osteopathy; Doctor of Oratory.
Do. (Ital. *ditto*), The same.
Dols. Dollars.
Dom. Econ. Domestic Economy.
Doz. Dozen.
Dpt. Deponent; Department.
Dr. Debtor; Doctor; Dram, drams.
D. S. (Ital. *dal segno*), From the sign.
D. S., D. Sc. Doctor of Science.
D. S. C. Distinguished Service Cross.
D. S. M. Distinguished Service Medal.
D. S. O. Distinguished Service Order.
D. T. (Lat. *doctor theologiæ*), Doctor of Theology.
Du. Dutch; Duke.
Duo., 12mo. Duodecimo (twelve folds).
D. V. (Lat. *Deo volente*), God willing.
D. V. M. Doctor of Veterinary Medicine.
D. V. S. Doctor of Veterinary Surgery.
dwt. (Lat. *denarius*, and English *weight*), Pennyweight, pennyweights.
Dyn., Dynam. Dynamics.

E. East, Eastern; English.
Ea. Each.
Eben. Ebenezer.
Eccl., Eccles. Ecclesiastical.
Econ. Economy, economics.
Ed. Editor; Edition; Edinburgh.
Ed., Edm. Edmund.
Edin. Edinburgh.
Edw. Edward.
E. E. Errors excepted; Electrical Engineer.
e. g. (Lat. *exempli gratia*), For example.
E. I. B. Export-import Bank of Washington.
Elec., Elect. Electric, electricity.
Eliz. Elizabeth, Elizabethan.
e. m. f. Electromotive force.
Emp. Emperor, empress.
Enc., Encl. Enclosure.
Ency., Encyc. Encyclopedia.
E. N. E. East northeast.
Eng. England, English.
Eng., Engin. Engineer, engineering.
Eng. Dept. Department of Engineers.
Ent., Entom. Entomology, entomological.
E. & O. E. Errors and omissions excepted.
Eph. Ephesians; Ephraim.
Epiph. Epiphany.
Epis., Episc. Episcopal.
Epis., Epist. Epistle, epistolary.
Eq. Equal, equivalent.
Equiv. Equivalent.
E. S. E. East southeast.
Esq., Esqr. Esquire.
et al. (Lat. *et alibi*), And elsewhere.
et al. (Lat. *et alii, aliæ*, or *alia*), And others.
etc., &c. (Lat. *et cetæri, cæteræ*, or *cætera*), And the others, and so forth.
Ethnol. Ethnology, ethnological.
E. T. O. European Theater of Operations, World War II.
Etym. Etymology.
Ex. Example; Examined; Exception; Exodus; Export; Executive.
Exch. Exchange; Exchequer.
Exd. Examined.
Ex. Doc. Executive Document.
Exec., Exr. Executor.
Execx., Exrx. Executrix.
Ex. Gr. (Lat. *exempli gratia*), For example.
Exod. Exodus.
Exon. (Lat. *Exonia*), Exeter.
exp. Express; Export; Expense.
Ezek. Ezekiel.

F. Fellow; Fahrenheit; France.
f. Farthing, farthings; Folio; Feminine.
f. Franc, francs.
Fahr. Fahrenheit.
F. & A. M. Free and Accepted Masons.
f. a. s. Free alongside ship.
F. B. I. Federal Bureau of Investigation.
F. C. A. Farm Credit Association.
F. C. C. Federal Communications Commission.
F. C. I. C. Federal Crop Insurance Corporation.
Fcp. Foolscap.
F. D., Fid. Def. (Lat. *fidei defensor*), Defender of the Faith.
F. D. I. C. Federal Deposit Insurance Corporation.
Feb. February.
Fec. (Lat. *fecit*), He (or she) did it.
Fem. Feminine.
F. F. V. First Families of Virginia.
F. G. S. Fellow of the Geological Society.
F. H. A. Federal Housing Administration.
F. I. A. Fellow of the Institute of Actuaries.
F. I. C. Fellow of the Chemical Institute.
Fig. Figure, figurative, figuratively.
Finn. Finnish.
Fl. Flemish; Florin, florins; Flourished.
Fla. Florida.
F. L. A. Federal Loan Administration.
F. M. Field Marshal; Frequency Modulation.
fo., fol. Folio.
f. o. b. Free on board.
fol. Folio; Following.
For. Foreign.
for'd., fwd. Forward, forwarded.
Fort. Fortification.
F. P. C. Federal Power Commission.
Fr. France, French; Francis; Francs.
F. R. A. S. Fellow of the Royal Astronomical Society.
Fred. Frederick.
F. R. G. S. Fellow of the Royal Geographical Society.
F. R. Hist. S. Fellow of the Royal Historical Society.
Fri. Friday.
F. R. S. Fellow of the Royal Society.
F. R. S. L. Fellow of the Royal Society of Literature.
frt. Freight.
F. S. A. Federal Security Administration.
ft. Foot, feet.
F. T. C. Federal Trade Commission.
Fth. Fathom.
Fur. Furlong.
F.W. A. Federal Works Administration.

G. Genitive; Guinea, guineas; Gulf.
Ga. Georgia.
Gael. Gaelic.
Gal. Galatians.
Gal., Gall. Gallon.
G. A. R. Grand Army of the Republic.
G. B. Great Britain.
G. C. B. Grand Cross of the Bath.
G. C. L. H. Grand Cross of the Legion of Honor.
G. C. M. G. Grand Cross SS. Michael and George.
G. C. S. I. Grand Commander of the Star of India.
G. C. V. O. Grand Cross of the Royal Victorian Order.
G. D. Grand Duke, Grand Duchess.
Gen., Genl. General.
Gen. Genesis; Genitive.
Gend. Gender.
Geo. George.
Geog. Geography, geographical.
Geol. Geology, geological.
Geom. Geometry, geometrical.
Ger., Germ. German, Germany.
G. H. Q. General Headquarters.
Gi. Gill, gills.
G. I. Government Issue.
G. L. Grand Lodge.
G. M. Grand Master.
Gm. Gram.
Go., Goth. Gothic.
G. O. P. Grand Old Party (applied to Republican party).
Gov. Governor, government.
Gov.-Gen. Governor-General.
Govt. Government.
Gr. Grain, grains; Great; Greek; Gross.
Gram. Grammar, grammatical.
Gro. Gross.
G. T. Good Templars; Grand Tyler.

Gtt. (Lat. *guttæ*), Drops.
H., *hr.* Hour, hours.
Hag. Haggai.
Hants. Hampshire.
H. C. House of Commons.
h. e. (Lat. *hoc est*), That is or this is; (*hic est*), Here is.
Heb., *Hebr.* Hebrew, Hebrews.
H. H. His (or Her) Highness; His Holiness (the Pope).
Hhd. Hogshead, hogsheads.
H. I. H. His (or Her) Imperial Highness.
Hind. Hindu, Hindustan, Hindustani.
Hist. History, historical.
H. J. (Lat. *hic jacet*), Here lies.
H. J. S. (Lat. *hic jacet sepultus*), Here lies buried.
H. M. His (or Her) Majesty.
H. M. S. His (or Her) Majesty's service, ship, or steamer.
Hon., *Honble.* Honorable.
Hor., *Horol.* Horology, horological.
Hort., *Hortic.* Horticulture, horticultural.
H. P. Half pay; High priest; Horse power.
H. R. House of Representatives.
H. R. H. His (or Her) Royal Highness.
H. S. (Lat. *hic situs*), Here lies.
H. S. H. His (or Her) Serene Highness.
Hun., *Hung.* Hungary, Hungarian.
Hyd., *Hydros.* Hydrostatics.
Hydraul. Hydraulics.
Hypoth. Hypothesis, hypothetical.

I., *Isl.* Island.
Ia., *Io.* (unofficial) Iowa.
Ib., *Ibid.* (Lat. *ibidem*), In the same place.
I. C. C. Interstate Commerce Commission.
Ice., *Icel.* Iceland, Icelandic.
Ich., *Ichth.* Ichthyology.
Id. (Lat. *idem*), The same.
Ida. (unofficial) Idaho.
i. e. (Lat. *id est*), That is.
I. H. S. Greek contraction for Jesus, —used as abbrev. for Lat. *Jesus Hominum Salvator*, "Jesus, the Savior of Men," and *In hoc signo*, "In this sign (cross)."
Ill. Illinois.
I. L. O. International Labor Organization.
Imp. (Lat. *imperator*), Emperor; Imperial; Impersonal.
In. Inch, inches.
Incog. (Ital. *incognito*), Unknown.
Ind. India, Indian; Indiana.
Ind. Ter. Indian Territory.
In lim. (Lat. *in limine*), At the outset.
In loc. (Lat. *in loco*), In its place.
in re. In regard to.
I. N. R. I. (Lat. *Jesus Nazarenus Rex Iudæorum*), Jesus of Nazareth, King of the Jews.
Ins. Insurance.
Ins. Gen. Inspector General.
Inst. Instant; The present month; Institute, institution.
Int. Interest.
Int. Dept. Department of the Interior.
Intrans. Intransitive.
In trans. (Lat. *in transitu*), On the passage; In transit.
Int. Rev. Internal Revenue.
Intro., *Introd.* Introduction.
I. O. F. Independent Order of Foresters.
I. O. G. T. Independent Order of Good Templars.
I. O. O. F. Independent Order of Odd Fellows.
I. O. R. M. Improved Order of Red Men.
I. O. S. M. Independent Order of Sons of Malta.
I. O. U. I owe you.
I. Q. Intelligence Quotient.
i. q. (Lat. *idem quod*), The same as.
Ir. Ireland, Irish.
I. R. O. Internal Revenue Officer.
Is., *Isa.* Isaiah.
I. S. Irish Society.
I. S. M. (Lat. *Jesus Salvator Mundi*), Jesus, Savior of the World.
It., *Ital.* Italy, Italian; Italic.
Itin. Itinerary.
I. W. W. Industrial Workers of the World.
J. Judge; Justice.
J. A. Judge Advocate.
Jac. Jacob, Jacobus (=James).
J. A. G. Judge, Advocate, General.
Jan. January.
Jav. Javanese.
J. C. Jesus Christ.
J. C. D. (Lat. *juris civilis doctor*), Doctor of Civil Law.
J. D. (Lat. *jurum doctor*), Doctor of Laws.
Jer. Jeremiah.
J. H. S. See *I. H. S.*
Jno. John.
Jon., *Jona.* Jonathan.
Jos. Joseph.
Josh. Joshua.
Jour. Journal; Journey.
J. P. Justice of the Peace.
Jr. Juror; Junior.
J. R. Joint Resolution.
Jr. O. U. A. M. Junior Order United American Mechanics.
J. U. D. (Lat. *Juris utriusque doctor*), Doctor of both laws (of civil and canon law).
Jud. Judith; Judicial.
Judg. Judges.
Jul. July; Julius, Julian.
Jun., *Je.* June.
Jurisp. Jurisprudence.
K. King; Knight.
k. Karat.
Kans., *Kan.* Kansas.
K. B. Knight of the Bath; King's Bench.
K. C. King's Counsel; Knights of Columbus.
kg. Kilogram.
Ki. Kings.
Kingd. Kingdom.
K. L. H. Knight of the Legion of Honor.
K. M. Knight of Malta.
km. Kilometer.
K. P. Knight of St. Patrick.
K. of P. Knights of Pythias.
Kt. Knight.
K. T. Knight Templar.
Kw. Kilowatt.
Kwh. Kilowatt hour.
Ky. Kentucky.
L. Latin; Lake; Lord; Lady.
L., *l.*, *£.* (Lat. *libra*), Pound, pounds (sterling).
L., *lb.*, ℔. (Lat. *libra*), Pound, pounds (weight).
La., *Lou.* Louisiana.
Lam. Lamentations.
Lat. Latin; Latitude.
L. c. Lower case (in printing).
L. c., *loc. cit.* (Lat. *loco citato*), In the passage cited.
l/c. Letter of credit.
L. D. S. Licentiate of Dental Surgery; Latter Day Saints.
Leg., *Legis.* Legislature, legislative.
Lev., *Levit.* Leviticus.
Lex. Lexicon.
Lexicog. Lexicography, lexicographer, lexicographical.
L. G. Life Guards; Low German.
L. H. D. (Lat. *Litterarum Humanarum Doctor*), Doctor of Humanities.
L. I. Light Infantry; Long Island.
Lib. (Lat. *liber*), Book; Library, librarian.
Lieut., *Lt.* Lieutenant.
Lieut. Col. Lieutenant Colonel.
Lieut. Gen. Lieutenant General.
Lieut. Gov. Lieutenant Governor.
Linn. Linnæus, Linnæan.
Liq. Liquor, liquid.
Lit. Literally, literature, literary.
Lit. D., *Litt. D.* (Lat. *literarum doctor*), Doctor of Literature.
Lith., *Lithog.* Lithography.
LL. B. (Lat. *legum baccalaureus*), Bachelor of Laws.
LL. D. (Lat. *legum doctor*), Doctor of Laws.
LL. M. Master of Laws.
L. M. Long meter.
loc. cit. In the place quoted.
Lon., *Lond.* London.
Lon., *Long.* Longitude.
Loq. (Lat. *loquitur*), He (or she) speaks.
L. S. (Lat. *locus sigilli*), Place of the seal.
L. s. d. (Lat. *libræ*, *solidi*, *denarii*), Pounds, shillings, pence.
Lt. Lieutenant.
Lt. Inf. Light Infantry.
Luth. Lutheran.
m. Married; Masculine; Meter, meters; Mile, miles; Minute, minutes.
M. Marquis; Middle; Monday; Morning; Monsieur.
M. (Lat. *mille*), Thousand.
M. (Lat. *meridies*), Meridian; Noon.
M. A. Master of Arts.
Mac., *Macc.* Maccabees.
Mad., *Madm.*, *Mme.* Madam.
Mag. Magazine.
Maj. Major.
Maj. Gen. Major General.
Mal. Malachi; Malay, Malayan.
Man. Manitoba.
Manuf. Manufactures, manufacturing.
Mar. March; Maritime.
Marq. Marquis.
Mas., *Masc.* Masculine.
Mass. Massachusetts.
M. Ast. S. Member of the Astronomical Society.
Math. Mathematics, mathematical.
Matt. Matthew.
M. B. (Lat. *medicinæ baccalaureus*), Bachelor of Medicine.
M. B. (Lat. *musicæ baccalaureus*), Bachelor of Music.
M. C. Member of Congress; Master of Ceremonies.
M. D. (Lat. *medicinæ doctor*), Doctor of Medicine.
Md. Maryland.
Mdlle., *Mlle.* (Fr. *mademoiselle*), Miss.
Mdse. Merchandise.
M. E. Most Excellent; Military Engineer; Mining Engineer; Mechanical Engineer; Methodist Episcopal.
Me. Maine.
Meas. Measure.
Mech. Mechanics, mechanical.
Med. Medicine, medical; Medieval.
Med. Lat. Medieval Latin.
Mem. Memorandum, memoranda.
Messrs., *MM.* (Fr. *messieurs*), Gentlemen.
Met. Metaphysics, metaphysical.
Metal., *Metall.* Metallurgy.
Metaph. Metaphysics; Metaphorically.
Meteor. Meteorology, meteorological.
Meth. Methodist.
Mex. Mexico, Mexican.
Mfd. Manufactured.
Mfg. Manufacturing.
Mfrs. Manufacturers.
Mfs. Manufactures.
M. H. Most Honorable.
M. H. G. Middle High German.
M. I. C. E. Member of the Institute of Civil Engineers.
Mich. Michaelmas; Michigan.
Mid. Middle; Midshipman.
Mil., *Milit.* Military.
M. I. M. E. Member of the Institute of Mining Engineers.
Min. Mineralogy, mineralogical; Minute, minutes.
Minn. Minnesota.
Min. Plen. Minister Plenipotentiary.
Miss. Mississippi.
M. L. Latin of the Middle Ages; Master of Laws.
mm. Millimeters.
M. N. A. S. Member of the National Academy of Sciences.
M. N. S. Member of the Numismatical Society.
M. O. Money order.
Mo. Missouri; Month.
Mod. Modern.
Mon. Monday.

Mons. (Fr. *monsieur*), Sir; Mr.
Mont. Montana.
M. P. Member of Parliament; Military Police.
M. P. P. Member of Provincial Parliament.
Mr. Master, Mister.
M. R. G. S. Member of the Royal Geographical Society.
M. R. I. Member of the Royal Institute.
Mrs. Mistress.
M. S. Master of Surgery; Master of Science.
M. S. (Lat. *memoriæ sacrum*), Sacred to the memory of.
Ms. Manuscript.
Mss. Manuscripts.
Mt., Mts. Mount, mountains.
mth., mo. Month.
Mus. Museum; Music, musical.
Mus. B. (Lat. *musicæ baccalaureus*), Bachelor of Music.
Mus. D., Mus. Doc., Mus. Doct. (Lat. *musicæ doctor*), Doctor of Music.
M. V. O. Member of the Royal Victorian Order.
M. W. A. Modern Woodmen of America.
Myth. Mythology, mythological.
N. Noon; North; Noun; Number; New; Neuter.
N. A. North America, North American.
Nah. Nahum.
N. A. M. National Association of Manufacturers.
Nat. Natural; National.
Nat. Hist. Natural History.
Naut. Nautical.
N. B. New Brunswick.
N. B. (Lat. *nota bene*), Note well; Take notice.
N. C. North Carolina.
N. Dak., N. D. North Dakota.
N. E. New England, Northeast.
N. E. A. National Education Assoc.
Nebr., Neb. Nebraska.
Neg. Negative, negatively.
Neh. Nehemiah.
Nem. con. (Lat. *nemine contradicente*), No one contradicting, unanimously.
Nem. diss. (Lat. *nemine dissentiente*), No one dissenting, unanimously.
Neth. Netherlands.
Neut. Neuter.
Nev. Nevada.
New Test., N. T. New Testament.
N. F. Newfoundland.
N. H. New Hampshire.
N. H. A. National Housing Agency.
N. J. New Jersey.
N. L., N. Lat. North Latitude.
N. L. R. B. National Labor Relations Board.
N. M. B. National Mediation Board.
N. Mex., N. M. New Mexico.
N. N. E. North northeast.
N. O. New Orleans.
No., Nos. Number, numbers.
nol. pros. (Lat. *nolle prosequi*), To be unwilling to prosecute.
Nom., Nomin. Nominative.
non-com. Non-commissioned officer.
Non con. Non-content, dissentient. (The formula in which Members of the House of Lords vote.)
Non obst. (Lat. *non obstante*), Notwithstanding.
Non pros. (Lat. *non prosequitur*), He does not prosecute.
Non seq. (Lat. *non sequitur*), It does not follow (as a consequence).
Nor., Norm. Norman.
Nor. Fr., Norm. Fr. Norman French.
Norw. Norway, Norwegian, Norse.
Nov. November.
N. P. Notary Public.
N. S. New style; Nova Scotia.
N. S. J. C. (Fr. *Notre Seigneur Jesus Christ*), Our Lord Jesus Christ.
N. S. W. New South Wales.
Num., Numb. Numbers.
Numis. Numismatic, numismatology.
N. V. M. Nativity of the Virgin Mary.
N. W. Northwest, northwestern.
N. W. S. B. National Wage Stabilization Board.
N. Y. New York.
N. Z., N. Zeal. New Zealand.

O. (unofficial) Ohio; Old.
ob. (Lat. *obiit*), He (or she) died.
Obj. Objective.
Obs. Obsolete.
Oct. October.
Oct., 8vo. Octavo.
O. F. Odd Fellows.
O. K. "All correct."
Okla. Oklahoma.
Old Test., O. T. Old Testament.
Olym. Olympiad.
O. M. Order of Merit.
O. M. I. Order of Mary Immaculate.
Ont. Ontario.
Op. Opposite, opposition.
Opt. Optative; Optics, optical.
Ord., Ordn. Ordnance.
Oreg., Ore. Oregon.
Orig. Original, originally.
Ornith. Ornithology, ornithological.
O. S. Old Style; Old Saxon.
O. S. A. Order of St. Augustine.
O. S. B. Order of St. Benedict.
O. S. F. Order of St. Francis.
O. U. A. M. Order of United American Mechanics.
O. W. M. R. Office of War Mobilization and Reconversion.
Oxf. Oxford.
Oxon. (Lat. *Oxonia, Oxoniensis*), Oxford, of Oxford.
Oz. Ounce. (The *z* in this contraction and in *viz.* represents an old symbol (ʒ), used to mark a terminal contraction.)

P. Page; Participle; Past; Pole; Port.
Pa. Pennsylvania.
Pal., Palæont. Palæontology, palæontological.
Par. Paragraph.
Parl. Parliament, parliamentary.
Part. Participle.
Pass. Passive.
Pathol. Pathological.
Payt. Payment.
Pd. Paid.
Pd. D. Doctor of Pedagogy.
P. E. Protestant Episcopal.
P. E. I. Prince Edward Island.
Penn. Pennsylvania.
Pent. Pentecost.
Per., Pers. Persian; Person, personal.
Per. an. (Lat. *per annum*), Yearly.
Per cent., per ct. (Lat. *per centum*), By the hundred.
Peruv. Peruvian.
pfd. Preferred.
P. G. M. Past Grand Master.
Phar., Pharm. Pharmacy.
Ph. B. (Lat. *philosophiæ baccalaureus*), Bachelor of Philosophy.
Ph. D. (Lat. *philosophiæ doctor*), Doctor of Philosophy.
Phil. Philip; Philippians; Philosophy, philosophical.
Phil., Phila. Philadelphia.
Philem. Philemon.
Philol. Philology.
Philos. Philosophy, philosophical.
Ph. M. Master of Philosophy.
Photog. Photography, photographic, photographer.
Phys. Physics, physical; Physiology, physiological.
Physiol. Physiology, physiological.
P. I. Philippine Islands.
Pinx., Pxt. (Lat. *pinxit*), He (or she) painted it.
Pk. Peck.
Pl. Place; Plate; Plural.
Plf., Plff., Pltff. Plaintiff.
Plur. Plural.
P. M. (Lat. *post meridiem*), Afternoon.
P. M. Past Master; Peculiar meter; Postmaster.
P. M. A. Production and Marketing Administration.
P. M. G. Postmaster-General.
P. O. Post Office.
Pol. Polish, Poland.
Polit. Econ. Political Economy.
P. O. O. Post-office order.
Pop. Population.
Port. Portugal, Portuguese.
Pp. Pages.
P. P. Parish Priest.
P. P. C. (Fr. *pour prendre congé*), To take leave. See *T. T. L.*
Pph. Pamphlet.
Pr. Present; Priest; Prince.
Pr. par. Present participle.
P. R. (Lat. *Populus Romanus*), The Roman People; Puerto Rico.
P. R. C. (Lat. *post Roman conditam*), After the building of Rome.
Pref. Prefix; Preface.
Pres. President; Present.
Prim. Primary.
Prin. Principal.
Print. Printing.
Prob. Problem; Probable, probably.
Prof. Professor.
Pron. Pronoun; Pronounced, pronunciation.
Pro tem. (Lat. *pro tempore*), For the time being.
Prov. Proverbs, proverbial, proverbially; Provincial; Provost.
Prox. (Lat. *proximo*), Next; Of the next month.
Prus. Prussia, Prussian.
P. S. (Lat. *post scriptum*), Postscript.
Ps., Psa. Psalm, psalms.
pseud. Pseudonym.
Psychol. Psychology.
Pt. Part; Payment; Point; Port.
Pub. Public; Published, publisher.
Pub. Doc. Public documents.
Pvt., pte. Private.
Pwt. Pennyweight.
Pyro., Pyrotech. Pyrotechnics.

Q., Qu. Query; Question.
q. e. (Lat. *quod est*), Which is.
Q. E. D. (Lat. *quod erat demonstrandum*), Which was to be proved.
Q. E. F. (Lat. *quod erat faciendum*), Which was to be done.
Q. E. I. (Lat. *quod erat inveniendum*), Which was to be found out.
Q. M. Quartermaster.
Q. M. Gen. Quartermaster-General.
Qr. Quarterly; Quire.
Qt. Quart.
Quar., quart. Quarterly.
Quar., 4to. Quarto.
Que. Quebec.
Ques. Question.
q. v. (Lat. *quod vide*), Which see.

R. Réaumur; River.
R. (Lat. *rex*), King; (Lat. *regina*), Queen.
R. A. Royal Academy, Royal Academician; Rear Admiral; Royal Arch; Royal Artillery; Royal Art.
Rad. (Lat. *radix*), Root.
R. C. Roman Catholic; Red Cross.
R. E. Reformed Episcopal.
R. E. A. Rural Electrification Administration.
Réaum. Réaumur.
Rec. Recipe; Receipt.
Recd. Received.
Recpt. Receipt.
Ref. Reference; Referee.
Ref. Ch. Reformed Church.
Ref. Pres. Reformed Presbyterian.
Reg. Regular; Registered.
Reg., Regr. Registrar.
Reg., Regt. Regiment.
Rel. Religion, religious.
Rel. Pron. Relative Pronoun.
Rem. Remark, remarks.
Rep. Report; Representative.
Rep., Repub. Republic; Republican.
Res. Reserve; Residence.
Retd. Returned.
Rev. Revelation; Revenue; Reverend; Review; Revise.
Revd. Reverend.
Rev. Stat. Revised Statutes.
R. F. C. Reconstruction Finance Corporation.
R. F. D. Rural Free Delivery.
Rhet. Rhetoric, rhetorical.
R. I. Rhode Island.
R. I. P. (Lat. *requiescat in pace*), May he (or she) rest in peace.
Riv. River.

R. N. Royal Navy.
Rom. Roman, Romans.
Rom. Cath. Roman Catholic.
R. O. T. C. Reserve Officers' Training Corps.
R. R. Railroad.
R. S. V. P. (Fr. *Répondez s'il vous plaît*), Please reply.
Rt. Right.
Rt. Hon. Right Honorable.
Rt. Rev. Right Reverend.
Russ. Russia, Russian.
R. V. Revised Version.
Ry. Railway.

S. Saint; Saturday; Section; Shilling; Sign; Signor; Solo; Soprano; South; Sun; Sunday; Sabbath.
s. Second, seconds; See; Singular; Son; Succeeded.
S. A. South Africa; South America; Salvation Army.
Sab. Sabbath.
Sam. Samuel.
Sans., Sansc., Sansk. Sanscrit, Sanskrit.
Sask. Saskatchewan.
Sat. Saturday.
Sax. Saxon, Saxony.
S. C. South Carolina.
S. caps., Sm. caps. Small capitals (in printing).
Sc. B. (Lat. *scientiæ baccalaureus*), Bachelor of Science.
Sc. D. (Lat. *scientiæ doctor*), Doctor of Science.
Sch. (Lat. *scholium*), A note.
Sch. Schooner.
Sci. Science.
Scil., Sc. (Lat. *scilicet*), Namely, to wit.
S. C. L. Student in Civil Law.
Scot., Sc. Scotland, Scotch, Scottish.
Scrip., Script. Scripture, scriptural.
Sculp. Sculpture.
Sculp., Sculpt., Sc. (Lat. *sculpsit*), He (or she) engraved it.
S. D. Doctor of Science.
S. Dak., S. D. South Dakota.
S. D. U. K. Society for the Diffusion of Useful Knowledge.
S. E. Southeast.
S.E.C. Securities and Exchange Commission.
Sec. Second.
Sec., Sect. Section.
Sec., Secy. Secretary.
Sec. Leg. Secretary of Legation.
Sen. Senate, senator.
Sen. Doc. Senate Document.
Sep., Sept. September.
Seq. (Lat. *sequentes, sequentia*), The following, or the next.
Serg., Sergt. Sergeant.
Sess. Session.
SHAEF. Supreme Headquarters Allied Expeditionary Forces.
Sing. Singular.
S. J. Society of Jesus.
S. J. C. Supreme Judicial Court.
Skr. Sanskrit.
Slav. Slavonic.
S. M. Sergeant Major.
Soc., Socy. Society.
Sol. Gen. Solicitor-General.
S. O. S. Wireless distress signal at sea.
Sp. Spain, Spanish; Spirit.
s. p. (Lat. *sine prole*), Without issue.
S. P. A. R. (Lat. *Semper parati* [æ]), Always ready; Coast Guard motto and translation, initials being used as designation for women's Coast Guard reserve.
S. P. C. A. Society for the Prevention of Cruelty to Animals.
S. P. C. C. Society for the Prevention of Cruelty to Children.
Spec. Special, specially.
sp. gr., s. g. Specific gravity.
S. P. Q. R. (Lat. *Senatus Populusque Romanus*), The Senate and the People of Rome.
sq. Square; *sq. ft.* Square foot, feet; *sq. in.* Square inch, inches; *sq. m.* Square mile, miles; *sq. yd.* Square yard; *sq. rd.* Square rod.
Sr. Senior.
S. R. Senate Resolution.
SS. Saints.
S. S. Sunday School; Steamship.
S. S. C. Solicitor before the Supreme Court.
S. S. E. South-southeast.
S. S. W. South-southwest.
St. Saint; Stone; Strait; Street.
st. (Lat. *stet*), Let it stand (in printing).
S. T. Sons of Temperance.
Stat. Statute, statutes; Statuary.
S. T. B. Bachelor of Sacred Theology.
S. T. D. (Lat. *sacræ theologiæ doctor*), Doctor of Sacred Theology.
ster., stg. Sterling.
Str. Steamer.
Subst. Substantive; Substitute.
Sun., Sund. Sunday.
Sup. Superior; Superlative; Supplement; Supine.
Sup. Ct. Supreme Court.
Sup. Sgt. Supply Sergeant.
Supt. Superintendent.
Surg. Surgeon, surgery.
Surg.-Gen. Surgeon-General.
Surv. Surveying, surveyor.
Surv.-Gen. Surveyor-General.
S. V. Sons of Veterans.
S. W. Southwest.
Sw. Sweden, Swedish.
Swit., Switz. Switzerland.
Syn. Synonym, synonymous.
Syr. Syria, Syriac.

T. Tenor; Ton; Tun; Tuesday.
Tab. Table; Tabular statement.
Tart. Tartaric.
Tcs. Tierces.
Tech. Technical, technically.
Tenn. Tennessee.
Ter. Territory.
Term. Termination.
Teut. Teutonic.
Tex. Texas.
Text. rec. (Lat. *textus receptus*), The received text.
Th. Thomas; Thursday.
Theo. Theodore.
Theol. Theology.
Tho., Thos. Thomas.
Thu., Thur., Thurs. Thursday.
Tim. Timothy.
Tit. Title; Titus.
T. N. T. Trinitrotoluene, an explosive.
Tob. Tobit.
Tom. Tome, volume.
Tonn. Tonnage.
Topog. Topography, topographical.
Tp. Township.
Tr. Translation, translator, translated; Transpose; Treasurer; Trustee.
Trans. Transaction; Translation, translator, translated.
Trav. Travels.
Treas. Treasurer.
Trig., Trigon. Trigonometry, trigonometrical.
Trin. Trinity.
T. S. Transport Ships.
T. T. L. To take leave. See *P. P. C.*
Tu., Tues. Tuesday.
Turk. Turkey, Turkish.
T. V. A. Tennessee Valley Authority.
Typ. Typographer.
Typog. Typography, typographical.

U. C. (Upper Case) Capital letters in printing.
U. C. V. United Confederate Veterans.
U. D. C. United Daughters of the Confederacy.
U. J. D. See *J. U. D.*
U. K. United Kingdom.
Ult. (Lat. *ultimo*), Last; Of the last month.
U. N. United Nations.
Unit. Unitarian.
Univ. University.
U. N. R. R. A. United Nations Relief and Rehabilitation Administration.
U. P. United Presbyterian.
U. S. United States.
U. S. A. United States of America; United States Army.
U. S. L. United States Legation.
U. S. M. United States mail; United States marine.
U. S. M. A. United States Military Academy.
U. S. N. United States Navy.
U. S. N. A. United States Naval Academy.
U. S. S. United States Senate; United States ship or steamer.
U. S. S. Ct. United States Supreme Court.
U. S. S. R. Union of Soviet Socialist Republics (Russia).

V. Verb; Verse; Victoria; Violin.
V. (Lat. *vide*), See.
V. A. Vicar Apostolic; Vice Admiral; Veterans Administration.
Va. Virginia.
V. A. D. Voluntary Aid Department.
Val. Valve; Value.
Vat. Vatican.
V. C. Victoria Cross.
V. D. M. (Lat. *Verbi Dei Minister*), Minister of the Word of God.
V-E Day. Official date of Germany's surrender in World War II.
V. F. W. Veterans of Foreign Wars.
V. G. Vicar General.
Vice pres. Vice President.
Vid. (Lat. *vide*), See.
Vis., Visc. Viscount.
Viz. (Lat. *videlicet*), Namely; To wit. See *Oz.*
V-J Day. Official date of Japan's surrender in World War II.
Voc. Vocative.
Vol., Vols. Volume, Volumes.
V. P. Vice President.
V. Rev. Very Reverend.
V. S. Veterinary surgeon.
vs., v. (Lat. *versus*), Against.
Vt. Vermont.
Vul., Vulg. Vulgate.

W. Wednesday; Week; Welsh; West, western.
W. A. A. War Assets Administration.
W. A. C. Women's Army Corps.
Wash. Washington.
W. A. V. E. S. Women Appointed for Volunteer Emergency Service, women's naval reserve.
W. C. A. Women's Christian Association.
W. C. T. U. Women's Christian Temperance Union.
W. D. War Department.
Wed. Wednesday.
Wel. Welsh.
w. f. Wrong font (in printing).
Whf. Wharf.
W. I. West Indies, West Indian.
Wis., Wisc. Wisconsin.
Wk. Week.
W. Long. West Longitude.
Wm. William.
W. N. W. West northwest.
W. R. C. Women's Relief Corps.
W. S. W. West southwest.
Wt. Weight.
W. Va. West Virginia.
Wyo. Wyoming.

X., Xt. Christ.
Xm., Xmas. Christmas.
Xn., Xtian. Christian.
Xnty. Christianity.
Xper., Xr. Christopher.

Y. Year.
Yd. Yard.
Yds. Yards.
Y. M. C. A. Young Men's Christian Association.
Y. M. Cath. A. Young Men's Catholic Association.
Y. M. H. A. Young Men's Hebrew Association.
Y. P. S. C. E. Young People's Society of Christian Endeavor.
Yr. Year; Younger; Your.
Yrs. Years; Yours.
Y. W. C. A. Young Women's Christian Association.

Zach. Zachary.
Zech. Zechariah.
Zeph. Zephaniah.
Z. G. Zoological Gardens.
Zool. Zoology, zoological.

WRITING AND SPEAKING

THE power to use effective language brings to its possessor ability to lead in social and civic affairs. Besides, more often than we commonly realize, personal success depends upon a command of good English.

Putting your thoughts together well in the sentences you speak or write is, therefore, always important. The social, professional, or business world measures you by the fitness of your language for the work you intend it to do. On the other hand, through persistent effort to adapt your language to your purposes, you gain a sense of self-command, an ease of manner, and a satisfying confidence in meeting people socially and in business.

Effective Language. Four requirements measure this fitness of language: *correctness, clearness, force, beauty.* Language is *correct* when it expresses thought in approved form. It is *clear* when those who hear or read it understand readily the thought of the speaker or writer. It is *forceful* when it interests those who hear or read it and impels them to respond according to the purposes of the speaker or writer. It is *beautiful* if it is correct, clear, and forceful, and also pleasing in sound or suggestion.

The art of expressing thought or feeling in effective language is called Rhetoric. The principles that govern the use of this effective language are rhetorical principles. One great principle underlies all others; namely, that true effectiveness of language depends upon the sincerity of the speaker or writer.

Choosing and Arranging Words. Words are wisely chosen when they express our thoughts and can be understood by our audience. Language has no value apart from the thought it expresses, the purpose of the speaker or writer, and the effect produced on his audience. If you are going to talk or write, you should have something to say and a motive for saying it, and you should understand your audience.

You want to find pleasure in carrying on conversation with a friend or a stranger. You may have to make a report upon some work. You may want to sell a house or secure the interest and the support of voters in an election. You may want to persuade a friend to give up a harmful habit. You may have to convince a hostile audience of the truth of your opinions. In conversation you will be alert, interested, and responsive; in reporting, cool and accurate; in persuasion, positive, earnest, and impassioned. These are your personal problems. They will make you prize every help toward mastery of language.

Ordering of Thought. Both in speaking and in writing it is of the utmost importance to marshal the parts of a discourse into an effective order. This careful observance of arrangement should be followed both in regard to the discourse as a whole and in regard to each portion of it which deals with a single thought. The divisions into which a discourse falls when thus logically ordered are usually indicated by some more or less mechanical means. In speech, a judicious use of pauses and of vocal inflections serves the purpose, and in written compositions we employ the device of paragraphing.

The Paragraph. This term means a group of sentences in which a single subject is discussed, its beginning being marked usually by indention, or setting the first word a little to the right of the usual margin. This group of sentences may make a separate unit, as in the editorial columns of a newspaper, or it may serve as a division of a longer article. The structure and the length of the paragraph are matters of logic and convenience. Too long a paragraph, as well as a succession of very short ones, is to be avoided.

There are three important rhetorical requirements for a paragraph. The first requirement is *unity,* which means that there must be in the paragraph only one main thought. The second requirement is *coherence,* which implies that the sentences in the paragraph must be well connected and arranged so that each added thought helps to make the main idea clearer and more forceful. The third requirement is *emphasis,* which demands that the more important sentences shall be so placed in relation to the others as to draw immediate attention. Arranging sentences in contrasting pairs, or in order of climax, and alternating long and short sentences—these are means of securing emphasis. The beginning and the end of a paragraph are usually the most emphatic positions for sentences.

The purpose of the paragraph is to develop an idea, or, as often in stories, a single situation. Development means, literally, unfolding the subject so that the reader may understand the topic better or see the situation more clearly. To this end, give details, comparisons, and examples, or repeat ideas in slightly different words. Clearness is frequently effected by using vivid contrasts. The main idea should be stated in a single sentence, preferably either near the beginning or near the close of the paragraph. The following paragraph from *Ancient Times* by James H. Breasted illustrates well these methods of development:

"The Phœnicians learned the methods of manufacturing their goods, in almost all cases, from Egypt. There they learned to make glass and porcelain, to weave linen and dye it, to cast and hammer and engrave metal. On the other hand, we find that the *designs* employed in their art were international. Their metal platters they engraved with designs which they found in both Egypt and Asia. The art of Phœnicia was thus a kind of oriental composite or combination, drawn chiefly from the Nile and the Two Rivers. We remember that it was Phœnician workmen whom the Assyrian kings employed to make furniture and metal work for the royal palace. King Solomon likewise employed Phœnician workmen to build for him the Hebrew temple at Jerusalem (I Kings, V). After 1000 B. C. the Phœnicians were thus the artistic manufacturers of a great world extending from Nineveh on the east to Greece on the west."

GENERAL FORM OF DISCOURSE

Expression in language assumes, in relation to the purposes for which it is used, several well-recognized forms or types of discourse. We give talks or addresses, or we write papers or articles; we argue, explain, describe, or tell a story. Practical methods for everyday use of these various forms are given in the following paragraphs:

EXPLANATION

A pencil seems to be a simple, everyday thing, but you may sometime ask yourself: *How is this pencil made? What is it made of? Could it be made better?* You discover a problem that needs explanation or clearing up. This problem concerns the parts of the pencil and the relations between them. Other questions arise: *Why are these particular materials used in the pencil? What is the history of pencil making? Why is this thing called "pencil"?* Similarly, such subjects as *How is a gas engine made?* or *What is a bank?* call for explanation. *The clear, orderly answering of these questions is explanation.*

The first step in explanation is to divide the subject into topics to be discussed. The purpose of division is to give logical orderliness and simplicity, and consequently clearness, to your composition. The method to be followed is that of the outline, as illustrated in the following examples.

The headings in these specimen outlines are numbered in several different ways, any one of which may properly be used. In any outline, however, the numbering must be consistent throughout.

Subject. The Pencil.

Introduction.

1. The pencil is a thing of common use, but its nature, history, and manufacture are little understood.
2. The study of the pencil under these heads may be both interesting and suggestive.

Body.

1. Taking a common pencil apart.
   a. The case of wood, paper, or metal.
   b. The "lead."
2. The history of the pencil.
   a. Early forms.
   b. The word "pencil."
3. Process of manufacture.
   a. Preparation of materials.
   b. Construction.

Conclusion.

1. Skill with the pencil.
2. A stock of pencils in a store and the occupations it may suggest.

Such an outline may serve for a single treatment of the subject, or any one of the headings may be used as a separate topic. It should then be outlined in this same form. For example:

Subject.—A Stock of Pencils.
1. Pencils for drawing.
2. Pencils for various kinds of writing.
3. Pencils of different shapes and sizes.

The following is another common form of outline:

HOW TO USE CONCRETE

I. What is concrete?
   A. Elements.
   B. Mixtures.

II. Uses of concrete.
   A. Substitute for stone and wood.
   B. Unique uses.

III. Mixing concrete.
   A. Proportions.
   B. Method.

IV. Forms.
   A. Construction.
   B. Method of use.

The second step is to look up information. A common and practical method for preserving facts is to copy information on cards about 3 by 5 inches in size, one fact or topic to a card, with a reference to book and page where the facts were secured. The habit of thus looking up and noting facts will help to develop careful and trustworthy thinking.

The third step in planning explanation is the finding of apt comparisons; for we learn by observing likenesses and differences between things. The unknown or unfamiliar thing should be compared with something known or familiar. For example, to make dimensions clear, use comparisons in addition to figures. Compare a length of 15 or 20 feet to the length of a room, the extent of a small surface to a table top. Such expressions as *T-shape, S-shape, U-shape* are useful. More imaginative comparisons are suggested by figures of speech.

DESCRIPTION

Generally speaking, the purpose of description is to appeal so vividly to the senses through language that the reader or hearer feels as if he were actually in the presence of the object described. To produce good description: (1) Indicate clearly your point of view, that is, your position with reference to the thing described. A railroad wreck may be described by one who was a passenger on the wrecked train or by a reporter who was sent to the wreck. Their mental points of view will be different. A building or a mountain may be described as seen from a nearby or from a distant point. These different physical points of view determine the nature of the description. (2) Choose words to convey sense impressions, as of *sight, sound, smell, taste, touch.* (3) Select and use only such details as help to make the total impression clear and vivid. Notice the indications of the point of view and the appeals to the senses of sight, touch, and hearing in the italicized words of the following paragraphs:

"It was *close on noon*: there was no *breath* of wind, and the heat was scarce *bearable* when the two men came on deck, had the boat manned, and *passed down*, one after another, into the stern sheets. A *white* shirt at the end of an oar served as a flag of truce; and the men, by direction, and to give it the better chance to be observed, *pulled* with extreme slowness. The isle *shook* before them like a place *incandescent:* on the face of the lagoon *blinding copper* suns, no bigger than *sixpences,* danced and *stabbed* them in the eyeball. There went up from sand and sea, and even from the boat, a *glare* of *scathing* brightness; and as they could only peer abroad from between closed lashes, the excess of light seemed to be changed into a *sinister* darkness, comparable to that of a *thundercloud* before it bursts."—Stevenson: *The Ebb Tide.*

"There could not be a more *somber* aspect of external nature than as then seen *from the windows of my study.* The great *willow tree* had caught and retained among its leaves a whole cataract of water, to be shaken down at intervals by the frequent *gusts* of wind. All day long, and for a week together, the rain was *drip-drip-dripping* and *splash-splash-splashing* from the eaves and *bubbling* and *foaming* into the tubs beneath the spouts. The old, *unpainted* shingles of the house and outbuildings were *black* with moisture, and the mosses of ancient growth upon the walls looked *green* and *fresh,* as if they were the newest things and afterthought of Time. The usually *mirrored* surface of the *river* was *blurred* by an infinity of raindrops. The whole landscape had a completely *water-soaked* appearance, conveying the impression that the earth was wet through *like a sponge*; while the summit of a *wooded hill,* about a *mile distant,* was enveloped in a dense mist, where the demon of the tempest seemed to have his abiding-place, and to be plotting still direr inclemencies."—Hawthorne: *Mosses from an Old Manse.*

NARRATION

This most interesting form of composition is simply the telling of stories.

Narration without Plot. This is telling about a series of actual events,—a day's travel, the course of an investigation, or a report of some piece of work. For telling such a story the most important directions are these: Select carefully the details to be told. Make a connected account that moves straight forward in the time order of events and is not lost in little, unimportant matters.

The carefully written news story furnishes a good example. It usually begins with a *lead,* that is, a first sentence that summarizes the most important features of the account. Then the connected story, consisting of several sentences or paragraphs, follows. See *The Book or Article Review.*

Description finds its chief use in helping to make narration or explanation vivid and interesting.

Narration with Plot. The telling of a story in such a way as to arouse interest and hold the hearer or reader in suspense and uncertainty as to the outcome of events. You can spoil an *anecdote* or a *story* by giving the "point" too soon. Even anecdotes have miniature plots. Give the setting or background and introduce the characters first, then bring in their action or conversation, and finally "come to the point or climax." This method secures suspense while your audience waits for the climax. A master of English fiction is credited with the following recipe for story-telling: "Make them laugh; make them cry; but make them wait."

For the composition of other story forms, see *Forms of Literary Composition; The Book or Article Review,—Plot; The Scenario.*

SPECIAL FORMS OF DISCOURSE

We find the General Forms of Composition most frequently useful in the immediate telling of a story or in the preparation of a talk, a paper, or an essay. These occasions usually call for combinations of argument, explanation, description, and narration. The following suggestions are helps in real problems. They serve to answer the questions: What shall I put into the toast, the talk, or the club paper? What shall I leave out? How shall I begin? Getting started is often the hardest problem. See *Public Speaking.*

THE CLUB PAPER

As a member of some organization, a club or society, you are often expected to read papers upon various subjects. The theme or subject is usually given in the program or course of reading. Frequently, however, your topic is too big or too general. When you come to the task of preparing the paper, you must narrow the theme to something that you can treat interestingly in fifteen to thirty minutes. Here are four important principles:

a. Two or three important points, not more, can be treated well in a brief time. The attention of an audience is easily exhausted by too many details.

b. Perfection in speaking and writing is achieved by leaving out superfluous matter.

c. Statements of principles, conditions, or definitions must be made plain by clear illustrations or examples.

d. A brief anecdote or story is often worth pages of laborious explanation.

Suggestion.—Suppose, then, that you have your subject. Whatever it may be, remember that many of the most interesting facts and illustrations for most subjects are things right around you, things that you can see and hear. Any given topic is related to many other themes and to many other fields of knowledge. To point out some of these relations is to enhance the clearness as well as the interest of your paper.

A topic in art, for example, as you begin to look it up, will suggest related topics in literature, in history, in geography, in biography. As you follow these suggestions you will find your paper growing, not as a task, but as a pleasant interest. Make notes of what you find in your reading. Follow each hint of a related topic. Make more notes.

The Working Plan

Always prepare an *outline*, or *working plan*. An outline shows a general sketch or an indication of a plan, a system, or a course of thought. See *Explanation for suggestions about reading and cards. For suggestions as to interesting order of topics*, see *The Advertisement. For suggestions as to presenting the paper*, see *Public Speaking*.

The following plans represent typical ways of dealing with various kinds of subjects:

Subjects which fall under the general theme, *Community Plans*, are very frequently used in club programs. They may be concerned with material improvements in streets or buildings, or with political or social plans and organizations. The following well-tested general order of discussion is appropriate and effective. Either a single paper or a whole program may be built upon this plan. In the latter case, the subordinate topics become the titles of separate papers.

a. The situation outlined,
   1. By a summary of facts, or
   2. By a story or description.

b. Analogies, or comparisons with
   1. Other communities, or
   2. Other local projects or plans.

c. Proposals for action,
   1. Clearly stated, and
   2. Urged persuasively by appeal to such motives as the following: (1) community pride; (2) rivalry; (3) self interest; (4) duty; (5) moral ideals involved in religion and education.

An interesting type of paper is one which discusses *new discoveries* or *inventions* or *new ideas* put into action in society. In such a paper, do at least these four things:

a. Give a clear, brief statement of the discovery or idea or plan.

b. Illustrate with examples the meaning of a discovery or an idea, to make the matter clear and interesting.

c. Give the circumstances of the discovery or statement of the idea as nearly as possible in story form.

d. Show plainly how the thing affects the everyday interests of your audience. See *Suggestions* in the following outlines. This last point should never be neglected. Anything worth writing or talking about has a bearing on everyday life.

Specimen Outlines

The following outlines illustrate the application of the general plan to the discussion of special themes:

I. Subject. Advertising.

Suggestion: This topic needs to be narrowed or divided as follows:

1. What Use Do I Make of Advertisements?

Suggestion.—An intimate chat with two or three friends on the subject of advertising and its uses will help you. You will get their points of view, which will suggest to you a greater variety of topics and a better balanced treatment of your theme.

2. Some Interesting Advertising Pages.

Suggestion.—You need not depend merely upon description. Have the actual pages to show to your audience. Then you can better explain why they are interesting.

3. Art in Advertising.

a. The Printer's Work.
b. Opportunities for Artists.

4. The Store Window.

Window Dressing.

Suggestion.—An interesting way to begin such a topic is to describe an actual window, especially if your audience may have seen it. If you have studied it carefully, you can surprise your audience and arouse interest by showing what they have failed to notice.

5. Advertising Associations and Ad Clubs.

Suggestion.—Any topic about organizations raises at least four questions: (1) How did they come to be formed? (2) What are their purposes? (3) What do they do? (4) Of what use are they to us?

6. The Responsible Advertiser.

Suggestion.—This kind of topic raises such questions as the following: (1) What gives the advertiser power? (2) For what is he responsible? (3) Do advertisers acknowledge this responsibility? (4) What are the reasons for your answer to (3)? (5) What personal experiences have you had with advertisers?

II. Subject. The Health of a Community.

The field of this theme is so large that a single paper should, as a rule, be restricted to one of the subordinate topics:

1. The Food Supply.

a. Sources.

Suggestion.—To make a paper on this topic interesting, you should get some first-hand facts from your local market. Such investigation will enable you to use more intelligently the material from magazines and books.

b. Markets.
   (1) Prices.
   (2) Handling the Food Supply.

2. Sanitation.

a. Housebuilding.
b. Water Supply.
c. Sewerage.
d. Waste and Garbage Removal.
e. Flies, Microbes, and Vermin.

3. Control of Diseases.

Public Health Service.
   (1) School Inspection.
   (2) Hospital Service.
   (3) Quarantine Regulations.

4. Public Parks and Playgrounds.

THE BOOK OR ARTICLE REVIEW

Treatments of historical, scientific, or literary themes frequently involve the reviewing of books or articles from magazines. In writing a book or article review, try (1) to convey a truthful, distinct impression of the outline—the plot, if the original is a story, or the logical plan, if it is a discussion—(2) to give a more specific idea of some notable feature of the work, and (3) to interest and instruct your audience so thoroughly that they will know whether they want to read the book or article.

By way of preparation, *read the material you are to review.* Then make sure that you have some general *reaction,* that is, some opinion or feeling about the book. Stating your own opinion or feeling furnishes a personal element which adds much to the worth and to the interest of your work.

Plot Outline. Remember that the outline or plot of a short story or of a novel concerns itself with the answers to six questions: *Who? What? When? Where? Why? How?* Usually the answers to the first four may be found very readily in a first reading of a story; they form the obvious framework for any tale. The writer of stories exercises his skill in cleverly managing the "How" and the "Why" of events and actions. Sometimes the answers to these two questions are reserved to the very end of the story and there made clear; in other cases one must draw one's own conclusions from the course of the narrative.

In planning a story review, especially for a rather brief paper, take a lesson from the *lead* of the newspaper reporter. The *lead* is an opening sentence in a news story, which summarizes accurately and concisely the substance of the article. It answers the six questions mentioned above. Such an opening sentence places the whole story briefly and concisely before the audience. Practice in writing such *leads* is a most valuable means of improving one's style of speaking or writing. Follow the lead with a brief outline of the plot. Then comment upon some especially interesting or important part of the book.

Suggestive Outlines

St. Ives, a novel by Robert Louis Stevenson.

Lead.—Viscount Anne de St. Ives, a poor private soldier of Napoleon, escapes from the military prison in Edinburgh, becomes heir, through his uncle's will, to a great English estate which had been settled on the older line of his family, marries a Scotch girl who had visited the prison, and becomes an English country gentleman.

I. Beginning.

1. *Setting.*—
   a. The French prisoners in Edinburgh Castle beguile their time by making souvenirs and toys to sell to the visitors from the city.
   b. One of the prisoners, St. Ives, is a gentleman of attractive manners, but a bungling craftsman.
2. *Inciting moments.*—
   a. St. Ives, by his handiwork and his courtesy, attracts the attention of a girl, Flora, who, with certain relatives, visits the prison.
   b. A London lawyer appears, gives St. Ives news, leaves him money and the address of his wealthy uncle.
3. *Complications.*—
   a. St. Ives fights a duel, killing his opponent, who had used vile language about Flora.
   b. The English lieutenant, in command of the prison, suspects St. Ives's part in the duel and threatens to become a rival for Flora.
   c. On the eve of escape through a tunnel, St. Ives incurs the hatred of a soldier who knows of the duel. A threat of trial for murder hangs over St. Ives.

II. The Story of a Fugitive.

1. By the aid of Flora's aunt, St. Ives escapes to England in the company of two drovers.
   Complication.—In a fight he kills or severely injures a third, a rival drover.
2. In England he is invested with his uncle's estate.
   Complication.—This brings on him the deadly hatred of his disinherited cousin.
3. With a carriage and a valet he goes back to Scotland to find Flora and to save his drover friends from prosecution.
   Complication.—His cousin follows and they meet at a ball. But St. Ives escapes in a balloon.

III. The End.

1. After sundry adventures St. Ives gets to Paris.
   Complication.—His cousin tries to trap him.
2. The London lawyer, his uncle's solicitor, appears just in time to discomfit the spy and save the hero.
3. Back to Scotland and Flora.

Any story may be reviewed in this manner, by answering the six questions in an outline of about three main divisions.

Abstract. Many books and articles upon scientific, historical, or social themes call for the writing of abstracts. These are connected condensed statements of the theme and contents of the book or essay. Four qualities must be aimed at: (1) *accuracy,* that is, truth to the ideas presented in the original work; (2) *completeness,* that is, treatment of all essential parts of the original; (3) *clearness,* which is a matter of especial difficulty, because, in the effort merely to condense the matter, one is tempted to leave out words essential to the meaning; (4) *brevity,* which is to be desired and yet may be sacrificed to the other three qualities.

Remember that people who have not seen the original writing must be able to understand your abstract. Observe the following directions for planning your work:

(1) Following the idea suggested in connection with the *lead,* select a title or a topic sentence which will summarize the entire article.

(2) Choose similar titles or topic sentences for each section of the article.

(3) Separate the essential points and necessary illustrations from the unessential and unnecessary. The abstract must omit most of the merely illustrative content of the original article.

(4) Write the new condensed version of the article.

(5) Review the new version in order to condense it further.

(6) Be careful to give the last part of the article as full treatment as you give the first part.

Paraphrase. This is a method of interpreting a writing by turning it into simpler or more common language. It is a much more widely used kind of writing than many people suppose. The preacher and the teacher use paraphrase constantly. Commentaries on the Scriptures and upon the writings of many great authors, Dante or Shakspere for example, consist very largely of paraphrase.

Four kinds of writings usually call for paraphrase: the work of (1) old authors, such as Spenser or Chaucer, whose language has become unfamiliar; (2) such learned authors as Darwin or Emerson, whose expressions need simplifying; (3) writers like Francis Bacon, whose style is very condensed and therefore needs enlargement and illustration; (4) poets like Browning, whose language is obscure or figurative and therefore needs to be rendered into plain and literal expression.

The writer of paraphrase should first determine to which of these classes his author belongs; then he can suit his manner to the need. The preacher and the Sunday school teacher may find it necessary to render the language of the Bible in more familiar forms. They may wish to enlarge a parable or a proverb by some simple illustration or to turn the figurative language of a psalm into plain, everyday speech. Again, the teacher of science may be obliged to simplify certain paragraphs found in a very condensed textbook. He will develop single sentences into paragraphs and add illustrations. The general method of planning the *abstract* applies also to making the paraphrase.

THE ADVERTISEMENT

The purpose of an advertisement is persuasion. In general, the successful writer of advertising "copy" uses simple, direct language and keeps the reader and his interests most prominent in the advertisement. He maintains what is called the "*you* attitude." For a full discussion and helpful suggestions regarding the writing of an advertisement, see *Preparation of Advertising Copy* on page 1239.

RADIO WRITING

A demand for this form of writing appeared for the first time in the decade 1920-30, when the radio audience came into being. Radio writing differs from other forms of composition by reason of the following facts. The words are written not to be read but to be spoken. The listener hears the speaker but does not see him. The potential audience comprises people of all ages, conditions, beliefs, prejudices, and levels of intelligence.

Simplicity of Language. The mixed character and educational attainments of the radio audience necessitate the use of the simplest possible language. Long and unusual words should be avoided. Sentences should be short and contain vivid word pictures. Words of varied meanings are undesirable. In short, one who prepares script for radio broadcasting should write not merely so that he may be understood but so that he cannot be misunderstood.

Sentences which look well on paper may not be effective when spoken. Hence one who writes for the radio should be "ear minded." Sentences should have a pleasing rhythm. Moreover, certain sounds are apt to be distorted by the microphone and should be avoided as far as possible. Thus a succession of sibilants, "explosive" consonants, and words like "herd" with its obscure "r" sound are difficult to enunciate intelligibly over the radio. Other words which are often heard unsatisfactorily include apathetic, incessantly, statistics, inimitable, egregious, indubitably, perpendicular, and population.

THE EDITORIAL

This is a special form of writing used in newspapers and magazines to interpret items of news or to give opinion about subjects of current interest. The editorial may be a mere summary of information gathered from any source for the convenience of the reader. It may be an argument in support of some policy, or an informing essay on a political, social, moral, historical, literary, or scientific theme. The editorial should be timely. The judgments expressed should be based upon accurate knowledge of facts and upon sincere belief, and the style should be at once popular and dignified. The methods of writing given under *Argument*, *Exposition*, and *The Paragraph* apply to the composition of the editorial.

THE SCENARIO

This is a succinctly written sketch or outline of the scenes, situations, characters, and action of a story or play. Writers of fiction generally use it in planning their work. Producers of moving pictures, however, have developed a special form and technique of the scenario. Scenario making has come to be the business of specially trained writers employed by the producers.

Parts of the Scenario. An approved form of the scenario includes the following parts:

1. *A summary or synopsis of the story.*—This is the form in which producers require that stories be submitted. The synopsis should be written in ordinary direct narrative style. Each paragraph should present the essential characters of a scene in clear, vivid, descriptive language and tell the action in words that mean action. Thoughts and feelings should be conveyed through the suggested acts and movements of the characters. Each succeeding paragraph must carry the story straight toward its culmination. Action should, as far as possible, be written in the present tense. Titles and subtitles may be put in, preferably in capital letters, but all other technical directions should be omitted.

2. *A list of characters*, with the scenes in which each appears, thus: *Old Man, 3, 8, 15.*

3. *A "scene plot,"* or schedule of the various stage settings, with the numbers of the scenes in which each setting is used, thus: *Hotel Entrance, 4, 10, 11, 18.*

A "scene," in moving picture studio language, is a part of the action that can be taken from one position of the camera. A move of the camera ushers in a new scene, except where the camera moves along with the actors or follows them, as in a race or some street scene.

4. *A list of properties*, or "props."

5. *An outline of the scenes, numbered in order.*—This is called the "continuity." The paragraph devoted to each scene gives (a) place or setting, (b) the characters, (c) the attitudes and actions of the characters (pantomime), (d) the thought or feeling these are intended to convey. The following is an approved short form of such a paragraph:

SCENE 5

Railroad Station. College boys and girls leaving after graduation. A send-off. Margaret and Winston meet. Realization of parting, long to speak; both too proud, part stiffly. Train pulls in. Boys and girls enter cars, waving good-byes. Margaret, assisted by Jim, enters end coach, her eyes following Winston, who enters adjoining car. Train pulls out. *Dissolve* into:

SCENE 6

Winston Library. Winston gazing at picture.—

Producers now employ professional continuity writers to work up synopses into the finished action plot, or continuity. The best authorities, however, advise writers to prepare their own continuities before writing synopses to submit to producers. This method gives clearer and firmer structure to the story, because the writer has followed his characters through all the details of the action that makes the story for the screen.

VERSE

For many people the writing of verse is an interesting and amusing pastime. It is also one of the best means of improving one's command of language: (1) It calls for condensed and vivid expression and for a selection of words to produce good measure and rime; (2) it gives one occasion for searching out figurative language that will give variety, point, and concreteness to expression; (3) it improves one's appreciation of verse, which today forms so large a part of our current literature.

There is a wide and pleasant field for agreeable, witty, humorous, and fanciful verse. You may use it for a short, pointed speech. Often an unexpected "hit" is made in this way. Many epigrams, proverbs, mottoes, and sentiments are more vivid and more easily memorized, if expressed in couplets or quatrains.

Observe the following suggestions: (1) Verse must have a rhythm more striking and regular than that of prose or spoken conversation. (2) In English verse this rhythm is marked by the succession of beats or strong accents. Each *line* in English verse is made up of a number of feet. A *foot* consists of an accented syllable with one or more unaccented syllables closely connected with it. Several kinds of verse are named from the kinds of feet used and the number of accents to the line. (3) Select a model that you wish to imitate; read it over, beating out the accents with a pencil, until you get the swing of the lines. Such attention to a model will cure many a set of limping feet.

Rhythms. Recent writers of verse employ a wide variety of rhythms. They also use great freedom in choosing different lengths of line within the same poems. The best popular verse, however, keeps close to the well-established rules. The most common feet in English verse are the following:

a. Iambic (*ī-ăm'bĭk*), composed of two syllables, an accented preceded by an unaccented syllable;
b. Trochaic (*trō-kā'ĭk*), which is an accented syllable followed by an unaccented.

Two other types of feet, sometimes used, are:
a. Dactylic (*dăk-tĭl'ĭk*), which is an accented syllable followed by two unaccented;
b. Anapæstic (*ăn'ȧ-pĕs'tĭk*), which is an accented syllable preceded by two unaccented.

A line of two accents is called a *dimeter* (*dĭm'ē-tẽr*); a line of three accents is called *trimeter* (*trĭm'ē-tẽr*); one of four accents, *tetrameter* (*tĕt-răm'ē-tẽr*); one of five accents, *pentameter* (*pĕn-tăm'ē-tẽr*).

Specimens of Feet and Meter

(Accented syllables are marked with ‾; unaccented, with ˘.)

Iambic.—

As flowers that bloom at morn, at eve decay.

Trochaic.—

Curls and ringlets of her tresses.

Dactylic.—

This is the story the sailorman told.

Anapæstic.—

Not a word, not a whisper, to soothe the sharp pain.

Mixed meter.—

Though it lashed the shallows that lined the beach.

Afar from the great sea deeps.

Dimeter.—

O'er folded blooms
On swirls of musk.

Trimeter.—

The lustrous blue of morn.

The night has a thousand eyes.

Tetrameter.—

They tempt the taste and charm the sight.

The crest and crowning of all good,
Life's final star, is Brotherhood.

Pentameter.—

Oft have I traveled in the realms of gold,
And many goodly states and kingdoms seen.

Bowed by the weight of centuries he leans
Upon his hoe and gazes on the ground.

Rime. The agreement of syllables in sound. A syllable in the middle of a line may be rimed with one at the end: this is called *internal rime.* Usually, syllables are rimed at the ends of lines: this is called *end rime.* Lines of poetry are commonly written in groups of two or more, forming stanzas. The lines may rime in couplet or alternately or in some other of the patterns illustrated below. *Blank verse* is unrimed, usually iambic pentameter. *Free verse* is unrimed; and its rhythm is said to be a rhythm of thought rather than of accent. It is difficult to distinguish from rhythmical prose. At best, it is not a form for the amateur.

Specimens of Rime

Couplet.—

Why has not man a microscopic eye?
For this plain reason,—man is not a fly.

Bubble, Bubble, flows the stream,
Like an old tune through a dream.

Alternate rime.—

We, in some unknown power's employ,
Move on a rigorous line;
Can neither, when we will, enjoy
Nor, when we will, resign.

Quatrain with two rimed lines.—

I think that saving a child
And bringing him to his own
Is a derned sight better business
Than loafing round the throne.

Quatrain with two rimes.—

Why should I stay? Nor seed nor fruit have I
But, sprung at once to beauty's perfect round,
Nor loss nor gain nor change in me is found,—
A life—complete in death—complete to die.

Six-line stanza with two rimes.—

The hollow sea-shell, which for years hath stood
On dusty shelves, when held against the ear
Proclaims its stormy parent, and we hear
The faint, far murmur of the breaking flood
We hear the sea. The Sea? It is the blood
In our own veins, impetuous and near.

Four lines with one rime.—

A little peach in an orchard grew,—
A little peach of emerald hue;
Warmed by the sun and wet by the dew
It grew.

Sonnet.—

What is a sonnet? 'Tis a pearly shell
That murmurs of the far-off murmuring sea,
A precious jewel carved most curiously;
It is a little picture painted well.
What is a sonnet? 'Tis the tear that fell
From the great poet's hidden ecstasy;
A two-edged sword, a star, a song—ah me!
Sometimes a heavy-tolling funeral bell.
This was the flame that shook with Dante's breath,
The solemn organ whereon Milton played,
And the clear glass where Shakspere's shadow falls;
A sea this is—beware who ventureth!
For like a fiord the narrow floor is laid
Deep as mid-ocean to sheer mountain walls.

Richard Watson Gilder.

The *Limerick* is a form of nonsense stanza, made up of five lines with two rimes. The first, second, and fifth lines rime, and the third and fourth lines. The following specimen well represents the limerick:

Said the Snail to the Tortoise: "You may
Find it hard to believe what I say;
You will think it absurd,
But I give you my word,
They fined me for speeding today."

Oliver Herford.

The following school songs illustrate a method of adapting sentiment and words to a popular tune:

Tune: Come Back to Erin.

Come back to Normal, Good English, Good English!
Back to the ones who have missed you so long.
Come back to Normal, Good English, Good English!
And all the building will ring with our song.

Tune: Row Your Boat.

Watch, watch, watch your speech,
Every word you say.
Carefully, carefully, carefully, carefully
Watch it every day.

PUBLIC SPEAKING

Public speaking, as commonly understood, though it does not lay claim to the more formal title of oratory, is nevertheless a term which includes that art. As oratory is the appeal of a high order of eloquence to the understanding and to the emotions, so, too, the province of public speaking is not only to entertain and inform, but also to convince and persuade.

Possibilities and Probabilities. Although it is not given to every one to become an orator, nevertheless, it is well within the scope and the power of the average intelligent person to become a good public speaker. Moreover, there never was a time when public speaking formed a more important factor in American life than it does today, nor was there ever a time when this talent brought to the individual more social and political influence.

Every citizen is likely at any time to be called upon to express his views on any topic which may be exercising the minds of the public. As an efficient member of the community, he should be ready to respond to the claim thus made upon him and be able to lay before his fellow-citizens or townsmen, in language at once clear and forceful, his opinions and his judgment on the question put before him for discussion.

Fundamentals. "What then," it will be asked, "is necessary in order to prepare one's self to become a successful public speaker?"

1. The first essential is a knowledge of one's fellow-men. By this is not meant that one must necessarily be a psychologist. He must, however, have an all-round knowledge of people in general, especially of the man in the street, with his prejudices to be overcome, his rights to be defended, and his wrongs to be rectified. Only in this way can a speaker get in touch with an audience. He must understand his audience before they will understand him.

2. In the second place, the speaker should have a knowledge of books. He should become acquainted with good literature. Not every intending speaker has had the advantages of a college training. He may not have enjoyed the privilege of extensive travel, and he may be wanting in that broader knowledge that comes only to those of wide and practical experience. But books are always open to him; they will furnish him with facts, ideas, and all that is needed for the illustration of his

subject. It was Bacon who said, "Reading maketh a full man." It is the man full of his subject, and thereby confident, who will interest and impress his audience.

3. As language is the chief means of conveying thought, it is a matter of the greatest importance to possess a ready command of words. To enlarge his vocabulary, the student of public speaking should make notes of all the new or strange words he meets in his general reading, or that he may hear in listening to lectures given by others. He should then make a point of using such words whenever opportunity offers; for it is by continuous use that they become his own.

The above three points sum up what may be regarded as the *remote preparation* for public speaking, in which lies in great measure the secret of success in this practical art. We now come to the *immediate preparation*, or the method to be followed in the actual planning and in the making of a speech.

Choice of Subject. Let the subject you choose be one of interest to yourself and one that is likely to be of interest to your audience. Remember you are to deliver a message. Unless you win the interest of your audience, your efforts to deliver a message will be in vain. Know beforehand the manner of audience you are about to address and adapt your subject to their capacity. In this way you will not be speaking "over their heads," and your purpose of convincing and persuading will be achieved.

The Plan. No matter how confident you may feel after you have gathered your material, always make in advance a plan or an outline of your intended talk or address. No builder undertakes the erection of a building until he has made a working plan of its different divisions, stories, and apartments. The same principle applies to an address. By making a plan you will put into your speech what you want to say, and will save time in saying it. Moreover, this much is due your audience. The habit of planning, if conscientiously cultivated, will enable you eventually to make a *mental* plan when opportunity will not allow of a penciled outline.

A speech to be convincing must be logical,—that is, it must be made up of an *introduction*, a *body*, and a *conclusion*. This rule is applicable to the formal address, to the simple talk at a club meeting, to an after-dinner speech, or to the toast at a wedding breakfast.

Introduction or Beginning. This should be a brief and clear forecasting of what the speaker proposes to discuss before or prove to his audience, and it should contain the logical scheme of his entire address. In plain words, he should let his hearers know how he intends to deal with his subject. In opening his speech his manner should be easy and natural. This end may be achieved in several ways; for instance, (1) by some happy compliment paid to the audience; (2) by reference to some interesting topic of the moment; (3) by an anecdote relating to some well-known character, or by a brief and apt quotation. In this simple manner a speaker may get in touch with his audience and at the same time may lead up to his subject.

Body of the Speech. This consists in the gradual and logical development of the proposition already set forth in your introduction. As you proceed in the unfolding of your main statements, make free use of illustration and comparison from other themes and topics familiar to your audience. This tends to greater clearness and insures interest. It is thus that you imperceptibly paint a background from which your word-picture will stand out in more sharply defined and vivid lines. As you pass from one point to another, revert occasionally to the argument already put forward, so that your audience may hold in mind the main divisions of your talk.

The Conclusion. The conclusion should be a careful summing up and welding together of the chief arguments developed in the body of the speech. They must be made to stand out lucidly and forcefully, and in such order that, by the presentation of their combined strength, conviction is driven home to the minds of those listening.

As has already been pointed out, public speaking may serve either to entertain, inform, convince, or persuade. The formal speech will always have dignity of form and of diction. So much will not be expected of the informal, short address, though the structure of each is essentially the same, both being built on the basis of logical thought. This being true, the informal speech is here dealt with, for practical purposes.

Informal Speeches. You may be called upon suddenly to say "a few words" in public, to propose a toast or to make an after-dinner speech, to take part in a discussion, or to talk as an executive to employees. A hundred different occasions may arise and demand from you some kind of address. You have to win the attention of your audience on the spur of the moment, and make your points as quickly. If you know the essentials that go to the making of a speech, as already stated above, a few hurried notes will be sufficient for the skeleton outline of what you intend to say.

A useful suggestive outline for the short talk or informal address is furnished by the following questions: 1—What is the fact or situation under discussion? 2—How has it come to be as it is? 3—How does it affect you? 4—What are you going to do about it?

Nucleus of an Informal Address. The nucleus, or concentrated matter, of a short talk may often be found (1) in the statement of some striking fact or incident, (2) in the presentation of clear and up-to-date statistics concerning a topic of real interest, (3) in the clever recital of a new story, or of an old one dressed in a new garb, and calculated to raise a laugh or a smile. The last method of beginning an address is perhaps the happiest of all, as by it the audience is warmed to sympathy with the speaker, the knowledge of which fact is no small aid to eloquence.

SOME STYLES OF SHORT TALKS

The occasions for the short talk are many, and there are almost as many styles as there are occasions. On the other hand, there are certain similarities to be noted in each, as the following examples will illustrate:

After-Dinner Speech. Usually, you have first to express some pointed sentiment in reference to the occasion, the host, or the guest of honor. A happy quotation or an adage which contains the gist of what you are about to say, will often serve as an appropriate *beginning*. Again, a half serious, half humorous comment will help in the development of the sentiment itself. Also, the flash light of a good crisp story will illumine your remarks so that your audience will see the point, and be won at once to your favor. As brevity is the soul of wit, so is it the essence of a good after-dinner speech.

The Wedding Toast. A short speech proposing the health of the bride and the bridegroom follows lines similar to those of the after-dinner speech. (1) You may begin felicitously by describing some pleasant journey, made more delightful by reason of congenial companionship. (2) The description of such a journey will be apt as a simile to describe life's journey, which the bride and the bridegroom have decided to make together. A few remarks on the ups and downs of life will add the humorous touch. (3) In the conclusion of your speech, leading to the drinking of the toast, you will voice the earnest wishes of the company for the welfare of the happy couple.

Impromptu Discussion. It may be that you are asked to take part in a running debate or discussion at which you happen to be present. In such a case you will have time to make a mental plan only. Nevertheless, you may adroitly begin your talk by referring to some salient fact or idea already mentioned in the debate, and thus gain time to put your thoughts in order. This is called a "point of contact" to which you may gradually attach your own trend of argument. Thus, often by an *impromptu* speech you can add to the interest of a debate by the orderly and well balanced presentment of your personal views. This happy facility comes from the persistent habit of making plans. To illustrate:

The debate is on the question of *safety*—an important topic to be discussed. Your opinion as an employer of labor, or as an employee, is sought on this subject. Possibly you will find a starting point for your talk by relating some accident which has taken place at the works or store in which you are employed. From this proceed to expand and make interesting your informal speech by putting forward your personal ideas on the best methods for preventing similar accidents in the future.

Again, the discussion may be on the question of *co-operation*. Once more you are asked to join in the debate. In such a case, a possible improvement in an industrial process, or a suggestion as to the better management of your business, may well supply you with a good opening and with excellent matter for an effective talk.

The examples given above illustrate some of the forms that a short address may take. It will be seen how some concrete and definite incidents, or accidents, may become the nucleus of your whole talk, and how, in time, you may find all the points you need to make a telling and striking address. If you have trained yourself in the habit of making plans, you will find that in an exigency you can do so without the aid of paper and pencil. You will unconsciously have taught yourself to make a hurried mental digest of what you are about to say, and so be enabled to speak *extempore* both with ease and with confidence.

FORMS OF PUBLIC SPEAKING

The Expository Speech or Lecture. The aim of the expository speaker is to make something clear to his audience. It is usually the aim of the teacher. But there are many occasions outside of the school where a speaker has as his basic purpose the presentation of clarifying ideas. A new system of handling personnel may be set forth by a personnel director or a new plan for organized recreation may be presented by the chairman of the program committee. It is important for the speaker who is called upon to give clarifying information to keep his talk on an expository basis; that is, he must see to it that he does not bring in his own ax to grind and thus try to straddle exposition with persuasion. There are some six methods of exposition, any or all of which may be employed in a speech for clearness:

(1) *Comparison.* This is, perhaps, the most useful expository device. The audience is made to understand something new by having it compared with that which they already know. Analogy, which is a comparison of ratios, is a most useful form of comparison. When analogy is used the audience is enabled to understand a new relationship or process by seeing it compared to one with which they are familiar.

(2) *Analysis.* Through this device we come to understand something by having it taken apart for us. Thus we come to see the whole in terms of its parts. It is a good idea to remember that talks making use of analysis should end up with synthesis, so that the hearers see the relationship of the parts to the whole.

(3) *Definition.* Many effective speeches with clearness as the end are based on the elaboration of a definition. We might, for instance, make an expository talk on Public Speaking by elaborating on the terms, and the relationship of the terms, in this definition: Public Speaking is the useful art of influencing human behavior through the medium of purposive speech.

(4) *Cause and Effect Relationship.* This method is often used where the material is of a historical character. A speaker might, for instance, explain Fascism by tracing its development in Germany.

(5) *Restatement.* When a speaker uses the expression, "in other words," and then goes on to give his audience another view of the same thing, he is using Restatement. It is different from *repetition* in that the same words are said over again in the latter.

(6) *Example.* The expository speaker uses *example* when he gives a demonstration, actually showing the thing he is explaining. The use of movies in teaching is an application of this method. It can also be said that illustrations by means of pictures or drawings on a blackboard are applications of the method. In the last few years, with the development of various techniques of visual education, expository presentations have been given added effectiveness by use of the example method.

Occasional and Commemorative Speeches. The purpose of the speaker in giving speeches at special occasions or in commemoration of some event or person is *Impressiveness.* The term Impressiveness is used to describe the purpose of those speeches in which the audience, already in agreement as to the concepts presented, is made to feel more deeply about them. Speeches of welcome, farewell speeches, speeches given when a gift is presented, and when one is accepted, have impressiveness as the purpose. Also those speeches given at dedication ceremonies and at anniversary gatherings have that purpose. Usually these speeches are eulogistic in character, that is, they are dominated by the mood of praise. Some of our finest oratory has been delivered at such occasions. The speakers have endeavored to catch the spirit of the hour, to voice the feelings of the listeners, to make the audience feel that their best thoughts and sentiments have been beautifully and effectively expressed.

It is in speeches of this kind that the expression comes close to the art of the poet. Metaphor, which is said to be the essence of poetry, is well employed in this form of speech composition. There also may be something of the rhythmic cadence of poetry. When the poetic element in such speech compositions springs from a genuine feeling of admiration of the subject being spoken of, there need be no fear of indulging in old-fashioned oratorical language. Love, affection, admiration, veneration, *when sincerely expressed*, is never out of date.

The Speech of Introduction. The function of the *speech of introduction* is to bring the speaker and the audience together in a proper spirit of acquaintanceship. It should meet this need and go no further. The listeners should be given that information about the speaker and his topic which will help them and the speaker. The introduction should be warm and friendly in spirit but should not embarrass the speaker by being eulogistic. It should be as short as possible and certainly should not encroach upon the speaker's topic. All too frequently the introducer is inclined to bask in the limelight of the main speaker, giving a speech of his own, indulging in oratorical flourishes, and generally stealing the main speaker's thunder.

DISCUSSION AND DEBATE

These two kinds of speaking are closely related in that they are a part of a general process, the process of arriving at a new point of view in regard to some public question. It can be said that *debate* picks up where discussion leaves off. Through the group discussion of a question or problem, a gathering of people may arrive at a point where it must decide whether or not to adopt a new policy in conducting its affairs. At this point debate begins: Should the new policy be adopted or not? For example, in group discussion the general question of obtaining proper medical care for the American people might be given consideration. At a certain point in the discussion the members of the group decide that the matter has reduced itself to the question: Should we or should we not adopt some form of nationalized health insurance? From that point on the gathering is on a debate basis. Following this line of thought, we shall give consideration first to the topic, group discussion.

Group Discussion. For hundreds of years the rhetoric of debating has been clearly set forth by textbook writers and followed by students in school debates and by lawyers and legislators. It is only in the last decade or so that the art of public discussion has been treated effectively in speech textbooks. However, public discussion of community and state problems has been effectively carried on in this country since the country's beginnings. The democratic method of open discussion of public questions was followed in New England Town Meetings in the 17th century. In the 18th century the same process of group thinking was to be observed in the Constitutional Convention. The delegates to the convention did not come to Philadelphia in 1787 to debate clearly defined issues nor to impress the gallery with persuasive oratory; they came to find a solution to a problem and to reach that solution by "negotiation and accommodation." We find the group discussion method manifested in the 19th century in the Lyceum and Chautauqua movements, the former being at its height in the middle of the century and the latter by the end of the century. The modern *open forum* movement had its beginnings in 1897 as a part of the adult education activities of Cooper Union in New York City. The movement was given fresh impetus in 1933 under the leadership of J. W. Studebaker, then superintendent of the Des Moines Public Schools. The Des Moines public Forums set the pattern for the discussion of public problems by citizens of a community. With the development of nationwide interest in this form of group thinking has come a substantial literature on the technique of discussion.

Today it is more important than ever that people be able to think through their problems in some co-operative fashion. We are no longer a world of isolated communities; the world itself is a community. This world community is endeavoring to find solutions to its problems in group discussions at the United Nations, in peace conferences, in industrial management-labor conferences, in organizations seeking racial harmony, and in international forums conducted by public spirited citizens.

The Process of Group Thinking. There are basically five steps in the process of thinking through to the solution of a problem. While it hardly can be said that any particular group discussion clearly follows the sequence, upon analysis it will be seen that the steps are involved. The steps are:

(1) Defining the problem.

(2) Analysis of the problem with the purpose of finding what values will be sought for in a solution.

(3) Suggestion of possible solutions or hypotheses.

(4) Consideration of relative merits of suggested solutions in the light of the values or criteria established in step two. Arrival at a tentative solution.

(5) Testing out the solution by visualizing it in operation.

A forum or discussion leader should keep these steps in mind in guiding a group in its problem solving efforts. He should have thought about the problem sufficiently beforehand and be sufficiently informed as to the basic aspects of the question so that he can detect tendencies to jump to conclusions, to reason in a circle, to generalize from insufficient evidence, to ignore minority interests, to fasten on trivial points, to indulge in personalities, and the many other all too human weaknesses to be found in our endeavors to be rational. When the leader sees that a member or members of the group are suggesting a solution before the problem has been adequately analyzed (step two) he should tactfully raise the question whether there are not values to be looked for in a solution which have not been considered and lead the members back to the second phase of the thought process. It will be found that this phase, the analysis step, is the one that is most difficult and which groups are prone to pass over too quickly. On the other hand, the leader must be on guard against having a preconceived solution to the problem and toward which he inflexibly directs the assembly. When that happens the discussion is no longer a co-operative, democratic process. The leader has become something of a dictator.

Types of Group Discussion. The type of group discussion taken up in the foregoing paragraphs is the type most commonly used. It is simple in its organization, there being only the chairman, or leader, and the gathering of people who sit before the leader, or with him around a table. This kind of discussion might be called the *conference* type. The unqualified word, *forum*, is also used as a term to describe this form of discussion.

Planning the Conference. The chairman or leader of the *conference* type of discussion must be imbued with the democratic principle of agreement in a group arrived at through full, free, and informed discussion. Collaboration for a common end should be the controlling objective. There are some things the leader can do to facilitate the attainment of that objective. He, himself, should command the respect of the group by being fair, tolerant, gracious, and firm, withal. He should be informed as regards the subject matter of the conference and as regards the process of democratic discussion. He should oversee the arrangements for the meeting, making sure that the room is a pleasant one, that the scheduled time for the meeting is a convenient one for the participants, that enough time is allotted for the meeting or meetings so that the group can arrive at a deliberative decision. When the discussion is going on he should carefully gauge the progress of the group, and if he sees that opposing interests are bringing about an impasse, he may well suggest a recess, in which heated tempers may cool off. Frequently, important concessions are made during recesses, especially if during the recess the members can get together on a good-fellowship basis.

Besides the conference type of discussion there are six others, each type having a distinguishing characteristic. They are similar to each other in one respect, all being more formal than the conference type of discussion. The six types are: the *Panel-Forum*, the *Symposium-Forum*, the *Lecture-Forum*, the *Colloquy* or *Dialogue*, the *Public Hearing*, and the *Debate-Forum*.

The Panel-Forum. In this type of discussion a panel of two to six speakers sit on the platform along with the chairman and converse on some chosen topic for the benefit of the audience facing the platform. This is a popular form of discussion especially in educational circles. Usually the group, the panel and chairman, have a meeting beforehand at which an outline covering the material for discussion is worked out and each member of the panel is assigned some part of the outline on which to talk. The chairman should keep these points in mind in directing the discussion: No member of the panel should talk for more than one minute at a time. All discussion should be directed toward the audience. The chairman and panel members should remain seated, for the sake of informality. Spontaneity should be encouraged in the panel members. If two speak up at the same time, the chairman designates who shall talk first.

After the panel members have finished their conversation and the chairman has made a summary of the discourse, the audience should be called upon to participate in an open-forum discussion. They may contribute ideas or ask questions of the panel members. It is a good idea to allow as much as half of the meeting time for audience participation and to inform the audience beforehand that they will have that time for discussion.

The panel-forum, as are the remaining types to be presented here, is better suited to the conveying of information than to problem solving. When a problem is to be solved, it is best to use the *conference* type of discussion.

The Symposium-Forum. This type is similar to the panel-forum in that it is made up of a panel of speakers, from two to four, and who have designated points upon which to speak. It differs from it in that each member of the panel gives a set speech, running from five to ten minutes in length. After the panel members have spoken and the chairman has summarized, the chairman invites the audience to participate as in the panel-forum.

The Lecture-Forum. Here one speaker takes the place of a panel of speakers. There may be a chairman, who opens the meeting, introduces the speaker, and conducts the open forum when the speaker finishes. However, the lecturer himself may act as chairman. This type is better suited to the conveying of information than to problem solving.

The Colloquy or Dialogue. Three units are found on the platform in this type of discussion, a panel of experts, an audience panel, and the chairman. The audience panel is usually chosen from the audience at the time of the meeting. The chairman and the panel representing the audience begin the discussion, after the manner of the ordinary panel-forum. The members of the expert panel are called upon to supply evidence when the need for it becomes apparent and to give opinions when they are desired. The *colloquy* is well suited for conventions where experts in a particular field are available and where the audience-members have a specialized interest in the subject-matter.

The Public Hearing. There are two types of public hearings, that which is held by legislative committees and that held by representatives of governmental agencies. In both types a legislative committee or government representatives seek information, evidence, and existing opinion from members of organizations, pressure groups, or individual citizens. At hearings the committee members and the audience face each other and the space between them is allotted to the particular speaker who happens to be speaking. He addresses the committee with his back to the audience. In the legislative hearing, members of the committee ask questions of the speaker. In the second type, audience and speakers usually ask questions of the governmental representatives. The chief problem for the speaker in hearings is to make himself heard by the audience at his back without shouting to the committee.

The Debate-Forum. This type is similar to the Symposium-Forum except for the fact that in the former the panel of speakers is broken up into two units each taking the affirmative or negative on some debatable question. When the two sides have presented their arguments, the chairman invites the audience to participate. After perhaps twenty minutes of open-forum discussion a final summary is made by the opponent of the proposed solution and by the advocate of the proposed solution. The debate-forum is best used when the audience is familar with the problem and almost ready to decide what to do about it.

ARGUMENT AND PERSUASION

An *argument* is a reason given in support of a proposition. As a form of composition, argument is also the logical arrangement of a proposition and the reasons urged in support of it. Sometimes we merely defend an opinion; sometimes we try to convince others that certain opinions are true or false. When we use arguments to make people believe or act as we want them to, we use *persuasion.* Persuasion is the means by which a speaker or writer tries to move his audience to belief or action.

We succeed in persuasion partly through logical argument and partly through personal appeal to the sympathies and interests of an audience. Both these elements are necessary. Sometimes one plays the larger part, sometimes the other. Sincere human interest, added to a logical argument, is as necessary to a salesman as to a lawyer before a jury or to a preacher in his pulpit.

Debate. The best way to learn to argue well is to practice in formal discussions or debates. Free discussion of public questions is necessary to the welfare of people in a democracy. Therefore, schools, clubs, and societies should encourage such discussion and give opportunity for debate. Any debate centers in a question about which two opposing propositions can be made and supported by arguments. We cannot debate words or phrases. We may speak of discussing "taxes" or "freedom of speech"; but the discussion cannot proceed until we have put together a sentence or proposition about the subject. Preparation for debate calls first for selecting a debatable question. This is a question (1) on which opinions may reasonably differ, (2) on which material for evidence and proof is available, (3) which is of real interest.

The steps in planning an argument or a debate are the following:

1. State the question clearly and definitely. Propositions should be stated affirmatively, and should be so worded as to throw the burden of proof upon the affirmative. For example:

"*Should the City of X purchase the local electric lighting plant?*" or "*Should James W. go to college?*" Sometimes the question is stated in the form of a resolution: "*Resolved, That the City of X should purchase the local electric lighting plant.*" The following form also is recommended by some teachers as a title for a debate: "*For and against the election of B. as mayor*"; "*For and against James W. going to college.*"

2. Define concisely the terms used in the question. For instance, the terms "purchase" and "plant," in the first question, and the term "college," in the second, need definition.

3. Find the main *issues*, or special subordinate questions, on which the decision may turn. This discovery of issues is really a most vital part of argument; for clear statement of main issues eliminates useless talk about unimportant details. The following is the best method of finding the issues: (1) set down a number of opposing statements upon the question; (2) analyze these to find what are the exact points on which they conflict; (3) state these points as questions. These questions are the issues. Such an analysis of arguments on the question as to the electric lighting plant would probably reveal the following issues:

Is the present electric service unsatisfactory? Is owning and operating public utilities a wise policy for this city? Is some other management to be preferred?

These issues appear in the form of questions, to which the affirmative answers *yes* and the negative, *no.* The skillful debater takes account of these questions and sifts them until he has found those which seem really essential. Then, by answering these essential questions, he answers the main question. Such an argument may be outlined as follows:

The body, or *brief*, for the affirmative or negative side of the argument should thus take up the issues in order and answer each question, with reasons and evidence. Then, on the basis of the reasoning given, the *conclusion*, or final answer to the main question should be stated.

In a debate on any question, certain of the apparent issues may be set aside, by mutual agreement, before opening the discussion. They are then called "admitted matter," and the discussion, for the sake of brevity and clearness, takes up only the issues on which there is clear difference of opinion.

Logic. "*Why?*" is the student's most troublesome question, but no progress in argumentative thinking can be made without clear answers to questions beginning with *Why*. The corresponding word in answers is *because*. One thing is true because another thing is true.

All reasoning must be based on long and careful observation of facts. *Logic*, which is the science or art of exact reasoning, teaches us how to arrange and test our propositions so that our conclusions shall be warranted.

The *syllogism* is a common form of logical reasoning. It may be represented as follows:

Major premise (general statement): Wooden houses can be burned.

Minor premise (particular statement): Mr. A's house is wooden.

Conclusion: Therefore, Mr. A's house can be burned.

To make this reasoning true, a sufficient number of cases must have been observed to justify the general statement. It must be certain also that Mr. A's house belongs to the general class of wooden houses.

If we said, "*Plants are good for food; geraniums are plants; therefore, geraniums are good for food,*" our reasoning would be faulty, because not all plants are good for food. Our general statement is untrue though our particular statement is true. If we said, "*Lumber is expensive; houses are made of lumber; therefore, houses are expensive,*" our reasoning would be faulty because not all houses are made entirely or mainly of lumber. The particular statement is untrue though the general statement and the fact stated in the conclusion are true. Therefore, in the first example, we would *distinguish* or *question* the *major* premise, *grant* the *minor*, and *deny* the *conclusion*; in the second, we would *grant* the *major*, *distinguish* the *minor*, and *deny* the *conclusion*.

Evidence and Proof. Answering these *why* questions involves evidence and proof. *Evidence* is any fact, testimony, or accepted principle, which tends to bring about a belief in the proposition which is being urged. Evidence may be direct or circumstantial. Direct evidence is such as immediately supports the proposition. For instance, a theft may have been committed, the thief pursued and caught; his possession of the stolen property and the testimony of the person who saw him steal would be *direct evidence*. If, however, no such evidence as this were available, *circumstantial evidence* might be used. This would be made up of facts about the suspected person and his movements, which would tend to show that he probably committed the deed. *Proof* is convincing evidence.

Formal Debate: Rules. In a formal debate each side must know which are the most important of the issues raised, and the debaters must remember that the decision depends upon the balance of argument. Every argument advanced by one side must be answered by the other. Unanswered argument stands, no matter how weak the evidence presented by the side using it. *Refutation*, or the answering of opponents' arguments, is very important.

The debating leagues of colleges and high schools have developed certain customs and rules for the conducting of debates. The most important of these follow:

1. *Selection of the Question.*—Usually one team proposes a question and the other team is allowed to choose to support either the affirmative or the negative side.

2. *Teams.*—Each side of the argument is maintained by a team of two (or three) members. An additional member, or alternate, is sometimes chosen. He may take one of the regular places in an emergency. Otherwise, he helps in the preparation of the debate.

3. *Teamwork.*—All members of the team should work together in preparing the debate. They should confer upon the selection of the important issues and the arrangement of material. Before the debate, each member of the team should be familiar with the entire argument, but the actual presentation should be divided among the three debaters. Each one should have a definite part of the case to present.

4. *Division of Work.*—The first speaker on each side has to state the position of his side, make one strong point, and win the attention and the interest of his audience. The second speaker has to maintain interest, make at least one striking argument, and refute some of his opponents' arguments. The last speaker has to drive home the strongest argument of his side, answer some of his opponents' arguments, and sum up the case.

5. *Organization of a Debate.*—A formal debate is organized with a chairman, a timekeeper, and usually three judges. The chairman calls the meeting to order, announces the question and any special rules for the discussion, and introduces the speakers. The timekeeper gives each speaker a signal one minute or two before his speech is to close and another, if necessary, when his time has expired.

6. *Order of Speaking.*—The speakers on the two sides alternate, first an affirmative and then a negative speaker. Usually the debaters give two series of speeches. The first consists of direct argument; the second, entirely of refutation. This second series of speeches is called rebuttal. The order of speakers in rebuttal may be changed from that followed in the direct argument. The affirmative may elect either to open or to close the rebuttal.

7. *Time.*—Each speaker in direct argument is allowed a definite time—six, eight, or ten minutes—for his direct speech and a shorter time for rebuttal. The first direct speakers and the last rebuttal speakers are sometimes allowed two or three minutes more than the others.

8. *Intermission.*—At the close of the direct speeches the debaters are allowed a brief intermission for conference before beginning the rebuttal.

9. *Limitations of Rebuttal.*—In rebuttal a speaker must confine himself to refuting his opponents' arguments. He is not allowed to bring in new material.

10. *Decision of the Judges.*—At the close of the debate the judges render their decision, usually without conferring. The chairman announces the decision, which is accepted as final.

RADIO SPEAKING

The importance of radio in our everyday life hardly needs emphasis. There are approximately 30 million radio sets in use in the United States today. Over a period of 25 years the broadcasting of radio programs has become a large and very profitable enterprise. The large national networks reach most of the 30 million homes and dwelling places where radio sets are to be found. Practically every American home depends upon radio for news, entertainment, instruction, and useful information.

Listening to Radio. In 1934 the Communications act was passed by Congress. This act established a permanent regulatory body, the Federal Communications Commission. It is the function of this body to regulate radio, acting for the American people, who own the title to the wave lengths of the air and whose interests must be protected in such a way that their property is not abused. The F.C.C. is charged by the Communications act to grant and, later, to renew a temporary license to operate a radio station only after it is satisfied that the applicant will operate "in the public interest, convenience, or necessity."

Since the radio wave lengths are the property of the people, it is important that they get the greatest value from their possession. This they can do through creative listening and by constructive criticism of what they hear. There are fine programs on the air today, of great value educationally and for recreation, and there are programs which are trashy and even of a harmful nature. The listener should seek out the good programs and listen to them creatively, responding to them freely, imaginatively, and intellectually.

The listener can enhance the value of his property by actively criticising programs. He can give praise or blame to programs by writing to radio column editors, by discussing them in Parent-Teacher Association meetings and other organizations, and by communicating his suggestions to the F.C.C. itself. It is particularly true in the case of American radio that you must "get what you like or you will grow to like what you get."

Performing on the Radio. There are two classes of radio performers, the professionals, who are on a paid basis, and the non-professionals, who more and more frequently are being called upon to broadcast, especially for those programs which are of an educational or documentary nature. When *Frequency Modulation*, a new technique for the transmission of sound over the air, is generally adopted in this country, and the majority of radio sets are equipped to receive this kind of transmission, there will be a far greater demand for non-professional broadcasters. With Frequency Modulation it is technically possible to have from 3500 to 5000 more stations in this country. This means that eventually, through F.M., there will be far more local stations, which will probably put greater emphasis on educational and documentary broadcasts. Twenty channels for F.M. broadcasting have been reserved by the F.C.C. for state and municipal authorities and already a number of channels have been applied for. As these new stations are set up, there will be an increasing demand for non-professional performers. Such performers will be called on for local forum discussions, for interviews at their place of work, for broadcasts of courts and legislatures in session, for meetings of industrial and union leaders, for broadcasts from the local schools and colleges. The basic techniques as required for broadcasting, whether on a professional or non-professional basis, will be presented here.

Radio Speaking. While basic public speaking techniques are involved in radio speaking, there is one fundamental difference. Radio differs from the normal public speaking situation in that the performer must reach his audience entirely through their auditory sense. The give-and-take of a speaker before an actual audience is, of course, not possible. There is an absence of what psychologists call circular audience-speaker responses, the subtle, but vital, cycle of influences that speaker and audience have upon each other.

This lack of a visible audience intensifies the need for observing the rules for good speech. He should have good articulation and enunciation; that is, the consonants and vowels should be clearly but not laboriously spoken. Mispronunciation of words, which might be excused in a speaker when he is before an audience, is always distracting on the radio and should be avoided. Conversational variety in pitch, as opposed to the sing-song, must be sought for, and a normal resonant quality, as opposed to such qualities as nasality and throaty harshness, is highly desirable. The speaker's rate and volume should be that of normal social conversation, with an absence of fumbling pauses, "uhs," "and uhs" and "wells." The all important techniques of phrasing and emphasis, which has been taken up in the section, Oral Reading, should be evident in his speaking.

The radio speaker must keep foremost in his mind that almost invariably his audience is made up of small family groups averaging between three and four in number. Many speakers come to the microphone with the idea that they must expand their mode of speaking to reach the great mass of potential listeners that radio affords. These speakers must be disabused of this idea and come to realize that a formal, oratorical style would not only be out of place but also in bad taste when heard in the average American living room.

The special character of the radio audience puts other demands upon the radio speaker. The fact that this audience can shut the broadcast off at will and without the embarrassment of leaving a hall in the presence of a visible speaker requires that the speaking hold interest continuously. This audience, because it listens only, pays closer attention to the auditory characteristics of the speaker and catches many elements that would be missed in a visible speaker. For some reason the voice is more revealing of the character of a speaker than are the visible elements. Insincerity, affectation, self-complacency are quickly sensed by hearers and usually with justification. The radio performer cannot afford to be elocutionary, to consciously direct the melody of his speech. His listeners will turn to another program.

Delivery. The radio speaker almost invariably reads from a manuscript. Consequently it is essential that he be able to read well from the printed page. As is pointed out in the Oral Reading section he must have caught the gist of a whole speech phrase before he starts to read the first word of that phrase. This guards against his falling into the stilted manner of reading words rather than speaking ideas. The radio speaker should not hesitate to use gestures and other movements that go with lively conversation. Even though the movements are not seen, the total bodily response that those movements bespeak makes for spontaneousness in the voice.

One cannot wisely specify the distance a speaker should be from the microphone. The distance changes with different types of microphones, with different voice qualities and voice-placing, with acoustics of different studios, and with varying numbers of people on a program. If, however, a speaker is alone, and he has learned to control his volume, 18 inches is about the right distance to keep from the modern type of microphone. His speaking volume should be that used in speaking to a person who is about four feet away. The rate of speech should average about 140 words per minute. Franklin D. Roosevelt spoke between 110 and 135 words per minute.

Extraneous noises are especially distracting when heard over the radio. Breathing into the microphone should be avoided and so should gasping noises which come with inadequate breath control. The speaker should turn away from the microphone if it is necessary to cough, clear the throat, or sneeze. Rattling of the manuscript comes over very loud.

A good standing position to take is one in which the feet are flat on the floor, the body erect, the shoulders back, and the chin up and away from the throat. The microphone should be high enough so that it is necessary to talk up to it slightly. At all times the radio speaker should aim for an alert, friendly, spontaneous quality of delivery.

The Manuscript. Instant intelligibility should be the aim in writing for radio. Devices which make for this are: Use of Anglo-Saxon words, use of concrete rather than abstract words, avoiding long sentences, giving of quick summaries at frequent intervals, making careful transitions, setting main headings forth clearly, use of synonyms for restatement of a new idea, and endeavoring to talk in terms of the common experience of the audience.

The manuscript itself should be prepared so that it is easy to read. It should be typewritten, double-spaced, and on paper of soft texture so that it won't rattle. The pages should be numbered but not clipped together.

Radio As A Vocation. The National Broadcasting Company, in the pamphlet on *The Selection and Training of Radio Announcers* indicates that the candidate should average well in the following:

A good voice, clear enunciation, and pronunciation free of dialect or local peculiarities; ability to read well; sufficient knowledge of foreign languages for the correct pronunciation of names, places, titles, etc.; some knowledge of musical history, composition, and composers; ability to read and interpret poetry; facility in extempore speech; selling ability in the reading of commercial continuity; ability to master the technical details in operating the switchboard; a college education.

Small local stations or colleges which have well organized radio departments are best places for training. In small stations (there are 881 stations in the U.S.) the newcomer can get experience in the various aspects of radio. He can work as announcer, actor, musician, writer, technician, and in the sales and office staff.

The radio field is a popular one today and many people are competing for positions in it. But if a man or woman has the proper training, has the ability to get on with people, can think clearly and quickly on occasions, is healthy, and has a good voice, and has the desire to make radio his profession, he should not be discouraged.

FORMS OF ORAL INTERPRETATION

In schools, in clubs, in social gatherings, and in the home, there are occasions when we desire to read, recite, act out, or tell about something from the printed page. Many of us hesitate to do so for fear of being elocutionary. It is true that the exhibitionary kind of recitation that flourished in the nineties and in the first decade of this century has gone out of style and is heard today only when it is being satirized. But there is no reason why one should be fearful of communicating to others what he has found worth-while in our literature. The sincere expression of fine literature is never out of date.

There are four forms of oral interpretation which are frequently used, the characteristics of which will be presented here. They are: *Interpretative Reading*, *Recitation*, *Impersonation*, and *Story Telling*. These forms might be called patterns of delivery. Each form is made up of certain factors of delivery which are so integrated that they make a characteristic pattern. It is well for the speech student to know these patterns. When he does he will be able to be judicious in his oral interpretations. He will know when to act out and when to recite. He will avoid the mistake frequently made of acting out in a literal fashion that which should be suggested. In other words, he can avoid being told he is "elocutionary."

Principles of Oral Reading. There are certain techniques in oral interpretation which are applicable to all the forms mentioned in the foregoing paragraph and which we take up here preliminary to our discussion of the four specific forms.

Phrasing. A speech phrase is different from a grammatical phrase. In the sentence, "While John was walking up the hill, he stopped and looked back at the sunset," there are two grammatical phrases, "up the hill" and "at the sunset." These grammatical phrases are only a part of the two speech phrases which go to make up the sentence. A speech phrase is a unit of speech expression which presents some element of experience for the audience to grasp. That element may be an idea, an image, an action, an emotion, an attitude. Thus, in the sentence about John we have two elements of experience, that of John walking up the hill, and John's turning to look at the sunset.

Characteristics of a Speech Phrase. The speech phrase is a *unit* in several respects. It is a unit in its separateness. Usually it is separated from other phrases by a pause. Sometimes, however, a change in pitch or volume or rate may indicate the end of one phrase and the beginning of another. It is a unit in its presenting one pattern of experience, something which can be grasped and reacted to by the listeners. It is a unit in its cohesiveness. The words in the phrase, "while John was walking up the hill," tie up with each other much in the same way as the syllables of a polysyllabic word are related. In fact, we can say one speaks a speech phrase just as he would pronounce a many-syllabled word, such as *unconstitutional*. Finally, it is a unit in that it has a beginning, a middle, and an end. Almost always it has a key word or combination of words which form the backbone of the phrase. The reader, both in voice and bodily movement, leads up to this key word, emphasizes it, and returns from it.

Phrasing in Oral Reading. Once a reader gets a command of phrasing, most of the battle for good reading is won. He will be reading ideas and images rather than words. His voice will have the spontaneous character of conversation, because he is really thinking and responding to the content of his phrase units. He must always remember to look ahead, grasp the meaning of the phrase he is to read, and speak that phrase, with the aim of stirring up the same meaning in his audience.

Emphasis. It would seem that if one had caught the meaning of a phrase he would give the proper emphasis to the words. But this does not always follow, since we are inclined, at least in reading aloud, unconsciously to give less emphasis to important words when we, the readers, are no longer reading the material for the first time. In other words, because the content is no longer fresh to us, the kind of emphasis which comes with the spontaneous realization of ideas and feelings is lost.

Three Kinds of Emphasis. The voice should give prominence, usually through raising the pitch of the voice, to that which is new or which advances the thought of the material; to that which involves contrast or comparison; and to that which is given emotional intensification because of its importance. The first two in the above have to do with new ideas; the third, intensifying emphasis, has to do with old ideas. Terms used to designate these three kinds of emphasis are (in the order given above): *Assertive*, *Antithetic*, and *Intensive*. In the sentence which follows, those words which require *assertive* emphasis will be italicized; those requiring ANTITHETIC will appear in lightface caps; and those requiring **intensive** will be in boldface:

There abides *faith*, *hope*, and *charity*, **these three;** but the *greatest* of these is CHARITY.

"Faith, hope, and charity" are *new* ideas; that is, it is the first time they have been spoken of by the reader, and consequently they get the downward stroke in the pitch of the voice that goes with *Assertive* emphasis. "These three" involves the giving of emotional significance to something already taken up and is consequently given *Intensive* emphasis. In the word "greatest" the thought is advanced with a new *assertion* and that kind of emphasis is given the word. When "charity" is repeated at the end of the sentence it is used in a comparative sense and consequently receives *Antithetic* emphasis. We have already pointed out that the voice takes a downward stroke in pitch for assertive emphasis. For antithetic emphasis it does likewise, but before starting down it takes a slight upward turn giving the voice what is called a *circumflex* inflection. For intensive emphasis the voice remains on a high level of pitch until the whole idea has been intensified. Thus, in "these three" the voice remains on the same high pitch for both words.

In applying these principles of emphasis the important thing to remember is that the reader must be constantly on the alert so that he distinguishes between that which is *new* or *important* and that which is *old*. On the new and important ideas his voice jumps to a high level and descends with a quick stroke; on that which is old, his voice remains on the neutral, "taken-for-granted" level. We mention again here that "new" and "old" are always used in terms of the audience. Good oral reading involves the constant fluctuation of the voice between the level of stress and the level of words which have been referred to before. If the reader effectively applies the two techniques taken up in the foregoing paragraphs, namely, *phrasing* and *emphasis*, he will have the necessary oral reading fundamentals for performing in the specialized forms to be taken up below.

Interpretative Reading. In the reading of literature from the printed page for the benefit of a listening audience, the reader acts as a mediator between his material and his audience. His aim is to recreate the material in the minds and imaginations of his listeners. Therefore, it is important that he subordinate himself as a personality and a performer to that end. If he calls too much attention to himself by displaying his elocutionary facility or by literally acting out the happenings of his material, his listeners will be distracted from their imaginative activity and pay attention to what is happening on the platform. If he concentrates on stirring up the imaginations of his listeners through the use of *suggestion* (as opposed to the literal portrayal of acting) he will be properly carrying out his function as an Interpretative Reader.

The following points should be kept in mind as important in the technique of Interpretative Reading:

1. The reader's relationship to the audience is a *mediate* one.

2. The reader's activities are on a *suggestive* basis, as opposed to the *literal*.

3. Because it is the literature being read which is the audience's chief concern, the manuscript or book *must* be used. It is best to have the book on a reading-stand, thus freeing the reader for suggestive activity.

4. What the reader does with his voice and body must always be *spontaneous* or *extemporaneous* in character. Conscious control of the voice and body to the extent that we in the audience listen to the reader's interesting inflections and notice his graceful gestures interferes with imaginative activity in the audience.

Interpretative Reading Today. This form of oral reading was developed at the end of the last century as a reaction to the elocutionary display of the *recitation* vogue, which had swept the country. It is a form of speech activity, which when understood and not confused with recitation or acting, has a real place in our everyday life. We can use it in our clubs and in church meetings and in library reading-hours. It is particularly adaptable to the reading of plays and novels.

Recitation. While it is true that Recitation easily turns into a display of the performer's elocutionary virtuosity, it need not be so, if the reciter appreciates the true character of the form. When one recites he is doing much the same thing as when one sings a song. The beauty and story of a poem is being conveyed to an audience through the reciter's body and personality. The more interesting the personality of the reciter, the more interesting will be the performance as a whole. As William Butler Yeats has said, the reciter is "an interesting and exciting messenger." It can be seen that the reciter's rôle is somewhat different from that of the interpretative reader's. Whatever the reciter can do to make more interesting what he has to report, he is at liberty to do. But he must make sure that what he does always pertains to what he is reporting. It was when the old "elocutionists" indulged in exaggerated graceful movements and poses and when they overused their vocal variations that the message was lost in the process.

Characteristics of Recitation.

1. The material is *memorized.*

2. Poetry of a musical nature and ballads are especially suited to recitation.

3. *Literal elements* are not out of place. What the performer does is not subordinated to the material as it is in Interpretative Reading.

4. *Formalized elements* in delivery are permissible. The reciter may consciously attend to the musical patterns of his material. He may also take on the formal movements of stylized behavior, when the material permits of it.

5. The reciter's relationship to his audience is *direct.* There may be an element of *display* in the relationship.

Choral Speaking as a Kind of Recitation. The speaking of a piece of literature by a group is a popular activity in our schools today. Usually the material used is strongly musical in character. The director of the choral speaking choir strives for a clear-cut unison in the voices and for interesting variations in the use of the bass and alto voices in the group. There are several good books to be found now which explain the technique of speech choir directing and which give suggested methods for handling poetry on a choir basis.

Impersonation. This form of speaking is closely related to *acting.* When a performer takes a dramatic monologue, such as Browning's *My Last Dutchess,* memorizes it, and acts out the character of the duke in that famous piece of literature, he is *impersonating.* Monologues, long speeches from plays, and short scenes from plays having few characters are best suited to impersonation.

Characteristics of Impersonation.

1. The material is *memorized.*

2. *Literal elements* predominate over *suggested elements.* What the audience sees before them is of primary importance; their own imaginative activity is subordinated.

3. The performer's personality is *submerged* in the character he is portraying. In Recitation the performer's personality is very much in evidence.

4. Impersonation differs from *acting* in that costumes, scenery, and make-up are seldom used and the activity on the platform is usually limited to an area about four feet in diameter.

5. The impersonator tries to create an *illusion.* Through literal activity and through suggestion he tries to give the audience a picture of life, sometimes realistic, sometimes idealized.

Story Telling. This form of oral interpretation is closest to public speaking in its character. In preparing to tell a story the performer should go about it much in the same way as he would prepare an extemporaneous speech. He should read the story carefully and set the gist of it down in outline form. Then he should rehearse the telling of the story just as he would rehearse an extemporaneous speech. In telling the story to his audience he should have the same spontaneous quality which is so desirable in speech-making.

Characteristics of Story Telling.

1. The story is *not memorized.* Only those parts of the story which the public have come to know and expect to hear should be spoken from memory. The dialogue in the story of *The Three Bears* would be well given as it is found on the printed page.

2. Story telling is *not reciting.* The story teller is conversing *with* an audience rather than performing *for* it. His relationship to his audience is that of social intercourse.

3. The *literal* and the *suggested* go hand in hand in this form. At times the speaker may appeal to the imaginations of his listeners and at times he may act out his characters quite completely.

4. The story teller's personality should play the same part it does in public speaking. It should enhance what he has to say.

DELIVERY

The following words of Quintilian, the famous Roman orator and teacher of rhetoric, contain advice for the speaker which is as appropriate now as when they were written:

"In all kinds of public speaking, but especially in popular assemblies, it is a capital rule to attend to all the decorum of time, place, and character. No warmth of eloquence can atone for the neglect of this. That vehemence which is becoming in a person of character and authority may be unsuitable to the modesty expected from a young speaker. That sportive and witty manner which may suit one assembly is altogether out of place in a grave cause and solemn meeting. No one should ever rise to speak in public without forming to himself a just and strict idea of what suits his own age and character; what suits the subject, the hearers, the place, the occasion; and adjusting the whole train and manner of his speaking to this idea."

There are, in general, four methods of delivering speeches. Each has its especial strength and its peculiar weakness. It is important that a speaker should adopt for his main dependence the method to which his abilities are best suited.

Speaking from Manuscript. The use of a carefully prepared manuscript is the most certain method of delivering a speaker's thought completely, logically, and economically. It is especially appropriate for formal occasions, such as lectures, when the speaker's chief purpose is to convey information to his hearers. The weakness of this method lies in the tendency of the speaker to keep his eyes too closely riveted to his manuscript and thus lose the attention of his audience. The speaker who uses manuscript usually sacrifices some of the directness of address which is so important a quality of oratory. For the speaker of small experience, however, the use of manuscript during delivery is to be recommended.

Speaking from Notes. The speaker who uses notes, that is, an outline of the previously prepared manuscript, has the advantage of possessing a ready guide through his argument, while at the same time he is freer to meet unexpected situations than is the man who must follow a complete manuscript. This is a weighty consideration in discussion or debate. All notes, however, should be clearly written, so that the speaker's eyes will not be taken from his audience for too long a time, while he attempts to decipher his outline.

Speaking from Memory. The memorized speech has the distinct advantage of permitting the speaker to look constantly at his audience. It does not, however, allow him to adapt himself readily to unforeseen circumstances, such as disturbances in an assembly or the necessity of answering unexpected arguments in debate. It is appropriate to formal occasions; for it permits the attainment of highly finished style both in composition and in delivery. The chief weakness of the method is that his effort to recall the memorized words may rob the speaker of directness and spontaneity. The ideal in the use of the memorized speech is to combine finished perfection of form with the appearance of that naturalness which marks the extemporaneous address.

Speaking Extemporaneously. Undoubtedly, the most effective form of public speaking is the extemporaneous address. This is to be defined as the presentation of thoroughly prepared thought in language which is the product of the occasion. As extemporaneous speaking is the most effective type of oratory, so it demands the most exacting and long-continued preparation and practice. However, the reward of the master of extemporaneous oratory is the consciousness of the most thorough command over his audiences. Extemporaneous speaking does not preclude the use of notes, and, for the short, informal address, the preparation of notes, outlining the thought to be clothed in extemporaneous language, is usually advisable.

Whichever of these general methods of speaking you choose to employ, you must observe certain well established principles pertaining to manner and to voice. The total effect of a speech is compounded of the words, the bodily attitudes, and the voice of the speaker. He must know how to adapt these elements to each other and to the spirit of his audience. It has well been said that the best oratorical style for a given individual is that of his best conversation.

The attainment of an effective manner before an audience is worthy of long and careful effort. Each speaker must study his own problems. However, there are two means which you will find to be fundamental:

1. Know your subject and your plan so well that you show *confidence* (a) by looking at your audience—letting them see your eyes, (b) by speaking directly to your audience—letting them see your lips move. The audience is entitled to this directness of address.

2. Be so thoroughly interested in your talk that you show ease (a) by standing so firmly *on both feet* that you can change your position without "teetering," (b) by such gestures with arms or body as are prompted by your thought and feeling *at the time,* (c) by directing your eyes and your voice at some time to every one in your audience, (d) by deep, steady breathing.

Gesture. The name for the bodily attitudes and movements and facial expressions by which a speaker supplements and emphasizes his words. Every speaker will use gesture in some way, because bodily movements are a fundamental mode of expressing ideas and feelings; and the more earnest and emphatic the speaker is, the more frequent and vigorous will be his gestures. Two rules you may well observe: (1) Do not try to repress all gesture. (2) Strive to make every gesture mean something definite. Superfluous gestures take the attention of your audience from what you are saying. Notice the gestures that you make spontaneously in conversation. Try to employ these and adapt them to the "enlarged conversation" of your public speech. We usually think of gestures as movements of the arms and hands. But remember that you can make many of your most effective gestures with your facial muscles, your head, or your whole body. This caution will help you to avoid the windmill method of gesture, or merely throwing your arms about. In gesture, as in every other phase of speaking, sincerity of thought and purpose is the best guard against meaningless expression.

Enunciation. For *good speech,* in uttering your own thoughts or reading orally the words of another, the first essential is this: *Carefully think* your words and phrases. Your voice will respond with wonderful accuracy to your understanding of the words you use. The second essential is this: Pronounce your words *distinctly and correctly.* This includes the true forming and arrangement of the sounds, faultless accent, and clear quality of voice. The list of words in the section entitled Correct Pronunciation will give you the precise sounds and accents for many words commonly used. For other words, consult unabridged dictionaries. Further, learn how to form these sounds exactly.

Voice Qualities. Pleasing and effective speech is very largely a result of the speaker's mastery of good voice qualities, the fundamental principle of which is proper breathing. Individual voices differ in quality because of the varied forms and conditions of the vocal cords and the resonance chambers of the mouth and nose. Each person has a normal quality of voice, which he uses in conversation, and by which it is possible to recognize him even when his features cannot be seen. But, by altering the shape of the mouth cavity or by opening or restricting the nasal and throat passages, each individual can produce several other qualities besides this normal one.

Eight qualities of the speaking voice are usually distinguished. Three of these the public speaker should cultivate: (1) *Normal,* which is a clear, resonant quality produced by the natural position of the vocal organs and the simple enunciation of vowels and consonants, the ordinary conversational voice. (2) *Orotund,* a fuller, clearer, and more resonant quality. It is appropriately used to express grandeur, sublimity, and similar thoughts and ideas of a lofty and impressive nature. The speaker should be careful not to use this quality too frequently, as it may easily pass into bombast and become unconvincing. (3) *Aspirate,* which is a breathy utterance either devoid of vocalization, as in a whisper, or partially vocalized, as in the so-called "stage whisper." The quality may suggest weakness or excessive emotion. It is sometimes used effectively in public speaking to give striking emphasis to an expression.

The remaining five qualities are generally undesirable and to be avoided in public speaking. They are confined to the art of the actor in portraying characters or in suggesting emotions with which they are associated. (4) *Guttural,* a throaty sound. (5) *Pectoral,* a hollow, breathy quality. (6) *Oral,* the result of a rather thin, mouth resonance. (7) *Nasal,* a quality characterized by a harsh twang. (8) *Falsetto,* a quality of tone above the speaker's natural range.

Cautions.—Three very common faults of American speech are *high pitch, nasality,* and *throatiness.* Too high a pitch of voice is due to nervousness and to lack of self-control. Nasality is not talking through the nose but failure to use the nasal cavity properly in speaking. It is frequently due to some obstruction of the nasal passages. Throatiness, or making sounds too low down in the throat, is usually caused by contraction of throat muscles.

Inflection. What punctuation is to written language, *inflection, change of pitch,* and *pauses* are to spoken language. The importance of changes of pitch in indicating emphasis was discussed under *emphasis* in the section on Oral Reading.

Change of Pitch. By pronouncing one of the words in a sentence with a decidedly high or low pitch as compared with the pitch of the others, you can give several additional meanings to the sentence. For instance: If *you* is given a higher pitch than *are going,* the sentence means that you are going and not some one else; pronouncing *are* with a higher pitch than *you* and *going* may indicate either surprise or decided determination. This abrupt shifting of the key, or tone, of speech *between* words, phrases, clauses, or sentences is called *change of pitch.*

Practice will show you the importance of this means of emphasis. It is, in fact, the natural method of marking off one idea from another in speech. If you think clearly, you can hardly keep such changes out of your voice.

Pauses. Plan your pauses as carefully as you arrange your words. Silences are the wells of thought. Definite pauses serve at least four main purposes: (1) They give your audience time to grasp important ideas. (2) They enable your audience to make the necessary transition from one thought to another and so to "follow" you. (3) They convey the impression that you are choosing your words carefully. (4) They impress your audience with a sense of your consideration for them. Thus, directly and indirectly, pauses serve to give emphasis to your speech.

Rate of Speaking. Just as the natural qualities of voice vary among individuals, so too their natural rates of speaking differ. Some people are naturally quick and nervous; others are slow and phlegmatic. It should be remembered, however, that the brain of the listener is capable of receiving and registering only a limited number of words in any given unit of time, and that a speaker should adjust his rate to the ability of the audience to take in what he says. Generally, it is unwise to exceed 125 words a minute in ordinary speaking. On the other hand, it is tiresome to listen to slow, drawling delivery. Hence, rate should be adapted (1) to the capability of the audience to grasp the speaker's meaning, as well as (2) to the nature of what is spoken.

It is important that, in the course of any speech or address, one should, from time to time, alter his rate of speaking. Change of rate (1) relieves monotony, (2) helps in emphasis, (3) suggests certain emotions or movements.

That which will quicken or retard a man's footsteps will also quicken or retard his rate of speaking. Narration, for example, is flowing, easy, and graceful; vehemence is firm and accelerated; anger and joy are sudden, sometimes hysterical. Again, dignity, authority, sublimity, and awe assume deeper tones and a slower movement. One may often hear a good speaker, at some sudden turn of thought or feeling, check himself in the full tide of utterance and give indescribable power to a passage by slackening his rate and by adopting a slow, deliberate enunciation.

Breathing. Breathe deeply and steadily, using the diaphragm and chest walls. Learn to feel your diaphragm, which is the flexible floor of your chest, expanding and moving downward as you "take in" breath. You can then control and steady its movement, keeping it expanded, and give *carrying power* to your voice. Practice this breathing. It will help you to avoid "stage fright." Take a "deep breath" before you begin to speak.

Correct Speech Sounds. These are secured by right breathing, proper shaping of the mouth, and correct placing of the various sounds. The voice is produced by vibrations, or waves, set up by the vocal cords in the column of air reaching from the lungs up into the mouth and the nose. The different shapes that the mouth cavity may take give special forms to these waves. The forms, thus produced, give rise to the *vowels,* or open voice sounds. Each vowel sound is made with the jaws and the flexible palate, lips, tongue, and cheeks in a definite position.

The cavities of the throat, nose, and mouth act as a *resonance chamber,* like an organ pipe or the body of a violin, to give volume and tone to the voice. Any obstruction, such as the mucus from a "cold," enlarged tonsils, or adenoids, interferes with the volume of the voice as well as with the purity and the clearness of its tone.

The *consonant sounds* we form by partially or entirely closing the mouth cavity with the teeth or tongue or lips. We thus, to some extent, shut off the vowel sound; at the same time, the friction or explosive force of the moving breath makes sounds which join or articulate with the vowels to form syllables.

CORRECT PRONUNCIATION

For key to pronunciation, see page 19.

Correct spelling is the outward mark of education in attention and accuracy. But English spelling is not phonetic—the same letters do not always represent the same sounds. Consequently, we fall easily into habits of incorrect pronunciation. The price of correctness is constant reference to correct standards.

In a living language, spoken by so many people and in so many different parts of the world, some variety in the pronunciation of many common words may be expected. For not a few words, various dictionaries give three or four pronunciations, all of which are current in the English-speaking world. The pronunciations here given are those most commonly approved by standard authorities. Where two pronunciations are given, the first is a preferred pronunciation, the second is widely and correctly used.

In the following list will be found more than 1600 words concerning which many questions in regard to pronunciation frequently arise.

abbé, *ȧ'bā'; ăb'ā*
abdomen, *ăb-dō'mĕn*
abhor, *ăb-hôr'*
abhorrent, *ăb-hôr'ĕnt*
abject, *ăb'jĕkt*
abjection, *ăb-jĕk'shŭn*
absent (adj.), *ăb'sĕnt*
absent (v.), *ăb-sĕnt'*
abstemious, *ăb-stē'mĭ-ŭs*
accent (n.), *ăk'sĕnt*
accent (v.), *ăk-sĕnt'; ăk'sĕnt*
accessory, *ăk-sĕs'ô-rĭ*
acclimate, *ă-klī'măt; ăk'lĭ-māt*
accompaniment, *ă-kŭm'pȧ-nĭ-mĕnt*
accuracy, *ăk'ū-rȧ-sĭ*
acetylene, *ă-sĕt'ĭ-lēn*
acorn, *ā'kôrn; ā'kẽrn*
acoustic, *ȧ-ko͞os'tĭk; ȧ-kous'-*
actor, *ăk'tẽr*
acts, *ăkts*
acumen, *ă-kū'mĕn*
adagio, *ȧ-dä'jō*
address, *ă-drĕs'*
adieu, *ȧ-dū'*
adios, *ä'dyōs'*
adjourn, *ă-jûrn'*
adobe, *ȧ-dō'bĭ*
adult, *ȧ-dŭlt'*
adventure, *ăd-vĕn'chŭr; -tûr*
adverse, *ăd-vûrs'*
advertisement, *ăd-vẽr'tĭz-mĕnt*
advertiser, *ăd'vẽr-tīz'ẽr*
aeroplane, *ā'ẽr-ô-plān'; âr'ô-*
a fortiori, *ā fōr'shĭ-ō'rī*
aft, *ȧft*
after, *ȧf'tẽr*
again, *ȧ-gĕn'*
agile, *ăj'ĭl; īl*
alas, *ȧ-lȧs'*
alder, *ôl'dẽr*
algebra, *ăl'jē-brȧ*
alias, *ā'lĭ-ăs*
alien, *āl'yĕn; ā'lĭ-ĕn*
allegro, *äl-lā'grō*
allies, *ă-līz'; ăl'īz*
allopathist, *ă-lŏp'ȧ-thĭst*
alloy, *ă-loi'*
alma mater, *ăl'mȧ mā'tẽr*
almond, *ä'mŭnd; ăm'ŭnd*
alpaca, *ăl-păk'ȧ*
alpine, *ăl'pīn; -pĭn*
alterative, *ôl'tẽr-ā'tĭv*
alternate (v.), *ôl'tẽr-nāt; ăl*
alternate (adj.), *ôl-tẽr'nĭt; ôl'*
alternate (n.), *ôl-tẽr'nĭt; ôl'*
alternately, *ôl-tẽr'nĭt-lĭ*
aluminum, *ȧ-lū'mĭ-nŭm*
alumnæ, *ȧ-lŭm'nē*
alumni, *ȧ-lŭm'nī*
amateur, *ăm'ȧ-tûr'; ăm'-*
ambrosia, *ăm-brō'zhĭ-ȧ; -zĭ-ȧ*
ameliorate, *ȧ-mēl'yô-rāt*
amenable, *ȧ-mē'nȧ-b'l*
amenity, *ȧ-mĕn'ĭ-tĭ*
ammonia, *ă-mō'nĭ-ȧ*
amortization, *ȧ-môr'tĭ-zā'shŭn*
amortize, *ȧ-môr'tīz*
ampere, *ăm'pēr; ăm-pâr'*
anarchist, *ăn'ȧr-kĭst*
ancestor, *ăn'sĕs-tẽr*
ancestral, *ăn-sĕs'trăl*
anchor, *ăng'kẽr*
ancient, *ān'shĕnt*
and, *ănd*
anemone, *ȧ-nĕm'ô-nē*
aniline, *ăn'ĭ-lĭn*
annihilate, *ă-nī'ĭ-lāt; hĭ-lāt*
answer, *ȧn'sẽr*
antarctic, *ănt-ärk'tĭk*
anxiety, *ăng-zī'ĕ-tĭ*
anxious, *ăngk'shŭs*
aperient, *ȧ-pē'rĭ-ĕnt*
aperture, *ăp'ẽr-chûr; -tūr*
aphelion, *ă-fē'lĭ-ŏn; fēl'yŏn*
apostle, *ȧ-pŏs''l*
apotheosis, *ăp'ô-thē'ô-sĭs; ȧ-pŏth'ē-ō'sĭs*
apparatus, *ăp'ȧ-rā'tŭs*
appellate, *ă-pĕl'ăt*
appendicitis, *ă-pĕn'dĭ-sī'tĭs*
applicable, *ăp'lĭ-kȧ-b'l*
appreciation, *ă-prē'shĭ-ā'shŭn*
apricot, *ā'prĭ-kŏt; ăp'rĭ-kŏt*
apron, *ā'prŭn; ā'pûrn*
apropos, *ăp'rô-pō'*
aqua, *ā'kwȧ; ăk' wȧ*
aquarium, *ȧ-kwâr'ĭ-ŭm*
aqueduct, *ăk'wē-dŭkt*
archangel, *ärk'ān'jĕl*
archbishop, *ärch'bĭsh'ŭp*
archipelago, *är'kĭ-pĕl'ȧ-gō*
architect, *är'kĭ-tĕkt*
archives, *är'kīvz*
arctic, *ärk'tĭk*
area, *ā'rē-ȧ; âr'ē-ȧ*
aria, *ä'rē-ȧ; âr'ĭ-ȧ*
arid, *ăr'ĭd*
armada, *är-mā'dȧ; mä'dȧ*
armistice, *är'mĭ-stĭs*
aroma, *ȧ-rō'mȧ*
arras, *ăr'ăs*
arroyo, *ă-roi'ō*
artisan, *är'tĭ-zăn*
asafetida, *ăs'ȧ-fĕt'ĭ-dȧ*
ascetic, *ă-sĕt'ĭk*
ask, *ȧsk*
askance, *ȧ-skăns'*
asphalt, *ăs'fôlt; -fălt*
aspirant, *ăs-pīr'ănt*
assay, *ă-sā'*
associate (v.), *ă-sō'shĭ-āt*
associate (n.), *-ăt*
associate (adj.), *-ăt*
association, *ă-sō'sĭ-ā'shŭn; -shĭ-ā'shŭn*
assume, *ă-sūm'*
asthma, *ăz'mȧ; ăs'mȧ*
atheneum, *ăth'ē-nē'ŭm*
athletics, *ăth-lĕt'ĭks*
attaché, *ȧ'tȧ'shā'*
attorney, *ă-tûr'nĭ*
audacious, *ô-dā'shŭs*
audience, *ô'dĭ-ĕns*
au gratin, *ō'grȧ'tăɴ'*
aunt, *änt*
au revoir, *ō'rē-vwär'*
aurora borealis, *ô-rō'rȧ bō'rē-ā'lĭs*
authority, *ô-thŏr'ĭ-tĭ*
automobile, *ô'tô-mô-bēl'; mō'bĭl*
auxiliary, *ôg-zĭl'yȧ-rĭ*
avenue, *ăv'ē-nū*
aviator, *ā'vĭ-ā'tẽr*
avoirdupois, *ăv'ẽr-dŭ-poiz'*
axiom, *ăk'sĭ-ŭm*
aye, (yes) *ī*

bacchant, *băk'ănt*
bacilli, *bȧ-sĭl'ī*
bacillus, *bȧ-sĭl'ŭs*
bade, *băd*
badinage, *băd'ĭ-näzh'; băd'ĭ-näzh*
balcony, *băl'kô-nĭ*
ballad, *băl'ăd*
ballade, *bȧ-lȧd'*
ballet, *băl'ā; bă-lā'*
balm, *bäm*
banquet, *băng'kwĕt; -kwĭt*
baptism, *băp'tĭz'm*
baptize, *băp-tīz'*
bargain, *bär'gĭn*
barrage, *bȧ-räzh'; băr'äzh*
barrel, *băr'ĕl*
basin, *bā's'n*
basket, *bȧs'kĕt; bȧs'kĭt*
bath, *bȧth*
baton, *bȧ'tôɴ'; băt'ŭn*
bayou, *bī'o͞o*
because, *bē-kôz'*
bedstead, *bĕd'stĕd*
been, *bĭn; bēn*
begonia, *bē-gō'nĭ-ȧ*
believe, *bē-lēv'*
belles-lettres, *bĕl'lĕt'r'*
belligerent, *bĕ-lĭj'ẽr-ĕnt*
bellows, *bĕl'ōz; -ŭs*
beloved (adj.), *bē-lŭv'ĕd; bē-lŭvd'*
beloved (part.), *bē-lŭvd'*
beneficent, *bē-nĕf'ĭ-sĕnt*
bequeath, *bē-kwēᴛʜ'*
bestial, *bĕs'chăl; bĕst'yăl*
betrothal, *bē-trŏth'ăl; -trōᴛʜ'ăl*
bicycle, *bī'sĭ-k'l*
biennial, *bī-ĕn'ĭ-ăl*
bijou, *bē'zho͞o; bē'zho͞o'*
billet-doux, *bĭl'ā-do͞o'*
bindery, *bīn'dẽr-ĭ*
biography, *bī-ŏg'rȧ-fĭ*
biology, *bī-ŏl'ô-jĭ*
biparous, *bĭp'ȧ-rŭs*
bipartite, *bī-pär'tīt*
bismuth, *bĭz'mŭth; bĭs'mŭth*
blackguard, *blăg'ärd*
blanch, *blȧnch*
blanc mange, *blȧ-mänzh'*
blasé, *blȧ'zā'*
blaspheme, *blȧs-fēm'*
blasphemous, *blȧs'fē-mŭs*
blast, *blȧst*
blessed (adj.), *blĕs'ĕd*
blessed (part.), *blĕst; blĕs'ĕd*
blouse, *blouz*
blue, *blo͞o*
bodega, *bô-dē'gȧ*
boisterous, *bois'tẽr-ŭs*
bolero, *bô-lâr'ō*
boll weevil, *bōl wē'v'l*
bomb, *bŏm*

bona fide, *bō'nȧ fī'dḗ*
bon marché, *bôN'mär'shā'*
bonnet, *bŏn'ĕt; -ĭt*
borax, *bō'răks*
borrow, *bŏr'ō*
bosom, *bo͝oz'ŭm*
boudoir, *bo͞o' dwär'*
bouquet, *bo͞o-kā'*
bourn, (bound), *bōrn; bo͞orn*
bourn (brook), *bōrn; bôrn*
bourse, *bo͞ors*
bovine, *bō'vīn; -vĭn*
bow-legged, *bō'lĕg'ĕd; bō'lĕgd'*
brand-new, *brănd'nū'*
brassière, *brȧs'ĭ-âr; brȧ-zēr'*
breviary, *brē'vĭ-ā-rĭ*
brigand, *brĭg'ănd*
bristle, *brĭs''l*
brochure, *brō-shūr'*
brogan, *brō'găn*
bromide, *brō'mīd*
bromine, *brō'mĭn; -mēn*
bronchitis, *brŏn-kī'tĭs; brŏng-*
brusque (brusk), *brŭsk; bro͞osk*
bungalow, *bŭng'gȧ-lō*
buoy, *boi; bo͞o'ĭ*
bureaucracy, *bū-rŏk'rȧ-sĭ; bū-rō'krȧ-sĭ*
burlesque, *bûr-lĕsk'*
bursar, *bûr'sẽr*
business, *bĭz'nĕs*
butcher, *bo͝och'ẽr*

cabal, *kȧ-băl'*
caballero, *kä'bäl-yā'rō*
cabaret, *kăb'ȧ-rĕt; kăb'ȧ-rā'*
cache, *kȧsh*
cadaver, *kȧ-dā'vẽr*
café, *kȧ'fā'*
cafeteria, *kăf'ē-tēr'ĭ-ȧ*
calf, *kăf; kȧf*
caliph, *kā'lĭf; kăl'ĭf*
caliphate, *kăl'ĭ-fāt*
calk, *kôk*
calliope, *kă-lī'ō-pē*
calm, *käm*
caloric, *kȧ-lŏr'ĭk*
calorie, *kăl'ō-rĭ*
calve, *käv; kȧv*
calyx, *kā'lĭks; kăl'ĭks*
camembert, *kăm'ĕm-bâr'*
campanile, *kăm'pä-nē'lā; kăm'pȧ-nē'lē*
cancel, *kăn'sĕl*
candelabra, *kăn'dē-lā'brȧ*
canine, *kȧ-nīn'; kā'nīn*
cañon, *kăn'yŭn*
cant, *kănt*
can't, *känt; kȧnt*
cantilever, *kăn'tĭ-lē'vẽr; kăn'tĭ-lĕv'ẽr*
cantonment, *kăn-tŏn'mĕnt; kăn'tŏn-mĕnt*
capitulate, *kȧ-pĭch'ū-lāt; kȧ-pĭt'yū-lāt*
capon, *kā'pŏn*
caprice, *kȧ-prēs'*
carafe, *kȧ-răf'*
carburetor, *kär'bū-rĕt'ẽr*
caricature, *kăr'ĭ-kȧ-chūr*
carillon, *kăr'ĭ-lŏn*
cartridge, *kär'trĭj*
cashmere, *kăsh'mēr; kăsh'mēr'*
casino, *kȧ-sē'nō*
caste, *kȧst*
catalogue, *kăt'ȧ-lŏg*
catalpa, *kȧ-tăl'pȧ*
catch, *kăch*
catchup, *kăch'ŭp*
catechize, *kăt'ē-kīz*
catsup, *kăt'sŭp*
caveat, *kā'vē-ăt*

celestial, *sē-lĕs'chăl*
cello, *chĕl'ō*
celluloid, *sĕl'ū-loid*
cemetery, *sĕm'ē-tĕr-ĭ*
centenary, *sĕn'tē-nĕr'ĭ*
centennial, *sĕn-tĕn'ĭ-ăl*
centime, *sän'tēm; säN'tēm'*
century, *sĕn'chū-rĭ; sĕn'tū-rĭ*
ceramic, *sē-răm'ĭk*
cerebrum, *sĕr'ē-brŭm*
chagrin, *shȧ-grĭn'*
challis, *shăl'ĭ; chăl'ĭs*
chamois, *shăm'ĭ*
champagne, *shăm-pān'*
chaos, *kā'ŏs*
chaperon, *shăp'ẽr-ōn; -ŏn*
character, *kăr'ăk-tẽr*
chargé d'affaires, *shär'zhā' dȧ'fâr'*
chassis, *shă'sĭ*
chasten, *chās''n*
chastise, *chăs-tīz'*
chastisement, *chăs'tĭz-mĕnt*
chatelaine, *shăt'ē-lān*
chauffeur, *shō'fûr'; shō'fẽr*
chef, *shĕf*
chemise, *shē-mēz'*
chemisette, *shĕm'ĭ-zĕt'*
chenille, *shē-nēl'*
chestnut, *chĕs'nŭt*
cheviot, *shĕv'ĭ-ŭt; chĕv'ĭ-ŭt*
chew, *cho͞o*
chic, *shēk*
chicane, *shĭ-kān'*
chicken, *chĭk'ĕn; -ĭn*
chiffon, *shĭf'ŏn; shĭ-fŏn'*
chiffonier, *shĭf'ō-nēr'*
children, *chĭl'drĕn*
chimera, *kĭ-mē'rȧ; kī-*
chirography, *kī-rŏg'rȧ-fĭ*
chiropodist, *kī-rŏp'ō-dĭst*
chisel, *chĭz''l*
chocolate, *chŏk'ō-lĭt*
choleric, *kŏl'ẽr-ĭk*
chorister, *kŏr'ĭs-tẽr*
chorus, *kō'rŭs*
christen, *krĭs''n*
chyle, *kīl*
chyme, *kīm*
cinchona, *sĭn-kō'nȧ*
cinematograph, *sĭn'ē-măt'ō-grăf*
circuit, *sẽr'kĭt*
circuitous, *sẽr-kū'ĭ-tŭs*
citadel, *sĭt'ȧ-dĕl*
civil, *sĭv'ĭl*
civilization, *sĭv'ĭ-lĭ-zā'shŭn*
clairvoyant, *klâr-voi'ănt*
clandestine, *klăn-dĕs'tĭn*
clapboard, *klăp'bōrd*
clasp, *klȧsp*
class, *klȧs*
cleanly (adj.), *klĕn'lĭ*
cleanly (adv.), *klēn'lĭ*
clematis, *klĕm'ȧ-tĭs*
clew, *klo͞o*
clientele, *klī'ĕn-tĕl'; -tĕl'*
clique, *klēk*
clothes, *klōTHz*
coagulate, *kō-ăg'ū-lāt*
cocaine, *kō'kȧ-ĭn; kō-kān'*
coccyx, *kŏk'sĭks*
codeine, *kō'dē-ēn; -ĭn*
coffee, *kŏf'ĭ*
cognac, *kō'nyăk*
cognizance, *kŏg'nĭ-zăns; kŏn'ĭ- (legal)*
cognomen, *kŏg-nō'mĕn*
coiffure, *kwä-fūr; koif'ūr*
colander, *kŭl'ăn-dẽr*
collation, *kŏ-lā'shŭn*
collect (n.), *kŏl'ĕkt*
collect (v.), *kŏ-lĕkt'*
colloquial, *kŏ-lō'kwĭ-ăl*

colosseum, *kŏl'ŏ-sē'ŭm*
colporteur, *kŏl'pōr'tẽr*
column, *kŏl'ŭm*
combatant, *kŏm'bȧ-tănt*
combine (v.), *kŏm-bīn'*
combine (n.), *kŏm'bīn; kŏm-bīn'*
comeliness, *kŭm'lĭ-nĕs*
comely, *kŭm'lĭ*
comity, *kŏm'ĭ-tĭ*
commiserate, *kŏ-mĭz'ẽr-āt*
communal, *kŏm'ū-năl; kŏ-mū'năl*
commune (v.), *kŏ-mūn'*
commune (n.), *kŏm'ūn*
comparable, *kŏm'pȧ-rȧ-b'l*
complex (n.), *kŏm'plĕks*
complex (adj.), *kŏm-plĕks'; kŏm'plĕks*
comport, *kŏm-pōrt'*
compromise, *kŏm'prō-mīz*
comptroller, *kŏn-trōl'ẽr*
concave, *kŏn'kāv*
concerto, *kôn-chĕr'tō; kŏn-sẽr'-*
conclude, *kŏn-klo͞od'*
conclusive, *kŏn-klo͞o'sĭv*
concourse, *kŏn'kōrs; kŏng'-*
concrete (n. and adj.), *kŏn'krēt; kŏn-krēt'*
concrete (v.), *kŏn-krēt'*
condolence, *kŏn-dō'lĕns*
conduit, *kŏn'dĭt*
confidant, *kŏn'fĭ-dănt'; kŏn'fĭ-dănt'*
confiscate, *kŏn'fĭs-kāt; -fĭs'-*
congé, *kôN'zhā'; kŏn'jē*
congenial, *kŏn-jēn'yăl*
congeries, *kŏn-jē'rĭ-ēz*
congregate, *kŏng'grē-gāt*
congress, *kŏng'grĕs*
congruous, *kŏng'gro͞o-ŭs*
conjure (implore), *kŏn-jo͞or'*
conjure (enchant), *kŭn'jẽr*
connoisseur, *kŏn'ĭ-sûr'; -sūr'*
conquest, *kŏng'kwĕst*
conscientious, *kŏn'shĭ-ĕn'shŭs*
considerable, *kŏn-sĭd'ẽr-ȧ-b'l*
consignee, *kŏn'sī-nē'; -sĭ-nē'*
conspiracy, *kŏn-spĭr'ȧ-sĭ*
constable, *kŭn'stȧ-b'l; kŏn'-*
consul, *kŏn'sŭl*
contemplate, *kŏn'tĕm-plāt; -tĕm'-*
contemplative, *kŏn-tĕm'plȧ-tĭv*
continuity, *kŏn'tĭ-nū'ĭ-tĭ*
contractor, *kŏn-trăk'tẽr*
contrary, *kŏn'trĕr-ĭ; kŏn'trâr-ĭ*
contumely, *kŏn'tū-mē-lĭ*
conversant, *kŏn'vẽr-sănt*
coquet, *kō-kĕt'*
coquetry, *kō'kĕ-trĭ*
coral, *kŏr'ăl*
cordial, *kôr'jăl; kôrd'yăl*
cornet, *kôr'nĕt*
corolla, *kō-rŏl'ȧ*
corps, *kōr*
corral, *kŏ-răl'*
corridor, *kŏr'ĭ-dôr; -dōr*
corrugate, *kŏr'o͞o-gāt*
cortège, *kôr'tĕzh'*
cosmetic, *kŏz-mĕt'ĭk*
costume (n.), *kŏs'tūm; kŏs-tūm'*
costume (v.), *kŏs-tūm'*
costumer, *kŏs-tūm'ẽr; kŏs'-*
cotillion, *kō-tĭl'yŭn*
coup, *ko͞o*
coupé, *ko͞o'pā'*
coupon, *ko͞o'pŏn*
courier, *ko͞or'ĭ-ẽr*
courteous, *kûr'tē-ŭs; kōrt'yŭs*
courtier, *kōr'tĭ-ẽr; kōrt'yẽr*
cousin, *kŭz''n*
covetous, *kŭv'ĕ-tŭs*
crabbed, *krăb'ĕd*

cranberry, *krăn'bĕr-ĭ*
crèche, *krāsh; krĕsh*
credence, *krē'dĕns*
credulous, *krĕd'ū-lŭs*
creek, *krēk*
crêpe de Chine, *krāp'dē-shēn'*
crescendo, *krĕ-shĕn'dō; -sĕn'-*
crew, *kro͞o*
crucial, *kro͞o'shăl*
cruel, *kro͞o'ĕl*
crux, *krŭks*
cuisine, *kwê-zēn'*
culinary, *kū'lĭ-nĕr'ĭ*
culture, *kŭl'chûr; kŭl'tūr*
cuneiform, *kû-nē'ĭ-fôrm*
cupboard, *kŭb'ẽrd*
cupola, *kū'pô-lȧ*
curator, *kû-rā'tẽr*
cycle, *sī'k'l*
cynosure, *sī'nô-sho͝or; sĭn'ô-*

daguerreotype, *dȧ-gĕr'ô-tīp*
dahlia, *däl'yȧ; dāl'yȧ*
damage, *dăm'ĭj*
dance, *dȧns*
data, *dā'tȧ*
daub, *dôb*
deaf, *dĕf*
debenture, *dê-bĕn'chûr; -tūr*
débris, *dĕ'brē'; dĕb'rē*
début, *dā-bü'; dĕ-bū'*
debutante, *dĕb'û-tänt'*
decade, *dĕk'ăd*
decent, *dē'sĕnt*
décolleté, *dā-kŏl'tā;* F. *dā'kôl'tā'*
decorous, *dê-kō'rŭs; dĕk'ô-rŭs*
dedicatory, *dĕd'ĭ-kȧ-tô-rĭ*
defalcate, *dê-făl'kāt; dē'făl-kāt*
defamation, *dĕf'ȧ-mā'shŭn; dē'fȧ-*
deficit, *dĕf'ĭ-sĭt*
deign, *dān*
delicatessen, *dĕl'ĭ-kȧ-tĕs'ĕn*
delirious, *dê-lĭr'ĭ-ŭs*
de luxe, *dê lo͝oks'; lŭks'*
demagogic, *dĕm'ȧ-gŏj'ĭk; gŏg'ĭk*
demi-tasse, *dĕm'ĭ-tȧs';-tăs'*
democratize, *dê-mŏk'rȧ-tīz*
demon, *dē'mŭn*
demonetization,
  dê-mŏn'ê-tĭ-zā'shŭn; dē-mŭn'-; -tī-zā'shŭn
demurrage, *dê-mûr'āj*
dénouement, *dā-no͞o'mäɴ*
depths, *dĕpths*
derisive, *dê-rī'sĭv*
deshabille, *dĕz'ȧ-bēl'*
desist, *dê-zĭst'*
despicable, *dĕs'pĭ-kȧ-b'l*
dessert, *dĭ-zûrt'*
destine, *dĕs'tĭn*
detail (n.), *dê-tāl'; dē'tāl*
detail (v.), *dê-tāl'*
detour, *dê-to͞or'*
devoir, *dĕ-vwär'*
dew, *dū*
dexterous, *dĕk'stẽr-ŭs*
diagnostician, *dī'ăg-nŏs-tĭsh'ăn*
diastole, *dī-ăs'tô-lē*
dictator, *dĭk-tā'tẽr*
dictionary, *dĭk'shŭn-ĕr'ĭ*
dietetics, *dī'ê-tĕt'ĭks*
dietitian, *dī'ê-tĭsh'ăn*
different, *dĭf'ẽr-ĕnt*
diffuse (adj.), *dĭ-fūs'*
diffuse (v.), *dĭ-fūz'*
digest (v.), *dĭ-jĕst'; dī-*
digest (n.), *dī'jĕst*
digestion, *dĭ-jĕs'chŭn*
digitalis, *dĭj'ĭ-tā'lĭs*
digraph, *dī'grăf*
dilettante, *dĭl'ĕ-tăn'tĭ*
diphtheria, *dĭf-thēr'ĭ-ȧ*

diphthong, *dĭf'thŏng*
diploma, *dĭ-plō'mȧ*
direct, *dĭ-rĕkt'*
disaster, *dĭ-zȧs'tẽr*
disburse, *dĭs-bûrs'*
discern, *dĭ-zûrn'; dĭ-sûrn'*
discipline, *dĭs'ĭ-plĭn*
discourse, *dĭs-kōrs'*
discretion, *dĭs-krĕsh'ŭn*
disdain, *dĭs-dān'*
disease, *dĭ-zēz'*
dishabille, *dĭs'ȧ-bēl'*
dishevel, *dĭ-shĕv'ĕl*
dispersion, *dĭs-pûr'shŭn*
disputant, *dĭs'pû-tănt*
district, *dĭs'trĭkt*
divan, *dĭ-văn'*
diverge, *dĭ-vûrj'; dī-*
divulge, *dĭ-vŭlj'*
domain, *dô-mān'*
domicile, *dŏm'ĭ-sĭl*
donkey, *dŏng'kĭ*
douche, *do͞osh*
drama, *drä'mȧ*
drawer, *drô'ẽr; drôr*
dromedary, *drŭm'ê-dâ-rĭ; drŏm'-*
drought, *drout*
drowned, *dround*
dubious, *dū'bĭ-ŭs*
due, *dū*
duty, *dū'tĭ*
dyspepsia, *dĭs-pĕp'shȧ; sĭ-ȧ*

eau de cologne, *ō dē kô-lōn'*
ebullition, *ĕb'ŭ-lĭsh'ŭn*
éclat, *ā'klä'*
eczema, *ĕk'zê-mȧ*
edible, *ĕd'ĭ-b'l*
education, *ĕd'û-kā'shŭn*
effigy, *ĕf'ĭ-jĭ*
effort, *ĕf'ẽrt; ôrt*
ego, *ē'gō; ĕg'ō*
egret, *ē'grĕt; ĕg'rĕt*
electrometer, *ē-lĕk'trŏm'ê-tẽr*
elegiac, *ĕl'ê-jī'ăk; ĕ-lē'jĭ-ăk*
eleven, *ê-lĕv'ĕn*
élite, *ā'lēt'*
elm, *ĕlm;* not *ĕl'ŭm*
elongate, *ê-lŏng'gāt; ē'lŏng-gāt*
embrasure, *ĕm-brā'zhẽr*
emeritus, *ê-mĕr'ĭ-tŭs*
emolument, *ê-mŏl'û-mĕnt*
employee, *ĕm-ploi-ē'; ĕm-ploi'ē*
enchant, *ĕn-chȧnt'*
encore, *äng-kōr'; -kôr'*
encyclical, *ĕn-sī'klĭ-kăl;*
  ĕn-sĭk'lĭ-kăl
endive, *ĕn'dīv; -dĭv*
enema, *ĕn'ê-mȧ*
enfranchise, *ĕn-frăn'chīz*
engine, *ĕn'jĭn*
ennui, *än'wē*
en route, *än ro͞ot'*
ensign (n.), *ĕn'sīn*
entente, *äɴ'täɴt'*
entrée, *än'trā'*
entrepôt, *än'trĕ-pō*
enunciate, *ê-nŭn'shĭ-āt; ê-nŭn'sĭ-āt*
envelope (n.), *ĕn'vĕ-lōp*
epaulet, *ĕp'ô-lĕt*
epistle, *ê-pĭs''l*
epitome, *ê-pĭt'ô-mê*
equine, *ē'kwīn*
equitable, *ĕk'wĭ-tȧ-b'l*
era, *ē'rȧ*
erasure, *ê-rā'zhûr*
erratum, *ĕ-rā'tŭm*
erysipelas, *ĕr'ĭ-sĭp'ê-lăs*
esquire, *ĕs-kwīr'*
etiquette, *ĕt'ĭ-kĕt*
étude, *ā'tüd'*
euphonic, *û-fŏn'ĭk*

evasive, *ê-vā'sĭv*
exaggeration, *ĕg-zăj'ẽr-ā'shŭn*
examine, *ĕg-zăm'ĭn*
example, *ĕg-zȧm'p'l*
excise, *ĕk-sīz'; ĕk'sīz*
exemplary, *ĕg-zĕm'plâ-rĭ;*
  ĕg'zĕm-plĕr'ĭ
exhalation, *ĕks'hȧ-lā'shŭn*
exist, *ĕg-zĭst'*
exit, *ĕk'sĭt; ĕg'zĭt*
exogenous, *ĕks-ŏj'ê-nŭs*
exorbitant, *ĕg-zôr'bĭ-tănt*
expedient, *ĕks-pē'dĭ-ĕnt*
exponent, *ĕks-pō'nĕnt*
exquisite, *ĕks'kwĭ-zĭt*
extant, *ĕks'tănt*
extempore, *ĕks-tĕm'pô-rê*
extraordinary, *ĕks-trôr'dĭ-nĕr'ĭ;*
  ĕks'trȧ-ôr'-

facet, *făs'ĕt; -ĭt*
facile, *făs'ĭl*
facsimile, *făk-sĭm'ĭ-lē*
factory, *făk'tô-rĭ*
falcon, *fôl'kŭn; fô'kŭn*
fallen, *fôl'ĕn*
falsetto, *fôl-sĕt'ō*
family, *făm'ĭ-lĭ*
fancy, *făn'sĭ*
far, *fär*
fast, *fȧst*
faucet, *fô'sĕt; fô'sĭt*
favorite, *fā'vẽr-ĭt*
fecund, *fē'cŭnd; fĕk'ŭnd*
fellow, *fĕl'ō*
feminine, *fĕm'ĭ-nĭn*
fête, *fāt*
fiancé, *fē'än-sā'; fē-än'sā*
fiancée, *fē'än-sā'*
fibril, *fī'brĭl*
fichu, *fĭsh'o͞o*
fidelity, *fĭ-dĕl'ĭ-tĭ; fī-*
figure, *fĭg'ûr*
fillet, *fĭl'ĕt; fĭl'ā*
film, *fĭlm*
finale, *fê-nä'lā*
finance, *fĭ-năns'; fī-*
financier, *fĭn'ăn-sēr'; fĭ-năn'sĭ-ẽr*
finis, *fī'nĭs*
fleur-de-lis, *flûr'dē-lē'*
flew, *flo͞o*
floral, *flō'răl*
florid, *flŏr'ĭd*
florin, *flŏr'ĭn*
flute, *flo͞ot*
food, *fo͞od*
forbade, *fŏr-băd'*
forehead, *fŏr'ĕd*
forest, *fŏr'ĕst*
forum, *fō'rŭm*
fountain, *foun'tĭn*
foyer, *fwȧ'yā; foi'ā; fŏy'ẽr*
fragile, *frăj'ĭl*
franchisement, *frăn'chĭz-mĕnt*
frappé, *frȧ'pā'*
fraternize, *frăt'ẽr-nīz*
fricassee, *frĭk'ȧ-sē'*
friends, *frĕndz*
friendship, *frĕnd'shĭp*
frontier, *frŭn'tēr; frŏn'tēr*
fuel, *fū'ĕl*
fulminate, *fŭl'mĭ-nāt*
funereal, *fû-nēr'ê-ăl*
fungi, *fŭn'jī*
furniture, *fûr'nĭ-chûr; -tūr*
fusillade, *fū'zĭ-lād'*

gala, *gā'lȧ; gä'lȧ*
gallery, *găl'ẽr-ĭ*
gangrene, *găng'grēn*
gape, *gāp; găp*
garage, *gȧ-räzh'; găr'äzh*

garrulous, *găr'ū-lŭs;-ōō-lŭs*
gaseous, *găs'ē-ŭs*
gastritis, *găs-trī'tĭs*
gather, *găTH'ẽr*
gazetteer, *găz'ĕ-tēr'*
geisha, *gā'shȧ*
genealogy, *jĕn'ē-ăl'ō-jĭ; jē'nē-*
generally, *jĕn'ẽr-ăl-ĭ*
genii, *jē'nĭ-ī*
genre, *zhäN'r'*
gentleman, *jĕn't'l-măn*
genuine, *jĕn'ū-ĭn*
geranium, *jē-rā'nĭ-ŭm*
gerrymander, *gĕr'ĭ-măn'dẽr*
gerund, *jĕr'ŭnd*
gest, *jĕst*
gesture, *jĕs'chůr; -tūr*
get, *gĕt*
ghastly, *gȧst'lĭ*
ghoul, *gōōl*
gibber, *jĭb'ẽr; gĭb'ẽr*
gibbet, *jĭb'ĕt*
gin, *jĭn*
giraffe, *jĭ-răf'*
girl, *gûrl*
gist, *jĭst*
gladiolus, *glăd'ĭ-ō'lŭs;*
glȧ-dī'ô-lŭs
glycerin, *glĭs'ẽr-ĭn*
gneiss, *nīs*
golf, *gŏlf*
gondola, *gŏn'dô-lȧ*
gone, *gŏn*
gospel, *gŏs'pĕl*
government, *gŭv'ẽrn-mĕnt*
granary, *grăn'ȧ-rĭ*
granddaughter, *grănd'dô'tẽr*
grandeur, *grăn'jůr; grăn'dūr*
grasp, *grȧsp*
grass, *grȧs*
gratis, *grā'tĭs*
grimace, *grĭ-mās'*
grimy, *grīm'ĭ*
gripe, *grīp*
grisly, *grĭz'lĭ*
grotesque, *grô-tĕsk'*
grovel, *grŏv''l*
guardian, *gär'dĭ-ăn*
guillotine (n.), *gĭl'ô-tēn*
guillotine (v.), *gĭl'lô-tēn'*
gymnasium, *jĭm-nā'zĭ-ŭm*
gyroscope, *jī'rô-skōp*

habitant, *hăb'ĭ-tănt;* Fr. *ȧ'bē'täN'*
habitué, *hȧ-bĭch'û-ā'*
hacienda, *ä-syĕn'dä;*
hä'sĭ-ĕn'dä
handbook, *hănd'bŏŏk'*
handkerchief, *hăng'kẽr-chĭf*
hangar, *hăng'ẽr; hăng'gär*
harass, *hăr'ăs*
harbinger, *här'bĭn-jẽr*
harem, *hā'rĕm; hâr'ĕm*
hasten, *hās''n*
haunt, *hônt; hänt*
hearth, *härth*
heaven, *hĕv'ĕn*
height, *hīt*
heinous, *hā'nŭs*
helm, *hĕlm*
hemoglobin, *hē'mô-glō'bĭn;*
hĕm'ô-
heroine, *hĕr'ô-ĭn*
hesitate, *hĕz'ĭ-tāt*
heteronym, *hĕt'ẽr-ô-nĭm'*
hieroglyphic, *hī'ẽr-ô-glĭf'ĭk*
highwayman, *hī'wā'măn*
hilarious, *hĭ-lâr'ĭ-ŭs; hī-*
hirsute, *hûr'sūt; hẽr-sūt'*
history, *hĭs'tô-rĭ*
hoist, *hoist*
holocaust, *hŏl'ô-kôst*
holograph, *hŏl'ô-grȧf*
homage, *hŏm'āj*
homeopathic, *hō'mē-ô-păth'ĭk*
homeopathist, *hō'mē-ŏp'ȧ-thĭst;*
hŏm'ē-
homestead, *hōm'stĕd*
homogeneous, *hō'mô-jē'nē-ŭs;*
hŏm'ô-
homonym, *hŏm'ô-nĭm; hō'mô-*
honest, *ŏn'ĕst*
honorable, *ŏn'ẽr-ȧ-b'l*
honorarium, *ŏn'ô-râr'ĭ-ŭm*
hoof, *hōōf*
horrid, *hŏr'ĭd*
horse-radish, *hôrs'răd'ĭsh*
hospitable, *hŏs'pĭ-tȧ-b'l*
hovel, *hŏv'ĕl; hŭv'ĕl*
humble, *hŭm'b'l*
humor, *hū'mẽr*
hundred, *hŭn'drĕd*
hydraulics, *hī-drô'lĭks*
hydrometer, *hī-drŏm'ē-tẽr*
hygiene, *hī'jĭ-ēn; hī'jēn*
hygienic, *hī'jĭ-ĕn'ĭk*
hypocrisy, *hĭ-pŏk'rĭ-sĭ*
hysteria, *hĭs-tēr'ĭ-ȧ*
hysterical, *hĭs-tĕr'ĭ-kăl*

idea, *ī-dē'ȧ*
ideal, *ī-dē'ăl*
idiosyncrasy, *ĭd'ĭ-ô-sĭng'krȧ-sĭ*
ignoramus, *ĭg'nô-rā'mŭs*
illusory, *ĭ-lū'sô-rĭ*
illustrate, *ĭl'ŭs-trāt;ĭ-lŭs'trāt*
imbroglio, *ĭm-brōl'yō*
impious, *ĭm'pĭ-ŭs*
importune, *ĭm'pŏr-tūn';*
ĭm-pôr'chůn
impotent, *ĭm'pô-tĕnt*
improvise, *ĭm'prô-vīz'; ĭm'prô-*
inaugurate, *ĭn-ô'gû-rāt*
incise, *ĭn-sīz'*
incisive, *ĭn-sī'sĭv*
incognito, *ĭn-kŏg'nĭ-tō*
incomparable, *ĭn-kŏm'pȧ-rȧ-b'l*
incredulous, *ĭn-krĕj'ū-lŭs;*
ĭn-krĕd'yū-
incursion, *ĭn-kûr'zhŭn; -shŭn*
indisputable, *ĭn-dĭs'pū-tȧ-b'l;*
ĭn'dĭs-pūt'ȧ-b'l
industry, *ĭn'dŭs-trĭ*
inertia, *ĭn-ûr'shĭ-ȧ; ĭn-ûr'shȧ*
inexplicable, *ĭn-ĕks'plĭ-kȧ-b'l*
inextricably, *ĭn-ĕks'trĭ-kȧ-blĭ*
infamous, *ĭn'fȧ-mŭs*
infantile, *ĭn'făn-tīl; -tĭl*
influence, *ĭn'flōō-ĕns*
ingénue, *ăN'zhā'nü'*
innocent, *ĭn'ô-sĕnt*
inopportune, *ĭn-ŏp'ŏr-tūn'*
inquiry, *ĭn-kwīr'ĭ*
insatiable, *ĭn-sā'shĭ-ȧ-b'l;*
-shȧ-b'l
insect, *ĭn'sĕkt*
insignia, *ĭn-sĭg'nĭ-ȧ*
instead, *ĭn-stĕd'*
insulate, *ĭn'sū-lāt; ĭn'sū-*
integer, *ĭn'tē-jẽr*
interesting, *ĭn'tẽr-ĕst-ĭng*
intermezzo, *ĭn'-tẽr-mĕd'zō*
international, *ĭn'tẽr-năsh'ŭn-ăl*
interpellate, *ĭn'tẽr-pĕl'āt*
interpellation, *ĭn'tẽr-pĕ-lā'shŭn*
interpolate, *ĭn-tûr'pô-lāt*
intricacy, *ĭn'trĭ-kȧ-sĭ*
intrigue, *ĭn-trēg'*
inundate, *ĭn'ŭn-dāt; ĭn-ŭn'dāt*
inveigle, *ĭn-vē'g'l;-vā'g'l*
iodine, *ī'ô-dīn; -dĭn; -dēn*
irony, *ī'rô-nĭ*
irrefragable, *ĭ-rĕf'rȧ-gȧ-b'l*
irrefutable, *ĭr'ē-fūt'ȧ-b'l;*
ĭ-rĕf'ū-tȧ-b'l
irremediable, *ĭr'rē-mē'dĭ-ȧ-b'l*
irrevocable, *ĭ-rĕv'ô-kȧ-b'l*
isinglass, *ī'zĭng-glȧs'*
isolate, *ī'sô-lāt; ĭs'ô-*
italic, *ĭ-tăl'ĭk*
ivory, *ī'vô-rĭ*

jardinière, *zhȧr'dē'nyâr';*
jär'dĭ-nēr'
jocose, *jô-kōs'*
jocund, *jŏk'ŭnd; jō'kŭnd*
jostling, *jŏs'lĭng*
judgment, *jŭj'mĕnt*
jugular, *jōō'gû-lȧr; jŭg'û-lẽr*
jujitsu, *jōō-jĭt'sōō*
junta, *jŭn'tȧ*
just, *jŭst*
jute, *jōōt*

kaleidoscope, *kȧ-lī'dô-skōp*
kept, *kĕpt*
kettle, *kĕt''l*
khaki, *kä'kē*
khedive, *kĕ-dēv'*
kiln, *kĭl; kĭln*
kimono, *kĭ-mō'nō; kĭ-mō'nȧ*
kindergarten, *kĭn'dẽr-gär't'n*
kinetoscope, *kĭ-nē'tô-skōp;*
-nĕt'ō-skōp
kiosk, *kē-ŏsk'*
kismet, *kĭs'mĕt; kĭz'mĕt*
kitchen, *kĭch'ĕn; -ĭn*
knout, *nout; nōōt*
kopje, *kŏp'ĭ*
kumiss, *kōō'mĭs*
kurd, *kōōrd*

label, *lā'bĕl; -b'l*
laboratory, *lăb'ô-rȧ-tō-rĭ*
laborer, *lā'bẽr-ẽr*
lamentable, *lăm'ĕn-tȧ-b'l*
language, *lăng'gwĭj*
largess, *lär'jĕs*
laryngitis, *lăr'ĭn-jī'tĭs*
larynx, *lăr'ĭngks*
laths, *lȧTHz; lȧths*
lattice, *lăt'ĭs*
laudanum, *lô'dȧ-nŭm; lŏd'nŭm*
laugh, *läf; lȧf*
lava, *lävȧ; lăv'ȧ*
lavaliere, *lăv'ȧ-lẽr*
layette, *lā-ĕt'*
leaped, *lēpt*
leapt, *lĕpt; lēpt*
learned (adj.), *lûr'nĕd*
learned (v.), *lûrnd*
legate, *lĕg'ĭt*
legislature, *lĕj'ĭs-lā'chůr; -tūr*
leisure, *lē'zhẽr; lĕzh'ẽr*
length, *lĕngth*
lenient, *lē'nĭ-ĕnt; lēn'yĕnt*
leper, *lĕp'ẽr*
lese majesty, *lēz măj'ĕs-tĭ*
lethal, *lē'thăl*
lettuce, *lĕt'ĭs*
leverage, *lē'vẽr-āj; lĕv'ẽr-*
liaison, *lē'ā'zôN'*
libel, *lī'bĕl*
libertine, *lĭb'ẽr-tĭn*
librarian, *lī-brâr'ĭ-ăn*
library, *lī'brĕr'ĭ*
lichen, *lī'kĕn*
licorice, *lĭk'ô-rĭs*
lief, *lēf*
lilac, *lī'lăk*
limn, *lĭm*
lineament, *lĭn'ē-ȧ-mĕnt*
lingerie, *lăN'zh'-rē'*
linoleum, *lĭ-nō'lē-ŭm*
linotype, *līn'ô-tīp'*

liqueur, *lē'kûr'; lĭ-kūr'*
liquor, *lĭk'ĕr*
literati, *lĭt'ē-rā'tī*
literatim, *lĭt'ē-rā'tĭm*
literature, *lĭt'ĕr-ȧ-chŭr; -tūr*
lithographer, *lĭ-thŏg'rȧ-fĕr*
livelong, *lĭv'lŏng'*
loath, *lōth*
loathe, *lōTH*
loggia, *lŏj'ȧ; lô'jĭ-ȧ*
longevity, *lŏn-jĕv'ĭ-tĭ*
long-lived, *lŏng'līvd'*
lower (threaten), *lou'ĕr*
lure, *lūr*
lurid, *lū'rĭd*
lyceum, *lī-sē'ŭm*

machination, *măk'ĭ-nā'shŭn*
mackerel, *măk'ĕr-ĕl*
madras, *mȧ-drȧs'*
madre, *mä'drā*
maestro, *mä-ĕ'strō*
magazine, *măg'ȧ-zēn'*
magna charta, *măg'nȧ kär'tȧ*
magnolia, *măg-nō'lĭ-ȧ; -nōl'yȧ*
malaria, *mȧ-lâr'ĭ-ȧ*
malefactor, *măl'ē-făk'tĕr*
malign, *mȧ-līn'*
mallow, *măl'ō*
malpractice, *măl-prăk'tĭs*
mama, *mä'mȧ; mȧ-mä'*
mañana, *mä-nyä'nä*
mandamus, *măn-dā'mŭs*
mandatory, *măn'dȧ-tō-rĭ*
mange, *mānj*
mania, *mā'nĭ-ȧ*
maniacal, *mȧ-nī'ȧ-kăl*
manor, *măn'ĕr*
manufactory, *măn'ū-făk'tō-rĭ*
manzanita, *măn'zȧ-nē'tȧ*
maraschino, *măr'ȧ-skē'nō*
margarine, *mär'gȧ-rĭn;*
mär'jȧ-rēn
maritime, *măr'ĭ-tīm; -tĭm*
marquis, *mär'kwĭs*
marshmallow, *märsh'măl'ō*
masculine, *măs'kū-lĭn*
mask, *mȧsk*
massacred, *măs'ȧ-kĕrd*
massage, *mȧ-säzh'*
masseur, *mă-sûr'*
masseuse, *mă-sûz'*
maté (drink), *mä'tā; măt'ā*
matinée, *măt'ĭ-nā'*
matron, *mā'trŭn*
mattress, *măt'rĕs; -rĭs*
mausoleum, *mô'sô-lē'ŭm*
mauve, *mōv*
mavournin, *mȧ-vōōr'nēn*
mayonnaise, *mā'ō-nāz'*
mayoralty, *mā'ĕr-ăl-tĭ*
measure, *mĕzh'ĕr*
mechanician, *mĕk'ȧ-nĭsh'ăn*
medicament, *mē-dĭk'ȧ-mĕnt;*
mĕd'ĭ-kȧ-
medicinal, *mē-dĭs'ĭ-năl*
medieval, *mē'dĭ-ē'văl; mĕd'ĭ-*
mediocre, *mē'dĭ-ō'kĕr*
megrim, *mē'grĭm*
melee, *mā-lā'; mā'lā*
memoir, *mĕm'wär*
memory, *mĕm'ô-rĭ*
ménage, *mā-näzh'*
meningitis, *mĕn'ĭn-jī'tĭs*
menu, *mĕn'ū; mā'nū*
mercantile, *mûr'kăn-tĭl; -tīl*
mere (lake), *mēr*
meringue, *mē-răng'*
mesa, *mā'sä; mĕ'sä*
mésalliance, *mā'zȧl'yäɴs'*
mesdames, *mā'dȧm'*
mesmerism, *mĕz'mĕr-ĭz'm; mĕs'-*
messieurs, *mĕs'ĕrs; -yĕrz*
metric, *mĕt'rĭk*
mezzo, *mĕd'zō*
microscopic, *mī'krô-skŏp'ĭk*
microscopy, *mī-krŏs'kô-pĭ*
migraine, *mī'grān; mĭ-grān'*
milch, *mĭlch*
militia, *mĭ-lĭsh'ȧ*
mime, *mīm*
mineralogy, *mĭn'ĕr-ăl'ō-jĭ*
mirage, *mĭ-räzh'*
misanthrope, *mĭs'ăn-thrōp*
miscellany, *mĭs'ĕ-lā-nĭ*
mischievous, *mĭs'chĭ-vŭs*
misconstrue, *mĭs'kŏn-strōō';*
mĭs-kŏn'strōō
miserable, *mĭz'ĕr-ȧ-b'l*
mitten, *mĭt''n*
mnemonics, *nē-mŏn'ĭks*
mock, *mŏk*
moderate (adj.), *mŏd'ĕr-ĭt*
modiste, *mô'dēst'*
modus vivendi, *mō'dŭs vĭ-vĕn'dī*
moiré, *mwä'rā'; mō'rā*
monetary, *mŏn'ē-tĕr'ĭ; mŭn'-*
monogram, *mŏn'ô-grăm*
monologue, *mŏn'ô-lŏg*
monomania, *mŏn'ô-mā'nĭ-ȧ*
monsieur, *mĕ-syû'*
monsignor, *mŏn-sē'nyôr*
morale, *mô-rȧl'; -räl'*
mountain, *moun'tĭn*
mountainous, *moun'tĭ-nŭs*
municipal, *mū-nĭs'ĭ-păl*
museum, *mū-zē'ŭm*
mushroom, *mŭsh'rōōm*
musicale, *mū'zĭ-kȧl'*
muskellunge, *mŭs'kĕ-lŭnj*
muskmelon, *mŭsk'mĕl'ŭn*
mustache, *mŭs-tȧsh'*
muzhik, *mōō-zhĭk'; mōō'zhĭk*
mystery, *mĭs'tĕr-ĭ*
mythology, *mĭ-thŏl'ô-jĭ*

naïve, *nä-ēv'*
nape, *nāp*
napery, *nā'pĕr-ĭ*
naphtha, *năf'thȧ; năp'thȧ*
nasal, *nā'zăl; -z'l*
nascent, *năs'ĕnt*
natatorium, *nā'tȧ-tō'rĭ-ŭm*
natural, *năch'ū-răl; năt'yū-*
nature, *nā'chŭr; nā'tūr*
nausea, *nô'shē-ȧ; -sē-ȧ*
necessarily, *nĕs'ĕ-sĕr'ĭ-lĭ*
necrology, *nĕ-krŏl'ō-jĭ*
née, *nā*
negligee, *nĕg'lĭ-zhā'; nĕg'lĭ-zhā'*
nephritis, *nē-frī'tĭs*
nepotism, *nĕp'ô-tĭz'm*
nervine, *nûr'vēn; -vīn*
neuralgia, *nū-răl'jĭ-ȧ; -răl'jȧ*
neuritis, *nū-rī'tĭs*
neurosis, *nū-rō'sĭs*
nicety, *nī'sĕ-tĭ*
niche, *nĭch*
nomad, *nŏm'ăd; nō'măd*
nom de plume, *nŏm'dĕ plōōm'*
nominative, *nŏm'ĭ-nȧ-tĭv*
nonchalant, *nŏn'shȧ-lănt*
nonpareil, *nŏn'pȧ-rĕl'*
nostalgia, *nŏs-tăl'jĭ-ȧ*
nostrum, *nŏs'trŭm*
notice, *nō'tĭs*
novice, *nŏv'ĭs*
noxious, *nŏk'shŭs*
nuance, *nū'äns'*
nuisance, *nū'săns*
nuncio, *nŭn'shĭ-ō*
nuptial, *nŭp'shăl*
nymph, *nĭmf*
oasis, *ô-ā'sĭs; ō'ȧ-sĭs*
oaths, *ōTHz*
oatmeal, *ōt'mēl'*
obedient, *ô-bē'dĭ-ĕnt*
obeisance, *ô-bā'săns; ô-bē'-*
obelisk, *ŏb'ē-lĭsk*
obesity, *ô-bĕs'ĭ-tĭ; ô-bēs'ĭ-tĭ*
obiter dicta, *ŏb'ĭ-tĕr dĭk'tȧ*
obscenity, *ŏb-sĕn'ĭ-tĭ; -sē'nĭ-tĭ*
occult, *ŏ-kŭlt'*
octave, *ŏk'tāv*
office, *ŏf'ĭs*
often, *ŏf''n*
olden, *ōl'dĕn;-d'n*
oleander, *ō'lē-ăn'dĕr*
oleomargarine, *ō'lē-ô-mär'gȧ-rēn;*
-jȧ-rēn
olfactory, *ŏl-făk'tō-rĭ*
on, *ŏn*
onerous, *ŏn'ĕr-ŭs*
opponent, *ŏ-pō'nĕnt*
oral, *ō'răl*
orange, *ŏr'ĕnj; -ĭnj*
orchestra, *ôr'kĕs-trȧ*
orchestral, *ôr-kĕs'trăl; ôr'-*
orchid, *ôr'kĭd*
ordeal, *ôr'dē-ăl; ôr-dē'ăl*
ordinance, *ôr'dĭ-năns*
ordinarily, *ôr'dĭ-nĕr'ĭ-lĭ*
ordnance, *ôrd'năns*
orgy, *ôr'jĭ*
oriental, *ō'rĭ-ĕn'tăl*
orifice, *ŏr'ĭ-fĭs*
oriole, *ō'rĭ-ōl*
orthoepist, *ôr'thô-ē-pĭst; ôr-thō'-*
orthopedic, *ôr'thô-pē'dĭk*
ostler, *ŏs'lĕr*
overalls, *ō'vĕr-ôlz'*

pacifist, *păs'ĭ-fĭst*
padre, *pä'drĭ*
padrone, *pä-drō'nā*
pageant, *păj'ĕnt; pā'jĕnt*
pagination, *păj'ĭ-nā'shŭn*
pajama, *pȧ-jä'mȧ; -jăm'ȧ*
palatial, *pȧ-lā'shăl*
palette, *păl'ĕt*
palladium, *pă-lā'dĭ-ŭm*
palm, *päm*
palmistry, *päm'ĭs-trĭ; păl'mĭs-*
paltry, *pôl'trĭ*
panacea, *păn'ȧ-sē'ȧ*
panegyric, *păn'ē-jĭr'ĭk*
panorama, *păn'ô-rä'mȧ; răm'ȧ*
papa, *pä'pȧ; pȧ-pä'*
papier-mâché, *pā'pĕr-mă-shā';*
pȧ'pyā'mä'shā'
papyrus, *pȧ-pī'rŭs*
paraffin, *păr'ă-fĭn*
paramour, *păr'ȧ-mōōr*
parasitic, *păr'ȧ-sĭt'ĭk*
parasol, *păr'ȧ-sŏl'*
paresis, *păr'ē-sĭs; pȧ-rē'sĭs*
parliament, *pär'lĭ-mĕnt*
parotid, *pȧ-rŏt'ĭd*
participle, *pär'tĭ-sĭ-p'l*
particularly, *pĕr-tĭk'ū-lȧr-lĭ; pär-*
partner, *pärt'nĕr*
partridge, *pär'trĭj*
passé, *pä'sā'*
pasteurize, *pȧs'tĕr-īz; pȧs-tûr'-*
path, *pȧth*
pathos, *pā'thŏs*
patience, *pā'shĕns*
patio, *pä'tĭ-ō; pät'yō*
patois, *păt'wä; pȧ'-twä'*
patriot, *pā'trĭ-ŏt; păt'rĭ-*
patrol, *pȧ-trōl'*
patron, *pā'trŭn, păt'rŭn*
pecan, *pē-kăn'; -kän'*
peculiar, *pē-kūl'yĕr*
peculiarity, *pē-kū'lĭ-ăr'ĭ-tĭ*
pedagogue, *pĕd'ȧ-gŏg*

pedagogy, *pĕd′ȧ-gō′jĭ; -gŏj′ĭ*
pedal, *pĕd′ăl*
pedometer, *pē-dŏm′ē-tẽr*
penal, *pē′năl*
penchant, *päɴ′shäɴ′; pĕn′chănt*
penitentiary, *pĕn′ĭ-tĕn′shȧ-rĭ*
peon, *pē′ŏn*
peony, *pē′ô-nĭ*
peremptory, *pĕr′ĕmp-tô-rĭ; pĕr-ĕmp′-*
pergola, *pûr′gô-lȧ*
perhaps, *pẽr-hăps′*
peril, *pĕr′ĭl*
period, *pēr′ĭ-ŏd*
periodic, *pēr′ĭ-ŏd′ĭk*
peritoneum, *pĕr′ĭ-tô-nē′ŭm*
peritonitis, *pĕr′ĭ-tô-nī′tĭs*
perpetuity, *pûr′pē-tū′ĭ-tĭ*
persist, *pẽr-sĭst′*
perspicuity, *pûr′spĭ-kū′ĭ-tĭ*
perspiration, *pûr′spĭ-rā′shŭn*
peso, *pā′sō*
petard, *pē-tärd′*
petiole, *pĕt′ĭ-ōl*
petite, *pē-tēt′*
petrel, *pĕt′rĕl*
pharmaceutic, *fär′mȧ-sū′tĭk*
pharyngitis, *făr′ĭn-jī′tĭs*
phial, *fī′ăl*
philology, *fĭ-lŏl′ō-jĭ*
phlegmatic, *flĕg-măt′ĭk*
photogravure, *fō′tô-grȧ-vūr′; -grā′vûr*
phraseology, *frā′zē-ŏl′ô-jĭ*
physicist, *fĭz′ĭ-sĭst*
pianist, *pĭ-ăn′ĭst; pē′ȧ-nĭst*
piano, *pĭ-ăn′ō*
picture, *pĭk′chûr; pĭk′tūr*
pillow, *pĭl′ō*
pincers, *pĭn′sẽrz*
piquant, *pē′kănt*
pique, *pēk*
piqué, *pē-kā′*
pistachio, *pĭs-tä′shĭ-ō; pĭs-tā′-*
pith, *pĭth*
placard, *plăk′ärd*
placer, *plăs′ẽr*
plagiarist, *plā′jĭ-ȧ-rĭst*
plague, *plāg*
plait, *plāt*
plant, *plȧnt*
plebiscite, *plĕb′ĭ-sĭt;-sīt*
plenary, *plē′nȧ-rĭ; plĕn′ȧ-rĭ*
plethora, *plĕth′ô-rȧ*
plural, *ploo͝′răl*
pneumonia, *nû-mō′nĭ-ȧ*
poem, *pō′ĕm*
poignant, *poin′yănt; -ănt*
poilu, *pwȧ′lü′; pwä′loo͞*
poinsettia, *poin-sĕt′ĭ-ȧ*
poll, *pōl*
polonaise, *pō′lô-nāz′*
pomegranate, *pŏm′grăn′ĭt′; pŭm′-*
poniard, *pŏn′yẽrd*
poor, *poo͝r*
porcine, *pôr′sīn; -sĭn*
portiere, *pôr′tyâr′; -tĭ-âr′*
posse, *pŏs′ē*
posterior, *pŏs-tēr′ĭ-ẽr*
postern, *pōs′tẽrn*
posthumous, *pŏs′chŭ-mŭs; pŏst′hû-*
potato, *pô-tā′tō*
precedence, *prē-sēd′ĕns*
precedent (adj.), *prē-sēd′ĕnt*
precedent (n.), *prĕs′ē-dĕnt*
precise, *prē-sīs′*
predicament, *prē-dĭk′ȧ-mĕnt*
preface, *prĕf′ĭs*
preferable, *prĕf′ẽr-ȧ-b′l*
prelate, *prĕl′ĭt*
prelude (n.), *prĕl′ūd; prē′lūd*
premature, *prē′ma-tūr′; prē′mȧ-chûr*
premier, *prē′mĭ-ẽr; prĕm′yẽr*
premise (n.), *prĕm′ĭs*
premise (v.), *prē-mīz′*
preparatory, *prē-păr′ȧ-tō-rĭ*
presentation, *prĕz′ĕn-tā′shŭn*
president, *prĕz′ĭ-dĕnt*
presidio, *prē-sĭd′ĭ-ō; prā-sē′dyō*
presumptuous, *prē-zŭmp′chû-ŭs*
pretense, *prē-tĕns′; prē′tĕns*
pretext, *prē′tĕkst*
pretty, *prĭt′ĭ*
prima donna, *prē′mȧ dŏn′ȧ*
prima facie, *prī′mȧ fā′shĭ-ē*
primates, *prī-mā′tēz*
pristine, *prĭs′tĭn; -tēn*
prodigious, *prô-dĭj′ŭs*
produce (n.), *prŏd′ūs*
produce (v.), *prô-dūs′*
profile, *prō′fēl; -fīl*
profuse, *prô-fūs′*
program, *prō′grăm*
progress (n.), *prŏg′rĕs*
projectile, *prô-jĕk′tĭl*
proletarian, *prō′lē-târ′ĭ-ăn*
promenade, *prŏm′ē-näd′*
pronunciation, *prô-nŭn′sĭ-ā′shŭn; -shĭ-*
propinquity, *prô-pĭng′kwĭ-tĭ*
propitious, *prô-pĭsh′ŭs*
pro rata, *prō rā′tȧ*
prosperous, *prŏs′pẽr-ŭs*
protégé, *prō′tē-zhā; prô′tā′zhā′*
protein, *prō′tē-ĭn; tēn*
protestant, *prŏt′ĕs-tănt*
protrude, *prô-tro͞od′*
prussic, *prŭs′ĭk; pro͞o′sĭk*
psalm, *säm*
pseudonym, *sū′dô-nĭm*
psychiatry, *sī-kī′ȧ-trĭ*
psychic, *sī′kĭk*
psychosis, *sī-kō′sĭs*
ptomaine, *tō′mān; tō-mān′*
publicist, *pŭb′lĭ-sĭst*
puerile, *pū′ẽr-ĭl*
pumpkin, *pŭmp′kĭn*
punitive, *pū′nĭ-tĭv*
purée, *pû-rā′; pū′rā*
pursue, *pŭr-sū′*
pyrites, *pĭ-rī′tēz*
pyrometer, *pī-rŏm′ē-tẽr*

quaff, *kwȧf*
quarrel, *kwŏr′ĕl*
quarter, *kwôr′tẽr*
quatrain, *kwŏt′rān*
quay, *kē*
queue, *kū*
quietus, *kwī-ē′tŭs*
quinine, *kwī′nīn; kwĭ-nēn′*
qui vive, *kē vēv′*
quixotic, *kwĭks′ŏt′ĭk*
quoit, *kwoit*
quorum, *kwō′rŭm*

rabies, *rā′bĭ-ēz; -bēz*
raceme, *rȧ-sēm′; rā-*
radish, *răd′ĭsh*
ragout, *rȧ-goo͞′*
raillery, *rāl′ẽr-ĭ; răl′-*
raja, *rä′jȧ*
rancor, *răng′kẽr*
ransack, *răn′săk*
rapier, *rā′pĭ-ẽr*
raspberry, *răz′bĕr-ĭ*
rather, *răth′ẽr; rä′thẽr*
ratio, *rā′shĭ-ō; -shō*
ration, *rā′shŭn; răsh′ŭn*
rational, *răsh′ŭn-ăl*
rationale, *răsh′ŭn-ā′lē*
recipe, *rĕs′ĭ-pē*
recitative (n.), *rĕs′ĭ-tȧ-tēv′*
reclamation, *rĕk′lȧ-mā′shŭn*
recluse, *rē-klo͞os′*
recognizance, *rē-kŏg′nĭ-zăns; rē-kŏn′ĭ-* (legal)
recognize, *rĕk′ŏg-nīz*
reconnaissance, *rē-kŏn′â-săns*
reconnoiter, *rĕk′ŏ-noi′tẽr*
referable, *rĕf′ẽr-ȧ-b′l*
referee, *rĕf′ẽr-ē′*
regalia, *rē-gā′lĭ-ȧ; -gāl′yȧ*
régime, *rā′zhēm′*
regular, *rĕg′û-lẽr*
reiterate, *rē-ĭt′ẽr-āt*
renaissance, *rĕn′ē-säns′; rē-nā′săns*
rendezvous, *rän′dĕ-vo͞o; rĕn′-*
reparable, *rĕp′ȧ-rȧ-b′l*
repertoire, *rĕp′ẽr-twär; -twôr*
replica, *rĕp′lĭ-kȧ*
reputable, *rĕp′û-tȧ-b′l*
requiem, *rē′kwĭ-ĕm; rĕk′wĭ-*
requital, *rē-kwīt′ăl*
research, *rē-sûrch′*
reservoir, *rĕz′ẽr-vwôr; -vwär*
residue, *rĕz′ĭ-dū*
resin, *rĕz′ĭn*
resolute, *rĕz′ô-lūt*
resonance, *rĕz′ô-năns*
resource, *rē-sōrs′*
respite, *rĕs′pĭt*
restaurant, *rĕs′tô-rănt*
restaurateur, *rĕs′tō′rä′tûr′*
résumé, *rā′zû-mā′*
reveille, *rē-vāl′yĭ; rĕv′ē-lē′*
revenue, *rĕv′ē-nū*
reversion, *rē-vûr′shŭn*
revocable, *rĕv′ô-kȧ-b′l*
rheumatism, *ro͞o′mȧ-tĭz′m*
rhythm, *rĭth′m*
ribald, *rĭb′ăld*
ridiculous, *rĭ-dĭk′û-lŭs*
rind, *rīnd*
rinse, *rĭns*
ripeness, *rīp′nĕs*
rise (n.), *rīz*
risk, *rĭsk*
robust, *rô-bŭst′*
roil, *roil*
romance, *rô-măns′*
roof, *ro͞of*
room, *ro͞om*
root, *ro͞ot*
roquefort, *rōk′fẽrt; rôk′fôr′*
roseate, *rō′zē-āt*
rostrum, *rŏs′trŭm*
route, *ro͞ot*
routine, *ro͞o-tēn′*
rude, *ro͞od*
rutabaga, *ro͞o′tȧ-bā′gȧ*

sabot, *sȧ′bō′; săb′ō*
sabotage, *săb′ô-täzh′; săb′ō-tĭj*
saccharin, *săk′ȧ-rĭn; rīn*
sachem, *sā′chĕm*
sachet, *sȧ′shā′*
sacrament, *săk′rȧ-mĕnt*
sacrilegious, *săk′rĭ-lē′jŭs;-lĭj-ŭs*
sagacious, *sȧ-gā′shŭs*
said, *sĕd*
salary, *săl′ȧ-rĭ*
saline, *sā′līn*
salmon, *săm′ŭn*
salve, *säv; săv*
sanatorium, *săn′ȧ-tō′rĭ-ŭm*
sanguine, *săng′gwĭn*
sarcasm, *sär′kăz′m*
sarcophagus, *sär-kŏf′ȧ-gŭs*
sarsaparilla, *sär′sȧ-pȧ-rĭl′ȧ*
satin, *săt′ĭn*
satire, *săt′īr*
satyr, *săt′ẽr; sā′tẽr*

savage, *săv'ĭj*
savant, *să'väɴ'; săv'ănt*
says, *sĕz*
scallop, *skŏl'ŭp; skăl'-*
scared, *skârd*
scenario, *shā-nä'rĭ-ō; sē-nä'rĭ-ō*
schism, *sĭz'm*
scilicet, *sĭl'ĭ-sĕt*
scion, *sī'ŭn*
scrofula, *skrŏf'ū-lȧ*
séance, *sā'äns; sā'äɴs'*
seckel, *sĕk''l*
secretary, *sĕk'rē-tĕr'ĭ*
sedative, *sĕd'ȧ-tĭv*
seidlitz, *sĕd'lĭts*
seismic, *sīz'mĭk; sīs'-*
semiannual, *sĕm'ĭ-ăn'ū-ăl*
senile, *sē'nīl; -nĭl*
señora, *sā-nyō'rä*
separable, *sĕp'ȧ-rȧ-b'l*
separate (v.), *sĕp'ȧ-rāt*
separate (adj.), *sĕp'ȧ-rĭt*
sesame, *sĕs'ȧ-mē*
several, *sĕv'ẽr-ăl*
shampoo, *shăm-pōō'*
shan't, *shänt; shȧnt*
shillelagh, *shĭ-lā'lȧ; lā'lē*
shrievalty, *shrēv'ăl-tĭ*
shrill, *shrĭl*
shrine, *shrīn*
sibilant, *sĭb'ĭ-lănt*
sidereal, *sī-dēr'ē-ăl*
signora, *sē-nyō'rä*
silhouette, *sĭl'ōō-ĕt'*
simultaneous, *sī'mŭl-tā'nē-ŭs; sĭm'ŭl-*
since, *sĭns*
sinecure, *sī'nē-kūr; sĭn'ē-kūr*
sirup; syrup, *sĭr'ŭp*
ski, *skē*
skiing, *skē'ĭng*
slake, *slāk*
sleek, *slēk*
slept, *slĕpt*
slough (n.), *slou; slōō*
slough (v.), *slŭf*
snout, *snout*
sofa, *sō'fȧ*
soften, *sŏf''n*
soirée, *swä-rā'*
solace, *sŏl'ĭs*
solarium, *sō-lâr'ĭ-ŭm*
solemn, *sŏl'ĕm*
sombrero, *sŏm-brā'rō*
sonata, *sō-nä'tȧ*
soprano, *sō-prä'nō; prăn'ō*
souvenir, *sōō'vē-nēr'; sōō'vē-nēr*
specie (coin), *spē'shĭ*
species, *spē'shĭz; spē'shēz*
spinach, *spĭn'ĭch;-ĭj*
spirit, *spĭr'ĭt*
splenetic, *splē-nĕt'ĭk; splĕn'ē-tĭk*
spouse, *spouz*
stalactite, *stȧ-lăk'tīt; stăl'ăk-tīt*
stalagmite, *stȧ-lăg'mīt; stăl'ăg-mīt*
static, *stăt'ĭk*
status, *stā'tŭs*
steady, *stĕd'ĭ*
stipend, *stī'pĕnd*
stirrup, *stĭr'ŭp; stûr'ŭp*
stoicism, *stō'ĭ-sĭz'm*
stomach, *stŭm'ăk*
strata, *strā'tȧ; străt'ȧ*
strategic, *strȧ-tē'jĭk;-tĕj'ĭk*
strew, *strōō*
strychnine, *strĭk'nĭn; -nēn*
student, *stū'dĕnt*
suave, *swāv; swäv*
subdue, *sŭb-dū'*
submarine(n), *sŭb'mȧ-rēn'*
subpœna; subpena, *sŭb-pē'nȧ; sŭ-pē'-*
subtile, *sŭb'tĭl; sŭt''l*
subtle, *sŭt''l*
suburb, *sŭb'ûrb*
suède, *swād;* Fr. *swĕd*
suggest, *sŭg-jĕst'; sŭ-jĕst'*
suit, *sūt*
suite, *swēt*
sumac, *sū'măk; shōō'măk*
sumptuous, *sŭmp'chŭ-ŭs; sŭmp'tū-ŭs*
superfluous, *sū-pûr'flōō-ŭs*
supple, *sŭp''l*
suppose, *sŭ-pōz'*
surcease, *sûr-sēs'*
surprise, *sẽr-prīz'*
surveillance, *sûr-vāl'ăns; -vāl'yăns*
swan, *swŏn*
swept, *swĕpt*
syndicate, *sĭn'dĭ-kāt*
synod, *sĭn'ŭd*
syringe, *sĭr'ĭnj*

table d'hote, *tȧ'blĕ dōt'*
taciturn, *tăs'ĭ-tûrn*
tallyho, *tăl'ĭ-hō'*
tapestry, *tăp'ĕs-trĭ*
task, *tȧsk*
teat, *tēt*
technique, *tĕk'nēk'*
tedious, *tē'dĭ-ŭs; tēd'yŭs*
teething, *tēᴛʜ'ĭng*
telephonic, *tĕl'ē-fŏn'ĭk*
temperament, *tĕm'pẽr-ȧ-mĕnt*
temperature, *tĕm'pẽr-ȧ-chŭr; -tūr*
temporarily, *tĕm'pō-rĕr'ĭ-lĭ*
tenet, *tĕn'ĕt; -ĭt*
tepid, *tĕp'ĭd*
terrain, *tĕ-rān'; tĕr'ān*
tête-à-tête, *tāt'-ȧ-tāt'*
textile, *tĕks'tĭl; -tīl*
theater, *thē'ȧ-tẽr*
thermostat, *thûr'mō-stăt*
thresh, *thrĕsh*
tiara, *tī-âr'ȧ; tē-ä'rȧ*
tincture, *tĭngk'chŭr; -tūr*
tolerable, *tŏl'ẽr-ȧ-b'l*
tomato, *tō-mä'tō; tō-mā'tō*
tongs, *tŏngz*
tonsorial, *tŏn-sō'rĭ-ăl*
tortoise, *tôr'tŭs; -tĭs*
toupee, *tōō-pē'*
tourniquet, *tōōr'nĭ-kĕt*
toward, *tō'ẽrd; tōrd*
transmigrate, *trăns-mī'grāt; trăns'mĭ-grāt*
transparent, *trăns-pâr'ĕnt*
travail, *trăv'āl*
travel, *trăv'ĕl*
traveler, *trăv'ĕl-ẽr*
traverse (n. v. adj.), *trăv'ẽrs*
treacle, *trē'k'l*
tribune, *trĭb'ūn*
trichina, *trĭ-kī'nȧ*
triumph, *trī'ŭmf*
trough, *trŏf*
trousseau, *trōō'sō'*
truculent, *trŭk'ū-lĕnt; trōō'kū-*
trustworthy, *trŭst'wûr'ᴛʜĭ*
tube, *tūb*
tulip, *tū'lĭp*
tune, *tūn*
turnip, *tûr'nĭp*
turquoise, *tûr-koiz'; tûr'kwoiz*

ukulele, *ū'kŭ-lā'lē*
ultimatum, *ŭl'tĭ-mā'tŭm*
umbrella, *ŭm-brĕl'ȧ*
unaccented, *ŭn'ăk-sĕn'tĕd*
undersigned, *ŭn'dẽr-sīnd'*
unfrequented, *ŭn'frē-kwĕn'tĕd*
uninterested, *ŭn-ĭn'tẽr-ĕs-tĕd*
unprecedented, *ŭn-prĕs'ē-dĕn-tĕd*
untoward, *ŭn-tō'ẽrd; -tōrd'*
usage, *ūz'ĭj; ūs'-*
used, *ūzd*
usually, *ū'zhōō-ăl-lĭ*
usurp, *ū-zûrp'*
usury, *ū'zhōō-rĭ*

vagary, *vȧ-gâr'ĭ; -gā'rĭ*
vagrant, *vā'grănt*
valance, *văl'ăns*
valuable, *văl'ū-ȧ-b'l*
vanquish, *văng'kwĭsh*
vase, *vās; vāz; väz*
vast, *vȧst*
vaudeville, *vōd'vĭl; vô'dē-vĭl*
vehement, *vē'ē-mĕnt*
veinous, *vān'ŭs*
velvet, *vĕl'vĕt; -vĭt*
venison, *vĕn'ĭ-z'n*
venous, *vē'nŭs*
ventriloquist, *vĕn-trĭl'ō-kwĭst*
veracious, *vē-rā'shŭs*
verbatim, *vûr-bā'tĭm*
verdigris, *vûr'dĭ-grēs;-grĭs*
version, *vûr'shŭn*
veterinary, *vĕt'ẽr-ĭ-nĕr'ĭ*
via, *vī'ȧ*
vicar, *vĭk'ẽr*
vice versa, *vī'sē vûr'sȧ*
victim, *vĭk'tĭm*
victual, *vĭt''l*
vicuna, *vĭ-kōōn'yȧ; vĭ-kū'nȧ*
vignette, *vĭn-yĕt'*
villain, *vĭl'ĭn*
vindictive, *vĭn-dĭk'tĭv*
vinous, *vī'nŭs*
vis-à-vis, *vē'zȧ-vē'*
viscid, *vĭs'ĭd*
viscount, *vī'kount'*
vise, *vē'zā; vē-zā'*
vitriol, *vĭt'rĭ-ŭl*
vituperation, *vī-tū'pẽr-ā'shŭn*
viva voce, *vī'vȧ vō'sē*
volatile, *vŏl'ȧ-tĭl*
volume, *vŏl'ūm*
voluntarily, *vŏl'ŭn-tĕr'ĭ-lĭ*

waft, *wȧft*
wainscot, *wān'skŏt*
warily, *wâr'ĭ-li*
was, *wŏz*
wash, *wŏsh*
wasp, *wŏsp*
weird, *wērd*
well-bred, *wĕl'brĕd'*
when, *hwĕn*
where, *hwâr*
whisk, *hwĭsk*
whistler, *hwĭs'lẽr*
whole, *hōl*
whooping (cough), *hōōp'ĭng*
whortleberry, *hwûr't'l-bĕr'ĭ*
widow, *wĭd'ō*
window, *wĭn'dō*
wiseacre, *wīz'ā-kẽr*
wistaria, *wĭs-tā'rĭ-ȧ*
withes, *wĭths; wĭᴛʜz*
women, *wĭm'ĕn; -ĭn*
wondering, *wŭn'dẽr-ĭng*
wont (custom), *wŭnt; wōnt*
wrath, *răth; räth*
wrestler, *rĕs'lẽr*

xenia, *zē'nĭ-ȧ*
xylophone, *zī'lō-fōn; zĭl'ō-*

yacht, *yŏt*
yolk, *yōk; yōlk*

zealot, *zĕl'ŭt*
zenana, *zē-nä'nȧ*
zenith, *zē'nĭth*
zodiacal, *zō-dī'ȧ-kăl*
zoo, *zōō*
zoology, *zō-ŏl'ō-jĭ*

FORMS OF LITERARY COMPOSITION

Enjoyment in Reading. A good book is like an excellent dinner in good company, to which you bring a good digestion, a keen appetite, alert attention, and as ready a wit as you can muster. It is easy to indulge oneself in drifting idly through a maze of moving pictures. But some effort is necessary to keep the mind alert to the procession of thoughts on the printed page. If the author has written something worth while, he has taken much time to select the right words and set them in order. There is no higher pleasure than that of the reader who follows such an author through his pages and re-creates from the printed symbols his thought, his pictures, and his fancies. The book that you enjoy in this way becomes a part of your life.

Journals and Magazines. Business and professional people read the journals of their special interests. Members of churches, societies, and orders should read at least some of the papers and magazines published in their interest. Such reading is necessary to intelligent membership, as the reading of daily newspapers and weekly journals is necessary to efficient citizenship. But no one need read all of any paper or review. Let your special interest select and direct your attention. Reading the news that prompts to reflection upon the issues of the day is worth while; but trying to read the entire newspaper only produces a confused impression of many things, which serves to weaken the judgment. One should not, however, confine his reading to newspapers and magazines.

Books and Taste. The magazines offer, at small expense, acquaintance with the best literary work of the day. The novels of Charles Dickens were originally published in magazines. But the wise man will spend something for the sake of possessing at least a few good books. Even the public library cannot take the place of books on a shelf at home, whether home be a single room or a mansion. You may select your books according to your taste, but you should take pains to cultivate your taste.

A useful distinction has been drawn between the *literature of knowledge* and the *literature of power*. Keep this in mind in filling your bookshelf. Reliable volumes that contain the things one needs to know, or should be able to refer to on occasion, are of great importance; for exact information is indispensable. These make up the literature of knowledge. This class includes dictionaries, encyclopedias, histories, and books upon special sciences. Of even greater value are the books of power. These feed the imagination and inspire ideals. Such are the great biographies, classic stories, essays, and poetry. The wise man will value these, not for all they contain, but for what they actually bring to *him*. A single article in a work of reference, a single idea or fact in a history, one little poem out of a large volume, may be worth to you many times the cost of the book.

STORY OR NARRATIVE

Both of these words are derived from roots which mean simply *see* or *know*, but they have come to be applied to all accounts of events. The order of telling a story is either: (1) the time order in which things happen, as in history; or (2) an "arrangement" different from the time order. This "arrangement" may be made for the sake of (a) holding attention or (b) making clearer the relations of cause and effect among the events. Such an "arrangement" is called a plot, and stories so planned are fiction.

For plot outlines, refer to *The Book or Article Review, The Scenario.*

Ancient Stories. Everybody likes a good story, and story-telling is very nearly, if not quite, the most ancient of the arts. The oldest discoverable collections of writing contain well-developed narratives in the form of myths and legends. A *myth* is an ancient tale which usually conveys some imaginative account of the origin of gods, various human arts, or natural phenomena. The *legend* is similar to the myth, but it is more directly concerned with the deeds of men. In the course of centuries, many of these tales were combined by master story-tellers into *epics*, which are stories of the lives and deeds of heroes, such as the *Iliad* and the *Odyssey*. The word epic comes from the Greek *epos*, meaning "speech" or "song," because these great stories were told or chanted for generations before the poems were actually written.

Medieval Romance. During the middle ages, long *romances* about the careers and conquests of Alexander and Charlemagne and their followers took shape from the tales and songs of minstrels who wandered from court to court and were welcomed in the castles for the entertainment they brought. The name *romance* was given to these stories because they were composed in the common Romance, or French, tongue rather than in the Latin of scholars. In similar manner, the romances of King Arthur and of the Holy Grail were built. Upon this fund of romance many modern writers have drawn. Tennyson embodied the Arthurian legends in the *Idylls of the King*.

In their early form, these stories were told in verse. Later they were recast in prose form by various writers. With these poems in prose there grew side by side the *prose tale*, which was a story of adventure, in which the events were strung together loosely and the interest depended on the strangeness of the events or the unforeseen outcome of the adventures. Several romantic prose tales were produced by Greek writers in the early Christian centuries. One of the most famous was *Apollonius of Tyre*. From this tale came Shakspere's plot for *Pericles, Prince of Tyre*. To this general type of story belongs the series of tales known as the *Arabian Nights*. Washington Irving's *Tales of the Alhambra* furnish a more modern instance. Out of these loosely constructed legends there have developed in modern times the novel and the short story.

The Novel. Of the *novel* there are two general types. In the *romantic novel*, of which the stories of Sir Walter Scott are examples, the story is placed at a distance from the reader, in either time or space, and the strangeness of events and places contributes much to its interest. In romance our dreams come true. The *realistic novel* takes its subject matter from everyday affairs. The usual motives of people form the story, and the outcome must be made to seem reasonable and likely. William Dean Howells's work is among the best in the realistic style. The love motive is almost universal in the novel. The *psychological novel*, exemplified in Joyce's *Ulysses*, is primarily interested in recording the thoughts and feelings of the characters. The novel may vary in length from several thousand words to several hundred thousand.

The Short Story. The modern *short story* has been developed within the last hundred years. Its ancestors were many,—the Greek romances, the *fabliaux* in France, such tales as Boccaccio told in prose in Italy and Chaucer retold in verse in England; but it is a form clearly distinguished from all these. Edgar Allan Poe may be credited with the first characteristic work in the new form in America, and his stories are still reckoned among the best. The short story takes a small group of characters, carries them through a brief time, and, in rapid action, with a minimum of description, works out their fortunes and interactions. The story may vary in length from a few hundred to six or seven thousand words. The explanation of the plot must usually be cleverly concealed until the end of the story is reached, but it must then be made to seem reasonable and convincing. The works of Bret Harte, Francis R. Stockton, R. L. Stevenson, and Rudyard Kipling furnish examples of various types of the short story.

Special Forms of Prose Fiction. Both the novel and the short story appear in various special forms. The *mystery story,* for example, may be either long or short, but its plot turns upon some skillfully concealed relation between the events narrated. When this relation is revealed, in the end, as something very simple and commonplace, we have what is sometimes called a *surprise plot.* Or the mystery may be left as an unexplained something in the borderland of fancy or superstition, which human science has not yet mapped out. The mystery story is really a very primitive sort of tale, and many examples of it are to be found in early folklore. It carries all the thrills of unexpected and unexplained fortunes. Poe's *Gold Bug* and *Fall of the House of Usher* are classic examples of the modern mystery story.

The extraordinarily popular *detective story* is one sort of mystery tale, in which such a fascinatingly keen, questioning mind as that of Sir Arthur Conan Doyle's creation, Mr. Sherlock Holmes, is seen at work unraveling the tangled threads of the mystery. It is really a story built backward; for the real story is assumed to be already finished, and the detective is set to going over the obscure trail to discover the origin of the train of events. What we get is really two stories in one, the first being that of the original characters and events, the second, that of the detective and his discoveries. Such a story is *The Leavenworth Case.* The *adventure story* is more nearly like the old-fashioned tale. Its interest depends mostly upon the succession of unexpected and more or less complicated incidents calling for courage and address in the characters. *Robinson Crusoe, Treasure Island,* and *Kidnapped* are favorite examples of this kind.

Both the novel and the short story may be so written as to carry a special interest derived from the *location of the events,* from the *type of industry* in which the characters are engaged, or from the *class of society* in which they move. This last kind may involve only the people of one class of society. But more commonly it follows the ancient instinct of story-tellers for the effect of contrast. Then the clash of high and low, of rich and poor, which has interested mankind from the time of Aladdin and King Cophetua, furnishes the moving impulse.

The *historical novel* involves historical events as a necessary part of the story, and pictures some historical period. When it is based upon real scholarship and gives a trustworthy picture of the time in which its action is placed, it is not only interesting in itself but valuable as an aid to the study of history. *Hugh Wynne, The Crisis, The Cloister and the Hearth, Ivanhoe, Quentin Durward, The Last Days of Pompeii, The Conqueror, Quo Vadis,* and *Ben Hur* are excellent examples.

History. The almost universal desire for the true story finds satisfaction in *history,* the story of man's life from the beginning to the present time. Indeed, it is out of this material that most fiction and poetry are made. A knowledge of history is essential to a true education. An impartial and readable history, therefore, entitles its author to very high regard. The following works are masterpieces in this field: James F. Rhodes's *History of the United States*; Theodore Roosevelt's *Winning of the West*; Green's *History of England*; Ferrero's *Greatness and Decline of Rome*; Prescott's *Conquest of Mexico* and *Conquest of Peru*; Parkman's *France and England in the New World*; J. L. Motley's *Rise of the Dutch Republic.*

Biography. Second only to history in importance as a part of education, and in its masterpieces equally fascinating, is *biography,* or the life histories of important personages. To know the great thinkers and workers of the world through their biographies is not only interesting but of incalculable worth as an influence in developing character. The list of true and readable biographies is long. Many short lives have been written and published in such series as *American Statesmen* and *English Men of Letters.* The following are of high rank: Boswell's *Life of Johnson,* unique among biographies; Plutarch's *Parallel Lives of Illustrious Greeks and Romans,* an ancient work still full of interest; Morley's *Life of Gladstone*; Thayer's *Life of Cavour*; Carlyle's *Oliver Cromwell*; Palmer's *Life of Alice Freeman Palmer*; Booker Washington's *Up from Slavery*; Jacob Riis's *Making of an American*; Beveridge's *Life of John Marshall. Letters* and *journals* supplement biography.

Travel. Always and everywhere people are interested in *travelers' stories,* and many most entertaining books have been written to satisfy this appetite. A very large part of the *Odyssey* is made up of the wanderings of Odysseus, the Greek hero; the adventures of Sindbad the Sailor are proverbial; the book of the travels of Marco Polo through Asia is a classic. Among recent books, those of Harry Franck about his walking trips in various parts of the world are unique and interesting. The *Reminiscences of Rafael Pumpelly* contain some charming stories of travel in the 19th century. The stories of Arctic exploration by Peary and Stefansson, Roosevelt's travel and hunting narratives, the lives of Stanley and Livingstone, and Stevenson's chronicles of the South seas furnish mines of fascinating reading.

Folk Stories. The *folk tale,* or *folk story,* is what its name implies, a tale which has been told over and over again among the common people. This type of story is common to all peoples, and it is worthy of note that such stories circulated among widely separated peoples tell of similar adventures and teach similar truths. Many of these legends may be found in the collections made by Andrew Lang.

The *fairy tale* may be thought of as a type of folk story. Most fairy stories are of very ancient origin; some are modern. They are always concerned with a fanciful explanation of events and with the fate of people. The fairies are the little people of the air and the trees and the caves, who are either friendly or unfriendly to human folk. Some of these stories are very beautiful, while others are marred by the savage cruelty of barbarous times. Andersen's original tales and the *Märchen* gathered by the brothers Grimm offer excellent specimens of the fairy tale.

Stories That Teach. A very engaging type of story, of ancient origin, widely current in medieval times in Europe, and still to be found among remote and untutored peoples, is the *animal story,* in which the animals are personified, or endowed with human faculties. Frequently each sort of animal is supposed to embody a particular human trait, and the stories take on a moral flavor. In America, the finest examples of these tales are the Uncle Remus and Br'er Rabbit stories, retold in the negro dialect by Joel Chandler Harris.

Closely related to these animal stories are *fables,* pointed anecdotes in which animals are endowed with human qualities and are made to illustrate moral lessons. The fables of Æsop and of La Fontaine are universally popular.

The *parable* is a story of common events or happenings of every day, used to illustrate moral or religious truths. As the typical beginning of the old-fashioned story is "Once upon a time," so the typical beginning of the parable is "It is like." The New Testament affords us the best examples of the parable, though in one form or another a parable appears wherever any teaching of moral or social truth is to be done.

The *allegory* is a development of the story of common things which conveys moral and spiritual meanings. The allegory extends metaphor and personification into a story, in which the characters represent qualities, motives, or types of character. The morality plays of early English literature, such as *Everyman*, and many modern short, poetic plays are really allegories. Indeed, the short allegory may be found frequently in fiction.

In English, the great prose allegory is Bunyan's *Pilgrim's Progress*. Dante's *Divine Comedy* is perhaps the greatest of the world's allegories. There is also much allegory in Tennyson's *Idylls of the King*.

DESCRIPTIVE PROSE

This type of composition appears as an important part of books on travel, art, architecture, cities, and natural scenery. The books of travel referred to under *Travel* contain many fine examples of this graphic style of writing.

EXPOSITION AND ARGUMENT

The logical development of themes is to be found in the form of *essays* on literary, historical, and scientific subjects, and in *speeches* and *orations*. The *essay* presents, either in serious or in light style, a writer's thoughts upon a subject, to inform, convince, explain, or entertain. The essays of Bacon, Addison, and Macaulay are English classics. Huxley was the great scientific essayist of the 19th century. Lord Bryce's *American Commonwealth* is a long essay, combining exposition and argument. Current magazines contain many essays upon a wide variety of subjects, in the form of editorials, special articles, and studies. The *speech* or *oration* is usually a discussion of a theme of public human interest, argumentative and persuasive in character, and prepared for a particular public occasion. The works of Edmund Burke, William Pitt, Patrick Henry, Daniel Webster, Abraham Lincoln, Stephen A. Douglas, Henry W. Grady, and Rufus Choate furnish examples of English and American oratory.

POETRY

When emotion and the creative imagination rule expression in language, we have poetry. The province of poetry is to kindle the imagination and inspire fine sentiments and high enthusiasms through beautiful language. English literature is rich in poetry that does just these things.

The Lyric. This is the simplest and most familiar form of poetry. The word *lyric* implies singing, but the lyric poem need not be set to music. It is simply the poet's personal expression of feeling, and it may be written upon any theme that arouses in him an emotional response. This theme is usually suggested by some person, place, or natural object. Usually the lyric is short, not more than a few stanzas, so that it can be read easily in a short time and grasped as a whole.

The songs of Robert Burns are among the purest lyrics in the English language. Tennyson's work includes many separate lyrics of very great beauty as well as numerous short songs inset in some of his longer poems. Rudyard Kipling's poetry should be read for a more rugged and vigorous type. Sidney Lanier produced several very beautiful lyrics, among which are *The Woods and the Master* and *The Marshes of Glynn*. James Whitcomb Riley's verses, even when he is telling a story, often seem to sing themselves. Riley is the great American master of the lyric in popular language. Joaquin Miller, among American poets, is to be read for his *Songs of the Sierras*. Among present day poets, also, the works of Alfred Noyes and John Masefield, in England, and of Richard Le Gallienne and Bliss Carman, in America, should be read.

The Sonnet. A lyric poem of the fixed length of fourteen iambic pentameter lines. Usually it has a first section of eight lines and a second section of six, though the sonnets of Shakspere do not conform to this rule. The sonnet was adopted into English from the Italian. It is a form that requires the finest mastery both of language and of thought. Every reader of literature should be acquainted with some of the greater sonnets of Shakspere and Milton and also with sonnets by poets of the present day. As fine examples of the English sonnet, one may read Wordsworth's *To Milton*, Keats's *On Chapman's Homer*, and Rupert Brooke's series of sonnets under the title "*1914*."

The Ode. A lyric adopted from the Greek, but altered greatly in form by various English poets. Today it is simply a poem written in dignified and elevated style, often for some set occasion. It varies, in length and metrical form, from such poems as Wordsworth's *Ode to Duty* and Shelley's *Ode to a Skylark* to a poem of the length of Lowell's *Commemoration Ode* or Tennyson's *Ode on the Death of the Duke of Wellington*.

Hymns and Songs. Hymns are written in stanzas usually of four or six lines with three or four accents to the line, though there is no special rule for these. *Popular songs* have most frequently the trochaic meter because of its lightness and rapidity of movement.

Elegies. These are funeral laments, often of a reflective character. Gray's *Elegy Written in a Country Churchyard* is an English classic.

Narrative Poetry. Aside from the great epics—the *Iliad*, the *Odyssey*, the *Æneid*, and *Paradise Lost*—and the metrical romances, such as those about Charlemagne and King Arthur, the most interesting form of narrative poetry is the *ballad*. This is really a folk story in lyric verse, though in modern use "ballad" means any short simple lyric. The manner of telling the story is frequently dramatic, that is, the characters are allowed to speak for themselves. The ballads of Robin Hood are perhaps the most familiar in English. These and many others may be found in such a collection as *English and Scottish Popular Ballads*, made by Francis J. Child.

Geoffrey Chaucer's *Canterbury Tales* mark the beginning of modern English narrative poetry. The stories of *Miles Standish* and *Evangeline*, as told by Longfellow, are familiar examples of the narrative poem of modern times. For many years the prose novel and the short story have crowded out the narrative poem, but recently it seems to be returning to favor in the work of several English and American poets. In America, Robert Frost is master of a type of short dramatic narrative, several examples of which are to be found in his volume *North of Boston*. John Masefield's *Dauber* and *Everlasting Mercy* and Alfred Noyes's *Drake* are excellent examples of recent poetic narratives.

Anthologies. The word means collections of flowers and was anciently used for compilations of short Greek poems and epigrams. Now it applies mostly to collections which represent the finest poetry of a given country, as an "American anthology," or poems about a certain class of subjects, as an "anthology of war poetry," or poems representing a certain type, as an "anthology of lyrics" or of hymns.

Vers libre, "Free Verse." This name is applied to a type of modern poetry in which the strict meters of the older verse do not appear and in which rime is rather deliberately rejected. Apart, therefore, from its arrangement in lines of irregular length, it is often difficult to distinguish this form of poetry from rhythmical prose. The writers of "free verse" attempt to make the rhythm of their poetry reflect truthfully the emotions that prompt them to write. Obviously, a poet must possess great skill to do this successfully. Hence very few pieces of good "free verse" have been written, the more successful being found in the works of Carl Sandburg, Amy Lowell, and Edgar Lee Masters.

DRAMA

A drama, or play, is essentially a story arranged to be told in action on the stage. This method of telling a story is very ancient, dating back to early

festivals, when legends connected with the god or patron of a feast were represented with music, dancing, and recitation. The history of the stage and the drama in all countries shows more or less intimate connection with the service of religion as well as with the human love of entertainment.

English dramas are written either in verse or in prose. Sometimes the dramatists may use both forms in the same play, as Shakspere did. At the present day, however, most plays that are to be both staged and printed are written in prose, for the modern public calls for a more "natural" mode of speech. The subject of the drama may be drawn from almost any source, according to the genius of the playwright, and, like the novel or short story, its manner may be romantic or realistic.

Tragedy and Comedy. Tragedy signifies a play of serious action and motive usually representing some human struggle having an adverse outcome. This struggle may be against the gods or fate, as in the ancient drama, against their own passions, as in the Shaksperian tragedies, or against their passions and social conditions, as in more modern plays. Comedy implies a lighter, more pleasant story, with a happy ending in place of the sad or disastrous close of tragedy. Few plays of the present day answer strictly to this classification, most of them exhibiting both tragedy and comedy.

Various Forms. We may have a *play of incident,* in which we are interested chiefly in what happens, or a *play of character,* in which we are interested chiefly in the people to whom things happen. The play may be said to belong either to *serious drama,* in the course of which some essential change or development in one or more characters is required, or to the *lighter drama,* in which there is frequently only change of situation or of relations among the characters. The *farce* is a light play of incident, carried to the extreme of artificial or ridiculous situations. The modern *melodrama* is, as the name implies, a play often accompanied with music, but characterized always by exaggerated sensational features together with a happy ending.

Goldsmith in the 18th century produced what is known as *comedy of manners.* He was followed by several playwrights in the same fashion. Plays in this class to be read are *The Good-Natured Man, She Stoops to Conquer, The Rivals,* and *The School for Scandal.*

A very large number of English and American plays of the last thirty years are to be classed as *social drama.* In these the method of the playwright is realistic, and his object is to portray the working of everyday human motives. Sometimes he rises to a discussion or criticism of modern social life and customs.

In America, William Vaughn Moody, Clyde Fitch, William Gillette, and Augustus Thomas have produced plays that are suitable for reading as well as for stage presentation. Among English playwrights, Sir Arthur W. Pinero, Henry Arthur Jones, and John Galsworthy have done notable work.

There are in English several dramas which, while not successful on the stage, should be read by the student. Among these may be mentioned Tennyson's *Becket* and *Mary* and Browning's *The Falcon* and *Pippa Passes.*

The modern play rarely goes beyond three or four acts, and at the present time there is a marked interest in short plays of one act or two acts. The short plays of Lady Gregory, Lord Dunsany, and Sir James Barrie represent the best in this type of drama. There is a widespread interest also in the *pageant,* which is simply an outdoor play with much action but with very little text. Its most frequent use is for portraying poetically the life and customs of past times, in celebrations of historical events. Much attention is being given to the religious play.

For further references, see *Family Library, articles and tables on the various national literatures,* and the *Table of Modern World Literature.*

FIGURES OF SPEECH

Apt figures of speech are pictures of one's thoughts. A good comparison throws light on an idea, thereby helping people to understand it. For this reason, the language of the plain, matter-of-fact man is full of comparisons and figures, which he has inherited or unconsciously learned from those around him. He says, "plain as day," "heavy as lead," "level headed," as naturally as he says "see," "lift," or "think."

A *figure of speech* is a deviation from the usual application of words in order to impart clearness, force, and beauty to the composition. By saying "an army of ants" we give a vivid impression both of orderliness and of vastness in number. When David says "they were swifter than eagles" and "stronger than lions," we at once get a graphic description of the physical qualities of Saul and of Jonathan. Figures may be grouped in the four following classes:

I. Figures that picture a hidden resemblance or make use of a close association.

Simile (*sĭm'ĭ-lē*). In this figure, a likeness between things is expressed, usually by *like* or *as,* in the form of a comparison: "Sweet *as the morning air.*" One may recount the kind words and acts and cheerfulness of a visitor and thus describe her prosaically very well, but if one says, "Her presence was *like a ray of sunshine* in a darkened room," the whole story is pictured in a single phrase. Other examples: "Quick *as lightning*"; "Abundant *as the light of the sun*"; "Deaf *as any tradesman's dummy*"; "A baby's feet, *like sea-shells pink*"; "Jolted *like a solitary penny* in an iron bank"; "White *as chalk.*"

Metaphor (*mĕt'ȧ-fŏr*). The word means "carrying over," "transfer." In this figure, the word *like* or *as,* used in *simile,* is omitted, and, by an implied comparison, a new meaning or picture is transferred directly to the word: "He was a *tower* of strength"; "*Seeds* of truth"; "Lowliness is young ambition's *ladder*"; "Sail on, O *Ship* of State"; "Hours and minutes are *dollars* and *cents.*"

The next two figures, *synecdoche* and *metonymy,* are similar in that the things suggested for comparison are more closely associated than those used in *simile* or *metaphor.* They are not uncommon in everyday speech, and their skillful use is a secret of much that is fascinating in literature. It is often difficult to classify an expression definitely as one or other of these figures. The name "metonymy" is often used for both.

Synecdoche (*sĭ-nĕk'dô-kē*). A figure in which a striking part of the object is used to signify the whole, or sometimes the whole to signify the part: "A thousand *hands* waved farewell"; "This *roof* (house) protects you"; "Now the *year* (the summer) is beautiful"; "*Ten thousand swords* would have leaped from their scabbards"; "The *hearths* (homes) of the nation"; "The *city* welcomed him."

Metonymy (*mē-tŏn'ĭ-mĭ*). A figure by which we put the cause for the effect, or the effect for the cause, as when we say, "He reads Milton," i. e., Milton's works; "Gray hairs should be respected," meaning old age; "My son, give me thy *heart*" (affection); "He was the *sigh* of his mother's soul" (the boy she loved).

Personification. The figure by which inanimate things or ideas are endowed with the qualities of human beings: "*Wisdom crieth* in the streets"; "*Hope* hath never lost *her* youth"; "The little *Road says,* Go";

"The *Worm* aware of his intent
Harangued him thus, right eloquent";

"Hark! *Truth proclaims,* thy triumphs cease"; "The *Sea saw* it and *fled.*"

Allusion. A figure in which reference, direct or indirect, is made to some personage, incident, expression, or custom, with which the reader is familiar, to convey a vivid picture of the subject in hand: "A *Daniel* come to judgment"; "A *Napoleon* of finance"; "*They shall not pass.*"

II. Figures that depend for their force partly upon the arrangement of words in the sentence and partly upon the mental attitude of the speaker or writer.

Interrogation. This figure consists in asking a question with an implied contrary answer. Its force amounts to a vigorous denial: "*Am I a dog?*" "Hath the Lord said it, *and shall He not do it?*" "Hath He spoken it, *and shall He not make it good?*" "He that planted the ear, *shall He not hear?*" "He that formed the eye, *shall He not see?*" The figure is appropriate in intense expression, especially in oratory.

Apostrophe (*ȧ-pŏs′trô-fē*). Another figure which is appropriate in oratory or in exalted poetry. It consists in turning aside from the usual order of words and addressing an object, an absent person, or a personified idea, thus bringing the object or idea vividly to the reader or audience: "O *Duty*, if that name thou love!" "O *Death*! where is thy sting?" "O *Grave*! where is thy victory?"

Vision. A figure closely akin to apostrophe but less forceful. This figure consists in describing a scene, an object, or an event as if it were immediately in view: "*I see before me the gladiator lie.*" The value of the figure consists in its vividness. The use of the historical present is a form of vision: "*I remember well the day I entered the room, the familiar objects are all before me, but my mother is not there.*"

Irony (*ī′rô-nĭ*). This consists in saying the opposite of what is meant. A classical illustration of irony is to be found in the repeated phrase of Mark Antony in *Julius Cæsar*: "They are *honorable* men"; "We have, to be sure, great reason to believe the *modest* man would not ask him for a debt, when he pursues his life." Modern writing is characterized rather by touches of irony than by a full development of the figure. It is a dangerous tool to use even occasionally and not at all fit for habitual employment.

Litotes (*lī′tô-tēz*). A figure of speech by which a strong affirmative is expressed simply by the negative of the contrary: "a citizen of *no mean city*," i. e., "of an important city"; "A storm of *no small force* drove our vessel before it"; "To be polite in word and in deed is a matter of *no slight significance.*"

Hyperbole (*hī-pẽr′bô-lē*). An exaggeration for the purpose of compelling attention: "*Every word that Webster used weighed a pound*";

"The sky *shrunk upward with unusual dread*
And trembling Tiber *div'd beneath his bed*";

"My song *shall blossom at your feet*
My heart *your throne shall be.*"

Euphemism (*ū′fē-mĭz′m*). A mild or inoffensive expression used in place of what is regarded as an unpleasant statement. It is generally to be avoided: "*He is a little careless when handling the truth*"; "*He was in the habit of removing people's goods out of their houses without previous arrangement with the owners*"; "*He passed away.*" These are euphemisms for lying, for stealing, and for death.

III. Figures that are simply arrangements of well-chosen words to produce packed and pointed expression.

Antithesis (*ăn-tĭth′ē-sĭs*). This figure depends for its force upon vivid contrast of opposite terms or ideas. It gains power through the balanced construction involved in the sentence: "If one would be rich, *should he labor to increase his possessions, or to diminish his desires?*" "The Puritans hated bear baiting, *not because it gave pain to the bear, but because it gave pleasure to the spectators.*" Many catch phrases are antitheses: "*rich and poor*"; "*capital and labor.*"

Climax. An arrangement of words or groups of words in ascending order of force or importance: "*I know it, I concede it, I confess it, I proclaim it.*" "*Force, force to the utmost; force without stint or limit; the righteous, triumphant force which shall make right the law of the world and cast every selfish dominion down in the dust.*" The strongest expression must be placed last in order.

Epigram. A short, forceful expression which depends for its value upon its brevity and upon some surprise involved in it. The best epigrams imply some antithesis: "*The silence was audible*"; "*So good that he is good for nothing*"; "*Some laborious orators mistake perspiration for inspiration.*"

Epithet (*ĕp′ĭ-thĕt*). A descriptive word or phrase into which has been packed an important meaning or a vivid picture. The epithet is an important element in poetry, and many epithets have become common words. There are two kinds of epithets:

1. *Essential Epithets*, or names of qualities always associated with the thing described: "*green* grass"; "*bright* sword."

2. *Conventional Epithets*, such as adjectives which become commonly associated with certain names: "*honest* Abe"; "*doubting* Thomas"; "*bright-eyed* Athena." The Greek poems, the *Iliad* and the *Odyssey*, are particularly rich in epithets: "the *wine-dark* sea"; "*hollow* ships"; "*rosy-fingered* dawn." Other examples: "our *honored* dead"; "*daisied* fields."

IV. The following names are given to certain uses of words for their sound values:

Euphony (*ū′fô-nĭ*). A name applied to the pleasing effects of sounds produced by the combination of words in sentences or of phonetic elements in spoken words. Euphony is a fundamental requirement of poetry: "The most sounding and euphonic surname that English history or topography affords";

"The bells of Shandon that sound so grand on
The pleasant waters of the river Lee."

Onomatopœia (*ŏn′ô-măt′ô-pē′yȧ*). The word means name-making. Onomatopœia is the use of a word or phrase formed to imitate the sound of the thing signified. Many words in common use furnish examples: We say *rat tat tat* to denote a knocking at the door, *bow wow* to express the barking of a dog, or *buzz, buzz* to indicate the sound made by bees. Onomatopœia is frequently used in poetry where the sound of certain words is used to convey the sense; thus,

"When Ajax strives some rock's vast weight to throw
The line too labors, and the words move slow";

"And the *light Latin tripped* along her tongue
Amid the *roar of Irish gutturals.*"

Alliteration (*ă-lĭt′ẽr-ā′shŭn*). The use of a succession of words having the same initial letter or sound. The chief value of alliteration is in challenging attention. Alliterative phrases, also, are easily memorized: "*babbling babes*"; "*feathered fowl.*" Early English poetry used alliteration in place of rime and meter. The device is frequently used in modern poetry; as, for example, "*Still stands* the forest primeval"; "*Lisp* of *leaves* and *ripple* of *rain.*"

Assonance (*ăs′ô-năns*). A name applied to the recurrence of the same vowel sound in a group of words. Assonance is likely to become monotonous and disagreeable in prose or even in poetry, though sometimes it is used with good effect: "*So all* day *long* the *noise* of battle *rolled*"; "*Hark*! *Hark*! the *lark.*"

LETTER WRITING

Among the arts of everyday life there is none more important than that of letter writing. Our business and social relations are so dependent upon our written communications that the ability to write a clear letter in correct form is regarded as an essential mark of an ordinary English education. No accomplishment is more highly prized than skill in writing tactful, effective business letters, unless it be the ability to write a graceful personal letter of friendship. The general principles that govern the writing of letters and many suggestions that will help the student of the art to perfect his work are given in the following pages. The very fact that a letter is taken as an index of the personal character of the writer should prompt us all to most careful study of this art which is at once so practical and so easy to master.

We all know the kind of letters we like to receive—social letters that are really sincere and hearty, like the personal talk of friends, business letters that are frank and clear and that bring the writers, as we say, face to face with us. The telephone conversation, instead of taking the place of the letter, has served to emphasize the importance of the personal, direct, well-planned letter, and to increase the demand for it. Telegrams often require "letters to follow," which state more completely the contents of the messages. Good business records demand letters to "confirm" important telephone conversations.

THE BUSINESS LETTER: PRINCIPLES

We judge people and business houses by the letters they write. First, the appearance of the letterhead, the quality of the paper, and the outward form or display of the letter attract or repel us; then the substance of the message and its style and its tone make their impression. All these elements contribute to the general effect of any letter and determine what the response to it shall be.

As we judge others, so we are judged. If our letters are to be worthy representatives of us and fulfill the missions on which they are sent, we must plan and construct them carefully and intelligently. No detail either of material or of dress can safely be neglected.

How do you plan your letters? Do you organize the ideas so that they can be quickly and easily understood? Do you present them with the ease of manner and with the touch of individuality that you would put into a personal interview? Do the sentences you write and the order in which you write them so clearly express what you wish to say that the reader will naturally make the response you want? Do you use the tone of courtesy and of respect that will leave in the reader's mind a pleasant impression and build his good will for you?

BUILDING YOUR LETTER

The object of practically every business letter is to secure action, either immediate or remote. But the reader is not likely to act as the writer wishes, unless it appears to his own advantage to do so. Hence, it is wise to study the merits of the proposed action from the reader's viewpoint, and to present them in such a light that he can see them plainly. In every legitimate transaction both sides profit, but it is necessary to lay greatest stress upon the reader's profit, since his self-interest is his most powerful incentive to action.

It is true that we all act upon suggestions, either in the form of commands or in the gentler forms of persuasion. First, however, our attention must be secured, our interest must be aroused, and we must have inducements to action. Hence, the following steps in the building of a business letter are well established and are of almost universal application: (1) Get the attention of the reader; (2) Give him definite information; (3) Arouse his interest; (4) Offer him an inducement to act or to respond to you; (5) Give him a positive suggestion or direction; (6) Close your letter with a courteous expression that leaves a good feeling behind it.

The following example illustrates one way of building the letter. The headings in the left margin are, of course, not a part of the letter.

(LETTERHEAD)

FOREST PRODUCTS ASSOCIATION
LUMBERMAN'S EXCHANGE
LASALLE AND MADISON STREETS, CHICAGO, ILLINOIS

HOMES BUILDING DEPARTMENT
WALTER C. HINES, *Manager*

June 17, 194–

Mr. Thomas C. Parsons *Subject: Expert Service*
22 Elm Street
Utica, New York

Dear Sir:

ATTENTION AND INTEREST (the receiver's point of view)

As you say in your interesting reply to our advertisement, the time was, not so long ago, when a man built his house just as his neighbors built theirs. He used wood or brick or stone, because these were the only materials to be had. For the same reason, his roof was either shingle or slate.

Nowadays, however, as you suggest, a man tries to express his taste in a home. He wants also to fit his house artistically to its location. In response to these demands, the variety of available materials and of plans for their combination has been increased beyond the range of any one man's knowledge.

INFORMATION

Right here is where we can help you. Our business is to bring to the solution of your problem the best possible expert knowledge of materials and construction. This service we are able to supply economically through our large co-operative organization.

INTEREST AND INDUCEMENT

We enable you to save money on the cost of building and to realize with greater satisfaction your ideals of convenience, quality, and beauty.

Two booklets, "Some How's of Houses" and "Forest to Finish," which we are mailing to you today, will give you a suggestion as to our method of service. You will notice that we propose to furnish unbiased advice about ALL *kinds of building materials.*

POSITIVE SUGGESTION AND COURTESY

When you have examined these booklets, just fill out and sign the enclosed card. It will bring our nearest expert representative for a personal conference at any time you suggest.

Very truly yours,
Walter C. Hines

Enclosure

This letter, to be sure, is a sales letter and therefore exemplifies more clearly the steps mentioned above than does a collection letter or letter of adjustment. All business letters, however, are in a sense sales letters, since all attempt at least to "sell" the writer's viewpoint and to secure the reader's favorable response.

Of course you can make these several steps in ways as varied as the kinds of people concerned and as the nature of the services involved. So, the particular contents of letters will vary with circumstances. Many very short notes, such as orders or brief acknowledgments, will not show all the steps. In general, however, the opening of the letter should recognize the reader's viewpoint. Beyond this very important approach to the recipient, the contents of the letter should further prepare him for the letter's real message by impressing upon him a sense of the writer's reliability, thus arousing his confidence. The next step is either direct statement or tactful suggestion of the writer's viewpoint. Persuasion of the reader to accept and to act according to that viewpoint is the final step.

The Letter as a Talk. You may think of the letter as a substitute for face to face talk. Hence, imagine as clearly as you can the characteristics of your reader, his immediate problems, and those features of his surroundings which you might see clearly in a personal interview. You will thus be able to put into your letter the welcome personal element. For instance, a letter planned to sell an article to a lawyer or to a doctor will be different in its appeal from letters designed to reach a farmer or a merchant. *Plan your letter for your reader.*

It should be noted that the letters quoted here are only illustrations of principles and methods and are not offered as models or guides. Since conditions vary greatly and every letter should be written with its particular reader definitely in mind, no set of letters, however extensive, could safely be copied or closely imitated. Imitation of models, moreover, destroys the element of personal character that is so important a part of the good business letter.

The Letter as a Record. The letter is a more permanent thing than the conversation. (1) It serves as a ready means of confirmation and of record. (2) In it matters may be elaborated, or treated more definitely and more connectedly than in a conversation. (3) Most people find it easier to understand an object or a statement if they can see it. They have more confidence in their eyes than in their ears. Besides, they can take more time to study the thing or the word that is before their eyes. Hence the letter frequently offers an occasion for clear, detailed explanation, which the reader may have before him for continuous study or for repeated examination.

In modern practice, clear explanation is recognized as the best means of persuasion through letters. Argument is generally regarded as out of place in a business letter, except as it appears in the form of a conclusion based upon clear explanation. This is a principle also of the best modern advertising; for an advertisement is really an "open letter" of business.

STYLE: QUALITIES

The preceding paragraph will suggest that the business letter is not necessarily brief. In practice, however, it is usually, if possible, limited to one page. But it must always be *clear, concise, positive,* and *courteous.*

I. Clearness. This is a quality to be secured through right order, simple, direct statements, and pleasing mechanical form. If you first arouse attention and interest, the way to understanding is open; clearness means ease of understanding for the reader, but nothing is clear to an inattentive mind. Clearness through style involves: (1) the use of accurate, definite, familiar words and phrases; (2) the use of well-made and well-punctuated sentences; (3) good paragraphing.

1. Words and Phrases. The words in your letter should be "loaded"—each one should carry a definite meaning. The habit of using a limited stock of words is easy to fall into, but it is fatal to clearness, except in the narrow circle of persons familiar with them. Every business has its peculiar set of *stock phrases,* its *cant* or *jargon,* which is unfamiliar to many people. For them, it must be translated into expressions they can understand readily. The letter writer should study *Usage* and *Synonyms.* This is the way to learn to adapt language to the reader. The following suggestions with respect to certain commonly used expressions are approved by good writers:

Advise, in the sense of *inform* or *tell.* The word is used too often. *Inform* or *notify,* except in formal writing, would be better.

Along these lines. A good phrase, but, when used too often, *lines* becomes indefinite. *In this way* or *following these plans* may be more definite.

And oblige, as in the phrase, "*and oblige* Yours truly." An obvious short-cut in courtesy, and therefore lacking in courtesy. Write "We (or I) shall be greatly obliged."

As per. Use *according to,* or some other phrase. See *Good Usage.*

At all times, At this time. The false formality in these phrases often repeated robs them of force. Prefer *always* and *now.*

At hand or **Has come to hand.** An obsolete phrase. Write "We have your letter—," or leave the fact to be understood.

Attached hereto. Appropriate only in the briefest, routine forms.

At the present writing. Prefer *now* or *at present.*

Beg, as in "We *beg* to state." An expression to be used only in the most formal correspondence. Otherwise it suggests a false humility.

Complaint. The word has been displaced in favor of *claim* and *adjustment.* The business advantage is obvious.

Contents carefully noted. A dead phrase. Use some words that will really convey the personal interest intended: "We have read with particular care, etc."

Enclosed herewith or **We enclose herewith.** *Herewith* is unnecessary.

Enclosed please find. *Please* is superfluous. Write "You will find enclosed" or "We enclose."

Earliest convenience. A faulty choice of words assumed to be courteous because of their indefiniteness. "As soon as possible" or "as soon as convenient for you" is the meaning usually intended.

Esteemed, as in "your *esteemed* favor." This and the following word are old forms of courtesy worn out by too frequent use. Say simply "your letter."

Favor, as in "*favor* us with a reply." Save the word for times when a reply is a real favor or courtesy.

Hand you herewith. Originally supposed to suggest personal presence in a letter, this phrase has lost its meaning through too frequent repetition. To say simply "inclose," or "enclose," is usually sufficient.

Inst., Ult., Prox. These are not now in good use to indicate present, last, or next month.

Kindly, as in "thanking you *kindly.*" Superfluous. Kindness is implied in thanks.

Our Mr......... No longer good form. Omit *our,* or say "our representative," or use his official title; as, "our manager."

Participial Construction, as in "*Hoping* for an early reply." In English, the present participle frequently gives a weak form of expression. Its use in the conclusion of letters is to be avoided. Write, "We hope for."

Party, meaning *person.* See *Good Usage.*

Passive Construction, as in "goods *were not able to be shipped.*" Use active form of expression: "It was not possible to ship" or "We could not ship."

Permit me to say. This phrase is too formal for ordinary use. It seems to imply some straining of relations.

Pronouns or Articles Omitted, as in "*Received yours and contents noted.*" The pronoun *I* or *we* is good form and should be used.

Proposition, meaning *affair.* See *Good Usage.*

Recent date, as in "yours of *recent date.*" Exactness is preferable. Give precise date.

Same, as in "the *same* shall receive prompt attention." The word is overworked. Use regular pronouns, except in formal papers.

State, meaning *say.* See *Good Usage.*

The writer. People are not so much afraid of the first personal pronoun as they used to be. Use *I* or *we,* instead of *the writer* or *the undersigned,* except in official letters, reports, and other formal documents.

Valued, as in "your *valued* communication." False formality, except on special occasions.

Would say or **Wish to say.** Too frequently these are mere wasteful, roundabout phrases. Omit them.

Your obedient servant. Another worn-out form. Many of these business forms are relics of the old servant attitude of the shopkeeper toward a patron. Let your phrases of courtesy express self-respect.

2. Sentences. The sentence is the common unit of thought expression. In some special types of letters the separate phrase may be used to challenge attention, but good sentence structure is necessary to the good letter. See *Sentence Building.*

Three rhetorical types of sentences are recognized.

(1) *The loose sentence* simply adds idea to idea; it can be closed at any one of several different points and still be a complete sentence. Example: "Students from Central and South America are already coming to our colleges and universities in considerable numbers—and nothing has done so much to make Latin America acquainted with the United States."

(2) *The periodic sentence* is more rarely used and must be definitely planned in advance. It piles up one subordinate idea after another, preparatory to the main statement. Its advantage is in its effect of climax. Example: "That there is a serious housing shortage today, not only in the United States but throughout the civilized world, is a generally known fact."

(3) *The balanced sentence* is so called because it is built of contrasting clauses of similar form, which seem to balance each other like a pair of scales. This sentence is much used in advertising and in business letters. Its value lies in the emphasis and clearness which come from the contrasts in the sentence. Example: "Not only is order Heaven's first law, but it is the first and last law of Earth."

The skillful writer will adapt his sentence form to the subject in hand and to the purpose in view. He will vary the forms of his sentences to avoid monotony, for monotony is the foe of attention and, therefore, of clearness.

See *Punctuation.*

3. Paragraphs. The paragraph is the common form for the relating and the developing of ideas. In its construction, we must consider logic, style, and form. For *Paragraph Development*, refer to *Speaking and Writing* and see below under *Form.* The skillful letter writer will study the psychology of the paragraph. Good paragraph arrangement enables the reader to see the relationship of sentences that belong together as parts of the treatment of a single topic. It enables him also to get the intended emphasis by observing the position of the various sentences in the paragraph. The beginning and the end of a paragraph, as of a sentence, are the emphatic points.

The following is an excellent example of a business paragraph:

"Saving should be more than the accumulation of money. It should include the use of money to add to the total; in other words, investment. Reckless investment is speculation, but careful investment is the best form of saving."

The first sentence states a topic clearly; the second enlarges on the topic; the third, a balanced sentence, develops the "investment" idea and repeats, for emphasis, the word "saving," which thus is kept the most emphatic word in the paragraph.

II. Conciseness. One attains conciseness through using the exact word, and by using no more words than necessary. The quality is the result of precision and of economy in diction. Skill in this matter is to be attained through study of *Synonyms* and of *Usage*. Conciseness is not improved by omitting the pronoun subject from a sentence; as, "Received yours of the 24th." Always put the subject into the sentence. (The imperative sentence is an exception.)

III. Positiveness. This is a matter of *contents* and of *style*. It means direct, definite, unmistakable meaning in directions and suggestions.

1. Strive for positiveness in the *contents* of a business letter. The reason for this rule is psychological. We know how the mind works. Desired action is best secured by positive suggestion; undesired action is best prevented, not by negative suggestion, but by positive suggestion of the opposite action. For example: instead of saying, "Do not delay writing us," say, "Write to us at once"; instead of "We hope you will not read this until the rest of your morning's mail is out of the way," write, "This letter will repay careful attention. Please get the rest of your morning's mail out of the way. Then read what we have written."

2. In *style*, positiveness is emphasized (1) by avoiding the passive construction wherever the active will convey the thought and (2) by avoiding the use of the loose present participle at the beginning of sentences. Use straightforward simple or balanced sentences. Instead of "Finding that we have had no orders from you for some time, we write to inquire," write, "Our records show that recently we have not had our usual orders from you. Naturally, we wonder why."

IV. Courtesy. The true quality of courtesy arises from the writer's consideration for the interests and feelings of his reader. It is usually manifested, however, in the choice and in the use of expressions of politeness that have been well established by convention. It is often made even more evident by what the letter leaves unsaid. Words and phrases that might wound or irritate or might suggest lack of respect for the reader should be scrupulously avoided. The quality of courtesy should pervade the whole letter, but it is especially vital at the beginning and at the end. Most of the specimen letters quoted here illustrate the value of courtesy.

FORM

Good psychology prompts attention to the *mechanical form* of the letter as a means of securing attention and favorable consideration. Not only must the letter be easy to read, but it must invite reading. No matter how important or interesting the contents of a letter may be, if its form is not attractive, it may be a failure.

Quality and Form of Stationery. This is the first consideration. Select good stationery; then write letters of corresponding quality. Generally, commercial letter paper is about 8½ by 11 inches in size. A half sized sheet, 6 by 10 or 5½ by 8, is sometimes used, although the best form is the full sized sheet for all letters. For mailing, this full sized sheet should be folded from the bottom so as to bring the bottom edge within about a half inch of the top. This folding makes the opening of the letter easy. If a letterhead is used, this folding may be made so as to leave a part of the letterhead visible. The folded sheet is then again folded twice, the first fold beginning about one-third of the distance from the right, bringing the sheet to a convenient size for the ordinary business envelope.

For the long or legal envelope, fold the bottom third of the page upward, then the top third down. This folding allows the reader, on opening the letter, to see the heading at once. Folding the top third down first and the bottom third upward makes insertion in the envelope easier. Formal official letters are frequently written on stationery of the social form, that is, on a four-page, folded sheet adapted for folding once to fit either an envelope of commercial size or the square type of envelope. It may carry a short form of letterhead either printed or engraved.

The envelope should, of course, match the paper in color and in quality. A short form of letterhead or return address is printed in the upper left-hand corner of the envelope, or sometimes on the flap of the envelope, as on social stationery.

In general, white paper of the "bond" type is always good form. If tinted papers are used, the color should be such as will not interfere with ease of reading.

Placing the Letter Upon the Page. This is very important. For the positions of the various parts there are set rules. The reader habitually looks for the address of the writer in the upper right-hand part of the page, for his own address and the salutation at the upper left-hand part, on lines slightly below the writer's address, and for a formal conclusion at the bottom. Examples of these rules and of permissible variations are shown in the following specimens.

CORRECT BUSINESS LETTER FORMS

I. The Heading. This contains the address of the sender and the date of writing. It is the first item in the business letter. A printed or engraved letterhead should contain the address of the individual or firm. The address so given need not be repeated. The following forms are approved to be placed in the upper right-hand part of the page. Care should be taken that this heading is not too near the right-hand side. When the heading takes two lines or three, the second and third lines may be indented; as,—

810 Jefferson Ave.,
Cleveland, Ohio,
June 28, 194-.

or, in block,

810 Jefferson Ave.,
Cleveland, Ohio,
June 28, 194-.

or,

725 Tremont St., Boston,
June 28, 194-.

To give a personal or social *tone* to the letter, numbers and dates may be written out. The following form for dates, in both heading and body of the letter, finds favor with some writers:

15 May, 194-.

II. The Introduction, or **Address.** This is the second item in the letter. It should be placed one or two lines below the heading and at the left of the page. The following forms are in good use:

1. Addressing a firm,—

Messrs. Jones & Black,
480 Main St.,
Buffalo, N. Y.

or, *The Aetna Company,*
7 Archer St.,
Omaha, Neb.

or, *Smith, Marks, & Co.,*
Boston, Mass.

2. Addressing an individual, as a member of a firm,—

Mr. James T. Girard,
President Girard Steel Company,
St. Louis, Mo.

3. Addressing an individual,—

Mr. Thomas Brown,
513 Sacramento St.,
San Francisco, Calif.

Note.—These addresses may be written in block. Some writers prefer not to use commas at the ends of lines in the heading or address. This practice is permissible. Periods also, except after abbreviations, may be omitted from the ends of these lines. Omission of marks must, however, be consistent:

16 Park St., Denver
December 14, 194-

Miss Jean Phillips
1014 Chamber of Commerce
Cleveland, Ohio

The method of open punctuation, used in the above example, may be seen illustrated in the letter by Walter C. Hines on page 120.

When the firm is addressed, but it is intended that the letter should go to some particular person, *Attention of Mr. . . . .* may be written at the right below the heading, or on a line with the salutation. Frequently, the *subject* of the letter is written at the right in line with the name of the firm or person addressed:

The Aetna Company, — *Subject: Flour Shipment*
7 Archer St.
Omaha, Neb.
Gentlemen: — *Attention of Mr. Brown*

4. Military Form,—

The following form is prescribed for U. S. Army correspondence:

U. S. ARMY RECRUITING STATION,
5 EAST SWAN STREET, BUFFALO, N. Y.

825 — *November 22, 194-.*
From: *Recruiting Officer.*
To: *The Adjutant General of the Army, Washington, D. C.*
Subject: Enlistments.

This is called the "brief." It occupies the upper third of the ordinary sheet and is folded back so as to be immediately visible in files or on opening the envelope. The usual *salutation* and the usual *complimentary close* are omitted. The number (825) refers to the office files.

Many business houses use a similar form, especially for routine letters between departments.

5. Addressing a firm of women,—

Mesdames Trigg & New,
5314 Michigan Ave.,
Chicago, Ill.

Note.—Some authorities permit omission of the period after *Mr.* and *Messrs.*

III. The Salutation. This is the third item.

1. In addressing a firm, *Gentlemen* is preferred to *Dear Sirs* by most writers. This form is used also in addressing firms made up of men and women.

2. In addressing a firm made up of women, *Ladies* is the usual salutation.

3. For individuals, *Dear Sir* is the usual form. *My dear Sir* is regarded as rather more formal. A little more informal, according to occasion, is *Dear Mr. Girard* or *My dear Mr. Girard.*

4. *Dear Madam* or, more formal, *My dear Madam* is appropriate in addressing either a married or an unmarried woman. *Dear Mrs. Smith* or, more formal, *My dear Mrs. Smith* may be used if the degree of acquaintanceship permits.

5. In addressing an unmarried woman, use such a form as *Dear Miss Walker* or, more formal, *My dear Miss Walker.*

6. In addressing a letter to a man *and* a woman, use the form *Dear Sir and Madam.*

Note.—The husband's title, as, *Doctor, Professor,* or *Reverend,* should never be prefixed to the wife's name.

In a letter to a doctor or a professor, the address may be *Dr. James Martin* or *James Martin, M. D.* (or *D. D., Ph. D., D. O., D. D. S.*), or *Professor Wm. James.* If *Dr.* precedes the name, the abbreviation for the degree should not follow. In such cases, the salutation may be *Dear Sir* or, less formal, *Dear Doctor Martin* or *Dear Professor James.*

Note.—In general, good taste seems to approve, even in business letters, the spelling out of a title in the salutation, although the abbreviation may be used.

Note.—In the punctuation of the salutation, usage varies. The colon is always correct. In short, informal letters, the comma may be used. The dash is superfluous. However, if the address takes more than three lines, the salutation may be made part of the first line of the letter and may be followed by colon and dash or by comma and dash:

Gentlemen:—In your letter of June 26, etc.

IV. The Body of the Letter. This should be well centered on the page. The margins at top and bottom should be approximately equal, and the margins at the sides should be kept, as nearly as possible, equal. It is easy to keep the left-hand margin regular, but some care is necessary to get an even right-hand margin. Wide margins at right and left are advisable for two reasons: (1) Short lines are easier to read than long ones; (2) the contrast of blank and filled spaces makes reading easier.

The Paragraphing of a Business Letter. This is perhaps the most important feature of its form. First of all, the paragraphs should be reasonably short, for a well broken page is more inviting to the eye and easier to read than solid masses of type. Secondly, the paragraphs should not have too great a contrast in length. Absolute uniformity is, of course, impossible and undesirable as well. Variety in the matter of length, however, should be only great enough to avoid monotony. Generally speaking, the paragraphs at the beginning and at the end of the letter should be somewhat shorter than those in the middle.

The following paragraph forms are in use:

The indented paragraph, like this one. The first line is set in from the margin a number of spaces approximately equal to the margin allowed.

The hanging paragraph, like this. The first line begins at the margin, and all other lines are indented a number of spaces equal to the margin allowed for the first line.

The blocked paragraph, like this. No line is given extra indention. This last type of paragraph calls for very wide margins. Examples of these various forms of paragraphing are given in the specimen letters on the following pages. Margins should be not less than one inch in width.

V. The Complimentary Close. In business letters this should be *Yours truly*, or *Yours very truly*, or *Respectfully yours*, *Very respectfully yours*, except in cases where the writer, because of close acquaintance, may prefer a more informal phrase, such as *Sincerely yours*, *Faithfully yours*. Never write *respectively* for *respectfully*. Some authorities permit omission of comma after the complimentary close.

Such an expression as *With sincerest regards, I am* should begin a new, indented line, just above the complimentary close.

Envelope. *The address on the envelope* and that in the letter should correspond accurately, although some authorities permit the omission of the street address in the letter. On the envelope, the first line of the address should be placed approximately halfway between the top and the bottom of the envelope, beginning about one-fourth of the length of the envelope from the left-hand end.

Additional directions, such as *in care of*, *c/o*, or *introducing*, may be placed at the lower left-hand corner. A post-office box number is usually placed in this position, to avoid having more than three, or at most four, lines in the address. Neither the abbreviation *No.* nor the sign # should be placed before the street address. The address may be punctuated with commas at the ends of lines, except the last line, where a period should be used; or punctuation may be omitted entirely, except after abbreviations.

In *street numbers* involving *second* or *third*, it is sufficient to write *d* after the figures instead of *nd* or *rd*; as 32d, 23d. Many writers do not use *d* or *th*. To insure the return of a letter in case of failure of delivery, the writer's address should be placed on the outside of the envelope, either in the upper left-hand corner on the front of the envelope or on the flap at the back of the envelope.

Cautions. Certain things the careful writer will always do: (1) He will use the *correct* address of the person to whom he is writing and will make the salutation *appropriate*; (2) he will have the complimentary close *appropriate* and his own signature *legible*. If the writer of the letter is a woman, she will add to her signature whatever may be necessary to indicate whether or not she is married, as in the following:

(*Mrs.*) or (*Miss*) *Anna M. Worden.*

or,

(*Mrs. J. C. Truman*) *Mary V. Truman.*

If there are "enclosures" in the letter, such as stamps, money, or papers, these should always be mentioned; and it is customary to write in the lower left-hand corner either the word *Enclosure* or the abbreviation *Enc.*; similarly, *Inclosure* or *Inc.*

Letters sent in the name of a firm by an official or employee may be signed as follows:

Knight, Lymmes, and Co.
By (or *Per*) *L. R. Parsons.*

APPROPRIATE FORMS IN ADDRESSING OFFICIALS AND DIGNITARIES

The President of the United States.
Name and address,—The President, White House (or Executive Mansion), Washington, D. C.
Salutation,—*Mr. President:* or *Sir:*
Close,—*Respectfully yours*, or *Very truly yours*,

The Vice President of the United States.
Name and address,—The Honorable.........., Vice President of the United States, Washington, D. C. or, To the Vice President of the United States, Washington, D. C.
Salutation,—*Sir:* or *Dear Sir:*
Close,—*Very truly yours*, or *Respectfully yours*,

Member of Cabinet.
Name and address,—The Secretary of State, Washington, D. C.
Salutation,—*Dear Mr. Secretary:*
Close,—*Yours very truly*,

or,
Name and address,—The Honorable the Secretary of the Treasury, Washington, D. C. or, The Honorable A............ B............, Secretary of the Treasury, Washington, D. C.
Salutation,—*Sir:* or *Dear Sir:*
Close,—*Very respectfully yours*,

Members of Congress.
Name and address,—The Hon. Martin Warren, Senate Chamber, Washington, D. C. or, The Hon. Martin Warren, House of Representatives, Washington, D. C.
Salutation,—*Sir:* or *Dear Sir:*
Close,—*Very truly yours*,

Foreign Ministers.
Name and address,—His Excellency,........, Ambassador to the Court of St. James, London, England.
Salutation,—*Your Excellency:* or *Sir:*
Close,—*Very truly yours*,

Governors.
Name and address,—His Excellency, the Governor of New York, Albany, N. Y. or, His Excellency, the Governor, Albany, N. Y. or, His Excellency, Governor S. M. Smith, Albany, N. Y.
Salutation,—*Your Excellency:* or *Sir:*
Close,—*Very truly yours*,

Mayors.
Name and address,—The Honorable ...., Mayor of New York City, New York City, N. Y.
Salutation,—*Sir:* or *Dear Sir:*
Close,—*Very truly yours*,

State Officers.
Name and address,—The Honorable Attorney-General of New York, Albany, N. Y. or, The Honorable ...., Attorney-General of New York, Albany, N. Y.
Salutation,—*Sir:* or *Dear Sir:*
Close,—*Very truly yours*,

Judge of Supreme Court (or highest court of a State).
Name and address,—The Hon. William V. Hinton, State Capitol, Columbus, Ohio.
Salutation,—*Dear Mr. Justice:*
Close,—*Yours very truly*,

Judge (other than Supreme Court).
Name and address,—The Hon. Henry A. Freeman, State Circuit Court Building, Chicago, Ill.
Salutation,—*Dear Sir:* or (less formal) *Dear Judge Freeman:*
Close,—*Yours very truly*,

Minor Officials (City or County).
Name and address,—Mr. James Wingate, City Treasurer, City Hall, Des Moines, Iowa.
Salutation,—*Dear Sir:*
Close,—*Yours very truly*,

President of a University.
Name and address,—President James B. Conant, Harvard University, Cambridge, Mass.
Salutation,—*Dear Sir:* or (more formal) *My dear Sir:*
Close,—*Yours very truly*,

College or University Professor.
Name and address,—Professor Arthur K. Rimer, Ph. D. (or other proper degree), University of Denver, Denver, Colo.
Salutation,—*Sir:* or *Dear Sir:*
Close,—*Yours very truly,* or *Yours sincerely,*

Superintendent of Schools.
Name and address,—Superintendent Edward Jones, School Headquarters (or Department of Education), Cleveland, Ohio.
Salutation,—*Sir:* or *Dear Sir:* or *My dear Sir:* or (very informally) *Dear Mr. Jones:*
Close,—*Yours very truly,* or *Yours sincerely,*

Protestant Clergyman.
Name and address,—The Rev. Thomas L. Warner, 1645 East Avenue, Harrisburg, Pa.
Salutation,—*Sir:* or *Dear Sir:* or *My dear Sir:* or (very informally) *Dear Mr. Warner:*
Close,—*Yours very truly,* or *Yours sincerely,*

Parish Priest.
Name and address,—The Rev. Frederick E. Kane, 276 Francis Street, Detroit, Mich.
Salutation,—*Reverend and dear Father:* or *Dear Reverend Father:*
Close,—*Yours sincerely,*

Jewish Rabbi.
Name and address,—Rabbi Stephen S. Wise, 340 W. 57th St., New York, N. Y.
Salutation,—*Dear Sir:*
Close,—*Yours very truly,* or *Yours sincerely,*

Protestant Doctor of Divinity (or of Laws).
Name and address,—The Rev. Charles A. McArthur, D. D. (or LL. D.), 5927 Dorchester Avenue, Boston, Mass.
Salutation,—*Sir:* or *Dear Sir:* or *My dear Sir:* or (very informally) *Dear Dr. McArthur:*
Close,—*Yours very truly,* or *Yours sincerely,*

The Pope.
Name and address,—His Holiness, Pope Pius XII, The Vatican, Rome.
Salutation,—*Your Holiness:*
Close,—*Sincerely yours in Christ,*

Cardinal.
Name and address,—His Eminence, William Cardinal O'Connell, Archbishop of Boston, 25 Granby Street, Boston, Mass.
Salutation,—*Your Eminence:*
Close,—*Faithfully your Eminence's servant,* or *Sincerely yours;* if the writer is a Catholic, the words "in Christ" are usually added.

Bishop.
Name and address,—The Rt. Rev. Moses E. Kiley, D. D., Bishop of Trenton, Trenton, N. J.
Salutation,—*Right Reverend and dear Bishop:* or *Right Reverend Bishop:* or, simply, and perhaps more commonly, *Sir:*
Close,—any of the ordinary forms, such as *Very truly yours,* or *Yours sincerely;* if the writer is a Catholic, the words "Sincerely yours in Christ" should be used.

Women in Religious Orders.
Name and address,—(1) The Reverend Mother Angela (in the case of the Mother Superior); (2) Sister Constance (in the case of a Sister); followed in each case by the address.
Salutation,—(1) *Reverend Mother:* (2) *Reverend Madam:* or *Dear Madam:*
Close,—*Yours sincerely,* or any of the more formal phrases.

Military Officer.
Name and address,—General George C. Marshall, War Department, Washington, D. C.
or, The Commanding Officer, Fort Niagara, N. Y.
Salutation,—*Sir:* or *Dear Sir:*
Close,—any of the ordinary forms.

Naval Officer.
Name and address,—Admiral William D. Leahy, Naval Observatory, Washington, D. C.
or, if at sea, U. S. S. *Pennsylvania*, c/o Postmaster, New York, N. Y.
Salutation,—*Sir:* or *Dear Sir:*
Close,—any of the ordinary forms.

Note.—The salutation *Sir*, in nearly all cases, is used in formal official letters. This is also an approved salutation to use in addressing a letter to the editor of a newspaper or other journal. See *Official Letters*.

TYPES OF BUSINESS LETTERS

The following are the common types of letters. Each type has its own peculiar problems.

I. The Simple Order and Reply. This type, supplemented by the letter of inquiry and explanation, is the kind that most people have frequent occasion to use. Out of this simple exchange, however, may develop the elaborate system of *claim, adjustment,* and *follow-up* letters. Claim and adjustment letters, in particular, should be tactfully written. The wording should make plain the writer's intention to be accurate and fair.

1. Order for Goods.

572 East Avenue,
Rochester, N. Y.,
April 3, 194–.

Messrs. Rowen, Winstead, & Co.,
437 State Street,
Chicago, Ill.

Gentlemen:

Will you please send me by freight, addressed to James Wilson, Alva, N. Y., the following:

1 French row-motor;
1 set Franklin garage door tracks and hangers.

I enclose check for $96.25, net price as listed in your special March bulletin.

The building materials purchased from you last summer have proved so satisfactory that I am very glad to send you this further order. I hope that it can be shipped very promptly.

Yours very truly,
Enc. *Robert T. Vane.*

2. Request for Adjustment.

572 East Avenue,
Rochester, N. Y.,
July 6, 194–.

Messrs. Rowen, Winstead, & Co.,
437 State Street,
Chicago, Ill.

Gentlemen:

I have had shipped to you today from Cayuga, N. Y., by insured parcel post, the propeller and housing from the row-motor which I recently purchased from you.

We have used this motor a very few times only. Yesterday, while we were on the river, the housing broke, and it was only by the merest accident that I was able to recover it at all. I do not know that the machine was subjected to any extraordinary strain, though, of course, it may have been. However, the metal looks to me as if it had been defective at the break. Will you please examine the housing and make such adjustment as you think is right.

I shall be glad to have this matter attended to promptly in order that we may have the engine to use as soon as possible.

Yours very truly,
Robert T. Vane.

3. Reply to Adjustment Request.

(LETTERHEAD)

July 8, 194–.

Mr. Robert T. Vane,
572 East Avenue,
Rochester, N. Y.

Dear Sir:

We are very sorry to learn from your letter of July 6 that you have had trouble with the row-motor. We have not yet received the broken parts, but we appreciate the fact that during vacation time you will want a motor to use. Accordingly, we will ship by today's parcel post a propeller and housing to replace the broken parts.

When your shipment arrives, we will have an examination made and will make adjustment such as we think will thoroughly satisfy you. We appreciate your patronage and your good offices in our favor.

Yours very truly,
Rowen, Winstead, & Co.
By J. C. Marcus.

4. Order for Magazine.

24 Winfield Street,
Oswego, Ill.,
October 15, 194–.

Time, the Weekly Newsmagazine,
350 East 22nd Street,
Chicago, Ill.

Gentlemen:

I enclose money order for $5.00 in payment for renewal of my subscription to Time, the Weekly Newsmagazine, for the year 194–.

Please note the change of address indicated at the head of this letter.

Former address: 371 Otis Ave., Kenmore, Ohio.

Yours very truly,

Enc. *(Miss) Myra V. Killian.*

5. Letter to College Officer.

622 Plymouth Ave.,
Harrisburg, Pa.,
July 13, 194–.

Mr. James Harvey, Registrar,
Fairmount University,
Fairmount, Pa.

Dear Sir:

Will you please send me a copy of your application blank for entrance to the engineering school in Fairmount. I completed my high school course in June, and I am planning to enter Fairmount this fall. I should be glad to receive also a copy of your catalogue and other information that would be useful.

Very respectfully yours,
William D. Brown.

II. Letters of Agreement. These usually supplement contracts of various sorts, and should be worded as nearly as possible in the terms of the accompanying contract.

III. The Sales or Advertising Letter. This has been very highly developed within the last few years. It is really the standard or type of all business letters. The psychological principles of the business letter, as stated before, apply with special force to this type, which has for its immediate purpose the securing of business. In present day practice, sales letters are frequently prepared in series, the whole series being planned to cover the steps already given for the typical business letter. The first letter is designed, for instance, to get attention; the last in the series is written as the "clincher," or final persuasive letter.

A short series of four or five letters may be used, each one distinctly different in contents and purpose. Again, a long series, sometimes called "continuous," may be employed, each letter differing only slightly from the others in point of view, all aimed at persuading the "prospect."

These series are the common form of the *follow-up systems*. The writer has a definite object in view, usually either to secure a new field of business or to maintain interest and good will among his present clients. If his first letter fails to produce the result at which it was aimed, he follows it up with others, in which the methods of approach or the inducements offered differ somewhat from those of the first. For example, the letter of the Forest Products Association, page 120, if the prospect fails to return the card, might be followed by one giving some more definite, *interesting* details about the special uses of woods, to arouse the attention and the interest of the man. If Mr. Parsons returns the card promptly, a second letter should precede the representative's call, introducing him and encouraging the fullest use of his services.

Such letters as the following (6, 7), when prepared as circular or form letters, should be so printed that the type style used in filling in the individual addresses shall be like that in the body of the letter. The whole then will have the appearance of a personal letter and will command attention.

6. Sales Letter.

(LETTERHEAD)

April 6, 194–.

Mrs. Marion T. Archer,
1432 Delavan Ave.,
Altoona, Ind.

Dear Madam:

ATTENTION — *On that auto trip last summer, you enjoyed tremendously the road and the ride through beautiful scenery. But when you came to the inn at the end of the day, did you find your gowns in the smooth, dainty condition you could have wished for? Isn't it annoying to find the only things you have to "change to" all rumpled and creased?*

INTEREST — *The answer, of course, is a wardrobe trunk. It is a compact, dust-proof trunk in your car, and a handy, complete wardrobe in your hotel room.*

INFORMATION — *Through an unusually large purchase of the widely known Plico trunks, we are able to offer, during the next*
INDUCEMENT — *week, a full stock at prices that mean to you a saving of more than one-third the usual cost of these high-grade trunks.*

POSITIVE SUGGESTION — *One look at the sturdy build of these trunks and their complete and dainty arrangement of trays and hangers for every sort of hat and garment will convince you that certainly, at these prices, you cannot afford another trip without such a convenience.*

Members of our sales staff are enthusiastic about these new Plico trunks, especially as regards the wide variety of types, conveniences, and styles offered. They will do their best to show you a wardrobe trunk which will best meet your individual traveling needs and your requirements in color and decorative treatment.

Come in early and make your selection before the present full stock is picked over by other buyers.

Very truly yours,
Eldridge, Warren, and Co.,
Per B. F. Warren,
Manager.

7. Sales Letter.

(LETTERHEAD)

THE SECRETARY OF THE TREASURY
Washington

October 1946

To Newspaper Publishers,
Editors and Ad Managers:

The first lesson in a democracy is that the Government belongs to its millions of citizens. It belongs to you—all of us. The Nation can be only as prosperous as are its cities, farms and communities of the individual families which inhabit them.

When you help to promote the sale of U. S. Savings Bonds, you help check inflation and subsequent depression. You help to maintain stable economy.

Stability alone is not enough. The ownership of Savings Bonds does more. It gives people an actual share in America. It presents the possibility of providing the funds for homes and higher education of your children, for old age security, and for emergencies. In other words, your effort in securing bond advertising provides for the security and prosperity of the individual and his family. Prosperous families mean prosperous communities. Prosperous communities mean a prosperous Nation.

That is how you help your Government—that is how you help yourself—when you assist in the U. S. Savings Bond Program.

I urge you to be of all the help you can.

Sincerely,
John W. Snyder
Secretary of the Treasury

IV. The Collection Letter. Collection letters are of two main types,—personal notifications of indebtedness, and personal requests for payment. Both kinds should be courteous and should avoid the use of threats or other offensive measures except as a last resort. Collection letters are usually prepared as a series which begins with a very mild suggestion that payment would be appreciated and ends with an insistent demand. The orderly and systematic mailing of such a series is often of more importance in making the work of collection effective than is the construction of any individual letter. Every letter, however, should have the double purpose of securing the money due and also of retaining the good will of the debtor.

8. Collection Letter.

(LETTERHEAD)

June 20, 194-.

Mr. M. C. Harris,
12 Arthur St.,
Conneaut, Ohio.

Dear Sir:

We find on our books a charge against you of $15.87, under date of May 14. We wish to call your attention to the fact that this is past due.

If there is no error in the account, your prompt remittance will be appreciated.

Very truly yours,
Owen, James, and Co.

9. Collection Letter (*a little more insistent*).

(LETTERHEAD)

June 1, 194-.

Mr. L. R. Converse,
156 Oliver St.,
Owanda, Md.

Dear Sir:

According to our books, your account for invoice of April 7 amounting to $47.60 is unpaid and past due. We wrote you about this account on May 20, but we have had no reply. We wish again to call your attention to the need for payment.

In case of any misunderstanding, we hope you will at once write us fully.

Very truly yours,
Owen, James, and Co.

V. The Letter of Application. The letter of application is in most respects similar to the sales letter. The writer is attempting to sell his own services. To be sure, he must be somewhat more modest and restrained in talking about himself than he is in talking about commodities and the services of others. He should not, however, run the risk of making his letter awkward as well as hypocritical by avoiding the use of the first personal pronoun *I* or by any other device that has its basis in false modesty. If the reader is to desire the writer's services, he must know enough about them to be able to judge their value to him in his business.

10. Direct Application for Commercial Position.

419 Marshall St.,
Syracuse, N. Y.,
February 3, 194-.

Messrs. G. A. Case & Son,
193 Broad Street,
Syracuse, N. Y.

Gentlemen:

I wish to apply for the position in your engineering office which you mention in your advertisement in this morning's "Standard."

I am nineteen years old, a graduate of the Technical High School in the class of 19—. I have also completed a course in drafting in the Mechanics' Institute of Rochester. At present I am employed in the shops of the J. W. Atkins Company, Machinists.

I should be glad to be granted a personal interview at your convenience.

Yours very truly,
James Manson.

11. Application Letter, with Side Heads.

311 East Walker Street,
Buffalo, N. Y.,
October 1, 194-.

Box 176,
Buffalo News.

Gentlemen:

Will you please consider me an applicant for the position mentioned in your advertisement in the Buffalo News of October 1. My qualifications are as follows:

Education. I am a graduate of the Bennett High School of this city, in the class of 19—. My course included commercial work in bookkeeping, typewriting, and stenography. In all these subjects my standing was high.

Experience. During the last two years, I have been employed in the office of R. D. Ward & Son, Ellicott Square Building. My work has included stenography and general office assistance.

References. I can refer you, for information as to my ability and my character, to R. D. Ward & Son, and also to the following: Mr. J. W. Archer, head of Commercial Department, Bennett High School; Mr. Martin B. Allen, Supreme Court Judge.

Very truly yours,
Thomas R. Stafford.

VI. Letter of Resignation. The conclusion of an employee's services should be brought about in a courteous, businesslike manner, and this should be reflected in the correspondence. Although formal, in that it is a record of proceedings, the letter of resignation is usually somewhat personal in tone. Whereas the letter of application is nearly always directed to strangers, the letter terminating one's employment is addressed to persons with whom one has become acquainted. Also *consideration*, which is an important characteristic of "separation correspondence," can best be expressed in language that is more or less informal.

12.

Columbus, Ohio
November 20, 194-

Mr. James B. Wilson, President
The Midwest Supply Company
Columbus 15, Ohio

Dear Mr. Wilson:

Circumstances have arisen which make it necessary for me to be at home with my family in Cleveland. I am therefore submitting my resignation, effective January first, 194-. This will give you a month in which to find a successor for my position. Meanwhile, I will do everything I can to train the new person and otherwise insure the continuation of the work without loss of efficiency.

My stay with your firm has been very pleasant, and I regret the necessity of making a change. I am grateful to you and your associates for many courtesies that have been shown me. It is a privilege to have been a member of your organization.

Yours sincerely,
Susan T. Woodruff

VII. Notes of Introduction. The writer should aim to make it easy for two of his friends to become acquainted with each other. The note may either be sent directly to the person whose good offices it bespeaks, or be given to the person introduced. In the latter case, the envelope is usually left unsealed. The wording should be frank and sincere and should suggest the opening for conversation.

13.

Trenton, Oklahoma,
May 7, 194-.

Mr. Chas. R. Andrews, Trustee,
School District No. 9,
Trenton, Oklahoma.

My dear Mr. Andrews:

Miss Emily Smith desires to secure a position as assistant in your school. She holds a first grade certificate and has had three years of successful experience in our school. We regret to lose her, but she prefers your district because it is nearer to her home. I can recommend Miss Smith as a skillful teacher. She will exert an excellent influence in any school.

Very truly yours,
Charles J. Major,
Trustee of School District No. 4.

14.

North Cornwall, Vermont,
July 6, 194–.

Mr. Walter C. Strong,
84 Arlington Ave.,
Pittsburgh, Pa.

My dear Mr. Strong:
It gives me great pleasure to introduce to you my friend, Mr. Weston Beach, who is to become a resident in your city. You will find him an affable person. I shall greatly appreciate whatever courtesy you may show him in helping him to become acquainted.

Cordially yours,
Henry B. Johnson.

VIII. Letters of Recommendation. Recommendations are sometimes included in notes of introduction, but often they are written as separate letters. They may be written as general letters addressed "To whom it may concern," or as special letters to some definite person.

15. General Recommendation.

Weymouth, Va.,
May 10, 194–.

To Whom It May Concern:
This is to certify that the bearer of this note, Miss Lillian Glades, was graduated from The Teachers' College, Cumberland University, and has since taught in the schools of this city. For the past three years she has taught in the Straymore School, and I have had opportunity to observe her work closely. I can recommend her as capable of filling any position in a city graded school.

John W. Grove,
Principal of Straymore School.

16. General Recommendation.

To Whom It May Concern:
Mr. Henry Laird has been in our employ as bookkeeper the past six years. He is a skilled accountant and a loyal man; in every way he has served us well. We regret to part with him. He goes at his own request because he feels that he should receive a higher salary than we can afford to pay.

We wish Mr. Laird every success.
Jones, Martin, and Co.

Birmingham, Ala.,
June 26, 194–.

17. Special Recommendation.

Lehigh University,
Bethlehem, Pa.,
January 1, 194–.

Mr. Harvey W. Jonson,
Superintendent of Public Works,
Topeka, Kansas.

My dear Mr. Jonson:
We have in our junior class a young man, Mr. Thomas Redding, who has done excellent work in the engineering department. He is a fine, clean young man and has commanded the respect of instructors and students, alike. His home is in Nebraska, and he is anxious, on account of the illness of his father, to get employment for the next year or two near home.

I shall greatly appreciate it if you will interest yourself in him and help him to get work.

Very truly yours,
Thomas Benedict.

IX. The Formal or Official Letter. In formal or official letters, the heading is placed as in the business letter, but the best usage approves the spelling out of the date instead of the use of numerals.

In such letters, also, the address of the person to whom the letter is sent may be placed at the close of the letter, in the lower left-hand part of the sheet. The title of the person addressed, as *Reverend* or *Honorable*, should be spelled out and the initials or given name used. "The" is not necessary before these titles, although good formal usage approves such expressions as *The Reverend Mr. Thomas* in the body of the letter, and many good writers prefer this form for the address. The salutation in such a letter may be *Dear Sir* or simply *Sir*.

18. Note of Appreciation.

October eleventh,
Nineteen-forty ——.

Dear Sir:
By formal vote the Rivoli Club last night instructed me, as secretary of the club, to convey to you their very sincere appreciation of your courtesy and genuine service in the address which you delivered before the club members and their guests on Friday evening, October 10.

I desire the privilege of adding also my own word of grateful acknowledgment.

Very sincerely yours,
James Wakefield.

The Honorable Thomas Downing,
7 Harcourt Street,
Denver, Colorado.

X. Excuse for Absence from School.

19.

Will Miss Stringer please excuse Frances Prescott's absence from school, March 4 and 5, on account of illness in the family.

Sarah C. Prescott.

(Mrs. J. W. Prescott),
March 6, 194–.

20.

Dear Miss Townsend,
Please excuse James's absence from school, October tenth to fourteenth, on account of illness.

Very truly yours,
(Mrs.) James T. Orcutt.

Post Cards or **Postal Cards.** These are appropriate only for brief notices sent out by individuals or organizations, or for impersonal notes. They are not suitable for personal messages. Even the shortest note of any degree of intimacy should always be written as a letter and enclosed in an envelope. *The Picture Post Card* is no exception to this rule.

Telegrams. The rates for sending telegrams are based upon a message of ten words, without punctuation. If punctuation is essential for clearness, the words *comma*, *period*, etc. may be inserted and paid for at regular word rates. No charge is made for the date, address, or signature. A message may be repeated back from the receiving office to the sender, for the sake of accuracy, at established rates.

Other classes of telegraphic service, known as night telegrams, night letters, and day letters, are also available. They offer the advantage either of lower rates or of greater length, but delivery is less prompt.

Cablegrams. Cablegrams, on account of higher cost, are more highly abbreviated than telegrams. The use of code words, that is, either ordinary words given unusual meanings by agreement of the sender and of the receiver, or artificial words whose meanings have been agreed upon, is common. Since the use of codes is governed by certain restrictions, however, the regulations of the cable companies should be consulted before writing a code message for transmission over their wires.

TAKING CARE OF THE DAILY MAIL

1. *Read carefully* letters received. Where the daily mail is heavy, have letters sorted into groups according to subject, as *orders*, *inquiries*, *adjustment*, etc. You can then deal with them more economically.

2. Keep incoming letters and envelopes together until you are certain that the writer's proper local address is *in the letter*. The omission of this item is a frequent offense.

3. Have your own local address on your letterhead. Omission of this often arouses in your correspondents the feeling that you are not a responsible business man.

4. *Reply promptly* to letters, usually within a day. If delay for full reply is necessary, acknowledge briefly the letter received, giving reasons for delay. Then, keep a reminder or "tickler file" to bring the matter again to your attention at the proper time.

5. *Plan your replies* to cover all points called for. Keep before you, while writing or dictating, the letter you are answering or a memorandum of its contents. An incomplete reply is annoying and unfair to your correspondent and to yourself.

6. *File together* in some orderly system the letters received and duplicates of your replies.

7. When replies are made by telegraph, *supplement and confirm* them by brief letters. These letters make useful records.

8. *Form letters*, printed on your regular stationery, to imitate typewriting, are convenient and economical when the same message is to go to a large number of people.

9. *Guide Forms.*—If your business does not call for much dictation of letters, you will find it worth while to prepare a few guide forms. These are letters prepared at leisure as carefully as possible, applying to various cases that arise frequently in your correspondence. Then, in the hurry of dictation, by making in the form letter only such changes as the particular case calls for, you can be certain of getting out a good letter.

10. *Filing.*—The purpose of filing correspondence is to keep an accurate, convenient record of past business and a guide for future correspondence. Any system used should be accurate, compact, readily accessible. There are in common use three systems:

a. *The Alphabetical System*, which is the simplest. In this system, letters are filed according to the names of the writers or the addressees; for example, letters received from and sent to *Williams* would be filed in a paper folder under *W*.

b. *The Subject System.*—The divisions of the file are made to correspond to the important items of the business: furnishings, clothing, etc. Usually an alphabetical order is kept within each subject.

c. *The Numerical System.*—In this system various subjects or correspondents are given numbers, and all papers connected with them are filed under the proper numbers in the file. The advantage of this is that it will take care of a file of any size and of any number of subjects. But a separate card index of names must be kept as a key. Each card carries the name of a subject or of a person and also the corresponding file number. The cards are arranged alphabetically.

Combination Systems are used also. Adapt your system to the requirements of your business, not your business to a system.

SOCIAL CORRESPONDENCE: FORMS

Stationery. Good usage approves a wide variety of forms and the indulgence of personal taste in the choice of stationery and in the writing of social letters and notes. The principles governing the form and appearance of business correspondence apply generally to social letters, but many informal variations from these rules are permitted.

White, unruled paper and envelopes to match are always in good taste, although pale-tinted papers which do not interfere with the clearness of the writing are permissible. Social note paper is usually a folded four-page sheet adapted to fold again once for the envelope. This paper, as well as the correspondence card, is prepared in various sizes and styles.

The Written Page. *The various parts of the letter*, as shown in the specimens, should be placed properly on the page, with due allowance for margins; no writing should be done in the margins. The heading should be placed as in the business letter, or, informally, the street address of the writer may be omitted, the date alone being written at the top of the sheet. An approved custom is to write out the date fully instead of using figures. The address of the recipient may be omitted in very familiar notes; that of the writer may be placed at the top of the paper or at the end of the letter in the lower left-hand part of the page.

Beginning and **End.** In the *salutation*, whatever form seems appropriate to the writer is permissible, except that certain abrupt and uncouth forms, such as *James* or *Friend John*, are ruled out, and the name of the person is preferred by many to the old form *Dear Friend*. *My dear Friend*, in this case, seems to be regarded as informal. *The complimentary close* may take any one of several forms, according to the degree of formality or familiarity in the letter. In such expressions as *Sincerely yours, Truly yours, Affectionately yours*, the first word only is capitalized.

TYPES OF SOCIAL NOTES AND LETTERS

The social note, written either upon the usual note-size paper or upon the commonly used correspondence card, is an important form of social writing. Such notes are brief, and the best taste dictates that the language should be as cordial and courteous as it can be made. The following specimens will suggest forms of expression appropriate for these notes. The heading is placed as in business or social letters, generally as follows:

439 East 23d Street,
June 7, 194–.

or,

Lyons Place,
November the Thirteenth.

The salutation may be as follows: *My dear Mr. Martin, My dear Mrs. Smith,* or *My dear Mary.* Best usage requires the addressing of a married woman by her husband's given name: *Mrs. Henry T. Myers*, not *Mrs. Laura Myers*. A widow may use her own given name or her husband's, as she pleases. The address of the recipient is placed at the lower left-hand corner of the sheet or card, or the date and the address of the writer may occupy this position. The complimentary close may be as for the social letter.

INFORMAL NOTES

1. Invitation.

515 Martin Place,
Thursday Evening.

Dear Frank,

If you are free to accept an invitation for Saturday afternoon, Mrs. Archer and I shall be very glad to have you with us in a little auto party out at Fort Beach. We shall take luncheon with us, and I know you will enjoy the trip. We will call for you at two.

Very cordially yours,
William S. Archer.

2. Reply.

Friday Morning.

My dear Archer:

I shall be more than glad to be one of your delightful party for tomorrow afternoon, and I shall be ready at two o'clock.

Sincerely yours,
Frank Adams Bates.

or,

3. Reply.

Friday Morning.

Dear Will,

I am very sorry to miss the pleasant party I am sure you will have at the Fort, but, as I leave for Chicago at six this evening upon very important business, I shall not be able to be with you.

Very truly yours,
Frank Adams Bates.

4. Invitation.

My dear Mrs. Graham:

How about Thursday afternoon for a little theater party in honor of your guest, Miss Smith? If you and she are at liberty, I shall take pleasure in making the necessary arrangements for the play, and for tea at Huyler's later.

Sincerely yours,
Marie Langs.

909 Fountain Avenue,
June the sixth.

5. Reply.

My dear Miss Langs:

I thank you very much for your kind thoughtfulness for my guest. Miss Smith and I are delighted to set aside Thursday afternoon as you suggest.

Sincerely yours,
Julia Graham.

314 Kingsley Place,
June the seventh.

6. Note of Regret.

My dear Marie:

Such fascinating suggestions of "cake and tea and other things" you contrive to put into your note. I wonder if that same imagination of yours can help you to understand our disappointment at not being able to accept your invitation for Thursday afternoon. We have not words to express it. And all on account of an out-of-town appointment of such long standing that it must be kept on that particular afternoon.

Please try to imagine us just as "sorry as we can be."

Cordially yours,
Julia Graham.

314 Kingsley Place,
June 7.

or,

7. Regrets.

My dear Miss Langs:

I regret that a previous engagement on the part of Miss Smith makes it impossible for us to accept your kind invitation for next Thursday afternoon.

Sincerely yours,
Julia Graham.

314 Kingsley Place,
June seventh.

8. Invitation.

Sunnyslope Farm,
October 1, 194—

My dear Mrs. Walters,

My sister Margaret and I are inviting a few friends, quite informally, to meet our cousin, Mary Arthur, on Thursday afternoon. May we count on the pleasure of having you and your daughter, Miss Esther, with us?

Sincerely,
Sara Beeman.

9. Invitation.

The Poplars,
April 10, 194—.

My dear Mrs. James:

Our Village Circle meets at our home on Monday evening next, April fifteenth. Mr. Williams and I shall be very glad to have you and Mr. James as our guests for the evening, that you may have an opportunity to meet some of your new neighbors.

Very cordially,
Harriet Williams.

10. Note with Birthday Gift.

My dear Miss Burns,

Please accept these flowers with my love and with the wish that you may enjoy many returns of this happy day.

Sincerely yours,
Helen Harvey.

73 Wellington Road,
September tenth.

Such a note, from a younger to an older person, accompanying a gift that gives so much pleasure, will naturally call forth a cordial letter of warm appreciation.

11. Reply.

Thursday Morning.

My dear Miss Helen,

Your note and gift of beautiful flowers completed a day of perfect happiness. It is good to grow old when friends emphasize the years with increasing kindness. Thank you, dear friend, for the love which has never failed me.

Cordially yours,
Celia Burns.

The Bread-and-Butter Note. A short letter to some one whose informal hospitality one has enjoyed should never be neglected or postponed. Something like the following is appropriate, though the matter should vary according to the relations and hearts of people. The language of friendship and courtesy is none too familiar to our pens.

12.

My dear Mrs. Hartley,

Back at routine again, I catch myself fancying that I am yet in the little circle of your guests of last week.

That is the joy of such hospitality as yours,—that the memory of it lingers so long and happily.

Sincerely yours,
John W. Dare.

10 Martin Street,
October 15, 194—.

13.

My dear Alice:

I wish I could tell you how much I have benefited from the physical relaxation and mental stimulus of my week-end with you. I have come back to the good old grind with real enthusiasm, and it is all a result of your cleverly planned hospitality. Saturday's picnic alone put enough new life into me to last for some time. Thank you so much for all your thoughtfulness from beginning to end.

Remember that you have promised to come to me for Christmas. I shall try to take a leaf out of your book and be as nearly as possible the perfect hostess that you are.

Cordially,
Marion.

35 Main Street, Overton,
August 17, 194—.

Letters of Condolence. Letters of condolence and sympathy are always difficult to write. Write only what is in your heart to say. In many instances the kindest thing is silence. The following letter of sympathy, now preserved in Oxford University, is a classic of this kind of expression, and appeals to us all.

14.

Executive Mansion,
Washington, November 21, 1864.

Dear Madame:

I have been shown on the file of the war department a statement of the Adjutant General of Massachusetts, that you are the mother of five sons who have died gloriously on the field of battle. I feel how weak and fruitless must be any word of mine which should attempt to beguile you from the grief of a loss so overwhelming, but I cannot refrain from tendering to you the consolation that may be found in the thanks of the republic they died to save. I pray that our Heavenly Father may assuage the anguish of your bereavement and leave only the cherished memory of the loved and lost, and the solemn pride that must be yours to have laid so costly a sacrifice upon the altar of freedom.

Yours very sincerely and respectfully,
A. Lincoln.

To Mrs. Bixby,
Boston, Mass.

15.

December 7, 194-.

Dear Margaret,

In the mail this morning came the sad news from Gertrude that your mother had passed away.

I wish I could be near you at this time to be of some comfort to you. But the greatest comfort you must have is the knowledge and feeling that your mother lived a full and happy life and left this world serene, largely because you and Emma and John did everything to make it so.

My thoughts and sympathy are with you at this time of sorrow.

Affectionately,
Henry Jerome.

To Miss Margaret Jones.

16.

My dear Tom:

I am very sorry to hear that business affairs have been apparently "going into reverse" for you lately. Be sure that I believe your difficulties are only temporary. They can't be otherwise, with your ability and faithfulness. Here is my hand. If I can be of any help, call on me at once.

Sincerely yours,
Robert.

September 10, 194_.

Letters of Congratulation. A letter of congratulation is easier to write. Here again let the letter come from your heart.

17.

My dear old Jack:

Could anything be finer than the result of yesterday's election? I don't know which to congratulate more, you or the city. The voters were satisfied with your past record and have acknowledged your worth by giving you this greater honor.

Continue to live up to your high ideals, and you will soon go to Washington to protect the people in their rights.

Remember me to the little woman at the head of the house, and accept my warmest congratulations and heartiest wishes for success.

Very sincerely yours,
Andrew Langtry.

November 10, 194_.

18.

My dear Martin,

Heartiest congratulations on the good news. Of course I know you don't entirely deserve such good fortune as the promise of Frances to become your wife, but fortunately we are not always treated strictly according to our deserts. We shall all be happy in the happiness that is to be yours.

Sincerely your well-wisher,
Robert Howard.

April 8, 194_.

19.

384 Linden Ave.,
August 18, 194_.

My dear Louise,

We are all greatly delighted over the announcement in the newspaper that you have won a scholarship in the university. You have our heartiest congratulations on your success in this severe test, as well as our sincere good wishes for your enjoyment of college life and work.

Sincerely yours,
Arlene Benham.

FORMAL INVITATIONS AND REPLIES

Formal invitations are written in the third person and, for large affairs, are usually engraved or printed and mailed about two weeks in advance. An invitation sent out by a school, or a class in the school, a club, or any group of persons, is usually in the third person; and, if the invitation be to an entertainment, as at a church or a commencement program, no formal reply is needed. Formal replies, however, should always be sent where entertainment is to be provided for each individual, for the host or hostess will need to know how to provide.

The letters *R. S. V. P.* are sometimes put in the lower left-hand corner of an invitation. They stand for the French phrase, *Répondez s'il vous plaît*, meaning "Reply, if you please." The English words, *An answer will oblige* or *An answer is requested*, are now much used.

Invitations to class commencements furnish happy occasions for friends to send notes of congratulation. The feeling of obligation to present gifts is very much to be regretted. No gifts should be expected unless it may be from near family friends. The formal wording of engraved cards or invitations may best be left to the engraver, as the fashions change slightly from year to year.

The reply to an invitation should follow the form of the note received, and should repeat the date and the hour mentioned in the invitation. In declining an invitation it is not necessary to repeat the hour.

1. Invitation to Commencement Exercises.

The Senior Class of
Columbia Seminary
requests the pleasure of your presence at the
Commencement Exercises
June fifteenth to eighteenth
nineteen hundred forty _
Washington, District of Columbia

2. Invitation to Commencement Exercises.

The Faculty and Graduating Class
of the
Boston Teachers' Training School
invite you to attend the
Seventeenth Annual Commencement Exercises
*Friday evening, April fifteenth, 194_*
at half past eight o'clock
Teachers' Training School
1124 Tremont Avenue

3. Formal Invitation to a Reception and Dance.

The Epsilon Mu Sorority
invites you to be present at a
reception and dance to be held at the
COLONIAL CLUB
Tuesday evening, April nineteenth
at half after eight o'clock

4. Wedding Invitation and Announcement.

Mr. and Mrs. Joseph Suffolk
request the honor of your presence at the
marriage of their daughter
Mabel Grace
to
Mr. Andrew Jackman
Wednesday afternoon, June fifteenth
at three o'clock
Saint-Mary's-on-the-Hill Church
Baltimore

5. Announcement.

Mr. Andrew Jackman
Miss Mabel Grace Suffolk
Married
on Wednesday, June the fifteenth
Nineteen hundred and forty _
Baltimore

6. Announcement.

Mrs. George Sampson
announces the marriage of her daughter
Margaret Louise
to
Mr. William Randolph Holmes
of Roxbury, Massachusetts
Saturday, December the twenty-fourth
nineteen hundred and forty _

Note.—At home cards are often inserted in the same envelope with the announcements.

7. For a Formal At Home.

Mrs. Jacques Randolph Stearns
At Home
on Wednesday, the seventh of December
from three until six o'clock
1106 Ballston Heights
to meet
Mrs. James Winchell Toynbee

8. Formal Note of Invitation.

Miss Belle Coe requests the pleasure of Miss Hinman's company on Thursday evening at eight o'clock.

128 Fremont St., January nine.

9. The Invitation Accepted.

Miss Hinman accepts with pleasure Miss Coe's invitation for Thursday evening at eight o'clock.

Wellington Place, January ten.

10. The Invitation Declined.

Miss Hinman sincerely regrets that she cannot accept Miss Coe's invitation for Thursday evening at eight o'clock.

Wellington Place, January ten.

11. A Less Formal Invitation. Calling cards are often used for small informal gatherings of friends.

At Home
Mrs. James Winchell Toynbee
Wednesday, January 14, 3 to 4.
40 College St.

12. Dinner Invitation.

1432 Lincoln Avenue
Mr. and Mrs. Thomas Dowd
request the pleasure of
Mr. James Morley's
company at dinner
On Wednesday evening, March the fifth
at eight o'clock

February the twenty-fifth

13. Acceptance.

415 Martin St.

Mr. James Morley accepts with pleasure the invitation of Mr. and Mrs. Thomas Dowd for Wednesday evening, March the fifth, at eight o'clock.

February the twenty-seventh.

14. Regrets.

Mr. James Morley sincerely regrets that a professional engagement made several months since prevents his acceptance of Mr. and Mrs. Thomas Dowd's kind invitation for Wednesday evening, March the fifth.

415 Martin St.,

February the twenty-seventh.

LETTERS OF FRIENDSHIP

The joy of letter writing is in letters of friendship, for which, most fortunately, there can be no exact rules. Write to your friend as if you were talking—good, bright, happy talk about the things in which you both are interested. No friendship can be so close as to excuse one for indifference or carelessness. Models of good letter writing are found in the memoirs of noted men and women. They form a valuable body of literature and will repay the reading.

Letter writing has been rightly called the "gentlest art." It is the art of giving joy to those who are dear to us, yet far away. An interchange of letters between members of the same family or between friends does more than anything else to keep alive the deep affections. Even brothers and sisters drift apart and hopelessly lose sight of each other when they forget to be faithful in their letters. Whatever the pressure of pleasure or of duties, the absent ones should take time for at least one letter every week to those who are left at home. Write cheerfully, never sharply or pettishly. The word once committed to paper may remain when the irritation has passed away. Never write unnecessarily of bad news. Letter writing, you remember, in its highest mission, is the "blessed art of giving joy." Answer home letters in detail. Many questions are asked which seem trifling, but they tell the very things about your life that the home people want to know.

The chief charm in letters of friendship is their naturalness. They should make the person who receives them feel that he has had a delightful visit with his friend who wrote. The following passage, taken from a letter written by Henry W. Longfellow, is full of the charm of simplicity: "I have just had the pleasure of receiving your photograph. It is so good, it could hardly be better. I wish the one I send you in return were as good. But that is wishing I were a handsome man, six feet high, and we all know the vanity of human wishes." Again he writes in a letter: "If 'Long Pond' were called Loch Long, it would be a beautiful lake. This and Sebago are country cousins to the Westmoreland lakes in England, quite as lovely, but wanting a little more culture and good society." This is simple language, but the thought is by no means commonplace. Our best thoughts belong to our friends, whether in conversation or in letters. Of Hawthorne's letters it is said, "They were full of passages of beauty and of details of his own plans and purposes, hopes and disappointments."

Bayard Taylor thus commends a friend for his naturalness in writing: "You somehow manage to bring your own bodily self before me when you write; I see your eyes and the changing expression of your face, as I read, and the sound of your voice accompanies the written word." Who would not, if he could, write letters that by their naturalness recall both face and voice? Charles Dickens thanks a friend for his letter "which is like a pleasant voice coming across the Atlantic, with that domestic welcome in it that has no substitute on earth." The following letter to Dickens from Thomas Hood carries such homelike, intimate qualities:

"Only thinking of the pleasure of seeing you again, with Mrs. Dickens, on Tuesday or Wednesday, I never remembered till I got home to my wife, who is also my flapper (not a young wild duck, but a remembrancer of Laputa), that I have been booked to shoot some rabbits—if I can—at Wantage, in Berks; a reverend friend, called 'Peter Priggins,' will be waiting for me, by appointment, at his railway-station on Tuesday. But I must and can only be three or four days absent; after which, the sooner we have the pleasure of seeing you the better for us. Mrs. Hood thinks there ought to be a ladies' dinner to Mrs. Dickens. I think she wants to go to Greenwich, seeing how much good it has done me, for I went really ill, and came home well, so that occasionally the diet of Gargantua seems to suit me better than that of Panta-gruel. Well, adieu for the present. Live, fatten, prosper, write, and draw the mopuses (money) wholesale through Chapman and *Haul*."

One likes letters written for the very joy of correspondence and not because the time has come and one must write. How welcome this passage must have been in one of Lowell's letters: "Somehow, this cool, beautiful summer day I feel my heart go out towards you all, and am not writing because I ought." Of the closeness and the intimacy of written thoughts that may be exchanged in letters, Lowell again writes: "I think it fortunate to have dear friends far away. For not only does absence have something of the sanctifying privilege of death, but we dare speak in the little closet of a letter what we should not have the face to at the corner of the street."

Occasions multiply for writing letters to our friends: birthdays, festivals, anniversaries, betrothals, weddings, funerals; any occasion for peculiar joy or sorrow when sympathy and love are called into expression. One of the most pleasing of the growing customs is the writing of letters to friends to accompany them on their journeys. Nowadays, those who go abroad in ships are showered with "steamer" letters, which keep them mindful of home and friends throughout their long voyage. The brightness and the sweetness of such letters enrich a whole lifetime with pleasant memories.

The mission of the letter has been summed up by Whittier in a letter to a friend: "I am thankful every day of my life that God has put it into the hearts of so many whom I love and honor to send me so many messages of good will and comfort."

In this day of complex living, when so much is said but so little realized of the "simpler life," we sometimes forget the joy which these simple "messages of good will and comfort" bring, and unnecessarily burden ourselves to overload our friends with purchased gifts; whereas, Christmas letters, birthday letters, any letters into which we put our best selves, are the most acceptable gifts that we can choose. Beyond compare is the joy of such written words as these sent as a Christmas offering by a young girl to an older friend:

"What can I wish for you that you have not already? Your heart is so full of good things that it needs no wish. Some day I may tell you just what you have done for me, my dear friend. Many a door have you opened for me, and these things cheapen in the telling.

"A blessed Christmas time to you and a New Year rich with God's best gifts."

The gift of "things" is forgotten but the gift of such words, never.

THE FAMILY LIBRARY

Every household should have a collection of books. In it there should be some books for all, and some that belong to individual members of the family. Such a library is not made all at once. It grows. But its growth can be directed so that it will contain books that tell something of all the great interests of men and women. We want, of course, good fiction and poetry, some picture books for the little folks, and a few books about inventions and discoveries. Then the heads of the household need some of the useful books about their business of housekeeping and of bringing up the children. Finally, histories, biographies, and books of travel should be on the shelves.

Of the many books of all kinds a short suggestive list is given here. The Reading Lists that follow will supply more titles that will help to make your bookshelves useful and interesting.

Sir John Lubbock's choice of the 100 best books and Theodore Roosevelt's "pigskin library" are useful guides for the young man or woman who is gathering a library. None of these is a "best list" for everybody. They are merely helps toward choosing the kinds of books that ought to be in every library.

Reference Books

Title	*Author or Publisher*
A good English dictionary.	
A good encyclopedia.	
The Lincoln Library of Essential Information,	The Frontier Press Co.
Dictionary of the Bible (1 vol.)	James Hastings
Dictionary of American Biography	New York Times
Dictionary of National Biography	Sidney Lee
Century Dictionary of Names	Century
Thesaurus of English Words	Roget
Dictionary of Music and Musicians	Grove
An Atlas of the World	
World Almanac and Encyclopedia	New York World
The Statesman's Year-Book	Macmillan
Reader's Handbook of Famous Names	Brewer
Dictionary of Phrase and Fable	Brewer
Familiar Quotations	Bartlett
A Practical Medical Dictionary	Thomas L. Stedman
Dyke's Auto and Gasoline Engine Encyclopedia,	A. L. Dyke
Dictionary of Photography	E. J. Ward
Bryant's Practical Bookkeeping	Henry W. Bryant
Essentials of Advertising	F. L. Blanchard
American Banking Practice	W. H. Kniffin
Robert's Rules of Order	Scott Pub. Co.
Handy Book of Curious Information	Wm. S. Walsh
Dictionaries of Foreign Languages, as required.	

Literature

Title	*Author or Publisher*
The Bible, with concordance.	
The Bible for Children	Kent
Classic Myths	C. M. Gayley
Shakspere (1 vol.)	Ed.—Craig
Volumes of Poets (choice limited by personal preferences).	
Oxford Book of English Verse	Oxford Univ. Press
Oxford Book of American Verse	Oxford Univ. Press
Golden Treasury of Verse	F. H. Palgrave
Prose and Poetical Quotations	Wm. S. Walsh
Our Familiar Songs	Johnson
Modern American Poetry	Louis Untermeyer
Cambridge History of English Literature,	Cambridge Univ. Press
History of English Literature	Garnett and Gosse
Studies in Literature	Frederick W. Tisdale
Chief Contemporary Dramatists (2 vols.)	T. H. Dickinson
Companionable Books	Henry van Dyke
The World's Greatest Short Stories	Sherwin Cody
A selection of best novels chosen by personal preference.	
Selected essays from Bacon, Lamb, Macaulay, Emerson, Huxley, Crothers (and others by personal preference).	
Valley of Democracy	Meredith Nicholson
Four on a Tour in England	Robert and Eliz. Shackleton
History of Everyday Things in England,	Marjorie and H. B. Quennell
Holy Days and Holidays	Edward M. Deems
American Pictures and Their Painters	L. M. Bryant
History of Painting in Italy	Ed.—Hutton
A Book of Opera	H. E. Krehbiel

History and Biography

Title	*Author or Publisher*
General History	P. V. N. Myers
The Outline of History	H. G. Wells
The Story of Mankind	H. W. Van Loon
Greatness and Decline of Rome	G. Ferrero
Modern Times and the Living Past	H. W. Elson
The Changing Chinese	E. A. Ross
Principles of Human Geography.	Huntington and Cushing
Industrial and Commercial Geography	J. Russell Smith
Modern History	Hayes and Moon
The Making of Modern England	Gilbert Slater
History of the Maya	Gann and Thompson
Discovery of America	John Fiske
France and England in the New World	Francis Parkman
Critical Periods in American History	John Fiske
Our Nation in the Building	Helen Nicolay
The Epic of America	James T. Adams
Presidents of the United States (4 vols.).	Ed.—James Grant Wilson
Civil Government of the United States	John Fiske
Riverside History of the United States (4 vols.),	Houghton, Mifflin, and Co.
History of the Civil War	James Ford Rhodes
A New History of the United States	H. W. Elson
Stories of the Great West	Theodore Roosevelt
Four American Leaders	Chas. W. Eliot
Select Orations Illustrating American History.	Harding
The American Commonwealth	James Bryce
Congressional Government	Woodrow Wilson
The American Revolution	Sir George Otto Trevelyan
The True George Washington	Paul Leicester Ford
Abraham Lincoln	Lord Charnwood
Short Life of Abraham Lincoln	J. G. Nicolay
The Boyhood of Abraham Lincoln	J. Rogers Gore
Lincoln's Own Stories	Ed.—Anthony Gross
Theodore Roosevelt: An Autobiography,	Theodore Roosevelt
Life of John Marshall	Albert J. Beveridge
The Making of an American	J. A. Riis
The Americanization of Edward Bok	Edward Bok
Lives of Poor Boys Who Became Famous	Sarah Bolton
Heroines of Modern Progress	Adams and Foster
Famous Scouts	Charles H. L. Johnston

Home and Education

Title	*Author or Publisher*
A-B-C of Correct Speech and the Art of Conversation,	Mrs. F. M. Hall
Self-Cultivation in English	G. H. Palmer
Everyday Good Manners for Boys and Girls,	Laird and Lie
How to Use Your Mind: A Psychology of Study,	Harry Dexter Kitson
The Psychology of Achievement	Walter B. Pitkin
Philosophy of Play	Luther H. Gulick
Health through Self Control	W. A. Spinney
Heredity and Christian Problems	Amory Bradford
What Men Live by	Richard C. Cabot
Health, Strength, and Happiness	C. W. Saleeby
First Aid in Emergencies	E. L. Eliason
Manual of Home-Making,	Van Rensselaer and Rose and Canon
The Effective Small House	Green and Bayliss
The House in Good Taste	Elsie de Wolfe
Home Economics	Maria Parloa
1000 Shorter Ways around the House	Mae Bell Croy
Better Meals for Less Money	Mrs. Lilian Green
Food Facts for the Home-Maker	L. S. Harvey
Care and Feeding of Children	L. E. Holt
Among Country Schools	O. J. Kern
All the Children of All the People	Wm. H. Smith
Roads to Childhood	Annie Carroll Moore
Guide to Literature	Starbuck and Shuttleworth
The Backward Child	Barbara Spofford Morgan
The Gifted Child	Guy Montrose Whipple
Problems of Childhood	Angelo Patri
On Our Hill	Josephine Daskam Bacon
Mothers and Children	D. F. Fisher
Profitable Vocations for Boys	Weaver and Byler
From Youth into Manhood	W. S. Hall
The Boy Problem in the Home	W. B. Forbush
Training the Boy	W. A. McKeever
Training the Girl	W. A. McKeever
Girl and Woman	Caroline Latimer
Coming of Age in Samoa	Margaret Mead
The High School Boy and His Problems	T. A. Clark
Vesper Talks to Girls	Laura Knott
Yule-Tide in Many Lands	Mary P. Pringle
Principles of Agriculture	L. H. Bailey
Manual of Gardening	L. H. Bailey
Law for the American Farmer	John B. Green

Home and Community

Title	*Author or Publisher*
Outlines of Sociology	Blackmar and Gillin
Political Economy	Sidney John Chapman
Our Cities Awake	Morris Cooke
City, State, and Nation	Wm. L. Nida
America's Creed and Its Meaning	Matthew Page Andrews
Land of Tomorrow	Wm. B. Stephenson

Title	*Author or Publisher*
The Land of Fair Play: How America is Governed,	Parsons and Geoffrey
The New Voter: Things He and She Ought to Know about Politics and Citizenship	Chas. Willis Thompson
The Community Health Problem	A. C. Burnham
Science of Home and Community,	Trafton, Gilbert, and Haven
Village Improvement	P. T. Farwell
Good Neighbors in the Modern City	Mary E. Richmond
The Promised Land	Mary Antin
Twenty Years at Hull House	Jane Addams
From Alien to Citizen	E. A. Steiner
Americans by Adoption	Joseph Husband
Use Your Government: What Your Government Does for You	Alissa Franc
Democracy and Ideals	John Erskine
Uncle Sam's Modern Miracles—His Gigantic Tasks That Benefit Humanity	William Atherton Du Puy
The Other Side of Government	D. Lawrence

Popular Science

The Outline of Science	Ed.—Thomson
A New Astronomy	David Todd
Astronomy with the Naked Eye	G. P. Serviss
The Universe of Stars	Harlow Shapley
Rural Science Series	Ed.—L. H. Bailey
The Science of Life, H. G. Wells, J. S. Huxley, G. P. Wells	
Pets for Pleasure and Profit	A. Hyatt Verrill
Studies in Arcady	R. L. Gales
Field and Study	John Burroughs
Nature's Garden	Neltje Blanchan
Handbook of Nature Study	A. B. Comstock
Book of Birds for Young People	F. Schuyler Mathews
The Holy Earth	L. H. Bailey
Sharp Eyes	Katherine Gibson
Wake Robin	John Burroughs
Maine Woods	Henry D. Thoreau
Our Insect Friends and Enemies	John B. Smith
Bird Life	F. M. Chapman
How to Know the Butterflies	J. H. and A. B. Comstock
Our Trees and How to Know Them	Arthur Emerson
Our Own Weather	E. C. Martin
Familiar Features of the Roadside	F. Schuyler Mathews
Secrets of Earth and Sea	Sir Ray Lankester
Face of the Fields	D. L. Sharp
World Minerals	L. J. Spencer
The Romance of Modern Invention	Archibald Williams
Miracles of Science	H. S. Williams
Men against Death	P. H. De Kruif
Chemistry and Civilization	A. S. Cushman
Story of the Engine from Lever to Liberty Motor,	Decker
Wings for Men	Frank Wead
Behemoth: the Story of Power	Hodgins and Magoun
Principles Underlying Radio Communication,	Signal Corps, U. S. Army

Travel

Pioneering Where the World is Old	Alice Tisdale
Out of Doors in the Holy Land	Henry van Dyke
The People of Palestine	Elihu Grant
Certain Delightful English Towns	Wm. Dean Howells
Unvisited Places of Old Europe	Robert Shackleton
The Joyful Heart	Robt. Haven Schauffler
Vagabond Journey around the World	Harry Franck
The Innocents Abroad	Mark Twain
Some Strange Corners of Our Own Country,	Chas. Lummis
Far Away and Long Ago	W. H. Hudson
Through the Brazilian Wilderness	Theodore Roosevelt
An Indian Journey	Waldemar Bonsels
Abroad at Home, American Ramblings	Julian L. Street
Literary Pilgrimages in New England	E. M. Bacon
Our National Parks	John Muir
Travels in Alaska	John Muir

Sir John Lubbock's List of 100 Books

The Bible.
The Meditations of Marcus Aurelius.
Epictetus.
Aristotle's Ethics.
Analects of Confucius.
St. Hilaire's Le Bouddha et sa Religion.
Wake's Apostolic Fathers.
Thomas à Kempis's Imitation of Christ.
Confessions of St. Augustine.
The Koran (portions of).
Spinoza's Tractatus Theologico-Politicus.
Comte's Catechism of Positive Philosophy.
Pascal's Pensées.
Butler's Analogy of Religion.
Taylor's Holy Living and Dying.
Bunyan's Pilgrim's Progress.
Keble's Christian Year.
Plato's Dialogues; at any rate, the Apology, Phædo, and Republic.
Xenophon's Memorabilia.
Aristotle's Politics.
Demosthenes' De Corona.
Cicero's De Officiis, De Amicitia, and De Senectute.
Plutarch's Lives.
Berkeley's Human Knowledge.
Descartes's Discours sur la Méthode.
Locke's On the Conduct of the Understanding.
Homer.
Hesiod.
Virgil.
Mahabharata.
Ramayana.
The Shah Nameh.
The Nibelungenlied.
Malory's Morte D'Arthur.
The Sheking.
Æschylus' Prometheus.
Trilogy of Orestes.
Sophocles' Œdipus.
Euripides' Medea.
Aristophanes' Knights and Clouds.
Horace.
Lucretius.
Chaucer's Canterbury Tales.
Shakspere.
Milton's Paradise Lost, Lycidas, and the shorter poems.
Dante's Divina Commedia.
Spenser's Faery Queen.
Dryden's Poems.
Scott's Poems.
Wordsworth (Mr. Arnold's selection).
Southey's Thalaba the Destroyer.
The Curse of Kehama.
Pope's Essay on Criticism.
Essay on Man.
Rape of the Lock.
Burns.
Byron's Childe Harold.
Gray.
Herodotus.
Xenophon's Anabasis.
Thucydides.
Tacitus' Germania.
Livy.
Gibbon's Decline and Fall.
Hume's History of England.
Grote's History of Greece.
Carlyle's French Revolution.
Green's Short History of England.
Lewes's History of Philosophy.
Arabian Nights.
Swift's Gulliver's Travels.
Defoe's Robinson Crusoe.
Goldsmith's Vicar of Wakefield.
Cervantes' Don Quixote.
Boswell's Life of Johnson.
Molière.
Sheridan's School for Scandal, The Critic, and The Rivals.
Carlyle's Past and Present.
Smiles's Self-Help.
Bacon's Novum Organum.
Smith's Wealth of Nations (part of).
Mill's Political Economy.
Cook's Voyages.
Humboldt's Travels.
White's Natural History of Selborne.
Darwin's Origin of Species.
Naturalist's Voyage.
Mill's Logic.
Bacon's Essays.
Montaigne's Essays.
Hume's Essays.
Macaulay's Essays.
Addison's Essays.
Emerson's Essays.
Burke's Select Works.
Voltaire's Zadig.
Goethe's Faust, and Autobiography.
Miss Austen's Emma, or Pride and Prejudice.
Thackeray's Vanity Fair.
Pendennis.
Dickens's Pickwick.
David Copperfield.
Lytton's Last Days of Pompeii
George Eliot's Adam Bede.
Kingsley's Westward Ho!
Scott's Novels.

Roosevelt's Pigskin Library

The following list of books was selected by Theodore Roosevelt for his famous African trip:

The Bible; Apocrypha.
Borrow—Bible in Spain; Zingali; Lavengro; Wild Wales; The Romany Rye.

Shakspere—Dramas.
Spenser—Faery Queen.
Marlowe—Dramas.
Mahan—Sea Power.
Macaulay—History; Essays; Poems.
Homer—Iliad; Odyssey.
La Chanson de Roland; Nibelungenlied.
Carlyle—Frederick the Great.
Bacon—Essays.
Shelley—Poems.
Lowell—Literary Papers; Biglow Papers.
Emerson—Poems.
Longfellow—Poems.
Tennyson—Poems.
Poe—Tales; Poems.
Keats—Poems.
Milton—Paradise Lost.
Dante—Inferno (Cary's trans.).
Holmes—Autocrat; Over the Teacups.
Bret Harte—Poems; Tales of the Argonauts; Luck of Roaring Camp.
Browning—Selections.
Crothers—Gentle Reader.
Twain—Huckleberry Finn; Tom Sawyer.
Bunyan—Pilgrim's Progress.
Euripides—Hippolytus; The Bacchæ.
The Federalist.
Gregorovius—Rome.
Scott—Legend of Montrose; Guy Mannering; Waverley; Rob Roy; Antiquary.
Cooper—Pilot; Two Admirals.
Froissart—Chronicles.
Percy—Reliques.
Thackeray—Vanity Fair; Pendennis.
Dickens—Mutual Friend; Pickwick.

THE CHILDREN'S LIBRARY

The following list of books embodies the considered judgment of many experts and the results of careful scientific inquiry. These books may, in fact, be confidently accepted as those most likely to attract young people to the enchanted gates that lead into the world of literature. The list consists of two groups.

The first comprises books suitable for children of the "story-telling" age, before they are able to interpret readily the printed page.

The second is a list for children who have learned to read and is based mainly on the preferences of the children themselves. It contains the best titles from about 9000 selected through a systematic investigation financed by the Carnegie corporation and carried out by the American Library association. Over 36,000 children co-operated in the choosing of the books. Those titles marked with an asterisk (*) were considered of superior literary merit by a jury of expert children's librarians. The titles are grouped by grades and are arranged according to the preference shown by the children of each grade.

In the second group will be found forty titles printed in italics. These forty have been specially recommended by the Office of Education, Washington, D. C.

The list should be accepted as an authoritative guide rather than as a complete selection of the best books for children. New children's books are continually being written, frequently placing old tales in a setting more familiar to generations largely urban in character. Those selecting reading for the young should be alert for the new but give chief weight to those books whose appeal has stood the acid test of childhood choice.

I. STORY-TELLING AGE

Title	*Author or Publisher*
Art of the Story-Teller	Shedlock
Baby Days	Dodge
Book of Nursery Rhymes	Welsh
Caldecott Books (Illus.)	Caldecott
Child Stories and Rhymes	Poulsson
Clean Peter and the Children of Grubbylea	Adelborg
Days and Deeds, a Book of Prose	Stevenson
Fanciful Tales	Stockton
Farm Book (Illus.)	Smith
Firelight Stories	Bailey
Five Mice in a Mouse Trap	Richards
Five Minute Stories	Richards
For the Children's Hour	Bailey
Golden Goose	Brooke
Goops and How to Be Them	Burgess
Great Panjandrum	Caldecott
Here and Now Story Book (Illus.)	Mitchell
How to Tell Stories	Bryant
In Sunshine Land	Thomas
In the Child's World	Poulsson
Kindergarten Stories	Hoxie
Lazy Matilda and Other Tales	Pyle
Little Folk Lyrics	Sherman
Little Mother Goose (Illus.)	Dodd, Mead & Co.
Little Sunshine	De Wolf
Lullaby Land	Field
Marigold Garden	Greenaway
Once upon a Time	Perrault
Pied Piper (Illus.)	Greenaway
Pinafore Palace	Wiggin and Smith
Rhymes and Jingles	Norton
Six Nursery Classics	Welsh
Some Great Stories and How to Tell Them	Wyche
Songs for Little Children	Smith
Star People	Johnson
Stories to Tell	Bryant
Stories to Tell the Little Ones	Bryant
Story of the Three Bears (Illus.)	Brooke
Tale of Pigling Bland	Potter
Tales of Laughter	Wiggin and Smith
Telling Bible Stories	Houghton
Through the Farmyard Gate	Poulsson
Toby Tyler or Ten Weeks with a Circus	Otis
Treasury of Stories, Jingles, and Rhymes	Humphrey
With Trumpet and Drum	Field
Wonder Clock	Pyle

II. GRADES THREE TO TEN

THIRD GRADE

Eskimo Stories	Mary E. Smith
Red Feather	Margaret E. Morcomb
Cherry Tree Children	E. A. and M. F. Blaisdell
Boy Blue and His Friends	E. A. and M. F. Blaisdell
Good Times on the Farm	Ethel C. Dietz
Twilight Town	Mary F. Blaisdell
Reynard the Fox	Louise Smythe
Tommy Tinker's Book	E. A. and M. F. Blaisdell
Five Little Friends	Sherred W. Adams
Stories of the Red Children	Dorothy Brooks
Work-a-day Doings on the Farm	E. Serl & V. Evans
Lost Monkey	Lucia W. Rice
Under the Story Tree	Mabel La Rue
So-fat and Mew-mew	Georgiana Craik

FOURTH GRADE

Dutch Twins	Lucy F. Perkins
**Grimm's Fairy Tales*	*Grimm*
**Child's Garden of Verses*	*Robert Louis Stevenson*
Japanese Fairy Tales	Teresa P. Williston
Old Mother West Wind	Thornton W. Burgess
About Harriet	C. W. Hunt
Pilgrim Stories	Margaret Pumphrey
*Little Black Sambo	Helen Bannerman
Peter Pan	Sir James M. Barrie
Peter and Polly in Autumn	Rose Lucia
Around the World with the Children,	Frank G. Carpenter
Peter and Polly in Summer	Rose Lucia
Early Cavemen	Katherine E. Dopp
Story of Mrs. Tubbs	Hugh Lofting
*At the Back of the North Wind	George MacDonald
Peter and Polly in Spring	Rose Lucia
Peter and Polly in Winter	Rose Lucia
Jack the Giant Killer	Andrew Lang
Tree-dwellers	Katherine E. Dopp
*Tale of Peter Rabbit	Beatrix Potter
Mother Goose Village	Madge A. Bigham
Merry Animal Tales	Madge A. Bigham
Cinderella	Andrew Lang
Little Folks of Many Lands	Lulu Maud Chance
Stories of Great Americans	Edward Eggleston
Little Red Riding Hood	Andrew Lang
Overall Boys	Eulalie Osgood Grover
Four Wonders	Elnora E. Shillig
Polly and Dolly	Mary Frances Blaisdell
Book of Nature Myths	Florence Holbrook
Fairy Stories and Fables	James Baldwin
Jan and Betje	Mary Emery Hall
Cock, Mouse, and the Little Red Hen	Felicite Lefevre
Six Little Ducklings	Katharine Pyle
Sleeping Beauty in the Woods and Other Stories,	Andrew Lang

FIFTH GRADE

Black Beauty	Anna Sewell
*Pinocchio	Collodi
**Story of Dr. Dolittle*	*Hugh Lofting*
**Little Lame Prince*	*Craik*
**Andersen's Fairy Tales*	*Dutton*

Title	Author or Publisher
**Alice's Adventures in Wonderland*	*Lewis Carroll*
Japanese Twins	Lucy F. Perkins
French Twins	Lucy F. Perkins
Fifty Famous Stories Retold	James Baldwin
Belgian Twins	Lucy F. Perkins
*King of the Golden River	John Ruskin
*East o' the Sun and West o' the Moon,	Gudrun T. Thorne-Thomsen
Eskimo Twins	Lucy F. Perkins
*Princess and the Goblin	George MacDonald
Irish Twins	Lucy F. Perkins
**Just So Stories*	*Rudyard Kipling*
Cave Twins	Lucy F. Perkins
Swiss Twins	Lucy F. Perkins
*Adventures of a Brownie	Craik
Viking Tales	Jennie Hall
Lonesomest Doll	Abbie F. Brown
Puritan Twins	Lucy F. Perkins
Moni the Goat Boy	Johanna Spyri
Mexican Twins	Lucy F. Perkins
Mother West Wind's Animal Friends,	Thornton Burgess
Mother West Wind's Children	Thornton Burgess
Clematis	B. & E. Cobb
*Peter Pan and Wendy	Sir James M. Barrie
Wee Ann	Ethel C. Phillips
*Jataka Tales of India	Ellen C. Babbitt
Golden Goose	Eva M. Tappan
*Granny's Wonderful Chair	Frances Browne
Pinocchio in Africa	Cherubini
Mother West Wind's Neighbors	Thornton Burgess
Peggy in Her Blue Frock	Eliza O. White
*English Fairy Tales	Joseph Jacobs
Adventures of Odysseus (a)	*Padraic Colum*

Sixth Grade

Title	Author or Publisher
**Heidi*	*Johanna Spyri*
Toby Tyler	James Otis
**Robinson Crusoe*	*Daniel Defoe*
Beautiful Joe	Marshall Saunders
Five Little Peppers and How They Grew.	Margaret Sidney
Katrinka	Helen Haskell
Blue Bird for Children	Maurice Maeterlinck
Birds' Christmas Carol	Kate D. Wiggin
Voyages of Dr. Dolittle	Hugh Lofting
Dog of Flanders	*Ouida*
**Jungle Book*	*Rudyard Kipling*
Scotch Twins	Lucy F. Perkins
*Blue Fairy Book	Andrew Lang
Doctor Dolittle's Circus	Hugh Lofting
Doctor Dolittle's Post Office	Hugh Lofting
Green Fairy Book	Andrew Lang
Spartan Twins	Lucy F. Perkins
Italian Twins	Lucy F. Perkins
**Water Babies*	*Charles Kingsley*
**Merry Adventures of Robin Hood*	*Howard Pyle*
Mr. Stubbs's Brother	James Otis
Red Fairy Book	Andrew Lang
John of the Woods	Abbie F. Brown
Monkey That Would Not Kill	Henry Drummond
Nancy Rutledge	Katharine Pyle
Yellow Fairy Book	Andrew Lang
*Peterkin Papers	Lucretia P. Hale
*Rip Van Winkle	Washington Irving
Five Little Peppers Midway	Margaret Sidney
**Tanglewood Tales*	*Nathaniel Hawthorne*
Arkansaw Bear	Albert B. Paine
Arlo	B. and E. Cobb
*Mopsa, the Fairy	Jean Ingelow
Burgess Bird Book for Children	Thornton W. Burgess
Magic Forest	Stewart Edward White
**Wonderful Adventures of Nils*	*Selma Lagerlof*
**Boy's King Arthur*	*Sir T. Mallory*
**Arabian Knights*	*Frances J. Olcott*
**Gulliver's Travels*	*Jonathan Swift*
**Æsops Fables*	*Æsop (Jacobs)*

Seventh Grade

Title	Author or Publisher
**Adventures of Tom Sawyer*	*Mark Twain*
**Little Women*	*Louisa M. Alcott*
**Hans Brinker*	*Mary Mapes Dodge*
Huckleberry Finn	*Mark Twain*
Call of the Wild	Jack London
**Treasure Island*	*Robert Louis Stevenson*
Secret Garden	Frances Hodgson Burnett
Little Men	*Louisa M. Alcott*
*Kidnapped	Robert Louis Stevenson
**Story of a Bad Boy*	*Thomas Bailey Aldrich*
Little Lord Fauntleroy	Frances H. Burnett
*Hoosier School Boy	Edward Eggleston
**Swiss Family Robinson*	*Johann David Wyss*
Anne of Green Gables	Lucy Maud Montgomery
Mrs. Wiggs of the Cabbage Patch	Alice Hegan Rice
Rebecca of Sunnybrook Farm	*Kate Douglas Wiggin*
Dandelion Cottage	Carroll Watson Rankin
Old Fashioned Girl	Louisa M. Alcott
*Biography of a Grizzly	Ernest Thompson Seton
Understood Betsy	*Dorothy Canfield*
Uncle Tom's Cabin	Harriet B. Stowe
Eight Cousins	Louisa M. Alcott
Jack and Jill	Louisa M. Alcott
*Merrylips	Beulah Marie Dix
Penrod and Sam	Booth Tarkington
Sara Crewe	Frances Hodgson Burnett
Sapphire Signet	Augusta H. Seaman
Under the Lilacs	Louisa M. Alcott
Young Trailers	Joseph A. Altsheler
Daddy Long Legs	Jean Webster
*Jim Davis	John Masefield
Two Little Confederates	Thomas Nelson Page
Widow O'Callaghan's Boys	Gulielme Zollinger
Nelly's Silver Mine	Helen Hunt Jackson
Covered Wagon	Emerson Hough
*Tales from Shakespeare	Charles and Mary Lamb
*Christmas Carol	Charles Dickens
**Man Without a Country*	*Edward Everett Hale*
**Uncle Remus*	*Joel Chandler Harris*
**Boy's Life of Abraham Lincoln*	*Helen Nicolay*

Eighth Grade

Title	Author or Publisher
Penrod	Booth Tarkington
**Prince and the Pauper*	*Mark Twain*
*Wild Animals I Have Known	Ernest Thompson Seton
**Ivanhoe*	*Sir Walter Scott*
**Master Skylark*	*John Bennett*
White Fang	Jack London
*Black Arrow	Robert L. Stevenson
**Captains Courageous*	*Rudyard Kipling*
**Men of Iron*	*Howard Pyle*
Twenty Thousand Leagues Under the Sea	Jules Verne
*Last of the Mohicans	James F. Cooper
Jo's Boys	Louisa M. Alcott
Little Shepherd of Kingdom Come	John Fox, Jr.
Lucky Sixpence	E. B. and A. A. Knipe
Wildfire	Zane Grey
Crimson Sweater	Ralph H. Barbour
Emmeline	Elsie Singmaster
Just Patty	Jean Webster
Oliver Twist	Charles Dickens
When Patty Went to College	Jean Webster
Hoosier Schoolmaster	Edward Eggleston
Young Pitcher	Zane Grey
*Stickeen	John Muir
Anne of Avonlea	Lucy M. Montgomery
Lad, a Dog	Albert P. Terhune
*David Copperfield	Charles Dickens
Baby Elton, Quarter-back	Lesley W. Quirk
Rose in Bloom	Louisa M. Alcott
Track's End	Hayden Carruth
Story of My Life	Helen Keller
Timothy's Quest	Kate D. Wiggin
Jacqueline of the Carrier Pigeons	Augusta H. Seaman
Ungava Bob	Dillon Wallace
Lass of the Silver Sword	Mary C. DuBois
*Evangeline	Henry W. Longfellow
*Dark Frigate	Charles B. Hawes

Ninth Grade

Title	Author or Publisher
*Jim Davis	John Masefield
Janice Meredith	Paul Leicester Ford
Adventures of Sherlock Holmes	Arthur Conan Doyle
*Two Years Before the Mast	Richard Henry Dana
*Bob, Son of Battle	Alfred Ollivant
Continental Dollar	E. B. and A. A. Knipe
*Lorna Doone	Richard Dodderidge Blackmore
Mysterious Island	Jules Verne
*Tale of Two Cities	Charles Dickens
*Ramona	Helen Hunt Jackson
Ben-Hur	Lew Wallace
Connecticut Yankee in King Arthur's Court,	Mark Twain
Captain Blood	Rafael Sabatini
*Silas Marner	George Eliot
Diantha's Quest	E. B. and A. A. Knipe
Boys' Life of Theodore Roosevelt	Herman Hagedorn
Black Wolf Pack	Daniel Beard
Bar Sinister	Richard Harding Davis
*Lives of the Hunted	Ernest Thompson Seton
*Westward Ho!	Charles Kingsley
Gold Seekers of '49	Edwin L. Sabin
Blue Magic	Edith Ballinger Price

Tenth Grade

Title	Author or Publisher
*Three Musketeers	Alexandre Dumas
Seventeen	Booth Tarkington
Buff, a Collie	Alfred Payson Terhune
Virginian	Owen Wister
That Year at Lincoln High	Joseph Gollomb
White Fire	Mary Constance DuBois
Oregon Trail (a)	*Francis Parkman*
Joan of Arc (a)	*L. M. Boutet de Monvel*

(a) Does not appear among books chosen through Carnegie Corporation survey but is recommended by the Bureau of Education. See the note at the head of this list.

SYNONYMS AND ANTONYMS

SYNONYMS are words having the same or nearly the same meaning: *custom, habit, fashion,* and *practice*; *enough* and *sufficient.* Antonyms are words of opposite meaning: *sharp, dull*; *long, short*; *high, low*; *weak, strong.*

There is probably no language which has not some synonyms; but the English language in particular abounds in synonymous terms. There are several reasons for this fact.

English is a highly developed language. In the course of its history the meanings of many words have changed, slowly, of course, but none the less surely. It is not surprising, therefore, that two or more words, having originally different meanings, should eventually come to signify the same thing. For example, *to refuse* and *to reject* an offer have essentially the same meaning. If we trace the words back to their origins, however, we find that to reject a thing was to throw it back and to refuse it was to pour it back, as if it were water that had been put into a glass before us. Thus from words which originally differed in meaning we have obtained two synonyms, which express the same idea. Such synonyms are to be found in all languages which have passed through long periods of development.

Numerous synonyms in English exist also in consequence of the fact that the language has received additions from many different sources. Upon no language has English drawn more freely for its vocabulary than upon Saxon and Latin. For this reason we often find a word of Saxon origin and another of Latin origin existing side by side and possessing the same meaning, as in the case of *help,* which is Saxon, and *assist,* which is Latin. Similarly, *sympathy,* derived from the Greek, occurs as a synonym of *compassion,* which has come into the language from the Latin.

While a few synonyms differ so imperceptibly that they are almost identical in signification, by far the greater number are definitely distinguishable in meaning.

Words are in some respects like living things; they bear the marks of their origin and of their history. Two words, therefore, which at first sight appear to be interchangeable, often show, on a closer examination, differences which they have acquired from the company they have kept. Thus *axiom* and *byword* are sufficiently alike to be classed as synonyms; but axiom cannot shake off the air of learning, which clings to it after its 25 centuries of use in Greek mathematical treatises. Similarly, *conclude* means *to close.* It may be used of a speech, but it would never suffer itself to be found in the humble company of a door. We must *close* a door; we cannot *conclude* it. It is only by practice and by the exercise of some care that we learn whether one word will exactly replace another or whether it will not.

The Study of Synonyms. Ability to use English comes in great part from hearing others use it and from reading what others have written. This is an easy method of learning; but it may fail of being effective because we do not always hear and read the best English and because the results of such a method come very slowly. It has been found that no method is more effective than the careful observation of the way in which closely related words differ in meaning. A man who cannot distinguish a Ford car from a Rolls-Royce would be highly incompetent to choose a car for himself. In the same way, a person who cannot tell the difference between *affect* and *effect* is sure to make blunders in his speech. It is necessary, therefore, to study the distinctions between words which are synonymous, if we would be precise in our choice of words.

The Value of Synonyms. A thorough acquaintance with English synonyms carries with it several practical advantages. It relieves one from the necessity of repeatedly using the same word to express several distinct ideas; for example, to say *grand,* when one means to say *great, fine, beautiful,* or *impressive.* Once we have acquired the habit of distinguishing words and of using the right one, we are able to speak much more justly and exactly, having at our command a variety of words which express distinctive qualities. We shall be able, for instance, by means of our diction, to discriminate between a person's *air* and his *manner.* Although *active* and *diligent* are synonymous, there is a real difference between an active and a diligent person. Similarly, *brave, courageous,* and *gallant* are synonyms, but each carries a precise meaning peculiar to itself.

The habit of using words accurately begets the habit of thinking accurately. By examining and comparing various synonymous expressions, one is able to select from among them such words as exactly convey the meaning and nothing more or less. It is this discriminating use of words which at once denotes the scholar and imparts the finest effect to composition.

The Value of Antonyms. Much that has been said regarding the study and the value of synonyms is true also of antonyms. The study of antonyms has other practical values, however. A knowledge that a word has two antonyms of different meanings will show us that the word itself has two meanings and will prevent us from using it ambiguously. For example, if we speak of a *poor* student, other people cannot tell whether we mean that the student is not clever or that he is not rich. But, if we recall that *poor* may have as antonyms *clever* or *good* and also *rich,* we shall be more careful to speak in a manner that will leave no doubt of our meaning.

A ready command of antonyms also enables us to contrast vividly two ideas or two facts and so to convey our meaning in a more impressive fashion. For example, in praising a statesman we may say that he is *always first,* but it is more effective to say that he is first in peace and first in war. By this use of contrasted words either in speaking or in writing, an instant and vivid impression is created.

How to Use. To get the greatest amount of value from the following dictionary of synonyms and antonyms, it is necessary that one should understand clearly the use of the index or key. Let us suppose, for example, that you are writing a letter in which you have used the word *trouble.* You may desire to repeat the idea of this word and yet you do not wish to employ the same word again. Perhaps you do not recall another word which will exactly express the thought you wish to convey.

Turn to the index or key beginning on page 172 and find the word *trouble* with a reference to page 170. You will also find *trouble* occurring twice followed by words in italics: once by *affliction* with a reference to page 139 and once by *difficulty* with a reference to page 153. First turn to page 170 and there you will find *disturb* and *molest* as variant words. It may be that one of these will suit your purpose. But, if both words fail, next refer to page 139 and look for *affliction.* Under it, in addition to *trouble,* are the words *distress, grief,* and *sorrow.* If up to this point you are not satisfied, you may turn to page 153 and look for *difficulty.* Under it you find the additional synonyms *obstacle, impediment,* and *embarrassment,* with an explanation of how each word is used. Among all these synonyms, you are almost certain to find a word to suit the need. But, in the very rare case that you do not find the precise word, you will have received many suggestions which will enable you to convey the desired idea in a different manner; for, by glancing at the antonyms under the three paragraphs you have read, you will have seen *soothe, quiet, compose, caress, happiness, comfort, satisfaction, cheer, aid, help, assistance, relief,* and *encouragement.*

DICTIONARY OF SYNONYMS AND ANTONYMS

Abandon, desert, forsake, relinquish. The idea of leaving or separation is common to these terms, which differ in the circumstances of the action; the first two are more positive acts than the last two. To abandon may be an act of necessity or discretion, as a captain abandons a vessel when it is no longer safe to remain in it. Abandoning may imply a violation of the most sacred ties, exposing the object to every misery; desertion is a breach of honor and fidelity, depriving a person of the assistance or the countenance which he has a right to expect. By forsaking, the kindly feelings are hurt, and the social ties are broken. A bad mother abandons her offspring; a soldier deserts his comrades; a man forsakes his companions. Things as well as persons may be abandoned, deserted, or forsaken; things only are relinquished. To relinquish may be an act of prudence or imprudence; men often inadvertently relinquish the fairest prospects in order to follow some favorite scheme which terminates in their ruin.

Antonyms.—Adopt, maintain, protect, uphold, keep.

Abase, humble, humiliate, degrade, disgrace, debase. Abase expresses the strongest degree of self-humiliation. To humble, marks a prostration to the ground, and figuratively a lowering of the thoughts and feelings. Abase and humble have regard to persons considered absolutely; degrade and disgrace, to their relative situation. To degrade signifies to lower in the estimation of others. Disgrace is always attended with circumstances of more or less ignominy. To debase is to reduce from a higher to a lower state or grade of worth, dignity, value, etc. The penitent man humbles himself; the contrite man abases himself; the man of rank degrades himself by a too familiar deportment with his inferiors; he disgraces himself by his vices; he debases his character by crime. Humiliation implies a feeling of disgrace. Coinage is debased by too much alloy.

Antonyms.—Exalt, honor, dignify, promote.

Abhor, detest, abominate, loathe. These terms equally denote a sentiment of aversion. What we abhor is repugnant to our moral feelings; what we detest is opposed to our moral principles; what we abominate does violence to our religious and moral sentiments; what we loathe offends our taste. We abhor what is base and ungenerous; we detest hypocrisy; we abominate profanation and open impiety; we loathe food when we are sick.

Antonyms.—Admire, approve, esteem, desire, love.

Abide, sojourn, dwell, live, reside, inhabit. Abide implies an indefinite stay in a place. Sojourn literally means to pass the day, or, generally, a portion of one's time in a place. Dwell, like abide, somewhat archaic, means to live in a place, implying a degree of permanence. Live and reside mean to have a permanent home in a place. Inhabit, unlike the other words, is used actively, meaning occupy, as a country or district, as a home; it is used of both men and animals.

Antonyms.—Move, migrate, depart, abandon.

Ability, capacity, faculty, talent. Ability is to capacity as the genus is to the species. Ability comprehends the power of doing in general, without specifying the quality or degree; capacity is a particular kind of ability. Ability may be either physical or mental; capacity, when used of persons, is mental only. Ability implies action, capacity refers to thought. Ability relates to human power generally, by which a man is enabled to act; it may vary in degree and quality with times, persons, and circumstances. Health, strength, and fortune are abilities; faculty is a gift of nature directed to a certain end and following a certain rule. An ability may be acquired, and consequently is properly applied to individuals, as an ability to speak extempore or an ability to write; but a faculty belongs to the species, as a faculty of speech or of hearing, etc. Talent signifies a particular type of ability; it imitates but does not originate.

Antonyms.—Inability, incompetence, ineptitude, stupidity.

Abolish, abrogate, repeal, revoke, annul, cancel. The word abolish conveys the idea of putting a total end to a thing, and is applied properly to those things which have been long in existence and are firmly established. An abolition may be effected by an act of power, as in abolishing an institution; or it may be a gradual act, or effected by indirect means, as in the case of doing away with a custom or practice. Laws are either repealed or abrogated, but repealing is a term of modern use, applied to the acts of public councils or assemblies, where laws are made or unmade by the consent or open declaration of numbers. Abrogate is a term of less definite import; to abrogate a law is to render it null by any act of the legislature: thus, the making of a new law may abrogate the old one. Revoking is an act of individual authority—edicts are revoked; annulling is an act of discretion, as official proceedings or private contracts are annulled; canceling is a species of annulling, as in the case of canceling bonds, obligations, etc.

Antonyms.—Establish, authorize, institute, confirm.

Absolute, despotic, arbitrary, tyrannical. Absolute power is independent of and superior to all other power: an absolute monarch is uncontrolled, either by men or by things. Despotic power is power exercised as by a master or lord. Despotic power is, therefore, as complete as absolute power but carries the added idea that the ruler has the right to treat his subjects according to his will or pleasure. With arbitrariness are associated the ideas of caprice and selfishness. With tyranny are associated the ideas of oppression and injustice. In modern use, both arbitrariness and tyranny are associated with despotism.

Antonyms.—Limited, constitutional, accountable, mild, lenient, just.

Acceptable, grateful, welcome. Acceptable signifies worthy to be accepted. Grateful signifies altogether pleasing; that which recommends itself is grateful. The acceptable is a relative good, the grateful is positive; the former depends upon our external condition, the latter on our feelings and taste. Welcome signifies come well or in season for us; it refers to whatever happens according to our wishes. It is a grateful task to be the bearer of welcome intelligence to our friends.

Antonyms.—Unwelcome, disappointing, saddening, painful, distasteful.

Accomplish, effect, execute, achieve. To accomplish an object signifies more than simply to effect a purpose, both as to the thing aimed at and the means employed in bringing it about. Extraordinary means are requisite for accomplishing and ordinary means, for effecting. To accomplish is properly said of that which a person sets before himself; but to effect, execute, and achieve do not relate to the views of a person acting, but to the thing brought about. What is executed is complicated in its nature, as to execute a design or project; what is achieved is of greater and worthier conception, as to achieve success in a profession.

Antonyms.—Fail, come short, default, give up.

Accuse, charge, impeach, arraign. The idea of asserting something to the prejudice of another is common to these terms. But accuse is said of acts; charge, of moral qualities constituting the character. We accuse a person of murder; we charge him with dishonesty. High officials are impeached; criminals are arraigned.

Antonyms.—Clear, discharge, exonerate, acquit.

Act, do, make. We always act when we do, but we do not always do when we act. Act is applied to either persons or things, as a spring or a lock acts; do applies in this sense to persons only. Act is generally used intransitively, as to act well or ill in this or that manner; do is usually transitive, as to do right or wrong, to do one's duty. To make is to bring a thing to being or form as to make a pen.

Act, work, operate. A machine works, but each of its parts is said to act; so beer works, and bread works. Sometimes act as well as work is taken in the sense of exerting a power upon other bodies and producing changes, as the sun acts on the plants. Operate is applied to matters of a general nature in science or morals, as a measure operates, or words may operate on the mind, or reasons may operate on the understanding.

Action, gesture, gesticulation, posture, attitude. All these terms are applied to the state of the body; the first three indicate a state of motion, the last two a state of rest. Action respects the movements of the body in general; gesture is an action indicative of some particular state of mind; gesticulation is the act of making gestures. Raising the arm is an action; bowing is a gesture. Actions may be ungraceful; gestures, indecent. Posture and attitude both imply a mode of placing the body, but the posture is either natural or assumed; the attitude is always assumed or represented. We assume a sitting posture or an attitude of prayer.

Active, diligent, industrious, assiduous, laborious, busy, officious. We are active if we are only ready to exert our powers, whether to any end or not; we are diligent when we are active for some specific end; we are industrious when no time is left unemployed in some serious pursuit; we are assiduous if we do not leave a thing until it is finished; we are laborious when the bodily or mental powers are regularly employed in some hard labor. Busy implies continuous occupation. Officious implies being busy without discretion, especially about other people's affairs.

Antonyms.—Inert, indolent, lazy, trifling, idle, shiftless.

Actual, real, positive, true. What is actual has proof of its existence within itself, and may be exposed to the eye; what is real may be satisfactorily proved to exist; and what is positive precludes the necessity of a proof. That is true which is genuine, in accord with evident facts or susceptible of proof.

Antonyms.—Supposititious, imaginary, doubtful, uncertain, false, artificial.

Actuate, impel, induce. One is actuated by motives, impelled by passions, and induced by reason or inclination. Whatever actuates is the result of reflection—it is a steady and fixed principle. Whatever impels is momentary and vehement, and often precludes reflection. Whatever induces is not vehement, though often momentary.
Antonyms.—Restrain, inhibit, impede, check.

Acute, keen, shrewd. In the natural sense, a fitness to pierce is predominant in the word acute; that of cutting, or a fitness for cutting, in the word keen. The shrewd man exposes follies. Arguments may be acute, reproaches keen, and replies or retorts shrewd. A shrewd understanding is quicker at discovering new truths than at distinguishing truth from falsehood.
Antonyms.—Dull, obtuse, shortsighted, stupid.

Adhere, attach. A thing adheres to another by reason of some quality in itself; a person adheres to a party for some reason of his own. Things are attached to others by external means; a person may be attached to a church or his home by sentiment.
Antonyms.—Detach, loosen, separate.

Adjacent, adjoining, contiguous. Buildings or farms may be adjacent or contiguous without being joined or touching. Adjoining lands or buildings meet at a boundary line. Things that so meet may be called contiguous.
Antonyms.—Distant, separated, disjoined.

Admit, allow, permit, suffer, tolerate. Admit in this sense is used mostly of ideas and propositions, usually used with *of*. Allow is of more general application, frequently implying no more than a tacit refraining from refusal. We admit that which concerns ourselves; we allow that which is for the convenience of others, or what they wish to do. What is suffered may be burdensome to the sufferer, if not morally wrong; what is tolerated is contrary to one's desires, and is suffered only because it cannot be prevented. Permit implies a positive grant of privilege.
Antonyms.—Forbid, refuse, withstand, prevent, deny.

Admit, receive. Persons are admitted to the tables, and into the familiarity or confidence of others; they are hospitably received by those who wish to be their entertainers. We admit willingly or reluctantly; we receive politely or rudely.
Antonyms.—Shut out, forbid, exclude.

Adoration, worship, reverence, veneration. Adoration is the service of the heart toward a superior being, in which we acknowledge our dependence and obedience by petition and thanksgiving; worship consists in the outward form of showing reverence to some supposed superior being. Reverence differs from adoration inasmuch as it has a mixture of awe, arising from consciousness of weakness and dependence, or of obligations for favors received. The contemplation of any place rendered sacred by its antiquity awakens veneration.
Antonyms.—Contempt, dishonor, impiety, sacrilege.

Advance, proceed. Advance implies movement forward; proceed, movement from one point to another, also resumption of movement after a pause.
Antonyms.—Recede, retire, withdraw.

Advantage, benefit, utility. Advantage refers to external or extrinsic circumstances of profit, honor, and convenience; benefit, to the consequences of actions and events; utility respects the good which can be drawn from the use of any object. A large house or a particular situation may have its advantages; suitable exercise is attended with benefit; the utility of motor cars consists in their supplying means of rapid travel.
Antonyms.—Disadvantage, futility, worthlessness.

Adverse, contrary, opposite, inimical, hostile. Adverse is used of the feelings and interests of persons: contrary, in respect to their plans and purposes; opposite refers to the situation and relative nature of things. Fortune is adverse; an event turns out contrary to what was expected; sentiments are opposite to each other. Inimical implies positive harmful opposition. Lack of harmony in an organization is inimical to its success. Inimical is applied to private, personal unfriendliness; hostile, chiefly to public conflict.
Antonyms.—Auspicious, favorable, helpful, friendly.

Advice, counsel, instruction. Advice flows from superior professional knowledge, or from an acquaintance with things in general; counsel implies superior wisdom, or a superior acquaintance with moral principles and practice; instruction involves superior local knowledge in particular transactions. A medical man gives advice to his patients; a father gives counsel to his children; in points of law a counselor gives advice to his client and receives instructions from him in matters of fact.

Affect, assume, pretend. To affect is to use forced efforts to appear to have that which one has not; to assume is to appropriate to oneself that which one has no right to have. One affects to have fine feelings, and assumes great importance. We pretend by making a false declaration. One affects indifference to praise and pretends to have wealth.

Affect, concern. Things affect us which produce any change in our outward circumstances; they concern us if connected with our circumstances in any way. The price of corn affects the interest of the seller; therefore it concerns him to keep it up, without regard to the public good or injury.

Affectionate, kind, fond. Affectionate characterizes the feelings; kind usually has reference to action. Affectionate describes an attitude toward a particular object; kind a manner of acting toward objects generally. Fond implies tender, indulgent, often unreasoning, liking.
Antonyms.—Unkind, ill-disposed, indifferent.

Affirm, assert. Affirm is said of facts; assert, of opinions. We affirm what we know; we assert what we believe.
Antonyms.—Deny, retract, repudiate.

Affliction, distress, trouble, grief, sorrow. Affliction is applied both to severe misfortune and to the deep sorrow of heart that may come from it. Grief is keen, poignant sorrow springing from a definite cause. Distress implies severe, painful trouble from physical or mental causes. Trouble may imply merely confusion of mind, or it may signify deep-seated disturbance.
Antonyms.—Happiness, comfort, satisfaction, cheer.

Affront, insult, outrage. To affront is to show reproach in the presence of others—it piques and mortifies; to insult is to attack with insolence—it irritates and provokes; to outrage is to combine all that is offensive, to add insult to injury.
Antonyms.—Honor, gratify, please, benefit.

Afraid, fearful, timorous, timid. Afraid is the most general of these words, implying either a slight or a high degree of fear. Fearful is a stronger word than afraid: one may be fearful of defeat and yet not afraid in a discreditable sense. Timid and timorous imply constitutional liability to fear, even of slight matters.
Antonyms.—Brave, bold, fearless, intrepid.

Agree, accede, consent, comply, acquiesce. Agree is the general term, meaning to fall in with. We accede by becoming a party to a thing; those who accede are on equal terms; one objects to that to which one does not accede. We consent to a thing by authorizing it, we comply with a thing by allowing it; those who consent or comply are not on equal terms with those in whose favor the consent is given or compliance made. Consenting is an act of authority, complying an act of good nature or weakness. To acquiesce is quietly to admit; it is a passive act, dictated by prudence or duty.
Antonyms.—Disagree, dissent, refuse, decline, oppose.

Agreeable, pleasant, pleasing. Agreeable expresses a less vivid feeling than pleasant; pleasing marks a sentiment less vivid and distinct than either. A pleasing countenance denotes tranquillity and contentment; a pleasant countenance bespeaks happiness.
Antonyms.—Disagreeable, repulsive, irritating.

Aim, aspire. We aim at a certain proposed point by endeavoring to gain it; we aspire after that which we think ourselves entitled to, and which we flatter ourselves with gaining. Many men aim at riches and honor; it is the lot of but few to aspire to a throne.

Aim, object, end, view. The aim is that which the person has in his own mind; it depends upon the character of the individual whether it be good or bad, attainable or otherwise. The object lies in the thing; it is a matter of choice; it depends upon accident as well as design, whether it be worthy or unworthy. The end is that which follows or terminates any course or proceeding; the nature of the end determines to some degree the means to be used to reach it. It is the aim of the Christian to live peaceably; it is a mark of dullness or folly to act without an object; it is sophistry to suppose that the end will justify the means. View refers primarily to the end or purpose as conceived by the person. One does business with a view of making money.

Air, manner, mien, look, carriage, gait. Air lies in the whole person; manner refers to movement or action or expressive gesture. A man has the air of a common person; it discovers itself in all his manners. An air is noble or simple—it marks an elevation or simplicity of character; a manner is rude, rustic, or awkward, for want of culture, good society, and good example. We assume an air, and affect a manner. Mien implies the whole outward appearance, carriage and bearing: noble mien, frightful mien. Look refers especially to the facial expression—an honest look. Carriage applies to the manner of holding or carrying the body. Gait is the manner of walking.

Alarm, terror, fright, consternation. Alarm is felt at the sudden approach of danger or signs of danger. Terror may arise from any appearance or event suggesting great harm or catastrophe; alarm prompts us to defense, and terror disarms us. Fright is a less vivid emotion than either, as it arises from the simple appearance of danger; we may be alarmed or terrified for others, but we are mostly frightened for ourselves. Consternation springs from the view of some very serious evil, and commonly affects many. Alarm affects the feelings, terror the understanding, and fright the senses; consternation seizes the whole mind and benumbs the faculties.

Antonyms.—Calmness, repose, confidence, self-command.

Alertness, alacrity. Alertness signifies an attitude and manner of keen readiness, promising prompt, spirited action. Alacrity implies a quick, willing response to impulse or demand from without.

Antonyms.—Inertness, sluggishness, languidness, apathy.

Allay, soothe, appease, mitigate, assuage. All these terms indicate a lessening of something painful. In a physical sense an irritating pain is allayed; a wounded part is soothed by affording ease and comfort. Extreme heat or thirst is allayed; extreme hunger is appeased; a punishment or suffering is mitigated. Temper or enthusiasm that is fervid and vehement is allayed; one soothes a mind that is distressed or irritated; one appeases what is tumultuous and boisterous; one mitigates the pains of others or what is rigorous and severe; one assuages grief or afflictions.

Antonyms.—Arouse, irritate, intensify, kindle, excite.

Alleviate, relieve. A pain is alleviated by making it less burdensome; a necessity is relieved by supplying what is wanted. Alleviate refers to internal feelings only; relieve, to either internal feelings or external circumstances. That alleviates which affords ease and comfort; that relieves which removes the pain.

Antonyms.—Aggravate, intensify.

Alliance, league, confederacy. Alliances are formed for the mutual convenience of parties, as between states to promote commerce. Leagues and confederacies are entered into mostly for purposes of self-defense or for common safety against the attacks of a common enemy; but a league is usually a solemn act between states and for general purposes of safety,—it may, therefore, be both defensive and offensive. A confederacy is commonly a temporary union to resist a common adversary in a season of actual danger.

Allot, appoint, destine. Allot is used only for things; appoint and destine for persons or things. A space of ground is allotted for cultivation; a person is appointed as steward or governor; a youth is destined for a particular profession. Allot and appoint imply immediate purposes; destine implies remote purposes.

Allow, grant, bestow. That is allowed which may be expected, if not directly required; that is granted which is desired, or directly asked for; that is bestowed which is wanted as a matter of necessity. A grant comprehends in it something more important than an allowance, and passes between persons in a higher station; what is bestowed is of less value than either. A boy is allowed money for expenses; a king grants pensions to his officers; relief is bestowed on the indigent.

Antonyms. —Refuse, withhold, disallow.

Allowance, stipend, salary, wages, hire, pay. All these terms denote a stated sum paid according to certain stipulations. An allowance is gratuitous—it ceases at the pleasure of the donor. All the rest are the requital for some supposed service—they cease with the engagement made between the persons. Stipend is more fixed and permanent than salary, and salary than wages, hire, or pay; a stipend depends upon the fulfilling of an engagement rather than on the will of an individual. A salary is a matter of contract between the giver and the receiver; an allowance may be given in any form or at any stated times. Stipend and salary are paid yearly or at even portions of a year; wages, hire, and pay are estimated by days, weeks, or months, as well as by years.

Allude, refer, hint, suggest. To allude is not so direct as to refer, but it is more clear and positive than either hint or suggest. We allude to a circumstance by introducing something collaterally allied to it; we refer to an event by expressly introducing it into our discourse; we hint at a person's intentions by darkly insinuating what may possibly happen; we suggest an idea by some expressions relative to it.

Alone, solitary, lonely. Alone, compounded of all and one, signifies altogether one, or single, that is, by oneself. Alone marks the state of a person, solitary and lonely, the quality of a person or a thing. A person walks alone, or he takes a solitary walk in a lonely place. One may feel lonely in company; one is solitary in the absence of companions.

Ambiguity, equivocation. An ambiguity arises from a too general form of expression, which leaves the sense of the words indeterminate; an equivocation lies in the power of particular terms used, which admit of a double interpretation or an application to two different things. The ambiguity leaves us in entire uncertainty as to what is meant; the equivocation misleads us through the use of a term in the sense which we do not suspect.

Antonyms.—Clearness, plainness, definiteness.

Amend, correct, emend, improve, mend, better. Amend, emend, and correct are all applied to works of the understanding, with these distinctions: amend signifies to remove faults or defects generally, either by adding, taking away, or altering, as to amend a law; to emend is to remove particular faults in any literary work by the alteration of letters or single words; to correct is to remove faults, as to correct the copy. Mend is employed in respect to any works in the sense of putting that right which either is or has become faulty; to improve is said either of persons or things which are made better, as to improve the mind, morals, etc.; to better is usually applied to the outward condition on familiar occasions.

Antonyms.—Corrupt, impair, harm, mar.

Amicable, friendly. Amicable implies a negative sentiment, a freedom from discordance; friendly implies a positive feeling of regard, the absence of indifference. We make an amicable settlement and have a friendly understanding.

Antonyms.—Ill-tempered, unfriendly, hostile.

Amuse, divert, entertain. Whatever amuses serves to kill time, to lull the faculties, and to banish reflection; whatever diverts causes mirth and provokes laughter; whatever entertains acts on the senses, and awakens the understanding.

Antonyms.—Annoy, disquiet, bore.

Anger, resentment, wrath, ire, indignation, rage, fury. Anger is a sudden sentiment of displeasure; resentment is a continued anger; wrath is a heightened sentiment of anger, which is poetically expressed by the word ire. Indignation is a sentiment awakened by the unworthy and atrocious conduct of others; as it is exempt from personality it is not irreconcilable with the temper of a Christian. Rage is a vehement show of anger, and fury is an excess of rage.

Antonyms.—Patience, acquiescence, gentleness, self-control, serenity, calmness.

Animadversion, criticism, stricture. Animadversion includes censure and reproof; criticism implies scrutiny and judgment, whether for or against; and stricture comprehends a partial investigation mingled with censure.

Antonyms.—Praise, approval, commendation.

Animate, inspire, enliven, cheer, exhilarate. To be animated in the physical sense is simply to possess animal life in however small a degree; to be animated in the moral sense is to receive the smallest portion of the sentiment or thinking faculty; to inspire expresses the communication of a strong moral sentiment or passion; to enliven respects the mind; cheer relates to the heart; exhilarate regards the spirits, both animal and mental. To be animated, in action, conversation, etc., is to show signs of vigorous life. One is inspired by strong sentiment, often conveyed by another. The mind is enlivened by music or wit; the heart is cheered by good news; one is exhilarated physically by a keen air, spiritually or mentally by success, joy, enthusiasm.

Antonyms.—Deaden, dull, dishearten, depress.

Announce, proclaim, publish. We announce an event that is expected and just at hand; we proclaim an event that requires to be known by all the parties interested; we publish what is supposed likely to interest all who know it.

Antonyms.—Conceal, suppress, withhold.

Answer, reply, rejoinder, response. An answer is given to a question; a reply is made to an assertion; a rejoinder is made to a reply; a response is made in accordance with the words of another. We answer either for the purpose of affirmation, information, or contradiction; we always reply, or rejoin, in order to explain or confute; responses are made by way of assent or confirmation.

Antonyms.—Question, query, interrogation.

Answerable, responsible, accountable, amenable. Answerable and responsible convey the idea of a pledge given for the performance of some act, or the fulfillment of some engagement, a breach of which subjects the defaulter to loss, punishment, or disgrace. A person is accountable to his employer for the manner in which he has conducted any business intrusted to him. To be amenable is to be accountable as far as laws and regulations bind a person; one is amenable to the laws of society, or he is amenable to the rules of the house in which he is only an inmate.

Antonyms.—Free, irresponsible, absolute.

Apologize, defend, justify, exculpate, excuse, plead. We apologize for an error by acknowledging ourselves guilty of it; we defend ourselves against a charge by proving its fallacy; we justify our conduct against any imputation by proving that it was blameless; we exculpate ourselves from all blame by proving that we took no part in the transaction. Excuse and plead are not grounded on any idea of innocence; a plea is frequently an idle or unfounded excuse, a frivolous attempt to lessen displeasure; we excuse ourselves for a neglect by alleging indisposition.

Apparent, visible, clear, plain, obvious, evident, manifest. That which is simply an object of sight is visible; that which presents itself to our view in any form, real or otherwise, is apparent. The stars themselves are visible to us; but their size is apparent. What is clear is to be seen in all its parts and in its proper colors; what is plain is seen by a plain understanding; what is obvious presents itself readily to the mind of every one; what is evident is unquestionably seen, and leaves no hesitation in the mind. What is manifest is so openly shown as to admit of no doubt and to force conviction.

Antonyms.—Obscure, hidden, latent, doubtful.

Applause, acclamation. These terms express a public demonstration, the former by means of a noise with the hands or feet, the latter by means of shouts and cries. The former is employed as a testimony of approbation, the latter as a sanction or an indication of respect.

Antonyms.—Censure, hissing.

Appoint, order, prescribe, ordain. To appoint is the act of either an equal or a superior; we appoint a meeting with any one at a given time and place; a king appoints his ministers. To order is the act of one invested with a partial authority; a master gives his orders to his servant. To prescribe is the act of one who is superior by virtue of his knowledge; a physician prescribes for his patient. To ordain is an act emanating from the highest authority; kings and councils ordain, but their ordinances must be conformable to what is ordained by the Divine Being.

Antonyms.—Forbid, prohibit, veto.

Apprehend, conceive, suppose, imagine. To apprehend is simply to take an idea into the mind,—thus we may apprehend any object that we hear or see. To conceive is to form an idea in the mind, as to conceive the idea of doing anything, to conceive a design. What one supposes may admit of a doubt; it is frequently only conjectural. What one imagines may be altogether improbable or impossible; that which cannot be imagined may be too improbable to admit of being believed.

Approach, access, admittance. Approach signifies the coming near or toward an object, and consequently it is an unfinished act, but access and admittance are finished acts; access is coming to, or as close to, an object as is needful; admittance is coming into any place, or into the presence or society of any person. An approach may be quick or slow, an access easy or difficult, an admittance free or conditional.

Antonyms.—Recession, withdrawal, exclusion.

Approach, approximate. Approach means to draw or come nearer to, although the distance at any time may still be great. Approximate implies a very close approach—as close as conditions will permit.

Antonyms.—Avoid, miss, shun, evade.

Argue, evince, prove. To argue is to establish an indication amounting to probability; to evince denotes an indication so clear as to remove doubt; to prove marks an evidence so positive as to produce conviction.

Argument, reason, proof. An argument serves for defense; a reason, for justification; a proof, for conviction. Arguments are adduced in support of a hypothesis or a proposition; reasons are assigned in matters of belief and practice; proofs are collected to determine truth as to alleged facts.

Arise, rise, mount, ascend, climb, scale. Arise is used only in the sense of simply getting up, but rise is employed to express a continued motion upward. A person arises from his seat or his bed; a bird rises in the air; a person mounts a hill, and ascends a mountain. To climb is to rise step by step by clinging to a certain body; to scale is to rise as by an escalade, or species of ladder, employed in mounting the walls of fortified towns. Trees and mountains are climbed; walls are scaled.

Antonyms.—Settle, fall, descend, sink.

Arrogance, presumption. Arrogance is the act of the great; presumption, that of the little. The arrogant man takes upon himself to be above others; the presumptuous man strives to be on a level with those who are above him.

Antonyms.—Modesty, meekness, humility.

Artist, artisan, artificer, mechanic, craftsman. The artist ranks higher than the artisan,—the former requires intellectual refinement, the latter nothing but to know the common, mechanical practice of an art or trade. The sculptor is an artist; the sign-painter is an artisan. An artificer is a master artisan. Mechanic and artisan are used interchangeably. Craftsman implies technical skill and judgment; it is used of both artist and artisan. The mechanic is one whose work involves manual skill, or skill in the use of tools.

Ask, inquire, question, interrogate. We perform all these actions in order to get information; but we ask, for general purposes of convenience; we inquire from motives of curiosity; we question and interrogate from motives of discretion. Indifferent people ask of each other whatever they wish to know; learners inquire the reasons of things that are new to them; masters question their servants, or parents their children, when they wish to ascertain the real state of any case; magistrates interrogate criminals when they are brought before them.

Antonyms.—Answer, reply, respond.

Assemble, muster, collect. To assemble is to bring together by a call or invitation or, as machine parts, by mechanical process according to a plan; to muster is to bring together by an act of authority, or by a particular effort, into one point of view at one time, and from one quarter; to collect is to bring together at different times, and from different quarters.

Antonyms.—Adjourn, dismiss, scatter, disperse.

Assent, consent, approbation, concurrence. Assent concerns matters of judgment; consent, matters of conduct. We assent to what we admit to be true; we consent to what we allow to be done. Approbation is a species of assent, concurrence, of consent. To approve is not merely to assent to a thing as right, but to determine upon it positively; concurrence is properly the consent of many. Assent is given by equals or inferiors; consent, by superiors; approbation, by equals or superiors; concurrence, by equals.

Antonyms.—Dissent, refusal, disapproval, disagreement.

Association, society, company, partnership, corporation. Associations and societies are organizations for the promotion of literary, scientific, religious, or benevolent objects. Companies and partnerships are formed for business purposes. The partnership is the least stable of business organizations. A corporation is a more permanent organization, chartered by the state. It persists irrespective of the particular individuals owning or controlling its stock.

Asylum, refuge, shelter, retreat. Asylum is chosen by him who has no home; refuge by him who is apprehensive of danger. Shelter is a cover or a protection. Fatigues and toils of life make us seek retreat.

Atone for, expiate. Both these terms express a satisfaction for an offense: atone is general; expiate is particular. We may atone for a fault by any form of suffering; we expiate a crime only by suffering a legal punishment.

Attack, assail, assault, encounter, charge. To attack is to make an approach in order to do some violence to the person; to assail or assault is to make a sudden and vehement attack; to encounter is to meet the attack of another. One assails by means of missiles, reproaches, or invective; one assaults by direct personal violence. To charge is to attack from a particular quarter.

Antonyms.—Resist, withstand, sustain, defend.

Attempt, endeavor, effort, essay. An attempt is the act of setting about a thing with a view of effecting it; an endeavor is a continued attempt. An effort is to an attempt as a means is to an end; it is the act of calling forth those powers which are required in an attempt. An essay is an attempt with the idea of testing one's own powers. It is applied either to material or intellectual matters.

Attend, hear, listen. To attend is to have the mind intently engaged on what we hear; to listen is to strive to hear. People attend when they are addressed. Listen implies a lesser degree of heed than attend. To hear is merely to be conscious of sound.

Attentive, careful. We are attentive in order to understand and to improve; we are careful to avoid mistakes. Attentive refers to mental attitude; careful relates to mechanical action: we listen attentively; we read or write carefully.

Antonyms.—Inattentive, careless, heedless, indifferent.

Attract, allure, invite, engage. That is attractive which draws the attention toward itself; that is alluring which awakens desire; that is inviting which offers persuasion; that is engaging which takes possession of the mind.

Antonyms.—Repel, deter, estrange, disgust.

Augur, presage, forebode, betoken, portend. Augur signifies either to serve or to make use of as an augury; to forebode or presage is to form a conclusion in one's own mind; to betoken or portend is to serve as a sign. Persons or things augur; persons or things forebode or presage; things only betoken or portend. Auguring is a calculation of some future event, in which the imagination seems to be as much concerned as the understanding. Presaging is rather a conclusion or a deduction of what may be from what is; it lies in the understanding more than in the imagination. Foreboding lies altogether in the imagination. Things which present natural signs are said to betoken; those which present extraordinary or supernatural signs are said to portend.

Auspicious, propitious. Those things are auspicious which are regarded as indicative of good omen. Persons are propitious to the wishes of others who listen to their requests and contribute to their satisfaction; favoring, helpful influences are propitious.

Antonyms.—Untoward, adverse, forbidding, ominous.

Austere, rigid, severe, rigorous, stern. The austere man is severe with himself; the rigid man binds himself to a rule. The manners of a man are austere when he refuses to take part in any social enjoyments; his probity is rigid, that is, inaccessible to the allurements of gain or the urgency of necessity. Severe is used with reference to conduct,—a man is severe in the restraints he imposes and the punishments he inflicts. Rigorous implies harshness, severity, as, rigorous treatment, a rigorous officer of justice. Sternness is a species of severity more in manner than in direct action: a commander may issue his commands sternly, or a despot may issue his stern decrees.

Antonyms.—Affable, gentle, indulgent, mild.

Avaricious, miserly, parsimonious, niggardly. An avaricious man shows his love of money in his ordinary dealings; but the miser lives for his money and suffers every privation rather than part with it. The avaricious man indulges his passion for money by parsimony, that is, by excessive personal saving, or by niggardly ways in his dealings with others.

Antonyms.—Unselfish, generous, lavish, free.

Awaken, excite, provoke, rouse, stir up. We awaken by a simple effort; we excite by repeated efforts or forcible means; we provoke by words, looks, or actions. The tender feelings are awakened; affections, or the passions in general, are excited; the angry passions are commonly provoked. We are roused from an extraordinary state by extraordinary means; we are stirred up from an ordinary to an extraordinary state.

Antonyms.—Calm, quiet, pacify, restrain.

Awe, reverence, dread. Awe and reverence both denote a strong sentiment of respect, mingled with some emotions of fear; but the former marks the much stronger sentiment of the two. Dread is an unmingled sentiment of fear for one's personal security.

Antonyms.—Familiarity, assurance, contempt.

Awkward, clumsy, bungling. Awkward applies to outward deportment; clumsy, to the shape and make of the object. A person has an awkward gait; he is clumsy in his whole person. Bungling applies to the result of awkwardness and clumsiness in performing work.

Antonyms.—Adroit, dexterous, neat, skillful.

Axiom, maxim, aphorism, apothegm, saying, adage, proverb, byword, saw. The axiom is a truth of the first value, a self-evident proposition which is the basis of other truths. A maxim is a truth of the first moral importance for all practical purposes; an aphorism is a truth set apart for its pointedness and excellence. Apothegm is, in respect to the ancients, what saying is in regard to the moderns; it is a pointed sentiment pronounced by an individual and adopted by others. Adage and proverb are common sayings, the former among the ancients, the latter among the moderns. The byword is a casual saying, originating in some local circumstance, frequently used in contempt; saw is an archaic word for saying.

Babble, chatter, chat, prattle, prate. Babbling denotes rapidity of speech, which renders it unintelligible; chatter is an imitation of the noise of speech properly applied to magpies or parrots, and figuratively to a corresponding mode of speech in human beings. The winter's fireside invites neighbors to assemble and chat away many an hour which might otherwise hang heavy on hand, or be spent less inoffensively. The prattling of babes has an interest for every feeling mind, but for parents it is one of the highest enjoyments; prating, on the contrary, is the consequence of ignorance and childish assumption. A prattler has all the unaffected gayety of an uncontaminated mind; a prater is forward, obtrusive, and ridiculous.

Band, company, crew, gang. All these terms denote a small association for a particular object. A band is an association in which men are bound together by some strong obligation, whether taken in a good or a bad sense, as a band of soldiers, a band of robbers; a company marks an association for convenience, without any particular obligation, as a company of travelers, a company of strolling players. A crew marks an association collected by some external power, or by coincidence of plan and motive; in the former case it is used for a ship's crew, in the latter and bad sense of the word it is employed for any number of evil-minded persons met together from different quarters and co-operating for some bad purpose. Gang and crew are applied to companies of workmen under one leader or on one job, or to bands brought together for boisterous or disorderly purposes. Gang is applied to groups of boys who play together under a leader.

Banishment, exile, expulsion. Banishment follows from a decree of justice; exile, either by the necessity of circumstances or by an order of authority; banishment is a disgraceful punishment inflicted by tribunals upon delinquents; exile is a disgrace incurred without dishonor; exile removes us from our country; banishment or expulsion drives us from it ignominiously.

Antonyms.—Recall, reinstatement, repatriation.

Be, become, grow. Be is positive; become is relative: a person is what he is without regard to what he was; he becomes that which he was not before. To grow is to become by a gradual process. A man may become a good man from a vicious one, in consequence of a sudden action of his mind; but he grows in wisdom and virtue by means of an increase in knowledge and experience.

Antonyms.—Die, stagnate, diminish.

Be, exist, subsist. We say of qualities, of forms, of actions, of arrangement, of movement, and of every different relation, whether real, ideal, or qualificative, that they are; we say of matter, of spirit, of body, and of substances, that they exist. Man is man, and will be man under all circumstances and changes of life; he exists under every known climate and variety of heat or cold in the atmosphere. Subsist implies generally dependence upon outside aid for existence. Cities subsist on the productivity of the country.

Bear, yield. Both words mean to produce: bear respects animals and plants, which bear young or fruit; yield respects plants and inanimate objects, which yield increase.

Beat, defeat, overpower, rout, overthrow. An army is beaten in important engagements; it is defeated and may be routed in partial attacks; it is overpowered by numbers, and overthrown in set engagements. These words are similarly applied to the fortunes of persons.

Antonyms.—Aid, help, succor, befriend.

Beautiful, fine, fair, handsome, pretty. Beautiful implies a certain perfection of form, correctness of proportion, unity of impression, harmony of details. Applied to human beings it connotes some spiritual excellence. Fine implies perfection of finish and design, both interior and exterior. Fair conveys the idea of external smoothness and freedom from blemish. Handsome implies superficial excellence, of proportion in particular. Pretty is confined to objects of refinement, especially those small and dainty: a beautiful landscape; a pretty fancy; a pretty child.

Antonyms.—Plain, uncouth, coarse, deformed, ugly.

Becoming, comely, graceful. Becoming applies to the decorations of the person and to the deportment; comely refers to natural embellishments; graceful, to natural or artificial accomplishments. Manner is becoming; figure is comely; air, figure, or attitude is graceful.

Antonyms.—Unsuitable, awkward, homely, uncouth.

Beg, beseech, solicit, entreat, supplicate, implore, crave. To beg denotes a state of want; to beseech, entreat, and solicit, a state of urgent necessity; supplicate and implore, a state of abject distress; crave, the lowest state of physical want. One begs with importunity, beseeches with earnestness, entreats by the force of reasoning and strong representation; one solicits by virtue of one's interest, supplicates by a humble address, implores by every mark of dejection and humiliation.

Antonyms.—Command, demand, claim, extort, refuse.

Begin, commence, enter upon. To begin has reference to the order of time; to commence implies the exertion of setting about a thing. A person begins a thing with a view of ending it; he commences a thing with a view of completing it. To enter upon implies a first doing of what has not been tried before.

Antonyms.—End, finish, complete, terminate, conclude, consummate.

Behavior, conduct. Behavior is more specific, and refers to acts, especially in the presence of or in reference to others. Conduct is more general and inclusive; it implies moral or ethical considerations governing behavior.

Belief, credit, trust, faith. Belief and credit are particular actions or sentiments; trust and faith are permanent dispositions of the mind. Things are entitled to our belief; persons are entitled to our credit; but people repose trust in others, or have faith in others. Belief is intellectual and may be quite impersonal. Faith and trust are personal and have immediate reference to conduct. Trust in God serves to dispel all anxious concern about the future.

Antonyms.—Doubt, denial, distrust, skepticism.

Beneficent, bountiful or **bounteous, munificent, generous, liberal.** The sincere well-wisher to fellow creatures is beneficent according to his means; he is bountiful in providing for the comfort and happiness of others; he is munificent in dispensing favors; he is generous in imparting his property; he is liberal in all he does. Beneficence and bounty are characteristics of the Deity as well as of his creatures.

Antonyms.—Stingy, niggardly, petty, mean.

Benevolence, benignity, humanity, kindness, tenderness. Benevolence lies in the will; benignity, in the disposition or frame of mind. Humanity lies in the heart; kindness and tenderness, in the affections. Benevolence indicates a general good will to all mankind; benignity, particular goodness or kindness of disposition. Humanity is a general tone of feeling; kindness and tenderness are particular modes of feeling.

Antonyms.—Malevolence, malignity, churlishness, harshness, brutality, ill will.

Bereave, deprive, strip. To bereave expresses more than deprive, but less than strip, which denotes a total and violent bereavement. One is bereaved of children, deprived of pleasures, and stripped of property. We are bereaved of that on which we set most value; the act of bereaving does violence to our inclination. We are deprived of the ordinary comforts and conveniences of life,—they cease to be ours. We are stripped of the things which we most want; we are thereby rendered, as it were, naked.

Antonyms.—Restore, supply, comfort, endow.

Blame, censure, condemn, reprove, reproach, upbraid. To blame is simply to ascribe a fault to; to censure is to express disapprobation. The former is less personal than the latter. The thing more than the person is blamed; the person more than the thing is censured. A person may be blamed for his good nature and censured for his negligence. That which is condemned is of a more serious nature, and it produces a stronger and more unfavorable expression of displeasure or disapprobation than that which is blamed; reprove is even more personal than censure. A reproof passes from one individual to another, or to a certain number of individuals. Reproaching and upbraiding are as much the acts of individuals as reproving, but the former denote the expression of personal feelings and may be just or unjust; the latter is presumed to be divested of all personal feelings.

Antonyms.—Praise, approve, abet, applaud, countenance.

Blemish, stain, spot, speck, flaw, defect, fault. Whatever detracts from the seemliness of appearance is a blemish. In works of art the slightest dimness of color or want of proportion is a blemish. A stain or spot sufficiently characterizes itself as that which is superfluous and out of its place; a speck is a small spot; a flaw is a defect that prevents the substance from holding together properly, as a flaw in glazing on china, in a steel rail, in an argument. A blemish tarnishes; a stain spoils; a spot, speck, or flaw disfigures. Defect consists in the want of some specific essential in an object; fault conveys the idea not only of something wrong, but also of its relation to the author. There is a blemish in fine china, a defect in the springs of a clock, and a fault in the contrivance.

Blot out, expunge, erase, efface, cancel, obliterate. Letters are blotted out, so that they cannot be seen again; they are expunged, so as to signify that they cannot stand for anything; they are erased, so that the space may be used for other writing. Efface does not designate either the manner or the object; inscriptions on stone may be effaced, that is, rubbed off so as not to be visible. Cancel is principally confined to written or printed characters; they are canceled by striking through them with the pen. Letters are obliterated which are in any way made illegible.

Antonyms.—Write, record, confirm, perpetuate.

Bold, fearless, intrepid, undaunted. Boldness is a positive characteristic of the spirit; fearlessness is a negative state of the mind, that is, simply an absence of fear. A person may be bold through fearlessness, but he may be fearless without being bold; he may be fearless where there is no apprehension of danger or no cause for apprehension, but he is bold only when he is conscious or apprehensive of danger, and prepared to encounter it. A man is intrepid who has no fear where the most fearless might tremble; he is undaunted whose spirit is unabated by that which would make the stoutest heart yield.

Antonyms.—Afraid, fearful, cowardly, timid, faint-hearted.

Booty, spoil, prey. Booty and spoil are used as military terms in attacks on any enemy; prey, in cases of particular violence. The soldier gets his booty; the combatant, his spoils; the carnivorous animal, his prey. Booty implies something of personal service to the captor; spoils, whatever serves to designate his triumph; prey includes whatever gratifies the appetite and is to be consumed.

Bound, limit, confine, circumscribe, restrict, enclose. Bound applies to the natural or political divisions of the earth: countries are bounded by mountains and seas. Limit applies to any artificial boundary,—landmarks in fields serve to show the limits of one man's ground. To confine is to shut within limits,—in this manner we confine cattle in a yard by means of walls. To circumscribe is literally to write or draw around, as a circle around a square or limits about our desires. To restrict is to exercise a strong degree of control: a person is restricted in his movements by the narrowness of a room; laws often restrict privileges. To inclose is to bound or limit on all sides, as a garden is inclosed.

Boundless, unbounded, unlimited, infinite. Space is boundless so long as no bounds to it have been discovered; desires are often unbounded which ought always to be bounded; power is sometimes unlimited which would be better limited. That is infinite which is without bound or end, as: the power of God; the series of figures in the decimal expression of the fraction $\frac{1}{3}$.

Antonyms.—Confined, restricted, circumscribed, finite.

Bravery, courage, valor, gallantry. Bravery lies in the blood; courage lies in the mind. The latter depends on the reason, the former on the physical temperament. The first is a species of instinct; the second is a virtue. A man is brave in proportion as he is without thought of danger; he has courage in proportion as he reasons or reflects. Valor is a higher quality than either bravery or courage—it combines the fire of bravery with the determination and firmness of courage. Gallantry is extraordinary bravery combined with high-spirited manner, particularly on unusual occasions.

Antonyms.—Fear, cowardice, dismay, effeminacy.

Breach, break, gap, chasm. A breach and a gap are the consequence of a violent removal which destroys the connection; a break and a chasm may arise from the absence of that which would form a connection. A breach in a wall is made by means of cannon; gaps in fences are commonly the effect of some violent effort to pass through; a break is made in a page of printing by leaving off in the middle of a line; a chasm is left when an earthquake causes a gaping fissure.

Break, bruise, squeeze, pound, crush. Break always implies the separation of the component parts of a body; bruise denotes simply to injure without separation of parts. Hard, brittle substances, as glass, are broken; soft, pulpy substances, as flesh or fruits, are bruised. Squeeze is used for soft substances or for gentle compression. To pound is properly to crush in a mortar, so as to produce a separation of parts. To crush is the most violent and destructive of all operations, which amounts to the destroying of the structure of a body.

Break, burst, crack, split. To break does not specify any particular manner or form of action,—what is broken may be broken in two or more pieces, broken short or lengthwise, and the like; to burst is to break suddenly and with violence, frequently also with noise. To crack and to split are modes of breaking lengthwise: the former in application to hard or brittle objects, as clay, or the things made of clay; the latter in application to wood or substances like coal or rock that have seams or lines of cleavage.

Antonyms.—Join, attach, mend, unite, weld.

Breeze, gale, blast, gust, storm, tempest, hurricane. A breeze is gentle; a gale is brisk, but steady: we have breezes on a calm summer's day; the mariner has favorable gales, which keep the sails on the stretch. A blast is impetuous. The blare of a trumpet, the breath of bellows, are blasts. A gust is sudden and vehement; storm, tempest, and hurricane include other particulars besides wind. A storm throws the whole atmosphere into commotion; it is a war of the elements, in which wind, rain, hail, and the like conspire to disturb the heavens. Tempest is a violent storm. Hurricane is a species of storm which exceeds all the rest in violence and duration.

Antonyms.—Lull, calm, stillness, fair weather.

Brightness, luster, splendor, brilliancy. Brightness and luster are applied properly to natural lights; splendor and brilliancy have been more commonly applied to that which is artificial or unusual. There is always more or less brightness in the sun or moon; there is an occasional luster in all the heavenly bodies when they shine in their unclouded brightness; there is splendor in the eruptions of flame from a volcano or from an immense conflagration; there is brilliancy in a collection of diamonds.

Antonyms.—Dullness, dimness, shadow, obscurity, gloom.

Bring, fetch, carry. To bring is simply to take with oneself from one place to another; to fetch is to go first to a place and then bring a thing. To fetch, therefore, is a sort of bringing: whatever is near at hand may be brought; whatever is at a distance must be fetched. To carry implies taking with one, without reference to any particular place or destination.

Bulky, massive. Whatever is bulky is large, unwieldy, often awkward to handle, whether heavy or not; what is massive is compact in substance and combines solidity with large size.
Antonyms.—Compact, small, slight, slender.

Burial, interment, sepulture. We bury in order to conceal. Interment and sepulture are accompanied with religious ceremonies. Burial is confined to no object or place; interment refers properly to burial in the earth; sepulture is an abstract term confined to particular cases, as in speaking of the rites and privileges of sepulture.

Business, occupation, employment, engagement, avocation, vocation. Business occupies all a person's thoughts as well as his time and powers. Occupation and employment occupy only his time and strength; the first is mostly regular, the object of our choice; the second is casual, depending on the will of another. Engagement is a partial employment; avocation, a particular engagement. Vocation is applied to one's regular work; avocation, to the occupation with which one occupies his time outside the regular routine of work.
Antonyms.—Recreation, amusement, relaxation, pastime.

Business, trade, profession, art. Buying or selling of merchandise is inseparable from trade; but the exercise of one's knowledge and experience for purposes of gain constitutes a business. A profession implies scholarship and skill in application of principles. An art involves skill in the practice of accepted rules and methods of work to produce practical results with definite materials. We speak of the profession of letters, but of the art of writing. Trade is used also of mechanical occupation, as the carpenter's trade.

Bustle, tumult, uproar. Bustle has most of hurry in it; tumult, most of disorder and confusion; uproar, most of noise: the hurried movements of one, or many, cause a bustle; the disorderly struggles of many constitute a tumult. The loud elevation of many opposing voices produces an uproar; uproar is the consequence either of general anger or of mirth.
Antonyms.—Calm, quietness, order, tranquillity.

Calamity, disaster, misfortune, mischance, mishap. A calamity is a great disaster or misfortune; a misfortune is a great mischance or mishap. Whatever is attended with destruction is a calamity; whatever occasions mischief to the person, or defeats or interrupts plans, is a disaster; whatever is accompanied with a loss of property or the deprivation of health is a misfortune; whatever diminishes the beauty or utility of objects is a mischance or a mishap.
Antonyms.—Success, blessing, boon, achievement.

Calculate, reckon, compute, count. To calculate denotes any numerical operation in general, but is particularly applicable to the abstract science of figures. The astronomer calculates motions of the heavenly bodies; the mathematician makes arithmetical calculations. To reckon is to enumerate and set down things in detail. Reckoning is applicable to the ordinary business of life: tradesmen keep their accounts by reckoning; children learn to reckon by various simple processes. Calculation is therefore the science; reckoning, the practical art of enumerating. To compute is to come at the result by calculation. We count one by one,—we count the minutes.

Calendar, almanac, ephemeris. The calendar is a book which registers events under every month; the almanac is a book which registers times or the divisions of the year; an ephemeris is a book which registers the planetary movements every day.

Call, cry, exclaim. Call is used on all ordinary occasions in order to draw a person to a spot, or for any other purpose, when one wishes to be heard. To cry is to call loudly on particular occasions. A call draws attention; a cry awakens alarm. To exclaim implies the expression of some particular feeling.
Antonyms.—Hush, listen, be silent.

Call, invite, bid, summon. In the act of calling, any sounds may be used; we may call by simply raising the voice. Inviting may be a direct or indirect act; we may invite by looks or signs as well as by words, by writing as well as by speaking. To bid and summon require the express use of words; the former is always directly addressed to the person, the latter may be conveyed by an indirect channel. To summon is an act of authority, as to summon witnesses.
Antonyms.—Dismiss, disperse, send away.

Calm, placid, serene, composed, collected. Physically, calm means free from violent action; mentally, free from disturbing emotion or passion. Placid implies ease and contentment of mind. We speak also of a calm sea and a placid lake. Serene implies clearness and composure of mind. A sky is serene when free from clouds and clear. The mind is composed when excitement has been allayed; it is collected when all its powers are at command.
Antonyms.—Agitated, stormy, violent, passionate.

Candor, openness, sincerity. Candor obliges us to acknowledge even that which may make against ourselves; it is disinterested. Openness impels us to utter whatever passes in the mind—it is unguarded. Sincerity assures that our words and actions are true to our thoughts and feelings—it is positive.
Antonyms.—Cunning, deceit, craft, duplicity.

Captious, cross, peevish, petulant, fretful. Captious marks a readiness to find fault; cross indicates a readiness to offend or go contrary to the wishes of others; peevish expresses a strong degree of crossness; fretful, a complaining impatience. Captiousness is the consequence of ill will or pique; crossness, of ill humor; peevishness and fretfulness, of a painful irritability. Petulance is the result either of a naturally hasty temper or of a sudden irritability.
Antonyms.—Considerate, good-natured, appreciative, thoughtful, patient.

Capture, seizure, prize. A capture is made by force of arms; a seizure is made by direct and personal force. Prize relates only to the thing taken and its value to the captor.

Care, charge, management. Care will include both charge and management; but, in the strict sense, it comprehends personal labor. Charge involves responsibility; management includes regulation and order. A gardener has the care of a garden; a nurse has the charge of children; a steward has the management of a farm.

Care, solicitude, anxiety. Care is the most indefinite of the three; it may be accompanied with pain or not, according to the nature of the object or the intensity of the application. Solicitude and anxiety are accompanied with a positive degree of pain—the latter still more than the former. Care may be exercised with or without feeling; solicitude has desire, mixed with fear; anxiety has distress for the present, mixed with fear for the future.
Antonyms.—Satisfaction, indifference, unconcern, trust.

Careful, cautious, provident. Careful, or full of care, that is, having care, is the general term. To be cautious is to be careful in guarding against danger; to be provident is to be careful in preventing straits and difficulties. The term careful is applied for the most part to present matters, but provident only to that which is future. One is careful of his money, but provident toward a time of need.
Antonyms.—Careless, neglectful, reckless, heedless, spendthrift.

Carnage, slaughter, massacre, butchery. Carnage pictures heaped corpses; slaughter, the wholesale taking of lives as in battle. Butchery is the brutal word for killing men and women as cattle are killed. Massacre implies the killing or butchery of defenseless men, women, and children.

Case, cause. The case is matter of fact; the cause is matter of question. A case involves circumstances and consequences; a cause involves reasons and arguments. A case is something to be learned; a cause is something to be decided.

Cause, occasion, create. What is caused seems to follow naturally. What is occasioned follows incidentally, or what occasions may be incidental, but necessary. What is created receives its existence arbitrarily. A wound causes pain; accidents occasion delay; busybodies create mischief.

Cause, reason, motive. A cause is that which brings about any event, act, or fact. "The Creator is the first cause of all things." A reason is an explanation devised by the mind for a fact, an event, or an action. We give reasons also for our beliefs, that is, the grounds for them. A motive is an influence that determines choice or action. Effects follow causes, conclusions follow reasons, and actions spring from motives.

Cautious, wary, circumspect. We must be cautious on all occasions where there is danger, but we must be wary where there is great danger. A tradesman must be cautious in his dealings with all men, but he must be wary when he has to deal with designing men. Circumspect implies attention to all the conditions and probable consequences of action. A man must be circumspect when he transacts business of particular importance and delicacy.
Antonyms.—Rash, impulsive, audacious, precipitate.

Cease, leave off, discontinue. Cease is used for either particular actions or general habits; leave off, more usually and properly for particular actions; discontinue, for general habits. A restless, spoiled child never ceases crying until it has obtained what it wants; it is a mark of impatience not to cease lamenting when one is in pain. A laborer leaves off his work at any given hour. A sensitive person discontinues his visits when they are found not to be agreeable.
Antonyms.—Continue, persist, persevere.

Celebrate, commemorate. Everything is celebrated which is distinguished by any marks of attention, without regard to the time of the event, whether present or past;

nothing is commemorated but what has already passed in point of time.
Antonyms.—Forget, ignore, disregard.

Celestial, heavenly. Celestial is applied mostly in the natural sense of the heavens; heavenly is employed more commonly in a spiritual sense. Hence, we speak of the celestial globe as distinguished from the terrestrial, and of the celestial bodies. But we speak of the heavenly habitation, of heavenly joys or bliss, of heavenly spirits and the like.
Antonyms.—Terrestrial, earthly, mundane.

Censure, carp, cavil. To censure respects positive errors; to carp and cavil have regard to what is trivial or imaginary. The former is employed for errors in persons; the latter, for supposed defects in things. Carping and caviling are resorted to only to indulge ill nature or self-conceit: party politicians carp at the measures of administration; infidels cavil at the evidences of Christianity, because they are determined to disbelieve.
Antonyms.—Praise, approve, sanction, uphold.

Cessation, stop, rest, intermission. Cessation refers to the course of things; whatever does not go on has ceased; things cease of themselves. Stop implies an abrupt cessation, as if due to an outside force. Rest is cessation from labor or exertion—whatever does not move or exert itself is at rest. Intermission is cessation only for a time or at certain intervals. That which ceases or stops is supposed to be at an end; rest or intermission supposes a renewal.
Antonyms.—Stir, work, persistence, continuance.

Chance, fortune, fate. Chance applies to all things personal or otherwise; fortune and fate are applied most often to that which is personal. Chance neither forms, orders, nor designs; neither knowledge nor intention is attributed to it; its events are uncertain and variable. Fortune forms plans and designs, but without choice; we attribute to it an intention without discernment; it is said to be blind. Fate forms plans and chains of causes; intention, knowledge, and power are attributed to it—its views are fixed; its results are decisive.
Antonyms.—Choice, free will, purpose.

Chance, hazard. As between chance and hazard, chance implies that the balance of probability inclines toward good fortune; hazard, that the chances of good or ill are about even, or inclining toward misfortune.

Change, exchange, barter, substitute. To change in respect to persons is to take one for another, without regard to whether they are alike or different,—as a king changes his ministers, or any person may change his servants. To exchange is to take one person in return for another who is in like condition, as prisoners are exchanged in time of war. In respect to things, to change is to take anything new or fresh, whether alike or different; clothes may be changed. To exchange is to take one thing for another, that is, either of the same kind or equivalent in value, as to exchange one commodity for another. To change may often be the result of caprice, but to exchange is always an act of either discretion or necessity. To barter is to give any commodity for other commodities. To substitute is to put one person or thing in the place of another for the purpose of doing any service or filling any office, as to substitute one for another in military service, or to substitute wood for steel in building.
Antonyms.—Keep, hold, retain.

Change, variation, vicissitude. Change consists simply in ceasing to be the same; variation consists in being different at different times; vicissitude consists in being alternately or reciprocally different and the same.
Antonyms.—Sameness, uniformity, permanence.

Character, letter. Character is any written or printed mark that serves to designate something; a letter is a species of character which is a constituent part of a word.

Character, reputation. Character lies in the man; it is the mark of what he is; it shows itself on all occasions. A person's reputation depends upon others; it is what they think of him.

Chasten, chastise. Chasten is used only of spiritual correction, as the chastening of men by God. Chastise implies physical pain or punishment with a corrective purpose.

Cheat, defraud, trick. One cheats by direct and gross falsehood or artifice; one defrauds by a settled plan or contrivance; one tricks by a sudden invention.

Check, chide, reprimand, reprove, rebuke. A person is checked that he may not continue to do what is offensive; he is chidden for what he has done, that he may not repeat it. People are checked by actions and looks, as well as by words; they are chidden by words only. A person may chide or reprimand in anger; he reproves and rebukes with coolness; great offenses call forth chidings. Omissions or mistakes occasion or require a reprimand; irregularities of conduct give rise to reproof; and improprieties of behavior demand rebuke.
Antonyms.—Allow, indulge, abet, approve, laud.

Check, hinder, stop. Check signifies to impede the course of a body in motion, that is, to cause it to move slowly; to stop is to cause it not to move at all. Hinder implies interference in a greater or less degree with action or motion.
Antonyms.—Accelerate, urge, quicken, expedite.

Cheer, encourage, comfort. To encourage is to give heart or courage for action, to strengthen resolution. To cheer and to comfort apply to the spirits or feelings; but to cheer expresses more than to comfort, the former signifying to produce a lively sentiment, the latter to lessen or remove a painful one. We are cheered in the moments of despondence, whether from real or imaginary causes; we are comforted in the hour of distress; we are encouraged in times of timidity and fear.
Antonyms.—Sadden, grieve, hurt, dishearten.

Chief, leader, chieftain, head. Chief denotes precedence in tribal or civil matters; leader regards the direction of enterprises; chieftain is a kind of leader; and a head is the superior in general concerns.
Antonyms.—Follower, aide, lieutenant.

Chief, principal, main. Chief respects order and rank; principal has regard to importance and respectability; main, to degree or quantity. We speak of a chief clerk, of a commander in chief, of the chief person in a city, but of the principal people in a city, of the principal circumstances in a narrative, and of the main object.
Antonyms.—Subordinate, minor, inferior, attendant.

Choose, prefer, pick, select. We may choose whatever comes in our way, without regard to the number of the objects to be chosen from, but we pick or select out of a number only, as to pick or select books from a library. We may pick one or many out of a number, but we mostly select a number. We select with even greater care than we pick. Prefer implies more definitely the mental comparison of one thing with others.
Antonyms.—Reject, disregard, ignore, dismiss.

Circumstance, incident, fact. A circumstance occurs or exists in connection with facts or incidents. Incidents occur or happen in the course of action, but are aside from the main plan or design. Whatever is or is produced or happens is a fact; it may be an incident or a circumstance, if it is thought of as merely attendant to some main fact.

Circumstance, situation. Circumstance is to situation as a part is to a whole: many circumstances constitute a situation; a situation is an aggregate of circumstances. A person is said to be in circumstances of affluence who has an abundance of everything essential to his comfort; he is in an easy situation when nothing exists to create uneasiness.

Circumstantial, particular, minute. Circumstantial expresses less than particular, and particular less than minute. A circumstantial account contains all leading events; a particular account includes every event and movement, however trivial; a minute account omits nothing as to person, time, place, form, and includes every trivial circumstance connected with the events.
Antonyms.—General, cursory, indefinite, vague.

Cite, quote. We quote exact words or the substance of a passage. We cite an author or a passage in his work by giving the exact location or reference, as line and page, so that the words may be found readily.

Civil, polite, obliging, complaisant. Polite expresses more than civil; it is possible to be civil without being polite. Civility is contented with pleasing when the occasion offers. Politeness seeks the opportunity to please: it prevents the necessity of asking by anticipating the wishes; it is full of delicate attentions, and is an active benevolence in the minor concerns of life. Civil applies to words or manner as well as to the action; obliging, to the action only. As civil is indefinite in its meaning, so it is often used indiscriminately in its application; obliging, on the other hand, is confined to what passes between particular persons or under particular circumstances. Civil and obliging both imply a desire to do a kindness; complaisant signifies the desire of pleasing others by being agreeable.
Antonyms.—Rude, discourteous, ill-mannered, churlish.

Clandestine, secret. To do a thing clandestinely is to elude observation; to do a thing secretly is to do it without the knowledge of anyone. What is clandestine is unallowed, which is not necessarily the case with what is secret.
Antonyms.—Authorized, public, open.

Clasp, hug, embrace. To clasp is the act of enclosing another in one's arms when it is performed with the warmth of true affection. To hug is to clasp tightly to the bosom. The more refined term, to embrace, is to infold in the arms in token of friendship or affection.

Classify, arrange, range. The general qualities and attributes of things are to be considered in classifying; their fitness to stand by each other must be considered in arranging; their capacity for forming a line is the only thing to be attended to in ranging. Classification serves the purposes of either public policy or science; arranging is a matter of convenience to the individual himself; ranging is a matter of convenience for others.

Antonyms.—Mix, disorder, jumble, confuse, scatter.

Clean, cleanly, pure. Clean expresses a freedom from dirt or soil; cleanly, the disposition or habit of being clean. A person who keeps himself clean is cleanly. Pure is used in a moral sense, as a pure heart; it is used also to mean free from other substances, as a solution is chemically pure.

Antonyms.—Soiled, dirty, foul, filthy.

Clearly, distinctly. That is seen clearly of which one has a clear view independent of anything else; that is seen distinctly which is seen so as to distinguish it from other objects. We see the moon clearly whenever it shines; but we cannot see the spots in the moon distinctly without the help of glasses.

Antonyms.—Dimly, vaguely, confusedly.

Clearness, lucidity, brightness, vividness. A mere freedom from stain or dullness constitutes clearness; a shining clearness, as of crystal, constitutes lucidity; brightness supposes a certain strength of light; vividness, a freshness combined with strength, and with a degree of brilliancy.

Antonyms.—Dimness, dullness, cloudiness, darkness.

Clearness, perspicuity. Clearness springs from right distinguishing of the ideas discussed. Perspicuity is a quality of the style in which thought is expressed. The argument is clear; the language, perspicuous.

Antonyms.—Obscurity, indefiniteness, ambiguity, vagueness.

Clever, skillful, expert, dexterous. Cleverness is mental power employed in the ordinary concerns of life—a person is clever in business. Skill implies both mental and physical ability, especially in mechanical operations and in science: a physician, a lawyer, or an artist is skillful; one may have a skill in divination or a skill in painting. Expertness and dexterity require more physical than mental power exerted in minor arts and amusements—one is expert at throwing the quoit, dexterous in the management of horses.

Antonyms.—Awkward, bungling, stupid, slow.

Cloister, convent, monastery. The proper idea of cloister is that of seclusion; the proper idea of convent is that of community; the proper idea of a monastery is that of solitude. One is shut up in a cloister, enters a convent; one retires to a monastery. Whoever wishes to take an absolute leave of the world shuts himself up in a cloister; whoever wishes to attach himself to a community that has renounced all commerce with the world goes into a convent; whoever wishes to shun all human intercourse retires to a monastery. In the cloister our liberty is sacrificed; in the convent our worldly habits are renounced, and, those of a regular religious community being adopted, we submit to the yoke of established orders; in a monastery we impose a voluntary exile upon ourselves, with the view of living only to God.

Close, conclude, finish. We may close anything, as a discourse or a meeting, at any point by simply ceasing to have any more to do with it; but we conclude in a definite and positive manner. To conclude is to bring to an end by determination; to finish is to bring to an end by completion. What is settled by arrangement and deliberation is properly concluded; what is begun and ended on a certain plan is said to be finished.

Antonyms.—Begin, open, start, commence, initiate.

Close, near, nigh. Close is more definite than near; houses which are almost joined stand close to each other; men stand close when they touch each other. Objects are near which are within sight; persons are near each other when they can converse together. Near and nigh, which are but variations of one root-word, admit of little or no difference in their use.

Antonyms.—Distant, far, remote, removed.

Coarse, rough, rude. In the physical sense, coarse refers to the composition and materials of bodies, as coarse bread, coarse meat, coarse cloth; rough applies to the surface of bodies, as rough wood and rough skin; rude respects the make or fashion of things,—as a rude bark, a rude utensil. The application of these words to manners and conduct follows their physical sense. A person's language may be coarse, his appearance rough, and his manner rude.

Antonyms.—Fine, refined, smooth, pleasant, suave, polished, civil, polite.

Cogent, forcible, strong. Cogency applies to reasons individually considered; force and strength, to modes of reasoning or expression. Cogent reasons impel to decisive conduct; strong conviction is produced by forcible reasoning conveyed in strong language.

Antonyms.—Feeble, ineffectual, unconvincing, weak.

Colleague, partner, associate. Colleague is used properly of people associated in high office, as in court or in legislature. It is used popularly by debaters associated on teams. Associate is a more general term. Used officially, it implies subordination, as an associate professor. Partner is used popularly of men associated for business and sharing common risks, especially in some hazardous undertaking.

Antonyms.—Opponent, rival, foe, adversary, competitor.

Colorable, specious, ostensible, plausible. The first three of these words are figures of speech drawn from what naturally pleases the eye; plausible is drawn from what pleases the ear. What is colorable has an aspect or face upon it that lulls suspicion and affords satisfaction; what is specious has a fair outside when contrasted with that which it may possibly conceal; what is ostensible is that which presents such an appearance as may serve for an indication of something real. The plausible sounds true, but may be false.

Antonyms.—Genuine, candid, open, unmistakable, ingenuous.

Combat, oppose. A person's views or attitudes are combated; his interests or his measures are opposed.

Antonyms.—Advocate, aid, promote, support.

Come, arrive. To come specifies neither time nor manner; to arrive is employed with regard to some particular period or circumstances. Guests arrive; trains arrive; what is to come is uncertain.

Antonyms.—Go, leave, depart, set out, take leave.

Comfort, pleasure, happiness. Comfort implies a freedom of the whole person from annoyance or pain, a positive feeling of contentment. Pleasure lies in a vivid and intense activity of the mind and is fleeting in its nature. Happiness is an abiding state of agreeable feeling.

Antonyms.—Uneasiness, pain, heartache, sorrow.

Command, direction, order, injunction, precept. A command is an exercise of power or authority; it is imperative and must be obeyed. Direction contains the idea of instruction; order, that of authority. Directions should be followed; orders, obeyed. An order serves to direct—it is instructive and must be executed. A superior issues his commands. Orders may be given by a subordinate or by a body, as orders of a court. Order is applied to the common concerns of life; injunction and precept, to the moral conduct or duties of men. Injunction imposes a duty by virtue of the authority which enjoins. The precept lays down or teaches such duties as already exist.

Antonyms.—Consent, leave, license, permission.

Commission, authorize, empower. We commission in matters where our own will and convenience are concerned; we authorize in matters where our personal authority is requisite; we empower in matters where the authority of the law is required.

Antonyms.—Refuse, prohibit, forbid, disallow, enjoin.

Commodious, convenient. Commodious is most often applied to that which contributes to the bodily ease and comfort; convenient, to whatever suits the purposes of men in their various transactions.

Antonyms.—Narrow, restraining, ill-contrived, awkward.

Commonly, generally, frequently, usually. What is commonly done is an action common to all; what is generally done is the action of the greatest part; what is frequently done is either the action of many, or an action many times repeated by the same person; what is usually done is done regularly by one or many.

Antonyms.—Rarely, occasionally, sometimes, seldom.

Communicate, impart. A thing may be communicated directly or indirectly, and to any number of persons, as to communicate intelligence by signal or otherwise. Impart is a direct action that passes between individuals, as to impart instruction.

Communion, converse. Both these terms imply a communication between minds; but the former may take place without corporeal agency, the latter never does. Spirits hold communion with each other; people hold converse.

Compatible, consistent. Compatibility has a reference principally to plans and measures; consistency, to character, conduct, and station. Everything which does not interrupt its prosecution is compatible with a plan; everything by which it is neither degraded nor elevated is consistent with a person's station.

Antonyms.—Discordant, incongruous, contradictory, inharmonious.

Compel, force, oblige, necessitate. To compel denotes moral rather than physical force; but to force is properly applied to the use of physical force or a violent degree of

moral force. A man may be compelled to walk if he have no means of riding; he may be forced to go at the will of another. Oblige expresses only an indirect influence, which may be resisted or yielded to at discretion. We are compelled to do that which is repugnant to our will and our feelings. That which one is obliged to do may have the assent of the judgment, if not of the will. We are necessitated by circumstances, or by anything which puts it out of our power to do otherwise.
Antonyms.—Induce, persuade, invite, tempt, lead.

Compensation, amends, satisfaction, recompense, remuneration, requital, reward. A compensation is a return for a loss or a damage sustained; amends is a return for anything that is faulty in ourselves or toward others. Satisfaction is that which satisfies the individual requiring it—it is given for personal injuries; a recompense is a voluntary return for a voluntary service—it is made from a generous feeling. Remuneration is estimated rather according to the condition of the person and the dignity of the service than for its positive worth. Authors often receive for their works a remuneration according to the reputation they have previously acquired and not according to the real merit of the work. A reward conveys no idea of an obligation on the part of the person making it—whoever rewards, acts optionally. When evil is returned for good, that is a bad requital, and, as a proof of ingratitude, wounds the feelings.

Competent, fitted, qualified. Competent especially regards the mental endowments and attainments; fitted, the disposition and character; qualified, the artificial acquirements or natural qualities.
Antonyms.—Unprepared, unsuitable, ill-adapted.

Complain, lament, regret. Complaint implies dissatisfaction; lamentation, grief; regret, pain. Complaint is expressed verbally; lamentation, either by words or signs; regret may be felt without being expressed. Complaint is made of personal grievances; lamentation and regret may be made on account of others as well as of ourselves. We complain of our ill health, of our inconveniences, or of troublesome circumstances; we lament our inability to serve another; we regret the absence of one whom we love.
Antonyms.—Rejoice, welcome, hail, approve.

Complaint, accusation. A complaint is usually made in matters that personally affect the complainant; an accusation is made of matters in general, but especially those of a moral nature. A complaint is made for the sake of obtaining redress; an accusation is made for the sake of ascertaining a fact or for the sake of bringing to punishment.
Antonyms.—Defense, justification, exoneration, acquittal.

Complaisance, deference, condescension. Complaisance signifies the act of complying with or pleasing others; deference marks the inclination to defer, or acquiesce in the sentiments of another in preference to one's own; condescension marks the act of conceding one's point, to yield to the satisfaction of others rather than rigorously to exact one's rights. The necessities and the allurements of society and of intimacy lead to complaisance; it makes sacrifices to the wishes, tastes, and personal feelings of others. Complaisance is the act of an equal; deference, that of an inferior; condescension, that of a superior.
Antonyms.—Refractoriness, discourtesy, impertinence, inconsiderateness, ungraciousness.

Complete, finish, terminate. The characteristic idea of completing is that of making a thing altogether what it ought to be; that of finishing, the doing all that is intended to be done toward a thing; and that of terminating, simply putting an end to a thing.
Antonyms.—Begin, commence, initiate.

Complete, perfect, finished. That is complete which has no deficiency; that is perfect which has positive excellence; and that is finished which is at an end.
Antonyms.—Deficient, faulty, marred, unaccomplished.

Compliant, yielding, submissive. A compliant person may want command of feeling; a yielding person may want fixedness of principle; a submissive person may want resolution. A too compliant disposition will be imposed upon by the selfish and the unreasonable; a too yielding disposition is unfit to exercise command; a too submissive disposition exposes a person to the exactions of tyranny.
Antonyms.—Stubborn, resolute, determined, recalcitrant, rebellious.

Comply, conform, yield, submit. To comply is to act from inclination; to conform is to act from judgment. Compliance is altogether optional—we comply with a thing or not, at pleasure. Conformity is binding on the conscience—it relates to matters in which there is a right and a wrong. To yield is to give way to another, either with one's will, judgment, or outward conduct. To submit is to give up oneself altogether—it is the substitution of another's will for one's own.
Antonyms.—Refuse, resist, differ, dissent, oppose, withstand.

Compose, settle. We compose that which has been disjointed and separated, by bringing it together again; we settle that which has been disturbed and put in motion, by setting it at rest.
Antonyms.—Disturb, disarrange, confuse.

Composed, sedate. Composed implies a temporary state of mental quiet and calm, arising from mastery of the emotions. Sedate signifies a permanent habit of calm steadiness of temper.
Antonyms.—Agitated, disturbed, flighty, indiscreet, frolicsome, sparkling.

Compound, compose. Compound applies in a physical sense only and refers especially to the mixing of substances in fixed proportions. Compose, in a physical, social, or moral sense, refers to the fact of a mixture of elements. The chemist compounds medicines carefully; society is composed of various classes.
Antonyms.—Resolve, analyze, dissect, break up.

Comprise, comprehend, embrace, contain, include. A library comprises a variety of books; the whole is comprised within a small compass. Laws comprehend a number of cases. A discourse embraces a variety of topics. A society contains very many individuals; it includes none but those of a certain class, or it includes some of every class.
Antonyms.—Exclude, debar, except, omit.

Conceal, dissemble, disguise. To conceal is simply to abstain from making known what we wish to keep secret; to dissemble and disguise signify to conceal by assuming some false appearance. We conceal facts; we dissemble feelings; we disguise sentiments.
Antonyms.—Reveal, discover, divulge, show, unveil.

Conceal, hide, secrete. To conceal is to keep from observation; to hide is to put under cover; to secrete is to set at a distance or in unfrequented places.
Antonyms.—Show, expose, exhibit, disclose.

Concealment, secrecy. Concealment has to do with what concerns others; secrecy, with that which concerns ourselves. What is concealed is kept from the observation of others; what is secret is known only to ourselves.
Antonyms.—Openness, frankness, ingenuousness.

Conceit, fancy. Conceit applies only to internal objects; it is mental in the operation and the result; it is a species of invention. Fancy is applied to external objects, or whatever acts on the senses. Nervous people are subject to strange conceits; timid people fancy they hear sounds or see objects in the dark which awaken terror.
Antonyms.—Actuality, reality, fact.

Conceive, understand, comprehend. Conception is the simplest operation of the three: when we conceive we may have but one idea; when we understand or comprehend we have all the ideas which the subject is capable of presenting. The builder conceives plans; the scholar understands languages; the metaphysician attempts to explain many things which are not to be comprehended.

Conception, notion, idea, image. Conception is the general, scientific word for idea, the product of the mind's relating and constructive work. Notion implies more direct reference to the thing known. Idea is used popularly and vaguely for conception, fancy, and image. An image is the product of the picturing activity of the mind. We speak of the conception of immortality, of the idea of God, of a notion of proper conduct, of an image of a face.

Concert, contrive, manage. There is a secret understanding in concerting, invention in contriving, execution in managing. Measures are concerted; schemes are contrived; affairs are managed.

Conciliate, reconcile. To conciliate is to get good will and affection for oneself; to reconcile is to unite the affections of two persons to each other.
Antonyms.—Disaffect, estrange, alienate.

Conclusion, inference, deduction, induction, demonstration. Demonstration is the most complete form of proof, but it is, strictly, not attainable outside of such deductive reasoning as is found in mathematics. A conclusion is a necessary consequence of certain admitted facts or statements. An inference is a probable conclusion; it may be hastily drawn from incomplete data. Induction is a process of reasoning from particular facts toward a general principle. Deduction is reasoning from a general principle, from which conclusions are drawn regarding particular facts to which the principle applies. Scientific conclusions are reached through the alternate use of induction and deduction.

Conclusive, decisive, convincing. Conclusive applies either to practical or theoretical matters; decisive, to what is practical only; convincing, to what is theoretical only. It is necessary to be conclusive when we deliberate, and decisive when we command. An argument is convincing, a chain of reasoning conclusive, a piece of evidence may be decisive.
Antonyms.—Uncertain, dubious, questionable, hypothetical.

Concord, harmony. Concord is generally employed for the union of wills and affections; harmony respects the aptitude of minds to agree. Harmony may be used in the sense of adaptation to things generally.
Antonyms.—Discord, disagreement, variance, dissension.

Condition, station. Condition commonly refers to circumstances, education, birth, and the like; station refers rather to rank, occupation, or fixed mode of life.

Conduce, contribute. To conduce signifies to serve the full purpose; to contribute signifies only to serve a secondary purpose. Exercise conduces to health; it contributes to give vigor to the frame.
Antonyms.—Counteract, contravene, hinder, defeat.

Conduct, manage, direct. Conducting requires most wisdom and knowledge; managing, most action; direction, most authority. A lawyer conducts the cause intrusted to him; an agent manages the mercantile concerns for his employer; a superintendent directs the movements of all the subordinate agents.

Confederate, accomplice. A confederate is a partner in a plot or a secret association; an accomplice is a partner in some active violation of the laws.
Antonyms.—Rival, adversary, betrayer.

Confer, bestow. Conferring is an act of authority; bestowing, an act of charity or generosity. Men in power confer; people in private station bestow.
Antonyms.—Deprive, withhold, retain, keep from.

Confidence, trust. Confidence is an extraordinary trust, but trust is always ordinary unless the term be otherwise qualified. Confidence involves communication of a man's mind to another, but trust is confined to matters of action.
Antonpms.—Doubt, mistrust, suspicion, misgiving.

Confident, dogmatic, positive. Confidence implies a general reliance on our abilities in whatever is undertaken; dogmatism implies a reliance on the truth of our opinions, positiveness, a reliance on the truth of our assertions. A confident man is always ready to act, as he is sure of succeeding; a dogmatic man is always ready to speak, as he is sure of being heard; a positive man is determined to maintain what he has asserted, as he is convinced that he has made no mistake.
Antonyms.—Uncertain, reluctant, doubtful, hesitant, vacillating.

Confirm, corroborate. Confirm is the stronger word, implying support by established facts or assured knowledge. Corroborate implies support of a statement or belief by added statements or attendant circumstances.
Antonyms.—Refute, confute, invalidate, annul, weaken.

Confirm, establish. Confirm is applied to what is partial, if not temporary; establish, to that which is permanent and of importance; as, to confirm a report, to establish a reputation, to confirm a treaty or alliance, to establish a trade or a government.
Antonyms.—Annul, abrogate, destroy, unsettle.

Conformable, agreeable, suitable. Conformable is employed for matters of obligation; agreeable, for matters of choice; suitable, for matters of propriety and discretion. What is conformable accords with some prescribed form or given rule of others; what is agreeable accords with the feelings, tempers, or judgments of ourselves or others; what is suitable accords with outward circumstances.
Antonyms.—Inconsistent, ill-adapted, unwelcome, unfitted.

Confound, confuse. A person confounds one thing with another; objects become confused, or a person confuses himself. It is a common error among ignorant people to confound names, and among children to have their ideas confused on commencing a new study.
Antonyms.—Distinguish, separate, discriminate.

Confront, face. Confront implies to set face to face, face signifies to set the face toward any object. Witnesses are confronted; a person faces danger.
Antonyms.—Avoid, evade, shun, dodge.

Confusion, disorder. Confusion supposes the absence of all order; disorder, the derangement of order where it exists or is supposed to exist.
Antonyms.—Method, regularity, orderliness.

Confute, refute, disprove, oppugn. Confute applies to what is argumentative; refute, to what is practical and personal; disprove, to whatever is represented or related; oppugn, to what is held or maintained. An argument is confuted by proving its fallacy; a charge is refuted by proving the innocence of the party charged; an assertion is disproved by proving that it is incorrect; a doctrine is oppugned by a course of reasoning.
Antonyms.—Prove, substantiate, support, uphold, defend.

Connect, combine, unite. Things connected and combined remain distinct, but things united lose all individuality. Things the most dissimilar may be connected or combined; things of the same kind only can be united. Houses are connected by means of a common passage; the armies of two nations are combined; two armies of the same nation are united.
Antonyms.—Separate, sever, disjoin, part.

Connection, relation. Families are connected with each other by the ties of blood or marriage; persons are connected with each other in the way of trade or business; objects stand in a certain relation to each other, as persons stand in the relation of giver and receiver, or of debtor and creditor.

Conqueror, victor. A conqueror is always supposed to add something to his possessions; a victor gains nothing but the superiority. Those who take possession of other men's lands by force of arms make a conquest; those who excel in any trial of skill are the victors.

Consent, permit, allow. As the act of an equal, we consent to that in which we have a common interest with others. We permit or allow what is for the accommodation of others: we allow by not opposing; we permit by a direct expression of our will. Contracts are formed by the consent of the parties who are interested. The proprietor of an estate permits his friends to sport on his grounds; he allows a passage through his premises. A parent consents to the requests of his children; he permits them to read certain books; he allows them to converse with him familiarly.
Antonyms.—Refuse, forbid, prohibit, interdict.

Consequence, effect, result, issue, event. A consequence is that which follows of itself, without any qualification or restriction; an effect is that which is effected or produced, or which follows from the connection between the thing effecting, as a cause, and the thing effected. A result is general, following from a whole; there may be many consequences from the same thing, with one result only. We speak of the issue of a negotiation or a battle, and the event of a war. The fate of a nation sometimes hangs on the issue of a battle; the measures of government are often unjustly praised or blamed according to the event.
Antonyms.—Cause, reason, condition, occasion, antecedent.

Consider, reflect. To consider is employed for practical purposes; to reflect, for matters of speculation or moral improvement. Common objects call for consideration; the workings of the mind itself or objects purely spiritual occupy reflection.

Consider, regard. There is more of caution or thought in considering, more of personal interest in regarding. To consider is to bear in mind all that prudence or propriety suggest; to regard is to bear in mind all that our wishes or interests suggest.

Consideration, reason. The consideration influences particular actions; the reason determines a line of conduct.

Consonant, accordant, consistent. Consonant (with, to) implies such agreement as would avoid discord. Consistent (with) applies to agreement that avoids contradiction. Consonant and accordant are applied to matters of belief and sentiment; consistent, also to matters of conduct.
Antonyms.—Dissonant, discordant, incongruous, incompatible.

Constancy, stability, steadiness, firmness. Constancy involves the affections; stability, the opinions; steadiness, the action or the motives of action; firmness, the purpose or resolution.
Antonyms.—Variableness, fickleness, capriciousness.

Constitute, appoint, depute. To constitute is the act of a body; to appoint and depute, either of a body or of an individual: a community constitutes anyone their leader; a monarch appoints his ministers. Whoever is deputed has private and not public authority; his office is partial, often confined to the particular transaction of an individual, or of a body of individuals.

Consult, deliberate. Consultations always require two persons at least; deliberations may be carried on either with a man's self or with others. An individual may consult with one or many; assemblies commonly deliberate.

Consummate, complete. Consummate refers to desires or plans or movements brought to fulfillment. Complete is applied in the sense of finishing according to design.
Antonyms.—Fail, fall short.

Contagion, infection. Contagion implies the manner of spreading from one body to another; infection, the act of working into the system in such a way as to affect it, as by disease. Whatever acts by contagion acts by direct personal contact or by means of the clothing, breath, etc. Whatever acts by infection acts indirectly, the source of the infecting organisms not being definitely known.

Contagious, epidemic, pestilential. The word contagious applies to that which is capable of being caught, and which ought therefore to be avoided; epidemic, to that which is already caught or circulated and which requires therefore to be stopped; pestilential, to that which may breed an evil, and which is therefore to be removed. Diseases are contagious or epidemic; the air or breath is pestilential.

Contaminate, defile, pollute, taint, corrupt. Whatever is impure contaminates; what is gross and vile, in the natural sense, defiles and, in the moral sense, pollutes; what is contagious or infectious corrupts; what is corrupted may taint other things.
Antonyms.—Wash, purify, cleanse, disinfect.

Contemn, despise, scorn, disdain. Contemn signifies to view or think of as worthless, to hold in contempt. Despise signifies to look down upon, which is a strong mark of contempt; scorn implies stripping of all honors and exposure to derision; disdain signifies to hold altogether unworthy.
Antonyms.—Esteem, value, admire, covet.

Contemplate, meditate, muse. Different species of reflection are marked by these terms. We contemplate what is present or before our eyes; we meditate on what is past or absent. The heavens and all the works of the Creator are objects of contemplation; the ways of Providence are fit subjects for meditation. One muses on events or circumstances which have recently passed.

Contend, contest, dispute. To contend is simply to exert a force against a force; to contest is to struggle with an opponent for an object; to dispute, according to its original meaning, applies to opinions only and is distinguished from contend in this,—that the latter signifies to maintain one's own opinion, the former to call in question the opinion of another.
Antonyms.—Yield, give up, surrender, admit, acknowledge.

Contentment, satisfaction. Contentment lies in ourselves; satisfaction is derived from external objects. One is contented when one wishes for no more; one is satisfied when one has obtained all one wishes. Contentment is within the reach of the poor man, to whom it is a continual feast; but satisfaction has never been procured by wealth, however enormous, or by ambition, however boundless.
Antonyms.—Desire, distress, trouble, regret, mourning.

Continual, continuous, perpetual, constant, continued. Continual implies possible intermission but also regular beginning again. Continuous admits of no pause or interruption. What is perpetual admits of no termination. There may be an end to that which is continual, and there may be intervals in that which is perpetual. Constant, like continuous, admits of no interruption, and it also admits of no change. What is continual may not always continue in the same state; but what is constant remains in the same state; what is continued ceases for a time, only to be taken up again.
Antonyms.—Changing, intermittent, desultory, broken, concluded.

Continuance, continuation, duration. Continuance is said of that which itself continues; continuation, of that which is continued by some other agency, as the continuance of the rain, the continuation of a history, work, line, etc. Things are of long or short duration by comparison.
Antonyms.—Cessation, interruption, termination.

Continue, persevere, persist. We continue from habit or circumstances; we persevere from reflection and the exercise of our judgment; we persist from attachment to a desire or purpose. A child perseveres in a new study until he has mastered it; he persists in making a request until he has obtained the object of his desire.
Antonyms.—Pause, stop, give up, desist, forbear.

Continue, remain, stay. Continue is associated with a state of action; remain, with a state of rest. We are said to continue to speak or to do anything, to remain stationary or in a position. Stay is a voluntary act, as to stay at a friend's, or with a friend.
Antonyms.—Cease, leave off, depart, remove.

Contracted, confined, narrow. Contracted signifies drawn into a smaller compass than it might otherwise be in; confined signifies brought within unusually small bounds. Narrow is the opposite of broad, in extent, scope, views, and resources. A limb is said to be contracted when it is drawn up by disease; a situation is confined which has not the necessary or usual degree of open space; a road or a mind is narrow.
Antonyms.—Extended, roomy, free, unbounded, broad.

Contradict, deny. One contradicts in direct terms by asserting something contrary; one denies by advancing arguments or by suggesting doubts or difficulties. Both these terms may therefore be used in reference to disputations. We may deny the truth of a position by contradicting the assertions that are advanced in its support.
Antonyms.—Admit, assert, corroborate, support, maintain.

Controvert, dispute. To controvert has regard to speculative points; to dispute respects matters of fact: there is more of opposition in controversy, more of doubt in disputing. A sophist controverts; a skeptic disputes.
Antonyms.—Agree, accord, harmonize, concur, unite.

Contumacious, rebellious. The contumacious resist only occasionally; the rebellious resist systematically. The contumacious stand only on certain points and oppose the individual; the rebellious set themselves up against the authority itself. Contumacious implies a proud, contemptuous air.
Antonyms.—Compliant, deferential, obedient.

Convenient, suitable, proper. Convenient regards the circumstances of the individual; suitable, the ends or purposes in view and the things or persons to be affected. Proper is closely connected with moral fitness and a regard to generally received opinion.
Antonyms.—Inconvenient, unfit, unseemly, unbecoming.

Conversant, familiar. A person is conversant in matters that come frequently before his notice; he is familiar with such as form the daily routine of his business.
Antonyms.—Unacquainted, strange, ignorant, unversed.

Conversation, dialogue, conference, colloquy. A conversation is always something actually held between two or more persons; a dialogue is usually fictitious and written as if spoken: any number of persons may take part in a conversation, but a dialogue always refers to the two persons who are expressly engaged. A conference is always specifically appointed and is usually on public concerns. The colloquy has the same character as the dialogue but is not confined to two people.

Convert, proselyte. Convert is more extensive in its sense and application than proselyte,—in its full sense it includes every change of opinion, without respect to the subject. Proselyte, in its original application, denoted changes only from one religious belief to another; it now means a new convert to a religion, a religious sect, or to some particular system or party.

Convict, convince, persuade. A person may be convicted of heresy, if it be proved to the satisfaction of others; he may be convinced that the opinion which he has held is heretical. So a person may be convicted who is involuntarily convinced of his error, but he is convinced if he is made sensible of his error without any force on his own mind. What convinces binds; what persuades attracts,—our persuasion respects matters of belief or practice.
Antonyms.—Mystify, puzzle, perplex, unsettle.

Convivial, social. The prominent idea in convivial is that of sensual indulgence; the prominent idea in social is that of enjoyment through intercourse with society. We speak of convivial meetings, convivial enjoyments, or the convivial board; but we say social intercourse, social pleasure, social amusements, and the like.
Antonyms.—Temperate, retiring, cold, solitary.

Copy, model, pattern, specimen. The term copy is applied to that which is delineated, as writings or pictures, which must be taken faithfully and literally; a model is that which may be used as a guide or a rule; the pattern regards solely the outward form or the color of anything that is made or manufactured; the specimen is any portion of a material which serves to show the quality of that of which it forms a part.

Copy, transcribe. To copy respects the matter; to transcribe respects simply the act of writing. What is copied must be taken immediately from the original, with which it must exactly correspond; what is transcribed may be taken from the copy, but not necessarily in an entire state. A copier should be very exact; a transcriber should be a good writer.

Coquette, jilt. The coquette makes a traffic of her own charms by seeking a multitude of admirers; the jilt sports with the sacred passion of love, and lightly casts off those previously accepted as lovers.

Correct, accurate. What is done by the exercise of the judgment is said to be correct, as a correct style, a correct writer; what is done by the effort of the individual is more properly accurate, as accurate observations, an accurate survey.

Antonyms.—Faulty, careless, imperfect, erroneous.

Correction, discipline, punishment. As correction and discipline have commonly required punishment to render them efficacious, custom has affixed to them a strong resemblance in their application, although they are distinguished from each other by obvious marks of difference. The prominent idea in correction is that of making right what has been wrong. In discipline, the leading idea is that of instructing or regulating. In punishment, the leading idea is that of inflicting pain. We remove an evil by correction; we prevent it by discipline.

Correspond, accord. To correspond is to answer or conform to the description of something else. Things that correspond must be alike in size, shape, color, and every minute particular. Appearance and reality seldom correspond. To accord is to agree or to be in harmony and without conflict. Things that accord must be suited to each other. His disposition accords with his looks.

Antonyms.—Differ, vary, disagree.

Cost, expense, price, charge. The cost is what a thing costs, or what is to be laid out for it; the expense is that which a person actually lays out; the price is that which a thing may fetch or which it may be worth; the charge is that which a person or thing is charged with. We do a thing at our own cost, but at another's expense; we can never set a price on anything until we have ascertained what it has cost us, nor can we know or defray the expense until the charge be made. In the moral acceptation, the attainment of an object is said to cost much pains; a thing is persisted in at the expense of health, of honor, or of life. The sacrifice of a man's quiet is the price which he must pay for the gratification of his ambition.

Countenance, sanction, support. Persons are countenanced; things are sanctioned; persons or things are supported. Persons or proceedings are countenanced by the apparent approbation of others; measures are sanctioned by the consent or the approbation of others who have due authority; measures or persons are supported by every means which may forward the object.

Antonyms.—Expose, denounce, oppose, disapprove.

Courage, fortitude, resolution. Courage respects action; fortitude respects passion: a man has courage to meet danger, fortitude to endure pain. Resolution simply marks the will not to recede; we require resolution not to yield to the first difficulties that offer.

Antonyms.—Fear, timidity, pusillanimity.

Cover, hide. The ruling idea in the word cover is that of throwing or putting something over a body; in the word hide is that of keeping carefully to one's self, from the observation of others.

Antonyms.—Show, reveal, expose.

Cover, shelter, screen. Cover includes the idea of concealing; shelter comprehends that of protecting from some immediate or impending evil; screen includes that of warding off some trouble.

Antonyms.—Discover, betray, expose, disclose, exhibit.

Credit, favor, influence. These terms mark the state we stand in with regard to others as flowing out of their sentiments toward ourselves. Credit arises from esteem; favor from good will or affection; influence from credit or favor or external circumstances. Influence is employed in directing others; weak people easily give their credit or bestow their favor, by which an influence is gained over them to bend them to the will of others.

Crime, vice, sin. A crime is a social offense; a vice is a personal offense. Every action which does injury to others, either individually or collectively, is a crime; that which does injury to ourselves is a vice. Crime consists in a violation of human laws; vice, in a violation of moral law; sin, in a violation of the Divine law.

Criminal, culprit, malefactor, felon, convict. When we wish to speak in general of those who by offenses against the laws or regulations of society have exposed themselves to punishment, we denominate them criminals; when we consider them as already brought before a tribunal, we call them culprits; when we consider them in regard to the moral turpitude of their character, as the promoters of evil rather than of good, we entitle them malefactors; when we consider them as offending by the grosser violations of the law, they are termed felons; when we consider them as already under the sentence of the law, we denominate them convicts.

Criterion, standard. The criterion is employed only in matters of judgment; the standard is used in the ordinary concerns of life. The former serves for determining the characters and qualities of things; the latter, for defining quantity and measure.

Cruel, inhuman, barbarous, brutal, savage. A person is cruel who neglects the creature he should protect and take care of; he is inhuman if he withholds from him the common marks of tenderness or kindness which are to be expected from one human being to another; he is barbarous if he finds amusement in inflicting pain; he is brutal or savage according to the circumstances of aggravation which accompany the act of torturing.

Antonyms.—Kind, humane, gentle, refined, tender, civilized.

Crying, weeping. Crying arises from an impatience in suffering bodily pains; weeping is occasioned by mental grief.

Cultivation, culture, civilization, refinement. Civilization implies for a people a high state of economic and social life. Cultivation primarily applies to the treatment of soil and plants to encourage growth. Applied to the human mind and character, it denotes the possession of training and refinement of which culture is the outcome. Culture comprehends the intellectual phases of civilization; in persons it implies a high mental, moral, and æsthetic development, with possession of graces and niceties of word and manner. Refinement connotes especially fineness and delicacy of feeling.

Antonyms.—Rusticity, rudeness, coarseness, crudity, savagery.

Cure, heal, remedy. To cure is employed for what is out of order; to heal for that which is broken. Diseases are cured, wounds are healed; the former is a complex process, the latter is simple. Whatever requires to be cured is wrong in the system; whatever requires to be healed is occasioned externally by violence, and requires external applications. To remedy, in the sense of applying remedies, has a moral application; an omission, a deficiency, or a mischief, requires to be remedied.

Antonyms.—Injure, irritate, inflame, aggravate.

Curious, inquisitive, prying. Curious implies an interest in learning about things generally, especially matters not of immediate concern to the person. Inquisitive connotes a rather persistent and impertinent curiosity. Prying applies to an officious, unwelcome, disagreeable inquisitiveness.

Antonyms.—Uninterested, indifferent, apathetic, nonchalant.

Cursory, hasty, slight, desultory. An author will take a cursory view of those points which are not necessarily connected with his subject; an author who takes a hasty view of a subject will mislead by his errors; he who takes a slight view will disappoint by the shallowness of his information. Between cursory and desultory there is the same difference as between running and leaping: we run in a line, but we leap from one part to another; so remarks that are cursory have more or less connection, but remarks that are desultory are without any coherence.

Antonyms.—Detailed, careful, thorough, methodical, coherent.

Custom, habit, fashion, practice. Custom is the practice of doing a thing in like circumstances and in a uniform manner for definite reasons. Social customs regulate many important concerns of men. Habit is the series of acts, which, through practice, has become involuntary or reflex. Fashion is arbitrary and capricious, and is applied to matters of minor importance. Practice signifies actual doing or the thing done: it may be the practice of a person to do acts of charity, as the occasion requires; but, when he uniformly does a particular act of charity at any given period of the year, it is properly denominated his custom.

Danger, peril, hazard. Danger signifies the chance of a loss; peril signifies imminent, threatening danger, as a critical situation, a rude trial, which may terminate in one's ruin. In all walks of life we are in danger; the explorer undergoes perils. Hazard respects the possibility of either good or evil. When we accept the hazard of battle, we may either win or lose.

Antonyms.—Safety, security, immunity, protection.

Daring, bold. He who is daring provokes resistance and courts danger; but the bold man is contented to overcome the resistance that is offered to him. A man may be bold in the use of words only; he must be daring in actions; he is bold in the defense of truth; he is daring in military enterprise.

Antonyms.—Fearful, hesitating, timorous, faint-hearted.

Dark, obscure, dim, mysterious, abstruse. Dark is opposed to light; obscure, to bright. What is dark is altogether hidden; what is obscure is not to be seen distinctly, or without an effort. Dim expresses a degree of darkness, but it is employed more in relation to the person seeing than to the object seen. Any intricate affair, which involves the characters and conduct of men, may be mysterious. Obscure may be applied to things or ideas; abstruse to ideas only.

Antonyms.—Light, bright, clear, distinct, plain.

Deadly, mortal, fatal. Deadly is applied to what is productive of death; mortal, to what terminates in or is liable to death; fatal applies not only to death, but to everything which may be of serious consequence.
Antonyms.—Vital, life-giving, wholesome.

Debate, deliberate. These terms equally mark the acts of pausing or withholding the decision, whether applicable to one or many. To debate supposes always a contrariety of opinion; to deliberate supposes simply the weighing or estimating the value of the opinion that is offered.

Debt, due. Debt is commonly applied to that which is owing from the person spoken of; due is always applied to that which is owing to the person: to pay one's debts, to receive one's due.

Deceit, deception, guile, art, cunning. Deceit is the habit of intentional falsehood. Deception is the act of misleading through false appearance. A person is deceitful; his look and manner may be deceptive. Guile implies crafty, insidious deceit. Art implies a disposition of the mind to use circumvention or artificial means to attain an end; cunning marks the disposition to practice disguise in the prosecution of a plan.
Antonyms.—Honesty, truth, candor, sincerity, straightforwardness.

Deceiver, impostor. A deceiver is anyone who practices any sort of deception; but an impostor is a deceiver who studiously deceives by putting on a false appearance.

Decency, decorum. Decency respects a man's conduct; decorum, his behavior.
Antonyms.—Unseemliness, impropriety, unfitness.

Decided, decisive. Decided marks that which is actually fixed and settled; decisive, that which appertains to decision. A person's aversion or attachment is decided; a sentence, a judgment, or a victory, is decisive.
Antonyms.—Indecisive, unsettled, doubtful.

Decided, determined, resolute. A man who is decided remains in no doubt; he who is determined is uninfluenced by the doubts or questions of others; he who is resolute is uninfluenced by the consequences of his actions.
Antonyms.—Irresolute, doubting, wavering, uncertain.

Decision, judgment, sentence. A decision has no respect to the agent; it may be said of one or many; it may be the decision of the court, of the nation, of the public, of a particular body of men, or of a private individual. But a judgment is given in a public court or among private individuals. A sentence is passed in a court of law or at the bar of a public assembly.

Declaim, inveigh. Declaim signifies literally to cry aloud in a set form of words; inveigh involves injurious censure or reproach. Public men and public measures are subjects for the declaimer; private individuals afford subjects for inveighing against.

Decree, edict, proclamation. A decree is a more solemn and deliberative act than an edict; on the other hand, an edict is more authoritative than a decree. A decree is the decision of one or many; an edict speaks the will of an individual. Councils and courts, as well as princes, make decrees; despotic rulers issue edicts. An edict is peculiar to a despotic government; a proclamation is any statement of will or information issued by authority. It may contain a decree or an edict.

Dedicate, devote, consecrate, hallow. There is something more solemn in the act of dedicating than in that of devoting, but less than in that of consecrating. To dedicate and devote may be employed in both temporal and spiritual matters; to consecrate and hallow, only in the spiritual sense. We may dedicate or devote anything that is at our disposal to the service of some object; but the former is employed mostly in regard to superiors, and the latter to persons without distinction of rank. An author dedicates a book to a friend or patron by prefacing it with the name and the complimentary inscription. We dedicate a house to the service of God; we devote our time to the benefit of our friends or to the relief of the poor. We may dedicate or devote ourselves to an object: the former always implies a solemn setting apart springing from a sense of duty; the latter, an entire application of oneself from zeal and affection. To consecrate is to declare sacred by means of religious ceremony. The church is consecrated; particular days are hallowed.
Antonyms.—Alienate, pervert, desecrate, profane.

Deduction, abatement. Both these words imply a taking from something. A person may make a deduction in an account for various reasons, but he makes an abatement in a demand when it is objected to as excessive.
Antonyms.—Increase, addition, augmentation.

Deface, disfigure, deform. Deface implies marring of the surface, frequently by destroying some of it, as letters or inscriptions. Disfigure applies to the deeper injury which mars beauty of form or shape. Deform means so to alter the structure as to produce a misshapen thing.
Antonyms.—Amend, better, improve, rectify.

Defective, deficient. Defective implies the quality or characteristic of lacking something or of being incomplete. Deficient is used with regard to the measure or character of the defect. A book may be defective in consequence of lacking some leaves. A man may be deficient in courage. Persons markedly deficient in some physical, mental, or moral quality are called defectives.
Antonyms.—Perfect, complete, unimpaired, whole.

Defend, protect, vindicate. A person may be defended in any particular case of actual danger or difficulty; he is protected from what may happen as well as what does happen. Defense respects the evil that threatens; protection involves the supply of necessities and the affording of comforts. Vindicate implies successful defense against a charge or accusation.
Antonyms.—Endanger, imperil, expose, betray.

Defendant, defender. The defendant is one called on to answer or defend or be defended in a suit or case in a law court; defender is the general word for one who defends another.
Antonyms.—Prosecutor, plaintiff, accuser, assailant.

Defender, advocate, pleader. A defender exerts himself in favor of one that wants support. An advocate signifies one who is called to speak in favor of another—he exerts himself in favor of any cause that offers. A pleader, from plea or excuse, signifies him who speaks or writes in behalf of one who is accused or in distress.
Antonyms.—Adversary, informer, complainant.

Definite, positive. Definite signifies that which is defined, or has limits drawn or marked out; positive, that which is placed or fixed in a particular manner. Definite is said of things as they present themselves or are presented to the mind, as a definite idea, a definite proposal. Positive is said of a person's temper of mind; a person is positive as to his opinions, or an assurance is positive.
Antonyms.—Doubtful, ambiguous, vague, uncertain.

Deity, divinity. Deity signifies a divine person; divinity signifies the divine essence or power.

Dejection, depression, melancholy. Depression is but a degree of dejection. Slight circumstances may occasion a depression; distressing events occasion dejection: the death of a near and dear relative may be expected to produce dejection in persons of the greatest self-possession. Melancholy is a severe form of depression which amounts to a mental disease.
Antonyms.—Rapture, happiness, elation, felicity, cheerfulness.

Delegate, depute—Delegate, deputy. To delegate is applied to the power or the office which is given; depute, to the person employed. Parents delegate their office to the instructor; persons are deputed to act for others. A delegate is the person commissioned, who is bound to act according to his commission; the deputy is the person deputed, who acts in the place of another, but may act according to his own discretion or otherwise, as circumstances require.
Antonyms.—Chief, master, principal.

Deliver, rescue, save. One may be delivered from any evil, whether great or small, and in any manner. To rescue is to deliver from a great impending danger or immediate evil, as to rescue from the hands of robbers or from the jaws of a wild beast. To save signifies to keep from evil.
Antonyms.—Abandon, destroy, surrender, lose.

Demand, require. We demand that which is owing and ought to be given; we require that which we wish and expect to have done. The creditor makes a demand on the debtor; the master requires a certain portion of duty from his servant.
Antonyms.—Appeal (for), entreat, request, beg.

Demur, doubt, hesitation, objection. Demurs often occur in matters of deliberation; doubt, in regard to matters of fact; hesitation, in matters of ordinary conduct; and objections, in matters of common consideration. Artabanes made many demurs to the proposed invasion of Greece by Xerxes. Doubts have been suggested respecting the veracity of Herodotus as a historian. It is not proper to ask that which cannot be granted without hesitation. There are but few things which we either attempt to do or recommend to others that are not liable to some kind of an objection.
Antonyms.—Certainty, approval, promptness, consent.

Demur, hesitate, pause. We demur from doubt or difficulty; we hesitate from an undecided state of mind; we pause from circumstances. Demurring is a matter of prudence, it is always grounded on some reason—a lawyer for the defense demurs to evidence presented by the prosecution, in the hope of throwing doubt upon its contents. Hesitating is rather a matter of feeling, and is oftener faulty than otherwise. When a request of a dubious nature is made of us, we hesitate in complying with it; one hesitates to voice objection to a plan about the wisdom of which his friends have no doubts.

Antonyms.—Assent, acquiesce, decide, proceed.

Denote, signify. Denote is employed with regard to things and their characters; signify, with regard to the thoughts or movements. A letter or character may be made to denote any number, as words are made to signify the intentions and wishes of the person.

Deny, refuse. Deny applies both to matters of fact and to matters of wish or request; refuse, only to the latter. We deny a report or we deny or refuse a request.

Antonyms.—Grant, accede (to), allow.

Deplore, lament. Deplore is a stronger expression than lament; it calls forth tears from bitterness of heart, though it may not find expression in words. Lament always implies an expression of intense grief. Deploring indicates despair; lamenting marks pain or distress.

Antonyms.—Rejoice (at), exult or glory (in).

Deponent, evidence, witness. All these words are properly applied to judicial proceedings, where the deponent testifies generally to facts either in causes or otherwise. The evidence consists either of persons or things, which are brought before the court for the purpose of making a doubtful matter clear; the witness is always a person who testifies to any fact for or against another.

Deposit, pledge, security. Pledge is the general term applying to anything given as assurance of fulfillment of an agreement. It may be a deposit, a term now generally used of money as commonly paid "to bind a bargain," or security, now usually some form of commercial paper, such as bonds, notes, etc.

Depravity, depravation, corruption. All these terms are applied to characters marked by a deep-seated tendency toward evil. But the term depravity characterizes the thing as it is; the terms depravation and corruption designate the making or causing it to be so. Depravity, therefore, excludes the idea of any cause; depravation always carries us to the cause or external agency. Hence we may speak of depravity as natural, but we speak of depravation as the result of circumstances. There is a depravity in man which nothing but the grace of God can correct. The introduction of obscenity on the stage tends to the corruption of a young man's morals.

Antonyms.—Virtue, goodness, correction, purifying.

Depth, profundity. Depth is indefinite in its signification; profundity is a positive and considerable degree of depth. Moreover, the word depth is applied to objects in general; profundity is confined in its application to matters of thought or feeling.

Antonyms.—Shallowness, superficiality.

Derive, trace, deduce. The act of deriving is immediate and direct; that of tracing, a gradual process; that of deducing, a reasoning process. We discover causes and sources by derivation; we discover the course, progress, and commencement of things by tracing; we discover the grounds and reasons of things by deduction.

Desert, merit, worth. Desert is taken for that which is good or bad; merit, for that which is good only. We deserve praise or blame; we merit a reward. Worth is that which is absolutely valuable—it must be sought for on its own account.

Antonyms.—Demerit, worthlessness.

Design, purpose, intend, mean. To design is to plan in a steady, methodical manner; to purpose is to propose to oneself, with some degree of determination; to intend is to have in mind to do something—a less definite expression than the others. Mean still has a colloquial flavor, signifying a vague intention.

Desire, wish, long for, hanker for or **after, covet.** To desire is imperious—it demands gratification; to wish is less vehement—it consists of a strong inclination. To long for expresses strong and continued desire; to hanker after is to desire with marked uneasiness; to covet is to desire that which belongs to another, or what it is in his power to grant.

Antonyms.—Dislike, detest, be averse to, spurn.

Desist, leave off. To desist is voluntary or involuntary; to leave off is voluntary. We are frequently obliged to desist, but we leave off at our option. He who annoys another must be made to desist; he who does not wish to offend will leave off when requested.

Antonyms.—Persist, continue, keep on.

Despair, desperation, despondency. Despair is a state of mind produced by the view of external circumstances; desperation and despondency may be the fruit of the imagination. The former therefore always rests on some ground; the latter are sometimes ideal. Desperation marks a state of vehement and impatient feeling; despondency is hopelessness, and is often a disease of the mind.

Antonyms.—Assurance, hopefulness, confidence, courage.

Destiny, destination. Destiny is the point or line marked out in the walk of life; destination is the place fixed upon in particular: as every man has his peculiar destiny, so every traveler has his particular destination. Destiny is altogether set above human control; destination is, however, under the specific control of an individual, either for himself or for another.

Destiny, fate, lot, doom. Destiny is used in regard to one's station and walk in life; fate, in regard to what one suffers; lot, in regard to what one gets or possesses; doom is the final destiny which terminates unhappily and depends mostly upon the will of another. Destiny is marked out; fate is fixed; a lot is assigned; a doom is pronounced or decreed.

Destroy, consume, waste. To destroy is to break or shatter or by other means put anything beyond hope of restoration. A house may be destroyed by fire or it may fall to ruin. To consume is to use up, as to consume food or merchandise; to waste is to expend unnecessarily, extravagantly, to spend to no purpose, as to waste time or property.

Antonyms.—Build, repair, restore, supply, preserve.

Destruction, ruin. Destruction is an act of immediate violence; ruin is a gradual process. A thing is destroyed by some external action upon it; a thing falls to ruin of itself. A reputation is destroyed; a character is ruined.

Antonyms.—Construction, upbuilding, preservation.

Determine, resolve. We determine how or what we shall do—this requires examination and choice. We resolve that we will do what we have determined upon—this requires a firm spirit.

Antonyms.—Hesitate, waver, question, vacillate.

Deviate, wander, swerve, stray. Deviate always supposes a direct path which is departed from; wander includes no such idea. The act of deviating is commonly faulty; that of wandering is indifferent. To swerve is to deviate from that which one holds right; to stray is to wander in the same bad sense. Men swerve from their duty to consult their interest; the young stray from the path of rectitude to seek that of pleasure.

Antonyms.—Continue, advance, progress.

Devise, bequeath. In the technical sense, to devise is to give lands by a will duly attested according to law; to bequeath is to give personalty for possession after one's death by a less formal instrument.

Dictate, prescribe. Dictate, from the Latin *dictatus* and *dictum*, "a word," literally signifies to make a word for another; prescribe signifies to write down for another. Thus the former of these terms is used technically for a principal who gets his secretary to write down his words as he utters them; the latter, for a physician who writes down for his patient what he wishes him to take as a remedy. They are used figuratively for a sort of counsel given by a superior; to dictate is however a greater exercise of authority than to prescribe.

Dictate, suggestion. Dictate signifies the thing uttered, and has an imperative sense; the suggestion signifies the thing intimated, and conveys the idea of its being proposed secretly or in a gentle manner. These terms are both applied, with this distinction, to acts of the mind. When conscience, reason, or passion present anything forcibly to the mind, it is called a dictate; when anything enters the mind in a casual manner, it is called a suggestion.

Dictionary, encyclopedia. The definition of words, with their various changes, modifications, uses, acceptations, and applications, are the proper subjects of a dictionary; the nature and properties of things, with their construction, uses, powers, etc., are the proper subjects of an encyclopedia.

Dictionary, lexicon, vocabulary, glossary. We speak of a lexicon of Greek or Latin, of a dictionary of a modern language. A vocabulary is a partial kind of dictionary, which may comprehend a simple list of words, with or without explanation, arranged in order or otherwise. A glossary is an explanatory vocabulary, which commonly serves to explain the obsolete terms employed in any old author.

Die, expire, perish. Die is the general word for cessation of life or extinction of being. Expire is a softened expression for die. Trees die and a flame expires; figuratively, a lease expires. Perish signifies utter decay and disappearance.

Antonyms.—Live, survive, persist, exist.

Difference, dispute, altercation, quarrel. A difference, as distinguished from the others, is generally of a less serious and personal kind; a dispute consists not only of angry words, but of much ill blood and unkind action; an altercation is a wordy dispute, in which difference of opinion is drawn out into a multitude of words; a quarrel is the most serious of all differences, which leads to every manner of violence.

Difference, distinction. Difference lies in the thing; distinction is the act of the person—the former is therefore to the latter as the cause is to the effect. The distinction rests on the difference: those are equally bad logicians who make a distinction without a difference, or who make no distinction where there is a difference. A careful writer will make a distinction between words that may have slightly different meanings.
Antonyms.—Similarity, likeness, agreement, identity.

Difference, variety, diversity, medley. Difference and variety seem to lie in the things themselves; diversity and medley are created either by accident or by design. A difference may lie in two objects only; a variety cannot exist without an assemblage. A difference is discovered by means of a comparison which the mind forms of objects to prevent confusion; variety strikes on the mind, and pleases the imagination with many agreeable images. Diversity arises from an assemblage of objects naturally contrasted; a medley is produced by a casual assemblage of objects often so illy suited as to produce a ludicrous effect.
Antonyms.—Likeness, sameness, correspondence, orderliness.

Difficulty, obstacle, impediment, embarrassment, trouble. A difficulty is something or a circumstance that interferes with ease of action. Obstacle means anything directly opposed to one's effort toward an end. Impediment is like a clog or brake in hindering movement or progress. An embarrassment is any condition or circumstance that gives rise to confusion or perplexity, and so proves an obstacle or difficulty. Trouble is a general word applied to the circumstances or to feelings aroused by them. Embarrassment may result from failure to deal with troubles effectively.
Antonyms.—Aid, help, assistance, relief, encouragement.

Diffuse, prolix. Both mark defects of style opposed to brevity. A diffuse writer is fond of amplification, the prolix writer is fond of circumlocution, minute details, and trifling particulars.
Antonyms.—Brief, concise, succinct, condensed.

Digress, deviate. Both in the original and the accepted sense, these words express going out of the ordinary course. We digress only in a narrative, whether written or spoken; we deviate in actions as well as in words, in our conduct as well as in writings.

Dilate, expand. Dilate implies enlargement, as a circular ripple on water widens; expand suggests enlargement in every direction, as a flower expands. A speaker dilates upon a theme, dwells upon it with many words; he expands his argument by discussing points in greater detail.
Antonyms.—Contract, condense, narrow, compress.

Diligent, expeditious, prompt. Diligent marks the interest one takes in doing something; he is diligent who loses no time, who keeps close to the work from inclination. Expeditious marks the desire one has to complete the thing begun. Prompt marks one's desire to get ready; he is prompt who sets about a thing without delay, so as so make it ready.
Antonyms.—Inattentive, neglectful, slow, hesitant, dilatory.

Disappear, vanish. A thing disappears either gradually or suddenly; it vanishes of a sudden: it disappears in the ordinary course of things; it vanishes by an unusual effort or as if by supernatural or magic power.
Antonyms.—Appear, arise, emerge.

Disapproval, dislike, disinclination. Disapproval is an act of the judgment; dislike, a matter of feeling and sentiments. Disinclination implies a mild or careless dislike, usually of something to be done.

Disapprove, dislike. Disapprove is an act of the judgement; dislike is an act of the will or of the affection. To approve or disapprove is peculiarly the part of a superior, or of one who determines the conduct of others; to dislike is altogether a personal act, in which the feelings of the individual are consulted.
Antonyms.—Approve, like, enjoy, delight in.

Disbelief, unbelief. Disbelief properly implies the believing that a thing is not, or refusing to believe that it is. Unbelief properly implies skepticism or a withholding of belief. As generally applied to religion, unbelief signifies disbelief of dogmas or doctrines, usually with the indication of willfulness. Disbelief is most properly applicable to the ordinary events of life; unbelief, to serious matters of opinion.

Disclaim, disown. One may disclaim responsibility for an act; he may disown his children.
Antonyms.—Claim, acknowledge, own, recognize.

Discord, strife, dissension, contention. Discord consists mostly in the feeling; strife consists mostly in the outward action. Discord evinces itself in various ways —by looks, words, or actions; strife displays itself in words or acts of violence. A collision of opinions produces dissension; a collision of interests produces contention; a collision of humors produces discord.
Antonyms.—Concord, peace, agreement.

Discover, manifest, declare. We discover by any means direct or indirect; we manifest by unquestionable marks; we declare by express words. Talents and dispositions discover themselves; particular feelings and sentiments manifest themselves; facts, opinions, and sentiments are declared.
Antonyms.—Conceal, hide, suppress, dissemble.

Discredit, disgrace, reproach, scandal, dishonor, shame. Discredit interferes with a man's respectability; disgrace marks him out as an object of unfavorable distinction; reproach makes him a subject of adverse criticism; scandal makes him an object of offense or even of abhorrence. Dishonor connotes loss of dignity and favor; disgrace expresses positive reproach and fall from honorable regard; a consciousness of guilt and of the resulting disgrace will bring shame to a person. Shame, the consequence of open moral guilt, is the strongest of these words.
Antonyms.—Honor, favor, regard, respect, dignity.

Discuss, examine. Discuss signifies to shake asunder or to separate thoroughly so as to see the whole composition; examine is used where the judgment holds the balance. Discussion is altogether carried on by verbal and personal communication; examination proceeds by reading, reflection, and observation.

Disgust, loathing, nausea. Disgust is less than loathing, and loathing than nausea. When applied to sensible objects, we are disgusted with dirt; we loathe the smell of food if we have a sickly appetite; we nauseate medicine. When applied metaphorically, we are disgusted with affectation; we loathe the endearments of those who are offensive; we are nauseated by all the enjoyments of life, after having made an intemperate use of them and discovered their inanity.
Antonyms.—Desire, relish, craving.

Dishonest, knavish. What is dishonest violates the established laws of man; what is knavish supposes peculiar art and design in the accomplishment.
Antonyms.—Honorable, straightforward, upright.

Disjoint, dismember. Disjoint means to put out of joint, to dislocate, as a dislocated ankle, or to separate as the joints, as a tool or mechanism. Speech, when not well connected or when hesitating, may be called disjointed. Dismember implies mutilating or tearing apart of the animal or human body.
Antonyms.—Join, unite, assemble.

Dismay, daunt, appall. We are dismayed by alarming circumstances; we are daunted by terrifying circumstances; we are appalled by horrid circumstances.
Antonyms.—Hearten, encourage, incite, rouse.

Disorder, disease, distemper, malady. Disease connotes any deviation from health, whether in plants or animals. Disorder implies usually a slight, temporary sickness. Distemper is now used only of animal diseases. Malady carries the sense of lingering, deep-seated diseases, often with the idea of a morbid state of mind or spirits.

Disparity, inequality. Disparity applies to two objects which should meet or stand in coalition with each other; inequality is applicable to those that are compared with each other. The disparity of age, situation, and circumstances is to be considered with regard to persons entering into a matrimonial connection; the inequality in the portion of labor which is to be performed by two persons is a ground for the inequality of their recompense.
Antonyms.—Parity, equality, equivalence.

Dispassionate, cool. Dispassionate is taken negatively —it marks merely the absence of passion. Cool is taken positively—it marks an entire freedom from passion. When we meet with an angry disputant it is necessary to be dispassionate in order to avoid quarrels; in the moment of danger our safety often depends upon our coolness.
Antonyms.—Hasty, hot, choleric, passionate.

Dispel, disperse. Dispel means to drive away, as doubt or gloom. It applies only to intangible things. Disperse means to drive apart, to scatter, as a crowd.
Antonyms.—Collect, gather, accumulate.

Dispense, distribute. Dispense is an indiscriminate action; distribute is a particularizing action: we dispense to all; we distribute to each individually. One dispenses charity, but he distributes gifts.
Antonyms.—Hold, keep, retain, withhold.

Displeasure, anger, disapprobation. Displeasure is always a softened and gentle feeling. Anger is the intense feeling of dissatisfaction and resentment, rising often to vehement expression. Displeasure may be slight or intense, but it lacks the element of resentment and may not reveal its true intensity in words. Disapprobation is a definite sentiment of censure or of disapproval.
Antonyms.—Satisfaction, pleasure, approval.

Disposal, disposition. Disposal implies merely the removal of things; disposition implies their orderly or appropriate placing or arrangement.

Dispose, arrange, digest. We may dispose ordinary matters by simply assigning a place to each—in this manner trees are disposed in a row. We arrange and digest by an intellectual effort. We arrange by putting those together which ought to go together; we digest by both separating that which is dissimilar, and bringing together that which is similar. Books are arranged in a library according to their size or their subject; the materials for a literary production are digested.
Antonyms.—Muddle, confuse, disorder, derange.

Disposition, inclination. We may always expect a man to do that which he is disposed to do; but we cannot always calculate upon his executing that to which he is merely inclined. We indulge a disposition; we yield to an inclination. The disposition comprehends the whole state of the mind at the time; an inclination is particular, referring always to a particular object.

Disposition, temper. Disposition is permanent and settled; temper may be transitory and fluctuating. The disposition comprehends the springs and motives of actions; the temper influences the action of the moment. It is possible and not infrequent to have a good disposition with a bad temper, and vice versa.

Disregard, neglect, slight. We disregard the warnings, the words, or opinions of others; we neglect their injunctions or their precepts. To disregard results from the settled purpose of the mind; to neglect, from a temporary forgetfulness or oversight. Slight is altogether an intentional act toward an individual.
Antonyms.—Attend to, regard, observe, respect, defer to.

Distant, far, remote. Distant is used to designate great space; far, only that which is ordinary. Astronomers estimate that the sun is nearly 93 million miles distant from the earth; a person lives not very far off, or a person is far from the spot. Remote expresses the relative idea of having disappeared from sight.
Antonyms.—Near, close, neighboring, contiguous.

Distinguish, discriminate. To discriminate is in fact to distinguish specifically; hence we speak of a distinction as true or false, but of a discrimination as nice. We distinguish by means of the senses as well as by the understanding; we discriminate by the understanding only.
Antonyms.—Overlook, confound, confuse.

Distinguished, conspicuous, noted, eminent, illustrious. A thing is distinguished in proportion as it is distinct or separate from others; it is conspicuous in proportion as it is easily seen; it is noted in proportion as it is widely known. Eminent applies to those things which set a man high in the circle of his acquaintances; illustrious applies to that which makes him shine before the world.
Antonyms.—Ordinary, common, unknown, humble.

Distress, anxiety, anguish, agony. Distress is the pain felt when in a strait from which we see no means of extricating ourselves; anxiety is that pain which one feels on the prospect of an evil. Distress always depends upon some outward cause; anxiety often lies in the imagination; anguish arises from the reflection on the evil that is past; agony springs from witnessing or suffering intense mental or bodily pain.
Antonyms.—Comfort, calm, apathy, indifference, tranquillity.

Distress, harass, perplex. A person is distressed either in his outward circumstances or in his feelings; he is harassed in mind or body; he is perplexed in his understanding more than in his feelings. A deprivation distresses; provocations and hostile measures harass; stratagems and ambiguous measures perplex.
Antonyms.—Soothe, console, comfort, compose.

Distrust, suspicion, diffidence. Distrust is said either of ourselves or of others; suspicion is said only of others; diffidence, only of ourselves. To be distrustful of a person is to impute no good of him; to be suspicious of a person is to impute positive evil to him. As regards oneself, a person may distrust his own powers for the execution of a particular office, or have a distrust of himself in company; he has a general diffidence, or he is naturally diffident.
Antonyms.—Trust, confidence, faith, self-confidence.

Disturb, interrupt. Disturb implies more or less constant or continued breaking up of the settled or orderly state of affairs or action. Interrupt connotes a sharp, sudden break, as of a flow of water or a course of action. One's mind may be disturbed from within, but one's thinking is interrupted by something from without.
Antonyms.—Quiet, pacify, let alone.

Divide, distribute, share. We divide the thing; we distribute to the person. To share is to make into parts, the same as divide, and it is to give those parts to some persons, the same as distribute. The person who shares takes a part himself; he who distributes gives it all to others.
Antonyms.—Keep, reserve, withhold, retain.

Divide, separate, part. That is divided which has been or has been conceived to be a whole; that is separated which might be joined. An army may be divided into two or three divisions or portions; the divisions are frequently separated in their march. To part is to divide or separate into distinct portions or pieces.
Antonyms.—Join, connect, unite, unify, coalesce, fuse.

Doctrine, dogma, tenet. A doctrine rests on the authority of the individual by whom it is framed; a dogma, on the authority of the body by whom it is maintained; a tenet rests on its own intrinsic merits. A tenet is a species of principle maintained in matters of opinion by persons in general.

Doctrine, precept, principle. A doctrine requires a teacher; a precept requires a superior with authority; a principle requires only a maintainer or a holder. A doctrine is always framed by some one; a precept is enjoined or laid down by some one; a principle lies in the thing itself. A doctrine is composed of principles; a precept rests upon principles or doctrines.

Doubt, question. Doubt lies altogether in the mind; it is a less active feeling than question: by the former we merely suspend decision; by the latter we actually demand proofs in order to assist us in deciding. We may doubt in silence; we cannot question without expressing doubt, directly or indirectly. We doubt the truth of a position; we question the veracity of an author.
Antonyms.—Accept, believe, assume.

Doubt, suspense. Doubt respects that which we should believe; suspense, that which we wish to know or ascertain. We are in doubt for lack of decisive, positive evidence; in suspense for lack of certainty about the future. Doubt interrupts our progress in the attainment of truth; suspense impedes us in the attainment of our objects.
Antonyms.—Confidence, certainty, assurance.

Draw, drag, haul, pull, pluck, tug. Draw expresses here the idea common to the first three terms, namely, that of putting a body in motion from behind oneself or toward oneself. To drag is to draw a thing with violence, or to draw that which makes resistance; to haul is to drag it with still greater violence. To pull signifies only an effort to draw without the idea of motion; horses pull very long sometimes before they can draw a heavily laden cart uphill. To pluck is to pull with a sudden twitch in order to separate; to tug is to pull with violence, frequently without moving the object.

Dream, vision, reverie (revery). Primarily, dreams are visions, thoughts, or images passing in the mind during sleep. One's imagined ideals in life when far from realization are called dreams. A vision may come to one during waking hours. A reverie is a loose train of thought or imagery, running through the mind when one is awake but given over to musing—a waking dream or daydream.

Dull, gloomy, sad, dismal. When applied to natural objects, dull and gloomy denote the want of necessary light or life; in this sense metals are more or less dull according as they are stained with dirt. The weather is dull when the sun is obscured by clouds, and gloomy when the atmosphere is darkened by fogs or thick clouds. Dismal denotes not merely the want of that which is necessary, but also the presence of that which is repugnant to the senses. Dismal carries the sense of evil omen or unlucky foreboding. Sad implies a gloomy or downcast countenance and suggests grief.
Antonyms.—Bright, happy, joyous, merry, cheerful.

Durable, lasting, permanent. Durable is naturally said of material substances; lasting, of those which are spiritual, although in ordinary discourse sometimes they exchange offices. Permanent connotes fitness to endure or remain. We make permanent improvements of lasting or durable materials. That which perishes quickly is not durable; that which ceases quickly is not lasting; that which is only for a time is not permanent.
Antonyms.—Perishable, flimsy, unstable, temporary.

Duty, obligation. Duty has to do with the conscience, and arises from the natural relations of society; an obligation arises from circumstances and is a species of duty. He who guarantees to pay a sum of money contracts an obligation. He who marries contracts new duties.

Ease, quiet, rest, repose. Ease and quiet respect action on the body; rest and repose respect the action of the body. Ease denotes an exemption from any painful agency in general; quiet denotes an exemption from that in particular which noise, disturbance, or the violence of others may cause; rest simply denotes the cessation of motion; repose is that form of rest which is agreeable after labor.
Antonyms.—Disturbance, disquiet, toil, strain.

Ease, readiness. Ease implies freedom from strain or effort, with application especially to the thing done. Readiness applies to the doer, and implies promptness, alertness, and preparedness. A machine always in readiness may be operated with ease.
Antonyms.—Difficulty, annoyance, awkwardness, constraint.

Eclipse, obscure. Heavenly bodies are eclipsed by the passing of other bodies between them and the beholder; things are in general obscured which are in any way rendered less striking or visible. So, figuratively, real merit is eclipsed by the intervention of superior merit; it is often obscured by an ungracious exterior in the possessor or by his unfortunate circumstances.
Antonyms.—Reveal, show, illuminate.

Education, instruction, breeding. Instruction and breeding are to education as parts to a whole. Instruction implies the communication of knowledge, and breeding connotes the manners or outward conduct. Education comprehends not only both these, but the formation of the mind, the regulation of the heart, and the establishment of the principles. Good instruction makes one wiser; good breeding makes one more polished and agreeable; good education makes one really good.

Effect, produce, perform. To produce signifies to bring something forth or into existence, to perform, to do something completely. To effect is to produce a result by performing. Whatever is effected is the consequence of a specific design; it always requires, therefore, a rational agent to effect. What is produced may follow incidentally, or arise from the action of an irrational agent or an inanimate object; what is performed is done by specific efforts.

Effusion, ejaculation. An effusion commonly flows from a heated imagination uncorrected by the judgment; it is therefore, in general, not only incoherent but extravagant and senseless. An ejaculation is produced by the warmth of the moment, but never without reference to some particular circumstance. Enthusiasts are full of extravagant effusions; contrite sinners will often express their penitence in pious ejaculations.

Elderly, aged, old. The elderly man has passed the meridian of life; the old man is fast approaching the term of our existence; the aged man has already reached this term, or has exceeded it.
Antonyms.—Youthful, young.

Embarrassments, perplexities, entanglements. Embarrassments depend altogether on ourselves; want of prudence and of presence of mind is the common cause. Perplexities depend on extraneous circumstances as well as on ourselves; extensive dealings with others are mostly attended with perplexities. Entanglements arise mostly from the evil designs of others.

Emissary, spy. Both these words designate a person sent out by a body on some public concern among their enemies; but they differ in their office according to the etymology of the words. The emissary is sent so as to mix with the people to whom he goes, to be in all places, and to associate with every one individually, as may serve his purpose. The spy takes his station wherever he can best perceive what is passing; he keeps himself at a distance from all but such as may particularly aid him in the object of his search. The emissary is generally employed by those who have some illegitimate object to pursue; spies, on the other hand, are employed by all regular governments in a time of warfare.

Empire, reign, dominion. Empire signifies command, or the power exercised in commanding; it properly refers to the country or the people commanded. Reign signifies the act of reigning; it refers to the individual sovereign. Dominion may be applied in the proper sense to the power which man exercises over the brutes or inanimate objects, and, figuratively, to the power of the passions.

Employ, use. We employ either persons or things; we use only things, unless, in an evil sense, we use persons. One may be employed in his own or another's affairs.
Antonyms.—Reject, discharge, overlook.

Encomium, eulogy, panegyric. We bestow encomiums upon any work of art or production of genius, without reference to the performer; we bestow eulogies on the exploits of a hero, who is of another age or country; but we write panegyrics either in a direct address or in direct reference to the person who is panegyrized. The encomium is called forth by merit, real or supposed; the eulogy may spring from admiration of the person eulogized; the panegyric may be mere flattery, resulting from servile dependence.
Antonyms.—Dispraise, condemnation, invective.

Encourage, embolden. To encourage is to give courage, and to embolden is to make bold; the former impels to action in general, the latter incites to that which is more difficult or dangerous.
Antonyms.—Discourage, frighten, intimidate.

End, terminate, close. End is a general term; an end may come by chance or intention. A discussion may end without being finished, closed, or properly terminated. Close implies a preceding opening in the sense of beginning, as we open and close meetings. Terminate implies usually a purposed end or definite means of ending. His visit was terminated by an abrupt departure. The lane terminated in a high wall.
Antonyms.—Begin, open, commence, initiate.

Endeavor, aim, strive, struggle. An endeavor springs from a sense of duty; we endeavor to do that which is right and avoid that which is wrong. Aiming is the fruit of an aspiring temper—the object aimed at is always something superior either in reality or imagination. Striving is the consequence of an ardent desire—the thing striven for is always conceived to be of importance. Struggling is the effect of necessity—it is proportioned to the difficulty of attainment; the thing struggled for is indispensably necessary.

Endeavor, effort, exertion. Exertion is any strong exercise of power, whether toward a definite end or not. Effort implies exertion of will and ability toward a purpose. Endeavor signifies continued, sustained effort.
Antonyms.—Rest, laxity, slackness, negligence.

Energy, force, vigor, power. Energy is power, thought of or expressed in terms of actual or possible work,—as electrical energy, the energy of his words. Force implies resistance to be overcome. Vigor connotes physical or mental power in daily use, as vigorous growth of a plant. Power is the most general term for ability to do,—as a powerful engine, a speaker of great power.
Antonyms.—Weakness, inefficiency, impotence, incapacity.

Enlarge, increase, extend. Enlarge is applied to dimension and extent; increase is applicable to quantity, signifying to become greater in size by the junction of other matter; extend signifies to make greater in space. We speak of enlarging a house, a room, premises, or boundaries; of increasing an army, or property, capital, expense; of extending the boundaries of an empire.
Antonyms.—Lessen, decrease, contract.

Enmity, animosity, hostility. Enmity lies in the heart; it is deep and malignant. Animosity, from *animus*, a spirit, lies in the passions—it is fierce and vindictive. Hostility, from *hostis*, a political enemy, lies in the action—it is mischievous and destructive. Enmity is altogether personal; hostility respects public or private measures; enmity often lies concealed in the heart and does not betray itself by any open act of hostility.
Antonyms.—Friendliness, love, affection, amity.

Enormous, prodigious, monstrous. The enormous goes beyond our rules of estimating and calculating; the prodigious raises our minds beyond their ordinary standard of thinking; the monstrous contradicts nature and the course of things.
Antonyms.—Small, minute, usual, natural, reasonable.

Enough, sufficient. Sufficient sometimes implies, more distinctly than enough, the idea of an end or purpose, but in general the words are used without distinction of meanings. Sufficient may be thought more elegant than enough.
Antonyms.—Scanty, sparing, meager.

Enterprising, adventurous. The enterprising character conceives great projects and pursues objects that are difficult to obtain. The adventurous character is contented with seeking that which is new and with placing himself in dangerous and unusual situations.
Antonyms.—Shrinking, contented.

Epithet, adjective. Epithet is the technical term of the rhetorician; adjective, that of the grammarian. The same word is an epithet as it qualifies the sense; it is an adjective as it is a part of speech. Thus, in the phrase, "Alexander the Great," great is an epithet, inasmuch as it designates Alexander in distinction from all other persons; it is an adjective as it expresses a quality in distinction from the noun, Alexander, which denotes a thing.

Equal, even, equable, like, alike, uniform. Equal is said of degree, quantity, number, and dimensions, as equal in years; even is said of the surface and position of bodies—a board is made even with another board. Like is said of accidental qualities in things, as alike in color or in feature; uniform is said of things only as to their fitness to correspond; those which are unlike in color, shape, or make, are not uniform, and cannot be made to match as pairs. Equable signifies free from sudden or violent changes,—as an equable climate, equable temper.
Antonyms.—Variable, irregular, unlike, different.

Error, mistake, blunder, fault. Error is the general term, applied to the judgment or to conduct. Mistake is an error of choice; blunder, an awkward error of action. Fault is more serious error, implying frequently a flaw in character or habits.

Eruption, explosion. Eruption is the coming into view by a sudden bursting; explosion signifies bursting out with a noise. Hence, of flames there will be properly an eruption, but of gunpowder an explosion.

Estimate, compute, rate. To estimate is to obtain the aggregate sum in one's mind either by an immediate or a progressive act; estimate allows for some inaccuracy in results. To compute is to obtain the sum by the gradual process of putting together items; to rate is to fix the relative value in one's mind by deduction and comparison. A builder estimates the expense of building a house on a given plan; a proprietor of houses computes the probable diminution in the value of his property in consequence of wear and tear; the surveyor rates the present value of lands or houses.

Eternal, endless, everlasting. The eternal is set above time; the endless lies within time. That is properly eternal which has neither beginning nor end; that is endless which has a beginning but no end; that which is everlasting has neither interruption nor cessation.
Antonyms.—Finite, temporary, transitory, passing.

Evade, equivocate, prevaricate. We evade by artfully turning the subject or calling off the attention of the inquirer; we equivocate by the use of expressions of double interpretation; we prevaricate by the use of loose and indefinite expressions. We avoid giving satisfaction by evading; we give a false satisfaction by equivocating; we give dissatisfaction by prevaricating.
Antonyms.—Meet, face, be frank.

Event, incident, accident, adventure, occurrence. These terms are expressive of what passes in the world, which is the sole signification of the term event, while to that of the other terms are annexed some accessory ideas. An incident is a personal event; an accident, an extraordinary event; an occurrence, an ordinary or domestic event. Event, in its ordinary and limited acceptation, excludes the idea of chance; accident excludes that of design; incident, adventure, and occurrence are applicable in both cases.

Exact, extort. To exact is to demand peremptorily—it is commonly an act of injustice. To extort is to get with violence—it is an act of tyranny.

Exact, nice, particular, punctual. To be exact is to arrive at perfection; to be nice is to be free from faults; to be particular is to be nice in certain particulars; to be punctual is to be exact in certain points. We are exact in our conduct or in what we do; nice and particular in our mode of doing it; punctual as to the time and the season for doing it.
Antonyms.—Inexact, heedless, crude, careless, dilatory.

Example, instance. The example is set forth by way of illustration or instruction; the instance is adduced by way of evidence or proof.

Example, pattern. The example must be followed generally; the pattern must be followed particularly, not only as to what but how a thing is to be done. The former serves as a guide to the judgment; the latter, to the actions.

Excite, incite, provoke. To excite is said more particularly of the inward feelings; incite is said of the external actions; provoke is said of both. A person's passions are excited; he is incited by any particular passion to a course of conduct; a particular feeling is provoked, or one is provoked to a particular step by some feeling.
Antonyms.—Calm, inhibit, deter, restrain.

Excursion, ramble, tour, trip, jaunt. Excursion is properly a journey out of one's usual range of travel. It may be long or short. A tour is usually a more carefully planned "round trip" of some length, as a tour of the lakes. Trip, formerly a short journey on foot, is now applied generally. Ramble is a purposeless, pleasant walk. Jaunt is a short ramble or journey.

Excuse, pardon. We excuse a person by exempting him from blame; we pardon by giving up the punishment of the offense one has committed. We excuse a small fault; we pardon a great fault; we excuse that which personally affects ourselves; we pardon that which offends against morals. Pardon is also conventionally used as a courteous term in place of excuse, as in "pardon the suggestion," excuse being understood to imply withdrawal of the person from a place, as in "excuse us for a moment."
Antonyms.—Blame, condemn, convict, punish.

Execute, fulfill, perform. To execute is to bring about an end; it involves active measures and is peculiarly applicable to that which is extraordinary, or to that which requires particular spirit and talents. Schemes of ambition are executed. To fulfill is to satisfy a moral obligation. We fulfill the duties of citizens. To perform is to carry through by simple action or labor; it is more particularly applicable to the ordinary and regular business of life. We perform a work or a task.

Exercise, practice. Exercise is action for the purpose of stimulating or developing power; practice is regular exercise for the purpose of acquiring or increasing skill and ease of action.

Exigency, emergency. The exigency is more common but less pressing; the emergency is imperious when it comes, but it comes less frequently. A prudent traveler will never carry more money with him than will supply the exigencies of his journey; in case of an emergency he will borrow of his friends rather than risk his property.

Exonerate, exculpate. The first is the act of another; the second is one's own act. We exonerate him upon whom a charge has lain or who has the load of guilt; we exculpate ourselves when there is any danger of being blamed. Circumstances may sometimes tend to exonerate; the explanation of some person is requisite to exculpate.
Antonyms.—Inculpate, accuse, blame, incriminate.

Expediency, fitness. The expediency of a thing depends altogether upon the outward circumstances; the fitness is determined by a moral rule.

Expedient, resource. The expedient is an artificial means; the resource is a natural means. A cunning man is fruitful in expedients; a fortunate man abounds in resources.

Explain, expound, interpret. Single words or sentences are explained; a whole work, or a considerable part of it, is expounded; the sense of any writing or symbolical sign is interpreted.

Explain, illustrate, elucidate. To explain is simply to render intelligible; to illustrate and elucidate are to give additional clearness. Everything requires to be explained to one who is ignorant of it; but the best informed will require to have abstruse subjects illustrated and obscure subjects elucidated. See *Dark*.

Expostulate, remonstrate. We expostulate in a tone of authority; we remonstrate in a tone of complaint. He who expostulates passes a censure and claims to be heard; he who remonstrates presents his case and requests to be heard.
Antonyms.—Abet, countenance, urge (on).

Extraneous, extrinsic, foreign. The extraneous is that which forms no necessary or natural part of anything. The extrinsic is that which forms a part or has a connection with a thing, but only in an indirect form; it is not an inherent or component part. The foreign is that which forms no part whatever, and has no kind of connection with an object or an incident.
Antonyms.—Essential, intrinsic, native.

Extraordinary, remarkable. The extraordinary is that which is out of the ordinary course, but it does not always excite remark and is not therefore remarkable, as when we speak of an extraordinary loan; on the other hand, when the extraordinary conveys the idea of what deserves notice, it expresses what is remarkable.
Antonyms.—Ordinary, usual, commonplace.

Extravagant, prodigal, lavish, profuse. The extravagant man spends his money without reason; the prodigal man spends it in excesses. One may be extravagant with a small sum where it exceeds one's means; one can be prodigal only with large sums. Lavish and profuse are properly applied to particular actions,—the former to denote an expenditure more or less wasteful or superfluous, the latter to denote a full supply without any sort of scant.
Antonyms.—Careful, thrifty, provident, sparing.

Exuberant, luxuriant. These terms are both applied to any flourishing growth or abundance: exuberance expresses the excess; luxuriance, the profusion. Luxuriant is the more usual and of wider application,—as luxuriant foliage, hair, fancy. Exuberant is applied specifically to the feelings,—as exuberant spirits, fancy, joy.
Antonyms.—Impoverished, scanty, poor, deficient, short.

Facetious, pleasant, jocular, jocose. Facetious may be employed either for writing or for conversation; the rest, only in conversation. The facetious man deals in that kind of discourse which may excite laughter. The pleasant man says everything in a pleasant manner; his pleasantry even on the most delicate subject is without offense. The person speaking is jocose; the thing said, or the manner of saying it, is jocular.
Antonyms.—Serious, solemn, literal, crabbed.

Factious, seditious. Factious is an epithet to characterize the tempers of men; seditious characterizes their conduct. The factious man attempts to raise himself into importance; he aims at authority, and seeks to interfere in the measures of government. The seditious man attempts to excite others and to provoke their resistance to established authority. The first wants to be a lawgiver; the second does not hesitate to be a lawbreaker.
Antonyms.—Loyal, complaisant, governable.

Fair, clear. Fair is used in a positive sense; clear, in a negative sense. There must be some brightness in what is fair; there must be no spots in what is clear. The weather is said to be fair, which is not only free from what is disagreeable, but somewhat enlivened by the sun; it is clear when it is free from clouds or mists.
Antonyms.—Dark, cloudy, murky, dull, stormy.

Faith, creed. These words are synonymous when taken for the thing trusted in or believed; but they differ in this: faith has always a reference to the principle in the mind; creed respects the doctrine which is the object of belief.

Faith, fidelity. Faith here denotes a mode of action, namely, in acting true to the faith which others repose in us; fidelity, a disposition of the mind to adhere to that faith which others repose in us. We keep our faith; we show our fidelity.
Antonyms.—Untruth, faithlessness, treachery.

Faithless, perfidious, treacherous. A faithless man is faithless only for his own interest; a perfidious man is expressly so to the injury of another. Perfidy may lie in the will to do; treachery lies altogether in the thing done. A friend is perfidious whenever he evinces his perfidy; but he is said to be treacherous only in the particular instance in which he betrays the confidence and interests of another.
Antonyms.—Faithful, true, trustworthy, dependable.

Fall, downfall, ruin. Fall applies generally to decline from erectness or to descent from high position or state—it applies to things, institutions, and persons. Downfall now generally applies to descent from rank, place, or position—it implies destruction and ruin. The fall of Sedan brought the downfall of Napoleon and the ruin of French hopes.
Antonyms.—Elevation, ascent, rise.

Fallacious, deceitful, fraudulent. Fallacious applies to falsehood in opinion; deceitful, to that which is externally false: our hopes are often fallacious; the appearances of things are often deceitful. Fallacious, as characteristic of the mind, excludes the idea of design; deceitful excludes the idea of mistake; fraudulent describes a gross species of the deceitful.
Antonyms.—Logical, true, real, genuine.

Fame, report, rumor, hearsay. Fame serves to form or establish a reputation either of a person or of a thing; it will be good or bad, according to circumstances,—the fame of our Savior's miracles went abroad through the land. A report serves to communicate information of events; it may be more or less correct according to the veracity or authenticity of the reporter. A rumor serves the purposes of fiction; it is more or less vague according to the temper of the times and the nature of the events. The hearsay is an indefinite report, passed from mouth to mouth, its origin quickly lost.

Famous, celebrated, renowned, illustrious. Famous signifies having fame or being of conspicuous note. It is applicable to that which causes a noise or sensation, to that which is talked of, written upon, discussed, and thought of, or to that which is circulated among all ranks and orders of men. Celebrated signifies kept in the memory by a celebration or memorial and is applicable to that which is praised and honored with solemnity. Renown means named again or repeatedly and signifies wide and exalted fame. Illustrious implies conspicuous nobility or worth.
Antonyms.—Unknown, obscure, commonplace, humble.

Fanciful, fantastic, whimsical, capricious. Whatever is dictated by or arranged by fancy, independently of serious thought, is fanciful; the fantastic adds exaggeration and oddity to the fanciful. Whimsical implies eccentric, quaint turns of fancy and inclination. Capricious implies a certain willfulness in sudden, unreasonable changes of mind or temper. The light, fanciful account of things may be pleasant or easily amusing; a fantastic tale will intrigue by its strangeness.
Antonyms.—Serious, logical, reasonable, regular.

Fancy, imagination. The fancy employs itself about things without regarding their nature; but the imagination aims at tracing a resemblance and getting a true copy. The fancy consequently forms combinations, either real or unreal, as chance may direct; but the imagination is less often led astray. The fancy is busy in dreams, or when the mind is in a disordered state; but the imagination is supposed to act when the intellectual powers are in full play.

Fatigue, weariness, lassitude. Fatigue is an exhaustion of the animal or mental powers; weariness is a wearing out of the strength, or a breaking of the spirits; lassitude is a general relaxation of the animal frame.
Antonyms.—Freshness, strength, endurance, elasticity.

Fearful, dreadful, frightful, tremendous, terrible, terrific, horrible, horrid. A contest is fearful when the issue is important, but the event doubtful; the thought of death is dreadful to one who feels himself unprepared. The frightful is less than the tremendous; the tremendous, less than the terrible; the terrible, less than the horrible. Shrieks may be frightful; thunder and lightning may be tremendous; the roaring of a lion is terrible; the glare of his eye terrific; the actual spectacle of killing is horrible or horrid. We may speak of a frightful, dreadful, terrible, or horrid dream, of a frightful, dreadful, or terrible tempest, of dreadful, terrible, or horrid consequences.
Antonyms.—Pleasant, agreeable, inspiriting, encouraging.

Feel, be sensible, conscious. Feel is generally an indefinite word for a function of the senses and the emotions. Sensible has a more definite use in both cases, always with reference to some object, as to be sensible of light or of error, or of a friend's sympathy. One is aware of external things; conscious refers to the working of the mind in respect to either inner or outer purposes. The expression "conscious of a fault" may refer to the intellectual grasp of it; "sensible of a fault," to the emotion aroused by it.
Antonyms.—(Be) apathetic, indifferent, insensible, unconscious.

Feign, pretend, simulate. Pretend, or pretend to, is the general word for assuming a false appearance or character. Feign implies more careful invention; simulate, more specific representation of resemblance. One pretends to be occupied; he feigns illness; but he simulates the action of a lunatic. Feign and simulate are very close synonyms.
Antonyms.—(Be) frank, sincere, open, ingenuous.

Felicitate, congratulate. Felicitate is the more formal term; congratulate, the more hearty word. Properly, we congratulate others only; we may felicitate others or ourselves.

Female, feminine, effeminate. Female applies to animal and human species. Feminine connotes the qualities and characteristics peculiar to woman. Effeminate implies reproach for men marked by weak or womanish qualities.
Antonyms.—Male, masculine, mannish, manly.

Ferocious, fierce, savage. All these imply predominance of brute passion. Ferocious signifies a settled, bloodthirsty cruelty or the appearance of it. Fierce connotes blazing, angry temper or sometimes simply an intense purpose or determination. Savage, whether applied to nature, animals, or men, signifies a disposition or character untamed, heartless, of a natural cruelty.
Antonyms.—Gentle, mild, tame, civilized.

Fervent, ardent. Fervent implies warmth of feeling, earnestness. Ardent connotes keenest passion, burning enthusiasm in a cause or in pursuit of a purpose. We may speak of fervent prayers and ardent lovers.
Antonyms.—Cold, dispassionate, sluggish, phlegmatic.

Final, conclusive. Final designates simply the circumstance of being the last. Conclusive implies fitness to be final because of being convincing. Final proof may be the last introduced in a discussion; conclusive proof shuts off further argument. If the reasoning is conclusive the conclusion will be final.
Antonyms.—Temporary, tentative, partial, inconclusive.

Find, discover, invent. Find is the general word for coming to know or bringing to knowledge what was not known before. We discover the things not before known to exist; we invent combinations or processes. Iron was discovered; processes for making steel were invented. The principles of flying were discovered; the airplane was invented.
Antonyms.—Imitate, copy, reproduce.

Fine, delicate, nice. Fine, in the natural sense, denotes smallness in general. Delicate denotes a degree of fineness that is agreeable to the taste. Thread is said to be fine; silk is said to be delicate, when to fineness of texture it adds softness. Nice is said of what is agreeable to a discriminating taste and judgment.
Antonyms.—Coarse, crude, uncouth, unrefined.

Finite, limited. Finite is the natural property of things; limited is the artificial property. The former is opposite only to the infinite; but the latter, which lies within the finite, is opposed to the unlimited or the infinite. This world is finite and space infinite; one's powers or resources are limited.

Antonyms.—Infinite, illimitable, boundless.

Firm, fixed, solid, stable. Firm implies steadiness. Fixed denotes the state of being secure; solid implies power of resisting deforming forces; stable implies ability to maintain a constant position. That is firm which is not easily shaken; that is fixed which is fastened to something else, and not easily torn away; that is solid which is able to bear and does not easily give way; that is stable which is able to make a stand against resistance or the effects of time.

Antonyms.—Insecure, unstable, shaky, loose.

Fit, apt, meet. A house is fit for the accommodation of the family, according to the plan of the builder; the young mind is apt to receive either good or bad impressions. Meet is a term of rare use, except in spiritual matters or in poetry: it is meet to offer our prayers to the Supreme Disposer of all things.

Antonyms.—Ill-adapted, inappropriate, unsuitable.

Flatterer, sycophant, parasite. The flatterer is one who flatters by words. The sycophant and the parasite are flatterers and something more; for the sycophant adopts every mean artifice by which he can ingratiate himself, and the parasite submits to every degradation and servile compliance by which he can obtain his base purpose.

Antonyms.—Critic, scorner, slanderer.

Flexible, pliable, pliant, supple, limber, lithe. Flexible implies ease of bending or of being changed in shape—figuratively, susceptible to external impression. Pliable suggests ease of bending, folding, or working (as with the hands). Pliant implies more distinctly an inherent quality of easy bending to meet resistance. Figuratively, pliable suggests readiness for control (especially by evil influence); pliant suggests a temper of easy complaisance or accommodation. Supple implies freedom of easy movement. Limber applies to flexible material objects. Lithe suggests grace of motion.

Antonyms.—Rigid, stiff, cross-grained, unyielding, stubborn, unbending, intractable.

Fluctuate, waver. To fluctuate conveys the idea of alternate movement; to waver, that of constant motion backward and forward. When applied in the moral sense, to fluctuate designates the action of the spirits or the opinions; to waver is said of the will or of the opinions.

Antonyms.—Stand, (be) firm, determined, resolute.

Follow, pursue. The idea of going after any object in order to reach or obtain it is common to these terms, but under different circumstances: to follow a person implies usually a friendly intention; to pursue, a hostile intention.

Antonyms.—Lead, go ahead of, flee from.

Follow, succeed, ensue. Follow and succeed are used of persons and things; ensue, of things only. Follow, in respect of persons, denotes going in order; succeed denotes going or being in the same place immediately after another. Many persons may follow one another at the same time, but only one individual properly succeeds another. Ensue is used in specific cases,—quarrels too often ensue from the conversations of violent men who differ either in religion or politics.

Antonyms.—Lead, precede, occasion.

Follower, adherent, partisan. A follower is one who follows a person generally; an adherent is one who holds to his cause; a partisan is the follower of a party.

Antonyms.—Independent, rival, opponent.

Folly, foolery. Folly is the general word for inconsiderate, foolish conduct, especially when leading to easily foreseen disaster. Foolery implies absurd, nonsensical, though frequently amusing, performances.

Antonyms.—Sense, sobriety, prudence, judgment.

Fool, idiot, buffoon. Fool, as commonly used, signifies one who acts or talks senselessly or foolishly, or one who uses no judgment. Buffoon—a word, like fool, connected in origin with wind, windbag—signifies a stage fool or clown. Idiot implies lack of reasoning powers; imbecile, meaning weak-minded, is the proper synonym for this word.

Foolhardy, adventurous, rash. The foolhardy man ventures in defiance of consequences; the adventurous man ventures from a love of the arduous and the bold; the rash man ventures for want of thought.

Antonyms.—Calculating, hesitating, cautious, careful.

Force, violence. The arm of justice must exercise force in order to bring offenders to a proper account; one nation exercises violence against another in the act of carrying on war. Force is mostly conformable to reason and equity; violence is always resorted to for the attainment of that which is unattainable by law. Force is often something desirable; violence is always something hurtful. We ought to listen to arguments which have force in them; we endeavor to correct the violence of all angry passions.

Antonyms.—Indulgence, clemency, gentleness, kindness.

Foretell, predict, prophesy, prognosticate. Foretell frequently implies some occult powers; predict generally implies reasonable inference from facts, though the words are used loosely to mean merely "tell before." Prophesy implies inspiration or great assurance on the part of the speaker that his predictions are true. Prognosticate means to predict from observation of symptoms, as a physician prognosticates. The word is sometimes used humorously for predict.

Forgetfulness, oblivion. Forgetfulness characterizes the person or that which is personal; oblivion, the state of the thing. The former refers to him who forgets; the latter to that which is forgotten.

Antonyms.—Remembrance, memory, recollection.

Forgive, pardon, absolve, remit. Individuals forgive each other personal offenses; they pardon offenses against law and morals. The former is an act of Christian charity; the latter, an act of clemency. To remit is to refrain from inflicting—it has more particular regard to the punishment. Remission is granted by an authority—it arrests the execution of justice. To absolve is to free from penalty either by the civil judge or the ecclesiastical minister—it re-establishes the accused in the rights of innocence.

Antonyms.—Condemn, convict, punish, inflict.

Form, ceremony, rite, observance. Form respects all determinate modes of acting and speaking, adopted by society at large, in every transaction of life; ceremony respects those forms of outward behavior which are made the expressions of respect and deference; rite and observance are applied to ceremonies, especially those of religion.

Form, fashion, mold, shape. Form conveys the idea of producing. When we wish to represent a thing as formed in any distinct or remarkable way, we may speak of it as fashioned. God formed man out of the dust of the ground; he fashioned him after his own image. When we wish to represent a thing as formed according to a precise rule, we should say it is molded. Thus the habits of a man are molded at the will of a superior. When we wish to represent a thing as receiving the qualities which distinguish it from others, we talk of shaping it.

Antonyms.—Break, destroy, demolish, mutilate.

Formidable, dreadful, terrible, shocking. The formidable acts neither suddenly nor violently; the dreadful may act violently but not suddenly. Thus the appearance of an army may be formidable, but that of a field of battle is dreadful. The terrible and the shocking act both suddenly and violently, but the former acts both on the senses and the imagination, the latter on the moral feelings. Thus the glare of the tiger's eye is terrible; the unexpected news of a friend's death is shocking.

Antonyms.—Weak, trivial, commonplace, insignificant.

Forsaken, forlorn, destitute. To be forsaken is to be deprived of the company and the assistance of those we have looked to; to be forlorn is to be forsaken in time of difficulty—to be without a guide in an unknown road; to be destitute is to be deprived of the first necessaries of life.

Antonyms.—Protected, cherished, cared for, supported, supplied.

Forswear, perjure, suborn. To forswear is applied to all kinds of oaths; to perjure is employed only for such oaths as have been administered by the civil magistrate. A soldier forswears himself who breaks his oath of allegiance by desertion; a man perjures himself in a court of law who swears to the truth of that which he knows to be false. Suborn signifies to make to forswear. A perjured man has all the guilt upon himself; but he who is suborned shares his guilt with the suborner.

Foster, cherish, harbor, indulge. These terms are all employed here in the moral acceptation, to express the idea of giving nourishment to an object. To foster in the mind is to keep with care and positive endeavors, as when one fosters prejudices by encouraging everything which favors them; to cherish in the mind is to hold dear or set a value upon, as when one cherishes good sentiments by dwelling upon them with inward satisfaction. To harbor is to allow room in the mind, and it is generally taken in the worst sense of giving admission to that which ought to be excluded, as when one harbors resentment by permitting it to have a resting place in the heart. To indulge in the mind is to give the whole mind to it, to make it the chief source of pleasure, as when one indulges an affection by making the will and the outward conduct bend to its gratifications.

Antonyms.—Cast off, reject, refrain from, abjure, forswear.

Foundation, ground, basis. A report is said to be without any foundation when it has taken its rise in mere conjecture or in some arbitrary cause independent of all fact. A man's suspicion is said to be without ground when not supported by the shadow of external evidence. Foundation and base are the lowest parts of a structure; but the former lies underground, the latter stands above. Basis is used now only in the figurative sense. Rumor which has no basis in fact may be called baseless fabrication.

Fragile, frail, brittle. That is fragile which, like a flower or a vase, is easily broken or destroyed; brittle implies liability to crack or shatter, as an eggshell. Frail is close to fragile in meaning, but it is applied to weak physical or mental natures. The human body is frail or a person's virtue shows frailty.
Antonyms.—Tough, strong, firm, unbreakable.

Frank, candid, ingenuous, free, open, plain. The frank man is under no constraint; his thoughts and feelings are both set at ease, and his lips are ever ready to give utterance to the dictates of his heart. The candid man has nothing to conceal; he speaks without regard to self-interest or to any like consideration—he speaks only the truth. The ingenuous man throws off all disguise; he scorns all artifice and brings everything to light—he speaks the whole truth. Free, open, and plain have not so high an office as the first three. Frank, free, and open men all speak without constraint, but the frank man is not impertinent nor indiscreet. The plain man speaks plainly but truly—he gives no false coloring to his speech.
Antonyms.—Insincere, disingenuous, close, reserved, shuffling.

Free, exempt. Free is applied to everything from which anyone may wish to be free; exempt, on the contrary, is applied to those burdens which we might share with others.
Antonyms.—Bound, restricted, liable, amenable.

Free, familiar. To be free is to be disengaged from the constraints which the ceremonies of social intercourse impose; to be familiar is to be upon the footing of a friend or a relative or of one of the same family.
Antonyms.—Restrained, reserved, distant.

Free, liberal. To be free signifies to act or think at will; to be liberal is to act according to the dictates of a large heart and an enlightened mind.
Antonyms.—Narrow, constrained, conservative.

Frequent, resort to, haunt. Frequent is generally used only of resorting often or repeatedly to a place and applies either to one person or to several together. Resort implies the gathering of a number of people in a place. Haunt implies frequenting continually or pertinaciously when unwelcome. He haunted the neighborhood or the memory haunts him.

Frighten, intimidate. Danger immediately present or evident to the senses frightens; danger distant but apprehended intimidates.
Antonyms.—Attract, encourage, stimulate.

Funeral, obsequies. We speak of the funeral as the last sad office which we perform for a friend; it is accompanied by nothing but mourning and sorrow. We speak of obsequies as the tribute of respect paid to the person of one who was high in station or public esteem.

Gape, stare, gaze. Gape and stare are taken in an ill sense. The former indicates the astonishment of gross ignorance; the latter, not only ignorance but impertinence. Gaze is taken in a good sense, as indicating a feeling of astonishment, pleasure, or curiosity.

Gather, collect. To gather signifies to bring things of a kind together; to collect annexes also the idea of binding or forming into a whole. We gather that which is scattered in different parts, as stones are gathered into a heap; vessels are collected so as to form a fleet.
Antonyms.—Scatter, disperse, separate.

General, universal, generic. What is general includes the greater part or number; what is universal includes every individual or part. Generic applies to the larger group or class; specific, to the individual example.
Antonyms.—Particular, specific, exceptional.

Genteel, polite. Gentility respects rank in life; politeness, the refinement of the mind and outward behavior. Genteel indicates now a pretension of superiority. All decent, intelligent people are polite; a decayed gentleman may be genteel.
Antonyms.—Common, uncouth, unpolished.

Gentle, tame. Gentle implies quietness, kindness; tame implies obedience and willingness, often with some lack of spirit.
Antonyms.—Fierce, wild, spirited.

Gift, present, donation. The gift is an act of generosity or condescension—it contributes to the benefit of the receiver. The present is an act of kindness, courtesy, or respect—it contributes to the pleasure of the receiver. The gift is private and benefits the individual; the donation is public and serves some general purpose. What is given to relieve the necessities of any poor person is a gift; what is given to support an institution is a donation.

Give, grant, bestow, present, confer. The idea of communicating to another what is our own or in our power is common to these terms; this is the whole signification of give. To grant is to give at one's pleasure; to bestow is to give from a certain degree of necessity. We give money, clothes, food, or whatever is transferable. Granting is confined to such objects as afford pleasure or convenience; bestowing is applied to such objects only as are necessary to supply wants. Present is to give formally; confer is to transfer something of value.
Antonyms.—Withdraw, refuse, deny.

Give up, abandon, resign, forego. To give up is applied to familiar cases; abandon, to matters of importance. One gives up an idea, an intention, a plan, and the like; one abandons a project, a scheme, a measure of government. A man gives up his situation by a positive act of his choice; he resigns his office when he feels it inconvenient to hold it. So, likewise, we give up expectations and resign hopes; we resign that which we have, and we forego that which we might have.
Antonyms.—Hold fast, guard, retain, enjoy, seize.

Glaring, barefaced. Glaring designates the thing; barefaced characterizes the person. A glaring falsehood is that which strikes the observer in an instant as a falsehood; a barefaced lie or falsehood betrays the effrontery of him who utters it.

Glimpse, glance. Glimpse is a casual or fleeting view determined by the position or movement of the object or the observer; a glance is a hasty look, determined by the eye alone. From a moving car one, glancing at the landscape, catches glimpses of trees.

Glory, boast, vaunt. To glory is to exult or to rejoice; to boast is to set forth to one's advantage; to vaunt is to set oneself up before others. To glory is more particularly the act of the mind, the indulgence of the internal sentiment; to boast denotes rather the expression of the sentiment; to vaunt is properly to proclaim praises aloud and is taken either in an indifferent or in a bad sense.

Glory, honor. Glory is something dazzling and widely diffused; honor is something less splendid but more solid. Glory impels to extraordinary efforts and to great undertakings; honor induces to a discharge of one's duty.
Antonyms.—Shame, discredit, disgrace.

Godlike, divine, heavenly. Godlike is a more expressive but less common term than divine. The former is used only as an epithet of peculiar praise for an individual; divine is generally employed for that which appertains to a superior being, in distinction from that which is human. A heavenly being denotes an angel or inhabitant of heaven, in distinction from earthly beings.
Antonyms.—Human, earthly.

Good nature, good humor. Good nature and good humor both imply the disposition to please and be pleased, but the former is habitual and permanent while the latter is temporary and partial. The former lies in the nature and frame of the mind, the latter in the state of the spirits.
Antonyms.—Ill nature, ill humor, sullenness, petulance.

Govern, rule, regulate. The exercise of authority enters more or less into the signification of these terms, but to govern implies the exercise likewise of judgment and knowledge. To rule implies rather the unqualified exercise of power, the making the will the rule. A king governs his people by means of wise laws and an upright administration; a despot rules over a nation according to his arbitrary decision. To regulate is to govern or control simply by judgment; the word is applicable to things of minor moment, where the force of authority is not so requisite. One governs the affairs of a nation or a large body where great interests are involved; we regulate the concerns of an individual.

Government, administration. Both these terms may be employed to designate either the act of governing and administering or the persons governing and administering. In both cases government has a more extensive meaning than administration. The former includes every exercise of authority; administration implies only that exercise of authority which consists in putting the laws or the will of another in force. When we speak of the government, as it respects the persons, it implies the whole body of constituted authorities; but the administration implies only that part which puts in execution the intentions of the whole.

Grace, charm, elegance. Grace is altogether physical; charm is either physical or mental. Grace qualifies the action of the body; charm is an inherent quality in the person. A lady moves, dances, and walks with grace; the charms of her person are equal to those of her mind. A graceful figure is rendered so by the deportment of the body. A comely figure has that in itself which pleases the eye. Grace is a quality pleasing to the eye, but elegance is a quality of a higher nature and inspires admiration. Elegance implies niceties and polish of manner. All these words are extended in meaning, figuratively, to language and dress.

Gratify, indulge, humor. To gratify is a positive act of the choice; to indulge is a negative act of the will, a yielding of the mind to circumstances. One gratifies his desires or appetites; he indulges his humors or indulges in pleasures. We gratify and indulge others as well as ourselves, and mostly in the good sense. To gratify, when directed toward others, is an act of generosity. To indulge is to yield to the wishes or to be lenient to the infirmities of others—it is an act of kindness or good nature. To humor is taken mostly in an unfavorable sense.
Antonyms.—Restrict, mortify, discipline, restrain.

Gratuitous, voluntary. Gratuitous implies a giving or conferring beyond what is required; voluntary connotes free, willing, uncompelled action.
Antonyms.—Obligatory, compulsory, necessary, demanded.

Grave, serious, solemn. Grave expresses more than serious. It bespeaks not merely the absence of mirth, but that heaviness of mind which is displayed in all the movements of the body. Serious, on the other hand, bespeaks no depression but simply steadiness of action and a refraining from all that is jocular. A judge pronounces the solemn sentence of condemnation in a solemn manner; a preacher delivers many solemn warnings to his hearers.
Antonyms.—Light, cheery, frivolous, gay.

Great, grand, sublime. These terms are synonymous only in their moral application. Great simply designates extent; grand includes likewise the idea of excellence and superiority. A great undertaking characterizes only the extent of the undertaking; a grand undertaking bespeaks its superior excellence. Sublime designates the dimensions of height. A scene may be either grand or sublime. It is grand as it fills the imagination with its immensity; it is sublime as it elevates the imagination beyond the surrounding and less important objects.
Antonyms.—Mean, petty, unimpressive, ordinary.

Great, large, big. Great applies to all sorts of dimensions by which things are measured; large usually refers to magnitude, bulk, or scope. Big denotes great as to expansion or capacity. Great suggests the impression on the speaker, and is used more often of abstract ideas. Large suggests absolute size, and is used mostly of things. Big is in loose colloquial use for all these meanings of great and large.
Antonyms.—Little, small, diminutive, inconsiderable.

Groan, moan. Groan is a deep sound produced by hard breathing; moan is a plaintive, long-drawn sound produced by the organs of utterance. The groan proceeds involuntarily as an expression of severe pain, either of body or mind; the moan proceeds often from the desire of awakening attention or exciting compassion.

Gross, coarse. These terms are synonymous in their moral application. A person becomes gross by an unrestrained indulgence of his sensual appetites, particularly in eating and drinking; he is coarse from the want of polish either as to his mind or manners.
Antonyms.—Refined, polished, delicate, elegant.

Guard, defend, watch. To guard, in its largest sense, comprehends both watching and defending, that is, both preventing the attack and resisting it when it is made. In the restricted sense, to guard is properly to keep off an enemy; to defend is to drive him away when he makes the attack. Watch, like guard, consists in looking to the danger, but it does not necessarily imply the use of any means to prevent the danger—he who watches gives an alarm.

Guard, guardian. The guard defends only against external evils; the guardian takes upon him the office of parent, counselor, and director.

Guess, conjecture, surmise, divine. We guess when we have no means or facts from which to reason. Conjecture is to conclude upon incomplete evidence. Surmise implies still slighter foundation for opinion. Divine implies some mysterious or particularly keen power of knowing. Some people divine motives or secrets.
Antonyms.—Reason, calculate, compute, conclude.

Guest, visitor, or visitant. Guest signifies one who is entertained; visitor or visitant is the one who pays the visit. The visitor simply comes to see the person and enjoy social intercourse, but the guest partakes also of hospitality. Visitant implies a visitor from outside one's sphere or usual environment, as a supernatural visitant. Migratory birds are commonly said to be summer or winter visitors; properly they are visitants.

Guise, habit. The guise is that which is unusual and often only occasional; the habit is that which is usual among particular classes. A person sometimes assumes the guise of a peasant, in order the better to conceal himself; he who devotes himself to the clerical profession puts on the habit of a clergyman.

Habitation, home, house, residence. Habitation implies merely a dwelling place; house refers to a building constructed purposely for dwelling. Home is usually restricted to mean a dwelling endeared as the scene of domestic ties and family life. Residence is a more formal term than house, though less exact.

Happen, chance. Happen applies to all events, without including any collateral idea; chance comprehends likewise the idea of lack of causation in events. Whatever comes to pass happens, whether regularly in the course of things or particularly and out of the order; whatever chances happens altogether without concert or intention and often without apparent relation to any other thing.

Happy, fortunate. Both words are applied to the external circumstances of a man. The former conveys the idea of that which is abstractly good; the latter implies rather what is agreeable to one's wishes. A man is happy in his marriage; he is fortunate in his trading concerns. Happy excludes the idea of chance; fortunate excludes the idea of personal effort.
Antonyms.—Unlucky, unsuccessful, infelicitous.

Harbor, haven, port. The idea of a resting place for vessels is common to these terms. Harbor carries with it little more than the common idea of affording a resting or anchoring place; haven conveys the idea of security; port conveys the idea of an enclosure. A haven is a natural harbor; a port is an artificial harbor.

Hard, firm, solid. That is hard which will not yield to a closer compression; that is firm which will not yield so as to produce a separation. Ice is hard, so far as respects itself, when it resists every pressure; it is firm, with regard to the water which it covers, when it is so closely bound as to resist every weight without breaking. Hard and solid respect the internal constitution of bodies and the adherence of the component parts, but hard denotes a much closer degree of adherence than solid.
Antonyms.—Soft, yielding, fluid.

Hasten, hurry, accelerate, speed, expedite, dispatch. To hasten expresses little more than the general idea of quickness in moving toward a point: he hastens who runs to get to the end of his journey. Hurry implies planless and restless or perturbed haste. Accelerate expresses the idea of definite increase in speed. The word speed includes not only quick but forward movement. He who speeds goes effectually forward and comes to his journey's end the soonest. This idea is excluded from the term haste, which may often be a planless, unsuitable quickness. Hence the proverb, "The more haste, the worse speed." Expedite and dispatch are terms of higher import, in application to the most serious concerns in life. Expedite expresses a process, a bringing forward toward an end; dispatch implies a putting an end to, making a clearance. We do everything in our power to expedite a business; we dispatch a great deal of business within a given time.
Antonyms.—Impede, retard, clog, check.

Hate, detest. Hate implies a personal feeling directed toward the object, independently of its qualities; detest implies a feeling independent of the person and altogether dependent upon the nature of the thing. One may hate because of enmity and ill will. He detests when he has strong aversion.
Antonyms.—Love, admire, esteem.

Hateful, odious. Hateful is properly applied to whatever violates general principles of morality: lying and swearing are hateful vices. Odious is more commonly applied to such things or persons as excite especial repugnance by their nature or conduct.
Antonyms.—Pleasing, attractive, desirable.

Haughtiness, disdain, arrogance. Haughtiness is founded on the high opinion we entertain of ourselves; disdain, on the low opinion we have of others; arrogance is the result of both, but, if anything, more of the former than of the latter. Haughtiness and disdain are properly sentiments of the mind; arrogance, a mode of acting resulting from a state of mind.
Antonyms.—Modesty, respectfulness, consideration, courtesy.

Have, possess. One may be said to have what is in one's hand or within one's reach, but to possess is to have as one's own. A clerk has the money which he has fetched for his employer; the latter possesses the money which he has the power of turning to his use.

Hazard, risk, venture. He who hazards an opinion or an assertion does it from presumptuous feelings and upon slight grounds; chances are rather against him than for him that it may prove erroneous. He who risks a battle does it often from necessity; he chooses the lesser of two evils although the event is dubious—yet he fears less from a failure than from inaction. One ventures on a business speculation from desire of gain, though the outcome may be uncertain.

Healthful, wholesome, salubrious, salutary. Healthful is applied to exercise, to air, situation, climate, and most other things except food, to which wholesome is commonly applied. The life of a farmer is reckoned the most healthful; the simplest diet is the most wholesome. Healthful and wholesome are rather negative in their sense; salubrious and salutary are positive. That is healthful and wholesome which does no injury to the health; that is salubrious which serves to improve the health; that is salutary which serves to remove a disorder.
Antonyms.—Hurtful, deleterious, unwholesome.

Heap, pile, accumulate, amass. To heap is an indefinite action—it may be performed with or without order. To pile is a definite action done with design and order—we heap stones, or pile wood. To accumulate is properly to bring or add heap to heap, which is a gradual and unfinished act; to amass is to form into a mass, which is a single complete act. A man may accumulate dollars or anything else in small quantities, but he properly amasses wealth.

Hearty, warm, sincere, cordial. There are cases in which it may be peculiarly proper to be hearty, as when we are supporting the cause of religion and of virtue; there are other cases in which it is peculiarly proper to be warm, as when our affections ought to be roused in favor of our friends. In all cases we ought to be sincere when we express either a sentiment or a feeling; it is peculiarly happy to be on terms of cordial regard with those who stand in any close relation to us. The man himself should be hearty; his heart should be warm; professions should be sincere; a reception, cordial.
Antonyms.—Formal, cold, insincere, indifferent.

Heed, care, attention. Heed applies to matters of importance to one's moral conduct; care, to matters of minor import. A man is required to take heed; a child is required to take care. The former exercises his understanding in taking heed; the latter exercises his thoughts and his senses in taking care. We speak of giving heed and paying attention. The former is applied only to that which is conveyed to us by another, in the shape of a direction, a caution, or an instruction; the latter is said of everything which we are said to perform.
Antonyms.—Heedlessness, carelessness, oversight, neglect, rashness.

Heinous, flagrant, flagitious, atrocious. A crime is heinous which seriously offends against the laws of men; a sin is heinous which seriously offends against the will of God. An offense is flagrant which is in direct defiance of established opinions and practice. It is flagitious if a gross violation of the moral law, or coupled with any grossness. A crime is atrocious which is attended with any aggravating circumstances.

Help, assist, aid, succor, relieve. Help signifies to do good to; assist signifies to place oneself by another so as to give him strength; aid signifies to profit toward a specific end; succor signifies to run to the help of anyone; relieve signifies to bring ease to. We help a person to prosecute his work or help him out of a difficulty; we assist in order to forward a scheme, or we assist a person in the time of his embarrassment; we aid a good cause, or we aid a person to make his escape; we succor a person who is in danger; we relieve him in time of distress.
Antonyms.—Oppose, obstruct, interfere with, aggravate.

Hesitate, falter, stammer, stutter. A person who is not in the habit of public speaking or of collecting his thoughts into a set form will be apt to hesitate even in familiar conversation; he who first addresses a public assembly will be apt to falter. Children who first begin to read will stammer at hard words; one who has an impediment in his speech will stutter when he attempts to speak in a hurry.

Heterodoxy, heresy. Heterodoxy means a belief different from an accepted doctrine; heresy usually implies pernicious erroneous doctrine. But one who has heterodox opinions is a heretic.
Antonyms.—Orthodoxy, conformity.

High, tall, lofty. High expresses the idea of extension upward. What is tall is high, but what is high is not always tall; that which attains considerable height by growing is tall; a thing may be high because on a pedestal. Lofty is said of that which is extended in breadth as well as in height. We say that a house is high, a chimney tall, a room lofty.
Antonyms.—Low, short, dwarfed.

Hinder, stop. To hinder is to interfere with the progress of a person or a thing; to stop implies entire, and usually sudden, cessation of motion.
Antonyms.—Further, promote, advance.

Hold, keep, detain, retain. To hold is a physical act and requires a degree of bodily strength, or at least the use of the limbs; to keep is simply to have by one at one's pleasure. Detain and retain are modes of keeping. The former signifies keeping back what belongs to another; the latter signifies keeping a long time for one's own purpose.
Antonyms.—Give up, surrender, return, restore.

Hold, occupy, possess. We hold a thing for a long or a short time; we occupy it permanently; we hold it for ourselves or others; we occupy it only for ourselves. We hold it for various purposes; we occupy only for the purpose of converting it to our private use. To occupy is to hold only under a certain compact; to possess is to hold as one's own.

Holiness, sanctity. Holiness implies inherent qualities of piety and godliness; sanctity is a character given or conferred upon persons or places because of relation to holy men or things. A priest should be holy; there is an air of sanctity about a church.
Antonyms.—Profaneness, impiety.

Hollow, empty. That is hollow which has an empty space, or cavity, as a hollow tree. That which has nothing in it is empty, as an empty chair.
Antonyms.—Solid, full.

Holy, sacred, divine. Whatever is most intimately connected with religion and with religious worship, in its purest state, is holy, uncontaminated by any worldly thought, and elevated in the greatest possible degree, so as to suit the nature of an infinitely perfect and exalted Being. The sacred derives its sanction from human institutions, and is connected rather with our moral than our religious duties. What is holy is altogether spiritual and abstracted from the earthly. The divine is often contrasted with the human, but there are many human things that are denominated divine. What is divine, therefore, may be so superlatively excellent as to be conceived of as having the stamp of inspiration from the Deity.
Antonyms.—Human, profane, secular.

Honor, reverence, respect. To honor is only an outward act; to reverence either is an act of the mind or is the outward expression of a sentiment; to respect is mostly an act of the mind, though it may admit of being expressed by some outward act. We honor God by adoration and worship; we honor our parents by obeying them and giving them our personal service; we reverence our Maker by cherishing in our minds a dread of offending him; we respect a person or a thing that is lofty, worthy, or honorable.
Antonyms.—Scorn, contemn, despise, disdain.

Hot, fiery, burning, ardent. In the figurative application, a temper is said to be hot or fiery; rage is burning; the mind is ardent in pursuit of an object. Zeal may be hot, fiery, burning, or ardent; but in the first three cases it denotes the intemperance of the mind when heated by religion or politics. The last is admissible so long as it is confined to a good object.
Antonyms.—Cool, calm, stolid, dispassionate.

Human, humane. The human race or human beings are opposed to the irrational part of the creation; a humane race or a humane individual is opposed to one that is cruel and fond of inflicting pain.
Antonyms.—Animal, divine, beastly, inhuman, cruel.

Humble, modest, submissive. A man is humble from a sense of his comparative inferiority to others in point of station and outward circumstances; he is humble from a sense of his imperfections, and a consciousness of not being what he ought to be. He is modest, inasmuch as he sets but little value on his qualifications, acquirements, and endowments. Between humble and submissive there is this prominent feature of distinction,—that the former marks a temper of mind, the latter a mode of action. We may be submissive because we are humble; but we may likewise be submissive from fear, from interested motives, and the like.
Antonyms.—Haughty, arrogant, vain, conceited, obstinate.

Humor, temper, mood. Humor is fluctuating, so that it varies continually in the same mind; temper is a more permanent quality, showing itself to be the same whenever it appears at all. Humor makes a man appear different at different times; temper makes him different from others. Hence we speak of the humor of the moment, the temper of youth or old age. Humor and mood denote temporary states of feeling, but mood is of a rather more pervasive, controlling nature than humor, which seems more capricious. There is no calculating on the humor of the man; it depends upon his mood whether he does work ill or well.

Hurtful, pernicious, noxious, noisome. Between hurtful and pernicious there is the same distinction as between hurting and destroying: that which is hurtful may hurt in various ways; but that which is pernicious necessarily tends to destruction. Confinement is hurtful to the health; bad company is pernicious to the morals. Noxious and noisome are forms of the hurtful. That which is noxious inflicts a direct injury; that which is noisome inflicts it indirectly. Noxious insects are such as wound; noisome vapors are such as tend to create disorders.

Antonyms.—Healthful, wholesome, salutary, salubrious.

Ideal, imaginary. The ideal is not directly opposed to, but is abstracted from, the real; the imaginary, on the other hand, is directly opposed to the real—it is the unreal thing formed by the imagination. Ideal happiness is based on that which is conceived in the mind without having any direct and actual reality in nature; the imaginary is that which is opposite to some positive, existing reality. The pleasure which a lunatic derives from the conceit of being a king is based on something altogether imaginary.

Antonyms.—Real, actual, practical.

Idle, lazy, indolent. One is termed idle who will do nothing useful; one is lazy who will do nothing at all without great reluctance; one is indolent who does not care to do anything or set about anything.

Antonyms.—Busy, industrious, energetic, active.

Illuminate, illumine, enlighten. We illuminate by means of artificial lights; the sun illuminates the world by its own light. Preaching and instruction enlighten the minds of men. Illumine is but a poetic variation of illuminate. Figuratively, we speak of an illuminating remark. Illuminating examples are an aid to understanding principles.

Antonyms.—Darken, shadow, obscure, cloud.

Imminent, impending, threatening. All these terms are used in regard to some evil that is exceedingly near. Imminent conveys no idea of duration; impending excludes the idea of what is momentary. A person may be in imminent danger of losing his life in one instant, and the danger may be over the next instant; but an impending danger is that which has been long in existence and gradually approaching. A threatening evil gives intimations of its own approach—we perceive the threatening tempest in the blackness of the sky.

Antonyms.—Doubtful, unexpected, improbable, unheralded, unlikely.

Impair, injure. To impair is a progressive mode of injuring; to injure is to do harm either by degrees or by an instantaneous act. Straining of the eyes impairs the sight, but a blow injures rather than impairs the eye.

Antonyms.—Benefit, help, remedy, repair.

Imperious, lordly, domineering, overbearing. A person's temper or his tone is said to be imperious; his air or deportment is lordly; his tone is domineering. Overbearing is employed for men in the general relations of society, whether superiors or equals. A man of an imperious temper and some talent will frequently be so overbearing in the assemblies of his equals as to awe the rest into silence.

Antonyms.—Servile, submissive, humble, pliant.

Implicate, involve. Implicate denotes folding into a thing; involve, rolling into a thing. To implicate therefore marks something less entangled than to involve; for that which is folded may be folded only once, but that which is rolled is turned many times. In application to human affairs, therefore, people are said to be implicated who have taken ever so small a share in a transaction; they are involved only when they are deeply concerned. Implicate is now always used in an unfavorable sense. Involve may have this sense also, but is of more general use.

Antonyms.—Extricate, disentangle.

Impugn, attack. He who impugns may sometimes proceed insidiously and circuitously to undermine the faith of others; he who attacks always proceeds with more or less violence. When there are no arguments wherewith to impugn a doctrine, it is easy to attack it with ridicule and scurrility.

Antonyms.—Defend, uphold, vindicate.

Inability, disability. The inability lies in the nature of the thing and is irremediable; the disability lies in the circumstances and may sometimes be removed.

Antonyms.—Ability, competence, capacity.

Inadvertency, inattention, oversight. Anyone may be guilty of inadvertencies, since the mind that is occupied with many subjects equally serious may be turned so steadily toward some that others may escape notice; but inattention, which designates a direct want of attention, is always a fault and belongs only to the young or to such as are thoughtless by nature. An oversight is properly a species of inadvertency, which arises from looking over or passing by a thing. We must be guarded against oversights in business, as their consequences may be serious.

Inclination, tendency, propensity, proneness. All these terms are employed to designate the state of the will toward an object. Inclination denotes its first movement toward an object; tendency is a continued inclination; propensity denotes a still stronger leaning of the will; proneness characterizes a habitual and fixed state of the will toward an object. Propensity and proneness both designate a downward direction and consequently refer only to that which is reprehensible or low. A person has a propensity to drinking or a proneness to lying.

Antonyms.—Aversion, repugnance, abhorrence, distaste.

Include, enclose (inclose). A yard is enclosed by a wall; particular goods are included in a reckoning.

Inconvenience, annoy, molest. We inconvenience in small matters or by omitting such things as might be convenient; we annoy or molest by doing that which is positively painful. Molest implies malicious or hostile annoyance. We are inconvenienced by a person's absence; we are annoyed by his presence if he renders himself offensive; we are molested by that which is weighty and oppressive. The rude insults of ill-disposed persons may molest.

Antonyms.—Accommodate, soothe, appease, gratify.

Increase, grow. To increase is either a gradual or an instantaneous act; to grow is a gradual process. A stream increases by the addition of other waters; but, if we say that the river or the stream grows, it is supposed to grow by some regular and continual process of receiving fresh water, as from the running in of different rivulets or smaller streams.

Antonyms.—Decrease, diminish, shrink.

Indebted, obliged. Indebted is more binding and positive than obliged. We are indebted to whoever confers an essential service; we are obliged to him who does us any service. A man is indebted to another for the preservation of his life; he is obliged to him for an ordinary act of civility.

Indifferent, unconcerned, regardless. Indifferent applies only to the will; unconcerned, to either the will or the understanding; regardless, to the understanding only. We are indifferent about matters of minor consideration; we are unconcerned about, or regardless of, serious matters that have remote consequences. An author will seldom be indifferent about the success of his work; he ought not to be unconcerned about the influence which his writings may have on the public, or regardless of the estimation in which his own character as a man may be held.

Antonyms.—Heedful, anxious, careful, mindful, observant.

Indubitable, unquestionable, indisputable, undeniable, incontrovertible, irrefragable. When a fact is supported by such evidence as admits of no kind of doubt, it is termed indubitable; the authority of a man whose character for integrity stands unimpeached, is termed unquestionable authority; when a thing is believed to exist on the evidence of every man's senses, it is termed undeniable; when a sentiment has always been held as either true or false, without dispute, it is termed indisputable; when arguments have never been refuted in any degree, they are termed incontrovertible; when arguments have never been satisfactorily answered, they are termed irrefragable.

Antonyms.—Doubtful, questionable, uncertain, dubious, debatable.

Indulgent, fond. Indulgence lies more in forbearing from the exercise of authority; fondness, in the outward behavior and endearments. They may both arise from an excess of kindness or love. An indulgent parent is seldom a prudent parent; a fond parent is foolishly tender and loving. All who have the care of young people should occasionally relax from the strictness of the disciplinarian and show an indulgence where a suitable opportunity offers. A fond mother takes away from the value of indulgences by an invariable compliance with the humors of her children.

Antonyms.—Strict, stern, exacting.

Infamous, scandalous. Infamous and scandalous are both said of that which is liable to excite great displeasure in the minds of all who hear it, and to degrade the offenders in the general estimation. But the infamous seems to be that which produces greater publicity and more general reprehension than the scandalous, consequently it is more serious in its nature and a greater violation of good morals.

Antonyms.—Honorable, respectable, creditable.

Inform, instruct, teach. To inform is the act of persons in all conditions; to instruct and teach are the acts of superiors, either on one ground or another. One informs by virtue of an accidental superiority or priority of knowledge; one instructs by virtue of superior knowledge or superior station; one teaches by virtue of superior knowledge rather than of station.

Antonyms.—Misinform, delude, mislead.

Ingenuity, wit. Ingenuity comprehends invention; wit in this sense implies only quickness of apprehension. He had the ingenuity to make good use of the opportunity if he had had the wit to see it.

Antonyms.—Dullness, slowness, stupidity.

Injustice, injury, wrong. The violation of justice or a breach of the rule of right constitutes injustice; but the amount or degree of ill that falls on the person constitutes injury. A wrong partakes of both injustice and injury; it is, in fact, an injury done by one person to another in express violation of justice.

Antonyms.—Justice, right, benefit.

Inside, interior. The term inside may be applied to bodies of any magnitude, small or large; interior is peculiarly appropriate to bodies of great magnitude. We may speak of the inside of a nutshell but not of its interior. The interior of the church was beautifully decorated.

Antonyms.—Outside, exterior.

Insinuate, ingratiate. A person who insinuates adopts every art to steal into the good will of another; but he who ingratiates adopts natural means to conciliate good will. Both are used in a bad sense.

Insinuation, reflection. An insinuation always deals in half words; a reflection is commonly open. They are both leveled at the individual with no good intent. The insinuation is general and may be employed to convey any unfavorable sentiment; the reflection is particular and commonly passes between intimates and persons in close connection.

Insist, persist. Both these terms express the idea of resting or keeping to a thing; but insist signifies to rest on a point, and persist signifies to keep on with a thing, to carry it through. We insist on a matter by maintaining it; we persist in a thing by continuing to do it.

Antonyms.—Desist, yield, abandon, forego, cease.

Insolvency, failure, bankruptcy. Insolvency is a state; failure, an act flowing out of that state; bankruptcy, an effect of that act. Insolvency is a condition of not being able to pay one's debts; failure is a cessation of business, from the want of means to carry it on; bankruptcy is a legal surrender of all one's remaining goods into the hands of one's creditors, in consequence of a real or supposed insolvency.

Antonyms.—Solvency, soundness.

Instant, moment. A dutiful child comes the instant he is called; a prudent person embraces the favorable moment. When both words have respect to the present time, instant expresses a much shorter space than moment.

Insurrection, sedition, rebellion, revolt. There may be an insurrection against usurped power, which is always justifiable; but sedition and rebellion are leveled against power universally acknowledged to be legitimate. Insurrection is always open,—it is a rising up of many in a mass, but it does not imply any concerted, or any specifically active, measure. Rebellion is the consummation of sedition; the scheme of opposition which has been digested in secrecy breaks out into open hostilities and becomes rebellion. Revolt is mostly taken either in an indifferent or a good sense for resisting a foreign dominion which has been imposed by force of arms, or for sudden rebellion.

Antonyms.—Subjection, obedience, submission, acquiescence, allegiance.

Intellect, genius, talent. Intellect is the power or faculty of knowing, improved by cultivation and exercise,—in this sense we speak of a man of intellect, or of a work that displays great intellect. Genius is the particular bent of the intellect which is born with a man, as a genius for poetry, painting, or music. Talent is a particular mode of intellect which qualifies its possessor to do some things better than others, as a talent for learning languages, a talent for the stage, etc.

Interchange, reciprocity. Interchange is an act; reciprocity is an abstract property. By an interchange of sentiment, friendships are engendered; the reciprocity of good services is what renders them doubly acceptable to those who do them and to those who receive them.

Interest, concern. We have an interest in whatever touches or comes near to our feelings or our external circumstances; we have a concern in that which demands our attention. Interest may be slight or intense; concern implies a serious care about something.

Antonyms.—Indifference, apathy, unconcern, insensibility.

Interval, respite. The term interval respects time only; respite includes the idea of ceasing from action for a time. Intervals of ease are a respite to one who is oppressed with labor.

Intervention, interposition. The light of the moon is obstructed by the intervention of the clouds; the life of an individual is preserved by the interposition of a superior.

Intrude, obtrude. To intrude is to go into any society unasked and undesired; to obtrude is to put oneself in the way of another by joining the company and taking a part in the conversation without invitation or consent.

Antonyms.—Recede, withdraw, remove.

Invalid, patient. An invalid is so called because he lacks his ordinary share of health and strength; the patient is one who is laboring under some bodily suffering for which he is receiving care and treatment.

Invest, endue, or **endow.** One is invested with that which is external; one is endued with that which is internal. We invest a person with an office or a dignity; a person is endued with good qualities. Endow carries the sense of bestowing upon, supplying, or equipping. One may endow a college; a man is richly endowed with intellect or ability; but he is endued with piety or virtue.

Antonyms.—Divest, deprive, strip, dispossess.

Irrational, foolish, absurd, preposterous. Irrational is applicable more frequently to the thing than to the person, to the principle than to the practice. Foolish, on the contrary, is commonly applicable to the person as well as to the thing, to the practice rather than to the principle; absurd is applied to anything, however trivial, which in the smallest degree offends our understanding. The conduct of children is therefore often foolish, but not absurd and preposterous. It is absurd for a man to persuade another to do that which he in like circumstances would object to do himself; it is preposterous for a man to expose himself to the ridicule of others, and then be angry with those who will not treat him respectfully.

Antonyms.—Reasonable, rational, sensible, consistent.

Irreligious, profane, impious. All men who are not positively actuated by principles of religion are irreligious. Profanity and impiety are, however, of a heinous nature; they consist not in the mere absence of regard for religion, but in a positive contempt for it and open outrage against its laws. The profane man treats what is sacred as if it were profane. The impious man is directly opposed to the pious man. The former is filled with defiance and rebellion against his Maker; the latter is filled with love and fear.

Antonyms.—Religious, pious, God-fearing, reverent.

Jealousy, envy, suspicion. We are jealous of what is our own; we are envious of what is another's. Jealousy fears to lose what it has; envy is pained at seeing others have that which it wants for itself. Suspicion denotes an apprehension of injury and has more of distrust in it than jealousy; the suspicious man is altogether fearful of the intentions of another.

Antonyms.—Friendliness, magnanimity, generosity, trust.

Journey, travel, voyage. Journey signifies the course that is taken in the space of a day or, in general, any comparatively short passage from one place to another. Travel signifies such a course or passage as requires labor and causes fatigue; in general, any long course. Voyage is now confined to passages by sea.

Joy, gladness, mirth. What creates joy and gladness is of a permanent nature; that which creates mirth is temporary. Joy is the most vivid sensation in the soul; gladness is the same in quality but inferior in degree. Joy is awakened in the mind by the most important events in life.

Antonyms.—Sorrow, sadness, distress, mourning.

Judgment, discretion, prudence. Judgment is conclusive,—it decides by positive inference, and it enables a person to discover the truth. Discretion is intuitive,—it discerns or perceives what is in all probability right. A person who exercises prudence does not inconsiderately expose himself to danger; a measure is prudent that guards against the chances of evil; the impetuosity of youth naturally impels to imprudence.

Antonyms.—Foolishness, recklessness, injudiciousness.

Justness, correctness. We estimate the value of remarks by their justness, that is, by their accordance to certain admitted principles. Correctness of outline is of the first importance in drawing; correctness of dates enhances the value of a history.

Antonyms.—Looseness, inexactness, inaccuracy, partiality.

Keep, preserve, save. The idea of having in one's possession is common to all these terms, which is, however, the simple meaning of keep. To preserve signifies to keep with care and free from all injury; to save is to keep laid up in a safe place and free from destruction.

Antonyms.—Lose, neglect, waste.

Keeping, custody. Keeping amounts to little more than having purposely in one's possession; but custody is a particular kind of keeping, for the purpose of preventing an escape. Inanimate objects may be in one's keeping; but a prisoner or that which is in danger of getting away is placed in custody.

Know, be acquainted with. We may know things or persons in various ways; we may know them by name only, or we may know their internal properties or characters. One is acquainted with either a person or a thing only in a direct manner, and by an immediate intercourse in one's own person.

Knowledge, science, learning, erudition. Knowledge is a general term which simply implies the thing known; science is the department of systematized knowledge; learning is that kind of knowledge which one derives from schools or through the medium of personal instruction; erudition is scholastic knowledge obtained by profound research.
Antonyms.—Illliteracy, ignorance, smattering.

Land, country. The term land, in its proper sense, excludes the idea of habitation; the term country excludes that of the earth or the parts of which it is composed. Hence we speak of the land as rich or poor according to what it yields; of a country as rich or poor according to what its inhabitants possess.

Large, wide, broad. A field is said to be wide both from its shape and from the extent of its space in the cross directions. In like manner, a house is large from its extent in all directions; it is said to be wide from the extent of its front. What is broad is in sense, and mostly in application, wide.
Antonyms.—Small, narrow, close, confined.

Laudable, praiseworthy, commendable. Things are laudable in themselves; they are praiseworthy or commendable in this or that person. That which is laudable is entitled to encouragement and general approbation. An honest endeavor to be useful to one's family or oneself is at all times laudable. What is praiseworthy obtains the respect of all men.
Antonyms.—Censurable, reprehensible, blameworthy.

Lay or **take hold of, catch, seize, snatch.** To lay or take hold of is here the generic expression; it denotes simply getting into one's possession, which is the common idea in the signification of all these terms, which differ in regard to the motion in which the action is performed. To catch is to lay hold of with an effort; to seize is to lay hold of with violence; to snatch is to lay hold of by a sudden effort.
Antonyms.—Let go, let slip, miss, lose.

Lead, conduct, guide. One leads by helping a person onward in any manner, as to lead a child by the hand; conduct and guide are different modes of leading,—the former by virtue of one's office or authority, the latter by one's knowledge or power, as to conduct an army, to guide a traveler in an unknown country.

Lean, incline, bend. In the proper sense, lean and incline are both said of the position of bodies; bend is said of the shape of bodies. That which leans rests on one side or in a sideward direction; that which inclines, leans or turns only in a slight degree; that which bends, forms a curvature.
Antonyms.—Rise, be erect, straighten.

Leave, quit, relinquish. We leave that to which we may intend to return; we quit that to which we return no more; we relinquish something unwillingly. We leave persons or things; we quit and relinquish things only.
Antonyms.—Stay by, retain, keep, hold.

Leavings, remains. Leavings are the consequence of a voluntary act; they signify what is left. Remains are what follow in the course of things; they are the residue.

Letter, epistle. Letter is a term altogether familiar; it may be used for whatever is written by one friend to another, even those which were written by the ancients, as the letters of Cicero, Atticus, and Pliny. In strict propriety, epistle is more formal than letter. An epistle is a written message or communication usually of serious import; it is applied generally to the ancient letters of sacred character or of literary excellence, as the epistles of St. Paul.

Lift, heave, hoist. We lift with or without an effort; we heave and hoist always with an effort. We lift a child up to let him see anything more distinctly; workmen heave the stones or beams which are used in a building; they hoist materials to the upper parts of the structure.
Antonyms.—Drop, lower, let fall.

Likeness, resemblance, similarity, or **similitude.** Likeness refers to either external or internal properties; resemblance, only to the external properties; similarity applies to the circumstances or properties. We speak of a likeness between two persons, of a resemblance in the cast of the eye, of a similarity in age and disposition. Similitude is a higher term than similarity; it implies a moral comparison, as in a parable.
Antonyms.—Unlikeness, dissimilarity, contrast, difference.

Linger, tarry, loiter, lag, saunter. To linger is to stop altogether, or to move but slowly forward; to tarry is properly to suspend one's movements: the former proceeds from reluctance to leave the spot on which we stand; the latter, from motives of discretion. To loiter is to move slowly and reluctantly. To lag is to move more slowly than others. To saunter is altogether the act of an idler; those who have no object in moving either backward or forward will saunter if they move at all.
Antonyms.—Hasten, hurry, press forward, rush, march.

Little, small, diminutive. What is little is so in the ordinary sense in respect to size; it is properly opposed to great. The small is that which is less than others in point of bulk; it is opposed to the large. The diminutive is that which is less than it ought to be, as a person who is below the ordinary stature is said to be diminutive in stature.
Antonyms.—Large, great, big, huge, immense.

Lodging, apartment. A lodging, or a place to dwell in, comprehends single rooms or many rooms, or in fact any place which can be made to serve the purpose; apartment applies to suites of rooms.

Look, appearance. Look or looks refers to an impression a person or thing makes; appearance implies outward characteristics. He presented a travel-stained appearance, but he had the look of a gentleman.

Lose, miss. What is lost is supposed to be entirely and irrecoverably gone; what is missed may be only out of sight or not at hand at the time when it is wanted.
Antonyms.—Find, hold, have.

Madness, frenzy, rage, fury. Madness is a confirmed derangement in the organ of thought; frenzy is only a temporary derangement from the violence of any disease or from any other cause. Rage refers more immediately to the agitation that exists within the mind; fury refers to that which shows itself outwardly. A person contains or stifles his rage, but his fury breaks out into some external mark of violence.
Antonyms.—Sanity, calmness, patience, self-control.

Magnificence, splendor, pomp. Magnificence lies not only in the number and the extent of the objects presented, but in the degree of richness as to their coloring and quality. Splendor is but a characteristic of magnificence, attached to such objects as dazzle the eye by the quantity of light or by the beauty and strength of coloring. Pomp signifies, in general, formality and ceremony.
Antonyms.—Plainness, meanness, simplicity, somberness.

Make, form, produce, create. To make is the most general and unqualified term; to form signifies to make after a given shape or pattern; to produce is to bring forth into the light, to call into existence; to create is to bring into existence by an absolute exercise of power.

Malevolence, maliciousness, malignity. Malevolence has a deep root in the heart and is a settled part of the character; we denominate the person malevolent, to designate the ruling temper of his mind. Maliciousness may be applied as an epithet to particular parts of a man's character or conduct; one may have a malicious joy or pleasure in seeing the distresses of another. Malignity is not so often employed to characterize the person as to describe the thing; the malignity of a design is estimated by the degree of michief which was intended.
Antonyms.—Good will, kindness, good nature, benevolence.

Manly, manful. Manly, or like a man, is opposed to juvenile, and of course applied properly to youths; manful, or full of manhood, is opposed to effeminate and is applicable more properly to grown persons.
Antonyms.—Boyish, unmanly, womanish, weak.

Manners, morals. Manners applies to the minor forms of acting with others and toward others; morals includes the important duties of life. By an attention to good manners we render ourselves good companions; by an observance of good morals we become good members of society.

Mark, trace, vestige, footstep, track. Mark implies a fresh and uninterrupted line; trace, a more or less temporary mark left by something passing. A carriage driven along the sand leaves marks of the wheels, but in a short time all traces of its having been there will be lost. The vestige is a species of mark or trace caused by the feet of men, or, which is the same thing, by the works of active industry, as the vestiges of buildings. Footstep is employed only for the steps of an individual. The track is made by the steps of many.

Martial, warlike, military, soldierlike. We speak of martial array, martial preparations, martial law, a court-martial, but of a warlike nation, meaning a nation which is fond of war, of a warlike spirit or temper, or a warlike appearance. We speak of military in distinction from naval, as military expeditions, military movements, and the like. The conduct of an individual is soldierlike or otherwise.
Antonyms.—Peaceful, unwarlike, civilian, unsoldierly.

Meeting, interview. Meeting is the act of coming into the company of anyone; interview is a personal conference, usually a formal meeting for consultation, as an interview with the president. A meeting is an ordinary concern and its purpose familiar; meetings are daily taking place between friends.

Memory, remembrance, recollection, reminiscence. Memory is the power of recalling images once made in the mind; remembrance is the exercise of memory by a conscious agent, and may be the effect of repetition or of habit; recollection carries us back to distant periods. Reminiscence implies a ratner indefinite recalling of past experiences.
Antonyms.—Forgetfulness, oblivion.

Mercantile, commercial. Mercantile applies to the actual transaction of business or to a transfer of merchandise by sale or by purchase. Commercial comprehends the theory and practice of exchange; hence we speak in a peculiar manner of a mercantile house, a mercantile situation, and the like, but of a commercial education, a commercial people, and the like.

Mix, mingle, blend, confound. Mix is here a general and indefinite term, signifying simply to put together, but we may mix two or several things. We mingle several objects; things are mixed so as to lose all distinction, but they may be mingled and yet retain a distinction. To blend is only partially to mix, as colors blend which shade into each other. To confound is to mix in a wrong way, as separate objects of sight are confounded when they are erroneously taken to be joined.
Antonyms.—Distinguish, separate, segregate, sort.

Modesty, bashfulness, diffidence. Modesty is a proper distrust of ourselves; bashfulness is a state of feeling which betrays itself in a downcast look or a timid air; diffidence is a culpable distrust. Diffidence altogether unmans a person and disqualifies him for his duty.
Antonyms.—Boldness, self-confidence, forwardness, egotism.

Moisture, humidity, dampness. Moisture is used in general to express any small degree of infusion of a liquid into a body; humidity is employed scientifically to describe the state of holding any portion of such liquid. Hence we speak of moisture on a table, moisture on paper, but of the humidity of the air. Dampness is the popular term for the condition resulting from a permeating of a substance by moisture, as a wall or the earth may be damp.
Antonyms.—Aridity, drought, dryness.

Money, cash. Money is applied to everything which serves as a circulating medium; cash is, in ordinary use, coin or paper, legal tender, actually in hand for use.

Motion, movement. We speak of a state of motion as opposed to a state of rest, of perpetual motion, the laws of motion, and the like. On the other hand, we use movement generally in speaking of change of position, as an upward movement, a person's movements. As applied to a person, motion implies gesture.
Antonyms.—Rest, quiet, pause.

Moving, affecting, pathetic. The good or bad feelings may be moved; the tender feelings only are affected. A field of battle is a moving spectacle; the death of a friend is an affecting spectacle. The pathetic applies only to what is addressed to the heart; hence an address is pathetic.

Name, call. Name is employed for distinguishing or addressing one by name. To call signifies properly to address one loudly; consequently, we may name without calling, when we only mention a name in conversation, and we may call without naming.

Native, natural. Of a person we may say that his worth is native, to indicate that it is some valuable property which is born with him; we may say that it is natural, as opposed to that which is acquired.
Antonyms.—Acquired, adventitious, affected.

Necessity, necessary. Necessity is the quality or state of circumstances or things that admits of no choice or alternative; the necessary is that which is absolutely and unconditionally indispensable for some end or purpose.
Antonyms.—Choice, contingency, freedom, possibility.

Neglect, omit. To neglect is to disregard, to treat with little or no attention or respect; to omit is to leave out, to leave unnoticed or undone. We neglect an opportunity, we neglect the means, the time, the use, and the like; we omit a word, a sentence, or a figure, and we may omit an item from the day's work. To omit does not always involve the censure that attends neglect.
Antonyms.—Attend to, notice, grasp, insert.

Neighborhood, vicinity. Neighborhood is employed in reference to the inhabitants, or in regard to inhabited places, to denote nearness of persons to each other or to objects in general; but vicinity is employed to denote nearness of one object to another, whether person or thing.

New, novel, modern, fresh, recent. All these epithets are applied to what has not long existed. New expresses this idea simply without any qualifications; novel is something strange or unexpected; the modern is the thing of today, as distinguished from that which existed in former times; the fresh is that which is so new as not to be the worse for use, or that which has not been before used or employed; the recent is that which is so new as to appear as if it were just made or done.
Antonyms.—Old, familiar, accustomed, ancient, stale.

News, tidings, information, intelligence, advice, notice. News is the general term for communicated knowledge of happenings. Tidings is used poetically in the same sense. Information implies knowledge of some particular thing or event. Intelligence implies that the knowledge has been gained systematically or through organized agencies. Advice in this sense is a formal, an official, or a business term. Notice involves announcement, especially of a formal nature.

Nominate, name. To nominate and to name are both to mention by name. The former is to mention for a specific purpose; the latter is to mention for general purposes. Persons only are nominated; things as well as persons are named. One nominates a person in order to propose him, or appoint him, to an office; but one names a person casually, in the course of conversation, or one names him in order to make some inquiry respecting him.

Notice, remark, observe. To notice is a more cursory action than to remark; we may notice a thing by a single glance, or on merely turning the head. To remark supposes a reaction of the mind on an object. We observe things in order to judge of, or draw conclusions from, them, as to observe the condition of the weather. We remark things as matters of fact, as to remark the manner of a speaker.
Antonyms.—Overlook, pass over, disregard, slight.

Numeral, numerical. Numeral, or belonging to number, is applied to a class of words in grammar, as a numeral adjective or a numeral noun. Numerical, or containing number, is applied to whatever involves number or calculation of numbers, as a numerical difference, where there is a difference between any two numbers or a difference expressed by numbers.

Obedient, submissive, obsequious. One is obedient to command, submissive to power or the will, obsequious to persons. Obedient is always taken in a good sense; submissive, in a humble sense; obsequious, in a mean sense.
Antonyms.—Rebellious, stubborn, recalcitrant, self-respecting.

Object, oppose. To object to a thing is to propose or start something against it; but to oppose it is to set oneself up steadily against it.
Antonyms.—Support, maintain, promote, encourage.

Obnoxious, offensive. In the sense of giving offense, obnoxious implies as much as hateful, offensive little more than displeasing. A man is obnoxious to a party, whose interest or principles he is opposed to; he may be offensive to an individual merely on account of his manners or on account of any particular actions.
Antonyms.—Acceptable, agreeable, pleasing, attractive.

Occasion, opportunity. The occasion is that which offers us the possibility of doing an act or the chance of giving rise to a result. The opportunity is that which invites to action—it tempts us to embrace the moment for taking the step.

Occasional, casual. Occasional carries with it the idea of infrequency; casual, that of unfixedness or the absence of all design. Our acts of charity may be occasional, but they ought not to be casual.
Antonyms.—Regular, systematic, frequent, periodic.

Offender, delinquent. Those who do forbidden or prohibited acts are offenders; those who fail in required or prescribed conduct are delinquents.

Offspring, progeny, issue. Offspring is a familiar term applicable to one or many children; progeny is employed only as a collective noun for a number; issue is used in an indefinite manner without particular regard to number. When we speak of the children themselves we call them the offspring; when we speak of the parents we call the children their progeny. Issue is used only in regard to a man that is deceased.

Antonyms.—Parents, parentage, stock.

Opinionated, conceited, egotistical. An opinionated man is not only fond of his own opinion but full of his own opinion; he has an opinion on everything, which is the best possible opinion. A conceited man has an inordinately high opinion of his own talent,—it is not only high in competition with others, but it is so high as to be set above others. The egotistical man makes himself the darling object of his own contemplation; he admires and loves himself to such a degree that he can talk and think of nothing else.

Antonyms.—Modest, generous, simple, unassuming.

Option, choice. The option or the power of choosing is given; the choice itself is made. Hence we say a thing is at a person's option, or it is his own option, or the option is left to him, in order to designate his freedom of choice more strongly than the word choice itself expresses it.

Antonyms.—Necessity, compulsion.

Outward, external, exterior. Outward signifies tending out from or appearing on the outside. Exterior applies to the outer side or face, as the exterior of a building. External adds to the idea of exterior the notion of whatever is outside and separate from a thing.

Antonyms.—Inward, internal, interior.

Paint, depict. To paint is employed either literally to represent figures on paper, or to represent circumstances and events by means of words; to depict is used mostly in this latter sense, but the former word expresses a greater exercise of the imagination than the latter. It is the art of the poet to paint nature in lively colors; it is the art of the historian or the narrator to depict in strong colors a real scene of misery.

Part, piece, patch. Things may be divided into parts without any express separation; but when divided into pieces they are actually cut asunder. Hence we may speak of a loaf as divided into twelve parts when it is only conceived to be so, and divided into twelve pieces when it is really so. The patch is that which is always broken and disjointed, a something imperfect; many things may be formed out of a piece, but the patch serves only to fill up a rent or break.

Particular, individual. Particular is much more specific than individual. The particular confines us to one object only of many; the individual may be any one object among many.

Antonyms.—General, collective, common.

Peace, quiet, calm, tranquillity. Peace implies an exemption from public or private broils; quiet implies a freedom from noise or interruption. Calm is a form of quiet which applies to objects in the natural or the moral world; it indicates the absence of violent motion as well as violent noise; it is that state which more immediately succeeds a state of agitation Tranquillity expresses the situation as it exists in the present moment, independently of what goes before or after; it is sometimes applicable to society, sometimes to natural objects, and sometimes to the mind.

Antonyms.—War, disturbance, noise, commotion, storm, violence.

Pellucid, translucent, transparent. Pellucid is a word of poetic use, implying a crystal clearness, as of a clear stream. A substance is translucent which permits the passage of light but does not permit objects to be seen through it. A substance through which objects can be seen is transparent.

Antonyms.—Turbid, unclear, opaque.

Penurious, economical, saving, sparing, thrifty, niggardly. To be economical is a virtue in those who have but narrow means. Saving implies care in the use of money. To be sparing is to use frugally or stintingly; thrifty suggests careful management; penurious means miserly or sparing in regard to the use of money; niggardly implies spending grudgingly or letting go in the smallest possible quantities.

Antonyms.—Generous, lavish, extravagant, unthrifty, wasteful.

Perpetrate, commit. One may commit offenses of various degrees and magnitude; but one perpetrates crimes only, and those of the more heinous kind.

Pillar, column. The word pillar is the more general in its application to any structure, whether rude or otherwise; the term column, on the other hand, is applied to whatever is ornamental, as the columns in the Grecian orders.

Piteous, doleful, woeful, rueful. Piteous is applicable to one's external expression of bodily or mental pain; a child makes piteous lamentations when it suffers from hunger or has lost its way. Doleful applies to those sounds which convey the idea of pain; there is something doleful in the tolling of a funeral bell or in the sound of a muffled drum. Woeful applies to the circumstances and situations of men; a scene is woeful in which we witness a large family of young children suffering under the complicated horrors of sickness and want. Rueful applies to the outward indications of inward sorrow depicted in the looks or countenance.

Antonyms.—Happy, joyous, merry, cheerful.

Pity, compassion. Pity is excited principally by the weakness or degraded condition of the subject; compassion, by his uncontrollable and inevitable misfortunes.

Antonyms.—Pitilessness, hardness, antipathy.

Playful, gamesome, sportive. Playful is applicable to youth or childhood, when there is the greatest disposition to play. Gamesome and sportive are applied to persons of maturer years, the former in the bad sense, and the latter in the good sense. A person may be said to be gamesome who gives in to idle jests, or sportive who indulges in harmless sport.

Antonyms.—Sober, dull, serious, gloomy.

Poise, balance. To poise is properly to keep the weight from pressing on either side; to balance is to adjust or equalize two forces. The idea of bringing into an equilibrium is common to both terms. A thing is poised as respects itself; it is balanced as respects other things.

Antonyms.—Mispoise, unbalance, tilt, upset.

Poison, venom. Poison is the general word for substances deadly when introduced into the human system. Venom now means the particular poison of serpents, etc. It applies figuratively to hatred or malignity as blighting to life.

Politeness, polish, refinement. Politeness and polish do not extend to anything but externals; refinement applies as much to the mind as to the body. Rules of conduct and contact with good society will make a man polite; lessons in dancing will serve to give a polish; refined manners or principles will naturally arise out of refinement in mind.

Antonyms.—Impoliteness, rudeness, crudity, boorishness.

Pour, spill, shed. We pour with design; we spill by accident. We pour water over a plant or a bed; we spill it on the ground. Shed is applied specifically to blood and tears; it is also sometimes used of clouds.

Powerful, potent, mighty. Powerful is applicable to strength as well as to power: a powerful man is one who by size and make can easily overpower another; a powerful person is one who has much in his power. Potent is used only in this latter sense, in which it expresses a larger extent of power; a potent monarch is much more than a powerful prince. Mighty expresses a still higher degree of power; might is power unlimited by any consideration or circumstance. A giant is called mighty in the physical sense; genius which takes everything within its grasp is said to be mighty.

Antonyms.—Weak, impotent, powerless, feeble.

Press, squeeze, pinch, grip. The forcible action of one body on another is included in all these terms. In the word press this is the only idea; the rest differ in the circumstances. We may press with the foot, the hand, or any particular limb. One squeezes commonly with the hand. One pinches either with the fingers or with an instrument constructed in a similar form; one grips with teeth, claws, or any instrument that can gain hold of the object.

Antonyms.—Ease, let go, relieve, relax.

Presumptive, presumptuous, presuming. A presumptive heir is one presumed or expected to be heir; presumptive evidence is evidence founded on some presumption or supposition; so likewise presumptive reasoning. But a presumptuous man, a presumptuous thought, a presumptuous behavior, all indicate an overconfidence in regard to one's own powers; a man is presuming when he is disposed to take unwarranted liberties.

Previous, preliminary, preparatory, introductory. Previous applies to actions and proceedings in general, as a previous question, a previous inquiry, a previous determination. Preliminary is employed only for matters of contract; a preliminary article and a preliminary condition are what precede the final settlement of any question. Preparatory is employed for matters of arrangement; the disposing of men in battle is preparatory to an engagement. Introductory is employed for matters of science or discussion; remarks are introductory to the main subject in question.

Antonyms.—Following, succeeding, concluding, final.

Principle, motive. The principle lies in conscious and unconscious agents; the motive, only in conscious agents. All nature is guided by certain principles; man is put into action by certain motives.

Privacy, retirement, seclusion. Privacy is opposed to publicity; he who lives in privacy is one who follows no public line, who lives so as to be little known. Retirement is opposed to openness or freedom of access: he who lives in retirement withdraws from the society of others; he lives by himself. Seclusion is the excess of retirement: he who lives in seclusion bars all access to himself and shuts himself from the world.
Antonyms.—Publicity, prominence, notoriety.

Proceeding, transaction. Proceeding signifies literally going forward; transaction, the thing carried through. The former implies therefore something that is going forward; the latter, something that is already done. We are witnesses to the whole proceeding; we inquire into the whole transaction.

Production, performance, work. The term production cannot be employed without specifying or referring to the source from which it is brought forth or the means by which it is brought forth, as the production of art, the production of the inventive faculty. A performance cannot be spoken of without referring to the individual by whom it has been executed; hence we speak of this or that person's performance. When we wish to specify anything that results from work or labor, it is termed a work; in this manner we speak either of the work of one's hands, or of a work of the imagination.

Profligate, abandoned, reprobate. A profligate man has lost all by his vices, and consequently to his vices alone he looks for regaining the goods or the fortune which he has squandered; as he has nothing to lose and everything to gain in his own estimation by pursuing the career of his vices, he surpasses all others in his unprincipled conduct. An abandoned man gives way to his passions, which, having the entire sway over him, naturally impel him to every excess. The reprobate man is one who has been reproved until he becomes insensible to reproof, and becomes a prey to the malignity of his own vices.
Antonyms.—Virtuous, high-principled, self-controlled, conscientious.

Prominent, conspicuous. What is prominent is, in general, on that very account conspicuous; but many things may be conspicuous which are not expressly prominent. Nothing is prominent except that which projects beyond a certain line; everything is conspicuous which may be seen by many. A man is prominent by reason of an outstanding place in a community; his services might be conspicuous by reason of their difference from those of others.
Antonyms.—Ordinary, insignificant, unimportant, trivial.

Promise, engagement, word. In promises the faith of an individual is admitted upon his word, and built upon as if it were a deed; in engagements the intentions of an individual for the future are all that are either implied or understood. As a promise and an engagement can be made only by words, word is often used for either, or for both, as the case requires.

Proportionate, commensurate, adequate. Proportionate implies an adaptation to some assumed proportion, as a reward may be proportionate to an act. Commensurate connotes greater accuracy of measurement, as a man's powers may be commensurate with his task. Adequate signifies sufficient, without the implications of the other words.
Antonyms.—Disproportionate, incommensurate, unequal, inadequate.

Provide, procure, furnish, supply. Provide and procure are both actions that have a special reference to the future; furnish and supply are employed for that which is of immediate concern. One provides a dinner in the contemplation that some persons are coming to partake of it; one procures help in the contemplation that it may be wanted. We furnish materials for a building as they are needed. One supplies a family with any article of domestic use.
Antonyms.—Miss, fail of, withhold, deprive of.

Publish, promulgate, divulge, reveal, disclose. To publish is the most general of these terms, conveying in its extended sense the idea of making known; it is in many respects indefinite,—we may publish to many or few. To promulgate is always to make known to many. We may publish that which is a domestic or a national concern; we promulgate properly only that which is of general interest; we divulge things intended to be kept secret; we commonly divulge the secrets or the crimes of another; we reveal the secret or the mystery of a transaction; we disclose from beginning to end an affair which has never before been known or accounted for.
Antonyms.—Hide, conceal, suppress, hush up.

Put, place, lay, set. To put is a general term meaning to bring to a position,—we may put a thing into one's room, one's desk, one's pocket, and the like. To place is to put in a specific manner, and for a specific purpose, as one places a book on a shelf. To lay and to set are still more specific than place, the former being applied only to such things as can be made to lie, and set only to such as can be made to stand. A book may be said to be laid on the table when placed in a downward position, and set when placed on one end.
Antonyms.—Take up, move, remove, disturb.

Qualification, accomplishment. The qualification serves the purpose of utility; the accomplishment serves to adorn. By the first we are enabled to make ourselves useful; by the second we are enabled to make ourselves agreeable.

Quarrel, broil, feud. Quarrel is the general and ordinary term; broil and feud, including active hostility, are particular terms. The idea of a variance between two or more persons is common to these terms; but the first involves the complaints and charges which are reciprocally made. Broil implies the confusion and the entanglement which arise from a contention and a collision of interests; feud, the mutual hostilities which arise out of the variance.

Question, query. Questions and queries are both put for the sake of obtaining an answer. A question may be for a reasonable or an unreasonable cause; a query is mostly a rational question. Idlers may put questions from mere curiosity; learned men put queries for the sake of information.
Antonyms.—Answer, reply, response.

Radiance, brilliancy. Radiance denotes the emission of rays and is therefore peculiarly applicable to bodies naturally luminous, like the heavenly bodies; brilliancy denotes the whole body of light emitted, and it may therefore be applied equally to natural and artificial light. Radiance implies the activity of the shining source of light; figuratively we speak of a radiant face or personality. Brilliancy applies specifically to the appearance; figuratively we speak of a brilliant wit.
Antonyms.—Dullness, murkiness, darkness, dimness.

Rapacious, ravenous, voracious. Rapacious is the quality peculiar to beasts of prey, or to what is like beasts of prey. A lion is rapacious when it seizes on its prey; it is ravenous in the act of consuming it. The word ravenous respects the haste with which one eats; the word voracious respects the quantity which one consumes. A ravenous person is loath to wait for the dressing of his food; he consumes it without any preparation. A voracious person not only eats in haste, but he consumes great quantities, and continues to do so for a long time.
Antonyms.—Frugal, fastidious, dainty.

Rashness, temerity, haste, precipitancy. Rashness is a general and indefinite term, in the signification of which an improper celerity is the leading idea; in the signification of temerity the leading idea is want of consideration, springing mostly from an overweening confidence, or from a presumption of character. Haste and precipitancy are but modes or characteristics of rashness and are consequently employed only in particular cases, as haste in regard to our movements and precipitancy in regard to our measures.
Antonyms.—Prudence, deliberation, caution, circumspection.

Ready, prompt, apt. Ready is in general applied to that which has been intentionally prepared for a given purpose; prompt is applied to that which is at hand so as to answer the immediate purpose; apt is applied to that which is fit, or from its nature has a tendency to produce effects.
Antonyms.—Unprepared, unfit, dilatory, unavailable.

Reclaim, reform. Reclaim signifies to call back to its right place that which has gone astray; reform signifies to form anew that which has changed its form; the words are allied only in their application to the moral character. A man is reclaimed from his vicious courses by the force of advice or exhortation; he may be reformed by various means, external or internal.
Antonyms.—Corrupt, degrade, impair, vitiate, confirm.

Recover, retrieve, repair, recruit, restore. We repair that which has been injured; we recruit that which has been diminished; we recover that which has been taken away; we retrieve our misfortunes or our lost reputation; we restore that which has been lost or misplaced, as health or money.
Antonyms.—Lose, lessen, wreck, diminish, injure.

Reform, reformation. Whatever undergoes such a change as to give a new form to an object occasions a reform; when such a change is produced in the moral character, it is termed a reformation. The concerns of a state require occasional reform; those of an individual require reformation.

Refuse, decline, reject, repel, rebuff. We refuse what is asked of us, for want of inclination to comply; we decline what is proposed, from motives of discretion;

we reject what is offered to us, because it does not fall in with our views. To repel is to reject with violence; to rebuff is to refuse with contempt or with what may be considered as such.

Antonyms.—Accept, receive, acquiesce, comply, welcome.

Relax, remit. In regard to our attempts to act, we may speak of relaxing our endeavors and remitting our labors or exertions; in regard to our dealings with others, we may speak of relaxing in discipline, of relaxing in the severity or strictness of our conduct, and of remitting a punishment or a sentence.

Antonyms.—Intensify, maintain, exact, enforce.

Repeat, recite, rehearse, recapitulate. To repeat is to say or utter again; to recite is to repeat in a formal manner; to rehearse is to repeat or recite by way of preparation; to recapitulate is to repeat the chapters or principal heads of any discourse.

Repress, restrain, restrict, suppress. Repress implies usually a temporary holding back of something from action; restrain is a stronger word, frequently implying physical force and more permanent holding back. Restrict adds to restrain the idea of bounds within which the restricted activity is free. Suppress implies permanent repression or stifling of activity.

Antonyms.—Release, loose, arouse, set free, incite.

Reproach, contumely, obloquy. The idea of contemptuous or angry treatment of others is common to all these terms; reproach is the general term, contumely and obloquy are the particular terms. Reproach is either deserved or undeserved; the name of Puritan is applied as a term of reproach to such as affect greater purity than others. Contumely is always undeserved; it is the insolent resistance to authority. Obloquy is always supposed to be deserved; it is applicable to those whose conduct has rendered them objects of general censure, and whose name, therefore, has almost become a reproach.

Antonyms.—Praise, sanction, commendation, honor, laudation.

Reputation, fame, renown. Reputation is the estimate formed by others. It may be good or bad. Fame often means widespread reputation. Renown is both widespread and favorable.

Antonyms.—Ignominy, infamy.

Restore, return, repay. We restore upon a principle of equity; we return upon a principle of justice and honor; we repay upon a principle of undeniable right. We cannot always claim that which ought to be restored; but we cannot only claim but enforce the claim in regard to what is to be returned or repaid.

Antonyms.—Withhold, retain, default.

Retard, hinder. We retard or make slow the progress of any scheme toward completion; we hinder or keep back the person who is completing the scheme. We often retard a person, therefore, by hindering his progress; but we frequently hinder a person without expressly retarding him.

Antonyms.—Accelerate, advance, further, help.

Right, claim, privilege. Right, in its full sense, is altogether an abstract thing which is independent of human laws and regulations; claims and privileges are altogether connected with the establishments of civil society. We have often a claim to a thing which is not in our power to substantiate; and, on the other hand, claims are set up in cases which are totally unfounded on any right. Privileges are rights granted to individuals, depending either on the will of the grantor, on the circumstances of the receiver, or on both; privileges are, therefore, partial rights transferable at the discretion of persons individually or collectively.

Antonyms.—Duty, obligation, responsibility.

Royal, regal, kingly. Royal signifies belonging to a king, in its most general sense; regal signifies appertaining to a king, in its particular application; kingly properly signifies like a king. A royal carriage, a royal residence, royal authority—all designate the general and ordinary appurtenances of a king. Regal government, regal state, regal power, denote the peculiar properties of a king; kingly always implies what is becoming a king, or after the manner of a king—a kingly crown is such as a king ought to wear.

Rural, rustic. Rural applies to all country objects except man; it is, therefore, often connected with the charms of nature. Rustic, as here compared, applies only to persons or to what is personal, with reference to the country—it is generally associated with the want of culture.

Antonyms.—Urban, refined, cultured, urbane.

Safe, secure. We may be safe without using any particular measures; but none can reckon on any degree of security without great precaution. A person may be very safe on the top of a coach; but, if he wish to be secure from falling off, he must be fastened.

Antonyms.—Unsafe, insecure, endangered.

Salute, salutation, greeting. A salute may consist of either a word or an action; salutations pass from one friend to another. The salute may be either direct or indirect; the salutation is always direct and personal. Guns are fired by way of a salute. Bows are given in the way of a salutation. Greeting is frequently a particular mode of salutation adopted on extraordinary occasions, indicative of great joy or satisfaction in those who greet.

Satisfy, please, gratify. What satisfies is not always adapted to please; nor is that which pleases that which will always satisfy: plain food satisfies a hungry person; it does not please him when he is not hungry. To gratify is to please in a high degree, to produce a vivid pleasure; we may be pleased with trifles; but we are commonly gratified with such things as act strongly either on the senses or the affections.

Antonyms.—Displease, offend, disgust, anger.

Seaman, waterman, sailor, mariner. All these words denote persons occupied in navigation. The seaman, as the word implies, follows his business on the sea; the waterman is one who gets his livelihood on fresh water. The sailor and the mariner are both specific terms to designate the seaman; every sailor and every mariner is a seaman, although every seaman is not a sailor or a mariner. The former is one who is employed about the work of the vessel; the latter is one who traverses the ocean to and fro, and passes his life upon it.

Secret, hidden, latent, occult, mysterious. What is secret is known to some one; what is hidden may be known to no one. It rests in the breast of an individual to keep a thing secret; it depends on the course of things if anything remains hidden. The latent is the secret or the concealed, especially forces which give no hint of their presence by external appearances; a latent fury may exist in an apparently gentle tiger. An occult science is one that is hidden from the view of persons in general, and is attainable by but few; occult causes or qualities are those which lie too remote to be discovered by the inquirer. The operations of Providence are said to be mysterious, as they are altogether past our finding out.

Antonyms.—Open, revealed, evident, plain, understandable.

See, perceive, observe. The eye sees when the mind is absent; the mind and the eye or other senses perceive in conjunction. Hence, we may say that a person sees, but does not perceive. We observe not by a mere simple act of the mind, but by its positive and fixed exertion.

Seem, appear. Seem is said of that which is dubious, contingent, or future; appear, of that which is actual, positive, and past. A thing seems strange which we are led to conclude is strange from what we see of it; a thing appears clear when we have a clear conception of it.

Sensualist, voluptuary, epicure. The sensualist lives for the indulgence of his senses; the voluptuary is devoted to his pleasures, and, as far as these pleasures are the pleasures of sense, the voluptuary is a sensualist. The epicure as one who makes the pleasures of sense his god, and in this sense he is a sensualist and a voluptuary. In the application of these terms, however, the sensualist is one who is a slave to the grossest appetites; the voluptuary is one who studies his pleasures so as to make them the most valuable to himself; the epicure is a kind of voluptuary who practices more than ordinary refinement in the choice of his pleasures, especially of food.

Antonyms.—Stoic, ascetic, hermit.

Servant, domestic, menial, drudge. In the term servant is included the idea of service performed; in the term domestic, the idea of one belonging to the house or family; in the word menial is included the idea of servile labor; and in the term drudge, that of wearisome labor.

Antonyms.—Master, mistress, employer, boss.

Shade, shadow. Both these terms express that darkness which is occasioned by the sun's rays being intercepted by any body; shade simply expresses the absence of light; shadow signifies also the figure of the body which intercepts the light.

Antonyms.—Light, brightness, sunshine.

Sharp, acute, keen. The general property expressed by these epithets is that of sharpness, or an ability to cut. The term sharp is generic and indefinite; the two others are modes of sharpness differing in circumstance or in degree. Acute is not only more than sharp in the common sense, but signifies also sharp-pointed; a knife may be sharp, but a needle is properly acute. Things are sharp that have either a long or a pointed edge; but keen is applicable only to the long edge, and that in the highest degree of sharpness. A common knife may be sharp; a razor or a lancet is properly said to be keen. All these words are applied figuratively to mental ability, their meanings corresponding to their literal senses.

Antonyms.—Dull, blunt, obtuse.

Short, brief, concise, succinct, summary. We may term a stick, a letter, or a discourse, short. We speak of brevity only in regard to the mode of speech. Conciseness or succinctness applies to the matter of speech; summary, to the mode either of speaking or of acting.
Antonyms.—Long, prolix, full, diffuse, extended, developed, detailed.

Show, exhibition, representation, sight, spectacle. A show consists of that which merely pleases the eye—it is not a matter either of taste or art, but merely of curiosity. An exhibition, on the contrary, presents some effort of talent or some work of genius; a representation sets forth the image or imitation of something by the power of art. Hence we speak of a show of wild beasts, an exhibition of paintings, and a theatrical representation; sights and spectacles present themselves to view. Whatever excites notice is a sight; a spectacle, on the contrary, is that kind of sight which has something in it to interest either the heart or the head of the observer. Processions are sights; battles or bullfights are spectacles.

Sick, sickly, diseased, morbid. Sick denotes a partial state; sickly, a permanent state of the body, a proneness to be sick. He who is sick may be made well; but he who is sickly is seldom really well. Sickly expresses a permanent state of indisposition unless otherwise qualified; but diseased expresses a violent state of derangement without specifying its duration. Sickly and morbid are applied to the habitual state of the feelings or character: a sickly sentimentality; a morbid sensibility. Morbid is used in no other sense, except technically.
Antonyms.—Well, healthy, whole, cheerful.

Sign, signal. The sign enables us to recognize an object; it is, therefore, sometimes natural. Signal serves to give warning; it is always arbitrary.

Simple, single, singular. We may speak of a simple matter as something easily grasped or understood. A single instance or circumstance is unaccompanied by any other; a singular instance is one that rarely has its like.
Antonyms.—Complex, complicated, accompanied, common.

Simulation, dissimulation. Simulation is making oneself like what one is not; dissimulation is making oneself appear unlike what one really is. The hypocrite puts on the semblance of virtue to recommend himself to the virtuous; the dissembler conceals his vices when he wants to gain the simple or the ignorant to his side.
Antonyms.—Truth, frankness, sincerity, ingenuousness.

Slack, loose. Slack is said only of that which is tied, or of that with which anything is tied; loose is said of any substances, the parts of which do not adhere closely.
Antonyms.—Taut, tight, stretched, compact.

Slant, slope. Slant is said of small bodies only; slope is said indifferently of all bodies, large and small. A book may be made to slant by lying in part on another book on a desk or a table; but a piece of ground is said to slope.
Antonyms.—Be perpendicular, erect, level.

Slip, slide, glide. Slip is an involuntary, and slide a voluntary, motion. Those who go on the ice in fear will slip; boys slide on the ice by way of amusement. To slip and slide are lateral movements of the feet; but to glide is the movement of the whole body, and just that easy motion which is made by slipping, sliding, flying, or swimming. A person glides along the surface of the ice when he slides; a vessel glides along through the water.

Soak, drench, steep. A person's clothes are soaked in rain when the water has penetrated every thread; he himself is drenched in the rain when it has penetrated, as it were, his very body. Steep respects a manner of soaking employed as an artificial process. Soak is, however, a permanent action by which hard things are rendered soft; steep is a temporary action by which soft bodies become penetrated with a liquid. Dried fruits are prepared for eating by soaking; herbs are steeped to extract their essences or flavors.
Antonyms.—Dry, dehydrate, desiccate, evaporate.

Social, sociable. Social people seek others; sociable people are sought for by others.
Antonyms.—Solitary, retiring, uncompanionable.

Solicitation, importunity. Solicitation is general; importunity is particular. Solicitation itself may give trouble to a certain extent, but it is not always unreasonable; importunity is troublesome, insistent solicitation. There may be cases in which we may yield to the solicitations of friends, to do that which we have no objection to being obliged to do; but importunity is that solicitation which never ceases to apply for that which it is not agreeable to give.

Solitary, desert, desolate. Solitary simply denotes the absence of all beings of the same kind—a place is solitary to a man where there is no human being but himself. Desert conveys the idea of a place made solitary by being shunned, because of its unfitness as a place of residence. Desolate conveys the idea of a place made solitary or bare of inhabitants and of all traces of habitation by violent means.
Antonyms.—Populous, peopled, cultivated, inhabited, fruitful.

Sound, sane, healthy. Sound is extended in its application to all things that are in the state in which they ought to be to preserve their vitality. A horse is said to be sound in mind and limb; a tree is sound when not decayed in any part. Healthy expresses more than either sound or sane; we are healthy in every part, but we are sound in that which is essential to life. He who is sound may live, but he who is healthy enjoys life. Sane is applicable to human beings, in the same sense, but with reference to the mind; a sane person is one of sound mind.
Antonyms.—Decayed, diseased, flawed, corrupt.

Speak, say, tell. To speak may simply consist in uttering an articulate sound; but to say is to communicate some idea by means of words. A child begins to speak the moment it opens its lips to utter any acknowledged sound; but it will be some time before it can say anything. To say is to communicate that which passes in our own minds, to express our ideas and feelings as they rise. To tell is to communicate events or circumstances respecting ourselves or others.

Spread, expand, diffuse. To spread may be said of anything which comes to occupy more space than it has done, whether by a direct separation of its parts or by an accession to the substance; but to expand is to spread by means of extending or unfolding the parts. A mist spreads over the earth; a flower expands its leaves. To diffuse is to scatter, to cause to spread, as to diffuse information.
Antonyms.—Contract, condense, restrict, close, draw in.

Staff, stay, prop, support. Anything may be called a staff which holds up after the manner of a staff, particularly as it relates to persons, as bread is said to be the staff of life. The stay makes a thing secure for the time being—it keeps it in its place. A prop is usually of a temporary nature; a support is more permanent. Every pillar on which a building rests is a support; the timbers which keep a damaged structure from falling are props. Whatever supports, that is, bears the weight of an object, is a support, whether in a state of motion, like a staff, or in a state of rest, like a stay or a prop.

Stain, soil, sully, tarnish. All these terms imply the act of diminishing the brightness of an object, but the term stain denotes something grosser than the other terms, and is applied to inferior objects. Things which are not remarkable for purity or brightness may be stained, as hands when stained with blood. Nothing is sullied or tarnished but what has some intrinsic value. A fine picture or piece of writing may be easily soiled by a touch of the finger. The finest silver is the soonest tarnished; a man's life may be stained by the commission of some gross immorality; his honor may be sullied, or his glory tarnished.
Antonyms.—Cleanse, clean, brighten, polish, clear.

State, realm, commonwealth. The ruling idea in the sense and application of the word state is that of government in its most abstract sense; affairs of state may involve either the internal regulations of a country or the arrangements of different states with each other. The term realm is employed for the nation at large, but it is confined to such nations as are monarchical. The term commonwealth refers rather to the aggregate body of men, their possessions and common interests, than to the government of a country.

Stir, move. We may move in any manner, but to stir is to move so as to disturb the rest and composure of either the body or the mind.

Story, tale. Story is an account of events either real or fictitious. Children often use story to mean falsehood. Tale is used of a longer, more wandering narrative, frequently in the sense of a deceptive or malicious account. Implying the evil sense, we say that one should not tell tales and that one has made up a story.

Stream, current, tide. All rivers are streams, more or less gentle according to the nature of the ground through which they pass. The force of the current is very much increased by the confinement of any water between rocks, or between artificial embankments. The tide is high or low, strong or weak, at different hours of the day; when the tide is high, the current is strongest. Stream is the general term implying flow; current implies a more or less definite direction and rate of flow; tide applies to a regular flow, alternating in direction. In these senses the words are applied figuratively to human affairs.

Strengthen, fortify, invigorate. Whatever adds to the strength, be it in ever so small a degree, strengthens; exercise strengthens either body or mind. Whatever gives strength for a particular emergency fortifies; religion fortifies the mind against adversity. Whatever adds to the strength, so as to give a positive degree of strength, invigorates—morning exercise in fine weather invigorates.

Antonyms.—Weaken, enfeeble, enervate.

Strict, severe. He who has authority over others must be strict in enforcing obedience, in keeping good order, and in encouraging attention to duty; but it is possible to be very severe in punishing those who are under us, and yet to be very lax in all matters that our duty demands of us.

Antonyms.—Lax, indulgent, mild, compliant.

Successive, alternate. The successive may be accidental or intentional; the alternate is always intentional. It may rain for three successive days, or a fair may be held for three successive days. Trees are placed sometimes in alternate order, when every other tree is of the same size and kind.

Surround, encompass, environ, encircle. We may surround an object by standing at certain distances all round it; in this manner a person may be surrounded by other persons; a garden is surrounded by a wall. To encompass is to surround in the latter sense; it applies to objects of a great or indefinite extent, as the earth is encompassed by the air. To surround is to extend around an object of any form, whether square or circular, long or short; but to environ and to encircle carry with them the idea of forming a circle round an object. Thus a town or a valley may be environed by hills, a basin of water may be encircled by trees, or the head may be encircled by a wreath of flowers.

Sympathy, compassion, commiseration, condolence. Sympathy has the literal meaning of fellow feeling, that is, a kindred or like feeling, or feeling in company with another. Compassion, commiseration, and condolence signify a like suffering, or a suffering in company. Sympathy preserves its original meaning in its application, for we laugh or cry because of sympathy. Compassion is altogether a moral feeling, which makes us enter into the distresses of others. We may sympathize with others without essentially serving them; but, if we feel compassion, we naturally turn our thoughts toward relieving them. Commiseration is awakened toward those who are in an abject state of misery. Condolence is expressed sympathy.

Antonyms.—Antipathy, harshness, mercilessness, unkindliness, inhumanity.

Tease, vex, taunt, tantalize, torment. To tease is applied to that which is most trifling; torment, to that which is most serious. We are teased by a fly that buzzes in our ears; we are vexed by the carelessness and stupidity of our servants; we are taunted by the sarcasms of others; we are tantalized by the fair prospects which present themselves only to disappear again; we are tormented by the importunities of troublesome beggars or by the pain of anxious fears.

Antonyms.—Calm, comfort, gratify, satisfy, console, relieve.

Tenacious, pertinacious. To be tenacious is to hold a thing close, to let it go with reluctance; to be pertinacious is to hold out in spite of obstacles. Each is used in a bad or a good sense.

Antonyms.—Yielding, inconstant, irresolute, pliant.

Thick, dense. We speak of thick in regard to hard or soft bodies, as a thick board or thick cotton; we speak of thick in regard to solid or liquid bodies, as a thick cheese or thick milk. Dense specifically adds the idea of great closeness of parts and consequent weight and solidity. Applied to mind, dense is a stronger term than thick.

Antonyms.—Thin, tenuous, rarefied, quick, clever.

Think, suppose, imagine, believe, deem. We think a thing right or wrong; we suppose it to be true or false; we imagine it to be real or unreal. In regard to moral points, in which case the word deem may be compared with the others, to think is to draw a conclusion from certain premises. I think that a man has acted wrongly. To suppose is to take up an idea arbitrarily or at pleasure; to imagine is to take up an idea by accident, or without any connection with the truth or reality. To deem is to form a conclusion; things are deemed hurtful or otherwise in consequence of observation. We think as the thing strikes us at the time; we believe as the result of a course of thought.

Antonyms.—Know, prove, demonstrate.

Threat, menace. We may be threatened with either small or great evils; but we are menaced only with great evils.

Antonyms.—Attraction, allurement, enticement.

Timely, seasonable. The former signifies within the time, that is, before the time is past; the latter, according to the season, or what the season requires. A timely notice prevents that which would otherwise happen; mercy and kindness are seasonable in the time of affliction.

Antonyms.—Inopportune, untimely, ill-timed, unseasonable.

Torment, torture. Torture is an excess of torment. We may be tormented by a variety of indirect means; but we are mostly said to be tortured by the direct means that may be compared to the rack or a similar instrument.

Antonyms.—Comfort, ease, solace.

Transfigure, transform, metamorphose. Transfigure is to make to pass over into another figure; transform and metamorphose are to put into another form. Transfigure is used only of spiritual beings, particularly in reference to our Savior; the other two terms are applied to physical form. Transformation is commonly applied to that which changes its outward form; in this manner a harlequin transforms himself into all kinds of shapes and likenesses. Metamorphosis is applied to the form internal as well as external, that is, to the whole nature.

Trembling, tremor, trepidation. Trembling expresses any degree of involuntary shaking of the frame, from the affection of either the body or the mind; cold, nervous affections, fear, and the like are the ordinary causes of trembling. Tremor is a slight degree of trembling, which arises mostly from a mental affection; when the spirits are agitated, the mind is thrown into a tremor by any trifling incident. Trepidation is more violent and springs from fear or alarm; it shows itself in the action, or the different movements of the body, rather than in the body.

Antonyms.—Firmness, immobility, steadiness, self-command.

Trouble, disturb, molest. Trouble is the most general in its application; we may be troubled by the want of a thing, or troubled by that which is unsuitable; we are disturbed and molested only by that which actively troubles. Trouble may be permanent; disturbance and molestation are temporary, and both refer to the peace which is destroyed. A disturbance ruffles or throws out of a tranquil state; a molestation burdens or bears hard on either the body or the mind.

Antonyms.—Soothe, quiet, compose, caress.

Truth, veracity. Truth belongs to the thing; veracity to the person. The truth of a story is admitted upon the veracity of the narrator.

Antonyms.—Deception, falsehood, falsity.

Turn, bend, twist, distort, wring, wrest, wrench. We turn a thing by moving it about a fixed point; thus we turn the earth over. To bend is simply to change direction; thus a stick is bent, or a body may bend its direction to a certain point. To twist is to bend many times, to make many turns. To distort is to turn or twist out of the right form; thus the face is distorted in convulsions. To wring is to twist with violence; thus linen that has been wetted is wrung. To wrest or wrench is to separate from a body by means of twisting; thus a stick may be wrested out of the hand, or a hinge wrenched off the door.

Turn, wind, whirl, twirl, writhe. To turn is to cause to rotate; wind is to turn a thing around in a regular manner; whirl, to turn it around in a violent manner; twirl, to turn it around in an irregular and unmeaning way. Writhe implies a twisting about within the thing itself, a contortion, as writhing in pain.

Unbelief, infidelity, incredulity. Unbelief implies a settled doubting state of mind; infidelity carries the idea of unfaithfulness to vows or responsibilities; incredulity is a doubting attitude toward tales more or less strange. In religion both unbelief and infidelity convey a sense of failure in duty, the latter being the stronger word.

Antonyms.—Belief, faith, faithfulness, credulity.

Understanding, intellect, intelligence. Understanding is employed to describe a familiar and easy power or operation of the mind in forming distinct ideas of things. Intellect is employed to mark the same operation in regard to higher and more abstruse objects. Understanding applies to the first exercise of the rational powers; it is therefore aptly said of children and savages that they employ their understandings on the simple objects of perception. Intellect, being a matured state of the understanding, is most properly applied to the efforts of those who have their powers in full vigor. Intelligence is less abstract, and is used of a particular person, often to denote large understanding.

Unspeakable, ineffable, unutterable, inexpressible. Unspeakable is sometimes used in religion to refer to those objects which are above human conception and surpass the power of language to describe, as the unspeakable goodness of God. Ineffable is said of such objects as cannot be painted in words with adequate force, as the ineffable sweetness of a person's look. Unspeakable is now applied especially to things too evil for utterance; ineffable is used of things too high or good for utterance. Unutterable and inexpressible are extended in their signification to that which is incommunicable by signs from one being to another. Grief is unutterable which it is not in the power of the sufferer by any sounds to bring home to the feelings of another; grief is inexpressible that is not to be expressed by looks, or words, or any sign.

Antonyms.—Common, commonplace, obvious, trivial.

Unworthy, worthless. Unworthy is a term of less reproach than worthless: the former signifies not to be worthy of praise or honor; the latter signifies to be without all worth, and consequently in the fullest sense bad. There are many unworthy members in every religious community; but every society that is conducted upon proper principles will take care to exclude worthless members.

Antonyms.—Worthy, estimable, admirable, noble.

Usage, custom, prescription. Usage is what one has been long accustomed to do; custom is what one generally does; prescription is what is indicated by usage to be done. The usage acquires force and sanction by dint of time; the custom acquires sanction by the frequency of its appearance or by the numbers following it; the prescription acquires force by the authority which prescribes.

Antonyms.—Innovation, novelty, fancy.

Utter, speak, articulate, pronounce. Utter signifies to put out; that is, to send forth a sound. This, therefore, is a more general term than speak, which is to utter an intelligible sound. We may utter a groan; we speak words only, or that which is intended to serve as words. Speak, therefore, is only a form of utterance—a dumb man has utterance, but not speech. Articulate and pronounce are modes of speaking. To articulate, from *articulum*, "a joint," is to pronounce distinctly the letters or syllables of words; this is the first effort of a child beginning to speak. To pronounce is to speak words intelligibly.

Antonyms.—Be silent, make signs, mutter, mumble.

Value, prize, esteem. To value is to estimate the worth, real or supposed, relative or absolute, of a thing; in this sense men value gold above silver, or an appraiser values goods. Prize and esteem are taken only as mental actions; the former is taken in reference to sensible or moral objects, the latter, only to moral objects. We may value books according to their market price, or we may value them according to their contents; we prize books only for their contents; in this sense prize is a much stronger term than value.

Antonyms.—Contemn, disregard, depreciate, disprize, despise.

Venial, pardonable. Venial implies trivial offense. Pardonable implies a more serious guilt. The venial fault may be overlooked; the pardonable offense, though not escaping censure, allows of clemency.

Antonyms.—Deadly, unpardonable.

View, survey, prospect. We take a view or survey; the prospect presents itself. The view is of an indefinite extent; the survey is always comprehensive in its nature. Ignorant people take but narrow views of things; the capacious mind of a genius takes a survey of all nature. Prospect, used literally, signifies an outlook as from a window; figuratively, it implies a person's outlook or view toward the future.

Violent, furious, boisterous, vehement, impetuous. A man is violent in his opinions, violent in his measures, violent in his resentments; he is furious in his anger, or has a furious temper; he is vehement in his affections or passions, vehement in love, vehement in zeal, vehement in pursuing an object. Violence transfers itself to some external object on which it acts with force; but vehemence respects that manner of violence which is confined to the person himself; we may dread violence, because it is always liable to do mischief. Impetuosity is rather the extreme of violence or vehemence. An impetuous attack is an excessively violent attack; an impetuous character is an excessively vehement character. Boisterous is said of the manner and of the behavior rather than of the mind.

Antonyms.—Mild, quiet, gentle, cool, collected, self-restrained.

Wakefulness, watchfulness, vigilance. Wakefulness is an affair of the body and depends upon the temperament; watchfulness is an affair of the will and depends upon the determination. Some persons are more wakeful than they wish to be; few are as watchful as they ought to be. Vigilance expresses a high degree of watchfulness. A sentinel is watchful who on ordinary occasions keeps good watch; but it is necessary for him, on extraordinary occasions, to be vigilant in order to detect whatever may pass.

Antonyms.—Drowsiness, heedlessness, inattention, negligence.

Want, need, lack. To want is to be without that which contributes to our comfort or is an object of our desires; to need is to be without that which is essential to our existence or our purposes. To lack expresses little more than the general idea of being without, unaccompanied by any collateral idea; it is usual to consider what we want as artificial, and what we need as natural and indispensable. What one man wants is a superfluity to another; but that which is needed by one is in like circumstances needed by all.

Antonyms.—Have, share, possess.

Wave, billow, surge, breaker. Waves which swell more than ordinarily are termed billows; waves which rise higher than usual are termed surges; waves which dash against the shore, or against vessels, with more than ordinary force, are termed breakers.

Weak, feeble, infirm. We may be weak in body or in mind; we are feeble and infirm only in the body; we may be weak from disease, or weak by nature—both words convey the gross idea of a defect. But the terms feeble and infirm are qualified expressions for weakness. An old man is feeble from age; he may likewise be infirm in consequence of sickness.

Antonyms.—Strong, sound, healthy, well.

Weight, burden, load. A person may sink under the weight that rests upon him; a platform may break down from the weight upon it; a person sinks under his burden or load; a cart breaks down from the load.

Whole, entire, complete, total, integral. Whole excludes subtraction; entire excludes division; complete excludes deficiency. A whole orange has had nothing taken from it; an entire orange is not yet cut; a complete orange is grown to its full size. Total is the opposite of partial. Integral is applied now to parts or to numbers not broken.

Wicked, iniquitous, nefarious. It is wicked to deprive another of his property unlawfully, under any circumstances; but it is iniquitous if it be done by fraud and circumvention; the act is nefarious if it involves any breach of trust.

Antonyms.—Good, moral, right, just.

Will, wish. We can will nothing but what we can effect; we may wish for many things which lie above our reach.

Wisdom, prudence. Wisdom directs all matters present or to come; prudence, which acts by foresight, directs what is to come. Rules of conduct are framed by wisdom, and it is the part of prudence to apply these rules to the business life.

Antonyms.—Unwisdom, imprudence, indiscretion, folly.

Wonder, miracle, marvel, prodigy, monster. Wonders are natural; miracles are supernatural. The whole creation is full of wonders; the Bible contains accounts of miracles. Wonders are real; marvels are often fictitious; prodigies are extravagant and imaginary; monsters are violations of the laws of nature. The production of a tree from a grain of seed is a wonder; but a calf with two heads is a monster.

Wonder, surprise, astonishment, amazement. Wonder is the feeling induced by something strange or unusual. Surprise has the idea of sudden wonder. Astonishment is stronger, and includes failure to understand. Amazement adds the idea of bewilderment at something strange or unexpected.

Antonyms.—Comprehension, coolness, composure.

Work, labor, toil, drudgery, task. Every member of society must work for his support, if he is not in independent circumstances. The poor are obliged to labor for their daily subsistence; some are compelled to toil incessantly for the pittance which they earn. Drudgery falls to the lot of those who are the lowest in society. A man wishes to complete his work; he is desirous of resting from his labor; he seeks for a respite from his toil; he submits to drudgery. Task is a work imposed by others, and it is, consequently, more or less burdensome.

Antonyms.—Play, ease, relaxation, recreation, amusement.

Writer, author. Writer refers us to the act of writing; author, to the act of inventing. There are, therefore, many writers who are not authors; but there is no author of books who may not be termed a writer. Compilers and contributors to periodical works are properly writers, though not always entitled to the name of authors. Poets and historians are properly termed authors rather than writers.

Youthful, juvenile, puerile. Youthful signifies full of youth or in the complete state of youth; juvenile signifies the same; but puerile signifies childish. The first two terms are taken in an indifferent sense; the last is taken in the sense of what is suitable to a child only. Thus we speak of youthful vigor, youthful employments, juvenile performances, juvenile years, and the like, but of puerile objections, puerile conduct, and the like. We expect nothing from a youth but what is juvenile; we are surprised and dissatisfied to see what is puerile in a man.

***Antonyms.*—Mature, adult, manly, womanly.**

KEY TO THE DICTIONARY OF SYNONYMS

The following is an index or a key to the synonyms which occur in the preceding section. It will be noticed that some words are in italics, while others are in roman type. The words in italics are *key* words; that is, each italicized word is the first word of a group of synonyms. By reference to the page indicated, the key word can be quickly found by reason of the alphabetic arrangement which has been observed in the text of the section. Words in roman type in the index are not key words but are synonyms of the key word. Each word in roman type is immediately followed by a word in italics, which is always the *key* word under which the word in roman type is to be found.

DICTIONARY OF LATIN WORDS AND PHRASES

A considerable number of Latin words and phrases have found their way into English. Some of these are familiar legal terms; some are church terms; some are quotations from poets; and some are merely convenient expressions without an exact English equivalent. Often they cannot be understood without some information in regard to the manner in which they were used in the past. It is frequently necessary to know the meaning which was attached to such phrases by those who spoke Latin and also to know the precise sense in which they have come to be employed in English. Such information is seldom given in the ordinary Latin dictionaries and yet it is necessary for an adequate understanding of the terms. The following is a list of Latin words and phrases which are frequently met with; it is particularly valuable in that it contains the pronunciation and the meaning of all terms used.

Roman Pronunciation. The Roman method of pronunciation is an approximation to the ancient pronunciation of the Latin language, or to that used by the Romans themselves in the days of Cicero and Augustus. It is the system now used almost exclusively in the public schools, and is the one employed in the preparation of the following list.

But many Latin words and phrases have become so thoroughly anglicized that it would be pedantic to disregard their customary English pronunciation. Therefore, the English pronunciation of an anglicized word or phrase is given in parenthesis immediately after the Roman.

The key to the English pronunciation will be found on page 19.

The key to the Roman method is as follows:

Vowels and Diphthongs

Long vowels (marked ¯) are supposed to take twice as long to utter as short vowels (marked ˘). All diphthongs are long. The following table shows the *approximate* sound of the Latin vowels and diphthongs:—

ā is pronounced like *a* in *father*
ă is pronounced like *a* in *what*
ē is pronounced like *e* in *prey*
ĕ is pronounced like *e* in *met*
ī is pronounced like *i* in *machine*
ĭ is pronounced like *i* in *pin*
ō is pronounced like *o* in *note* (close *o*)
ŏ is pronounced like *aw* in *law* (open *o*—uttered very rapidly)
ū is pronounced like *u* in *rude*
ŭ is pronounced like *u* in *pull*
ȳ is pronounced like *French u* or *German ü*
y̆ is pronounced like *French u* or *German ü* (but uttered very rapidly)
ae is pronounced like *ai* in *aisle*
au is pronounced like *ow* in *how*
eu is pronounced like *eh-oo* (run rapidly together)
oi is pronounced like *oi* in *boil*

Consonants

The consonants have *approximately* the same sounds as in English, with the following exceptions:—

c is pronounced like *k* (never like *s*)
g is pronounced like *g* in *get* (never like English *j*)
j is pronounced like *y* in *yet* (never like English *j*)
s is pronounced like *s* in *sin* (never like *z*)
t is pronounced like *t* in *tin* (never like *sh*)
v is pronounced like *w* in *win* (never like *v* in *very*)
ch* is pronounced like *k-h* (in *back home*)
ph* is pronounced like *p-h* (in *up hill*)
th* is pronounced like *t-h* (in *at home*)

* But these three aspirates are commonly, if improperly, pronounced as *k*, *f*, and *th* (in *thin*) respectively.

AB EXTRA, *ăb ĕx′tră.* Without, from outside; as, influence *ab extra.*

AB IMO PECTORE, *ăb ī′mō pĕc′tŏ-rĕ.* From the bottom of one's heart.

AB INITIO, *ăb ĭn-ĭ′tĭ-ō (ăb ĭn-ĭsh′ĭ-ō).* From the beginning.

AB OVO AD MALA, *ăb ō′vō ăd mā′lă.* From the eggs to the apples; from beginning to end. The Roman dinner began with eggs and ended with apples.

ABSIT OMEN, *ăb′sĭt ō′mĕn.* May no harm come from it, that is, from a word just used.

AB UNO DISCE OMNES, *ăb ū′nō dĭs′cĕ ŏm′nēs.* From one specimen, judge of the rest.

AB URBE CONDITA, *ăb ŭr′bĕ cŏn′dĭ-tā.* From the foundation of the city,—Rome.

ABUSUS NON TOLLIT USUM, *ă-bū′sŭs nōn tŏl′lĭt ū′sŭm.* Abuse of a thing does not argue its uselessness.

AD ASTRA PER ASPERA, *ăd ăs′tră pĕr ăs′pĕ-ră.* To the stars through difficulties. Motto of Kansas.

AD CALENDAS GRÆCAS, *ăd că-lĕn′dās græ′cās.* At the Greek calends; never. The Greeks had no calends.

AD CAPTANDUM VULGUS, *ăd căp-tăn′dŭm vŭl′gŭs.* To attract the rabble, like "playing to the gallery."

AD INFINITUM, *ăd ĭn′fĭ-nī′tŭm (ăd ĭn′fĭn-ī′tŭm).* To infinity; without end.

AD LIBITUM, *ăd lĭb′ĭ-tŭm.* At one's pleasure.

AD MULTOS ANNOS, *ăd mŭl′tōs ăn′nōs.* For many years to come; long life! (a toast).

AD NAUSEAM, *ăd nau′sĕ-ăm (ăd nô′sē-ăm).* To the point of disgusting or nauseating.

AD REM, *ăd rĕm.* To the purpose; to the point.

AD UNGUEM, *ăd ŭn′guĕm.* To the finger nail; to a nicety. The ancient sculptors used the nail to put the finishing touches when modeling.

AD USUM, *ăd ū′sŭm.* For the use of.

AD VALOREM, *ăd vă-lō′rĕm (ăd văl-ō′rĕm).* According to value.

ADVORSUM STIMULUM CALCES, *ăd-vŏr′sŭm stĭm′ŭ-lŭm căl′cēs.* To kick against the pricks.—Terence.

ÆQUO ANIMO, *æ′quō ăn′ĭ-mō.* With a calm mind; with equanimity.

ÆTATIS SUÆ, *æ-tā′tĭs sū′æ.* Aged; in the year of his or her age.

ÆTERNUM VALE! *æ-tĕr′nŭm vă′lē.* Farewell forever!

A FORTIORI, *ā fŏr′tĭ-ō′rī (ā fôr′shĭ-ō′rī).* For the stronger reason; all the more.

ALIAS, *ă′lĭ-ăs (ā′lĭ-ăs).* Otherwise; generally indicating the variant of a name.

ALMA MATER, *ăl′mă mā′tĕr (ăl′mà mā′tẽr).* Beloved or foster mother; one's college or university.

ALTER EGO, *ăl′tĕr ĕ′gŏ (ăl′tẽr ē′gō).* Another or second self.

ANNO DOMINI, *ăn′nō dŏ′mĭ-nī (ăn′ō dŏm′ĭ-nī).* In the year of our Lord. *A. D.*

ANNO HEGIRÆ, *ăn′nō hĕ-gī′ræ (ăn′ō hē-jī′rē).* In the year of the Hegira (622 A. D.). A Mohammedan method of dating.

ANNO URBIS CONDITÆ, *ăn′nō ŭr′bĭs cŏn′dĭ-tæ.* In the year of the founding of the city (Rome, 753 B. C.). A Roman method of dating. *A.U.C.*

ANTE BELLUM, *ăn′tĕ bĕl′lŭm (ăn′tē bĕl′ŭm).* Before the war.

A POSSE AD ESSE, *ā pŏs′sĕ ăd ĕs′sĕ.* From possibility to actuality.

A POSTERIORI, *ā pŏs′tĕ-rĭ-ō′rī (ā pŏs′tē-rĭ-ō′rī).* By induction; an *a posteriori* argument,—inferring causes from effects.

A PRIORI, *ā prī-ō′rī (ā prī-ō′rī).* Deductively; an *a priori* argument,—one which infers effects from known causes.

AQUÆ POTORIBUS, *ă′quæ pō-tō′rĭ-bŭs.* By water drinkers. Horace wrote that their poems could not live.

ARS ARTIUM, *ărs ăr′tĭ-ŭm.* Art of arts,—logic.

ARS ARTIUM OMNIUM CONSERVATRIX, *ărs ăr′tĭ-ŭm ŏm′nĭ-ŭm cōn′sĕr-vā′trĭx.* The art preservative of all arts,—printing.

ARS EST CELARE ARTEM, *ărs ĕst cē-lā′rĕ ăr′tĕm.* Art is to conceal art.

ARS LONGA, VITA BREVIS, *ărs lŏn′gă vī′tă brĕ′vĭs.* Art is long, life is short. A Latin translation from Hippocrates.

ARTIUM MAGISTER, *ăr′tĭ-ŭm mă-gĭs′tĕr (är′shĭ-ŭm mà-jĭs′tẽr).* Master of arts.

ASINUS AD LYRAM, *ăs′ĭ-nŭs ăd ly̆′răm.* An ass at the harp; an awkward fellow.

ASINUS AISNUM FRICAT, *ăs′ĭ-nŭs ăs′ĭ-nŭm frī′căt.* One donkey rubs another. Used of two people extravagantly flattering each other.

AUDACES FORTUNA JUVAT, *au-dā′cēs fŏr-tū′nă jŭ′văt.* Fortune favors the bold. A paraphrase from Virgil.

AUDI ALTERAM PARTEM, *au′dī ăl′tĕr-ăm păr′tĕm.* Hear the other side (of an argument).

AUREA MEDIOCRITAS, *au′rĕ-ă mĕ′dĭ-ŏ′crĭ-tās.* The golden mean. A paraphrase from Horace.

AURES HABENT ET NON AUDIENT, *au′rēs hă′bĕnt ĕt nōn au′dĭ-ĕnt.* They have ears and will not hear. Applicable to obstinate people.

AURI SACRA FAMES, *au′rī să′cră fă′mēs.* The cursed hunger for gold.—Virgil.

AUSTRIÆ EST IMPERARE ORBI UNIVERSO, *aus′trĭ-æ ĕst ĭm′-pĕ-rā′rĕ ŏr′bī ū′nĭ-vĕr′sō.* Austria shall rule the world. The ambitious device of Austria, written AEIOU.

AUT CÆSAR AUT NIHIL, *aut cæ′săr aut nĭ′hĭl.* Either Cæsar or nothing. A saying attributed to Cæsar Borgia and applicable to those unduly ambitious.

AUT VINCERE AUT MORI, *aut vĭn′cĕ-rĕ aut mŏ′rī.* To conquer or die.

AVE, IMPERATOR! MORITURI TE SALUTANT, *ă′vē ĭm′pĕ-rā′tŏr mŏ′rĭ-tū′rī tē să-lū′tănt.* Hail, Emperor! Those about to die salute thee.—Suetonius. Cry of the Roman gladiators on entering the arena.

BEATÆ MEMORIÆ, *bĕ-ā′tæ mĕ-mŏ′rĭ-æ.* Of blessed or happy memory.

BELLA MATRIBUS DETESTATA, *bĕl′lă mā′trĭ-bŭs dĕ′tĕs-tā′tă.* Wars hated by mothers.—Horace.

BIS DAT QUI CITO DAT, *bĭs dăt quī cĭ′tŏ dăt.* He gives twice who gives in a trice.

BIS PECCARE IN BELLO NON LICET, *bĭs pĕc-cā′rĕ ĭn bĕl′lō nōn lĭ′cĕt.* One must not blunder twice in war.

BIS PUERI SENES, *bĭs pŭ′ĕ-rī sĕ′nēs.* Old men are in second childhood.

BONA FIDE, *bŏ′nă fĭ′dē (bō′nà fī′dē).* In good faith.

BONA FIDES, *bŏ′nă fĭ′dēs (bō′nà fī′dēz).* Good faith; word of honor.

BONUM VINUM LÆTIFICAT COR HOMINIS, *bŏ′nŭm vī′nŭm læ-tĭ′fĭ-căt cŏr hŏm′ĭ-nĭs.* Good wine gladdens man's heart.

CACOETHES SCRIBENDI, *că′cŏ-ē′thĕs scrī-bĕn′dī.* The incurable passion for scribbling.—Juvenal.

CÆLUM, NON ANIMUM, MUTANT QUI TRANS MARE CURRUNT, *cæ′lŭm nōn ă′nĭ-mŭm mū′tănt quī trāns mă′rĕ cŭr′rŭnt.* They change their sky, not their mind, who run across the sea.—Horace.

CARCERE DURO, *căr′cĕ-rĕ dū′rō.* In durance vile; at hard labor.

CARPE DIEM, *căr′pĕ dĭ′ĕm.* Seize the day, enjoy life.—Horace.

CASUS BELLI, *cā′sŭs bĕl′lī (kā′sŭs bĕl′ī).* The cause that brings about war.

CAVEAT EMPTOR, *kā′vĕ-ăt ĕmp′tŏr.* Let the buyer beware. An old maxim of the common law, which still applies to titles of real estate transferred.

CEDANT ARMA TOGÆ, *cē′dănt ăr′mă tŏ′gæ.* Let arms give place to the toga.—Cicero. Let the statesman's glory outshine the soldier's.

CENSOR DEPUTATUS, *cēn′sŏr dē′pŭ-tā′tŭs.* A deputed censor; one empowered to examine books, plays, etc., before publication.

CETERA DESUNT, *cē′tĕ-ră dē′sŭnt.* The rest is wanting; an incomplete work.

CETERIS PARIBUS, *cē′tĕ-rĭs păr′ĭ-bŭs.* Other things being equal,—expressing a condition.

CIVIS ROMANUS SUM, *cī′vĭs rō-mā′nŭs sŭm.* I am a Roman citizen.

CLARUM ET VENERABILE NOMEN, *clā′rŭm ĕt vĕ′nĕ-rā′bĭ-lĕ nō′mĕn.* Illustrious and venerable name. Used when that of some celebrated person is mentioned.

COGITO, ERGO SUM, *cō′gĭ-tō ĕr′gō sŭm.* I think, therefore I exist. The basis of Descartes's philosophy.

CONSENSUS OMNIUM, *cōn-sēn′sŭs ŏm′nĭ-ŭm.* Universal agreement.

CONSILIO MANUQUE, *cōn-sĭl′ĭ-ō mă-nū′quĕ.* By deftness and the hand. Motto of the Barber of Seville.

CONSUETUDO PRO LEGE SERVATUR, *cōn′suĕ-tū′dō prō lē′gĕ sĕr-vā′tŭr.* Custom is held as law. The basis of English common law.

CORAM POPULO, *cō′răm pŏ′pŭ-lō.* Before the people; publicly.

CORPUS DELICTI, *cŏr′pŭs dē-lĭc′tī.* The body of a crime; anything which serves to prove its commission; essential proof in a case.

CREDAT JUDÆUS APELLA, NON EGO, *crē′dăt jū-dæ′ŭs ă-pĕl′lă nōn ĕ′gŏ.* The Jew, Apella, may believe it, not I.—Horace. The Jews were regarded by the Romans as highly superstitious.

CREDO QUIA ABSURDUM, *crē′dō quĭ′ă ăb-sŭr′dŭm.* I believe because it is absurd; the conquest of reason by faith.

CRESCIT AMOR NUMMI, QUANTUM IPSA PECUNIA CRESCIT, *crēs′cĭt ă′mŏr nŭm′mī quăn′tŭm ĭp′să pĕ-cū′nĭ-ă crēs′cĭt.* As wealth increases, so does the love of it.

CRUX, *crŭx.* A cross, a difficulty; as, the crux of the matter.

CUCULLUS NON FACIT MONACHUM, *cŭ-cŭl′lŭs nōn fă′cĭt mŏ′nă-chŭm.* The cowl does not make the monk; appearances are deceiving.

CUI BONO? *cŭ′ī bŏ′nō (kī bō′nō).* To whose advantage? The criminal may possibly be traced by the answer to the question.

CUI FORTUNA IPSA CEDIT, *cŭ′ī fŏr-tū′nă ĭp′să cē′dĭt.* To whom Fortune herself yields; that is, a lucky person.

CUIQUE SUUM, *cŭ′ī quĕ sū′ŭm.* Let each one have his own.

CUM GRANO SALIS, *cŭm grā′nō să′lĭs.* With a pinch of salt; not to be taken seriously.

CURIOSA FELICITAS, *cū′rĭ-ō′să fē-lī′cĭ-tās.* The happy knack (of writing). Said of Horace.

CURRENTE CALAMO, *cŭr-rĕn′tĕ că′lă-mō.* With a running pen; without much reflection.

DA LOCUM MELIORIBUS, *dā lŏ′cŭm mĕ′lĭ-ō′rĭ-bŭs.* Give place to your betters.

Date obolum Belisario, *dā'tē ŏb'ō-lŭm bĕl'ĭ-sā'rĭ-ō.* Give an alms to Belisarius; lend a helping hand to one who has known better days.

Dat veniam corvis, vexat censura columbas, *dăt vē'nĭ-ăm cŏr'vĭs vĕx'ăt cĕn-sū'ră cō-lŭm'băs.* Censure spares the crows and persecutes the doves. Applied to unfair or partial criticism.

De auditu, *dē au-dĭ'tū.* From hearsay.

De facto, *dē făc'tō.* Actually; as a matter of fact.

De gustibus et coloribus non est disputandum, *dē gŭs'tĭ-bŭs ĕt cŏ-lō'rĭ-bŭs nōn ĕst dĭs'pŭ-tăn'dŭm.* There's no use disputing about tastes or colors,—an old scholastic proverb.

Dei gratia, *dē'ī grā'tĭ-ā (dē'ī grā'shĭ-ȧ).* By the grace or favor of God. Part of the inscription on British coinage.

De jure, *dē jū'rĕ (dē jū'rē).* Lawfully, by right.

Delenda est Carthago, *dē-lĕn'dȧ ĕst căr-thā'gō.* Carthage must be destroyed. Applicable to the intention of overcoming a difficulty.

De mortuis nil nisi bonum, *dē mŏr'tŭ-īs nīl nĭ'sī bŏ'nŭm.* Say nothing but good of the dead.

De minimis non curat lex, *dē mĭ'nĭ-mīs nōn cū'răt lēx.* The law pays no attention to trifles.

Dente lupus, cornu taurus petit, *dĕn'tĕ lŭ'pŭs cŏr'nū tau'rŭs pĕ'tĭt.* The wolf attacks with his teeth, the bull with his horns.—Horace. Use the gifts you have to best advantage.

Dente superbo, *dĕn'tĕ sŭ-pĕr'bō.* With disdainful tooth. —Horace. Used of accepting a gift gracelessly, especially from an inferior.

Dentibus albis, *dĕn'tĭ-bŭs ăl'bīs.* With white teeth; biting satirically without drawing blood—without hurting; jocosely.

Deo adjuvante, *dĕ'ō ăd'jŭ-văn'tĕ.* With the help of God.

Deo gratias, *dĕ'ō grā'tĭ-ās (dē'ō grā'shĭ-ăs).* Thanks be to God. Used in the liturgy of the Mass.

De omni re scibili et quibusdam aliis, *dē ŏm'nī rē scĭ'bĭ-lī ĕt quĭ-bŭs'dăm ă'lĭ-īs.* About everything knowable and more besides. A sarcasm attributed to Voltaire in reference to a young writer.

Deo volente, *dĕ'ō vŏ-lĕn'tĕ.* God willing. *D. V.*

De profundis, *dē prŏ-fŭn'dīs.* Out of the depths. An appeal made *de profundis*, that is, in dire distress.

Deus ex machina, *dĕ'ŭs ĕx măch'ĭn-ā.* A god from a machine; an artificial solution of a problem, from the practice in the Greek drama of introducing a god by stage machinery to bring an otherwise insoluble plot to a satisfactory end.

Dies iræ, *dĭ'ēs ī'rœ.* The day of wrath; the judgment day. The title of a celebrated Latin hymn.

Dii penates, *dĭ'ī pĕ-nā'tēs (dī'ī pē-nā'tēz).* Household gods. Said of valuable ornaments, furniture, etc.

Disjecta membra poetæ, *dĭs-jĕc'tă mĕm'bră pŏ-ē'tœ.* The scattered remains of the poet.—Horace. The fate of poetry transformed into prose.

Displicuit nasus tuus, *dĭs-plĭc'ŭ-ĭt nā'sŭs tŭ'ŭs.* Your nose has displeased you.—Juvenal. Said of one annoyed at trifles; a victim of caprice.

Divide et impera, *dĭ'vĭ-dĕ ĕt ĭm'pĕ-rā.* Divide and rule. A motto of Roman imperialism.

Doctus cum libro, *dŏc'tŭs cŭm lĭ'brō.* Learned with the aid of a book.

Dominus vobiscum, *dŏm'ĭ-nŭs vō-bĭs'cŭm.* The Lord be with you,—words used frequently in the Roman liturgy.

Donec eris felix multos numerabis amicos, *dō'nĕc ĕ'rĭs fē'līx mŭl'tōs nŭ'mĕ-rā'bĭs ă-mī'cōs.* While you are happy, you will count many friends.—Ovid.

Dulce et decorum est pro patria mori, *dŭl'cĕ ĕt dĕ-cō'rŭm ĕst prō pă'trĭ-ā mŏ'rī.* It is sweet and glorious to die for one's country.—Horace.

Dura lex sed lex, *dū'ră lēx sĕd lēx.* 'Tis a hard law, but it's law. Said of a harsh and unnecessary measure.

Dux femina facti, *dŭx fē'mĭ-nă făc'tī.* A woman was the leader in the adventure.—Virgil.

Ecce homo! *ĕc'cĕ hŏ'mō (ĕk'sē hō'mō).* Behold the man! Applied specifically to any picture of Christ wearing the crown of thorns.

Ecce iterum Crispinus! *ĕc'cĕ ĭ'tĕ-rŭm crĭs-pī'nŭs.* Here comes Crispin again!—Juvenal. Used in reference to an unwelcome bore.

Editio princeps, *ē-dĭ'tĭ-ō prĭn'cĕps (ē-dĭsh'ĭ-ō prĭn'sĕps).* A first edition of a printed work.

Ego sum Qui sum, *ĕ'gō sŭm quī sŭm.* I am who I am.—Exodus III:14. The answer of the Supreme Being to Moses.

Eheu! fugaces labuntur anni, *ē'heu fŭ-gā'cēs lā-bŭn'tŭr ăn'nī.* Alas! how the years slip by.—Horace.

Ejusdem farinæ, *ē-jŭs'dĕm fă-rī'nœ.* Of the same flour or dough. Used disparagingly of people having the same faults or failings.

Epicuri de grege porcum, *ĕp-ĭ-cū'rī dē grĕ'gĕ pŏr'cŭm.* A pig from the sty of Epicurus.—Horace. Said of those who love good things, the sensuous.

E pluribus unum, *ē plū'rĭ-bŭs ū'nŭm* From many, one. Motto of the United States of America.

Errare est humanum, *ĕr-rā'rĕ ĕst hū-mā'nŭm.* To err is human.

Esse quam videri, *ĕs'sĕ quăm vĭ-dē'rī.* To be, rather than to seem.

Est modus in rebus, *ĕst mŏ'dŭs ĭn rē'bŭs.* There's a measure in all things.—Horace. Meaning,—excess in anything is a fault.

Esto quod esse videris, *ĕs'tō quŏd ĕs'sĕ vĭ-dē'rĭs.* Be what you seem to be.

Et cetera, *ĕt cē'tĕ-ră (ĕt sĕt'ē-rȧ).* And the rest; *etc., &c.*

Etiamsi omnes, ego non, *ĕt-ĭ-ăm'sī ŏm'nēs ĕ'gŏ nōn.* Even should all fail thee, I will not. A phrase expressive of undying friendship.

Et in Arcadia ego! *ĕt ĭn ăr-cā'dĭ-ā ĕ'gō.* I, too, once lived in Arcadia! An exclamation of regret for happiness no longer possessed.

Et sequentia, *ĕt sĕ-quĕn'tĭ-ă.* And what follows; *et seq.*

Et sic de similibus, *ĕt sīc dē sĭ-mĭl'ĭ-bŭs.* And so of similar things.

Et tu, Brute! *ĕt tū brū'tĕ.* And thou also, Brutus! Usually given as the last words of Julius Cæsar, when he saw Brutus among his murderers.

Ex abrupto, *ĕx ă-brŭp'tō.* Suddenly, unexpected; as, an argument *ex abrupto*.

Ex æquo, *ĕx œ'quō.* Equal in merit; a prize won by two.

Ex cathedra, *ĕx că'thĕ-drā (ĕks kă'thē-drȧ).* "From the chair." A statement bearing unquestionable authority.

Ex dono, *ĕx dō'nō.* As a gift. Used preceding the name of a public benefactor on what he has presented.

Exegi monumentum ære perennius, *ĕx-ē'gī mŏn'ŭ-mĕn'tŭm œ'rĕ pĕr-ĕn'nĭ-ŭs.* I have executed a monument more lasting than brass.—Horace. The poet's work will outlast all material monuments.

Exempli gratia, *ĕx-ĕm'plī grā'tĭ-ā (ĕg-zĕm'plī grā'shĭ-ȧ).* By way of example,—written *e.g.*

Exeunt omnes; exit, *ĕx'ĕ-ŭnt ŏm'nēs ĕx'ĭt (ĕks'ē-ŭnt ŏm'nēz ĕk'sĭt).* All go out; he or she goes out.

Ex nihilo nihil fit, *ĕx nĭ'hĭ-lō nĭ'hĭl fĭt.* From nothing, nothing comes.

Ex ore infantium veritas, *ĕx ō'rĕ ĭn-făn'tĭ-ŭm vē'rĭ-tās.* Truth from the mouths of children,—an adage sometimes too true.

Ex parte, *ĕx păr'tĕ.* On one side only. An *ex parte* argument.

Expende Hannibalem, *ĕx-pĕn'dĕ hăn-nĭ'bă-lĕm.* Weigh Hannibal.—Juvenal. How much for human glory?

Experto crede, *ĕx-pĕr'tō crē'dĕ.* Believe one who has tried it.—Virgil.

Ex tempore, *ĕx tĕm'pŏ-rĕ (ĕks tĕm'pō-rē).* Offhand; without preparation.

Ex ungue leonem, *ĕx ŭn'guĕ lĕ-ō'nĕm.* From the claw you tell the lion. A great artist is recognized by the slightest detail of his work.

Facile princeps, *fă'cĭ-lĕ prĭn'cĕps (făs'ĭ-lē prĭn'sĕps).* The acknowledged chief; one who stands indisputably first.—Cicero.

Facilis descensus Averni, *fă'cĭ-lĭs dē-scĕn'sŭs ă-vĕr'nī.* The descent to hell is easy.—Virgil. It is easy enough to get into trouble.

Fama volat, *fā'mă vŏ'lăt.* Fame flies,—expressing the rapidity with which news is spread.

Favete linguis, *fă-vē'tĕ lĭn'guīs.* Favor with your tongues; preserve a religious silence.

Favores sunt ampliandi, *fă-vō'rēs sŭnt ăm'plĭ-ăn'dī.* Favors should be taken in an enlarged sense.

Felix culpa, *fē'līx cŭl'pă.* Happy fault.—St. Augustine. Applicable when a mistake turns out to be a benefit.

Feræ naturæ, *fĕ'rœ nā-tū'rœ.* Of a wild nature. Applied to wild beasts.

Fervet opus, *fĕr'vĕt ŏ'pŭs.* The work goes feverishly on.—Virgil. Used in reference to bees; said of one who loves his work.

Festina lente, *fēs-tī'nă lĕn'tē.* Make haste slowly; don't rush serious work.

Fiat justitia ruat cælum, *fī'ăt jūs-tĭ'tĭ-ă rŭ'ăt cœ'lŭm.* Let justice be done though the heavens should fall.

Fiat lux, *fī'ăt lūx.* Let there be light.

Fidei defensor, *fĭ'dĕ-ī dē-fĕn'sŏr.* Defender of the faith.

Fidus Achates, *fī'dŭs ă-chā'tēs (fī'dŭs ȧ-kā'tēz).* Faithful Achates.—Virgil. A trusty friend.

Fieri facias, *fī'ĕ-rī fă'cĭ-ās (fī'ē-rī fā'shĭ-ăs).* A legal paper authorizing execution on the goods of a debtor.

Finis coronat opus, *fī'nĭs cŏ-rō'năt ŏ'pŭs.* The end crowns the work; you judge the work by the result.

Flagrante delicto, *flă-grăn'tĕ dē-lĭc'tō.* The crime blazing; red-handed; in the very act.

Fluctuat nec mergitur, *flŭc'tŭ-ăt nĕc mĕr'gĭ-tŭr.* Wave-tossed but does not sink. Motto of the city of Paris. One unaffected by failures.

Fœnum habet in cornu, *fœ'nŭm hă'bĕt ĭn cŏr'nū.* He has hay on his horns.—Horace. Meaning,—a dangerous fellow.

Fortiter, fideliter, feliciter, *fŏr'tĭ-tĕr fĭ-dĕl'ĭ-tĕr fē-lĭc'ĭ-tĕr.* Boldly, faithfully, successfully.

Fortiter in re, *fŏr'tĭ-tĕr ĭn rē.* With firmness in action.

Fugit irreparabile tempus, *fū′gĭt ĭr′rē-pă-rā′bĭ-lĕ tĕm′-pŭs.* Time flies, never to be recalled.—Virgil.
Fuit Ilium, *fū′ĭt ĭ′lĭ-ŭm.* Troy *has* been; it no longer stands.—Virgil.

Gaudeamus igitur, *gaud-ē-ā′mŭs ĭ′gĭ-tŭr.* Therefore, let us rejoice,—the burden of a macaronic song.
Gens togata, *gēns tŏ-gā′tă.* Civilians. The toga was the national dress of the Romans in time of peace.
Genus irritabile vatum, *gĕ′nŭs ĭr′rĭ-tā′bĭ-lĕ vā′tŭm.* Irritable race of poets.—Horace. Used to express the sensitiveness of men of letters.
Gloria in excelsis Deo, *glō′rĭ-ă ĭn ĕx-cĕl′sĭs dĕ′ō (glō′rĭ-á ĭn ĕk-sĕl′sĭs dē′ō).* Glory to God in the highest.
Gradus ad Parnassum, *grā′dŭs ăd păr-nās′sŭm.* A step to Parnassus; aid in writing Latin poetry; a work on Latin verse-making containing rules and examples.
Græcum est, non legitur, *græ′cŭm ĕst nōn lĕ′gĭ-tŭr.* It is Greek, so skip it; don't meddle with what you know nothing about.
Gratis pro Deo, *grā′tĭs prō dĕ′ō.* Freely for God,—the manner in which charity should be bestowed.

Habeas corpus, *hă′bĕ-ās cŏr′pŭs (hā′bē-ăs côr′pŭs).* Have the body. A writ issued for the purpose of bringing a person before a court or a judge, usually to determine whether he should be retained in custody or given his freedom.
Hannibal ad portas, *hăn′nĭ-băl ăd pŏr′tās.* Hannibal at the gates; the enemy is at hand.
Hic et nunc, *hĭc ĕt nŭnc.* Here and now.
Hic jacet, *hĭc jă′cĕt (hĭk jā′sĕt).* Here lies. Inscribed on tombstones.
Hinc illæ lacrimæ, *hĭnc ĭl′læ lă′crĭ-mæ.* Hence these tears.—Terence. This is the cause of the trouble.
Hodie mihi, cras tibi, *hŏ′dĭ-ē mĭ′hĭ crās tĭ′bĭ.* Today me, tomorrow you,—a warning to prepare for trouble.
Homo homini lupus, *hŏ′mō hŏm′ĭ-nĭ lŭ′pŭs.* Man is a wolf toward his fellow man.—Plautus.
Homo sum; humani nihil a me alienum puto, *hŏ′mō sŭm hū-mā′nĭ nĭ′hĭl ā mē ă′lĭ-ē′nŭm pŭ′tō.* I am a man; there is naught which touches man that is not my concern.—Terence.
Honos alit artes, *hŏn′ōs ă′lĭt ăr′tēs.* Honor nourishes the arts.—Cicero. It is indifference that kills them.
Horresco referens, *hŏr-rēs′cō rĕ′fĕ-rēns.* I tremble telling it.—Virgil. Words often used jocosely.
Hortus siccus, *hŏr′tŭs sĭc′cŭs.* A dry garden; a collection of dried plants; a herbarium.

Impavidum ferient ruinæ, *ĭm-păv′ĭ-dŭm fĕr′ĭ-ĕnt rŭ-ĭ′næ.* The ruins of the world strike but leave him undaunted.—Horace. Said of a man of resolute character.
Imperium in imperio, *ĭm-pĕ′rĭ-ŭm ĭn ĭm-pĕ′rĭ-ō.* A government existing within another. Said of a power set up against constituted authority.
Imprimatur, *ĭm′prĭ-mā′tŭr.* It may be published. A censor's permission at the beginning of certain Catholic works.
In articulo mortis, *ĭn ăr-tĭc′ŭ-lō mŏr′tĭs.* At the point of death; the same as *in extremis.*
In camera, *ĭn că′mĕ-rā.* In the judge's chamber; in secret.
In cauda venenum, *ĭn cau′dā vĕ-nē′nŭm.* Poison, sting in the tail; a speech beginning blandly and ending bitingly.
Incidis in Scyllam cupiens vitare Charybdin, *ĭn′cĭ-dĭs ĭn scy̆l′lăm cŭ′pĭ-ēns vĭ-tā′rĕ chă-ry̆b′dĭn.* You fall into Scylla trying to avoid Charybdis; from the frying pan into the fire.
Inde iræ, *ĭn′dĕ ĭ′ræ.* Hence the reason of his anger.—Juvenal.
In esse, *ĭn ĕs′sĕ.* In being.
In extenso, *ĭn ĕx-tēn′sō (ĭn ĕks-tĕn′sô).* Entirely, at full length; as, to treat a subject *in extenso.*
In extremis, *ĭn ĕx-trē′mĭs (ĭn ĕks-trē′mĭs).* In very bad circumstances; at the point of death.
Infandum, Regina, jubes renovare dolorem, *ĭn-făn′dŭm rē-gĭ′nă jū′bēs rĕ′nŏ-vā′rĕ dŏ-lō′rĕm.* You command me, O Queen, to renew unspeakable sorrow.—Virgil.
In foro conscientiæ, *ĭn fŏ′rô cōn′scĭ-ĕn′tĭ-æ.* In the tribunal of one's own conscience; privately.
Infra dignitatem, *ĭn′frā dĭg′nĭ-tā′tĕm.* Beneath one's dignity, *infra dig.*
In globo, *ĭn glŏ′bō.* Altogether; taken as a whole.
In hoc signo vinces, *ĭn hōc sĭg′nō vĭn′cēs (ĭn hŏk sĭg′nô vĭn′sēz).* In this sign thou shalt conquer. The motto is said to have been adopted by Constantine after his vision of a cross in the heavens just before his decisive battle with Maxentius, 312 A. D.
Initium sapientiæ timor Domini, *ĭ-nĭ′tĭ-ŭm să′pĭ-ĕn′tĭ-æ tĭm′ŏr dŏm′ĭ-nī.* The fear of the Lord is the beginning of wisdom.
In loco parentis, *ĭn lŏ′cō pă-rĕn′tĭs (ĭn lō′kô pá-rĕn′tĭs).* In the place of a parent.
In medias res, *ĭn mĕ′dĭ-ās rēs.* Into the middle of the subject; without wasting words.
In medio stat virtus, *ĭn mĕ′dĭ-ō stăt vĭr′tŭs.* Virtue stands in the middle,—equally distant from extreme views.

In memoriam, *ĭn mĕ-mŏ′rĭ-ăm (ĭn mē-mō′rĭ-ăm).* In memory of.
In perpetuam rei memoriam, *ĭn pĕr-pĕt′ŭ-ăm rĕ′ĭ mĕ-mŏ′rĭ-ăm.* In everlasting remembrance of the event.
In poculis, *ĭn pŏ′cŭ-lĭs.* In his cups; while drunk; also *inter pocula.*
In posse, *ĭn pŏs′sĕ.* In possible existence.
In propria persona, *ĭn prŏ′prĭ-ā pĕr-sŏ′nā.* In one's own person.
(In) re, *ĭn rē (ĭn rē).* In the matter of, concerning; as, *(in) re* the election.
In situ, *ĭn sĭ′tū (ĭn sī′tû).* In position; the actual spot. A phrase especially employed in mineralogy.
In solido, *ĭn sŏl′ĭ-dō.* In the lump; as, to condemn a thing *in solido.*
Instar omnium, *ĭn′stăr ŏm′nĭ-ŭm.* Like every one; as, to follow the fashion *instar omnium.*
In statu quo, *ĭn stă′tū quō (ĭn stā′tû kwō).* In its former state.
Integer vitæ scelerisque purus, *ĭn′tĕ-gĕr vī′tæ scĕ′lĕ-rĭs′quĕ pū′rŭs.* A man upright in life and free from blame.—Horace.
Intelligenti pauca, *ĭn-tĕl′lĭ-gĕn′tī pau′că.* But few words necessary for one who is intelligent (also *verbum sapienti, verb. sap.*).
In tempore opportuno, *ĭn tĕm′pŏ-rĕ ŏp′pŏr-tū′nō.* At the right moment.
Inter alia, *ĭn′tĕr ă′lĭ-ă (ĭn′ tĕr ā′lĭ-á).* Among other things.
Inter nos, *ĭn′tĕr nōs (ĭn′tĕr nōs).* Between, among ourselves.
In toto, *ĭn tō′tō.* In the whole; entirely.
Intus et in cute, *ĭn′tŭs ĕt ĭn cŭ′tĕ.* Inside and under the skin. Applicable to a good judge of character.
In vacuo, *ĭn vă′cŭ-ō (ĭn văk′ū-ô).* In a vacuum.
In vino veritas, *ĭn vī′nō vĕr′ĭ-tās.* In wine there's truth; a man becomes more confidential when he drinks.
Invita Minerva, *ĭn-vī′tā mĭ-nĕr′vā.* In spite of Minerva.—Horace. Said of one who writes without the necessary talent.
Ipse dixit, *ĭp′sĕ dĭx′ĭt (ĭp′sê dĭk′sĭt).* He himself has said it; a mere assertion.
Ipsissima verba, *ĭp-sĭs′sĭ-mă vĕr′bă.* The identical words.
Ipso facto, *ĭp′sō făc′tō (ĭp′sô făk′tô).* By the very fact; actually.
Ira furor brevis est, *ī′ră fū′rŏr brĕ′vĭs ĕst.* Anger is a short madness.—Horace.
Ita est, *ĭ′tă ĕst.* It is so.

Jacta alea esto, *jăc′tă ā′lĕ-ă ĕs′tō.* Let the die be cast.—Julius Cæsar. It is probable that the exact words uttered by Julius Cæsar on crossing the Rubicon were from a Greek play of Menander, the Latin being a translation.
Jus civile, *jūs cī-vī′lĕ (jŭs sĭ-vī′lê).* The law of citizens. The Roman law applied to citizens. See *Jus gentium.*
Jus est ars boni et justi, *jūs ĕst ărs bŏ′nī ĕt jūs′tī.* Right is the art of the good and of the just.
Jus et norma loquendi, *jūs ĕt nōr′mă lŏ-quĕn′dī.* The law and rule of language. Horace says that usage decides both.
Jus gentium, *jūs gĕn′tĭ-ŭm (jŭs jĕn′shĭ-ŭm).* The law of nations. The Roman law applied to foreigners, or between foreigners and citizens. See *Jus civile.*

Labor omnia vincit improbus, *lă′bŏr ŏm′nĭ-ă vĭn′cĭt ĭm′prŏ-bŭs.* Stubborn labor overcomes all things.—Virgil.
Lapsus calami, *lăp′sŭs că′lă-mī (lăp′sŭs kăl′â-mī).* A slip of the pen.
Lapsus linguæ, *lăp′sŭs lĭn′guæ (lăp′sŭs lĭng′gwē).* A slip of the tongue.
Lares et penates, *lă′rēs ĕt pĕ-nā′tēs (lā′rēz ĕt pē-nā′têz).* Household gods.
Latet anguis in herba, *lă′tĕt ăn′guĭs ĭn hĕr′bā.* A snake lies hid in the grass.—Virgil. Said by way of warning.
Lato sensu, *lā′tō sēn′sū.* In a broad sense; with a wide meaning.
Laudator temporis acti, *lau-dā′tŏr tĕm′pŏ-rĭs āc′tī.* One who praises the good old days,—generally to the disparagement of the present.—Horace.
Laus Deo, *laus dĕ′ō.* Praise to God.
Levius fit patientia quidquid corrigere est nefas, *lĕ′vĭ-ŭs fĭt pă′tĭ-ĕn′tĭ-ā quĭd′quĭd cŏr-rĭ′gĕ-rĕ ĕst nĕ′fās.* What cannot be cured may be lightened by patience.—Horace.
Lex talionis, *lēx tăl′ĭ-ō′nĭs.* The law of retaliation.
Loco citato, *lŏ′cō cĭ-tā′tō (lō′kô sĭ-tā′tō).* In the place quoted. (*loc. cit.*)
Loco dolenti, *lŏ′cō dŏ-lĕn′tī.* To the sore spot. Said of applying kind words to soothe a grievance.
Locum tenens, *lŏ′cŭm tĕ′nēns (lō′kŭm tē′nĕnz).* One occupying a place; a substitute; a proxy.
Locus classicus, *lŏ′cŭs clăs′sĭ-cŭs (lō′kŭs klăs′ĭ-kŭs).* A classical passage; the acknowledged place of reference.
Locus sigilli, *lŏ′cŭs sĭ-gĭl′lī (lō′kŭs sĭ-jĭl′lī).* The place for the seal. Usually abbreviated to *L.S.*
Lucidus ordo, *lū′cĭ-dŭs ŏr′dō.* A clear style in speaking or writing.
Lusus naturæ, *lū′sŭs nā-tū′ræ.* A sport of nature.

Magister dixit, *mă-gĭs'tĕr dĭx'ĭt (mȧ-jĭs'tĕr dĭks'ĭt).* The master has said it,—hence no more argument.

Magna cum laude, *măg'nă cŭm lau'dĕ.* With high honors.

Magni nominis umbra, *măg'nī nōm'ĭ-nĭs ŭm'bră.* The shadow of a great name.—Lucan. Said of one whose greatness is but a memory.

Magnum opus, *măg'nŭm ŏ'pŭs (măg'nŭm ō'pŭs).* A great undertaking; the great work of a man's life.

Major e longinquo reverentia, *mā'jŏr ē lŏn-gĭn'quō rĕv'ĕr-ĕn'tĭ-ă.* Distance increases reverence. To admire at a distance; used in a humorous sense.

Malesuada fames, *măl'ĕ-suā'dă fā'mēs.* Hunger is a bad adviser.—Virgil. Often it prompts to crime.

Manibus date lilia plenis, *măn'ĭ-bŭs dă'tĕ lĭl'ĭ-ă plē'nĭs.* Give lilies in handfuls,—said of one deeply mourned, especially a child.—Virgil.

Mater familias, *mā'tĕr fă-mĭ'lĭ-ās (mā'tĕr fȧ-mĭl'ĭ-ăs).* The mother of the family.

Materiam superabat opus, *mā-tē'rĭ-ăm sŭ'pĕ-rā'băt ŏ'pŭs.* The workmanship surpassed the materials.—Ovid.

Maxima debetur puero reverentia, *măx'ĭ-mă dē-bē'tŭr pŭ'ĕr-ō rĕv'ĕr-ĕn'tĭ-ă.* Greatest reverence is due to a child. —Juvenal. Nothing should be said to tarnish innocence.

Mea culpa, *mĕ'ă cŭl'pă (mē'ȧ kŭl'pȧ).* Through my fault.

Medice cura teipsum, *mĕd'ĭ-cĕ cū'ră tē-ĭp'sŭm.* Doctor, cure yourself; practice what you preach.

Melioribus annis, *mĕ-lĭ-ō'rĭ-bŭs ăn'nĭs.* In better years.—Virgil.

Memento homo quia pulvis es, *mĕ-mĕn'tō hŏ'mō quĭ'ă pŭl'vĭs ĕs.* Remember, man, thou art but dust.

Memento mori, *mĕ-mĕn'tō mŏ'rī.* Remember death.

Mens agitat molem, *mĕns ă'gĭ-tăt mō'lĕm.* The mind moves the mass; it's brains that count.

Mens sana in corpore sano, *mĕns sā-'nă ĭn cŏr'pŏ-rĕ sā-nō.* A sound mind in a sound body.—Juvenal. Often wrongly interpreted to mean that the one depends on the other.

Minima de malis, *mĭn'ĭ-mă dē mă'lĭs.* Of evils, choose the least.

Mirabile dictu, *mĭ-rā'bĭ-lĕ dĭc'tū.* Wonderful to relate.

Mirabile visu, *mĭ-rā'bĭ-lĕ vĭ'sū.* A wonderful sight.

Modus operandi, *mŏ'dŭs ŏ'pĕ-răn'dī (mō'dŭs ŏp-ĕr-ăn'dī).* Mode, or manner, of working.

Modus vivendi, *mŏ'dŭs vī-vĕn'dī (mō'dŭs vĭ-vĕn'dī).* Mode, or manner, of living.

Mors ultima ratio, *mŏrs ŭl'tĭ-mă ră'tĭ-ō.* Death is the last reason; it solves all riddles of life.

Multa paucis, *mŭl'tă pau'cĭs.* Many things in few words; conciseness.

Multi sunt vocati, pauci vero electi, *mŭl'tī sŭnt vō-cā'tī pau'cī vē'rō ē-lĕc'tī.* Many are called, but few are chosen.

Multum in parvo, *mŭl'tŭm ĭn păr'vō.* Much in little.

Mutato nomine, *mū-tā'tō nōm'ĭ-nĕ.* The name being changed; the story fits you.

Natura non facit saltus, *nā-tū'ră nōn fă'cĭt săl'tūs.* Nature does not leap or bound,—you cannot force her except at your own peril.

Necessitas non habet legem, *nĕ-cĕs'sĭ-tās nōn hă'bĕt lē'gĕm.* Necessity knows no law.

Nec mortale sonans, *nĕc mŏr-tā'lĕ sŏ'nāns.* 'Tis not a mortal voice that sounds. Applicable to great orators and poets.

Nec temere, nec timide, *nĕc tĕm'ĕ-rē nĕc tĭm'ĭ-dē.* Neither rashly nor timidly.

Ne plus ultra, *nē plūs ŭl'trā (nē plŭs ŭl'trȧ).* Nothing beyond. The *ne plus ultra* of elegance; also *nec* or *non plus ultra.* Hercules engraved these words on the summits of Abyla and Calpe, the modern Iebel Musa and Gibraltar, the "Pillars of Hercules."

Neque semper arcum tendit Apollo, *nĕ'quĕ sĕm'pĕr ăr'cŭm tĕn'dĭt ă-pŏl'lō.* Apollo is not always stretching his bow.—Horace. Apollo is not always the angry god of pestilence and sudden death; he is sometimes the kindly god of art and of healing.

Ne quid nimis, *nē quĭd nĭ'mĭs.* Let there be nothing too much; excess is a fault.

Nescit vox missa reverti, *nĕ'scĭt vōx mĭs'să rē-vĕr'tī.* A word uttered cannot be recalled.

Nihil obstat, *nĭ'hĭl ŏb'stăt.* Nothing prevents; there is no objection. A phrase sometimes placed at the beginning of books. See *Imprimatur.*

Nil admirari, *nīl ăd'mī-rā'rī.* To be astonished at nothing. —Horace. A *nil admirari* state of mind.

Nil desperandum, *nīl dē'spē-răn'dŭm.* Never despair.—Horace.

Nil medium est, *nīl mĕ'dĭ-ŭm ĕst.* There is no middle course.

Nil novi sub sole, *nīl nŏ'vī sŭb sō'lĕ.* Nothing new under the sun.

Nolens volens, *nō'lĕns vŏ'lĕns (nō'lĕnz vō'lĕnz).* Whether one will or not.

Noli me tangere, *nō'lī mē tăn'gĕ-rĕ.* Touch me not.

Nolle prosequi, *nŏl'lĕ prō'sĕ-quī (nŏl'ē prŏs'ē-kwī).* To be unwilling to proceed. A legal phrase to indicate the abandonment of a suit.

Non decet, *nōn dĕ'cĕt.* It is not proper, feasible.

Non est, *nōn ĕst (nŏn ĕst).* It is not; wanting; minus.

Non ignara mali miseris succurrere disco, *nōn ĭg-nā'ră mă'lī mĭs'ĕ-rīs sŭc-cŭr'rĕ-rĕ dĭs'cō.* Knowing misfortune, I hasten to help the unfortunate.

Non licet omnibus adire Corinthum, *nōn lĭ'cĕt ŏm'nĭ-bŭs ăd-ī'rĕ cō-rĭn'thŭm.* Every one cannot go to Corinth; we cannot all take a holiday, through want of funds.

Non liquet, *nōn lĭ'quĕt.* It does not flow; it is obscure, not quite clear.

Non multa, sed multum, *nōn mŭl'tă sĕd mŭl'tŭm.* Not many things, but much; quality, not quantity.

Non nova sed nove, *nōn nŏ'vă sĕd nŏ'vē.* Not new things, but old things in a new manner.

Non omnia possumus omnes, *nōn ŏm'nĭ-ă pŏs'sŭ-mŭs ŏm'nēs.* We cannot all of us do everything.—Virgil.

Non omnis moriar, *nōn ŏm'nĭs mŏ'rĭ-ăr.* I shall not altogether die; my good works will survive me.—Horace.

Non possumus, *nōn pŏs'sū-mŭs (nŏn pŏs'ū-mŭs).* We cannot,—an irrevocable refusal; as, to utter a *non possumus.*

Non sequitur, *nōn sĕ'quĭ-tŭr (nŏn sĕk'wĭ-tŭr).* It does not follow; an unwarranted conclusion.

Nosce teipsum, *nōs'cĕ tē-ĭp'sŭm.* Know thyself. From the Greek inscription written over the entrance to the Delphian temple.

Nota bene, *nŏ'tă bĕ'nĕ (nō'tȧ bē'nē).* Mark well; give good heed. *N. B.*

Novissima verba, *nō-vĭs'sĭ-mă vĕr'bă.* The last (dying) words; often, the latest news.

Novus homo, *nŏ'vŭs hŏ'mō (nō'vŭs hō'mō).* A new man; one who has raised himself from obscurity.

Numero deus impare gaudet, *nŭ'mĕ-rō dĕ'ŭs ĭm'pă-rĕ gau'dĕt.* There's luck in odd numbers.—Virgil.

Nunc est bibendum, *nŭnc ĕst bĭ-bĕn'dŭm.* It is time for a drink.—Horace.

Obiit, *ŏb'ĭ-ĭt.* He (or she) died.

Obiter dicta, *ŏb'ĭ-tĕr dĭc'tă.* Things said incidentally; an unofficial expression or opinion.

Oculos habent et non videbunt, *ŏc'ŭ-lōs hă'bĕnt ĕt nōn vĭ-dē'bŭnt.* They have eyes but will not see. Said of those who are obstinate.

Oderint dum metuant, *ō'dĕr-ĭnt dŭm mĕt'ŭ-ănt.* Let them hate as long as they fear me.—Cicero.

Odiosa sunt restringenda, *ŏ'dĭ-ō'să sŭnt rĕ'strĭn-gĕn'dă.* Vexatious rules should be taken in a restricted sense.

Odi profanum vulgus, *ō'dī prō-fā'nŭm vŭl'gŭs.* I hate the vulgar crowd.—Horace.

Odium theologicum, *ŏ'dĭ-ŭm thĕ'ō-lŏ'gĭ-cŭm (ō'dĭ-ŭm thē'ō-lŏ'jĭ-cŭm).* The hatred of theologians.

O fortunatos nimium! *ō fŏr'tū-nā'tōs nĭm'ĭ-ŭm.* O you who are too well off (and don't know it)!—Virgil.

Oleum perdidisti, *ŏ'lĕ-ŭm pĕr'dĭ-dĭs'tī.* You have wasted your oil; trouble for nothing.

Omne ignotum pro magnifico est, *ŏm'nĕ ĭg-nō'tŭm prō măg-nĭ'fĭ-cō ĕst.* Everything unknown is magnified; distance lends enchantment.—Tacitus.

Omnia mecum porto, *ŏm'nĭ-ă mē'cŭm pŏr'tō.* I carry all my belongings (my brains) with me.

Omnia vincit amor, *ŏm'nĭ-ă vĭn'cĭt ă'mŏr.* Love conquers all things.—Virgil.

Onus probandi, *ŏ'nŭs prō-băn'dī (ō'nŭs prō-băn'dī).* The burden of proving. It rests with him who makes a gratuitous statement.

Ora pro nobis, *ō'rā prō nō'bīs.* Pray for us.

Ore rotundo, *ō'rĕ rō-tŭn'dō.* With rounded mouth; with polished words.—Horace

O sancta simplicitas! *ō sănc'tă sĭm-plĭ'cĭ-tās.* O blessed simplicity!—said ironically.

Os magna sonaturum, *ōs măg'nă sŏ'nā-tū'rŭm.* A mouth for sublime speech.—Horace. One who possesses the gift of eloquent utterance.

O tempora! O mores! *ō tĕm'pŏ-ră ō mō'rēs.* Alas, for the age we live in and its manners!—Cicero.

O terque quaterque beati! *ō tĕr'quĕ quă-tĕr'quĕ bē-ā'tī.* O thrice and again happy!—Virgil. Meaning,—those who die for their country.

Otium cum dignitate, *ō'tĭ-ŭm cŭm dĭg'nĭ-tā'tĕ.* Ease with dignity.—Cicero. A phrase applied humorously to stout people.

O ubi campi! *ō ŭ'bī căm'pī.* O where are the green fields! —Virgil. A cry of regret after one's holidays.

Palma non sine pulvere, *păl'mă nōn sĭ'nĕ pŭl'vĕ-rĕ.* The palm (of victory) is not gained without dust; no excellence without great labor. A paraphrase from Horace.

Panem et circenses, *pā'nĕm ĕt cĭr-cēn'sēs.* Bread and the games.—Juvenal. Words applied contemptuously to those who think only of pleasure.

Par pari refertur, *păr pă'rī rē-fĕr'tŭr.* Like is paid by like; an eye for an eye.

Particeps criminis, *păr'tĭ-cĕps crī'mĭ-nĭs (păr'tĭ-sĕps crĭ'mĭ-nĭs).* An accomplice.

PARTURIUNT MONTES, NASCETUR RIDICULUS MUS, *păr-tŭ'rĭ-ŭnt mŏn'tēs năs-cē'tŭr rī-dĭ'cŭ-lŭs mūs.* The mountains labor, a ridiculous mouse will be born; big boasting results in nothing.—Horace.

PATER FAMILIAS, *pā'tĕr fă-mĭl'ĭ-ās (pā'tẽr fȧ-mĭl'ĭ-ȧs).* The father of the family.

PATER NOSTER, *pă'tĕr nŏs'tĕr (pā'tẽr nŏs'tẽr).* Our father.

PATER PATRIÆ, *pă'tĕr pă'trĭ-œ.* The father of his country.

PATRES CONSCRIPTI, *pă'trēs cōn-scrĭp'tī (pā'trêz kŏn-skrĭp'tī).* The conscript fathers; the Roman senate. The words are often jocularly applied to the members of a town council.

PAUCA SED BONA, *pau'că sĕd bŏ'nă.* A few things, but good things.

PAULO MAJORA CANAMUS, *pau'lō mā-jō'ră că-nā'mŭs.* Let us sing of things more elevating.—Virgil. Let us change the subject.

PAX VOBISCUM! *pāx vō-bĭs'cŭm.* Peace be with you!

PECCAVI, *pĕc-cā'vī.* I have sinned. Used to acknowledge one's mistake.

PECTUS EST QUOD DISERTOS FACIT, *pĕc'tŭs ĕst quŏd dĭ-sĕr'tōs fă'cĭt.* 'Tis the heart that speaks eloquently.—Quintilian.

PEDE PŒNA CLAUDO, *pĕ'dĕ pœ'nă clau'dō.* Punishment follows on a lame leg.—Horace. Punishment may lag, but it seldom fails to overtake the criminal.

PER FAS ET NEFAS, *pĕr fās ĕt nĕ'fās.* By fair means and foul; by hook or by crook.

PERINDE AC CADAVER, *pĕr-ĭn'dĕ ăc că-dā'vĕr.* Just as a corpse; to have no will of one's own. The rule of obedience among the Jesuits except in cases of conscience.

PER JOCUM, *pĕr jŏ'cŭm.* For fun.

PER JOVEM! *pĕr jŏ'vĕm.* By Jove! By Jupiter!

PER SALTUM, *pĕr săl'tŭm.* By a jump.

PER SE, *pĕr sē.* Of itself; without other support.

PERSONA GRATA, *pĕr-sō'nă grā'tă.* A favored person; one always welcome.

PISCEM NATARE DOCES, *pĭs'cĕm nă-tā'rĕ dŏ'cēs.* You are teaching a fish to swim,—an absurd task because he knows all about it.

PLERUMQUE FIT, *plē-rŭm'quĕ fĭt.* What happens oftenest; the rule, not the exception.

PLURIMA MORTIS IMAGO, *plū'rĭ-mă mŏr'tĭs ĭ-mā'gō.* Death under a thousand aspects.—Virgil.

PLUS ÆQUO, *plūs œ'quō.* More than what is reasonable.

POETA NASCITUR, ORATOR FIT, *pō-ē'tă năs'cĭ-tŭr ō-rā'tŏr fĭt.* The poet is born, the orator made. The French say: "You can learn to cook but not to grill."

PONS ASINORUM, *pōns ă'sĭ-nō'rŭm (pŏnz ăs'ĭ-nō'rŭm).* The bridge of asses. Applied to first difficult proposition in Euclid's textbook of geometry.

POST EQUITEM SEDET ATRA CURA, *pōst ĕ'quĭ-tĕm sĕ'dĕt ā'tră cū'ră.* Dark care is in the saddle behind the rider.—Horace. Wealth and position cannot rid one of care.

POST HOC ERGO PROPTER HOC, *pŏst hōc ĕr'gō prŏp'tĕr hōc.* After that, therefore, on account of that; bad logic, taking an antecedent as a cause.

POTIUS MORI QUAM FŒDARI, *pŏ'tĭ-ŭs mŏ'rī quăm fœ-dā'rī.* Death before dishonor.

PRIMA FACIE, *prī'mă fă'cĭ-ē (prī'mȧ fā'shĭ-ê).* At the first glance; as, *prima facie* evidence.

PRIMO MIHI, *prī'mō mĭ'hĭ.* First of all myself. Motto of the egotist.

PRIMUM VIVERE DEINDE PHILOSOPHARI, *prī'mŭm vĭv'ĕ-rĕ dē-ĭn'dĕ phĭ-lŏ'sŏ-phā'rī.* Earn your living first, then you may talk.

PRIMUS INTER PARES, *prī'mŭs ĭn'tĕr pā'rēs.* First among equals; for example, the president of a republic.

PRINCIPIA, NON HOMINES, *prĭn-cĭ'pĭ-ă nōn hŏ'mĭ-nēs.* Principles, not men.

PRO ARIS ET FOCIS, *prō ā'rīs ĕt fŏ'cīs.* For altars and hearths; for faith and fatherland.

PRO BONO PUBLICO, *prō bŏ'nō pŭb'lĭ-cō (prō bō'nô pŭb'lĭ-kô).* For the public good.

PRO FORMA, *prō fŏr'mā.* As a matter of form.

PROH PUDOR! *prōh pŭ'dŏr.* For shame!

PROPAGANDA FIDE, *prō'pā-găn'dā fĭ'dē (prō'pȧ-găn'dȧ fī dê).* For extending the faith.

PRO REGE SÆPE, PRO PATRIA SEMPER, *prō rē'gĕ sœ'pĕ prō pă'trĭ-ā sĕm'pĕr.* For the king often, for my country always.

PRO TEMPORE, *prō tĕm'pŏ-rĕ (prō tĕm'pô-rê).* For the time being. *Pro tem.*

PULCHRE, BENE, RECTE! *pŭl'chrē bĕ'nĕ rēc'tē.* Beautiful, splendid, perfect!—Horace. A phrase implying that those who use exaggerated praise are to be distrusted.

PULSATE ET APERIETUR VOBIS, *pŭl-sā'tĕ ĕt ă-pĕr'ĭ-ē'tŭr vō'bīs.* Knock and it shall be opened to you; perseverance is the key to success.

PUNICA FIDES, *pū'nĭ-că fĭ'dēs (pū'nĭ-kȧ fī'dêz).* Carthaginian faith; a worthless something.

QUÆRENS QUEM DEVORET, *quœ'rēns quĕm dē'vŏ-rĕt.* Seeking whom he may devour. Said of one who is fond of wrangling.

QUALIS PATER TALIS FILIUS, *quā'lĭs pă'tĕr tā'lĭs fī'lĭ-ŭs.* Like father, like son; a chip of the old block.

QUANDOQUE BONUS DORMITAT HOMERUS, *quăn-dō'quĕ bŏ'nŭs dŏr-mĭ'tăt hŏ-mē'rŭs.* Even the good Homer sometimes nods.—Horace. Not even the greatest always excel.

QUID NUNC? *quĭd nŭnc (quĭd nŭnc).* What now? A newsmonger or gossip.

QUOD ERAT DEMONSTRANDUM, *quŏd ĕ'răt dē'mŏn-străn'dŭm (kwŏd ĕr'ăt dĕ'nŏn-străn'dŭm).* Which was to be proved. *Q.E.D.*

QUOD ERAT FACIENDUM, *quŏd ĕ'răt fă'cĭ-ĕn'dŭm.* Which was to be done. *Q.E.F.*

QUOD SCRIPSI SCRIPSI, *quŏd scrĭp'sī scrĭp'sī.* What I have written, I have written. To express an unalterable decision. Words attributed to Pontius Pilate.

QUOMODO VALES? *quō'mŏ-dŏ vă'lēs.* How are you?

QUOT HOMINES, TOT SENTENTIÆ, *quŏt hŏ'mĭ-nēs tŏt sĕn-tĕn'tĭ-œ.* As many opinions as there are persons.—Terence. Too many cooks spoil the broth.

RARA AVIS IN TERRIS, *rā'ră ă'vĭs ĭn tĕr'rīs.* A rare bird on earth.—Juvenal. Sometimes used of a sly or knowing person.

RARI NANTES IN GURGITE VASTO, *rā'rī năn'tēs ĭn gŭr'gĭ-tĕ văs'tō.* Wreckage floating here and there in the vast abyss.—Virgil.

REDUCTIO AD ABSURDUM, *rĕ-dŭc'tĭ-ō ăd ăb-sŭr'dŭm (rê-dŭk-shĭ-ô ăd ăb-sŭr'dŭm).* A reducing to an absurdity.

RELIGIO LAICI, *rĕ-lĭ'gĭ-ō lā'ĭ-cī (rē-lĭj'ĭ-ô lā'ĭ-sī).* The religion of a layman.

RELIGIO MEDICI, *rĕ-lĭ'gĭ-ō mĕ'dĭ-cī (rê-lĭj'ĭ-ô mĕd'ĭ-sī).* The religion of a physician.

REQUIESCAT IN PACE, *rĕ'quĭ-ĕs'căt ĭn pā'cĕ (rĕk'wĭ-ĕs'kăt ĭn pā'sê).* May he rest in peace. *R.I.P.*

RES ANGUSTA DOMI, *rēs ăn-gŭs'tă dŏ'mī.* The poverty at home,—which a man hides, and on account of which he fails to succeed.—Juvenal.

RES JUDICATA, *rēs jū'dĭ-cā'tă.* A matter decided; a case already settled. The French phrase is *chose jugée.*

RES, NON VERBA, *rēs nōn vĕr'bă.* Deeds not words. The secret of success.

RES SACRA MISER, *rēs să'cră mĭ'sĕr.* Misfortune is sacred; that is, we should respect it.—Seneca.

RISUM TENEATIS? *rī'sŭm tĕn'ĕ-ā'tĭs.* Can you help laughing (the thing is so absurd)?—Horace.

RUS IN URBE, *rūs ĭn ŭr'bĕ (rŭs ĭn ŭr'bê).* A residence in or near town, with many of the advantages of the country.

SALUS POPULI SUPREMA LEX, *să'lūs pŏ'pŭ-lī sŭ-prē'mă lēx.* The welfare of the people is the first law.—From the Laws of the XII Tables.

SANCTUM SANCTORUM, *sānc'tŭm sānc-tō'rŭm (sănk'tŭm sănk-tō'rŭm).* The holy of holies.

SAPIENS NIHIL AFFIRMAT QUOD NON PROBET, *să'pĭ-ēns nĭ'hĭl ăf-fĭr'măt quŏd nōn prŏ'bĕt.* A wise man says nothing he cannot prove.

SEDET ÆTERNUMQUE SEDEBIT, *sĕ'dĕt œ'tĕr-nŭm'quĕ sĕ-dē'bĭt.* There he sits and will sit forever.—Virgil. Jocosely applied to one who likes to see *others* work.

SEMPER FIDELIS, *sĕm'pĕr fĭ-dē'lĭs.* Always faithful.

SERVUS SERVORUM DEI, *sĕr-vŭs sĕr-vō'rŭm dĕ'ī.* Servant of the servants of God. A title used by the pope.

SESQUIPEDALIA VERBA, *sĕs'quĭ-pĕ-dā'lĭ-ă vĕr'bă.* Words a foot and a half long.—Horace. Pompous twaddle with little meaning.

SIC SEMPER TYRANNIS, *sĭc sĕm'pĕr tÿ-răn'nĭs (sĭk sĕm'pẽr tĭ-răn'ĭs).* Ever thus to tyrants. The motto of Virginia.

SIC TRANSIT GLORIA MUNDI, *sĭc trăn'sĭt glō'rĭ-ă mŭn'dī.* Thus passes the glory of the world. Words addressed to the pope on his election,—accompanied by the burning of flax.

SIC VOS NON VOBIS, *sĭc vōs nōn vŏ'bīs.* You work, others reap the benefit.—Virgil.

SILENT LEGES INTER ARMA, *sĭ'lĕnt lē'gēs ĭn'tĕr ăr'mă.* The laws are silent in the midst of arms.—Cicero.

SIMILIA SIMILIBUS CURANTUR, *sĭ-mĭl'ĭ-ă sĭ-mĭl'ĭ-bŭs cū-răn'tŭr.* Like things are cured by like. The principle of homeopathy.

SI MONUMENTUM REQUIRIS, CIRCUMSPICE, *sī mŏn'ŭ-mĕn'tŭm rĕ-quī'rĭs cĭr-cŭm'spĭ-cĕ.* If you seek my monument, look around. The epitaph of Sir Christopher Wren in St. Paul's Cathedral, of which he was the architect.

SINE DIE, *sĭ'nĕ dĭ'ē (sī'nê dī'ê).* Without a day; finally. E.g., an adjournment *sine die.*

SINE QUA NON, *sĭ'nĕ quā nōn (sī'nê kwā nŏn).* Without which, not; essential; as, a *sine qua non* condition.

SINITE PARVULOS VENIRE AD ME, *sĭ'nĭ-tĕ păr'vŭ-lōs vĕ-nī'rĕ ăd mē.* Let the little ones come to me.

SI PARVA LICET COMPONERE MAGNIS, *sī păr'vă lĭ'cĕt cŏm-pō'nĕ-rĕ măg'nīs.* If it be allowed to compare small things with great.—Virgil.

SIT PRO RATIONE VOLUNTAS, *sĭt prō ră'tĭ-ō'nĕ vŏ-lŭn'tās.* Let my wish stand for the reason.—Juvenal.

SIT TIBI TERRA LEVIS, *sĭt tĭb'ĭ tĕr'ră lĕ'vĭs.* May the earth lie light on thee. Said in touching reference to one who is dead.

SI VIS PACEM PARA BELLUM, *sī vīs pā'cĕm păr'ă bĕl'lŭm.* If you wish peace, prepare for war. A specious maxim.

SOLITUDINEM FACIUNT, PACEM APPELLANT, *sŏ'lĭ-tū'dĭ-nĕm fā'cĭ-ŭnt pā'cĕm ăp-pĕl'lănt.* They make a wilderness and call it peace.—Tacitus.

SOL LUCET OMNIBUS, *sōl lū'cĕt ŏm'nĭ-bŭs.* The sun shines for all; even the poorest have certain natural rights.

SOLVE SENESCENTEM, *sŏl'vĕ sĕ'nĕs-cĕn'tĕm.* Unharness your horse, he's getting old; those advanced in age should retire from business.—Horace.

SPIRITUS PROMPTUS EST, CARO AUTEM INFIRMA, *spĭr'ĭ-tŭs prŏmp'tŭs ĕst că'rō au'tĕm ĭn-fĭr'mă.* The spirit is willing, but the flesh is weak; good-natured but indolent.

SPLENDIDE MENDAX, *splĕn'dĭ-dē mĕn'dăx.* Nobly untruthful; untrue for a good object.—Horace. Often used ironically of an unblushing liar.

STANS PEDE IN UNO, *stāns pĕ'dĕ ĭn ū'nō.* Standing on one leg; performing a task with ridiculous ease.—Horace.

STATU QUO ANTE BELLUM, *stă'tū quō ăn'tĕ bĕl'lŭm (stă'tū kwō ăn'tē bĕl'ŭm).* As things were before the war, or in *statu quo.* Used to express the unchanged state of things in general.

STULTORUM INFINITUS EST NUMERUS, *stŭl-tō'rŭm ĭn'fĭ-nī'tŭs ĕst nŭ'mĕr-ŭs.* The number of fools is infinite.

SUB LEGE LIBERTAS, *sŭb lē'gĕ lī-bĕr'tās.* Liberty under the law; the only freedom compatible with order.

SUB PŒNA, *sŭb pœ'nă (sŭb pē'nȧ).* Under a penalty. A judicial writ requiring attendance at a certain time and place under penalty.

SUB ROSA, *sŭb rŏ'să (sŭb rō'zȧ).* Under the rose; secretly

SUB SPECIE, *sŭb spĕ'cĭ-ē.* Under the appearance of.

SUFFICIT DIEI MALITIA SUA, *sŭf'fĭ-cĭt dĭ-ē'ī mă-lĭ'tĭ-ă sŭ'ă.* Sufficient for the day is the evil thereof; don't meet trouble halfway.

SUI GENERIS, *sŭ'ī gĕ'nĕ-rĭs (sū'ī jĕn'ĕr-ĭs).* Of its own kind; unlike any other.

SUMMA CUM LAUDE, *sŭm'mā cŭm lau'dĕ.* With highest honors.

SUMMUM JUS, SUMMA INJURIA, *sŭm'mŭm jūs sŭm'mă ĭn-jū'rĭă.* Excess of justice is excess of injustice; the law applied too vigorously.—Cicero.

SUNT LACRIMÆ RERUM, *sŭnt lă'crĭ-mæ rē'rŭm.* There are tears for suffering.—Virgil.

SUNT VERBA ET VOCES PRÆTEREAQUE NIHIL, *sŭnt vĕr'bă ĕt vō'cēs præ-tĕ'rĕ-ā'quĕ nĭ'hĭl.* Words and sounds and nothing else; empty talk.

SUO TEMPORE, *sŭ'ō tĕm'pŏ-rĕ.* In its own time.

SUPREMUM VALE, *sŭ-prē'mŭm vă'lē.* Farewell for the last time.—Ovid.

SURSUM CORDA, *sŭr'sŭm cŏr'dă.* Lift up your hearts; take courage.

SUTOR NE SUPRA CREPIDAM, *sū'tŏr nē sŭ'prā crĕ'pĭ-dăm.* Let the cobbler stick to his last.—Pliny.

TÆDIUM VITÆ, *tæ'dĭ-ŭm vī'tæ (tē'dĭ-ŭm vī'tē).* The weariness of life, which comes from doing nothing.

TARDE VENIENTIBUS OSSA, *tăr'dē vĕ'nĭ-ĕn'tĭ-bŭs ŏs'să.* The bones for the late comers; negligence is its own reward.

TE DEUM LAUDAMUS, *tē dĕ'ŭm lau-dā'mŭs (tē dē'ŭm lô-dā'mŭs).* We praise thee, O God.

TELUM IMBELLE SINE ICTU, *tē'lŭm ĭm-bĕl'lĕ sĭ'nĕ ĭc'tū.* A toy arrow without force; an insult to a man of integrity.

TEMPORA SI FUERINT NUBILA, SOLUS ERIS, *tĕm'pŏ-ră sī fŭ'ĕr-ĭnt nŭ'bĭ-lă sō'lŭs ĕr'ĭs.* If times be cloudy, you will be alone (in reference to fair-weather friends).—Ovid.

TEMPUS EDAX RERUM, *tĕm'pŭs ĕ'dāx rē'rŭm.* Time is the devourer of all things.—Ovid.

TEMPUS FUGIT, *tĕm'pŭs fŭ'gĭt (tĕm'pŭs fū'jĭt).* Time flies.

TEMPUS OMNIA REVELAT, *tĕm'pŭs ŏm'nĭ-ă rĕ-vē'lăt.* Time reveals all things.

TENERE LUPUM AURIBUS, *tĕn-ē'rĕ lŭ'pŭm au'rĭ-bŭs.* To take the wolf by the ears, the bull by the horns; to overcome a difficulty courageously.

TERES ATQUE ROTUNDUS, *tĕ'rēs ăt'quĕ rō-tŭn'dŭs.* Smooth and round; polished and complete,—said of a wise man.

TERMINUS AD QUEM, *tĕr'mĭ-nŭs ăd quĕm.* The limit to which; the goal.

TERMINUS A QUO, *tĕr'mĭ-nŭs ā quō.* The limit from which; the starting point.

TERRA FIRMA, *tĕr'ră fĭr'mă (tĕr'ȧ fēr'mȧ).* The firm land; the continent.

TERRA INCOGNITA, *tĕr'ră ĭn-cŏg'nĭ-tă (tĕr'ȧ ĭn-kŏg'nĭ-tȧ).* An unknown land.

TERTIUM QUID, *tĕr'tĭ-ŭm quĭd (tĕr'shĭ-ŭm kwĭd).* A third something, produced by the union of two different things or the collision of two opposing forces.

TESTIS UNUS TESTIS NULLUS, *tĕs'tĭs ū'nŭs tĕs'tĭs nŭl'lŭs.* One witness is no witness,—a legal axiom.

TIBI GRATIAS, *tĭb'ĭ grā'tĭ-ās.* Thank you.

TIMEO DANAOS ET DONA FERENTES, *tĭm'ĕ-ō dă'nă-ōs ĕt dō'nă fĕ-rĕn'tēs.* I fear the Greeks even when they bring gifts. The guileful should never be trusted.—Virgil.

TIMEO HOMINEM UNIUS LIBRI, *tĭm'ĕ-ō hŏm'ĭnĕm ū-nī'ŭs. lĭ'brī.* I fear the man of one book; he who possesses thorough knowledge of a book is a redoubtable adversary. —St. Thomas Aquinas.

TROS TYRIUSQUE MIHI NULLO DISCRIMINE AGETUR, *trōs tĭr'ĭ-ŭs'quĕ mĭ'hī nŭl'lō dĭs-crī'mĭ-nĕ ă-gē'tŭr.* Trojan and Tyrian shall have the same treatment from me.

TU ES ILLE VIR! *tū ĕs ĭl'lĕ vĭr.* Thou art that man! Used often by way of comic denouncement.

TU QUOQUE, *tū quō'quĕ (tū kwō'kwē).* Thou also; a *tu quoque* argument, that is, a weak and worthless one.

UBI BENE IBI PATRIA, *ŭ'bĭ bĕ'nĕ ĭ'bĭ pă'trĭ-ă.* Where one is well off, there is his country. A paraphrase of Pacuvius.

ULTIMA RATIO REGUM, *ŭl'tĭ-mă ră'tĭ-ō rē'gŭm.* The last argument of kings,—engraved on French cannon by order of Louis XIV.

ULTRA VIRES, *ŭl'trā vī'rēs (ŭl'trȧ vī'rēz).* Beyond power; transcending authority. A phrase used frequently in relation to acts by corporations in excess of their legal rights.

UNGUIBUS ET ROSTRO, *ŭn'guĭ-bŭs ĕt rōs'trō.* With claws and beak; tooth and nail.

URBI ET ORBI, *ŭr'bī ĕt ŏr'bī.* To the city (of Rome) and to the universe. The pope gives a blessing *urbi et orbi.*

USQUE AD NAUSEAM, *ŭs'quĕ ăd nau'sĕ-ăm (ŭs'kwē ăd nô'sē-ăm).* To disgust.

UT INFRA; UT SUPRA, *ŭt ĭn'frā ŭt sŭ'prā.* As below; as above (quoted). Direction notes in books.

VADE MECUM, *vā'dĕ mē'cŭm (vā'dē' mē'cŭm).* Go with me; a constant companion.

VADE RETRO SATANA! *vā'dĕ rĕ'trō săt'ă-nă.* Get behind me, Satan! Used jocosely to refuse a tempting invitation.

VÆ VICTIS, *væ vĭc'tīs.* Woe to the conquered. Said to have been the exclamation of Brennus, when he threatened to exterminate the Romans.

VANITAS VANITATUM ET OMNIA VANITAS, *văn'ĭ-tās văn'ĭ-tā'tŭm ĕt ŏm'nĭ-ă văn'ĭ-tās.* Vanity of vanities and all is vanity.

VARIORUM, *vă'rĭ-ō'rŭm.* Of various things. With the comments of various critics; as, a *variorum* edition of Shakspere.

VELUT ÆGRI SOMNIA, *vĕl'ŭt æ'grī sŏm'nĭ-ă.* Like the dreams of a sick man.—Horace. Said of a book written incoherently.

VENI, VIDI, VICI, *vē'nī vī'dī vī'cī (vē'nī vī'dī vī'sī).* I came, I saw, I conquered. The laconic dispatch in which Julius Cæsar announced to the Senate his victory in Asia Minor.

VERA INCESSU PATUIT DEA, *vē'ră ĭn-cĕs'sū păt'ŭ-ĭt dĕ'ă.* In her walk was revealed the true goddess.—Virgil. Applied to a woman of great dignity.

VERBA VOLANT SCRIPTA MANENT, *vĕr'bă vŏ'lănt scrĭp'tă mă'nĕnt.* Spoken words fly; those written remain.

VERITAS ODIUM PARIT, *vēr'ĭ-tās ŏ'dĭ-ŭm păr'ĭt.* Truth engenders hatred.—Terence.

VESTIGIA NULLA RETRORSUM, *vĕs-tĭ'gĭ-ă nŭl'lă rĕ-trŏr'sŭm.* No footsteps backward.—Horace.

VIA MEDIA, *vĭ'ă mĕ'dĭ-ă (vī'ȧ mē'dĭ-ȧ).* A middle course.

VICE VERSA, *vĭ'cĕ vĕr'să (vī'sē vĕr'sȧ).* The terms being interchanged.

VIDEO LUPUM, *vĭd'ĕ-ō lŭ'pŭm.* I see a wolf. Said as a warning against an approaching parasite.

VI ET ARMIS, *vī ĕt ăr'mīs.* By main force.

VIR BONUS DICENDI PERITUS, *vĭr bŏ'nŭs dī-cĕn'dī pĕ-rī'tŭs.* A good man skilled in the art of speaking. The Roman definition of an orator.

VIRES ACQUIRIT EUNDO, *vī'rēs ăc-quī'rĭt ĕ-ŭn'dō.* It gathers strength as it goes.—Virgil. Calumny; scandal.

VIRTUS POST NUMMOS, *vĭr'tūs pŏst nŭm'mōs.* Virtue after wealth. Virtue is not a bad thing to acquire, but money is more important.—Horace.

VIS A TERGO, *vīs ā tĕr'gō.* Force from the rear.

VIS COMICA, *vīs cŏm'ĭ-că.* The comic element or power; the gift of causing laughter.—Julius Cæsar.

VIS INERTIÆ, *vīs ĭn-ĕr'tĭ-æ (vĭs ĭn-ĕr'shĭ-ē).* The power of inertia.

VIVA VOCE, *vī'vā vō'cĕ (vī'vȧ vō'sē).* With the living voice; by word of mouth.

VIVE VALEQUE! *vī'vĕ văl-ē'quĕ.* Long life and prosperity!—Horace. Used at the end of letters.

VIVIT SUB PECTORE VULNUS, *vī'vĭt sŭb pĕc'tŏ-rĕ vŭl'nŭs.* The wound is still in her heart.—Virgil. An unforgetable sorrow.

VOLENTI NON FIT INJURIA, *vŏ-lĕn'tī nōn fĭt ĭn-jū'rĭ-ă.* No injury is done to a consenting party.

VOX CLAMANTIS IN DESERTO, *vōx clā-măn'tĭs ĭn dē-sĕr'tō.* A voice crying in the wilderness. Said of one whose advice is not heeded.

VOX ET PRÆTEREA NIHIL, *vōx ĕt præ-tĕ'rĕ-ā nĭ'hĭl.* A voice and nothing more; sound without sense.

VOX FAUCIBUS HÆSIT, *vōx fau'cĭ-bŭs hæ'sĭt.* My voice stuck in my throat.—Virgil. Used to express horror in speaking about a certain subject.

VOX POPULI VOX DEI, *vōx pŏ'pŭ-lī vōx dĕ'ī (vōks pŏp'ŭ-lī vōks dē'ī).* The voice of the people, God's voice.

VULNERANT OMNES, ULTIMA NECAT, *vŭl'nĕ-rănt ŏm'nēs ŭl'tĭ-mă nĕ'căt.* They all wound, the last kills. An inscription found on old clocks referring to the hours.

WORDS AND PHRASES FROM MODERN LANGUAGES

All phrases from the Italian are marked (It.); those from the Spanish, (Sp.); and those from the German, (Ger.). The unmarked phrases are from the French.

The key to pronunciation of the following list of words and phrases will be found in the introductory pages of this volume.

Abandon, *ȧ'bän'dôɴ'*. Unconstraint; an amiable negligence in speech or manner.

À bas, *ȧ bä'*. Down with (disapproving).

À bas l'injustice, *ȧ bä' lăɴ'zhüs'tēs'*. Down with injustice.

À bout portant, *ȧ bōō' pôr-täɴ'*. Quite close; point blank.

Absence d'esprit, *ȧp'säɴs' dĕs'prē'*. Absence of mind.

À cheval, *ȧ shĕ-väl'*. On horseback.

A chi vuole, non mancano modi (It.), *ä kē vwô'lĕ nōn mäng'kä-nō mô'dē*. Where there's a will, there's a way.

A chico pajarillo chico nidillo (Sp.), *ä chē'kō pä-hä-rēl'yō chē'kō nē-thēl'yō*. Little bird, little nest; adapt your manners to your company.

A compte, *ȧ kôɴt'*. On account.

À corps perdu, *ȧ kôr' pĕr'dü'*. Headlong; desperately.

À couvert, *ȧ kōō'vĕr'*. Under cover; protected; sheltered.

À deux mains, *ȧ dû' măɴ'*. With or for both hands; having a double office or employment.

Adieu, la voiture, adieu, la boutique, *ȧ'dyû' lȧ vwȧ'tür' ȧ'dyû' lȧ bōō'tēk'*. Good-by, carriage; good-by, shop,—all is over.

À discrétion, *ȧ dēs'krā'syôɴ'*. At discretion; unrestrictedly.

A donde fueres haz lo que vieres (Sp.), *ä dôn'dä fwā'rĕs äth lō kā vyā'rĕs*. Where you are, do what you see; when in Rome, do as Rome does.

À droite, *ȧ drwät'*. To the right.

Affaire d'amour, *ȧ'fâr' dȧ'mōōr'*. A love affair.

Affaire d'honneur, *ȧ'fâr' dō'nûr'*. An affair of honor; a duel.

Affaire de cœur, *ȧ'fâr' dē kûr'*. An affair of the heart; a love affair.

A fin, *ȧ făɴ'*. To the end or object.

À fond, *ȧ fôɴ'*. To the bottom; thoroughly.

À gauche, *ȧ gōsh'*. To the left.

À genoux, *ȧ zhĕ-nōō'*. On one's knees; kneeling.

À grands frais, *ȧ gräɴ' frĕ'*. At great expense.

À haute voix, *ȧ ōt' vwȧ'*. Aloud.

À huis clos, *ȧ üē' klō'*. With closed doors; secretly.

À l'abandon, *ȧ lȧ'bäɴ'dôɴ'*. In confusion; uncared for.

À la belle étoile, *ȧ lȧ bĕl' ā'twäl'*. Under the canopy of heaven; in the open air at night.

A la bonne heure, *ȧ lȧ bô'nûr'*. Well done! That's something like!

À l'abri, *ȧ lȧ'brē'*. Under shelter.

À la campagne, *ȧ lȧ käɴ'pȧn'y'*. In the country.

À la carte, *ȧ lȧ kȧrt'*. By the bill of fare; to dine *a la carte*.

À la créole, *ȧ lȧ krā'ōl'*. With tomatoes.

À la dérobée, *ȧ lȧ dā'rō'bā'*. Stealthily.

À la française, *ȧ lȧ fräɴ'sâz'*. In the French fashion.

À la grecque, *ȧ lȧ grĕk'*. After the Greek fashion.

À la mode, *ȧ lȧ môd'*. In the fashion; according to the custom or fashion.

À la Tartuffe, *ȧ lȧ tȧr'tüf'*. Like Tartuffe, the hypocritical hero of Molière's comedy, *Tartuffe*,—hence, hypocritically.

Á la tempestad sigue la calma (Sp.), *ä lä tĕm-pĕs-täth' sē'gä lä käl'mä*. After the storm comes the calm.

Al buen entendedor pocas palabras bastan (Sp.), *äl bwān ĕn-tĕn'dē-thōr' pō'käs pä-lä'bräs bäs'tän*. For a good listener but few words are needed; a word to the wise.

Al buon vino non bisogna frasca (It.), *äl bwôn vē'nō nōn bē-zōn'yä fräs'kä*. Good wine needs no bush.

Al contado (Sp.), *äl kōn-tä'thō*. For cash; ready money.

À l'envi, *ȧ läɴ'vē'*. In emulation of one another.

Al fresco (It.), *äl fräs'kō*. In the open air.

À l'improviste, *ȧ lăɴ'prô'vēst'*. Unawares; on a sudden.

Alla vostra salute (It.), *äl'lä vôs'trä sä-lōō'tē*. To your good health.

Allez-vous-en, *ȧ'lā'vōō'zäɴ'*. Away with you; be off.

Allons, *ȧ'lôɴ'*. Come; now then!

Al più (It.), *äl pyōō'*. At most.

À main armée, *ȧ măɴ'nȧr'mā'*. By force of arms.

Am Anfang (Ger.), *äm än'fäng*. In the beginning.

Amar y saber no puede ser (Sp.), *ä-mär' ē sä-bĕr' nō pwā'thā sĕr*. No one can love and be wise at the same time.

Amende honorable, *ȧ'mäɴd'dō'nō'rȧ'bl'*. Fit reparation; a satisfactory apology.

À merveille, *ȧ mĕr'vā'y'*. Marvelously; to perfection.

Ami de cour, *ȧ'mē' dĕ kōōr'*. A friend of the court; a false friend; one who is not to be depended on.

Ami du peuple, *ȧ'mē' dü pû'pl'*. Friend of the people.

Ami en voie, *ȧ'mē' äɴ vwä*. A friend at court; one who has influence.

Amor con amor se paga (Sp.), *ä-môr' kōn ä-môr' sā pä'gä*. Love is paid with love; one good turn deserves another.

Amour propre, *ȧ'mōōr' prô'pr'*. Vanity; self-respect.

Antes de que te cases mira lo que haces (Sp.), *än-tĕs' dā kā tā kä'sĕs mē'rä lō kā ä'thĕs*. Before you marry 'tis well to tarry.

Ancien régime, *äɴ'syăɴ' rā'zhēm'*. The former condition of things; of French government before 1789.

À outrance, *ȧ ōō'träɴs'*. To the death; to the last extremity.

À pas de géant, *ȧ pä' dē zhā'äɴ'*. With a giant's stride.

À pas de loup, *ȧ pä' dē lōō'*. With stealthy steps.

À perte de vue, *ȧ pĕrt' dē vü'*. Till out of sight.

À peu près, *ȧ pû' prā'*. Nearly.

À pied, *ȧ pyā'*. On foot.

À point, *ȧ pwăɴ'*. Just in time; to a turn; exactly right.

Après nous le déluge, *ȧp'rā' nōō' lē dā'lüzh'*. After us, the deluge.

À prima vista (It.), *ä prē'mä vĭs'tä*. At the first glance.

À propos, *ȧ prō'pō'*. To the point; pertinently.

À propos de rien, *ȧ prō'pō' dē ryăɴ'*. Apropos to nothing; motiveless; for nothing at all.

Á quien madruga, Dios le ayuda (Sp.), *ä kyān mä-thrōō'gä dyōs lā ä-yōō'thä*. Those who get up early God helps; God helps those who help themselves.

Aquí se habla español (Sp.), *ä-kē' sä ä'blä ĕs-pä-nyōl'*. Spanish is spoken here.

Argent comptant, *ȧr'zhäɴ' kôɴ'täɴ'*. Ready money.

Armuth ist keine Schande (Ger.), *är'mōōt ĭst kī'nĕ shän'dē*. Poverty is no disgrace.

Arrière pensée, *ȧ'ryâr' päɴ'sā'*. Mental reservation; unavowed purpose.

À tort et à travers, *ȧ tôr'tā ȧ trä'vâr'*. At random.

Au bout de son latin, *ō bōō' dē sôɴ' lȧ'tăɴ'*. At the end of his Latin; at one's wit's end; in a fix.

Au contraire, *ō kôɴ'trâr'*. On the contrary.

Au courant, *ō kōō'räɴ'*. Well acquainted with; well informed.

Au désespoir, *ō dā'zĕs'pwär'*. In despair.

Au fait, *ō fĕ'*. Expert; up-to-date.

Au fond, *ō fôɴ'*. At bottom; at heart; really.

Au gratin, *ō grȧ'tăɴ'*. With cheese or bread raspings to form a crust.

Au jus, *ō zhü'*. With the natural juice.

Au pas de charge, *ō pä dē shȧrzh'*. Double quick time.

Au pis aller, *ō pē' zȧ'lā'*. At the very worst; let the worst come to the worst. *Un pis aller* means a last resource, a makeshift.

Au reste, *ō rĕst'*. As for the rest.

Au revoir, *ō rē-vwär'*. Till we meet again.

Aussitôt dit, aussitôt fait, *ō'sē'tō' dē' ō'sē'tō' fĕ'*. No sooner said than done.

Autant d'hommes, autant d'avis, *ō'täɴ' dôm' ō'täɴ' dȧ'vē'*. Many men, many minds.

Autre fois, *ō'tr' fwä'*. Another time.

Aux armes, *ō zȧrm'*. To arms.

À volonté, *ȧ vô'lôɴ'tā'*. At pleasure.

À votre santé, *ȧ vô'tr' säɴ'tā'*. To your health.

Á vuestra salud (Sp.), *ä vwās'trä sä-lōōth'*. To your health; good health!

Ballon d'essai, *bȧ'lôɴ' dĕs'sĕ'*. A balloon sent up to test the direction of air currents,—hence, anything said or done to gauge public feeling on any question.

Bas bleu, *bä' blû'*. A bluestocking; a woman who seeks a reputation for learning.

Beaux yeux, *bō' zyû'*. Handsome eyes, a fair face.

Bel esprit, *bĕl' ĕs'prē'*. A wit; a genius.

Benedetto è quel male che vien solo (It.), *bĕn-ĕ-dāt'tō ĕ kwāl mä'lĕ kā vyĕn sō'lō*. Blessed is the misfortune that comes alone.

Ben trovato (It.), *bĕn trō-vä'tō*. Well invented.

Bête noire, *bât' nwär'*. A black beast; a bore; a nuisance.

Billet doux, or billet d'amour, *bē'yĕ' dōō'* or *bē'yĕ' dȧ'mōōr'*. A love letter.

Bizarre, *bē'zär'*. Odd; fantastic.

Blasé, *blȧ'zā'*. Surfeited; term applied to a pose of indifference.

Bon ami, *bôɴ'nȧ'mē'*. Good friend.

Bon gré, mal gré, *bôɴ' grā' mȧl' grā'*. With good or bad grace; willing or unwilling.

Bonhomie, *bôn'nô'mē'*. Good nature; simplicity.
Bon jour, *bôn' zhōōr'*. Good day; good morning.
Bon mot, *bôn' mô'*. A witticism.
Bonne et belle, *bôn' nā-bĕl'*. Good and handsome,—said of a woman.
Bonne foi, *bôn' fwä'*. Good faith.
Bon soir, *bôn' swär'*. Good evening.
Bon ton, *bôn' tôn'*. Good breeding; the style and manner of gentlefolk.
Boute-en-train, *bōō' tän trăn'*. Mirth inspirer, merry companion.
Breveté, *brĕv'-tā'*. Patented.
Buenas noches (Sp.), *bwā'näs nō'chĕs*. Good evening.
Buenas tardes (Sp.), *bwā'näs tär'dĕs*. Good afternoon.
Bueno (Sp.), *bwā'nō*. Good; all right.
Buenos dias (Sp.), *bwā'nōs dē'äs*. Good morning.

Ça vaut mieux voir le dessous des cartes, *sä vō myû' vwär' lē dĕs-sōō' dā kärt'*. 'Tis best to see the face of the cards; to be in the secret.
Cada oneja con su pareja (Sp.), *kä'thä ō-nā'hä kôn sōō pä-rā'hä*. Every sheep with its like; birds of a feather flock together.
Cada uno es como Dios le hizo, y aun peor, muchas veces (Sp.), *kä'thä ōō'nō ĕs kō'mō thē'ôs lā ē'thō ē ä-ōōn pā-ôr' mōō'chäs vā'thĕs*. Every one is as God made him and often much worse.
Cada uno sabe donde le aprieta el zapato (Sp.), *kä'thä ōō'nō sä'bĕ dôn'dä lā ä-pryā'tä ĕl thä-pä'tō*. Each one knows where his own shoe pinches.
Carte blanche, *kärt' blänsh'*. Full power; full permission.
Castello che dà orecchia si vuol rendere (It.), *käs-tĕl'lō kā dä ō-räk'kyä sē vwôl rĕn'dĕ-rĕ*. The fortress that parleys soon surrenders.
Cela va sans dire, *sē-lä' vä' sän' dēr'*. That goes without saying; that is understood.
Ce n'est que le premier pas qui coûte, *sē nĕ' kē lē prē-myā' pä' kē kōōt'*. It is only the first step that is difficult.
C'est à dire, *sĕ' tä' dēr'*. That is to say.
C'est une autre chose, *sĕ'tün' ō'tr' shōz'*. That is quite another thing.
Chacun à son goût, *shä'kûn' nä sôn' gōō'*. Every one to his taste.
Chacun tire de son côté, *shä'kûn' tēr' dē sôn' kō-tā'*. Every one inclines to his own side or party.
Chanson de geste, *shän'sôn' dē zhĕst'*. A song of heroic deeds; medieval French epic poem.
Chapeau de bras, *shä'pō' dē brä'*. A military cocked hat.
Chapelle ardente, *shä'pĕl' är'dänt'*. The chamber where a dead body lies in state.
Château, *shä'tō'*. A castle
Chauviniste, *shō'vē'nēst'*. Over-aggressive patriot; "jingo."
Chef-d'œuvre, *shĕ'dû'vr'*. A masterpiece; a crowning piece of work.
Chemin de fer, *shē-măn' dē fâr'*. Iron road; a railway.
Chère amie, *shâr' ä'mē'*. A dear (female) friend.
Che sarà, sarà (It.), *kä sä-rä' sä-rä*. What will be, will be.
Cheval de bataille, *shē-väl' dē bä'tä'y'*. A war horse; chief dependence or support; one's strong point.
Chi lo sa? (It.), *kē lō sä*. Who knows?
Chi tace confessa (It.), *kē tä'chĕ kōn-fĕs'sä*. He who keeps silent admits his guilt.
Chi va piano va sano (It.), *kē vä pyä'nō vä sä'nō*. Who goes slowly goes surely.
Ci gît, *sē zhē'*. Here lies. (A common inscription on tombstones.)
Comme il faut, *kô mēl fō'*. Proper; as it should be.
Comment vous portez vous? *kô'män' vōō' pôr'tā' vōō'*. How are you?
Como se dice en ingles—? (Sp.), *kō'mō sā dē'thä ĕn ēn'glĕs*. How do you say in English—?
Como se escribe en español? (Sp.), *kō'mō sā ĕs-krē'bā ĕn ĕs'pä-nyôl'*. How is it written in Spanish?
Como se pronúncia esa palabra? (Sp.), *kō'mō sā prō-nōōn'thyä ā'sä pä-lä'brä*. How is this word pronounced?
Como va (colloq. Sp.), *kō'mō vä*. How are you?
Compagnon de voyage, *kôn'pä'nyôn' dē vwä'yäzh'*. A traveling companion.
Compte rendu, *kônt' rän'dü'*. An account rendered; a report.
Concierge, *kôn'syârzh*. A portress, hall porter, lodge keeper.
Concours, *kôn'kōōr'*. Competition (as for a prize); contest.
Con diligenza (It.), *kōn dē-lē-jĕn'tsä*. With diligence.
Con dolore (It.), *kōn dō-lō'rĕ*. With grief; sadly.
Con mucho gusto (Sp.), *kôn mōō'chō gōō'stō*. With great pleasure.
Conseil de famille, *kôn'sĕ'y' dē fä'mē'y'*. A family council or consultation.
Conseil d'état, *kôn'sĕ'y' dā'tä'*. A council of state; a privy council.
Consommé, *kôn'sô'mā'*. A clear soup.
Con trabajar adelantamos (Sp.), *kôn trä-bä-här' ä' thĕl-än-tä'mōs*. By working we progress.
Contretemps, *kôn'tr'-tän'*. An awkward mishap.
Cordon sanitaire, *kôr'dôn' sä'nē'târ'*. A line of sentries to prevent, as far as possible, the spread of contagion or pestilence. (Used also of other precautionary measures.)
Couleur de rose, *kōō'lûr' dē rōz'*. Rose color.
Coup, *kōō*. A stroke; a blow; a thrust; a dig.
Coup de grace, *kōō' dē gräs'*. A finishing-stroke. (Formerly applied to the fatal blow by which the executioner put an end to the torments of a culprit broken on the wheel.)
Coup de main, *kōō' dē măn'*. A sudden attack; an enterprise (military); an undertaking; a helping hand.
Coup de maître, *kōō' dē mâ'tr'*. A master stroke.
Coup d'essai, *kōō' dā'sĕ'*. A first attempt; an experiment.
Coup d'état, *kōō' dā'tä'*. A stroke of policy, bringing about a sudden change of government (usually by unconstitutional means).
Coup d'œil, *kōō' dû'y'*. A rapid glance; a view.
Coup de pied, *kōō dē pyā'*. A kick.
Coup de poing, *kōō dē pwăn'*. A blow of the fist; a punch.
Courage sans peur, *kōō'räzh' sän pûr'*. Fearless courage.
Courant d'air, *kōō'rän' dâr'*. A draft.
Course de chevaux, *kōōrs' dē shē-vō'*. A horse race.
Coûte que coûte, *kōōt' kē' kōōt'*. Cost what it may; at any price.
Cuisine, *küē'zēn'*. A kitchen; cookery.

Dame d'honneur, *däm' dô'nûr'*. A maid of honor.
Dar la mano a (Sp. and It.), *där lä mä'nō ä*. To give the hand to; to shake hands with.
Dar un paseo (Sp.), *där ōōn pä-sā'ō*. To take a walk.
Das geht Sie nichts an (Ger.), *däs gāt zē nĭkts än*. That does not concern you.
De bonne grâce, *dē bôn' gräs'*. With good will; willingly.
Début, *dā'bü'*. First appearance.
Débutante, *dā'bü'tänt'*. A young lady just entering society.
De but en blanc, *dē bü' tän blän'*. Bluntly; right off.
Décolleté, *dā'kô'l'-tā'*. Wearing a low-necked dress.
Dégagé, *dā'gä'zhā'*. Free; easy; without constraint.
De gaieté de cœur, *dē gā'tā' dē kûr'*. In sport; sportively.
Déjeuner à la fourchette, *dā'zhû'nā' ä lä fōōr'shĕt'*. A meat breakfast; a lunch.
De la fama el atajo se entra por el trabajo (Sp.), *dā lä fä'mä ĕl ä-tä'hō sā ĕn'trä pōr ĕl trä-bä'hō*. The path of fame begins by work.
De mal en pis, *dē mäl' än pē'*. From bad to worse.
Déme la mano (Sp.), *dā'mā lä mä'nō*. Give me your hand; shake hands.
De moda (Sp.), *dā mō'thä*. Fashionable.
Dénouement, *dā'nōō'män'*. An unraveling or disclosure, as of a plot in a play; a wind-up; a catastrophe.
Dernier ressort, *dĕr'nyā' rē-sôr'*. The last resource.
Désagrément, *dā'zä'grā'män'*. Something disagreeable or unpleasant.
De sol á sol (Sp.), *dā sôl ä sôl*. From morning till night.
Di buona volontà sta pieno l'inferno (It.), *dē bwôn'ä vō-lōn-tä' stä pyĕ'nō lēn-fĕr'nō*. Hell is full of good intentions.
Dieu est toujours pour les plus gros bataillons, *dyû'ĕ' tōō'zhōōr' pōōr lā plü' grō' bä'tä'yôn'*. God is always on the side of the largest battalions; the largest army has the best chance.
Dieu et mon droit, *dyû' ā môn' drwä'*. God and my right. Motto on the British royal coat of arms.
Dieu vous garde, *dyû' vōō' gärd'*. God protect you.
Di grado in grado (It.), *dē grä'dō ĭn grä'dō*. Step by step; gradually.
Dios me libre de hombre de un libro (Sp.), *dē'ōs mā lē'brā dā ôm'brā dā ōōn lē'brō*. God deliver me from a man of one book.
Dir l'orazione della bertuccia (It.), *dēr lō'rä-tsyō'nĕ dāl'lä bĕr-tōōt'shä*. To pray like a monkey; to chatter.
Di salto (It.), *dē säl'tō*. By leaps.
Dispénseme usted (Sp.), *dēs-pĕn'sā-mā ōōs-tĕth'*. I beg your pardon; allow me.
Di tutti novello par bello (It.), *dē tōōt'tē nō-vĕl'lō pär bĕl'lō*. Everything new seems beautiful.
Dolce far niente (It.), *dōl'chĕ fär nyĕn'tĕ*. The sweet do-nothing; sweet idleness.
Donnant donnant, *dôn'nän' dôn'nän'*. Give and take.
Dorer la pilule, *dô'rā' lä pē'lül'*. To gild the pill.
Double entente, *dōōb'län'tänt'*. Double meaning.
Durante vita (It.), *dōō-rän'tä vē'tä*. During life.

Eau de cologne, *ō' dē kô-lôny''*. Cologne water.
Eau de vie, *ō' dē vē'*. Water of life—applied usually to brandy.
Éclat, *ā'klä'*. Splendor, brilliancy.
Édition de luxe, *ā'dē'syôn' dē lüks'*. A costly edition of a book, handsomely bound, and usually well illustrated.
Ehrlich währt am längsten (Ger.), *âr'lĭk vârt äm lĕngs'tĕn*. Honesty is the best policy.
Eile mit Weile (Ger.), *ī'lĕ mĭt vī'lĕ*. Make haste slowly.
Eine Schwalbe macht keinen Sommer (Ger.), *ī'nĕ shväl'bĕ mäkt kī'nĕn zō'mĕr*. One swallow does not make a summer.

Ein gebranntes Kind scheut das Feuer (Ger.), *in gä-brän'tĕs kĭnt shoit däs foi'ĕr*. A burnt child dreads the fire.
Élan, *ā'läɴ'*. Military dash; quick, sudden movement.
El árbol se conoce por su fruto (Sp.), *ĕl är'bōl sā kō-nō'thā pôr sōō frōō'tō*. The tree is known by its fruit.
El ejercicio hace maestro (Sp.), *ĕl ĕh-ĕr-thē'thyō ä'thā mä-ĕs'trō*. Exercise makes the master; practice makes perfect.
Élite, *ā'lēt'*. A select body of persons; society.
El trabajo hace la vida agradable (Sp.), *ĕl trä-bä'hō ä'thā lä vē'thä ä-grä-thä'blā*. Work makes life worth living.
Embarras des richesses, *äɴ'bä'rä' dā rē'shĕs'*. The plague of riches; difficulty of choice.
Embonpoint, *äɴ'bôɴ'pwăɴ'*. Roundness; corpulence; mostly used in humorous reference.
En ami, *äɴ nȧ'mē'*. As a friend.
En arrière, *äɴ nȧ'ryâr'*. In the rear; behind.
En attendant, *äɴ nȧ'täɴ'däɴ'*. In the meantime.
En avant, *äɴ nȧ'väɴ'*. Forward.
En badinant, *äɴ bȧ'dē'näɴ'*. In sport; jestingly.
En casa (Sp.), *ĕn kä'sä*. At home.
En cueros, en cueros vivos (Sp.), *ĕn kwä'rōs vē'vōs*. Naked; without clothing.
Ende gut, Alles gut (Ger.), *ĕn'dĕ gōōt ä'lĕs gōōt*. All's well that ends well.
En déshabillé, *äɴ dā'zȧ'bē'yā'*. Carelessly dressed as at early morning; unprepared.
En Dieu est tout, *äɴ dyû' ĕ tōō'*. In God are all things.
En effet, *äɴ nĕ'fĕ'*. Indeed; really; in effect.
En famille, *äɴ fȧ'mē'y'*. With one's family; at home.
Enfant gâté, *äɴ'fäɴ' gä'tā'*. A spoiled child.
Enfants perdus, *äɴ'fäɴ' pĕr'dü'*. Lost children; a forlorn hope.
Enfant terrible, *äɴ'fäɴ' tĕ'rē'bl'*. A child or person whose acts or remarks are embarrassing.
Enfant trouvé, *äɴ'fäɴ' trōō'vā'*. A foundling.
Enfin, *äɴ'făɴ'*. In short; finally; at last.
En grande tenue or toilette, *äɴ' gräɴd' tĕ-nü'* or *twȧ'lĕt'*. In full official, or evening, dress.
En masse, *äɴ' mȧs'*. In a body or mass.
Ennui, *äɴ'nwē'*. Weariness; boredom.
En passant, *äɴ' pä'säɴ'*. In passing; by the way.
En plein jour, *äɴ' plăɴ' zhōōr'*. In broad daylight.
En queue, *äɴ' kû'*. Immediately after; in the rear. Used especially of persons waiting in line, as at the door of a theater or at the ticket office of a railway station.
En rapport, *äɴ' rȧ'pôr'*. In harmony, relation, or agreement.
En règle, *äɴ' rĕg'l'*. Regular; in order.
En route, *äɴ' rōōt'*. On the way.
Ensemble, *äɴ'säɴ'bl'*. The whole; together.
En suite, *äɴ' süēt'*. In company; in a set.
Entente cordiale, *äɴ'täɴt' kôr'dyȧl'*. A good understanding, especially between two states.
Entêté, *äɴ'tĕ'tā'*. Headstrong.
Entourage, *äɴ'tōō'räzh'*. Surroundings; associates.
Entre amigos honrados cumplimientos excusados (Sp.), *ĕn'trä ä-mē'gōs ōn-rä'thōs kōōm'plē-myĕn'tōs ĕks'kōō-sä'-thōs*. Among honorable friends compliments are superfluous.
Entre deux feux, *äɴ'tr' dû' fû'*. Between two fires.
Entre deux vins, *äɴ'tr' dû' văɴ'*. Between two wines; half drunk.
Entrée, *äɴ'trā'*. Entry; first course.
Entremets, *äɴ'tr'-mĕ'*. Small and dainty dishes set between the principal ones at table.
Entre nous, *äɴ'tr' nōō'*. Between ourselves; in confidence.
En venir aux coups, *äɴ' vĕ-nēr' ō kōō'*. To come to blows.
En verité, *äɴ' vā'rē'tā'*. In truth; really.
En vez de oro es dorado (Sp.), *ĕn vāth dā ō'rō ĕs dō-rä'thō*. In place of gold 'tis only gilt; a false friend.
En voiture! *äɴ' vwȧ'tür'*. All aboard!
E pur si muove! (It.), *ā pōōr sē mwô'vĕ*. Nevertheless it moves! (Supposed words of Galileo after his condemnation; referring to the motion of the earth.)
Es freut mich sehr (Ger.), *ĕs froit mĭk zār*. I am very glad.
Est ist nicht Alles Gold, was glänzt (Ger.), *ĕs ĭst nĭkt ä'lĕs gōlt väs glĕntst*. All is not gold that glitters.
Esprit de corps, *ĕs'prē' dē kôr'*. The animating spirit of a collective body of persons, as of a regiment, the bar, the clergy, a school.
Esprit des lois, *ĕs'prē' dā lwä'*. Spirit of the laws.
Es thut mir leid (Ger.), *ĕs tōōt mēr līt*. I am sorry.
Ewigkeit (Ger.), *ā'vĭk-kīt*. Eternity.

Façon de parler, *fȧ'sôɴ' dē pär'lā'*. Manner of speaking; phrase; locution.
Faire bonne mine, *fâr' bôn' mēn'*. To look pleasant.
Faire les cent coups, *fâr' lā säɴ' kōō'*. To play all sorts of tricks.
Faire sans dire, *fâr' säɴ' dēr'*. To act without ostentation.
Faire son devoir, *fâr' sôɴ' dē-vwär'*. To do one's duty.
Fait accompli, *fĕ'tȧ'kôɴ'plē'*. An accomplished fact.
Faux pas, *fō' pä'*. A false step; an act of indiscretion.
Femme de chambre, *fȧm' dē shäɴ'br'*. A chambermaid.
Femme de charge, *fȧm' dē shȧrzh'*. A housekeeper.
Fendre un cheveu en quatre, *fäɴ'dr' ûɴ shē-vû' äɴ' kȧ'tr'*. To split a hair in four; to make subtle distinctions.
Fête, *fât*. A feast; festival; holiday.
Fête champêtre, *fât' shäɴ'pâ'tr'*. A rural out-of-door feast; a festival in the fields.
Feu de joie, *fû' dē zhwä'*. A bonfire or discharge of firearms as a sign of rejoicing.
Fille de chambre, *fē'y' dē shäɴ'br'*. A chambermaid.
Fille d'honneur, *fē'y' dô'nûr'*. A maid of honor; a lady in waiting.
Fleur-de-lis, *flûr'dē-lē'*. The flower of the lily. The coat of arms of France (a heraldic iris).
Fra Modesto non fu mai priore (It.), *frä mō-dĕs'tō nōn fōō mä'ē prē-ō'rĕ*. Friar Modest never became prior. "Push" is necessary to succeed.
Frisch begonnen, halb gewonnen (Ger.), *frĭsh bĕ-gôn'nĕn hälp gĕ-vôn'nĕn*. Well begun is half done.
Froides mains, chaude amour, *frwäd' măɴ' shō'dȧ'mōōr'*. Cold hands, warm heart.
Front à front, *frôɴ'tȧ frôɴ'*. Face to face.
Fuyez les dangers du loisir, *füē'yā' lā däɴ'zhā' dü lwä'zēr'*. Fly from the dangers of leisure.

Gaieté de cœur, *gā'tā' dē kûr'*. Gaiety of heart.
Garçon, *gȧr'sôɴ'*. A lad; a waiter.
Garde à cheval, *gȧr'dȧ shē-vȧl'*. A mounted guard.
Garde du corps, *gȧrd' dü kôr'*. A bodyguard.
Gardez la foi, *gȧr'dā' lȧ fwä'*. Keep the faith.
Gardez-vous-en bien, *gȧr'dā' vōō' zäɴ' byăɴ'*. Don't you do it; do nothing of the kind.
Gendarme, *zhäɴ'dȧrm'*. Policeman; a turbulent woman; a flaw (as in a diamond).
Gens de condition, *zhäɴ' dē kôɴ'dē'syôɴ'*. People of rank.
Gens de même famille, *zhäɴ' dē mâm' fȧ'mē'y'*. People of the same family; birds of a feather.
Gentilhomme, *zhäɴ'tē'yôm'*. A gentleman; a nobleman.
Gibier de potence, *zhē'byā' dē pô'täɴs'*. A gallows bird; one who deserves hanging.
Giovine santo, diavolo vecchio (It.), *jô'vē-nĕ sän'tō dyä'vō-lō vĕk'kyō*. A young saint, an old devil.
Gleich und gleich gesellt sich gern (Ger.), *glīk ōōnt glīk gĕ-zĕlt' zĭk gȧrn*. Birds of a feather flock together.
Gli assenti hanno torto (It.), *lyē äs-sĕn'tē än'nō tôr'tō*. The absent are in the wrong.
Gota á gota el mar se apoca (Sp.), *gō'tä ä gō'tä ĕl mär sā ä-pō'kä*. Drop by drop the sea can be emptied.
Goutte à goutte, *gōō'tȧ-gōōt'*. Drop by drop.
Gouvernante, *gōō'vĕr'näɴt'*. A governess; housekeeper.
Grâce à Dieu, *grä'sȧ dyû'*. Thanks be to God.
Grande chère et beau feu, *gräɴd' shâr' ā bō' fû'*. Good fare and a good fire; comfortable quarters.
Grand merci, *gräɴ' mĕr'sē'*. Many thanks.
Grosse tête et peu de sens, *grōs' tât' ā pû' dē säɴ'*. A big head and little sense.
Guerra á cuchillo (Sp.), *gär'rä ä kōō-chēl'yō*. War to the knife.
Guerra cominciata, inferno scatenato (It.), *gwĕr'rä kô'mēn-chä'tä ēn-fĕr'nō skä'tĕ-nä'tō*. War begun, hell unchained.
Guerre à mort, *gâr ȧ môr'*. War to the death.
Guten Morgen (Ger.), *gōōt'ĕn môr'gĕn*. Good morning.

Hace buen tiempo (Sp.), *ä'thā bwān tyĕm'pō*. It is fine weather.
Hasta luego (Sp.), *äs'tä lwā'gō*. Until by and by; I'll see you later.
Hasta otra vez (Sp.), *äs'tä ō'trä vāth*. Until another time; till we meet again.
Hasta mañana (Sp.), *äs'tä män-yä'nä*. Good-by; until tomorrow.
Haut goût, *ō' gōō'*. High flavor; elegant taste.
Haut ton, *ō' tôɴ'*. Highest fashion.
Homme d'affaires, *ôm' dȧ'fâr'*. A man of business; an agent.
Homme de robe, *ôm' dē rôb'*. A person in a civil office.
Homme d'esprit, *ôm' dĕs'prē'*. A wit; a genius.
Homme d'état, *ôm' dā'tä'*. A statesman.
Honi soit qui mal y pense, *ô'nē' swä' kē' mȧl' ē päɴs'*. Shame be to him who thinks evil of it. (The motto of the Order of the Garter.)
Hors de combat, *ôr' dē kôɴ'bȧ'*. Out of the fight; disabled; unfit to continue a contest.
Hors de la loi, *ôr' dē lȧ lwä'*. Outlawed.
Hors de propos, *ôr' dē prô'pō'*. Wide of the point; inapplicable.
Hors de saison, *ôr' dē sĕ'zôɴ'*. Out of season; unseasonable.
Hors d'œuvre, *ôr' dûv'r'*. Out of course; a side dish; a digression.
Hôtel de ville, *ô'tĕl' dē vēl'*. A town hall.
Hôtel Dieu, *ô'tĕl' dyû'*. The chief hospital of a town.
Hôtel garni, *ô'tĕl' gȧr'nē'*. Furnished lodgings.

Ich dien (Ger.), ĭk dēn. I serve.
Idée fixe, ē'dā' fēks'. A fixed idea; a mental conviction or attitude.
Ignorance crasse, ēn'yô'räns' kräs'. Gross ignorance.
I gran dolori sono muti (It.), ē grän dō-lō'rē sō'nō mōō'tē. Great griefs are silent.
Il a le diable au corps, ēl ä' lē dyäb'l' ō kôr'. The devil is in him.
Il faut de l'argent, ēl fō' dē lär'zhäN'. Money is needed.
Il n'a ni bouche ni éperon, ēl nä' nē bōōsh' nē äp'-rôN'. He has neither mouth nor spur; he has neither wit nor courage.
Il ne faut jamais défier un fou, ēl nē fō' zhä'mĕ' dā'fyā' ûN fōō'. One should never provoke a fool.
Il ne faut point disputer des goûts, ēl nē fō' pwăN' dĕs'pü'tā' dā gōō'. There is no accounting for tastes.
Il n'est sauce que d'appétit, ēl nĕ' sōs' kē dä'pā'tē'. Hunger is the best sauce.
Il souffle le chaud et le froid, ēl sōōf'l' lē shō ā lē frwä'. He blows hot and cold; he's a timeserver.
Impoli, ăN'pō'lē'. Unpolished; rude.
In un giorno non si fe' Roma (It.), ēn ōōn jōr'nō nōn sē fā rō'mä. Rome was not built in a day.
Ir por lana, y volver trasquilado (Sp.), ēr pôr lä'nä ē vôl-vĕr' träs'kē-lä'thō. To go for wool, and come back shorn.

Jamais bon coureur ne fut pris, zhä'mĕ' bôN kōō'rûr' nē fü' prē'. A good runner is not to be taken; old birds are not to be caught with chaff.
Je ne sais quoi, zhē nē sā' kwä'. I know not what; hard to describe; used humorously, as a "je ne sais quoi."
Je n'oublierai jamais, zhē nōō'blyā'rā' zhä'mĕ'. I will never forget.
Je suis prêt, zhē süē' prĕ'. I am ready.
Jet d'eau, zhĕ' dō'. A fountain; a jet of water.
Jeu de mots, zhû' dē mō'. A play upon words; a pun.
Jeu d'esprit, zhû' dĕs'prē'. A witticism.
Jeu de théâtre, zhû dē tā'ät'r'. A stage trick; claptrap.
Jeunesse dorée, zhû'nĕs' dô'rā'. Gilded youth.
Jouer de bonheur, zhwä' dē bô'nûr'. To be in luck.

L'addition, lä'dē'syôN'. The bill.
L'addition s'il vous plaît, lä'dē'syôN' sē vōō' plĕ'. Give me my bill please.
La carga andando crece (Sp.), lä kär'gä än-dän'dō krā'thā. The farther we walk, the heavier becomes our burden.
La caridad bien ordenada empieza por uno mismo (Sp.), lä kä-rē-thäd' byān ôr-dā-nä'thä ĕm-pyā'thä pôr ōō'nō mēs'mō. Charity well directed begins with oneself; charity begins at home.
La costumbre es otra naturaleza (Sp.), lä kôs-tōōm'brā ĕs ō'trä nä'tōō-rä-lā'thä. Custom is second nature.
La critique est aisée, l'art est difficile, lä krē'tēk' ĕ'tā'zā' lär'ĕ' dē'fē'sēl'. Criticism is easy enough, but art is difficult.
Lade nicht Alles in ein Schiff (Ger.), lä'dē nĭkt ä'lĕs ĭn īn shĭf. Do not load all in one ship; do not put all your eggs into one basket.
L'adversité fait les hommes, et le bonheur les monstres, läd'vĕr'sē'tā' fĕ' lä'zôm' ā lē bô'nûr' lā môN'str'. Adversity makes men, and prosperity, monsters.
La fortuna aiuta i pazzi (It.), lä fôr-tōō'nä ä-yōō'tä ē pät'sē. Fortune helps fools.
La fortune passe partout, lä fôr'tün' päs' pär'tōō'. Fortune passes everywhere; all men are subject to the vicissitudes of fortune.
Laissez faire, lĕ'sā' fâr'. Let it alone.—A *laissez faire* (careless) attitude.
L'amour et la fumée ne peuvent se cacher, lä'mōōr' ā lä fü'mā' nē pûv' sē kä'shā'. Love and smoke cannot be hidden.
Langage des halles, läN'gäzh' dā' äl'. The language of the markets; Billingsgate.
La patience est amère, mais son fruit est doux, lä pä'syäN' sĕ'tä'mâr' mĕ sôN' früē' tĕ' dōō'. Patience is bitter, but its reward is sweet.
La pluma es lengua del alma (Sp.), lä plōō'mä ĕs lĕn'gwä dĕl äl'mä. The pen is the tongue of the mind.
La pointe du jour, lä pwăNt dü zhōōr'. Daybreak.
La povertà è la madre di tutte le arti (It.), lä pō-vĕr-tä' ĕ lä mä'drĕ dē tōōt'tā lä är'tē. Poverty is the mother of all the arts.
L'argent, lär'zhäN'. Silver; money.
L'art pour l'art, lär' pōōr lär'. Art for art's sake.
Lasciate ogni speranza, voi ch'entrate (It.), lä-shä'tĕ ōn'yē spĕr-än'tsä vō'ē kān-trä'tē. All hope abandon, ye who enter here. The inscription over the gates of hell in Dante's "Inferno" (III.9).
L'avenir, läv''nēr'. The future.
La verdad es amarga (Sp.), lä vĕr-däTH' ĕs ä-mär'gä. Truth is bitter.
La vertu est la seule noblesse, lä vĕr'tü' ĕ lä sûl' nō'blĕs'. Virtue is the sole nobility.

Le beau monde, lē bō' môNd'. The world of fashion; society.
Le bon temps viendra, lē bôN' täN' vyăN'drä'. There's a good time coming.
Le coût en ôte le goût, lē kōō'täN' ōt' lē gōō'. The expense takes away the pleasure.
Le demi-monde, lē dē-mē'môNd'. The half-world, that is, of women of equivocal reputation, demimondaines.
Le jeu n'en vaut pas la chandelle, lē zhû'näN' vō' pä' lä shän'dĕl'. The game is not worth the candle; the object is not worth the trouble.
Le malheur ne vient jamais seul, lē mäl'ûr' nē vyăN' zhä'mĕ' sûl'. Misfortune never comes alone.
Le monde est le livre des femmes, lē môN'dĕ' lē lēv'r' dā fäm'. The world is woman's book.
L'empire des lettres, läN'pēr' dā lĕt'r'. The empire of letters.
Le parole son femmine, e i fatti son maschi (It.), lā pä-rō'lĕ sōn fäm'mē-nē ĕ ē fät'tē sōn mäs'kē. Words are feminine, and deeds are masculine.
Les absents ont toujours tort, lā zäp'säN' zôN' tōō'zhōōr' tôr'. The absent are always wrong.
Les convenances, lā kôN'v'-näNs'. The proprieties; the rules of politeness.
Lèse majesté, lĕz' mä'zhĕs'tā'. High treason.
Les murailles ont des oreilles, lā mü'rä'y'-zôn' dā zô'rā'y'. Walls have ears.
Les plus sages ne le sont pas toujours, lā plü' säzh' nē lē sôN' päs tōō'zhōōr'. The wisest are not always wise.
Le tout ensemble, lē tōō'täN'säN'bl'. The whole taken together.
Lettre de cachet, lĕt'r' dē kä'shā'. A sealed letter containing orders; a royal warrant, usually authorizing the imprisonment, without trial, of a person named therein.
Le vrai n'est pas toujours vraisemblable, lē vrĕ' nĕ' päs' tōō'zhōōr' vrĕ'säN'blä'bl'. Truth is not always probable.
L'homme propose, et Dieu dispose, lôm' prô'pōz' ā dyû' dēs'pōz'. Man proposes and God disposes.
L'inconnu, lăN'kô'nü'. The unknown.
L'incroyable, lăN'krwä'yä'bl'. The incredible; the marvelous. (The word incroyable was applied substantively to the fops of the Directory period in the great French Revolution.)
Lingerie, lăN'zh'-rē'. Linen goods; also, collectively, all the linen, cotton, and lace articles of a woman's wardrobe.
Littérateur, lē'tā'rä'tûr'. A literary man.
Lo barato es caro (Sp.), lō bä-rä'tō ĕs kä'rō. A bargain is dear.
L'occhio del padrone ingrassa il cavallo (It.), lôk'kyō dāl pä-drō'nē ēn-gräs'sä ēl kä-väl'lô. The master's eye fattens the horse.
Lo más pronto posible (Sp.), lō mäs prôn'tō pō-sē'blā. As soon as possible.
Lo que no se puede remediar se ha de aguantar (Sp.), lō kā nō sā pwā'thā rā-mā'thē-är' sā ä' thā ä-gwän-tär'. What cannot be cured must be endured.
Loyauté m'oblige, lwä'yō'tā' mô'blēzh'. Loyalty binds me.

Ma chère, mä' shâr'. My dear (fem.).
Mademoiselle, mäd'mwä'zĕl'. Miss.
Maestro di color che sanno (It.), mä-ĕs'trō dē kō-lōr' kā sän'nō. Master of those that know. (Applied by Dante to Aristotle.)
Ma foi, mä' fwä'. Upon my faith; upon my word.
Maintiens le droit, măN'tyăN' lē drwä'. Maintain the right.
Maison de campagne, mā'zôN' dē käN'pän'y'. A country house.
Maison de santé, mā'zôN' dē säN'tā'. A private asylum or hospital.
Maison de ville, mā'zôN' dē vēl'. A town hall.
Maître d'hôtel, mā'tr' dō'tĕl'. A house steward.
Maladie du pays, mä'lä'dē' dü pē'ē'. Homesickness.
Mal à propos, mäl' ä' prô'pō'. Out of place; ill suited.
Mal de mer, mäl' dē mâr'. Seasickness.
Malentendu, mäl'äN'täN'dü'. A misunderstanding; a mistake.
Malgré nous, mäl'grā' nōō'. In spite of us.
Malheur ne vient jamais seul, mä'lûr' nē vyăN' zhä'mĕ' sûl'. Misfortunes never come singly.
Mardi gras, mär'dē' grä'. Shrove Tuesday.
Mariage de conscience, mä'ryäzh' dē kôN'syäNs'. A private marriage.
Mariage de convenance, mä'ryäzh' dē kôN'v'-näNs'. A marriage of convenience, or from interested motives.
Marquer le pas, mär'kā' lē pä'. To mark time.
Marzo ventoso y abril lluvioso sacan á mayo hermoso (Sp.), mär'thō vĕn-tō'sō ē ä-brēl' lyōō'vyō'sō sä'kän ä mī'ō ĕr-mō'sō. Windy March and showery April bring flowery May.
Más quiero asno que me lleve que caballo que me derrueque (Sp.), mäs kyā'rō äs'nō kā mā lyā'vā kā kä-bäl'yō kā mā dĕr-rwā'kā. I prefer the ass that carries me to the horse that throws me.

MÁS SABE UN NECIO PREGUNTAR QUE PUEDEN CIEN SABIOS CONTESTAR (Sp.), *mäs sä'bä o͞on nĕ'thyō prä-go͞on'tär kä pwä'thĕn thyĕn sä'byōs kōn-tĕs-tär'.* One fool can ask more questions than a hundred learned men can answer.

MÁS VALE PÁJARO EN MANO QUE CIENTO VOLANDO (Sp.), *mäs vä'lā pä'hä-rō ĕn mä'nō kā thyĕn'tō vō-län'dō.* A bird in the hand is worth two in the bush (a hundred flying).

MÁS VALE TARDE QUE NUNCA (Sp.), *mäs vä'lā tär'dā kā no͞on'kä.* Better late than never.

MÁS VALE UN TOMA QUE DOS TE DARÉ (Sp.), *mäs vä'lā o͞on tō'mä kā dôs tĕ dä-rā'.* One "take" is better than two "I'll give."

MAUVAISE HONTE, *mō'vâz' zônt'.* False modesty.

MAUVAIS GOÛT, *mō'vĕ' go͞o'.* False taste.

MI CARO AMIGO (Sp.), *mē kä'rō ä-mē'gō.* My dear friend.

MIR IST ALLES EINERLEI (Ger.), *mēr ĭst ä'lĕs ī'nĕr-lī.* It's all the same to me.

MISE-EN-SCÈNE, *mē'zäN'sân'.* The staging of a play.

MON AMI, *môn' nä'mē'.* My friend.

MON CHER, *môn' shâr'.* My dear (fellow).

MONSIEUR, *mē-syû'.* Sir; Mr.; gentleman.

MOT DU GUET, *mō' dü gĕ'.* A watchword.

MOTS D'USAGE, *mō' dü'zäzh'.* Words in common use.

MUCHOS POCOS HACEN UN MUCHO (Sp.), *mo͞o'chōs pō'kōs ä'thĕn o͞on mo͞o'chō.* Many littles make much; many a mickle makes a muckle.

MURAGLIA BIANCA, CARTA DI MATTO (It.), *mo͞o-räl'yä byän'kä, kär'tä dē mät'tō.* A white wall is the fool's paper.

NAÏVE, *nä'ēv'.* Having unaffected simplicity.

NAÏVETÉ, *nä'ēv''tā'.* Native simplicity.

NÉE, *nā.* Born; maiden name.

NÉGLIGÉ, *nā'glē'zhā'.* A morning dress.

NESSUN MAGGIOR DOLORE CHE RICORDARSI DEL TEMPO FELICE NELLA MISERIA (It.), *nĕs-so͞on' mä-jōr' dō-lō'rĕ kā rē-kōr-där'sē dāl tĕm'pō fē-lē'chĕ näl'lä mē-zä'rē-ä.* No greater sorrow than to remember happy days when in misery.—Dante.

NEUE BESEN KEHREN GUT (Ger.), *noi'ĕ bā'zĕn kā'rĕn go͞ot.* A new broom sweeps clean.

NI FIRMES CARTAS QUE NO LEAS, NI BEBAS AGUA QUE NO VEAS (Sp.), *nē fĕr'mĕs kär'täs kā nō lā'äs nē bā'bäs ä'gwä kä nō vä'äs.* Sign no letter you have not read, nor drink water you cannot see; be very cautious.

NI L'UN NI L'AUTRE, *nē lûN' nē lō'tr'.* Neither the one nor the other.

N'IMPORTE, *năN'pôrt'.* It is of no consequence.

NOBLESSE OBLIGE, *nô'blĕs' ô'blēzh'.* Nobility imposes obligations; much is expected from persons of good position.

NO ES ORO TODO QUE RELUCE (Sp.), *nō ĕs ō'rō tō'thō kā rā-lo͞o'thä.* All is not gold that glitters.

NO HAY BIEN NI MAL QUE CIEN AÑOS DURE (Sp.), *nō ī byān nē mäl kā thyān än'yōs do͞o'rā.* No good or evil lasts a hundred years.

NO HAY DE QUE (Sp.), *nō ī dā kā.* You are welcome; don't mention it.

NO IMPORTA (Sp.), *nō ēm-pōr'tä.* No matter; 'tis all the same.

NO LAS MERECE (Sp.), *nō läs mā-rā'thā.* It is not worth it (in answer to *Gracias*).

NOM DE GUERRE, *nôN' dē gâr'.* A war-name; an assumed name in controversy.

NOM DE PLUME, *nôN dē plüm'.* An assumed title; a pen name.

NON MI RICORDO (It.), *nōn mē rē-kōr'dō.* I do not remember.

NON OGNI FIORE FA BUON ODORE (It.), *nōn ōn'yē fyō'rĕ fä bwōn ō-dō'rĕ.* It is not every flower that smells sweet.

NON VENDER LA PELLE DELL' ORSO PRIMA DI PIGLIARLO (It.), *nōn vän'dĕr lä pĕl'lĕ däll ōr'sō prē'mä dē pēl-yär'lō.* Don't sell the bearskin before you have caught the bear.

NO SE GANÓ ZAMORA EN UNA HORA (Sp.), *nō sā gä-nō' thä-mō'rä ĕn o͞o'nä ō'rä.* (Zamora was not won in an hour), Rome was not built in a day.

NO SE PERMITE HURTAR PARA DAR POR DIOS (Sp.), *nō sā pĕr-mē'tā o͞or-tär' pä'rä där pôr dē'ōs.* It is not lawful to steal in order to give to God.

NOT KENNT KEIN GEBOT (Ger.), *nōt kĕnt kīn gā-bōt'.* Necessity knows no law.

NOTRE DAME, *nô'tr' dàm'.* Our Lady; the Virgin Mary; the great cathedral of Paris.

NOUS AVONS CHANGÉ TOUT CELA, *no͞o'zä'vôN' shäN'zhā' to͞o' sē-là'.* We have changed all that.

NOUS VERRONS, *no͞o' vĕ'rôN'.* We shall see.

NOUVELLES, *no͞o'vĕl'.* News.

NO VALE LA PENA (Sp.), *nō vä'lā lä pā'nä.* It is not worth the trouble.

NO VALE NADA (Sp.), *nō vä'lā nä'thä.* It is worthless; no use; no matter.

NUL BIEN SANS PEINE, *nül' byăN' säN pân'.* No pains, no gains.

NULLA NUOVA, BUONA NUOVA (It.), *no͞ol'lä nwō'vä, bwō'nä nwō'vä.* No news is good news.

OGNI BOTTEGA HA LA SUA MALIZIA (It.), *ōn'yē bŏt-tā'gä ä lä so͞o'ä mä-lē'tsyä.* Every shop has its trick; there are tricks in all trades.

OJOS QUE NO VEN, CORAZÓN QUE NO SIENTE (Sp.), *ō'hōs kā nō vĕn' kō-rä-thōn' kā nō syĕn'tā.* Eyes that see not, heart that feels not; out of sight, out of mind.

OLLA PODRIDA (Sp.), *ôl'yä pō-thrē'thä.* A heterogeneous mixture; a stew of meat and vegetables.

ON CONNAÎT L'AMI AU BESOIN, *ôN kô'nâ' lä'mē' ō bē-zwăN'.* A friend is known in time of need; a friend in need is a friend indeed.

ON DIT, *ôN' dē'.* They say; a rumor.

ORO È CHE ORO VALE (It.), *ō'rō ĕ kā ō'rō vä'lĕ.* That is gold which is worth gold.

OUBLIER JE NE PUIS, *o͞o'blyā' zhē nē püē'.* I can never forget.

OUÏ-DIRE, *o͞o-ē' dēr'.* Hearsay.

OUVRAGE DE LONGUE HALEINE, *o͞o'vräzh' dē lôN'gà'lăn'.* A work of time.

PARA TRABAJAR HACEN FALTA LOS BURROS (Sp.), *pä'rä trä-bä-här' ä'thĕn fäl'tä lōs bo͞or'rōs.* For work you must have the donkeys; let others do the work while you pocket the results.

PAR CI, PAR LÀ, *pär sē' pär là'.* Here and there.

PAR EXCELLENCE, *pär ĕk'sĕ'läNs'.* Pre-eminently.

PAR EXEMPLE, *pär ĕg'zäN'pl'.* For instance.

PAROLE D'HONNEUR, *pà'rôl' dô'nûr'.* Word of honor.

PARTOUT, *pàr'to͞o'.* Everywhere.

PARVENU, *pàr'vē-nü'.* An upstart.

PAS À PAS, *pä'zà'pä'.* Step by step.

PASSÉE, *pä'sā'.* Worn; faded, said of a woman no longer young.

PÂTÉ DE FOIE GRAS, *pä'tā' dē fwä' grä'.* A pie made from the livers of geese.

PEINE FORTE ET DURE, *pân' fôr'tā dür'.* Very severe punishment; a kind of judicial torture.

PENSÉE, *päN'sā'.* A thought expressed in terse, vigorous language.

PÈRE DE FAMILLE, *pâr dē fà'mē'y'.* The father of the family.

PERDU, *pĕr'dü'.* Lost.

PER PIÙ STRADE SI VA A ROMA (It.), *pār pyo͞o' strä'dĕ sē vä ä rō'mä.* There are many roads to Rome.

PERRO QUE LADRA NO MUERDE (Sp.), *pĕr'rō kā lä'thrä nō mwĕr'dā.* His bark is worse than his bite.

PETIT, *pē-tē'.* Small.

PETIT À PETIT L'OISEAU FAIT SON NID, *pē-tē' tà pē-tē' lwä'zō' fâ sôN nē.* Little by little the bird builds its nest.

PETIT COUP, *pē-tē' ko͞o'.* A small mask; a domino.

PETIT-MAÎTRE, *pē-tē' mâ'tr'.* A little master; a fop.

PEU À PEU, *pû'à pû'.* Little by little; by degrees.

PEU S'EN FAUT, *pû' säN fō'.* Nearly so; very near.

PIED À TERRE, *pyā' tà târ'.* A resting place; a temporary lodging.

PIGLIAR DUE COLOMBI A UNA FAVA (It.), *pēl-yär' do͞o'ĕ kō-lōm'bē ä o͞o'nä fä'vä.* To catch two pigeons with one bean; to kill two birds with one stone.

PIS ALLER, *pē' zà'lā'.* The worst or last shift.

POCO A POCO (It.), *pô'kō ä pô'kō.* Little by little; by degrees.

POINT D'APPUI, *pwăN' dà'püē'.* Prop; point of support.

POMMES DE TERRE, *pôm' dē târ'.* Potatoes (apples of the earth).

POR DONDE MENOS SE PIENSA SALTA EL LIEBRE, *pôr dôn'dā mā'nôs sā pyĕn'sä säl'tä ĕl lyā'brā.* The hare leaps whence you least expect; never be surprised.

PORTER UN COUP FUNESTE, *pôr'tā' ûN ko͞o' fü-nĕst'.* To deal a fatal blow.

POT-POURRI, *pō'po͞o'rē'.* A medley.

POUR ACQUIT, *po͞or à'kē'.* Paid; settled. (The usual form of receipt.)

POUR FAIRE RIRE, *po͞or fâr' rēr'.* For fun; for a joke.

POUR FAIRE VISITE, *po͞or fâr' vē'zēt'.* To pay a visit,—written in the corner of a visiting card to notify of a formal call.

POUR PASSER LE TEMPS, *po͞or pä'sā' lē täN'.* To while away the time.

POUR PRENDRE CONGÉ, *po͞or präN'dr' kôN'zhā'.* To take leave. Usually abbreviated to P.P.C. on a visiting card.

PRENDRE LA LUNE AVEC LES DENTS, *präN'dr' là lün' à'vĕk' lā däN'.* To seize the moon in one's teeth; to aim at impossibilities.

PRESTO MATURO, PRESTO MARCIO (It.), *prĕs'tō mä-to͞o'rō prĕs'tō mär'chō.* Soon ripe, soon rotten.

PRÊT D'ACCOMPLIR, *prĕ' dà'kôN'plēr'.* Ready to accomplish.

PRÊT POUR MON PAYS, *prĕ' po͞or môN' pĕ'ē'.* Ready for my country.

PREUX CHEVALIER, *prû' shē-vâ'lyā'.* A brave knight.

PROTÉGÉ, *prô'tā'zhā'.* One protected by another; one to whom patronage is given.

PURÉE, *pü'rā'.* A thick soup, or mashed potatoes.

PURÉE AUX CROUTONS, *pü'rā' ō kro͞o'tôN'.* A thick soup with small cubes of toasted bread.

QUELQUE CHOSE, *kĕl'k' shōz'*. Something; a trifle.
QUÉ QUIERE DECIR ESO? *kā kyā'rā dā-thēr' ā'sō.* What does that mean?
QUERIDO AMIGO MIO (Sp.), *kā-rē'THō ā-mē'gō mē'ō.* My dear friend.
QUI A BU BOIRA, *kē' ȧ' bü' bwȧ'rȧ'.* The tippler will go on tippling; it is hard to break off bad habits.
QUIEN ABROJOS SIEMBRA, ESPINAS COGE (Sp.), *kyān ä-brō'-Hōs syām'brä ĕs-pē'näs kō'Hā.* He who sows brambles reaps thorns.
QUIEN CALLA OTORGA (Sp.), *kyān käl'yä ō-tôr'gä.* Silence gives consent.
QUIEN MÁS TIENE MÁS QUIERE (Sp.), *kyān mäs tyā'nā mäs kyā'rā.* The more one has, the more one wants.
QUIEN MUCHO DUERME, POCO APRENDE (Sp.), *kyān mōō'chō dwĕr'mā pō'kō ä-prĕn'dā.* He who sleeps much learns little; the indolent make little headway.
QUIEN POCO SABE, PRESTO LO REZA (Sp.), *kyān pō'kō sä'bā prĕs'tō lō rā'thä.* He who knows little soon tells it.
QUIEN QUITA LA OCASIÓN, QUITA EL PECADO (Sp.), *kyān kē'tä lä ō-kä-syōn' kē'tä ĕl pā-kä'THō.* He who avoids the occasion avoids sin.
QUIÉN SABE? (Sp.), *kyān sä-bā.* Who knows?
QUIEN TODO LO QUIERE TODO LO PIERDE (Sp.), *kyān tō'THō lō kyā'rā tō'THō lō pyĕr'dā.* Who wants all loses all.
QU'IL SOIT COMME IL EST DÉSIRÉ, *kēl' swȧ' kō'mē' lē' dā'zē'rā'.* Let it be as desired.
QUI AIME BERTRAND AIME SON CHIEN, *kē'âm' bĕr'trăN' âm' sôN' shyăN'.* Love me, love my dog.
QUI N'A SANTÉ, N'A RIEN, *kē' nȧ' săN'tā' nȧ' ryăN'.* He who has not health, has nothing.
QUI PRÊTE À L'AMI PERD AU DOUBLE, *kē' prât' ȧ lȧ'mē' pĕr' tō' dōō'bl'.* Loan oft loses both itself and friend.
QUI VA LÀ? *kē' vȧ' lȧ'.* Who goes there?
QUI VIVE? *kē' vēv'.* Who goes there? On the "qui vive," adroit, watchful.

RAISON D'ÉTAT, *rĕ'zôN' dā'tȧ'.* Interest of the state.
RAISON D'ÊTRE, *rĕ'zôN' dâ'tr'.* The reason for a thing's existence.
RÉGIME, *rā'zhēm'.* Mode or style of rule or management.
RENDEZVOUS, *răN'dā'vōō'.* A place of meeting.
RENDEZ MES DEVOIRS, *răN'dā' mā' dē-vwär'.* Pay my respects.
RENTRER EN GRÂCE, *răN'trā' äN gräs'.* To be restored to favor.
RÉPONDEZ S'IL VOUS PLAÎT (R. S. V. P.), *rā'pôN'dā' sēl vōō' plĕ'.* Reply if you please, written on invitation cards.
RÉPONDRE EN NORMAND, *rā'pôN'dr' äN nôr'măN'.* To answer in Norman; to speak evasively.
RÉSUMÉ, *rā'zü'mā'.* A summing up.
RETE NUOVA NON PIGLIA UCCELLO VECCHIO (It.), *rā'tĕ nwô'vä nōn pēl'yä ōōt-shĕl'lō vĕk'kyō.* A new net won't catch an old bird.
REVENONS À NOS MOUTONS, *rē-vnôN' ȧ nō' mōō'tôN'.* Let us return to our sheep; let us come back to our subject.
RIEN N'EST BEAU QUE LE VRAI, *ryăN' nĕ' bō' kē lē vrâ'.* There is nothing beautiful but truth.
RIRA BIEN QUI RIRA LE DERNIER, *rē'rȧ' byăN' kē' rē'rȧ' lē dĕr'nyā'.* He laughs best who laughs last.
RIRE ENTRE CUIR ET CHAIR; RIRE SOUS CAPE, *rēr' äN'tr, küēr' ā shâr'; rēr' sōō' kȧp'.* To laugh in one's sleeve.
ROBE DE CHAMBRE, *rôb' dē shäN'br'.* A dressing gown; a morning gown.
ROBE DE NUIT, *rôb' dē nüē'.* A nightdress.
RÔLE, *rōl.* A part in a performance.
RUSE DE GUERRE, *rüz' dē gâr'.* A military stratagem.

SALUD Y PESETAS! (Sp.), *sä-lōōTH' ē pā-sā'täs.* Health and money (a toast).
SANAN CUCHILLADAS, MÁS NO MALAS PALABRAS (Sp.), *sä'nän kōō'chēl-yä'THäs mäs nō mä'läs pä-lä'bräs.* Wounds from a knife will heal, but not those from the tongue.
SANS CÉRÉMONIE, *săN sā'rā'mô'nē'.* Without ceremony.
SANS PEUR ET SANS REPROCHE, *săN pûr' ā săN rē-prôsh'.* Fearless and stainless.
SANS RIME ET SANS RAISON, *săN rēm'ā săN rĕ'zôN'.* Without rime or reason.
SANS SOUCI, *săN sōō'sē'.* Free from care.
SAUVE QUI PEUT, *sōv' kē' pû'.* Save yourselves; let each one look out for himself; headlong flight.
SAVOIR FAIRE, *sȧ'vwär' fâr'.* Tact.
SAVOIR VIVRE, *sȧ'vwär' vē'vr'.* Good breeding.
SDEGNO D'AMANTE POCO DURA (It.), *zdān'yō dä-män'tĕ pô'kō dōō'rä.* A lover's anger is short-lived.
SÉANCE, *sā'äNs'.* A sitting given for a painting; an assembly gathered for some set purpose.
SE FAIRE JOUR, *sē fâr' zhōōr'.* To force one's way.
SELON LES RÈGLES, *sē-lôN' lā rĕg'l'.* According to rule.
SEMPRE IL MAL NON VIEN PER NUOCERE (It.), *sĕm'prĕ ēl mäl nōn vyĕn pär nwôt'shä-rĕ.* Misfortune is not always an evil.
SE NON È VERO, È BEN TROVATO (It.), *sĕ nōn ĕ vā'rō ĕ bĕn trō-vä'tō.* If it is not true, it is cleverly invented.
SÍ GRACIAS (Sp.), *sē grä'thyäs.* Yes, thank you.

SI JEUNESSE SAVAIT, SI VIEILLESSE POUVAIT, *sē zhû'nĕs' sȧ'vâ' sē vyâ'yĕs' pōō'vâ'.* If youth but knew, if age but had strength.
SI JUVENTUD SUPIERA Y SI VEJEZ PUDIERA (Sp.), *sē Hōō-vĕn-tōōTH' sōō-pyā'rä ē sē vā-Häth' pōō-THyā'rä.* If youth but knew, if age but had strength; lost chances.
SOIRÉE, *swä'rā'.* An evening party.
SOUFFLER LE CHAUD ET LE FROID, *sōō'flā' lē shō' ā lē frwä'.* To blow hot and cold.
SOUS UN FAUX JOUR, *sōō' zûN fō' zhōōr'.* In a bad light.
SO VIEL ICH WEISS (Ger.), *zō fēl ĭK vīs.* As far as I know.
STURM UND DRANG (Ger.), *shtōōrm ōōnt dräng.* Storm and stress.

TABLE D'HÔTE, *tȧ'bl' dōt'.* Table of the host; a meal served entire, not from separate orders.
TÂCHE SANS TACHE, *täsh' săN tȧsh'.* A work without a stain.
TANT MIEUX, *täN' myû'.* So much the better.
TANT PIS, *täN' pē'.* So much the worse.
TEL MAÎTRE, TEL VALET, *tĕl mâ'tr' tĕl vȧ'lā'.* Like master, like man.
TÊTE-À-TÊTE, *tâ'tȧ-tât'.* A conversation between two parties.
TOUJOURS PERDRIX, *tōō'zhōōr' pĕr'drē'.* Always partridges; the same thing over and over again; too much of a good thing.
TOUJOURS PRÊT, *tōō'zhōōr' prĕ'.* Always ready.
TOUR DE FORCE, *tōōr' dē fôrs'.* A feat of strength or skill.
TOUT À FAIT, *tōō'tȧ-fĕ'.* Wholly; entirely.
TOUT À L'HEURE, *tōō'tȧ-lûr'.* Presently; just now.
TOUT AU CONTRAIRE, *tōō'tō-kôN'trâr'.* Quite the contrary.
TOUT À VOUS, *tōō'tȧ-vōō'.* Entirely yours.
TOUT BIEN OU RIEN, *tōō' byăN'nōō ryăN'.* All well or nothing.
TOUT DE SUITE, *tōō'dē-süēt'.* Immediately.
TOUT ENSEMBLE, *tōō'täN'säN'bl'.* All together, entire effect (of a work of art).
TOUT LE MONDE EST SAGE APRÈS COUP, *tōō' lē môN'dĕ'sȧzh' ȧ'prĕ' kōō'.* Everybody is wise after the event,—when it's too late.
TRADUTTORI, TRADITORI (It.), *trä-dōōt-tō'rē trä-dē-tō'rē.* Translators are traitors,—they often give a wrong meaning to an author.
TRAVAUX FORCÉS, *trä'vō' fôr'sā'.* Hard labor (legal sentence).
TUTTE LE STRADE CONDUCONO A ROMA (It.), *tōōt'tĕ lĕ strä'dĕ kōn-dōō'kō-nō ä rō'mä.* All roads lead to Rome.

UEBUNG MACHT DEN MEISTER (Ger.), *ü'bōōng mäKt dĕn mīs'tĕr.* Practice makes perfect.
UN BIENFAIT N'EST JAMAIS PERDU, *ûN byăN'fĕ' nĕ' zhȧ'mĕ' pĕr'dü'.* A kindness is never lost.
UN SOT À TRIPLE ÉTAGE, *ûN sō'ȧ trē'pl' ā'tȧzh'.* A consummate fool.
UN "TIENS" VAUT MIEUX QUE DEUX "TU L'AURAS," *ûN tyăN' vō' myû' kē dû tü lō'rȧ'.* One "take it" is worth two "you shall have it"; a bird in the hand is worth two in the bush.

VALET DE CHAMBRE, *vȧ'lā' dē shäN'br'.* An attendant.
VAMOS (Sp.), *vä'mōs.* Let us go; now, then!
VAYA USTED CON DIOS (Sp.), *vä'yä ōōs-tĕTH' kōn dē'ōs.* Go with God; good-by and good luck!
VEDI NAPOLI E POI MORI (It.), *vā'dē nä'pō-lē ĕ pō'ē mō'rē.* See Naples and then die.
VERDADES Y ROSAS TIENEN ESPINAS (Sp.), *vĕr-dä'THĕs ē rō'säs tyā'nĕn ĕs-pē'näs.* Truth and roses have their thorns.
VÉRITÉ SANS PEUR, *vā'rē'tā' săN pûr'.* Truth without fear.
VIELE HÄND' MACHEN BALD EIN END' (Ger.), *fē'lĕ hĕnt' mäk'ĕn bält īn ĕnt'.* Many hands make quick work.
VIGUEUR DE DESSUS, *vē'gûr' dē dē-sü'.* Strength from on high.
VINO DENTRO, SENNO FUORI (It.), *vē'nō dān'trō sān'nō fwō'rē.* When the wine is in, the wit is out.
VIS-À-VIS, *vē'zȧ vē'.* Face to face.
VIVE LA BAGATELLE, *vēv' lȧ bȧ'gȧ'tĕl'.* Success to trifles! Said on hearing something ridiculous related.
VIVE LE ROI, *vēv' lē rwä'.* Long live the king.
VOILÀ, *vwȧ'lȧ'.* See there; there is; there!
VOILÀ TOUT, *vwȧ'lȧ' tōō'.* That's all; there you are!
VOILÀ UNE AUTRE CHOSE, *vwȧ'lȧ' ü'nō'tr' shōz'.* That's quite another thing.
VOIR LE DESSOUS DES CARTES, *vwär lē dē-sōō' dā kärt'.* To see the face of the cards; to be in the secret.
VOUS Y PERDREZ VOS PAS, *vōō'zē pĕr'drā' vō' pȧ'.* You will have your walk for nothing; you will lose your labor over it.

WAS FEHLT IHNEN? (Ger.), *väs fält ē'nĕn.* What ails you? What is the matter with you?
WIE DIE ARBEIT, SO DER LOHN (Ger.), *vē dē är'bīt zō dâr lōn.* As the labor, so the reward.

ZEITGEIST (Ger.), *tsīt'gīst.* The spirit of the age.

TEST QUESTIONS

The following list of *test* questions has been prepared to serve as a *review* of the preceding subject matter on the English language. As the questions have been arranged in logical order for the proper development of each subject, they should serve also to suggest a thorough and systematic *course of study* for those who desire to improve their everyday English.

Although the list contains more than 1300 questions, it includes but a small fraction of the thousands of questions which the English department will answer. A similar list will be found at the end of each of the other 11 departments of the book.

HISTORY AND DEVELOPMENT OF THE ENGLISH LANGUAGE

How did the English language come to be so generally spoken? . . . 25

Explain the relationship of the English language to other tongues . . . 25

What is meant by the Aryan language? . . . 25

What early tongue is called the basis of the English language? . . . 25

Tell the story of the beginning of the Anglo-Saxon language . . . 25–26

Mention four Anglo-Saxon words . . . 26

What occasioned the introduction of a foreign element into the pure Saxon speech of England? . . . 26

What kind of words were brought into the English language by the introduction of Christianity? . . . 26

Name some words introduced by the Romans into the language spoken by the inhabitants of Britain . . . 26

What effect had the conquest of the Danes upon the culture and the language of the people of England? . . . 26

Mention six words of Danish origin . . . 26

Who were the Northmen? . . . 26

What was the language of the Northmen? . . . 26

What country was called Normandy? Why? . . 26

What effect did the Norman conquest have on the English language? . . . 26

After the Norman conquest, which classes spoke the Saxon language? Which spoke French? . 26

In what qualities did the Norman language surpass the Saxon? . . . 26

What is meant by Middle English? How did Middle English differ from the Anglo-Saxon of earlier years? . . . 26

What influences made the Latin element in the English language so large? . . . 26

Describe the development of the English language during the Middle English period . 26

What great literary works mark the beginning of the modern English period? . . . 26

How did the printing press affect the growth of the English language? . . . 26

Do changes in the English language still occur? Give a reason for your answer . . . 26

Mention two things which have contributed greatly to the growth of modern English . . 26

From what language are most of our modern scientific words derived? . . . 26

By a comparison of the synonyms *royal, regal, kingly,* explain the way in which many words have found their way into English . . . 26

In what two ways were Latin words brought into the English language? . . . 26

Mention two words which have come directly from the Latin . . . 26

Give two words which have come from the Latin through the French . . . 26

From what language is each of the following synonyms: *breeze, gale, storm, gust, tempest, hurricane*? . . . 27

Give three English words which are of Dutch origin . . . 27

What kind of words for the most part are those which have been taken over into English from the Hebrew? . . . 27

What is the earliest Italian word incorporated into the English language? . . . 27

From what language do we get most of our musical terms? . . . 27

What effect has exploration had upon the English language? Explain . . . 27

Give four English words acquired from the Spanish; two from the French . . . 27

Mention three words taken from languages of American Indians . . . 27

From what languages do we get the following words: *law, castle, acute, pattern, crime, sin, pull, depot, wigwam*? . . . 26–27

Of what practical value is a knowledge of the sources of the words from which the English language is built? . . . 27

How may one better his command of language? 28

GOOD USAGE

Which is correct, *a historical society* or *an historical society*; *such a one* or *such an one*? . 30

Before two adjectives qualifying a noun, what is the rule for the use of the article *a*? . . . 30

In *a secretary and treasurer,* how many persons are implied? What change in the expression will increase the number implied? . . . 30

Jane bought *a black and a white dress.* How many dresses did she buy? Change the sentence to mean one dress . . . 30

Explain the use of the word *is* in the sentence, "Acoustics *is* a science." . . . 30

Which is correct, "Two and three *are* five" or "Two and three *is* five"? . . . 30

Distinguish between *admittance* and *admission* by using these words correctly in sentences . 30

In what sense is the word *adore* correctly used? 30

Correct the following sentence: "Agreeable to your request, I am writing you." . . . 30

Is it correct to say, "They are both just alike"? Explain the reason . . . 30

Explain the distinction in meaning between *all together* and *altogether* . . . 31

Distinguish between being *almost* killed and being *nearly* killed. Illustrate these words correctly used . . . 31

Illustrate the correct use of the words *alone* and *only* . . . 31

Explain the use of *all ready* and *already* . . 31

Point out the error in the following sentence: "If he is satisfied, I am satisfied also." What is the rule for the use of the word *also*? . . 31

In regard to usage, compare the following words: *alumni, alumna, alumnus, alumnæ* . 31

What is wrong in this sentence: "Whenever I see her, I always think of mother"? . . . 31

Explain the difference between *amateur* and *novice* . . . 31

Correct the error in the following sentence and give a reason for your answer: "He was there among the rest." . . . 31

Do we say correctly, "a large amount of people"? Explain . . . 31

Which word suggests the greater quantity, *ample* or *sufficient*? . . . 31

Distinguish between *answer* and *reply* . . . 31

Is there any difference between *antiquated, ancient, antique,* and *old*? Illustrate by using these words correctly in sentences . . . 31

What is wrong in this sentence: "All came but not a one was on time"? . . . 32

What is the difference between *appear* and *seem*? Show the correct use of these words . 32

Give accurately the use of each of the following words: *apt, likely, liable* . . . 32

Explain the difference in meaning between the following sentences: "James is not *as* tall *as* Tom"; "James is not *so* tall *as* Tom." . . 32

WORD BUILDING

DERIVATION OF ENGLISH WORDS FROM THE LATIN

SPELLING

SENTENCE BUILDING

PREPOSITIONS AND CONJUNCTIONS

CAPITAL LETTERS

PUNCTUATION

WRITING AND SPEAKING

PUBLIC SPEAKING

Of what practical value is a knowledge of public speaking? 97
Mention three requisites of the successful public speaker 97
What is the first step in planning a speech? Why is this important? 98
Of what three chief divisions must a well arranged speech consist? 98
What is a practical preparation for the impromptu speech? 98
Give two appropriate suggestions for the beginning of an after-dinner speech. 98
What is the most certain aid to the delivery of an address? 98
Mention an advantage and a disadvantage in speaking from a manuscript 98
What is considered the most effective form of public speaking? 99
Upon what combined forces does the total effect of a speech depend? 99
In the use of *comparison* as a method of exposition, why is it important to know something of the audience's experience? 99
Why should *synthesis* follow *analysis* in expository speaking? 99
What are the six basic methods of exposition? 99
Give a definition of Public Speaking 99
What method of exposition is being used when a speaker gives another view of the object explained? 99
What method of exposition is used when a blackboard drawing is shown? 99
Speeches with the purpose of *Impressiveness* are akin to poetry. Why? 99
Name three speech occasions for which the *purpose* may be *Impressiveness* 99
What is the essential function of the speech of introduction? 99
List three common faults of speeches of introduction 99
Why may we say *debate* is one of the final steps in the discussion process? 99
In what New England gatherings were *open forum discussions* first held in America? . . . 100
When and where did the modern *open-forum* movement have its beginnings? 100
What is the significance of J. W. Studebaker in the open forum? 100
Give the *five steps* in the process of group thinking? 100
Which step in the process is likely to be neglected in group discussion? 100
What is the essential duty of the leader in group discussion? 100
What must the leader guard against in forum directing? 100
List five points for the leader of a *conference* to keep in mind 100
In conference directing why is it sometimes a good idea to call a *recess*? 100
List the seven types of group-discussion . . . 100
What type of discussion is best suited to *problem-solving?* 100
In the *panel-forum* how much time should be allowed for audience participation? 100
When is it best to use the *debate-forum* type of discussion? 101
What is the purpose of argumentative discourse? 101
State the aim of *persuasion* 101
How does the appeal made by *argument* differ from the appeal made by *persuasion?* . . . 101
What constitutes *debate*? 101
Mention three important steps in planning a debate 101
What place has *logic* in argumentative discourse? 102
Outline the steps necessary in conducting a debate 102

RADIO SPEAKING

About how many radio sets are in use in America today? 102
What is the significance of the Federal Communications Commission in radio? 102
How can Americans go about getting better programs? 103
What does *frequency modulation* offer to the future of American radio? 103
With extension of F.M. why will there be greater opportunity for non-professionals in radio broadcasting? 103
What is the essential difference between radio speaking and public speaking? 103
Why is good oral reading important in radio speaking? 103
What is the average size of the radio audience? 103
Should radio speakers use gestures? 103
What are the qualities looked for in a professional announcer? 104
What are the two best ways through which one can get training for the radio profession? . 104

FORMS OF ORAL INTERPRETATION

What is the difference between a *speech* phrase and a grammatical phrase? 104
Why is a *speech phrase* essentially a unit? . . 104
Why is phrasing so important in oral reading? 104
What are the three forms of speech emphasis? 104
What does the voice do in the respective forms? 104
Why is it so important to distinguish between the *new* and the *old* in reading? 104
List four commonly used forms of oral interpretation 105
Should one memorize in *interpretative reading?* 105
Why is *literal activity* out of place in Interpretative Reading? 105
What type of material is best suited to Recitation? 105
What type of material is best suited to Impersonation? 105
Should one memorize for Impersonation? . . 105
Should one memorize for Story Telling? . . 105
In what ways is Story Telling similar to Public Speaking? 105
What is the best means of obtaining an effective manner in delivery? 106
Explain the part which gesture should play in public speaking 106
Name two well established rules for the use of gestures 109
How can one acquire *good speech* in delivery? . 107
What is the fundamental principle in the mastery of good voice quality? 107
Explain what is meant by *change of pitch* . . 107
Of what value is a *change of pitch* in the voice? . 107
Mention eight qualities of the speaking voice 107
In changing the pitch of the voice, what should one be careful to avoid? 107
In general what words should receive particular emphasis? 107
Should the *rate of speaking* remain the same? Explain 107
Show how the inflection of the voice may alter the meaning of a sentence 107
State four advantages of definite pauses in public speaking. 107
Name five means of securing emphasis in oratory 107
Of what importance in public speaking is the habit of right breathing? 107

PRONUNCIATION

Give the correct pronunciation of abdomen, address, adult, asphalt, column, conduit, cheviot, chiropodist 108–109
Is your pronunciation of each of the following words correct: exit, financier, diphtheria, élite, interesting, gratis? 110–111
How should the following words be pronounced: longevity, mischievous, municipal, protein, senile, root? 112–113

Pronounce correctly the following: chauffeur, décolleté, entente, masseur, masseuse, menu, morale, passé, protégé, résumé, seidlitz, suite, ukulele 109–114
What is the correct pronunciation of each of the following words: clique, clematis, forehead, khaki, jardinière, monetary? 109–112

FORMS OF LITERARY COMPOSITION

Mention several sources of good literature . . 115
Name the principal forms of prose composition 115–116
What are the distinguishing features of the *romance*, the *novel*, and the *short story*? 115
Distinguish between *history* and *biography*. Name some well-known histories 116
What are folk stories? To what form of composition do they belong? 116
Mention some well-known specimens of the *fairy tale* 116
Explain the difference between a *parable* and an *allegory*. Give examples of each 116–117
What book furnishes the best examples of the parable? 116
Of what form of prose composition is *Robinson Crusoe* an example? 116
Mention three historical novels 116
Name five forms of poetry 117
What is the character of lyric poetry? Give two examples of lyric poetry 117
Distinguish the ode from other forms of poetry. Mention two English odes 117
What is the nature of an elegy? Give a well-known example of elegy 117
Name four great epics 117
Of what form of poetry are *Miles Standish* and *Evangeline* examples? 117
Name two authors who have written notable essays 117
Explain the difference between an essay and an oration 117
Mention two writers whose works furnish examples of American oratory 117
What is a sonnet? Name two authors who have composed sonnets 117
Explain the characteristics of the drama . 117–118
Are English dramas written in verse or in prose? Explain 118
How does tragedy differ from comedy? . . . 118

FIGURES OF SPEECH

What is a *figure of speech*? Illustrate 118
What is a *simile*? By what words is it usually introduced? Give two examples of *simile* . 118
How does a *metaphor* differ from a *simile*? Give sentences to show this difference . . . 118
Define and illustrate *synecdoche* 118
What is *metonymy*? Give two examples of *metonymy* 118
How does *synecdoche* differ from *metonymy*? Illustrate 118
In the following sentence, change the *simile* to a *metaphor*: "He shall be like a tree planted by the rivers of water." 118
State what figure of speech is employed in the following sentence: "The sea was covered with sails." 118
Give three examples of *personification* 118
Explain the following figures and illustrate each: *apostrophe, irony, alliteration* 119
Tell what figure of speech is used in each of the following sentences: "Caesar leaves Gaul." "His steel gleamed on high." "The more haste, the less speed." "Give us this day our daily bread." 118–119

LETTER WRITING

Why is the study of letter writing of so great importance? 120
Name four requisites of a business letter . . . 120
Should one say "Enclosed please find"? Give a reason for your answer 121
Explain the importance of the mechanical form of a letter 122
Name the first three items in the building of a business letter 123
What should the *heading* of a business letter contain? Explain its position on the page . 123
Illustrate three forms of *heading* for a business letter 123
Should the word *street* or *avenue* in the address begin with a capital? 123
Show a correct form of *introduction* to a business letter 123
Give three forms of *salutation* used for business letters 123
Which is the more formal salutation, "My dear Mr. Brown" or "Dear Mr. Brown"? Which is proper in writing to a stranger? . 123
Illustrate two forms of *address* and of *salutation* used in writing to a doctor 123
Is it permissible in addressing a letter to write Mrs. Dr. Bennett? 123
In the punctuation of the salutation, is the colon or the comma to be preferred? Explain . . 123
Explain the position of the *body of the letter*, and show the margins which should be left . 123
Give several forms of complimentary closing used in business correspondence 124
Where should the signature of a letter be written? If one wishes to sign "Miss" or "Mrs." to a business letter, within what marks should such words be enclosed? 124
Explain the proper position of the address on the envelope 124
Should the address on the envelope be punctuated? Explain and illustrate 124
Illustrate the correct forms of *introduction, salutation*, and *close*, in writing to the mayor of New York City 124
Write a letter ordering a magazine; a letter of application for a position; a note of introduction 126, 127
How may a letter of recommendation be addressed? Write a letter of recommendation. 128
For what purposes may postal cards be used? Is it permissible to write a personal message on a postal card? 128
Mention six general rules concerning the care of daily mail 128–129
Distinguish between the business letter and the friendly letter. 120–132
Write an informal invitation to a luncheon; an informal letter acknowledging a gift of flowers 130
In what person are formal invitations always written? In what person should the reply to a formal invitation be written? 131
Write a formal invitation to an afternoon reception. Write a reply of acceptance . . . 131
What is the meaning of *R. S. V. P.*, sometimes placed in the lower left-hand corner of an invitation? 131
What is the chief charm in a letter of friendship? 132

SYNONYMS AND ANTONYMS

What is the meaning of the word *synonym*? of the word *antonym*? 137
Explain the correct use of *abandon, desert, forsake, relinquish* 138
How does *ability* differ from *talent*? 138
By means of a sentence, show the correct use of *loathe*. Mention a word of opposite meaning. 138
Show the difference between *affirm* and *assert*. 139
In meaning, which is the stronger word, *afraid* or *fearful*? What word is an antonym of *afraid*? of *fearful*? 139
How does *carriage* differ from *gait*? 139
What is the difference between a person's *air* and his *manner*? 139
When is pain *alleviated* and when is it *relieved*?. 140
Compare the meanings of *alone, solitary, lonely* 140

How is *applause* shown? How is *acclamation* shown? What word is opposed in meaning to *applause*? to *acclamation*? 141
Explain the difference between being *attentive* and being *careful*. Which may be used in reference to an action? 141
Do we *assent* or *consent* to matters of conduct? 141
Make a careful distinction between the meanings of *beautiful, fine, fair, handsome, pretty*. Would you call a landscape *handsome*? . . . 142
In meaning, which is the broader term, *conduct* or *behavior*? Explain. 142
Distinguish between *begin, commence, enter upon*. 142
Give an antonym of each of the following: *belief, credit, trust, faith*. 142
Explain the words *bravery* and *courage*. How does *valor* compare with *bravery* or *courage*? . 143
Which applies to the greater distance, *bring* or *fetch*? Explain the use of these words . . . 143
What is a *calamity*? a *disaster*? Was the sinking of the Titanic a *calamity* or a *disaster*? . 144
How does *capture* differ from *seizure*? 144
Explain accurately the use of each of the following words: *business, occupation, employment* . 144
Distinguish between things *heavenly* and things *celestial*. Give an antonym of each word . . 145
Explain the difference between one's *character* and one's *reputation* 145
Is it possible for a person to be *civil* without being *polite*? Give a reason for your answer. . 145
Give sentences showing the correct use of the words *clearly* and *distinctly* 146
Mention two synonyms of *close*; an antonym of *close* 146
State the difference between a thing that is *finished* and a thing that is *complete* 147
Compare the meanings of *consent, permit, allow* 148
Distinguish between *effect* and *result* 148
Name two words which are synonyms and give an antonym of each 148
How does *contagion* differ from *infection*? . . 149
When is a disease said to be *contagious*? when *epidemic*? 149
Do *accurate* and *correct* mean the same? Give a reason for your answer 149–150
When do we *cry* and when do we *weep*? . . . 150
Contrast the meanings of *crime, vice,* and *sin* . 150
What is the difference between a *remedy* and a *cure*? 150
What words are antonyms of *dark, obscure, dim*? 150
In what way is *habit* formed? How does *custom* differ from *habit*? 150
Distinguish between *correction, discipline, punishment*. Do we remove an evil by *correction* or by *discipline*? 150
Compare the meanings of *cost, expense, price, charge* 150
Of what word is *plaintiff* an antonym? Of what word is it a synonym? 151
Is *deity* the same as *divinity*? Explain 151
When is a thing said to be *defaced*? when *disfigured*? How do *disfigure* and *deform* compare in meaning? 151
The cathedral at Reims was seriously bombarded during the World War. Was it *destroyed* or *ruined*? 152
Give the difference between *intend* and *purpose*. Which is the stronger in meaning, *purpose* or *design*? 152
When does one properly *merit* a reward? . . . 152
Is there any difference in meaning between *die* and *expire*? 152
Mention a synonym of *difficulty*; an antonym of *nausea* 153
Explain the distinction between *disappear* and *vanish* 153
Is it possible to have a bad *temper* with a good *disposition*? Give a reason for your answer . 154
State the difference between a *durable*, a *lasting*, and a *permanent* thing 154
Which word implies the more, *education* or *instruction*? Explain their relation to each other. 155
To what is the word *enlarge* correctly applied? *increase*? 155
Give two synonyms of *eternal* and explain the meaning of each. What word is of opposite meaning to *eternal*? 156
Upon what does the *expediency* of a thing depend? What determines its *fitness*? 156
What is the difference between *discover* and *invent*? Did Marconi *invent* or *discover* wireless telegraphy? 157
Mention an antonym of each of the following: *female, feminine, effeminate* 157
When do we *forgive* and when do we *pardon*? . 158
How do *free* and *liberal* differ in usage? Mention an antonym of each word 159
Is one *intimidated* or *frightened* by present danger? Explain the correct use of each word . 159
Distinguish between *guard* and *guardian* . . . 160
Of what word is *happen* a synonym? Of what word is *unlucky* an antonym? 160
Explain the difference between *habitation* and *home*; between *house* and *residence* 160
Mention two synonyms of *hard* and give an antonym of each 160
Distinguish between *human* race and *humane* race 161
Is a tree *high* or *tall*? Is the bird's nest in the top of the tree *high* or *lofty*? Give a sentence in which *lofty* is used correctly. 161
Compare the meanings of *hollow* and *empty* and mention an antonym of each word. 161
When is a person properly termed *idle* and when *lazy*? What does *indolent* mean? 162
A man saved a boy's life. Is the boy *indebted* or *obliged* to the man? 162
State the difference between *imminent* danger and *impending* danger 162
Are *inability* and *disability* the same? Explain. 162
Distinguish between *inside* and *interior*. . . . 163
In speaking of time, which is of greater duration, *instant* or *moment*? 163
How does *intellect* differ from *talent*? What is the difference between *talent* and *genius*? . . 163
Is there any difference between *joy* and *gladness*? Explain 163
Mention a synonym and an antonym of *large* . 164
What is an *apartment*? How do *lodging* and *apartment* compare in meaning? 164
Explain the difference between a person's *manners* and his *morals* 164
Contrast the meanings of the words *meeting* and *interview* 165
Distinguish between *native* worth and *natural* worth 165
When is a thing *poised* and when is it *balanced*? 166
Mention a word opposed in meaning to each of the following: *powerful, mighty, peace, politeness* 166
Of what word is *unprepared* an antonym? . . . 167
Can a person be *conspicuous* without being *prominent*? Explain 167
Contrast the meanings of the words *rural* and *rustic* 168
What word is a synonym of *sharp*? an antonym of *sharp*? 168
State the difference between a *sign* and a *signal*. 169
In regard to usage, compare the following words: *speak, say, tell* 169
What is the difference between *truth* and *veracity*? 170
Do we *cite* authors or do we *quote* them? Illustrate the distinction 145
Are all authors writers? Are all writers authors? Explain 171
Explain the correct use of each of the following words: *want, need, lack* 171
Give an antonym of each of the following words: *weak, feeble, infirm* 171

BIBLIOGRAPHY

HISTORY OF THE ENGLISH LANGUAGE

Baugh, A. C.—A History of the English Language. *Appleton-Century*
Bloomfield, L.—Language. . . . . *Holt*
Graff, W. L.—Language and Languages. *Appleton*
Greenough, J. B. and Kittredge, G. L.—Words and Their Ways in English Speech. . . . *Macmillan*
McKnight, G. H.—English Words and Their Background. . . . . *Appleton*
Robertson, S.—The Development of Modern English. . . . . *Prentice-Hall*
Wyld, H. C. K.—The Best English. *Clarendon Press*

GOOD USAGE

Canby, H. S. and Opdycke, J. B.—Handbook of English Usage. . . . . *Macmillan*
Fowler, H. W.—A Dictionary of Modern English Usage. . . . . *Oxford*
Horwill, H. W.—A Dictionary of Modern American Usage. . . . . *Oxford*
Hutchinson, Lois I.—Standard Handbook for Secretaries. . . . . *McGraw-Hill*
Kennedy, A. G.—Current Usage. *Ginn and Company*
Partridge, Eric—Usage and Abusage. . . *Harper*
Vizetelly, F. H.—A Desk-book of Errors in English. *Funk and Wagnalls*
Woolley, E. C.—Handbook of Composition. *Heath*

WORD BUILDING

Brown, Ivor J.—A Word in Your Ear. . . *Dutton*
Chadsey, Charles P.—Words. . *Grosset and Dunlap*
Hart, Archibald—Twelve Ways to Build a Vocabulary. . . . . *Dutton*
Weekley, Ernest—An Etymological Dictionary.
—The Romance of Words.. . *Dutton*

SPELLING AND PRONUNCIATION

Bender, J. F.—NBC Handbook of Pronunciation. *Crowell*
Betts, Emmett A.—Spelling Vocabulary Study. *American Book Co.*
Foran, Thomas George—The Psychology and Teaching of Spelling. . *Catholic Education Press*
Masters, Harry V.—A Study of Spelling Errors. *University of Iowa Studies*
Phyfe, W. H. P.—Eighteen-thousand Words Often Mispronounced. . . . . *Putnam*

DICTIONARIES

New Standard Dictionary. . *Funk and Wagnalls*
Webster's New International Dictionary. *Merriam*
Oxford English Dictionary. . . . . . . *Oxford*
Craigie, Sir Wm. A.—A Dictionary of American English. . . . . . . *Univ. of Chicago Press*
Desk Dictionaries for Ready Reference:
American College Dictionary. . . . . . *Harper*
College Standard Dictionary. *Funk and Wagnalls*
Webster's Collegiate Dictionary . . . . *Merriam*
The Winston Simplified Dictionary. . . *Winston*
Foreign Language Dictionaries:
Cassell's New German Dictionary. *Funk and Wagnalls*
Edgren, A. H.—Italian-English Dictionary. *Holt*
Harrap's Standard French and English Dictionary. . . . . *Heath*
New English-Spanish Dictionary. . . *Appleton*

SENTENCE BUILDING

Aiken, Janet R.—Commonsense Grammar. *Crowell*
Curme, G. O.—Parts of Speech and Accidence. *Heath*
Dakin, Dorothy—The Mastery of the Sentence. *Harper*
Fernald, J. G.—English Grammar Simplified. *Funk and Wagnalls*
Fries, Charles O.—American English Grammar. *Appleton-Century*
Frost, Minnie—Correct English Through Practice. *Scribner*
Jespersen, J. O. H.—Essentials of English Grammar. *Holt*

PUNCTUATION AND CAPITALIZATION

Collins, F. H.—Authors' and Printers' Dictionary. *Milford*
Knoettge, Rebecca W. and Van Duzen, Mabel—How Shall I Punctuate It? *Farrar and Rinehart*
Manual of Style. . . . . . *Univ. of Chicago Press*
Monro, Kate M.—English for Secretaries. *McGraw-Hill*
Sumney, George, Jr., and Abbott, J. P.—A Manual for College English. . . . . *Ronald Press*

WRITING AND SPEAKING

Appel, Francis S.—Write What You Mean . *Holt*
Archer, William—Playmaking. *Small, Maynard & Co.*
Baldwin, Charles Sears—Writing and Speaking. *Longmans Green*
Blackiston, E.—Teach Yourself to Write. *The Writer*
Canby, H. S.—Better Writing. . *Harcourt Brace*
Canby, H. S. and Opdycke, J. B.—A Modern English Course. . . . . *Macmillan*
Flesch, R.—The Art of Plain Talk. . . . *Harper*
Foerster, N. and Steadman, J. M.—Writing and Thinking. . . . . *Houghton Mifflin*
Lawton, S. P.—Radio Continuity Types. *Expression Co.*
Opdycke, J. B.—The English of Commerce. *Macmillan*
Palmer, G. H.—Self-cultivation in English. *Houghton Mifflin*
Quiller-Couch, Sir Arthur—On the Art of Writing. *Putnam*
Williams, Arnold—Modern Exposition. . . *Crofts*
Wylie, Max—Radio Writing. *Farrar and Rinehart*

FORMS OF SPEAKING

Abbott, Waldo—Handbook of Broadcasting. *McGraw-Hill*
Borden, Richard C.—Public Speaking—As Listeners Like It! . . . . *Harper*
Eubank, H. L. and Auer, J. J.—Discussion and Debate. . . . . *Crofts*
Farma, Wm. J.—Prose, Poetry and Drama for Oral Interpretation. . . . . *Harper*
Gullan, M.—Choral Speaking . . . *Expression Co.*
Johnson, Gertrude E.—Modern Literature for Oral Interpretation. . . . . *Century*
Monroe, A. H.—Principles and Types of Speech. *Scott-Foresman*
O'Neill, J. M.—Extemporaneous Speaking. *Harper*
—Models of Speech Composition. . *Century*
Sarett, L. R. and Foster, W. T.—Basic Principles of Speech. . . . . *Houghton Mifflin*
Weaver, A. T.—The New Better Speech (Rev.) *Harcourt Brace*
Wicks, Sidney—Public Speaking for Business Men. *Methuen*

LETTER WRITING

Aurner, Robert R.—Effective English in Business. *Southwestern Pub. Co.*
Hotchkiss, G. B., Kilduff, E. J., and Janis, J. H.—Advanced Business Correspondence. . . *Harper*
Lucas, E. V.—The Gentlest Art. . . . *Methuen*
Williams, Cecil B.—Effective Business Writing. *Ronald Press*

SYNONYMS AND ANTONYMS

Allen, F. S.—Synonyms and Antonyms. . *Harper*
Baker, Josephine T.—The Correct Word. *Correct English Pub. Co.*
Fernald, J. C.—Standard Handbook of English Synonyms, Antonyms and Prepositions. *Funk and Wagnalls*
March, Francis A.—Thesaurus Dictionary of the English Language. . . . *Historical Pub. Co.*
Mawson, C. O. S.—The Dictionary Companion. *Garden City Pub. Co.*
Roget, Peter—Thesaurus of English Words and Phrases. . . . . *Grossett and Dunlap*
Trench, R. C.—On the Study of Words. . *Dutton*

II

Literature

SUBJECT GUIDE

LINCOLN LIBRARY INDEXES

• • •

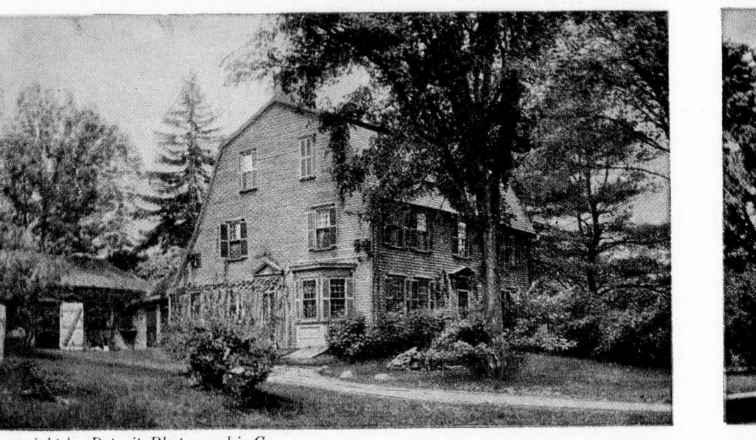

HOMES OF NOTED AMERICAN WRITERS

"Craigie," Longfellow's House at Cambridge, Mass.
"The Old Manse," Hawthorne's House, Concord, Mass.

Emerson's House, Concord, Mass.
Lowell's House, Cambridge, Mass.

INTRODUCTORY

The meaning of the term literature has been so widely extended during the past century that careless writers have sometimes used it to cover in rough-and-ready fashion all that has been written or printed. Thus we sometimes hear men in highly specialized professions speak of the "literature" of their subjects, and officers of corporations will speak of distributing their "literature." Such uses of the word are not only extreme, they are certainly incorrect. A chronological list of the presidents of the United States would contain many facts and would constitute a valuable historical record, but it would not be literature. On the other hand, the brief address which President Lincoln delivered at the dedication of the Gettysburg battlefield is imperishable literature. It differs from the historical list in both purpose and form.

Literature an Art. In order to be properly designated as literature, subject matter must be so arranged and ordered that it will appeal to the heart and mind of man, or, as we sometimes say, to the imagination. When any work, whether a musical score or a book, a painting, a statue, or a monument, succeeds in making this appeal, we say that it has the qualities of art. This, then, is the first requisite of literature. The appeal of art can be made only by works that have form. For a literary work to have form it is necessary that its creator shall be a master of language and construction. The author must have "style." He must be able to express or communicate effectively the emotion or idea that possesses him, and in ranking works of literature this must be one of our criteria. We shall give them a higher or a lower ranking in proportion as they have greater or less perfection of form. A work of art, like a story of the Greek gods, like a fable or a fairy tale, or a play or novel about an imagined character, may dispense with facts and still be great; but it cannot dispense with form.

Literature an Interpretation of Life. In addition to form, literature must have significant content. A statement of the rules of Latin grammar in perfect verse will not be great poetry. Without form, a work is not literature at all; without significance, it cannot be great literature. If, then, we assume that the form is adequate, a work of literature will be entitled to a higher ranking in proportion as the truths with which it deals are of greater significance to humanity.

Literature "Truer than History." Literature which meets these demands upon form and content constitutes our most valuable record of the inner life of man. Nowhere is the life of humanity, that is, the history of man's spiritual existence as distinguished from his mere animal existence, so thoroughly and fundamentally presented to us as in the world's great masterpieces; for, though literature is not valuable in proportion to the number of isolated facts presented, it is valuable because of the truths of life which it sets before us. It deals, not with what may once have chanced to happen, but with man's most vital, permanent, and significant relationships. It studies society and evaluates all those allegirnces which man has found most fitting and necessary, the ties that bind him to his fellows, to his country, to nature. It provides, therefore, a standard of values for our human activities. It gives us, not the facts primarily, but, what is much more important, it gives us in beautiful form the meaning of human history and what may be called the logic of life. For this reason, Aristotle said that "poetry is truer than history." Literature may be studied with the greatest profit, therefore, not only by those who are interested in art, but also by those who wish to understand humanity's progress.

Three Types of Literary Excellence. Because of this dual appeal of literature we find that there are three types of literary excellence.

1. Judged from the point of view of construction and style, a certain work may stand in its formal perfection as a representative of one of the art forms—the epic, the elegy, or the short story, for instance. Such is the case with Milton's *Paradise Lost*, Gray's *Elegy Written in a Country Churchyard*, or a tale of De Maupassant's.
2. On the other hand, we may have other works not so perfect in form, which nevertheless give us profound insight into the life of men at certain periods of history. Such poems are the German *Nibelungenlied*, the French *Chanson de Roland*, and the Spanish *Poem of the Cid*.
3. In rare cases both of these elements—the artistic form and the historic or spiritual significance—will be present in the highest degree. This is true of the *Iliad* and the *Odyssey* of Homer, the *Divine Comedy* of Dante, and the *Hamlet* or *Macbeth* of Shakspere. Such works will naturally constitute the world's greatest masterpieces.

Modern Literature largely Western European. When we speak of "the world's" greatest literature, it should be remembered that we generally include in our survey only the literature and literary tradition which, first developed in Europe by the Greeks, has been passed down through the Romans to the modern European nations, from whom it has spread to the colonies which these nations founded. This literature, to be sure, includes the Bible, which comes to us from farther East, and there have been thin streams of influence from Persia and India. As a matter of fact, however, the literary traditions of the Hindus, of the Persians, or of the Chinese, for instance, have remained largely alien to us and are therefore not considered as constituting a part of our literary heritage.

The Test of Greatness. It is, of course, extremely difficult to give final rank to all the great works which have been passed down to us, and many works which enjoyed a great vogue in their day, like *Ossian* for instance, have been found subsequently to contain but little that is permanently valuable either as art or as a criticism of human ideals. Occasionally, a work like *Uncle Tom's Cabin*, appearing at a particular juncture, has exercised great immediate influence on history but is of relatively little permanent value as art. In so far as the critic himself applies principles, they should be the principles which we have stated: the degree of perfection exemplified in the construction of the work, and the significance of its content. The safest test, however,—and this should always be used as a corrective of personal judgment—is the sifting of time. Humanity has naturally taken to itself those works which it has found to express the great lessons of life.

MODERN LITERATURE IN THE WESTERN NATIONS FROM ABOUT 500 A. D. TO ABOUT 1900 A. D.

The table given below aims to present summarily the following points: (1) The general inheritance of the modern from the ancient world; (2) Important influences at work in each period; (3) The most important general types of literature developed in each period or century; (4) The characteristic contributions of each country to general world literature in each period; (5) The origin and flourishing of the chief types of literature; (6) The names of the greatest and most characteristic authors in each period. Necessarily many worthy names are omitted, and it is very difficult, especially in ages of great literary activity, to tell just where the line of exclusion should be drawn. Authors who belong only to their particular national literature will be found in the separate tables and sketches of the literatures of the world. A relative ranking of authors and books in point of greatness and world influence is indicated by different styles of type, as: (1) *PSALMS*, (2) CICERO, (3) *Juvenal*, (4) Pliny.

EUROPE'S COMMON INHERITANCE: WORKS MORE GENERALLY KNOWN OR WHOSE INFLUENCE IS STILL FELT AT THE BEGINNING OF THE SIXTH CENTURY

Poetry	Sources	Prose
PSALMS, also in Latin and Greek.	***From the Hebrew***	*OLD TESTAMENT*, also in Latin and Greek.
Epic: *HOMER'S ILIAD* and *ODYSSEY*. Known through references in Latin literature, by reputation as the work of the greatest of the poets, but in original unknown even to Petrarch. Tragedy: ÆSCHYLUS, SOPHOCLES, and EURIPIDES, the great Greek dramatists, will remain unknown until the Renaissance, except in so far as they influence Seneca. Comedy: *Menander*, through Latin adaptations and influence on Latin comedy. ARISTOPHANES, seemingly unknown until time of Renaissance. Lyrics: Lyric poets SAPPHO and ANACREON, and particularly the anthologies, known through their influence on Latin poetry and verse forms and through translations or imitations by Latin poets. PINDAR becomes an important influence only in the Renaissance and later period. Pastoral: *Theocritus* and Bion, known through Latin imitations but will become models in Renaissance.	***From the Greek*** At the beginning of the so-called dark ages, Greek culture, and knowledge of and interest in Greek literature, become virtually extinct. Greek is known and sometimes used in commerce in southern Gaul during the 6th century, and later many Greek monks driven out by the Eastern Church take refuge in Italy. Charlemagne is supposed to have known it, and there are sporadic centers, especially monasteries, where Greek is taught as far west as Ireland up to the period of the Renaissance. But it may be safely said that the spirit of Greek literature is unknown, and Greek literature as such has little direct influence until after Petrarch.	Religion: *NEW TESTAMENT*, in Latin translations. *The Church Fathers*, known through influence on Latin Church fathers. Philosophy: *ARISTOTLE*. Known only in part, through fragmentary Latin translations, and, during Mohammedan occupation of Spain, through influence of Arabian schools and teachers. After 1000 A. D. the most important influence on medieval philosophy. *PLATO*. Known through Boethius and Latin translation of the *Timæus*. His influence early enters the Church through the Greek fathers, from whom it passes to the Latin fathers. His is the strongest philosophical influence on the early Church, and tends to give literature first its allegorical turn and later its idealistic tendency. Biography and morals: PLUTARCH. Though not read in Greek, subject matter known in Latin. Will become one of most popular works of the Renaissance period because of subject matter and conception of the heroes of antiquity. Late Greek romances: Greek romances and tales of Greek mythology and Greek life pass into tradition, and at a later period Greek materials will enter through trade with Byzantium and through contacts during time of the Crusades. History and oratory: Historians like *Herodotus*, *Xenophon*, and *Thucydides*, and orators like DEMOSTHENES will become known as such and enter literary tradition in period of Renaissance. Fables: *Æsop*. Well known in popular tradition and in Latin versions used in medieval schools.

Poetry	Sources	Prose
Epic: *VIRGIL'S ÆNEID*; Statius. Pastoral: VIRGIL: ECLOGUES and BUCOLICS. Lyric: HORACE; *Catullus* (almost unknown). Elegiac: Tibullus; Propertius; OVID. Narrative: Lucan; OVID. Philosophical: *Lucretius*. Didactic: HORACE. Tragedy: *Seneca*. Comedy: Plautus; *Terence*. Satire: HORACE; *Juvenal*; *Martial*. Fables: Phædrus.	***From the Latin*** The Latin authors fare much better than the Greek. Many of them are available, and some of them, like Ovid, Horace, and Virgil, have their readers, even during the dark ages. Latin itself continues to be the language of the Church. It is the failure to comprehend the spirit and the form of Latin literature, and occasionally the hostility of the Church, that leads to the disappearance of ancient culture in its Latin form. Knowledge of the language and the letter will remain, but the spirit of Latin culture will become moribund for some centuries. It will not, however, be so nearly extinguished as the Greek; consequently Latin culture will be the first to revive. Most of the great Latin poets, and particularly Virgil, will be known to Dante (1265–1321). He will take Virgil as his master and will know him by heart. ***From the East*** Persian ideas and faint Persian influence are apparent in later books of the Old Testament and in later Greek philosophy. During the middle ages there will be some contact with the East, especially during the Crusades; the Hindu story of Buddha, for instance, will be found in the old French *Barlaam and Josaphat*. ***From the North*** During the invasion of the barbarians, folklore and folk tales and possibly unwritten songs are brought by the Germanic tribes into southern Europe.	Oratory: CICERO, great master of style for Renaissance. Philosophy: Cicero; *Boethius*, *Consolations of Philosophy*. History: *Cæsar*; *Livy*; Sallust; *Tacitus* (little known). Natural history: Pliny the Elder. Religion: Church Fathers: Tertullian; *St. Augustine*,—*Confessions*, *City of God*.

THE MEDIEVAL PERIOD

6th TO 12th CENTURY—The Disappearance of Classical Culture

COUNTRY	POETRY	PROSE	IMPORTANT MOVEMENTS AND INFLUENCES
Europe	Latin hymns.	Sermons, Latin chronicles.	The "dark ages," particularly the 7th to the 10th century.
France	Saints' lives. Beginnings of liturgical drama, about 10th century. Epic: Chansons de Gestes,—CHANSON DE ROLAND.	The Oaths of Strasbourg, 842, first document written in Old French.	Disappearance of urban and development of feudal civilization. Romance languages supersede vulgar Latin as spoken language. Continuance of Latin tradition. Dominance of Church.
Germany	Nibelungen sagas, unwritten.		
Scandinavia and Iceland	"*Elder Edda*" and *sagas* in oral tradition, written in 12th and 13th centuries.		Development of monasteries as centers of learning, 9th to 12th century. Charlemagne crowned, 800.
Ireland	Growth of tale and folklore.		Development of schools.
England	Epic: *Beowulf*, 7th century(?). Religious poems. Songs of sea and travel: The Wanderer; The Seafarer.	Bede's Ecclesiastical History, 731, in Latin. Translations: King Alfred. Chronicles: Anglo-Saxon Chronicle.	Norman conquest, 1066. The introduction of Nordic element into literary tradition from Scandinavia, Germany, and Britain. First Crusade, 1095.

12th CENTURY—The Great Age of Medieval Romance

COUNTRY	POETRY	PROSE	IMPORTANT MOVEMENTS AND INFLUENCES
France	Religious poetry: Bernard of Cluny, in Latin; Bernard of Clairvaux, in Latin; medieval hymns, in Latin. Drama: Early miracle plays in Latin and French. Lyric: Provençal poetry; songs of troubadours and trouvères. Epic: Later Chansons de Gestes celebrating Charlemagne and French heroes. Romances of chivalry and adventure, dealing with "matter of Britain," King Arthur, etc. *Christian of Troy.* Beast epic: *Reynard the Fox.*	Romance, in prose and verse: *Aucassin and Nicolette.*	Founding of universities of Paris and Oxford. The development of modern lyric verse forms in Provence. Woman comes to occupy a more important place in courtly life, and love becomes the theme of poets. Development of Arabic civilization, particularly in Spain, through which knowledge of Aristotle is spread.
England		Chronicles and legendary history: Geoffrey of Monmouth,—History of the Kings of Britain, including stories of King Arthur and King Lear.	
Germany	Epic: NIBELUNGENLIED, written; *Gudrun.*		
Scandinavia		History: Saxo Grammaticus, includes story of Hamlet.	

13th CENTURY—High Point of Medieval Civilization

COUNTRY	POETRY	PROSE	IMPORTANT MOVEMENTS AND INFLUENCES
France	Folk song and satire: *The Fabliaux.* Allegory: *The Romance of the Rose.* Religious poetry: Saints' lives; Gautier de Coincy,—The Miracles of Our Lady. Drama: Beginnings of secular drama and farce.	Chronicles: Joinville.	Gothic art reaches its point of perfection. Epics gradually succeeded by romances in verse. Popularity of stories of King Arthur, Lancelot, and the Grail. Beginnings of romance in prose.
Italy	Poems of courtly love: The Sicilian School. Lyrics: *Dante.* Hymns: THOMAS OF CELANO,—DIES IRÆ, Latin.	Biography: *Dante,—The New Life.* Travel: *Marco Polo.* Theology: *Thomas Aquinas*, in Latin. Saints' lives: JACOPO DA VORAGINE,—THE GOLDEN LEGEND, in Latin.	Struggle for supremacy between popes and emperors. Growth of cities and development of guilds and municipal government.
Spain	Epic: THE CID.		
Germany	Romances: *Wolfram von Eschenbach,—Parzival*; Hartmann von Aue; Gottfried von Strassburg. Lyrics: *Walther von der Vogelweide.*	Encyclopedia: Albertus Magnus, in Latin.	
England	Romances: Imitations of Norman-French romances. Layamon's Brut. Songs and ballads.		The rise of parliaments. Magna Charta. Fusion of Saxon and Norman peoples and of English and Norman-French speech.

14th CENTURY—End of the Literature of Feudalism

Country	Poetry	Prose	Important Movements and Influences
France	Drama: Miracle plays,—The Miracles of Notre Dame. Mystery plays.	Chronicles: Froissart.	Societies for the production of plays become more numerous. Froissart shows the decay of feudalism and the end of chivalry. He marks the end of knighthood. Civilization will soon become urban.
Italy	Epic: *DANTE,—DIVINE COMEDY.* Love sonnets: PETRARCH.	Prose tales: BOCCACCIO,—THE DECAMERON. Politics: Dante,—On Monarchy, in Latin.	Petrarch introduces that enthusiasm for the study of the classical authors and intimate acquaintance with them which marks the beginning of the Revival of Learning. His interests and curiosities have earned him the title of "the first modern man." His younger admirer, Boccaccio, is the first modern man really to learn Greek.
England	Miracle plays. Allegory: Langland,—Piers Plowman. Narratives: CHAUCER,—CANTERBURY TALES. Romances: Sir Gawain and the Green Knight.	Religion: Wiclif,—Translation of Bible. Travels: Sir John Mandeville, originally in French (?).	Chaucer visits Italy and meets Petrarch.

THE RENAISSANCE

15th CENTURY—The Period of Transition

Country	Poetry	Prose	Important Movements and Influences
France	Poems in the medieval forms: Ballades. Charles of Orleans. VILLON. Religious drama: Mysteries,—The Mystery of the Passion. Farce: *Master Pathelin.*	Memoirs: Commines.	The Renaissance is sometimes taken to begin with the discovery of America, though the movement is under way before this time. Beginnings of modern personal poetry.
Italy	Romantic and burlesque epic: Pulci; Boiardo. Sonnets and songs: Lorenzo the Magnificent.	Translations: Boiardo's translation of Apuleius and Lucian; Bruni's renderings of Demosthenes, Æschines, Plutarch, Xenophon, Plato, Aristotle; Valla's Iliad, Thucydides, Herodotus, Æsop. Pastoral romance: Sannazzaro.	Early in century Greek masterpieces are brought to Italy, and the literature of the ancient Greek world begins strongly to influence modern literary tradition. Enthusiasm for art, literature, and science for their own sakes and not as subsidiary to theology. Struggle for dominance in literature between writing in Latin and Greek and writing in the modern languages.
Germany	Satire and allegory: Brant,—The Ship of Fools.	Popular romance: Till Eulenspiegel.	Gutenberg's invention of printing.
England	Morality plays.	Religion: *Thomas à Kempis,—Imitation of Christ.* Tales of chivalry: *Malory's Morte D'Arthur.*	Caxton prints first book in England, 1477. Fall of Constantinople, 1453.

16th CENTURY—The Reformation

Country	Poetry	Prose	Important Movements and Influences
France	Lyric: The Old School: Marot. The New School: *Ronsard*; Du Bellay.	Humor: RABELAIS. Essays: MONTAIGNE. Theology: *Calvin.* Translation: *Amyot's Plutarch.*	Enthusiasm for study and worship of ancients. Reform in religion, and wars of religion.
Italy	Epic: *Ariosto*; *Tasso.* Lyric and sonnet: *Michelangelo.*	Politics: *Machiavelli.* Biography: *Cellini*; Vasari.	The influences of classical drama,—of Plautus and Terence in comedy and of Seneca in tragedy,—as well as of the theories of critics like Aristotle and Horace, make themselves felt in modern drama.
Germany	Meistersinger: Hans Sachs. Hymns: *Luther.*	Translation: LUTHER'S BIBLE.	The end of Humanism.
Holland		Letters and colloquies: *Erasmus*, in Latin.	The Renaissance passes from Italy to France and England.
Spain	Drama: *Lope de Vega.* Ballads: The *Romancero General.*	Romances of chivalry: Montalvo's Amadis de Gaula. *Romances of Roguery.*	
Portugal	Epic: *Camoëns,—The Lusiad.*		
England	Allegory: *Spenser's Faery Queen.* Sonnets: Sidney; SHAKSPERE. Drama: *Marlowe*; SHAKSPERE'S EARLY PLAYS.	Politics: More's Utopia. Defense of Poesy: Sidney. Voyages: Hakluyt. Romance: Lyly's Euphues.	Age of adventure and discovery.

THE MODERN ERA

17th CENTURY—The Great Age of Drama

Country	Poetry	Prose	Important Movements and Influences
France	Poets of the French Classical Period: Tragedy: *Corneille*; RACINE. Comedy: *MOLIÈRE*. Fables: LA FONTAINE. Criticism: *Boileau*.	Drama, comedy: *MOLIÈRE*. Philosophy: *Descartes*; *Pascal*. Religion: *Pascal*; Bossuet. Letters: *Mme. de Sévigné*. Critics and moralists: *La Rochefoucauld*; La Bruyère.	Golden age of French literature; Richelieu, Louis XIV, and the "century of authority." French Academy founded and strict standards established.
Germany		Picaresque novel: Grimmelshausen's Simplicissimus. Religion: Jacob Böhme.	
Holland		Philosophy: *Spinoza*, in Latin. Law: Grotius, in Latin.	
Spain	Drama: *Lope de Vega*; CALDERÓN.	Novel: *CERVANTES' DON QUIXOTE*.	
England	Drama: *SHAKSPERE,—THE GREAT TRAGEDIES*; *Jonson*; Webster; Otway; Beaumont and Fletcher. Lyric: Donne; Herrick. Cavalier poets: Lovelace. Epic: MILTON. Satire: *Dryden*.	Translation: *KING JAMES VERSION OF THE BIBLE*; Chapman's Homer. Essays: *Bacon*. Religion: Jeremy Taylor. Politics: *Milton*. Walton's Compleat Angler. Diary: Pepys. Philosophy: *Locke*. Science and philosophy: Bacon's Novum Organum, in Latin, and The Advancement of Knowledge.	End of the Age of Elizabeth and rise of the Puritans. Settlement of America. The Commonwealth and the Restoration. Growth of political liberalism.

18th CENTURY, FIRST HALF—The Age of Reason

Country	Poetry	Prose	Important Movements and Influences
France	Drama: Voltaire.	Politics: *Montesquieu,—Spirit of Laws*. Novel: *Lesage,—Gil Blas*; *Abbé Prévost,—Manon Lescaut*. Drama: Marivaux. Translation: Abbé Galland's translation of the Arabian Nights. Morals: Fénelon.	Beginnings of cosmopolitan attitude. Rise of public opinion as a force in social and political affairs. English influence strong in France.
Italy		Philosophy: Vico.	
England	Poet of Classicism: POPE. Nature poetry: Thomson.	Translation: Sale's Koran. Novel: DEFOE; *Richardson*; Fielding. Essay: *Addison*. Satire: SWIFT. Philosophy: Hume; Berkeley.	Increasing importance of novel. Great advances in science by Newton and others.

18th CENTURY, SECOND HALF—Development of the Idea of Progress

Country	Poetry	Prose	Important Movements and Influences
France	The end of Classicism. Lyric, satire: Voltaire; Chénier.	The Encyclopedia: *Diderot*. Return to nature; Beginnings of Romanticism: ROUSSEAU. Novel: *Rousseau*; Saint-Pierre. Critic and satirist: VOLTAIRE. Natural history: Buffon. Drama: *Beaumarchais*.	Age of criticism and unrest preparing for overthrow of the existing order in the French Revolution. Beginnings of Romanticism, and return to nature. Increasing interest in human history, political and social problems. The French Revolution. Growth of individualism and lyricism.
Italy	Drama: Alfieri.	Drama: *Goldoni*.	
Germany	Lyric and ballad: GOETHE; *Schiller*; Bürger. Drama: *Goethe*; *Schiller*; Lessing.	Novel: *Goethe*. Criticism: *Lessing*. History: Herder. Philosophy: *Kant*.	Great age of German literature.
England	Narrative poetry: Goldsmith. Romantic songs and folk poetry: Percy's Reliques; BURNS; "Ossian"; Blake. Elegy: *Gray*.	History: *Gibbon*. Criticism: *Samuel Johnson*. Politics: Burke. Novel: *Goldsmith*; Sterne. Drama: Goldsmith; Sheridan. Biography: *Boswell*.	Beginnings of English Romanticism.
America		Autobiography: Franklin. Politics: Jefferson; Hamilton.	The American Revolution.

19th CENTURY, FIRST HALF—Romanticism and Beginnings of Realism

Country	Poetry	Prose	Important Movements and Influences
France	Romantic School: *Lamartine*; *De Vigny*; HUGO; *De Musset*. Drama: Hugo.	Religion: Chateaubriand. Criticism: Mme. de Staël; *Sainte-Beuve*. Romantic novel and novel with social thesis: *Hugo*; George Sand. Psychological novel: Stendhal. Realistic novel: BALZAC. Drama: Dumas the Elder; Scribe; De Musset. History: Michelet; Guizot.	Era of social and political reconstruction, following French Revolution. Development of nationalism and the spirit of nationalism in literature. Glorification of individualism. Increasing liberalism in politics, soon turning to humanitarianism.
Italy	Poetry of pessimism: Leopardi.	Historical novel: Manzoni.	The romanticists turn to the "rich and strange," and present with enthusiasm pictures of the middle ages, using "local color." With this comes the development of the historical novel and of history. Under the influence of science there develops an increased respect for the facts, even the brutal facts of life, and many novelists turn more and more toward realism. Invention of steamboat and railroad, and application of steam to industry.
Germany	Lyric poetry: *GOETHE*; Heine; Uhland. Poetry of Romantic School: Novalis. Drama: *GOETHE'S FAUST*; *Schiller*.	Novel: *Goethe*. Tale: Hoffmann. Philosophy: *Hegel*; Schelling; *Schopenhauer*. Criticism: A. W. von Schlegel.	
England	Poets of liberty: BYRON; *Shelley*. Poets of beauty and romance: *Keats*; Coleridge; Scott. Nature poetry: WORDSWORTH.	Essay: *Lamb*. Historical novel: *Scott*; *Thackeray*. Novel of contemporary life: *Dickens*; *Thackeray*; Austen. History and criticism: *Carlyle*.	
America	Lyrics: Poe.	Philosophy: Emerson. Essay and tale: Irving. Frontier and sea stories: Cooper. Romance and psychological tales: Hawthorne. Short story: *Poe*.	
Poland	Poet of liberty: Mickiewicz.		
Russia	National poet: Púshkin.	Novel: Gógol.	
Hungary	Lyric poetry: Petöfi.		

19th CENTURY, SECOND HALF—The Age of Science and Evolution

Country	Poetry	Prose	Important Movements and Influences
France	*Later work of Victor Hugo*. The Parnassian School: Leconte de Lisle. Art for art's sake: Gautier and Baudelaire. The Symbolists: Paul Verlaine. Drama: Rostand.	Novel: *Hugo's Les Misérables*; *Flaubert*; Anatole France; Bourget. Naturalistic novel: Zola. Short story: *Maupassant*; Daudet. History: Renan; *Taine*. Criticism: Brunetière; Anatole France; *Taine*. Drama: Dumas the Younger; Maeterlinck.	The development, formulation, and spread of evolution, and its application, not only to the study of biology, but also to that of the social sciences and even to literature, constitute the most striking phenomenon of this time. There arises a bitter quarrel between the older theology and the newer science. For this reason two opposed tendencies appear in literature. One, the idealistic, emphasizes the life of the spirit; the other, the materialistic, attempts to explain everything in terms of matter and scientific laws. Widespread application to industry of new discoveries in electrical and other sciences. The basis of wealth and society becomes more and more industrial. Profound unrest and beginnings of strife between capital and labor. As America extends itself to the West, with Whitman and Mark Twain a newer and more characteristically American note appears. Unification of Germany and Italy. The further development of the idea of nationality.
Italy	Lyric poetry: Carducci; D'Annunzio. Drama: D'Annunzio.	Novel and drama: D'Annunzio.	
Spain		Drama: Echegaray. Novel: Galdós; Pereda; Valera.	
Germany	Drama: Hauptmann.	Novel, short story: Heyse. Drama: Hauptmann; Sudermann. Philosophy: *Nietzsche*. National history: Treitschke. History: Mommsen.	
England	Poets of the Victorian age: *Tennyson*; *Browning*; Swinburne. Love sonnets: Elizabeth Barrett Browning. The Pre-Raphaelites: William Morris; Christina Rossetti; D. G. Rossetti.	Science: DARWIN'S ORIGIN OF SPECIES; Huxley. Novel: George Eliot; *George Meredith*; *Thomas Hardy*. Religion: Newman. Romance and short story: Stevenson; Kipling. Scholarship and criticism: Ruskin; *Matthew Arnold*; Pater.	
America	Poet of democracy: Whitman. New England poets: Longfellow; Lowell; Whittier; Holmes.	Novel: *Mark Twain*; Henry James; W. D. Howells. State papers: Lincoln.	
Poland		Historical novel: Sienkiewicz.	
Russia	Realistic poet: Nekrásov.	Novel: *Tolstóy*; *Turgéniev*; Dostoiévsky. Short story and drama: Chékov.	
Norway		Drama: *Ibsen*. Novel: Björnson.	
Sweden		Prose tale: Selma Lagerlöf.	
Denmark		Fairy tales: *Hans Christian Andersen*. Criticism: Georg Brandes.	

AMERICAN MEN OF LETTERS

William Dean Howells
Photo by Brown Bros.

Francis Marion Crawford
Photo by Brown Bros.

Samuel Langhorne Clemens
Copyright by Rockwood, N. Y.

John Bigelow

Thomas Wentworth Higginson

Edward Everett Hale
Photo by Soule Art Co.

Winston Churchill
Photo by Brown Bros.

George Washington Cable
Photo by Brown Bros.

Thomas Nelson Page
Photo by P. Thompson

AMERICAN POETS

James Whitcomb Riley — James Russell Lowell
Ralph Waldo Emerson — Henry Wadsworth Longfellow — Oliver Wendell Holmes
William Cullen Bryant — John Greenleaf Whittier

AMERICAN LITERATURE

AMERICAN literature, like the literatures of all peoples who have emigrated from lands already in an advanced stage of culture, is not an original native growth. On the contrary, from the very first, American writers began with a long tradition behind them. They brought with them an intimate familiarity with a rich literature and a deep interest in certain burning problems of religion and conduct. Faced with a new and stubborn land to conquer, they had at first little leisure to write, and, even when the leisure was available, it was long before they wrote with the consciousness that they belonged to a people having an individuality and a life of its own.

Colonial Period (1608–1775). Literary history in America begins with such accounts of life, travels, and adventures as appear in the simple, direct narrative of John Smith's *True Relation of Virginia* (1608). Smith followed this with a more pretentious work, *A Map of Virginia, with a Description of the Country* (1612). Of all the early accounts of explorers, this *Description* has made the greatest appeal to the popular imagination. It is fairly representative of many English pamphlets, written to draw attention to America and other distant parts of the world, and published in London during the 17th century. In New England, also, there were some who wrote narratives similar to John Smith's *True Relation*. One of these was Edward Winslow, whose *Good News from New England* was published in 1624.

Colonial Journals and Diaries.—To these published works there must be added numerous diaries and journals which long remained unpublished. The most important of these in New England were written by William Bradford and Edward Winslow of Plymouth and John Winthrop of Massachusetts Bay. The *Journal of Bradford and Winslow* is vivid and full of interesting incidents. Bradford's *History of Plymouth Plantation*, bringing the story of that colony down to the year 1646, is a book of dignity, reflecting the best qualities of early Puritanism. Less interesting but no less valuable is the journal of John Winthrop. This diary was faithfully kept by the first governor of Massachusetts Bay from 1630 until a few months before his death in 1649. Although it bears the title *A History of New England*, it is concerned with little outside the author's own colony.

In the 18th century, the greater degree of leisure and comfort attained in the older settlements gave opportunity for journeys, of which several accounts have survived. These are frequently illuminated with comment upon the life of the times that gives them literary flavor. One of the most interesting of these narratives is the journal kept by a New England woman, Mrs. Sarah Knight, on a trip from Boston to New York in 1704-05. The *History of the Dividing Line* (between Virginia and North Carolina) by William Byrd of Westover in Virginia, which recounts his experiences and observations on a surveying expedition in the region of the Great Dismal Swamp in 1729, is of great value. Not only does it supply information, but, like other journals of this Virginia gentleman, it bears the impress of a genial and humane personality. Byrd was, in his European education, in his knowledge of the ancient and modern classics, and in his interest in public affairs, a typical Virginia aristocrat, while in his vivacious style and quaint humor he was one of the best colonial writers.

Of the more ambitious attempts to write colonial history, the most notable are the unfinished *Chronological History of New England*, by the Reverend Thomas Prince, of Boston, and the *History of the Colony of Massachusetts Bay*, likewise incomplete, by Thomas Hutchinson.

Religion.—In connection with the religious writing which was so important in colonial New England, the names of Roger Williams, Thomas Hooker, and John Wise should be mentioned as defenders of democratic church polity and of freedom of thought. These men stood in clear opposition to the powerful family of the Mathers,—Richard, Increase, and Cotton, father, son, and grandson. Of all the voluminous works published by this extraordinary family succession, only the *Magnalia Christi Americana* (1702), by Cotton Mather, retains today any real interest. It is a useful collection of material for the study of early New England, which reflects the curious compound of power, scientific spirit, and superstition that marked the character of its author.

Philosophers.—The 18th century produced, apart from the group of political thinkers and writers of the Revolutionary period, two outstanding figures, Jonathan Edwards and Benjamin Franklin. Edwards, descended from families of high standing and culture in New England, was educated at Yale college. After a stormy period as minister of the church at Northampton, Mass., he was sent as a missionary to the Indians at Stockbridge. Here he wrote his famous treatise upon the *Freedom of the Will*, which is widely known as one of the greatest of American contributions to philosophical thought. Edwards was also one of the leaders in the religious movement in New England, known as the Great Awakening.

Franklin, the son of a tallow chandler in Boston, inherited a sound taste for life and letters, was largely self-educated, and became the best exponent of the average American's practical philosophy of life. He wrote on many themes, political, scientific, and commercial, but his literary fame rests now upon his *Autobiography* and upon the proverbial sentences of *Poor Richard's Almanac.*

Two other names should be noted in this time. Samuel Johnson, an Episcopal clergyman of Connecticut and a friend of Franklin, is reckoned one of the clearest of American thinkers in religion and philosophy. John Woolman, a Quaker, who lived at Mt. Holly, New Jersey, where he was a tailor "by the choice of providence," left a *Journal* which is remarkably attractive in its sincerity.

Newspapers.—During the first half of the 18th century, newspapers and magazines multiplied in America. These publications encouraged discussion of public questions and contributed largely to that growth of public opinion which resulted in the Revolution. The first newspaper published in the colonies was *Public Occurrences* (Boston, 1690). The *Boston News Letter* was first issued in 1704, and the *Boston Gazette* was founded in 1719 by James Franklin, an older brother of Benjamin Franklin. He also started the *New England Courant* in 1721. Benjamin was employed upon both papers as a printer.

Colonial Verse.—What has been called the "one really American poem" of the 17th century is an epitaph of 44 lines on Nathaniel Bacon, the insurrectionary leader in Virginia. This poem belongs to the class of elegies, of which a large number were produced in the colonies, especially by the New England clergy. The best one credited to New England is a "Funeral Song" by the Reverend Samuel Wigglesworth. His father, Michael Wigglesworth, was the author of the most widely read poem of colonial times, "The Day of Doom," a vivid résumé of the main tenets of Calvinism.

An attractive figure in this period is Anne Bradstreet. Amid her family of eight children on a frontier farm in the town of Andover, she found time to write many verses. These were published in London in 1650, by her brother, in a volume entitled *The Tenth Muse, Lately Sprung Up in America.*

Revolutionary Period (1775–1800). Ballads and satirical verses mark the next notable stage in American poetry. Among all the patriotic ballads of the Revolution, one on the death of Nathan Hale is notable for its real poetic quality. Francis Hopkinson's "Battle of the Kegs" is the best-known of the purely humorous ballads of the time. Joel Barlow's mock-heroic "Hasty Pudding" is one of the best longer pieces of humorous verse in early American literature. The same author's *Columbiad* is an attempt to write an American epic, but it fails to reach the level of poetry. John Trumbull's "McFingal" is the most effective of the many political satires of the period.

The Hartford Wits.—From about 1780 to 1800 a group of talented and versatile men, known as the "Hartford Wits," formed a literary center at New Haven and Hartford. The chief of these were Timothy Dwight, John Trumbull, Joel Barlow, David Humphreys, Richard Alsop, Lemuel Hopkins, and Theodore Dwight. Timothy Dwight, afterward president of Yale, wrote a long poem, *Greenfield Hill*, in which he imitated the English poets from Milton to Goldsmith. His *Conquest of Canaan* represents a type of biblical epic which was popular at this time.

Freneau.—In quality and range of subject and style, Philip Freneau is equaled by none in the Revolutionary period, and is in fact the first of American poets. He first acquired reputation by his satirical verse, but his fame now rests upon his romantic lyrics, especially of the sea and of nature. In such poems as "The Indian Burying Ground," "Eutaw Springs," and "The Wild Honeysuckle," he anticipates the spirit of the English romantic poets.

Politics.—The political literature of the Revolutionary period includes the speeches of James Otis, Samuel Adams, Patrick Henry, and others, as well as many pamphlets and letters which appeared during the period of controversy ushered in by the opposition to the Writs of Assistance in 1761. These publications discussed trenchantly, from both sides, the pressing problems of the times. The passage of the Townshend acts brought forth John Dickinson's *Letters from a Farmer in Pennsylvania to the Inhabitants of the British Colonies*, which were widely copied and translated. In his earlier days Franklin did much to bring about the union of the colonies, and the letters and published papers of his later life helped to interpret his country to Europe. From the loyalist point of view, the best statements came from Myles Cooper, president of King's college, and from Jonathan Boucher, at one time a clergyman in Maryland and Virginia, who wrote *A View of the Causes and Consequences of the American Revolution* (1797). Thomas Paine's pamphlet entitled *Common Sense* probably contributed more powerfully than any other single utterance to bring about the final break between the colonies and England. Paine wrote also the most effective of the war time pamphlets, *The Crisis* (1776–83), a series of stirring appeals, the first of which was published just after Washington's disastrous retreat across New Jersey. Jefferson gave classic form to the statement of the case for the colonies in the *Declaration of Independence*.

Of all the writings of this period, however, the most important are the 85 essays included in the collection known as *The Federalist*. These papers, written by Alexander Hamilton, James Madison, and John Jay, were first published in the *Independent Journal* of New York in 1787-88. They did more than any other one thing to bring about the adoption of the Constitution, and they remain of the highest value in American political history and literature.

Early American Drama.—The first American drama was *The Prince of Parthia*, a romantic tragedy by Thomas Godfrey, first acted at the Southwark theater in Philadelphia, 1767. The first American comedy to be presented by a professional company was *The Contrast* by Royall Tyler. It was produced in New York, 1787. Tyler was the author of more than 50 plays, most of which were successful. His immediate successors were James N. Barker and John Howard Payne. Barker used American Material in *The Indian Princess* (1808) and *Superstition* (1824). During the next 25 years, many national themes were used by playwrights, of which R. P. Smith's *William Penn* is a good example. In 1855 George H. Boker's *Francesca da Rimini*, notable for literary and acting quality, was first presented. In *The Forest Rose* (1825) by Samuel Woodworth, the first permanent Yankee character, "Jonathan Plowboy," was developed.

First National Period (1800–1840). Two centuries of American writing had prepared the way for rapid development in the first decades of the 19th century. After Philip Freneau, the next American poet is William Cullen Bryant, lawyer, successful journalist, and publicist. His literary career extended over almost 70 years,—from "Thanatopsis," which he produced when he was but 18 years of age, to his translation of Homer, the work of his old age. Like Freneau, Bryant hewed his own paths and produced distinctively American work. Minor poets of Bryant's early years were Samuel Woodworth, author of "The Old Oaken Bucket," Joseph Rodman Drake, who wrote "The Culprit Fay," the first fairy story in American verse, and Fitz-Greene Halleck, whose "Marco Bozzaris" is still popular.

The Knickerbocker Group.—In the first two decades of the 19th century, when the tempest of harsh criticism of American writers was at its height, a group of young men in New York were cultivating the informal, humorous, and half-satiric essay. The leaders were James K. Paulding and Washington Irving. They, with William Irving, published the *Salmagundi* papers. Washington Irving's literary career, however, really began with the *History of New York* (1809). This work attracted the attention of Walter Scott and afterward helped to secure for the author much-needed assistance in England. The *Sketch Book* was issued in New York and London (1819-20). Irving's writings established the prestige of American letters in Europe and at the same time interpreted the charm of Europe, especially of England, to the new nation. He was recognized as continuing in America the fine tradition of Addison. His early successes were followed by a long series of works in biography and travel.

First American Novelists.—American fiction in the longer novel form began with the work of Charles Brockden Brown, who was deeply influenced by the English writer, Godwin. He was a romancer. His first work was *Wieland* (1798); *Edgar Huntley*, his best. He anticipated Cooper in adventure and Poe in his use of mystery and horror.

James Fenimore Cooper made his reputation with *The Spy* (1821), a romance of the Revolution. *The Pilot* is a sea story. His greatest work is a series of five novels published between 1823 and 1841 called "The Leatherstocking Tales," of which *The Last of the Mohicians* is the most gripping. The series deals in a romantic fashion with frontier life and centers around a great trapper and his Indian friends. The books won wide European approval. Less significant romantic novelists were Daniel Pierce Thompson (*The Green Mountain Boys*) and John Pendleton Kennedy of Baltimore, author of *Swallow Barn*. William Gilmore Simms of South Carolina wrote *The Yemasee* (1835) dealing with Colonial Indian warfare. *The Partisan* is the best of his revolutionary tales.

Transcendentalism.—In New England, during the third and the fourth decade of the 19th century, interest centers in the group of literary and religious leaders who reacted from rigid Puritanism toward Unitarianism and Transcendentalism. W. E. Channing, the leader of the Unitarians, was the greatest figure in the religious thought of the time. About 1836 the Transcendental Club, an informal group, was founded. It included Bronson Alcott, Margaret Fuller, Theodore Parker, and Ralph Waldo Emerson.

This Transcendentalist movement, partly philosophical, partly literary, attracted a large number of the best minds of the period; *The Dial*, published from 1840 to 1844, was their medium of expression. One phase of the movement is exemplified in the Brook Farm experiment (1841). This was an attempt to put into practice certain ideal communistic plans. Its failure brought ridicule upon Transcendentalism. But out of the emphasis which this movement placed upon ideals in life came the moral tone of the literature of America in the middle years of the 19th century.

Second National Period (1840-1870). *Prose.*—Emerson became the prophet of the idealism which ruled the literature of the three decades just before the Civil War. His essays, poems, and addresses assert the importance of the individual as a spirit. His Phi Beta Kappa address, *The American Scholar*, has been called our "literary declaration of independence." Many of Emerson's essays were given as lectures, the vigor and sincerity of his personality adding to their effect. Henry David Thoreau's *Walden*, which tells of his effort to withdraw to a simple life, is rich with reflection. Thoreau was one of the most sturdily individualistic of the "Concord Group." Hawthorne and Melville are the two great novelists of the period. Hawthorne is haunted by his puritan background with its sense of sin and retribution. His ethical import is conveyed through symbolic devices. Chief volumes are *The Scarlet Letter* (1850), *The House of Seven Gables* (1851). Herman Melville, after youthful years as a seaman, published *Typee* (1846), the record of four months in the Marquesas. His *Moby Dick* (1851) with its philosophic sweep is open to rich interpretation. Against a universe inscrutable and unfathomable is hurled a tremendous human defiance symbolized in the pursuit of the white whale. Only recently has Melville been truly appreciated.

Poetry.—Henry W. Longfellow and John G. Whittier belong to New England. Longfellow's narratives and simple didactic poems have made him a household poet. As a translator, teacher,and diligent gatherer of material from the literatures of the world, he had a profound influence on this culture of his time. Whittier, with a scanty formal education was more limited. Poems such as "Snowbound," focussed upon New England life, give him a permanent place in American literature. He was also active in liberal movements, notably anti-slavery. James Russell Lowell, ambassador to England, was our second literary ambassador to Europe (Irving having gone to Spain). He was a distinguished essayist and critic. His poetry includes *The Bigelow Papers*, dialect satire and his famous "Commemoration Ode," though some prefer his less formal lyrics to the "Ode." Oliver Wendell Holmes maintained through many years his hold upon a wide public with his polished verse of humor and sentiment, as well as by his witty essays published as *The Autocrat of The Breakfast Table*.

But of all the poets to emerge in mid-century, Edgar Allan Poe and Walt Whitman are by far the greatest. Poe's poems such as "The Raven," "Israfel," "Ulalume," "The City of the Sea," achieve their effects by a haunting music and an eerie power of suggestion which evoke an atmosphere quite irrespective of the intellectual content. Whitman (*Leaves of Grass*, 1855) was more robust and created a sensation. He is the first of the free verse poets and his long crashing lines disturbed many. His frankness of expression disturbed more. He aspired to be the poet of democratic America— a dynamic land full of healthy men and women. He came into poetry like a great wind and now his genius is fully recognized.

Oratory and History.—Among the orators and statesmen of this period are Daniel Webster, Edward Everett, Rufus Choate, Wendell Phillips, and Charles Sumner. Contemporary with these were the great orators of the South,—Henry Clay, Robert Y. Hayne, and John C. Calhoun. To these must be added the name of Abraham Lincoln, not the least of whose titles to immortality is his *Gettysburg Speech*. The writing of history has employed the pens of many Americans whose work rises to the plane of literature. Most notable among these are George Bancroft, Francis Parkman, John Lothrop Motley, William Hickling Prescott, and John Fiske.

Humor.—The humorous writing of the 19th century began with Seba Smith's *Letters of Major Jack Downing* (1830). Benjamin P. Shillaber created the character of "Mrs. Partington." George Horatio Derby (1823–61) is credited with originating the type of humor which ruled in the works of Henry W. Shaw ("Josh Billings"), David Ross Locke ("Petroleum V. Nasby"), and Charles Farrar Browne ("Artemus Ward"). The chief of all American humorists was Samuel L. Clemens ("Mark Twain") with his numerous sketches and books like *Innocents Abroad* and *Roughing It.* Novels such as *Huckleberry Finn* and others, because of their vivid sense of the American scene and their expression, both picturesque and natural, put him in the front rank of American novelists, probably one of the three or four greatest of the century.Under his good humor there was also a genuine social seriousness.

Later Poetry.—The Civil War period was productive of many inspiring lyrics from minor poets. Two of these are especially notable, "Maryland, My Maryland" by James Ryder Randall, and "Battle Hymn of the Republic" by Julia Ward Howe. To the South in this period belong Paul H. Hayne, Henry Timrod, and Sidney Lanier, whose lives were shortened as a result of the war. Lanier achieved a rare music in his verse, matched with thought and imagery of peculiar beauty. "The Marshes of Glynn" has given him a permanent place in American poetry.

Paul Laurence Dunbar, the poet of the colored race, had the lyric charm that belongs to true poetry. Another poet of lyric genius was John Bannister Tabb. With these names we must include James Whitcomb Riley, the beloved Hoosier poet, Eugene Field, writer of delightful children's verse, and Cincinnatus Heine ("Joaquin") Miller, poet of the Sierras.

Turn of the Century to the Present. *The Novel.*—There is always a taste for the novel of free action in far times or places. Lew Wallace's *Ben Hur* (1880) is still widely read. Jack London's stories were of this type and, vastly superior in literary quality, Nordhoff and Hall's recent *The Mutiny on the Bounty* has the same basic appeal. At the turn of the century there were many romantic novels, usually dealing with the Revolutionary or Civil War. Paul Leicester Ford, Winston Churchill, and Mary Johnston wrote in this pattern, and Thomas Nelson Page with his feeling for the South is especially notable. But there is always a contrary trend. Henry James (1843–1916), the third great American novelist, explored a subtle realism of the mind and in doing so often showed different national cultures operating on one another. Among his important books are *The American*, *Portrait of a Lady*, *The Golden Bowl.* Edith Wharton (*The Age of Innocence*) followed his manner. A more forthright style of realism developed, closer to the common life, a style which later in some cases became increasingly sordid. Hamlin Garland (1860–1940) wrote true but happy accounts of post-pioneer days on the plains. Frank Norris (1870–1902) died young, yet in *The Octopus* and *The Pit* he had written two strong novels, dealing with the railroad trust and the power of the wheat market of Chicago. His less known *McTeague* is equal in strength. William Dean Howells (1837 - 1920), a middle westerner who settled in Boston, tells stories well and is a realist within his limits. Theodore Dreiser (*Sister Carrie*, 1900, *The American Tragedy*, 1925) by his initial daring made later extreme realism possible. Sinclair

Lewis (*Main Street*, 1920, *Babbitt*, 1922) made his reputation by satires on the small town and business. In his best novel, *Arrowsmith* (1925), although Lewis is free for satire, his central figure is victorious instead of frustrated. He is a very accurate observer. Sherwood Anderson in *Winesburg Ohio* wrote a collection of unhappy sketches with sympathy. Ernest Hemingway is a novelist of range and seriousness. In *Farewell to Arms* (1929), his description of the retreat from Caporetto is brilliant. *For Whom the Bell Tolls* is his latest. James Farrall completed his trilogy *Studs Lonigan* in 1935 and John Dos Passos finished *U.S.A.* in 1937. Dos Passos writes with discontent about social conditions. Ole Edvart Rolvaag (*Giants in the Earth*) tells the terrible struggle of a homesteading family in the Northwest. Willa Cather wrote of farm life on the plains but turned to the more romantic subject of French Colonial Quebec (*Shadows on the Rock*). Thomas Wolfe (1900–1938) with *Look Homeward Angel* and *Time and the River* created a sensation by his expansive style with both realistic and poetic qualities. During the 1940's, in revolt against more gloomy realism, a series of books such as *Old Doc's Girl* (1942) by Mary Medearis, appeared, which though honest in statement are happier in tone.

Drama.—Such dramatists as Bronson Howard, David Belasco, Augustus Thomas, William Vaughn Moody, and Clyde Fitch had produced successful plays, Fitch being especially skillful, but the American stage lacked greatness until the triumph of Eugene O'Neill in the 1920's. There is a somber fury to O'Neill's plays together with a great sense of pity for men caught in the web of circumstance. He also was a great experimentalist, testing out the possibilities of the stage. His effect was electric. A great creative burst followed and New York rather than London became the theater capital. Chief plays: *The Emperor Jones* (1920), *The Hairy Ape* (1922), and the long plays *Strange Interlude* (1928), *Mourning Becomes Electra* (1931), and *The Ice Man Cometh* (1946). Maxwell Anderson (*Both Your Houses, Mary of Scotland, Winterset, High Tor*) is another great figure. He is sometimes a strict realist, but has turned to historical themes and sometimes has interspersed loose verse lines. Other noteworthy dramatists are Elmer Rice (*Street Scene*), Robert Sherwood (*The Petrified Forest*), Marc Connelly (*Green Pastures*), Clifford Odets (*Awake and Sing*), and Philip Barry (*The Animal Kingdom*).

Short Story.—Irving in *The Sketch Book* produced the first enduring short stories in American literature. Poe was the greatest short story writer of the mid-century. His tales of terror (*The Fall of the House of Usher*) are written in a sumptuous, haunting style. His detective stories (*The Purloined Letter, The Mystery of Marie Roget*) are the ancestors of all modern detective fiction. Also, in a review of Hawthorne's tales, Poe discussed the laws which govern this literary form. By nature the short story is ephemeral, likely to be read and put aside, and few writers have built important reputations by short stories alone. Among those to do so are Bret Harte with his effective but shallow stories of the Far West; Joel Chandler Harris with his retelling of Negro folk-tales; Mary Wilkins Freeman with her stories of New England; and William S. Porter (O. Henry). O. Henry's stories of "Babylon on the Hudson" (New York), written with surprise endings, were highly popular early in this century. Since the 1930's Katherine Porter and Wilbur Daniel Steele have become notable. Among novelists to use the form are George W. Cable with his pictures of Creole life in Louisiana and Henry James with psychological studies. Two distinguished collections publish annually a volume of the best stories of the year. *Best American Short Stories* has appeared since 1915; *O. Henry Memorial Award Prize Stories*, since 1919.

Recent Poetry.—With the publication in 1912 of *Poetry: A Magazine of Verse*, which was followed by many other small magazines, there began a revival of interest in poetry. From the Middle West Carl Sandburg, Edgar Lee Masters, and Vachel Lindsay became prominent. Freedom in choice of subject and form increased. In the East, Amy Lowell took the lead of a free verse group called The Imagists. Edwin Arlington Robinson with his psychological studies and Robert Frost with his thoughtful poems of the soil preferred the traditional forms. In 1917 T. S. Eliot published his first volume. Both his poetry and criticism have been of great influence. Hart Crane, another experimentalist, rich in style but obscure, became important in the 1920's. Elinor Wylie wrote exquisite lyrics and Edna St. Vincent Millay excelled in the sonnet. A very important figure is Stephen Vincent Benét whose best work is on American themes written in a direct style. Archibald MacLeish, since the success of his *Conquistador* (1932), has been one of the most distinguished figures in American poetry.

TABLE OF AMERICAN LITERATURE

Authors		Representative Works	
Time	Name	Prose	Poetry and Drama
1588–1649	John Winthrop	History of New England	
1590–1657	William Bradford	History of Plymouth	
1604–1690	John Eliot	Bible in Indian Language	
1608–1683	Roger Williams	Religious Controversy	
1612–1672	Anne Bradstreet		Poems.
1631–1705	Michael Wigglesworth		Poems (The Day of Doom).
1663–1728	Cotton Mather	New England Church History	
1674–1744	William Byrd	History of the Dividing Line	
1687–1758	Thomas Prince	History of New England	
1696–1772	Samuel Johnson	Philosophy	
1703–1758	Jonathan Edwards	Freedom of the Will	
1706–1790	Benjamin Franklin	Poor Richard's Almanac	
1711–1780	Thomas Hutchinson	History of Massachusetts	
1720–1772	John Woolman	Journal	
1725–1783	James Otis	Orations	
1736–1763	Thomas Godfrey		Prince of Parthia, Poems.
1736–1799	Patrick Henry	Orations	
1737–1791	Francis Hopkinson		Battle of the Kegs.
1737–1809	Thomas Paine	Common Sense, The Crisis	
1743–1826	Thomas Jefferson	Notes on Virginia, State Papers	
1750–1831	John Trumbull		Satire (McFingal).
1752–1817	Timothy Dwight		Conquest of Canaan.
1752–1832	Philip Freneau		Lyrics (Eutaw Springs).
1754–1812	Joel Barlow		The Columbiad, Hasty Pudding.
1757–1804	Alexander Hamilton	State Papers	
1757–1826	Royall Tyler	Stories	Drama (The Contrast).
1771–1810	Charles B. Brown	Novels (Wieland, Clara Howard).	
1777–1852	Henry Clay	Orations	
1779–1843	Washington Allston	Lectures on Art	Poems.

TABLE OF AMERICAN LITERATURE—Con.

Authors		Representative Works	
Time	Name	Prose	Poetry and Drama
1779–1860	James K. Paulding	Novels (The Dutchman's Fireside)	Poems (The Backwoodsman).
1780–1842	William E. Channing	Essays, Addresses	
1780–1843	Francis Scott Key		Star-Spangled Banner.
1782–1850	John C. Calhoun	Orations	
1782–1852	Daniel Webster	Orations	
1783–1859	Washington Irving	History of New York, Sketch Book	
1785–1842	Samuel Woodworth		Poems (The Old Oaken Bucket), Plays.
1787–1879	Richard H. Dana	Lectures on Shakspere	The Buccaneer.
1789–1841	James A. Hillhouse		Dramas (Percy's Masque, Hadad).
1789–1851	James F. Cooper	The Pilot, Leatherstocking Tales.	
1789–1867	Catherine M. Sedgwick	Novels (A New England Tale)	
1790–1867	Fitz-Greene Halleck		Poems (Marco Bozzaris).
1790–1870	Augustus B. Longstreet	Humor (Georgia Scenes)	
1791–1852	John Howard Payne		Home, Sweet Home, Plays.
1791–1865	Lydia H. Sigourney		Poems (Pocahontas).
1792–1868	Seba Smith	Humor (Letters of Major Jack Downing)	
1793–1860	Samuel G. Goodrich	Peter Parley Books	
1793–1868	Daniel P. Thompson	Novels (Green Mountain Boys)	
1794–1865	Edward Everett	Orations	
1794–1878	William C. Bryant		Poems (Thanatopsis).
1795–1820	Joseph R. Drake		Poems (The Culprit Fay).
1795–1856	James G. Percival	History	Prometheus.
1795–1870	John P. Kennedy	Novels (Horse-Shoe Robinson).	
1796–1859	William H. Prescott	History (Ferdinand and Isabella, Conquest of Mexico)	
1799–1854	Richard Penn Smith		Dramas (William Penn).
1799–1859	Rufus Choate	Orations	
1799–1888	Amos Bronson Alcott	Philosophy	
1800–1891	George Bancroft	History of the United States	
1802–1864	George P. Morris	Journalism	Lyrics (Woodman, Spare That Tree).
1802–1870	George D. Prentice	Journalism, Humor (Prenticiana).	Poems.
1802–1876	Horace Bushnell	Nature and the Supernatural.	
1803–1882	Ralph W. Emerson	Philosophy, Conduct of Life, Representative Men	
1804–1864	Nathaniel Hawthorne	Novels (Blithedale Romance, Scarlet Letter), Tales	
1806–1867	Nathaniel P. Willis	Sketches of Travel and Biography	Scriptural Poems.
1806–1870	William G. Simms	Novels (The Scout), Biography	Poems (Atalantis).
1807–1882	H. W. Longfellow	Outre-Mer	Poems (Hiawatha).
1807–1892	John G. Whittier		Poems (Maud Muller, Snowbound).
1808–1895	Samuel F. Smith	Biographies, Sketches	Poems (America).
1809–1849	Edgar Allan Poe	Tales (The Gold Bug)	Poems (The Raven).
1809–1865	Abraham Lincoln	Addresses (Gettysburg Speech)	
1809–1894	Oliver W. Holmes	Autocrat of the Breakfast Table	Poems (Chambered Nautilus).
1810–1850	Margaret Fuller	Essays	
1810–1860	Theodore Parker	Essays, Sermons	
1811–1874	Charles Sumner	Orations	
1811–1884	Wendell Phillips	Orations	
1811–1896	Harriet B. Stowe	Novels (Uncle Tom's Cabin)	
1814–1877	John L. Motley	History (Rise of the Dutch Republic)	
1814–1890	Benjamin P. Shillaber	Humor	
1815–1882	Richard H. Dana, Jr.	Two Years before the Mast	
1816–1887	John G. Saxe		Humorous Poems (The Proud Miss MacBride).
1817–1862	Henry D. Thoreau	Essays (Walden)	Poems.
1818–1885	Henry Wheeler Shaw, "Josh Billings"	Humor	
1819–1881	J. G. Holland	Novels (Sevenoaks), Essays	Poems (Kathrina).
1819–1891	James R. Lowell	Essays (Among My Books)	Poems (Commemoration Ode).
1819–1891	Herman Melville	Typee, Moby Dick	Poems.
1819–1892	Walt Whitman		Poems (Leaves of Grass).
1819–1910	Julia Ward Howe	Essays	Battle Hymn of the Republic.
1822–1897	W. T. Adams, "Oliver Optic"	Juvenile Stories	
1822–1908	Donald G. Mitchell	Novels, Essays	
1822–1909	Edward E. Hale	The Man without a Country	
1823–1890	George H. Boker		Francesca da Rimini, Poems.
1823–1893	Francis Parkman	History (Conspiracy of Pontiac).	
1823–1911	Thomas W. Higginson	Essays (Outdoor Papers)	
1824–1892	George W. Curtis	Essays (Potiphar Papers), Biography	
1824–1906	Adeline D. Whitney	Novels (The Gayworthys)	Poems.
1825–1878	Bayard Taylor	Travel, Novels (Hannah Thurston)	Poems, Translation (Faust).
1825–1903	Richard H. Stoddard	Criticism	Poems (Songs of Summer).
1827–1892	Rose Terry Cooke	Stories	Poems.
1827–1905	Lew Wallace	Novels (The Fair God, Ben Hur)	
1829–1867	Henry Timrod		The Cotton Boll.
1829–1900	Charles D. Warner	Essays (Backlog Studies, Being a Boy)	
1829–1914	Silas Weir Mitchell	Essays, Novels (Hugh Wynne)	
1830–1886	Emily Dickinson		Lyrics.
1830–1896	Mary A. Dodge	Essays (Country Living)	
1831–1885	Helen Hunt Jackson	Novels (Ramona)	Poems.
1831–1886	Paul H. Hayne		Poems (Legends and Lyrics).
1831–1922	Mary V. Terhune	Novels (Alone, Hidden Path)	
1832–1888	Louisa M. Alcott	Stories (Little Women)	

TABLE OF AMERICAN LITERATURE—Con.

Authors		Representative Works	
Time	Name	Prose	Poetry and Drama
1833–1888	David Ross Locke, "Petroleum V. Nasby"	Humor	
1833–1908	Edmund C. Stedman	Criticism	Poems (Alice of Monmouth).
1834–1867	Charles Farrar Browne, "Artemus Ward"	Humor	
1834–1902	Francis R. Stockton	Stories (The Lady or the Tiger)	
1835–1910	Samuel L. Clemens, "Mark Twain"	Humor (Huckleberry Finn)	
1836–1907	Thomas B. Aldrich	Stories (Marjorie Daw)	Songs, Sonnets.
1836–1917	William Winter	Dramatic Criticism	Poems (Thistledown).
1837–1902	Edward Eggleston	Novels (The Hoosier Schoolmaster, Roxy)	
1837–1920	William D. Howells	Novels (The Rise of Silas Lapham)	
1837–1921	John Burroughs	Essays (Wake Robin, Signs and Seasons)	
1838–1888	Edward Payson Roe	Novels (Barriers Burned Away)	
1838–1905	Albion W. Tourgee	Novels (A Fool's Errand)	
1838–1905	Mary Mapes Dodge	Stories (Hans Brinker)	
1838–1914	John Muir	Story of My Boyhood and Youth.	
1838–1915	F. Hopkinson Smith	Stories (Colonel Carter of Cartersville)	
1838–1918	Henry Adams	The Education of Henry Adams.	
1839–1886	Abram Joseph Ryan		Civil War Poems.
1839–1902	Bret Harte	Stories (Luck of Roaring Camp)	Poems (The Heathen Chinee).
1839–1908	James Ryder Randall		Maryland, My Maryland.
1841–1887	Edward Rowland Sill		Poems (The Venus of Milo).
1841–1913	Cincinnatus H. Miller		Songs of the Sierras.
1842–1881	Sidney Lanier	Essays, Criticism	Poems (The Marshes of Glynn).
1842–1901	John Fiske	Histories, Essays	
1842–1908	Bronson Howard		Plays (The Henrietta, Shenandoah).
1843–1904	Lawrence Hutton	Dramatic Criticism	
1843–1916	Henry James	Novels (Daisy Miller, Portrait of a Lady)	
1844–1909	Richard W. Gilder		Poems (The Great Remembrance).
1844–1911	Elizabeth S. P. Ward	Gates Ajar	
1844–1925	George W. Cable	Novels (Old Creole Days)	
1845–1909	John B. Tabb		Lyrics.
1847–1930	Arthur S. Hardy	Novels (Passe Rose)	
1848–1908	Joel Chandler Harris	Uncle Remus Tales, The Tar Baby	
1848–1927	James Ford Rhodes	Histories, Essays	
1849–1887	Emma Lazarus		Songs of a Semite.
1849–1925	James Lane Allen	Novels (The Choir Invisible)	
1849–1924	Frances H. Burnett	Little Lord Fauntleroy	Plays.
1850–1895	Eugene Field		Poems (With Trumpet and Drum).
1850–1922	Mary N. Murfree	Novels (The Prophet of the Great Smoky Mountains)	
1852–1940	Robert Grant	Novels (The Chippendales), Essays	Humorous Verse.
1852–1932	John B. McMaster	Histories, Biographies	
1852–1940	Edwin Markham		Poems (Lincoln).
1852–1929	Brander Matthews	Essays, Criticism (Aspects of Fiction)	
1852–1933	Henry van Dyke	Essays, Stories (The Blue Flower)	Poems.
1853–1916	James W. Riley		Poems (Pipes o' Pan).
1853–1922	Thomas Nelson Page	Novels (In Ole Virginia)	
1854–1909	F. Marion Crawford	Novels (Saracinesca)	Ballads.
1854–1931	David Belasco		Plays (The Return of Peter Grimm).
1855–1930	George E. Woodberry	Essays, Criticism	Poems.
1856–1939	Edward S. Martin	Essays (In a New Century)	Poems (A Little Brother of the Rich).
1856–1924	Woodrow Wilson	History, Essays	
1857–1934	Augustus Thomas		Plays (Alabama, Arizona).
1857–1948	Gertrude Atherton	Novels (Ancestors)	
1857–	Alice Brown	Novels (The Prisoner)	Plays (Children of Earth).
1857–1927	S. M. Crothers	Essays (The Gentle Reader)	
1857–1945	Margaret W. Deland	Old Chester Tales, Novels	
1858–1919	Theodore Roosevelt	History, Travel, Politics	
1858–	Agnes Repplier	Essays (Points of View)	
1859–1929	Katharine L. Bates	Essays, Criticism	Poems.
1859–1923	William R. Thayer	History, Biography	Poems.
1859–1923	Kate Douglas Wiggin	Rebecca of Sunnybrook Farm	
1860–1940	Hamlin Garland	Stories (Main-traveled Roads)	
1860–	Bliss Perry	Novels, Stories, Essays	
1860–1932	Clinton Scollard		Pictures in Song, Lyrics.
1860–1938	Owen Wister	Novels (The Virginian)	Poems.
1860–1946	Ernest Thompson Seton	Wild Animals I Have Known	
1861–1925	John Herbert Quick	Novels (Vandemark's Folly)	
1862–1910	William S. Porter "O. Henry"	Short Stories (The Four Million)	
1862–1930	Mary E. W. Freeman	Stories, Novels	Poems.
1862–1937	Edith Wharton	Novels (Ethan Frome)	Poems.
1863–1932	Gamaliel Bradford	Biographical Essays	
1863–	George Santayana	Essays (The Life of Reason)	Poems (The Hermit of Carmel).
1863–1936	James Harvey Robinson	History, Essays	
1864–1937	Paul Elmer More	Shelburne Essays	
1865–1902	Paul Leicester Ford	Novels (Janice Meredith)	
1865–1909	William Clyde Fitch		Plays (Beau Brummell, The Truth).
1865–1943	William Lyon Phelps	Criticism, Autobiography	
1865–	Logan Pearsall Smith	Essays (Trivia, More Trivia)	
1866–1944	George Ade	Humor (Fables in Slang)	Plays (The College Widow).
1867–1936	Finley Peter Dunne	Humor (Mr. Dooley's Philosophy)	

TABLE OF AMERICAN LITERATURE—Con.

Authors		Representative Works	
Time	Name	Prose	Poetry and Drama
1868–1938	Robert Herrick	Novels (The Common Lot)	
1868–1924	Gene Stratton Porter	Stories (Freckles)	
1868–1944	William A. White	Novels (A Certain Rich Man)	
1869–1910	William V. Moody		Poems, Dramas (The Great Divide).
1869–1935	Edwin A. Robinson		Poems (Merlin), Dramas (Van Zorn).
1869–1946	Booth Tarkington	Novels (The Plutocrat)	Plays (The Intimate Strangers).
1869–1934	Brand Whitlock	Novels (The Turn of the Balance)	
1869–	Edgar Lee Masters	Novels (Mitch Miller)	Poems (Spoon River Anthology).
1870–1902	Frank Norris	Novels (The Octopus)	
1870–1936	Mary Johnston	Novels (To Have and to Hold)	
1870–1942	Alice Hegan Rice	Novels, Stories (Lovey Mary)	
1871–1947	Winston Churchill	Novels (Richard Carvel)	
1871–1900	Stephen Crane	Novels (The Red Badge of Courage)	Poems (Black Riders).
1871–1945	Theodore Dreiser	Novels (American Tragedy)	
1871–	Charles Rann Kennedy		Dramas (The Servant in the House).
1872–1906	Paul Laurence Dunbar	Stories	Dialect Poems.
1872–1943	Cale Young Rice		Poems (Earth and New Earth).
1872–1946	Gertrude Stein	Novels (The Making of Americans)	Poems (Tender Buttons).
1873–	Stewart Edward White	Novels (The Blazed Trail)	
1874–1922	Josephine P. Peabody	Folk Stories	Poetic Dramas (The Piper).
1874–1938	Zona Gale	Stories (Friendship Village)	Plays (Miss Lulu Bett).
1874–1945	Ellen Glasgow	Novels (The Sheltered Life)	
1874–1925	Amy Lowell	Criticism	Poems (What's O'clock).
1875–	Robert Frost		Poems (North of Boston).
1875–1939	Zane Grey	Novels (Riders of the Purple Sage)	
1875–	Percy Mackaye	Essays	Poetic Dramas (The Scarecrow).
1876–1916	Jack London	Novels (The Sea Wolf)	
1876–1931	Ole Edvart Rolvaag	Novels (Giants in the Earth)	
1876–1941	Sherwood Anderson	Stories, Novels (Marching Men)	
1876–1947	Willa Sibert Cather	Novels (My Antonia), Stories	
1876–	Mary Roberts Rinehart	Stories (The Circular Staircase)	Plays (Double Life).
1877–	William Beebe	Nature Essays (Jungle Peace)	
1878–1927	James Oliver Curwood	Novels	
1878–1937	Donald Marquis	Humor (The Old Soak)	
1878–	James Truslow Adams	The History of New England	
1878–	Carl Sandburg	Biography (Abraham Lincoln)	Poems (Smoke and Steel).
1879–	James Branch Cabell	Novels (Jurgen)	
1879–	Dorothy Canfield Fisher	Novels (The Brimming Cup)	
1879–1931	N. Vachel Lindsay	The Golden Book of Springfield	Poems (The Congo).
1879–	John Erskine	Essays, Novels	
1879–	Simeon Strunsky	Essays (Sinbad and His Friends)	
1880–1930	Henry Sydnor Harrison	Novels (Queed; St. Teresa)	
1880–	Joseph Hergesheimer	Novels (Java Head)	
1880–	Kathleen Norris	Novels (Lucretia Lombard)	
1880–	Ernest Poole	Novels (The Harbor)	
1880–	Henry L. Mencken	Essays, Social Criticism	
1881–	Witter Bynner		Poems (Songs for Celia).
1882–	Susan Glaspell	Novels (Brook Evans)	Plays (Alison's House).
1882–1932	James Oppenheim	Novels and Short Stories	Poems (Songs for the New Age).
1882–1944	Hendrik Willem Van Loon	History (Story of Mankind)	
1883–	Coningsby Dawson	Novels (Garden without Walls)	The Worker, and Other Poems.
1884–1933	Sara Teasdale		Helen of Troy, and Other Poems.
1885–1928	Elinor Wylie	Novels (Jennifer Lorn)	Poems (Nets to Catch the Wind).
1885–	Sinclair Lewis	Novels (Main Street; Babbitt)	
1885–	Louis Untermeyer	Criticism	The Younger Quire.
1885–	Will Durant	Essays (Story of Philosophy)	
1885–	Carl Van Doren	Biography (Benjamin Franklin)	
1886–1918	Joyce Kilmer		Rouge Bouquet, and Other Poems.
1886–1941	Elizabeth Madox Roberts	Novels (Great Meadow)	Poems (Under the Tree).
1886–	John Gould Fletcher		Goblins and Pagodas.
1886–	Edward B. Sheldon		Dramas (Romance).
1886–	Wilbur Daniel Steele	Novels, Stories (Land's End)	
1886–	Van Wyck Brooks	The Flowering of New England	
1887–	Mary Ellen Chase	The Bible and the Common Reader	
1887–	Floyd Dell	Novels (Moon-Calf)	
1887–	Robinson Jeffers		Poems (Thurso's Landing).
1887–	Edna Ferber	Novels (So Big, Show-Boat)	
1888–	Eugene G. O'Neill		Plays (Mourning Becomes Electra).
1888–	Maxwell Anderson		Plays (High Tor, Winterset).
1888–	John Crowe Ransom	Criticism (The World's Body)	Selected Poems (1945).
1888–	Thomas Stearns Eliot	Criticism (The Sacred Wood)	Poems (The Wasteland).
1889–	W. Hervey Allen	Novels (Anthony Adverse)	Poems (New Legends).
1890–	Christopher Morley	Essays, Novels (Thorofare)	Poems (Song for a Little House).
1892–	Archibald MacLeish	Essays (A Time to Speak)	Poems (Conquistador).
1892–	Edna St. Vincent Millay		Poems (Renascence), Plays.
1893–	John P. Marquand	Novels (The Late George Apley)	
1896–	John Dos Passos	Novels (U.S.A.)	
1897–	Thornton Wilder	Novels (Bridge of San Luis Rey)	Plays (Our Town).
1898–	Ernest Hemingway	Novels (Farewell to Arms)	
1898–1943	Stephen V. Benét	Stories	Poems (John Brown's Body).
1899–1932	Hart Crane		Poems (The Bridge).
1900–1938	Thomas Wolfe	Novels (Of Time and the River)	
1900–	John Steinbeck	Novels (The Grapes of Wrath)	
1906–	Margaret Mitchell (Mrs. Marsh)	Novels (Gone with the Wind)	
1908–	William Saroyan	Stories (My Name Is Aram)	Plays.

ENGLISH LITERATURE

When the Angles and Saxons went from the continent to Britain in the 5th and the 6th century, they had no written language, but they carried with them the love of song. Bards and gleemen accompanied them and sang the tales of the Northland. The oldest of the ancient songs which have been preserved for us is *The Far-Traveler*. *Beowulf* is their epic song. At the time of their invasion of Britain, these Anglo-Saxons were heathen, but when, after two long centuries of struggle, they had become possessed of the land, they came under the softening influence of Christianity. Monasteries were built, and in these safe shelters literature had a beginning. The glory of this beginning belongs to Northumbria in the 7th century. For nearly two centuries, this was the seat of learning.

Old English Period. The poem *Beowulf* is Anglo-Saxon, but it is not native to English soil. Cædmon's *Paraphrase of the Scriptures* is the first great native British poem. With Christianity a new spirit entered into English poetry.

Old English prose also began in the monastery of Northumbria with Bede. His learning was famed throughout Europe. How industrious he was is indicated by the tradition that he wrote no less than 45 works in Latin. His last work was a translation of the Gospel of St. John into English.

During the 9th century the greater part of England was laid waste by the Danes, and literature was almost extinguished. The long battle against these invaders was lost in Northumbria, but was gained for a time by Alfred the Great in Wessex. The center of learning was transferred from the North to the South, and as Whitby was the cradle of English poetry in the North, so Winchester became the seat of English prose in the South. Alfred gathered scholars about him, who translated the Latin works of Bede and the *Chronicles* of Orosius, adding an account of the voyages of Othere and Wulfstan. Many other works were rendered into the vernacular in Alfred's time. "At Winchester the king took the English tongue and made it the tongue in which history, philosophy, law, and religion spoke to the English people." He also established schools and wrote textbooks for these schools, so that every free-born youth might attend to his books till he "could read English writing perfectly."

The next great name in literature after King Alfred is Ælfric. He wrote numerous ecclesiastical works and was the first translator of any considerable portion of the Bible. His translations of the Pentateuch, Joshua, Judges, and part of Job are the best examples we possess of the language at the beginning of the 11th century. Indeed, our greatest Old English prose is perhaps to be found in the sermons and saints' lives by Ælfric. The *Old English Chronicle* records the most significant happenings of history, chiefly English history, and was continued in Peterborough Abbey down to the death of King Stephen in 1154.

Middle English Period. The overthrow of Saxon rule in England by William the Conqueror is an event of vast importance in literature as well as in history. For a hundred years after the conquest, literature was inert. A foreign king and an aristocracy of a foreign people ruled the land; an alien language had been introduced. However, after a few generations of such domination there were signs of returning life. The language could not die while the bulk of the people remained Saxon, but it underwent a great change. England was still to remain the land of the Saxon tongue, but the language was to be greatly modified by its contact with the Latin of the clergy and with the French of the Norman conquerors. For 300 years after the conquest these languages contended with the Saxon English for supremacy in England. In the reign of Edward III it had been fully demonstrated that the English were to be the ruling people, and Parliament enacted important laws making English the official language of law courts and schools.

But the English of King Edward's time was quite unlike the rude Saxon speech of *Beowulf* and Cædmon's *Paraphrase* or the later chronicles. Pure Anglo-Saxon was an energetic language, able to express with vigor the practical common thoughts of every day, but it lacked delicacy and flexibility of expression. The Saxon mind, too, was lacking in quickness of thought and in the creative play of the imagination. It has been well said that in this blending of languages the Saxon furnished the dough and the Norman French the yeast. Out of the combined product we get a strength and flexibility of language that belonged to neither element alone.

Chronicles and Romances.—The literature of England during the 12th century was almost entirely Latin and French, but we reckon it as a rich source of our story-telling. Geoffrey of Monmouth wrote twelve short books in Latin, which he called *History of the Kings of Britain*. It is a clever compilation of Welsh legends, a source to which we go for some of our King Arthur stories. These stories were afterward translated into French and were later brought back into English verse by Layamon in his *Brut d'Angleterre*. Later many other stories were added, and other cycles of romance were introduced into English literature. There were four of these great romantic cycles: (1) the King Arthur legends, to which later stories were added, such as *Quest of the Grail*, *Le Morte D'Arthur*, *Romance of Sir Tristram*; (2) Charlemagne and his Twelve Peers, containing the stories of Roland, Charlemagne, Roland and Otuel, the *Siege of Milan*, and others; (3) the *Life of Alexander*, romantic wonder stories from the East; (4) the *Siege of Troy*, derived from Latin sources. Popular ballads, such as "Robin Hood," Robert of Gloucester's *Rhyming Chronicles*, and lyrics sung among the people, kept the love of poetry alive until the greater burst of song in the 14th century.

Mandeville and Wiclif.—In the three centuries following the conquest there was very little prose writing done in England, but in the 14th century there appeared a book of stories entitled *The Voiage and Travaile of Sir John Mandeville.* We do not know who is the author of this book. Many of the stories seem to be translations. The exaggerations in the book make it valueless as a record of travel, but it did establish the love of story-telling. It is the first example of a definitely achieved prose style, and after the invention of printing it long remained one of the most popular books. John Wiclif, next to Chaucer, is the greatest literary name of the century. He and his friend, John Purvey, were the first to give a complete version of the Scriptures to the English people in their own tongue. The influence of such a translation read by all the people was to raise a dialect to the dignity of a national language. Besides this great work, Wiclif is the author of a large number of sermons and polemical writings. Contemporary with these religious tracts which Wiclif distributed so freely was *Piers Plowman*, by William Langland. It was a satire in verse upon certain ecclesiastical corruptions of the period and remained the greatest allegory in the language until the publication of Bunyan's *Pilgrim's Progress*.

Chaucer.—The most distinguished name in the literature of the 14th century is that of Geoffrey Chaucer. Some critics maintain that before him there was no permanent English verse. He is therefore often called the "Father of English Poetry." Chaucer's earlier poems are "Romaunt of the Rose," "The Book of the Duchess," and "Parlement of Foules." His greatest work is *Canterbury Tales*, the plan of which was suggested by Boccaccio's *Decameron*. The Prologue to the *Canterbury Tales* is one of the finest pieces of descriptive poetry in our language. Before Chaucer's time English was a language of dialects. He wrote in the Midland dialect and made that the language of the nation. Chaucer died in 1400, just 334 years after the Norman Conquest. To sum up the most important literary events of these years, we note the development of the English language, the translation of the Bible, and the creation in English of one of the world's supreme masterpieces, *Canterbury Tales.*

There was but little progress in the development of literary art in the century following Chaucer. Social conditions were changing, and there was intellectual and political unrest. The struggle between the houses of York and Lancaster absorbed men's minds. These are the reasons assigned for the dearth of literature. To the genius of Chaucer there arose no successor.

Printing and the Bible.—The greatest prose work of the 15th century is Sir Thomas Malory's *Morte D'Arthur.* This is a prose epic of the deeds of King Arthur and his knights of the Round Table. In 1476 Caxton established his printing press and, in 1477, issued the first printed book in England,—the *Dictes and Sayings of the Philosophers.* He had already printed in English on the continent his *Recuyell of the Histories of Troy* and the *Game and Playe of the Chesse.* The 16th century was a period of Bible translation. Wiclif had made his rendering from the Latin, but, in the early years of the 16th century, Greek was being taught in the English universities, and William Tyndale made the first translation of the New Testament directly from the Greek text. He later translated the Pentateuch from the Hebrew, and in 1535 Miles Coverdale published the first printed copy of the whole Bible. In 1560 a new translation, called the Genevan Bible, was issued from Geneva in Switzerland. This was long the popular Bible among Protestants, even after the publication of the King James Version. In 1582, scholars in the Catholic college at Reims in France issued a translation of the New Testament.

The Elizabethans. The Elizabethan age is marked by features so distinct and so superior that it has been called the "Golden Age in English literature." Two mighty forces, the Renaissance and the Reformation, combined to make this a great intellectual age. Men's minds were stimulated, and a language completely formed was ready at their hand. There was freedom for thought to express itself, and there was variety in life and freshness of experience to nourish the mind. The printing press, travel, and social intercourse all stimulated intellectual activity. The great period began with Spenser and Marlowe, reached its climax in Shakspere, but was still capable of producing Donne and Webster.

Spenser.—Spenser had a rich, dreamy music and a skill in poetic form which has caused him to be called "the poet's poet." Later such poets as Byron, Shelley, and Keats used the "Spenserian Stanza." His first great work, *The Shepherd's Calender*, was an exercise piece in which he tried out and stabilized certain metrical forms. *The Faery Queen*, although incomplete, is one of the longest poems in the language. It is a combination of Reformation moral thinking, of the Renaissance sense of luxury, of Aristotle's ethics, and of Spenser's own great musical genius. To some modern readers, however, his style is cloying.

The Drama.—The beginnings of the drama in England may be traced to the *miracle plays* and *mysteries* which were introduced soon after the Norman Conquest. Following these were the later dramatic recitals, the *moralities, interludes, masks,* and *pageants.*

As early as the 11th century, *miracle plays* were performed in the monasteries by monks and choristers. Later, companies of professional players traveled about the country and enacted their plays in the yards of inns. In 1575 the Puritans expelled the players from the city, and theaters were built outside the limits. Shakspere was born in 1564. Twenty-two or twenty-three years later he made his way to London, where he was attracted by one of these forbidden theaters. Already English drama had attained classical utterance in the great plays of Christopher Marlowe, *Tamburlaine the Great, Faustus, The Jew of Malta.* The greatest of these plays is *Faustus.* Marlowe established the use of blank verse in the English drama, a form of verse which Shakspere adopted and brought to technical perfection.

Shakspere.—That Shakspere quickly rose to prominence in his art, we may judge from the fact that in 1592, when he had been in London not more than five or six years, he was already writing plays and was the object of a jealous attack by a rival playwright. At the age of 49 he was able to leave London with a competence and to return to his home at Stratford-on-Avon. This also argues for his success as a dramatist. In 1598 Francis Mere writes of the growing fame of Shakspere and prints the titles of a number of his plays. Ben Jonson, the second dramatist of the age, was his intimate friend. These are facts worth knowing about the personality of the man who is the greatest figure in English literature, perhaps in all literature.

Attributed to Shakspere are 34 plays, counting as single plays those written in several parts. His dramatic work may be divided into three classes: comedies, histories, tragedies. The following are a few of the best in each class. Every reader should be familiar with them:

Comedies: *Midsummer Night's Dream, As You Like It, Merchant of Venice, Winter's Tale, Twelfth Night, The Tempest.*

Histories: *Richard III, Henry IV, Henry V, Henry VIII, King John, Julius Cæsar.*

Tragedies: *Hamlet, Macbeth, King Lear, Othello, Romeo and Juliet, Antony and Cleopatra.*

In addition to his dramas, Shakspere wrote two long narrative poems and 154 sonnets. It is said that the measure of Shakspere's greatness is his universality; he was "not of an age, but for all time." Other writers have equaled Shakspere in some one quality, but he excels them all in the combination of these diverse qualities.

Even without Shakspere, the age of Elizabeth and James I would be considered a great dramatic period. Beaumont and Fletcher with a long series of tragedies and romantic comedies, among which *The Maid's Tragedy* and *Philastor* are notable, rivalled Shakspere in popularity. They had a genuine dramatic sense and wrote beautiful blank verse but their sense of character was inferior and their morals dubious. Ben Jonson, writing according to the classical "three unities," scored successes with comedies such as *Volpone, The Alchemist,* and *Every Man in His Humor.* Jonson's figures are exaggerated, each being dominated by a special bias, or "humor" of the mind, a device which enabled Jonson to satirize the foibles of human nature. John Webster's few plays are somber and haunted by death and disaster. He is notable for the creation of two great heroines, The Duchess of Malfi and The White Devil, in plays of those names. The one is a gentle and generous woman, the other all that the title implies.

Elizabethan Prose.—One of the most remarkable of the men who adorned the court of Queen Elizabeth was Sir Francis Bacon, the greatest prose writer of the age. As courtier and scholar he adorned both this and the succeeding reign of James I. His political success and his political disgrace are familiar stories in history. His enduring work is in literature. He was both poet and philosopher. His great work in philosophy is magnificent in scope, as may be inferred from the title *Instauratio Magna*, or "The Great Institution of True Philosophy." This monumental work was designed to be written in six parts, but it was never finished.

The second part, *Novum Organum*, or the "New Instrument," is described as "the science of a better and more perfect use of reason in the investigation of things, and of the true aids of the understanding." It sets forth the methods to be adopted in searching after truth, points out sources of error, and suggests the means of avoiding errors in the future. His entire philosophy is built upon the idea of inductive investigation. Bacon had so little respect for the English language that he wrote his great philosophy in Latin. His *New Atlantis*, like Sir Thomas More's *Utopia*, pictures in romance an ideal commonwealth. The most important among his English works is his volume of essays, clear, concise, practical in observation, and of profound wisdom. Sir Walter Raleigh contributed to prose his ambitious *History of the World*, and to poetry a few beautiful lyrics.

Transition.—With the death of Bacon in 1626, we pass from the glory of the Elizabethan age into the Puritan age. There are some characteristics which sharply separate this age from the preceding. Intense patriotism, peace within the realm, general prosperity, and much worldliness characterized the reign of Elizabeth. The Stuart reign was characterized by controversy in religion and politics; the open rupture between the king and Parliament was protracted into the great Civil War. Puritan standards became triumphant during this period. Literature, which always reflects life, presented the somber tone of the age and was in large part religious. In 1609 the Roman Catholic English version of the Bible, the *Douai Bible*, was issued from Douai, France. The *King James Version of the Bible* was printed in 1611. It is impossible to overestimate the influence of both translations upon the lives of the people and upon the language of the day. The study of the Bible became more universal, so much so that it colored the imagination and the speech of the common people. Even those who were irreligious in their lives spoke in the language of the Scriptures.

The Puritan Age. The great literature of the Elizabethan age was in poetry. With one exception, John Milton, the main achievement of the Puritan age was in prose. But the prose writers of the Puritan age were not without imagination and delicacy of humor. Bunyan's *Pilgrim's Progress*, thought by some to be the crowning work of the Puritan imagination, is a product of this age. During the same period, Thomas Fuller brightens his *History of the Worthies of England* by irresistible touches of humor, and Izaak Walton gives expression to delight in nature and rustic pastimes in his *Compleat Angler*; but for the most part the world was looked upon seriously.

Milton.—John Milton is usually regarded as the second greatest name in English literature. He was born eight years before the death of Shakspere. It may be that Shakspere saw the boy Milton,—perhaps on Bread street as the great dramatist strolled past Milton's doorstep on his way to the Mermaid Tavern. One likes to think so. Milton's childhood was very happy. He had every advantage of a liberal education and of long quiet years of study at his father's country home in Horton. Here he stored up strength of mind and soul for the years of struggle that followed. Milton's literary career may be divided into three periods: his youth, his manhood, and his old age. It has been called "a drama in three acts." The first may be stated in years as extending from 1623 to 1640; the second, from 1640 to 1660; and the third, from 1660 to 1674.

The first period, that of his youth, was spent at school and with his family at Horton. During this period he wrote the "Hymn on the Morning of Christ's Nativity," the *Masque of Comus*, "Lycidas," "L'Allegro," "Il Penseroso," and a number of his sonnets. Some critics consider *Comus* Milton's finest poem. It is perfect in lyric qualities and, as an apotheosis of virtue, is lofty in conception. "If virtue feeble were, Heaven itself would stoop to her."

"Lycidas," an elegy on Milton's classmate, Edward King, ranks as one of the great elegies in our language. "L'Allegro" and "Il Penseroso" are companion poems; one describes the delights of social life, the other the deep enjoyment of the scholar in seclusion. These poems will always remain favorites for their beautiful imagery and for their truthful study of the emotions. Milton's sonnets have for their theme such subjects as religion, patriotism, domestic affection; whereas the older poets, Shakspere, Spenser, Wyatt, Surrey, and their imitators, preferred to write sonnets on love.

The second period of Milton's life may be called the time of "storm and stress." For 20 years, from 1640 to 1660, his life was filled with religious and political controversy. He was forced to turn from poetry to prose, and lamenting it he says: "I have the use, as I may account it, but of my left hand." His prose works are voluminous. They are upon varied subjects but upon one theme, liberty. He struck heavy blows for liberty in church and state and in all the relations of life. He pleaded for more freedom of speech and for more liberal ideas in education. His greatest prose work is the *Areopagitica: A Speech for the Liberty of the Press.* In 1652, at the age of 43, Milton became totally blind; but, even in his blindness, he served the Commonwealth as secretary for foreign tongues under Oliver Cromwell, the lord protector, and continued to write his burning pamphlets against the royalists, who were struggling to regain power.

The third period is that which succeeds the Restoration, in 1660. With the return of Charles II, the leaders of the Commonwealth had to flee for their lives. Milton's life was at first endangered, and he was concealed by friends. Later, he preferred retirement where he might have leisure to do the great work of his life, the writing of *Paradise Lost*, *Paradise Regained*, and *Samson Agonistes.*

The beauty of *Paradise Lost* has been compared to that of a stately temple; its style is the loftiest in the whole range of English poetry. Its scenes are laid in heaven and earth and hell, its characters are God and the holy angels, Satan and his legions, and the newly created race of man. In *Paradise Regained* Christ is tempted in the wilderness and resists Satan. In *Samson Agonistes* we have a choral drama modeled upon the form of a Greek tragedy. In the noble grandeur of his work, Milton can be compared only to the great classic writers, Homer and Virgil.

Bunyan.—The second notable name in the Puritan age is that of John Bunyan, the prince of prose writers for his time. *Pilgrim's Progress* has been pronounced the greatest of all allegories. Bunyan's pre-eminence is undoubted. It is no exaggeration to approve this estimate of him: "What Shakspere is to English dramatists, what Milton is to English epic poets, that John Bunyan is to writers of English allegory." From extreme poverty and ignorance and years of imprisonment in Bedford jail, he rose to the respected position of pastor over a large church. His biographer says of him, "The fame of his sufferings, his genius as a writer, his power as a speaker, gave him unbounded influence among the Baptists; while the beauty of his character and the catholic liberality of his views secured him universal esteem. His ministrations extended over the whole region between Bedford and London."

Pepys and Hyde.—One of the most interesting prose works of the century is Samuel Pepys's *Diary.* It is a gossipy record of nine years and gives a lifelike picture of the gay and profligate portion of society, engaged in vigorous and not always edifying reaction against Puritanism, which fell under the diarist's observation. The chief historical work of the age is the *History of the Great Rebellion* by Edward Hyde, Earl of Clarendon. A curious coincidence marks the life and the death of Clarendon. His life (1609–74) is virtually coextensive with that of John Milton, his principal opponent in the great civil strife. Clarendon has been called the "Cavalier-prince of historic portrait painters," and Milton the "Puritan-prince of epic poets."

Poetic Transition. *Dryden.*—Milton, whose life overlapped Shakspere's, belongs because of his splendor of style to the Renaissance; Dryden (d. 1700), whose life overlapped Milton's, is the precursor of a new period, a somewhat cynical period which prided itself on its "commonsense" and its epigrammatic wit. Dryden's greatest works are his satires, *MacFlecknoe*, directed against a personal literary enemy, and especially his *Absalom and Achitophel*, a political satire on the Whigs which he wrote in support of the court party of Charles II. Both poems were deadly in effectiveness. English satire to Dryden's time had been rough-and-tumble but he "substituted the rapier for the bludgeon" and his crisp, biting couplets prepared the style that Pope, his successor, was to use. Dryden also wrote rather dull didactic poems such as *The Hind and the Panther* and *Religio Laici*, in which he argued religious questions with himself. As a critic, he ranks very highly but his criticism is scattered through many prefaces and essays. *The Essay on Dramatic Poetry* is most quoted. Also, he wrote many successful plays in a fashion which is now outmoded. One play, *All for Love*, just misses true greatness.

The English revolution of 1688 secured peace for the realm and an opportunity for the development of arts and sciences. The investigations of Newton and the development of philosophy under Locke mark this period.

The Eighteenth Century. Alexander Pope is the literary successor of John Dryden and the representative poet of his time. He was a precocious boy whose life was "one long disease," and as an adult, he was so frail that he had literally to be laced into a canvas corset in order to sit erect. To understand Pope, one must remember his deformity and the spirit of the time in which he lived. The first half of the 18th century is marked by a low standard of morals. Political unrest and political double-dealing, coarse social life,—dull, unimaginative, brutal,—these are the common characteristics ascribed to it. Drunkenness was common and morality was laughed at. Out of such conditions, Pope, Swift, and Steele gathered the material for their satires. Of this distinguished group of writers, Addison and Steele, although very serious, kept a genial and gentle tone.

Pope.—As a boy, Pope heard that there had been many poets but no "perfect poet" and he set out to be one, driving his sickly body and brain to the effort. He became the literary dictator of his age. Dryden's sharpness in the couplet Pope improved upon so well that he is one of the most quoted authors of the language. Scholars dispute whether the Bible, Shakspere, or Pope is most frequently quoted. Pope was treacherous personally and his intelligence was limited, but he had an uncanny skill in saying the obvious, such as "A little learning is a dangerous thing." As the "perfect poet" he wrote "What's oft been thought but ne'er so well expressed."

Gray's "Elegy," Collins's *Odes*, and Cowper's hymns belong in date to the 18th century, as do the works of Burns and Blake, but their spirit is more that of the following Romantic Period.

Steele and Addison.—The first half of the 18th century is far more remarkable for its prose than for its poetry. A new and excellent field for essayists was found in the *Tatler*, planned by Richard Steele. Periodical papers containing news had existed in England from the time of the Commonwealth, but this was the first periodical designed to have literary merit, to discuss questions of common, everyday interest, and to include lively sketches, anecdotes, and humorous discussions. It was succeeded by the *Spectator*, which appeared every week day morning in the shape of a single leaf, from March 1, 1711 to December 1712; after a suspension it reappeared three times a week in 1714 and extended to 635 numbers. The *Guardian* was begun in 1713 but ceased after the 176th number. Steele was the principal contributor to the *Tatler* and to the *Guardian*, and Addison to the *Spectator*, but papers were also furnished by Swift, Pope, Berkeley, and Hughes. The essays, especially those of Addison, were often models of grace and delicacy and were highly influential in correcting and refining the tone of society.

The Novel.—Prose fiction is another development of the 18th century. Daniel Defoe (1661–1731) first gave to English fiction a simple, direct, matter-of-fact human interest, and the narrative of *Robinson Crusoe* has never been excelled. The *Tale of a Tub* and *Gulliver's Travels*, by Swift, and *The History of John Bull*, by Arbuthnot, are satires in the form of fictitious narratives. Swift's style is famous for its ease and clarity. One of the ironies of history is that *Gulliver's Travels*, the bitterest and most comprehensive satire in the language, has become a favorite children's book. The novel proper became more complex, showing greater diversity in the handling of plot and character, and giving realistic pictures of the social life of the time. *Joseph Andrews*, *Tom Jones*, and *Amelia*, by Fielding, and *Pamela*, *Clarissa Harlowe*, and *Sir Charles Grandison*, by Richardson, were published near the middle of the century. *Peregrine Pickle*, *Humphrey Clinker*, and other novels by Smollett are distinguished for coarse, comic incidents and broad humor. *Tristram Shandy* and *Sentimental Journey*, by Sterne, contain passages sparkling with wit and humor and full of rare tenderness of sentiment. The *Vicar of Wakefield*, by Oliver Goldsmith, is a most delightful romantic novel. It is not a book without artistic faults, but it combines delicate humor with sweet human emotion. Goldsmith was a writer in every field of invention, but he will be remembered chiefly because of the Vicar and his family. His "Deserted Village" and his "Traveler" contain passages that cannot be forgotten.

History and Oratory.—The 18th century, which gave us the modern essay and the novel, also produced writers of carefully elaborated and finished history: *History of England* by David Hume; *History of the Decline and Fall of the Roman Empire* by Gibbon; and Robertson's histories of Scotland, Germany, and America. This century produced great orators, like Burke, Fox, and Pitt, and great philosophers, like Berkeley, Paley, and Hume, besides the economist, Adam Smith, and the great lawyer, William Blackstone.

Samuel Johnson.—In striking personality and in power to make others think, Doctor Samuel Johnson was, without doubt, the foremost man of later 18th century literary London. He was the central figure around whom all the literary men and women gathered, the Nestor of his age. Doctor Johnson founded and carried on as sole editor two periodicals, the *Rambler* and the *Idler*, in the style of the *Spectator*, which Addison had made so popular. His most famous work was a *Dictionary of the English Language*. His critical estimates of poetry must be read with caution, and his criticisms are often stilted and overstrained in language. His best prose is his romance, *Rasselas, the Prince of Abyssinia*. Johnson is better known because of the intimate record of his life, written by his biographer, Boswell, than for what he wrote.

Romanticism. At the turn of the century a new spirit which might be called the quality of wonder—a sense of the richness and mystery of life—in contrast to the skeptical temper of the 18th century became dominant. There had been gropings toward this new spirit in such men as Gray, Collins, and Blake. Robert Burns, probably the greatest writer of song lyrics, had written in Scottish dialect. He was thoroughly familiar with the tunes of the countryside and he put into his lyrics the natural things—girls and love and laughter, mice and men.

In 1798 Wordsworth and Coleridge published *Lyrical Ballads*—a dramatic announcement of a new era. Like Burns, Wordsworth drew on the simple things of life for materials but added a philosophic comprehension of what can lie behind or within little things. Wordsworth is known as a "nature poet" because of his awareness and sense of communion with the physical world in which men move and have their emotions. Wordsworth also insisted on honest language and, although he wrote some silly verses, he killed once and for all the idea that there is such a thing as "poetic diction"—a language for poetry distinct from the speech of men. Among his more representative poems are "Tintern Abbey," "Ode on Intimations of Immortality," "Expostulation and Reply," and "Resolution and Independence." *The Prelude*, in fourteen books, describes the development of a poetic personality.

Coleridge had only a brief period of poetic production but for magic and flair of imagination he is unequalled. Unlike Wordsworth, in his best work such as "The Ancient Mariner," "Kubla Khan," and "Christabel," he took for his subject matter the far away in time and space. He also was a great critic, in his lectures and *Biographia Literaria*. These two poets with their friend Southey are called *The Lake Poets* because of their residence in the Lake district.

Often called *The Revolutionary Poets* are Byron and Shelley. Wordsworth and Coleridge had in their youth been in sympathy with the French Revolution but later turned reactionary. Byron in the later cantos of *Childe Harold*, with smashing rhetoric expresses the individual's defiance of the world in which he finds himself. In the great and rollicking satire *Don Juan*, he makes fun of that world. Byron's earlier cantos of *Childe Harold* so completely eclipsed Scott's poetry (*Lady of the Lake*, *Marmion*) that Scott turned to the novel. Another popular poet was Thomas Moore whose oriental romance *Lalla Rookh* is not read today although his song lyrics retain a well deserved popularity. Shelley equalled Byron in revolutionary ardor. His personal lyrics are intense and beautiful. Politically, he believed in the possibility of a perfect world and preached it with unquenchable optimism. The world he desired and its way of attainment he pictures in *Prometheus Unbound*. When he wrote his magnificent "Ode to the West Wind," he knew he would not see that perfect world in his lifetime but he builds up in the last stanza to a burst of symphonic music and triumphant hope.

Keats, another great poet of the period, was not indifferent to political ideas but his greatest quality is amazing responsiveness to the beauty of the physical world in which we live and his skill in making his reader also respond. "The Eve of St. Agnes," "Ode to a Nightingale," and "Ode on A Grecian Urn" all show his richness of appreciation.

The Victorian Age. The prose of this first half of the 19th century also takes high rank. Scott will always be remembered as the creator of the historical novel; Charles Lamb, for his rare humor and delicate use of language. His *Essays of Elia* have been called the best representative of the personal, chatty essay in English. De Quincey's *Opium Eater* and his *English Mail Coach* are also brilliant specimens of English. Mill, Bentham, and Malthus are the chief contributors to philosophical prose.

In 1837 Queen Victoria ascended the throne. The rest of the century is usually called the Victorian age. This age is remarkable, not for the development of any new type of literature, but for the quantity and general excellence of literature in every department. Representative names of the Victorian age are Browning, Tennyson, Matthew Arnold, the Rossettis, in poetry; Thackeray, Dickens, George Eliot, Trollope, in prose fiction; Carlyle, Macaulay, Ruskin, Matthew Arnold, Leslie Stephen, in essay writing; Spencer, Newman, Hamilton, Darwin, Tyndall, Huxley, Faraday, Mill, in philosophy and science; Milman, Grote, Froude, Freeman, Buckle, Green, and Lecky, in history.

Novelists.—Problems of life occupy the minds of the Victorian writers. It is an age of scientific thought and of practical reform. There is an upward struggle of the masses, a striving for better government, for higher moral ideals. Prose and poetry alike are imbued with an ethical purpose. Dickens desired to bring out what he called "the romantic aspect of familiar things," and he began with the study of "vicious poverty." Most of Dickens's novels were inspired by a firm purpose to accomplish some reform. His social creed has been formulated in these words: "Banish from earth some few monsters of selfishness, malignity, and hypocrisy, set to rights a few obvious imperfections in the machinery of society, inspire all men with a cheery benevolence, and everything will go well with this excellent world of ours." While Dickens with inimitable humor and exuberant optimism was presenting the cause of the submerged poor, Thackeray wrote of the follies of the upper classes of society, and George Eliot pictured the English middle class. These great novelists, with their deep human sympathies, pictured the interdependence of human beings, the relation that every man bears to his surroundings. Thus fiction kept in close touch with the social ideas of the time, reflecting not only its mood but also its important changes. Later in the century, Meredith wrote brilliantly in a mannered style not much approved today and Stevenson wrote his romantic yarns, of which *Treasure Island* is one of the best "boy's books" in existence.

Poets and Critics.—Alfred Tennyson carried on the richness of Keats allied to the moral seriousness of his own age. It has been said that all of his Knights of King Arthur (*Idylls of the King*) are Victorian gentlemen on the way to church. Nevertheless he did retell the old stories effectively, and his *In Memoriam*, with its expression of grief and ultimate faith, is one of the great English elegies. His best lyrics, although sometimes thin in emotional content, are technically nearly perfect. Robert Browning was more robust in style and adventurous of mind. His greatest contribution is his effort to understand human motive, which he attempted through his "dramatic monologues," a literary form which he perfected. *The Ring and the Book* (1868), which is an extreme elaboration of the form, is unquestionably one of the great books of the century. Here he allows a whole set of characters to interpret differently exactly the same set of events—a famous murder which occurred in Rome in 1698. Matthew Arnold as a poet published little, but that of such high quality that it places him as one of the great poets. His critical and controversial works are numerous. He was the champion of the cosmopolitan outlook and of "sweetness and light." *The Essays in Criticism* which came out over a series of years and *Culture and Anarchy* (1869) are his most important prose works. Thomas Carlyle was crusty and dyspeptic of temper but he believed in personal integrity, the essential spirituality of the world and above all, in the destruction of shams. *Sartor Resartus* and *Past and Present* are his great works. Ruskin saw a relationship between economics, art, and daily life. His art criticism is not now highly esteemed but his basic idea of good workmanship under good conditions has never been challenged. A chapter in one of his books later led William Morris into founding a semi-socialistic company which was to produce beautiful household goods to replace the ugly Victorian products.

In 1847, still in his teens, Dante Gabriel Rossetti wrote the first version of *The Blessed Demozel* but he matured and revised his work and published his *Poems* in 1870. His younger sister Christina wrote lyrics of great delicacy. In 1886, Algernon Charles

Swinburne scandalized Victorian England with his *Poems and Ballads*. He is famous for his skillful control of every device known to English prosody and for his luxuriousness which might be summed up in his own line "In a twilight where virtues are vices."

Transition. According to modern standards, the "naughty nineties" were neither so naughty nor so gay as they were supposed to be, but there was a revolt from Victorian formalism and a great deal of talk about "Aestheticism" and "beautiful sins." As early as the seventies Gilbert and Sullivan with their operettas had begun making fun of almost everything. Less healthy was the brilliant conversationalist Oscar Wilde, who put his wit to advantage in such plays as *Lady Windermere's Fan* (1892) and his drollery in *The Importance of Being Earnest* (1895), one of the best farces in English. His *Salome*, written in French, was illustrated in black and white by the brilliant but sinister artist Aubrey Beardsley. Arthur Symons wrote poetry; as an editor of *The Savoy* he encouraged artistic adventure but his proper stand is best described in the dedication of a volume to his wife (1906), *Studies in Seven Arts*, "In my endeavor to master what I have called the universal science of beauty, I owe more to you than to technical books... because in you there is some instinct which turns toward beauty unerringly." John Davidson, Ernest Dowson, and Lionel Johnson were writing skillful verse and Francis Thompson wrote "The Hound of Heaven," a great religious poem. In the nineties there existed in London The Rhymer's Club whose membership is not perfectly clear. Somewhere in the late seventies or eighties Gerard Manley Hopkins was writing but he received no recognition until the publication of his poems in 1918. Most significant in the late 1800's was the sense of stir and the beginning of recognition of such diverse figures as Kipling, Hardy, and Yeats.

Twentieth Century. *Prose and Drama.*—Thomas Hardy must be considered a remarkable man. He began publishing novels in 1873 and through the beginning of the next century they were treated with increasing respect. From 1904 to 1908 he published *The Dynasts*, a poetic drama in 19 acts and 130 scenes plus prologues and epilogues, dealing with the Napoleonic Wars, and in 1909, when over 70, he began publishing poetry. His most significant novels are *The Return of the Native* (1878), *Tess of the D'Urbervilles* (1891), and *Jude the Obscure* (1895). He is unsparing in his realism; he has been called a "philosophic realist" because his general gloominess is drawn largely from the unhappy thinking of Schopenhauer. If any central thread of thought can be found in his novels, play, and poems, it is that of the willingness of human beings to be decent, and the tricks by which fate betrays them. Kipling was a young newspaper correspondent in India selling his books cheaply on newspaper stalls in the late eighties. The news of him spread and he became a sensation. His stories are adroit; his vocabulary, no matter what subject he deals with, is accurate. *Kim* is his best book. *The Jungle Books* have been loved by generations of children. When he was awarded the Nobel prize in 1907 it was "in consideration of the power of observation, originality of imagination, and also the manly strength . . .". His poetry varies. Everyone knows "Mandalay." His "Tommy Atkins" poems (and stories in the same temper) have endeared him to the British army all around the world. Kipling also wrote deeper poetry as in "Recessional," where he asks "Lord God of Hosts, be with us yet!"

Joseph Conrad, Polish by birth, learned English "the language of his secret choice" only after he was 21 but became one of the most remarkable stylists in the language. His novels frequently have far Eastern or shipboard settings which reflect his long experience in the merchant marine before he became a writer. They are, however, predominantly psychological, involving very subtle analysis of human motive and "fine consciences." *Lord Jim* (1900) is his greatest, but *Youth*, *Chance*, and *Victory* also display his genius admirably.

John Galsworthy had published a series of distinguished novels before he developed the theme upon which his fame must really rest. In 1906 he published *The Man of Property*; in 1920 he returned to the Forsyte family, adding in subsequent years two more novels which were combined into the trilogy *The Forsyte Saga*. Later he wrote six more novels ending with *One More River* (1933) and a volume of short stories dealing with the Forsytes. The character delineation is superb and the narrative tension consistently maintained. In addition to being first class novels, the Forsyte series is a remarkable social document, showing as it does through the history of a family the changes in life and thought in England from 1888 until just before World War II. He also wrote more than 25 plays. *Old English* exhibits the same sense of character he showed in *The Forsyte Saga*. As a dramatist he mainly is concerned with social questions: the true nature of justice in *Justice*, personal obligations in *Loyalties*.

Arnold Bennett wrote much. His best work is *The Old Wives Tale*, although a series of novels dealing with the industrial cities (*Clayhanger*, etc.) is preferred by some critics. H. G. Wells also was a prolific writer. He made his reputation with pseudo-scientific romances such as *The Time Machine* but at the time of his death in 1946 he himself felt them outmoded, as science had gone beyond him. Some novels such as *Tono Bungay* retain their freshness. *Mr. Britling Sees It Through* was popular in World War I but is now not much read. Nevertheless there was an energy and comprehensiveness to Wells's mind which influenced his age. To his *The Outline of History* scholars object on details but concede that it would be hard to do the large plan better. In his late years, he also wrote *Experiment in Autobiography* (1934).

William DeMorgan (1839–1917) wrote his first and best novel *Joseph Vance* when he was 66 and then wrote eight more. His books are leisurely and have considerable charm. W. H. Hudson (1841–1922) had a great vogue in the 1920's. His appreciation of nature and the grace of his writing in *Green Mansions* was recognized but he is a naturalist rather than a novelist. C. M. Doughty (1843–1926), in his *Travels in Arabia Deserta*, wrote one of the great travel books. After World War I, H. M. Tomlinson wrote another, *The Sea and the Jungle*, spicy with humanity and gifted phrase. T. E. Lawrence (Lawrence of Arabia), who had been the leading British agent in the Near East, re-enlisted as a private because he wanted to be "anonymous" and wrote *The Seven Pillars of Wisdom*, a book whose deep value still has to be estimated. D. H. Lawrence (1885–1930) is marked by power and ruthlessness in his stories and novels. Fundamentally he feels that modern life has become too artificial and that a return to the more primitive—which of course involves sex—is essential. *Lady Chatterley's Lover* is his most sensational novel; *Women in Love* perhaps his best.

Somerset Maugham is versatile. His comedies, such as *The Circle*, are sophisticated and sparkling; the dramatization of his story *Rain* is stark and dreadful. *Of Human Bondage* is one of the best examples of the autobiographical novel in English. The half century has produced many other novelists of ability. Notable are E. M. Forster (*Passage to India*); J. B. Priestly (*The Good Companion*); C. S. Forester, whose *Captain Horatio Hornblower* is an excellent historical novel. P. G. Wodehouse is a master of English foolery, and Dorothy S. Sayers is a modern master of detective fiction. Lytton Strachey with his *Eminent Victorians* set a fashion in "debunking" biography. G. K. Chesterton, a master of paradox, and Hilaire Belloc were important essayists and critics. Max Beerbohm was a cartoonist as well as a writer and his caustic wit, always fair, was notable.

Drama. The English stage early in the century was dominated by George Bernard Shaw, an Irishman, and James Barrie, a Scotsman. Shaw began to attain prominence in the nineties but with the appearance of *Man and Superman* (1901–03) his position was established. He is sharp of tongue, paradoxical of thought, and has a real genius for stage surprises. Among other plays of his are *Arms and the Man, Caesar and Cleopatra, Androcles and the Lion,* and *St. Joan* (1923). Barrie, in contrast, is tender and sentimental. *Peter Pan* really established his reputation. *What Every Woman Knows* is a favorite. During World War I, a group of his one act plays toured America and a whole continent wept at *The Old Lady Shows Her Medals.* His *Dear Brutus* had a somewhat similar effect. Maugham, Milne, and Galsworthy brought out distinguished plays between the two wars. John Van Druten, now a naturalized American, produced *The Young Woodley,* a play dealing with English public school life. The thirties saw the emergence of the brilliant Noel Coward of whom it is said, "he never had a failure." His wit is his best asset but he is not afraid of seriousness. His best plays are *Cavalcade, Bittersweet, Tonight at Eight-thirty,* the last a collection of nine short plays. Terence Rattigan (*O Mistress Mine,* 1945) seems one of the most promising of the recent men.

Poetry. The skill of Tennyson and the frail and beautiful lyrics of the 1890's stifled poetry at the turn of the century but there was a change coming. Masefield published his *Everlasting Mercy* (1911) in which a drunkard gains grace in some very intentionally crude verses and some beautiful pages. In 1918 the poet laureate Robert Bridges published the poems of Gerard Manley Hopkins (d. 1889). Also in operation were the Imagists and the old traditional formality was shaken. Masefield wrote some exquisite sonnets in traditional form, notably "On Growing Old" and vigorous narratives such as *Dauber.* Masefield had been a merchant seaman and a barkeeper in New York before he reached his position as poet laureate, in succession to Bridges. Bridges' *The Testament of Beauty* will probably stand as his greatest work but his publication in 1918 of his old classmate's poems (Hopkins and Bridges were together at Oxford in 1863) had a profound influence on the course of modern poetry. Hopkins advanced a technique called "sprung rhythm" and insisted on intensity of phrase. Alfred Housman (*The Shropshire Lad,* 1896, and *Last Poems,* 1922), with his perfectly written lyrics of great charm in spite of their pervading melancholy, was a distinguished figure. In the years prior to World War I, the series of *Georgian Anthologies* printed such poets as Walter de la Mare, a master of music, Wilfred Gibson, William H. Davies, Ralph Hodgson, and Rupert Brooke, all of whom went on to distinction. Brooke, killed in the war, is justly famous for his sonnets. His war poetry may be contrasted with the bitter poems of Gibson and Siegfried Sassoon. Hardy's reputation as a poet continued to increase.

In the late 1930's, the most striking new poets to emerge were H. W. Auden, Stephen Spender, C. Day Lewis, and Louis MacNeice. Of these Auden and Spender, because of their aggressiveness, are best known, but Lewis has perhaps the most sensitive talent.

TABLE OF ENGLISH LITERATURE

AUTHORS		REPRESENTATIVE WORKS	
Time	Name	Prose	Poetry and Drama
?	Unknown		The Far-Traveler.
?	Unknown		Beowulf.
665 (about)	Cædmon		Paraphrase of the Scriptures.
673–735	Bede	Ecclesiastical History	Poems.
750 (about)	Cynewulf		Christ, Elene, Andreas.
849–901	Alfred the Great	Translations	
1095–1143	William of Malmesbury	History of Kings of England	
1100–1154	Geoffrey of Monmouth	History of English Kings	
1200 (about)	Layamon		Chronicles of Britain, Brut.
1324–1384	John Wiclif	Translation of Bible, Sermons	
1325–1408	John Gower		Ballads, Lover's Confession.
1332–1400	William Langland		Piers Plowman.
1340–1400	Geoffrey Chaucer		Canterbury Tales, Short Poems.
1422–1491	William Caxton	Translation (History of Troy)	
1430–?	Thomas Malory	Le Morte D'Arthur	
1478–1535	Sir Thomas More	Utopia	
1484–1536	William Tyndale	Translation of New Testament	
1488–1568	Miles Coverdale	Translation of Bible	
1503–1542	Sir Thomas Wyatt		Sonnets, Lyrics.
1536–1608	Thomas Sackville		Mirror for Magistrates.
1552–1599	Edmund Spenser		Faery Queen, Shepherd's Calender.
1554–1586	Sir Philip Sidney	Arcadia	Sonnets.
1559–1634	George Chapman		Translation of Homer, Dramas.
1561–1626	Francis Bacon	Essays, Philosophy	
1564–1593	Christopher Marlowe		Dramas (Faustus), Poems.
1564–1616	William Shakspere		Dramas, Poems, Sonnets.
1573–1631	John Donne	Sermons	Lyrics, Sacred Sonnets.
1573–1637	Ben Jonson		Dramas (The Alchemist, Volpone).
1577–1640	Robert Burton	Anatomy of Melancholy	
1579–1625	John Fletcher }		Dramas (Philaster, Maid's Tragedy).
1584–1616	Francis Beaumont }		
?1580–?1625	John Webster		Dramas (The Duchess of Malfi).
1591–1674	Robert Herrick		Poems.
1593–1633	George Herbert		Poems (The Temple).
1593–1683	Izaak Walton	The Compleat Angler	
1608–1674	John Milton	Areopagitica	L'Allegro, Comus, Paradise Lost.
1609–1674	Edward Hyde	History of the Great Rebellion	
1612–1680	Samuel Butler		Hudibras.
1613–1667	Jeremy Taylor	Holy Living	
1628–1688	John Bunyan	Pilgrim's Progress, Holy War	
1631–1700	John Dryden	Essays, Prefaces	Absalom and Achitophel.
1632–1704	John Locke	Philosophy	
1633–1703	Samuel Pepys	Diary	
1661–1731	Daniel Defoe	Robinson Crusoe	
1667–1745	Jonathan Swift	Gulliver's Travels, Tale of a Tub	
1672–1719	Joseph Addison	Essays (The Spectator)	Dramas, Poems.

TABLE OF ENGLISH LITERATURE—Con.

Authors		Representative Works	
Time	Name	Prose	Poetry and Drama
1672–1729	Sir Richard Steele	Essays (The Tatler)	
1685–1753	Bishop Berkeley	Philosophy	
1688–1744	Alexander Pope		Poems (Essay on Man).
1689–1761	Samuel Richardson	Novels (Clarissa Harlowe, Pamela)	
1700–1748	James Thomson		The Seasons.
1707–1754	Henry Fielding	Novels (Tom Jones, Amelia)	
1709–1784	Samuel Johnson	Dictionary, Rasselas, Essays	
1711–1776	David Hume	History of England	
1713–1768	Laurence Sterne	Novels (Tristram Shandy)	
1716–1771	Thomas Gray	Criticism	Poems.
1721–1759	William Collins		Odes.
1721–1771	T. George Smollett	Novels (Humphrey Clinker)	
1728–1774	Oliver Goldsmith	Vicar of Wakefield, Essays	Plays (She Stoops to Conquer), Poems.
1729–1797	Edmund Burke	Essays, Speeches (On Conciliation)	
1731–1800	William Cowper		Poems (The Task, John Gilpin).
1737–1794	Edward Gibbon	Decline and Fall of the Roman Empire	
1740–1795	James Boswell	Life of Samuel Johnson	
1745–1833	Hannah More	Cœlebs in Search of a Wife	Sacred Dramas.
1748–1832	Jeremy Bentham	Political Essays	
1749–1806	Charles James Fox	Orations	
1751–1816	Richard B. Sheridan	Speeches	Plays (The Rivals).
1757–1827	William Blake		Songs of Innocence and Experience.
1759–1796	Robert Burns		Lyrics.
1759–1806	William Pitt	Orations	
1767–1849	Maria Edgeworth	Novels (Castle Rackrent)	
1770–1835	James Hogg	Shepherd's Calendar	Pastorals.
1770–1850	William Wordsworth		Poems (Tintern Abbey).
1771–1832	Sir Walter Scott	Waverley Novels	Lady of the Lake.
1771–1845	Sydney Smith	Sermons, Essays	
1772–1834	S. T. Coleridge	Essays	Poems (The Ancient Mariner).
1774–1843	Robert Southey	Biographies of Nelson and Wesley	Poems (Madoc).
1775–1817	Jane Austen	Pride and Prejudice, Emma	
1775–1834	Charles Lamb	Essays of Elia	
1775–1864	Walter S. Landor	Imaginary Conversations	Count Julian, Heroic Idyls.
1776–1850	Jane Porter	Scottish Chiefs	
1777–1844	Thomas Campbell		Pleasures of Hope, Lyrics.
1777–1859	Henry Hallam	History	
1778–1830	William Hazlitt	Table Talk, English Poets	
1779–1852	Thomas Moore	Biographies	Lalla Rookh, Irish Melodies.
1784–1859	Leigh Hunt	Essays, Sketches, Memoirs	Poems.
1785–1854	John Wilson	Noctes Ambrosianæ	Poems.
1785–1859	Thomas De Quincey	An English Opium Eater	
1788–1824	Lord Byron	Letters	Poems (Childe Harold).
1791–1868	Henry H. Milman	History	Poems, Poetical Dramas.
1792–1822	Percy B. Shelley	Essay on Poetry	Poems (Prometheus Unbound).
1792–1848	Frederick Marryat	Mr. Midshipman Easy	
1793–1835	Felicia Hemans		Lyrics.
1795–1821	John Keats	Letters	Poems and Odes.
1795–1881	Thomas Carlyle	French Revolution, Cromwell	
1797–1868	Samuel Lover	Handy Andy, Rory O'More	Songs, Ballads.
1798–1827	Robert Pollock	Tales of the Covenanters	Course of Time.
1799–1845	Thomas Hood		Poems.
1800–1859	Thomas B. Macaulay	Essays, History of England	Lays of Ancient Rome.
1801–1890	John H. Newman	Essays (The Idea of a University)	Poems, Hymns.
1803–1873	Edward Bulwer-Lytton	Last Days of Pompeii	
1804–1881	Benjamin Disraeli	Novels (Lothair, Vivian Grey)	
1806–1861	E. B. Browning		Poems (Aurora Leigh).
1806–1872	Charles Lever	Novels (Charles O'Malley)	
1809–1892	Alfred Tennyson		In Memoriam, Idylls of the King.
1811–1863	William M. Thackeray	Novels (Vanity Fair, The Newcomes)	
1812–1870	Charles Dickens	David Copperfield, Oliver Twist	
1812–1889	Robert Browning		Poems (The Ring and the Book).
1814–1884	Charles Reade	The Cloister and the Hearth	Plays (Peg Woffington).
1815–1882	Anthony Trollope	Novels (Barchester Towers)	
1816–1855	Charlotte Brontë	Novels (Jane Eyre, The Professor)	
1818–1894	James A. Froude	Essays, History of England	
1819–1875	Charles Kingsley	Novels (Hypatia)	Poems.
1819–1880	George Eliot	Novels (Silas Marner)	Poems (Spanish Gypsy).
1819–1900	John Ruskin	Essays (Modern Painters)	
1820–1897	Jean Ingelow		Poems.
1821–1862	Henry T. Buckle	History of Civilization in England.	
1822–1888	Matthew Arnold	Essays, Criticism	Poems (Sohrab and Rustum).
1822–1896	Thomas Hughes	Tom Brown at Oxford	
1823–1892	Edward A. Freeman	Histories	
1824–1889	Wilkie Collins	Novels (Woman in White)	
1825–1895	Thomas H. Huxley	Essays (Man's Place in Nature)	
1825–1900	R. D. Blackmore	Novels (Lorna Doone)	
1826–1887	Dinah Maria Mulock	Novels (John Halifax, Gentleman)	Poems.
1828–1882	Dante G. Rossetti		Poems (The Blessed Damozel).
1828–1909	George Meredith	Novels (Diana of the Crossways).	Poems (Modern Love).
1834–1896	William Morris	Essays (Mural Painting)	Poems (Earthly Paradise).
1835–1902	Samuel Butler	Novel (The Way of all Flesh)	
1837–1909	A. C. Swinburne	Essays (Study of Shakspere)	Poems, Ballads.
1838–1903	William E. H. Lecky	History	
1838–1922	James Bryce	American Commonwealth	
1838–1923	John Morley	Essays, Biography	

TABLE OF ENGLISH LITERATURE—Con.

Authors		Representative Works	
Time	Name	Prose	Poetry and Drama
1839–1917	Wm. F. De Morgan	Novels (Joseph Vance)	
1840–1928	Thomas Hardy	Novels (Wessex Tales)	Poems, Drama (The Dynasts).
1843–1926	Charles Montagu Doughty	Travels (Arabia Deserta)	Poems (Dawn in Britain).
1844–1889	Gerard Manley Hopkins	. . . .	Poems.
1844–1930	Robert Bridges	. . . .	Poems, Shorter Poems, Plays (Ulysses).
1850–1894	Robert L. Stevenson	Essays, Romances	Child's Garden of Verses.
1851–1920	Mrs. Humphrey Ward	Novels (Robert Elsmere)	
1853–1931	Hall Caine	Novels (The Christian)	
1855–1934	Arthur W. Pinero	. . . .	Plays (The Second Mrs. Tanqueray)
1856–	George B. Shaw	Essays	Plays (Man and Superman).
1857–1924	Joseph Conrad	Novels (Lord Jim, Victory)	
1859–1930	Sir A. Conan Doyle	Novels (Sherlock Holmes)	
1860–1937	Sir James Barrie	Novels (The Little Minister)	Plays (Peter Pan).
1861–1941	Sir Rabindranath Tagore	Essays, Stories (Gitanjali)	Poems.
1865–1936	Rudyard Kipling	Tales (Jungle Book, Kim)	Barrack-room Ballads, Poems.
1866–1946	Herbert G. Wells	Novels, History	
1867–1931	Arnold Bennett	Novels (The Old Wives' Tale)	Plays.
1867–1933	John Galsworthy	Novels, Stories, Essays	Plays (Loyalties).
1868–1915	Stephen Phillips	. . . .	Poems, Dramas (Herod).
1870–	Hilaire Belloc	Essays, Stories	Poems.
1873–	Walter de la Mare	Novels (Memoirs of a Midget)	Poems (Peacock Pie).
1874–1936	G. K. Chesterton	Essays, Fiction	Poems.
1874–	W. Somerset Maugham	Novels	Plays (Rain).
1875–	John Masefield	Novels, Stories	Poems, Plays.
1879–	Edward Morgan Forster	Novels (Passage to India)	
1880–1932	Lytton Strachey	Biography (Eminent Victorians)	
1880–	Alfred Noyes	Essays, Criticism	Poems (The Loom of Years).
1882–1937	John Drinkwater	Essays	Poems, Plays (Lincoln).
1882–1941	Virginia Woolf	Novels (Mrs. Dalloway)	
1882–	A. A. Milne	Novels, Essays	Poems, Plays (The Dover Road).
1885–1930	David H. Lawrence	Novels (Women In Love)	Poems, Plays.
1888–1923	Katherine Mansfield	Stories (The Garden Party)	
1888–1935	Thomas E. Lawrence	Memoirs (Seven Pillars of Wisdom)	
1892–	Richard Aldington	Novels (All Men Are Enemies)	Poems (Images of Desire).
1894–	John Boynton Priestley	Novels (Good Companions)	Plays (Laburnum Grobe).
1894–	Aldous Huxley	Novels (Eyeless In Gaza)	Poems.
1899–	Noel Coward	. . . .	Plays (Hay Fever, Cavalcade).
1899–	Cecil Scott Forester	Novels (Captain Hornblower)	
1907–	Wystan Hugh Auden	. . . .	Poems (Collected Poems).
1909–	Stephen Harold Spender	. . . .	Ruins and Visions (Poems 1934–42).

CANADIAN LITERATURE

Canada, as she has developed from a colony to a nation and acquired the measure of material prosperity essential to artistic creation, has had, besides her native-born authors, writers that, according to the extent of their association with the country, may be divided into four classes. There have been those whose residence in Canada was only incidental and temporary; those who came to Canada in maturity and retained an old-world point of view; those who, though they came to Canada in maturity, became thoroughly Canadian in sentiment; those who, though foreign born, came to Canada in their childhood and grew up under Canadian influences. This applies to English Canada and in a measure to French Canada, each of which has its own literature.

French Canadian Literature. The most important French Canadian prose writings are *Les relations des Jesuits; Les anciens canadiens*, by Philippe Aubert de Gaspé, a mine of information about life under the old Régime, translated into English by Charles G. D. Roberts; *Histoire du Canada*, by François Xavier Garneau, which started the first school of French Canadian literature; *Un pèlerinage au pays d'Evangeline*, by Abbé Casgrain. The first school of French Canadian poetry developed in Quebec between 1860 and 1870. Gérin-Lajoie wrote a truly national poem, *Un canadien errant*, voicing the homesickness of a French Canadian exiled on account of the rebellion of 1837. Octave Crémazie, regarded as the father of French Canadian poetry, wrote verse of distinct merit, including colorful, sentimental descriptions of the Canadian scene. Pamphile Le May translated Longfellow's *Evangeline* into French. Louis Fréchette, who married a sister of William Dean Howells and who is regarded as the greatest French Canadian poet, approached epic grandeur in his chief poem, *La légende d'un peuple*. The second school of French Canadian poetry began in Montreal in 1895. To it belong in fact Emile Nelligan and Albert Lozeau, and in spirit Paul Morin.

English Canadian Literature. In the main, the British settlers in Canada upheld the literary tradition of the British romanticists; the United Empire Loyalists, that of the English pseudo-classicists.

Miscellaneous Prose. The Honorable Joseph Howe, of the Loyalist tradition, whose published speeches are the best political literature in Canada, powerfully influenced Canadian prose by publishing in his paper, the *Novascotian*, his own sketches, the papers of the *Club*, of which he and Haliburton were members, and the series of sketches by Haliburton that constitute *The Clockmaker*.

Thomas Chandler Haliburton, a native of Nova Scotia, after a long career in that province as lawyer and judge, removed to England in 1856, where he was elected to the British House of Commons. *The Clockmaker, or The Sayings and Doings of Sam Slick of Slickville*, the first edition of the first series of which appeared in book form at Halifax in 1836, was the first Canadian work to achieve widespread fame and translation. Through the conversations of a country squire and Sam Slick, an itinerant Yankee clock seller who frequently quotes his New England parson, Haliburton discussed and criticized local and imperial politics and government. The remarks of his characters became widely current for their homely shrewdness. Later volumes in the Slick series were less successful.

The greatest Canadian humorists in nonfictional prose since Haliburton are Peter McArthur and Stephen Leacock.

As to history and biography, the older Canadian historians, whether writing voluminously like William Kingsford or on a smaller scale like James Hannay, tended to lack style when they were accurate or to fall short of fairness and proportion when they wrote with imaginative power. In recent years, Canadian scholars have done much diligent and careful work in organizing and writing the history of their country. Of those who have written somewhat extensively and have combined good material and style, William Wood is one of the best. There have been at least a dozen good biographers, but none of high distinction.

As literary essayists may be mentioned Sir William Osler, Sir Andrew MacPhail, and Professor Archibald M. MacMechan.

Canada has a good literature of voyages, travels, and color writing. This includes Alexander Mackenzie's *Voyages from Montreal through the Continent of North America* (1801); Alexander Henry's *Travels and Adventures in Canada and the Indian Territories* (1807); Mrs. Jameson's *Winter Studies and Summer Rambles in Canada* (1838); Mrs. Moodie's *Roughing It in the Bush* (1852); Lady Edgar's *Ten Years of Peace and War in Upper Canada* (1890); L. J. Burpee's *Search for the Western Sea* (1907); and the recent color writing of Arthur Heming, W. H. Blake, "Katherine Hale" (Mrs. J. W. Garvin), and F. P. Grove.

Fiction. What is regarded as the first Canadian novel, Mrs. Frances Brooke's *Emily Montague*, a story of frontier life, was published in 1769. In 1832, John Richardson published *Wacousta*, the earliest Canadian novel that has secured and held a place in Canadian fiction. To the middle of the 19th century belong several stories of pioneer life by Catherine Parr Traill and her sister, Susanna Moodie. James De Mille wrote voluminously,—humorous, romantic, and juvenile fiction. William Kirby was the first Canadian novelist to use with great power the romantic material in early Canadian history. His *Golden Dog* (1877), an excellent novel of 18th century life in Quebec, has been widely read in English and in translation into French.

Edward William Thompson did good work in short juvenile fiction. William McLennan wrote habitant tales in prose that correspond somewhat to Drummond's poetic stories, and essayed longer fiction. "Ralph Connor" (Rev. Charles William Gordon) has written novels of the West that have been widely read throughout the English-speaking world. Sara Jeanette Duncan (Mrs. Everard Cotes) wrote clever, humorous novels of travel and of life in India. Sir Gilbert Parker, most popular and productive of Canadian novelists, has set his novels and short stories in every part of the British Empire, but his Canadian fiction is probably his best.

Norman Duncan wrote successful travel sketches, atmosphere stories of land and sea, and juvenile fiction. Margaret Marshall Saunders and Grace Dean McLeod Rogers have attracted attention to Nova Scotia by their fiction. Lucy Maud Montgomery has done a similar work for Prince Edward Island. Gordon Hill Grahame has written fiction set in early French Canada. Robert Stead and Arthur J. Stringer interpret understandingly the Canadian West. William Alexander Fraser, Ernest Thompson Seton, and Charles G. D. Roberts have given Canada great animal fiction. A new school of realism of great promise is represented by Laura Goodman Salverson, Frederick Phillip Grove, and Martha Ostenso writing of the West.

Writing of the East, Mazo de la Roche produced a cycle of novels centering around an imaginary ancestral estate, Jalna, and around the characters who lived there. The popularity of these novels bore witness to the power of her inventive imagination and to its rise above regional limitations. Morley Callaghan belongs likewise to the school of realistic observers, his *Strange Fugitive* and *They Shall Inherit the Earth* being characterized by an incisive directness rare among Canadian authors.

Poetry. The first English Canadian verse of note is credited to Nova Scotia. Joseph Howe wrote some good poems. Oliver Goldsmith, a kinsman of the English Oliver, published *The Rising Village* at London in 1825. Charles Heavysege, an emigrant from England to Montreal, wrote several volumes of verse. His dramatic poem *Saul* was highly praised by Bayard Taylor and Longfellow in the United States and by Coventry Patmore in England. Alexander McLachlan, a disciple of Burns, was widely read in pre-Confederation Canada. Canadian natural scenery appears as poetic subject matter in Charles Sangster's *The St. Lawrence and the Saguenay, and Other Poems* (1856); in Charles Mair's *Dreamland and Other Poems* (1868) and collected poems (1901) (containing his poetic drama *Tecumseh*); and in Isabella Valancy Crawford's *Old Spookses' Pass, Malcolm's Katie, and Other Poems* (1884) and collected poems (1905). Miss Crawford, compared in intensity to Emily Brontë, was an artist in dialect narrative and in original handling and delicate workmanship in lyric.

Charles G. D. Roberts, most versatile of Canadian writers, was the leader of the greatest school of Canadian poetry, the first post-Confederation school. In his poetry he is an exquisite painter of Canadian scenes, a singer of ideals learned from nature, and a lyrist of love. Archibald Lampman, a great admirer of the poetic gift of George Frederick Cameron (most like Shelley of all Canadian poets), throughout his career wrote poetic descriptions of nature that in appreciation of beauty and felicity of diction rival the best work of Keats. Duncan Campbell Scott, who prefixed an excellent memoir to the 1900 edition of Lampman's poems, is one of Canada's greatest poets. Since his first volume in 1893, he has published several volumes of poetry of versatility and range. He images every aspect of the Canadian year, and expresses in apt meters the thoughts, sentiments, or emotional experiences of vastly different characters. William Wilfred Campbell, of the same stock as the poet Thomas Campbell and the novelist Henry Fielding, was chiefly interested in human life, but wrote some good nature poems in addition to his poetry of man. He wrote poetic dramas as well as lyrics and narratives, and essays and novels. Bliss Carman was a worshiper of beauty, especially in nature, and a master of melodious verse. Beginning with *Low Tide on Grand Pré* (1893), he wrote a large amount of excellent poetry and several volumes of prose. Some critics rank him as Canada's major poet. Frederick George Scott published several volumes of poetry, the first in 1888. As a nature poet, he is especially associated with the Laurentians. His broad human sympathy manifests itself in poems on old literary themes, on the subject of empire, and on love and brotherhood. Pauline Johnson, the Indian poetess whose mother belonged to the Howells family, in striking verse interpreted the spirit of Indian life. Ethelwyn Wetherald wrote charming nature poetry.

Somewhat apart are two poets of Irish birth. Thomas D'Arcy McGee, enamored of the cause of freedom, at length came to think that it could not be realized in Ireland, but saw for it a future in Canada. William Henry Drummond in a unique form of dialect monologue has most sympathetically interpreted the French Canadian *habitant* and *voyageur* from his contact with them as a telegrapher and, later, a country doctor.

Of many later women poets, such as Jean Blewett, Helena Coleman, Virna Sheard, "Katherine Hale," Jean Graham, Louise Morey Bowman, Norah M. Holland, Marjorie Pickthall, the greatest artist is the last. Among the later men to attract considerable attention by their verse are Tom MacInnes, Robert W. Service, Robert Norwood, John McCrae, and Bernard Freeman Trotter.

TABLE OF CANADIAN LITERATURE

Authors		Representative Works	
Time	Name	Prose	Poetry and Drama
1739–1824	Alexander Henry	Travels	
1745–1789	Frances Brooke	Emily Montague	
1763–1820	Alexander Mackenzie	Travels	
1781–1861	Oliver Goldsmith		The Rising Village
1786–1871	Philippe A. de Gaspé	Les Anciens Canadiens	
1794–1860	Mrs. Anna Jameson	Color Writing	
1796–1852	John Richardson	Fiction, History	
1796–1865	Thomas C. Haliburton	Satiric Humor, History	
1802–1899	Catherine P. Traill	Stories	
1803–1885	Susanna Moodie	Stories, Color Writing	Poems
1804–1873	Joseph Howe	Essays, Orations	Poems
1809–1866	François X. Garneau	History of Canada	
1816–1876	Charles Heavysege		Saul
1817–1906	William Kirby	The Golden Dog	Poems
1818–1896	Alexander McLachlan		Poems
1819–1898	William Kingsford	History of Canada	
1822–1893	Charles Sangster		Poems
1824–1882	Gérin-Lajoie		Poems (French)
1825–1868	Thomas D'A. McGee	History, Oratory	Poems
1827–1879	Octave Crémazie		Poems (French)
1833–1880	James de Mille	Fiction	
1837–1918	Pamphile Le May		Poems (French)
1838–1927	Charles Mair		Poems, Poetic Drama
1839–1908	Louis Fréchette		Poems (French)
1842–1910	James Hannay	History of Acadia	
1844–1910	Lady Edgar	History, Biography	
1849–1919	Sir William Osler	Essays, Orations	
1850–1887	Isabella V. Crawford		Poems
1854–1885	George F. Cameron		Poems
1854–1907	William H. Drummond		Habitant Poems
1856–1904	William McLennan	Habitant Tales	
1860–	E. Thompson Seton	Animal Tales	
1860–1937	"Ralph Connor" (C. W. Gordon)	Novels	
1860–1943	Sir Charles G. D. Roberts	Fiction, Animal Tales	Poems
1861–1899	Archibald Lampman		Poems
1861–1918	W. Wilfred Campbell	Essays, Novels	Poems, Poetic Dramas
1861–	M. Marshall Saunders	Fiction	
1861–1929	Bliss Carman	Essays	Poems
1861–	Frederick G. Scott		Poems
1861–1924	W. H. Blake	Color Writing	
1862?–1922	Sara J. Duncan (Mrs. E. Cotes)	Novels	
1862–1913	Pauline Johnson		Poems
1862–1932	Sir Gilbert Parker	Fiction	Poems
1862–	Duncan C. Scott	Stories	Poems
1865–	Grace D. McLeod Rogers	Stories, Novels	
1866–1924	Peter McArthur	Humor	Poems
1869–1944	Stephen Leacock	Essays, Stories, Humor	
1871–1916	Norman Duncan	Fiction	
1872–1918	John McCrae		Poems
1873–	L. J. Burpee	Search for the Western Sea	
1874–	Robert W. Service		Rhymes of a Rolling Stone
1875–1924	Albert Lozeau		Poems (French)
1877–1942	Lucy M. Montgomery	Novels (Anne of Green Gables)	
1883–1922	Marjorie L. C. Pickthall	Stories, Novels	Poems, Poetic Drama
1885–	Mazo de la Roche	Novels (Jalna)	
1903–	Morley Callaghan	Novels (Strange Fugitive)	

AUSTRALIAN LITERATURE

The past forty years have seen a notable development of literature, both poetry and prose, in Australia. Before this period, but few writers succeeded in freeing themselves from the trammels of imitation imposed by the conditions of a young settlement, in which a distinctive literature is a plant of slow growth. Yet, in the vividly alternating kindness and cruelty of nature in the new country, in the adventurous life of the bush and the mining camp, in the swing and clatter of horsemen, and in the varied moods of the sea, never left far behind by the earliest settlers, there was matter for poetry and romance that could not long remain unsung.

The chief strength of Australian literature lies in its poetry, which often in its meters suggests the gallop of horses or the rolling of high ocean waves. It is frequently humorous, showing a particularly keen appreciation of the unusual types of character which mark the unstable conditions of life in a new country. A gloomy view of life is, however, not infrequent in the earlier serious verse. The development of Australian poetry may be divided, roughly, into four periods.

Early Pioneer Period. The first poems actually written and published in Australia were the *Royal Birthday Odes* (1810–21) of Michael Robinson. These were broadsides, of which few are extant. The work of this period, with the exception of the poems of Charles Harpur (1817–68), is a washy overflow from England. Harpur was born in New South Wales, and spent much of his life in the bush. He was the first to give sincere poetic expression to the life around him. In narrative and description he reflected truly, with a certain largeness and simplicity, the pioneer land and people, and his work had a great influence on his younger contemporary, Kendall. *The Creek of the Four Graves* is his best-known poem.

Beginnings of Australasian Literature. The discovery of gold marked a new era in the life of Australia, and the establishment of a periodical entitled *The Australasian* in 1854 gave to Melbourne a literary pre-eminence, which it held for many years. Gordon, Kendall, Marcus Clarke, R. H. Horne, George G. McCrae (1833–1927), and others, in the South, James Brunton Stephens (1835–1902) in Queensland, Thomas Bracken (1843–98) and Alfred Domett (1811–87) in New Zealand, were founding a really Australasian literature. Several of them made considerable use of aboriginal and Maori legends,—Domett, for instance, in *Ranolf and Amohia*. The humorous poetic sketches of Brunton Stephens won for him the title of the Bret Harte of Australia, and his more serious work, such

CANADIAN WRITERS

William Drummond
Octave Cremazie
Charles William Gordon
Photo by Brown Bros.

Duncan Campbell Scott
Sir Gilbert Parker
Photo by Brown Bros.
Lucy Maud Montgomery

Bliss Carman
Charles G. D. Roberts
Stephen B. Leacock
Photo by Keystone View Co.

MODERN WORLD WRITERS

Anatole France
Photo by Brown Bros.
Maurice Maeterlinck
Photo by Keystone View Co.
Frédéric Mistral
Photo by P. Thompson

Selma Lagerlöf
Photo by P. Thompson
Rabindranath Tagore
Copyright by P. Thompson
Vicente Blasco Ibáñez
Copyright by Harris & Ewing

Gerhart Hauptmann
Photo by Underwood & Underwood
Romain Rolland
Photo by Keystone View Co.
Gabriele d'Annunzio
Photo by Underwood & Underwood

as "Convict Once," shows a technical mastery and a depth of thought only too rare in his time and place. Horne was the mentor and guide of several young poets. The greatest names in this period, however, and possibly the greatest Australia has yet to show, are those of Gordon and Kendall.

Adam Lindsay Gordon (1833–70), whose adventurous disposition drove him through a short and tumultuous career, came to Australia in 1853. He had been educated at Cheltenham college, Woolwich, and Oxford in a desultory way, which yet gave him the technical capacity to write greatly of the horses he loved, and to breathe the pride and defiance of his spirit in poems which are certainly the most widely known in Australia. To many a rough unlettered man Gordon represents the very spirit of poetry. And his work is the expression of a truly poetic soul. His best themes are actions of gallant and stirring adventure. It was from the race-meeting that he drew inspiration for the first poems that brought him fame. A despairing melancholy, however, the atmosphere of an unhappy life, tinges his reflective poems. "The Sick Stockrider," "How We Beat the Favourite," and the Swinburnian "A Dedication" are his most characteristic works.

The quieter genius of Henry Clarence Kendall (1841–82) expresses itself in descriptions of delicate and haunting beauty, rising to its height in "Orara" and "After Many Years." Kendall was born in New South Wales, and he was the first Australian poet to win critical recognition in England, where his work was praised in the *Athenaeum*, as early as 1862. He was a lover of country life, and he gave enduring expression to the beauty of the mountains, rivers, and forests of Australia. These two true poets, each in his way, continued the work which Harpur had begun.

The Later Nineteenth Century. With the establishment of the *Bulletin* in 1880, the literary center shifted to Sydney. The racy cynicism of the *Bulletin*, though original and, in some respects, salutary, was not really a favorable atmosphere for contemplative poetry. A school of writers arose, however, inspired by genuine national feeling and capable of both refined and vigorous poetic expression. Victor James Daley (1858–1905), with his singing note of Celtic romance, is perhaps entitled to the highest rank. But the characteristic figure of the school in regard to both prose and verse is Henry Archibald Lawson (1867–1922), whose work is "honest Australian," vivid and truthful, often grim, full of sympathy with the poverty and struggle of the drover and the shearer. The same life, physical rather than mental, and occupied largely with horses, is depicted in a happier light by Andrew Barton Paterson (1864–). Terse narrative is the main achievement of this group,—good ringing rimes, written not only about the man outback, but for him.

Contemporary Poetry. The popularity of these bush verses had somewhat waned, when in 1900 Bernard O'Dowd (1866–) won a prize offered by the *Bulletin* for the best sonnet on Australia. At the present time, a great deal of serious, and sometimes excellent, work is being done in both Australia and New Zealand. O'Dowd and "Furnley Maurice" (Frank Wilmot) in Victoria, Arthur Adams and Dorothea MacKellar in New South Wales, Jessie Mackay and Blanche Baughan in New Zealand, are only a few of those who are worthy of mention. In another vein C. J. Dennis's *Songs of a Sentimental Bloke*, in slang, have been deservedly popular.

Australian Prose. Some interesting work has been done lately in drama, and there is a certain amount of novel writing, though the short story and the sketch predominate. The earliest Australian novels were *Clara Morison* and others by Catherine Helen Spence (1825–1910), but the best-known are *For the Term of His Natural Life* by Marcus Andrew Hislop Clarke (1846–81), published in 1874, a grim tale of the convict days, and *Robbery under Arms*, by "Rolf Boldrewood" (Thomas Alexander Browne, 1826–1915), a thrilling story of bushranging. "Steele Rudd" (Arthur Hoey Davis, 1861–) gives a humorous picture of country life, rich in local color, in *On Our Selection* and in kindred books.

"Ada Cambridge" (Mrs. G. F. Cross, 1844–1927) wrote many successful novels, notably *The Three Miss Kings*; and Mrs. Æneas Gunn (1870–) has gained an international reputation with her stories of the Northern Territory, *We of the Never-Never* and *The Little Black Princess*. The latter, though full of ethnological interest, is ostensibly a children's book, a field in which "Ethel Turner" (Mrs. H. R. Curlewis, 1872–) holds pride of place. To these should be added the name of Louise Mack, magazine writer and critic.

A considerable amount of literary criticism is written in Australia, the most delightful to read being that of Walter Murdoch, professor of English literature in the University of Western Australia. The literature of the country owes much to the high quality and the vigorous and independent character of Australian newspapers.

The keynote of Australian literature is sincere endeavor. Though as yet it has not attained to the heights, it has not striven after superficial technical achievement nor lost its way in affectation. Its crudeness is the crudeness of a youth that holds rich promise of maturity.

TABLE OF AUSTRALIAN LITERATURE

Authors		Representative Works	
Time	Name	Prose	Poetry and Drama
?	Michael Robinson	. . . .	Poems (Royal Birthday Odes).
1811–1887	Alfred Domett	. . . .	Poems (Ranolf and Amohia).
1817–1868	Charles Harpur	. . . .	Poems (The Creek of the Four Graves).
1825–1910	Catherine Helen Spence	Novels (Clara Morison)	
1826–1915	Thomas Alexander Browne	Novels (Robbery under Arms)	
1833–1870	Adam Lindsay Gordon	. . . .	Poems (The Sick Stockrider, How We Beat the Favourite, A Dedication).
1833–1927	George Gordon McCrae	. . . .	Poems.
1835–1902	James Brunton Stephens	. . . .	Poems (Convict Once).
1841–1882	Henry Clarence Kendall	. . . .	Poems (Orara, After Many Years).
1843–1898	Thomas Bracken	. . . .	Poems (Not Understood).
1844–1927	Mrs. G. F. Cross	Novels (The Three Miss Kings)	
1846–1881	Marcus Clarke	Novels (For the Term of His Natural Life)	
1858–1905	Victor James Daley	. . . .	Poems (At Dawn and Dusk).
1861–	Arthur Hoey Davis	Novels, Humor	
1864–1941	Andrew Barton Paterson	Novels (An Outback Marriage)	Poems (Man from Snowy River).
1866–	Bernard O'Dowd	. . . .	Poems.
1867–1922	Henry Archibald Lawson	. . . .	Poems (While the Billy Boils).
1870–	Mrs. Æneas Gunn	Novels (We of the Never-Never, The Little Black Princess)	
1872–	Mrs. H. R. Curlewis	Children's Stories	
1874–	Walter Murdoch	Criticism, Essays (Loose Leaves)	
1876–1938	Clarence James Dennis	. . . .	Poems (Songs of a Sentimental Bloke).

IRISH LITERATURE

Since the disappearance of Gallic, the ancient language of Gaul, the Celtic, or westernmost group of the Indo-European family of languages, has been represented by: (1) the Goidelic, or Gaelic, which includes the Irish, the Scotch Gaelic, and the Manx; (2) the Brythonic, which includes the Welsh or Cymric, the Cornish, and the Celtic dialects of Brittany, these last being the language of refugees from Britain at the time of the Anglo-Saxon invasion.

In the Scotch Gaelic there is a very rich store of ballads, folklore, and proverbs, besides versions of the Ossianic cycle of Ireland. The two most famous monuments of earlier Scotch Gaelic are (1) *The Book of the Dean of Lismore*, compiled by James and Duncan Macgregor, and (2) *The Book of Femaig*, compiled by Duncan Macrae. The Cymric of Wales is the language of large collections of poetry, dating from the poets Aneurin of the 12th and Taliessin of the 13th century. The *Mabinogion* are poetic tales which were told by men during their training for admission to the guilds or societies of bards. The Eisteddfod, or annual poetry and music contest, is still maintained in Wales, and today more printing is done in this language than in all other Celtic languages combined.

The Saga Cycles. The manuscripts which contain the remains of early Irish literature show that Irish writers used their native legends, religious themes, and the mythology and legends of other nations. But the best contributions of the Irish to the world's literature are the heroic sagas, prose tales interspersed with poetry, recounting the early myths and legends of the Celtic inhabitants of Ireland and Scotland. These are preserved in such manuscript collections as the *Book of the Dun Cow*, of the 11th century, the *Speckled Book*, of the 14th century, and the *Yellow Book of Lecan*, of the 15th century. Although through the sacking of monasteries and the destruction of libraries by the viking invaders, in the 9th and the 10th century, many of the very early manuscripts perished, the production of the stories in the manuscripts that remain can be traced back to the 8th or the 9th century A. D.

These stories were composed and transmitted orally by guilds of trained story-tellers and poets, whom the early kings and chiefs of Ireland maintained at their courts. These guilds were organized into classes for the purpose of carefully training their members. The chief of the story-tellers (the *ollam, ollave*) was supposed to know 250 principal tales and 100 of secondary importance.

These early poets arranged their stories in several different series, probably for the sake of aiding their memories. Modern scholars have grouped them into three great cycles of saga-telling, the Mythological Cycle, the Red Branch or Ulster Cycle, and the Fenian or Leinster-Munster (sometimes also called the Ossianic) Cycle.

The earliest, or Mythological, Cycle introduces us to the gods of the early Irish as we are introduced to the gods of Greece, Rome, and Scandinavia in classical literature and northern saga. In these tales we meet Lugh, the long-handed, and Balor of the Evil Eye, who doubtless represent good and evil deities. But there is little or nothing about a so-called race of gods for, as Doctor Douglas Hyde points out, the gods came to be thought of as men, and "the Firbolgs, Fomorians,....Tuatha de Dananns, etc., are spoken of, both by annalists and historians, as ordinary human tribes." The best-known, as well as the most complete and interesting of these cycles, is that of Ulster, variously called the Heroic, Ultonian, or Red Branch, Cycle. Its dominating theme is the rivalry and warfare between Ulster and Connaught, which had its origin in the murder of the sons of Usnach. The events narrated possibly took place about the beginning of the Christian era. The greatest tale in the collection, and one of the world's great early stories, is the *Táin Bó Chuailgne*, or "Cattle Raid of Cooley," which tells of the attempt of the queen of Connaught, Maeve, daughter of Eochy, *Ard-Righ*, or "High King," of Ireland, to carry off the great brown bull of Cooley (in Louth) from the Ultonians who were captained by Cuchulain, Maeve leading her own forces. Fact and myth are mingled in this tale, which, because it lacks high poetic finish, has been called "an epic in the making." Of the other tales of this cycle, probably the most famous are *The Wooing of Emer*, *The Death of the Children of Usnach*, and *The Death of Cuchulain*.

The third great cycle is the Ossianic, sometimes called the Fenian Cycle. The stories center around the exploits of Fionn (Finn MacCool) or, as he is known in the Scotch versions, Fingal, which may mean Finn the Stranger. Ossian (or Oisin) is the son of Fionn and also his poet. Fionn appears to have been a leader of warriors, possibly mercenaries, in the 2d or the 3d century A. D., when Britain was under the rule of the Romans.

Another smaller group of stories includes the tales of sea voyages undertaken by pious pilgrims, apparently in the 6th or the 7th century, when the Irish missionary spirit was most fervent. The most famous of these are *The Voyage of St. Brendan* and *The Voyage of Maeldune*.

In ancient Irish literature, the attention of almost all the leading modern scholars of the subject has hitherto been given mainly to the epic tales. In style these tales are forcible and abrupt, but they are shot through with gleams of strange, fierce tenderness, and are relieved, at unexpected moments, by the emergence of the unique humor of the Celt. Hardly less attractive is the early Christian poetry of the Irish, which is full of a beautiful awareness of all the natural loveliness of sea wave and cloud and tree and star. Such sensitive response to the changing moods of nature is unique in the earliest European poetry. "The bardic order," in W. B. Yeats's words, "....had gone down in the wars of the 17th century, and poetry had found shelter amid the turf smoke of the cabins."

Poetry and prose in Irish never quite ceased to be written. The 18th century produced the poems of Red O'Sullivan, blind O'Heffernan, John MacDonnell of Claragh, Turlough O'Carolan, who has been called "the last of the bards," and Anthony Raftery, of whom Lady Gregory writes fully in her *Poets and Dreamers*. The distinct success, in our own day, of the Gaelic League (an Irish organization having for object the restoration of Gaelic as the spoken language of the people) has greatly increased the number of speakers and writers of Irish in Ireland. Among significant modern Gaelic writers are Canon O'Leary, Reverend P. S. Dinneen, Thomas Hayes, P. J. O'Shea (Conán Máol), and the late Padraic Pearse.

Irish Writers in English; Prose. The achievement of Irish writers in English is by no means the least glory of English literature. Richard Steele (1672–1729), Jonathan Swift (1667–1745), Oliver Goldsmith (1728–74), Edmund Burke (1729–97), and Richard Brinsley Sheridan (1751–1816) are the most famous names of an earlier day. But there was little in the writings of these men from which their nationality might be deduced. An indubitable entrance of Irish national sentiment into the work of Irish men of letters, a movement toward the restoration of a national literature, is hardly noticeable until after the passing of the act of Union (1801).

But the externals of Irish life are described with vigor and skill by Maria Edgeworth (1767–1849), whose best-known novels are *Castle Rackrent* and *The Absentee*, and whose work influenced Scott not a little. The name of Samuel Lover (1797–1868) will always be kept alive by the boisterous verve of his *Handy Andy*, and Charles James Lever

(1806–72) is still read for his rollicking records of soldier and squireen life. His masterpiece is *Charles O'Malley*. Gerald Griffin (1803–40) has written, in *The Collegians*, one of the tenderest and most delightful of Irish novels. The Banim brothers, Michael (1796–1876) and John (1798–1844), wrote in conjunction a powerful series of *Tales by the O'Hara Family* which do not deserve the oblivion into which they seem to have fallen. Charles J. Kickham (1830–82) displayed a subtle understanding of the Irish peasant in *Knocknagow, or the Homes of Tipperary*. William Carleton (1798–1869) is, however, generally esteemed the greatest of all Irish novelists and has been called "the prose Burns of Ireland." His *Traits and Stories of the Irish Peasantry*, a series of tales of which the finest is *The Poor Scholar*, is his best-known contribution to fiction, but *The Black Prophet*, a novel of the great famine of '49, is harrowing in its tragic intensity, and *Fardorougha the Miser* is reminiscent of the genius of Balzac at its greatest.

More recent novelists who have achieved fame are Canon P. A. Sheehan (1852-1913), (author of *My New Curate, The Triumph of Failure*, and *The Blindness of Dr. Gray*), the finest interpreter in fiction of the Irish priest; James Stephens (b. 1882), who has displayed his mastery of realistic fantasy in *The Charwoman's Daughter* (American title *Mary, Mary*), in his volume of sketches, *Here are Ladies*, and in his best and most characteristic work, *The Crock of Gold*; and George Moore (1853-1931), who in *The Lake* evokes delicately and beautifully the spirit of the Western Irish countryside, and in the three volumes (*Ave, Salve*, and *Vale*) of his trilogy *Hail and Farewell* has recorded his participation in the Irish Literary Revival "of which they are the indispensable glossary and the sentimental history" (E. A. Boyd in *Ireland's Literary Renaissance*). Most of George Moore's major works (*Esther Waters, Evelyn Innes, A Mummer's Wife*, etc.) belong, however, to English rather than to Irish literature.

James Joyce (1882-1941) became internationally famous by his autobiographical novel, *A Portrait of the Artist as a Young Man* (1916), a merciless and morbid study in self-analysis set forth in prose of rare beauty; also by the privately-printed *Ulysses* (1922) which has been severely criticized for its unprecedented liberation of suppressions. St. John Ervine (1883-) is most widely known for his *Changing Winds*, a "war novel" which includes a description of the Irish insurrection of 1916. Seumas O'Kelly (1881-1918) won well-deserved recognition by his *Waysiders* (1917), a volume of sketches of Connaught life, and by two posthumously published tales, *The Golden Barque* and *The Weaver's Grave* (1919), which contain some of the best writing that has been done in Ireland for many years. Daniel Corkery, (1878-), author of *A Munster Twilight* (1916), a collection of sketches of Munster life, and of *The Threshold of Quiet* (1917), a long novel, has written in his *Hounds of Banba* (1920) a series of remarkable studies of life in Ireland during the months of conflict between the Irish Republican forces and the Black and Tans. This writer is hardly less distinguished as poet and as dramatist.

Irish Writers in English; Poetry. Irish poetry written in English may be divided into four somewhat overlapping classes:

First, the work of such poets as Goldsmith, Oscar Wilde (1856–1900), and Edward Dowden (1843–1913), which is distinctly English in matter and manner.

The second class embraces that poetry of the closing 18th and the opening 19th century which was Irish in sentiment. Examples of this are the patriotic songs of Thomas Moore (1779–1852), author of the famous *Irish Melodies*, the poems of Wm. Drennan (1802–73), of Gerald Griffin, of James Joseph Callanan (1795–1829). The work of all these men is characterized by grace and tenderness, while the songs of Charles Lever, Samuel Lover, and "Father Prout" (Francis Sylvester Mahony, 1804–66) exhibit the gaiety and exuberance which is so marked an element in the Irish temperament.

To the third division belong the poets of *The Nation*, the organ of the Young Ireland party, founded in 1842 by Sir Charles Gavan Duffy. Irish patriotism is almost exclusively their theme, and to inspire a love of country or a hatred of foreign domination, their object. Chief among these poets were Thomas Davis (1814–45) and Richard Dalton Williams (1822–62).

To the fourth division belong the poets of the modern Irish Literary Revival, who are essentially and pervasively Irish, but whose concern is with poetry primarily as a fine art. The great precursor of this movement was James Clarence Mangan (1803–49), author of *My Dark Rosaleen*. The initiator of it was Sir Samuel Ferguson (1810–86), who wrote *Lays of the Western Gael*. The chief contemporary figure in the movement is William Butler Yeats (1865-1939), whose place is conceded to be the highest among Irish artists in verse who have used English as their medium.

Among the younger Irish poets of today, especial mention must be made of Padraic Colum (b. 1881), whose *Wild Earth* is the finest of all books of Irish poetry dealing with peasant types; "Seumas O'Sullivan" (James Starkey, b. 1879), author of *The Twilight People*; James Stephens (b. 1882), who strikes out a sturdy full-bodied music in his *Insurrections*; Joseph Campbell (b. 1879), a poet of mystic and brooding intensity, at his best in *The Mountainy Singer*; Winifred Letts, who sings simple and delightful *Songs from Leinster*; and "Moira O'Neill" (Nesta Higginson, Mrs. John Skrine) whose voice rises no less clearly and sweetly in *Songs from the Glens of Antrim*.

Irish Drama. There is no drama of literary significance to be found in modern Irish literature before the Irish Literary Theatre was established in 1899 by William Butler Yeats, Augusta Lady Gregory, and Edward Martyn (1859-1923). The most interesting plays produced by these pioneers were Yeats's *Cathleen Ni Houlihan*, *Deirdre* by "Æ" (George Russell, 1867-1935), and *The Heather Field* by Edward Martyn. The story of the foundation and early struggles of the modern Irish movement in the theater has been told finally by Lady Gregory in *Our Irish Theatre*. The latent powers of John Millington Synge (1871–1909), the most vivid and powerful genius of the new drama, were suspected and evoked by W. B. Yeats. Synge then left Paris to live in loneliness upon the Aran Islands, listening to the rich peasant idiom. While his greatest single work, *Riders to the Sea*, is the expression in dramatic form of a tragedy of frequent occurrence in those bleak, storm-swept coasts, his fantastic comedy, *The Playboy of the Western World*, has given rise to the most violent controversy in America no less than in Ireland.

The prevailing theme of Padraic Colum's plays is "the land" and the influence exercised by it and the passions connected with it. His dramatic characterization is consistently fine and searching, and in his three most important dramas, *The Land, The Fiddler's House*, and *Thomas Muskerry*, he displays an Ireland which one may take to be Ireland "on the average, as one cannot take it that what we have in the plays of Synge or Lady Gregory is Ireland on the average" (Professor Weygandt in *Irish Plays and Playwrights*). The best plays of Augusta Lady Gregory (1852-1932) are probably *The Rising of the Moon* and *Spreading the News*. W. B. Yeats's *The Countess Cathleen* perhaps best represents the essentially lyrical quality of his dramatic energy. Other Irish dramatists of today are Lord Dunsany, St. John Ervine, and William Boyle.

FRENCH LITERATURE

The colloquial speech of Rome was the Latin that Cæsar's legions and their following of colonists and traders carried into Gaul. Absorbing possibly forty Celtic words there and, later, several hundred Germanic, this speech developed, clipping its unaccented syllables and changing vowel sounds, until by the 8th century the average Gallo-Roman could not understand the church offices, and preachers were ordered to preach in the "rustic, Roman tongue." In 842 it was used for the oath of an armistice; by 900, for the translation of a Latin hymn. In the 11th century it was called "French" from the kingdom of "France," around Paris and Orleans.

Medieval Verse and Story. The 11th century saw hymns to saints, secular lyrics, and war songs against the Moors who were barring the way to St. James's tomb at Santiago in Galicia, which French pilgrims were seeking. Minstrels (*jongleurs*) may have begun these songs, but they were soon aided by the monks, who found in Latin chronicles of Charlemagne's day the record of invasions of Spain, and of that emperor's wars against the infidels. So racial pride was added to religious zeal, and, these factors being given the environment of the newly formed feudal system, the national French epic was created. It grew until no less than eighty specimens of it (*chansons de gestes*—"songs of deeds") were known. Its masterpiece, in style and plot, was the *Song of Roland,* that told (about 1106) of the destruction of Charlemagne's rear guard and his Peers, by treason and overwhelming numbers, in a pass of the Pyrenees.

The 12th century witnessed the bloom of medieval French literature. There were didactic and narrative poems, often from the Latin, like *Saint Brendan's Voyage.* There were poems praising Alexander, the longest being in lines of twelve syllables that were henceforth known as "alexandrines." And there were romances of love and war, based on Virgil's *Æneid* and other epics of antiquity. The folklore and legends of the Celts, often called the "matter of Britain," also went into French poetry. Marie de France rimed short *lais* in octosyllabic couplets, on the loves of fairies for mortals; the story of Tristan and Isolt was expanded into long poems; and Chrétien de Troyes, choosing for his heroes the knights of Arthur's Round Table, emphasized knightly gallantry in his *Lancelot* and *Story of the Grail.* At the same time, following the example of the troubadours of southern France and profiting by the development of the art of music, lyric poetry claimed many writers.

Fables and Plays.—Animal fables, generally about the quarrels of the fox and the wolf, were rimed into the long *Romance of Reynard.* Jocose and coarse stories, often of wanton wives tricking their dull husbands, were made into poems called *fabliaux.* Good comedy in verse appeared at Arras after 1200. But the main effort of the playwrights was spent on the liturgical drama, which had begun centuries before in the churches, by interpolations of Scripture into the liturgy of Easter and Christmas. These interpolations had grown. They had become real scenes, too long for church services; they had been translated from Latin into French; and their stage had been removed from the choir to the front of the church. Continuing to expand, they presented to admiring crowds many of the leading events of the Old and New Testaments.

Prose.—In the early 12th century the Psalter had been translated into French prose. By 1200, Latin lives of saints and didactic and dogmatic treatises had followed in its train. History also was being written in French prose, notably Villehardouin's picturesque account of the Fourth Crusade with its capture of Constantinople. Huge prose romances on Lancelot's guilty love and the quest for the Grail were written, while in the quaint *chantefable* of *Aucassin and Nicolette* only the chapter headings were in verse.

Devout poetry and allegory developed in the 13th century. Guillaume de Lorris's *Romance of the Rose* (about 1235) told how the lover, aided by Friendly Greeting, would pluck the bud that Resistance defended. It also laid down Love's commands. The Parisian poet, Rutebeuf, composed saints' lives and saints' plays for pious patrons, and tried realistic, personal verse also. Jean de Meung, continuing the *Romance of the Rose,* made almost an encyclopedia of it, criticizing abuses and enjoining naturalness. Adam de la Halle, of Arras, produced in Italy the operetta "Robin and Marion" (1285). A farce written about the tricks played on a blind beggar by his boy guide was acted, while all kinds of learned and moral works went into prose.

The early 14th century saw Joinville's sympathetic memoirs of Louis IX, besides various short stories. Later, lyric poetry, which had survived the Hundred Years' War under the lead of the musician, Guillaume de Machaut, produced Deschamps, Froissart, Christine de Pisan, and Chartier, author of *La Belle Dame sans Merci.* Plays on Christ's Passion and dramatized *miracles* of the Virgin, together with a play on Griselda, represent the stage. Then came Froissart's dazzling chronicles of court and camp life, written by a gifted author from personal observation of events and intimate association with warring princes in the long 14th century struggle between France and England.

The old epic went into storybooks in the 15th century, short tales abounded, and the *Cent Nouvelles Nouvelles,* salacious anecdotes from the Italian and from native wit, offered models of clarity and conciseness. La Salle may have written them, as he did that amusing novel of manners, *Little John of Saintré.* Sermons, often abusive of the higher classes, moral treatises, and chronicles were numerous. And Commines compiled his philosophical memoirs of Louis XI.

Drama.—The liturgical drama had now grown into enormous plays called "mysteries," as the *Mystery of the Old Testament.* Paid for from the public purse and requiring crowds of actors, these plays would entertain entire populations with their mixture of Scriptural scenes and rough horseplay. In Paris they were performed by the Fraternity of the Passion, chartered in 1402. Associations of amateurs, as the *Basoche,* formed of law clerks, or the *Sots,* "Fools," improved the *farces,* invented diverting or instructive *monologues,* and played allegorical *moralities* in which personified vices and virtues edifyingly dealt with themes of daily existence. But the best medieval play was the farce of *Pathelin* (about 1470), where a seedy lawyer, who had wheedled a cloth merchant and then confused him by appearing in court as attorney for the merchant's thievish shepherd, was cheated of his fee through the very trick he had taught his client.

The larger part of the century's poetry is too rhetorical, too extravagant in its rimes. But Charles d'Orléans wrote pleasing society verse, and there was François Villon, the penniless, dissipated student, the best poet, the most human writer of them all. Having nothing in the world of his own, he amused himself and delighted posterity with a series of pretended legacies, written in separate stanzas that were formed into the *Little* and *Great Testaments.* To his ill-wishers he left his worthless garments or whatever else they could get; to his friends, his gratitude and his pity; to his mother, a *ballade* in honor of the Virgin. Of his other poetry, the "Ballade of the Hung," on the Montfaucon gibbet at Paris, and the "Ballade of the Ladies of Olden Time," with its haunting refrain, "Where are the snows of yesteryear?" would alone make him famous.

The Renaissance. Printing, the immigration of Greek scholars, the French invasion of Italy, and Luther's schism, all contributed to the intellectual and spiritual upsetting of the 16th century. Rabelais' *Gargantua and Pantagruel*, a romance of giants, father and son, of a lively, gluttonous monk and the tricky Panurge, told in ludicrous language, with much coarseness, erudition, and mother wit, well illustrated the prevailing confusion of thought, impatience of dogma, and desire for new standards of living. Pantagruel's education comprised bodily exercise, visits to workshops, and direct observation of nature, as well as study of books. A reformer also, yet rigidly logical, was Calvin, who translated his *Institutes of the Christian Religion* (1541) from its original Latin into French, in order to reach the laity. Lighter prose came with Marguerite of Navarre's *Heptameron*, suggested by Boccaccio's *Decameron*, and the romance, *Amadis of Gaul*, which Francis I brought back from Spain.

The liturgical drama, attacked by both the Reformers and the lovers of good literature, was killed in 1548 by an edict of the Paris parliament. That year also saw Ronsard and Du Bellay form a group of seven writers, the "Pléiade," for the purpose of renewing poetry and the theater after classical and Italian models. Marot had already written sonnets. Now odes and elegies were composed, while five-act tragedies in twelve-syllable lines, with an action which did not last over 24 hours, replaced the forbidden *mysteries*. The public taste was improved also by Bishop Amyot's translations of Greek novels and Plutarch's *Lives*. Then Montaigne summed up the efforts of the age in his rambling, piquant *Essays*, replete with human experience, fortified by copious quotations from the ancients, yet constantly postulating the skeptical query "What do I know?"

The Seventeenth Century. To reduce the confusion of the Renaissance to reason and order was the first task of the 17th century. Malherbe, arguing that poetry should express universal ideas in general terms and harmonious phrases, and that the rime should always emphasize the sense, was supported by Madame de Rambouillet's *salon* and by the French Academy, founded by Richelieu in 1634. Malherbe's views were also adopted by Corneille in his comedies and tragedies. Corneille's *Cid* (1636), with its theme of love struggling with honor and duty, was so perfect rhythmically that "beautiful as *The Cid*" became a popular saying.

The Great Dramatists.—Molière, the greatest of French dramatists, learned his art from Corneille and the Italian farces. In 1658 he established himself at Paris with a satire, *The Affected Misses*, on women of the trades class who tried to copy the refinements in language practiced at the *salon* of Madame de Rambouillet. The success won with this comedy was increased by plays that ranged from amusing skits to studies of character, like *The Misanthrope* and *Tartufe*, on hypocrisy, and studies of manners, like *The Learned Ladies*. In all his work he preached the favorite doctrines of the French people,—moderation, common sense, avoidance of extremes.

Racine, Molière's contemporary, wrote tragedies which dealt especially with woman. In *Andromache* he showed the heroine divided between maternal love and respect for her husband's memory. In *Phædra* he pictured the result of unrestrained jealousy. In *Athaliah*, written for the girls' school of St. Cyr, he painted an ambitious, yet irresolute, woman vanquished by a more determined man.

Writers of Prose.—Descartes had affirmed the dominance of reason in his *Discourse on Method* (1637) which, with its dictum, "I think, therefore I exist," introduced philosophy to the public. Pascal's biting *Provincial Letters*, against hypocrisy, and his unfinished *Thoughts*, on man's need of God, offered genuinely classical prose. La Rochefoucauld's *Maxims*, on human selfishness, were most cutting, while La Bruyère tellingly painted man's foibles in his *Characters*. Madame de Sévigné's sprightly *Letters* chronicled court doings, as did Saint-Simon's *Memoirs* later. Pulpit oratory reached its height with Bossuet's sermons and funeral orations, on the vanity of the world.

Fiction had developed many long romances, with pen portraits of society folk in disguise as a leading feature. But Madame de La Fayette's *Princess of Cleves* is modern in its theme of self-renunciation. Perrault, who preferred modern writers to ancient, wrote down the nursery *Tales of Mother Goose* (1697).

Poetry, outside the drama, was found mainly in society verse. But the critic, Boileau, used it for his attacks on other poets and for his defense of Malherbe's ideas. La Fontaine, advocating naturalness, like Boileau, Molière, and Racine, chose poetry for his famous *Fables*.

The Eighteenth Century. Newtonian science and increasing humanitarianism characterized the 18th century. Bayle's *Dictionary*, partly encyclopedic, foreshadowed the one. The other appeared in Fénelon's *Telemachus*, a romance of adventure, filled with wise counsels for his pupil, the Dauphin. Voltaire, skeptical and argumentative, preached religious tolerance and the equality of man in his plays, studied national movements in his *Essay on Manners*, and attacked abuses in tales and pamphlets. Brilliant, clever, daring, he advanced both scientific thought and political freedom. His vast correspondence remains a model of epistolary style.

Montesquieu was more philosophical, discussing social changes in his *Causes of the Greatness and Decline of the Romans*, and arguing in his *Spirit of Laws* (1748) for a division of governmental authority into the executive, the legislative, and the judicial—a plan adopted later in the Constitution of the United States. The *Encyclopedia*, edited mainly by Diderot and D'Alembert, was the mouthpiece of scientific criticism. It exerted an enormous influence. Buffon's *Natural History* (1748), through its excellent style, gave to the science of zoology the charm of literature.

Molière and Racine were followed by many playwrights. Marivaux created light comedies of intrigue. Destouches, La Chaussée, and Diderot undertook the problems of the family. But Beaumarchais, master of stage effects and witty dialogue, excelled all, making his valet, Figaro, who was a most merry jester in the *Barber of Seville*, a defender of the rights of man in *Figaro's Marriage*, a play which anticipated some of the ideas of the French Revolution.

Rousseau.—Fiction was much cultivated in short stories and novels. Lesage's *Gil Blas* and Marivaux's *Life of Marian* studied manners. Prévost's *Manon Lescaut* is a faithful history of love's errors. Rousseau's *New Heloïse* (1760) is as much a thesis as a romance. Hating social restraints and hostile to science and civilization, Rousseau had appealed in various essays for a return to the primitive state of man, when all property was held in common. His *Social Contract* was communistic, anarchical. His *New Heloïse* carried on the same warfare, with much praise of nature and the simple life. His *Emile* advocated education through nature and experience, before books are studied. Rousseau had most intense convictions. He expressed them in burning language. Pleading for justice, he inaugurated the present social unrest. Egotistical, a lover of nature, he was the father of French Romanticism. Saint-Pierre's delightful idyl, *Paul and Virginia*, is a concrete illustration of his theories.

Throughout this century, poetry was neglected, its best specimens being Chénier's odes and elegies, at the century's end, and Rouget de Lisle's "Marseillaise" (1792).

The Nineteenth Century. Chateaubriand described with marvelous colors the savannas of the Mississippi as seen by the sorrowful eyes of his characters, Atala and René, whose careers form two episodes of his *Genius of Christianity*, a book which attacked modern science and eulogized medieval and Christian art. Madame de Staël, in her novels, *Delphine* and *Corinne*, pleaded for woman's freedom, while her *Germany* introduced German thought and literature to France and England. George Sand, a most fluent writer, sided with Madame de Staël in various novels, and in her peasant stories drew charming pictures of her home province.

Romanticism.—Romantic fiction as a whole, however, imitated Scott. De Vigny's *Cinq-Mars*, Hugo's *Notre Dame de Paris*, Dumas's *Three Musketeers* are instances. Later, Hugo's *Les Misérables* and *Toilers of the Sea* described man's futile efforts against society and nature. Romanticism, with its insistence on what is individual and peculiar in races and epochs, transformed historical studies. Thierry was both picturesque and dramatic in his essays on French and English history, and Michelet most eloquent and democratic in his *History of France*. Guizot, who discussed the chief factors of national development in his *Courses on Modern History*, was more philosophical, as was De Tocqueville in his *Democracy in America* (1835). Renan's numerous works on religious history were more critical and scientific.

Romanticism was at its best in lyric poetry,—individualistic, emotional. Lamartine, De Vigny, Hugo, and De Musset have few equals. Admirers of form, of "art for art's sake," such as Gautier and Baudelaire, followed them. Then came the Parnassians (1866) with Leconte de Lisle and Coppée, who had more kindliness. Later still were Verlaine—lewd, devout, human—and the Symbolists, who would carry poetry back again to its origin in music, appealing to the ear rather than to the eye.

The Romantic drama, taking Shakspere for its guide, discarded the unities of time and place and mingled the comic with the tragic. But it produced few good plays, the elder Dumas's historical tragedies, Hugo's *Hernani* and *Ruy Blas*, and De Musset's comedies being the best. It was soon supplanted by the broader theater of Scribe, a master of dramatic construction. Scribe's ideas were carried on by the next generation of playwrights, Dumas *fils* and Augier, who found their subjects in contemporary life, and Sardou, who began with comedy of manners, to continue with tragedies intended chiefly for Madame Bernhardt. But Rostand, with *Cyrano*, *L'Aiglon*, and *Chantecler*, went back to the praise of the homely virtues.

The Realists.—Realism, the offspring of scientific study, had given Dumas *fils* and Augier their especial bent. But it had taken possession of fiction even earlier. Stendhal's *Red and Black* and Balzac's *Human Comedy* showed men fighting for wealth and power, while Mérimée's *Colomba* and *Carmen* described the influence of race and environment. More positive and agnostic after 1850, realism produced Flaubert, a pathologist who, pitilessly impersonal, endowed with an exceptional style, traced human decadence in *Madame Bovary* and other works. Zola, choosing his characters from a lower social class, emphasized heredity in his series of the *Rougon-Macquart*, while Maupassant surpassed even Flaubert in exactness of description. Less extreme, more human, Daudet, "the French Dickens," wrote up the trades class, the politician, and the adventurer in Parisian life.

The Present Day. A less harsh realism still holds in fiction. Anatole France, ironical, learned, protests against injustice, defending liberty of thought and action. Rolland's *Jean Christophe* is the careful biography of a talented musician. Loti, atheistic, seeing death at the end of everything, imbues his many-hued descriptions of customs and peoples with an atmosphere of melancholy foreboding. The psychological novels of Marcel Proust, carrying introspection to the extreme limit, have enlarged the scope of the novel.

Jules Romains' *Men of Good Will* is a social novel which depicts with uncanny realism modern French life at every level, from the consciousness of the pet dog to that of the statesman. In André Malraux appears the active revolutionist as writer, whose lean, tragic tales evoke poignantly the tragedy of class warfare.

The drama, under Ibsen's influence, continued the study of manners with Hervieu, Brieux, and their compeers. Poetry developed free verse and offers in the rhythms of Paul Fort most charming pages, while the emotional Comtesse de Noailles returned to traditional forms.

Throughout her entire career France has maintained a high standard of literary excellence, characterized by a sense of order, an objective point of view, and an insistence on clarity.

TABLE OF FRENCH LITERATURE

Authors		Representative Works	
Time	Name	Prose	Poetry and Drama
1140–?	Chrétien de Troyes		Arthurian Romances.
1150–?	Marie de France		Lais.
1160–1213	Villehardouin	Conquest of Constantinople	
1210–1235	Guillaume de Lorris		Romance of the Rose.
1224–1317	Joinville	Chronicles	
1230–1287?	Rutebeuf		Poems.
1240–1287	Adam de la Halle		Robin and Marion.
1240–1305	Jean de Meung		Romance of the Rose.
1300?–1377?	Guillaume de Machaut		Poems.
1336–1406	Eustache Deschamps		Poems.
1338–1410	Jean Froissart	Chronicles	
1364–1430?	Christine de Pisan		Poems.
1385–1432	Alain Chartier		Poems.
1387–1460	Antoine de la Salle	Stories	
1394–1465	Charles d'Orléans		Poems.
1431–1465	François Villon		Ballads.
1445–1511	Philippe de Commines	Memoirs	
1492–1549	Marguerite of Navarre	Heptameron	
1495–1553	François Rabelais	Lives of Gargantua and Pantagruel	
1497?–1544	Clément Marot		Sonnets.
1509–1564	John Calvin	Institutes of the Christian Religion	
1513–1593	Jacques Amyot	Translations of Plutarch's Lives and of Greek Novels	
1524?–1560	Joachim du Bellay		Poems.
1524–1585	Pierre de Ronsard		Sonnets, Odes.
1533–1592	Michel de Montaigne	Essays	
1555–1628	François de Malherbe		Poems.
1596–1650	René Descartes	Philosophy	

TABLE OF FRENCH LITERATURE—Con.

Authors		Representative Works	
Time	Name	Prose	Poetry and Drama
1606–1684	Pierre Corneille		Plays (The Cid, Le Menteur).
1613–1680	Duke de La Rochefoucauld	Maxims, Memoirs	
1621–1695	Jean de la Fontaine		Fables, Contes.
1622–1673	Molière		Comedies (The Misanthrope, Tartufe).
1623–1662	Blaise Pascal	Mathematics, Thoughts	
1626–1696	Mme. de Sévigné	Letters	
1627–1704	Jacques Bossuet	Sermons, Funeral Orations	
1628–1703	Charles Perrault	Tales of Mother Goose	
1634–1693	Mme. de La Fayette	Princess of Cleves	
1636–1711	Nicolas Boileau-Despréaux		Poems, Art Poétique.
1639–1699	Jean Racine		Tragedy (Andromache, Athaliah).
1645–1696	Jean de la Bruyère	Characters	
1647–1706	Pierre Bayle	Dictionary	
1651–1715	François de Fénelon	Telemachus	
1657–1757	Bernard Fontenelle	Dialogues of the Dead	Tragedies.
1668–1747	Alain René Lesage	Gil Blas, Translations	
1675–1755	Saint-Simon	Memoirs	
1680–1754	Destouches		Plays.
1688–1763	Marivaux	Novels	Comedy.
1689–1755	Montesquieu	Spirit of Laws	
1692–1754	P. C. Nivelle de La Chaussée		Plays.
1694–1778	Voltaire	Critical Essays, Satires, Letters	Poems, Dramas.
1697–1763	Abbé Prévost	Manon Lescaut	
1707–1788	Buffon	Science	
1712–1778	Rousseau	The New Heloïse, Confessions	
1713–1784	Denis Diderot	Fiction, Encyclopedia	Plays.
1717–1783	D'Alembert	Essays, Encyclopedia	
1723–1799	Marmontel	Memoirs, Stories	
1732–1799	Pierre de Beaumarchais		Comedies (The Marriage of Figaro).
1737–1814	Bernardin de Saint-Pierre	Paul and Virginia	
1760–1836	Rouget de Lisle		Marseillaise.
1762–1794	André Chénier		The Girl Captive, Iambes.
1766–1817	Mme. de Staël	Delphine, Corinne, Germany	
1768–1848	Chateaubriand	René, Genius of Christianity	
1780–1857	Pierre Jean de Béranger		Popular Songs.
1783–1842	Stendhal	Novels	
1787–1874	François P. G. Guizot	Courses on Modern History	
1790–1869	Alphonse de Lamartine	History of the Girondists	Poems.
1791–1861	Eugène Scribe		Comedy (Bataille de Dames).
1795–1856	Augustin Thierry	History of France	
1798–1857	Auguste Comte	Philosophy	
1799–1850	Honoré de Balzac	Novels ("Comédie Humaine")	
1799–1863	Alfred de Vigny	Novels (Cinq-Mars)	"Poèmes Antiques et Modernes."
1802–1870	Dumas the Elder	Novels (Three Musketeers)	Dramas.
1802–1885	Victor Hugo	Novels (Les Misérables)	Lyrics, Dramas (Hernani).
1803–1870	Prosper Mérimée	Novels (Colomba), Letters	
1804–1857	Eugène Sue	Wandering Jew, Mysteries of Paris	
1804–1869	C. A. Sainte-Beuve	Criticisms	
1804–1876	George Sand	Novels (Indiana), Peasant Tales	
1805–1859	Alexis de Tocqueville	Democracy in America	
1810–1857	Alfred de Musset	Short Stories	Poems, Comedies.
1811–1872	Théophile Gautier	Criticisms, Novels	Poems.
1811–1883	Jules Sandeau	Novels (Marianna)	Plays.
1818–1894	Leconte de Lisle		Poems, Dramas.
1821–1867	Charles Baudelaire		Poems.
1821–1880	Gustave Flaubert	Novels (Madame Bovary)	
1821–1890	Octave Feuillet	Novels, "Feuilletons"	Dramas.
1822–1899	Emile Erckmann	Novels, with Chatrian	
1823–1892	Ernest Renan	Life of Jesus	
1824–1895	Dumas the Younger	Novels	Dramas.
1826–1890	Alexandre Chatrian	Novels, with Erckmann	
1828–1885	Edmond About	Novels (Le Roi des Montagnes)	
1828–1893	Hippolyte Taine	Criticism	
1830–1914	Frédéric Mistral		Provençal Poetry (Mireille).
1831–1908	Victorien Sardou		Dramas (Patrie).
1839–1907	Sully-Prudhomme	Criticism	Poems (Les Solitudes).
1840–1897	Alphonse Daudet	Novels, Short Stories	
1840–1902	Emile Zola	Novels (La Débâcle)	
1844–1896	Paul Verlaine		Poems.
1844–1924	Anatole France	Novels, Essays	Poems.
1850–1893	Guy de Maupassant	Short Stories (The Necklace)	
1850–1923	Pierre Loti	Novels, Travel	
1852–1935	Paul Bourget	Novels (La Terre Promise)	
1853–1932	René Bazin	Novels	
1857–1915	Paul Hervieu	Novels	Dramas (The Labyrinth).
1858–1932	Eugène Brieux	Essays	Dramas (The Red Robe).
1859–1941	Henri Bergson	Creative Evolution	
1859–1940	Henri Lavedan	Novels	Dramas.
1862–1923	Maurice Barrès	Novels (Le Voyage de Sparte)	
1862–	Maurice Maeterlinck	Essays (Life of the Bee)	Poems, Dramas.
1866–1944	Romain Rolland	Novels (Jean Christophe), Essays	Plays.
1868–1918	Edmond Rostand		Dramas (Cyrano de Bergerac).
1869–1940	André Gide	Novels, Travel Books	
1872–	Paul Fort		Free Verse.
1873–1922	Marcel Proust	Psychological Novels	
1876–1933	Comtesse M. de Noailles	Novels	Poems (The Quick and the Dead).
1885–	André Maurois	Biographical Novels	
1885–	Jules Romains	Novels (Men of Good Will)	
1895–	André Malraux	Novels (Man's Fate)	

ITALIAN LITERATURE

For convenience, the history of Italian literature may be divided into five periods: (1) beginning about 1230 with the Sicilian poets gathered at the court of the emperor Frederick II and including the three writers of cardinal importance, Dante, Petrarch, and Boccaccio (d. 1375); (2) the Revival of Learning, initiated by Petrarch and extending through the age of Lorenzo de' Medici (1449–92); (3) the mature Renaissance, to the death of Tasso (1595); (4) a period of decline extending to the middle of the 18th century; (5) the period of the regeneration of Italy, extending to the present.

The Early Period. The poetry of the Sicilians is mainly amatory as to subject, but the individualities of the poets are not strongly marked. The writer of courtly lyrics celebrates the perfections of his lady in an emphatic but somewhat conventional manner that does not often convince us of the sincerity of his emotions. However, it should be borne in mind that this poetry depended for no small part of its effect upon the music to which it was set. Nor is it by any means all artificial; a number of poems have survived, which bear a partially popular stamp, and which charm through their evident genuineness of feeling. Such poems are a girl's lament for her lover who has gone on a crusade overseas; and a dialogue between a lover and his beloved—the so-called *Contrasto* (debate), attributed to an otherwise unknown Cielo d'Alcamo—famous enough to have been quoted by Dante. A notable achievement as to form was the invention of the sonnet by Giacomo da Lentino, a member of this group.

Among poets of continental Italy, who continued the work of the Sicilians but broadened their range of subjects, was Guittone d'Arezzo, who was regarded as a leader by a considerable group of minor writers in central Italy, and who is noteworthy besides for a collection of letters written about 1260 as models for prose writing. Italian prose was then in its infancy, but it developed speedily, largely through translations, from Latin and French, of lives of saints, religious treatises, romances of chivalry, and Latin classics, but also through original works, such as chronicles and collections of short stories.

The wave of intense religious emotion which swept over Italy in the 13th century, in the wake of the Franciscan movement, found expression in religious poetry of deep sincerity, such as the *laudi* (hymns) of Jacopone da Todi. These, being sometimes written in the form of dialogues, became the starting-point of the religious drama which reached the climax of its development in the Florentine religious plays of the 15th century.

Outside of the more or less faithful followers of the Sicilian poets in central Italy, there arose, in opposition to them, two groups of writers that were powerful forces in advancing the rapid development of Italian poetry.

The earlier group was composed mainly of Florentine poets of the middle class, in whom the courtly, artificial idealism of the Sicilians and their adherents provoked a reaction, out of which came a quantity of realistic and often broadly humorous verse. The second group includes a number of Florentine poets whose work began around 1280. To them came a new lyric impulse from an ode by a distinguished poet of Bologna, Guido Guinizelli, beginning "Love e'er betakes him to the gentle heart." Guinizelli's theory of the source of love differed from that of his predecessors in declaring that love, instead of being merely communicated from the eyes to the heart—as had been held by the earlier poets—has its natural home in the "gentle heart," and that none but gentle hearts can know true love. Such a conception of a company of elect souls, to whom alone true love can be known, was bound to prove a kindling spark to this young and enthusiastic group, who are referred to in the *Divine Comedy* as the writers of the "sweet new style."

Their leader was for a time the noble and scholarly Guido Cavalcanti, a member of one of the most powerful Florentine families, to whom Dante dedicated his first great work, the *Vita Nuova*, "New Life." On the appearance of this little book, however, its young author speedily took the first rank.

Dante.—The *Vita Nuova* is at once a selection from the lyric poetry of the writer's youth and early maturity (interspersed with explanatory and narrative prose passages), the story of his spiritual awakening through the love of a gentle lady, Beatrice, and the forerunner of his greatest work, the *Divine Comedy.*

The ten years between 1292, when the *Vita Nuova* was probably completed, and 1302, when Dante was forced into exile, were the period of the poet's preparatory studies for his masterpiece; likewise, of his political career, that ended in disaster. In spite of the handicap of lifelong banishment, he not only wrote some lesser though highly important works, but planned and brought to a triumphant conclusion the *Divine Comedy*, one of the most monumental achievements of the poetic imagination in the world's literature. See *Divine Comedy*.

The purpose of helping his fellow men, by diffusing among them useful knowledge which might otherwise have remained inaccessible to them, is revealed in several of the poet's minor works, particularly the *Convivio*, "Banquet," a philosophical commentary, preceded by an introduction, on three of the poet's own odes. The *Monarchia* is a treatise in Latin, setting forth the necessity of a universal temporal monarchy coexistent with the spiritual sovereignty of the pope. *De Vulgari Eloquentia* is another Latin treatise on Italian language and poetry, of great value though unfinished. The most important of Dante's Latin letters defines the structure and purpose of the *Divine Comedy.*

Petrarch.—Francesco Petrarca, the second of Italy's great writers, came into prominence about a dozen years after the death of Dante, and was for more than forty years the undisputed leader in Italian poetry and scholarship. The main inspiration of his lyric poetry was his love for Laura, a French lady of Avignon; but patriotic and religious sentiments find noble expression in his work. His shorter Italian poems number well over 300, the majority of which are sonnets.

Petrarch wrote many treatises, poems, and letters in Latin. An enthusiastic student of the Latin classics, he broke away from the medieval method of seeking in them allegorical meanings wholly foreign to their spirit, and tried to understand them by striving to put himself back in the times in which they were written. He thus probably unconsciously initiated a new era in the study of the classics, and is rightly regarded as the pioneer of the movement known as the Revival of Learning. He has been styled, on the whole justly, the "first modern man." His discovery, in a northern Italian library, of some letters of Cicero, hitherto believed lost, started the search for vanished literary treasures, and, from his time on, the monastery libraries of Europe were ransacked with diligence and notable success by generations of scholars, mostly Italians.

Petrarch, after an honored and varied career, died peacefully (1374) in his little country home in the Euganean hills in northern Italy.

Boccaccio.—The third great figure of this period is Giovanni Boccaccio, to whom the Italians owe their first masterpiece of prose,—the collection of 100 stories known as the *Decameron.* The materials for this famous collection were derived from a variety of sources, European and Oriental. The tales are as varied in character as in origin, ranging from gay anecdote to tragic story, and reveal the author's great gift of lifelike portrayal of human types from every class of society. Whatever the alleged scenes of their action, it was the life of his country and time that Boccaccio put into his tales, in such profusion and variety as to suggest to some its characterization as the "Human Comedy," in contrast to the *Divine Comedy* of Dante.

A devoted admirer of Dante, Boccaccio made with his own hand a copy of the *Divine Comedy*, and wrote a life of the poet. Later, he publicly read and expounded Dante's great work, appointed to the task by the government of Florence, which thus strove to make amends for its injustice to its greatest citizen. Like his friend Petrarch, Boccaccio was an eager student of the Latin classics, and wrote in Latin numerous treatises that were useful to generations of scholars.

As a result of the work of Dante, Petrarch, and Boccaccio, the prestige acquired by Tuscan Italian established it definitely as the literary language of Italy.

The Revival of Learning. The second period of Italian literature, extending until nearly the end of the 15th century, is more remarkable for the vigorous development of classical studies, fostered by the fresh impulse given them by Petrarch, Boccaccio, and their followers, than for the production of great works in Italian; although such were by no means lacking, especially toward the close of the period. In this age the field of studies was immeasurably extended by the revival of the knowledge of Greek. Even Petrarch and Boccaccio had been able to acquire but the merest smattering of this language, owing to the lack of competent teachers. In 1397, however, Coluccio Salutati (1331–1406), a friend and the worthiest successor of Petrarch in the domain of scholarship, who had risen to be chancellor of the Republic of Florence, extended, in the name of the government, an invitation to a Greek scholar in Constantinople—then still in Greek hands—to come to Florence as official instructor in Greek. This scholar, Manuel Chrysoloras (1350?–1415), was the first of a notable line of Greek men of learning who, after the break of nearly seven centuries between the Greek and the Roman world, brought back to western Europe the language, literature, and philosophy of ancient Greece.

Enthusiasm for these studies was not confined to scholars alone, but spread rapidly and widely. The rulers of many Italian states—including the popes, several of whom were famous scholars—invited humanists, as these men of learning came to be called, to grace their courts; wealthy merchants fitted out ships to sail for Constantinople and to return with cargoes of precious manuscripts. The collections made in this age formed the nuclei of many famous libraries, such as those of Venice, Florence, and Rome.

It was natural that during this intensive revival of classical studies the cultivation of Italian should have been relatively neglected. In the end, however, Italian literature, far from losing, was incalculably benefited by the widening of the intellectual horizon achieved through the scholarship of this time. Indeed, the masterpieces of the ensuing age, in both poetry and prose, could never have been written without the background of classical culture derived from the humanistic period.

The neglect of Italian was also, as has been said, only relative. From about 1465, we come upon a generation of admirable poets, some of whom, like Pulci, Boiardo, Poliziano, and the great Lorenzo de' Medici, were themselves classical scholars of high attainments. Of these writers, Pulci and Boiardo wrote mainly narrative poetry; the others, chiefly lyric and dramatic.

The Renaissance. In the third period of Italian literature, the elements of classical culture, blended with those of the brilliant life of the epoch, combined to produce the ripest fruits of the age of the Renaissance, a term broader than humanism, as it is not, like the latter, applied exclusively to literary activities, but to those in all the arts—painting, sculpture, architecture, and music—which flourished with incomparable splendor at this time in Italy. A further aid to men of letters of this time was the art of printing, which, invented during the preceding age, incalculably multiplied the resources and opportunities of literary production.

Ariosto.—Among the remarkable number of distinguished writers brought forth by this age, the greatest are the following: (1) Ludovico Ariosto, author of the *Orlando Furioso*, "Orlando in Madness," a romance of chivalry in verse (46 cantos) continuing the *Orlando Innamorato*, "Orlando in Love," of his predecessor Boiardo. The hero is the medieval Roland, whom legend made into a nephew of Charlemagne. Vividness of imagination, fertility of invention, skill in character drawing, and a rich, mellow style, through which the attractive personality of the author is pleasantly revealed, have combined to insure the permanent vitality of the work, in which the life of Renaissance Italy is mirrored as faithfully as is that of the end of the middle ages in the tales of Boccaccio's *Decameron*. Ariosto wrote, besides, five comedies—mostly free adaptations of the Latin plays of Plautus and Terence—and seven partly autobiographical satires, as well as some lyric poetry in Italian and in Latin.

Machiavelli.—(2) Niccolo Machiavelli, the first great modern writer on statecraft and the art of war. His treatise entitled *The Prince*—an examination of the methods of acquiring and maintaining sovereign power—has been discussed more than any other single work of this period. Written for its time, when might usually made right, and intended as a practical guide for the ruler, its advocacy of expediency and ruthlessness over justice and good faith naturally laid it open to the harsh criticism of later ages that have witnessed vast improvements in methods of government. Machiavelli's *History of Florence* shows his characteristic political and historical insight, as do his *Discourses on Livy*, which deal with popular forms of government. Besides minor works, he wrote, in a lighter vein, several comedies, a fantastic, satirical short story, and some poetry.

Castiglione.—(3) Baldesar Castiglione, the author of the *Cortegiano*, "Courtier," the best treatise in dialogue form since those of Plato and Cicero. The discussions of the qualifications of the courtier are represented as having taken place during four successive evenings in 1506 at the court of Urbino, the capital of a diminutive duchy in central Italy. The artistic handling of one of the most difficult literary forms, and the realistic and pleasing picture of Italian society of the Renaissance at its best, unite to make the *Cortegiano* perhaps the most delightful prose work of 16th century European literature.

Tasso.—(4) Torquato Tasso, the last great figure of this age. The son of a minor but not negligible poet and scholar, Bernardo Tasso (1493–1569), he achieved fame at eighteen with *Rinaldo*, a romance of chivalry in verse. In 1573 he obtained another great success with *Aminta*, a pastoral drama, a form to which the popularity of this work gave a great vogue. His highest achievement, however, was in the field of epic poetry. His *Gerusalemme Liberata*, "Jerusalem Delivered," first published complete in 1581 (20 cantos), is the last truly great work of Italian poetry until the middle of the 18th century. Tasso chose for his subject the stirring story of the First Crusade (1095–99), handling it imaginatively, but still preserving the dignity of the theme.

Minor Writers.—Besides these four principal writers, there are many others of distinction and influence: Bembo, scholar, poet, and historian; Vasari, the biographer of painters, sculptors, and architects; Guicciardini, the historian; Bandello and Giraldi Cinthio, authors of voluminous collections of tales, drawn upon for plots by many dramatists of the 16th and 17th centuries, including Shakspere. The "Othello" story was derived from Cinthio, who himself wrote tragedies, but never rose above mediocrity in this form. Among the most picturesque figures of the time was the Florentine sculptor and goldsmith, Benvenuto Cellini, whose autobiography, one of the most original works of its kind, is of inestimable value to the student of the life of the Renaissance. This work is likewise accessible in English, having been finely translated by John Addington Symonds, an authority on the Renaissance.

The Period of Decline. In the interval between 1595, the year of Tasso's death, and the middle of the 18th century, there are no writers of enduring significance in the purely literary field. National life was at a low ebb, and the official censorship of books, which had been established about the middle of the 16th century, increasingly hampered free expression of thought. Poetry declined notably, not in quantity of production, but in quality. In this era of Italy's political weakness and dependence, her writers could derive no inspiration from the life of the nation. Literature, as a consequence, lost contact with life; its subjects, especially in poetry, became artificial and futile; taste and style deteriorated in a welter of exaggeration, sensationalism, and affectation. Toward the end of the century a reaction led to an attempt at reform; but this ended in puerile artificialities of pseudo-Arcadian simplicity. The Muse of Poetry was all powder and rouge.

Until a regeneration of the national life could set in, and contact between writing and reality could be restored, nothing great in literary production was to be expected.

Even during this time, however, the Italian genius was by no means dormant in all fields. The 17th century is the period of the development of a hybrid but still vital compound of poetry and music, the opera—originally planned as a revival of the Greek tragedy; and it was likewise in this time that the spirit of scientific investigation was nobly embodied in the imposing figure of Galileo. The early part of the age, moreover, produced one historical masterpiece, the *History of the Council of Trent* (1619), by the brilliant and fearless Venetian ecclesiastic, Fra Paolo Sarpi.

The Regeneration. About the middle of the 18th century, signs of a change appear. The Treaty of Aix-la-Chapelle (1748) brought relief from protracted wars and inaugurated a long era of peace for Italy, during which the currents of liberal ideas and the spirit of investigation characteristic of the 18th century manifested their quickening influence there as elsewhere. Aspirations toward the moral progress of the individual and toward the social betterment of the people as a whole began to find expression in writings of enduring value.

One of the most striking literary reforms belonging to the middle of the 18th century is that which was effected in comedy, through the efforts of Carlo Goldoni, who became the founder of modern Italian comedy. His great achievement was to substitute written-out comedy, as we know it, for the unwritten improvisations based upon stock scenarios and characters—the so-called *commedia dell' arte* (professional comedy)— which had monopolized the Italian comic stage for 200 years.

Parini.—In lyric poetry, amid the long-cultivated futilities of unreal Arcadianism, the note of moral earnestness and sincerity finally makes itself heard in the work of Giuseppe Parini, who, more than any other Italian writer, joined again the broken links between literature and life. A man of humble origin but of genuine nobility of soul, he felt keenly the moral laxity and social injustices of his age, and, throughout his life, he devoted himself to combating these with the powerful weapon of satire. Some of the contemporary abuses he attacked in powerful odes; in a longer poem, *Il Giorno*, "The Day," he treats, in a mock-heroic vein, of a day in the life of a young Italian nobleman, a representative of the prevailingly corrupt privileged class of his time. The whole constitutes one of the most effective and cleverly handled pieces of satire in all literature.

Alfieri.—Parini's endeavors toward the moral reform of his contemporaries were extended to the political field by the dramatic poet, Vittorio Alfieri. Nobody felt more deeply than he the degradation of the national life of his country. The task he set before himself was the reawakening of the national consciousness, deadened in the majority of his countrymen by ages of foreign domination. This he strove to achieve through a series of tragedies glorifying champions of liberty against oppression. He tells us himself that, unable to fight alone, in the literal sense, against tyranny in rulers and apathy in the ruled, he is forced to content himself with the "mimic warfare of the stage." He chose the drama as the most appropriate vehicle for his propaganda, in order to reach the Italians through their passion for the theater, and for the purpose of reforming their taste in the drama by substituting the spoken tragedy for the song of the long popular opera, which he considered effeminate and demoralizing. The poet at whom he particularly struck was the popular Pietro Metastasio, whose sentimental tragedies, set to music by two generations of Italian composers, were sung all over Europe.

Alfieri was not so richly endowed with poetic gift as with energy and determination, and his tragedies are not dramatic masterpieces—with the possible exception of the biblical tragedy *Saul*, which is still occasionally revived in Italy. Nor was he able to wean his countrymen from their love of opera. His tragedies were widely read, however, and his principal aim was attained. Furthermore, he inspired greater poets, who followed him, with his passion for the national regeneration of Italy, to which they were able to give higher artistic expression than he could attain.

The Nineteenth Century. Among the successors of Alfieri were Ugo Foscolo, Giacomo Leopardi, and Alessandro Manzoni.

Foscolo.—In a much read epistolary novel, *The Last Letters of Jacopo Ortis* (1802), Foscolo eloquently voiced his sorrow over the fate of the ancient republic of Venice, which had been traded to Austria by Napoleon in 1797. His best lyric poem is *I Sepolcri*, "The Graves," in which he feelingly expresses his reverence for Parini, Alfieri, and other great Italians. His odes and sonnets, while not numerous, are of a very high poetic quality. His collected correspondence gives interesting pictures of himself and of his time. Unwilling to take the oath of allegiance to Austria in 1815, he went into exile, first to Switzerland and then, in 1817, to England, where he died in 1827.

Leopardi.—Leopardi, the greatest of modern Italian poets, achieved renown at twenty with two remarkable odes. The first of these, beginning "O Italy, I see thy walls, arches, columns, statues and solitary towers, but thy glory I do not see," contains the keynote of his patriotic poetry, which echoed widely among his contemporaries and maintains its appeal to this day. After three or four further odes, he discarded the patriotic strain and devoted what little strength remained to him during a long period of distressing invalidism to the expression of his personal disillusionments with life, which he came to consider not worth living.

In spite of the sterile pessimism of the poet's thought, the later odes live through their unsurpassed beauty of style. Among miscellaneous prose works, he wrote a series of essays—some in dialogue form—which display the learning for which he was as famous as for his poetry, and in which the pessimistic theme reappears in many variations. Leopardi's personality, as revealed in his poems, essays, and correspondence, has the quality of haunting the imagination of his reader as does that of his contemporary, Keats, different as were their natures.

Manzoni.—In proportion to the length of his life, the amount of Manzoni's literary output is small.

He belongs among those writers whose vein of inspiration is not copious but is intense while it lasts, and who have the restraint not to force it. He wrote when deeply stirred, with a resultant sincerity which his readers cannot help but feel. His conversion from a skeptical attitude in religion to an abiding faith he voiced in hymns (*inni sacri*) of deep feeling. In the discouraging, reactionary period of the so-called restoration which followed Napoleon's fall and the Congress of Vienna, he contributed two plays and a historical novel to the national and patriotic literature of his country.

In both novel and plays the background is historical. In the first of the latter, the *Conte di Carmagnola* (1820), Manzoni pictures the disastrous policy of the Italian states of the 15th century, whose internecine strife only prepared the way for foreign domination. The scene of the other play, the *Adelchi* (1822), is laid in northern Italy of the 8th century, during the struggle for supremacy between the Lombards and the Franks, neither of whom were of Italian stock. The moral of the play is that an oppressed people can hope for no improvement of its lot from a mere change of masters, but solely from its own efforts. In the *Promessi Sposi*, "The Betrothed," the application of the rule of force in government and the petty tyranny of the nobles over the weak are exhibited in a series of vivid pictures from 17th century life in the Milanese district. The story is unified by the adventures of three or four humble characters, victims of the forces of injustice. Manzoni's insight into human nature, his power to create living characters, his descriptive force, and his sustained excellence of style make of this work perhaps the greatest historical novel of the 19th century. Among his nonreligious minor poems, that on the abortive revolution of 1821 and the ode on the death of Napoleon are the finest.

Manzoni's life was prolonged until well into the period when the aspirations of his predecessors and contemporaries with respect to Italy's unity and independence were happily fulfilled. The stirring years leading up to the great campaign of 1859, when, with French help, the Austrian grip on the country was loosened, and that of 1866, when it was finally broken—except in limited areas recovered by Italy after the World War—produced numerous writers whose work, while valuable and effective at the time, is hardly of permanent vital quality. There are, however, five outstanding figures in this period who should be mentioned. Giuseppe Giusti, Giuseppe Mazzini, Francesco de Sanctis, Pasquale Villari, and Giosuè Carducci.

Giusti's field was political satire. A number of his poems possessed intrinsic value sufficient to preserve their vitality long after the causes they advocated or condemned had passed into history.

Mazzini's power and versatility as a writer on political and miscellaneous subjects ensure him a place in the literary as well as in the political history of his time. De Sanctis is the greatest literary critic yet produced in Italy. His numerous essays on various literary subjects, as well as his *History of Italian Literature*, have attained the rank of classics.

Carducci.—Beginning to write in 1850, Carducci became the leading poet of Italy from about 1870 until his death in 1907. As was natural in one who had lived through one of his country's greatest crises, his inspiration was largely derived from history. No great poet of recent times has written so little about himself. His great historical odes, some of them in meters adapted from Greek and Latin lyric poetry, are the finest in Italian literature since Leopardi. He excels also in the smaller forms, such as the sonnet. For over a generation he was professor of Italian literature at the University of Bologna, and in this period he published many volumes of critical essays. His style, in both poetry and prose, is characterized by nervous vigor.

Villari.—Like Carducci, Villari, whose literary career covered nearly 70 years, was a link between the Italy of the old order and that of the new. An admirable historian, he treated early Florentine history, the life and times of the reformer Savonarola (1452–98), and the life and times of Machiavelli, in highly readable and accurate books that are indispensable to students of those periods. They are available in English translations.

Recent Literature. Among men of letters no longer living, whose work was done chiefly or wholly after the establishing of Rome as the capital of the Kingdom of Italy (1870), the most notable are the following: Giovanni Verga, Antonio Fogazzaro, Renato Fucini, Edmondo de Amicis, Giuseppe Giacosa, and Giovanni Pascoli.

Verga, a powerful realist, excels in depicting in a peculiarly intense but restrained manner, the peasant and middle-class life of his native Sicily. His best work is in the short story or sketch, in which he has achieved highly original and artistic effects with outwardly simple means.

As both poet and prose-writer, Fogazzaro reveals a noble, generous, sympathetic nature, endowed with keen psychological insight and ability to create a great variety of characters. His *Piccolo Mondo Antico*—translated into English under the title of "The Patriot"—is the best Italian historical novel since Manzoni's *Promessi Sposi*. It vividly portrays life in northern Italy during the period culminating in 1859.

Fucini, blending humor and pathos, wrote delightful and penetrating sketches of Tuscan peasant life, that are likely to stand the test of time. He produced also a set of sonnets, mostly in dialect.

De Amicis was a versatile and popular writer, mainly of short stories and books of travel. His clever and kindly personality, which one easily distinguishes through his work, has endeared him to a host of readers.

Giacosa was the author of a number of successful plays that, in an effective, if not always especially original, way, usually deal with modern social life. His best work is *Come le Foglie*, "Like Falling Leaves," which has been published in English.

Pascoli was looked upon as the legitimate successor to Carducci in poetry, but survived him only a few years. He was a poet of great delicacy of feeling, a lover of nature and of country life.

Of writers living or very recently deceased, the following are the most noteworthy:

Roberto Bracco, a Neapolitan playwright of considerable power, but seemingly obsessed by themes of rarely relieved gloom.

Gabriele d'Annunzio, a prolific poet, novelist, and playwright. His main asset is a colorful style, which he uses with effect in descriptive passages—always the best parts of his work, as his powers of thought are insignificant.

Benedetto Croce, a Neapolitan critic and philosopher, vigorous, prolific, and influential. A follower of De Sanctis, he is at the head of the younger school of æsthetic criticism, which has lately arisen in Italy in opposition to the historical method of criticism, of which Carducci was an exponent.

Luigi Pirandello, a novelist and dramatist whose theme is the necessity and vanity of illusion.

Giovanni Papini, a brilliant and versatile writer, who became widely known as an iconoclast. To the great surprise of his readers, he subsequently evolved into a mystic with his famous *Life of Christ*.

Besides the foregoing men, there are several women who have attained distinction as writers. Matilde Serao successfully portrayed Neapolitan life and character, and Grazia Deledda, recipient of a Nobel prize, similarly described the people of her native Sardinia.

As in other lands, literary activity in Italy is stimulated to overproduction through the ever-increasing commercialization of bookmaking. Nevertheless, there is no reason to apprehend that the Italian genius will not continue to enrich the world of literature with works of power and beauty.

TABLE OF ITALIAN LITERATURE

Authors: Time	Authors: Name	Representative Works: Prose	Representative Works: Poetry and Drama
1230?–1276	Guido Guinizelli		Sonnets, Canzoni (odes).
1230–1290	Poets of the Sicilian School		
1230?–1294	Guittone d'Arezzo	Letters	Sonnets, Canzoni.
1230–1306	Jacopone da Todi		Hymns.
1250?–1300	Guido Cavalcanti		Sonnets, Canzoni.
1255?–1336	Cino da Pistoia		Sonnets, Canzoni.
1265–1321	Dante Alighieri	Monarchia (Latin), De Vulgari Eloquentia (Latin), Letters (Latin)	Divina Commedia, Vita Nuova (poetry and prose), The Banquet (poetry and prose), Various Lyric Poems.
1270?–1348	Giovanni Villani	Chronicles	
1304–1374	Francesco Petrarca (Petrarch)	Letters (Latin), De Viris Illustribus (Biographies in Latin), De Vita Solitaria (Latin), De Contemptu Mundi (Latin), Epistola ad Posteros (Autobiographical Letter to Posterity, Latin)	Sonnets, Canzoni, Madrigals, Sestinas, Ballads, Triumphs, Latin Epic Poem (Africa).
1313–1375	Giovanni Boccaccio	Decameron, Filocolo, Fiammetta, Corbaccio	Narrative Poems (Teseide, Filostrato), Ameto (Pastoral, poetry and prose).
1432–1484	Luigi Pulci		Romance of Chivalry (partly burlesque), Il Morgante.
1440–1494	Matteo Maria Boiardo	Translation of Herodotus	Romance of Chivalry (Orlando Innamorato), Lyric Poems.
1449–1492	Lorenzo de' Medici		Sonnets, Canzoni, Ballads, Carnival Songs, Pastoral Poems, a Sacred Drama.
1454–1494	Angelo Poliziano	Letters, Critical Works (Latin)	Lyric Poetry, Drama (Orfeo), Stanze per la Giostra.
1458–1530	Jacopo Sannazzaro		Arcadia (Pastoral, poetry and prose), Sonnets, Canzoni, Latin Poetry.
1469–1527	Niccolo Machiavelli	The Prince, The Discourses on Livy, The Art of War, History of Florence	Comedies (La Mandragola, La Clizia).
1470–1547	Pietro Bembo	History of Venice, Asolani	Poems (Sonnets, Canzoni).
1474–1533	Ludovico Ariosto		Romance of Chivalry (Orlando Furioso, continuation of Boiardo's work), Lyric Poems.
1478–1529	Baldesar Castiglione	Il Cortegiano (The Courtier)	
1483–1540	F. Guicciardini	History of Italy, Political Writings	
1490–1547	Vittoria Colonna		Sonnets and Canzoni, commemorating her husband, and on religious subjects.
1500–1571	Benvenuto Cellini	Autobiography	
1504–1573	Giraldi Cinthio	Tales	
1512–1574	Giorgio Vasari	Lives of Celebrated Artists	
1544–1595	Torquato Tasso	Treatises, Dialogues, Letters	Romance of Chivalry (Rinaldo), Pastoral Play (Aminta), Epic on First Crusade (Jerusalem Delivered).
1548–1600	Giordano Bruno	Scientific Treatises	Comedy (Il Candelaio).
1552–1623	Fra Paolo Sarpi	History of the Council of Trent	
1564–1642	Galileo Galilei	Scientific Treatises	
1568–1639	Tommaso Campanella	Philosophical Treatises, The City of the Sun (System of Ideal Government)	
1672–1750	L. A. Muratori	Annals of Italy, Italian Antiquities, Publication of Medieval Chronicles	
1698–1782	Pietro Metastasio		Dramas (used as opera librettos).
1707–1793	Carlo Goldoni		Comedies.
1729–1799	Giuseppe Parini		Odes, Il Giorno (satirical mock-heroic).
1731–1794	Girolamo Tiraboschi	Literary History	
1749–1803	Vittorio Alfieri	Autobiography	Lyric Poetry, Tragedies (Saul).
1754–1828	Vincenzo Monti		Poems, Tragedies, Epic (Mascheroniana).
1766–1837	Carlo Botta	History of Italy (continuation of Guicciardini)	
1778–1827	Ugo Foscolo	The Last Letters of Jacopo Ortis	Odes, I Sepolcri.
1785–1873	Alessandro Manzoni	I Promessi Sposi	Dramas, Odes, Hymns.
1788–1854	Silvio Pellico	My Prisons	Tragedies (Francesca da Rimini).
1789–1853	Cesare Balbo	History, Politics	
1798–1837	Giacomo Leopardi	Moral Essays	Odes.
1804–1895	Cesare Cantù	History, Novels	
1805–1872	Giuseppe Mazzini	Essays (Political and Literary)	
1809–1850	Giuseppe Giusti	Letters	Poems (Political Satire).
1817–1883	Francesco de Sanctis	History of Italian Literature, Essays	
1827–1917	Pasquale Villari	History, Biography, Essays	
1835–1907	Giosuè Carducci	Essays	Poems.
1840–1922	Giovanni Verga	Short Stories, Novels	
1842–1911	Antonio Fogazzaro	Novels (The Patriot)	Poems, Dramas.
1843–1921	Renato Fucini	Short Stories	Sonnets.
1846–1908	Edmondo de Amicis	Novels, Travel	
1847–1906	Giuseppe Giacosa		Dramas (Triumph of Love).
1856–1927	Matilde Serao	Novels, Short Stories	
1862–1943	Roberto Bracco		Dramas.
1863–1938	Gabriele d'Annunzio	Novels (Il Piacere)	Poems, Dramas (Francesca da Rimini).
1866–	Benedetto Croce	Criticism, Philosophy, Æsthetics	
1867–1936	Luigi Pirandello	Short Stories	Dramas.
1875–1936	Grazia Deledda	Novels, Short Stories	
1881–	Giovanni Papini	Criticism, Autobiography	Poems.

SPANISH LITERATURE

The Spanish language, like the French, is a descendant of the popular Latin spoken by soldiers and colonists brought into Spain by the Roman conquest. This conquest, completed by Augustus, changed the language of the country as thoroughly as it changed the customs. During the period of the Empire, Spain gave to Rome not a few Latin writers, the greatest of whom were Martial, Quintilian, Lucan, and the Elder and the Younger Seneca. The languages of Germanic origin, introduced into Spain by the barbarian invasions of the 5th century, gradually changed the character of the Latin spoken in the peninsula. The Arabian occupation of the country, begun in the 8th century and continued for seven centuries, also left important traces in the language of the population.

Early Writers. The oldest manuscript in Spanish is a fragment of a mystery play of the Magi, written for the Church of Toledo about the middle of the 12th century. Allusions in later literature suggest that the early heroic poetry of Spain may have been quite rich, and from prose passages in the *Crónica General*, or "Universal Chronicle," begun by Alfonso X, scholars have been able to reconstruct parts of several early poems. But the only work of any length from this period is the *Poema del Cid*, which was composed probably about the middle of the 12th century, though our earliest manuscript copy is of the 14th. A later manuscript, *Crónica rimada del Cid*, or "The Rimed Chronicle of the Cid," supplements the poem with a story of the youth of this hero, who was a certain Rodrigo Díaz de Bivar of the 11th century, called "El Cid" or "Lord" by the Moors.

Many ballads of later centuries also give clear evidence that early minstrels sang of Roderick the Goth and several other popular heroes.

Side by side with the school of heroic poetry, whose subjects were chosen from history and legends, there grew up in the 13th century one of religious and narrative verse written mostly by monks and of much greater bulk than was that of the romantic school. Among these monastic writers was Gonzalo de Berceo, who wrote poetical lives of the saints, devotional poems, and religious hymns. To this century belong the *Book of Apollonius*, from a Latin version, and a *Life of St. Mary of Egypt*, translated from the French. The miracle play, *El Auto de los Reyes Magos*, or "The Drama of the Three Kings," said to have appeared as early as 1120, is regarded as the oldest drama extant in any modern literature.

King Alfonso X (1221–84), better known to history as Alfonso the Wise, was author of that admirable compilation of laws known as the *Siete Partidas*, from which is derived all subsequent Spanish legislation, and of which traces are found in the state laws of Florida and Louisiana. Under his patronage many scientific compilations were made, and he is honored as the founder of history written in Spanish. The *Crónica General*, begun under his direction, tells of universal history from the creation of the world. The parts of it devoted to Spanish history, called *Historia de España*, form a veritable treasure house of Spanish tradition.

King Alfonso's example encouraged the production of various prose works, chronicles, biographies, romances, and translations of many foreign works, particularly proverbs and sayings from the Arabic. To the beginning of the 15th century belongs the most famous of the tales of chivalry, the *Amadis de Gaula*, translated from the Portuguese by Montalvo. There is also evidence that the principal themes of French romance were familiar to the Spanish writers of this time.

Don Juan Manuel, a nephew of Alfonso X, is one of the foremost prose writers of the 14th century. Both soldier and statesman, he found time to write didactic and historical treatises, but his most famous work is the *Conde Lucanor*, a collection of 51 tales drawn from various Spanish and foreign sources, each one intended to illustrate some principle of conduct or to point a moral. Juan Manuel's style is simple, dignified, and unpretentious.

Development of Poetry and Fiction. In the 14th century appeared the first of the genuine Spanish poets, Juan Ruiz, a wayward priest, who called his work *The Book of Good Love*. The genius and the skill of this Spanish poet, though lacking the dignity and tenderness of Chaucer, have nevertheless won for him a comparison to the great English master. Pedro López de Ayala, who lived in the 14th century, is the author of the didactic poem, *Rimado de Palacio*, "Court Rimes," which is a grim satire on the society of the period. He wrote also the *Chronicles of the Kings of Castile*, a narrative of great vividness and historic accuracy.

It was the 15th century which saw a full development of poetry. In the reign of John II of Castile (1406–54) there appeared a court poetry, written in short fragments and in complicated verse form. It was made up of love ditties, debates, repartees, burlesques, and satirical songs. To understand or appreciate these poems, one must read them in connection with the history of the time. Mendoza, marquis of Santillana, stands first among these courtiers and poets, and some of his lighter poems are very graceful and full of melody. Not less fascinating are those of Enrique de Villena, a scion of the royal houses of both Castile and Aragon, who is justly celebrated as being the chief propagator of the Provençal style of verse. He was, moreover, the forerunner of the Spanish humanists. Juan de Mena belongs to a succeeding phase of this period, when the influence of Italy, and especially that of Dante, began to dominate lyrical writing in general and such allegorical poems as *The Labyrinth*, from the pen of De Mena.

The 16th century produced a long line of artificial and religious epics, numerous novels of the pastoral and chivalric type, and also the first of the realistic picaresque (roguery) tales. Such tales as *El Lazarillo de Tormes*, *Guzmán de Alfarache*, *La Pícara Justina*, and *Marcos de Obregón* set the pace for all nations in the novel of adventure and intrigue. At the beginning of the 17th century, Miguel de Cervantes Saavedra produced in *Don Quixote* the supreme example in this kind of literature and put an end to the vogue of the exaggerated romance of chivalry. *Don Quixote* is Spain's greatest contribution to universal literature and remains one of the world's indestructible treasures.

The Drama. As the beginning of Spanish drama during these centuries, liturgical representations, or miracle plays, had been given at church festivals, with the object of explaining the ritual to the lay folk. Gradually, dialogue was added and plays were enacted in the public squares. Near the close of the 15th century appeared *La Celestina*, a book written by Fernando de Rojas, a most astonishing work, exhibiting for the first time persons of all classes, particularly the lowest, talking in harmony with their natural surroundings. This work, consisting of 21 acts or parts, could not have been represented on the stage, but nevertheless it left its mark on the later drama and romance of Spain.

Cervantes wrote in the great period of the Spanish drama, and he had some degree of success with play-writing, as well as with the short story. But the two great names of this period are Lope de Vega and Calderón.

The life of Lope de Vega (1562–1635) is profoundly interesting. He was a prodigy of learning and imagination. Besides tales, poems, and dramatic sketches, he produced about 1500 regular dramas, with a very large proportion of real masterpieces among them. His themes ranged from history to everyday life, the latter to be found in his comedies of character and manners. Calderón de la Barca (1600–81) succeeded Lope de Vega as head of the Spanish drama. His plays are of four kinds: sacred dramas from Scriptural sources, historical dramas, classic dramas, and pictures of society and manners. The most celebrated are *La vida es sueño*, "Life Is a Dream," and *El Mágico Prodigioso*. Calderón was attached to the court for the purpose of furnishing dramas for the royal theater. But it is as a writer of the Sacramental drama, *auto sacramental*, that his fame as a Spanish playwright stands imperishable.

The work of Lope de Vega, Calderón, Tirso de Molina, Moreto, Rojas, and others produced for Spain one of the three great dramatic literatures of the world, destined to exercise a considerable influence on other literatures, especially on the French classic drama.

History. With the celebrated Jesuit Juan de Mariana (1536–1623), a new manner of writing history appeared. In place of merely recording one fact after another, with no apparent connection, he wrote a general survey of the history of Spain, his *Historia de España*, surpassing in achievement any work of either Ribadeneira or Sigüenza. Garcilaso de la Vega, a descendant of the Incas, wrote a history of Florida, based upon the adventures of De Soto. To the historian, Antonio de Solís y Ribadeneira, above mentioned, belongs a *Conquest of Mexico*, a flattering picture, and very successful. López de Gomara, Oviedo y Valdéz (1478–1557), and Bartolomé de las Casas (1474–1566) left records of adventures in the New World, and on these records all history of early Spanish settlements in America is founded. Among numerous writers of letters and memoirs, none surpasses Antonio Pérez (1539–1611) in style and interest. Pérez was minister to Charles V and secretary to Philip II. His *Relaciones* give a most vivid picture of the intrigues, policies, and vices of the court of Philip.

Lyric Poetry. Juan Boscán (1493?–1542?) and Garcilaso de la Vega, born in 1503, were the leaders in Spain of the Italian school of lyric poetry, led by Petrarch, and very much in vogue at the time. Other lyric poets of great merit are Fray Luis Ponce de León (1527–91) and Fernando de Herrera, born in 1534. De León, recognized as the prince of all Spanish lyrists, is the first to have freed himself from Italian influence. Much of their verse shows a mystical inspiration drawn from the Hebrew Scriptures. To the category of mystic writers must also be added such brilliant masters of style as Fray Luis de Granada, St. John of the Cross, and St. Theresa, whose prose and verse rank them among the shining lights of Spanish literature. Nor are the popular ballads (*romances*) of this period to be overlooked. These have always been the delight of the Spanish people. No poetry of modern times has been more widely known or has so thoroughly influenced national life. The earliest collections of ballads, in praise of the valorous deeds of national heroes, date from the 15th century. From the 16th century, all poets who have sought fame or distinction among the Spanish people have written ballads. Wherever Spaniards have settled in new colonies, there they have kept the old ballads and produced many new ones.

The Eighteenth Century. With the coming of the Bourbons to the throne of Spain in 1700, France gained a large place in Spanish thought; French customs crept into use, and French became the language of the court.

Native Spanish literature had, in the 17th century, followed in the path of the poet Luis de Góngora y Argote (1561–1627), who had introduced freaks of style and meaningless obscurity into his work. The result was a decay which left the first three decades of the 18th century practically barren, but for the establishment of the Royal Academy (1713) and the publication of its dictionary, which had no equal in any other European language. Ignacio de Luzán attempted to reform the Spanish theater upon French principles, and his *Poética* (1737), a work dealing with the French system of dramatic unities, marks the beginning of this renovation, which was assiduously promulgated by his followers, Nasarre, Montiano, and Luis Velásquez, in their subsequent productions. Ramón de la Cruz delighted the Spanish public at this time with witty, vivacious *sainetes*, short dramatic pieces imitated or freely translated from the French.

Leandro Fernández de Moratín, an enthusiastic disciple of Molière and a son of Nicolás de Moratín, himself a writer of some repute, produced *El Sí de las Niñas*, a still popular masterpiece of comedy. José Francisco de Isla, a Jesuit, in his novel *Fray Gerundio*, ridiculed the extravagant pedantry of the pulpit of his day, and succeeded in bringing about some wholesome reform. Tomás Iriarte, a contemporary of De Isla, evoked the spirit of La Fontaine in fabled verse of a high degree of poetic excellence.

The Nineteenth Century. Imitation of the French Classicists still persisted in the opening decades of the 19th century. Two poets, Manuel José Quintana and Juan Nicasio Gallego, acknowledge French models, even while, as patriotic Spaniards, in their heroic odes they assail the Napoleonic invaders. The highly gifted Mariano Jose de Larra (1809–37), famous as a political writer and satirist under the pseudonym "Fígaro," shows in some of his novels and plays a tendency toward Romanticism, as may be seen in his *El doncel de Don Enrique El Doliente* and his *Macías*.

The romantic movement reached Spain in the third decade of the 19th century through a group of patriotic writers. These men looked to the middle ages for inspiration, and in their writings voiced the enthusiasm for social and political freedom which marked this movement in other countries. Angel de Saavedra, author of *Don Alvaro*, the most celebrated of the romantic plays, José Zorrilla, author of the popular *Don Juan Tenorio*, and Antonio García-Gutiérrez, upon whose play *El Trovador* Verdi's opera "Il Trovatore" is founded, are notable writers of this period. But in 1850 the romantic movement gave way to realism, which continues to be the mood of present day Spanish literature.

Contemporary Writers. Within recent years Spain has witnessed a remarkable revival of letters which evokes the best phases of the classic period. In Echegaray, in Pérez Galdós, in Benavente, in the brothers Alvarez Quintero, in Martínez Sierra, the Spanish dramatic instinct finds itself anew and bows to no superior in originality, in resourcefulness of invention, or in the colorful portrayal of life. Spain's literary prowess has also been seen to advantage in the novel, especially in the realistic depiction of life in various regions of the country. Among the earlier significant names of the period may be mentioned Fernán Caballero (Cecilia Böhl von Faber), pioneer in the regional novel; Juan Valera, who produced *Pepita Jiménez*; Palacio Valdés, the creator of *Marta y María* and *La hermana San Sulpicio*; Pérez Galdós, whose monumental *Episodios nacionales* rivals Balzac's *Comédie Humaine*. Blasco Ibáñez, author of *The Four Horsemen of the Apocalypse*, was more popular outside his own country.

Of more recent writers, the novelist, Pío Baroja and the brilliant dramatist Jacinto Benavente are among the best-known. Such writers as Valle-Inclán, Jiménez, the Machado brothers, Azorín, Ortega, and Pérez de Ayala represent so many phases of the literary and intellectual awakening which came over Spain in the 20th century; while Miguel de Unamuno, in his searching revaluation of the Spanish soul, sought to draw the modern world into a deeper and more sympathetic understanding of Spain. Unamuno's masterpiece is generally conceded to be *Del Sentimiento Tragico de la Vida* (*The Tragic Sense of Life*).

TABLE OF SPANISH LITERATURE

Authors		Representative Works	
Time	Name	Prose	Poetry and Drama
1176–1250	Juan Lorenzo de Segura		Poem on Alexander the Great.
1198–1268	Gonzalo de Berceo		Religious Poems.
1226–1284	Alfonso X	Works on Laws, Astronomy, Spanish History	Canticles of the Virgin.
1282–1349	Don Juan Manuel	Tales (Conde Lucanor)	Poems.
1300–1360	Juan Ruiz de Hita		Poems (The Book of Good Love).
15th Cent.	Fernando de Rojas	La Celestina	
1411–1456	Juan de Mena		The Labyrinth.
1474–1566	Las Casas	History of the Indies.	
1478–1557	Oviedo y Valdéz	History of the Indies.	
1493?–1542?	Juan Boscán		Poems.
1503–1536	Garcilaso de la Vega		Poems, Pastorals, Sonnets.
1503–1575	Diego de Mendoza	History, Fiction	
1512–1581	Jerónimo de Zurita	Annals of Aragon	
1527–1591	Fray Luis de León		Religious Lyrics.
1533–1595	Alonso de Ercilla		La Araucana.
1534–1597	Fernando de Herrera		Lyrics.
1535–1616	Garcilaso de la Vega, the Inca	History of Florida.	
1536–1623	Juan de Mariana	History of Spain.	
1539–1611	Antonio Pérez	Letters, Memoirs, Revelations.	
1547–1616	Cervantes	Novels (Don Quixote, Galatea)	Short Dramatic Pieces.
1561–1627	De Góngora y Argote		Sonnets, Odes, Ballads, Songs.
1562–1635	Lope de Vega	Tales	Dramas (La Moza de Cántaro).
1569–1631	Guillén de Castro		Dramas.
1580–1645	Gómez de Quevedo	Theology, Satires	Poems.
1590–1639	Ruiz de Alarcón y Mendoza		Dramas (Truth Suspected).
1600–1681	Calderón		Dramas (Life Is a Dream, El Magico Prodigioso, The Constant Prince).
1610–1686	Antonio de Solís	Conquest of Mexico	
1702–1754	Don Ignacio Luzán	Art of Poetry (Poética).	Poems.
1703–1781	José Francisco de Isla	Fray Gerundio, Translations	
1731–1799	Ramón de la Cruz		Dramas.
1750–1791	Tomás de Iriarte	Proverbs	
1760–1828	Leandro F. Moratín		Dramas (El Sí de las Niñas), Poems.
1772–1857	Manuel José Quintana		Poems.
1791–1865	Angel de Saavedra		Dramas, Poems (Don Alvaro).
1796–1877	Fernán Caballero (Cecilia Böhl von Faber)	Novels (La Gaviota)	
1796–1873	M. Bretón de los Herreros		Comedy of manners.
1799–1867	S. Estébanez Calderón		Sketches of manners.
1803–1882	R. de Mesonero Romanos		Sketches of manners.
1808–1842	Jose de Espronceda		Poems (Canto a Teresa).
1809–1837	Mariano José de Larra	Political Satires, Novels	Plays.
1817–1893	José Zorrilla y Moral		Poems (Don Juan Tenorio).
1824–1905	Juan Valera y Alcalá	Long and Short Stories (Pepita Jiménez)	Poems.
1829–1898	Manuel Tamayo y Baus		Dramas (Un drama neuvo).
1832–1916	José Echegaray		Plays (The Great Galeoto).
1833–1891	Antonio de Alarcon	Novels (The Three-Cornered Hat)	Poems.
1833–1906	José M. de Pereda	Novels (Sotileza)	
1845–1920	Benito Pérez Galdós	Novels (Doña Perfecta)	Dramas.
1851–1921	Emilia Pardo Bazán	Criticism, Novels	
1853–1938	Armando Palacio Valdés	Novels (Marta y María)	
1864–1937	Miguel de Unamuno	Novels, Essays	Poems (El Cristo de Velazquez).
1866–	Jacinto Benavente		Dramas (Los Intereses Creados).
1867–1928	Blasco Ibáñez	Novels (The Four Horsemen)	
1872–	Pío Boroja	Novels	
1880–	G. Martínez Sierra.	Novels	Dramas (The Cradle Song).

LATIN AMERICAN LITERATURE

Latin American literature of the colonial period represents the life of the colonies with its adventures, its strong religious element, and its close relation with the mother country. It interprets also the life of the native Indians. Long before the arrival of the Spanish conquerors, we find from fragments still preserved that the Aztecs, Mayas, and other tribes possessed literatures of oratory and story-telling in which are disclosed both grandeur of conception and transcendent power of imagery.

Mexico. After the conquest, numbers of native Indians acquired proficiency in the Spanish tongue, but, under the fierce oppression of their new masters, this activity was ruthlessly checked. Yet, in the latter part of the 16th century, native-born Mexicans, some of Spanish, others of Indian, blood, manifested an extraordinary enthusiasm for literature, and we are told of literary contests taking place in which as many as 300 competitors strove for the laurels of poetry alone.

One of the most popular writers of this period was Fernán González de Eslava, whose *autos sacramentales*, or "sacred dramas," became so popular when presented on festival occasions that they continued to be performed for over a hundred years. Francisco Terrazas, a contemporary of De Eslava's, was another poet of prominence, whose rich and polished style won for him the praise of the great Cervantes.

A poet of rare excellence among those of the 17th century, whose name is well worthy of recording, was Sister Juana Inés de la Cruz, a nun of the Convent of St. Jerónimo. She was known in her time as "The Tenth Muse." Her writings are full of exquisite tenderness, spiritual beauty, and grace. Indeed, it may be remarked that most of the Mexican poetry of this and the following century was imbued with the deep religious feeling of the age.

José Fernandez de Lizardi (1771–1817) belongs to the transition period which marks the passing of Mexico from beneath the sway of the Spanish crown. He was the fiery evangelist, who evoked in his writings the spirit of Mexican independence. He is known as "The Mexican Thinker," and his

El Periquillo Sarniento is regarded as a classic wherever the Spanish language is spoken.

Manuel de Gorostiza (1789–1851) wrote mainly for the Spanish public, although he adapted some of his comedies to please the Mexican public. It was Ignacio Rodríguez Galván (1816–42) who first drew on national themes for his dramas. Fernando Calderón and Manuel Carpio were other contemporary writers who attained distinction, the former as a playwright and the latter as an epic and lyric poet.

The latter half of the 19th century in Mexico is remarkably prolific of literary genius. Undoubtedly, the most striking figure among the many brilliant writers of this period is Guillermo Prieto (1818–97). He was the leading spirit of republicanism. In his lyrics and novels, as well as in his political and historical works, he wrote with a flaming pen and did much to reform the abuses of his time. His style is seen to best advantage in his work *El Romancero Nacional*.

In the field of the drama, it will be noted, Mexico has ever been exceedingly rich and fertile. Nor in recent times has this fecundity shown any signs of weakening. So true is this that today Mexico City is the stronghold of a dramatic talent surpassing, it is said, that which produced the *autos sacramentales* of former times.

Among present day writers, Juan Tablada ranks high as a lyrist of tender melodies. In much of his poetry is to be found a wealth of imagery and oriental coloring strongly reminiscent of Moore's *Lalla Rookh*. Both Francisco Bulnes and Luis Obregón won distinction as historical writers. The genius of Antonio Plaza, realist and anticlerical in tendency, brought him into conflict with conservative circles.

Argentina. As in other colonies, the early literature of the Argentine Republic is full of that revolutionary spirit that gave birth to the nation. Pre-eminent among these early Argentine poets was Estéban Echeverría (1805–51). A cultured linguist, he wrote profusely, and in one of his poems, "La Cautiva," established new literary ideals which in great measure influenced the later writers of Latin America.

Ricardo Gutiérrez (1836–96) is the best interpreter of *criollo* life in Argentina. He possesses an intimate knowledge of the lower classes on the plains and has portrayed the strong characteristics of these people with great vividness and imagination. In the list of contemporary writers are to be found the names of Carlos María Ocantos, whose novels are read throughout Spain as well as Latin America, and Emma de la Barra, who draws her characters from society life in Buenos Aires. Leopoldo Lugones stands out as the greatest of recent poets, his writings being a manifesto for social and political reform.

Chile. The Spaniard José Joaquín de Mora (1783–1864) and the Venezuelan Andrés Bello (1780–1865) first gave impetus to Chilean literature, which had languished since the early days of independence. Due to the sturdy homogeneity of their race and to their comparative geographical isolation, Chilean writers have excelled particularly in the more objective type of literature, such as history, the chronicle, the general essay, and historical fiction. In history and the general essay, such writers as José Victorino Lastarria (1817–88), the brothers Amunátegui, Benjamin Vicuña Mackenna (1831–86), and Diego Barros Arana (1830–1907), author of the monumental *Historia general de Chile*, have imparted to Chilean letters a note of seriousness and scholarship which richly compensates for the more brilliant but uneven literature of most of the other Spanish American countries. In the field of fiction, Alberto Blest Gana (1830-1920) is undoubtedly the greatest novelist Chile has yet produced, and perhaps the greatest in Spanish America. His realistic manner betrays keen powers of observation and bold characterization. His best work is *Martín Rivas*. Among his followers may be mentioned Martín Palma (1821–84), Vicente Grez (1843–1909), and, more recently, Luis Orrego Luco (b. 1866), all well known for their keen studies of Chilean life.

Although poetry has had many clever devotees, it has flourished more as a cultivated plant than as one of spontaneous growth. The grandiloquent patriotic note and the narrative form set in classic molds have been especially dominant in Chilean poetry. Of late, however, romantic and *modernista* influences have inspired the verse of such writers as Eduardo de la Barra, Pedro Antonio González, Diego Dublé Urrutia, Miguel Luis Rocuant, and others. In 1945, the Chilean poetess Gabriela Mistral (Lucila Godoy Alcayaga) was awarded the Nobel Prize for Literature, the first such honor to come to a Latin American.

Uruguay. The literatures of Uruguay and Argentina have always been intimately related because of the geographical propinquity of the two countries. Each country has given refuge to literary men exiled from the other. The most brilliant name in the literature of Uruguay is unquestionably that of Alejandro Magariños (1825–93), who was at once diplomat, dramatist, poet, and novelist. Not only in his native Uruguay, but throughout Latin America and Spain, was he the object of unstinted and enthusiastic admiration. *Caramarú*, a novel of great constructive power, is looked upon as his finest work. Juan Zorilla de San Martín (1857–1931) is admitted to be the leading figure among romantic poets, as Eduardo Ocevedo Díaz (1851–1921) is the chief of story-writers, while with pungent realism Carlos Reyles depicts ranch life in the interior of the country.

Peru. For a considerable period the disturbed conditions in Peru and Bolivia retarded an otherwise natural development of native literature. Yet despite this fact the land of the Incas has shown signs of rejuvenation throughout the years of the 19th century and onward. Peru claims Carlos Agusto Salaverry (1831–90) as essentially a lyric poet with depth of feeling and great attractiveness. Manuel González Prada (1848–1918), albeit displaying a wayward and turbulent fanaticism, shows himself a past master in beauty of style. Clorinda Matto de Turner, the Peruvian wife of an Englishman, has written much patriotic poetry besides several stories and novels. Her *Aves sin Nido*, "Birds without a Nest," in which she portrays the distress of the native Indians, has been compared to *Uncle Tom's Cabin*.

Colombia. Colombia has, in the short span of its national life, produced a goodly number of literary men. The figure which looms largest among those of the 19th century is that of José María Samper (1828–98), a dramatist and novelist of rare versatility and of a high order. Rafael Núñez (1825–94), president of Colombia for many years, was a writer of polished verse as well as of political prose at once dignified and trenchant. Jorge Isaacs (1837–1895) is the author of *María*, one of the best novels in Spanish American literature.

Venezuela. In Venezuela, as in Argentina, we find literature in its earlier stages chiefly political and revolutionary. Of distinctively literary fame, however, Rafael María Baralt (1810–60), historian, poet, and scholar, is known to every student of literature in Venezuela as well as in Spain, where his talents received the recognition of membership in the Spanish Academy. Cecilio Acosta, orator and poet, is justly famous as a prose writer of great dignity and power, no less than as a master of verse full of simple grace and beauty, recalling at times the quaint and fascinating rhythm of the native Indian writers. Julio Calcana, essayist and novelist, whose work *The Castilian Language in Venezuela* has done much to inspire literary progress among his countrymen, was well known in both Europe and America. As a delineator of Venezuelan life with all its local details, Manuel Romero

García became the model for later writers. The modernist verse and political tracts of Rufino Blanco and the colorful, dramatic novels of Romulo Gallegos made them outstanding figures in recent Venezuelan literature.

Brazil. The freedom of the press and the abolition of the censorship in Brazil (1821) opened up a new era for the literature of the country. Previously, literature had been gagged and bound by political partisans, and at best there existed but a desultory spirit of dilettantism among those who were educated. Once the shackles were removed, the real soul of the Portuguese awoke and began to express itself in prose and verse. Intellectual activity was aroused, and a band of brilliant journalists and polemic writers proceeded to exert a wholesome influence on a hitherto intractable government. Tavares Bastas by his forceful *Cartas do Solitario*, "Letters of a Solitary," brought about the abolition of slavery and forced the hands of those in power to throw open the Amazon to the world's commerce. Francisco Adolpho Varnhagen is a historian of eminence, whose *Historia do Brazil* ranks high as a standard work. José de Alencar holds first place among writers of romance, to which list may be added the names of Escragnolle Taunay and Machado de Assis. The most popular of the poets are Bernardo Guimarães, Thomaz Gonzaga, António Dias, and Olovo Bilac. There are many minor poets whose lyric writing is full of winsome grace and singular sweetness.

Cuba. Cuba has contributed to literature mainly through her verse. "Every one in Cuba," writes a celebrated critic, "makes verses." The first of the great Cuban poets in the order of time is Manuel de Zequeira (1760–1846), whose patriotic odes breathe the intensive fervor of the Spaniards, Quintana and Gallego. Next, but greater than De Zequeira, comes José María de Heredia (1803–39), noted not only for his political poems, but for his descriptive verse such as "Niágara" and "Tempestad," full of glowing imagery shot with a dark and fateful melancholy.

Gabriel de la Concepción Valdés (1809–44), if a lesser light, was a poet of true worth. A mulatto foundling, his lyrics will live as long as the Spanish tongue is spoken. Of Gertrudis Gómez de Avellaneda (1814–73), it is said she has no rival of her sex as a lyric poet in any literature, unless we go back to Sappho and Corinna or to the Italian Renaissance and Vittoria Colonna.

Cuba shows a lamentable dearth of prose writers, and the work of the few that can be mentioned ranks much inferior to that of her poets. In the list of historians, the names of Arrati and Urrutia in the 18th century and those of Valdés and Arrango y Castillo in the 19th are perhaps the most prominent and noteworthy. Outstanding among Cuban novelists is Cirilo Villaverde, known especially for his *Cecilia Valdez*. Carlos de la Torre's *Historia Natural de Cuba* is well and favorably known.

An interesting essay by Menéndez y Pelayo on the lyric poets of Cuba forms the preface to the *Antología de poetas hispano-americanos*, in which may be found an excellent selection of the works of the more important.

No literary sketch of Latin America as a whole would be complete without touching upon the *modernista* movement, which has not only transcended the several Spanish American nationalities, but has extended also to the mother country. The *modernistas*, finding their source of inspiration in the French Parnassians, decadents, and symbolists, and in Poe and Walt Whitman, have enriched the Spanish language and made it more lucid and vigorous. The leader of this important movement is the Nicaraguan Rubên Darío, whose *Azul*, published in 1888, set the pace for a brilliant galaxy of poets and essayists, of whom the Peruvian José Santos Chocano and the Uruguayan José Enrique Rodó are perhaps the best-known representatives.

GERMAN LITERATURE

The origins of German literature are shrouded in obscurity, but it is certain that the Germans were the last important people of western Europe to achieve international literary repute. This was due partly to their geographical isolation from Roman and Gallic culture (the Alps, the Rhine), partly to the great migrations which swept across the German lands again and again (Visigoths, Vandals, Huns) and which diverted the minds of the people from literary pursuits, partly to certain characteristic traits of the German people—great physical energy combined with a somewhat sluggish mentality, making them a warlike but backward folk.

Early Medieval Epics. The bases of their literary beginnings were the same as in other Western lands: songs and epic lays celebrating their military triumphs, written in rugged alliterative verse, such as that of *Beowulf*, and sung in the halls of the chiefs by professional bards. These were orally transmitted, and are largely lost to us, for the great collection which Charlemagne caused to be made was subsequently destroyed by pious zealots. Only a fragment is preserved for us in very nearly its original form: a bit of the *Hildebrandslied* (about 800), which relates in crude but powerful alliterative verse the widely popular story of a father who is forced to do battle with a knight and slay him, knowing it is his own unsuspecting son.

Ancient saga material, though in a modernized form, comes to us in the *Nibelungenlied*, the greatest national epic of Germany, and one of the great epics of the world. Crude in form, it tells a story which for primitive dramatic power can hardly be surpassed. It is the story of Siegfried, who wins Brunhild for his master Gunther; of his death at the hands of Gunther's henchman Hagen because Siegfried's wife, Kriemhild, boasts of his triumph over Brunhild; and of Kriemhild's vengeance on her kinsmen, Gunther and the Burgundians.

From the monasteries, which alone kept literature alive in the 9th and the 10th century, we have two interesting literary figures. One is Otfried von Weissenburg, who (about 868), using rime for the first time in Germany, wrote a Gospel harmony to show his disapproval of "the obscene songs of the laymen." The other was the nun Hroswitha of Gandersheim (10th century), who wrote Latin plays dealing with the struggle between the virtues and the vices. *Dulcitius* is a typical example of her art, which derives from the Latin poet Terence.

The Crusades, that ushered in the age of chivalry (11th to 13th century), fostered a new narrative literature that grew out of the old epics and sagas, but was adapted to a courtly audience and a modern taste. Among the many writers of the so-called court epic, the three outstanding figures are Hartmann von Aue, Wolfram von Eschenbach, and Gottfried von Strassburg. Hartmann (d. 1220?) takes his *Erec* and *Iwein* from the French romances of the Arthurian cycle, and tells in *Der Arme Heinrich* (see Hauptmann's drama) one of the most affecting tales of medieval literature: a peasant girl offers her lifeblood to cure her master's leprosy; his refusal of her sacrifice purifies his soul and his body.

Gottfried (1165?–1215?) writes in *Tristan und Isolde* a story of forbidden love, with a tragic outcome, which Wagner's opera has made famous. Nowhere else in medieval German literature do we find so convincing a study of the love-passion.

Wolfram (d. 1225) is the greatest thinker and philosopher of the three. He gets the theme of *Parzival* from the French, but deepens and broadens it until it becomes the epitome of the development of the human soul. The raw youth Parzival sins and errs, is purified by suffering, and finally becomes worthy to be lord of the castle of the Holy Grail.

Minnesinger and Meistersinger. With the Crusades and chivalry came the development of the feudal system, one of whose happier by-products was the so-called *minnesong,* in which poets embodied in lyric verse a chivalric conception of love. Scores of noble knights turned to song in praise of their ladyloves, until such lyrics became almost a standard product. One poet, however, Walther von der Vogelweide (d. 1230), succeeded in making the conventional love song the vehicle for some of the most charming lyrics in the German language. Nor did Walther confine himself to songs of courtly *minne* or "love"; he also wrote lines glowing with religious fervor, and some of the earliest patriotic verses in German come from his pen. He was also a master of humor, as are all who come close to life.

The rapid bloom of this great epoch faded as rapidly, and German literature entered upon a long decline (1350–1650). The minnesong grew more and more conventional and empty, and in its place rose the *Meistergesang,* or "mastersong," so deliciously satirized in Wagner's "Meistersinger." Poetry and song were to be produced by rule of thumb, like shoes or bricks, and judged by pedantic criteria. Yet there were powerful forces at work; only they found no master minds to bring them to full fruition. The natural fondness of the common people for songs of love and war and history, of religious fervor and the joys of wine, burst forth in the artless but vigorous folk song, in which Germany still stands pre-eminent. The religious spirit of the time and of the German people found expression in the mysticism of Meister Eckhart (about 1260–1328), and in the only less powerful Heinrich Suso (1295–1366) and Johannes Tauler (1290–1361). Aside from their own writings, their importance lies in the fact that their individualistic trend was preparing for the struggle in which the Protestants battled for the rights of the individual conscience; and their early translation of the Bible paved the way for Martin Luther.

At this period the drama begins to emerge as a special literary category, growing out of the so-called mystery plays, which were at first given in the churches as genuine religious performances, then gradually became secularized. The influence of Latin comedy, brought in by the humanists, was especially marked in the form of the German plays. One of the most productive writers of short comedies was Hans Sachs (1494–1576), the famous cobbler of Nuremberg, who deserves more notice, however, as singer and story-teller.

Mention might be made, too, of Sebastian Brant (1458–1521) and his *Ship of Fools,* a bitter and widely influential satire on the gross ignorance of the common people. Grotesque and often coarse practical jokes were collected as the pranks of *Till Eulenspiegel,* and the animal fables of the middle ages developed into the fascinating epic of *Reynard the Fox* (printed 1498).

The Reformation. Great importance in the history of German literature must be accorded to Philipp Melanchthon (1497–1560), Ulrich von Hutten (1488–1523), and Martin Luther (1483–1546). Hutten and Melanchthon were reformers of the intellect, Luther a reformer of the spirit. The labors of the former, who were leaders in the humanistic movement in Germany, sharpened men's wits and polished their speech through the study of the classics; the labors of the latter came to work a profound change in the relations of men to God. Luther's prime literary service, however, apart from his stirring and devout hymns, was the great translation of the Bible into the language of the Saxon chancelleries, whereby he created a classic that set the standard for the literary speech of his country.

On the other hand, Luther's work brought upon the literature of Germany the most disastrous blight it had ever known, when the deluge of the Thirty Years' War (1618–48) left Germany at a lower stage of political and moral degradation than that reached by any European people since the middle ages. The crushing of the middle classes destroyed all political and religious liberty; the country was impoverished; its population was reduced by three-fourths; the best energies of its citizens were needed in the indispensable work of restoration.

For nearly one hundred years German literature sank into utter insignificance. One great novel did indeed result from the turmoil: Grimmelshausen (1625–76) bequeathed to us in his *Simplicissimus,* a story of life in Germany during the Thirty Years' War, that is worthy of its place among the great books of the world. But otherwise we have mediocrities: Opitz (1597–1639) with his unsuccessful efforts to reform German poetry; Gryphius (1616–64) with his two farce-comedies, of which *Peter Squentz* alone has any vitality; and other lesser lights, such as Gellert, writer of fables and odes, Haller, author of the didactic poem *The Alps,* Gessner, whose pastoral idyls were widely read in his day, and Gottsched (1700–66), the advocate of French classicism on the German stage.

The German Revival. By an odd paradox, it is with the reign of Frederick the Great of Prussia (1740–86), who himself spoke and wrote only French and had nothing but contempt for the best German writers of his day, that we associate the renaissance of German letters. The German people were recovering from the effects of the Thirty Years' War; conditions had become more settled, and were more favorable to the leisure that literary production requires. The stage was set for the most dramatic literary development that any European literature has witnessed. Three men stand out as leaders of the German people toward the brilliance of its classical period in letters. Klopstock (1724–1803), in his *Messiah,* was the first German poet to attempt the sublime, and he succeeded in voicing the religious idealism of the German people of his time; in his *Odes* he sounds the note of cosmopolitanism coupled with genuine patriotism. Wieland (1733–1813) attempted, in his *Agathon,* to exemplify by an object lesson the true way toward individual perfection, and gave expression in it to the same spirit that was to underlie Goethe's *Faust*—faith in the innate goodness and the unwearied aspiration of the human soul. His graceful, charming style and manner cultivated German taste as Klopstock's work had promoted German idealism and moral sentiment. Greater than either is Lessing (1729–81), whose versatility and keenness of intellect hardly yield the palm to Goethe's own. He it was whose fierce polemic freed German letters from the fallacies that hemmed its growth, and who set up the new canons of theory and technique that the literary world has subsequently justified. But not only was he a critic; he could produce. *Minna von Barnhelm* is the first great play of German life, the first German comedy to outlive its author, and the first German work to voice the plea for national unity. *Emilia Galotti* is a bitter indictment of the evils of monarchic absolutism. *Nathan the Wise* champions, in the very teeth of intolerance, the now universally accepted principle of free inquiry in religious as in other matters.

The seeds of the doctrine of individualism which the Mystics had preached and the Protestants had died to defend, which Lessing had championed and Rousseau had made into a passionate slogan, became as grains of dynamite in France, whereas in Germany they flowered out in a golden age of literature. The frenzy of "Storm and Stress"—the term is the title of a play by Maximilian Klinger—soon gave place to the restrained symmetry of the classic writers.

The Classic Period. There are four men that guide the peaceful triumph of this German revolution. Herder (1744–1803) defended individualism, but viewed it as an element in national character, thus enforcing the patriotic lesson of *Minna von Barnhelm.* He drove home the theory of the embodiment of national traits in all significant literature, and made the first studies in what we now call comparative literature. As Herder showed history to blend individual and collective forces, Kant (1724–1804) revealed a similar ideal in the mental and moral life of man. First proving that all human knowledge is subjective, in his *Critique of Pure Reason,* he proceeded to formulate, in his *Critique of Practical Reason,* religious and ethical principles which still sway the civilized world. Our individual freedom, Kant says, lies in obedience to the moral law that speaks within us.

What Kant and Herder taught, one as critic, the other as philosopher, was creatively embodied in the works of the two great poets of the age. Goethe (1749–1832) saw life as an organic whole, like Herder; Schiller (1759–1805) saw it as a continual struggle for perfection. Goethe strove for æsthetic universality; Schiller, for moral freedom. Both began as poets of "Storm and Stress": Goethe's *Götz von Berlichingen, Werther,* and *Faust,* Schiller's *Robbers, Love and Intrigue,* and *Fiesco*—all deal with excessively emotional and impulsive natures, and all are more or less tragically conceived. Their influence and their appeal to contemporaries were unexampled: utter strangers embraced and wept on each other's necks at the first performance of *The Robbers.*

But this early individualism was soon transmuted into a classic collectivism, partly under Italian influence. Goethe produced *Iphigenia, Wilhelm Meister,* and *Hermann und Dorothea;* Schiller, his great dramas,—*Wallenstein, Mary Stuart, William Tell.* Still later, at the very close of his life, Goethe embodied in the second part of *Faust* a supreme utterance of one of the fundamental tendencies of all modern life.

Romanticism. The individualistic note of the closing 18th century rings through the discordant harmonies of the Romantic school, in the unrestrained imaginings and fantastic self-assertiveness of Tieck (*William Lovell*), F. Schlegel (*Lucinde*), Novalis (*Henry of Ofterdingen*), and J. P. Richter (*Quintus Fixlein, Siebenkäs*).

On the other hand, the collectivistic humanism of Goethe and Schiller was held fast by Kleist (*Prinz von Homburg*) and by Uhland, author of many of the best-known lyrics and ballads in the language; while the speculative genius of Kant found worthy successors in Fichte, Schelling, Hegel, and Schleiermacher.

The reaction from the liberalizing tendencies of the late 18th century was fateful for German literature, and a fresh decline set in, which reached almost as low a level between 1850 and 1870 as it had a hundred years before. The Austrian censorship stunted the growth of Grillparzer (*Sappho, The Golden Fleece*); political pressure forced Rückert, a patriotic lyric poet, into retirement; Schopenhauer, the pessimistic thinker, Lenau, the morbid poet, and Platen, the morose one, are characteristic results of this discordance. Gravest harm was done to Heine (1797–1856), one of the most original lyric poets Germany has had, who, despite his patriotic fervor, was virtually driven into exile, a humiliated, embittered, disappointed man.

Recent and Contemporary Writing. With the turn of the mid-century, however, there began a steady rise of German letters. Friedrich Hebbel (*Agnes Bernauer, Herodes und Mariamne*) writes some of the most powerful dramas of the 19th century; Richard Wagner combines drama and music with surpassing genius in creations of overwhelming power. There is a new school of novelists: Freytag (*Debit and Credit*), Ludwig (*Between Heaven and Earth*), K. F. Meyer (*The Saint*), Spielhagen (*Storm and Flood*), Anzengruber (*Meteor Farm*), Sudermann (*Dame Care*), Frenssen (*Jörn Uhl*), Thomas Mann (*Buddenbrooks*), including the women writers Böhlau (*The Switching-Station*), Ebner-Eschenbach (*The Child of the Parish*), and Viebig (*Our Daily Bread*). And of short story writers several are notable —Gottfried Keller (*Seldwyla Folk*), Heyse (*The Fury*), Storm (*Immensee*), Rosegger, and others. Foremost in the field of biography is Emil Ludwig.

Lyric poetry remains at a high level throughout. One might mention, as outstanding figures of recent years, Liliencron, Dehmel, Hofmannsthal, and some of the above-mentioned novelists, notably Keller, Meyer, and Storm.

With the eighteen-nineties, German drama entered into a new period of success and eminence, under the influence of Zola, Ibsen, Tolstóy, and other naturalistic writers. Chief among the dramatists are Gerhart Hauptmann (*The Weavers, Lonely Lives, Rose Bernd, Henry the Wretched, The Sunken Bell*), who cultivates both a romantic and a realistic vein, and Sudermann (*Heimat, Sodom's End*), a playwright rather than a dramatist. Mention might also be made of Hofmannsthal (*The Adventurer and the Singer*), Schnitzler (*Light o' Love*), and Wedekind (*Spring's Awakening*).

The third decade of the 20th century brought an abrupt change in the course of German literature. Jewish writers were mostly exiled, and the works of many others were blacklisted by the Nazi regime. Thomas Mann took refuge abroad as did the younger writers whose works were forged in the fiery furnace of the World War period. Prominent among them were Feuchtwanger (*Power*), Zweig (*Education before Verdun*), and Remarque (*All Quite on the Western Front*).

TABLE OF GERMAN LITERATURE

Authors		Representative Works	
Time	Name	Prose	Poetry and Drama
About 865	Otfried		Rimed Gospel Harmony.
About 967	Hroswitha		Latin Comedies (Dulcitius).
?–1225	Wolfram von Eschenbach		Court Epics (Parzival).
?–1230	Walther von der Vogelweide		Love Songs, Hymns, Patriotic Poems
1165?–1215?	Gottfried von Strassburg		Epic (Tristan).
1170–1220?	Hartmann von Aue		Epics (Der Arme Heinrich).
1458–1521	Sebastian Brant		Satiric Poem (Ship of Fools).
1483–1546	Martin Luther	Bible Translation	Hymns (Ein Feste Burg).
1494–1576	Hans Sachs		Verse Tales, Plays (The Hot Iron).
1597–1639	Martin Opitz	Literary Theory (Von der Deutschen Poeterei)	Songs, Odes, Sonnets.
1607–1676	Paul Gerhardt		Hymns (O Haupt voll Blut und Wunden).
1609–1640	Paul Fleming		Lyrics, Hymns.
1616–1664	Andreas Gryphius		Comedies (Peter Squentz).
1625–1676	H. J. K. von Grimmelshausen	Novel (Simplicissimus)	
1700–1766	J. C. Gottsched	Criticism (Versuche einer Kritischen Dichtkunst)	
1708–1777	A. von Haller		Odes, Didactic Poems (The Alps).
1715–1769	Christian Gellert	Story (Swedish Countess)	Fables, Religious Poems.
1724–1803	F. G. Klopstock		Messiah, Odes.

TABLE OF GERMAN LITERATURE—Con.

Authors		Representative Works	
Time	Name	Prose	Poetry and Drama
1724–1804	Immanuel Kant	Philosophy (Critique of Pure Reason)	
1729–1781	G. E. Lessing	Criticism (Laokoön)	Dramas (Minna von Barnhelm).
1730–1788	S. Gessner	Idyls	
1733–1813	C. M. Wieland	Novels (Agathon)	Epic (Oberon).
1744–1803	Johann G. von Herder	Criticism	Translations (Cid, Folk Songs).
1747–1794	G. A. Bürger		Ballads (Lenore), Lyrics.
1749–1832	Wolfgang von Goethe	Novel (Wilhelm Meister)	Dramas (Faust), Lyrics, Epic.
1751–1826	Johann H. Voss		Translation (Iliad), Idyl (Luise).
1759–1805	F. von Schiller	History of Thirty Years' War	Dramas (William Tell), Ballads.
1762–1814	Johann G. Fichte	Philosophy (System of Ethics).	
1763–1825	Jean P. Richter	Humorous Novels (Awkward Age, Quintus Fixlein).	
1767–1845	A. W. von Schlegel	Criticism	Translations (Shakspere, Calderón).
1768–1834	F. E. D. Schleiermacher	Philosophy of Religion.	
1769–1860	Ernst M. Arndt	History (Spirit of the Times)	Patriotic Songs.
1770–1831	Georg W. F. Hegel	Philosophy (Logic, Science of Philosophy)	
1772–1801	Novalis	Novels (Henry of Ofterdingen)	Lyrics (Hymns to Night).
1772–1829	F. von Schlegel	Criticism, Novel (Lucinde)	
1773–1853	Ludwig Tieck	Satire, Fancy (Puss in Boots, Blond Eckbert)	Dramas (Genoveva).
1775–1854	F. von Schelling	Philosophy (Transcendental Idealism)	
1777–1811	H. von Kleist	Tales (Michael Kohlhaas)	Dramas (Prinz von Homburg).
1781–1838	A. von Chamisso	Tales (Peter Schlemihl)	Ballads.
1785–1863	Jakob Grimm	Fairy Tales	
1786–1859	Wilhelm Grimm	Fairy Tales	
1787–1862	Ludwig Uhland		Ballads, Lyrics.
1788–1860	Arthur Schopenhauer	Pessimistic Philosophy	
1791–1813	Karl Theodor Körner		War Lyrics (Lyre and Sword).
1791–1872	Franz Grillparzer	Tale (The Poor Fiddler)	Dramas (Sappho).
1796–1835	August von Platen		Polished Lyrics.
1797–1854	Jeremias Gotthelf	Peasant Novels	
1797–1856	Heinrich Heine	Pictures of Travel (Harz Journey)	Love Songs, Ballads (Lorelei).
1802–1850	Nikolaus Lenau		Somber Lyrics.
1812–1882	Berthold Auerbach	Novels (Black Forest Stories)	
1813–1863	Friedrich Hebbel		Dramas (Maria Magdalena).
1813–1865	Otto Ludwig	Novel (Between Heaven and Earth)	Dramas (Der Erbförster)
1816–1895	Gustav Freytag	Novels (Debit and Credit)	Plays (Journalists).
1817–1888	Theodor Storm	Stories (Immensee)	Lyrics.
1817–1903	Theodor Mommsen	History (Roman History)	
1819–1890	Gottfried Keller	Novels (Der Grüne Heinrich)	Poems.
1819–1898	Theodor Fontane	Novels (Effi Briest)	
1825–1898	K. F. Meyer	Novels (The Saint)	Poems.
1829–1911	F. Spielhagen	Novels (Storm and Flood).	
1830–1914	Paul Heyse	Stories (The Fury)	
1830–1916	Marie von Ebner-Eschenbach	Novel (Child of the Parish).	
1839–1889	Ludwig Anzengruber	Novel (Meteor Farm)	
1843–1918	Peter Rosegger	Stories of Peasant Life	
1844–1900	F. Nietzsche	Philosophy	
1844–1909	D. von Liliencron	Stories (Kriegsnovellen)	Lyrics.
1846–1926	R. C. Eucken	Philosophy	
1857–1928	Hermann Sudermann	Novels (Dame Care)	Dramas (Heimat).
1860–	Clara Viebig	Novels (Our Daily Bread).	
1862–	Gerhart Hauptmann	Novels (Emanuel Quint)	Dramas (Sunken Bell).
1862–1931	Arthur Schnitzler	Stories (Sterben)	Dramas (Liebelei).
1863–1920	Richard Dehmel		Poems (Zwei Menschen), Lyrics.
1863–1945	Gustav Frenssen	Novels (Jörn Uhl)	
1864–1918	Frank Wedekind		Dramas (Spring's Awakening).
1864–	Ricarda Huch	Novels (Ludolf Ursleu).	
1874–1929	H. von Hofmannsthal		Lyrics, Dramas (Death and the Fool).
1875–	Thomas Mann	Novels (Buddenbrooks)	
1880–1936	Oswald Spengler	Philosophy (Decline of the West)	
1881–	Emil Ludwig	Biography (Napoleon)	
1884–	Lion Feuchtwanger	Novels (Power, Success)	
1887–	Arnold Zweig	Novels (Education before Verdun)	
1898–	Erich Remarque	Novels (All Quiet on the Western Front)	

DUTCH LITERATURE

Dutch literature, including Flemish, begins with the rise of the Low Frankish dialect, or *Niederdeutsch*, about the middle of the 13th century. The first writing of literary rank is said to be a version of the French romance of Floris and Blanchefleur. Very soon several Dutch authors gave their countrymen tales from the romances of Charlemagne and Arthur. In the latter part of the 13th century, the language was used with such skill and vigor by Jakob van Maerlant that to him has been assigned the title "Father of Dutch Poetry." His most notable work is his *Spiegel Historiæ*, or "Mirror of History." He used subjects from the Arthurian cycle, and at the same time freed the Dutch language from undue French influence.

Popular Drama. Like that of England and France, the drama of the Netherlands began in the medieval mystery and miracle plays. In the 14th and 15th centuries, burgher literary guilds or clubs arose in the towns from the organizations that produced these sacred dramas. Poetic and dramatic contests, held by these clubs on popular festivals, served to popularize literature among the people. However, virtually no important original work came out of this period of comparative barrenness, which corresponds to the Burgundian and Spanish supremacy in the Netherlands. The publication of the *Staatenbijbel*, the Dutch authorized version of the Scriptures, in the 16th century, exerted a powerful influence in stabilizing the language. One cultured writer, Dirk Potter (d. 1428), who had traveled to Italy, wrote a long poem, *Der Minnen Loep*, "Course of Love," after the manner of Boccaccio.

Renaissance and Reformation. The 16th century saw, along with the Reformation, a revival of classical learning. Three names in this century are notable. Anna Bijns (1494–1575) is said to have been the "first writer to use the Dutch tongue with grace and precision of style." Dirk Volkertszoon Coornhert (1522–90), a man of philosophic bent, wrote poetry, drama, and prose, all of considerable merit. Philip van Marnix (1538–98) produced a famous folk song, "William of Nassau," and satirized the Roman Church. To this period belongs the famous Dutch scholar, Erasmus (1466?–1536); and in the following century the works of Spinoza, the philosopher (1632–77), and those of Grotius, the great jurist and theologian (1583–1645), imparted luster to Dutch scholarship. But these authors wrote mostly in Latin.

Amsterdam, with its freedom of thought, was the center of Dutch literary activity in its Augustan age, the 17th century. Pieter Corneliszoon Hooft (1581–1647), author of a valuable history of the Netherlands, is regarded as the prose master of this period, as Joost van den Vondel, his contemporary (1587–1679), is the greatest of all Dutch dramatists. His powers were well adapted to the treatment of sublime conceptions. Of 32 tragedies that he wrote, half are founded upon biblical subjects. The influence of his drama *Lucifer* is discoverable in Milton's *Paradise Lost.* Two other great lyric poets worthy of mention are Dirk Camphuizen (1586–1627) and Constantine Huygens (1596–1687). Other dramatists of the century were Geeraerdt Brandt (1626–85) and Antonides van der Goes (d. 1684), the latter noted for a beautiful descriptive poem called *De Ystroom.* The popular poet of the time was Jakob (Father) Cats (1577–1660). He took his themes from everyday life, and through his verse there runs a vein of homely wit mingled with shrewd common sense that appealed to the people.

Decadence and Revival. After the close of the wars in the late 17th century, there began a period of literary decadence. For nearly a century, Dutch writers were, for the most part, mere imitators under French influence. The literary society "Nil volentibus arduum," established by Andries Pel, followed strictly the French school of drama, while Johann Oudaen (d. 1692), Van Focquenbrock, and Rotgans held to traditions of a more native cast. Voltaire's *Henriade* was translated with elaborate detail by Sybrand Feitama (1694–1758); Hoogvliet produced the remarkably fine epic, *Abraham* (1763); and Van Waagenaar, his great history of Holland. In the last quarter of the 18th century, however, the influence of the great literary awakening in Germany touched the Dutch genius. A fresh stream of romantic and patriotic poetry flowed in the verse of Jan Helmers (1767–1813) and Hendrik Tollens (1780–1856). Willem Bilderdijk (1756–1831),—after Vondel the most powerful among Dutch writers,—and likewise his successor, Isaac da Costa (1798–1860), showed themselves in brilliant opposition to the classic spirit.

The Nineteenth Century. After the resplendency of Bilderdijk, a new period of Dutch literature begins with the 19th century. Jakob van Lennep (1802–68), poet, dramatist, and romancer, has been called the "Dutch Sir Walter Scott." He was followed by Mrs. Bosboom-Toussaint, Schimmel, and a host of other excellent writers. In the work of Nikolaas Beets (1814–1903), who is reckoned the greatest Dutch humorist, the influence both of Scott and of Dickens may be seen. Edward Dekker (1820–87), known by his pen name of "Multatuli," is celebrated outside of the Netherlands for his romance, *Max Havelaar*, in which he attacked Dutch rule in Java.

The novel is still the most representative phase of Dutch literature. Adèle Opzoomer (A. S. C. Wallis) and Louis Couperus are both well-known authors of popular stories. Among several poets who have attained distinction since 1880 are the lyrist Hélène Lapidoth-Swarth, M. Emants, and F. Van Eeden, the last a writer of both lyrics and drama. The feminist writer and novelist, Jo van Ammers-Küller, wrote many novels, short stories, and plays, some of which became popular outside the Netherlands. Her writings include *The House of Joy* and *Rebel Generation.*

DANISH LITERATURE

Outside of the runic inscriptions, no literary monument from pagan times (before 1000) has been preserved in Denmark. The first half of the middle age (1000–1500) was a period of growing power and influence culminating in the age of the Waldemars, while the second half shows decline. The earliest written literature is in Latin, the most famous Latin work being *Gesta Danorum*, the early history of Denmark, written by Saxo. The provincial laws of Scania and Zealand and the later law of Jutland (1241) were in Danish. The famous Danish ballads had their beginning in the 12th century. This popular literature reached its highest development in the 14th century but continued for many generations after that.

At the time of the Reformation (1530), the most important name is that of Kristiern Pedersen, who contributed an important part to the first complete Danish translation of the Bible (1550). The early leaders of the Lutheran Reformation tried to reach the common people by publishing, in the mother tongue, polemical writings, songs, and satires. The first Danish hymn book was printed in 1528. In the Age of Learning, following the Reformation, Latin was again used by the learned. The sciences have brilliant representatives in this age: Tyge (Tycho) Brahe, Thomas Bartholin, Steno, Ole Römer. A. S. Vedel, who translated Saxo's work, and A. Huitfeldt were historians. To the 17th century belongs the famous hymn writer, Thomas Kingo. Toward the close of the century there was a revival of interest in the Danish language.

The greatest name of the 18th century is that of the Norwegian Ludvig Holberg, the real father of modern Dano-Norwegian literature. He towers far above his contemporaries. Yet, in his age lived the great hymn writer, A. Brorson, and Ambrosius Stub shows his love of nature in poems that still are popular. The latter half of the century is the Age of Enlightenment. The Norwegian Tullin wrote his highly admired *May Day*, the Norwegian Brun wrote *Zarine* in imitation of the French classical drama, the Norwegian Wessel wrote his immortal parody *Love without Stockings*, which cleared the atmosphere of bombast and artificiality. The outstanding Danish genius of the time is Johannes Ewald, author of the Danish national hymn "King Christian."

With the 19th century came the Age of Romanticism, beginning the golden age of Danish literature. A. G. Oehlenschläger is the greatest name of the period. His *Poems* of 1803 were epoch making, and after that he published one successful work after another, among them *Hakon Jarl* and *Aladdin.* Contemporary with him was N. F. S. Grundtvig, one of the most powerful men Denmark has produced, exerting great and lasting influence. Ingemann is Denmark's Walter Scott, Blicher portrays life in Jutland in masterly fashion, Hauch is a prominent writer, Winther a great lyric poet. J. L. Heiberg created the popular form of comedy, technically called "vaudeville," and was an eminent literary critic. *The Soul after Death* is his best-known work. Henrik Hertz was a versatile dramatist and a master of style. H. C. Andersen won world fame through his fairy tales, and Paludan-Müller was an author of great power and depth. Ploug became the poet of the historical movement called Scandinavianism; Goldschmidt, the great prose writer, attacked absolutism in politics unsparingly, till Denmark adopted her constitution in 1849. The most generally popular author in this period is Hostrup, whose comedies are most entertaining, rivaling the works of Heiberg and Hertz. In the period of 1850–70, several new men of talent appear, winning much popularity, but there is no outstanding genius.

With the famous lectures of 1871 by Georg Brandes, for over fifty years Europe's best-known literary critic, begins the Age of Realism. Of the new men, the best-known are Drachmann, who was Denmark's greatest lyric poet, Schandorph, and J. P. Jacobsen, two of whose novels have recently been translated into excellent English. Somewhat later appear K. Gjellerup, H. Pontoppidan—these two are the Danish writers who have won the Nobel prize—H. Bang, G. Wied, Karl Larsen. Of other recent writers, the best-known are K. Michaelis, J. Jörgensen, V. Rördam, L. C. Nielsen, J. Aakjær, J. V. Jensen. The last mentioned is a master of style and is endowed with a superior creative imagination. Andersen-Nexö has powerfully depicted the life of the proletariat.

TABLE OF DANISH LITERATURE

Authors		Representative Works	
Time	Name	Prose	Poetry and Drama
1200–?	Saxo Grammaticus	History of Denmark	
1480–1554	Kristiern Pedersen	Tales, Translation of Bible	
1494–1561	Hans Tausen	Religion	
1495–?	Broder Niels		Rimed Chronicle.
1587–1637	Anders Arrebo		World's First Week, Poetic Version of David's Psalms, Hexameron.
1634–1703	Thomas Kingo		Psalms, Hymns, Winter Psalter.
1684–1754	Ludvig Holberg	History of the World, Philosophy	Comedies, Comic Poetry.
1694–1764	Hans A. Brorson		Hymns.
1743–1781	Johannes Ewald		King Christian, Lyrics, Tragedies.
1744–1812	Werner Abrahamson	Criticism	
1760–1830	Knud Lyne Rahbek	Novels, Essays	Dramas, Songs.
1764–1826	Jens Baggesen	Novels, Essays, Travels	Humorous Poems, Lyrics, Rimed Letters.
1769–1826	Adolph Schack-Staffeld		Lyrics.
1773–1856	Baroness Gyllembourg	Novels	
1775–1854	Bishop Mynster	Theology	
1777–1817	Peter T. Foersom		Translation of Shakspere.
1779–1850	A. G. Oehlenschläger	Romances	Tragedies, Poems (Hakon Jarl, Aladdin).
1783–1872	N. F. S. Grundtvig	Theology, Politics	Poems, Hymns.
1789–1862	Bernhard S. Ingemann	Historical Novels	Lyrics, Epics.
1791–1860	Johan L. Heiberg		Lyrics, Dramas.
1791–1862	Niels M. Petersen	History, Mythology	
1793–1877	H. N. Clausen	Criticism	
1794–1838	Poul Möller	Novels	Poems, Student Songs.
1796–1876	Christian Winther	Tales	Poems.
1798–1865	A. N. de Saint-Aubain	Romances	
1798–1870	Henrik Hertz		Lyrics, Satire, Dramas, Epics.
1805–1875	Hans C. Andersen	Fairy Tales, Novels (Only a Fiddler)	Dramas, Poems.
1809–1876	Frederik Paludan-Müller		Dramas, Poems.
1813–1855	Sören A. Kierkegaard	Philosophy	
1818–1892	J. C. Hostrup		Comedies, Popular Songs.
1819–1887	Meir Goldschmidt	Journalism, Novels, Short Stories.	
1840–1921	T. F. Troels-Lund	History, Biography, 16th Century	
1842–1927	Georg Brandes	Criticism (Main Currents in 19th Century Literature)	
1846–1908	Holger Drachmann	Novels	Lyrics, Dramas.
1857–1919	Karl Gjellerup	Novels	
1857–1943	Henrik Pontoppidan	Novels	Plays.
1869–	Martin Andersen-Nexö	Novels (Palle the Conqueror)	
1872–	Karin Michaelis	Novels (The Dangerous Age)	

NORWEGIAN LITERATURE

The earliest Norwegian literary monuments are the runic inscriptions, of which the oldest are from about 400. At the beginning of the 9th century, the viking age brought the Norwegians into contact with western Europe. Their religious views had by this time found their final form in all essentials, but influence from Christian Britain and Ireland may also be traced in the *Elder Edda*, a collection of poems dealing with gods and heroes. While the manuscript was preserved in Iceland, the greater number of the poems are of Norwegian origin. These poems are all anonymous. Also the oldest lays of known *scalds*, or poets, are Norwegian. The greatest of Norwegian scalds was Eyvind Skaldaspillir, whose mighty *Hakonarmal*, "Poem about Hakon," was composed in memory of Hakon the Good (961). In 874 the first settler came to Iceland from Norway, and in the following centuries this island became the center of Norwegian-Icelandic literature. While the Icelandic sagas to a great extent treat of persons and happenings in the mother country, Norway herself contributed only a smaller part of the Norwegian-Icelandic literature.

Among Norwegian works may be mentioned an excellent translation of (a part of) the Bible, a translation of a collection of sermons, and *The King's Mirror* (13th century), the remarkable handbook of court customs, which has since become a gold mine of knowledge concerning the highly developed culture of that period. During the reign of Hakon IV and his successors (13th century), numerous French poems and stories were translated in Norway into old Norwegian (Icelandic). Other Norwegian works of importance to be mentioned are the provincial laws and King Magnus's law for the whole country (1274). The most important work in Latin produced in Norway was *About the Old Norwegian Kings* by Theodoricus Monachus.

When the old royal house became extinct in the 14th century, and Norway later was united with Denmark, the fellowship in culture between Norway and her colony Iceland ceased, and the upper classes gradually acquired a Danish and North German stamp of culture. In this period, preceding the Lutheran Reformation of the 16th century, the old literary language of Norway was broken up into dialects; the ballads, folk stories, and fairy tales produced were not reduced to writing, but were handed down from generation to generation until they were printed in the 19th century.

After the Reformation the writers of Norway used the Danish language. This Dano-Norwegian period lasted until the two countries separated in 1814. The most prominent name in this period is that of the Norwegian Ludvig Holberg (1684–1754). He produced excellent historical works and his comedies are immortal. He is a representative of the farseeing and liberal men of his times.

After the separation from Denmark, Norway declared her independence and adopted a constitution, May 17, 1814. In a general way, it may be said that the great literary men Norway has produced in the 19th century have served the historical mission of making the two fundamental principles of the constitution a reality: national independence and democracy.

Henrik Wergeland (1808–45), the most beloved and honored of all Norwegian writers, was the very embodiment of the aspirations of the rejuvenated nation. No Scandinavian has written more beautiful, more strongly felt, more powerfully conceived, or more luxuriously formed, lyrics. But, because so much of his verse is well-nigh untranslatable, his fame has not spread as that of some other writers of his country. The poetry of his contemporary, Welhaven, is harmonious and perfect in form and shows the reflection of a more critical nature. The central figure in the succeeding period is the historian, P. A. Munch, whose monumental work is *The History of the Norwegian People.* Around him are arrayed many talented men who brought into the light of day the hidden treasures of national poetry, music, and dialects. Most important were the fairy tales, edited by Asbjörnsen and Moe, fresh and full of humor, truly reflecting the national character, creating a new style and infusing new life into the language. Out of the dialects, descendants of the old Norwegian language, Aasen created the idiom called *Landsmaal,* which he himself used for literary work, and in which he was later succeeded by such masters as Vinje, Garborg, and others. At this period appeared Wergeland's famous sister, Camilla Collett, whose *The Governor's Daughters* made her the leader of the woman's emancipation movement.

With the appearance of Björnson (1832–1910) and Ibsen (1828–1906), comes the great era of Norwegian literature. From Björnson's *Synnöve Solbakken* (1857) until the end of the century, the Norwegians took the lead in Scandinavian literature, and many of their works, through translations, became known throughout the world. Björnson, winner of the Nobel prize in 1903, excelled as poet, story-teller, and dramatist. As an orator he was without a peer in his age. Ibsen became the leading dramatist of the 19th century, and his dramatic technique has been imitated by authors of many lands. Contemporary with these giants of the North were Jonas Lie, whose stories of sea life, of the Northland, and of family life made him very popular; and Alexander Kielland, whose charm and wit at once won the reading public. Of recent authors, the best-known outside of Norway are Knut Hamsun, whose *Growth of the Soil* won the Nobel prize in 1920, and Johan Bojer, the author of *The Great Hunger* and *The Last Viking.* Sigrid Undset, winner of the Nobel prize for 1928, shows remarkable insight into feminine psychology and into the medieval mind.

Other prominent writers are Gunnar Heiberg, Hans Kinck, Nils Kjær, Peter Egge, Olav Duun, Sigurd W. Christiansen; among women writers, Barbra Ring and Nini R. Anker; and the poets Th. Caspari, N. C. Vogt, Olaf Bull, H. Wildenwey

TABLE OF NORWEGIAN LITERATURE

Authors		Representative Works	
Time	Name	Prose	Poetry and Drama
800?–?	Bragi Boddason		Poem on Ragnar's Shield.
850–933	Harold Haarfagre		Poem on Snefrid.
9th Century	Thorbjörn Hornklovi		Poem on King Harold.
9th Century	Thjodolf of Hvin		Ynglingatal, Genealogy of Royal Family.
910–995	Eyvind Finnson Skaldaspillir		Poem on Hakon the Good.
1200–?	Anonymous	King's Mirror	
1545–1623	Peder Clausen (Friis)	Description of Norway	
1647–1708	Petter Dass		Poems (Northland's Trumpet).
1684–1754	Ludvig Holberg	History, Philosophy	Comedies, Comic Poetry.
1722–1780	Gerhard Schöning	History of Norway	
1728–1780	C. B. Tullin		Poems.
1742–1785	J. H. Wessel		Lyrics, Play (Love without Stockings).
1746–1791	Claus Fasting		Poems.
1749–1794	Edv. Storm		Poems.
1751–1833	Niels Treschow	Philosophy	
1792–1842	H. A. Bjerregaard		Dramas, Poems (Sons of Norway).
1794–1842	M. C. Hansen	Novels	
1802–1880	M. B. Landstad		Hymn Book, Ballads.
1803–1864	R. Keyser	History	
1807–1873	J. S. C. Welhaven		Poems (The Dawn of Norway).
1808–1845	H. A. Wergeland		Patriotic Poems, Dramas.
1810–1863	P. A. Munch	History (Scandinavian)	
1811–1884	A. Munch		Lyrics, Translations, Dramas.
1812–1885	Peter Asbjörnsen	Folk Tales	
1813–1882	J. I. Moe	Folk Tales	Poems, Lyrics.
1813–1895	Camilla Collett	Novels, Essays	
1813–1896	Ivar Aasen	Philology	Dramas, Poems.
1818–1870	A. O. Vinje	Journalism	Lyrics.
1828–1906	Henrik Ibsen		Dramas (A Doll's House), Poems.
1832–1910	B. Björnson	Novels	Dramas (Sigurd Slembe), Lyrics.
1833–1908	Jonas Lie	Novels	
1835–1917	J. E. Sars	History, Essays	
1849–1906	Alexander Kielland	Novels	
1851–1924	Arne Garborg	Novels	Lyrics.
1856–1925	Gerhart Gran	Literary Criticism, Essays	
1859–	Knut Hamsun	Novels (Growth of the Soil)	
1869–	Peter Egge	Novels (Hansine Solstad)	
1872–	Johan Bojer	Novels (The Great Hunger)	
1876–1939	Olav Duun	Novels (The People of Juvik)	
1882–	Sigrid Undset	Novels (Kristin Lavransdatter)	
1891–	Sigurd W. Christiansen	Novels (Two Living and one Dead)	

SWEDISH LITERATURE

Traces of ancient Swedish literature are very rare and consist principally of inscriptions on the rune stones. There are about 2000 of these in Sweden, the oldest from the 6th century, the majority belonging to the period of transition from paganism to Christianity. Some of the inscriptions are in alliterative versification, the most famous being *Rökstenen,* the longest known in the world, consisting of 750 runes.

The oldest of the written provincial laws is the *Västgöta Law,* "Westgothian Law," from the beginning of the 13th century. St. Bridget (1302–73) is the most eminent Swedish author of the middle ages; her *Revelations,* first written in Swedish, then translated into Latin, are distinguished by glowing fancy and imagery. The purest national poetry of medieval times consists of what we call national ballads, which have survived on the lips of the people to the present day.

The greatest name of the time of the Reformation is that of Olaus Petri (1497–1552), a personal disciple of Luther. All his writings are marked by a powerful genius, and his style bears the stamp of simplicity coupled with erudition and an exceptionally keen insight. After the Thirty Years' War, poetry for the first time became an art with patriotic aims, and not merely a handmaid of religion. Stiernhielm (1598–1672) is the most prominent author of the 17th century. Efforts were made to prove that the ancient history of Sweden could be traced as far back as that of any other nation, or still further. O. Rudbeck (1630–1702) has given a good expression of these ideas in his brilliant and learned though fantastic *Atland.*

In the Period of Liberty, after the fall of Charles XII, scientific interests were uppermost. It is the age of Linnæus and Scheele. In literature the principal name is O. von Dalin (1708–63), pre-eminent because of his prose style and because he opened the way for the ideas of the Age of Enlightenment.

K. M. Bellman (1740–95) is the most original and perhaps the greatest of Sweden's poets and is entirely national. He has especially an eye for the beauties of nature, and he has depicted the scenery around Stockholm as no other poet has. French influence reached its climax during the reign of Gustavus III (1771–92). With the French Academy as a model, the king founded the Swedish Academy, now awarding the Nobel literary prize. Gustavus himself took a great interest in the drama. Kellgren is, side by side with the king, the most typical representative of the period. His contemporaries were K. G. Leopold and Anna M. Lenngren.

T. Thorild (1759–1808) was a follower of Rousseau and advocated the rights of feeling and of nature. J. O. Wallin (1779–1839) is the greatest hymnologist of the country.

After the revolution of 1809 and the loss of Finland, the Romantic school appears. Atterbom's *The Island of Felicity* is one of the most beautiful works created by Romanticism. Other writers are Stagnelius and Sjöberg. The men through whom Swedish literature attained almost classical perfection were Esaias Tegnér (1782–1846) and E. G. Geijer (1783–1847). Geijer's poems are not numerous, but possess a manly and national ring. He was also a philosopher and composer and is above all the greatest historian of Sweden. The best-known of Tegnér's works is his lyrical epic *Frithjof's Saga,* which has been translated by some fifty different hands into eleven foreign languages. Almqvist (1793–1866) is an exponent of Romanticism in a state of dissolution. His chief literary works are the two collections called *The Book of the Thorn Rose.*

In the following age of Liberalism, several noted names appear in literature: Sturzen-Becker is the finest and most brilliant Swedish publicist; Blanche is known by his comedies and novels; Strandberg was a great lyric poet and a distinguished translator; Malmström produced poems born of patriotism and ancient classical studies; Witterbergh wrote short, highly appreciated sketches.

The realistic tendencies of the age found expression in the ever-increasing predominance of prose in literature. Fredrika Bremer (1801–65) wrote many novels, advanced the emancipation of women, and gained fame outside of Sweden. A very popular novelist was Emilie Flygare-Carlén (1807–92). Living in Finland but of Swedish descent was the great writer, J. L. Runeberg (1804–77). His most famous work is *The Tales of Ensign Stål.* Another Finnish writer using the Swedish language was Topelius (1818–98), whose *The Surgeon's Tales* is extremely popular.

In the middle of the 19th century, Viktor Rydberg (1829–95) gradually obtained the position of intellectual leader in modern Swedish literature. His contemporaries were the lyrical poets, Count Snoilsky and C. D. af Wirsén. The greatest name afterward is that of August Strindberg (1849–1912), a genius of extraordinary dimensions and overwhelming production. He is Sweden's greatest dramatist, but he produced great works in many other fields. Geijerstam (1858–1909) portrayed the life of the peasantry and the middle classes in a fresh and good-natured style and also wrote comedies. Heidenstam produced *Karolinerna,* "The Heroes of Charles XII," inspired by love of nation and the history of Sweden. G. Fröding (1860–1911) showed a masterly handling of rimes and meters and was as great a poet as was Bellman. The foremost of all recent Swedish authors is Selma Lagerlöf (1858–1940), who won the Nobel prize in 1909. Ellen Key (1849–1926) aroused attention by her treatment of social problems. Others are Gellerstedt, Österling, Karlfeld, F. Hedberg, T. Hedberg, Ossiannilsson. Very popular in most recent times is the dialect literature. Among authors cultivating this style are Dahlgren and Bondeson.

TABLE OF SWEDISH LITERATURE

Authors		Representative Works	
Time	Name	Prose	Poetry and Drama
1302–1373	St. Bridget (Birgitta) . . .	"Revelations"	
–1484	Johannes Budde.	Translation of Bible	
1497–1552	Olaus Petri	Chronicle of Swedish History, Religious Works, History . .	Hymns.
1499–1573	Laurentius Petri	. . . .	Psalms.
1579–1636	Johannes Messenius . . .	History of Sweden	Poems, Lyrics.
1594–1632	Gustavus Adolphus . . .	Speeches, History	Hymns.
1598–1672	Georg Stiernhielm	Works on Language and Mathematics	Masques, Poems.
1605–1669	Lars Wivallius	. . . .	Lyrics.
1688–1772	Emanuel Swedenborg . . .	Philosophy	
1707–1778	Karl von Linné (Linnæus) .	Botany, Travels	
1707–1787	Sven Lagerbring	History of Sweden	
1708–1763	Olof (von) Dalin	History of Sweden, Journalism, Swedish Freedom	Poems, Dramas.
1714–1763	Jakob Henrik Mörk . . .	Novels	

TABLE OF SWEDISH LITERATURE—Con.

Authors		Representative Works	
Time	Name	Prose	Poetry and Drama
1718–1763	Charlotta Nordenflycht		Lyrics.
1731–1785	Gustav Filip Creutz		Poems.
1731–1808	G. F. Gyllenborg		Poems.
1740–1795	Karl M. Bellman		Odes, Lyrics, Songs.
1751–1795	J. H. Kellgren	Journalism	Poems.
1754–1817	Anna Maria Lenngren		Household Poems.
1759–1808	Thomas Thorild	Criticism	
1772–1847	Frans Franzén		Lyrics, Hymns.
1779–1839	Johan Olof Wallin		Hymns.
1782–1846	Esaias Tegnér	Speeches	Poems (Frithjof's Saga).
1783–1847	Erik Gustaf Geijer	History, Philology	Poems.
1789–1877	Gustav W. Gumaelius	Historical Novels	
1791–1844	K. F. Dahlgren	Novels, Short Stories	Poems.
1793–1823	E. J. Stagnelius		Dramas, Lyrics, Sonnets.
1793–1866	K. J. L. Almqvist	Novels (Thorn Rose), Essays	Poems.
1795–1881	Anders Fryxell	History	
1800–1877	Per Wieselgren	History of Swedish Literature	
1801–1865	Fredrika Bremer	Novels	
1804–1877	J. L. Runeberg		Poems, Dramas.
1811–1868	August Blanche	Novels, Short Stories, Sketches	Comedy.
1818–1898	Zakarias Topelius	Historical Novels	
1829–1895	Viktor Rydberg	Historical Novels, Philosophy, Mythology, History	Poems.
1829–1907	King Oscar II	Criticism	Poems.
1841–1903	Karl Snoilsky		Poems.
1849–1912	August Strindberg	Novels, Short Stories	Dramas (The Father), Lyrics.
1858–1940	Selma Lagerlöf	Novels, Tales (Wonderful Adventures of Nils)	
1859–1940	V. von Heidenstam	Novels, Essays, Short Stories	Poems.
1860–1911	Gustav Fröding		Lyrics.
1862–1906	Oskar Levertin	Short Stories, Essays	Poems.
1866–	Per Hallstrom	Novels, Short Stories	Lyrics, Dramas.

ICELANDIC LITERATURE

The Icelandic literature is a continuation of the Old Norwegian literature. Most of the poems of the *Edda* were composed in Norway, but they were preserved in Iceland, where the art of poetry flourished after it had all but disappeared from Norway. The Icelandic scalds, or poets, were welcomed at the courts of the British Isles and in the Scandinavian countries. In honor of the princes and chieftains, they composed poems and songs, which are now of historic as well as of poetic value. The first great Icelandic poet is Egil Skallagrimson (about 900). He was both poet and warrior. Glum Geirason was the first poet at the court of the Norwegian king (10th century), and from that time on practically all of the poets at the royal court are Icelanders. Many of them are prominent. Most famous is Sigvat Tordson, a friend of St. Olaf and his son Magnus the Good.

The first historical saga is Are Frode's *Islendingabok* (beginning of 12th century). Soon after follows *Landnamabok*, which tells about the settlement of Iceland. This is succeeded by a long series of family sagas. These, for the most part, tell of persons and events in the period from the first settlement of the island until about the year 1030. The most important are *Egil's Saga*, *Gunlaug's Saga*, *Laxdölasaga*, *Vatsdölasaga*, *Njal's Saga*. The series ends with the very comprehensive *Sturlungasaga*. Another series deals with the history of Norway: *Morkinskinna*, "Rotten-skin" (so called from the appearance of the manuscripts), *Fagrskinna*, "Fairskin" (the Icelandic authors of which are unknown), and Snorre's famous *Sagas of the Kings of Norway* (to 1177), often called "Heimskringla" from the first words in the original text. Snorre is the greatest writer among the Icelanders. Abbot Jonson wrote *Sverri's Saga*; Sturla Tordson, *Hakonarsaga*. In connection with these there are historical descriptions of the Faroe islands, the Orkney islands, Greenland—all old Norwegian settlements—and Denmark. In addition to these, sagas which were mostly fiction were written. Best-known among these are *Frithjof's Saga* and the *Volsung Saga*. From this period (1100–1300) is also Snorre's *Edda*—the *Younger* or *Prose Edda*—dealing with mythology and the art of poetry.

In the following period (1300–1550), the day of the old scald, or bard, is passed. A new form of narratives in verse form, called *rimur*, arises, taking its material from the earlier sagas and the *Eddas*. Religious poetry has several notable representatives, the most important of whom are Eysteinn Asgrimson, the author of *Lilja*, and Jon Arason, the last Catholic bishop, who was executed in 1550.

With the introduction of the Lutheran Reformation, the last remnants of political independence in Iceland are lost, and, as far as literature is concerned, the following period (1550–1780) is one of even greater decline than the preceding period. Of outstanding writers there are only few. Reverend Hallgrimur Pjetursson has become famous because of his hymns. After 1600 there is a revival of interest in the early history and literature of Iceland, and a number of learned works in Latin, dealing with these subjects, were produced. Best known among the men of this period is Professor Arni Magnusson, who made a large collection of manuscripts, which he presented to the University of Copenhagen.

It is only from about 1830 that one can speak of a real revival of Icelandic literature. The famous Dane, Rasmus Rask, one of the world's greatest philologists, had been a great influence in awakening the new interest. Four prominent Icelanders started a new periodical whose object was to purify the language, elevate the literature, and arouse the national sentiment. Hallgrimsson's beautiful poem *Island*, "Iceland," may be said to contain the program of the new movement. A number of poets produced lyric poetry, some have excelled as writers of novels, and in most recent times powerful dramas have been produced by Icelanders. Of poets who made their home in America, the best-known name is that of Stephan G. Stephansson. Jon Sigurdsson, most beloved of Icelanders in recent times and the champion of Icelandic independence, which was finally won in 1918, has written much on politics and history. Björn Olsen became the first president of the Icelandic university at Reykjavik (established 1911); Gudbrandur Vigfusson has done much to acquaint the English-speaking world with Iceland; Professor Finnur Jonsson of the University of Copenhagen, besides being a very learned philologist, has written the most important works on Icelandic literature.

RUSSIAN LITERATURE

Russia, the vague territory known to the ancients as the land of wandering Scythian tribes and the Hyperboreans, enters the pale of history in the 9th century. Rurik, a Norse chieftain of the same group of adventurers who were making new homes for themselves in France and England, came to Novgorod. At the invitation of the people, who were beset by neighboring enemy tribes, he established himself as prince. Out of this dim period of tribal warfare, there has come down to us only oral tradition in the form of *skazki* (prose folk tales) and *byliny* (tales of old time).

Early Folk Tales. There was no writing in the Russian language before the time of Peter the Great. A few of the byliny, which are rude, epic songs depending for rhythm upon a certain cadence and the endless repetition of stock figurative phrases, were first written down by an Oxford scholar who in the early 17th century was secretary of legation in Russia. A Cossack writer made another collection early in the 18th century, and the romantic interest in common life and tradition prompted the publication of this in the year 1800. These songs reflect native Russian history and beliefs as well as some foreign elements. They cover in all a long period, some of the latest dealing with Napoleon.

Differences of subject matter and locality, as well as of time, mark off several distinct groups of stories. (1) The earliest of them, belonging to the period before 1000 A. D., represent a nature mythology, the characters depicted being monstrous creatures, such as the Giant of the Mountain and Gorinich, a serpent who guards metals in caves of the earth. Other more human characters are Pagan Idol, a glutton, and Nightingale, the robber, who has a nest in six oaks and is the terror of travelers. (2) Kiev, one of the most famous and beautiful of medieval cities, and her great prince, Vladimir, of the 10th century, are the center of a large group of these byliny, in which one of the main characters is Ilya Muromets, a giant who performs prodigies of valor. (3) A third group of stories arose around the northern merchant republic of Novgorod. In these, the adventures of Sadko, a rich merchant, figure largely. (4) Another group of tales reflects the Tatar conquest and the transfer of the government to Moscow. (5) The Cossack group pictures with vigorous realism the life of the times and the surrender of the Cossack republic to the czars, and tales about the exploits of Peter the Great are numerous. In addition to the phases of life embodied in these tales, the beliefs and religious customs of the middle ages in Russia are reflected in a large number of religious poems that have been preserved in various collections.

Slavic Writings. With the introduction of the Greek Church into Russia through the conversion of Vladimir of Kiev in the 10th century, the old church Slavic (a Bulgarian language) came into use for the liturgy. Very soon this imported language was used for all official and literary purposes. From this period and from the following centuries, we have numerous sermons, lives of the saints, accounts of pilgrimages, some real and some imagined, and a great variety of books of instruction, as well as some romances and chronicles, such as the *Chronicle of Kiev*. An edition of the Slavonic Gospels dates from the years 1056-57. Hilarion's discourse concerning the Old and New Testaments is a famous piece of medieval writing. The *Chronicle of Kiev* becomes more than a dry record of events through its sprinkling of picturesque incidents and quaint stories of daily life and adventure. The most interesting of these productions, however, is the story of the Raid of Igor, a 12th century epic, which recounts the expedition of Prince Igor of Novgorod against his troublesome neighbors, the Polovtzes. This was first published in the year 1800.

The period from the 13th century to the middle of the 17th is the time of Tatar supremacy. Under a pernicious Oriental tyranny in Moscow, literature and learning as well as piety and morality disappeared. During this time, Kiev was united with the kingdom of Lithuania and became a center of learning from which scholars and teachers afterward went into Russia. Reform began in the middle of the 17th century with Simeon Pólotsky of Kiev, the pioneer of modern culture and the first Russian versifier. His writings include secular as well as religious subjects, with several religious plays which he composed in his attempt to introduce Western culture as he knew it. The first Russian theater was opened in 1674, and the first newspaper was issued in manuscript shortly after this date.

Royal Patronage of Letters. Peter the Great, who came to the throne in 1689, undertook, in connection with all his other radical reforms, to modernize and purify the Russian language. In this task he had the assistance of Bishop Prokopovitch, a very learned and politic scholar. The most important work in this reform of the language was done by Lomonósov in the early 18th century. He wrote extensively upon grammar, rhetoric, and versification, besides producing some original verse and prose. A remarkable work was produced in this time by a peasant, Pososhkóv, entitled *Poverty and Riches*. Pososhkóv may be called the Russian Adam Smith.

The latter part of the 18th century in Russia was a period of French influence, especially during the reign of Catherine II (1762–96), who herself wrote much. Catherine gathered around her a group of poets, mediocre for the most part, whom she exhorted to imitation of the classics, especially Ovid and Virgil, but whose real models were the French pseudo-classicists. To her court she invited many French scholars and writers who, because of their liberal ideas, were threatened in their own country. This classical influence, however, was not in harmony with Russian genius and soon passed away before the coming of the Romantic movement.

Sumarókov deserves an important place in the early history of literature in Russia. His writings were of various kinds, but he was most successful in the drama, both prose and verse. He was made director of the first theater opened in Petrograd in the year 1766, just a year after the founding of the University of Moscow. Before this time only religious plays had been permitted, but Sumarókov both wrote and produced in the theater work after the style of Racine, Corneille, and Voltaire. Other members of Catherine's court circle were Denis von Visin, who produced a real national comedy keenly satirizing Russian life, especially the treatment of the serfs, and Gabriel Derzhávin, who has been called Catherine's poet laureate, and whose poems, "Ode to God," "The Nobleman," and "The Taking of Warsaw," are well known.

But, in spite of her encouragement of these men of letters, Catherine held a tight rein upon real literary development, fearing the spread of modern ideas among the people. In a small book entitled *A Journey to St. Petersburg and Moscow*, Alexander Radístchev was unfortunate enough to criticize severely the treatment of the serfs. So he was banished to Siberia. Nicholas Nóvikov was an enthusiastic and hard-working journalist who did much for education in Russia, but he too overstepped the bounds that Catherine thought proper, and she put him in prison.

Karamzín, under the reign of Alexander I (1801–25), was more fortunate in his opportunity. He refined the Russian language and developed a reading public in Russia through his writings on history and travel, and by his fiction and translations.

Translation from Western languages was in this time an important contribution to Russia. Vasilii Zhukóvsky translated numerous works from the English, including poems by Gray and Byron. Out of the German he translated selections from

Goethe and Schiller, and he also rendered into Russian some German translations from the Indian *Mahabharata* and the Persian *Shah Nameh.* Through these translations the Romantic movement, which was dominant elsewhere in Europe in the early years of the 19th century, came into Russia, but, like the classical influence, it soon disappeared before the rise of the peculiarly Russian realistic style. Alexander Púshkin (1799–1837) in his short life made good his title to the place that has been assigned him as the father of Russian literature. He first truly expressed the Russian spirit, drawing upon Russian antiquity and legends for subject matter, as in his verse novel *Eugene Onegin*, probably his greatest work. Ivan Kozlóv translated Burns's "Cottar's Saturday Night." He is sometimes called the Russian Burns because of his expression of the peasant life of Russia in his own poetry.

The Novel and the Drama. The greatest work of Russian writers has been in the field of the novel. Russia may be said to have contributed to the world's literature the realistic method in prose fiction, and it is notable that this development took place within a very few years after 1840. There is in Russian prose literature no such long development as is to be seen in the history of either English or French prose. The first of the Russian novelists is Nikolai Gógol. His *Taras Bulba* is a story of the Cossack and Polish wars; his other masterpiece, *Dead Souls*, which he did not live to finish, is a vivid realistic picture of the peasant life of Russia and a bitter satire upon the official class.

Some critics give the highest place in Russian literature to Ivan Turgéniev. His work, which began with a volume of short stories, entitled *A Sportsman's Sketches*, depicting life on the great estates, furnishes an unsurpassed record of the Russian life of his time, and his prose in style and structure is unequaled among Russian writers. Dostoiévsky is the greatest psychological novelist of Russia. Probably his masterpiece is *Crime and Punishment*, a work which grew out of his experiences during his period of imprisonment and exile in Siberia. His analysis of character is very skillful, but he is rough in point of style. Count Liov Tolstóy is recognized as a great genius in various fields. He became famous in the last two decades of the 19th century for his social and religious opinions, which led him to adopt a life of asceticism. His *Anna Karenina* and *War and Peace* rank among the world's masterpieces of fiction. In recent years the folk life of the lower classes in Russia has been portrayed in a masterly fashion in the stories of Grigoróvitch and "Maxim Gorky."

The Russian drama, although not so important as the novel, has had a remarkable development since the work of Sumarókov in the 18th century. *The Woes of Wit* by Griboiédov and *The Inspector General* by Gógol are still reckoned as the greatest Russian comedies, though the greatest dramatist is Ostróvsky. His masterpieces are *Poverty Is No Vice* and *The Thunderstorm.* Anton Chékov is famous as a writer of both comedies and short stories, particularly the latter. *The Cherry Orchard* probably represents his best work in the drama. His numerous stories are crowded with brilliantly drawn characters from humble life. The short story has been developed notably in recent years by "Gorky" (Alexei Pyéshkov), Andréiev, and Chékov. They have influenced Western short story writing in both form and matter.

But the Russian short story, while it is powerful in its condensation and realism, is frequently a closed field to the foreign reader whose insight into Russian life and character is too limited. This difficulty, however, is obviated in proportion as the reader realizes that in Russian literature, as in no other, there is a deep sense of seriousness and social purpose. To an American, a novel is a novel, intended to amuse, seldom to instruct or to arouse. To a Russian, literature is a social instrument, one of the few he had in the old days, whose purpose, beneath all its art and power. was to solidify social purpose and desire.

The Bolshevist revolution of 1918 and its aftermath divided Russian writers into two hostile groups,—those who remained in Russia and those who took refuge abroad. Of those who, like Gorky, remained in Russia, Sergei Esenin (1895–1925) was a poet with a wide appeal to the intelligensia. The greatest among the exiles was Ivan Bunin, whose tales of peasant life, of young love, and of the Orient were honored by an award of the Nobel prize.

Bunin was an exception among the writers who divided violently in their reaction to the revolution. Neither in subject nor spirit do his works reveal any response to the storm which swept over his country and which left literature largely a handmaid to the official rulers. One consequence of this change was that sincere literature reflecting personal experience could be published only outside the country and probably did less than justice to those who sought to remake a society on new lines.

TABLE OF RUSSIAN LITERATURE

Authors		Representative Works	
Time	Name	Prose	Poetry and Drama
900–1200	Numerous	Annals	
About 1200	Unknown		Lay of Igor's Raid.
1629–1680	Pólotsky		Mystery Drama.
1712–1765	Lomonósov	Science, Philosophy, History	Odes.
1718–1777	Sumarókov		Poems, Fables.
1743–1816	Derzhávin		Poems.
1744–1818	Nóvikov	Essays, Philosophy	
1749–1802	Radístchev	Political Essays	
1766–1826	Karamzín	Historical Novels	
1768–1844	Krylóv		Fables.
1779–1840	Kozlóv		Poems, Translations.
1783–1852	Zhukóvsky		Poems, Translations.
1795–1829	Griboiédov		Drama.
1799–1837	Púshkin	Novels	Odes, Lyrics, Drama.
1809–1852	Gógol	Novels, Satire	Comedies.
1814–1841	Lérmontov	Novels, History	Nature Poetry, Odes, Drama.
1817–1875	A. K. Tolstóy		Poems, Drama.
1818–1883	Turgéniev	Novels, Sketches	Comedies.
1821-1877	Nekrásov	Essays	Poems.
1821–1883	Dostoiévsky	Novels, Essays	
1823–1886	Ostróvsky		Comedies, Tragedy.
1828–1910	L. N. Tolstóy	Novels, Tales, Essays, Criticism	Poems, Drama.
1860–1904	Chékov	Short Stories, Sketches, Novels	Plays.
1865–1941	Merezhkóvsky	Criticism, Novels, Essays	Poems.
1868–1936	"Gorky"	Tales, Short Stories	Poems, Plays.
1870-	Ivan Bunin	Novels (The Grammar of Love)	Poems.
1871–1919	Andréiev	Short Stories, Tales	Plays.

POLISH LITERATURE

The language of Poland belongs to the Western family of Slavic tongues and possesses the same pliancy and power of composition as does the Russian. It has preserved certain nasal sounds which are traceable to the Paleo-Slavonic, once the language of the Polish Church, but now extinct.

Of Polish literature before the advent of Christianity (965), but few fragments have been left to us. Chroniclers, such as Gallus, Kadlubek, and Boguchwal, appearing between the 12th and 13th centuries, wrote in Latin. However, we have a version of the Psalms in Polish dating from 1292 and also a manuscript copy of the Psalter, known as that of Queen Margaret, belonging to the 14th century.

The Renaissance. The University of Cracow, which had its origin in the famous academy founded by Casimir the Great in the year 1400, attracted many students within its walls. A great number of young Poles also went abroad to foreign universities, returning later as humanists and pioneers of the Renaissance.

As a consequence of this development of national intellectual life, the Polish language superseded the Latin tongue in literary usage. A printing press was established at Cracow in 1474, and the first book printed in Polish was *The Sayings of the Wise King Solomon.* Other books—translations, paraphrases, versions of the Bible—now followed in rapid succession. The influence of Italian culture was notably nurtured under the patronage of Queen Bona, and many young writers like Modrzewski, Rey, and Orzechowski sprang into fame.

Poland's Golden Age. The period between 1548 and 1600 is known as the golden age of Polish literature. Jan Kochanowski (1530–84), called the prince of Polish poets, in 1557 wrote the first of his poems which for beauty and tenderness have never been surpassed save perhaps by those of Mickiewicz. Especially notable are his *Lamentations* on the death of his daughter Ursula. Two other writers, Rey and Bielski, wrote didactic poems and satires of considerable merit. Peter Skarga, a Jesuit (1536–1612), the embodiment of all that is pure in Polish patriotism, by the fiery intensity and clarity of his style in preaching and in writing, did much to enhance the literature of his country.

Decadence. After the beginning of the 17th century, a decadence in Polish literature became evident. The period between 1606 and 1764 has been styled *macaronic,* owing to the fashion, in vogue among writers, of introducing Latin words into their compositions. At best, it was a period of imitation when poets who affected the style of Jan Kochanowski mistook imitation for inspiration. The writers of this time certainly lacked originality, though the name of Potocki (1622–96) should be excepted for his *War of Chocim,* and that of Kochowski (1633–99), for many spirited odes instinct with true patriotic feeling.

Polish literature may now be said to have reached its lowest ebb, and, between the years 1696 and 1763, but few writers can lay claim to any distinction. Among the few may be mentioned Druzbacka (1695–1760), the first Polish authoress, who wrote many poems showing both grace and depth of feeling. With her name may be coupled those of Krasicki (1735–1801), called the Alexander Pope of his period, and Trembecki (1722–1812), whose writings are marked by wit, humor, and clearness of style.

The Nineteenth Century. The period of the last division of Poland (1796–1822) saw a vigorous revival of the native literature. The instinct of national self-preservation prompted a united effort to save the language from obloquy and destruction. Such effort, fostered by the Society of the Friends of Learning at Warsaw, resulted in a glorious achievement for Polish literature. The first promulgator of the Romantic movement was Kasimir Brodzinski (1791–1835), author of the idyl *Wieslau.* Following him came Adam Mickiewicz (1798–1855), the sublimest of all Polish poets, from whom the Romantic period rightly takes its name.

With Mickiewicz, Slowacki (1809–49) and Krasiński (1812–59) form a transcendent trio of lyric and idyllic writers. Alexandro Fredo (1793–1876) appeared as a writer of successful comedies. His work was characterized by purity of style and strong dramatic quality. Another popular playwright of this period was Zablocki, noted as a writer of comedy and satire.

Among numerous poets writing since the middle of the 19th century, Adam Asnyk (1838–97) and Marya Konopnicka are two of the most notable. The outstanding master of prose fiction of recent times was Henryk Sienkiewicz (1846–1916), famous for his *Quo Vadis* and for his great trilogy of Polish history, *With Fire and Sword.* Glowacki (1847–1912), under the pen name of "Boleslaw Prus," was a writer of romances, notably *The Outpost* and *The Doll.* Wladislaw Reymont (1868–1925), a writer of the realistic school, is known especially as the author of *The Peasants,* which has been translated into English, French, and German.

Such is a brief outline of Polish literature, in which may be seen the admirable perseverance with which it has striven to preserve its integrity and to attain to still higher and nobler ideals of development. In such an endeavor Poland has given to the world a proof of its full comprehension of the meaning of Christian civilization.

CZECH (BOHEMIAN) LITERATURE

The Czech language was the first of the Slavonic tongues to be developed scientifically. The earliest literary impulse came with the introduction of Christianity into Moravia and Bohemia by Cyril and Methodius in 863. With the exception of the Bulgarian, Czech is the oldest among all Slav literatures and, until the 17th century, was the richest and most copious. Cyril adapted the characters of the Greek alphabet to the demands of the Czech speech and originated what is known as the Cyrillic alphabet. For a long period, however, the influence of the Latin churchmen gave Latin precedence over the native language. Literary remains from the period before the 14th century include various chronicles and a few national songs. The famous Reims Gospel is said to date from the 11th or 12th century; what is known as the newer part of it, however, was written in 1395 and is the only remnant of Old Slavonic extant. The church song *Hospodine pomiluj ny,* "Lord, have mercy," belongs to the 11th century and is the most precious relic of this period,—unsurpassed save by the beautiful hymn in honor of St. Wenceslas.

The Awakening. About the year 1250, through the crusaders and wandering minstrels from the Western lands, Bohemia came into touch with the manners and customs of the world outside her boundaries. Crusaders' tales of the East and troubadours' songs of chivalry and knightly adventure profoundly influenced the Bohemian spirit and imagination. The *Book of Marco Polo* and the *Travels of John Mandeville* were translated, and an adaptation of the *Alexandreis* of Walter de Chatillon testifies to the eager rendering of episodes from the Alexandrian and Arthurian cycles of romance. Original didactic and satirical poems also characterize this period. Under the emperor Charles I the use of the Bohemian language was encouraged. In 1348 the University of Prague, the first institution for higher learning in central Europe, was founded, and in a short time it became one of the most noted establishments of learning and culture in the whole continent.

The Reformation Period. The period from 1410 to 1620 is looked upon as the greatest age of Czech literature. The era opened with religious discussion which gave rise to sermons and controversial prose, as well as to translations of the Bible. John Huss (1370?–1415), a thorough Latin scholar, used the Bohemian language for writings designed to reach the people. He employed the dialect of Prague and its surrounding territory. In addition to his sermons, addresses, and letters, Huss composed and translated many beautiful hymns. To his genius and scholarship is due also the present system of accents used with the Czech vowels and consonants.

The schools of learning were at this period thrown open to all classes in Bohemia, as was the case in but few other countries. A group of brilliant writers belonging to the Bohemian Brethren appeared (about 1457) and added a new luster to the native literature. Printing was introduced in 1468, the *Trojan Chronicle* being the first book printed. In the 15th and 16th centuries many translations were made from Latin and Greek. The first printed Bible appeared in 1488. The Kralická Bible, translated from the original Hebrew and Greek languages, under the supervision of Jan Blahoslav, and published 1579–93, took in Bohemia a place similar to that held in England by the King James Version. In the 17th century, Bishop Jan Komenský, better known as Comenius (1592–1670), attracted international attention by his writings on education. His masterpiece, *The Labyrinth of the World and the Paradise of the Heart*, was a forerunner of *Pilgrim's Progress*. He prepared also the *World in Pictures*, probably the first illustrated textbook ever published for children.

Decline and Revival. The year 1620, notable in Bohemian history for the battle of the White Mountain, saw the end of this glorious development in Czech literature. A period of decadence, occasioned by the desolation of Bohemia in the Thirty Years' War, continued until about 1774. The German language came to be in the ascendant for official and school use. Not a single literary work of any particular merit appeared in Bohemia during the 17th century. However, near the close of the reign of the emperor Joseph II, Bohemian writers were again encouraged. The Bohemian Society of Sciences was established, and the emperor founded professorships of the Czech language in the universities of Vienna and Prague. Joseph Jungmann, leader of a group of national poets, translated *Paradise Lost*, in addition to his renderings of Goldsmith, Pope, Goethe, and many other Western writers.

The Nineteenth Century. The years from 1820 to 1848 form a period of brilliant activity. In poetry, the two greatest names are Kollar, author of *The Daughter of Slava*, a collection of poems in praise of Slavic life and speech, and Čelakovský (1799–1852), a diligent collector of folk songs and a popular writer of lyric and epic verse.

After 1848 a rich revival of Czech literature took place. The impulse of this movement has been continued to the present day in the production of a strong and varied literature. Karel Havlichek, in journalism, and Ján Néruda and Vitezslav Hálek (1835–74), in poetry, were leaders in the first enthusiastic years of the new era. In the field of the drama, Joseph Jiri Kolar was the first Czech to translate and stage Shakspere's plays. He followed this work with popular original dramas.

Jaroslav Vrchlický (1853-1912) is recognized as the most versatile and prolific of modern Czech writers, having to his credit no less than 67 volumes of original verse, and a vast number of translations from almost every language in Europe. Eliska Krasnohorska has long been a leader in the modern women's educational movements, and is a skillful writer of verse and stories. The foremost historical novelist is Alois Jirasek (1851-1930), who draws his inspiration from the hopes and struggles of his native land.

Among other prominent writers of recent years should be mentioned Karel Rais (1859-1926); Brodsky (b. 1862); Jan Havlasa (b. 1883); and the Bohemian American poet Jan Vránek, of Omaha, Nebraska.

It is a matter of no small interest to note how, in the short space of little more than a century, Czech literature has grown to such dignity of stature, grace, and beauty, that it can today take its place worthily among the literatures of civilized countries. The native of Czechoslovakia certainly owes a debt of lasting gratitude to that small group of patriotic priests and teachers who, in its darkest hour, saved their language from threatened dissolution and became the heralds of its glorious resurrection.

HUNGARIAN (MAGYAR) LITERATURE

The Hungarian language, spoken at the present day by nearly twelve millions of people, is terse, cogent, and full of rich vowel sounds, lending itself readily both to oratory and to serious poetry. Differing essentially from the majority of literary tongues, it belongs to the Ural-Altaic group of languages, in which are included the Lapp, the Finnish, and the Turkish.

Its literary development was long retarded, owing chiefly to the fact that Latin was, up to comparatively recent times, the official language of Hungary. Not until 1840, after a struggle dating from a literary movement begun in 1780 against the Germanizing efforts of Austria, did Hungarian receive official recognition as the dominant language of the country.

Reformation and Counter-Reformation. Before the year 1450, there is little to record of vernacular literature, save a few scanty remnants of the elusive songs of the bards and gypsies who sang in praise of Attila and the Arpáds. Scattered legends of the saints are here and there also to be found. Two of the oldest literary monuments of this era are *Halotti Beszéd*—a funeral oration (1230)—and a hymn to the Virgin dating from 1300. Literary productions during the period between 1570 and 1711 are notably influenced by the spirit both of the Renaissance and of the Reformation as well as imbued with the fiery enthusiasm called forth by Matthew Hunyadi. Impetus too was given to the vernacular literature of this age by the establishment of a printing press at Buda (1473) and the founding of the Pozsony university with the Corvina library. Many controversial writings, spiritual books, and volumes of sermons were the natural outcome of the Reformation. A complete translation, for the first time, of the Protestant Bible by Karolyi appeared in 1589, as did one of the Catholic Bible by Kaldi, a Jesuit, in 1626.

Profane literature in the 16th and 17th centuries is represented by the following writers: Michael Sztarai, who produced the first Hungarian drama, *The Marriage of Priests* (1550); the epic poet and wandering minstrel Tinodi (d. 1557); Balassi, the author of many beautiful lyrics, including the notable *Flower Songs* (1551–94); and Albert Gergei, who wrote the well-known and still popular *Argivius Kiralyfi*. Hungarian literature throughout the 17th century was considerably hampered, owing to the preference affected by Latin Schoolmen and by the upper classes for Italian and French productions. The two outstanding figures in the prose of this epoch are Cardinal Pazmany (1570–1637) and Molnar de Szenick (1574–1634). The publication of an encyclopedia (1655) and that of a dictionary (1708) mark the close of what may be called the Reformation and Counter-Reformation period.

The Modern Revival. After the Peace of Szatmar, 1711, began an age of peaceful development for Hungary. But not until the third quarter of the 18th century is there anything of notable interest in the native literature to be chronicled. In 1772 a revival set in, fostered by the influence of the French Revolution. Journals and periodicals of great repute were founded, and notable establishments arose, such as the Magyar and Classical schools and that known as the Hungarian Guard, which produced many brilliant writers, among others, Kazinczy (1759–1831), Alexander Kisfaludy (1772–1844), and Daniel Berzsenyi (1776–1826)—three poets of the foremost rank.

Modern Hungarian literature owes much in particular to Count Stephen Széchenyi, through whose efforts and inspiration it may be said to have reached its acme of perfection. Through his instrumentality, also, the Academy was founded in 1830 and the National Theater at Pest in 1837. It was the eloquence of Count Széchenyi in Parliament which finally succeeded in banishing Latin from the Hungarian Diet in 1844.

Among a galaxy of brilliant writers, may be mentioned, in particular, Charles Kisfaludy (1788–1830), regarded as founder of the modern Hungarian drama; Vörösmarty, composer of the national hymn, *Szózat*; Petöfi (1823-49), author of *Rise O Magyar*; and John Arany (1817–82), who wrote the *Toldi Trilogy, Flower Fables*, and the humorous poem, *The Lost Constitution.* A few of the more notable novelists are Nicolas Jósika (1796–1865), author of *The Bohemians in Hungary*; Joseph Eötvös (1813-71), who wrote *The Carthusian* and *The Village Notary*; and Mór Jókai (1825–1904), writer of no less than 250 novels, the best of which are *A Hungarian Nabob, Black Diamonds*, and *Love's Fools.*

Katona comes first in order among the dramatists, followed by Szigligeti (1814–78), a writer of folk-plays, Charles Bernstein (1817–77), author of *Banker and Baron*, and Gregory Gsiky (1842–90). The name of Joseph Bajza (1804–58), director of the National Theater, ranks high as that of poet, historian, and critic.

In the 20th century, Hungarian writers were divided into two groups. Of these the so-called traditionalists drew their inspiration from the East, the early home of the Magyar race. The other group, led chiefly by Endré Ady (1877-1919), comprised the moderns, who accepted gladly the industrial, cosmopolitan world of today.

Native periodical literature is fully represented in the United States, where between twenty and thirty periodicals are published in Hungarian. In Canada likewise are published several Hungarian periodicals.

CHINESE LITERATURE

Four important and clearly distinguished epochs should be noticed in the history of Chinese literature. The first is the classical period, distinguished by the work of Confucius (551–478 B. C.) and Mencius (372–289 B. C.) and by that of Lao Tzu (604 B. C.) and Chuang Tzu (330 B. C.).

The Classical Period. Confucius modestly declared that he was merely a lover of the ancients, a transmitter and not a creator, but he was really an original thinker and he did an important work. He gathered together the fragmentary records of antiquity and edited them: (1) the Book of History; (2) the Book of Changes, used in divination; (3) a selection from the ancient odes, including those few of religious character, used in sacrifices; and (4) perhaps a collection of the Rites,—a sort of Leviticus which prescribed the ceremonies to be used in private and public worship, in marriages, in funerals, and upon all other important occasions in life. His collection, if made, was not identical with the extant Book of Rites. In addition (5) he wrote the Spring and Autumn Annals, drawn from the official records of his native state, which, with the commentary by Tso, forms a continuation in brief outline of the chronicles of the Book of History.

Mencius, although a devoted disciple of Confucius, surpassed his master in his comprehension of the principles of government. In his teaching he emphasized the rights of the people. "The people," he said, "are the foundation of the state; the national altars are second in importance, and the sovereign is the least important of all."

Some deny to Lao Tzu the authorship of the *Tao Te King*, but the greatness of Lao Tzu is evidenced by the teachings of his disciple, Chuang Tzu, the idealist. The *Tao Te King*, no matter who wrote it, is one of the most remarkable books of this period. It preserves many striking sayings ascribed to Lao Tzu, rejoices in paradox, declaims against war, preaches the simple life, and urges us to "recompense evil with kindness."

The Reconstructive Period. The second period begins with the overthrow of the Chou dynasty (249 B. C.). The greatest monarch of the new dynasty called himself the "First Emperor." He tried to destroy all Confucian literature and was guilty of the murder of many scholars because their bigoted conservatism hindered the reforms he sought to introduce.

The Han dynasty which followed restored Confucius to honor, but the period was one given very generally to the things which Confucius contemned,—tales of the marvelous. The philosopher's stone, the elixir of immortality, and the isles of the blessed, where the elixir was to be found, were the objects of search. It was probably at this time that the *Shan Hai King*, or "Classic of Mountains and Seas," was written. Although its tales are ridiculous to us, it undoubtedly has a certain value as preserving much of the folklore and many of the traditions of the Chinese.

The time was one, too, during which foreign influences crept in. Alexander's conquests in central Asia and Chinese exploration of adjoining lands created a channel of communication between the East and the West. Buddhism spread into Turkestan in the 3d century B. C. In the early years of the Christian era it received imperial recognition in China. In the following centuries, a great volume of Hindu literature was translated into Chinese by Buddhist missionaries,—not only Buddhist religious works, but Hindu mathematical, astronomical, and philosophical treatises. Chinese thought was profoundly affected.

This age may very properly be called the reconstructive period. In striking contrast to the credulity of the masses of the people were the works of two men: Ssu-ma Ch'ien (163–85 B. C.), the Herodotus of Chinese history, whose careful method and love of accuracy have become the model of later historians; and Wang Ch'ung (19–90 A. D.), whose originality and boldness won praise in spite of his heretical attacks upon the sages of antiquity and in spite of his denial of the immortality of the soul.

The Golden Age. This period of reconstruction prepared the way for what has sometimes been called the "golden age" of Chinese literature, which may be said to begin with the T'ang dynasty (618 A. D.) and include the Sung (960–1278). For our purposes it will cover also the period of the Mongol rule (to 1368). The T'ang period was noted for its poets, conspicuous among whom were Li Po, also called "Li T'ai Po" (699–762), whose verses in form and sentiment remind one of Omar the "tentmaker." Scarcely second to him was Tu Fu (712–770).

The Sung dynasty was adorned by its love of philosophy. The speculations of Buddhists and Taoists had produced a reaction. Confucianism separated itself entirely from their metaphysical theorizing. Chou Tun-i (1017–1073), the brothers Ch'eng (1032–1107), and, greatest of all, Chu Hsi (1130–

1200), although calling themselves Confucianists, departed far from the cautious views of the master. Their philosophy, which has generally been regarded as materialistic but has also been interpreted otherwise, has dominated Confucian thought from that day to this. The Sung period also had its poets, among whom Su Tung-po (1036–1101) may be mentioned as justly celebrated.

The Mongol dynasty, glorified by the praise given to it by Marco Polo, was distinguished in its literature chiefly for its attention to the drama and the novel. Because the drama and the novel use the spoken rather than the written style of language, the Confucianist of the old school was disposed to regard these forms of literature as beneath his notice. Yet the Chinese are among the most confirmed playgoers in the world. The most popular plays are representations of historical incidents, and this is true also of many of the novels.

Period of Western Influence. The fourth period in the history of Chinese literature, the period of Western influence, may be said to begin with the close of the 15th century, after the discovery by the Portuguese of the sea route to the Far East around the Cape of Good Hope. From that date, European intercourse with China increased rapidly.

Foreign missionaries aided both the Mings and the Manchus by preparing mathematical and scientific works, and since the beginning of the 19th century they have published an enormous mass of literature, both religious and secular. Chinese, educated abroad or in mission schools, have added greatly to the volume of translations. Original works by native authors have not been lacking. Poetry and fiction flourished both under the Mings and during the Manchu dynasty. One of the most celebrated novels, the *Hung Lou Meng*, commonly translated "The Dream of the Red Chamber," was written about the beginning of the Manchu period. The *Liao Chai*, by P'u Sung-ling, is a collection of stories that dates from about the same time. The splendid K'anghsi Dictionary belongs to this period, which is distinguished also for its topographical histories, in which China excels, and for its voluminous encyclopedias.

The influence of Western thought increased greatly after China's defeat by Japan in 1894-95. China saw her former pupil transformed by the new learning. The old viceroy, Chang Chih-tung, in a small volume appealed to his countrymen to take up the study of the sciences. The advice was not taken by the Manchu government until after further humiliation through the suppression of the Boxer rising. Chang Chih-tung was called to assist in creating a new system of public education. This caused a demand for translations of Western literature, particularly treatises on political science, economics, engineering, and medicine. A new impetus was given to literary effort. The stilted style, once so popular, with its penchant for literary allusion and empty verbiage, is giving way to a simple, direct expression. The invention and adoption of a syllabary is supplementing, but not supplanting, the use of ideograms and thus is popularizing learning. Polite literature is not neglected, but urgent need prompts discussion of political and economic problems. Newspapers and magazines abound; the periodical press is a powerful engine of reform.

JAPANESE LITERATURE

There is some reason to believe that the Japanese in the island of Kyushu had come into possession of the Chinese written characters some centuries before the time of Christ, yet the oldest Japanese literary works extant today are the *Kempo*, a constitution of 17 articles (604 A. D.); the *Kojiki*, a record of ancient events (612); the *Rokkokushi*, which consists of six works on national history, including the famous *Nihongi* or *Nihon Shoki* (620–901); and the *Manyoshu*, a collection of renowned ancient poets and poetesses (756). All these works were written in the Chinese characters. The *Kempo* and the *Rokkokushi* were written in pure Chinese classical style. The *Kojiki* and the *Manyoshu* used the Chinese characters as phonetics.

Early Poetry. Japanese poetry, which has neither meter nor rime, is peculiarly a native product. Its form is the same as in ancient times. The essential feature of a popular poem is that it consists of 5 successive lines of 5, 7, 5, 7, and 7 syllables respectively, that is, a total of 31 syllables. Longer poems are sometimes written, but the present tendency is toward shorter ones. Near the close of the 17th century, *Hokku* poems, which consisted of 3 lines of 5, 7, and 5 syllables respectively, a total of 17 syllables, became very popular. The poets Basho and Kikaku are rightly regarded as originators of this style. The poetry of Japan, like her pictorial art, gives strong impression and suggestion, rather than the description and narration so characteristic of Occidental poetry.

Many Japanese believe that poetry has declined since the *Heian* era (9th and 10th centuries). Yet the poets Tsurayuki and Katei and the poetess Murasaki-Shikibu rank as high as do Hitomaru and Akahito of the golden age of Japanese poetry, during which period many poetic works were compiled in accordance with imperial decree.

The Drama. The period from the 13th to the 17th century is known as the dark ages of Japanese literature. Because most men were engaged in warfare, literature was neglected. Only one or two schools in the entire empire remained open. Yet, even under such conditions, many famous works were produced, such as the *Hojoki*, a journal of important events, and the *Tsurezuregusa*, a collection of essays and anecdotes. In this period appeared also the splendid type of classical drama known as the *Noh*, which somewhat resembles the drama of ancient Greece. Singers, dancers, and musicians plied their arts both at Shinto shrines and at imperial and shogunate courts. In the *Noh* drama, Chinese and Japanese historical narrations are frequently delivered in conversational tone. The singing part of the *Noh*, which is often performed by itself, is called *Yokyoku* or *Utai*. In the same period, the *Kyogen*, a sort of farce or comedy, had its beginning. Most of the *Noh* and the *Kyogen* were composed by Buddhist priests along the lines of the drama of the Yuan dynasty of China (12th century). They were both enacted and patronized chiefly by the nobility. Even at the present time, these types are very popular with the higher classes. In their presentation, magnificent costumes are worn.

Toward the end of the 16th century, the *Kabuki*, a type of popular drama, was introduced. Notwithstanding that the *Kabuki* was originated by a woman, and was for some time enacted only by women of the courtesan class, yet from the early 18th to the latter part of the 19th century, because actors and actresses were strictly forbidden by law to play on the same stage, the higher type of *Kabuki* productions came to be presented entirely by men, who took the part of both sexes. The *Kabuki* has recently been subjected to critical reform and has become a popular amusement with all classes. Amateurs and professionals both play the *Kabuki*, and men and women appear together now on the same stage. This has led to the translation and presentation of many Western plays.

Another popular drama is the marionette play, accompanied by songs which are called *joruri*. Such songs also form an essential part of the *Kabuki*, taking the place of the orchestra in Western plays. The marionette plays originated in a chant (*Gidayu*) telling a love story, to which the marionettes were added. The development of this since the 17th century has produced most skillful performers. The chanters sit in one corner of the stage, while the marionettes are worked by players in harmony with the chant. These plays always aim at the encouragement of good and at the condemnation of evil.

The words of the *Kabuki* are frequently changed and are often impromptu, but the text for the marionette chant must be carefully finished. It is the marionette play, therefore, rather than the *Kabuki* that has given rise to a literary form most nearly like the Western drama.

Modern Fiction. Since the beginning of the 18th century, Japan has produced a large body of fiction. Children's stories, in particular, have been very popular and have frequently been translated into Western languages. Many novels and romances with a great variety of settings and a wide range of subjects have been produced.

In all periods of Japanese literature the work of women has been notable. It is said that the *Kojiki* and *Nihongi* were produced under the patronage of empresses. During the 10th and the 11th century, feminine authorship was at its best. In the 11th century, a woman produced the first novel, "a prose epic of real life." To the same century belongs the *Makura no Zoshi,* "Pillow Sketches," a realistic picture of social life in Kyoto of that time.

The distinction attained by women in Japanese literature may be ascribed to the fact that in the 8th and 9th centuries the two forms of the Japanese syllabary, the Katakana and the Hiragana, were brought to perfection. This enabled the women to write without having to learn the Chinese ideograms, and they were quick to seize upon the new style of writing, while the men still clung to the Chinese classical models.

Western Influence. Contact with the West during the past century has greatly influenced Japanese literature as well as politics. Men of Western education have taught in the universities. English has become very largely the language of learning. Much translation from English and other European languages has been done. Political and historical romances have been produced upon both native and Western models. Much writing has been done with the motive of interpreting Japan to the outside world and the outside world to Japan.

The growth of newspapers and other periodicals is a remarkable feature of this period. About 1800 periodicals are published in the empire, and in Tokyo alone there are several newspapers which have a daily circulation of 1,000,000 each.

The greatest problem in the Japanese literary world at present is to find a way to get rid of the use of Chinese characters. Japanese literature was founded in the Chinese written language, and the best has been embellished with quotations from the Chinese classics. At present, publishers are discouraging the use of these ideograms and have practically agreed to reduce the number employed to about 2000. But, after Japan has rid herself of the use of Chinese characters, the question will arise whether it would not be better to employ the Roman alphabet rather than the Japanese syllabary.

ASSYRO-BABYLONIAN LITERATURE

The literature of Babylonia and Assyria has for us a threefold interest, because of (1) the romantic progress of discovery in the last century, (2) the revelations of a rich and ancient civilization given us by the excavations in the Tigris and Euphrates valley, and (3) the light these discoveries have thrown on the Old Testament.

Deciphering the Inscriptions. In 1835 Henry C. Rawlinson, an English officer, found at Behistun, in Persia, a long inscription on the smoothed face of a high rock. The writing was in three languages, old Persian, Elamite, and Babylonian. Although these tongues belong to different families of languages, the cuneiform characters were used for all. Rawlinson succeeded first in deciphering the old Persian, and during the next twenty years he, with other scholars, particularly a German named Grotefend, whose researches had in fact preceded those of Rawlinson by a few years, penetrated the secrets of the other two languages of the inscription. Thus we were given the means of studying the culture and the literature of Babylonia in its records on rocks, walls, and vast collections of clay tablets.

Early Sumerians and Babylonians. The cuneiform writing, which consists of wedge-shaped characters placed at various angles and in groups of from two to thirty, probably originated among the Sumerians at a quite remote date. The Sumerians were a non-Semitic people who migrated into the fertile Mesopotamian valley, probably from the northeast, before 4000 B. C. They early developed a high civilization, a complex nature religion, and an elaborate system of writing. Most of the inscriptions found in the temple libraries at Telloh and Nippur are in Sumerian. The oldest Sumerian inscriptions are short, historical in character, and were probably composed shortly after 4000 B. C.

Commencing apparently about 4000 B. C., Semites from the southwest also settled in Mesopotamia. Gradually they conquered and absorbed their Sumerian neighbors. But, although the Babylonian people resulting from this fusion was predominantly Semitic, and the Babylonian language was Semitic, nevertheless the superior Sumerian civilization prevailed. The Babylonian religion contains many elements of Sumerian origin. Sumerian survived for over thirty centuries as the language of religious documents, while the Semitic Babylonian, or Akkadian as it is commonly called, became the language of daily intercourse and profane literature. And Sumerian cuneiform writing was employed in all Babylonian documents.

Babylonian and Assyrian Libraries. The libraries, like the very ancient one in the temple of En-Lil, the Sumerian god, at Nippur, provided a record department and an educational department, equipped with grammars, dictionaries, commentaries, and interlinear translations. The great Babylonian period lasted from about the 22d to the 13th century B. C. After this time the Assyrians, a kindred people, succeeded to power. Among them, warfare and conquest were held in honor, and the works of culture were but little regarded. In consequence, their literary work shows little originality. They copied the Babylonian writings and preserved them in libraries, notably that of Assurbanipal (668–626 B. C.)—better known perhaps by the Greek version of his name, Sardanapalus—at Nineveh, which contained about 30,000 clay tablets. This library, explored by Layard and George Smith, was our first great source of information about Babylonian literature. It contained histories, grammars, lexicons, law books, works on astrology and astronomy, mathematics, epic poems, books of magic and incantations, omens, liturgies, psalms, and prayers. With the fall of Nineveh (607 B. C.), the library was buried in the ruins of the palace.

The Gilgamesh Epic. But, while these libraries are rich in all manner of writings, their principal treasures are the great mythological epics of the Babylonians. Chief of these is the Gilgamesh epic. It is the story of Gilgamesh, semimythical king of the ancient city, Erech. Ishtar, the Babylonian Venus, tries to win his love. But he rejects her advances and, instead, with his faithful companion En-Gidu, goes forth to seek immortal life. After many adventures, during which En-Gidu is killed, Gilgamesh finds his ancestors, Ut-Napishtim and his wife, enjoying immortality upon the Isle of the Blessed far to the west across the waters of death. Ut-Napishtim tells Gilgamesh the story of the great flood brought by the gods, from which only he and his companions in the ship escaped, while all the rest of mankind perished. This Babylonian flood story parallels the biblical flood story so exactly that it is probable that the biblical story was borrowed from the Babylonian. Ut-Napishtim tells Gilgamesh that at the bottom of the sea grows a magic plant which will restore his youth. But, just as he is about to possess it, a serpent steals it, and thus gains immortality for serpents, while Gilgamesh and all mankind forfeit it. The epic concludes with the account of the bringing up of the ghost of En-Gidu, who describes for Gilgamesh the abodes of death and the nature of life after death and informs him that his search is vain, that for mankind there is no escape from death. This Gilgamesh epic has a peculiar literary significance. It is written in twelve books or tablets, corresponding seemingly to the twelve months of the year, and must have initiated the custom of composing epic poems in twelve books or multiples thereof.

Epic of Creation. Another epic of almost equal interest tells the story of Creation. Marduk, the great god, slays Tiamat, the dragon of Chaos. Out of one half of her body he forms the heaven, out of the other half the earth. He then creates plants, animals, and man on earth. This story is strikingly similar to the biblical Creation story, and again it is likely that borrowing has taken place. This epic is arranged in seven tablets, corresponding probably to the seven days of the week, or else to the seven days of creation.

Other poems of epic character exist, chief among them being the legend of Adapa and the South Wind, the descent of Ishtar into Hell, the legend of Etana and the Eagle, the legend of the Zu-bird and the tablets of destiny, and the myth of Ura, the plague god.

Code of Hammurabi. Of equal literary and historical significance is the Law Code of Hammurabi, king of Babylon about 2100 B. C. It is engraved upon a large diorite column which was found at Susa in 1898. It contains almost 300 laws dealing with all manner of subjects, and is probably the oldest law code in the world's history.

Up to the present time, about 150,000 tablets and inscriptions have been discovered in Babylonia. Comparatively few of these have been deciphered, but scholars are continually at work, and each year adds to our knowledge and understanding of this great ancient literature.

The principal collections of tablets are in the British Museum at London, in the Louvre at Paris, in the Royal Museum at Berlin, in the National Museum at Istanbul, and in America in the museums of the universities of Pennsylvania, Chicago, and Yale.

HEBREW LITERATURE

The people of Israel form a part of the Semitic branch of the Caucasian race. Their language, Hebrew, belongs to the Western group of Semitic languages. Cradled in the great Arabian desert, they migrated to Palestine about 1400–1200 B. C. and established a nation which endured until overthrown by the Romans in 70 A. D. Since then, Israel has been scattered throughout the world.

In the solitudes of the Arabian desert the Israelite mind pondered over the deep mysteries of life. Gradually there was revealed to it through the long course of its history the knowledge of one, only God, sole Creator of the universe, who has fashioned all things in infinite wisdom, goodness, and love, and has ordained laws of justice and righteousness for human guidance. This ethical monotheism is the foundation principle of Judaism. It became the eternal and unquenchable passion of the Jewish people and the keynote of Hebrew literature.

Early Songs and Legends. Hebrew literature began, like almost every other ancient literature, in folk songs and legends probably recited in camp and village gatherings by tribal bards. As civilization developed, some of these poems were written down. The Bible mentions two collections of ancient Hebrew songs, *The Book of Yashar* and *The Book of the Wars of Yahwe*. Unfortunately, both books have been lost, and only a few fragments of these ancient poems, such as the "Song of Lamech" (Genesis IV:23-24), the "Song of the Well" (Numbers XXI: 17), and the "Song of Deborah" (Judges V) survive.

By the time of David (1000 B. C.), Israelite culture had advanced materially. One of David's court officials was the scribe, who recorded the important events of Israelite history. This marks the definite beginning of literary activity in Israel.

The history of Hebrew literature may be divided into four periods: (1) the Biblical (from the earliest times to 70 A. D.); (2) the Rabbinic (70 to about 1000); (3) the Medieval (1000 to about 1800); and (4) the Modern.

The Bible. This constitutes the sacred book of Christian peoples. To the Jews, however, only the Old Testament is so regarded. It is far from being the whole of Hebrew literature. Unlike the Koran, the sacred book of the Mohammedans, the Bible was not composed at any one period. It is, rather, a collection of books, a small library, a national literature—all that survives of the quite considerable mass of writings composed during the national period of Israel's history. Therefore, it naturally contains many kinds of writing, including historical sketches and unhistorical or semihistorical legends, religious and social laws, the inspired utterances and visions of the prophets, liturgical and lyric poems (the Psalms), didactic poetry (Proverbs and Ecclesiastes), pragmatic fiction (Ruth), and even a pure love poem (Song of Songs) and two dramas (Job and Esther).

Pentateuch and Hexateuch. After the ancient poems referred to above, the oldest biblical writings are found in the Pentateuch and in Judges and Samuel. They were composed during the 10th and 9th centuries B. C. Science has established that, contrary to tradition, the Pentateuch is not the work of Moses, nor of any one man, but was composed by different groups of writers between 900 B. C. and 400 B. C., or even somewhat later. It has proved also that the book of Joshua was composed by these same writers; therefore, science speaks of the *Hexateuch*, "the six books," rather than of the *Pentateuch*, "the five books."

The oldest document of the Hexateuch, composed probably in 899 B. C. in the Southern Kingdom, is found in Exodus XXXIII:12–XXXIV:28. It contains an interesting and historically important tradition about Moses and also a little code of laws, which Exodus XXXIV:28 calls explicitly the "Ten Commandments." These are by no means identical with the Ten Commandments of Exodus XX, which were composed much later, probably in the 8th century B. C.

About a half century after this first document, a similar work was composed in the Northern Kingdom. It is found in Exodus XX:23–XXIV:8, and is generally designated by the name applied to it in Exodus XXIV:7, "The Book of the Covenant." It contains a code of laws, of greater extent than the code in the older document. In fact, several of the laws of the Book of the Covenant were borrowed from this older book, with minor changes to meet conditions obtaining in the Northern Kingdom.

Following these two oldest writings came the so-called Yahwist and Elohist documents, composed in the Southern and the Northern Kingdom respectively. The former, the product of the 8th and 7th centuries B. C., is so called by scholars because it uses only the name Yahwe (usually, but mistakenly, pronounced Jehovah) for the Deity. The Elohist Document, written during the 8th century B. C., is likewise so designated because it employs the word Elohim for God. The vast majority of the narratives of Genesis, Exodus, Numbers, and Joshua belong to the Yahwist and Elohist documents.

The Book of Deuteronomy. II Kings XXII and XXIII tell of the finding of a book in the Temple at Jerusalem in the eighteenth year of Josiah. This pious king, persuaded that this was the law of Moses, made it the basis of a far-reaching religious, social, and economic reformation. Scholars have established conclusively that this book was the book of Deuteronomy, or rather the greater part thereof. But, instead of having been written by Moses, then lost for centuries, and suddenly found again, it was composed by prophetic writers at this very time, 621 B. C., and the story of its discovery was merely a pious fiction designed to induce the devout and credulous king to institute the legal provisions of Deuteronomy as the law of the land. The plan succeeded, and the ensuing reformation brought about a greatly needed, thoroughgoing purification of the Israelite religion, and an abolition of the idolatrous rites. The book of Deuteronomy is animated by the fine religious spirit of the prophets. It adapts many of the laws of the Book of the Covenant to the conditions of the end of the 7th century B. C., and reveals a deep humanitarian spirit and a marked progress in civilization.

The Priestly Code. One unforeseen result of this Deuteronomic reformation was the centralization of the worship in the Temple. Gradually the priestly influence overshadowed that of the prophets, and the religion of Israel became steadily more ritualistic. This tendency grew during the Babylonian Exile (586–536 B. C.). This spirit of ritualism and formal religion characterizes the last main stratum of the Hexateuch, which is known, therefore, as the Priestly Code. This was composed, partly in Babylonia and partly in Palestine, between 570 and 400 B. C. or somewhat later. The main body of the Priestly Code is found in Exodus XXV–XXXI and XXXV–XL, the whole of Leviticus, and Numbers I–X:28, while other portions are scattered through Genesis, the early chapters of Exodus, and the latter chapters of Numbers and Joshua.

Sometime after 400 B. C., these various documents were woven together into a kind of running narrative that purported to recount the history of Israel in the period preceding its entrance into Palestine. In this way the Pentateuch, or better, the Hexateuch, came into being.

The Prophets. The prophetic writings, in the main, come from the same period as the Hexateuch. Amos, oldest of the literary prophets, lived about 760 B. C. A generation later came Hosea, Isaiah, and Micah. Nahum wrote about the middle of the 7th century B. C.; Zephaniah, Habakkuk, and Jeremiah, in the last quarter of the same century. Both Jeremiah's style and the content of his prophecy show a marked affinity to the book of Deuteronomy. Ezekiel wrote in Babylon at the very beginning of the Exile. His writings, in turn, exhibit a significant relationship to the Priestly Code. The great anonymous prophet, called Deutero-Isaiah because his supremely rhapsodic utterances are found in Isaiah XL–LVI, lived at the end of the Exile.

The Hagiographa. To the postexilic period belong the books of Zechariah, Haggai, Obadiah, Malachi, Jonah, and Joel. All the books of the Hagiographa, the third division of the Old Testament, were composed during the Exile or in the postexilic period, with the possible exception of a few pre-exilic psalms. Many of the Psalms, however, and also the book of Daniel, were written as late as the 2d century B. C. The book of Job, written about 400 B. C., is generally regarded as one of the masterpieces of the world's literature.

Apocryphal Writings. The Old Testament, in its present arrangement, came into being in the 2d century A. D. through a clear-cut distinction made by the rabbis between those books that were pronounced sacred and those that were declared profane. The latter were forbidden to be read, and gradually disappeared from use in Palestine. Many, however, continued to be regarded as sacred by the Greek-speaking Jews of Alexandria, and have been preserved in Greek translations in two collections known as the Apocrypha and the Pseudepigrapha. The books of the Apocrypha are included in Catholic editions of the Bible. Of the Apocryphal writings, the three books of Maccabees, Esdras, Judith, Tobit, Ben Sirach, and the Wisdom of Solomon are the most important. Recently a large portion of the Hebrew original of Ben Sirach was discovered in Egypt. Of the Pseudepigrapha, Enoch, Jubilees, The Testaments of the Twelve Patriarchs, the Sibylline Oracles, and the Psalms of Solomon are best known. All these works were composed between 200 B. C. and 200 A. D.

The Mishna. With the destruction of the Temple at Jerusalem by the Romans in 70 A. D., the religious life of Israel underwent a complete transformation. Without altar and priesthood, sacrifice and elaborate ritual were impossible. Prayer, reading of the Scriptures, and ceremonies in synagogue and home became the main elements of religious practice. The biblical laws were carefully studied, commented upon, and amplified by the rabbis in the great schools of the land. New laws that regulated all the activities of daily life were devised. Eventually they became so numerous that codification was necessary. This work was successfully accomplished by the great teacher and leader, Rabbi Judah the Prince, about 200 A. D. His work, called the *Mishna*, or "Teaching," is a systematic compilation in six books of all the laws evolved by the rabbis up to that time.

The *Mishna* almost immediately came to be regarded as second in authority only to the Bible. Along with the Bible it became the chief object of discussion by the rabbis in the schools of Palestine and Babylonia. Constantine the Great closed the schools in Palestine in 327, but not until the discussions of the laws of the Bible and *Mishna* had been compiled into a large work known as the *Palestinian* or *Jerusalem Talmud*.

The Talmuds. About the middle of the 6th century, a similar compilation of the rabbinical discussions of the laws of the Bible and *Mishna* in the Babylonian schools was made. This is known as the *Babylonian Talmud*. Hence there are, actually, two *Talmuds*. But, since the *Babylonian Talmud* was compiled two centuries after the *Palestinian*, it is naturally a far larger work, and contains practically everything found in the latter, with much new material. When the *Talmud* is referred to, the *Babylonian Talmud* is usually meant.

But it must not be imagined that these *Talmuds* are purely legalistic works. They abound in information about diverse matters,—folklore, medicine, history, geography, religion and ethics, legends, stories, wise maxims, and the like. This material constitutes a good half of the content of the *Talmud* and is known as *Haggada*, or "Narrative," in contrast to the legalistic matter, called *Halacha*, "Rule." Moreover, a vast store of additional Haggadic material is contained in various collections known as *Midrashim*, or "Expositions" (of biblical texts). Of these, the *Midrash Rabba* is the largest and most popular. The many well-known stories and sayings of the rabbis are taken from the *Haggadic* portions of the *Talmud* and the *Midrashim*.

Medieval Hebrew Literature. After the year 1000 A. D., the center of Jewish life shifted from Babylonia to southwestern Europe. During this period the Jews transmitted much of Arabic science and culture to the European nations and thus contributed mightily to the Renaissance. Hebrew literature during the medieval period dealt with a wide range of subjects,—philosophy, ethics, biblical commentaries, history, mathematics, astronomy, geography, travel, Hebrew grammar, poetry, and the like. The leading Jewish philosopher, Moses Maimonides, exerted a strong influence upon medieval scholasticism. The best-known medieval Hebrew poets were Judah Halevi and Solomon ibn Gabirol.

The Modern Period. During the 16th, 17th, and 18th centuries, Hebrew literature declined noticeably both in extent and in the value of its content. The last century, however, has witnessed a remarkable revival of Hebrew literature, due chiefly to the Zionist movement, which has sought, with some success, to revive Hebrew as a spoken language. This modern Hebrew literature deals with the same wide range of themes as do other modern literatures. Of the present day Hebrew dramatists, David Pinski is perhaps the foremost. The most gifted modern Hebrew poet is H. N. Bialik, while Asher Ginzberg, better known by his pseudonym, *Achad Haam*, "One of the People," is recognized as the leading essayist.

SYRIAC LITERATURE

The Syriac language belongs to the Aramaic group of Semitic languages, and is, therefore, akin to Hebrew. Syriac was the vernacular of Syria and Iraq until after the Arab conquest (7th century), when Arabic gradually superseded it. Today, Syriac survives as a spoken language only in a few isolated communities in Iraq.

Syriac literature had its beginnings early in the Christian era, and reached its zenith between the 4th and the 7th century. Thereafter it gradually declined and eventually ceased about 1300. It is largely a church literature, and was cultivated chiefly in the Jacobite and Nestorian ecclesiastical schools, particularly those of Edessa and Nisibis. It is rich in hymns, homilies, martyrologies, church histories, and the like.

Of especial interest are the early Syriac versions of the Bible. At least three such are known, composed probably between the 2d and the 5th century. Most important is the version known as the *Peshitta* (the "simple" text). Of some biblical books it is a literal translation, of others a free translation, and of still others merely a paraphrase. In those books of which it is a literal translation, its text frequently varies materially from the Hebrew. It is therefore much used by biblical scholars in determining the original and correct text of the Bible.

Besides church writings, Syriac literature contains many important scientific works, such as treatises on the Syriac grammar and language, histories, and translations, chiefly from the Greek. Some of the works in Aristotle's *Organon* were known to Europe, prior to the Revival of Learning, only by translation from Syriac versions.

Among the leading Syriac writers may be mentioned Bardesanes (b. 154), seemingly the father of Syriac literature, author of an interesting account of the heathen religions of the Orient; Ephraem Syrus (d. 373), the homilist and hymnologist; and Gregory Abulfarag bar Hebræus (1226–86), one of the last and probably the greatest Syriac writer. His extant works are exceedingly numerous and treat a great variety of subjects, mostly scientific. Of particular value is his *Chronikon*, one of the earliest attempts at a universal history in the world's literature.

ARABIC LITERATURE

The Arabic language commands the attention of students of the history of civilization because (1) with the exception of English it is spoken by more people than is any other language; (2) it is the language of the *Koran*, and therefore the sacred tongue of one of the world's great religions; (3) it is the instrument of expression of a vast and varied literature, through which the elements of science and philosophy were communicated to European scholars during the middle ages, thus, in large part, giving rise to the Renaissance; and (4) through it many familiar stories, such as those of the *Thousand and One Nights*, were brought to the Western world.

Arabic is a Semitic language, with a vocabulary far larger probably than that of any other language, and possessing a flexibility that permits the utmost delicacy and imagery of expression. It is primarily the language of the nomad tribes of the Arabian desert, but through the rapid development and spread of Mohammedanism it became the language of a very large part of the Orient.

Pre-Islamic Poetry. Arabic literature began, as might be expected, in the songs of tribal bards extolling the glories of their respective tribes. At the great gatherings of the tribes, and notably at the annual fair at Ukaz, when the tribes came together each year in peaceful intercourse, contests of skill were regularly held between the poets of the various tribes. Poems were first committed to writing in the 6th century A. D., shortly before the birth of Mohammed and the rise of Islam. The greatest of pre-Islamic poets was Imru-'l-Qais, though others, notably Labid and Amr-ibn-Kultum, rank with him. Antar, another famous poet of this time, was the hero of a very long, romantic poem that goes by his name.

The Koran. The *Koran*, the Bible of Islam, contains the inspired utterances of Mohammed, the supposed revelations of God through the prophet to his people. It is written in rimed prose, which produces a rhythmic, dignified, and impressive effect. It is divided into 114 sections or *suras*. For a time after Mohammed's death (632) various versions of the *Koran* were current, but under Caliph Uthman (644–656) these were collected into the present official text. Since then the *Koran* has served as the chief model and inspiration of all Arabic literature. It has been widely studied and commented upon by Mohammedan scholars, and commentaries upon it form an extensive branch of Arabic literature. Baidawi (d. 1282) is the best-known and most authoritative commentator of the *Koran*.

Forms of Arabic Poetry. Pre-Islamic poetry likewise exerted an important and lasting influence upon subsequent Arabic literature, particularly upon its poetry. The poems of the five greatest pre-Islamic poets were collected and hung up, as the lasting glories of the Arab tribes, in the Kaaba, the great temple at Mecca. Hence they were known as the *muallakat*, "the suspended ones." They served as the models of later Arabic poetry. Therefore it happens that the Arabic *qasida*, or long poem, usually begins with a description of a camping ground and with a lamentation for the fallen or absent companions of the poet. After this introduction the poet takes up the story of his love, his sufferings, and his journey, and adds many details in praise of his horse, his arms, and the like. And then he usually concludes, in typical Oriental manner, with fulsome praise of some influential man, from whom a substantial reward is expected in return.

After the time of Mohammed, when cities and courts developed, these early literary forms, which had sprung out of wandering tribal life, were retained for a time. But in the atmosphere of the cities they became so artificial that, about the 8th century, poets began to employ new forms and treat new subjects. In this century, Abu Nuwas is the most distinguished name in Arabic poetry.

A closely related type of Arabic literature is the *maqama* (assembly), consisting of stately rimed prose interspersed with metrical passages. It therefore exhibits the influence of both pre-Islamic poetry and the *Koran*. It is a combination of legend and story, in which the writer tells how in various places he meets a wandering scholar who puts all his rivals to shame. This type of writing was practiced as late as the 19th century. Hamadhani in the 10th century was the originator, and Hariri in the 11th century is regarded as the most brilliant writer, of the *maqama*.

Arabic Fables and Stories. From the 8th through the 15th century, and particularly during the brilliant reign of the caliph Haroun-al-Raschid (786–809), Arabic literature reached the height of its development. Arabic writers drew largely upon outside sources. Thus the fables of Bidpai were borrowed from the Persian, and the story of Kalilah and Dimnah, from Indian literature. Best-known of this class of writing is the widely read collection of stories known as the *Thousand and One Nights*, or, less correctly, the *Arabian Nights*. These have been translated into almost every European language.

History and Science. Historical composition has been diligently cultivated by Arabic writers. Their method is peculiar. The historian follows the principle that, if a thing has once been told well, the words of this account can be used again; therefore he keeps as close as possible to his sources. Moreover, if two or more accounts of an incident are current, instead of attempting to determine which is the correct, or at least the most probable, account, he usually cites all the accounts, scrupulously stating his sources for each, and leaves it to his readers to choose whichever tradition pleases him best. In this way thirty or more accounts of a single incident are frequently recorded by Arabic historians.

Other sciences besides history were diligently cultivated by Arabic sages, and the literature is extremely rich in important works on mathematics, astronomy, chemistry, grammar, and philosophy.

Recent Literary Revival. With the advent of the Turks into western Asia and Europe and the conquest of the Moors in Spain in the 15th century, Arabic literature began to decline. The 19th century, however, saw numerous attempts to revive and modernize Arabic literature, due to the increasing contact between Arabic and Western writers and thinkers. Large printing presses have been set up and numerous works of poetry and history as well as historical novels by both Mohammedan and Christian writers have been published. The Latin alphabet has been officially adopted by order of the Turkish government.

ETHIOPIC LITERATURE

Ethiopic is a Semitic language, closely related to Arabic. The Ethiopians were Semites who, about the beginning of the Christian era, were driven from their home in Sheba in southern Arabia by kindred tribes pushing in from the Arabian desert. They crossed over the narrow strait of Bab el Mandeb at the southern end of the Red Sea and settled in Abyssinia, where they established a powerful kingdom. Today Ethiopic has resolved itself into several dialects spoken by the Abyssinians, the modern descendants of the Ethiopians.

The introduction of Christianity into Ethiopia in the 4th century marks the systematic beginning of Ethiopic literature. The Bible and other writings of the ancient Church were early translated from Greek, Coptic, and Syriac into Ethiopic. Although quite extensive, Ethiopic literature is almost entirely religious in character, occasionally varied by some work of historic or semihistoric nature. Ethiopic writers have been, almost without exception, devoid of distinctive individual merit.

None the less, the literature is important because it contains several important Jewish and early Christian pseudepigraphic writings which have survived only in Ethiopic. Chief of these are the books of Enoch (one version) and Jubilees, the Apocalypse of Ezra, the Ascension of Isaiah, and the Life of Adam and Eve.

There are a few modern works of secular character in the Amhari and Geez dialects.

EGYPTIAN LITERATURE

Egyptian literature presents to modern readers several unusual features: (1) the long history of the Egyptian language, from 4000 B. C. to 1500 or 1600 A. D. (including the Coptic period); (2) the very slight connection of ancient Egyptian literature with that of neighboring countries; (3) an almost total lack of progress in style or subject matter; (4) the fragmentary and inaccurate manuscripts in which the large mass of writings have come down to us.

Three forms of writing were used in ancient Egypt: (1) the hieroglyphic (priestly writing), consisting of pictures to represent ideas, a system in use for inscriptions down to the 2d or 3d century B. C.; (2) the so-called hieratic, an abbreviated form of the hieroglyphic, used by the priests for writing manuscripts; (3) the demotic (popular) script, which came into use very late. The key to these forms of writing was found on the famous Rosetta Stone, discovered in 1798-99 in Fort St. Julien de Rosetta near the Rosetta mouth of the Nile. Knowledge of writing, however, was apparently never widely distributed in Egypt, and the numerous errors and corruptions in the most beautiful of existing papyri show that the copyists were more interested in making accurate characters to be placed with the dead in tombs than in reproducing the thought for living readers.

The remains of Egyptian literature include inscriptions upon monuments and in tombs and a vast mass of papyri which, well preserved in the dry Egyptian climate, have been gathered into the various museums of the world. Most of this literature was produced during the period of the Middle Kingdom (3000 to 1600 B. C.), and the papyri were copied in later times. In general, although the records reveal an ancient, busy, and religious civilization, they are devoid of significance as literature.

Herodotus remarked the devotion of the Egyptians to their gods, and modern scholars find that much of the literature that has survived is concerned with the religious beliefs of the people and with accounts of ceremonies and magical charms and incantations. These are gathered into collections, such as the *Book of the Dead*, portions of which are found on tombs and sarcophagi.

The mythology of the Egyptians seems to have been very rich. It is said that every sanctuary had local legends of the gods, which the priests presented in dramatic form at the local festivals. But very little of such material has survived.

In philosophy, nothing has been found except a few collections of proverbs, sayings such as those ascribed to Ptah Hotep. One such collection, known as the *Papyrus Prisse*, is assigned to the 12th dynasty (about 2500 B. C.) and is called the oldest book in the world.

In poetry a few hymns and some graceful love songs have survived; and one epic poem, celebrating the victory of Rameses II over the Hittites in the battle of Kadesh, is well known. But the Egyptian verse, while it sometimes resembles Hebrew poetry, has very little of real poetic quality and was never highly developed.

The largest body of literary remains, other than the religious works, consists of tales and stories, such as are found in the *Arabian Nights*. These bear evidence of having been passed down through many generations. Some of them are in the form of fables, such as the story of *The Lion and the Mouse*; among fairy tales a Cinderella story appears. For the most part these are written in a simple and unaffected style. Fairly representative of these collections is the story of King Cheops of the Middle Kingdom, who, to relieve his insomnia, called upon his sons for entertainment. They, in obedience, narrated in turn tales of wonders wrought by famous magicians.

In the time of the Middle Kingdom another more

artificial or rhetorical type of story developed, in which the interest centers rather in the semipoetical passages than in the plot. The most famous of such stories have been called *The Fated Prince*, *The Tale of Two Brothers*, and *The Eloquent Peasant*. In the last of these the peasant has been robbed of his ass and applies to an official of his district for redress. The official is so charmed by the peasant's speech that he makes report to the king, and the case is carried on from term to term to give occasion for the peasant to make more of his eloquent speeches. This rhetorical narrative gave place under the New Kingdom to a simpler style of tales of magic and adventure.

After the Greek conquest (about 300 B. C.) Egyptian literature ceased. Its place was taken by the work of Greek authors, and Alexandria became a center of Greek learning. From the 3d to the 16th century A. D., Coptic, a descendant of the ancient Egyptian language, was the tongue of Christian Egypt, but it gave way to Arabic, which is now the popular language of the country. Except for a few unimportant fragments, the only Coptic literary remains are religious,—stories of saints and martyrs, and translations of parts of the Bible. The Gospels and Epistles are still taught to children in Coptic Christian schools in both the Coptic and the Arabic language.

PERSIAN LITERATURE

Persian literature has for Western readers three chief points of interest: (1) its long history and great works; (2) its influence on the later Greek and Hebrew writers; (3) its transmission of Hindu thought and story to the West.

Zoroaster, living probably in the 11th century B. C., did so thoroughly his work of religious teaching and reform, that but scant traces of earlier Persian religion and customs survive. But he and his followers left the world one of its noblest bodies of religious writing, the *Avesta*, which is our earliest example of Persian literature. The language of the *Avesta* is called *Zend*, a word which means literally "interpretation," *Zend-Avesta* meaning "commentary and text." This language and the Vedic Sanskrit were dialects of an earlier Aryan or Indo-European language spoken on the highlands of Iran. Both very early passed out of general use and knowledge.

With the conquest of Persia by the Greeks under Alexander in the 4th century B. C., the "middle" period of Persian literature begins. The *Avesta* was translated into Pehlevi, the language of this period, a mixture of Persian and Arabic. Other literary remains of the time are very scanty.

The successive waves of conquest and tyranny which passed over Persia during the next few centuries, as well as the introduction of Mohammedanism, severely restricted the variety of themes for Persian writers, but these very influences enriched their stock of materials through contact with Greece, Arabia, and especially India, where for several centuries Persian was the official language. From the winning of a partial independence from the caliphs in the 9th century A. D. dates modern Persian literature, written in an Aryan language mixed with many Arabic words.

The 10th century brought the first high tide of Persian literature. Chief among a multitude of writers stands the name of Firdousi, whose greatest work, the *Shah Nameh* or "Book of Kings," is ranked as one of the world's great epics. This poem is a source from which Persian and Western poets and story-tellers have drawn much material. Matthew Arnold made Rustan or Rustum, Firdousi's greatest hero, familiar to English readers in his narrative poem *Sohrab and Rustum*. Firdousi also produced the earliest poetic treatment of the biblical story of Joseph, which has been retold by many of his followers.

Firdousi is counted the originator of romantic, didactic, and mystic Persian poetry. A contemporary of his, a mystic poet, originated the form of the *ruba'i* or "quatrain," peculiarly adapted for the writing of moral and ethical reflections in the skeptical strain characteristic of Persian poetry. It is familiar to Western readers through Fitzgerald's translation of the *Rubaiyat* (Quatrains) of Omar Khayyam, the fascinating freethinker and ironist of the 11th century.

Rather strangely, the next great period of Persian literature falls in the fearful time of conquest and devastation under the Mongolian conqueror, Jenghis Khan. In the 14th century, Hafiz wrote what are called the most perfect of Persian lyrics. The last of the great Persian poets is Djami, who wrote epic, lyric, and mystic verse. These poets, perhaps because of the tyranny of government, did not attempt new themes but gave themselves to treating old themes in new ways; hence their elaborate system of figures, synonyms, and rimes, which in translation often produce an effect monotonous to Western taste. It should be noted that romantic passion, as known among Western nations, does not appear in Persian poetry.

The three centuries after 1500 produced a great wealth of prose in the form of fables, fairy tales and myths, novels and short stories, as well as folklore and history. This Persian telling of many of these stories is the first stage of their journey from India toward the West. Many of them find a place in the collection known as the *Arabian Nights*.

The 19th century in Persia was marked by the late beginnings of the drama. As in other countries, this found its origin in religious ceremonies. The range of themes is very small, although some biblical stories and Christian legends have been used upon the stage. Although much restricted as compared with earlier periods, there is today in Persia literary activity which produces both prose and poetry.

INDIAN LITERATURE

The literature of India (Sanskrit and Hindustani) claims our interest for three reasons: (1) its antiquity; (2) its peculiarly rich development; (3) its vast contributions to Western literature, especially in the form of proverbs, fairy stories, and fables.

This ancient literature, so amazingly vigorous and luxuriant, was opened up to the Western world by the discovery of the Sanskrit language in the 18th century. The discovery revealed the *Vedas*, the most ancient sacred books of the Brahman religion. The contents of these four *Vedas* or "Books of Knowledge," an elaborate body of religious ritual and legend, had been handed down by tradition through many centuries before they were committed to writing perhaps ten centuries before the Christian era. The language in which they are written is called Vedic (knowledge) or Vedic Sanskrit, and it is the ancestor of the Classic Sanskrit. The name Sanskrit (formed, refined) was given to this "older sister" of the western Aryan tongues by grammarians about the 4th century B. C. Since that time, at least, it has been the special language of the high literary and priestly classes, distinguished from the Prakrit (common) dialects of medieval India and from the modern Hindi and Urdu.

The immense literature of this Classic Sanskrit is very rich in epic, didactic, lyric, and dramatic poetry, as well as in prose fables, fairy tales, and romances.

There are two classes of Sanskrit epics. Of the *puranas* (ancient tales) the greatest are the *Mahabharata* (great poem or tale of the Bharatas) and the later and more artistic *Ramayana* (poem concerning Rama). These are partly legendary histories and partly mythical accounts of the universe, all with a religious motive. The greater ones antedate the Christian era, but lesser puranas were written in the first and following centuries A. D. to promote special Brahman beliefs. The *kavyas* (court epics) are artificial epics, most of which belong to the period between 500 and 1300 A. D. Of these the two best-known are *The Family of Rama* and *The Birth of the War God.* These epics mingle many grotesque fancies with passages of high poetic grace and power. Their delineation of the sentiments of love and forgiveness make an appeal to Western readers that is not always found in the Greek epic.

All forms of Sanskrit literature are strongly lyric, but long lyric poems are rare, their place being taken by series of little poetic pictures. Many poets are known only through some of these detached stanzas, which are commonly intensely sensuous in feeling and full of elaborate figures drawn from natural scenery. A very famous long lyric is *The Cloud Messenger* of Kalidasa. Bhartrhari in the 7th century was a much admired writer of both long and short lyrics.

In didactic and proverb verse, the Sanskrit literature is very prolific. It is said that practically all the proverbs and sayings to be found in other languages can be matched in the Sanskrit. One collection of about eight thousand of these didactic stanzas, representing all periods of the Sanskrit, has been made.

In the 5th or 6th century A. D., the Sanskrit drama began to develop from the pantomime dances connected with religious service. Although rather meager in extent, it is very noteworthy in theme and style. In several points it is similar to the romantic Shaksperian drama; the jester is there, and both comic and serious actions are included in the same play. Its themes are taken from heroic legend or contemporary court life, and its action always ends happily. The most famous of the dramatists, as he was the most illustrious poet of his time, is Kalidasa, whose best-known play is the *Sakuntala.*

The 4th century B. C. saw the earliest collection of fables, made for the purpose of instruction. Assigning of manlike parts to animals and mingling of prose and poetry are characteristic of these stories. We may trace the beast fable, so popular in medieval Europe, to the *jatakas* or Buddhist birth stories, in which the chief character is identified with some previous existence of Buddha. The most famous collection of fairy tales was put together in verse by Somadeva in the 11th century A. D. The titles of three story collections of this period are interesting: *Seventy Stories Told by the Parrot, The Great Cluster of Stories,* and the *Ocean of the Streams of Story.*

The 6th or 7th century A. D. may mark the beginnings of prose romances somewhat like the earlier English novels. One of the best-known is *The Adventures of the Ten Princes.* These romances are sometimes classed with the *kavyas.*

In modern times, two principal dialects, Hindi and Urdu, both of which contain a large Persian element, have achieved the standing of literary languages. The literature in Hindi is said to permeate all classes of the people more thoroughly than is the case with any literature of Europe. Its great poetic period was the 16th century, the Elizabethan period of English. Both Hindi and Urdu have been encouraged by the schools established in India during the 19th century, and they are adapting themselves in style and vocabulary to the expression of modern native and foreign thought. Native presses issue large numbers of books and periodicals. The newspapers of India are of unusual literary importance, because through them rather than through books, modern thought is disseminated among the people.

Extended instruction in English in the schools of India has been accompanied by the rise of numerous Hindu writers of English, several of whom have attained very high rank. The best-known to Western readers is Rabindranath Tagore, teacher and author, to whom the Nobel prize for literature was awarded in 1913.

GREEK LITERATURE

Greek literature is the living record of a great people, comprising works in many fields, which have served as models for all succeeding ages. This remarkable contribution was made possible by the sheer force and originality of the Greek genius, which displayed extraordinary creative power. For the literature of Greece is in the truest sense original; it is the unhampered expression of her great men in a language unsurpassed in grace and dignity.

Epic Poetry. The literature of Greece, as we know it, begins with epic poetry which is plainly the finished product of a society long familiar with this form of literary expression. When these poems were written, the Greeks already possessed, besides the myths of the gods, a large body of so-called historical myths,—of Thebes, of Troy, of the Argonauts, of Theseus, and of Heracles, or Hercules. These myths had long been the subject of the songs of the bards, or wandering minstrels, before Homer composed the two greatest of the world's epic poems. The *Iliad* tells the story of the incidents in the tenth year of the Trojan War; the *Odyssey* recounts the adventures of the return of Odysseus, one of the Trojan heroes, to his home in Ithaca after ten years' wandering. From both their matter and their style, most scholars conclude that a great master poet, Homer, living probably in the neighborhood of Smyrna in Asia Minor, in the 9th century B. C., gave final form in these poems to the stories and songs of a long line of earlier poets. The degree of originality shown by Homer in composing the *Iliad* and the *Odyssey* can only be estimated, and will probably never be known with certainty.

In the two centuries following Homer's time, there flourished a number of writers, known as the cyclic poets, who told and retold in the language of Homer many early legends and hero stories from the well-known "cycles," or groups of myths. During this epic age the Greeks created a larger body of literature of myth and legend than has been developed by any other people, but the most of this literature has not been preserved.

About 100 years after Homer, Hesiod, who wrote the *Works and Days*, a sort of farmer's almanac, wrote also a *Theogony*, an account of old beliefs about the gods and the origin of the world; in the former work he set forth an account of the five ages, beginning with the age of gold and passing through the ages of silver, of bronze, and of heroes, coming finally to the present wicked age of iron.

Reflective and Lyric Poetry. In the next period of Greek literature (about 700–475 B. C.) the turbulent growth of democracy seems to have encouraged reflective and lyric verse, though we know the early writers of this poetry only in tantalizing fragments of their work; these, however, are sufficient to prove its exquisite beauty. Pure lyric poetry was written early in the Æolian island of Lesbos, and the local dialect was one of the first used for lyric expression. This poetry was always sung to the accompaniment of the harp, just as the songs of the epic writers had been sung. At about the same time, lyrics were produced in the Dorian city of Sparta, where life was still free and natural, and not yet hardened into the rigid artificiality which was the blight of Sparta in the 5th century. Sappho and Alcæus, both of Lesbos, are the greatest of the Æolian school of lyric poetry. Toward the end of the period under consideration, a Dorian poet, Pindar, born in the Æolian city of Thebes, rose to the distinction of a national lyric poet of all Greece, and his works are for the most part preserved.

Reflective poetry, with its calmer mood, adopted the elegiac couplet for the treatment of a great variety of subjects. This measure, derived from the Homeric hexameter, was accompanied by a strain of flute music, the "elegy," which had been heard by the Greeks in Asia in songs of mourning. Simonides employed this measure in epitaphs honoring the Greek heroes who fell in the Persian wars. Solon, the lawgiver, used the elegy to publish his political precepts.

The Drama; *Origin.*—After the Persian wars in the beginning of the 5th century, Athens became one of the chief political centers of Greece, and she maintained a position of intellectual and literary leadership in the Mediterranean world for over 200 years. The drama is the most important literary development of this period, and it belongs peculiarly to Athens. It had its origin in very ancient religious observances, and its performance always remained essentially an act of worship of the god Dionysus. It grew out of a dance-song performed annually in honor of the god; this simple dance-song, rendered by a large group of men, came to be called a *dithyramb*, and at Corinth it became dignified into a literary form. Arion is said to have been the first to introduce this improvement, limiting the number of dancers to fifty and dressing them in goatskins as satyrs. At first they sang only of Dionysus and his adventures as he first journeyed into Greece, but later the theme was taken at will from any of the stories of the heroic *saga*.

Tragedy.—The beginning of the tragic drama, as distinguished from the dithyramb, is ascribed to Thespis of Icaria, a village near Athens, in the 6th century; he introduced an actor or speaker distinct from the chorus of singers, so that a legendary story might be enacted by the single actor and the chorus leader, supported by the chorus. Because of the satyr-like dress of the chorus (goatskins) the performance came to be called *tragœdia* or "goat-song"—hence *tragedy*. Æschylus, the first great tragic poet, added a second actor to the one used before his time. Of the eighty or more tragedies which he wrote, only seven remain. He took all his stories from the Homeric and cyclic poems, except that of the *Persians*, in which he celebrated the victory of the Greeks over Xerxes. His greatest work is the *Agamemnon*, which tells the story of the return of Agamemnon from Troy and of his treacherous murder. Sophocles we know through eight plays, the greatest of which is the *Œdipus Tyrannus*, a story taken from the epic cycle of Thebes. Sophocles is held to be the greatest of the Greek writers of tragedy in portrayal of character, and his work holds an unchallenged position among the world's greatest masterpieces. Euripides closely followed Æschylus and Sophocles, but, while the work of his predecessors was marked by profound religious feeling, that of Euripides was characterized by a rationalizing or "modern" spirit. He was regarded with suspicion during his lifetime, but after his death he became the most popular of the three tragedians, so that more tragedies of Euripides have been preserved than of Æschylus and Sophocles together. His is a realistic art, and it was well said by an ancient that, while Sophocles represents men as they should be, Euripides represents them as they are. His songs are particularly admired for their beautiful lyric quality.

Comedy.—Soon after tragedy had been molded by Æschylus into a noble literary form, another kind of dramatic performance came to the front, inspired by the same god. This grew out of the boisterous revels which took place during the festivals in honor of Dionysus—hence the name, *comœdia*, or "revel-song." The earliest comedy is known as the "old comedy"; in this, Aristophanes was the master; he used it as a vehicle of satire, both personal and political. The "middle comedy," which succeeded this Aristophanic comedy, became an instrument of social satire. The "new comedy," beginning about the end of the 4th century, was a light comedy of manners. The greatest writer of this type of comedy was Menander, of whose plays large fragments have recently been discovered in Egypt. This was the comedy which was adopted and imitated in Rome by Plautus and Terence.

Prose Literature; *History.*—The story of Greek prose begins after many centuries during which poetry was the only form of literary expression. The earliest prose, in the 6th century, recorded the speculations of philosophers or the monotonous records of chroniclers; the first prose of lasting importance is the history written by Herodotus in the 5th century, telling the story of the wars between Persia and Greece. Thucydides later wrote a history of the Peloponnesian war, in which he showed the critical insight of a philosophic historian. Xenophon, master of a simple, delightful style, wrote a continuation of Thucydides' history and also the *Anabasis*, an account of the expedition of the Greeks under Cyrus; besides recollections of Socrates and minor essays.

Oratory.—The free Athenian democracy of the 5th century was bound to encourage the art of public speaking and the study of rhetoric. Pericles himself was an orator of pre-eminent ability, and by this gift he maintained his leadership. The art of writing speeches for delivery by clients in the Athenian courts was perfected by Lysias, the master of the plain style, and he was himself an orator of no mean ability. In the following century, the greatest Athenian orators, Isocrates and Demosthenes, pleaded eloquently, but vainly, for a Greece united against the barbarian.

Philosophy.—The profound speculations of mature Greek philosophy are recorded in the writings of Plato, who stands pre-eminent among the writers of Greek prose. Socrates, the teacher of Plato, left no writings; and Aristotle's work, though characterized by the acute penetration of one of the greatest minds of all time, lacks the imaginative quality and the literary value of Plato's writings.

The Alexandrian Age. The productive period of Greek literature ends with the Alexandrian age. The center of intellectual life had shifted from Athens to Alexandria, and great scholarly industry took the place of creative work. Theocritus was the one outstanding exception. He, as the first writer of pastoral poetry, has furnished models and inspiration to many poets of succeeding ages, beginning with the Roman, Virgil. In this period the Hebrew Scriptures were translated into Greek in the version known as the Septuagint.

The Roman Period. In the Roman period, which extends from the middle of the 2d century B. C. to the beginning of the 6th century A. D., among a host of writers we find one of conspicuous ability, Lucian, who wrote in a clear and sparkling style a number of works on a variety of subjects, always handled in a light or playful manner. His *Veracious History* is a story of adventure such as Swift later produced in his *Gulliver's Travels*. His work often assumed a satiric tone, as in his *Dialogues of the Dead*. Plutarch, the father of biography, placed all succeeding centuries in his debt with his *Parallel Lives of the Illustrious Greeks and Romans*, while Strabo wrote on geography, and Josephus produced his *History of the Jews*. It was in this period that the modern novel had its beginning in such writings as the romance of *Daphnis and Chloe*, ascribed to Longus.

The Byzantine Period. From the 6th to the 15th century, the time of the fall of Constantinople, Greek, in the form of a stereotyped literary dialect imitating the Attic, continued to be the language of the culture which centered at Byzantium (Constantinople), as Latin was the language of Rome and the West. Apart from the work of a few able historians, such as Procopius of Cæsarea, most of the writings produced are of theological interest only, being the work of the Church fathers, such as Eusebius and Chrysostom. But it was during this period that the collection of short poems known as the *Greek Anthology* was completed. This collection includes thousands of poems, some of universal interest, and others inspired by some particular occasion, ranging in date from the 5th century B. C. to the 6th century A. D.

MODERN GREEK LITERATURE

Greek literature in the modern period, beginning about 1453, has been written partly in classical Greek, partly in the vernacular, but mainly in a literary language based on the classical tongue but modified by the vernacular and given definiteness through the work of the philologian Cortaës (1748–1833). The literary language was not spoken, but until the early years of the 20th century it was employed generally in prose writing. The use of the vernacular, or Romaic, language spread from poetry to all other types and had virtually completed its conquest of the literary tongue by 1925.

Before the national revival in the 18th century, few modern works were produced in Greek. A number of philosophical tracts in the classical tongue appeared during the 15th century, and an anonymous ballad poetry expressed in the vernacular arose in the mountainous districts of Greece. Crete too was represented by a number of poems in the local dialect, of which the *Eratocritus* by Cornaro (16th century) was the most noted. Several chronicles appeared in the literary tongue, which do not, however, attain to the distinction of histories.

The period of the revolution in the 18th century is represented by many writers, among whom the more noted were Rhigas (1760–89), who wrote stirring patriotic odes, and Trikoupis (1788–1873), the author of *History of the Revolution.*

Like other Western literatures, that of Greece in the 20th century has been especially rich in novels and short stories. Best known of modern Greek poets is Kostes Palamas (1859–), whose *Immutable Life* won him international recognition. His influence was one of the most powerful factors leading to the triumph of the vernacular over the literary tongue in Greek letters.

TABLE OF GREEK LITERATURE

Authors		Representative Works	
Time	Name	Prose	Poetry and Drama
B. C.			
About 900	Homer		Iliad, Odyssey.
About 800	Hesiod		Works and Days, Theogony.
About 700	Tyrtæus		Elegies.
About 600	Sappho		Lyrics.
About 600	Alcæus		Lyrics.
639–559	Solon		Elegies.
6th Cent.	Thespis		Tragedy.
About 563	Anacreon		Lyrics.
556–468	Simonides		Choral Lyrics, Elegies.
525–456	Æschylus		Tragedy (Prometheus Bound, Agamemnon).
522–443	Pindar		Choral Poetry.
500–428	Anaxagoras	Natural Philosophy	
495–406	Sophocles		Tragedy (Antigone, Œdipus Tyrannus).
484–424	Herodotus	History (Persian Wars)	
480–406	Euripides		Tragedy (Medea, The Bacchæ).
454–399	Thucydides	History (Peloponnesian War)	
445–385	Aristophanes		Comedy (The Birds, The Frogs)
445–378	Lysias	Oratory (Eratosthenes)	
436–338	Isocrates	Oratory (Panegyricus)	
434–355	Xenophon	History (Hellenica, Anabasis)	
429–347	Plato	Philosophy (Republic, Phædo)	
389–314	Æschines	Oratory (Against Ctesiphon)	
385–322	Demosthenes	Oratory (Philippics, On the Crown)	
384–322	Aristotle	Philosophy (Organon)	
372–287	Theophrastus	Philosophy (Characters)	
342–291	Menander		Comedy.
342–270	Epicurus	Philosophy	
About 300	Euclid	Geometry	
About 300	Theocritus		Pastoral Lyrics (Idyls).
287–212	Archimedes	Mechanics	
276–196	Eratosthenes	Astronomical Geography	
205?–122?	Polybius	History of world, 264-146 B. C.	
B. C. A. D. 64– 21	Strabo	Geography	
A. D. 37–100	Josephus	History (Jewish War)	
46–125	Plutarch	Biography (Parallel Lives of the Illustrious Greeks and Romans).	
125–192	Lucian	Dialogues of the Dead, Veracious History	
264–340	Eusebius	Church History (Chronicle)	
347–407	Chrysostom	Sermons	
5th Cent.	Longus	Pastoral Romance (Daphnis and Chloe)	

LATIN LITERATURE

Latin literature is to be prized because it contains such masterpieces as the poems of Lucretius, Virgil, and Horace, and the prose writings of Cicero and Livy. It has also transmitted to the Western world and adapted for it much of Greek thought and culture. Thus it has had an abiding influence on the form and content of the literatures of Europe and America. It deserves careful study also because the Latin language is one of the most perfect vehicles of literary expression that man has ever perfected, and because Latin is not only the predominant element in French, Spanish, and Italian, but also a very powerful factor even in the English language.

Early Epic and Drama. The early development of pure literature among the Romans is closely related to their political and military history. Southern Italy and Sicily were Greek. The war which the Romans carried on in the South against Pyrrhus and later in Sicily against the Carthaginians gave them a better acquaintance with the Greek people, Greek literature, and the Greek theater than they had had before. It was a Greek teacher, Livius Andronicus, brought to Rome as a captive from Tarentum in southern Italy in 272 B. C., who composed the first piece of formal Latin literature. It was a translation of the *Odyssey*. Later, in 241 B. C., to celebrate the successful conclusion of the long war with Carthage, a festival was held, and for this festival Andronicus adapted a Greek tragedy and a comedy. Nævius, the successor of Andronicus, and a native Italian, broke away in part from the Greek tradition by writing in verse the story of the first Punic war, and by basing some of his plays on Roman subjects.

Ennius also chose a Roman theme for his great epic, the *Annals*, which Virgil has followed here and there in the *Æneid.* Ennius used the hexameter verse too for the first time in Roman epic poetry. Greek tragedy in a Roman dress flourished in the early period, but it never attained great popularity with the Romans, and the writing of it for the stage ceased before the time of Cicero. The drama was best represented by the comedies of Plautus and Terence, in the latter part of the 3d and the early part of the 2d century B. C. Twenty of the plays of Plautus and six plays of Terence have come down to us. These two writers contented themselves with adapting Greek plays to their Roman audiences, but, in the century after them, plays based on Italian life made their appearance and won a place on the stage.

Oratory and History. While some native themes appeared in comedy and satiric verse, the practical Latin genius found best expression in this period in the prose of history and oratory. Cato the Censor is called the first of the orators, as he was the first historian in Latin. One hundred and fifty of his speeches are said to have been extant in the time of Cicero. He wrote also on agriculture and country life, and his *Origines* furnished Virgil with much material on the local history of Italian towns.

The following century (about 150–50 B. C.) witnessed the development of a Latin prose which combined the earnestness of the Roman temperament with something of the Greek artistic skill. The republican form of government was friendly to political discussion and furnished the motive for reflective political and historical prose. Sallust wrote history of the philosophic type found in the Greek historian, Thucydides. Cæsar, in his *Commentaries on the Gallic War*, created a model of direct, simple prose narrative.

Cicero. But the greatest figure of this time is Cicero, whose career falls in the first half of the 1st century B. C. Cicero was the greatest orator of his time, both in training and in performance. He developed a temperate style of oratory in contrast to the more florid Asiatic style then in vogue, and set a high standard for all orators of later centuries. His best-known speeches are those delivered against the conspirator Catiline. But, besides being a master of oratory, Cicero was a practical interpreter of the Greek philosophers. He was a finished critic and a graceful writer of letters which, in historical interest and personal charm, have perhaps never been surpassed. Among his famous books on criticism and philosophy are those *On the Orator*, *On Old Age*, and *On Friendship.*

The Augustan Age. To this "age of Cicero" belong two poets,—Lucretius, who wrote what has been called the world's greatest didactic poem, *De Rerum Natura*, an exposition of the atomic theory of Epicurus, and Catullus, the first great lyric poet of Rome. But the half century immediately following Cicero, called the Augustan age, saw the great outburst of Roman poetry. Loss of political freedom brought about the decline of oratory and political writing. Livy is the only great historian of the time, and he devoted his attention to giving the world splendid pictures, especially of the earlier periods of Roman history. Horace, for whom Catullus had prepared the way, wrote satires, epistles in verse, and odes, producing the finest Latin lyric verse. Ovid is best known through his *Metamorphoses*, in which he retold many Greek myths.

Virgil. The work of these men, as well as that of their greater contemporary, is still a living influence. The greatest of Roman poets is Virgil, whose earlier work, prompted by his own love of country life and perhaps by a suggestion of Augustus that he might kindle a like enthusiasm among the people, consisted of *Eclogues*, that is, shepherd or pastoral poems, and *Georgics*, or poems of farming, which have inspired many later poets. But Virgil's greatest theme was the glorification of Rome and through Rome the praise of the empire and Augustus. In his crowning work, the *Æneid*, which he modeled upon the Greek *Iliad* and *Odyssey*, he gave deathless form to the story, first attempted by Nævius and Ennius 200 years before, of the adventures of Æneas and his companions from the fall of Troy to the founding of Rome.

The Period of Decline. After the Augustan age, Latin literature begins to decline. In the years following the death of Virgil, we have in the drama only Seneca, whose artificial, closet-tragedies were taken as models by early French and English dramatists. Pliny the elder left a great name as an encyclopedist. Martial, who was the court poet of Domitian, is known as the creator of the epigram. Juvenal is the great satirist of the period. By an age that had lost creative power much attention was given to rhetoric, in which Quintilian was, for many centuries, the highest authority. In the reigns of Nerva and Trajan, Tacitus, embittered by the persecutions of the reign of Domitian, wrote independently and with some republican bias upon the early empire. He is the last of the great historians of antiquity.

Up to the time of Tacitus, Rome had been the center of literary activity. All the great writers had been born there or had come there to live. In the later period, Rome and Italy lose their primacy in the literary as well as in the political world. Their vitality is gone. But literature springs up afresh in the new soil of the Western provinces, especially in Africa and in Gaul, and flourishes there from the 2d to the 6th century. In this latter century we find the last piece of pure literature which seems to belong to the old civilization, the *Consolations of Philosophy* of Boethius. It is to the 6th century also that we owe the *Code* of Justinian, which has served as a basis for all later jurisprudence. It does not fall within the field of pure literature, but it is the most characteristic product of the Roman genius. It summarizes in its *Institutes* the great principles of law which the Romans had developed through the generations; in the *Digests* it sets forth the opinions of distinguished jurists on important points of law; while in the *Code* proper and in the *Novels* edicts and decrees of the emperors are grouped together.

It is quite impossible to fix any point as marking the end of Latin literature, but, by the 7th century, French, Italian, and Spanish were beginning to develop, and it is convenient to take Isidore, the bishop of Seville, who died in the year 636, as marking the end of the long line of Latin authors. As if conscious of the fact that he closed the series of writers in Latin, he tried to sum up in his great work on *Etymologies* all the learning of past generations of Romans.

Medieval Latin. Even after French, Italian, and Spanish came into use in everyday life, Latin continued to be the language employed by the scholar, by the diplomat, and especially by the churchman, even in the services of the Church and in the sermons of the clergy. The rapid spread of Christianity from the 3d century on made radical changes in both the form and the content of Latin literature, and to the scholars of the Church and to her institutions we owe such learning as the middle ages had and the transmission of the masterpieces of Latin literature to us. So far as literary form was concerned, Christian writers brought in accentual, rimed poetry in place of the quantitative blank verse of pagan literature. This new form of verse was used especially in their hymns, which St. Hilary of Poitiers introduced into the Latin Church in the 4th century.

Shortly afterward, in 405 A. D., St. Jerome completed his translation of the Bible into Latin, the Vulgate so called, perhaps the most widely used book that the world has ever known. A contemporary of his, St. Augustine, wrote his great treatise on the *City of God,* the first philosophic interpretation of history from the Christian point of view. As we come into the later period, we find in the 6th century the valuable *History of the Franks* by Gregory, bishop of Tours, and, corresponding to this work, the *Ecclesiastical History of the English People* by Bede, the monk of Jarrow. The classical tradition is kept alive in the Latin plays of the German nun, Hroswitha, in the 10th century, and in the works of John of Salisbury, the great English scholar of the 12th century.

Manuscripts in Monasteries. The preservation of the classics also is due primarily to the Church. In 540 Cassiodorus established a monastery in southern Italy, in which he employed the monks in copying Latin authors. When the rest of Europe was sunk in ignorance and poverty, the Irish monks kept up this practice, until order was restored on the continent by Charlemagne, and the copying of manuscripts was again taken up there, in the great monastery and school of Tours. When, in the time of the Renaissance, the works of Cicero, Virgil, and the other great writers of the early period were found in the monasteries and carefully studied, their Latin appeared so much finer than that in current use, that the latter fell into disrepute, and consequently the humanists may be said to have put an end to Latin as the accepted vehicle of literary expression.

Roman literature as we have it owed much to the Greeks, but it may well have been a misfortune to it that in the very beginning it was brought under the influence of so highly perfected a literature as was that of the Greeks. As a consequence, it never had an opportunity to develop along the lines of the Roman national genius. In the writing of satire, in letter writing, and in the realistic romance, the Romans found fields essentially new and especially adapted to their talent; but all the other literary *genres*—the epic, the lyric, the pastoral, the drama, oratory, history, biography, and the essay,—they found represented by finished Greek productions. That their prose literature in the last century B. C. and their verse in the Augustan age did attain such a high degree of excellence, is an indication that the Romans had a marked strain of originality and made themselves masters of literary technique.

TABLE OF LATIN LITERATURE

Authors		Representative Works	
Time	Name	Prose	Poetry and Drama
B. C.			
3d Cent.	Livius Andronicus		Translation of the Odyssey, Tragedy.
269?–199	Nævius		Comedy, Tragedy, Epic (The Punic War).
254–184	Plautus		Comedy, (Aulularia, Captivi, Pseudolus).
239–169	Ennius		Epic (The Annals), Tragedy, Miscellanies.
234–149	Cato the Censor	De Re Rustica, Origines	
220–130	Pacuvius		Tragedy.
190?–159	Terence		Comedy (Andria, Phormio, Adelphi).
180–103	Lucilius		Satires.
170– 90?	Accius		Tragedy.
116– 27	Varro	On Agriculture, Antiquities	
106– 43	Cicero	Orations, Letters, Essays	
100– 44	Julius Cæsar	Commentaries on the Gallic War and the Civil War	
99?– 55	Lucretius		De Rerum Natura.
87– 54	Catullus		Lyrics.
86– 34	Sallust	History (Conspiracy of Catiline, War with Jugurtha)	
70– 19	Virgil		Eclogues, Georgics, Æneid.
65– 8	Horace		Odes, Satires, Epistles, Epodes.
1st Cent.	Nepos	Biographies	
B. C. A. D.			
59 – 17	Livy	History of Rome	
54?– 19?	Tibullus		Elegies.
50?– 15?	Propertius		Elegies.
43 – 18	Ovid		Heroides, Metamorphoses, etc.
4?– 65	Seneca	Investigations, Moralistic Essays.	Dramas.
A. D.			
23– 79	Pliny the Elder	Natural History	
35– 95?	Quintilian	Rhetoric	
39– 65	Lucan		Pharsalia.
40?–104?	Martial		Court Poetry, Epigrams.
55?–120?	Tacitus	Germany, History, Annals	
60?–140?	Juvenal		Satire.
61–113?	Pliny the Younger	Letters	
70?–150?	Suetonius	Lives of the Cæsars	
125?–200?	Apuleius	Romance	
?–366	Hilary		Hymns.
340–420	St. Jerome	The Vulgate	
354–430	St. Augustine	Confessions, City of God	
480?–524	Boethius	De Consolatione Philosophiæ, Translations	
490?–580?	Cassiodorus	History, Rhetoric	
538–593	Gregory of Tours	History (of the Franks)	
540?–604	Gregory the Great	Commentaries, Letters	
560?–636	Isidore of Seville	Theology, Encyclopedia	
673–735	The Venerable Bede	Ecclesiastical History	
About 967	Hroswitha	Legends	Epics, Plays.
1100–1156	Bernard of Cluny		Hymns (Jerusalem the Golden; For Thee, O Dear, Dear Country; The World Is Very Evil).
1118–1180	John of Salisbury	Encyclopedia, Letters	Elegies.
?–1192	Adam of St. Victor		Hymns.

LITERARY PLOTS, CHARACTERS, AND ALLUSIONS

No one can hope to be conversant with all the stories that have been told and with all the characters that have been depicted in literature.

Not even the more famous books can be familiar to those who have limited time to devote to reading. Nevertheless, one cannot go far in reading, or even in conversation, without being confronted with some allusion or some reference to a great literary work or to a story or a character drawn from such a book.

The following dictionary is intended to make such allusions more intelligible: to *outline* the stories in a few words; to *place* the characters; to *explain* terms that get their meaning from their connection with celebrated works; and, in general, to be a *guide* through that complex, imaginary world built up by the literatures of all lands.

Abbot, The. Sir Walter Scott. A story of thrilling adventures and vivid historic scenes around Lochleven Castle, north of Edinburgh, where Mary Queen of Scots was imprisoned. The story centers about the fortunes of Mary. A famous scene in the book is Mary's signing of her abdication, at the insistence of Lindsay and Ruthven, the royal commissioners.

Abdallah. Life of Mohammed, Washington Irving. A hero in Mohammedan legend. It is said that Abdallah, the father of Mohammed, was so beautiful that, when he married Amina, 200 virgins died of broken hearts.

Abdiel (*ăb'dĭ-ĕl*). **Paradise Lost, Milton.** The name, meaning "servant of God," of the seraph, who, when Satan stirred up a revolt, boldly withstood him.

Abou ben Adhem (*ä'bōō bĕn ä'dĕm*). Title and hero of a short poem by Leigh Hunt. An angel appearing to him, inscribes his name first among those "whom love of God hath blessed," since he loved, not God, but his fellow men.

Abou Hassan (*ä'bōō hăs'ăn*). **Arabian Nights.** According to *Arabian Nights*, a merchant of Bagdad who was carried in his sleep to the bed of Caliph Haroun-al-Raschid and on waking was made to believe himself the caliph, a deception which occurred twice. He afterward became in reality the caliph's favorite and companion.

Abraxas. In Persian literature a word denoting a supreme being. In Greek notation it stands for the number 365. In old tales or romances Abraxas presides over 365 impersonated virtues, one of which is supposed to prevail on each day of the year. In the 2d century the word was employed by the Basilidians for the deity; it was also the principle of the Gnostic hierarchy, and that from which sprang their numerous Æons. The word is found on stones used as talismans in the middle ages, called abraxas stones.

Absalom. Absalom and Achitophel, Dryden. A name given by Dryden, in his satirical poem "Absalom and Achitophel," to the duke of Monmouth, a natural son of Charles II. Like Absalom, the son of David, Monmouth was remarkable for his personal beauty, his popularity, and his undutifulness to his father.

Absolute, Captain. The Rivals, Sheridan. The hero in Sheridan's comedy *The Rivals*. He is distinguished for his gallant, determined spirit, his quickness of speech, and his dry humor.

Absolute, Sir Anthony. The father of the hero in Sheridan's *Rivals*. He is represented as testy, positive, impatient, and overbearing, but yet of a warm and generous disposition.

Abudah (*ä-bōō'dä*). A merchant of Bagdad. He finds the only way to rid himself of the torment of an old hag by whom he is haunted is "to fear God and keep his commandments." In James Ridley's *Tales of the Genii* (1764).

Acadia. The original, now the poetic, name of Nova Scotia. The name is derived from the Micmac Indian word *akade*, meaning plenty; in old documents the territory was called L'Acadie or La Cadie. It was granted by Henry IV of France, November 8, 1603, to De Monts, a Frenchman, and a company of Jesuits. They were finally expelled from the country by the English governor and colonists of Virginia, who claimed all that coast by virtue of its prior discovery by the Cabots in 1497. In 1621, Sir William Alexander, a Scotchman, applied to and obtained of James I a grant of the whole peninsula, which he renamed Nova Scotia, in honor of his native land. In 1755, the French inhabitants were seized, forcibly removed, and dispersed among the English colonists on the Atlantic coast. Longfellow has made this event the subject of his poem "Evangeline."

Achitophel (*ȧ-kĭt'ō-fĕl*). **Absalom and Achitophel, Dryden.** Achitophel, a nickname given to the first earl of Shaftesbury by his contemporaries, and made use of by Dryden in his poem "Absalom and Achitophel," a satire designed as a defense of Charles II against the Whig party. There is said to be a striking resemblance between the character and career of Shaftesbury and that of Achitophel, or Ahithophel, the treacherous friend and counselor of David, and the fellow conspirator of Absalom.

Acrasia (*ȧ-krā'zhĭ-ȧ*). **Faery Queen, Spenser.** A witch represented as a lovely and charming woman, whose dwelling is the Bower of Bliss, situated on an island floating in a lake or a gulf, and adorned with everything in nature that can delight the senses. The word signifies intemperance. She is the personification of sensuous indulgence and intoxication. Sir Guyon, who represents the opposite virtue, is commissioned by the faery queen to bring her into subjection and to destroy her residence.

Acres, Bob. The Rivals, Sheridan. A character in *The Rivals*, celebrated for his cowardice and his peculiar method of allegorical swearing.

Acrostic (*ȧ-krŏs'tĭk*). A form of verse in which the first letters of the lines form a word, usually a name. The Hebrews wrote a form of acrostic poetry in which the initial letters made their alphabet in regular order. Some of the psalms of the Old Testament are on this plan, especially the 119th Psalm.

Adam. Meaning "the made one." (1) A character frequently alluded to in the *Talmud*. Many strange legends are related of him. He was buried, so Arabian tradition says, on Aboncais, a mountain of Arabia. (2) In Shakspere's *As You Like It*. An aged servant to Orlando, who offers to accompany Orlando in his flight and to share with him his carefully-hoarded savings of 500 crowns. (3) In Shakspere's *Comedy of Errors*. An officer known by his dress, a skin-coat.

Adamastor. Lusiad, Camoëns. A hideous phantom described by Camoëns as the spirit of the stormy cape (Cape of Good Hope).

Adams, Parson. Joseph Andrews, Fielding. A character in Fielding's story *Joseph Andrews*. He is distinguished for his goodness of heart, poverty, learning, and ignorance of the world, combined with courage, modesty, and a thousand oddities.

Adelphi (*ȧ-dĕl'fī*), "The Brothers." A play by Terence. Two brothers are brought up, one under stern parental discipline, the other under a scheme of indulgence. The play shows neither plan by itself to be successful. A golden mean between the extremes is suggested as the right method of education.

Adonais (*ăd'ō-nā'ĭs*). A poetical name given by Shelley to the poet Keats, on whose untimely death he wrote an elegy bearing this name for its title. The name was coined by Shelley probably to hint an analogy between Keats's fate and that of Adonis.

Adrastus. (1) *Jerusalem Delivered*, Tasso. An Indian prince from the banks of the Ganges, who aided the king of Egypt against the crusaders. He was distinguished by his garment, a serpent's skin. Adrastus was slain by Rinaldo. (2) A mythical king of Argos. While in exile in Sicyon, he instituted the Nemean games.

Æneas (*ē-nē'ăs*). A Trojan prince, son of Anchises and the goddess Venus. When Troy fell, he quitted the city with his followers, accompanied by his father and son, visited various countries, settled in Latium, and married Lavinia, the daughter of Latinus. To him tradition ascribes the founding of the Roman state. Virgil tells his story in the *Æneid*.

Æneid. An epic of Latin national life. Virgil introduces into his poem the outlines of the Roman history and a number of interesting episodes. The first three books are not arranged in the order of time. The second book, which relates the downfall of Troy, and is the basis of the poem, is the first in time. The third, which relates the voyage of Æneas until after his departure from Sicily for Italy, follows. The first, which relates the dispersion of his fleet and his arrival in Africa, with his kind reception by Dido, succeeds the third. By this change the hero relates the downfall of his country, and the fortunes of his long and eventful voyage. The idea which underlies the whole action of the poem is the great part played by Rome in the history of the world.

Æsop's Fables. In the 5th century B. C., fables were in circulation in Athens, which were attributed to a certain Æsopus. Nothing is known for certain of his career. Probably he did not write the stories, but merely told them. The common collections bearing the name "Æsop" are versions of a book made by Phalereus in Athens about 320 B. C. and translated into Latin by Phædrus in the 1st century A. D.

Agamemnon. A Tragedy by Æschylus. The first of a trilogy consisting of *Agamemnon, Choëphori,* and *Eumenides.* In the play, Clytemnestra, wife of Agamemnon, aided by Ægisthus, kills him, ostensibly to avenge their daughter Iphigenia, whom he had sacrificed.

Agapida (*ä-gä-pē'THä*), **Fray Antonio.** The imaginary chronicler of the *Conquest of Granada,* written by Washington Irving.

Agib. Arabian Nights. The third Calendar in the story of "The Three Calendars," in the *Arabian Nights.* Also, in "The Story of Noureddin Ali and Bedreddin Hassan," the son of the latter.

Agnes. (1) A young girl in Molière's *L'Ecole des Femmes,* who affects to be remarkably simple and ingenuous. The name has passed into popular use, and is applied to any young woman unsophisticated in affairs. (2) A strong, womanly character in *David Copperfield,* who proves a true friend to David's "childwife," Dora, and to David himself. Later, Dora dies and David marries Agnes.

Agramante (*ä'grä-män'tä*) or **Agramant** (*ăg'rȧ-mănt*). King of the Moors in Ariosto's poem *Orlando Furioso.*

Aguecheek (*ā'gū-chēk'*), **Sir Andrew. Twelfth Night, Shakspere.** A simpleton to whom life consists only of eating and drinking. He is stupid even to silliness, but so devoid of self-love or self-conceit that he is delightful in his simplicity.

Ahmed, Prince. Arabian Nights. A hero who possessed a magic tent which would cover a whole army but might be carried in the pocket. He also possessed a magic apple which would cure all diseases.

Al Aaraaf (*ăl ä-räf'*). The Mohammedan limbo, or abode of souls who have been about equally good and bad. The subject of an uncompleted poem by Edgar Allan Poe.

Aladdin. One of the best-known characters in the *Arabian Nights.* Aladdin becomes possessed of a wonderful lamp and ring. On rubbing them, two genii appear, who are the slaves of anyone who possesses the lamp and ring, They obey Aladdin and perform incredible deeds by their magic.

Alasnam. The hero of a story in the *Arabian Nights* entitled "The History of Prince Zeyn Alasnam and the Sultan of the Genii." Alasnam had eight diamond statues, but had to go in quest of a ninth more precious still, to fill the vacant pedestal. The prize was found in the lady who became his wife, at once the most beautiful and the most perfect of her race.

Alastor, the Spirit of Solitude, Shelley. A poem in which he pictures an uncorrupted youth who, in seeking sympathy in the world, finds only the solitude of the crowd. In Greek story, Alastor is the avenger who follows the guilty man.

Albany, Albainn. A name given to Scotland or the Scottish Highlands in old romances and early histories. The title "Duke of Albany" has been frequently conferred since the 14th century. The "Duke of Albany" is the husband of Goneril in Shakspere's *King Lear.*

Alberich, Dwarf. In the *Nibelungenlied* the dwarf "Alberich" is the guardian of the famous "hoard" won by Siegfried from the Nibelungs. The dwarf is twice vanquished by the hero, who gets possession of his "Tarnhelm," or cap of invisibility.

Albion. An ancient name of Britain, now used only in poetic allusion. Some say the name is derived from the lofty white cliffs on the south coast. Others derive it from the name of a fabulous giant, Albion, son of Neptune, who called the island after his own name and ruled it 44 years.

Albracca (*äl-bräk'kä*). **Orlando Innamorato, Boiardo.** A castle of Cathay to which Angelica retires in grief at being scorned and shunned by Rinaldo, with whom she is deeply in love. Here she is besieged by Agricane, king of Tartary, who resolves to win her, notwithstanding her indifference to his suit.

Alceste (*ăl-sĕst'*). **Le Misanthrope, Molière.** A noble but misanthropic man, the hero of Molière's comedy.

Alchemist, The, Ben Jonson. A comedy. The alchemist is Subtle, a quack, who makes dupes of Sir Epicure Mammon and others. He leads them to believe that he has discovered the philosopher's stone. The best of Jonson's dramas.

Alcina. Orlando Innamorato, Boiardo. A fairy represented as carrying off Astolfo. She reappears in great splendor in Ariosto's *Orlando Furioso.*

Aldiborontiphoscophornio. A character in Henry Carey's burlesque tragedy *Chrononhotonthologos.*

Aldine (*ăl'dĭn*) **Edition.** This name is now applied to some editions of English works. The original Aldine editions were books from the press of Aldus Manutius, printed in the years 1490–1597 in Venice. These books have been highly prized for both their literary value and their handsome exterior. The distinguishing mark of the Aldine books is an anchor entwined with a dolphin. Collections of these books have been made. Many of the works are now very rare and are highly prized.

Aldingar (*ăl'dĭn-gär*), **Sir.** A character in an ancient legend, and the title of a celebrated ballad, preserved in Percy's *Reliques.* This ballad relates how the honor of Queen Eleanor, wife of Henry Plantagenet, impeached by Sir Aldingar, her steward, was submitted to the hazard of a duel, and how an angel, in the form of a little child, appeared as her champion and established her innocence.

Alexandrian Codex (*kō'dĕks*). A manuscript of the Scriptures in Greek, which belonged to the library of the patriarchs of Alexandria, in Africa, A. D. 1098. In 1628 it was sent as a present to Charles I and was placed in the British Museum. It is on parchment, in uncial letters, and contains the Septuagint version (except the Psalms), a part of the New Testament, and the Epistles of Clemens Romanus It is much consulted by biblical scholars, especially in the critical study of the epistles.

Alhambra (*ăl-hăm'brȧ*), **The, Washington Irving.** A series of legends of this famous Moorish fortress and palace near Granada, Spain. The book contains the finest descriptions of the palace. The name means "Red Castle."

Alice Brand. Lady of the Lake, Scott. Alice signed Urgan the dwarf thrice with the sign of the cross, and he became "the fairest knight in all Scotland." Then Alice recognized in him her own brother.

Alice's Adventures in Wonderland. A popular children's story by Lewis Carroll (C. L. Dodgson). In the story Alice, in a dream, in which she follows a rabbit into his burrow, comes out in a marvelous land underground where the animals act and talk like human beings. Her later adventures are given in *Through the Looking-Glass.*

Allan-a-Dale. A friend of Robin Hood's in the ballad. He is introduced into Sir Walter Scott's *Ivanhoe* as Robin Hood's minstrel.

All's Well that Ends Well. A comedy by Shakspere. The hero and heroine are Bertram, count of Rousillon, and Helena, a physician's daughter, who are married by the command of the king of France, but separate because Bertram thinks the lady not sufficiently well born for him. Ultimately, however, all ends well.

Allworthy. Tom Jones, Fielding. Tom's foster father. He is distinguished for his benevolence. This character is said to be drawn from Fielding's friend, Ralph Allen.

Alph. Kubla Khan, Coleridge. A name invented by Coleridge and applied to a river mentioned in this poem.

Alquife (*äl-kē'fä*). A personage that figures in all the books of the lineage of Amadis as a powerful wizard.

Al Rakim (*ăl rȧ-kēm'*). A fabulous dog connected with the legend of the "Seven Sleepers." The Mohammedans have given him a place in paradise.

Al Sirat (*ăl sē-rät'*). A bridge from this world to the next, extending over the abyss of hell. This narrow bridge, less than the thread of a famished spider, must be passed over by every one who would enter the Mohammedan paradise.

Amadis (*ăm'ȧ-dĭs*) **of Gaul.** The hero of a celebrated medieval romance. The first part of the story is said to have been written by Lobeira of Portugal in the 14th century. Other portions were added later in Spain and France. Amadis, the hero, is a prince of Gaula, or Wales. He is exposed to the sea in his cradle, is rescued, brought up in Scotland, and, finally, after numerous adventures, marries the princess Oriana, in some versions daughter of a king of England, in others, of a king of Denmark.

Amaimon or **Amaymon.** An imaginary king of the East, one of the principal devils who might be bound or restrained from doing hurt from the third hour till noon, and from the ninth hour till evening. He is alluded to in Shakspere's *Merry Wives of Windsor.*

Amanda. A young woman who impersonates spring in Thomson's "Seasons."

Amaurot. Utopia, Sir Thomas More. Amaurot was the chief city in Utopia.

Amaurote. A bridge in Utopia. The word means "faintly seen."

Amelia. The title of one of Fielding's novels, and the name of its heroine, who is distinguished for her tenderness and affection. The character of Amelia is said to have been drawn from Fielding's wife.

Amine (*ăm'ĭ-nē*). In *Arabian Nights* a female character who leads her three sisters by her side as a leash of hounds.

Aminte (*ä'mäNt'*). **Les Précieuses Ridicules, Molière.** A contradictory character in this comedy. She dismisses her admirers for proposing to marry her, scolds her uncle for not carrying himself as a gentleman, and marries a valet whom she believes to be a nobleman.

Amlet, Richard. The name of a gamester in Vanbrugh's *Confederacy*.

Amoret. (1) The name of a lady married to Sir Scudamore, in Spenser's *Faery Queen.* She is the type of a devoted, loving wife. (2) The heroine of Fletcher's pastoral drama, *The Faithful Shepherdess.*

Amys and Amylion. Two faithful friends. The Pylades and Orestes of the feudal ages. Their adventures are the subjects of ancient romances. An abstract of this early romance is found in Ellis's *Specimens of Early English Metrical Romances.*

Anabasis (*ȧ-năb'ȧ-sĭs*). A Greek work by Xenophon, which describes the expedition of the 10,000 Greeks, allies of Cyrus, particularly their retreat after the defeat and the death of Cyrus in 401 B. C.

Anacreontic (*ȧ-năk'rē-ŏn'tĭk*) **Verse.** Commonly of the jovial or Bacchanalian strain, named after Anacreon of Teos, the Greek lyric poet, born at Teos, an Ionian city in Asia Minor. He died at the age of 85, probably about the year 550 B. C. In his poems Anacreon sang chiefly the praises of love and wine, to the enjoyment of which his life appears to have been dedicated. Many fragments of his songs are preserved, which are models of delicate grace, simplicity, and ease.

Anagram. A transposition of the letters of a name or sentence, the change of one word or phrase into another, by reading the letters backward or by transposing them.

Anastasius (*ăn'ăs-tā'shĭ-ŭs*). **Anastasius, Thomas Hope.** The hero of this novel purports to be a Greek, who, to escape the consequences of his own crimes and villainies, becomes a renegade, and passes through a long series of the most extraordinary vicissitudes.

Ancient Man. Idylls of the King, Tennyson. Merlin, the old magician, King Arthur's protector and teacher.

Ancient Mariner. Rime of the Ancient Mariner, Coleridge. The ancient mariner, for the crime of having shot an albatross, a bird of good omen to voyagers, is doomed to undergo terrible suffering. Dreadful penalties are visited upon his companions, who have made themselves accomplices in his crime. The penalties are at last remitted in consequence of his repentance. When pity enters his heart he can pray, and the dead albatross, bound about his neck, falls off. The ship moves on, and he returns to his home port. There he encounters a hermit to whom he relates his story. At certain times the agony of remorse returns and drives him on, like the Wandering Jew, from land to land, compelled to relate the tale of his suffering and crime as a warning to others, and as a lesson of love and charity toward all God's creatures.

Andrews, Joseph. The hero in a novel of the same name, written by Fielding, to ridicule Richardson's *Pamela.* Fielding presents Joseph as a brother to the modest and prudish Pamela, and pictures him as a model young man.

Androclus or **Androcles** (*ăn'drô-klēz*) **and the Lion.** A story of a runaway slave who extracted a thorn from the paw of a lion. Later the slave, Androclus, was condemned to fight with a lion in the arena at Rome. The lion let out against him, turning out to be the animal he had befriended, expressed affection for him. G. B. Shaw wrote a satirical play on the subject.

Angel of the Schools, Angelic Doctor. Epithets applied to the medieval philosopher, Thomas Aquinas.

Angelica (*ăn-jĕl'ĭ-kȧ*). An infidel princess of exquisite beauty in Boiardo's *Orlando Innamorato* and Ariosto's *Orlando Furioso.* A beautiful heiress in Congreve's *Love for Love.*

Anna Karenina (*kä-rä'nē-nä*), **Count Tolstóy.** One of Tolstóy's most powerful books. The story of an attractive and, in many points, admirable woman, who forsakes her husband for a lover. The end, for her, is tragic suicide.

Antipholus of Ephesus, Antipholus of Syracuse. Twin brothers, sons of Egeon and Emilia, in Shakspere's *Comedy of Errors.*

Antiquary, The, Scott. One of the Waverley novels. The Antiquary is Sir Jonathan Oldbuck, who has William Lovel as his guest at Monkbairns. Lovel there meets the daughter of Sir Arthur Wardour. He reveals himself as the earl of Glenallan and marries her.

Antonio. A frequent name in Shakspere's plays. (1) In *The Merchant of Venice,* the friend to Bassanio, and the object of Shylock's hatred. (2) The usurping duke of Milan, and brother to Prospero, in *The Tempest.* (3) The father of Proteus, in *Two Gentlemen of Verona.* (4) A minor character, in *Much Ado about Nothing.* (5) A sea captain, friend to Sebastian, in *Twelfth Night.*

Antony and Cleopatra (*klē'ô-pā'trȧ*). Historical tragedy by Shakspere, which may be considered as a continuation of *Julius Cæsar.* In the opening scene of *Julius Cæsar* absolute power is lodged in one man. In the conclusion of *Antony and Cleopatra* a second Cæsar is again in possession of absolute power, and the entire Roman world is limited under one imperial ruler. There are four prominent characters in this play: Cleopatra, voluptuous, fascinating, gross in her faults, but great in the power of her affections; Octavius Cæsar, cool, prudent, calculating, avaricious; Antony, quick, brave, reckless, prodigal; Enobarbus, a friend of Antony, at first jocular and blunt, but transformed by penitence into a grief stricken man who dies in the bitterness of despair.

Aonian Mount. Milton says his muse is to soar above "the Aonian Mount," i. e., above the flight of fable and classic themes, because his subject was "Jehovah, lord of all." Mount Helicon, home of the Muses, was in Aonia in Greece.

Apemantus (*ăp'ê-măn'tŭs*). A churlish philosopher in Shakspere's play *Timon of Athens.*

Apocalypse (*ȧ-pŏk'ȧ-lĭps*). The Greek name of the last book of the New Testament, termed in English "Revelation." It has been generally attributed to the apostle St. John, but some wholly reject it as spurious. In the first centuries many churches disowned it, and in the 4th century it was excluded from the sacred canon by the council of Laodicea, but was again received by other councils, and confirmed by that of Trent, held in the year 1545. Most commentators suppose it to have been written after the destruction of Jerusalem, about A. D. 96, while others assign it an earlier date. Its figures and symbols are impressive.

Apocrypha (*ȧ-pŏk'rĭ-fȧ*). The word originally meant secret or hidden. The books of the Apocrypha are not found in either the Aramaic or the Hebrew language. The Old Testament apocryphal writings are fourteen in number: Baruch, Ecclesiasticus, Wisdom of Solomon, Tobit, Judith, two books of the Maccabees, Song of the Three Children, Susannah, Bel and the Dragon, The Prayer of Manasses, Esdras 1 and 2, parts of Esther found only in Greek. Their style proves that they were a part of the Jewish-Greek literature of Alexandria, within 300 years before Christ; as the Septuagint Greek version of the Hebrew Bible came from the same quarter, it was often accompanied by these Greek writings, and they gained a general circulation. No trace of them is found in the *Talmud*; they are mostly of legendary character, but some of them are of value for historical information, for their moral and maxims, and for the illustrations they give of ancient life. Several of these books were received as canonical by the Roman Catholic Church, at the Council of Trent. Protestant churches differ in the use of them. New Testament Apocrypha are certain letters and gospels, mostly of the 2d century, written to supplement the canonical books.

Apollyon. An evil spirit introduced by Bunyan in his allegorical romance *Pilgrim's Progress.*

Arabian Nights Entertainments. A series of one thousand and one stories, told by the sultana of the Indies to divert the sultan from the execution of a bloody vow which he had made to marry a lady every day and have her head cut off next morning, to avenge himself for the disloyalty of the first sultana. The story on which all the others hang is familiar. Scheherazade, the generous, beautiful young daughter of the vizier, like another Esther, resolves to risk her life in order to save the poor maidens of her city whom the sultan is marrying and beheading at the rate of one a day. She plans to tell an interesting story each night to the sultan, breaking off in a very exciting place in order that the sultan may be tempted to spare her life so that he may hear the sequel.

Arcadia, Sir Philip Sidney. The full title of this prose romance is "The Countess of Pembroke's Arcadia." Shakspere, at times, borrowed matter from this popular book. The word had long stood for a country of simple life and customs.

Archer. The Beaux' Stratagem, Farquhar. A servant to Aimwell and an amusing fellow.

Archimago (*är'kĭ-mā'gō*) or **Archimage. Faery Queen, Spenser.** The name implies a hypocrite or deceiver. He is an enchanter in the *Faery Queen,* opposed to holiness embodied in the Red Cross Knight. In the disguise of a reverend hermit, he wins the confidence of the knight, and, by the help of Duessa, or Deceit, separates him from Una, or Truth.

Arcite (*är′sīt*). **Palamon and Arcite, Chaucer.** "Palamon and Arcite" is the first story told by Chaucer in his *Canterbury Tales.* Chaucer borrowed this story from Boccaccio, who, in his turn, borrowed it from a more ancient medieval tale. Dryden later put the same story into verse. Dryden pronounced the word Ar′cite′ or Ar-ci-te′. Arcite, a young Theban knight, made prisoner by Duke Theseus, is shut up in a prison in Athens with Palamon. Both the captives fall in love with Emily, the duke's sister-in-law. Both gain their liberty, and Emily is promised by the duke to the one who wins in a tournament. Arcite wins but is killed by a fall from a horse, and Emily marries Palamon.

Arden, Enoch. The hero of Tennyson's poem of the same name, a seaman who is wrecked on an uninhabited, tropical island, where he spends many years. He returns home at last only to find that his wife, believing him to be dead, has married his old playfellow and rival, and is prosperous and happy. In a spirit of heroic self-sacrifice, he determines not to undeceive her, and soon dies of a broken heart.

Arethusa. The name of a sylph in Pope's "Rape of the Lock." A reference to the Greek story of the love of Alpheus for Arethusa.

Argalia (*är′gȧ-lē′ȧ*). **Orlando Innamorato, Boiardo.** A brother to Angelica in this romantic poem. He is celebrated as the possessor of an enchanted lance which threw whomsoever it touched. Ferraù eventually killed him, and Astolfo obtained the lance.

Argalus. An unhappy lover in Sir Philip Sidney's *Arcadia.*

Argan. The hero of Molière's comedy *Le Malade Imaginaire.*

Argonauts of '49. A literary name applied to the gold seekers who made the long overland trip or the longer sea journey to California in 1849 in search of gold. A reminiscence of the ancient Greek search for the golden fleece.

Ariel. (1) In the demonology of the cabala, a water spirit. (2) In the fables of the middle ages, a spirit of the air, the guardian angel of innocence. (3) In Shakspere's *Tempest,* a bright, airy spirit whom Prospero had released from a tree to do his bidding and work his magical spells. By obedience Ariel is to win freedom when Prospero leaves the island.

Ariodantes (*ăr′ĭ-ō-dăn′tēz*). A lover in Ariosto's *Orlando Furioso.*

Armageddon. The name of the field in the plain of Esdraelon where the Israelites fought many battles with their enemies. Now applied to any great, decisive conflict.

Armida (*är-mē′dȧ*). **Jerusalem Delivered, Tasso.** A beautiful sorceress whom Rinaldo loved. By a talisman he is disenchanted. Not being able to allure him back, Armida rushes into the midst of a combat, is defeated, and, after conversion to Christianity, regains his love.

Arnolphe (*är′nôlf′*). **L'Ecole des Femmes, Molière.** A selfish and morose cynic.

Aroundight (*ȧr′ŭn-dīt*). The sword of Lancelot of the Lake.

Arrow-Maker, The, Mary Austin. A drama of Indian life. The story is that of Chisera, a Piute medicine woman. Wearying of the loveless rôle she is compelled to play, she gives her love to Simwa, the "arrow-maker." He deserts her for the chief's daughter. Chisera ceases to serve as intermediary between the gods and the Indians. Disaster for the tribe follows. Chisera dies by one of her own magic arrows.

Arsinoe (*är-sĭn′ō-ē*). **Le Misanthrope, Molière.** A prudish character in this comedy.

Artegal. Also written Artegall, Arthegal, and Artegale. (1) A legendary king of Britain mentioned by Geoffrey of Monmouth in his chronicles and by Milton in his *History of Britain.* (2) A character in Spenser's *Faery Queen,* representing justice. (3) The hero in a poem by William Wordsworth, entitled "Artegal and Elidure."

Artful Dodger. See *Dawkins.*

Arthur, King. A poetical character, based on historical traditions. The Arthur of the old Welsh bards was a warrior chieftain ruling over fierce and warlike tribes. Every generation of poets has added something to this picture, until the Arthur of modern romance is the Christian gentleman as Tennyson pictures him in his *Idylls of the King* surrounded by his chivalrous knights, all bound together in one quest for the Holy Grail.

Arthurian Romances. These may be divided into six parts: (1) The romance of the "San Graal." (2) "Merlin," which celebrates the birth and exploits of King Arthur. (3) "Lancelot." (4) The search or "Quest of the San Graal." (5) "Le Morte D'Arthur," or death of Arthur. (6) "Sundry Tales."

Arthur's Drinking-Horn. No one could drink from this horn who was either unchaste or unfaithful.

Arthur's Round Table. It contained seats for 150 knights. Three were reserved,—two for honor, and one, called the "siege perilous," for Sir Galahad, destined to achieve the quest of the Holy Grail.

Arthur's Sword. Excalibur or Excaliber. Geoffrey of Monmouth calls it Caliburn and says it was made in the isle of Avalon, by Merlin.

Ascapart. The name of a giant whom Bevis of Southampton conquered. This is a favorite story of the old British romancers. The effigy of Ascapart may be seen on the city gates of Southampton. He is said to have been thirty feet high, and to have carried Sir Bevis, his wife, and his horse, under his arm. Allusions to him occur in Shakspere, Drayton, and other English poets.

Ashton, Sir William. The lord keeper of Scotland; a prominent character in Scott's *Bride of Lammermoor.*

Asmodeus (*ăz′mō-dē′ŭs*). (1) In the Jewish demonology, an evil spirit, sometimes the demon of vanity, or dress. One legend makes him the destroyer of seven husbands of Sara, daughter of Roguel, on their bridal nights. In modern times he has been spoken of as the destroying demon of matrimonial happiness. (2) The demon hero of *Le Diable Boiteux* by Lesage, from which Foote took his play *The Devil on Two Sticks.*

Aspasia (*ăs-pā′shĭ-ȧ*). A woman of ancient Athens, celebrated, in the age of Pericles, for wit, beauty, and influence.

Aspatia (*ăs-pā′shĭ-ȧ*). The unfortunate heroine of Beaumont and Fletcher's play *The Maid's Tragedy.*

Astolat. The home of Elaine, "the lily maid of Astolat," in Tennyson's *Idylls of the King.*

Astolfo or **Astolpho.** A boastful and generous English knight in the tales of the adventures of Charlemagne and his Paladins. He was the possessor of a magic horn and book.

Astoria, Irving. A book of rambling sketches of Western trading and exploration, centering about the founding of Astoria, at the mouth of the Columbia, by John Jacob Astor in 1811. Still interesting and valuable.

As You Like It. A comedy by Shakspere. A French duke, driven from his dukedom by his brother, sought a refuge in the forest of Arden with a few of his followers. Here they lived a free and easy life. Rosalind, the daughter of the banished duke, remained at court with her cousin Celia. At a wrestling match Rosalind fell in love with Orlando, who threw his antagonist, a giant and professional athlete. The usurping duke, Frederick, now banished her from the court, but her cousin Celia resolved to go to Arden with her; so Rosalind in boy's clothes, and Celia, as a rustic maiden, started to find the deposed duke. Orlando, being driven from home by his elder brother, also went to the forest of Arden, and was taken under the duke's protection. Here he met the ladies, and a double marriage was the result—Orlando married Rosalind, and his elder brother Oliver married Celia. The usurper retired to a religious house, and the deposed duke was restored to his dominions.

Athalie (*ăt′ȧ-lē*). **Athalie** (Anglicized, **Athaliah**), **Racine.** Daughter of Ahab and Jezebel, and usurping queen in Jerusalem, in Racine's famous tragedy by this name.

Attic Salt. The phrase is used to mean a certain wit or vigor of style in writing, in reference to the superior quality anciently attributed to Athenian works. The Roman style was heavier, less spirited.

Auburn. The name of a village immortalized by Oliver Goldsmith in his "Deserted Village." Some critics are disposed to connect it with Lissoy near Athlone in Ireland; but Goldsmith's "Auburn" is purely poetical.

Aucassin and Nicolette (*ō′kȧ′săɴ′*) (*nē′kō′lĕt′*). The delicate and vivid love story of Aucassin, son of the French count of Beaucaire, and Nicolette, a captive daughter of a king of Carthage. A product of the 12th century, it is the best of early French tales. Translated into English by Andrew Lang.

Audrey. A country wench, in Shakspere's *As You Like It.*

Aulularia (*ô-lōō-lā′rĭ-ȧ*). A comedy by Plautus, in which a miser, Euclion, is the central character. The name comes from *aulula,* meaning "a pot." This play has influenced several modern "miser" plays.

Autolycus. The craftiest of thieves. He stole the flocks of his neighbors and changed their marks. Sisyphus outwitted him by marking his sheep under their feet. Shakspere introduces him in *The Winter's Tale* as a peddler, and says he was called the son of Mercury.

Avalon or **Avilion.** The earthly paradise of the Britons. In medieval romance the name of an ocean island and of a castle. It is represented as the abode of Arthur and Oberon and Morgan le Fay. It is most fully described in the old French romance of *Ogier le Danois*. It is the island kingdom to which King Arthur is finally borne by the mysterious barge in Tennyson's "Passing of Arthur." Some identify Avalon with the modern Glastonbury.

Avare, L' (*lȧ'vȧr'*). A comedy by Molière. The old miser, Harpagon, who has planned to marry a young girl, Marianne, finds his son, Cléante, a rival for her affection. Cléante obtains possession of Harpagon's gold and gives his father a choice of girl or gold. He chooses the gold.

Aymer (*ā'mĕr*), **Prior.** A Benedictine monk, prior of Jorvaulx Abbey, in Sir Walter Scott's *Ivanhoe*.

Aymon (*ā'mŏn*). The family name of four brothers who lived in France in the 8th century. Their exploits are celebrated in many chivalric tales of the middle ages.

Azazel (*ȧ-zā'zĕl*). **Paradise Lost, Milton.** Represented in this poem as Satan's standard bearer. According to the *Koran*, when God commanded the angels to worship Adam, Azazel replied, "Why should the son of fire fall down before a son of clay?" and God cast him out of heaven.

Azo. The name given by Byron to the prince of Este, in his poem "Parisina."

Bab Ballads, The. A collection of light satiric and comic verses by W. S. Gilbert which appeared as occasional poems in "Fun" (1866–71), and were published in volumes as "The Bab Ballads" (1869) and "More Bab Ballads" (1873). They have been issued later in several editions. The "Yarn of the Nancy Bell" and "Bob Polter" are famous examples of these pieces.

Babbitt. The central character in Sinclair Lewis's novel of the same name. Babbitt is a type of the successful business man whose viewpoint and sympathies are determined solely by his business interests and personal pride and comfort. Lewis depicted this type so convincingly that the term Babbitt has passed into popular use to designate a person of this character.

Babes in the Wood. See *Children in the Wood*.

Baboon, Lewis. History of John Bull, Arbuthnot. A name given to Louis XIV of France. The name Philip Baboon was given in the same writing to Philip Bourbon, duke of Anjou.

Babu or **Baboo** (*bä'bōō*). A Hindu title equivalent to "Mr." Often used of a native official or clerk who writes English.

Backbite, Sir Benjamin. School for Scandal, Sheridan. A vacantly busy man who peddled scandal.

Bagstock, Joe. Dombey and Son, Dickens. The insistent and selfish "J. B.," "old J. B.," and "Joey B." of the story.

Baillie, Harry. Canterbury Tales, Chaucer. The jolly landlord at Tabard Inn, where the Canterbury Pilgrims gathered in making ready for their journey.

Balafré, Le (*lĕ bȧ'lȧ'frā'*). **Quentin Durward, Scott.** Nickname given to an old archer belonging to the Scottish guards. The name means "the man with a scar."

Balderstone, Caleb. Bride of Lammermoor, Scott. The butler of the Ravenswoods, who tries to conceal the poverty of the family. A type of faithful servant. His pretentions have often been laughingly quoted.

Baldwin. Jerusalem Delivered, Tasso. The brother of Godfrey of Bouillon. In the tale of *Reynard the Fox* the name Baldwin is given to one of the beasts.

Balmawhapple (*băl'mȧ-hwăp''l*). **Waverley, Scott.** An obstinate, stupid-faced, blundering Scotch laird.

Balthazar (*băl-thā'zȧr*). (1) In Shakspere's *Comedy of Errors*, a merchant, ordered to furnish impossible merchandise. (2) In *Much Ado about Nothing*, Balthazar appears as servant to Don Pedro. (3) Portia takes the name in the *Merchant of Venice*. (4) Chaucer, in "The Monk's Tale," gives this name to Belshazzar. (5) Balthazar is also the traditional name of one of the wise men who followed the star to Bethlehem.

Balwhidder (*băl'hwiтн-ẽr*). **Annals of the Parish, Galt.** A sincere, kind, talkative Scotch Presbyterian clergyman. With natural prejudices and old-fashioned ways he is too "easy" to carry on his parish work with zeal. His friends enjoy Balwhidder's jokes.

Banquo. Macbeth, Shakspere. A thane of Scotland, said to belong to the 11th century and to be ancestor of the Stuarts. In fiction, made immortal as the innocent laird murdered by Macbeth. Banquo's ghost is more famous than Banquo himself.

Barabas (*băr'ȧ-băs*). **The Jew of Malta, Marlowe.** A monster, the hero of the tragedy, who wears a big nose and invents infernal machines.

Barbara Frietchie, Whittier. A poem based on an alleged incident at Frederick, Md., in the Civil War. It exhibits the patriotism of the aged Barbara Frietchie, who dared to fly the Union flag in the presence of Confederate troops, and the chivalry of Stonewall Jackson, who forbade punitive measures against her.

Barber of Seville, Beaumarchais. A witty comedy. The plot, in which Bartolo, who wants to marry his ward Rosina, is duped and outwitted by her lover, Almaviva, and the ex-valet and barber, Figaro, serves to carry brilliant dialogue and satire. First presented in 1775.

Bardell, Mrs. Pickwick Papers, Dickens. The landlady, a widow, who sues Mr. Pickwick for breach of promise to marry her.

Bard of Avon. Name given to Shakspere, who was born and buried in Stratford-on-Avon.

Bard of Ayrshire. A name often given to Robert Burns, the great poet of Scotland, who was a native of the county of Ayr.

Bard of Rydal Mount. An epithet sometimes applied to the poet Wordsworth, who resided at Rydal Grasmere, in the county of Westmoreland from 1813 to 1850. His dwelling overlooked a beautiful view of the lake.

Bardolph. Merry Wives of Windsor, Shakspere. A follower of Falstaff, known as the "knight of the burning lamp," from his red nose.

Barkis. David Copperfield, Dickens. Remembered by the much-quoted "Barkis is willing," his form of proposing marriage to his beloved Clara Peggotty.

Barleycorn, Sir John. Tam O'Shanter, Burns. Name given to the personification of a malt liquor made from barley. Sir Barleycorn has also been noticed by Scott and Hawthorne. The name comes down to us from an old English pamphlet in which Sir John Barleycorn is arraigned in court, tried by jury, and acquitted.

Barmecide (*bär'mē-sīd*) **Feast.** The phrase, which means a feast with little or nothing to eat, refers to a Persian story. One of the Barmecide family invited a poor man to dine, but, while the host called for the most delicious dishes and urged his guest to eat, there was nothing to eat. The poor man played the game, even feigning to get drunk on the make-believe wine and knocking his host down. This so pleased the Barmecide that he provided a real banquet and took the poor man into his household.

Barnaby Rudge. Barnaby Rudge, Dickens. A half-witted lad who wanders about with a pet raven. They experience together many adventures, including a no-popery riot.

Barry Lyndon, The Memoirs of, W. M. Thackeray. A famous story of the picaresque, or roguery, type. The hero, Barry Lyndon, is represented as telling his own story of scoundrelly adventure. Throughout his revelations of rascality and villainy in gaming and in illtreatment of his wife, he maintains a confident air of gentility. His life ends in imprisonment and a sordid death. Thackeray wrote the story in a vein of sustained irony.

Basilisco (*băs'ĭ-lĭs'kō*). **Soliman and Persida, Old Play.** A boasting knight who became so popular with his foolish bragging that his name grew into a proverb.

Bassanio (*bȧ-sä'nĭ-ō*). **Merchant of Venice, Shakspere.** The lover of Portia, who won her when he chose a leaden casket in which her portrait was hidden.

Bath, Major. Amelia, Henry Fielding. A noble-minded gentleman, pompous in spite of poverty, and striving to live according to the "dignity and honor of man." He tries to hide his poverty under bold speech even when found doing menial service.

Battle, Sarah. Essays of Elia, Lamb. Sarah considered whist the business of life, and literature one of the relaxations. When a young gentleman, of a literary turn, told her he had no objection to unbending his mind for a little time by taking a hand with her, Sarah declared "Whist was her life business, her duty, the thing she came into the world to do. She unbent her mind afterwards over a book."

Battle of the Books, The, Jonathan Swift. A famous satire, in which Swift discusses the endless controversy over the comparative merits of ancient and modern writers.

Battle of the Kegs, Francis Hopkinson. A humorous poem. It ridiculed the British, who are represented as firing at all the kegs floating in the river at Philadelphia, because some explosive machines had been sent among their ships. The ballad was one of the greatest sources of inspiration to the colonists in the trying revolutionary crises.

Bayard (*bā'ärd*). **Old Poems and Romances.** Bayard was a famous horse belonging to the four sons of Amyon, a semimythical character. He seemed but an ordinary horse when one person rode, but, if the four mounted, the horse accommodatingly grew in length. Among wonderful things related of him is that his hoofprints have been found on rocks and in deep forests. Bayard is also known as the property of Amadis of Gaul in an old Portuguese romance. He was found under the watch of a dragon whom a wizard knight charmed in order to rescue the horse. In French tales Bayard is represented to be yet living in some of the forests of France but disappearing when disturbed. Bayard is also the name of the horse belonging to Fitz-James in Scott's poem "Lady of the Lake." He appears as Bayardo in *Orlando Furioso* and other poems. It is said that Rinaldo was riding on his favorite steed, when a demon sprang behind him, but the animal in terror took three tremendous leaps and unhorsed the fiend.

Bayes. The Rehearsal, George Villiers, second duke of Buckingham. This farce, or satire, was brought out in 1671, and its wit has been much quoted. In its present form the hero, Bayes, is intended to represent Dryden as at the head of heroic rimes. He is shown as greedy for applause, impatient of censure or criticism, inordinately vain, yet obsequious to those who, he hopes, will gratify him by returning his flattery, and, finally, as anxiously mindful of the minute parts of what, even as a whole, is scarce worthy of attention.

Bay Psalm Book, The. The first book printed in the British American colonies (1640). A metrical version of the psalms, prepared by Richard Mather, Thomas Wilde, and John Eliot.

Beatrice. (1) Daughter of an illustrious family of Florence, for whom Dante had a great love. In the *Divine Comedy* she is represented as being his guide through paradise. (2) Beatrice is also the name of the heroine of Shakspere's *Much Ado about Nothing*. Of her Mrs. Jameson says: "The extraordinary success of this play in Shakspere's own day, and ever since, in England, is to be ascribed more particularly to the parts of Benedick and Beatrice, two humorsome beings, who incessantly attack each other with all the resources of raillery. In Beatrice, high intellect and high animal spirits meet, and excite each other like fire and air. But Beatrice, though willful, is not wayward; she is volatile, not unfeeling."

Beau Brummell. This was the nickname of George Bryan Brummell, a dandy and "glass of fashion" of the time of George IV. He finally fell from royal favor and lived in exile in Calais. His life was made the subject of a play by William Blanchard Jerrold (1859) and the subject of another by Clyde Fitch (1891).

Beauty and the Beast. Fairy Tale, Mme. Villeneuve. Often repeated in stories for children. "Beauty and the Beast" is known in many forms and in many languages. In the tale referred to, young and lovely Beauty saved the life of her father by putting herself in the power of a frightful, but kind-hearted, monster, whose respectful affection and deep melancholy finally overcame her aversion to his hideousness, and induced her to consent to marry him. By her love, Beast was set free from enchantment and allowed to assume his own form, that of a handsome and graceful young prince.

Bede, Adam. Adam Bede, George Eliot. An ideal workman, hero of the novel.

Bedivere (*bĕd'ĭ-vēr*). **Tales of the Round Table.** Bedivere was the last knight of King Arthur's Round Table. He had served as a butler, was of much importance, and was sent by the dying king to throw his sword, Excalibur, into the lake. A hand and an arm rose from the lake, caught the sword, flourished it three times, and sank. Bedivere watched King Arthur's departure for Avalon, the "Isle of the Blest." This knight is noticed, under the name Bedver, in Geoffrey's British History.

Beggar's Daughter. Reliques, Percy. First known as the Beggar's Daughter of Bethnal Green, a beautiful girl named Bessie, who is wooed by a knight, and whose father turns out to be a son of Simon de Montfort, living in disguise as a blind beggar. The story was dramatized by James Sheridan Knowles.

Beggar's Opera, The. This work, by John Gay, with music by Dr. Pepusch, was given in London in 1728. It satirized the polite society and the opera of the day. The characters are mostly thieves and highwaymen, among them Captain Macheath and his wife, Polly Peachum. It is said that three actresses who played the part of Polly won marriages into the English nobility. The play with the original music was reproduced in England and in the United States and Canada with the greatest success in 1919-20.

Bel and the Dragon. (1) Two stories, apocryphal additions to the book of Daniel, telling how Daniel convinced Cyrus of the fraud imposed upon him and his people in the worship of the god, Bel, and the Dragon. (2) A story found in the Babylonian cuneiform tablets, which is thought to resemble closely the account of the struggle of Michael and the Dragon in the Book of Revelation.

Belch, Sir Toby. Twelfth Night, Shakspere. Uncle to Olivia, a jolly, care-free fellow, type of the roisterers of Queen Elizabeth's days.

Belinda. Rape of the Lock, Pope. Poetical name of the heroine whose real name was said to be Arabella Fermor. In a frolic Lord Petre cut a lock from the lady's hair. This was so much resented that it broke the great friendship between the two families. The poem, "Rape of the Lock," was written to bring them into a better temper and lead to reconciliation. Belinda is also the name of the heroine in a novel written by Maria Edgeworth.

Bell, Adam. Old Ballad. A famous wild outlaw belonging to the north country and celebrated for his skill as an archer.

Bell, Laura. Pendennis, Thackeray. One of the sweetest heroines in English literature.

Bell, Peter. Peter Bell, a Tale in Verse, Wordsworth. A wandering tinker, subject of Wordsworth's poem, whose hard heart was touched by the fidelity of an ass to its dead master. Shelley wrote a burlesque of this poem, entitled "Peter Bell the Third," intended to ridicule the ludicrous puerility of language and sentiment which Wordsworth often affected. This burlesque was given the name of the Third because it followed a parody, already published as "Peter the Second."

Bellman. L'Allegro, Milton. The watchman who patrolled the streets and called out the hour of night. Sometimes he repeated scraps of pious poetry in order to charm away danger.

Bell-the-Cat. Name given to a nobleman at Lauder, Scotland, early in the 16th century. King James II called an assembly of Scottish barons to resist a threatened invasion of his realm by Edward IV of England. After long discussion one of the barons related the nursery tale of a convention of mice in which it was proposed to hang a bell on the cat's neck, to give warning of her presence. No one would serve on the mouse committee. To the story Archibald Douglas responded by saying, "I will bell the cat" and was afterwards known by the name, Bell-the-cat.

Beloved Physician. Bible. Name given to St. Luke and first used in the Apostle Paul's epistle to the Colossians.

Belphœbe (*bĕl-fē'bē*). **Faery Queen, Spenser.** A delicate and graceful flattery offered to Queen Elizabeth through the huntress, Belphœbe, intended to represent the queen. The name is taken from *belle*, meaning beautiful, and Phœbe, a name sometimes bestowed on Diana.

Belvawney, Miss. Nicholas Nickleby, Dickens. She belonged to the wonderful Portsmouth theater, always took the part of a page, and gloried in silk stockings.

Belvidera (*bĕl'vĭ-dē'rȧ*). **Venice Preserved, Otway.** The beautiful heroine of this almost forgotten tragedy. Sir Walter Scott said, "More tears have been shed, probably, for the sorrows of Belvidera and Monimia than for those of Juliet and Desdemona."

Benedick. Much Ado about Nothing, Shakspere. A young lord of Padua who is gentleman, wit, and soldier. He was a pronounced bachelor, but after a courtship full of witty sayings and coquetry he marries the lovely Beatrice. From this gentleman comes the name Benedick or Benedict, applied to married men who had thought they never were going to marry. See *Beatrice*.

Benengeli, Cid Hamet (*sĭd hăm'ĕt bĕn'ĕn-gē'lĭ*). **Don Quixote, Cervantes.** Supposed to be a writer of chronicles among the Moors and claimed as authority for the tales of adventure recorded by Cervantes. The name, Cid Hamet, has been often quoted by writers.

Ben Hur, General Lew Wallace. Messala, the Roman playmate and young friend of Ben Hur, afterward became his remorseless enemy. Ambitious, hard, and cruel, when he came into power he made Ben Hur a galley slave, confiscated his property, and imprisoned his mother and sister. Ben Hur escaped, returned later as a wealthy Roman, and entered in the famous chariot race against Messala who had put up enormous sums in wagers. Messala recognized Ben Hur and hoped to win the race and bring him to final ruin; but Messala himself was thrown and seriously injured. His cruelties were made known, and he was at last slain by his wife, Isas, the daughter of Balthasar.

Benvolio (*bĕn-vō'lĭ-ō*). **Romeo and Juliet, Shakspere.** One of Romeo's friends who would "quarrel with a man that had a hair more or a hair less in his beard than he had." Mercutio says to him, "Thou hast quarreled with a man for coughing in the street."

Beowulf (*bā'ô-wōōlf*). **Anglo-Saxon Poem.** He was a Gothic warrior who slew the monster Grendel, which infested the great hall of Hrothgar, king of the West Danes. This great poem of over 6000 lines is divided into two parts. The first part describes the beautiful palace of King Hrothgar, the ravages wrought by the fiend Grendel and his mother, and the deliverance wrought by the hero Beowulf. The second part describes the combat between the aged king Beowulf and the dragon which was wasting the land of the Goths. The Beowulf who took part in Hygelac's historical expedition against the Hetware is probably historical, but the Beowulf of the four great exploits of the poem, the swimming match with Breca, and the contests with Grendel, with his dam, and with the dragon, is more probably a character allied to the Norse divinities.

Bergerac, Cyrano de (*sē'rä'nō' dẽ bĕr'zhĕ-räk'*). In history, he was a French poet, a contemporary of Molière. Edmond Rostand makes him the exaggerated hero of the play named for him. The hero is violently in love with Roxane, but aids Christian de Neuvillette to win her, writing letters for the rather dull gallant. After the death of Christian, Cyrano plays the part of platonic friend to the widow, revealing the truth of his feelings only in the immediate prospect of death.

Bertram. Guy Mannering, Scott. The character was suggested by James Annesley, rightful heir of the earldom of Anglesey, of which he was dispossessed by his uncle Richard. He died in 1743. Bertram was also the name of a haughty and dissolute count, who was the husband of Helena in Shakspere's comedy *All's Well that Ends Well.*

Bianca (*bĭ-ăng'kȧ*). **Othello, Shakspere.** Cassio's sweetheart.

Bibliomania. A passion for rare and curious books. The word means book madness, and is usually applied by people unsympathetic toward those who collect books for their rarity rather than for their value in use. The term bibliophile, "lover of books," is the more complimentary word for amateur or professional book collectors.

Big-endians (*bĭg'ĕn'dĭ-ănz*). **Gulliver's Travels, Swift.** The name of a religious party in the imaginary empire of Lilliput who made it a matter of duty and conscience to break their eggs at the large end. They were regarded as heretics by the law, which required all persons to break the smaller end of their eggs, under pain of heavy penalties in case of disobedience.

Birch, Harvey. The Spy, Cooper. The chief character of the novel.

Black Beauty, Anna Sewell. Full title, "Black Beauty, His Grooms and Companions." The story of a horse. Written in the form of a horse's autobiography, it is a strong plea for kind treatment of animals.

Black-eyed Susan. Ballad, John Gay. The heroine of the popular sea song.

Blatant Beast. Faery Queen, Spenser. A bellowing monster typical of slander; or, an impersonation of what we now call "*vox populi,*" or the "voice of the people."

Blifil (*blĭ'fĭl*). **Tom Jones, Fielding.** Allworthy's nephew, a talebearer and consummate hypocrite.

Blimber, Miss Cornelia. Dombey and Son, Dickens. The daughter of Dr. Blimber, the head of a first-class educational establishment conducted on the forcing or cramming principle. She is a very learned, grave, and precise young lady, "no light nonsense about her," who has become "dry and sandy with working in the graves of deceased languages."

Blouzalinda (*blouz'ȧ-lĭn'dȧ*). **Shepherd's Week, John Gay.** The country girl, heroine of this pastoral poem written over 200 years ago, and quoted as a picture of the poverty and rudeness of rural life at that time.

Bluebeard. A fairy tale by Perrault (1697). The ugly, blue-bearded rich man has for his seventh wife Fatima. One day, when he is away, she finds in a closet the bodies of the former wives. Bluebeard discovers her disobedience of his command, and is about to kill her, when her brothers rescue her. Earlier Italian and Arabian stories resemble this tale.

Bluebird, The. (1) A fairy tale by Countess d'Aulnoy. A prince, refusing to marry the ugly one of two sisters, is changed into a bluebird. Finally, a friendly fairy restores him to his former shape and to his sweetheart. (2) A fairy play by Maurice Maeterlinck, in which two children, Mityl and Tyltyl, set out to seek for happiness, the bluebird. They wander in a dream through the lands of Memory, Night, and the Future. At last, when Tyltyl gives up his dove to a neighbor's sick child, they find happiness for a moment. The bird turns blue and then flies away.

Bob, Son of Battle, Alfred Ollivant. The hero and title of a popular dog story. Bob is the last of a famous breed of shepherd dog; his adventures are most realistic.

Bobadil (*bŏb'ȧ-dĭl*), **Captain. Every Man in His Humor, Jonson.** A boasting coward, who passes himself off with young and simple people for a Hector.

Bois Guilbert, Brian de (*brē-äɴ' dẽ bwä gēl'bĕr'*). **Ivanhoe, Scott.** A brave but cruel, crafty, and dissolute commander of the Knights Templars.

Boniface (*bŏn'ĭ-fās*). **The Beaux' Stratagem, Farquhar.** A fine representation of an English landlord. Hence, the name is applied to landlords generally.

Bontemps, Roger (*rô'zhā' bôɴ'täɴ'*). **Song, Béranger.** Known in France as the personification of care-free leisure. The equivalent, among the French peasantry, for the English proverb, "There's a good time coming," is "Roger Bontemps," one of Béranger's most celebrated songs written in 1814.

Bottom, Nick. A Midsummer Night's Dream, Shakspere. A man who fancies he can do everything, and do it better than anyone else. Shakspere has drawn him as profoundly ignorant, and with an overflow of self-conceit. Oberon, the fairy king, desiring to punish Titania, his queen, commissioned Puck to watch her till she fell asleep, and then to anoint her eyelids with the juice of a plant called "love-in-idleness," the effect of which, when she awoke, was to make her dote upon Bottom, upon whom Puck had fixed an ass's head.

Bowling, Tom. Roderick Random, Smollett. A name made almost famous as hero of the novel. Critics have said, "The character of Tom Bowling, in *Roderick Random*, will be regarded in all ages as a happy exhibition of those naval heroes to whom Britain is indebted for so much of her happiness and glory." The Tom Bowling referred to in Dibdin's famous sea song was Captain Thomas Dibdin, brother of Charles Dibdin, who wrote the song.

Box and Cox. Farce, Morton. Principal characters in the farce known as a "dramatic romance of real life." The two men, Box and Cox, rent the same room from a Mrs. Bouncer. One works in the daytime, the other at night, so they do not meet until a holiday reveals the situation. The conflict, however, is adjusted amicably.

Brag, Jack. Jack Brag, Theodore Hook. Hero of the novel and a spirited embodiment of the arts employed by a vulgar pretender to creep into aristocratic society, and of his ultimate discomfiture. General Burgoyne figures in an old ballad known as "Sir Jack Brag."

Bramble, Matthew. Humphrey Clinker, Smollett. Noted character in the novel, described as "an odd kind of humorist," afflicted with the gout, and "always on the fret," but full of generosity and benevolence.

Brass, Sally and Sampson. Old Curiosity Shop, Dickens. Brother and sister, well mated, he a "shystering" lawyer and she outreaching him in villainy. Sampson was dishonest, sentimental, and affected in manner, and both are interesting characters to read about.

Brentford, The Two Kings of. The Rehearsal, Villiers. Much question has been raised as to who was to be ridiculed under these characters. The royal brothers, Charles II and James II, have been suggested; others say the fighting kings of Granada. In the farce the two kings are represented as walking hand in hand, as dancing together, as singing in concert, and, generally, as living on terms of the greatest intimacy and affection.

Br'er Rabbit. In the plantation stories of Uncle Remus, he is the personification of mental agility and craft, by which he vanquishes Br'er Fox.

Brick, Mr. Jefferson. Martin Chuzzlewit, Dickens. A ranting American politician who makes a ridiculous figure as editor.

Britomart. Faery Queen, Spenser. The embodiment of chastity. Having seen in a magic mirror the face of Sir Artegal, who embodies justice, she falls in love with him. After a long search and many adventures, she at last finds him and they are united.

Brook Farm. The full name was "Brook Farm Institute of Agriculture and Education," a stock company of nearly 70 members, located on a farm of 200 acres at West Roxbury, Mass. Among the members were George Ripley, Charles A. Dana, George William Curtis, Margaret Fuller, and Nathaniel Hawthorne. Among their frequent visitors were Ralph Waldo Emerson, Theodore Parker, Bronson Alcott. This idyllic life lasted about five years, from 1841 to 1846. Brook Farm was a financial failure, but it was important in intellectual results. Hawthorne took from it some suggestions for his *Blithedale Romance*.

Brown, Tom. Tom Brown's School Days and **Tom Brown at Oxford, Thomas Hughes.** The hero of these stories of school days, a typical English schoolboy and undergraduate.

Brunhild (*broon'hilt*). **Nibelungenlied.** The story of Brunhild figures largely in ancient German romance. She was, herself, a warrior, proud and skillful, and she promised to be the bride of the man who could conquer her in three trials: in hurling the lance, in throwing the stone, and in leaping after the stone when thrown. By the arts and bravery of Siegfried, she was deluded into marrying Gunther, king of Burgundy; but, discovering the trick, she planned and accomplished the destruction of Siegfried and the humiliation of Kriemhild, his wife.

Bumble, Mr. Oliver Twist, Dickens. A pompous, disagreeable beadle who figures largely in the beginning of the story. The name Bumble has since attached itself to the office.

Bunsby, Jack. Dombey and Son, Dickens. A commander of a ship, looked up to as an oracle by his friend, Captain Cuttle. He is described as wearing a "rapt and imperturbable manner" and seeming to be "always on the lookout for something in the extremest distance."

Bunthorne. Patience, Sullivan. A gloomy poet shown most distinctly in his gloom when surrounded by the characters of a comic opera. He was inserted as a satire on the æsthetic cult affected at the time by Oscar Wilde and his imitators.

Burchell, Mr. Vicar of Wakefield, Goldsmith. A prominent character who passes himself off as a poor man, but is really a baronet in disguise. He is noted for his habit of crying out "Fudge!" by way of expressing his strong contempt for the opinions of others.

Burd, Helen. Scotch Ballad. A traditional name standing for constancy. She was carried to England by fairies and imprisoned in a castle. The youngest brother of the fair Helen was guided by the enchanter Merlin and accomplished the perilous task of rescuing his sister. This is recited in the line "Childe Roland to the dark tower came," quoted by Shakspere. Only a fragment of the old ballad has been preserved.

Buskin. A name used to mean "tragedy." Known in English since the 16th century. The word means "boot." It early took on the sense given here. The Greek tragic actors used to wear a sandal some two or three inches thick, to elevate their stature. To this sole was attached a very elegant boot top. The whole boot was called *cothurnus*. Milton uses the phrase "buskined stage" in *Il Penseroso*.

Buzfuz, Serjeant. Pickwick Papers, Dickens. A pompous, chaffing lawyer, who bullies Mr. Pickwick and the witnesses in the famous breach of promise suit, Bardell *v.* Pickwick.

Byfield. A New England parish, the scene of a historical novel by John Lewis Ewell. Here lived the ancestor of Longfellow, to whom the poet dedicated "The Village Blacksmith," himself a blacksmith, keeping his accounts in peculiar orthography. According to the deed of sale in 1681, the Byfield Indians got a larger price from the first English settlers than was paid for Manhattan island.

Cabala (*kăb'ȧ-lȧ*). The oral law of the Jews handed down from father to son by word of mouth. It is the usual belief that God instructed Moses, and Moses his brother Aaron, and so on from age to age. The cabalists developed an elaborate system of mystic symbolism, in which combinations of letters and numbers are important.

Cadmean (*kăd-mē'ăn*) **Victory.** A victory purchased at great expense of life. The allusion is to the armed men who sprang out of the ground from the teeth of the dragon sown by Cadmus. These men fell foul of each other, and only five of them escaped death.

Caius (*kā'yŭs*), **Doctor. Merry Wives of Windsor, Shakspere.** A physician in the comedy, who adds a touch of humor. He is conspicuous as the lover of Anne Page.

Calandrino (*kä-län-drē'nō*). A simpleton frequently introduced in Boccaccio's *Decameron*; expressly made to be befooled and played upon. His mishaps, as Macaulay states, "have made all Europe merry for more than four centuries."

Caleb. (1) The enchantress who carried off St. George in infancy. (2) A character in Dryden's satire of "Absalom and Achitophel," meant for Lord Grey, one of the adherents of the duke of Monmouth.

Caleb Quotem. A parish clerk or jack-of-all-trades, in Colman's play *The Review*, or *Wags of Windsor*. Colman borrowed the character from *Throw Physic to the Dogs*, an old farce.

Caliban. (1) A savage and deformed slave of Prospero in Shakspere's *Tempest*. He is represented as being the "freckled whelp" of Sycorax, a foul hag, who was banished from Argier, or Algiers, to the desert island afterward inhabited by Prospero. From his rude, uncouth language we get the phrase "Caliban style," "Caliban speech," meaning the coarsest possible use of words. (2) A character in Browning's *Caliban on Setebos*.

Calidore. A knight in Spenser's *Faery Queen*, typical of courtesy, and said to be intended for a portrait of Sir Philip Sidney.

Calipolis. Battle of Alcazar, George Peele. A character in the *Battle of Alcazar*, used by Sir Walter Scott and others as a synonym for ladylove, sweetheart, charmer. Sir Walter always spells the word Callipolis.

Calista. The name of a celebrated character in Rowe's *Fair Penitent*.

Calydon. A forest celebrated in the romances relating to King Arthur and Merlin. Also an ancient city of Ætolia, in Greece, celebrated in the stories of the Calydonian Hunt.

Camacho (*kä-mä'chō*). **Don Quixote, Cervantes.** A character in an episode in *Don Quixote*, who gets cheated out of his bride after having made great preparations for their wedding.

Camaralzaman (*kăm'ȧ-răl'zȧ-măn*), **Prince. Arabian Nights.** One of the stories of the *Arabian Nights* and the name of a prince who fell in love with Badoura, princess of China, the moment he saw her.

Cambalo or **Cambel. Faery Queen, Spenser.** A brother of Canace. He challenged every suitor to his sister's hand, and overthrew all except Triamond, who married the lady.

Cambalu (*kăm'bȧ-lōō*). In the *Voyages* of Marco Polo, the chief city of the province of Cathay.

Cambuscan (*kăm-bŭs'kăn*). A Tatar king identical with Jenghis Khan. The king of the Far East sent Cambuscan a "steed of brass, which, between sunrise and sunset, would carry its rider to any spot on the earth." All that was required was to whisper the name of the place in the horse's ear, mount upon his back, and turn a pin set in his ear. When the rider had arrived at his destination, he had to turn another pin and the horse instantly descended, and, with another screw of the pin, vanished till it was again required. This story was begun by Chaucer in the *Squire's Tale* but was never finished. Milton refers to Chaucer as the poet who "left half told" this story (*Il Penseroso*).

Camelot. A parish in Somersetshire, England, now called Queen's Camel, where King Arthur is said to have held his court. In this place there are still to be seen vast intrenchments of an ancient town or station—called by the inhabitants "King Arthur's Palace." Several other localities dispute the tradition, notably Winchester.

Camille (*kȧ-mēl'*). English adaptation of *La Dame aux Camēlias*, a play by Dumas the younger. Also known in America as *The Lady of the Camellias*. The story is that of Marguerite Gautier, a courtesan, whose genuine love for Armand Duval prompts her to live only for him. But his father persuades Marguerite that such a union would wreck Armand's career. Therefore she deliberately estranges him, and really sacrifices her life for him. The meaning of her acts Armand learns too late.

Canace (*kăn'ȧ-sē*). **Faery Queen, Spenser.** A paragon among women, the daughter of King Cambuscan, to whom the king of the East sent as a present a mirror and a ring. The mirror would tell the lady if any man on whom she set her heart would prove true or false, and the ring, which was to be worn on her thumb, would enable her to understand the language of birds and to converse with them. Canace was courted by a crowd of suitors, but her brother announced that anyone who aspired to her hand must encounter him in single combat and overthrow him. She ultimately married Triamond, son of the fairy Agape.

Candide (*käɴ'dēd'*). The hero of Voltaire's work of the same name. All sorts of misfortunes are heaped upon him, and he bears them all with philosophical indifference.

Candour, Mrs. A most energetic slanderer in Sheridan's *School for Scandal*.

Canidia. A sorceress, alluded to by Horace, who could bring the moon from heaven.

Canterbury Tales, Chaucer. The Prologue to the "tales" introduces the reader to "full nine and twenty" pilgrims, each of whom, on the way to and from Canterbury, is to tell two stories, the one telling the best tale to be treated to a dinner on their return to the Tabard Inn in Southwark, whence they start. Only 24 of the 58 tales called for in the scheme have come down to us. These are:

"The Knight's Tale," "The Miller's Tale," "The Reeve's Tale," "The Cook's Tale," "The Man of Law's Tale," "The Wife of Bath's Tale," "The Friar's Tale," "The Summoner's Tale," "The Clerk's Tale," "The Merchant's Tale," "The Squire's Tale," "The Franklin's Tale," "The Doctor's Tale," "The Pardoner's Tale," "The Shipman's Tale," "The Prioress's Tale," "Chaucer's Tale of Sir Thopas," "Chaucer's Tale of Melibœus," "The Monk's Tale," "The Nun's Priest's Tale," "The Second Nun's Tale," "The Canon's Yeoman's Tale," "The Manciple's Tale," "The Parson's Tale." The plan of the work affords artistic scope for introducing a company of pilgrims on their way to the shrine of Thomas Becket. It represents all classes of society and presents a series of tales of great interest set in the midst of beautiful descriptions of nature. Perhaps the most interesting tales by which to gain introduction to Chaucer are: "The Clerk's Tale" (Griseldis); "The Knight's Tale" (Palamon and Arcite); "The Man of Law's Tale" (Constance); "The Prioress's Tale" (Hugh of Lincoln); "The Nun's Priest's Tale" (Chanticleer and Pertelote).

Caora. Description of Guiana, Raleigh. A river, on the banks of which are a people whose heads grow beneath their shoulders. Their eyes are in their shoulders, and their mouths in the middle of their breasts. The original picture is found in Hakluyt's *Voyages* 1598.

Cape Cod Folks. The group of characters drawn from Cape Cod life in the stories of Joseph C. Lincoln.

Captains Courageous, Kipling. One of the best stories for boys. The young son of a wealthy American family is lost overboard from an Atlantic liner. He is picked up by a fishing boat off Newfoundland. The captain sets him to work. He learns much of fishing and fishermen. When the boat returns to Gloucester, his parents come, and the family are reunited.

Capulet (*kăp'ū-lĕt*). The head of a noble Veronese house in Shakspere's tragedy *Romeo and Juliet*—hostile to the house of Montague. He is at times self-willed and tyrannical, but a jovial and testy old man.

Capulet, Lady. The proud and stately wife of Capulet, and mother of Juliet.

Carabas, Marquis of. (1) The master of the cat in the nursery tale of *Puss in Boots.* (2) In a lyric by Béranger, Carabas is an emigré who comes back after the battle of Waterloo to reclaim his property. (3) In Disraeli's *Vivian Gray*, a servile and pompous character, the Marquess of Carabas.

Caradoc (*kȧ-răd'ŏk*). A knight of the Round Table. Also in history, the British chief whom the Romans called Caractacus. Caradoc is the hero of an old ballad entitled "The Boy and the Mantle."

Carker. A scoundrel clerk in Dickens's *Dombey and Son.*

Carpetbaggers. Name applied to Northerners who, after the enfranchisement of the negroes, went into the South for the purpose of representing the negroes in state and national offices. Since most of these men held no property in the South, their possessions were all supposed to be in their "carpetbags" or grips. Hence the name. *A Fool's Errand* by A. W. Tourgee is a story of the period.

Carrasco, Sanson (*săn-sōn' kăr-răs'kō*). A waggish bachelor of Salamanca, in Cervantes' *Don Quixote.*

Carton, Sidney. A hero transformed by unselfish love in Dickens's *Tale of Two Cities.* He voluntarily goes to the guillotine to save his successful rival in love.

Casca. Julius Cæsar, Shakspere. A blunt-witted Roman, one of the conspirators against Julius Cæsar.

Casella. The name of a musician and old friend of Dante, immortalized by him in his *Divine Comedy.*

Cassandra. A daughter of Priam, king of Troy, gifted with the power of prophecy; but Apollo, whom she had offended, brought it to pass that no one believed her predictions, consequently now a name applied to one who makes gloomy forecasts. Shakspere makes use of this character in *Troilus and Cressida.*

Cassibelan. Great-uncle to Cymbeline, in Shakspere's play by that name.

Cassio (*kăsh'ĭ-ō*). A Florentine lieutenant of Othello and a tool of Iago, in Shakspere's tragedy *Othello.* Iago made Cassio drunk, and then urged on Roderigo to quarrel with him. Cassio wounded Roderigo. Othello suspended Cassio, but Iago induced Desdemona to plead for his restoration. This interest in Cassio aroused the jealous rage of Othello and moved him to murder Desdemona and to kill himself. After the death of Othello, Cassio was appointed governor of Cyprus.

Castle Dangerous. A keep belonging to the Douglas family, which gives its name to one of Sir Walter Scott's *Tales of My Landlord.* It was so called by the English because it was always retaken from them by the Douglas.

Castle of Indolence. The title of a poem by Thomson, and the name of a castle described in it as situated in a pleasing land of drowsiness, where every sense was steeped in the most luxurious and enervating delights.

Castlewood, Beatrix. The heroine of Thackeray's novel *Henry Esmond,* a picture of splendid, lustrous, physical beauty.

Cattle Raid of Cooley. An early Irish story. Queen Maeve of Connaught, to make her herd equal to that of her husband Ailill, asked Daré Mac Fiachne, of Ulster, for the loan of his wonderful "Brown Bull of Cooley." He at first granted the request, but later, in anger, refused. Upon this, the queen invaded Ulster, to take the bull by force. It happened that a disease unfitted the Ulstermen for battle during the winter. A youth of 17, Cuchulain, exempt from the disease, faced the foe alone. Agreement was made that each day a Connaught warrior should fight with him, and that when he had killed this opponent Queen Maeve's forces should halt and camp for the night. Day after day Cuchulain was victorious, until, when the queen impatiently broke her agreement, the Ulstermen were able to do battle. They drove the invaders out, but not until Queen Maeve had captured and carried off the "Brown Bull."

Caudle, Mrs. Margaret. The feigned author of a series of curtain lectures delivered to her husband, Job Caudle, who was a patient sufferer under this form of persistent nagging by his wife. The real author of these humorous lectures was Douglas Jerrold.

Cauline, Sir. The hero of an ancient English ballad preserved in Percy's *Reliques.*

Cave of Mammon. The abode of the god of riches, described in the second book of Spenser's *Faery Queen.*

Caxton, Pisistratus (*pĭ-sĭs'trȧ-tŭs*). The hero of Bulwer-Lytton's novel *The Caxtons,* and of its sequel *My Novel.*

Cecilia (*sē-sĭl'ĭ-ȧ*), **St.** A patron saint of the blind, also patroness of musicians, and "inventor of the organ." According to tradition, an angel fell in love with her for her musical skill, and used nightly to visit her. A crown of martyrdom was bestowed upon both her and her husband. Dryden and Pope have written odes in her honor, and both speak of her charming an angel by her musical powers.

Cedric (*sĕd'rĭk*). A Saxon thane in Scott's *Ivanhoe.* Father of Ivanhoe and uncle of Rowena.

Celia. (1) In Spenser's *Faery Queen,* the mother of Faith, Hope, and Charity. She was herself known as Heavenliness and lived in the hospice Holiness. (2) Celia, cousin to Rosalind, in Shakspere's comedy *As You Like It.* Celia is a common poetical name for a lady or a ladylove.

Cephalus (*sĕf'ȧ-lŭs*) **and Procris** (*prŏk'rĭs*). Cephalus was the husband of Procris, who, out of jealousy, deserted him. Cephalus went in search of her, and rested awhile under a tree. Procris discovered him, and crept through some bushes to ascertain if a rival was with him. Cephalus heard the noise and, thinking it to be made by some wild beast, hurled his javelin into the bushes and slew Procris. When the unhappy man discovered what he had done, he slew himself in anguish of spirit with the same javelin. This story is alluded to in "Pyramus and Thisbe," in Shakspere's *Midsummer Night's Dream,* where they are humorously miscalled "Shafalus and Procus."

Chadband, The Rev. A clerical character in Dickens's *Bleak House.* He will always stand as a type of hypocritical piety.

Chanticleer. The cock, in the tale of "Reynard the Fox" and in Chaucer's "Nun's Priest's Tale."

Characters, "Caractères." A work by Jean de la Bruyère, in which he sketches with great skill the men and women and manners of the 17th century in France. The work is based in part upon the "Characters" of Theophrastus, which La Bruyère had translated. John Earle wrote similar studies in English.

Charge of the Light Brigade, The, Tennyson. A famous descriptive lyric celebrating the tragic charge of the brigade of light cavalry at Balaklava in the Crimean war.

Charlemagne (*shär'lē-mān*). The romance of Charlemagne and his Paladins is of French origin, as the romances of King Arthur and the Knights of the Round Table are of Celtic or Welsh origin. According to one tradition, Charlemagne is not dead, but waits, crowned and armed, in Odenberg, near Salzburg, till the time of antichrist, when he will wake up and deliver Christendom. According to another tradition, Charlemagne appears in seasons of plenty. He crosses the Rhine on a golden bridge and blesses both cornfields and vineyards.

Charmian. A kind-hearted but simple-minded female attendant on Cleopatra in Shakspere's play *Antony and Cleopatra.*

Chauvinism (*shō'vĭn-ĭz'm*). An attitude of exaggerated, unreasoning patriotism. The word is said to be derived from the name of Nicolas Chauvin, a soldier in the army of Napoleon and a person in Cogniard's *Cocarde Tricolore* (1831). The equivalent English word is "jingoism," derived from a jocular oath, "By Jingo," which came into vogue through a popular patriotic song.

Cheeryble Brothers, The. A firm of benevolent London merchants in Dickens's *Nicholas Nickleby.*

Cherry Orchard, The, Chekov. A play of Russian life, portraying the reversal of relations between the old landed families and the freed serfs. Through the futile wastefulness of Madame Ranévsky and her brother Leonid Gayef, their estate, on which is a cherry orchard, has become hopelessly involved in debt. Their sentimental love for the place blinds them to practical matters. Lopákhin, son of a former serf on the estate, suggests that the orchard be cut up into building lots, since it is near the city, but his suggestion is ignored. Finally, he buys the place at auction, and the family, including Anya, Madame Ranévsky's daughter, and her adopted daughter Barbara, are scattered. The tragic element is heightened by the presence of Firs, an old servant, who, forgotten by all, lies down to die in the abandoned house.

Chery and Fair-Star. Countess d'Aulnoy's Fairy Tales. Two children of royal birth, whom their father's brothers and their mother's sisters cast out to sea. They are found and brought up by a corsair and his wife. Ultimately they are told of their birth by a green bird and marry each other. A similar tale is found in the *Arabian Nights.*

Chevy Chase. The subject and the title of a famous old English ballad. Percy Hotspur entered the domain of Douglas, in Scotland, slew 100 deer, and was attacked by Douglas. The ensuing combat resulted in the slaughter of both leaders and many of their bravest followers. The ballad is apparently intended to commemorate the battle of Otterburn in 1388, but it is impossible to reconcile the incidents of the poem with history.

Childe. A title of honor often used in old English ballads, as "Childe Harold," "Childe of Ellechilde Waters," "Childe Roland," "Childe Tristram," "Childe Arthur." Use is made of the term in Byron's poem entitled *Childe Harold's Pilgrimage.* See *Harold, Childe.*

Children in the Wood. Two characters in an ancient and well-known ballad entitled "The Children in the Wood, or The Norfolk Gent's Last Will and Testament," which is said to be a disguised recital of the alleged murder of his nephews by Richard III. This is the story as related in Percy's *Reliques.* The master of Wayland Hall, Norfolk, on his deathbed left a little son, three years old, and a still younger daughter, named Jane, to the care of his wife's brother. If the children died before they came to their majority, their uncle was to inherit their estate. After twelve months had elapsed, the uncle hired two ruffians to murder the two babes. As they went along, one of the ruffians relented and killed his fellow; then, putting down the children in a wood, left them. The poor babes gathered blackberries to allay their hunger, but died during the night, and "Robin Redbreast" covered them over with strawberry leaves. Addison says of the ballad referred to, that it is "one of the darling songs of the common people."

Children of the Abbey, The, Regina Maria Roche. A famous novel (1798). The heroine, Amanda, daughter of the earl of Dunreath by his first wife, is cast out through the influence of her stepmother. After rather more than her share of misfortune and slander, she triumphs over her enemies and lives happily.

Chillingly, Kenelm. The hero in a novel of this name by Bulwer-Lytton.

Chillon (*shĭl'ŏn*; Fr., *shē'yôɴ'*). A castle in Vaud, Switzerland, at the eastern end of Lake Geneva. It covers an isolated rock on the edge of the lake, and is a very picturesque combination of semicircular and square towers and machicolated curtains grouped about a higher central tower. It is famous in literature and song, especially as the prison of Bonnivard, a defender of Swiss liberties against the duke of Savoy in the 16th century. This is the theme of Byron's "Prisoner of Chillon."

Chimmie Fadden. The hero of a series of stories by E. M. Townsend. The character is drawn from that of Patrick O'Connell, or "Chuck Conners," known as "The White Mayor of Chinatown" in New York. Chimmie Fadden's career has been dramatized.

Chingachgook. A sagamore of the Mohicans, and father of Uncas, in Cooper's *Leatherstocking Tales.*

Chloe. (1) In *Daphnis and Chloe,* by Longus, the shepherdess loved by Daphne. (2) *Paul and Virginia* by St. Pierre is founded on this romance. (3) Chloe is also a shepherdess in Shakspere's *As You Like It.* (4) The heroine in George Meredith's *Tale of Chloe.*

Chœreas. The lover of Callirrhoë, in Chariton's Greek romance.

Choir Invisible, The, James Lane Allen. A story of the pure love of a man and a woman who were separated by marriage. The scene is Kentucky in the period following the Revolution. A story of the inner life, with little action.

Chouans, Les (*lā shōō'äɴ'*), **Balzac.** This romance is a story of the Chouans, or bands of Vendean peasants, who maintained a guerrilla warfare against the French Republican forces from 1792 to 1800. Their leader, Cottereau, a salt-smuggler, had acquired the title "Chouan" from the screech owl cry he used as a signal.

Christabel. (1) The subject and heroine of an old romance by Sir Eglamour of Artois. (2) The heroine of an ancient ballad "Sir Cauline." (3) The lady in Coleridge's poem "Christabel."

Christian. The hero of John Bunyan's allegory *Pilgrim's Progress.* He flees from the City of Destruction and journeys to the Celestial City. He starts with a heavy burden on his back, but it falls off when he stands at the foot of the cross. All his trials on the way are depicted.

Christiana. The wife of Christian, who started with her children and Mercy from the City of Destruction, forms the subject of Bunyan's *Pilgrim's Progress,* part II. She was placed under the guidance of Mr. Greatheart, and met her husband at the Celestial City.

Christmas Carol. See *Scrooge, Ebenezer.*

Christopher, St. The giant that carried a child over a brook and said, "Chylde, thou hast put me in grete peryll. I might bere no greater burden." The Chylde was the Christ and the burden was the "sin of the world." This has been a favorite theme for painters.

Christus, a Mystery. A dramatic trilogy by Henry W. Longfellow: Part I, "Divine Tragedy"; Part II, "The Golden Legend"; Part III, "New England Tragedies."

Chrysalde (*krē-säld'*). A character in Molière's *L'Ecole des Femmes*; a friend of Arnolphe.

Chrysale (*krē'zäl'*). An honest, simple-minded, henpecked tradesman, in Molière's *Les Femmes Savantes.*

Chuzzlewit, Jonas. A miser and murderer, the opposite type of character from Martin.

Chuzzlewit, Martin. The hero of Dickens's novel of the same name.

Cid, The, Corneille. This play established Corneille's fame, although it was bitterly criticized. He borrowed material from many Spanish sources. The play tells the story of the love of Rodrigue, "the Cid," and Chimène. Rodrigue, to defend his father's honor, kills Chimène's father. She demands his life, though not concealing her love. Meanwhile, Rodrigue has defeated the Moors. Chimène accepts Don Sanche as her champion, but when he returns from the duel with a bloodstained sword, she scorns him and plans to enter a convent. It then appears that Rodrigue has merely disarmed Don Sanche, refusing, because of his love, to injure a champion of Chimène. After this proof of loyalty the lovers are wedded.

Cid Campeador (*thēth käm'pā-ä-thōr'*). The name given in histories, traditions, and songs to the epic hero of Spain. So greatly was he honored that he was called *Mio Cid el Campeador,* "my lord the champion." Relics of the "Blessed Cid," as he is still called in Spain, such as his sword, shield, banner, and drinking-cup, are still held in great reverence by the populace. The numerous "Cid romances" that were first published in the 16th century contain the most romantic improbabilities concerning the life and deeds of the Cid. The most interesting chronicle of the Cid for English readers was written by Robert Southey.

Cinderella. Heroine of a fairy tale. She is the drudge of the house, while her elder sisters go to fine balls. At length a fairy enables her to go to the prince's ball; the prince falls in love with her, and she is discovered by means of a glass slipper which she drops. This will fit no foot but her own. She is represented as returning good for evil and heaping upon her half sisters every kindness a princess can show.

Cipango (*sĭ-păng'gō*). A marvelous island, described in the *Voyages* of Marco Polo, the Venetian traveler. It is represented as lying in the Eastern seas, some 1500 miles from land, and of its beauty and wealth many stories are related. Columbus and early navigators made a diligent search for this island.

Clare, Ada. The wife of Carstone, and one of the most important characters in Dickens's *Bleak House*.

Clayhanger, Arnold Bennett. The hero of the novel *Clayhanger* is a shy, average young man of the Five Towns in the Potteries district of England, in which Bennett places his stories of common life. He marries Hilda Lessways.

Clementina, The Lady. An accomplished woman who appears in Richardson's novel, *Sir Charles Grandison*.

Clifford, Paul. An attractive highwayman and an interesting hero in Bulwer's novel of the same name. He is familiar with the haunts of low vice and dissipation but afterward is reformed and elevated by the power of love.

Clinker, Humphrey. The hero of Smollett's novel entitled *The Expedition of Humphrey Clinker*, a philosophic youth who meets with many adventures. Brought up in the workhouse, put out by the parish as apprentice to a blacksmith, he was afterward employed as a hostler's assistant. Having been dismissed from the stable, and reduced to great want, he at length attracts the notice of Mr. Bramble, who takes him into his family as a servant. He becomes the accepted lover of Winifred Jenkins, and at length turns out to be a natural son of Mr. Bramble.

Cloister and the Hearth, The, Charles Reade. The great historical novel of the Renaissance. The time is the close of the 15th century. Gerard Eliassoen, a humble Dutch boy, is betrothed to Margaret, daughter of a wealthy alchemist-physician. But their marriage is prevented and Gerard flees to Rome. There he hears that Margaret is dead. Hopeless of love, he becomes a monk. Returning to Holland, he finds Margaret alive and the mother of a boy. But Gerard, devoted to the Church, cannot return to Margaret. The son grew up to be the great scholar Erasmus.

Clorinda. Jerusalem Delivered, Tasso. Clorinda, the heroine of this poem, is represented as an Amazon inspiring the most tender affection in others, especially in the Christian chief Tancred; yet she is herself susceptible of no passion but the love of military fame.

Cloten. A rejected lover of Imogen, in Shakspere's play *Cymbeline*.

Clout, Colin. A name that Spenser applies to himself in the *Faery Queen* and "Shepherd's Calendar." Colin Clout also is introduced into Gay's pastorals.

Cœlebs (*sē'lĕbz*). The hero of a novel by Hannah More, *Cœlebs in Search of a Wife*.

Collean, May. The heroine of a Scottish ballad.

Cologne, The Three Kings of. A name given to the three Magi who visited the infant Savior, and whose bodies are said to have been brought by the empress Helena from the East to Constantinople, whence they were transferred to Milan. Afterward, they were removed to Cologne and placed in the principal church of the city, where, says Cressy, "they are to this day celebrated with great veneration." Their names are commonly said to be Gaspar, Melchior, and Balthazar.

Colonel Carter of Cartersville, F. Hopkinson Smith. A story of an old Virginia gentleman set down among New York financiers, and involved in railroad building schemes.

Comédie Humaine (*kô'mā'dē' ü'mân'*). The uncompleted series of nearly a hundred novels by Balzac, designed to give a panoramic picture of the manners and morals of his time. He began the work in 1829, adopting the general title in 1842. The appearance of the same characters in various stories binds them into a single series.

Comedy of Errors. Shakspere. Twin brothers of exact likeness, named Antipholus, are served by attendant slaves named Dromio, also of striking resemblance. The humor of the play lies in the complications that arise. The two brothers are lost at sea with their servants and are picked up by different vessels. After long separation they all reappear in Ephesus. There is great entanglement of plot until both brothers face each other in a trial before the duke and all is explained.

Common Sense, Thomas Paine. The title of a famous pamphlet published by Paine in Philadelphia in 1776, in which he urged separation of the colonies from England. The work helped to crystallize American sentiment for independence.

Compleat Angler, The. A famous book by Izaak Walton. It was first published in 1653, and it is said to have been issued in a new edition, on the average, every two and a half years since. The "compleat angler" is the fisherman who loves peaceful nature and seasons his hours by the stream with wise philosophy. The book is written in the form of a prose pastoral, the chief characters being "Piscator" and "Venator."

Comus. In Milton's poem entitled *Comus: a Masque*, he is represented as a base enchanter, who endeavors, but in vain, to beguile and entrap the innocent by means of his enchantments. The name in Greek means "a revel."

Concord Bridge. The old bridge at Concord, Mass., made famous by the battle between Americans and British, April 19, 1775, and celebrated in Emerson's "Concord Hymn," written for the dedication of the Concord monument, April 19, 1836.

Concord, Mass. The town of Concord, noted in revolutionary history, became famous later as the residence of several literary men and women,—Hawthorne, Emerson, Thoreau, Bronson Alcott, Louisa May Alcott, William Ellery Channing, and others. Here was the center of the so-called Concord school of philosophy.

Consuelo (*kŏn'sü-ā'lō*). The heroine of George Sand's novel of the same name, an impersonation of noble purity sustained amid great temptations.

Cooperstown. A village in Otsego county, New York. It was for many years the home of James Fenimore Cooper, where he wrote most of his novels. In *The Pioneers* he wrote of the wilderness life about Cooperstown, introducing the place under the name of Templeton.

Cophetua (*kô-fĕt'ů-ȧ*). An imaginary African king, of whom a legendary ballad told that he fell in love with a beggar maid and married her. This ballad is found in Percy's *Reliques*. Many poets have made use of the story. Tennyson has given us a modern version in "The Beggar Maid."

Copperfield, David. The hero of Dickens's novel of the same name. This is said to be Dickens's favorite among his works and somewhat autobiographic.

Cordelia. King Lear, Shakspere. The youngest of Lear's three daughters, and the one who truly loved him.

Corydon. A shepherd in one of the idyls of Theocritus and in one of the eclogues of Virgil. Used by Shakspere and later poets to designate a rustic swain.

Costard. A clown, in Shakspere's *Love's Labor's Lost*, who apes the display of wit and misapplies, in the most ridiculous manner, the phrases and modes of combination in argument that were then in vogue.

Cotter's Saturday Night, Robert Burns. This famous poem was published in 1786. Celebrated for its beautiful picture of humble Scotch life. One of the most frequently quoted of English poems.

Count of Monte Cristo, The, Dumas. A young sailor, Edmond Dantes, with the world and hopeful love before him, is imprisoned on a false charge of being a Bonapartist emissary. The time is 1815. In prison he is told by a fellow prisoner of a treasure buried on the island of Monte Cristo. He escapes, finds the treasure, and spends the rest of his life as the mysterious count, bringing punishment upon his enemies and rewarding his friends.

Crabtree. A character in Smollett's novel *The Adventures of Peregrine Pickle*.

Crane, Ichabod. The name of a Yankee schoolmaster, whose adventures are related in the *Legend of Sleepy Hollow*, in Irving's *Sketch Book*.

Crawley, Rawdon. The husband of Becky Sharp in *Vanity Fair*, Thackeray's novel without a hero.

Creakle, Mr. A tyrannical and cruel schoolmaster in Dickens's *David Copperfield*.

Cressida. The heroine of Shakspere's play *Troilus and Cressida*, also the heroine of one of Chaucer's *Canterbury Tales*. She was a faithless lover.

Cricket on the Hearth, The, Dickens. A Christmas story. The title is suggested by the singing-match between the kettle and the cricket on Dot Peerybingle's immaculate and snug little hearth. The cricket wins the match. A love story is woven in. Edward, son of old Caleb Plummer, the toy maker, comes home from South America just in time to save his sweetheart, May Fielding, from marriage to Tackleton, a toy merchant.

Crisis, The, Churchill. A story of Civil War times, the scenes located for the most part in St. Louis. A Yankee and a Southern girl are the lovers. Lincoln, Grant, and Sherman are brought into the tale.

Cris Kingle (*krĭs' kĭng'l*). Also variously spelled Kriss Kingle, and Kriss Kringle, has been corrupted from the German word, *Christ-Kindel*, meaning the "little *Christ-child*." Later uses, especially among German peoples, have identified the name with that of Santa Claus and Saint Nicholas.

Croaker. A character in Goldsmith's comedy *The Good-natured Man.*

Crocodile Tears. False tears, often affected for a purpose. The expression appears first in Greek and Latin proverbs and is based on the erroneous belief that the crocodile weeps in order to arouse the pity of a human being who, on approaching, is promptly devoured.

Crossing, The, Churchill. A historical tale of a boy's adventures in the westward movement of settlers across the Alleghenies after the Revolution. George Rogers Clark is the hero of the story.

Crummles, Vincent. A theatrical head of a theatrical family in Dickens's *Nicholas Nickleby.*

Crusoe, Robinson. See *Robinson Crusoe,* page 310.

Cuchullin, Cuchulain (*kōō-hōō'lĭn*). See *Cattle Raid of Cooley.*

Cuneiform (*kū-nē'ĭ-fôrm*) **Writing.** So called from the wedge shape of the characters (Latin *cuneus,* wedge). The signs, to represent objects and also sounds, were composed of the wedge-shape marks arranged in groups. These marks were impressed on soft clay tablets with a stylus or cut into rock with a chisel. This system was in use in Babylonia from 7000 B. C. to 300 B. C. and in neighboring countries, including that of the Hittites.

Cuttle, Captain. A character in Dickens's *Dombey and Son,* good-humored, eccentric, pathetic in his simple credulity.

Cymbeline. A mythical king of Britain and the titular hero of Shakspere's play of the same name. Imogen, daughter of Cymbeline, king of Britain, married clandestinely Posthumus Leonatus; and Posthumus, being banished for the offense, retired to Rome. One day, in the house of Philario, the conversation turned on the merits of wives, and Posthumus bet his diamond ring that nothing could tempt the fidelity of Imogen. Through the villainy of Iachimo, Posthumus was forced to believe Imogen untrue. The villainy was in time disclosed and the beautiful character of Imogen revealed.

Daddy-Long-Legs, Jean Webster. The story of an orphan girl who is sent to school by an unknown benefactor. She writes to him under the name of "Daddy-Long-Legs."

Dagonet, Sir. In the romance *Le Morte D'Arthur* he is called the fool of King Arthur.

Dalgetty, Rittmaster Dugald. A soldier of fortune in Sir Walter Scott's *Legend of Montrose,* distinguished for his pedantry, conceit, valor, vulgar assurance, knowledge of the world, greediness, and a hundred other qualities, making him one of the most amusing, admirable, and natural characters ever drawn by the hand of genius.

Damocles (*dăm'ō-klēz*). A flatterer in the court of Dionysius of Syracuse. By way of answer to his constant praises of the happiness of kings, Dionysius seated him at a royal banquet, with a sword hung over his head by a single horsehair. In the midst of his magnificent banquet, Damocles, chancing to look upward, saw the sharp and naked sword suspended over his head. A sight so alarming instantly changed his views of the felicity of kings. "Sword of Damocles" signifies now a dread foreboding of evil or tantalizing apprehension.

Damon and Pythias or **Phintias.** Two noble Pythagoreans of Syracuse, who have been remembered as models of faithful friendship. Pythias, having been condemned to death by Dionysius, the tyrant of Syracuse, begged to be allowed to go home, for the purpose of arranging his affairs, Damon pledging his own life for the reappearance of his friend. Dionysius consented, and Pythias returned just in time to save Damon from death. Struck by so noble an example of mutual affection, the tyrant pardoned Pythias, and desired to be admitted into their sacred fellowship.

Dandie Dinmont. A jovial, true-hearted store farmer, in Sir Walter Scott's *Guy Mannering.*

Dantesque (*dăn-tĕsk'*). Dante-like—that is, a minute, lifelike representation of the infernal horrors, whether by words, as in the "Inferno," or in visible form, as in Doré's illustrations of the poem.

Daphnis and Chloe (*klō'ē*). A pair of lovers in the pastoral romance of the same name written by Longus in Greek prose probably in the 5th century.

Darby and Joan. A married couple said to have lived in the village of Healaugh, in the West Riding of Yorkshire, and celebrated for their long life and conjugal felicity. They are the hero and the heroine of a ballad called "The Happy Old Couple," which has been attributed to Prior but is of uncertain authorship. Timperley says that Darby was a printer in Bartholomew Close, who died in 1730, and that the ballad was written by one of his apprentices named Henry Woodfall.

Dares (*dā'rēz*). One of the competitors at the funeral games of Anchises in Sicily, described in the fifth book of Virgil's *Æneid.*

Dark Rosaleen. A poetical name for Ireland. See James Clarence Mangan's beautiful poem of that name.

Darrel of the Blessed Isles, Irving Bacheller. A story of an old clock-mender whose imagination traveled through a country of poetry, the "blessed isles," fashioned out of his familiarity with Shakspere, Milton, and the Bible.

David. In Dryden's satire called "Absalom and Achitophel," the character representing Charles II; Absalom, his beautiful but rebellious son, represents the duke of Monmouth.

David, Saint. He was said to be the uncle of King Arthur. St. David first embraced the ascetic life at Witland in Carmarthenshire, but subsequently removed to Menevia, in Pembrokeshire, having founded twelve convents in West Britain.

Davy. Henry IV, Shakspere. The varlet of Justice Shallow, who so identifies himself with his master that he considers himself half host, half varlet. Thus, when he seats Bardolph and Page at table, he tells them they must take "his" good will for their assurance of welcome.

Dawfyd. The Betrothed, Scott. The one-eyed freebooter chief.

Dawkins. Oliver Twist, Dickens. Known by the sobriquet of the "Artful Dodger." He is one of Fagin's tools. Jack Dawkins is a scamp, but of a cheery, buoyant temper.

Deadwood Dick. The adventurous character to be found in many dime novels of the middle of the 19th century. In real life, he was Robert Dickey (1840–1912), who had a romantic career as Indian scout, trapper, and fur trader.

Deans, Douce Davie. A poor herdsman at Edinburgh, and the father of Effie and Jeanie Deans, in Sir Walter Scott's novel *The Heart of Midlothian.*

Deans, Effie. A beautiful but unfortunate character in Sir Walter Scott's *The Heart of Midlothian.*

Deans, Jeanie. The heroine of *The Heart of Midlothian,* characterized by her kindness, sturdiness, and good sense. She journeys from Edinburgh to London and obtains pardon for her sister Effie, condemned for child murder.

Debon. One of the heroes who accompanied Brut, or Brutus, to Britain. According to British fable, Devonshire is the county or share of Debon.

Decameron (*dē-kăm'ẽr-ŏn*). A volume of 100 tales told by Boccaccio. Seven ladies and three gentlemen, assembled in one place, agree that each shall tell one story every day for the entertainment of the rest. Thus ten stories daily are told for ten consecutive days. Chaucer borrowed the plan but reconstructed it for his *Canterbury Tales.*

De Coverley, Sir Roger. One of the members of the imaginary club under whose direction the *Spectator* was professedly edited. He represents a kind-hearted, simple-minded English squire in the time of Queen Anne. He figures in thirty papers of the *Spectator.*

Dedlock, Sir Leicester and Lady. Bleak House, Dickens. Sir Leicester was an honorable and truthful man but of such fixed ideas that no one could shake his prejudices. He had an idea that the one thing of greatest importance to the world was a certain family by the name of Dedlock. He loved his wife, Lady Dedlock, and believed in her implicitly. His pride had a terrible fall when he learned the secret of her life before her marriage and knew the fact that she had been hiding from him, that she had a daughter. Lady Dedlock, beautiful, but apparently cold and heartless, suffered from constant remorse. The daughter's name is Esther Summerson, the heroine of the novel. Volumnia Dedlock was a cousin of Sir Leicester, a young lady of sixty, who had the disagreeable habit of entering into other people's business.

Deerslayer. The hero of a novel of the same name, by James Fenimore Cooper. A strong fine character, honorable, truthful, brave, without cultivation but without reproach. This character appears under different names in five of Cooper's novels,—*The Deerslayer, The Pathfinder, The Last of the Mohicans, The Pioneers,* and *The Prairie.*

Defarge (*dē-färzh'*), **M. Tale of Two Cities, Dickens.** Keeper of a wine shop in the Faubourg St. Antoine, in Paris. He is a bull-necked, implacable-looking man. His wife, a dangerous woman, was "everlastingly knitting" before the guillotine as heads fell.

Defarge, Madame. Wife of the wineseller, a dangerous woman, "everlastingly knitting."

Delectable Mountains. In Bunyan's *Pilgrim's Progress*, a beautiful range of hills from the summit of which the pilgrim could see the Celestial City.

Delphin Classics. For the use of the dauphin, son of Louis XIV (1674–91), the writings of 39 Latin authors were collected and published in sixty volumes. Notes and an index were added to each work. An edition of the Delphin classics was published in London in the year 1818. The name comes from Latin *delphinus*, meaning "dolphin," from which "dauphin" also is derived, because of the device of a dolphin worn on his helmet.

Delphine. The title of a novel by Mme. de Staël, and the name of its heroine.

Delphine, Madame. Old Creole Days, George W. Cable. A free quadroon connected with the splendor of Lafitte, the smuggler and patriot. Madame Delphine disowned her beautiful daughter Olive in order to assure to her the rights of a white woman.

Demetrius (*dē-mē'trĭ-ŭs*). **A Midsummer Night's Dream, Shakspere.** The young Athenian to whom Egeus promised his daughter Hermia in marriage.

De Profundis (*dē prō-fŭn'dĭs*), "Out of the Depths." (1) The 130th Psalm is so called from the first two words in the Latin version. In the Roman Catholic Church it is sung when the dead are committed to the grave. (2) Title of a poem by Oscar Wilde.

Deronda, Daniel. One of George Eliot's strongest character sketches in her novel of the same name.

Der Tag, "The Day." For many years this was a favorite toast in the German army and navy, the day when war should come.

Deserted Village. A poem by Goldsmith in which he describes rural England. He calls the village Auburn, but tells us it was the seat of his youth, every spot of which was dear and familiar to him. He pictures familiar persons, the preacher, the teacher, pastimes, and favorite haunts.

Desmas. The repentant thief is so called in "The Story of Joseph of Arimathea." Longfellow, in "The Golden Legend," calls him Dumachus. The impenitent thief is called Gestas, but Longfellow calls him Titus.

Despair, Giant. Pilgrim's Progress, Bunyan. A giant who is the owner of Doubting Castle, and who, finding Christian and Hopeful asleep upon his grounds, takes them prisoners and thrusts them into a dungeon.

Deus Ex Machina, "A god from the machine." Used of some external power or idea brought into a story or argument to resolve a difficulty. An allusion to the custom of the ancient theater, where a god was brought in by machinery to explain or resolve situations past the power of human actors to understand or control.

Dhu, Roderick. A Highland chieftain and outlaw in Scott's poem "Lady of the Lake," cousin of Ellen Douglas, and also her suitor. He is slain by James Fitz-James.

Diana of the Crossways, George Meredith. This was the first of Meredith's novels to gain popularity, and it is still ranked as a masterpiece. The heroine, Diana Merion, the victim of a youthful, unhappy marriage, plunges into the gaiety of London and becomes unfortunately involved in the betrayal of a political secret. Sobered and disillusioned, she finally, after the death of her first husband, marries a strong, sensible man, Redworth, who had been devoted to her.

Dido. The daughter of Belus, king of Tyre, and the wife of Sichæus, whom her brother Pygmalion murdered for his riches. Not far from the Phœnician colony of Utica she built the city of Carthage. According to Virgil, when Æneas was shipwrecked upon her coast, in his voyage to Italy, she hospitably entertained him, fell in love with him, and, because he did not requite her passion, stabbed herself in despair.

Dies Iræ (*dī'ēz ī'rē*). The name generally given, from the opening words, to the famous medieval hymn on the Last Judgment. On account of the solemn grandeur of the ideas which it brings before the mind, as well as the deep and trembling emotions it is fitted to excite, it soon found its way into the liturgy of the Church. The authorship of the hymn has been ascribed to Gregory the Great, St. Bernard of Clairvaux, Umbertus, and Frangipani, the last two of whom were noted as hymnists. The consensus of recent hymnologists, however, is in favor of Thomas of Celano.

Diggon, Davie. A shepherd in the "Shepherd's Calendar," by Spenser. He tells Hobbinol that he drove his sheep into foreign lands, hoping to find better pasture; but he was amazed at the luxury and profligacy of the shepherds whom he saw there and the wretched condition of the flocks.

Dimmesdale (*dĭmz'dāl*), **Arthur.** In Hawthorne's romance *The Scarlet Letter*, a Puritan minister of great eloquence and spirituality, in colonial New England, who secretly commits adultery and afterward makes a public confession.

Dinah. (1) Aunt of Walter Shandy in Sterne's novel *Tristram Shandy*. She leaves Mr. Walter Shandy £1000, which he fancies will enable him to carry out all the schemes that enter into his head. (2) A character in Mrs. Stowe's *Uncle Tom's Cabin*. (3) *St. Ronan's Well*, Scott. Daughter of Sandie Lawson, landlord of the Spa hotel.

Dingley Dell. Pickwick Papers, Dickens. The home of Mr. Wardle and his family, and the scene of Tupman's love adventure with Miss Rachel.

Dirlos, Count. One of Charlemagne's paladins, an ideal of valor, generosity, and truth.

Divine Comedy. The immortal work of Dante Alighieri, written between 1300 and 1321, the year of the poet's death. It consists of a vision of the world beyond the grave, and depicts the final destiny of the human soul in accordance with its exercise of free will during life, by which it has chosen to follow the way of evil or of good.

The structure of the sublime poem is based upon the dual scheme of the *De Monarchiâ*. It is made up of a hundred cantos in metrical lines of eleven syllables, written in *terza rima*, a form of the popular poetry of the day but distinctly modified in an especial manner by the poet.

The vision of which Dante writes is one which was vouchsafed to him for his salvation's sake twenty years previously when leading an evil life. During the year of Jubilee, 1300, commencing on the morning of Good Friday and continuing for six consecutive days, the poet passed through the confines of hell, purgatory, and paradise. He held converse with the souls in each of the three realms and learned the future purposes of Divine Providence in his own regard and in that of the world at large.

The poet relates how, by special grace, while yet in the flesh, he was permitted to travel through these three realms of the After Life. Virgil appears to him, typifying human wisdom, informed by the moral and intellectual virtues. He guides Dante by the light of reason, from the dark forest, wherein the beasts of pride, avarice, and lust keep men from ascending the Holy Mount, through hell and purgatory as far as the earthly paradise. Here the poet realizes how the state of temporal happiness is reached through purgatorial travail which regains for the soul its spiritual liberty.

Beatrice, representing divine philosophy, illumined by revelation, leads him next up through the nine heavens of spiritual preparation of the mind. Then slowly, before the eyes of Dante, is opened up the true paradise, limitless, timeless, wherein is found the eternal happiness of the sight of God.

Here the place of Beatrice is taken by St. Bernard who typifies divine contemplation, which is the eternal life of the soul. The saint commends the poet to the patronage of the Blessed Virgin, through whose intercession Dante is awarded a foretaste of the Beatific Vision.

The poem closes in ineffable grandeur and majesty, showing how Faith is lost in Vision, Hope in Fruition and with nothing remaining but that "Charity which moves the sun and the other stars." The powers of the soul are consumed in their union with the Divine Essence and the finite will at last has become one with the Infinite.

In this stupendous allegory, we have in truth the transcendent vision of a god-given genius, who unfolds before us what has been revealed to him of the unspeakable justice, mercy, and glory of the Most High. In spiritual wisdom, dramatic force, infallible confidence of touch, and terseness of expression, the *Divine Comedy* has never been excelled. It is the culminating and crowning glory of medieval culture, which rivals in splendor that of the classical world at any period of its history.

Dobbin, Captain William. The awkward, plodding, patient, faithful friend of George Osborne in *Vanity Fair* by Thackeray. After years of unselfish devotion, he finally wins Amelia, George's widow, and marries her.

Doctor Syntax. The hero of a work entitled *The Tour of Dr. Syntax in Search of the Picturesque.* Doctor Syntax is a simple-minded, pious, henpecked clergyman, but of excellent taste and scholarship, who left home in search of the picturesque. His adventures are told in eight-syllable verse by William Combe.

Doctour of Phisikes, Tale of the. The Roman story of Virginius, given by Livy. Told by Chaucer in *Canterbury Tales.*

Dods. The old landlady in Scott's novel *St. Ronan's Well.* An excellent character, a mosaic of oddities, all fitting together, and forming an admirable whole. She was so good a housewife that a cookery book of great repute bears her name.

Dodson. The Three Warnings, Mrs. Thrale. A youth called upon by Death on his wedding day. Death told him he must go with him. "With you!" the hapless youth cried, "young as I am." Death then told him he would not disturb him yet, but would call again after giving him three warnings. When he was 80 years of age Death called again. "So soon returned?" old Dodson cried. "You know you promised me three warnings." Death then told him that as he was "lame, and deaf, and blind" he had received his three warnings.

Dodson and Fogg. The lawyers employed by the plaintiff in the famous case of "Bardell *v.* Pickwick," in the *Pickwick Papers* by Charles Dickens.

Doeg (*dō'ĕg*). **Absalom and Achitophel, Dryden.** Doeg was Saul's herdsman, who had charge of his mules and asses. He told Saul that the priests of Nob had provided David with food; whereupon Saul sent him to put them to death, and 85 were ruthlessly massacred.

Dogberry and Verges. Two ignorant, conceited constables, in Shakspere's *Much Ado about Nothing.*

Dolly Varden. Barnaby Rudge, Dickens. Daughter of Gabriel Varden, locksmith. Dolly dressed in the Watteau style, and was lively, pretty, and bewitching.

Dolopatos. Sandabar's Parables. The Sicilian king, who placed his son Lucien under the charge of "seven wise masters." Because the queen, Lucien's stepmother, had wrongfully accused him of violence toward her, he fell under his father's fury and was condemned to death. By astrology the prince discovered that if he could tide over seven days his life would be saved; so the wise master amused the king with seven tales, and the king relented. The prince himself then told a tale which embodied his own history; the eyes of the king were opened, and the queen was condemned to death.

Dombey. Dombey and Son, Dickens. Mr. Dombey, a self-sufficient, purse-proud, frigid merchant, who feels satisfied there is but one Dombey in the world, and that is himself. When Paul was born, his ambition was attained, his whole heart was in the boy, and the loss of the mother was but a small matter. The boy's death turned his heart to stone.

Dombey, Florence. A motherless child, hungering and thirsting to be loved, but regarded with indifference by her father, who thinks that sons alone are worthy of regard.

Dombey, Little Paul. A pathetic child in Dickens's novel *Dombey and Son.* He is a delicate, thoughtful boy, the only son of a rich and pompous London merchant.

Domdaniel (*dŏm-dăn'ĭ-ĕl*). A cave in the region adjoining Babylon, the abode of evil spirits. By some traditions said to have been originally the spot where the prophet Daniel imparted instruction to his disciples. In another form, the Domdaniel was a purely imaginary region, subterranean, or submarine, the dwelling place of genii and enchanters. Arabian mythology.

Domesday Book or **Doomsday Book.** The name of one of the oldest and most valuable records of England, containing the results of a statistical survey of that country made by William the Conqueror, and completed in the year 1086. The origin of the name—which seems to have been given to other records of the same kind—is somewhat uncertain; but it has obvious reference to the supreme authority of the book in doom or judgment on the matters contained in it.

Dominical Letter or **Sunday Letter.** One of the seven letters A, B, C, D, E, F, G, used in almanacs, etc., to mark the Sundays throughout the year. The first seven days of the year are marked in their order by the above corresponding letters. The following seven, and all consecutive sets of seven days to the end of the year are similarly marked; so that the 1st, 8th, 15th, 22d, etc., days of the year are all marked by A; and the 2d, 9th, 16th, 23d, etc., by B; and so on. The days being thus marked, it is evident that on whatever date the first Sunday of the year falls, the letter which marks it will mark all the other Sundays in the year, as the number of the letters and of the days in the week is the same. As the common year consists of 52 weeks and one day over, the dominical letters go backwards one day every common year. If the dominical letter of a common year be G, F will be the dominical letter for the next year.

Don Adriano de Armado (*dŏn äd'rĭ-ä'nō dā är-mä'dō*). A pompous, fantastical Spaniard in Shakspere's *Love's Labor's Lost,* "who has a mint of phrases in his brain." His language is fantastically out of proportion to the thought. He uses "examples suited only to the gravest propositions and impersonations, or apostrophes to abstract thoughts impersonated, which are, in fact, the natural language only of the most vehement agitations of the mind."

Donatello. The hero of Hawthorne's romance *The Marble Faun.* He is a young Italian with a singular likeness to the "Faun of Praxiteles." He leads an innocent but purely animal existence, until a sudden crime awakens his conscience and transforms his whole nature.

Don Cherubim. The "Bachelor of Salamanca" in Lesage's novel of this name; a man placed in different situations of life and made to associate with all classes of society, in order to give the author the greatest possible scope for satire.

Donegild. Man of Law's Tale, Chaucer. Mother of Alla, king of Northumberland, hating Constance, the wife of Alla, because she was a Christian, placed her on a raft with her infant son, and turned her adrift. When Alla returned from Scotland and discovered this cruelty of his mother, he put her to death. The tradition of St. Mungo resembles the "Man of Law's Tale" in many respects

Donet (*dō'nĕt*). The first Latin grammar put into the hands of scholars. It was that of Donatus the grammarian, who taught in Rome in the 4th century and was the preceptor of St. Jerome.

Don Juan (*dŏn jŭ'ăn*). A legendary and mythical personage like Dr. Faustus. Don Juan is presented in the life of a profligate who gives himself up so entirely to the gratification of sense, especially to the most powerful of all the impulses, that of love, that he acknowledges no higher consideration, and proceeds to murder the man that stands between him and his wish, fancying that in so doing he had annihilated his very existence. He then defies that spirit to prove to his senses his existence. The spirit returns and compels Don Juan to acknowledge the supremacy of spirit and the worthlessness of a merely sensuous existence. The traditions concerning Don Juan have been dramatized by Tirso de Molina; thence passed into Italy and France. Glück has a musical ballet of Don Juan, and Mozart has immortalized the character in his opera "Don Giovanni." His adventures form the subject of a half-finished poem by Byron.

Don Quixote (*dŏn kwĭk'sôt*). The hero of a celebrated Spanish romance of the same name by Cervantes. Don Quixote is represented as "a gaunt country gentleman of La Mancha, full of genuine Castilian honor and enthusiasm, gentle and dignified in his character, trusted by his friends, and loved by his dependents," but "so completely crazed by long reading the most famous books of chivalry, that he believes them to be true, and feels himself called on to become the impossible knight-errant they describe, and actually goes forth into the world to defend the oppressed and avenge the injured, like the heroes of his romances." The fame of Cervantes will always rest upon this incomparable satire upon the foolish and extravagant romances of chivalry.

Dooley, Mr. The Irish American character made popular by F. P. Dunne in humorous monologues of comment on men and affairs. Mr. Dooley, a saloon-keeper of Archey Road, appeared first in a series of sketches in the Chicago *Times-Herald.*

Doorm. Idylls of the King: Enid, Tennyson. An earl called "the Bull," who tried to make Enid his handmaid; but, when she would neither eat, drink, nor array herself in bravery at his bidding, "he smote her on the cheek"; whereupon Geraint slew the "russet-bearded earl" in his own hall.

Dora. David Copperfield, Dickens. The childwife to David, affectionate and tender-hearted. She was always playing with her poodle and saying simple things to her "Dody." She could never be his helper, but she looked on her husband with idolatrous love. While quite young she died.

Dorastus. The hero of an old popular "history" or romance, upon which Shakspere founded his *Winter's Tale.* It was written by Robert Greene, and was first published in 1588, under the title of *Pandosto, the Triumph of Time.*

Dorothea. The heroine of Goethe's celebrated poem "Hermann und Dorothea."

Dorrit, Edward and "Little." Little Dorrit, Dickens. The "father" of the Marshalsea prison and his interesting daughter. It is a fine picture of innocent, affectionate child life in the midst of the trying circumstances of a debtor's prison.

Dory, John. (1) Hero and title of an old English ballad. (2) A character in *Wild Oats,* or *The Strolling Gentleman,* a comedy by John O'Keefe.

Dotheboys (*dōō'THē-boiz'*) **Hall. Nicholas Nickleby, Dickens.** A school for boys kept by a Mr. Squeers, a puffing, ignorant, overbearing brute, whose system of education consisted of alternately beating and starving.

Doubting Castle. The castle of the giant Despair, in which Christian and Hopeful were incarcerated, but from which they escaped by means of the key called "Promise," which was able to open any lock in the castle.

Dousterswivel. A German schemer, in Sir Walter Scott's novel *The Antiquary.*

Drac (*drăk*). A sort of fairy in human form, whose abode is the caverns of rivers. "Faire le drac," same as "Faire le diable." Irish, "Play the Puck"; English, "Play the deuce."

Drama of Exile, A. A poem by Elizabeth Barrett Browning (1844). The exile is Eve, driven out of paradise into the wilderness. Lucifer, Gabriel, and Christ are introduced into the poem, as well as Adam and Eve.

Dramatic Unities, The Three. One catastrophe, one locality, one day. These are Aristotle's unities of time, place, and action. To these the French added a fourth, the unity of uniformity; i. e., in tragedy all the *dramatis personœ* should be tragic in style, in comedy comic, and in farce farcical.

Drap. Drayton. One of Queen Mab's maids of honor.

Drawcansir (*drô'kăn-sẽr*). The name of a blustering, bullying fellow in the celebrated mock-heroic play *The Rehearsal*, written by George Villiers, duke of Buckingham, assisted by Sprat and others. He is represented as taking part in a battle, where, after killing all the combatants on both sides, he makes an extravagantly boastful speech. From the popularity of the character, the name became a synonym for a braggart.

Driver. Guy Mannering, Scott. Clerk to Mr. Pleydell, advocate, Edinburgh.

Dromio. The Brothers Dromio. Two brothers exactly alike, who serve two brothers exactly alike, in Shakspere's *Comedy of Errors*, based on the *Menœchmi* of Plautus.

Dryasdust, The Rev. An imaginary personage who serves to introduce Scott's novels to the public.

Dudu. One of the three beauties of the harem into which Juan, by the sultana's order, had been admitted in female attire.

Duessa (*dû-ĕs'ȧ*). A foul witch, in Spenser's *Faery Queen*, who, under the assumed name of Fidessa and the assumed character of a distressed and lovely woman, entices the Red Cross Knight into the House of Pride. The knight, having left the palace, is overtaken by Duessa, and drinks of an enchanted fountain, which paralyzes him. In this state he is attacked, defeated, and imprisoned by the giant Orgoglio. Duessa becomes the paramour of Orgoglio, who decks her out in gorgeous ornaments, gives her a gold and purple robe to wear, puts a triple crown on her head, and sets her upon a monstrous beast with seven heads. Prince Arthur slays Orgoglio and rescues the knight. Duessa is stripped of her gorgeous disguise and is found to be a hideous hag.

Duff, Jamie. Guy Mannering, Scott. The idiot boy attending Mrs. Bertram's funeral.

Dulcinea del Toboso (*dōōl'thê-nā'ä dĕl tô-bō'sō*). A country girl whom Don Quixote courts as his ladylove.

Dumaine. A lord attending on the king of Navarre, in Shakspere's *Love's Labor's Lost.*

Duncan. (1) A king of Scotland immortalized in Shakspere's tragedy *Macbeth.* Shakspere represents him as murdered by Macbeth, who succeeds to the Scottish throne, but according to history he fell in battle. (2) A Highland hero in Scott's "Lady of the Lake."

Dunder, Sir David, of Dunder Hall. A conceited, whimsical old gentleman, who forever interrupts a speaker with "Yes, yes, I know it," or "Be quiet, I know it." *Ways and Means*, by Colman.

Dundreary, Lord. A grotesque character in Taylor's comedy *Our American Cousin*; noted for his aristocratic haughtiness of manner. The part, insignificant in the first form of the play, was enlarged and made famous by the actor, E. A. Sothern.

Durandal. Written also Durandart, Durindana, and Durlindana. The name of the marvelous sword of Orlando, the renowned hero of romance. It is said to have been the workmanship of the fairies, who endued it with such wonderful properties that its owner was able to cleave the Pyrenees with it at a blow.

Durandarte (*dōō'rän-där'tā*). A fabulous hero of Spain, celebrated in the ancient ballads of that country and in the romances of chivalry. Cervantes has introduced him, in *Don Quixote*, in the celebrated adventure of the knight in the cave of Montesinos.

Durden, Dame. (1) The heroine of a popular English song. She is described as a notable housewife, and the mistress of five serving girls and five laboring men. The five men loved the five maids. (2) A sobriquet playfully applied to Esther Summerson, the heroine of Dickens's *Bleak House.* (3) Mistress of the Inn of Sherwood in the opera "Robin Hood."

Dwarf, Peter. An allegorical romance by Ludwig Tieck. The dwarf is a castle specter that advises and aids the family; but all his advice turns out evil, and all his aid productive of trouble.

Dwarf, The Black. A novel by Sir Walter Scott. The black dwarf is a fairy of the most malignant character; a genuine northern Duergar, and once held by the dalesmen of the border as the author of all the mischief that befell their flocks and herds. In Scott's novel the "Black Dwarf" is introduced under the "aliases" of Sir Edward Mauley; Elshander, the recluse; Cannie Elshie; and the Wise Wight of Mucklestane Moor.

Earnscliffe, Patrick. The Black Dwarf, Scott. The young laird of Earnscliff.

Earthly Paradise, The, William Morris. A narrative poem, the scene of which is laid in a "nameless city in a distant sea" to which come a band of Norse rovers fleeing from the Black Death and seeking a paradise. In this city they linger and find freedom from fear. During the year of waiting they tell 24 tales. These stories are gathered from Greek, Norse, French, and Arabian sources. They are connected by lyric passages of landscape poetry.

Eckhardt, The Faithful. A legendary hero of Germany, represented as an old man with a white staff, who, in Eisleben, appears on the evening of Maundy Thursday and drives all the people into their houses, to save them from being harmed by a terrible procession of dead men, headless bodies, and two-legged horses, which immediately after passes by. Other traditions represent him as the companion of the knight, Tannhäuser, and as warning travelers from the Venusberg, the mountain of fatal delights in the old mythology of Germany. Tieck has founded a story upon this legend, which has been translated into English by Carlyle, in which Eckhardt is described as the good servant who perishes to save his master's children from the seducing fiends of the mountain. The German proverb, "Thou art the faithful Eckhardt; thou warnest every one," is founded upon this tradition.

Eclecta. The "Elect" personified in "The Purple Island," by Phineas Fletcher. She is the daughter of Intellect and Voletta (free will).

Ecole des Femmes, L' (*lā'kōl' dā fȧm*), "The School of Wives," **Molière.** The dramatist in this comedy developed an Italian story. Arnolphe adopts a young girl, Agnes, whom he proceeds to educate in a school where distinctions of sex and social class are ignored. When her education is finished, he plans to marry her, but she betrays her training in her very naïve treatment of men as if they were schoolgirls. The upshot is that a young fellow, Horace, falls in love with her and they are married. Arnolphe's experiment has failed.

Ecole des Maris, L' (*lā'kōl' dā mä'rē'*), "The School of Husbands," **Molière.** In this comedy, Sganarelle appears as a surly despot. To him and his brother Ariste, the father of two girls, Isabelle and Léonor, has given the care of them until they have grown up. With marriage in view, the brothers set out to educate their charges. Sganarelle restricts Isabelle severely, and as a consequence she deceives him and marries Valère. Ariste, on the other hand, through giving Léonor liberty and trusting her, gains a loving, dutiful wife.

Ector or **Hector, Sir.** The foster father of King Arthur, and lord of many parts of England and Wales. Father of Sir Kay, seneschal to King Arthur.

Edda. There are two religious codes, so called, containing the ancient Scandinavian mythology. One is in verse, composed in Norway and Iceland by various unknown authors; the other is written in prose, attributed to Snorre Sturleson, who wrote a commentary on the first edda.

Edenhall, The Luck of. A painted goblet in the possession of the Musgrave family of Edenhall, Cumberland, said to have been left by the fairies on St. Cuthbert's Well. The tradition runs, that the luck of the family is dependent on the safe-keeping of this goblet. The German poet Uhland embodied the legend in a ballad, translated into English by Longfellow.

Edgar. Son of Gloucester, in Shakspere's tragedy *King Lear.* He was disinherited for his half brother Edmund.

Edgar or **Edgardo.** Master of Ravenswood, in love with Lucy Ashton in Scott's *Bride of Lammermoor.*

Edith. The "Maid of Lorn" in Scott's *Lord of the Isles*, who married Ronald when peace was restored after the battle of Bannockburn.

Edith Granger. Dombey and Son, Dickens. Daughter of the Hon. Mrs. Skewton, married to Colonel Granger of "Ours," who died within two years. Edith became Mr. Dombey's second wife, but the marriage was altogether unhappy.

Edith, The Lady. Ivanhoe, Scott. Mother of Athelstane "the Unready," thane of Coningsburgh.

Edith Plantagenet (*plăn-tăj'ē-nĕt*), **The Lady. The Talisman, Scott.** Called "The Fair Maid of Anjou," a kinswoman of Richard I, and attendant on Queen Berengaria.

Edmund. A bastard son of Gloucester in Shakspere's tragedy *King Lear*.

Edward. Count Robert of Paris, Scott. Brother of Hereward, the Varangian guard. He was slain in battle.

Edward, Sir. The Iron Chest, Colman. He commits a murder, and keeps a narrative of the transaction in an iron chest. Later, he trusts the secret to his secretary. Wilfred, and the whole transaction becomes public.

Edwin. (1) The hero of Goldsmith's ballad entitled "The Hermit." (2) The hero of Mallet's ballad "Edwin and Emma." (3) The hero of Beattie's "Minstrel."

Edyrn. Idylls of the King: Enid, Tennyson. Son of Nudd. A suitor for the hand of Enid and an evil genius of her father, who opposed him. Later, Edyrn went to the court of King Arthur and became quite a changed man,—from a malicious "sparrow hawk" he was converted into a courteous gentleman.

Egeus (*ē-jē'ŭs*). Father of Hermia in Shakspere's *Midsummer Night's Dream*.

Egil. Brother of Weland, a great archer. The story related is similar to the William Tell story. There are many such stories. One day, King Nidung commanded him to shoot at an apple placed on the head of his own son. Egil selected two arrows, and being asked why he wanted two replied, "One to shoot thee with, O tyrant, if I fail." Such stories, though probably not true to fact, are true to the spirit of patriotism, and are worth repeating.

Eglamour. (1) A character in Shakspere's *Two Gentlemen of Verona*, who is an agent of Silvia in her escape. (2) A valiant knight of the Round Table, celebrated in the romances of chivalry, and in an old ballad. Written also Eglamore.

Eglantine (*ĕg'lăn-tīn*), **Madame.** The prioress in Chaucer's *Canterbury Tales*, who was "full pleasant and amiable of port." She was distinguished for the ladylike delicacy of her manners at table, for her partiality to "small hounds," and for a peculiar mixture in her manner and dress of feminine vanity and slight worldliness, together with an ignorance of the world. She is noted for her delicate oath, "by Seint Eloy," her "entuning the service swetely in her nose," and her speaking French "after the scole of Stratford atte Bowe."

Egoist, The. George Meredith. A psychological novel in which the intense egoism of the central figure, Sir Willoughby Patterne of Patterne Hall, is analyzed. The cruelty of such egoism or egotism appears in Willoughby's treatment of Laetitia Dale, daughter of a retired officer living on the Patterne estate. Its comic side is revealed through the conduct of Clara Middleton, daughter of a learned clergyman. After fancying herself in love with Sir Willoughby, she is awakened to a clear understanding of his character and administers severe and appropriate punishment to him.

Egyptian Thief. A personage alluded to by the duke in Shakspere's *Twelfth Night*. The reference is to the story of Thyamis, a robber chief and native of Memphis.

Eivir. Harold the Dauntless, Scott. A Danish maid who assumes boy's clothing and waits on Harold "the Dauntless" as his page.

Elaine. A mythic lady in the romances of King Arthur's court. She is called "the lily maid of Astolat" in Tennyson's *Idylls of the King*. For love of Sir Lancelot she died, and then according to her request was borne on a barge to the castle of King Arthur, holding a lily in one hand and a letter to Lancelot in the other. Sir Thomas Malory states that Elaine was sister of King Arthur by the same mother. She married Sir Nentres of Carlot and was by King Arthur the mother of Modred.

Elbow. A constable, in Shakspere's *Measure for Measure*, modest and well-meaning, though of simple mind and the object of wit among those who are wiser but not better.

El Dorado (*ĕl dō-rä'dō*). Spanish, meaning "the gilded." A name given by the Spaniards to an imaginary country, supposed, in the 16th century, to be situated in the interior of South America, between the rivers Orinoco and Amazon, and abounding in gold and all manner of precious stones. Expeditions were fitted out for the purpose of discovering this fabulous region; and, though all such attempts proved futile, the rumors of its existence continued to be believed down to the beginning of the 18th century. El Dorado is used proverbially for any ideally rich territory.

Electra. See *Mythology*. The name of this classical figure was used in the title of one of O'Neill's trilogies. The "Electra Complex" is a term of Freudian psychology.

Elfland. The realm ruled over by Oberon, king of Fairies.

Elgitha. Ivanhoe, Scott. A female attendant on the Lady Rowena at Rotherwood.

Elia, Essays of. Elia was an assumed name of Charles Lamb, who so signed a number of articles which he contributed to the London Magazine between 1820 and 1825. These, known as the essays of Elia, constitute the chief foundation of Lamb's fame as a critic and essayist.

Elidure. A legendary king of Britain, fabled to have been advanced to the throne in place of his brother Artegal, or Arthgallo. Returning to the country after a long exile, Artegal accidentally encountered his brother, who received him with open arms, took him home to the palace, and reinstated him in his old position, abdicating the throne himself. Wordsworth has taken the story of these two brothers for the subject of a poem.

Elim. The Messiah, Klopstock. The guardian angel of Libbeus the Apostle. Libbeus, the tenderest and most gentle of the apostles, at the death of Jesus also died from grief.

Elliott, Hobbie. There are seven Elliotts in Scott's *Black Dwarf*. The farmer Elliott himself, whose bride-elect is Grace Armstrong; Mrs. Elliott, Hobbie's grandmother; John and Harry, Hobbie's brothers; Lilias, Jean, and Arnot, Hobbie's sisters.

Elope. Milton gives this name to the dumb serpent which gives no warning of its approach.

Elsie. The daughter of Gottlieb, a farm tenant of Prince Henry of Hoheneck, who offered her life as a substitute for the prince. She was rescued as she was about to make the sacrifice. Longfellow has told this story in "The Golden Legend."

Elsie Venner. The heroine of a novel of the same name by O. W. Holmes. The story tells of the gradual humanizing of a girl whose moral and physical system had been poisoned by a snake bite suffered by her mother before the girl's birth. Love is the correcting force, but the severe struggle results only in Elsie's death.

Elspeth. Scotch, shortened from Elizabeth. (1) A character in Sir Walter Scott's *Antiquary*. (2) An old servant to Dandie Dinmont, in Scott's *Guy Mannering*. (3) The housekeeper in Stevenson's *Weir of Hermiston*.

Elzevir or **Elzevier.** The name of a celebrated family of printers at Amsterdam, Leyden, and other places in Holland, whose beautiful editions were published chiefly between the years 1583 and 1680. These editions are unrivaled for both beauty and correctness. It is said that the Elzevirs generally employed women to correct the press, under the conviction that they would be less likely than men, on their own responsibility, to introduce alterations into the text. They printed in all about 2000 books, of which 968 were in Latin, 44 in Greek, 126 in French, 32 in Flemish, 11 in German, 10 in Italian, and 22 in Oriental languages. Rare editions of the Elzevirs are highly valued by collectors.

Emerald Isle. The author of this epithet was Dr. William Drennan, of Belfast, who died 1820. It occurs in a poem entitled "Erin," of which the fourth stanza runs thus:

"Arm of Erin! prove strong, but be gentle as brave,
And, uplifting to strike, still be ready to save,
Not one feeling of vengeance presume to defile
The cause, or the men of the Emerald Isle."

Emile (*ā'mēl'*). The hero of Jean Jacques Rousseau's novel of the same name, in which he has depicted his ideal of a perfectly educated young man.

Emilia. (1) The sister-in-law of "Duke Theseus," beloved by the two knights, Palamon and Arcite. (2) A lady attending Hermione in Shakspere's *Winter's Tale*. (3) Wife of Iago, and waiting woman to Desdemona, in the tragedy *Othello*, a woman of thorough vulgarity and loose principles, united to a high degree of spirit, energetic feeling, strong sense, and low cunning. (4) The sweetheart of Peregrine Pickle in Smollett's novel *The Adventures of Peregrine Pickle*.

Em'ly, Little. David Copperfield, Dickens. Orphan daughter of Tom, the brother-in-law of Dan'el Peggotty, a Yarmouth fisherman, by whom she was brought up, David Copperfield and Em'ly were at one time playfellows. While engaged to Ham Peggotty, Dan'el's nephew. Little

Em'ly runs away with Steerforth, a friend of David's, who was a handsome but unprincipled gentleman. Being subsequently reclaimed, she emigrates to Australia with Dan'el Peggotty and old Mrs. Gummidge.

Empyrean. According to Ptolemy, there are many heavens, the earth being surrounded by the spheres of the planets and fixed stars. The Empyrean is the ultimate and last, the seat of the deity.

Encyclopedists or **Encyclopædists** (*ĕn-sī'klō-pē'dĭsts*). The collaborators in the encyclopedia of Diderot and D'Alembert (1751–65). The Encyclopedists as a body were the exponents of the French skepticism of the 18th century.

Endell, Martha. David Copperfield, Dickens. A poor girl, to whom Em'ly goes when Steerforth deserts her.

Enid. The wife of Geraint, one of the Knights of the Round Table in the legends of King Arthur. The story was elaborated by Tennyson in his *Idylls of the King.* Falsely suspected of infidelity by Geraint, she nevertheless nursed him back to health after he had been desperately wounded in combat. His faith in her restored, he implored and received her forgiveness. In the older legends, Geraint supposed that Enid had lost her love for him because of his indolence at the court, and he therefore set out to win back her love by some brave deed.

Epimenides (*ĕp'ĭ-mĕn'ĭ-dēz*). A philosopher and poet of Crete, who probably lived in the 6th or 7th century, B. C. He is said to have fallen asleep in a cave, when a boy, and to have remained in that state for 57 years. On waking and going out into the broad daylight, he was greatly perplexed and astonished to find everything around him altered. But what was more wonderful still, during his long period of slumber, his soul, released from its fleshly prison, had been busily engaged in the study of medicine and natural philosophy, and, when it again became incarnated, Epimenides found himself a man of great knowledge and wisdom. Goethe has written a poem on the subject, "Des Epimenides Erwachen." See *Klaus, Peter*, and *Rip Van Winkle.*

Epithalamium (*ĕp'ĭ-thȧ-lā'mĭ-ŭm*). A species of poem which it was the custom among the Greeks and Romans to sing in chorus near the bridal chamber of a newly married couple. Anacreon, Stesichorus, and Pindar composed poems of this kind, but only scanty fragments have been preserved. Spenser's "Epithalamium," written on the occasion of his marriage, is one of the finest specimens of this kind of verse.

Eppie. (1) In George Eliot's *Silas Marner*, the child of Godfrey Cass, brought up and adopted by Silas Marner, whose love transformed him from a miser into a tender, loving father. (2) *St. Ronan's Well,* Scott. One of the servants of the Rev. Josiah Cargill. (3) In the same novel is Eppie Anderson, one of the servants at the Mowbray Arms, Old St. Ronan's, kept by Meg Dods.

Erlking. King of the elves, who prepares mischief for children, and even deceives men with his seductions. He is said to haunt the Black Forest. Goethe has a ballad called "The Erlking."

Ermangarde of Baldringham, Lady. The Betrothed, Scott. Aunt of the Lady Eveline Berenger, "the betrothed."

Ermeline. The wife of Reynard, in the tale of *Reynard the Fox.*

Erminia (*ĕr-mē'nyä*). The heroine of Tasso's *Jerusalem Delivered,* who fell in love with Tancred. When the Christian army besieged Jerusalem, she dressed herself in Clorinda's armor to go to Tancred, but, being discovered, fled, and lived awhile with some shepherds on the banks of the Jordan. Meeting with Vafrino, sent as a secret spy by the crusaders, she revealed to him the design against the life of Godfrey, and, returning with him to the Christian camp, found Tancred wounded. She cured his wounds, so that he was able to take part in the last great day of the siege.

Ernest, Duke. A poetical romance by Henry of Veldig (Waldeck), contemporary with Frederick Barbarossa. It is a mixture of Greek and Oriental myths and hero adventures of the crusader.

Error. Faery Queen, Spenser. A monster who lived in a den in "Wandering Wood," and with whom the Red Cross Knight had his first adventure. She had a brood of 1000 young ones of sundry shapes, and these cubs crept into their mother's mouth when alarmed. The knight was nearly killed by the stench which issued from the foul fiend, but he succeeded in "rafting" her head off, whereupon the brood lapped up the blood, and burst with satiety.

Escalus. An ancient and kind-hearted lord, in Shakspere's *Measure for Measure,* whom Vincentio, the duke of Vienna, joins with Angelo as his deputy during a pretended absence on a distant journey.

Escanes. A lord of Tyre, in Shakspere's *Pericles.*

Esmeralda (*ĕs'mȧ-räl'dä*). **Notre Dame de Paris, Victor Hugo.** A beautiful gipsy girl, who, with tambourine and goat, dances in the "place" before Notre Dame.

Esmond (*ĕz'mŭnd*), **Henry.** A cavalier and a fine-spirited gentleman in the reign of Queen Anne. Hero of Thackeray's novel of the same name.

Estella. The heroine of Dickens's novel *Great Expectations.*

Esther Summerson. Bleak House, Dickens. The unacknowledged daughter of Lady Dedlock. She becomes the notably skillful housekeeper of Bleak House for Mr. Jarndyce and finally marries Allan Woodcourt. Her character is said to have been drawn from life. She is the narrator of a large part of the story.

Estotiland (*ĕs-tŏt'ĭ-lănd*) or **Estotilandia.** An imaginary region in America, near the Arctic circle, referred to by Milton as "cold Estotiland," and variously fabled to have been discovered by Frisian fishermen in the 14th century, and by a Pole named John Scalve, in 1477.

Ettrick Shepherd, The. He is one of the characters in the *Noctes Ambrosianæ* of Christopher North. Identified as James Hogg, the Scotch poet, who was in early life a shepherd in the parish of Ettrick.

Etzel or **Attila.** King of the Huns, a monarch ruling over three kingdoms and more than thirty principalities; being a widower he married Kriemhild, the widow of Siegfried. In the *Nibelungenlied,* where he is introduced, he is made very insignificant.

Eulalie, Eulalia, St. In the calendar of saints there is a virgin martyr called Eulalie. She was martyred by torture, February 12, 308. Longfellow calls Evangeline the "Sunshine of St. Eulalie."

Eulenspiegel, Till (*tĭl oi'lĕn-shpē'gĕl*). The hero of a German tale, which relates the pranks and drolleries of a wandering cottager of Brunswick. The name means "owlglass."

Euphrasy. Paradise Lost, Milton. The herb eyebright; so called because it was once supposed to be efficacious in clearing the organs of sight. Hence, the archangel Michael purged the eyes of Adam with it, to enable him to see into the distant future.

Euphues (*ū'fū-ēz*). The principal character in Lyly's two famous works, entitled *Euphues, or the Anatomy of Wit,* and *Euphues and His England.* These works are remarkable for their pedantic and fantastical style, and for the monstrous and overstrained conceits with which they abound. Euphues is represented as an Athenian gentleman, distinguished for the elegance of his person and the beauty of his wit, and for his amorous temperament and roving disposition. He gained a bosom friend, Philautus, and then robbed him of his lover, Lucilla. The lady is false to both, the friends are reconciled, and Euphues returns to Athens and philosophy. The peculiarities of Lyly's style are a perpetual striving after alliteration and antithesis, and a most ingenious stringing together of similes. This book immediately became the rage in the court circles, and for many years was the court standard. From it we get our word *euphuism,* meaning an affected, bombastic style of language.

Evan Dhu M'Combich. Waverley, Scott. The foster brother of MacIvor.

Evan Dhu of Lochiel (*lŏĸ-ēl'*). **Legend of Montrose, Scott.** A Highland chief in the army of Montrose.

Evangeline. The heroine of Longfellow's poem. The subject of the tale is the expulsion of the inhabitants of Acadia (Nova Scotia) from their homes by order of George II, and the lifelong wanderings of Evangeline in search of her lover, Gabriel. It is a story of a woman's love and devotion.

Evangelist. In Bunyan's *Pilgrim's Progress,* he represents the effectual preacher of the Gospel, who opens the gate of life to Christian.

Evelina. The heroine in a novel of the same name, by Miss Burney.

Eve of St. Agnes, The, Keats. The Lady Madeline, on St. Agnes's Eve, goes supperless to bed, trying the old superstition that thus a maid might see her future husband on awaking. An old servant admits Porphyro, Madeline's lover, to her chamber. After arranging a dessert by her bed, he wakens her with a favorite air, and persuades her to leave the castle with him while the festivities are going on in the great hall.

Every Man in His Humor. A comedy by Ben Jonson. Every person in the play is liable to be duped by his special humor: Captain Bobadil's humor is bragging; Kitelly's is jealousy; Stephen's is stupidity; Knowell's is suspicion; Dame Kitelly's, like her husband's, is jealousy.

Evir-Allen. Fingal, Ossian. The white-armed daughter of Branno, an Irishman. "A thousand heroes sought the maid; she refused her love to a thousand. The sons of the sword were despised, for graceful in her eyes was Ossian."

Excalibur. Meaning of the words: "liberated from the stone." The name of Arthur's far-famed sword, which he unfixed from a miraculous stone, though previously two hundred and one of the most puissant barons in the realm had singly been unable to extract it. In consequence of this remarkable feat, Arthur was chosen and proclaimed king by general acclamation. When about to die, he sent an attendant to throw the weapon into a lake hard by. Twice eluding the request, the squire at last complied. A hand and arm arose from the water, caught the sword by the hilt, flourished it thrice, and then sank into the lake and was seen no more. Written also Excalibor, Escalibar, Escalibor, and Caliburn.

Eyre (*âr*), **Jane.** The heroine of Charlotte Brontë's novel of the same name, a governess in the family of a Mr. Rochester, to whom she is finally married.

Ezzelin, Sir. Lara, Byron (1814). The gentleman who recognizes Lara at the table of Lord Otho, and charges him with being Conrad the Corsair. A duel ensues, and Ezzelin is never heard of more. A serf used to say that he saw a huntsman one evening cast a dead body into the river which divided the lands of Otho and Lara, and that there was a star of knighthood on the breast of the corpse.

Faa, Gabriel. Guy Mannering, Scott. Nephew of Meg Merrilies. One of the huntsmen at Liddesdale.

Fabliaux (*fȧ'blē'ōz'*). The metrical fables of the trouvères, or early poets north of the Loire, in the 12th and the 13th century. The word fable, in this case, is used very widely, for it includes not only such tales as *Reynard the Fox*, but all sorts of familiar incidents of knavery and intrigue, as well as legends and family traditions. The fabliau *Aucassin and Nicolette* is full of interesting incidents and contains much true pathos and beautiful poetry.

Fada. A fee or kobold of the south of France, sometimes called "Hada." These house spirits, of which, strictly speaking, there are but three, bring good luck in their right hand and ill luck in their left.

Fadladeen. The hypercritical grand chamberlain in Thomas Moore's poem *Lalla Rookh*. Fadladeen's criticism upon the several tales which make up the romance are very racy and full of humor; and his crestfallen conceit when he finds out that the poet was the prince in disguise is well conceived.

Faery or **Fairy Land.** The land of the fays or fairies. The chief fay realms are Avalon, an island somewhere in the ocean, Oberon's dominions, situated "in wilderness among the holtis hairy," and a realm somewhere in the middle of the earth, where was Pari Banou's palace.

Faery Queen. A metrical romance, in six books of twelve cantos each, by Edmund Spenser. The hero, Prince Arthur, arriving at the court of Gloriana, the queen in Faeryland, finds her holding a solemn festival during twelve days. At the court there is a beautiful lady, for whose hand twelve most distinguished knights are rivals, and in order to settle their pretensions these twelve heroes undertake twelve separate adventures. The first book contains the legend of the Red Cross Knight, who is the allegorical representative of "holiness," while his mistress Una represents true "religion"; and the action of the knight's exploit shadows forth the triumph of holiness over the enchantments and deceptions of heresy. The second book is the legend of Sir Guyon. The third book is the legend of Britomartis—a female champion—or "chastity." Britomartis is Diana, or Queen Elizabeth the Britoness. The fourth book is the legend of Cambel and Triamond (fidelity). The fifth book is the legend of Artegal (justice). The sixth book is the legend of Sir Calidore (courtesy). The remaining books were never completed. The plan of the *Faery Queen* is borrowed from the *Orlando Furioso*, but Spenser's creative power is more original, and his imagery more striking, than Ariosto's.

Fag. A lying servant to Captain Absolute in Sheridan's *Rivals*.

Fagin. An old Jew in Dickens's *Oliver Twist*, who employs young persons of both sexes to carry on a systematic trade of robbery.

Fainall, Mr. and Mrs. Noted characters in Congreve's comedy *The Way of the World*.

Fainéant, Le Noir (*lĕ nwär' fā'nā'äɴ'*), "The Black Idler." In Sir Walter Scott's *Ivanhoe*, a name applied to Richard Cœur de Lion, in disguise, by the spectators of a tournament, on account of his indifference during a great part of the action, in which, however, he was finally victorious.

Fairies. Fairy lore of the nursery grows out of belief in unseen powers of good and of evil. Good fairies are called fairies, elves, elle-folks, and fays; the evil ones are urchins, ouphes, ell-maids, and ell-women.

Fair Maid of Perth. The title of a novel by Sir Walter Scott, and the name of the heroine.

Fairservice, Andrew. A shrewd Scotch gardener at Osbaldistone Hall in *Rob Roy*, by Sir Walter Scott.

Fairy of the Mine. A malevolent being supposed to live in mines, busying itself with cutting ore, turning the windlass, etc., and yet effecting nothing.

Faithful. One of the allegorical personages in Bunyan's *Pilgrim's Progress*, who dies a martyr before completing his journey.

Faithful, Jacob. The title and hero of a sea tale, by Captain Marryat.

Faith Healer, The, William Vaughn Moody. A play. In a farmhouse in the Middle West live Matthew Beeler, his invalid wife Mary, who has not walked for several years, Annie, their little daughter, Martha, sister of Matthew, and Rhoda Williams, a niece. Ulrich Michaelis, a spiritual healer, has come as a lodger to the farm. The time is just before Easter. Under his treatment, Mrs. Beeler walks. Then Michaelis falls in love with Rhoda. and, since he believes earthly love inconsistent with his mission, his power fails for a time. But, when he sees that his love for Rhoda and hers for him are good, his power of healing returns in even greater effectiveness than before.

Fakenham Ghost. A ballad by Robert Bloomfield, author of "The Farmer's Boy." The ghost was a donkey.

Fakreddin's Valley. Over the several portals of bronze were these inscriptions: (1) "The Asylum of Pilgrims"; (2) "The Traveler's Refuge"; (3) "The Depository of the Secrets of All the World."

Falkland. In Godwin's novel called *Caleb Williams*. He commits murder, and keeps a narrative of the transaction in an iron chest. Williams, a lad in his employ, opens the chest, and is caught in the act by Falkland. The lad runs away, but is hunted down. This tale, dramatized by Colman, is entitled *The Iron Chest*.

Falstaff (*fôl'stȧf*), **Sir John.** A famous character in Shakspere's comedy *Merry Wives of Windsor*, and in the first and second parts of his historical drama *Henry IV*. He is as perfect a comic portrait as was ever sketched. In the former play, he is represented as in love with Mrs. Ford and Mrs. Page, who make a butt and a dupe of him; in the latter, he figures as a soldier and a wit; in both he is exhibited as a monster of fat,—sensual, mendacious, boastful, and cowardly. In *Henry V* his death is described by Mrs. Quickly.

Fang. (1) A sheriff's officer, in the second part of Shakspere's *King Henry IV*. (2) Dickens's *Oliver Twist*. A bullying, insolent magistrate, who would have sent Oliver Twist to prison, on suspicion of theft, if Mr. Brownlow had not interposed.

Fata Alcina (*fä'tä äl-chē'nä*). **Orlando Innamorato, Boiardo.** Sister of Fata Morgana. She carried off Astolfo on the back of a whale to her isle, but turned him into a myrtle tree when she tired of him.

Fata Morgana (*fä'tä môr-gä'nä*). The name of a potent fairy, celebrated in the tales of chivalry and in the romantic poems of Italy. She was a pupil of the enchanter Merlin, and the sister of Arthur, to whom she discovered the intrigue of his queen, Geneura, or Guinever, with Lancelot of the Lake. In the *Orlando Innamorato* of Boiardo, she appears at first as a personification of Fortune, inhabiting a splendid residence at the bottom of a lake, and dispensing all the treasures of the earth, but she is afterward found in her proper station subject to the all potent Demogorgon.

Fat Boy, The. A laughable character in Dickens's *Pickwick Papers*; a youth of astonishing obesity, whose employment consists in alternate eating and sleeping.

Father, The, Strindberg. A drama exploiting the conflict between the sexes. A cavalry captain, intensely interested in science, and his wife, outwardly a pious churchwoman, are divided over the kind of education their daughter Bertha shall have. To gain her end, the control of the daughter, the wife Laura sows in her husband's mind a suspicion that Bertha is not his child. She has already intercepted the captain's letters so that he is robbed of the fruits of his scientific studies. Then she so plays upon his violent temper and his fear of becoming insane that he falls ill and dies. The woman has demonstrated, to her own satisfaction, her superiority and has won control of her daughter.

Father Brown, The Innocence of, G. K. Chesterton. Father Brown is the hero of an interesting series of detective stories. He attains results through his unusual insight into the workings of the ordinary mind.

Fathom, Ferdinand, Count. The title of a novel by Smollett, and the name of its principal character, a complete villain, who proceeds step by step to rob his benefactors and finally dies in misery and despair.

Fatima (*făt'ĭ-mȧ*). (1) An enchantress, in the story of Aladdin, in the *Arabian Nights' Entertainments.* (2) The last of the wives of Bluebeard, and the only one who escaped being murdered by him. (3) The favorite daughter of Mohammed.

Faust. The hero and title of a celebrated tragedy by Goethe, the materials of which are drawn in part from the popular legends of Dr. Faustus, a famous magician of the 16th century. Faust is a student who is toiling after knowledge beyond his reach, and who afterwards deserts his studies and makes a pact with the Devil, Mephistopheles, in pursuance of which he gives himself up to the full enjoyment of the senses, until the hour of his doom arrives, when Mephistopheles reappears upon the scene, and carries off his victim as a condemned soul. This mythical personage dates back to the time of the Reformation.

Faustus. The hero of Marlowe's tragedy of the same name; represented as a vulgar sorcerer tempted to sell his soul to the Devil, Mephistopheles, on condition of having a familiar spirit at his command for 24 years, the possession of earthly power and glory, and unlimited gratification of his sensual appetites. At the end of that time, when the forfeit comes to be exacted, he shrinks and shudders in agony and remorse, imploring yet despairing of the mercy of heaven. This has been the theme of many writers. It is the subject of an opera by Gounod.

Faw, Tibbie. Redgauntlet, Scott. The ostler's wife, in Wandering Willie's tale.

Feeble. In Shakspere's *Henry IV*, a starveling tailor, whom Falstaff calls "most forcible Feeble."

Felton, Septimius. Septimius Felton is the mystical hero in Hawthorne's novel of the same name.

Femmes Savantes, Les (*lā făm sȧ'văNt'*), "The Learned Ladies," **Molière.** This comedy is a satire upon women who pretend to literature and learning. The plot concerns the plans of Philaminte for the marriage of her daughter Henriette. She wishes her to marry Trissotin, but Henriette loves Clitandre. In the end, when Henriette's father is nearly bankrupt, Trissotin loses interest in the match, and the lovers are wedded. The "learned ladies" are Philaminte and her friends, Armande and Bélise.

Fenella. A fairylike creature, a deaf and dumb attendant on the countess of Derby, in Sir Walter Scott's *Peveril of the Peak.*

Fenton. A character in Shakspere's *Merry Wives of Windsor*, who woos the rich Anne Page for her money, but soon discovers treasures of character in her which quite transform him.

Feramorz (*fĕr'ȧ-mŏrz*). **Lalla Rookh, Thomas Moore.** Feramorz in *Lalla Rookh* is the young Cashmerian poet, who relates poetical tales to Lalla Rookh, in her journey from Delhi to Lesser Bucharia. Lalla Rookh is going to be married to the young sultan, but falls in love with the poet. On the wedding morn she is led to her future husband, and finds that the poet is the sultan himself, who had gallantly taken this course to win the heart of his bride and beguile her journey.

Ferdinand. (1) A character in Shakspere's *Tempest.* He is a son of the king of Naples, and falls in love with Miranda, the daughter of Prospero, a banished duke of Milan. (2) King of Navarre, a character in *Love's Labor's Lost.*

Ferrars. Endymion, Benjamin Disraeli. The story tells of the progress of the colorless hero who, by the aid of his wife and sister, rises to the position of prime minister.

Ferrex and Porrex. Two sons of Gorboduc, a mythical British king. Porrex drove his brother from Britain, and when Ferrex returned with an army he was slain, but Porrex was shortly after put to death by his mother. The first tragedy in the English language was *Gorboduc*, or *Ferrex and Porrex*, by Thomas Norton and Thomas Sackville.

Fib. Nymphidia, Drayton. One of the fairy attendants of Queen Mab.

Fidele (*fĭ-dē'lē*). **Cymbeline, Shakspere.** (1) The name assumed by Imogen, when, attired in boy's clothes, she started for Milford Haven to meet her husband, Posthumus. (2) Subject of an elegy by Collins.

Fidelio (*fē-dā'lĭ-ō*). In Beethoven's opera of the name, the heroine Leonore, disguised as a man under the name of Fidelio, serves the jailor of the prison in which her lover, Florestan, is confined. She is thus enabled to save Florestan's life.

Fidessa. Faery Queen, Spenser. The companion of Sansfoy; but, when the Red Cross Knight slew that "faithless Saracen," Fidessa turned out to be Duessa, the daughter of Falsehood and Shame. See *Duessa.*

Fine-ear. Fairy Tales (Fortunio), Countess d'Aulnoy. One of the seven attendants of Fortunio. He could hear the growing of the grass and of the wool on a sheep's back. This is an old, old story. It is also found in Grimm's *Fairy Tales.* There the heroine is Fortunio. In the German tale *Fortunio*, the fairy gives her a horse named Comrade, not only of incredible swiftness, but all-knowing, and endowed with human speech; she also gives her an inexhaustible turkey-leather trunk, full of money, jewels, and fine clothes. By the advice of Comrade, she hires seven gifted servants, named Strongback, Lightfoot, Marksman, Fine-ear, Boisterer, Tippler, and Gormand. Fortunio goes forth disguised as a warrior, meets her king, and marries him.

Finetta, The Cinder Girl. A fairy tale by the Countess d'Aulnoy. This is merely the old tale of Cinderella slightly altered.

Fingal. A mythical hero, whose name occurs in Gaelic ballads and traditions, and in Macpherson's *Poems of Ossian.*

Fires of St. John. A representative play of the school to which Sudermann belongs. The whole group of plays of which *The Fires of St. John* is a type reflect a revolt against the conventionalities of life in Germany, as Ibsen's dramas express the revolt against the conventionalities of life in northern Europe.

Firmin, Philip. The hero of Thackeray's novel *The Adventures of Philip.*

Fleance. A son of Banquo, in Shakspere's tragedy *Macbeth.* The legend relates that after the assassination of his father he escaped to Wales, where he married the daughter of the reigning prince, and had a son named Walter. This Walter afterwards became lord high steward of Scotland, and called himself Walter the Steward. From him proceeded in a direct line the Stuarts of Scotland, a royal line which gave James VI of Scotland, James I of England. This is myth.

Fledgeby. Our Mutual Friend, Dickens. An overreaching, cowardly sneak who pretends to do a decent business under the trade name of Pubsey and Co.

Fleet Street. Formerly called Fleet Bridge street. A London street running from Ludgate Hill to the east end of the Strand. It is named from the Fleet river. In the early chronicles of London many allusions are made to the deeds of violence done in this street. By the time of Elizabeth the street had become a favorite spot for shows and processions of all descriptions. It was noted formerly for its taverns and coffeehouses, frequented by many persons of literary fame. Among these were Ben Jonson, later, Goldsmith, Doctor Samuel Johnson, and Charles Lamb. It is now the chief center of British journalism.

Flite, Miss. Bleak House, Dickens. The poor little old woman who haunts the Chancery Court in hope of a judgment in her favor, and becomes insane from long waiting.

Florentius (*flō-rĕn'shĭ-ŭs*). A knight whose story is related in the first book of Gower's *Confessio Amantis.* He bound himself to marry a deformed hag, provided she taught him the solution of a riddle on which his life depended.

Florian. The Foundling of the Forest, W. Dimond. Discovered in infancy by Count de Valmont, and adopted as his own son. Florian was light-hearted and volatile, but with deep affection, very brave, and the delight of all who knew him.

Florimel. A female character in Spenser's *Faery Queen*, of great beauty, but so timid that she feared the "smallest monstrous mouse that creeps on floor," and was abused by every one. She was noted for sweetness of temper amid great trials. The word Florimel signifies "honey flower."

Florizel. (1) A prince of Bohemia, in Shakspere's *Winter's Tale*, in love with Perdita. (2) Character in Stevenson's *New Arabian Nights.*

Fluellen. A Welsh captain, who is an amusing pedant, in Shakspere's *Henry V.*

Flying Dutchman. A spectral ship, seen in stormy weather off the Cape of Good Hope, and considered ominous of ill luck. Captain Marryat has taken this theme for his novel *The Phantom Ship.*

Folk, Good. Fairies, also called good people, neighbors, wights. The Germans have their *kleine volk*, "little folk," the Swiss their hill people and earth people. See *Fairies.*

Ford. Mr. and Mrs. Ford are characters in *The Merry Wives of Windsor.* Mrs. Ford pretends to accept Sir John Falstaff's protestations of love, in order to punish him by her devices.

Fortinbras (*fôr'tĭn-brăs*). Prince of Norway, in Shakspere's tragedy *Hamlet.*

Fortunatus. You have found Fortunatus' purse. You are in luck's way. The nursery tale of Fortunatus records that he had an inexhaustible purse. It is from the Italian fairy tales.

Fortunio's Horse. Comrade not only possessed incredible speed, but knew all things and was gifted with human speech. See *Fine-ear.*

Forty Thieves. In the tale of Ali Baba in *Arabian Nights' Entertainments.* Represented as inhabiting a secret cave in a forest, the door of which would open and shut only at the sound of the magic word "Sesame," the name of a kind of grain. One day, Ali Baba, a woodmonger, accidentally discovered the secret, and made himself rich by carrying off gold from the stolen hoards. The captain tried several schemes to discover the thief, but was always outwitted by Morgiana, the woodcutter's female slave.

Four Horsemen of the Apocalypse, The, Blasco Ibáñez. A story of the German invasion of France in 1914. In the panorama presented, a wealthy Argentinian settled in France, with a passion for "collecting," is the central figure. His family are connected with German families by marriage, and this circumstance complicates the story. The family represent the country of France under the scourge of the four horsemen, War, Famine, Pestilence, and Death.

Four Million, The. The title of a volume of short stories by O. Henry. The stories reflect the common life of the people in the great city of New York.

Foxley, Squire Matthew. Redgauntlet, Scott. A magistrate who examines Darsie Latimer (Sir Arthur Darsie Redgauntlet), after he had been attacked by the rioters.

Francesco. The "Iago" of Massinger's *Duke of Milan.*

Frankenstein. The hero in Mrs. Shelley's romance of the same name. As a young student of physiology he constructs a monster out of the horrid remnants of the churchyard and dissecting-room, and endues it, apparently through the agency of galvanism, with a sort of spectral and convulsive life. This existence, rendered insupportable to the monster by his vain craving after human sympathy, and by his consciousness of his own deformity, is employed in inflicting the most dreadful retribution upon the guilty philosopher. It is a parody on the creature man, powerful for evil, and the instrument of dreadful retribution on the student, who usurped the prerogative of the Creator.

Freeport, Sir Andrew. The name of one of the members of the imaginary club under whose direction the *Spectator* was professedly published. He is represented as a London merchant of great eminence and experience, industrious, sensible, and generous.

Friar Lawrence. The Franciscan monk who attempted to befriend the lovers in *Romeo and Juliet.*

Friar's Tale, The. Canterbury Tales, Chaucer. An archdeacon employed a summoner as his secret spy to find out offenders, with the view of exacting fines from them. In order to accomplish this more effectually, the summoner entered into a compact with the Devil, disguised as a yeoman. Those who imprecated the Devil were to be dealt with by the yeoman-devil, and those who imprecated God were to be the summoner's share.

Friar Tuck. Chaplain and steward of Robin Hood. Introduced by Scott in *Ivanhoe.* He is a self-indulgent, combative Falstaff, a jolly companion to the outlaws in Sherwood Forest. Also in *Sherwood*, by Alfred Noyes.

Friday. Robinson Crusoe's faithful man Friday pictured by De Foe.

Friendly, Dinah. The Bashful Man, Moncrieff. Daughter of Sir Thomas Friendly.

Frollo, Archdeacon Claude. A noted character in Victor Hugo's *Notre Dame de Paris*, absorbed in a bewildering search after the philosopher's stone.

Front de Bœuf (*frôɴ' dē bĕf'*). **Ivanhoe, Scott.** A follower of Prince John of Anjou, and one of the knight's challengers.

Froth, Master. A foolish gentleman in Shakspere's *Measure for Measure.* His name explains his character.

Fudge Family. A name under which the poet Moore satirized the absurdities of his traveling countrymen, who, having been long confined at home by the wars waged by Napoleon, flocked to the continent after his defeat at Waterloo. The family is composed of a hack writer and spy, his son, a young dandy of the first water, his daughter, a sentimental damsel, and Madame Le Roy, in love with a Parisian linen draper, whom she has mistaken for one of the Bourbons in disguise. The tutor, a "poor relation" of this egregious family, is an ardent Bonapartist and Irish patriot.

Fusbos. In "Bombastes Furioso," the minister of state to the king of Utopia. This was a burlesque opera by W. B. Rhodes.

Fuzzy-Wuzzy. The name applied by Kipling to the Sudanese native in a ballad of the same name. The "big, black, boundin' beggar" that "broke the British square."

Fyrapel, Sir. The leopard, the nearest kinsman of King Lion, in the beast epic of *Reynard the Fox.*

Gabriel. The name of an angel described in the Scriptures as charged with the ministration of comfort and sympathy to man. In the New Testament, he is the herald of good tidings, declaring the coming of the predicted Messiah and of his forerunner. In Jewish and Christian tradition he is one of the seven archangels. Gabriel has the reputation, among the rabbis, of being a distinguished linguist, having taught Joseph the 70 languages spoken at Babel. The Mohammedans hold him in even greater reverence than the Jews. He is called the spirit of truth, and is believed to have dictated the *Koran* to Mohammed. Milton posts him at "the eastern gate of paradise," as "chief of the angelic guards," keeping watch there. The *Talmud* describes him as the prince of fire, and as the spirit who presides over thunder.

Gadshill. A companion of Sir John Falstaff, in the First Part of Shakspere's *King Henry IV.*

Galahad, Sir. A celebrated knight of the Round Table who achieved the quest of the Holy Grail. Tennyson has made him the subject of one of his idylls. In Malory he is also represented as the perfect knight clad in wonderful armor. He was the only knight who could sit in the "siege perilous," a seat reserved for the "knight without a flaw."

Galapas. A giant of marvelous height in the army of Lucius, king of Rome. He was slain by King Arthur.

Galaphrone or **Galafron.** A king of Cathay and father of Angelica in Boiardo's *Orlando Innamorato* and Ariosto's *Orlando Furioso.*

Galatea, Galathea (*găl'ȧ-tē'ȧ*). The Greek legend is of an artist, Pygmalion, who carved a figure, Galatea, so beautiful that he fell overwhelmingly in love with his own creation; his own passion wakens the statue to life. The story has been frequently used in literature. Shaw's *Pygmalion* is a modern modification of the theme.

Gamp, Mrs. A nurse who is a prominent character in Dickens's novel *Martin Chuzzlewit.* She is celebrated for her constant reference to a certain Mrs. Harris, a purely imaginary person, for whose feigned opinions and utterances she professes the greatest respect, in order to give the more weight to her own.

Gandercleugh (*găn'dẽr-klŭk*), "Folly-cliff." That mysterious place where a person makes a goose of himself, in *Tales of My Landlord*, by Sir Walter Scott.

Ganelon, Gan, or **Gano.** A count of Mayence, and one of the paladins of Charlemagne, whom he betrayed at the battle of Roncesvalles; always represented as a traitor, engaged in intrigues for the destruction of Christianity. His character was marked by spite, dissimulation, and intrigue, but he was patient, obstinate, and enduring. He loved solitude, disbelieved in the existence of moral good, and has become a byword for a false and faithless friend. He figures in the romantic poems of Italy, and is placed by Dante in his "Inferno." He is introduced into Chaucer's "Nun's Priest's Tale."

Garcias, Pedro (*pā'drō gär-thē'äs*). A mythical personage, of whom mention is made in the preface to *Gil Blas*, in which it is related that two scholars of Salamanca discovered a tombstone with the inscription, "Here lies interred the soul of the Licentiate Pedro Garcia," and that, on digging beneath the stone, they found a leathern purse containing a hundred ducats.

Gareth (*gȧr'ĕth*). In Arthurian romance a knight of the Round Table, who was first a scullion in King Arthur's kitchen, but afterward became champion of Lady Linet, or Lynette, whose sister Lionês, or Lyonors, he delivered from Castle Perilous.

Gargamelle (*gär'gȧ'mĕl'*). The mother of Gargantua in Rabelais' celebrated romance, *Gargantua.*

Gargantua (*gär-găn'tŭ-ȧ*). The hero of Rabelais' celebrated romance of the same name, a gigantic personage, about whom many wonderful stories are related. He lived for several centuries, and at last begot a son, Pantagruel, as wonderful as himself. The *Pleasant Story of the Giant Gargantua and of his Son Pantagruel* so satirized the monastic orders of his time that it was denounced by the spiritual authorities. Francis I, however, protected the author, and allowed him to print the third part of it in 1545.

Gargery, Mrs. Joe. Great Expectations, Dickens. Pip's sister. A virago, who kept her husband and Pip in constant awe. Joe Gargery, a blacksmith, married to Pip's sister. A noble-hearted, simple-minded young man, who loved Pip sincerely. Joe Gargery was one of nature's gentlemen.

Gaspar or **Caspar.** The white one, one of the three Magi or kings of Cologne. His offering to the infant Jesus was frankincense, in token of divinity.

Gaunt, Griffith. Hero of a novel by Charles Reade, of the same title.

Gawain (*gô′wân*), **Sir.** A nephew of King Arthur, and one of the most celebrated knights of the Round Table; noted for his sagacity and wonderful strength. He was surnamed "the courteous." His brothers were Agravaine, Gaheris, and Gareth.

Gebir (*jē′bēr*). A legendary Eastern prince, said to have invaded Africa and to have given his name to Gibraltar. He is the subject of a poem of the same name by Walter Savage Landor.

Gellatley, Davie. The name of a poor fool in Sir Walter Scott's novel *Waverley.*

Genevieve. (1) The heroine of a ballad by Coleridge. (2) Under the form "Genoveva," the name occurs in a German myth as that of the wife of the Count Palatine Siegfried, in the time of Charles Martel. Upon false accusations her husband gave orders to put her to death, but the servant intrusted with the commission suffered her to escape into the forest of Ardennes, where she lay concealed, until by accident her husband discovered her retreat and recognized her innocence. This legend is often repeated in the folk tales of Germany. Tieck and Miller have given it in modern versions.

Genevra. A lady in Ariosto's *Orlando Furioso.* Her honor is impeached, and she is condemned to die unless a champion appears to do combat for her. Her lover, Ariodantes, answers the challenge, kills the false accuser, and weds the dame. Spenser has a similar story in the *Faery Queen,* and Shakspere availed himself of the main incident in his comedy *Much Ado about Nothing.* From Italian romances "Genevra" has been taken as subject of "The Mistletoe Bough," by T. Haynes Bayly, and as both title and subject of a metrical tale by Samuel Rogers, in which he tells of a young Italian, who, upon her wedding day, secreted herself, from motives of frolic, in a self-locking oaken chest, the lid of which shut down and held her captive. Many years afterward the chest was opened and the skeleton was revealed.

Genius (*jē′nĭ-ŭs*) pl. genii. Tutelary spirits believed by the Romans to attend each individual from the cradle to the grave, determining his character and governing his fortunes. They were two in number for each person, a "good genius" bringing good fortune and an "evil genius" being responsible for his ill luck. In some translations of *The Thousand and One Nights* the word genius is used for Jinn, a fallen angel under the dominion of Eblis, the Evil One.

Georgics (*jôr′jĭks*). Bucolic poetical compositions, treating of farm-husbandry and the tillage of the soil. The most famous examples of the kind are those by Virgil, 31 B. C., in four books.

Geraint (*gĕ-rānt′*), **Sir.** One of the knights of the Round Table. His story is told in Tennyson's *Idylls of the King* under "Geraint and Enid."

Geraldine. A name frequently found in romantic poetry. The name is said to have been adopted from the heroine, connected with Surrey, whose praises he celebrates in a famous sonnet, and who has been the occasion of much controversy among his biographers and critics. There is no doubt that the lady called Geraldine was an Irish lady named Elizabeth Fitzgerald, the daughter of Gerald Fitzgerald. This sonnet led to the adoption of the name into the class of romantic names. Used by Mrs. Browning in "Lady Geraldine's Courtship."

Gertrude of Wyoming. Heroine of a poem by Thomas Campbell, which tells the story of the Indian massacre of Americans in the Wyoming valley of Pennsylvania in 1778.

Gesta Romanorum (*jĕs′tȧ rō′mȧ-nō′rŭm*). A collection of old romances and tales, mostly from Roman sources, which has been the storehouse for our best story-writers. Shakspere, Spenser, Gower, and many later writers have gone to this source. Compiled probably about the close of the 13th century. Moralizing paragraphs and other religious and mystical tales are said to have been added by Pierre Bercaire, a Benedictine prior of Poitou.

Giaour (*jour*). Byron's tale called "The Giaour" is represented as told by a Turkish fisherman, who had committed a crime which haunted him all his life. *Giaour* means "unbeliever." See *Hassan.*

Gibbie, Goose. A half-witted boy in Scott's *Old Mortality.*

Gibbie, Sir. A simple-hearted, fine character in George Macdonald's novel of the same name.

Gifts of the Magi, O. Henry (W. S. Porter). The title of one of O. Henry's most successful and typical stories. A young husband and wife, living in a little New York flat, with little to spend, plan each to give the other a perfect Christmas gift. They have two most treasured possessions,—a watch, inherited from his grandfather, and her long, beautiful hair. The husband covets a fob, the wife a set of combs. Christmas Eve, pawning the watch to buy the combs, he comes home to find that she has cut off and sold her hair to buy him a fob.

Gil Blas (*zhēl bläs*). The title of a famous romance by Lesage, and the name of its hero. The tale is full of adventures, and Gil Blas is represented as squire to a lady and as brought up by his uncle, Canon Gil Peres Gil Blas went to Dr. Godinez's school of Oviedo and gained the name of being a great scholar. He had fair abilities, wit and humor, and good inclinations, but was easily led astray by his vanity and became lax in his morals. Duped at first, he afterwards played the same devices on others. As he grew in years, his conduct improved, and when his fortune was made he became an honest man.

Gilgamesh (*gĭl′gȧ-mĕsh*). The hero of an ancient Babylonian epic, who searches for the secret of immortality. He fails in his search, receiving, at the end, only some vague information about the abode of the shades.

Gilpin, John. A citizen of London, and "a trainband captain," whose adventures are related in Cowper's humorous poem, "John Gilpin's Ride." After being married twenty years his wife proposed a holiday. They agreed to make a family party and dine at the Bell, at Edmonton. Mrs. Gilpin, her sister, and four children went in the chaise, and Gilpin promised to follow on horseback. The horse, being fresh, began to trot, and then to gallop, and John, a bad rider, grasped the mane with both his hands. On went the horse, off flew John Gilpin's cloak, together with his hat and wig. He flew through Edmonton, and never stopped till he reached Ware, when his friend the calender furnished him with another hat and wig, and Gilpin galloped back again, till the horse stopped at his house in London.

Glastonbury (*glȧs′tŭn-bĕr-ĭ*). A town in Somerset, England, 21 miles south of Bristol. Its abbey, founded in Roman times, was refounded under Ine in the 8th century. Glastonbury is associated in legend with Joseph of Arimathea, who is said to have visited it, and, in sign of possession, to have planted his staff, which took root and became the famous Glastonbury thorn that is reputed to burst into leaf on Christmas Eve. The Isle of Avalon, to which King Arthur was taken, is supposed to have been here.

Gloriana (*glō′rĭ-ā′nȧ*). In Spenser's *Faery Queen,* the "greatest glorious queen of Faeryland."

Gloss. In biblical criticism, an explanation of purely verbal difficulties of the text, to the exclusion of those which arise from doctrinal, historical, ritual, or ceremonial sources. These explanations were frequently inserted between the lines of the text, or in the margins; and many modern critics of the Bible explain certain passages there as due to "glosses." From an early period, these verbal difficulties were the object of attention, and the writers who devoted themselves to the elucidation were called "glossatores," and their works "glossaria."

Glumdalca. Tom Thumb the Great, Fielding. Queen of the giants, captive in the court of King Arthur.

Glumms. Peter Wilkins, Robert Paltock. The male population of the imaginary country Nosmnbdsgrsutt, visited by Peter Wilkins. Both males and females had wings which served both for flying and for clothes.

Gnome (*nōm*). (1) A pithy and sententious saying commonly in verse, embodying some moral sentiment or precept. The gnome belongs to the same generic class with the proverb; but it differs from a proverb in wanting the common and popular acceptance. The use of gnomes prevailed among all the early nations, especially the Orientals, and the literatures of most countries abound with them. In the Bible, the book of Proverbs, part of Ecclesiastes, and still more the apocryphal book of Ecclesiasticus, present numberless illustrations of the highest form of this composition. (2) In ancient times the name gnome represented one of the classes of imaginary beings which are supposed to be the presiding spirits in the mysterious operations of nature in the mineral and vegetable world. They are introduced in Pope's "Rape of the Lock."

Gobbo, Launcelot. A clown in Shakspere's *Merchant of Venice*. He left the service of Shylock the Jew for that of Bassanio, a Christian. Launcelot Gobbo is one of the famous clowns of Shakspere.

Gobbo, Old. Father to Launcelot Gobbo in *Merchant of Venice*. He was stone-blind.

God Save the King. The national anthem of Great Britain, and formerly that of Prussia and the German states. Its words are apparently imitated from the *Domine Salvum* of the Catholic Church service.

Gold Bug, The. Found in Poe's most successful tale of the same name. Scene laid on Sullivan's island, near Charleston, S. C., and the cipher made to concern Captain Kidd's buried treasure.

Golden Ass. A celebrated romance by Apuleius, a Latin writer of the 2d century. Lucius, the hero, changed by enchantment into an ass, has many adventures and is finally restored to his human form by the priests of Isis. The story of Cupid and Psyche is found in this book. Many modern writers have borrowed from it.

Golden Legend, The. (1) The title of an ecclesiastical work in 177 sections, dating from the 13th century, written by Jacopo da Voragine, a Dominican monk, and descriptive of the various saints' days in the Roman calendar. It is deserving of study as a literary monument of the period, and as illustrating the religious habits and views of the Christians of that time. (2) A poem by Longfellow, second part of his *Christus*.

Gold of Nibelungen, The. Unlucky wealth. "To have the gold of Nibelungen" is to have a possession which seems to bring a curse with it. See *Nibelung, King*.

Goneril (*gŏn'ẽr-ĭl*). The oldest of the three daughters of King Lear, in Shakspere's tragedy. Having received her moiety of Lear's kingdom, the unnatural daughter first abridged the old man's retinue, then gave him to understand that his company was not wanted and sent him out, a despairing old man, to seek refuge where he could find it. Her name is proverbial for filial ingratitude.

Gonzalo (*gŏn-zä'lō*). An honest old counselor in Shakspere's *Tempest*, a true friend to Prospero.

Good-natured Man, The, Oliver Goldsmith. The hero of this comedy, Honeywood, tries to order his life on the principle of "universal benevolence," giving indiscriminately and disagreeing with no one. Because he believes his friend Jack Lofty to be in love with Miss Richland, he even abstains from telling her of his own love. His uncle, Sir William Honeywood, and Miss Richland finally cure the young man of his folly.

Goody Blake. A character in Wordsworth's poem entitled "Goody Blake and Harry Gill." A farmer forbids old Goody Blake to carry home a few sticks, which she had picked up from his land, and in revenge she invokes upon him the curse that he may "never more be warm"; and ever after "his teeth they chatter, chatter still."

Goody Two-shoes. The name of a well-known character in a nursery tale by Oliver Goldsmith. Goody Two-shoes was a very poor child, whose delight at having a pair of shoes was unbounded. She called constant attention to her "two shoes" which gave her the name.

Gordian Knot. A great difficulty. Gordius, a peasant, chosen king of Phrygia, dedicated his wagon to Jupiter, and fastened the yoke with a rope so ingeniously that no one could untie it. Alexander was told that "whoever undid the knot would become king," and he cut the knot with his sword.

Gotham (*gŏt'ăm*). At one time the term was applied to a parish of Nottingham, England. The people here were famed for their stupidity and simplicity, which obtained for them the satirical appellation of the "wise men of Gotham." Many nations have designated some particular locality as the paradise of fools; for example, Phrygia was the fools' home in Asia, Abdera of the Thracians, Bœotia of the Greeks, Swabia of the modern Germans, etc. To Americans it is chiefly significant as a colloquial term (pron. *gō'thăm*) for the city of New York. Thus applied, it first appeared in *Salmagundi*, by Washington Irving and James K. Paulding, and is supposed to hint sarcastically at the worldly wisdom of its inhabitants.

Graal, Grail, or **Greal** (a word derived probably from the old French, through the medieval Latin, *gradalis*, a cup or platter). In the legends and poetry of the middle ages, we find accounts of the Holy Graal—San Gréal—a miraculous chalice, made of a single precious stone, sometimes said to be an emerald, which possessed the power of preserving chastity, prolonging life, and other wonderful properties. It is fabled to have been the dish from which Christ ate at the Last Supper and in which Joseph of Arimathea received His blood at the Cross, later preserving it and carrying it to England. It remained there many years, an object of pilgrimage and devotion, but at length it disappeared, one of its keepers having violated the condition of strict virtue in thought, word, and deed, which was imposed upon those who had charge of it. The quest of this cup forms the most fertile source of adventures to the knights of the Round Table. The story of the Sangreal or Sangraal was first written in verse by Troyes in the 12th century. The legend of the graal was introduced into German poetry in the 13th century by Wolfram von Eschenbach, who filled his *Parzival* with deep allegorical meanings. Malory embodied the story in his *Morte D'Arthur*, and Tennyson told it in his *Idylls of the King*.

Graciosa (*grā'shĭ-ō'sȧ*). A princess in an old and popular fairy tale,—the object of the ill-will of a stepmother named Grognon, whose malicious designs are perpetually thwarted by Percinet, a fairy prince, who is in love with Graciosa.

Gradgrind. A hardware merchant in Dickens's *Hard Times*. He is a man of hard facts and cultivates the practical. His constant demand in conversation is for "facts." He allows nothing for the weakness of human nature, and deals with men and women as a mathematician with his figures.

Gradgrind, Mrs. Wife of Thomas Gradgrind. A little thin woman, always taking physic, without receiving from it any benefit.

Grandison, Sir Charles. The hero of Richardson's novel *The History of Sir Charles Grandison*. Designed to represent his ideal of a perfect hero,—a union of the good Christian and the perfect English gentleman.

Gratiano (*grā'shĭ-ä'nō*). A friend to Antonio and Bassanio in Shakspere's *Merchant of Venice*. He "talks an infinite deal of nothing, more than any man in Venice." (2) Brother to Brabantio, in Shakspere's tragedy *Othello*. (3) A character in the Italian popular theater called "Commedia del' Arte." He represents a Bolognese doctor, wearing a mask with black nose and forehead and red cheeks.

Gray, Auld Robin. The title of a popular Scotch ballad written by Lady Anne Lindsay, and name of its hero. Auld Robin Gray was a good old man married to a poor young girl whose lover was thought to have been lost at sea, but who returns to claim her hand a month after her marriage.

Great Divide, The, William Vaughn Moody. A three-act play. Ruth Jordan, alone on a ranch in Arizona, is menaced by three men who broke into the house. She promises one of them, Stephen Ghent, to marry him if he will save her from the others. This he does, buying off a Mexican with a chain of gold nuggets. Her New England conscience prevents her going through with the bargain, which she tries to buy her way out of by attempting to redeem the nuggets. She returns to her New England home, burdened with a sense of guilt. Stephen follows her and eventually leads her to see the folly of her inhibitions. She goes back West with him.

Great Galeoto (*gä-lā-ô'tō*), **The, José Echegaray.** The title of this tragedy is derived from the saying placed in the mouth of Francesca da Rimini in Dante's "Inferno," that Galeoto was the book that prompted her sin and Paolo's. Echegaray makes Galeoto a kind of personification of common gossip. Julian, at first, is deaf to gossip about his young wife, who is thrown daily with Ernest, his secretary and adopted son. He is fatally wounded in a duel over the matter and is borne to Ernest's chamber. Here he finds his wife and dies believing her guilty, although she is really innocent. In the end, Ernest kills the slayer of Julian, marries Julian's widow, and upbraids the world for its stupid, tragic chatter.

Greatheart, Mr. In Bunyan's *Pilgrim's Progress*, the guide of Christian's wife and children upon their journey to the Celestial City.

Greek Fire. An inflammable liquid first used by the Greeks in defense of Constantinople in 668 A. D. It is believed to have consisted of a mixture of sulphur, naphtha, and quicklime, the last ingredient developing sufficient heat when wet to ignite the other substances.

Gremio. In Shakspere's *Taming of the Shrew*, an old man who wishes to wed Bianca.

Grendel. Beowulf. The half brute, half man monster from which Beowulf delivered Hrothgar, king of Denmark. Night after night Grendel crept stealthily into the palace called Heorot, and slew sometimes as many as thirty of the inmates. At length Beowulf slew it in single combat.

Gretna Green Marriages. A term for runaway marriages. It alludes to marriages performed at Gretna Green, in Scotland, just across the border from England. Until the law was altered in 1856, the sole requirement for a valid marriage there was a mutual declaration before witnesses of willingness to marry.

Griffin-Feet. Fairy Tales, Countess d'Aulnoy. The mark by which the Desert Fairy was known in all her metamorphoses.

Grim, Giant. A giant, in *Pilgrim's Progress*, who seeks to stop the march of the pilgrims to the Celestial City, but is slain in a duel by Mr. Greatheart, their guide.

Grimalkin (*grĭ-măl'kĭn*). A cat, the spirit of a witch. Any witch was permitted to assume the body of a cat nine times.

Grimwig. Oliver Twist, Dickens. An irascible old gentleman, who hid a very kind heart under a rough exterior. He was always declaring himself ready to "eat his head" if he was mistaken on any point on which he passed an opinion.

Griselda (*grĭ-zĕl'dȧ*), **The Patient.** A lady in Chaucer's "Clerk of Oxenford's Tale," immortalized by her virtue and her patience. The model of womanly and wifely obedience, she comes victoriously out of cruel and repeated ordeals. The story of Griselda is first told in the *Decameron*. Boccaccio derived the incidents from Petrarch, who seems to have communicated them also to Chaucer, as the latter refers to Petrarch as his authority. The story has been told by many modern writers.

Grub Street. Thus described in Dr. Johnson's Dictionary: "Originally the name of a street near Moorfields, in London, much inhabited by writers of small histories, dictionaries, and temporary poems, whence any production is called Grub Street." The name in its appropriate sense was freely used by Pope, Swift, and others.

Grundy. "What will Mrs. Grundy say?" What will our rivals or neighbors say? The phrase is from Tom Morton's *Speed the Plough*, but "Mrs. Grundy" is not introduced into the comedy as one of the dramatis personæ. The solicitude of Dame Ashfield, in this play, as to "what will Mrs. Grundy say," has given the latter great celebrity, the interrogatory having acquired a proverbial currency.

Gudrun (*gŏŏd'rōōn*). (1) Norse Edda. A lady married to Sigurd by the magical arts of her mother; and, on the death of Sigurd, to Atli (Attila) whom she hated for his cruelty, and murdered. She then cast herself into the sea, and the waves bore her to the castle of King Jonakun, who became her third husband. (2) Low German Saga. A model of heroic fortitude and pious resignation. She was the daughter of King Hettel (Attila), and the betrothed of Herwig, king of Helgoland.

Guildenstern (*gĭl'dĕn-stĕrn*). The name of a courtier in Shakspere's tragedy *Hamlet*.

Gulliver, Lemuel. The imaginary hero of Swift's celebrated satirical romance known as *Gulliver's Travels*. He is represented as being first a surgeon in London, and then a captain of several ships. After having followed the sea for some years he makes in succession four extraordinary voyages.

Gunga Din. The hero of Rudyard Kipling's poem of this name. He is a water carrier for the regiment, a Hindu, who meets heroic death in devotion to his duty.

Guppy, Mr. Bleak House, Dickens. A weak, commonplace youth, who has the conceit to propose to Esther Summerson, the ward in Chancery.

Gurth. Ivanhoe, Sir Walter Scott. The swineherd of Rotherwood.

Gurton, Gammer. The heroine of an old English comedy *Gammer Gurton's Needle*, first acted at Christ's college, Cambridge, in 1566.

Guy, Sir, Earl of Warwick. The hero of a famous English legend, which celebrates the wonderful achievements by which he obtained the hand of his ladylove, the Fair Felice, as well as the adventures he subsequently met with in a pilgrimage to the Holy Land. He is reputed to have lived in the reign of the Saxon king, Athelstan. The romance of Sir Guy, mentioned by Chaucer in the *Canterbury Tales*, was written in French in the 12th century, in English in the 14th.

Guy Mannering. The second of Scott's historical novels. It contains the excellent characters, Dandie Dinmont, the shrewd and witty counselor Pleydell, and also the desperate, seabeaten villainy of Hatteraick, the uncouth devotion of that gentlest of all pedants, poor Dominie Sampson, and the savage, crazed superstition of the gypsy dweller in Derncleugh.

Guyon (*gī'ŏn*). The impersonation of Temperance or Self-government in Spenser's *Faery Queen*. He destroyed the witch Acrasia, and her bower, called the "Bower of Bliss." His companion was Prudence. "Sir Guyon represents the quality of Temperance in the largest sense: meaning the virtuous self-government which holds in check not only the inferior sensual appetites but also the impulses of passion and revenge."

Hagen (*hä'gĕn*). The murderer of Siegfried, in the German epic, the *Nibelungenlied*. He is a pale-faced dwarf, who knows everything and whose sole desire is mischief. After the death of Siegfried he seized the "Nibelung hoard" and buried it in the Rhine, intending to appropriate it. Kriemhild invited him to the court and had him slain.

Haidee (*hī-dē'*). A beautiful young Greek girl in Byron's poem, "Don Juan." She is called the "beauty of the Cyclades."

Hakim (*hä-kēm'*). **The Talisman, Scott.** Saladin, in the disguise of a physician, visited Richard Cœur de Lion in sickness, gave him a medicine in which the "talisman" had been dipped, and the sick king recovered.

Hamlet. In Shakspere's tragedy of the same name, son to the former, and nephew to the reigning king of Denmark. The ghost of his father appears to him, and urges him to avenge his murder upon his uncle. But the prince feigns madness, and puts off his revenge from day to day by "thinking too precisely on the event." Hamlet's mother had married Claudius, king of Denmark, after the death of her former husband. Claudius prepared poisoned wine, which he intended for Hamlet; but the queen, not knowing it was poisoned, drank it and died. Hamlet, seeing his mother fall dead, rushed on the king and killed him almost by accident, and is killed himself by a poisoned rapier in the hands of Laertes. See *Ophelia*.

Hamlin, Jack. The gentlemanly gambler in *Gabriel Conroy* and other tales by Bret Harte. The appearance of this character revolutionized the gambler of popular story and drama.

Hanswurst. A pantomimic character formerly introduced into German comedies. It corresponds to the Italian "Macaroni," the French "Jean Potage," and the English "Jack Pudding."

Hardcastle, Mr. A character in Goldsmith's comedy *She Stoops to Conquer*, represented as prosy and hospitable. Father of Kate, the pretty heroine.

Hardcastle, Mrs. A very "genteel" lady indeed. Tony Lumpkin is her son by a former husband.

Hard Times. A novel by Dickens, dramatized under the title of *Under the Earth* or *The Sons of Toil*. Bounderby, a street arab, raised himself to banker and cotton prince. When past fifty years of age, he married Louisa, daughter of Thomas Gradgrind. The bank was robbed, and Bounderby believed Stephen Blackpool to be the thief, because he had dismissed him from his employ. The culprit was Tom Gradgrind, the banker's brother-in-law, who escaped out of the country. In the dramatized version the bank was not robbed, but Tom removed the money to another drawer for safety.

Harlequin. The name of a well-known character in the popular extemporized Italian comedy.

Harlowe, Clarissa. The heroine of Richardson's novel entitled *The History of Clarissa Harlowe*. In order to avoid a marriage urged upon her by her parents, she casts herself on the protection of Lovelace, who grossly abuses the confidence thus reposed in him. He subsequently proposes to marry her, but Clarissa rejects the offer.

Harold, Childe. Childe Harold's Pilgrimage, Byron. A man of gentle birth and peerless intellect, who exhausted all the pleasures of youth and early manhood, and loathed his fellow-bacchanals and the "laughing dames in whom he did delight." To banish his disgust and melancholy, he determines to travel; but, though he traverses some of the fairest portions of the earth, the feelings of bitterness and desolation still prey upon him.

Haroun-al-Raschid (*hä-rōōn'äl-rä'shēd*). Caliph of the Abbasside race, contemporary with Charlemagne, and, like him, a patron of literature and the arts. Many of the tales in the *Arabian Nights* are placed in the caliphate of Haroun-al-Raschid.

Harpagon (*är'pȧ'gôɴ'*). The hero of Molière's comedy *L'Avare*, represented as a wretched miser.

Harpier or **Harper.** Some mysterious personage referred to by the witches in Shakspere's tragedy *Macbeth*.

Harum, David, Edward Noyes Westcott. A novel. David Harum is a shrewd country banker in a central New York town. The deeper springs of humor and goodness in his nature are revealed in the story, in contrast to his unprincipled trading. The love story of his clerk, a young city man, is woven into the narrative.

Hassan. The Giaour, Byron. Caliph of the Ottoman empire, noted for his hospitality and splendor. In his seraglio was a beautiful young slave named Leila, who loved a Christian called the Giaour. Leila is put to death by an emir, and Hassan is slain by the Giaour. Caliph Hassan has become the subject of popular romance.

Hassan, Al. The Arabian emir of Persia, father of Hinda, in Moore's *Fire-Worshippers.*

Hatto. In German legend, an archbishop of Mentz in the 10th century, who, for his hard-heartedness to the poor in time of famine, was eaten by mice in the "Mouse Tower" on an island in the Rhine near Bingen. Robert Southey has made this legend the subject of a poem.

Havelok (*hăv'lŏk*) **the Dane.** A fisherman, known as Grim, rescued an infant named Havelok, whom he adopted. This infant was the son of the king of Denmark, and, when the boy was restored to his royal sire, Grim was laden with gifts. He built the town which he called after his own name. This is the foundation of the medieval tales about "Havelok the Dane."

Hazard of New Fortunes, A, Howells. A story of New York City life, involving Mr. and Mrs. March, the principal figures in *Their Wedding Journey* and *Their Silver Wedding Journey.* In this story Mr. March has come to New York to conduct a magazine.

Hazlewood, Sir Robert. The old baronet of Hazlewood, in Scott's *Guy Mannering.* In the story, Charles, son of Sir Robert, is in love with Lucy Bertram, whom he marries.

Headstone, Bradley. Our Mutual Friend, Dickens. The schoolmaster, in love with Lizzie Hexam. He tries to murder Eugene Wrayburn, whom he throws into the river. Lizzie rescues Eugene and nurses him back to life. Headstone tries to throw suspicion of the crime on Roger Riderhood, but fails, and both are drowned when, during a fight, they fall into the river lock.

Heart of Midlothian, The. The tollbooth, or old jail of Edinburgh, which is the county town of the county of Midlothian. It is the title of one of Sir Walter Scott's novels.

Heep, Uriah. David Copperfield, Dickens. A detestable character who, under the garb of the most abject humility, conceals diabolic malignity. Mrs. Heep, Uriah's mother, was a character equally to be despised for her hypocritical assumption of humility.

Heinrich, Der Arme, Hartmann von Aue. A court epic written about 1200. Prince Henry, smitten with leprosy, takes refuge in the house of one of his tenants, whose twelve-year old daughter cared for him. One day she learned that her prince could be cured by the blood of an innocent maiden. She determined to make the sacrifice. But at Salerno, when she was about to submit to the operation, Prince Henry refused to accept her sacrifice. On the homeward journey he was healed, and he afterward made the girl his wife. Longfellow used the story in his "Golden Legend," and Gerhart Hauptmann has written a poetic drama about the subject.

Helena. (1) A lady in Shakspere's *Midsummer Night's Dream,* in love with Demetrius. (2) The heroine of Shakspere's *All's Well that Ends Well,* in love with Bertram, who marries her against his will and leaves her, but is finally won by the strength of her affection. (3) A character in an old popular tale, reproduced in Germany by Tieck. (4) A Greek tragedy by Euripides.

Helvetia (*hĕl-vē'shĭ-ȧ*). The old Latin name of Switzerland; often used as a poetical appellation in modern literature. The country is often mentioned as the "Helvetic Republic," which was formerly the official name.

Hermann and Dorothea. The hero and heroine of Goethe's poem of the same name.

Hermengild (*hĕr'mĕn-gĭld*). **Canterbury Tales, Chaucer.** The wife of the lord-constable of Northumberland. She was converted by Constance, but was murdered by a knight. Hermengild at the bidding of Constance restored sight to a blind Briton.

Hermia. A lady in Shakspere's *Midsummer Night's Dream,* in love with Lysander.

Hermione (*hĕr-mī'ō-nē*). The heroine of the first three acts of Shakspere's *Winter's Tale.*

Hernani (*ĕr-nä'nē*) or **Ernani.** The hero of Victor Hugo's tragedy of the same name, and of Verdi's opera, founded on the play. He was a Spanish noble in revolt against the emperor Charles V and killed himself from a high sense of honor.

Hero and Leander. See *Leander.*

Hexam, Lizzie. The heroine of Dickens's novel *Our Mutual Friend.*

Hiawatha (*hī'ȧ-wô'thȧ*). A mythical person believed by the North American Indians to have been sent among them to clear their rivers, forests, and fishing-grounds, and to teach them the arts of peace. When the white man came, then Hiawatha knew that the time of his departure was at hand, when he must go "to the kingdom of Ponemah, the land of the Hereafter." These legends of Hiawatha were used and given a literary form by the poet Longfellow in his "Hiawatha."

Hilda. A New England girl of the most sensitive delicacy and purity of mind, in Hawthorne's romance *The Marble Faun.* She is an artist, living in Rome, and perhaps typifies the conscience.

Hildebrand. (1) The Nestor of German romance, a magician and champion. (2) The famous pope, Gregory VII, whose stern dealings with Henry IV have given rise to the phrase "a regular Hildebrand."

Hildesheim (*hĭl'dĕs-hīm*). In an old German legend, the monk of Hildesheim, doubting how a thousand years with God could be "only one day," listened to the melody of a bird, as he supposed, for only three minutes, but found that in reality he had been listening to it for the space of a hundred years.

Hobbididance. The name of one of the fiends mentioned by Shakspere in *King Lear,* and taken from Harsnett's *Declaration of Egregious Popish Impostures* (1603).

Holofernes (*hŏl'ō-fĕr'nēz*). (1) The pedantic schoolmaster of Italian comedy. (2) A pedant living in Paris, under whose care Gargantua is placed for instruction. (3) A pedantic schoolmaster in Shakspere's *Love's Labor's Lost.* (4) The Assyrian general slain by Judith.

Holt, Felix. The hero of George Eliot's novel of the same name.

Holy Grail. See *Graal.*

Honeycomb, Will. One of the members of the imaginary club by whom the *Spectator* was professedly edited. He is distinguished for his graceful affectation, courtly pretension, and knowledge of the gay world.

Honeyman, Charles. A fashionable preacher in Thackeray's novel *The Newcomes.*

Hoosier Schoolmaster, The, Edward Eggleston. A realistic story of life in southern Indiana about the middle of the 19th century.

Hopeful. A pilgrim in Bunyan's *Pilgrim's Progress,* who accompanies Christian to the end of his journey.

Hop-o'-my-Thumb. A character in the tales of the nursery. Tom Thumb and Hop-o'-my-Thumb are not the same, although they are often confounded. Tom Thumb was the son of peasants, knighted by King Arthur, and was killed by a spider. Hop-o'-my-Thumb was a nix, the same as the German "daumling," the French "le petit pouce," and the Scotch "Tom-a-lin" or "Tamlane." He was not a human dwarf, but a fay.

Horatio (*hō-rā'shĭ-ō*). **Hamlet, Shakspere.** An intimate friend of Hamlet, a prince, a scholar, and a gentleman.

Horatius Cocles (*hō-rā'shĭ-ŭs kō'klēz*). Captain of the bridge-gate over the Tiber. He and two men to help him held the bridge against vast approaching armies. Subject and title of a poem by Lord Macaulay.

Hornbook. The primer or apparatus for learning the elements of reading, used in England before the days of printing, and common down to the time of George II. It consisted of a single leaf, containing on one side the alphabet, large and small, in black letter or in roman, with perhaps a small regiment of monosyllables. Then followed a form of exorcism and the Lord's Prayer, and, as a finale, the Roman numerals. The leaf was usually set in a frame of wood, with a slice of transparent horn in front,—hence the name of "hornbook." Copies of the hornbook are now exceedingly rare.

Horner, Jack. The name of a celebrated personage in the literature of the nursery. A Somersetshire tradition says that the plums which Jack Horner pulled out of the Christmas pie alluded to the title deeds of the abbey estates at Wells, which were sent to Henry VIII in a pasty, and abstracted on the way by the messenger, a certain Jack Horner.

Hortense. Bleak House, Dickens. The vindictive French maidservant of Lady Dedlock. In revenge for the partiality shown by Lady Dedlock to Rosa, Hortense murdered Mr. Tulkinghorn, and tried to throw the suspicion of the crime on Lady Dedlock.

Hourglass, A Morality, The, W. B. Yeats. The Wise Man has taught in his village that the visible world is all. Suddenly, an angel appears and tells the Wise Man that in an hour he must die, but that, if within that time he can find one person who believes in God and heaven, he shall enter paradise. In haste he sends out, but all his pupils and his children have lost all belief. At last comes Teigue the Fool, who has learned, not in the Wise Man's school, but on the hills. He believes, and in joy at finding the believing fool the Wise Man dies.

Houris (*hōō'rĭz*). In the fairy tales found in the *Koran*, these are the black-eyed daughters of paradise. They are created from musk and are free from all physical weakness and are always young. It is held out to every male believer that he will have 72 of these girls as his household companions in paradise. See Tom Moore's *Lalla Rookh*.

House of Fame. Of this poem it has been said that of itself it might have given fame to Chaucer. Under the form of a dream, it gives a picture of the "Temple of Glory," crowded with aspirants for immortal renown, and adorned with statues of great poets and historians.

Houssain (*hōō-sän'*). A prince in the *Arabian Night*, who had a flying carpet which would carry him whithersoever he wished.

Hubbard, Old Mother. A well-known nursery rime. "Mother Hubbard's Tale," by Edmund Spenser, is a satirical fable in the style of Chaucer.

Hubert de Burgh. Justice of England, created earl of Kent, introduced by Shakspere into *King John*. He is the one to whom the young prince addresses his piteous plea for life. The lad was found dead soon afterwards, either by accident or foul play.

Hubert, Saint. The legend of Saint Hubert makes him a patron saint of huntsmen.

Hudibras. The title and hero of a celebrated satirical poem by Samuel Butler. Hudibras is a Presbyterian justice of the time of the Commonwealth.

Hugh of Lincoln. A legendary personage who forms the subject of Chaucer's "Prioress's Tale," and also of an ancient English ballad. Wordsworth has given a modernized version of this tale.

Hugh Wynne. Hero of Dr. S. Weir Mitchell's novel of the American Revolution, *Hugh Wynne, Free Quaker*. Hugh, born of a French mother, defies his father's nonresistance principles, joins Washington's army, and gains rank on the general's staff. A love story of interesting complications runs through the book.

Hugo Hugonet. Castle Dangerous, Scott. Minstrel of the earl of Douglas.

Humphrey. The imaginary collector of the tales in *Master Humphrey's Clock*, by Charles Dickens.

Humpty Dumpty. The hero of a well-known nursery rime. The name signifies humped and dumpy, and is the riddle for an egg.

Huon of Bordeaux, Sir. A hero of one of the romances of chivalry bearing this name.

Hypatia (*hī-pā'shĭ-ȧ*). Of this romance its author, Charles Kingsley, said: "My idea in the romance is to set forth Christianity as the only really democratic creed and philosophy; above all, spiritualism as the most exclusively aristocratic creed." Hypatia was a beautiful and learned woman of Alexandria, who was murdered by jealous, fanatical monks.

Hyperion. Keats's incomplete *Hyperion*, in magnificent verse, deals with plans of the fallen gods to revolt against Jupiter. Hyperion is the sun god, identified with Apollo.

Hypocrites' Isle. An island described by Rabelais in one of his satires. He pictures this island of "Hypocrites" as wholly inhabited by people of low and defiled natures, by sham saints, spiritual comedians, seducers, and "suchlike sorry rogues who live on the alms of passengers like the hermit of Lamont."

Iago (*ē-ä'gō*). **Othello, Shakspere.** Othello's ensign and the villain of the play. Iago is said to be a character next to a devil, yet not quite a devil, such as Shakspere alone could delineate with skill.

Idleness, The Lake of. Faery Queen, Spenser. Who ever drank thereof grew instantly "faint and weary." The Red Cross Knight drank of it and was readily made captive by Orgoglio.

Idylls of the King. Tennyson has told the purpose and the meaning of these idylls. Taken together they form a parable of the life of man. Each idyll taken as a separate picture represents the war between sense and soul. In Lancelot and Guinevere the lower nature leads them astray, and there is intense struggle before the higher nature prevails. In Vivien, Ettarre, Tristam, and Modred, the base and sensual triumph. In Arthur, Sir Galahad, and Percival, it is the victory of the spiritual.

Ignaro (*ĭg-nä'rō*). **Faery Queen, Spenser.** Foster father of Orgoglio. Spenser says this old man walks one way and looks another, because ignorance is always "wrong-headed."

Iliad. The tale of the siege of Troy, an epic poem in 24 books. It is written in Greek hexameters, and commemorates the deeds of Achilles and other Greek heroes at the siege of Troy. The date of its composition may, with much probability, be assigned to the 9th century B. C., and the poem is so deficient in continuity, and contains so much that is inconsistent and irrelevant with the main topic, that it has been thought by many critics to have been the performance of several persons, although its authorship is still nominally accredited to Homer. Books one, two, and three are introductory to the war. Paris proposes to decide the contest by single combat, and Menelaus accepts the challenge. Paris, being overthrown, is carried off by Venus, and Agamemnon demands that the Trojans shall give up Troy in fulfillment of the compact, and the siege follows. The gods take part and frightful slaughter ensues. At length Achilles slays Hector and the battle is at an end. Old Priam, going to the tent of Achilles, craves the body of his son Hector; Achilles gives it up, and the poem concludes with the funeral rites of the Trojan hero. Virgil continues the tale from this point, shows how the city was taken and burned, and then continues with the adventures of Æneas, who escapes from the burning city, and makes his way to Italy. See *Æneid*.

Illuminating. The art of adorning manuscripts and books with ornamented letters and paintings, which was practiced by artists, generally monks, called "illuminators," in the middle ages, prior to the introduction of printing. Manuscripts, containing portraits, pictures, and emblematic figures, form a valuable part of the riches preserved in the principal libraries in Europe and America.

Il Penseroso, Milton. Title of one of two companion poems. The name is shortened from Italian *Il Pensieroso*, meaning "The Thoughtful Man." The poem pictures a day in the life of such a person.

Imogen (*ĭm'ō-jĕn*). The wife of Posthumus, and the daughter of Cymbeline in the play *Cymbeline*. "Of all Shakspere's women," says Hazlitt, "she is, perhaps, the most tender and the most artless."

Improvvisatori (*ēm'prôv-vē'zä-tō'rē*). Poets who utter verses without previous preparation on a given theme. Among the ancients, Greece was the land of improvisation. In modern times, it has been almost entirely confined to Italy, where Petrarch introduced the practice of singing improvised verses to the lute.

Incantation. Derived from a Latin root meaning simply "to sing." It is the term in use to denote one of the most powerful and awe-inspiring modes of magic, resting on a belief in the mysterious power of words solemnly conceived and passionately uttered.

Inchcape Rock. A rock in the North Sea, off the Firth of Tay. It is dangerous for navigators, and therefore the abbot of Aberbrothock fixed a bell on a float, which gave notice to sailors. Southey says that Ralph the Rover, in a mischievous joke, cut the bell from the buoy, and it fell into the sea, but on his return voyage his boat ran on the rock, and Ralph was drowned. Precisely the same tale is told of St. Goven's bell.

Inferno, The. Divine Comedy, Dante. Epic poem in 34 cantos. Inferno is the place of the souls who in life were wholly given up to sin. The ascent is through Purgatorio to Paradiso.

Ingoldsby Legends, The, Rev. R. H. Barham, "Thomas Ingoldsby." A collection of laughable tales in prose and verse first printed in magazines and published later in a volume in 1840. A second and a third series appeared in 1847. They treat all sorts of ancient, medieval, and modern matters of society and superstition in a burlesque fashion that has made them famous.

In Memoriam, Tennyson. An elegy, or philosophical poem, in memory of the poet's friend, Arthur Hallam, who died at the beginning of a seemingly brilliant career. It is reckoned as one of the great literary expressions of faith.

Innocents Abroad, Mark Twain. Travelers seeing Europe without any illusions. The fun consists in an irreverent application of modern common sense to historic associations, and in ridiculing sentimental humbug. An air of innocence and surprise adds to the drolleries of their adventures.

Interludes, The. Springing from the moralities and bearing some resemblance to them, though nearer the regular drama, are the interludes, a class of compositions in dialogue, much shorter and more merry and farcical. They were generally played in the intervals of a festival.

Iphigenia (*ĭf'ĭ-jē-nī'ȧ*). The heroine of Euripides' tragedy *Iphigenia in Aulis*, and of Goethe's tragedy *Iphigenie auf Tauris*. She was placed on the altar because of her father's rash vow. Artemis at the last moment snatched her from the altar and carried her to heaven, substituting a hind in her place. The similarity of this legend to the Scripture stories of Jephthah's vow and of Abraham's offering of his son Isaac is noticeable.

Iras. (1) A strongly delineated character in *Ben Hur, a Tale of The Christ,* by Lew Wallace. (2) A female attendant in Shakspere's play *Antony and Cleopatra.*

Iron Mask, The Man with the. Alexander Dumas wrote his *Viscomte de Bragelonne* around this personage. The real person was a mysterious prisoner of the time of Louis XIV. He wore at all times a mask of iron. His identity has remained a profound secret.

Iron Woman, The, Margaretta Deland. A novel describing Sarah Maitland, who, on her husband's death, managed his iron factory. The title characterizes her attitude also toward her son, whom she disinherited because of an ill-considered marriage.

Isaac of York. A wealthy Jew, the father of Rebecca, in Sir Walter Scott's novel *Ivanhoe.*

Isabella. (1) The heroine in Shakspere's comedy *Measure for Measure.* (2) A character of absorbing grief in Keats's *Isabella.*

Iseult (*ĭ-sōōlt'*) or **Isolt.** Iseult of the White Hands (Iseult of Brittany) was the unloved wife of Sir Tristram in the Arthurian romances. Iseult the Fair, whom Tristram loved, was the bride of his uncle, Sir Mark.

Island of Lanterns. In the celebrated satire of Rabelais, an imaginary country inhabited by false pretenders to knowledge. The name was probably suggested by the "City of Lanterns," in the Greek romance of Lucian.

Island of St. Brandan. A flying island, the subject of a widely-spread legend of the middle ages. Though the Island of St. Brandan has been a disappointment to voyagers, it has been a favorite theme with poets.

Israfel. In the *Koran* the archangel commissioned to blow the trumpet of the resurrection. Poe, in his poem "Israfel," uses the Mohammedan legend of the sweet-voiced Israfel.

Italics. The name applied to printed type sloping from left to right, as exemplified *thus.* Ordinary vertical type is called roman. Italics were first used by Aldus Minutius in printing an edition of Virgil in 1501. They are now used principally for emphasis, although in the ordinary versions of the Bible they indicate words supplied by the translators, corresponding words not being present in the original.

Ithuriel (*ĭ-thū'rĭ-ĕl*). In Milton's *Paradise Lost,* an angel commissioned by Gabriel to search through paradise, in company with Zephon, to find Satan, who had eluded the vigilance of the angelic guard, and effected an entrance into the garden. It is related that Ithuriel found Satan "squat like a toad, close at the ear of Eve," and transformed him by a touch of his spear to his proper shape.

Ivanhoe. The hero of Sir Walter Scott's novel of the same name. He figures as Cedric of Rotherwood's disinherited son, the favorite of King Richard I, and the lover of the Lady Rowena, whom, in the end, he marries. The scene is laid in England in the reign of Richard I, and we are introduced to Robin Hood in Sherwood Forest, banquets in Saxon halls, tournaments, and all the pomp of ancient chivalry. Rowena, the heroine, is quite overshadowed by the gentle, meek, yet high-souled Rebecca.

Ivanovitch, Ivan (*ē-vän' ē-vän'ō-vĭch*). An imaginary personage, who is the embodiment of the peculiarities of the Russian people, in the same way as John Bull represents the English, Jean Crapaud the French, and Brother Jonathan the American character.

Ivory Gate of Dreams. A passage in Virgil's *Æneid* tells of twin gates of sleep, one of horn, the other of ivory. Dreams which delude are said to pass through the ivory gate, but those which come true, through the horn gate. The fancy is introduced at the beginning of Sir William Watson's poem "The Dream of Man." The fancy depends upon two Greek puns: ivory in Greek is *elephas,* and the verb *elephairo* means "to cheat with empty hopes"; the Greek for horn is *keras,* and the verb *karanoö* means "to accomplish."

Ivy Green, The. Dickens published this song in *Pickwick Papers.* The theme is the creeping of the ivy over old buildings and ruins.

Jack and the Beanstalk. A nursery legend said to be an allegory of the Teutonic Alfadur; the "red hen" representing the all-producing sun, the "moneybags" the fertilizing rain, and the "harp" the winds.

Jack-in-the-Green. A prominent character in Maypole dances.

Jack Robinson. A famous comic song by Hudson.

Jack Sprat. The hero of a nursery rime. Jack and his wife form a fine combination in domestic economy.

Jack the Giant Killer. The name of a famous hero in the literature of the nursery, the subject of one of the many Indo-European legends which celebrate the triumph of skill over brute force.

Janice Meredith, Paul L. Ford. A historical novel of the American Revolution. Janice, daughter of a New Jersey Tory, falls in love with a young Englishman indentured to her father. She persists in her attachment and gets into many adventures. Finally, when her lover, whose real name is Brereton, has risen to the rank of general in Washington's army, they are betrothed.

Jaquenetta (*jăk-ĕ-nĕt'ȧ*). **Love's Labor's Lost, Shakspere.** A country wench courted by Don Adriano de Armado.

Jaques (*jā'kwēz*). A lord attending upon the exiled duke, in Shakspere's *As You Like It.* A contemplative character who thinks and does—nothing. He is called the "melancholy Jaques," and affects a cynical philosophy. He could "suck melancholy out of a song, as a weasel sucks eggs."

Jarley, Mrs. The proprietor of a waxworks' show in Dickens's *Old Curiosity Shop.* She has lent her name to a popular game of parlor tableaux.

Jarndyce. A prominent figure in Dickens's *Bleak House,* distinguished for his philanthropy, easy good nature and good sense, and for always saying, "The wind is in the east," when anything went wrong with him. The famous suit of "Jarndyce *v.* Jarndyce," in this novel, is a satire upon the court of Chancery.

Jarvie, Baillie Nicol. A prominent character in Sir Walter Scott's novel *Rob Roy.* He is a magistrate of Glasgow.

Jekyll (*jē'kĭl*), **Doctor, and Mr. Hyde.** The duplex hero of Robert Louis Stevenson's singular romance of the same name. Doctor Jekyll is a benevolent and upright physician, who by means of a potion is able to transform himself for a time into a second personality, Mr. Hyde, of a brutal and animal nature.

Jellyby, Mrs. A character in Dickens's novel *Bleak House,* a type of sham philanthropy. She spends her time and energy on foreign missions, to the neglect of her family. Mrs. Jellyby is quite overwhelmed with business correspondence relative to the affairs of Borrioboola Gha.

Jenkins, Winifred. The name of Miss Tabitha Bramble's maid in Smollett's *Expedition of Humphrey Clinker.* She makes ridiculous blunders in speaking and writing.

Jenkinson, Ephraim. A green old swindler, whom Dr. Primrose met in a public tavern. Dr. Primrose sold the swindler his horse, Old Blackberry, for a draft upon Farmer Flamborough.

Jeroboam Sermon. One of Dr. Emmons's sermons which made a great noise at the time. It was known as his Jeroboam Sermon. It was written on the occasion of Jefferson's inauguration as president, and, although Jefferson is not named, the delineation of the character of Jeroboam is such that no one can doubt Emmons's intention.

Jerusalem Delivered. An epic in twenty books, by Torquato Tasso (1544–1595). The crusaders, encamped on the plains of Tortosa, chose Godfrey for their chief, and Alandine, king of Jerusalem, made preparations of defense. The Christian army having reached Jerusalem, the king of Damascus sent Armida to beguile the Christians. It was found that Jerusalem could never be taken without the aid of Rinaldo. Godfrey, being informed that the hero was dallying with Armida in the enchanted island, sent to invite him back to the army; he returned, and Jerusalem fell. Armida fled into Egypt, and offered to marry any knight who slew Rinaldo. The love of Rinaldo returned; he pursued her and she relented. The poem concludes with the triumphant entry of the Christian army into the Holy City, and their devotions at the tomb of the Redeemer. The two chief episodes are the loves of Olindo and Sophronia, and of Tancred and Clorinda.

Jessamy Bride. A by-name given to Miss Mary Horneck, afterward Mrs. Gwyn. She was a contemporary and friend of Goldsmith. Also title of a novel by F. F. Moore. Jessamy means "Jasmine."

Jessica. The beautiful daughter of Shylock, in Shakspere's *Merchant of Venice.*

Jew, The Wandering. An imaginary person in a legend connected with the history of Christ's Passion. As the Savior was on the way to the place of execution, overcome with the weight of the cross, he wished to rest on a stone before the house of a Jew, who drove him away with curses. Driven by fear and remorse, he has since wandered, according to the command of the Lord, from place to place, and has never yet been able to find a grave. Romances, ranking among the best in literature, have been founded on this character. The best-known is the story by Eugène Sue *Le Juif Errant.*

Job. The central figure in the dramatic poem which forms the biblical book of the same name. The theme of the book is the question of why trouble comes to men. Because of his endurance of great woes, Job has become a synonym for patience.

Jones, Tom. The hero of *The History of Tom Jones, a Foundling*, by Henry Fielding. One of the first English novels. The hero is represented as a model of generosity, openness, and manly spirit, though thoughtless and dissipated.

Joseph Vance, William De Morgan. The novel is named for the hero. His life in London streets and his rise in his career form the central theme of the story, which involves a varied crowd of characters.

Joyeuse (*zhwȧ'yēz'*), **La.** The sword of Charlemagne as mentioned in romances of chivalry.

Joyeuse Garde, La. The residence of the famous Lancelot du Lac.

Judith. The heroine in the book of the same name in the Apocrypha. She was a beautiful Jewess of Bethulia, who, when her town was besieged by Holofernes, the general of Nebuchadnezzar, attended him in his tent, and, when he was drunk, killed him, whereupon her townsmen fell upon the Assyrians and defeated them with great slaughter. The tale is not mentioned by Josephus, and has, from an early period, been held to be an allegory. It has frequently furnished poets and painters with subjects.

Jungle Books, Kipling. The title of two series of tales of animal life in the Indian jungles. The animals use the language of men, yet they always are animals, never personified. See *Mowgli.*

Justice, Galsworthy. A play in which the author attacks certain abuses in the administration of justice. The drama involves a terrible portrayal of the effect of solitary confinement upon a prisoner.

Just So Stories, Kipling. A series of animal stories for children, *How the Leopard Got His Spots, How the Elephant Got His Trunk*, etc.

Kadr, Al. The night on which the *Koran* was sent down to Mohammed. Al Kadr is supposed to be the seventh of the last ten nights of Ramadan, or the night between the 23d and 24th days of the month.

Kalevala (*kä'lä-vä'lä*). One of the so-called "artificial epics," or modern poems made up of more or less ancient popular song and story. It belongs to Finland, the name meaning "the country of Kaleva," who is one of the heroes. The work, consisting of 22,800 verses, was put together first in 1835 and revised in 1849 by Dr. A. Lönnrot. It contains a vast treasure of Finnish popular songs, magic and mythical lore, and heroic tales.

Karma. A Sanskrit word, meaning "action" or "sequence." The Buddhist uses the word to mean a judgment on actions. The Theosophist uses it to mean the connected sequence of things as causes and effects.

Kay. A foster brother of King Arthur, and a rude and boastful knight of the Round Table. He was the butt of King Arthur's court. Called also "Sir Queux." He appears in the "Boy and the Mantle," in Percy's *Reliques*. Sir Kay is represented as the type of rude boastfulness, Sir Gawain of courtesy, Sir Lancelot of chivalry, Sir Modred of treachery, Sir Galahad of chastity, Sir Mark of cowardice.

Kehama (*kē-hä'mȧ*). A Hindu rajah, who obtains and sports with supernatural power. His adventures are related in Southey's poem entitled "The Curse of Kehama."

Kenilworth (*kĕn'ĭl-wẽrth*). A town in Warwickshire, England, five miles north of Warwick. The castle is one of the most admired of English feudal monuments, and was long of note as a royal residence. The chief scene of Sir Walter Scott's novel *Kenilworth*. The story is based on a ballad called "Cumnor Hall." The earl of Leicester, favorite of Queen Elizabeth, had secretly married Amy Robsart. For fear of Elizabeth's displeasure, he conceals her in Cumnor Hall. During a visit to Leicester's Castle of Kenilworth, the queen encourages Leicester to believe that she might marry him. Persuaded that Amy has been unfaithful, he commands her death. Later, finding that he has been deceived, Leicester confesses the truth, but messengers reach Cumnor Hall after Amy has been killed by falling through a trapdoor arranged by Varney, Leicester's retainer.

Kent, Earl of. A rough, plain-spoken, but faithful nobleman in Shakspere's *King Lear*, who, disguised as a servant and under the assumed name of Caius, follows the fallen fortunes of the king.

Kentucky Cardinal, A, James Lane Allen. A delicate story of Kentucky. A misunderstanding creeps into the romance of two young people through an unkind act toward a cardinal bird. The sequel is *Aftermath.*

Kenwigs. A family in Dickens's novel *Nicholas Nickleby*, which includes a number of little girls who differed from one another only in the length of their frilled pantalettes and of their flaxen pigtails tied with bows of blue ribbon.

Kilkenny Cats. Two cats, in an Irish story, which fought till nothing was left but their tails. It is probably a parable of a local contest between Kilkenny and Irishtown, which impoverished both boroughs.

Kim, Kipling. A story of India. The hero, Kimball O'Hara, nicknamed "Kim," orphaned while a baby, "grows up" to the precocious "age of indiscretion" in the native quarter of Lahore. He attaches himself to a Tibetan pilgrim, with whom he wanders over India, learning much of native ways. Eventually, the Irish regiment to which his father had belonged find and adopt Kim. He is sent to school and inducted into the Indian Secret Service.

King Cambyses (*kăm-bī'sēz*). The hero of "A Lamentable Tragedy" of the same name, by Thomas Preston, contemporary of Shakspere. A ranting character known to modern readers by Falstaff's allusion to him in Shakspere's *Henry IV.*

King Estmere. The hero of an ancient and beautiful legend, which, according to Bishop Percy, seems to have been written while a great part of Spain was in the hands of the Saracens, or Moors, whose empire was not fully extinguished before the year 1491.

King Horn. A metrical romance which was very popular in the 13th century. King Horn is a beautiful young prince who is carried away by pirates; but his life is spared, and after many wonderful adventures he weds a princess, and regains his father's kingdom.

King Log and King Stork. Characters in a celebrated fable of Æsop, which relates that the frogs, grown weary of living without government, petitioned Jupiter for a king. Jupiter accordingly threw down a log among them, which made a satisfactory ruler till the frogs recovered from their fright and discovered his real nature. They, therefore, entreated Jupiter for another king, whereupon he sent them a stork, who immediately began to devour them.

Klaus, Peter. The hero of an old popular tradition of Germany—the prototype of Rip Van Winkle. He is represented as a goatherd.

Knickerbocker, Diedrich. The imaginary author of a humorous fictitious *History of New York*, written by Washington Irving.

Knights of the Round Table. A name given to King Arthur's knights. They were so called because they sat with him at a round table made by Merlin for King Leodegraunce. This king gave it to Arthur on his marriage with Guinevere, his daughter.

Knight's Tale, The. Canterbury Tales, Chaucer. Two Theban knights, Palamon and Arcite, captives of Duke Theseus, were accustomed to see from their dungeon window the duke's sister-in-law, Emily, and fell in love with her. Both captives having gained their liberty contended for the lady by single combat. Arcite was victor, but being thrown from his horse was killed, and Emily became the bride of Palamon.

Koppenberg. The mountain of Westphalia to which the pied piper (Bunting) led the children when the people of Hamelin refused to pay him for killing their rats. Browning's poem, "The Pied Piper," tells the tale. Josephine Preston Peabody has dramatized it in her poetic play *The Piper.*

Kriemhild or **Chriemhild.** A beautiful Burgundian lady, daughter of Dancrat and sister of Gunther. She first marries Siegfried, king of the Netherlands, and next Etzel, king of the Huns. In the first part of the *Nibelungenlied*, Kriemhild brings ruin on herself by a tattling tongue. In the second part of the great epic she is represented as bent on vengeance, and, after a most terrible slaughter of both friends and foes, she is killed by Hildebrand.

Kubla Khan (*kōōb'lȧ kän*). A poem by Coleridge. Coleridge says that he composed the poem in a dream immediately after reading a description of "Cublai Can's" palace in Purchas's *Pilgrimage* and that he wrote it down upon waking.

Laconic. Very concise and pithy. The name came from the Spartan manner of curt speech. A Spartan was called a Lacon from the name of his country, Laconia.

La Débâcle (*lȧ dā'bäk'l'*), **Zola.** A realistic novel portraying the horrors of the breakdown of France before the German invasion in the Franco-Prussian War. One of the most powerful novels ever written.

Lady Day. The 25th day of March, anniversary of the Annunciation.

Lady of Lyons, The, Bulwer-Lytton. Pauline Deschappelles, daughter of a Lyonese merchant, rejected the suits of Beauseant, Glavis, and Claude Melnotte, who therefore combined on vengeance. Claude, who was a gardener's son, aided by the other two, passed himself off as Prince Como, married Pauline, and brought her home to his mother's cottage. The proud beauty was very indignant, and Claude left her to join the French army. He became a colonel, and returned to Lyons. His father-in-law was on the eve of bankruptcy, and Beauseant had promised to satisfy the creditors if Pauline would consent to marry him. Pauline was heartbroken; Claude revealed himself, paid the money required, and carried home the bride.

Lady of the Lake, The. The heroine in the poem by Sir Walter Scott. She was Ellen Douglas, once a favorite of King James; when her father fell into disgrace, she retired with him to the vicinity of Loch Katrine.

Lady of the Lake and Arthur's Sword. The heroine who gave to King Arthur the sword "Excalibur." She ordered King Arthur to sail out into the lake and take the sword as it was seen rising from the water. He sailed out with a knight and Merlin, came to the sword that a hand held up, and took it by the handles. The arm and hand went under the lake again. This Lady of the Lake asked in recompense the head of Sir Balin, because he had slain her brother; but the king refused the request. Balin, who was present, exclaimed: "Evil be ye found! Ye would have my head; therefore ye shall lose thine own." With his sword he smote off her head in the presence of King Arthur.

Lady or the Tiger, The, Stockton. A famous short story, the conclusion of which is left to the reader. The hero, in the arena, stands before two doors. Behind one stands the lady he loves, behind the other a tiger. The princess, who loves him but cannot wed him, is to give him a sign indicating which door he shall open.

Laertes (*lâ-ûr'tēz*). The son of Polonius, lord chamberlain of Denmark, and brother of Hamlet's beloved Ophelia. The king persuades him to challenge Hamlet, after Ophelia wanders in mind, and he calls him out in "friendly" duel, but poisons his own rapier. He wounds Hamlet, and, in the scuffle which ensues, the combatants change swords, and Hamlet wounds Laertes, so that both die.

Lagado (*lȧ-gä'dō*). **Gulliver's Travels, Swift.** The name of a city belonging to the king of Laputa. Lagado is celebrated for its grand academy of projectors, who try to extract sunbeams from cucumbers, and to convert ice into gunpowder. In the description of this fancied academy, Swift ridicules the pretenders in philosophy and science.

Lake District, English. A region in Westmoreland and Cumberland, England, which abounds in lakes enclosed by mountains. The district is a celebrated tourist center, and is associated with the poetry of Wordsworth. The lakes include Windermere, Ullswater, Derwentwater, and Bassenthwaite Water; and Skiddaw, Helvellyn, and Scafell Pike are the principal mountains. See *The Lake Poets*.

Lake Poets, The. Wordsworth, Southey, and Coleridge, who lived about the lakes of Cumberland. The name was applied also to other contemporary poets, who took subjects and inspiration from nature.

Lalla Rookh (*lă'lȧ rōōk'*). Poem by Thomas Moore. The name of the heroine, daughter of the emperor Aurungzebe, gives the title. On the journey to meet Aliris, her betrothed, in the Vale of Cashmere, she is entertained by a young Persian poet, Feramorz. She falls in love with him, and her delight is unbounded to find at the end of the journey that the poet is Prince Aliris.

L'Allegro, Milton. Title of a poem in which is sketched the life of a contented, happy man through one day. A companion poem to *Il Penseroso*. *L'Allegro* means "The Happy Man."

Lame Dog's Diary. A clever diary in which the provincial life of a little English village is reflected. It is supposed to be kept by an invalid officer who returned crippled from the Boer war. The suggestion of the diary came from a winning, tantalizing young widow, who cheered the invalid by her amusing, paradoxical talk. The diarist and his sister Palestrina are true English types—quiet gentlefolk.

L'Ami Fritz (*lȧ'mē' frĭts*), **Erckmann-Chatrian.** A quiet tale of Bavaria, which carries a lesson of peace and tolerance. Fritz Kobus, a bachelor of 36, proud of his escape from matrimony, gradually falls victim to the housewifely charms of Suzel, daughter of one of the tenants. The story was dramatized and translated as "Friend Fritz."

Lampoon. A personal satire, often bitter and malignant. These libels, carried to excess in the reign of Charles II, acquired the name of lampoons from the burden sung to them: "Lampons, lampons, camerades lampons." From a French slang verb, meaning "to drink, booze."

Lamps of Sleep. Magic lamps. A wonderful knight of a mythical land had an equally wonderful black castle. In the mansion of the knight of the black castle were seven lamps, which could be quenched only with water from an enchanted fountain. So long as these lamps kept burning, all within the room fell into a deep sleep, from which nothing could rouse them.

Landlady's Daughter. Longfellow's Hyperion. She rowed Fleming "over the Rhine-stream, rapid and roaring wide," and told to him the story of the Liebenstein.

Land of Beulah. The paradise in which souls wait before the resurrection. In *Pilgrim's Progress* the land from which the pilgrims enter the Celestial City. The name is found in Isaiah LXII: 4.

Land of Bondage. Name given to Egypt in the Bible, because of the oppression of Israel in that country.

Land of Cakes. A name sometimes given to Scotland, because oatmeal cakes are a common national article of food, particularly among the poorer classes. The title has become popular through its use by Burns and Scott.

Land of Nod. In common speech, sleepy-land or land of dreams, as if an unknown land. Cain fled to Nod, east of Eden.

Land of Promise. The land of Canaan; so called because it was promised to Abraham.

Land of Shadows. A place of unreality, sometimes meaning land of ghosts.

Land o' the Leal. An unknown land of happiness, loyalty, and virtue. Carolina Oliphant, Baroness Nairne, meant heaven in her song, and this is now its accepted meaning. Leal means "faithful," and "Land of the Leal" means the "land of the faithful."

Land of Veda. Name often given to India.

Lanternland. The land of literary charlatans, whose inhabitants, graduates in arts, doctors, professors, and artists of all grades, waste time in displaying their wonderful learning. See *Island of Lanterns*.

Laodicean (*lâ-ŏd'ĭ-sē'ăn*). One indifferent to religion, like the Christians of that church mentioned in the Book of Revelation.

Laputa (*lȧ-pū'tȧ*). The name of a flying island described by Swift in *Gulliver's Travels*. It is said to be "exactly circular, its diameter 7837 yards or about four miles and a half, and consequently contains ten thousand acres." The inhabitants are chiefly speculative philosophers, devoted to mathematics and music; and such is their habitual absent-mindedness, that they are compelled to employ attendants, called "flappers," to rouse them from their profound meditations. This is done by striking them gently on the mouth and ears with a peculiar instrument consisting of a blown bladder with a few pebbles in it, fastened to the end of a stick.

Last Days of Pompeii, The, Bulwer-Lytton. A historical novel of the time of the destruction of the city by the eruption of Mount Vesuvius, 79 A. D. The vivid descriptions of life in the Græco-Roman city are the most interesting features of the book. The lovers, Glaucus and Ione, are aided to escape by the blind flower girl, Nydia. They become Christians and go to live in Greece.

Last of the Mohicans (*mô-hē'kănz*). A romantic novel of North American Indian life by James Fenimore Cooper, the second of his Leatherstocking series. The title of the work is descriptive of the character Uncas, son of Chingachgook and the last of the Mohican line. Represented as gallant, swift, courteous, and a noble lover, he makes the perennial appeal of youth cut off in the flower.

Latitudinarians. Persons who hold very loose views of Divine inspiration and of what are called orthodox doctrines. A common name in England for the less strict groups in the Anglican Church.

Launfal, Sir. Steward of King Arthur. Detesting Queen Guinevere, he retired to Carlyoun, and fell in love with a lady named Tryamour. She gave him limitless money and told him if he wished to see her he was to retire into a private room, and she would be with him. Sir Launfal now returned to court, and excited much attention by his great wealth. Guinevere made advances to him; he would not turn from the lady to whom he was devoted but sang her praises. At this repulse, the angry queen complained to the king, and declared to him that she had been insulted by his steward. Arthur bade Sir Launfal produce this paragon of women. On her arrival, Sir Launfal was allowed to accompany her to the isle of Oleron; and no one ever saw him afterwards. James Russell Lowell has written a poem entitled "The Vision of Sir Launfal."

Laus Deo (*lôs dē'ō*), "Praise to God." A poem by Whittier, inspired by the passing of the Constitutional amendment abolishing slavery, and suggested to the poet as he sat in the Friends' meetinghouse in Amesbury and heard the bells proclaiming the fact.

Lavaine. Son of the lord of Astolat, who accompanied Sir Lancelot when he went to tilt for the ninth diamond. Lavaine is described as young, brave, and a true knight. He was brother to Elaine.

Lavender, Dr. A wise and lovable old clergyman in Margaret Deland's Old Chester stories.

Lavinia and Palemon. Thomson's Seasons. Lavinia was the daughter of Acasto, patron of Palemon. Through Acasto, Palemon gained a fortune and wandered away from his friend. Acasto lost his property and, dying, left a widow and daughter in poverty. Palemon often sought them, but could never find them. One day, a lovely modest maiden came to glean in Palemon's fields. The young squire was greatly struck with her exceeding beauty and modesty, but she was known as a pauper, and he dared not give her more than a passing glance. Upon inquiry, he found that the beautiful gleaner was the daughter of Acasto; he proposed marriage, and Lavinia was restored to her rightful place. Similarity between this story and that of Ruth in the Bible is notable.

Lawyer's Alcove. Name given to a volume of poems selected from the best poems by lawyers, for lawyers, and about lawyers. Included in this volume are Shakspere's "Sonnet CXXXIV"; Blackstone's "A Lawyer's Farewell to his Muse"; "Justice," by John Quincy Adams; Landor's "At the Buckingham Sessions"; "The Judicial Court of Venus," by Jonathan Swift; Saxe's "Briefless Barrister" and "The Lawyer's Valentine"; "General Average," by William Allen Butler; "The Festival of Injustice," by Carlton, and Riley's "Lawyer and Child."

Lay of the Last Minstrel, Scott. Lady Margaret of Branksome Hall, "the flower of Teviot," was beloved by Baron Henry of Cranstoun, but a deadly feud existed between the two families. A goblin lured Lady Margaret's brother into a wood, where he fell into the hands of the English. At the same time an army of 3000 English marched to Branksome Hall to take it; but, hearing that Douglas was on the march against them, the two chiefs agreed to decide the contest by single combat. Victory fell to the Scotch, when it was discovered that "Sir William Deloraine," the Scotch champion, was in reality Lord Cranstoun, who then claimed and received the hand of Lady Margaret as his reward. This united the two houses.

Lazy Lawrence. Name and description of a character in one of Miss Edgeworth's stories. Probably derived from a chapbook *The Infamous History of Sir Lawrence Lazy.* This hero of Lubberland had served the schoolmaster, his wife, the squire's cook, and the farmer, which, by the laws of Lubberland, was accounted high treason. He was arraigned and tried, but acquitted of the many treasons laid to his charge.

Leander (*lē-ăn'dẽr*). A young man of Abydos, who swam nightly across the Hellespont to visit his ladylove, Hero, a priestess of Sestos. One night he was drowned in his attempt, and Hero leaped into the Hellespont also. The story of Hero and Leander is so old and so well known as nearly to belong to mythology.

Lear. A legendary king of Britain, and the hero of Shakspere's tragedy of the same name. He had three daughters, and when four score years old, wishing to retire from the active duties of sovereignty, resolved to divide his kingdom among them. By elaborate but false professions of love and duty on the part of two daughters, Goneril and Regan, King Lear was persuaded to disinherit the third, Cordelia, who had before been deservedly more dear to him, and to divide his kingdom between her sisters. The tragedy is wrought out in the ungrateful conduct of the older sisters and the suffering of Lear. The beauty of the play is the exquisite character Cordelia.

Leatherstocking Tales. Five stories or romances written by James Fenimore Cooper. The same hero, Leatherstocking, or Natty Bumppo, figures throughout in his life among the Indians. Natty had learned wood-lore as the young Indian learned it. He knew the calls of the wild animals far across the wilderness. He could follow the deer and bear to their haunts. He could trace the path of the wolf by the broken cobwebs glistening in the sunlight; and the cry of the panther was a speech as familiar as his own tongue. When he was thirsty he made a cup of leaves and drank in the Indian fashion. He lay down to rest with that sense of security that comes only to the forester. These tales take Leatherstocking from young manhood to old age, following the fortunes of the American Indian tribes. The order in which his story is told in these volumes is *The Deerslayer, The Last of the Mohicans, The Pathfinder, The Pioneers,* and *The Prairie.* He is also known by the name of Hawkeye in one part of his story. The best writers on the American Indian are thus quoted in our literature: **James F. Cooper, the romancer of the Indian; Henry W.** Longfellow, the poet of the Indian; Francis Parkman, the historian of the Indian; Helen Hunt Jackson, the novelist of the Indian.

Leaves of Grass. The title of a small volume of poems published by Walt Whitman in 1855. It contained his first unconventional work. Later, other poems were included under the same title.

Legend. Anciently, a kind of rubric containing the prayers appointed to be read in Roman Catholic churches. In later times, the word was employed to denote a chronicle or register of the lives of saints, because they were to be read on the festivals of the saints. The manner in which credulous love of the wonderful, exaggeration of fancy, and ecclesiastical enthusiasm, at times even pious fraud, were mixed up with true history in these narrations caused stories of a religious or ecclesiastical nature generally to be designated as "legends," to distinguish them from real history. The word has come to mean a tale handed down by tradition, unauthentic, but popularly believed. Among the medieval collections of legends, that drawn up by the Genoese archbishop, Jacopo da Voragine, in the second half of the 13th century, under the title of *Legenda Aurea,* "Golden Legends," or *Historia Lombardica,* is the most celebrated.

Leonine Verse. This form of verse was used in the middle ages in Latin hymns and in secular verse. Said to derive its name from Leonius, a canon of the church of St. Victor, in Paris. In English, any verse which rimes middle and end is called a Leonine verse.

Les Misérables (*lā mē'zä'rä'bl'*), **Victor Hugo.** This great work is the story of a sturdy, courageous peasant, who, sent to the galleys for a minor offense, becomes a hardened convict. He is reclaimed through the kindness of a saintly bishop and becomes a respected manufacturer and town official. Discovered and hunted by his enemies, he becomes once more an outlaw. But he bears his misfortunes with heroism. His noble death is one of the great episodes in fiction.

Letterpress. Printed matter. The word is often used to distinguish printed words from engraving, or matter printed from types instead of from plates.

Lexicon. A vocabulary, or book containing an alphabetical arrangement of the words of a language, with an explanation of the meaning or sense of each. The term is used chiefly with reference to dictionaries or wordbooks of the Greek, Hebrew, Arabic, or Syriac languages.

Libations. With the prayers among all ancient peoples were usually joined the libations, or drink offerings. These consisted generally of wine, part of which was poured out in honor of the gods, and part of it drunk by the worshiper. The wine must be pure, and offered in a full cup. Sometimes there were libations of water, of honey, of milk, and of oil.

Ligeia. A story written by Poe. Suggested by a dream in which the eyes of the heroine produced the wonderful effect described in the story. Its theme is the conquest of death through the power of will.

Light of the Harem. Name given to the bride of Selim in the poem *Lalla Rookh.* She was the sultana Nourmahal, afterwards called Nourjeham, "light of the world."

Light that Failed, The, Kipling. The hero of the novel, Dick Hildar, after years of military campaigns in Egypt, goes back to London, where, in the midst of success as an artist, he meets Maisie, his boyhood sweetheart. She, bound up in her hopes of success in art, cannot or will not return his whole-hearted love. Suddenly, Dick goes blind, and Maisie is incapable of sacrificing anything for him. He returns to Egypt and is killed. The tragic ending of the story was, for one publication, changed into a happy ending, which was used in a dramatization of the novel.

Lilliput. An imaginary country described in *Gulliver's Travels,* where an ordinary man becomes a great giant beside the small people of the land. Lilliputian is used to designate small ways of expressing malice or jealousy. Among amusing characters in Lilliput land were the Little-endians and the Big-endians who made up two religious factions, which waged incessant war on the subject of the right interpretation of the 54th chapter of the "Blundecral": "All true believers break their eggs at the convenient end." The godfather of Calin, the reigning emperor of Lilliput, happened to cut his finger while breaking his egg at the big end, and therefore commanded all faithful Lilliputians to break their eggs in future at the small end. The Blefuscudians called this decree rank heresy, and determined to exterminate the believers of such an abominable practice from the face of the earth. Hundreds of treatises were published on both sides, but each sect put all those books opposed to its own views into the "Index Expurgatorius," and not a few of the more zealous sort died as martyrs for daring to follow their private judgment in the matter.

Limbo. From Latin *limbus*, meaning "edge" or "border." A place where the souls of good men not admitted into heaven wait the general resurrection. A similar place exists for the souls of unbaptized children. Still another limbo is a fool's paradise, a place for all nonsense. This old belief has been used by Dante and Milton in their poems.

Lincoln's Inn Fields. A square in London near the junction of High Holborn and Chancery Lane. It is surrounded by lawyers' offices, Lincoln's Inn, the Royal College of Surgeons, and the Soane Museum. It was laid out by Inigo Jones, the celebrated architect. The square is named from Lincoln's Inn, one of the legal societies of England through which men are called to the bar. The buildings occupied by the society formerly belonged to the earl of Lincoln. Hence their name.

Literati (*lĭt'ê-rā'tī*). (1) Men of letters, scholars of note. (2) "The Literati" was the title of a series of comments by Edgar Allan Poe on 38 New York authors which appeared in *Godey's* from May to October, 1846.

Lithgow's Bower. A favorite residence of the kings and queens of Scotland, especially of Mary of Guise; and here the unfortunate Mary Queen of Scots was born in 1542.

Little Billee. Trilby, Du Maurier. The nickname of the hero, William Bagot, an impulsive, boyish art student in Paris, who falls in love with Trilby, an artist's model. The match is broken off by Little Billee's mother. Trilby, under the tutelage of Svengali, musician and hypnotist, becomes a great singer. At the death of Svengali, her power leaves her and she dies. After the death of Little Billee, Taffy, one of his Paris friends, marries his sister.

Little Breeches, John Hay. The title of a poem published in *Pike County Ballads* in 1871.

Little Brother. An appellation made popular through the tale bearing the name. Josiah Flynt ran away from home when he was three years old and continued to do so frequently ever after. His first piece of fiction was naturally based on trampdom. His hero is a boy-tramp, a little fellow whose irresistible impulse to view the great world around him causes him to become a "Prushun" to an old inhabitant of Hoboland. He wished people to see where a number of stray boys land, for he had found out that a great many of the so-called "kidnapped" youngsters are in reality simple runaways with romantic temperaments.

Little Citizens, Myra Kelly. A New York schoolteacher's stories of her East Side Jewish charges. Human nature and American Yiddish dialect are alike faithfully rendered.

Little Dorrit. The heroine and title of a novel by Dickens. Little Dorrit was born and brought up in the Marshalsea prison, where her father was confined for debt.

Little John. A big, stalwart fellow, named John Little, who encountered Robin Hood and gave him a sound thrashing, after which he was rechristened, and Robin stood godfather. Little John is introduced by Sir Walter Scott in *The Talisman.*

Little Lord Fauntleroy. The seven-year-old hero of the story of this title by Frances Hodgson Burnett. He is the son of an Englishman who has been disinherited by his father, an English earl, for marrying an American. Upon the death of the boy's father, the old earl has the boy brought to England, but on condition that his mother, "Dearest," shall not accompany him to the family home. Gradually, the boy wins for himself and his mother a place in the old man's heart.

Little Men, Louisa May Alcott. A story of the boys in the school at Plainfield, kept by "Jo" and her husband, Mr. Baer. *Jo's Boys* is a sequel to this story.

Little Minister, The, Barrie. A romantic "Thrums" story. An Auld Licht minister's love for the beautiful "Egyptian," a lady in disguise, is the theme.

Little Nell. Old Curiosity Shop, Dickens. The prominent character of the story, pure and true, though living in the midst of selfishness and crime. She was brought up by her grandfather, who was in his dotage, and who tried to eke out a narrow living by selling curiosities. At length, through terror of Quilp, the old man and his grandchild stole away and led a vagrant life.

Little Women, L. M. Alcott. A story of the girlhood life of Louisa May Alcott and her three sisters, at Concord, Mass A sequel to the story is *Little Men.*

Llewellyn. A legendary Welsh prince who, on returning from hunting, found his baby boy missing and his favorite greyhound, Gelert, covered with blood. Thinking that the hound had eaten him, he killed it. But, on searching more carefully, the child was found alive under the cradle clothes, and near him the body of a huge wolf which had been killed by the faithful hound.

Lochiel (*lŏk-ēl'*). The title of the head of the clan Cameron. Thomas Campbell's poem, "Lochiel's Warning," is a prophecy of the battle of Culloden.

Lochinvar (*lŏk'ĭn-vär'*). The hero—a young Highlander—of an incidental song in "Marmion," who was much in love with a lady whose fate was decreed that she should marry a "laggard." Young Lochinvar persuaded the too-willing lassie to be his partner in a dance; and while the guests were intent on their amusement he swung her into his saddle and made off with her before the bridegroom could recover from his amazement.

Locksley. So Robin Hood is sometimes called, from the village in which he was born. He appears as an archer in *Ivanhoe.*

Locksley Hall. A poem by Tennyson, in which the hero, the lord of Locksley Hall, having been jilted by his cousin Amy in favor of a rich boor, pours forth his feelings in a flood of scorn and indignation. Many lines from this poem have passed into common speech, such as "In the spring a young man's fancy lightly turns to thoughts of love."

Locrin or **Locrine.** Father of Sabrina, and eldest son of the mythical Brutus, king of ancient Britain. On the death of his father he became king of Loegria.

Loegria (*lô-ē'grĭ-ȧ*) or **Logres** (*lō'grĕs*). England is so called by Geoffrey of Monmouth, from Logrine, or Locrine, eldest son of the mythical King Brute, or Brutus.

Logos. This word, occurring at the beginning of the gospel of St. John, was early taken to refer to the "second person of the Trinity, i. e., Christ." Yet the apostle's precise meaning—who alone makes use of the term in this manner, and only in the introductory part of his gospel,—whether he adopted the symbolical usage in which it was employed by the various schools of his day, which of their differing significations he had in view, or whether he intended to convey a meaning quite peculiar to himself,—these are some of the innumerable questions to which the word has given rise, and which, though most fiercely discussed ever since the first days of Christianity, are far from having found a satisfactory solution.

Lohengrin. The Knight of the Swan; the hero of a romance written by a disciple of Wolfram von Eschenbach, in the 13th century, and also of a modern music drama by Richard Wagner. He was the son of Parsifal, and came to Brabant in a ship drawn by a white swan, which took him away again when his bride, disobeying his injunction, pressed him to discover his name and parentage.

Lord Jim, Joseph Conrad. The hero of this novel, a young ship's officer, had been dismissed from the merchant marine service because he had erred in a serious emergency. Self-exiled among Malaysian savages, he tries to redeem himself by devoted service. Among these people he gains the title of "Lord Jim."

Lorna Doone, R. D. Blackmore. A novel. Lorna, child of the outlaw family of the Doones in Exmoor, saves John Ridd, a fourteen-year-old boy, from capture by them. Seven years later, grown to manhood, John becomes her champion against her own people, and finally they are married. It is a story of England in the 17th century, and involves the infamous Judge Jeffrey.

Lothario (*lô-thä'rĭ-ō*). The name has come to stand in literature for the type of the gay, handsome, and gallant libertine. The original is a Florentine cavalier in Cervantes' story *The Curious Impertinent.* Rowe, in *The Fair Penitent,* gave the name to a Genoese noble, and Richardson developed the character in Robert Lovelace of his novel *Clarissa Harlowe.*

Lotos-Eaters. Tennyson wrote a poem called "The Lotos-Eaters," describing a set of islanders who live in dreamy idleness, weary of life, and regardless of all its stirring events.

Love Doctor, The. L'Amour Médecin (*lȧ-mōōr' mād"săɴ'*). A comedy by Molière, written about the year 1665. Lucinde, the daughter of Sganarelle, is in love, and the father calls in four doctors to consult upon the nature of her malady. They see the patient, and retire to consult together, but talk about Paris, about their visits, about the topics of the day; and, when the father enters to know what opinion they have formed, they all prescribe different remedies, and pronounce different opinions. Lisette then calls in a "quack" doctor, Clitandre, the lover, who says that he must act on the imagination, and proposes a seeming marriage, to which Sganarelle assents. The assistant being a notary, Clitandre and Lucinde are married.

Lover's Vows. Altered from Kotzebue's. Baron Wildenhaim, in his youth, seduced Agatha Friburg, and then forsook her. She had a son, Frederick, who became a soldier. While on furlough, he came to spend his time with his mother, and found her in abject poverty and almost starved. A poor cottager took her in, while Frederick, who had no money, went to beg charity. Baron Wildenhaim was out with his gun, and Frederick asked alms of him. The count gave him a shilling; Frederick demanded more, and, being refused, seized the baron by the throat. The keepers arrived and put him in the castle dungeon. Here he was visited by the chaplain, and it came out that the count was his father. The chaplain, being appealed to, told the count the only reparation he could make would be to marry Agatha and acknowledge the young soldier to be his son. This advice he followed, and Agatha Friburg, the beggar, became the Baroness Wildenhaim of Wildenhaim castle.

Love's Labor's Lost, Shakspere. Ferdinand, king of Navarre, with three lords named Biron, Dumain, and Longaville, agree to spend three years in study, during which time no woman was to approach the court. The compact signed, all went well, until the princess of France, attended by Rosaline, Maria, and Katharine, besought an interview respecting certain debts said to be due from the king of France to the king of Navarre. The four gentlemen fell in love with the four ladies. The love of the king sought the princess, by right, Biron loved Rosaline, Longaville admired Maria, and Dumain adored Katharine. In order to carry their suits, the four gentlemen, disguised as Muscovites, presented themselves before the ladies; but the ladies, being warned of the masquerade, disguised themselves also, so that the gentlemen in every case addressed the wrong lady. A mutual arrangement was made that the suits should be deferred for twelve months and a day; and, if, at the expiration of that time, they remained of the same mind, the matter should be taken into serious consideration.

Loves of the Angels. A poetical story written by Thomas Moore. It may be called the stories of three angels, and was founded on the Eastern tale of "Harût and Marût," and the rabbinical fictions of the loves of "Uzziel and Shamchazai." (1) The first angel fell in love with Lea, whom he saw bathing. She returned love for love, but his love was carnal, hers heavenly. He loved the woman, she loved the angel. At last the angel gave to her the password which should open the gates of heaven. She pronounced it, and rose through the air into paradise. The angel degenerated and became no longer an angel of light, but "of the earth, earthy." (2) The second angel was Rubi, one of the seraphs. He loved Liris, who asked him to come in all his celestial glory. He did so; and she, rushing into his arms, was burned to death; but the kiss she gave him became a brand on his face forever. (3) The third angel was Zaraph, who loved Nama. It was Nama's desire to love without control, and to love holily; but, as she fixed her love on a creature and not on the Creator, both she and Zaraph were doomed to live among the things that perish. When the end of all shall come, Nama and Zaraph will be admitted into the realms of everlasting love.

Loving Cup. A large cup passed round from guest to guest at state banquets and city feasts. On the introduction of Christianity, the custom of wassailing was not abolished, but it assumed a religious aspect. The monks called the wassail bowl the loving cup. In the universities the term "Grace Cup" is more general. Immediately after grace the silver cup, filled with wine, is passed round. The master and wardens drink welcome to their guests; the cup is then passed to all the guests. A loving or grace cup should have two handles, and some have four. This ceremony, of drinking from one cup and passing it round, was observed in the Jewish paschal supper, and our Lord refers to the custom in the words, "Drink ye all of this."

Lubberland. An imaginary country of idleness and luxury. The name has been applied to certain cities in burlesque.

Luck of Roaring Camp, The, Bret Harte. A story of the softening influence of a child's presence among the men of an early mining camp in California. The poem, published in the second number of the *Overland Monthly* (1868), brought Harte his first real fame and popularity.

Luggnagg. Gulliver's Travels. An imaginary island whose inhabitants have the gift of eternal life, lacking with it the gift of immortal health and strength.

Lumbercourt, Lord. Character in Macklin's comedy *The Man of the World*. A voluptuary, greatly in debt, who consented, in return for considerable money, to give his daughter, Lady Rudolphe, to Egerton McSycophant. Egerton, however, had no fancy for the lady, but married Constantia, the girl of his choice. His lordship was in alarm lest this should be his ruin; but Sir Pertinax told him the bargain should still remain good if Egerton's younger brother, Sandy, were accepted by his lordship instead. To this his lordship and the lady readily agreed.

Lure of the Labrador Wild, The, Wallace. A recital of the ill-fated expedition to Labrador undertaken by Leonidas Hubbard, Jr., during the summer of 1903. The party consisted of Mr. Hubbard, Mr. Wallace, and a half-breed Cree Indian named Elson, who proved himself a veritable hero. As is generally known, the object of the party was to reach the interior of Labrador over a portion of that country unexplored, or at least unmapped by white men. This purpose was only partially carried out. The winter came on long before Hubbard was ready to turn back, the provisions were exhausted, game was scarce, and the fish failed to rise to the fly. On the return journey toward the coast, Hubbard gave out and had to be left behind until aid could be brought. Wallace succeeded in finding some provisions which had been thrown aside on the inland trip and had returned within a few hundred feet of Hubbard's tent, but without finding it. Elson, the half-breed, managed to reach a trapper's camp and sent back a relief expedition, which picked up Wallace, and later found the body of Hubbard, who had died of starvation.

Lusiad (*lū'sĭ-ăd*), **The.** The only Portuguese poem that has gained a world-wide celebrity. It was written by Luiz de Camoëns, appeared in 1572, and was entitled *Os Lusiadas*, the "Lusitanians," that is, the Portuguese—the subject being the conquests of that nation in India. It is divided into ten cantos, containing 1102 stanzas. Among English translations, that by Sir Richard Burton is especially notable. *The Lusiad* celebrates the chief events in the history of Portugal, and is remarkable as the only modern epic poem which is pervaded by anything approaching the national and popular spirit of ancient epic poems. Bacchus was the guardian power of the Mohammedans, and Venus or Divine Love, of the Lusians. The fleet first sailed to Mozambique, then to Melinda (Africa), where the adventurers were hospitably received and provided with a pilot to conduct them to India. In the Indian Ocean, Bacchus tried to destroy the fleet; Venus, however, calmed the sea, and Gama arrived at India in safety. Having accomplished his object, he returned to Lisbon. Among the most famous passages are the tragical story of Inez de Castro, and the apparition of the giant Adamastor, who appears as the Spirit of the Storm to Vasco da Gama, when crossing the cape. The versification of *The Lusiad* is extremely charming. The best edition was published in Paris (1817), reprinted in 1819, and again in 1823. *The Lusiad* has been translated into Spanish, French, Italian, English, Polish, and German.

Lusitania (*lū'sĭ-tā'nĭ-ȧ*). The ancient name of Portugal; so called from Lusus, the companion of Bacchus in his travels. He colonized the country, and called it "Lusitania," and the colonists "Lusians."

Lustrum. The solemn offering made for expiation and purification by one of the censors in the name of the Roman people at the conclusion of the census. The animals offered in sacrifice were a boar, a sheep, and a bull. They were led round the assembled people on the Campus Martius before being sacrificed. As the census was quinquennial, the word lustrum came to signify a period of five years.

Luther's Postil (*pŏs'tĭl*) **Gospels.** Advent, Christmas, and Epiphany sermons, first published in Latin in 1521, and dedicated to his protector, the elector Frederick. Translated immediately into German, Luther's postils, or homilies, on the gospels are esteemed the best of his sermons. "Postils" was a common name in the 16th century for expositions of the gospels and epistles for Sundays and holydays. The word is explained from the fact that the gospels and epistles were printed first and that after them (*post illa*) came the commentary.

Lycidas (*lĭs'ĭ-dăs*). The name under which Milton celebrates the untimely death of Edward King, who was drowned in the passage from Chester to Ireland, August 10, 1637. He was the son of Sir John King, secretary for Ireland.

Lydia Languish. The heroine of Sheridan's comedy *The Rivals*, distinguished for the extravagance of her romantic notions.

Lydia. Orlando Furioso. A daughter of the king of Lydia, who was sought in marriage by Alcestes, a Thracian knight; his suit was refused, and he repaired to the king of Armenia, who gave him an army, with which he laid siege to Lydia. He was persuaded by the king's daughter to raise the siege. The king of Armenia would not give up the project, and Alcestes slew him. Lydia now set him all sorts of dangerous tasks to "prove his love," all of which he surmounted. Lastly, she induced him to kill all his allies, and when this was done she mocked him. Alcestes pined and died, and Lydia was doomed to endless torment in hell, where Astolfo saw her, to whom she told her story.

Lygia. The Christian bride of the pagan, Vinicius, in *Quo Vadis*, a historical novel treating the age of Nero, written by Sienkiewicz, a Polish novelist.

Lyric. Literally, pertaining to the lyre. In poetry a name originally applied to what was sung or recited to the accompaniment of the lyre, but it is now applied to odes, ballads, and other verses, such as may be set to music. Lyrics were originally employed in celebrating the praises of gods and heroes, and their characteristic was melodiousness. The Greeks cultivated them with effect, particularly Anacreon and Sappho, but among the Romans Horace was the first and principal lyric poet. It has been said that all poets are singers and these singers are divided into three classes. First, the lyric poet, who can sing but one tune with his one voice. Second, the epic poet, who with his one voice can sing several tunes. Third, the true dramatist, who has many tongues and can sing all tunes.

Mab, Queen. Romeo and Juliet, Shakspere. The origin of the name is obscure. By some it is derived from the Midgard of the Eddas. The name is given by the English poets of the 15th and succeeding centuries to the imaginary queen of the fairies.

Mabinogion (*măb′ĭ-nō′gĭ-ŏn*). A series of Welsh tales, chiefly relating to Arthur and the Round Table. A manuscript volume of some 700 pages is preserved in the library of Jesus college, Oxford.

Macbeth. The tale of Macbeth and Banquo was borrowed from the legendary history of Scotland, but the interest of the play is not historical. It is a tragedy of human life, intensely real, the soul, with all its powers for good or evil, deliberately choosing evil. The three witches in the desert place, in thunder, lightning, storm, strike the keynote of evil suggestion. The awfulness of soul destruction is felt in Macbeth and Lady Macbeth as in no other of Shakspere's dramas.

Maccabees, The. This Jewish family led the struggle of their people against Antiochus Epiphanes, B. C. 168–135. The two Books of the Maccabees give an account of this struggle.

Macheath, Captain. A highwayman who is the hero of Gay's *Beggar's Opera.*

Machiavellism (*măk′ĭ-ă-vĕl′ĭz′m*). The name came from a writing by Machiavelli, under the title *The Prince*, a famous treatise, in which are expounded those principles of political cunning and artifice, intended to promote arbitrary power, ever since designated "machiavellism."

MacIvor. Waverley, Scott. Fergus MacIvor is a prominent character in the novel, and his sister, Flora MacIvor, is the heroine. They belong to a Scotch chieftain's family.

Macreons, The Island of. Pantagruel, Rabelais. The title is given to Great Britain, derived from a Greek word, meaning long-lived, "because no one is put to death there for his religious opinions." Rabelais says the island "is full of antique ruins and relics of popery and ancient superstitions."

Madasima, Queen. An important character in the old romance called *Amadis of Gaul*; her constant attendant was Elisabat, a famous surgeon, with whom she roamed in solitary retreats.

Madge Wildfire. The Heart of Midlothian, Scott. A poor, wandering, fantastically dressed girl, driven insane by the profligate abuse of George Staunton. She is the daughter of old Meg Murdochson, the gypsy thief.

Madoc (*mā′dŏk*). A poem by Southey; founded on one of the legends connected with the early history of America. Madoc, a Welsh prince of the 12th century, is represented as making the discovery of the Western world. His contests with the Mexicans form the subject.

Madrigal. (1) A short lyric poem, generally on the subject of love, characterized by epigrammatic terseness or quaintness, and composed of a number of free and unequal verses, confined neither to the regularity of the sonnet, nor to the subtlety of the ode. The madrigals of Tasso are noted in Italian poetry. (2) In music, a part song for several voices, properly with contrapuntal imitation and without musical accompaniment.

Magi (*mā′jī*). The three "Wise Men" who followed the star to Bethlehem. The traditional names of the three Magi are Melchior, represented as an old man with a long beard, offering gold; Gaspar, a beardless youth who offers frankincense; Balthazar, a black, or Moor, who tenders myrrh.

Magic Rings. These are mentioned by Plato, Cicero and other writers and are supposed to make the wearer invisible.

Magic Staff. The story of the magic staff belongs to the days of legends and seems to be of French origin, but has found its way into other lands. This staff would guarantee the bearer safety from all the perils and mishaps incidental to travelers. According to earliest traditions the staff was a willow branch cut on the eve of All Saints' Day.

Magic Wands. These are found in many old tales or writings. In Tasso's *Jerusalem Delivered* the hermit gave to Charles the Dane and Ubaldo a wand, which, being shaken, infused terror into all who saw it, and in Spenser's *Faery Queen* the palmer who accompanied Sir Guyon had a wand of like virtue. It was made of the same wood as Mercury's caduceus.

Magnalia. The best-known in the long list of Cotton Mather's works was his *Magnalia Christi Americana* (1702), purporting to be an ecclesiastical history of New England, from its first planting in 1620 to the year 1698, but including also civil history, an account of Harvard college, the Indian wars, the witchcraft troubles, and a large number of biographies. The work is of no historical value, but has an important place in puritan psychology.

Magnano. Hudibras, Butler. One of the leaders of the rabble that attacked Hudibras at a bear baiting.

Magnificat (*măg-nĭf′ĭ-kăt*). In the ritual of the Roman Catholic Church, the name given to the "Song of the Virgin Mary," in Luke I:46–55. The name is derived from the opening word of the song in the Vulgate or Latin New Testament.

Maiden Lane. A street in London, between Covent Garden and the Strand. Andrew Marvell, Turner, the landscape painter, and Voltaire lived here at different times. The name is said to have been given from an image of the Virgin which once stood there.

Maidens' Castle. An allegorical castle mentioned in Malory's *Morte D'Arthur.* It was taken from a duke by seven knights, and held by them till Sir Galahad expelled them. It was called "The Maidens' Castle," because these knights made a vow that every maiden who passed it should be made a captive.

Maid Marian. (1) A half mythical character, but the name is said to have been assumed by Matilda, daughter of Robert Lord Fitzwalter, while Robin Hood remained in a state of outlawry. The name Maid Marian is connected with the morris dance, or May-day dance, at which she was said to appear. (2) The title of a charming novel by Thomas Love Peacock (1822).

Maid of Athens. Made famous by Lord Byron's song of this title. Twenty-four years after this song was written, an Englishman sought out "the Athenian maid," and found a beggar without a vestige of beauty.

Maid of Saragossa. Childe Harold, Byron. A young Spanish woman distinguished for her heroism during the defense of Saragossa in 1808-09. She first attracted notice by mounting a battery where her lover had fallen, and working a gun in his place.

Malaprop, Mrs. A character in Sheridan's *Rivals*, noted for her blundering use of words.

Malbecco. Faery Queen, Spenser. The husband of a young wife, Helinore, and himself a crabbed, jealous old fellow.

Malengrin. A character in Spenser's *Faery Queen*, who carried a net on his back "to catch fools with." The name has grown to mean the personification of guile or flattery.

Malepardus. The castle of Master Reynard the Fox, in the beast epic *Reynard the Fox.*

Malvoisin. Ivanhoe, Scott. One of the challenging knights at the tournament, Sir Philip de Malvoisin. Sir Albert de Malvoisin was a preceptor of the Knights Templars.

Mambrino (*măm-brē′nō*). (1) In *Orlando Furioso* by Ariosto, a king of the Moors, who was the possessor of an enchanted golden helmet, which rendered the wearer invulnerable, and which was the object of eager quest to the paladins of Charlemagne. This helmet was borne away by the knight Rinaldo. (2) In *Don Quixote* we are told of a barber who was caught in a shower of rain, and who, to protect his hat, clapped his brazen basin on his head. Don Quixote insisted that this basin was the helmet of the Moorish king, and, taking possession of it, wore it as such.

Managarm. Prose Edda. The largest and most formidable of the race of giants. He dwells in the ironwood, Jamvid. Managarm will first fill himself with the blood of man, and then will he swallow up the moon. This giant symbolizes war, and the "ironwood" in which he dwells is the wood of spears.

Man and Superman, G. B. Shaw. Called by many the most important of Shaw's plays. It is a comedy in which he "modernizes" the Don Juan motive. John Tanner, a social revolutionist, of spotless character and a foe of convention, is determined to escape love and marriage. But he is overtaken and captured by Ann Whitefield, who personifies the demands of the Life Force. Other clearly drawn characters add to the keen comedy of the piece.

Manfred. The hero of a poem by Byron. Manfred is a melancholy and defiant soul, haunted by a mysterious past crime. He visits the court of Arimanes and causes to be evoked the vision of his lost love, Astarte. She gives him no answer to his question. At the conclusion, when he is dying in his lonely castle in the Alps, devils come to claim his soul and he defies them.

Manon Lescaut (*mä'nôɴ' lĕs'kō'*), **Prévost.** One of the first of modern novels, published in 1733. Chevalier des Grieux, who tells the story, is disgraced through his association with Manon. But she proves her love by going with him into exile in America.

Mantalini (*măn'tä-lē'nē*). **Nicholas Nickleby, Dickens.** The husband of madame; he is a man-doll, noted for his white teeth, his oaths, and his gorgeous morning gown. This "exquisite" lives on his wife's earnings, and thinks he confers a favor on her by spending. Madame Mantalini is represented as a fashionable milliner near Cavendish Square, London.

Man with the Hoe, The, Edwin Markham. The subject of a famous poem, suggested by the picture by J. F. Millet. The theme is the hopelessness of the toiler.

Marble Faun, The, Nathaniel Hawthorne. A romance. Miriam, a beautiful art student in Rome, whose origin and relations are mysterious, is loved by Donatello, a young count, whose striking resemblance to the "Faun of Praxiteles" suggests his descent from the woodland fauns. Donatello is singularly unsophisticated. One night, at a sign from Miriam, he throws Brother Antonio, who has been following Miriam, over the Tarpeian rock to his death. Miriam disappears, but Donatello, awakened to responsibility, gives himself up to justice.

Marcellus. Hamlet, Shakspere. An officer of Denmark, to whom the ghost of the murdered king appeared before it presented itself to Prince Hamlet.

Marchioness, The. Old Curiosity Shop, Dickens. A half-starved maid-of-all-work, in the service of Sampson Brass and his sister Sally. She was so lonesome and dull that it afforded her relief to peep at Mr. Swiveller even through the keyhole of his door. Mr. Swiveller called her the "marchioness," when she played cards with him, "because it seemed more real and pleasant" to play with a marchioness than with a domestic. While enjoying these games they made the well-known "orange-peel wine."

Mariana in the Moated Grange. (1) In Tennyson's poem of this name, a young damsel who sits in the moated grange, looking out for her lover, who never comes. (2) In Shakspere's *Measure for Measure*, Mariana is a lovely and lovable lady, betrothed to Angelo, who, during the absence of Vincentio, the duke of Vienna, acted as his lord deputy.

Mark Tapley. Martin Chuzzlewit, Dickens. A young man with an ambition to be "jolly" under adverse conditions. He accompanies young Martin Chuzzlewit to America, is constantly the good genius of that heedless youth, and on his return marries Mrs. Lupin, thus becoming landlord of the Blue Dragon, where he had formerly worked.

Marplot. "The busy body." A blundering, good-natured, meddlesome young man, very inquisitive, too officious, and always bungling anything with which he interferes. Character found in comedies written by Mrs. Centlivre.

Marriage of Figaro (*fē'gä'rō'*), **The, Beaumarchais.** This play is the sequel to the *Barber of Seville*. It was presented in 1784, and was immediately popular. It helped forward the Revolution. In the play, Almaviva and Rosine are weary of married life. The husband has turned his fancy to Suzanne. But Figaro is in love with her, and he succeeds in checkmating the noble gallant. Brilliant wit and careless mockery both adorn and mar the play.

Marse Chan, T. N. Page. A short story, told in the language of the hero's negro servant. A Virginia gentleman loves a lady, who, though loving him, is cold and haughty. He is killed in battle, and she mourns him as a husband during the rest of her life.

Martin's Summer, St. Halcyon days; a time of prosperity; fine weather. Mentioned by Shakspere in *Henry VI*, etc.

Masora or **Massorah** (*mȧ-sō'rȧ*). A critical work or canon, whereby is fixed and ascertained the reading of the text of the Hebrew Bible. The word means "tradition."

Masques (*mȧsks*). Dramatic representations made for a festive occasion, with a reference to the persons present and the occasion. Their *dramatis personæ* were allegorical. They admitted of dialogue, music, singing, and dancing, combined by the use of some ingenious fable into a whole. They were made and performed for the court and the houses of the nobles, and the scenery was gorgeous and varied. According to Holinshed's *Chronicle*, the first masque performed in England was at Greenwich, in 1512. Shakspere, as well as Beaumont and Fletcher, have frequently introduced masques into their plays. Milton himself made them worthier by writing *Comus*. H. W. Longfellow wrote the "Masque of Pandora," taking the story from Hawthorne's *Wonder Book*.

Master Builder, The, Ibsen. A drama which embodies the dangers of selfish ambition and the struggle of age against youth. Sollness, a master builder, has gained success through sacrificing his wife and his business associates. He thinks himself secure from the competition of younger folk, when Hilda Wangel appears and tempts him to climb a high tower "as he did in his youth." He falls to his death.

Master of Ballantrae, The, Stevenson. A novel of the time of the Stuart Pretender, about 1745. The story is told by the old steward of Ballantrae. The older son of the house, James Durrie, espouses the Stuart cause, the younger, Henry, staying at home, the decision being made on the turn of a coin. Alison Graeme, in love with James, marries Henry when James is reported dead. But James returns, with a disgraceful record behind him, and takes advantage of the situation to persecute the family with diabolical persistence. Henry, with Alison and their son, at last emigrates to her estate in New York. James follows. Both brothers die on an ill-fated search for treasure which James claims to have hidden in the northern woods, and are buried side by side.

Mauth Dog. Lay of the Last Minstrel, Scott. A black specter spaniel that haunted the guardroom of Peeltown in the Isle of Man. A drunken trooper entered the guardroom while the dog was there, but lost his speech, and died within three days.

Mavournin or **Mavourneen.** Irish for "my darling."

Mayeux (*mä'yē'*). The name of a hunchback, who figures prominently in numberless French caricatures and romances.

Mayfair (*mā'fâr'*). A fashionable locality in London, east of Hyde Park. All streets north of Piccadilly now lead into the district of Mayfair, which takes its name from a fair which used to be held in Shepherd's Market and its surrounding streets.

Mayor of Casterbridge, The, Thomas Hardy. One of the most famous of Hardy's Wessex stories. Michael Henchard, a hay trusser by trade, comes one day with his wife and little daughter, Elizabeth Jane, to a village fair. While drunk he offers the wife and daughter for sale. The offer is taken up by a young sailor, who takes them away with him. The next morning, Michael, sobered, takes a vow to touch no liquor for twenty years. He comes to the town of Casterbridge, and in time becomes wealthy in the grain trade and is made mayor of the town. One evening the wife he had sold, with her daughter, comes to Casterbridge. To avoid discovery of his old folly, Henchard provides them a cottage, and after a time marries his wife again. But she soon dies, when Henchard discovers that Elizabeth Jane is not his child, but the child of the sailor. His old character comes to the surface, and disaster overtakes him. He dies miserably in a moorland cottage, after the sailor, now wealthy himself, has returned to claim his child, who marries Donald Farfrae.

Mazeppa, Byron. Mazeppa, in a poem under the same title, was a Cossack of noble family who became a page in the court of the king of Poland. While in this capacity, he intrigued with Theresia, the young wife of a count, who discovered the amour, and had the young page lashed to a wild horse and turned adrift.

McFingal. The hero of Trumbull's political poem of the same name; represented as a burly New England squire, enlisted on the side of the Tory party of the American Revolution, and constantly engaged in controversy with Honorius, the champion of the Whigs.

Measure for Measure, Shakspere. There was a law in Vienna that made it death for a man to live with a woman not his wife, but the law was so little enforced that the mothers of Vienna complained to the duke of its neglect. So the duke deputed Angelo to enforce it and, assuming the dress of a friar, absented himself awhile to watch the result. Scarcely was the duke gone, when Claudio was sentenced to death for violating the law. His sister Isabel went to intercede on his behalf, and Angelo told her he would spare her brother if she would become his Phryne. Isabel told her brother he must prepare to die, as the conditions proposed by Angelo were out of the question. The duke, disguised as a friar, heard the whole story, and persuaded Isabel to "assent in words," but to send Mariana, the divorced wife of Angelo, to take her place. This was done, but Angelo sent the provost to behead Claudio, a crime which "the friar" contrived to avert. Next day, the duke returned to the city, and Isabel told her tale. The end was, the duke married Isabel, Angelo took back his wife, and Claudio married Juliet.

Médecin Malgré Lui, Le (*lĕ mād″săɴ′ màl′grā′ lwē*), "The Doctor in Spite of Himself," **Molière.** In this comedy Sganarelle, Molière's frequently used character, appears as a woodcutter whom Geronte summons as a physician to cure his daughter's dumbness. When Sganarelle discovers that Lucinde is pretending dumbness to avoid marriage with Horace, her father's choice, he brings in an apothecary who soon effects a cure. The apothecary turns out to be Léandre, Lucinde's lover, and all ends happily.

Meeting of the Waters. Title of a poem by Moore, better known under the name "Sweet Vale of Avoca." "The Meeting of the Waters" forms a part of that beautiful scenery which lies between Rathdrum and Arklow, in the county of Wicklow, Ireland. The poem was suggested by a visit to this romantic spot in the summer of 1807.

Meg Merrilies. A half-crazy gypsy or sibyl, a prominent character in Scott's *Guy Mannering*. Keats wrote a ballad about her.

Meister, Wilhelm. Hero and title of a philosophic novel by Goethe. The object is to show that man, despite his errors and shortcomings, is led by a guiding hand, and reaches some higher aim at last. This is considered to be the first true German novel.

Meistersinger. In Germany an association of master tradesmen, to revive the national minstrelsy, which had fallen into decay with the decline of the minnesinger or love-minstrels (1350–1523). Their poems were chiefly moral or religious, and were constructed according to rigid rules.

Melissa. Orlando Furioso, Ariosto. The prophetess who lived in Merlin's cave. Bradamant gave her the enchanted ring to take to Rogero; so, assuming the form of Atlantes, she not only delivered Rogero, but disenchanted all the forms metamorphosed in the island, where he was captive.

Melnotte, Claude. Lady of Lyons, Bulwer. The son of a gardener in love with Pauline, "the Beauty of Lyons," but treated by her with contempt. Beauseant and Glavis, two other rejected suitors, conspired with him to humble her.

Melyhalt. A powerful female subject of King Arthur's court. Sir Galiot invaded her domain, but she forgave his trespass and chose him for her knight and chevalier.

Menard. The Road to Frontenac, Merwin. The hero of the novel, a leader among Indians and white men during the making of New France. From Quebec he goes west, holding control of affairs in spite of treachery in both races. His companions are chiefly French, amid whom figure a Jesuit and two Indians, and the story contains much of that romantic charm peculiar to early French pioneer life, whence Longfellow and other poets and story-tellers have drawn inspiration.

Mengtsu (*mŭng-tsû′*). One of the sacred "four books" of China, so called from its author, Mengtse, Latinized into Mencius. This great work was written in the 4th century B. C., and contains the wisdom of the age. These are some of its teachings: "Humanity, righteousness, propriety, knowledge, are as natural to man as his four limbs." "Humanity is internal, righteousness is external." In this same book Mencius taught that government is from God, but for the people, whose welfare is the supreme good. The phrase "mother of Meng," which has been borrowed from the Chinese, signifies "a great teacher."

Menteur, Le (*lĕ măɴ′tĕr′*), "The Liar," **Corneille.** The propensities of the leading character give the play its name and lead to the complications of the plot. This is generally considered Corneille's best comedy and the most important before the time of Molière.

Merchant of Venice. Antonio, the merchant, in Shakspere's play, signs a bond in order to borrow money from Shylock, a Jew, for Bassanio, the lover of Portia. If the loan were repaid within three months, only the principal would be required; if not, the Jew should be at liberty to claim a pound of flesh from Antonio's body. The ships of Antonio being delayed by contrary winds, the merchant was unable to meet his bill, and the Jew claimed the forfeiture. Portia, in the dress of a law doctor, conducted the defense, and saved Antonio by reminding the Jew that a pound of flesh gave him no drop of blood.

Merchant's Tale, The, Chaucer. Substantially the same as the first Latin metrical tale of Adolphus, and not unlike a Latin prose tale given in the appendix of Wright's edition of *Æsop's Fables*. It is the story of the betrayal of an old husband by a young wife. The story is evidently of Oriental origin and very old. Boccaccio and Chaucer may have borrowed it from the *Commedia Lydiæ*. The well-known incident of the pear tree is found in all these sources, an interesting account of which has been given by the Chaucer Society Publications under *Origins and Analogues of the Tales*. Pope used this story as his basis for "January and May."

Merlin. (1) The name of an ancient Welsh prophet and enchanter. He is often alluded to by the older poets, especially Spenser, in his *Faery Queen*, and also figures in Tennyson's *Idylls of the King*. In *Le Morte D'Arthur* by Malory, Merlin is the prince of enchanters and of a supernatural origin. He is said to have built the Round Table and to have brought from Ireland the stones of Stonehenge on Salisbury Plain. (2) A dramatic poem by E. A. Robinson, in which the poet embodies modern life and problems in the story of Merlin, Vivian, and Arthur.

Merlin's Cave. In Dynevor, near Carmarthen, noted for its ghastly noises of rattling iron chains, groans, and strokes of hammers. The cause is this: Merlin set his spirits to fabricate a brazen wall to encompass the city of Carmarthen. Leaving to call on the Lady of the Lake, he bade them labor till he returned; but he never did return, for Vivian held him prisoner by her wiles.

Merry Wives of Windsor, The, Shakspere. A rollicking farce. The merry wives are Mrs. Ford and Mrs. Page, to whom Falstaff makes love. The two ladies set traps and tricks for him, making him the laughing stock of the town. The booby love of Slender for Anne Page parallels Falstaff's adventures. Justice Shallow, Bardolph, Pistol, and Mistress Quickly find place in the play.

Messiah, The. An epic poem in fifteen books, by F. G. Klopstock. The subject is the last days of Jesus, His crucifixion and resurrection.

Micawber, Mr. Wilkins. David Copperfield, Dickens. This character has become a by-word for improvidently "waiting for something to turn up." He is thought to have been modeled on Dickens's father.

Michael and His Lost Angel, H. A. Jones. Michael Feversham, a young, mystical, ascetic clergyman, has insisted upon a public confession in the village church by the daughter of his secretary, who has been concealing an illicit love affair. Within a few months he himself falls deeply in love with a woman, Audrie Lesden, who has recently come to his parish and who gives the money to rebuild his church. He makes public confession at the dedication of the rebuilt church and leaves the parish. In Italy, as Michael is about to enter a monastery, Audrie, very ill, appears and dies in his arms. Seeing his life as a tissue of blunders, he seeks the monastery for peace.

Midsummer Night's Dream, A, Shakspere. Egeus promised his daughter Hermia to Demetrius. She loved Lysander and fled from Athens with her lover. Demetrius went in pursuit of her, followed by Helena, who doted on him. All four came to a forest and fell asleep. Oberon and Titania had quarreled, and Oberon, by way of punishment, dropped on Titania's eyes during sleep some lovejuice, or "love in idleness," the effect of which is to make the sleeper fall in love with the first thing seen when waking. The first thing seen by Titania was Bottom the weaver, wearing an ass's head. In the meantime King Oberon dispatched Puck to the lovers, and with the juice Puck changed their vision and made all content. It has been suggested that in this play Shakspere may have borrowed hints from Chaucer.

Mildendo. Gulliver's Travels, Swift. The metropolis of Lilliput, the wall of which was two feet and a half in height and at least eleven inches thick. The emperor's palace, called Belfaborac, was in the center of the city.

Miles Standish. In Longfellow's *Courtship of Miles Standish*, the Puritan captain is too shy to propose. He sends John Alden, and the girl Priscilla says, "Speak for yourself, John Alden."

Miller, Daisy. Name of heroine and title of the story by Henry James. An American girl traveling in Europe, where her innocence, ignorance, and disregard of European customs and standards of propriety put her in compromising situations and frequently expose her conduct to misconstruction.

Mill on the Floss, The, George Eliot. Maggie Tulliver, living with her brother Tom and their parents at the mill, as she grows up, becomes confused and entangled in the mysteries and disappointments of existence. Separated from her lover, Philip Wakeham, she is estranged from her family through her imprudent conduct with Stephen Guest. She welcomes death, which comes to her and Tom in a tidal wave that sweeps away the old mill.

Mincing Lane. A street in London connecting Fenchurch street with Great Tower street; the center of colonial (wholesale) trade. It received its name from the "minchens" (nuns) of St. Helen's, a part of whose domain it once was.

Minnehaha. Hiawatha, H. W. Longfellow. The daughter of the arrow-maker of Dacotah, and wife of Hiawatha. She was called Minnehaha from the waterfall of that name.

Minnesänger or **Minnesinger.** A name given to the German lyric poets of the middle ages, on account of love being the principal theme of their lays, the German word *minne* being used to denote a pure and faithful love.

Miranda. The Tempest, Shakspere. The daughter of Prospero, the exiled duke of Milan, and niece of Antonio, the usurping duke. She is brought up on a desert island, with Ariel, the fairy spirit, and Caliban, the monster, as her only companions.

Miriam. A beautiful and mysterious woman in Hawthorne's romance *The Marble Faun*, for love of whom Donatello commits murder, thus becoming her partner in crime.

Misanthrope, Le (*lĕ mē'zäɴ'thrōp'*), **Molière.** The hero of this comedy, Alceste, wearied with society, has grown misanthropic. He loves Célimène, but she will not share his seclusion, and he gives her up. The play is famous for its vivid contrasts among the characters, as for example, that between Alceste and his friend Philinte.

Miserere (*mĭz'ē-rē'rē*). A title given in the Roman Catholic Church to the 51st Psalm, usually called the "psalm of mercy," and derived from the opening word in the Latin version.

Monsieur Beaucaire (*mē-syû' bō'kâr'*), **Booth Tarkington.** The plot is laid at Bath, in England, in the time of Beau Nash. A young French barber has the temerity to fall in love with an aristocratic English woman. He gives a good account of himself with gentlemen's weapons, and turns out to be Louis Philippe of Valois, who had fled from France to escape marriage with a princess.

Morality, The. An old play in which the characters were the Vices and Virtues, with the addition afterwards of allegorical personages, such as Riches, Good Deeds, Confession, Death, and any human condition or quality needed for the play. These characters were brought together in a rough story at the end of which Virtue triumphed.

Morituri Salutamus. Latin, meaning "We about to die salute you." A "hymn to age," written by H. W. Longfellow, for the jubilee reunion of Bowdoin's Class of 1825. It contains a number of classic allusions and an entire tale from the *Gesta Romanorum*.

Morris Dance. The name is derived from "Moorish dance," introduced into England in the reign of Edward III. It was a prominent feature of the May-day and other outdoor festivities.

Mortality, Old. Old Mortality, Scott. A religious itinerant, who frequented country churchyards and the graves of the Covenanters. He was first discovered at Gandercleugh, clearing the moss from the grey tombstones, renewing with his chisel the half-defaced inscriptions, and repairing the decorations of the tombs.

Morte D'Arthur, Le. (1) A prose version of the Arthurian romances, made by Sir Thomas Malory before 1470 and printed by Caxton in 1485. The classic English version of these stories. Tennyson drew on this source. (2) Title of a poem by Tennyson, *Morte d'Arthure.*

Mother Goose. The origin of this name has been variously explained. *Mother Goose's Melodies* was published in Boston by Thomas Fleet in 1719. His mother-in-law is said to have been Mother Goose. But the suggestion of the name may have come from the *Mother Goose's Tales* published in French by Perrault in 1697. These contained the stories of Cinderella, Little Red Ridinghood, and others.

Mother Hubbard, Old. The subject of this nursery rime has been rather reasonably traced to the work of some untutored rimester, who mistook a picture of St. Hubert, patron of dogs, for that of an old woman. The saint was often represented with long hair and a loose, long gown. He was often besought to cure the illnesses of pet dogs. Spenser used the name simply as that of any old dame in "Mother Hubbard's Tale." This is a tale of a fox and an ape in human form, out for adventures.

Mowgli (*mou'glĭ*). **Jungle Books, Kipling.** The name given to the man-cub suckled and brought up in the jungle by Mother Wolf. He runs with the pack and learns the law of the jungle. But, in the end, he is forced to seek a home among men, where he marries the daughter of Abdul Gafur.

Mualox. The Fair God, Lew Wallace. The old paba or prophet who assured Nenetzin that she was to be the future queen in her father's palace.

Much Ado about Nothing, Shakspere. One of the dramatist's most successful comedies. The play is located in Messina. Claudio, deceived by Don John into thinking his affianced bride, Hero, unfaithful, repudiates her at the altar. Friar Francis, suspicious, reports her dead. Don John, who had bribed Hero's maid to dress in her mistress' clothes and meet him, thus imposing upon Claudio, flees, and the maid confesses. The lovers are happily married. Beatrice and Benedick, whose linked names have become proverbial, are also wedded. In this play appear Dogberry and Verges, ignorant police officers.

Mucklebacket. The Antiquary, Scott. Name of a conspicuous family, consisting of Saunders Mucklebacket, the old fisherman of Musselcrag; Old Elspeth, mother of Saunders; Maggie, wife of Saunders; Steenie, the eldest son, who was drowned; Little Jennie, Saunders' child.

Mugwump. A celebrated cartoon pictured the independent voter as having his mug on one side of the fence and his wump on the other.

Munchausen (*mŭn-chô'zĕn*), **The Baron.** A hero of most marvelous adventures, and the fictitious author of a book of travels filled with most extravagant tales. The name is said to refer to Hieronymus Karl Friedrich von Münchhausen, a German officer in the Russian army, noted for his marvelous stories.

Mussel Slough Affair. The Octopus, Norris. The basis of plot for the novel, and name given to an actual though little-known piece of California history. The story of the conflict between the wheat growers of the San Joaquin valley and the railroad trust, which they believed was trying to defraud them of their land.

My Prisons, Silvio Pellico. Italian *Le Mie Prigioni* (1832). The poignant story of the author's experiences in Austrian prisons. He had been condemned to death and then to fifteen years' imprisonment, for conspiracy. The simple recital of the author's experiences, with no word of personal condemnation, has made the book one of great influence in Italy.

Mystery of Edwin Drood, The, Dickens. A novel unfinished at the time of the author's death. The scene of the story is laid in the cathedral town of Cloisterham. The choirmaster, John Jasper, secretly an opium addict, is guardian for his nephew, Edwin Drood, who is just about to come of age. During the Christmas holidays, Edwin and an orphan girl at school in Cloisterham decide to break off the engagement their parents had arranged for them. Then, after a dinner in Jasper's rooms, Edwin disappears. His watch is found in a weir near the town, but the body cannot be found. Consequently, a young man with whom Edwin had had a dispute is freed from the charge of murder. Numerous hints point to Jasper as the villain, but no satisfactory conclusion has ever been offered for the book, though many people have tried their hands at it.

Natty Bumppo. Called "Leatherstocking." He appears in five of Cooper's novels: (1) *The Deerslayer*; (2) *The Pathfinder*; (3) "The Hawkeye," in *The Last of the Mohicans*; (4) "Natty Bumppo," in *The Pioneers*; and 5) as "The Trapper," in *The Prairie*, in which he dies.

Neæra (*nê-ē'rà*). The name of a girl mentioned by the Latin poets, Horace, Virgil, and Tibullus; sometimes also introduced into modern pastoral poetry as the name of a mistress or sweetheart, as in Milton's "Lycidas."

Nerissa. Merchant of Venice, Shakspere. The bright, lively maid to Portia. She marries Gratiano.

Nest of Linnets. Title given to a story by F. F. Moore, a sequel to his *Jessamy Bride*, and noted for the group of people collected. Richard Brinsley Sheridan may be called its hero, inasmuch as he is the lover of its heroine, Miss Linley, the famous singer, who became Sheridan's first wife. The whole remarkable group to which she belonged gave title to the book,—Garrick, Goldsmith, Sir Joshua Reynolds, Mrs. Thrale, Dr. Johnson, Burke, Thomas Sheridan, the father of Richard, and others.

New Atlantis, The. An imaginary island in the middle of the Atlantic. Bacon, in his allegorical fiction so called, supposes himself wrecked on this island, where he finds an association for the cultivation of natural science and the promotion of arts. Called the "New" Atlantis to distinguish it from Plato's Atlantis, an imaginary island of fabulous charms.

Newcome, Colonel. A gallant, simple-hearted retired East Indian officer, in Thackeray's novel *The Newcomes.* His unworldliness leads to the loss of his fortune, and he finally dies, poor and broken-hearted, in the Charter House hospital.

New England Primer. This book, of which it is estimated that 2,000,000 copies were sold in the 18th century, was published by Benjamin Harris, a printer of Boston, shortly before 1690. A copy of the New England Primer, published in Walpole, N. H., in 1814, contains an illustrated alphabet. The letter "L" is illustrated by a lion with one of its paws resting upon a lamb, which is lying down. Accompanying the picture are the following lines:

"The Lion bold
The Lamb doth hold."

New England Tragedies. Among the poems of H. W. Longfellow are the "New England Tragedies" and the "Divine Tragedy." These, taken in connection with "The Golden Legend," form one connected work of art, *Christus, a Mystery*.

New Jerusalem. The name by which, in the Christian faith, heaven, or the abode of the redeemed, is symbolized. The allusion is to the description in the 21st chapter of the book of Revelation.

New Pastoral. A poem by T. B. Read, truly American in character, like its companion poem, "The Wagoner of the Alleghanies."

News. This word is made up of the first letter of each point of the compass: North, East, West, South. This fanciful explanation is frequently given as the origin of the term "news," as something coming from all points of the compass. Actually, however, the word probably comes from the French *nouvelles*, meaning "news," or medieval Latin *nova*, neuter plural of *novus*, meaning "new things." Some authorities would trace it to Anglo-Saxon, but, in the sense of "tidings" or "information," it has been in common use only since 1500.

Nibelung (*nē′bĕ-lōōng*), **King.** A king of the Nibelungen, a mythical Burgundian tribe, who gives name to the great medieval epic of Germany, the *Nibelungenlied*. He bequeathed to his two sons a hoard or treasure beyond all price and incapable of diminution, which was won by Siegfried, who made war upon the Nibelungen and conquered them.

Nibelungenlied. A historic poem generally called the German "Iliad." It is the only great national epic that European writers have produced since antiquity, and belongs to every country that has been peopled by Germanic tribes, as it includes the hero traditions of the Franks, the Burgundians, and the Goths, with memorials of the ancient myths carried with them from Asia. The poem is divided into two parts, and 32 lieds, or cantos. The first part ends with the death of Siegfried, and the second part with the death of Kriemhild. The death of Siegfried and the revenge of Kriemhild have been celebrated in popular songs dating back to the lyric chants now a thousand years old. These are the foundation of the great poem.

Nickleby, Mrs. Nicholas Nickleby, Dickens. The mother of the hero Nicholas, a widow fond of talking and of telling long stories with no connection. She imagined that her neighbor, a mildly insane man, was in love with her because he tossed cabbages and other articles over the garden wall. She had a habit of introducing, in conversation, topics wholly irrelevant to the subject under consideration, and of always declaring, when anything unexpected occurred, that she had expected it all along and had prophesied to that precise effect on divers (unknown) occasions. Nicholas Nickleby has to make his own way in the world. He first goes as usher to Mr. Squeers, schoolmaster at Dotheboys Hall; but leaves in disgust with the tyranny of Squeers and his wife, especially to a poor boy named Smike. Smike runs away from the school to follow Nicholas, and remains his humble follower till death. At Portsmouth, Nicholas joins the theatrical company of Mr. Crummles, but leaves the profession for other adventures. He falls in with the brothers Cheeryble, who make him their clerk; and in this post he rises to become a merchant, and ultimately marries Madeline Bray.

Nils, The Wonderful Adventures of, Selma Lagerlöf. A delightful story of the dreams of a boy about birds and animals.

Nine Worthies, The. Famous personages often alluded to, and classed together, rather in an arbitrary manner, like the Seven Wonders of the World, the Seven Wise Men of Greece, etc. They have been counted up in the following manner:

Three Gentiles.	1. Hector, son of Priam. 2. Alexander the Great. 3. Julius Cæsar.
Three Jews.	4. Joshua, conqueror of Canaan. 5. David, king of Israel. 6. Judas Maccabeus.
Three Christians.	7. Arthur, king of Britain. 8. Charlemagne. 9. Godfrey of Bouillon.

Noctes Ambrosianæ (*nŏk′tēz ăm-brō′zhĭ-ā′nē*), "Ambrosian Nights." The name of a famous series of literary and political disquisitions which appeared in *Blackwood's Magazine* from 1822 to 1835. These articles, consisting of supposed conversations, purported to be a verbatim report of convivial gatherings held at Ambrose's tavern, Edinburgh, by several literary celebrities of the time. At first these brilliant dialogues were the work of several writers, among them J. G. Lockhart and William Maginn. Those appearing after 1825 were nearly all contributed by John Wilson, under the pen name "Christopher North." Of the 71 "Noctes" 49 were afterward published separately as being entirely Wilson's work. By reason of their inexhaustible humor and trenchant wit, these imaginary discussions enjoyed an immense vogue and were largely responsible for the success of *Blackwood's Magazine*. Their great permanent literary creation is Wilson's delineation of the character of the Ettrick Shepherd, an idealized portrait of James Hogg, who is described as one of the frequenters of the "Ambrosian" feasts.

No Man's Land. The name given to the strip of territory between the trenches of opposing armies in the World War. A proverbial phrase for disputed ground or the borderland between two opinions.

North Americans of Yesterday. Name given to the Indians of North America by recent writers, among them F. S. Dellenbaugh, in a work under same title. This work, a comparative study of North American Indian life and customs, is written on the theory that the races are of ethnic unity.

Notre Dame de Paris (*nō′tr′ dȧm′ dĕ pä′rē′*), **Victor Hugo.** English title, "The Hunchback of Notre Dame." A romance. The time is the reign of Louis XI; the scene, Paris. Esmeralda, a dancing girl, is loved by Quasimodo, the hunchback bell ringer, but she, repelled by his deformity, only pities him. She is condemned as a witch, but Quasimodo hides her in the church. Claude Frollo, the archdeacon, to whose passion she will not surrender, betrays her to the mob, and she is hanged. The hunchback throws Claude over the battlements of Notre Dame. Years afterward, Quasimodo's skeleton is found beside that of Esmeralda in the charnel cave.

Nourmahal (*nōōr-mȧ-häl′*). **Lalla Rookh, Moore.** "Light of the Harem." She was for a season estranged from the sultan, till he gave a grand banquet, at which she appeared in disguise as a lute player and singer. The sultan was so enchanted with her performance, that he exclaimed, "If Nourmahal had so played and sung, I could forgive her all"; whereupon the sultana threw off her mask.

Novum Organum (*nō′vŭm ôr′gȧ-nŭm*). Published by Francis Bacon in 1620 under a general title *Instauratio Magna*, but having, after the preface, a second title: "The second part of a work called Novum Organum, or certain opinions on the Interpretation of Nature." It outlines his scientific, or inductive, method, that is, reasoning from observed facts to general laws.

Nucta. Paradise and the Peri, Moore. The name given to the miraculous drop which falls from heaven, in Egypt, on St. John's Day, and is supposed to stop the plague.

Nun of Nidaros. Tales of a Wayside Inn, Longfellow. The abbess of the Drontheim convent, who heard the voice of St. John while she was kneeling at her midnight devotions.

Nut-brown Maid. Reliques, Percy. The maid who was wooed by the "banished man." The "banished man" described to her the hardships she would have to undergo if she married him; but, finding that she accounted these hardships as nothing compared with his love, he revealed himself to be an earl's son, with large hereditary estates, and married her.

Oakhurst, John. The Outcasts of Poker Flat, Bret Harte. Oakhurst, the hero of the story, is a gambler who has been driven out of the mining camp in winter, with three other "undesirable citizens." He kills himself that the others may have a chance to live and escape.

Oberon. King of the Fairies, whose wife was Titania. Shakspere introduces both Oberon and Titania in his *Midsummer Night's Dream*. Oberon and Titania, his queen, are fabled to have lived in India, and to have crossed the seas to northern Europe to dance by the light of the moon.

Oberon the Fay. A humpty dwarf only three feet high, but of angelic face, lord and king of Mommur.

Octopus, The, Frank Norris. A California story of a struggle between the wheat growers and the railroads. See *Mussel Slough Affair*. The first of a trilogy, the story of a wheat crop. The second in the series, *The Pit*, a tale of gambling in grain, is a story of the middleman. Mr. Norris, when he died, had planned the third story, to be called *The Wolf*, which was to have dealt with the consumption in Europe.

Odyssey (*ŏd′ĭ-sĭ*). Homer's epic, recording the adventures of Odysseus, or Ulysses, in his voyage home from Troy. The poem opens in the island of Calypso, with a complaint against Neptune and Calypso for preventing the return of Odysseus to Ithaca. Telemachus, the son of Odysseus, starts in search of his father, accompanied by Pallas in the guise of Mentor. He goes to Pylos, to consult old Nestor, and is sent by him to Sparta, where he is told by Menelaus that Odysseus is detained in the island of Calypso. In the meantime, Odysseus leaves the island,

and, being shipwrecked, is cast on the shore of Phæacia. These wanderings of Odysseus occupied ten years after the close of the ten years of the Trojan War. Penelope is tormented by suitors. To excuse herself, Penelope tells her suitors he only shall be her husband who can bend Odysseus' bow. None can do so but the stranger, who bends it with ease. Odysseus is recognized by his wife, and the false suitors are all slain and peace is restored to Ithaca.

Œdipus Tyrannus (*ĕd'ĭ-pŭs tī-răn'ŭs*), **Sophocles.** One of a group of three tragedies. Œdipus, or "Swollen-feet," son of Laius, king of Thebes, and Jocasta, is exposed on a mountain, but found and brought up by a shepherd. Grown to manhood, and learning the prophecy that he should kill his father and marry his mother, he leaves Corinth. Journeying toward Thebes, he unwittingly fulfills all the prophecy. A plague is sent on the city, which can be averted only by banishment of the king. Tiresias, a seer, reveals the truth to Œdipus. Jocasta hangs herself, and Œdipus, led by his daughter Antigone, wanders forth. *Œdipus at Colonna* and *Antigone* are the other two plays of the trilogy.

Offertory. In the Roman Catholic Church that portion of the Mass, with accompanying prayers and chants, which consists of the oblation, or offering, of bread and wine. In Protestant religious services, the word is frequently used to indicate the collection of money and the music which accompanies it.

Ogham or **Ogam** (*ŏg'ăm*) **Inscriptions.** These are mostly ancient Celtic names found on stones in Ireland, Scotland, Wales, the Shetlands, and England. A peculiar alphabet is used, consisting of straight vertical or slant lines arranged along a middle horizontal line. Different letters are represented by groups of lines, of varying number and direction. They are referred to in T. W. Rolleston's world-famous Irish lyric "The Dead at Clonmacnoise."

Ogier (*ō'jĭ-ēr*) **the Dane.** One of the paladins of the Charlemagne epoch. Also made the hero of an ancient French romance, and the subject of a ballad, whose story is probably a contribution from the stores of Norman tradition, Holger, or Olger Danske, being the national hero of Denmark. He figures in Ariosto's *Orlando Furioso*.

O'Groat. A name often alluded to in early English parables or sayings coming from the legend of "John O'Groat's House." This ancient building was supposed to stand on the most northerly point in Great Britain. John of Groat and his brothers were originally from Holland. According to tradition, the house was of an octagonal shape, being one room with eight windows and eight doors, to admit eight members of the family, the heads of eight different branches of it, to prevent their quarrels for precedence at table, which, on a previous occasion, had well-nigh proved fatal.

Old Bailey, The. The central criminal court of London, England, situated on the street named Old Bailey, which runs from Newgate to Ludgate Hill, not far from St. Paul's, London. It was the site of the Roman *vallum*, forming part of the city's fortifications external to the wall, hence Ballium and Bailey. A *vallum* was a rampart of palisades, so called from *vallus*, a "stake," and was planted on the top of the *agger*, or "mound," thrown up for the purposes of defense. Vividly described in Dickens's *Tale of Two Cities*.

Oldbuck, Jonathan. Antiquary, The, Scott. The character whose whimsies gave name to the novel. He is represented as devoted to the study and accumulation of old coins, medals, and relics. He is irritable, sarcastic, and cynical from an early disappointment in love, but he is full of humor and is a faithful friend.

Old Chester Tales, Margaret Deland. A series of artistic tales of the vicissitudes of old-fashioned people in a quiet old New England village. The series is extended in *Dr. Lavender's People*.

Old Creole Days, George W. Cable. A collection of tales of New Orleans life in the early 19th century. It contains some of the best of modern stories, for example, *Jean-ah Poquelin* and *Café des Exilés*.

Old Curiosity Shop, The, Dickens. See *Little Nell*.

Old Grimes. The New England character in a popular American ballad by Albert G. Greene. The name probably is borrowed from George Crabbe's Peter Grimes in "The Borough," though resemblance ends here.

Old Man of the Sea. In the *Arabian Nights*, a monster encountered by Sindbad the Sailor in his fifth voyage. After carrying him upon his shoulders a long time, Sindbad at last succeeds in intoxicating him, and effects his escape. The "Old Man of the Sea" was also made the title of a humorous and well-known poem by O. W. Holmes.

Old Mortality, Scott. A novel which tells a story of the days of the Covenanters of Scotland in the latter part of the 17th century. "Old Mortality" is an old man who makes it his business to clean the gravestones of old Covenanters and to keep the inscriptions on them clear. The love story is that of Edith Bellenden, an heiress, who marries Henry Morton, a Covenanter, after the death of her betrothed, Lord Evendale.

Old Red Sandstone. One of the most noted of Hugh Miller's famous writings on geological subjects. It revealed his discovery of fossils in a formation which, up to that time, had been deemed almost destitute of them.

Oliver Twist, Dickens. The hero, Oliver, is an orphan, born in a workhouse, of a mother who did not reveal her name. Starved and illtreated, he runs away to London, falls in with Fagin's gang of thieves, and finally, in the house of the Maylie's, which he has been forced to enter for robbery, finds, in their adopted daughter, his aunt. Her name, as his, had been Fleming.

Olivia. Twelfth Night, Shakspere. A rich countess, whose love was sought by Orsino, duke of Illyria; but, having lost her brother, Olivia lived for a time in entire seclusion, and in no wise reciprocated the duke's love. Olivia fell in love with Viola, who was dressed as the duke's page, and sent her a ring. Mistaking Sebastian, Viola's brother, for Viola, she married him out of hand.

Opal, The Story of. The diary of a child, Opal Whitely, whose parents had died while she was very small, leaving her to the care of a family in the backwoods of Oregon. Gifted with acute powers of observation, a vivid imagination, and a naïve command of words, she wrote and printed on scraps of paper her daily play life. These sheets were afterward torn into fragments, but, with the encouragement of a publisher, Miss Whitely laboriously pieced together the torn bits. The result is an interesting picture of natural child life.

Ophelia. Hamlet, Shakspere. Daughter of Polonius, the chamberlain. Hamlet fell in love with her, but, after his interview with the ghost, finds that his plans must draw him away from her. During his real or assumed madness, he treats her with undeserved and angry rudeness, and afterward, in a fit of inconsiderate rashness, kills her father, the old Polonius. The terrible shock given to her mind by these events completely shatters her intellect, and leads to her accidental death by drowning.

Opium Eater, Confessions of an English. A famous series of papers or essays, which describe the effect of opium upon the mind and body. The writer, Thomas De Quincey, had become a victim of the opium habit.

Ordeal of Richard Feverel, The, George Meredith. The story of a youth brought up by his father on an abstract theory of education. The "system" fails when Richard comes to manhood and falls in love with Lucy, an innocent girl of great nobility of character. This period is the "ordeal" of Richard. The story ends in bitter tragedy.

Organon. The name given to the first work on logic by Aristotle. He is said to have created the science of logic. The *Organon* has been enlarged and recast by some modern authors, especially by Mr. John Stuart Mill in his *System of Logic*, into a structure commensurate with the vast increase of knowledge and extension of positive method belonging to the present day.

Orlando Furioso (*ôr-lăn'dō fōō'rē-ō'sō*). An epic poem in 46 cantos, by Ariosto, which occupied his leisure for eleven years, and was published in 1516. This poem, which celebrates the semimythical achievements of the paladins of Charlemagne, in the wars between the Christians and the Moors, became immediately popular, and has since been translated into all European languages, and passed through innumerable editions.

Ormulum. The *Ormulum*, as originally planned, was to consist of English paraphrases of the gospels for the church year as arranged in the missal, with an exposition for English readers at the end of each. The result embodies only thirty paraphrases with the corresponding homilies. There are very few French words in the poem, but Scandinavian words and constructions abound. The writer, Orm, or Ormin, belonged to the East of England, and he and his brother Walter were Augustinian monks. He makes no use of rime or of alliteration, and he handles his verse form—the iambic *septenarius*—mechanically and with no freedom or license.

Osbaldistone. Rob Roy, Scott. A family name in the story which tells of nine of the members: (1) the London merchant and Sir Hildebrand, the heads of two families; (2) the son of the merchant is Francis; (3) the offspring of the brother are Percival, the sot; Thorncliffe, the bully; John, the gamekeeper; Richard, the horse-jockey; Wilfred, the fool; and Rashleigh, the scholar, by far the worst of all. This last worthy is slain by Rob Roy, and dies cursing his cousin Frank, whom he had injured.

Osman. Sultan of the East, conqueror of the Christians, a magnanimous man. He loved Yara, a young Christian captive. This forms the subject of a once famous ballad.

Osric. A court fop in Shakspere's *Hamlet*. He is made umpire by Claudius in the combat between Hamlet and Laertes.

Osseo. Hiawatha, Longfellow. Son of the Evening Star. When broken with age, he married Oweenee, one of ten daughters of a North hunter. She loved him in spite of his ugliness and decrepitude, because "all was beautiful within him." As he was walking with his nine sisters-in-law and their husbands, he leaped into the hollow of an oak tree and came out strong and handsome; but Oweenee at the same moment was changed into a weak old woman. But the love of Osseo was not weakened. The nine brothers and sisters-in-law were transformed into birds. Oweenee, recovering her beauty, had a son, whose delight was to shoot the birds that mocked his father and mother. An Algonquin legend gave the foundation of the story.

Ossian (*ŏsh'ăn*) or **Oisin.** A bard of Gaelic legend, son of the hero, Finn. In the middle of the 18th century, James MacPherson, a Scotch schoolmaster, published what he said were translations from ancient Gaelic poetry. These he collected as *The Poems of Ossian*. The poetry was meritorious, but it has been proved that MacPherson had misrepresented matters in calling his verses "translations."

Othello. A Moor of Venice, in Shakspere's play of the same name. He marries Desdemona, the daughter of a Venetian senator, and is led by his ensign Iago, a consummate villian, to distrust her fidelity and virtue. Iago hated the Moor both because Cassio, a Florentine, was preferred to the lieutenancy instead of himself, and also from a suspicion that the Moor had tampered with his wife; but he concealed his hatred so well that Othello wholly trusted him. Iago persuaded Othello that Desdemona intrigued with Cassio, and urged him on till he murdered his bride.

Othello's Occupation's Gone. A phrase much quoted from the play *Othello*, meaning "the task is ended," or that one has retired from active work.

O'Trigger, Sir Lucius. The Rivals, Sheridan. A volatile, fortune-hunting Irishman, fighting and forgiving with equal readiness.

Outre-Mer (*ōō'trẽ-mâr'*). A "Pilgrimage beyond the Sea." This title was given to the work by H. W. Longfellow, published in 1835, and written before European travel was much known to Americans. It is a poetical prose work, not unlike the *Sketch Book* of Washington Irving.

Over the Top. The phrase used by soldiers in the World War to mean going over the high front of the trench to a charge. Generally applied to the successful attainment of a goal or aim.

Pacolet. In *Valentine and Orson*, an old romance, a character who owned an enchanted steed, often alluded to by early writers. The name of Pacolet was borrowed by Steele for his familiar spirit in the *Tatler*. The French have a proverb, "It is the horse of Pacolet," that is, it is one that goes very fast.

Page. Merry Wives of Windsor, Shakspere. Name of a family of Windsor, conspicuous in the play. When Sir John Falstaff made love to Mrs. Page, Page himself assumed the name of Brook. Sir John told the supposed Brook his whole "course of wooing."

Page, Anne. Daughter of Mrs. Page, in love with Fenton. Slender calls her "the sweet Anne Page."

Page, Mrs. Wife of Mr. Page, of Windsor. When Sir John Falstaff made love to her, she joined with Mrs. Ford to dupe and punish him.

Palimpsest (*păl'ĭmp-sĕst*). A parchment on which the original writing has been effaced and something else has been written. The monks and others used to wash or rub out the writing in a parchment and use it again. As they did not efface it entirely, many works have been recovered by modern ingenuity. Thus Cicero's *De Republica* has been restored from an ancient manuscript which had been partly erased. There are relics of ancient learning of which even the mutilated members have an independent value. This is especially true of biblical manuscripts for criticism, and, in a still broader sense, of all the remains of the ancient historians.

Palinurus. The pilot of Æneas, in Virgil's *Æneid*, who fell asleep at the helm and tumbled into the sea. The name is employed as a generic word for a steersman or pilot, and sometimes for a chief minister. Thus, Prince Bismarck was called the palinurus of William, emperor of Germany.

Palladium (*pă-lā'dĭ-ŭm*). Something that affords effectual protection and safety. The Palladium was a colossal wooden statue of Pallas in the city of Troy, said to have fallen from heaven. The statue was carried away by the Greeks, and the city was burned. The Scotch had a similar tradition attached to the great stone of Scone, near Perth. Edward I removed it to Westminster, and it is still framed in the coronation chair of England. Stories connected with the palladium of a nation or a family are common in literature, as "Luck of Edenhall," a poem by Longfellow. Matthew Arnold uses the Trojan idea in a moral sense for the individual soul in his beautiful lyric "Palladium."

Pallet. A painter in Smollett's novel *Peregrine Pickle*. The absurdities of Pallet are painted in lurid colors.

Pamela (*păm'ē-lȧ*). Name of heroine and title of novel by Richardson. She is a simple country girl, and maidservant of a rich young squire. She resists every temptation, and at length marries the young squire and reforms him. Pamela is very modest, bears her afflictions with much meekness, and is a model of maidenhood. The story is told in a series of letters which Pamela sends to her parents.

Pamphlet. This word seems to be derived from *Pamphilus seu de Amore*, a well-known 12th century amatory poem in Latin, colloquially known as "Pamphilet." Other little books were similarly named, as *Æsopet*, the "Fables of Æsop."

Pandarus. A son of Lycaon, and leader of the Lycians in the Trojan War, celebrated by Homer in the *Iliad*. In medieval romances, and by Shakspere in *Troilus and Cressida*, he is represented as procuring for Troilus the love and good graces of Chryseis,—hence the word "pander."

Panegyric (*păn'ē-jĭr'ĭk*). A eulogistic harangue or oration, written or uttered in praise of a person or body of persons.

Panjandrum, The Grand. A sort of mythical nonentity invented by Foote, the comic dramatist. The word occurs in Foote's farrago of nonsense, which he composed to test the memory of a person who said he had brought his memory to such perfection that he could remember anything by reading it over once.

Pantagruel (*păn-tăg'rōō-ĕl*). A character in a famous romance by Rabelais. The name is said to have been given him because he was born during the drought which lasted thirty and six months, three weeks, four days, thirteen hours, and a little more, in that year of grace noted for having "three Thursdays in one week." His father was Gargantua, the giant, who was four hundred fourscore and forty-four years old at the time. He was chained in his cradle with four great iron chains, like those used in ships of the largest size. Being angry at this, he stamped out the bottom of his bassinet, which was made of weavers' beams. When he grew to manhood he knew all languages, all sciences, and all knowledge of every sort. The character has originated the English phrase "pantagruelian humor," that is, extravagant, coarse mirth like that of Pantagruel.

Pantagruelian Law Case. Pantagruel, Rabelais. This case, having nonplused all the judges in Paris, was referred to Lord Pantagruel for decision. After much "statement" the bench declared, "We have not understood one single circumstance of the defense." Then Pantagruel gave sentence, but his judgment was as unintelligible as the case itself. So, as no one understood a single sentence of the whole affair, all were perfectly satisfied.

Pantaloon. The character in old Italian comedy. He is represented as a wizened old man in dressing gown and slippers. See *As You Like It*, act 2, scene 7, "the lean and slippered Pantaloon."

Panurge (*păn-ûrj'*). A celebrated character in Rabelais' *Pantagruel*, and the real hero of the story; represented as an arrant rogue, a drunkard, a coward, and a libertine, but learned in the tongues, an ingenious practical joker, and a boon companion. He was the favorite of Pantagruel, who made him governor of Salmygondin, and finally set out with him in quest of the oracle of the Holy Bottle.

Paolo and Francesca (*pä'ō-lō*) (*frän-chĕs'kä*), **Stephen Phillips.** A tragedy based upon the story in Dante's "Inferno." Giovanni, tyrant of Rimini, occupied with his wars, leaves his young bride and his brother Paolo much together in his castle. Though both wish to be loyal to the husband and brother, youth and love overmaster them. The old housekeeper arouses Giovanni's suspicions. Discovering their guilt, he slays both, though he thus destroys all that he loves.

Paracelsus (*păr'ȧ-sĕl'sŭs*). The name of the hero in Browning's poem of the same name. Paracelsus, at twenty, starts out to find the supreme good in knowledge, but after eight years of study, he is disappointed. Then, after being again disillusioned in the search for good in love, he gives himself to such happiness as he may get from material things. The historical Paracelsus was a famous Swiss doctor and alchemist (1493–1541).

Paradise and the Peri. The second tale in Moore's poetical romance *Lalla Rookh.* The peri laments her expulsion from heaven, and is told she will be readmitted if she will bring to the gate of heaven the "gift most dear to the Almighty." After several failures the peri offered the "repentant tear," and the gates flew open to receive the gift.

Paradise Lost. The poem by Milton under this name opens with the awakening of the rebel angels in hell after their fall from heaven, the consultation of their chiefs how best to carry on the war with God, and the resolve of Satan to go forth and tempt newly created man to fall. Satan reaches Eden, and finds Adam and Eve in their innocence. This is told in the first four books. The next four books contain the archangel Raphael's story of the war in heaven, the fall of Satan, and the creation of the world. The last four books describe the temptation and the fall of man, and tell of the redemption of man by Christ and the expulsion from paradise.

Paradise Regained. In this poem Milton tells of the journey of Christ into the wilderness after his baptism, and its four books describe the temptation of Christ by Satan.

Pardoner's Tale. Canterbury Tales, Chaucer. Three rioters agreed to kill Death, and were directed to a tree under which he was to be found. At the foot of the tree they came upon a treasure, which all coveted. The youngest of the three went to buy wine and the other two conspired to kill him on his return. He poisoned the wine and was slain by his brothers, who soon died from the effect of the poison. Thus all found Death under the tree.

Parian Chronicle. A chronological register of the chief events in the mythology and history of ancient Greece, kept in the island of Paros. It is engraved on marble tablets now in the collection of Oxford university.

Parian Verse. Ill-natured satire; so called from Archilochos, a native of Paros.

Parizade (*pä'rē-zä'dä*). A princess whose adventures in search of the Talking Bird, the Singing Tree, and the Yellow Water, are related in the "Story of the Sisters" in the *Arabian Nights' Entertainments.*

Parley, Peter. Name assumed by Samuel Griswold Goodrich, an American (1793–1860). His series of *Peter Parley* books, popular and juvenile, included more than a hundred volumes.

Parody. A kind of writing in which the words of an author or his thoughts are, by some slight alterations, adapted to a different purpose.

Parthian Shaft. An unexpected and effective witticism, especially when satirical. The phrase refers to a custom of the ancient Parthians, who in battle would feign retreat and then shoot backward with unerring aim. It has come to mean "parting shot" or "last word" in a controversy.

Partington, Mrs. An imaginary old lady whose laughable sayings have been recorded by an American humorist, B. P. Shillaber.

Partlet. The hen in "The Nun's Priest's Tale," and in the famous animal epic *Reynard the Fox.*

Parzival or **Parsifal.** The German name of Perceval the hero and title of a metrical romance of the 13th century, by Wolfram von Eschenbach, and of a modern music drama by Richard Wagner. Parzival was brought up by a widowed mother in solitude, but, when grown to manhood, two wandering knights persuaded him to go to the court of King Arthur. His mother consented to his going if he would wear the dress of a common jester. This he did, but soon accomplished such noble deeds that Arthur made him a knight of the Round Table. Sir Parzival went in quest of the Holy Graal, which was kept in a castle called Graalburg, in Spain. He reached the castle, but, having neglected certain conditions, he was shut out, and, on his return to court, the priestess of Graalburg insisted on his being degraded from knighthood. Parzival then led a new life, and a wise hermit became his instructor. At length he reached such a state of purity and sanctity that the priestess of Graalburg declared him worthy to become lord of the castle. Lohengrin, "Knight of the Swan," was the son of Parzival.

Pasquinade (*păs'kwĭ-nād'*). A widely used name for a lampoon or satire. A certain free-spoken, witty tailor, Pasquino by name, is said to have lived in Rome in the 15th century. He was locally famous for his epigrams, directed especially at the popes. About the time of his death a mutilated statue was discovered and set up in one of the squares. Its origin was unknown, though it was recognized as part of a masterpiece. The populace gave it the name of the dead tailor. The custom grew up of hanging placards carrying satiric epigrams upon this statue. Hence the name.

Pastoral. Something descriptive of a shepherd's life, or a poem in which any action or passion is represented by its effects on a country life. The characteristics of this type of poetry are simplicity, brevity, and delicacy.

Pastor Fido (*päs-tōr' fē'dō*). "The Faithful Shepherd." Title of a pastoral drama by Guarini, first played in Turin in 1585. A very famous piece, which has been translated into many modern languages.

Paternoster Row (*pā'tēr-nŏs'tēr rō*). A street in London, north of St. Paul's, long famous as a center of book pubshing. See *Amen Corner.*

Patterne, Sir Willoughby. See *The Egoist.*

Pattieson, Peter. An imaginary assistant teacher at Gandercleuch, and the feigned author of Scott's *Tales of My Landlord,* which were represented as having been published posthumously by his pedagogue superior, Jedediah Cleishbotham.

Paul and Virginia, Bernardin de St. Pierre. A pastoral romance. The scene of the story is the island of Port Louis in the Mauritius. Virginia, daughter of a French widow who had been disowned by her family, and Paul, an illegitimate son of a woman betrayed by a lover, were brought up in complete ignorance of the outside world. An aunt of Virginia has the girl taken to France to be educated, but, on her refusal to marry according to dictation, sends her back to the island. Within sight of the eager Paul the ship is wrecked and Virginia is drowned. Paul soon dies, broken-hearted. The story has been used with variations in operas and plays.

Pauline (*pô-lēn'*). (1) The "Lady of Lyons" in Bulwer-Lytton's play of this name. She was married to Claude Melnotte, a gardener's son, who pretended to be a count. (2) Heroine of Browning's dramatic poem of the same name.

Paul Pry. Paul Pry, John Poole. An idle, inquisitive, meddlesome fellow, who has no occupation of his own, and is forever poking his nose into other people's affairs. He always comes in with the apology, "I hope I don't intrude."

Peeping Tom of Coventry. A tailor of Coventry, the only soul in the town mean enough to peep at the Lady Godiva as she rode naked through the streets to relieve the people from oppression. Tradition says he was stricken blind. See Tennyson's *Lady Godiva.*

Peer Gynt (*pā'ĕr günt*), **Ibsen.** A poetic drama in which is presented the career of a reckless, irresponsible dreamer. His motto is "To thyself be enough." At last, realizing that he has been a bungler and failure in life, he finds a healing influence in the love of the heroine, Solveig. Ibsen seems to have intended this work for reading rather than for the stage.

Peggotty, Clara. The nurse of David Copperfield in Dickens's novel of this name. Being very plump, whenever she makes any exertion some of the buttons on the back of her dress fly off.

Peggotty, Dan'el. Brother of David Copperfield's nurse. Dan'el was a Yarmouth fisherman. His nephew, Ham Peggotty, and his brother-in-law's child, "Little Em'ly," lived with him.

Peggotty, Em'ly. She was engaged to Ham Peggotty; but being fascinated with Steerforth she eloped. She was afterwards reclaimed, and emigrated to Australia.

Peggotty, Ham. Represented as the very beau ideal of an uneducated, simple-minded, honest, and warm-hearted fisherman. He was drowned in his attempt to rescue Steerforth from the sea.

Pelléas and Mélisande (*pĕl'ē-ăs*) (*mĕl'ĭ-sănd'*), **Maurice Maeterlinck.** An exquisite romantic tragedy. Mélisande, discovered in a forest, is married, unwillingly, to Goland in the gloomy castle in Allemonde. She and Goland's younger brother Pelléas fall in love. Goland murders Pelléas and wounds Mélisande. She dies after giving birth to a child.

Pendennis. Name of title and hero of a novel by Thackeray, published in 1849 and 1850,—the immediate successor of *Vanity Fair.* Literary life is described in the history of Pen, Arthur Pendennis, a hero of no very great worth.

Pendennis, Laura. Cousin of Arthur Pendennis. She has been regarded as one of the best of Thackeray's characters.

Pendennis, Major. A gentlemanly dandy, who fawns on his patrons for the sake of insinuating himself into their society. Uncle of Arthur.

Pendragon. A title conferred on several British chiefs in times of great danger, when they were invested with dictatorial power; thus Uther and Arthur were each appointed to the office to repel the Saxon invaders. The word means "chief of the kings."

Pennsylvania Farmer. A name given to John Dickinson, a citizen of Pennsylvania. In the year 1768 he published his *Letters from a Pennsylvania Farmer to the Inhabitants of the British Colonies.* These were republished in London, with a preface by Dr. Franklin, and were subsequently translated into French.

Penny-a-liner. A contributor to the local newspapers, but not on the staff. At one time these collectors of news used to be paid a penny a line on English newspapers. Applied to cheap literary work.

Penny Dreadfuls. Cheap sensational papers and books.

Penrod, Booth Tarkington. A story of the life and adventures of a twelve-year-old boy in a town of the Middle West. One of the most successful studies of the boy and his contacts with the adult and child worlds around him.

Pentateuch (*pĕn'tȧ-tūk*). A name given by Greek translators to the first five books of the Old Testament. The Pentateuch describes the origin and history of the Hebrew people up to the conquest of Canaan, and the theocracy founded among them. Genesis, Exodus, Leviticus, Numbers, and Deuteronomy—these form the Pentateuch, and, with Joshua, are called the Hexateuch.

Pepys' (*pēps*) **Diary.** A work which brought fame to Samuel Pepys, the author, was written in shorthand. It was deciphered and published in 1825. It extends over the nine years from 1660 to 1669, and is the gossipy chronicle of that gay and profligate time. We have no other book which gives so lifelike a picture of that period.

Père Goriot (*pâr' gō'ryō'*), "Father Goriot," **Balzac.** A novel. The tale is that of King Lear and his ungrateful daughters, brought down to the plane of a bourgeois grocer, but lacking the light of a Cordelia for comfort.

Peregrine Pickle. The hero and title of a novel by Smollett (1751). Peregrine Pickle is a savage, ungrateful spendthrift, fond of practical jokes, and suffering with evil temper the misfortunes brought on himself by his own willfulness.

Peronella. The subject of a fairy tale, represented as a pretty country lass, who, at the offer of a fairy, changes places with an old and decrepit queen, and receives the homage paid to rank and wealth, but afterward gladly resumes her beauty and rags.

Peter Pan. The hero and title of a children's drama by J. M. Barrie. Peter Pan runs away to Never-Never-Land to escape growing up. The play relates his adventures among his fairy playmates. Three of them, including Wendy Darling, return home with him for a time and meet with many adventures of a serio-comic nature.

Petruchio (*pē-trōō'chĭ-ō*). A gentleman of Verona, in Shakspere's *Taming of the Shrew.* A very honest fellow, who hardly speaks a word of truth, and succeeds in all his tricks. He acts his assumed character to the life, with untired animal spirits, and without a particle of ill humor.

Phædo (*fē'dō*). An ancient and well-known work by Plato, in which the doctrine of the immortality of the soul is most fully set forth. It is in the form of a dialogue which combines with the abstract philosophical discussion a graphic narrative of the last hours of Socrates, which, for pathos and dignity, is unsurpassed.

Phantom Rickshaw, The, Kipling. A ghost story of India. An English woman, who had been cruelly treated by her lover, returns and haunts him in Simla.

Philax. Fairy Tales, D'Aulnoy. Philax was cousin to the Princess Imis. The fay Pagan shut them up in the "Palace of Revenge," a palace containing every delight except the power of leaving it. In the course of a few years Imis and Philax longed as much for a separation as at one time they had wished for a union.

Philip. The Madness of Philip, Josephine Daskam Bacon. A representation of "the child of strong native impulses who has not yet yielded to the shaping force of education; the child, therefore, of originality, of vivacity, of humor, and of fascinating power of invention in the field of mischief."

Philippic. A word used to denote any discourse or declamation full of acrimonious invective. It derives its name from orations made by Demosthenes against Philip of Macedon, in which the orator bitterly attacked the king as the enemy of Greece.

Philistines (*fĭ-lĭs'tĭnz*). Meaning the ill-behaved and ignorant. German students gave meaning to the word by calling all outside the universities "Philisters." The idea goes back to the conflicts of Israelites and Philistines in Palestine. Matthew Arnold, in his *Culture and Anarchy,* applied the term Philistine to the middle class in England.

Philo. The Messiah, Klopstock. A Pharisee, one of the Jewish Sanhedrin, who hated Caiaphas, the high priest, for being a Sadducee. Philo made a vow that he would take no rest till Jesus was numbered with the dead. He commits suicide, and his soul is carried to hell by Abaddon, the angel of death.

Philtra. Faery Queen, Spenser. A lady of large fortune, betrothed to Bracidas; but, seeing the fortune of Amidas daily increasing, and that of Bracidas getting smaller, she attached herself to the more prosperous younger brother.

Phineas. Uncle Tom's Cabin, Mrs. Stowe. The Quaker, an "underground railroad" man who helped the slave family of George and Eliza to reach Canada, after Eliza had crossed the river on cakes of floating ice.

Phyllis. In Virgil's "Eclogues," the name of a rustic maiden. This name, also written Phillis, has been in common use as meaning any unsophisticated country girl.

Pickaninny. A young child. A West Indian negro word, derived from Spanish *pequeño.*

Pickwick, Mr. Samuel. The hero of the *Pickwick Papers,* by Charles Dickens. He is a simple-minded, benevolent old gentleman, who wears spectacles and short black gaiters. He founds a club, and travels with its members over England, each member being under his guardianship. They meet with many laughable adventures.

Pied Piper of Hamelin. Old German legend. Robert Browning, in his poem entitled "The Pied Piper," has given a metrical version. The legend recounts how a certain musician came into the town of Hamelin, in the county of Brunswick, and offered, for a sum of money, to rid the town of the rats by which it was infested. Having executed his task, and the promised reward having been withheld, he in revenge blew again his pipe, and drew the children of the town to a cavern in the side of a hill, which, upon their entrance, closed and shut them in forever.

Piers Plowman. The hero of a satirical poem of the 14th century. He falls asleep, like John Bunyan, on the Malvern Hills, and has different visions, which he describes, and in which he exposes the corruptions of society, the dissoluteness of the clergy, and the allurements to sin. The author is supposed to be Robert or William Langland, No other writings so faithfully reflect the popular feeling during the great social and religious movements of that century as the bitterly satirical poem, *The Vision of Piers Plowman.* In its allegory, the discontent of the common people with the course of affairs in church and state found a voice.

Pietro (*pyĕ'trō*). **The Ring and the Book, Browning.** The professed father of Pompilia, criminally assumed as his child to prevent certain property from passing to an heir not his own.

Pilgrim's Progress. Written by Bunyan in the form of a dream to allegorize the life of a Christian, from his conversion to his death. His doubts are giants, his sins a pack, his Bible a chart, his minister Evangelist, his conversion a flight from the City of Destruction, his struggle with besetting sins a fight with Apollyon, his death a toilsome passage over a deep stream, which flows between him and heaven.

Pillars of Hercules. In ancient geography, the two opposite promontories Calpe (Gibraltar) in Europe and Abyla in Africa, situated at the eastern extremity of the Strait of Gibraltar, sentinels, as it were, at the outlet from the Mediterranean into the unknown Atlantic.

Pilot, The. Title of a sea-story by Cooper, which was called the "first sea-novel of the English language." It was published in the year 1823 and was soon translated into Italian, German, and French. It is founded on the adventures of John Paul Jones.

Pinch, Tom. A character in Dickens's *Martin Chuzzlewit,* distinguished by his guilelessness, his oddity, and his exhaustless goodness of heart.

Pippa Passes. The title of a dramatic poem by Robert Browning. Pippa is a light-hearted peasant maiden, who resolves to enjoy her holiday. Various groups of persons overhear her as she passes by singing, and some of her stray words act with secret but sure influence for good.

Place in the Sun, A. A phrase used by the German emperor in 1901 with reference to the commercial concessions secured for Germany in China. It became the slogan of the Pan-German party, with the meaning of a larger share of the colonial and commercial opportunities of the world. Hitler called it "Lebensraum."

Platonic Love. Spiritual love between persons of opposite sexes. It is the friendship of man and woman, without mixture of what is usually called love. Plato strongly advocated this pure affection, and hence its distinctive name.

Playboy of the Western World, The, J. M. Synge. An extravagant, boisterous play of Irish peasant life. In a lonely public house, Christy Mahon, under questioning, confesses that he is a fugitive, because he has killed his tyrannical father with a spade. His hearers convince themselves and Christy that he is a hero. So inspired he makes love to Pegeen. But suddenly his old father appears, only a little the worse for the blow. Christy's fame is shattered, and Pegeen, enraged at her broken romance, leads the attack upon the fallen hero.

Pocket, Matthew. Great Expectations, Dickens. A real scholar, educated at Harrow, and an honor man at Cambridge; but, having married young, he had to take up the calling of "grinder" and literary fag for a living. Pip was placed in his care.

Pocket, Mrs. Daughter of a city knight, brought up to be an ornamental nonentity, helpless, shiftless, and useless. She was the mother of eight children, whom she allowed to "tumble up" as best they could, under the charge of her maid Flopson.

Pocket, Sarah. Sister of Matthew Pocket, a little, dry, old woman, with a small face that might have been made of walnut shell, and a large mouth.

Poet Laureate. A poet appointed by the English crown to compose odes and other verses in honor of grand state occasions. The name seems to have originated in the custom at the English universities of presenting a laurel wreath to a graduate, who was then called *laureatus.* The king's laureate, then, would be a graduated rhetorician, or poet, in the king's service. The early history of the laureateship is obscure, and statements conflicting. Chaucer and Spenser received royal pensions. They were unofficial laureates. The offices of Historiographer and Master of the Revels were united at times with that of Poet Laureate. The stipend of the office was formerly £100 a year, with a tierce of canary, but this latter emolument was commuted in Pye's time to an annual payment of £27. The present salary is equivalent to $360 a year. Formerly it was the duty of the laureate to write an ode on the birthday of the sovereign and on the occasion of a national victory, but this custom ceased with the death of James Pye. The appointment is now simply an official recognition of a poet as worthy to represent English letters. Ben Jonson was the first laureate to be formally appointed. He held the appointment at his death in 1637. William Davenant succeeded him. Later appointments have been as follows: John Dryden, 1670–1688; Thomas Shadwell, 1688–1692; Nahum Tate, 1692–1715; Nicholas Rowe, 1715–1718; Lawrence Eusden, 1718–1730; Colley Cibber, 1730–1757; William Whitehead, 1757–1785; Thomas Warton, 1785–1790; Henry James Pye, 1790–1813; Robert Southey, 1813–1843; William Wordsworth, 1843–1850; Alfred Tennyson, 1850–1892; Alfred Austin, 1896–1913; Robert Bridges, 1913-1930; John Masefield, 1930. The first real history of the office and its holders was issued from the Clarendon Press in 1922.

Poilu (*pwä'lü'*). The word means "hairy." As a noun, it was applied to the French soldiers in the World War, because of their bearded faces.

Polyglot (*pŏl'ĭ-glŏt*). The word means, in general, an assemblage of versions in different languages of the same work, but is almost exclusively applied to manifold versions of the Bible. Besides the Bible, many other works, or small pieces, have been published in polyglot. Of smaller pieces, the Lord's Prayer has been the favorite, of which many collections have been published since the 15th century. Of these, the most comprehensive, and the most valuable, is the well-known *Mithridates* of Adelung, which contains the Lord's Prayer in more than 400 languages.

Ponte Vecchio (*pŏn'tĕ vĕk'kyō*). A bridge in Florence, over the Arno; a picturesque structure with three wide arches, rebuilt in 1345. The roadway is bordered on both sides by quaint little shops, except over the middle arch, where there is an opening. Over the south row of shops is carried a gallery, built by Vascari, connecting the Pitti Palace with the Uffizi and the Palazzo Vecchio.

Poor Richard's Almanac. From 1732 to 1757 Benjamin Franklin issued in Philadelphia a yearly almanac, under the name of Richard Saunders, or "Poor Richard." The publication was popular throughout the colonies for its comments and sayings. These have been translated into all languages.

Popinjay. A butterfly man, a fop; so called from the popinjay or figure of a bird shot at for practice. The title is used by Scott in *Old Mortality*, by Shakspere in *Henry IV*, and by others.

Porterhouse Steak. The name is of American origin, said to be derived from "porterhouse," a kind of tavern, because the proprietor of such a house in New York made the cut popular. There is a story that Charles Dickens christened it because an innkeeper of the name of Porter served him such excellent steak at one town during his first American tour.

Portia. Merchant of Venice, Shakspere. A rich heiress whom Bassanio loved and who defended Antonio.

Potboilers. Articles written and pictures of small merit drawn or painted for the sake of earning daily bread.

Potiphar Papers. A series of brilliant satiric sketches of society written by George W. Curtis in the year 1852, and afterward collected in book form.

Prester John. The name given, in the middle ages, to a supposed Christian sovereign and priest of the interior of Asia, whose dominions were variously placed. He has been the subject of many legends and is mentioned by Shakspere in *Much Ado about Nothing.*

Pride and Prejudice, Jane Austen. A novel of domestic life. The plot turns upon the struggle of Elizabeth's love with her pride and the prejudice aroused in her by Darcy's rather proud consciousness of family position. Love triumphs in the end.

Primrose, Rev. Charles. Vicar of Wakefield, Goldsmith. A clergyman, rich in heavenly wisdom, but poor indeed in all worldly knowledge.

Primrose, George. Son of the vicar. He went to Amsterdam to teach the Dutch English, but never once called to mind that he himself must know something of Dutch before this could be done.

Primrose, Moses. Brother of George, noted for giving in barter a good horse for a gross of worthless green spectacles with copper rims.

Primrose, Mrs. Deborah. The doctor's wife, full of motherly vanity, and desirous to appear genteel. She could read without much spelling, and prided herself on her housewifery, especially on her gooseberry wine.

Primrose, Olivia. The eldest daughter of the doctor. Pretty, enthusiastic, a sort of Hebe in beauty. "She wished for many lovers," and eloped with Squire Thornhill.

Primrose, Sophia. The second daughter of Dr. Primrose. She was "soft, modest, and alluring."

Prince and the Pauper, The, Mark Twain. A humorous tale, exploiting the possibilities of an exchange of places between Prince Edward and a poor man.

Priscilla. Courtship of Miles Standish, Longfellow. A Puritan maiden who is wooed by Captain Standish through the mediation of his friend John Alden, who is in love with Priscilla. She prefers John Alden and marries him after the captain's supposed death. The captain, however, appears at the close of the wedding service, and the friends are reconciled.

Prospero. Tempest, Shakspere. Rightful duke of Milan, deposed by his brother. Exiled on a desert island, he practiced magic, and raised a tempest in which his brother was shipwrecked. Ultimately, Prospero "broke his wand," and his daughter married the son of the king of Naples.

Puck of Pook's Hill, Kipling. A delightful book of history stories. The children, Dan and Una, in the fields around their country home, meet Puck, "the oldest old thing in England." The little man tells them fascinating tales of Roman, Saxon, and Norman times, often calling up his friends, characters from early times, to talk to the children.

Pudd'nhead Wilson, Mark Twain. A tale of a little Missouri town of the middle 19th century. A son of a slave, almost pure white, substituted for the master's son, grows up in luxury, but displays peculiarly mean traits. He is, by means of finger prints, detected in a crime and punished. Wilson is the lawyer.

Punch. Name of a famous London comic weekly. Derived from the puppet-show character, Punch.

Punch and Judy. The name of a popular puppet show. Punch is shortened from the Italian "Pulcinella," the character in 17th century *commedia.* Judy, or Joan, was added later, probably from an English ballad of the 18th century. In the play, the hunchback Punch strangles his infant child, beats his wife Judy to death, throws a policeman into the street, and is finally carried off by the Devil. Punch's dog Toby is usually in the play.

Puss in Boots. The subject and title of a well-known nursery tale derived from a fairy story in the *Nights* of the Italian author Straparola, and Charles Perrault's *Contes des Fées.* The wonderful cat secures a princess and a fortune for his master, a poor young miller, whom he passes off as the rich marquis of Carabas.

Pyncheon. The name of an ancient but decayed family in Hawthorne's romance *The House of the Seven Gables.* There are: (1) Judge Pyncheon, a selfish, cunning, worldly man; (2) His cousin Clifford, a delicate, sensitive nature, reduced to childishness by long imprisonment and suffering; (3) Hepzibah, the latter's sister, an old maid who devotes herself to the care of Clifford; (4) A second cousin, Phœbe, a fresh, cheerful young girl, who restores the fallen fortunes of the family and removes the curse which rested on it.

Quasimodo (*kwăs'ĭ-mō'dō*). **Notre Dame de Paris, Hugo.** A misshapen dwarf, one of the prominent characters in the story. He is brought up in the cathedral of Notre Dame de Paris. One day he sees Esmeralda, who had been dancing in the cathedral close, set upon by a mob, and he conceals her for a time in the church. When, at length, the beautiful gypsy girl is gibbeted, Quasimodo disappears mysteriously, but a skeleton corresponding to the deformed figure is found after a time in a hole under the gibbet.

Quaver. The Virgin Unmasked, Fielding. A singing master, who says, "if it were not for singing masters, men and women might as well have been born dumb." He courts Lucy by promising to give her singing lessons.

Queen Labe (*lä'bā*). **Arabian Nights.** The queen of magic, ruler over the Enchanted City. Beder, prince of Persia, is connected with her in the tale. She transforms men into horses, mules, and other animals. Beder marries her, defeats her plots against him, but is himself turned into an owl for a time.

Quentin Durward, Scott. A historical romance of about 1470. The hero, Quentin Durward, a young Scottish guardsman in the service of Louis XI of France, after a series of adventures leading here and there in the monarch's maze of activities, wins the love of Countess Isabelle of Croye. When Liége is assaulted, Quentin and the countess, who has been put into his charge, escape on horseback. The countess publicly refuses to marry the duke of Orleans, to whom she has been promised, and ultimately marries the young Scotchman.

Quidnunkis. Title and name of hero in a fable found or written by Gay in 1726. This hero was a monkey which climbed higher than its neighbors and fell into a river. For a few moments the monkey race stood panic-struck, but the stream flowed on, the monkeys continued their gambols. The object of this fable is to show that no one is of sufficient importance to stop the general current of events or cause a gap in nature.

Quilp. Old Curiosity Shop, Dickens. A hideous dwarf, cunning, malicious, and a perfect master in tormenting. Of hard, forbidding features, with head and face large enough for a giant. He lived on Tower Hill, collected rents, advanced money to seamen, and kept a kind of wharf, containing rusty anchors, huge iron rings, piles of rotten wood, and sheets of old copper, calling himself a ship breaker. He was on the point of being arrested for felony, when he was drowned.

Quilp, Mrs. Wife of the dwarf, a young, obedient, and pretty little woman, treated like a dog by her husband, whom she loved but more greatly feared.

Quintessence, "the fifth essence." In the modern and general sense, an epithet applied to an extract which contains the most essential part of anything. The ancient Greeks said there are four elements or forms in which matter can exist: fire, or the imponderable form; air, or the gaseous form; water, or the liquid form; and earth, or the solid form. The Pythagoreans added a fifth, which they call "ether," more subtle and pure than fire, and possessed of an orbicular motion. This element, which flew upwards at creation, and out of which the stars were made, was called the "fifth essence"; quintessence, therefore, means the most subtle extract of a body that can be procured.

Quintus Fixlein. Title of a romance by Jean Paul Richter and the name of the principal character.

Quixote. See *Don Quixote.*

Quixote of the North. Charles XII of Sweden, sometimes called in derision the Madman, was also called the Quixote of the North.

Quixotic (*kwĭk-sŏt'ĭk*). Like Don Quixote, or one who has foolish and impractical schemes—a would-be reformer.

Quiz. A word of uncertain origin. It is said that Daly, the manager of a Dublin playhouse, laid a wager that a new word of no meaning should be the common talk and puzzle of the city in 24 hours. In consequence of this the letters *q u i z* were chalked by him on the walls of Dublin, with an effect that won the wager. But the word appears in literature some years before the date given for this episode.

Quodling, The Rev. Mr. Peveril of the Peak, Scott. Chaplain to the duke of Buckingham.

Quo Vadis? Sienkiewicz. Lygia, a Christian girl in a Roman household, who will not yield her virtue to Vinicius, is by him denounced as a Christian. She is condemned to the arena, but her attendant, Ursus, saves her from death on the horns of the bull. Later, she marries Vinicius, who has been converted by Paul and Peter.

Radigund. Faery Queen, Spenser. Queen of the fabled Amazons. Having been rejected by Bellodant "the Bold," she revenged herself by degrading all the men who fell into her power by dressing them like women, and giving them women's work.

Ramona. Name of heroine and title of romance by Helen Hunt Jackson. Ramona saw the American Indian followed by "civilization" while retreating slowly but surely toward his own extinction, and had herself a share in the tragedy. Ramona is considered the great romance of Indian life.

Rappaccini. Mosses from an Old Manse, Hawthorne. A doctor in whose garden grew strange plants whose juices and fragrance were poison. His daughter, nourished on these odors, became poisonous herself. Her lover found an antidote which she took, but the poison meant life and the antidote meant death to her.

Rasselas (*răs'ĕ-lăs*). An imaginary prince, hero of the romance by Dr. Johnson, bearing same title. According to the custom of his country, Abyssinia, he was confined in paradise, with the rest of the royal family. This paradise was in the valley of Amhara, surrounded by high mountains. It had only one entrance, a cavern concealed by woods and closed by iron gates. He escaped with his sister Nekayah and Imlac the poet, and wandered about to find what condition or rank of life was the most happy. After careful investigation, he found no lot without its drawbacks, and resolved to return to the "happy valley."

Raud the Strong. Tales of a Wayside Inn, H. W. Longfellow. The viking who worshiped the old gods and lived by fire and sword. King Olaf went against him, sailing from Drontheim to Salten Fiord.

Ravenswood. Bride of Lammermoor, Scott. The lord of Ravenswood, an old Scotch nobleman and a decayed royalist. His son Edgar falls in love with Lucy Ashton, daughter of Sir William Ashton, lord keeper of Scotland. The lovers plight their troth, but Lucy is compelled to marry Frank Hayston, laird of Bucklaw. The bride, in a fit of insanity, attempts to murder the bridegroom and dies. Bucklaw goes abroad. Colonel Ashton, seeing Edgar at the funeral of Lucy, arranges a hostile meeting; and Edgar, on his way to the place appointed, is lost in the quicksands. A prophecy, noted as a curse, hung over the family and was thus fulfilled.

Raymond. Jerusalem Delivered, Tasso. Raymond was known as the Nestor of the crusaders, slew Aladine, king of Jerusalem, and planted the Christian standard upon the tower of David.

Realism. In literature, realism is opposed to idealism and romanticism. Realism aims at depicting things as they actually appear in ordinary human experience. Hence the realistic writer will choose familiar subjects and will take pains to emphasize accuracy in details.

Rebecca. Ivanhoe, Scott. Daughter of Isaac the Jew, in love with Ivanhoe. Rebecca, her father, and Ivanhoe, as prisoners, are confined in Front de Bœuf's castle. Rebecca is taken to the turret chamber and left with the old sibyl, but when Brian de Bois Guilbert comes to her she spurns him with heroic disdain. Ivanhoe, who was suffering from wounds received in a tournament, is nursed by Rebecca. After escape and adventure, and being again prisoner, the Jewish maiden is condemned by the Grand Master to be tried for sorcery, and she demands a trial by combat. The demand is granted, and Brian de Bois Guilbert is appointed as the champion against her. Ivanhoe undertakes her defense, slays Brian, and Rebecca is set free. In contrast with this strong character, Rowena seems insignificant even when she becomes the bride of Ivanhoe. Scott is said to have named Rebecca from the beautiful Rebecca Gratz of Philadelphia, described to him by Washington Irving.

Rebecca of Sunnybrook Farm, Kate Douglas Wiggin. The pathetic and humorous experiences of an imaginative little girl who, on account of the poverty of her home, is sent to live with two maiden aunts. The story has been dramatized.

Recessional, The, Kipling. A poem written for the celebration of the 60th anniversary of Victoria's accession to the throne of England.

Red Cross Knight. The Red Cross Knight is St. George, the patron saint of England, and, in the obvious and general interpretation, typifies holiness, or the perfection of the spiritual man in religion. In Spenser's *Faery Queen* the task of slaying a dragon was assigned to him as the champion of Una.

Redgauntlet. One of the principal characters in Sir Walter Scott's novel of the same name, a political enthusiast and Jacobite, who scruples at no means of upholding the cause of the Pretender, and finally accompanies him into exile. His race bore a fatal mark resembling a horseshoe, which appeared on the face of Redgauntlet as he frowned when angry.

Red Riding Hood. This nursery tale is, with slight variations, common to Sweden, Germany, and France. In Charles Perrault's *Contes des Fées* it is called "Le Petit Chaperon Rouge."

Regent Street. One of the principal streets of the West End of London, extending from Portland Place to Waterloo Place.

Representative Men, R. W. Emerson. A series of essays on the characters of certain great men, in which Emerson embodied his philosophy of manhood. The topics are: (1) Plato, the Philosopher; (2) Swedenborg, the Mystic; (3) Montaigne, the Skeptic; (4) Shakspere, the Poet; (5) Napoleon, the Man of the World; (6) Goethe, the Writer. The mental portraits sketched under these six heads give us Emerson himself, so far as he is capable of being formulated at all.

Republic, The, Plato. This work, in the form of a dialogue, is usually regarded as the finest product of Plato's genius. It is ostensibly an inquiry into the nature of justice, but actually sets forth, in a lucid and convincing form, Plato's views on the ideal state, education, and morality. It contains analyses of, and searching comments on, the major political and social problems connected with democracy and other forms of government. In the broad sweep of its argument, it undertakes to give a systematic answer to the fundamental questions of psychology, economics, science, religion, and philosophy. Its literary form and its intellectual grasp combine to make it one of the enduring masterpieces of the world's literature.

Return of Peter Grimm, The, David Belasco. A play made famous by David Warfield in the part of Peter. Peter, an old nurseryman, makes, in sport, an agreement with his Scotch doctor that whichever one dies first will try to communicate with the other. Peter has arranged the marriage of his niece and his grandson Frederick, who turns out to be a cheat and scapegrace. To correct this fleshly blunder, Peter "returns." He succeeds in "getting his message over" through the little illegitimate son of Frederick, and takes the little fellow "back with him."

Reveries of a Bachelor. Name of a writing by D. G. Mitchell. A collection of sketches of life and character, painted in such a dreamlike, delicate manner as to make the reader lose for the time being the full consciousness of his own reality.

Reynard (*rā'nård*) **the Fox.** The hero in the animal epics, celebrated *fabliaux* of the middle ages, belonging to the series of poems in which "beasts" are the speakers and actors. The "beast fable" goes back to the remotest antiquity, and is a common inheritance of the Aryan or Indo-Germanic races. This story of Reynard the Fox, certainly known as early as the 12th century, is the great creation of the people of the Netherlands, northern France, and western Germany. Its source was Flanders, where, apparently, the beasts were named. Few contributions to it were made in England; but Odo of Cheriton made use of the stories, and an English *fabliau*, "The Fox and the Wolf," belongs to the Reynard family and is the best example of comic satire before Chaucer. Reynard means "strong in counsel." According to many authorities, this prose poem, in its later form, is a satire on the state of Germany in the middle ages. Reynard typifies the Church; his uncle, Isengrin the Wolf, typifies the baronial element; and Nobel the Lion, the regal. However that may be, in the real fable, Reynard the Fox has a constant impulse to deceive and victimize everybody, whether friend or foe, but especially Isengrin; and, though the latter frequently reduces him to the greatest straits, he generally gets the better of it in the end.

Rhapsody. Means songs strung together. The term was originally applied to the books of the *Iliad* and *Odyssey*, which at one time were in fragments. Certain bards collected a number of the fragments, enough to make a connected "ballad," and sang them as our minstrels sang the deeds of famous heroes.

Rhoda Fleming. The heroine of George Meredith's novel of this name. Of a proud nature, she sets out to right the wrong done to her sister Dahlia, who has fled from home. At last she finds she has really destroyed her sister's last chance of happiness. Humbled and chastened, she repents of her obstinacy. In the end she marries her deserving lover, Robert Armstrong.

Richelieu, Bulwer-Lytton. The action of the play hinges upon the attempt of certain courtiers, among them the duke of Orleans and the count of Baradas, to displace the old cardinal. But their plots are revealed to Richelieu by Marion de Lorme, and he crushes them successfully. The pretty love story of Julie, Richelieu's ward, is involved in the main plot.

Riders to the Sea, J. M. Synge. A one-act tragedy of peasant life in the Aran islands. Maurya, who already has lost in the sea five of her sons, entreats the last, Bartley, not to go to the boat with his horses for the Connemara fair. He persists in going, and he too is lost. The mother's revolt turns to utter resignation. "There isn't anything more the sea can do to me," she says.

Rights of Man, Thomas Paine. The title of this work was suggested by the *Declaration of the Rights of Man* issued by the French National Assembly. It was a reply to Edmund Burke's *Reflections on the French Revolution.* In it Paine vigorously defended the French.

Rigolette. The name of a female character in Eugène Sue's *Mysteries of Paris.* It has acquired a proverbial currency, and is used as a synonym of "grisette," or shop-girl.

Rimmon, The House of. A biblical play by Henry van Dyke. The story of the Hebrew slave girl Ruahmah in the house of Naaman the Syrian, who persuades her master to go to the prophet in Israel for healing.

Rinaldo (*rē-näl'dō*). A character in Tasso's *Jerusalem Delivered.* He belonged to the army of the Christians. He was the son of Bertoldo and Sophia, and nephew of Guelpho, but was brought up by Matilda. The name Rinaldo is also found in Boiardo's *Orlando Innamorato,* in Ariosto's *Orlando Furioso,* and in other romantic tales of Italy and France. He was one of Charlemagne's paladins, and cousin to Orlando. Having killed Charlemagne's nephew Berthelot, he was banished and outlawed. After various adventures and disasters, he went to the Holy Land, and, on his return, succeeded in making peace with the emperor.

Ring and the Book, The. An epic by Robert Browning. It is founded on Italian history. Guido Franceschini, a Florentine count of shattered fortune, married Pompilia, thinking her to be an heiress. Finding this a mistake the count treated Pompilia so brutally that she left him, under the protection of Caponsacchi, a young priest. Pompilia sued for a divorce, but, pending the suit, gave birth to a son. The count murdered Pompilia, and Pietro and Violante, her supposed parents, but, being taken red-handed, was brought to trial, found guilty, and executed.

Rip Van Winkle. Sketch Book, Irving. An indolent, good-natured fellow, living in a village on the Hudson. While shooting among the Catskill mountains he meets with a stranger whom he helps in carrying a keg over rocks and cliffs; with him he joins a party who are silently rolling ninepins. Rip Van Winkle drinks deeply of the liquor they furnish, and falls into a sleep which lasts twenty years, during which the Revolutionary War takes place. After awaking, Rip returns to the village, finds himself almost forgotten, and makes friends with the new generation. The name of the great actor, Joseph Jefferson, became so identified with this character, in the dramatic version of the story, that to the English-speaking world he was Rip Van Winkle.

Rise of Silas Lapham, The, Howells. The story of the business and social fortunes of a wealthy paint manufacturer and his family in Boston in the middle of the 19th century. Silas, a coarse, crowding man, already rich when the story opens, loses his fortune, but in his adversity he rises in moral power.

Rivals, The, R. B. Sheridan. A comedy. Miss Lydia Languish, niece of Mrs. Malaprop, has two suitors, Bob Acres, a young country man, and Ensign Beverley, the latter of whom she loves and hopes to elope with. Meanwhile Sir Anthony Absolute and Mrs. Malaprop arrange that she shall marry Captain Absolute, son of Sir Anthony. Sir Lucius O'Trigger sets Bob on to challenge Beverley. When they meet for the duel, and Bob finds Beverley to be Captain Absolute and his best friend, he refuses to fight. Lydia, though deprived of the romantic elopement, accepts the captain.

Roast Pig, A Dissertation on, Charles Lamb. In *Essays of Elia.* Ho-ti, a careless Chinese swineherd, one day allowed the pigsty to burn. Desperately searching in the smoking ruins, he burned his fingers in the charred remains of a pig. But, on putting them involuntarily to his mouth, he found clinging to them some bits of meat of a most enticing flavor, "crackling." This discovery led to the burning of many pigsties, until the further discovery that the toothsome morsel, roast pig, could be produced by less wasteful means.

Robert the Devil. The hero of an old French metrical romance of the 13th century, the same as Robert, first duke of Normandy, who became an early object of legendary scandal. Having been given over to the Devil before birth, he ran a career of cruelties and crimes unparalleled until he was miraculously reclaimed, did penance, became a shining light, and married the emperor's daughter. In the 14th century the romance was turned into prose, and of the prose story two translations were made into English. There was also a miracle play on the same subject. The opera "Robert le Diable" was composed by Meyerbeer, in 1826.

Robin Goodfellow. A domestic spirit. He is sometimes called Puck, son of Oberon. He attends the English fairy court; he is full of tricks and fond of practical jokes. He is also considered the same as Lob-lie-by-the-fire, in some tales. His character and achievements are recorded in the well-known ballad beginning "From Oberon in Fairyland."

Robin Hood. A famous English outlaw whose exploits are the subjects of many ballads, but of whose actual existence little or no evidence can be discovered. Various periods, ranging from the time of Richard I to near the end of the reign of Edward II, have been assigned as the age in which he lived. He is usually described as a yeoman, and his chief residence is said to have been the forest of Sherwood, in Nottinghamshire. Of his followers, the most noted are: Little John; his chaplain, Friar Tuck; and his companion, Maid Marian. The popular legends extol his personal courage and generosity, and his skill in archery. Scott introduces Robin Hood in two novels, *Ivanhoe* and *The Talisman*. In the former he first appears at the tournament as Locksley the archer. Robin Hood's adventures are the theme of an opera by De Koven, "Robin Hood."

Robinson Crusoe. A tale by Daniel Defoe. Robinson Crusoe went to sea, was wrecked, lived on an uninhabited island of the tropics, and relieved the weariness of life by numberless contrivances. At length he met a young Indian, whom he saved from death. He called him his "man Friday," and made him his companion and servant. This story has been translated into more languages than any other English book.

Rob Roy. The title and hero of a novel by Sir Walter Scott. It signifies "Rob the Red," and was the sobriquet of a famous Scottish outlaw, Robert MacGregor, the chief of the clan MacGregor.

Roderick Dhu. Lady of the Lake, Scott. An outlaw and chief of a band of Scots who resolved to win back what had been lost to the Saxons. In connection with Red Murdock he sought the life of the Saxon, Fitz-James.

Roderick Random. The Adventures of Roderick Random, Tobias Smollett. Random, hero of the novel, is a reckless, mischievous, thankless young Scot who, apprenticed to an apothecary, goes to sea as surgeon's mate. His adventures run the gamut of the sea and of English town and country life. Hugh Strap, his devoted attendant, he treats heartlessly. Finally, he marries Narcissa, a wife much too good for him.

Roderigo (*rŏd'ĕr-ē'gō*). In Shakspere's *Othello*, a Venetian in love with Desdemona. He, when the lady eloped with Othello, hated the "noble Moor."

Roger Drake. Name of hero and title of novel by H. K. Webster. "Captain of Industry" is the title added to the name of the hero, who is interested in the working of a copper mine, the founding of a trust, the change from the old-fashioned trust to the simple plan of one monster corporation, and the deadly business fight for supremacy found in modern industrial struggles.

Roland. The hero of one of the most ancient and popular epics of early French or Frankish literature was, according to tradition, the favorite nephew and captain of the emperor Charlemagne. In Italian romance he is called Orlando. He was slain in the valley of Roncesvalles as he was leading the rear of the army from Spain to France. The oldest version of the "Song of Roland," forming part of the *chansons de gestes*, which treat of the achievements of Charlemagne and his paladins, belongs to the 11th century. Throughout the middle ages, the "Song of Roland" was the most popular of the many heroic poems. William of Normandy, when on his way to conquer England, had it sung at the head of the troops, to encourage them on their march. At the present day, the traditionary memory of the heroic paladin is still held in honor by the hardy mountaineers of the Pyrenees, among whose dangerous defiles the scene of his exploits and death is laid. Roland is the hero of Théroulde's *Chanson de Roland*; of Turpin's *Chrŏnique*; of Boiardo's *Orlando Innamorato*; of Ariosto's *Orlando Furioso*.

Romance of the Rose. A poetical allegory, begun by Guillaume de Lorris in the latter part of the 13th century and continued by Jean de Meung in the first half of the 14th century. The poet dreams that Dame Idleness conducts him to the palace of Pleasure, where he meets many adventures among the attendant maidens, Youth, Joy, Courtesy, and others, by whom he is conducted to a bed of roses. He singles out one, when an arrow from Love's bow stretches him fainting on the ground. Fear, Slander, and Jealousy are afterward introduced. The part written by De Lorris is the greatest embodiment of French romance; De Meung's continuation is a rambling allegorical satire especially against women. The whole work had a profound influence on early English poetry, especially that of Gower and Chaucer.

Romances. The French troubadours composed romances and sang them at the courts of the Norman kings. Richard I was himself a troubadour. The subjects of the romances were generally the deeds of Charlemagne and his knights, or of King Arthur and his knights. A little later, tales of the crusaders became popular. Old tales were retold, and the incidents were transferred to Eastern lands. From the time of Edward II many of these tales were translated into English.

Romanticism. The name of both a spirit and a method in art and literature. As contrasted to *classicism*, it means the introduction of the artist's hopes and ideals, his personality, into his work, and the attempt to suggest more than can be definitely expressed. The ideal of the classicist is harmonious objective beauty. As contrasted to *realism*, romanticism means the treatment of distant, strange themes and scenes, while realism handles the near and familiar.

Romeo. In Shakspere's tragedy *Romeo and Juliet*, a son of Montague, in love with Juliet, the daughter of Capulet, who was the head of a noble house of Verona, in feudal enmity with the house of Montague.

Romeo and Juliet, Shakspere. Romeo, of the house of Montague, and Juliet, of the house of Capulet in Verona, are lovers. But between their families is a deadly feud. Juliet takes a sleeping draft, that she may be borne to the family tomb, later released and married to Romeo by Friar Lawrence. Romeo, coming to keep the appointment, sees what he thinks is Juliet's dead body. He at once kills himself, and Juliet, awaking, follows his example. Over the dead bodies of their children, the two families are reconciled.

Rosetta Stone. A stone found at Rosetta in the delta of the Nile. It contains equivalent inscriptions in hieroglyphics and in Greek letters. The meaning of the Greek text being known, the hieroglyphics were translated.

Rotten Row. A fashionable promenade in London. The origin of the name is found in its older form, *rottan raw* or lane of the rats, from the rodents which formerly infested the unsavory banks of the near-by Serpentine canal.

Round Table, The. Le Morte D'Arthur, Malory. A table made by Merlin for Uther pendragon. Uther gave it to King Leodegraunce of Camelyard, and when Arthur married Guinevere, the daughter of Leodegraunce, he received the table with a hundred knights as a wedding present. The table would seat 150 knights, and each seat was appropriated. What is usually meant by Arthur's Round Table is a smaller one for the accommodation of twelve favorite knights. King Arthur instituted an order of knighthood called "the knights of the Round Table," the chief of whom were Sir Lancelot, Sir Tristram, and Sir Lamerock or Lamorake. The "siege perilous" was reserved for Sir Galahad, the son of Sir Lancelot by Elaine.

Roussillon, Alice. The heroine of the romance, *Alice of Old Vincennes*, by Maurice Thompson. Her guardian was Gaspard Roussillon, a successful trader with the Indians. "Eat frogs and save your scalps" was the plan of the Latin Creoles. "Papa Roussillon" was a frog eater and the ruling spirit in his little village. The English and their Indian allies arranged their attack on the fort at Vincennes, and the American flag was in danger. Alice, with the help of a crippled boy, Jean, stole the flag. No search or questioning could reveal the whereabouts of either flag or thief. At the end of the siege it was produced, much to the amazement of General Hamilton. Alice forgot her flag for a moment in the appearance of her lover, Beverly, whom she had mourned as dead, but Jean raised it on a staff from which the stars and stripes still floats.

Ruach (*rōō'äk*). **Pantagruel, Rabelais.** The isle of winds, visited by Pantagruel and his companions. The people of this island live on wind, such as flattery, promises, and hope. The poorer sort are very ill-fed, but the great are stuffed with huge mill-drafts of the same unsubstantial puffs.

Rubaiyat (*rōō-bī-yät'*). The word means "quatrains." Omar Khayyam, a famous Persian astronomer of the 11th century, wrote, in this four-line stanza form, his reflections upon life. Edward Fitzgerald translated and adapted about a hundred of the many quatrains attributed to Omar. The later editions of this work differ in many points from the first edition of 1859.

Rübezahl (*rü'bĕ-tsäl'*). The name of a famous spirit of the Riesen-Gebirge in Germany, corresponding to the Puck of England. He is celebrated in innumerable sagas, ballads, and tales, under the various forms of a miner, hunter, monk, dwarf, giant, etc. He is said to aid the poor and oppressed, and to show benighted wanderers their road, but to wage incessant war with the proud and wicked.

Rubric. From the Latin *ruber*, meaning "red." A portion of the type in a book distinguished by being printed in red ink, or, nowadays, by a type-face different from the rest of the print. The use of the rubric arose in the custom of old copyists of making the first letter of a new passage or paragraph red. The usage was extended to whole sentences, and it persists today in prayer books and other books of religious service.

Rudge. Barnaby Rudge, Dickens. Barnaby, a half-witted lad, with pale face, red hair, and protruding eyes, dressed in tawdry finery including peacock feathers in his hat, is the hero of the novel. His inseparable companion is a raven. Barnaby joined the Gordon rioters for the proud pleasure of carrying a flag and wearing a blue bow. He was arrested and lodged in Newgate, whence he made his escape, with other prisoners, when the jail was burned. But both he and his father were recaptured, brought to trial, and condemned to death. By the influence of Gabriel Varden, the locksmith, the poor half-witted lad was reprieved. Mr. Rudge, the father of Barnaby, was supposed to have been murdered the same night as Mr. Haredale, to whom he was steward. Rudge himself was the murderer both of Mr. Haredale and also of his faithful servant, to whom the crime was attributed. After the murder, he was seen by many, haunting the locality, and was supposed to be a ghost. He joined the Gordon rioters. Mrs. Mary Rudge, mother of Barnaby, was very like him, "but where in his face there was wildness and vacancy, in hers there was the patient composure of sorrow."

Ruggiero (*rōōd-jä'rō*). **Orlando Furioso, Ariosto.** A young Saracen knight born of Christian parents, who falls in love with Bradamante, a Christian Amazon, and sister to Rinaldo. After numerous adventures and crosses, they marry and found the house of Este. Ruggiero is noted for the possession of a hippogriff, or winged horse, and also a veiled shield, the dazzling splendor of which when suddenly disclosed, struck with blindness and astonishment all eyes that beheld it.

Rumpelstilzchen. Old German Tales. According to Grimm, this name is a compound, but the spirit represented is one familiar to all German children. The original story tells of him as a dwarf who spun straw into gold for a certain miller's daughter. He has since done favors for many people and paid visits known only by the results of his helpfulness.

Runes. The earliest alphabet in use among the nations of northern Europe The exact period of their origin is not known. They are found engraved on rocks, crosses, monumental stones, coins, medals, rings, brooches, and the hilts and blades of swords. There is no reason to believe that they were at any time in the familiar use in which we find the characters of a written language in modern times, nor have we any traces of their being used in books or on parchment.

Rupert, Knight. Formerly in the villages of northern Germany, a personage clad in high buskins, white robe, mask, and enormous wig, who at Christmas time distributes presents to the children. Like St. Nicholas, he keeps watch over naughty children. The horseman in the May pageant is in some parts of Germany called Ruprecht, or Rupert.

Rustam. Persian Romances. He is the chief of the Persian mythical heroes, son of Zal, king of India, and descendant of Benjamin, the beloved son of Jacob. He delivered King Caicaus from prison, but afterwards fell into disgrace because he refused to embrace the religious system of Zoroaster. Caicaus sent his son Asfendiar to convert him, and, as persuasion availed nothing, single combat was resorted to. The fight lasted two days, and then Rustam discovered that Asfendiar bore a "charmed life." The valor of these two heroes is proverbial, and the Persian romances are full of their deeds. *Sohrab and Rustum* is the title of a poetical romance by Matthew Arnold.

Ruydera. Don Quixote, Cervantes. A duenna who had seven daughters and two nieces. They were imprisoned for 500 years in a cavern in Spain. Their ceaseless weeping stirred the compassion of Merlin, who converted them into lakes in the same province.

Sabrina. English legend. The daughter of King Locrine and his mistress Estrildis. Gwendolen, the queen, jealous, after the death of Locrine in war, caused Sabrina and Estrildis to be thrown into a river, called since, Sabrina or Severn. Sabrina became the nymph of the stream. Refer to Milton's *Comus* and Fletcher's *Faithful Shepherdess*.

Sacripant, King. (1) King of Circassia, and a lover of Angelica, in Boiardo and Ariosto. (2) A personage introduced by Alessandro Tassoni, the Italian poet, in his mock-heroic poem entitled the "Rape of the Bucket," represented as false, brave, noisy, and hectoring. The name is quoted as a synonym for vanity and braggart courage.

Sagas. Scandinavian myths or hero stories, in prose or poetry. "Saga" is also the name of a goddess of history in Norse mythology. The name given to those ancient traditions which form the substance of the history and mythology of the Scandinavian races; the language in which they are written is supposed to be the old Icelandic. In the *Edda* there are numerous sagas. As our Bible contains the history of the Jews, religious songs, moral proverbs, and religious stories, so the *Edda* contained the history of Norway, religious songs, a book of proverbs, and numerous stories. The original or *Elder Edda* was compiled in the 9th century in Iceland. It contains 28 parts or books, all of which are in verse. In the 12th century, Snorre Sturleson of Iceland abridged, rearranged, and reduced this *Edda* to prose, and his work was called *The Younger Edda*. In this we find parts of the famous *Nibelungenlied*. Besides the sagas contained in the *Eddas*, there are numerous others, and the whole saga literature makes over 200 volumes. Among them are the *Volsung Saga*, a collection of lays about the early Teutonic heroes. The *Saga of St. Olaf* is the history of this Norwegian king. *Frithjof's Saga* contains the life and adventures of Frithjof of Iceland. Snorre Sturleson, at the close of the 12th century, made the second great collection of chronicles in verse, called the *Heimskringla*, or "World-Circuit," *Saga*.

St. Leon. The hero and title of a novel by William Godwin. St. Leon obtains the elixir of life and the secret of the transmutation of metals, acquisitions which only bring him misfortunes and misery.

St. Nicholas. The patron saint of boys and girls, of the poor and the weak, and of mariners. He is said to have been bishop of Myra, and to have died in 345 or 352. The young were universally taught to revere him, and the popular fiction which represents him as the bearer of presents to children on Christmas Eve is well known. His name, "Santa Claus" or Klaus, is of Dutch origin

St. Patrick's Purgatory. The subject and locality of a legend long famous throughout Europe. The scene is laid in Ireland, upon an islet in Lough Derg. The punishments undergone here are analogous to those described by Dante in his *Divina Commedia*. The story was made the subject of a romance in the 14th century; and, in Spain, in the 17th century, it was dramatized by Calderón.

St. Swithin. Rain on St. Swithin's day, July 15, is said to entail rain for 40 days thereafter. St. Swithin was the bishop of Winchester, who died in 862. He requested burial in the churchyard. When he was canonized, the monks thought to honor him by removing his body into the church. The ceremony was set for July 15 but was prevented by rain for 40 days. The saint was believed thus to show disapproval of the project, and it was abandoned.

Sakuntala (*sȧ-kōōn'tȧ-lä*). Drama by Kalidasa, famous dramatist of India. The heroine, Sakuntala, left at birth in the forest, is fed by the birds until the king, Dushyanta, finds her and marries her. A ring he had given her she loses while on her way to join him. When, without this ring, the king refuses to acknowledge her, she is compelled to return to the forest. A fisherman who had found the ring is brought before the king on a charge of theft. Recognizing the ring, Dushyanta sends for Sakuntala and proclaims her his queen.

Sally in Our Alley. This popular song was written by Henry Carey in 1734. The author tells of getting the material for the poem by watching a shoemaker's apprentice and his sweetheart on a holiday.

Salmagundi. The name of a periodical started by Washington Irving, his brother, and James K. Paulding, in the year 1807. The object of the paper was the same as that of the *Spectator*, to "correct the town." The publishers became tired of their venture before their subscribers did, and only twenty-two numbers were issued. The political pieces were full of humor, but were not in support of any party. The wit and satire were connected with things local and would not be thoroughly understood or appreciated now. The writers touched upon the follies of fashionable life as well as other follies of their day.

Salt-Box House. Title of book by J. D. Shelton and name given to an imaginary house supposed to stand in a Connecticut hill town more than a century ago. The life of the family to whom the house belonged is followed for three generations. The people, like most families of the same social station, have no sympathy with the war for colonial independence. They have little to do with political life, but in their everyday concerns, work and play, school and church, love and marriage, sickness and death, with their old-time customs, traditions, and habits of thought, they are very interesting. Miss Mary, the last mistress of the Salt-Box House, is a most attractive old maid.

Salt River. American political slang. An imaginary river, up which defeated political parties are supposed to be sent to oblivion. The name and application said to have originated in connection with a river of Kentucky where, for one reason or another, travelers were lost.

Sambo. This term and the name Cuffey used to designate the negro race. Both were used by Mrs. Stowe in her stories.

Samian (*sā'mĭ-ăn*) **Letter, The.** The letter Y used by Pythagoras as an emblem of the paths of virtue and of vice.

Samian Sage. Pythagoras, said to have been born at Samos.

Samian Wine. The cup of despair and regret over the decay of Greece in Byron's *Isles of Greece.*

Sampson, Dominie. Guy Mannering, Scott. A village schoolmaster and scholar, poor as a church mouse, and modest as a girl. He cites Latin like a "porcus literarum," and exclaims "Prodigious!" He has fallen to the leeward in the voyage of life. He is no uncommon personage in a country where a certain portion of learning is easily attained by those who are willing to suffer hunger and thirst in exchange for acquiring Greek and Latin.

Samson Agonistes (*săm'sŭn ăg'ō-nĭs'tēz*). The principal character in Milton's sacred drama *Samson Agonistes* or *Samson the Combatant.* Samson, blind and bound, triumphs over his enemies. As in the Bible story, he grasps two of the supporting pillars and perishes in the general ruin.

Sancho Panza (*săng'kō păn'zȧ*). The esquire and counterpart of Don Quixote in Cervantes' famous novel. He has much shrewdness in practical matters and a store of proverbial wisdom. He rode upon an ass which he dearly loved, and was noted for his proverbs.

Sandals of Theramenes (*thĕ-răm'ĕ-nēz*). Theramenes, one of the Athenian oligarchy, was nicknamed "the trimmer," from the name of a sandal or boot which might be worn on either foot, because no dependence could be placed on him. The proverb, "He walks in the sandals of Theramenes," is applied to those who speak fairly but do the things that promise to profit themselves.

Sandford and Merton. Harry Sandford and Tommy Merton, the two heroes of Thomas Day's once popular tale for the young, the *History of Sandford and Merton* (1783–1789).

Sanskrit. The ancient language of India, now extinct, from which most of the languages there spoken are derived. It belongs to the Aryan or Indo-European group of tongues. It was declared by Sir William Jones to be more perfect than the Greek, more copious than the Latin, and more refined than either. The earliest existing work is the *Vedas.* These and the *Puranas* are religious writings; but there are also epic poems, dramas, and philosophical compositions.

Santa Claus. In fable he was first known as patron saint of children. The vigil of his feast is still held in some places, but for the most part his name is now associated with Christmastide. The old custom used to be for some one, on December 5th, to assume the costume of a bishop and distribute small gifts to "good children." See *St. Nicholas.*

Santiago (*săn-te-ä'gō*). The war cry of Spain; adopted because St. James (Sant Iago) rendered, according to tradition, signal service to a Christian king of Spain in a battle against the Moors.

Satan. Hebrew, "the adversary." One of the names of the Devil, and that by which in the Bible, in poetry, and in popular legends, he is often designated. Those medieval writers who reckoned nine kinds of demons, placed Satan at the head of the fifth rank, which consisted of cozeners, as magicians and witches. Milton represents him as the monarch of hell. His chief lords are Beelzebub, Moloch, Chemosh, Tammuz, Dagon, Rimmon, and Belial. His standard bearer is Azazel.

Satyrane. Faery Queen, Spenser. A noble knight who delivered Una from the fauns and satyrs. The meaning seems to be that Truth, driven from the towns and cities, took refuge in caves and dens, where for a time she lay concealed. At length Sir Satyrane rescues Una from bondage; no sooner is she free than she falls in with Archimago, who poses as the Red Cross Knight, but whose falsehood is later exposed.

Saunders, Clerk. The hero of a well-known Scottish ballad.

Sawney. A sportive designation applied by the English to the Scotch. It is a corruption of "Sandie," the Scottish abbreviation of "Alexander."

Sawyer, Bob. Pickwick Papers, Dickens. A drinking young doctor who tries to establish a practice at Bristol, but without success. Sam Weller calls him "Mr. Sawbones."

Scalds or **Skalds.** Court poets and chroniclers of the ancient Scandinavians. They resided at court, were attached to the royal suite, and attended the king in all his wars. These bards celebrated in song the gods, the kings of Norway, and national heroes. Few complete scaldic poems have survived, but a multitude of fragments exist.

Scarecrow, The, Percy Mackaye. A New England phantasy. Farce. Goody Rickby, reputed a witch, at her forge making a scarecrow for her cornfield, is persuaded by her "familiar," Dickon, to fashion a figure of cornstalks and pumpkin, animate it with a brimstone pipe, and send it as Lord Ravensbane to ask for the hand of Rachel, niece of Justice Gilead Merton. Dickon tells Merton that this young "lord" is really his own son by Goody Rickby, whom he has thought dead. Rachel, who is betrothed to young Squire Talbot, falls in love with the scarecrow "lord." The scarecrow, through love of her, gradually wins enough manhood to break his pipe, thus giving up life and leaving Rachel to Richard. Goody Rickby disappears, but she has had revenge on Justice Merton.

Scarlet Letter, The. Title of a romance by Nathaniel Hawthorne. The heroine, Hester Prynne, was condemned to wear conspicuously the letter "A" in scarlet, token of her sin as mother of her child, Pearl, whose father was not known. She was first exposed in disgrace on a raised scaffold, then served a term in prison, and afterward gained a moderate support for herself and child by embroidering. She refused to reveal the name of the father, although she might then be allowed to lay aside the letter. He was always near, held an important position, and lived a life of wearing remorse. After his death Hester Prynne took her child to another country, but returned to spend her old age in seclusion and comfort in the same place that had witnessed her punishment. She always bore herself proudly but not defiantly and brought to herself such love and respect that the scarlet letter became a badge of honor. Roger Chillingworth, Hester's husband, appeared as a learned foreign physician, visited her in prison, but promised not to reveal his relation to her, and devoted his life to learning her secret. The characters in the story are intense and the analysis of motives subtle.

Schahriah. Arabian Nights. The sultan of Persia. His reign was a despotism and his decrees absolute.

Scheherazade (*shĕ-hä'rȧ-zä'dĕ*). **Arabian Nights.** The fabled relater of the stories in these "Entertainments." Among other decrees the sultan had decided upon a new wife for every day. Tradition or fable tells that Scheherazade, wishing to free Persia of this disgrace, requested to be made the sultan's wife. She was young and beautiful, of great courage and ready wit, had an excellent memory, knew history, was poet, musician, and dancer. Scheherazade obtained permission for her younger sister, Dinarzade, to sleep in the same chamber, and instructed her to say, "Sister, relate to me one of those stories." Scheherazade then, under pretense of speaking to her sister, told the sultan a story, but always contrived to break off before the story was finished. The sultan, in order to hear the end of the story, spared her life till the next night. This went on for a thousand and one nights, when the sultan's resentment was worn out, and his admiration of his sultana was so great that he revoked his decree.

Schlemihl, Peter. The title of a little work by Chamisso (1781–1838), and the name of its hero, a man who sells his shadow to an old man in gray (the Devil) who meets him just after he has been disappointed in an application for assistance to a nobleman. The name has become a byword for any poor, silly, and unfortunate fellow.

Scholar-Gipsy. The subject of one of Matthew Arnold's greatest poems.

Scotland Yard. A short street in London, near Trafalgar Square. Here formerly were the headquarters of the metropolitan police, now removed to New Scotland Yard on the Thames embankment, near Westminster bridge. The detectives are known as Scotland Yard men. Often mentioned in the detective stories of Conan Doyle and others.

Scourge of God. Attila, king of the Huns. A. P. Stanley says the term was first applied to Attila in the Hungarian Chronicles. It is found in a legend belonging to the 8th or 9th century.

Scrap of Paper, A. A phrase used by the German chancellor, von Bethmann-Hollweg, with reference to England's entry into the World War in 1914. He is quoted as saying that England was going to war for Belgian neutrality, "just for a scrap of paper." But his phrase was widely understood as expressing the German attitude toward the Belgian treaty and hence toward all treaties.

Scrooge, Ebenezer. Christmas Carol, Dickens. The prominent character, made partner, executor, and heir of old Jacob Marley, stockbroker. When first introduced, he is a grasping, covetous old man, loving no one and by none beloved. One Christmas, Ebenezer Scrooge sees three ghosts: The Ghost of Christmas Past; the Ghost of Christmas Present; and the Ghost of Christmas To-come. The first takes him back to his young life, shows him what Christmas was to him when a schoolboy, and when he was an apprentice. The second ghost shows him the joyous home of his clerk, Bob Cratchit, who has nine people to feed on what seems a pittance, and yet could find wherewithal to make merry on this day; it also shows him the family of his nephew, and others. The third ghost shows him what would be his lot if he died as he then was, the prey of harpies, the jest of his friends on 'Change. These visions wholly change his nature, and he becomes benevolent, charitable, and cheerful, and makes Christmas a happy day for many within his reach.

Seasons. A well-known poem said to be the foundation of Thomson's literary fame. Its description of the phenomena of nature during an English year is minute, and the poem has been much read by foreigners. Its real value today is largely historical, in that Thomson represents, in relation to nature, the transition in English literature from the classicism of Pope and his school to the romanticism of the Lake School.

Sedley, Mr. Vanity Fair, Thackeray. A wealthy London stockbroker, brought to ruin in the money market just prior to the battle of Waterloo. The old merchant tried to earn a living by selling wine, coals, or lottery tickets by commission, but his bad wine and cheap coals found but few customers. Mrs. Sedley, wife of Mr. Sedley, a homely, kind-hearted woman, soured by adversity, and quick to take offense. Amelia Sedley, daughter of the stockbroker, educated at Miss Pinkerton's academy, and engaged to Captain George Osborne, son of a rich London merchant. After the ruin of Mr. Sedley, George marries Amelia, and old Osborne disinherits him. George is killed in the battle of Waterloo. Amelia is reduced to great poverty, but is befriended by Captain Dobbin, and after many years of patience and great devotion she consents to marry him. Joseph Sedley, vain, shy, and vulgar. He told of his brave deeds, and made it appear that he was Wellington's right hand; so that he obtained the sobriquet of "Waterloo Sedley." He became the "patron" of Becky Sharp, who fleeced him of all his money, and in six months he died under suspicious circumstances. Interest in the novel is centered on Amelia, an impersonation of virtue without intellect as contrasted with Becky Sharp, who is an impersonation of intellect without virtue. The one has no head, the other no heart. Amelia and Becky afforded brilliant contrasts in acting in the dramatized version of *Vanity Fair*,—"Becky Sharp."

Selim (*sē'lĭm*). **Bride of Abydos, Byron.** The character of Selim is bold, full of enterprise, and faithful. The story runs that Selim was the son of Abdallah and cousin of Zuleika. When Giaffir murdered Abdallah, he took Selim and brought him up as his own son. The young man fell in love with Zuleika, who thought he was her brother; when she discovered he was Abdallah's son, she eloped with him. As soon as Giaffir discovered this he went after the fugitives, and shot Selim. Zuleika died broken-hearted, and the old pasha was left childless. Selim, son of Akbar, in Arabian tales, marries Nourmahal, the "Light of the Harem."

Selith. The Messiah, Klopstock. One of the two guardian angels of the Virgin Mary and of John the Divine.

Sellers, Colonel Mulberry. A famous character in *The Gilded Age*, a novel by Mark Twain and C. D. Warner. John T. Raymond made a dramatized version popular. The colonel is a Southern gentleman of visionary but invincible optimism. Mark Twain wrote that he had drawn the character from the life of James Lampton, a cousin of his mother.

Sellock. Peveril of the Peak, Scott. A servant girl in the service of Lady and Sir Geoffrey Peveril of the Peak.

Senena. Madoc, Southey. A Welsh maiden in love with Caradoc. Under the assumed name of Mervyn she became the page of the princess Goervyl, in order that she might follow her lover to America, when Madoc colonized Caer-Madoc. Senena was promised in marriage to another; but, when the wedding day arrived, the bride was nowhere to be found.

Sentimental Journey, The, Laurence Sterne. It was intended to be sentimental sketches of his tour through Italy in 1764, but he died soon after completing the first part.

Sentimental Tommy, Barrie. The story of a "Thrums" boy with an insuppressible insincerity and habit of posing. The story is continued in *Tommy and Grizel*. The two stories form a comedy of sentimentality.

Septuagint (*sĕp'tū-ȧ-jĭnt*). A Greek version of the books of the Old Testament; so called because the translation is supposed to have been made by 72 Jews, who, for the sake of round numbers, are usually called the "seventy interpreters." It is said to have been made at the request of Ptolemy Philadelphus, king of Egypt, about 280 B. C. It is that out of which all the citations in the New Testament from the Old are taken and from which the Psalter in the English Book of Common Prayer is translated. It was also the ordinary and canonical translation made use of by the Christian Church in the earliest ages; and is still retained in the churches of both the East and the West.

Serena. Faery Queen, Spenser. Allured by the mildness of the weather, she went into the fields to gather wild flowers for a garland, when she was attacked by the Blatant Beast, who carried her off in its mouth. Her cries attracted to the spot Sir Calidore, who compelled the beast to drop its prey.

Sesame (*sĕs'ȧ-mē*). In Arabian tales given as the talismanic word which would open or shut the door leading into the cave of the forty thieves. In order to open it, the words to be uttered were, "Open, Sesame!" and in order to close it, "Shut, Sesame!" Sesame is a plant which yields an oily grain, and hence, when Cassim forgot the word, he substituted "barley," but without effect. Sesame has come into general use in connection with any word or act which will open the way for accomplishment of the thing desired. "Sesame and Lilies" is one of the most important and beautiful of Ruskin's works.

Seven Sleepers, The. The tale of these sleepers is told in divers manners. The best accounts are those in the *Koran*; *The Golden Legend*, by Jacopo da Voragine; the *De Gloria Martyrum*, by Gregory of Tours; and the *Oriental Tales*, by Caylus. According to one version they were seven noble youths of Ephesus, who fled in the Decian persecution to a cave in Mount Celion, the mouth of which was blocked up by stones. After 230 years they were discovered, and awoke, but died within a few days, and were taken in a large stone coffin to Marseilles. Another tradition is, that Edward the Confessor, in his mind's eye, saw the seven sleepers turn from their right sides to their left, and whenever they turn on their sides it indicates great disasters to Christendom. This idea was introduced by Tennyson in his drama *Harold*.

Seven Wise Masters. The title of a medieval collection of novels, important from both its contents and its widespread popularity. The work is undoubtedly of Oriental origin, yet neither the period when it was composed, nor how far it spread through the East, is known, but it existed in Arabic as a translation from Indian sources before the 11th century. The work became known in literature, sometimes in a complete form; sometimes only particular novels were reproduced, under all sorts of names, in verse and in prose. Latin versions began to appear about the beginning of the 13th century and parts have been translated into English.

Seven Wise Men. The collective designation of a number of Greek sages, who lived about 620–548 B. C. and devoted themselves to the cultivation of practical wisdom. Their moral and social experience was embodied in brief aphorisms, expressed in verse or in prose.

Sganarelle (*z'gȧ'nȧ'rĕl'*). The hero of Molière's comedy *Le Mariage Forcé*. He is represented as a humorist of about 53, who, having a mind to marry a fashionable young woman, but feeling a doubt, consults his friends upon this momentous question. Receiving no satisfactory counsel, and not much pleased with the proceedings of his bride elect, he at last determines to give up his engagement, but is cudgeled into compliance by the brother of his intended.

Shallow. A braggart and absurd country justice in Shakspere's *Merry Wives of Windsor*, and in the second part of *King Henry IV*.

Shalott, The Lady of. The heroine of Tennyson's poem of the same name. She weaves into her web all the sights reflected in the mirror which hangs opposite her window; but, when Sir Lancelot passes, she leaves her mirror and looks out of the casement at the knight himself, whereupon a curse comes upon her. She entered a boat bearing her name on the prow, floated down the river to Camelot, and died heartbroken on the way.

Shandy, Mrs. The mother of Tristram Shandy in Sterne's novel of this name. She is the ideal of nonentity, a character individual from its very absence of individuality.

Shandy, Tristram. The nominal hero of Sterne's *The Life and Opinions of Tristram Shandy, Gent.*

Shandy, Walter. The name of Tristram Shandy's father in Sterne's novel of this name, a man of an active and metaphysical, but at the same time a whimsical, cast of mind, whom too much and too miscellaneous learning had brought within a step or two of madness. The romance, *Tristram Shandy*, is not built on a regular plot. The hero has no adventures, and the story consists of a series of episodes which introduce the reader to the home life of an

English country family. This family is one of the most amusing.

Sharp, Rebecca. The prominent character in Thackeray's *Vanity Fair*, the daughter of a poor painter, dashing, selfish, unprincipled, and very clever, who manages to marry Rawdon Crawley, afterwards his excellency Colonel Crawley, C. B. He was disinherited on account of his marriage with Becky, then a poor governess, but she taught him how to live in splendor on no income. Lord Steyne introduced her to court, but her conduct with this peer gave rise to scandal, which caused a separation between her and Rawdon. She joins her fortunes with Joseph Sedley, a wealthy "collector," of Boggley Wollah, in India. Having insured his life and lost his money, he dies suddenly under very suspicious circumstances. Becky at last assumes the character of a pious, charitable Lady Bountiful, given to all good works.

Shaving of Shagpat, The, George Meredith. A burlesque version of an Oriental tale. The style suggests the *Arabian Nights*.

Shepherdess, The Faithful. A pastoral drama by John Fletcher. The "faithful shepherdess" is Corin, who remains faithful to her lover although he is dead. Milton has borrowed from this pastoral in his *Comus*.

Shepherd of Banbury. The ostensible author of a work entitled "The Shepherd of Banbury's Rules to judge of the Changes of Weather, Grounded on Forty Years' Experience, etc.," a work of great popularity among the English poor.

Shepherd of Salisbury Plain, The. The hero and title of a religious tract by Hannah More. The shepherd is noted for his homely wisdom and simple piety.

Shepherd's Calendar, The. Twelve eclogues in various meters, by Spenser, one for each month. January: Colin Clout (Spenser) bewails that Rosalind does not return his love. February: Cuddy, a lad, complains of the cold, and Thenot laments the degeneracy of pastoral life. March: Willie and Thomalin discourse of love. April: Hobbinol sings a song on Eliza. May: Palinode exhorts Piers to join the festivities of May, but Piers replies that good shepherds who seek their own indulgence expose their flocks to the wolves. June: Hobbinol exhorts Colin to greater cheerfulness. July: Morrel, a goatherd, invites Thomalin to come with him to the uplands. August: Perigot and Willie contend in song, and Cuddy is appointed arbiter. September: Diggon Davie complains to Hobbinol of clerical abuses. October: On poetry. November: Colin, being asked by Thenot to sing, excuses himself because of his grief for Dido, but finally sings her elegy. December: Colin again complains that his heart is desolate. Thenot is an old shepherd bent with age, who tells Cuddy, the herdsman's boy, the fable of the oak and the briar, one of the best-known fables included in the calendar.

Shepherd's Pipe. Pan, in Greek mythology, was the god of forests, pastures, and flocks, and was the reputed inventor of the shepherd's flute or pipe, a series of graduated tubes set together, open at one end and closed at the other, played by blowing across the open ends.

Sheridan's Ride. A lyric by T. B. Read, one of the few things written during the heat of the Civil War that have survived.

Sherlock Holmes, The Adventures of, Conan Doyle. A series of clever and popular detective stories in which the hero, Holmes, a private detective, employs his extraordinary fund of scientific knowledge and unusual powers of reasoning to solve many baffling mysteries of crime. The stories are told by Holmes's friend and companion, Dr. Watson. The plan of these stories was suggested by Poe's *Murders in the Rue Morgue*. The methods of Holmes are said to have been suggested to Doyle by the work of Dr. Joseph Bell, a physician of Edinburgh and at one time an instructor of the novelist.

Sherwood Forest. A forest in Nottinghamshire, England, fourteen miles north of Nottingham. It was formerly of large extent. It is the principal scene of the legendary exploits of Robin Hood.

She Stoops to Conquer. This well-known comedy by Oliver Goldsmith is said to have been founded on an incident which actually occurred to its author. When Goldsmith was sixteen years of age, a wag residing at Ardagh directed him, when passing through that village, to Squire Fetherstone's house as the village inn. The mistake was not discovered for some time, but all concerned enjoyed the joke. *She Stoops to Conquer* is one of the gayest, pleasantest, and most amusing pieces of English comedy.

Shingebis. In Longfellow's "Hiawatha," the diver who challenged the North Wind and put him to flight in combat.

Shocky. The Hoosier Schoolmaster, Edw. Eggleston. The little lad from the poorhouse who adores the schoolmaster and early warns him of plans for upsetting his authority. He is also somewhat of a poet, not in versification, but in the comprehension of things about him and in his way of looking at life, and he grows to be a helper in the "Church of the Best Licks," founded by the schoolmaster. He is brother to Hannah whom the master loves. Shocky and Hannah and their companions in the story bring the speech and life of their people and their time into American literature.

Shylock. The Jew, in Shakspere's *Merchant of Venice*.

Siege Perilous, The. The Round Table contained sieges, or seats, in the names of different knights. One was reserved for him who was destined to achieve the quest of the holy grail. This seat was called "perilous," because if any one sat therein except him for whom it was reserved it would be his death. This seat finally bore the name of Sir Galahad.

Siegfried. The hero of various Scandinavian and Teutonic legends, particularly of the old German epic poem, the *Nibelungenlied*. He is represented as a young warrior of physical strength and beauty, and in valor superior to all men of his time. He cannot easily be identified with any historical personage.

Sikes, Bill. A brutal thief and housebreaker in Dickens's novel *Oliver Twist*. He murders his mistress, Nancy, and, in trying to lower himself by a rope from the roof of a building where he had taken refuge from the crowd, he falls and is choked in a noose of his own making. Sikes had an ill-conditioned savage dog, the beast-image of his master, which he kicked and loved, illtreated and fondled.

Silas Marner. The principal character in George Eliot's story *Silas Marner, the Weaver of Raveloe*. Silas, a cataleptic, lived his younger life in a little religious community of weavers in Lantern Yard. Robbed of his sweetheart and his good name by his best friend, Silas withdrew to the village of Raveloe. Here in his lonely hut he hoards his earnings. Robbed of these, he is saved from utter despair by finding a baby girl. On her he spends his love. In the end the shattered man is remade by this influence, and the stolen savings are found and restored to him.

Silken Thread. Gulliver's Travels. In the kingdom of Lilliput, the three great prizes of honor are "fine silk threads six inches long, one blue, another red, and a third green." The thread is girt about the loins, and no ribbon of the Legion of Honor, or of the Knight of the Garter, is won more worthily or worn more proudly.

Simon Pure. The real thing. In Mrs. Centlivre's comedy, *A Bold Stroke For A Wife*, (1718), another man impersonates the Quaker, Simon Pure, who asserts that he is the genuine article.

Sindbad the Sailor. A character in the *Arabian Nights*, in which is related the story of his strange voyages and wonderful adventures.

Singed Cat. An allusion found in Haliburton's *Old Judge*. "That crittur is like a singed cat, better nor he seems." Found also in Ramsay's *Scotch Proverbs* (1750). "He's like a singed cat, better than he's likely." Applied to one whose looks belie his real quality.

Sinon (*sī'nŏn*). In Virgil's *Æneid*, the cunning Greek who, by a false tale, induced the Trojans to drag the wooden horse into Troy.

Slay-Good, Giant. A giant, in *Pilgrim's Progress*, slain in a duel by Mr. Greatheart.

Sleeping Beauty. The heroine of a celebrated nursery tale which relates how a princess was shut up by fairy enchantment, to sleep a hundred years in a castle, around which sprang up a dense, impenetrable wood. At the expiration of the appointed time, she was delivered from her imprisonment and her trance by a gallant young prince, before whom the forest opened itself to afford him passage. Grimm derives this popular and widely diffused tale from the old northern mythology.

Slender. A silly youth in Shakspere's *Merry Wives of Windsor*, who is an unsuccessful suitor for the hand of "Sweet Anne Page."

Slick, Sam. The title and hero of various humorous narratives, illustrating and exaggerating the peculiarities of the Yankee character and dialect, written by Judge Thomas C. Haliburton, chief justice of Nova Scotia. Sam Slick is represented as a Yankee clockmaker and peddler, full of quaint drollery, unsophisticated wit, knowledge of human nature, and aptitude in the use of what he calls "soft sawder." Haliburton's *Sam Slick* may be said to originate the American school of humor.

Slough of Despond. Pilgrim's Progress, Bunyan. A deep bog, which Christian had to pass on his way to the Wicket Gate. Neighbor Pliable would not attempt to pass it, and turned back. While Christian was floundering in the slough, Help came to his aid and assisted him over.

Sly, Christopher. Taming of the Shrew, Shakspere. A keeper of bears and a tinker, son of a peddler and a sad drinker.

Sohrab and Rustum, Matthew Arnold. A narrative poem. The story is Persian. Sohrab, son of Rustum, long an adventurer, is a warrior who appalls the Persian armies. At last, in a fight with Rustum, he is mortally wounded. Rustum, discovering in Sohrab his son, is inconsolable.

Soldiers Three, Kipling. The title of a series of tales of army life in India, which recount the adventures of three private soldiers, whose portraits are perhaps Kipling's best work. Of them he writes in beginning their story, "Mulvaney, Ortheris, and Learoyd are privates in B Company of a Line Regiment and personal friends of mine."

Song of Roland. An ancient song recounting the deeds of Roland, the renowned nephew of Charlemagne, slain in the pass of Roncesvalles. At the battle of Hastings, Taillefer advanced on horseback before the invading army, and gave the signal for onset by singing this famous song. See *Roland*.

Songs of the Sierras. A collection of poems by Joaquin Miller, which made him known on two continents within a year of their publication. The title explains the chief subject of the songs.

Spanish Main. The southern banks of the West India islands, and the water extending for some distance into the Caribbean Sea, so called from the fact that the Spaniards confined their buccaneering enterprises to this locality.

Spectator, The. A periodical famous in literature, in which most of the articles were written by Addison or Sir Richard Steele. The first number was published in London in the year 1711, the last, No. 635, was issued in December 1714. The most noted of Addison's writings is said to be the series of sketches in *The Spectator*, of which Sir Roger de Coverley is the central figure, and Sir Andrew Freeport and Will Honeycomb the side ones. Sir Roger himself is an absolute creation; the gentle yet vivid imagination, the gay spirit of humor, and the keen, shrewd observation mark it a work of pure genius. In this, Addison has given a delicacy to English sentiment and a modesty to English wit which it never knew before. Dr. Johnson says, "To attain an English style, familiar but not coarse, and elegant but not ostentatious, one must give his days and nights to the volumes of Addison."

Sphinx. A Greek word, applied to certain symbolical forms of Egyptian origin. The most remarkable sphinx is the Great Sphinx at Giza, a colossal form, hewn out of the natural rock. Immediately in front of the breast is a small naos, or chapel, formed of three hieroglyphical tablets. Votive inscriptions of the Roman period, some as late as the 3d century, were discovered in the walls and constructions. On the second digit of the left claw of the Sphinx, an inscription, in pentameter Greek verse, by Arrian, was discovered. Another metrical and prosaic inscription was also found. In Assyria and Babylonia, representations of sphinxes have been found, and they are not uncommon on Phœnician works of art.

Spoon River Anthology, Edgar Lee Masters. The best-known work of this poet. It is a collection of poems in free verse, in the form of realistic epitaphs on the citizens of a village of the Middle West. The plan was suggested by Masters' reading of the *Greek Anthology*.

Squeers. Name of a family prominent in Dickens's *Nicholas Nickleby*. Wackford Squeers, master of Dotheboys Hall, Yorkshire, a vulgar, conceited, ignorant schoolmaster, overbearing and mean. He steals the boys' pocket money, clothes his son in their best suits, half starves them, and teaches them next to nothing. Ultimately he is transported for theft. Mrs. Squeers, a rawboned, harsh, heartless virago, with no womanly feeling for the boys put under her charge. Miss Fanny Squeers, daughter of the schoolmaster. Miss Fanny falls in love with Nicholas Nickleby, but later hates him because he is insensible to her tender passion. Master Wackford Squeers, overbearing, self-willed, and passionate. The picture of this family and their ways had great influence on the schools of England, by rousing the people to a knowledge of their management.

Squire of Dames. A personage introduced by Spenser in the *Faery Queen*, whose curious adventures are there recorded. A phrase often used to express a person devoted to the fair sex.

Stalky and Company, Kipling. A series of stories of English school life. Corkran (Your Uncle Stalky), McTurk, and Beetle, who is probably the author, combine to play pranks, victimizing both masters and boys.

Steerforth. David Copperfield, Dickens. The young man who led Little Em'ly astray. When tired of his toy, he proposed to her to marry his valet. Steerforth being shipwrecked off the coast of Yarmouth, Ham Peggotty tried to rescue him, but both were drowned.

Stentor. A Grecian herald in the Trojan War, whom Homer describes as "great-hearted, brazen-voiced Stentor, accustomed to shout as loud as fifty other men." Hence our adjective "stentorian."

Stephano. (1) A drunken butler, in Shakspere's *Tempest*. (2) A servant to Portia, in Shakspere's *Merchant of Venice*.

Stickeen, John Muir. The story of a dog.

Stiggins, Rev. Mr. A red-nosed, hypocritical "shepherd," or Methodist parson, in Dickens's *Pickwick Papers*, with a great appetite for pineapple rum. He is the spiritual adviser of Mrs. Weller and lectures on temperance.

Stone of Sardis. The Great Stone of Sardis, Stockton. In this stone the imaginary science of the future is joined to the actual science of today in an extremely plausible way. The north pole is visited by a submarine vessel, a light is found capable of penetrating for miles into the interior of the earth, and finally the center of that earth is discovered to be an enormous diamond.

Storm and Stress Period. In the literary history of Germany, the name given to a period of great intellectual convulsion, when the nation began to assert its freedom from the fetters of an artificial literary spirit. The period derives its name from a drama of Klinger (1753–1831), whose high-wrought tragedies and novels reflect the excitement of the time.

Strife, John Galsworthy. The scene of this play is the Trenartha Tin Works. A strike is on, led by David Roberts, determined foe of the owners. John Anthony, founder and president of the company, is all for fighting. Among the directors, called down from London, and also among the workers are those who are for compromise. These finally come to agreement, in spite of Roberts and Anthony, the strong men and "bitter enders." At the close of the play, these two evince their sense of a common defeat and a reluctant respect for each other's strength, mixed with contempt for the weak compromisers. The action of the play is confined to one day.

Sunken Bell, The, Hauptmann. A fairy drama which portrays the bitter struggles of a bell-founder, Heinrich, against the forces that thwart his ambition. A fairy will not endure the ringing of a bell he wants to place in a mountain chapel. The bell is sunk in a deep abyss. Discouraged, he finds help in a mountain elf, Rautendelein. With her, he plans new things. But the eternal strife between the low and the high wears him out at last.

Swallow Barn. The three novels, *Swallow Barn*, *Horse-Shoe Robinson*, and *Rob of the Bowl*, besides their value as works of art, are all careful historical studies giving admirable pictures of life in the southern states in the earlier days of the republic. They were written by John P. Kennedy, who holds a place among American novelists not far removed from that of Cooper.

Swiveller, Dick. A careless, light-headed fellow in Dickens's novel *Old Curiosity Shop*, whose flowery orations and absurdities of quotation provoke laughter, but whose real kindness of heart enlists sympathy.

Tabard, The, Chaucer's Inn. The old London tavern, immortalized by Chaucer as the "Tabard" in *Canterbury Tales*. It took its name from its sign, a tabard, or loose, sleeveless jacket. From this hostelry in Southwark, on the south side of the Thames, the "pilgrims" started on the famous journey to Canterbury, "the holy blissful martyr for to seek." The inn was burned in the great fire of 1676. Upon its restoration the name was changed to the "Talbot," or Dog, which name it retained until about 1873, when it was demolished.

Tales of a Wayside Inn. Name given by Longfellow to a collection of his short poems arranged in much the same form as Chaucer's *Canterbury Tales*. These "tales" were mostly gathered from old literatures and translated into Longfellow's own verse. Only one, "The Birds of Killingworth," is said to be entirely original. Seven narrators are represented: the Landlord, the Student, the Spanish Cavalier, the Jew, the Sicilian, the Musician, and the Theologian. Four colonial tales are included in the work: "Paul Revere's Ride," "Elizabeth," "Lady Wentworth," and "The Rhyme of Sir Christopher."

Tales of My Landlord, Scott. A series of novels in which the stories are told by the landlord of the Wallace Inn, parish of Gandercleugh, and edited by Jedediah Cleishbotham, schoolmaster. The series includes, besides others, *The Black Dwarf* and *Count Robert of Paris*.

Talmud. A Hebrew word meaning "doctrine." It is the name applied to a work containing traditions respecting the usages and laws of the Jewish people. The law, among that people, was divided into the written and the unwritten. The written law embraced the five books of Moses; the unwritten was handed down orally; the oral being, in fact, explanatory of the written. But, in time, the oral came, also, to be put in writing, and formed the text of the *Talmud*. This was first done, it is believed, about the year 200. There are two separate commentaries on this text, which are distinguished as the Babylonian and the Jerusalem. The *Talmud* of Jerusalem consists of two parts, the "Mishna" and the "Gemara." The "Mishna" gives a simple statement of a law; the "Gemara" presents the discussion upon it. The *Talmud* of Babylon, which is of higher authority among the Jews than that of Jerusalem, was composed by Rabbi Aser, who lived near Babylon; he did not live to finish it, but it was completed by his disciples about 500 years after Christ.

Taming of the Shrew, Shakspere. A farce-comedy. Katherine, the shrewish daughter of Baptista Minola of Padua, is transformed by Petruchio, a good-humored but determined gentleman, into a model of the obedient wife. By thwarting her every wish, under the pretense of the most thoughtful care for her comfort, he brings her to terms through sheer weariness of strife.

Tam O'Shanter. The title of a poem by Burns, and the name of its hero, a farmer, who, riding home very late and very drunk from Ayr, in a stormy night, had to pass by the kirk of Alloway, a place reputed to be a favorite haunt of the Devil and his friends and emissaries. On approaching the kirk, he perceived a light gleaming through the windows; but, having got courageously drunk, he ventured on till he could look into the edifice, when he saw a dance of witches. His presence became known and in an instant all was dark, and Tam, recollecting himself, turned and spurred his horse to the top of her speed, chased by the whole fiendish crew. It is a current belief that witches, or any evil spirits, have no power to follow a poor wight any farther than the middle of the next running stream. Fortunately for Tam, the River Doon was near, and Tam escaped while the witches held only the tail of his mare, Maggie. It has been said of "Tam O'Shanter" that in no other poem of the same length can there be found so much brilliant description, pathos, and quaint humor, nor such a combination of the terrific and the ludicrous.

Tancred. The hero of the First Crusade. The love of woman was his one besetting weakness. Tasso follows his career in *Jerusalem Delivered*, and he appears in Scott's *Count Robert of Paris*. Disraeli uses the name for the hero of his novel *Tancred, or the New Crusade*.

Tannhäuser. A famous legendary hero of Germany, and the subject of an ancient ballad of the same name. The noble Tannhäuser is a knight devoted to valorous adventures and to beautiful women. In Mantua, he wins the affection of a lovely lady, Lisaura, and of a learned philosopher, Hilario, with whom he converses frequently upon supernatural subjects. Enchanted by marvelous tales, he wishes for nothing less than to participate in the love of some beauteous elementary spirit, who shall, for his sake, assume the form of mortal woman. Hilario promises to grant even more than he has wished, if he will have courage to venture upon the Venusberg. Tannhäuser ascends the mountain, and, hearing of his departure, Lisaura dies. Tannhäuser stays long on the enchanting mountain, but at last, moved to repentance, he obtains permission to depart. He hastens to Mantua, weeps over the grave of Lisaura, and thence proceeds to Rome, where he makes public confession of his sins to Pope Urban. The pope refuses him absolution, saying he can no more be pardoned than the dry wand which he holds can bud and bear green leaves. Tannhäuser flees from Rome, and vainly seeks his former preceptor, Hilario. Venus appears before him and lures him back to the mountain, there to remain until the day of judgment. Meanwhile, at Rome the dry wand bears leaves. Urban, alarmed at this miracle, sends messengers in search of the unhappy knight; but he is nowhere to be found. This Tannhäuser legend is very popular in Germany, and is often alluded to by German writers. Tieck has made it the subject of a narrative, and Wagner, of an opera which has gained great celebrity.

Tartarin. The quixotic hero of a series of humorous, half-satiric masterpieces by Alphonse Daudet. Tartarin, at his home in Tarascon, in southern France, is continually dreaming of travel and adventure. By reading of distant lands and viewing the guns in his collection, he persuades himself that he actually has had the adventures he imagines. Finally, he does journey to Africa to hunt lions, and to Switzerland to climb mountains. The stories of these exploits and others Daudet makes a source of neverfailing entertainment.

Tartufe (*tär-to͞of'*), "The Hypocrite." (1) A comedy by Molière, in which the leading character is Tartufe (*Fr. tär'tüf'*). Tartufe, an adventurer, masquerading under a cloak of piety, worms his way into the household of Orgon, a well-to-do merchant. Orgon, with the connivance of his mother, goes so far as to make Tartufe a deed to his estate and promises him his daughter Mariane, already affianced to Valère. But Tartufe really wants Elmire, Orgon's second wife. She arranges that Orgon shall overhear the hypocrite's declaration of love to her. Tartufe meets Orgon's anger by claiming his property under the deed. Louis XIV intervenes, saves Orgon's estate, and imprisons Tartufe. (2) A common nickname for a hypocritical pretender to religion. It is derived from the name of the character in Molière's comedy.

Teazle, Lady. The heroine of Sheridan's comedy *The School for Scandal*, and the wife of Sir Peter Teazle, an old gentleman who marries late in life. She is represented as being "a lively and innocent, though imprudent, country girl, transplanted into the midst of all that can bewilder and endanger her, but with enough of purity about her to keep the blight of the world from settling upon her."

Teazle, Sir Peter. A character in Sheridan's play *The School for Scandal*, husband of Lady Teazle.

Tel-el-Amarna Letters. A collection of several hundred clay tablets with cuneiform inscriptions found at Tel-el-Amarna, a village on the Nile. Official correspondence of about 1400 B. C., between Egypt and Syria.

Tempest, The. This has been called one of Shakspere's fairy plays. The story of it runs: Prospero, duke of Milan, was dethroned by his brother Antonio, and left on the open sea with his three-year-old daughter Miranda, in "a rotten carcass of a boat." In this they were carried to an enchanted island, uninhabited except by a hideous creature, Caliban, the son of a witch. Prospero was a powerful enchanter, and soon had not only Caliban, but all the spirits of the region under his control, including Ariel, chief of the spirits of the air. Years afterward Antonio, Alfonso, Sebastian, and other friends of the usurper came near the island. Prospero, by his magic, raises a storm which casts their ship on the shore, and the whole party are spellbound and brought to Prospero. Plots and counterplots follow, bringing in Caliban and clowns, but all are made ridiculous and defeated by Prospero and Ariel.

Tenson (*tĕn'sŏn*). A kind of poem among the troubadours which carries on a contention or dispute, apparently serious, and often concerning love. The tenson was usually recited by two persons in alternating stanzas. The greater number of these are found in early Italian and French literature.

Ten Times One. A writing in story form by E. E. Hale. It is said that the inspiration of this story led to the founding of the "King's Daughters" society.

Tess of the D'Urbervilles, Thomas Hardy. A tragic novel. Tess Durbeyfield, whose father fancies himself related to the great family of D'Urberville, is employed by them. Alec, the eldest son, seduces her. Her child dies. Several years afterward, Angel Clare, who has married Tess, deserts her on learning her past secret. Later, he tries to win her back, but Alec treacherously meddles, and Tess, in anger, murders him and is executed for the crime.

Thaddeus of Warsaw. The hero and title of a novel by Jane Porter.

Thangbrand. Tales of a Wayside Inn, H. W. Longfellow. King Olaf's drunken priest, "short of stature and large of limb," who was sent to Iceland, found the people poring over their books, and sailed back to Norway to say to Olaf that there was "little hope of those Iceland men."

Thekla. The daughter of Wallenstein, in Schiller's drama of this name. She is one of the poet's own creations.

Theodorus. The name of a physician, in Rabelais' romance *Gargantua*. At the request of Ponocrates, Gargantua's tutor, he undertook to cure the latter of his vicious manner of living, and accordingly purged him canonically with Anticyrian hellebore, by which medicine he cleared out all the foulness and perverse habit of his brain, so that he became a man of great honor, sense, courage, and piety.

They Shall Not Pass. During the World War, this phrase became the watchword of the defenders of Verdun. It has become the symbol of determined resistance.

Thomas the Rhymer or **Thomas Rhymer.** The popular name in Scotland of an old prophet, supposed to have been inspired by the fairies. Thomas Rhymer's real name is supposed to have been Thomas Learmount of Ercildoune (Earlston). He lived in the 13th century. A metrical romance called *Sir Tristram* is attributed to him. He is also the subject of one of the best-known English ballads.

Thorberg Skafting. Tales of a Wayside Inn, H. W. Longfellow. The master builder ordered by King Olaf to build a ship twice as long and twice as large as the *Dragon* built by Raud the Strong, which was stranded. Thorberg built the ship, watching his workmen closely, and when she was ready for launching, King Olaf and the workmen were amazed to see every plank down her sides cut with deep gashes and more amazed to find that Thorberg had done the deed. From these gashes he then chipped and smoothed the sides, to the delight of all; she was christened the *Long Serpent* and the name of her builder recited in the saga.

Thorpe, Harry. The Blazed Trail, S. E. White. The hero of the novel, a vigorous young man, who, as a "landlooker," finds and takes up a valuable timber tract, against the crafty old corporation which seeks first to steal the timber, then to forestall him in buying it, and finally to ruin him. The true romance of the story is that of the forest and the titanic struggle of man against nature and against man.

Three Kings, Feast of the. A famous medieval festival, identical with the Epiphany. But the name is more particularly given to a kind of dramatic or spectacular representation of the incidents recorded in the second chapter of Matthew: the appearance of the wise men in splendid pomp at the court of Herod; the miraculous star; the manger at Bethlehem; the solemn and costly worship of the Babe. This was long very popular.

Three Musketeers, The, Dumas the Elder. A romance of the time of Richelieu. Also called "The Three Guardsmen." The three are Athos, Porthos, and Aramis. Their adventures, with those of D'Artagnan, make up this popular story. Dumas is said to have taken material for the story from a manuscript, *The Memoirs of D'Artagnan*, in the National Library of Paris. The story hinges on the successful attempt of the four soldiers to recover certain jewels that the queen had given to the Englishman, Buckingham. In doing this, they not only free the queen from a trap Richelieu had set for her, but they rid Richelieu, the queen's opponent, of a dangerous woman messenger, and D'Artagnan is rewarded by the cardinal with a promotion.

Thrums. The market town of Kirriemuir, in which J. M. Barrie places many of his stories and sketches, *A Window in Thrums, Auld Licht Idylls*, etc.

Thunderer, The. Name popularly given to the English newspaper, *The Times*. The accepted version of the way in which the great journal got its name of "The Thunderer," is that Captain Sterling, one of the "staff," once wrote a sort of apology in reference to a mistaken assertion and used the phrase "We thundered out." This caught the public fancy, hence the name. Captain Sterling was a well-known figure in London political circles and was father of the more famous John Sterling, critic, essayist, and friend of Wordsworth, Coleridge, and De Quincey.

Thwackum, Parson Roger. The learned and honest, but selfish and hot-tempered, pedagogue in Fielding s novel *The History of Tom Jones, a Foundling*.

Thyrsis (*thûr'sĭs*). (1) Corydon and Thyrsis are favorite names given to shepherds by writers of pastoral poetry. So also, Phyllis and Thestylis are names often applied to rustic maidens or shepherdesses. (2) The title of one of the most beautiful elegies in English literature in which Matthew Arnold mourns the loss of his friend, the poet Clough.

Tibbs or **Tibs.** A character in Goldsmith's *Citizen of the World*, quoted as a "most useful hand." He will write you a receipt for the bite of a mad dog, tell you an Eastern tale to perfection, and understands the business part of an author so well that no publisher can humbug him.

Tigg, Montague (*mŏn'tā-gū*). **Martin Chuzzlewit, Dickens.** A clever impostor, who lives by his wits. He starts a bubble insurance office and makes considerable gain thereby. Having discovered the attempt of Jonas Chuzzlewit to murder his father, he compels him to put his money in the "new company," but Jonas afterwards murders him.

Timon. Timon of Athens, Shakspere. The drama begins with the joyous life of Timon and his hospitable extravagance, launches into his pecuniary embarrassment and the discovery that his "professed friends" will not help him, and ends with his flight into the woods, his misanthropy, and his death. Introduced into the play is "Timon's Banquet." Being shunned by his friends in adversity, he pretended to have recovered his money, and invited his false friends to a banquet. The table was laden with covers, but, when the contents were exposed, nothing was provided but lukewarm water.

Tintern Abbey. (1) A noted ruin of great beauty on the Wye in Monmouthshire, England. The abbey was founded by Cistercian monks in 1131. (2) The shortened title of a reflective poem by William Wordsworth,—one of his finest works. The complete title is "Lines Composed a Few Miles above Tintern Abbey, on Revisiting the Banks of the Wye during a Tour, July 13, 1798."

Tiny Tim. Christmas Stories, Dickens. A striking character, the little son of Bob Cratchit, whose family were made happier by gifts from the converted Scrooge. See *Scrooge, Ebenezer*.

Tippecanoe. Name given to William Henry Harrison during the political canvass which preceded his election, on account of the victory gained by him over the Indians in the battle which took place on the 6th of November 1811, at the junction of the Tippecanoe and Wabash rivers.

Tirzah. Ben Hur, General Lew Wallace. A beautiful Jewish maiden, sister of Ben Hur. Their father had been a prince of Jerusalem, and died leaving a large estate. At the age of fifteen, Tirzah, with her mother, was imprisoned through the cruelty of Messala who coveted their property. They both became lepers and when released from prison were forced to live among the outcasts. They were healed by Jesus, Ben Hur himself witnessing the miracle. As soon as the change in their look had taken place he recognized them, and, when the Jewish statutes had been complied with, Tirzah and her mother were united with their brother in their former home.

Toby, Uncle. A character in Sterne's *Tristram Shandy*. A captain who was wounded at the siege of Namur, and was obliged to retire from the service. He is the impersonation of kindness, benevolence, and simple-heartedness; his courage is undoubted, his gallantry delightful for its innocence and modesty.

Token, The. A collection of original articles, prose and poetry, by various contributors, issued first in the year 1824. This was the first "annual" in America; it became popular and was continued for fifteen years under the supervision of S. G. Goodrich, or "Peter Parley." To it Hawthorne owed his first hold on the public.

Tom, Dick, and Harry. An appellation very commonly employed to designate a crowd or rabble.

Tommy Atkins. Barrack-room Ballads, Kipling. The name is here used in its general meaning, a British soldier. The name came from the little pocket ledgers served out, at one time, to all British soldiers. In these manuals were to be entered the name, the age, the date of enlistment, etc. The War Office sent with each little book a form for filling it in, and the hypothetical name selected was "Thomas Atkins." The books were instantly so called, and it did not require many days to transfer the name from the book to the soldier.

Tom Sawyer. Adventures of Tom Sawyer, Mark Twain. An "elastic" youth whose performances delight both old and young readers. Queer enterprises influenced by the old superstitions among slaves and children in the Western states give reliable pictures of boy-life in the middle of the 19th century.

Tom the Piper. One of the characters in the ancient morris dance, represented with a tabor, tabor-stick, and pipe. He carried a sword and shield, to denote his rank.

Tom Thumb. In legendary history, a dwarf no larger than a man's thumb. He lived in the reign of King Arthur, by whom he was knighted. He was killed by the poisonous breath of a spider in the reign of the successor of King Arthur. Among his adventures it is told that he was lying one day asleep in a meadow, when a cow swallowed him as she cropped the grass. At another time, he rode in the ear of a horse. He crept up the sleeve of a giant, and so tickled him that he shook his sleeve, and Tom, falling into the sea, was swallowed by a fish. The fish being caught and carried to the palace gave the little man his introduction to the king. The oldest version of his nursery tale is in rime. P. T. Barnum named a celebrated midget "General Tom Thumb." The "General" had an audience with Queen Victoria.

Tonio. Daughter of the Regiment, Donizetti. The name of the youth who saved Marie, the sutler girl, from falling down a precipice. The two fall in love with each other, and the regiment consents to their marriage, provided Tonio will enlist under its flag. No sooner is this done than the marchioness of Berkenfeld lays claim to Marie as her daughter, and removes her to the castle. In time, the castle is besieged and taken by the very regiment into which Tonio had enlisted, and, as Tonio had risen to the rank of a French officer, the marchioness consents to his marriage with her daughter.

Topsy. Uncle Tom's Cabin, Mrs. Stowe. A young slave girl, who never knew whether she had either father or mother, and, being asked by Miss Ophelia St. Clare how she supposed she came into the world, replied, "I 'spects I growed." Topsy illustrates the amusing and humorous side of the African character.

Touchstone. A clown in Shakspere's *As You Like It.*

Townley Mysteries. Certain religious dramas; so called because the manuscript containing them belonged to P. Townley. These dramas are supposed to have been acted at Widkirk Abbey, in Yorkshire.

Traddles. David Copperfield, Dickens. A simple, honest young man, who believes in everybody and everything and who is never depressed by his want of success. He had the habit of brushing his hair up on end, which gave him a look of surprise. Traddles was generally accompanied by "the dearest girl" and her numerous sisters.

Treasure Island, Stevenson. A story of pirates' gold. After the death of an old seaman in the Admiral Benbow inn, a map is found in his chest. Squire Trelawney, Dr. Livesey, men of the neighborhood, and Jim Hawkins, the young son of the innkeeper, go on a voyage in search of the island shown on the map. Unluckily, they ship some of the original pirates in their crew, chief of them, Long John Silver, ship's cook. Mutiny and fighting arise at the island. But in the end, through a sailor long marooned on the island, they find the treasure.

Triads. The Welsh triads, known in literature, are collections of historic facts, mythological traditions, moral maxims, or rules of poetry, disposed in groups of three.

Trilby. See *Little Billee.*

Trim, Corporal. Uncle Toby's attendant, in Sterne's novel *The Life and Opinions of Tristram Shandy, Gent,* distinguished for his fidelity and affection, his respectfulness, and his volubility.

Tristram, Sir. One of the most celebrated heroes in medieval romance. His adventures form an episode in the history of Arthur's court. He appears in Tennyson's "The Last Tournament."

Trotwood, Betsey. David Copperfield, Dickens. A great-aunt to David, whose daily trial seemed to be donkeys. A dozen times a day would she rush on the green before her house to drive off the donkeys and donkey-boys. She was a most kind-hearted woman, who concealed her tenderness under a snappish manner. Miss Betsey was the true friend of David Copperfield.

Troubadours. Minstrels of southern France in the 11th, 12th, and 13th centuries. They were the first to discard Latin and use the native tongue in their compositions. Their poetry was about either love and gallantry or war and chivalry. In northern France, similar minstrels were called trouvères.

Truth, The, Clyde Fitch. Becky Warder, who has been in the habit of telling fibs, "white lies," about all sorts of things, suddenly finds herself involved in disaster. Her husband, whose faith in her has been complete, finds she has lied to him about money sent to her father, a gambler, about bills, and about meeting the husband of a friend. He leaves the house, offering her a divorce if she wants it. She goes to her father in Baltimore. He telegraphs Warder that Becky is dying, and Warder hastens to Baltimore. Becky resents the lie in the message and faces her husband with the truth. The two are reconciled, with the prospect of the wife's sincere attempt to tell the truth thereafter. The subtle interplay of the lie and the truth is skillfully presented in the drama. The problem as to whether Becky can tell the truth remains unsolved.

Truthful James. The character whom Bret Harte makes the narrator of a number of his poetic stories, among them "The Society on the Stanislaw" and "The Heathen Chinee."

Tuck, Friar. Ivanhoe, Scott. The father-confessor of Robin Hood and connected with Fountain Abbey. He is represented as a clerical Falstaff, very fat and self-indulgent, very humorous, and somewhat coarse. His dress was a russet habit of the Franciscan order. He was sometimes girt with a rope of rushes. Friar Tuck also appears in the "morris dance" on May Day.

Tulkinghorn, Mr. Bleak House, Dickens. The family lawyer of Sir Leicester Dedlock. He is murdered by Lady Dedlock's French maid.

Tulliver, Maggie. See *Mill on the Floss, The.*

Turveydrop. Bleak House, Dickens. A conceited dancing master, who imposes on the world by his majestic appearance and elaborate toilette. He is represented as living upon the earnings of his son, who has a most slavish reverence for him as a perfect "master of deportment."

Twelfth Night. A drama by Shakspere. The story is said to have come from a novelette written early in the 16th century. A brother and sister, twins, are shipwrecked. Viola, dressed like her brother, becomes page to the duke Orsino. The duke was in love with Olivia, and, as the lady looked coldly on his suit, he sent Viola to advance it, but the willful Olivia, instead of melting towards the duke, fell in love with his beautiful page. Sebastian, the twin brother of Viola, was attacked in a street brawl before Olivia, who, thinking him to be the page, invited him in. The result was the marriage of Sebastian to Olivia and of the duke to Viola.

Twice Told Tales. This name was given by the author, Nathaniel Hawthorne, to the tales included under its title, because some of them had been already published in the *Token* and other periodicals. They are mystical and, though in prose form, are the work of a poet. The tales are nearly all American in subject but treated from the spiritual rather than the practical side.

Two Gentlemen of Verona, The, Shakspere. One of the early comedies. The two gentlemen, Valentine and Proteus, go to Milan. Both fall in love with Sylvia. Proteus persuades the duke to banish Valentine, who gathers a following of bandits to capture Sylvia, who is affianced to Thurio. But Proteus had forgotten Julia, his Veronese sweetheart, who, following to Milan, serves him, unrecognized, as a page. In the end, Thurio proving unworthy, Sylvia is married to Valentine, while Proteus, repenting, takes Julia as his bride.

Two Noble Kinsmen, The, Shakspere and **Fletcher.** The story of this play is that of Palamon and Arcite, told by many poets. The two young men, prisoners, fall in love with Emilia, sister-in-law of Duke Theseus, who rules that she shall be the bride of the victor of a combat. Arcite wins, but is later killed by a fall from his horse, and Palamon marries the lady.

Ubaldo. Jerusalem Delivered, Tasso. One of the older crusaders, who had visited many regions. He and Charles the Dane went to bring back Rinaldo from the enchanted castle.

Ubeda. Don Quixote, Cervantes. A noted artist who one day painted a picture, but was obliged to write under it, "This is a cock," in order that the spectator might know what was intended to be represented.

Ulin. Tales of the Genii, Ridley. An enchantress, who had no power over those who remained faithful to Allah and their duty; but, if any fell into error or sin, she had full power to do as she liked. Thus, when Misnar, sultan of India, mistrusted the protection of Allah, she transformed him into a toad.

Ulrica. Ivanhoe, Scott. An old woman, one-time mistress of Front de Bœuf. She gets revenge for all his illtreatment of her in the burning of the castle of Torquilstone.

Ultima Thule. The extremity of the world; the most northern point known to the ancient Romans. Pliny and others say it is Iceland. See William Black's novel *A Princess of Thule.* Also applied to Ireland.

Una. Faery Queen, Spenser. The personification of truth. She goes, leading a lamb and riding on a white ass, to the court of Gloriana, to crave that one of her knights might undertake to slay the dragon which kept her father and mother prisoners. The adventure is accorded to the Red Cross Knight. Being driven by a storm into "Wandering Wood," a vision is sent to the knight, which causes him to leave Una, and she goes in search of him. In her wanderings a lion becomes her attendant. After many adventures, she finds St. George, the Red Cross Knight, but he is severely wounded. Una takes him to the house of Holiness, where he is carefully nursed, and then leads him to Eden.

Uncle Remus. The old plantation negro, whom Joel Chandler Harris makes the narrator of the fascinating animal fables in his fourteen "Uncle Remus" books (1881–1908).

Uncle Tom. Uncle Tom's Cabin, Mrs. Stowe. A negro slave of unaffected piety, and most faithful in the discharge of all his duties. His master, a humane man, becomes embarrassed in his affairs, and sells Tom to a slave dealer. After passing through various hands and suffering intolerable cruelties, he dies.

Underground Railroad, The. A popular embodiment of the various ways in which fugitive slaves from the Southern states of the American Union were assisted in escaping to the North, or to Canada; often humorously abbreviated U. G. R. R. H. D. Thoreau, the naturalist and philosopher, is said to have aided escaping slaves at his cottage on Walden Pond. "The Underground Railway" is the title of an absorbing historical work on the struggle of the slaves by Professor W. H. Siebert (N. Y. 1898).

Undine (*ŭn-dēn'*). In a German fairy romance by Fouqué, a water nymph, who was exchanged for the young child of a fisherman living near an enchanted forest. One day, Sir Huldbrand took shelter in the fisherman's hut, fell in love with Undine, and married her. By marrying a mortal she obtained a soul, and with it all the pains and penalties of the human race.

Unicorn. The name means "one horn." The origin of the belief in the existence of this fabulous animal has been assigned to the animal profiles on Egyptian sculptures. Travelers in the middle ages often reported having seen unicorns. But the spirit and prowess of the animal were said to be such that it never could be taken alive. These qualities probably induced James III of Scotland to adopt the unicorn as supporter for the royal arms. Later, James VI, who was James I of England, adopted the unicorn and the lion for the royal shield of the united realms.

Urgan. Lady of the Lake, Scott. A human child stolen by the king of the fairies, and brought up in elfland. He said to Alice Brand, the wife of Lord Richard, "If any woman will sign my brow thrice with a cross, I shall resume my proper form." Alice signed him thrice, and Urgan became at once "the fairest knight in all Scotland," and Alice recognized in him her own brother Ethert.

Urganda. In the romance of *Amadis of Gaul*, a powerful fairy sometimes appearing in all the terrors of an evil enchantress.

Uther (*ū'thẽr*). Son of Constans, one of the fabulous or legendary kings of Britain, and the father of Arthur.

Utopia. The name of an imaginary island described in the celebrated work of Sir Thomas More, in which was found the utmost perfection in laws, politics, and social arrangements. More's romance obtained a wide popularity, and the epithet "Utopian" has since been applied to all schemes for the improvement of society which are deemed impracticable.

Valentine. (1) One of the heroes in the old romance *Valentine and Orson*, which is of uncertain age and authorship. (2) One of the *Two Gentlemen of Verona*, in Shakspere's play of that name. (3) A gentleman attending on the duke in Shakspere's *Twelfth Night*. (4) One of the characters in Goethe's *Faust*. He is a brother of Marguerite.

Valerian or **Valirian. Canterbury Tales, Chaucer.** The husband of St. Cecilia. Cecilia told him she was beloved by an angel, who constantly visited her; and Valirian requested to see this visitant. Cecilia replied that he should do so, if he went to Pope Urban to be baptized. This he did, and, on his return, the angel gave him a crown of lilies and to Cecilia a crown of roses, both from the garden of paradise.

Valley of Humiliation. Pilgrim's Progress, Bunyan. The place where Christian encountered Apollyon, just before he came to the "Valley of the Shadow of Death."

Vanity Fair. Pilgrim's Progress, Bunyan. (1) A fair established by Beelzebub, Apollyon, and Legion, for the sale of all sorts of vanities. It was held in the town of Vanity, and lasted all the year round. Here were sold houses, lands, trades, honors, titles, kingdoms, and all sorts of pleasures and delights. Christian and Faithful had to pass through the fair, which they denounced. (2) Thackeray gave the name *Vanity Fair* to the first of his famous works. It has been called "a novel without a hero." See *Sedley*.

Varden, Dolly. In Dickens's *Barnaby Rudge*, the pretty, coquettish daughter of the locksmith, Gabriel Varden. She marries Joe Willet, and is for many years the mistress of the Maypole Inn. Her name was formerly applied to certain styles of gay dress stuffs.

Veck, Toby. The Chimes, Dickens. A ticket porter who went on errands and bore the nickname Trotty. One New Year's Eve he had a nightmare and fancied he had mounted to the steeple of a neighboring church, and that goblins issued out of the bells. He was roused from his sleep by the sound of the bells ringing in the new year.

Veda (*vā'dȧ*). The technical name of those ancient Sanskrit works on which the first period of the religious belief of the Hindus is based.

Veiled Prophet. Lalla Rookh, Moore. He assumed to be a god, and maintained that he had been Adam, Noah, and other representative men. Having lost an eye, and being otherwise disfigured in battle, he wore a veil to conceal his face, but his followers said it was done to screen his dazzling brightness.

Veni Creator Spiritus (*vē'nī crē-ā'tôr spĭr'ĭ-tŭs*). An ancient and very celebrated hymn of the Roman breviary, which occurs in the offices of the Feast of Pentecost, and which is used in many of the most solemn services of the Roman Catholic Church. Its author is not known with certainty.

Vernon, Die or **Diana. Rob Roy, Scott.** The heroine of the story, a highborn girl of great beauty and talents. She is an enthusiastic adherent of a persecuted religion and an exiled king. She is excluded from the ordinary wishes and schemes of other girls by being predestined to a hateful husband or a cloister, and by receiving a masculine education, under the superintendence of two men of talent and learning.

Vicar of Wakefield. A novel by Goldsmith, praised by Goethe as one of the best ever written. Its title refers to the hero, Dr. Primrose, whose experiences and naïve observations are frequently to be understood as those of the author himself. The tale abounds in amusing episodes, as memorable as proverbs. These include the purchase, by the vicar's son Moses, of a pair of green spectacles at the price of a horse; also the painting of the family portrait, which, when completed after great care and expense, was found to be too large to be hung. The chief charm of the work lies in its easy movement of idyllic events recorded in language at once homely and felicitous. Many of the incidents verge on melodrama, but the work as a whole leaves an inescapable impression of reality. See *Primrose*, page 307.

Vincentio (*vĭn-sĕn'shĭ-ō*). The duke of Vienna in Shakspere's *Measure for Measure*. He commits his scepter to Angelo, under the pretext of being called to take an urgent and distant journey, and, by exchanging the royal purple for a monk's hood, observes incognito the condition of his people.

Viola (*vī'ō-lȧ*). **Twelfth Night, Shakspere.** A sister of Sebastian. They were twins, and so much alike that they could be distinguished only by their dress. When they were shipwrecked, Viola was brought to shore by the captain, but her brother was left to shift for himself. Being in a strange land, Viola dressed as a page, and, under the name of Cesario, entered the service of Orsino, duke of Illyria. The duke greatly liked his beautiful page, and, when he discovered her true sex, married her.

Violenta. All's Well that Ends Well, Shakspere. A character in the play who enters upon the scene only once and then neither speaks nor is spoken to. The name has been used to designate any young lady nonentity; one who contributes nothing to the amusement or conversation of a party.

Virginian, The, Owen Wister. A story of the cattle country of Wyoming in the '80's of the 19th century. The hero is a young Virginian, in love with a school-teacher from Vermont. The Virginian "cow-puncher" character is said to have been drawn from the ranch life of Theodore Roosevelt.

Virginians, The, Thackeray. The story of the two grandsons of Henry Esmond. They take opposite sides in the Revolution. The action lies in both America and England. The gallery of characters includes George Washington, Dr. Johnson, and Richardson and Fielding, the novelists.

Vision of Sir Launfal, J. R. Lowell. A poetic story of a dream of the knight on the eve of his setting out on a quest. In this vision he sees the opportunity for best service at his own gates in giving himself with his alms. In Arthurian story Sir Launfal was a knight of the Round Table and a steward of King Arthur.

Vivien or **Vivian. Idylls of the King, Tennyson.** She is also known as the Lady of the Lake, and according to early legends was of a high family. These legends tell that Merlin, in his dotage, fell in love with her. She then persuaded Merlin to show her how a person could be imprisoned by enchantment without walls, towers, or chains and, after he had done so, she put him to sleep. While he slept, she performed the needful ceremonies, whereupon he found himself enclosed in a prison stronger than the strongest tower, and from that imprisonment was never again released.

Walden. A record of the experiences of the author, Thoreau, while living near Walden Pond on nine cents a day. He read Homer, watched the birds, bees, ants, and the animals that came within his range, describing the results of his acute powers of observation in a characteristic, quaint form.

War and Peace, Count Tolstóy. The title of a long philosophical novel. The action centers in the Napoleonic invasion of Russia. The story includes a vast number of characters, drawn with minute care and great realism. The author tries to show even the great leaders as creatures in the hands of overpowering fate or chance.

Waverley. Name of hero and title of novel by Scott. Scott had won great triumph as a narrative poet with such poems as *Marmion* and *The Lady of the Lake*. Byron eclipsed him in the field of romantic poetic narrative, and Scott picked up his unfinished manuscript of a novel, *Waverley*, and finished it. It was a great success. It was published anonymously, Scott not wishing to admit his withdrawal from the field of poetry. Many of the great Scott novels were published by "The Author of *Waverley*" but it was an "open secret" after a few years as to who the real author was. Few writers have really triumphed in two fields as Scott did.

Waverley Novels. General name given to Scott's historical novels. Those founded on English history are *Ivanhoe, Kenilworth, Peveril of the Peak, Betrothed, Talisman,* and *Woodstock.* Founded on Scotch history are *Waverley, Old Mortality, Monastery, The Abbott, Legend of Montrose, Fair Maid of Perth,* and *Castle Dangerous.* Treating of continental history are *Quentin Durward, Anne of Geierstein,* and *Count Robert of Paris.* Twelve others in the series, including *Rob Roy, Heart of Midlothian, Bride of Lammermoor,* are connected with historical events, but are more personal and deal mainly with Scottish character.

Weird Sisters, The. Three witches, in Shakspere's tragedy *Macbeth.*

Weller, Samuel. In Dickens's celebrated *Pickwick Papers,* a servant to Mr. Pickwick, to whom he becomes devotedly attached. Rather than leave his master, when he is sent to the Fleet, Sam Weller gets his father to arrest him for debt. He is an inimitable compound of wit, simplicity, quaint humor, and fidelity. "Tony Weller," father of Sam; a coachman of the old school, who drives between London and Dorking. On the coach box he is a king, elsewhere a mere London "cabby." He marries a widow and his constant advice to his son is, "Sam, beware of the vidders." Everybody was merry over Mr. Pickwick and Sam Weller, and everybody was eager to read this entertaining author.

Werewolf (*wēr′wo͝olf′*), **"Man-Wolf."** The notion of the changing of men into wolves is very old in literature. The Romans fancied the change made by magic. The Norse tales employ the wolfskin shirt, by which the man becomes a wolf for nine days out of ten.

When Knighthood Was in Flower, Charles Major. A historical novel, which tells the love story of Mary Tudor, sister of Henry VIII, and Charles Brandon.

Whittington, Dick. The hero of a famous old legend, in which he is represented as a poor orphan boy from the country, who went to London, where, after undergoing many hardships, he obtained a penny and bought a cat. Shortly after, he sent his cat on a venture in his master's ship; and the king of Barbary, whose court was overrun with mice, gladly bought the cat at a high price. With this money Whittington commenced business, and succeeded so well that he finally married his former master's daughter, was knighted, and became lord mayor of London.

Wife of Bath. One of the pilgrims in Chaucer's *Canterbury Tales.* She tells, in her turn, the story of Midas. The prologue to her story is famous for the wife's naïve revelation of her own story and character.

Wild Duck, The, Ibsen. An ironic play, its leading idea being that sometimes it is unwise to tell the entire bald truth.

Wilfer. Name of a family prominent in *Our Mutual Friend,* by Dickens. Reginald Wilfer, called by his wife R. W., and by his fellow clerks Rumty. He was clerk in the drug house of Chicksey, Stobbles, and Veneering. Mrs. Wilfer, wife of Mr. Reginald, a most majestic woman, with an exalted idea of her own importance. Bella Wilfer, daughter of Mr. and Mrs. Wilfer, a wayward, playful, affectionate, spoiled beauty, so pretty, so womanly, and yet so childish that she was always captivating. She spoke of herself as "the lovely woman." Bella married John Harmon. Lavinia Wilfer, a younger sister of Bella, and called "The Irrepressible."

William Tell. The hero of a Swiss legend, which has been told in many poems and dramas. He obeys the command of Gessler, the governor, to shoot an apple from his son's head. Asked by Gessler why he had put a second arrow in his belt, he replies, "To kill you with, had I slain my son." He is then placed in a boat as prisoner, but escapes and kills the governor, thus opening the Swiss War of Liberation from Austria. The date is placed in 1307. But the fact seems to be that, in the middle of the 15th century, an unknown author introduced into Switzerland a Danish archer and apple story, which fitted local needs so well that it grew into a national legend. Schiller's *William Tell* is the best-known telling of the story in drama.

Winter's Tale, The, Shakspere. Leontes, king of Sicily, invites his friend Polixenes to visit him, becomes jealous, and commands Camillo to poison him. Camillo warns Polixenes and flees with him to Bohemia. Leontes casts his queen, Hermione, into prison, where she gives birth to a daughter. Hermione is reported dead, and the child is brought up by a shepherd, who calls it Perdita. Florizel sees Perdita and falls in love with her; but Polixenes, his father, tells her that she and the shepherd shall be put to death if she encourages the suit. Florizel and Perdita flee to Sicily and are introduced to Leontes. It is soon discovered that Perdita is his lost daughter. Polixenes tracks his son to Sicily and consents to the union. The party are invited to inspect a statue of Hermione, and the statue turns out to be the living queen.

Witching Hour, The, Augustus Thomas. A play upon the theme of hypnotism and telepathy. In the rooms of Jack Brookfield, a professional gambler of Louisville, Ky., Clay Whipple strikes Tom Deming with a heavy paper cutter. Deming, who while drunk has been pursuing Clay with a cat's-eye stickpin, to which Clay has an inherited aversion, falls dead. A jury convicts Clay of murder. The prosecutor is Hardmuth who is Clay's rival for the hand of Brookfield's niece, Viola Campbell. On a retrial Clay is acquitted. Between the two trials, Brookfield has come, under the tutelage of Supreme Court Justice Prentiss, to believe in the effectiveness of his own powers of telepathy. He makes use of these powers to influence the trial jury. Believing that much of his gambling success has been due to these powers, he quits that business. Further, he has publicly charged Hardmuth, on good evidence, with having planned the murder of a governor of the state. But, believing that his own previous thought may have influenced Hardmuth, he helps him to escape from the state. Under his suggestion also, Clay is freed from his morbid fear of the "cat's-eye."

Worldly Wiseman, Mr. One of the characters in Bunyan's *Pilgrim's Progress,* who converses with Christian by the way, and endeavors to deter him from proceeding on his journey.

Wrayburn, Eugene. Our Mutual Friend, Dickens. Barrister at law. He is an indolent, moody, whimsical young man, who loves Lizzie Hexam. After he is nearly killed by Bradley Headstone, he reforms, and marries Lizzie, who saved his life.

Yahoo. A name given by Swift, in his satirical romance *Gulliver's Travels,* to one of a race of brutes having the form and all the vices of man. The Yahoos are represented as being subject to the Houyhnhnms, or horses endowed with reason.

Yarpe. The Gray Horse Troop, Hamlin Garland. The resolute leader of the cowboy gang that undertook to drive the Tetons from their reservation lands in the Far West. The real hero of the story, Captain Curtis, is in charge of the Indians. His fight against the political ring that would defraud his wards and his courageous handling of a serious crisis show him to be a different power from that with which these cowboys generally met, when they "shot up" towns and raced the Tetons across the hills, making of themselves a lynching party on Federal territory. United States soldiers appear on the scene and Yarpe and his men depart.

Yeast. A romance by Charles Kingsley. It was the outcome of his interest in the Chartist riots and disturbances, and it gives some of the most powerful delineations of the sufferings of the poor, found in English literature.

Yemassee. A historical tale founded on personal knowledge of the American Indian character. It was written in the first half of the 19th century by W. G. Simms, of whom it has been said, "He has done for the historical traditions of the Carolinas what Cooper did for those of the North and West."

Yeo. Westward Ho! Chas. Kingsley. A character in the novel, prominent as a bold mariner, a true friend, a terrible foe. He was a lifelong sailor, and made voyages to New Guinea for negro slaves that were sold in the West Indies. He joined in the search for fabulous wealth in New Spain, crossed the Isthmus of Panama, was pursued, and wandered in the woods of the isthmus for some months. *Westward Ho!* is a historical novel of the Elizabethan English period.

Yorick. (1) The king of Denmark's jester, mentioned in Shakspere's *Hamlet.* Hamlet picks up his skull in the churchyard and apostrophizes it. (2) A humorous and careless parson in Sterne's *Tristram Shandy.*

Zarathustra (*zär′ȧ-tho͞os′trȧ*). *Thus Spake Zarathustra* is the title of a work by Frederick Nietzsche, in which he embodied his philosophy. Zarathustra is a form of the name of Zoroaster, the Persian sage.

Zenobia. Blithedale Romance, Hawthorne. A strong-minded woman, beautiful and intelligent, who was interested in playing out the pastoral of the life at Brook Farm. She is represented as disappointed in love; at last she drowned herself.

Zero Hour. The name given in the World War to the moment set for a charge from the trench. Generally used to mean the instant for beginning any important move or work.

Zuleika (*zo͞o-lā′kä*). (1) In Byron's "Bride of Abydos," the pasha's daughter in love with her cousin Selim. They elope, but are pursued. Selim is killed, and Zuleika dies of a broken heart. (2) A character in the Persian story of Joseph and Zuleika.

MYTHOLOGY

The term mythology is applied to the body of stories current among ancient and primitive peoples regarding their gods and heroes. Many of these myths, particularly those of the Greeks and Romans, have been woven into the literatures of the world, from which, to no small degree, they have passed into common knowledge.

This section is a guide to mythology from two separate and distinct approaches—the literary and the practical.

The student of literature is continually meeting allusions to myths which must be understood if the author's meaning is to be intelligible. In such instances, the reader is already in possession of the name of the mythical character or place and he wishes to learn the story connected with it. For this purpose he will find a trusty guide in the Dictionary of Mythology on the following pages.

On the other hand, there are many purposes for which it is desirable to know the mythical names and stories associated with certain ideas, qualities, or the like. Beginning with such terms as love, war, friendship, or fleetness, for instance, one may wish to know what deities or mythical characters are associated with them. The answers to such questions are quickly found by consulting the Table of Mythological Associations given below. For every mythological name in this table a descriptive article will be found in the Dictionary of Mythology. If the reader wishes to know, for example, what mythical names and stories are associated with beauty, he finds in the table the term Beauty, followed by the names Adonis, Aphrodite, and others. Then by referring to each of these names in the Dictionary of Mythology, he learns the principal stories connected with them.

TABLE OF MYTHOLOGICAL ASSOCIATIONS

Agriculture. See *Earth, Fruit, Harvest, Sheep, Woods.*
Art. Apollo, Muses, Parnassus.
Aviation. Dædalus, Icarus, Pegasus.
Beauty. Adonis, Aphrodite, Apollo, Graces, Freya, Helen, Hyperion, Krishna, Phaon, Rambha, Venus.
Birds. Æsacus, Alectryon, Blue Jay, Coronis, Leda, Paupukkeewis, Philomela, Phœnix.
Bravery. Achilles, Deiphobus, Euphorbus, Fortitudo, Pyrrhus, Tyr.
Celestial Regions. Asgard, Bilskirnir, Cauther, Elysium, Gladsheim, Glasir, Islands of the Blest, Valhalla.
Civilization. Cadmus, Cecrops, Egeria, Hou Chi, Italapas, Melissa, Old One, Prometheus, Votán.
Cold. Elivagar, Fafnir, Gerda, Ginungagap, Hymir, Lord of Cold Weather, Mowis, Niflheim, Ymir.
Creation. Afraid of Nothing, Chaos, Dagan, Earth-Namer, Embla, Iapetus, Ormuzd, Pandora.
Dance. Corybantes, Silenus, Terpsichore.
Dawn. Aurora.
Death. Azrael, Giallar, Hell Shoon, Lethe, Libitina, Manes, Pauguk, Ponemah, Valkyries.
Demons, Spirits, and Dwarfs. Azazel, Barguest, Beelzebub, Berg Folk, Diatyas, Dives, Elf, Galar, Gian ben Gian, Gnome, Goblins, Kelpie, Kobold, Lilith, Mammon, Mephistopheles, Moakkibat, Nickneven, Nix, Trolls.
Destruction. Apollo, Nickar, Ragnarok, Siva.
Earth or Soil. Demogorgon, Duergar, Frigga, Great Turtle, Midgard, Pachacamac.
Education. Athena, Minerva.
Eloquence. Bragi, Mercury.
Evil. Ahriman, Akuman, Belphegor, Dahak, Eblis, Hobomoko, Hugon, Loki, Nickar, Rakshasas.
Fairies. Befana, Elf, Hodeken, Melusina, Peri.
Faithfulness. Penelope.
Fate. Atropos, Clotho, Fates, Lachesis, Norns.
Fertility. Danu, Draupnir, Frey, Isis, Mithra, Ops.
Fire. Agni, Fire People, Fire Spirit, Nanabozho, Vulcan.
Fleetness. Ajax, Atalanta, Hippomenes.
Flood. Coxcox, Deucalion and Pyrrha.
Flowers. Clytie, Flora, Hyacinthus, Narcissus.
Food and Drink. Ambrosia, Nectar.
Fountains. Aganippe, Arethusa, Camenæ, Castilia, Hippocrene, Naiads, Pirene.
Friendship. Iolaus, Lofen, Nisus, Patroclus, Pylades.
Fruit. Feronia, Golden Apples, Iduna, Pomona.
Gardens. Pomona, Priapus.
Giants. Antæus, Atlas, Briareus, Egia, Enceladus, Giants, Læstrygonians, Ogre, Orion, Ravana, Tityus.
Good Fortune. Felicitas, Fortuna.
Guardians. Bertha, Heimdall, Irus, Jizo, Melic Nymphs, Mentor, Palladium, Polias, Radegaste.
Happiness. Nepenthe.
Harvest. Ceres, Consus, Demeter, Paimosaid, Saturn.
Health. Æsculapius, Apollo, Eira, Hygeia, Podalirius.
Heroes. See Kings.
Heroines. Antigone, Camilla, Electra, Hecuba, Helle, Hermione, Hippolyta, Ismene, Nausicaa.
Home and Hearth. Hestia, Lares, Penates, Vesta.
Hunting. Actæon, Artemis, Diana, Herla, Orion.
Immortality. Ambrosia, Calypso, Nectar, Tithonus.
Infidelity. Clytemnestra, Cressida.
Islands. Atlantis, Ithaca.
Jealousy. Helice, Io, Juno, Latona.
Justice. Æacus, Minos, Orlog, Rhadamanthus, Themis.
Kings and Heroes. Agamemnon, Anchises, Bellerophon, Baldud, Diomedes, Hector, Idomeneus, Ion, Ixion, Laertes, Laius, Laomedon, Lycomedes, Meleager, Memnon, Menelaus, Neleus, Neoptolemus, Œdipus, Orestes, Palamedes, Peleus, Pelops, Perseus, Polydorus, Priam, Romulus, Telamon, Theseus, Ulysses.
Light. Agni, Amida, Diana, Janus, Lucifer, Mithra.
Love. Aphrodite, Astarte, Cupid, Derceto, Dione, Eros, Freya, Hylas, Hymen, Kama, Lofua, Venus.
Love Lure. Fata Morgana, Lilinau, Lorelei, Sirens.
Lovers. Acis, Alcestis, Ariadne, Echo, Eurydice, Laodamia, Nala, Narcissus, Parthenope, Pasiphaë, Phædra, Philemon and Baucis, Psyche, Pyramus, Tithonus.
Magic. Circe, Hecate, Medea, Paupukkeewis.
Memory. Mnemosyne.
Messenger. Hermes, Hofvarpnir.
Monsters. Argus, Centaurs, Cerberus, Chimæra, Chiron, Cyclopes, Fenris, Geryon, Gorgons, Harpies, Hydra, Lamia, Laomedon, Medusa, Minotaur, Nemean Lion, Nithhogg, Polyphemus, Scylla, Sphinx.
Moon. Astarte, Diana, Endymion, Luna, Mani, Phœbe.
Mountains. Calpe, Cybele, Helicon, Ida, Koppenberg, Latmus, Mænalus, Meru, Olympus, Parnassus, Pelion.
Music. Amphion, Apollo, Arion, Bran, Chibiabos, Israfel, Marsyas, Orpheus, Pan.
Nature. Mendes, Pan.
Navigation. Argo, Argonauts, Pleiades.
Night. Hecate, Hoder, Nox.
Ocean and Sea. Ægir, Mermaids, Mimir, Neptune, Nereids, Oceanids, Oceanus, Poseidon, Thetis, Triton.
Peace. Balder, Concordia, Frey, Frodi, Harmonia, Irene, Janus, Pax, Pukwana.
Poetry. Apollo, Bragi, Bran, Brigit, Calliope, Daphnis.
Pride. Arachne, Niobe, Thersites.
Prophecy. Apollo, Augurs, Brigit, Calchas, Cassandra, Delphi, Dodona, Gripir, Helenus, Pythia, Silenus.
Purity, or Chastity. Artemis, Diana.
Rain and Rainbow. Frey, Hyades, Iris, Pluvius.
Revelry. Comus.
Riches and Gain. Kubera, Mercury, Midas, Plutus.
Rivers. Alpheus, Elivagar, Enipeus, Ifing, Pactolus.
Robbery and Thieving. Cacus, Charybdis, Mercury.
Rulers of Gods. Amen, Ammon, Anu, Baal, Brahma, Cronus, Frigga, Grid, Hera, Juno, Jupiter, Manitou, Odin, Ormuzd, Rhea, Zeus.
Seasons. Æstas, Glooskap, Horæ, Ostara, Peboan.
Serpents. Adissechen, Laocoön, Midgard Serpent, Python.
Sheep and Cattle. Pales, Pan.
Sleep and Dreams. Morpheus.
Stars and Constellations. Ariadne, Callisto, Cassiopeia, Gemini, Hyades, Orion, Pleiades, Sirius.
Strength. Chou, Hercules, Megingiard.
Strife. Discordia, Eris.
Sun. Ama-Terasu, Aten, Frey, Helios, Horus, Hyperion, Ipalnemohuani, Phaëthon, Ra, Rama Chandra, Sol.
Thunder. Donar, Haskah, Mjöllnir, Thor, Thunder Bird.
Treasure. Cluricaune, Golden Fleece, Hesperides.
Trees. Daphne, Lotis, Phyllis, Sedrat, Yggdrasil.
Underworld. Aralu, Avernus, Cerberus, Charon, Cocytus, Dis, Elbegast, Erebus, Garm, Giall, Hades, Hecate, Hel, Naraka, Persephone, Pluto, Styx, Tartarus.
Vengeance. Alecto, Diræ, Eumenides, Furies, Nemesis.
War. Ares, Bellona, Mars.
Winds. Æolus, Auræ, Boreas, Feng, Zephyrus.
Wine. Bacchus, Dionysus, Icarius, Liber, Mæra.
Wisdom. Athena, Mimir, Minerva, Nestor, Odhrerir.
Woods. Artemis, Dryads, Fauns, Satyr, Silvanus.
Youth. Agni, Hebe, Iduna, Jamshid.

MYTHOLOGICAL PERSONS, PLACES, AND STORIES

Acheron (*ăk'ẽr-ŏn*). One of the four rivers of the lower regions. See *Styx*.

Achilles (*ȧ-kĭl'ēz*). The son of Peleus and Thetis. In the Trojan War he was the most distinguished of the Greeks for his strength and bravery. When Achilles was born, Thetis plunged him in the river Styx, which made him invulnerable in every part except the heel by which she held him. And in this heel later he received a fatal wound.

Acis (*ā'sĭs*). The handsome shepherd loved by the nymph Galatea, whose favor the monstrous Cyclops, Polyphemus, sued for in vain.

Acrisius (*ȧ-krĭs'ĭ-ŭs*). Son of King Abas of Argos, grandson of Lynceus, and great-grandson of Danaus. An oracle had declared that Danaë, the daughter of Acrisus, would give birth to a son who would kill his grandfather. For this reason Acrisius kept Danaë shut up in a brazen tower. But here she became the mother of Perseus, by Zeus, who visited her in the form of a shower of gold.

Actæon (*ăk-tē'ŏn*). The son of Aristæus and Autonoë, daughter of Cadmus. He was reared by Chiron, and, becoming passionately fond of the chase, passed his days chiefly in pursuit of wild beasts that haunted Mount Cithæron. There, having accidentally come upon and seen Diana taking a bath, he was turned into a stag by her and killed by his own dogs.

Adad (*ȧ-dăd'*). An Assyrian and Babylonian god of the storm, identified with Ramman and Rimmon, the latter of whom is mentioned in the Old Testament. His weapons were flood, lightning, and famine.

Adissechen (*ȧ-dĭs'ĭ-kĕn*). In Hindu mythology, the serpent of a thousand heads which holds the universe in place.

Admetus (*ăd-mē'tŭs*). See *Alcestis* and *Apollo*.

Adonis (*ȧ-dō'nĭs*). A beautiful youth, loved by Venus and slain by a wild boar which he was hunting. Venus was inconsolable at his loss, and at last obtained from Proserpina consent that Adonis should spend six months on earth with her and six months among the shades.

Adrammelech (*ȧ-drăm'ê-lĕk*). A god of the people of Sepharvaim, to whom infants were burned in sacrifice. He was later known as one of the fallen angels.

Æacus (*ē'ȧ-kŭs*). Son of Jupiter and grandson of the river god Asopus. He was renowned throughout Greece for his justice and piety, and after his death he became one of the judges in Hades.

Æetes (*ē-ē'tēz*). Father of Medea and king of Colchis when Phrixus brought there the golden fleece.

Ægæon (*ê-jē'ŏn*). Another name for Briareus, the giant.

Ægeus (*ē'jê-ŭs*). King of Athens, and father of Theseus. In grief at the supposed loss of his son he threw himself into the sea, thereafter called Ægean.

Ægir (*ē'jĭr*). God of the ocean, whose wife is Ran. They had nine daughters, the billows, who were clad in colored, diaphanous robes and whose moods varied with that of their brother, the wind.

Ægis (*ē'jĭs*). The shield of Jupiter made by Vulcan.

Ægle (*ĕg'lê*). The mother of the Graces. Also the name of one of the sisters of Phaëthon.

Æolus (*ē'ô-lŭs*). A son of Neptune, or, according to others, of Hippotes, an ancient lord of the Lipari Isles. Jupiter made him keeper of the winds, which, having previously been represented as mythical persons, under the names Zephyrus, Boreas, Notus, and Eurus, were afterwards considered the servants of Æolus. He held them imprisoned in a cave of an island in the Mediterranean Sea, and let them loose only to further his own designs or those of others, in producing storms. He is usually described by the poets as virtuous, upright, and friendly to strangers, and is represented pictorially as a vigorous man supporting himself in the air by wings, and blowing into a shell trumpet, like a Triton, while his short mantle waves in the wind.

Æsacus. A son of Priam, who was enamored of the nymph Hesperia and, on her death, threw himself into the sea. He was changed by Thetis into a cormorant.

Æsculapius (*ĕs'kû-lā'pĭ-ŭs*). The son of Apollo and of Coronis, the daughter of a Thessalian king. By his father he was committed to the care of the wise centaur, Chiron, who taught him botany, together with the secret efficacy of plants. He became a great physician, even restoring the dead to life on one occasion. For this, Jupiter, at the request of Pluto, struck the physician dead with lightning. After his death, at the request of Apollo, he was placed among the stars. In later centuries he was worshiped as the god of healing.

Æsir (*ē'sĭr*). The name of the thirteen celestial gods of Scandinavia, who lived in Asgard, accessible only by the bridge of the rainbow. The chief was Odin.

Æson (*ē'sŏn*). The father of Jason. In extreme old age he was restored to youth by the magic arts of Medea.

Æstas. Personification of summer; he is crowned with corn and generally holds a sickle in his hand. So he appears on reliefs, medals, and gems, usually in company with the representations of the other three seasons. He is depicted as youthful and sprightly, while Ver, "spring," is infantile and tender; Autumnus, "autumn," is mature and manly; and Hiems, "winter," is old and decrepit.

Afraid of Nothing. Among some North American Indian tribes, the goddess dwelling in the East, who created the world and prepared it for the dwelling of men.

Agamemnon (*ăg'ȧ-mĕm'nŏn*). King of Argos in Greece and commander in chief of the allied Greeks who went to the siege of Troy. Agamemnon married Clytemnestra, the daughter of Tyndareus, by whom he became the father of Iphianassa (Iphigenia). On his return home from Troy, he was killed by Clytemnestra and her paramour.

Aganippe (*ăg'ȧ-nĭp'ē*). A fountain at the foot of Mount Helicon, in Bœotia, consecrated to Apollo and the Muses. It was supposed to have the power of inspiring those who drank of it. From it the Muses were called Aganippides.

Agni. A Vedic god of light and fire. He appears under many characters, but chiefly embodies eternal youth. Sometimes he is regarded as a beneficent household god and a protector against the horror of darkness.

Ahriman (*ä'rĭ-mȧn*). In early Persian, Angra Maïnyu (*ăn'grä mī'nū*). A deity of the ancient Persians, representing the principle of evil. Unlike Ormuzd, the principle of good, who is eternal, Ahriman is created and will one day perish.

Ajax (*ā'jăks*). The son of Telamon, and one of the Greek heroes in Homer's *Iliad*. He was of great stature, strength, and courage, but dull in mind. He killed himself out of vexation because, in a competition for the armor of Hector, the prize was awarded to Ulysses.

Akuman. The most malevolent of all the Persian gods.

Alcestis or **Alceste** (*ăl-sĕs'tĭs*) (*-sĕst*). A daughter of Pelias, and the wife of Admetus. By request of Apollo, the gods had granted eternal life to Admetus, but on the condition that, when the appointed time came for the good king's death, some one should be found willing to die in his stead. This decree was reported to Alcestis, Admetus' beautiful young wife, who offered herself as substitute and cheerfully gave her life for her husband. But immortality was too dearly bought at such a price. Admetus mourned until Hercules, pitying his grief, descended into Hades and brought back Alcestis.

Alecto (*ȧ-lĕk'tō*). One of the Furies. She is represented with her head covered with serpents, and breathing vengeance, war, and pestilence.

Alectryon (*ȧ-lĕk'trĭ-ŏn*). A servant of Mars, who was changed by him into a cock because he did not warn his master of the rising of the sun.

Alfadur or **Alfadir** (*äl-fä'dĭr*). In Scandinavian mythology, one of the many names of Odin. It means "father of all."

Alpheus (*ăl-fē'ŭs*). A river god who fell in love with the nymph Arethusa and pursued her. Diana came to her rescue and changed her into a fountain.

Althæa (*ăl-thē'ȧ*). Sister of Atalanta, and mother of Meleager. She caused the death of her son and killed herself in remorse.

Ama-Terasu. A Japanese sun goddess. She figures in myths which represent her as hiding in a cave and coming out only after the other gods exhaust their powers of persuasion. Thus the alternation of night and day is portrayed. Ama-Terasu is the fabled ancestress of the royal house of Japan.

Amazons. A nation of women warriors who lived in Scythia. Early traditions tell of their appearance at the siege of Troy, under Penthesilea, their queen, who was eventually slain by Achilles. Hercules defeated them when, as one of his labors, he was required to obtain the girdle of their queen Hippolyta. Theseus later made an expedition against them and carried off their queen Antiope. In revenge they invaded Greece and were defeated on the site of Athens. A similar story was told among the Caribs in regard to a tribe of women warriors in South America and accounts for the name of the river Amazon.

Ambrosia (*ăm-brō'zhĭ-ȧ*). The food of the gods; so called because it preserved their immortality.

Amen (*ä'mĕn*). An ancient Egyptian god, identified with Ammon and also with the Greek Zeus. Under the name Amen-Ra, he was worshiped as king of the gods. He is at different times represented as a ram with large twisted horns; a human figure with a ram's head; a king seated on a throne and wearing a disk surmounted by two tall ostrich feathers.

Amida. One of the principal Buddhist gods of Japan, originally a god of light. Usually he is represented as seated cross-legged on a lotus flower. The "Great Buddha" at Kamakura is an image of Amida.

Ammon. A cult name of Jupiter, under which he was worshiped at Thebes in Egypt. As Jupiter Ammon he was represented as having the horns of a ram. See *Amen*.

Amphion (*ăm-fī'ŏn*). Son of Jupiter and Antiope, and brother of Zethus. He and Zethus were born on Mount Cithæron and grew up among the shepherds. When they had learned their origin they marched against Thebes, where reigned Lycus, the husband of their mother Antiope, who had married Dirce in her stead. They took the city and killed Lycus and Dirce, because they had treated Antiope with great cruelty. After they had obtained possession of Thebes, they fortified it by a wall. Amphion had received a lyre from Mercury, on which he played with such magic skill that the stones moved of their own accord and formed the wall.

Ancæus (*ăn-sē'ŭs*). A son of Neptune who, having left a cup of wine untasted to pursue a wild boar, was killed in his attempt to destroy it. With this story is connected the proverb, "There's many a slip 'twixt the cup and the lip."

Anchises (*ăn-kī'sēz*). King of Dardanus and, by his union with Venus, father of Æneas. On the capture of Troy by the Greeks, Æneas carried his father on his shoulders from the burning city.

Andromache (*ăn-drŏm'ȧ-kē*). The wife of Hector, prince of Troy. After the death of Hector, she was given to Neoptolemus of Epirus. Later, she married a Trojan, Helenus. She is the subject of a tragedy by Euripides.

Andromeda (*ăn-drŏm'ē-dȧ*). Daughter of Cepheus, king of Ethiopia. The sea nymphs, offended by her mother, had sent to ravage the coast a sea monster which, according to an oracle of Jupiter Ammon, would not desist until Andromeda had been offered to it as a sacrifice. Perseus beheld the maiden fastened with chains to a rock and the monster rising out of the sea ready to devour her, while her parents stood on the shore in despair. He rushed down upon the monster, struck it a deadly blow, delivered the maiden, and obtained her as his wife.

Angurvadel. The sword of the Norse hero Frithjof, which, inscribed with Runic letters, blazed in time of war, but gleamed with a dim light in time of peace.

Antæus (*ăn-tē'ŭs*). One of the giants, sons of Neptune, whose home was in Libya. His strength was invincible so long as he remained in contact with his mother, the earth, but when he was lifted from it his strength decreased. One of the exploits ascribed to Hercules was his conquest of Antæus, whose weakness he had discovered.

Antigone (*ăn-tĭg'ō-nē*). Daughter of Œdipus, king of Thebes. When Œdipus had put out his eyes and was exiled, she shared his misfortunes and acted as his guide until his death at Colonus. After her return to Thebes one of her brothers, Polynices, leading an attack on Thebes, was slain. Creon, the new king, forbade him burial. Antigone, disobeying the prohibition, was sentenced to be buried alive, but committed suicide in anticipation of the execution.

Anu. The chief of the Babylonian triad of gods, the others being Bel and Ea. He was the king of heaven and the father of the gods. In Hindu mythology, Anu was a son of King Yayati, who cursed him for refusing to bear the burden of his old age.

Aphrodite (*ăf'rō-dī'tē*). The Greek goddess identified by the Romans with Venus. She was said to be the daughter of Zeus, but later poets frequently relate that she was sprung from the foam of the sea, whence they derive her name.

Apis. One of the Egyptian gods worshiped under the form of a man with a bull's head.

Apollo. According to both Greeks and Romans, Apollo was the son of Jupiter and Latona, born on the island Delos. He was regarded as the god of the sciences and the arts, especially poetry, music, and medicine. They ascribed to him the greatest skill in the use of the bow and arrow, which he proved in killing the serpent Pytho, the sons of Niobe, and the Cyclopes. The last achievement incensed Jupiter, and he was banished from Olympus. During his exile Apollo abode as a shepherd with Admetus, king of Thessaly. All sudden deaths were believed to be the effect of his arrows; and with them he sent the plague into the camp of the Greeks before Troy. As he had the power of punishing men, so he was also able to deliver men, if duly propitiated. From his being the god who afforded help, he was the father of Æsculapius, the god of healing. As a god of inspiration and prophecy he gave oracles and communicated this gift to other gods and to men. He was often referred to by his cult name Phœbus.

Arachne (*ȧ-răk'nē*). A Mæonian maid who, proud of the skill in weaving and embroidery imparted to her by Minerva, ventured to challenge her patron goddess to a trial of skill. Minerva accepted the challenge. Arachne produced a piece of cloth in which the amours of the gods were woven, and, as the goddess could find no fault with it, she tore the work to pieces. Arachne, in despair, tried to hang herself. Minerva, however, loosened the rope and saved her life, but the rope was changed into a cobweb, and Arachne herself, into a spider.

Aralu. The Babylonian underworld. It was described as a melancholy place, where the dead wandered with only clay and dust for food.

Ares (*ā'rēz*). The Greek god of war, identified by the Romans with Mars. He is often represented as the lover of Aphrodite, or Venus.

Arethusa (*ăr'ē-thū'sȧ*). A wood nymph of Elis, in Greece, who, pursued by the river god Alpheus, was changed into a spring and ran under the sea. The waters of this spring, mingling with the river, rose again in the fountain of Arethusa in the island of Ortygia near Syracuse.

Argo. A fifty-oared ship in which Jason and his companions made their voyage to Colchis in search of the golden fleece. This ship was built of pines cut from Mount Pelion, and, although larger than any other previously constructed, it moved lightly and easily, and was therefore called the *Argo*, "swift-sailing." From her name, those who embarked in her were called Argonauts. The mast of the *Argo* was taken from the forest of Dodona, where the oaks were endowed with the power of making predictions; therefore, the ship was regarded as an animated being, in accord with fate, to which a man might commit himself with confidence.

Argonauts (*är'gō-nôts*). The participants in the so-called Argonautic expedition. It was a voyage from Greece to Colchis undertaken by Jason in order to obtain the golden fleece. The task had been imposed upon Jason by his uncle Pelias, in the hope of destroying the hero. Jason, however, invited the most illustrious heroes of Greece to join him, among them Hercules, Castor and Pollux, Peleus, Pirithous, and Theseus. The vessel built for the purpose was named *Argo*. After various adverse events it arrived at Æeta, the capital of Colchis, where Jason, with the help of Medea, was successful in his quest.

Argus. A fabulous being of enormous strength, who had a hundred eyes, of which only two were closed in sleep at the same time. Juno, jealous of Io, whom her husband, Jupiter, loved, changed her into a heifer and set Argus to guard her. Jupiter had Mercury slay him, and Juno placed his hundred eyes in the tail of her favorite bird, the peacock.

Ariadne (*ăr'ĭ-ăd'nē*). Daughter of Minos, second king of Crete, and of Pasiphaë. She fell in love with Theseus, who was shut up in the labyrinth to be devoured by the Minotaur, and gave him a clew of thread by which, after he had killed the monster, he extricated himself from the windings of the labyrinth. He took Ariadne back with him but deserted her on the island of Naxos, where Bacchus found and married her. Bacchus gave her a crown of gems which on her death he placed as a constellation in the sky.

Arion (*ȧ-rī'ŏn*). A Greek bard, who, while passenger on a ship, was made to leap overboard and leave his money with the crew. He was taken up by dolphins, and carried on their backs safe to land.

Artemis (*är'tē-mĭs*). Daughter of Zeus and Latona, and twin sister of Apollo. She was the goddess of chastity, the chase, and the woods. Artemis was identified by the Romans with Diana.

Asgard. In Scandinavian mythology Asgard represents the city of the gods, situated at the center of the universe, and accessible only by the bridge Bifröst, or the rainbow.

Astarte (*ăs-tär'tē*). An ancient Syrian deity, noticed in the Old Testament under the name Ashteroth. She was a goddess of love, women, and the moon, and hence corresponds to Aphrodite or Venus.

Atalanta (*ăt'ȧ-lăn'tȧ*). A maid of Arcadia with athletic tastes who joined in the Calydonian hunt, and, at the funeral games of Pelias, won the prize in wrestling. Warned not to marry, she offered her hand to any suitor who could overcome her in a race. The penalty of failure was death. Hippomenes won by the strategem of throwing three golden apples before her which she paused to pick up. They were married, but the pair was transformed into lions by Cybele and continued to accompany her.

Aten. The name of the winged solar disk, the worship of which was introduced into Egypt by Amenhotep IV in the 14th century B. C. Hymns addressed to Aten hail him as creator and lord of love. No image of this deity was permitted to be made.

Athena. The Greek goddess of wisdom, identified by the Romans with Minerva. She was claimed by Athens as its guardian deity and in that character was usually known as Pallas Athena.

Atlantis. A mythical island in the West, mentioned by Plato, Pliny, and other ancient writers, and said to have sunk beneath the ocean.

Atlas. One of the Titans, son of Iapetus and Clymene. Being conquered by Jupiter, he was condemned to the labor of bearing on his head and hands the heaven he had attempted to destroy.

Atropos (*ăt'rô-pŏs*). The one of the three Parcæ, or Fates, that cuts the thread of life. Her name signifies "the inexorable one." The other two Fates were Clotho, who spins the thread, and Lachesis, who determines its length. See *Fates*.

Augean (*ô-jē'ăn*) **Stables.** The stables of Augeas, king of Elis, in Greece. In these stables he had kept 3000 oxen, and the stalls had not been cleansed for thirty years. When Hercules was required to cleanse these stables, he caused two rivers to run through them and afterward slew Augeas.

Augurs. Men whose principal business was to observe and interpret the entrails of animals and other phenomena which were regarded by the Romans as omens of the future.

Auræ (*ô'rē*). The breezes, nymphs of the air, a species of sportive, happy beings and well-wishers to mankind. They were represented as winged.

Aurora. The goddess of the morning or the dawn, sometimes described as the goddess of day. She is represented as standing in a magnificent chariot, drawn by winged steeds. A brilliant star sparkles upon her forehead, and from her rosy finger tips drops dew; with one hand she grasps the reins, and she holds in the other a lighted torch.

Avatar (*ăv'ȧ-tär'*). The incarnations or descents of the deity Vishnu, of which nine are believed to be past. The tenth is yet to come when Vishnu will descend from heaven on a white-winged horse, and will introduce on earth a golden age of virtue and peace.

Avernus (*ȧ-vûr'nŭs*). A small, deep lake in Campania, occupying the crater of an extinct volcano, and almost completely shut in by steep and wooded heights. It was supposed to be the entrance to the infernal regions, which were therefore sometimes called Avernus.

Azazel (*ȧ-zā'zĕl*). According to Ewald, a demon belonging to the pre-mosaic religion. Another opinion identifies him with Eblis, or the devil, who refused to prostrate himself before Adam. Milton makes him the standard bearer of the infernal hosts.

Azrael (*ăz'rȧ-ĕl*). In the Jewish and the Mohammedan mythology, the name of an angel who watches over the dying, and separates the soul from the body. It means in Hebrew "help of God."

Baal or **Bel.** The chief god of the Phœnicians and Carthaginians.

Bacchus (*băk'ŭs*). The god of wine; he taught the cultivation of the grape and the preparation of its juice. Greek drama developed from festivals in honor of Dionysus, the name usually given to him by the Greeks.

Balder (*bôl'dēr*). The god of peace, son of Odin and Frigga. He was killed by the blind war god, but was restored to life at the general request of the gods.

Balmung. In Norse mythology, the sword of Siegfried forged by Wieland, or Völund.

Barguest. A frightful goblin among fairies. It was armed with teeth and claws and was an object of terror in the north of England.

Bast or **Pasht.** A goddess of ancient Egypt, represented as a lion-headed or cat-headed woman and worshiped especially at Bubastis.

Beelzebub (*bē-ĕl'zē-bŭb*). The name of a Moabite or Syrian deity. The name means "god of flies." It came to be applied to the chief of evil spirits.

Befana (*bā-fä'nä*). The fairy of Italian children, who is supposed to fill their stockings with toys on Twelfth Night if they have been good. The name is a juvenile corruption of the word *Epifania*, meaning *Twelfth Night*.

Bellerophon (*bĕ-lĕr'ô-fŏn*). A prince who rode the winged horse, Pegasus, and controlled him with a golden bridle, the gift of Minerva. By aid of Pegasus, he killed the lion-headed monster, the Chimæra.

Bellona. Roman goddess of war. She prepared the chariot of her brother Mars when he was going to war, and appeared in battles armed with a whip and holding a torch.

Belphegor (*bĕl'fē-gôr*). A god of evil, worshiped by the Moabites. He was represented as an archfiend who had been an archangel.

Berenice (*bĕr'ē-nī'sē*). The name of several famous princesses and queens. (1) The wife of Mithridates the Great. He had her killed after his defeat by Lucullus, lest his enemies should capture her. (2) The wife of Ptolemy III, Euergetes. When her husband was absent in a Syrian war, she vowed her beautiful hair to the gods if he should return safe. Accordingly, her hair was cut off and left in the temple of Venus. Soon afterward it disappeared. The astronomer, Conon of Samos, declared it had been wafted to heaven. Hence the constellation *Coma Berenices*, "hair of Berenice," near that of Leo.

Berg Folk. Pagan spirits doomed to live on the Scandinavian hills till the day of redemption.

Bertha. The white lady who guards good German children, but is the terror of the bad, who fear her iron nose and big feet. She corresponds to the Italian Befana. She was often identified also with Frigga or Ostara, goddess of the earth and spring.

Bhima (*bē'mȧ*). In Hindu mythology, son of the wind god, Vayu. He is remarkable for his great size and strength, his voracious appetite, and his fiery temper.

Bifröst (*bēf'rŏst*). In Norse mythology, the rainbow bridge between earth and heaven, over which none but the gods could travel.

Bilskirnir. A wonderful palace built by Thor for the use of peasants after death.

Bladud. A mythical king of England, who built the city of Bath, and dedicated the medicinal springs to Minerva.

Blue Jay. In the myths of the Chinook Indians of the Columbia River country, this animal-like god plays a part similar to that of Loki in the Norse tales. He is a mischief-maker. He and his sister Ioi have many adventures among the supernatural beings.

Boreas (*bō'rē-ăs*). The north wind, represented as a son of Astræus and Aurora.

Bragi (*brä'gē*). The Scandinavian god of poetry and eloquence, son of Odin and Frigga. He is represented as an old man with a flowing white beard.

Brahma. The supreme god of the Hindus, represented with four heads and four arms, the source of the universe and of other gods, who will again be absorbed into him. He forms, with Vishnu the preserver and Siva the destroyer, the divine triad.

Bran. An ancient Welsh Celtic god of the underworld. His care was poetry and music. He is later represented as "Bran the Blessed," who first brought the cross from Rome to Britain.

Briareus (*brī-ā'rē-ŭs*). A giant with fifty heads and a hundred hands. He hurled a hundred rocks at Jupiter in a single throw, and Jupiter bound him under Mount Etna with a hundred chains.

Brigit. An ancient Irish Celtic goddess of poetry and prophecy, daughter of the god Dagda the Great. She was later transformed into the female patron saint of Ireland.

Bukadawin. The god of famine among certain North American Indians.

Cacus. A famous robber, son of Vulcan, said to have inhabited a cave on Mt. Aventine, the later site of Rome. He robbed Hercules of some cattle, but Hercules discovered him, killed him, and established on the site of his cave the ox market and altar, "ara maxima," which existed for ages in Rome.

Cadmus (*kăd'mŭs*). A Phœnician hero, son of King Agenor. His father sent him to seek his sister Europa, whom Jupiter in the guise of a bull had carried over the sea on his back. Unable to find her and afraid to return, he was directed by an oracle to build a city and call it Thebes. This he did with the help of the five survivors of the warriors who grew up from a dragon's teeth which Cadmus had planted after taking them from a dragon he had slain. He is said to have introduced the worship of heroes and the use of the alphabet, which at first consisted of sixteen letters. This last tradition expresses the fact that the Greek alphabet was developed from the Phœnician.

Caduceus (*kȧ-dū'sē-ŭs*). The fabled wand carried by Hermes. It was represented as entwined with two serpents and having two wings at the top.

Calchas (*kăl'kăs*). The wisest of the soothsayers among the Greeks at Troy. He died from grief on meeting with a soothsayer who proved wiser than he.

Calliope (*kă-lī'ō-pē*). The Muse who presided over epic poetry. She is generally depicted using a stylus and wax writing tablet, or a scroll.

Callisto. A nymph of Arcadia, whose son Arcas was changed into a bear and placed in the heavens as a constellation.

Calpe. One of the two pillars of Hercules. The other was named Abyla. These two were originally only one mountain, which Hercules tore asunder; he then poured the sea between them. Calpe is now called Gibraltar.

Calypso. One of the daughters of Atlas. When Ulysses was shipwrecked on her coasts, she received him with hospitality. She offered him immortality if he would become her husband, but he refused. After remaining with her seven years, he was summoned by Hermes to continue his voyage homeward.

Camenæ (*kȧ-mē'nē*). Italian nymphs or fountain deities, identified later by Roman poets with the Greek Muses. Egeria was one of the Camenæ.

Camilla. Virgin queen of the Volscians, poetically described by Virgil as so swift that she could run over a field of corn without bending a blade, or make her way over the sea without wetting her feet.

Cassandra (*kă-săn'drȧ*). Daughter of Priam and Hecuba. She was passionately loved by Apollo, who, as the price of her love, gave her the gift of prophecy, but, when she deceived him, added the condition that her prophecies should never be believed.

Cassiopeia (*kăs'ĭ-ō-pē'yȧ*). The mother of Andromeda. Placed at her death in the heavens, she forms a constellation, the chief stars of which suggest by their arrangement the outline of a chair.

Castalia. A fountain on Mount Parnassus, sacred to Apollo and the Muses. Whoever drank of its waters was endowed with the gift of poetry.

Castor and Pollux. Twin brothers, sons of Leda. Mercury carried them to Pallena, where they were educated. As soon as they arrived at manhood, they embarked with Jason in quest of the golden fleece. Pollux was the son of Jupiter; Castor, of Tyndareus. Hence Pollux was immortal, while Castor, like other men, was subject to old age and death.

Cauther. In Mohammedan mythology, the lake of paradise, whose waters are as sweet as honey, as cold as snow, and as clear as crystal; any believer who tastes of them is said to thirst no more.

Cecrops (*sē'krŏps*). The mythical founder of Athens, who is said to have also divided Attica into twelve communities, and to have introduced the first elements of civilized life. He instituted marriage, abolished bloody sacrifices, and taught his subjects how to worship the gods. He is represented with the upper part of his body human and the lower part like that of a dragon.

Centaurs (*sĕn'tôrz*). Monsters, half horse, half human. They are especially celebrated for their contest with the giants in the mountains of Thessaly, and for their assault on the bride at the wedding of Peleus and Thetis. On the latter occasion they were defeated and driven away by the Lapithæ.

Cerberus (*sûr'bĕr-ŭs*). The three-headed dog that keeps the entrance of the infernal regions. He prevents the living from entering and the shades from escaping. Orpheus lulled Cerberus to sleep with his lyre; and the sibyl who conducted Æneas through Hades threw the dog into a sleep also by a cake treated with an opiate.

Ceres (*sē'rēz*). The daughter of Saturn, sister of Jupiter and Neptune. She was the goddess of corn, flowers, and the harvest. She is represented as crowned with poppies and riding in a chariot drawn by dragons. She was the mother of Proserpina, who while gathering flowers was seized by Pluto.

Chaos (*kā'ŏs*). The formless void preceding the genesis of an orderly universe and out of which the gods, men, and all things arose.

Charon (*kā'rŏn*). A god of the infernal regions, son of Nox, "Night," and Erebus. He conducted the souls of the dead in a boat over the rivers Styx and Acheron.

Charybdis (*kȧ-rĭb'dĭs*). A woman who robbed travelers and was turned by Jupiter into a dangerous whirlpool on the coast of Sicily, opposite Scylla, a six-headed monster which lived in a rock and seized passing sailors. Scylla and Charybdis are generally mentioned together to represent alternative dangers.

Chibiabos. A musician, ruler in the land of spirits, and friend of Hiawatha. Personification of harmony in nature.

Chimæra, Chimera (*kĭ-mē'rȧ*). A celebrated monster, having the combined semblance of a goat, lion, and dragon, which continually vomited flames. It was destroyed by Bellerophon.

Chiron (*kī'rŏn*). A centaur, son of Saturn and Philyra. He was famous for his knowledge of medicine, and taught mankind the use of plants and herbs.

Chou. An Egyptian god in many respects similar to the Roman Hercules.

Cimmerians (*sĭ-mē'rĭ-ănz*). A half mythical people, first described in the *Odyssey* as dwelling in perpetual gloom beyond the ocean stream. A people with this name was said by the Greeks to live along the Black Sea.

Circe (*sûr'sē*). A sorceress, daughter of Sol and Perse, celebrated for her knowledge of magic and venomous herbs. Ulysses, on his return from the Trojan War, visited her coasts, and his companions were changed by her potions into swine.

Clio (*klī'ō*). The Muse who presided over history.

Clotho (*klō'thō*). The youngest of the three Fates, daughters of Jupiter and Themis, and supposed to preside over the moment of birth. She held the distaff and spun the thread of life.

Cluricaune (*klo͞o'rĭ-kôn*). An Irish elf, who guarded a hidden treasure.

Clytemnestra (*klī'tĕm-nĕs'trȧ*). The wife and murderer of Agamemnon.

Clytie (*klī'tē*). A water nymph who loved the sun god Apollo and was changed into a sunflower. In this form, she turns always toward the sun.

Cocytus (*kō-sī'tŭs*). A river of the infernal regions. The unburied dead wander on its banks for 100 years. The name means the river of lamentation. See *Styx*.

Colchis or **Colchos** (*kŏl'kĭs*) (*-kŏs*). A country of Asia, bordering the Black Sea, famous in connection with the expedition of the Argonauts, and as the birthplace of Medea.

Comus (*kō'mŭs*). The god of revelry, presiding over feasts. See Milton's *Comus*.

Concordia (*kŏn-kôr'dĭ-ȧ*). The Roman goddess of peace and concord. She is represented holding a horn of plenty and a scepter budding with fruit.

Consus. An early Italian god of harvests. Mules were under his protection and mule races were held in his honor.

Cora. A name sometimes given to Proserpina.

Coronis (*kō-rō'nĭs*). (1) Mother of Æsculapius by Apollo. (2) A king's daughter, who was transformed into a crow by Minerva when asking for protection from Neptune.

Corybantes (*kŏr'ĭ-băn'tēz*). Priests who served at the worship of Cybele, the mother of the gods, and were in the habit of striking themselves in their religious dances.

Coxcox. The Noah of the Mexican tribes, who, with his wife Xochiquetzal, alone escaped the deluge. They took refuge in a hollow cypress tree which floated until the water subsided and then ran aground on a mountain of Culhuacan. Two of their children, who were taught speech by the Great Spirit, were the ancestors of the Toltecs and the Aztecs.

Coyote (*kī-ō'tē*). See *Italapas*.

Cressida. Daughter of Calchas, the Greek, and beloved by Troilus, son of Priam. They vowed eternal fidelity, and as pledges Troilus gave the maiden a sleeve, while Cressida gave the Trojan prince a glove. Cressida proved false and her name has since stood as a byword for faithlessness.

Creusa. Daughter of Priam and wife of Æneas. She was lost in the city of Troy when her husband escaped from its flames.

Cronus. The youngest of the Titans. He was said to be the son of Uranus and Gæa, "the heavens and the earth," and to have exercised the first government over the universe. His wife was Rhea, who was also his sister. Cronus and his five brothers were called Titans. Rhea and her five sisters were called Titanides. Cronus seized upon the government of the universe by his superiority over his father and brothers, yet pledged himself to rear no male children; accordingly, he is represented as devouring his sons as soon as born. But three of them, Jupiter, Neptune, and Pluto, escaped this fate through the artifice of Rhea, their mother, who gave Cronus stones to devour instead of the children at their birth. Jupiter aided Cronus in recovering his throne, after he had been driven from it by his brothers, the Titans, and bound in Tartarus. But soon Jupiter himself made war upon Cronus and seized the government. See *Saturn*.

Cupid. God of love, son of Jupiter and Venus. He is represented as a winged boy, naked, armed with a bow and arrows, and often with a bandage covering his eyes. He shot his arrows into the hearts of both gods and men, thus infecting them with love. Like all the gods, he put on different forms to suit his plans. He became the husband of Psyche.

Cybele (*sĭb'ē-lē*). A goddess, daughter of Uranus and Terra, and identified by the Romans with Ops, wife of Saturn. On her birth she was exposed on a mountain, where she was tended and fed by wild beasts, receiving the name of Cybele from the mountain. She is represented on a throne with lions at her side. See *Atalanta*.

Cyclopes (*sī'klŏps*). One-eyed giants who forged the thunderbolts of Jove. Homer describes them as wild, insolent, lawless shepherds, who devoured human beings. A later tradition represents them as Vulcan's assistants.

Cyparissus (*sĭp-ȧ-rĭs'ŭs*). A beautiful youth, who, grief-stricken at having inadvertently killed his favorite stag, was metamorphosed into a cypress by Apollo.

Dædalus (*dĕd'ȧ-lŭs*). A great architect and sculptor. He invented the wedge, the ax, the level, and the gimlet, and was the first to use sails. He made himself wings with feathers and wax, and fitted them to his body and to that of his son Icarus They sailed in the air, but the heat of the sun melted the wax on the wings of Icarus, who flew too high, and he fell into the sea, which after him has been called Icarian.

Dag. In Scandinavian mythology, (1) a god representing day, the son of Nott, "night," and (2) the last survivor of a treacherous race, the Hundings.

Dagan. In Hindu mythology, a god who reconstructed the world when it had been destroyed after creation.

Dagon (*dā'gŏn*). A Syrian divinity who, according to the Bible, had richly adorned temples in several of the Philistine cities. He was a national god of the Philistines, formed in human shape upwards from the waist, his lower extremity resembling that of a fish.

Dahak. In Persian mythology, a wicked deity who is destined to break the chains in which he is bound, and to bring upon men the most terrible calamities for 1000 years. After this period the reign of Ormuzd will begin, when men will be good and happy.

Daikoku. A mythical god invoked by Japanese workers. He is represented as holding a full sack which he beats to bring from it all useful articles, and the sack never becomes empty.

Daityas. Hindu titans or demons who made war on the gods and prevented sacrifices to them.

Danaë (*dăn'ȧ-ē*). The daughter of Acrisius, king of Argos, who became by Jupiter the mother of Perseus. An Italian legend related that Danaë came to Italy. built the town of Ardea, and married Pilumnus, by whom she became the mother of Daunus, the ancestor of Turnus.

Danaides (*dȧ-nā'ĭ-dēz*). The fifty daughters of Danaus, king of Argos, who married the fifty sons of their uncle Ægyptus, and murdered them on their wedding night. They were condemned in Hades to pour water into sieves.

Danu. Among the ancient Irish Celts, the mother of the gods. She was a goddess of fertility and so associated with the underworld.

Daphne. Daughter of the river god Peneus. Apollo courted her, but she fled from him and was, at her own request, turned into a laurel tree.

Daphnis. A Sicilian shepherd, son of Hermes, or Mercury, by a nymph. He was taught by Pan to play on the flute, and was regarded as the inventor of bucolic poetry.

Deiphobus (*dē-ĭf'ō-bŭs*). A son of Priam and Hecuba. After the death of Paris, he married Helen, but was betrayed by her to the Greeks. Next to Hector, he was the bravest among the Trojans. On the capture of Troy by the Greeks he was slain and fearfully mangled by Menelaus.

Deirdre (*dā'THră*). An Irish heroine, fated to be the cause of misfortune. King Conchobar secluded her as his intended bride. Accidentally meeting with Noisi, she loved him and, fleeing, lived with him and his two brothers in Alba. The king brought about the death of the brothers, and Deirdre committed suicide.

Delphi (*dĕl'fī*). A town at the foot of Mount Parnassus, famous for its oracle and for a temple of Apollo.

Demeter (*dē-mē'tẽr*). A goddess of the earth, of seedtime, and of harvest. By Zeus she became the mother of Persephone, or Proserpina.

Demogorgon (*dē'mō-gôr'gŏn*). The tyrant genius of the soil or earth, the life and support of plants. He was depicted as an old man covered with moss and was said to live underground. He is a figure of medieval European mythology.

Derceto (*dûr-sē'tō*). A Syrian mermaid goddess who had analogies with Dagon of the Philistines and who was regarded by the Romans as identical with Venus.

Deucalion and Pyrrha (*dū-kā'lĭ-ŏn*) (*pĭr'ȧ*). Jupiter and Neptune once destroyed the race of men with a flood. Only Deucalion and Pyrrha, his wife, escaped, finding refuge on Parnassus. At the behest of an oracle, they took up stones and cast them behind them. These stones took form as a new, hardy race of men and women, who peopled the earth again.

Diana (*dī-ăn'ȧ*). An ancient Italian goddess of light, of virginity, and of childbirth. Identified with Artemis, she became also goddess of the chase. She was often represented as the moon goddess, and, identified with Hecate, as a deity presiding over incantations. Her worship is said to have been introduced at Rome by Servius Tullius, who dedicated a temple to her on the Aventine. As Artemis, she was a daughter of Jupiter, and was born of Latona, or Leto, on the island Delos, at the same time as Apollo.

Dictynna (*dĭk-tĭn'ȧ*). One of the names of the Cretan goddess Britomartis, identified by the Greeks with Artemis.

Dike (*dī'kē*). One of the three guardians of life appointed by Themis, whose names are Eunomia, "order," Dike, "justice," Irene, "peace." Their office was to promote unanimity by the exercise of equity and justice. They likewise stand around the throne of Zeus, and their regular occupation is to open and shut the gates of heaven, and to yoke the steeds to the chariot of the sun.

Dindymus. Mountains between Phrygia and the frontiers of Galatia, near the town Pessinus, sacred to Cybele, the mother of the gods.

Diomedes (*dī'ō-mē'dēz*) or **Diomed.** (1) A Greek hero of the Trojan War, son of Tydeus, and king of Argos. He was a favorite of Minerva, who, according to Homer, encouraged him to attack and wound both Mars and Venus, who were engaged on the side of the Trojans. He survived the siege of Troy, but on his return home found his wife untrue to him. He fled to Italy and remained in exile. (2) The cruel tyrant of Thrace, who fed his mares on the flesh of his guests. He was overcome by Hercules, and was given to the same horses as food.

Dione. The youngest of the Titan sisters, and reputed mother of Venus.

Dionysus (*dī'ō-nī'sŭs*). Son of Jupiter and Semele, the daughter of Cadmus. He was the god of wine and is generally represented crowned with vine leaves, drawn in a car by tigers, and accompanied by satyrs and many revelling women, called Bacchantes. See *Bacchus*.

Diræ. The avenging goddesses, or Furies.

Dis. A name sometimes given to Pluto, and hence also to the lower world.

Discordia. A malevolent deity corresponding to the Greek Eris, the goddess of contention. She was driven from heaven by Jupiter because she sowed dissensions among the gods. At the nuptials of Peleus and Thetis she threw an apple among the gods inscribed with the words "For the fairest," which, stirring up a quarrel between Juno, Venus, and Minerva, led eventually to the Trojan War.

Dives (*dēvs*). Demons of Persian mythology. According to the *Koran*, they are ferocious and gigantic spirits under the sovereignty of Eblis.

Dodona. The most ancient oracle in Greece, by which Jupiter used to make known his will. It was said to have been built by Deucalion.

Donar. A name sometimes given to Thor, the thunder god in Norse mythology.

Dragon. A fabulous snake-like monster, thought originally to typify the life-giving and also the destructive aspect of water and of nature generally. It was for many years the national symbol of China. In some religions, including Christianity, it represented the power of evil.

Draupnir. The magic ring, symbolic of fertility, which belonged to Odin. It was burned on the funeral pyre of his son Balder.

Droma. The chain forged for the purpose of binding the wolf Fenris, but which he broke. Hence the proverbial phrase, "to dash out of Droma."

Dryads. Wood nymphs. The dryads were sometimes distinguished from the hamadryads in that the latter were supposed to be attached to some particular tree, with which they came into being, lived, and died, while the former had the care of the woods and trees in general.

Duergar (*dwĕr'gär*). In Norse mythology, dwarfs who dwelt in rocks and hills. They were noted for their strength, subtlety, magical powers, and skill in metallurgy, and were regarded as the personification of the subterranean powers of nature.

Durga or **Doorga.** A ten-armed goddess worshiped among the Hindus. She was the principal wife of Siva.

Earth-Namer. Earth-namer or Codoyanape, in some Indian legends, is represented as working with Coyote to prepare the earth for the first people. Defeated by the tricky Coyote, he withdrew to the bright Eastern-land after the coming of men. See *Italapas.*

Eblis. The name given by the Arabians to the prince of the apostate angels, whom they represent as exiled to the infernal regions for refusing to worship Adam at the command of God. Eblis alleged, in justification of his refusal, that he himself had been formed of ethereal fire, while Adam was only a creature of clay. See *Azazel.*

Echo. A nymph who engaged the attention of Juno by her never-ceasing talk, meanwhile allowing Jupiter his freedom. Juno found out her trick and punished her by taking away from her all power of speech except repetition of words just spoken by others. Echo loved Narcissus; as her love was not returned, she pined away until nothing remained but her beautiful voice.

Egeria (*ē-jē'rĭ-ȧ*). A nymph from whom King Numa Pompilius received his instructions respecting the forms of public worship which he established in Rome.

Egia. One of the nine beautiful giantesses seen by Odin along the seashore, known as wave maidens. Her son became guardian of Bifröst, the rainbow bridge.

Egil (*ā'gĕl*). A giant in Norse mythology. Thor left his goats in the care of Egil while he went to secure a kettle in which to brew ale for the gods.

Eira (*ār'ȧ*). An attendant of the goddess Frigga, and a skillful nurse. She gathered curative herbs and plants and taught the science to women.

Elbegast. King of the dwarfs in Scandinavian mythology, who dwelt in a magnificent underground palace and drew their servants from the earth above.

Electra. A daughter of Agamemnon and Clytemnestra, rulers of Argos. When Agamemnon returned after the siege of Troy, Clytemnestra, aided by her lover Ægisthus, slew her husband. Electra concealed her young brother Orestes, who later returned and aided Electra in avenging their father's murder by slaying their mother and Ægisthus.

Eleusinian Mysteries. Secret religious rites performed at Eleusis, near Athens, which later became part of the state religion of Athens. The rites celebrated the earth goddess Demeter, her daughter Persephone, and Iacchus. The initiates obtained, through the rites, both communion with the deities and the assurance of immortality.

Elf. The water sprite, known also as Elb, from which the name of the river Elbe is said to be derived. Elves are more properly known as mountain fairies or those airy creatures that dance on the grass or sit on the leaves of trees and revel in the light of the full moon.

Elivagar (*ĕ-lĭv'ȧ-gär*). In Norse mythology, the name of an ice-filled river in Chaos, flowing from a fountain in the land of mist.

Elysium (*ē-lĭzh'ĭ-ŭm*). The paradise of the Greeks, known also as the islands of the blest: Departed mortals were adjudged to Elysium or to Tartarus by the sentence of Minos and his fellow judges in the "Field of Truth." Elysium is described as abounding in beautiful gardens, meadows, and groves; where birds ever warble; where the river Eridanus winds between banks fringed with laurel, and "divine Lethe" glides through silent valleys; where the air is always pure, and the day serene.

Embla. In Norse mythology, the name of the first woman, so called because the gods made her of an *embla,* "elder," as they made man of an *aske,* "ash."

Enceladus (*ĕn-sĕl'ȧ-dŭs*). A Titan, son of Terra, and the most powerful of all the giants who conspired against Jupiter and attempted to scale heaven. He was struck by Jupiter's thunderbolts and chained beneath Mount Etna.

Endymion. In Greek mythology, the setting sun with which the moon is in love. One of the many renderings of his story is that Endymion was a beautiful youth who fed his flock on Mount Latmus. One clear night, Diana, the moon, looked down and saw him sleeping. The cold heart of the goddess was warmed by his beauty, and she came down to him, kissed him, and watched over him while he slept. Another story was that Jupiter bestowed on him the gift of perpetual youth united with perpetual sleep. One version of this myth made sleep a reward for piety, while another version made it a punishment for presuming to fall in love with Juno.

Enipeus (*ē-nī'pūs*). A fabled river in Thessaly. Poseidon assumed the form of the god of this river in order to obtain possession of Tyro, who was in love with Enipeus. She became the mother of Pelias and Neleus.

Enyo (*ē-nī'ō*). (1) One of the gray maidens, or hoary witches. (2) Daughter of Mars, a goddess of war, who delights in bloodshed and the destruction of towns, and accompanies Mars in battles.

Epaphus. The son of Zeus and Io, born on the river Nile, after the long wanderings of his mother. He became king of Egypt and built Memphis.

Erebus (*ĕr'ē-bŭs*). A name applied to the dark and gloomy space under the earth through which the souls of the dead were obliged to pass on their way to Hades, with which it and Tartarus are often synonymous.

Eris. The goddess of discord; a sister of Mars, and a daughter of Night; identified with the Roman Discordia.

Eros. The son of Aphrodite and Hermes, with whom the Romans identified Cupid. See *Cupid.*

Erytheis or **Erythea** (*ĕr'ĭ-thē'ĭs*) (*-ȧ*). One of the daughters of Night, appointed to guard the golden apples in the garden of the Hesperides.

Esangetuh Emissee. "Master of Breath." A chief deity of the Creek Indians.

Eumæus (*ū-mē'ŭs*). The faithful swineherd of Ulysses, whom Ulysses consulted upon his return to Ithaca.

Eumenides (*ū-mĕn'ĭ-dēz*). A euphemistic name given by the Greeks to the Erinyes, or Furies. They are represented as the daughters of Earth, or of Night, and as fearful winged maidens, with serpents twined in their hair and with blood dripping from their eyes. They dwelt in the depths of Tartarus, dreaded by gods and men.

Euphorbus. The son of Panthous and one of the bravest of the Trojans. He was slain by Menelaus, who dedicated his victim's shield in the temple of Hera near Mycenæ. Pythagoras asserted that he had once been Euphorbus, and in proof of his assertion took down at first sight the shield from the temple of Hera.

Euphrosyne (*ū-frŏs'ĭ-nē*). One of the three Graces. She represented joy, as her sisters stood for splendor and for pleasure.

Europa. Daughter of the Phœnician king Agenor, or, according to the *Iliad,* daughter of Phœnix. Jupiter in the form of a bull carried her on his back across the sea to Crete, where by him she became the mother of Minos, Rhadamanthus, and Sarpedon. See *Cadmus.*

Eurydice (*ū-rĭd'ĭ-sē*). Orpheus's wife, who died from the bite of a serpent. Orpheus, disconsolate at her loss, determined to descend to the lower world and obtain permission for his beloved Eurydice to return to the regions of light. Armed only with his lyre, he entered the realms of Hades and gained an easy admittance to the palace of Pluto. Orpheus was promised she should return on condition that he should not look back till she had reached the upper world. When the musician reached the confines of his journey, he turned his head to see if Eurydice were following, and she was instantly caught back again into Hades.

Eurylochus. One of the companions of Ulysses in his wanderings, and the only one of them who was not changed by Circe into a hog.

Evadne (*ē-văd'nē*). Wife of Capaneus, and mother of Sthenelus. Her husband having been killed at the siege of Thebes, she threw herself upon the funeral pile and was consumed with him.

Fafnir. In Scandinavian mythology, the eldest son of the dwarf king Hreidmar. The slaying of Fafnir represented the destruction of the demon of cold or darkness who had stolen the golden light of the sun.

Fahfah. Name given to one of the rivers of paradise in the mythology of the East.

Fata Morgana. In Italian folklore, a wraith who, in the guise of a beautiful woman, lured her pursuers into dangerous spots where they perished.

Fates. In Greek and Roman mythology the Fates are identical with the Parcæ. They were three sisters, daughters of Night, whom Jupiter permitted to decide the fortune and the duration of mortal life. They were viewed as inexorable, and ranked among the inferior divinities of the lower world. They were generally represented as three women, with chaplets made of wool and interwoven with the flowers of the narcissus, wearing long robes, and employed in their works: Clotho with a distaff; Lachesis having near her sometimes several spindles; and Atropos holding a pair of scissors. See *Atropos.*

Fauns. Among the Romans, a class of rural deities corresponding to the Greek satyrs. They were the demigods of woods and forests and hence included among the so-called "sylvan deities." They are represented with horned heads, sharp-pointed ears, and with their bodies below the waist resembling those of goats.

Felicitas. A symbolical, moral deity of the Romans. She was the personification of good fortune, and is frequently seen on Roman medals, in the form of a matron, with the staff of Mercury and a cornucopia.

Feng. The name taken by Odin in the capacity of wave-stiller. Under this name he teaches mortals to distinguish between good and bad omens and to know the moods of the winds.

Fenrir or **Fenris.** In Scandinavian mythology, the wolf, offspring of Loki, which, because of his sinister growth in size and strength, the gods bound with a magic chain. When he gapes, one jaw touches earth and the other, heaven.

Ferohers (*fĕr-ō'hĕrz*). The guardian angels in Persian mythology. They were countless in number, and their chief tasks were to ensure the well-being of man.

Feronia. A goddess of fruits, nurseries, and groves among the Romans. She had a very rich temple and a grove consecrated to her. She was honored as the patroness of enfranchised slaves, who ordinarily received their liberty in her temple.

Fire People. A people mentioned in a Pacific Coast Indian legend as possessing fire before other peoples did. Raven stole a baby belonging to them and refused to exchange it for anything less than fire. Finally, the fire people taught him the use of fire.

Fire Spirit. A spirit which, according to certain North American Indian myths, jealously guarded fire. Many people tried to steal the fire from him. Finally, Nanabozho, taking the form of a hare, reached the wigwam of the fire spirit. He succeeded in seizing a firebrand and returned with it to his people. Like Hiawatha, Nanabozho stands in legend as a benefactor of the race.

Flora. The Roman goddess of blossoms and flowers.

Fortitudo. A personification of courage and bravery, worshiped as a goddess by the Romans.

Fortuna. The goddess of chance, to whom was ascribed the allotment of prosperity and adversity among men.

Freki and Geri (*frä'kē*) (*gĕr'ē*). The two wolves of Odin, which lie at his feet as he overlooks heaven and earth.

Frey. In Scandinavian mythology, the god of the sun and of rain, and also of fertility and of peace. He was one of the most popular of the Norse divinities. No weapons were ever allowed in Frey's temple, although oxen and horses were sacrificed to him.

Freya. The Scandinavian goddess of beauty and love, sister of Frey, and wife of Odur, who deserted her for a while but was found again by her and won back. Plants were called Freya's hair, and the butterfly, Freya's hen.

Frigga. In Scandinavian mythology, the wife of Odin, and so the queen of the gods. She was the mother of Balder, Thor, and others. She sometimes typifies the earth, as Odin does the heavens. She is often confounded erroneously with Freya, in very early stories. Her name survives in "Friday."

Frodi. The son of Frey, a god of peace. Under his direction two giantesses turned a pair of magic millstones which ground out gold according to his wish and filled his coffers. Excited by greed he forced them to labor, allowing rest only long enough for the singing of one verse. When Frodi himself slept, the giantesses changed their song and proceeded to grind out an army of troops to invade the land. These troops represent the vikings.

Furies. Three divinities of the lower world, whose office it was to torment the guilty in Tartarus, and often to inflict vengeance upon the living who had slain their relatives. They are also known as Erinyes and Eumenides. See *Megæra.*

Fylgie. Guardian spirits treated of in Norse mythology. Besides the Norns or Dises, who were regarded as protective deities, one of the Fylgie was ascribed by the Norsemen to each human being as a guardian spirit to attend him through life.

Galar. One of the dwarfs who, with his fellow dwarf Fialar, slew the giant Kvasir and drained every drop of his blood.

Gangler. The gatekeeper in Odin's palace who gave the explanation of the Norse mythology that it might be recorded.

Ganymede (*găn'ĭ-mēd*). A son of Tros, king of Troy, who, according to Homer, was the most beautiful of all mortals, and was carried off by the gods that he might fill the cup of Zeus, or Jupiter, and live among the immortal gods. Later writers state that Jupiter, in the form of an eagle, carried him away from Mount Ida.

Garm. A fierce dog that kept guard at the entrance of Hel's kingdom, the realm of the dead. He could be appeased by the offering of a Hel-cake, which always appeared in the hand of one who, on earth, had given bread to the needy.

Gemini (*jĕm'ĭ-nī*). A name meaning "the twins," applied to Castor and Pollux and to the constellation formed by them when transported to the heavens to dwell among the stars.

Gerda, Gerdhr, or **Gerth.** Wife of Frey, and daughter of the frost giant, Hymir. She was so beautiful that the brightness of her naked arms illuminated both air and sea. The marriage of Frey and Gerda represented the conquering of winter by the sun god.

Geryon (*jē'rĭ-ŏn*). A monster, said to be the offspring of Chrysaor and Callirrhoë and to have three bodies and three heads. His residence was in the island of Gades, where his numerous flocks were kept by the herdsman Eurythion and guarded by a two-headed dog, called Orthos. The destruction of this monster was one of the twelve labors of Hercules.

Giall (*yäl*). The infernal river of Scandinavian mythology.

Giallar. The bridge of death, over which all must pass.

Giallarhorn, The. Heimdal's horn, the sound of which went out into all worlds whenever he chose to blow it. He blew a long-expected blast as a rallying call to the battle which ended the reign of the gods, Odin, Frey, and Tyr.

Gian ben Gian. King of the Jinn or Genii in Arabian mythology, and founder of the pyramids. He was overthrown by Azazel, or Eblis.

Giants. In Greek mythology, beings of monstrous size, with dragons' tails and fearful countenances. They attempted to storm heaven, being armed with huge rocks and the trunks of trees, but were killed by the gods with the assistance of Hercules, and were buried under Mount Etna and other volcanoes. They probably symbolized the great forces of nature. In Scandinavian mythology they are described as evil genii of various forms and races, enemies of the gods. They dwelt in a territory of their own, called Giant-land. They had the power of assuming divers shapes and of increasing or diminishing their stature at will.

Ginungagap (*gĭn'nōōng-gä-gäp'*). In Norse mythology, the vast chaotic gulf of perpetual twilight, which existed before the present world and separated the region of fog from the region of heat. Giants were the first beings who came to life among the icebergs and filled this vast abyss.

Gladsheim. A great hall in the palace of Odin, where were the twelve seats occupied by the gods when holding council.

Glasir. A marvelous grove in the land of Asgard, in which the leaves were all of shimmering red gold.

Glaucus. (1) Son of Hippolytus. Being smothered in a tub of honey, he was restored to life by Æsculapius. (2) A fisherman of Bœotia who became the fisherman's patron deity.

Glendoveer. In Hindu mythology, a kind of sylph, the most lovely of the good spirits.

Glooskap. In an Iroquois legend, a man who fell asleep in the land of the guardian of winter. After six months he awoke and journeyed southward. Finding the little summer-woman, he ran away with her from the summer-land people and came again to the land of the guardian of winter. The old guardian tried once more to put Glooskap into slumber, but the summer-woman used her magic to melt the snow and ice and winter had to flee to the North. Since that time the summer-people journey to the Northland every year.

Gnome (*nōm*). Dwarfs which were supposed to tenant the interior parts of the earth, and in whose charge mines, quarries, etc., were left. Rübezahl, of the German legends, is often cited as a representative of the class.

Goblins and Bogies. Familiar demons of popular superstition which lurk about houses. They are also called hobgoblins.

Golden Apples, The. A great treasure in the garden of the Hesperides watched by a monstrous dragon. Hercules secured them in obedience to the command of Eurystheus.

Golden Fleece. A treasure celebrated in Greek myth. Ino persuaded her husband, Athamas, that his son Phryxus was the cause of a famine which had desolated the land, and he ordered him to be sacrificed to the angry gods. Phryxus made his escape over sea on a ram which had a golden fleece. When he arrived at Colchis, he sacrificed the ram to Zeus and gave the fleece to King Æetes, who hung it on a sacred oak and set an ever-watchful dragon to guard it. It was afterwards stolen by Jason.

Gorgons. Three hideous monsters, whose faces turned to stone whoever looked on them. One of these creatures, Medusa, was slain by Perseus, and the head was presented to Minerva. She attached it to her shield, where the face continued to retain its petrifying power.

Graces. To the retinue of Venus belonged the Graces, servants and companions of the goddess. They were said to be three daughters of Jupiter and Eurynome, or, according to others, of Bacchus and Venus herself. They were honored especially in Greece. See *Euphrosyne.*

Great Turtle. According to some North American Indian tribes, the upholder of the world. When earthquakes are felt, Great Turtle is said to be weary or moving his feet.

Grid. Wife of Odin and mother of Vitharr. She lent Thor her girdle, staff, and glove, warning him to beware of treachery when he went to visit the giant Geirrödhr.

Griffin. A mythical animal, resembling an eagle in front and a lion behind. It had four legs, wings, and a beak. Sacred to the sun, it guarded gold mines and hidden treasures.

Gripir. A horse trainer, servant of Odin, who could foretell events of the future and could teach a young hero all that he might need to know.

Hades. An earlier name for Pluto. Later it was applied to the lower world itself.

Hamadryad. See *Dryads.*

Harmonia. A daughter of Mars and Venus, and wife of Cadmus.

Haroeris. An Egyptian god, whose eyes are the sun and moon.

Harpies. "Robbers" or "spoilers," described by Homer as carrying off persons who had mysteriously disappeared. Hesiod represents them as fair-locked and winged maidens; but subsequent writers describe them as disgusting monsters, birds with the heads of maidens, with long claws, and faces pale from hunger, who tormented an old man, Phineus, by stealing his food as he tried to eat.

Haskah. A thunder god of the Sioux Indians, who used the winds as sticks to beat the thunder-drum.

Hebe (*hē'bē*). The goddess of youth, daughter of Zeus and Hera. She was employed by her mother to prepare her chariot and harness her peacocks, and she was cupbearer to all the gods until, on her marriage with Hercules, Ganymede took over the task.

Hecate (*hĕk'ȧ-tē*). A goddess of magic and of the lower world. Having powers also on the earth and above it, she was identified not only with Proserpina but also with Diana and Luna. She was worshiped at night and invoked to produce enchantments.

Hector. The most prominent hero of the Trojans in their war with the Greeks, eldest son of Priam and Hecuba, and the husband of Andromache. He slew Patroclus, the friend of Achilles, and thereby roused Achilles to the fight. The other Trojans fled into the city, and Hector alone remained without the walls. But when Achilles approached, Hector's heart failed him, and he too took to flight. Thrice he ran round the city, pursued by Achilles, and fell at last, pierced by Achilles' spear. Achilles tied Hector's body to his chariot and thus dragged him into the camp of the Greeks. At the command of Zeus, he surrendered the body in response to the prayers of Priam, who buried it at Troy with great pomp. Hector is one of the noblest characters depicted in the *Iliad.*

Hecuba (*hĕk'ū-bȧ*). The second wife of Priam, king of Troy, and the mother of Paris and Hector. After the fall of Troy, she fell into the hands of the Greeks as a slave, and, according to one account, threw herself in despair into the sea.

Heimdal or **Heimdallr.** In Norse tales, a god, the son of nine giantesses. He lived in the celestial fort Himinbiorg, under the farther extremity of the bridge Bifröst, and kept the keys of Asgard. He could see even in sleep, could hear the growing of grass, and even of the wool on a lamb's back. He was appointed to wake the gods with his trumpet at the end of the world.

Hel. The name of the world of the dead and of its goddess, in early Norse mythology. The word means "the coverer or hider." Later myths represented Hel as the abode of all save those who had not fallen by the sword. Under the influence of Christian dogma Hel came to be associated with punishment. The goddess or demon, Hel, was a daughter of Loki.

Helen. A daughter of Jupiter and Leda, and the wife of Menelaus, king of Sparta. She was the most beautiful woman of her age, and chose Menelaus among many suitors. She afterward eloped with Paris, her husband's Trojan guest, and thus brought on the war between the Greeks and Trojans. After the fall of Troy she was restored to Menelaus.

Helenus. Son of Priam and Hecuba, celebrated for his prophetic powers.

Helice. A maid beloved of Zeus, and by jealousy of Hera changed into a she-bear.

Helicon (*hĕl'ĭ-kŏn*). A mountain in Bœotia sacred to the Muses, from which place the fountain Hippocrene flowed. It is part of the Parnassus, a mountain range in Greece.

Helios (*hē'lĭ-ŏs*). The Greek sun god, who rode to his palace in Colchis every night in a golden car furnished with wings. This god gives light to both gods and men. He sees and hears everything and discovers all that is kept secret.

Helle (*hĕl'ē*). Daughter of Athamas and Nephele, and sister of Phrixus. When Phrixus was to be sacrificed, Nephele rescued her two children, who rode away through the air upon the ram with the golden fleece, the gift of Hermes; but Helle fell into the sea. The episode gave the name of the Hellespont to the part of the sea where Helle was drowned. It is now called the Dardanelles.

Hellen. The son of Deucalion and Pyrrha, and father of Æolus, Dorus, and Xuthus. He was king of Phthia in Thessaly, and was succeeded by his son Æolus. He was the mythical ancestor of all the Hellenes.

Hell Shoon. In Icelandic mythology, shoes indispensable for the journey to Valhalla, as the obolus was for crossing the Styx.

Helmet of Hades. A helmet worn by Perseus, rendering him invisible, and which, with the winged sandals and magic wallet, he took from certain nymphs who held them in possession. After he had slain Medusa he restored them again, and presented the Gorgon's head to Minerva, who placed it in the middle of her shield.

Hera (*hē'rȧ*). Greek name for the wife of Zeus or Jupiter, with whom the Romans identified Juno. See *Juno.*

Heraclidæ (*hĕr'ȧ-klī'dē*). Name given to the descendants of Hercules, who, together with the Dorians, conquered the Peloponnesus eighty years after the destruction of Troy. This legend represents the conquest of the Achæan population by Dorian invaders, who thereafter appeared as the ruling race in the Peloponnesus.

Herculean Knot. A snaky complication on the rod or caduceus of Mercury, adopted by the Grecian brides as the fastening of their woolen girdles. The loosing of the girdle symbolized the surrendering of their virginity.

Hercules (*hûr'kū-lēz*). Son of Jupiter and Alcmene and most famous of the Greek heroes. Wonderful strength was ascribed to him even directly after his birth, when he squeezed to death two serpents sent by Juno to destroy him. Since he was the offspring of her husband's infidelity, Juno compelled him to be subject to the commands of Eurystheus, who imposed upon him many difficult enterprises, known as the "twelve labors" of Hercules. They were as follows: to kill the Nemean lion; to destroy the Lernæan hydra; to catch alive the stag with golden horns; to catch the Erymanthean boar; to cleanse the stables of Augeas; to exterminate the birds of Lake Stymphalus; to bring alive the wild bull of Crete; to seize the man-eating horses of Diomedes; to obtain the girdle of Hippolyta, queen of the Amazons; to destroy the monster Geryon; to plunder the garden of the Hesperides, which was guarded by a sleepless dragon; and to bring from the infernal world the three-headed dog, Cerberus. He accomplished them all successfully, as well as many other exploits ascribed to him, by which he gave proof of his extraordinary strength and exhibited himself as an avenger and deliverer of the oppressed. Such were: his slaying the robber, Cacus; the deliverance of Prometheus, bound to a rock; the killing of Busiris; and the rescue of Alcestis from the infernal world. His last achievement was the destruction of the centaur, Nessus. Nessus dying, gave his poisoned tunic to Deianira, telling her that his blood would preserve her husband's love. Hercules afterwards, receiving it from her and putting it on, suffered such torment that as soon as he slew Nessus he cast himself in despair upon a funeral pile on Mount Œta.

Herla. A mythical king, the supposed leader of the Wild Hunt of Scandinavian mythology. This hunt was known as the Raging Host in Germany and in England as Herlathing.

Hermes (*hûr'mēz*). The Greek god with whom the Romans identified Mercury. In early times he was represented, like Priapus, as a bearded, ithyphallic figure, likenesses of which were erected before private dwellings.

Later, he became beardless, and of a more beautiful form. His business was to carry messages for Zeus, and his pleasure to pursue and woo nymphs.

Hermione (*hĕr-mī'ô-nē*). The beautiful daughter of Menelaus and Helen. She had been promised in marriage to Orestes before the Trojan War, but Menelaus, after his return home, married her to Neoptolemus. She later married Orestes.

Hesperides (*hĕs-pĕr'ĭ-dēz*). The daughters of Hesperus or of Erebus and Nox, who were appointed along with a never-sleeping dragon to watch the golden apples in the garden of the Hesperides in an island beyond Mount Atlas.

Hesperus. A son or brother of Atlas enrolled among the deities after death, and made identical with the Evening Star.

Hestia. The Greek name for Vesta, the goddess of the domestic hearth.

Hippocrene (*hĭp'ô-krēn*). A fountain on Mount Helicon, which sprang up where the winged horse Pegasus pawed the ground. He had been sent up by Poseidon to still the merriment of the Muses, and to accomplish this it was sufficient for him to strike the ground with his hoof. The name means "fountain of the horse."

Hippolyta (*hĭ-pŏl'ĭ-tȧ*). Queen of the Amazons, and daughter of Mars. It was her girdle that Hercules was required by Eurystheus to obtain. He captured her and brought her to Athens, where he gave her to the ruler, Theseus, as a wife.

Hippolytus. Son of Theseus and Hippolyta; his stepmother, Phædra, loved him but being repulsed accused him before Theseus of an attempt on her chastity. Theseus called down a curse on his head and was heeded by Poseidon, who sent up a great bull and so frightened Hippolytus' horses, as he was driving, that he was killed in the runaway. Artemis, whom he worshiped as a goddess of chastity, later induced Æsculapius to bring him to life and transferred him under the name of Virbius to a grove in Italy.

Hippomenes (*hĭ-pŏm'ĕ-nēz*). Son of Megareus, and great-grandson of Poseidon, or Neptune, who conquered Atalanta in a foot race. He had three golden apples, which he dropped one by one, and which she stopped to pick up. By this delay she lost the race, and was bound to marry Hippomenes. See *Atalanta*.

Hobomoko. An evil spirit known among certain North American Indians.

Hodeken. A famous German kobold, or domestic fairy servant; so called from wearing a little felt hat pulled down over his face.

Hoder. In Norse mythology, a blind god who, at the instigation of Loki, destroyed his brother Balder. He personifies night and darkness, as Balder does light and day.

Hofvarpnir. The fleet steed of Gna, in Scandinavian legend, which traveled through fire and air and enabled this messenger of Frigga to see all that was happening on the earth.

Honir. In Norse tales, a name given to the god of mind or thought.

Horæ or **Hours.** Daughters of Zeus and Themis, the goddesses of the order of nature and of the seasons. They guarded the doors of Olympus and promoted the fertility of the earth.

Horus. The Egyptian god of the sun, who was also worshiped in Greece and at Rome.

Hou Chi. A Chinese divinity, said to have been the founder of the royal house of Chou. He is said to have taught the arts of agriculture to the Chinese. For this service he was deified.

Hugin (*hōōg'ĭn*). One of Odin's two ravens which carried him news from earth, and which, when not thus employed, perched upon his shoulders. The other was called Munin. They were personifications of thought or intellect.

Hugon (*ü'gôɴ'*). An evil spirit, in the folklore of France, made use of to frighten children.

Hyacinthus. A youth beloved by Apollo, and accidentally slain by him while playing at quoits. From his blood sprang the flower which bears his name.

Hyades (*hī'ȧ-dēz*). A group of nymphs to whom was given the care of Dionysus, the god of wine and of fertility. They were later placed among the stars. As rainstars, they symbolize nourishing rains.

Hydra. A monstrous serpent. Of especial note was the hydra in the lake Lerna, which was slain by Hercules. It had many heads and when one of these heads was cut off, two others immediately grew in its place, unless the blood of the wound was stopped by fire. Hercules accomplished its destruction by the aid of Iolaus, who applied lighted brands as each head was removed. The blood of the monster formed a poison into which Hercules dipped his arrows, in order to inflict mortal wounds on his enemies.

Hygeia (*hī-jē'yȧ*). The goddess of health and a daughter of Æsculapius, though some traditions make her the wife of the latter. In works of art she is represented in a long robe, feeding a serpent from a cup.

Hylas. A beautiful boy, beloved by Hercules. He was drawn into a spring by nymphs, who were enamored of him. The story has been treated by Bayard Taylor, and by William Morris in his "Life and Death of Jason."

Hymen or **Hymenæus.** A companion of Venus who presided over marriage.

Hymir. In Scandinavian mythology, the frost giant from whom Thor took and carried off the great kettle called "Mile-deep."

Hyperboreans (*hī'pĕr-bō'rê-ănz*). A fabulous people, supposed to live in a state of perfect happiness in a land of perpetual sunshine beyond the caverns of the north wind.

Hyperion. Son of Cœlus and Terra, and, like Apollo, a model of manly beauty. Hyperion was the father of the sun, moon, and dawn, and may be regarded as the original Greek sun god.

Iacchus (*ī-ăk'ŭs*). The solemn name of Bacchus in the Eleusinian mysteries, derived from a boisterous song of the same name. In these mysteries Iacchus was regarded as the son of Zeus and Ceres, not of Zeus and Semele.

Iapetus (*ī-ăp'ê-tŭs*). The father of Atlas and ancestor of the human race.

Icarius (*ī-kā'rĭ-ŭs*). An Athenian, who hospitably received Dionysus in Attica and was taught the cultivation of the vine.

Icarus (*ĭk'ȧ-rŭs*). See *Dædalus*.

Ida. A mountain range of Mysia in Asia Minor, celebrated in mythology as the scene of the rape of Ganymede and of the judgment of Paris. In Homer, the summit of Ida is the place from which the gods watch the battles in the plain of Troy. It is an ancient seat of the worship of Cybele. A mountain in Crete, known as Mount Ida, was closely connected with the worship of Jupiter.

Idæan Mother. Cybele, who had a temple on Mount Ida in Asia Minor.

Idomeneus (*ī-dŏm'ê-nūs*). The heroic leader of the Cretans against Troy. He vowed to sacrifice to Poseidon whatever he should first meet on his landing, if the god would grant him a safe return. This was his own son, whom he accordingly sacrificed. As Crete was thereupon visited by a plague, the Cretans expelled Idomeneus, who went to Italy.

Iduna or **Idun.** Daughter of the dwarf Ivald, and wife of Bragi. She kept in a box the golden apples which the gods tasted as often as they wished to renew their youth. Loki on one occasion stole the box, but the gods compelled him to restore it. Iduna seems to personify that part of the year when the sun is north of the equator. Her apples indicate fruits generally. Loki carries her off to Giant-land, when the sun descends below the equator, and he steals her apples. In time, Iduna makes her escape, in the form of a sparrow, when the sun again rises above the equator and fruits return.

Ifing. In Scandinavian mythology, the great stream, between the earth and the sacred lands, whose waters never froze.

Inachus (*ĭn'ȧ-kŭs*). One of the river gods, a son of Oceanus and Tethys, and father of Phoroneus and of Io. He was the legendary first king of Argos.

Indra. In Hindu mythology, the ever youthful god of the firmament, and the omnipotent ruler of the elements. In the Vedic period of the Hindu religion, he occupied a foremost rank, and, though degraded to an inferior position in the Epic period, he long enjoyed a great legendary popularity. In works of art, he is represented as riding on an elephant.

Io. The daughter of Inachus, beloved by Zeus, and changed by him, because he feared Hera's jealousy, into a heifer. Wandering in this form she crossed the sea named after her, Ionian.

Iolaus (*ī'ô-lā'ŭs*). The son of Automedusa and of Iphicles, who was the half brother of Hercules. Iolaus is known as the latter's faithful companion and charioteer.

Iole (*ī'ô-lē*). The daughter of Eurytus of Œchalia, beloved by Hercules. Eurytus promised his daughter to the man who should conquer him and his sons in shooting with the bow. Hercules defeated them; but Eurytus and his sons, with the exception of Iphitus, refused to give Iole to the victor, on the ground that he had, in a fit of insanity, murdered his own children.

Ion. The fabulous ancestor of the Ionians, son of Apollo and Creusa, and grandson of Erechtheus. According to some traditions he reigned in Attica.

Ipalnemohuani. The sun god and supreme deity of the Toltecs. Human sacrifices were offered to him.

Iphigenia (*ĭf′ĭ-jē-nī′ȧ*). A daughter of Agamemnon and Clytemnestra, and sister to Orestes. Iphigenia was about to be sacrificed at Aulis to obtain fair sailing for the expedition against Troy; but she was rescued by Diana, who carried her to the Tauri, where she became a priestess in her temple. She was afterwards recognized by her brother Orestes, who, with his friend Pylades, was wrecked on the Taurian coast and brought, according to local custom, to be sacrificed to Diana as shipwrecked sailors. Iphigenia succeeded in saving them.

Irene (*ī-rēn′*). Goddess of peace, called Pax by the Romans, daughter of Zeus and Themis, and one of the Horæ.

Iris. Name given among the Greeks to the rainbow, as personified and considered a goddess. Her father was said to be Thaumas, and her mother, Electra, one of the daughters of Oceanus. Her residence was near the throne of Juno, whose commands she bore as messenger to the rest of the gods and to mortals. Sometimes, but rarely, she was Jupiter's messenger and was employed even by other deities.

Irus. The beggar of gigantic stature, who kept watch over the suitors of Penelope and carried their messages for them. His real name was Arnæus, but the suitors nicknamed him Irus, by analogy with Iris.

Isis. In Egyptian mythology, the sister-wife of Osiris. She was the type of motherhood and fertility in nature. The Greeks identified her with Demeter. Her worship as a nature goddess, in various forms, spread over most of the ancient world.

Islands of the Blessed. The early Greeks, as we learn from Homer, placed the Elysian fields, into which favored heroes passed without dying, at the extremity of the earth, near the river Oceanus. In poems later than Homer, an island is spoken of as their abode; hence, when certain islands were discovered in the ocean, off the western coast of Africa, the name of *Fortunatæ Insulæ* was applied to them. They are now called the Canary and the Madeira islands.

Ismene (*ĭs-mē′nē*). Daughter of Œdipus and Jocasta. When her sister Antigone was condemned to be buried alive by the order of King Creon for defying his edict and burying her brother Polynices, Ismene declared that she had aided her sister, and requested to be allowed to share the same punishment. Denied this, she is said to have died from grief. The story is told by Sophocles, and the modern artist, Teschendorf, has made a noted picture of the two sisters.

Israfel. Known among Arabians as the angel of music, who possessed the most melodious voice of all God's creatures. It was his duty to sound the resurrection trump and make music for the saints in paradise. Israfel, Gabriel, and Michael were the three angels that warned Abraham of Sodom's destruction.

Italapas, the Coyote. Among the Chinook Indians the Coyote was regarded as a helper of Ikanam, the creator, and as a teacher of men. Among certain Californian tribes, Coyote was a mischievous god.

Ithaca. In Greek mythology, the island kingdom of Ulysses.

Ixion (*ĭk-sī′ŏn*). A fabled king of Thessaly, who became father of the centaurs. The story by which he is most noted runs: When Deioneus demanded of Ixion certain gifts he had promised, Ixion treacherously invited him to a banquet and contrived to make him fall into a pit filled with fire. Zeus pardoned Ixion, but later for an insult to Hera he was chained by his hands and feet to an ever-revolving wheel.

Jamshid (*jăm-shēd′*). King of the genii, who owned a golden cup full of the elixir of life. This cup, hidden by the genii, was said to have been discovered by those who dug the foundations of Persepolis.

Janus. One of the superior gods of the Romans. The myths represent him as reigning over the earliest inhabitants of Italy, where he received Saturn driven from Crete by Jupiter. The two reigned in Italy throughout what was known later as the golden age. To Janus, Numa dedicated that celebrated temple, which was always open in time of war, and was closed with much solemnity whenever there was general peace in the Roman Empire, a thing which happened but three times during 700 years. From this deity the month of January was named, and the first day of each month was sacred to him. He was a god of beginnings, of doors, and perhaps, originally, of light. He was represented with two faces looking in opposite directions.

Jason. The son of Æson, king of Iolcus. Æson appointed his half brother Pelias as guardian to the young Jason, whom Pelias tried to get rid of by sending him to get the golden fleece. Enlisting a number of famous heroes in the quest, Jason set sail on the ship *Argo* from Iolcus and came to King Æetes in Colchis, who promised him the fleece if he would use certain fire-breathing bulls to plow a field. With the help of Medea, the daughter of Æetes, who fell in love with Jason and offered the use of her magic art, he overcame all obstacles and obtained the fleece. Medea fled with him. Later, angered by Jason's intention to take a new wife, she accomplished his death and that of their two children.

Jinn or **Genii.** Fairies in Arabian mythology, the offspring of fire. They were governed by a race of kings named Suleyman, one of whom built the pyramids. Their chief abode is the mountain Kaf, and they appear to men under the forms of serpents, dogs, cats, monsters, or even human beings, and become invisible at pleasure. The evil jinn are ugly, but the good are beautiful. They were created from fire 2000 years before Adam lived.

Jizo. A Japanese Buddhist god. He is represented as a kindly priest, a protector of travelers, women, and children. His image is frequently placed at crossroads.

Jörd (*yĕrd*). Daughter of Night, wife of Odin, and mother of Thor.

Jove. A form of the name Jupiter.

Juggernaut or **Jagannath** (*jŭg′ẽr-nôt*) (*-ȧ-nät*). A Hindu god, worshiped in the town of Puri in Orissa. On festival days the throne of his image is placed on a sixty-foot tower on wheels, which is drawn through the streets. Devout worshipers are said to throw themselves in front of this car to be crushed.

Juno. The Roman goddess of women, who was identified with the Greek goddess Hera. As such she was the wife of Jupiter and queen of heaven. The amours of her husband gave her many occasions for jealousy which she often indulged with vindictive cruelty against his paramours.

Jupiter. The supreme god of the Romans, who was identified with the Greek god Zeus. Both were probably at first gods of light. As identified by poets with Zeus, he ruled over gods and men on his throne in Mount Olympus, but often came down to visit mortals and make love to mortal women. The Capitol at Rome was dedicated to him as guardian of the city. See *Zeus*.

Kama (*kä′mȧ*). The Hindu god of love. His wife is Rati, "voluptuousness," and he is represented as riding on a sparrow, holding in his hand a bow of flowers and five arrows, each tipped with the bloom of a flower supposed to conquer one of the senses. His power is so much exalted that even the god Brahma is said to succumb to it.

Kami. The gods of ancient Japan. The name, in modern times, designates any saintly person and may also be applied to a prince.

Kaswa. The favorite camel of Mohammed, admitted into the Moslem paradise because it fell on its knees in adoration when the prophet delivered the last clause of the *Koran* to the assembled multitude at Mecca.

Kelpie. In the mythology of Scotland, a spirit of the water seen in the form of a horse, and believed to appear to those who are about to be drowned. Each lake has its kelpie.

Kobold (*kō′bŏld*). A house spirit in German folklore. In northern Europe the name is sometimes used in place of elf or dwarf, representing an underground spirit. It is probably the same as the Scotch brownie.

Koppenberg. The hill which miraculously opened to receive the children who followed Odin under the form of the Pied Piper. The rats, which he previously lured into the river and drowned, were the restless souls of the dead, which were thus released.

Krishna. A popular hero-god of the ancient Hindus. He is represented as one of the incarnations, or *avatars*, of Vishnu. One of the stories regarding him relates that, when the people of the earth appealed to Vishnu against the tyranny of the king Kansa, Vishnu took the form of Krishna to destroy the king. Kansa, forewarned, killed all the other children of Vasudeva and Devaki, the parents of Krishna. But Krishna was concealed by a cowherd. He is represented as a beautiful and gifted youth, somewhat like the Greek Apollo.

Kubera (*kōō-bā′rȧ*). In Hindu mythology, the god of riches, represented as frightfully deformed, and as riding in a car drawn by hobgoblins.

Lachesis (*lăk'ĕ-sĭs*). The one of the three Fates who fixed the length of the thread of life. See *Fates*.

Læding. In Norse mythology, a strong chain with which the wolf Fenris was bound. He easily broke the chain and from this legend has grown the saying, "to get loose out of Læding." A stronger chain, known as Droma, was also broken by Fenris. See *Droma*.

Laertes (*lā-ûr'tēz*). Mythical king of Ithaca and father of Ulysses. Laertes took part in the Calydonian hunt and in the expedition of the Argonauts. He was still alive when Ulysses returned to Ithaca, after the fall of Troy. During the absence of Ulysses he had withdrawn to the country in grief and bowed with age. It was his shroud which Penelope, the wife of Ulysses, was weaving and on the completion of which she promised to choose one of her suitors as husband. But each night she raveled what she had woven in the day.

Læstrygonians (*lĕs'trĭ-gō'nĭ-ănz*). A mythical race of giants who lived in Sicily. Ulysses sent two of his men to request that he and his crew might land, but the king ate one and the other fled. The Læstrygonians assembled on the coast and threw stones against Ulysses and his crew. Ulysses escaped after losing many of his companions.

Laius. King of Thebes, son of Labdacus, husband of Jocasta, and father of Œdipus, by whom he was slain.

Lamia (*lā'mĭ-ȧ*). A daughter of Belus, king of Egypt, who, because she was loved by Jupiter, was transformed by the jealous Juno into a monster devouring human flesh. Greek and Roman children were often frightened by stories of her.

Laocoön (*lā-ŏk'ō-ŏn*). Son of Priam, and priest of Apollo. He opposed the reception of the wooden horse into Troy, thinking it some artifice of the deceitful Greeks, whereupon he and his two sons were killed by two monstrous serpents which came from the sea at the instance of Apollo, whom Laocoön had offended by offering sacrifice to Poseidon. The Trojans, however, interpreted the occurrence as evidence that Laocoön should not have opposed taking the horse into the city.

Laodamia (*lā-ŏd'ȧ-mī'ȧ*). The wife of Protesilaus, who was slain before Troy. She begged to be allowed to converse with her dead husband for only three hours, and her request was granted. Hermes, or Mercury, led Protesilaus back to the upper world; when, at the end of the three hours, Protesilaus died a second time, Laodamia died with him.

Laomedon. The king that built the walls of Troy assisted by Neptune and Apollo, who had displeased Jupiter and were sent to work for wages. Neptune built the walls, while Apollo tended the king's flocks on Mount Ida. When the two gods had done their work, Laomedon refused the reward he had promised and expelled them from his dominions. Neptune sent to ravage the country a sea monster which could be propitiated only by the sacrifice of Laomedon's daughter, Hesione. When she was chained to a rock and the monster came to devour her, Hercules appeared and rescued her.

Lapithæ (*lăp'ĭ-thē*). A mythical people of Thessaly, noted for their defeat of the centaurs at the marriage feast of Peleus and Thetis.

Lares. Those deities which Romans chose as the protectors of their houses or cities and statues of whom were set up over the hearth. Each house chose two gods as its lares.

Latinus. A king of Latium, son of Faunus and of the nymph Marcia. He was the father of Lavinia, whom he gave in marriage to Æneas. Æneas built a town which he called Lavinium, capital of Latium. According to one account, Latinus, after his death, became Jupiter Latiaris, just as Romulus became Quirinus.

Latmus. A mountain in Caria. It was the mythological scene of the story of Selene, or Luna, and Endymion.

Latona. Daughter of Cœus, a Titan, and of Phœbe, and, by Jupiter, the mother of Apollo and Diana. The love of the king of the gods procured for her the hatred of Juno.

Lavinia. The daughter of Latinus and Amata, betrothed to Turnus, but married to Æneas. Æneas founded the town of Lavinium, called after Lavinia.

Leda. The mother of Helen. Jupiter visited her in the form of a swan, and "Leda and the Swan" has been a favorite subject with artists.

Leprechaun (*lĕp'rĕ-ĸôn'*). In Irish mythical tales a fairy shoemaker resembling an old man, who resorts to out-of-the-way places, where he is discovered by the noise of his hammer. Besides making shoes, he grinds meal and in other ways assists people who are kind to him. While any one keeps his eye fixed upon him, he cannot escape, but the moment the eye is withdrawn he may vanish.

Lethe (*lē'thē*). The river that separates Hades from the Elysian fields. The souls of the dead drink of this river and straightway forget all their past.

Liber. A name frequently given by the Roman poets to the Greek Bacchus, or Dionysus. But the god Liber and the goddess Libera were ancient Italian divinities, presiding over the cultivation of the vine and the fertility of the fields. Hence they were worshiped in early times in conjunction with Ceres. The vine and ivy and the panther were especially sacred to him, and goats were usually offered in sacrifice to him.

Libertas. The deification of liberty, to whom as a goddess several temples were erected at Rome. She is represented in works of art as a matron wearing a wreath of laurel and holding in her hand the pileus, the cap given to freed slaves as a symbol of their emancipation.

Libitina (*lĭb'ĭ-tī'nȧ*). An ancient goddess of Rome who presided over the burial of the dead. At her temple in Rome everything necessary for funerals was kept, and might be bought or hired for use. As goddess of death she was often identified with Proserpina but, as she had originally been a goddess of gardens and of voluptuous joy, she was sometimes identified with Venus.

Lif (*lēf*). In Norse mythology, the name given to man in the state in which he is to occupy the purified earth when goodness resumes its sway.

Lilinau. In the folklore of certain North American Indians, a woman wooed by a phantom. She followed his green waving plume through the forest and was never seen again.

Lilith (*lĭl'ĭth*). In Hebrew mythology, a female specter who lies in wait for children in order to destroy them. The older traditions tell of Lilith as a former wife of Adam and the mother of demons. Amulets were worn as protection from her powers.

Lofen. The Scandinavian god who guards friendship.

Lofua. The Scandinavian goddess who reconciles lovers.

Loki (*lō'kē*). In Norse mythology, the contriver of all mischief among the gods. He is the father of Fenris the wolf, of the Midgard Serpent, and of Hel, "death."

Lord of Cold Weather. Among the Blackfeet Indians, a tall, old man, who sits and smokes in his white tepee far in the north country.

Lorelei (*lō'rĕ-lī*). In German legend, a bewitching maiden who haunted a rock of the same name on the right bank of the Rhine. She combed her hair with a golden comb, and sang a wild song which enticed fishermen and sailors to destruction on the rocks and rapids at the foot of the precipice. In Norse mythology, Lorelei is represented as immortal, a daughter of the Rhine, and dwelling in the river bed.

Lotis. A nymph, who, to escape the embraces of Priapus, was metamorphosed into a tree, called, after her, "lotus."

Lubins. A species of goblins in Normandy that take the form of wolves and frequent churchyards. They are very timorous and take flight at the slightest noise.

Lucifer (*lū'sĭ-fēr*). (1) "Light-bearer." The name of the planet Venus, when seen in the morning before sunrise. The equivalent Greek is "Phosphor." The same planet was called "Hesperus," when it appeared in the heavens after sunset. (2) By a false etymology the church fathers connected the Hebrew word for Lucifer with a word meaning "to lament." He thus became the fallen angel who lamented his original glory, which was bright as the morning star, and he was identified with Satan by Dante and Milton, following the earlier writers.

Luna. The daughter of Hyperion and Thea. She was distinct in name, descent, and story, from Diana, who was regarded as goddess of the moon. To Luna was ascribed great influence in relation to the birth of children.

Lycomedes (*lĭk'ō-mē'dēz*). A king in the island of Scyros, to whose court Achilles, disguised as a maiden, was sent by his mother, Thetis, who was anxious to prevent her son from going to the Trojan War.

Mænalus (*mĕn'ȧ-lŭs*). A mountain in Arcadia, extending from Megalopolis to Tegea, celebrated as the favorite haunt of the god Pan.

Mæra. The dog of Icarius. Icarius, having made wine, gave it to some shepherds, who, thinking themselves poisoned, killed him; recovering themselves, they buried him. His daughter Erigone, being shown the spot by his faithful dog Mæra, hanged herself through grief.

Mammon. In demonology, a spirit placed at the head of nine ranks of demons. Also a Syriac word used in the Scriptures to signify either riches or the god of riches. Milton made Mammon one of the fallen angels.

Manes (*mā'nēz*). In Roman mythology, spirits of the dead, which were often supposed to hover about their former abodes and needed to be pacified by ceremonies.

Mani. Name given in ancient Norse mythology to a personification of the moon. He was later known as the son of Mundilfori, and was taken to heaven by the gods to drive the moon-car. He was followed by a wolf, which, when time should be no more, would devour both Mani and Mani's sister Sol.

Manitou. The great spirit of certain North American Indians.

Mars. A Roman god, originally of husbandry and later god of war, in which character he was identified with the Greek Ares. The Romans regarded him as the father of Romulus, and the founder and protector of their nation.

Marsyas. The Phrygian flute player who challenged Apollo to a contest of skill and, being beaten by the god, was flayed alive for his presumption. From his blood arose the river Marsyas. The flute on which Marsyas played was one Athena had thrown away, and, being filled with the breath of the goddess, gave forth such music as enabled him at least to compete with Apollo.

Medea. A daughter of Æetes, skilled in charms and witchcraft. She had scarcely beheld Jason, when, through the influence and disposal of the gods, a tender affection for the hero was raised in her bosom, and soon kindled to a flame of the most violent passion. Jason went to the temple of Hecate to supplicate the mighty goddess, where he was met by Medea. She disclosed her love to him, at the same time promising her assistance in the dangers which threatened him, and offering her help in accomplishing his glorious undertaking, provided he would swear fidelity to her. Jason complied, and Medea, reciprocating the oath, rendered the hero invincible by means of her magical incantations. She was later deserted by him and in revenge slew his children, his intended bride, and his father.

Medusa (*mē-dū'sȧ*). One of the three Gorgons whose hair was entwined with hissing serpents, and whose bodies were covered with impenetrable scales; they had wings, brazen claws, and enormous teeth, and whoever looked upon them was turned to stone. Medusa, who alone of the sisters was mortal, was, according to some legends, at first a beautiful maiden, but her hair was changed into serpents by Athena, or Minerva, in consequence of her having become by Poseidon, or Neptune, the mother of Chrysaor in one of Athena's temples. She was killed by Perseus, and her head was fixed on the shield of Minerva. From her blood sprang the winged horse, Pegasus.

Megæra (*mē-jē'rȧ*). One of the Furies, the author of insanity and murders. The others were: Tisiphone, whose particular work was to originate fatal epidemics and contagion; Alecto, to whom were ascribed the devastations and cruelties of war.

Megingiard (*mĕg'ĭn-yärd*). A magic belt worn by the god Thor, which, as it was tightened, rendered its wearer more powerful. The god was accustomed to show his strength by lifting great weights, but on one occasion the belt failed him, when he was challenged to pick up from the ground a cat belonging to a certain giant. He tugged and strained, only to succeed in raising one paw from the floor.

Meleager (*mĕl'ē-ā'jẽr*). Son of the Calydonian king Œneus. He took a prominent part in the Argonautic expedition and distinguished himself among his companions, especially by reason of his skill in throwing the javelin.

Melia (*mē'lĭ-ȧ*). One of the daughters of Oceanus and the mother of Phoroneus, a fabulous king of Argos.

Melicertes (*mĕl'ĭ-sûr'tēz*). A son of the Theban king Athamas by Ino. He was metamorphosed into a sea god.

Melic (*mĕl'ĭk*) **Nymphs.** Maidens of the ashen spear, sprung from the blood of Uranus. Two of them, Adrastea and Ida, cared for the infant Jupiter in a cave on Mount Ida.

Melissa. A nymph, said to have discovered the use of honey, and from whom bees were said to have received their Greek name.

Melpomene (*mĕl-pŏm'ē-nē*). The Muse of the tragic drama.

Melusina (*mĕl'ū-sē'nȧ*). The most noted among French fairies. She was condemned to become every Saturday a serpent from the waist downward, as a punishment for having, by means of a charm, enclosed her father in a high mountain, in order to avenge an injury her mother had received from him. She married Raymond, count of Toulouse, who in violation of a promise he gave her never to visit her on Saturdays came and saw her during her loathsome transformation. For his breach of faith she left him. The story has analogies with legends of the mermaids, and of Cupid and Psyche.

Memnon. A son of Tithonus and Aurora, and king of Ethiopia. After the fall of Hector, he went to the assistance of his uncle Priam with 10,000 men, and displayed great courage in the defense of Troy, but he was at length slain by Ajax, in single combat, whereupon he was changed into a bird.

Mendes (*mĕn'dēz*). An Egyptian god similar to Pan. He was worshiped in the form of a goat.

Menelaus (*mĕn'ē-lā'ŭs*). A son of Atreus, and younger brother of Agamemnon. He was king of Lacedæmon, and was married to the beautiful Helen, by whom he became the father of Hermione. When Paris seduced and took to Troy his wife Helen, he enlisted the help of Agamemnon, his brother, and many other Greek princes to win back his wife by sacking Troy. In the war Menelaus killed many Trojans, and would have slain Paris also in single combat had not the latter been carried off in a cloud by Venus.

Menœceus (*mē-nē'sūs*). (1) A Theban, grandson of Pentheus, and father of Hipponome, Jocasta, and Creon. (2) Grandson of Menœceus, and son of Creon. When the seven Argive heroes marched against Thebes, he put an end to his life because Tiresias had declared that his death would bring victory to his country.

Mentor. A friend of Ulysses in Ithaca, whose form Minerva assumed in order to give instructions to Ulysses' son Telemachus, whom she accompanied to Pylos and Lacedæmon.

Mephistopheles (*mĕf'ĭs-tŏf'ē-lēz*). One of the seven chief devils in the old demonology, the second of the fallen archangels, and after Satan the most powerful among the infernal legions. He figures in the old legend of Dr. Faustus as the familiar spirit of that magician. To modern readers he is chiefly known as the cold, scoffing, relentless fiend of Goethe's *Faust*, and as the attendant demon in Marlowe's *Faustus*. The name is said to be a corruption of a Greek word meaning "one who hates what is helpful."

Mercury. A Roman god, identified with the Greek Hermes. In Rome, however, he continued to carry a sacred branch as the emblem of peace instead of the caduceus. Like Hermes he was the messenger of Jupiter, the god of eloquence, of gain, and of thievery, and conducted souls to the lower world.

Mermaids (*mûr'mādz*). Wave maidens of medieval folklore. They were generally represented as young and beautiful women, fish-form below the waist, who used their charms to lure men to destruction in the sea. Sometimes they are said to have quit the sea, temporarily acquiring complete human form, and marrying, only to bring disaster upon their husbands and upon themselves.

Meru (*mā'rōō*). In Hindu mythology, a sacred mountain, 80,000 leagues high, situated in the center of the world. It was the abode of Indra, god of the air, and abounded with every charm that can be imagined.

Midas. The king of Phrygia, who restored to Bacchus the god's nurse and preceptor, Silenus, and received as a compensation the power of turning into gold everything he touched. But this proved to be very inconvenient, as it prevented him from eating and drinking, and he prayed that the gift might be revoked. At the command of the god, he washed in the Pactolus, the sands of which became, in consequence, mixed with gold. Another tradition is that, in a musical contest between Pan and Apollo, he gave judgment in favor of the satyr; whereupon Apollo in contempt gave the king a pair of ass's ears. Midas hid them under his Phrygian cap; but his servant, who used to cut his hair, discovered them, and was so pleased with the "joke," which he dared not mention, that he dug a hole in the earth and relieved his mind by whispering in it, "Midas has ass's ears."

Midgard (*mĭd'gärd*). In Scandinavian mythology, the name given to the earth, meaning "middle yard or enclosure." It was formed in the middle of *Ginnungagap*, or "gaping abyss," out of the eyebrows of the giant Ymir and joined to heaven by the rainbow bridge Bifröst. The solid portion of Midgard was surrounded by the giant's blood or sweat, which now formed the ocean, while his bones made the hills, his flat teeth became the cliffs, and his curly hair took the form of the trees and all vegetation.

Midgard Serpent. The great serpent, offspring of Loki, which grew to such a length that it surrounded the earth and bit its tail. Odin cast it into the sea.

Mimir (*mē'mẽr*). In Scandinavian mythology, the god of wisdom. Also god of the ocean, called "Mimir's well," in which wit and wisdom lay hidden, and of which he drank every morning from the Giallarhorn. Odin once drank from this fountain, and by doing so became the wisest of gods and men; but he purchased the privilege and distinction at the cost of one eye, which Mimir exacted from him.

Minerva. Under the name of Minerva among the Romans and of Athena among the Greeks was personified and deified the idea of intelligence and wisdom. Minerva was a daughter of Jupiter, sprung from his head. The Greeks ascribed to this goddess the invention of many arts and sciences, which had a great influence on their civilization. She was regarded as inventress of the flute, of embroidery and spinning, of the use of the olive, and of various instruments of war; in short, of most works indicating superior intelligence or skill. See *Arachne.*

Minos (*mī'nŏs*). A semimythical king and lawgiver of Crete. In order to avenge the wrong done to his son Androgeos at Athens, he made war against the Athenians, and compelled them to send to Crete every year, as a tribute, seven youths and seven maidens, to be devoured in the labyrinth by the Minotaur.

Minotaur (*mĭn'ô-tôr*). A celebrated monster with the head of a bull and the body of a man, kept by Minos in the famous labyrinth constructed by Dædalus. The monster devoured a tribute of young people from Athens each year until he was slain by Theseus, with the assistance of Ariadne, the daughter of Minos.

Mithra. A Persian deity whose worship spread over western Asia and through the Roman world. This cult was the most formidable rival of early Christianity. Mithra was a god of light, heat, and fertility, a giver of all good things. He was popularly represented as a sun god, and in many respects he resembled Apollo.

Mjölnir (*myûl'nêr*). In the mythology of Scandinavia, the name of Thor's celebrated hammer — a type of the thunderbolt — which, however far it might be cast, was never lost, as it always returned to his hand. Whenever he wished, it became so small that he could put it in his pocket.

Mnemosyne (*nē-mŏs'ĭ-nē*). Mother of the Muses and goddess of memory. She was courted by Jupiter in the guise of a shepherd.

Moakkibat. A class of angels, according to the Mohammedan mythology. Two angels of this class attend every child of Adam from the cradle to the grave. At sunset they fly up with the record of the deeds done since sunrise. Every good deed is entered ten times by the recording angel on the credit or right side of his ledger, but when an evil deed is reported the angel waits seven hours in the hope that the evildoer may repent.

Mœræ (*mē'rē*). The Greek name for the Fates.

Morpheus (*môr'fūs*). The son of Sleep and the god of dreams. The name signifies the fashioner or molder, because he shapes or forms the dreams which appear to the sleeper.

Mowis. The snow bridegroom who, according to a certain North American Indian tradition, wooed and won a beautiful bride; but, when morning dawned, Mowis left the wigwam and melted into the sunshine. The bride hunted for him night and day in the forests, but never saw him again.

Muses. Nine daughters of Jupiter and Mnemosyne. They were goddesses of poetry, of history, and of other arts and sciences. Calliope was the Muse of eloquence and heroic poetry, and to her the ancients gave precedence; Clio, of history; Erato, of amorous poetry; Euterpe, of music; Melpomene, of tragedy; Polyhymnia, of eloquence and of imitation; Terpsichore, of dancing; Thalia, of comic and lyric poetry; and Urania, of astronomy. Their usual abode was Mount Parnassus in Helicon.

Myrmidons (*mûr'mĭ-dŏnz*). The trusty followers of Achilles. They are said to have inhabited originally the island of Ægina, and to have emigrated with Peleus into Thessaly; but modern critics, on the contrary, suppose that a colony of them emigrated from Thessaly into Ægina. The Myrmidons disappeared from history at a later period. The ancients derived their name either from a mythical ancestor, Myrmidon, son of Zeus and father of Actor and Eurymedusa, or from the ants in Ægina, which were supposed to have been metamorphosed into men in the time of Æacus.

Mysterious Three, The. In Scandinavian mythology, "Har" (the Mighty), the "Like-Mighty," and the "Third Person," who sat on three thrones above the rainbow. Below them ranked the "Æsir," of which Odin was chief, who lived in Asgard between the rainbow and the earth; and below them, the "Vanir," or gods of the ocean, air, and clouds, of which deities Niord was chief.

Naiads (*nā'yădz*). The nymphs of fresh water, whether of rivers, lakes, brooks, or springs. See *Nymphs.*

Nala. A legendary king of India, whose love for Damayanti and whose subsequent misfortunes have supplied subjects for numerous poems.

Nanabozho. A North American Indian hero who, like Hiawatha, showed himself a benefactor of mankind. He stole fire from the fire spirit.

Naraka (*năr'à-kà*). The hell of the Hindus. It has 28 divisions, in some of which the victims are torn by ravens and owls; in others they are compelled to swallow cakes boiling hot, or are made to walk over burning sands.

Narcissus. The beautiful youth, son of the river god Cephissus and of the sea nymph Liriope. Echo, whose love he refused, died of grief. But Nemesis, to punish him, caused him to see his own image reflected in a fountain, whereupon he became so enamored of it that he gradually pined away, until he was metamorphosed into the flower which bears his name. According to another tradition, Narcissus had a sister of remarkable beauty, to whom he was tenderly attached. She resembled him in features, was similarly attired, and accompanied him in the hunt. She died young, and Narcissus, lamenting her death, frequented a neighboring fountain to gaze upon his own image in its stream. The strong resemblance that he bore to his sister made his own reflection appear to him, as it were, the form of her whom he had lost. The gods looked with pity upon his grief, and changed him to the flower that bears his name.

Nausicaa (*nô-sĭk'â-à*). A daughter of Alcinous, king of the Phæacians, and of Arete. She discovered the shipwrecked Odysseus (Ulysses) on the shore and conducted him to the court of her father.

Nectar. Wine conferring immortality, which was, according to Homer, drunk by the gods.

Neleus (*nē'lūs*). Son of Neptune and Tyro, and brother to Pelias. He became king in Peloponnesus; his twelve sons were all killed by Hercules.

Nemean (*nê-mē'ăn*) **Lion.** A monstrous lion, near the forest of Nemea, which wasted the surrounding country and threatened destruction to the herds. Hercules promised to deliver the country of the monster, and Thespius rewarded Hercules by making him his guest so long as the chase lasted. Hercules slew the lion, and thereafter wore its skin as his garment and its head as his helmet.

Nemesis (*nĕm'ē-sĭs*). A Greek goddess, who measured out to mortals happiness and misery, and visited with losses and sufferings all who were blessed with too many gifts of fortune. This is the character in which she appears in the earlier Greek writers; but subsequently she was regarded, like the Erinyes or Furies, as the goddess who punished crimes.

Neoptolemus. The son of Achilles. He was reared in Scyros, in the palace of Lycomedes, and was brought thence by Ulysses, because it had been prophesied that Neoptolemus and Philoctetes were necessary for the capture of Troy. At Troy Neoptolemus showed himself worthy of his great father. He was one of the heroes concealed in the wooden horse, and at the capture of the city he killed Priam, and sacrificed Polyxena to the spirit of his father. He was also called Pyrrhus. See *Pyrrhus.*

Nepenthe (*nê-pĕn'thê*). A care-dispelling drug, which Polydamna, wife of Thonis, king of Egypt, gave to Helen. A drink containing this drug "changed grief to mirth, melancholy to joyfulness, and hatred to love." Homer mentions this drug nepenthe in his *Odyssey.*

Neptune. A Roman god of water, identified with Poseidon, the Greek god of the ocean. To him as god of the ocean, myths assign the following activities: his assistance to Jupiter against the Titans; the building of the walls and ramparts of Troy; the creation and taming of the horse; the raising of the island Delos out of the sea; and the destruction of Hippolytus by a monster sent from the deep. He was feared also as the author of earthquakes and deluges, which he caused or checked at pleasure by his trident.

Nereids (*nē'rê-ĭdz*). Sea nymphs, generally regarded as belonging to the Mediterranean. The chief characteristics of these minor deities of the sea were the power of divination and the ability to change their forms at pleasure. They were daughters of Nereus and Doris, fifty in number, and usually followed in the train of Neptune.

Nereus (*nē'rūs*). A son of Pontus and Gæa, and husband of Doris, by whom he became the father of the fifty Nereids.

Nestor. A son of Neleus and Chloris, and king of Pylos in Triphylia. He took a prominent part in the Trojan War, acting as counselor of the other Grecian chiefs, but he was equally distinguished for his valor in the field of battle. Homer extols his wisdom, justice, bravery, and eloquence. He lived to so great an age that his advice and authority were deemed equal to those of the immortal gods. Hence the name is often found in literature as an appellation denoting wisdom.

Nickar or **Hnickar.** The name assumed by Odin when he impersonated the destroying principle.

Nickneven. A gigantic and malignant female spirit of the old popular Scottish mythology. The hag is represented as riding at the head of witches and fairies at Halloween.

Niflheim (*nēv″l-hām*). "Mist home" of old Norse mythology, the region of endless cold and everlasting night, ruled over by Hel, daughter of Loki. It consisted of nine worlds, to which were consigned those who died of disease or of old age. This region existed "from the beginning" in the North, and in the middle of it was the well Hvergelmir, from which flowed twelve rivers.

Nina. The ancient patron goddess of Nineveh. The Babylonian word sign for her name and that of the city meant "house of the fish."

Niobe (*nī′ō-bē*). The daughter of Tantalus and the wife of Amphion, king of Thebes. Niobe offended Latona, the mother of Apollo and Diana, by boasting that she had more children than Latona, and the latter engaged both her children to avenge her; they, by their arrows, slew the seven sons and seven daughters of Niobe, who by grief was changed into stone. She was transported in a whirlwind to the top of Mount Sipylus, where she has ever since remained, her tears flowing unceasingly.

Nisus. A Trojan youth who accompanied Æneas to Italy after the fall of Troy. He is celebrated for his devoted attachment to his friend Euryalus.

Nithhogg (*nēTH′hŏg′*). The dragon that gnaws at the root of Yggdrasil, the tree of the universe in Scandinavian mythology.

Nix. Little creatures not unlike the Scotch brownie and German kobold. They wear a red cap, and are ever ready to lend a helping hand to the industrious and thrifty.

Nokomis (*nō-kō′mĭs*). Daughter of the moon in North American Indian myths. Sporting one day with her maidens on a swing made of vine canes, a rival cut the swing, and Nokomis fell to earth, where she gave birth to a daughter named Wenonah. Wenonah later became the mother of Hiawatha.

Norns. The three Fates of Scandinavian mythology, past, present, and future. They spin the events of human life, sitting under the ash tree Yggdrasil, which they carefully tend. Their names are Urd, "the past," Verdandi, "the present," and Skuld, "the future." Besides these three Norns, every human creature has a personal Norn or Fate. The home of the Norns is called in Scandinavian mythology, "Doomstead."

Nox. The goddess of night, considered among the ancients as one of their oldest divinities and worshiped by them with great solemnity. In the temple of Diana, at Ephesus, was a famous statue of her. She became the mother of Æther, "air," and Dies, "day." She is likewise, according to some, the mother of the inexorable Parcæ; of the avenging Nemesis, who punishes hidden crime; of the Furies, who torment the wicked; of Charon, the ferryman of hell; and of the twin brothers, Sleep and Death.

Nymphs. The nymphs of ancient fiction were viewed as holding an intermediate place between men and gods as to the length of life, not being absolutely immortal, yet living a vast length of time. Oceanus was considered as their common father, although the descent of different nymphs varies. Their usual abode was in grottoes. Special groups had their own peculiar duties, each group being distinguished by special names according to the several objects of their patronage, or the regions in which they chiefly resided. Thus, there were the Oreads, or nymphs of the mountains; Naiads, Nereids, and Potamids, nymphs of the fountains, seas, and rivers; Dryads and Hamadryads, nymphs of the woods; Napææ, nymphs of the vales.

Oceanids (*ō-sē′ȧ-nĭdz*). Daughters of Oceanus, sea nymphs said to be 3000 in number.

Oceanus. The god of the river which was thought to surround the whole earth, in early times believed flat and round. He was the son of heaven and earth, the husband of Tethys, and the father of all the river gods and water nymphs. Out of and into this river the sun and the stars were supposed to rise and set; and on its banks were the abodes of the dead.

Odhrerir. In Scandinavian mythology, the name of the cauldron containing mead or nectar made of honey mingled with the blood of Kvasir, wisest of men. This potion conferred wisdom and the poetic faculty on those who drank of it.

Odin. The king of gods and men, and the reputed progenitor of the Scandinavian kings. He corresponds both to the Jupiter and to the Mars of Græco-Roman mythology. As god of war, he held his court in Valhalla, surrounded by all warriors who had fallen in battle, and attended by two wolves, to whom he gave his share of food; for he himself lived on wine alone. On his shoulders he carried two ravens, Hugin, "mind," and Munin, "memory," whom he dispatched every day to bring him news of all that was being done throughout the world. He had three great treasures: Sleipnir, an eight-footed horse of marvelous swiftness; Gungnir, a spear, which never failed to strike what it was aimed at; and Draupnir, a magic ring, which every ninth night dropped eight other rings of equal value. The German tribes worshiped Odin under the name of "Woden."

Odur. In Scandinavian mythology, husband of Freya, whom he deserted. After a long search she found him again and was restored to happiness by his love.

Odysseus (*ō-dĭs′ūs*). Greek form of the name Ulysses.

Œdipus (*ĕd′ĭ-pŭs*). The son of Laius, king of Thebes. Laius, having been warned by an oracle that his throne and life were in danger from this son, gave him immediately after birth to a herdsman to be killed. But the child was saved, and reared by a peasant. Having grown up he ransomed Thebes from the sphinx by answering her riddle, unwittingly killed his own father, and, on becoming king of Thebes, married his father's wife, that is, his own mother, Jocasta. Subsequently discovering his parentage, he destroyed his eyesight and wandered away from Thebes, attended by his daughter Antigone, who remained with him till his death.

Ogre (*ō′gẽr*). In nursery mythology, a giant of very malignant disposition, who lives on human flesh.

Old One. Among the Thompson River Indians, the god who created the earth and taught the people how to hunt and fish and to do all the other things needful for living.

Olympus. A range of mountains in Thessaly, the abode of the gods. A gate of clouds, kept by the goddesses named the Seasons, unfolded to permit the passage of the deities to earth, or to receive them on their return.

Ops. A Roman goddess of plenty, and of fertility, the wife of Saturn, and the patroness of husbandry.

Orestes (*ō-rĕs′tēz*). The son of Agamemnon and Clytemnestra. On the murder of his father by Ægisthus and Clytemnestra, Orestes was saved from the same fate by his sister Electra. She caused him to be secretly carried to Strophius, king of Phocis, who was married to Anaxibia, the sister of Agamemnon. There he formed a close and intimate friendship with the king's son Pylades; and, when he had grown up, he repaired secretly to Argos with his friend, and avenged his father's death by slaying Clytemnestra and Ægisthus. After the murder of his mother he was seized with madness, and fled from land to land, pursued by the Erinyes, or Furies. At length, on the advice of Apollo, he took refuge in the temple of Athena at Athens, where he was acquitted by the court of the Areopagus, which the goddess had appointed to decide his fate.

Orion. A mighty giant and hunter, famous for his beauty. Having come to Chios, he fell in love with Merope, the daughter of Œnopion; his treatment of the maiden so exasperated her father, that, with the assistance of Dionysus, he deprived the giant of his sight. Being informed by an oracle that he should recover his sight if he exposed his eyeballs to the rays of the rising sun, he followed the sound of a Cyclops's hammer, and at Lemnos he found Vulcan, who gave him Cedalion as a guide to the abode of the sun. After the recovery of his sight he lived as a hunter with Artemis, or Diana. Orion was slain by Diana, or, as some say, by Jupiter, and placed among the stars.

Orithyia. A daughter of Erechtheus, beloved by Boreas, who carried her off as she was wandering near the river Ilissus.

Orlog. A god of Norse fable personifying the eternal law of the universe. From his decree there was no appeal.

Ormuzd (*ôr′mŭzd*). In the *Avesta*, called Ahura Mazda (*ä′hōō-rȧ-mȧz′dȧ*). The name of the supreme deity of the ancient Persians, and of their descendants, the Parsees and Ghebers. He is, according to them, an embodiment of the principle of good, and is in perpetual conflict with Ahriman, the principle of evil. He created the earth, moon, sun, and stars, and continues to regulate their motion. See *Ahriman.*

Orpheus (*ôr′fūs*). The son of Apollo or of Œagrus, a river god, and of Calliope. Presented with the lyre by Apollo, and instructed by the Muses in its use, he enchanted with its music not only the wild beasts, but the trees and rocks upon Olympus, so that they moved from their places to follow the sound of his golden harp. He accompanied the Argonauts in their expedition. After his return, he took up his abode in Thrace, where he married the nymph Eurydice. His wife having died of the bite of a serpent, he followed her into the abodes of Hades. Here his lyre so charmed King Pluto that Eurydice was released from death, but on the condition that Orpheus should not look back until he had reached the earth. He was just about to place his foot on the earth when he turned round, and Eurydice vanished from him in an instant.

Osiris (*ō-sī′rĭs*). An Egyptian god, said to have been the son of Jupiter by Niobe, to have ruled first over the Argives, and afterwards to have become king of the Egyptians. His wife was Isis, who is by many said to be the same as Io, daughter of Inachus. Osiris was at length slain by Typhon, and his corpse was concealed in a chest and thrown into the Nile. Isis, after much search, by the aid of keen-scented dogs, found the body and placed it in a monument on an island near Memphis. The Egyptians paid divine honor to his memory, and chose the ox to represent him, because, according to one account, a large ox appeared to them after the body of Osiris was interred, or, according to others, because Osiris had instructed them in agriculture. Osiris was generally represented with a cap on his head like a miter, and with two horns; he held a stick in his left hand, and in his right a whip with three thongs. Sometimes he appears with the head of a hawk.

Ostara or **Eástre.** Saxon goddess of spring and returning life. At her festival it was customary to exchange gifts of painted eggs. Christianity adopted the festival as Easter and gave it a new meaning.

Otus. One of the two giants who were usually called the Aloadæ. The other was Ephialtes. The two were renowned for their extraordinary strength and courage.

Pachacamac. The name of an ancient Peruvian god of earthquakes, which were regarded as his voice. The meaning of this name is "earth-generator." He was worshiped as a god of fertility also, and as a civilizer.

Pactolus. The river whose sands turned to gold when Midas by order of Bacchus washed in the waters.

Paimosaid. In certain North American Indian myths, a wandering thief who walks through cornfields about harvest time to pluck the ears of corn.

Palæmon. Son of Ino, originally called Melicertes, until he was made a sea god. The Roman god of harbors, Portunus, was identified with him.

Palamedes (*păl'ȧ-mē'dēz*). A Greek hero sent by the Greek princes to induce Ulysses to join in the Trojan War, when Ulysses sought to avoid going by pretending insanity. Palamedes soon penetrated the deception, and Ulysses was obliged to join in the war.

Pales (*pā'lēz*). The goddess of shepherds, presiding over cattle and pastures, whose festival, the Palilia, was celebrated on the 21st of April, the anniversary of the day on which Rome was founded. The Palatine hill at Rome was sacred to her. Later the Roman emperors built on it their residence, called the Palatium, from which comes our word palace.

Palladium (*pă-lā'dĭ-ŭm*). A Trojan statue of the goddess Pallas Athena, which represented her as sitting with a spear in her right hand, and in her left a spindle or distaff. It is said to have fallen from heaven near the tent of Ilus at the time when that prince was employed in building the citadel of Troy; and Apollo, by an oracle, declared that the city should never be taken as long as the Palladium was contained within its walls. Ulysses and Diomedes captured the statue for the Greeks and not long afterwards the city was taken.

Pallas. (1) One of the giants. (2) The father of Athena, according to some traditions. (3) Son of Lycaon and grandfather of Evander. (4) Son of Evander and an ally of Æneas.

Pallas Athena (*păl'ȧs ȧ-thē'nȧ*). See *Athena.*

Pan. The god of shepherds and herdsmen, of groves and fields, and of rural life generally. He was said to be the son of Mercury and Dryope. His favorite residence was in the woods and mountains of Arcadia, where he was frequently heard playing on his pipe or flute of seven reeds, called a syrinx. It was fabled that this pipe was a metamorphosis of a nymph named Syrinx, whom he had loved. His pride in this invention led him into an unlucky contest with Apollo. His festivals were introduced by Evander among the Romans, and by them called Lupercalia. Goats, honey, and milk were the usual offerings to Pan. Pan, like other gods who dwelt in forests, was dreaded by travelers, to whom he sometimes appeared, and whom he startled by his uncanny presence. Hence sudden fright, without any visible cause, was ascribed to Pan and was called a panic. See *Mendes.*

Pandora. The first woman, according to Greek mythology. She was made of clay by Vulcan, and all the gods made presents to her. Venus gave her beauty and the art of pleasing; the Graces gave her the power of captivating; Apollo taught her how to sing; Mercury instructed her in eloquence and brought her to Epimetheus, who made her his wife, forgetting the advice of his brother Prometheus, not to receive gifts that came from Jupiter. In her home she found a box which she was forbidden to open. Disobeying the injunction she allowed to escape from it all the evils of life except hope. According to another version, all the blessings of life escaped from it except hope, which remained to solace mortals.

Parcæ (*pär'sē*). See *Fates.*

Paris. The son of Priam, king of Troy, and of Hecuba; he was also called Alexander. The tradition is that, at the marriage of Peleus and Thetis, the goddess of discord, who had not been invited, showed her displeasure by throwing into the assembly of the gods, who were at the nuptials, a golden apple on which were the words "For the fairest." The apple was claimed by Hera, Aphrodite, and Athena. Zeus ordered Hermes to take the goddesses to Mount Ida, and to intrust the decision of the dispute to the Trojan shepherd Paris. The goddesses accordingly appeared before him. Hera promised him the sovereignty of Asia; Athena, renown in war; and Aphrodite, the fairest of women for his wife. Paris decided in favor of Aphrodite, and gave her the golden apple. Under her protection, Paris sailed to Greece, and was hospitably received in the palace of Menelaus at Sparta. Here he succeeded in carrying off to Troy Helen, the wife of Menelaus, who was the most beautiful woman in the world. Menelaus enlisted the support of many other Greek chieftains and proceeded to besiege Troy. Paris fought with Menelaus before the walls of Troy, and, though defeated, was carried off by Aphrodite. He slew Achilles by wounding him in his heel, where alone he was vulnerable, while Achilles was engaged in a peaceful mission in Troy.

Parnassus. A well-wooded mountain ridge near Delphi in Greece. At its foot grew myrtle, laurel, and olive trees, and, higher up, firs; its summit was covered with snow during the greater part of the year. It contained numerous caves, glens, and romantic ravines and had two summits, one of which was consecrated to Apollo and the Muses, the other to Bacchus. It was anciently called Larnassus, from *larnax,* "an ark," because Deucalion's ark was stranded there after the flood. After the oracle of Delphi was built at its foot it received the name of Parnassus and was celebrated as one of the chief seats of Apollo and the Muses.

Parthenope (*pär-thĕn'ō-pē*). One of the sirens, who threw herself into the sea out of love for Ulysses, and whose dead body was washed ashore on the present site of Naples. Naples itself was anciently called Parthenope, which name was changed to *Neapolis,* "the new city," by a colony of Cumæans.

Pasiphaë. The wife of Minos, king of Crete, and, by a bull, the mother of the Minotaur, to which human captives were given as food.

Patroclus (*pȧ-trō'klŭs*). The gentle and amiable friend of Achilles in Homer's *Iliad.*

Pauguk. Name given to the great power, death, in the mythology of certain North American Indians.

Paupukkeewis (*pô'pŭk-kē'wĭs*). In North American Indian folklore, a mischievous magician, who, pursued by Hiawatha, went through a series of wonderful transformations in his endeavors to escape, and finally became an eagle.

Pax. The goddess of peace, worshiped in Greece under the name Irene. Pax wore a crown of laurel and held in her hand the branch of an olive tree.

Peboan. In North American Indian folklore, the personification of winter in the form of a great giant who shook the snow from his hair and turned water into stone by his breath.

Pegasus (*pĕg'ȧ-sŭs*). The winged horse which sprang from the blood of Medusa when her head was struck off by Perseus.

Peleus (*pē'lūs*). King of the Myrmidons at Phthia in Thessaly. Having, in conjunction with his brother Telamon, murdered his half brother Phocus, he was expelled by Æacus from Ægina, and went to Thessaly. He was purified from the murder by Eurytion, who then gave Peleus his daughter Antigone in marriage, and a third part of his kingdom.

Pelion (*pē'lĭ-ŏn*). A high mountain in Thessaly near whose summit was the cave of the centaur Chiron. The giants, in their war with the gods, are said to have attempted to heap Pelion and Ossa on Olympus, in order to scale heaven.

Pelops (*pē'lŏps*). A Phrygian prince, grandson of Jupiter and son of Tantalus. Expelled from Phrygia, he came to Elis, where he married Hippodamia, daughter of Œnomaus, whom he succeeded on the throne. By means of the wealth he brought with him, his influence became so great in the peninsula that it was called after him the Peloponnese, "the island of Pelops."

Penates (*pē-nā'tēz*). Roman gods who were supposed to preside over the welfare and prosperity of the family. The storehouse, or *penus,* was sacred to them.

Penelope (*pē-nĕl'ō-pē*). The faithful wife of Ulysses, who, being importuned during his long absence by numerous suitors for her hand, postponed making a decision among them until she should have finished weaving a funeral pall for her father-in-law, Laertes. Every night she secretly unraveled what she had woven by day, and thus put off the suitors till Ulysses returned.

Peri (*pē′rĭ*). In Persian mythology, delicate, gentle, fairylike beings, begotten by fallen spirits. They direct with a wand the pure in mind along the way to heaven. These lovely creatures, according to the *Koran*, are under the sovereignty of Eblis; and Mohammed was sent for their conversion, as well as for that of man.

Perse. A daughter of Oceanus, and wife of Helios (the sun), by whom she became the mother of Æetes, Circe, Pasiphaë, and Perses.

Persephone (*pẽr-sĕf′ō-nē*). The Greek name of Proserpina. Homer describes her as the wife of Hades, or Pluto, and the formidable and majestic queen of the shades, who, with her husband, rules over the souls of the dead.

Perseus (*pûr′sūs*). One of the most distinguished of the early heroes. He was the son of Jupiter and Danaë, and was educated by Polydectes on the island of Seriphus. His chief exploit was the destruction of the Gorgon Medusa, whose head he struck off with a sword given to him by Vulcan. From the blood that fell, sprang the winged horse Pegasus, on which Perseus afterwards passed over many lands. Of his subsequent achievements, the most remarkable were his changing King Atlas into a high rock or mountain by means of Medusa's head, and his deliverance of Andromeda when she was bound and exposed to be devoured by a sea monster.

Phædra (*fē′drȧ*). Daughter of Minos, and wife of Theseus, who, finding her love rejected by her stepson Hippolytus, falsely accused him of making improper advances toward her, and so induced her husband to bring about his son's death.

Phaëthon. A son of Phœbus and Clymene. Anxious to display his skill in horsemanship, he was so presumptuous as to request his father to allow him to drive the chariot of the sun across the heavens for one day. Helios was induced by the entreaties of his son and of Clymene to yield, but the youth, being too weak to check the horses, permitted them to go too close to the earth, thereby scorching it. To save mankind Zeus killed Phaëthon with a thunderbolt, and hurled him down into the river Eridanus. His sisters wept for him until they were metamorphosed into poplars, and their tears became amber.

Phaon. A boatman of Mytilene, ugly in appearance, who once carried Aphrodite across the sea without accepting payment. In return the goddess gave him a box of ointment with which, when he anointed himself, he grew so beautiful that Sappho became enamored of him; but when the ointment had all been used Phaon returned to his former condition, and Sappho, in despair, drowned herself.

Philemon and Baucis (*fĭ-lē′mŏn*) (*bô′sĭs*). An aged couple, who alone in Phrygia honored two travelers with hospitality. The travelers proved to be Jupiter and Mercury in disguise and in acknowledgment of the kindness they had received, they changed into a temple the house of Philemon and Baucis. The two old people were granted the privilege of caring for the temple and of leaving life together. One day, as they stood before the door, they were suddenly transformed into trees, an oak and a linden, which stood side by side.

Philoctetes (*fĭl′ŏk-tē′tēz*). The most celebrated archer in the Trojan War. He was the friend and armor-bearer of Hercules, who bequeathed to him his bow and his poisoned arrows in return for setting fire to the pile on Mount Œta on which Hercules perished.

Philomela (*fĭl′ō-mē′lȧ*). A daughter of Pandion, king of Athens. Her sister Procne had married Tereus, king of Thrace. Becoming tired of her after she had given birth to a son, Itylus, he cut out her tongue and told that she had died. Philomela became his next wife, and, learning the truth from her sister, served up, with her sister's help, the cooked flesh of Itylus for Tereus to eat. The gods in anger turned Philomela into a nightingale, Procne into a swallow, and Tereus into a hawk.

Phœbe. The goddess of the moon, and sister of Phœbus; a name of Diana.

Phœbus. See *Apollo*.

Phœnix. (1) A fabulous bird described as being as large as an eagle. Its head was finely crested with a beautiful plumage, its neck covered with gold-colored feathers, its tail white, and its body purple or crimson. It was said to appear once every 500 years, each bird rising from the ashes of its sire, who voluntarily cremated himself. (2) Father of Europa and reputed ancestor of the Phœnicians.

Phyllis. A daughter of King Sithon of Thrace. She hanged herself, thinking that she was deserted by her lover, Demophon, who had failed to appear on the day appointed for their marriage. She was changed by the gods into an almond tree.

Pirene (*pī-rē′nē*). A celebrated fountain of Corinth, at which Bellerophon is said to have caught the horse Pegasus. It gushed forth from the rock in the Acrocorinthus, was conveyed down the hill by subterraneous conduits, and fell into a marble basin, from which the greater part of the town was supplied with water.

Pleiades (*plē′yȧ-dēz*). The seven daughters of Atlas and Pleione, named Electra, Alcyone, Celæno, Maia, Sterope, Taygeta, and Merope. They were transformed into stars, one of which, Merope, is invisible out of shame, because she alone married a human being. Some call the invisible star "Electra," and say she hides herself from grief for the destruction of the city and royal race of Troy. The name means "sailing stars," because navigation was considered safe after their appearance.

Pluto (*plōō′tō*). A brother of Jupiter and Neptune. He received, as his portion in the division of empire, the infernal regions. His wife was Persephone, or, as the Romans called her, Proserpina, the daughter of Demeter, whom he carried by force from the upper world and made queen of the lower regions. The nymph Mintho, whom he loved, was metamorphosed by Proserpina into the plant called mint; and the nymph Leuce was changed by him after her death into a white poplar. The ensign of his power was a staff, with which, like Hermes, he drove the shades into the lower world. He possessed a helmet which rendered the wearer invisible, and which he sometimes lent to men or to other gods. The Furies were said to be his daughters. Being the king of the lower world, Pluto was regarded as giver of the blessings that come from the earth, such as the metals.

Plutus. The god of riches, and son of Iasion and Demeter. Jupiter blinded him so that he would bestow his gifts irrespective of merit.

Pluvius. A surname of Jupiter among the Romans meaning, "the sender of rain." Sacrifices were offered to him in this capacity during long-protracted droughts.

Podalirius. The son of Æsculapius, and brother of Machaon, with whom he led the Thessalians of Tricca against Troy. He was, like his brother, skilled in the medical art.

Polias. A cult name of Athena at Athens meaning "protectress of the city."

Pollux. A son of Jupiter and Leda, and brother to Castor.

Polydorus. (1) King of Thebes, son of Cadmus and Harmonia, husband of Nycteus, and father of Labdacus. (2) Son of Priam and Hecuba. When Ilium was on the point of falling into the hands of the Greeks, Priam intrusted Polydorus and a large sum of money to Polymnestor, king of the Thracian Chersonesus.

Polyhymnia (*pŏl′ĭ-hĭm′nĭ-ȧ*). See *Muses*.

Polyphemus. A son of Neptune, and one of the Cyclopes who dwelt in Sicily. He was a cruel monster of immense size and strength, and had but one eye, which was in the middle of his forehead. He dwelt in a cave near Mount Etna, and fed his flocks upon the mountain. He fell in love with the nymph Galatea, but, as she rejected him for Acis, he destroyed the latter by crushing him under a huge rock. When Ulysses landed in Sicily, he, with twelve of his companions, was caught in the cave of Polyphemus, and six of the number were eaten by the terrible cannibal. The rest were in expectation of the same fate, but their cunning leader enabled them to escape by contriving to intoxicate Polyphemus, and then destroying his single eye with a firebrand.

Polyxena (*pō-lĭk′sē-nȧ*). The daughter of Priam and Hecuba, beloved by Achilles. She was sacrificed by the Greeks on Achilles' tomb.

Pomona. A nymph at Rome, who presided over gardens and fruit trees.

Ponemah. In North American Indian mythology, the name of the spirit land, to which the souls of the dead go.

Poseidon (*pō-sī′dŏn*). The Greek god of the sea, identified by the Romans with Neptune. He was a brother of Jupiter and Pluto. The palace of Poseidon was in the depth of the sea near Ægæ, where he kept his brazen-hoofed and golden-maned horses. With these horses he used to ride in a chariot over the waves, which became smooth as he approached, while the monsters of the deep played around his chariot. Poseidon, in conjunction with Apollo, is said to have built the walls of Troy for Laomedon.

Priam. King of Troy when that city was sacked by the allied Greeks. His wife's name was Hecuba; she was the mother of nineteen children, the eldest of whom was

Hector. When the Greeks landed on the Trojan coast, Priam was advanced in years and took no active part in the war. Once only did he venture upon the field of battle, to conclude the agreement respecting the single combat between Paris and Menelaus. After the death of Hector, Priam went to the tent of Achilles to ransom his son's body for burial, and obtained it. When the gates of Troy were thrown open by the Greeks concealed in the wooden horse, and the hostile army without was admitted, the aged Priam was slain by Pyrrhus, the son of Achilles.

Priapus. An Italian god of gardens. Images of him were often placed in vineyards or before houses to frighten away thieves.

Procne. See *Philomela.*

Prœtus (*prē'tŭs*). Twin brother of Acrisius and son of Abas. In the dispute between the two brothers for the kingdom of Argos, Prœtus was expelled. He fled to Iobates in Lycia, and married Antea, the daughter of the latter. With the assistance of Iobates, Prœtus returned to his native land, and Acrisius gave him a share of his kingdom, surrendering to him Tiryns, Midea, and the coast of Argolis.

Prometheus (*prô-mē'thūs*). A son of Iapetus and Clymene, the brother of Epimetheus, and the father of Deucalion. He made men of clay, and animated them by means of fire which he stole from heaven; for this he was chained by Jupiter to Mount Caucasus, where an eagle, or, as some say, a vulture, preyed by day upon his liver, which grew again by night. His name means forethought, and that of his brother, afterthought.

Proserpina (*prô-sûr'pĭ-nȧ*). See *Persephone.*

Psyche (*sī'kē*). Psyche was the youngest of the three daughters of a king, and excited by her beauty the jealousy and envy of Venus. To avenge herself, Venus ordered Cupid to inspire Psyche with a love for the most contemptible of all men; but Cupid was so stricken with her beauty that he himself fell in love with her. He conveyed her to a charming spot, where unseen and unknown he visited her every night, and left her as soon as the day began to dawn. But her jealous sisters made her believe that in the darkness of night she was embracing some hideous monster, and, accordingly, once, while Cupid was asleep, she drew near to him with a lamp, and, to her amazement, beheld the most handsome and the most lovely of the gods. In the excitement she let fall a drop of hot oil from her lamp upon his shoulder. This awoke Cupid, who censured her for her mistrust and fled. Psyche's happiness was now gone, and, after attempting in vain to throw herself into a river, she wandered about from temple to temple, inquiring after her lover, and at length came to the palace of Venus. There her real sufferings began, for Venus retained her, treated her as a slave, and imposed upon her the hardest and most humiliating labors. Psyche would have perished under the weight of her sufferings had not Cupid, who still loved her in secret, invisibly comforted and assisted her in her toils. With his aid she at last succeeded in overcoming the jealousy and hatred of Venus; she became immortal and was united to him forever. In works of art Psyche is represented as a maiden with the wings of a butterfly. Her name is the Greek word for soul and representations of her frequently have an allegorical meaning based on this fact.

Pukwana. The smoke from the Calumet, or peace pipe, among certain North American Indians. The pipe was made from stone found near the headwaters of the Mississippi at a spot which the Indians agreed to make neutral ground. To apply the stone to any other use than that of pipe making would have been sacrilege in their eyes. From its color, they fancied it to have been made at the great deluge out of the flesh of the perishing Indians.

Pukwudjies. The pygmies of North American Indian folklore, who haunted the woods.

Pygmalion. A grandson of Agenor. He made a beautiful statue with which he fell so deeply in love that Venus, at his earnest petition, gave it life.

Pylades (*pĭl'ȧ-dēz*). Son of Anaxibia, sister of Agamemnon. His father was king of Phocis, to whose court, after the death of Agamemnon, Orestes was secretly carried. Here Pylades contracted that friendship with Orestes which became proverbial.

Pyramus (*pĭr'ȧ-mŭs*). The lover of Thisbe, who stabbed himself on account of her supposed death. Thisbe, afterwards, finding the body of her lover under the mulberry tree where he fell, killed herself on the same spot with the same weapon; and the fruit of the mulberry has ever since been as red as blood.

Pyrrhus. A son of Achilles, remarkable for his bravery at the siege of Troy. He was known also as Neoptolemus. He was slain at Delphi, at the request of his own wife, Hermione, who later married his slayer, Orestes.

Pythia (*pĭth'ĭ-ȧ*). The priestess of Apollo at Delphi. Crowned with laurels she was seated on a tripod and placed over a chasm whence arose a peculiar vapor. As she inhaled the intoxicating fumes, she was thrown into convulsive ravings, which were thought to be an evidence of divine inspiration and were interpreted by priests and conveyed as intelligible, but usually ambiguous, messages to those who came to consult the oracle.

Python (*pī'thŏn*). The monster serpent hatched from the mud of the deluge. He lived in the caves of Mount Parnassus, but was slain by Apollo, who founded the Pythian games in commemoration of his victory and received in consequence the surname Pythius.

Ra (*rä*). Egyptian sun god and principal diety of historical Egypt, from whom most of the Pharaohs claimed descent.

Radegaste. In Slavonic mythology, a tutelary god of the Slavs. His head was that of a cow, his breast was covered with a shield, his left hand held a spear, and a cock surmounted his helmet.

Ragnarok (*räg'nȧ-rŏk'*). "Twilight of the Gods." The day of doom, when the present world and all its inhabitants will, according to Scandinavian mythology, be annihilated. Vitharr and Vali will survive the conflagration, and reconstruct the universe. After this time the earth or realm will become imperishable and happiness sure.

Rahu (*rä'hōō*). In Hindu mythology, the demon that causes eclipses of the sun and of the moon. One day Rahu stole into heaven to quaff some of the nectar of immortality. He was discovered by the sun and the moon, who informed against him, and Vishnu cut off his head. As he had already taken some of the nectar into his mouth, the head was immortal, and he ever afterwards hunted the sun and the moon, which he caught occasionally, causing eclipses.

Rakshasas (*rŭk'shȧ-sȧz*). Evil spirits, in Hindu myths, who guard the treasures of Kubera, the god of riches. They haunt cemeteries and devour human corpses, they assume any shape at will, and their strength increases as the day declines. Some are hideously ugly, but others, especially the female spirits, allure by their beauty.

Rama Chandra. The seventh incarnation of Vishnu in Hindu mythology. He is the hero of the *Ramayana.* Rama probably represents the sun, as Sita, his wife, represents the earth, or "the furrow."

Rambha. In Hindu mythology, a nymph born of the churning of the ocean. She is a type of female beauty.

Ravana (*rä'vȧ-nȧ*). According to Hindu mythology, a demon giant with ten faces, who was fastened down between heaven and earth for 10,000 years by Siva's leg for attempting to move the hill of heaven to Ceylon.

Rhadamanthus (*răd'ȧ-măn'thŭs*). A son of Jupiter and Europa, brother of Minos, and king of Lycia. He was so renowned for his justice and equity, that, after death, he was made one of the three judges in the underworld.

Rhamnusia. A daughter of Nox, and otherwise known as Nemesis.

Rhea. The wife of Cronus and the mother of the gods.

Romulus (*rŏm'ū-lŭs*). The mythical founder of the city of Rome.

Saturn. An ancient Italian deity, identified with the Greek Cronus. His wife was Ops. He was the god of seedtime and harvest and was represented as bearing a sickle or scythe. As he was later confused with the Greek *chronos* "time," Father Time is still represented with a scythe. Before becoming a god he is said to have ruled in Italy during the golden age.

Satyr (*săt'ēr*). A sylvan deity, or demigod, represented as a monster, half man and half goat; having horns on his head, a hairy body, and the feet and tail of a goat. The satyrs belong to the train of Bacchus, and are distinguished for lasciviousness and riotousness. Although mortal, they are superior to the cares and sorrows of mortal life.

Scylla (*sĭl'ȧ*). A maiden whose body Circe, in a fit of jealousy, transformed so that the heads of hideous barking dogs grew about her haunches. She later inhabited the rock opposite the whirlpool Charybdis and lay in wait to snatch sailors from ships which came too near her haunt.

Sedrat (*sĕd'răt*). The lotus tree which stands on the right-hand side of the invisible throne of Allah. Its branches extend wider than the distance between heaven and earth. Its leaves resemble the ears of an elephant. Each seed of its fruit encloses a houri, and two rivers issue from its roots. Numberless birds sing among its branches, and numberless angels rest beneath its shade.

Silenus (*sī-lē'nŭs*). The older satyrs were generally termed sileni; but the one who always accompanied Dionysus and who brought up and instructed him is commonly known as the Silenus. He is represented as a jovial old man, with a bald head, pug nose, and rubicund visage, and generally as intoxicated, riding on an ass or supported by satyrs. He was fond of music and dancing. It is a peculiar feature in his character that he was an inspired prophet, yet, when he was drunk and asleep he was in the power of mortals, who might compel him to prophesy and sing by surrounding him with chains of flowers.

Silvanus or **Sylvanus** (*sĭl-vā′nŭs*). An Italian deity presiding over woods, forests, and fields.

Sirens. Sea goddesses, said by some to be two in number, by others, three, and even four. Homer mentions but two, and describes them as maidens, dwelling upon an island and detaining with them every voyager who was allured thither by their captivating music. They would have decoyed even Ulysses on his return to Ithaca, had he not commanded his sailors to tie him to the mast and fill their own ears with wax. By others they were described as daughters of the river god Achelous, and companions of Proserpina, after whose seizure they were changed into birds, that they might fly in search of her. In an unhappy contest with the Muses in singing, they lost their wings as a punishment. Others make them sea nymphs, with a form similar to that of the Tritons, with the faces of women and the bodies of flying fish. Their fabled abode was placed by some on an island near Cape Pelorus in Sicily, by others, on the islands or rocks called Sirennusæ, not far from the promontory of Surrentum on the coast of Italy.

Sirius. Known in mythology as the faithful dog of Orion, and set in the heavens as a bright star by Diana when she mourned the display of her archery which caused Orion's death. See *Orion.*

Siva. The third of the great triad of Hindu deities, regarded as the destroyer. See *Vishnu.*

Sol (*sŏl*). Although the Greeks and Romans worshiped Apollo as the god and dispenser of light, and in view of this attribute named him Phœbus, yet they conceived another divinity distinguished from Apollo, especially in the earlier fables, under the literal name applied to designate the sun, viz., Sol, or Helios.

Specter of the Brocken. Among German myths, a singular colossal apparition seen in the clouds at certain times of the day by those who ascend the Brocken, or Blocksberg, the highest of the Harz mountains.

Sphinx. A monster said to be a daughter of Chimæra, and living in the neighborhood of Thebes. Seated on a rock, she put a riddle to every Theban that passed by, and whoever was unable to solve it was killed by the monster. This calamity induced the Thebans to proclaim that whoever should deliver the country of the sphinx should obtain the kingdom and marry the recently widowed Theban queen, Jocasta. The riddle ran as follows: "What is that which has one voice, and at first four feet, then two feet, and at last three feet, and when it has most is weakest?" Œdipus explained the enigma by saying that it was man, who, when an infant, creeps on all fours, when a man, goes on two feet, and, when old, uses a staff, a third foot. The monster immediately flung herself into the sea and perished. The form of the so-called Egyptian sphinxes is that of a winged lion with a human head and bust, always in a lying attitude, whereas the Greek sphinxes are represented in any attitude which might suit the fancy of the artist.

Styx. One of four rivers of the lower world, often called the river of hate, because its name comes from a Greek word meaning "to hate." It was said to flow nine times round the infernal regions. The second river was Acheron, river of woe. The third river, Cocytus, flowed out of the river Styx, and the murmur of its waters, the sound of which resembled howlings, was inexpressibly dismal; Phlegethon, the fourth river, rolls slowly along with waves of fire. As a mythical being, Styx is described as a daughter of Oceanus and Tethys. As a nymph, she dwelt at the entrance of Hades in a lofty grotto which was supported by silver columns. She was the divinity by whom the gods took oath. On such an occasion Iris fetched a cup full of water from the river Styx, and the god confirmed his oath by drinking the draught.

Tantalus. The son of Jupiter and king of Lydia, who, according to some legends, was punished for betraying the secrets of his father. He was placed in a lake whose waters fled from him when he sought to quench his thirst, and amid trees laden with fruit whose boughs avoided every effort he made to seize them. Another version represents him as in dread of a rock hanging over his head and always about to fall.

Tartarus. A dark abyss under the earth in which the Titans were chained when their father feared their strength. The music of Orpheus at one time penetrated its depths and caused the condemned to cease their toil. The name has come to signify the lower regions generally.

Telamon. A son of Æacus and Endeis, and brother of Peleus. Having assisted Peleus in slaying their half brother Phocus, Telamon was expelled from Ægina, and came to Salamis, where he was made king. He afterward became the father of Atlas. Telamon himself was one of the Calydonian hunters and one of the Argonauts. He was also a great friend of Hercules, whom he joined in an expedition against Laomedon of Troy, which city he was the first to enter. Hercules, in return, gave to him Hesione, a daughter of Laomedon.

Telemachus (*tē-lĕm′ă-kŭs*). The son of Ulysses and Penelope. He was an infant when his father went to Troy; when Ulysses had been absent nearly twenty years, Telemachus went to Pylos and Sparta to gather information concerning him. He was hospitably received by Nestor, who sent his own son to conduct Telemachus to Menelaus at Sparta. Menelaus also received him kindly, and communicated to him the prophecy of Proteus concerning Ulysses. From Sparta Telemachus returned home; on his arrival there he found his father, whom he assisted in slaying the suitors. See *Penelope.*

Terpsichore (*tûrp-sĭk′ō-rē*). The muse of dancing and of lyric poetry. The name means "delighting in the dance."

Themis. The goddess of justice and one of the daughters of Uranus and Gæa. To her is ascribed the first uttering of oracles, and also the introduction of sacrifices.

Thersites (*thĕr-sī′tēz*). The ugliest and most scurrilous of the Greeks before Troy. He spared, in his revilings, neither prince nor chief, but directed his abuse principally against Achilles and Ulysses. He was slain by Achilles for deriding his grief for Penthesilea. The name is often used to denote a calumniator.

Theseus (*thē′sūs*). An early heroic king of Athens. Of the many adventures of Theseus, one of the most celebrated was his expedition against the Amazons. He is said to have assailed them before they had recovered from the attack of Hercules, and to have carried off their queen, Antiope. The Amazons, in their turn, invaded Attica, and the final battle, in which Theseus overcame them, was fought in the very midst of the city.

Thespian Maids, The. The nine Muses. So called from Thespia, in Bœotia, near Mount Helicon.

Thetis (*thē′tĭs*). A marine divinity, who, like her sisters, the Nereids, dwelt in the depths of the sea with her father Nereus. She there received Dionysus on his flight from Lycurgus, and the god in his gratitude presented her with a golden urn. When Vulcan was thrown down from heaven, he was likewise received by Thetis. Thetis rejected the advances of Zeus, because she had been brought up by Hera, and the god, to avenge himself, decreed that she should marry a mortal. She became the wife of Peleus and the mother of Achilles.

Thisbe. See *Pyramus.*

Thor. In Scandinavian mythology, the eldest son of Odin and Frigga. The strongest and bravest of the gods, he launched the thunder, presided over the air and the seasons, and protected man from lightning and evil spirits. His wife was Sif, "love"; his chariot was drawn by two he-goats; he had a hammer, called *Mjöllnir*, and a belt, *Megingiard*, the wearing of which doubled his strength. His palace, called *Thrudvangr*, contained 540 halls. Thursday is Thor's day.

Thunder Bird. A culture god of the North American Indians, represented as a helper of man, and the personification of thunder and lightning.

Titans. Members of the early régime of Greek gods ruled over by Cronus, who with his adherents was overthrown by Zeus, one of his sons.

Tithonus. A son of Laomedon, king of Troy. He was so beautiful that Aurora became enamored of him, and persuaded the gods to make him immortal; but, as she forgot to ask for eternal youth, he became decrepit and ugly, and was, therefore, changed by her into a cicada.

Tityus (*tĭt′ĭ-ŭs*). A giant, son of Jupiter and Terra. His body was so vast that it covered nine acres of ground. He had dared to offer an insult to Juno and in punishment was chained like Prometheus while a vulture feasted on his liver.

Triton. Son of Neptune, who dwelt with his father and mother in a golden palace at the bottom of the sea. Later writers describe him as riding over the sea on sea horses or other monsters. By a blast on his horn of seashell he roused or calmed the waves.

Trolls (*trōlz*). Dwarfs of Scandinavian mythology, living in hills or mounds; they are represented as stumpy, misshapen, and humpbacked, inclined to thieving, and fond of carrying off children or substituting their own offspring for children of a human mother. They are called hill people, and are especially averse to noise, from a recollection of the time when Thor used to fling his hammer after them.

Troy. The city on the west coast of Asia Minor made famous by the Trojan War. It was ruled by Priam at the time of the war, and its chief defender was Hector. The attacking Greeks were led by Agamemnon and Menelaus, supported by many heroes, the most famous of whom was Achilles. The city fell after a ten-year siege. Among the inhabitants who escaped was Æneas. After wandering for some years, he settled in Italy and, according to legend, became the founder of the Roman race.

Tyr. In Norse mythology, a warrior deity and the protector of champions and brave men. When the gods wished to bind the wolf Fenris, Tyr put his hand into the demon's mouth as a pledge that the bonds would be removed. But Fenris found that the gods had no intention of keeping their word, and revenged himself in some degree by biting off the hand. Tyr was the son of Odin and brother of Thor.

Ulysses. Called "Odysseus" by the Greeks. One of the principal Greek heroes in the Trojan War, a son of Laertes, or, according to a later tradition, of Sisyphus. He married Penelope, the daughter of Icarius, by whom he became the father of Telemachus. During the siege of Troy he distinguished himself by his valor, prudence, and eloquence, and after the death of Achilles contended for that hero's armor with Telamonian Ajax and gained the prize. He is said by some to have devised the stratagem of the wooden horse. The most celebrated part of his story comes in connection with his ten-year voyage home after the Trojan War. Among his adventures he entered the cave of Polyphemus and escaped with some sheep. One of the gods gave him a bag of winds which should carry him home, but the winds were let loose without his permission and his ships driven to an island inhabited by the sorceress Circe. After many wanderings and strange adventures, he arrived at his home in Ithaca. During his absence his father, Laertes, in grief and old age, had withdrawn into the country, and his mother, Anticlea, had died. His wife, Penelope, had been importuned by suitors but had rejected them all. In order that he might not be recognized on his arrival, Athena metamorphosed Ulysses into an unsightly beggar. He was kindly received by Eumæus, the swineherd, to whom he made himself known, and a plan of revenge was resolved on. Penelope, with great difficulty, was made to promise her hand to him who should conquer the others in shooting with the bow of Ulysses. As none of the suitors were able to draw this bow, Ulysses himself took it up, and, directing his arrows against the suitors, slew them all with the help of his son Telemachus, to whom he had previously made himself known. Ulysses now revealed himself to Penelope. The people rose in arms against Ulysses; but Athena, who assumed the appearance of Mentor, brought about a reconciliation.

Valhalla (*văl-hăl'ȧ*). In Scandinavian mythology, the gold and silver palace of Odin, wherein were received the souls of heroes slain in battle. Each morning the heroes went out of the palace and fought until noon. All wounds were then healed, and the heroes, under the presidency of Odin, assembled to feast, being served by the battle maidens, or Valkyries.

Valkyries (*văl-kĭr'ĭz*). The battle maidens of Scandinavian mythology. Mounted on swift horses, they rushed into battle with drawn swords and, selecting those destined to death, they conducted them to Valhalla. The number of Valkyries differs greatly according to the various mythologists, and ranges from three to sixteen. They are generally mentioned, however, as being only nine.

Vayu (*vä'yo͞o*). The spirit of the air in Hindu mythology. His wife Angana was a celestial nymph, who was compelled by a curse to assume the form of a monkey. Their son was the monkey god Hanuman, who led the monkeys in support of the god Rama when the latter was battling to recover his wife Siva from the demon Ravana.

Venus. The Roman goddess of women, identified with the Greek Aphrodite, goddess of beauty and love. She is said to have sprung from the foam of the sea, and to have been immediately carried to the abode of the gods on Olympus, where they were all charmed with her extreme beauty. According to other legends she was the daughter of Jupiter and Dione. Sparrows and doves were customarily yoked to her chariot; the sight of her girdle inspired all hearts with passion for the wearer; and her son Cupid was her attendant and minister. The myrtle was sacred to her. Her favorite residence was at Cyprus. Venus was represented often as the wife of Vulcan and frequently as the paramour of Mars. Among mortal men, she loved Anchises, by whom she became the mother of Æneas, and Adonis, whose untimely death left her inconsolable. One of her tasks was to restore harmonious relations for couples who had quarreled.

Vesta. The Roman goddess of the hearth-fire. Æneas was believed to have brought the eternal fire of Vesta from Troy, along with the images of the penates; the prætors, consuls, and dictators, before entering upon their official functions, sacrificed, not only to the penates, but also to Vesta at Lavinium. Similarly, in the house, sacrifices were offered to Vesta at the hearth, and the common meal eaten about the hearth was regarded as an act of worship for her. At Rome, six maidens were chosen to serve for 30 years as priestesses of Vesta. They were known as vestal virgins and took a vow of chastity, the breaking of which involved the penalty of being buried alive. The duty of the vestal virgins was to tend the sacred fire of the city. If the fire went out as a result of their negligence, the penalty was scourging. This custom was probably a survival from the days when it was difficult to obtain fire and when, consequently, the fire once kindled had to be guarded with the utmost care. The office of vestal virgin was highly honored in Rome and was much sought after by distinguished families.

Vishnu. One of the great deities of the Hindu triad, ranking as the "Preserver," after Brahma, the "Creator," and before Siva, the "Destroyer." It is believed that he has appeared on earth nine times, his tenth *avatar*, or incarnation, having yet to come.

Votán. The deity supposed to have taught the people of Chiapas (Mexico) the arts of civilization.

Vulcan. The Roman god of fire, identified with the Greek Hephæstus. He was the son of Jupiter and Juno and became lame by being thrown out of heaven by Jupiter for taking Juno's part in a quarrel. He wrought skillfully at a forge, where he produced tripods that came and departed automatically and many other wonders, including Pandora, the first woman. Venus is usually represented as his wife. Vulcan is represented in art as a middle-aged man having a beard and unkempt hair. Relay torch races were sometimes held in his honor, probably to symbolize the bringing of fire from heaven to mankind or the transference of the sacred element to replace a fire that had become extinguished. Such ceremonies hark back to a time when fire was difficult to kindle.

Woden. The Anglo-Saxon form of the Scandinavian god Odin. Wednesday is called after him.

Xipe. The Mexican god of sowing and of vegetation. Also the god of the goldsmiths and the silversmiths.

Yacatecutli, "He-who-guides." The Mexican god of commerce. His symbol was a traveler's staff.

Yggdrasil (*ĭg'drȧ-sĭl*). The giant ash tree of Norse mythology. It overspreads the earth and binds earth, hell, and heaven together. From beneath it springs a fountain, and under its branches sit the Norns or Fates.

Ymir (*ü'mêr*). In Norse mythology, the ancient frost giant. The gods slew him and out of his body formed the earth. From it, too, grew the mighty ash tree, Yggdrasil, which was thought to support the universe.

Zamzam. The sacred well situated in the heart of the city of Mecca. According to Arab tradition, it is the very well that was shown to Hagar when she was wandering with Ishmael in the desert.

Zephyrus. A personification of the west wind. He was the mildest and gentlest of the sylvan deities.

Zethus. One of the twin sons of Antiope and Zeus. See *Amphion.*

Zeus (*zūs*). The greatest of the Olympian gods, father of gods and men, a son of Cronus, or Saturn, and of Rhea. He was identified by the Romans with Jupiter. When Zeus and his brothers distributed among themselves the government of the world by lot, Poseidon obtained the sea; Hades received the lower world; and Zeus, the heavens and the upper regions; but the earth became common to all. According to Homer, Zeus dwelt on Mount Olympus in Thessaly, which was believed to penetrate into heaven itself. By his counsel he managed everything; he founded law and order, so that Dike, Themis, and Nemesis came to be regarded as his assistants. According to his own choice he used to assign good or evil to mortals. Zeus had an ancient oracle at Dodona in Greece, where, by means of speaking oaks, he made known his will to mortals. His wife was Hera. Many stories are told of her jealous pursuit of mortal women who had been loved by Zeus and visited by him, usually in a disguised form. By such unions Zeus became the father of many heroes. Europa, receiving him in the form of a white bull, had several sons by him, one of whom was Minos, the famous lawgiver of Crete. Zeus came to Leda as a swan and by her was the father of Helen and of Pollux. Gaining admittance to Danaë in the form of a shower of gold, he begot Perseus. His greatest son was Hercules, the offspring of Alcmene, to whom Zeus obtained access by impersonating her husband.

PEN NAMES

Pen Name	Real Name
Adams, Moses	Geo. Wm. Bagby
Adeler, Max	Charles Heber Clark
Æ	George Russell
Akers, Elizabeth	Mrs. E. M. Allen
Alexander, Mrs.	Mrs. Annie French Hector
Allen, F. M.	Edmund Downey
A. L. O. E. (A Lady of England)	Charlotte M. Tucker
Amyand, Arthur	Major E. A. Haggard
Angell, Norman	Ralph Norman Angell Lane
Anstey, F.	F. Anstey Guthrie
Armstrong, Regina	Mrs. C. H. Niehaus
Arnold, Birch	Mrs. J. M. D. Bartlett
Arp, Bill	Charles H. Smith
"Ashmont"	J. Frank Perry
"Aunt Elmira"	Mrs. Isaac Slenker
Ayres, Alfred	Thomas E. Osmun
Barnaval, Louis	Charles De Kay
Bart	Charles L. Bartholomew
Beard, Dan	Daniel Carter Beard
Beard, Frank	Thos. Francis Beard
Beaumont, Averil	Mrs. Margaret Hunt
Bede, Cuthbert	Rev. Edward Bradley
Bell, Acton	Anne Brontë
Bell, Currer	Charlotte Brontë
Bell, Ellis	Emily Brontë
Bell, Lilian	Mrs. Arthur Hoyt Bogue
Bell, Nancy	Mrs. A. Geo. Bell
Belloc, Marie Adelaide	Mrs. Frederick S. Lowndes
Bentzon, Thérèse	Marie Thérèse Blanc
Bibliophile	S. A. Allibone
Bickerdyke, John	Charles H. Cook
Bickerstaff, Isaac	Swift and Steele
Biglow, Hosea	J. R. Lowell
Billings, Josh	Henry W. Shaw
Birmingham, George A.	James Owen Hannay
Blanchan, Neltje	Mrs. F. N. Doubleday
Boldrewood, Rolf	Thos. Alex. Browne
Bonehill, Capt. Ralph	Edw. Stratemeyer
Boyce, Neith	Mrs. Hutchins Hapgood
Boyd, Barbara	Agnes Rush Burr
Boz	Charles Dickens
Braddon, Miss M. E.	Mrs. John Maxwell
Brannigan, Calvin	Jas. Jeffrey Roche
Breitmann, Hans	Charles Godfrey Leland
Briscoe, Margaret Sutton	Mrs. A. J. Hopkins
Bruce, Arthur Loring	Francis W. Crowninshield
"Brunswick"	Jeannette Leonard Gilder
Brydges, Harold	James Howard Bridge
"Bunny"	Carl E. Schultze
Cambridge, Ada	Mrs. Geo. F. Cross
Canfield, Dorothy	Dorothy Canfield Fisher
Carey, Charles	Charles Carey Waddell
Carroll, Lewis	Rev. C. L. Dodgson
Carton, R. C.	R. C. Critchett
Cartwright, Julia	Mrs. Henry Ady
Caskoden, Edwin	Charles Major
Castlemon, Harry	Charles A. Fosdick
"Champ"	Jas. W. Champney
"Chicot"	Epes Winthrop Sargent
Collins, Mabel	Mrs. Keningale Cook
Collins, Percy	Price Collier
Connor, Marie	Marie Connor Leighton
Connor, Ralph	Rev. C. W. Gordon
Conway, Hugh	F. J. Fargus
"Coo-ee"	W. S. Walker
Coolidge, Susan	Sarah C. Woolsey
Corelli, Marie	Eva Mary Mackay
Cornwall, Barry	Bryan W. Procter
Craddock, Charles Egbert	Mary N. Murfree
Crayon, Geoffrey	Washington Irving
Crinkle, Nym	Andrew C. Wheeler
Crowfield, Christopher	Harriet Beecher Stowe
Cushing, Paul	Roland A. Wood-Seys
D'Ache, Caran	Emmanuel Poire
Dacre, J. Colne	Mrs. A. S. Boyd
"Dagonet"	George R. Sims
Dale, Alan	Alfred J. Cohen
Dale, Darley	Francesca Maria Steele
Danbury, Newsman	J. M. Bailey
Danby, Frank	Mrs. Julia Frankau
D'Anvers, N.	Mrs. A. Geo. Bell
Daring, Hope	Anna Johnson
Dean, Mrs. Andrew	Mrs. Cecily Sidgwick
Devoore, Ann	Mrs. R. P. Walden
D'Istria, Dora	Helena Ghika
Dix, Dorothy	Elizabeth M. Gilmer
Dobson, Austin	Henry A. Dobson
Donovan, Dick	Joyce Emerson Muddock
Dooley, Martin	Finley Peter Dunne

Pen Name	Real Name
Douglas, Marian	Annie D. G. Robinson
Drinkwater, Jennie Maria	Jennie Conklin, M. D.
"Droch"	Robert Bridges
"Duchess, The"	Mrs. Hungerford
Duncan, Sara Jeannette	Mrs. Everard Cotes
Dunning, Charlotte	Charlotte D. Wood
Edwards, Albert	Arthur Bullard
Elia	Charles Lamb
Eliot, George	Marian Evans
Eliot, Max	Mrs. Granville Alden Ellis
Ettrick, Shepherd	James Hogg
Fair, Frank	Jane Frances Winn
Fairfax, Marion	Mrs. Tully Marshall Phillips
Fairfield, Clarence	Edwin Ross Champlin
Fane, Violet	Lady Currie
Farquharson, Martha	Martha F. Finley
Fern, Fanny	Sara P. Parton
Finn, Mickey	Ernest Jarrold
Fitzboodle, George	W. M. Thackeray
"Fitznoodle"	B. B. Vallentine
Fleming, George	Julia Constance Fletcher
Flynt, Josiah	Josiah Flynt Willard
Fontenoy, Marquis de	Frederick Cunliffe-Owen
Forrester, Francis	Daniel Wise
Forrester, Frank	Henry Wm. Herbert
Forrester, Izola	Mrs. Reuben Merrifield
F. P. A.	Franklin Pierce Adams
"Fra Elbertus"	Elbert Hubbard
France, Anatole	Jacques Anatole Thibault
Francis, M. E.	Mrs. Francis Blundell
Gates, Eleanor	Mrs. Richard Walton Tully
"Gath"	George Alfred Townsend
Gerard, Morice	Rev. J. Jessop Teague
Gibbons, Lucy	Lucy G. Morse
Gift, Theo.	Mrs. G. S. Boulger
Gilman, Winona	Mrs. F. Schœffel
Glaspell, Susan	Mrs. George Cram Cook
Glyndon, Howard	Mrs. Laura C. R. Searing
Goodman, Maude	Mrs. A. E. Scanes
Gordon, Julien	Mrs. Van Rensselaer Cruger
Gorki, Maxim	Alexel Maximovitch Peshkov
Graduate of Oxford	John Ruskin
Graham, John	David Graham Phillips
Grand, Sarah	Mrs. McFall
Gray, Maxwell	Miss M. G. Tuttiett
Green, Anna Katharine	Mrs. Charles Rohlfs
Greenwood, Grace	Sara Jane Lippincott
Greville, Henri	Mme. Durand
Grile, Dod	Ambrose Bierce
"Gyp"	Countess de Martel
Haam, Achad	Asher Ginzberg
Haliburton, Hugh	James Logie Robertson
Hall, Holworthy	Harold E. Porter
Hamilton, Gail	Mary Abigail Dodge
Hardinge, E. M.	(Ellen) Maud Going
"Hard Pan"	Geraldine Bonner
Hardy, Francis H.	Edward James Cattell
Harland, Marion	Mrs. Mary V. Terhune
Harrod, Frances	Frances Forbes-Robertson
Hawthorne, Alice	Septimus Winner
Hayes, Henry	Ellen Olney Kirk
Hazeltine, Horace	Charles Stokes Wayne
Hegan, Alice Caldwell	Mrs. Cale Young Rice
Henry, O.	William Sydney Porter
Heron, E. and H.,	Mrs. Kenneth and Mr. Hesketh Prichard
"H. H."	Helen Hunt Jackson
Hickson, Mrs. Murray	Mrs. S. A. P. Kitcat
Hill, Headon	F. Grainger
"Historicus"	Sir W. Vernon Harcourt
Hobbes, John Oliver	Mrs. Pearl Craigie
Hoffman, Prof.	Angelo Lewis
Hope, Anthony	Anthony Hope Hawkins
Hope, Ascot R.	R. Hope Moncrieff
Hubbard, Kin	Frank McKinney Hubbard
Huntington, Faye	Theodosia T. Foster
Hutchinson, Ellen M.	Ellen M. H. Cortissoz
"Iota"	Mrs. Mannington Caffyn
Iron, Ralph	Mrs. S. C. Cronwright
James, Martha	Mrs. James R. Doyle
Jay, W. L. M.	Julia L. M. Woodruff
Jean Paul	J. P. F. Richter
Johnson, Benjamin F.	James Whitcomb Riley
Johnson, Effie	Mrs. Orson Richmond
Johnson, Fanny Kemble	Mrs. Vincent Costello
"Josiah Allen's Wife"	Marietta Holley
J. S. of Dale	Frederick J. Stimson
"June, Jenny"	Mrs. David G. Croly

Pen Name	Real Name
Keith, Leslie	Grace L. K. Johnston
Kerr, Orpheus C.	Robert H. Newell
Kerr, Sophie	Mrs. S. K. Underwood
Kirk, Eleanor	Eleanor K. Ames
Kirke, Edmund	James R. Gilmore
Knickerbocker, Diedrich	Washington Irving
"Kron, Karl"	Lyman Hotchkiss Bagg
Laurie, Annie	Mrs. Chas. A. Bonfils
Lea, Fannie Heaslip	Mrs. H. P. Agee
Lee, Hoeme	Harriet Parr
Lee, Vernon	Violet Paget
L. E. L.	Letitia E. Landon
Leslie, Amy	Lillie West Brown Buck
Lessing, Bruno	Rudolph Block
Logan, Olive	Mrs. W. Wirt Sikes
Lope de Vega	Lope Felix de Vega Carpio
Lothrop, Amy	Mrs. Anna Bartlett Warner
Loti, Pierre	L. M. Julien Viaud
Ludlow, Johnny	Mrs. Henry Wood
Luska, Sidney	Henry Harland
Lyall, Edna	Ada Ellen Bayly
Lys, Christian	Percy Jas. Brebner
Maartens, Maarten	J. N. W. van der Poorten Schwartz
Maclaren, Ian	Rev. John Watson
Macleod, Fiona	William Sharp
Maitland, Thomas	Robert Buchanan
Malet, Lucas	Mary St. Leger Harrison
"Maori"	James Inglis
Marbourg, Dolores	Mary Schell Hoke Bacon
Marlitt, E.	Henriette Eugenie John
Marlowe, Charles	Harriet Jay
"Marshes, A Son of the"	Mrs. Owen Visger
Martin, Ellis	Marah Ellis Ryan
Martin, George Madden	Mrs. Atwood R. Martin
Marvel, Ik	Donald G. Mitchell
Mathers, Helen	Mrs. Henry Reeves
May, Sophie	Rebecca Sophia Clarke
McManus, Blanche	Mrs. M. F. Mansfield
Meade, L. T.	Mrs. F. Toulmin Smith
Meredith, Owen	Lord Lytton
Merriam, Florence A.	Mrs. Florence M. Bailey
Merriman, Henry Seton	Hugh Stowell Scott
"M. E. W. S."	Mrs. Jno. Sherwood
Mignon, August	John A. Darling
Miller, Joaquin	Cincinnatus Heine Miller
Miller, Olive Thorne	Harriet Mann Miller
Miln, Louise Jordan	Mrs. George Crichton Miln
Moore, Mollie E.	Mollie Evelyn Moore Davis
Mowbray, J. P.	Andrew C. Wheeler
Mulholland, Rosa	Lady Gilbert
Mulock, Miss	Mrs. G. L. Craik
Nasby, Petroleum V.	David Locke
Nesbit, E.	Mrs. Hubert Bland
Nordau, Max	Simon Sudfeld
North, Barclay	William C. Hudson
North, Christopher	John Wilson
Nox, Owen	Charles B. Cory
Nye, Bill	Edgar Wilson Nye
O'Dowd, Cornelius	Charles Lever
Ogden, Ruth	Fannie Ogden Ide
Ogilvy, Gavin	J. M. Barrie
O. H. K. B.	Rev. Oliver H. K. Boyd
"O. K."	Mme. Ulga Kireef Novikoff
Oldcastle, John	Wilfred Meynell
"Old Sleuth"	Harlan P. Halsey
Oliver, Temple	Jeanie Oliver Smith
O'Neill, Rose Cecil	Mrs. Harry Leon Wilson
Optic, Oliver	Wm. T. Adams
O'Reilly, Miles	Charles G. Halpine
O'Rell, Max	Paul Blouet
Otis, James	James Otis Kaler
"Ouida"	Louise de la Ramée
Owen, Jean A.	Mrs. Owen Visger
Oxenham, John	Mr. Dunkerley
Palmer, Lynde	Mrs. A. A. Peebles
"Pansy"	Isabella Macdonald Alden
Parker, Maude	Mrs. Richard Washburn Child
Parley, Peter	Samuel G. Goodrich
Partington, Mrs.	Benj. P. Shillaber
Paston, George	Miss E. M. Symonds
Paul, John	Chas. Henry Webb
Peabody, Josephine Preston	Mrs. L. S. Marks
Perkins, Eli	Melville de Lancey Landon
Phiz	H. K. Browne
Phœnix, John	George H. Derby
Pindar, Peter, Esq.	John Wolcott
Plymley, Peter	Rev. Sydney Smith
Poor Richard	Benjamin Franklin
"Porte Crayon"	David H. Strother
Powell, Richard Stillman	Ralph Henry Barbour

Pen Name	Real Name
Prescott, Dorothy	Agnes Blake Poor
Prevost, Francis	Harry F. P. Battersby
Prout, Father	Rev. Francis S. Mahony
"Q."	Arthur T. Quiller-Couch
Quad, M.	C. B. Lewis
Quinn, Dan	Alfred Henry Lewis
Quirinus	Dr. Döllinger
Raimond, C. E.	Elizabeth Robins (Mrs. George R. Parks)
Reid, Christian	Frances F. Tiernan
Rheinhardt, Rudolph H.	George Hempl
"Rita"	Mrs. E. M. J. von Booth
Rives, Amélie	Princess Troubetskoi
Robins, Elizabeth	Mrs. Joseph Pennell
Robinson, Agnes Mary F.	Mme. Emile Duclaux
Ross, Adrian	Arthur Reed Ropes
Ross, Albert	Linn Boyd Porter
"Rover"	Alfred Gibson
Rowe, Bolton / Rowe, Saville	Clement Scott
Roy, Rob	John Macgregor
Rudd, Steele	Arthur Hoey Davis
Rutherford, Mark	Wm. Hale White
St. Aubyn, Alan	Frances Marshall
St. Clair, Victor	G. Waldo Browne
St. Laurence, A.	Alfred Laurence Felkin
Sand, George	Mme. Dudevant
Sanghamita, Sister	Countess M. A. de S. Canavarro
Saunders, Marshall	Margaret M. Saunders
Sawyer, Ruth	Mrs. Albert C. Durand
Schreiner, Olive	Mrs. S. C. Cronwright
Scriblerus, Martinus	Pope, Swift, and Arbuthnot
Setoun, Gabriel	Thomas Nicoll Hepburn
"Sevenoaks"	Alfred S. Edwards
Sharp, Luke	Robert Barr
Sidney, Margaret	Harriet Mulford Lothrop
Siegerson, Dora	Mrs. Clement Shorter
Siegvolk, Paul	Albert Mathews
Sinjohn, John	John Galsworthy
Slick, Sam	T. C. Haliburton
Smith, T. Carlyle	John Kendrick Bangs
Spinner, Alice	Mrs. Augusta Zelia Fraser
"Spy"	Leslie Ward
Steele, Alice Garland	Mrs. T. Austin-Ball
Stepniak	S. Kartcheffsky
Sterne, Stuart	Gertrude Bloede
Stevens, Margaret Dean	Bess Streeter Aldrich
"Stonehenge"	J. H. Walsh
Strange, Michael	Mrs. John Barrymore (second)
Stretton, Hesba	Hannah Smith
Stuart, Cosmo	Cosmo Chas. Gordon-Lennox
Stuart, Eleanor	Mrs. Harris Robbins Child
Sturgis, Dinah	Mrs. Belle A. Whitney
Swan, Annie S.	Mrs. Burnett Smith
Swift, Benjamin	William Romaine Paterson
Sylva, Carmen	Elizabeth, queen of Rumania
Tasma	Madame Couvreur
Temple, Hope	Mme. André Messager
Thanet, Octave	Alice French
Thomas, Annie	Mrs. Pender Cudlip
Thompson, Wolf	Ernest Thompson Seton
Thorpe, Kamba	Elizabeth Whitfield Bellamy
Titmarsh, M. A.	W. M. Thackeray
"Tivoli"	Horace W. Bleackley
"Toby, M. P."	Sir Henry W. Lucy
Tower, Martello	Commander F. M. Norman
T. P.	Thomas Power O'Connor
Trask, Katrina	Mrs. Spencer Trask
"Trois-Etoiles"	E. C. Grenville-Murray
Turner, Ethel	Mrs. H. R. Curlewis
Twain, Mark	Samuel L. Clemens
Tynan, Katherine	Mrs. H. A. Hinkson
"Uncle Remus"	Joel Chandler Harris
Vaka, Demetra	Demetra Kenneth Brown
Vandegrift, Margaret	Margaret T. Janvier
Van Dine, S. S.	Willard Huntington Wright
Varley, John Philip	Langdon E. Mitchell
Verne, Jules	M. Olchewitz
Voltaire	François Marie Arouet
Vorse, Mary Heaton	Mrs. Joseph O'Brien
Ward, Artemus	Charles F. Browne
Warde, Margaret	Edith Kellogg Dunton
Warden, Florence	Mrs. Florence James
Watanna, Onoto	Winnifred Eaton Babcock
Wetherell, Elizabeth	Susan Warner
Wildwood, Will	Frederick E. Pond
Wilson, Charlotte	Karle Wilson Baker
Winfield, Arthur M.	Edw. Stratemeyer
Winter, John Strange	Mrs. H. E. V. Stannard
Yechton, Barbara	Lyda Farrington Krause

TEST QUESTIONS

What are the two essential characteristics of great literature? Upon what grounds can it be said that "poetry is truer than history"? 201

State three types of literary excellence. What is the safest test of the greatness of a work of literature? 201

From what ancient peoples did the principal literary inheritances of the modern world come? 202

Name three ancient works of the first rank of greatness 202

What are reckoned as the greatest literary works of Europe during the medieval period? In what countries were they produced? 203–204

Name the two dramatists who are assigned first rank in the 17th century 205

What idea characterizes the literature of the second half of the 18th century? of the second half of the 19th century? 205–206

AMERICAN LITERATURE

What were the subjects of the earliest writings in American literature? Name two representative writers and the title of a work by each. 207

What early New England men wrote journals that are valuable? 207

What new subject appeared in the colonial diaries of the 18th century? For what is William Byrd notable? 207

Who were the first writers of colonial history? What is the title of Cotton Mather's principal work? Of what value is this book today? . . 207

Name four 18th century American philosophers. 207

What are the principal works of Jonathan Edwards and of Benjamin Franklin? . . . 207

What was the first newspaper in the American colonies? Where was it published? On what newspaper did Benjamin Franklin begin his career as a printer? 207

Who were the best-known writers of colonial verse? 207

Whose poems were published under the title *The Tenth Muse?* 207

What kind of verse was characteristic of the Revolutionary period? Give the titles of two examples and the names of their authors . 208

Who were the Hartford Wits? Give two reasons for recognizing Philip Freneau as an important name in American literature . . 208

Name four important American political writings of the 18th century. Name three of the most notable orators of the Revolutionary period 208

Where and when was the first American drama acted? What was the first American comedy presented by professional players? 208

Who was the first American novelist? What is the greatest work of James Fenimore Cooper and what is the subject? 208

Who were the leaders of the Transcendentalist movement? What service did this movement render to American literature? 208–209

What was Ralph Waldo Emerson's chief service to American life? 209

Name two novels by Hawthorne, two by Melville. What background haunted Hawthorne? 209

Name two great poets that belong to New England 209

What influence did Longfellow exert on the culture of his time? 209

Who wrote "Snowbound"? "The Bigelow Papers"? "The Autocrat of the Breakfast Table"? 209

Who was the first free verse poet? What did he aspire to be? How do Poe's poems achieve their effects? 209

Name three orators and four historians of the Second National Period 209

What work marks the beginning of American humorous writing? Who created the character of "Mrs. Partington"? Who was Josh Billings? Artemus Ward? Mark Twain? . . 209

Who wrote "Maryland, My Maryland"? 209

Name three authors who wrote novels of interest in far times or places. Who is the third great American novelist? Who wrote "The Pit"? What did Sinclair Lewis write? . 209–210

Characterize O'Neill's dramatic skill and its effect. Name three other dramatists and their important plays 210

Who produced the first enduring American short story? 210

What stories were the ancestors of modern detective fiction? Who wrote about "Babylon on the Hudson"? 210

Who wrote short stories of the Far West? Of New England? Of Louisiana? Who retold Negro folk tales? 210

Characterize the poetic themes of Frost, Robinson, Benet. Who was the leader of the Imagists? 210

Name two women who wrote poetry in the 20th Century 210

ENGLISH LITERATURE

To what district of England and to what institutions do we trace the beginnings of English literature? Name the first native British poem 214

Who was Bede? What service did Alfred the Great render to English letters? For what are Whitby and Winchester notable? What is the position of Ælfric in English literature? . 214

What change in language took place in England after the Norman Conquest? In what languages was most literary writing done in the 12th century in England? Name the four great romantic cycles 214

For what reason is *The Voiage and Travaile of Sir John Mandeville* important? 214

Who first translated the entire Bible into English? Who wrote *Piers Plowman?* 214

Who is called the "Father of English Poetry"? What is his greatest work? 214

In what year was the first book printed in England? Who was the printer? Give titles of two of his publications 215

What was William Tyndale's part in translating the Bible? What was the Genevan Bible? . 215

Characterize the Elizabethan age. Who were the greatest poets of the period? Who established blank verse in English drama? . . . 215

Outline briefly the career of Shakspere. What kinds of poetry did he write? 215

Name three plays by Ben Jonson. Characterize his work 215

Who was the greatest prose writer of the Elizabethan period? 215

What literary work bears the name of Sir Walter Raleigh? 215–216

Compare the Elizabethan with the Puritan period. When was the *King James Version of the Bible* published? the *Douai Bible?* . . 216

Into what three periods can you divide the life of John Milton? Name two of his earlier poems. What is his greatest poem? his greatest prose work? 216

What is *Pilgrim's Progress?* Who is the author? Who was the most notable diarist of the 17th century? the chief historian? 216–217

What are Dryden's greatest satires? Does he have any influence on a following poet? Who? 217

Characterize the life of the early 18th century in England. What were the literary faults of the age? Mention a characteristic contribution of Pope to English letters 217

CANADIAN LITERATURE

AUSTRALIAN LITERATURE

IRISH LITERATURE

FRENCH LITERATURE

Sketch briefly the origin and early history of the French language 228

Trace the origin of the French epic of Charlemagne. What is the *Song of Roland*? . . . 228

Name two French poets of the 12th century. Upon what subjects were the romances of this time written? What was "matter of Britain"? 228

Discuss the origin of the liturgical drama . . 228

Of what subject did Villehardouin write? Guillaume de Lorris? Froissart? 228

Describe the production of the "mysteries" in the 14th and 15th centuries. What was the best medieval play? What is its theme? . . 228

Characterize François Villon. What were his *Testaments*? Give a famous line from one of his poems 228

What were the disturbing influences in 16th century France? Of what did Rabelais write? Who was Calvin? 229

What was the "pléiade"? What was its purpose? Who translated Plutarch's *Lives*? What was Montaigne's characteristic query? 229

What was the task of the 17th century? Who founded the French Academy? What was the origin of the phrase "beautiful as *The Cid*"? 229

Name three plays by Molière. What are the chief lessons taught in his works? Give the themes of three plays by Racine 229

Give the names and the chief themes of three writers of French prose in the 17th century. Who was Boileau? La Fontaine? 229

Name two tendencies that characterized French thought in the 18th century. What two authors embodied these tendencies? Characterize Voltaire and his work 229

What especial importance attaches to Montesquieu's writing? Who edited the *Encyclopedia*? Who was the chief French dramatist of the 18th century? 229

Summarize the work and influence of Rousseau. Who wrote "The Marseillaise"? 229

Upon what themes did the following authors write: Chateaubriand? Madame de Staël? George Sand? Who was the model for French romantic fiction? Give two examples. 230

Name three French historians. What was the theme of De Tocqueville's best-known work? 230

Whom did the French romantic dramatists take as their guide? Who wrote *Hernani*? *Cyrano*? 230

Who were the chief French writers of realist fiction in the 19th century? To whom is the phrase "the French Dickens" applied? . . 230

Characterize the work of the following: Anatole France; Rolland; Loti; Romains. What have been the chief literary merits of French Literature? 230

ITALIAN LITERATURE

Name five periods of Italian literature. To which of these periods does Dante belong? Tasso? 232

Upon what kind of subjects did the early Sicilian poets write? What was the *Contrasto*? Name the inventor of the sonnet 232

For what work is Guittone d'Arezzo notable? To what movement can we trace the origin of religious drama in Italy? 232

Quote a notable line from an ode of Guinizelli. Why is the thought of this line important in Italian literature? Who was Cavalcanti? . 232

Characterize the *Vita Nuova* of Dante. What was Dante's purpose in writing the *Convivio*? Name two other minor works of Dante. Upon what themes were they written? 232

Why is Petrarch called "the first modern man"? Who was the Laura of Petrarch's sonnets? What service did the poet render to the study of ancient classics? 232

Who is the author of the *Decameron*? Where did he get the stories for this book? Why has it been called the "Human Comedy"? Describe Boccaccio's work in explaining Dante's *Divine Comedy* 232–233

What is the chief characteristic of the second period of Italian literature? What Greek scholar was invited to teach Greek in Florence? Who were the humanists? Describe the collecting of libraries in Italian cities . . 233

Distinguish between the terms "Renaissance" and "humanism." Who wrote *Orlando Furioso*? Characterize the literary quality and the historic value of this poem 233

What place does Machiavelli hold in modern literature? Why has his *Prince* been harshly criticized? 233

In what city is the scene of Castiglione's *Courtier* laid? What is the literary rank of this work? Of what historic value is it possessed? 233

What is the theme of Tasso's *Jerusalem Delivered*? Name Tasso's earliest work and also a pastoral drama from his pen 233

Name three minor writers of the Italian Renaissance. From what writer did the Othello story, used by Shakspere, come? Of what value is the autobiography of Cellini? 233–234

What historical conditions account for the decline of Italian literature after 1595? Name two great Italians of this period 234

What connection is there between the Treaty of Aix-la-Chapelle (1748) and the revival of Italian literature? Characterize the work of Carlo Goldoni 234

Who was Parini? What are the theme and purpose of his long poem *The Day*? What was the life purpose of Alfieri? Did he attain his goal? 234

Outline the life story of Foscolo. What is his best lyric poem? Quote the line which gives the key to Leopardi's patriotic verse. What was his general attitude toward life? . . . 234

What three works constitute Manzoni's gift to Italy's patriotic literature? State the themes of these works. Name five outstanding literary figures in Italy of the middle 19th century 235

What is Carducci's rank in Italian literature? From what source did he draw his chief inspiration? Of what periods did the historian Villari write? 235

Characterize the work of the following recent Italian writers: Fogazzaro; De Amicis; Verga; D'Annunzio; Croce. Name two contemporary women writers. What is the present outlook for Italian literature? 235

SPANISH LITERATURE

From what speech is the Spanish language descended? What other tongues have affected the language of Spain? Name four Roman writers who were natives of Spain 237

What is the oldest Spanish manuscript? Who was the original of "the Cid"? Name two early works written about his exploits . . . 237

What place in modern literature is assigned to the Spanish *Drama of the Three Kings*? Summarize the service of Alfonso the Wise to literature and history. From what language was the *Amadis de Gaula* translated? 237

Describe the *Conde Lucanor*. Who is the author of this famous work? What was the purpose of the stories in this work? . . . 237

Who is counted as the first genuine Spanish poet? What is the title of his work? . . . 237

Describe the poetry written at the court of John II of Castile. Who was the "forerunner of the Spanish humanists"? What Italian poet's work influenced Juan de Mena? Name De Mena's chief work 237

Describe the beginning of Spanish drama. Of what importance is *La Celestina*? 237

What types of writing characterized the 16th century in Spain? When and by whom was *Don Quixote* written? What is the rank of this book in world literature? 237

Who were the two greatest Spanish dramatists of the 16th and 17th centuries? Upon what themes did they write? What is the rank of Spanish drama among the literatures of the world? 237–238

Who began modern writing of history in Spain? What Spanish historian was a descendant of the Incas? Of what importance are the records of Las Casas, López de Gomara, and Oviedo y Valdéz? 238

Who is reckoned as the "prince of all Spanish lyrists"? Tell something of the importance of ballads in Spanish literature 238

Account for the decay of Spanish literature in the 18th century. Who wrote *El Sí de las Niñas*? Of what importance was De Isla's novel *Fray Gerundio*? 238

When did the 19th century romantic movement reach Spain? Name two notable writers of this period. When did the realistic movement in Spanish literature begin? 238

Name three recent Spanish dramatists. Note a peculiar feature of the popularity of Blasco Ibáñez 238

LATIN AMERICAN LITERATURE

What were the themes of Spanish American writers of the colonial period? 239

State a fact that shows the popular interest in literature in Mexico of the 16th century. Who, in the 17th century, was called "The Tenth Muse"? Who was called "The Mexican Thinker"? Characterize his work . 239–240

Of what importance was the work of Guillermo Prieto? How does present day Mexican drama compare with that of former times? Characterize the writing of Juan Tablada . 240

What spirit animated early Argentine literature? Characterize the writing of Ricardo Gutiérrez and that of Emma de la Barra . 240

In what types of literature have Chilean writers done the best work? Who is the greatest novelist of Chile? 240

Whose is the most brilliant name in Uruguayan literature? Name Uruguay's leading romantic poet; chief story writer 240

Characterize the work of the Peruvian writer, Clorinda Matto de Turner. What Colombian author wrote the best Latin American novel? 240

What two political acts about the year 1821 profoundly influenced Brazilian literature? What political effect did *Letters of a Solitary* produce? Characterize modern Brazilian lyric poets and poetry 241

What has been said about verse writing in Cuba? Estimate the importance of the *modernista* movement in Latin America . . . 241

GERMAN LITERATURE

Why was the development of German literature so long delayed? What were the earliest forms of literature in Germany? Who used rime for the first time in German literature? . 241

What change of theme did the period of the Crusades produce in German literature? Name the three greatest poets of this period. What are their most important poems? . . 241

Describe the *minnesong*. Characterize the work of Walther von der Vogelweide 242

Of what importance was the work of Eckhart, Suso, and Tauler? 242

Trace the origin of German drama. Who was Hans Sachs? Who wrote the *Ship of Fools*? What was the theme of this work? 242

Distinguish between the work of Hutten and Melanchthon and that of Luther. What was Luther's greatest literary contribution to Germany? Estimate the effect of the Thirty Years' War on German literature 242

Who were the three leaders in the revival of German literature in the 18th century? Name their greatest works and give the theme of each 242

Who are the four leaders of the Classic Period? Who made the first studies in comparative literature? What does Kant say is the way to individual freedom? What was the ideal goal of Goethe? of Schiller? 242–243

Name three leaders of the Romantic school. Who were the successors of Kant? Account for the decline of German literature between 1850 and 1870. What foreign writers aided the revival of drama in the 1890's? 243

What untoward influence put a blight on German literature in the 1930's? Name three writers who took refuge abroad. 243

OTHER GERMANIC LITERATURES

What were the earliest stories written in the Dutch language? Who is called the "Father of Dutch Poetry"? Why is this title bestowed upon him? What is his most notable work? 244

Trace the origin of Dutch drama. Who is the greatest of Dutch dramatists? What is the distinction of Anna Bijns in Dutch writing? Name three great Dutch scholars of the 16th and 17th centuries. What city was the Dutch literary center of this period? Upon what themes did "Father" Cats write? . . . 244–245

Name two leaders of the Dutch literary revival in the 18th century. Who has been called the "Dutch Sir Walter Scott"? Who is the greatest Dutch humorist? What literary form is most representative of Dutch literature? . . 245

In what language is the earliest written literature of Denmark? When did Danish ballads first appear? In what century did the ballad literature reach its highest development? 245

When was the first Danish translation of the Bible made? Who contributed most to this work? 245

Whose is the greatest literary name in Denmark of the 18th century? in the early 19th century? Who is Denmark's "Walter Scott"? For what is H. C. Andersen most famous? 245–246

For what literary work are the following most notable: Goldschmidt? Hostrup? Georg Brandes? 246

What are the earliest Norwegian literary monuments? Who is the greatest of Norwegian *scalds*, or poets? 246

Of what historic value is *The King's Mirror*? What change in Norwegian culture took place in the 14th and 15th centuries? 246–247

What was the language of Norway from the Reformation to the 19th century? What is the rank of Henrik Wergeland in modern Norwegian letters? 247

Estimate the rank of Björnson and that of Ibsen in Scandinavian literature 247

Of what do the earliest traces of Swedish literature consist? Give an interesting fact about the *Rökstenen* 248

Who was St. Bridget? What is the title of her chief work? 248

What change in the purpose of Swedish poetry took place after the Thirty Years' War? Who is the most original of Sweden's poets? What institution confers the Nobel literary prizes? Who founded the institution? 248

State the variety of E. G. Geijer's work. What is his rank among Swedish authors? Who is Sweden's greatest dramatist? Name two noted Swedish women authors 248

How are the early literatures of Iceland and Norway related? Name the first great Icelandic poet 249

What are subjects of the early family sagas? Who is the greatest of Icelandic writers? . 249

Who were the chief writers of religious poetry in the period from 1300 to 1550? Name the two most notable literary men of the period from 1550 to 1780 and characterize their work . . 249

When did the modern revival of Icelandic literature begin? Give the names of two influential men connected with this movement . 249

SLAVONIC LITERATURES

What are the two kinds of oral tradition handed down from the early period of Russian history? Distinguish the five groups of early Russian folk tales. What two medieval cities figure in these stories? Who is Sadko? Vladimir? . . 250

How was the Slavic language introduced into Russia? What is the story of the Raid of Igor? 250

When did Kiev become the center of Russian learning? Who was the pioneer of modern culture in Russia? When was the first Russian theater opened? 250

What part did Peter the Great play in Russian literary history? Who is called the "Russian Adam Smith"? How did Catherine II attempt to encourage Russian letters? Give the titles of three poems by Derzhávin . . 250

State the importance of Sumarókov in Russian literature. For what are the years 1765 and 1766 notable? What was Karamzín's most effective work? 250

Name some important works translated into Russian by Zhukóvsky. What was the influence of these translations? What is the rank of Púshkin in Russian literature? Who has been called the "Russian Burns"? . . 250–251

In what field have Russian writers done the greatest work? What may be said to be Russia's contribution to prose fiction? Name three great Russian novelists 251

Name three great Russian dramatists and give the title of a play by each. Who are the representative Russian writers of the short story? 251

How may the intense realism of the Russian short story be accounted for? Into what two groups did the revolution of 1918 divide Russian writers? 251

To what family of languages does Polish belong? What existing book shows the literary use of Polish in the 13th century? 252

What influences caused the Polish language to supersede Latin in literary use? What was the first book printed in Polish? 252

What period is known as the "golden age" of Polish literature? Who is called the "prince of Polish poets"? 252

Who was the first Polish authoress? To what English poet was Krasicki compared? . . . 252

What is the period of the modern revival of Polish literature? To what rank in Polish letters is Adam Mickiewicz assigned? Who is the greatest recent Polish writer of prose fiction? Name one of his books 252

What influence first gave a literary impulse to the Czech language? What are the chief literary remains from the period before the 14th century? 252

What was the effect of the Crusades upon Bohemia? When was the University of Prague founded? 252

What period is the greatest age of Czech literature? Tell something of the varied work of John Huss. Compare the educational advantages in Bohemia at this period with those of other countries. Who was Comenius? Give two interesting facts about his writings . . 253

From about what year do we date the modern revival of Czech literature? Who are the two greatest poets of the early 19th century? Who first translated and staged Shakspere's plays in Czech? Give two facts to indicate the vastness of the literary work done by Vrchlicky. Name a prominent woman writer. 253

HUNGARIAN LITERATURE

What particularly strong qualities are possessed by the Hungarian language? To what languages is it most closely related? Why was its literary development so long delayed? . . 253

What literary fragments remain from the period before 1450? Name three events which encouraged vernacular literature in the 15th century. What influences hampered Hungarian literature in the 17th century? 253

When did the modern revival of Hungarian literature begin? Name three important services of Count Stephen Széchenyi to the Hungarian language and culture 254

Who is the founder of the modern Hungarian drama? Name two novels by Mór Jókai. Who wrote *Banker and Baron*? 254

ANCIENT AND ORIENTAL LITERATURES

Into how many epochs do we divide Chinese literature? What are the great names in the first period? 254

Name the works written or edited by Confucius. What was the chief political teaching of Mencius? Quote a maxim from the *Tao Te King*. 254

When did the Reconstructive Period begin? What kind of beliefs and superstitions prevailed during the Han dynasty? Of what value is the *Classic of Mountains and Seas*? When was Buddhism recognized in China? . 254

What is the extent of the "golden age" of Chinese literature? What poet of this period is compared to the Persian poet Omar? . 254–255

To what two literary forms did the Mongol dynasty give encouragement? What themes are most popular in Chinese dramas? 255

What historical event opens the fourth period of Chinese literature? Trace the influence of missionaries and Western schools upon the literary development of this period. What change in Chinese literary style is taking place? 255

What is the date of the oldest extant literary work in Japanese? Give the essential features of Japanese poetry. What are *Hokku* poems? 255

What centuries are called the "dark ages" of Japanese literature? Name the two kinds of drama that originated in this period. Give four interesting facts about the origin and acting of the *Kabuki*. Describe the production of the Japanese marionette plays . 255–256

Sketch the work of women in Japanese literature. 256

How has Western culture influenced Japanese literature? What is the greatest problem of the Japanese literary world at present? . . . 256

Tell how Rawlinson found the key which enabled scholars to decipher the Assyro-Babylonian inscriptions. What is cuneiform writing? Who were the Sumerians? the Babylonians? 256

Describe the contents of the famous library of Assurbanipal. What is the story of the Gilgamesh epic? For what biblical story does it contain a parallel? 256–257

According to the Babylonian Creation epic, who created heaven and earth? of what were they made? Describe the code of Hammurabi . . 257

To what group of languages does Hebrew belong? What idea is the keynote of Hebrew literature? How did Hebrew literature begin? What two ancient collections of songs are mentioned in the Bible? 257

Into what four periods is Hebrew literature divided? Name five kinds of literary writing found in the Bible. What is the oldest document in the *Hexateuch*? What are its contents? What is "The Book of the Covenant"? 257

What are the Yahwist and Elohist documents? Why are they so called? Describe the effect of the book of Deuteronomy in the reign of King Josiah 257–258

GREEK LITERATURE

LATIN LITERATURE

LITERARY PLOTS, CHARACTERS, AND ALLUSIONS

MYTHOLOGY

What is the meaning of the name Atropos? Describe the representation of Aurora. What were the Augean stables? 324
Define avatar. Where and what was Avernus? What is the meaning of Beelzebub? 324
Who was Bellerophon? What constellation derives its name from a story of Berenice? . . 324
Identify the following: Bhima; Blue Jay; Brahma; Brigit; Cacus. Recount the adventures and achievements ascribed to Cadmus. 324
What fate overtook the soothsayer Calchas? Who was Calypso? Camilla? Cassandra? . 325
Under what forms were the following represented: Cecrops? centaurs? Cerberus? Charybdis? Chimera? 325
What powers were ascribed to the following: Circe? Clotho? Cluricaune? 325
What is the story of Clytie? 325
Who was Coxcox? Cressida? Creusa? . . . 325
Give the story of Cronus; of Dædalus . . 325–326
Identify the following: Dagon; Dahak; Daikoku; Danu; Daphnis 326
What is the story of Deucalion and Pyrrha? . 326
Characterize the goddess Diana; Discordia . 326
To the mythologies of what peoples do the following belong: Durga? Earth-Namer? Eblis? Egeria? Egil? 327
Describe Elysium. Recount the story of Endymion 327
Recount the story of Eurydice 327
Characterize the following: the Eumenides; the Fates; the fauns 327–328
What were the Indian beliefs about the Fire People? about the Fire Spirit? 328
What qualities and processes of nature and human life did the following Scandinavian deities represent: Frey? Freya? Frodi? . . 328
Who was Ganymede? Geryon? Glaucus? Glooskap? 328
Distinguish between the giants of Greek mythology and those of Norse myths 328
Tell the story of the Golden Fleece . . . 328–329
What were the Gorgons? the Graces? the Harpies? Who was Hebe? Hector? Hecuba? Helen? 329
What were the twelve labors of Hercules? . . 329
Describe the fortunes of Hippolytus; of Hippomenes; of Hyacinthus 330
Who was Honir? Horus? Hou Chi? Hugin? . 330
Identify the following: Hydra; Hygeia; Hyperion 330
For what was Mount Ida noted in Greek mythology? What does Iduna represent in Norse mythology? What is the significance of Indra in Hindu myths? 330
Recount the story of Iphigenia 331
What were the position and function of Iris? Isis? Israfel? Italapas? Jamshid? Janus? . 331
Explain the following allusions: Jason; Jinn; Juggernaut 331
Explain the mythological importance of Juno; of Jupiter; of Kama; of Krishna 331
Who was Laertes? What adventures did Ulysses have among the Læstrygonians? 332
What fate overtook Laocoön? Laodamia? . . 332
What is the character ascribed to the leprechaun? to the Lorelei? to Lucifer? to Mammon? 332
Tell the stories of the following: Marsyas; Medea; Medusa; Melusina 333
What parts did Memnon and Menelaus play in the Trojan War? 333
With what characteristics do myth and poetry endow Mephistopheles? 333
Recount two tales about King Midas 333
What was the position of Minerva among the gods? What were her especial powers? . 333–334
What was the Minotaur? 334
Who was Mithra? 334
Explain the following references: Morpheus; Muses; Myrmidons; Narcissus; Nemesis; nepenthe 334

What achievements were ascribed to the god Neptune? What qualities of character attached to Nestor? 334
What and where was Niflheim? 335
What is the meaning of the Babylonian word sign for Nina? 335
Explain a reference to the tears of Niobe . . 335
To what Greek mythological personages do the Scandinavian Norns correspond? What were the different groups of the nymphs? . . . 335
Describe the Scandinavian representation of the god Odin 335
Recount the tragic story of Œdipus; the story of Orestes. What was the fate of Orion? . . 335
Describe the character of the Persian deity Ormuzd. What is the story of the Egyptian god Osiris? 335–336
Describe the character and the festivals of Pan. 336
Who was Pandora? What decision did Paris render in a dispute among the goddesses? What consequences followed? 336
Where was Parnassus? What was its significance in Greek mythology? 336
What city was anciently named for Parthenope? 336
Explain the mythological reference in the phrase "to heap Pelion and Ossa on Olympus" . . 336
Why was the peninsula of southern Greece named for Pelops? 336
Who was Penelope? 336–337
Recount some of the adventures of the hero Perseus; of Phaëthon 337
Relate the story of Phaon and Sappho; that of Philemon and Baucis 337
For what deed was Philomela transformed into a nightingale? Explain the mythological references attaching to the word Phœnix . . . 337
What is the meaning of the name Pleiades? . 337
What was the office assigned to the god Pluto? Explain the epithet Pluvius, applied to Jupiter 337
Relate the story of Polyphemus and Galatea; that of Ulysses and Polyphemus 337
Of what city was Priam the king? What fate overtook him? 337–338
What is the meaning of the name Prometheus? Why did Jupiter wreak terrible vengeance upon Prometheus? 338
Relate the story of Psyche and Cupid. What is the meaning of the name Psyche? 338
Explain the Indian name Pukwana 338
What is the fabled relation between Pyramus and the color of the mulberry? 338
How were the oracles of the priestess Pythia delivered? 338
Explain the following names from Hindu mythology: Rahu; Rakshasas; Ravana . . . 338
With what Greek god is the Italian deity Saturn identified? 338
Who was Silenus? 338–339
Explain the mythological references implied in the following: Sirens; Sphinx; Styx; Tantalus; Tartarus 339
Relate the story of the journey of Telemachus. What was the most celebrated of the adventures of Theseus? 339
What Greek hero was the son of the goddess Thetis? 339
What was the character, and what were the functions of Thor? 339
Explain: Titans; trolls. Who was Tyr? . 339–340
Recount the story of the wanderings of Ulysses. 340
What was Valhalla? Who were the Valkyries? What duties were they said to perform on the battlefield? 340
What were the principal legends of the birth of Venus? Explain the Roman mode of worship of Vesta 340
State a Hindu belief about Vishnu 340
How was the lameness of Vulcan explained? What works were ascribed to him? 340
Describe the character and powers of Zeus. With what Roman god was he identified? . 340

BIBLIOGRAPHY

Brandes, Georg—Main Currents of Nineteenth-Century Literature. . . . . *Liveright*
Elton, O.—The Augustan Age. . . . . *Scribner*
Gayley, C. M.—Classic Myths. . . . *Ginn & Co.*
Gordon, C. S.—English Literature and the Classics. *Oxford*
Hannay, D.—The Later Renaissance. . *Blackwood*
Ker, W. P.—The Dark Ages. . . . . . . *Oxford*
Millar, J. H.—The Mid-Eighteenth Century. *Blackwood*
Omond, T. S.—The Romantic Triumph. *Blackwood*
Thrall, Wm. F. and Hibbard, Addison—Handbook to Literature. . . . . *Doubleday Doran*
Vaughan, C. S.—The Romantic Revolt. . .*Scribner*

AMERICAN LITERATURE

Cambridge History of American Literature. *Putnam*
Boynton, Percy H.—A History of American Literature. . . . . *Ginn & Co.*
Macy, John—The Spirit of American Literature. *Modern Library*
Pattee, F. L.—The New American Literature. *Century*
Quinn, A. H.—American Fiction. . . . *Appleton*

ENGLISH LITERATURE

Cambridge History of English Literature. *Putnam*
Courthope, W. J.—History of English Poetry. *Macmillan*
Garnett, Richard and Gosse, E.—English Literature: An Illustrated Record. . . . *Macmillan*
Harvey, Sir Paul—The Oxford Companion to English Literature. . . . . *Clarendon*
Legouis, Emile H. and Cazamian, Louis—A History of English Literature. . . . . . *Macmillan*
Ward, A. W.—A History of English Dramatic Literature. . . . . *Macmillan*

IRISH LITERATURE

Hyde, Douglas—A Literary History of Ireland. *Unwin*
Welsh, Charles—The Golden Treasury of Irish Songs and Lyrics. . . . . *McBride*

FRENCH LITERATURE

Bradley, R. F. and Michell, R. B.—French Literature of the Nineteenth Century. . . . *Crofts*
Nitze, W. A. and Dargan, E. P.—A History of French Literature to 1914. . . . . . . *Holt*
Smith, H. E.—Masters of French Literature. *Scribner*
Wright, C. H. C.—A History of French Literature. *Oxford*

ITALIAN LITERATURE

Fletcher, J. B.—Literature of the Italian Renaissance. . . . . *Macmillan*
Kuhns, Oscar—The Great Poets of Italy. *Houghton*
MacClintock, L.—The Contemporary Drama of Italy. . . . . *Little*
Symonds, J. A.—The Renaissance in Italy. *Holt*
Wilkins, E. H.—Dante: Poet and Apostle. *Univ. of Chicago Press*

SPANISH AND LATIN AMERICAN LITERATURE

Bell, Aubrey F.—Castilian Literature. . . *Oxford*
Farnell, Ida—Spanish Prose and Poetry, Old and New, with Translated Specimens. . . . *Oxford*
Fitzmaurice-Kelly, J.—A New History of Spanish Literature. . . . . *Oxford*
Ford, J. D. M.—Main Currents in Spanish Literature. . . . . *Holt*
Goldberg, Isaac—Brazilian Literature. . *Brentano*
Walsh, Thomas (Ed.)—Hispanic Anthology. *Putnam*

GERMAN LITERATURE

Francke, Kuno—A History of German Literature. *Holt*
Robertson, J. G.—A History of German Literature. *Putnam*
Thomas, Calvin—The History of German Literature. . . . . *Appleton*

SCANDINAVIAN LITERATURES

Blankner, Frederika (Ed.)—The History of the Scandinavian Literatures. . . . . *Dial Press*
Friis, Oluf—A Book of Danish Verse. *American Scandinavian Foundation*
Gosse, E.—The Oxford Book of Scandinavian Verse. *Clarendon*
Topsoe-Jensen, H. G.—Scandinavian Literature from Brandes to Our Day (tr. by Isaac Anderson). *Norton*

RUSSIAN, POLISH, CZECH LITERATURES

Brückner, Alexander—A Literary History of Russia. *Unwin*
Dyboski, R.—Modern Polish Literature. . *Oxford*
Hrbkova, S. B.—Czechoslovak Stories. *Duffield*
Kropotkin, P.—Ideals and Realities in Russian Literature. . . . . *Duckworth*
Lavrin, J.—An Introduction to the Russian Novel. *Whittlesey House*
Lützow, Franz (Count)—A History of Bohemian Literature. . . . . *Appleton*
Wiener, Leo—Anthology of Russian Literature. *Putnam*

CHINESE AND JAPANESE LITERATURES

Aston, W. G.—History of Japanese Literature. *Appleton*
Chamberlain, Basil H.—Japanese Poetry. *Murray*
Giles, H. A.—A History of Chinese Literature. *Heineman*
Legge, James—The Chinese Classics (8 vols.). *Trübner*
Lyall, L. A. (tr.)—The Sayings of Confucius. *Longmans*

SEMITIC LITERATURES

Abrahams, I.—Chapters on Jewish Literature. *The Jewish Publication Society of America*
Fowler, H. T.—A History of the Literature of Ancient Israel. . . . . *Macmillan*
Harper, R. F.—Assyrian and Babylonian Literature. *Univ. of Chicago Press*
Lyall, C. J.—Translations of Ancient Arabian Poetry. . . . . *Williams and Norgate*
Nicholson, R. A.—A Literary History of the Arabs. *Cambridge University Press*
Slouschz, Nahum—The Renascence of Hebrew Literature. *The Jewish Publication Society of America*

INDIAN AND PERSIAN LITERATURES

Browne, Edward G.—A Persian Anthology. *Dutton*
Frazer, R. W.—A Literary History of India. *Scribner*
Macdonnell, Arthur A.—A History of Sanskrit Literature. . . . . *Appleton*
Sidhanta, Nirmal Kumar—The Heroic Age of India. *Knopf*

GREEK AND LATIN LITERATURES

Capps, E.—From Homer to Theocritus. *Scribner*
Croiset, Alfred—Hellenic Civilization. . . *Knopf*
Duff, J. W.—A Literary History of Rome from the Origins to the Close of the Golden Age. *Scribner*
Fowler, H. W.—A History of Ancient Greek Literature. . . . . *Macmillan*
Laing, Gordon J.—Masterpieces of Latin Literature. *Houghton*
Loeb Classical Library (Translated classics). *Putnam*
Moulton, R. G.—The Ancient Classical Drama. *Oxford*
Murray, Gilbert—History of Ancient Greek Literature. . . . . *Appleton*
Wright, W. C.—A Short History of Greek Literature. . . . . *American Book Company*

III

History

SUBJECT GUIDE

LINCOLN LIBRARY INDEXES

• • •

HIGH LIGHTS IN OUR HISTORY

1609 – HENRY HUDSON DISCOVERED MANHATTAN ISLAND AND THEN SAILED UP THE HUDSON RIVER

1776 – THE FIRST CONSTITUTION OF AN INDEPENDENT AMERICAN STATE ADOPTED AT WILLIAMSBURG, VA

1848 – THE DISCOVERY OF GOLD IN CALIFORNIA ACCELERATED SETTLEMENT OF WESTERN STATES

1861 – FORT SUMTER FIRED ON, BEGINNING THE WAR BETWEEN THE NORTHERN AND SOUTHERN STATES

1903 – FIRST SUCCESSFUL AIRPLANE FLIGHT MADE BY WRIGHT BROTHERS AT KILL DEVIL HILL, KITTY HAWK, N. C.

1945 – THE JAPANESE FORMALLY SURRENDERED TO THE ALLIES ON THE U. S. S. MISSOURI AT TOKYO

HISTORY

INTRODUCTORY

THE word history is sometimes used to mean all that has happened in the past. In this sense we speak of the history of the earth, of rocks, or of plants, as well as of the history of man. In the narrower sense, however, history is an account of the actions and the fortunes of mankind. Such an account must be based upon reliable records which can be understood and interpreted by the writers of history. The records may be in the form of buildings, products of art, manufactured objects, or writings. They may even be institutions, language, or survivals of customs. But, so long as they throw light upon man's activity in the past, such records are material for the writing of history.

Unfortunately, it has been the exception for people to try consciously to hand down to their successors information about their own day. It often happens that certain records are preserved by the merest chance, while others, which would have been much more valuable, are lost. These conditions, it will be seen, make it a very difficult task to obtain a true picture of a past age, to recover the habits and the customs of a society, to trace the effects of its actions upon later times, and to understand the motives and the feelings of people who ceased to live many years or even centuries ago. Yet these are the things which the writers of history aim to do. To accomplish their purpose, historians have worked out an elaborate science of evidence. The more successful historians have also brought to bear upon the task consummate gifts of art and of understanding.

The Use of History. To study history is to live over again this story of the past, to meet familiarly great men and notable women, and to see the outcome of their actions more clearly than the actors saw it themselves. It is to have at one's disposal authentic facts about the past. More than this, the reading of history enlarges our experience, and enables us to judge of present issues and to forecast the future of situations through our knowledge of similar situations in the past. For these reasons, history is a study of the utmost importance for every one, and especially for citizens of a democracy, who have to make up their minds about issues of government, in order that they may help to determine public policies and actions.

The Task of the Historian. The first requisite for all sound historical writing is the careful establishment of facts. This object is attainable only if the historian has full knowledge of the sources of information in regard to the period to be described. Furthermore, he must possess the gift of critically estimating the value of his sources according to the rules of historical evidence. But something more than mere chronicling of facts is expected of the historian. We look to him for interpretation of movements and of events.

To this task the historian must bring an insight into the motives which actuate men in various situations. He needs a power of discernment in state affairs and a due appreciation of the parts which economic, social, and religious interests play in human affairs. Moreover, the historian should keep himself free from considerations of self-interest, that his interpretation may be objective, reasonable, and as free from bias as is humanly possible. In style, he should be candid and unimpassioned, avoiding both panegyric and satire. To truth alone must he offer sacrifice. He must be fearless, incorruptible, untrammeled, conceding nothing either to hatred or to friendship, a citizen of no city, recognizing no ruler, and setting forth the result of his researches in a diction which the many may understand and the more educated approve. Only by such a method can the integrity of a writer be established and his reputation as a historian be justified.

Earlier Historians. Such demands have not always been met. The earliest historian was probably Herodotus, but he had not learned to test his sources critically. However, Thucydides, another Greek historian, showed a spirit so scientifically rigorous that his work has seldom been equaled. Later Greeks and the Romans, with the possible exception of Tacitus, gave history a vicious turn in the direction of rhetoric, by an excessive interest in style rather than in matter. During the middle ages, histories were seldom more than chronicles, devoid alike of artistic form and of scrupulous care for fact. With the Renaissance and in early modern times an interest in genuine history was roused by controversy over facts connected with religion. The histories in that period were written, however, by people who were familiar with religious wars and with struggles between dynasties, and who were acquainted only with a royalist form of government. These circumstances made it difficult for them either to understand records of democratic institutions in the past or to estimate justly social and economic changes in their own day.

Modern Writing of History. In more recent times a different problem has confronted the historian. Broadening interests in his readers have made it necessary for him to treat more aspects of life, and this means that for the history of the past more material must be collected. In the present also an extraordinarily great amount of material is being produced, largely because of the wide use of the printing press. The result is that sifting and selection of material has become one of the chief tasks of the historian. In fact, the increasing complexity of the historian's work has proceeded to such a point that no one man is equal by himself to the task of writing a comprehensive history of even a short period. All great histories now are corporate undertakings. Historical societies as well as governments encourage the collection of facts; periodicals are published to print what researches, carried on in all parts of the world, succeed in bringing to light; and experts in various fields write the parts of the history with which they are competent to deal.

Prehistory. The life of man on the earth may be divided into two periods: historic and prehistoric. The researches of ethnologists and anthropologists continue to teach us more of prehistoric man, but from this early period few records were left which can be used by historians.

Primitive man's struggle for existence claimed and consumed all his energies, so that he had neither time, inclination, nor faculty to concern himself consciously with works that would long survive his death. Our knowledge of these primitive tribes is drawn from the examination of objects belonging to the ages of stone and of bronze, such as have been found in caves, mounds, graves, and other places. Man's slow and difficult progress toward civilization is marked by the various tools and weapons which he left behind him. Each step of his labored advance is apparent from the successive improvements in his implements, which show how he passed in turn through the hunting and fishing stage, the pastoral and the agricultural period, onward and upward through the eras of picture writing and of sound writing, of early drawing, of carving, and of painting. At length, in various parts of the world, societies attained to such mastery over the means of life that they could give attention to those improvements in living which would entitle them to be called civilized. At this point, history proper may be said to begin.

Divisions of History. In treating of history, an arbitrary division is commonly made into three periods,—ancient, medieval, and modern.

Ancient history deals with the course of the Eastern and Western civilizations up to 476 A. D., the year in which the last Roman emperor of the West was deposed. The civilizations of the East included Babylonia, Elam, Assyria, Mesopotamia, Egypt, Palestine, Phœnicia, Persia, India, China, and Japan; those of the West were Greece, Carthage, and Rome. India, China, and Japan, though having a historical past corresponding to the period we call ancient, are less intimately connected with European civilization than are the other Oriental nations mentioned, and so are usually treated separately.

The history of the medieval period takes up the story of civilization at the fall of Rome. Throughout the course of a thousand years, it traces the gradual development of the old world into the new. Beginning with the almost complete cessation of governmental authority and of learning, it proceeds to describe the growth and power of Christianity, to narrate the rise of the feudal system, and to reveal the origin of the states which developed into the various nations of today. This era comes to an end with the fall of the Byzantine Empire in 1453.

Modern history may be said to begin with the time of the invention of printing and with the discovery of America. It is largely the story of the internal development and of the outward expansion of nations, together with their conflicts—a story ever lengthening as the improved means of communication bring nations, east and west, into more intimate relations with each other and make the actions and the policies of each people the concern of all.

These divisions have been found useful, but they should not be allowed to obscure the fact that in reality history is continuous, and that, in particular, European and American history exhibits an unbroken chain of development in culture and ideas from the dawn of civilization to the present time. The grand and well ordered empire of Rome passed by insensible degrees into an age of less significance, which, however, served as a period of incubation for the astonishing improvements that were later elaborated in the economic and political organization of modern society.

The Study of History. For various reasons, the history of certain periods or nations may be more attractive or more enlightening to the reader than that of other times and peoples. This fact has led to the placing of a certain emphasis on those eras which show the growth of political power, or which reveal a high development of art, of learning, and of culture. Some ages are of especial interest because we see in them the unfolding of religious ideas or the spread of democratic views and practices; or they may gain significance from the sheer force of great personalities which they produced.

The Hebrews.—In the history of the Hebrews we follow the evolution of an ethical religious faith and the rise of a conception of a just and universal god. We see the worshipers of Jehovah clinging tenaciously to their beliefs in spite of the successive waves of conquest that swept over their heads, and even, by means of their faith, maintaining their identity for 2000 years, though deprived of a national habitation and a government.

Greece.—The history of Greece in the 5th century B. C. shows a people so inspired by an ideal of freedom as to defy a despotic empire of much greater power. This too was a period prolific in inventions, rich in literature and in art—a period which has had something to teach to every nation.

Rome.—The history of Rome, on the other hand, from the Punic wars to the widest extent of the Empire, shows the overmastering power of organization. It describes a time in which was built up a system of law that underlies the legal customs of Western Europe and of Latin America.

The Crusades.—Next come the Crusades. Though the military result was the defeat of the Christian nations and a diminution of their prestige, yet the enterprise widened the horizon of the people of Western Europe, and began for a second time to unite the destinies of Europe and Asia.

The Renaissance.—After the Crusades, we arrive at the period of the Renaissance—the rebirth of literature, art, philosophy, and science. Allied to this was the Reformation, from which dates the origin of the Protestant Church.

The Commonwealth.—One of the most instructive periods is that of the struggle between Parliament and the Stuart monarchs in England during the 17th century. It was in this period that the power of Parliament was first made paramount over the authority of the king.

Medieval France.—A quite different development is seen in the history of France from the time of Charlemagne. In this period France became differentiated from the rest of Europe and passed through a long process of constitutional change, which culminated in the monarchy of Louis XIV.

The Modern World.—Finally, we see history take a new direction as a result of the growth of knowledge and the heightening of the sense of individual human worth, which had been going on ever since the time of the Renaissance. The widespread conviction of the value of personality led to a growth of democratic sentiment and to the overthrow of absolute forms of government. This process was attended with much bloodshed and great violence in the French Revolution, but it proceeded more peacefully in many other countries because of its success in France. In Russia, however, where it met with more determined resistance, it was attended by unprecedented convulsions throughout the fabric of social and political life.

The increase of knowledge led to a few simple inventions which were vastly elaborated and applied widely by means of complex organization. This development occasioned profound changes in the ways in which goods were produced and in which human needs were satisfied. These changes necessitated, for workers, a more rigid routine of life, and thus tended to undo the efforts that had been made in the direction of individual freedom. The impersonal power of the industrial master weighed more heavily upon the workman than the personal authority to which men had formerly been accustomed, so that political agitation came to be overshadowed by industrial conflict. For nations, it often became a matter of life and death to have access to raw materials and markets. Thus a period of desperate attempts to parcel off the productive, but little developed, parts of the world was succeeded by struggles among the strongest nations for the control of markets. These struggles culminated in the World War.

Thus two factors, the impulse toward democratic institutions and the compulsory transformation of the means of livelihood, serve today so to involve in one destiny all the nations of the earth, that in the future the history of one nation cannot be written apart from the history of all.

AMERICAN HISTORY

The discovery and the colonization of the American continent were immediate consequences of the intellectual movements of the Renaissance and of the political and economic conditions of Western Europe at the close of the 15th century. Europe, by that time, had fairly passed from the middle ages to the modern period. With equal truth it may be said that the creation of the United States of America was one of the first great results of the growth of liberal political thought in Western Europe during the 17th and 18th centuries. A brief survey of the European conditions of these periods is, therefore, a necessary preliminary to the study of American colonial and national history.

European Background of American History. The Renaissance, which had created a new world of literature, painting, sculpture, and architecture, had also prepared the way for scientific discovery. Western Europe was thus made ready to enter upon an era of search for new modes of living and for new lands. The movement toward geographic discovery found its enthusiastic and inspiring apostle in Prince Henry of Portugal.

At the same time, the opening of the modern period was signalized by the appearance of national states—England, France, and Spain being the first to rise from the disorder of medieval feudalism. The emergence of these countries from long periods of war left many adventurous spirits free to engage in voyages of exploration. The ranks of the merchant adventurers, too, were swelled, and the demands of commercial enterprises gave impetus to the search for a new route to the Indies, whence came the goods for the most profitable traffic of the times. Not only were the Western merchants chafing under the large tolls taken by the Italian cities, but the Ottoman conquests had resulted either in the imposition of ruinous exactions upon commerce or in the practical closing of the ancient overland trade routes to the East.

Another important influence was due to the fact that, in England particularly, the 16th century saw a very large increase in population. The industrial and agricultural methods of the time, which had changed but little in many centuries, were proving inadequate to provide for the needs of the people. Moreover, a land system that restricted land ownership to a few was becoming irksome to the common people. These conditions caused thousands to welcome an opportunity for life in a new country.

From Imperialism to Popular Government. The questions as to the character and the rights of the state and as to its relation to the lives and happiness of the people occupied the attention of many European thinkers in the 17th and the 18th century. Moreover, these same centuries had seen in Europe the struggle among the powers to unite large areas into imperial states. But the governing classes and the "benevolent despots" of Europe remained generally indifferent to the intellectual movement of the period, while, among the political leaders in the American colonies, this liberal thought found hospitable minds. The political mission of the united colonies in 1776 was to withdraw from the arena of imperial rivalry, and to initiate a movement which should endow with modern liberal meanings the ideas of the state and of political union of states. The realization of this ideal continues to be the task of the American people.

Early Voyages of Discovery. In the latter half of the 15th century, Portuguese sailors attempted the sea route around the Cape of Good Hope. Numerous scholars, however, had come to believe that the earth was round and that, consequently, the Indies could be reached by sailing directly westward from Europe. The credit for putting these theories to a practical test belongs to Christopher Columbus, a Genoese sailor.

After years of fruitless endeavor to gain a hearing for his proposals, Columbus at length appealed to Isabella, the Spanish queen, through her interest in Christianizing the natives of heathen lands. With her aid, he finally secured three small ships and money with which to fit out his first expedition. Toscanelli, an Italian geographer, probably supplied Columbus with a map, on which Japan was represented in a position about 2500 miles west of the Canary islands. This error of distance was fortunate, for it is doubtful that Columbus could have found the men or the means for an undertaking which was likely to involve a longer time and greater danger than the voyage down the west coast of Africa.

Thus equipped with ships, and thoroughly acquainted, through years of study, with the scientific knowledge of geography and navigation that his age afforded, Columbus sailed westward from Palos, Spain, on August 3, 1492. On October 12, the explorers sighted land, probably one of the Bahama islands, which they called San Salvador. In the belief that they had found the East Indies, they took possession of San Salvador, Hispaniola (Haiti), and other islands in the name of the king of Spain. The report carried home by Columbus in 1493 prompted the sailors of other nations to make similar attempts to reach the East. He himself made three more voyages, in 1493, 1498, and 1502, touching at length the northern coast of the continent of South America. But the significance of his discovery was not appreciated until after his death.

The Portuguese redoubled their efforts, and in 1498 Vasco da Gama actually reached India, following the eastward route, by way of the Cape of Good Hope. Henry VII of England, who had refused the offer of Columbus to sail under the English flag, commissioned John Cabot, another Genoese, to set out in search of a new westward route to the Indies. Cabot sailed from Bristol in 1497, and reached the coasts of Labrador and Newfoundland. England, however, lacked money and ships to follow up the discoveries of John Cabot and his son Sebastian, and American exploration was left for the time to Spain.

In 1513 Balboa crossed the Isthmus of Panama and discovered the Pacific Ocean. Magellan, in 1520, entered the Pacific through the strait, which now bears his name, at the southern end of the American continent, sailed up the west coast of South America, and thence westward to the Philippines, where he met his death. One of his ships, however, finally reached Spain by way of the Cape of Good Hope, thus completing the first circumnavigation of the globe. Magellan had reached the goal in Asia toward which Columbus had sailed, and which he believed he had gained.

Exploration. During the early part of the 16th century, Spain was without a rival in the exploration of America. In 1513 Ponce de León visited Florida. While Cortés and Pizarro were gathering fabulous wealth in Mexico and Peru, other Spaniards, inspired by the hope of similar fortune, led expeditions into the country which now forms the southern part of the United States. De Soto marched inland from Florida and explored the country westward to the Mississippi river and the present state of Arkansas. About the same time, Coronado, in search of the rich cities of Cibola, led an expedition northward from the west coast of Mexico as far as the present state of Kansas. Within the latter half of the century, Spaniards visited points on the Pacific coast northward to the Strait of Juan de Fuca.

Meanwhile, French ambitions had been aroused. In 1493-94, Pope Alexander VI had confirmed to Spain possession of all new lands to the westward of a meridian drawn 370 leagues west of the Cape Verde islands, and to Portugal similar discoveries east of that line. Ignoring this division, the French king, Francis I, sent an Italian sailor, Verrazano, westward across the Atlantic. He explored the coast in the neighborhood of the present harbor of New York. Ten years later (1535), Jacques Cartier found the entrance to the St. Lawrence river, and sailed up that stream until his further progress was stopped by the rapids which were later called Lachine, or Chinese. Charmed by the beauty of the situation, he gave the name Mount Royal to the eminence which now crowns the city of Montreal.

In the opening years of the reign of Queen Elizabeth, English merchants and sailors, stirred to emulation by the commercial monopoly enjoyed by Spain, and, being in religious and political conflict with that power, began to think of possessing the New World. Their activities took two directions: (1) the search for a passage to India around the northern shore of America; (2) a direct attack on Spanish commerce in the Caribbean. The most valuable immediate results of English attempts to find the northwest passage were the discovery and the exploration of Hudson bay, in whose tributary land basin the powerful Hudson's Bay Company gained its first foothold upon the American continent.

The harrying of Spanish commerce was carried on most effectively by Francis Drake. In 1577 Drake, who had already played the pirate with great success, passed through the Strait of Magellan, took several rich prizes from the Spanish fleets on the west coast of America, and put in at a harbor north of the bay of San Francisco for repairs. Thence he continued his voyage of three years by way of the Cape of Good Hope, around the world to England and to the prize of knighthood (1580).

During this same period, persistent efforts toward more permanent possession and colonization of the New World were made by Englishmen. In 1578, Sir Humphrey Gilbert attempted to colonize Newfoundland. His first expedition failed to reach America, but a second, in 1583, entered St. John's harbor, Newfoundland. The colonists became discouraged, however, and soon returned to England. Sir Walter Raleigh, under a charter obtained from Queen Elizabeth in 1584, made three attempts to settle a colony on Roanoke island, off the coast of that part of Virginia which later was included in North Carolina. All three of his attempts failed, largely because supplies could not be sent from England.

The failures of Gilbert and Raleigh proved that the founding of colonies was too expensive a venture for individuals. Further attempts at settlement were postponed until after the close of the wars with Spain in 1604.

The French, meanwhile, had followed up the explorations of Cartier on the St. Lawrence river. The greatest of the French explorers in the 16th century was Champlain, who pushed boldly westward from Quebec into the interior. He initiated that movement of French missionaries and settlers which at length planted a line of missions, forts, and settlements, stretching from the St. Lawrence west and south through the Mississippi valley to New Orleans.

Colonization. Nevertheless, while their leaders were the boldest and most successful explorers of the time, most of the Frenchmen who came to the New World were little interested in real colonizing. They ignored the advantage which early French discoveries on the middle Atlantic coast would have given them, and pressed back into the interior along the line of the St. Lawrence river. As the Spaniards in the South sought for wealth in the mines, so the Frenchmen in the North developed the fur trade, penetrating very early as far west as Lake Superior and north to Hudson bay.

French colonial government, moreover, was despotic. This governmental policy and the dearth of suitable colonists lost the New World to France. The French claims, which at the opening of the 17th century stretched from the latitude of Philadelphia to that of Quebec, overlapped those of the English. But the only French settlements of importance were made at Port Royal, the present city of Annapolis, Nova Scotia (1604), and at Quebec (1608).

Frenchmen were, however, the first to attempt settlements within the present territory of the United States. In 1562 a group of Huguenots settled at Port Royal on the coast of what is now known as the state of South Carolina. Upon the failure of this colony, they planted another on the St. Johns river in Florida in 1565. The Spanish retaliated by founding St. Augustine in the same year and by then destroying the French colony.

The Spaniards were able rapidly to conquer large and rich territories in Mexico and in South America. Their policy of exploitation reduced to slavery many of the natives, whom they used in working the mines. However, an important feature of Spanish colonization is the fact that Spanish settlers intermarried with the natives and produced a mixed race of people who proved themselves capable of a culture which rivaled that of Spain itself. They built cities, with parks and churches and notable public buildings. They established universities and encouraged literature; the first printing press in North America was set up in Mexico. But the government of the Spanish colonies was military, under governors who carried out instructions from the despotic home government in Spain. Under Spanish rule, neither democracy nor representative government appeared.

The English victory over the Spanish *Armada* in 1588 had so checked the growth of Spanish power that, while Spain was able to keep her colonies in Mexico and South America, she was not able to extend settlements into the northern territory which she had already explored. Moreover, this territory did not appeal to the Spaniards, because it did not appear to be rich in mineral wealth. At the beginning of the 17th century, therefore, the settlement of the eastern coast of North America, between Florida and Nova Scotia, approximately the present Atlantic coast of the United States, was left to the English and the Dutch.

In 1609 Henry Hudson, sailing under the Dutch flag, discovered and explored the Hudson river, and in 1613 a Dutch trading company established a post on the site of the city of New York, calling it New Amsterdam. In 1621 the Dutch West India Company secured the right to colonize in territory adjoining New Amsterdam and the Hudson river. The company granted large estates to patroons, who were given feudal rights over whatever settlers they chose to send out. These settlements remained under Dutch control until 1664, when they were surrendered to the English. Meanwhile, a colony of Swedes and Finns was established at Fort Christina on the present site of Wilmington, Delaware, in 1638, but this territory was seized by the Dutch in 1644, and it passed later, with the other Dutch holdings, to England.

England in the Seventeenth Century. English colonization of America was profoundly influenced by the political and the religious conditions dominant in England in the 17th century. Following the brilliant reign of Elizabeth, which ended in 1603, came the period of the Stuart kings, interrupted by Cromwell and the Commonwealth from 1649 to 1660. The leading political movement of the century arose out of the demand of the middle classes to be heard in affairs of government. It resulted in the temporary overthrow of the Stuarts in 1649 and in the effectual restriction of royal power through the revolution of 1688-89. In the domain of religion, the Puritan movement gathered strength until it controlled the established church of England during the Cromwellian period and, after the Restoration of 1660, maintained itself in the Nonconformist churches, which secured toleration and political privilege after the revolution of 1688-89. The Puritan and Cavalier migrations to America reflect the influence of these great struggles.

Motives for Colonization. A desire to outdo the Spaniard had been the motive of English explorers in the 16th century. The attempts of such men as Gilbert and Raleigh to establish colonies had been prompted by mixed patriotic, commercial, and religious motives. When, after some disastrous experiments, it became clear that colonization was a business for companies of men who could supply large capital, the commercial motive became supreme. After 1660, the influence of this incentive became noticeable in the grants of territory for commercial purposes, especially in connection with the Carolinas (1663) and, to a less extent, with Georgia and Pennsylvania. It is worthy of note, however, that the religious ideal of Christianizing the natives was never quite lost.

London and Plymouth Companies. In 1606 a group of London merchants formed a company of two divisions,—one called the London Company, the other, the Plymouth Company. Their purpose was to colonize the coast of America between the Spanish claims on the south and the French claims on the north. The London Company was granted a tract of land 100 miles along the coast and extending inland 100 miles, located somewhere between Cape Fear (Carolina) and the Hudson river. The Plymouth Company had a similar grant somewhere between the Potomac and Maine. The result was that the country lying between the Potomac and the Hudson, in which the grants overlapped and which was to go to the company that should first occupy it, was avoided by both companies. The London Company planted a settlement at Jamestown in 1607, and in 1620 the Pilgrims settled at Plymouth, within the Plymouth Company's grant.

Virginia Colonial Government. The first charter granted to the London Company, giving them the privilege of making settlements in Virginia, divided the powers of government between the king and the company, or the proprietors, as the company was called. It conferred no privileges of self-government on the colonists, although it did grant them the privileges of Englishmen, which meant jury trial, the right of habeas corpus, and free speech. The colony at Jamestown was really a great plantation. The colonists were servants and employees of the company. All cultivation of the soil was done in common. Products went into the company's storehouse, from which food and clothing and other articles needed by the settlers were issued to them, and such products as might find ready sale in England were taken for shipment. The profits from these sales went to the members of the company who had invested in the enterprise.

Some changes in the charter were made in 1609 and in 1612. The government was placed in the hands of the company. The first governor was Sir Thomas Dale, a soldier who ruled the colony with an iron hand from 1611 to 1616. Severe martial law was in force during this time, and Dale's governorship was known as the "time of slavery." Whatever his faults of undue severity, Dale maintained order in the colony and made one very important change in the government. This was the allotment of three-acre plots to private holders in 1614.

First Representative Assembly. The year 1618 brought the chief power in the London Company into the hands of Sir Edwin Sandys and the earl of Southampton. These men were Puritans and bitter opponents of King James I and his Stuart policies. They seized the opportunity to grant a larger measure of freedom to the colonists. In 1618 they issued a charter, or contract, and appointed Governor Yeardley to carry out this contract in the colony. The new governor abolished the system of common industry and granted 100-acre tracts to free immigrants. Then he formed an assembly made up of representatives from each plantation. In this act of Governor Yeardley, we see the beginning of representative government in America.

The date of the first meeting of the assembly, or House of Burgesses, as it came to be called, was July 30, 1619. This assembly soon fell into the ways of the English Parliament. It sat for six days and did most of its work in committees. It passed laws, which today would be called "blue laws," against drunkenness, gambling, absence from church, and excess in fine clothing. Although the governor possessed veto power, there was no occasion for its use. But the most important act of the Virginia assembly was that of 1624, which asserted the right of the assembly to control taxation. This right was reasserted upon the appointment of later governors.

The Founding of Maryland. The settlement of the colony of Maryland was due to the enterprise of a Catholic gentleman, George Calvert. Calvert had secured from King James in 1623 a title to Newfoundland, but his attempt to plant a colony there failed on account of the harsh climate of the island. He then petitioned for territory farther south, and Maryland was granted to him. In 1633, after his death, the title was confirmed to his son, Cecil Calvert, second baron of Baltimore. This charter made the baron really a constitutional king over the settlers in the new colony, but it provided for a representative assembly to be composed of freeholders, or freemen.

The Maryland assembly proved to be as progressive and tenacious as the House of Burgesses in Virginia. In 1635 it passed a code of laws, which Calvert vetoed. In 1638 the assembly rejected a code of laws which Calvert presented to it for acceptance; by 1650 it had won the right to initiate legislation.

The most notable feature of the Maryland government was its provision for religious toleration. Catholics were at this period severely persecuted in England, but Calvert secured for his colony the privilege of toleration. An act of the assembly, passed in 1649, declared that all persons professing belief in Jesus Christ should not be molested nor discountenanced for their religion. Although this act excluded Jews, it was far in advance of English practice or that of other English colonies.

New England. The Plymouth Company, formed by gentlemen in the west of England, attempted in 1607 to plant a colony at the mouth of the Kennebec river, but the venture was a failure, and for several years this company did nothing. Then some of its members formed the Council for New England. They did not send out colonists, but granted lands to individuals who would undertake to make settlements. Their policy, however, was unsuccessful. Only seven little settlements were made before 1630, the chief one being at Salem.

The Settlement of Plymouth. Meanwhile, a little band of Separatists,—Puritans who had withdrawn from the Church of England and, because of persecution, had settled at Leyden,—became desirous of leaving Holland and finding more favorable conditions under the English flag. Through the influence of the Puritan members of the London Company, these people secured a grant of land from that company and also obtained a loan of several thousand pounds from a company of London merchants. After many delays, 102 persons embarked on the *Mayflower* at Plymouth, England, in September 1620. Driven out of their course by autumn storms, they landed in America at a point to which Captain John Smith had already given the name of Plymouth. But Plymouth was outside the London Company's territory, and, consequently, the Pilgrims' grant of land was of no value. In this situation, 41 members of the company joined in signing an agreement known as the Mayflower Compact. This agreement bound the signers to co-operate in providing such government as might be necessary for the colony. The next year (1621) they secured a grant from the Council for New England.

The agreement of the Plymouth colonists with the London merchants provided that industry should be carried on in common for seven years. Supplies were to be sent out from London each year. After two years' trial, Governor Bradford found that the system of common industry was not working well, and he therefore granted parcels of land to individuals for temporary use. Under this new arrangement the colony began to prosper. In 1627 the term of agreement with the London merchants expired. Bradford and a few others assumed the debt of the colony, on condition of being allowed a monopoly of the fur trade. It took them fourteen years to repay the loan.

During the first few years of the Plymouth colony, government was carried on by an assembly which was virtually a town meeting. But as other settlements were formed near by, the need of a different legislature became insistent, and in 1636 a representative assembly was first convened. It provided the first written code of laws in the portion of America that later became the United States. As in other colonies, the franchise was not conferred even upon all freemen. An act of 1671 provided that a voter must give evidence of upholding the orthodox faith. During all this time, the colony of Plymouth had no charter, nor was it ever recognized by the home government. Probably this condition was due to the disturbed state of affairs in England. In 1691, the colony was annexed to Massachusetts.

Colony of Massachusetts Bay. The first settlements around Massachusetts bay were due to the activity of the Dorchester Company, made up of west of England men, who were interested in the fishing trade. A station was established at Cape Ann in 1623, largely through the influence of John White, a member of the company, to provide a home for the extra crews necessary on the fishing vessels. The settlement was moved to Salem in 1628. The Massachusetts Bay Company was formed, and in the following year a large body of settlers was added to the group already at Salem. The danger to English Puritanism, which appeared now in the policy of Charles I, brought a number of the members of the Massachusetts Bay Company to make the famous Cambridge Agreement, by which they secured control of the company and agreed to transfer the charter and all the government of their colonies to America. In this way the commercial company became an organized government and the promoter of the great Puritan migration.

The Puritan Migration. In the course of the next eleven years, during which period no Parliament was summoned in England, 25,000 selected English colonists were transferred to New England at a cost of about $4,000,000. The leader of this movement was John Winthrop. With a company of 900 he came to Massachusetts in 1630. In this year six new towns were founded in the neighborhood of Massachusetts bay. In 1640, when Parliament was again summoned in England, many colonists returned to the mother country, and New England received very few immigrants until after the American Revolution (1775–82).

Colonial Conditions. In the early years of the 17th century, glowing accounts of the climate and productiveness of the region of English settlement had been carried back to England, and all the early colonists, including the Pilgrims who landed at Plymouth, had visions of rapid rise to wealth. It took but a few years to dissipate these visions and to teach the colonists that they were dealing with a country of greater extremes of climate than they had known in England, and a land whose soil yielded returns only to labor. John Smith, the restless soldier and explorer, when he was president of the council at Jamestown in 1608-09, grappled sternly with this problem. He enforced regulations as to industry and social organization which probably saved the colony from utter extinction within the first three years of its existence.

While the colonists in New England at first drew some profit from the fur trade, they soon learned that the prosperity of the colonies was dependent upon the utilization of the fisheries and upon the cultivation of the soil. They learned from the Indians how to raise Indian corn, or maize, the food which saved the lives of the Pilgrims in the first difficult years of the settlement at Plymouth. Raleigh had brought back to England from Virginia the first tobacco which he had secured from the Indians. The growing of tobacco was for many years discouraged by the London Company, but it formed the basis of the wealth of the colonists in Virginia, as the cultivation of maize gave them their staple food.

The severe climate in New England came near proving fatal to the first settlements. Half of the first company of 102, who landed at Plymouth in the winter of 1620, died before spring. The colony of Jamestown in Virginia was planted on low, unhealthful ground, and in the first year two-thirds of the immigrants perished. It is said that for twenty years each new body of immigrants lost one-half their number within the first season.

Popular Government in New England. The charter of the Massachusetts Bay Company provided that eighteen assistants, freemen of the corporation, should be elected each year, to carry on the government with the governor, but only twelve of the elected assistants came to the colony. These men were all of the rank of English gentlemen and had been made magistrates before leaving England. According to the charter, four general courts were to be held each year for the making of laws. At first, the magistrates—the governor and the assistants—themselves constituted this court. Very soon after the first settlements were made, however, a movement arose for the extension of political power. A group of about 100 settlers demanded a share in the lawmaking, and a considerable number of new freemen were admitted to the corporation. In 1634 a delegation composed of men from each of eight towns met in Boston and asked to see the charter. Out of this action came representative government for the colony. The charter, they found, granted the lawmaking power to the whole body of freemen. The next step was taken by the towns in sending delegates to represent them in the general court. Furthermore, the freemen demanded voting in the general court by ballot instead of by a show of hands. Thus the ballot was introduced into American politics.

It is important to remember that there were in the colony five classes of people: (1) gentlemen, who were addressed as Master; (2) skilled artisans and freeholders, usually addressed as Goodman; (3) unskilled laborers, addressed by their given names; (4) servants; (5) slaves. The three lowest classes were never admitted to political citizenship, while, of the first two, only those who were approved church members were given the franchise.

During the 17th century, about one-fourth of the adult males in the colony of Massachusetts bay could vote. The struggle between the freemen and the assistants continued until, in 1644, the general court was divided into two houses, the Upper House of the Assistants, the Lower House of the Deputies. This was the first two-chamber legislature in America.

Town Government. Meanwhile, new machinery of local government was being contrived in the villages or towns. In these towns the people did not live on widely separated farms or plantations as they did in Virginia, but the houses were grouped closely together in the village, around which lay the farms. The town meeting came into use first in Dorchester and Watertown in 1633. It was a clumsy and often a slow means of government, but it proved to be the greatest of all schools of political liberty. All residents of the town might attend the town meeting and speak, but only the "inhabitants," that is, the gentlemen, artisans, and freeholders, might vote. Usually, the possession of a certain amount of property was necessary to entitle one to vote in the town meeting. Outside the pale of the governing classes, there was a lower class of "cottagers," made up of strangers and day laborers, to whom the town meeting had not given any rights.

This form of town government became characteristic of New England, and was perhaps the most significant contribution of that section to the practice of government in the United States, just as the county organization was the peculiar contribution of the southern colonies. As the town meeting developed through its appropriateness to the needs of people who lived close together and farmed small areas of land, so the county government flourished in the circumstances arising from the custom of farming large plantations and from the consequent separation of homes in Virginia.

Massachusetts Laws. The colony of Massachusetts did not have a written code of laws until 1641, when, after several years of deliberation, the Body of Liberties was drawn up and adopted by the general court. The government of the colony, while it came gradually to provide a considerable degree of political freedom, never allowed religious liberty. The founders of the colony intended to provide a place where they could practice their own forms of religion and develop a "City of God" after their own pattern. They were acting consistently with their principles when they expelled from the colony Roger Williams and Anne Hutchinson, with their followers.

Rhode Island. Roger Williams opposed the union of church and state as it was practiced in the colony of Massachusetts, and Anne Hutchinson questioned the authority of some of the ministers. Williams escaped to the Narragansett Indians and later founded the colony of Rhode Island. His great purpose was to prove that a colony could be governed successfully while complete religious freedom was allowed to all its citizens. In this experiment he succeeded, being fortunate in getting encouragement both from the Long Parliament in 1644 and from Charles II after the Restoration.

Connecticut. As the founding of Rhode Island was a protest against the lack of democracy in religion in the colony of Massachusetts, so the founding of Connecticut was a protest against the aristocratic tendencies in Massachusetts politics. The inhabitants of Watertown, Dorchester, and Newtown had been leaders in the first opposition to the oligarchy set up by the assistants at the founding of the colony. In 1635, citizens of these towns began the first of those westward migrations which were to mark the next two centuries of American history. They moved into the Connecticut valley and established the towns of Hartford, Wethersfield, and Windsor. In 1639, they drew up a document which may be called the first written constitution in America, the Fundamental Orders. The new colony still maintained control of the churches, but in politics it was far more democratic than the mother colony. Voting was not restricted to church members, but was regulated by the towns until, in 1659, the general court declared that no one could be made a freeman or allowed to vote unless he possessed property to the value of 30 pounds.

New England Confederation. The next stage in the political history of New England was marked by the formation of the New England Confederation in 1643. This provided for a firm and perpetual league of the colonies of Massachusetts, Connecticut, New Haven, and Plymouth. With the restoration of the Stuarts in England in 1660, a new period of colonial history began, which was marked by efforts of the English government to draw the growing colonies into closer relations with the home government. Charles II organized a colonial department under various names. This was a wise act of statesmanship, but it aroused the colonists to greater insistence upon their right of popular government.

British Colonial Policies. During the thirty years from 1660 to 1690, several important changes occurred in the situation of the American colonies. The Dutch and Swedish possessions, which had separated the two large English settlements, were brought under English control, the wealthy colony of Pennsylvania was founded, and the Carolinas, including the territory which later became the colony of Georgia, were added to the English domain. By the year 1690, therefore, England controlled the entire coast from the Penobscot river in the North to the Savannah in the South. During these thirty years the population of the colonies increased from 60,000 to 250,000. Under the advice of his Council for Foreign Plantations, the policy of Charles II took two forms.

Navigation Acts. First came the passage of the Navigation acts, which were designed to hold the trade of the colonies for the mother country. Such a trade policy was in accord with the practices of all the nations of the time, and the English methods were far less oppressive than those of Spain or of France. The first Navigation act provided that all trade with the colonies should be carried in either English or colonial vessels. This was a positive benefit to New England, for it gave the first impetus to the great New England industry of shipbuilding. A later act restricted imports. All goods imported by the colonists had to pass through English ports. This requirement gave rise to smuggling. It is estimated that in the year 1700 one-third of the trade at the port of New York was in smuggled goods.

Colonial Charters. The second part of the policy of Charles II was concerned with controlling more closely the colonies already in existence. It is interesting to note that, in spite of the tyrannical character of the Stuart government in England, very liberal charters were granted to the heretofore unauthorized governments of Connecticut (with New Haven) and Rhode Island. On the other hand, there was continual trouble between the English government and Massachusetts, arising chiefly from the unwillingness of that colony to tolerate churches other than Puritan. So many complaints were made about this denial of civil and religious rights, that Charles sent a commission, in 1664, to hear appeals from the colonial courts. The authority of the commissioners was recognized in Connecticut, Rhode Island, and Plymouth, but the magistrates of Boston forbade recognition of the commissioners, and they were forced to leave the colony without hearing any appeals whatever. Matters dragged on until the year 1684, when the highest English court declared the Massachusetts charter of 1629 forfeited.

Consolidation of Colonies. The next move of the English government was to consolidate New England into one province. This was done by James II, who appointed Sir Edmund Andros governor-general of New England. Andros was already proprietor of New York and New Jersey, and these colonies were consolidated with New England. James struck out of the new charter all provision for any representative government, and made the governor virtually a despot. What would have been eventually the result of continuing this policy we can only imagine, for within three years the revolution of 1688 occurred in England, and in 1689, upon the accession of William III to the English throne, the colonists revived their old governments. The people of Boston and near-by towns seized the fort in the harbor and imprisoned Andros. In 1691

Massachusetts was given a new charter, which provided, among other things, that all Protestants should have religious freedom and that the franchise should be based upon a property qualification. These were important changes from the earlier government of the colony. Maine, Plymouth, and Nova Scotia were included in what was now the royal province of Massachusetts.

Cavalier Migration. During this same period the government of Virginia was subjected to important changes. Between 1650 and 1670 the colony grew rapidly and became very prosperous. A royalist immigration set in, which raised the population of the colony from 15,000 to 40,000. This was the second great colonial migration of the century. Virginia became the land of the Cavaliers. At this time the Lee family, the Masons, and the Washingtons came to Virginia, — families which were later to furnish great leaders of the Revolution. Berkeley was again appointed governor, and the colonial democracy, which had been growing in power, was changed into an oligarchy made up of the governor and a council entirely subservient to him. Under this influence, the franchise was restricted to freeholders, and for a long period even they were practically disfranchised, because, between 1660 and 1676, Berkeley permitted no election for his Cavalier assembly.

Struggles for Popular Government. The local government units in Virginia had been counties and parishes. The parish rendered such social service as taking care of the poor, and sometimes even punished minor offenses. Until 1645 the parish vestry meeting had been opened to all free white males, but in that year the parishes began to elect vestrymen. Berkeley, however, made the vestrymen's office a life position, providing that vacancies were to be filled by the vestrymen themselves. County affairs had been managed by a county court, which was a meeting of all free white males. Under Berkeley, this court was displaced by a board of eight justices, appointed by the governor. Along with these changes went serious abuses in taxation and expenditure. At the same time, Berkeley's government failed to protect the frontier against the Indians.

Out of this situation grew the uprising known as Bacon's Rebellion. As a result of this movement, some of the worst abuses introduced by Berkeley were corrected, but the aristocratic organization in both colonial and local government became permanent in Virginia. In 1686, however, the House of Burgesses, in opposition to Governor Effingham, insisted upon its right to levy taxes in spite of any veto by governor or king. This right was confirmed by William III.

The Carolinas. In response to the interest which some of his courtiers had shown in colonization, Charles II, in 1663, granted to eight proprietors the colony of Carolina. The grant, as amended in 1665, included territory between the parallels of 29° and 36° 30′ north latitude. In the case of this colony, the expected returns from trade were realized. Government of the colony, however, under various methods, including the famous plan drawn up by John Locke, proved difficult. At length, the proprietors were willing to sell their rights to the crown. In 1729 the territory was reorganized into two royal provinces, North Carolina and South Carolina; thus the more democratic northern part of the original colony was separated from the more aristocratic southern portion.

The Colony of Pennsylvania. Pennsylvania was founded as a proprietary colony, but the proprietor, William Penn, a man of large wealth and of great influence at the English court, was a friend to popular government. He had already aided some of his Quaker friends to organize the colony of New Jersey. In 1681 he received a charter for a new colony. This charter provided for religious toleration, for appeal from the colonial courts to the king, and for the right of the colonists to tax themselves. From the first, the population of Pennsylvania differed from that of the other colonies in being at least one-third non-English. It contained large settlements of German Mennonites, Moravians, Amish, and Dunkards, besides some Swedes and Dutch.

Thanks to the wise dealing of Penn, the colony was free from Indian troubles, and the large resources of English and Welsh Quakers saved it from the biting poverty that the other colonies had experienced. Nevertheless, its political history for a number of years was stormy. At length, a new charter was granted in 1701. This has been called one of the most important of American governmental documents, for it was the first written constitution to provide for its own amendment. Under this charter a single house assembly was organized, which could be dissolved only by its own vote.

Government in New York. In the matter of popular government, the colony of New York was distinctly behind its neighboring colonies. During the period of Dutch rule, there was no self-government in the colony except what was insisted upon by English settlers on Long Island. They demanded a measure of self-government from the Dutch director, Stuyvesant, in 1653, but, before any important action was taken, the colony fell into the hands of the English. King Charles gave the province to his brother James, duke of York, with arbitrary power. The insistence of the English towns on Long Island compelled the introduction of a representative assembly in 1682, though the governor of New York still retained more power than the governor in any other of the colonies.

Growth of Population. The period from 1690 to 1760 in America was one of very remarkable growth in wealth and population. At the beginning of this period, the total population of the colonies, including Georgia, was about 250,000; at the end of the period, about 1,600,000. It has been noted already that Pennsylvania had in the beginning a large German population. Many of these Germans had been driven from their homes in South Germany by religious persecution. After 1683, a great many Huguenots, exiled from France by the persecutions of Louis XIV, came to the English colonies. Most of them settled in the Carolinas, but many historic names indicate their presence in the northern colonies also. Among such names are those of Paul Revere, the hero of Lexington, and Peter Faneuil, the builder of Faneuil Hall.

Another large element of the 18th century immigration was made up of the so-called Scotch-Irish, who between 1730 and 1750, it is said, came to America at the rate of 12,000 a year. They settled principally in what was then the back country of Virginia and Pennsylvania. Later, they were in the van of migration across the mountains into the territory of Kentucky and Tennessee. It has been remarked that these people, descendants of Saxon English who had lived for centuries in the Scottish lowlands, were the first of the American colonists to turn their faces away from the Old World, thus marking the real beginnings of America.

Contest for the Continent. During this period, Spain still held a strip of territory in Florida and along the coast of the Gulf of Mexico, and her missionaries were beginning their settlements on the coast of California. She was, however, clearly out of the race for control of the North American continent. The struggle for this lay between England and France. At the close of the 17th century, the English held a narrow domain between the Appalachian mountains and the Atlantic coast and a district around Hudson bay. The French were in control of the St. Lawrence valley. In 1682, moreover, the intrepid La Salle, after having made the long journey from Lake Ontario southwest to the mouth of the Mississippi, had taken possession of the Mississippi valley for the French king, Louis XIV,

COLONIAL WARS

Remote and Immediate Causes: (1) The Colonial wars in America were incidents in the general European wars which involved England and France upon opposite sides. (2) They were immediately occasioned by the unavoidable struggle of the two nations to control the continent of North America.

Historic Name	Chief Battles	Leaders		Victor	Results
		English	French		
King William's War, 1689-97.	Schenectady, Feb. 8, 1690	Colonists	Iberville	French	War terminated by Treaty of Ryswick (1697), each side retaining the territory held prior to the war. French retain Quebec. The "Five Nations" subdued.
	New Eng'nd Massacres, March 1690-97	Colonists	Frontenac	French	
	Siege of Quebec, April 1690	Phipps	Frontenac	French	
	Attacks on the "Five Nations," 1693-97	Indians	Frontenac	Indians	
Queen Anne's War, 1702-13.	Deerfield Massacre, Feb. 29, 1704	Colonists	Indians	Indians	Settled by Treaty of Utrecht. Hudson Bay and its borders, Acadia and Newfoundland, ceded to England by France.
	Haverhill Massacre, Aug. 29, 1708	Colonists	Hertel		
	Conquest of Nova Scotia, 1710	Nicholson	Subercase	English	
King George's War, 1744-48.	Capture of Louisburg, June 17, 1745	Pepperell	Duchambon	English	Louisburg was returned to the French by the Treaty of Aix-la-Chapelle, Oct. 7, 1748.
French and Indian War, 1754-63.	Surrender of Fort Necessity, July 4, 1754	Washington	Villiers	French	In 1763, by the Treaty of Paris, France ceded to England, Canada and all her possessions lying east of the Mississippi river; to Spain, New Orleans and all her possessions west of the Mississippi. The transfer from the French to the British of the posts between the Great Lakes and the Ohio river led to a war with the Indian tribes, in which the leading figure was Pontiac. The French and Indian war convinced the colonists of the necessity of union.
	Expedition against Fort Duquesne, July 9, 1755	Braddock	Beaujeu	French	
	Deportations of Acadians, June 16-17, 1755.				
	Capture of Louisburg, July 26, 1758	Amherst	Drucour	English	
	Capture of Fort Duquesne, Nov. 25, 1758	Forbes	?	English	
	Capture of Fort Niagara, July 1759	Johnson	D'Aubry	English	
	Capture of Fort Ticonderoga, July 26, 1759	Amherst	Bourlamaque	English	
	Capture of Quebec, Sept. 13, 1759	Wolfe	Montcalm	English	

naming it Louisiana. The contest began in the way of peaceful penetration, but the Indians were frequently stirred up by both sides, and between 1689 and 1763 four wars were fought by the contending parties. At length, by the treaty of 1763, at the close of the French and Indian war, France lost Canada and, consequently, her line of outposts in the Mississippi valley. After this event, England's position in America was to depend entirely upon her treatment of the colonies.

Movement toward Self-Government. The defeat of the French in Canada removed from the colonies all feeling of dependence upon England for protection against any foreign power. They were free to insist upon their rights. But, apparently oblivious of this fact, England, in her colonial policy, blundered continuously and stupidly, until the patience of the colonists was exhausted and American independence became a fact. These blunders in the policy of England are clearly revealed in the two fields of industry and politics.

English Restriction on Industry. First, the development of industry in the colonies occasioned several restrictions which were designed to eliminate colonial competition with England. In 1696, colonists were forbidden to export any woolen manufactures. Later acts limited the fabrication of iron products. Even when these restrictions were not burdensome, they gave rise to irritation and to the suspicion that the English government did not look with favor upon the rise of a free people in America.

Political Control. The most important movements of the 18th century, however, were those concerned with the form of colonial government and the control of taxes. The English Board of Trade, which had taken the place of Charles II's Council for Foreign Plantations, found many things to criticize in the conduct of the colonists. The Navigation laws were evaded; smuggling, as well as trade with pirates, was a general practice; and the colonies were notably careless in provision for their own defense. In 1701 a proposal was introduced in Parliament to unite all the colonies in one province. This aroused great opposition in America, and the bill was never passed. Steady progress was made, however, in converting the colonies into royal provinces. Only Connecticut and Rhode Island, at the outbreak of the Revolution, possessed the privilege of electing all branches of their governments. On the whole, in spite of the attempt at greater royal control, and notwithstanding increases in the authority of royal governors, the colonial assemblies maintained their rights of taxation and even somewhat enlarged them. They used without stint their power over the governor through their control of his salary. It was the custom to make the fixing of the governor's salary the last business of the legislative session, a practice which proved effective in preventing a governor from vetoing bills.

Colonial Life. Life in the English colonies during the latter part of the 17th century and during the 18th exhibited great variety in customs and industry. This diversity was due, in the first place, to the variant native characteristics of the different groups of people who made up the colonies, and, in the second place, to the wide range of conditions of soil and climate. In the South, industry was almost entirely agricultural. Tobacco raising was the chief occupation of the people upon large plantations worked by slaves. The Virginia plantation was an industrial unit in itself, and the product of the plantation, mostly tobacco, was loaded on ships at the plantation wharf and sent to England. The ships brought back supplies of various kinds, but most of the clothing and the simpler utensils of the workers on the plantations were made in the plantation shops. Each great farm had its blacksmith and woodworking shops. The mistress of the plantation supervised the spinning and weaving and the preparation and preserving of food.

In the middle colonies, such as Pennsylvania, foodstuffs were raised, and the German colonists maintained, upon a small scale, many industries, including the manufacture of linen, pottery, and clothing. New England was the real district of the small farm, although its two most characteristic industries were fishing and shipbuilding. New Englanders also carried on a rich trade with the other colonies, and indeed with all parts of the world. The possession of water power to operate sawmills enabled them to build up a particularly large trade in lumber.

Slaves and Servants. There were negro slaves in all the colonies, though in New England most of the labor was free. The middle colonies had a large number of white bond servants, some of whom had sold their time to the extent of from four to seven years as the price of the voyage to America, while others were convicts who had been transported from England. While some of these convicts were of an undesirable class and made much trouble in the colonies, the severe English laws caused the "transportation" of many persons who proved themselves good citizens. One of these, a convicted thief, later became attorney-general of Virginia, and it is said that most of the tutors and teachers in Maryland, just before the Revolution, had come to America under sentence for offenses against English law.

Education. Education in most of the colonies was sadly neglected. Although parents were required by law to have their children taught the rudiments of knowledge, many of them lacked the ability and the time to carry out these requirements. In some parts of the colonies, church schools were established. The wealthy planters of the South employed private tutors for their families. At the very beginning of their history, Massachusetts and Connecticut had established school systems, but the work of these schools was severely limited by the primitive conditions of life and by the poverty of many settlements. The most important service of these early institutions in New England was the preservation of the ideal of an educated citizenship. Nine colleges were established in the colonies in the 17th and the 18th century, up to the period of the Revolution.

Questions of Taxation. The close of the wars with France left the English government with a serious financial problem on its hands. The cost of the wars had been heavy. It seemed that the colonists, who were highly prosperous and had scarcely any public debt, should help to carry the load. Unfortunately for the English government, however, the antagonism of the colonists had already been aroused when, in 1755, the writs of assistance came into use. These were warrants by which an English officer might search any house or place of business, merely upon suspicion that the owner had been trading with the French and furnishing them with supplies. The prevalence of such trade was not denied, but the colonists were alive to the danger which lay in the use of general search warrants. In 1761, when application was made to the superior court of Massachusetts for renewal of the writs of assistance in that colony, James Otis, the advocate-general, resigned his office and opposed the granting of the writs. He lost his case, but his argument opened the whole question of Parliamentary government of the colonies.

The Sugar Act. In 1733 a sugar act had been passed as a part of the Navigation laws, whose purpose was to restrict colonial trade to England. The colonists had never seriously objected to these Navigation laws, and many of the acts had been helpful. But now, in 1764, a new sugar act was passed, not as a trade law, but as a means of taxing the colonies for revenue. The act laid a tax upon sugar imported from the French West Indies, and the tax was made so heavy as practically to stop this very profitable trade of the New England and middle colonies. The tax did not, however, affect the southern colonies, and, therefore, it was not a means of unifying the sentiment of the colonists, as the Stamp act, passed in 1765, proved to be.

The Stamp Act. The English government insisted that it must have revenue and proposed the stamp tax method in 1764, giving the agents of the colonies a year to propose some other means of raising money. But the absence of any general government or central authority in the colonies, as well as the great differences of sentiment among the colonists themselves, made any counter proposal impossible. Protests were sent to the English ministry from all the colonies, but without producing any effect. The law was enacted in March 1765. Opposition to the sugar act had been based upon its interference with trade; it resulted in actual money loss to the colonists. The stamp tax ushered in a new era of opposition, for now the colonists contended against the principle of the tax. They were not concerned with the immediate money burden placed upon them, but with the possible future use of such a tax, if once they permitted the English government to impose it.

Opposition to England. Several of the colonial assemblies passed resolutions, condemning the Stamp act and asserting their right to be taxed only by a body in which they were represented. The most forcible of these resolutions were introduced by Patrick Henry in the Virginia assembly, when he used the expressions, "Cæsar had his Brutus, Charles I his Cromwell, and George III—may profit by their example." At the invitation of the Massachusetts assembly, the Stamp Act Congress met in New York, October 7, 1765. This congress drew up a petition to the British government, together with a statement of the rights and liberties of the colonists. The society of the Sons of Liberty was organized for the purpose of compelling people to comply with the agreements not to import British goods. It was at first a secret society, but later it became public and very effective.

The Townshend Acts. So intense was the opposition that, in 1766, a new ministry secured the repeal of the Stamp act, with the provision, however, that Parliament still retained its authority to tax the colonies. In 1767 the prime minister, Townshend, secured the passage of a series of acts which placed duties on several articles of import into the colonies, among which glass, paper, and tea were included. Previous attempts at taxation had been justified by the plea that money was needed to protect the colonies. The proceeds of the Stamp act had been pledged beforehand for this purpose. Now, however, the revenue from the Townshend duties was to be used for the payment of colonial governors and judges. This proposal struck at the very heart of the independence of colonial assemblies, because the principle was well recognized, that the governor and judge served the party who appointed and paid them. Trials for evasion of the Townshend acts were to be held in courts of admiralty without juries. This again was a violation of a cherished principle in colonial government.

Further Provocation and Controversy. Throughout the three years during which the Townshend acts remained in force, the opposition of the colonists, through their legislatures and by mob violence, never ceased. In 1769 Parliament provided by a treason act that a colonist accused of treason should be taken to England for trial. The assembly of Virginia, which had not been seriously affected by the Townshend acts themselves, was aroused by this violation of the principle of jury trial. It adopted unanimously a resolution condemning both the Townshend laws and the treason act. This was followed by agreements among the colonies not to import merchandise from England until the objectionable acts were repealed. Fuel was added to the flames by the sending of troops to Boston in 1768, to aid the governor in maintaining order. The immediate result of this attempt to overawe the colonists was a settled hostility between citizens and soldiers, which resulted in the Boston Massacre of 1770.

Committees of Correspondence. The revenue collected under the Townshend acts amounted to about one-tenth of the cost of collecting it. On the day of the Boston Massacre, Lord North moved the repeal of these acts, except that providing a tax on tea. The tea tax was kept as a mark of the supremacy of Parliament. During the next two years, the British ministry persisted in various arbitrary orders which interfered with the liberties of the colonial legislatures. The assemblies protested, and the governors dissolved them. The result was the organization of provisional governments. Under the leadership of Samuel Adams, the towns of Massachusetts organized town committees of correspondence in 1772. Virginia in the following year took a further step, prompted thereto by the incident of the *Gaspee*. English officers had attempted to arrest some Rhode Islanders, suspected of burning the revenue ship *Gaspee*, and to take them to England for trial. On March 12, 1773, the Virginia House of Burgesses appointed a committee for intercolonial correspondence and invited the other colonies to take similar measures.

Boston Tea Party and the First Congress. Meanwhile, the English government attempted to force upon the colonists the tea of the British East India Company. The duty on tea was lowered to such a point that the company could sell it to the colonists more cheaply than they could buy smuggled tea. Under this arrangement, large cargoes were sent to the American ports. At Charleston, South Carolina, the tea was seized and stored. At New York, Annapolis, and Philadelphia, the authorities were compelled to send the tea ships back to England. But a group of the people of Boston held the famous "tea party," when large quantities of tea were thrown from the East India ships into the harbor.

To punish the Bostonians, the English government passed the Boston Port bill in 1774, closing the port to all commerce. This was deemed as harsh a blow as could be delivered to any commercial, maritime town. But the result was that food and supplies were poured in from all parts of the colonies, the merchants of Salem offered Boston merchants the use of their wharves, and the committees of correspondence in the colonies immediately proceeded to consider means of redress. The House of Burgesses in Virginia set apart June 1, 1774, on which day the port bill became effective, as a day of fasting and prayer. The governor dissolved the assembly two days later, but the burgesses met at a tavern, and recommended an annual congress of delegates from all the colonies to consider their united interests. On August 1, at Williamsburg, they appointed delegates to such a congress. Other colonies took similar action, some in the regular assemblies, but many of them in irregular meetings of legislators or citizens. Thus the members of the First Continental Congress were chosen to meet at Philadelphia on September 5, 1774.

Self-Government. English authority had now broken down in the colonies. The colonists were governing themselves through agencies which were really revolutionary legislatures and committees. Actual independence, however, was not yet considered, and the congress which had been called was to be only an informal conference. This was its actual character. Its most important act was to recommend agreements among the colonies neither to import nor to export English goods. This recommendation and others were considered and adopted by the revolutionary bodies in the various colonies. Before its adjournment, the First Continental Congress arranged for calling a second congress to meet in May 1775, if the grievances of the colonies had not been redressed before that time.

Concord and Lexington. Most of the members of the First Continental Congress, in common with the majority of the people in the colonies, believed that a peaceful settlement of the difficulties with England was possible, but, before the second congress met, trouble had broken out in Massachusetts and war had become a fact. The leaders in Massachusetts had organized a revolutionary body called the Provincial Congress, within which was created a committee of safety. This committee, among its varied activities, organized a body of militia called minutemen.

General Howe, who was in command of the British garrison at Boston, planned to arrest John Hancock and Samuel Adams, the leaders of the patriots. For the purpose of seizing the two men and also of destroying some military stores of the patriots at Concord, a force of 800 men was sent out from Boston on the night of April 18, 1775. Warning of this movement was carried through the countryside by Paul Revere and other riders, and, when the British appeared at Lexington on the morning of April 19, they found a small body of minutemen drawn up on the village green. Seven of the patriot force were killed and nine were wounded by the fire of the British troops. Later in the morning, the minutemen made a stand at the North bridge at Concord. The British were forced to retreat, and during the day the militia took revenge in harassing the British column on its march from Concord back to Boston. In this running fight, 273 British and 93 Americans were killed. The result of the day's conflict was to encourage the people in the other colonies to drive out their governors and to proceed more rapidly with the formation of revolutionary congresses and conventions.

The Second Congress. When the Second Continental Congress, composed of representatives from all of the thirteen colonies, met in Philadelphia on May 10, 1775, it had to set about the business of organizing for war. The congress had no formal authority from the colonies, but depended altogether upon their general good will and assent. It must be remembered that the Revolutionary War was not a struggle of united colonists in America against a united England, but rather, in reality, a civil war in the colonies, both sides having sympathizers in the mother country. It is estimated that at least one-third of the colonists were Tories or Loyalists, while many of the other two-thirds were only half-hearted in their support of resistance to English authority. Nevertheless, the Second Continental Congress ordered the colonies to be put into a state of defense, organized a post office, voted to raise an army, appointed George Washington commander in chief, and began to consider Franklin's proposal of a federal constitution.

Bunker Hill. Massachusetts, however, had acted without authority from Congress. Twenty thousand militia laid siege to the British in Boston. Patriots intrenched themselves on Bunker Hill, June 17, 1775, but were driven out by the British. This battle of Bunker Hill, however, was really a victory for the colonists, since it showed that they could fight the British regulars and inflict severe losses upon them. Washington took command of the force of militia intrenched around Boston, and in the early spring of 1776 he fortified Dorchester Heights and compelled the British force of 10,000 to leave the city. Meanwhile, General Montgomery and Benedict Arnold led two small detachments of troops into Canada, but they failed to get the support of the Canadians.

The story of the Revolution from this time forward has two phases. The military history is made up of a long series of conflicts on sea and land, with but few important pitched battles. The civil history is concerned with the struggle of the various colonies to maintain their new governments, to suppress or expel the Tories, and to agree upon a plan of union.

REVOLUTIONARY WAR

Contributing Causes: Unjust Legislation; Taxation without Representation; Infringements of the Rights of the Colonists by Great Britain.

Campaigns	Chief Battles	American Leaders	American Troops	British Leaders	British Troops	Victor	Results
Contest for control of Boston.	Lexington and Concord, April 19, 1775	Parker, Heath	500	Smith, Lord Percy	1,700	Amer.	British besieged in Boston after battle of Bunker Hill.
	Bunker Hill, June 17, 1775.	Prescott, Warren	1,500	Howe	2,500	Brit.	
	Dorchester Heights, Mar. 4, 1776	Washington, Thomas	2,500	Howe	10,000	Amer.	Howe and his army evacuate Boston March 17, 1776, leaving guns and supplies.
American invasion of Canada.	Ticonderoga, May 10, 1775.	Ethan Allen	83	Delaplace	48	Amer.	Ticonderoga captured. Fruitless siege of Quebec. Ethan Allen captured. Invaders dispersed.
	Montreal, Nov. 12, 1775	Montgomery	2,000	Carleton	?	Amer.	
	Quebec, Dec. 31, 1775	Arnold	900	Carleton	1,200	Brit.	
Attack on Charleston.	Fort Moultrie, June 28, 1776	Moultrie	435	Clinton	?	Amer.	British abandon the attack and sail for New York.
Struggle for control of the City of New York and for New Jersey.	Long Island, Aug. 27, 1776.	Sullivan, Putnam	5,000	Howe	20,000	Brit.	Americans forced across the Hudson. British occupy New York City. American forces inspired to renewed efforts. British forces evacuate New Jersey.
	Harlem Heights, Sept. 15, 1776	Washington.	12,000	Howe	25,000	Brit.	
	White Plains, Oct. 28, 1776.	Washington.	1,400	Howe	4,000	Brit.	
	Fort Washington, Nov. 16, 1776	Magaw	3,000	Howe	5,000	Brit.	
	Trenton, Dec. 25, 1776	Washington.	2,400	Rall	1,600	Amer.	
	Princeton, Jan. 3, 1777	Washington.	5,000	Mawhood	1,200	Amer.	
British attempt to control the Hudson and to divide the colonies. Burgoyne's invasion from the north.	Ticonderoga, July 6, 1777.	St. Clair	2,500	Burgoyne.	7,500	Brit.	Americans control the Hudson valley, New York, and New England. Burgoyne's surrender, Oct. 17, 1777, marks the turning point of the war.
	Oriskany, Aug. 6, 1777	Herkimer	800	St. Leger	1,200	Amer.	
	Bennington, Aug. 16, 1777.	Stark	2,000	Baum	1,200	Amer.	
	Fort Stanwix, Aug. 22, 1777	Arnold	800	St. Leger	?	Amer.	
	Bemis Heights, or Stillwater, Sept. 19, 1777	Gates, Lincoln, Arnold	2,500	Burgoyne.	6,000	Amer.	
	Bemis Heights, Oct. 7, 1777	Gates, Arnold	8,000	Burgoyne.	5,000	Amer.	
British attack on Philadelphia.	Brandywine, Sept. 11, 1777.	Washington.	11,000	Howe	17,000	Brit.	Howe's army enters and occupies Philadelphia during the winter.
	Germantown, Oct. 4, 1777.	Washington.	10,000	Howe	15,000	Brit.	
British retreat from Philadelphia, begun June 18, 1778.	Monmouth, June 28, 1778.	Washington.	12,000	Clinton	10,000	Amer.	British return to New York.
Indian massacres.	Wyoming, July 4, 1778	Zeb. Butler	400	Butler	1,100	Brit.	
	Cherry Valley, Nov. 11, 1778	Alden	?	Butler, Brant	800?	Brit.	
Expedition for control of the Western frontier.	Kaskaskia, July 4, 1778	Clark	200	Indians.	?	Amer.	Americans establish claim to possession of the Northwest.
	Vincennes, Feb. 14, 1779	Clark	170	Hamilton	500	Amer.	
Campaign for control of the South by British.	Savannah, Dec. 29, 1778	R. Howe	900	Campbell	2,000	Brit.	Georgia reduced to submission.
	Savannah, Oct. 9, 1779	Lincoln	4,500	Prevost	2,500	Brit.	
Battle for control of the Hudson.	Stony Point, July 15, 1779.	Wayne	1,200	Clinton	600	Amer.	Continental army encouraged.
Naval operations.	*Bon Homme Richard* and *Serapis*, Sept. 23, 1779	J. Paul Jones		Pearson		Amer.	
American expedition against the Indians.	Newtown (Elmira, N. Y.), Aug. 29, 1779	Sullivan	5,000	Johnson, Brant	1,500	Amer.	"Six Nations" weakened.

REVOLUTIONARY WAR—Con.

Campaigns	Chief Battles	American Leaders	American Troops	British Leaders	British Troops	Victor	Results
Campaigns for control of the South; conflict in North and South Carolina.	Charleston, May 12, 1780.	Lincoln	3,700	Clinton	9,000	Brit.	British in possession of the South.
	Camden, Aug. 16, 1780	Gates	3,000	Cornwallis	2,000	Brit.	
	King's Mountain, Oct. 7, 1780	Shelby, Sevier	1,000	Ferguson	1,100	Amer.	
	Cowpens, Jan. 17, 1781	Morgan	900	Tarleton	1,100	Amer.	British forced to retire towards Charleston.
	Guilford Court House, March 15, 1781	Greene	4,400	Cornwallis	2,200	Brit.	Americans in control of the South.
	Hobkirk's Hill, April 25, 1781	Greene	940	Rawdon	900	Brit.	
	Eutaw Springs, Sept. 8, 1781	Greene	2,000	Stuart	2,500	Amer.	
Invasion of Virginia.	Siege of Yorktown; surrender, Oct. 19, 1781	Washington, Rochambeau, De Grasse (navy)	20,000	Cornwallis, Graves (navy)	8,000	Amer.	Surrender of Cornwallis. Contest terminated.

Result of War: Preliminary treaty of peace signed at Paris, November 30, 1782. Final and definitive treaty signed at Versailles, September 3, 1783, by which the United States were formally acknowledged by Great Britain to be free, sovereign, and independent. United States territory extended from the Atlantic to the Mississippi, from Florida to Canada.

Independence. Sentiment in favor of independence was crystallized during the spring of 1776 by the publication of Thomas Paine's pamphlet entitled *Common Sense.* Virginia's convention, which met on May 6, 1776, instructed its representatives to move in the Continental Congress for a declaration of independence.

Following instructions, Richard Henry Lee, on June 7, 1776, moved that the united colonies should be free and independent states. The first vote, taken on July 1, showed nine states in favor; on the following day twelve voted yes, and the declaration was adopted on July 4. The delegates from New York did not vote, because they had no instructions from the provisional congress of that colony. New York's approval was given on the 9th of July. On August 2 the official copy was signed by the members of the Congress who were present.

State Constitutions. In reality, the colonies had been acting independently even before the declaration of independence. After the battle of Lexington, several colonies applied to the Congress for advice. The Congress advised New Hampshire to set up such a government as seemed necessary "during the continuance of the present dispute between Great Britain and the colonies." In May 1776, a general resolution was adopted, advising the colonies to form governments for themselves whenever the old government had broken down. Virginia adopted its constitution in June 1776. The first part of this Virginia constitution was a bill of rights, the first document of its kind drawn up in America. This became a model for the bills of rights in the later state constitutions. It stated the rights of man as general principles, rather than as particular privileges, such as that of self-taxation. Jefferson placed similar statements in the Declaration of Independence.

Provisions of First State Constitutions. Several characteristics of these constitutions deserve notice. Some of them were made under the impression that the colonies would remain under the rule of England, but they were all republican in form. They provided for an executive, who was called either governor or president, and for courts and legislatures. The legislatures, however, were given large powers of control over both the executive and the judiciary. Nearly every constitution contained a bill of rights. Several of them had no provision for amendment, although today this is regarded as one of the most important parts of a constitution. All maintained some sort of religious discrimination. Throughout the colonies, the suffrage for local elections was made more general than it had been, but the privilege of voting was still restricted in some way in all the colonies. The most democratic provisions permitted only taxpayers to vote.

Officeholding and Voting. Nor did the privilege of voting carry the privilege of holding office, at least in respect to colonial offices. In North Carolina, to be elected governor, it was required that a man must own real estate to the value of 1000 pounds. In Massachusetts, a member of the lower house of the general court had to own at least 1000 pounds in real estate or 200 pounds in other property; a senator, three times as much. Most of these constitutions were drawn up and adopted by conventions or congresses in the colonies. In Massachusetts, a referendum was demanded, and it was not until 1780 that the constitution of that state was adopted. The mechanics of New York City, who were largely of New England descent, demanded a referendum in New York, but none was ever held.

Military Movements. Meanwhile, the military campaigns were dragging on under most discouraging conditions for Washington and his little army. From the first, the colonies were unwilling to enlist troops for long service. Consequently, the number of troops at Washington's command varied considerably from time to time. The Continental Congress proved weak and undependable in its provision of funds and supplies. This was due in part to the very nature of a government which had no central authority. Washington was continually subject to interference and slights, which he bore with an admirable patience and self-control. He never had more than 40,000 men under arms at one time, and his forces often dwindled to four or five thousand. This condition persisted in a country that might with ease have put 300,000 men in the field. On the other hand, the British had hired 30,000 Hessians for service in the colonies. Both sides enlisted the Indians, but the British had the greater number of them in their service, because both the Iroquois in New York and the Indians of the West recognized that the colonists were their real enemies.

Following the evacuation of Boston in the spring of 1776, the British were defeated in an attempt to take the city of Charleston, South Carolina. In this battle, Sergeant Jasper, by his rescue of the colors of Fort Moultrie, began his brave and romantic career. In August, however, the British landed an army of 25,000 men on Long Island, and the Americans were compelled to withdraw after severe defeats in the battles of Long Island and White Plains. It appears that only the heroic work of Robert Morris, who raised funds on his private credit to supply the army, prevented the collapse of the Revolution at this point. Washington was able to encourage the patriots by his victories at Trenton and Princeton in the early winter.

In the spring of 1777, the British planned to divide the colonists by bringing a force under General Burgoyne from Canada down Lake Champlain and the Hudson, to be joined by General Howe. Burgoyne advanced and issued very boastful proclamations, but the colonists rallied from all sides. General Howe embarked from New York in August 1777, to attempt the capture of Philadelphia. He defeated Washington at the battle of Brandywine in September. Washington, however, in addition to keeping Howe occupied around Philadelphia, sent men north to Schuyler, who was obstructing Burgoyne's progress, while a body of patriots under General Herkimer defeated a British expedition from Canada at the battle of Oriskany on August 6. Burgoyne was thus deprived of expected help from the West, and, as Clinton failed to move up the Hudson to meet him, while the farmers of Vermont, New Hampshire, and Massachusetts rose to attack him, he was compelled to surrender his entire force at Saratoga in October 1777. This defeat of Burgoyne is generally reckoned as the turning point of the Revolution, because it aroused in the French government sufficient confidence in the colonial cause to prompt the aid which came from France in the next year.

French Alliance. During the winter of 1777, Washington's troops endured great suffering at Valley Forge, while the British held the capital, Philadelphia. Benjamin Franklin secured a treaty of alliance with France early in 1778, and the coming of French forces compelled the English to evacuate Philadelphia. Washington pursued them across New Jersey, but by treachery he was prevented from completely defeating them at Monmouth, and they succeeded in regaining their base at New York City.

War in the South. The war was now transferred in the main to the southern colonies, and became largely a series of raids against towns and countrysides, directed by colonial Loyalists who were familiar with the country. The patriots, Marion and Sumter, maintained a vigorous guerrilla warfare. General Gates was defeated by the British at the battle of Camden in August 1780, but the battle of King's Mountain was won in October by the settlers from west of the mountains.

Surrender of Cornwallis. In 1781 General Nathanael Greene was put in command of the American forces in the South. Cornwallis withdrew into Virginia, and was besieged at Yorktown by Greene and Lafayette. A French fleet blockaded Chesapeake bay and prevented re-enforcements from reaching Cornwallis. Washington, with a French force under Rochambeau, went to the aid of Greene, and Cornwallis was compelled to surrender his whole army, October 19, 1781. His capitulation virtually ended the war.

Efforts at Confederation. The effort to secure a formal union of the states began almost as soon as the Second Continental Congress met, and a plan was at length drawn up and proposed under the title of Articles of Confederation. The ratification of these articles was not completed until 1781, the chief cause of the delay being the questions which arose over the disposition of the western lands. While the war was going on, along the Atlantic seaboard, important events were happening in the West, which affected the negotiations for peace and the whole history of the country thereafter.

Occupation of Western Lands. The territory west of the Allegheny mountains, as far as the Mississippi, formerly in the hands of the French, had come into British possession by the treaty of 1763. After the war with Pontiac in 1763-64, the British government had proclaimed this section closed to settlement and reserved for the Indians. Detroit was made the seat of government for the region. The principal French settlements were at Vincennes on the Wabash river and at Kaskaskia on the Mississippi. The town of Pittsburgh had been founded on the site of Fort Pitt shortly after the close of the French and Indian war. Frontiersmen of Scotch-Irish and of German blood, together with some Huguenots, ignored the British proclamation and crossed the mountains into the western wilderness. In 1774, Parliament, by the Quebec act, united to the Province of Quebec all the region between the Ohio river and the Great Lakes, thus indicating that new colonies were not wanted in that territory.

Kentucky Pioneers. Just as the Revolution was breaking out, Daniel Boone blazed the pack trail, known as the "wilderness road," through the Cumberland gap into Kentucky, and a little later Boonesboro and Harrodsburg were founded. People of this region petitioned Congress to admit them as a fourteenth state of the Confederation, but Virginia organized the country south of the Ohio in 1776 as Kentucky county. Farther south, the Watauga settlement was made, in a region included in North Carolina's western claims.

During the next few years, the frontier was subjected to the horrors of Indian warfare, in spite of the efforts of Congress to placate the Indians. The Iroquois in New York were finally subdued by General Sullivan in 1779.

George Rogers Clark. In 1778-79, George Rogers Clark led a notable expedition down the Ohio river and into the Illinois country, where he took the towns of Kaskaskia, Cahokia, and Vincennes, enlisting the aid of the French residents. Clark had been commissioned by Virginia, and that state now erected the territory between the Ohio and the Mississippi and the Great Lakes into the county of Illinois.

The Confederation. The Articles of Confederation went into effect on March 1, 1781. Congress then proceeded to authorize the survey of the western territory by the Land act of 1785, and the Ordinance of 1787 provided for the government of the Northwest Territory. The disputed lands south of the Ohio river were soon formed into the states of Kentucky and Tennessee.

Despite the late date for the adoption of the Articles of Confederation, Congress, under the necessity of providing for war, had long been acting on the assumption that the articles would certainly be ratified; the executive and judicial offices had already been organized.

Treaty of Peace. It now fell to the United States to conclude a treaty of peace with England. Benjamin Franklin, John Adams, John Jay, and Henry Laurens were appointed to conduct the negotiations. They were instructed, in accordance with the alliance of 1778, to take no step without the approval of the French government, but, when it appeared that the French, owing to Spanish influence, did not desire to make boundary concessions west of the Appalachians, the American envoys agreed to ignore their instructions. As a consequence, they secured a very favorable treaty, which was signed in preliminary form, November 30, 1782. The final treaty was completed in 1783. The United States of America was at last recognized by Great Britain as independent.

Weakness of the Confederation. Very soon the serious weaknesses of the Confederation began to appear. Congress was merely a body of delegates elected by the legislatures of the states. It possessed no adequate powers for dealing with foreign nations; it had no real authority over the people themselves; it could not control commerce either between the states or with foreign countries. Moreover, Congress had no adequate means of raising funds to carry on its work. And, finally, amendment of the Articles of Confederation proved impossible.

Need for Strong Central Government. Washington and other leaders saw the conditions clearly, and urged provision for a stronger government. Not only was the power of Congress at a low ebb, but the rapid changes in state governments had in some cases weakened the authority of the law within the states themselves. The conditions in many places could be described only as anarchy. Both the Confederation and the states were deeply in debt. Both had issued paper money to the extent of many millions of dollars, which had so depreciated that, at the end of the war, one specie dollar would purchase a thousand dollars in the continental currency. In 1786, delegates from several states met at Annapolis to consider questions of common interest. One result of this meeting was a call for the states to elect delegates to a convention for the purpose of revising the Articles of Confederation. All the states except Rhode Island finally sent delegates.

The Constitutional Convention. The convention met in Philadelphia in May 1787. Its members represented the ablest men in America, including such leaders as Benjamin Franklin, Alexander Hamilton, William Patterson of New Jersey, James Wilson of Pennsylvania, John Jay, George Washington, and James Madison. Of these men, Madison probably did the most to secure agreement among the sharply divided parties in the convention. Three great difficulties presented themselves: (1) adjustment of the interests of the small and the large states; (2) treatment of slavery; (3) control over commerce. No more thorough discussion of the fundamentals and details of a great instrument of government has ever occupied the minds of legislators than that which was conducted in Philadelphia between May 25, 1787 and September 17 following, when the Constitution was signed by 39 of the original 55 members of the convention.

Compromises. A series of compromises had made possible the framing of the new constitution. (1) The differences between the small and the large states were reconciled by giving to all the states equal representation in the Senate, and by apportioning membership in the House of Representatives according to the population of each state. (2) The slavery compromise provided that the slave trade should not be prohibited before the year 1808 and also that, in the apportionment of representation and direct taxes according to population, five slaves should count as three free persons. (3) In respect to commerce, Congress was empowered to lay duties upon imports and to regulate interstate commerce, but was forbidden to levy taxes upon exports.

Ratification. There remained the difficult task of getting the Constitution ratified by the states. Its supporters went out to work for its ratification, under the name of Federalists. To their opponents the name Antifederalists was applied. Alexander Hamilton, James Madison, and John Jay published in New York newspapers a series of articles in defense of the Constitution, signed "Federalist." Their discussion was very influential in the campaign which was waged with great bitterness, especially in Massachusetts, Virginia, and New York. The assent of nine states was necessary to adoption, and New Hampshire ratified as the ninth state, May 23, 1788. Others followed, Rhode Island finally in 1790. Certain objections urged by the Antifederalists were removed by the adoption of the first ten amendments (1791), which added to the Constitution a bill of rights.

Population. A glimpse at the diversities of population and at the conditions of intercourse and industry in the United States about the year 1790 helps one to understand some of the difficulties which threatened the new union, as well as the elements of strength which promised well for it. In 1790 the total population of the United States was 3,930,000, excluding 80,000 Indians. Sixty thousand of the inhabitants were free negroes and 700,000 were slaves. In all the states, the English race was predominant. About 300,000 Scotch-Irish were scattered throughout the colonies, chiefly on the frontier. New York had a small Dutch population. Most of the 175,000 Germans lived in Pennsylvania and in the great valley to the southward. There was a small Huguenot group in the Carolinas. Nine-tenths of the people lived in the country. Philadelphia was the largest city, with about 42,000 people, and Louisville on the Ohio river was the town farthest west.

Agriculture. Some changes in agriculture had taken place since the middle of the 18th century. The most valuable crop in 1790 was wheat. Rice was becoming an important crop in the South. Cotton was not yet extensively raised, because of the great expense in the employment of hand labor to separate the fiber from the seed. This situation was changed by Whitney's invention of the cotton gin in 1793. Cotton growing then became profitable.

Manufactures. By the year 1800, manufacturing had increased considerably in the middle and northern states. Philadelphia exported about 300,000 barrels of flour a year. In New England the spinning and weaving industries had not yet developed. There was no power loom in America until 1814, when one was set up at Waltham, Massachusetts, by F. C. Lowell.

Commerce. Large numbers of New Englanders were engaged in the China and East India trade. American inventors had begun to show the ability for which they later became famous. John Fitch ran a steamboat on the Delaware river in 1787. Communication between the colonies was difficult because of the lack of good roads, but between 1790 and 1800 many roads were built from the East across the mountains, and in the eastern parts of the colonies numerous turnpikes or stone roads were constructed. A few canals were built, but, for the most part, such improvements in the means of communication and transport were left to later years.

Culture. The Revolution was followed by rapid extension of education. The Northwest Ordinance had made provision for popular education in the Northwest Territory before that great area had any English inhabitants. This act reflected the interest in education that was general in the colonies. The University of North Carolina, the first state institution of its kind, was founded in 1795. There was as yet no American literature, but several artists, notably John S. Copley and Gilbert Stuart, were very successful. Their work enables us today to be familiar with the faces of most of the leaders of the Revolutionary era. Throughout the states, there were to be found numerous private residences and public buildings of excellent architecture, which perhaps constitute America's best contribution to art, previous to the 19th century.

Political Ideas. The assertions about the rights of men, which had been found in many of the state constitutions and had been put into the Declaration of Independence, were widely discussed, and out of this discussion grew a more humane spirit in the treatment of workers and criminals. In politics, most of the state governments were still aristocratic, though the influence of the Western communities and of Vermont, in which manhood suffrage prevailed, was beginning to make itself felt.

Religion. The moral and religious life of the 18th century in the colonies cannot be said to have been of a high order. After the Revolution, the churches of America began to organize in forms appropriate to the new national life. In 1785 the first general convention of the Protestant Episcopal Church was held. The Methodist Episcopal Church was organized in 1784. The first diocese of the

Roman Catholic Church was established with the appointment of Bishop Carrol (Baltimore) in 1789. In the same year, the Presbyterian synods united in a general assembly of the Presbyterian Church. The Congregational churches in New England had no general government, and they were nearly all supported by taxation. These and several other denominations enjoyed religious freedom, and within a few years the states removed most of the religious qualifications formerly required for voters and officials. In this matter the Federal Constitution had been in advance of the states.

The New National Government. The first presidential election was held in 1788. George Washington was the unanimous choice for president, and John Adams was elected vice president. Congress, meeting in New York City, was organized on April 6, 1789, with Frederick Muhlenberg of Pennsylvania as speaker of the House. The committees of the House of Representatives were at first elected, but after 1790 the speaker was instructed to appoint all committees, and he retained this power until 1911. Washington was inaugurated as president on April 30, 1789. Congress created three executive departments: (1) the department of state; (2) the war department; (3) the treasury department. The office of attorney-general was created and also that of postmaster-general. Washington then formed the chiefs of the departments, with the attorney-general, into an advisory body which came to be called the president's cabinet. He originated the cabinet meeting.

The secretary of the treasury was Alexander Hamilton, and to him is due much of the credit for the successful organizing of the government. He succeeded in maintaining the confidence of the business world by insisting upon the honorable payment of the government's obligation in full, not in depreciated currency. To Hamilton also is to be attributed the plan of chartering the Bank of the United States. The discussion upon this proposal brought about the first clash between Hamilton, who believed in a strong central government, and Jefferson, who argued against what he thought to be an unwarranted extension of the Federal authority. Out of this dispute was to grow within a few years the division of the people into two great parties, the Federalists and the Republicans or Democratic-Republicans.

Foreign Difficulties. The outbreak of the French Revolution brought Washington's administration face to face with a serious foreign problem. Many Americans wanted the United States to support France against the other European powers. The French minister, Genet, violated the privileges of his office by attempting to force Washington into calling an extra session of Congress. Washington stood firmly for neutrality, and issued a proclamation which made it clear that the United States would not take sides. Trouble arose also with England over the rights of American vessels on the high seas, and Congress was on the point of declaring war. Washington, however, sent John Jay to England to negotiate a treaty, by which war with England was averted. In 1795 a treaty with Spain opened the mouth of the Mississippi river to navigation by American boats.

The Presidency of John Adams. With the retirement of Washington, real party struggles began in the United States, but the system of election then in vogue put the two leading presidential candidates into office at once, making the Federalist, Adams, president and the Democratic-Republican, Jefferson, vice president. John Adams was the first president to occupy the White House at Washington (1800).

The new administration was beset with foreign troubles. France had been resentful over the Jay treaty with Great Britain, and the French government warned the American minister, Charles C. Pinckney, to leave Paris. President Adams tried to arrive at an understanding with the French government, but the only result was a demand for bribes. This demand was refused, and for a time America and France were virtually at war. Bonaparte, however, soon came into power in France, and a treaty of peace was negotiated in 1800. The French behavior gave rise to the passage of the Alien and Sedition acts in Congress in 1798. The enforcement of these acts intensified the conflict between the Federalists and the Republicans.

Jefferson's Administration. The most important result of this political situation was the so-called revolution of 1800, when the Republican (Democratic-Republican) candidates, Thomas Jefferson and Aaron Burr, were elected president and vice president respectively. The dispute in this election led to the passing of the 12th amendment, requiring that president and vice president be voted for separately.

Jefferson's administration is notable for two things: (1) the personal influence of the president in the direction of greater democracy in government; (2) the remarkable foresight which he displayed in connection with the purchase of the Louisiana territory and its exploration by Lewis and Clarke. His second term as president was troubled by the conspiracy of Aaron Burr and by the stoppage of American trade, due to the European war measures. Jefferson believed that if American foodstuffs and exports were cut off from Europe, the belligerents would be compelled to make peace. He proposed the Embargo act, with the main result that American ships were tied up at their wharves and American commerce seemed strangled, although Europe did suffer to some extent by the policy.

The War of 1812. Ever since the signing of the Treaty of Paris in 1783, the policy of Great Britain toward American shipping had occasioned friction between the two governments. As the war between Napoleon and the allies dragged on, American commerce was robbed under Napoleonic decrees and English orders in council. The failure of such retaliatory policies as the Embargo act of 1807 and the Nonintercourse acts of 1809 and 1810 became clear, and there grew up in Congress a strong party which favored war against Great Britain. This hostile feeling was intensified by British impressment of American seamen.

The Republican party drew much of its strength from the West, and many Westerners believed it would be easy to strike at England through Canada, although the United States maintained but a small regular army, and had made no provision for a larger one. Finally, war was declared on June 18, 1812. At first the American forces were defeated on land, but American ships won brilliant victories at sea. The year 1813 was less favorable to the American ships, although Perry's victory on Lake Erie opened the way for a campaign in western Canada. In 1814 the British seized Astoria in Oregon, burned public buildings in the city of Washington, and made an attack upon Baltimore. The Americans failed in an attempt to invade Canada, but Andrew Jackson successfully defended his position at New Orleans against the British forces under General Pakenham.

The war had brought no especial credit to either side, but English shipowners were impatient at their losses, and their influence prompted the English government to make a favorable treaty with America. Within the United States, the war had been made the occasion of party conflict. When President Madison called for state troops, Federalist New England refused to send them. The climax of this opposition to the government was the Hartford Convention, the action of which was virtually a threat to withdraw from the Union. But just before the report of this convention was issued, the treaty of peace had been signed at Ghent, December 24, 1814.

WAR OF 1812

Causes, direct and remote: England's asserted right to search American vessels; Impressment of American seamen; Inciting of Indian hostilities by British agents; Blockades and other arbitrary practices under the British orders in council; Neglect on the part of England to transfer to the United States the posts on the western frontier.

Campaigns	Chief Battles	American		British		Victor	Results
		Leaders	Troops	Leaders	Troops		
On the Canadian frontier.	Fort Dearborn, Aug. 15, 1812	Heald	67	Indians	1,300	Ind.	Americans surrender to British and abandon Michigan territory. Ends first attempt to invade Canada.
	Detroit, Aug. 16, 1812	Hull	1,400	Brock	1,300	Brit.	
	Queenston Heights, Oct. 13, 1812	Van Rensselaer	1,100	Brock	1,500	Brit.	
Harrison in the Northwest and Perry on Lake Erie.	River Raisin, Jan. 22, 1813.	Winchester	900	Proctor	1,100	Brit.	Americans regain Michigan territory. British and Indian alliance broken. Tecumseh slain. British fleet on Lake Erie annihilated.
	Fort Meigs, May 5, 1813.	Harrison	1,100	Proctor	2,200	Amer.	
	Fort Stephenson, Aug. 2, 1813	Croghan	160	Proctor	391	Amer.	
	Naval Battle of Lake Erie, Sept. 10, 1813	Perry	54 guns	Barclay	63 guns	Amer.	
	The Thames, Oct. 5, 1813.	Harrison	3,500	Proctor, Tecumseh	1,700	Amer.	
Lake Ontario and Niagara frontier.	York, April 27, 1813	Pike	1,600	Sheaffe	600	?	Americans convinced that their troops could successfully cope with trained veterans of Europe.
	Fort George, May 27, 1813.	Chauncey	4,500	Vincent	2,500	?	
	Sackett's Harbor, May 29, 1813	Brown	650	Prevost	800	Amer.	
	Stony Creek, June 6, 1813.	Winder, Chandler	1,400	Vincent	750	Brit.	
	Beaver Dams, June 24, 1813	Boerstler	600	Kerr, Brant	500	Brit.	
	Crystler's Farm, Nov. 11, 1813	Wilkinson	2,000	Morrison	1,000	Brit.	
	Chippewa, July 5, 1814	Brown	3,200	Riall	2,500	Amer.	
	Lundy's Lane, July 25, 1814	Brown	3,100	Drummond	3,500	?	
	Fort Erie, Aug. 15, 1814	Gaines	2,400	Drummond	3,600	Amer.	
	Fort Erie, Sept. 17, 1814	Brown	3,000	Drummond	4,000	Amer.	
Prevost attempts to invade New York via Lake Champlain.	Plattsburg, Sept. 11, 1814.	Macomb	2,000	Prevost	13,000	Amer.	British retreat, leaving northern frontier clear for remainder of the war.
	Lake Champlain, Sept. 11, 1814	MacDonough	14 vessels 86 guns	Downie	16 vessels 92 guns	Amer.	
Destruction of Washington; attack on Baltimore.	Bladensburg, Aug. 24, 1814.	Winder.	6,000	Ross	5,000	Brit.	Washington abandoned to the British. British retire to Halifax.
	Fort McHenry, Sept. 13, 1814	Armistead	3,200	Ross	5,000	Amer.	
Jackson's victory at New Orleans.	New Orleans, Jan. 8, 1815.	Jackson	5,500	Pakenham	10,000	Amer.	British withdraw.

ON THE SEA

Location	Date	American		British		Victor
		Vessels	Commanders	Vessels	Commanders	
Off Newfoundland	Aug. 13, 1812	Essex	Porter	Alert	Langharne	Amer.
Off Massachusetts Bay	Aug. 19, 1812	Constitution	Hull	Guerrière	Dacres	Amer.
Off North Carolina	Oct. 18, 1812	Wasp	Jones	Frolic	Whinyates	Amer.
Off Canary Islands	Oct. 25, 1812	United States	Decatur	Macedonian	Carden	Amer.
Off Brazil	Dec. 29, 1812	Constitution	Bainbridge	Java	Lambert	Amer.
Off Demerara	Feb. 24, 1813	Hornet	Lawrence	Peacock	Peake	Amer.
Off Massachusetts coast	June 1, 1813	Chesapeake	Lawrence	Shannon	Broke	Brit.
Off English Channel	Aug. 14, 1813	Argus	Allen	Pelican	Maples	Brit.
Off Maine coast	Sept. 5, 1813	Enterprise	Burrows	Boxer	Blythe	Amer.
At Valparaiso	Mar. 28, 1814	Essex	Porter	Phoebe, Cherub	Hillyar, Tucker	Brit.
In English Channel	June 28, 1814	Wasp	Blakeley	Reindeer	Manners	Amer.
Off Africa	Sept. 1, 1814	Wasp	Blakeley	Avon	Arbuthnot	Amer.
At Fayal, Azores	Sept. 26, 1814	Gen'l Armstrong	Reid	Plantagenet, Carnation, Rota	Floyd, Bentham, Somerville	?
Off Long Island	Jan. 15, 1815	President	Decatur	Endymion, Pomone, Tenedos, Majestic	Hope, Lumly, Parker, Hayes	Brit.
Off Madeira	Feb. 20, 1815	Constitution	Stewart	Cyane, Levant	Falcon, Douglass	Amer.
In South Atlantic	Mar. 23, 1815	Hornet	Biddle	Penguin	Dickenson	Amer.

Results of War: The independence of the United States was definitely insured. Respect for American seamen was fully established. Treaty of Ghent terminated war, Dec. 24, 1814, but did not definitely settle questions of its cause. Owing to lack of facilities for transmission of news, the battle of New Orleans and some naval battles were fought after date of signing the treaty of peace.

TERRITORIAL GROWTH OF THE UNITED STATES

Territory	Year Acquired	How Acquired	Occasion of Acquisition	Area in Square Miles	Cost
Original Thirteen States, including claims in the Northwest Territory	1783	. . . . . .	. . . .	892,135	
Louisiana Territory. .	1803	Purchase . .	Negotiations for Purchase of New Orleans. French Offer.	827,987	$15,000,000
West Florida	1810–13	Occupation .	Boundary Dispute	13,435	
Florida	1819	Cession, indemnity	Settlement of Border Troubles	58,666	5,000,000
Texas	1845	Annexation .	Petition of Republic of Texas	389,166	
Oregon Territory . . .	1846	Treaty . . .	Settlement of Boundary Dispute	286,541	
Mexican Cession . . .	1848	Cession, indemnity	Close of Mexican War	529,189	15,000,000
Gadsden Purchase . .	1853	Purchase . .	Boundary Dispute	29,670	10,000,000
Alaska	1867	Purchase . .	Pacific Coast Interest in Alaska Fisheries. Russian Offer	590,884	7,200,000
Midway Islands . . .	1867	Annexation .	Fitness for Coaling Station		
Hawaiian Islands. . .	1898	Annexation .	Petition of Hawaiian Government	6,449	
Guam	1898	Annexation .	Close of Spanish War	210	
Palmyra Island . . .	1898	. . . . . .	Obtained with Hawaii		
Puerto Rico	1898	Cession . .	Close of Spanish War	3,435	
Philippine Islands . .	1898	Cession, indemnity	Close of Spanish War	114,400	20,000,000
Samoan Islands . . .	1899	Annexation .	Treaty with Germany and Great Britain	58	
Add. Philippine Islands	1901	Indemnity .	Boundary Adjustment	68	100,000
Canal Zone	1903	Lease . . .	Canal Construction and Control	436	{ 10,000,000 250,000 annually
Virgin Islands	1917	Purchase . .	Need of Naval Base	149	25,000,000

The Monroe Doctrine. In European affairs, after the close of the Napoleonic wars, there was much unrest and domestic discord, which directly affected the United States chiefly through immigration. But to the southward, throughout the American continent, there was a general movement of revolution in the Spanish colonies, tending toward the establishment of independent republican states. During the administration of President Monroe, Canning, the English prime minister, had suggested that England and the United States should join in preventing the annexation of any American state to Spain, France, or Portugal. The president responded to this suggestion with the famous Monroe Doctrine.

A New National Period. With the close of the War of 1812, a new period opened in American history. This era was to be marked by several notable features: (1) the expansion of United States territory in the West; (2) the beginnings of the slavery dispute; (3) the tariff question; (4) the rise of new political parties; (5) the rise of humanitarian and educational societies and movements.

Expansion. In 1800 the western boundary of the United States was the Mississippi river, access to which from the sea was still controlled by Spain. The western half of the Mississippi valley was claimed by France. Within a few years, New Orleans had passed from Spain to France and from France, together with Louisiana, to the United States. Settlers poured into the valley of the Ohio and began to fill up the Northwest. Ohio was admitted as a state in 1803. The expedition of Lewis and Clark revealed the greatness of the Western country, and John Jacob Astor, a New York merchant, by establishing his trading post at Astoria, began competition in the fur trade with the Hudson's Bay Company.

Both Great Britain and the United States claimed the territory now included in the states of Washington and Oregon. The planting of Indian missions in the valleys of the Columbia and Willamette rivers was followed before 1840 by an immigration of United States citizens. Spain still held the California coast and territory now known as New Mexico and Arizona. The increasing travel, incident to the immigration from all sections of the East into the Mississippi valley, necessitated further building of roads and canals. By the year 1825 the Erie canal was finished from Albany to the Niagara river. The Cumberland road from Maryland westward through Wheeling and Columbus to St. Louis was built about the same time. After 1812, steamers began to appear on the Western rivers.

Slavery. The settlement of the Western country raised at once the question of the extension of slavery. In the Northwest Territory, slavery was forbidden by the Ordinance of 1787, but this prohibition did not extend to the vast lands of the Louisiana Purchase, out of which new states would be formed. The consequent dispute reached its first crisis in 1819 with the discussion over the admission of Missouri, the first state to be formed out of the Louisiana Purchase. The immediate result was the passage of the Missouri Compromise, by which a line was drawn across the Louisiana Purchase, north of which there were to be no slaveholding territories and no slaveholding states except Missouri.

From this time, slavery was a sectional question between the North and the South. States were admitted in such an order as to maintain a kind of balance between the two forces. The general growth of humane sentiment throughout the country gave rise to the formation of antislavery societies and encouraged an increasing agitation of the question. Abolition societies were at first general in both the North and the South, but about the year 1830 those in the South disappeared, and the societies in the North were largely increased in membership and vigor. The second great crisis came in 1850, when the question of admitting California and New Mexico arose. Following the resulting compromise, came the famous Kansas-Nebraska bill.

New Parties. Politically, the period from 1815 to 1860 saw the break-up of the old party alignment of Federalists and Republicans and the formation of new parties. From 1800 to 1828 the government was in the hands of the Republicans (Democratic-Republicans), who gradually, under the stress of expansion and war, adopted the policies of the Federalists to such an extent that the Federalist party disappeared. The administration of Monroe was known as the "era of good feeling." As a matter of fact, it was a time of factional strife.

At the close of Monroe's administration, several candidates for the presidency were put into the field by various means. Nominations were made by some of the state legislatures; other nominations were made by small political groups. John Quincy Adams, now a Republican, although he had begun his political life as a Federalist, was elected. He represented the old aristocratic line of presidential succession.

New Political Elements. Several conditions in the country contributed to the development of new parties. First, the growth of the West, with its democratic ideas and its popular organization of local government, gave rise to a political group which looked with suspicion on the growing financial interests of the East. In the second place, there had taken place in all the states, since the formation of the Union, a wide extension of the suffrage, which had brought into the ranks of voters the growing class of mechanics in Eastern cities and towns. Moreover, the close of the period of wars in Europe left the industries and commerce of the United States open to a new competition. This situation gave rise to the demand for higher tariffs to protect "infant industries." Upon this question the southern states, which were mainly agricultural, the middle states, in which factories had grown up, and the New England states, interested chiefly in shipping, were divided. And, finally, the question of slavery, in its various phases, was more and more frequently injected into political contests, until, linked with the question of state rights, it finally became the ruling issue in American politics.

Political Leaders. Political organizations were being developed in the states during this period, particularly in New York and Pennsylvania, and these contributed to the general uncertainty of politics during the decade from 1830 to 1840. Several notable leaders came to the front. Henry Clay early became the champion of the protective tariff under the name of the "American system." Daniel Webster at first opposed, and then favored, the tariff. John C. Calhoun of South Carolina, in the beginning a friend of the tariff, soon changed to opposition and became the great exponent of the nullification idea. Andrew Jackson, who belonged by birth to the so-called "poor whites" of the Carolinas, had gone to Tennessee as a young man and had gained prominence in politics and in the military operations of the War of 1812. During the administration of John Quincy Adams, he became the leader of the opposition and of the democratic movement. He was looked upon as the man of the people, and the combination of the South and West elected him president in 1828. His is the first administration controlled by the Democratic party.

The Presidency of Jackson. The two great issues of Jackson's administration were the question of the United States bank and the question of the right of states to nullify tariff acts. He attacked the bank as an instrument of dangerous commercial monopoly and succeeded in destroying it as a government institution. On the question of nullification, he took the position that the Federal Union must be preserved. The tariff which had aroused the opposition of South Carolina was modified, and this issue disappeared. It was in connection with this discussion upon the question of a state's right to nullify Federal acts that the great debate between Daniel Webster of Massachusetts and Senator Hayne of South Carolina took place in 1830. Webster was from this time recognized as the great champion of Federal supremacy.

The Whigs. Between 1830 and 1840 several political groups drew together into a party which took the name of Whigs. They became strong enough to elect William Henry Harrison in 1840 over Martin Van Buren, the Democratic candidate, who had served one term as president. Harrison died very soon after his inauguration, and the vice president, John Tyler, of Virginia, who was not in reality a Whig, began a stormy administration.

Texas and Mexico. The most important issues of the period between 1840 and 1850 grew out of the expansion of the United States toward the west and south. Party strife became especially bitter because of the relationship of this expansion to the Monroe Doctrine and to the extension of slavery. A strong demand arose for the annexation of territory belonging to Mexico, which was now independent of Spain.

A considerable number of Americans had moved into Texas and had set up an independent state in which slavery was legal. A treaty of annexation was proposed in 1844, but it was rejected by the Senate. In the election of that year, Clay was the Whig nominee, opposed to annexation, and James K. Polk was the Democratic nominee, in favor of annexation. Polk was elected. As a consequence, just before the close of Tyler's administration, Texas was annexed by joint resolution of Congress.

In 1846 President Polk settled with England the boundary of the Oregon country and thus completed the adjustment of the boundary between Canada and the United States. Several exploring expeditions, such as that led by John C. Frémont in 1842–45, had been sent by Americans into California, and President Polk was determined that not only Texas but also the remaining Mexican territory north of the line of the Rio Grande, should be taken for the United States. He finally ordered General Taylor to advance into the disputed territory north of the Rio Grande, where Taylor's forces were attacked by the Mexicans. In a message

Causes: (1) Dispute over the western boundary of Texas; (2) The desire of the United States government to annex the Mexican territory, southwest of the boundary fixed by treaty in 1819, which included the present states of Arizona, Nevada, Utah, New Mexico, and California, with parts of Wyoming and Colorado.

Campaigns	Chief Battles	American		Mexican		Victor	Results
		Leaders	Troops	Leaders	Troops		
Along the Rio Grande.	Palo Alto, May 8, 1846	Taylor	2,000	Arista	6,000	Amer.	
	Resaca de la Palma, May 9, 1846	Taylor	2,200	Arista	6,800	Amer.	
	Monterey, Sept. 20–24, 1846	Taylor	6,600	Ampudia	10,000	Amer.	
	Buena Vista, Feb. 23, 1847.	Taylor	5,000	Santa Anna	20,000	Amer.	
Expedition from Vera Cruz to the City of Mexico.	Vera Cruz, March 10–25, 1847	Scott	12,000	?	?	Amer.	The Treaty of Guadalupe Hidalgo added 522,568 sq. mi. of territory to the United States, awarding to Mexico payment of $15,000,000. Rio Grande made boundary between Texas and Mexico.
	Cerro Gordo, April 18, 1847	Scott	8,500	Santa Anna	12,000	Amer.	
	Contreras, Aug. 20, 1847	Scott	4,500	Valencia, Santa Anna	19,000	Amer.	
	Churubusco, Aug. 20, 1847.	Scott	7,300	Santa Anna	25,000	Amer.	
	Molino del Rey, Sept. 8, 1847	Scott	3,500	Santa Anna	10,000	Amer.	
	Chapultepec, Sept. 12-13, 1847	Scott	7,500	Bravo	4,800	Amer.	

to Congress, May 11, 1846, Polk declared that a state of war existed, and Congress passed a declaration of war. The campaign of the American troops was entirely successful. Mexico ceded New Mexico and California and gave up all claim to Texas.

New States and Slavery. These western additions of territory had been reckoned as valuable chiefly for their furs, but the discovery of gold in California revealed far greater wealth in the new territory than anybody had hoped to find there. In 1849, immigrants began to pour into California, and the question of its admission to the Union as a state came to the fore in the administration of Zachary Taylor, who was elected as the Whig candidate in 1848. He encouraged the Californians to adopt a constitution, and determined to bring California into the Union. The miners, who were working with their own hands, declared against slavery in the new constitution.

In 1849 the Union consisted of fifteen slave states and fifteen free states. There was no slave territory ready to be admitted. The annexation of California would give the free states a majority in the Senate. This situation led to the Compromise of 1850, urged by Henry Clay, "the great pacificator." Under this compromise, California came into the Union as a free state, while New Mexico and Utah were organized as territories with the privilege of determining whether they would be slave or free.

Continuance of the Slavery Issue. The Compromise of 1850 failed to settle the great dispute which was gradually dividing the North from the South, and which was raising to national importance an issue in respect to which neither the Democratic nor the Whig party took a decided position. In the election of 1852, Franklin Pierce of New Hampshire, the Democratic candidate, was elected. President Pierce's first step was in pursuit of a policy looking to the annexation of Cuba. This project was viewed with great favor in the South, because Cuba was a rich slave territory. But the scheme failed, largely because of the rise of the Kansas and Nebraska difficulty over slavery. The Missouri Compromise of thirty years before had forbidden slavery in the territory out of which Kansas and Nebraska were to be formed. Stephen A. Douglas, one of the greatest debaters of the day, supported the theory of squatter sovereignty, virtually embodied in the Kansas-Nebraska bill, which would give the settlers in the territories the right to decide whether or not they would have slavery. Settlers from both North and South poured into the country in dispute, and civil war broke out.

The Republican Party. Out of this discussion over the Kansas-Nebraska bill came the new alignment of parties under the names of Republicans and Democrats. In the election of 1856, the Republicans, whose candidate was John C. Frémont, were defeated by the Democrats, and James Buchanan became president. Far more significant than the outcome of this election, however, was the political contest and great debate between Douglas and Lincoln in 1858. The two men were candidates for the senatorship from Illinois. Douglas won the election, but Lincoln had compelled him to announce his Freeport Doctrine, which cost him the support of Southern Democrats. This series of debates was largely influential in making Lincoln the Republican candidate for president in 1860.

Social Movements, 1820–1860. In order to comprehend thoroughly the course of events which, in the period succeeding the War of 1812, gradually brought the states to the verge of civil war, we must take account of the remarkable contemporary growth of enthusiasm for humanitarian and religious reforms in America. The churches in this period began their extensive missionary efforts in the West and in foreign countries. The circuit rider was a common and important figure on the frontier. The Sunday school movement for the education of poor children, which had begun in England, was adopted in America. American missions were started in the Hawaiian islands, in Asia, and in Africa. The churches began also to emphasize social duties and to found many schools and academies. In the Eastern cities, trade-unions began about 1830 to call attention to the cruel conditions of labor for both adults and children in the factories of New England and of the middle states.

Aside from these organized movements, many individual reformers arose, who spent their lives in efforts for better social conditions. Dorothea Dix brought about the establishment of public asylums for the insane. The treatment of prisoners in jails and penitentiaries was generally brutal at the beginning of the 19th century. In 1830 the Eastern penitentiary at Philadelphia marked a great advance in this respect by providing separate cells for prisoners. The harsh laws against poor debtors were modified also in the course of this period.

The great vice of Americans in the colonial period and throughout the early years of the republic was drunkenness. Agitation for reform of drinking customs gave rise to temperance societies in Boston in 1824; in 1840 the Washingtonian societies began in Baltimore the more widespread movement for temperance. The first state prohibition law was adopted in Maine in 1846.

About 1830 the woman's rights movement began. Its first fruits were seen in the founding of good schools and academies for girls. In 1833 Oberlin college opened its doors to women. The demand for woman suffrage was part of this movement, but it was not to attain success for nearly a hundred years.

The idea of popular education was growing. The mechanics' organizations in Eastern cities protested against the prevalent idea of pauper schools to educate the children of those who could not afford private instruction. About 1830 the policy of a general public school system supported by taxation began to gain favor. This entire educational movement was enlarged and vitalized through the lecture tours of such intellectual leaders as Ralph Waldo Emerson and Edward Everett, and by the establishment of "circulating" libraries in many small towns throughout the country.

Economic Progress. American industry had been progressing by leaps and bounds during this period. The great cotton and woolen mills grew up in New England; coal and iron had been discovered in the neighborhood of Pittsburgh; and the beginnings of the giant steel industry were made. Many inventions of labor-saving machinery appeared between 1830 and 1860. By the invention of his reaper in 1831, Cyrus McCormick made possible a revolution in methods of farming. Railroads were built on lines running westward from the Atlantic seaboard and, to a less extent, southward from the Potomac and Ohio rivers. Canals were constructed by states and by private companies. The foundations of many large individual fortunes were laid through the granting of land for railroad building and by the rapid growth of cities. Industry received a severe check in the panic of 1837, but business organization was greatly strengthened through the economic lessons taught by this disaster.

Immigration. The era under review was also a time of great increase in immigration. Between 1820 and 1840, about 600,000 people came from the Old World and were scattered over all sections of the country. Most of the immigrants were English, Scotch, and Irish. After the unsuccessful revolutionary movement of 1848 in Germany, a large German immigration began, which included many highly educated and able men, such as Carl Schurz. Famine conditions in Ireland sent more than a million Irishmen to America between 1845 and 1855. Immigrants of these groups furnished the labor with which cities, roads, canals, and factories were built, and they occupied much of the new farming land in the West.

The South. Most of this industrial development took place in the North and West, where the laborer was free. In the South, the main change from colonial conditions was the abandonment of much of the worn-out tobacco land of the East and the movement of planters into the black belt of the Carolinas, Georgia, Alabama, and Mississippi, for the raising of cotton. Cotton was the one staple Southern crop, and so much of the land was given up to its production that the South had to draw its food supplies in large amounts from the North.

South and North. Thus, at the opening of the war of secession, the Southern states were behind the North in industrial development and in population. When the crisis came, Maryland, Delaware, Kentucky, and Missouri—all slaveholding states—remained in the Union, and many of the people of eastern Tennessee—descendants of the early English pioneers, and opponents of slavery—were loyal. The South, therefore, entered the war with about 9,000,000 people as opposed to 22,000,000 in the North. It is estimated that the South had 1,300,000 white men available for military service, while the North had 5,500,000, about half of whom were foreign born. The Southern society was aristocratic, and its leaders were generally highly educated men. In the North, democracy, together with popular education, had become more general.

The Election of 1860. The controversy over the Dred Scott decision, the constitutional struggle in Kansas, and the Lincoln-Douglas debates helped to weld together various elements into the new Republican party, as the party of opposition to slavery. Between 1859 and 1861 this party had a small majority in the House of Representatives, but the Senate was strongly Democratic. In February 1860, Jefferson Davis, senator from Mississippi, introduced in the Senate a number of resolutions, which were passed. They declared for the protection of slavery by Congress, for the suppression of abolitionist agitation in the North, and for the sovereignty of the states. This action was interpreted as a notice that the election of an antislavery president would be the signal for possible withdrawal of the Southern states from the Union.

The Democratic party met in a convention at Charleston, South Carolina, in April 1860, and divided upon the policy of extending slavery. A second convention, held at Baltimore, nominated Douglas, while the extreme Southern Democrats nominated John C. Breckinridge, who was at that time vice president. A Constitutional Union party, made up of Southern and Northern Whigs, nominated John Bell of Tennessee. The Republican party, meeting at Chicago in May, nominated Abraham Lincoln.

Lincoln and Secession. Lincoln was elected, although he received a minority of the total popular vote. The Republicans had a majority in every Northern state except California, Oregon, and New Jersey. On the day after the national election, steps were taken in South Carolina to call a secession convention. By unanimous vote, this convention, on December 20, 1860, declared South Carolina no longer a part of the Union. Before the first of February 1861, six other states—Mississippi, Florida, Alabama, Georgia, Louisiana, and Texas—had followed the example of South Carolina. In the month of February, a convention of delegates from six states drew up a provisional constitution for the Confederate States of America, and elected Jefferson Davis president and Alexander H. Stephens vice president. Preparations for war began immediately. Southern citizens resigned their civil and military offices under the United States government, thus demoralizing, to a large degree, the Union army and navy.

The sentiment in the North during these months was divided. Strong pressure was brought by such leaders as Horace Greeley in favor of acquiescing in the action of the Southern states and of recognizing the independent Confederacy. Lincoln was inaugurated on March 4, 1861, and his inaugural address stated clearly his position. He declared himself opposed to interference with the institution of slavery in the states where it existed, but he expressed equal determination to maintain the Union unbroken, and he clearly stated his belief in the utter unwisdom of secession. Lincoln had already lent his aid to efforts at reconciliation, but these efforts had failed, and he now placed upon the South the responsibility for war.

Opening of the War. On April 12, 1861 the Confederate forces began the bombardment of Fort Sumter in Charleston harbor. On April 15, Lincoln issued his call for 75,000 volunteers. The president's stand in his inaugural address and his action in calling for recruits for the army crystallized sentiment in the North as well as in the South. North Carolina and Virginia, Tennessee and Arkansas joined the Confederacy. The two sides stood 22 Union states and 11 Confederate. There was a general belief in the North that the conflict could be ended with one blow. But this opinion reckoned without the gallant spirit and unanimous determination of the Southern people. To the Southern mind, loyalty to the state came first. This ingrained belief accounts for the action of such men as Alexander H. Stephens and Robert E. Lee. Stephens fought against secession in Georgia, but, when once the majority of his fellow citizens of that state had decided against him, he threw in his influence with them. Robert E. Lee, a Virginian, was an officer in the army of the United States and was offered command of the Union armies, but, when Virginia decided for secession, he remained true to his state.

The Opposing Forces. Both sides misjudged and underestimated each other's powers. The men of the South were accustomed to outdoor life, to the use of firearms, and to the management of horses. Their leaders had been trained in their own military schools and at West Point. The South could put a larger proportion of its white men into service, because the labor on the plantations would be done by the slaves. On the other hand, the North had less of military spirit than the South; a larger proportion of its white population was engaged in the labor of farming and in factories. Moreover, its labor at home had to be done by freemen, and, therefore, a smaller proportion could be spared for military service. As a matter of fact, during the war, about nine men out of every ten in the South served in the army, while in the North one man out of two bore arms at some period of the war. Both sides had to put forth tremendous efforts to equip and maintain armies and navies. One very great advantage the North possessed; namely, its factories and its developed resources in coal and iron. Added to this was the wide distribution of labor-saving machines on the farms, without which it is doubtful whether the North could have maintained itself throughout the war. One other advantage was that, in the decade between 1850 and 1860, railroad lines had been completed, which bound together the Mississippi valley and the Atlantic seaboard, thus directing the products of the Western farms toward the East, rather than toward the South.

The Siege of the South. The military problem of the war was simple. The Southern armies had to protect a border running from the Potomac river westward across the mountains through Tennessee to the Mississippi river. In order to succeed, they had also to keep communications open through their ports for the shipment of their cotton and for the importation of food supplies and arms. The first task of the Northern army and navy was to draw a line around the Confederate states and, by means of the armies on the north and west and the navy on the south and east, to isolate the Confederacy from the outside world. In the second place, the Northern armies had to invade the South and defeat the Southern forces on their own territory.

At first, a blockade of the Southern ports was impossible, for the Federal government had only twelve ships at its disposal. But it had shipyards, and blockading squadrons were rapidly gathered until an effective blockade was secured. Cotton was piled up on the wharves of Southern ports, where it became valueless, and food and medicines grew scarce.

War in the West. The northern frontier of the Confederacy was well protected by the mountains of western Virginia, Kentucky, and Tennessee. There were strongly fortified points on the Kentucky and Tennessee rivers and along the Mississippi. But several railroad lines penetrated southward from the Potomac in the East and from Louisville, on the Ohio, in the West. The campaigns of the Northern armies were determined by these approaches. The first three years of the war were consumed by a stubborn struggle in the West for control of the Mississippi and of the railroad lines leading southward into Georgia and Alabama. This struggle was finally won by the Union armies through the capture of Vicksburg and the defeat of General Bragg at Chickamauga and Chattanooga in the summer and fall of 1863.

War in the East. In the East, the better fortune of war was with the Confederate armies commanded by General Lee, until their defeat at the battle of Gettysburg. General Grant was placed in command of the army of the Potomac in the spring of 1864, and for a year the war settled down to a contest between the armies of Lee and Grant in Virginia. The Northern losses were terrific and discouraging. Lee handled his army in masterly fashion, and he surrendered at Appomattox, April 9, 1865, only after his resources in men and equipment were exhausted. The material resources of the South had been seriously crippled by the march of Sherman from Atlanta to Savannah in the fall and winter of 1864.

Reconstruction. Lincoln's diplomacy had already laid the basis for wise reconstruction to follow the war, but his assassination removed the only man who could lead wisely in this process. Andrew Johnson, who became president, lacked the tact and skill to carry out Lincoln's policy, although he set himself to the task. Under Lincoln's plan, the Southern states were viewed as never having been outside the Union. Governors were appointed for the states which recognized the conditions laid down by the president for the restoration of government. Conventions in these states adopted new constitutions, elected legislatures and governors, and ratified the 13th amendment, which abolished slavery. Civil government was then declared to be fully restored.

CIVIL WAR OR WAR OF SECESSION

Causes: (1) The conflict between the North and the South upon the question of slavery; (2) The state rights controversy, involving the right of secession; (3) The lack of understanding between the North and the South, due to differences of economic development.

Campaigns	Chief Battles	Union		Confederate		Victor	Results
		Leaders	Troops	Leaders	Troops		
Opening conflicts.	Fort Sumter, S. C., April 12–14, 1861	Anderson	75	Beauregard	?	Confed.	Both sides realize the seriousness of the conflict and prepare for a long war.
	First Battle of Bull Run (Manassas), Va., July 21, 1861	McDowell	18,000	J. E. Johnston, Beauregard	22,000	Confed.	
	Ball's Bluff, Va., Oct. 21, 1861	Baker	1,700	Evans	1,600	Confed.	
Western campaigns, 1862. To close the northern frontier in Kentucky and Tennessee; to control the Mississippi; to open routes of invasion into the South.	Mill Spring, Ky., Jan. 19-20, 1862	Thomas	4,000	Crittenden	4,000	Union	
	Ft. Henry, Tenn., surrender, Feb. 6, 1862	Grant, Foote(navy)	20,000	Tilghman	4,000	Union	
	Ft. Donelson, Tenn., surrender, Feb. 14–16, 1862.	Grant, Foote(navy)	20,000	Pillow, Floyd, Buckner	14,000	Union	
	Shiloh (Pittsburg Landing), Tenn., April 6-7, 1862	Grant, Buell	38,000	A.S. Johnston, Beauregard	40,000	Union	
	Island No. 10 (Miss. river), surrender, April 7, 1862.	Pope, Foote(navy)	?	Mackall	6,000	Union	Union troops in control of the upper Mississippi and of the Tennessee river.
	Corinth, Miss., Oct. 3-4, 1862	Rosecrans	20,000	Van Dorn, Price	22,000	Union	
	Perryville, Ky., Oct. 8, 1862	Buell	54,000	Bragg	68,000	Union	
Eastern campaigns, 1862. First contest for capture of Richmond. Peninsular campaign.	Yorktown, Va., siege, April 5–May 3, 1862	McClellan	110,000	J. E. Johnston	50,000	Union	
	Williamsburg, Va., May 5, 1862	McClellan	110,000	J. E. Johnston	50,000	Union	
T. J. (Stonewall) Jackson's Valley campaign.	McDowell, Va., (now W. Va.), May 8, 1862	Schenck	2,600	Jackson	?	Union	
	Fair Oaks (Seven Pines), Va., May 31–June 1, 1862	McClellan	51,000	J. E. Johnston	42,000	Union	
	Seven Days' Battles before Richmond, Va., June 25–July 1, 1862	McClellan	92,000	Lee	80,000	Confed.	McClellan retreats to Malvern Hill.

CIVIL WAR OR WAR OF SECESSION—Con.

Campaigns	Chief Battles	Union		Confederate		Victor	Results
		Leaders	Troops	Leaders	Troops		
Shenandoah Valley campaign.	Second Battle of Bull Run, Va., Aug. 28–30, 1862	Pope	65,000	Lee, Jackson	54,000	Confed.	Union armies fail in attempt to capture Richmond.
First Confederate invasion of the North.	Antietam (Sharpsburg), Md., Sept. 16-17, 1862	McClellan	75,000	Lee	40,000	Union	Lee's invasion of the North defeated.
	Fredericksburg, Va., Dec. 13, 1862	Burnside	116,000	Lee	78,000	Confed.	
Coast and Harbors campaign.	Hampton Roads, Va., *Merrimac* and *Monitor*, March 9, 1862	Worden	?	Buchanan	?	Union	
Effort to blockade the Southern ports.	New Orleans, La., surrender, April 29, 1862	Farragut (navy), Butler (army)	11,000	Mitchell (navy), Lovell (army)	?	Union	Effective blockading of Southern commerce assured.
Western campaigns, 1863. For control of the Mississippi and to open the way for invasion to Atlanta. J. H. Morgan's raid across the Ohio ended at Salineville, July 26, 1863.	Murfreesboro (Stone River), Tenn., Dec. 31, 1862–Jan. 2, 1863	Rosecrans	43,000	Bragg	37,000	Union	
	Vicksburg, Miss., surrender, July 4, 1863	Grant, Porter (navy)	75,000	Pemberton	40,000	Union	
	Port Hudson, Miss., July 9, 1863	Banks	13,000	Gardner	6,000	Union	
	Chickamauga, Ga., Sept. 19-20, 1863	Rosecrans, Thomas	57,000	Bragg	71,000	Confed.	Complete control of the Mississippi and of the approaches to Atlanta by Union forces.
	Battle of Chattanooga, Lookout Mountain, Missionary Ridge, Tenn., Nov. 23–25, 1863	Grant, Sherman, Thomas	60,000	Bragg	40,000	Union	
Eastern campaign, 1863. Second Confederate invasion of the North, "High Tide of the Confederacy."	Knoxville, Tenn., siege, Nov. 17–Dec. 4, 1863	Burnside, Sherman	12,000	Longstreet	20,000	Union	
	Chancellorsville, Va., May 1-4, 1863	Hooker	60,000	Lee	40,000	Confed.	Lee's second attempt to invade the North fails.
	Gettysburg, Pa., July 1–3, 1863	Meade	93,000	Lee	70,000	Union	
Western campaign, 1864-65. To break the industrial power of the South. Sherman's march through Georgia and the Carolinas.	Battles before Atlanta, Ga., July 20, 22, 29, 1864. Capture of Atlanta, Sept. 2, 1864.	Sherman	(max'm) 112,000	J.E.Johnston, Hood	(max'm) 71,000	Union	Resources of the Confederacy exhausted. J. E. Johnston surrenders to Sherman at Durham Station, N. C., April 26, 1865.
	Savannah, Ga., surrender, Dec. 21, 1864	Sherman	60,000		?	Union	
Eastern campaigns, 1864-65. Final struggle for control of Richmond.	Battle of the Wilderness, Va., May 5–7, 1864	Grant	(max'm) 116,000	Lee	(max'm) 61,000	?	
	Spottsylvania Court House, Va., May 8–18, 1864	Grant	66,000	Lee	?	?	
The Valley campaign.	Opequon (Winchester), Va., Sept. 19, and Fisher's Hill, Va., Sept. 22, 1864	Sheridan	(max'm) 43,000	Early	(max'm) 20,000	Union	Fall of Richmond, April 2, 1865.
	Cedar Creek, Va., Oct. 19, 1864	Sheridan	31,000	Early	13,000	Union	Complete defeat of the Confederate armies through exhaustion of man power and supplies. Capital of the Confederacy in Union hands. Lee surrenders at Appomattox C. H., April 9, 1865.
	Cold Harbor, Va., June 3, 1864	Grant	103,000	Lee	78,000	Confed.	
	Petersburg, Va., June 15–18, 1864	Grant	(max'm) 110,000	Lee	(max'm) 66,000	Confed.	
	Siege of Petersburg and Richmond, June 22, 1864–April 2, 1865	Grant	(max'm) 124,000	Lee	(max'm) 57,000	Union	
	Five Forks, Va., March 31, 1865	Sheridan	?	Pickett	?	Union	

Results of the War: The institution of slavery was abolished within the United States. The Union was preserved, and the supremacy of the Federal government over the states was established.

Congressional Policies. Congress, however, was jealous of the power of the president, and a large Northern element became alarmed at the speedy restoration of the Southern states. In 1865 Congress ignored the work of the president and proceeded to treat the Southern states as rebel territory. This movement was led by Charles Sumner, who was determined at all hazards to do justice to the Negro, and Thaddeus Stevens, who was equally determined to establish Republican power in the South through the command of Negro votes. The 14th amendment was passed, and ratification of this was made a condition of the admission of states to the Union.

Then began, in 1867, the passage of a series of reconstruction acts. The former Confederacy was divided into five military districts. The commanders of these districts had supervision of elections. The result was to bring into power a large, ignorant Negro vote. Anarchy and misgovernment grew throughout the South. The legislatures, without competent leadership and largely influenced by the "carpetbaggers" and "scalawags," made enormous appropriations of money and laid heavy taxes, the proceeds of which were largely wasted by irresponsible adventurers. Enormous state debts were piled up. Most of the taxpaying classes were disfranchised, a condition which intensified the general disturbance.

Restoration of the South. The result of thus displacing Lincoln's moderate diplomacy by an arrogant Congressional scheme of reconstruction was to provoke a countermovement on the part of the Southern whites. This movement was prevented from using legal means of redress, and therefore such organizations as the Ku-Klux Klan were resorted to. During the administration of President Grant, the arbitrary means necessary to maintain Southern Republican and Negro influence became more and more distasteful to the president and to the country. Political rights were restored to all save a few ex-Confederates in 1872, and after the election of 1876 President Hayes withdrew the military forces that had been in control of the elections. The abuses which had attended the Ku-Klux Klan subsided, and white rule was established in all the Southern states.

Impeachment of President Johnson. The conflict between Congress and President Johnson grew more and more intense, until impeachment proceedings were brought against the president in 1868. He was acquitted, though by a very narrow margin, and the country was saved this dangerous precedent of removing a president because he disagreed with Congress.

The Presidency of Grant. The most important feature of Grant's first term was an agreement with England for the settlement of the Alabama claims. President Grant was unfortunate in his selection of officials, but he himself was a vigorous foe of abuses, such as the passing of private pension and relief bills and the wholesale removing of civil officers, a practice which had begun in Jackson's time. He secured a civil service act in 1871, but three years later Congress cut off appropriations for its enforcement, and so destroyed its effect. President Grant's second term was a period of humiliation on account of the inefficiency and corruption revealed in the government. Congressmen and officials were found to have been involved in frauds in connection with Indian affairs, in the financing of the Union Pacific railway, and in the Whisky Ring. One result of these revelations was the appearance of a Democratic majority in the House of Representatives in 1874.

Contested Election of 1876. The presidential election of 1876 proved to be a critical event in American history. On the morning after the election, a Democratic victory was announced by newspapers of both parties, but "carpetbagger" governments were still in control in Louisiana, Florida, and South Carolina. From these states and from Oregon, rival electors secured credentials, which threw doubt upon the election. The matter was finally referred to an electoral commission of fifteen, which decided all contests by a strictly party vote in favor of the Republicans. Historians generally remark the notable restraint which characterized the people of the United States in this trying situation. The peaceable settlement of the election dispute furnishes a strong assurance of the strength of popular government.

The New Industrial Period. The ten years following the Civil War constituted a period of very rapid commercial and industrial growth throughout the country. It is true that the South had been ruined and devastated by the war, but one of the most admirable features of American history is the heroic manner in which the Southern people returned after defeat to take up the work of rebuilding their homes and industry and of maintaining their civilization. They still had the soil which produced large cotton crops. Soon Northern and foreign capital began to flow in. This made possible the development of water power by which cotton mills could be operated. Alabama possesses large deposits of iron and coal, and the larger use of these resources in manufacturing was begun. Thus a new industrial era was introduced in the South.

The Northern states had developed industrially and commercially under the stress of war necessities. Railroad building had been pushed westward, initiated by the chartering of the Union Pacific in 1862.

Banking and Currency. This was a period of change in banking conditions, through the extension of the national banking system and the organization of trust companies. Large amounts of money became available for investment in land and for savings in the form of savings bank deposits and of life insurance. Soon after the Civil War, also, a period of speculation set in, which contributed to the bringing on of the panic of 1873. The problem of national currency was difficult after the Civil War, for the greenbacks, or paper money, which had been issued, depreciated in value when the government would not redeem them in gold. But from the government surplus a sum was gradually accumulated in the treasury to redeem the greenbacks, and what is called resumption of specie payment was begun in 1879. About the same time, a demand arose in the West for the restoration of silver coinage, which had been discontinued by act of Congress in 1873. An act providing for a limited coinage of silver was passed in 1878.

Invention and Discovery. The discovery of oil and the invention of new processes for making steel gave rise to the great organizations for producing these two commodities. The inventive genius of Americans, which has been noted before, produced a multitude of new inventions and processes, especially in electricity. The system of making machine parts of standard dimensions led to the specialization and division of labor. The wonders of all this tide of invention and discovery gave occasion for the exposition of 1876 in Philadelphia, where thousands of people saw for the first time the wealth of their own country and of foreign lands. This was also the era of the invention of the telephone and of the rapid extension of the telegraph.

The organization of capital into large units was followed by organizations of labor and by contests between employers and employees, which led to serious disturbances, such as the railroad strike of 1877.

Immigration, which had been checked during the Civil War, was largely increased. Immigrants from Asia as well as from Europe were received. Chinese laborers by the thousand were employed on the new railroads of the West. In 1879, however, a policy of Chinese exclusion was initiated.

Garfield and Civil Service. The election of 1880 placed James A. Garfield in the White House. The Democratic candidate, General Hancock, was supported by the "solid South," the first occasion of a united Southern Democratic vote. Garfield was shot by a half-crazed office seeker, and died September 19, 1881. The vice president, Chester A. Arthur, succeeded to the presidency, and in 1883 a civil service act was passed, which provided for the classified service and for competitive examinations. President Arthur began the enforcement of this act.

Cleveland and the Tariff. In the election of 1884 the Republican candidate, James G. Blaine, was defeated by Grover Cleveland, who became the first Democratic president since Buchanan. Blaine was opposed by the "Mugwumps," the reform element in the Republican party. Cleveland extended the scope of the classified civil service in the face of intense opposition within his own party. He also aroused antagonism by his vetoes of pension bills and of bills for public buildings and for rivers and harbors which he deemed extravagant. His message of December 1887 brought the tariff forward as the dominant issue. A high tariff had been imposed during the Civil War and many of its rates remained even after revision in 1883, the revenue resulting in a surplus accumulating in the national treasury,—an encouragement to extravagance. The real issue was not so much a matter of rates as of policy, whether the tariff should be for protection or primarily for revenue.

The Presidency of Harrison. Cleveland raised the issue of a lower tariff, or a tariff for revenue only, in the campaign of 1888. The Republicans responded by a platform which declared for high protection as a party policy. The Democrats were defeated, and Benjamin Harrison was elected president with a Republican majority in both houses of Congress. Appropriations for pensions were greatly enlarged, as were expenditures for public buildings, and the building of a new navy was carried forward. In October 1890, the McKinley tariff was passed, which raised some duties, but provided a large free list and arranged for reciprocity treaties with foreign nations.

Second Administration of Cleveland. Under the new tariff, prices on many commodities suddenly rose, and, in 1892, in a campaign waged over the tariff issue, Grover Cleveland was again elected president,—this time with a majority in both houses of Congress during the first two years of his term. Cleveland's second administration was an era of hard times. Government revenues dropped. There were many commercial failures throughout the country, and in the West a new movement for free coinage of silver arose. The Democratic Congress passed a new tariff act, which President Cleveland refused to sign, because it contained so many protective duties. Congress also passed an income tax law, which, in 1895, the supreme court declared unconstitutional. A notable feature of Cleveland's second administration was the stand taken by the president and his secretary of state, Richard Olney, upon the Venezuelan boundary question, in maintaining that the interests of the United States under the Monroe Doctrine were involved in Great Britain's refusal to arbitrate. In the election of 1896 the Democratic party was split on the silver question, and William McKinley, the Republican candidate, was elected by a large plurality over the Democratic candidate, William J. Bryan.

Cities. The period from 1860 to 1885 brought before the American people a new set of problems. One serious question was that of city government, rendered more acute by the growth of large cities in the period following the Civil War. With the opportunities for private gain at the expense of the community, corruption was rife in city governments. The infamous Tweed Ring in New York plundered that city of millions of dollars. Since 1890 much has been done to provide efficient systems of city management.

Trusts and Trade-Unions. The second great problem which appeared in this time grew out of the organizing of so-called trusts for the control of certain industries, forming monopolies and able, at their pleasure, to extort high prices and rates. Control of these evils in connection with the railroads began with the Interstate Commerce act of 1887. In 1890 the Sherman Antitrust law was passed. Closely related to the rise of huge industrial combinations of capital were questions connected with the rapid growth of the labor unions and with increasing agitation for the improvement of working conditions.

Immigration. In the last quarter of the 19th century, a marked change came about in respect to the nationalities and the numbers of immigrants who came to America. About 1880, they began to come from southern and central, rather than from northern, Europe. A large number of French Canadians also came into the New England states. Numerous laws were passed, beginning in 1885, to prevent the immigration of "contract labor," paupers, the insane or disabled, or anarchists. Nevertheless, the number of immigrants admitted kept increasing until, in 1907, and again in 1914, it reached its maximum of well over a million.

World Power. The administration of President McKinley was marked by the outbreak of the war with Spain. The most important question which arose out of this short conflict concerned the disposition of the Philippine Islands. The country was sharply divided over the policy of retaining the islands,—one group favoring it, the other opposing such an "imperial policy." In the end, the Philippines were retained under the control of the United States. Another outcome of the war with Spain and the consequent acquisition of the Philippines, together with the annexation of the Hawaiian islands, was the rise of the United States as a world power, with important territorial interests in the Pacific, bringing United States troops into the Boxer Rebellion in 1900 in China.

The New West. No feature of the history of the United States since the Civil War is more important than the building up of the Middle West, the Southwest, and the Far West. During the Civil War a new policy of homesteading was adopted, and after the close of the war great numbers of ex-soldiers took advantage of this act to settle beyond the Mississippi and the Missouri. Gradually, the land was taken up as far as the Rocky Mountain slopes. Several military campaigns were necessary to settle Indian difficulties, as white settlement encroached upon Indian lands. Cattle raising became the great industry upon the plains of the West and Southwest, while the states immediately west of the Mississippi rapidly became the vast granary of the nation.

Several railroad lines were soon completed to the Pacific coast, and a steady tide of migration followed these lines into California, Oregon, and Washington. Out of these newly settled sections, new states were formed after 1888, the last being New Mexico and Arizona in 1912. The settlement of the West opened up new and large sources of wealth. Mines of lead and silver were discovered in the Black hills and in Colorado; large copper deposits were opened in Montana; and the vast forests of the Pacific coast were made available.

Presidency of Theodore Roosevelt. After the assassination of President McKinley, the vice president, Theodore Roosevelt, came into the presidency. Roosevelt was a courageous and outspoken leader in affairs, a man of large experience in city, state, and national government. He increased the classified civil service list until it included about half the civil employees of the government, and during his

WAR WITH SPAIN

Causes: (1) Disorders in Cuba under Spanish rule; (2) Destruction of the battleship *Maine* in Habana harbor.

Campaigns	Chief Battles	American		Spanish		Victor	Results
		Leaders	Troops	Leaders	Troops		
In the Philippines.	Manila Bay, May 1, 1898.	Dewey . .	(navy)	Montojo . .	(navy)	Amer.	
	Siege of Manila, July 31–Aug. 13, 1898	Merritt . Dewey .	11,000	Jaudenes. .	13,000	Amer.	
		Aguinaldo (insurgents)	12,000				Treaty of peace by which Cuba was freed from Spain; Puerto Rico, Guam, and the Philippines were ceded to the United States. The United States paid to Spain $20,000,000.
In Cuba.	El Caney and San Juan Hill, June 30, 1898 . .	Shafter . Wheeler . Lawton . Kent . .	6,600 8,000	Linares . . Toral . . .	500 4,200	Amer.	
	Santiago Harbor, July 3, 1898	Sampson. Schley . .	(navy)	Cervera . .	(navy)	Amer.	

administration the consular service was improved by the application of the merit system and by the more general appointment and promotion of experienced men. Roosevelt probably represented the people at large more completely than any president since Jackson, and he acted upon that theory. He used his influence to settle a great coal strike in 1902, and he took an active interest in the direction of prosecution for violations of the Sherman Antitrust act and of other laws dealing with corporations.

Progressive Measures. Probably the most far-reaching influence of the Roosevelt administration is the impulse that the president gave to the conservation of national resources in forests, water power, and other natural forms of wealth. The diplomatic negotiations and the beginning of actual construction in connection with the Panama canal form part of the achievements of Roosevelt's administration. Two very important enlargements of government activity belong to this period: (1) the giving of greater powers to the Interstate Commerce Commission; (2) the extension of government control over the preparation of food products, through what are known as the pure food laws.

Foreign Relations. In international affairs, President Roosevelt brought about the Treaty of Portsmouth between Russia and Japan in 1905. In 1907–09 a fleet of United States battleships made a cruise around the world. American naval prestige was heightened by this demonstration. United States delegates to the Hague Conference in 1907 exerted their influence strongly in favor of proposals for world peace. The president also gave some important applications to the Monroe Doctrine, which he interpreted as implying for the United States a kind of police power in the Western world.

The Presidency of Taft. On the expiration of Roosevelt's second term, William H. Taft was elected president. Mr. Taft came into the presidency with a party divided into two sharply opposed factions,—the progressives, who were strong supporters of the policies urged by Roosevelt, and the conservatives, who were definitely opposed to these policies. The first task of the new administration was the revision of the tariff. The conservative elements of both parties combined to pass the Payne-Aldrich tariff, and Mr. Taft gave the act his approval, thereby alienating progressive Republicans.

Mr. Taft, nevertheless, by his executive orders and through encouragement of legislation, did much to enforce the conservation policy. To this administration belong also the establishment of the parcel post and the postal savings system. Many treaties of arbitration were negotiated, and the constitutional amendments providing for the Federal income tax and for direct election of senators were submitted to the states by Congress. In 1912, the "standpat" Republicans nominated Mr. Taft, while the progressive Republicans, or Progressives, nominated Theodore Roosevelt, for president. The Republican vote was thus split, and the Democratic candidate, Woodrow Wilson, was elected.

Wilson's Administration. President Wilson's first term was occupied with legislation upon three principal matters: (1) the tariff,—Congress was called in a special session, and the Underwood tariff, intended to produce revenue and to discourage monopoly, was passed in October 1913; (2) banking,—the discussion of this question resulted in the formation of the Federal Reserve banking system; (3) control of corporations,—the president secured the passing of a law which provided for the Federal Trade Commission, and also the Clayton Antitrust act. Mr. Bryan, as secretary of state, initiated an enlarged program of arbitration treaties.

In 1913, the 16th amendment to the Constitution, authorizing an income tax, and the 17th amendment, providing for the election of United States senators by direct vote, were ratified by the states.

World War I. In 1914 the World War broke out. The United States government took a position of strict neutrality. Nevertheless, without any adequate preparation, it was being surely drawn into the circle of the war. Germany's decisive act in the matter was the declaration of unrestricted submarine warfare, January 31, 1917. On April 6, 1917, the United States declared war. At the end of the war, the Versailles Treaty was rejected through a deadlock between the president and the Senate, centering on the question of the League of Nations. See *World War I*.

Constitutional Amendments. In January 1919 the 18th amendment to the Constitution, forbidding the manufacture and sale of intoxicants for beverage purposes, was ratified. In 1920 the 19th amendment, granting equal suffrage to men and women, became a part of the fundamental law of the nation. Of these amendments, the former occasioned ceaseless controversy. A rising tide of opposition bore fruit in 1933 with its repeal by the ratification of the 21st amendment. By the 20th amendment, ratified also in 1933, the presidential and Congressional terms begin in the January following elections.

The Presidency of Harding. In 1920 the Republican candidate, Warren G. Harding, was elected on the issues of oppositions to the League of Nations and "return to normalcy."

Prominent among the achievements of the new administration was the provision for a bureau of the budget. The first general budget was submitted to Congress by President Harding on December 5, 1921. In the same year an international conference was called to consider limitation of armaments. It met at Washington, November 12, 1921. See *Washington Conference*. A treaty of peace with Germany was signed in Berlin on August 25, 1921. President Harding died suddenly on August 2, 1923. Vice President Calvin Coolidge succeeded him.

Coolidge's Administration. The first months of this administration were clouded by irregularities in connection with the leases of the Teapot Dome oil properties. Coolidge was reelected in 1924. Features of his administration were the refunding of the Allied war debts; a measure in 1924 restricting immigration to 150,000 annually; and the multilateral Kellogg treaty of 1928, renouncing war as an instrument of national policy.

Herbert Hoover. Coolidge was succeeded in 1929 by another Republican, Herbert Hoover. He was successful in negotiating a naval limitation treaty with England, Japan, France, and Italy. A serious economic depression, beginning in 1929, was in no way helped by the Smoot-Hawley upward revision of the tariff and little mitigated by measures establishing a Federal Farm Board and the Reconstruction Finance Corporation. In 1932, his democratic opponent, Franklin D. Roosevelt, promising a "new deal," was elected by a landslide.

The New Deal. Roosevelt's inauguration coincided with a collapse of the banking system. Receiving extraordinary powers from Congress, he speedily effected changes touching every aspect of economic life. To meet the emergency, he initiated measures for caring for the needy, halting bankruptcies, and increasing employment. These were followed by changes designed to guard against recurrence of such crises. Among them were efforts to reopen the channels of foreign trade by reciprocal tariff concessions, taxation policies to prevent concentration of wealth, policing the securities markets, and establishment of a program of social security. The Republican party, opposing these changes and the general trend toward the centralization of national power, was decisively defeated in 1936, its candidate carrying only two states.

The supreme court had declared unconstitutional some of the new deal measures for controlling agriculture and manufacturing. Roosevelt's proposal for conditional enlargement of the supreme court failed in Congress, but changes in the court (between 1937 and 1941 seven of the nine justices died or retired) resulted in more favorable decisions. The presidential campaign of 1940 resulted in the unprecedented election of President Roosevelt for a third term by an electoral vote of 449 to 82 for his Republican opponent, Wendell L. Willkie.

World War II. At the outbreak of the war in Europe in September 1939, the president issued the usual proclamations of neutrality, although both public opinion and the administration were strongly favorable to the Allies. The stringent Neutrality act of 1937 was amended, November 3, 1939, to the advantage of Great Britain and France, allowing sales of munitions on a "cash and carry" basis.

The course of the war in the Atlantic, the danger from Axis influence in Latin America, and above all the fall of France in July 1940, emphasized the nation's weakness in the face of modern war. In January 1940, President Roosevelt asked for nearly two billion dollars for national defense, and special taxes were levied to meet it. Congress passed acts in September 1940 calling out the national guard and reserves and increasing the regular army. A conscription act called men between 21 and 36 into service for one year's training. Arms production was speeded up. The principle of a two-ocean navy was put into operation.

From the beginning the United States adopted a policy of conference and cooperation with Canada and the Latin American nations. In August 1940, the United States and Canada set up a Permanent Joint Board of Defense. Conferences at Panama in September 1939 and at Havana in July 1940, arranged for common action of the American nations. They laid out neutrality zones adjoining the American continent, and would not permit a transfer of other American colonies to non-American powers.

Measures for Defense. Acting on the assumption that American interests lay with the victory of the Allies, and wishing to promote that victory by "measures short of war," President Roosevelt, in September 1940, transferred 50 over-age destroyers to Great Britain, in return for leases of sites for naval and air bases in the Atlantic.

Congress, on the president's recommendation, passed in March 1941 the "Lend-Lease Act," authorizing the president to transfer to other countries, whose defense he regarded as vital to the defense of the United States, war materials and other commodities under arrangements providing for their return or "recompense." The United States was to be an "Arsenal of Democracy." Naturally only a small part of the articles "lent" would ever be returned. By the end of hostilities in 1946 the United States had loaned goods and munitions amounting to $50,692,000,000, and received in return something over ten billion dollars.

After the invasion of Denmark, the United States assumed control of Greenland and sent troops to Iceland. The "neutrality patrol" of our coasts was extended. All these transactions involved clashes with the Axis submarine blockade.

Other defense measures included the registration of aliens; the closing of German and Italian consulates to check espionage and propaganda; and the "freezing" of the assets of Axis and Axis-occupied countries. Embargoes were laid on the export of war materials required for the national defense.

The War and War Measures. When war came with the Japanese attack on Pearl Harbor, December 7, 1941, it fused the nation into an unprecedented unity of purpose. Japan's allies, Germany and Italy, immediately declared war, and their declarations were answered in kind. The draft age was extended, and 11 million men were drawn into the armed forces. Despite heavy initial losses the navy's strength was tripled. The national debt, on February 15, 1946, reached a peak of $279,496,760,104.49, or $1991.52 per capita.

The special commissions already existing were enlarged and new ones created: the war production board (WPB), organizing production, the war manpower commission (WMC); and the war labor board (WLB), regulating labor and wages; and, with the same purpose of preventing inflation, the office of price administration (OPA) tried to hold down prices, and administered the rationing system. And, as the overlapping and duplication inseparable from piecemeal legislation appeared, the Office of War Mobilization and Rehabilitation (OWMR) was created in 1944 in an attempt to co-ordinate their activities. The number of government employees increased from 932,000 in 1939 to approximately three million in 1945. American production increased phenomenally, supplying America and her allies. (For the military history, see *World War II.*)

President Roosevelt was reelected for a fourth term in 1944, with an electoral vote of 432 to 90 for the Republican candidate, Thomas E. Dewey.

War's End and After. President Roosevelt died on April 12, 1945, and was succeeded by the vice president, Harry S. Truman. But without regard to changes in Washington, the war moved on to a victorious conclusion. In May came the surrender of Germany. On August 14, 1945, President Truman announced to the nation the unconditional surrender of Japan. On December 31, 1946, he declared the legal cessation of hostilities.

Nor could the United States escape its commitments to the Old World. A part of these were embodied in its adhesion to the United Nations, in whose formation at San Francisco the United States had taken a leading part. (See *World War II.*) The United States had contributed two-thirds of the cost of UNRRA, and had made loans to Great Britain and other countries.

Growing Opposition to Russia. A split was developing in the United Nations. Russia had entered upon a policy of expansion. She would tolerate in

HISTORICAL STATISTICS OF THE UNITED

Name of State or Territory	Origin and Meaning of Name	Date of Admission or Acquisition	Settlement*			Area in Square Miles	Population When Admitted or Acquired
			Where	When	By Whom		
Alabama	Indian—Thicket Cutters. Erroneously thought to mean, "Here We Rest."	1819	Mobile Bay	1702	French	51,609	127,901
Alaska	Indian—Al-ay-ek-sa, meaning Great Country	1867	Kodiak	1783	Russians	590,884	30,000‡
Arizona	Indian—Place of Little Springs	1912	Tucson	1776	Spanish	113,909	204,354
Arkansas	From a tribe of Indians	1836	Arkansas Post	1685	French	53,102	97,574
California	First used in a Spanish romance, 1510	1850	San Diego	1769	Spanish	158,693	92,597
Canal Zone	Strip of land bordering Panama Canal	1904	Panama	1519	Spanish	436	......
Colorado	Spanish—Red, or Colored	1876	Auraria	1859	Americans	104,247	39,864
Connecticut	Indian—Long Tidal River	1788†	Windsor	1633	English	5,009	237,946
Delaware	Named for Lord Delaware	1787†	Wilmington	1638	Swedes	2,057	59,096
District of Columbia	From poetic name of United States	1791	Georgetown	1695	Scotch and Irish	69	......
Florida	Spanish—Flowery	1845	St. Augustine	1565	Spanish	58,560	87,445
Georgia	Named for George II	1788†	Savannah	1733	English	58,876	82,548
Guam	Spanish Guajan—Juan	1898	....	1688	Spanish	210	......
Hawaii	Hawaii—Big Island	1898	Honolulu	1820	Americans	6,449	109,020
Idaho	Indian—Gem of the Mountains	1890	Cœur d'Alene	1842	Americans	83,557	88,548
Illinois	Indian—The People	1818	Kaskaskia	1700 ?	French	56,400	55,211
Indiana	Indian's Ground	1816	Vincennes	1727	French	36,291	147,178
Iowa	Indian—Drowsy Ones	1846	Dubuque	1833	Americans	56,280	192,214
Kansas	From a tribe of Indians	1861	Leavenworth	1854	Americans	82,276	107,206
Kentucky	Indian—Prairie. Not "Dark and Bloody Ground."	1792	Boonesboro	1775	English	40,395	73,677
Louisiana	Named for Louis XIV	1812	New Orleans	1718	French	48,523	76,556
Maine	The Main Land	1820	Saco, Monhegan	1622 ?	English	33,215	298,335
Maryland	Named for Queen Henrietta Maria	1788†	St. Mary's	1634	English	10,577	319,728
Massachusetts	The Place of Great Hills	1788†	Plymouth	1620	English	8,257	378,787
Michigan	Indian—Great Water or Lake	1837	Sault Ste. Marie	1668	French	58,216	212,267
Minnesota	Indian—Cloudy Water	1858	St. Paul	1838	Americans	84,068	172,023
Mississippi	Indian—Great River, or Father of Waters	1817	Biloxi	1699	French	47,716	75,448
Missouri	Indian—Great Muddy	1821	St. Genevieve	1735	French	69,674	66,586
Montana	Spanish—A Mountain	1889	Yellowstone River	1809	Americans	147,138	142,924
Nebraska	Indian—Shallow Water	1867	Bellevue	1847	Americans	77,237	122,993
Nevada	Spanish—Snow-covered	1864	Genoa	1850	Americans	110,540	42,491
New Hampshire	Hampshire, England	1788†	Portsmouth	1623	English	9,304	141,885
New Jersey	Named in compliment to the governor of Jersey Island	1787†	Elizabethtown	1617	Dutch	7,836	184,139
New Mexico	Mexitl, Aztec war god	1912	San Gabriel	1598	Spanish	121,666	327,301
New York	Named for the duke of York	1788†	New York	1613	Dutch	49,576	340,120
North Carolina	Named for Charles II	1789†	Albemarle Sound	1653	English	52,712	393,751
North Dakota	Indian—Allied	1889	Pembina	1859	Americans	70,665	190,983
Ohio	Indian—Beautiful River	1803	Marietta	1788	Americans	41,222	45,365
Oklahoma	Indian—Land of Red Men	1907	Guthrie	1890	Americans	69,919	1,414,042
Oregon	Spanish—Wild Marjoram	1859	Astoria	1811	Americans	96,981	52,465
Pennsylvania	Latin—Penn's Woodland	1787†	Chester	1638	Swedes	45,333	434,373
Puerto Rico	Spanish—Rich Port	1898	Pueblo Viejo	1508	Spanish	3,435	813,937
Rhode Island	Rhodes, an island in the Ægean Sea	1790†	Providence	1636	English	1,214	68,825
Samoan Islands, Tutuila and Manua	From Sa-ia-moa, meaning Sacred to Moa	1899	....	1830	English	58	5,000‡
South Carolina	Named for Charles II	1788†	Ashley River	1670	English	31,055	393,751
South Dakota	Indian—Allied	1889	Southeast part	1859	Americans	77,047	348,600
Tennessee	Indian—Cherokee Indian Town, Tennassee	1796	Watauga	1769	Americans	42,246	35,691
Texas	Indian—Hello, Friend	1845	San Antonio	1692	Spanish	267,339	212,592
Utah	Indian—Mountain Dwellers	1896	Salt Lake City	1847	Americans	84,916	210,779
Vermont	French—Green Mountain	1791	St. Anne	1665	French	9,609	85,425
Virgin Islands	Named in honor of St. Ursula and her companions	1917	St. Croix	1625 ?	Dutch and English	149	26,051
Virginia	Named for Elizabeth, the Virgin Queen	1788†	Jamestown	1607	English	40,815	747,610
Washington	Named for George Washington	1889	Columbia River	1811	English	68,192	357,232
West Virginia	From Virginia	1863	Berkeley County	1726-7	Americans	24,181	442,014
Wisconsin	Indian—Meaning unknown	1848	Green Bay	1745	French	56,154	305,391
Wyoming	Indian—The Plain	1890	Cheyenne	1867	Americans	97,914	62,555

* Exact dates and places of first permanent settlements are frequently difficult to determine; authorities differ.
† Dates of ratification of the Constitution by the Thirteen Original States.
‡ Estimate.

STATES—STATE AND TERRITORIAL

Original Name, or Territory from which Derived	Numbers Furnished for Army and Navy During World War I				Name of State or Territory
	Under Selective Service Act		Volunteers		
	Registrations	Inductions	Army	Navy*	
Louisiana and Georgia, Mississippi Territory, Alabama Territory	444,842	64,405	11,705	4,814	Alabama
Russian America	16,061	2,090	163	95	Alaska
Mexico	94,310	9,580	1,689	1,574	Arizona
Louisiana, Louisiana Territory, Missouri Territory, Arkansas Territory	365,904	55,419	10,849	4,657	Arkansas
New Albion, Upper California	839,614	79,593	39,675	26,774	California
Republic of Panama	....	....	174	....	Canal Zone
Louisiana and Mexican Cession, Colorado Territory	216,820	25,950	9,088	5,130	Colorado
North Virginia, New England	374,400	36,010	14,864	11,884	Connecticut
New Sweden, New Netherland, Pennsylvania, Three Lower Counties on the Delaware	55,277	5,527	2,150	1,041	Delaware
Prince George's County, Maryland	90,361	11,029	4,567	5,670	District of Columbia
Florida Territory	209,248	27,988	7,734	5,334	Florida
One of the Thirteen Original States	549,235	72,383	16,421	8,059	Georgia
San Juan	....	....	....	248	Guam
Sandwich Islands	71,800	6,008	2,964	381	Hawaii
Oregon Territory, Washington Territory, Idaho Territory	105,337	13,824	4,603	2,100	Idaho
Northwest Territory, Indiana Territory, Illinois Territory	1,574,877	193,338	66,072	38,393	Illinois
Northwest Territory, Indiana Territory	639,834	77,440	34,664	12,253	Indiana
Louisiana, Missouri Territory, Michigan Territory, Wisconsin Territory, Iowa Territory	524,456	74,512	25,494	10,597	Iowa
Louisiana, Kansas Territory	382,065	49,757	19,080	8,081	Kansas
Virginia	486,739	60,617	18,906	8,430	Kentucky
Louisiana, Territory of Orleans	392,316	61,623	7,970	7,131	Louisiana
New England, Laconia, and Massachusetts	159,631	17,659	8,333	5,239	Maine
One of the Original States	313,489	36,334	11,429	8,791	Maryland
North Virginia, New England, Massachusetts Bay	886,728	93,960	44,754	44,385	Massachusetts
Northwest Territory, Indiana Territory, Michigan Territory	873,383	106,802	31,323	16,453	Michigan
Louisiana and Northwest Territory, Minnesota Territory	541,607	79,383	19,773	10,863	Minnesota
Louisiana and Georgia, Mississippi Territory	344,724	47,319	8,448	4,791	Mississippi
Louisiana, Louisiana Territory, Missouri Territory	765,045	104,591	34,020	17,862	Missouri
Louisiana, Nebraska Territory, Idaho Territory, Dakota Territory, Montana Territory	201,256	29,446	7,225	2,663	Montana
Louisiana, Nebraska Territory	287,414	34,783	14,784	6,138	Nebraska
Upper California, Utah Territory, Nevada Territory	30,808	3,384	1,582	257	Nevada
North Virginia, New England, Laconia	95,158	9,665	5,072	2,513	New Hampshire
New Netherland	762,485	78,615	30,050	23,826	New Jersey
Mexico	81,013	9,508	2,740	1,516	New Mexico
New Netherland	2,511,046	279,875	98,994	75,856	New York
Albemarle Colony	482,463	62,557	13,845	7,124	North Carolina
Louisiana, Minnesota Territory, Nebraska Territory, Dakota Territory	160,292	20,680	6,199	1,692	North Dakota
Northwest Territory	1,389,474	154,236	48,850	16,908	Ohio
Indian Territory, Oklahoma Territory	435,668	71,926	13,838	6,955	Oklahoma
Oregon Territory	179,436	19,617	12,312	6,588	Oregon
Original State	2,069,407	223,122	83,740	37,571	Pennsylvania
Borinquén	240,886	16,901	2,263	418	Porto Rico
North Virginia, New England, Isles of Rhodes, Providence and Rhode Island Plantations	134,515	12,554	6,400	7,264	Rhode Island
Navigators' Islands	....	....	....	90	Samoan Islands
Carteret Colony	307,350	47,341	8,085	5,127	South Carolina
Louisiana, Minnesota Territory, Nebraska Territory, Dakota Territory	145,706	22,423	7,357	1,976	South Dakota
North Carolina, Territory south of the Ohio River	474,347	66,064	16,186	6,184	Tennessee
Republic of Texas	990,522	127,797	36,224	18,217	Texas
Mexican Cession, Deseret, Utah Territory	103,052	12,309	4,483	1,955	Utah
New Netherland, New Hampshire Grants	71,484	7,450	3,789	1,603	Vermont
Danish West Indies	....	....	....	55	Virgin Islands
South Virginia	465,439	61,878	13,539	11,854	Virginia
Oregon Territory, Washington Territory	328,466	33,257	13,138	11,887	Washington
Virginia	325,266	46,596	9,431	3,203	West Virginia
Northwest Territory, Illinois Territory, Michigan Territory, Wisconsin Territory	586,290	79,012	24,387	13,391	Wisconsin
Louisiana and Oregon Territory (chiefly), Nebraska Territory, Dakota Territory, Idaho Territory, Wyoming Territory	59,977	8,790	2,807	668	Wyoming
Totals	24,237,323	2,952,927†	964,003‡	549,314**	

*Includes the Naval Reserve Force. †Includes 2,944,357 Army, 1911 Navy, and 6659 Marine Corps. ‡About 80 per cent of total. Includes Regular Army, National Guard, and Enlisted Reserve Corps. **Includes 12,493 men obtained under the Selective Service act.

the immediately neighboring states only Communist-controlled governments which would take their orders from Moscow. Winston Churchill in the "Iron Curtain" speech at Fulton, Missouri, sounded a warning. Poland, Rumania, and Bulgaria came first. Hungary and Czechoslovakia were seized by Communist minorities in 1947 and 1948. The Comintern was revived as the Cominform. All this might mean that the Soviet Union had returned to its old policy of spreading Communist doctrines over the whole world. In such a conflict of ideologies the United States inevitably was brought forward as the champion of free enterprise and democracy.

The opposition of the two ideologies appeared in the matter of the atomic bomb. The United States was willing to place the bomb under the control of the United Nations, but Russia vetoed the American plan in the Security Council, and her own proposals were insufficient. On other matters, such as the admission of member nations, Russia persistently interposed her veto against the majority of the council.

The Truman Doctrine. In March 1947 the "Truman Doctrine" was stated. It arose from the situation in Greece, where there was danger that the Communist minority, with foreign assistance, would seize the government (not too respectable, but favored by the majority of the Greeks) and bring Greece under Soviet control. This would put Turkey and the Dardanelles in danger. President Truman declared that the United States must assist free peoples, "striving to maintain their freedom and independence," and resisting pressure from armed minorities or foreign powers. He asked and Congress gave $400,000,000 for economic assistance to Greece and Turkey. The United States was now committed to oppose Communism in all quarters.

The Marshall Plan. As in Greece, the economic dislocation and social demoralization of the war had created conditions in the countries of western Europe which rendered them a fertile field for Communist propaganda. To remedy these conditions, relief was not enough. A better way was suggested by Secretary Marshall in his Harvard address in June 1947. Let the countries of Europe, as a unit, take account of their own resources and find out what they could do toward rehabilitation. America would make a survey of what it could give. The aim was to be European reconstruction, not continued American relief. The Russians, invited to the preliminary conference, denounced the proposal as "American imperialism," and Communist parties in all countries opposed it.

Great Britain and France called the Conference for European Economic Co-operation at Paris in July 1947. Sixteen countries took part. Russia and the Russian satellites were not represented. The final statement of their needs amounted to fifteen billion dollars, over a period of four years.

In April 1948 Congress accepted the European Recovery Program (ERP), and appropriated five billion, three hundred million dollars for the first year's work. The program was to be handled by the Economic Co-operation Administration (ECA), with Paul G. Hoffman as administrator, and W. Averell Harriman as chief European representative.

The Western Alliance. A Security Alliance of Great Britain, France, and the Benelux countries expanded in 1949 into the North Atlantic Defensive Alliance, including at its inception also the United States, Canada, and Norway. This alliance, following the principle laid down by the treaty of Rio de Janeiro, signed in 1947 by 19 American republics, declared that an attack on one member would be resisted by all. Russia denounced the plans for co-operation as "warmongering."

Meantime, the Cold War was waging in all quarters, but especially in Germany. Here Berlin became the storm center. The Russians, attempting to drive the western representatives from Berlin, blockaded their quarters of the city by road, rail, and water. The Anglo-American answer was the "airlift," bringing food and fuel to the city by air. It began operations in June 1948, and brought in its millionth ton of supplies—it happened to be dried carrots and potatoes—on February 18, 1949—the most gigantic operation in air freight in history.

Nor was Europe the only field of America's new foreign activity. She had claimed and received from the United Nations the trusteeship for the mid-Pacific islands taken from Japan. In southern Korea she was supporting a democratic government. In China she was aiding the Nationalist government with economic relief, but not with military support.

Domestic Affairs. After President Truman's accession the cabinet was gradually reorganized. (See *Government and Politics*.) In response to public demand, the armed forces were rapidly demobilized—too rapidly, some thought. Industry absorbed the veterans, with no serious increase in unemployment, but the housing situation became acute.

Inflation. Wages, prices, and the cost of living became outstanding issues. Reconversion was stimulated by the demand for "consumer goods," and hindered by an epidemic of strikes which affected most of the large industries in 1945 and 1946, as powerful unions sought to maintain the high pay of war times. The strikes affected the automobile, steel, and electric industries, coal mining, railroad and marine transportation. They were settled largely through the efforts of the president. The general effect was an increase in wages of about 18 per cent. Naturally, prices increased and the first round of the "inflation spiral" was started.

The Office of Price Administration had done good service in keeping down prices during the war, but its methods had made it unpopular. Congress, against the president's protests, materially reduced its power. The controls, except upon rents, were gradually removed by the end of 1946. All these factors contributed to a higher range of prices, which reached its peak in September 1948, and then slowly sank.

The Eightieth Congress. In the elections of 1946 the Republicans carried both Houses of Congress for the first time since 1930. The result was a bitter contest between Congress and the president, in which party feeling accentuated the traditional opposition of executive and legislature. The Republicans wished to reduce expenditures and taxation. They cut down appropriations and reduced the income tax. Their tax bill was passed over the president's veto by a bi-partisan vote. The Taft-Hartley labor bill, amending the Wagner act, was bitterly opposed by the labor leaders, and vetoed by the president, but passed over his veto, again with bi-partisan support. The various measures of social reform proposed by the president received little attention.

Since the disclosure of Soviet wartime espionage in Canada, the House Committee on Un-American Activities has brought out some unpleasant facts about espionage and the activities of foreign agents within the government service. Its disclosures made a great public impression.

The Election of 1948. Three conventions were held at Philadelphia. The Republicans again nominated Governor Dewey, with Governor Warren of California for vice president; the Progressive party nominated Henry A. Wallace; the Democrats, after unsuccessful efforts of some prominent leaders to induce him to withdraw, renominated President Truman, with Senator Barkley of Kentucky for vice president. Some of the Southern delegates withdrew, and later nominated Governor Thurmond of South Carolina as candidate of the States Rights party. President Truman took the stump in a fighting campaign. Contrary to all predictions and expectations, President Truman was re-elected. He received 49 per cent of the popular vote and 304 electoral votes, to 189 for Dewey and 38 for Thurmond.

HISTORIC AMERICA. I

The Mayflower, Plymouth Harbor, 1620.
Old Bridge, Concord, Mass.
Washington Elm, Cambridge, Mass. (Fell in 1923)
Old City Gates, St. Augustine, Fla.

Plymouth Rock under canopy.
Minute Men Memorial, Lexington, Mass.
House of Cornwallis' Surrender, Yorktown, Va.
St. Xavier Mission, Tucson, Ariz.

HISTORIC AMERICA. II

1 Custis-Lee Mansion, Arlington, Va. 2 King's Chapel, Boston. 3 Bunker Hill Monument, Charlestown (Boston), Mass. 4 Faneuil Hall, Boston. 5 Washington Monument, Washington, D. C. 6 Grant's Tomb, New York City. 7 Independence Hall, Philadelphia. 8 Jefferson Davis Mansion, Richmond, Va. 9 Fort Mackinac, Michigan.

AMERICAN FLAGS

The origin of the device of stars and stripes in the flag of the United States has occasioned much discussion. Several theories have been advanced to account for the alternating red and white stripes. Some writers have derived these from the Dutch flag, which had flown over New Netherlands from 1609 to 1664. Others point out that the so-called Union or Great Union flag, raised on Prospect hill, in what is now Somerville, Mass., January 1, 1776, followed the design of a contemporary British merchant marine flag. This flag which had thirteen alternating red and white stripes, with a union in which appeared the crosses of St. George and St. Andrew on a blue field. The thirteen stripes symbolized the union of the colonies, while the union jack represented their allegiance to Great Britain.

Throughout the Revolution many different colonial and regimental flags were used, in which red and white stripes, stars, and the blue field appear in various combinations. Contemporary prints show the stripes but no stars until the year 1780. It appears, therefore, that the elements which entered into the final design of the national flag were already in common use in the colonies.

The Stars and Stripes. After the declaration of independence, the design of the Grand Union flag was inappropriate. The design of stars and stripes, known as the Betsy Ross flag, was therefore presented to the Congress for consideration. On June 14, 1777, the Continental Congress passed the following resolution: "Resolved, That the flag of the United States be thirteen stripes, alternate red and white, that the union be thirteen stars, white in a blue field, representing a new constellation." But this resolution seems to have been generally disregarded for a long time. A communication to Washington from the war board in May 1779 contained the statement that "it is not yet settled what is the standard of the United States."

On January 15, 1794, Congress, in order to adapt the flag to the new number of states, fifteen after the admission of Vermont and Kentucky, enacted "that from and after May 1, 1795, the flag of the United States be fifteen stripes, alternate red and white and the union be fifteen stars, white in a blue field." In 1818 the number of stripes was reduced to the original number, and Congress ordered that the number of stars should correspond to the number of states, a star to be added on the 4th of July next following the admission of a new state.

Various arrangements of the stars were used until 1896, when Secretary of War Daniel Lamont ordered that they should be placed in six rows. An executive order of President Taft, in 1912, fixed the arrangement of stars as six rows of eight stars each, the stars symbolizing the states in the order of their ratification of the Constitution and their admission to the Union, as follows: Delaware, Pennsylvania, New Jersey, Georgia, Connecticut, Massachusetts, Maryland, South Carolina, New Hampshire, Virginia, New York, North Carolina, Rhode Island, Vermont, Kentucky, Tennessee, Ohio, Louisiana, Indiana, Mississippi, Illinois, Alabama, Maine, Missouri, Arkansas, Michigan, Florida, Texas, Iowa, Wisconsin, California, Minnesota, Oregon, Kansas, West Virginia, Nevada, Nebraska, Colorado, North Dakota, South Dakota, Montana, Washington, Idaho, Wyoming, Utah, Oklahoma, New Mexico, Arizona.

The inspiring name of *Old Glory* was given to the American flag by Captain William Driver of Salem, Mass., in 1831. The words were his salute to a beautiful new flag presented to his ship when starting on a voyage around the world. This flag is preserved in the Smithsonian institution, Washington, but with its union incorrectly restored. It shows 34 stars, instead of the correct number of 24.

The symbolic meanings of the colors in the flag are suggested in a "remark" which Will Barton, the designer of the seal of the Confederation, attached to the description of his design in 1782: "White signifies purity, innocence; red, hardiness and valor. Blue is the ground of the American uniform, and this color signifies vigilance, perseverance, and justice."

Instruction in the symbolic and historical meanings of the national banner has come to be recognized as part of the work of every American school. The first recorded raising of the flag over a school, now so general a custom, took place on Catamount hill, Colrain, Mass., in May 1812. A suitable monument marks the site of the old log schoolhouse. June 14, the anniversary of the Congressional adoption of the stars and stripes, is widely observed as Flag Day. The following pledge, as adopted by Congress on December 22, 1942, is a part of the daily school program, as well as a part of the Flag Day exercises:

"I pledge allegiance to the flag of the United States of America and to the Republic for which it stands, one Nation indivisible, with liberty and justice for all."

Official flag etiquette requires that, when floating horizontally or hanging vertically, the flag should show the stars to the left of the observer. When the flag is hung across a street, the stars should be to the north in an east-and-west street; to the east in a north-and-south street. The flag should not be used for bunting.

The following flags are of interest for historical reasons.

Bunker Hill Flags. As early as the year 1737, a recognized flag of the New England colonies had a blue field with a white union quartered by a red cross. Such a flag, with the addition of a green pine tree in the upper inner quarter of the union, was carried at the battle of Bunker Hill. Another flag of the same design, but having a red field, also appears to have been used in that battle. Some authorities say that each of these flags had, on one side, the words "An Appeal to Heaven," on the other, *Qui Transtulit Sustinet,* meaning "He who transplanted us will care for us."

Flag of Lexington and Concord. In the fight at Concord and Lexington, Captain Nathaniel Page, of the Bedford Minutemen, carried a maroon-colored flag, upon which was the motto *Vince Aut Morire,* meaning "Conquer or Die." This flag is preserved in the town of Bedford, Mass., and is known as the Bedford flag.

Rattlesnake Flags. The device of a rattlesnake, usually represented coiled and ready to strike, was popular with the American colonists just before the Revolution. The origin of its significance as an American emblem can only be surmised. The flag of the Culpepper Minutemen carried this symbol, together with the two inscriptions,—"Don't Tread on Me" and "Liberty or Death." It appeared also on a yellow banner presented to Congress by Colonel Gadsden on February 8, 1776.

Crescent Flags. In the southern colonies, during the early part of the Revolution, a blue flag, having in its upper inner corner a white crescent, was popular. The first use of this design as a distinctively American emblem is credited to Colonel William Moultrie, who hoisted a crescent flag over Fort Johnson, on James island, South Carolina, September 13, 1775. The crescent flags sometimes bore the word "Liberty" in white letters. This is said to have been the design of the flag which Sergeant Jasper gallantly replaced on Fort Sullivan during the British attack of June 28, 1776.

Pine Tree Flags. The design of a green pine tree was a favorite emblem in colonial New England. It was used on coins as early as 1652. The Sons of Liberty are said to have unfurled on Harvard College campus in 1770 a plain red flag, upon which later a green pine tree design was sewed. On some New England flags, the tree had a serpent coiled around the trunk. Below the design were the words "Don't Tread on Me," and above was the inscription "An Appeal to Heaven." In 1776 the Massachusetts Council provided that the naval colors of the colony should be a white flag bearing a green pine tree and the inscription "An Appeal to Heaven."

Flag of Philadelphia Light Horse. It is believed that this flag was carried by the troop that escorted General Washington from Philadelphia to New York, in June 1775, when he was on his way to take command of the army at Cambridge. The banner, now in possession of the Philadelphia City Cavalry, derives especial interest from the fact that its canton is formed of thirteen stripes, alternating blue and silver,—probably the earliest use of stripes on an American flag.

The Continental Flag. This name is applied to the flag raised on Prospect Hill, Somerville, Mass., January 1, 1776, by a unit of the continental army. The navy is known to have used it on January 4, 1776. The flag, which was apparently formed from a contemporary British merchant marine flag, was called also the Great Union. It contained the thirteen stripes, one for each colony, as in the present flag, but in place of the stars it displayed the crosses of St. George and St. Andrew. This was the first occasion when thirteen alternating stripes of white and of red were made the foundation of the national standard.

The Betsy Ross Flag. This was the first flag combining the stars and stripes. It contained thirteen five-pointed stars arranged in a circle on a blue field. This is said to have been the design authorized for the official flag by the Continental Congress, June 14, 1777. The design was produced by a committee of Congress, consisting of General Washington, Robert Morris, and Colonel George Ross, with the assistance of Mrs. Elizabeth Ross.

The Bennington Flag. This banner was unique among Revolutionary flags. It was made of homespun linen; its union was nine stripes in depth instead of seven; its stars were seven-pointed instead of five-pointed, and they were arranged in an arch rather than in a circle. It was probably made near Bennington and carried into the battle of Bennington by Nathaniel Fillmore, August 16, 1777.

Eutaw Flag. A crimson banner with a romantic history, presented in 1780 to Colonel William A. Washington by Miss Jane Elliott, of South Carolina, whom he later married. It was carried in the battles of Cowpens and Eutaw Springs. Mrs. Washington later presented this flag to the Washington Light Infantry of Charleston, S. C., and it is now in their possession.

Flag of the Bon Homme Richard. It is said that some young women of Portsmouth, N. H., made this flag for Captain John Paul Jones from pieces of their silk gowns. The name of the *Bon Homme Richard* attaches to this flag because of the fact that it was the ensign of that ship in the famous battle with the *Serapis*, September 23, 1779, when Captain Jones captured the *Serapis*, although he lost his own unseaworthy vessel. When the *Bon Homme Richard*, riddled with shot, sank beside the *Serapis*, the flag was still flying at her masthead, as a symbol of the gallant victory her crew had won.

Commodore Perry's Flag. This flag, flown at the battle of Lake Erie, September 10, 1813, contained the words of the dying Lawrence, "Don't give up the ship," which have become the watchword of the American navy.

Flag of Fort McHenry. The flag which waved over the American defenses during the British bombardment on the night of September 13, 1814, inspired the writing of the "Star-Spangled Banner." The pattern of this flag, fifteen stripes and fifteen stars, is that authorized by Congress in 1794.

THE DEMOCRATIC PARTY

The Democratic party had its origin coincidently with the beginning of the republic. Thomas Jefferson was the first leader and spokesman. The elements of the party were in existence when the Constitution was adopted, as, for example, the Constitutionalist party in Pennsylvania. The opponents of the Constitution maintained that the government was being centralized and that it was organized in the interests of the privileged classes. Those who took this position called themselves Antifederalists. By 1792, the term Democratic-Republican party was used. This designation was generally shortened,—members of the party calling themselves "Republican," their opponents applying to them the term "Democratic."

This party was made up of men who, like Jefferson, were theoretical believers in the rights of the people, and of those without wealth or position, many of whom had previously been disfranchised. Jefferson stated their principles as follows: "* * * to maintain the will of the majority. We believed that man was a rational animal endowed by nature with rights and with an innate sense of justice; and that he could be restrained from wrong and protected in right, by moderate powers confided to persons of his own choice, and held to their duties by dependence on their own will."

Early Power and Principles. The "Republican" party opposed the Federalists. In 1792, it carried Congress and numerous local elections, but did not oppose Washington for his second term as president. In 1797, it received 68 electoral votes in comparison with the Federalists' 71, and Jefferson became vice president. The party opposed the Alien and Sedition laws of 1798 as dangerous assertions of power by the central government. It elected Jefferson president and Burr vice president in 1800, and re-elected Jefferson in 1804.

The "Republican" party ceased to oppose the Constitution after the first ten amendments were made. However, it insisted that, in respect to the powers granted to the general government by the Constitution, that instrument should be construed very strictly. In consequence, the party continually opposed such extensions of Federal power as were construed by Chief Justice John Marshall to be constitutional.

The elections of 1808 and 1812, when Madison was elected president, indicated general acceptance of the Republican party. The Federalist party nearly disappeared in most of the states, and it ceased to exist as a national body after its futile opposition to the War of 1812. At the close of that conflict, the country was in a strong financial condition. The Republicans accepted the idea of a national government, and the former Federalists generally acted with the only party now in existence. The lack of organized opposition gave to the administration of President Monroe the name "Era of Good Feeling." Monroe was elected president in 1816 and again in 1820; John Quincy Adams, a former Federalist, was elected in 1824.

The Democratic Party of Jackson. Up to this period in American history, nearly every one elected to conspicuous public office, no matter what his belief in the rights, powers, and privileges of the common people, had been a man of wealth, education, and family. From some of the newer districts, however, especially of the West, men who owed little to such advantages had come to Congress. In 1828, Andrew Jackson, a man of this style, was elected to the presidency. His followers were first called "Jackson men" and then "Democrats." Democracy was no longer a theory, but was exemplified. Although the principles of Jefferson continued to be followed, the agents were new.

Jackson, re-elected in 1832, put down nullification, secured a lowering of the tariff, and destroyed the Bank of the United States. Van Buren, his trusted friend, followed him in the presidency. But, in 1840, after the panic of 1837 had occasioned widespread dissatisfaction with the Democrats, the representative of a new party, the Whigs, was elected.

Democrats and Whigs. Until 1856 the Democrats and Whigs contested the elections. There was no sharp sectional division, but everywhere there were Democratic districts alongside the more conservative or aristocratic regions which voted Whig. In principle, the Democrats opposed high tariffs and Federal aid for internal improvement. After 1840 the Democratic party definitely aligned itself as opposed to interference with slavery.

The Divided Party. The slavery question finally overshadowed all others. It caused a split in Democratic ranks in 1848, when Lewis Cass became the regular Democratic candidate, while antislavery Democrats joined with the Free Soilers in supporting Van Buren. In the years from 1852 to 1856, the same issue broke up the Whig party. The new opposition party was called Republican. It drew most of its supporters from the North and West; the Democratic party was strongest in the South.

In 1860 the Democratic party had two candidates, one Northern, one Southern. The Republicans won. The Southern states seceded, but the ensuing Civil War resulted both in the preservation of the Union and in the destruction of slavery. At the end of the struggle, the Northern Democrats were weak and discredited; the Southern Democrats were disfranchised. Not until 1874 was there much chance of victory. In that year the party won in the Congressional elections. In 1876, it won a popular victory for the presidency, but was not awarded the electoral votes by the electoral commission.

Cleveland and Bryan. In the '80's, the question of civil service reform and of reform of the tariff became prominent. In 1884, the Democrats won, largely on these issues. They received a large Republican vote, dubbed Mugwump, made up chiefly of men who feared and disliked Blaine and approved Cleveland's record on civil service. Cleveland was the victor. He was defeated in 1888 only to be elected again in 1892, the only president to be re-elected after an interim. In his second term came financial depression. Dissatisfaction with the capitalists, moneyed interests, banks, and railroads was rife among large sections of the people. Free coinage of silver was seized upon as a method of relief. The silver men, under the lead of William Jennings Bryan, captured the Democratic party, and in the 1896 campaign it included the Silver Republicans and won most of the Western states as well as the South.

But the conservatives or standpatters, especially in the East, went solidly into the Republican party. The term "sound money" won the election for the Republicans in 1896. By 1900, the Spanish American war had been fought, and the demand for the retention of the Philippines was so strong that the anti-imperialistic and free silver platform of the Democrats carried but few states. In 1904, the Democrats swung to a conservative candidate, but the progressive measures adopted by the Republicans gave Roosevelt the victory, and the success of the progressive policy of the Republicans carried the country in 1908.

Wilson and Roosevelt. Between 1908 and 1912, the progressive element revived in the Democratic party, and the Republicans were divided. In the election of 1912, the Republicans split, and Wilson was elected. In a close election in 1916 he was re-elected. In his second administration occurred the participation of the United States in the World War, with the resulting Peace Treaty. The end of the war left a widespread feeling of unrest, and the Democrats were severely defeated in 1920. Some prophesied the dissolution of the party, but in 1928 the Democratic candidate, Alfred E. Smith, received more votes than had ever before been cast for a presidential candidate of that party. He was defeated by Hoover on a platform of "prosperity." But Hoover's term was one long fight against ever deepening economic depression. In 1932, the country turned decisively to the Democratic party and elected Franklin D. Roosevelt. He was reelected in 1936, 1940, and 1944. After losing control of Congress in 1946, the party was able, contrary to all predictions, to elect President Truman two years later.

Democratic Principles. In all its history, the party has stood for the rights of the people. It opposed the "rich, the well-born, and the able" in Washington's time; it advocated extension of the suffrage; it opposed the manufacturers and the bankers. It was strong on the frontier and on the farms and among the mechanics. When it became associated with the slave interests, it had an aristocratic element that came to dominate the party. After the Civil War, the party reverted to its old principles, although with a tendency to adopt radical proposals in opposition to the Republicans.

The Democratic party throughout most of its history opposed a loose construction of the Constitution. Its leaders felt that those in control of capital would find the Federal government easier to influence than the numerous state governments. Consequently they opposed enlargement of Federal power, a result most easily secured through a loose interpretation of the language of the basic law. In the party's first years, its leaders could see no justification for a national bank, for protective tariffs, or for government interference with state functions. The party believed also in state rights, although it was not willing to go as far as nullification in 1832.

On the other hand, the Democratic party, under strong leaders, has been vigorous in its national policy. Jefferson, having purchased Louisiana, found the leaders of his party in Congress prepared to surpass him in a broad construction of the Constitution to justify an act not expressly provided for. Jackson, faced by the threat of nullification in South Carolina, declared: "The Federal Union, it must and shall be preserved." Cleveland and Wilson were strong leaders in national policies. Democrats, like Dix, Douglas, Logan, Palmer, and McClellan, emphatically repudiated secession, and fought for the Union. Finally Franklin D. Roosevelt went beyond all earlier leaders of either party in finding ways for the central government to handle problems of national importance.

The Party Constituency. In the course of its history, the constituency of the party has changed. There have always been in its ranks, among the wealthy and among men of position, the theoretical or doctrinaire democrats, like Jefferson himself and Gallatin. But the frontier developed men of character who were democratic by nature. Up to the Civil War practically all the immigrants who had escaped from autocracy in Europe were Democrats by instinct. The cities ceased to be controlled by merchants and bankers, and elections were carried by the votes of the masses.

Several changes are notable in the period since the Civil War. The South became solidly Democratic except in the Appalachian Mountain region. In 1936, this tendency was so pronounced that every state in the Union with the exception of Maine and Vermont joined the Democratic column in support of Roosevelt's New Deal. In recent years, immigrants have been distributed among all political parties. The number of independent voters has increased, and they have usually voted for the party with a liberal platform. The economically discontented have seemed to look to the Democratic party for relief, and most third parties of the period have eventually been absorbed by the Democrats,—as Greenbackers, Grangers, Populists, Silverites.

THE REPUBLICAN PARTY

The Republican party has been, since 1854, one of the two chief political parties in the United States. It developed out of the political and territorial disputes occasioned by the question of slavery. This question had forced one of the compromises in the formation of the Constitution, but did not appear as a political issue so long as free states and slave states were evenly balanced in the Senate. In 1819, the question of the admission of Missouri arose, because Missouri comprised a part of the new Louisiana territory and, although in the region far enough north to be included in the free states, was proposing to come in as a slave state.

Rise of the Slavery Issue. By Clay's compromise of 1820, Missouri was admitted as a slave state, but slavery was not to exist in the territories north of its southern border. This compromise remained in force for 34 years. In the meantime, abolition societies had grown up in the North, a Free Soil party had been formed to prevent the extension of slavery into the territories, and the slavery question had become political. The Democratic party, under the control of its Southern portion, was definitely committed to noninterference with slavery in the states, and the Whig party was divided, its main body holding to the compromises secured by its great leader, Henry Clay.

In 1854, the Missouri Compromise of 1820 was broken by the Kansas-Nebraska act, which proposed the principle of squatter sovereignty for the territories which were north of the line laid down in 1820 as the dividing line between slave and free regions. The slavery party was strengthened by the Dred Scott decision of 1857.

The opponents of the Kansas-Nebraska act were the Free Soilers, the Northern Democrats, and the Northern Whigs. The Free Soil party, though small, had been fighting for a principle in its opposition to slavery. The Northern Whigs belonged to a national party which had for years carefully refrained from agitating the slavery question, until the Kansas-Nebraska act seemed to repudiate the act of one of their great leaders, Henry Clay, and to arouse the long suppressed antislavery feeling of the North. The Anti-Nebraska Democrats felt that their consciences could not accept a betrayal of the compact of 1820, in favor of the slaveholding aristocracy of the South. Their number was increased in 1858 by anti-Lecompton Democrats who protested against forcing the Lecompton constitution on Kansas. Later, the American or Know-Nothing party of the '50's, which had not been long in existence, and was found chiefly in free states, dissolved. These elements united to form a new party.

The New Party. The Republican party sprang up simultaneously in different states. The date usually given for its founding is June 1854, and the place, Jackson, Michigan. It entered the Congressional campaign of 1854, elected a plurality in the House of Representatives, and, by a combination with the American party, elected the speaker of the House. The Republican strength was in the north Atlantic and north central states.

In the presidential campaign of 1856, the Republicans nominated Frémont for president, and won New England, New York, and the West—114 votes; but Buchanan carried Pennsylvania and the South—174 votes. In the senatorial campaign of 1858 in Illinois, Lincoln and Douglas debated the slavery question, and the issue was clearly defined, with the result that a break between the Northern and the Southern Democrats became inevitable. In 1860, the Republicans, instead of nominating a radical antislavery man, turned to Lincoln. The Democrats split, and the remnant of the Whigs nominated a candidate. Lincoln secured 180 votes against 123 for all others.

War and Reconstruction. The Civil War broke out almost immediately. Lincoln took the ground that the North would fight for the preservation of the Union. The War Democrats supported him, while the abolitionist element in the Republican party tried to urge more rapid action against slavery, and the Peace Democrats favored no action. The Republican party was essentially the antislavery party, and the friend of the Negro, but it needed the support of the former Democrats. In 1864, it called itself the Union party, and the War Democrats continued with the party in the reelection of Lincoln. Opportune war successes helped. The vote was 212 for Lincoln to 21 for McClellan. Lincoln's assassination resulted in Johnson's succession; the extreme antislavery element of the Republicans controlled Congress for four years and opposed the president. The three Civil War amendments to the Constitution were passed, and the control of the Southern states was placed under Northern troops. In 1868, Grant was elected president by the Republicans.

By 1872, the liberal element in the Republican party had become restive under the domination of the extremists, and they broke away, nominating Horace Greeley for president. The Democrats also nominated Greeley, but the vote was 286 for Grant to 63 for his opponent. In 1873, however, came a business panic, and there were political and financial irregularities in Grant's administration, so that the Republicans lost Congress in 1874.

In 1876, the presidential election was disputed. The electoral commission declared Hayes elected by one vote over Tilden. The administration was liberal and was opposed by the Stalwarts. In 1880, the latter desired Grant for a third term, and the fight in the convention resulted in the nomination of Garfield, a "dark horse," who was elected, 214 to 155, but was assassinated a few months after his inauguration.

Tariff and Civil Service Issues. Arthur succeeded, and during his term the tariff and civil service became important issues. By this time the Southern states had become solidly Democratic, as, after the withdrawal of the Federal troops in 1877, the Negroes and the Northerners known as "carpetbaggers" had no more chance to carry the elections. The Republicans still favored "force bills" to preserve the civil rights of the Negroes, but the Southern whites were in control, and, after 1889, wrote into most of the Southern state constitutions "grandfather" clauses which effectually disfranchised the Negroes.

In 1884, the weakness occasioned by the certain loss of the South to the Republicans was aggravated by the movement within the party of those who felt that the high moral plane of the early days of the Republican party had been distinctly lowered, and who favored an exponent of civil service reform in the person of Cleveland. The Republican position upon the tariff question, also, in respect to which the party had succeeded to the earlier position of the Whigs (and their predecessors, the Federalists), in favor of a high tariff for protection of American industries, was alienating a considerable number of voters. The result was that the Republicans lost Congress in 1882 and the presidency in 1884. Blaine was defeated by Cleveland, 182 to 219, although the vote was in doubt until the last moment.

During the next twelve years, when economic and industrial questions were prominent, it was claimed that the Republican party was in the hands of the moneyed classes, including the banks, the railroads, Wall Street, and the manufacturers. In the West, the Farmers' Alliance entered politics, and then the People's party, later called the Populists, arose. These drew votes away from the Republicans. The presidential elections varied. In 1888, Harrison defeated Cleveland, 233 to 168, largely on the issue of the tariff; but in 1892 Cleveland again became president. Changes in the tariff took place in each of these administrations.

Free Silver. In 1893 came a financial depression which, being charged to the Democratic tariff, gave Congress to the Republicans in 1894. Between the election of 1894 and that of 1896, the question of free silver came to the fore as the summing up of the prevailing economic discontent. There were free silver advocates in both parties. The Democrats declared in favor of free and unlimited coinage of silver at the ratio of 16 to 1. The Republicans were not extreme advocates of gold as a single standard, but became known as the "sound money" men, and attracted the conservative economic elements. The Silver Republicans voted with the Democrats, who nominated Bryan, and the Populists nominated the same candidate. The Gold Democrats nominated a ticket of their own, although most of the conservative Democrats voted for McKinley, the Republican nominee.

During McKinley's term, the gold standard was adopted, and the Spanish American war was fought. Out of the war there arose a new issue of imperialism, the main question being the retention of the Philippines. The Republican and the Democratic candidate of 1896 ran again in 1900, and McKinley won, 292 to 155. As a result of the alignment of the parties in 1900, the Republicans became the "standpat," almost reactionary, party.

Conservatives and Progressives. Upon the assassination of McKinley, Roosevelt succeeded to the presidency, and in 1904 he was elected president over Parker. In Roosevelt's term the liberal element of the party was in control, and the Republicans favored measures providing for government regulation of industry and demanding the "square deal." In 1908, Taft was elected president. During his term, the policies pursued with respect to the tariff and conservation of natural resources indicated that the "old guard," "standpat," reactionary element had again secured control of the party. In 1912, the two elements, progressive and conservative, split. The conservatives nominated Taft; the progressives formed a new party, the Progressive, and nominated Roosevelt. Wilson, the Democratic nominee, was elected.

The World War broke out in 1914. In 1916, the Republicans and Progressives united again, but Wilson defeated Hughes, 277 to 254. After the war, the Republicans came into power again in 1920 by a very large majority, with the reactionary element uppermost. In 1924, the progressive group nominated La Follette, but he received only 13 electoral votes. Coolidge in 1924 and Hoover in 1928 continued the succession of Republican presidents. In the depression years the Progressive wing turned to the Democrats and helped them in their victories in 1932 and 1936. In 1940 and 1944 the party gained strength, but not enough to win the presidency. In 1946 it won control of both Houses of Congress, but was again defeated in the presidential election of 1948.

Republican Principles. From Civil War days the Republican party supported a broad construction of the Constitution, but it abruptly reversed its position in 1936. Favoring centralized power in an era when this meant high tariffs, an imperialistic foreign policy, and Federal aid for railroads, waterways, and reclamation, the party declared for state rights when the Federal government, under Franklin D. Roosevelt, introduced a program declared by Republicans to mean interference with private initiative and ruinous taxation on business.

In general, the Republican party has been a party of the North and West. The "solid South" is Democratic because of Civil War memories, although the Republicans won some temporary successes there in 1928. In the election of 1936, when voters divided more on class lines, the Republican party was largely that of "big business."

COMPARATIVE PARTY STRENGTH IN CONGRESS

Congress		President	Democrats		Republicans		Other Parties
			Senate	House	Senate	House	Abbreviations Used: A.L., AmericanLabor; F-L., Farmer-Labor; H, House; Ind., Independent; Pop., Populist; Pg., Progressive; Proh., Prohibition; S, Senate; Soc., Socialist.
43d	1873–1875	Grant	19	88	51	198	Liberal Rep., S, 4; H, 5
44th	1875–1877	Grant	29	181	47	107	Ind., H, 3
45th	1877–1879	Hayes	36	156	39	137	Ind., S, 1
46th	1879–1881	Hayes	43	156	33	133	
47th	1881–1883	Garfield, Arthur .	37	130	37	152	Ind., S, 2. Greenback, H, 11
48th	1883–1885	Arthur	36	200	40	119	Greenback, H, 6
49th	1885–1887	Cleveland . . .	34	183	42	139	Greenback, H, 3
50th	1887–1889	Cleveland . . .	37	169	39	152	Ind., H, 4
51st	1889–1891	Harrison	37	161	45	169	
52d	1891–1893	Harrison	39	235	47	88	Ind., S, 2. Farmers' Alliance, H, 9
53d	1893–1895	Cleveland . . .	44	218	37	127	Ind., S, 4; H, 11
54th	1895–1897	Cleveland . . .	39	104	43	248	Ind., S, 6; H, 7
55th	1897–1899	McKinley . . .	34	130	47	202	Silver and Pop., S, 8; H, 25
56th	1899–1901	McKinley . . .	26	159	50	189	Silver and Pop., S, 10; H, 8
57th	1901–1903	McKinley . . . Roosevelt. . . .	29	151	53	198	Pop. and Ind., S, 8; H, 8
58th	1903–1905	Roosevelt. . . .	33	178	57	208	Union Labor, H, 2
59th	1905–1907	Roosevelt. . . .	32	136	58	250	
60th	1907–1909	Roosevelt. . . .	31	166	60	220	
61st	1909–1911	Taft	32	175	60	214	Unionist, H, 1
62d	1911–1913	Taft	42	227	49	162	Soc., H, 1
63d	1913–1915	Wilson	51	290	45	127	Progressive, H, 18
64th	1915–1917	Wilson	55	230	41	201	Pg., H, 5. Ind., H, 1. Soc., H, 1
65th	1917–1919	Wilson	51	209	42	212	Pg., S, 1; H, 3. Soc., H, 1. Ind., H, 2
66th	1919–1921	Wilson	47	190	49	240	Ind., H, 2. Proh., H, 1
67th	1921–1923	Harding	37	132	59	300	Soc., H, 1
68th	1923–1925	Harding, Coolidge	42	206	53	223	F-L., S, 1; H, 1. Soc., H, 1. Ind., H, 1
69th	1925–1927	Coolidge	39	183	56	247	F-L., S, 1; H, 3. Soc., H, 2
70th	1927–1929	Coolidge	47	195	48	237	F-L., S, 1; H, 2. Soc., H, 1
71st	1929–1931	Hoover	39	165	55	268	F-L., S, 1; H, 1
72d	1931–1933	Hoover.	47	216	48	218	F-L., S, 1; H, 1
73d	1933–1935	Roosevelt . . .	59	313	36	117	F-L., S, 1; H, 5
74th	1935–1936	Roosevelt	69	322	25	102	Pg., S, 1; H, 7. F-L., S, 1; H, 3. Vac., 1
75th	1937–1938	Roosevelt	76	334	16	88	Pg., S, 1; H, 8. F-L., S, 2; H, 5. Ind., S, 1
76th	1939–1940	Roosevelt . . .	69	262	23	170	Pg., S, 1; H, 2. F-L., S, 2; H, 1. Ind., S, 1
77th	1941–1942	Roosevelt . . .	66	268	28	162	Pg., S, 1; H, 3. F-L., H, 1. Ind., S, 1; H, 1
78th	1943–1944	Roosevelt . . .	59	222	36	208	Pg., S, 1; H, 2. F-L., H, 1. A.L., H, 1
79th	1945–1946	Roosevelt, Truman	56	243	39	190	Pg., S, 1; H, 1. A.L., H, 1
80th	1947–1948	Truman	45	188	51	246	A.L., H. 1
81st	1949–1950	Truman	54	275	42	162	A.L., H. 1

PRESIDENTS OF THE

Name	Born: When	Born: Where	Parents: Father	Parents: Mother	Paternal Ancestry
1. George Washington	Feb. 22, 1732	Bridge's Creek, Va.	Augustine	Mary Ball	English
2. John Adams	Oct. 30, 1735	Quincy, Mass.*	John	Susanna Boylston	English
3. Thomas Jefferson	Apr. 13, 1743	Shadwell, Va.	Peter	Jane Randolph	Welsh
4. James Madison	Mar. 16, 1751	Port Conway, Va.	James	Nelly Conway	English
5. James Monroe	Apr. 28, 1758	Westmoreland Co., Va.	Spence	Eliza Jones	Scotch
6. John Quincy Adams	July 11, 1767	Quincy, Mass.*	John	Abigail Smith	English
7. Andrew Jackson	Mar. 15, 1767	Waxhaw Settl'nt, S.C.†	Andrew	Elizabeth Hutchinson	Scotch-Irish
8. Martin Van Buren	Dec. 5, 1782	Kinderhook, N. Y.	Abraham	Maria Hoes	Dutch
9. William H. Harrison	Feb. 9, 1773	Berkeley, Va.	Benjamin	Elizabeth Bassett	English
10. John Tyler	Mar. 29, 1790	Charles City Co., Va.	John	Mary Armistead	English
11. James K. Polk	Nov. 2, 1795	Mecklenburg Co., N.C.	Samuel	Jane Knox	Scotch-Irish
12. Zachary Taylor	Sept. 24, 1784	Orange Co., Va.	Richard	Sarah Strother	English
13. Millard Fillmore	Jan. 7, 1800	Summer Hill, N. Y.	Nathaniel	Phebe Millard	English
14. Franklin Pierce	Nov. 23, 1804	Hillsborough, N. H.	Benjamin	Anna Kindreck	English
15. James Buchanan	Apr. 23, 1791	Stony Batter, Pa.	James	Elizabeth Speer	Scotch-Irish
16. Abraham Lincoln	Feb. 12, 1809	Nolin Creek, Ky.	Thomas	Nancy Hanks	English
17. Andrew Johnson	Dec. 29, 1808	Raleigh, N. C.	Jacob	Mary M'Donough	English
18. Ulysses S. Grant	Apr. 27, 1822	Point Pleasant, Ohio	Jesse Root	Hannah Simpson	Scotch
19. Rutherford B. Hayes	Oct. 4, 1822	Delaware, Ohio	Rutherford	Sophia Birchard	Scotch
20. James A. Garfield	Nov. 19, 1831	Orange, Ohio	Abram	Eliza Ballou	English
21. Chester A. Arthur	Oct. 5, 1830	Fairfield, Vt.	William	Malvina Stone	Scotch-Irish
22. Grover Cleveland	Mar. 18, 1837	Caldwell, N. J.	Richard F.	Anna Neal	English
23. Benjamin Harrison	Aug. 20, 1833	North Bend, Ohio	John Scott	Elizabeth Irwin	English
24. Grover Cleveland	Mar. 18, 1837	Caldwell, N. J.	Richard F.	Anna Neal	English
25. William McKinley	Jan. 29, 1843	Niles, Ohio	William	Nancy C. Allison	Scotch-Irish
26. Theodore Roosevelt	Oct. 27, 1858	New York City, N. Y.	Theodore	Martha Bullock	Dutch
27. William H. Taft	Sept. 15, 1857	Cincinnati, Ohio	Alphonso	Louise M. Torrey	English
28. Woodrow Wilson	Dec. 28, 1856	Staunton, Va.	Joseph R.	Jessie Woodrow	Scotch-Irish
29. Warren G. Harding	Nov. 2, 1865	Corsica, Ohio	George T.	Phebe E. Dickerson	Scotch-Dutch
30. Calvin Coolidge	July 4, 1872	Plymouth, Vt.	John C.	Victoria J. Moor	English
31. Herbert Hoover	Aug. 10, 1874	West Branch, Iowa	Jesse Clark	Hulda R. Minthorn	Germ.-Swiss
32. Franklin D. Roosevelt	Jan. 30, 1882	Hyde Park, N. Y.	James	Sara Delano	Dutch
33. Harry S. Truman	May 8, 1884	Lamar, Mo.	John Anderson	Martha Ellen Young	Eng. Scotch-Ir.

PRESIDENTS OF THE

Name	Married	Wife's Name	Children: Boys	Children: Girls	Inaugurated	Residence When Elected	Age When Inaugurated
1. George Washington	1759	Mrs. Martha Custis	..	..	1789	Mt. Vernon, Va.	57
2. John Adams	1764	Abigail Smith	3	2	1797	Quincy, Mass.	61
3. Thomas Jefferson	1772	Mrs. Martha Skelton	..	6	1801	Monticello, Va.	57
4. James Madison	1794	Mrs. Dorothy Todd	..	..	1809	Montpelier, Va.	57
5. James Monroe	1786	Eliza Kortwright	..	2	1817	Oakhill, Va.	58
6. John Quincy Adams	1797	Louisa C. Johnson	3	1	1825	Quincy, Mass.	57
7. Andrew Jackson	1791	Mrs. Rachel Robards	..	..	1829	Hermitage, Tenn.	61
8. Martin Van Buren	1807	Hannah Hoes (Goes)	4	..	1837	Kinderhook, N. Y.	54
9. William H. Harrison	1795	Anna Symmes	6	4	1841	North Bend, O.	68
10. John Tyler	1813 1844	Letitia Christian Julia Gardiner	3 4	4 2	1841	Williamsburg, Va.	51
11. James K. Polk	1824	Sarah Childress	..	..	1845	Nashville, Tenn.	49
12. Zachary Taylor	1810	Margaret Smith	1	3	1849	Baton Rouge, La.	64
13. Millard Fillmore	1826 1858	Abigail Powers Mrs. Caroline McIntosh	1 ..	1 ..	1850	Buffalo, N. Y.	50
14. Franklin Pierce	1834	Jane Means Appleton	3	..	1853	Concord, N. H.	48
15. James Buchanan	....	Unmarried	..	..	1857	Wheatland, Pa.	65
16. Abraham Lincoln	1842	Mary Todd	4	..	1861	Springfield, Ill.	52

*Formerly a part of Braintree. † Jackson stated that he had been told this was his birthplace. Some authorities give Mecklenburg county, N. C.

UNITED STATES—TABLE I

Father's Business	Educational Advantage	Early Vocation	Politics	Profession	Religious Connections	NAME	
Planter	Common School	Surveyor	Fed.	Planter	Episcopalian	Washington.	1
Farmer	Harvard College, 1755	Teacher	Fed.	Lawyer	Unitarian	Adams.	2
Planter	Entered College, William and Mary	Lawyer	Rep.	Lawyer	Liberal	Jefferson.	3
Planter	Princeton College, 1771	Lawyer	Rep.	Lawyer	Episcopalian	Madison.	4
Planter	Entered College, William and Mary	Lawyer	Rep.	Politician	Episcopalian	Monroe.	5
Lawyer	Harvard College, 1787	Lawyer	Rep.	Lawyer	Unitarian	Adams, J. Q.	6
Farmer	Self Taught	Lawyer	Dem.	Lawyer	Presbyterian	Jackson.	7
Farmer	Academy	Lawyer	Dem.	Lawyer	Reformed Dutch	Van Buren.	8
Statesman	Entered Hampden-Sidney College	Medicine	Whig	Army	Episcopalian	Harrison.	9
Jurist	College, William and Mary, 1807	Lawyer	Dem.	Lawyer	Episcopalian	Tyler.	10
Farmer	University of North Carolina, 1818	Lawyer	Dem.	Lawyer	Methodist‡	Polk.	11
Planter	Common School	Soldier	Whig	Army	Episcopalian	Taylor.	12
Farmer	Public School	Tailor	Whig	Lawyer	Episcopalian	Fillmore.	13
Farmer	Bowdoin College, 1824	Lawyer	Dem.	Lawyer	Episcopalian	Pierce.	14
Merchant	Dickinson College, 1809	Lawyer	Dem.	Lawyer	Presbyterian	Buchanan.	15
Farmer	Self Taught	Farmer	Rep.	Lawyer	Liberal	Lincoln.	16
Sexton	Self Taught	Tailor	Rep.	Politician	Liberal	Johnson.	17
Farmer	West Point Military Academy, 1843	Tanner	Rep.	Army	Methodist	Grant.	18
Merchant	Kenyon College, Ohio, 1842	Lawyer	Rep.	Lawyer	Methodist	Hayes.	19
Farmer	Williams College, 1856	Teacher	Rep.	Lawyer	Disciples	Garfield.	20
Clergyman	Union College, 1848	Teacher	Rep.	Lawyer	Episcopalian	Arthur.	21
Clergyman	Common School	Teacher	Dem.	Lawyer	Presbyterian	Cleveland.	22
Farmer	Miami University, Ohio, 1852	Lawyer	Rep.	Lawyer	Presbyterian	Harrison.	23
Clergyman	Common School	Teacher	Dem.	Lawyer	Presbyterian	Cleveland.	24
Iron Manfr.	Entered Allegheny College	Lawyer	Rep.	Lawyer	Methodist	McKinley.	25
Merchant	Harvard, 1880	Publicist.	Rep.	Publicist.	Reformed Dutch	Roosevelt.	26
Lawyer	Yale, 1878	Lawyer	Rep.	Lawyer	Unitarian	Taft.	27
Clergyman	Princeton, 1879	Lawyer	Dem.	Teacher	Presbyterian	Wilson.	28
Physician	Attended Ohio Central College	Editor	Rep.	Publisher	Baptist	Harding.	29
Farmer	Amherst College, 1895	Lawyer	Rep.	Lawyer	Congregationalist	Coolidge.	30
Blacksmith	Stanford University, 1895	Engineer	Rep.	Engineer	Quaker	Hoover.	31
Capitalist	Harvard, 1904	Lawyer	Dem.	Lawyer	Episcopalian	Roosevelt.	32
Farmer	Kansas City School of Law, 1923-25	Business	Dem.	Pub. service	Baptist	Truman.	33

UNITED STATES—TABLE II

Served as President	Died	Age at Death	Cause of Death	Place of Death	Place of Burial	
7 yr., 10 m., 4 d.	1799	67	Acute laryngitis	Mt. Vernon, Va.	Mt. Vernon, Va.	1
4 yr.	1826	90	Natural decline	Quincy, Mass.	Quincy, Mass.	2
8 yr.	1826	83	Chronic diarrhœa	Monticello, Va.	Monticello, Albemarle Co., Va.	3
8 yr.	1836	85	Natural decline	Montpelier, Va.	Montpelier, Orange Co., Va.	4
8 yr.	1831	73	Natural decline	New York City	Originally, N. Y. Removed, 1858, to Hollywood Cemetery, Richmond, Va.	5
4 yr.	1848	80	Paralysis	Hall of Congress, Washington, D. C.	Unitarian Church, Quincy, Mass.	6
8 yr.	1845	78	Dropsy	Hermitage, near Nashville, Tenn.	Hermitage, near Nashville, Tenn.	7
4 yr.	1862	79	Asthma	Kinderhook, N. Y.	Kinderhook, N. Y.	8
1 m.	1841	68	Pleurisy	White House, Washington, D. C.	North Bend, Ohio.	9
3 yr., 11 m.	1862	71	Bilious attacks, with bronchitis	Ballard House, Richmond, Va.	Hollywood, Richmond, Va.	10
4 yr.	1849	53	Chronic diarrhœa	Nashville, Tenn.	Nashville, Tenn.	11
1 yr., 4 m., 5 d.	1850	65	Cholera morbus and typhoid fever	White House, Washington, D. C.	Near Louisville, Kentucky.	12
2 yr., 7 m., 26 d.	1874	74	Paralysis	Buffalo, N. Y.	Forest Lawn, Buffalo, N. Y.	13
4 yr.	1869	64	Dropsy and inflammation of stomach	Concord, N. H.	Minot Cemetery, Concord, N. H.	14
4 yr.	1868	77	Rheumatic gout	Lancaster, Pa.	Woodward Hill Cemetery, Lancaster, Pa.	15
4 yr., 1 m., 11 d.	1865	56	Assassinated	Washington, D. C.	Oak Ridge Cemetery, Springfield, Ill.	16

‡ Baptized on death bed by minister of Methodist Episcopal Church, South. His wife was a member of the Presbyterian Church, which he sometimes attended with her.

PRESIDENTS OF THE

Name	Married	Wife's Name	Children: Boys	Children: Girls	Inaugurated	Residence When Elected	Age When Inaugurated
17. Andrew Johnson	1827	Eliza McCardle	3	2	1865	Greenville, Tenn.	56
18. Ulysses S. Grant	1848	Julia Dent	3	1	1869	Washington, D. C.	46
19. Rutherford B. Hayes	1852	Lucy Ware Webb	7	1	1877	Fremont, Ohio	54
20. James A. Garfield	1858	Lucretia Rudolph	4	1	1881	Mentor, Ohio	49
21. Chester A. Arthur	1859	Ellen Lewis Herndon	1	1	1881	New York City	50
22. Grover Cleveland	1886	Frances Folsom	2	3	1885	Buffalo, N. Y.	47
23. Benjamin Harrison	1853	Caroline Lavinia Scott	1	1	1889	Indianapolis, Ind.	55
	1896	Mary Scott (Lord) Dimmick	..	1			
24. Grover Cleveland	....	(See above)	..	..	1893	New York City	55
25. William McKinley	1871	Ida Saxton	..	2	1897	Canton, Ohio	54
26. Theo. Roosevelt	1880	Alice Lee	..	1	1901	Oyster Bay, N. Y.	42
	1886	Edith Carow	4	1			
27. William H. Taft	1886	Helen Herron	2	1	1909	Cincinnati, Ohio	51
28. Woodrow Wilson	1885	Helen Louise Axson	..	3	1913	Princeton, N. J.	56
	1915	Mrs. Edith Bolling Galt	..	..			
29. Warren G. Harding	1891	Florence Kling	..	..	1921	Marion, Ohio	55
30. Calvin Coolidge	1905	Grace A. Goodhue	2	..	1923	Northampton, Mass.	51
31. Herbert Hoover	1899	Lou Henry	2	..	1929	Stanford Univ., Cal.	54
32. Franklin D. Roosevelt	1905	Anna Eleanor Roosevelt	4	1	1933	Hyde Park, N. Y.	51
33. Harry S. Truman	1919	Bess Wallace	..	1	1945	Independence, Mo.	61

VICE PRESIDENTS OF THE

Name	Born: When	Born: Where	Parents: Father	Parents: Mother	Ancestry	Educational Advantages
1. John Adams (1, 5)	1735	Quincy, Mass.	John	Susanna Boylston	English	Harvard, 1755.
2. Thomas Jefferson (1)	1743	Shadwell, Va.	Peter	Jane Randolph	Welsh	Wm. and Mary, 1762.
3. Aaron Burr	1756	Newark, N. J.	Aaron	Esther Edwards	English	New Jersey, † 1772.
4. George Clinton (2, 5)	1739	Little Britain, N. Y.	Charles	Elizabeth Denniston	English	Academy.
5. Elbridge Gerry (2)	1744	Marblehead, Mass.	Thomas	Elizabeth Greenleaf	English	Harvard, 1762.
6. Daniel D. Tompkins (5)	1774	Scarsdale, N. Y.	Jonathan G.	Sarah Hyatt	English	Columbia, 1795.
7. John C. Calhoun (3, 5) (2 terms)	1782	Abbeville Dist., S.C.	Patrick	Martha Caldwell	Scotch-Irish	Yale, 1804.
8. Martin Van Buren (1)	1782	Kinderhook, N. Y.	Abraham	Mary Hoes	Dutch	Kinderhook Acad.
9. Richard M. Johnson	1781	Bryant's Station, Ky.	Robert	Jemima Suggett	English	Transylvania.
10. John Tyler (4)	1790	Greenway, Va.	John	Mary Armistead	English	Wm. and Mary, 1807.
11. George M. Dallas	1792	Philadelphia, Pa.	Alexander J.	Arabella M. Smith	Scotch-Eng.	New Jersey, † 1810.
12. Millard Fillmore (4)	1800	Summerhill, N. Y.	Nathaniel	Phebe Millard	English	Public School.
13. Wm. Rufus King (2)	1786	Sampson Co., N. C.	William	Margaret Devane	Irish-Hug'n't	Univ. of N. C. 1803.
14. John C. Breckinridge	1821	Lexington, Ky.	John C.	Mary C. Smith	Scotch	Centre, 1839.
15. Hannibal Hamlin	1809	Paris, Me.	Cyrus	Anna Livermore	English	Hebron Acad.
16. Andrew Johnson (4)	1808	Raleigh, N. C.	Jacob	Mary McDonough	English	Self-taught.
17. Schuyler Colfax	1823	New York City	Schuyler	Hannah Stryker	Eng.-Dutch	Public School.
18. Henry Wilson* (2)	1812	Farmington, N. H.	Winthrop*	Abigail Witham	Scotch-Irish	Academy.
19. William A. Wheeler	1819	Malone, N. Y.	Almon	Eliza Woodward	English	Vermont.
20. Chester A. Arthur (4)	1830	Fairfield, Vt.	William	Malvina Stone	Scotch-Irish	Union, 1848.
21. Thomas A. Hendricks (2)	1819	Zanesville, O.	John	Jane Thomson	Sc'h-Hug'n't	Hanover, Ind., 1841.
22. Levi P. Morton	1824	Shoreham, Vt.	Daniel O.	Lucretia Parsons	English	Shoreham Acad.
23. Adlai E. Stevenson	1835	Christian Co., Ky.	John T.	Eliza Ewing	Scotch-Irish	Centre.
24. Garret A. Hobart (2)	1844	Long Branch, N. J.	Addison W.	Sophia Vanderveer	Eng.-Hug'n't	Rutgers, 1863.
25. Theodore Roosevelt (1,4)	1858	New York City	Theodore	Martha Bullock	Dutch	Harvard, 1880.
26. Charles W. Fairbanks	1852	Unionville Center, O.	Loriston M.	Mary A. Smith	English	Ohio Wesleyan, 1872.
27. James S. Sherman (2)	1855	Utica, N. Y.	Richard U.	Mary F. Sherman	English	Hamilton, 1878.
28. Thomas R. Marshall (5)	1854	N. Manchester, Ind.	Daniel M.	Martha A. Patterson	English	Wabash, 1873.
29. Calvin Coolidge (1, 4)	1872	Plymouth, Vt.	John C.	Victoria J. Moor	English	Amherst, 1895.
30. Charles Gates Dawes	1865	Marietta, O.	Rufus R.	Mary Beman	English	Marietta, 1884.
31. Charles Curtis	1860	N. Topeka, Kans.	Oran A.	Helen Pappan	Kaw Indian	Public School.
32. John Nance Garner (5)	1869	Red River Co., Tex.	John N.	Sarah	English	Public School.
33. Henry Agard Wallace	1888	Adair Co., Ia.	Henry A.	May Brodhead	Scotch-Irish	Iowa State Coll.
34. Harry S. Truman (1, 4)	1884	Lamar, Mo.	John A.	Martha Ellen Young	Eng.-Sco.-Ir.	Kans. City Law Sch.
35. Barkley, Alben William	1877	Graves Co., Ky.	John W.	Electa Smith	Eng.-Sco.-Ir.	Marvin, Emory Coll., U. of Va. Law Sch.

* Born Jeremiah Jones Colbath, son of Winthrop Colbath; changed his name to Henry Wilson. † Now Princeton.

(1) Vice presidents thus marked were later elected president (Adams, Jefferson, Van Buren, Roosevelt, Coolidge, Truman). (2) These vice presidents died while in office (Clinton, Gerry, King, Wilson, Hendricks, Hobart, Sherman). (3) Resigned from office (Calhoun).

UNITED STATES—TABLE II

Served as President	Died	Age at Death	Cause of Death	Place of Death	Place of Burial	
3 yr., 10 m., 19 d.	1875	66	Paralysis	Greenville, Tenn.	Greenville, Tenn.	17
8 yr.	1885	63	Cancer of the tongue	Mt. McGregor, N. Y.	Riverside, New York City.	18
4 yr.	1893	70	Neuralgia of heart	Fremont, Ohio	Fremont, Ohio.	19
6½ m.	1881	49	Assassinated	Elberon, Long Branch, N. J.	Lake View Cemetery, Cleveland, Ohio.	20
3 yr., 5½ m.	1886	56	Bright's disease	New York City	Rural Cemetery, Albany, N. Y.	21
8 yr.	1908	71	Heart failure	Princeton, N. J.	Princeton, N. J.	22
4 yr.	1901	67	Pneumonia	Indianapolis, Ind.	Crown Hill Cemetery, Indianapolis, Ind.	23
4 yr., 6 m., 10 d.	1901	58	Assassinated	Buffalo, N. Y.	Cemetery, Canton, Ohio.	25
7 yr., 5 m., 20 d.	1919	60	Embolism	Oyster Bay, N. Y.	Young's Memorial Cemetery, Oyster Bay, N. Y.	26
4 yr.	1930	72	Hardening of arteries	Washington, D. C.	Arlington National Cemetery.	27
8 yr.	1924	67	General breakdown	Washington, D. C.	Washington, D. C.	28
2 yr., 4 m., 30 d.	1923	57	Apoplexy	San Francisco, Cal.	Marion, Ohio.	29
5 yr., 7 m., 1 d.	1933	60	Coronary thrombosis	Northampton, Mass.	Plymouth, Vt.	30
4 yr.						31
12 yr., 1 m., 8 d.	1945	63	Cerebral hemorrhage	Warm Springs, Ga.	Hyde Park, N. Y.	32
						33

UNITED STATES

Profession	Politics	Served as Vice President: Length of Time	Served as Vice President: Administration of	Died	Place of Burial	
Lawyer	Fed.	7 yr., 10 mo., 4 d. (1789–1797)	Washington	1826	Quincy, Mass.	1
Lawyer	Rep.	4 yr. (1797–1801)	Adams, John	1826	Monticello, Va.	2
Lawyer	Rep.	4 yr. (1801–1805)	Jefferson	1836	Princeton, N. J.	3
Politician	Rep.	4 yr. (1805–1809)	Jefferson	1812	Washington, D. C.	4
		3 yr., 1 mo., 16 d. (1809–1812)	Madison			
Politician	Rep.	1 yr., 8 mo., 19 d. (1813–1814)	Madison	1814	Washington, D. C.	5
Lawyer	Rep.	8 yr. (1817–1825)	Monroe	1825	New York City.	6
Lawyer	Rep.	4 yr. (1825–1829)	Adams, J. Q.	1850	Charleston, S. C.	7
		3 yr., 9 mo., 24 d. (1829–1832)	Jackson			
Lawyer	Dem.	4 yr. (1833–1837)	Jackson	1862	Kinderhook, N. Y.	8
Lawyer	Dem.	4 yr. (1837–1841)	Van Buren	1850	Frankfort, Ky.	9
Lawyer	Dem.	1 mo. (1841)	Harrison	1862	Richmond, Va.	10
Lawyer	Dem.	4 yr. (1845–1849)	Polk	1864	Philadelphia, Pa.	11
Lawyer	Whig	1 yr., 4 mo., 5 d. (1849–1850)	Taylor	1874	Buffalo, N. Y.	12
Lawyer	Dem.	1 mo., 14 d. (1853)	Pierce	1853	Selma, Alabama.	13
Lawyer	Dem.	4 yr. (1857–1861)	Buchanan	1875	Lexington, Ky.	14
Lawyer	Rep.	4 yr. (1861–1865)	Lincoln	1891	Bangor, Maine.	15
Politician	Rep.	1 mo., 11 d. (1865)	Lincoln	1875	Greenville, Tenn.	16
Journalist	Rep.	4 yr. (1869–1873)	Grant	1885	South Bend, Ind.	17
Politician	Rep.	2 yr., 8 mo., 18 d. (1873–1875)	Grant	1875	Dell Park, Natick. Mass.	18
Lawyer	Rep.	4 yr. (1877–1881)	Hayes	1887	Malone, N. Y.	19
Lawyer	Rep.	6 mo., 15 d. (Mch. 4–Sept. 19, 1881)	Garfield	1886	Albany, N. Y.	20
Lawyer	Dem.	8 mo., 21 d. (Mch. 4–Nov. 25, 1885)	Cleveland	1885	Indianapolis, Ind.	21
Banker	Rep.	4 yr. (1889–1893)	Harrison	1920	Rhinebeck, N. Y.	22
Lawyer	Dem.	4 yr. (1893–1897)	Cleveland	1914	Bloomington, Ill.	23
Banker, Lawyer	Rep.	2 yr., 8 mo., 17 d. (1897–1899)	McKinley	1899	Paterson, N. J.	24
Publicist	Rep.	6 mo., 10 d. (Mch. 4–Sept. 14, 1901)	McKinley	1919	Oyster Bay, N. Y.	25
Lawyer	Rep.	4 yr. (1905–1909)	Roosevelt	1918	Indianapolis, Ind.	26
Lawyer	Rep.	3 yr., 7 mo., 26 d. (1909–1912)	Taft	1912	Utica, N. Y.	27
Lawyer	Dem.	8 yr. (1913–1921)	Wilson	1925	Indianapolis, Ind.	28
Lawyer	Rep.	2 yr., 5 mo. (1921–23)	Harding	1933	Plymouth, Vt.	29
Banker	Rep.	4 yr. (1925–1929)	Coolidge			30
Lawyer	Rep.	4 yr. (1929–1933)	Hoover	1936	Topeka, Kans.	31
Lawyer	Dem.	7 yr., 10 mo., 17 d. (1933–1941)	Roosevelt			32
Editor	Dem.	4 yr. (1941–1945)	Roosevelt			33
Pub. serv.	Dem.	2 mo., 23 d. (1945)	Roosevelt			34
Lawyer	Dem.		Truman			35

(4) Succeeded to the presidency at death of president (Tyler, Fillmore, A. Johnson, Arthur, Roosevelt, Coolidge, Truman). (5) Elected as vice president two terms (Adams, Clinton, Tompkins, Calhoun, Marshall, Garner).

PRESIDENTIAL ELECTIONS

Showing the States Carried by Each Party Since 1864

R, Republican; D, Democratic; P, Populist; Pr., Progressive; S., States Rights.

STATE	1864	1868	1872	1876	1880	1884	1888	1892	1896	1900	1904	1908	1912	1916	1920	1924	1928	1932	1936	1940	1944	1948
Alabama	..	R	R	D	D	D	D	D	D	D	D	D	D	D	D	D	D	D	D	D	D	S
Arizona	..	..	..	..	..	..	..	..	..	..	..	..	D	D	R	R	R	D	D	D	D	D
Arkansas	..	R	R	D	D	D	D	D	D	D	D	D	D	D	D	D	D	D	D	D	D	D
California . . .	R	R	R	R	D *g*	R	R	D *h*	R *i*	R	R	R	Pr *n*	D	R	R	R	D	D	D	D	D
Colorado	..	..	..	R *a*	R	R	R	P	D	D	R	D	D	D	R	R	R	D	D	R	R	D
Connecticut. . .	R	R	R	D	R	D	D	D	R	R	R	R	D	R	R	R	R	R	D	D	D	R
Delaware . . .	D	D	R	D	D	D	D	D	R	R	R	R	D	R	R	R	R	R	D	D	D	R
Florida	..	R	R	R	D	D	D	D	D	D	D	D	D	D	D	D	R	D	D	D	D	D
Georgia	..	D	D	D	D	D	D	D	D	D	D	D	D	D	D	D	D	D	D	D	D	D
Idaho	..	..	..	..	..	..	..	P	D	D	R	R	D	D	R	R	R	D	D	D	D	D
Illinois	R	R	R	R	R	R	R	D	R	R	R	R	D	R	R	R	R	D	D	D	D	D
Indiana	R	R	R	D	R	D	R	D	R	R	R	R	D	R	R	R	R	D	D	R	R	R
Iowa	R	R	R	R	R	R	R	R	R	R	R	R	D	R	R	R	R	D	D	R	R	D
Kansas	R	R	R	R	R	R	R	P	D	R	R	R	D	D	R	R	R	D	D	R	R	R
Kentucky . . .	D	D	D	D	D	D	D	D	R *b*	D	D	D	D	D	D	R	R	D	D	D	D	D
Louisiana . . .	..	D	R	R	D	D	D	D	D	D	D	D	D	D	D	D	D	D	D	D	D	S
Maine	R	R	R	R	R	R	R	R	R	R	R	R	D	R	R	R	R	R	R	R	R	R
Maryland . . .	R	D	D	D	D	D	D	D	R	R	D *j*	D *k*	D	D	R	R	R	D	D	D	D	R
Massachusetts .	R	R	R	R	R	R	R	R	R	R	R	R	D	R	R	R	D	D	D	D	D	D
Michigan . . .	R	R	R	R	R	R	R	R *c*	R	R	R	R	Pr	R	R	R	R	D	D	R	D	R
Minnesota . . .	R	R	R	R	R	R	R	R	R	R	R	R	Pr	R	R	R	R	D	D	D	D	D
Mississippi . . .	..	..	R	D	D	D	D	D	D	D	D	D	D	D	D	D	D	D	D	D	D	S
Missouri	R	R	D	D	D	D	D	D	D	D	R	R	D	D	R	R	R	D	D	D	D	D
Montana	..	..	..	..	..	..	..	R	D	D	R	R	D	D	R	R	R	D	D	D	D	D
Nebraska . . .	..	R	R	R	R	R	R	R	D	R	R	D	D	D	R	R	R	D	D	R	R	R
Nevada	R	R	R	R	D	R	R	P	D	D	R	D	D	D	R	R	R	D	D	D	D	D
New Hampshire	R	R	R	R	R	R	R	R	R	R	R	R	D	D	R	R	R	R	D	D	D	R
New Jersey. . .	D	D	R	D	D	D	D	D	R	R	R	R	D	R	R	R	R	D	D	D	D	R
New Mexico . .	..	..	..	..	..	..	..	..	..	..	..	..	D	D	R	R	R	D	D	D	D	D
New York . . .	R	D	R	D	R	D	R	D	R	R	R	R	D	R	R	R	R	D	D	D	D	R
North Carolina .	..	R	R	D	D	D	D	D	D	D	D	D	D	D	D	D	R	D	D	D	D	D
North Dakota .	..	..	..	..	..	..	..	P *d*	R	R	R	R	D	D	R	R	R	D	D	R	R	R
Ohio	R	R	R	R	R	R	R	R *e*	R	R	R	R	D	D	R	R	R	D	D	D	R	D
Oklahoma . . .	..	..	..	..	..	..	..	..	..	..	..	D	D	D	R	D	R	D	D	D	D	D
Oregon	R	D	R	R	R	R	R	R *f*	R	R	R	R	D	R	R	R	R	D	D	D	D	R
Pennsylvania . .	R	R	R	R	R	R	R	R	R	R	R	R	Pr	R	R	R	R	R	D	D	D	R
Rhode Island . .	R	R	R	R	R	R	R	R	R	R	R	R	D	R	R	R	D	D	D	D	D	D
South Carolina .	..	R	R	R	D	D	D	D	D	D	D	D	D	D	D	D	D	D	D	D	D	S
South Dakota .	..	..	..	..	..	..	..	R	D	R	R	R	Pr	R	R	R	R	D	D	R	R	R
Tennessee . . .	..	R	D	D	D	D	D	D	D	D	D	D	D	D	R	D	R	D	D	D	D	D *r*
Texas	..	..	D	D	D	D	D	D	D	D	D	D	D	D	D	D	R	D	D	D	D	D
Utah	..	..	..	..	..	..	..	..	D	R	R	R	R	D	R	R	R	D	D	D	D	D
Vermont	R	R	R	R	R	R	R	R	R	R	R	R	R	R	R	R	R	R	R	R	R	R
Virginia	..	..	R	D	D	D	D	D	D	D	D	D	D	D	D	D	R	D	D	D	D	D
Washington . .	..	..	..	..	..	..	..	R	D	R	R	R	Pr	D	R	R	R	D	D	D	D	D
West Virginia . .	R	R	R	D	D	D	D	D	R	R	R	R	D	R *q*	R	R	R	D	D	D	D	D
Wisconsin . . .	R	R	R	R	R	R	R	D	R	R	R	R	D	R	R	Pr	R	D	D	D	R	D
Wyoming . . .	..	..	..	..	..	..	..	R	D	R	R	R	D	D	R	R	R	D	D	D	R	D

a Electors chosen by the Legislature. *b* Rep., 12; Dem., 1. *c* Rep., 9; Dem., 5. *d* Rep., 1; Dem., 1. *e* Rep., 22; Dem., 1. *f* Rep., 3; People, 1. *g* Dem., 5; Rep., 1. *h* Dem., 8; Rep., 1. *i* Dem., 1; Rep., 8. *j* Dem., 7; Rep., 1. *k* Dem., 6; Rep., 2. *n* Dem., 2; Prog., 11. *q* Hughes, 7; Wilson, 1. *r* Dem., 11; States Rights, 1.

AMERICAN GENERALS AND ADMIRALS

David Glasgow Farragut	Fred Funston *Photo by Harris-Ewing*	George Dewey *Photo by Clinedinst*
William Tecumseh Sherman	Ulysses Simpson Grant	Philip Henry Sheridan *Copyright by Taber Art Co.*
Joseph Eggleston Johnston	Thomas Jonathan Jackson	Robert Edward Lee

Photos for 1 and 9 copyright by Ewing Galloway; 3 copyright by Underwood & Underwood; 2, 4, and 8 copyright by Detroit Photographic Co.; 5, 6, and 7 Halliday Historic Photos.

HISTORIC AMERICA. III

1 The Alamo, San Antonio, Tex. 2 Ancient Church, Pueblo of Acoma, N. M. 3 Statue of Massasoit, Plymouth, Mass. 4 Liberty Bell, Independence Hall, Phila. 5 Old North Church, Boston. 6 Alden House, Duxbury, Mass. 7 Birthplace of John Adams (*left*) and of John Quincy Adams (*right*), Quincy, Mass. 8 Old Custom House, Monterey, Cal. 9 Washington Inn, Valley Forge, Pa.

DICTIONARY OF AMERICAN HISTORY

THE following section deals with topics in the history of the American people, both in regard to the nation's development at home and in regard to its relations with other peoples. Some of these topics have already received mention in the article on the history of the United States but are here treated with greater completeness than is possible in the continuous narrative. The majority of the items, however, are concise accounts of parties, events, and other phases of national life which have not received specific mention in the connected narrative of the country's history, being reserved for a more adequate treatment in special articles.

Abolitionists. The group of Northerners who, in the period from 1830 to 1850, advocated immediate emancipation of slaves without compensation to owners. William Lloyd Garrison was a leading figure in the early period of this movement. Through his militant journal, the *Liberator*, he aroused the North to the moral evil of slavery. To further their aim, Garrison and his associates organized in 1832 the New England Antislavery Society, which in 1833 was expanded into the American Antislavery Society. The purpose of the organization was to establish antislavery societies throughout the country and to spread antislavery propaganda. The society, however, in its beginnings, recognized the Constitutional limitations which prevented the Federal government from interfering with the institution of slavery so far as it existed and remained within the bounds of the particular states.

The abolitionists aroused intense antagonism both in the South and in the North, many Northerners believing that such agitation unnecessarily antagonized the South and endangered the peace and security of the Union. Abolitionist meetings were frequently broken up; Garrison was mobbed; and Lovejoy, a leading abolitionist, was killed. In 1840 the American Antislavery Society split into two factions: the more radical group, which followed Garrison in his extreme views; and the more conservative faction, which formed the Liberty party, and whose purpose was confined to bringing the national government under the control of those opposed to the extension of slavery.

Alabama Claims. A series of claims for indemnity made upon Great Britain by the United States, based upon alleged failure of Great Britain to observe certain obligations of international law. These claims arose chiefly from damages inflicted by vessels in the Confederate service, which vessels had been fitted out or built in English waters. The history of the Confederate cruiser *Alabama* is typical of the more flagrant cases. This vessel was built at Birkenhead, England, and, although the attention of the British government was repeatedly called to suspicious circumstances, "No. 290," as the ship was called, sailed July 29, 1862, without register or clearance papers. After taking on equipment in the Azores from two English vessels, she assumed the name *Alabama* and began her famous career of destruction. She is said to have destroyed 70 vessels, before being sunk by the *Kearsarge*, June 19, 1864.

The determination of the extent to which the government of Great Britain was responsible for the damage inflicted by the *Alabama* and other vessels of similar history was the most important problem of diplomacy resulting from the Civil War. By the Treaty of Washington, 1871, the *Alabama* claims were submitted to the decision of five arbitrators,—one named by England, one by the United States, and one each by the king of Italy, the emperor of Brazil, and the president of Switzerland. The arbitrators met at Geneva, December 15, 1871, and, on September 14, 1872, signed the final award. By unanimous vote, England was adjudged responsible for the depredations of the cruiser *Alabama* and, in full satisfaction of this and all other claims, was directed to pay an indemnity of $15,500,000.

Alamo, Defense of the. In the year 1835, the people of Texas, then a department of the Republic of Mexico, revolted against the Mexican government. Their ultimate purpose was annexation to the United States. In 1836, Santa Anna, with an army of several thousand, undertook to crush the revolution. For a time his campaign was successful. It was the heroic defense of the old fort of the Alamo, at San Antonio, by 183 Texans under W. B. Travis, that inspired the people to successful efforts at resistance. The little band endured a siege of thirteen days. When all but six of the garrison had been killed, the Mexicans took the place by storm, and the survivors were shot by order of Santa Anna. The war cry of Texas became "Remember the Alamo."

Alaska Boundary Commission. A commission of six jurists appointed under the treaty of 1903 to determine the eastern boundary of the Alaska "Panhandle." The boundary was admitted to be ten marine leagues from the sea. Canada claimed that the distance should be measured from a straight line from headland to headland; the United States, that the boundary should follow the windings of the coast. A majority decision, rendered October 20, 1903, supported the United States contention.

Alaska Highway. A road from Dawson Creek, B. C., about 250 miles west of Edmonton, Alta., to White Horse, Y.T., and thence to Fairbanks, Alaska, on the east of the Rocky Mountains. Between March and November 1942, it was built as a war measure by the United States Army Engineers under an agreement between the United States and Canada in order to give a land route to Alaska. Its cost was $138,000,000; its length, 1671 miles. In April 1946 the Canadian portion, about 1000 miles, was turned over to Canada.

Alaska Purchase. By a treaty between the United States and Russia, in 1867, the latter power surrendered all her possessions on the continent of North America, approximately the present great territory of Alaska, together with the Pribilof islands, in consideration of a payment of $7,200,000.

Albany Regency. The first well organized American political machine. A coterie of Democrats who, from 1820 to 1854, exercised a controlling influence over the politics of the State of New York, and had consequently considerable power in national politics. Their headquarters were at Albany. Chief among this regency were Martin Van Buren and W. L. Marcy.

Alien and Sedition Acts. A series of four acts passed by the Federalist party in Congress in 1798, after the publication of the "X Y Z" letters. The Alien acts (1) raised the residence period for naturalization from five to fourteen years, (2) authorized the president for two years to order out of the country any aliens he might judge dangerous, (3) authorized the president to expel from the country citizens of any nation with which the United States might be at war. The Sedition act provided penalties of fine and imprisonment for combining to oppose governmental measures and for any false, scandalous, or malicious writing against the government or its high officials, with intent to bring them into disrepute. A few prosecutions took place under this Sedition act. These acts provoked the first assertions of the doctrine of state rights. See *Virginia and Kentucky Resolutions*.

Amana (ăm'ȧ-nȧ) **Society.** A religious community established in 1855 at Amana, Iowa, in which all land and factories were owned by the community, which practiced certain principles of communism. The chief interest of the community was the religious society, which was founded by Eberhard Gruber in Württemberg in 1714. The community was reorganized as a joint stock company in 1932.

America. This name was first applied, with little warrant, to the continental regions of the western hemisphere by Martin Waldseemüller, a young geographer at Saint-Dié, a town in the Vosges mountains. In a Latin work, *Cosmographiæ Introductio*, which Waldseemüller edited in 1507, he used the name America in honor of Amerigo (Americus) Vespucci, whose narrative of the latter's voyages of discovery to the New World Waldseemüller had read. "Because Americus discovered it," wrote the geographer, "it ought to be called the land of Americus, or America."

America, Discovery of. According to the Norse sagas, the discovery of America should be placed to the credit of the vikings who made five expeditions to the coast between 985 and 1011, the first being that of Eric the Red, who settled in Greenland in 986, and the most famous that of Thorfinn Karlsefne, about 1007. Madoc, a Welsh prince, is said to have established a colony in the Western world in 1170. A Norse expedition penetrated into western Minnesota, leaving an inscription dated 1362 on a stone which was discovered in 1898. But the real discovery that opened the continent to colonization was made by Columbus in 1492.

America Act. An act passed by the British Parliament in 1775, consolidating all the previous penal acts relating to the American colonies. It declared that all American vessels were lawful prizes, and that all Americans captured in them, or elsewhere, could be forced to take service against America. Commissioners were appointed to receive the submission of the revolted colonies, but no provisions were made for the redress of grievances.

American Antislavery Society. See *Abolitionists*.

American Customs Act. An act passed by the British Parliament in 1764, levying customs duties on goods imported into the American colonies. These duties were to be levied for the benefit of England, and the proceeds thereof were to be paid into the English treasury. The assertion of this right to tax the colonies for the benefit of the mother country was a main cause of the Revolutionary War.

American Legion. An organization of World War veterans. It sponsored the creation of the United States Veterans' bureau at Washington, and a program for the establishment of government hospitals for the care of the disabled was put into effect. The Legion secured the passage of soldier-bonus laws in the Federal and a number of state legislatures. By 1936, over 10 billion dollars had been appropriated by the Federal government for the benefit of the World War veterans. The Legion led in preparing a code of national flag etiquette, aided in finding employment for veterans out of work, and carried out a program for the care of war orphans. In 1921, two years after its organization, its membership stood at 759,779. Ten years later it exceeded 1,300,000. For an account of its organization, see *American Legion*, page 2047.

American Party. Name adopted in 1854 by a faction of the Whigs who sought to crush the power of the foreign-born in politics, particularly through opposition to the Irish and to the Roman Catholic Church. From about 1835 there had been an organized movement aimed at keeping Roman Catholics out of public office. The early "Native American" movement, which later passed into the "Know-Nothing" movement, was occasioned by the political ascendancy of certain foreign groups in Eastern cities. The so-called American party was formed by the merging of the "Know-Nothings" with a faction of the Whigs. In 1855 the American party swept the elections in New York, Massachusetts, Rhode Island, Connecticut, and New Hampshire, and elected a number of its candidates in other states. In 1856 the party nominated Millard Fillmore for president and Andrew Jackson Donelson for vice president. These nominees were adopted by the Whig party as its candidates. Among the provisions in the platform of the American party were such declarations as the following: "Americans must rule America"; "Native-born citizens should be selected for all state, Federal, and municipal offices." A further provision of the platform was that a residence of 21 years should be required for citizenship in the United States. In 1860 the American party virtually dissolved, and the major part of its members joined the Constitutional Union party.

American Protective Association, "A. P. A." A secret organization formed in 1887. Its avowed purpose was to curb the political power of the Roman Catholic Church, to keep Catholics out of public office, and to protect the public school system from subversion by the Roman Church. The society fell into desuetude soon after its organization. It has, however, been revived in various parts of the country from time to time and has endeavored to make itself felt in local elections in some of the larger municipal centers. At times it has been also a factor of some consequence in state and national elections.

American System. The name applied to the policies advocated by the National Republicans under Clay from 1829 to 1833. Primarily, it designated the policy of a high protective tariff; but it was extended to include the establishment of a national bank and the construction of internal improvements by the Federal government, particularly the construction of national highways.

Annapolis Convention, The. A small conference which met at Annapolis, September 11, 1786, and was attended by delegates from five states, New York, New Jersey, Pennsylvania, Delaware, and Virginia. The meeting was originally suggested for discussion of matters relating to roads for commerce and to uniform duties on imports, but the members found it necessary to consider the entire subject of the weakened Confederation. As a result, they issued a call for a meeting of delegates from all the states, to be held at Philadelphia in the following May. This action brought about the Constitutional Convention of 1787.

Antifederalists. The "small states" party which opposed the adoption of the Constitution, taking their name from their opposition to the group which favored adoption. The Antifederalists became the party of state rights, and consistently opposed the expansion of the powers of the Federal government. After the adoption of the Constitution, this party merged into the Republican, or, as it was later called, the Democratic-Republican, party, under the leadership of Jefferson and Madison.

Anti-Imperialists. The political group which, after the close of the Spanish war in 1898, opposed the retention of the Philippine Islands by the United States. They maintained that holding this territory or any other, on the terms contemplated by the treaty with Spain, would be a violation of the principles and institutions of the United States. The leading figures in this group were Senator George F. Hoar of Massachusetts, Republican, and Senator Arthur P. Gorman of Maryland, Democrat. After the ratification of the treaty which provided for the acquisition of the Philippines, those who sympathized with the antiannexation view organized the Anti-Imperialist League, embracing numerous societies throughout the country, whose purpose was to secure the early recognition of Philippine independence.

Antimasonic Party. A third party which exercised considerable power in state and in national elections from 1828 to 1840. One William Morgan, a resident of Batavia, N. Y., who announced in 1826 that he was about to publish the secrets of the Masonic order, was said to have been abducted and murdered. The popular indignation over the reported outrage crystallized in 1827 into a political organization opposed to the election of Masons to office.

In the State of New York the party polled a very strong vote in 1830, and in 1831 the movement had spread so far throughout the country that a national nominating convention was called to meet in Philadelphia,—the first meeting of its kind in the United States. The convention named an Antimasonic candidate for the presidency, but his decisive defeat in 1832 marked the end of the movement as a national party. In various states, however, the party continued to exercise a definite influence until 1840.

Anti-Nebraska Men. Whigs and Democrats who in 1854 were opposed to the repeal of the Missouri Compromise and to the extension of slavery to the territories. This group had a large part in forming the Republican party. See *Kansas-Nebraska Bill.*

Antirent Riots. Disturbances attending the movement in New York to abolish certain survivals of feudal land tenure which persisted in the 19th century on the so-called patroon estates along the Hudson river, which were owned by the Van Rensselaers and other families of Dutch origin. The tenants banded together in 1839 to resist the collection of arrears of rents and of other perquisites due the estate owners. A state of virtual rebellion existed in 1844 and 1845. For some years the tenants commanded sufficient votes to make them a force in the legislature, but their real victory was due to a decision of the court of appeals in 1852, which declared that agreements of sale entailing the feudal obligations to which the tenants objected were illegal. Settlements between the landlords and the tenants were accordingly effected, so that the titles to the land were placed on the same basis as that on which land titles elsewhere in the country rested. See *Patroons.*

Antisaloon League. A nonpartisan organization formed in 1893. The purposes of the league were to spread propaganda and to exert a united nonpartisan influence at elections within the major political parties, in order to bring about the eradication of the saloon and the ultimate suppression of the manufacture and sale of intoxicating liquor. After the enactment of prohibition laws in the states, and particularly after the adoption of the 18th amendment, the Antisaloon League constituted itself a private committee of citizens seeking to aid the authorities in securing the proper enforcement of the prohibition laws.

Anti-Snappers. Supporters of Grover Cleveland, who in 1892 withdrew from the regular state convention of the Democratic party in New York. They held a separate convention and chose delegates to the Democratic national convention to contest the seats of the delegates from the regular state convention, all of whom were opposed to the presidency of Cleveland. See *Snappers.*

Army, The United States. The military history of the United States must take account of the development of the regular army and of the militia. In the colonies, before the Revolution, the volunteer militia gave excellent service in the Indian wars. Not infrequently, as at the defeat of Braddock, they saved the British troops from utter destruction. The minutemen of Massachusetts fought the battles of Concord and Lexington, and, as long as ammunition lasted, held the British regulars at bay on Bunker Hill. Washington, whose military training had been received in the militia of Virginia, took command of an army of the same character at Cambridge in 1775.

But, as the militia was the source of strength at the beginning of the war, it was a source of weakness later on. Washington found the militia difficult to organize into a compact fighting force, and undependable because of the short terms of enlistment and general aversion to military discipline. He urged the formation of an army directly under the authority of the Congress and with an enlistment period of several years.

The nucleus of such a force had been provided for by the Congress on June 14, 1775, when the enlistment of a corps of ten companies of riflemen for one year in the service of the United Colonies was authorized. From this act dates the history of the regular army of the United States. Washington found the militia effective for short periods but unreliable for longer operations. The United States had inherited the English preference for militia over the standing army. The states have maintained the militia, now known as the National Guard. The regular army, under Federal control, has provided, in time of war, the nucleus of officers and the skeleton of organization.

In 1802 the Military Academy was established at West Point for the training of officers. The first national militia law was passed by Congress in 1792. It remained in force until 1903, when it was supplemented by the National Defense act of 1916, which reorganized the National Guard.

In the War of 1812, neither the small force of regulars nor the much larger body of volunteers registered many notable successes. In the early Indian wars, regulars, volunteers, and militia cooperated. The Mexican war was fought by a force of about 100,000, of which approximately 30,000 were regulars, 60,000 were volunteers and rangers, and the remainder were militia. Just before the Civil War the regular army numbered but 67,000.

After the Civil War, the Indian campaigns were made the business of detachments of regulars, operating from various frontier military posts. The sudden outbreak of the Spanish war necessitated the mobilization of the National Guard, and the results showed lack of training for modern warfare.

The outbreak of war with Germany in 1917 found the United States unprepared to participate effectively in extensive military operations. Through unprecedented efforts, by mobilizing of National Guard units, by volunteering, and under the Selective Service act, an army of four million was raised.

At the outbreak of World War II, the United States army included (1) the Regular Army; (2) the National Guard while in the service of the United States; (3) the Organized Reserves, including the Officers' Reserve Corps and the Enlisted Reserve Corps. To these were added, after September 1940, the men drafted under the Selective Service act. These organizations were merged for the war period into the Army of the United States.

The actual strength of the army on October 9, 1941, was 1,588,000 officers and men. At the peak of enrollment in World War II, May 1945, it was 8,300,000. Its enrollment at the end of 1948 was 664,464, a large part of them overseas. A new Selective Service act (June 1948) was to be applied if voluntary enlistments proved insufficient.

The army, under the president as commander in chief, is commanded by the chief of staff. In March 1942, it was organized into three great commands: the Army Air Forces, Army Ground Forces, and Army Service Forces (formerly Service of Supply). The old distinctions of infantry, cavalry, and artillery disappeared, the cavalry becoming mechanized squadrons. The ground forces were organized in "triangular" divisions, each including all arms. New elements were added, including tanks and antitank forces, parachutists, and port engineers for landing operations and port construction. Since the field of operations extended all over the world, men were specially trained and conditioned for all climates and for mountain, desert, and jungle terrain. In May 1942, the enlistment of women was authorized in an auxiliary force, which later became the Women's Army Corps (WAC) for service in the camps and posts and behind the lines.

Bacon's Rebellion. The armed uprising in Virginia in 1676 against the arbitrary, "special privilege" rule of Governor Berkeley. Its immediate occasion was the governor's failure to authorize protection of the plantations from Indian attacks. Nathaniel Bacon, a young planter, took matters into his own hands, raised a force, and punished the Indians. Berkeley was forced to call a new assembly, which passed several acts, known as Bacon's Laws, restoring a degree of representative government. The sudden death of Bacon robbed the movement of leadership. Berkeley took so fiendish a revenge in executions that Charles II recalled him in disgust.

Barbary War. From the 16th to the 19th century the Barbary states—Morocco, Algiers, Tunis, and Tripoli—carried on systematic piracy and levied blackmail upon the powers that wished to trade in the Mediterranean. The United States paid several millions in tribute and for ransom of prisoners. Finally, in 1815, Commodore Decatur with his fleet forced the rulers of Algiers, Tunis, and Tripoli to give up all claims to payments from the United States and to release Christian prisoners of all nationalities.

Barnburners. A name given by their opponents, the Hunkers, to the antislavery faction of the Democratic party in New York from 1844 to 1848. The name has reference to the faction's indifference to all issues but slavery, which suggested the conduct of the man who is said to have burned his barn to rid it of rats. This faction opposed James K. Polk, the party's presidential candidate in 1844, and in 1848 they nominated for president, Van Buren, who was later nominated by the Free-Soil party. The Barnburners in part joined the Free-Soil party, but many, known later as the Soft-Shell Democrats or merely the Softs, returned to the Democratic ranks. See *Hunkers*.

"Battle above the Clouds," The. Popular name given to a part of the battle of Chattanooga, November 23-24-25, 1863. While General Hooker's troops were ascending the slopes of Lookout mountain on the 24th, a heavy fog hung over them, concealing the battle from the view of troops in the valley.

Bering Sea Controversy. The question as to the right of Canadian sealers to capture seals in Bering Sea (known as pelagic sealing), after being long in dispute, was submitted to arbitration in 1892. The right to conduct land sealing on the Pribilof islands had been leased by the United States to the North American Commercial Company. Pelagic sealing by Canadians and other nationalities involved killing of females and young. This threatened extinction of the seal herd. To prevent this calamity, the United States asserted a claim to the right to control all sealing in Bering Sea. In 1893 the arbitrators decided against this claim, and declared Bering Sea to be open ocean. But, as authorized by the terms of the reference, they made the following regulations: (1) all sealing within sixty maritime miles of the Pribilof islands to be forbidden; (2) a closed time for seals to be established; (3) all sealing vessels to be licensed. These regulations proved worthless. In 1898 Americans were forbidden by law to do pelagic sealing. Finally, in 1911, the United States, Great Britain, Russia, and Japan agreed to suspend pelagic sealing for a period of fifteen years.

Bill of Rights, The. The name given to the first ten amendments to the Constitution, which restrict the power of the Federal government with respect to certain rights of the individual citizen and of the separate states. Precedent for this statement of "rights" was found in the Bill of Rights presented by the English Parliament to William and Mary in 1689. Similar bills or declarations of rights are attached to the constitutions of most of the states of the Union.

Black and Tans. About 1892–96, this name was applied to Southern Republicans who believed in giving to the Negro an equal opportunity with the whites in holding party and political office. They were opposed by the Lily-white Republicans, who favored the exclusion of the Negro from public and party affairs.

Black Hawk War. Two short campaigns in 1831-32 in Illinois. Black Hawk, chief of the Sac Indians, after his tribe had ceded their lands to the United States and moved west of the Mississippi, returned and began massacres of white settlers. He was captured in August 1832. Abraham Lincoln was a captain of militia in the campaign of 1832.

Black Republicans. Name applied by Democrats to members of the newly created Republican party during the years immediately preceding the Civil War, by reason of the new party's apparent solicitude for the interests of the Negro race. Those who thus contemptuously applied the name distinguished the new Republican party from the old Republican or Democratic-Republican party, which had been the predecessor of the Democratic party. Other appellations used of the new party were Negro Worshipers and Abolitionist Republicans.

Black Warrior Case. An incident which almost brought about a war between the United States and Spain in 1854. An American vessel was seized at Havana, Cuba, for alleged violation of customs regulations. The ship and cargo were confiscated despite the protest of the American consul. The United States demanded restoration of the property. Hostilities between the two countries, however, were avoided by the disavowal by Spain of the acts of the Havana officials and by payment of the value of the ship and its cargo to the American owners. The case acquired especial importance from its connection with attempts of filibusters to force the annexation of Cuba to the United States. The entire annexationist movement ceased at about the time of this incident.

Bloody-Shirts. A term applied after the Civil War to those Northerners who, prompted by petty political motives, persisted in denouncing Southerners as traitors to their country, and who, in political parlance, thus sought to keep alive the Southern issue by "waving the bloody shirt."

Blue Laws. Laws which seek to regulate the moral conduct of individuals in the community. Blue was the color adopted by the Scotch Covenanters in the 17th century in England, and it became also the Whig color. The term blue was applied to those who decried the licentious freedom of the Restoration period, and to Puritans in general. In New England it came to be attached to certain rigorous laws, passed at various times and in different colonies, for the regulation of religious and personal conduct. The "blue laws of Connecticut" became proverbial. The title "Blue Laws" seems to have attached to the earliest code of the colony of New Haven (about 1640). The list of 45 such laws, published in 1781, in a *History of Connecticut* by S. A. Peters, a fugitive Tory clergyman, was compiled mostly from the codes of various New England colonies. It did not represent the laws of Connecticut.

Blue Light Federalists. A name applied first to Federalists, and later to all New Englanders who were opposed to the war with England in 1812. The term originated from the charge that blue light signals had been flashed by Federalists at New London in 1813 as a warning to the British, when Commodore Decatur was trying to escape through the blockade.

Booth's Conspiracy. A conspiracy headed by John Wilkes Booth, at the end of the Civil War, having for its object the assassination of the president, the vice president, and members of the cabinet. President Lincoln was shot by Booth on April 14, 1865, and on the same date Seward, the secretary of state, was wounded by Payne, another of the conspirators. Booth was shot while in hiding. Four of the other conspirators were hanged, the rest being sentenced to various terms of imprisonment.

Border Ruffians. The name applied in Kansas before the Civil War to the lawless element, coming largely from Missouri, which menaced the settlers from the North and attempted to prevent the establishment of a free state government.

Border States. Before the Civil War, this name was applied to the five slave states—Delaware, Maryland, Virginia, Kentucky, and Missouri—bordering on the free states.

Boston Massacre. A conflict of citizens and British soldiers in Boston on the evening of March 5, 1770, in which five persons were killed and six were injured. The affair grew out of the quartering of soldiers on the townspeople for purposes of intimidation. Blame attaches, not to the soldiers, but to the government that made the trouble possible. John Adams and Josiah Quincy volunteered as counsel for the soldiers at their trial. Two were given light punishment, the others were acquitted.

Boston Port Bill. An act passed by the British Parliament in 1774, closing the custom house and port of Boston. It was a measure of retaliation for the action of the inhabitants in preventing the importation of tea by the British East India Company. The bill failed of its purpose through the ready aid given to the city by the rest of the country.

Boston Tea Party. The American colonists had determined not to pay the tea duty imposed by Parliament. On December 16, 1773, the tea ships of the British East India Company, which were lying in Boston harbor, were boarded by a party of men disguised as Indians, who threw into the harbor the entire cargo of the three ships, 342 chests of tea, valued at about £18,000. The immediate result of this action was the passing of the Boston Port bill.

Bounty Jumping. During some periods of the Civil War, the government paid "bounties" to volunteers. Unprincipled men would enlist, go to the front and serve long enough to get the "bounty money," and then desert, afterward re-enlisting under assumed names, thus getting another "bounty." Such men were called "bounty jumpers."

Braddock's Defeat. The utter rout of the combined English and colonial forces under General Edward Braddock by a small body of French and Indians near Fort Duquesne, July 9, 1755. The defeat was due to Braddock's refusal to adopt the methods of frontier warfare, with which he was unfamiliar. English losses were nearly 900 out of 1400. Washington accompanied Braddock as an aide, and he, with Virginia troops, saved the remnant of the retreating army from massacre.

Buck Stove and Range Case. A case on which, from 1906 to 1940, reliance was placed for limiting action of labor unions in industrial disputes. In 1906 the American Federation of Labor, acting in conjunction with the striking employees of the Buck Stove and Range Company, placed on a widely circulated "unfair list" the names of all retailers who sold the company's stoves. The company brought action in the Federal courts to enjoin the federation from circulating the list. The injunction was granted on the ground that the federation's action was a "secondary boycott," that is, a boycott not of the company itself, but of those who dealt with the company. A series of decisions in 1940–41 by the supreme court declared the advertising of a labor dispute to be under the protection of the free speech guarantee of the constitution. Thereafter the earlier precedent lost its force. See *Danbury Hatters' Case.*

Bucktails. Nickname popularly applied to members of the Tammany Society during its early years, by reason of the buck's tail worn in the hat as a part of the costume of members of the society. The term was later indiscriminately applied to all opponents of Governor Clinton's canal project in New York, since the Tammany men constituted the most aggressive of these opponents.

Bull Moose. Nickname applied to the Progressive party in 1912, the name originating from Theodore Roosevelt's remark upon one occasion: "I feel as fit as a bull moose." The bull moose was taken up as the emblem of the party, and the party itself came to be called popularly the "Bull Moose party."

Burrites (*bûr'īts*). Political followers of Aaron Burr, for the most part members of the Tammany Society of New York, who were opposed to the regular or Jeffersonian branch of the Democratic-Republican party.

Butternuts. Northerners who sympathized with the South during the Civil War. The term was suggested by the "butternut" color of the Confederate uniform.

Canadian Fisheries Question. A long-standing dispute between Canada and the United States, dating from the treaty of peace of 1783, which recognized American fishing rights off the coast of Canada. The Americans claimed that this right was inalienable; England, that it was forfeited during the second war. In 1818 a treaty was made by which the Americans were allowed to fish outside the three-mile limit, but friction as to the meaning of "three-mile limit" continued till 1871, when a treaty was signed at Washington giving the two countries reciprocal rights. Canada maintained that her fisheries were more valuable than those off the American coast. In 1877 a commission, which met at Halifax, awarded Canada and Newfoundland $5,500,000 as compensation. The United States abrogated the reciprocity treaty in 1885. The whole question was settled acceptably by an arbitration board appointed by the Hague Tribunal in 1910. This decision cleared up disputed points in the treaty of 1818 and provided a commission to decide future disputes about fishing regulations.

Cannonism. The term applied by Progressive Republicans in 1910–12 to the arbitrary methods of Joseph G. Cannon in his use of the great power of the speaker of the House of Representatives. The Progressives accused him of giving committee appointments only to members who agreed with him, thus directing legislation in the interests of a few people.

Carpetbaggers. A term of opprobrium justly applied to Northern politicians who, after the Civil War, went to the Southern states with no more baggage than a carpetbag, and, by fraud and manipulation of the votes of the newly enfranchised Negro, obtained control of several of the state governments. Through misgovernment by these carpetbaggers, some of the Southern states were run deeply into debt. The term later came to be applied to all whites who sought to enlist the aid of the colored vote in the South.

Chinese Exclusion Acts. In 1881 a treaty with China gave the United States power to "regulate, limit, or suspend" immigration of Chinese laborers. Successive acts suspended such immigration from 1882 to December 1943, when the existing act was repealed. The naturalization of Chinese already in the United States was permitted, and new immigrants were admitted on a quota basis, 105 in a year.

Clintonians (*klĭn-tō'nĭ-ănz*). The political followers of members of the Clinton family, who, together with the Livingston and the Schuyler families, controlled the government of the State of New York from 1777 to 1827. This group formed a powerful support for the Democratic-Republican or Antifederalist party, which secured the election of Jefferson to the presidency in 1800. George Clinton was elected vice president of the United States in 1804. His nephew, Dewitt Clinton, leading a Republican faction opposed to the Virginian domination of the party, was nominated for the presidency in 1812 and, with Federalist support, unsuccessfully opposed Madison.

Compromise of 1850. The name given to a group of bills passed by Congress in 1850. These measures were modifications of the omnibus bill proposed by Henry Clay. They contained the following provisions: (1) The admission of California as a free state; (2) the organization of Utah and New Mexico, with the question of slavery left to the people of those territories; (3) payment of $10,000,000 to Texas for her claims to portions of New Mexico; (4) prohibition of the slave trade in the District of Columbia; (5) a more drastic fugitive slave law.

Confiscation Acts. During the Civil War, two so-called Confiscation acts were passed by Congress, the first in 1861, and the second in the following year. Under the first act, all property of rebels, used in furthering the rebellion, was subjected to forfeiture or confiscation by the Federal government, the proceeds thereof to be used to support the Northern armies.

By the act of 1862, the penalty of confiscation was extended to cover all property, including slaves, of rebels and of traitors to the Union. Although the validity of the Confiscation acts was never questioned in the courts, they probably were unconstitutional as violative of article I, section IX (III), which forbids the passing of bills of attainder and of *ex post facto* laws.

Congress, Meeting Places of. The First Continental Congress met at Philadelphia in 1774, continuing in session from September 5 to October 26. The Second Continental Congress met at Philadelphia on May 10, 1775; this Congress continued as the national government until 1781. With the ratification of the Articles of Confederation in that year, it became the Congress of the Confederation. From 1775 to 1785 the Congress convened ten times in eight different places, as follows:

Philadelphia, May 10, 1775–December 12, 1776.
Baltimore, December 20, 1776–March 4, 1777.
Philadelphia, March 4, 1777–September 18, 1777.
Lancaster, Pa., September 18, 1777–September 27, 1777.
York, Pa., September 30, 1777–June 27, 1778.
Philadelphia, July 2, 1778–June 21, 1783.
Princeton, N. J., June 30, 1783–November 4, 1783.
Annapolis, Md., November 26, 1783–June 3, 1784.
Trenton, N. J., November 1, 1784–December 24, 1784.
New York, January 11, 1785–November 4, 1785.

Its later sessions in New York were held as follows:

November 7, 1785–November 3, 1786.
November 6, 1786–October 30, 1787.
November 5, 1787–October 21, 1788.

From this time until March 1789, the Confederation Congress was kept alive by the occasional attendance of a few members. The last entry in the journal, March 2, 1789, records the presence of Mr. Philip Pell, from New York.

The first Congress under the Constitution met in New York, March 30, 1789. On June 28, 1790, an act was passed which provided that, from the year 1800, the capital should be established on the Potomac river, at a point between the mouth of the East Branch and that of the Connogocheague. In the intervening ten years the Congress met in Philadelphia. The first session in Washington was opened on November 17, 1800.

Conscience Whigs. A name applied about 1850 to members of the Whig party in New England who felt so strongly upon the subject of the moral evils of slavery that they were willing to sacrifice political office and the interests of their party rather than violate the dictates of their consciences by sanctioning the extension of slavery into Federal territory. Together with the Democratic "Barnburners" of New York, the Conscience Whigs formed the nucleus of the Free-Soil party, which developed into the Republican party. Their opponents in the Whig party were called Cotton Whigs.

Constitutional Union Party. Remnant of the old Whig party, composed largely of Southerners who favored conciliation upon the slavery issue. In 1860 this party nominated an independent national ticket headed by John Bell of Tennessee and by Edward Everett of Massachusetts, upon an evasive platform of adherence to "the Constitution and the Union" and law enforcement.

Conway Cabal. A petty intrigue against Washington in the year 1777-78. It was headed by General Horatio Gates, Charles Lee, Thomas Mifflin, James Lovell, and Thomas Conway. Their object was to put Gates in Washington's place. They succeeded in having Gates made president of the board of war in November 1777. But his first acts were so inefficient and puerile that he was soon removed, and the cabal broke up.

Copperheads. A term of opprobrium applied by Northerners during the Civil War to fellow Northerners who sympathized with the Southern Confederacy and were suspected of secretly aiding the South. The allusion suggested in the name was to the venomous copperhead snake, which strikes without warning. Some of the partisans of the peace policy wore badges of heads cut from copper cents. Their leader was Clement L. Vallandigham, Congressman from Ohio, 1853–63. Lincoln banished him to the South.

Cotton Whigs. "Old-line" Whigs who preferred to have their party side-step the question of slavery rather than to endanger the integrity of their party and of the Union. They were accused of failing to take a stand in opposition to slavery because of their personal interest in fostering the cotton trade. See *Conscience Whigs.*

Countervailing Legislation. The series of acts passed by Congress at the close of the War of 1812, discriminating against British shipping and commerce because of the injuries inflicted upon American shipping by the British navigation acts.

Credit Mobilier (*mô-bĕl'yẽr*). The "inside" construction company formed in 1867 by a group of the leading stockholders of the Union Pacific Railroad Company. The latter company had received from the United States government, in land grants and loans, far more than the cost of the railroad to be built from Omaha to California. The Credit Mobilier was used by the manipulators of the Union Pacific to construct the road at an excessive cost. In this way, both the railroad and the government were defrauded. The participation of congressmen and government officials in the profits of this scheme was the occasion of one of the greatest scandals in American political history.

Crime of '73. The characterization given by the free silver advocates to the demonetization of silver by Congress in 1873. It was alleged that the provision in the act of 1873, which omitted silver from the freely coined metals, was passed surreptitiously and with the design of injuring the farmer and debtor classes of the West and of the South. In fact, no silver had been brought to the mint for coinage for more than twenty years before the act was passed, because, during that period, silver, in relation to gold, was more highly valued for industrial purposes than for coinage at the mint. In providing that silver should no longer be freely coined, therefore, Congress was merely repealing a provision which had been a dead letter for many years. See *Free Silver Movement.*

Custer's Last Fight. The battle of the Little Big Horn, June 25, 1876. General George A. Custer, in command of a cavalry regiment of 600 men, had been sent in advance of the main body of United States troops in pursuit of Sitting Bull and his band. In the belief that he was attacking only a part of the Indian force, Custer divided his regiment and, with 260 men, attacked the Indian center. Instead of encountering 1000 Indians he found himself surrounded by 5000. The general and every man in his troop were killed. One Indian scout attached to the force is said to have escaped. The field is marked by marble monuments, each placed where a man fell.

Danbury Hatters' Case. The popular name of a case on the strength of which, from 1908 to 1941, boycotts of interstate manufacturers by labor unions were held illegal.

The United Hat Makers' Union, supported by the American Federation of Labor, declared a boycott of the products of a firm of hat manufacturers in Danbury, Connecticut, who insisted on maintaining an open shop. The action of the union was declared by the supreme court in 1908 to be a violation of the Sherman Antitrust act. The Clayton act, in 1914, declared that, if workmen entered into combinations to further their interests by lawful means, such combinations should not be regarded as unlawful. In 1941, the supreme court, in the case of U. S. v. Hutcheson, decided that this law made the earlier ruling untenable.

Dark Horse. One who has not been prominently in the public eye as a candidate, but who is brought forward at the psychological moment as a compromise candidate when a nominating convention has reached a deadlock. Often a so-called "dark horse" is in fact the candidate who has been the favorite of the party manager from the beginning, but for strategic purposes has been held in reserve. Presidents Polk, Pierce, Hayes, Garfield, and Harding were all "dark horse" candidates.

Dartmouth College Case. A celebrated case, in regard to which the supreme court in 1819 handed down a decision, declaring that charters given to private corporations were contracts and, as such, inviolable. The decision also demonstrated for the first time the method by which the sovereignty of the individual states could, through the supreme court, be limited by the Federal Constitution.

The legislature of New Hampshire had attempted to take the control of Dartmouth college out of the hands of the trustees chosen according to its charter and to intrust the college to other trustees chosen by the legislature. The original trustees brought suit against the officers of the new board of trustees, who had obtained possession of the college property. The case for the regularly appointed trustees was argued by Daniel Webster before the supreme court, which decided for the inviolability of the charter. Since this decision, it has been the custom for the states, in granting charters, to insert clauses reserving to the legislature the right of amendment.

Democratic-Republican Party. The name given to the party, at first called Republican, founded by Thomas Jefferson soon after the adoption of the Federal Constitution. The party inherited from the Antifederalists their opposition to a strong centralized government and set its face against the broad-constructionist and nationalist tendencies of Hamilton. Its members sympathized strongly with the French revolutionists and, like them, glorified the rights of man.

The party succeeded in having Jefferson elected to the presidency in 1800. It continued to hold power until 1828, but departed so far from the principles of its founders that after 1816 there was no longer any apparent difference between its position and that of its former opponents, the Federalists, who had long ceased to exist as a separate group. In 1828 the Democratic-Republicans split into two parts: one, under the leadership of Andrew Jackson, called the Democratic party; the other, under the leadership of Clay, which took the appellation of National Republicans. The Democratic party has continued until the present day, but the National Republican party dissolved after the defeat of its ticket in 1832. This Republican party must not be confused with the Republican party which was formed in 1854 on quite different issues and which has continued until the present time.

Deseret (*dĕz'ĕr-ĕt*), **The State of.** The name is from the *Book of Mormon* and means "land of the honeybee." A convention of Mormons in 1849 organized an independent state with this name. Congress refused them recognition and in 1850 organized the territory under the name of Utah.

Donkey, Democratic. Popular symbol of the Democratic party. It was originated by Thomas Nast in a celebrated cartoon published January 15, 1870.

Dorr's Rebellion. An insurrection in Rhode Island, headed by Thomas W. Dorr, 1841-42, having for its object the extension of the suffrage, which, according to the charter of 1663, was restricted to holders of real estate and to their eldest sons. Dorr, chosen governor by an irregular election, seized the statehouse at Providence. His forces, however, were dispersed, and he himself was tried for treason and sentenced to life imprisonment. In 1845 he was released. The movement resulted in the adoption in 1842, of a constitution providing for extended suffrage.

Doughfaces. A name used by John Randolph in 1820 in reference to the Northerners in Congress who voted with the South on the Missouri Compromise. It was taken up and applied by abolitionists to Northerners with Southern sympathies during the decades preceding the Civil War.

Draft Riots. An outbreak in New York City in 1863, occasioned by resistance to the drafting of New Yorkers into the Union army. The mob held possession of the city for four days, the absence of the militia at the front having left only the police available for the protection of the city. It is estimated that more than 1000 persons were killed, and that damage to the extent of $1,500,000 was done during the riots.

Dred Scott Case. A case of notable importance in American history, decided in 1857 by the supreme court of the United States. Dred Scott, a negro, claimed that, having lived with his owner in a free state, he could not legally be sold back into slavery on his master's death. The action was first brought in the state circuit court of St. Louis county, Missouri, and was later carried to the supreme court. The supreme court decided against Scott, and it was further laid down that he had no standing before the court, as no person who had been a slave, or was the descendant of a slave, could claim rights of citizenship. After the decision, Scott, having been transferred to a new owner, was freed. The utterances of the court with respect to these points were received in the North as challenges from the slave power, and they did much to hasten the crisis of war.

Drys. A name popularly applied to members of the Prohibition party, and later to persons of any political affiliation who advocated the prohibition or restriction of the manufacture and the sale of intoxicating liquor.

El Caney (*ĕl kä-nā'*). A small town located four miles northeast of Santiago de Cuba. It was made famous during the Spanish American war. On July 1, 1898, a force of about 4500 Americans fought a sharp battle here with a force of about 525 Spaniards. The American troops were commanded by General Lawton, while the Spaniards were under the command of General Vara del Rey. The Spanish force was thoroughly intrenched and desperately resisted the attacks of the Americans. The battle was finally won by the American force, the casualties amounting to more than 400 on each side. The battlefield is now a public reservation owned by the United States.

Elephant, Republican. Symbol of the Republican party, originated by Thomas Nast in a cartoon published November 7, 1874.

Emancipation Proclamation. A first proclamation was issued by President Lincoln on September 22, 1862, announcing that on the first of the following January "all persons held as slaves within any state or designated part of a state the people whereof shall then be in rebellion against the United States, shall be then, thenceforward, and forever free"; and that on that day he would, by proclamation, "designate the states and parts of states, if any, in which the people thereof" should be in "rebellion against the United States." The final emancipation proclamation was issued January 1, 1863.

Embargo Act. An act of Congress, passed December 22, 1807, forbidding any ship to sail with cargo from an American port to any foreign port. It was a reply to the English orders in council and to the Napoleonic decrees, which made lawful prizes of American ships on the high seas. These threatened to destroy American commerce. The embargo, however, served only to bring distress at home. The act was replaced in 1809 by a Nonintercourse act applying only to France and England.

Equal Rights Party. A faction which arose within the Democratic party of New York in 1835. This group opposed the granting of special privileges and exemptions to state banks and to other corporations, in many of which the regular or Tammany leaders of the Democratic party were personally interested. The Equal Rights men were also called "Locofocos." See *Locofocos.*

Era of Good Feeling. The period of Monroe's administration (1816–24), during which there was a truce between Republicans and Federalists. The latter party's doctrines had been adopted in large part by the Republicans (Democratic-Republicans).

Faneuil (*făn'’l*) **Hall.** The famous market house and hall in Boston, built and given to the city in 1742 by Peter Faneuil. During the Revolutionary period it was the meeting place of the patriots and came to be called "the cradle of American liberty." In 1805 the hall was enlarged to a capacity of 3000 people. Here the great speakers of the country have been heard, from the days of Webster and Wendell Phillips to our own time.

Farmers' Alliance. A national organization for the bettering of agricultural conditions through social and legislative activity. The first state organization of societies out of which the alliance grew is credited to Texas in 1876. Similar organizations were developing about the same time in the Southern, Western, and Central states. The earlier activity of these alliances was chiefly nonpolitical. In 1887, however, the National Farmers' Alliance was formed, and its energies were directed into political channels, its chief strength being in Kansas and Nebraska. An agreement with the Knights of Labor in 1889 resulted in the formation of the National Farmers' Alliance and Industrial Union. The political phases of this movement were soon transferred to the Populist party. The Farmers' Alliance ceased to be political, but has survived as an agricultural organization. It joined in the Farmers' National Congress of 1914, as a body of about three million farmers.

Federalists. The party of Alexander Hamilton and John Marshall, which favored the creation of a strong national government and urged the adoption of the Federal Constitution. The party drew its supporters from the commercial classes, who looked for a strong government to afford greater security to person and property than the discarded Confederation had supplied, and from other farsighted, patriotic groups, who desired a government that would command international respect and fair treatment. The strength of the party lay mainly in the large states—Massachusetts, New York, Pennsylvania, and, for a time, Virginia. The smaller states feared that they would be eclipsed by the overwhelming influence of the large states in the new Union.

The Federalists were in control of the national government for 12 years—from 1789 to 1801. The death of Alexander Hamilton in 1804 robbed the party of its only great political leader, and its disintegration speedily set in. The Democratic-Republicans, however, during a supremacy which lasted for the next two decades, appropriated the main Federalist principles. The supreme court, too, under the influence of Chief Justice Marshall, continued, until his death in 1835, to exert a dominant nationalist influence in keeping with the principles that had been upheld by the Federalist party. Thus the Federalists, by means of their influence both in the legislature and in the judiciary, impressed themselves deeply on the early history of the country and determined the direction of its subsequent development toward a strongly centralized Federal government.

Federal Republicans. A name applied at different times to two different groups: (1) the followers of George Clinton in New York, who, in 1787, organized to oppose the adoption of the Constitution; (2) the supporters of President Monroe who had formerly been Federalists.

Fiat (*fī'ăt*) **Money Party.** Another name for the Independent National or Greenback party organized in 1874. See *Free Silver Movement, Greenbackism, Greenback Party.*

Fifty-Four Forty or Fight. Slogan of those Americans who from 1842 to 1846 demanded that the boundary line between American and British territory in the Northwest be established at 54° 40′. This was the southern boundary of Alaska, agreed to by Russia and by the United States in 1824. The phrase is ascribed to Senator William Allen of Ohio. The line was in fact established at the 49th parallel to a point in the Strait of Georgia, thence through the Haro canal and the Juan de Fuca strait to the Pacific.

Finality (*fī-năl'ĭ-tĭ*) **Men.** A term applied by abolitionists to those Northerners who, in the decade before the Civil War, sought to avert the pending danger to the Union by a "conspiracy of silence" upon the question of slavery. The group received the name in allusion to its contention that the Compromise of 1850 constituted a final solution of the slavery question.

Fire Eaters. The extreme supporters of slavery and of state rights in the South were so called by their political opponents before the Civil War.

Five Nations, The. The five tribes of Indians who formerly ranged the east coast of America, along the Hudson, and as far south as the Delaware. They were always on the English side in the wars with France. The designation included the Mohawks, Oneidas, Onondagas, Cayugas, and Senecas. See *Six Nations.*

Force Bill. The popular name given to several acts of Congress applying to the South: (1) a bill of March 2, 1833, to enforce the tariff law which had been challenged by nullification acts in South Carolina; (2) acts passed in 1870 and 1871 authorizing the president to use troops to protect election places in the South; (3) the Lodge Election bill providing for efficient enforcement of United States election laws, passed by the House July 2, 1890, but defeated in the Senate.

Fort Duquesne (*doo-kān'*). A colonial fort on the present site of Pittsburgh, at the junction of the Allegheny and Monongahela rivers. The work was begun in 1754 by a party of Virginians sent out by Governor Dinwiddie. They were driven away by French and Indians before completing the fort. It was then finished by the French and named *Du Quesne.* After being burned by the French in 1758, it was rebuilt by the English and named Fort Pitt. Only a blockhouse now remains, preserved by the Daughters of the American Revolution.

Fort Niagara. A masonry fort built by the French governor Vandreuil in 1725-27 at the mouth of the Niagara river, on the American side. Fort Niagara was the most important French military station and trading post on the Great Lakes. The English leader Sir William Johnson captured it in 1759 and there negotiated treaties with numerous Indian tribes. The Wyoming and Cherry Valley expeditions set out from this fort during the Revolutionary War. The British relinquished it to the United States by the Treaty of 1783, but actual evacuation was delayed until 1796. Canadian forces held it in the War of 1812 from December 19, 1813, until March 27, 1815. Through the activities of a patriotic association, a beginning was made in 1928 toward restoring the fort in its original form from plans preserved in archives at Paris, France.

Fort Sumter. A brick-walled fortification built on a shoal in the narrowest part of the harbor of Charleston, South Carolina. When that state seceded, December 20, 1860, this fort was in process of completion. Guns were being mounted, but no garrison had been assigned to it. On December 26, 1860, Major Anderson, expecting an attack, transferred his 75 men from Fort Moultrie to Fort Sumter. On April 12, 1861, the attack came in a bombardment from the other harbor batteries; on the 14th, Anderson and his little garrison, whose supplies were exhausted, evacuated the place. Not a man had been killed on either side during this engagement, which opened the Civil War.

Four Freedoms. In his annual message of January 6, 1941, President Roosevelt announced as essentials of the post-war world "four essential human freedoms": freedom of speech and of expression; freedom of worship; freedom from want, secured to the world by economic understandings; freedom from fear, secured by limitation of armaments to prevent aggression.

Freeport Doctrine. Called also "Freeport heresy." The proposal, advocated by Stephen A. Douglas in his debate with Lincoln at Freeport, Ill., in 1858, was that any territory had the right to stamp out slavery by "unfriendly" police laws. It was suggested that this policy would in time do away with the institution of slavery.

Free Silver Movement. An agitation, supported by the farmers and the silver mining industry, for the free minting of silver with a fixed valuation of sixteen ounces of silver for one of gold.

The Bland-Allison act of 1878 provided for the coinage of silver dollars in a limited amount, and in 1890 by the Sherman act the purchases of silver were increased and treasury certificates were issued against the silver acquired. In 1893, however, the further purchase of silver was stopped. In 1900, by the Gold Standard act, the coinage of the country was established on a gold basis. The agitation died down as a result of an increase in general prosperity.

In the earlier stages of the free silver movement its supporters were not confined to any one party, but in 1891 the Populist party was organized mainly for the purpose of furthering the policy. In 1896 and in 1900 the Democratic party espoused the cause and were joined by the Populists in the support of their presidential candidate, William J. Bryan. He attained to national prominence as the champion of free silver. He was defeated, however, in both elections, and with the passage of the Gold Standard act in 1900 the movement ceased to be a political issue.

Free-Soil Party. A party organized in 1840 by the amalgamation of the Liberty party with Antislavery or Conscience Whigs of New England and Antislavery Democrats, or Barnburners, of New York, upon a platform of opposition to the extension of slavery. By nominating Van Buren, an old-line Democrat, for president in 1848, the new party lost the support of many Antislavery Whigs who otherwise would have joined its ranks. By 1856 the Free-Soil party had practically disintegrated, and the remnant of the party was ready to join with the now swelling number of Antislavery Whigs and Antislavery Democrats of the North, to form the new Republican party, which represented the principles for which the Free-Soilers had stood.

Fries's (*frēs'ĕz*) **Rebellion.** An uprising in Pennsylvania, led by a man named Fries. It was a protest against the tax placed by the Federal government, in July 1798, on slaves and real estate. It was sometimes called the "Window Tax War" because houses were assessed according to the size and number of their windows. President Adams called out troops to suppress the rioters, who, at Bethlehem, had forced a United States marshal to release prisoners. Fries and other leaders were captured. In 1800 President Adams proclaimed an amnesty for all who had participated in the "rebellion."

Fugitive Slave Laws. The fugitive slave law of 1793, amended in 1818, failed to accomplish its purpose because its enforcement was left to the states. Free states refused to carry out the provisions of the law. In the Compromise of 1850 a new law was included, which made it the duty of Federal officers to capture and to return to their owners all fugitive slaves. The slave was denied jury trial, and a citizen who refused to aid an officer was declared guilty of treason. Attempts to enforce the provisions of this act served to arouse more intense opposition in the free states, and its repeal was demanded by the Republican party. The law, which had thus become a leading immediate cause of the Civil War, was repealed in 1864.

Full Dinner Pail. Campaign slogan adopted by the Republican party in 1900 and used occasionally in national campaigns since that time. It symbolized the promise of employment and a fair wage for the laborer, and the outlook of industrial prosperity for the country under a Republican administration.

Gadsden Purchase. The United States purchased from Mexico, for $10,000,000, about 45,000 square miles now forming the southern part of Arizona and New Mexico. This was known as the Gadsden Purchase. It was negotiated by James Gadsden while he was United States minister to Mexico in 1853. This transaction gained immediate importance from the fact that the treaty accompanying it settled questions of boundary and Mexican damage claims, which grew out of the provisions of the Treaty of Guadalupe Hidalgo (1848).

Gag Rules. The name applied to the series of rules adopted by the House of Representatives during the period from 1836 to 1844 to prevent reception of antislavery petitions. John Quincy Adams fought this policy as a violation of the Constitution and finally won his long battle in 1844.

Geneva Award. The decision of the board of five arbitrators appointed by the United States, Great Britain, Italy, Switzerland, and Brazil, in the matter of the Alabama claims. This tribunal met in Geneva, December 15, 1871. In the final award, signed September 14, 1872, allowance was made for an indemnity of $15,500,000, to be paid by Great Britain to the United States. This decision greatly strengthened the principle of arbitration as a means of settling serious international differences. See *Alabama Claims*.

Goldbugs. A nickname applied by the Free Silver partisans in the campaign of 1896 to Democrats and Republicans who favored the single gold monetary standard. See *Free Silver Movement, Populist Party.*

Gold Democrats. "Sound money" Democrats, largely from the Eastern states, who were opposed to the free coinage of silver, and who bolted the regular Democratic national convention in 1896, when William J. Bryan was nominated on a free silver platform. Under the name of the National Democratic party, the Gold Democrats nominated a national ticket of their own, with John M. Palmer for president and Simon Buckner for vice president. The party disappeared upon the passage of the Gold Standard act in 1900.

Grandfather Clauses, The. This name is popularly applied to certain clauses written into the constitutions of some Southern states, providing that certain educational tests for voters shall not apply to white persons whose fathers or grandfathers were voters before the year 1867. The effect of the literacy tests is to decrease the colored vote, while the "grandfather clause" prevents a corresponding decrease of the white vote.

Grand Old Party. Characterization given by Republican campaign orators to the Republican party in 1880. It was abbreviated to Gop in the Cincinnati *Gazette* in 1884 for typographical reasons. Thereafter G. O. P. became the accepted abbreviated form.

Grangers. See *Patrons of Husbandry.*

Greenbackism. A term applied to the doctrine of those who, in the decades following the Civil War, opposed the deflation of the large and unredeemable paper issues of government notes (greenbacks) and advocated the further inflation of the currency. The amount of the notes issued had reached the total of half a billion dollars, but was subsequently considerably reduced. The supporters of the doctrine organized the Independent National or Greenback party in 1874 and, in 1878, succeeded in having a law passed in Congress, which provided that the amount of government notes should not be reduced beyond the point which it had reached at that time. The amount of outstanding government notes stood then at $346,681,016, and, through the renewal of worn-out notes, has remained at the same figure. The notes were made redeemable in gold in 1879. See *Greenback Party.*

Greenback Labor Party. The name of the party formed in 1878 by the merging of the Greenback party with certain labor groups, who had much in common with the Greenback party, particularly a belief in the desirability of an inflated currency. In 1880 the Greenback Labor party nominated James B. Weaver for president, and in 1884 it nominated Benjamin F. Butler. The party soon disintegrated, many of its members joining the Populist party, organized in 1891.

Greenback Party. The popular name of the Independent National party, which held its first national convention at Indianapolis in 1874. In 1876 it nominated Peter Cooper for the presidency. The party opposed further retirement of the greenback or paper money issue, which had been authorized during the Civil War but was not redeemable in gold. Hoping thereby to increase the price of farm products, they even advocated the further inflation of the currency. In 1878 the party incorporated with itself certain labor groups and took the name of the Greenback Labor party. See *Greenbackism.*

Green Mountain Boys. An organized band of settlers in Vermont, formed in 1773 to resist the encroachments of the New Yorkers, who claimed Vermont as part of the colony of New York under the charter of Charles II. At the head of a regiment of Green Mountain Boys, Ethan Allen made his famous and effective demand for the surrender of Fort Ticonderoga "in the name of the Great Jehovah and the Continental Congress," May 10, 1775.

Half-Breeds. The name applied in 1877 to President Hayes and those Republicans who supported him in his policy of withdrawing troops from the South, thus permitting Democratic officials to take office. The suggestion in the epithet was that the followers of the president were not "full-blooded" Republicans. The term was applied later (1880) to the New York Republicans who failed to support Senator Conkling.

Halifax Fishery Commission. A commission appointed in 1877 to assess the compensation to be awarded to the British-American colonies, in return for the recognition of American fishing rights in colonial waters. Canada was awarded $4,500,000 and Newfoundland $1,000,000. See *Canadian Fisheries Question.*

Hampton Roads Conference. A conference held on February 3, 1865, on board the ship *River Queen* in Hampton Roads, between President Lincoln and representatives of the Confederacy, with the object of bringing about a suspension of hostilities. The conference was barren of results.

Hard-Shell Democrats. See *Hunkers.*

Hartford Convention. A secret convention of prominent members of the peace party in New England, who, in 1814, objected to the energetic prosecution of the war with England. The chief proposals of the convention involved such amendment of the Constitution as would diminish the control of Congress over questions of peace and war.

Hawley-Smoot Tariff Act. Signed by President Hoover on June 17, 1930, this act increased tariff rates on the average by about 20 per cent, the largest increases being on agricultural products. By a so-called flexible tariff provision, the president was empowered, on the recommendation of a tariff commission, to increase or decrease rates on individual commodities by a maximum of 50 per cent. The act bars goods made by convict or forced labor.

Hay-Herran Canal Treaty. A treaty between the United States and Colombia, signed January 22, 1903. By this treaty, the United States was to secure a strip of territory six miles wide along the route of the canal, against a payment to Colombia of $10,000,000 and an annual subsidy. This was granted on a lease for a hundred years, renewable at the option of the United States. Colombia failed to ratify the treaty, and within a few months the independent Republic of Panama was set up.

Hearst Party. See *Independence League.*

"Higher Law," Seward's. A speech delivered by William H. Seward during the debates on the Compromise of 1850 is referred to as Seward's "higher law" speech. He used the following words: "The Constitution devotes the domain to union, to justice, to defense, to welfare, and to liberty. But there is a higher law than the Constitution, which regulates our authority over the domain, and devotes it to the same noble purpose." The South interpreted this to mean that the Constitution, which recognized slavery as existing, was set aside by this "higher law."

Homestead Act. The first of a series of acts and amendments, which make up the national homestead law, was passed by Congress in 1862. This act provided that a tract not exceeding 160 acres of unappropriated portions of the public domain should be given to any head of a family who would live on the tract for five years and improve it. The provisions of the law extend also to any person 21 years of age, who is a citizen of the United States or has filed declaration of his intention to become a citizen. Within ten years, 28 million acres were "homesteaded" under this act. Later laws permitted withholding of grants and all unappropriated land was withdrawn from settlement in 1935.

Hunkers. A contemptuous name of uncertain origin applied by the Barnburners to the proslavery section of the Democratic party in New York from 1844 to 1848. They supported the party's presidential candidate, James K. Polk, in 1844, and after his election they received most of the offices. After 1848 this section was called the Hard-Shell Democrats or merely the Hards. See *Barnburners.*

Icarian (*ī-kā'rĭ-ăn*) **Community.** A communistic society founded by Cabet, a Frenchman, in 1849, after the plan set forth in his novel *Voyage en Icarie.* The community was first established in Texas, but later migrated to Nauvoo, Illinois. Cabet himself was expelled from the community in 1856, and soon thereafter the society moved to Iowa, where it continued to exist until about 1895. In 1881, some of the members of the society went to California and there established the Icaria Speranza, a co-operative business association.

Impeachment of President Johnson. As a result of his long quarrel with Congress, the House of Representatives presented articles of impeachment against President Johnson in 1868. The special charge voted upon in the Senate was that the president had tried to remove Secretary Stanton, contrary to the Tenure of Office act passed by Congress over the president's veto. The impeachment failed for lack of one vote to make the two-thirds necessary to convict. The constitutional right for which Johnson contended was upheld by a decision of the Supreme Court in 1926.

Impressment and Search. Impressment was forcible recruiting for the English navy. Search was the right, claimed by England after the Revolution, to stop American ships and search their crews for English deserters or English citizens liable to naval service. Frequently, Americans were thus impressed along with the real deserters. This practice was one of the occasions of the War of 1812.

Independence League. A political organization initiated by William Randolph Hearst in 1905 in New York City. It extended also for a brief period to Boston, Chicago, and San Francisco. Out of it grew the national Independence party, sometimes called the Hearst party, which held a national convention at Chicago in 1908. Its program called for government ownership of public utilities, for the referendum and the recall, and for other radical reforms. The party did not survive the election in 1908.

Independent National Party. An official name adopted by the Greenback party in 1876, when it placed in the field an independent national ticket, headed by Peter Cooper for president. See *Greenback Party.*

Indian Population of Early America. It is estimated that full blooded Indians in North and South America number approximately 26,000,000, making allowance for mixed bloods at proportional value. As a result of the archeological researches of Dr. H. J. Spinden and others, it would appear that the Indian population reached its maximum about 1200 A. D., with a total of from 50 to 75 million, although the peak of population in Mexico and Central America was attained about 550 A. D. When Europeans arrived in America, the Indians were still much more numerous than at the present time. A rapid depopulation took place, chiefly as a result of the introduction of smallpox and measles. In the West Indies the aborigines were virtually exterminated. In Mexico, however, and in many parts of South America the Indians have increased. With better living conditions and lessened infant mortality, most Indian tribes in the United States have grown in numbers in the last 20 years.

Insurgents. Progressive Republicans in the Senate and the House of Representatives who, during the second administration of Theodore Roosevelt and the administration of Taft, rebelled against the methods of Speaker Cannon and the control of legislation by conservative Republican leaders in the House and in the Senate. They sought to secure the enactment of progressive measures looking to the more effective government regulation of railways and "big business." In 1910, with the aid of the Democratic members, the House insurgents were successful in bringing about a drastic change in the rules, depriving the speaker of many of the powers which he had previously exercised.

Intolerable Acts. A name often applied to four (sometimes five) acts of Parliament, passed in 1774, in retaliation for the destruction of tea in Boston harbor, December 1773: (1) The Boston Port bill, which closed the port of Boston; (2) the Regulating act, which virtually abolished the charter of Massachusetts; (3) the Quebec act, extending the boundary of Quebec to the Ohio river; (4) an act providing that officers or soldiers accused of murder should be tried in England or in some colony other than that in which the murder had been committed; (5, sometimes included) an act compelling citizens to supply with shelter, wood, drink, bedding, soap, and candles, the soldiers quartered among them. See *Boston Port Bill, Boston Tea Party, Quebec Act.*

Ironclad Oath. The oath required by Congress from 1862 to 1871 for Federal officeholders. It was designed to exclude from office any possible enemy of the Union, and received its name because of its very stringent character. After the close of the war, this oath was required of officeholders in the "reconstructed" states.

Jacksonian Democracy. A term applied to an ideal of popular government to which Andrew Jackson gave expression and which he applied during his presidential term. To its hostility toward aristocracy of all kinds the ideal adds a belief in the capability of the common people to rule by direct participation in government.

The election of Jackson in 1828 was regarded as a triumph for this democratic ideal. It had become politically effective for the first time, through the strong sentiment of equality prevalent in the pioneer communities of the South and the West, and by reason of the general extension of the suffrage in the East, whereby citizens who did not own property were given a direct voice in government.

Jackson Men. Supporters of Andrew Jackson for the presidency during the so-called period of "personal politics" in the United States, from 1822 to 1828. During this period there was but one recognized national political party—the Democratic-Republican party—and such political divisions as existed were based merely upon adherence to one national leader or another. Thus the followers of Clay during this period were called "Clay Men," and the followers of Adams and Calhoun were called "Adams Men" and "Calhounites" respectively.

Jeffersonian Democracy. A term applied to an ideal of popular government advocated by Jefferson. The ideal was based upon faith in the political wisdom of the common people, who could be relied upon to choose those of ability to rule for them. Jeffersonian democracy differs from Jacksonian democracy in that it recognized a natural aristocracy of ability, whereas Jacksonian democracy emphasized the right of the common people to participate directly in government.

With Jeffersonian democracy was associated an advocacy of a broad sovereignty for the individual states and of a restricted province for the Federal government.

Jeffersonian Republican. A term used to designate the member of the Republican or Democratic-Republican party founded by Thomas Jefferson in the last decade of the 18th century. See *Democratic-Republican Party.*

John Brown's Raid. The seizing of the U. S. arsenal at Harpers Ferry, Va., by John Brown and a company of 22 men, October 16, 1859. The purpose of the raid was to start a slave insurrection. But the slaves did not respond. Brown was captured by U. S. Marines under Colonel Robert E. Lee. He was tried in a Virginia court, convicted of murder and treason, and hanged. Although Brown's whole enterprise was madly fanatical and utterly failed of its immediate aim, yet it did serve his ultimate purpose of furthering the fight against slavery.

Jones & Laughlin Case. A case, decided by the supreme court April 12, 1937, which established the validity of the National Labor Relations act as applied to manufacturing. By ruling that interruption in operations of a business whose raw materials and finished products cross state lines interferes with interstate commerce, the decision radically enlarged the authority of Congress.

Kansas Border Warfare. The armed conflict between slavery and free state settlers in Kansas in 1856. The Kansas-Nebraska bill put into the hands of the settlers the decision as to slavery in the territory. Immigrants poured into the country from both North and South. Rival governments were set up. Elections for the proslavery government were fraudulently carried by raiders from Missouri. In the murder and open warfare that followed, about 200 lives were lost. President Pierce supported the proslavery legislature and broke up the free state government, July 4, 1856.

Kansas-Nebraska Bill. An act of Congress, May 30, 1854, by which Kansas and Nebraska were admitted to the Union as territories. This act was a breach of the Missouri Compromise, as it left to each of the new territories the settlement of the question of slavery within its borders.

King Philip's War. The name given to the series of battles and Indian massacres in New England in 1675–76. The conflict was precipitated by the slaying of an Indian interpreter who had revealed to the Plymouth authorities a plot to exterminate the white settlers. The Indians who, at the instance of King Philip, a son of the great sachem, Massasoit, killed the informer were executed. This action provoked Indian retaliations, which grew into a terrible series of atrocities. The war ended with the killing of King Philip at Bristol, August 12, 1676.

Kitchen Cabinet. The name given by their political opponents to the unofficial advisers of President Andrew Jackson, 1829–37. Among these men, whose influence with the president was believed to be greater than that of his official advisers in the cabinet, were Amos Kendall, Isaac Hill, and General Duff Green.

Knights of the Golden Circle. A secret political order organized shortly before the Civil War. It was composed of Northerners with proslavery sentiments. It was suspected during the war of secretly aiding, and of negotiating with, the Confederacy. In 1863 the order was dissolved, and its members reorganized, first as the order of American Knights, and later as the Sons of Liberty. At the close of the war a number of the leaders of the order were convicted of treason for their part in the Northwest conspiracy, an attempt to disrupt the North by organizing a confederacy in the Northwest.

Its name has reference to a slaveholding empire which the order hoped to set up, centering in Habana and including the territory within a "golden circle" which should have a radius of 1200 miles.

Know-Nothings. A name given to the members of a secret political organization which had as its purpose the exclusion from political offices of Catholics and of foreign-born citizens. The name arose from the usual reply of members to inquiries about the nature or aims of the organization, "I know nothing about it." The movement, rising soon after 1840, became prominent in 1852, and, being joined in 1854 by a large part of the Northern Whig party, the organization assumed the name of the American party. It held a national convention in 1856 but disintegrated as a national party in the controversies over the slavery question, although in separate states it continued to be a force until 1860.

Koszta (*kô'stä*) **Incident.** The diplomatic dispute between Austria and the United States in 1853 over the citizenship of Martin Koszta. Koszta, a Hungarian refugee who had taken out first citizenship papers in 1850, was seized at Smyrna by Austrian officers. Instructed by the American minister at Istanbul, Captain Ingraham of the *Saint Louis* demanded surrender of Koszta, who was held on the Austrian ship *Huzar*. His demand was complied with. The Austrian government called upon the United States for apology and satisfaction. But Secretary of State Marcy held that Koszta was an American citizen. Congress awarded Captain Ingraham a medal for his services in the case.

Ku-Klux Klan (*kū'klŭks' klăn*). An organization which was formed in the South after the Civil War, in order to check the threatened Negro supremacy. Its methods involved the terrorizing of Negroes and of white "carpetbaggers" by bands of night riders. It achieved its purpose, but eventually it became so powerful and abuse of power under its name became so flagrant that Congress was influenced to pass the Force bill of 1871. Restoration of political rights to ex-Confederates gave the whites electoral power, and the Klan gradually died out. The name is adapted from Greek *kyklos*, in the sense of "circle" or "society," and from English *clan*. A secret organization of national scope, bearing the name of Ku-Klux Klan, and having headquarters at Atlanta, Ga., was established in 1915.

Labor Party. The first American labor party of national scope, the Labor Reform party, or National Labor Reform party, as it was later called, was organized in 1869 as an outgrowth of the National Labor Union. The party inveighed against both major parties as dominated by the capitalist class, and called upon laborers to unite behind a party of their own which would enact legislation favorable to the laborer. The party advocated a protective tariff imposing a tax on the importation of luxuries only, and also advocated a national, legal tender, paper currency issued by, and under the control of, the national government as the basic currency of the country. In 1872 the National Labor party nominated Charles O'Connor, of New York, as its candidate for president. The party polled comparatively few votes at this election, and in 1878 merged with the Greenback party to form the Greenback Labor party. See *Socialist Labor Party, Union Labor Party, United Labor Party*.

Lewis and Clark Expedition, The. The exploring expedition conducted by Meriwether Lewis, private secretary to President Jefferson, and by Captain William Clark into the Oregon country. The success of this expedition furnished a part of the basis for the claim of the United States to the Oregon territory. The enterprise was due primarily to Jefferson's keen scientific interest in determining the extent and character of the country west of the Mississippi. One of his first acts upon becoming president was to secure from Congress an appropriation for such an exploration. The explorers left River Dubois, near St. Louis, May 14, 1804, and reached the mouth of the Columbia river on November 15, 1805. Beginning the return journey on March 23, 1806, they arrived at St. Louis on September 23 in the same year.

Liberal Republicans. A party which appeared in 1872, caused by a schism in the Republican party. The new party favored removing political disabilities from those who had favored the South in the Civil

War and advocated conciliation rather than force in dealing with the defeated states. The ticket adopted was chosen also by the Democrats, but it was defeated, and the party dissolved.

Liberty Bell. This famous bell was originally cast in England in 1752 for the Pennsylvania statehouse. In transport it was so injured that its tone was ruined. It was therefore recast in Philadelphia in 1753, when the words, "Proclaim Liberty throughout the land unto all the inhabitants thereof," were inscribed on it. On July 8, 1776, the bell was rung to summon the people of Philadelphia to the first public reading of the Declaration of Independence. During the British occupation of Philadelphia, the bell was hidden beneath the floor of the Zion Reformed church at Allentown, Pa. It was broken while being tolled for the death of Chief Justice Marshall, July 8, 1835. Since 1854 it has rested in the hall of the Old Statehouse on a thirteen-sided pedestal, each side representing one of the original thirteen colonies.

Liberty Party. The name given to a new national party, formed in 1840 by the more conservative abolitionists, who refused to adopt the extreme position of the Garrisonians. Their purpose was to bring about by political means the abolition of slavery in all territory under the jurisdiction of the national government. This party merged with the Free-Soilers in 1848 and with the Republicans in 1856.

Lincoln-Douglas Debates. A series of joint debates to which Abraham Lincoln challenged Stephen A. Douglas in 1858. Lincoln was the Republican candidate for the Senate in Illinois; Douglas, the Democratic candidate. Lincoln's position was antislavery; Douglas championed the Popular Sovereignty doctrine, and won the senatorial election. However, Lincoln's conduct of this discussion helped to make him president.

Little Giants. Political followers of Stephen A. Douglas, who had been nicknamed the "Little Giant," because of his short stature and because of his great mental and oratorical powers.

Locofocos (*lō'kō-fō'kōs*). The nickname given in 1835 to members of the Equal Rights faction of the Democratic party in New York, and later to members of the Democratic party itself. At a meeting in Tammany Hall, October 29, 1835, the Tammany men withdrew, turning off the gas as they left. The Equal Rights party, however, were supplied with candles and "locofoco" matches. The meeting proceeded, and from that time the faction was dubbed the "Locofocos."

Lost Colony. The name applied to a colony of 121 persons sent out by Sir Walter Raleigh from England under John White, which settled on Roanoke island July 22, 1587. White, who went back to England for supplies, returned in 1590 after unavoidable delays only to find no trace of the colony except the word "Croatan" carved on a tree, a name designating an Indian tribe. Virginia Dare, granddaughter of White, was born in the colony August 18, 1587, the first child of English parents to be born in America.

Twenty-four stones were reported to have been discovered in 1937-39 bearing inscriptions purporting to be by Eleanor Dare, mother of Virginia, dated 1591, 1592, and 1593. If authentic, the inscriptions would indicate that the colonists settled for a while in Greenville county, S. C., and then went on to the Chatahoochee river in northern Georgia. In 1591, 64 persons, including Virginia Dare and her father Ananias, are declared to have been massacred by Indians.

The buildings occupied by the colony in 1587 were restored in 1936 on the basis of drawings taken back to England by a prior colony of 108 men who erected the buildings and abandoned them in 1586. A play based on the colony's fate is presented periodically in an open air theater built near by.

Louisiana Purchase. In 1803 the United States purchased from France the (then) city of New Orleans and the territory west of the Mississippi, extending to the eastern spurs of the Rocky mountains and to the British frontier on the North. The price paid was $15,000,000.

Lynch Law. Originally, on the western frontier in and after 1819, lynch law was a necessary substitution of an irregular trial for the regular process of law. It is now understood as mob rule and action effecting the summary execution of an offender, without even the form of trial. The most frequent use of it is in the case of Negroes charged with offenses against white women. The origin of the name is uncertain. Charles Lynch of Virginia, through his flogging of Tories during the Revolution, is said to have given his name to the practice. Another explanation is that the Carolina Regulators, about 1770, administered whippings to offenders on Lynch's creek.

McKinley Tariff Act. The high protective tariff act passed by Congress in 1890. William McKinley, as chairman of the Ways and Means committee, was chief sponsor for the bill. It fixed import duties at an average of 49 per cent. Its novel feature was a "reciprocity" provision. See *Reciprocity Treaties*.

Mason and Dixon's Line. The boundary line fixed between the colonies of Pennsylvania and Maryland in 1767; so called from the two English surveyors, Charles Mason and Jeremiah Dixon, who determined the line, thereby ending a long-standing controversy between the two colonies. Later, this line was regarded as the boundary between the free states and the slave states.

Mayflower. The ship of 180 tons which carried the Pilgrims, the first colonists of New England, to the shores of America. This vessel, which had been chartered from her London owner, sailed from Southampton, England, August 5, 1620, in company with the *Speedwell*. The latter ship proved unseaworthy, and both vessels put into the port of Plymouth, whence the *Mayflower* sailed alone on September 17. The original intention had been to reach the mouth of the Hudson river, but the captain of the *Mayflower* laid his course for Cape Cod. Accordingly, the first landing was made near the present site of Provincetown. After some exploration the site of the present town of Plymouth was chosen for the settlement. The landing at this point took place on December 21, 1620. The event is celebrated on Forefathers' Day, December 22.

According to the list of passengers, given by Governor William Bradford, 102 persons, including two children born on shipboard, arrived at Plymouth in the *Mayflower*. While the ship lay in Provincetown harbor, 41 of the men joined in signing the agreement as to the government of the colony, known as the Mayflower Compact. The following is a list of the names signed to this historic document:

Alden, John	Hopkins, Stephen
Allerton, Isaac	Howland, John
Allerton, John	Lister, Edward
Billington, John	Margeson, Edmond
Bradford, Wm.	Martin, Christopher
Brewster, Wm.	Mullins, William
Britteridge, Richard	Priest, Degory
Brown, Peter	Ridgedale, John
Carver, John	Rogers, Thomas
Chilton, James	Soule, George
Clarke, Richard	Standish, Miles
Cook, Francis	Tilley, Edward
Crackston, John	Tilley, John
Doty, Edward	Tinker, Thomas
Eaton, Francis	Turner, John
English, Thos.	Warren, Richard
Fletcher, Moses	White, William
Fuller, Edward	Williams, Thomas
Fuller, Samuel	Winslow, Edward
Gardiner, Richard	Winslow, Gilbert
Goodman, John	

Mecklenburg Declaration. A document resembling in its phraseology the Declaration of Independence, and dated May 20, 1775, supposed to record the action of a body of citizens of Mecklenburg county, North Carolina, in declaring their independence of Great Britain. Historians regard this document as having been written from memory some time after the event it purports to record. The generally accepted facts are that, on the occasion of a militia muster at Charlotte, May 31, 1775, the citizens present, having heard of the conflict at Lexington and Concord, adopted a vigorous set of patriotic resolutions. In effect, they declared all civil and military commissions void and set up a local administration to serve "until laws shall be provided for us by Congress." A copy of this notable document, known as the Mecklenburg Resolves, was sent to England, where it is preserved. The loss by fire of the original copy of the Resolves is supposed to have occasioned the writing of the document known as the Declaration. The variance in date between the two documents is usually ascribed to the difference between the old and the new style of reckoning time. Since 1831, the 20th of May has been a legal holiday in North Carolina.

Middle of the Roaders. Populists who refused to merge with the Democratic party in 1896, preferring to "keep to the middle of the road" as a separate political organization. See *Populist Party*.

Minuit's Purchase of Manhattan. Peter Minuit (1580–1638) was governor of the Dutch settlements in North America, known as New Amsterdam, from 1625 to 1631. Some time between July and September 1626, he negotiated with Indian chiefs on Manhattan island for the purchase of the entire island for merchandise valued at 60 guilders, about $24.12. Three centuries later, this same island was valued at more than 7 billion dollars.

Minutemen. The organization of provincial militia in Massachusetts in 1775. They were under the orders of the Committee of Safety, and were so called because they were supposed to be ready to march at a minute's notice. Minutemen met the British at Lexington, April 19, 1775.

Missouri Compromise. An agreement between the slavery and antislavery parties in 1820. The act passed by Congress in 1820, admitting Missouri to statehood, determined that, west of the Mississippi river, slavery should be lawful only south of 36° 30′ north latitude, except in Missouri. This arrangement was maintained until 1854, when it was violated by the admission of Kansas and Nebraska as territories, with the right to decide the slavery question for themselves.

Modoc (*mō′dŏk*) **War.** The conflict between U. S. troops and the Modocs, a warlike tribe of northern California Indians, in 1872–73. Entrenched in the lava beds, the Indians defied the troops, inflicting severe losses and murdering two peace messengers. Finally, their chief, "Captain Jack," was captured and hanged. Part of the tribe were allowed to remain in California; the rest, about 150, were sent to Indian Territory.

Monitor and Merrimac, Battle of the. The decisive engagement between these two new armored vessels in Hampton Roads, March 9, 1862. The *Merrimac* was a wooden U. S. frigate which had been rebuilt and christened the *Virginia* by the Confederates. The hull was covered with a roofing of iron plates and was equipped with a heavy iron prow for "ramming" enemy vessels. She was expected to break the blockade of Southern ports. On March 8, 1862, this "ironclad" destroyed the Union vessels *Congress* and *Cumberland*.

The *Monitor* was a new type of war vessel, built low in the water, with nothing above the deck but smokestacks and a turret 20 feet in diameter. She was the Northern reply to the Southern challenge of the formidable *Merrimac*. Arriving at Hampton Roads in the night of March 8, before she had been accepted by the government, she engaged the *Merrimac*, or *Virginia*, on the 9th. The Confederate ship, unable to ram or hit with shot the "Yankee cheesebox on a raft," was so seriously damaged by the *Monitor's* 11-inch shells that she withdrew to Norfolk. The battle left the blockade intact and demonstrated the superiority of ironclads over wooden warships.

Monroe Doctrine. A statement of policy in President Monroe's message to Congress in 1823, to the effect that the United States could not regard with indifference any further territorial expansion on the part of European powers on the American continent. The occasion for the pronouncement was the suspected intention of the Holy Alliance to interfere on behalf of Spain in her struggle with her revolted colonies. The doctrine was somewhat broadened in later interpretations, and the United States sought the cooperation of other American nations, as when, in July 1940, a conference of the American nations at Habana took steps to prevent the transfer of American possessions of European powers to other non-American nations as a consequence of World War II.

Morgan's Raid. The marauding expedition of the Confederate general, John H. Morgan, with 2400 men, into Indiana and Ohio, July 2–26, 1863. Morgan had been ordered by General Bragg to destroy railroads and the public works at Louisville. He exceeded his orders and crossed the Ohio into Indiana from Brandenburg, Ky., on July 8–9. The Union general, Hobson, pursued him, and local militia blocked and harried his troops. Near Pomeroy, Ohio, Morgan tried to escape across the Ohio, but he was attacked and lost a third of his force, killed and prisoners. A second attempt to cross the river was checked after a large number of the raiders had succeeded in escaping into Kentucky, Morgan, with the remaining third of his force started northeast through Athens and Washington counties. He was finally captured, with a small remnant of followers, near New Lisbon.

Mormons. A sect founded in 1830, at Fayette, New York, by Joseph Smith, the son of a Vermont farmer. The Mormons moved westward and, after several years' wanderings, settled on Great Salt lake in 1847, under the leadership of Brigham Young. Their advocacy of polygamy was for a long time a bar to the admission of Utah to the Union, but the enforcement of the Edmunds act of 1882 led to the formal abandonment of polygamy as a tenet by the Mormons in 1890, and Utah was admitted to statehood in 1896.

Mossbacks. The name given during the Civil War to men who hid themselves in swamps and elsewhere to avoid conscription for the Southern army. The fancy was that they would stay hidden till the moss grew on their backs. The name was later applied to extreme conservatives in politics.

Mountain Meadows Massacre. The massacre by Indians, under alleged Mormon leadership, of a party of 140 emigrants, who were crossing Utah on their way to California in 1857. Only 17 children were spared. They were distributed among Mormon families, but were restored to relatives by the U. S. government. The leader of the band, J. D. Lee, an Indian agent, was executed for the crime, in 1877, on the actual site of the massacre.

Mugwumps. A name applied by Blaine supporters to those who, in 1884, supported Cleveland, the Democratic candidate for president, owing to his advocacy of civil service reform. The word later came to be applied to independent voters. It had been used ironically as early as 1832 to mean a person of superior views. In Eliot's Indian Bible the original *mugquomp* meant "big chief" or leader.

Mulligan Letters. A series of letters written by James G. Blaine to a business associate, Warren

Fisher. It was alleged that these letters proved Blaine's share in some corrupt railroad transactions. The letters were presented to a congressional committee by James Mulligan, a clerk employed by Fisher. Blaine obtained possession of the letters, and in a dramatic defense before the House of Representatives, June 5, 1876, read parts of them. He defied the committee to compel him to give them up. The suspicion engendered by the incident was used effectively against him in the campaigns of 1876 and 1884.

Nationalists. Those who, during the period preceding the adoption of the Federal Constitution, favored the creation of a strong national government resting upon proportionate representation, possessing broad national powers, and acting directly upon individuals rather than upon or through the state governments. Their policy was adopted by the Federalist party and was supported by the supreme court decisions in the early decades of the nation's existence. This doctrine of centralization was carried further under the name of the New Nationalism and the New Deal. See *Federalists, New Deal, New Nationalism.*

National Union Party. See *War Democrats.*

Navy, The United States. To Silas Deane, John Adams, and John Langdon, the phrase "Fathers of Our Navy" has been applied. These three men constituted a committee appointed by the Continental Congress on October 13, 1775, with power to fit out two warships for service against the British. Several small craft had been in use in Boston harbor to prevent the bringing of supplies to the British forces in the city, and, in the summer of 1775, American coasting vessels had captured three British ships. However, it was in January 1776 that Lieutenant John Paul Jones hoisted the first flag unfurled aboard an American warship. On February 17, 1776, the first regular naval expedition under the authority of the United States put to sea under the command of Captain Esek Hopkins. The little fleet was successful in capturing military stores at New Providence, in the Bahamas.

In the course of the Revolution, the United States had 64 vessels regularly in commission, including the fleet on Lake Champlain. The most romantic and daring exploits were those performed by John Paul Jones. It is said that, at the close of the Revolution, at least two of the American vessels, the *Alliance* and the *Confederacy,* were the equals of any warships afloat. But all vessels were sold or scrapped, so that the new government under the Constitution came into existence without any navy.

The first naval act was passed in 1794, authorizing the construction of six frigates, one of which was the *Constitution.* During the two years of quasi war with France, 1798–1800, the number of vessels was increased. At the close of hostilities, the naval force was again depleted. During the war with the Barbary pirates, however, the American navy came into its own. At the close of the conflict the fleet was accorded full formal honors by the warships of other nations.

The War of 1812 was marked by a series of brilliant American naval victories. During the conflict, 23 regularly commissioned vessels were in service, besides numerous privateers. After the Peace of Ghent, the strength of the navy was fixed at 35 ships, frigates, and smaller vessels.

In 1844 the *Princeton,* the first screw steam war vessel ever built, was constructed. The year 1845 saw the establishment of the Naval Academy at Annapolis. In spite of some shipbuilding, the opening of the Civil War found the navy altogether inadequate. In the course of the conflict, a sufficient force was built up, the most important achievement being the building of the *Monitor,* the success of which revolutionized naval architecture.

Again, in the years following the Civil War, the navy was suffered to deteriorate in respect to ships and armament. In 1881, a program of steel construction for the new navy was laid out. In 1884, the *Dolphin,* the first ship of the steel fleet, was completed. The opening of the Spanish war found the country in possession of an adequate fleet.

In 1906 the United States entered upon an enlarged naval building program, signalized by the cruise of the battleship fleet around the world in 1907–09. The World War led to a further expansion of the fleet to a fighting strength of 2,400,000 tons at its close. From 1922 to 1936 the American navy was limited by agreements with Great Britain and Japan, (See *Washington Conference*) but after abrogation of the treaty enlargement began.

As a result of developments in World War II, the United States adopted the policy of a two-ocean navy and began to lay more stress on aircraft carriers and naval aviation. On July 1, 1945, the navy included 91,209 vessels of all types, 1100 of which were combat ships. The personnel stood at 3,389,000. At the end of 1948 the Navy included 800 active ships, with 1888 in reserve, of which 290 were combat ships. These included 11 heavy and 2 light aircraft carriers, with 7 escort carriers; 1 battleship; 30 cruisers; 147 destroyers, with 12 destroyer escorts; and 80 submarines. The personnel was 421,125, with 8782 selective service men. In July 1942 Congress authorized the enlistment of women in the Women's Reserve of the Navy (Women Appointed for Volunteer Emergency Service—WAVES). By the act of 1948 this was integrated with the Navy.

New Deal. A term used of the political and economic program sponsored by President Franklin D. Roosevelt. Suggested by the title of a book, *A New Deal,* published by Stuart Chase in 1932, the term came into wide use in the electoral campaign of that year. The New Deal signified, in its broadest aspects, a change in the accepted function of the Federal government, no longer merely an arbiter, but an active agent to guide economic activities.

Its principal measures adopted were: 1. relief of the destitute by providing work at a living wage; 2. adjustment of agricultural production in line with demand; 3. strengthening the bargaining power of labor; 4. limiting cut-throat competition carried on with the help of sweat shops and child labor; 5. insurance of bank deposits; 6. protection of investors against market manipulation; 7. taxation policies designed to decrease concentration of wealth; 8. extension of the use of electric power at low rates partly by direct competition through publicly owned plants and partly by policing utility holding companies to prevent exaction of unduly high rates; 9. conserving natural resources by discouraging wasteful use of land and its products; 10. encouraging balanced commerce with foreign nations by mutual tariff concessions; 11. safeguarding neutrality by licensing export of munitions; 12. regulating the use of credit to check deflation and inflation; 13. control of the dollar's value in foreign exchange with a view to stabilizing domestic prices; 14. provision of old age pensions and unemployment compensation.

New Nationalism. Name given to the views advanced by Theodore Roosevelt in 1910 and 1911 with respect to the powers of the Federal government. According to this doctrine, the government is looked upon, not as one of limited, delegated powers, but as a sovereign government possessing jurisdiction over all matters with respect to which the Federal government can act more effectively than the states. The field in which these powers were to be immediately exercised was in the national regulation of all corporations doing interstate business. Associated with the theory as to the national scope of the powers of the Federal government was a system of reforms which included the graduated income and inheritance taxes, conservation of natural resources, revision of the banking system, direct primaries, and a strong army and navy. The so-called New Nationalism became a central feature of the platform of the Progressive party.

New Orleans, Battle of. An engagement, January 8, 1815, between the British forces under General Pakenham and the Americans under General Andrew Jackson. The Americans, 5500 in number, were well commanded and thoroughly intrenched at Chalmette, below the city. They repulsed the attack of 10,000 British troops, inflicting a loss of 2000. The battle took place after the signing of the peace treaty at Ghent. Means of communication were few and slow, and the news of the signing of the treaty in December had not reached America. Some authorities believe that, if the transatlantic cable had been in use at the time, not only this battle but the entire War of 1812 would have been avoided.

Nonintercourse Act. An act passed March 1, 1809, forbidding all commerce with France and Great Britain. It was part of a scheme of retaliation against French and British interference with American ships. Enforcement of the law proved impossible.

Nullification, Right of. A constitutional principle asserted by the Southern states before the Civil War, to the effect that "a state under the Constitution retained the right to judge for itself the extent of the powers vested in the Federal government." Under this so-called right of nullification, it was further maintained that if, in the opinion of any state, the Federal government had exceeded its constitutional powers, such state could itself declare that act to be inoperative, and nullify its effect within the borders of that state. The right was first asserted in the Kentucky Resolutions of 1799. The climax of the discussion and also the virtual abandonment of the principle came in 1832 in connection with the protest of South Carolina against the tariff bill passed in that year. The outcome of this contest, which was virtually compromised, left doubtful the decision upon the principle of nullification. However, after 1832 in the Southern states the more fundamental doctrine of state sovereignty displaced the nullification doctrine, until the entire discussion was terminated by the Civil War.

Old Ironsides. A popular name for the 44-gun U. S. frigate *Constitution.* This famous ship was launched October 21, 1797; took part in three bombardments of Tripoli in 1805; in 1812, escaped from a British squadron in July, defeated the frigate *Guerrière* in August, and captured the *Java* in December; took the *Picton* with a convoy in 1814 and the *Cyane* and *Levant* in 1815. She was reported unseaworthy in 1828, but her proposed dismantling was prevented through popular sentiment aroused by O. W. Holmes's "Old Ironsides." Rebuilt in 1833, she was in active service till 1855 and was then used as a training ship, being again partially rebuilt in 1877; crossed the Atlantic for the last time in 1878; and was stored at the Boston Navy yard in 1897. In 1927-30, she was reconditioned in order to be converted into a U. S. Navy museum afloat.

Omnibus Bill. A name applied to bills covering several different matters, to be voted upon as a whole. The most noted of such bills in American history is that reported out by a compromise committee of the U. S. Senate on May 8, 1850. See *Compromise of 1850.*

Ordinance of 1787. An act of the Congress of the Confederation making provision for the government of the Northwest Territory, providing for religious toleration and popular education, and forbidding slavery in the territory.

Panama Canal Commission. The board of engineers and officials appointed to govern the Canal Zone and to construct the Panama canal. The commission was first organized in May 1904 with Major General Whitfield Davis as chairman. After disagreements and change of plans, Theodore P. Shonts was made chairman of a reorganized body. In 1907 a new commission was formed with Lieutenant Colonel George W. Goethals as chairman. It was abolished when the canal was completed in 1914.

Pan-American Congress. A congress of the various states of North, of South, and of Central America, organized by James G. Blaine during the term of office of President Harrison, and held at Washington in 1890. Similar congresses were held in 1901 at the City of Mexico, in 1906 at Rio de Janeiro, in 1910 at Buenos Aires, in 1923 at Santiago, in 1928 at Habana, in 1933 at Montevideo, and in 1938 at Lima.

Conferences of foreign ministers to deal with the conditions created by World War II were held at Panama, September 1939; at Habana, July 1940; and at Rio de Janeiro, January 1941.

Pan-American Union. The name of the international organization formerly known as the International Bureau of the American Republics. The bureau was established in 1890, pursuant to resolutions adopted by the first Pan-American conference, held at Washington in 1889-90. At the fourth conference, in Buenos Aires in 1910, the name of the organization was changed. In the same year the headquarters building of the union was dedicated in Washington. The purpose of the union is to promote better cultural, political, and commercial understanding among the 21 American republics: Argentina, Bolivia, Brazil, Chile, Colombia, Costa Rica, Cuba, Dominican Republic, Ecuador, Guatemala, Haiti, Honduras, Mexico, Nicaragua, Panama, Paraguay, Peru, Salvador, United States, Uruguay, and Venezuela.

The union maintains a staff of specialists, at the head of which is the director general, who publish and distribute information upon the progress and development of the member states. The expenses of the union are defrayed by contributions from the various countries, in proportion to population.

Patrons of Husbandry. A fraternal organization called The National Grange of the Patrons of Husbandry, formed in 1867 for the promotion of agricultural interests in the United States. Between that date and 1876, when the society reached its zenith, the number of lodges or "granges" increased in number from 90 to 19,000. *Grange* means "farm," and the members of the society are known as Grangers. The discussion of political questions was strictly forbidden at their meetings, but, as the organization grew in strength, its members became a considerable political force. The political phases of their activity soon passed to the Farmers' Alliance and later to the Populist party. The Grange was thus freed for its original purpose of social, educational, and industrial influence.

Patroons. A Dutch term meaning "patron" or "protector." It was popularly applied to certain large landholders under Dutch West India Company grants of 1629 and 1640. The grants really gave to any good citizen of the Netherlands feudal authority over large tracts of land bordering the seacoast or navigable streams, on condition of settlement with a colony of fifty or more. Some of the estates thus created along the Hudson river were held until the middle of the 19th century. See *Antirent Riots.*

Payne-Aldrich Tariff. The law enacted by Congress August 5, 1909, providing a comprehensive system of taxes on imports. The bill was severely attacked by its opponents as operating to raise import duties rather than to lower them, contrary to what was deemed to be the public demand. The measure provided also for the creation of a tariff board to advise the president in determining the specific rates, between designated maximums and minimums provided in the act itself, which should be imposed upon certain articles.

Pearl Harbor. Large American naval base near Honolulu, Hawaii. A surprise attack on Pearl Harbor by the Japanese, Sunday morning, December 7, 1941, brought the United States into World War II as a belligerent. Two battleships and three destroyers were sunk, other vessels were damaged, about 500 planes were destroyed on the ground, and 2897 men were killed or wounded, all by air attacks launched from Jap aircraft carriers. This was the greatest naval disaster in American history.

Peonage (*pē′ŏn-āj*) **Act.** The law passed by Congress in 1867, forbidding peonage in the states and territories. Peonage is a kind of slavery under which a person is held in debt to another and is forced to labor to pay the debt.

"Permanent" Generals. During war officers and men of the United States Army (Regular Army) may be given temporary higher rank in the Army of the United States, that is, the Army as expanded for war purposes. Only four such commissions have been made permanent—those of Grant, Sherman, Sheridan, and Pershing.

Personal Liberty Party. An organization formed in New York and Pennsylvania in 1887 to secure the repeal of laws requiring Sunday closing of saloons by voting on candidates of the regular parties according to their position on this question. Later "personal liberty" associations were formed to secure the repeal of the prohibition amendment.

Philippine Insurrection. The outbreak of Filipinos under Aguinaldo against the American authorities. Manila was attacked February 4, 1899, and fighting continued until the capture of the rebellious leader, Aguinaldo, by General Funston in March 1901. This disturbance was really a continuance of a former insurrection under Spanish rule in 1897, when Aguinaldo, for a payment of 600,000 pesos, agreed to leave the islands.

Pilgrim Fathers. The name applied to the band of English Separatists who became the first colonists of New England. They belonged to a group of dissenters who had previously emigrated to Leyden, in Holland. Preferring to be under the English flag, they founded the settlement of Plymouth, in New England, in 1620. Early New England writers referred to them as "pilgrims and strangers on the earth," and before the end of the 18th century the name Pilgrims had come to signify the original Plymouth colonists.

Platt Amendment. The body of regulations passed by Congress, March 2, 1901, for the government of Cuba. By the terms of this amendment, Cuba agreed (1) to make no agreements with foreign governments contrary to the interests of the United States, (2) to keep its debts within reasonable bounds, (3) to cede lands for United States naval stations, (4) to maintain sanitary conditions in ports. Finally, the United States was given right of occupation to maintain order in the island. The agreement was abrogated in 1934.

Popular Sovereignty. The doctrine, championed by the Northern element of the Democratic party, and particularly by Stephen A. Douglas, during the period from 1850 to 1854, that the settlers of each Federal territory should determine for themselves whether slavery should be permitted in that territory and also whether that territory should be admitted to the Union as a free or as a slave state. The policy was derisively termed "squatter sovereignty" by its opponents, because, in practice, it left the question of slavery to be decided by "squatters," that is, by individuals who rushed to the territory and took up a temporary residence there for the single and express purpose of affecting the slavery issue within that territory.

The Democratic party, from 1852 to 1856, advocated popular sovereignty as a solution of the slavery question so far as it related to the territories, and the Kansas-Nebraska act embodied an attempt to put that policy into practice. It was upon this issue that Lincoln and Douglas squarely met in the senatorial contest in Illinois in 1858. The Dred Scott decision, rendered by the supreme court in 1857, held, in effect, that the doctrine of popular sovereignty was unconstitutional; that it was beyond the power of Congress and of the government of any territory to exclude slavery from its limits. Despite this decision, however, the Democratic party continued to insist upon that principle as the solution of the slavery question in its relation to the territories, and the doctrine did not disappear from American politics until the problem of slavery itself was wiped out by the Civil War.

Populist Party. The popular name for the People's party, organized in 1891, which drew its support largely from the earlier Farmers' Alliance, from the Greenback party, and from the Union Labor party. The principal policy advocated by the party was the expansion of the currency, especially by the free coinage of silver. This was part of a revolt against the alleged advantages enjoyed by the financiers of the East, by the railroads, and by the capitalists generally. It was expected that the free coinage of silver would offset these advantages by increasing the prices of farm products and by making it easier for farmers to obtain money.

In 1892 the People's party carried four states: Colorado, Nevada, Idaho, and Kansas. In 1894 the party polled nearly two million votes in the Congressional elections. In 1896, however, the Democratic party adopted the chief item of the Populists' program, the unlimited coinage of silver, and the Populists indorsed William J. Bryan, the presidential candidate of the Democratic party. Rather than fuse entirely with the Democrats, however, a majority of the Populists, accepting the name "Middle of the Road" Populists, voted to nominate a vice presidential candidate of their own. After the defeat of Bryan, the Populist party split into the Fusionists, who favored co-operation with the Democrats and with the "Middle of the Road" branch. After the election of 1900, when Bryan, as the candidate for the Democratic party and the Fusion Populists, was again unsuccessful, increasingly conservative control of the Democratic party led the Fusionists to seek union with the "Middle of the Road" Populists. The united party put a presidential candidate in the field in 1904 and again in 1908, but, in the latter year, polling only 29,100 votes, the party ceased to exist. See *Free Silver Movement*.

Privateering (*prī′vȧ-tēr′ĭng*). The operations of a privately owned and armed vessel which, under permission of a government, makes war on hostile shipping. The permission is in the form of "letters of marque." In the Revolution and in the War of 1812, American privateers inflicted heavy damage on British shipping. In the Civil War the president was given power to commission privateers, but the authority was not used. See *Declaration of Paris*.

Progressive Party. Organized in 1912 as a result of the split in the Republican party between the conservative, "standpat," group and the more liberal or progressive members of the party. The immediate occasion of the formation of the Progressive party was the success of the old-line leaders in controlling the convention party machine and in renominating Taft for the presidency, to the exclusion of Roosevelt. The principles advocated by the Progressive party were fundamentally similar to those which the insurgent group in Congress had advocated during the Roosevelt and Taft administrations. These policies included a greater measure of government control of the railroads and large industrial combinations, a radical reduction of the tariff, adoption of the direct primary, and the initiative and referendum, as well as the application of the recall both to officials and to judicial decisions.

The Progressive party nominated Theodore Roosevelt for president and Senator Hiram Johnson, of California, for vice president. In the election which followed, the Progressive party polled nearly one million more votes than the Republican party, and its candidates received 88 electoral votes, as against 8 for the Republican ticket. The split in the Republican party enabled the Democratic candidates to win in the election, the combined popular vote of the Republican and Progressive parties exceeding by nearly 1½ million the vote cast for the Democratic. With the return of its leader, Theodore Roosevelt, to the Republicans in 1916 the party rapidly disintegrated. The name was also used by a party headed by Henry A. Wallace in 1948, which received about one million votes.

Prohibition Party. The national Prohibition party was organized in 1869 upon a platform advocating the prohibition of the manufacture and sale of intoxicating liquor except for religious and medicinal purposes. In 1872, the party nominated candidates for president and vice president, and it has placed a presidential ticket in the field at every national election since that time. The party polled its largest presidential vote in 1892, when John Bidwell, of California, received 271,000 votes.

The Prohibition party was the first of the regular national parties to advocate woman suffrage. It has also advocated numerous constructive reforms which were later adopted by other parties, and which have since been enacted.

Puritans. The name applied to the group of people within the Established Church of England, in the 16th and 17th centuries, who disapproved of certain usages and ceremonies which were derived from the Roman Catholic Church, and which were being used in the Church of England. Because of their purpose to "purify" the English Church by eliminating these customs, the name Puritan was applied to this party.

Among the Puritans, there were some groups, called Separatists, who withdrew entirely from the state church and set up independent congregations. One such group left England and settled in Holland in 1609, whence a number of them emigrated to America, founding in 1620 the colony at Plymouth. These colonists were later known as the Pilgrims.

The unrelenting persecution visited upon the Puritans by the Stuart kings at length drove most of them out of the Established Church. Many left England altogether. Among these were the Puritans who, in 1630 and later, settled the country around Massachusetts bay, known as Massachusetts Bay Colony. Here they established their churches upon the congregational plan, each church being independent in faith and organization, and having neither priest nor bishop. See *Mayflower*, *Pilgrim Fathers*, *Separatists*.

Quebec Act. An act passed by the British Parliament in 1774 to provide for the government of the Province of Canada, which had come under British authority by the Treaty of Paris in 1763. In this act, three features particularly aroused the attention of the thirteen English colonies: (1) The act extended the boundaries of Quebec to include the territory between the Ohio river and the Great Lakes, westward from the Allegheny mountains to the Mississippi; (2) It established French civil law in the province; (3) It withheld from the inhabitants such representative institutions of government as existed in the English colonies. The English colonists regarded the act as a blow at their free institutions. It was consequently a factor in precipitating the Revolutionary War.

Quids (*kwĭds*). Followers of John Randolph, of Virginia, in Congress, who opposed the policies of the Jeffersonian administration and favored Monroe over Madison to succeed to the presidency. They were the first "third party" in the United States and were called quids from the phrase *tertium quid*, "a third thing," because they supported neither the administration forces nor their Federalist opponents.

Rag Baby. During the currency expansion agitation of the late 70's, this term was applied by the "sound money" advocates to the greenbacks, the government fiat currency issued during the Civil War. The term originated in a series of cartoons by Thomas Nast, published in *Harper's Weekly* in 1876, in which the greenback was depicted as a rag baby.

Rainbow Division, The. The 42d division of the American Expeditionary Force in the World War. The insignia of the division was a rainbow superimposed on a black field. The 42d was made up of National Guard troops drawn from almost all the states of the Union,—hence its name. The last units of the division arrived in France, December 7, 1917, and it soon was sent to the front. In Champagne, at Château-Thierry, at St. Mihiel, and in the Argonne, it served brilliantly. After the armistice, it remained in the occupation forces.

Readjusters. The name of a faction of the Democratic party in Virginia, formed in 1878. Its main issue was that of a readjustment of the state debt by means of refunding at 3 per cent.

Red Herring. Originally a herring cured by smoking, used in English hunting practice to train dogs. "To drag a red herring across the trail," became used later in political argument for the practice of raising an obscure issue to draw attention away from a more important one.

Rum, Romanism, and Rebellion. A phrase used by Reverend Samuel D. Burchard as descriptive of the membership of the Democratic party, at a banquet given on October 30, 1884, in honor of James G. Blaine, the Republican candidate for president. Blaine promptly repudiated it, but the phrase was used to draw away Irish Catholic votes.

Salary Grab. Popular name for an act of Congress of March 4, 1873, which made the salary increase for members of Congress, provided in the general salary act of March 3, effective for the preceding two years. Popular indignation was so intense that both acts were repealed, except the parts increasing the salaries of the president and of court justices.

Salem Witchcraft. An extraordinary outbreak of the medieval witchcraft superstition occurred in Salem, Massachusetts, in 1692. In the summer of that year, 19 persons were convicted and executed on the charge of exercising witchcraft. It appears that the community had been prepared for such a mania by the attention given to the subject by the Mathers and other clergy. The belief had become prevalent that some evil influences abroad in the colony were responsible for certain military and political disasters. In 1689, Cotton Mather had published his study of the symptoms of two girls upon whose testimony an Irish laundress in Boston had been convicted of witchcraft and executed.

The Salem delusion broke out in a village, now Danvers, where several girls who had read some accounts of witchcraft accused various friendless old people of bewitching them. After a time, accusations were lodged against prominent citizens, including even the wife of the governor. The very excess of the proceedings at length produced a revulsion of sentiment, and release of accused people was speedily followed by disapproval of those who had pressed the charges.

Sand Lotters. Anti-Chinese and anti-capitalist agitators in California in 1887–89 so called because their regular meeting place was a sand lot in San Francisco. The movement, led by Denis Kearney, was known as Kearneyism. Kearney called a convention to have his principles written into the state constitution. His influence waned rapidly thereafter.

San Juan (*săn hwän'*) **Arbitration.** The question as to the ownership of the island of San Juan, lying between Vancouver and the American coast, arose out of the wording of the Treaty of Ghent in 1814, by which instrument the middle of the channel between Vancouver and the mainland was fixed as the boundary. San Juan being in the middle of the channel, the question of ownership was a doubtful one. Emperor William I of Germany, acting as arbitrator in 1872, decided in favor of the United States.

Scalawags. Nickname applied by Southerners to Southern whites who, like the Northern carpetbaggers after the Civil War, were willing to use the Negro vote to gain political office and political spoils for themselves.

Secession, Ordinance of. The declaration issued by South Carolina, December 20, 1860, dissolving its union with the United States. The other Southern states followed with similar declarations.

Sedition Act. See *Alien and Sedition Acts.*

Seminole (*sĕm'ĭ-nōl*) **War, The.** The longest and most severe conflict between United States forces and the Indians. In 1835, the Seminoles under their chief, Osceola, refused to cede lands in Florida and to remove to Indian Territory. The war continued until 1842, when the Indians were completely subdued. In 1843, about 4000 were removed to form one of the five nations in Indian Territory. A few of the tribe fled to the Everglades, and there a small number still maintain themselves, unconquered.

Separatists. This was the name which attached to the more radical and democratic groups of Puritans in England, during the reigns of Elizabeth and James I. In obedience to their belief that the English Church had not gone far enough in Protestantism, they withdrew, as many more moderate Puritans were forced later to do, and set up their own independent congregations. To the Separatists belonged the congregation of Scrooby, in Nottinghamshire, some of whom became the Pilgrims of Plymouth. See *Mayflower, Pilgrim Fathers, Puritans.*

Seward Whigs. Members of the Whig party in New York who approved the conduct of Seward, when, as United States senator, he came out flatly in opposition to any further extension of slavery and opposed the Compromise of 1850. This group joined the ranks of the Republican party soon after its formation. See *Silver Grays.*

Shays's Rebellion. A rising in Massachusetts, in 1786-87, headed by an ex-officer named Daniel Shays, in protest against the increasing burdens of court fees, lawsuits, and imprisonment for debt. It was part of the general unrest of the times, due to weaknesses in state governments and in the Confederation. At the head of 1100 men, Shays attacked the Springfield arsenal, December 25, 1787, but his forces were repulsed and scattered. Minor outbreaks occurred in the course of several following months, but the unrest gradually died down. A general amnesty was extended to the leaders. Shays himself was pardoned.

Sheridan's Ride. The famous ride of General Philip H. Sheridan, from Winchester, Va., to Cedar Creek. His army had been surprised and routed, October 19, 1864. When the news reached him, he rode the distance of twenty miles, rallied his retreating forces, and attacked and defeated the Confederates under General Early. This exploit is celebrated in a stirring poem by T. B. Read.

Sherman Silver Act. An act of Congress, passed in 1890, by which the treasury was obliged to purchase, at market price, 4½ million ounces of silver monthly. Treasury notes payable in coin were to be issued against this silver. The act was repealed in 1893.

Sherman's March. The famous march of General William T. Sherman, during the Civil War, through the state of Georgia from Atlanta to Savannah. His purpose, in which General Grant concurred, was to complete the invasion of the South by destroying the sources of Confederate supplies. Before starting on his march, Sherman ordered the evacuation of Atlanta and burned the city. The army left a wide swath of devastation over the entire distance of 300 miles. Sherman entered Savannah on December 23, 1864. This campaign, which really ended only with the surrender of General Johnston at Durham Station, N. C., on April 18, 1865, combined with Grant's victory over Lee to end the Civil War.

Silver Grays. The Whig faction in New York which, in 1850, approved Fillmore's compromise course with respect to slavery and disapproved Seward's opposition to slavery extension.

Silver Party. Republicans who favored the free coinage of silver, and who, in 1896, bolted the Republican national convention, and endorsed Bryan and Sewall. See *Free Silver Movement.*

Silver Purchase Act. The purpose of this act of 1934 was to increase the proportion of silver to gold in the monetary stock of the country to one-fourth of the whole, an object never attained. Under the act the Treasury was required to pay for newly mined domestic silver 64.64 to 77.58 cents per ounce; against a market price of 35.3 to 42.5 cents. Amendments in 1939 fixed the price at 71.11 cents. The procedure was a mild inflationary factor.

Six Nations, The. The name by which the Iroquois Indian confederacy was known after the Tuscaroras were united with the original "five nations" in 1722. The confederacy or league was first formed about 1570 among the tribes occupying territory now in northern and northeastern New York. In it were included the Mohawks, Oneidas, Onondagas, Cayugas, and Senecas. The name Iroquois was given them by French explorers. They called themselves "the people of the long house." They extended their authority southward to the Susquehanna and to the Ohio, westward to Lake Michigan, and northward over Upper Canada. The league, which superseded the tribal organization, was a true federal union, providing for a central council at Onondaga and for independence of the tribes in local affairs.

The social organization of the Iroquois was much more highly developed than that of other Indians. The recognition of the mothers was notable. The titles to chiefship, the lands and their products, and the lodges belonged to the mothers.

The Iroquois tribes were agricultural in their occupations. General Sullivan, on his raid into central New York in 1779, found well developed plantations of corn and fruit trees. They were noted also for their skill in building their lodges and fortifications. In the fields of warfare, handicrafts, and government they were the most advanced tribes north of Mexico.

Because of the mistaken policy of the early French explorers, the Iroquois became partisans of the English. During the Revolution the league was neutral, but the tribes, with the exception of the Oneidas and some of the Tuscaroras, sided with the British. Chief Brant, at length, led the Mohawks and Cayugas into Canada, whither parts of the other tribes also went. The Canadian government gave them reservations.

The Iroquois in the United States are now on reservations in New York, except part of the Oneidas in Wisconsin and some Senecas in Oklahoma.

Sixteen to One. A phrase expressive of the ratio at which silver and gold were to be valued by the mint under the bimetallic system, or free coinage of both silver and gold, advocated by the Free Silver men. See *Free Silver Movement.*

Slavocrats (*slāv'ô-krăts*). A term applied, during the abolitionist controversy, to those who approved of the institution of slavery, and even to those who were willing to acquiesce in its continuance and extension. See *Doughfaces.*

Snappers. Machine Democrats in New York who convened at a "snap" convention in 1892 at the call of "Boss" Hill, and who picked a solid anti-Cleveland delegation to the Democratic national convention. See *Anti-Snappers*.

Social Democrats. Original name of the present Socialist party, organized in 1897 by Eugene V. Debs. The ultimate aim of the party was the abolition of the capitalist system by peaceful means, its program resting flatly upon the economic doctrines of Karl Marx. In 1900, with Debs as its candidate for president, it received the support of most of the members of the Socialist Labor party, and after 1900 became known as the Socialist party.

Socialist Labor Party. The name adopted in 1877 by an organization to promote an economic rather than a political program. It adopted a platform of opposition to the capitalist system, and advocated, among other reforms, immediate government ownership and operation of all basic industries, and an elastic paper currency issued and controlled by the government. In 1892, it designated its first national ticket, and has placed in nomination candidates for president and vice president at every election since that time, although it has never polled any considerable number of votes.

In 1900 most of the members of the party joined the ranks of the Social Democratic party, the present Socialist party. The more radical members of the Socialist Labor group, however, continued their separate organization, maintaining their identity as distinct from the Socialist party upon a more thoroughgoing adherence to the Marxian doctrines of economic and social revolution. The Socialist Labor party holds the view that the abolition of private property can be achieved only as a result of the class war predicted by Marx and through the economic revolution which is to follow in its train. The 1928 platform of the party declared that the desired revolution is to be effected by constitutional means.

Socialist Party. The party formed in 1900 by the union of the Social Democratic party and most of the members of the Socialist Labor party. The party has advocated, in addition to state ownership of public utilities and of basic industries, the initiative, referendum, and recall, and a strict limitation of the power of the courts, particularly with respect to declaring laws unconstitutional. This party has nominated a national ticket at each presidential election since 1900, Eugene V. Debs being its candidate for president five times. Norman Thomas was nominated in 1928 and 1932. He became leading spokesman for American socialism.

The party showed a steady increase in strength from 1900 to 1912, when nearly 900,000 votes were cast for the Socialist candidates. This total was slightly bettered in 1920.

Softs. See *Barnburners*.

Solid South. A phrase used to express the consistency of the Southern states in their support of the Democratic party. It appears to have been first applied during the presidential campaign of 1876.

Sons of Liberty. A society of Americans, which arose in New York and Connecticut in 1765, and pledged to work for liberty in the American colonies. After the close of the Revolution, the members became part of the Tammany Society.

Spoils System, The. Popular name for the practice, inaugurated by Andrew Jackson, of turning out officeholders of a preceding administration and of filling their places with political friends. In 1820 a bill had been passed by Congress which provided that many Federal offices should automatically become vacant at the end of a four-year term. The purpose was to provide against "bureaucracy." President Adams (1825–29) made only twelve removals during his term. But this law and the constitutional powers of the president gave Jackson and the new Democratic party a convenient means for punishing enemies and rewarding friends. Their slogan, "To the victors belong the spoils of the enemy," was furnished by Senator Marcy of New York. The spoils system has been the fruitful source of inefficiency and corruption in city and in state as well as in the national government. See *Civil Service*.

Spoliation Claims, French. Claims of American merchants and shipowners against the United States government for damages inflicted by French privateers in 1798-99, when the two countries were virtually at war. No indemnity was ever obtained from France. But descendants of the original claimants continued to press their demands until 1885. At that time the matter was referred to the court of claims, which awarded $4,800,000 in satisfaction of damages.

Squatter Sovereignty. The principle of leaving the slavery question in a state or territory to the decision of the settlers. It was first applied to the districts acquired from Mexico in 1848, on their admission to the Union as territories. It was afterward extended, in spite of the Missouri Compromise, to Kansas and Nebraska in 1854. See *Popular Sovereignty*.

Stalwarts. New York Republicans, led by Senator Conkling, who were opposed to President Garfield in 1881 on the question of civil service reform. Guiteau, the assassin of Garfield, was a Stalwart, and gave as his reason for the crime that he could see no other way to bring about a reunion of the Republican party. The word had come into political use early in the presidency of Hayes, to designate those Republicans who opposed his policy in the Southern states. See *Half-Breeds*.

Stamp Act. An act passed by the British Parliament in 1765, for the purpose of raising revenue from the colonies. It was even more unpopular in America than was the American Customs act, and it proved almost impossible to enforce. It was repealed in 1766.

Standpat Policy. A phrase used to describe the general conservative attitude of the regular or old guard wing of the Republican party in Congress, particularly during the second administration of President Roosevelt and during the administration of President Taft. The term is supposed to have originated in a declaration of Senator Mark Hanna in 1900, to the effect that the Republican party should "stand pat" upon the high protective tariff plank which had served the party well during the previous two and a half decades. The supporters of this policy were called "standpatters." See *Progressive Party*.

Strict Constructionists. A general name applied to all those who advocated a narrow construction of the powers granted to the Federal government by the Constitution. The Antifederalists, the Jeffersonian Republicans, the State Rights men, and the Southern Secessionists were all strict constructionists, believing in a minimum of Federal authority and activity and in a maximum of state rights.

Tammany Hall. A political organization in New York City. It originated in the Society of St. Tammany, founded by William Mooney in 1789 and incorporated in 1805 as a fraternal aid association. Its name is adapted from that of an Indian chief, Tamanend, of the Delaware tribe, famous for his virtues and for his wisdom. The society long affected Indian organization and Indian ceremonies; the building which it leases to the political organization known as Tammany Hall is still frequently called the wigwam.

The society, under the guidance of Aaron Burr, took an interest in politics, and in 1798 threw in its lot with the Democratic-Republicans as opposed to the Federalists and was mainly instrumental in carrying the State of New York for Jefferson in 1800. It later identified its fortunes with the national Democratic party, which succeeded the Democratic-Republican party, and has claimed ever since to represent the Democrats in New York City.

Tammany Hall as a political organization early became distinct in form from the Society of St. Tammany, yet in reality the control of the political organization has remained in the hands of leaders of the society.

Tammany Hall's political influence was based on its charitable activities and on the advantages that its friends might hope to receive when it was in power. Before 1830 it supported a pure Americanism, but, with the extension of the franchise and with the influx of numerous immigrants, it came later to identify its interests with those of the foreign-born citizens. Its control of the foreign vote and its strongly centralized organization have made it during many years the dominant factor in local politics.

In 1872 William M. Tweed, the "boss," or head, of Tammany Hall, was convicted upon the charge of having stolen many millions of dollars from the city of New York. The unpopularity resulting from this exposure compelled Tammany to relax for a time its political control. Later revelations of improper methods and activities have resulted in temporary reverses for the society, but Tammany has had the vitality to recover its power on each occasion, so that it remains both the oldest and the strongest organization in American civic politics.

Tariff for Revenue Only. Tariff policy advocated by the Democratic party during the period of the tariff controversy from 1876 to 1912. Under this policy, taxes on imports were to be levied only for the purpose of raising revenue to meet the expenses of the government, as distinguished from the Republican policy of a protective tariff, the chief purpose of which was to promote American industry by barring or handicapping foreign competition.

Thirteen States. The thirteen American colonies which became the original thirteen states of the Union were New Hampshire, Massachusetts, Connecticut, Rhode Island, New York, New Jersey, Delaware, Pennsylvania, Maryland, Virginia, North Carolina, South Carolina, and Georgia.

Tippecanoe and Tyler Too. Refrain of a campaign ballad composed by A. C. Ross, which became the campaign slogan of the Whigs in the picturesque national campaign of 1840. The Whig candidates in that election were William H. Harrison, who had been nicknamed "Tippecanoe" from the battle in which he first gained national fame, and John Tyler.

Tories. The party in colonial politics which supported the authority of the English king and of the royal government. After the Revolution the Tories disappeared as a political party. Some of those who had belonged to it emigrated to Canada, where they were known as the United Empire Loyalists, while others returned to England. The remainder joined the Nationalists, and later the Federalists, who favored a strong central government which could be relied on to enforce law and order and to protect property rights.

Treaties of United States. The following list includes the most important treaties and agreements between the United States and foreign powers. Besides these major pacts, the United States has entered into many treaties with the Indians. It is also a party to many international agreements upon matters of commerce and trade, as well as to treaties providing for international arbitration. See *Treaties* under *Dictionary of World History*.

1782-83 Treaty of Paris. The treaty with Great Britain which terminated the Revolutionary War and recognized the independence of the United States. The treaty recognized the rights of United States fishermen in Newfoundland waters; it also provided that the Mississippi river, at that time the western boundary of the United States, should be open equally to British and to American navigation.

A preliminary agreement was signed at Paris, November 30, 1782. The definitive treaty was signed, also at Paris, on September 3, 1783. The American negotiators were Benjamin Franklin, John Adams, John Jay, and Henry Laurens.

1794 Jay's Treaty. The treaty between Great Britain and the United States negotiated by John Jay. It provided for the withdrawal of British military posts south of the Canada boundary in the Northeast, and settled certain boundary and financial questions. The assertion in the treaty that a neutral flag did not protect enemy merchandise, as well as its vague recognition of the right of search, aroused opposition. Only Washington's personal influence secured its ratification, June 24, 1795.

1795 Treaty with Spain. An agreement which provided for free navigation of the Mississippi, with privilege of deposit at New Orleans, and established a boundary between the United States and the Spanish possessions on the south.

1803 Louisiana Treaty. The treaty with Napoleon which provided for the purchase of the Louisiana territory. The acquirement of the area included in the purchase price of $15,000,000 more than doubled the area of the United States. See *Louisiana Purchase*.

1814 Treaty of Ghent. A treaty between Great Britain and the United States. It provided (1) for the restoration of all territory seized during the war, except certain islands near Passamaquoddy bay, the disposition of which was referred to a commission; (2) for a commission to settle boundary lines between the United States and Canada; (3) for co-operation between the United States and Great Britain in suppressing the slave trade.

1817 Rush-Bagot Convention. Between Great Britain and the United States. It restricted the building, arming, and use of naval vessels on the Great Lakes.

1818 Convention with Great Britain. This agreement provided for fishing rights off Newfoundland and Labrador, for establishing the boundary line between Canada and the United States, from Lake Superior to the Rockies, on the parallel of 49°, and for joint occupation of the Oregon country.

1819 Treaty with Spain. By this treaty, Spain surrendered all claim to West Florida and ceded East Florida. The United States gave up all claim to Texas and agreed to pay to American citizens claims against Spain to the amount of $5,000,000.

1842 Webster-Ashburton Treaty. The treaty with Great Britain which settled the question as to the boundary between Maine and Canada.

1846 Oregon Boundary Treaty. Negotiated with Great Britain. This treaty settled the question of the boundary between Canada and the United States, from the Rocky mountains westward. The dividing line was fixed at the 49th parallel.

1848 Treaty of Guadalupe Hidalgo. A treaty between the United States and Mexico at the close of the Mexican war. It provided for the cession to the United States of New Mexico and California, in return for a cash payment of $15,000,000. The United States also took over the debts of Mexico to American citizens, amounting to about $3,250,000. The territory acquired by the United States included the present states of Arizona, Nevada, Utah, New Mexico, and California, with parts of Wyoming and Colorado.

1850 Clayton-Bulwer Treaty. A treaty between Great Britain and the United States, providing for joint control of a canal to connect the Atlantic and the Pacific by the Nicaragua or any other route. The treaty stipulated that neither party should erect fortifications on the line of the canal, nor assume any sovereign rights over any portion of Central America. This treaty was abrogated by the Hay-Pauncefote Treaty in 1901.

1854 American-Japanese Treaty. Also called Perry's Treaty. A treaty negotiated between the shogun, for Japan, and Commodore Perry, on behalf of the United States, in 1854, by which Japan opened the ports of Yokohama, Kobe, Nagasaki, and Hakodate to foreign commerce. Foreigners had been excluded from Japan for 216 years before this date, with the exception of the Dutch, who, however, were strictly confined to their factory at Deshima.

1868 Burlingame Treaty. The treaty of the United States with China which first provided for recognition of international law by China. It stipulated certain important reciprocal privileges for the signatories.

1871 Treaty of Washington. A treaty negotiated with Great Britain. It provided for arbitration of the Alabama claims, of the San Juan (Vancouver) boundary question, of British Civil War claims, and of the Nova Scotia fisheries dispute.

1898 Treaty of Paris. The treaty with Spain which terminated the Spanish American war. It provided for the independence of Cuba and for the cession of the Philippines, Guam, and Puerto Rico to the United States. The United States paid to Spain, under the treaty, $20,000,000.

1901 Hay-Pauncefote Treaty. A treaty signed November 18, 1901, between Great Britain and the United States, with respect to the Panama canal. This treaty abrogated the Clayton-Bulwer Treaty of 1850. It maintained the general principle of neutralization of the canal, but the United States alone was charged with the maintenance of its neutrality. General rights of control and fortification were left undefined. The United States reserved the right to maintain a military police force along the line of the canal for protective purposes, and it was not required to keep the canal open in time of war.

1903 Hay-Bunau-Varilla Convention. A treaty between the United States and Panama, in lieu of the Hay-Herran convention between the United States and Colombia (1903). It provided that the United States should guarantee the integrity of Panama, and that, for a cash payment of $10,000,000 and annual payments of $250,000, the United States should receive full sovereignty over a strip of land 10 miles wide across the isthmus, within which the interoceanic canal should be constructed.

1921 Peace Treaty with Germany. This treaty provided for peace relations, reserving to the United States any rights and advantages which would have accrued under the Treaty of Versailles, and recognizing that the United States was not bound by any provisions of that treaty relating to the League of Nations.

1921 Four-Power Pacific Treaty. A treaty negotiated at Washington with England, Japan, and France. It provided for diplomatic adjustment of disputes occasioned by possessions of these powers in the Pacific.

1922 Five-Power Armament Treaty. A treaty negotiated with England, Japan, France, and Italy. It provided for limitation of naval armaments.

1923 North Pacific Fisheries Treaty. The first convention made directly by Canada with the United States. It provided measures for the preservation of the halibut fisheries in the north Pacific Ocean.

1924 "Twelve-Mile Limit" Treaty. A treaty negotiated with Great Britain extending the right of search on British ships suspected of carrying liquor. By international law, the authority of United States officers extends three miles from the coast. By treaty, this zone was increased to an hour's sailing distance from the coast. Similar treaties were signed with a number of other nations.

1945 United Nations Treaty. On July 28, 1945, the Senate ratified, by a vote of 89 to 2, the Charter of the United Nations, framed by the San Francisco conference.

Trent Affair. In 1861, Captain Wilkes of the United States sloop *Jacinto* intercepted the British steamer *Trent* at sea and removed two Confederate envoys, Mason and Slidell, who were accredited to France. The two men were released, January 1, 1862, on the protest of the British government. Secretary Seward held the British demand to be a recognition of the American doctrine which denied the right of search. See *Impressment and Search.*

Tuscarora (*tŭs′kȧ-rō′rȧ*) **War.** The conflict waged between the Tuscarora Indians and the white settlers on the Roanoke river and Pamlico sound in North Carolina. An expedition made up of colonial troops and friendly Indians defeated the hostile Indians in a battle, January 28, 1712. The remnant of Tuscaroras migrated to New York State and later joined the Iroquois confederacy.

Tweed Ring. A group of politicians, led by William M. Tweed, the "boss" of Tammany Hall, who in 1871 were shown to have defrauded New York City of many millions of dollars. The disclosures were effected through the activity of the *New York Times, Harper's Weekly,* and a so-called Committee of Seventy. Tweed and Mr. A. O. Hall, mayor of the city, were indicted and convicted of fraud. See *Tammany Hall.*

Underground Railroad, The. Popular name applied to the system used by Northern abolitionists before the Civil War, to aid the escape of fugitive slaves. More than 3000 people had a part in the system, and between 1830 and 1860 at least 60,000 slaves escaped by this route. Once across the border between slave and free states, the slave was sure of secret transportation northward. Many hiding places in houses and in out-of-the-way localities where the fugitives were concealed are still to be seen. If pursuit grew too close, the slaves were helped across the Great Lakes into Canada.

Union Labor Party. A party organized in 1886 by members of the newly developing trade-unions, to further the interests of the laboring class. A national ticket was nominated in 1888. The party was the successor of the Greenback Labor party, and it favored a national greenback currency with free coinage of silver. Other planks in its platform were the state ownership of transportation lines, no monopoly of land, woman suffrage, a graduated income tax, and arbitration in labor troubles. After 1888 the majority of this group joined the Populist party. See *Greenback Labor Party, Populist Party.*

Union Party. Organized in 1936, this party was composed of three elements. The first consisted of followers of Dr. Francis E. Townsend, who advocated pensions of $200 monthly for all over 60 years of age, the money to be spent within 30 days. The second group looked to Father Charles E. Coughlin, who proposed to equalize opportunity by depriving banks of note-issuing privileges. The third group was the remnants of the following of Senator Huey P. Long, who, promising a sharing of the nation's wealth, had made himself "dictator" of Louisiana but was assassinated in 1936. The party's candidate for president in 1936 was Representative William Lemke, who had worked for a plan under which all existing farm mortgages would be retired by a currency issue, the government taking in return new mortgages bearing very low interest rates. Mr. Lemke polled about 800,000 popular votes. See also *War Democrats.*

Union Savers. Group of Northerners, including both Whigs and Democrats, who, during the pre-war slavery agitation, placed the preservation of the Union above the question of slavery. They were willing to permit slavery to be extended to the territories, if that should be necessary in order to preserve the Union. Henry Clay and Stephen A. Douglas were typical leaders of this group.

United Labor Party. Organized in 1886 as a result of an independent labor movement. In New York City, with Henry George as its candidate for mayor on a single tax platform, the party came close to scoring a notable victory. In 1888, like the less radical Union Labor party, the party nominated a national ticket. It advocated, besides most of the policies supported by the other labor party, the single tax and the public ownership of land. Most of the members of this party joined the People's or Populist party. See *Populist Party.*

Valley Forge. A village on the Schuylkill river, 24 miles west of Philadelphia, famous for the heroic conduct of Washington, Baron Steuben, and the American army of 11,000 men in the winter of 1777-78. After a masterly campaign, which allowed Howe to occupy Philadelphia but kept him from giving aid to Burgoyne, Washington went into winter quarters at Valley Forge, December 17, 1777. The troops suffered from lack of food and clothes; for the people of the neighboring country were not entirely loyal, and supplies stored near by could not be brought to the camp. A fifth of the army, influenced by the glamour of life among the well-fed British in Philadelphia and by the apparent weakness of Congress, deserted. But the large majority of the troops endured their hardships nobly in the little village of log huts, and Baron Steuben drilled the men into capable soldiers.

Venezuela Boundary Arbitration. In January 1895, Venezuelan troops crossed the Cuyuni river, part of the Schomburgk line, into British Guiana, and hoisted the Venezuelan flag in territory which had been in dispute since 1814. The British government issued an ultimatum, whereupon Venezuela appealed to the United States to intervene, in support of the Monroe doctrine. President Cleveland, under authority of Congress, appointed an American commission to examine into the boundary question. The commission concluded its work when Great Britain and Venezuela agreed in February 1897 to submit their claims to arbitration. The award of the arbitrators confirmed most of the British claims.

Vinland (*vĭn′lănd*) or **Wineland.** The name given to the region on the American continent visited by the Norsemen in the early part of the 11th century. The leaders of the principal Norse expeditions mentioned in the sagas were Leif and Thorfinn. The latter is said to have established a colony which survived for three years. The location of this settlement has long been debated. Recent studies point to Nova Scotia and to the neighborhood of the St. Lawrence river as the most probable scene of early Norse explorations in America.

Virginia and Kentucky Resolutions. These were passed by the Republican legislatures of the two states in 1798 and 1799 in protest against the Federal Alien and Sedition acts. The Virginia Resolutions asserted the duty of the states to *interpose* when the central government exercised dangerous power. The Kentucky Resolutions of 1799 declared *nullification* by the sovereign states to be a proper action in such a case.

War Democrats. Members of the Democratic party in the North who, at the outbreak of the Civil War, pledged the national government their wholehearted co-operation in the conduct of war and in the effort to preserve the Union. Stephen A. Douglas was the most conspicuous leader of this group in the early period of the war. In a number of state elections and in the national election of 1864, many of these Northern Democrats combined with the Republicans, who, in that year and in the years immediately following, adopted the name of the Union or National Union party. Coalition tickets were nominated, resting upon a platform of prosecution of the war to a successful conclusion.

Wars, American. Since 1775, the United States has engaged in seven major wars—the Revolution, the War of 1812, the Mexican War, the Civil War, the Spanish War, and two World Wars. In addition, the army was used in the Whisky Insurrection. (See *Whisky Insurrection.*) During the greater part of the 19th century there was almost constant fighting with the Indians. The army was used to intervene in Mexico in 1916. The navy, with the marine corps, has likewise been used for intervention in Latin-American countries. It fought minor wars against France in 1798–99 and against the Barbary pirates in the early 19th century.

Watauga (*wȧ-tô′gȧ*) **Articles.** The *Articles of Association* drawn up in 1772 by the settlers on the Watauga, one of the headwaters of the Tennessee river. This settlement had been made in 1769 by emigrants from Virginia, led by James Robertson and John Sevier. Moved by the need for self-protection, the men of the thirteen forts or "stations" organized a local government at Robertson's station in the spring of 1772. They drew up in *articles* the first written constitution "ever adopted west of the mountains, or by a community of American-born freemen." These articles established religious freedom and manhood suffrage. A court of thirteen representatives, one from each station, was chosen, which in turn selected a commission of five to manage the affairs of the colony. After six years of this independent existence, Watauga, in 1778, became Washington county in North Carolina.

Whigs. During the Colonial period of American history, the colonists naturally tended to align themselves politically along the lines which marked political divisions in the mother country. The Whigs among the colonists included those who sought to vest greater authority in the colonial assemblies. The Tories, on the other hand, who desired a strong government which would protect them in the property and special privileges which they had acquired by special grants from the crown, supported the authority of the king and the royal government. With the close of the American Revolution, the Tories and the Whigs disappeared as political divisions in the United States, and in their places arose the Federalist and Antifederalist parties. Those who formerly had aligned themselves with the Whigs split into two groups, some of which joined the Federalist party and others the Antifederalist, later the Democratic-Republican, party.

In 1834, the term Whig came into use again, being adopted by a party composed of various elements, including the former members of the National Republican party. United under the leadership of Henry Clay, this party arose in opposition to the Democratic party under the leadership of Andrew Jackson. The platform of the new Whig party centered about a protective tariff, national internal improvements, and a national bank. In 1840, the Whigs elected their presidential ticket, Harrison and Tyler; they were again successful in 1848, when Taylor and Fillmore were elected. With the increasing tension over the slavery issue and the failure of the Whig party to take a positive stand in opposition to slavery, its strength rapidly diminished, and by 1860 the party had practically dissolved.

Whisky Insurrection. A serious rising in western Pennsylvania in 1794, caused by an attempt of the authorities to suppress illicit distillation, which was rife in that region. Some six or seven thousand insurgents were in arms, and the outbreak was suppressed only after 15,000 militia had been called out.

Wilmot Proviso. An amendment to the bill for the purchase from Mexico in 1846 of California and New Mexico, which under Mexican law were "free" territory. This amendment was proposed by David Wilmot of Pennsylvania. It provided that neither slavery nor involuntary servitude should ever exist in the territory to be acquired. Passed by the House, the amendment was defeated in the Senate. The proviso derives its historical importance from its statement of antislavery principle and from its being a center around which the free state and slave state struggle was waged for several years.

Woman's Rights Party. A group which nominated a presidential ticket in 1884 with Belva A. Lockwood for president and Marietta L. Stow for vice president, on a platform of women's political equality with men. In 1888, the party again designated a presidential ticket, with Mrs. Lockwood for president and Alfred H. Love for vice president.

Wyoming Massacre. During the Revolutionary War, in 1778, the settlement in the Valley of Wyoming, Pennsylvania, was attacked by a body of British soldiers, together with a band of Seneca Indians and some Tories who had been expelled from the valley. Most of the able-bodied men were in the field under Washington, and the remaining settlers had taken refuge in Forty Fort, near Wilkes-Barre. About 400, mostly old men and boys, opposed the British force of 1100. They surrendered after losing two-thirds of their number. Many were tortured and killed by the Indians.

X Y Z Mission. An American mission dispatched to France in 1797. Demands were made on them for bribes to the French officials. In the report of the American commissioners to Congress, the initials, X, Y, Z, were substituted for the real names of the French agents.

Yamassee (*yä′mȧ-sē*) **War.** A series of Indian outbreaks in South Carolina in 1714-15, in the course of which several hundred white settlers were killed. The Yamassees were driven from South Carolina into Florida, which was Spanish territory. The hostility of these Indians has been credited to Spanish instigation.

HISTORICAL PERIODS, EVENTS, AND MOVEMENTS IN THE NEW WORLD

From the Discovery of America by Columbus to the Settlement of Jamestown—1492–1607

1492	Columbus sails from Palos, Spain, and discovers West India islands.
1493	Columbus, on his second expedition, founds town of Isabella on the island of Haiti.
	Cattle first brought to America.
1494	Columbus discovers Jamaica.
1497	John Cabot discovers the North American continent, probably Labrador.
1498	Columbus, on his third voyage, discovers mainland of South America.
	Sebastian Cabot explores Atlantic coast, Labrador to Carolina.
1499	Voyage of Amerigo Vespucci to coast of Venezuela.
1500	Cortereal explores Labrador and Newfoundland.
	Cabral touches coast of Brazil, and claims the country for Portugal.
	Amazon river discovered.
1502	Columbus, on his fourth voyage, explores Panama coast.
1504	French fishermen reach the banks of Newfoundland.
1511	Velásquez subjugates Cuba; Havana founded.
1513	Florida discovered by Ponce de León.
	The Pacific Ocean discovered by Vasco de Balboa.
1516	Solis discovers Rio de la Plata.
1517	Cordova rediscovers Yucatan.
1519	Hernando Cortés lands in Mexico; Panama settled.
1520	Magellan sails through the Strait of Magellan.
1521	Cortés captures the City of Mexico.
1524	Verrazano explores Atlantic coast northward from Cape Fear.
1525	Pizarro explores coast of Peru.
1526	Cabot explores in South America for Spain.
1527	Spaniards, under Narváez, land in Florida.
1533	Cuzco conquered by Pizarro.
	Lower California discovered by Jiminez.
1534	Jacques Cartier enters Gulf of Saint Lawrence.
1535	Cartier ascends Saint Lawrence river to Montreal.
	Lima founded by Pizarro; Buenos Aires, by Mendoza.
1540	Coronado discovers the Grand Canyon of the Colorado and the Pueblos of New Mexico.
	California coast explored by Spaniards.
1541	De Soto discovers the Mississippi.
	Santiago de Chile founded.
1548	La Paz founded.
1549	Bahia established as capital of Brazil.
1562	Jean Ribault explores coast of Florida.
1565	Saint Augustine, Florida, founded by Menéndez.
1567	Caracas and Rio de Janeiro founded.
1572	Drake makes a voyage to South America.
1576	Frobisher, searching for northwest passage, discovers Frobisher's straits.
1583	Sir Humphrey Gilbert takes possession of Newfoundland.
1584	Raleigh's first expedition lands in Virginia.
	First book printed at Lima, Peru.
1585	John Davis discovers Davis strait.
	English settlers left on Roanoke island.
1586	Sir Francis Drake visits Roanoke Inlet; burns Saint Augustine.
1587	Virginia Dare, first English child born in America.
1590	English settlement at Roanoke island disappears.
1602	Bartholomew Gosnold discovers Cape Cod.
	San Diego bay discovered.
1603	Martin Pring explores New England coast.
	Champlain's first voyage up the Saint Lawrence river.
1604	Founding of Port Royal (Annapolis), Nova Scotia.
1605	De Monts takes possession of Maine.

From the Settlement of Jamestown to the Declaration of Independence—1607–1776

	British America	French America	Spanish America
1607	English settlement at Jamestown. First settlement in Maine; lasted one year.	1608. Champlain settles Quebec.	
1609	Second charter of Virginia. Henry Hudson discovers Hudson river.	1609. Champlain discovers Lake Champlain.	
1610	The "starving time" in Virginia.	1610. Discovery of Hudson bay. French Jesuits settle at Port Royal.	1610. León, Nicaragua, established at present site.
1612	Third charter of Virginia, including Bermudas.	1612. Champlain, lieutenant governor of Canada.	
1613	French settlement at Mt. Desert island; destroyed by Virginians.		1613. Dutch settle Demerara.
1614	Fort built by Dutch at Manhattan. Captain John Smith explores New England coast.		
1615	Dutch build Fort Orange (Albany).	1615. Champlain and Le Caron visit the Huron country.	
1619	First colonial assembly in Virginia. Dutch ship brings first slaves to Virginia.		
1620	First women brought to Virginia. Pilgrims land at Plymouth, Mass. Peregrine White, first white child born in New England.		
1621	Death of John Carver, first governor of Plymouth colony; succeeded by William Bradford. Treaty between Plymouth colony and Massasoit. Dutch West India Company founded.	1621. Acadia granted to Sir Wm. Alexander, as Nova Scotia, by James I. Newfoundland granted to Lord Baltimore.	
1622	Settlement at Portsmouth and Dover, N. H.		
1623	First settlement on Manhattan island.		
1624	Lord Baltimore founds a colony at Ferryland, Newfoundland.		1624. The Dutch capture Bahia. 1625. The Spanish and Portuguese retake Bahia.
1627	Governor Bradford and associates assume debt of Plymouth colony to London merchants.	1627. Colony of Quebec given to the Hundred Associates.	
1628	Settlement at Salem under John Endicott as governor.	1628. The English take possession of Port Royal.	
1629	The company of Massachusetts bay organized.	1629. Sir David Kirke captures Quebec.	
1630	Settlement of Charlestown and Boston; John Winthrop, governor.		1630. The Dutch capture Pernambuco.
1632	Lord Baltimore receives the grant of Maryland.	1632. Richelieu obtains restoration of Canada and Acadia.	Discovery of silver at Cerro de Pasco.
1634	English Catholics settle at Saint Marys, Maryland.		

From the Settlement of Jamestown to the Declaration of Independence—1607-1776—Con.

	British America	French America	Spanish America
1635	First English settlement of Connecticut.	1635. Death of Champlain.	
1636	Roger Williams settles Rhode Island.	1639. Jesuit mission at Ste. Marie.	
1637	Pequot war begins in Massachusetts.	Ursuline convent established at Quebec.	
1638	Swedes settle Delaware. Harvard college founded. New Haven settled.	The French attempt a settlement at Green bay, Wisconsin.	
1639	Printing press established by Stephen Daye at Cambridge, Mass. First constitution of Connecticut.	1642. Montreal founded by Maisonneuve. 1644. Iroquois attack on Montreal.	
1643	New England Confederation formed.	1649. Iroquois massacre of Huron Indians.	
1644	Indians massacre 300 colonists in Virginia.		
1647	Peter Stuyvesant comes to New Amsterdam as governor.	1659. Laval, first bishop of New France.	
1652	Mint established in Boston. Coinage of "Boston shillings."	1660. Dollard's defense of the Long Sault.	1662. Dutch give up Brazil.
1655	Delaware brought under Dutch rule.	1662. French West India Company grant.	
1656	Quakers arrive in Boston; they meet persecution.	1663. Canada made a royal province.	1663. Grant of Guiana by Charles II to Lord Willoughby.
1662	Connecticut charter granted.	Great earthquakes in Canada.	
1663	Patent for Carolina colony granted by Charles II. Rhode Island charter granted.	1668. Marquette establishes mission at Sault Sainte Marie. 1669. La Salle sails down the Ohio to Louisville.	1665. Saint Augustine pillaged by English buccaneers.
1664	New Amsterdam surrendered to the English. Grant to duke of York. Name changed to New York.	Father Allouez begins a mission at Green bay. 1672. Count Frontenac, governor of Canada.	1671. Danes occupy Saint Thomas.
1669	Fundamental Constitutions of Carolina.	1673. Marquette and Joliet discover the Mississippi.	
1670	South Carolina settled; Charleston. Hudson's Bay Company founded.	Fort Frontenac (Kingston, Ont.) built.	
1671	Mackinac island founded.	1679. La Salle launches the *Griffin* on Niagara river and sails to southern end of Lake Michigan.	
1675	King Philip's war in Massachusetts.		
1676	Nathaniel Bacon's rebellion in Virginia.	1680. Discovery of the Mississippi by Hennepin.	
1680	New Hampshire made separate colony.		
1681	William Penn receives charter for Pennsylvania.	1682. La Salle descends the Mississippi to the Arkansas, and names the valley Louisiana.	
1682	Founding of Philadelphia.		
1683	First assembly in New York under English rule.		1685. Dampier, English buccaneer, sacks León.
1684	Charter of Massachusetts forfeited.	1685. French in Texas under La Salle.	
1686	Andros appointed governor of New England.	1689. Iroquois capture Lachine.	
1689	Andros deposed; former governments resumed. King William's war breaks out.	1691. Nova Scotia retaken by the French.	
1690	French and Indian massacre of settlers at Schenectady, Salmon Falls, and Casco. Colonial congress called in New York.	1699. French colony under Iberville at Biloxi, in Louisiana.	
1691	New charter for Massachusetts (Plymouth and Maine included).	1702. Biloxi colony moved to Mobile.	1693. Gold mining begins in Brazil.
1692	Salem witchcraft. College of William and Mary founded in Virginia.	1710. Port Royal captured by English fleet.	1697. France secures western half of Haiti from Spain. 1698. Scotch attempt a settlement on Isthmus of Panama.
1701	Philadelphia incorporated as a city. Yale college founded.	1713. Hudson bay, Nova Scotia, and Newfoundland ceded to England.	
1702	Queen Anne's war breaks out.	1718. New Orleans founded.	
1711-12	Tuscarora Indian war in Carolina.	1729. Massacre of French at Natchez by Indians.	1711. French capture Rio de Janeiro.
1714-15	Yamassee Indian war in Carolina.	1745. Louisburg captured by New England troops and British naval force.	
1729	North and South Carolina separated; become royal provinces.		
1732	First stage between Boston and New York.	1748. Louisburg restored to France.	1719. French capture Pensacola.
1733	Settlement of Georgia.		
1744	King George's war breaks out.	1749. Fort Rouille (Toronto) built. 1754. Halifax founded.	1723. Pensacola restored to Spain. 1726. Spaniards establish themselves at Montevideo.
1750	First theater opened in New York.		
1753	George Washington sent by Virginia to the Ohio region.	1755. French defeat Braddock near Fort Duquesne.	
1754	Albany Congress. French and Indian war begins.	1758. Louisburg captured by the English.	1740. Governor Oglethorpe attacks Florida.
1755	Braddock defeated at Fort Duquesne. Battle of Lake George.	1759. Quebec surrenders to the English.	1750. Treaty between Spain and Portugal marking boundaries in South America.
1758	Fort Frontenac surrendered to the English.	1760. Montreal surrendered to the British.	
1759	Battle of Quebec—Wolfe and Montcalm killed.	1762. Louisiana ceded to Spain. 1763. Nova Scotia and Canada permanently ceded to the British.	1759. Royal edict expelling Jesuits from Brazil. 1763. Florida ceded to Great Britain.
1761	James Otis argues against writs of assistance in Massachusetts.	1764. English settle in New Brunswick.	French Guiana colonized. Rio de Janeiro made capital of Brazil.
1763	Pontiac's war begins.		

From the Settlement of Jamestown to the Declaration of Independence—1607-1776—Con.

	British America	French America	Spanish America
1765	Delegates of the colonies assemble in New York to resist the Stamp act.		
1766	Stamp act repealed.		1766. Large colony of Acadians arrive in Louisiana.
1767	Parliament passes Townshend revenue acts.		1767. Jesuits expelled from Spanish America.
1768	British troops arrive in Boston; selectmen refuse quarters for them.		1768. Revolt of the French against Spanish rule in Louisiana. 1769. Spanish missions established in California; San Diego settled; San Francisco bay discovered.
1770	Boston Massacre.		
1772	Destruction of the *Gaspee*.		
1773	Tea thrown overboard in Boston harbor. Virginia appoints committees of correspondence.		1773. Santiago, Guatemala, destroyed by an earthquake.
1774	Boston Port bill. The Continental Congress adopts a declaration of rights.	1774. Passage of the Quebec act.	
1775	Beginning of the Revolutionary War with the battle of Lexington. Battle of Bunker Hill. Washington appointed commander in chief of the American forces.	1775. Gen. Montgomery captures Montreal and Saint John. Death of Montgomery at Quebec and failure of American campaign.	
1776	First Union flag unfurled at Cambridge, Mass. British evacuate Boston. Declaration of Independence adopted by Congress at Philadelphia.		1776. Paraguay placed under the jurisdiction of Buenos Aires. Buenos Aires made capital of the viceroyalty.

From the Declaration of Independence to the Adoption of the Constitution—1776-1789

	United States	Canada	Spanish North America	South America
1777	Landing of Lafayette at Charleston. Battle of Princeton. Battle of Brandywine. British army occupies Philadelphia. Surrender of Burgoyne at Saratoga. Washington and his army at Valley Forge.			1777. Treaty of San Ildefonso, establishing Spanish and Portuguese boundaries in South America.
1778	Treaty of alliance with France. Evacuation of Philadelphia by the British. Battle of Monmouth.	1778. Frederick Haldimand, governor of Canada. *Montreal Gazette* published.		
1779	War in the South. British overrun South Carolina. Stony Point captured by Wayne. Paul Jones gains naval victory over the British off the coast of Scotland.	1779. Library founded at Quebec.	1779. Baton Rouge captured from the British.	
1780	Benedict Arnold bargains treasonably to surrender West Point. Major André hanged as a spy. Battle of King's Mountain, S. C.	1780. Coteau du Sack canal built.		1780. Insurrection of Peruvians under Amaru.
1781	Battles of Cowpens, Guilford Court House, and Eutaw Springs. Cornwallis surrenders at Yorktown. Articles of Confederation ratified.			1781. The English admiral Rodney takes possession of Guiana.
1781	Bank of North America established at Philadelphia.			
1782	Holland recognizes the independence of the United States. Preliminary articles of peace signed at Paris.	1782. United Empire Loyalists settle in Nova Scotia.		1782. France takes Guiana from England.
1783	Denmark, Sweden, Spain, and Russia recognize the independence of the United States. Treaty of peace signed with Great Britain.	1783. Saint John, N. B., founded. Kingston founded. United Empire Loyalists settle in Upper Canada.		1783. Dutch colonies restored to Holland. Spain regains Florida from England.
1784	Connecticut and Rhode Island adopt slave emancipation measures. New Hampshire constitution antislavery.	1784. Province of New Brunswick formed.	1784. Island of Saint Bartholomew transferred to Sweden.	
1785	Thomas Jefferson appointed minister to France; John Adams to Great Britain.			
1786	Daniel Shays's rebellion in Massachusetts. Annapolis Convention.			1786. Pacifications of the Negroes and tribes in Dutch Guiana.
1787	Constitutional Convention assembles at Philadelphia; adopts constitution for the United States. Ordinance for Northwest Territory passed by Continental Congress.	1788. King's college, Windsor, Nova Scotia, founded.		

From the Adoption of the Constitution of the United States to the Close of the Civil War—1789–1865

	United States of America	Canada	Spanish and French North America	South America
1789	**George Washington,** president; John Adams, vice president. First Congress meets in New York. First tariff bill passed.	1789. Sir Alexander Mackenzie discovers Mackenzie river.	1789. Settlers from North Carolina arrive in Louisiana.	
1790	Indian war in Northwest Territory. Census enumeration ordered.			1796. Guiana again in British possession.
1791	Bank of the United States established. Vermont admitted as a state.	1791. Quebec divided into Upper and Lower Canada.	1791. Negroes of Haiti revolt against France.	
1792	Corner stone of White House laid. Kentucky admitted as a state. Decimal system of coinage adopted. First mint established at Philadelphia.	1792. First parliaments of Upper and Lower Canada meet.	1792. First refined cane sugar made in Louisiana.	
1793	**Washington re-elected;** receives all electoral votes. Whitney invents the cotton gin. Corner stone of United States Capitol laid by Washington. Political parties assume names of Republican and Federalist.	1793. Slavery Abolition act passed in Upper Canada.		1802. The Dutch resume possession of British Guiana.
1794	First ships of United States Navy authorized. Whisky insurrection in Pennsylvania. Jay's Treaty with England.	1794. Jay's Treaty provides agreements relative to commerce, navigation, and boundary. York founded.	1794. Refined sugar produced on commercial scale.	1803. British Guiana finally acquired.
1795	Antirent troubles in New York.		1795. Maroon war in Jamaica. France secures Spanish portion of Haiti.	
1796	Tennessee admitted as a state. Washington issues his Farewell Address.			
1797	**John Adams,** president; Thomas Jefferson, vice president. X Y Z mission to France.	1797. York (Toronto) becomes capital of Upper Canada.		1806. Miranda's expedition against Caracas.
1798	Alien and Sedition laws passed. Commercial intercourse with France suspended. Naval conflict results.	1798. Northwest Fur Company completes canal at Sault Sainte Marie.		1806-07. Argentina repels two British attacks.
1798-99	Virginia and Kentucky Resolutions.			1808. Royal family of Portugal arrive in Brazil.
1799	Death of George Washington.			
1800	Capital removed from Philadelphia to Washington.			1809. Ecuador makes unsuccessful attempt to secure independence.
1801	**Thomas Jefferson,** president; Aaron Burr, vice president. Congress establishes the District of Columbia. Tripoli declares war against the United States.	1803. Slavery illegal in Lower Canada.	1801. Louisiana transferred to France by Spain. Toussaint L'Ouverture founds republic of Santo Domingo.	1810. Movement for independence begins in Argentina and in Chile.
1803	Louisiana purchased for $15,000,000. Ohio admitted as a state.		1803. French quit Haiti.	1811. Paraguay declares its independence. Venezuela proclaims its independence; forms constitution. New Granada declares independence. Spanish defeated in Uruguay.
1804	Vice president Burr kills Hamilton in a duel.			
1805	**Jefferson re-elected;** George Clinton, vice president.			
1807	Embargo act passed. Fulton's steamboat *Clermont* steams from New York to Albany.	1809. Steamer *Accommodation* arrives at Quebec from Montreal.		
1808	Importation of slaves prohibited.		1808. Rebellion against France in Santo Domingo.	
1809	**James Madison,** president; George Clinton, vice president. Embargo act repealed.			1812. Great earthquake in Caracas. Battle of Tucumán. San Martín begins his revolutionary career.
1811	Trading posts first established among the Indians. Battle of Tippecanoe with Indians. First steamboat on the Ohio.	1812. Sir George Prevost, governor. Capture of Detroit by General Brock. Battle of Queenston Heights; Americans defeated; Brock killed. Red River settlement, led by Lord Selkirk.	1810. Mexican revolt begins under Hidalgo.	
1812	Louisiana admitted as a state. War declared against Great Britain. American successes at sea: *Constitution* defeats *Guerrière*; *Wasp* defeats *Frolic*; *United States* defeats *Macedonian*; *Constitution* defeats *Java*. Canada invaded unsuccessfully.			1813. Bolivar begins his military career in New Granada.
1813	**Madison re-elected;** Elbridge Gerry, vice president. Perry captures the English fleet on Lake Erie. Battle of the Thames.	1813. York (Toronto) captured and burned by Americans. American fleet defeated on Lake Ontario. Americans defeated at Chrystler's Farm. Buffalo burned by British.	1813. Mexico declares independence.	1814. Chile temporarily reconquered by Spain. Montevideo captured by the revolutionary army of Buenos Aires. French Guiana restored to France by Portugal.
1814	Battle of Lundy's Lane. British capture and burn Washington. Hartford Convention meets to oppose war. Stonington, Conn., bombarded by British fleet.		1814. Provisional constitution formed for Mexico. Spain receives Santo Domingo from France.	

From the Adoption of the Constitution of the United States to the Close of the Civil War—1789–1865—Con.

	United States of America	Canada	Mexico, Central America, and West Indies	South America
1815	Jackson defeats the British at New Orleans. Treaty of Peace with Great Britain ratified. Algerian war. Decatur negotiates Treaty.	1816. Half-breeds assault Fort Douglas in Red River settlement.	1817. Unsuccessful insurrection in Mexico ends.	1815. Brazil becomes a kingdom.
1816	Second Bank of the United States chartered. The *Ontario*, first steamboat on Great Lakes. Indiana admitted as a state. American Colonization Society formed; founds Liberia (1822).	1817. First bank note issued at Montreal. 1818. United States and Great Britain make agreement to limit war vessels on Great Lakes.	1821. Mexico becomes independent of Spain. Santo Domingo revolts from Spain. Costa Rica independent.	1816. Buenos Aires declares its separation from Spain. Francia made perpetual dictator of Paraguay. 1817. Chileans defeat Spanish. Bolivar leads another revolt in New Granada.
1817	**James Monroe,** president; Daniel D. Tompkins, vice president. Mississippi admitted as a state. First instruction of deaf-mutes in America by T. H. Gallaudet, at Hartford, Conn. Seminole war.	1820. Earl of Dalhousie, governor. 1821. McGill college founded.	1822. Mexico, an empire under Iturbide. Costa Rica united to Mexico. 1823. Federation of Central American states.	1818. Chileans declare independence; O'Higgins, supreme director.
1818	Illinois admitted as a state. Pensions granted Revolutionary soldiers.		1824. Federal republic proclaimed for Mexico.	1819. New Granada and Venezuela form Republic of Colombia. Bolivar, president.
1819	The *Savannah*, the first transatlantic steamship. Alabama admitted as a state. Florida purchased by the United States from Spain. Maine separated from Massachusetts.			1820. Revolt in Peru. 1821. San Martín, protector of Peru.
1820	Maine admitted as a state. Missouri Compromise bill passed.		1826. First survey for Nicaragua ship canal. Panama congress.	1822. Brazil declares its independence. Pedro I, emperor. Ecuador joins Republic of Colombia.
1821	**Monroe re-elected;** Tompkins, vice president. Missouri admitted as a state. Andrew Jackson appointed governor of Florida.	1826. Canada Company chartered. Bytown (now Ottawa) founded.	1827. Expulsion of Spaniards from Mexico decreed.	
1822	Independence of Spanish South American states recognized. Gaslight introduced into Boston.			1824. Bolivar, dictator of Peru. Ayacucho, last battle in wars of independence.
1823	President Monroe proclaims the "Monroe Doctrine."	1827. King's college founded at York.		
1824	General Lafayette arrives in New York. Protective Tariff law.			1825. Argentine constitution decreed. Upper Peru, independent, takes the name of Bolivia. Uruguay declares itself independent.
1825	**John Quincy Adams,** president; John C. Calhoun, vice president. Treaty with Russia ratified. Erie canal finished.	1829. Welland canal from Port Dalhousie to Port Robinson completed.		
1827	First railroad in United States built at Quincy, Mass.			1826. Callao, last Spanish stronghold, surrenders.
1828	"Tariff of Abominations."			
1829	**Andrew Jackson,** president; John C. Calhoun, vice president.			1827. Treaty between Buenos Aires and Brazil, acknowledging independence of Uruguay.
1830	Great speeches of Webster and Hayne delivered in the United States Senate on "nullification." First steam railroad for passengers opened at Charleston, S. C.			1829. Venezuela separates from New Granada.
1831	The *Liberator* established by William Lloyd Garrison. First national nominating convention (Antimasonic).	1832. Newfoundland obtains a colonial legislature.	1833. Santa Anna, president of Mexico.	1830. Death of Bolivar. Ecuador separates from Colombia; first constitution.
1832	Black Hawk war. Nullification in South Carolina. United States Bank bill vetoed by the president.	1833. Constitutional government in Newfoundland.		1831. Revolution in Brazil. Dom Pedro abdicates. 1832. Charles Darwin visits Patagonia. Constitution for New Granada, Santander, president.
1833	**Jackson re-elected;** Martin Van Buren, vice president. Bank deposits removed from the National Bank.		1836. Texas declares her independence. Spain and Mexico sign a treaty.	1833. Sixth Chilean constitution formed.
1834	Whig party first takes its name.	1836. First railway in Canada opened.		
1835	Seminole war begins.			
1836	Massacre at the Alamo, Texas. Arkansas admitted as a state. Sam Houston elected president of Texas.	1837. Papineau and Mackenzie rebellion.		1835. Rosas becomes supreme ruler in Argentina.
1837	**Martin Van Buren,** president; Richard M. Johnson, vice president. Great commercial panic. Morse system of telegraphy patented. Michigan admitted as state.	1838. Canadian rebellion suppressed.	1838. Mexico declares war against France. Slavery abolished in British West Indies.	1836. Confederation of Peru and Bolivia under Santa Cruz. Dissolved, 1839.
1838	*Great Western* and *Sirius* cross the Atlantic.		1839. Termination of the Mexican-French war.	
1839	Vulcanized rubber patented by Goodyear.	1839. Issuance of Lord Durham's report on Canada.	Dissolution of Central American Confederation.	1839. Dissolution of Confederation of Peru and Bolivia.

From the Adoption of the Constitution of the United States to the Close of the Civil War—1789–1865—Con.

	United States of America	Canada	Mexico, Central America, and West Indies	South America
		1840. Upper and Lower Canada re-united.		1840. Death of Francia in Paraguay. Spain acknowledges Ecuador's independence.
1841	**William H. Harrison**, president; John Tyler, vice president. Harrison dies April 4; **John Tyler**, president.	1841. First Parliament of Canada meets at Kingston.	1841. Santa Anna, dictator of Mexico.	
1842	Dorr's rebellion in Rhode Island. Webster-Ashburton Treaty with England signed.			1842. Independence of Argentine Republic recognized by Spain. Republic established in Paraguay.
1843	Bunker Hill monument dedicated.	1843. McGill university, Montreal, opened.		
1844	Morse telegraph completed from Baltimore to Washington.	1844. Toronto *Globe* first published.	1844. Dominican Republic set up by revolt from Haiti.	1844. López, president of Paraguay. Spain acknowledges Chilean independence.
1845	**James K. Polk**, president; George M. Dallas, vice president. Florida admitted as a state. United States Naval Academy established at Annapolis. Texas admitted as a state. Petroleum discovered near Pittsburgh.			1845. England and France blockade Buenos Aires, pending civil war. Venezuela's independence recognized by Spain.
1846	Mexican war begins. Wilmot Proviso. Smithsonian Institution established. Oregon Treaty with Great Britain. Iowa admitted as a state. Elias Howe patents his sewing machine.	1846. Earl of Cathcart, governor.	1846. Gen. Mejía of Mexico issues proclamation of hostility to the United States; War with United States.	1846. Civil war period of 15 years begins in Ecuador. Spain recognizes Bolivian independence.
1847	Settlement on Great Salt lake, Utah, founded by the Mormons.			1847. Slavery prohibited in New Granada.
1848	Gold discovered near Colonia, Cal. Peace signed with Mexico; Acquisition of New Mexico and California. Wisconsin admitted as a state. Corner stone of Washington monument laid.	1848. Responsible government established.	1848. Peace between the United States and Mexico; treaty of Guadalupe Hidalgo.	1848. Belzu, president of Bolivia; liberal policy.
1849	**Zachary Taylor**, president; Millard Fillmore, vice president. Rush of gold hunters to California begins.		1849. Soulouque, emperor of Haiti.	1849. First export of guano from Peru.
1850	Death of President Taylor, July 9; **Millard Fillmore**, president. California admitted as a state. Clayton-Bulwer Treaty with Great Britain signed. Fugitive Slave bill passed. Clay's compromise bills passed.	1850. Riots in Montreal; Parliament House burned.	1850. Cuba invaded by American filibusters under López. Spain acknowledges independence of Costa Rica and Nicaragua.	1850. Steamship line from Brazil to Europe inaugurated. Jesuits expelled from New Granada.
1851	Vigilance committee organized in San Francisco.		1851. Second invasion of Cuba; López shot.	1851. Manuel Montt, president of Chile.
1852	United States mint authorized at San Francisco. Deaths of Henry Clay and Daniel Webster.	1852. Laval university chartered.		1852. Slave trade suppressed in Brazil.
1853	**Franklin Pierce**, president; Wm. Rufus King, vice president. Gadsden Purchase.		1853. Santa Anna again president of Mexico.	1853. Rosas defeated in Argentina.
1854	Treaty between United States and Japan. Kansas-Nebraska bill approved. Ostend Manifesto issued.	1854. First petroleum wells bored. Clergy reserves abolished. Seigniorial land tenure abolished.	1854. Carrera proclaimed president for life in Guatemala.	1854. Buenos Aires separates from Argentine confederacy. First railway in Brazil. Slavery abolished in Venezuela.
1855	Completion of Panama railroad.	1855. Suspension bridge at Niagara Falls opened.	1855–60. Central America invaded by American filibusters under Walker.	
1856	Civil strife in Kansas. First Republican national convention.	1856. Grand Trunk railroad opened. Allan steamship line established.		
1857	**James Buchanan**, president; J. C. Breckinridge, vice president. Dred Scott decision. Great financial panic in United States. First attempt to lay transatlantic cable. First state agricultural college established at Lansing, Mich.		1857. Mexican constitution established.	1857. Linares, president in Bolivia; in office four years.
1858	Minnesota admitted as a state. Second treaty with China signed. First message over Atlantic cable. Lincoln-Douglas debates in Illinois.	1858. Ottawa made the capital. Decimal system of coinage adopted.	1858. Mexican constitution annulled by church party. Civil war in Mexico. Haiti, a republic.	
1859	Oregon admitted as a state. John Brown's raid.		1859. Juárez of Mexico confiscates church property.	1859. Buenos Aires reunited to Argentine confederacy.

From the Adoption of the Constitution of the United States to the Close of the Civil War—1789-1865—Con.

	United States of America	Confederate States of America	Canada	Mexico, Central America, and West Indies	South America
1860	South Carolina passes ordinance of secession from the Union. Morrill high tariff bill passed.		1860. Prince of Wales visits Canada.		1860. Revolutions and insurrections prevail in Uruguay for next thirty years.
1861	**Abraham Lincoln**, president; Hannibal Hamlin, vice president. Secession of Mississippi, Florida, Alabama, Georgia, Louisiana, Texas, Virginia, North Carolina, Arkansas, and Tennessee. Attack on Fort Sumter. Kansas admitted as a state. Southern states form a confederacy. McClellan appointed commander in chief. Mason and Slidell taken from British vessel.	1861. Jefferson Davis, president; A. H. Stephens, vice president.	1861. Gold found in Nova Scotia.	1861. Juárez, president of Mexico. Mexican troubles with England, France, and Spain. Dominican Republic united to Spain.	1861. Pérez, president of Chile. In Bolivia, beginning of period of anarchy and loss of prestige. Mosquera, president in New Granada. New Granada becomes United States of Colombia.
1862	Slavery abolished in District of Columbia. Treaty with Great Britain for suppression of slave trade. Law to prevent polygamy in the territories. Greenbacks first issued.	1862. Capture of New Orleans by Farragut and Butler. Battle of Fair Oaks. Battles before Richmond. Battle of Fredericksburg. Battle of Murfreesboro.	1862. Macdonald, premier.	1862. England and Spain disapprove Mexican monarchy for Maximilian.	1862. General Mitre becomes president of Argentine Republic. The younger López elected president of Paraguay.
1863	Emancipation proclamation. W. Va. admitted as a state. Battle of Gettysburg. Draft riots in New York.	1863. Battle of Chancellorsville. Siege of Vicksburg. Battle of Chickamauga. Battle of Lookout Mountain.		1863. Mexico occupied by the French. Spain acknowledges independence of Guatemala.	1863. Falcon, president of Venezuela.
1864	Fight between *Kearsarge* and *Alabama*. Fugitive Slave law repealed. Premium on gold, 285 per cent. Nevada admitted as a state. President calls for 800,000 volunteers. Modoc Indian war begins.	1864. Grant's Virginia campaign. Battles of Wilderness, Spottsylvania, Cold Harbor. Atlanta campaign. Capture of Mobile. Sherman's march to the sea.	1864. Confederates in Canada plan raids.	1864. Maximilian, emperor of Mexico.	1864. Paraguayan war.
1865	**Lincoln re-elected;** Andrew Johnson, vice president. Hampton Roads Conference. President Lincoln shot, April 14; **Andrew Johnson**, president, April 15. Thirteenth amendment passed, prohibiting slavery.	1865. Confederate Congress adjourns *sine die*. Richmond evacuated by Confederates. Lee surrenders at Appomattox, April 9. Johnston, Morgan, Taylor, and Kirby-Smith surrender. Jefferson Davis captured.	1865. Quebec Resolutions favoring confederation of provinces passed in Quebec legislature.	1865. United States protests against French occupation of Mexico. Insurrection in Jamaica. Spain withdraws from Santo Domingo. Spain recognizes independence of Salvador. Carrera dies in Guatemala.	1865. Agassiz makes scientific expedition up the Amazon. American congress at Lima, Peru. Treaty between Brazil, Uruguay, and Argentina against Paraguay. Four years' war follows. Religious toleration begins in Chile. Chile declares war against Spain.
1866	Civil Rights bill passed over president's veto. Atlantic telegraph completed. Shoshone Indian war begins.		1866. Invasion of Canada threatened by Fenians.	1866. Napoleon III agrees with United States to withdraw French troops from Mexico.	1866. Spaniards bombard Valparaíso, Chile. Bolivia cedes territory to Chile.
1867	Nebraska admitted as a state. Alaska transferred by Russia to the United States. Reconstruction acts passed over president's veto.		1867. British North America act forms Dominion of Canada. Dominion Day, July 1. Lord Monck, first governor-general. New Parliament at Ottawa.	1867. Maximilian, Miramón, and Mejía tried in Mexico and shot. Republic re-established in Mexico.	1867. Bolivia cedes territory to Brazil.

From the Close of the Civil War, 1865, to the Present Time

	United States of America	Canada	Mexico, Central America, and West Indies	South America
1868	President Johnson impeached, tried, and acquitted. Readmission of Southern states to representation in Congress begins. Burlingame Treaty with China signed. Fourteenth amendment adopted.	1868. Agitation against confederation in Nova Scotia. Fenian raid repelled. Sir John Young, governor-general.	1868. Insurrection of Creoles in Cuba; beginning of ten years' war. Santo Domingo treaty for annexation to U. S.	
1869	**U. S. Grant,** president; Schuyler Colfax, vice president. Union Pacific and Central Pacific railroads opened for traffic. Financial panic in New York.	1869. Newfoundland refuses to join the Dominion. Hudson's Bay Co. territory purchased by Dominion.	1869. Filibusters again attack Cuba; repelled.	1869. Asunción occupied by allied troops of Argentina, Brazil, and Uruguay.
1870	Northern Pacific railroad begun. Fifteenth amendment ratified.	1870. Rupert's Land made the Province of Manitoba.	1870. Continual insurrections in Cuba.	1870. Guzmán Blanco begins 20 years of power as real ruler of Venezuela. First Peruvian railway opened.
1871	Legal Tender act declared constitutional. "Tweed Ring" in New York exposed. Great fire in Chicago. Treaty of Washington signed with Great Britain.	1871. British Columbia united to the Dominion. Uniformity of currency established.	1871. Juárez, president of Mexico. Present constitution of Costa Rica drawn up.	1871. Brazilian law passed for gradual emancipation of slaves.
1872	Geneva award of $15,500,000 made to the United States. Great fire in Boston; loss $80,000,000. Modoc war in California.	1872. Lord Dufferin, governor-general.	1872. Death of Juárez in Mexico.	
1873	**Grant re-elected,** Henry Wilson, vice president. Credit Mobilier investigation by Congress. One-cent postal cards issued. Financial panic sweeps entire country.	1873. Prince Edward Island joins the Dominion.	1873. Slavery abolished in Puerto Rico.	1873. Defensive alliance of Peru and Bolivia, against Chile.
				1874. Treaty between Bolivia and Chile about Atacama and the nitrate deposits.
1875	Act authorizing the resumption of specie payments, beginning January 1, 1879.	1875. Icelanders settle in Northwest Territories.		
1876	Massacre of Custer's troops by Sitting Bull. Centennial exposition at Philadelphia. Colorado admitted as a state.	1876. Intercolonial railway opened from Quebec to Halifax.		1876. Venezuela renounces papal authority. Beginning of Daza's notorious dictatorship in Bolivia.
1877	Electoral commission appointed. **Rutherford B. Hayes,** president; William A. Wheeler, vice president. Great railroad strike. "Molly Maguires" hanged in Pennsylvania. War with the Nez Percés Indians. Edison announces his phonograph.	1877. Great fire at Saint John, New Brunswick. Canadian fisheries award by Halifax commission.	1877. Porfirio Diaz, provisional president of Mexico.	
1878	Bland Silver bill passed over president's veto. Electric lighting introduced by Edison. First telephone exchange established.	1878. Marquis of Lorne, governor-general. Second premiership of Sir John A. Macdonald begins.	1878. Surrender of insurgent government in Cuba.	1878. President Hayes decides El Chaco boundary question in favor of Paraguay.
1879	United States government resumes specie payment. Women permitted to practice before United States courts. French Atlantic cable laid.	1879. Industrial exhibition at Ottawa.		1879. War of the Pacific, between Chile on one side and Peru and Bolivia on the other.
1880	Immigration treaty with China.	1880. Royal Canadian Academy of Arts founded.	1880. Manuel Gonzáles, president of Mexico.	1880. Buenos Aires made the capital of Argentina. Spain acknowledges Paraguay's independence.
1881	**James A. Garfield,** president; Chester A. Arthur, vice president. President Garfield shot, July 2; **Chester A. Arthur,** president, September 20. International Cotton exposition at Atlanta, Ga.	1881. Contract for Canadian Pacific railway ratified. Last British soldiers leave the Dominion.		1881. Lima occupied by the Chileans. United States mediates in boundary dispute between Chile and Argentina. Spain recognizes Colombia's independence.
1882	Star Route trials begin. War with the Apache Indians. Chinese Exclusion act passed.	1882. Northwest Territory beyond Manitoba divided into Assiniboia, Saskatchewan, Alberta, and Athabaska.	1882. Heureux, president of Dominican Republic. In power 17 years.	
1883	Northern Pacific railroad completed. Opening of the Brooklyn bridge. Pendleton Civil Service act passed.	1883. Standard time adopted. Marquis of Lansdowne, governor-general.	1883. Ancient city discovered in Sonora, Mexico.	1883. Peace treaty signed by Chile and Peru.
1884	Great floods in the Ohio valley. Financial crises in New York.		1884. Porfirio Diaz, president of Mexico (to 1911).	1884. Treaty of Valparaíso, establishing truce between Chile and Bolivia.

	From the Close of the Civil War, 1865, to the Present Time—Con.			
	United States of America	**Canada**	**Mexico, Central America, and West Indies**	**South America**
1885	**Grover Cleveland**, president; Thomas A. Hendricks, vice president. Apache war in New Mexico. World's industrial exposition at New Orleans.	1885. The Riel insurrection in Northwest.	1885. Concessions to the Nicaragua canal company granted by Nicaragua.	
1886	Railroad strikes and anarchistic riots. Silver certificates authorized. Bartholdi's Statue of Liberty unveiled.	1886. Fisheries dispute with United States. City of Vancouver founded.	1886. Slavery abolished in Cuba.	1886. Balmaceda, president of Chile. Colombia becomes a centralized republic. Politico-religious struggles begin.
1887	Interstate commerce commission created.	1887. Great railway bridge at Lachine completed.		
1888	Chinese immigration further restricted.	1888. Lord Stanley, governor-general.		1888. Slavery totally abolished in Brazil.
1889	**Benjamin Harrison**, president; Levi P. Morton, vice president. Johnstown flood. Pan-American congress meets in Washington. North and South Dakota, Washington, and Montana admitted as states. Oklahoma opened for settlement.	1889. Northwest Territories given responsible government.		1889. Revolution at Rio de Janeiro; emperor banished; republic declared.
1890	Idaho and Wyoming admitted as states. People's party convenes at Topeka, Kansas. McKinley tariff goes into effect. Sioux war; Sitting Bull killed.	1890. Dominion Commons passes a resolution of loyalty to Great Britain.		1890. First Brazilian congress meets. Great financial crisis in Argentina.
1891	Lynching of Italians in New Orleans. National People's party organized.	1891. Canadian Pacific railway completed. First Pacific mail steamer arrives at Vancouver from Yokohama.		1891. Civil war in Chile; Jorge Montt becomes president. Brazilian republican constitution adopted. Fonseca, president.
1892	Bering Sea dispute referred to arbitration.	1892. Dominion discriminates against United States in use of Welland canal.		Mutiny and insurrections. Peixoto becomes president.
1893	**Grover Cleveland**, president; Adlai E. Stevenson, vice president. Columbian exposition, Chicago. Chinese Exclusion bill approved. Great financial depression. Silver Purchase act repealed.	1893. Canal tolls arranged with U. S. Earl of Aberdeen, governor-general. Bering Sea arbitration.	1893. Zelaya elected president of Nicaragua (to 1910).	1893. Insurrections in Argentina. Naval revolt in Brazil.
1894	Wilson tariff bill passed. Coal and railroad strikes. Republic of Hawaii recognized. New treaty with Japan.	1894. Intercolonial Congress opened at Ottawa.	1894. Spain recognizes independence of Honduras.	1894. Moraes, president of Brazil.
1895	Free silver movement an important issue. Special message of the president on the Venezuelan question.	1895. First exhibition in Northwest opened at Regina.	1895. Cuba, in rebellion, demands autonomy from Spain. Weyler issues *reconcentrado* order in Cuba.	1895. Naval revolt in Brazil suppressed. Venezuela boundary dispute with England.
1896	Treaty with the Choctaw Indians. Utah admitted as state.	1896. Sir Wilfrid Laurier, Liberal, premier.		
1897	**William McKinley**, president; Garret A. Hobart, vice president. Universal postal congress meets in Washington. Strikes among coal and iron miners. Dingley tariff bill goes into effect.	1897. School question settled in Manitoba. Commission for Yukon gold region appointed.	1897. Weyler recalled from Cuba; Blanco appointed captain general.	1897. Venezuela ratifies boundary treaty with Great Britain.
1898	City government of Greater New York inaugurated. War with Spain. Admiral Dewey destroys the Spanish fleet at Manila. Naval battle at Santiago; destruction of Cervera's fleet. Treaty of Paris: United States acquires sovereignty over Puerto Rico and the Philippines. Annexation of Hawaii.	1898. Great influx of miners to Yukon gold region. Earl of Minto, governor-general. Joint high commission meets at Quebec to settle difficulties between Canada and U. S.	1898. United States battleship *Maine* blown up in Habana harbor. Invasion of Cuba and Puerto Rico by United States. 1898–1902. Cuba temporarily governed by the United States war department.	1898. Chile and Peru adopt convention in Tacna-Arica controversy. Campos Salles, president of Brazil; financial reforms. First Latin American scientific congress at Buenos Aires.
1899	Aguinaldo foments Philippine war. First Philippine commission named. General Wood, governor of Cuba.	1899. Adjournment of the joint high commission.		1899. Venezuelan boundary award. Castro in power in Venezuela.
1900	Civil government established in the Philippines under act of Congress. Galveston flood and hurricane. Civil government in Alaska. American forces sent to China.	1900. Great fire in Ottawa. Liberal ministry retains power.	1900. Mexican drainage canal completed.	Revolution in Colombia begins. Pando, a liberal, in power in Bolivia.
1901	**McKinley, re-elected;** Theodore Roosevelt, vice president. Platt amendment relating to Cuban independence passed. President McKinley shot at Buffalo, N.Y., Sept. 6; **Theodore Roosevelt,** president, September 14. Cuban autonomy granted.	1901. Toronto exhibition opened.	1901. Cuban constitution adopted. Second international American conference, in City of Mexico.	1901. War declared between Venezuela and Colombia. Riesco, a liberal, president of Chile.

From the Close of the Civil War, 1865, to the Present Time—Con.				
	United States of America	Canada	Mexico, Central America, and West Indies	South America
1902	President recommends Panama Canal purchase. Civil government established in the Philippines. Decision of United States supreme court in Northern Securities case.	1902. Canadian-Australian cable laid. Treaty between Newfoundland and United States.	1902. Revolution in Santo Domingo. Eruption of Mt. Pelée, Saint-Pierre.	1902. End of revolution in Venezuela. Civil war in Colombia ended. Boundary award on dispute between Argentina and Chile.
1903	Department of commerce and labor. Pacific cable completed. Alaskan boundary dispute decided. Hay-Bunau-Varilla canal treaty with Panama.	1903. Bill providing for new transcontinental railway passed.	1903. West Indian hurricane destroys many lives.	1903. Hay-Herran canal treaty rejected by Colombia. The Republic of Panama proclaimed.
1904	Commercial treaty with China. Arbitration treaty with France. Great fire in Baltimore. Louisiana Purchase exposition at Saint Louis.	1904. Earl Grey, governor-general.		1904. Hague Tribunal awards payments from Venezuela to European powers.
1905	**Theodore Roosevelt,** president; C. W. Fairbanks, vice president.	1905. Provinces of Alberta and Saskatchewan created.	1905. U. S. establishes financial protectorate over Dominican Republic.	
1906	Destruction of San Francisco by earthquake and fire. Interstate Commerce act. Second occupation of Cuba by U. S.	1906. British preferential tariff debated.	1906. Mexican agreement with U. S. on boundary and irrigation.	1906. Pan-American conference, at Rio de Janeiro. Earthquake at Valparaíso.
1907	Pure Food law becomes effective. Jamestown exposition opened. Oklahoma admitted as a state. Financial panic.	1907. Miners' strikes; anti-Asiatic riots in Vancouver.	1907. Central American conference at Washington.	
1908	General arbitration treaty with France. Conference of governors at the White House, to discuss conservation.	1908. Tercentenary held at Quebec.		1908. Railroad, Guayaquil to Quito, completed.
1909	**William H. Taft,** president; James S. Sherman, vice president. Payne-Aldrich tariff. Alaska-Yukon-Pacific exposition. Peary discovers north pole.	1909. Unusual immigration from the United States begins. Railway development.	1909. Meeting of presidents Taft and Diaz at El Chamizal. Gómez, president of Cuba. U. S. troops withdrawn.	1909. Boundary treaty between Brazil and Peru.
1910	Commerce court created. Postal savings banks established.	1910. Laurier's naval defense bill accepted by Parliament.	1910. President Diaz re-elected.	1910. Hermes da Fonseca, president of Brazil.
1911	Trust trials before United States supreme court; dissolution of Standard Oil company ordered. Arbitration treaties with Great Britain and France.	1911. Duke of Connaught, governor-general. Reciprocity with the U. S. defeated. Borden, Conservative, premier.	1911. Diaz forced to resign. Francisco I. Madero, president.	1911. "Bolivian Congress" of representatives from different South American states.
1912	Formation of Progressive party. Arizona and New Mexico admitted as states.	1912. Conservative emergency naval bill defeated.	1912. Insurrection in Mexico.	1912. Railroad across Andes completed.
1913	Parcel post established. Sixteenth amendment adopted. **Woodrow Wilson,** president; Thomas R. Marshall, vice president. Seventeenth amendment adopted. California anti-alien land law. Underwood-Simmons tariff law. Glass-Owen currency law.	1913. Unusual prosperity throughout the Dominion. Notable extension of rural free delivery system.	1913. Madero, president of Mexico, forced to resign. Madero is assassinated. Huerta, leader of insurrection in Mexico.	1913. Brazil: Coffee valorization dispute settled with United States. Ex-President Roosevelt visits South America.
1914	Neutrality of United States in European war proclaimed. Nicaragua canal treaty negotiated. Federal Reserve banks established.	1914. Death of Lord Strathcona. *Empress of Ireland* sinks.	1914. Revolution in Haiti. United States troops at Vera Cruz.	1914. "A. B. C." conference concerning Mexico. Panama canal opened to traffic.
1915	Federal trade commission. Pan-American financial conference at Washington. Naval advisory board established. Government railroad in Alaska begun.	1915. Canada sends troops and supplies to Europe.	1915. Carranza recognized president of Mexico.	1915. South American delegates at third Pan-American scientific congress, Washington.
1916	Philippine Independence bill. Military expedition in Mexico. National Guard mobilized. Purchase of Danish islands approved. Workman's Compensation act. Eight-hour Railway Wage law. Canal treaty with Nicaragua ratified.	1916. Duke of Devonshire, governor-general. Prohibition legislation in all provinces.	1916. United States lands marines in Santo Domingo. Villa's raid on Columbus, New Mexico.	1916. Ramón Valdéz chosen president of Panama. Irigoyen elected president of Argentina.
1917	Diplomatic relations with Germany severed. **Wilson re-elected;** T. R. Marshall, vice president. Senate adopts cloture rule. Congress declares war on Germany. Selective Conscription bill. Navy greatly increased. Government takes over railways.	1917. Woman suffrage granted, in limited form. Conservatives win election. Terrific explosion wrecks Halifax. Compulsory military service.	1917. Cuba declares war on Germany. Guatemala, Honduras, Haiti, and Nicaragua end diplomatic relations with Germany.	1917. Brazil declares war on Germany. Argentina, Bolivia, Ecuador, Peru, and Uruguay sever relations with Germany. Guerra elected president of Bolivia.

	From the Close of the Civil War, 1865, to the Present Time—Con.			
	United States of America	Canada	Mexico, Central America, and West Indies	South America
1918	Federal fuel administration. War Finance Corporation bill. Daylight Saving bill. Man power registration exceeds 23,000,000. Two million American troops overseas. Severe influenza epidemic. American troops in Rhenish Prussia.	1918. Dominion troops win distinction at second battle of the Somme, Quéant, Drocourt, Bourlon Wood, Cambrai, Douai, Valenciennes, and Mons.	1918. Guatemala, Nicaragua, Costa Rica, Honduras, and Haiti declare war on Germany. Mexico severs diplomatic relations with Cuba.	1918. Brazil gives Allies interned German ships. Railroad strike in Argentina. Territorial dispute between Peru and Chile revived.
1919	Death of Theodore Roosevelt. President Wilson heads American delegation to Peace Conference. Prohibition amendment ratified. Peace Treaty and League of Nations rejected by Senate.	1919. Premier Borden represents Dominion at Peace Conference. Death of Laurier.	1919. Mexico and Cuba resume diplomatic relations. Tension over foreign concession in Mexico.	1919. General strike in Argentina. Brazil excludes German banks.
1920	Woman Suffrage amendment ratified. Republican victory in presidential election. Army reorganized. Railways returned to private management.	1920. Arthur Meighen, Conservative, becomes premier. Prohibition an issue in the provinces.	1920. Carranza assassinated. General Obregon becomes president. Downfall of Cabrera in Guatemala.	1920. In Argentina, the Radicals win in elections. Irigoyen, president. Alessandri, president of Chile.
1921	**Warren G. Harding,** president; Calvin Coolidge, vice president. Congress restricts immigration. Agricultural *bloc* in Congress. Washington Conference meets. Peace Treaty with Germany ratified.	1921. Defeat of Conservatives. W. L. M. King premier. Opening of Queenston hydro-electric plant.	1921. Zayas declared president of Cuba. United States plans withdrawal from Santo Domingo.	1921. Saavedra, president of Bolivia.
1922	Four Power Pacific Treaty ratified by the United States. General coal strike. Supreme court declares Federal child labor law unconstitutional. Fordney-McCumber tariff law. Lincoln memorial temple at Washington dedicated.	1922. Coal strike. United Farmers party controls legislatures in Ontario, Alberta, and Manitoba.	1922. Nicaragua, Honduras, and Salvador renew treaty of peace with United States. Growth of labor organizations in Mexico.	1922. Peru and Chile submit Tacna-Arica dispute to arbitration by President Harding. Brazilian centennial exposition at Rio de Janeiro.
1923	Last American troops withdrawn from the Rhine. Great Britain refunds debt to the United States. First nonstop airplane flight across continent, from New York to San Diego. Death of President Harding; **Calvin Coolidge,** president, August 5.	1923. First treaty between Canada and U. S. signed; trade treaty with Italy. Murray, premier of Nova Scotia for 27 years, resigns.	1923. Crowder first ambassador from U. S. to Cuba. U. S. recognizes Obregon government in Mexico.	1923. Pan-American conference at Santiago, Chile. Peru and Chile present Tacna-Arica controversy before the arbiter, President Harding.
1924	Death of Woodrow Wilson. Lease of oil lands by Navy department cancelled by government. Jap immigrants excluded. United States navy fliers encircle globe. Soldier bonus bill passed.	1924. Liquor treaty with the United States ratified. Strike of postal employees.	1924. Calles elected president of Mexico. U. S. troops withdrawn from Dominican Republic.	1924. Constitutional curb placed on power of presidency in Chile. Insurrections in Brazil suppressed.
1925	**Calvin Coolidge,** president; Charles G. Dawes, vice president. Scopes "Evolution Trial" attracts world-wide attention. Italy and Belgium fund debts to the United States. Postal rates increased.	1925. Defeat of Liberal party. Premier retains office, governing with help of Progressives. United Church of Canada formed.	1925. Costa Rica announces intention of withdrawing from League of Nations.	1925. Revolution in Ecuador. Boundary dispute among Brazil, Colombia, and Peru settled through U. S. arbitration.
1926	Senate votes adherence to World Court but with unacceptable reservations. North pole reached by U. S. navy airplane from Spitzbergen. Sesquicentennial Exposition, Phila.	1926. First minister to the U. S. Liberal government elected. W. L. M. King premier.	1926. Chamorro dictator, Nicaragua. Church properties seized by Mexican government.	1926. Brazil blocks entry of Germany into League of Nations.
1927	Disastrous floods in Mississippi valley and in northern New England states. Lindbergh flies alone from New York to Paris. Federal Radio Commission appointed. Execution of Sacco and Vanzetti arouses protests.	1927. Canada elected to League of Nations Council. Canada protests U. S. order classifying as immigrants Canadian commuters to U. S. cities.	1927. Mexico seizes petroleum lands. Civil war in Nicaragua; U. S. supervises elections. Cuba elected to Council of League of Nations.	1927. Chile nitrate industry faced with crisis due to new processes of nitrogen fixation. Deportation of radicals from Chile.
1928	Mississippi flood control bill passed. President-elect Hoover makes tour of South America. Notable expansion in air transportation.	1928. Canada establishes diplomatic relations with France and Japan.	1928. Pan-American conference, Habana. Obregon, pres. of Mexico, slain; Portes Gil, pres.	1928. Paraguay-Bolivia dispute over Chaco.
1929	**Herbert Hoover,** president; Charles Curtis, vice president. Senate ratifies Paris pact. Naval increase voted by Congress. Census and reapportionment bill. Federal farm board established. Stock market panic.	1929. Canadian rum runner *Im Alone* sunk by U. S. coast guard under circumstances resulting in diplomatic protests.	1929. Rebellion suppressed in Mexico; church-state conflict compromised. Insurrection in Haiti suppressed by U. S. marines.	1929. Tacna-Arica dispute settled amicably, Tacna going to Peru and Arica to Chile.

From the Close of the Civil War, 1865, to the Present Time—Con.

	United States of America	Canada	Mexico, Central America, and West Indies	South America
1930	Admiral Byrd returns from Antarctic. London conference provides for Anglo-American naval parity. Hawley-Smoot tariff bill enacted.	1930. Conservative government elected on tariff increase issue; R. B. Bennett premier.	1930. Mexico severs diplomatic relations with Soviet Russia; Ortiz Rubio president. Revolution in Dominican Rep.	1930. Revolutions in Brazil, Peru, Argentina, Bolivia, due to economic crises. Vargas seizes Brazil presidency.
1931	Depression and bank failures. Moratorium on war debts for one year.	1931. Welland ship canal opened. Westminster statute, legalizing Canadian independence.	1931. Revolution in Salvador. Mexico joins League of Nations.	1931. Revolutions in Panama, Chile, Peru, Ecuador, Paraguay.
1932	Reconstruction Finance Corporation established to aid credit. St. Lawrence waterway treaty with Canada negotiated.	1932. Ottawa conference for imperial economic unity.	1932. Rodriguez president of Mexico; Mexico resigns from League of Nations.	1932. Chaco war between Paraguay and Bolivia resumed. Alessandri regime begins in Chile.
1933	**Franklin D. Roosevelt,** president; John N. Garner, vice president. All banks closed for 10 days; deposit insurance established. Gold standard suspended. New Deal—N R A, A A A, T V A established. "Lame duck" and prohibition repeal amendments ratified.	1933. Newfoundland accepts British control of finances. Royal commission recommends establishment of central bank for Canada.	1933. Revolution in Cuba; Machado driven out; Grau San Martin president.	1933. Revolution in Uruguay. Colombia-Peru dispute over Leticia. Pan-American conference at Montevideo.
1934	Dollar revalued. Securities exchange regulation begun. First reciprocal trade agreement with Cuba. Severe drought and dust storms.	1934. Dionne quintuplets born. Relief and recovery laws passed	1934. Mendieta president of Cuba. Cardenas president of Mexico.	1934. Brazil adopts new constitution. Contreras president of Venezuela.
1935	Supreme court holds N R A codes unconstitutional. Social security act passed. Reserve Board's control over banking system enlarged. National labor relations act. Philippine constitution approved.	1935. Bank of Canada opened. "Social credit" government elected in Alberta led by Aberhart.	1935. General strike in Cuba.	1935. Brazil and United States sign reciprocal trade treaty. Unsuccessful revolt in Brazil. Truce ends Chaco war.
1936	A A A declared unconstitutional; soil conservation act substituted. Labor movement splits, C. I. O. unions being suspended from A. F. of L. Inauguration of trans-Pacific airplane mail service to Manila. President Roosevelt reelected.	1936. Liberal government elected. W. L. Mackenzie King premier. Reciprocal trade agreement with the United States.	1936. Pres. Gomez of Cuba impeached, succeeded by Bru. Batista, controlling army, exercises power. Mexico resumes expropriation of Church property. New treaty negotiated by Panama with U. S. over canal.	1936. Pan-American conference at Buenos Aires, Monroe Doctrine tending to become "common front" policy. Bolivia and Paraguay ratify Chaco Truce terms, but army revolution follows in Paraguay.
1937	**Franklin D. Roosevelt,** president; John N. Garner, vice president. Ohio-Mississippi floods, more than a million homeless. President seeks enlargement of supreme court; plan defeated. Supreme court upholds social security act and Wagner labor law.	1937. Supreme court invalidates trade and social insurance acts. Commission appointed to study possible changes in constitution. Alberta's social credit government admits failure.	1937. Cardenas renews drive to create "democracy of workers" in Mexico; assumes control over oil industry. Batista of Cuba announces three-year plan of economic and social reconstruction.	1937. Bolivia reinstates constitution of 1880; seizes foreign oil concessions.
1938	Japan attacks American gunboat, *Panay*, in Chinese waters.	1938. Reciprocal trade agreement with United States extended.	1938. Mexico seizes foreign oil properties to enforce court decision growing out of labor dispute.	1938. Chaco dispute finally settled. Aguirre, president of Chile; forms "popular front" government.
1939	"Cash and Carry" neutrality act. Neutrality proclamations. Government Reorganization act.	1939. Declaration of war against Germany; establishment of training centers for British war aviators.	1939. Declaration of Panama for safety zone for neutral shipping.	1939. Venezuela-U. S. trade pact. German warship *Graf Spee* sunk at Montevideo.
1940	Defense measures: bases leased in British possessions; enlargement of army and navy; conscription act. President Roosevelt reelected for a third term.	1940. King government re-elected. Earl of Athlone governor-general.	1940. Act of Habana forbidding transfer of colonies. Camacho, president of Mexico.	
1941	**Franklin D. Roosevelt,** president; Henry A. Wallace, vice president. "Lend-Lease" act for aid to Britain. Pearl Harbor attacked; war declared on Japan, Germany, and Italy.	1941. Joint defense measures with U. S. planned. War declared against Japan.	1941. Nine republics declare war against Japan. Mexico cooperates with United States for defense.	
1942	Philippines taken by Japan. Battles of Coral Sea and Midway. Americans attack the Solomons; join in invasion of North Africa.	1942. Conscription for overseas service. Dieppe raid.		1942. Conference at Rio de Janeiro. All countries except Argentina and Chile sever diplomatic relations with Axis powers. Brazil declares war on Germany and Italy.
1943	Americans in Sicily and Italy. Victories in Southwest Pacific.	1943. Regulations for manpower control.	1943. French West Indies capitulate.	1943. Revolutions in Argentina and Bolivia.
1944	Americans invade Normandy; liberate France and Belgium. Ardennes attack: "Battle of the Bulge;" last German offensive. Philippines invaded. Japanese Navy smashed at Leyte.	1944. Conflict over applying overseas conscription.	1944. Dr. Grau San Martin elected president of Cuba.	
1945	**Franklin D. Roosevelt,** president; Harry S. Truman, vice president. Manila retaken. Death of President Roosevelt. **Harry S. Truman,** president, April 12. Americans invade southern France; advance into Germany. United Nations conference at San Francisco; U. S. ratifies charter. Iwo Jima and Okinawa taken. First use of atomic bomb. Surrender of Japan. Americans occupy Japan and southwestern Germany.	1945. King government re-elected.	1945. Inter-American conference at Mexico City. Act of Chapultepec.	1945. Vargas deposed in Brazil.

From the Adoption of the Constitution of the United States to the Close of the Civil War—1789-1865—Con.

	United States of America	Canada	Mexico, Central America and West Indies	South America
1946	General demand for return of troops from overseas. Reconversion of industry for peace. Strikes in steel, automobile, meat, and coal industries. Secretary Ickes resigns. Winston Churchill's "Iron Curtain" speech at Fulton, Mo. President Truman forces settlement of railroad strike. Fred M. Vinson, chief justice of the Supreme Court. Contest over extension of O. P. A. Most controls are removed. Atom bomb tests at Bikini. Philippines become independent. Secretary of Commerce Wallace removed for disagreement about foreign policy. Coal strike stopped by legal proceedings. Republicans gain control of Congress. State of hostilities ends December 31.	1946. Viscount Alexander of Tunis, governor-general. Reconversion to peace status; war controls are gradually lifted. Loan to Britain of $1,250,000,000. Exposure of "spy ring" within the government, giving information to Russian agents.	1946. Mexico elects Miguel Alemán president to succeed Camacho.	1946. Juan Perón elected president of Argentina; takes measures to control press. Revolution in Bolivia; President Villaroel murdered by a mob; Enrique Herzog elected president. 1947. Bolivia and Argentina make arbitration treaty. Brazil severs diplomatic relations with Russia. Argentina and Chile lay claim to Antarctic lands.
1947	U. S. ends intervention in China. General Marshall, secretary of state. "Truman Doctrine" stated; $400,000,000 aid to Greece and Turkey. Constitutional amendment limiting president to two terms sent to states. Agitation against Communists in government service. U. S. becomes trustee of Japanese Pacific islands. Peace treaties with Italy, Rumania, Hungary, and Bulgaria. Taft-Hartley labor bill and reduction of taxes passed over president's veto. Rise in prices and fear of inflation. Secretary Marshall announces plan for European relief. Armed forces merged under secretary of defense.	1947. President Truman visits Canada; warmly received at Ottawa. Lifting of war controls continues. Immigration laws broadened to favor displaced persons. Peace treaties with Italy, Rumania, Hungary, Finland.	1947. Presidents Truman and Alemán exchange visits. Mexico completes payments for U. S. oil properties expropriated in 1938.	1948. Communist movements in Brazil and Chile lead to outlawing the party in both countries. Sessions of the Inter-American Conference at Bogota, Colombia, are interrupted by political riots. President Bustamente of Peru deposed by a military uprising. In Venezuela the army assumes control of the country and promises new elections.
1948	Higher prices and increased cost of living, reaching a peak in September. Increasing tension in relations with Russia, "Cold War." Russian blockade of Berlin forces; supply of western zones by "Airlift." Disclosures of Russian spy activities increase anti-Communist feeling. Congress appropriates six billion dollars for Marshall plan (ERP). President Truman proposes "civil rights" legislation. Democrats renominate President Truman. Southern (States Rights) Democrats nominate Governor Thurmond. Republicans nominate Governor Dewey. President Truman re-elected; Democrats carry House and Senate.	1948. Question of "dollar exchange" causes limitation of trade with U. S. Mackenzie King retires as premier; succeeded by L. S. St. Laurent. Barbara Ann Scott, Olympic and world figure-skating champion, is named winner of the Marsh Memorial Trophy as Canada's outstanding athlete for 1948.	1948. Disputed election and civil war in Costa Rica leaves Figueres in power.	1949. Argentina publishes the draft of a new Constitution requiring that foreigners who have spent two years in Argentina must either become citizens or leave the country. Argentina redistributes the powers of the National Economic Council, preparatory to softening the "hard bargain" trade policy of Miguel Miranda. Paraguay's president Juan Natalicio Genzalez, after five months in office, is ousted in a coup led by defense minister General Raimondo Relon, who becomes temporary president for two months, pending an election. United States grants de facto recognition to new government in Venezuela.
1949	**Harry S. Truman,** president; Alben W. Barkley, vice president Truman inaugurated with exceptional display; his inaugural address attacks Communism, and makes proposals for improvement of world economic conditions Secretary of State Marshall retires; succeeded by Dean Acheson. Operation "Haylift" is organized by U. S. Air Force to drop feed for sheep and cattle in isolated blizzard areas of the West Central and Mountain states. Congress votes to increase the salaries of the president, vice president, and speaker of the House. Full recognition of the Israeli and Trans-Jordan governments is announced by President Truman. Congress approves bill to extend to June 30, 1951, the Government's power to control exports.	1949 Newfoundland admitted as tenth province. Canada renews agreement to supply Great Britain with wheat at $2 a bushel. Price guaranteed until July 31, 1950.	1949. United States grants de facto recognition to new government in San Salvador.	

AMERICAN FLAGS

1 Flag of Bunker Hill. 2 Continental Flag. 3 Betsy Ross Flag. 4 Bennington Flag. 5 Flag of the Bon Homme Richard. 6 Flag of Fort McHenry. 7 Old Glory. 8 Stars and Stripes—Present Flag.

FLAGS OF THE BRITISH COMMONWEALTH OF NATIONS

1 Canada. 2 Newfoundland. 3 Great Britain. 4 Irish Free State. 5 Australia. 6 New Zealand. 7 Union of South Africa.

THE BRITISH EMPIRE

The name British Empire, or Commonwealth of Nations, designates the group of states, colonies, protectorates, and other dependencies which acknowledge allegiance to the British Crown. The kingdom of Great Britain and Northern Ireland, which is the nucleus of the Empire, embraces the island of Great Britain (England, Scotland, and Wales) and the northern part of Ireland.

The Period of Commercial Foundations. The first stage of the Empire, from the annexation of Newfoundland in 1583 to the treaty of Paris in 1763, is marked by the predominance of commercial interests. The challenge of English private interests to the Spanish monopoly of the New World resulted in the occupation of some West Indian islands, and the establishment of colonies on the North American coast. In the 17th century England competed with the French for the fishing industry and the fur trade in America. In Asia she struggled unsuccessfully with the Dutch for the trade of the East Indies, but the East India Company laid the foundation for English control of India.

At the opening of the 18th century, France had superseded Spain and the Netherlands in the contest and remained England's chief colonial rival. Out of the consequent struggle, which was ended by the Treaty of Paris in 1763, England won supremacy in India and in North America.

The Second British Empire. The attempt to tighten political and commercial control over the colonies, in the face of their own economic and political growth, brought friction with the American colonies. This was accentuated by a new feeling of distinct nationality which neither party clearly comprehended, and with which the then British government was wholly incompetent to deal. The result was the American Revolution (1775-1783) and the fall of the first British Empire.

But immediately the growth of a Second Empire began. In America, Great Britain had held Canada and the West Indian islands. In India she had even made gains. In the Napoleonic wars she picked up bits of land of commercial and strategic significance. By exploration and colonization she made a start in Australia, New Zealand, and South Africa. Nevertheless, for a time the imperial spirit was dampened. However, economic conditions in England favored the exportation of people and capital, and the colonies grew stronger. As they grew, their demand for self-control became more insistent. Fortunately Britain had now produced statesmen who could meet the growing feeling of nationality and still keep the connection with the mother country. Canada, then Australia, New Zealand, and South Africa were given first self-government, then "Dominion Status." Soon after 1885 the new colonial rivalry, manifesting itself in the partition of Africa, gave Great Britain a large share of that continent. Her holdings were increased after World War I by most of the former German possessions.

The Commonwealth of Nations. After World War I the changed position of the Dominions in the Empire was recognized. By the Statute of Westminster (1931), putting in legal form the Balfour Report of 1926, Parliament declared that Great Britain and the six self-governing dominions were "equal in status, in no way subordinate one to another." They are independent in foreign as well as in domestic affairs but united by common allegiance to the British Crown and by the much stronger ties of common culture and interests. The name of British Commonwealth of Nations began to be preferred for the new body politic. The dominions, except Ireland, loyally supported the mother country in World War II. At its end, India, Pakistan, and Ceylon were given dominion status, and Burma was allowed to choose independence. The imperial position of the smaller, mostly tropical, colonies and outlying possessions remained unchanged.

ENGLAND

The British Isles have not been successfully invaded since the Norman Conquest of 1066 A. D., but their early history records a series of settlements by peoples from the continent of Europe. The earliest belong to the age of tradition. Before the Christian era, migrations of tall, fair-haired people largely displaced the aboriginal inhabitants of the islands. One migration brought over a bronze-using folk, probably the ancestors of the Gaels of Scotland and Ireland; another introduced the Brythonic, iron-using race, who gave their name to Britain and occupied the southern part of what is now England, when Cæsar's legions landed in 55 B. C. Greek travelers and traders are supposed to have visited Britain as early as the 4th century B. C., linking its trade with the Greek colony of Massilia (Marseille). The invasion by the Romans is the first of which a written record exists.

Germanic Tribes Invade Roman Britain. Roman generals and governors extended Roman authority until Agricola, by the year 84 A. D., completed a line of forts between the Forth and the Clyde as a barrier against the Caledonians. Roman colonists settled in the island, built towns around their military camps, connected these with roads, and introduced Roman law and civilization. Christianity likewise spread to this remote province. With the decline of the empire, however, the Roman legions were withdrawn to the continent, and the Britons were unable to defend themselves against the inroads of the barbarians from the North. They are said to have appealed for help to the Saxons, Angles, and Jutes, who lived along the North Sea to the south of Denmark. The response of these German folk developed into the Germanic invasion and settlement of Britain. The Anglo-Saxon chronicles date the principal migration at 449 A. D.

The Jutes were the first to form a settlement, taking possession of part of Kent and the Isle of Wight; but the more extensive conquests of the Saxons in the South and of the Angles in the North gave these two folk the lead. The struggle for occupation continued 150 years; at the end of that time the entire southern part of Britain, with the exception of Strathclyde, Wales, and West Wales (Cornwall), was in the hands of the new German kingdoms.

Before the common struggle with the Britons was settled, the small German kingdoms were at war with one another. In the middle of the 6th century, the West Saxons defeated the Jutes, who were pressing westward from Kent. The West Saxons, turning north, were probably faced by the Angles, already in possession in the valley of the Ouse, and so were diverted westward. They occupied the Severn valley. Meanwhile, in the North and the East, the Angles were making a slow advance. They formed three kingdoms: Mercia, in the upper valley of the Trent; Bernicia and Deira, together called Northumberland, or the country north of the Humber. These kingdoms, with those of the East Saxons, South Saxons, and Jutes, are sometimes called the Saxon Heptarchy; but they never formed such an organization as this name would indicate.

Christianity Established in Kent. While the Saxons and Angles, in the 6th century, were still struggling with the Britons, the men of Kent enjoyed a more settled life and carried on intercourse with the Latinized Gauls of the continent. Toward the end of the century, their king, Ethelbert, had become overlord of all the other kings south of the Humber. He had married a Christian wife, Bertha, daughter of a Frankish king. In 597 came Augustine and a band of Roman missionaries, sent by Pope Gregory. The legal and political changes immediately consequent upon the adoption of Christianity in the Germanic kingdoms in Britain were not great, but there began a more intimate relation with the continent and its Christian civilization. The introduction of Christian learning and culture, the formation of a written vernacular, and the fusion of the small kingdoms into a single large kingdom may be credited to the influence of the Roman clergy.

Upon the death of Ethelbert, the overlordship that he had maintained passed to the Anglian kings of the North. Northumbria had come under the influence of the Church, through first the Irish, and then the Roman, missionaries, and in the Northumbrian monasteries learning flourished. By the 7th century, the Church had regained all the Saxon kingdoms, which had previously all but obliterated the traces of the earlier British Church. Egbert of Wessex, before his death in 839, united the English kingdoms under his overlordship and may be considered the first king of England.

Danish Incursions. The land, meanwhile, was kept in a state of disturbance by the repeated incursions and attacks of the Danes. About half a century after Egbert's unification of the kingdom, the Danes acquired the mastery of nearly the whole of England. But the genius of Alfred the Great overcame the Danes at Ethandun (878). Guthrum, their king, embraced Christianity, acknowledged the supremacy of the English king, and received a strip of land including Northumbria on the east coast and known as the Danelaw. The two immediate successors of Alfred, Edward (899–925) and Athelstan (925–940), the son and the grandson of Alfred, both vigorous and able rulers, had in turn to direct their arms against these Danes of the Danelaw. The reigns of the next five kings, Edmund, Edred, Edwig, Edgar, and Edward the Martyr, are remarkable chiefly for the influence exerted by Dunstan, who was counselor to Edmund, minister of Edred, treasurer under Edwig, and virtual ruler during the reigns of Edgar and his successor. It was possibly due to Dunstan that from the time of Athelstan until after the death of Edward the Martyr (979) the country had comparative rest from the Danes.

During the 10th century many changes were altering the character of early English government. A feudal system was beginning to appear; the king's authority increased; the folkland was being taken over as the king's personal property; the nobles by birth, or ealdormen, were becoming of less importance in administration than the nobility of thegns, the officers of the king's court. Ethelred (978–1016), who succeeded Edward, was a minor. The government was feeble, and, no united action being taken against the Danes, their incursions became more frequent and destructive. Animosities between the English and the Danes who had settled among them became daily more violent, until a general massacre of the latter took place in 1002. The following year Svend invaded the kingdom with a powerful army and assumed the crown of England. Ethelred was compelled to take refuge in Normandy; though he afterwards returned, he found in Canute an adversary no less formidable than Svend. Ethelred left his kingdom to his son Edmund, who displayed great valor but was compelled to divide his kingdom with Canute. When Edmund died in 1016, the Danes succeeded to the sovereignty of the whole.

Canute (Knut), who espoused the widow of Ethelred that he might reconcile his new subjects, obtained the name of Great, not only on account of his personal qualities, but from the extent of his dominions, since he was master of Denmark and Norway as well as of England. In 1035 he died, and in England the reigns of two other Danish kings, Harold and Harthacnut, lasted till 1042, after which the English line was again restored in the person of Edward the Confessor.

The Norman Conquest. Edward was a weak prince; in the latter years of his reign, he had far less real power than his brother-in-law Harold, son of the great earl Godwine. On Edward's death in 1066, Harold accordingly obtained the crown. He found, however, a formidable opponent in the second cousin of Edward, William of Normandy, who instigated the Danes to invade the northern counties, while he landed in the South. Harold vanquished the Danes and, hastening southward, met the Normans at Senlac, near Hastings. Harold and his two brothers fell, October 14, 1066, and William (1066–87) immediately claimed the crown as lawful king of England. He is known in history as William I, the Conqueror. For some time he conducted the government with great moderation; but, being obliged to reward those who had assisted him, he bestowed the chief offices of the government upon Normans and divided among them a great part of the country. The consequent revolts of the native English were quickly crushed, continental feudalism in a modified form was established, and the English Church came under Norman influence through Lanfranc, archbishop of Canterbury.

At the death of the conqueror in 1087, his desire to have the strongest-willed of his sons rule England resulted in bestowing the throne upon William Rufus. The eldest son, Robert, was given the duchy of Normandy, while the third son, Henry, received a sum of money. The character of William II was vicious, and his rule in England, an unscrupulous tyranny. When, in 1100, he was found dead in the New Forest, with an arrow through his body, he was buried without funeral rites. He was succeeded by his younger brother, Henry, who set out to undo the evils of the previous reign. He allied himself with the English by marrying Eadgyth, or Matilda, a descendant of English kings. He subdued the Norman barons and wrested Normandy from his brother Robert. Henry's power being secured, he entered into a dispute with Anselm, the primate, and with the pope, concerning the right of granting investiture to the clergy. He supported his quarrel with firmness and brought it to a not unfavorable issue. In 1135 he died in Normandy, leaving behind him only a daughter, Matilda.

By the will of Henry I, his daughter Matilda, wife of Geoffrey Plantagenet, count of Anjou, was declared his successor. But Stephen, son of the count of Blois and of Adela, daughter of William the Conqueror, raised an army in Normandy, landed in England, and declared himself king. After years of civil war and bloodshed, an amicable arrangement was brought about, by which it was agreed that Stephen should continue to reign during the remainder of his life, but that he should be succeeded by Henry, son of Matilda and the count of Anjou. Stephen died in 1154, and Henry Plantagenet ascended the throne with the title of Henry II, the first of the Plantagenet, or Angevin, kings. A larger dominion was united under his sway than had been held by any previous sovereign of England, for at the time when he became king of England he was already in possession of Anjou, Normandy, and Aquitaine.

Beginnings of Constitutional Government. Henry II found far less difficulty in restraining the license of his barons than in abridging the special privileges of the clergy, who claimed exemption, not only from the taxes of the state, but also from its courts, and who were supported in their demands by the primate Becket. The king's wishes were formulated in the Constitutions of Clarendon (1164), which were first accepted and then repudiated by the primate. The assassination of Becket by the king's followers placed the king at a moral disadvantage in the struggle; after his conquest of Ireland (1174) he submitted to the Church and did penance at Becket's tomb. Henry contrived to associate the people of England with his new plan of government. The system of frankpledge was revived, trial by jury was sanctioned by the Assize of Clarendon, and the system of itinerant justices, twelve justices on circuit from the king's court, employed by Henry I, was revived. To lessen the power of the nobles he granted charters of incorporation to towns, freeing them from all obligation to any but himself, thus laying the foundation of a burgher or town class in society.

Richard I, called Cœur de Lion, who in 1189 succeeded his father, Henry II, spent most of his reign away from England. Having gone to Palestine to join in the Third Crusade, he proved himself an intrepid soldier. Returning homeward in disguise through Germany, he was made prisoner by Leopold, duke of Austria, but was ransomed by his English subjects. In the meantime, John, his brother, had aspired to the crown, and hoped, by the assistance of the French, to exclude Richard from his right. Richard's presence for a time restored matters to some appearance of order; but, having undertaken an expedition against France, he received a mortal wound at the siege of Châlus in 1199.

The reigns of Henry II and Richard were marked by an improved government. The kingdom became more orderly; the collection of taxes, more regular. The Church also was in large measure subject to royal control. The towns grew in wealth, and the merchant guilds became powerful. English churchmen promoted learning; in 1186 there were at Oxford faculties in several branches of study. The work of government and the law courts had made a demand for "clerks," that is, men skilled in writing and in law.

Magna Charta. At the death of Richard, John was at once recognized as king of England, and he secured possession of Normandy; but Anjou, Maine, and Touraine acknowledged the claim of Arthur, son of Geoffrey, second son of Henry II. On the death of Arthur, while in John's power, these four French provinces were lost to England. John's opposition to the pope in electing a successor to the see of Canterbury led to the pope's placing the kingdom under an interdict in 1208. On account of the disturbed condition of the nation, John was at last compelled to receive Stephen Langton as archbishop and to accept England as a fief of the papacy (1213). His exactions and misgovernment had equally embroiled him with the nobles. In 1213 they refused to follow him to France, and, on his return, defeated, they at once took measures to secure their own feudal rights and to limit the prerogatives of the crown. King and barons met at Runnymede, and, on June 15, 1215, the great charter (Magna Charta) was signed. It was speedily declared null and void by the pope, and war broke out between John and the barons, who were aided by the French king. In 1216, however, John died, and his turbulent reign was followed by the almost equally disturbed period of Henry III. Up to this time, the barons and the organized townspeople had entrenched themselves in a body of liberties, but no favor was shown the poor. Every town was surrounded by the miserable hovels of the poverty-stricken. It was to minister to these that the Franciscan friars came from Italy in the 13th century.

During the first years of the reign of Henry III, the ability of the earl of Pembroke, who was regent until 1219, retained the kingdom in tranquillity; but, when Henry assumed the reins of government in 1227, he showed himself incapable of ruling. The charter was three times reissued in a modified form, and new privileges were added to it, but the king took no pains to observe its provisions. The struggle over money grants, long maintained in the great council, henceforward called Parliament, reached an acute stage in 1263, when civil war broke out. Simon de Montfort, who had laid the foundations of the House of Commons by summoning representatives of the shire communities to the Mad Parliament of 1258, had by this time engrossed the sole power. He defeated the King and his son Edward at Lewes in 1264, and in his famous Parliament of 1265 he still further widened the representation of the people by summoning to it burgesses from the boroughs as well as knights from the shires. The escape of Prince Edward, however, was followed by the battle of Evesham (1265), at which Earl Simon was defeated and slain; the rest of the reign was undisturbed.

On the death of Henry III, in 1272, Edward I succeeded without opposition. From 1276 to 1284, he was largely occupied in the conquest and annexation of Wales, which had become practically independent during the barons' wars. In 1292, Balliol, whom Edward had decided to be rightful heir to the Scottish throne, did homage for his kingdom to the English king; but when, in 1294, war broke out with France, Scotland also declared war. The Scots were defeated at Dunbar (1296), and the country was placed under an English regent; but the revolt under Wallace (1297) was followed by that of Bruce (1306), and the Scots remained unsubdued.

The First Perfect Parliament. The reign of Edward was distinguished by many legal and legislative reforms, such as the separation of the king's court into the court of exchequer, the court of king's bench, and the court of common pleas. The passage of the statute of mortmain forbade the gift of land to clergy, because they paid no feudal dues. In 1295 the first "perfect parliament" was summoned, the clergy and barons by special writ, the commons by writ to the sheriffs directing the election of two knights from each shire and two burgesses from each borough. Two years later the imposition of taxation without consent of Parliament was forbidden by a special act, *De Tallagio non Concedendo*. The English constitution, in outline, was now complete. The great aim of Edward, however, to include England, Scotland, and Wales in one kingdom proved a failure, and he died in 1307, on an expedition against Robert Bruce.

Edward II made a feeble attempt to carry out his father's last and earnest request to prosecute the war with Scotland, but his army was constantly unsuccessful. At length, in 1314, it received at Bannockburn a defeat from Robert Bruce, which insured the independence of Scotland. The king proved incapable of ruling his baronage; and his consort, a woman of intrigues, joined in the confederacy against him, which resulted in his imprisonment and death in 1327.

Edward III and the French War. The reign of Edward III was as brilliant as that of his father had been the reverse. His main projects were directed against France, the crown of which he claimed in 1328. The victory won by Edward at Crécy (1346), the capture of Calais (1347), and the victory of Poitiers (1356) ultimately led to the Peace of Bretigny in 1360, by which he received all the West of France, on condition of renouncing his claim to the French throne. Before the close of his reign, however, these advantages were all lost, save for a few principal towns on the coast.

A Period of Political and Social Disorder. Edward III was succeeded in 1377 by his grandson Richard II, son of Edward the Black Prince. In 1379 an unjust and oppressive poll tax brought outstanding popular grievances to a head; 100,000 men, so accounts say, under Wat Tyler, marched toward London (1381). Wat Tyler was killed while conferring with the king, but the prudence and courage of Richard appeased the insurgents. Despite his conduct on this occasion, Richard was deficient in the vigor necessary to curb the lawlessness of his nobles. In 1398 he banished his cousin, Henry Bolingbroke; on the death of the latter's father, the duke of Lancaster, Richard unjustly appropriated his cousin's patrimony. To avenge the injustice, Bolingbroke landed in England, during the king's absence in Ireland, and, at the head of an army of malcontents, compelled Richard to surrender. Richard was confined in the Tower, and despite the superior claims of Edmund Mortimer, earl of March, Henry was appointed king (1399), the first of the house of Lancaster. Richard was, in all probability, murdered early in 1400.

The continued struggle of Parliament to retain control of taxation marked the constitutional side of the reign of Edward III. In 1341 the two houses of Parliament separated, the knights going with the burgesses into a lower house, or House of Commons. Social conditions in this period displayed marked contrasts in the distribution of wealth. On the one hand, the spoils of the French wars brought new luxuries to the nobles and upper classes. Larger and more comfortable houses were built, and the churches became more richly ornamented. On the other hand, the laborers had small share in this gain. When, after their ranks had been thinned by the Black Death, they attempted to secure higher wages, Parliament passed the Statute of Laborers, fixing wages at the old rate.

The manner in which the duke of Lancaster, now Henry IV, acquired the crown rendered his reign turbulent, but the vigor of his administration quelled every insurrection. The most important—that of the Percies of Northumberland, Owen Glendower, and Douglas of Scotland—was crushed by the battle of Shrewsbury (1403). During the reign of Henry IV, the government acquired a legal sanction for burning heretics, under the act *de haeretico comburendo,* passed in the second year of his reign. The act was directed chiefly against the Lollards, as the followers of Wiclif now came to be called. Henry died in 1413, leaving his crown to his son, Henry V, who revived the claim of Edward III to the throne of France in 1415 and invaded that country. The disjointed councils of the French rendered their country an easy prey; the victory of Agincourt was gained in 1415; and, after a second campaign, a peace was concluded at Troyes in 1420, by which Henry received the hand of Katherine, daughter of Charles VI. He was appointed regent of France during the reign of his father-in-law and, on the latter's death, was declared heir to his throne. The two kings, however, died within a few weeks of each other in 1422, and thus, at the age of nine months, the infant son of Henry became king of England and France.

English Defeat in France. England during the reign of Henry VI was subjected, in the first place, to all the confusion incident to a long minority, and afterwards to all the misery of a civil war. Henry allowed himself to be managed by anyone who had the courage to assume the conduct of his affairs, and the influence of his queen, Margaret of Anjou, a woman of uncommon capacity, was of no advantage either to himself or to the realm. In France (1422–53), the English forces lost ground and were finally expelled, Calais alone being retained. The withdrawal was the triumph of an attack begun by the heroic and inspired Joan of Arc, now Saint Joan of Arc since her canonization at the end of the World War. A rebellion under Jack Cade in 1450 was suppressed, only to be followed by more serious trouble. In that year, Richard, duke of York, the father of Edward IV, began to advance his pretensions to the throne which had been so long usurped by the house of Lancaster.

Wars of the Roses. The wars which resulted, called the Wars of the Roses, from the fact that a red rose was the badge of the house of Lancaster and a white one that of the house of York, lasted for thirty years, from the first battle of St. Albans, May 22, 1455, to the battle of Bosworth, August 22, 1485. This period, marked by the rapacity of the great landholders and by ferocious cruelty in the conduct of war, is, in some respects, the darkest in English history. A callous materialism, that found no place for the enthusiasms of Renaissance culture and despised the printing press, ruled the land. Henry VI was twice driven from the throne, in 1461 and in 1471, by Edward of York, whose father had previously been killed in battle in 1460. Edward of York reigned as Edward IV from 1461 till his death in 1483, with a brief interval in 1471. He was succeeded by two other sovereigns of the house of York,—first his son Edward V, who reigned for eleven weeks in 1483, and then his brother Richard III, who reigned from 1483 till 1485. Richard was defeated and slain on Bosworth field by Henry Tudor, of the house of Lancaster, who then became Henry VII.

Henry VII was at this time the representative of the house of Lancaster, and, in order at once to strengthen his own title and to put an end to the rivalry between the houses of York and Lancaster, he married, in 1486, Elizabeth, the sister of Edward V and heiress of the house of York. His reign was disturbed by insurrections attending the impostures of Lambert Simnel (1487), who pretended to be a son of the duke of Clarence, brother of Edward IV, and by the pretensions of Perkin Warbeck (1488), who affirmed that he was the duke of York, younger brother of Edward V; but neither of these disturbances attained any magnitude. The king's worst fault was his avarice, which led him to employ in schemes of extortion such instruments as Empson and Dudley. His administration throughout did much to increase the royal power and to establish order and prosperity. He died in 1509.

Henry VIII; The Reformation. The authority of the English crown, which had been so much extended by Henry VII, was, by his son Henry VIII, exerted in an exacting and capricious manner, though always for national and not merely for selfish ends. The most important event of the reign was undoubtedly the breach with Rome; though this had its official origin rather in Henry's personal caprice and in his relations with the court of Spain than in his conviction of the need of ending the pope's authority in England. Henry had been espoused to Catherine of Spain, the widow of his elder brother, Arthur, who died very shortly after marriage. Henry tired of his queen, who bore him no male heir, and became enamored of one of her maids of honor, Anne Boleyn. He had recourse to the pope, therefore, to dissolve a marriage which had at first been rendered legal only by a papal dispensation; but, failing in his desires, he broke entirely with the Holy See. In 1534 he got himself recognized by act of Parliament as supreme head of the Church of England. He died in 1547 while his court was sharply divided upon the question of further ecclesiastical and doctrinal changes.

In spite of adverse conditions and the lack of Renaissance enthusiasm in England, the new learning had secured a foothold in Oxford. Colet became a leader in the study of Greek. Out of this movement cameTyndale's translation of the New Testament. Thomas More founded St. Paul's School in 1510 to give boys an education in the spirit of the new learning. His criticism of the cynical policy of Henry VIII moved him to write his *Utopia.*

Henry was married six times and left three children, each of whom reigned in turn. These were: Mary, by his first wife, Catharine of Aragon; Elizabeth, by his second wife, Anne Boleyn; and Edward, by his third wife, Jane Seymour. Edward, who reigned first, with the title of Edward VI, was nine years of age at the time of his accession, and he died in 1553, when he was only sixteen. His short reign, or rather the government of the earl of Hertford, afterward duke of Somerset, who was appointed regent, was distinguished chiefly by the success which attended the measures of the Protestant reformers. The intrigues of Dudley, duke of Northumberland, caused Lady Jane Grey to be declared Edward's successor; but her reign, if it could be so called, lasted only a few days. Mary, daughter of Henry VIII, was placed on the throne, and Lady Jane Grey and her husband were both executed. Mary, a zealous Catholic, seems to have wished for the crown chiefly to restore papal authority. Persecution of the Protestant reformers drove many for safety to Geneva, to Holland, and to Scotland. Political motives had induced Philip of Spain to marry her; but she could never prevail on her subjects to allow him any share of power. She died in 1558.

The Reign of Elizabeth. Elizabeth, who succeeded her half-sister Mary, was attached to the Protestant faith, and she found little difficulty in re-establishing it in England, accomplishing her end partly by the relentless persecution of Catholics. Having concluded peace with France (1559), Elizabeth set herself to promote the confusion which prevailed in Scotland, to which country her cousin Mary Queen of Scots had returned from France in 1561. Mary was forced to seek asylum under Elizabeth's protection (1568) and, after many years' imprisonment, charged with plot and intrigue, was sent to the scaffold (1587). As a powerful Protestant nation and as a rival of Spain in the New World, England drifted into conflict with that country. The dispersion of the *Armada* (1588) by the English fleet under Howard, Drake, and Hawkins was the most memorable event of an era which first revealed the energy and daring of English seamanship.

Elizabeth's reign was for England a period of unprecedented commercial enterprise. Town industries increased; land that had been enclosed for pasture was turned back to grain production; the food and dwellings of the people improved. Imposing manor houses, often built in the form of the letter E, were erected by the more wealthy landowners. These had chimneys and glass windows, which were novelties. Many might be compared to the palaces of the Italian cities for luxury in service and appointments. Along with material prosperity, came a rich, spontaneous, original literature which of itself makes the Elizabethan era immortal.

The Stuart Struggle with Parliament. Elizabeth was succeeded in 1603 by James VI of Scotland and I of England, son of Mary Queen of Scots and Darnley. His accession to the crown of England in addition to that of Scotland began the union of the two nations. His dissimulation, however, ended in his satisfying neither of the discontented church parties,—the Puritans and the Catholics; and his insistence on his prerogative made his reign an unseemly struggle between the crown and the people. His extravagance kept him in constant disputes with Parliament, which would not grant him the sums he demanded and compelled him to resort to monopolies, loans, benevolences, and other unparliamentary methods. The nation at large, however, continued to prosper through the whole of this inglorious reign. Colonial enterprises in America marked a new departure in trade and in empire building.

Charles I, who succeeded James in 1625, inherited his father's exalted ideas of royal prerogative; his marriage with a Catholic, his arbitrary rule, and his unparliamentary methods of raising money provoked bitter hostility. Under the guidance of Laud and Strafford, partisanship grew inflamed in both Church and State. Civil war broke out at last in 1642 between the king's party and that of the Parliament. The royal government was overthrown, and in 1649 Charles was beheaded.

Cromwell and The Commonwealth. A commonwealth, or republican parliamentary government, was now established, in which the most prominent figure was Oliver Cromwell. Mutinies in the army among Fifth-monarchists and Levellers were subdued by Cromwell and Fairfax; and Cromwell, in a series of masterly movements, subjugated Ireland and gained the important battles of Dunbar and Worcester. At sea, Blake had destroyed the Royalist fleet under Rupert and was engaged in a struggle with the Dutch under Van Tromp. But, within the new government, matters had come to a deadlock. A dissolution of Parliament was necessary, yet Parliament shrank from dissolving itself, and in the meantime the reform of the law, a settlement with regard to the Church, and other important matters remained untouched. In April 1653, Cromwell cut the knot by forcibly ejecting the members and putting the keys of the house in his pocket. From this time, he was practically head of the government, which was vested in a council of ten. An attempt at a nominated parliament—the Little, or Barebone's Parliament—failed. The council then promulgated England's only written constitution, the Instrument of Government, under which, in December 1653, Cromwell was installed Lord Protector of the Commonwealth of England, Scotland, and Ireland. With more than the power of a king he controlled the confusion at home and made his government respected abroad. Cromwell died in 1658, his son Richard was a failure, and a year of uncertainty and unrest made England long for security under the old forms.

The Stuart Restoration. Charles II, son of Charles I, was called to the throne by the Restoration of 1660. He came without conditions, but he had learned the lessons of the Civil war. He took complete advantage of the popular reaction against the narrowness and intolerance of Puritanism; later, he even endeavored to carry it to the extreme of establishing the Catholic religion. The promises of religious freedom made by him in the declaration of Breda, before the Restoration, were broken by the Test and Corporation acts, and by the Act of Uniformity, which drove two thousand clergymen from the Church and created the great dissenting or nonconformist movement of modern times. The reaffirmation of the principle of habeas corpus, however, was a most praiseworthy step in the advance of the liberty of the subject.

The society of the court of Charles II was notoriously corrupt and profligate. This condition was reflected in the drama and literature of the period following the Restoration. Commercially, however, this was a prosperous time. More colonies were established in America, and English seaports grew upon the new trade thus built up. Country life remained dull, but London attracted the county families by its gaiety. The coffeehouses of London answered the purpose of informal clubs, promoting a more general political and literary discussion. The Royal Society was founded in 1660. England was hospitable to such foreign painters as Van Dyck, but her own architects designed her buildings, such as the new St. Paul's cathedral. In politics, this period saw the rise of the Whig and Tory parties. Macaulay, in his *History of England*, Chapter III, gives a description of this era; it is one of the most graphic delineations to be found in his writings.

The Revolution of 1688. As Charles II left no legitimate issue, his brother, the duke of York, succeeded him as James II (1685–89). The king's zealous support of Roman Catholicism and his attempts to force the Church and the universities to submission provoked a storm of opposition. Seven prelates were brought to trial for seditious libel, but they were acquitted amid general rejoicing. The whole nation was prepared to welcome any deliverance, and in 1688 William of Orange, husband of James's daughter Mary, was invited to come to England. James fled to France; and a convention settled the crown upon William and Mary. Annexed to this settlement was a declaration of rights, circumscribing the royal prerogative by depriving the king of the right to exercise dispensing power, or to exact money, or to maintain an army without the assent of Parliament. This placed the right of the British sovereign to the throne upon a purely statutory basis. A toleration act, passed in 1689, allowed nonconformists their own chapels and freedom of church worship.

An armed opposition to William lasted for a short time in Scotland but ceased with the fall of Viscount Dundee, the leader of James's adherents; though the struggle was prolonged in Ireland, it was brought to a close before the end of 1691. The following year saw the beginning of the national debt, the exchequer having been drained by the heavy military expenditure. A bill for triennial parliaments was passed in 1694, the year in which Queen Mary died. For a moment after her death, William's popularity was in danger, but his successes at Namur and elsewhere in the campaigns against Louis XIV, with the obvious exhaustion of France, once more confirmed his power. The Treaty of Ryswick followed in 1697, and the death of James II in exile in 1701 removed a not unimportant source of danger. Early in the following year William also died, and, by the Act of Settlement, Anne succeeded him.

Party and Cabinet Government. Several significant changes in politics and finance belong to William's reign. The Whig Junto, formed to stabilize the House of Commons, was the beginning of the "cabinet." The refusal of Parliament to renew licensing acts in 1695 freed the press from censorship. The great accumulations of capital in London brought about the founding of the Bank of England in 1694.

The closing act of William's reign had been the formation of the Grand Alliance, between England, Holland, and Austria, against Louis XIV. Queen Anne's rule opened with the successes of Marlborough at Blenheim (1704) and Ramillies (1706). Throughout the earlier part of her reign, Marlborough practically ruled the kingdom, the duchess of Marlborough, Sarah Jennings, being the queen's most intimate friend and adviser. From 1707 the history of England becomes the history of Great Britain, the Act of Union passed in that year having merged the parliaments and realms of England and Scotland into a single state. This has proved to be one of the most successful political experiments ever tried.

The wars with France ended in the Treaty of Utrecht in 1713, by which the British right of sovereignty over Hudson Bay Territory, Newfoundland, Acadia, Minorca, and Gibraltar was acknowledged, and the foundation of Great Britain's imperial and colonial power was securely laid. The remainder of Queen Anne's reign was distracted by the never-ending altercations of Whigs and Tories. She died on the 1st of August 1714, and with her ended the line of the Stuarts. The period is notable for the practice of securing skillful controversial writers for both government and opposition. Dean Swift was the ablest Tory writer, Addison the ablest Whig.

At the death of Anne, George I, elector of Hanover, descended from Elizabeth, daughter of James I, ascended the throne of Great Britain, according to the Act of Settlement. The Whigs under this prince regained in the national councils that superiority of which the Tories recently deprived them. Their extreme measures to destroy Tory power provoked retaliation. In 1715 the earl of Mar in Scotland and the earl of Derwentwater in England raised the standard of rebellion and proclaimed the Chevalier St. George, the "Old Pretender," king. But the insurrection, feebly supported by the people, was soon suppressed.

In 1716 the Septennial act was passed, making Parliament of seven instead of three years' duration. In 1720 occurred, after a phenomenal growth, the collapse of the South Sea Company. From this date until 1742 the government was in the hands of Sir Robert Walpole, the first of modern premiers, leading the cabinet and chiefly responsible for its acts. Walpole had great sagacity, prudence, and business ability, and could manage dexterously the king, Parliament, and the people alike. It is true that in the case of Parliament he achieved this by undue influence in elections and a scandalous use of bribery. But the power he thus acquired was, for the most part, wisely used. The failure of the war with Spain, into which he had reluctantly entered, drove him from office, and in 1742 his long ministry came to an end. In 1743, George II, frightened at the danger to Hanover, drew Great Britain into the wars between France, Prussia, and Austria, regarding the succession of the emperor Charles (War of the Austrian Succession). George himself fought at the head of his troops at Dettingen (1743), where he obtained a complete victory over the French. This victory was balanced later on, however, by the defeat at Fontenoy (1745).

The Young Pretender. A fresh attempt was made, while the war was in progress, to restore the Stuart family to the throne. Charles Edward, son of the Old Pretender, having been furnished by France with a small supply of money and arms, landed in the West Highlands in 1745 and was joined by a considerable number of the people. Marching southward with 1500 Highlanders, his forces increasing as he advanced, he entered Edinburgh without opposition; having defeated Sir John Cope near Prestonpans, he marched into England. Finding himself disappointed of expected succors from France, and the English Tories, contrary to his expectations, keeping aloof, he commenced his retreat into Scotland, closely pursued by the king's troops, whom he again defeated at Falkirk. With this victory his good fortune terminated. The duke of Cumberland arrived from the continent and put himself at the head of the forces which were destined to check the rebels. At Culloden, near Inverness, the Young Pretender was completely defeated. After lurking for six months amid the wilds of Inverness-shire, he at length, with much difficulty, escaped to France.

Eighteenth Century Life. During this period came notable changes in religion, philosophy, art, and literature. The 18th century is the Augustan or Classical age, with common sense, skepticism, and a belief in natural law as its chief traits. But, before the middle of the century, a reaction against the skeptical spirit set in. Butler defended Christianity in his *Analogy*. John Wesley led the evangelical religious movement, called Methodism, among the common people. The life of the times was realistically portrayed in the drawings of Hogarth. Fielding and Richardson created the modern, middle class, sentimental novel.

The War of the Austrian Succession, which was the cause of hostilities between the French and the British in India and America as well as in Europe, was terminated by the Treaty of Aix-la-Chapelle in 1748. During most of this period, Pelham and his brother, the duke of Newcastle, had been the ruling ministers; and in their hands the conduct of government reached, for modern times, a very low level of morality and statecraft.

The Seven Years' War. The French, uneasy at the growing colonial power of Great Britain, began after 1748 a determined effort against the British colonies and possessions in North America and in the East Indies. In 1756 fighting became general in the Seven Years' war. Austria and France were allied on the one side, and Prussia and England on the other. The advantage at first lay everywhere with France. But a great war minister, William Pitt, retrieved these early defeats. In 1758 the British made themselves masters of Louisburg, uncovering the approach to the Gulf of St. Lawrence, while the attack made by Wolfe on Quebec in 1759 was completely successful and gave Britain the mastery in Canada. In the same year the British and their allies defeated the French at Minden in Prussia. In the East Indies, the French were even less successful than in America. Clive's victory at Plassey (1757) and Coote's at Wandewash (1760) secured British ascendancy in the East. These successes, together with the naval victories of Hawke and Boscawen, made England the greatest of maritime and colonial powers.

On the accession of George III in 1760, hostilities were still carried on, generally to the advantage of the French as far as the theater of war in Germany was concerned, but still more to their loss in the other quarters of the world; and this notwithstanding the fact that Spain had now joined her forces to those of France. At length the success of the British arms induced France and Spain to accede to terms, and the hard-fought war ended by the Treaty of Paris in 1763. The French relinquished their possessions in North America; Minorca was restored to Britain; in the East Indies, the French got back their factories and settlements, on condition that they should maintain neither forts nor troops in Bengal; Cuba and Manila were resigned to the Spaniards.

The American Revolution. The close of the Seven Years' war ushered in a new and critical period in the history of the British Empire. The expenses of this war, which had been undertaken partly for the defense of the American colonies against the French, brought the amount of the national debt to more than 132 million pounds. It seemed to the British government to be just that the Americans should be taxed to assist in the payment of the interest. The Americans did not deny the justice of the claim, but replied that if they were to be taxed they had a right to be represented in Parliament, in order that, like other British subjects, they might be taxed only with their own consent. Grenville, then the prime minister, stood to his purpose, however, and introduced a bill for imposing certain stamp duties in the American colonies. The Americans protested and resisted; partly by the influence of the great Pitt, who had steadily opposed the measure, the act was repealed. On the illness of Pitt, now Lord Chatham, in 1767, Townshend became premier and revived the project of taxing the colonies indirectly by imposing duties on tea.

In 1770, Lord North, as Townshend's successor, set himself to carry out his scheme. The result was that in 1775 the thirteen colonies were in a state of rebellion, and a war began, in which both France and Spain joined the revolted colonies. The end was recognition of the independence of the United States. On the American side of this struggle, the great name is that of George Washington. On the British side, the war was unskillfully conducted; though some successes were gained, these were more than counterbalanced by such losses as the capitulation of Burgoyne at Saratoga (1777) and of Cornwallis at Yorktown (1781). Against France and Spain, the British could show such successes as that of Admiral Rodney off Cape St. Vincent (1780), the brilliant defense of Gibraltar by General Eliott (1779–82), and Admiral Rodney's victory over the French fleet in the West Indies (1782). The war closed with the Treaty of Versailles in 1783. Britain finally acquired several West Indian islands; Spain recovered Florida and Minorca; France secured Pondicherry and Chandernagore in India.

Industrial and Political Progress. In England, far-reaching changes were at the same time making their influence felt. In politics, freedom to criticize the king and the government and freedom to report and discuss Parliamentary debates in the press were being recognized. The way was thus prepared for Parliamentary reform. The latter part of the 18th century was a period of great economic progress. Population increased rapidly. Agricultural experiments were carried on; improved methods of farming were introduced; intelligent cattle breeding was undertaken. The invention of the steam engine and of labor-saving machinery brought about those great changes in management of industry, in factory production, and in the relation of labor to capital, known as the Industrial Revolution.

From 1783 to 1801, the government of Great Britain was directed by William Pitt, the younger son of Lord Chatham, who when only 24 years of age was made first lord of the treasury and chancellor of the exchequer. The affairs of Ireland and India and the impeachment of Warren Hastings were among the first subjects that occupied the attention of Pitt's ministry. In 1782, Ireland had been accorded legislative independence. There were thus two separate parliaments in the British Isles until 1800, when Pitt, who had in the interval experienced some of the difficulties arising out of two separate parliaments, contrived their union. Great Britain and Ireland became the United Kingdom, the two houses of lords and houses of commons being merged into the Imperial Parliament.

The Napoleonic Wars. In 1789, the French Revolution began. For a time there was in England general approval of this movement; but as the revolutionaries proceeded to extremes there was a reaction in English feeling, of which Edmund Burke became the exponent. The execution of Louis XVI was followed by the French declaration of war against Great Britain, on February 1, 1793. With one brief interval, the war lasted till 1815. At first, Britain co-operated with Prussia and Austria against France, and successes were gained on sea and on land. Later, the armies of the French Republic were everywhere victorious on the continent. In 1797 Britain stood alone in the conflict and indeed soon found a European coalition formed against her. The war was now largely maritime, and the naval success of Jervis off St. Vincent and of Duncan off Camperdown were followed by the victory of Nelson in Aboukir bay and of Abercromby at Alexandria.

In 1798, a rebellion in Ireland had to be crushed. Peace with France was made in 1802 by the Treaty of Amiens, only to be broken by another declaration of war in 1803, as the ambitious projects of Napoleon became evident. In spite of the efforts of Pitt, who died in 1806, in the way of forming and supporting a new coalition against France, the military genius of Napoleon swept away all opposition on land, though the naval victory of Trafalgar (1805) established England's supremacy on the seas.

Napoleon, who had assumed the title of emperor of the French in 1804, was now virtually the ruler of Europe. He put forth his Berlin Decree (1806), prohibiting all commerce with Great Britain wherever his power reached, set his brother Joseph on the throne of Spain, and occupied Portugal. But the spirit of resistance had now taken deep root in the British people; in 1808, troops were sent into Spain under Sir John Moore, and a year later Wellington, then General Wellesley, landed in Portugal. Then began that famous series of successful operations, the Peninsular war, which drove back the French into their own country and powerfully aided to undermine the fabric of Napoleon's empire.

The other chief European powers having united, Paris was occupied in 1814. Napoleon was deposed and exiled to Elba, and Louis XVIII was placed on the throne of France. Escaping in 1815, Napoleon appeared once more in the field with a large army. Wellington and Blücher hastened to oppose him, and at Waterloo his long career of conquest ended in a crushing defeat. The restoration of Louis followed, and Napoleon was sent to the island of St. Helena. Of her conquests, Britain retained Tobago, St. Lucia, Mauritius, the Cape of Good Hope, Demerara, Essequibo, Berbice, Helgoland, and Malta. Ceylon and Trinidad had been gained in 1802, and Britain emerged from this long struggle with a very great increase of territorial possessions and political importance.

Political and Economic Reform. After the termination of the wars with Napoleon, many things concurred to make a troublous era in the home administration. The new burden of debt which the wars had left on the nation, the bad harvest of 1816, a government which had no idea but that of absolute resistance to all reforms—all these contributed to increase popular discontent. The result was a strong Radical agitation, accompanied often by serious riots throughout the country, more especially in the large towns, and loud demands for reform in Parliament and in the system of representation. The death of George III and the accession of George IV in 1820 made little change in this respect. From 1822 a succession of able statesmen, Canning, Peel, and Huskisson, gave the government a more liberal turn and did much to satisfy the popular demands. The Catholics were admitted to Parliament; political restrictions on Dissenters were removed; and, in the face of a determined opposition, Earl Grey carried the Reform bill of 1832, which gave large manufacturing towns a representation in some proportion to their importance, practically transferring the basis of political authority from the upper to the middle classes. Similar changes affected all local government. The next great public measure was the abolition of negro slavery in every British possession in 1833. Even more important was the factory act of 1833, which began the correction of abuses in the factory system by limiting the hours of labor for women and children.

William IV died June 20, 1837, and was succeeded by Victoria. The year following is notable as that in which the Chartists began their movement for radical reform, which continued, with popular meetings, presentations of monster petitions, and occasional tumults, till 1848. This same period saw the struggle of the Anti-Corn-Law League (of which Cobden and Bright were the leaders), which was finally successful when Sir Robert Peel, the leader of the Tory party, himself proposed the repeal of the corn duties (1846). The principle of free trade had further success in the repeal of the navigation laws and in the general repeal of import duties made during Lord Aberdeen's ministry (1853).

The Crimean War. In 1852-53, dissension arose between Russia and Turkey, regarding the rights of the Latin and Greek Christians to access to the "holy places" in Palestine. The emperor of Russia, aiming at the possession of Constantinople and finding the concessions made to French devotees a sufficient pretext for war, sent Prince Menshikov to Constantinople to demand redress. Not being satisfied with the response secured, he declared war on Turkey in October 1853. On the plea that it was impossible to leave Russia a free hand in dealing with Turkey or in extending her influence in the Balkans, France and Great Britain formed an alliance against Russia in 1854. A joint invasion of the Crimea followed; Russia was defeated, and peace was signed in 1856 at Paris.

Immediately after the Crimean War came the mutiny of the sepoys in India. In 1858, sovereignty over the East India Company's possessions was transferred by Parliament to the crown. Wars with China (1857 and 1860) opened up five new Chinese ports to trade.

Extension of Suffrage. In 1867, Parliament passed the second Reform bill,—a measure establishing the principle of household suffrage. The act, by extending the franchise to the factory wage earner, made England politically democratic; and it has profoundly influenced all subsequent English history. Disraeli, who soon became official leader of the Conservative party, sought to attach the new voters to the Conservative interest by making the crown and the Church popular, and by a spirited foreign policy. But the next year put the Liberals in power. In 1869, Gladstone passed a bill for the disestablishment of the Irish Church. In 1870, an Irish land bill, for improving the relations between landlord and tenant, became law; and a national system of public elementary education for England was started. Early in 1874, Gladstone dissolved Parliament, and, a large Conservative majority being returned, Disraeli again became premier. His politics followed the lines of the new imperialism, with its interests in India, Africa, and the Near East. The Ashantee war, begun the previous year, ended early in 1874.

In 1876 the title, Empress of India, was added to the titles already held by the queen. During the Russo-Turkish war of 1877-78, Britain remained neutral; but she took an important part in the settlement by the Congress of Berlin and acquired from Turkey the right to occupy and administer Cyprus. Then followed war in Afghanistan, war with the Kafirs of Zululand, and a brief war with the Boers of the Transvaal.

Gladstone and Irish Home Rule. In 1880 Gladstone again became premier. By this time the Irish Nationalists in the House of Commons formed a third party, under the lead of C. S. Parnell. This party worked for Home Rule. Parliament passed another land act for Ireland (1881); an act for putting down crime in Ireland (1882), under which Parnell was arrested and imprisoned in Kilmainham jail; a third reform bill equalizing the borough and county franchise (1884)—all important. The intervention of Britain in Egypt led to the bombardment of Alexandria in July 1882 and the sending of an army into Egypt to quell rebellion. A rising in the Sudan caused British troops to be dispatched to Suakin; but another force, sent by way of the Nile to relieve General Gordon at Khartum, arrived too late for its object, and the Sudan was abandoned temporarily. For a brief period Lord Salisbury was premier in 1885; but in February 1886 he made way for Gladstone. In April, Gladstone proposed the first Home Rule bill, a bill which would establish a separate Irish legislative body. Against this a determined opposition was organized, and the bill was thrown out on its second reading. This gave rise to the Unionist party, which left the Liberals for the Conservatives. The Liberal remnant was mainly Radical and Irish.

Conservative-Unionist Government. A general election followed, in which the new Unionists and Conservatives had a great majority. The Conservative-Unionist party assumed office, with the marquis of Salisbury as head. A criminal law amendment act for Ireland (1887) and a local government act for England (1888) were passed. In 1887 the golden jubilee of the queen was celebrated. The Liberals won in the elections in 1892, Gladstone acting as premier until his retirement, when Lord Rosebery became premier. In 1895 Lord Salisbury, with the Conservative-Unionists, was returned to power. October 11, 1899, war was declared by the Boers of the Transvaal and Orange Free State, who hoped to destroy British paramountcy in South Africa; these states were annexed to the empire in 1900 and made part of the Union of South Africa in 1909. In 1900, a new Parliament was elected, with a slightly increased Conservative majority. Victoria died January 22, 1901, and was succeeded by Edward VII.

In 1902, on Lord Salisbury's retirement, the new ministry was reconstituted, with A. J. Balfour as premier. The Balfour ministry came to grief over Chamberlain's protective tariff controversy. It was succeeded in 1905 by a Liberal ministry headed by Sir Henry Campbell-Bannerman, who, at his death in 1908, was succeeded by Mr. Herbert Asquith.

The Conservative-Unionist, or, more briefly, the Unionist, party, which went out of office in 1905, had, with the slight interval of Liberal government from 1892 to 1895, been in power continuously since 1886. It inaugurated the Irish Land Purchase system, designed to do away with landlords in Ireland by advancing purchase money to peasants to enable them to buy outright the full title to their farms. Peasant proprietorship began a new era in Ireland's economic and social history. The ominous rivalry with Germany indirectly ended the Unionist government, for Mr. Chamberlain's protective tariff, which split the party, cut too deeply across the old free trade prejudices. The Unionists, nevertheless, had already formed the Anglo-Japanese alliance (1902) and had entered into the *Entente Cordiale* with France (1904).

Liberal Government. The Liberal government that came into office in 1905 drew its support from a strong intellectual radical element (Fabian Socialists, etc.) with its views of the "social uplift," discountenanced during the long Unionist ascendancy, also from the new Labor Party, and from the Irish Nationalists. It had to satisfy these three groups and to watch the threatening course of world politics.

The new Radicalism showed itself first in the act for old age pensions paid by the state (1908),—a controversy which marks the end of the Victorian school of Liberalism and the victory of the younger radical thinkers. Lloyd George, as chancellor of the exchequer. next (1909) framed a budget destined to have important consequences. It embodied a new scheme of taxation bearing heavily upon the "unearned" incomes of the well-to-do. When the House of Lords rejected this budget, a grave constitutional crisis was reached. For years Liberals and Radicals had resented the privileged hereditary position of the Peers and their indifferent rejection of popular measures passed by the Commons. But this was the first case of an entire budget being annulled. A general election (1910) gave popular endorsement to the rejected budget, which the Lords accordingly passed. They then, to ward off the impending crisis, put forward plans which would have modified the composition and privileges of their own house. But the government was bent upon a more radical constitutional alteration. Soon after the death of King Edward (1910) and the accession of George V, Parliament was dissolved, and a general election, largely on the House of Lords question, once more returned the Liberals to office. The Parliament act of 1911 followed,—passed by the Lords only when it was known that the king was prepared to create enough peers to assure its passage. Henceforth, if any measure passed the Commons in three successive sessions, it would become law regardless of the contrary vote of the Lords; at the same time, the duration of Parliament was reduced from seven to five years.

The bill for the disestablishment of the Church in Wales became law in 1914, without the consent of the Lords, after passing the Commons for the third time. The question of women's franchise was settled by the fourth Reform bill of 1918. With certain exceptions, women over thirty years of age were given the Parliamentary vote—a later act enabled them to sit in Parliament—while, by the same bill, the franchise for men approximates to manhood suffrage. At the same time, the Education bill made full time attendance at school compulsory to the age of 14, with compulsory continuation work until the age of 18. The further development of the views of the radical school will probably come from the Labor party, numerically already very strong, and comprising professional men as well as wage earners in its ranks.

Irish Home Rule. It required the new procedure of the Parliament act of 1911 to secure an Irish Home Rule bill. A measure passed the Commons for the third time, in 1914, and became law without the consent of the Lords. Certain counties in Ulster actually prepared for civil war rather than have the measure come into force. When the World War began, the enforcement of the act was suspended, and subsequent events caused it to lapse altogether. The war proved a most troublesome and chaotic period for Ireland, bringing to the surface all the latent antagonism between the two races. A further Home Rule bill, recognizing two separate parts and two separate governments for Ireland, was passed in 1920; but this was generally disregarded. The position of the Nationalists, who still hoped for favorable concessions from the Imperial Parliament, was complicated by the political program of the Sinn Fein, demanding an independent Irish Republic completely detached from the United Kingdom and from the empire. Late in 1921 Lloyd George succeeded in framing a "treaty" which the Imperial Parliament approved. The treaty, on the part of Great Britain, recognized the Irish Free State—the inclusion of the Ulster counties was left to their own consent—and the new Free State was to acquire the status of a self-governing dominion, analogous to that of Canada, within the empire. The treaty was ratified by the Irish representative assembly, the Dail Eireann, January 7, 1922.

The Approach of War. The rivalry with Germany took the direction (1) of a competition in naval armament, and (2) a diplomatic understanding with a group of powers which together should outbalance the Triple Alliance of Germany, Austria, and Italy. The naval competition had begun before 1905; but the victory of the Japanese fleet over the Russian in the battle of Tsushima in that year had demonstrated the advantage of the long range gun. The British admiralty at once laid the keel of the first modern dreadnought, a ship of high speed, with a few guns only and those of the largest caliber. Germany followed suit and took up the challenge which drove both powers to a naval program of overreaching dimensions.

To the alliance with Japan and the entente with France was added (1907) an understanding with Russia. This completed the diplomatic edifice intended to outmatch the German alliance. The main German objective, of which the Constantinople to Bagdad railway was a part, would have given the Central Powers a wide belt of influence and exclusive economic exploitation extending from the North Sea through the Balkan states and Asia Minor to the Persian Gulf, and impinging upon both Russian and English interests in western and central Asia. On the other hand, the French design of rounding out an empire in northwestern Africa by an inclusion of Morocco aroused German resentment. From either quarter, a reason for war might have come.

The annexation of Bosnia and Herzegovina by Austria (1908) found Russia not yet sufficiently recovered from the war with Japan to make this a crucial issue. The annexation was a diplomatic victory for the Central Powers; but it increased the tension between the two rival groups. The sending of the German gunboat *Panther* to Agadir in 1911 brought England at once to the diplomatic support of France, and Germany had to be content to leave France a free hand in Morocco, accepting territorial compensation elsewhere in Africa. The war of Italy against Turkey for territory in North Africa left the two groups of powers undisturbed. But the Balkan wars seemed to tell on the whole against the diplomatic prestige of the German group; and they left Serbia strengthened with Russian support against Austria's advance. While the memory of this diplomatic setback was fresh, the heir to the Austrian throne was assassinated at Sarajevo by Serbian nationalists. This event seemed to Germany to involve a further loss of prestige unless avenged by the complete humiliation of Serbia.

While Russia was mobilizing for the support of Serbia, England tried to have the impending conflict localized, and then to have it made the subject of a general European conference. Failing both, the full implications of the understanding with Russia and with France had to be met. When Germany declared war against Russia and then against France, England took the occasion of the violation of Belgian neutrality to enter the lists against Germany, and the World War had begun.

The World War. England's contribution to the combined operations of the Entente against the Central Powers and their allies was primarily naval. She resisted successfully, although with fearful loss of mercantile tonnage and food supply, the German submarine blockade of the British Isles. Her navy maintained to the end the counter blockade of all the maritime approaches of the Central Powers—a task which the adherence of Italy to the Entente in 1915 made the easier—thus cutting off all sea-borne war supplies and foodstuffs for the enemy. The naval battle of Jutland, the only large open engagement between the two high seas fleets (1916), ended in the safe withdrawal of the German squadrons to cover, whence they never emerged till the surrender after the armistice. After Turkey had joined the Central Powers, with Bulgaria, the attempt to force the Dardanelles, preparatory to taking Constantinople with the army quartered at Gallipoli, was foiled by the Turkish land batteries (1915). But Turkey was despoiled of most of her empire. England successfully defended the Suez canal and Egypt (severed definitely from the Turkish empire and declared a British possession, 1914), secured Jerusalem, and gained Mesopotamia.

England's share in military operations involved unprecedented disturbance of industrial and social activity at home. The English army, with a fighting service alone of over 4,000,000 men, assumed the proportions of the huge armies of the continental powers. See *World War*.

Post-War Period. After the Treaty of Versailles the government was faced by problems of demobilization, debt finance, and unemployment. Within the Empire, the Dominions, including Eire (Irish Free State), were given an equal status with Great Britain, extending to foreign relations, and India received a new constitution. Lloyd George was compelled to resign in 1922, when Greece, whose claims he had supported, was overcome by Turkey. A Conservative government succeeded, first under Bonar Law and later under Stanley Baldwin.

In 1923 a Labor government under Ramsay MacDonald held office for 10 months, Baldwin being returned to power again at the end of the year. The Labor government was returned to power in 1929 and was succeeded in October 1931 by a coalition government, preponderantly Conservative, led by Ramsay MacDonald. Elected to deal with a financial crisis, this government took the historic step of abandoning Britain's free trade policy. A system of preferential tariffs within the empire was adopted in 1932. The Conservatives won the election of 1935, Baldwin serving as prime minister until 1937. He was succeeded by Neville Chamberlain.

Edward VIII, who had succeeded George V in January 1936, abdicated in December because the Cabinet objected to his proposed marriage with Mrs. Wallis Simpson. He was succeeded by a younger brother, crowned May 12, 1937, as George VI.

Abroad England had been a leading supporter of the League of Nations and the limitation of armaments, as shown at the Washington Conference of 1921–22. The rising military strength of Germany under its totalitarian government, together with the aggressive policy of Japan and Italy, forced a change in 1936 to a rearmament program. Even after the Italian conquest of Ethiopia, however, the Insurgent victory in Spain with Italian and German assistance, the Japanese invasion of China, and the German annexation of Austria, England followed a policy of appeasement, climaxed by the Munich agreement in September 1938, which allowed Germany to take over the Sudeten lands of Czechoslovakia. England and France then guaranteed the integrity of Poland against German attempts to regain Danzig and the Polish Corridor. Russia signed a ten-year non-aggression pact with Germany; and, when Germany invaded Poland, England and France declared war, September 3, 1939.

World War II. In the first inactive months of the war, Britain established a strict blockade of the Continent, and sent an expeditionary force to France, and later to Norway. The German successes of 1940 left the enemy holding the whole coast of the Continent, and well supplied with bases for sea and air attacks, while British defense was hampered by the neutrality of Eire. Winston Churchill succeeded Chamberlain and a coalition ministry was formed. Parliament passed the Emergency Powers Defense act, authorizing the general conscription of persons and property for defense. Food production was encouraged. The people accepted a strict rationing system, stringent control of labor, and an unprecedented burden of taxation as necessary for ultimate victory. One third of the homes in England were destroyed or damaged, over 60,000 civilians were killed, and 86,000 injured, by the planes and robot bombs. Meantime, Britain, assisted by the United States, struck back with air raids and commandos; gave asylum to the governments-in-exile, who were directing resistance abroad; and furnished a base for the American forces already gathering for the invasion of the Continent. (See *World War II*.)

Post-War Problems. Victorious over Germany, Britain had to meet domestic and imperial problems. In July 1945 a general election, the first in ten years, unseated the war ministry. The Labor party came into power with 393 seats in the Commons, against 189 for the Conservatives. The new prime minister was Clement Attlee, with Ernest Bevin as foreign minister. The new ministry announced a policy of nationalization and social reforms.

The program of nationalization began with the Bank of England. The coal industry was taken over by the state, January 1, 1947, with compensation to the owners set at 659 million dollars. Legislation brought the development and use of land under government control. The electrical industries were nationalized. Inland transportation, including the four main railway systems with their appurtenances; the London Transport system; and the major canals were taken over on January 1, 1948, by the British Transport Commission. Medicine was taken under state control, and the nationalization of the iron and steel industry was proposed.

To meet the strain on national resources, it was vitally necessary to rebuild Great Britain's export trade, in order to make payments to foreign countries. Loans aggregating five billion dollars from the United States and Canada assisted, but labor troubles in the vital coal industry and the worst winter England had known in years aggravated the situation. In August 1947 the government was forced to ask for emergency powers, and initiate a policy of "austerity" almost equal to that of the war régime. In 1948 better weather, good harvests, and aid from the United States under the Marshall plan improved the situation, but threatening foreign complications made it necessary to suspend demobilization and reintroduced the draft.

In the field of imperial and foreign policy: Burma became independent; India, divided into Hindu India and Moslem Pakistan, received dominion status, as did Ceylon. Malaya was reorganized. In Palestine, after long-continued attempts to keep the peace between Jews and Arabs, Britain resigned its mandate to the United Nations, and withdrew in May 1948. It likewise withdrew military aid from Greece and Turkey. In the growing disagreements between the Western powers and Russia, Britain supported the United States in the reorganization of western Germany. She also supported France and the Benelux countries, in May 1948, in forming a western alliance against the encroachments of Russia.

An event of much personal interest to the English people was the marriage of Princess Elizabeth, heiress presumptive to the throne, and Lt. Philip Mountbatten, Duke of Edinburgh, and the birth of her son, Charles Philip Arthur George, on November 14, 1948.

SCOTLAND

Scotland in ancient times was known to the Romans as *Caledonia* The Romans, from 80 A.D., held parts of the lowlands. After their departure from Britain in 410 the country was occupied by the Picts, the Scots in the west, originating in Ireland, the Britons of Strathclyde in the southwest, and the Angles in the southeast.

Early Scottish Kings. In the year 844 the Scots and Picts were united under Kenneth MacAlpin. The new kingdom, now called *Scotland*, absorbed the Britons, and by the victory of Carham (1018), over Canute's forces, gained the district of Lothian. The line of Kenneth MacAlpin ruled until 1290, except for the reign of Macbeth (1040–57). The Norman Conquest of England and the marriage of Malcolm III with Margaret, a Saxon princess, tended to bring in the English language and Norman-English institutions. Of Malcolm's three sons, who succeeded him, David I (1124-53) was the most powerful and capable.

English Suzerainty Begun. The English kings since Athelstan had made vague claims of suzerainty over Scotland. In 1173, William the Lion of Scotland, after his defeat in Northumbria, was forced to become a liegeman of Henry II. This

English suzerainty, however, was relinquished by Richard Cœur de Lion in 1188.

From 1214 to 1285, under Alexander II and Alexander III, Scotland once more experienced a long period of national progress and prosperity. Alexander III was succeeded by his eight-year-old granddaughter, Margaret, in 1285. The child queen dying suddenly, the vacant throne was disputed among many rivals. Between two of these claimants, John of Baliol and Robert Bruce, Edward I was appointed arbiter. He decided in favor of Baliol, which decision implied once again suzerainty over Scotland.

In 1296, Edward defeated Baliol, who had chafed against his position as vassal, and forced him to abdicate, appointing a governor to administer the Scottish kingdom.

Wallace and Bruce. The Scots under Wallace rose in rebellion and won a decisive victory over the English at Stirling in 1297. The following year Edward again invaded Scotland, and at Falkirk the Scottish forces, after a brave but futile resistance, were broken. Wallace was later betrayed, and after a mock trial was condemned and executed, August 23, 1305.

Soon, however, another champion of the cause of Scotland was found in Robert Bruce, who, in 1314, at Bannockburn, drove the English into headlong flight and thus freed his country from foreign dominance. Bruce reigned fifteen years as Robert I of Scotland. After a period of civil war, his son, David II, gained the throne in 1342.

Rise of Stuart Dynasty. David died childless, and a new line of Scottish kings began in the person of Robert II, son of Marjorie (daughter of Bruce) and the high steward, from which hereditary office the new dynasty took its name. He was succeeded in 1390 by his son Robert III, and, on the death of the latter in 1406, James I became king, under the regency of the duke of Albany. Internal strife among his turbulent barons led to James's being held captive in England for eighteen years. He was subsequently liberated and crowned at Scone in 1423.

James I proved a capable and gifted monarch, but unfortunately he was assassinated at Perth in 1437, being succeeded by his young son, James II. After a long minority, James assumed the reins of government and showed signs of being a firm and prudent ruler. He was, however, accidentally killed in 1460, and was succeeded by his son James III, who was slain in 1488 at the battle of Sauchieburn. James IV, son and successor of James III, in 1503 married Margaret, daughter of Henry VII of England. When Henry VIII, in 1509, ascended the English throne, border troubles broke out between him and James IV, resulting in the defeat and death of the latter at Flodden Field (1513).

Mary Queen of Scots. James V, son of James IV, became king in 1513. He made war in turn on England and was defeated at Solway Moss in 1542, dying a few days later on December 14 at Caerlaverock Castle. He was succeeded by his infant daughter, pitifully famous in Scottish history as Mary Queen of Scots. Her unfortunate marriage with Lord Darnley, a worthless ingrate, lost her the support of the Reformed party in Scotland.

He was murdered, and Mary married Bothwell, who was suspected of complicity in the crime. A rebellion forced her to abdicate in favor of her infant son who, in 1567, became King James VI, with the earl of Moray as regent. After a thwarted attempt to regain her throne, Mary fled to England, where Elizabeth detained her as a state prisoner. As the head of the Catholic party and the next heir to the throne, Mary became the center of a series of plots against the queen, and Elizabeth finally ordered her execution. She was beheaded in Fotheringay Castle in 1587.

Union of Scotland and England. On the death of Elizabeth, James VI, as nearest heir, succeeded to the English throne in 1603 as James I of England, with the title of King of Great Britain, France, and Ireland. James I died in 1625 and was succeeded by his son Charles I, whose reign was marked by foreign wars and religious dissensions, which resulted in his execution, January 1, 1649. Six days later the Scots proclaimed his son, Charles II, king and invited him to Scotland. On two occasions he was defeated by Cromwell's troops, the second being at Worcester (1651), where his army was completely annihilated. In 1660 Charles was restored to the throne in Scotland and England. Charles II was succeeded at his death in 1685 by his brother James VII of Scotland and II of England. The Revolution of 1688 drove James from his kingdom and in 1689 placed on the throne William and Mary, who were succeeded by Anne in 1702.

Coalescence of Parliaments. Already a spirit of alienation was rife in Scotland, due to commercial jealousy of England. To prevent a more serious estrangement between the two countries, the Scottish and English parliaments in 1707 passed an act by which the two governments were amalgamated into one ruling body.

Subsequent history has shown that the Scottish people have been in no way fallible in the intuition that guided them to the acceptance of a political arrangement which has brought to them such lasting peace and prosperity.

WALES

The early inhabitants of Wales were a mixed race of Celtic and pre-Aryan peoples. They are largely represented in the small, dark, dolichocephalic (long-headed) types, still to be met in the coal valley districts of southern Wales. These "small dark" Welshmen, as they are known today, probably represent an early migration of Mediterranean peoples along the Atlantic coast. Their own name for themselves was *Cymri*, "men of the same country," in contrast to the Saxon invaders, who called them Welsh (Wälsch) or foreigners.

The Roman Occupation. The Romans, under Ostorius Frontinus and Agricola conquered Wales by 78 A.D. They received a veneering of Roman culture and were so far reconciled to Roman rule that their defense was left largely in their own hands. After the departure of the Romans, however, they reverted to their clan system and Celtic culture, with the addition of Christianity

Saxons and Normans. The Saxon invasion cut off the Welsh from their kinsmen to north and south. Against the Saxon kings they fought with varying success. The Norman kings, after 1072, allowed their barons to carve out feudal domains as they could in Wales, and by the end of the next century these "Marcher Lords" had occupied most of the level ground in the Severn valley and on the southwest coast, but they were less successful in the mountains.

Subjugation by Edward I. The princes of the house of Llewelyn attained some degree of unity among the clans, and had some success against the English. The last of them made the mistake of defying Edward I, who invaded Wales (1276–84) and conquered it. He divided the former Welsh lands into shires, and built castles to secure control. Wales, with its mixture of native clans, royal domain, and Marcher lordships, was far from stabilized, and even became an element of discord in English politics. In 1403, Owen Glendower, with Harry Hotspur, rose in rebellion against Henry IV, but was defeated.

Incorporation in England. In 1485 Henry VII, himself of Welsh stock, began a reorganization, which was completed by Henry VIII with the amalgamation of Wales with England. Local government was established on the English model, and Welsh members sat in the English parliament. The Welsh became and remained loyal adherents to the English crown, but they have always maintained their spirit of individual nationality, which in great measure has been kept alive by the preservation of their native tongue.

THE BRITISH COMMON-

Countries	Political Character	Form of Government	Executive Authority	Area in Sq. Miles
England (Great Britain)	Great Britain and Northern Ireland, represented in Parliament			50,874
Wales (Great Britain)		Constitutional monarchy	King through ministry	7,466
Scotland (Great Britain)				30,405
Northern Ireland (Ulster)		Responsible	King through ministry	5,237
Isle of Man		Representative	Governor	221
Channel Islands		Representative	Lt. Governor	75
Dominions				
Canada[1]	Dominion	Self-governing	Gov.-General	3,349,923
Australia	Commonwealth	Self-governing	Gov.-General	2,977,600
New Zealand	Dominion	Self-governing	Gov.-General	103,935
Union of South Africa	Legislative Union	Self-governing	Gov.-General	472,494
Irish Free State	Free State	Self-governing	Gov.-General	26,959
India	Dominion	Self-governing	Gov.-General	628,808[2]
Pakistan	Dominion	Self-governing	Gov.-General	236,638[2]
Ceylon	Dominion	Self-governing	Gov.-General	25,332
Dependencies and Possessions				
In Europe				
Gibraltar	Colony		Governor	1⅞
Malta and Gozo	Colony	Internally self-gov.	Governor	122
In Africa				
British East Africa				
Kenya	Colony and Protec'te	Part. representative	Governor	219,730
Tanganyika	Trusteeship		Governor	342,706
Somaliland	Protectorate		Governor	68,000
Uganda	Protectorate		Governor	80,292
Zanzibar and Pemba	Protectorate		Governor	1,020
Mauritius and Dep.	Colony		Governor	720
Nyasaland	Protectorate		Governor	37,596
St. Helena and dependencies	Colony		Governor	130
Seychelles	Colony		Governor	156
South Africa				
Basutoland	Colony		Res'd'nt Com's'n'r	11,716
Bechuanaland	Protectorate		Res'd'nt Com's'n'r	275,000
Northern Rhodesia	Protectorate		Governor	287,640
Southern Rhodesia	Colony	Responsible	Governor	150,333
Swaziland	Protectorate		Res'd'nt Com's'n'r	6,704
Southwest Africa (Under Union of South Africa)	Mandate	Mandatory	Administrator	317,725
West Africa				
Gambia	Colony and Protec'te		Governor	4,132
Gold Coast	Colony and Protec'te		Governor	78,802
Nigeria	Colony and Protec'te		Governor	338,593
Cameroon (British)	Trusteeship		Gov. of Nigeria	34,081
Sierra Leone	Colony and Protec'te		Governor	27,925
Togoland (British)	Trusteeship		Gov. of Gold Coast	13,041
Anglo-Egyptian Sudan	Condominium		Gov. General	967,500
In Asia				
Aden (and Hadramaut)	Colony and Protec'te		Governor	115,080
Cyprus	Colony		High Commissioner	3,572
Hong Kong	Colony		Governor	391
Maldive Islands	Protectorate			115
Malaya, Federation	Protectorate		High Com's'n'r	50,850
North Borneo	Colony		Governor	29,417
Brunei	Protectorate		British resident	2,226
Sarawak	Colony		Governor	50,000
Singapore	Colony		Governor	217
In Australasia and Oceania				
Papua (under Australia)	Colony		Administrator	90,540
New Guinea (under Australia)	Trusteeship		Administrator	91,000
Western Samoa (under New Zealand)	Trusteeship		Administrator	1,150
Fiji	Colony		Governor	7,083
Nauru	Trusteeship (under New Zealand, Austr., and Gt. Britain)		Administrator	8
Pitcairn Island	Colony		Chief mag. and council	2
Pacific Islands			High Commissioner	
Tonga (Friendly Islands)	Protectorate	Rep. monarchy	Queen; Br. agent	250
Gilbert and Ellice Is.	Colony		Res'd't com's'n'r	333
Solomon Islands (British)	Protectorate		Res'd't com's'n'r	11,500
New Hebrides	Condominium with Fr.		High com's'n'r	5,700
Canton and Enderbury Is.	Condomi'um with U.S.			
In America				
Bermuda	Colony	Representative	Governor	21
British Guiana	Colony	Part. representative	Governor	83,000
British Honduras	Colony		Governor	8,867
Falkland Is. (with So. Georgia)	Colony		Governor	5,618
West Indies				
Bahamas	Colony	Representative	Governor	4,375
Barbados	Colony	Representative	Governor	166
Jamaica	Colony	Representative	Governor-in-chief	4,411
Turks and Caicos Is.	Dep. of Jamaica		Commissioner	224
Leeward Islands	Colony		Governor	412
Trinidad, with Tobago	Colony		Governor	1,980
Windward Islands	Colony		Governor	821

1. Including Newfoundland, 154,000 sq. mi., pop. 321,000. 2. Approximate. 3. Before partition.

WEALTH OF NATIONS

Accession to the Empire		Foreign Trade		Population	Capital	Countries
Method	Date	Imports	Exports			
Conquest	449–1066	. . .	. . .	43,270,000	. . .	England
Conquest	1283	$4,447,882,790	$1,814,567,950	2,043,000	London	Wales
Political union	1603, 1707			5,139,000	. . .	Scotland
Conquest, settlement	1172–1494	. . .	. . .	1,295,000	Belfast	No. Ireland (Ulster)
Purchase	1827	. . .	. . .	49,308	Douglas	Isle of Man
Thro' duke of Norm'dy	1066	. . .	. . .	. . .	St. Peterport	Channel Islands
						DOMINIONS
Settlement, conquest	1627–1763	2,002,106,998	2,374,742,606	12,903,100	Ottawa	Canada
Settlement	1788–1828	749,749,260	497,640,050	7,580,800	Canberra	Australia
Settlement, treaty	1840	177,553,740	261,244,750	1,802,840	Wellington	New Zealand
Conquest, treaty	1814–1900	452,742,290	271,060,260	11,391,950	Pretoria	Union of So. Africa
Conquest, treaty	1494, 1922	163,851,740	140,836,410	2,953,450	Dublin	Irish Free State
Conquest, cession	1612–1857	869,827,040[3]	729,200,290	31,400,000	Delhi	India
Separated from India	1947	. . .	. . .	69,000,000	Karachi	Pakistan
Treaty, cession	1796–1815	178,827,220	178,025,250	6,695,605	Colombo	Ceylon
						IN EUROPE
Treaty, cession	1713	. . .	. . .	21,230	Gibraltar	Gibraltar
Treaty, cession	1814	36,977,030	270,010	285,600	Valletta	Malta and Gozo
						IN AFRICA
						Br. East Africa
Annexation	1920	55,485,040	61,598,550	4,053,280	Nairobi	Kenya
Conquest	1918	27,146,080	31,107,570	5,499,680	Dar-es-Salaam	Tanganyika
Treaty, cession	1914	. . .	. . .	700,000	Berbera	Somaliland
Occupation	1894	Included with	Kenya	3,997,690	Entebbe	Uganda
Treaty, cession	1890	5,973,030	4,114,630	250,000	Zanzibar	Zanzibar
Conquest, cession	1810–1814	17,570,800	7,769,840	428,270	Port Louis	Mauritius
Treaty, cession	1891	6,532,630	7,378,930	2,230,960	Zomba	Nyasaland
Conquest, occupation	1673	. . .	. . .	4,919	Jamestown	St. Helena
Treaty	1814	801,970	701,220	35,020	Victoria	Seychelles
						South Africa
Conquest	1884	14,540,240	. . .	556.390	Maseru	Basutoland
Conquest	1885–1895	. . .	. . .	265,760	Mafeking	Bechuanaland
Conquest	1889	29,116,750	46,155,590	1,658,810	Lusaka	No. Rhodesia
Conquest	1889	50,387,090	43,959,240	1,764,000	Salisbury	So. Rhodesia
Treaty	1894	. . .	. . .	185,210	Mbabane	Swaziland
Conquest	1920	20,359,560	32,598,670	341,000	Windhoek	Southwest Africa
						West Africa
Treaty, cession	1807	4,199,260	2,679,950	249,270	Bathurst	Gambia
Treaty, cession	1672	41,134,210	44,644,340	3,571,000	Accra	Gold Coast
Settlement, purchase	1861–1900	54,639,490	68,824,340	21,800,000	Lagos	Nigeria
Conquest, annexation	1916	Included under	Nigeria	800,000	Buea	Cameroons
Treaty, cession	1787	14,540,240	18,841,930	1,768,480	Freetown	Sierra Leone
Conquest	1914	Included under	Gold Coast	391,520	. . .	Togoland, *Br.*
Conquest	1899	41,488,850	41,363,170	6,590,000	Khartum	Anglo-Egyptian Sudan
						IN ASIA
Cession, settlement	1839–1876	46,212,410	34,757,155	730,880	Aden	Aden (and Hadramaut)
Annexation	1914	21,471,840	13,265,420	449,490	Nokpsia	Cyprus
Treaty, cession	1842	187,620.680	154,893,050	1,600,000	Victoria	Hong Kong
. . .	. . .	. . .	. . .	79,281	. . .	Maldive Is.
Treaty, cession	1786, 1948	. . .	. . .	5,250,000	. . .	Malaya, Fed. of
Cession, protectorate	1881–1888	. . .	. . .	269,970	Sandakan	North Borneo
Treaty	1888	. . .	. . .	48,634	Brunei	Brunei
Cession	1946	. . .	. . .	500,000	Kuching	Sarawak
Cession	1824	. . .	. . .	948,300	Singapore	Singapore
						IN AUSTRALASIA
Annexation	1884	2,172,783	1,984,883	300,000	Port Moresby	Papua
Mandate	1920	. . .	. . .	688,400	. . .	New Guinea
Mandate	1920	1,235,570	2,031,120	66,450	Apia	West Samoa
Cession	1874	9,514,830	5,057,650	259,640	Suva	Fiji
Conquest	1914	. . .	. . .	2,794	. . .	Nauru
Settlement	1790	. . .	. . .	126	. . .	Pitcairn Is.
Cession, conquest	1893–1915	. . .	. . .	. . .	Suva, Fiji	Pacific Islands
Protectorate	1900	717,340	652,860	40,670	Nukualofa	Tonga
Colony	1892–1915	. . .	. . .	35,300	Ocean Island	Gilbert & Ellice Is.
Protectorate	1893	. . .	. . .	94,970	Tulagi	Solomon Is.
Treaty	1906	914,810	1,128,400	48,900	. . .	New Hebrides
Treaty	1938	. . .	. . .	. . .	. . .	Canton & Enderbury Is.
						IN AMERICA
Settlement	1612	9,849,320	141,050	34,970	Hamilton	Bermuda
Conquest, cession	1803–1814	17,832,750	17,582,860	381,320	Georgetown	British Guiana
Conquest	1798	7,834,320	1,974,700	59,149	Belize	British Honduras
Treaty, cession	1771	2,873,390	3,272,360	2,590	Port Stanley	Falkland Islands
						West Indies
Settlement	1609	7,278,180	1,419,310	80,640	Nassau	Bahamas
Settlement	1625	19,287,580	13,923,650	195,400	Bridgetown	Barbados
Conquest	1655–1670	38,631,580	19,287,580	1,314,430	Kingston	Jamaica
Annexation	1705	378,820	84,630	6,148	Grand Turk	Turks and Caicos Is.
Settlement	1623–1659	6,045,000	4,333,000	108,850	St. Johns	Leeward Islands
Conquest	1797	54,598,440	15,725,060	558,610	Port of Spain	Trinidad
Cession	1763–1783	6,482,000	1.206,000	251,840	St. George's	Windward Islands

RULERS OF ENGLAND

Name	Lineage	Period of Reign		Birth	Death
		A. D.	A. D.	A. D.	A. D.
	Anglo-Saxon Kings				
Egbert	First King of all England	827	839	775?	839
Ethelwulf	Son of Egbert	839	857	....	858
Ethelbald	Son of Ethelwulf	857	860	....	860?
Ethelbert	Second son of Ethelwulf	860	866	....	866?
Ethelred I	Third son of Ethelwulf	866	871	....	871
Alfred the Great	Fourth son of Ethelwulf	871	899	849	899
Edward the Elder	Son of Alfred	899	925	870?	925
Athelstan	Eldest son of Edward	925	940	895?	941
Edmund I	Brother of Athelstan	940	946	923	946 or 8
Edred	Brother of Edmund I	946	955	....	955?
Edwy	Son of Edmund I	955	959	939?	959
Edgar	Second son of Edmund I	959	975	943?	975
Edward the Martyr	Son of Edgar	975	978	961?	978
Ethelred II	Half-brother of Edward	978	1016	968	1016
Edmund Ironside	Eldest son of Ethelred	1016	1017	989	1017
	Danish Kings				
Canute	By conquest and election	1017	1035	995	1035
Harold I (Harefoot)	Son of Canute	1035	1040	....	1040
Hardicanute	Another son of Canute	1040	1042	1019	1042
	Saxon Kings				
Edward the Confessor	Son of Ethelred II	1042	1066	1004	1066
Harold II	Brother-in-law of Edward	1066	....	1022	1066
	Norman Kings				
William I	Second cousin to Edward the Confessor; obtained the Crown by conquest	1066	1087	1027	1087
William II	Third son of William I	1087	1100	1056	1100
Henry I	Youngest son of William I	1100	1135	1068	1135
Stephen	Third son of Stephen, Count of Blois	1135	1154	1105	1154
	The Plantagenets				
Henry II	Son of Geoffrey Plantagenet by Matilda, d. of Henry I	1154	1189	1133	1189
Richard I, the Lion-hearted	Eldest surviving son of Henry II	1189	1199	1157	1199
John	Youngest son of Henry II	1199	1216	1166	1216
Henry III	Eldest son of John	1216	1272	1207	1272
Edward I	Eldest son of Henry III	1272	1307	1239	1307
Edward II	Eldest surviving son of Edward I	1307	1327	1284	1327
Edward III	Eldest son of Edward II	1327	1377	1312	1377
Richard II	Son of the Black Prince, eldest son of Edward III	1377	1399	1366	1400
	House of Lancaster				
Henry IV	Son of John of Gaunt, fourth son of Edward III	1399	1413	1367	1413
Henry V	Eldest son of Henry IV	1413	1422	1387	1422
Henry VI	Only son of Henry V	1422	1461	1421	1471
	House of York				
Edward IV	His grandfather was Richard, son of Edmund, fifth son of Edward III	1461	1483	1441	1483
Edward V	Eldest son of Edward IV	1483	....	1470	1483
Richard III	Younger brother of Edward IV	1483	1485	1452	1485
	House of Tudor				
Henry VII	Son of Edmund, eldest son of Owen Tudor, by Katharine, widow of Henry V; his mother was great-granddaughter of John of Gaunt	1485	1509	1457	1509
Henry VIII	Only surviving son of Henry VII	1509	1547	1491	1547
Edward VI	Son of Henry VIII by Jane Seymour	1547	1553	1537	1553
Mary I	Daughter of Henry VIII by Katharine of Aragon	1553	1558	1516	1558
Elizabeth	Daughter of Henry VIII by Anne Boleyn	1558	1603	1533	1603
	House of Stuart				
James I	Son of Mary Queen of Scots, granddaughter of James IV and Margaret	1603	1625	1566	1625
Charles I	Only surviving son of James I (executed)	1625	1649	1600	1649
Commonwealth and Protectorate	Oliver Cromwell, Lord Protector	1649	1658	1599	1658
	Richard Cromwell, third son of Oliver, Lord Protector	1658	1659	1626	1712
Charles II	Eldest son of Charles I	1660	1685	1630	1685
James II	Second son of Charles I	1685	1689	1633	1701
William III and	Son of William, Prince of Orange, by Mary, daughter of Charles I	1689	1702	1650	1702
Mary II	Eldest daughter of James II	1689	1694	1662	1694
Anne	Second daughter of James II	1702	1714	1665	1714
	House of Hanover				
George I	Son of Elector of Hanover, by Sophia, daughter of Elizabeth, daughter of James I	1714	1727	1660	1727
George II	Only son of George I	1727	1760	1683	1760
George III	Grandson of George II	1760	1820	1738	1820
George IV	Eldest son of George III	1820	1830	1762	1830
William IV	Third son of George III	1830	1837	1765	1837
Victoria	Daughter of Edward, fourth son of George III	1837	1901	1819	1901
	House of Windsor *				
Edward VII	Son of Victoria	1901	1910	1841	1910
George V	Son of Edward VII	1910	1936	1865	1936
Edward VIII	Son of George V	1936	1936†	1894	....
George VI	Son of George V	1936	....	1895	....

* Adopted in place of Saxe-Coburg by George V, July 1917. † Accession, January 20; abdication, December 10.

CANADA

After the voyages of the Norsemen, Bjarni Herjulfson and Leif Ericson, in the 10th century, when, as related in the Norse sagas, they probably explored much of the east coast of Canada, no European for five centuries left evidence of setting foot on the American continent. Impelled by his own surmises as to the longitude of the east coast of Asia, and also by news of the landfall of Columbus, John Cabot, in 1496, obtained a commission from King Henry VII of England for a westward voyage of discovery under the English flag. In the spring of 1497 Cabot sailed from Bristol; on June 24 he sighted land, possibly Cape Breton island. His discovery furnished a ground for England's later claim to North American territory. The English did not follow up the advantage offered by the later explorations of John Cabot and his son Sebastian, doubtless because the reports about the new found land confuted John Cabot's boast that the wealth of Asia should flow into the port of London.

First Explorations and Settlements. By the early 16th century, French fishermen, among others, began to frequent the codbanks off Newfoundland. By sailing around the northern extremity of Newfoundland they discovered the Straits of Belle Isle, and became aware of the vast body of water into which the straits led. It was Jacques Cartier, a sailor of St. Malo in Brittany, who discovered this body of water to be the gulf of a great river, and with this discovery the story of Canadian exploration really begins. In 1534 Cartier sailed into the Gulf of St. Lawrence and took possession of its shores in the name of the French king. On a second voyage, in 1535-36, he ascended the St. Lawrence as far as the rapids by the island of Montreal. Following Cartier, attempts were made by the French to plant colonies along the coast of Acadia and the shores of the Gulf of St. Lawrence (Canada). The penetration and occupation of this latter region awaited the genius and devotion of Samuel Champlain. Champlain made his first voyage to the St. Lawrence in 1603; he began the first permanent settlement at Quebec in 1608. His activities during the next twenty years left an indelible impress upon the fortunes of the French in Canada. To him is due the discovery of Lake Champlain (the link between the St. Lawrence and the Hudson) as well as of Lake Ontario, and the establishment of a trading post at Montreal. But Champlain committed the French to an alliance with the Algonquin and Huron Indians against the more powerful confederacy of the Iroquois, who thus became the allies of the English both in war and in the fur trade. To this alliance is due in some measure the failure of the French to hold their empire in North America.

The conversion and the civilizing of the Indians were undertaken in earnest by the Jesuit fathers, who began their great mission on their arrival in Quebec in 1625. Many suffered martyrdom when their converts, the Hurons, were practically exterminated by the vengeful Iroquois. The Jesuit fathers shared in the exploration of the interior of the continent, where many a distant mission center attests their pious labors; they made the Church the most powerful influence in shaping the history of New France in the 17th and the 18th century.

Government of New France. To correct the abuses attending the early government and commerce of the colony, Richelieu, in 1627, organized the Hundred Associates, a company that controlled New France and enjoyed a monopoly of the fur trade until 1663. In that year Louis XIV constituted Canada a royal province. Its civil government was administered by a governor, an intendant, who was usually a lawyer, and a council. These were all appointed by the crown; no trace of representative government ever appeared in New France, nor, it may be added, was any Huguenot or heretic ever permitted to settle. Sturdy French peasants were encouraged to migrate from France; they brought with them the traditions of the seignioral system of land tenure, which was used in Canada as the basis of land grants.

Large tracts of uncleared land, called seigniories, were bestowed upon seigniors, who thus formed a landed noblesse. The seigniors held their estates by the "tenure of fealty and homage"; they enjoyed social leadership and judicial powers over the tenant farmers under them. The farmers, or habitants, received from their seignior a tenure resting upon payment of small annual rentals in money or in produce, together with the customary seignioral dues. The seigniories, sometimes called côtes, usually had the bank of a river for a base line. Each habitant received a rectangular strip of land running from the river into the woodland behind. The houses, one to each rectangular strip, were built close to the river front; the village bore the appearance of a single line of houses placed at wide intervals instead of a cluster of cottages grouped around a church, as in the European manor or seigniory. Since each habitant was expected to divide his land fairly among his children, the original rectangular farm became subdivided into mere ribbons of land, such as are to be seen today in the St. Lawrence valley. The system with its seignioral dues survived in Lower Canada (Quebec) until 1854, when, by a statute of that year, seignioral rights were terminated and seignioral dues commuted.

English and French Rivalry. In 1689, with the beginning of the world-wide struggle between England and France for maritime and commercial supremacy, the wars of the French and the English colonies for the control of America were opened in earnest. The warfare was carried on by means of cruel, merciless border raids, in which the Indians shared. The Treaty of Utrecht in 1713 gave England Acadia (now the provinces of Nova Scotia and New Brunswick) and recognized the English title to Newfoundland and to Hudson Bay Territory. For the next forty years the French tried to hold the interior country of the Lakes and the Mississippi valley, and to confine the English to the Atlantic seaboard. English pioneers from Virginia and Pennsylvania, pushing west to the Ohio, were checked at the Alleghenies by forces of the French and of the Indians friendly to them. The Iroquois for long held the balance of power, seeing their own safety in the rivalry of the two contending white nations. The Seven Years' war, commencing in the Ohio valley in 1756, turned at the start in favor of the French, until the fall of Louisburg in 1758, and the capture of Quebec by Wolfe in 1759 put an end to French power in America. Canada, as well as all the territory between the Alleghenies and the Mississippi, was given to England by the Treaty of Paris (1763).

An area comprising the portion of the St. Lawrence valley already settled by the French Canadians was erected at the close of the war into the province of Quebec, the Ohio valley and beyond being administered separately as an Indian reservation. The ill-advised attempt to introduce English law and English courts among the French of the new province of Quebec provoked so much discontent that in 1774 the Quebec act restored the old French civil law, at the same time virtually establishing the Roman Catholic Church. Both have helped to perpetuate the French language, which with English is recognized as an official language in the Dominion. The Quebec act also extended the area of the province to include the Indian reservation, which became the Northwest Territory of the United States after the Treaty of 1783. The delimitation of the various portions of the long boundary between Canada and the United States from the Northeast Boundary of 1783, through the adjustment of the 49th parallel, to the Alaska Award of 1903, has been an example of arbitration and treaty negotiation in international disputes.

Growth of the Provinces. The Continental Congress at the outbreak of the American Revolution tried to secure the adherence of the French Canadians of Quebec; but these remained neutral during the struggle. After the independence of the thirteen colonies had been acknowledged, thousands of loyalists—known later as United Empire Loyalists—assisted by the English government, found asylum in Nova Scotia and Quebec. Those who settled in Nova Scotia, being refused adequate representation in the provincial assembly, which had been instituted in 1758, petitioned for a separate government. For them the province of New Brunswick was formed out of the western part of Nova Scotia in 1784. Those taken to Upper Quebec were settled in the vicinity of Lake Ontario. Between them and the French Canadians in the lower part of the province, differences in language, in religion, and in law provoked an estrangement which seemed to make impolitic the further inclusion of the two races under one provincial government. By the Canada act, or the Constitutional act of 1791, Quebec was divided: the French-speaking province took the name of Lower Canada; Upper Canada, with its English-speaking loyalist pioneers, began its separate history under Governor Simcoe. Public land was offered to pioneers upon terms which soon raised their number to 30,000. York, later Toronto, grew up as the center of industry and commerce.

In both provinces, to a governor responsible only to the Colonial office, and to a council appointed by the governor, was added by the Constitutional act an elective assembly. The governor and council together had no means of controlling the assembly; nor had the assembly any means of making the governor and council responsible to its wishes or to the wishes of the people of the province. This fatal adjustment of constitutional machinery precipitated the long struggle for responsible government—a struggle that did not end until provincial assemblies acquired a position and procedure similar to that enjoyed by the British House of Commons.

Expansion and Union. The defense of Canada in the War of 1812 was the first general or "national" venture of the four unrelated provinces; it bore with special hardship, however, upon Upper Canada. At the same time the exploration of the great Northwest, the prairies and the Rocky mountains, as well as the Pacific coast, by Mackenzie and Vancouver, gave the first glimpses of a "national" domain. Lord Selkirk founded the Red River settlement, the beginning of the province of Manitoba, in 1812. Immigration, likewise the concern of all the provinces, had begun to increase through the work of land companies and colonization societies which brought in more than 150,000 people before 1833. But no "national" policy was possible until the issue of responsible government was settled. The question inflamed the politics of both Canadas until, in 1837, the *Patriotes* under L. J. Papineau, in the lower province, and the Reformers under W. L. Mackenzie, in the upper province, set up the flag of revolt. The armed insurrections, slight enough in themselves, were easily suppressed, but they served to direct the attention of the British government to the two difficulties under which the Canadas labored; namely, race friction and irresponsible rule. The government took the momentous step after 1837 of dispatching to Canada as high commissioner the earl of Durham, well known for his great wealth and for his radical opinions. The statesmanlike report, which he and his secretaries prepared, exposed clearly the impolicy of continuing the irresponsible rule of governor and council.

Durham allowed himself to form an adverse judgment upon the special claims of the French Canadians, and he fancied that he could devise a political expedient to bring about their ultimate Anglicization. To this end he proposed the union of the two provinces, carried out by the Union act in 1841. The plan to obliterate the distinctiveness of the French could not in the nature of things be successful, for the inclusion of both races into a single union government merely intensified their mutual hostility, and in the end forced the two races apart, to come together again on the basis of confederation instead of union.

The Union, however, achieved responsible government. To the Assembly of the new government, Upper and Lower Canada each was to send an equal number of representatives, regardless of any differences in the population. While, at the outset, this device served to protect the interests of the English-speaking minority, in the end it turned to their disadvantage when the balance of population stood in their favor. An executive council, or cabinet, chosen by the governor from the Council and the Assembly, made the constitution parliamentary in form. But cabinet responsibility to the Assembly was not actually settled until 1849, when the governor, Lord Elgin, acting in the full spirit of Durham's report, signed a bill granting compensation for losses of property in the rebellion in Lower Canada,—a bill acceptable to the French and to the Reformers, who together had a majority in the Assembly, but extremely distasteful to the "Tories." The signing of this bill marks the supremacy of the Canadian Assembly in its control of the executive. For his action Lord Elgin was stoned at Montreal by a "Tory" mob, which also set fire to the Parliament house. Mob violence prompted the removal of the capital to Bytown, renamed Ottawa, on the Ottawa river, which has since remained the capital.

Confederation. The impracticability of the Union, as seen in the Parliamentary deadlock, and the apprehension that Canada might be involved in the American Civil War, led in 1864 to a convention of delegates from all the provinces, who met in Quebec to confer upon a confederation. Under the guidance of such statesmen as John A. Macdonald, Charles Tupper, George Brown, George E. Cartier, D'Arcy McGee, and others, known as the Fathers of Confederation, a set of resolutions was adopted, which served as the basis of the British North America act passed by the Imperial Parliament in 1867. By this act, the provinces of Upper and Lower Canada, of Nova Scotia, and of New Brunswick were formally confederated into the Dominion of Canada. Newfoundland preferred not to enter the Confederation and still remains a separate part of the empire. Upper Canada became Ontario; Lower Canada took the name of Quebec. The anniversary of confederation, July 1, is Dominion Day, the national political holiday.

The federal constitution provides for a governor-general, a privy council, a Senate, and a House of Commons; the system of executive and legislative procedure follows the English Parliamentary model. In contrast to the Constitution of the United States, the British North America act, in view of the state rights controversy in the United States, accords to the provinces certain specific and explicit rights only, reserving to the Federal government all the general and residuary rights and prerogatives of sovereignty. Constitutional law has been concerned chiefly with the respective powers assigned to the provinces and to the Federal government, the ultimate appeal being to the judicial committee of the privy council at Westminster.

Unifying the Dominion. To give the Dominion its continental scope from ocean to ocean and to unify its widely separated parts was the task of Canadian statesmen in the two decades following 1867. In 1869 the Dominion acquired by purchase from the Hudson's Bay Company its title to the Northwest Territories. Thus the prairies, hitherto guarded as an exclusive preserve for the Indian fur trade, were thrown open to settlers and proved to be among the richest wheat yielding areas of the continent. Railways were to bind together all these distant outlying parts. New Brunswick and Nova Scotia had been influenced to consent to confederation by an agreement, incorporated in the British North America act, to unite them with Quebec and Ontario by a railway. This promise was fulfilled by the completion of the Intercolonial railway in 1876. After the Oregon boundary had been settled, the Hudson's Bay Company procured the creation of Vancouver island into a crown colony. On the mainland, owing to the discovery of gold in 1856, New Caledonia became a crown colony in 1858, under the name of British Columbia. The union of the two crown colonies under the latter title came in 1866. British Columbia joined the Confederation in 1871. Prince Edward Island agreed to enter the Confederation in 1873.

A serious difficulty in taking over the Northwest was raised by the half-breed and Indian revolt of 1869–70, led by Louis Riel. The trouble arose over the half-breeds' fear that their holdings under the Hudson's Bay title might be disregarded. The disturbance subsided when the new province of Manitoba was taken into the Confederation.

Sir John A. Macdonald headed the first federal cabinet after confederation (1867–73). In this administration, the outstanding disputes between the Dominion and the United States were settled by arbitration or negotiation. The issues involved the Newfoundland and east coast fisheries, the adjustment of the 49th parallel on the Pacific coast, and the losses due to the Fenian raids of 1866 and 1870–71. Macdonald took the first steps toward the construction of the transcontinental railway; but a scandal connected with campaign funds subscribed by a company seeking the charter brought his resignation. The Liberal leader, Alexander Mackenzie, formed a new ministry.

As leader of the Conservative opposition, Macdonald found it opportune to champion the "National Policy" of protection for Canadian industries; in 1878 he was returned to office on this platform. He led the Conservative government from that year until his death in 1891. A protective tariff was established, and, largely as a direct consequence, the Dominion secured the right to negotiate directly her own commercial treaties with foreign states. The first transcontinental railway, the Canadian Pacific, was completed late in 1885. Two others, the Grand Trunk Pacific and the Canadian Northern, later consolidated in the Canadian National system, have been built since. As the Canadian Pacific was being completed, Louis Riel led a second revolt of half-breed settlers in the Saskatchewan valley. This outbreak, easily suppressed by a military force, served to direct public and newspaper attention to the Northwest Territories. Settlers poured in, brought by the railway, and the Territories received representation at Ottawa. The two provinces of Saskatchewan and Alberta were constituted in 1905.

After the death of Sir John A. Macdonald, several Conservative ministries followed in rapid succession. Then the general elections of 1896 brought the Liberals into office under Sir Wilfrid Laurier.

National Development. The period of Liberal government which lasted for fifteen years proved to be a time of rapid economic development, accompanied by signs of a very distinctive national spirit. The sending of a contingent to South Africa during the Boer war showed this. The Laurier government lowered duties on some manufactured goods and instituted a British preference, but still retained the principle of adequate protection for Canadian industries. In 1903 the Alaska boundary dispute and questions relating to the joint use of the Great Lakes and other boundary waters were settled with the United States. The Imperial government left Canada free to reach an agreement with Japan in 1907, upon the restriction of Japanese immigration into the Dominion. Reciprocity with the United States became a major political issue in 1910. Previously, in 1854, the two countries began a reciprocity agreement which continued until the United States abrogated it in 1866. In 1911 the Laurier government took the question to the country at a general election and were defeated. The Conservatives under Sir Robert Borden formed a ministry.

Canada in World War I. In 1912 the Borden government had proposed to contribute three dreadnaughts to the imperial navy at a cost of $35,000,000, as Canada's share of imperial defense. The measure was defeated by the Liberals in the Senate, who wanted an exclusively Canadian navy. But when war came Canada responded instantly and heroically to the challenge. The first contingent of the Canadian Expeditionary Force sailed from Quebec in September 1914, and half a million men followed them overseas. See *World War I*.

Post-War Period. The new status of Canada within the Empire was shown by the appointment in 1926 of a Canadian minister to Washington. Dissatisfaction with the railroad and tariff policies of the Conservatives and the rise of a new Farmers', or Progressive, party caused their defeat in 1921. The Liberal party, led by W. L. Mackenzie King, and supported by the Progressives, controlled Parliament until 1930. The Conservatives under R. B. Bennett were committed to a high tariff policy, and established a central bank, the Bank of Canada. Economic discontent brought back Mackenzie King and the Liberals in 1935. One of their first measures was a reciprocity agreement with the United States.

Following the World War, the liquor prohibitory laws were mostly repealed. In 1924 the United Church of Canada was formed, consisting of sections of the Methodist, Presbyterian, and Congregational communions. An imperial Economic Conference, held at Ottawa in 1932 arrived at agreements for granting mutual tariff and other trade concessions among the British nations. The governor-general, John Buchan, Lord Tweedsmuir, died in February 1940. He was succeeded by the Earl of Athlone, and he, in 1946, by Viscount Alexander of Tunis.

World War II. On September 10, 1939, a week later than Great Britain, Canada declared war on Germany; war followed with Italy in 1940 and with Japan in 1941. The King cabinet, returned to power in 1940, carried on. The National Resources Nationalization act placed all property at the government's disposal and conscripted all man power for home defense. In 1942, against the opposition of Quebec, conscription for overseas service was authorized. In 1943-44, Canadian troops figured prominently in Allied victories in Sicily and Italy. The First Canadian Army under General Crerar opened the battle for the Ruhr in February 1945. The navy concentrated on convoy work in the Atlantic.

In August 1940 a Permanent Joint Board of Defense brought about cooperation with the United States for hemisphere defense. The expense of the war was met by a threefold increase in taxation and the increase of the public debt to over 13 billion dollars. Careful control of man-power utilized nearly 60 per cent of the population above 14. By December 1943, 13.6 per cent were engaged in war work, and 8.6 per cent were in the armed forces. In 1944 the latter numbered 992,103, 40 per cent of those of military age. The casualties of the war were 104,-925, 41,371 killed; the cost, $20,255,865, 996, $1688 per capita.

Prime Minister King and the Liberals were returned to office in 1945, in spite of the rise of a new leftist party, the Co-operative Commonwealth Federation. A new law creating Canadian citizenship was enacted. The war controls were gradually relaxed, but in 1948 a stringency in foreign exchange forced the renewal of some restrictions. In 1946 revelations of widespread Russian espionage resulted in the trial and conviction of several Canadian citizens. Prime Minister King retired from office in November 1948, after a term of service longer than any other Dominion premier, and was succeeded by the new leader of the Liberal party, Louis Stephen St. Laurent. Newfoundland at last decided to join the Dominion, and became the tenth province in 1949.

GOVERNORS-GENERAL OF CANADA

Name	Title While in Office	Born	Parents: Father	Parents: Mother
Sir Charles Stanley	4th Viscount Monck, G. C. M. G.	1819	C. J. K. Monck, 3d Viscount	Bridget Willington
Sir John Young	1st Lord Lisgar, G. C. M. G.	1807	Sir William Young	Lucy Frederick
Frederick T. H. T. Blackwood	Earl of Dufferin, K. P., K. C. B., G. C. M. G., 1st Marquess of Dufferin and Ava	1828	Price Blackwood, 4th Baron Dufferin	Helen Sheridan
John Douglas S. Campbell	The Marquess of Lorne, K. T., G. C. M. G., 9th Duke of Argyll	1845	George S. Campbell, 8th Duke of Argyll	Elizabeth, dt. 2d Duke of Sutherland
Henry C. K. Fitz-Maurice	The 5th Marquess of Lansdowne, G. C. M. G.	1845	Henry Fitz-Maurice, 4th Marquess of Lansdowne	Emily Jane, dt. Comte de Flahault
Frederick A. Stanley	Lord Stanley of Preston, G. C. B., 16th Earl of Derby	1841	Edward Geoffrey, 14th Earl of Derby	Emma, dt. of 1st Baron Skelmersdale
John C. Gordon	The Earl of Aberdeen, K. T., G. C. M. G., 1st Marquess of Aberdeen and Temair	1847	George J. J. Gordon, 5th Earl of Aberdeen	Mary Baillie
Gilbert J. M. K. Elliot	The 4th Earl of Minto, G. C. M. G.	1845	William H. Elliot, 3d Earl of Minto	Emma, dt. of Sir T. Hislop, Bart.
Albert H. G. Grey	The 4th Earl Grey, G. C. M. G.	1851	Charley Grey, 2d son 2d Earl Grey	Mary, dt. 1st Baron Ponsonby
	Field Marshal His Royal Highness the 1st Duke of Connaught, K. G.	1850	H. R. H. The Prince Consort	H. M. Queen Victoria
Victor C. W. Cavendish	The 9th Duke of Devonshire, K. G., G. C. M. G., G. C. V. O.	1868	Lord Edward Cavendish, 3d son 7th Duke Devon	Lady Blanche, dt. 6th Earl of Carlisle
Julian H. G. Byng	General the 1st Lord Byng of Vimy, G. C. B., G. C. M. G., M. V. O.	1862	George S. Byng, 2d Earl of Strafford	Hon. Harriet, dt. 1st Baron Chesham
Freeman Freeman-Thomas	The 1st Lord Willingdon of Ratton, G. B. E., G. C. S. I., G. C. I. E.	1866	Frederick Freeman Thomas	Mabel, dt. of 1st Viscount Hampden
Vere Brabazon Ponsonby	The 9th Earl of Bessborough	1880	Edward Ponsonby, 8th Earl of Bessborough	Blanche Vere
John Buchan	1st Baron Tweedsmuir	1875	Rev. John Buchan	Helen Masterton
Alexander A. F. W. A. G. Cambridge	1st Earl of Athlone	1874	Duke of Teck	Princess Mary Adelaide
Harold R. L. G. Alexander	Viscount Alexander of Tunis	1891	James, 4th Earl of Caledon	Lady Elizabeth Graham Toler

PREMIERS OF CANADA SINCE

Name	Born: When	Born: Where	Parents: Father	Parents: Mother	Religious Connection	Educational Advantages
Sir John A. Macdonald	1815	Glasgow, Scotland	Hugh	Helen Shaw	Anglican	Grammar School, Kingston, Ontario
Alexander Mackenzie	1822	Logierait, Scotland	Alexander	Mary Fleming	Baptist	Parish School
Hon. Sir John A. Macdonald (Second Term)	1815	Glasgow, Scotland	Hugh	Helen Shaw	Anglican	Grammar School, Kingston, Ontario
Sir J. J. C. Abbott	1821	St. Andrews, Quebec	Joseph	Harriet Bradford	Anglican	McGill University
Sir J. S. D. Thompson	1844	Halifax, Nova Scotia	John S.	Charlotte Pottinger	Roman Catholic	Academy, Halifax
Sir Mackenzie Bowell	1823	Rickinghall, England	John	. . . . . .	Methodist	Printer's Apprentice
Sir Charles Tupper, Bart.	1821	Amherst, Nova Scotia	Charles	Miriam Lockhart	Baptist	Edinburgh University
Sir Wilfrid Laurier	1841	St. Lin, Quebec	Carolus	Mariette Martineau	Roman Catholic	L'Assomption College, McGill University
Sir Robert L. Borden	1854	Grand Pré, Nova Scotia	Andrew	Eunice Laird	Anglican	Academy, Horton, Nova Scotia
Arthur Meighen*	1874	Anderson, Ontario	Joseph	Mary Meighen	Presbyterian	Toronto University
W. L. Mackenzie King†	1874	Kitchener, Ontario	John	Isabel Mackenzie	Presbyterian	Toronto, Chicago, and Harvard Universities
Richard B. Bennett	1870	Hopewell, N. B.	Henry	Henrietta Stiles	United	Dalhousie University
Louis Stephen St. Laurent	1882	Compton, Quebec	J. B. Moise	Mary Broderick	Roman Catholic	St. Charles Coll. Laval Univ.

*Besides the term of office here indicated, Meighen was premier from July 13, 1926, following the resignation of Mackenzie King,

SINCE CONFEDERATION (1867)

Educational Advantages	Profession	Date Married	Wife's Name	Date of Appointment	Date of Assuming Office	Date of Death
Trinity College, Dublin	Lawyer	1844	Elizabeth, dt. Earl of Rathedown	June 1, 1867	July 1, 1867	Nov. 29, 1894
Eton, Oxford	Lawyer	1835	Adelaide Dalton	Dec. 29, 1868	Feb. 2, 1869	Oct. 6, 1876
Eton, Oxford	Diplomatist	1862	Harriot Hamilton	May 22, 1872	June 25, 1872	Feb. 12, 1902
Eton, St. Andrews, Cambridge	Author, Historian	1871	H. R. H. Princess Louise, 4th dt. Queen Victoria	Oct. 5, 1878	Nov. 25, 1878	May 2, 1914
Eton, Oxford	Statesman, Administrator	1869	Lady Maud Hamilton, dt. 1st Duke of Abercorn	Aug. 18, 1883	Oct. 23, 1883	June 3, 1927
Eton	Army	1864	Lady Constance, dt. 4th Earl of Clarendon	May 1, 1888	June 11, 1888	June 14, 1908
St. Andrews and Oxford	Statesman, Administrator	1877	Hon. Ishbel Marjoribanks, dt. 1st Baron Tweedmouth	May 22, 1893	Sept. 18, 1893	Mar. 7, 1934
Eton, Cambridge	Statesman, Administrator	1883	Mary, dt. Gen. Hon. Charley Grey	July 30, 1898	Nov. 12, 1898	Mar. 14, 1914
Harrow, Cambridge	Statesman, Administrator	1877	Alice Holford	Sept. 26, 1904	Dec. 10, 1904	Aug. 29, 1917
Royal Military Academy, Woolwich	. . . .	1879	H. R. H. the Princess Louise, 3d dt. H. R. H. Prince Frederick Charles of Prussia	Mar. 21, 1911	Oct. 13, 1911	Jan. 16, 1942
Eton, Cambridge	Statesman, Administrator	1892	Lady Evelyn Fitz-Maurice, dt. 5th Marquess of Lansdowne	Aug. 19, 1916	Nov. 11, 1916	May 6, 1938
. . . .	Army	1902	Marie, dt. Hon. Sir Richard Moreton	Aug. 2, 1921	Aug. 11, 1921	June 6, 1935
Eton, Cambridge	Administrator	1892	Hon. Marie Adelaide, dt. 1st Earl of Brassey	Aug. 5, 1926	Oct. 2, 1926	Aug. 12, 1941
Harrow, Cambridge	Lawyer	1912	Roberte de Neuflize, dt. Baron Jean de Neuflize	Feb. 9, 1931	Apr. 4, 1931	
Glasgow, Oxford	Publisher, Author	1907	Susan Charlotte, dt. Hon. Norman Grosvenor	Mar. 27, 1935	Nov. 2, 1935	Feb. 11, 1940
Eton, Sandhurst	Statesman, Soldier	1904	Princess Alice, dt. Duke of Albany	April 3, 1940	June 21, 1940	
Harrow, Sandhurst	Army	1931	Lady Margaret Diana Bingham	July 31, 1945	April 12, 1946	

CONFEDERATION (1867)

Profession	Date Married	Wife's Name	Party Connection	Appointed	Resigned	Died	Place of Death
Lawyer	1843 1867	Isabella Clark (d. 1857) Agnes Bernard	Conservative	July 1, 1867	Nov. 6, 1873	1891	Ottawa, Ontario
Stonecutter	 1853	Helen Neil (d. 1852) Jane Sym	Liberal	Nov. 7, 1873	Oct. 16, 1878	1892	Toronto, Ontario
Lawyer	1843 1867	Isabella Clark (d. 1857) Agnes Bernard	Conservative	Oct. 17, 1878	June 6, 1891 (Died)	1891	Ottawa, Ontario
Lawyer	1849	Mary Bethune	Conservative	June 16, 1891	Dec. 5, 1892	1893	Montreal, Quebec
Lawyer	1871	Annie Affleck	Conservative	Dec. 5, 1892	Dec. 12, 1894 (Died)	1894	Windsor Castle, England
Journalist	1847	Harriet L. Moore	Conservative	Dec. 21, 1894	April 27, 1896	1917	Belleville, Ontario
Physician	1846	Frances Morse	Conservative	May 1, 1896	July 8, 1896	1915	Bexley Heath, England
Lawyer	1868	Zoe Lafontaine	Liberal	July 11, 1896	Oct. 6, 1911	1919	Ottawa, Ontario
Lawyer	1889	Laura Bond	Conservative	Oct. 10, 1911	July 10, 1920	1937	Ottawa, Ontario
Lawyer	1904	Isabel Cox	Conservative	July 10, 1920*	Dec. 29, 1921*		
Publicist	. . . .		Liberal	Dec. 29, 1921†	Aug. 7, 1930†		
Lawyer	. . . .		Conservative	Aug. 7, 1930	Oct. 14, 1935	1947	Dorking, England
Lawyer	1908	Jeanne Renault	Liberal	Nov. 15, 1948			

until September 14, 1926. †Reappointed October 15, 1935, and served until November 15, 1948.

DEVELOPMENT OF THE PROVINCES OF CANADA—TABLE I

PROVINCE	Origin and Meaning of Name	Area Square Miles	Early Settlements: Where	When	By Whom	First Separate Gov't.	Entered Confed-eratio
Alberta . . .	In honor of H.R.H., Princess Louise Alberta, dt. of Queen Victoria, wife of marquis of Lorne, governor-general of Canada.	255,285	Ft. la Jonquière (Now Calgary) Ft. Athabaska	1752 1778	Sieur de Niverville Peter Pond	1882	1905
British Columbia . .	Devised and chosen by Queen Victoria (1858). "Columbia" on many old maps of this region.	355,855	Nootka	1788 1789	Capt. Meares Martinez	1858	1871
Manitoba . .	From Indian *Manito-Wabo*, meaning "narrows of the Great Spirit," from wind rushing through the narrows.	251,832	Ft. York (Nelson) Ft. Saint Charles Ft. Rouge	1686 1732 1736	Hudson's Bay Company Sieur de la Verendrye	1870	1870
New Brunswick . . .	In honor of English royal family, originally of German line of Brunswick-Luneburg.	27,985	Sainte Croix Port Royal	1604 1605	Sieur de Monts Sieur de Monts	1784	1867
Newfoundland	First called *Terra Nova*, New Land; Newfoundland appears about 1620.	42,734 (Labrador, 110,000)	Ferryland	1638	Sir David Kirke	1728	1949
Northwest Terr's: ** .	From geographical location.	1,309,682	. . . .	. . .	. . . .	1876	
Keewatin	Cree for "north wind."	. . .	. . . .	. . .	. . . .	1882	
Franklin	After Sir John Franklin.	. . .	. . . .	. . .	. . . .	1895	
Mackenzie	After Sir Alexander Mackenzie.	. . .	. . . .	. . .	. . . .	1895	
Nova Scotia	New Scotland.	21,428	Port Royal (Annapolis, 1710)	1605	Sieur de Monts	1710† 1713‡	1867
Ontario . .	After Lake Ontario,—Iroquois and Huron for "the beautiful or the great lake."	407,262	Ft. Rouille (Now Toronto) Ft. Frontenac	1749 1673	French traders Frontenac	1791	1867
Prince Edward Island . .	In honor of duke of Kent, Edward Augustus, father of Queen Victoria.	2,184	Port la Joie (Charlottetown)	1713	Acadians	1769	1873
Quebec . . .	In Algonquin, Kebec means "narrowing of the waters," referring to narrowing of the Saint Lawrence at the present city of Quebec.	594,434	Tadousac Quebec	1600 1608	Chauvin and Pont-Grave Champlain	1760† 1763‡	1867
Saskatchewan	From the river Saskatchewan. Cree for "rapid river."	251,700	Ft. Cumberland Ft. Chipewyan	1774 1788	Samuel Hearne R. Mackenzie	1882	1905
Yukon . . .	From Yukon river. Yukon is an Indian term for "the river."	207,076	Dawson	1896	Gold seekers	1898	

DEVELOPMENT OF THE PROVINCES OF CANADA—TABLE II

PROVINCE	Original Territory or District from which Derived	Population Entering Confederation ††	Pop. 1931	Pop. 1941	Per Cent Increase 1931-1941	Rural and Urban Population 1941	* Largest City and Capital
Alberta . . .	Formerly Alberta and part of Athabaska, Saskatchewan, and Assiniboia, districts of original N. W. Territories.	73,022 (1901)	731,605	796,169	8.8	(R) 489,583 (U) 306,586	Edmonton.
British Columbia . .	Vancouver island and New Caledonia (British Columbia after 1858) joined in 1866.	36,247 (1871)	694,263	817,861	17.8	374,467 443,394	Vancouver. Victoria.
Manitoba . .	Red River Settlement.	25,228 (1871)	700,139	729,744	4.2	407,871 321,873	Winnipeg.
New Brunswick . . .	Part of Acadia; later, county of Sunbury, Nova Scotia.	252,047 (1861)	408,219	457,401	12.0	313,978 143,423	Saint John. Fredericton.
Newfoundland	Separately settled for fisheries.	325,000	294,304 (1935)	320,101 (1945)	8.6	234,244 85,857	St. John's.
Northwest Terr's: ** . Keewatin Franklin Mackenzie	Prince Rupert's Land and Hudson's Bay Co's Territory.	. . . .	9,204	12,028	30.7	(R) 12,028	Administered from Ottawa. Land Office at Fort Smith.
Nova Scotia	A portion of Acadia.	330,857 (1861)	512,846	577,962	12.7	310,422 267,540	Halifax.
Ontario . .	Formerly Upper Canada, part of old province of Quebec.	1,396,091 (1861)	3,431,683	3,787,655	10.4	1,449,022 2,338,633	Toronto.
Prince Edward Island . .	Formerly Isle Saint Jean, attached to Acadia.	94,021 (1871)	88,038	95,047	8.0	70,707 24,340	Charlotte-town.
Quebec . . .	A portion of "Canada" under French rule before 1760.	1,111,566 (1861)	2,874,255	3,331,882	15.9	1,222,198 2,109,684	Montreal. Quebec.
Saskatchewan	From parts of Saskatchewan, Athabaska, and Assiniboia, districts of old Northwest Territories.	91,279 (1901)	921,785	895,992	−2.8	600,846 295,146	Regina.
Yukon . . .	Part of old Northwest Territories.	27,219 (1901)	4,230	4,914	16.7	3,871 1,043	Dawson.

* Where but one name is given, it indicates both the largest city and the capital; elsewhere, the second name is that of the capital. † Military rule. ‡ Province. ** Provisional districts. †† Figures in parenthesis indicate date of census.

PROMINENT CANADIANS

Robert Laird Borden
Lord Graham
Sir John William Dawson

Lord Strathcona
Sir Wilfrid Laurier
Sir Sandford Fleming

Sir Charles Tupper
Sir Robert Alexander Falconer
Sir John Alexander Macdonald

Photo for 1 copyright by Detroit Photographic Co.; for 2 from Brown Bros.; photos for 3 to 9 inclusive from Publishers' Photo Service.

HISTORIC CANADA

1 Church of Sainte Anne de Beaupré, Quebec. 2 Old Church, Grand Pré, N. S. 3 Northwest Mounted Police. 4 Champlain Monument, Quebec. 5 Evangeline Monument, Grand Pré, N. S. 6 Ancient Fort, Annapolis Royal, N. S. 7 Fort Garry, Winnipeg. 8 Martello Tower, Halifax. 9 Old Clock Tower, Halifax.

IRELAND

The history of no other country is so interwoven with mystery and legend as is that of Ireland. To the early classic writers, this island of mists and shadows was known under various names, such as *Ierne* or *Hibernia*, the "Land of Winter," *Ogygia*, the "Distant Land," *Ultima Thule*, the "Farthest Reach," and, to native historians, as *Innisfail*, the "Island of Destiny,"—this last, in the light of Ireland's manifold vicissitudes, perhaps the most appropriate name of all.

Early History. In the Annals of the Four Masters and in the chronicles of Keating, we read of certain tribes and races of people who invaded the island at different remote periods. We are told of the Partholans who came to Ireland about 1484 B. C., and of the Nemedians who succeeded them about 1154 B. C. The Firbolgs next are said to have divided the land into fifths about 738 B. C.; then the Tuatha Dé Danaan (*thōō'ă* THă THōōn-ŏn'), or the tribes of the god Danu, about 701 B. C., overcame the Firbolgs; and the Milesians or Scots from Scythia, about 504 B. C., in turn conquered the Tuatha Dé Danaan.

Heremon, who was of Milesian stock, is mentioned about this time as being sole and supreme ruler of Ireland, and he is believed to have been the head of a long line of Milesian monarchs who reigned over the land in unbroken succession down to the time of Roderick O'Connor (1116–98 A. D.), the last of the native Irish kings. But, between Heremon and O'Connor, the long list of kings is so legendary as to be unreliable, and their deeds of prowess often savor more of fiction than of fact. We may except from this judgment, however, Conn of the Hundred Battles in the 1st century after Christ, Cormac, who lived a century later, Tuathal (*tōōl*), who established the royal Feis (*fāsh*) at Tara, Niall of the Nine Hostages, who invaded Britain and scoured the seas off northern Gaul, and Dathi, who in the 5th century lost his life at the foot of the Alps.

Manners, Customs, and Laws. Though the ancient Irish were pagans, they were not barbarians. They were a pastoral people who tilled the land and tended their flocks; their houses were built of wickerwork made of reeds covered with clay. The common dress of the men was the kilt of saffron color, with shirt, tunic, and *brat* (*brŏtth*) or cloak buckled at the shoulder; the women wore a long outer garment reaching to the feet. Writing of their love of music and literature, Dr. Douglas Hyde says: "The love of literature of a traditional type in song, in poem, and in saga was more nearly universal in Ireland than in any other country of Europe." Their marvelous skill as metal workers in bronze, gold, silver, and enamel may be witnessed in the priceless treasures preserved today in the National Museum of Dublin.

An *ardri* (*ŏrd-rē'*), or "high king," ruled over the whole of Ireland, and the kings, princes, and chieftains of the various provinces were subject and paid tribute to him. The laws were made and dispensed by *brehons*, or "judges," who, with the poets and druids, belonged to the royal household. The pagan Irish worshiped the sun as the author of all life and paid an inferior homage to rivers and wells. They also believed in the "good people," or fairies; and the *beanside* (banshee), or "fairy woman," was known to come always to warn them of approaching death.

Dawn of Christianity. It was in such spiritual darkness that St. Patrick found the people of Ireland when he was sent by Pope Celestine to that country in 432 A. D. Forty-four years before, as a youth of sixteen, he had been taken a captive to Ireland and sold as a slave to a druid, with whom he dwelt six years. During his years of servitude, he had learned the Celtic tongue and had become familiar with the druidical rites and ceremonies. Thus equipped, he now began to preach the gospel of Christianity. He appeared before the high king at Tara, where he put the druid priests to confusion, with the result that the ardri and the chief *ollam* (*ŏl'lăv*), or "poet," were then and there converted to the new faith. Thenceforward until his death, which took place at Saul, March 17, 493, Patrick's progress throughout the island was a veritable triumph. Schools and monasteries arose throughout the land, and, from the 5th to the 8th century, Ireland was acknowledged as the center of Western culture, while her monks went forth to found monasteries and new schools of learning in almost every country of Europe.

Invasion of the Danes. But the progress of civilization brought about by religion and learning was fated to be checked at the close of the 8th century by the invasions of the Danes. These ruthless barbarians ravaged and destroyed wherever they went, and everywhere left smoking ruins in their trail to testify how well they had done their work. After 200 years of this career of savagery, they were completely overthrown (1014) at the battle of Clontarf by Brian Boroihme, who paid the price of victory with his life.

Anglo-Norman Period. The death of Brian now became the source of much dissension among the Irish, because of the partition of the land made by him in favor of his three sons. On the pretense of quelling such strife, Henry II sought to gain possession of Ireland. A bull or papal edict, purporting to have been sent by Adrian IV but now generally regarded as fictitious, lent color to his good intentions. In 1172 he arrived in the island and proceeded to divide the country into fiefs, which he gave to the Anglo-Norman knights who, but a few years before, had come to the assistance of MacMurrough, the deposed king of Leinster. For many years thereafter, the history of Ireland is one of plunder and persecution. In 1315, after the battle of Bannockburn, Edward Bruce hastened to the side of the Irish in an attempt to overthrow the English power. Though at first successful, he was slain at Faugart the following year. His gallant example, however, resulted in a general decline of English dominion in Ireland, and the descendants of the Anglo-Norman knights in a short time became *ipsis Hibernis hiberniores*, "more Irish than the Irish themselves." At the dawn of the 16th century, England's thralldom of Ireland might be said to have been on the wane. Unfortunately, as a result of the continuous feuds between the chiefs of Irish descent and those of English descent, lawlessness and irreligion had grown apace.

The Tudor Period. In 1547 the Parliament of Dublin gave Henry VIII the title of king of Ireland and also passed the Act of Supremacy, making him spiritual head of the Irish Church. However, neither clergy nor people could be won from their allegiance to Rome. As a consequence, Henry dissolved the monasteries and confiscated the church lands, large portions of which he divided among the most powerful of the chieftains in order to conciliate them. The religious changes under Edward VI and Mary had little effect on Ireland. Under Mary, the natives of King's county and Queen's county were deprived of their lands and driven from their homes to make room for English colonists. In the reign of Elizabeth, a series of rebellions took place under Shawn O'Neill, Desmond, and Hugh O'Neill, earl of Tyrone. After ten years' fighting, Hugh O'Neill was defeated in 1603, and the whole of the island passed into the hands of the English. No less than 600,000 acres of land belonging to Irish chieftains were divided among English colonists.

Under the Stuarts. In the reign of James I (1603–25) a similar confiscation of land took place, when 800,000 acres of Ulster land became forfeited to the crown and were planted with English

Protestants and Scotch Presbyterians. The policy of spoliation continued under Charles I, when the best lands in Wicklow, Wexford, County Leitrim, West Meath, and Longford were handed over to the English planters. Despairing of redress, the exasperated Irish rose in rebellion under Roderick O'Moore. It was planned by the rebels to take Dublin castle and the chief garrison towns. Their attempt on Dublin castle was frustrated, though they succeeded in capturing many of the towns, and it is said that in the course of the conflict 30,000 of the planters perished. This rebellion has been described by certain writers as the "massacre of 1641," but, according to the English historian Lingard, the appellation is as unjust as it is untrue.

In August 1649, Cromwell landed in Dublin with an army of 10,000 men. He laid siege to Drogheda and put to the sword 2000 Irish soldiers who formed the garrison. A month later a similar slaughter took place at Wexford. Within two years the whole country was subjugated, and the fairest portions of Ulster, Munster, and Leinster were divided among the Cromwellian soldiery. It is estimated that no fewer than 20,000 of the Irish were sold as slaves in America, while 40,000 took up military service in the various armies of Europe. Cromwell died in 1658, and Charles II (1660–85) was restored to the throne. With the best of intentions, he succeeded in doing but little to ameliorate the conditions of the impoverished Irish, except that, by Act of Settlement, 600 of them were restored to their lands.

William of Orange. In the English revolution of 1688, the Catholics of Ireland rallied to the side of James II, while the Protestants supported William of Orange. William crossed over to Ireland in 1689 and defeated the Irish forces under James at the battle of the Boyne, and, in the following year, Limerick, which had been gallantly defended by Sarsfield, capitulated. The treaty that was signed, giving to Catholics the privileges they enjoyed under Charles II, was callously broken, and Limerick came to be known as the "city of the violated treaty." The English Parliament decreed that one million acres of land should be divided among the Protestants, and a cruel code of penal laws was forthwith enacted. Though these laws were directed mainly against Catholics, they proved fatal alike to the Irish Protestants. All Irish trade with the English colonies was prohibited, and commerce and industries, including the great woolen trade which had been built up by Irish Protestants, were deliberately crushed. Thus it was that the best elements of the country were forced to emigrate,—the Catholics to serve in the armies of France and Spain, the Protestants to carry their industries to America. The elaboration of such infamous laws could have no other effect than embittering those against whom they were made. Secret societies sprang up over all the land, and in 1798 a rebellion was organized by the Society of United Irishmen. The peasantry rose in Wexford, but after a gallant fight they were overcome by the British soldiery at the battle of Vinegar Hill.

The Act of Union. The British government under Pitt now decided to unite the English and Irish parliaments. To effect this, $8,000,000 was spent in bribing and in buying up the petty boroughs which held the majority of the seats in the Irish House of Commons. The Act of Union was accordingly proclaimed in 1801.

George III refused to sign a measure introduced by Pitt to emancipate the Catholics of Ireland; thereupon the Catholic Association was inaugurated and, under the leadership of O'Connell, forced the government to bring in an emancipation bill which received the assent of George IV on the 13th of April, 1829. Following this victory, O'Connell founded an association for the repeal of the Union. The government, fearing sedition, suppressed the association.

In 1847-48 Ireland was stricken by an appalling famine due to the failure of the potato crop. Thousands died of hunger, while vast numbers emigrated, especially to America, with hatred for England in their hearts and vengeance on their lips. In 1848 the Young Ireland party made an attempt at revolt, which was immediately crushed and the leaders transported. In 1864 a conspiracy originating with the Fenians, having as its object the separation of England and Ireland, was discovered and likewise suppressed by the British government.

From this time onward there were two views taken among British politicians regarding Ireland, one favoring coercion, the other supporting a policy of conciliation. Gladstone, in 1869, disestablished the Protestant Episcopal Church of Ireland, but he was unable to carry the whole of the Liberal party with him on his Home Rule bill of 1886. Again, in 1892, with a small majority of forty, he failed to force his second Home Rule bill through an antagonistic House of Lords.

In August 1914, the World War broke out. Asquith was now prime minister. He had been elected on a Home Rule platform and had succeeded in placing his Home Rule bill on the statute book. But Ulster had to be reckoned with. Four of the Ulster counties, with Carson at their head, opposed the Act and threatened armed resistance. The government, thus intimidated, showed signs of vacillation, and it was arranged that the Act should not come into force until the termination of the war.

Sinn Fein's Proclamation. But those who knew Ireland from within were aware of two great forces which had long been silently leavening the life of the Irish people socially and intellectually. One of these forces was the Gaelic League, whose main object was the rejuvenation of the national language and the popularizing of all things Gaelic. The other and greater force, which had sprung from the League as a natural growth, was that of Sinn Fein (*shĭng fān*), a society of young Irish intellectuals. They had grown impatient of the Dead Sea fruits of constitutional methods and into the old bottles of Irish politics had poured a new wine. The Sinn Fein, in Easter week of 1916, rose in rebellion against England and proclaimed Ireland a republic.

After a week's severe fighting in Dublin, the republican army was defeated and fifteen of the leaders were executed. But the spirit of Sinn Fein did not die. In the general election of 1918, Sinn Fein swept the Nationalist party out of existence, and the Dail Eireann (*THô'il ârn*) was set up as the one and only parliament of Ireland. Once more they declared Ireland a republic, insisting on their right of self-determination and on that same independence which had been granted to Poland, Lithuania, and Czechoslovakia. Lloyd George took the position of Abraham Lincoln in the American Civil War as a precedent, and declared it was impossible to allow of Ireland's secession. To this, Sinn Fein replied that Ireland had never been willingly a part of the United Kingdom and that there was therefore no question of seceding. Such was the state of affairs in the autumn and winter of 1918 when, in reprisal for the guerrilla tactics of the Irish republican army, the Black and Tans, auxiliary mercenary troops, burned the city of Cork and sacked the town of Balbriggan.

The Irish Free State. At last, after two and a half years of unremittent fighting, outside influence was brought to bear so that a truce was proclaimed and the leaders of the provisional government of Ireland agreed to meet the representatives of the British government. After several months of conference, on December 6, 1921, at a memorable all-night sitting, a treaty was signed in which Ireland was given the status of a Free State in the British Commonwealth, and by which Ulster was left outside its provisions to choose her own path and destiny under the Parliament of Northern Ireland, which had already been opened in state by King George on June 22, 1921. Eamonn De Valera, president of the Irish Republic, dissatisfied with the terms of the treaty, resigned, and Arthur Griffith was elected president of the Irish Free State, with Michael Collins as head of the provisional government.

The republican extremists now, however, became filled with the bitterness of disappointment at what they considered the betrayal of Ireland's cause by the plenipotentiaries who had signed the treaty. They accordingly planned a *coup d'état* by which to overthrow the provisional government. This attempt was for a time averted by the action of Premier Michael Collins, who invited De Valera to form with him a coalition administration.

Winston Churchill, secretary for the colonies, denounced in the British House of Commons this Collins-De Valera agreement and warned the colonial secretary that it was "the intention of the British government to hold Dublin in the event of a republic being set up." This veiled threat put an end to all hopes of a conciliation, and the republican army proceeded to take the field against their former comrades in arms.

On December 4, the Irish Constitution bill was passed by the British Parliament, and Timothy M. Healy, the veteran Irish Nationalist, was appointed governor-general.

The Dail, as the Irish Parliament is called, on December 6, 1922, elected William Cosgrave president of the executive council. The establishment of the Irish Free State as a fact was inaugurated by the lowering of the Union Jack above Dublin castle and by hoisting in its stead the new Irish flag of orange, white, and green.

Hostilities between the Constitutional troops and the Republican irreconcilables under De Valera continued into 1923. In May, De Valera issued an order to his forces to cease resistance, and its complete cessation was definitely marked by the release of practically all political prisoners in 1924. The general election of that year resulted in strengthening the hands of the Constitutional party.

Early in 1925, railways formerly operated by 26 companies were consolidated as the Great Southern railway. Industrial development was encouraged through the application of a tariff and the completion in 1929 of a large hydroelectric project on the Shannon river. The process of land distribution, begun in 1870 by the British government, was completed in 1931, when 150,000 tenant farmers were made owners of their farms through a land purchase act reimbursing the former owners.

General elections in 1932 resulted in the choice of De Valera as president of the executive council. Under his leadership, the government abolished the oath of allegiance to the king and refused to continue payments due to Great Britain for land purchase advances made before the independence of the Irish Free State. Tariff war with Britain followed. Ensuing economic distress and internal dissension led to a gradual modification of this policy.

When De Valera returned to power in 1937 by a reduced majority he secured in the same election a new constitution which came close to establishing an independent republic. During his administration he had abolished the governor generalship, done away with the oath of allegiance to the king, and terminated the practice of appealing to a court of last resort in England. The new constitution renamed the country Eire. On the outbreak of war in 1939, Eire, alone of the Dominions, did not declare war upon Germany, but proclaimed its neutrality.

In the elections of February 1948 De Valera failed to hold his parliamentary majority, and John A. Costello became prime minister, with a coalition cabinet. The new government prepared to carry out De Valera's policy by severing the last connections between Eire and the British Empire.

AUSTRALIA

The Australian continent was not known to Europeans until after the Portuguese and the Dutch developed trade with the East Indies. The earliest maps of this region of the globe show a blank space where Australia actually lies. But gradually portions of the west coast were sighted and were added piece by piece to the map. Shakspere was alluding to such an addition when in *Twelfth Night* he made Maria say of Malvolio, "He doth smile his face into more lines than are in the new map with the augmentation of the Indies"—the "augmentation" including a portion of the northwest coast of Australia.

Dutch mariners made the principal additions to the world's knowledge of the continent in the 17th century. In 1606, the Dutch yacht *Duyfken*, "Little Dove," examined part of the north coast. After 1611, the west coast was frequently sighted by Dutch vessels; for the Dutch mariners had discovered that, on their voyages to Java, they obtained the aid of strong winds by steering due east for three thousand miles after leaving the Cape of Good Hope, and then striking north. This route brought them close to the Australian coast. But the Dutch never made an attempt to utilize their knowledge either for settlement or for commercial purposes. The natives of Australia were not traders, and the natural wealth of the country was not readily available. The most important of the Dutch voyages was that of Tasman, who in 1642 discovered Van Diemen's Land, now called Tasmania. He also discovered New Zealand, but believed it to be part of a great southern continent, the Terra Australis Incognita of early geographers. It is doubtful whether the Portuguese knew anything of Eastern Australia, though the Spaniard Torres sailed through Torres strait from the New Hebrides in 1606. By the Dutch, Australia was known as The Great Southland, or, more generally, as New Holland.

The English buccaneer, William Dampier, made an acquaintance with New Holland, in two voyages, of 1688 and 1699. But he made a mistake in not approaching the continent across the Pacific, from the east. As he saw only the western coasts, which the Dutch had already explored, he added little to the world's knowledge of Australia, though his narratives of his voyages were unusually picturesque. The voyage which really directed the attention of the English to the possibilities of Australia was that of James Cook in 1770. Cook discovered the entire eastern coast of the continent. He had with him the botanist, Sir Joseph Banks, who was able to speak with authority on the potentialities of the country.

First Settlements. Prior to the separation of the American colonies from the British Empire, it had been the practice to send convicted persons to that quarter of the globe. But after 1776 that policy was no longer possible. As, however, transportation was the punishment imposed for a long list of offenses, it became necessary to find some other place to which convicts might be sent. The first proposal made for the settlement of Australia by people from Great Britain was that the American "loyalists," victims of the War of Independence, should be sent to New South Wales, as Cook had named the eastern half of the continent. The British government, however, was at the time chiefly anxious to find a convenient place for continuing the transportation policy, and determined to use New South Wales for this purpose. The first settlement was made at Port Jackson, where the city of Sydney was founded under the command of Captain Arthur Phillip in 1788.

The settlement at Sydney provided quite sufficient accommodation for the convicts who were sent out from Great Britain, but the activities of French explorers in Australian waters generated the fear that rival settlements would be formed, and this fear led to the establishment of the first subsidiary colonies in other parts of the continent. Tasmania was occupied in 1803. Settlements were founded in what is now the state of Victoria, and in Western Australia in 1827. Fear of French rivalry was the motive in each of these cases.

Exploration and Industry. Meanwhile, the continent was completely mapped. The southern coast was discovered by Captain Matthew Flinders in 1802, and the same navigator was the first to circumnavigate Australia (1803). Flinders also made the first complete map of the continent, and he it was who gave to it the name Australia.

Inland exploration was mainly promoted by the necessity of finding pasture for sheep and cattle. John Macarthur, a military officer with a genius for improving the breed of domestic animals, imported some merino sheep and crossed them with Indian varieties. He produced a sheep bearing a fleece superior to any which British cloth weavers had known before. Sheep breeding became from about the beginning of the 19th century the principal Australian industry. In search of pasture land, explorers found a way over the extremely difficult barrier of the Blue mountains, rising like a wall at the back of Sydney, in 1813. Thence, extending their researches still farther towards the center of the continent, explorers opened up the watershed of the Murray and Darling rivers, and revealed the richness of the territory of Victoria.

The most important of these inland journeys of exploration were those of Oxley, who opened up the regions watered by the Lachlan and the Macquarie (1817-18); of Hume and Hovell, who explored the country south of the Murray to Port Phillip (1824); of Allan Cunningham, who crossed the Liverpool Range and discovered the Darling Downs, thus making possible the settlement of Queensland (1827); of Charles Sturt, who explored the great rivers Darling and Murray (1828–30); of Mitchell, who found the rich western plains of Victoria (1836); and of J. McDouall Stuart, who crossed the continent from south to north, and set the flag upon the central point of the vast expanse of the interior (1862).

As the first phase of Australian settlement was the convict phase, and the second the pastoral, so gold was the third. Important discoveries of the precious metal were made in 1851-52, at Ballarat and Bendigo. Enormous yields were obtained. In later years the gold discoveries of Western Australia proved to be exceedingly rich.

Colonial Government. The form of government was in the beginning necessarily despotic. But the convict system came to an end when the number of free settlers, attracted by the conditions of life in Australia, outnumbered the involuntary exiles. The transportation system was abolished in 1852, but, at the request of Western Australia, was revived for a few years to provide that state with labor.

From first to last, the convict system brought about 150,000 persons to Australia. Many of these were transported for offenses which would be considered comparatively trivial under the more humane criminal laws of a later age. Very many were youths under twenty-one, who were transported under the theory that their removal from a contaminating environment, together with the provision of opportunities for starting life afresh in a new country, would be morally salutary. There were a few thousand political prisoners, victims of the Irish rising of 1798, of the Chartist troubles of the 19th century, and of disturbances connected with the Industrial Revolution; some thousands also were transported under the extremely harsh game laws of the 18th and early 19th centuries.

The total number transported was small, however, in proportion to those who came voluntarily, attracted to Australia by the conditions of life and work in this country, or assisted to immigrate by the governments of the states, or lured by the richness of the gold fields. Demands for self-government were made from about 1820. A popular element was introduced into the government from 1823, and this element was extended from time to time, until, in 1855, the British government resolved to confer full responsible government upon the Australian colonies. They were thus equipped with legislatures elected by the people and with ministries responsible to these legislatures.

The Commonwealth. The six colonies of Australia which existed under responsible government were New South Wales, the oldest of the group, founded 1788; Tasmania, founded 1803; South Australia, founded to demonstrate the soundness of Wakefield's colonization principles in 1836; Victoria, colonized originally by "Squatters," in 1835, but not recognized as a separate colony till separated from New South Wales in 1851; Western Australia, colonized in 1829; and Queensland, which was proclaimed as a separate state in 1859.

These colonies maintained each a separate political existence and often the rivalry between them was acute. However, it was realized by thoughtful men that the separateness of these communities, scattered over a continent consisting of 2,900,000 square miles, was a source of weakness to Australia as a whole, and a federation movement was started quite soon after responsible government was inaugurated. Discussion educated the public as to the gain to be attained by union; and, as the outcome of several tentative efforts, a Federal convention in 1897-98 drafted a constitution which was accepted by the people of all the states, and was passed as an act of the Imperial Parliament in 1900. That act established the Commonwealth of Australia.

Lord Hopetoun (afterward Lord Linlithgow) was appointed the first governor-general of the new commonwealth. In March 1901, the members of the first Parliament under the new constitution were elected, and the Parliament was opened by the Prince of Wales on May 9 following.

Contemporary Australia. The policy of Australia under the Commonwealth has been directed mainly towards (1) keeping Australia "white," that is, keeping Asiatic and Pacific races out of Australia; (2) developing Australian industries by means of tariff protection; (3) strengthening the defenses of the country; (4) providing for the settlement of differences between capital and labor, by means of a court of conciliation and arbitration; (5) strengthening the ties with the British Commonwealth of Nations.

Australia gave whole-hearted support in World War I. From its first decades the Commonwealth had adopted the policy of building up an Australian-controlled navy. This was now placed under imperial control, while over 300,000 Australian troops fought on the various fronts. The "Anzacs" at Gallipoli won undying fame. Australia continued her cooperation after the peace.

World War II. Australia followed Great Britain in declaring war on Germany. A National Security act gave the government almost unlimited control over persons and property for war purposes. After some political wrangling the Labor party came into power in October 1941 under Prime Minister John Curtin. Australian troops served in Libya, Greece, and Malaya, and the navy was increased. Equally important was the development of the manufacture of munitions, tanks, and planes. Australia had from the first apprehended danger from Japan, and her declaration of war on December 9, 1941, was followed by redoubled efforts. Practically all able-bodied men were called on. As war went on Australia had drawn closer to the United States, and their relations were strengthened by the arrival of an American expeditionary force. Australian troops took part in the fighting in the Solomons and on New Guinea. Premier John Curtin died in July 1945 and was succeeded by John B. Chifley. See *World War II.*

NEW ZEALAND

The discovery and the naming of the two islands now included in the self-governing dominion of New Zealand is credited to the Dutch navigator, Tasman (1642). So far as is known, no other white man visited the country until Captain Cook arrived in 1769. He made several later visits and mapped the islands. In 1814, the Reverend Samuel Marsden established a mission in the Bay of Islands. Under this influence, the natives, the Maoris, began rapidly to adopt the outward forms of Christianity. At the same time, however, their intertribal wars were made more destructive through their use of firearms in place of the clubs and spears they had used before the coming of Europeans. It is estimated that their numbers were decreased by one-fourth within the following twenty years. Between 1830 and 1840, a comparatively peaceful period, large numbers of the Maoris accepted Christianity.

Colonization. Systematic emigration from Europe to New Zealand began in 1839. The first company of English settlers reached Wellington in January 1840, and the English government took formal possession of the islands in the same month. In spite of difficulties with the Maoris and with the home government, the colony, under the leadership of the governor, Sir George Grey, made substantial progress during the next ten years. In 1852 the colonists were granted self-government, and in 1856 the first responsible government came into power.

Several years of war with the Maoris followed, and the settlements in the North Island made little progress. At length, about 1871, a policy of conciliation toward the natives was adopted, provision was made for their education, and they were given representation in the colonial parliament. This peaceful policy ushered in a period of advance in industry and public improvements. Meanwhile, agriculture and sheep raising had made great strides in the South Island.

Political Development. The era of political progress for which New Zealand is famous began with the year 1877. Previous to that year, political power had been in the hands of the landholding and professional classes, under a limited franchise. Under the leadership of Sir George Grey, a popular, democratic party brought about the organization of a national system of public education. This has been developed until New Zealand has a national university with four co-operating colleges and a system of public schools in which elementary education is free and compulsory for children from 7 to 14 years of age. In the secondary and the special schools, the payment of fees is required for advanced instruction. The university is an examining body and conducts no courses of instruction.

In 1890, manhood suffrage was adopted, and, in the year 1893, women were given the ballot. The growth of industries other than farming and grazing gave rise to a notable series of legislative acts for the control of land and public utilities, and for the settlement of labor disputes. This legislation attracted world-wide attention. In 1891 the land tax system was adopted, which lays a tax upon the land rather than on improvements. In 1892 the government began the policy of buying large estates and leasing them for long periods in parcels of 2000 acres or less. Arbitration of labor disputes was made compulsory in 1894. Old age pensions were introduced in 1898, and a minimum wage law was passed in 1899. The leader in these liberal policies was Richard Seddon, a Lancashire mechanic, who was premier from 1893 to his death in 1906. The government of New Zealand has owned the railroads since 1870, and the policy of public ownership and operation has been extended to telegraphs and telephones, and to other utilities of public concern, such as coal mines. Co-operative production and marketing are popular and successful in the dominion.

The progressive policies of the New Zealand government have involved large expenditures for public works and the consequent incurring of a large public debt. But the general prosperity of the country has helped to make popular the governmental management of affairs. After a period of greater conservatism in social legislation, the Parliament of New Zealand in 1938 provided for health insurance and extended the country's earlier measures of socialism by taking over the steel industry.

New Zealand troops did notable service in World War I in Egypt and at Gallipoli, and on the western front. After the war, the government assisted several thousand returned soldiers to settle on farms. In September 1939 New Zealand declared war on Germany. Like Australia the Dominion feared possible Japanese encroachments. The government introduced conscription of men and property and sent 157,000 men to the imperial army. In 1941 New Zealand sent its first minister to the United States.

UNION OF SOUTH AFRICA

A self-governing dominion within the British Empire, made up of the four colonies, Cape of Good Hope, Natal, Transvaal, and Orange Free State, which, on their union, became provinces of the dominion. It was organized on May 31, 1910. The executive power is vested in a governor-general appointed by the crown, with an executive council. The seat of government is at Pretoria. The legislature, which meets at Cape Town, consists of the Senate and the House of Assembly.

During World War I, the Union supplied troops for European service and also for campaigns in East Africa and in German Southwest Africa. The latter was assigned as a mandate to South Africa under the name of Southwest Africa.

South African political alignments have turned largely on questions of race: the rivalry between whites of Dutch and English descent, with a serious native problem in the background. The Dutch are slightly in the majority, but the English connection has been sustained, though with occasional flashes of independence.

On the outbreak of war in 1939 Premier Herzog and his coalition cabinet favored neutrality. The influence of General Smuts, however, prevailed, and South Africa entered the war with General Smuts as premier. Without conscription, the Union raised 140,000 men. In May 1948 General Smuts and his party lost the elections, largely on racial issues, and Premier Malan succeeded, with a cabinet of separatist tendencies.

Cape of Good Hope. The colony of the Cape of Good Hope, or Cape Colony, was first settled by the Dutch in 1652. It remained under the control of the Dutch East India Company until 1795, when it was captured by the British. Under the terms of the Treaty of Amiens (1802), the British forces evacuated the territory in 1803, but reoccupied it in 1805 in order to prevent its falling into the hands of the French.

Since that date the colony has been British territory, England's possession having been confirmed by treaty, August 13, 1814. By annexation of neighboring areas during the 19th century, the extent of the colony was considerably enlarged.

In 1850, a Parliament, consisting of the governor, a Legislative Council, and a House of Assembly, was granted to the colony, and in 1872 responsible government was provided for. In 1910, the colony was merged in the Union of South Africa as the province of the Cape of Good Hope.

Natal (*nȧ-tăl′*). A South African province, named by Vasco da Gama, who discovered it on Christmas Day, 1497. It was settled by the English in 1824, and later by Boers from Cape Colony. The Boers declared themselves independent, but in 1843 the British reclaimed the territory. It now forms a province of the Union of South Africa.

Orange Free State. A province of the Union of South Africa. The Orange River Colony was settled in 1835-36 by Boers from Cape Colony. The British annexed it in 1848 but recognized its independence as the Orange Free State in 1854. After many years of peaceful development, it joined with the Transvaal against Great Britain in 1899. In 1910 it was finally merged in the South African Union.

Transvaal (*trăns-väl'*). The territory now included in this province of the Union of South Africa was settled by Boers from Cape Colony in 1836-37. In 1852 Great Britain recognized the independence of the Transvaal Republic, but, in 1877, because of financial troubles and difficulties with the natives, it was made a part of the British Empire. The Boers revolted in 1880, and in 1881 and 1884 conventions were signed which recognized the independence of the Transvaal under the name of the South African Republic. Foreign affairs, however, except with reference to Orange Free State, were left in British hands. The discovery of gold and the consequent large influx of English brought about conditions which resulted in the Boer war of 1899–1902. The republic was annexed to the British crown as the Transvaal, and in 1910 it was incorporated in the Union of South Africa.

NEWFOUNDLAND

The dominion of Newfoundland includes the island of Newfoundland and a part of Labrador. It is the oldest of English colonial possessions. The island of Newfoundland was discovered by John Cabot in 1497. Its rich fisheries soon attracted fishermen from Portugal, France, Spain, and the west of England. In 1583, Sir Humphrey Gilbert took formal possession and attempted a settlement, but without success.

In 1713 France conceded sovereignty of the island to England but reserved fishing rights on the west coast. For more than a century the English government discouraged settlement. However, the number of permanent settlers increased, and representative government was granted in 1832; responsible government in 1855; and dominion status in 1918. The area of its Labrador dependency was doubled in 1927 by the favorable outcome of a boundary dispute with Canada. As a result of the depression of 1929, the Dominion finances were so disorganized that in 1933 its fiscal affairs were entrusted to appointees of the British government, and Newfoundland assumed temporarily the status of a crown colony. Newfoundland's strategic position brought economic improvement in World War II. In 1948, after two years of negotiations, a popular vote decided upon union with the Dominion of Canada, as the tenth province.

INDIA

There is no authentic political history of India previous to the expedition of Alexander the Great into the Punjab in 327 B. C. Seleucus, Alexander's successor in Syria (312–280), maintained a limited authority in the Punjab and established relations with Chandragupta, ruler in the Ganges valley, whose dynasty established Buddhism in India. The Greek influence left a deep mark upon the art and science of India. In the 7th and again in the 8th century the Moslems invaded northern India, but they were driven out by the Hindus in 750. Their great invasion, led by Sultan Mahmud of Ghazni, Turkish ruler of Afghanistan, occurred late in the 10th century. In the 12th century, the Afghan Moslems rose to power, and, about the beginning of the 13th century, Delhi became the Mohammedan capital of India. In 1398 the great Mongol conqueror, Timur, or Tamerlane, invaded India, and, in 1526, Baber, a descendant of Timur, established there the Mogul Empire, which, enlarged and consolidated by Akbar the Great (1556–1605), lasted until 1857. The consequence of these invasions is that India is peopled by races speaking 222 different languages and practicing the rites of innumerable religious sects.

Beginning of Western Trade. In 1498 India was first visited by Vasco da Gama. From 1500 to 1600 the Portuguese had a monopoly of Indian trade, but toward the end of the period they aroused a religious struggle of Christian against Mohammedan, and their power declined. In the beginning of the 17th century the Dutch and English drove the Portuguese entirely from the field, and during the 17th century they were rivals, but gradually the Dutch withdrew from the mainland to the East Indian islands. The French, in the 18th century, under the skillful diplomacy of Dupleix, secured great influence in southern India, but in 1761, with the loss of Pondicherry to the British, their power was broken. Pondicherry was finally restored to France in 1815, and that country now holds it as well as Karikal and Yanaon on the eastern coast of India, Mahe on the west coast, and Chandernagore, near Calcutta, while Portugal retains Goa on the western coast.

The British East India Company. The first English trading post was established at Surat (1612–14). For more than a hundred years the British were in India simply as traders, but the decay of the Mogul Empire necessitated military action in self-defense. From the year 1750, however, when the military acquisition of territory began under Lord Clive, a succession of conquests, almost forced upon the British contrary to their inclinations, placed nearly all India under their sway. In 1773, by act of the British Parliament, the three provinces, or presidencies, of Madras, Bombay, and Bengal were placed under the administration of a governor-general, and Calcutta was made the seat of a supreme court of judicature. Hitherto, the affairs of India had been managed by the East India Company, but in 1784 a board of control was appointed by the government, the president of which became secretary of state for India. See *Sepoy Mutiny*.

India under British Sovereignty. In 1858 the direct sovereignty of India and the powers of government hitherto held by the East India Company were vested in the British crown. Since that time the history of India, under successive governors-general, has been marked by slow development in industry and agriculture, extension of education, more settled control of the frontiers, and provision for a wider native share in government. Agitation for self-government and for ultimate independence increased in those provinces under direct British rule. The princes of the numerous small states, independent except in the right to make war, strongly favored continued British suzerainty. In World War I India staunchly supported the Empire.

Thereafter pressure for independence was intensified. In 1917 the Montagu-Chelmsford reforms provided a rather shadowy legislature, elected by about 3 per cent of the population. During the decade of 1920–30, native protests took the form chiefly of a non-co-operative movement, headed by Mohandas Gandhi. In 1937 several years work by a British commission resulted in a new constitution, creating a federation still under British control.

During World War II the defense of India was hampered by the refusal of Indian leaders to cooperate, and their demand for immediate independence. At the close of the war the British government took steps to fulfill its promises. Religious differences between the All-India Congress party, representing the Hindus, and the Moslem League interposed a serious obstacle. The Moslems demanded a separate Moslem state, Pakistan. The British government, in August 1946, set up an interim government to draft a constitution and six months later announced its intention of withdrawing from India by June 1948. In June 1947 both parties at last accepted partition into Hindu India and Moslem Pakistan, and the two new dominions were proclaimed August 15, 1947. The process of organizing them was marred by religious rioting and the movement of some eight million refugees between the two countries. On January 30, 1948, Mohandas Gandhi was murdered by a Hindu fanatic. In the same year further disputes over Kashmir and Hyderabad.

LATIN AMERICA

The history of the countries which occupy the greater part of the North American continent is included in the two preceding sections, which tell the story of the United States and that of the British Empire. To the group of American states lying south of the Rio Grande, the term Latin America is customarily applied, because the languages and cultures of these countries are, in the main, of Latin origin—Spanish, Portuguese, French. Therefore, in this section, historical accounts of the Central and South American republics, as well as of Mexico and the independent states in the West Indies, are brought together under the title of *Latin America*.

Argentina (*är'jĕn-tē'nȧ*). In the year 1516 Juan Diaz de Solis, searching for a western route for Spanish trade to the East Indies, entered the estuary now known as the river Plata. De Solis and several of his company were killed by the Indians, and the discouraged remainder returned to Spain. In 1526 Sebastian Cabot, in charge of another Spanish expedition, established at the mouth of the Parana the fort Espiritu Santo, and named the estuary, then called Rio Solis, Rio de la Plata, or "silver river," because of the silver utensils he found in the possession of the Indians with whom he traded on the upper Parana. After his return to Spain, the fort was attacked and burned. The next settlement was made in 1535 by a Spanish nobleman, Mendoza, on the present site of the Argentine capital. He named it Santa Maria de Buenos Aires, or "St. Mary of the good breezes." This little town was soon destroyed. But many of the men of the expedition—Germans, French, Belgians, and Italians—remained and intermarried with the natives. These various expeditions had brought a few horses, cattle, and sheep, which formed the nucleus of the great herds of Argentina.

In the later years of the century, other colonies were founded, and, since military means failed to control the Indians, Jesuit missionaries were called upon for this work. They established, and long maintained, many very successful missions among the Guaranies.

Independence.—In 1580 Buenos Aires was reestablished. During the next two centuries, immigration was gradual, but many educated liberals fled from oppression in Spain to the colonies on the Plata and the seeds of independence were sown by books and papers smuggled from France and England. In 1776 the Viceroyalty of Buenos Aires was formed including the present states of Argentina, Paraguay, Uruguay, and Bolivia. The coming of an English force in 1806 roused the people to their need of self-protection, and, notwithstanding the flight of the Spanish governor, they repelled the attack. Many English prisoners, after the defeat of their forces, remained in the country and helped in the forming and directing of the independent government.

In 1816 a congress at Tucuman proclaimed the independence of the United Provinces of Rio de la Plata. But the union was weak, and years of anarchy followed, relieved by the strong and progressive work of Rivadavia, secretary of the government of Buenos Aires, in founding schools, building public works, and promoting commerce. During this time, however, forces from Argentina aided Chile and Peru to free themselves from Spain, and a war with Brazil resulted in the independence of Uruguay. In 1835 Juan Manuel de Rosas became dictator, and until 1852 his power was absolute. With stern cruelty he maintained a measure of order in Buenos Aires, the other provinces going their own ways, but his tyranny drove many of the industrial and educated classes into exile in Uruguay and Chile. Finally, a concerted effort of men of all the provinces, aided by Brazilian forces, overthrew De Rosas, and in 1853, the Argentine Republic was formed, with a constitution closely resembling that of the United States.

A New Period of Progress.—Immediately, the old jealousy between Buenos Aires and the other provinces broke out, and personal rivalries of military leaders added to the political confusion. A five years' war with Paraguay drew heavily on the resources of the nation; but the leadership of President Mitre strengthened the national spirit. His successor, Sarmiento, elected in 1868, wisely advanced the economic and educational affairs of the nation, and set it on the road to peaceful, democratic progress. Since 1880, the Republic has developed in wealth and political stability. Boundary disputes with Chile have been settled by arbitration.

From a very early period, Argentina has had a large and influential class of liberal, cultured citizens. Education in all grades has received generous government support. The entire school system was reorganized in 1916. In addition to the University of Cordoba, founded in 1613, the country now has four other national and five provincial universities.

In 1915, the first real treaty between Argentina, Brazil, and Chile—the "A B C powers"—was signed, in which they agreed, for a period of five years, to submit all disputes to impartial tribunals before engaging in war. During World War I, the discovery of dispatches from the German minister at Buenos Aires, Count Luxburg, advising that Argentine vessels should be "sunk without trace," led the legislature of Argentina to advise the president to sever diplomatic relations with Germany. President Irigoyen, however, remained neutral. Argentina suffered from the depression, but passed through it without changes in the basic laws. President Ortiz (1938–42) put forward a program of economic reform. In 1942, his successor, in opposition to popular feeling, refused to break off relations with the Axis powers. President Ramirez, placed in power by a "Palace revolution," continued the same policy. In 1945 Argentina broke off relations with the Axis powers, and was admitted to the San Francisco conference, but the fascist supporters of Colonel Juan Perón carried the presidential election of 1946.

Bolivia. The territory included in Bolivia was conquered by Pizarro in 1538. He and his successors subdued the Indians so thoroughly that no uprising occurred until 1780. The usual Spanish policy of compelling the Indians to work in the mines rapidly reduced their numbers. From 1809 to 1824 a bloody struggle for independence was waged, and in the latter year the Spanish army was defeated by a Colombian force under General Sucré. On August 6, 1825 the independence of Upper Peru, as the country was then called, was declared, and the Republic of Bolivia was organized five days later. A constitution, drafted by Bolivar, the Liberator, was adopted in 1826. General Sucré was offered the life presidency but held office two years only.

Since 1827 the history of Bolivia has been a story of chronic civil war. In that period it has had some 75 presidents and dictators. War with Chile, ended by treaty in 1884, robbed Bolivia of its Pacific seacoast and rich mineral deposits. In 1904, however, by a new agreement, Bolivia obtained access to the coast through Chilean territory and the right to establish customhouses at certain ports. A dispute with Paraguay over title to the Gran Chaco led to a bloody three-year war, which ended in 1935 with Paraguay in possession. Arbitration in 1938 gave Paraguay three-fourths of the disputed territory, reserving to Bolivia her rights of transit to the sea. Despite the fascist leanings of its government following a revolution in 1936, Bolivia broke off diplomatic relations with the Axis powers in 1942 and received aid from the United States in return for its tin. In 1943 a group with strong fascist leanings seized power. In 1946 they were unseated by a government of apparently more popular character.

Brazil (*brȧ-zĭl'*). The name of this South American country is derived from a Portuguese word, *braza*, meaning "live coal," in reference to the color of its dyewoods, the first cargo of which was taken to Portugal in 1503 by Amerigo Vespucci. He had been sent by the king of Portugal to take possession of the territory discovered by both a Spaniard, Pinzón, and a Portuguese commander, Cabral, in 1500. Vespucci, in 1503, left a small garrison at a point which he named *Todos os Santos*, "All Saints." Portugal was occupied with her Indian and African trade, however, so the settlement of Brazil was left to private grantees to whom were given large areas, called captaincies, with fifty leagues of seacoast each. Much trouble was encountered in dealing with the natives, although a young nobleman, Diogo Alvares (generally known as Caramarú), at Bahia, secured their favor by his enterprise and daring and took daughters of native chiefs as wives. To him, it is said, many of the best families of Bahia trace their ancestry.

The supposed poverty of Brazil spared her from the commercial rivalries of the next 150 years. In 1649 the Brazil Company of Portugal successfully repelled the encroaching Dutch West India Company. About the beginning of the 18th century, diamonds and gold were discovered in the South and West, and labor was withdrawn from the growing sugar industry, to the detriment of the country. Slaves were, at this period, brought in from Africa for plantation work.

Independence.—In 1789 an unsuccessful attempt was made to free the country from Portugal. Independence came finally as an indirect result of the French Revolution; for, in 1807, when Napoleon threatened Portugal, the prince regent, afterward King John, with the royal family, fled to Brazil. John opened Brazilian ports and brought in workmen and manufacturers from northern Europe and England. In 1821 he returned to Portugal, leaving his son, Dom Pedro, in Brazil. The latter proclaimed the independence of Brazil in 1822 and became constitutional emperor, but he lost his popularity, abdicated, and returned to Portugal in 1831. In 1840 his son, then fourteen years old, was declared of age, and in the following year as Dom Pedro II took possession of the throne, which he held until 1889. In that year a peaceful revolution exiled the emperor, and a provisional government was set up under Fonseca. In 1891 a national congress proclaimed the Constitution of the United States of Brazil, with Fonseca as first president. After a few months, Fonseca was forced to resign in favor of Peixoto.

Many difficulties faced the new government, the most serious being the disorder attending the final freeing of slaves. The heads of the state frequently resorted to arbitrary measures, and several attempts were made during the period from 1890 to 1900 to restore the monarchy. But the republic has grown considerably stronger, adopting progressive democratic institutions. Social organization, however, retains much of its earlier feudal character.

In World War I Brazil declared war on Germany, and her navy co-operated with the United States. In World War II she also declared war, and sent a contingent to the Italian front. In 1937 President Vargas proclaimed a new constitution, which, however, was not put into effect, and Vargas continued to rule as a benevolent dictator. On May 28, 1945, President Vargas proclaimed an election, to be held in the following December. Before the election Vargas was deposed with little disturbance, and was succeeded by the president of the supreme court. At the election, December 3, 1945, Gaspar Dutra, a moderate "rightist" was chosen.

British Guiana. A British colony on the north coast of South America. This territory was explored by Raleigh and others in the 16th century. During the 17th and the 18th century, it was by turns in the hands of the Dutch, the English, and the French. Treaties of 1814-15 gave to Great Britain the colonies of Essequibo, Demerara, and Berbice, and these were united in 1831. In 1899 a boundary dispute with Venezuela was settled by an international tribunal. Although larger than Kansas, British Guiana has only one-sixth as many people, representing many racial strains. In 1940 an airbase in British Guiana was among those leased by Great Britain to the United States.

Chile (*chē'lā*). In the 16th century, the Araucanians were the chief Indian tribe on the western slope of the Andes, south of the territory of the Incas. The Spaniards sent their first expedition against the Araucanians in 1535, but found them harder than the Incas to subdue. After 17 years of fighting, they obtained sufficient foothold in the country to found Valdivia. Until 1773, however, the Araucanians made good their claim to the southern part of Chile. Meanwhile, slow development of farming and mining had been going on in the colony. Napoleon's invasion of Spain brought to the Chileans their opportunity for independence. The Spanish governor was forced to resign in 1810, and, after eight years of struggle, with the aid of Argentine forces under San Martin, independence was proclaimed in 1818. A constitution was adopted in 1824. This was followed by several others, that of 1833 being in force with modifications made in 1925. It is similar to that of the United States, but provides for a more centralized government with provinces instead of states.

Several internal upheavals have occurred; but the country has been free from these, compared with other South American states. A war begun with Spain in 1865 led to the blockade of the coast by the Spanish fleet and to the bombardment of Valparaiso in 1866. In 1869 the American Minister secured a cessation of active hostilities, although formal peace was not established until 1879. In that year, a war broke out with Bolivia and Peru in reference to the rights of Chile in the mineral district of Atacama. This virtually came to an end in 1881, and the victorious Chileans gained a large accession of territory from both Bolivia and Peru. The dispute over the possession of the provinces of Tacna and Arica, held by Chile, long disturbed South American politics. It was settled in 1929, Tacna being assigned to Peru and Arica to Chile.

Recent Political Progress.—In 1885 Balmaceda, for many years a liberal leader, was elected president. Opposition to his proposals of reform in respect to education, relations of church and state, and other internal affairs helped to make him unpopular. This, together with dislike of his dictatorial methods, brought about his overthrow in 1891. The Chilean constitution demanded that both senators and deputies have a fixed yearly income, and that every voter, to be qualified, possess a certain amount of property and be able to read and write. As a consequence, political power was given to but a few. Serious abuses existed in the treatment of laborers on the large estates, which included most of the agricultural lands. It was this state of affairs which led to a general strike in 1913, after which most of the causes of dissatisfaction were removed. The constitutional president, Alessandri, was overthrown by a military *coup d' état* in 1924, but, in 1925, Alessandri was invited to return, a different group having seized power. A more liberal constitution came into force in October 1925.

Disorders in 1931-32 resulted in a succession of several dictators but with the final victory falling again to Alessandri. He was succeeded by Aguirre, who proceeded to promote the adoption of many social reforms. Aguirre was the first avowedly popular front president to be elected in the Americas.

Colombia. In 1499 Ojeda and Vespucci explored the north coast of Colombia, and, after Balboa's discovery of the Pacific, settlements were rapidly made on the Isthmus of Panama and along the west coast. Until the beginning of the 19th century this territory was a Spanish possession, known as New Granada. In 1810 the colony revolted, become independent in 1819, and joined with Venezuela and Ecuador, under Bolivar, the

Washington of South America, to form the Republic of Colombia. This union broke up on the death of Bolivar in 1830. The Republic of New Granada was formed in 1831. Civil wars followed, until, in 1863, eight states formed a federal union as the United States of Colombia. This was changed in 1886 into a centralized republic, with the former "states" as provinces. But this policy was unpalatable to the Liberals. A succession of rebellions and civil wars followed, the most serious breaking out in 1899. This extremely costly war raged until 1902 and resulted in the independence of the former province of Panama.

The issue at stake in this conflict was the policy of the government toward the disposal of the rights of the French canal company in Panama. This company had offered its rights to the United States for $40,000,000. A new congress, in August 1903, rejected the Hay-Herran treaty, which provided for construction of the canal by the United States. In November, Panama declared its independence, thus taking the canal question out of Colombia's hands. Colombia continued to insist on indemnity and apology for the alleged part played by the United States in the secession of Panama. Finally, in 1921, the United States Senate ratified a treaty which awarded to Colombia $25,000,000. In 1930, the first Liberal president since 1886 was elected in the person of Enrique Herrera. Dr. Alfonso Lopez, also a Liberal, was elected president in 1934.

Costa Rica. A Central American republic lying just north of Panama. The Spanish province of Costa Rica was established in 1540. For 250 years it was reckoned the poorest of Spanish possessions, a condition due to the inroads of Indians and buccaneers. Within the last century it has made great advance in industry and education. Independence of Spanish rule was declared in Costa Rica on Sept. 15, 1821. From 1824 to 1839 it formed part of the Central American union. Since 1839 it has been an independent state. The political life of the country has been comparatively peaceful and its government enlightened. The president is elected for four years. Costa Rica is primarily agricultural, and, by a system of limited holdings, land tenure is almost universal. Country schools provide instruction in rural industry and are a feature of the educational system.

Cuba (*kū'bȧ*). This island, called the "Queen of the Antilles," was discovered by Columbus in 1492, and called by him "the most beautiful land that eyes ever beheld." It was first settled by Spaniards at Baracoa. For two centuries, Cuba, regarded as the "Key of the New World" and the source of fabulous wealth, was in constant danger from French, Dutch, English, and West Indian pirates and buccaneers. Havana was twice burned, first in 1528 and again in 1556. In 1762 the English, under Lord Albemarle, took Havana, which, however, by the Treaty of Paris in the next year, was restored to Spain.

The early 19th century was a period of prosperity in the island, and the Cubans remained loyal to Spain, while other colonies fell away. But, as soon as the great value of her fertile soil was apparent, Cuba began to feel the selfish cruelty of Spanish policy. The captains general were, by the decree of 1825, given absolute power over the lives and property of Cubans. From the rebellion of 1829, through the slave insurrection in 1844 and the Ten Years' war (1868–78), to 1895, the story of Cuba is one of revolts and cruel reprisals. In 1848 the United States offered $100,000,000 to Spain for the island. At that period, the United States government withheld all encouragement of Cuban independence, because the Spanish colonies, on gaining their own freedom, emancipated all slaves, and the slave states of the South feared the effect of Cuban emancipation.

War with Spain.—The insurrection begun in 1895 gained formidable proportions by 1898. The United States battleship *Maine*, while on a friendly visit, was blown up in Havana harbor, February 15, 1898, and, on April 19, the Congress of the United States adopted resolutions declaring Cuba independent. War with Spain began at once. Cervera's Spanish fleet was destroyed at Santiago de Cuba, July 3, and Santiago and its large army were surrendered on July 17. The leading military events of the war, so far as Cuba was concerned, were the fights at El Caney and San Juan, the battle at Santiago, and the destruction of Cervera's fleet. From 1898 to 1902, the island was under United States military governors. During this time financial reforms were introduced, a free school system was organized, the island was freed from the scourge of yellow fever, and the general death rate was lowered by modern sanitation.

Recent History.—A constitutional convention assembled in November 1900 and adopted a constitution providing for a republican form of government, with a president, vice president, Senate, and House of Representatives. Thereupon, the United States Congress authorized the transfer of the government to the people of Cuba but subject to several important restrictions. Under the name of the Platt amendment, these restrictions were embodied in the Cuban constitution and in a treaty with the United States, dated May 20, 1902. They provided for American intervention in case of civil disorder, American occupation of certain naval stations, and prohibition of treaties impairing Cuban independence.

Democratic processes in Cuba were foredoomed to failure in view of the island's social organization. The country is largely dependent on a single crop, sugar. Production is carried on in large estates, with control of sugar mills and other enterprises concentrated in a small group operating chiefly with American capital. The bulk of the rural population is only one step removed from peonage.

The United States government intervened five times in all, ruling through provisional governors. In 1934, the Platt amendment was abrogated by the American government, leaving Cuba ostensibly free to pursue her own way. Although several elections have been held under constitutional forms, presidents have usually been dictators, relying on the power of the army. Without taking office but acting through elected officials, Fulgentio Batista, chief of staff of the army, rose to power in 1933 and, in 1940, was elected president, offering a three-year plan of radical social reforms.

Dominican (*dō-mĭn'ĭ-kăn*) **Republic** or **Santo Domingo** (*săn'tō dō-mĭng'gō*). A state formed in 1844 by separation of the Spanish or eastern section of the island of Haiti from the Republic of Haiti. In 1861 Spain took possession of her former colony, but in 1863 she gave it up in the face of a revolt. The republic has since maintained a troubled existence. In 1907 an agreement between the Dominican Republic and the United States was ratified, under which the latter undertook to collect the customs revenues, assist the Dominican government to maintain peace, and act as intermediary between the republic and its foreign creditors. In 1916, after a series of revolutionary outbreaks, American marines were landed on the island in force, and United States naval and marine officers took charge of the executive posts of the government. Toward the end of 1922, the military governor installed a provisional native government. In 1925 the United States forces were withdrawn, but customs were to be collected by an American-appointed commissioner until the Dominican debts were paid. In 1940 this arrangement was terminated, and the American commissioner also was withdrawn.

Dutch Guiana or **Surinam** (*sōō'rĭ-năm'*). A Dutch colony in South America, lying just east of British Guiana. It was first settled by the English in 1652, but, in 1667, by the Treaty of Breda, the colony was transferred to the Dutch. By the same treaty, New Amsterdam (New York) passed to the English.

Ecuador (*ĕk'wȧ-dôr'*). After the Spanish conquest of the Inca dominions, the kingdom of Quito remained under Spanish rule from 1533 to 1822. It achieved its independence by the battle of Pichincha, May 22, 1822. The territory was incorporated into the Republic of Colombia, on the disruption of which, in 1830, it became an independent republic under the name of Ecuador. But a series of civil broils among rival political leaders and wars with neighboring states ensued, lasting, almost without intermission, for more than twenty years. Since 1850 the political struggle between Clericals and Liberals has been continuous and bitter. Outstanding features have been the conservative dictatorship of Garcia Moreno, 1860–75; and the Liberal ascendancy of Alfaro, 1895–1911, during which the church was disestablished. A constitution adopted in 1945 was superseded by another in 1946.

French Guiana. The French colony lying east of Dutch Guiana. It was first settled by the French at Cayenne about 1636, but this settlement was abandoned in 1653. Ten years later a new company took over the venture, but progress was slow in the face of Portuguese attacks. Toward the end of the 18th century, many political prisoners were sent to the colony, and their complaints about the deadly effects of the climate gave the place an evil reputation. The English and Portuguese seized the colony in 1809, but it was restored to France in 1815. Since 1855, Devils island, off the coast, has been of notorious repute as a French penal colony. In 1931, the hinterland, believed to contain valuable natural resources, was erected into a separate administrative district, known as Inini.

Guatemala. The Central American republic which borders Mexico on the south. From 1524 to 1821 it was a Spanish possession. After a brief period of union with the Mexican empire, its independence of all powers was declared in 1823, and a union was effected with the other new republics of Central America. In 1839 Guatemala seceded from this union and assumed the name Republic of Guatemala on March 21, 1847. Its history has been marked by a series of long dictatorships: Carrera, 1842–65; Cabrera, 1898–1920; and Ubico, 1931–44. The effect has been to stabilize the government, but at the cost of extinguishing political freedom. President Ubico attempted some reforms, and accomplished the payment of the foreign debt, and his "authoritarian" tendencies led to a revolution. He was succeeded in 1945 by President Arevala. In World War II Guatemala declared war on the Axis powers, November 8, 11, 1941.

Haiti (*hā'tĭ*). The island of Haiti, or Santo Domingo, was discovered by Columbus in 1492. The inhabitants were rapidly exterminated by warfare and by the heavy labor imposed by their Spanish masters, who soon began to import Negroes from Africa. French adventurers occupied part of the island early in the 17th century, and the Treaty of Ryswick (1697) assigned the island to France. In 1789, the freedmen of the island began a movement for equal political rights. The French National Assembly granted their request, but a struggle ensued with the landlords, aided by the English.

At this juncture, Toussaint L'Ouverture took command of the freedmen's forces and drove English and Spanish alike from the island. The French government made him governor. Later, at Napoleon's orders, he was deposed and at length taken prisoner to France. In 1804, Haiti, under General Dessalines, proclaimed its independence. In 1844 the Spanish section of the island set up a separate government, as the Dominican Republic. The later history of Haiti has been a long series of rebellions and revolutions. In 1915, violent disturbances led to intervention by the United States. Under a treaty of that year, the control of customhouses and of a native constabulary, to continue for 10 years, later increased to 20, was given to the United States. Civil government was restored in 1930; the country had prospered under American control, but disliked it. Four years later American personnel was withdrawn with the exception of a fiscal representative. A new constitution was adopted in 1935. In 1937 a clash occurred with the Dominican government over the murder of some Haitian farmers. The country has a good school system in form, but about 85 per cent of the people are illiterate. See *Dominican Republic.*

Honduras. This republic is the third largest of the Central American states. On its shores, near the present Cape Honduras, Columbus made a landing in 1502. The conquest of the country was completed by Cortés, who came thither from Mexico in 1525. For three centuries the land suffered the usual fate of exploitation under Spanish rule. In 1821, after a successful revolt, Honduras became a part of the Mexican empire. It joined the Central American Confederation in 1823, and became independent in 1839. From 1849 to 1863, it shared in a union with Salvador and Nicaragua. The later history of the republic has been marked by frequent revolutions; those of 1910-11 were the occasion of intervention by the United States. The United States intervened also at the time of a threatened revolution in 1934; acted as a mediator in a boundary dispute with Guatemala in 1928; and in 1937 in a similar dispute with Nicaragua. President Carrias Andino took office in 1933 after some disturbances. A new constitution was adopted in 1936.

A large part of the natural resources of Honduras still await development, because of its constant political troubles. The country is mainly agricultural, with bananas the largest item of export.

The state supports several institutions for secondary and higher education, but the country as a whole suffers from lack of an adequate system of common schools.

Mexico. Ancient Mexican tradition tells of the passage of numerous tribes from the north to the south across the country and of the establishment of powerful states by some of these peoples. In this shadowy procession the accomplishments of two tribes, the Toltecs and the Aztecs, stand out boldly. The Toltecs, in the course of their migrations, are said to have reached Tulacingo, a little north of the City of Mexico, early in the 8th century. They appear to have been a commercial people who built great cities. Apparently, their government extended its authority over a large territory. Other kindred races shared the land of Mexico with the Toltecs, and all were skillful workers in textiles and metals. They possessed elaborate religious systems, the ceremonies of which centered around many vast temples.

The Aztecs.—After some 400 years, disaster in the shape of civil war and disease overtook the Toltecs. Their traditions and culture were preserved by the Texcocan people, whose city, Texcoco, situated on the lake of the same name, became the most famous center of culture in the later Aztec empire. In government, the Aztecs were the real successors of the Toltecs. They established their capital of Tenochtitlan, or Mexico, "the place of Mexitli," their war god, in the 14th century. The superior ability of their kings brought all central Mexico under the Aztec authority. It was this empire, ruled over by Montezuma (Moctezuma) II, that the Spanish adventurers met with in the beginning of the 16th century.

Cortés, led on by a dream of vast wealth, landed at Vera Cruz in 1519 and started on his daring march toward the Aztec capital. On the way, he recruited a native army from various states tributary to the Aztecs and contrived to so impress the emperor, Montezuma, that he was received into the royal palace. In 1520 he made Montezuma his prisoner. The death of the monarch and the desecration of their shrines roused the Mexicans to an attack on the little band of Spaniards. For a time Cortés and his followers were in desperate straits, but they rallied, and, on August 13, 1521, they captured the

City of Mexico. From that event dates the Spanish rule in Mexico, which continued to the year 1821.

Mexico under Spanish Rule.—The governors and viceroys of New Spain gave to Mexico a government which, in its tyranny, was not very different from the system to which they had been accustomed. The zeal of the churchmen stamped out the horrible practices that had attended the old Aztec worship; but, unfortunately, the system of exploiting the natives destroyed much that was valuable in their ancient culture. Mexico, however, became the most prosperous and progressive of Spain's colonies. The government encouraged settlement, built roads and harbors, and established schools and a university. But the restriction of trade and agriculture, to avoid all competition with Spain, and the enslaving of the natives were evils that far outweighed the good in Spanish government. The vast resources of a country stretching from Panama to Vancouver could never be realized, much less developed, under such a system.

Independence.—The revolt which led to Mexican independence was really opened by the patriot priest, Hidalgo, of Dolores, in 1810. He was defeated and executed, but, in 1821, under General Iturbide, the Spanish power was finally broken. For a brief period Iturbide ruled as emperor. Then followed many years of turmoil, during which the general, Santa Anna, exercised a predominant influence. During his ascendancy, Texas was lost in 1836, and the war with the United States (1846-47) resulted in the further loss of New Mexico and California.

The evils of constant internal warfare were overshadowed for a time when, in 1861, England, France, and Spain sent a fleet to Vera Cruz to compel a settlement of Mexico's foreign debt. This was followed by the French military expedition which placed Maximilian on the throne as emperor of Mexico. Diplomatic warning from the United States, in support of the Monroe Doctrine, moved France to withdraw her troops. Maximilian was captured by revolutionary forces and executed.

The Presidency of Diaz.—The next important period in Mexican history is that covered by the administration of Porfirio Diaz. Except for the presidency of Gonzales (1880–84), Diaz ruled Mexico as a sort of benevolent despot from 1876 to 1911. Diaz reformed the government, introducing an adequate tax system with modern methods of accounting which largely prevented dishonesty among officials. He encouraged public improvements, railroads, and manufactures, and developed the educational system of the country. But numerous abuses, incident to long holding of power by a small group of men, led to severe criticism and active opposition to the Diaz régime. He was compelled to resign in 1911, immediately after the centenary celebration of Mexican independence.

Revolution and Reform.—A period of disorder in Mexico was ushered in by the withdrawal of Diaz. Rival leaders kept the country in a state of civil war. The presidency of Madero was brief. His successor, Huerta, assumed a defiant attitude toward the United States over a demand for reparation for the arrest of American sailors at Tampico in 1914. This led to an attempt at mediation by the "A B C powers," Argentina, Brazil, and Chile, which produced no result. Meanwhile, various revolutionary and bandit forces were active, chiefly those of Carranza and Villa. Raids by the latter's troops into American territory led to the sending of a punitive expedition into Mexico under General Pershing in 1916.

A constituent assembly, in 1917, directed by Carranza, ushered in a new epoch for Mexico. It radically revised a former constitution dating from 1857. The earlier constitution had decreed the separation of church and state. The new one sought to make the separation effective by nationalizing all ecclesiastical property, limiting the number of priests, abolishing monastic orders, and forbidding public religious demonstrations. It provided also for expropriating large landed estates to be divided among small farmers or given to communal villages. Mineral resources were declared the property of the state, and curbs were placed on trusts.

Enforcement of the constitution awaited the presidency of Obregon in 1921 and of his successor Calles, in 1924. Calles, though in retirement after 1928, wielded the real power until exiled by President Cardenas in 1936.

The land program was the first to be put into operation. Then in 1926 the laws against the church began to be enforced, arousing intense bitterness. The government wished to nationalize church property and secularize education. A "Six-Year Plan," looking toward a cooperative economic system, was adopted in 1934. In March 1938, after previous restrictive legislation, Cardenas announced the expropriation of all oil properties owned by foreign companies, which had defied the new laws. In 1940 President Cardenas was succeeded by the government candidate, Avila Comacho.

Nicaragua (*nĭk'ȧ-rä'gwȧ*). The largest Central American republic. The coast of Nicaragua was discovered by Columbus in 1502. Until 1821 the country was a Spanish dependency, but in that year it declared its independence. It formed part of the United Provinces of Central America from 1823 to 1839, when it again assumed independence. Until 1860 the republic was the scene of constant war. In that year William Walker, who had made himself dictator in 1855, was captured and shot. Then followed a long period of peace, broken only in 1893 by a factional struggle for the presidency. In 1909 Zelaya, who had held the presidency since 1894, was forced to resign. From 1909 to 1933, the attempts of the United States to maintain order resulted in constant interventions, opposed by local factions. In 1916 to United States was given the right to build an interoceanic canal. After supervising an election in which President Sacasa was chosen, the United States forces were withdrawn in 1933.

Panama (*păn'ȧ-mä'*). Since 1513, when Balboa discovered the Pacific Ocean, Panama, the connecting link between North and South America, has been of great importance as a possible trade route. This peculiar commercial interest made its union with Colombia, both in the Spanish period and later, very insecure. The people attempted to set up an independent republic in 1840 but failed. In 1855 Panama was made a self-governing state dependent upon Colombia, but in 1885 direct government was restored. In 1903 a bloodless revolution secured independence from Colombia.

Paraguay (*păr'ȧ-gwā*). The territory included in this South American republic was first explored by Sebastian Cabot in 1526. A fort was built on the site of the present capital city of Asunción in 1536. The most notable feature of the Spanish period is the management of the country by the Jesuits from 1609 to 1768. Their mission communities, or *reductions*, were centers of education for the Guaranies, or native Indians. After the overthrow of the Spanish government in 1811, the state was governed by a triumvirate until 1816, when José Gaspar Francia made himself dictator. He ruled until 1840, maintaining a policy of national isolation. Carlos López established another dictatorship in 1844. He was succeeded by his son, Francisco López, whose territorial ambition plunged Paraguay into a disastrous war with Argentina, Brazil, and Uruguay. When the war closed in 1870, Paraguay had lost nearly half a million of its population. Since the war political revolutions have been frequent, with a fascist trend in recent years. Following a war with Bolivia over the Gran Chaco, in 1932–35, Paraguay received 70 per cent of the disputed area under an arbitration award in 1938.

Peru (*pē-rōō'*). A republic on the west coast of South America. Authentic history of this country begins with the coming of the Spaniards under

Pizarro in 1531. They found the land of the Incas engaged in a war between rival chiefs and took advantage of this situation to establish Spanish authority. The conquerors at once began to seize vast quantities of gold and silver and to enslave the natives for work in the mines. This policy aroused protest from the Spanish churchman, Las Casas, and a code of laws was framed in Spain, designed to protect the Indians. In 1551 a viceroy was sent to Peru to enforce these laws. But neither he nor his forty successors were able to prevent merciless exploiting of the natives.

After the first few years of Spanish control, no serious uprising of the Indians occurred until 1780. This rebellion was crushed with great cruelty. The Viceroyalty of Peru included at first all of Spanish South America, but in 1718 New Granada was separated from it, and in 1776 the Viceroyalty of Rio de la Plata was formed, including most of Argentina, Paraguay, Uruguay, and Bolivia.

Independence.—A movement for separation from Spain was started in 1820 under the leadership of General San Martin. Independence was declared at Lima, July 28, 1821. After several years of conflict, the Peruvians, led by General Bolivar, succeeded in defeating the Spanish forces. A constitution was adopted in 1828.

A dispute over the possession of the rich mineral territory of Tarapaca and the provinces Arica and Tacna brought on war with Chile in 1879. The Peruvians were defeated, Chile annexed Tarapaca, and Peru ceded Tacna and Arica to Chile for ten years. Permanent settlement of the dispute, which was to be made by popular vote in the provinces, was delayed, by disputes and disagreements over the conditions of the election, until 1929, when Tacna was assigned to Peru and Arica to Chile.

Recent political history has consisted largely of revolutions, with the dictatorships of Leguia (1919–30) and Benavides (1933–39). Agriculture and mining are the chief occupations. A good education law, passed in 1920, is moderately enforced. The oldest of Peru's four universities, and the oldest in the New World, is the University of San Marcos at Lima, founded in 1551.

Salvador (*săl'vȧ-dōr'*). The smallest and most thickly populated of Central American republics. In Salvador, as in Guatemala, the native Indian blood still predominates, more than a million of the million and a half inhabitants being of mixed or pure Indian ancestry. The country is progressive in government and industry, and, in spite of the practical necessity of providing against destruction by earthquakes, the people try to secure good architectural effects in their buildings. From 1524 until 1821 Salvador was part of the Spanish viceroyalty of Guatemala. After a period of union with Mexico and with the other Central American states, it became independent in 1839. Its constitution has been frequently revised. Education in Salvador is free and compulsory.

Uruguay (*ū'rōō-gwā*). This South American republic lies east of the Uruguay river and north of the river Plata. The district was known in Spanish times as the Banda Oriental, and the official title of the state is *Republica Oriental del Uruguay*, or "Eastern Republic of Uruguay." The native Indians prevented settlement by Europeans until 1624, when the first permanent colony was founded on the Rio Negro. The Portuguese claimed the territory and made numerous settlements, but after a series of conflicts during the 18th century they were compelled to give way to the Spaniards.

Independence.—An English fleet captured the city of Montevideo in 1807 but gave it up after the failure of their attack on Buenos Aires. The people of Uruguay joined the Argentinians in their revolt against Spain in 1810, and the Spanish forces were driven from Montevideo in 1814. Brazil took advantage of Uruguayan weakness following this struggle and annexed the country. A number of patriotic leaders took refuge in Buenos Aires, watching for an opportunity to drive the Brazilians out. Their opportunity came in 1825, and by 1828 the Brazilian forces were finally defeated. The republic was organized in 1830. Its history for many years was one of disorder and conflict between the *Colorado* and *Blanco*, or Colored and White, parties, for the color line between the whites and the people of mixed blood was drawn early. The traditional party names still remain, although their original significance has largely disappeared.

Uruguay, however, in spite of these internal troubles, has attained rank as a progressive state. A revised constitution was adopted in 1934. Attempts at economic reform were hampered by fears of interference by Soviet Russia and Germany. Much progress has been made recently in education. The illiteracy rate is among the lowest in South America. In Montevideo are numerous special and higher institutions and a university.

Venezuela (*vĕn'ē-zwē'lȧ*). A South American republic lying east of Colombia and bordering the Caribbean Sea. The name, meaning "little Venice," was given to the country probably on account of the pile dwellings built by the natives on Lake Maracaibo, which suggested Venice to the early explorers. These natives were living in a savage state when Columbus sailed along the coast in 1498. Settlers were very early attracted to the coast islands by the pearl fisheries, and by 1520 several Spanish colonies had been established on the mainland by Franciscan and Dominican monks. In 1731 most of the territory now known as Venezuela was placed under the authority of a captain general and all of it was so governed after 1777.

Independence.—The first serious revolt against Spanish rule occurred in 1797, but it failed, as did others in the first decade of the 19th century. A Venezuelan congress met and declared independence on July 5, 1811. Several years of intermittent conflict between republican and royalist forces ensued, and it was not until Oct. 8, 1823 that the royalists, who had drawn support largely from the half-breeds, finally surrendered. During this period, Simon Bolivar, a young Venezuelan aristocrat, had launched his great scheme for a Colombian republic, in which Venezuela was included. Venezuela, however, withdrew from the union in 1829, and in 1830 formed an independent republic with its capital at Caracas.

Political Difficulty.—After some years of peace, civil war broke out in 1846 between the Liberal and Conservative parties, which lasted almost continuously until 1870. Since that time several revolutions have marked the transfer of power from one party or dictator to another. Slavery in the republic was abolished in 1854. Two disturbing incidents in the later history of Venezuela took on international importance. The long-standing boundary dispute with Great Britain reached a critical stage in 1886, when the British fortified the mouth of the Orinoco. Settlement by arbitration was secured, at the insistence of the United States, in 1899. The despotic conduct of Cipriano Castro, who secured control of affairs as president in 1900, brought on a blockade of Venezuelan ports by Germany, England, and Italy in 1903, to force payment of Venezuelan indebtedness in Europe. This matter was submitted to the Hague Tribunal and settled in favor of the European claimants in 1904.

Recent Events.—Castro was overthrown in 1909 by Juan Vincente Gomez, who controlled politics, in and out of office, until his death in 1935. Material prosperity, in which the development of oil deposits played an important part, increased under Gomez and his successor, Lopez Contreras. In the cities of Venezuela much progress has been made in public works and education, but the rural districts are still very backward. In the city of Caracas is a university founded in 1721, besides normal schools and schools of arts and trades for boys and for women.

WORLD HISTORY

THE following section brings together, in alphabetical order, historical accounts of the states and nations which have not been included in the preceding separate treatments of American history, of the history of the British Empire, and of that of the Latin American countries. Here are included stories of the origin and progress of existing sovereign states not previously considered, as well as accounts of ancient and medieval states and countries, the stories of which are essential to a comprehensive view of world history. Certain minor divisions and dependencies of present day states, which of themselves have had important careers, also are treated in this connection.

Topics of such particular historical importance and interest as to demand special treatment are discussed farther on in the Dictionary of World History. These include accounts of parties, treaties, alliances, congresses, and especially such notable events as affected at once the history of several countries. In a separate section, beginning on page 513, the distinctive characters, the relationships, and the histories of races and peoples are treated.

The political natures and the governmental organizations of existing states are discussed in the department of Government. Geographical characteristics and relations of countries, which so notably affect the history of nations, will be found in the department of Geography, while, for those commercial and industrial facts and conditions which help to determine the course of history, the reader is referred to the department of Economics.

ABYSSINIA (ETHIOPIA)

Abyssinia (*ăb'ĭ-sĭn'ĭ-ȧ*) was, until 1936, one of the three independent states of Africa, the others being Egypt and Liberia. In that year it was conquered by Italy and made an Italian colony in a freshly proclaimed New Roman Empire. The official title, Ethiopia, reverts to the name of the country of which it anciently formed a part, the modern name Abyssinia being a corrupt Portuguese form of the Arabic word *habash* or *habeshi* meaning "mixture," applied in reference to the diverse tribes of the country. Abyssinia had never been subject to any foreign power until its conquest by Italy. Early traditions and some features of the language, known as Amharic, indicate contact with the Jews, and the Queen of Sheba is supposed to have ruled the land in Solomon's time.

In the 4th century, Christianity was introduced, and a bishop, called in the Abyssinian tongue, *Abuna Salamah*, "our father of peace," was consecrated by the patriarch of Alexandria. In spite of efforts to introduce other forms of Christian faith, this original Coptic church rite has been maintained. The abuna is appointed by the Coptic church at Alexandria and shares authority with the native head of the monastic orders.

In the 6th century, the Abyssinians conquered the Yemen, a district of Arabia on the Red Sea, opposite Abyssinian territory, and ruled it as a province for 60 years until it was lost to the Mohammedans, shutting off Abyssinia from the outer world. Up to the 19th century Abyssinia was known only through a few explorers. An English punitive expedition in 1868 left its internal condition unchanged. An Italian attempt at conquest was defeated in 1896. Abyssinia became a member of the League of Nations in 1923, but League protests and attempted sanctions did not prevent the Italian conquest in 1936.

Prior to the Italian conquest, the government of Abyssinia was feudal, with the emperor, or negus, at the head and governors in charge of the nine provinces. Menelek, who reigned from 1889 to 1913, was one of the strongest rulers. Under his authority, boundary treaties were concluded with England, a bank was established, a line of railroad between the Gulf of Aden and his capital, Addis Ababa, was begun (completed in 1917). Haile Selassie became emperor in 1928. He took refuge in England in 1936, but, in the early months of 1941, English expeditions from Kenya and the Sudan overcame the Italians and restored Haile Selassie.

AFGHANISTAN

Afghanistan (*ăf-găn'ĭ-stăn'*), a small Asiatic country, called by the natives Khorassan, lies between Iran and northern India and was among the conquests of Alexander in the 4th century B. C. In succeeding centuries it was the prey of many conquerors. About the middle of the 18th century, Ahmed Shah gave the country an independent status which it has maintained ever since. In 1809 Sujah, grandson of Ahmed, was dethroned and fled to India. Dost Mohammed established partial order in the country, but in 1838 the British government of India attempted to interfere in Afghan affairs, on the ground that Sujah was rightful ruler and Dost Mohammed was intriguing with Russia. This led to ten years of conflict terminating in Dost Mohammed's holding of the throne in friendly relations with the British. Further trouble arose in 1878 over the British demand that a British resident should be received at Kabul as a Russian had been.

In 1901, the British government acknowledged the independence of Afghanistan, which was later reaffirmed by a definite treaty in November 1921. Afghanistan is backward in the development of industry and transportation. In 1919, however, King Amanullah came to the throne and initiated a program of modernization, not only in transportation and communication, but also in customs, such as the unveiling of women and the adoption of Western dress. These changes antagonized many of his subjects, and he was deposed in 1929. His successor was Nadir Khan. Education has advanced markedly in recent years. The government workshops at Kabul provide public education in mechanical method and shop work. Most of the people are diligent cultivators, and all profitable soil is industriously utilized. See *Afghans*.

ALBANIA

As one of the political results of the Balkan wars, the independent state of Albania was set up in 1912. After a declaration of independence on November 28, the separate existence of the Albanian government was approved on December 20 by a conference of ambassadors held in London. An international commission was appointed to control the Albanian finances for a period of ten years. The crown was accepted by Prince William of Wied. He arrived in Durazzo, then capital of Albania, on March 7, 1914, but, at the outbreak of World War I, he left the country.

On June 3, 1917, Albania was proclaimed independent under Italian protection, and its complete independence was recognized on July 2, 1920. From 1925 to 1928 Albania was a republic. In 1928 its president, Ahmed Beg Zugu, became king, under the title of King Zog. In April 1939 Italian troops invaded Albania and annexed it. In World War II, it was invaded by the Greeks, and regained by the Germans, but popular resistance continued, and by the end of 1944 the Germans were driven out. In 1945 a republic was established under Enver Hoxha.

ALSACE-LORRAINE

Alsace-Lorraine (*ăl-säs' lō'rān'*) is the name applied to the combined portions of Alsace and Lorraine, which, after the war of 1870, the German government organized under a single imperial administration. The cession secured by Germany included all of the historic French province of Alsace, except the district around Belfort, and about one-fourth of the old province of Lorraine, a district rich in iron and including the fortified city of Metz.

Until their incorporation in the kingdom of France, the histories of these provinces had been quite distinct. The name Lorraine is derived from Lotharingia, the kingdom of Charlemagne's grandson Lothair. French Lorraine represented a district known in early medieval times as Upper Lorraine, which had been separated from Lower Lorraine—now part of Belgium and the Netherlands—in the middle of the 10th century. Though tributary to the Holy Roman Empire, Upper Lorraine became more and more closely related to France. Ruled by the dukes of Lorraine until the 18th century, it was then for a time in the possession of Stanislas, ex-king of Poland. At his death in 1766, it passed under the sovereignty of France.

Alsace, a territory lying in the upper Rhine valley, has been, throughout its history, disputed territory. The Romans, on entering Gaul, found this district inhabited by Celtic tribes. The Celts in time were supplanted by the Teutons, and the whole territory gradually came under German sway. From the 7th century, Alsace was governed by petty princes and other dignitaries, later by the dukes of Swabia, and finally by the Habsburgs. Between the years 1648 and 1697, Alsace became partly incorporated with France and was subsequently taken through force of arms by Louis XIV. Accordingly, by the Treaty of Ryswick, 1697, it came entirely under the dominion of France.

The French government made intermittent efforts to amalgamate the Teutonic element in Alsace with that of the French. But it was not until the Revolution that the German and the French peoples of the province were drawn close together in sentiment and sympathy—all classes of the German population becoming thoroughly reconciled to French rule. It is an incident here worthy of recording, that the "Marseillaise" was composed and first sung in the city of Strasbourg.

In 1790, in the process of reorganization of the realm of France in departments, Alsace was divided into the departments of Haut Rhin and Bas Rhin, while Lorraine was distributed among three—Moselle, Meurthe, and Vosges. The cession to Germany included Bas Rhin, most of Haut Rhin, the department of Moselle, and portions of Meurthe and Vosges. For administrative purposes, Germany divided Alsace-Lorraine into three civil districts—Lower Alsace, Upper Alsace, and Lorraine. Members of the legislative body, 58 in number, were elected by popular suffrage. But, at heart, the people in general were strongly opposed to the change in government. More than 150,000 proclaimed their adherence to France, and of this number no less than 50,000 chose exile rather than become German subjects.

For nearly half a century, the possession of Alsace-Lorraine by Germany had been a source of the keenest bitterness and resentment to the French. Neither had this sentiment grown less intense, nor had the loyalty of the people of Alsace-Lorraine became less devoted at the outbreak of World War I. By the Treaty of Versailles, in 1919, Alsace and Lorraine were returned to France. They were taken back by Germany on the fall of France in 1940, and reorganized as a part of the Reich, Lorraine becoming the Westmark, but on the defeat of the Axis were regained by France.

ANATOLIA

Anatolia (*ăn'à-tō'lĭ-à*), a name of Greek derivation, meaning sunrise, or eastern land, was anciently applied to Asia Minor, the land east of the Ægean Sea. Under the Eastern Empire, it designated one of the three Phrygian provinces. It is still used in a popular sense to designate this region, now territory of Turkey. The western part of this land, along the Ægean coasts, was the home of early Greek civilization. Here, in the 6th century B. C., arose the famous kingdom of Lydia, ruled by Crœsus. Persia extended its sway to the Ægean, to be superseded by the Macedonian power. Numerous states which arose after the death of Alexander, including the powerful realm of Pontus, succumbed to the advance of Rome in the 2d and the 1st century B. C. The power of the Eastern, or Byzantine, Empire in Asia Minor was shattered by the Turkish attacks begun in the 11th century A. D. Since 1453 the land has been ruled by the Ottoman Turks. After the close of the World War, the Turkish Nationalist movement fixed its political center at Ankara in Anatolia.

ANDORRA

Andorra is one of the two oldest and smallest republics in the world, the other being San Marino in Italy. It consists of 6 parishes in the diocese of the Spanish bishop of Urgel, lying in the valleys of the eastern Pyrenees, between France and Spain. Within its 175 square miles of territory, about 5000 people live, 1000 in the capital, Andorra. Charlemagne is said to have rewarded the little state for its help during his campaigns against the Moors by declaring it independent. Similar independence was enjoyed in feudal times by the people of many valleys of the Pyrenees. Fortunately for Andorra, the suzerainty over this territory was, in 1278, divided in perpetuity between the counts of Foix and the bishops of Urgel. The rights of the house of Foix descended to the French crown, and hence Andorra is now under the protection of the government of France and the bishop of Urgel. All citizens from 10 years of age to 60 are liable for military service. Inhabitants speak French and the Catalan dialect of Spanish.

ARABIA

The peninsula of Arabia has never been a political unit, although the recently established kingdom of Saudi Arabia embraces nearly all the territory. At a very early period, it was settled by two groups of Semitic people, one of which occupied the South, the other the North. The people of the South adopted a settled, agricultural life more readily than the northern tribes, and are said to have maintained a kingdom, perhaps that of Yemen, for 2000 years. It was a period of Semitic migrations eastward into Mesopotamia and northward into Syria. The Roman power affected only some portions of the North. In consequence, many sects of early Christians took refuge in Arabia, and from their monasteries many valuable ancient manuscripts have been recovered. The oldest known manuscript of the Bible (4th century) was found in a convent on Mt. Sinai.

With the coming of Mohammed arose the brilliant historic period of the Arabs. From the 7th to the 15th century they swept out in conquest, established many centers of civilization, and contributed to the progress of science and art among the Western nations. But their homeland was still a group of petty states around the interior of the peninsula.

In 1517 the Turks subdued Hejaz and Yemen on the Red Sea coast. Oman, on the Persian Gulf, maintained independence except during the 16th century, when for a time it was subject to Portugal. Its later history has been turbulent. It is now independent, but the sultan is pledged to cede no territory to any other power than Great Britain. Since 1839 the district of Aden, in the southwest corner of Arabia, has been a protectorate of Great Britain.

In 1916 the Grand Sherif of Mecca, or "Keeper of the Holy Places," proclaimed the independence of Hejaz and assumed the title of king. His troops co-operated with British forces in Syria and penetrated northward as far as Damascus. The king of Hejaz aspired to rule all Arabia but was conquered in 1924 by Ibn Saud, sultan of the Nejd. Saud captured also Jebel Shammar and created the sultanate of Hejaz and the Nejd, renamed Saudi Arabia in 1932. It was later extended to include almost the entire peninsula from the Red Sea to the Persian Gulf. See *Arabians*.

ARMENIA

As a state, Armenia first appears in history in the 6th century B. C., when the Armenian people were freed by Tigranes from the rule of the Assyrians and the Medes. About the beginning of the 2d century B. C., the division of Armenia into Armenia Major, east of the Euphrates, and Armenia Minor, west of the Euphrates, was made. The former was ultimately divided between Turkey, Persia, and Russia. The latter became Turkish territory in 1541.

Nationalist movements in Armenia led to cruel repressions and massacres, none of which exceeded in barbarity the "deportations" by the Turks during the World War. Armenian independence was recognized by the Allies in 1920. On April 2, 1921, Armenia declared itself a soviet republic. From 1922 to 1936, it formed part of Transcaucasia, a federated state of the Soviet Union. Armenia itself was then given the status of a federated state. See *Armenians.*

ASSYRIA

In ancient history, we hear of Assyria first as a northern province of the Babylonian Empire in the 19th century B. C. It grew in power until about 1100 B. C., when its king, Tiglath-Pileser I, taking advantage of Babylonian troubles with Arabian invaders, made himself master of the empire. After his death, the realm fell apart. In 745 B. C. an adventurer, Pul, who had been a gardener, seized the reins of authority and, as Tiglath-Pileser II, established the strongest empire the world had yet seen. He originated the organization of provinces, to take the place of the earlier principalities.

Sargon II, the next great king, used the favorite plan of the Assyrians for subduing rebellious people, when he carried the tribes of Northern Israel into captivity, 722-723 B. C. Sennacherib, son of Sargon, in the course of extending his power westward, met disaster in a siege of Jerusalem, celebrated in Byron's poem beginning, "The Assyrian came down like a wolf on the fold." His son Esarhaddon conquered Egypt in 672 B. C. But the murderous cruelty and oppressive taxation of this great empire roused hatred among its subject peoples. Egypt and Babylon revolted, the Scythians invaded from the north, and finally the Medes and Babylonians conquered Nineveh, the capital, the very site of which was forgotten until recent years. See *Assyrians.*

AUSTRIA

The history of Austria is chiefly the history of the house of Habsburg. When Rudolf of Habsburg became emperor of Germany, Ottokar, king of Bohemia and duke of Austria, Styria, and Carinthia, refused to take the oath of allegiance. The emperor succeeded in dispossessing Ottokar of his fiefs (1278) and subsequently conferred them on his own sons (1280). Thus the dynasty of Habsburg was founded. In the first half of the 16th century, Duke Ferdinand of Austria was elected king of Hungary by one party; John Zapolya of Transylvania was elected by another. After several wars, in which John was supported by the Turks, Ferdinand came out victorious and united Hungary to Austria. Possessed of a large territory, fertile and densely peopled, the house of Habsburg was for several centuries the richest and most powerful family in Europe. But humiliations came with Napoleon. Driven out of Germany, the emperor Francis assumed, August 11, 1804, the title of emperor of Austria.

After the fall of Napoleon, Austria was restored to its former size, and under the administration of Metternich it also regained its prestige in European politics. But its internal weakness became apparent, first by the revolution of 1848, when only the support of Russia prevented the whole fabric from falling to pieces; again, after the battle of Sadowa, 1866, when, for the second time, it was driven out of Germany and lost its hold on Italy. The empire was then constituted as a double state—Austria and Hungary. In 1878 the administration of Bosnia and Herzegovina was given to Austria. In 1882 the dual kingdom entered into the Triple Alliance with Germany and Italy. Thereafter, the policy of the Habsburg rule became more and more identified with the Hohenzollern ambition for world domination. In 1908 Austria annexed Bosnia and Herzegovina in defiance of Russia. With Germany's support in 1913, Austria, by securing a protectorate over Albania and by denying Serbia access to the sea, prevented the Balkan allies from realizing the fruits of their victory over the Turks.

Francis Ferdinand, Austrian heir apparent, was assassinated at Serajevo, June 28, 1914. Accusing Serbia of complicity, Austria demanded that Serbia punish the accomplices and suppress anti-Austrian influence. Rejecting Serbia's reply, Austria invaded Serbia, thereby beginning the World War. Following the utter defeat of the Austrian armies by the Italian forces in October 1918, Austria-Hungary, on Nov. 3, signed terms of truce equivalent to military surrender. On Nov. 11, Charles I abdicated his throne, thereby ending more than 600 years of Habsburg rule. The Republic of Austria was proclaimed on Nov. 12, 1918. A constitution was adopted in November 1920.

The Treaty of Versailles dismembered Austria-Hungary and left Austria a small inland state. Grave economic depression ensued. As Germany became stronger after her defeat in the World War, she pursued a policy looking toward union with Austria. This prospect not only divided Austrian opinion but for a time elicited aid from Italy for the party opposing union. Violent division led to a dictatorship. Unlike that in Germany, it was favorably disposed to the church. The former democratic constitution was replaced in 1934 by one which declared the country a Christian, German, federal state on a corporative foundation. Suppression by the Austrian chancellor of a movement for union with Germany led Hitler to invade the country. On March 13, 1938, Austria became part of the Reich under the name of Ostmark. At the end of World War II, Austria was separated from Germany, with a republican form of government.

BABYLONIA

At two periods the territory of Babylonia, located in the lower valley of the Tigris and Euphrates, was the center of an empire with the city of Babylon as its capital. The first Babylonian empire was organized from the Mesopotamian states by Hammurabi about 2000 B. C. About 1500 B. C. this empire in its growth came into conflict with Egypt, and later with the increasing power of its rival, Assyria. But the city of Babylon continued to be a center of political power and culture until the 8th century B. C., when it fell before the Assyrians.

The second Babylonian empire arose about 625 B. C., when the people rebelled against Assyrian tyranny and divided the Assyrian dominions with the Medes. This state lasted until 538 B. C., when the Persians captured Babylon. Within this period falls the brilliant reign of Nebuchadnezzar, who rebuilt Babylon with great magnificence and extended his power beyond the bounds of the first empire. In his reign the city of Jerusalem was sacked and many Jews were carried off as captives to Babylon. See *Sumerians.*

BARBARY STATES

The Barbary States are the North African lands of Morocco, Algeria, Tunis, and Tripoli. The name Barbary is derived from the Berbers, who were the earliest known inhabitants of the territory. In the 9th and the 10th century B. C. the Phœnicians colonized northern Africa, their principal city being Carthage. Their state was conquered and the city of Carthage destroyed by the Romans in 146 B. C. North Africa formed one of the most prosperous provinces of the Roman Empire, and the extensive ruins of great Roman towns and public works are still to be seen in many places. With the decline of the empire, a state of anarchy ensued, and the Vandals found the country an easy prey. The first tide of Mohammedan conquest swept over the country in 647. The Arabs mingled with the Berbers, and the combined races advanced into Spain, where they were known as Moors.

After the expulsion of the Moors from Spain, the fugitives settled on the African coast, and the states there formed became the home of piracy. Spain in the 16th century and France in the 17th made vigorous war on these Barbary pirates, but with little success. During the 18th century all the Christian states were paying tribute to the heads of the Barbary States, which were either independent or nominally under the government of the Turkish sultan. In 1815 the United States forced Algeria, Tripoli, and Tunis to cease attacks on American shipping. England took similar action in 1819. The French established control of Algeria in 1847. Tunis since 1881 and the greater part of Morocco since 1912 have been French protectorates. The Franco-Spanish treaty of 1912 recognized Spanish rights in Morocco, and confirmed Spain in control of a strip of Mediterranean coast about 60 miles wide and 200 miles long. Italy conquered Tripoli and Barca in 1912 and united them in one colony as Libya.

BAVARIA

Bavaria, the second largest state of the former states, and since 1934 an administrative unit, of Germany, has long been famous for its literature, art, and music. Its name is derived from the Latin *Boiarii*, the name given to the Germanic tribe that seized the land of the Boii (Bohemia) and drove out the Celtic people of the present Bavarian territory. These Celts were subject to Rome from 15 A. D. to the fall of the Western Empire. The Franks overran the country about the 6th century, and Charlemagne later made it part of his empire. In 1180 an imperial grant placed the count of Wittelsbach in power, and descendants of that family ruled as counts, dukes, and kings until the establishment of the republican Free State of Bavaria in 1918.

Bavaria sided with Napoleon against Austria, and in 1805 he made it a kingdom, a dignity which the king, by adroit changing of sides in 1813, managed to retain. In 1818 a constitution was adopted, but King Louis I was more interested in rebuilding and embellishing his capital, Munich, than in promoting popular liberty. His policy, followed by his successors, made Munich one of the most beautiful cities of Europe and enriched it with art and scientific collections. The year 1848 brought an uprising of the citizens of Munich, who demanded further political reform. Louis abdicated, and his son, Maximilian, acceded to the demands of the people.

In 1866 Bavaria sided with Austria, and after the Prussian victory she was compelled to cede territory to Prussia and form an alliance. This alliance as well as national feeling placed her by the side of Prussia against France in 1870 and brought her into the German Empire. After the collapse of Germany in 1918 a radical government was formed under the leadership of Kurt Eisner, an Independent Socialist.

After the assassination of Eisner by a reactionary army officer, the inability of any one group to maintain a government resulted in a period of great disorder. At length, with the military aid of the central German government, the city of Munich was wrested from the extremists. A moderate coalition government secured the adoption of a new constitution in August 1919.

Further difficulties arose over disarming the "home guards," but Bavaria became a part of the German Republic. In November 1923 Munich was the scene of an unsuccessful revolt which brought Adolf Hitler into prominence. At Munich, September 30, 1938, was signed the agreement by which England, France, and Italy allowed Germany to take the Sudeten lands from Czechoslovakia. See *Germany*.

BELGIUM

The name of this heroic little country comes from that of a division of the ancient Roman province of Gallia Belgica, of which modern Belgium includes only a small part. Throughout the middle ages this name, of which the French form is *Belgique* and the Flemish, *Belgie*, was used locally for the southern provinces of the Netherlands, which remained loyal to Catholicism and Spain when the northern Netherlands attained independence, in 1579, as the United Provinces. This territory, on account of its strategic military position and its agricultural, industrial, and commercial wealth, has been coveted and fought for by all the nations of western Europe. Its history has been colored by the rivalry of the Germanic and Celtic peoples who have occupied it, by their religious differences, and by the conflict of the agricultural interests of the South with the commercial interests of the North.

A Province of Spain and Austria. The earlier history of Belgium belongs to the story of Flanders and the Netherlands in the middle ages. After the successful revolt of the United Provinces in 1579, the duke of Parma diplomatically retained the Belgic provinces for Spain, but the oppressive and bigoted measures of the Spanish government put a blight upon the flourishing industries of the country and drove artisans and merchants to England and to the Dutch Republic. Grass grew in the once busy streets of Ghent and Bruges. From 1598 to 1633, under Archduke Albert and his wife Isabel, daughter of Philip II of Spain, the country was officially independent, but in 1633 it reverted to Spain, and, as the Spanish Netherlands, entered upon a long period of disaster. It was the pawn in the wars of the 17th century. As the battlefield of contending armies, it justified its name, the "cockpit of Europe." France seized much of its territory, and the closing of the Scheldt river to shipping in 1648 shut its cities out from the ocean and commerce.

A brief respite from disaster came when the Bavarian elector, Maximilian Emanuel, an able and enlightened ruler, was made governor in 1692. He endeavored to revive commerce by the building of canals to take the place of the Scheldt river. But at the opening of the 18th century the insatiable ambition of Louis XIV again made the country a battle ground. Louis's desire to annex Belgium was thwarted by the successful campaigns of the English, Dutch, and Austrians, under Marlborough, and the Peace of Utrecht in 1713 gave the country to Austria. For a century it was known as the Austrian Netherlands.

The Belgians were jealous of their local liberties, especially of the right of their own assemblies, or "states," to levy or approve taxes, and the Austrians for a time found their new subjects difficult to rule. But a liberal policy was maintained, first by the archduchess Mary Elizabeth and later by Charles of Lorraine, Austrian governors. The latter was known as the "Good Governor" for his efforts in enlarging the canal system, in developing agriculture, and in providing for education. Among other institutions, he founded the Academy of Science.

Belgian Independence. The victorious armies of the French Revolution brought the Belgians into the Republic in 1794, and until the fall of Napoleon in 1814 they were governed as French people. In 1815 the Congress of Vienna joined the country to Holland in the Kingdom of the Netherlands, a union which, in view of the commercial power of Holland and the industrial resources of Belgium, would seem wise. But the conflicting temper and interests of the two peoples at once became evident. Differences arising from history, religion, and language could not be settled. In spite of real progress and prosperity in this period under the rule of the Dutch king, the Belgians found grievances in the large number of Dutch officeholders, in the regulations set up for education, and in the government's policy of religious toleration. Liberal and Clerical parties joined in a demand for separate administration of the Belgian provinces. This was finally granted, but not until the extremists had forced a national revolt in 1830.

In 1831, with the approval of a conference of the Powers, called in London, the Belgians adopted a constitution providing for a Senate and a Chamber of Deputies, a ministry responsible to the legislature, and a king with restricted powers. Leopold of Saxe-Coburg was elected king of the Belgians. Belgium was made, by treaty among the powers, an independent, neutral state. Holland, however, withheld assent until 1839, when a final settlement of boundaries was effected.

Political and Economic Progress. The great confidence placed by the people in King Leopold carried Belgium through the revolutionary period of 1848 without disturbance, that year being marked only by an extension of the franchise by lowering the property qualification of voters. This question of the franchise has continued to share with the question of public education the first place in Belgian politics. Several reforms have been effected. In 1892 a system of plural voting was adopted, the right to more than one vote being dependent upon the possession of certain property or educational qualifications. In 1899 the system of proportional representation was put in force. But great inequalities in the suffrage still remained. In 1919 the Parliament ordered elections on a "one man, one vote" basis, and the new Parliament was required to legalize this system of election. Widows of soldiers killed before Jan. 1, 1919, who had not married again, or the mothers of such soldiers, widows or mothers of civilians shot by the enemy, and women who had been imprisoned for patriotic acts, were allowed to vote.

Belgium, in the 19th century, rapidly grew into an industrial country, and about 1886 Socialism became a political force. Frequent strikes led to extension of the suffrage already referred to and to the passing of much progressive legislation, providing, among other things, for industrial councils of employers and workmen, for regulating hours of labor, for old age pensions, and for better education.

At the death of Leopold I in 1865 his son was proclaimed king as Leopold II. The new king proved himself a shrewd business man and an able administrator. His influence was strong in extending Belgian trade, but his chief accomplishment was the acquiring of the Belgian Congo, or Congo Free State. He was succeeded in 1909 by his nephew, Albert I. Before Albert had been five years on the throne, the World War broke out, and the succeeding ordeal proved him a masterful man.

The World Wars. On Aug. 2, 1914, Germany demanded free passage of German troops through Belgium to attack France. Belgium refused, and a German invasion began in direct violation of Germany's treaty agreement of 1839. Belgian forces, bravely contending, were defeated and compelled to retreat. On Aug. 20 the Germans took Brussels, levying upon it a war tax of $40,000,000. The city of Louvain was burned, Aug. 27. Ghent and other cities were in turn occupied. On Oct. 8 Antwerp fell. Hundreds of thousands of refugees found shelter in England, Holland, France, and America. The remaining population was subjected to barbaric indignities. Cities and towns were fined, and their treasuries looted; the machinery of factories was removed or destroyed, and many citizens were deported to Germany. But the German policy of "frightfulness" failed to crush the national spirit. The army continued to fight heroically in the Allied lines, while the patriotism of the king and the loyalty of the people were unwavering. Finally, in the autumn of 1918 the invaders were forced to withdraw. On Nov. 22 King Albert re-entered Brussels at the head of the victorious army, and Belgium was proclaimed a free and independent nation. The Treaty of Versailles in 1919 abrogated the neutrality treaties of 1839 and provided for new agreements to take their place. After the conclusion of peace, the Belgian people made remarkably rapid progress in the work of reconstruction in their devastated areas. The government formed a defensive alliance with France. King Albert was killed by a fall while rock-climbing, February 17, 1934, and his son succeeded him as Leopold III. In October 1936, Belgium proclaimed her neutrality. Nevertheless, she was invaded and occupied by the Germans in 1940. King Leopold became a German prisoner, while the cabinet retreated to England and set up a government-in-exile there. Belgium was liberated by the British and Americans in September 1944 and the exiles returned. A regency was set up under Prince Charles, brother of King Leopold. See *Belgian Congo*, *Flanders*, *Netherlands*, *World Wars*.

BRITTANY

Brittany is the medieval and popular modern name applied to the district in the northwest peninsula of France, now included in the departments of Finistère, Côtes-du-Nord, Morbihan, Ille-et-Vilaine, and Lower Loire, called in ancient times *Armorica*, meaning "upon the sea." The Romans subdued this territory in 51 B. C. In the 5th century, Celtic people, fleeing before the Anglo-Saxon invasion of Britain, settled a large part of the peninsula. From the name of these people, Britons, came the names Brittany for the country and Bretons for the people. They built up a powerful aristocracy and fought off both Frankish kings and Norman dukes. In the 12th century, however, Conan IV, duke of Brittany, called on Henry II of England for help against rebellious Breton nobles. Henry forced Conan to give his daughter in marriage to Henry's son Geoffrey, who thus became duke of Brittany. But a French line soon succeeded this dynasty, and in 1532 Brittany was annexed to France. The Bretons, however, retained many special rights until the French Revolution.

BULGARIA

The modern kingdom of Bulgaria occupies virtually the territory of the ancient Roman province of Mœsia. In the 4th and 5th centuries A. D., a Slavic people invaded this district, and about a century later came the Bulgars, a people related to the Huns. A mingling of Bulgars and Slavs took place, and these racial elements have since been supplemented by mixture with neighboring peoples. About the middle of the 9th century, Christianity was introduced into the state, which had been growing into power. In addition to religious faith, the Bulgarians in this period borrowed many cultural elements from the Greeks, some of which they later transmitted to Russia.

In the 12th and 13th centuries, the Bulgarian state rose to great power, only to be surpassed by Serbia as the leading Slav state, and to fall a prey to the Ottoman Turks in the latter part of the 14th century. Not until the last quarter of the 19th century did Bulgaria again have a distinct national existence.

A revolt in 1876 against the crushing tyranny of the Turk was put down with the barbarously cruel measures known as the "Bulgarian atrocities." This was the occasion of the Russo-Turkish war of 1877–78, out of which Bulgaria emerged as an autonomous principality, tributary to Turkey. In 1885, through a revolution, Eastern Rumelia was united to Bulgaria. Prince Alexander abdicated in the following year, and in 1887 Prince Ferdinand of Coburg was elected by the people. In spite of opposition on the part of the European powers, Ferdinand, with the aid of his minister, Stambulov, so strengthened his power that, in 1896, he was recognized as prince of Bulgaria.

Under the rule of Ferdinand, the Bulgarian state made rapid progress in economic growth and in military power. In the midst of political disturbances in Turkey in 1908, Ferdinand proclaimed the independence of the Bulgarian kingdom. In 1912,

Bulgaria made common cause with her former enemies—Serbia, Montenegro, and Greece—against the Turk, but lost the greater part of her gains in the Second Balkan war. In 1915 Bulgaria entered World War I on the side of the Central Powers, and again suffered heavy losses.

Bulgaria was forced by the Axis powers into World War II, but changed sides when invaded by Russia in 1944. Two years later, September 8, 1946, the boy king, Simeon II, was deposed, and Bulgaria became a republic. The peace treaty, signed February 10, 1947, promised free elections and a democratic government, but in the following months the Communists gained control, suppressed all other political parties, executed their leaders, and set up a Communist régime under Russian control, against the protest of the Western signatory powers.

BURMA (UNION OF BURMA)

This recently created Asiatic republic is on the east coast of the Bay of Bengal. Burmese tradition suggests the immigration of a people from the northwest, about 2000 years ago, who conquered the earlier inhabitants and set up a kingdom. When European traders first entered the country, in the 15th century, the kings of Ava, who traced descent to the early Buddhist rulers of India, were supreme. Toward the close of the 16th century, power passed to the kings of Pegu, a southern capital, but the French and English, who began trading at the delta of the Irrawaddy, early in the 18th century, found a weak government. In 1753-54, Alompra, a village chief of Ava, made himself master of Burma and founded a peculiarly bloodthirsty and cruel dynasty. England gained control of southern Burma in 1853, by the annexation of Pegu. In 1885 the British deposed King Thebav, and in 1886 Burma became a part of the British Empire. It was made a province of India in 1895; a separate colony, with partial self government, in 1937. It was overrun by the Japanese in 1942. The British returned in 1945 but Burmese dissatisfaction led the British government to offer them a choice between Dominion status and independence. Burma chose the latter, and became independent January 4, 1948. See *Burmese.*

CEYLON

Ceylon (*sē-lŏn'*) is a British dominion in the Indian Ocean. The traveler of today in the island of Ceylon may see the ruined remains of temples, monasteries, and palaces of a size and splendor rivaling the structures of ancient Egypt, and gardens and baths as luxurious as those of Rome. The creation of this magnificence was the work of the Singhalese. Vijaya, a prince from the valley of the Ganges, invaded Ceylon in 543 B. C. and established a dynasty. The island was called Lankā in early Sanskrit works, but Vijaya called it Sinhala, and the colonists he brought from the neighboring mainland of India took the name of Sinhalese or Singhalese. In the reign of King Tissa (307 B. C.), Buddhism was made the state religion, and the famous sacred bo tree was planted (288 B. C.). After several centuries of conflict with invading Malabars, another notable era in the history of Ceylon began in 1155 A. D. with the reign of Parakrama, famed for the monuments of architecture he left behind him.

In 1505 the Portuguese reached Ceylon, and gradually conquered the coastal lowlands. In 1638 the Dutch invaded the island, and conquered the Portuguese after a 20-year struggle. Both were seeking a monopoly of the cinnamon trade. In 1796 the English took it from the Dutch, desiring mainly the naval base of Trincomalee. The island was ceded to England in 1802. In 1815 the English completed their occupation by conquering the Kingdom of Kandy, in the central highlands. The chief features of recent history have been the rise and fall of the coffee industry and the substitution of tea and rubber. In 1946 the island received a new constitution, providing for responsible government. On February 4, 1948, it received dominion status. See *Singhalese.*

CHINA

Chinese tradition carries the story of civilization in eastern Asia back to about the year 2852 B.C. The historical period, however, begins in 841 B.C. during the rule of the Chou dynasty (1122-256 B.C.).

The long period of the Chou kings was distinguished by remarkable progress in literature and the arts. It was during the reign of the Chou dynasty that Confucius lived (551-479 B.C.). Luxury and war had brought the Chinese people to a low ebb of moral and political life. The teachings of this great sage, with those of his older contemporary, Lao Tzu, and those of Mencius, a disciple of Confucius, who lived in the 4th and 3d centuries B.C. (372-289), are represented as an unavailing protest against the decay of their times.

The Chou dynasty fell into anarchy and was supplanted by the Ch'in, from which comes the name of China. The Ch'in dynasty abolished feudalism and built the Great Wall, but was short-lived. The Early and Later Han dynasties followed (206 B.C.-220 A.D.). During this period intercourse with Rome began and Buddhism was introduced.

The Golden Age. After a long series of divisions and civil wars, the great T'ang dynasty arose (618-907 A.D.). The empire was extended as far west as the Caspian Sea. Embassies came from Persia, from Tibet, from Annam, and from Japan. Nestorian missionaries introduced Christianity. The Arabs brought in Mohammedanism. The Chinese capital became a center of international influence. Commerce flourished, literature was encouraged, and the invention of printing from movable blocks gave a great impetus to bookmaking. It was the golden age of Chinese poetry and painting. The Sung period (960-1278) was distinguished for its philosophical speculation.

The Mongols, led by Genghis Khan, invaded China and ruled from 1280 to 1368. Marco Polo has described the glorious reign of Kublai Khan. His successors were unequal to the task of ruling so great an empire and soon lost the throne. Dramatic writing characterized the literature of the period.

The Manchus; Relations with the West. The Ming dynasty succeeded. Under its sway modern intercourse with Europe began. The Portuguese discovered the route via the Cape to the Far East and arrived in China in 1516. The Ming dynasty was replaced in 1644 by the Manchus. The mark of their mastery was the requirement that Chinese men should wear the queue. The Manchus adopted the language and general customs of the people they ruled. Russian aggression was stopped. By the treaty of 1689 the Muscovite was compelled to leave the Amur valley.

Gifts sent to the court by Western potentates were considered as tribute, and the refusal of the representatives of these powers to perform the kotow, as China's tributaries did, was regarded as insubordination. To the Europeans, this was an arrogant assumption of superiority, and it was met by an overbearing attitude upon their part.

Growth of Trade; Treaties with Western Powers. In spite of the political friction, trade at Canton flourished. The British East India Company enjoyed the largest share of it. This company was dissolved in 1834. Opium smuggling constituted a good part of the foreign trade. The attempt to suppress this smuggling, added to other causes of friction, brought on war with Great Britain.

The treaty of peace of 1842 and the commercial treaty of 1843 opened five ports to foreign trade and limited Chinese import and export duties to 5 per cent *ad valorem.* The first American treaty, that of 1844, provided definite arrangements for the exercise of extraterritorial jurisdiction.

The seizure of a Chinese vessel in 1856 by the Chinese, on the charge that acts of piracy had been committed by some of the crew, was the occasion of further trouble with Great Britain, for the vessel had had a British charter and was still flying the British flag. This, with the repeated refusal of the Chinese to revise the treaties and to redress various other grievances, brought on the second war with Great Britain, in which the French joined. It resulted in the revision of the treaties, the legalizing of the opium traffic, diplomatic representation at Peking, and the toleration of Christianity.

The Taiping rebellion had meanwhile been in progress. It was suppressed in great part by the "Ever Victorious Army," which was organized and led by the American general, Frederick Townsend Ward, and, after he had been killed in battle, was commanded for a short time by Charles George Gordon—whence his sobriquet of "Chinese Gordon."

In 1868 the United States entered into a treaty with China to encourage Chinese immigration. It was supplemented in 1880 by another permitting the suspension of labor immigration. In 1894 China agreed to a suspension for ten years. In 1904 China refused to extend the period, and Congress made Chinese coolie exclusion perpetual.

War with Japan. In 1894 Japan forced a war upon China over the control of Korea. China was defeated, and by the treaty of Shimonoseki she recognized the independence of Korea and ceded to Japan the Liaotung Peninsula, Formosa, and the Pescadores. Russia, Germany, and France protested against the Japanese holding of Liaotung and compelled its restoration to China, but they proceeded to take advantage of China's revealed weakness to press their own claims to compensation for their intervention. Russia obtained railway rights in Manchuria; Germany added to her claim that of compensation for the murder of two missionaries and secured the lease of Kiaochow; Russia then demanded and obtained further compensation in the lease of a portion of Liaotung; France secured Kwang-chow Wan; and Britain, to preserve the balance of power, obtained the lease of Weihaiwei and the enlargement of her Hongkong colony. These extorted leases were followed by the assertion, by various powers, of claims to spheres of interest in different regions.

The Boxer Rising. The United States took the position of insisting upon an "open door," or equality of opportunity, in these spheres of interest. The aggressive attitude of the European powers brought on the "Boxer" rising, which at first was a movement directed against the Manchu government because of its supineness, but subsequently was converted into an antiforeign rising.

The suppression of this disturbance brought about a few progressive changes in Chinese administration, which were given further impetus by the Japanese victory over Russia in 1905. Large numbers of Chinese students were sent to Japan, to Europe, and especially to the United States, whose remission of a portion of her share of the Boxer indemnity each year, as it was being paid, provided an annual fund for the American education of Chinese.

The Republic. In 1911 a dispute over the building of a railway by means of a foreign loan was the immediate cause of the revolt that swept the Manchus out of power in 1912. Dr. Sun Yat Sen, who had long worked for this result, became provisional president of the government set up in the South in January 1912. In March, a reconciliation of the North and the South was effected, and Yuan Shih-kai was elected to the office of president.

Yuan's government was republican only in name, and the division between the North and the South grew more pronounced. A threatened establishment of a new monarchy with Yuan as emperor was prevented in 1915 by the warning of Japan, who had never forgotten nor forgiven Yuan since, as imperial resident in Korea in 1894, he had striven to strengthen Chinese power there at the expense of Japanese influence. Yuan Shih-kai died in 1916, and Li Yuan Hung became president. The Parliament, which had been dissolved by Yuan Shih-kai, was reassembled.

China during the World War. Meanwhile, during the World War, Japan, assisted by Great Britain, had taken up the task of eliminating the Germans from their position in Shantung. She pushed her expedition beyond the limits of German occupation and forced demands on China, the acceptance of which gave Japan virtual control over the valuable province of Shantung. In March 1917, at the invitation of the United States, China broke off diplomatic relations with Germany and in the summer declared war.

A secret treaty between Chinese and Japanese militarists had alarmed the Parliament, which for a time refused to declare war. This led to an overthrow of the cabinet and an attempt by a Manchu general to re-establish the Manchu dynasty. Parliament was dissolved, but a portion reassembled at Canton and set up an opposition government. The dynastic movement was suppressed within six days. Representatives of the Canton faction and of the recognized government united in a refusal to sign the Versailles treaty, because it gave to Japan the territorial and economic rights formerly enjoyed by Germany in Shantung. The Shantung question was, at length, satisfactorily adjusted by a treaty between China and Japan signed during the Washington Conference, 1921-22.

Recent Developments. In 1923 Ts'ao K'un was elected president. Sun refused to recognize him. Sun had agreed to receive Russian political and military advisers with arms and money. In 1924 Peking signed a treaty with the Soviet government giving the latter the desired recognition. In the autumn of 1924 a coalition of the "Christian General" Feng, the War Lord of Manchuria, Chang, and Dr. Sun seized Peking, deposed President Ts'ao and made Tuan Chih-jui chief executive. Dr. Sun died March 12, 1925. An international conference on tariff autonomy was held at Peking in October 1925 and one on extraterritoriality in January following. Both conferences were broken up by a rupture of the alliance between the "Christian General" and the War Lord of Manchuria, who drove Feng out of Peking. Chang became dictator. Meantime the Russians at Canton had organized labor and peasant unions and schooled them in Communism and in antiforeign and anti-Christian propaganda. These paved the way for the easy triumph of the Nationalist army, which captured the Wuhan cities in the autumn of 1926 and took Nanking in March 1927. Shanghai had been occupied a few days earlier by another Nationalist force. The capture of Nanking was stained by outrages upon the foreign residents, chiefly Americans. A year later apology was made and duly accepted.

When General Chiang Kai-shek discovered that the Russian advisers of the political committee at Hankow were responsible for the outrages at Nanking, he repudiated the authority of that committee and set up a separate government at Nanking. In June 1927 he formed an alliance with the "Christian General" Feng in the North. Yen Hsi-shan, governor of Shansi, a northern province, joined this alliance. The Russian advisers were forced to leave Hankow, and their followers in south China, charged with Communism, were massacred in large numbers. General Chiang, having thus established himself in control and having secured the aid of his northern allies, moved northward in April 1928.

The Japanese had sent a considerable force into Shantung to protect Japanese lives and property. The Nationalist troops came into collision with them on May 3. Desultory fighting continued for eight days. On May 18 Japan warned both Chinese belligerents against war in Manchuria and later made a futile attempt to prevent the union of Manchuria with Nationalist China. Marshal Chang Tso-lin issued a statement that he had no quarrel with Nationalism and had seized Peking to check Communist activity there. He withdrew from Peking without fighting and the southern forces made no attempt to interfere with this movement. Chang was murdered by a bomb on his arrival at Mukden June 4. Peking was occupied by the forces of Governor Yen on June 8, 1928. The Nationalists moved the capital to Nanking and changed the name of Peking to Peiping.

New treaties with the principal powers in 1928 restored tariff autonomy to China. But the government was hampered by military revolts, and the advances of Communism. In 1931 Japan seized Manchuria and turned it into the puppet state of Manchukuo. China replied with a boycott of Japanese goods. In order to break this boycott, the Japanese occupied Shanghai, but later evacuated it. In 1935 Japan advanced into Inner Mongolia and Hopei, while Russian pressure in the west continued.

In 1937, however, Chinese resistance stiffened and regular, though undeclared, war broke out. The Japanese had the advantage of superior equipment and a unified command. By 1940, the Japanese had captured the six largest cities of China—Peiping, Tientsin, Shanghai, Nanking, Hankow, Canton—and had occupied eastern China. The Chinese under Generalissimo Chiang Kai-shek established a national government at Chungking, which also had to contend with "communistic" dissent in the north.

When Japan entered World War II in 1941, British and American aid to China was increased. Chinese troops continued the war in the south, and occupied the southern cities after Japan surrendered. China became a permanent member of the Security Council of the United Nations. Quarrels between the Nationalist (Kuomintang) government at Nanking under Chiang Kai-shek, and the Communists in the north under Chou En-lai still divided China. General Marshall's attempt at mediation in 1946 failed. The Nationalists framed a constitution under which Chiang Kai-shek was later elected president. Inflation was ruining the national economy, and the people were getting tired of war. Through 1947 and 1948 the Communists, now better equipped with the Japanese arms they had acquired in Manchuria, made steady gains. By the beginning of 1949 Mukden was in their hands, Peiping and Tientsin has fallen, they controlled North China, and were driving on Nanking and the line of the Yangtse. In January 1949 the Nationalist government abandoned Nanking for Canton, Chiang has resigned his power to the vice president and retired, probably to Formosa. The Communists, with Russia behind them, were triumphant.

CISALPINE REPUBLIC

This name attaches to the short-lived state in northern Italy which Napoleon created in 1797, to include Lombardy, the duchies of Parma and Modena, and some parts of Venetia and the papal states. In 1802 it took the name of the Italian Republic, choosing Napoleon as president; in 1805 Napoleon transformed it into the Kingdom of Italy, with himself as king, a status it held until 1814.

CORSICA

The Mediterranean island of Corsica, famous as the birthplace of Napoleon, received its first civilized colonists in a body of Phocæans from Ionia, who founded the town of Alalia in 560 B. C. These people were followed first by the Etruscans, then by the Carthaginians, and at length by the Romans, who established their power in the island about the middle of the 2d century B. C. In the early Christian centuries, Rome used Corsica as a place of banishment for political offenders, one conspicuous exile being the younger Seneca. After the decline of Rome, the island was the prey of Goths, Vandals, Lombards, Franks, and Moors.

To counteract the feudal anarchy which engulfed the country, a kind of republic, called the Terra di Comune, was set up in the north part of the island in the 11th century. This federation of parishes continued to exist until the French Revolution. Pisans, Genoese, and Aragonese fought for the island during the next four centuries. It is within this long period of anarchy and misgovernment that the vendetta, or blood feud, for which Corsica has been noted, is said to have arisen.

From 1568 until 1729, Corsica, exhausted by war, was peaceful under Genoese control. After another period of disturbance and a bold attempt at independence led by the most famous hero of Corsican freedom, Pasquale Paoli, France completed a conquest of the island in 1770. Paoli led another revolt in 1793, which was followed by a British occupation of two years. Under Bonaparte, French authority was again asserted. Since 1815, Corsica has been a department of France.

CRETE

A large island in the eastern Mediterranean. Extensive remains of palaces recently discovered in the island have established the fact that from about 2800 B. C. it was the seat of a highly developed civilization, to which the name Minoan has been given, after the name of a legendary lawgiver, Minos. By 2000 B. C. Crete exported vases to Egypt. About 1500 B. C. the island established control over the sea as far as Sicily to the west and Canaan to the east. The people were possessed of a system of writing, although, as late as the year 1923, scholars had not been able to decipher it. The ancient Cretans showed much skill in engineering and architecture; and the Greek legends of the labyrinth, from which Theseus could find his way out only by carrying one end of a silk thread given him by Ariadne, seem to find substantial verification in the remains of the elaborate palace in the former city of Cnossus. Carvings and paintings of great refinement have been discovered, such as might do credit to Daedalus, the legendary artificer of the labyrinth. The paintings indicate that bull fighting by young men and young women was a popular amusement. This custom may well have given rise to the story of the Athenians that Crete had once levied on them a tribute of youths and maidens to be devoured by the Minotaur or "bull of Minos." Greek legends made Minos a judge in Hades. The Greek myths regarding Crete, so remarkably confirmed by modern investigation, bear witness to the transmission by Crete to Greece of numerous arts.

In early historical times, Crete was conquered by a Greek race and had a government much like Sparta's. It became a great slave market and was a resort for pirates until the Romans conquered it in 67 B. C. The Saracens took it in 823 A. D. Held later by the Venetians, by the Turks from 1669, and claimed by the Greeks since 1830, the island has had an unhappy history of oppression and massacre. In 1912 it was recognized as part of Greece and in the person of Venizelos produced that nation's ablest statesman during the World War.

CZECHOSLOVAKIA

The republic of Czechoslovakia (*chĕK'ô-slô-vä'kĭ-ȧ*) in central Europe was formed from provinces of the former Austro-Hungarian empire. It came into existence October 28, 1918, when the National Council took over the government of the Czechoslovak countries—Bohemia, Moravia, Slovakia, and Austrian Silesia. Two of these countries, Bohemia and Moravia, before their absorption into the Habsburg empire, had attained independent national status. Slovakia formed an important part of the medieval Great Moravian kingdom.

Bohemia (*bô-hē'mĭ-ȧ*). A former crownland of the Austro-Hungarian empire. The name means "home of the Boii," but this Celtic tribe occupied the country for only a short time at the beginning of the Christian era, being driven out or killed by the German Marcomanni. In the 6th century, the territory was occupied by a Slavic people, the Czechs, who were converted to Christianity during the 9th century. Various houses of princes and kings ruled these Czechs, until, under Ottokar II reigning from 1253 to 1278, the kingdom of Bohemia became a powerful state, extending from the Elbe to the Adriatic. It fell before Emperor Rudolf of Habsburg, and became a crownland of the Austro-Hungarian empire.

In 1348, Emperor Charles IV founded the University of Prague, the first in the old German Empire. Under his successor, Wenceslas, the religious movement led by John Huss and Jerome of Prague took place. After 1526, when Ladislas II, king of both Bohemia and Hungary, lost his life in the battle with the sultan Soliman at Mohács, Bohemia became a possession of the house of Habsburg. It was a center of the Reformation struggle, and the bloodiest battle-ground of the Thirty Years' war, which began with the Defenestration of Prague, when the reformers threw three members of the council from a window 70 feet above the ground; they fell in a rubbish heap without serious injury.

Moravia (*mô-rā'vĭ-ȧ*). A district conquered by the Slavs in the 6th century A. D. In the 9th century the Moravian princes formed a powerful kingdom, Great Moravia, but the Magyar invasions reduced this territory. In 1029, Moravia was united to Bohemia, and in 1526 it came into the hands of the Austrian monarchs. The country was almost depopulated during the Thirty Years' war.

All of the districts included in Czechoslovakia had been subject to a determined policy of Germanization pursued by the Austrian government, but in the 18th century, in Bohemia and Moravia, a movement arose for the revival of the Czech language. This developed into a political movement for independence in the 19th century.

Period of Independence. On November 14, 1918, the National Assembly met in Prague, declared a republic, and elected T. G. Masaryk its first president. Masaryk continued, by re-election, to serve as president until 1935, when he was succeeded by Edward Benes. Under the leadership of its two presidents, Czechoslovakia maintained a democratic regime in the midst of neighbors which adopted totalitarian governments and took the lead in maintaining the independence of smaller states through organizing the Little Entente. Czechoslovak foreign policy was oriented toward France, which, with Russia, had agreed to protect Czechoslovakia's independence.

In 1937, the Sudetan Germans, on the border of Germany, led by Karl Henlein, and supported by the Reich, demanded independence. The result was the Munich agreement, and the eventual seizure of Bohemia and Moravia by Germany, while Slovakia became independent. (See *World War II.*) President Benes and his cabinet returned with the Russian armies in 1945. The pre-war constitution and boundaries (except Ruthenia) were restored; Germans and Hungarians were exiled. For the political changes since 1946, see *Government*.

DANZIG

As early as the year 997, Danzig was known as a town of importance. In succeeding centuries, it was held at different times by various states, including Denmark. The Teutonic Knights took possession of the city in 1308. In 1455, having revolted from the Teutonic Knights, it became nominally subject to Poland. It had, however, large privileges, and it was long virtually a free city, governing a considerable extent of neighboring territory, including about thirty villages, a status which was recognized at the first partition of Poland in 1772. In 1793, however, Danzig was annexed to Prussia. After regaining for a time, under Napoleon, its position as a free city, it was returned to Prussia in 1814. By the Treaty of Versailles, Danzig, together with its surrounding territory, was again made a free city, in order to provide a seaport, and commercial outlet for Poland. United to Germany, August 1939, the Potsdam agreement, August 1945, placed it under Polish administration.

DENMARK

Upon the Danish peninsula there are many remains which indicate the presence of man in the early Stone age. Norse sagas contain more or less mythical traditions of the movements of tribes in very early ages, but very little is certainly known of Danish affairs before the 9th century A. D. Probably about the 2d century the coast islands had become the home of the Angles, Saxons, and Jutes, who, in the 5th century, began their invasion of Britain, leaving their former territory to the Danes. The latter, in the following centuries, formed parts of the roving bands of Northmen. The monk Ansgar preached Christianity in Denmark in the 9th century, but the conversion of the country took place in the 10th century only after a bitter struggle between adherents of the old and the new faith. King Gorm the Old is said to have been a determined enemy of the Christians.

Svend (Sweyn) I (985 or 986-1014) was the first Danish king to exercise his power in England. Canute, his son, was the great king of both England and Denmark. His death in 1035 was followed by a period of internal dissensions and external wars, which weakened the country and brought about the introduction of a feudal system whence sprang a powerful nobility.

Reigns of the Waldemars. Waldemar I (1157-82), by the help of his minister, Bishop Absalon, subjugated the Wends and forced them to accept Christianity. During the time of Canute VI and in the early part of the reign of Waldemar II, the conquest of Denmark extended so far into German and Wendic lands that the Baltic was little more than an inland Danish sea. Envy and resentment on the part of the German princes, together with the perfidious conduct of his vassals, served to rob Waldemar II of these brilliant conquests. However, this period of the Waldemars was a time of great internal prosperity. National resources were developed, education spread, a vigorous middle class appeared, guilds were founded, and the yeomen were independent.

But the death of Waldemar in 1241 was followed by a century of misrule and inglorious decadence of the authority of the crown. Under Waldemar's great-grandson, Waldemar III (1340-75), Denmark made a quick but transient recovery of the conquests of the older Waldemars, and a system of national law was framed so as to form one thoroughly exhaustive and comprehensive code. This strong monarch revived the Danehof as a popular assembly and sharply curbed the power of the nobles. His daughter, the great Margaret (1375-1412), first as regent for her only and early lost son, Olaf, and later as sole monarch, ruled Denmark, Sweden, and Norway with such consummate tact and with so light yet firm a hand that, for once in the course of their history, the three rival Scandinavian kingdoms were content to act in harmony. Margaret's successor, Erik, for whose sake she had blended the three sovereignties into one, undermined her glorious work with fatal rapidity and was finally deposed by the nobles. The short reign of his nephew, Christopher of Bavaria, is notable for the ascendancy of the nobles and the oppression of the peasants to the point of serfdom.

The Oldenburg Kings. The Danes, on the death of Christopher in 1448, again exercised their long dormant right of election to the throne, and chose for their king Christian of Oldenburg, a descendant of the royal Waldemar family. As Christian I, he founded the Oldenburg line of Danish kings, which continued unbroken until the death of Frederick VII in 1863. Christian was at the same time elected duke of Schleswig and Holstein, and the resulting combined rule became the source of the later Schleswig-Holstein troubles. The insane tyranny of the otherwise able and enlightened Christian II cost him his throne. Denmark chose his uncle, Frederick I, as king, and Sweden became independent under Gustavus Vasa. Christian III (1534-59), in whose reign Protestantism was established, united the Schleswig-Holstein duchies in perpetuity to the crown. But he and his successor, Frederick II, made trouble by partitioning the duchies among members of their families.

Christian IV (1588–1648) was one of the ablest of Danish rulers. His liberal policy was, however, cramped by the nobles, through whose supineness Denmark and Norway lost some of their provinces to Sweden. During the reign of his son and successor, Frederick III, the last of the old Danish provinces on the eastern side of the sound were lost to Sweden (1658–60). The national abasement which followed led to the rising of the people against the nobles in 1660 and the surrender of the supreme power into the hands of the king. But the common people reaped little benefit from the autocracy they had thus set up. The abolition of serfdom was delayed until the reign of Christian VII. In 1797 it was begun, although the process was not completed until twenty years later. In 1804 the serfs were liberated in the duchies of Schleswig and Holstein.

During the period of the Napoleonic wars, Denmark's attempt to remain neutral brought her into disastrous conflict with England in the battle of Copenhagen (1801), which entailed the loss of her fleet, and in the destructive bombardment of Copenhagen (1807). Her subsequent alliance with Napoleon brought about the loss of Norway by the Peace of Kiel in 1814. After 1830 the discontent and animosity of the Danish and German peoples of Schleswig and Holstein increased and in 1848 broke out into open warfare. The disturbance came to an end in 1851 without settling the difficulty.

Parliamentary Government. Meanwhile, agitation for parliamentary government brought about the adoption of a new constitution in 1849. This provided for a national assembly composed of an upper house, or *Landsthing*, and a lower house, or *Folkething*. The 38 members of the upper house were partly to be appointed by the king, the 114 members of the lower house, elected by the people. But the Germans and other continental powers who had joined in the settlement of the royal succession in 1851 looked upon the new government as too democratic. Repeated futile attempts were made to arrange a constitution that would operate for Denmark and the duchies of Schleswig and Holstein. The matter was finally settled when Prussia and Austria took the duchies in 1864, after Christian IX had come to the throne.

After 1864 Danish history was for a number of years marked by the struggle for supremacy between the Landsthing and the Folkething. The political struggle centered from the first around the question of the control of financial measures. From 1874 to 1894 Estrup, the Conservative premier, was able to maintain his position. However, after his retirement the Radical party gained power. In 1913, after the accession of Christian X (1912), the Folkething narrowed somewhat the king's power and granted suffrage to women. Under the constitutional charter of 1915, universal and equal suffrage has been established and also a system of proportional election. All finance measures must be proposed first to the Folkething.

The past half century has seen a remarkable development of agriculture and commerce in Denmark. Manufacturing is still of minor importance, although home manufactures are notable. The basis of Danish commerce is agriculture and dairying. Most Danish farms are small and owned by the farmers. Nearly a hundred "people's high schools" give instruction in agriculture. Denmark enjoys a strong school system, headed by the University of Copenhagen. In World War I Denmark was neutral. In World War II it was occupied by the Germans, April 1940, and remained under their control, quiet but non-cooperative, until King Christian's authority was restored at the German surrender. King Christian died, April 20, 1947, and was succeeded by his son, Frederick IX.

EASTERN (BYZANTINE) EMPIRE

Constantine the Great, before his death in 337 A. D., divided the administration of the Roman Empire among his three sons and two nephews. In 395, at the death of Theodosius, this division of administration became a permanent division of the empire into East and West. Arcadius became emperor of the East, with his capital at Byzantium, or Constantinople. This Eastern Empire maintained itself for nearly 1000 years after the fall of the Roman power in the West. Such survival was made possible, despite weak frontiers, by the vast wealth at the command of the Eastern emperors, their strong armies, their despotic government, and the almost impregnable position of the city of Constantinople.

The greatest of the Eastern emperors was Justinian, who ruled from 527 to 565. His most notable work was the codifying of the Roman law. Before his death, his realm reached from Spain to the eastern end of the Black Sea and practically commanded all the shores of the Mediterranean, making it again a "Roman lake."

But the following centuries formed a period of almost continuous struggle against Slavs and other barbarians on the north and west, and Persians, Arabs, and Tatars on the east. In the 11th century the reigning emperor appealed to the Western Christians for help, and their answer was the First Crusade. After the Third Crusade, jealousy of the trade and wealth of Constantinople caused the knights of the Fourth Crusade to attack the Christian city instead of the Moslems and divide its diminished lands among Venetians, Genoese, and other Western peoples. After the crusaders had quarreled over their spoils for half a century, the Eastern throne was established again under the family of the Palæologi, the last of whom, Constantine, died heroically defending his capital against the final, irresistible onslaught of the Turks in 1453.

EGYPT

The earliest empire of the ancient world. Its political history begins with Menes, who reigned probably about 3400 B. C. He consolidated the whole Nile valley into a kingdom, with its capital at Memphis, in Lower Egypt. The next thousand years formed a period of rapid development of civilization. About 3000 B. C. King Cheops erected the Great Pyramid, and later kings followed his example, in building pyramids, temples, and tombs. From about 2400 to about 2000 B. C. the country was ruled by a new line of pharaohs, whose capital was Thebes, in Upper Egypt. This period is called the Middle Kingdom, or, by some, the Feudal age. It was a time of foreign conquest, of extended commerce, and of the development of great economic works, such as the irrigation systems and the canal from the Nile to the Red Sea. The Egyptian power reached into Ethiopia and Syria.

The Empire. About the year 2000 B. C. bands of roving invaders from Arabia established themselves in Egypt, and their chiefs at last ruled the land, from a capital in the delta of the Nile, as the Hyksos, or Shepherd Kings. They are said to have introduced the horse into Egypt. It was during this period that the Hebrews, in a time of famine in Syria, came to Egypt. However, the native monarchs of Thebes drove out the foreigners about 1600 B. C., and for about 500 years maintained a powerful military state. They made conquest of Syria and even had a short period of rule in Babylon. Thus came about the first contact of the two ancient civilizations of Egypt and Mesopotamia. Syria and northern Arabia became the routes of travel and commerce. The last and greatest of the strong pharaohs of this period was Rameses II, who waged war against the Hittites and finally made an alliance with them. Rameses was an ardent patron of architecture, and Thebes in his reign is said to have been the most magnificent city of the age, by reason of its wealth of statuary and the splendor of its temples.

Decline of Egyptian Power. About 1300 B. C. the power of Egypt steadily declined, until in 672 it became subject to Assyria. Early in this period, the Hebrews returned to Canaan, escaping from a weak pharaoh. After twenty years of Assyrian rule, Psammetichus, an aggressive leader of foreign blood, restored the independence of Egypt. His greatest service was in opening the country to travelers and colonists. Greeks thronged to his capital of Sais, and the treasures of Egyptian civilization were passed on to the new nations of the north and west. In the reign of his successor, Necho, about 600 B. C., Egyptian sailors are credited with having sailed around the coasts of Africa.

The Ptolemies. In 525 B. C. Persia conquered Egypt and ruled it until Alexander in 332 B. C. established his Greek empire. Egypt now became a Greek state, many Greeks having been already settled in the country, and the Egyptians were treated as an inferior race. Alexandria was founded as the new Greek capital. On the death of Alexander, his general, Ptolemy, took possession of the throne and became the first ruler of a Greek dynasty that for 300 years made Egypt one of the chief kingdoms of the world. The Ptolemies were magnificent patrons of arts and letters. Theocritus, Callimachus, Euclid the geometrician, the astronomers Eratosthenes and Aratus, with many others, flourished under their rule. But, while the Alexandrian Greeks managed to keep down the native Egyptians, they were themselves sinking under the Romans. Ptolemy Auletes, "the Flute Player" (81–51 B. C.), went to Rome to ask help against his subjects, and the famous Cleopatra maintained her power only through her personal influence with Julius Cæsar and Mark Antony.

Roman Rule. On the defeat of Mark Antony by Augustus, 30 B. C., Egypt became a province of Rome. It was still a Greek state, and Alexandria was the chief seat of Greek learning and science. On the spread of Christianity the old Egyptian doctrines lost their sway. Now arose in Alexandria the Christian catechetical school, which produced Clement and Origen. The sects of Gnostics united astrology and magic with religion. From the school of Alexandria emerged such neoplatonic philosophers as Plotinus and Proclus. Monasteries were built throughout Egypt, Christian monks took the place of the pagan hermits, and the Bible was translated into Coptic.

Mohammedan Conquest. On the division of the Roman Empire, in the time of Theodosius, into the Western and the Eastern Empire, Egypt became a province of the latter and sank deeper and deeper in barbarism and weakness. It was conquered in 640 A. D. by the Saracens under Caliph Omar. As a province of the caliphs it was under the government of the celebrated Abbassides, Haroun-al-Raschid and Al-Mamun, and that of the heroic sultan Saladin. The last dynasty was, however, overthrown by the Mamelukes (1250); and the Mamelukes in their turn were conquered by the Turks (1516-17). The Mamelukes made repeated attempts to cast off the Turkish yoke, and had virtually done so by the end of the 18th century. The French conquered Egypt in 1798 and held it till 1801, when they were driven out by the British.

On the expulsion of the French, a Turkish force under Mehemet Ali Bey took possession of the country. Mehemet Ali was made pasha and administered the country vigorously, greatly extending the Egyptian territories. At length he broke with the Porte, and, after gaining a decisive victory over the Ottoman troops in Syria, in 1839, was acknowledged by the sultan as viceroy of Egypt, with the right of succession. Mehemet Ali died in 1849, having survived his son Ibrahim, who died in 1848. He was succeeded by his grandson Abbas, who, murdered in 1854, was succeeded by his uncle Said, son of Mehemet. Under his rule, railways were opened and the cutting of the Suez canal was commenced. After Said's death, Ismail Pasha, a grandson of Mehemet Ali, obtained the government in 1863. His administration was vigorous but extravagant, and brought the finances of the country into disorder. In 1866, he obtained a royal license from the sultan, granting him the title of khedive. In 1879 he was forced to abdicate, under pressure of the British and French governments, and was replaced by his son Tewfik.

British Influence. In 1882 the "national party" under Arabi Pasha revolted and forced the khedive to flee. On July 11, a British fleet bombarded Alexandria and restored the khedive, and Arabi's forces were totally crushed at Tel el Kebir on September 13. A rebellion in the Sudan, under the leadership of Mohammed Ahmed, the so-called mahdi, now gave the government trouble. In 1883 the mahdi's forces annihilated an Egyptian force under Hicks Pasha in Kordofan. British troops dispatched to Suakin inflicted two severe defeats on the mahdi's followers. The British cabinet resolved to abandon the Sudan; General Gordon was sent to effect the safe withdrawal of the garrisons (1884). However, the mahdi's forces were strong enough to shut the general up in Khartum for nearly a year. He perished (January 1885) before the relief expedition could reach him. Since then Anglo-Egyptian troops have reoccupied it. Prince Abbas Hilmi succeeded as khedive in 1892, the British still retaining control. The predominant position of Great Britain in Egypt was formally recognized by France under the Anglo-French agreement of 1904.

British Protectorate. As a consequence of Great Britain's participation in the World War, Egypt was declared a British protectorate, Dec. 17, 1914. The following day Abbas II was deposed. He was succeeded by Hussein Kemal, with the title of sultan. In 1915 and 1916, British troops prevented the success of Turkish efforts to invade Egypt. In 1917 Hussein Kemal died, and his brother became sultan as Fuad I.

Independence. On March 14, 1922 the English House of Commons approved the policy of establishing Egypt as an independent state. Sultan Ahmed Fuad Pasha was proclaimed king on March 16. The terms of this treaty were broadened in 1936 to include the abandonment by the British of extraterritorial courts in Egypt. Egypt was given a share in administering the Anglo-Egyptian Sudan and agreed to facilitate British military action in defending the Suez Canal and Egypt which it did in World War II.

ESTONIA

Estonia is a republic lying north of Latvia and bordering on the Gulf of Finland. From about 1260 to 1560 it was included in a federal republic formed of several Baltic provinces. It then passed to Sweden. In 1710 it was annexed to Russia. On February 24, 1918 Estonia, made up of three provinces of Russia, declared its independence. A constituent assembly was for a time the supreme governing power. In December 1920 the constitution of the Estonian Republic went into force.

A temporary dictatorship, established in 1934, gave way again to parliamentary government in 1936. The "mutual assistance" treaty of September 1939 placed Estonia in Russia's hands; the Communists gained control, and on August 6, 1940, Estonia was admitted to the Soviet Union.

FINLAND

The country of Finland lies on the northwest border of Russia, along the eastern coast of the Gulf of Bothnia. It is called by the Finns *Suomi*. About the middle of the 12th century, the Swedes conquered the pagan tribes inhabiting this region and introduced Christianity among them. The Russians made frequent attempts at the conquest of Finland, and in 1809 it was annexed to Russia as a grand duchy. The Finns always resented Russian control, even while they were allowed local self-government. They were equally opposed to a dominance of Swedish language and culture in Finland. During the latter part of the 19th century, therefore, they bent their energies to revive and cultivate their own language, and to develop the Finnish state along native democratic lines. In these policies, they were remarkably successful, with the measure of self-government allowed by Russia. But in 1897 a policy of repression and thorough Russification was put into force.

This Russian policy was somewhat modified after the revolution of 1905. But the heavy indemnities demanded by Russia, in lieu of military service, occasioned continual friction. On the outbreak of the Russian revolution in 1917, the Finns declared their independence. A conflict ensued between the lower classes of the townspeople, who formed the Red Guards and sided with the Bolsheviki, and the White Guards, made up of the upper classes and the peasantry. With German assistance, the White Guards triumphed, and set up a republic, with a single chamber legislature and a president, in June 1919. Finland alone, of the indebted nations, has kept up its payments to the United States. For Finland's part in World War II, see *Finland*: *Government*; *World War II*.

FIUME

The city of Fiume (*fyōō'mā*) occupies the site of an ancient town of Roman times. From the year 799, the place was under Frankish rule for a long period. Later, it was governed by various feudal lords. In 1471, it passed to the emperor Frederick. From that time until the close of the World War, it lay within the domain of the Austrian empire.

By the Treaty of Rapallo, November 12, 1920, between Italy and Yugoslavia, the independence of the former Austrian city of Fiume was recognized. Equal commercial rights in the port were guaranteed to the Free State of Fiume, to Italy, and to Yugoslavia. Ratifications of the treaty were exchanged in February 1921. The history of the new state, however, was stormy. Fascist violence ousted the new government, March 3, 1922. The Italian government, in response to an appeal from the city, organized a provisional régime, and, in 1924, by agreement with Yugoslavia, the city was annexed to Italy. As a result of the Italian defeat in World War II Fiume became subject to Yugoslavia.

FLANDERS

Flanders was a medieval country of Europe, which comprised the present provinces of East and West Flanders in Belgium, the southern part of the province of Zealand in the Netherlands, and parts of the departments of Nord and Pas-de-Calais, in France. In the division of Charlemagne's empire, Flanders fell to the western Frankish kingdom, or France, while the rest of the country, known later as the Netherlands, went to the kingdom of Lothair. The important history of Flanders begins with Baldwin, called "Iron-arm," who was appointed to defend this Frankish seacoast country against the Northmen in the 9th century. In the 10th century his descendants became counts. They strengthened their position at Bruges, Ypres, Ghent, and other cities by bringing in weavers and laying the foundation of the industrial greatness of those cities. In the 12th century, Count Philip of Alsace further encouraged the growth of the towns by granting them special privileges. The struggles of these "communes" during the next three centuries, to maintain their freedom and political power, forms the most important part of Flemish internal history. They became most powerful in the 14th century, under the leadership of Ghent; but rivalries, especially between Ghent and Bruges, left them at the mercy of their foes. The popular party, called the White Hoods, led by Philip van Artevelde, was defeated by the French forces in 1382. Flanders then became a part of the powerful realm of Burgundy, ruled by Philip the Bold. See *Belgium*, *France*.

FRANCE

The history of France begins with the peoples who dwelt in Gaul long before the Christian era. The principal racial element of the French nation is Celtic. The Celts appear to have entered the country from the north and to have absorbed the scattered primitive tribes. Although the Gauls had a developed civilization when Cæsar began his conquests (58–51 B. C.), they soon became in language and in institutions as Roman as the Italians. Colonists from Italy, however, affected the Gallic population chiefly in the South.

Rise of the Capetian Dynasty. With the barbarian invasions, Roman Gaul fell away from the Empire and became a group of warring kingdoms. The Franks under Clovis were relatively few in number. So were the Goths and the Burgundians. These tribes were soon assimilated by the older population. When the Frankish empire, which Charlemagne (768–814) had created, fell to pieces in the 9th century, France in the narrower sense took its beginnings under the Capetian dynasty, the first of whose kings, Hugh Capet, was consecrated in 987. The Carolingian empire had fallen because it did not rest upon the solid foundation of an organized administration, an imperial revenue, and a law valid throughout its borders. These had been impossible since the decay of Roman power. For them had been substituted varying codes of local or tribal law, a meager income from landed estates, and a body of officials bound to their chiefs mainly by ties of personal loyalty. What is called "feudal anarchy" was coming into existence. The consequence was that when Hugh Capet ascended the throne he found himself master of only a small territory around Paris and Orleans. The great dukes and counts of Flanders, Burgundy, Aquitaine, Brittany, and Normandy recognized his nominal right to the usual feudal services, but held themselves independent in their own territories. The chief task of the kings from the time of Hugh to the reign of Charles VIII (1483–98) was to strengthen the royal power and unify the realm of France.

Several forces aided the kings in their task. One was the Church, which, in its canon law, reflected the old Roman ideal of universality, and in its principle of authority, the notion of an effective royal power. Another influence in the same direction was the towns, which began to grow strong with the revival of trade in the 12th century, for they were the sworn enemies of the feudal nobles. The Crusades also helped, stimulating a feeling of unity in a common cause. Incidentally they impoverished many noble families which exhausted their resources in distant expeditions. The crusades against the Albigenses in southern France during the reign of Philip Augustus (1180–1223) weakened the nobles of that region and enriched the monarchy. It was the same king who, in his wars with King John of England, annexed Normandy and other important fiefs which had belonged to the English crown. Later kings also, by fortunate marriage alliances, by war, by intrigue, and by purchase, added to the royal domain, until at last this was practically coterminous with the kingdom of France.

Philip Augustus is often styled the founder of the absolute monarchy. He allied himself with the lawyers and the clergy against the nobles. His jurists applied the principles of the old Roman law and provided for appeals from local to royal courts. His grandson Louis IX, or St. Louis, embodied in all his acts so high an ideal of justice that his very name grew to be a symbol of kingly authority. In 1302 a States-General was summoned by Philip IV, including delegates from the "good towns" along with the clergy and the nobles. Originating at the same time as the English Parliament, this assembly failed to develop into a strong representative body, capable of sharing with the king the government of the country.

Medieval Civilization in France. The development of royal power by no means sums up French activity in the middle ages. The breakdown of feudalism carried with it the freedom of the rural classes from serfdom as well as the growth of a flourishing body of merchants and artificers in the towns. Agricultural methods were primitive, but the peasant acquired more permanent tenant rights and began to show that love for the soil which has ever been one of the corner stones of French prosperity. Industry was organized under a guild system which lasted until the Revolution. Artistic skill and creative genius found its noblest manifestations in the cathedrals of Paris, Chartres, Amiens, and Reims, in great town halls and palaces of justice, not to forget the castles of wealthy nobles and the dwellings of merchant princes. A literature arose, first in the Latin tongue, afterward in French. Universities were organized, and Paris took its place as a center of light and learning.

England and France at War. The work of medieval civilization in France was menaced and marred by the Hundred Years' war, a struggle between the English heirs of the Angevin empire and their French rivals. It arose out of a disputed succession, after the death of the three sons of Philip IV without male heirs. A curious survival of Frankish times, the so-called Salic law, was given a new meaning by designing intriguers in order to exclude the daughters of the late kings. From this time forward it became the rule in France that succession was strictly in the male line. Accordingly, the throne passed to Philip VI of Valois, a nephew of Philip IV. But Edward III of England claimed the throne through his mother, a daughter of Philip IV. In reality, the conflict grew out of economic rivalries in Flanders and of the desire of the French kings to seize the fiefs which the English kings still held in France.

The Hundred Years' war was rendered illustrious by battles, Crécy (1346), Poitiers (1356), and Agincourt (1415), in which English bowmen proved more than a match for French knights; by the career of Bertrand du Guesclin, who reduced the English possessions to a few coast towns; and by the heroic conduct of Joan of Arc. Joan, when the English had again overrun the country and had conquered all the region north of the Loire, saved Orleans, conducted Charles VII to Reims for his coronation, and drove the English from half a dozen provinces, only to be captured and burned as a heretic and sorceress at Rouen. Shortly after the death of Joan, the duke of Burgundy, who had been driven into the arms of the English by the murder of his father in a factional struggle, made terms with Charles VII and assisted him in driving the English armies from the country. When the war ended in 1453 Calais alone remained under English control. The devastation of the land by armies and by partisan bands had been terrible. Hundreds of villages were reduced to heaps of ruins, haunted by wild animals. The monarchy, however, emerged stronger than before. The work of consolidating the royal domain went on rapidly under Louis XI, so that when he died the only great independent fief was Brittany. His successor, Charles VIII, secured that province by marriage and completed his father's work by creating a thorough military organization.

Expansion of French Power. The campaigns of Charles VIII in Italy marked the beginning of the French policy of expansion abroad, and the reign of Francis I (1515–47) brought into France from Italy the inspiration of the Renaissance. A new era of art and architecture began, rivaling that of the middle ages. This development, again, was retarded by the religious wars, partly a consequence of the Reformation, partly due to factional conflicts between the powerful house of Guise and Protestant nobles and princes. At this time the real ruler was not one feeble monarch after another, but their mother Catherine de' Medici, widow of Henry II, who made up in unscrupulousness what she lacked in strength. After the massacre of St. Bartholomew (1572) the leadership of the Huguenots passed to Henry of Navarre, a Bourbon prince who came to the throne in 1589 as Henry IV. On the principle that "Paris was well worth a Mass," Henry became a Catholic, thus pacifying his Catholic subjects. Then, in 1598, he issued the Edict of Nantes, which granted religious freedom to the Protestants.

With the religious question settled in such a way as to insure quiet at home and also to encourage the Protestant German states in their contest with the Habsburgs, Henry and his minister, Sully, set about the military and administrative strengthening of the crown, with the purpose of making France the first power in Europe, but in the midst of his work he was struck down by an assassin. Several years of regency under Marie de' Medici and a period of personal rule under Louis XIII followed. The States-General met in 1614 for the last time before 1789. In 1624 Cardinal Richelieu took direction of affairs; during the next sixteen years he crushed the Protestant political power and all Catholic oligarchical tendencies, hopelessly divided the German states, and made France a united nation with a highly centralized government. Cardinal Mazarin continued Richelieu's work and left to Louis XIV the machinery of the personal despotism which that monarch wielded for more than half a century. The policy of all the great French kings since the days of Hugh Capet could be carried no further than the absolutism of the Grand Monarch.

Reign of Louis XIV. With the financial genius of Colbert, the engineering skill of Vauban, the organizing gifts of Louvois, and the military talent of Turenne at his command, Louis was able to secure enormous revenue, to build magnificently, and to wage war splendidly. France advanced her frontier northward and eastward by annexations in the Netherlands, by the conquest of Alsace, and the seizure of Franche-Comté. French explorers and traders in America and India laid the foundations of a great colonial empire. In the arts of civilization, France achieved the leadership of Europe. Domestic and public architecture flourished. Poetry and the drama were adorned by the names of Corneille, Racine, and Molière; prose, by those of Bossuet, La Rochefoucauld, and Saint-Simon. But excessive taxation depleted the resources of the people, unprovoked wars set all the powers of Europe against France, and the bigotry and prodigal luxury of king and court sapped the moral foundations of the national life. Louis XIV left to his infant great-grandson, Louis XV, a decaying power.

The Eighteenth Century. The long and disastrous reign of Louis XV, intelligent, but nonchalant and corrupt, culminated in the loss of Canada and the abandonment of India. The discredit of the government abroad made more insistent the demands for reform at home. The great books of the period belong to the literature of criticism and revolution. Authority in State and Church was undermined. Writers like Montesquieu, Voltaire, Diderot, Rousseau, and Turgot were establishing new principles in public law and social economy. Even the monarchy began to take on the characteristics of a benevolent despotism, and it made belated efforts to correct a vicious system of taxation in which the burden rested mainly upon the industrious peasantry. To break down the dead wall of privilege, a Henry IV was needed, but the successor of Louis XV was his weak-willed, half-educated grandson, the unfortunate Louis XVI. He had no lack of able advisers in such finance ministers as Turgot, Necker, and even Calonne, but he had not the persistence of character to push through their schemes against the opposition of the privileged classes. If the country was to be saved from bankruptcy it was essential to abolish exemptions from taxation and to demand its proper share from every form of wealth. Upon Calonne's advice, an assembly of the notables was called in 1787, but this body, composed of privileged persons, was frightened at the thought of thoroughgoing reform. At last the king summoned the States-General and recalled Necker, in whom the public had great confidence.

The Revolution. The States-General, which met at Versailles on May 5, 1789, was composed of members elected by the three orders,—nobility, clergy, and commons. The *cahiers*, or "statements," drawn up by each order, gave promise of speedy agreement upon governmental reform, but the nobles and the higher clergy were opposed to the demand of the commons that all three orders should sit together and vote individually. A long deadlock ensued. After a majority of the clergy and many of the nobles had gone over to the side of the third estate, the king intervened with a declaration aimed at the preservation of the distinction between the three orders. Within four days he was obliged to yield and to sanction the union of all the orders in a single National Assembly. Influenced by the reactionary court nobles, he dismissed Necker. He also called several regiments to the neighborhood of Paris and Versailles. Popular suspicion credited the government with a plan to dissolve the National Assembly.

On July 12 Paris rose, and two days later a mob forced the surrender of the Bastille, a royal fortress and prison which seemed to symbolize the despotism of the old régime. Similar scenes of violence spread over France. This strengthened the hands of the reform party in the Assembly and intimidated their opponents. In a night session, on August 4, nobles, clergy, and commons seemed to vie with one another in renouncing every form of privilege. A few days later the Assembly drew up its famous Declaration of the Rights of Man and the Citizen, proclaiming the new gospel of human equality. The king believed the Assembly was going too far, and he determined to check its career with a royal veto. Again he summoned troops to protect himself against an outburst of popular violence. The result in October was the same as that in July. This time a mob led by several thousand women streamed out to Versailles, brought the royal family to Paris, and compelled the king to take up his residence in the Tuileries.

The National Assembly. In the period from October 1789 to June 1791, the National Assembly, also called the Constituent Assembly, carried through constructive reforms which lie at the foundation of modern French life. The country was redistributed into departments, and a uniform system of local government introduced. New courts with a more liberal mode of procedure protected innocence and reduced the expenses of justice. Landed property was freed from feudal dues, and peasant ownership was promoted. The taxes characteristic of the old régime gave place to a new system which distributed the burden fairly. Here the Assembly's fault was failure to secure prompt collection, with the consequence that revenues steadily failed. A more serious mistake was the attempt to reorganize the Church and to free it from papal control. This followed the confiscation or nationalization of the vast ecclesiastical landed estates, in the hope that by their sale the country could be saved from bankruptcy. The plan of issuing land scrip, or assignats based upon the proceeds of the expected sales, led to inflation, which multiplied the difficulties of the government, especially after 1792.

The king was forced to accept the changes which the Assembly made in the Church, but his conscience was so troubled that he lent himself to schemes of counter-revolution. In this pass of affairs, the king and queen made the fatal error of trying to escape from Paris to the frontier, where a zealous royalist, the Marquis de Bouillé, was in command of the army. They were arrested and brought back. This episode gained importance for two reasons: it confirmed popular suspicion of the king's disloyalty to the Constitution; it gave impetus to a hitherto slow movement toward republicanism.

The Legislative Assembly. The National Assembly adjourned on September 30, 1791, to give place to the Legislative Assembly provided for in the Constitution. But, in an excess of disinterestedness, the members passed a "self-denying ordinance," which declared all members of the Constituent Assembly ineligible for membership in either the new Legislative Assembly or the ministry. The new body, therefore, which met on October 1, was made up of inexperienced men and was subject to the vagaries of doctrinaire leaders and the sway of undisciplined groups among its members.

The evils arising from this lack of statesmanlike counsel in the government were increased by the rise of two radical clubs, the Jacobins and the Cordeliers. To these were added a group of ambitious, unpractical republicans in the Assembly, the Girondists. France was still monarchist; the French people did not desire a republic. But radicalism, spurred by the spirit of self-seeking and rivalry, was rapidly moving toward the destruction of the monarchy without being able to provide a stable government to take its place.

On the other hand, the king and the queen were plotting with the émigrés, or royalists who had fled from the country, and Austria had joined with Prussia during the summer of 1791 in a threat of intervention. The Assembly declared war against Francis II of Austria on April 20, 1792. This also involved Prussia by virtue of the alliance between Francis and Frederick William II. Only Robespierre and a few others opposed the move on the ground that war never helped democracy. But the tide of national feeling was running high, and the Jacobins proclaimed the conflict to be one of democracy against autocracy. When, in the late summer, the Prussian army crossed the French frontier, a manifesto was issued which confirmed this Jacobin view. The manifesto demanded the restoration of Louis XVI to complete liberty of action, under penalty of the sack and ruin of Paris. The Jacobins had their reply ready. They engineered a popular uprising, established a Revolutionary Commune in place of the regular city government, and made an assault on the palace of the Tuileries, compelling the king to take refuge in the hall of the Legislative Assembly. Intimidated by this new revolution, the Assembly, reduced to a third of its numbers, called a convention to draft a constitution on republican lines, and proclaimed universal suffrage. A ministry was elected, of which the leading member was Danton. But it was the Commune rather than the national government that seemed to control the course of events. It signalized its bloody career by permitting its Committee of Surveillance to organize a massacre of political prisoners, nobles, and priests. The butchery went on for four days, and more than a thousand persons perished.

The Convention. On September 20 the Convention, the third of the revolutionary assemblies, which was to last for three years, or until October 26, 1795, began its work. On the same day the army of Prussia was defeated at Valmy, more by its own failure to press home its attack than by the strength of the French armies.

The Convention must be recognized as one of the great governmental bodies of history. The bitter party rivalry between Girondists and Jacobins, resulting in the expulsion of the former, the execution of the king, the Terror with its especial ferocity in Lyons and the Vendée—these are incidents in the defensive and constructive work of that body. Terrible as were these excesses, tragic as was the fate of Madame Roland, the Girondist leader, of Danton, the vigorous compromiser, and of Robespierre, the austere fanatic, such things have not been confined to France of the Revolution.

The first act of the Convention was to declare unanimously that "royalty is abolished in France." Thus almost furtively was the French Republic ushered in. Constitution making was postponed by the bitter struggle between the Girondists, who represented the provinces, and the Jacobins, whose main strength was in Paris. Supported by the Commune, the Jacobins won. The invasion of the Austrian Netherlands and the menace to Holland alarmed the English. The execution of Louis XVI served as the occasion for an outbreak of war, not only with England, but also with Holland and Spain. Soon all Europe seemed united against the regicide republic. The Vendean peasants rose in behalf of king and Church. The Convention met the encircling perils by decreeing universal military service and by organizing a government under a committee of public safety. The opposition was cowed by the threat of trial before a revolutionary tribunal, from whose judgments there was no appeal. Such was the machinery of administration until the danger was past.

The Commune of Paris, led by Marat, forced the Convention to expel the Girondists; they retaliated by arousing a revolt in the departments. The Jacobin Convention hastily prepared a constitution so generous in its democratic provisions that the country ratified it by an overwhelming vote. This took the heart out of the revolt. Having served this purpose, the constitution of 1793 was never put into effect. France had need of a strong government, which was already provided for in the committees and the widely distributed and highly organized Jacobin clubs. The Committee of Public Safety became supreme; its members toiled tremendously. Their method was the appeal to fear, to impress by startling and ruthless action. Carnot raised and equipped a dozen armies, aggregating 750,000 men. Every commander, watched by representatives of the Convention on mission, had the alternative of victory or the guillotine. Under this stimulus, superhuman feats were accomplished. The armies were everywhere victorious against the allies, and civil war was stamped out at home.

Meanwhile, in affairs of peace the Convention wrought greatly. It gave France the metric system of weights and measures; it began the work of codifying the law; it planned an elaborate system of popular education; it created or enlarged many institutions, such as the Polytechnic School of Paris, the Museum of the Louvre, and the National Library. The Convention also devised a new calendar.

The revolutionary tribunal in Paris became increasingly the instrument of the violent elements of the Commune. The success of the Commune, which was wholly antichristian, attained its climax when it set up at Paris in 1793 the worship of Reason. Robespierre condemned this move and a few months later urged the worship of the Supreme Being as the only democratic religion. To enforce this virtuous régime, he seized control of the Tribunal and would have used it to destroy his political enemies, a corrupt group which discredited the Revolution. These men combined to bring about his fall and execution. The power of the Jacobins dwindled, and the Convention in 1795 drew up a new constitution.

The Rise of Napoleon Bonaparte. This third constitution of the Revolution placed the Republic in the hands of property holders, who alone could vote, thus striking a blow at the power of the Paris mob. The Convention added supplementary decrees, in accordance with which two-thirds of the new legislature should be chosen from the membership of the Convention itself. This provoked strong protests, especially in Paris. The conservative elements of the National Guard, with the aid of many royalists, planned an attack upon the Convention. Its defense was undertaken by Barras, one of its members, and he called to his aid an artillery officer, General Napoleon Bonaparte, who had won distinction at the siege of Toulon. Bonaparte turned his cannon upon the advancing insurgent columns, saved the Convention, and at the same time inaugurated a great career.

The time was auspicious for Napoleon. The Terror had robbed France of her natural leaders. The constitution of 1795 provided for a legislative body of two houses, the Council of Five Hundred and the Council of Elders. The executive power was lodged in the Directory composed of five men. Such extreme division of power, with its consequent weakness of decision, made Napoleon's opportunity. After four years of troubled history, the Directory and the Councils reached the verge of collapse. During these same years Napoleon had become the most renowned military commander in Europe. Dispatched to northern Italy in the struggle with Austria, he had won an astonishing series of victories and in 1797 had negotiated the Peace of Campo Formio. One of the consequences was the application in Italy of the French program of reform and the beginnings of the *Risorgimento.* In 1798 he was sent to Egypt, and the luster of Oriental conquest added to his name, although Nelson's destruction of the French fleet at the battle of the Nile deprived France of the fruits of the enterprise. Napoleon now left his army and returned to France. With the opportune and dramatic aid of his brother Lucien, president of the Council of Five Hundred, he executed his famous *coup d'état* in 1799. He dictated a new constitution which provided for three consuls (himself to be first consul with power to initiate all legislation), a tribunate to discuss bills, and a legislative body to vote them.

The Concordat. Now opened the period of the Consulate, a period of reorganization,—administrative, financial, and social. An efficient local government in the departments was put under the control of prefects. The taxes were collected and a bank of France was established. A civil code summed up the legal gains of the citizen during the Revolution, reconciling the new law with the older principles of French jurisprudence. By a concordat the schism, which had vexed the Catholic population since 1791, was brought to an end. New victories over Austria led to the Peace of Lunéville, and even Great Britain saw the necessity of agreeing to a treaty at Amiens in March 1802. All that lacked was political liberty, for the First Consul soon assumed the attitudes of a dictator. With the creation of the Consulate for Life in 1802, France, though still a republic in name, was in fact a monarchy. Two years later Napoleon was declared emperor of the French.

Napoleon, Emperor. Meanwhile, war broke out again with England, which country Napoleon could not reach across the channel. In 1805 the coalition of England, Russia, and Austria was formed against him. He struck at Austria, won the battle of Austerlitz, and dictated the Peace of Pressburg. He then organized the Confederation of the Rhine and destroyed the Holy Roman Empire. In 1806, at Jena and Auerstädt, the Prussian armies crumbled before the French, but the battle of Eylau, February 1807, was a disaster, only partially retrieved by the victory at Friedland in June. Napoleon was satisfied to make the Treaty of Tilsit with Alexander of Russia. England alone remained to be dealt with. The victory of Trafalgar in 1805 had left her supreme on the sea. Napoleon attempted to reach her through his Continental System, that is, by excluding her trade from continental ports and by attacking Portugal, an ally of England, through Spain. But here he went too far in attempting to reduce Spain also. Although he unseated an unpopular Bourbon monarch, he aroused national sentiment which he found unconquerable. This new power of national feeling was in the end the conqueror's undoing.

Leaving Spain hastily when Austria declared war in 1809, he again brought that power to her knees and dictated the Treaty of Vienna. England still was unconquered, even though her industries were feeling the effect of the continental blockade. In 1809 Napoleon was at the height of his career, but the anticlimax was approaching. The Russian campaign in 1812, ending in disaster and retreat, the battle of Leipzig in October 1813, which was a decisive defeat—these were the signals for the defection of the German states. On March 31, 1814 the allies entered Paris, and Louis XVIII was placed on the throne, reckoning himself to be in the 19th year of his reign, king "by the grace of God." He went too far, however, in ignoring the Revolution and Bonaparte, and the people were soon ready to receive their "emperor" again. But the battle of Waterloo sealed his doom. The Congress of Vienna, which had rearranged the states of Europe, trying vainly to forget the Revolution and Napoleon, had already come to a close.

The Restoration. Under Louis XVIII some beginnings toward a liberal government, such as periodical elections, annual voting of the budget, and liberty of the press, were made. But a reaction set in under Charles X, who attempted a *coup d'état* in 1830. He was defeated, and Louis Philippe of the house of Orleans was placed on the throne, with the title "King of the French," instead of "King of France." During his reign, manufacturing industries grew beyond precedent, and the power of the working classes was thereby increased. Socialist doctrines were widely taught, although they were resolutely opposed by the ministry. But Guizot, the prime minister, made the mistake of governing with too little regard for popular movements.

Revolution and the Second Empire. The storm broke in February 1848. The king abdicated and went into exile in England, and a provisional government was compelled by the workmen of Paris to establish "national workshops" and to guarantee employment. The experiment, never sincerely undertaken, turned out to be merely a scheme for occupying the unemployed, which drained the national treasury. When the National Assembly suddenly closed the shops, Paris was thrown into the hands of mobs of idle, half starved workmen, demanding "bread or lead." The terrible "June days" of 1848, when the military crushed the revolt with great severity, left an evil influence in the labor problem of France. But the peasants of the provinces were not in sympathy with the Paris workmen, and conservative republicans were able to put a new constitution in force. A single chamber legislature and a president, to be chosen by popular vote, were provided for. The election made Louis Napoleon president of the second French Republic, largely through the power of the reactionary royalists, made possible his *coup d'état* of 1851, and brought upon France the disaster of the Second Empire.

The new president was a nephew of Napoleon I. In 1832 he had put forward his claims to the throne of France, but, not meeting with encouragement, he had then retired to England. In 1840 he made a second attempt to seize the crown, but this time he was captured and shut up in a fortress, whence he escaped to England. He continued, however, to ingratiate himself with the people by posing as a democrat,—even professing sympathy with the projects of the socialist leader, Louis Blanc. In 1839 he had published a volume on *Napoleonic Ideas*, in which he represented his uncle as the devoted friend of democracy and a victim of tyrants. Now, on the eve of the election of 1848, he adroitly offered himself as the champion of the working classes, the middle classes, and the army. Elected by an overwhelming majority, he set to work at once to arouse enthusiasm for a restored empire. The Assembly refused to aid him, and on December 2, 1851, the anniversary of the battle of Austerlitz, he dissolved that body. A special election gave him a large vote of approval for this *coup d'état.* Another vote in 1852 approved a decree of the Senate making him emperor.

From 1852 to 1860 Napoleon III wielded a despotic rule, largely through the magic of his name. Yet during this period France made great industrial and scientific advance. Railroads were built, the city of Paris was modernized with broad streets and avenues, and institutions of charity and education multiplied. Little of this is to be credited to the emperor. His one real service to France was the acquisition of Nice and Savoy, and this was the outcome of Cavour's adroit use of Napoleon in driving the Austrians out of Italy. His weakness and indecision allowed a more liberal policy of government after 1860 but left France an easy prey to the Prussians in 1870.

Fall of Napoleon III. The Franco-Prussian war grew out of Napoleon's schemes for annexations on the northeastern frontier of France and Bismarck's conviction that only through a German triumph over the French Empire could the unification of Germany be assured. Bismarck seized the occasion of a dynastic controversy apropos of the succession to the crown of Spain to provoke the struggle. French armies crumbled before the German attack, the emperor was made prisoner, and the Empire collapsed like a house of cards. Léon Gambetta led in the proclamation of a republic in Paris,—he raised armies and prepared to defend the city. But adequate training of the troops was impossible, and after a siege of four months the Germans starved Paris into surrender. Bismarck, by the Treaty of Frankfort, May 10, 1871, forced France to cede Alsace and Lorraine to Germany and to agree to pay an indemnity of one billion dollars within three years.

The Third Republic. In this crisis, as in 1793 and 1848, Paris was the center of a radical movement, that of the "Communards." They were not supported outside of the city, and when the provisional government, headed by Thiers, had made peace with Prussia, the National Assembly, sitting at Versailles, suppressed the Commune after a second siege and a terrible week of arson and murder.

The National Assembly then proceeded to the work of framing a constitution. The republican minority gained time and gathered strength against the divided royalists, until they were able to set up the Third Republic in 1875. An unsuccessful attempt to check republican tendencies led to President MacMahon's resignation in 1879. From that time only two incidents seriously disturbed the political peace. In 1887, General Boulanger, a very popular army officer, was tempted to use his popularity to overthrow the Republic, but the attempt ended in his flight and suicide. The Dreyfus affair for a time divided the country. A strong anti-clerical movement led France in 1905 to abrogate the Concordat of 1801 and declare complete separation of church and state.

Economic and Political Growth. In spite of the seemingly crushing burden of the war indemnity of 1871, France speedily cleared the obligation. The Third Republic has been a period of large development in French industries and commerce. In 1870, French colonial possessions were limited to Algeria, the Senegal region, and some small stations on the Gulf of Guinea in Africa, besides a settlement in Cochin China. These have been largely extended until now France controls in her colonies and dependencies an area about twenty times as large as her home area in Europe.

After the Franco-Prussian war the army had been reorganized upon the principle of universal military service. In 1913, following upon large German military preparations, France made feverish efforts to strengthen her army. Within a few months, French territory was invaded and Europe was plunged into a prolonged war, fought chiefly on French soil. See *World War I*.

After the close of the war, French governmental policy was concerned mainly with (1) the problem of security against a renewal of German attack on the Rhine frontier; (2) enforcement of the reparation provisions of the Treaty of Versailles; (3) alliances with the new small states of central Europe; (4) development of French interests in Morocco and the Near East.

In 1922 Prime Minister Poincaré seized the Ruhr and held it for three years as security for reparations payments. Poincaré's successors had to meet a rapid trend toward financial collapse through currency inflation, aggravated by expensive wars in Syria and Morocco. Another Poincaré ministry balanced the budget and stabilized the franc.

Aristide Briand, in the next five years, secured somewhat better relations with Germany. Then came the depression. It brought an end of reparations, it brought the Hitler dictatorship in Germany, and, finally, in 1936, the "popular front" administration of Leon Blum, with its labor disorders.

After 1938 the German danger overshadowed all else. France acquiesced in the annexation of Austria and Czechoslovakia. When Germany invaded Poland France and Britain declared war, Sept. 3, 1939.

World War II. With the armistice of June 22, 1940, France withdrew from the war, completely defeated. See *World War II*. By the terms of the armistice, the Germans occupied northern France, Paris, and the western coast. A totalitarian government under Marshal Pétain and Pierre Laval, set up at Vichy, collaborated with Germany.

Meantime a "Free French" government, headed by General Charles De Gaulle, had been organized in London and recognized by the Allies. Under the name of the National Committee of Liberation, it secured possession of French Equatorial Africa, Syria, and Madagascar; and later of northern Africa.

On the invasion of France, the Committee proclaimed itself the Provisional Government of the French Republic and was accepted by the French people. French troops took part in the invasion and occupation of Germany. France became a member of the United Nations, with a permanent seat on the Security Council. The new government took vigorous steps against the "collaborators." Marshal Pétain was condemned to life imprisonment, and Laval and others executed.

After the rejection of one constitution, due largely to De Gaulle's opposition, a second constituent convention presented another, which was adopted by popular vote, October 13, 1946. De Gaulle had resigned the presidency in January; his successor, Felix Gouin, in June; and Georges Bidault, with the assistance of Leon Blum, carried on the government. Political conditions were highly unstable, owing to the even balance between the Moderate Republicans, the Socialists, and the Communists.

The Fourth French Republic went into operation in January 1947, with a socialist president, Vincent Auriol, and Paul Remadier as premier. In the next two years France had three more prime ministers, Schuman, Marie, and Queuille. Their cabinets had the same general character, a middle-way coalition between De Gaulle's strong government party on the right and the Communists on the left. The Communists were excluded from the Remadier cabinet April 30, 1947. All had to deal with economic problems: inflation, taxes, wages, cost of army and government, with danger from Russia and fear of Germany in the background. The former was manifested in the repeated strikes, largely political, by Communist-led trade unions. The most serious of these was a miners' strike in the fall of 1948, directed unsuccessfully against adherence to the Marshall plan. The latter appeared in disputes over reparations and the settlement of the Ruhr. In 1948 France joined with Great Britain and her smaller neighbors in the Western European alliance.

RULERS OF FRANCE

Name	Lineage	Period of Rule		Birth	Death
	THE OLD FRANKISH KINGDOM	A. D.	A. D.	A. D.	A. D.
	THE MEROVINGIANS				
Clodian	King of the Salian Franks	428?	448	?	?
Meroveus	Founder of the Merovingian dynasty	448	456	411?	456
Childeric I	Son of Meroveus; king of the Franks	456	481	?	481
Clovis I	Son of Childeric I	481	511	466?	511
	THE KINGDOM IN FOUR PARTS				
Childebert I	Son of Clovis I; king of Paris	511	558	495	558
Thierry I	Son of Clovis I; king of Austrasia	511	534	?	534
Clodomir	Son of Clovis I; king of Orleans	511	524	?	524
Clothaire I	Fourth son of Clovis I { king of Soissons	511	558		
	{ sole king	558	561	497	561
	SECOND DIVISION OF THE KINGDOM				
Charibert } Sons of Clothaire I	King of Paris	561	567	?	567
Guntram } Sons of Clothaire I	King of Orleans and Burgundy	561	593	?	593
Chilperic I } Sons of Clothaire I	King of Neustria at Soissons	561	584	?	584
Sigebert I } Sons of Clothaire I	King of Austrasia at Metz	561	575	?	575
Childebert II	Son of Sigebert I; king of Austrasia and Burgundy	575	596	570	596
Clothaire II	Son of Chilperic I; sole king	613	628	584	628
Dagobert I	Son of Clothaire II; sole king	628	638	602	638
Clovis II	Son of Dagobert I	638	656	633	656
Dagobert II	King of Austrasia	656	679	652	679
Clothaire III	King of Neustria	656	670	652?	670?
Childeric II	Son of Clovis II; sole king	670	673	?	673
Thierry III	Son of Clovis II; king of Burgundy	673?	691	652?	691
Clovis III	King of Neustria	691	695	681	695
Childebert III	King of Neustria	695	711	?	?
Dagobert III	King of Neustria	711	715	699	715
Chilperic II	Son of Childeric II	715	720	?	720
Thierry IV	Son of Dagobert III	720	737	712?	737
Childeric III	Son of Chilperic II; deposed by Pepin the Short	742	752	?	755
	THE CAROLINGIANS				
Pepin the Short	Son of Charles Martel	752	768	714?	768
Charlemagne, or Charles the Great	Son of Pepin the Short	768	814	742	814
Louis I, le Débonnaire	Son of Charles the Great	814	840	778	840
Charles the Bald	Younger son of Louis I, le Débonnaire	840	877	823	877
Louis II	Son of Charles the Bald	877	879	846	879
Louis III	Son of Louis II	879	882	863	882

RULERS OF FRANCE—Con.

Name	Lineage	Period of Rule		Birth	Death
		A. D.	A. D	A. D.	A. D.
Charles the Fat	Son of Louis the German	885	888	832?	888
Count Eudes (Odo)	Elected king at Compiègne	888	893	857?	893
Charles III, the Simple	Son of Louis the Stammerer	893	923	879	929
Raoul (Rudolf of Burgundy)	Elected king by the nobles	923	936	?	936
Louis IV	Son of Charles III, the Simple	936	954	921?	954
Lothair	Son of Louis IV	954	986	941	986
Louis V	Son of Lothair	986	987	966?	987
	THE KINGDOM OF FRANCE				
	HOUSE OF CAPET				
Hugh Capet	Son of Hugh the Great	987	996	939?	996
Robert II	Son of Hugh Capet	996	1031	971?	1031
Henry I	Son of Robert II	1031	1060	1011?	1060
Philip I	Son of Henry I	1060	1108	1052?	1108
Louis VI, the Fat	Son of Philip I	1108	1137	1078?	1137
Louis VII	Son of Louis VI	1137	1180	1120?	1180
Philip II, Augustus	Son of Louis VII	1180	1223	1165	1223
Louis VIII	Son of Philip II, Augustus	1223	1226	1187	1226
Louis IX, or St. Louis	Son of Louis VIII	1226	1270	1215?	1270
Philip III, the Bold	Son of Louis IX	1270	1285	1245	1285
Philip IV, the Fair	Son of Philip III	1285	1314	1268	1314
Louis X	Son of Philip IV	1314	1316	1289	1316
Philip V, the Tall	Second son of Philip IV	1316	1322	1293	1322
Charles IV, the Fair	Youngest son of Philip IV, the Fair	1322	1328	1294	1328
	HOUSE OF VALOIS				
Philip VI of Valois	Son of Count Charles of Valois	1328	1350	1293	1350
John the Good	Son of Philip VI	1350	1364	1319	1364
Charles V, the Wise	Son of John II	1364	1380	1337	1380
Charles VI	Son of Charles V	1380	1422	1368	1422
Charles VII, the Victorious	Son of Charles VI	1422	1461	1403	1461
Louis XI	Son of Charles VII	1461	1483	1423	1483
Charles VIII	Son of Louis XI	1483	1498	1470	1498
Louis XII	A descendant of the younger son of Charles V	1498	1515	1462	1515
Francis I	Son of Charles, count of Angoulême	1515	1547	1494	1547
Henry II	Son of Francis I	1547	1559	1519	1559
Francis II	Eldest son of Henry II	1559	1560	1544	1560
Charles IX	Second son of Henry II	1560	1574	1550	1574
Henry III	Third son of Henry II	1574	1589	1551	1589
	HOUSE OF BOURBON				
Henry IV	Son of Antoine de Bourbon, king of Navarre	1589	1610	1553	1610
Louis XIII	Son of Henry IV	1610	1643	1601	1643
Louis XIV	Son of Louis XIII and Anne of Austria	1643	1715	1638	1715
Louis XV	Great-grandson of Louis XIV	1715	1774	1710	1774
Louis XVI	Grandson of Louis XV	1774	1792	1754	1793
	REVOLUTIONARY PERIOD				
National Convention	September 21, 1792—October 26, 1795	1792	1795		
Directory nominated	October 27, 1795—November 10, 1799	1795	1799		
	THE CONSULATE				
Bonaparte				1769	1821
Cambacérès	Elected by the Elders and the Five Hundred	1799	1804	1753	1824
Lebrun				1739	1824
Bonaparte	Elected consul for life	1802			
	THE EMPIRE				
Napoleon I (Bonaparte)	Crowned emperor, December 2, 1804	1804	1814	1769	1821
	THE RESTORATION				
Louis XVIII	Brother of Louis XVI; proclaimed April 11, 1814.	1814	1824	1755	1824
Charles X	Younger brother of Louis XVIII; deposed 1830	1824	1830	1757	1836
	HOUSE OF ORLEANS				
Louis Philippe	Son of Philippe Egalité; abdicated 1848	1830	1848	1773	1850
	THE SECOND REPUBLIC				
Louis Napoleon	Nephew of Napoleon I; elected president	1848	1852	1808	1873
	THE SECOND EMPIRE				
Napoleon III (Louis Napoleon)	Elected emperor; deposed 1870	1852	1870	1808	1873
	THE THIRD REPUBLIC				
Louis Adolphe Thiers	Elected president	1871	1873	1797	1877
Marshal MacMahon	Elected president	1873	1879	1808	1893
Jules Grévy	Elected president	1879	1887	1807	1891
M. F. Sadi Carnot	Elected president	1887	1894	1837	1894
Jean Casimir-Périer	Elected president	1894	1895	1847	1907
Francois Félix Faure	Elected president	1895	1899	1841	1899
M. Emile Loubet	Elected president	1899	1906	1838	1929
Clément Armand Fallières	Elected president	1906	1913	1841	1931
Raymond Poincaré	Elected president	1913	1920	1860	1934
Paul Deschanel	Elected president, served Feb. 18–Sept. 16	1920	1920	1856	1922
Alexandre Millerand	Elected president, September 23, 1920	1920	1924	1859	1943
Gaston Doumergue	Elected president, June 13, 1924	1924	1931	1863	1937
Paul Doumet	Elected president, May 13, 1931	1931	1932	1857	1932
Albert Lebrun	Elected president, May 11, 1932; April 5, 1939	1932	1940	1871	
Henri Philippe Pétain	Chief of state, July 11, 1940	1940	1944	1856	

Heads of Provisional Government: Charles de Gaulle (1891-) rec. Oct. 23, 1944; Felix Gouin (1884-) elec. Jan. 23 1946; Georges Bidault (1899-) elec. June 24, 1946.

RULERS OF FRANCE—Con.

Name	Lineage	Period of Rule		Birth	Death
	THE FOURTH REPUBLIC	A. D.	A. D.	A. D.	A. D.
Vincent Auriol	Elected President, Jan. 16, 1947	1947		1884	

GEORGIA

As an independent kingdom in the Caucasus, Georgia, with occasional periods of submission to Turkish and also to Persian power, maintained its existence from the death of Alexander the Great (323 B. C.) to 1801, when it was annexed by Russia. After the Russian revolution, in 1918, Georgia declared its independence, but in 1920–21, under pressure from Russia, became a socialist soviet republic. For 14 years it was united with Armenia and Azerbaijan in the Transcaucasian Soviet Republic. In 1936 Georgia was made one of the federated states of the Soviet Union.

GERMANY

German history, perhaps better than that of any other country, exemplifies the conflict between internal dissension and the centralizing trend of human governments. In Roman days the country was inhabited by numerous tribes, one of which, the Cherusci, under their Roman-trained prince Arminius, drove the Roman invaders permanently back to the Rhine in the great battle of the Teutoburg Forest, 9 A.D. With the fall of the Roman Empire came a general westward movement of the German tribes, from which the Franks emerged as the dominant power. Charlemagne (Karl the Great, 768–814) ruled to the Atlantic, the Pyrenees, the Po, the Raab (Hungary) and the Elbe. The Franks were now Christians, and Charlemagne was crowned by Pope Leo III on Christmas Day 800 as Emperor of the Romans. This unity under Charlemagne saved European civilization, but it was premature, and his empire disintegrated under his weaker successors before racial and local separatism and new invasions.

Founding of a German State. German history proper begins with the Treaty of Verdun, 843, in which Charlemagne's grandsons partitioned his empire, conceding to Lewis the German the lands east of the Rhine. For the first time a German prince ruled German-speaking tribes. But unity was a different matter. The feudal system made rapid advances under weak rulers, and there were serious internal disturbances, which were terminated only under the Saxon Henry I (919–936), called the Fowler, who was a born statesman and warrior, and who not only established peace within the realm, but did much to insure it against foes from without, defeating the Magyars in 933.

Henry had established a federated state, anticipating German history by a thousand years. His son Otto I (936–973) the Great, increased the number of the German princes and the power of the prelates, but the latter turned against his successors in the struggle with the Papacy. Still more fateful was his attempted expansion into Italy, and his coronation in 962 by the Pope as head of the Holy Roman Empire. The power which might have united Germany was frittered away in Italian expeditions, and the imperial crown became a curse to the German kings and people. Otto's first Italian expedition, indeed, gave opportunity for a rebellion in Germany and a dangerous Magyar invasion. But the German people, with a dawning consciousness of national life, united in 955 to crush the Magyar peril forever in a great battle on the Lechfeld near Augsburg.

The history of subsequent reigns is largely a reaping of the evil harvest sown by Otto's misguided policies, a record of civil strife and of fruitless and often ignominious conflicts with Italian princes and the popes. The memorable scene at Canossa in 1077, when for three days the emperor Henry IV begged for admission to the pope's presence, has become one of the bywords of history. The struggle over the investitures, settled by the compromise Concordat of Worms in 1122, ended in an empty victory for the emperor.

The Hohenstaufens. One of the most interesting epochs in German history is the period of the Hohenstaufens (1138–1254), two of whom, Frederick I, called Barbarossa, or Redbeard, who died in 1190 by drowning while on a crusade, and Frederick II, his grandson, were among the most brilliant of German kings. It was the golden age of the minnesingers and other court poets, and marked a revival of culture which anticipated the Renaissance, while there were remarkable ideas of religious tolerance in Walther von der Vogelweide and Wolfram von Eschenbach. The Wartburg castle and many splendid cathedrals prove the wealth and good taste of the time. It was then that the cities made their great growth, partly owing to Barbarossa's policy, and the famous Hansa was only one of many leagues of cities. It was a time of great men and great ideas, of dramatic contrasts of character and opinion.

Important political changes took place. Prussia was conquered for Christianity by the Teutonic Order. The German kings, straining for world empire, lost control of Poland, Denmark, Burgundy, Prussia, and Schleswig-Holstein. Power passed more and more into the hands of the German princes, seven of whom now came to form the electoral college, which chose the successive emperors. These rulers, requiring powerful support for their foreign ventures, increased the control of the nobles, repressed the cities, and thus retarded for generations the development of a united nation.

The House of Habsburg. The Habsburgs, who came to the throne with the election of Rudolf in 1273, thus ending the Great Interregnum, pursued the same policies. Ambitious for their family rather than for Germany, they did indeed establish a powerful Austrian dynasty, but the fortunes of Germany sank to their lowest level under Frederick III (1440–93), who lost all influence at home and abroad, and for thirty years never attended the imperial diet. Wars were waged all over the land without interference, the most important being a four years' war between a league of cities and a number of princes, in which the victory of the latter was disastrous to German unity.

Frederick's son Maximilian I (1459–1519) ascended the throne in 1486, and gave the empire an authority in Europe which it had not had for centuries. Germany was as feeble as ever, but Maximilian was by inheritance and intermarriage one of the most powerful princes of Europe. His reign marks the end of the middle ages. Gunpowder destroyed the feudal system, through the development of mercenaries. The invention of printing, the discovery of America, the revival of learning, the recognition of peaceful industry as a higher ideal than warfare—these changed the face of the world. And the medieval relation of State and Church was about to undergo the fiery trial of the Reformation.

The Reformation; Thirty Years' War. Outwardly, the struggle began in Germany when Luther nailed to the church door at Wittenberg his 95 theses against the indulgences; inwardly, it had long been preparing, and was doubtless inevitable. The religious schism soon invaded the field of politics, and the princes were divided, the Protestants forming the Schmalkaldic League. The hostility maintained toward the League by Charles V (1520–58),

Maximilian's brilliant grandson, finally led to his crushing victory over it at Mühlberg in 1547; but the movement went on. The Peace of Augsburg (1555) secured freedom of worship; sectarian friction produced the strife of the Counter Reformation under Rudolf II (1576–1612); both parties prepared for war. A dispute over the succession to the throne of Bohemia precipitated the most devastating conflict Europe had known since the middle ages—the Thirty Years' war.

Germany suffered most. Plundering armies crossed and recrossed her; industry and trade were crippled; she lost three-fourths of her population, and the remainder were crushed by taxes; the solid middle classes were wiped out; the empire disintegrated. In the final peace, Switzerland, the Netherlands, Alsace, and other territory left the empire, which had fallen apart into a loose confederation of petty states.

The Rise of Prussia. It was reserved for Prussia to weld the fragments into a new and more powerful state. In the 15th century a Hohenzollern had received the March of Brandenburg; a series of able descendants gradually built up a considerable province. Prussia's greatness, however, begins with Frederick I; he laid the foundations of the military system, and saved the money to run it. His son, Frederick the Great (1740–86), had the genius to employ his heritage, and the ambition to increase it. No sooner had he ascended the throne than he advanced a claim of the house of Brandenburg to the Silesian principalities, and when Maria Theresa (1740–80) of Austria—which had tried to weaken Prussia's growing power—rejected the claim, he promptly seized the disputed territory. This seizure was confirmed, after the War of the Austrian Succession (1741–45) had ended in the recognition of Maria Theresa's husband, Francis I, as emperor, in the Peace of Dresden (1745). But Austria was still resentful, and the issue was finally fought out in the Seven Years' war (1756–63), in which Frederick's extraordinary military genius triumphed over apparently irresistible coalitions. Prussia was now a military power of the first rank, and in the foundation of the Princes' League (1785) assumed for the first time a leadership in German affairs.

This initial movement toward a union of the North German states was halted for many years by the French Revolution and the Napoleonic wars. Divided, Germany was an easy prey for the conqueror and lay helpless before him until 1813, when the war of liberation, in which Russia, Austria, and England participated, finally terminated his sway in the great battles at Leipzig and Waterloo (1815).

At the Congress of Vienna (1815) a German Confederation was formed, with Austria as president of the federal diet. Constant agitation for the recognition of popular sovereignty, encouraged by the Parisian revolutions of 1830 and 1848, led to constitutional government in several German states, and to the attempt to set up a federal constitution. The crown of the empire was indeed offered to Frederick William IV of Prussia, but on condition that the Prussian state should be broken up into its several provinces. To this the interests of Prussia were utterly opposed, and the entire plan met with shipwreck.

Founding of the German Empire. Enmity to Austria had already borne fruit in her exclusion from the new constitutional state; and when, after the Schleswig-Holstein campaign of 1864, Prussia and Austria could not agree on the partition of the acquired territory, the step to armed conflict was not great. Hence the war of 1866, in which Austria was decisively defeated, and which resulted in the formation of the North German Confederation. Neither Austria nor the South German states were members, but the latter had formed with Prussia a secret offensive-defensive alliance. The time was nearly ripe for a closer union of the German states, and it was a sudden political crisis that made it possible. The war of 1866 had brought Germany and France near to the breaking point, for the insensate ambition of Napoleon III saw a threat to his power in the imminent union of the German people. A point of honor, arising out of the disputed succession to the Spanish throne, led to a declaration of war in 1870, in which, however, Napoleon found himself opposed both by the North German Confederation and by the South German states, whereas neither Austria nor Italy was ready for war. The struggle was brief, and in 1871 William I of Prussia was proclaimed German emperor.

Industrial and Social Progress. Germany now entered upon a long period of peaceful growth, marked at the same time by extraordinary industrial activity. France had been compelled to pay as indemnity the enormous sum—as it was then considered—of five billion francs; and the investment of this money in Germany resulted in a fever of speculative enterprise in every direction. At the same time there were profound social changes going on. The rise of the industrial magnate had done two things: it had weakened the power of the old landed gentry (Junker); and it had developed a new class, the proletariat. Thence originated the spectacular rise to power of the Socialists, who, despite measures designed to limit their voting strength, rapidly grew to such proportions as a political party that they had to be seriously reckoned with. Only the astute policy of Bismarck, the "iron chancellor," prevented grave disturbances. His plan was, essentially, to steal the thunder of the Socialists by putting into effect the reforms which they advocated.

Less easily managed was the restlessness of the German people under the steadily increasing military expenditure of the government. But the Germans, as we have seen, are naturally warlike; they are also naturally ambitious. Until 1871 there had been a German people, but no German nation. Now they suddenly found themselves in the limelight of the world. German manufactures went into every land; German science became recognized as unexcelled if not unequaled; students from all countries came to learn of the professors in the German universities, in philology and literature, in science and medicine.

International Rivalry. It was not hard to suggest to this newly self-conscious nation an ideal of military prominence, if not of world domination, and such a program appealed to the young kaiser, William II, who ascended the Prussian throne in 1888. Gradually the entire foreign policy was shaped along lines of power and military action. The army was steadily strengthened, its organization improved; presently a navy came to the fore. And the German people approved, for they were convinced that their national life was threatened.

The European situation had indeed grown more and more tense. The Triple Alliance (1882), between Germany, Austria, and Italy, was balanced in 1892 by a similar understanding between France, which wanted revenge for the loss of Alsace-Lorraine (1871), and Russia, which had become estranged from Germany. The age-long desire of Russia to play a dominant rôle in the Balkans and to gain control of Constantinople threatened to force a conflict with Austria, which would bring in Germany.

Meanwhile, Great Britain also had been drifting into the hostile camp. In the year 1884 Germany had inaugurated a colonial policy which eventually led to the development of a large navy. In this step England saw a menace and a challenge which she could not ignore. The lifeblood of England is overseas commerce; her food is largely imported in ships; a naval blockade could starve her out in three months. Vainly she attempted to secure Germany's consent to a halt in the race of armaments. And Germany's attitude toward the efforts for international peace, signalized by the Hague Conferences, served to strengthen the suspicion that she was bent upon war. In another respect also Germany had crossed the lines of English policy. William II had cultivated the friendship of Turkey with a view to securing valuable concessions in Asia, the fruit of which was to be the famous "Berlin to Bagdad" railway, with its allied plans that threatened to imperil British interests in the Orient.

It was natural, then, that England should begin to feel a community of interest with France, one of the first fruits of which was the agreement of 1904 with respect to Morocco. Germany felt in this a blow at her commercial interests there, and forced the conference at Algeciras (1906) to grant her recognition as the price of peace. But Europe had now heard the rattling of the German sword, and plot and counterplot followed on each other's heels. The next dispute that threatened the peace of Europe arose from the annexation of Bosnia and Herzegovina by Austria in 1908. Serbia protested, and Russia supported the protest, but finally withdrew her opposition, feeling herself weakened by the disastrous war with Japan (1906), and hence not yet ready to try conclusions with the powerful military machine of Germany. Nevertheless, she remained secretly unreconciled, and proceeded on her part with military preparations.

World War I. By this time Germany had become the most efficient military power the world has ever seen. So great was the organized concentration of all the resources of the state, that one might compare the nation to a single huge battering-ram, with every ounce of national strength contributing to its driving power. The entire population was thoroughly conscious of this incomparable might.

Such was the situation when, in June 1914, the Austrian heir apparent and his wife were assassinated in the streets of the Bosnian capital. Within two months the pent-up enmities of western Europe had burst forth into armed conflict and produced the greatest war of recorded history. (See *World War I.*)

The German Republic. One of the most dramatic events attending the armistice was the German revolution of November 9, 1918. The disaffection on Germany's "home front," as von Hindenburg called it, had reached the point of open rebellion. The kaiser, forced to abdicate, fled to Holland, and within a short time every hereditary ruler in Germany had abdicated or been deposed. A temporary government provided for a constituent convention, which drew up a democratic constitution. Two armed attempts were made by communist groups to establish a socialist commonwealth similar to that in Russia. These were the so-called Spartacan revolts in Berlin and a communist revolt in Munich, all in the early months of 1919. They were ruthlessly suppressed, and the constitution was adopted on July 31, 1919.

There were two attempts by monarchist partisans to overthrow the democracy. Under the leadership of Kapp, in 1920, this group held Berlin for five days but was defeated by means of a general strike. In 1923, a similar insurrection broke out in Bavaria, led by Erich von Ludendorf and a young Austrian named Adolf Hitler. The leaders were captured, and Hitler was imprisoned.

Friedrich Ebert was the first president of Germany. His policy, pursued also after his death in 1925 by his successor, Paul von Hindenburg, was directed toward a peaceful defeat of the Versailles treaty by combined sabotage and conciliation.

Reparation Problem. The peace treaty fastened on Germany the payment of large annual sums as reparations. The result was a runaway inflation. The Allies declared Germany in default, and French troops, in January 1923, seized the Ruhr valley. Germany then refused all payments. The deadlock was broken by the Dawes plan, named from Charles G. Dawes, the American chairman of the commission framing it. The amount of the annuities was fixed, and the French left the Ruhr in 1925. Four years later a new arrangement fixed also total reparations. In 1931 came the depression, and the Allies cancelled their claims.

Nazi (*nä'tsê*) **Rule.** Hitler, having failed in the revolt of 1923, proceeded to organize a political party (Nazi), from the extremists of the right and the discontented middle class. It was anti-communistic and ultra-nationalistic. Its power grew phenomenally, and Hitler was a close rival of Hindenburg for the presidency in 1932.

In 1933, Hitler seized the opportunity of a fire in the Reichstag to ask for dictatorial power to suppress the communists, who were accused of causing the fire. Its origin was never satisfactorily explained.

Receiving the powers sought, Hitler proceeded to rule by decree and to establish a so-called totalitarian state, in which all parties except the Nazi were suppressed. His policy aimed at aggrandizement abroad and was based on glorification of the Nordic race. One aspect of this policy involved persecution of the Jews, and a revised form of Protestantism, based on the old Teutonic myths, was encouraged. In seeking to work out this change, however, Hitler, who had assumed the title of *Führer*, "Leader," and added that of Chancellor after the death of Hindenburg in 1934, encountered the determined opposition of the Lutheran clergy.

Under Hitler's leadership, Germany ignored the disarmament clauses of the Versailles treaty, withdrew from the League of Nations, and proceeded to build up her military might. One immediate aim of German foreign policy remained union with Austria, although consideration of Italian jealousy and of French opposition counselled delay in its realization. The methods used in seeking control of Austria and other countries was to foster the organization of a Nazi party, which, with German help, was expected eventually to obtain the reins of power. This technique facilitated the acquisition of both Austria and Czechoslovakia in 1938-39. France and Britain agreed, in a conference at Munich, to Germany's taking over a part of Czechoslovakia. But when the remainder was taken over contrary to agreement and Poland was next attacked in 1939, these countries declared war on Germany in the face of a German-Russian non aggression treaty.

World War II. During the first three years of the war, Germany was everywhere victorious. Poland, Denmark and Norway, The Netherlands, Belgium, and France were overrun. Great Britain was threatened with devastation by air, starvation by submarine blockade, and actual invasion. In the spring of 1941 Germany clinched her hold upon the Balkans —and upon Italy as well. In June she invaded Russia and swept over the western provinces; in 1942 her armies drove east to the Volga and the Caucasus oil fields. But in late 1941 Germany had declared war on the United States, whose power was destined to bring about German defeat.

In the fall of 1942 the tide turned. The Germans were repulsed with heavy losses at Stalingrad and were forced slowly back across Russia. Meantime, with the Allied invasion of North Africa and Italy, the control of the Mediterranean was lost, and a new front was opened on the south. In 1944 the Russians swept across Poland and invaded Hungary; Finland and the Balkan states were forced out of the war. In the west, the Allied invasion had liberated France and Belgium and opened the long-feared western front. Within Germany the pitiless air bombardment was wrecking industries and communications. The outworks were lost, and, early in 1945, with the Russians across the Oder and the Americans across the Rhine, the Reich itself lay open to attack.

In December a desperate attempt to break the American lines in the Ardennes failed. The counterattacks which followed broke the German defense, and carried the Allied armies to the Elbe, and over south Germany. Meantime the Russians on the eastern front had crossed the Oder. Berlin fell on May 2, and Hitler died in the ruins. The German armies surrendered on May 7, and the Reich was divided among the Allies for military occupation, until they should allow a German government to be formed which could make a treaty. See *Government.*

RULERS OF GERMANY

Name	Lineage	Period of Rule		Birth	Death
	CAROLINGIAN EMPERORS				
		A. D.	A. D.	A. D.	A. D.
Louis the German	Son of Emperor Louis I. He is regarded as the founder of the German Empire	843	876	804?	876
	Kingdom divided on death of Louis the German.				
Charles the Fat	Son of Louis the German; sole king through death of his brothers, Carloman and Louis; crowned emperor 881	876	887	832	888
Arnulf of Carinthia	Illegitimate son of Carloman; elected by the nobles	887	899	850?	899
Louis the Child	Son of Emperor Arnulf	899	911	893	911
	HOUSE OF FRANCONIA				
Conrad I	Duke of Franconia, elected king of Germany	911	918	?	918
	HOUSE OF SAXONY				
Henry I, the Fowler	Son of the duke of Saxony	919	936	876	936
Otto the Great	Son of Henry I; crowned emperor 962	936	973	912	973
Otto II	Son of Otto I	973	983	955	983
Otto III	Son of Otto II	983	1002	980	1002
Henry II, the Saint	Son of Henry the Quarrelsome of Bavaria	1002	1024	972?	1024
	SALIAN OR FRANCONIAN EMPERORS				
Conrad II	Crowned emperor 1027	1024	1039	990?	1039
Henry III	Son of Conrad II	1039	1056	1017	1056
Henry IV	Son of Henry III	1056	1106	1050	1106
Henry V	Son of Henry IV	1106	1125	1081	1125
	HOUSE OF SAXONY				
Lothair II	Crowned emperor 1133	1125	1137	1060?	1137
	THE HOHENSTAUFENS				
Conrad III	Duke of Franconia	1138	1152	1093	1152
Frederick I, Barbarossa	Nephew of Conrad III; crowned emperor 1155	1152	1190	1121?	1190
Henry VI	Son of Frederick Barbarossa; crowned emperor 1191	1190	1197	1165	1197
Otto IV } Double	Son of Henry the Lion; crowned emperor 1209	1198	1215	1174	1218
Philip of Swabia } Election		1198	1208	1177?	1208
Frederick II	Son of Henry VI; crowned emperor 1220	1215	1250	1194	1250
Conrad IV	King of Germany, not emperor	1250	1254	1228	1254
An Interregnum		1254	1273		
	HOUSE OF HABSBURG				
Rudolf I	Son of Albert IV, count of Habsburg	1273	1291	1218	1291
	HOUSE OF NASSAU				
Adolphus	Elected king of Germany and deposed	1291	1298	1252?	1298
	HOUSE OF AUSTRIA				
Albert I	Eldest son of Rudolf I	1298	1308	1250?	1308
	HOUSE OF LUXEMBURG				
Henry VII	Son of the count of Luxemburg, crowned emperor 1312	1308	1313	1262	1313
	HOUSE OF BAVARIA				
Louis IV } Double	Son of the duke of Bavaria	1314	1347	1286?	1347
Frederick the Fair } Election	Son of Albert I; minority choice	1314	1330	1286?	1330
	HOUSE OF LUXEMBURG				
Charles IV	Son of John of Luxemburg; crowned emperor 1355	1347	1378	1316	1378
Wenceslas	Son of Charles IV; elected king of Romans 1376, deposed from German throne	1378	1400	1361	1419
	HOUSE OF PALATINATE				
Rupert	Elector of the Palatinate	1400	1410	1352	1410
	HOUSE OF LUXEMBURG				
Sigismund	Son of Charles IV; crowned emperor 1433	1411	1437	1368	1437
	HOUSE OF HABSBURG				
Albert II	Son-in-law of Sigismund	1438	1439	1397	1439
Frederick IV	Son of Ernest, duke of Austria; crowned emperor (Frederick III) 1452	1440	1493	1415	1493
Maximilian I	Son of Frederick IV	1493	1519	1459	1519
Charles V	Son of Philip of Burgundy	1519	1556	1500	1558
Ferdinand I	Younger brother of Charles V	1556	1564	1503	1564
Maximilian II	Son of Ferdinand I	1564	1576	1527	1576
Rudolf II	Son of Maximilian II	1576	1612	1552	1612
Matthias	Younger son of Maximilian II	1612	1619	1557	1619
Ferdinand II	Son of Charles, duke of Styria	1619	1637	1578	1637
Ferdinand III	Son of Ferdinand II	1637	1657	1608	1657
Leopold I	Second son of Ferdinand III	1658	1705	1640	1705
Joseph I	Son of Leopold I	1705	1711	1678	1711
Charles VI	Son of Leopold I	1711	1740	1685	1740
	HOUSE OF BAVARIA				
Charles VII	Elector of Bavaria	1742	1745	1697	1745

RULERS OF GERMANY—Con.

Name	Lineage	Period of Rule		Birth	Death
	HOUSE OF LORRAINE	A. D.	A. D.	A. D.	A. D.
Francis I	Son of Leopold, duke of Lorraine	1745	1765	1708	1765
Joseph II	Son of Francis I	1765	1790	1741	1790
Leopold II	Third son of Francis I	1790	1792	1747	1792
Francis II	Son of Leopold II	1792	1806	1768	1835
	THE CONFEDERATION OF THE RHINE	1806	1815		
	THE GERMAN CONFEDERATION	1815	1866		
	THE NORTH GERMAN CONFEDERATION	1866	1871		
	THE HOUSE OF HOHENZOLLERN				
William I	Second son of Frederick William III of Prussia	1871	1888	1797	1888
Frederick III	Son of William I	1888	....	1831	1888
William II	Son of Frederick III and grandson of William I	1888	1918	1859	1941
	GERMAN REPUBLIC				
Friedrich Ebert	Chosen provisionally, later elected president	1918	1925	1871	1925
Paul von Hindenburg	Elected president	1925	1934	1847	1934
Adolf Hitler	Führer and Chancellor	1934	1945	1889	1945

GREECE

The history of Greece is the story of a group of tiny states which grew up as independent units and resisted to the end any plan of federation among themselves. Consequently, Greece never became a military power which could present a united front to the world, and her greatness did not lie in the field of political organization. Yet, despite the serious menace of foreign invaders and devastating wars between the states themselves, these states maintained their independence long enough to produce works of literature, philosophy, art, and architecture, which have been the priceless heritage of later civilizations.

The Coming of the Hellenes. Greece was occupied by the Hellenes, an Indo-European people, at some time after 2000 B. C. They came as undeveloped tribes in search of homes, and immediately demolished an earlier civilization which had flourished in the prehistoric period, established themselves as masters of the entire peninsula, and made it their home henceforth, while the earlier occupants were entirely driven out or annihilated. This was probably accomplished by a gradual process covering several hundred years; for the Hellenic people comprised different groups, who may be supposed to have swept down into the peninsula in successive waves. These groups were closely related to one another but showed different characteristics. They were known in later times, when the Greeks were reconstructing their own ancient history, as Achæans, Æolians, Dorians, and Ionians, and, with the development of the Hellenic civilization, the special characteristics of each group produced a peculiar culture easily distinguishable from that of the other groups.

The Hellenes, thus established in a permanent home, began immediately to display the vigor and aggressiveness of a virile race. They soon spread over the neighboring islands of the Ægean, and then passed over these as by stepping-stones to the western coast of Asia Minor and to Crete. The sea was their highway and they became essentially a seafaring people. They developed a vigorous commerce and were ultimately competing for the markets of the Mediterranean with the Phœnicians, whose powerful colony, Carthage, was dominant for a time in the West.

Greek Colonization. There followed a period of colonization which cannot be defined as to its beginning, but it was over by the end of the 6th century B. C. The colonies were founded as private enterprises by groups who were led to leave their native homes, sometimes through dissatisfaction with political conditions, sometimes through lack of land or by economic distress; they were not in the first instance commercial enterprises. The colonies thus established became independent units, but each maintained a close association with the mother state, reproducing its polity in a foreign land. Of course the colonies carried with them and preserved the Greek language and culture.

In this way colonies were sent to the shores of the Black Sea, to Egypt, to southern Italy, and to Sicily. A few of the important Greek colonies were: Byzantium (modern Constantinople), founded by Megarians in 660 B. C.; Naucratis, "Mistress of Ships," in Egypt, founded by Milesians about 640 B. C.; Cyrene on the northern coast of Africa, founded by Therans about ten years later; Syracuse in Sicily, founded by Corinthians in the 8th century B. C.; and Croton in southern Italy, founded by Achæans about 700 B. C. These and many other colonies were important trading centers for Greek commerce.

The large cluster of colonies established in southern Italy gave a distinctive character to this district, which was called by the Romans *Magna Græcia.* This was to the Greeks a land of promise and opportunity such as the American "great West" has been. Here wealth was accumulated in great abundance, and the colony of Sybaris came to be spoken of as typifying extravagance and luxurious living. It was from these particular colonies that the first gleams of Greek culture began to reach the vigorous Roman people, and hence came the mellowing influence which was destined to make over the Roman character and bring about Rome's willing acknowledgment of the supremacy of Greece in the world of the spirit.

Greek Division and Unity. The segregation of the Greeks into tiny political units was brought about, first and chiefly, by the character of the people themselves and, secondly, by the nature of the country in which they settled. The Greek was by instinct strongly individualistic, thoroughly devoted to the interests of his family and immediate community, but inclined to be jealous and suspicious of those not so closely connected with him, even though they might be Greeks like himself. He was also ready to defend his own views, with prolonged argument if necessary, and unwilling to let any other man do his thinking for him. The land of Greece, on the other hand, with its endless succession of mountains and narrow valleys, each with a limited area of arable land, made isolation natural and easy, and strongly encouraged—nay, almost made inevitable—the formation of small units which came to have a sense of independence and self-sufficiency.

Yet the centrifugal tendency was not the only one at work. The Greeks were led by a sort of national pride to designate all who were not Greeks as "barbarians," or people without the pale. This term was at first used without the opprobrium now attaching to the word, but it soon came to have a distinct suggestion of inferiority, and finally it indicated downright contempt. Then the songs of Homer, which were known and sung throughout Greece, strongly encouraged the same feeling; for in them the Greek states were represented as fighting together against a foreign power. Furthermore, the religious worship of the Greeks was, broadly speaking, the same; and so they came together at stated intervals to honor special divinities in great festivals which assumed a national character. Such festivals were held at Olympia and at Nemea, in honor of Zeus, at Delphi, in honor of Apollo, and at the Isthmus, in honor of Poseidon. While these festivals were going on, it was customary to observe a religious truce throughout Greece. Mention may also be made of a council or league of several states in northern Greece, called the Amphictyonic League, which met primarily to discuss and settle questions pertaining to religious matters, and which naturally fostered a close bond of sympathy between all the participating states.

The City-State. The political unit throughout Greece was the *polis*, or "city-state," an independent organization composed usually of the inhabitants of a single small town. Occasionally, a town associated neighboring villages with itself in a small federation; this was done by Athens with the country villages of Attica, and by Sparta with those of Laconia. The population of these city-states was astonishingly small, and this characteristic remained one of the determining factors in Greek political development. The typical city-state of early times was ruled by a king, and this was doubtless the only form of government known in Greece during several centuries, after the tribal organization was outgrown and before the time when the record of Greek history commences, about the 8th century B. C.

At this time we find a state of political unrest prevalent throughout the land, for the reigning families were being overthrown in many of the states. The power was being taken over by small groups of nobles, or by individuals who succeeded for a time in getting sufficient support to maintain themselves supreme; in the former case the government came to be called an *oligarchy*, in the latter, a *tyranny*. Many of the tyrants were men of real ability and proved to be excellent rulers.

The spirit of political unrest, however, did not always lead to violence. In some states men of conspicuous wisdom and integrity were designated to draw up and codify a new system of laws. Such a service was rendered by Draco, and later by Solon, at Athens, and by Pittacus at Mytilene. This, of course, implies that writing was by this time in common use throughout Greece. The alphabet had been adopted from the Phœnicians at some time after 1000 B. C.

Government in Athens. The fortunes of the city-state of Athens may be considered typical of what was taking place throughout Greece prior to the end of the 6th century B. C. The early Athenian monarchy was gradually transformed into an aristarchy, which finally gave place to a pure democracy. This was accomplished as follows: First, the king's power was curtailed by the introduction of two new magistrates, the *polemarch* and the *archon*, elected by the people. Later, the kingship became elective, and six new magistrates were added, making the "nine archons." Meanwhile, unfavorable economic conditions were causing distress among the common people. The introduction of money to replace the old system of barter produced serious disturbance in the economic development of Athens, as it did in all Greece. The first coinage is said to have come into the Greek world from the wealthy kingdom of Lydia in Asia Minor in the 7th century B. C. This and other causes brought about a situation which demanded a remedy, and Draco was appointed an extraordinary legislator (*thesmothetes*) and commissioned to draw up a new code of laws. This he did in 621 B. C., but the penalties imposed by his laws for wrongdoing were so severe that it was found difficult to use his code; in later times an Athenian orator said that Draco's laws were written in blood, not in ink.

About thirty years later Solon was chosen to perfect the work of Draco. He undertook his task with a statesman's skill and was remarkably successful. By his social legislation he relieved the poor of their unbearable burdens, and by his political reforms he erected the framework of the Athenian democracy, making the people the sovereign power of the state, with complete control over all their executives, and giving all free men some degree of right as citizens.

The Athenian democracy, however, was not even yet fully established. Party strife continued, and Pisistratus, a popular and successful general, backed by the discontented element of the population, was able to grasp the supreme power. He proved himself a wise and able ruler; for he kept the form of the constitution laid down by Solon, while holding the guiding power in his own hands. The diversity and importance of the various enterprises carried on by Athens during his rule bear testimony to his tireless activity. Among these, may be mentioned the re-editing of the poems of Homer, the foundation of a huge temple of Olympian Zeus,—which had to await the wealth of a Roman emperor to bring it to completion,—the establishment of the great annual festival of "Dionysus in the City," in which tragedy, one of the richest fruits of the Greek genius, was performed, and the prosecution of successful military operations on the Hellespont.

The rule of Pisistratus was carried on by his sons after his death, until the tyranny was brought to an end, with the help of Sparta, in 510 B. C., and the descendants of Pisistratus were forever debarred by law from the rights of citizenship. Athens now began her career as a democracy, first modifying the constitution of Solon by the reforms of Cleisthenes, which provided for a new and more satisfactory grouping of the citizens.

Sparta and Other States. The other states had meanwhile been working out practicable constitutions, each in its own way. In contrast to the pure democracy finally achieved by Athens, a constitution of a strangely mixed character was adopted in Sparta. Here there were two hereditary kings, holding office for life, and a board of five ephors, elected annually; these ephors exercised most of the important civil functions which had belonged to the kings, and represented the common people as against the nobility. The senate or *Gerusia*, however, was composed of nobles and naturally represented the interests of that class. The Spartans had grown to be a conservative people devoted to a strict military discipline—in fact, a military state composed of a limited number of free warriors imposed upon a larger number of serfs or *helots*. The strictness of the Spartan discipline, which has become proverbial, did indeed produce a remarkably efficient corps of fighting men, but it repressed rather than encouraged the free development of the individual citizen.

Thus, by the end of the 6th century B. C., all the Greek states had passed through the period of political readjustment, and, temporarily at least, tyrannies were at an end. The period under discussion had witnessed notable achievement in many fields of activity. There had been great commercial expansion, as noted above, with marked progress in local industry, and real achievement in architecture and in literature. Indeed, the Greeks had by this time attained a high level of culture which marked them out as a peculiarly gifted people.

Religious Conceptions. The Greek had been wrestling also with the problems of life as expressed in his religion. The old anthropomorphic gods of Homer, whose writings were to the Greeks almost sacred, were little better than humans and had ceased to fulfill the ideal of an awakening age, and a more spiritual interpretation of godhead than that found in Homer was coming to be adopted by thoughtful men. Yet the outward form of the old polytheistic religion remained, with its temples, its priests, and its ritual worship.

A widespread yearning for immortality is evidenced by the prominence of societies which gave promise of this boon to mortals. The Eleusinian

Mysteries, a kind of Passion Play of the sorrows of Demeter, were open to all, even the humblest. Here great numbers found comfort in the hope of salvation and purification from the sins of the world. There was also the Orphic Sect, of widespread influence, and, in southern Italy, Pythagoras had founded his brotherhood.

On the other hand, many had been turning to seek a rationalistic explanation of the universe, as a protest against the mysticism of such bodies as the Orphic Sect. This movement grew up in Ionia in Asia Minor, and it was here that Greece was saved from the tyranny of religion interpreted by a priestly class. Beginning with crude speculations upon the nature of the material composition of the world, and progressing very slowly at first, a succession of serious and able men prepared the way for the great achievement of Greek philosophy in the 5th and the 4th century B. C. Thales, the pioneer of this movement, proposed that water is the primary element of all things.

Athens, Sparta, Thebes. At the beginning of the 5th century B. C., the important Greek states were related as follows: Sparta, with her wonderfully efficient army and her iron discipline, was unquestioned leader in the Peloponnesus, having come to overshadow Argos, whose ancient importance was waning. This pre-eminent position of Sparta placed her automatically at the head of a kind of league of Peloponnesian states. Even Athens, as we have seen, was indebted to Sparta for deliverance from her tyrants, and was for a time strongly under her influence. Athens, at the head of the federation of the villages of Attica, had outstripped her near-by rivals and held a secure and easily defended position as a sea power. The rival of Athens on the north was Thebes, the dominant power in Bœotia.

Persian Wars. At this time a new age dawned on Greece. The expanding Persian power was turning toward European conquest. Meanwhile the Athenians had sent aid to the Ionian cities in Asia Minor during a revolt against Persian rule. With this revolt crushed, Darius planned to punish Athens. His first expedition, in 492 B. C., was destroyed by storms, but two years later he sent a fleet and an army across the Ægean, which landed on the plain of Marathon, about twenty-five miles distant from Athens. His forces were guided by Hippias, son of Pisistratus, former tyrant of Athens. The Greeks, remembering the terrible Persian punishment of Asiatic cities, were panic-stricken. But Miltiades, who was familiar with Persian methods of warfare, roused their courage by his confident plans for meeting the invader, and under his leadership the Greek citizen-soldiers, with their spears, broke the attack of the Persian bowmen. The Persians fled, leaving 6000 dead on the field, while the Greek loss was only about 200. The grateful Athenians, who had borne the brunt of the battle almost without assistance, raised a memorial mound, which may still be seen on the field of Marathon.

Ten years passed, and Xerxes, son of Darius, in 480 B. C., entered Greece with an army of overwhelming size, accompanied by a great fleet. Sparta, on this occasion, stood solidly with Athens, and the Persian advance was opposed at strategic points on land and sea. Treachery, however, enabled Xerxes to enter by the pass of Thermopylæ—but only over the dead bodies of the heroic Leonidas and his loyal band of Spartans. Athens was burned. But the Athenians, wisely advised by Themistocles, had built a navy, and in the strait of Salamis they crushed the Persian fleet. The next year, 479 B. C., the remnant of Xerxes' army was defeated by the Greek spearmen at Platæa. Never again did a Persian army enter Greece. In the West also, the year 480 B. C. saw the Hellenic world freed from an Asiatic menace through the overwhelming defeat of the Carthaginians by the Greeks of Syracuse.

The generous co-operation of Athens and Sparta ceased, unfortunately, as soon as the danger was passed, and the old spirit of jealous rivalry again manifested itself. The Spartans looked with apprehension upon the energetic preparations of Athens to meet another possible emergency; sullen distrust and mutual suspicions prepared the way for the internecine struggle which was destined to ruin the fairest city of Greece.

The Athenian Empire. The Athenians, led by Themistocles, rebuilt their city with strong fortifications and improved and protected the harbor of the Piræus. Next, in order to secure complete protection against the menace of Persia, they organized the Confederacy of Delos, whose guiding spirit was Aristides, known as "The Just." This was a union of Athens with the Greek cities of Asia Minor and the Ægean islands and was at first a purely co-operative league. Its name arose from the fact that its treasury was located on the island of Delos under the protection of Apollo. The allies at first contributed ships, with which Cimon, son of Miltiades, freed the entire Asia Minor coast from Persian control, as far as the mouth of the Black Sea. Under his leadership, Athens gradually brought the states of the league into the position of dependencies, while maintaining friendship with Sparta. In 454 B. C. the transfer of the treasury to Athens marked the beginning of the Athenian "empire." But Cimon's policy of co-operation with Sparta was unpopular with the radical, democratic party at Athens, and he was ostracized.

At this period most of the offices of the Athenian democracy were filled by lot; hence the men selected were often inefficient. But the ten generals were elected by the votes of the people, an arrangement which gave a single powerful man his opportunity to direct the state. For about thirty years this position in the Athenian state was maintained by Pericles. His supremacy coincided with the most brilliant era of Athenian culture, though this period was marred by the first of those contests with Sparta which finally resulted in the complete ruin of Athenian political power.

The Periclean Age. Pericles' ambitious plan of establishing an Athenian land empire led to conflict with Sparta, and after years of fruitless struggle the so-called Thirty Years' Truce, in 445 B. C., restored the *status quo*. Both sides were exhausted. Meanwhile Athens had carried on a disastrous campaign against the Persians in Egypt. The next fifteen years in Athens are known as the Periclean age. Commerce brought the wealth of the world to the port of the Piræus. Tribute from allied and subject cities filled the public treasury. Rich citizens and the state lavished money without stint upon festivals and public buildings. Sculptors and architects of genius were employed to raise statues and temples in honor of the gods and of great men, and to express in marble the beauty and dignity of the human form. Contests and public prizes stimulated poets and dramatists. The democracy, by opening offices to all save the poorest citizens, encouraged a keen interest in politics. Schools flourished, oratory became a fine art, and the sophists, disturbers though they were, challenged the skill of the cleverest by the subtleties of their art of dialectics. Athens had become the center of Greek culture, and her influence extended far beyond the limits of Greece.

The Fall of Athens. But the other cities of Greece were jealous and hostile, and in 431 B. C. the truce of 445 B. C. was broken. The armies of Sparta, Thebes, and Corinth, with their allies, entered Attica and devastated the country about Athens. The people who were thus driven within the city were stricken with a plague due to crowded, unsanitary conditions. Pericles fell a victim to the disease, and Athens, lacking capable leadership, was thrown into confusion. The war continued for ten years. Athens managed to maintain control of the sea, and in 421 B. C. a truce of fifty years was arranged. But this peace failed to settle any real issue or to check the brutal passions that the war had aroused.

At this stage of affairs, Alcibiades, a high-spirited young man of remarkable ability, rose to power as champion of those opposed to the peace party in Athens. He incited the Athenians to undertake an expedition against the Corinthian city of Syracuse in Sicily, 415 B. C. But Alcibiades, who sailed as a general with the expedition, found himself recalled to Athens to answer a charge of impiety. He promptly deserted to Sparta. By his advice a Spartan general and a few troops were sent to Syracuse. The Athenian fleet and army were annihilated, 413 B. C., and the Spartans, who had been making annual invasions of Attica during the early years of the war, now definitely locked her within her walls by occupying the fortress of Decelea, a few miles to the north. For ten years the city held out, though forced to see her flourishing farms devastated and to import all supplies by sea. At length, in the battle of Ægospotami, 405 B. C., the entire Athenian fleet was captured or destroyed by the Spartans, and Athens, faced by starvation, surrendered. Her fortifications were leveled, and she was forced to recognize the supremacy of Sparta. After enduring a reign of terror carried out under Spartan protection, her democratic constitution was again restored, but her strength was broken.

Sparta and Thebes. There followed a dreary period of negotiations with Persia, both Athens and Sparta bidding in turn for an alliance which would gain the support of Persian gold. The King's Peace, 387 B. C., gave Greek leadership to Sparta. She had won her final battle with Athens by means of Persian funds, under the guise of champion of the free Greek cities. Now she revealed her purposes by overturning every democratic government and establishing in each state an oppressive and irresponsible Spartan governor supported by a garrison of Spartan soldiers. On a fateful night, a young Theban noble entered Thebes with a band of followers, killed the leaders of the oligarchic party, and forced the Spartan garrison to an ignominious surrender. Pelopidas and his friend, Epaminondas, thus challenged Sparta and made Thebes, for a few years, supreme in Greece. Epaminondas, who gave evidence of possessing a high type of statesmanship, was killed at the battle of Mantinea in 362 B. C.

It is worth noting that, even during the stress of her life-and-death struggle with Sparta, Athens had still been able to continue the work on the noble buildings which crown her acropolis. The shameless mismanagement of Athenian affairs after the death of Pericles had been subjected to the biting satire of Aristophanes, the dramatist, and the sophists had been ably and fearlessly met by the challenge of Socrates. The story of the nations was being completed by Herodotus the very year in which Pericles succumbed to the plague, and Thucydides was engaged in setting forth in his history the lessons of the Greek wars while the greatest of them was actually in progress. In the years after the war, Plato, a pupil of Socrates, wrote of the ideal city-state, but he failed to see the larger problem of statesmanship, the union of cities. Isocrates, understanding the weakness of the Greek policies, pleaded for united action against the foreigner, and Xenophon endeavored to rouse Greek patriotism through his story of the Ten Thousand. But Greece was not to see political unity realized until her many quarreling states were welded into a dependency by the Macedonian power.

Alexander the Great. Macedonia, peopled by a race which was Greek in language as well as in blood, had been slowly assimilating the culture of its southern neighbors since the period of the Persian wars. In 360 B. C., Philip, a man of Greek education and military experience, came to the throne. He at once adopted a policy of Macedonian expansion. The battle of Chæronea in 338 B. C. gave him control of all Greece except Sparta. Death cut short his ambitious plan of invading Persia, but he left to his son Alexander a remarkable body of trained and devoted councilors and officers. Alexander, however, coming to the throne at the age of twenty, was soon to display a genius that outshone them all. He had been taught by Aristotle, who not only instructed him in history and science but also fired his imagination with the vision of a world empire resting on the firm basis of Greek culture and Greek traditions and headed by Macedonia.

In 334 B. C., after crushing a rebellion at Thebes, Alexander crossed the Hellespont and began the march which was to make his dream a reality. During the next twelve years he led his armies along the ancient highways of Asia, subjugating the cities which had been seats of civilization from hoary antiquity. He conquered Egypt, where he founded the great city of Alexandria, and penetrated the trackless desert as far as the shrine of Ammon, in order to win assurance from the god himself that he was, in very truth, son of Ammon; here he stood on the confines of the Carthaginian empire. His eastward march carried him into India, and only the restlessness of his army drew him back from the valley of the Ganges. In Babylon he made his capital with the magnificence of an Eastern potentate, and in that ancient city of the marshes, fever struck him down. He had brought Greek culture to the East; the Hellenistic age, which he ushered in, saw this culture thriving in many flourishing cities, from his own Alexandria in Egypt to the central plains of Asia.

The Greco-Roman World. But, if this age Hellenized the East, it also Orientalized the West. Oriental ideas of religion and statecraft found their way into the thinking and practice of the Greeks and of the Romans as well; for, although Alexander did not march into the West, Rome had long been under the spell of Greek influence. The religious cults of the Egyptian Isis and the Persian Mithra became widely popular in the Roman world, which was soon to include Greece among its provinces. Likewise, the Romans became acquainted with the notion of the divine character and right of kings, which may be traced to Alexander's practice of having himself proclaimed the son of Zeus. This may have seemed to him necessary in order to sustain his great authority, but it must be said that his assumption of divine right alienated loyal followers from him and, in the end, proved disastrous to his plans.

The death of Alexander destroyed the last hope of a unified Greek empire. Within a generation the vast realm he had conquered was divided among three of his generals. Macedonia and Greece fell to Antigonus; Syria, to Seleucus; and Egypt, to Ptolemy. One more attempt was made by a group of states in the Peloponnesus to assert Greek independence. But this Achæan League, as it was called, though led by able and patriotic men, was only partially and temporarily successful. For 150 years, under the Ptolemies, Alexandria was the center of that later widespread Greek civilization known as Hellenism. Here the Hebrew Old Testament was translated into Greek. The Museum of Alexandria was in effect a great state university. The schools of Alexandria were rivaled by those of Pergamum and of Rhodes; but it was an age of scholarship rather than of creative activity.

The strife and internal weakness of the Greek kingdoms left by Alexander gave Rome an opportunity to extend her power over all the East and to hammer the Greco-Roman world into a stable empire, a realm of Greek culture and Roman law.

Modern Greece. Greece was merged in the Eastern or Byzantine Empire when the Roman world was divided, and, after the fall of Constantinople in 1453, it became a part of the Turkish empire. From the 4th century B. C. until 1821, when the Greeks rose in revolt against the Turkish power, they were at no time a free people. During the 18th century an intellectual revival had taken place in Greece, and this had aroused national pride and brought about a restoration of the Greek language. This revival of the national consciousness of Greece had stirred the interest of enlightened people in all the nations of the West. Lord Byron was one of many who joined the Greeks and gave his life for the cause. England, France, and Russia finally intervened; by the treaty of Adrianople in 1829 Greek independence was acknowledged by Turkey, and guaranteed by the three powers. In 1833 Otto of Bavaria became king of the new Christian state of Greece.

Otto was deposed in 1862; in the next year a brother of the Danish king succeeded him as George I. England strengthened his hands by ceding the Ionian islands in 1864. In the same year a new constitution established a legislature, the *Boule*, elected by universal suffrage. In 1881 Greece gained Thessaly, but lost a part by the Turkish war of 1897. Greece participated in the Balkan wars, and made substantial gains, including Crete. King George was assassinated in March 1913.

World War and After. At the outbreak of the World War, the Greek prime minister, Venizelos, supported the cause of the Allies against the wishes of King Constantine, whose sympathies favored Germany. Venizelos was compelled to resign, Oct. 7, 1915. In October of 1916 he set up a provisional government at Saloniki, which was recognized by the Allies. After great pressure on the part of the Allies, Constantine abdicated on June 11, 1917, and his son Alexander ascended the throne. Venizelos now brought Greece officially into the war on the side of the Allies, and Greek troops took part in the Balkan campaign of 1918. The Treaty of Sèvres, which was never fully ratified, gave to Greece important accessions of territory. Venizelos, however, defeated at the polls, left the country. On King Alexander's death, Constantine was recalled. This act estranged the Allies, who consented to a revision of the Treaty of Sèvres. Constantine took the field to enforce against the Turks the favorable arrangements previously agreed to, but was defeated.

Greece was obliged to sign the humiliating peace of Lausanne in 1923, by which Turkey recovered her control of Istanbul and the Anatolian coast of the Ægean. Over 1,500,000 Greeks were expelled from Turkey and settled in Greece. Constantine was forced to abdicate a second time. His successor, George II, was later compelled to leave the country and, on May 1, 1924, a republic was proclaimed. A royalist movement, however, slowly gathered force and, after a futile revolt led by Venizelos, it succeeded in re-establishing the monarchy in 1935. George II returned to the throne. The next year power was seized by a military group under John Metaxis. Greece was forced into World War II by an Italian attack in 1940. She was conquered by the Germans the next year, and suffered until liberated by the British in 1944.

Internal dissension followed. King George II was recalled by popular vote, September 1, 1946, but revolts broke out in northern Greece, promoted by the leftist party, EAM, and supported, so the government asserted, by the communist regimes in Albania, Yugoslavia, and Bulgaria. Economically, Greece was on the verge of collapse, when in February 1947, Great Britain announced that she must withdraw her support. Greece appealed to the United States. In reply President Truman recommended to Congress the grant of 250 million dollars for her assistance. George II died in April, 1947, and was succeeded by his brother, Paul I.

GREENLAND

The discovery of Greenland is credited to the Norwegian, Eric the Red, who is said to have spent three years on the coast of the country (982–985). Within the next few years, several Norwegian settlements were made. These colonies, of which only a few ruins and tombstones remain, had originally a republican organization, such as prevailed in Iceland, but, like the latter country, they fell under the authority of the Norwegian kings about the middle of the 13th century. Christianity had already been established about the year 1000.

During the 15th and 16th centuries, Greenland disappeared from history, and, in 1585, the explorer John Davis found only Eskimos on the coast. After a lapse of 150 years, Hans Egede, a Norwegian clergyman, established a Lutheran mission settlement near Godthaab, under the authority of the king of Denmark. The religious and educational work thus begun among the natives is still conducted by the Danish government. Greenland, like Iceland, was left in Danish hands at the separation of Norway and Denmark in 1814.

Since 1774, trade with Greenland has been a Danish royal monopoly. Commerce and the administration of the various colonies, of which there are about sixty, is in the hands of the Greenland commission. In consequence of the invasion of Denmark by Germany, the United States in 1941 assumed temporary control of Greenland to prevent any transfer or hostile use of the colony.

HOLLAND

Holland is the popular name for the Kingdom of the Netherlands. Properly, the name applies to the medieval county of Holland, now represented by the provinces of North and South Holland, in the Netherlands. Holland was one of the provinces which in 1579 joined in the Union of Utrecht. See *Netherlands.*

HOLY ROMAN EMPIRE

The Roman Empire succeeded the republic and began its history with the rule of Augustus Cæsar in 29 B. C. After the death of Theodosius the Great in 395 A. D., the Western Roman Empire was separated from the Eastern, sometimes called the Byzantine, or Greek, Empire. Owing to the frequent incursions of the barbarians, the two empires became riven asunder. The Eastern Roman Empire lasted until the fall of Constantinople in 1453 A. D.; the Western had come to an end as early as 476 A. D. In the year 800, Charlemagne at Rome inaugurated anew this Western empire as the Holy Roman Empire and was crowned as its first emperor by Leo III. After the extinction of the Carolingian line, there ensued a period of feudal disturbance, when the empire existed only in name. The title of emperor was, however, again given substance by Otto I, king of the East Franks. At the invitation of the pope, he entered Italy with his victorious armies, and at Rome in 962 was crowned emperor. The Saxon line of emperors, founded by Otto, gave place in 1024 to the Franconian line, begun by Conrad II. In the reign of Henry IV (1056–1106) began the momentous contest for supremacy between the emperors and the popes.

On the death of Henry V in 1125, the imperial office became elective, the first elected emperor being Lothair II. In 1356, the emperor Charles IV promulgated the Golden Bull, which determined the imperial electors.

In 1273 Rudolf, the first emperor of the house of Habsburg, was elected, and from 1438 the succeeding emperors belonged to this house. Not until 1806, when the Empire was broken up by Napoleon, did Francis II relinquish his title as emperor of the Holy Roman Empire. See *Austria, Italy, Spain.*

HUNGARY

Hungary, a country in which the Magyar race is dominant, regained its independence as a result of the World War. The Magyars, an Asiatic people of Turanian race, allied to the Finns and the Turks, dwelt in what is now southern Russia before they descended, under Arpád, into the plain of the Danube, toward the end of the 9th century, and conquered the whole of Hungary and Transylvania. During the first half of the 10th century their invasions and incursions spread terror throughout Germany, France, and Italy; but at length their total defeat by Otto I of Germany put an end to their maraudings, and under their native Arpád dynasty they settled down to learn agriculture and the arts of peace. Stephen I (997–1038) was the first who was successful in extending Christianity generally among the Hungarians; and he was rewarded with a crown from Pope Sylvester II and the title "apostolic king" (1000). Stephen encouraged learning and literature, and under him Latin became not only the official language of the government, but the vehicle of Hungarian civilization, which it unfortunately continued to be for the next 800 years.

About the end of the 11th century the boundaries of Hungary were extended by the conquest of Croatia, Slavonia, and Dalmatia. In the 12th century the Hungarians first attained, through French connections, a certain refinement of life and manners. About the middle of the 13th century, King Bela induced many Germans to settle in the country, which had been depopulated by Mongol invasions. With Andrew III (1290–1301) the male line of the Arpád dynasty ceased, and the sovereignty now became dependent upon an electorate. Charles Robert of Anjou was the first to be thus chosen (1309). Louis I (1342–82) added Poland, Red Russia, Moldavia, and a part of Serbia to his kingdom.

Decline of the Kingdom. From the accession of Sigismund, elected emperor of the Holy Roman Empire, dates the beginning of the decline of Hungary. His reign (1387–1437) was marked by the Turkish invasion and the Hussite war. He nevertheless introduced various reforms and founded an academy at Buda. Matthias Corvinus (1458–90), surnamed the Great, combining the talents of diplomatist and general, proved successful against his enemies at home and abroad, and his name has been handed down in history as that of a just and firm ruler. He was an ardent patron of learning, and he founded a university at Pest.

During the early 16th century, domestic troubles and the rapacity of the magnates brought the power of Hungary to a low pass, and the battle of Mohács (1526) reduced a part of the country to a Turkish province. The rest was left to the opposing claims of Ferdinand of Austria and John Zapolya. Eventually, with the aid of the Protestants, the quarrel was settled in favor of Ferdinand, who was proclaimed king of Hungary. In 1687 the sovereignty was made hereditary and remained until 1918 under the scepter of the Habsburgs. In 1686 Leopold I took Buda and recovered most of Hungary and Transylvania from the Turks. In 1723 Charles VI, by a decree known as the Pragmatic Sanction, secured from his several hereditary states their promise of allegiance at his death to his daughter, Maria Theresa. In this way the Hungarian crown passed to the female descendants of the house of Habsburg. Charles died in 1740, and the loyalty of the Hungarians to his daughter was at once proved by the support they gave her in her struggle against the encroachments of Frederick of Prussia and the insidious designs of France.

Movement for Independence. Despite the War of the Austrian Succession, Maria Theresa did much for the improvement of Hungary, particularly in the founding of schools and colleges. Her son and successor, Joseph II (1780–90), in his zeal for an ideal enlightened despotism, tried to break down all the ancient Magyar institutions of self-government. Opposition to this policy was increased by his edict of 1784, making German the official language. However, on the advent of the French Revolution and during the wars that ensued, the Hungarians once more played a prominent part in support of the Habsburg crown. Leopold II (1790–92) had revived the power of the Hungarian diet. But the Revolution had given an impetus to ideas of national and popular rights, which the Hungarians, long stifled under the Germanic traditions and tendencies of their rulers, were among the first to feel. For a time, Francis I and Metternich stood stiffly out against all concessions, and tried to govern by pure absolutism, but they ended by summoning a new diet in 1823, controlled by Magyars.

Successive diets made new demands for religious equality, suffrage, and abolition of privileges. The Austrian government responded by imprisoning Deak, Kossuth, and other leaders, but the diet of 1839 forced their release and other concessions. The revolution of 1848 in Austria drove out Metternich and gave new force to the Magyar struggle.

The Dual Empire. Prince Metternich fled to London and the court at Vienna made concessions, but planned reprisals. In December 1848 the Austrian army, reinforced by the Slav dependencies of Austria, renewed the war. The Hungarians held their own, and the Austrians, in despair, called on Russia for assistance. "Nine nations are fighting against Hungary," said an old Magyar, "and yet they must call in the Russians." The Hungarian revolt was cruelly suppressed, but a constitutional agitation continued, and, after her defeat at Sadowa, in 1866, Austria, facing a nation as strong as herself, was compelled to make terms. In 1867 Hungary became an equal partner in the empire; the emperor and empress were crowned king and queen of Hungary.

The dualism of the Austrian empire was thus finally constituted. But Hungary itself was made up of people of several races, the Slavs constituting more than half of the population, although the Magyars, or rather the Magyar nobles, alone held political power. About 1875 this ruling class began a policy of "Magyarizing" the entire state through manipulating the suffrage laws and insisting on the universal use of the Magyar language. Until the outbreak of the World War, this policy was a source of increasing bitterness among the Hungarians.

Hungary in the World Wars. At the opening of World War I Hungary followed Austria and Germany. In the collapse of 1918 the Slav population went to the new states, Czechoslovakia and Yugoslavia; the Rumanians, with over a million Magyars, to an enlarged Rumania; leaving Hungary practically a Magyar state, with about half its former area. This arrangement was sealed by the Treaty of Trianon, upheld by the Little Entente, formed by Hungary's neighbors in 1920.

In November 1918, Hungary proclaimed the Hungarian People's Republic, with Count Karolyias provisional president. This government lasted until March 1919, when a soviet administration, under Bela Kun, was set up. A socialist government succeeded the soviet, and after an interim of seven months, Admiral Nicholas Horthy was elected regent, March 1, 1920, by the National Assembly. A "party of Unity," under Stephen Bethlen, succeeded in stabilizing the political situation. In 1921 Charles IV, former emperor of Austria and king of Hungary, attempted unsuccessfully to regain the throne.

In World War II Hungary was forced to side with the Axis powers. She recovered some of her territory, lost to Rumania and Yugoslavia, joined Germany in her wars against Yugoslavia and Russia, and declared war against the United States, December 13, 1941. Upon invasion by the Russians in 1944, her government was taken over by the Germans, but Russia occupied the country. A provisional anti-German government made an armistice with Russia. A republic was established November 1, 1945, after elections which had given a majority to a non-Communist Small Land Owners party. Under Communist pressure the economic situation grew steadily worse, and inflation ran rife. Hungary signed a peace treaty, prepared by the Allies, in February 1947.

In May the Communists holding key positions in the ministry discovered a "conspiracy against the government," implicating the leaders of the Small Land Owners party. The premier, Ferenc Nagy, was forced to resign. The usual machinery of arrests and purges followed, and a law disfranchising the non-Communists secured Communist control of the diet. With Russian sympathy and support, a Soviet régime was set up. February 1, 1949, Hungary was declared a "People's Republic."

ICELAND

Though the Culdees, an ancient order of Irish monks, are said to have settled in Iceland as early as 795 A. D., it was not until between 870 and 930 that Iceland was discovered and colonized by the Norsemen or Scandinavian vikings. The earliest immigrants came in three successive movements,—from Norway, then from the Norse kingdom of Dublin, the Orkneys, and the Hebrides, and, latest, again from the kingdom of Norway. Christianity established itself about the year 1000.

In the beginning the government of Iceland was a species of aristocratic republic made up of small landowners whose laws were framed and sanctioned by a national assembly called the *Althing*, which met once a year in summer time. But, between the years 1262 and 1271, a period of internecine strife brought the island under the sway of the Norwegian kings. From 1280, Iceland, through the union of the Scandinavian crowns, became a dependency of the Danish crown, though it was not until 1381 that it was constituted such by law.

This medieval period under foreign rule saw a sad decline in the spirit and enterprise of the Icelandic people. The Black Plague decimated the population. Ancient arts and crafts perished, and song and story languished. The Reformation kindled anew the intellectual life of the country, but this wrought little change in the economic state of the people. Moreover, throughout the 16th and 17th centuries the island was the prey of pirates and buccaneers. In the 18th century there fell disaster in the form of plagues of smallpox, famines, and volcanic eruptions, which caused the death of about a fourth of the population.

The early decades of the 19th century brought better fortune to Iceland. The intellectual movement that was stirring Europe touched the Icelandic people through an effort at popular education. When Norway was separated from Denmark in 1814, Iceland remained a dependency of the latter kingdom. A struggle for more liberal government began. In 1874, limited home rule was secured, followed in 1903 by provision for responsible government. Iceland in 1918 was joined in personal union with Denmark. On the German invasion of Denmark in 1940, the Icelandic parliament took charge. On June 17, 1944, Iceland, again a republic, formally separated from Denmark.

ITALY

The history of ancient Italy is the story of Rome down to 476, when Odoacer, the strongest of the German generals in Italy, having deposed the boy-emperor Romulus Augustulus, made himself master of the western half of the Roman Empire. In 493, however, he was overthrown by Theodoric, leader of the invading Ostrogoths (East Goths), a powerful and able man who established himself as king and ruled until his death in 526. The strong and statesmanlike policy of Theodoric seemed to promise order and the preservation of the remnants of ancient Italian civilization. But, just after his death, Justinian succeeded to the throne of the Eastern Empire, and he sent his general, Belisarius, to conquer the Goths. They were so completely defeated that they withdrew from Italy, and but meager accounts of them have been left to history.

The Lombard Supremacy. After the death of Justinian (565), his successors at Constantinople were unable effectively to protect their reconquest of the Western Empire, of which they lost a great part to the invading Lombards, who in 568 poured from the north over the Alps into the plain of northern Italy, which still bears the name of Lombardy. Originating from near the Baltic, these barbarians, unlike the Ostrogoths, had had little intercourse with the Empire and were consequently far less civilized. Their leader, Alboin, who came to a violent end in 573, was in no way comparable to Theodoric. Though the Lombards overran the North and strips of territory down the center of Italy without meeting serious resistance, they lacked military and administrative capacity—as well as control of the seas—to complete the conquest of the peninsula. Their kingdom, which endured two centuries (568-774), consisted of a loose confederation of over thirty duchies which the central authority at Pavia was too weak to weld together.

The period of the Lombard domination is noteworthy for the rise of the power of the papacy, especially in the time of Gregory the Great, bishop of Rome from 590 to 604, under whom was begun the conversion of the heathen Germanic tribes who had conquered Britain. The term "pope" (father), formerly the title of every Christian bishop, came to be applied exclusively to the successor of St. Peter; and as the bond between Rome and the Eastern Empire gradually weakened, the people of Rome came to look for protection more and more to the pope as their temporal as well as spiritual ruler.

The final rupture between Constantinople and Rome occurred following a rebellion in Italy, supported by the pope, against the image-breaking decree promulgated by the emperor Leo III in 726. In this strife the Lombards intervened in the hope of completing their conquest of Italy. They captured Ravenna and the coast cities that had been held by the Eastern Empire, and threatened Rome; but their king, Liutprand, out of deference to Pope Gregory II, desisted from an attempt on the city, and even presented the pope with some conquered towns, thus laying the foundation of papal temporal sovereignty, which was to have a profound influence on the history of Italy.

Overthrow of the Lombards. From this time on, the popes worked steadily and successfully to undermine the Lombard power. In 754, ten years after Liutprand's death, Pope Stephen II crossed the Alps and appealed in person to Pepin, the first king of the Franks of the Carolingian line, for aid against the Lombard king, Aistulf, who was threatening Rome. In requital for being anointed king of the Franks by the pope, Pepin twice made war on Aistulf, forcing him to surrender his conquest of the same coast cities that had been taken 26 years before by Liutprand, and handing them over to the pope, whose temporal sovereignty was thus notably increased.

Twenty years later, Pepin's son Charles, known to history as Charlemagne, for a personal grudge against Desiderius, then king of the Lombards and his own father-in-law, and in response to an appeal from the pope, led his army into Italy and made an end of the Lombard rule. In view of his great power in Italy, Gaul, and Germany, it seemed very natural and wise that the pope, on Christmas Day in the year 800, should crown him emperor of the Romans. This act, however, was to bring Italy little good, as it was the origin of frequent and far-reaching struggles between emperors and popes over supremacy of authority. For a time Italy found herself in close relationship with northern Europe, but the Treaty of Mersen in 870 established her once more as the Kingdom of Italy, and for many centuries this ancient land, the center of the Christian Church, was the battle-ground of her own jealous cities and of contending foreign armies. Southern Italy and Sicily were overrun by the Byzantines, Lombards, and Saracens, until the Normans drove them out in the 11th century and established the rich and strong Kingdom of the Two Sicilies.

In 962 Otto the Great, who had subdued the rebellious Lombards in the North, was crowned emperor, and later the rise of the Norman power in the South, the strengthening of the papal states, and the growth of the city-states, such as Florence and Venice, practically displaced the imperial authority. The northern Italian cities formed the Lombard League and successfully opposed the attempts of Emperor Frederick Barbarossa (reigned 1152-90) to establish his authority over their local affairs.

Italian City-States. These Italian cities were usually governed by an oligarchy composed of the wealthier citizens. They were continually at war with each other. But, in spite of all their disorder, they grew rich and powerful. Venice and Florence achieved rank among the important states of Europe. In the 14th and the 15th century, Italian cities became the centers of the revival of art and learning known as the Renaissance.

At the beginning of the 14th century the kingdom of Naples occupied southern Italy, the papal states extended in a diagonal band across the center of the peninsula, and the North was divided among the city-states. The greatest of these were Venice and Florence. Most of the cities fell at one time or another into the control of despots. Venice was a city of merchants, ruled by an aristocracy; Florence was a republic, but its government came to be directed by the family of the Medici. Rome was governed by the popes, and after the return of the papacy from Avignon (1417) they rebuilt the city and employed the greatest artists and architects of the time to adorn their capital with splendid buildings, paintings, and sculptures.

Period of Foreign Rule. The latter years of the 15th century mark the beginning of the long series of struggles of France, Spain, and Germany in the peninsula. Naples and Sicily were in the hands of the Spanish kings of Aragon. Charles VIII of France determined to seize the Spanish territory and, if possible, unite Italy under his authority. But, after a campaign in which he lost but one battle, he was compelled to withdraw. His successors, Louis XII and Francis I, endeavored to extend the French power in Italy, and protracted warfare ensued, especially between Francis I and the emperor Charles V, in which Francis I was repeatedly worsted. By the Peace of Cambrai in 1529 the Habsburgs secured a grip upon Italy that was not broken until the establishment of the Kingdom of Italy in the 19th century. The most important result of these campaigns, however, was the revelation of the treasures of Italian learning and art to the northern nations.

In the course of the struggle between France and Austria in the 17th century and the early part of the 18th, the house of Savoy secured Sardinia, and the duke of Savoy took the title of king of Sardinia. From the growth of this power in Piedmont sprang the modern national strength of Italy.

Napoleon in Italy. After the French Revolution, the French armies entered Italy and drove the Austrians out of the North, leaving them, however, in possession of Venice, where the ancient republican government was destroyed. The French set up the Cisalpine, Ligurian, Roman, and Parthenopean republics. But the democratic movements which were thus encouraged received sharp repression from Napoleon when he was firmly in power. He took for himself the iron crown of Lombardy and gave Naples first to his brother Joseph and later to Joachim Murat. Rome became part of the French Empire. After the fall of Napoleon, the Congress of Vienna restored, with few changes, the 18th century order.

Struggle for Italian Freedom. The despotisms maintained in Italy by Austria and the Holy Alliance met with continued opposition from patriotic Italians throughout the first half of the 19th century. The ideal of a unified and independent Italy, as preached by a group of notable and devoted men, gained more and more adherents. The strong movement toward the realization of this ideal began with the accession of Charles Albert to the throne of Sardinia in 1831. Mazzini called upon the new monarch to lead in the liberation of Italy. The liberal movement was given a strong impulse by the reforms introduced in the papal states by a new pope, Pius IX. In 1848 numerous uprisings throughout Italy secured constitutions in several states, and Charles Albert undertook a campaign against the Austrians in Lombardy. In this and in a second campaign, in 1849, he was defeated. Following this disaster, he abdicated in favor of his son, Victor Emmanuel II. Meanwhile, the people of Rome, led by Mazzini and Garibaldi, had abolished the temporal rule of the pope and set up a republic. This was overthrown by the French. The kingdom of Sardinia, now under a liberal constitution, became the rallying point for the party of United Italy. The statesmanship of Cavour (1810–61), the prime minister of Sardinia, secured attention to the claims of Italy in the Congress of Paris in 1856, on account of the help given by Sardinian troops in the Crimean war.

In 1858 Cavour secured the aid of Napoleon III in an attempt to drive the Austrians from Lombardy. After the victories of Magenta and Solferino (1859), Napoleon suddenly weakened and signed the preliminary treaty of Villafranca. However, in spite of Napoleon's lapse, Piedmont had acquired Lombardy. Soon the duchies of Tuscany, Parma, and Modena, and the papal state of Romagna united with Piedmont. On April 2, 1860 a parliament of the enlarged kingdom met at Turin.

On May 5, 1860 Garibaldi, already the popular hero of Italy, whose name was worth an army, embarked from Genoa with a thousand men for the conquest of Sicily and Naples. This was one of the most audacious and brilliant exploits of modern history. On September 6 Garibaldi, with a few companions, entered Naples by rail. The king had fled. Victor Emmanuel entered the city on Nov. 7. On the 18th of February 1861 a parliament representing all Italy, except Venetia and Rome, met at Turin, and the title of king of Italy was bestowed on Victor Emmanuel. Austria, crippled by her disastrous war with Prussia in 1866, was forced to yield Venice to Italy in that year, and when, in 1870, the French, at war with Prussia, withdrew their garrison from Rome, the sole support of the temporal rule of the popes was gone, and Italy could at last claim the Eternal City for her capital. The dream of a united Italy was now realized.

The Kingdom of United Italy. Many serious problems confronted the new state. The people, more than 75 per cent of whom were illiterate, had to be educated. A compulsory education law was passed in 1877, and since that time the percentage of illiteracy has been largely reduced. In 1881 and again in 1912 the suffrage was greatly extended; in 1920 it was made universal for men and women. Relations with the pope were difficult. The Law of Papal Guarantees, passed in 1871, gave the pope sovereignty over certain parts of the city of Rome and an annual grant of money. This arrangement was never accepted by the pope in its original form. In 1882 Italy joined the Triple Alliance. This entailed large expenditures for army and navy, and the financial problems of the country, already difficult, were further disturbed. In 1885 she embarked upon a colonial policy and became involved in a disastrous war with Abyssinia. Popular discontent increased under heavy taxation. In July 1900 King Humbert was assassinated, and Victor Emmanuel III came to the throne.

Great increase of population and consequent emigration to other countries turned the attention of the Italian government to the acquisition of colonies. In 1912, after a war with Turkey, Italy acquired Tripoli and twelve Ægean islands. She long looked upon the region around the city of Trent, Trieste, and Istria as properly Italian territory, *Italia Irredenta*, or "unredeemed Italy." On the outbreak of the World War, Italy remained neutral until May 1915, when she repudiated her treaty of alliance with Austria and entered the war on the side of the Allies. By the Treaty of St. Germain her territory was greatly enlarged at the expense of Austria, practically all of "unredeemed Italy" coming under Italian government.

Fascist Rule. The years 1920-21 were marked by conflicts between communist and nationalist groups. The latter, known as Fascisti, seized power in 1922, under the leadership of Benito Mussolini.

Dictatorial power was conferred on Mussolini. He established a form of modified capitalism which he described as a corporative state, Fascism. Mussolini made peace with the Vatican in 1929, yielding to the papacy the sovereignty over Vatican City.

In 1935–36 Italy conquered Ethiopia, in defiance of League of Nations sanctions, and assisted the insurgents in the Spanish civil war, 1936–39. For Italy's unfortunate war experiences see, *World War II*. When the Allies entered Rome the king retired, appointing crown prince Humbert lieutenant general of the realm. His formal abdication followed in May 1946. In a popular referendum, held in June, 54 per cent of the people declared for a republic, and the House of Savoy went into exile. A provisional government was set up, and a constituent assembly began the preparation of a constitution. Meantime unemployment increased, and famine was averted only by gifts from abroad.

In June 1947 Premier De Gasperi formed his fourth cabinet without Communist members. The constitution was completed and went into effect January 1, 1948. The interval before the April elections was marked by political strikes and rioting. The Vatican and the clergy worked against the Communists, and the prospect of American assistance helped De Gasperi. The elections returned a decisive majority for De Gasperi's Christian Democratic party and its allies. Luigi Einaudi was elected president, and De Gasperi continued as premier. In July, Italy accepted the European recovery program.

JAPAN

Early Japanese history is interwoven with myths and legends. Tradition says that Jimmu Tenno set up his government near the present Kyoto in 660 B. C. Modern historians place the event about the beginning of the Christian era. Koreans were the civilizers of Japan. Confucianism is thought to have been introduced about 415 A. D.; Buddhism, in 552. In 604 the earliest Japanese laws were written in Chinese. The government was modeled upon that of China.

Medieval Government. From the middle of the 8th century onward, the country was governed by military families or by armed monastic communities, whose heads exercised a regency, while the emperor, often a minor, was a mere figurehead.

Near the end of the 16th century, Nobunaga attempted to subjugate the armed Buddhist communities. He was assassinated. Hideyoshi followed and established peace. About 1600, Iyeyasu established a feudal government, known as the Tokugawa Shogunate, with its capital at Yedo, the present Tokyo. Nominally, the shogun was appointed by the emperor, but the emperor could not remove or punish him, so long as the shogun's family possessed the power. On the other hand, the shogun sometimes removed and exiled an emperor.

Early Relations with Western Nations. It was during the 16th century, too, that Europeans made their first acquaintance with Japan. Mendez Pinto, a Portuguese, was shipwrecked on the coast of Japan in 1542. This led to a visit by St. Francis Xavier in 1549. Thousands of Japanese became Christians. Missionaries and merchants of various nationalities followed the Portuguese. Much rivalry was created. Religious jealousy mingled with political intrigue and the strife of feudal clans. Hideyoshi, moved in part, perhaps, by the fear of foreign domination, sought to banish the missionaries. The attempt failed, and in 1596 the authorities, in order to terrify the Christians, seized several of them, together with a number of missionaries, and crucified them at Nagasaki. This persecution led to a rebellion of the Christians, which was punished in 1606 by an edict forbidding the exercise of the Christian religion. Another Christian conspiracy in 1611 brought about the expulsion of the missionaries in 1614. In 1636 an edict excluding all foreigners and prohibiting all intercourse with foreign countries was issued.

One exception was made,—the Dutch, who had no missionaries, were allowed to leave twenty men on a small island in Nagasaki harbor. For more than 200 years the gates of Japan remained closed to the world.

Commercial Treaties. In 1852 the American government, in order to secure the protection of American sailors shipwrecked on the coasts of Japan, and in the hope of opening ports where American vessels might obtain supplies, sent Commodore Perry to Japan to attempt to establish treaty relations. He arrived in Japan in July 1853 and delivered the president's letter to the shogun. In February 1854 he returned for a reply, and in March that year signed the treaty that opened Shimoda and Hakodate to the use of American vessels. A commercial treaty between the two countries was signed in 1858. The example of the United States was followed by other countries.

The signing of the treaties by the shogun provided a rallying cry for the clans that opposed the Tokugawa Shogunate. A civil war was followed in 1867 by the restoration of the emperor to real power and by the removal of the capital from Kyoto to Tokyo in 1868.

Modern Progress. In 1871 feudalism was abolished. Western laws and military organization were introduced. Teachers from America and Europe were invited to establish schools. A constitution was proclaimed in 1889, and the first Parliament assembled in 1890.

The extraterritorial jurisdiction enjoyed by foreign powers over their nationals resident in Japan was surrendered in 1899. Tariff autonomy was not fully recovered until 1911. These two accomplishments were perhaps aided by Japan's triumph over China in the war of 1894–95.

Russian intrigue in Korea led in 1904 to war with Russia, which secured for Japan a protectorate over Korea and the transfer to herself of Russian leases of railways and ports in southern Manchuria, together with certain mining rights. In 1910 Japan annexed Korea.

Japan in World War I. During World War I, Japan, assisted by Great Britain, expelled the Germans from Kiaochow, leased territory in China, and took possession of the former German rights in the province of Shantung. The Treaty of Versailles, which transferred these rights to Japan, was never signed by China, and the Shantung question remained unsettled until the meeting of the Washington Conference, when, on February 4, 1922, Japan agreed in a treaty with China to withdraw from that province. This withdrawal was accomplished in December 1922.

The World War gave Japan also a mandate over the islands north of the equator, formerly belonging to Germany. The mandate was not recognized by the United States until the Treaty of Yap was signed on February 11, 1922, in which Japan acknowledged certain American rights in Yap.

In 1918, Japan, with the other Allied and associated powers, sent troops into Siberia to protect their interests jeopardized through the Russian Revolution. In reprisal for the massacre of several hundred Japanese in Nikolaevsk in the autumn of 1920, Japan occupied several cities in the lower Amur valley and established civil government over all northern Sakhalin, which belongs to Russia. The last detachment of Japanese troops was withdrawn from northern Sakhalin on May 20, 1925.

Recent Developments. The Anglo-Japanese defensive alliance of 1902 was replaced in 1922 by an agreement between the United States, Great Britain, France, and Japan to respect one another's rights in their insular possessions in the Pacific. In 1924 the Japanese Diet abolished the dual nationality of Japanese born in foreign lands, thereby removing a serious objection in certain countries to Japanese immigration.

A serious earthquake, resulting in great loss of life and enormous destruction of property occurred September 1, 1923. Losses resulting from this, together with post-War economic unsettlement, were assigned as causes of a financial crisis in 1927, which was attended by the failure of 36 banks. The emperor, Hirohito, succeeded to the throne on Dec. 25, 1926. The first parliamentary election under a new manhood suffrage act was held in 1928.

In 1931, Japan began her career of expansion by attacking Manchuria, and turning it into a puppet state, called Manchukuo. Further aggressions on northern China followed, including the seizure of Peiping. From 1937 to 1940 Japan conquered, without a formal declaration of war, a half million square miles of China, including its six largest cities. (See *China.*) On December 7, 1941, Japan attacked the United States and Great Britain. For an account of her successes and ultimate failure, see *World War II; Japan: Government.*

Japan surrendered formally and unconditionally September 1, 1945. Complete authority now passed to the Allied Supreme Commander, General Douglas MacArthur, and the Allies began a complete reorganization of Japan. Emperor Hirohito abjured the myth of his divine origin and that of his race. The old feudalism and the modern monopolistic industrialism were attacked. The power of the ruling classes was broken, and their leaders excluded from office or brought to trial as "war criminals." Parliament was summoned and a new constitution was prepared and promulgated November 3, 1946.

JAVA

The modern inhabitants of the island of Java are said to be the highest type of Malays in the East Indies. They are, however, inferior in culture to their ancestors, as indicated by such structures as the temple at Boro Buddur, said to be the largest Buddhist temple in the world. In the 15th century the Mohammedans conquered the island.

The Portuguese were the first Europeans to settle in Java, in the year 1511. However, in 1595 they were driven out by the Dutch, who had established numerous trading stations in the coast towns. For a hundred years, Dutch occupation was confined to forts and small areas, but in the beginning of the 18th century a period of expansion began. In 1745, Dutch authority was dominant over the entire northeast coast. The kingdom of Bantam was subdued in 1808. From 1811 to 1818, the British were in possession of Java. By the middle of the 19th century, however, Dutch authority in the island was thoroughly established. Japan conquered Java in 1942. The Dutch returned after the Japanese surrender, but Javanese demands for independence delayed the settlement of the government. See *Netherlands.*

THE JEWS

The word *Jew*, derived from *Judah*, designates the Hebrew people as a religious group, a church, in contrast to the terms Israel and Israelites, which designate them as a racial and national group. The Hebrew people, like all the kindred Semites, were cradled in the Arabian desert. They migrated thence in small tribal groups between the 15th and 12th centuries B. C. and settled in Palestine. In this movement, Moses and Joshua were the main figures. Moses led a few small tribes forth from Egypt, where they had been dwelling, federated them with other small tribes of the desert, established for them the worship of Yahwe, founded certain legal institutions that became the nucleus of the later Israelite law code, and settled his followers in southern Palestine. Joshua was the leader of another group of tribes that settled in the central part of Palestine.

The Early Kingdom of Israel. There the Israelite tribes encountered powerful enemies, especially the Philistines. After a century-long struggle with them, Israel finally triumphed about 1000 B. C., chiefly through the able leadership of David. This struggle welded the originally independent tribes into one compact nation with many national traditions. Among these was the tradition of the descent of all the Israelite tribes from one common ancestor, Abraham, and his descendants, Isaac and Jacob. Many legends and traditions about these prehistoric figures are recorded in the book of Genesis. Some may possess a slight basis of historic truth, but otherwise all the narratives of Genesis are purely legendary. Furthermore, the historic figures of Moses and Joshua have been enveloped in legend, until the true story of these men and their times is involved in obscurity.

Israel's real history begins with the entrance of the tribes into Palestine. But we tread firm historical ground only when we reach the time of David. After his conquest of the Philistines, David subdued the surrounding nations. His empire was consolidated by his son Solomon. But a rebellion of the northern tribes, provoked by an obnoxious system of taxation, immediately after Solomon's death in 932 B. C., divided his dominion into the Northern and Southern kingdoms, called Israel and Judah respectively.

Northern and Southern Kingdoms. The Northern Kingdom lasted until 722 B. C., when the Assyrians destroyed the capital, Samaria, and deported a considerable number of people. These mixed eventually with other Eastern nations and disappeared. Tradition speaks of them, though incorrectly, as the Ten Lost Tribes. The Southern Kingdom endured until overthrown by the Babylonians in 586 B. C. Many of the people were carried away to exile in Babylonia, while others, among them the prophet Jeremiah, fled to Egypt.

The Prophets. But, while Israel's national existence was brief and ill-starred, during this period the beginning of Israel's chief contribution to human civilization was made. Amos, Hosea, Isaiah, Jeremiah, and their fellow-prophets gave to the old tribal and national religion a significant reinterpretation. They conceived of Yahwe, or Jehovah, as the word is usually but mistakenly pronounced, as Creator of the entire universe, the loving Father of mankind; all men, God's children, therefore, they regarded as brothers, forming one human family. They denounced idolatry, immorality, and social injustice, and proclaimed that above all else God desires that men do justice, love mercy, and walk humbly with Him. They thus established the eternal, universal foundations of true religion, ethical monotheism, a universalistic conception of both God and man, and justice and love as the basic forces of human conduct.

The Return from Exile. Cyrus, founder of the Persian empire, permitted the exiles in Babylonia to return to Palestine in 536 B. C., undoubtedly for political reasons. But only a comparatively few did so, and that no longer as an independent nation, Israel, but solely as a religious community. Henceforth they are known as Jews. Under Ezra and Nehemiah, Judaism was definitely established. From 536 B. C. on, the Jews of Palestine were successively vassals of Persia, Alexander the Great, Egypt, and Syria. During this entire period, with the exception of the short reign of Alexander, increasing political oppression and religious persecution were their lot.

The Dispersion. Finally, in 166 B. C., under the Maccabees, they revolted against Syria, and through marvelous heroism against tremendous odds they regained independence and set up their own kings, the Asmonean dynasty. But this new independent Jewish state was short-lived. It crumbled with the conquest of Syria by Pompey in 63 B. C. For a while it continued as a Roman vassal under a semi-Jewish dynasty, Herod and his successors. During this period Jesus of Nazareth lived and worked and Christianity arose. Finally, in 70 A. D., after a heroic but fruitless defense, the Romans under Titus captured Jerusalem, destroyed the Temple, massacred thousands of Jews, and sold other thousands as slaves throughout the world.

The nation Israel was destroyed forever. A heroic attempt to regain independence under Bar-Cochba in 132–135 A. D. shattered miserably. Hadrian completed Titus's work of dispersion. Since then the Jews have lived scattered throughout the world.

During the next two centuries the interest of the Jews remaining in Palestine centered in their religion. About the year 200 the *Mishna*, an extensive legal code, was compiled, and about 330 the *Palestinian Talmud*. At nearly the same time Constantine closed the great rabbinical schools; with this event, Jewish life and history in Palestine practically ceased until 1923.

Since the Babylonian Exile a large Jewish population had flourished in Babylonia. This now became the chief center of Jewish life and thought. There the *Babylonian Talmud* was compiled about 550. Under the Mohammedan rulers the lot of the Jews improved materially.

The Jews in Europe. But, with the decadence of Mohammedan power in the East, the center of Jewish life gradually shifted to Europe, particularly to Spain, where Jews attained great influence in both learning and commerce, and occasionally even became royal counselors. In southern Russia in the 7th century the entire Tatar kingdom of the Chazars was converted to Judaism. During this period Jewish scholars translated much of Arabic literature into European languages, thus communicating Arabic science and philosophy to Europe, and thereby contributing mightily to the Renaissance.

The religious zeal and bigotry fostered by the Crusades reacted unhappily upon the Jews. Increasing oppression became their lot. They were successively banished from England, France, Spain, Portugal, and many of the small German states. However, Italy, Poland, Turkey, and especially Holland granted them refuge. Cromwell finally permitted them to return to England. In Holland, Baruch Spinoza, the Jew, laid the foundations of modern philosophy. In many cities of Italy, however, and of other countries to which Jews were admitted, ghettoes were established—districts where Jews were required to dwell and out of which they might pass only if wearing a distinctive garb. See *Ghetto*.

The French Revolution and the rise of liberalism in England in the first half of the 19th century had a tendency to dissolve anti-Jewish animus. Since that time, two waves of anti-Semitism have swept over parts of Europe accompanied by persecution reminiscent of medieval times.

Anti-Semitism. The characteristic of more recent anti-Semitism is that it is based less on religious considerations than on national, racial, and economic ones. This turn was first given as a result of a pamphlet published in 1873 by a Hamburg journalist, *Jewry's Triumph over Germanism*. This book attributed to international Jewry a severe economic depression that followed three years after Germany's triumph over France, thus turning patriotism and economic interest into the service of an ancient prejudice. The book had a great influence throughout central Europe and Russia. Anti-Jewish political parties were formed in several countries, with which the more conservative and nationalistic interest allied themselves.

The movement was gradually discredited in Germany. In France it did not survive the Dreyfus Affair as a political factor. See *Dreyfus Affair*. In Russia, however, it exploded in the pogrom of Easter, 1881. This massacre was followed by restrictive laws against Jews, which remained in effect until the revolution of 1917.

The second wave of anti-Semitism likewise took its rise in Germany. Hitler rose to power in the 1930's by fanning the flames of German nationalism and pride of race, the chief enemies of which he declared were the twin evils of Jewry and Communism. His ascendency brought laws which deprived Jews of political rights, the right of marriage with "Aryans," and the right of entry into educational institutions and professions. A fine of a billion marks was imposed on German Jews in 1938 as reprisal for the assassination, by a Jew, of a German diplomatic representative in France. Anti-Semitism in Germany engendered similar movements in many other countries, their success frequently falling or rising with German influence.

The Jews in America. Already in the 17th century, Jews sought in North America a refuge from European persecution. The first notable migration was that of a group from Brazil to New Amsterdam, in 1654, while that colony was under Dutch rule. In 1658, a few Jews settled in Newport, R. I., under the conditions of religious toleration which prevailed in that colony. There were Jewish settlements in other colonies, before the Revolution, but the number of Jews in America increased very slowly before 1800. Jewish immigration in the 19th century, however, developed so rapidly that today nearly 5,000,000 Jews reside in the United States.

Zionism. An important recent development in world Judaism is Zionism. In general it was a plan to establish an autonomous Jewish state in Palestine. It had a twofold source, the ancient dream of a restored Israel and the need of an asylum for oppressed Jews. The Zionist Organization was founded in 1897, under the leadership of Theodore Herzl. Its aim was, with the consent of other governments, to secure from Turkey a charter for Jewish colonization of Palestine *en masse*. To many, however, this appeared remote or impossible of attainment. Accordingly a party of so-called practical Zionists urged an immediate beginning of gradual settlement in Palestine, in order eventually to bring about a Jewish majority in the population of the country and Jewish control of its religious, cultural, and economic development. A number of other parties, with somewhat variant programs, likewise sprang up within the Zionist movement.

Balfour Declaration. On November 2, 1917, Lord Balfour issued the following statement on behalf of the British government: "His Majesty's government view with favour the establishment in Palestine of a national home for the Jewish people, and will use their best endeavours to facilitate the achievement of this object, it being clearly understood that nothing shall be done which will prejudice the civil and religious rights of existing non-Jewish communities in Palestine or the rights and political status enjoyed by Jews in any other country."

A mandate for Palestine was assigned to Great Britain after the World War, and, in 1923, effect was given to the Balfour Declaration. See *Palestine*.

DISTRIBUTION OF JEWISH POPULATION

BY COUNTRIES

Algeria	110,127	Iraq	90,000
Argentina	260,000	Italy	57,629
Australia	23,553	Latvia	93,479
Belgium	60,000	Lithuania	155,125
Brazil	40,000	Mexico	20,000
Bulgaria	48,565	Morocco (Fr. and Sp.)	175,330
Canada	155,614	Netherlands	156,817
Chile	3,697	Palestine	399,807
China	19,850	Poland	3,113,900
Cuba	7,800	Rumania	900,000
Denmark	5,690	Russia	2,676,112
Egypt	72,550	South Africa	95,000
Eire	3,686	Spain	4,000
Estonia	4,302	Sweden	6,653
France	240,000	Switzerland	17,973
Germany	1,061,558	Tunis	59,485
Great Britain and N. Ireland	300,000	Turkey	81,872
		United States	4,832,376
Greece	72,791	Uruguay	12,000
Hungary	444,567	Yugoslavia	68,405
India	24,141	Other Countries	177,474
Iran	40,000	Total	16,190,928

BY CONTINENTS

America, North	5,018,251	Asia	815,243
America, South and Central	324,949	Africa	601,797
		Australasia	27,016
Europe	9,403,672	Total	16,190,928

KOREA (CHOSEN)

Tradition carries the story of the Asiatic country of Korea (*kô-rē'ȧ*) back to about 1122 B. C., when Ki-tse is said to have founded a state. The first authentic date marks the annexation of the country to China in 108 B. C. About 960 A. D. a period of great prosperity and progress began, which continued for several centuries. Art, religion, literary forms, and governmental methods were borrowed from China. In 1392 Buddhism was displaced in favor of Confucianism. In the 16th century the Japanese, led by Hideyoshi, the Japanese regent, occupied much territory for a time, being driven out finally by Chinese forces. Early in the 17th century the rising Manchu power overran the country and exacted tribute, which was afterward paid annually to the Manchu rulers of China until 1894.

Until very recently, most of our scanty knowledge of Korea was obtained from the narratives of Dutch sailors who were wrecked on the Korean coast in 1653 and detained in the country some years. For Korea was determined to seclude herself from the world. This persistent policy of isolation, the desire to be let alone by the *So Yang Saram,* "men from the Western Ocean," consecrated by time, became, in fact, a sort of Korean religion. From 1835 till 1860, several intrepid and devoted French missionaries contrived to find shelter, and, in spite of incessant persecutions, the Christian community, founded in the 18th century, continued to increase. In 1864 a violent reactionist was made regent, in the minority of the king, and he encouraged the persecution of Christians and the extermination of foreigners. Neither an unsuccessful attack by the French, in 1866, nor two successive American expeditions succeeded in breaking down the barriers.

In 1876, however, Korea made a treaty with Japan, and, later on, through Admiral Shufeldt, with the United States,—followed by others with England, Russia, France, Germany, and Italy. After Japan's victory over China, in 1895, Korea's independence was recognized by both powers. In 1907, pursuant to the recognition of Japan's interests by the Treaty of Portsmouth, Korea practically passed under a Japanese protectorate and in 1910 was annexed to that empire, under the ancient name of Chosen. In 1945 it was taken from Japan, and was promised ultimate independence. The Americans occupied southern Korea up to 38°; the Russians, the north. As a result of disagreements between the two powers, two governments were set up in 1948, a Communist government, sponsored by Russia, and a democratic constitution, under American protection, each claiming authority over all Korea.

LATVIA

A republic of northern Europe, situated in the basin of the Dvina river and bordering the Gulf of Riga. It includes practically all the territory of the former Russian province of Courland. The inhabitants are chiefly Letts. From about 1260 to 1560, Courland formed part of a federal republic organized by the Teutonic Knights among the Baltic provinces. Then, until 1795, it was an independent duchy tributary to the kingdom of Poland. In 1795 it joined Russia. On November 18, 1918 the Free State of Latvia was proclaimed. A period of conflict with combined Russian and German forces and also with Bolshevik armies followed. At length, with British and Esthonian aid, the country was freed from both bands of invaders, and, on August 11, 1920, a peace treaty with Russia was signed.

A constituent assembly, which was convened on May 1, 1920, formed a coalition government and adopted a constitution. In April 1923, a final boundary agreement between Russia and Latvia was signed. A mutual assistance pact with Russia was signed in 1939, under which Russia was given the right to establish air and naval bases in Estonia. The Communists gained control, and Latvia was admitted to the Soviet Union, August 5, 1940.

LIBERIA

Liberia is an independent Negro republic on the west coast of Africa. It had its origin in the plan of the American Colonization Society, founded in 1817, to colonize free Negroes from the United States. The name is derived from the Latin word *liber*, meaning "free." Settlement of the territory acquired by the Society began in 1822, and in 1838 a government called the Commonwealth of Liberia was organized. The independent Republic of Liberia was established in 1847. The entire population numbers over one million; 50,000 are civilized and Christians, and use English as their common language. Of these, 12,000 claim to be Americo-Liberians. Only persons of Negro blood may become citizens. Liberia declared war on Germany in 1917, and again in 1942. She has permitted the United States to establish military bases in her territory.

LIECHTENSTEIN

Liechtenstein (*lĭĸ'tĕn-shtīn*) is a principality lying between Austria and Switzerland. It consists of territory which came into the possession of the house of Liechtenstein at the beginning of the 18th century, and it was made a principality by the emperor Karl VI in 1719. From 1815 to 1866 it formed part of the German Confederation. Later it was practically a dependency of Austria, but in 1918 the Diet resolved to establish independence. In 1920 an agreement was reached under which Switzerland manages the postal system and telegraph lines of the principality, which is included in the Swiss customs union.

LITHUANIA

The Baltic republic of Lithuania (*lĭth'ū-ā'nĭ-ȧ*) lies between Latvia, Poland, and East Prussia. In the 11th century, the Lithuanians were tributary to Russia, but under Ringold and his successors, in the 13th century, they became independent. Eventually the Lithuanian power extended to the Black Sea. In the 14th century, by a royal marriage, Poland was united to Lithuania. A closer political union was effected in 1569. But the forces of disunion in the combined states were very strong, and, in the partitions of Poland, in the late 18th century, Lithuania was divided between Russia and Prussia. The independence of Lithuania was declared on February 16, 1918. A constitution, declaring the state to be a democratic republic, was adopted June 2, 1920.

The seat of government was located at Vilna, but, when the Poles occupied that city, Kaunas became the Lithuanian capital. Vilna was awarded to Poland by the League of Nations in 1923. When Russia overran part of Poland in 1939, she handed over to Lithuania an area which included Vilna. Russia received in return the right to establish air and naval bases in Lithuania. The Baltic port of Memel, placed by the Allied Powers under the control of a commission, was seized by Lithuania in 1923 but was handed over to Germany in 1939. Under the Communist party, Lithuania joined the Soviet Union, August 3, 1940.

LUXEMBURG

Luxemburg (*lŭk'sĕm-bûrg*) is a grand duchy bordering France, Belgium, and Germany. It was made a duchy within the German Empire by Charles IV in 1354. In 1814 it was raised to a grand duchy under the king of Holland but passed to the duke of Nassau in 1890. It was included in the German Confederation from 1815 to 1866. The Treaty of London in 1867 declared Luxemburg neutral territory and guaranteed its independence. It was overrun by the Germans in 1914, but regained its independence in 1919. On May 10, 1940, the Germans again occupied it, and Grand Duchess Charlotte took refuge in Canada. It was liberated by American troops in September 1944.

MONACO

Monaco (*mŏn'ȧ-kō*) is the smallest principality in Europe, about 370 acres in area. It borders the Mediterranean and on the landward side is entirely surrounded by French territory. The name is said to come from the Greek *Mónoikos*, a cult name for Hercules, who was worshiped here by the Greeks. The reigning prince is a descendant of the ancient Genoese Grimaldi family, with whom Monaco has been associated since the 10th century. The principality was placed under the protection of the kingdom of Sardinia in 1814, but in 1848 this protectorate ended. Monaco, though Italian in language, is now practically under French control, an agreement having been negotiated in 1932 giving France customs privileges and control of finances. In 1911 a constitution displaced the former absolute rule of the prince. The principality issues its own postage stamps. Its state expenses are paid by the income from the gambling concessions of Monte Carlo.

MOROCCO

The state of Morocco, sultanate and French protectorate of northwest Africa, is called by its inhabitants *Moghreh-el-Aksa*, meaning "The Extreme West." This country in ancient times was called Mauretania and its people, Mauri. Its early history is included in that of the Barbary States. In the 11th century a chief of the Morabites, or Marabouts, a warlike Berber sect, was proclaimed sovereign. Several dynasties followed, the present one being founded in 1648.

A war with Spain in 1859-60 resulted in the cession of land to Spain and the payment of a large indemnity. In 1894 occurred the Perdicaris incident, when an American citizen, Ion Perdicaris, was seized and held for ransom by Rais-Uli, a Moroccan chief. Perdicaris was released after pressure by the United States and European powers. But the occurrence revealed the weakness of the sultan. The country, except Tangier and the Spanish zone along the coast, has been since 1912 a French protectorate. About 30,000 Moors fought with the Allies in Europe during the World War. Spanish and French hold on Morocco was threatened, 1921-25, by Riff tribesmen under Abd-el-Krim. He was defeated and captured in 1926.

The sultanate in Morocco is elective, but only members of the reigning family are eligible. Each sultan is expected to designate his choice of a successor from among the members of the family. Usually, this person is elected, since he probably has control of military forces and the royal treasure. Once elected, he is an absolute ruler, though he must now respect the advice of the French resident-general. See *Algeciras Conference*, *Moors*, *Riff*.

THE NETHERLANDS

The northern European kingdom popularly called Holland. Originally, the name, meaning "low countries," applied to all the territory now included in Holland, Belgium, and northeastern France. Julius Cæsar found this country peopled by the Frisii in the north, the Batavi in the center along the lower Rhine, and the Belgæ in the south. Cæsar brought the Gallic Belgæ into subjection to Rome, but the Germanic tribes of the Batavi and the Frisii resisted Roman conquest somewhat longer. They finally made peace and were recognized as allies. The low-lying territory of the Batavi between the Waal and the Rhine, known as the "island of the Batavians," was long an important outpost of the empire. Batavian soldiers served in Roman armies and formed a large part of the Prætorian guard. By the end of the 3d century, when the Franks began their inroads, the Batavi, as well as the other tribes within the Roman frontier, had become Romanized. But the Frisii, or Frisians, allied with the Saxons, held the seacoast from the Scheldt to the Ems in defiance of the Franks, until the time of Charlemagne. They resisted Christianization as well as Frankish conquest, and their conversion was finally as much the result of armed compulsion as the outcome of missionary zeal.

The division of Charlemagne's empire in 843 gave the part of the Netherlands east of the Scheldt river to Lothair, to be known as Lothair's kingdom, or *Lotharii Regnum*, whence comes the name Lorraine. It finally passed to the East Frankish power, and in 953 Otto the Great transferred it to Bruno, archbishop of Cologne. Bruno divided his lands into Upper and Lower Lorraine, giving the charge of the latter to Godfrey of Verdun. This territory, difficult of access, far removed from both French and German seats of government, but open to the ravages of the Northmen on its rivers and coast line, now became for two centuries the scene of pirate raids and petty dynastic struggles.

Rise of Free Cities. At the close of the 11th century, stable government began in these feudal states, and then the Crusades opened a new era. The soldiers of the Netherlands distinguished themselves with a valor equal to that which had made their ancestors famous in Roman times. New avenues of trade were opened up, and the cities of the Low Countries began their wonderful growth in industry and commerce. Free cities and communes, governed by burgomasters and sworn councilors, flourished as practically self-governing republics. This development was slower in the North than in the South. The charters of the free cities of Holland and Zealand date from the 13th century, while those of the communes of Flanders date from the 12th. The latter also came earlier into conflict with the dukes of the great Burgundian power. In the 15th century the house of Burgundy brought all the Netherlands under its control; but lack of statesmanship wrecked the promising schemes of Duke Charles the Bold, and in 1477 the marriage of his daughter Mary to Maximilian of Austria threw the Netherlands into the power of the Habsburgs.

Period of Spanish Rule. In February 1477, the provinces secured Mary's signature to the Great Privilege, a charter confirming their political rights and local liberties. Her grandson, who in 1519 became emperor as Charles V, was born and brought up in the Netherlands, and his policy, administered first through his aunt, Margaret, and later through his sister, Mary, was moderate and progressive. But the notable spread of Protestantism, especially in the northern provinces, moved him to severe measures of restraint. His son, Philip II, a thorough Spaniard, who lacked sympathy with the Netherlands, used every means at his command to suppress both civil and religious liberty. By the year 1566 the most violent passions had been aroused, and fanatical mobs, called iconoclasts or "image breakers," spread ruin among the churches and religious houses. In 1567 Philip sent the duke of Alva to curb the disturbance with Spanish and Italian troops. Six years of pitiless, bloody severity served to bring him the curses of the Netherlands as well as the disfavor of Philip, and he was compelled to resign in 1573.

The most important result of Alva's rule was the revolt of the northern, Protestant provinces under the leadership of William of Orange. Their struggle for independence is one of the most splendid episodes in history. Again and again they cut their dikes and flooded hard-won land to baffle the foreign troops. The University of Leyden is a memorial founded in 1574 by the province of Holland in honor of the deliverance of the city of Leyden, accomplished by the help of a great flood over the broken dikes. In 1576 the southern provinces, terrified by the outrages of the mutinous Spanish troops, joined with the northern provinces in the Pacification of Ghent. But the policy of Alessandro Farnese won the southern, Catholic provinces back to Spain, and in January 1579 Holland, Zealand, Utrecht, Gelderland, Friesland, Overyssel, and Gröningen bound themselves together in the Union of Utrecht, thus founding the modern state of the Netherlands.

Independence of Dutch Republic. William, called "the Silent," was murdered in 1584, but the struggle was continued by his son, Maurice of Nassau, stadholder of Holland and Zealand. The merchants of these two provinces had prospered and achieved a Dutch supremacy in trade, which continued through the 17th century. They had no other thought but that of independence. In 1609 a twelve years' truce was concluded with Spain, but not until the close of the Thirty Years' war was the independence of the United Provinces finally recognized. During this time the Union was a confederacy of sovereign states, among which Holland was leader. In 1651 the office of stadholder was abolished, and the head of the Union was called the grand pensionary. For twenty years this office was held by the statesmanlike John de Witt; but in 1672, when Louis XIV attacked the Netherlands, the prince of Orange, afterward William III of England, was made stadholder and captain general. His diplomacy and military genius made possible a successful resistance to the plans of Louis.

The Kingdom of the Netherlands. During the 18th century the United Netherlands, or Dutch Republic, played a secondary rôle among the nations, and internal government with the old machinery was becoming more and more difficult when the French Revolution broke out. In 1795, under French direction, the Batavian Republic was organized on the wreck of the United Netherlands. In 1806 Napoleon made the country a kingdom, and in 1810 he incorporated it in the French Empire. The Congress of Vienna united it with Belgium in the Kingdom of the Netherlands, but the Belgians withdrew in 1830. Since the final adjustment of Dutch and Belgian boundary disputes in 1839, the Kingdom of the Netherlands, except for colonial wars in Sumatra, has had a steady, peaceful development. The people are devoted to the royal house of Orange, to which Queen Wilhelmina belongs.

The people of the United Netherlands, under their old republican, stadholder system of government, had been pioneers in many features of modern democracy. The ideas of a written constitution and a state-supported school system are rightly credited to them. Religious toleration made the Netherlands the refuge for the persecuted of all nations in the 17th century. The rights of the provincial states and the States-General had been jealously guarded. The Fundamental Law of 1815, however, quite in the spirit of the Congress of Vienna, provided for a constitutional monarchy in which the king was more powerful than the Parliament, or States-General, which could not originate or amend legislation. The personal, autocratic rule thus permitted was one cause of the Belgian separation of 1830. In 1848 the law was changed to make the upper house of the Parliament elective by the provinces, the lower elective by the people, and a ministry responsible to the Parliament was provided for. Later changes have extended the suffrage. An electoral reform act passed in 1917 provided for universal suffrage.

Agriculture and dairying are the principal industries of the kingdom, and, as in Denmark, co-operative organizations, aided by the government, have contributed largely to their growth. The colonial possessions of the Netherlands are extensive and valuable in both the East and the West Indies.

The Dutch maintained their neutrality in World War I under difficult conditions. In World War II they were less fortunate. The Germans invaded the country in May 1940. The queen and ministers escaped to England and carried on from there. (See *World War II*). The damage to the country was exceptionally great for, besides the usual ravages of war, the cutting of the dykes, in military operations or intentionally, laid some 450,000 acres of pasture and arable land under water.

Queen Wilhelmina returned in May 1945. On September 4, 1948, she abdicated the throne, and was succeeded by her daughter, Princess Juliana of Orange and Nassau.

NORWAY

The Norwegian people are mainly descended from a tall, blond Teutonic race which probably entered the Scandinavian peninsula in the late Stone age. A slight mixture with a shorter, dark type seems to have occurred very early. But the development of this sturdy, virile people was never affected by the waves of migration that swept over the continent of Europe.

Like the other Scandinavian peoples, the Norwegians have a long legendary story preserved in sagas. But the authentic history of Norway begins in the latter part of the 9th century A. D. in the time of Harold Fairhair, who united the petty tribal kingdoms under his authority and died about 933. This was the period of the Norse sea rovers. Contact with the more civilized peoples of Europe resulted in the establishment of Christianity in Norway in the 10th and the 11th century. Olaf the Saint, who was a zealous apostle of the new faith, ruled the turbulent chieftains from 1015 to 1028. He was slain in 1030 in war with rebellious subjects who invited Canute of Denmark and England to come to their aid. Olaf's son, Magnus I, recovered the throne from Canute's son Svein in 1035, and henceforth, till 1319, Norway was governed by native kings.

Union with Sweden and Denmark. During this period the country was prosperous. The small landholders gained political control, and Norse colonies were established in Iceland and Greenland. The death of Hakon V in 1319, without male heirs, threw the election of a new king into the hands of the National Assembly, who, after many discussions, made choice of Magnus VII of Sweden, the son of Hakon's daughter. He was in turn succeeded by his son Hakon and his grandson Olaf V, who, having been elected king of Denmark in 1375, became ruler of the sister Scandinavian kingdoms on the death of his father in 1380. This young king, who exercised only a nominal sway under the guidance of his mother, Queen Margaret, heiress of Waldemar IV of Denmark, died without issue in 1387. Margaret's love of power and capacity for government brought about her election to the triple throne of the Scandinavian lands, and from this period till 1814 Norway continued united with Denmark.

While Norway shared in the general fortunes of Denmark, it retained its own constitutional mode of government and exercised its right of electing its monarchs. After a time, like the sister kingdom, it agreed of its own free will to relinquish this privilege in favor of hereditary succession to the throne. The Napoleonic crisis may be said to have severed this union, which had existed for more than 400 years; for Denmark, after having given unequivocal proofs of adhesion to the cause of Napoleon, was compelled, after his defeat, to purchase peace at the cost of sovereignty over Norway. Crippled in her resources and almost bankrupt, she saw herself constrained to sign the Treaty of Kiel in 1814, by which it was stipulated by the allied powers that she should resign Norway to Sweden, receiving in return, by way of indemnity, some portion of Swedish Pomerania and the island of Rügen, which were subsequently exchanged with Prussia for Lauenburg.

Union of Norway and Sweden. The Norwegians, having refused to admit the validity of the Treaty of Kiel, nominated Prince Christian, heir presumptive to the throne of Denmark, as regent and subsequently king of Norway. This nomination was made by the Constitutional Assembly, which also drew up a constitution based on the French constitution of 1791. These measures found, however, neither supporters nor sympathizers among the other nations. With the sanction of the great allied powers, Charles John Bernadotte, crown prince of Sweden, led an army into Norway and, after taking Frederikstad and Frederikshald, threatened Christiania. Norway, being utterly destitute of the means necessary for prosecuting a war, accepted union with Sweden on the basis of equality of the two kingdoms. Norway retained self-government in internal matters under its own constitution.

Independence of Norway. The growth of parliamentary government brought about a desire on the part of the parliaments of both Sweden and Norway to control the king's selection of ministers and his foreign policy. This condition kept alive Norwegian impatience with the union. Besides, Sweden was aristocratic, while Norway was strongly democratic. In spite of the royal veto the Norwegian Parliament abolished the orders of nobility in that country. Meanwhile, Norway became prosperous and developed a large commerce. This led to demand for a separate consular service. After several years of dispute, the Norwegians declared the union with Sweden dissolved in 1905. Their decision was confirmed by the Treaty of Karlstad, and Prince Charles of Denmark was chosen king of Norway as Haakon VII.

The World Wars. Norway remained neutral and fairly prosperous during World War I. In World War II the Germans invaded Norway in April 1940, and conquered it after a stiff resistance. They set up a puppet government under Vidkun Quisling, which most of the people resisted passively, and sometimes actively. The great merchant fleet and all other resources outside of the kingdom were put at the service of the Allies. On June 7, 1945, King Haakon returned amid popular rejoicing.

PALESTINE

Previously to the 16th century B. C., it appears that Palestine was subject to the power of Babylon. Babylonian culture persisted even when the territory was mastered for a time by the Amorites. Early Egyptian records disclose the fact that the peoples of Canaan, as Palestine was at that time called, had commercial relations with Egypt. Canaan was conquered by the Egyptian king, Thothmes III, in the first half of the 15th century B. C.

The period of Egyptian supremacy was interrupted for some time by the inroads of the Hittites from the north. About 1350 B. C., however, the power of Egypt was again dominant in Canaan. It was within the following two centuries that the country was subjected to invasion by the Israelites, the Semitic race whose achievements lend to Canaan its chief historic interest.

For a brief period in the 10th century B. C., the entire land of Canaan, with some adjacent territory, was brought under the power of the independent kingdom of Israel and was ruled by David and by his successor, Solomon. The subsequent division of the realm between northern Israel and Judah left the land an easy prey to the Assyrian and the Babylonian empire. The northern kingdom fell in 722 B. C., and the southern, Judah, in 586 B. C. The inhabitants of the latter kingdom, known as Jews, were taken as captives to Babylon. Being permitted by Cyrus, the Persian, to return in 536, they became the nucleus of a small Jewish community in the land which their fathers had ruled.

The conquests of Alexander, at the end of the 4th century B. C., brought a strong Greek influence to bear on the country. Many places, such as Samaria, became virtually Macedonian cities. After the death of Alexander, Palestine passed first under the control of the Ptolemies of Egypt, and, later, in 197 B. C., it came into the power of Antiochus of Syria. In 168 B. C., the Jews, led by the Maccabean princes, threw off the tyranny of the Syrian ruler and set up an independent state extending throughout southern Palestine from the river Jordan to the sea.

In 63 B. C., internal strife opened the way for intervention and conquest by the Romans. A revolt of the Jews in 66-67 A. D. resulted in the destruction of Jerusalem (70 A. D.). A second rebellion, in 132–135 A. D., terminated in the final dispersion of the people.

For a brief period in the early part of the 7th century, Palestine was under Persian control. In 636, Jerusalem surrendered to Mohammedan armies under Omar, whose name was given to a famous mosque on the site of the Jewish temple.

Toward the end of the 11th century, Palestine became the goal of the crusaders, who, in 1099, established in the Holy Land the Latin kingdom of Jerusalem. This kingdom lasted barely a century. The country remained in the hands of Mohammedan powers until it was conquered by Allied troops in 1918, and assigned as a mandate to Great Britain.

Immigration under Zionist auspices increased the Jewish population to 400,000 against 1,000,000 Arabs by 1936, and in 1938 civil war broke out. British propositions for partition failed of acceptance. The disorders continued through World War II, complicated by the desire to open Palestine to displaced European Jews.

In 1946 and 1947 the British government endeavored to keep the peace in Palestine between Jews and Arabs, suppress Jewish terrorists, and stop illegal importation of Jews. At last they resigned their mandate to the United Nations, and announced that they would withdraw their troops by May 15, 1948. The United Nations in 1947 proposed a plan for partition which satisfied neither party. The British withdrew as announced, and the Jewish leaders at once proclaimed a new state of Israel. Count Folke-Bernadotte, sent by the United Nations as mediator, proposed some changes in the partition plan, among them, giving the southern desert, the Negab, to the Arabs. Meantime the war continued with Jewish successes, and many Arabs were driven from their homes. The Arab League intervened, while men and munitions were sent to the Jews from abroad. In September, Count Folke-Bernadotte was murdered by Jewish fanatics. See *Jews.*

PARTHIA

Parthia is the name of the ancient empire of the Parthians, a people related to the Mongols. Their original territory lay to the southeast of the Caspian Sea. They were conquered by Cyrus the Great of Persia in the 6th century B. C., but in 250 B. C. they revolted. From that time the empire of Parthia was rapidly extended as far as the Euphrates and Indus. It successfully repelled Roman attacks until 217 A. D., when, after the battle of Nisibis, both sides were ready to make peace. In 226 the Parthian empire, weakened by factional conflicts, passed to the Persian dynasty of the Sassanidæ.

PERSIA (IRAN)

The ancient Persians were an Aryan people who occupied territory to the east of the Persian Gulf and were for a time subject first to Assyria and then to Media. In 553 B. C., under the leadership of Cyrus the Great, they revolted against the Medes. Three years later, after the capture of the Median capital, Ecbatana, the union of the Persians and Medes began the Persian empire.

The Reign of Cyrus. Cyrus pushed the boundaries of his domain westward to the Mediterranean and the Ægean coasts, eastward almost to the Indus. He subdued Babylonia and Lydia. The return of the exiled Jews to Palestine was part of his scheme to have loyal colonists on the western borders of his empire. His successor, Cambyses (529–522 B. C.), brought Egypt within his control, and Darius the Great (521–485 B. C.) added Macedonia and Thrace in Europe and the Punjab in India to the Persian dominions. Darius organized the civil government of the vast empire under satraps, or governors, thus separating the civil from the military authority in each province. He built splendid roads, the most important of which, the Royal Road from Susa, the capital, to Sardis in Lydia, was 1500 miles long. The inns along these roads were post stations. Government couriers traveled from Susa to Sardis by relays of horses, within a week. "Nothing mortal is more swift than these messengers," wrote Herodotus. Darius had some reason for the inscription, which still survives, "the great king, king of kings, king of countries, king of all men."

Greco-Persian Wars. But the "great king," with his formidable masses of soldiery, met a new type of foe when he attempted to push his conquests farther into Europe. The Athenians, realizing the danger in the Persian advance, gave aid to the Ionian cities of Asia Minor in a revolt (499–493 B. C.). Darius crushed this rebellion and then set out to punish the Athenians. But at the battle of Marathon in 490 B. C. the Greeks, under Miltiades, gave the Persian forces a defeat that sent them back to Asia. Ten years later, Xerxes bridged the Hellespont with boats and built a canal through the promontory of Mt. Athos. Treachery alone gave his troops access to Greece through Thermopylæ, but the Greek fleet practically destroyed the Persian fleet in the strait between the island of Salamis and Attica. A land battle at Platæa and a naval engagement at Mycale, in 479 B. C., forced the final withdrawal of the Persians from Greece.

After Alexander's Conquest. One hundred and fifty years later the Persian empire yielded to Alexander, and at his death in 323 B. C. the greater part of it came under the family of the Seleucidæ. The Parthians ruled it for a time, until the dynasty of the Sassanidæ restored a large degree of Persian power about 226 A. D. This new Persian kingdom was long the chief foe of the Byzantine Empire. In the 7th century the Mohammedan conquests engulfed Persia; between the 11th and the 16th century the land was held by various dynasties of the Seljuk Turks and the Mongols. From 1501 to 1722 the Sufi dynasty, a native Persian family descended from the ancient Sassanidæ, ruled Persia. In the 18th century an Afghan dynasty ruled Persia.

Modern Persia. Modern official relations with Russia and Great Britain began in the 19th century, and the conflict of foreign interests injured Persia's development. In 1906 the first national assembly convened and a short-lived constitution was granted.

An Anglo-Russian treaty in 1907 divided Persia into three "spheres of influence," the north to be Russian, the southeast, English, the remaining section to be neutral. The finances of the country were chaotic, and in 1911 Mr. Morgan Shuster, an American, was selected to take control. His vigorous administration of eight months resulted in his dismissal under pressure from Russia. Anarchy increased, and at the opening of World War I, although Persia was neutral, German agents fomented uprisings. A British force was organized in 1916, which did much to restore order. Famine conditions were relieved in 1917-18 by the American Committee for Armenian and Syrian Relief.

In 1919 Persia made a favorable treaty with Great Britain. In 1921 she repudiated it, and made a more favorable treaty with Russia. A constituent assembly, in 1925, placed the government in the hands of a hereditary shah. In 1935 the name Persia was officially changed to Iran.

In World War II Iran became important as a corridor through which Britian and the United States could send munitions to Russia. Iranian oil deposits were also significant. By the Tehran agreement, Britain, Russia, and the United States guaranteed the independence of Iran, and agreed to withdraw their troops at the conclusion of hostilities.

PHILIPPINE REPUBLIC

The Republic of the Philippines occupies a group of islands, lying off the eastern coast of Asia, extending from Formosa to Borneo. Discovered by Magellen in 1521, they remained a Spanish colony for over three centuries, and then became an American dependency for nearly 50 years. In 1933 an act of Congress provided for their independence, after a ten-year transition period, as the Philippine Commonwealth. On July 4, 1946, the islands, with Manuel A. Roxas as their first president, became independent, although closely connected by treaties and economic relations with the United States.

PHŒNICIA

The ancient country of Phœnicia (*fē-nĭsh'ĭ-ȧ*) comprised a strip of land about 120 miles long and hardly more than 12 miles wide, between the Lebanon mountains and the eastern shore of the Mediterranean. The Phœnicians were probably a Semitic people, related therefore to the Hebrews. The name by which they are known is of Greek origin, derived perhaps from *phoinix*, the Greek name for the purple or crimson dye for which Phœnicia was famous.

Our earliest acquaintance with Phœnicia comes through records of Egyptian control from 1600 to 1300 B. C. The city of Sidon then became powerful and withstood the advance of the Israelites. Tyre assumed leadership about 1250 B. C. and held it for nearly 400 years. It was Hiram, king of Tyre, who furnished Solomon with ships, workmen, and building materials.

The forests of Phœnicia supplied excellent wood for shipbuilding, and its coast furnished good harbors. Under these conditions, with the smallness of the country, the Phœnicians became the greatest sailors and traders of the ancient world. They supplied ships to Egypt, and Phœnician vessels and sailors made up the sea forces with which Darius and Xerxes attacked Greece. It is probable that there were Phœnician colonies on the Ægean islands as early as 1500 B. C. By 1100 B. C. Phœnician ships had passed Gibraltar, and the coasts of Europe and Africa were dotted with colonies and trading posts. Cadiz in Spain, mentioned in the Old Testament as Tarshish, and Carthage, later a great maritime power, were Phœnician colonies.

Phœnician traders brought tin from Cornwall in England, silver from Spain, linen from Egypt, and copper from Cyprus. Phœnician mechanics knew how to work the metals skillfully and how to dye cloth in the purple hue so highly prized among the ancients, while Phœnician scholars gave to the Western peoples a simplified alphabet.

Assyria broke the power of Tyre in the 9th century B. C. Control by Egypt and Babylon followed, and under the Persians Tyre became important again as the center of their sea power. After a memorable siege in 332 B. C., in which Alexander captured the city of Tyre, the history of Phœnicia came to an end.

POLAND

The republic of Poland is a Slavic state created at the close of the World War.

Formerly, Poland was an important kingdom of Europe, with its capital at Krakow from about 1320 to the reign of Sigismund III (1587–1632), when it was removed to Warsaw. At the period of its greatest extent, previous to 1660, it had an area of about 375,000 square miles, extending northward to the Baltic Sea and the Gulf of Riga, westward to Brandenburg, southward to Hungary and almost to the Crimea, and eastward throughout most of the basin of the Dnieper.

Poland was a state of much influence and promise until it was weakened by serious factional troubles in the 18th century and fell a prey to the more powerful neighboring states of Russia, Prussia, and Austria. In 1772, 1793, and 1795 occurred the three successive partitions of Poland whereby all the territory of the kingdom was divided among these three great powers. Napoleon, in return for military support, promised to reconstruct an independent Poland, but accomplished little.

At the outbreak of the World War in 1914, about six-sevenths of this area was comprised in Russia, including Russian Poland, Lithuania, Volhynia, and a major part of Little Russia, Livonia, and Courland. The portion of Poland which belonged to Austria comprised the crownland of Galicia. The portion belonging to Prussia comprised Posen, West Prussia, and Ermland, in what is now known as East Prussia.

In November 1918 the independence of Poland was proclaimed at Warsaw, and the powers signatory to the Treaty of Versailles guaranteed the independence of the new state, within the limits of the 18th-century Polish Commonwealth. The success of Polish claims at the Paris peace conference was due in no small part to the diplomacy of the pianist Paderewski, who became the first prime minister. Poland attacked Russia in 1919 but in turn was invaded in 1920 by Russian forces, which were turned back with French aid when near Warsaw. The Treaty of Riga, in October 1920, terminated hostilities and increased Poland's territory by about one-third at the expense of Russia. An insurgent Polish army seized Vilna, the capital of Lithuania, in 1920. It later withdrew, but the city was re-occupied by Poland in 1922 after a plebiscite favorable to Poland and was awarded to her in 1923 by the League of Nations. A republican constitution was adopted in 1921. General Pilsudski, the hero of the war with Russia, made himself dictator in 1926. On his death in 1935 a new constitution was adopted. For the overthrow of Poland and its fourth partition, by Germany and Russia, see *Poland*: *Government.*

PORTUGAL

The Portuguese people are descended originally from the ancient Iberians, who occupied the country when Carthaginian and Greek settlers appeared on the west coast of the Iberian peninsula. The Romans conquered the country, and they were followed by the Visigoths and the Moors. The Portuguese of today bear traces of the mixture of all these bloods from imported slaves.

At the end of the 11th century, Portugal, then called Portucalia from the old Roman name of Oporto, *Portus Cale,* was an obscure fief of the kingdom of León. In 1095 Alfonso VI gave this fief to Henry of Burgundy, one of the northern adventurers who came to Spain to fight the Moors. Henry extended the boundaries of his realm, and his son, Alfonso I, became the first king of Portugal. Within the next two centuries, despite wars with the Moors and opposition from the pope, the boundaries of the kingdom were extended to their present limits, and Portugal became a power in Europe. The 13th century saw the end of war with the Mohammedans, and an era of prosperity and organization of government began in the 14th century. King Ferdinand, who came to the throne in 1367, was successful in correcting the abuses of the corrupt court and making war with Spain. On his death in 1383, the legitimate Burgundian line ended. In 1385 John I was chosen by the Cortes. His protracted reign is notable chiefly for the beginning of the long series of Portuguese discoveries and explorations inaugurated by his son, Prince Henry the Navigator.

The voyages of Portuguese sailors led to the building of a great commercial empire. Portugal secured possession of Madeira and the Azores, a part of Morocco, the Cape Verde islands, and the Guinea Coast. At the close of the 15th century, Vasco da Gama discovered the route to India by way of the Cape of Good Hope. The opening of the 16th century saw the establishment of Portuguese settlements in Brazil, India, Malacca, and the Sunda islands. Portugal then ranked as one of the strongest European states. But her decline was at hand, and was hastened by policies of bigoted oppression and tyranny at home and in the colonies. The Jews, who controlled the wealth of Portugal, were expelled, and other emigration weakened the state. In 1580 Philip II became king of Portugal, and the country was the victim of his imperial schemes. He robbed her to pay for his campaigns in the Netherlands; and the English, Dutch, and French avenged themselves on her colonies.

After sixty years of the Spanish tyranny, John, duke of Braganza, established a new Portuguese dynasty. In the course of the next century, Portugal established close commercial relations with England. In the 18th century, she experienced a period of great progress, broken only by the sad disaster of the Lisbon earthquake, November 1755, in which 40,000 persons perished.

Portugal's friendship with England brought her into the wars following the French Revolution. In 1807, at the approach of the armies of Napoleon, the regent, Prince John, transferred his government to Brazil. He returned to Portugal in 1821, although he had reigned as king of Portugal and Brazil since 1816, when the English forces had expelled the French invaders.

The 19th century was a period of almost continual struggle between the party of absolute monarchy and the friends of constitutional government. The reign of Carlos I, which began in 1889, was a period of demoralization. He and his son, the crown prince, were assassinated in Lisbon, Feb. 1, 1908. Prince Manuel came to the throne, but in 1910 he was deposed. A republican government was then set up, which survived several stormy crises but was at length overthrown by a military *coup d'état* in 1926. A modified dictatorship was set up in 1934 having many elements of the corporate state.

In World War I Portugal entered the war on the side of the Allies. In World War II she remained benevolently neutral.

PROVENCE

Provence (*prô'väNs'*) is the district of southeastern France which corresponds roughly to the ancient Roman province, *Provincia Romana,* whence the name. This province was organized in the 2d century B. C., after the Greek city of Massilia (Marseilles) had appealed to the Romans for protection against the invading Ligures. In the first four Christian centuries the province was the seat of a rich and cultured life which centered at Arles and Marseilles. Many interesting remains of this Roman period, such as the theater at Arles, are still preserved. Provence was the field of the conflict between Cæsar and Pompey, and between the Franks and the Saracens. It became a part of France under Louis XI. In the 12th and the 13th century Provence was the seat of a splendid poetic literature, and the Provençal dialect still persists, in both speech and writing.

ROME

The Roman Empire was built on the foundation of a strong local state in Italy. The geography of the peninsula and its ethnographic condition in the early period would scarcely have led us to predict a united Italy. The peninsula is not compact, but long and narrow. The Alps with their many easy passes set up no barrier to the north; a long coast line and frequent harbors along the southern coasts tempted immigrants from overseas. When recorded history begins, then, we are not surprised to find Italy occupied by six or seven peoples of entirely different racial stocks. The most important of these peoples were the Italians, who had entered the peninsula by a land route, and the Greeks and Etruscans, who had come by sea. The Etruscans held north central Italy; the Italians, the central and southwestern part of the peninsula; while the Greeks settled along the southern coast. The factors which gave unity to Italy and in the end made Rome mistress of the Western world were: the sturdiness of the Italic peoples; the strength of their compact political organization, when pitted against the lack of political unity which their principal rivals, the Greeks and Etruscans, showed; the convenient position of Rome near the center of the peninsula and on a navigable river; and the position of the broad fertile strip of Italy west of the Apennines, with the more important harbors on the western coast.

The Latin People. The people who were to build the Roman state were tribes of Indo-European stock, who very early descended through the Alpine passes into the valley of the Po and thence spread into the highlands of the East and the plains of the West and South. The tribes who occupied *Latium,* or the "flat lands" to the south of the Tiber, were the Latins, a hardy race. They were neighbors of the Etruscans, who lived north of the Tiber. From these people the Latins acquired many of the arts of civilization, but they were at the same time forced to defend themselves against the encroachments of the Etruscans and against the Sabines, a highland people in the upper valley of the Tiber. Perhaps it was this situation which brought about the formation of the Latin League, a union of several settlements whose peoples met annually at the town of Alba Longa, where there was a temple of Jupiter. His worship brought the tribes together.

At a ford of the Tiber, near the Palatine mount, was an ancient market, where the Latin peasants came to purchase the wares of the Etruscan merchants. Here the rude Latins had their first glimpse of the civilization and industry of the East, for the Etruscans did business with Greek and probably with Phœnician merchants. By this route too the alphabet may have come to the Latins, as they learned to spell out the accounts and invoices of traders. The earliest settlement to which we may properly give the name Rome was made on the Palatine and the neighboring hills, with its stronghold on the Capitoline. Recent excavations carry the foundation of the city back to a very early date; the Romans fixed 753 B. C. as the year of its founding, and they dated events from that year. The population of the early city was probably made up of Latins, Etruscans, and Sabines, but the Latins predominated.

The Early Latin Republic. For a time this Latin state was ruled by kings, assisted by a council of old men (*senes*), or a senate, but toward the close of the 6th century B. C. the monarchy was displaced by a republic. At the head of the state were two consuls, elected for a year. In an emergency, supreme power was sometimes granted to a single official, who was called a dictator. The two annually elected officials were chosen from among the patricians, as the governing class was called, and they did not treat the plebeians, or common people, fairly. With the establishment of the republic, therefore, began a struggle on the part of the plebeians to compel the patricians to grant them a share in the government. This contest lasted for more than two centuries. The first step in the progress of the plebeians was the election of tribunes of the people. The persons of these officers, ten of whom were elected annually, were declared inviolate, and they were given the power of vetoing any act of a magistrate that seemed to bear too hard upon a citizen. A long step toward securing the rights of the average citizen was taken in 449 B. C., when the laws, which previously had been known to the priests only, were codified, engraved on twelve bronze tablets, and set up in the Forum where they could be read by anyone. In course of time, these laws were developed into a system which has proved one of the richest legacies left to the world by the Romans.

By the middle of the 3d century B. C., the plebeians had won the right to hold the highest offices of the state and had attained equality with the patricians before the law. The republic was really what the words *res publica* implied,—an "affair of the people." Yet the popular assembly never had the right of discussion. It could only vote *yes* or *no* upon measures proposed by the magistrates; debate was reserved to the Senate, which, throughout the period of the republic, in the main, guided the state wisely.

Besides the tribunes and consuls, ancient Rome had also prætors, who served as judges; quæstors, who had charge of the treasury; and censors, whose business it was originally to take a census of the people and assess the taxes. The office of censor grew in importance, and after a time the censors assumed the power of expelling senators for immorality and of depriving citizens of their votes because of misconduct. These offices are interesting, not only for their original character in the republic, but also because the Roman emperors acquired their power by assuming the functions of some of them, and because the old Roman titles appear frequently in modern history, as in France and in the Latin states of South America.

Growth of the Roman State. The task of the Senate and the consuls in the growing Roman state was not an easy one. While the struggle for democracy within the republic was going on, constant warfare was the price of safety from attacks by the Etruscans and the neighboring highland tribes. In the midst of all this, the Gauls, in the early part of the 4th century, captured and burned the city of Rome. But when this danger had passed, the Roman armies pursued the business of conquest until, by the year 338 B. C., when Greece was surrendering her freedom to Philip of Macedon, Rome was supreme in Latium and had extended her power over southern Etruria. The beginning of the 3d century B. C. saw her victory over the Samnites in the South, and, in 264 B. C., Roman arms had triumphed over the Greek cities in the extreme South, or Magna Græcia. Italy was united, from the Strait of Messina on the south to the Arno and Rubicon rivers on the north.

Citizenship and Colonies. A new problem in government now presented itself to the Romans. The idea of citizenship was at this time confined to residence in Rome or the near-by territory. All elections were held in the city, and election days were numerous. Consequently, even those who held Roman citizenship but lived at a distance from Rome found attendance upon elections impossible. It thus came about that, even while Roman conquests were confined to Italy, elections and legislation were controlled by the Roman populace. This defect in the Roman system was never wholly corrected, and it led to grave evils. It might have been remedied by the introduction of a representative system. This concession, however, the city of Rome was unwilling to make. But immediate trouble was avoided by allowing the conquered peoples to manage their own local affairs, and by demanding only that they should furnish soldiers for the Roman armies in time of war. The loyalty of the new territory in Italy was secured by the planting of Latin and Roman colonies at various points. The Latin colonists were mainly poor plebeians and veterans who wanted their own farms. Although possessing the private rights of Roman citizens, they had not yet acquired the right to vote and hold office, whereas these rights and privileges were possessed by the members of the Roman colonies, who were able to exercise political power by going to Rome. Both classes of colonies, however, were loyal to Rome and served to spread Roman customs and the Latin language throughout Italy. Moreover, what was quite as important as anything else, the agricultural development of the land was assured through these farmer settlements.

These colonies were connected by splendid roads, which served both as a means of rapid military movements and, since they were free to the public, as arteries of trade and routes of travel. In later centuries this admirable system of roads was extended throughout the empire, from Britain to Asia Minor, and so well were the highways built that many stretches of them are even now in good condition. By such means, the people of Italy were brought to feel their national unity, even though they belonged to many separate tribes and spoke widely differing dialects and languages.

The long wars which had resulted in making Rome mistress of Italy had developed the Roman citizen army into a military machine of wonderful efficiency. The basis of it was the legion, in which all citizens from 17 to 46 years of age were liable to service. Added to this was a body of auxiliaries, recruited from the subject states. The severe discipline of these troops, their open order of fighting, and the skillful use of reserves carried the Roman standards to victory.

Rome and Carthage. Such was the preparation of the Roman state for its life and death struggle with its greatest rival, the commercial Carthaginian power. The first stage of this long contest was the fight for Sicily, begun in 264 B. C. The Romans remedied their one weakness, lack of sea power, by building a navy, with which in 241 B. C. they won a complete victory. During the next twenty years they prepared for a second contest by subjugating the Gauls in the Po valley and by seizing Sardinia and Corsica, while the Carthaginians were making good their losses by developing the resources of Spain. In the summer of 218 B. C. the Carthaginian commander, Hannibal, carried the war into Italy by successfully leading his army from Spain through Gaul and over the Alps. At first the rapid movements of this great captain took the Romans by surprise. They appointed Quintus Fabius Maximus dictator. He earned the title of "delayer" through his policy of avoiding a direct conflict until he could drill his troops. The Romans were impatient of delay, and the new consuls of 216 B. C., yielding to the popular demand for speedy action, joined battle with the numerically inferior force of Hannibal at Cannæ. They were disastrously defeated, and 35,000 of the 50,000 men who made up their army were killed or captured. For nearly fifteen years Hannibal maintained himself in Italy with forces inferior to those of the Romans, but he failed to arouse the Italians to revolt, and when, in 202 B. C., he was summoned to Africa, which Publius Scipio had invaded after driving the Carthaginians from Spain, he was defeated on the field of Zama. Carthage became a dependant ally of Rome, and Rome's political supremacy was assured.

But Carthage still remained a dangerous rival of Rome. For fifty years the Romans watched the city's growth and then determined to destroy it. In 146 B. C., after a heroic defense of three years, an adopted grandson of the conqueror of Zama carried out the order of the Senate to burn the city and declared its site accursed.

The difficult task of subjugating Spain was completed in 133 B. C., and all of the peninsula except the mountainous northwest part became gradually and thoroughly Romanized; a few years later the strip of southern Gaul, or France, which connects Italy with Spain, was made Roman territory. In 121 B. C., Rome had conquered Italy and the adjacent islands of Sicily, Sardinia, and Corsica, southern Gaul, Spain, and northern Africa. In other words, she was mistress of the western Mediterranean. In the eastern Mediterranean, Rome became involved in quarrels with Macedonia and Syria in the early part of the 2d century, and by 133 B. C. she had annexed Macedonia and the western portion of Asia Minor.

Economic Problems. As the domain of the republic became imperial in extent, it appeared that the old plan of making allies and citizens of conquered tribes, which had worked so well in Italy, was difficult to apply on distant and barbarous frontiers. Rome, therefore, began the policy of making provinces of the conquered lands outside of Italy, and of requiring them to pay tribute. The result was that these provinces were, in many instances, treated as mere opportunities for plunder. But the consequences of the vast influx of wealth from this new territory to Rome were even more disastrous for the city than for the provinces. The gulf between the rich, to whom the power and wealth of conquest went, and the citizen farmers, who fought the battles, became wider. Cheap wheat from the new provinces flooded the market of Italy, and the small farmer was forced to sell his land to the great landholder who could work it with slaves. These landless folk flocked to Rome, and they, with the quickly enfranchised slaves, who had been brought in great numbers to Italy as a result of the long wars, made up the Roman mob which was to be for centuries a constant menace to the peace of the city. Thus, while the richer classes of Italy were appropriating the wealth of the Mediterranean world and assimilating the culture of Greece, a difficult social problem arose in the state.

The Gracchi. The first serious attempt to meet this situation was made by the tribune Tiberius Gracchus, in 133 B. C. He proposed that the government should reclaim from the great landlords a part of the public lands and divide it into small holdings to be given to poor citizens. He even wanted to use public funds to stock these little farms. Tiberius at length secured the passing of a law covering these points, but the violent means used by him, added to the hatred aroused by his plan among the rich landholders, brought about his assassination and the repeal of the measure. Ten years later, Gaius Gracchus, the younger brother of Tiberius, was elected a tribune of the people. The means he took to carry out the reforms which he had in mind combined good and bad elements. His first move was to secure a law permitting sale of grain from the public storehouses to citizens at half the market price. This led directly to plain charity and disaster, but it gave Gaius the political support of the needy. He then projected a system of roads and began a policy of establishing colonies of poor citizens in the provinces. Here were the beginnings of wise policies, but the next measure proposed, although equally wise, proved his undoing. He wanted to bestow citizenship upon the people of the Latin colonies. But the Roman populace saw in this a possible curtailment of their privileges. They refused to re-elect him to the tribunate, and he was killed in an ensuing riot.

The Movement toward Monarchy. The work of the Gracchi had begun the revolution that was finally to make one man supreme in the Roman state. One element of weakness in their plans lay in their entire dependence upon the fickle, ignorant, selfish Roman populace. Later, men with trained legions at their command were able to master the mob and use it for their own purposes.

At the beginning of the 1st century B. C. the struggle between the aristocracy and the democracy centered around Marius and Sulla. Marius was of peasant birth, but his military ability, signalized in his victory over Jugurtha in Africa, in 105, and over the Germans, in 102 B. C., gave him great influence with the people. Sulla was a noble, who won his early military honors in the Social war (90-88 B. C.), a contest through which all Italians won Roman citizenship. Later he carried on a successful war against Mithridates in Syria. While he was in the East, the democratic faction, under Marius, was supreme in Rome, where it carried out a campaign of terror against the aristocrats. Marius died suddenly, and Sulla returned to defeat the democrats and wreak a bloody vengeance on their leaders. He ruled as "Perpetual Dictator" for three years.

The next stage in the march of the Roman state toward monarchy was marked by the ascendancy of Pompey, a friend of Sulla. He had won military laurels in Spain, in campaigns against the Mediterranean pirates, and in the final subjugation of Mithridates. He annexed Syria to the Roman domain and returned to Rome in 62 B. C. Three other men were also to be reckoned with in Rome. They were men of different types. Cicero was the leading lawyer of his day, champion of the Senate and of the traditions of the republic. Julius Cæsar was a young politician, popular with the masses because of his oratory and his lavish expenditure for public shows. When his own fortune was exhausted, the wealthy Crassus came to his aid. Cæsar and Crassus made a private compact with Pompey, known as the First Triumvirate. They were masters of Rome. But Cæsar was more daring and able than his colleagues, and fortune favored him. While he was engaged in the conquest of

Gaul, Crassus met defeat at the hands of the Parthians at Carrhæ in Mesopotamia.

Julius Cæsar. Pompey, fearful of Cæsar's ambition for despotic power, now sided with Cicero and the Senate. Cæsar was summoned to return to Rome without his army; his reply was the crossing of the Rubicon with his troops. Taken unawares, Pompey, with what forces he could collect, withdrew to Greece. Cæsar, after a brief campaign in Spain, followed and defeated him at Pharsalus in 48 B. C. Two years sufficed to subdue revolts in Egypt, Asia, and Africa. In 46 B. C., Cæsar returned to Rome. He now began a series of wise political and economic reforms. He struck at the worst abuses of public charity, reformed the system of tax collection, planned foreign colonies for landless Italians, and began the extension of Roman citizenship. But his political and personal enemies formed a conspiracy against him and brought about his death in 44 B. C.

The Rise of Octavius. Then followed a desperate struggle for power between the senatorial party, led by Cicero, Brutus, and Cassius, and the opposition, under the Triumvirs,—Antony, Octavius, and Lepidus. The battle of Philippi, in 42 B. C., put an end to the hopes of the senatorial oligarchy and the republicans. Of the three new masters of the Roman world, Lepidus, a weak man, quickly dropped out of sight; Antony was defeated at Actium, and the reins of power came into the hands of Octavius. But Octavius took care that the old governmental forms should be preserved. The Senate gave him the title of *Augustus*, "the majestic"; he called himself *Princeps*, "the first citizen"; his command of the army carried the title of *Imperator*, "commander." Here are the origins of modern royal titles, to which we may add Octavius' family name of *Cæsar*. Augustus, as he is known, held the tribunate, which gave him large authority in Rome, and he had the proconsul's power on the frontiers and in the provinces. In this way the new government was linked with the old.

The Early Empire. The reigns of Augustus and his successors to the year 180 A. D. cover the period of the Early Empire, the time of Rome's greatness. Except on the frontiers of the empire, the reign of Augustus was a period of general peace. The emperor gave his personal attention to the problems of ruling. He made the Rhine the boundary of the empire on the north; the Euphrates, on the east. He built splendid structures in Rome; he constructed long stretches of roadway in the provinces; and he made life and property more secure throughout the empire.

With few exceptions, the emperors of the first two centuries were able men, great builders, and strong administrators. The list includes Claudius, Vespasian, Trajan, Hadrian, and Marcus Aurelius. In the reign of Claudius the conquest of Britain was begun, a difficult task, which was not completed until the end of the 1st century A. D., after which time, for 300 years, Britain was a Roman province. Vespasian rescued the Roman state from the anarchy which threatened after the death of Nero. During his reign, his son Titus captured Jerusalem, 70 A. D. Trajan, one of the so-called "good emperors," pushed the frontiers of the empire to their extreme limit, but his conquest of the Tigris-Euphrates valley was abandoned by Hadrian, who found the difficulties of administration too great in so distant a province. With the reign of Marcus Aurelius, the philosopher-emperor, the barbarians began to show the growing strength that was at last to break through the Roman barriers.

Civic Life in the Empire. But the real story of this great period is to be read in the traces of Roman life that still remain in all parts of the wide territory that became the home of the Roman citizen. Massive and beautiful ruins of cities in Syria, in Dalmatia, in Africa, Spain, France, Germany, and England testify to a wealthy and luxurious civilization that appropriated the traditions and genius of its predecessors in sculpture and architecture. The rich commerce which sustained this civilization entered splendidly improved ports and passed over a vast system of paved roads. In hundreds of free, self-governing cities a vigorous political life developed, which left to medieval and modern times a lasting tradition of free local government. In these cities the industries were carried on largely by free workmen who were organized in guilds. Art and literature were cultivated, and the Latin language became the common tongue of the Western world. Roman law was supreme and became the basis of the modern legal systems of western Europe. With all this greatness, however, there grew up the social, political, and religious evils that accompany the rise of a luxury-loving society. Wealth was concentrated in the hands of a few. Cities grew at the expense of the country, and their citizens were divided into the very rich and the very poor.

The Later Empire. The period of the Later Empire extends from the year 180 to the year 395, when, on the death of Theodosius, the empire was divided. The first half of this period was marked by civil wars provoked by the strife of rival claimants for the imperial throne. Emperors were made and unmade by the legionaries from Rome or the provinces. This internal trouble was made more serious by the constant attacks of the northern barbarians and the Persians. Diocletian (284–305 A. D.) undertook to reorganize the government. He associated with himself a trusted officer, Maximian. Each was called *Augustus* and had all the honors of emperor. Diocletian ruled the East; Maximian, the West. Each *Augustus* selected a younger associate, or *Cæsar*, to aid him. The civil and the military authority were separated, and the empire was divided into more than one hundred provinces. By these means, Diocletian hoped to hold in check ambitious aspirants for the throne. His system prolonged the existence of the empire, but along with it went absolutism and all the old strife as to the succession.

Constantine, a man of ability in war and statecraft, became sole master of the empire in 324. He made his reign of thirteen years memorable by the recognition of Christianity and by moving his capital to the ancient Greek town of Byzantium, which became Constantinople, or the "city of Constantine." Both of these acts were founded upon good reasons of state. Byzantium was a better military center than Rome from which to repel the barbarian attacks, and it was well adapted to connect the eastern and western halves of the empire.

The death of Constantine, however, was the signal for another period of disorder in the empire. The barbarians were crowding in along the Danube and the Rhine, and the interests of the eastern and western parts of the empire were driving Rome and Constantinople farther apart. The slave system and childlessness sapped the vitality of the population. The Roman armies lacked free men. Expenses of government increased faster than revenues. The Roman Empire faced bankruptcy.

Rise of Christianity. Christianity, the latest of the religious faiths to come out of the East, in its principles and practice was not in perfect harmony with the religious and social conditions of the time. The Christians refused to worship the emperor or to share in any of the customary pagan rites. Their conduct brought many years of persecution until at last the emperor Constantine himself accepted Christianity. Slowly the new faith triumphed inside the empire over the old paganism and the newer Oriental faiths, such as the popular cult of Mithra. Christian missionaries had made converts among the Germans, so that the Roman world passed to their hands with less disturbance than otherwise would have occurred.

Germanic Invasions; Fall of Rome. A peaceful mingling of Romans and Germans was going on along the Danube, when the Huns suddenly appeared. The Germanic Visigoths were allowed refuge on the Roman side of the Danube. Here Roman officials robbed and persecuted them until they revolted. At the battle of Adrianople in 378 A. D. they overthrew the emperor Valens and his legions. They had now learned their power, and after the death of Theodosius in 395 the great Gothic invasion of Greece and Italy began. In 410 the Goths captured the city of Rome itself. Four years earlier a vast body of Germans had crossed the Rhine. A few years later (429–439) the Vandals conquered North Africa, and by the middle of the century the Angles and Saxons were masters of Britain, while the Franks controlled Gaul. The Huns were beaten back at the battle of the Mauric plains in 451 by a union of Romans and Germans. But in 455 the Vandals sacked the city of Rome. The government of the West by the Romans was now a thing of history. German officers made and unmade puppet emperors. The last claimant to the imperial throne was the boy, Romulus, nicknamed *Augustulus*, "the little Augustus." He was dethroned, and the German troops made Odoacer king. The date of his accession is sometimes taken to mark the end of the Roman Empire in the West, but no line can be drawn to mark the end of the old world and the beginning of the new. The new rulers of Italy, of Gaul, and of Spain still thought of their authority as coming from Rome. Roman law was followed, and the Latin language was still spoken for many centuries throughout the West.

ROMAN EMPERORS

Name	Lineage	Period of Rule		Birth	Death
	THE CÆSARS				
Augustus (Octavian)	The title of Augustus conferred by the Senate	B. C. 27	A. D. 14	B. C. 63	A. D. 14
Tiberius	Stepson of Augustus	A. D. 14	37	42	37
Caligula	Youngest son of Germanicus, nephew of Tiberius	37	41	A. D. 12	41
Claudius	Son of Drusus, stepson of Augustus	41	54	B. C. 10	54
Nero	Adopted son of his stepfather Claudius	54	68	A. D. 37	68
Galba	Was proclaimed emperor	68	69	B. C. 5	69
Otho	Was proclaimed emperor	69	....	A. D. 32	69
Vitellius	Was proclaimed emperor	69	....	15	69
Vespasian	Was proclaimed emperor	69	79	9	79
Titus	Son of Vespasian	79	81	41	81
Domitian	Second son of Vespasian	81	96	51	96
	THE FIVE GOOD EMPERORS				
Nerva	Was proclaimed emperor	96	98	32	98
Trajan	Adopted son of Nerva	98	117	53	117
Hadrian	Nephew of Trajan	117	138	76	138
Antoninus Pius	Adopted son of Hadrian	138	161	86	161
Marcus Aurelius Antoninus	Nephew and adopted son of Antoninus Pius	161	180	121	180
	THE PERIOD OF MILITARY DESPOTISM				
Commodus	Son of Marcus Aurelius	180	192	161	192
Pertinax	Was proclaimed emperor	193	....	126	193
Didius Julianus	Was proclaimed emperor	193	....	?	193
Septimius Severus	Was proclaimed emperor	193	211	146	211
Caracalla	Son of Septimius Severus	212	217	188	217
Macrinus	Was proclaimed emperor	217	218?	164	218
Elagabalus	First cousin of Caracalla	218	222	205?	222
Alexander Severus	Cousin of Elagabalus, by whom he was adopted	222	235	205	235
Maximin	Was proclaimed emperor by his soldiers on the Rhine	235	238	?	238
Gordianus I	Was elevated by insurgents in Africa	238	....	158	238
Gordianus II	Son and associate of Gordianus I	238	....	192	238
Pupienus and Balbinus	Were appointed by the Senate	238	....	?	238
Gordianus III	Grandson of Gordianus I	238	244	224?	244
Philip	Murdered Gordianus III and usurped the throne	244	249	?	249
Decius	Was proclaimed emperor by the army	249	251	?	251
Gallus	Was elected emperor by Senate and soldiers	251	253	?	253?
Æmilianus		253	....	208?	254
Valerian		253	260	?	269
Gallienus	Son of Valerian	260	268	?	268
Claudius II		268	270	214	270
Aurelian	Was designated by Claudius	270	275	212	275
Tacitus	Was chosen by the Senate	275	276	200	276
Florian	Was proclaimed emperor	276	....	?	?
Probus	Was chosen by the army	276	282	?	282
Carus	Was elevated to throne by soldiers	282	283	222	283
Carinus and Numerian	{ Elder son of Carus { Son of Carus	283	284	? ?	285 ?
Diocletian and	Was proclaimed emperor by the army	284	305	245	313
Maximian	Was made Augustus by Diocletian	286		?	310
Constantius I	Nephew of Claudius II — Had been Cæsars under the Augusti, Diocletian and Maximian	305	306	250?	306
Galerius		305	306	?	311
Constantine the Great	Eldest son of Augustus Constantius I	306	337	274	337
Constantine II	Eldest son of Constantine the Great	337	340	312?	340
Constans	Youngest son of Constantine the Great		350	320?	350
Constantius II	Second son of Constantine the Great		361	317	361
Julian the Apostate	Cousin of Constantius II, was proclaimed emperor by his soldiers	361	363	331	363
Jovian	Was elevated to the throne by the army	363	364	332	364

ROMAN EMPERORS—Con.

Name	Lineage	Period of Rule		Birth	Death
	ROMAN EMPERORS OF THE WEST	A. D.	A. D.	A. D.	A. D.
Valentinian I	Was proclaimed emperor by the army	364	375	321	375
Gratian	Son of Valentinian I	375	383	359	383
Valentinian II	Son of Valentinian I	375	392	372	392
Theodosius the Great	Was called by Gratian to share the empire { In the East / In East and West	379 / 392	395	346	395
Honorius	Second son of Theodosius	395	423	384	423
Valentinian III	Grandnephew of Valentinian II	425	455	419?	455
Maximus	By force of arms	455	....	395?	455
Avitus	....	455	456	?	456
Majorian	Was elected by Ricimer	457	461	?	461
Severus	Was raised to imperial dignity by Ricimer	461	465	?	465
Anthemius	Was made emperor through influence of Leo I.	467	472	?	?
Olybrius	Was made emperor by Ricimer	472	473	?	?
Glycerius	Was proclaimed emperor	473	....	?	?
Nepos	Was proclaimed emperor by order of Leo I	474	475	?	480
Romulus Augustulus	Son of Orestes	475	476	?	?

Augustulus was deposed and banished by Odoacer, who thus put an end to the line of Western Roman emperors.

RUMANIA

Rumania (*rōō-mā'nĭ-ȧ*) is a kingdom of southeastern Europe, bordering on the Black Sea. In ancient times this country was peopled by the Dacians, who were conquered by Trajan about 101 A. D. Roman colonists were introduced, and Dacia was made a Roman province in 106. As an outpost of the empire, Dacia was for several centuries a battleground of invading barbarians. Toward the end of the 13th century the principality of Wallachia was founded, and about the middle of the 14th century, Moldavia. In the 16th century both of these principalities were forced to acknowledge Turkish sovereignty. In 1861 they were united under the ancient name of Rumania. Prince Alexander John Cuza was chosen as head of this union. He introduced several reforms, but his despotic methods forced his abdication in 1866. Prince Charles of Hohenzollern was then elected. The independence of Rumania was recognized by the Congress of Berlin in 1878, and in 1881 the country was made a kingdom. Rumania is an agricultural country, with rich soil and fine grazing lands. Ownership of land has been one of its political problems.

Rumania took no part in the first Balkan war in 1912-13, but she secured additional territory through the second Balkan war of Serbia, Greece, and Rumania against Bulgaria. In 1914 Ferdinand became king on the death of his uncle. Rumania was drawn into World War I on the side of the Allies, and defeated. She was compensated at the peace with territory taken from Russia and Hungary.

King Ferdinand died in 1927. His son Carol had renounced his claim to the throne, which was conferred on Carol's infant son Michael. Carol seized the throne in 1930. In 1940, Rumania was forced to cede Bessarabia and northern Bukovina to Russia, a part of Transylvania to Hungary, and southern Dobruja to Bulgaria. Carol was again deposed in 1940. Prince Michael was proclaimed king with a pro-German ministry, and Rumania joined the Axis powers, sent contingents to the German army invading Russia, and occupied Odessa. When the Russian counterattack reached Rumania, in August 1944, Rumania promptly changed sides, and a pro-Communist government took office. It was recognized by Great Britain and the United States on promises of free elections and liberty of speech and press. These promises were not kept and the protests of the two countries were disregarded. Rumania signed her peace treaty, September 15, 1948, receiving back the territory she had formerly seized from Hungary, but not that taken by Russia. King Michael abdicated, December 30, 1947, under Communist pressure, and a "People's Republic" was proclaimed. By 1948 Rumania was completely under Russian control, economically and politically. The opposition was liquidated, and an attack on the Catholic Church began. See *Rumanians*.

RUSSIA

The story of Russia begins with the coming of the Norseman, Rurik, with a body of followers, to Novgorod in 862 A. D. The Norsemen, or Varangians, set up an orderly government among the warring Slavic tribes and, moving southward to Kiev, opened the country to trade and to the influence of Mediterranean civilization. By the middle of the 10th century, the Norsemen and the Slavs had become thoroughly united. One must not, however, judge that the Norsemen were more than a very small minority. Their influence helped the formation of early Russia, and even named the country, but the native race and culture always predominated. Under Vladimir the Great, Russian authority was extended in all directions. Vladimir was converted to Greek Christianity, and in 988 he and his followers were baptized.

The Tatar Conquest. During the next two centuries, Russia was a field of conflict among petty states. The land was therefore an easy prey to the Mongols in the 13th century. Despite the heroic resistance of the Russian princes, the superior numbers and generalship of the Mongols enabled them to take complete mastery of Russia in 1238. This Tatar conquest cut Russia off from contact with the Western nations of Europe for 300 years; the Renaissance and the Reformation, which remolded the rest of Europe, she did not share in. The conquerors appear to have been content to exact tribute from Russia. They did not interfere seriously with the language or customs of the Russians, but nevertheless they introduced many Oriental elements into Russian life.

The 14th century saw the rise of the principality of Muscovy, with its capital at Moscow. This state attained a position of supremacy among the Russians in the 15th century, and the grand prince, Ivan the Great (1462–1505), united the rival principalities and threw off the Tatar yoke. Under his son, Ivan the Terrible, the boyars, or nobles, were reduced to submission, western Siberia was conquered, and trade with England was opened up. Ivan took the title of czar. After the death of his grandson, Feodor, a long period of strife resulted in the choice of Czar Michael Romanov, the first of the dynasty that ruled until 1917.

Peter the Great; Catherine II. Modern Russian history begins with the accession of Peter the Great in 1689. He was a man of restless energy, and he attempted to modernize and Westernize Russia by main force. He enlarged his territory, built a new capital, Saint Petersburg, on land taken from the Swedes, and introduced Western industry and customs. After Peter's death, his schemes fell into abeyance until the vigorous and unscrupulous Catherine II came to the throne in 1762. In her reign of more than thirty years, she improved governmental methods, encouraged modern industry, and established schools. She directed the division of Poland and secured the Crimea from Turkey.

Extension of Russian Power. Czar Alexander I (1801-25) opened his reign by freeing the serfs in the Baltic provinces, but he later receded from his liberal position. In 1807 Alexander made the famous Treaty of Tilsit with Napoleon, in consequence of which he was able to take Finland from Sweden in 1809 and to wrest much territory from Turkey. The reign of his successor, Nicholas I (1825-55), was marked by the beginnings of the liberal movement in Russia and by a succession of wars with Turkey. Russian defeat of the Turkish fleet at Navarino in 1827 aided materially the cause of Greek independence. In 1832, after crushing a revolt in Poland, Nicholas began a policy of repression in that country.

Reform; Reaction; Nihilism. The liberal reform movement in Russia received great encouragement from the early policies of Alexander II (1855-81). Serfdom was abolished in 1861. Reforms in the administration of justice were introduced. But the period of vast extension of Russian power in Asia was marked by reaction at home. The government's repressive measures provoked nihilist activity. Alexander was killed by a bomb, March 13, 1881. His son, Alexander III (1881-94), pursued a reactionary policy. Repression of liberals and persecution of the Jews in Russia accompanied imperial policies in Asia. Nicholas II (1894-1917) continued the blind policy of his father. Intervention in the Chinese-Japanese war (1894-95) gave Russia possession of Port Arthur, and absorption of Manchuria followed the Boxer troubles of 1900.

Meanwhile, the large increase of manufacturing in Russia had been adding new elements to the revolutionary forces. The workers learned from Western factory managers and superintendents the superior conditions of their class in other countries. The government had tried to meet this rising tide of revolution by various kinds of paternalistic laws and by stirring up hatred between races in the empire. The trouble reached a climax in 1904 and 1905. The crushing defeat of Russian armies and fleets by Japan had clearly revealed the corruption of the government. In the midst of a series of strikes and riots, a congress of delegates from the zemstvos, or provincial assemblies, met in Petrograd and formulated demands for political and industrial reform. Bloody repression led to an outbreak of strikes in all industrial centers.

The Duma. At length, on October 30, 1905, the czar issued a manifesto which announced the speedy establishment of a representative assembly, the Duma, and real participation of the people in the government. But this announcement was immediately followed by a reign of terror, in which the people, and especially the Jews, were made to feel the iron hand of the autocracy. The first Duma met in the Winter Palace at Saint Petersburg on May 10, 1906. But this body and its successors found the imperial government unprepared to further any genuine reform. The following years, up to 1914, formed a period of virtual deadlock between the reactionary court party and the liberals, who were, by changed electoral laws, virtually excluded from even the Duma.

Upon the outbreak of war in the summer of 1914, the Russian people rallied to the support of the government. For a time the government held out promises of progressive reform, but military successes were accompanied by reactionary programs. When, in the summer of 1915, the government stood in need of popular support, a large progressive party in the Duma demanded a ministry responsible to that body. This demand was answered by a proroguing of the Duma.

Evidence of the same government corruption and traitorous intrigue that had been so disastrous in 1904-05 now began to accumulate. At the same time, the people, providing war supplies and hospitals through their zemstvos and municipal organizations, were learning their strength. The inevitable result was revolution, which broke out in 1917. The czar abdicated, and a government by an executive committee of the Duma was attempted.

The Bolsheviki. A temporary government under Alexander Kerensky, a socialist, was wrecked by the extreme radicals, or Bolsheviki, led by Nicolai Lenin and Leon Trotzky. In November 1917, the All-Russian Congress of Workmen's and Soldiers' Delegates made Lenin the premier, and Trotzky the foreign minister, of the Soviet Republic. On March 3, 1918, Lenin's envoys signed a peace with Germany at Brest-Litovsk. The Bolshevik government was set up at Moscow, and Trotzky, with his armies, proceeded to the task of suppressing rebellion. The avowed purpose of the Bolsheviki to support propaganda for the proletariat revolution in other countries led the Entente Allies and the United States to maintain troops in Russia, to support various anti-Bolshevik movements, and to refuse to trade with the Russians. Eventually all the anti-Bolshevik enterprises collapsed.

The government of Russia was dominated by the personality of Lenin until his death in 1924. Private property and the right to trade were at first abolished by decree, enforced through terrorism by the notorious *cheka*. The peasants, however, who had recently seized the land, had no intention of relinquishing it and refused to raise surplus grain to be confiscated by government agents. Economic maladjustment and widespread famine ensued and led to the development of a so-called new economic policy. Trade was permitted to individuals, although the government remained the chief property holder and trader. A sound currency replaced the paper currency, which had become worthless.

The Third International. Russia's foreign relations were based on the theory of world revolution, the Bolshevik party regarding itself as a branch of the so-called Third International. This organization, formally founded at Moscow in 1919, aimed at fomenting movements in every country that might lead toward a dictatorship of the proletariat.

After Lenin's death, Russian opinion became more and more divided on the relative value of fomenting world revolution and entering into helpful economic relations with other countries. Trotzky, who favored more unreservedly the policy of world revolution, was gradually forced out of important offices, and, in 1927, was expelled from the executive body of the Third International.

The revolution introduced drastic social changes, notably a new marriage code based on equality of men and women.

Five-Year Plans. In 1928 began a process momentous for Russian life. Under the dominating influence of Joseph Stalin, who had become absolute, though unofficial, dictator of Russia, a five-year plan of industrialization was initiated. This embraced both agriculture and manufacturing. With a combination of effective propaganda and ruthless compulsion, individual farming was transformed into large co-operative or state enterprises, huge factories were built, sources of power were developed, and transportation facilities were constructed on a scale and with a speed unmatched in the history of the world.

The first five-year plan, having been substantially completed in a little over four years, was succeeded by a second, in which more attention was given to raising the standard of living. Illiteracy by this time had largely disappeared. The strain of the process having engendered opposition, a "purge" of industrial and military leaders was carried through in 1937–38. A new constitution, democratic in form, was proclaimed in 1936. Actually, however, control lay within the Communist party, which nominated the candidates, and the party was ruled by Stalin. See *Russia*: *Government*.

RULERS OF RUSSIA

Name	Lineage	Period of Rule		Birth	Death
	HOUSE OF RURIK	A. D.	A. D.	A. D.	A. D.
Ivan III, the Great	Grand Duke of Moscow	1462	1505	1440	1505
Vasily IV	Son of Ivan, the Great	1505	1533	?	?
Ivan IV, the Terrible	Son of Vasily IV, assumed title of czar	1533	1584	1530	1584
Feodor I	Son of Ivan, the Terrible	1584	1598	1557	1598
Boris Godounov	Brother-in-law of Feodor, was elected to the throne	1598	1604	1552	1605
Demetrius	Usurped the throne (The "Time of Troubles")	1604	1606	?	1606
Zuiski (Vasily V)		1606	1610	?	?
An Interregnum		1610	1613		
	HOUSE OF ROMANOV				
Michael Romanov	Unanimously elected czar	1613	1645	?	1645
Alexis	Grandson of Czar Michael Romanov	1645	1676	1629	1676
Feodor II	Eldest son of Alexis	1676	1682	1656	1682
Ivan V and Peter the Great	Half brothers, sons of Alexis. Sophia Alexeyevna, sister of Ivan, ruled as regent	1682	1689	1666	1696
Peter the Great	Son of Alexis	1689	1725	1672	1725
Catherine I	Was married to Peter the Great in 1711	1725	1727	?	1727
Peter II	Grandson of Peter the Great	1727	1730	1715	1730
Anna	Daughter of Ivan V	1730	1740	1693	1740
Ivan VI	Grandnephew of Anna	1740	1741	1740	1764
Elizabeth	Daughter of Peter the Great	1741	1762	1709	1762
Peter III	Grandson of Peter the Great	1762	....	1728	1762
Catherine II	Wife of Peter III	1762	1796	1729	1796
Paul I	Son of Peter III	1796	1801	1754	1801
Alexander I	Son of Paul I	1801	1825	1777	1825
Nicholas I	Third son of Paul I	1825	1855	1796	1855
Alexander II	Son of Nicholas I	1855	1881	1818	1881
Alexander III	Son of Alexander II	1881	1894	1845	1894
Nicholas II	Son of Alexander III	1894	1917	1868	1918
	FEDERAL SOVIET REPUBLIC				
Nicolai Lenin	Chosen president of Council of People's Commissars	1917	1924	1870	1924
Joseph Stalin	Chosen General Secretary of Communist Party; became also premier in 1941	1922		1879	

Meanwhile Russia had definitely given up the idea of spreading socialism to other countries in advance of exploiting her own resources. This change was signalized by the exile of Trotzky in 1929. Treaties with neighboring nations were followed by her admission to the League of Nations in 1934. Her foreign policy changed sharply in 1939. For her alliance and subsequent war with Germany, and her advances on the Baltic, see *World War II*. Her position with the western powers was improved by the dissolution of the Third International (Comintern) and the recognition of the Greek Orthodox Church.

Soon after the surrender Russia set on foot a new 5-year plan for rehabilitation and new construction, especially in the districts beyond the Urals. The government also fostered scientific research, especially in the field of nuclear science. In the United Nations she pressed proposals for peace and the reduction of armaments. On the other hand, the organization (September, 1947) of the Communist Information Bureau (Cominform), for the exchange of information among Communist countries, looked very much like a revival of the Comintern, while her obstinate dissent in the administration of Germany, her action in the Security Council, and her dealings with neighboring states caused grave concern to the western powers. See *Government*.

SAN MARINO

The little independent state of San Marino (*sän mä-rē'nō*), lying in the Apennines near the Adriatic coast in northeastern Italy, is the smallest republic in the world and claims to be the oldest independent state in Europe. The city of San Marino is said to have been founded in the 4th century. In 1631 Pope Urban VIII formally acknowledged the independence of the state, which has an area of about 38 square miles. Undisturbed by Napoleon, its sentimental interest probably saved it from union with Italy in 1860-61. The government is in the hands of a Great Council, whose sixty members are elected by popular vote. From this council two are chosen every six months to act as regents. They share executive power with an executive council of twelve, chosen annually. The population of San Marino in 1947 was 12,100. Its chief exports are wine, cattle, and stone.

SAXONY

The name of Saxony was anciently applied to the entire northwestern district of Germany, extending from the Zuider Zee to the present neighborhood of Cassel and Magdeburg. By scattering the Saxons, who resisted bitterly, and by bringing in Frankish colonists, Charlemagne finally subdued the country. In the 10th century, Duke Henry of Saxony became king of Germany, and his son, Otto the Great, was crowned Roman emperor. The territory of Saxony was frequently changed during the following centuries. In 1485 the domain was divided between Elector Ernst and Duke Albert, the latter becoming the founder of the royal house of Saxony, which ruled until 1918. Frederick Augustus III was made king by Napoleon, and Saxony became the scene of Napoleon's struggle with the allies in 1813. In the Austro-Prussian war of 1866 Saxony sided with Austria and was compelled at the close of the war to join the North German Confederation. On November 9, 1918 Saxony was proclaimed a republic. See *Germany*.

SIAM (THAI)

Siam (*sī-ăm'*) is the only independent country in southeastern Asia. Its authentic history begins with the year 1350, when the old capital, Ayuthia, was founded. After a Burmese conquest, Siamese forces were rallied by a Chinese leader, Phya Tak, on whose death in 1782 the present dynasty came to the throne.

Under King Mongkut, who came to the throne in 1851, the development of Siam as a modern state began. Between 1855 and 1865, the principal foreign powers obtained the right by treaty to trade in Siam under a 3 per cent tariff, and they established their own extraterritorial courts there. In 1920-26, these courts were abolished by agreements, and the tariff was replaced by a most favored nation clause. Siam was an absolute monarchy until 1932, when King Prajadhipok granted a constitution. Siam changed its official name to Thai in 1939. In December 1941, Siam yielded to Japan, concluded a treaty of alliance, and declared war on Great Britain and the United States. Her submission was superficial, however, and with the collapse of Japan, Siam made peace with the Allies and became a member of the United Nations.

SIBERIA

Early Russian chronicles record expeditions into Siberia before the end of the 15th century, but the conquest of this vast Asiatic territory was not begun until the last quarter of the 16th century.

In the course of the 17th century, Russian traders and explorers penetrated eastward as far as Kamchatka, and all of northern Siberia was brought under Russian authority. The Russian advance had, however, generally avoided the more thickly settled and hostile southern area. In 1689, by the Treaty of Nerchinsk with China, further Russian occupation of the Amur valley was barred. For more than a century and a half after this date, Russian interest was directed westward. In 1710, Peter the Great began the practice of exiling political offenders to Siberia, and from the first part of the 19th century the country became notorious for its prison camps of exiled Russian criminals.

About the middle of the 19th century, the eastward movement of Russian power began once more. In 1847, by treaty with China, the Amur river was made the boundary between the two countries. In 1860, Vladivostok was founded. The building of the Trans-Siberian railway, to connect Moscow with Russia's distant Pacific port, was begun in 1891. The succeeding Russian advance brought about the conflict with Japan in the first decade of the 20th century.

Under the Soviet Russian government began an intensive development of Siberia which is rapidly transforming it into one of the richest territories in the world. The name Siberia, however, which formerly embraced nearly all Asiatic Russia, has now been narrowed to an intermediate region occupying about 1,731,000 square miles stretching from the Arctic Ocean to Mongolia.

SICILY

Recorded history of the island of Sicily begins with the establishment of the Greek city of Naxos in 735 B. C. This, with other Greek colonies established in the course of the following two centuries, became the center of thriving commerce. From the year 536 B. C. until the period of the Punic wars, Greeks and Carthaginians contended for mastery in the island. In 210 B. C., however, Sicily became the first of the Roman provinces.

During the middle ages, Goths, Byzantines, and Saracens in succession held sway. At length, in the year 1090, the Normans made conquest of the land, and Roger II became king of Sicily in 1130. From the close of the 13th century until the Treaty of Utrecht in 1713, Sicily was ruled by princes of Aragon and by the Spanish crown. In 1734, under Don Carlos, the Kingdom of the Two Sicilies arose, uniting Naples and Sicily under a Bourbon dynasty. Garibaldi's bold expedition in 1860 opened the way for the union of Sicily with the kingdom of Italy in 1861.

SPAIN

The original inhabitants of the Spanish peninsula, which was known to the Greeks and Romans as Hispania or Iberia, were probably a primitive race called Iberians. Upon these a host of Celts are supposed to have descended from the Pyrenees. The two races mingled and formed the mixed nation of the Celtiberians. About the middle of the 3d century B. C. the Carthaginians, deprived by Rome of their trading posts in Sicily and Sardinia, began to develop Iberia as a source of wealth and soldiers, and an extensive tract of territory was brought under subjection to Carthage by Hamilcar Barca, who is said to have founded the city of Barcelona.

Roman, Gothic, and Moorish Rule. The Romans had driven the Carthaginians from the peninsula in 206 B. C., and the country was erected into a Roman province. From this time until the end of the 2d century A. D., the condition of Spain was eminently prosperous. Everywhere throughout the country, Roman towns sprang up, and numerous aqueducts, bridges, and amphitheaters were built. Spain was for three centuries the richest province of the Roman Empire. Its fertile grainfields fed the imperial city, and its mines yielded enormous wealth. Many of the leading men of the later empire, in politics, military life, and literature, were natives of Spain.

In 409 A. D. hordes of barbarians, Alans, Vandals, and Suevi, crossed the Pyrenees and swept over the peninsula. About 412 the Visigoths invaded the country as agents of the weakened Roman government. After the fall of the Western Empire they maintained a show of authority with a monarchy organized in imitation of the Roman system. But they fell an easy prey to the Mohammedan invasion, and in 711–714 the Moors obtained mastery of nearly the whole of Spain. Under the Ommiad dynasty Spanish civilization far surpassed that of other European states. Systems of irrigation made a garden out of desert areas. Learning and literature were highly developed in great universities.

Castile and Aragon United. In 1031, however, the realm split into several small kingdoms, and the Christian kings of Castile, Aragon, and Navarre quickly took advantage of the divisions among the Moors to break their power. Ferdinand II, the last sovereign of Aragon, married Isabella, queen of Castile, in 1469. By the conquest of Granada in 1492 and that of Navarre in 1512, they united all the states of Spain under their joint rule.

It was under the auspices of the united kingdoms of Castile and Aragon, and especially under the protection of Queen Isabella, that Columbus started on his voyages of discovery, which laid the foundation for Spain's vast empire in the three Americas.

The kingdoms of Castile and Aragon had developed in the direction of constitutional government, with much power in the hands of the estates of the realm, or the Cortes. But Ferdinand and Isabella used the Cortes and other councils for their own purposes. At the great Cortes of Toledo in 1480 far-reaching reform and organization of the government were undertaken, the Inquisition was firmly established, and oppressive measures were adopted against the Jews. The free growth of industry, religion, and national life was checked by a vast system of taxation, supervision, and espionage.

Period of the Empire. At the death of Ferdinand in 1516, all Spain came under the single rule of his daughter Juana, called "the mad. But her son, the Habsburg Charles I, who in 1519 became emperor as Charles V, seized the throne, and Spain was dragged into the great scheme for aggrandizing the house of Austria. Charles V gave little attention to Spain, except as it served to supply him with treasure out of the newly acquired American territories. He even acknowledged the claim of the Cortes to the right of granting taxes, although he got what he wanted by bribery. Under his son, Philip II, the country was the victim of the worst vices of a bigoted absolutism. Its resources were exhausted in futile wars with every power of Europe. Spanish ships and soldiers won glory at the battle of Lepanto against the Turks, but the Protestant Netherlands were lost, the *Armada* was destroyed, and oppressive taxation served only to pile up disaster.

In 1680, the royal orders and laws relative to the Spanish colonies in America were compiled in the famous *Recopilación de las leyes de Indias*, "Laws of the Indies," a system of laws admirable so far as it went, and remarkably enlightened in its day. The system fundamentally failed, however, in looking upon the American possessions as a vast estate, closed to all the world and exploited only by Spain under a régime of the narrowest overlordship and the most exclusive of monopolies.

A Period of Decline. The reigns of Philip III and Philip IV witnessed a fearful acceleration in the national decline. That of Charles II was still more unfortunate, and his death was the occasion of the War of the Spanish Succession. Philip V was the first of the Bourbon dynasty who occupied the throne of Spain. Under Charles III (1759–88), one of the "enlightened despots" of the 18th century, a great industrial revival began, and for a time trade and commerce showed signs of returning activity. But, even though "enlightened," Charles III was a despot, and no sound national growth could come from his policy.

During the inglorious reign of Charles IV (1788–1808), a war broke out with Britain, which was productive of nothing but disaster to the Spaniards; and, by the pressure of the French, another arose in 1805 and was attended with similar ill success.

Charles's eldest son ascended the throne as Ferdinand VII. Forced by Napoleon to resign all claims to the Spanish crown, Ferdinand became a prisoner of the French, and Joseph, the brother of the French emperor, was declared king of Spain and the Indies. But before this time an armed resistance had been organized throughout the whole country. The various provinces elected juntas, or councils, consisting of the most influential inhabitants of the respective neighborhoods, and it was their business to administer local rule. The Supreme Council of Seville declared war against Napoleon and France in 1808. England, on solicitation, made peace with Spain, recognized Ferdinand VII as king, and sent an army to aid the Spanish insurrection. After many bloody campaigns the French were driven from the country.

Efforts toward Liberal Reform. The Cortes in 1812, during the absence of Ferdinand, had adopted a liberal constitution, but on his return this was abolished and the old abuses restored. But the struggle against tyranny, already on the road to success in her New World colonies, had now really begun in Spain. A revolution in 1820 formulated a remarkably liberal constitution, but a French invasion suppressed the movement. The only reform which survived was the abolition of the Inquisition.

The next hundred years was a continual struggle between the advocates of a liberal, constitutional government and the adherents of the old absolutist and clerical party. Of the latter group, the extremists were the Carlists who, on the death of Ferdinand VII in 1833, supported Don Carlos in opposition to Isabella, for whom Queen Maria Christina was ruling as regent. Civil war broke out and the Carlists were defeated. The absolutists then aligned themselves with the queen regent and later with Queen Isabella, who was declared of age in 1843.

The attempt to enforce an absolutist government provoked further liberal agitation, and in 1868 Isabella was compelled to flee from the kingdom. A liberal monarchical constitution was formulated, and in 1870 Amadeus, duke of Aosta, was induced to take the crown. But the chief supporter of the new government, Prim, had been assassinated, and after a troublous reign the king abdicated in 1873. A republic was then declared and Castelar was made president. But his course displeased the radicals. After his resignation Alfonso XII, son of Isabella, was proclaimed king.

A measure of parliamentary government was attained, but its effectiveness was rendered futile by an unfortunate political compromise whereby Liberals and Conservatives were to alternate in power as a matter of form rather than in response to an active public opinion.

Coming of the Republic. The last king of Spain was Alfonso XIII, who came to the throne in 1902. Spain was neutral during the World War. A serious revolt of the Riff tribes in Spanish Morocco, however, revealed grave weaknesses in the army and the government. Misrule and industrial disturbances culminated in a bloodless military revolt, led by General Primo de Rivera. He made himself dictator, with the king's aid, and ruled without constitutional sanctions from 1923 until 1930.

General Berenguer succeeded Rivera in 1930 and arranged for general elections. In March 1931, he was forced to resign; election plans were cancelled; and, on April 13, a group headed by Niceto Zamora declared Spain a republic. King Alfonso fled from the country, and Zamora issued a call for the election of a constitutional convention. Elections were held on June 29. The republican form of government received popular ratification. A new constitution was drawn up and adopted. The church and state were separated; women were enfranchised.

The Republican régime, though victorious in the election of 1936, encountered powerful opposition from the Church, the army, and the land-owning groups. A rebellion ensued, leading to full-scale civil war. In this struggle the Republicans received aid from France and Russia and were opposed by Germany and Italy. Great Britain and the United States maintained a nonbelligerent status. In 1939 the government forces were defeated, and a corporate state headed by General Francisco Franco was established. During World War II Spain remained neutral, but favored the Axis.

SWEDEN

When Sweden first appears in history, the country is inhabited by numerous tribes, kindred in origin but politically separate. Two principal groups are recognizable, Goths in the South and Swedes in the North. Ingiald Hrada, the last ruler of the old royal family of the Ynglingar, who drew their origin from Njord, sought to establish a single government in Sweden and perished in the attempt. Erik Edmundsson acquired the sovereignty of the whole of Sweden about 829. The dawn of Swedish history now begins. Efforts to introduce Christianity were made as early as 829, but it was not until the year 1000 that Olaf Sköttkonung, the Lapp king, was baptized. Erik undertook a crusade against the pagan Finns, compelling them to submit to baptism.

Growth of Swedish Power. The murder of Erik in 1160 by the Danish prince, Magnus Henriksen, who had made an unprovoked attack upon the Swedish king, was the beginning of a long series of troubles. In 1389 the throne was offered by the Swedish nobles to Margaret, queen of Denmark and Norway, who threw an army into Sweden, defeated the Swedish king, Albert of Mecklenburg, and, by the Union of Calmar, in 1397, brought Sweden under the same scepter with Denmark and Norway. In 1523 Sweden emancipated itself from the union with Denmark, which had become hateful to the Swedes, and rewarded its deliverer, the young Gustavus Vasa, by electing him king. Gustavus Vasa, on his death in 1560, left to his successor a hereditary and well-organized kingdom, a full exchequer, a standing army, and a well-appointed navy. Sigismund, grandson of Vasa, who had been elected king of Poland through the influence of his Polish mother, was compelled in 1599 to resign the throne to his uncle Charles, who was crowned as Charles IX in 1604. He renewed the policies of his great father, Gustavus Vasa, developing the power of the burghers at the expense of the aristocracy. He encouraged commerce and reorganized the legal system of the country.

The deposition of Sigismund gave rise to the Swedo-Polish War of Succession; on the death of Charles IX in 1611, his son, the great Gustavus Adolphus, found himself involved in hostilities with Russia, Poland, and Denmark. The young king soon concluded treaties of peace with his northern neighbors and placed the internal affairs of his kingdom in order. Although he ranks as one of the greatest military commanders of his age, the extraordinary number of benefits which he conferred on the administrative system of Sweden entitles him to still greater renown as the benefactor of his native country.

After the death of Gustavus, his great minister, Oxenstierna, ably directed the government during the minority of Christina, his daughter. Sweden became the leading power of northern Europe. The reign of Christina, however, was disastrous. Charles X was occupied in wars against Poland and

Denmark. The southern Swedish provinces, Danish up to that time (1658), were acquired by him. The long rule of his son, Charles XI (1660–97), was characterized by success abroad and the augmentation of the regal power. The military genius of Charles XII brought the climax of Swedish power, but his vast schemes of conquest left the country overburdened with debt. The male line of the Vasas expired with his death in 1718. His sister and her husband, Frederick of Hesse-Cassel, were called to the throne by election. During their reign the government was really in the hands of the nobles, who were divided into rival factions,—the Hats, or French party, and the Caps, or Russian party.

Union of Sweden and Norway. The weak Adolphus Frederick of Holstein-Gottorp, who was called to the throne on the death of Frederick in 1751, did little to retrieve the evil fortunes of the state; but his son, Gustavus III (1771–92), skillfully recovered the lost power of the crown. Gustavus IV was forcibly deposed in 1809 and obliged to renounce the crown in favor of his uncle, Charles XIII. The dominant party in Sweden, in order to win the favor of Napoleon, elected General Bernadotte to the rank of crown prince. Sweden's steady support of the allies against the French emperor, secured to her the promise of Norway, which, however, resulted in a purely personal union of the two kingdoms. Under the administration of Bernadotte, who in 1818 succeeded to the throne as Charles XIV John, the united kingdoms of Sweden and Norway made great advances in material prosperity and in political and intellectual development. Although the nation at large entertained very little personal regard for their alien sovereign, his son and successor, Oscar (1844–59), and his grandsons, Charles XV and Oscar II, the latter of whom came to the throne in 1872, so identified themselves with their subjects that the Bernadotte dynasty secured the loyal affections of the Swedish people.

Sweden, a Separate Kingdom. In the latter part of the 19th century serious difficulty arose between Norway and Sweden, owing to the desire of the former for a consular service of her own. In 1905 the two nations separated, and Oscar II continued monarch of Sweden until his death, December 8, 1907, when he was succeeded by his oldest son, Gustavus V. In 1909 manhood suffrage was introduced for elections to the lower house of the Parliament. Now there is in Sweden, as in Denmark and in Norway, universal and equal suffrage. During the World wars, Sweden maintained a neutral position.

SWITZERLAND

When the Romans began their conquest of Gaul (about 58 B. C.), they found in the Alpine territory two peoples, the Helvetians and the Rhætians. The country was conquered and connected with Italy by roads, and it became the center of a flourishing trade. About 400 A. D. the barbarian invasions brought the Burgundians and Alemanni into the country. They in turn were subdued by the Franks. The Burgundians accepted Christianity about the end of the 5th century, but the Alemanni retained their paganism until a group of Irish missionaries succeeded in converting them in the 7th century.

After the downfall of the kingdom of Burgundy, the entire country fell to the control of Germany and so became a part of the Holy Roman Empire. Switzerland remained a stronghold of feudalism for several centuries. Under the rule of the dukes of Zähringen in the 12th century, the Swiss towns grew very prosperous, and in the 13th century, when the Habsburgs were the most powerful among the princes of the country, many of the towns and some of the cantons obtained imperial charters of liberties. The three forest cantons, Uri, Schwyz, and Unterwalden, formed a league in 1291 to resist the tyranny of the Habsburgs. Allied with Zurich, the confederation fought and won the battle of Morgarten in 1315, thus securing their independence from Austria. The cantons of Glarus and Zug joined the confederation, which, with this added strength, defeated the Austrians at Sempach in 1386 and at Näfels in 1388. Early in the 15th century the cantons took the offensive, and a series of conflicts with Austria and Burgundy enlarged their territory and won them recognition from the states of Europe. Swiss independence was formally confirmed by the Peace of Westphalia in 1648.

Swiss mercenaries had long been famous in the armies of Europe, and in the 16th and the 17th century they played a large part in the European wars, especially in Italy and France. In 1516 an alliance was concluded with France, which lasted until the French Revolution. During these two centuries Switzerland was rent by civil and religious dissension.

The 18th century was a period of remarkable advance in Swiss agriculture and industry. Swiss scientists and scholars became famous. But the old struggle between the privileged aristocracy and the growing democratic element of the population continued. In 1798, under French direction, the Helvetic Republic was organized. This was changed to a confederation of cantons by Napoleon in 1803. A period of quiet and prosperity followed, and the Congress of Vienna in 1814-15 recognized the independence of the Swiss and guaranteed the perpetual neutrality of their state.

The 19th century was a period of steady advance in Swiss economic and political life. The confederacy and the cantons in 1848 finally became purely republican. Later revisions of the constitution have enlarged the powers of the central government, improved the educational system, and strengthened the machinery of the democracy. The Swiss use of the initiative and referendum in politics and Swiss army organization are notable.

The World wars placed Switzerland in a trying position. She maintained her neutrality, kept her army on a war footing, and served as a refuge for wounded prisoners and exiles.

TRANS-JORDAN

This Arab state (area, 34,750 square miles; population, 340,000) lies east of the Jordan, between Syria, Iraq, and Saudi Arabia. It was included in the British mandate of Palestine, but was given a separate administration under the Emir Abdullah in 1923. In 1946 the British recognized its independence, and the emir became King Abdullah-ibn-Hussein of the "Hashimite Kingdom of Trans-Jordan." As a member of the Arab League, it was concerned in the disputes over Palestine.

TURKEY

The name commonly applied to the Ottoman empire and the republic which succeeded it. In the Turkish language, *Turk* means "a rustic or clown" and is applied to the Turkomans of central Asia. The ruling people of the Ottoman empire called themselves Osmanli, from a chieftain, Osman or Othman, who established himself in western Asia Minor at the beginning of the 14th century. This Osman and his followers were the decendants of emigrants from central Asia, who, nearly a hundred years earlier, had sought safety among the Seljuk Turks from the advance of the Mongol conqueror, Genghis Khan. The Seljuks granted the newcomers land in Phrygia and converted them to the faith of Islam. But the Seljuk power declined, and the new Ottoman state rose in its place.

Ottoman Conquests. The first expansion of the Ottomans was westward. They mastered all the northwest coast of Asia Minor and crossed into Europe, where they seized Gallipoli and Adrianople. They closed steadily in on the Roman Empire of the East, until it had shrunk, in 1400, to the city of Constantinople and the small neighboring district of Thrace, Macedonia, and part of Greece. In 1389 the Turks had broken the Serbian power at the battle of Kossovo and had then made conquest of Bulgaria. They were now the first military power in Europe; their disciplined Janizaries, inspired by fanatic zeal, were irresistible. Macedonia, Hungary, and Greece were rapidly conquered, and in 1453 the city of Constantinople, deserted and weakened through the commercial jealousy of Western Christians, fell before the Mohammedan onslaught. The Turks moved their capital from Adrianople to Constantinople and proceeded to consolidate their European dominion. The Tatar khan of the Crimea became a vassal of the sultan. Albania, which had long held out, was at last subdued, and before the close of the 15th century the conquest of Otranto gave the Ottomans a foothold in Italy. Only Montenegro remained unconquered.

Selim I (1512–20) led the Ottoman arms in triumph through Syria to Persia, into Egypt, and down the western border of Arabia, where he assumed the power of the caliphs at Mecca. Under his successor, Soliman the Magnificent (1520–66), the height of the Ottoman power was reached. In his reign Belgrade was taken (1521), the island of Rhodes was captured (1522), the Hungarian power was broken at the battle of Mohács (1526), and in 1529 Vienna was besieged, a large part of Hungary being made a Turkish province. Algeria had already become tributary to the sultan, and Tripoli was taken in 1561. The Turks ruled the Mediterranean.

Decline of Turkish Power. But Western Christendom was now thoroughly alarmed. The pope, Venice, and Spain formed a Holy League, and, although Cyprus had fallen into the hands of the Turks, their sea power was broken by the defeat of Lepanto, off the coast of Greece. The decline of the Ottoman empire dates from this, the greatest naval battle the world had witnessed since the time of the Romans and Carthaginians. The rise of the Persian power checked the Ottoman advance in the East. The Polish monarch, John Sobieski, in 1683 turned back the Moslem force from Vienna, and in 1695 Peter the Great took up the Russian contest with Turkey, which was to last, with varying fortune, until the World War. In 1774 Russia secured the Crimea and other Tatar lands on the Black Sea; she was granted free navigation of Turkish waters and also a protectorate over Moldavia and Wallachia. The 19th century was a period of steady loss of territory. In 1854 only the intervention of England and France, who feared Russia, saved the Turks from being driven out of Europe. They were again saved from Russian destruction by the Congress of Berlin in 1878.

The Treaty of Paris in 1856, by which the Western Powers guaranteed the integrity of Turkey, was followed by the sultan's proclamation of civil rights to all races and creeds in the empire, and in 1876 a parliamentary constitution was proclaimed. But the real Turkish policy of persecution and massacre of non-Moslem peoples was carried out. The slaughter of Christians in Lebanon in 1860 and the Armenian atrocities in 1895-96 aroused angry but empty protests, significantly barren in results.

The Young Turks. At the opening of the 20th century, Turkey was rent by disorders and revolts in Europe and Arabia. In 1908 the Young Turk party, headed by men who had studied in Western universities, proclaimed the restoration of the constitution of 1876. In 1909 Sultan Abdul Hamid was deposed and Mohammed V was enthroned. But this widely-heralded "reform" movement proved to be only a transfer of tyranny from one group to another. The extermination of all peoples other than Ottomans within the empire soon appeared as the real policy of the Young Turks. Armenian atrocities before and during the World War appear as the characteristic conduct of the Turkish government toward non-Moslems. The Balkan wars of 1912-13 materially cut down Turkish territory in Europe. Italy in 1912 seized Tripoli, in Africa.

The World War. The World War revealed Turkey as the tool of Germany. Turkish troops successfully repelled Allied attacks on the Dardanelles, but the army, despite German leadership, was disastrously beaten in Palestine and Mesopotamia.

The Treaty of Sèvres between the Entente Allies and Turkey was signed by the Turkish representatives on August 10, 1920. The terms of this treaty left to the Turks in Europe only Constantinople and a small neighboring territory. Smyrna was placed under Greek control; Konia, given to Italy; and Cilicia, assigned to France. Armenia and Kurdistan were declared independent.

The Republic. This treaty was never ratified by Turkey. A strong nationalist movement began, led by Mustapha Kemal Pasha. A government was set up at Ankara (Angora), which demanded modification of the treaty. When Constantine was recalled to the Greek throne in December 1920 the Allies were displeased and agreed to a settlement more favorable to Turkey. Greece dissented but, in August 1922, suffered a disastrous defeat at the hands of the Turks. Kemel demanded the restoration of Smyrna, Istanbul, and the territory of Thrace east of the Maritza river, which he obtained by the treaty of Mudania, October 11, 1922.

With their prestige enhanced by victory, the Nationalist leaders abolished the office of sultan. A new constitution was adopted. Turkey became a republic with Mustapha Kemal Pasha as the first president clothed with wide powers. Ankara was made the capital, and the name of Constantinople was changed to Istanbul.

Kemal proceeded to modernize Turkey. Polygamy was forbidden. The law of the Koran was replaced by a civil code. The wearing of the fez, with its religious associations, was prohibited. Education was secularized. Arabic letters were replaced by the Latin alphabet. Railroad building and irrigation projects were undertaken with vigor, and state-sponsored industries were initiated. Kemal died in 1938, and was succeeded by Ismet Inönü, who persued a policy of neutrality until 1945 and then declared war on the Axis.

UKRAINE

The soviet republic of Ukraine (*ū'krān*) includes a large territory which, before the World War, was divided between Russia and Austria. The history of this area as a distinct and, at times independent, state dates back to the 9th century, when the city of Kiev was made the center of a government. After the Tatar invasions of the 13th century, the country was for 200 years a part of the Lithuanian state. In the 16th century it was incorporated with Poland, but in the middle of the 17th century the Ukrainians revolted from the Polish power, and, by the Treaty of Pereyaslavl, the greater part of Ukraine was joined to the territory of the Muscovite czars. The western portion of Ukraine passed later to Austria. After the close of the World War, both Russian and Austrian Ukraine declared their independence. A union of the two was effected in 1919, and in 1920 a soviet government was established. It joined the Russian Soviet Union in 1923. In 1945 the union of the Ukraine was completed by the Czechoslovak cession of Carpatho-Ruthenia to Russia.

VATICAN CITY

This papal territory of about 109 acres within the city of Rome was created in 1929 by an agreement between Pope Pius XI and Mussolini, dictator of Italy. When Italy took over the Papal States in 1871, the pope, by the so-called Law of Guarantees, was voted an annuity of $622,425. This was never accepted. As a further mark of protest against the arrangement, the pope never left the Vatican during the life of this law. The arrangement of 1929 involved a payment to the pope of about $90,000,000. Canon law in regard to marriage was recognized in Italy, and the teaching of the Catholic religion was made compulsory in Italian schools.

YUGOSLAVIA

The southern European state of Yugoslavia (*yōō′gō-släv′ĭ-ȧ*) was constituted in December 1918 by the union of Serbia with certain Croatian, Slovenian, and other Slav provinces of the former Austro-Hungarian empire. In March 1921, Montenegro joined the new state. A constitution, which provided for a limited monarchy, was put into effect on June 28, 1921. It was suspended in 1929 by King Alexander, who made himself dictator. In 1931, he promulgated a new constitution, but it left him still with supreme power in matters of state. In 1924 the disputed city of Fiume was assigned to Italy. King Alexander was murdered at Marseilles in 1934; his minor son, Peter, became king. In World War II Yugoslavia wished to remain neutral, but was invaded and overrun by Germany and Italy in April 1941. Yugoslavia was dismembered, but its people resisted vigorously. In 1945 a republic, headed by Marshal Tito, was established.

Serbia (*sẽr′bĭ-ȧ*). From the 7th to the 11th century the Serbs enjoyed virtual self-government in the Roman province of Mœsia in the northwestern part of the Balkan peninsula. When the Byzantine government attempted to place some restrictions on them, they revolted under their grand shupon, or patriarch, Michael, who took the title of king and made a successful fight for independence. By the middle of the 14th century the Serbian empire included Bosnia, Albania, Macedonia, Thessaly, and part of Bulgaria, and reached to Attica and the Peloponnesus. But the Serbian power fell before the Turks, who completed their conquest in 1459. In 1804 a revolt broke out, led by Kara George. The uprising was crushed, but during the 19th century the Serbians gradually won a measure of self-government under constitutional forms. The independence of Serbia was recognized by the Congress of Berlin (1878), and in 1882 it became a kingdom.

In 1893 Alexander I came to the throne. He began at once to assume the rôle of autocrat. In April 1903 he abrogated the constitution and made changes of law and ministry. This policy exasperated the liberal party. On June 11 the king, the queen, and about fifty others were assassinated. Peter, a grandson of Kara George, was made king.

Serbian national ambitions now brought the country into frequently strained relations with Austria and Turkey. Through the Balkan wars (1912-13) Serbia doubled her territory. But Serbian hatred of Austria was increased by the refusal of the latter to allow Serbia a port on the Adriatic. On June 28, 1914, Archduke Ferdinand, heir to the Austrian throne, was assassinated in Bosnia by Serb nationalist conspirators. Austrian demands on Serbia for reparation clearly involved violation of the country's sovereignty, and her refusal of abject surrender was made by Germany and Austria the occasion for war. In 1915, Austrian and Bulgarian troops drove the Serbian army from the country. In November 1918, however, the Serbs again occupied their capital, Belgrade.

Montenegro (*mŏn′tē-nē′grō*). Formerly a principality on the eastern shore of the Adriatic Sea, and united to the Serbian kingdom from 1159 to 1356. After the defeat of the Serbs by the Turks at Kossovo in 1389, the Montenegrins, in their mountain fastnesses, began in turn their long struggle with the same enemies. In 1484 Ivan the Black withdrew with his people to the mountain village of Cetinje, founded a monastery, and created a bishopric. In 1696 the offices of prince and bishop, or *vladika*, were combined under the title of vladika. The last and greatest ruler to hold this title was Peter II (1830–51). Danilo I took the title of prince. In 1878 the independence of Montenegro was recognized by the Treaty of Berlin. On Nov. 29, 1918 the National Skupshtina deposed King Nicholas, who had reigned since Aug. 28, 1860, and a decision was made to unite Montenegro with Serbia.

ANCIENT CITIES

In the course of the centuries, the various races and tribes of the world's population have shifted from region to region, and, as a result, many cities, once busy and prosperous, have become as so many desert places of the earth.

Most of the cities described below are today no longer existent. In the case of others, their sites are occupied by villages or small towns of little importance.

Antioch (*ăn′tĭ-ŏk*). This ancient capital of the Greek kings of Syria, on the Orontes, 21 miles from the sea, was built by Seleucus Nicator about 300 B. C. and named for his father. As a point of trade exchange between the caravans from the East and the Mediterranean shipping from the West, it became wealthy, and both Greeks and Romans so adorned it with public buildings that it was called the "Queen of the East." Here the disciples of Jesus were first called Christians. The modern Antioch, or Antakieh, is a small city with but little manufacturing and trade.

Baalbec (*bäl′bĕk*), "City of Baal," the sun god, called Heliopolis by the Greeks. A ruined city on the slope of the Antilibanus mountains, about forty miles northwest of Damascus. It was a very ancient center of sun worship, and in Greek and Roman times it became the most splendid of Syrian cities. Massive blocks of limestone and fragments of richly ornamented columns now mark the site of a great temple of the sun, built by Romans about 150 A. D. Pillaged by Arabs, Tatars, and Turks, and ruined by earthquakes, the city survives merely as a small village.

Babylon (*băb′ĭ-lŏn*). The ancient capital of Babylonia. The name probably means "gate of the gods." Already in existence in the time of Sargon, about 2800 B. C., the city grew in importance until Hammurabi made it his capital, about 2100 B. C. It was several times destroyed and rebuilt. Nebuchadnezzar enlarged it and brought it to its greatest splendor. Excavations in several mounds and villages, mostly on the east bank of the Euphrates, have recently revealed this city of Nebuchadnezzar (605–562), as well as scanty remains of earlier periods.

Carthage (*kär′thȧj*). An ancient Phœnician city in northern Africa, near the site of the modern Tunis. Probably it was originally founded in the 9th century B. C. as a trading post for Tyre and Utica. It grew in commercial power, extending its authority westward to the Atlantic and establishing trade in Sardinia, Gaul, Spain, and Britain. Conflict with Rome arose in the 3d century B. C. and, after the three Punic wars, it was utterly destroyed in 146 B. C. Carthage left no records of its own history. It was rebuilt by Augustus, and was for several centuries a great Roman city. In Christian times it was the seat of a bishop. Only a few ruins and small villages now mark its site. Recent excavations by French archeologists have revealed important remains dating from the earliest period of the city, which throw much light upon its culture.

Corinth. An ancient city of Greece, situated between the gulfs of Corinth and Ægina. It became proverbial for its luxuries and pleasures. Its fountains, statues, theaters, and other buildings were of a design which created the order of architecture known by its name. The Romans destroyed the city in 146 B. C., but Julius Cæsar rebuilt it in 46 B. C. St. Paul addressed his *Epistles to the Corinthians* to a Christian community which formed in Corinth under his ministrations. New Corinth was built on a site three miles distant, after an earthquake had destroyed the old city in 1858.

Ephesus (*ĕf′ē-sŭs*). The origin of this Ionic city of Asia Minor is lost in mythology. It was situated in Lydia, near the mouth of the river Cayster, at the western end of a great Asiatic trade route. Under the Romans, it was the capital of the Province of Asia and a prosperous trade center. Its greatest fame arose from its temple of Diana. St. Paul spent three years in the city, and the church of Ephesus was important in early Christian history. Several times destroyed and rebuilt, it sank to small importance in the middle ages. Recent excavations have uncovered the Roman city.

Gaza (*gä′zȧ*). An ancient Syrian town, situated near the seacoast, about fifty miles southwest of Jerusalem. The ancient city, which Herodotus regarded as equal in importance to Sardis, was a border fortress and a commercial center because of its position at the junction of trade routes between Egypt, Arabia, and Syria. The earliest notice of the place is in the Tel-el-Amarna letters, one of which was written by the local governor to his superiors in Egypt. The Israelite king, Hezekiah, held Gaza for a short time, but surrendered it to Assyria. It withstood a siege of five months by Alexander the Great. In 96 B. C. it was totally destroyed by Alexander Jannæus. Aulus Gabinius rebuilt the city on a new site in 57 B. C., the old location being spoken of as Desert Gaza. Gaza was famous for the long and bitter struggle to substitute Christianity for the local worship of *Marna*, "Lord." In 402, the new faith triumphed. The modern town is called Ghuzzeh.

Herculaneum (*hĕr'kû-lā'nē-ŭm*). A Roman city, situated about five miles southeast of Naples. In the eruption of Vesuvius, 79 A. D., it was buried under volcanic mud and lava. The site was forgotten, until in 1738 the digging of a well in the village of Portici uncovered its ancient theater. Later excavations have brought to light many relics of the city's life.

Memphis (*mĕm'fĭs*). A city of ancient Egypt, said to have been built by Menes, first king of Egypt. It was for a time the capital of Egypt, and, in the 6th century B. C., the chief commercial city. In the 7th century A. D., it was destroyed by the Arabs. The site of its ruins is the village of Metrahineh, twelve miles south of Cairo.

Mycenæ (*mī-sē'nē*). An ancient Greek city, on a steep hill six miles northeast of Argos. It was the home of Agamemnon before the Trojan war. Excavations begun by Schliemann in 1876 have revealed, through the relics recovered in this city, the life of the period of Greek civilization called, after the city, Mycenean.

Nineveh (*nĭn'ĕ-vĕ*). One of the ancient capitals of Assyria, first made important by Sennacherib, 705–681 B. C. It was destroyed about 606 B. C. by Babylonians and Medes. The site of the city is the present village of Kuoyinjik, opposite Mosul. Excavations by Layard and later explorers have uncovered splendid palaces, temples, and libraries in the mounds of this district. The name Nineveh may have been applied to a group of cities, which would account for the great size attributed to Nineveh by ancient writers.

Palmyra (*păl-mī'rȧ*), "City of Palms." A ruined city situated in an oasis of the Syrian desert, about 140 miles northeast of Damascus. It was enlarged by Solomon in the 10th century B. C. as an outpost of the kingdom of Israel. It is most famous as the residence of Zenobia, "Queen of the East," in whose reign the city was besieged and destroyed by Aurelian, 273 A. D.

Pergamum (*pĕr'gȧ-mŭm*). A city of Asia Minor, on the north bank of the Caicus, fifteen miles from the sea, the site of the modern Bergama. From the beginning of the 3d century B. C., it was famous for its library, second only to that of Alexandria, for its architecture, and for its manufacture of tapestries and pottery. Parchment (*Pergamenta Charta*) derives its name from the city. The church at Pergamum was one of the seven addressed in the Book of Revelation.

Persepolis (*pĕr-sĕp'ô-lĭs*), "City of the Persians." The capital of ancient Persia, most famous under Darius and Xerxes. The citadel was destroyed by Alexander about 330 B. C., but the rest of the city was important for two centuries more. The ruins of Persepolis, in the mountain-rimmed plain near the junction of the Kur and Polvar rivers, are among the most extensive and important remains of the ancient world.

Pompeii (*pŏm-pā'yē*). The ancient city, about twelve miles southeast of Naples, destroyed in the eruption of Vesuvius, 79 A. D. At this time it was covered by ashes and pumice in such a way that the entire city was preserved almost intact. For two centuries it had been a favorite seacoast resort for the Romans.

Sardis (*sär'dĭs*). The ancient capital of Lydia, in Asia Minor. Through its market place flowed the river Pactolus. Once the center of a rich trade, and the residence of Crœsus, nothing remains on its site today but a village and some mounds. Recent excavations conducted by Americans have uncovered a great temple of Artemis, of the 4th century A. D., and many inscriptions in the Lydian language.

Sidon (*sī'dŏn*). "Fishingtown." One of the chief commercial cities of ancient Phœnicia, situated on the coast midway between Tyre and Beirut. It is now called Saida. Many allusions to the city are found in Homer and in the Old Testament. It was famous for its manufacture of glass, linen, and purple dye. Many notable remains of the city's splendor have been found, among them a collection of sarcophagi from the best period of Greek art.

Susa (*sōō'sȧ*). A city, originally under Babylonian rule, which came under Persian authority in the time of Cyrus and was made a splendid capital. From Susa to Sardis, in Asia Minor, ran a royal road, 1500 miles in length. In the middle ages the city was still noted for its manufacture of sugar. It is mentioned in the Old Testament as Susa or Shushan, in connection with Esther and Daniel. From the ruins of the place, which lie in southern Iran about fifty miles west of Shuster, many inscriptions and remains of ancient art and building have been recovered.

Tarsus (*tär'sŭs*). An ancient city of Asia Minor, in Roman times the capital of the province of Cilicia. Some traditions ascribed its foundation to the Assyrian king, Sardanapalus. It was, however, very early colonized by Greeks, and Greek writers speak of it as an important and wealthy city. The situation of Tarsus, on the river Cydnus, placed it in the path of armies of conquest from the time of Cyrus to the ages of Alexander and the Cæsars. Under the Romans, the inhabitants of Tarsus enjoyed Roman citizenship and the city rivaled Alexandria as a center of culture. St. Paul proudly claimed it as his native city. After its capture by the Saracens in 640 A. D., it lost its former importance. Modern Tarsus is but a small town in the Turkish province of Adana.

Thebes (*thēbz*). Egypt. A city, about 350 miles southeast of the modern city of Cairo, which was the capital of ancient Egypt between the 16th and 12th and, again, in the 7th century B. C. It fell into insignificance later, and an earthquake, in 27 B. C., completed its ruin. Its remains, recently discovered near the villages of Karnak and Luxor, bear witness to its former magnificence and splendor, and include colossal statues, palaces and tombs of kings, and temples sacred to Ammon and to other gods. The most notable recent discovery near Thebes was the uncovering of the tomb of Tutankhamen, in the valley of the Tombs of the Kings. See *Egypt*.

Thebes. Greece. A city of Bœotia, probably one of the earliest centers of population in Greece. It owed its chief importance throughout its history to its strength as a fortress. Tradition ascribed the building of the first citadel, the Cadmeia, to Cadmus. In the 6th century B. C. the Thebans adopted a hostile attitude toward the Athenians. The outbreak of the Persian wars found them on the side of Sparta, but their ruling aristocracy soon went over to the Persians. In the Peloponnesian war Thebes fought on the side of Sparta, but in the early part of the 4th century B. C. the two cities were almost continuously at war with each other. At length, under the leadership of Epaminondas and Pelopidas, Thebes attained for a short period (371–362) to the position of the chief power in Greece, but speedily lost it after the death of Epaminondas. The resistance of the Thebans to the Macedonian and the Roman power brought severe reprisals upon the city. It sank into an insignificance relieved only by a transitory prosperity in the 11th and 12th centuries A. D., and was finally destroyed by the Catalans in 1311.

Troy. A city on the coast of Asia Minor, about three and a half miles from the Dardanelles. Troy was the most famous city of Greek legend, having been celebrated in the first instance by Homer in the *Iliad* as the prize of the Trojan war. The site is now known as Hissarlik. In 1870, Schliemann began a series of excavations there, which have revealed the remains of nine successive settlements made upon the spot. The sixth one is believed to be the city described by Homer, on account of the similarity of its remains to those found at Mycenæ. The other settlements range from a village of the Stone age to a Greco-Roman town which rose into prominence after 334 B. C. This last town passed under Roman protection in 189 B. C. and was honored as the city from which came Æneas, a reputed ancestor of the Romans. In 1306, the Turks plundered the city, which, since that time, has lain in ruins.

Tyre. The famous city of ancient Phœnicia. It attained its greatest glory under Hiram, in the 10th century B. C. It was celebrated by ancient poets for the beauty of its scenery, and its harbors were among the wonders of the world. The basis of its commerce, which reached all countries, was its dyed woolens. This trade it continued, though in diminished volume, until the 16th century A. D., when the discovery of the sea route to the East diverted trade from its old courses. A small town, called Sûr, now occupies the ruins of the ancient city.

Ur (*ûr*). The Bible story of Abraham mentions Ur of the Chaldees as the Mesopotamian home of the patriarch. The site of this ancient city bears the modern name of Mughair, meaning pitch-built and given in allusion to the large quantities of pitch which were used in the construction of its earliest buildings. The city, which stood about 140 miles southeast of Babylon, was the chief center of the worship of the moon god Sin. The ruins of the famous zikkurat, or stage tower, still rise impressively above the surrounding plain.

Recent excavations have revealed successive reconstructions of walls and temples, made in various periods from the 30th to the 4th century B. C. The earliest remains, however, which are of unbaked clay bricks, indicate Sumerian construction antedating by many centuries the year 3000 B. C. Conspicuous among the reconstructions is that carried out by Nebuchadnezzar, in which the early form of the temple of Sin was, for the first time, radically altered. The historical record of the city is now complete from about 2300 B. C. to about 400 B. C., when, under Persian rule, Zoroastrianism displaced the city's ancient religious cult and effected the destruction of its temples.

Photos from Publishers' Photo Service

AMERICAN INDIANS. I

1 Navajo Family and Dwelling (Hogan), Arizona. 2 Zuñi Village, New Mexico. 3 Hopi Basket Weavers, Arizona. 4 Navajo Girl Weaving Rugs. 5 Pueblo Indians Making Pottery, New Mexico. 6 Zuñi Jewel-maker Grinding Turquoise. 7 The Pueblo of Taos, New Mexico. 8 Children of Taos.

Photos for 1, 3, 4, and 5 from Publishers' Photo Service; 2 copyright by Underwood & Underwood; 6 copyright by E. M. Newman; 7 from Underwood & Underwood; 8 from Brown Bros.

AMERICAN INDIANS, II

1 Hopi Dwellings, Walpi, Ariz. 2 Hopi Indians. 3 Hopi Dancer. 4 Blackfeet Indians, Mont. 5 Navajo Indians, Ariz. 6 Typical Pueblo Indians, New Mex. 7 Relics of the Cliff Dwellers. 8 Sun Temple, Mesa Verde, Colo.

RACES AND PEOPLES

Men that have lived, or are living, on the earth may be readily divided, on the basis of striking physical characteristics, into large groups, called races. Skeletons, or parts of skeletons, dating from prehistoric times, have been found, which, in the skillful hands of scientists, have established the existence of such races. In some cases, indeed, we have only a part of one skeleton upon which to base our knowledge of a distinctive group. In historic times, however, we may distinguish not only races, characterized by physical differences, but peoples,—groups which are marked off from each other to some degree by less obvious variations of physical characteristics but mainly by cultural differences, that is, by divergences of language, customs, and institutions.

PREHISTORIC RACES

The most striking archeological discoveries of the 19th century were due to the unearthing of the remains of men who lived in the very remote past. Mounds of shells, bones, and other *dêbris*, called in Europe *kitchen middens* and, in America, *shell heaps*, have yielded evidence of the existence of very early tribes; but, besides these, skeletons have been found which appear to belong to manlike creatures of a different and more primitive build.

The succeeding articles indicate the most famous types discovered, together with certain of their characteristics and an estimate of the period when they lived. Their age is still open to controversy.

Cave Men, or **Cave Dwellers.** A name sometimes applied to Cro-Magnon men, described below. The period in which they lived is often called Mousterian from a cave in southern France, Le Moustier, where important remains of their race were found.

Cro-Magnon (*krō' mä' nyôN'*) **Man.** The prehistoric race which, in Europe and northern Africa, immediately preceded the present racial inhabitants. Their existence is believed to have spanned the last glacial age and extended into the post-glacial age, possibly from 25,000 to 10,000 B. C. This race has been called Cro-Magnard, because in the cave of Cro-Magnon, France, were discovered in 1858 the first remains of the race—the skeletons of a woman, a child, and three men. They indicate a tall people with broad faces, prominent noses, and very large brains. In fact, the brain capacity of the woman found is greater than that of the average man living today.

The Cro-Magnards, like the Neanderthal men, used stone for making implements, but, besides this, they employed horn and bone for making fishhooks and as material upon which designs were drawn. Caves, in which these men frequently lived, contain many other marks of artistic activity, such as drawings and paintings of animals and little images fashioned out of ivory or sometimes out of soapstone. The people of this race sometimes built timber houses roofed with hides which they obtained by hunting.

Heidelberg (*hī'dĕl-bûrg'*) **Man.** The man, or manlike creature, whose jawbone was found in 1907 about 80 feet below the surface of a sand pit near Heidelberg, Germany. Much more extensive remains were found at Mauer, Germany, in 1927. Anthropologists place the time of this creature's life at the second interglacial period, possibly 250,000 years ago. The jawbone is manlike, although it bears no trace of a chin. The teeth, which are remarkably well preserved, are unmistakably of human type.

Java Man. This is generally believed to be the earliest manlike animal. Its scientific name, Pithecanthropus erectus, means erect ape-man. Remains of the Java man were found first at Trinil, Java, in 1892 and consisted of the top of a skull, some teeth, and a thigh bone. A complete skull was discovered at the same place in 1926. This creature is believed to have lived before the first Ice Age, several hundred thousand years ago.

Lake Dwellers. Men of prehistoric, and also of historic, times, who built their huts on piles driven into the beds of lakes. Probably the chief motive of the builders was to secure an easily defensible situation. The most noted remains of such communities are those discovered in Switzerland in 1854. In that year, and again in 1921, very low water levels permitted the examination of the ancient village foundations. There, as well as in similar lake villages in Scotland and Ireland, many utensils of wood, of bone, and of earthenware have been recovered.

Mechta Race. This name is applied to a type of man whose remains were first discovered in the cave of Mechta el-Arbi, near Constantine, Algeria. The most important discovery of these remains, however, was made in 1928-29 in the commune of Oued Marsa, Algeria, where bones of over 50 individuals were unearthed, including 9 complete skeletons.

The skulls present a brutal appearance, having prominent ridges above the eyes uniting over the nose. The limbs are very stout with indications of large, powerful muscles. The upper front teeth were knocked out early in life, probably in a tribal rite. In stature, these people were below the average of modern man. It is estimated that they lived at least 25,000 years ago.

Mound Builders. The Stone Age people who built the extensive earthworks found in the Mississippi valley of North America and southward as far as Peru. The purpose of these mounds is still a matter of dispute. Many small conical mounds are supposed to have been used as altars. Mounds which were used as burial places are numerous; in some cases they contain single graves; in others the mound holds several separate tombs; while in still others large collections of bones are found.

Because of their location and form, several extensive mound structures may be looked upon as defensive works. Among these, the most famous is the Great Serpent mound in Adams county, Ohio. Here what have been walls extend in the form of a partially coiled serpent for a length of 1350 feet. On the banks of the Miami river in Warren county, Ohio, is a structure of earthen walls enclosing an area of about 100 acres, to which the name Fort Ancient has been given.

The great Cahokia mound, in Madison county, Illinois, 17 acres in extent at its base and having an extreme height of 100 feet, was apparently at the center of extensive groups of smaller mounds. The Etowah mound in Bartow county, Georgia, is similarly situated.

In the state of Wisconsin are found the most extensive remains of mounds. These are constructed in the forms of eagles, bears, serpents, and other animals, which probably represent various tribal totems, and were connected with the religious beliefs and ceremonies of the builders.

It used to be thought that the Mound Builders were an earlier agricultural and highly civilized race which the nomadic Indians exterminated. But it is generally held now that they were not conquered by, but were the ancestors of, the historic Indian tribes.

Neanderthal (*nä-än'dĕr-täl'*) **Man.** The name given to the race that inhabited Europe in the warm period between the third and fourth Ice Ages, probably from 20,000 to 40,000 years ago. Human remains of this period were first discovered in 1857, near Düsseldorf, Germany, in Neanderthal, after which this type of human being has been named. The bony structure as preserved indicates that this creature could not hold his head erect, and that his thumb was not as flexible as the true human thumb. The formation of his head and jaws makes it appear unlikely that he had a language. However, he used fire, and, as he made rough stone implements, he may be regarded as the earliest representative of the Stone age. He lived in caves, probably for shelter against the increasing rigors of the climate as the last glacial age approached.

Peking Man. A race of men believed to have lived in about the same period as the Heidelberg man, probably 250,000 years ago or more. The name assigned to the race by scientists is Sinanthropus pekinensis. Fossilized remains of 10 individuals were found in a cave about 40 miles from Peking (now Peiping) between 1926 and 1930 by W. E. Pei, a Chinese scientist, and Dr. Davidson Black. With the skeletons were many bones of animals now extinct, a fact which facilitated the dating of this race. The brain capacity is estimated to be about one-fourth larger than that of the Java man.

Piltdown Man or **Sub-Man.** The name given to the creature, otherwise known as Eoanthropus, "dawn-man," some pieces of whose skull were found in a gravel pit at Piltdown in Sussex, England, in 1911-15. The gravel deposit in which the skull was found belongs to the third interglacial period, which means that the skull is from 50,000 to 100,000 years old. This skull is of a much less definitely human character than is the jaw of the more ancient Heidelberg man. On the other hand, the brain capacity is much greater, exceeding that of the smaller brained races of the present day.

Rhodesian Man. The name applied to men whose existence is inferred from a skeleton unearthed at Broken Hill mine, Northern Rhodesia, in 1921. These men are believed to have been contemporary with Neanderthal man, but with somewhat smaller brain capacity. The individual found was 5 feet, 10 inches in height. Many of its facial features were gorilla-like, but its teeth were distinctively human.

HISTORIC RACES AND PEOPLES

It has been customary for anthropologists, that is, for those who make a study of the natural history of mankind, to distinguish, on the basis of color, five, or sometimes four, races, as follows: Caucasian (white); Negro (black); Indian (red); Mongolian (yellow); and Malay (brown). The last is sometimes included with the Mongolian. More recently, however, anthropologists have attempted to base distinctions of race on differences in the size and the proportions of skulls and on other physical differences found to follow these, such as the shape of the cross section of the hair and the composition of the blood. These attempts have resulted in a division into the dolichocephalic (long-skulled) and the brachycephalic (short-skulled) races.

The term race is often popularly applied to groups which are properly designated as peoples. Ethnologists, however, that is, those who devote themselves to the study of peoples, classify a group as a people when its distinguishing characteristics are cultural rather than physical. So it often happens that a people will include individuals of different or of mixed races. Moreover, since differences between groups are often vague, a third term, family, has come into use, which is intermediate between race and people. We find peoples grouped into families, which may be regarded roughly as branches of the race, as the Aryans are said to be a branch of the Caucasian race. Peoples and families, however, and even races, have tended to unite and fuse by intermarriage so as to produce new groups. As a result, an account of races and peoples is necessarily complex. Nevertheless, the characteristics of the various groups do persist in a surprising manner, even over a great many centuries, so that a knowledge of the racial origin of a nation is often helpful in understanding its qualities.

Afghans (*ăf'gănz*). The native Iranic people of Afghanistan. The Afghans are Caucasian in physical type and Mohammedan in religion. In language they are related to the Persians and to the northern Hindus. The origin of the Afghans is obscure, some writers supposing that they are descended from the soldiers of Alexander the Great, and others affirming that the Copts or the Chaldeans were their ancestors. The Afghans themselves hold that they are in Jewish descent, but there is no trace of Israelite origin of the Afghan language. As a race they are handsome and athletic, with fair complexions, aquiline features, and long, flowing beards. Familiar with the art of war from youth, the Afghan makes a valiant soldier. The present day Afghans are firm in the belief that they will become a great and powerful nation. See *Afghanistan*.

Albanians (*ăl-bā'nĭ-ănz*). The aboriginal people of Albania, on the southwest coast of the Balkan peninsula, where they have lived since very ancient times. They are probably descendants of the earliest Aryan immigrants into Europe. Their language seems to be Aryan, resembling the Slavic rather than the Greek. The Albanians are very backward in culture, having scarcely any literature, and their rate of illiteracy is one of the highest in Europe. Physically, they are tall and muscular, with rather blond and regular features which clearly show their Caucasian origin. Their chief distinction in history is the persistence with which they have maintained their customs, characteristics, and independence. The Moslems overran Albania in 1468, but their rule over the Albanians was only nominal even in the larger towns. While the Albanians are brave, they are somewhat turbulent in spirit and are warriors rather than workers. It is estimated that they number about 1,350,000. Of this number, some 250,000 are resident in eastern Greece and perhaps 100,000 in southern Italy and Sicily, where they colonized many centuries ago. In religion, about two-thirds of the Albanians are Mohammedans; the remainder belong chiefly to the Catholic and the Greek faith. See *Albania*.

Algerians (*ăl-jē'rĭ-ănz*). Natives of Algiers; a geographical term and not the name of a distinct race. About two-thirds of the population of Algiers are Berbers and one-third are Arabs. The former are the original inhabitants of the country; they speak their native language but write with Arabic characters. The Arab population is mostly nomadic, although a few are settled in villages along the coast. In the Algerian towns the population is largely Moorish.

AMERICAN INDIANS

Christopher Columbus gave the name Indians to the natives of America, because he thought he had reached India from Europe by the western route. The opinion is now very widely held that the Indians are the descendants of people who migrated from Asia at a very early period. In the course of many centuries they spread over the American continents and, under widely differing conditions, developed a great variety of manners and customs. At the time of Columbus some peoples in South and Central America had advanced to a level of culture approaching that of ancient Egypt or Babylon. Over the greater part of the northern continent, however, the natives were still in the Stone age. They lived in wigwams or log huts. Many still subsisted by hunting, although a few tribes had made notable progress in agriculture, especially in growing such crops as maize, tobacco, peanuts, and cotton; some of the Iroquois even planted fruit trees. They had no domesticated animals except the dog.

Indians of the United States and Canada. The Indians of the United States and Canada varied greatly in appearance, in degree of culture, and in habits. They used no less than 200 distinct languages. Apart from the short, fair Eskimos of the north, however, most of them were tall, bronze-colored, having black hair, high cheek bones, and little or no beard. Their weapons were bows and arrows, and axes, spears, or knives of stone or of bone. After the coming of Europeans, guns and other iron instruments were employed. For money, strings of shell beads, called wampum, were often used. Among some tribes there was a belief in a great spirit and in a future life spent in a "happy hunting ground." A confidence in the efficacy of magic was very widespread. There was little writing, although some tribes, like the Delawares, had a picture script to record their history and myths. On the plains an elaborate sign language was developed for intertribal communication. The Cherokees alone had a literature written in an alphabet of their own invention. There were many rich mythologies, however, handed down by word of mouth.

Social customs varied widely. In most tribes, affairs of common interest were managed by a chief, or sachem, advised by a council of elders. Women were highly respected in some tribes; in others they had scarcely any rights. Slavery, in the sense of the right of life and death over others, was rare, although it existed in some cases. Burial, cremation, and exposure were all used in different localities as means of disposing of the dead. Various games, such as lacrosse, football of a certain type, and hunt-the-button, were played by some tribes.

It is estimated that at the time of the discovery of the continent there were upwards of a thousand tribes in North America. A complete enumeration of these would be plainly impossible. A large number have not survived, and even those which are still known as tribes no longer inhabit the regions they once did, but are brought together into reservations or even divided up among different reservations. Most of the larger tribes, however, survive in the general regions over which they once ruled.

Tribal Groups and Cultures.—The land lying both north and south of the Great Lakes and extending from the Mississippi river to the Atlantic coast was formerly inhabited by numerous tribes described by the general name of Algonquin. They included, among others, the Delawares, Potawatamis, and Mohicans. The Algonquins to the north lived by hunting and fishing, while those to the south of the Lakes harvested wild rice and other grains, and made pottery.

The Iroquois, sometimes called the Five Nations, or, later, the Six Nations, inhabited what is now the state of New York and southern Ontario. Their agriculture was more intensive, and their manufacture of pottery was more skillful than that found among the Algonquins. They comprised the Mohawks, the Oneidas, the Cayugas, the Senecas, the Onondagas, and, later, the Tuscaroras. Organized into a "league of nations," they waged war systematically against their enemies.

South of the Algonquins and occupying territory which extended from the Carolinas and Georgia to Texas and Arkansas, dwelt a group of tribes of which the more important were the Creeks, the Choctaws, the Cherokees, and the Seminoles. They lived in permanent villages, cultivated the soil, made pottery, and even wove cloth. Among them the Busk, or corn dance ceremony, was most fully developed.

The Indians of the Mississippi plain were hunters, living principally on buffalo meat. They housed themselves in tepees and did not cultivate the soil. Before the 17th century, when horses were introduced, the dog, which they used as a beast of burden, was their only domesticated animal. In the northeastern part of the plain lived the Crees, the Chippewas, and the Ojibwas; in the eastern part were the Omahas and the Wichitas; and in the center dwelt the Sioux, the Assiniboins, and the Dakotahs.

Among the Pueblo Indians, inhabiting the southwestern part of the continent, were the Apache tribe and the

Navajos, who became famous for their blankets. Others in this region, who did not belong to the Pueblo tribes, were noted for their basket weaving, but in general were inferior in culture, neither producing as skillful pottery nor living in permanent dwellings. Certain Pueblo Indians used to build stone and mortar dwellings in cliffs as a protection against the fiercer Apaches and Navajos. This fact gave rise to the belief in a prehistoric race of "Cliff Dwellers." Many Pueblo tribes are made up of remnants of different stocks which have come together through migrations. These movements of tribes account for the many ruins of abandoned villages in the southwestern United States.

The California Indians, the so-called Diggers, represent the most primitive form of historic American culture. They subsisted on roots and acorns; they made neither pottery, baskets, nor cloth; and they had only the most rudimentary social and political organization. The chief tribes were the Washos, the Yumans, and the Maidu.

The tribes of the northwestern states and of British Columbia, on the other hand, showed great skill in woodwork and developed a system of barter and of credit, with which was connected the so-called potlatch. This was a festive occasion on which each family displayed all its wealth and even gave away much of it in a spirit of extravagant generosity. They lived in houses built of planks and erected totem poles of carved wood. Among the more prominent tribes were the Bannocks, the Snakes, and the Flatheads.

In the north Pacific area lived a number of tribes, including the Bellacoolas and the Chinooks. The Chippewas, the Slaveys, and other tribes in the Mackenzie area are still little molested by white men, but they live under hard conditions of climate. The caribou provides their principal food, as well as the material for their clothing and tents.

In the arctic region, the Eskimos formerly depended for food mainly on the seal, which they hunted from skin boats when the water was open, and at other times from sleds drawn by dogs. Reindeer, particularly in Alaska, now provide sustenance for many. The number of Eskimos is small in relation to the immense stretch of land over which they range, but they have shown extraordinary persistence in maintaining their language and habits. They are thought to be connected racially with the Algonquins.

Political and Economic Status of the Indian.—The number of Indians in North America north of Mexico about the year 1492 has been estimated by James Mooney, United States government expert, at 1,115,000. Dr. H. J. Spinden regards this estimate as too low. The number decreased rapidly, largely as a result of epidemics of measles and smallpox. Since 1900 an increase in the Indian population has been recorded, so that in 1931 it stood at approximately 471,000 for the United States and Canada.

The United States government dealt with the Indians by treaties up to 1878, and after that by Congressional enactment. In 1887, land formerly held by tribes in common was authorized for parceling out to individuals. That not so allotted was sold, so that many Indians coming of age later found themselves without a share. In 1906, permission was granted for sale of land allotted to individuals, and sale was obligatory if one heir of a tract so demanded. The result was a progressive diminution of land owned by Indians enrolled in tribes from 138 million acres in 1887 to 47 million in 1934, when a new policy was adopted.

The new policy was incorporated in the Wheeler-Howard act, under which each tribe may elect to organize as a species of political subdivision, and, if this course is chosen, it may also organize as a corporation. In either case, no further alienation of Indian land is permitted, except that individuals may sell their parcels to the incorporated tribe, receiving stock in return. The purpose is to permit Indian tribes to set their own pace in abandoning tribal organization for individual adaptation to industrial life.

Supervision of Indian welfare is the duty of the office of Indian affairs, created in 1832. In 1924, American citizenship was conferred on all non-citizen Indians born in the United States. The right to vote is subject to state limitations.

In Canada, the government each year pays a certain amount of money, known as "treaty money," and distributes a certain amount of provisions to every Indian on a reservation, in accordance with treaties made originally with the various tribes. Industrial schools, also, are provided by the government and are maintained by religious organizations. Indians on reservations are wards of the government, being educated and given medical attention free of charge. Their land cannot be sold without joint consent of "owner" and the government. Chief and councellors are elected and exercise powers similar to those of officers of rural municipalities.

In the following table for the United States the population is based on the census returns, the land area on the report of the office of Indian affairs. The latter, counting only those enrolled in tribes, reported a total of 235,270 in 1935 owning land totaling 50,496,606 acres and enjoying an estimated annual income of $17,270,000. In 1940 it reported an Indian population of 394,280. The Canadian table is based on official publications.

INDIANS OF THE UNITED STATES

State	Area of Indian Lands Acres	Population (1940)
Alaska		32,464
Arizona	19,224,717	55,076
California	666,817	18,675
Colorado	666,533	1,360
Florida	60,574	690
Idaho	817,659	3,537
Iowa	3,386	733
Kansas	35,678	1,165
Michigan	26,872	6,282
Minnesota	652,746	12,528
Montana	6,454,953	16,841
Nebraska	75,958	3,401
Nevada	1,127,171	4,747
New Mexico	7,153,109	34,510
New York		8,651
North Carolina	56,849	22,546
North Dakota	1,036,292	10,114
Oklahoma	2,844,431	63,125
Oregon	1,736,794	4,594
South Dakota	5,864,604	23,347
Utah	1,693,160	3,611
Washington	2,739,830	11,394
Wisconsin	445,443	12,265
Wyoming	2,013,409	2,349
All Other States	9,427	12,428
Total	55,406,412	366,433

INDIANS OF CANADA

Province	Indian Lands Acres (1941)	Income Dollars (1941)	Population (1939)
Alberta	1,348,527	876,949	12,163
British Columbia	780,854	2,474,447	24,276
Manitoba	529,432	566,220	14,561
New Brunswick	37,394	39,844	1,922
Northwest Territories	*5,474	*304,565	3,724
Nova Scotia	18,187	57,097	2,165
Ontario	1,326,503	2,258,551	30,145
Prince Edward Island	1,508	4,755	274
Quebec	175,049	617,009	14,578
Saskatchewan	1,200,806	652,751	13,020
Yukon			1,550
Total	5,423,734	7,852,188	118,378

*Includes Yukon.

Central and South American Indians. In Central and South America an even greater variety of culture is found than in North America. At the time of the discovery of the New World the Aztecs in Mexico had developed a political organization and an architecture of a fairly high order, while the Cariban tribe still practiced cannibalism. In fact, one of the companions of Amerigo Vespucci was overpowered by some women of this tribe and was eaten. Certain tribes on the Amazon are "lake dwellers," living in huts built on piles driven into the bed of the river. Many of the Arawakan tribes were good agriculturists when discovered. They made pottery, worked in stone and gold, and used cotton. From them, white people have adopted the use of the hammock and of tobacco. A large number of languages were spoken, from which a considerable number of words have been taken over into English and naturalized, such as: cannibal, coca, condor, hammock, hurricane, maize, potato, quinine, and tobacco. A curious custom, known as the *couvade*, is found among some tribes, according to which, when a child is born, the father takes to his bed as though he himself had suffered the pains of childbirth.

When America was discovered, these Indians had no iron implements, but silver and gold were very abundant. This condition invited conquests; the Spaniards, and later the Portuguese, waged wars with the natives for many decades and eventually established colonies. Over against the attempts at extermination, however, should be set the work of the missions, which aimed at Christianization. In the present population of the South American continent the Indian element is racially dominant instead of being negligible, as it is in North America.

For those Indians of Mexico and of Central and South America who developed distinct civilizations, see ***Aztecs***, ***Incas***, ***Mayas***, ***Toltecs***.

Angles (*ăng'g'lz*). A tribe originally from northern Germany, which, along with part of the Saxons, effected a settlement in England in the 5th century A. D. The Angles gave their name to the country.

Arabians (*ȧ-rā'bĭ-ănz*) or **Arabs** (*ăr'ăbz*). The Semitic people inhabiting Arabia and large portions of neighboring countries. Under the one name are included the settled Arabs and the wandering Bedouin tribes of the desert. After their adoption of Mohammedanism in the 7th century A. D., they spread far from the country which bears their name and settled in distant portions of Africa and Asia and also penetrated into Europe. Through the *Koran* they have given their language to vast populations of the Mohammedan faith. With the Persians, the Arabs took a leading part in developing Moslem civilization. They promoted commerce and geographical exploration, created a new order of architecture, and made the products of Greek culture accessible to European nations. During the middle ages the Arabs were far in advance of the rest of the world in the cultivation of the sciences, philosophy, literature, and art. As a race, they show great absorptive power, and, when intermingled with conquered or converted peoples, have impressed their characteristics upon these to a remarkable extent. While Syrians and Moors have long used the Arabic language, they are not Arabian in origin. The true Arab population of Arabia is between three and one-half and five millions. A much larger number live in northern Africa. See *Arabia.*

Armenians (*är-mē'nĭ-ănz*). The Aryan people who conquered the country of Armenia in the 7th century B. C. They mingled to some extent with the earlier inhabitants and also with the Persians; consequently, among modern Armenians there are great differences of physical type. Generally, they have swarthy complexions and dark eyes and hair, and Armenian women are noted for their delicate and regular features. The sturdy character of these people has enabled them to survive centuries of oppression and misrule. The Church of Armenia, established about 301 by Bishop Gregory the Illuminator, may be said to have been the first national Christian church. Since the Council of Chalcedon in 451, whose decrees it refused to acknowledge, the Church of Armenia has been independent of the Eastern Church and has had as its head the Catholicos, whose see is at a monastery near Erivan in Russia. The Armenian patriarch, however, residing at Constantinople, is the head of the Armenian Church in Turkey and is equal in importance to the Catholicos.

On account of their religious faith, the Armenians have been systematically persecuted by the Turks, and much of the ignorance and superstition to be found among the peasantry may be attributed to the persistently cruel treatment meted out to them by their inhuman tyrants. A deliberate plan of the Turkish government to exterminate the Armenians was set on foot at the beginning of the World War, and it is estimated that more than a million perished in this series of massacres. But the race, everywhere, shows a high capacity for education and culture, and many Armenians who have emigrated to different parts of Europe and America have proved this by their success, not only in industry and business, but also in the wider fields of art and learning.

Aryans (*är'yănz*). A family of peoples assumed to be of kindred race because their languages show common characteristics. The original home of the race is thought to have been either northern Europe or Asia. They had already domesticated the horse by 2500 B. C., at which time they first appear in history. Their descendants include the people of India, of Greece, of Italy, and of Albania, together with the Celtic, the Germanic, the Anglo-Saxon, and the Scandinavian peoples, and also the northern Russians or Slavs. The race is often known as Indo-European or Indo-Germanic.

Assyrians (*ă-sĭr'ĭ-ănz*). A Semitic people, calling themselves Assur, who, about 2000 B. C., settled in the valley of the Tigris, north of Babylonia. Here they occupied a former Hittite stronghold, built up a power which became a rival of Babylon, and finally gave the name of Assyria to the entire Tigris-Euphrates valley. The Assyrians were a strong, warlike people, speaking a language similar to that of the Babylonians, but lacking their capacity for culture. Their history was one of ruthless, cruel conquest and tyranny.

Aztecs (*ăz'tĕks*). The tribe or group of tribes that ruled southern Mexico at the time of the Spanish conquest in 1521. The name is derived from *Aztlan*, meaning "heron-place," "white place," or "seacoast," the earlier home of this people, which probably was located on the west coast of Mexico. Properly, the Aztecs, or "heron clan," were the tribe that built Tenochtitlan, now the City of Mexico. The name, however, is extended to include the seven tribes of the surrounding territory, which formed the Aztec Confederacy, and, more loosely, to designate all the ancient semicivilized tribes of central and southern Mexico and their modern descendants.

When Cortés came to Mexico, the Aztecs had been in power for two or three centuries. They had developed, in some respects, a high order of civilization. Their capital, Tenochtitlan, was a strong stone city, with palaces, baths and fountains, and an elaborate system of canals. They held regular weekly markets, in which trade was carried on by barter. Their temples were built in a form much like the Egyptian pyramids, and they showed great skill in agriculture and in industrial arts, especially metal working.

The Aztec tribe was organized in twenty clans, which were grouped in four phratries, or wards of the city. The supreme government was a council of twenty, the executive power being placed in the hands of two magistrates, one for civil, the other for military affairs. The council was called "speech-place," which is the literal meaning of our word parliament.

Yet, the purpose of all the Aztec organization seems to have been, not government, but the exacting of plunder and tribute from other tribes. Besides, with all their culture, the Aztecs were cannibals, and their religious rites called for human sacrifices of the most revolting character. The modern Aztecs, however, living in the neighborhood of the City of Mexico, are a quiet, peaceable people. They still retain their ancient language, but they have lost all the other features of ancient Aztec culture. See *Mexico.*

Bantus (*băn'to͞oz*). The sturdy group of African tribes, including the Kafirs, Zulus, and Bechuanas, living in Central and South Africa, who speak dialects of one language called Bantu. They are agriculturists, living in settled communities, most of the field work being done by the women, while the men hunt and care for the herds. They do good work in wood, metals, and pottery.

Basques (*bȧsks*). A remarkable and very ancient people inhabiting the Pyrenees of northern Spain and southwestern France. They are believed to be a fragment, perhaps the only distinct remnant, of the pre-Aryan race, or aboriginal people of Europe. The Basque tongue is the only non-Aryan language of western Europe. Formerly, it was thought to point to a Mongolian origin for this people, but recent investigations indicate connections with the Berbers of northern Africa, who are of Hamitic stock. The Basques are not now easily distinguishable in appearance from their Spanish and French neighbors, though they still speak their own strange language and adhere to their peculiar customs and laws.

Since the dawn of history the Basques have formed small exclusive republics ruled by duly elected chiefs, under their own special laws, with fierce independence and great patriotic pride. Although the Basques of Spain have not contributed in any prominent way to the country's history, their national code has been respected by every ruler. At all times they have constituted a sort of realm within the realm, having their own special parliament, tariffs and tolls, and, until recently, their own army and police; collecting their own taxes and paying a fixed annual levy or tribute to the Spanish government.

While, on the whole, the Basques are not keen minded or progressive, illiteracy is rare among them, and they possess many admirable traits. They are faithful and honest and show marked kindness and hospitality to strangers. It is said that no people on earth are prouder than the Basques, but they have no aristocracy among them, and no one will acknowledge a superior.

About a half million Basques still remain, chiefly on the Spanish side of the Pyrenees. Only about 150,000 now live in Gascony, the French province formerly called Vasconia after them. It is estimated that during the latter half of the 19th century 200,000 Basques emigrated to South America.

Bedouins (*bĕd'o͝o-ĭnz*). See *Arabians.*

Belgæ (*bĕl'jē*). The northernmost group of Celtic tribes which inhabited ancient Gaul. The Belgæ occupied the country between the Seine, Marne, and Moselle rivers and the ocean, which includes modern Belgium, together with portions of Holland and northern France. Some of the Belgæ settled in Kent and Sussex in southern Britain. In 57 B. C., Julius Cæsar conquered the Belgæ in a long, hard campaign, though part of the tribes revolted later. According to Cæsar, the Belgæ were the bravest of all the Gauls. See *Belgium.*

Belgians (*bĕl'jĭ-ănz*). The name applied to natives or citizens of Belgium, but not the name of a distinct race. Southern Belgians, for the most part, are Walloons, and northern Belgians are Flemish. See *Walloons, Flanders.*

Bengalese (*bĕn'gȧ-lēz'*). The principal race inhabiting Bengal, British India. Their language, a modern Hindu tongue called Bengali, is now spoken by a population of some 45 million. On account of their unusually broad heads, the Bengalese are thought to contain an admixture of Mongolian stock.

Berbers (*bûr'bĕrz*). The most important native people of northwest Africa, scattered over the whole space between Egypt and the shores of the Atlantic. The Berbers are of Hamitic origin and number at least 7,000,000 in Morocco and Algeria and 500,000 in Libya and Tunis. Physically, they are of middle height with brown or nearly black complexion. They are usually thin but strong and muscular, and their bodies are beautifully formed. Although illiterate, they are remarkably industrious, usually honest in their dealings, and of high natural intelligence. By working native iron they make various implements and utensils, including gun barrels, knives, and swords. The tribes of the plains breed sheep, cattle, goats, asses, and mules. The Berbers are Mohammedan in religion, and their language is said to be related to the Semitic group.

Bohemians. See *Czechs.*

Boii (*bō'ĭ-ī*). A Celtic people, who emigrated from transalpine Gaul into Italy, where they occupied the old seat of the Umbrians, between the Po and the Apennines. In 283 B. C. the Boii were defeated by the Romans at the Vadimonian lake, and thereafter they prolonged, through numerous campaigns, especially in support of Hannibal, but sometimes single-handed, their resistance to the Roman arms, till their complete defeat by Scipio Nasica, 191 B. C. They were subsequently compelled to recross the Alps, and dwelt for more than a century in a part of modern Bohemia, which derives its name from them, but they were ultimately exterminated by the Dacians. See *Bohemia.*

Bretons. About the 6th century B. C., the Celts of Gaul invaded Britain and, coalescing with the Iberians, founded the states later overthrown by the Romans. Upon the invasion of the Anglo-Saxons between the 5th and 6th centuries A. D., the British Celts who fled from England to avoid the Saxon domination crossed to the northwest of France and founded the Celtic state of Brittany, then called Armorica. These Celts are the direct ancestors of the modern Bretons, whose language is closely allied to the Welsh and the now extinct Cornish languages. It is spoken by over 1¼ million persons. Of its four dialects *León* is the purest and *Cornuallais* the most widely spread. See *Brittany.*

Britons. A people, largely of Celtic origin, who inhabited England at the time of Julius Cæsar's visit. They had a highly developed druidic religion. Young men in Gaul who wished to be priests were sent to Britain to be educated.

Bulgars. An Asiatic race akin to the Huns. When first known, they were nomadic horsemen, fierce and barbarous, who migrated westward behind the Huns. In the 4th century A.D., they conquered the region between the Volga and the Urals. Later they formed a state north of the Black Sea. In the 7th century, they menaced Constantinople. Settling down, they gave their name to the region now known as Bulgaria.

Burmese (*bûr'mēz'*). The principal native race of British Burma. The Burmese are Mongolian in origin, and their language is related to the Indo-Chinese of farther India. They are generally a well-formed race, with skin of a rich brown hue, black hair, and black eyes; the men are fond of athletics. The dress of the common people is a strip of cotton or silk cloth wound about the body. They are fond of personal decorations in bright colors, and expert native jewelers supply the demand for gold and silver ornaments. Their festivals are many and are celebrated with games, pageants, and plays. Life is very easy in their friendly climate, and the people are inclined to enjoy it as much as possible. They are Buddhists in religion, and Burma is rich in shrines and temples. In the temple schools all Burmese boys are educated. Travelers seem to find the romance suggested by the name of the Burmese capital, Mandalay, actually present in the country. See *Burma.*

Bushmen. A group of very primitive peoples of southern Africa, who live a wandering life in the desert and obtain their food by hunting.

Catalans (*kăt'ȧ-lănz*) or **Catalonians** (*kăt'ȧ-lō'nĭ-ănz*). The people inhabiting Catalonia, the northeastern division of Spain. They extend northward over the Spanish boundary into France, and their language, called Catalan, is distinct from both the Provençal of southern France and the Castilian of Spain. Castilians can understand the speech of Portuguese more easily than that of Catalans, and the rapid enunciation of the Catalan adds to the difficulty. The Catalans are the most energetic, industrious, and intelligent people of Spain.

Caucasian (*kô-kā'shăn*) **Race.** This name is applied to a large group of white peoples, including the most highly civilized nations. It was first used in the belief that the highest type of this race was to be found among the people of the Caucasus mountains. Most Europeans (excluding Turks, Hungarians, and Finns), the Hindus, Persians, Arabs, Hebrews, and ancient Phœnicians come under this classification.

Celts (*sĕlts*). A vague term which names the large group of peoples, of mixed race but using a common language, whose early home, about 1000 B. C., was in the upper valleys of the Rhine and the Danube. From this center they spread west, south, and east, one branch becoming the Galatians of Asia Minor, another, the Gauls of western Europe. In Italy, as early as the 4th century B. C., they made large settlements in the valley of the Po, a region from which afterward came Virgil, Catullus, and other men of note in Latin letters. In the East, they served as mercenaries in Africa and Asia. They were known to the ancients by many different names, and there seem to have been two distinct physical types among them, one tall and fair, the other short and dark. On the continent, the Celts succumbed to Roman and Germanic conquest. At the present day, they are represented most conspicuously by the Irish, the Welsh, and the Highland Scotch.

Chinese. In common use, the name of the native inhabitants of the country of China. The Chinese, properly, are the product of the fusion of several primitive races, most of which were Mongolian. Their traditions tell us that the original Chinese nation occupied a small territory near the present city of Si-an-fu, and that they extended their rule by peaceful and warlike means to the west and south. In general, the Chinese show the low stature, the square and flattened face, and markedly uniform expression of the Mongolians, but various types appear in the northern, central, and southern parts of the country. Yet, with many differences of disposition and wide variations of dialect, the Chinese show several uniform qualities which mark them as one people. They are courteous, peace loving, practical, temperate, and generally unimaginative, and they are highly endowed with the power of memory.

The heart of the Chinese social and religious life is filial piety, the worship of ancestors. The care of the dead seems often to be of more importance than provision for the living. In houses of the wealthier classes, rooms are set apart for tablets inscribed with the names of deceased ancestors, and ceremonies, prescribed by the classic Book of Rites, are performed before these. Indeed, the daily life of the Chinese, particularly of the upper classes, is a matter of minutely ordered etiquette.

Although the Chinese are not inclined to outdoor sports, especially vigorous athletics, they are fond of the theater and various entertainments given by traveling showmen. But in these tastes they are changing through contact with Western nations. They are adopting Western clothing, and foot binding and the wearing of the queue have been discarded. See *China.*

Circassians (*sẽr-kăsh'ănz*). The name applied to people inhabiting the northwestern part of the Caucasus. Their name for themselves is *Adighe*; the Turks and Russians call them *Tcherkasses*, or "brigands." Both Circassian men and women are noted for physical beauty, and many Circassian girls entered Turkish harems. After the Russian conquest of their territory, in 1864, several hundred thousand of them emigrated. Among the upper classes, Mohammedanism is the chief religion; among the lower classes, this is mixed with vestiges of earlier religions.

Copts. Egyptian Christians who separated from the Church in the 5th century on the question of the "nature" of Christ. Racially they are the purest representatives of the ancient Egyptians. They preserved their religion and customs against the persecution of their Moslem conquerors, retaining their own schools and the use of the Coptic language in church services. For many years they were compelled to wear black or blue turbans as a degrading distinction. The men were employed chiefly as clerks and secretaries. Under British rule, however, persecution ceased. Their economic position improved as they engaged in agriculture, banking, and other activities. Their children attended secular schools, and, in general, the lines of demarcation from their neighbors tended rapidly to break down. See *Egypt.*

Cossacks (*kŏs'ăks*). The inhabitants of the southern and eastern frontiers of Russia. The most important of these communities were those of the Dnieper and the Don. They retained a certain degree of independence with a kind of democratic government, at the head of which was their "hetman," until the reign of Catherine II. In lieu of taxes, they supplied the Russian empire with a most valuable military force of cavalry and scouts. In 1918 the Cossacks proclaimed the new Republic of the Don, but they were later overrun by the Soviet forces.

Croatians (*krô-ā'shănz*). A southern Slavic people whose language differs but slightly from that of the Serbians, with whom they are commonly grouped, as Serbo-Croatians. The Croatians are most numerous in Croatia, Slavonia, Dalmatia, and Bosnia, former provinces of the Austrian empire, now included in Jugoslavia.

Czechs (*chĕks*). A northern group of the Slavic peoples, who were living in Bohemia, Moravia, and Austrian Silesia, as early as the 5th century. Their struggle against Habsburg tyranny started the Thirty Years' war. After the French Revolution they began a revival of their literature, a movement which became political in 1848. The Czechs united in 1918 with their neighbors, the Slovaks, in forming a new republic, Czechoslovakia.

Danes. A northern tribe which, in the 5th century A. D., drove the Saxons and the Angles from Jutland and from the adjacent islands. Most of them remained in the country which has become Denmark, but others settled in England in the 9th and the 10th century.

Dorians (*dō'rĭ-ănz*). A race of people in ancient Greece who are believed to have come from the north and conquered the Peloponnesian peninsula. In Sparta, the leading Doric state, the conquerors held the subject population in rigorous servitude. Thence arose the conception of the Dorians as aristocratic and warlike in temper as opposed to the Ionian peoples, among whom the leading state was Athens, the extreme exponent of democracy.

Dravidians (*drȧ-vĭd'ĭ-ănz*). The non-Aryan people who inhabit the southern part of India and Ceylon. They occupied the country before the coming of the Aryans. Their languages, of which there are a dozen, belong to the Turanian group. Some of the tribes are of a very low type of civilization, but the Tamils and Telugus have attained a high culture and produced excellent literature and architecture. The religion of the Dravidians varies from rude nature worship to a borrowed Islamism or Hinduism. See *Ceylon, India.*

Egyptians (*ē-jĭp'shănz*). The ancient Egyptians maintained that they were a race of pure blood, native to the Nile valley, without foreign mixture. Modern study confirms this belief. They belonged to the Hamitic branch of the Caucasian or white race, and the modern *fellah,* or peasant, of Egypt is said to represent the ancient type with remarkable purity. The Egyptian language is in many points similar to the Semitic tongues, a fact for which no satisfactory explanation has been made. See *Egypt.*

Eskimos (*ĕs'kĭ-mōz*). The race inhabiting the arctic regions of America and the extreme northeastern part of Asia. They call themselves *Innuit,* or "men." The Algonquin Indians dubbed them *Eskimo,* or "raw fish eaters." They are believed to be of the same stock as the North American Indians and to have migrated from the north Atlantic coast to the districts they now occupy. The language used by widely separated groups of this people is remarkably uniform. In stature the Eskimos are about 5 feet in height, well built, and usually fat. Where they have not been in contact with the white race, they use the tools and weapons of the later Stone age. Their skill in carving fishbones is remarkable. The seal supplies them with food, clothing, boats, shelter, light, and heat. Their shelters are tents for summer and huts for winter. The latter are built of wood by some tribes; by others, of stone chinked with moss and snow. In Alaska, however, the Eskimos are largely civilized and depend for their living on reindeer.

Ethiopians (*ē'thĭ-ō'pĭ-ănz*). The ancestors of the present-day Abyssinians. They were Semites who migrated from southern Arabia about the 5th or 4th century B. C. and were in no way related to the Negro race, to which, through a mistaken identification, the name has been frequently applied.

Etruscans (*ē-trŭs'kănz*). An early people who inhabited Italy north of the Tiber, but whose culture and language were distinct from those of other Italian peoples. By some they are thought to have come from Asia Minor. They developed a considerable commerce and at one time conquered Rome. The inscriptions left by them have not yet been deciphered.

Fellahs (*fĕl'ȧz*) or **Fellahin** (*fĕl'ȧ-hēn'*). The name by which the settled, agricultural Arab tribes are known, in contrast to the wandering Bedouins. It is more familiar as applied to a class of agricultural laborers or peasants of Egypt and Palestine. They represent the ancient Egyptians in physical form and features. In temperament they are peaceful and unprogressive.

Filipinos (*fĭl'ĭ-pē'nōz*). The Malay inhabitants of the Philippine Islands. The earliest occupants of the islands are thought to have been the Negritos, or pygmy Negroes, about 25,000 of whom are still found in the interior of Luzon. At some remote period there occurred a series of Malay migrations. These immigrants scattered over the islands in small groups with different dialects and local customs. Like their modern descendants, such as the Igorots, they were head-hunters and warriors. In the northern highlands of Luzon, some of them developed a remarkable system of irrigated mountain terraces, on which they grow rice. Probably they brought with them a knowledge of ironworking.

Later Malay migrations brought the people represented by the three most important tribes of the present time, Visayans, Tagalogs, and Ilocanos, to whom the name Filipinos is often restricted. Of these, the Tagalogs, who are the most numerous of the inhabitants of Manila, central Luzon, and Mindanao, are the most highly civilized group. The Moros of the southern islands are Mohammedan Malays who followed the other migrations. Since the beginning of the Spanish occupation of the Philippines, intermarriage of Filipinos with Spaniards, Chinese, and Mexicans has produced a large group of mixed blood, called *mestizos,* who are the leaders in government and business.

The Filipinos of today present all stages of civilization, from the primitive life of the wild mountain tribes to the town and village communities where schools have been established. Most of the Filipinos are Christians. The schools introduced by the Americans, the cost of which has been borne by the Filipinos themselves, have done much to spread a knowledge of reading and writing and to develop habits of industry. See *Philippine Islands.*

Finns. A people inhabiting the area north and east of the Baltic Sea and in scattered areas throughout Russia. Their origin is the subject of wide differences of opinion. The traditional view is that they are related to the Mongols and ancient Scythians, having been driven from the Ural mountains near the Caspian Sea about 2000 years ago. Archeologists adduce evidence to show the Finns come from the Volga River valley. On the basis of physical traits, some anthropologists attribute a western European origin. The Finns are a sturdy, independent people. Among those residing in Finland, illiteracy of the adult population is less than 1 per cent. From the Finnish epic *Kalevala* Longfellow borrowed the meter used in his "Hiawatha." See *Finland.*

Franks. A group of Germanic tribes which from the 3d century was allied with the Romans and which, after the overthrow of the Empire, conquered Gaul. The Franks established a kingdom there under Clovis, and gave their name to the country which we now call France.

Frisians (*frĭzh'ănz*). An ancient Germanic people, who inhabited the extreme northwest of Germany, between the mouths of the Rhine and Ems, and were subjected to the Roman power under Drusus. They were subdued by the Franks, and, on the division of the Carlovingian empire, their country was divided into West Frisia (West Friesland) and East Frisia (East Friesland). The language of the Frisians is closely akin to the Anglo-Saxon. Our knowledge of the old Frisian is derived from certain collections of laws, called the "Asegabuch," composed about 1200. Modern Frisian is split into many dialects, but the greater part of its literature is written in West Frisian.

Gauls. See *Celts.*

Goths. A powerful German people, who originally dwelt on the Prussian coast of the Baltic, at the mouth of the Vistula, but afterwards migrated to the south. About the beginning of the 3d century we find them separated into two great divisions, the Ostrogoths or Eastern Goths, and the Visigoths or Western Goths. The meaning of *Goth* is said to be "nobly born."

Gypsies. The name given in England to the wandering tribes that since the beginning of the 15th century have been scattered over Europe. They were supposed by the English to be Egyptians. In France the gypsies are called *Bohémiens,* from the belief that they were originally Hussites driven from Bohemia. Scholars now believe that the Gypsies are remnants of a tribe from India. Their language is undoubtedly derived from Sanskrit, though it is mixed with many words from other languages. They call themselves *Roma,* and their language *Romany.* For several centuries they were a source of trouble in Europe because of their wandering and thieving habits, though they were protected in Scotland by royal authority.

Hamites (*hăm'īts*). A branch of the Caucasian race, thought to have inhabited northern Africa and to have been the ancestors of the Egyptians, the Berbers, and others. The name was chosen because the race was supposed to have been descended from Noah's son Ham.

Helvetii (*hĕl-vē'shĭ-ī*) or **Helvetians** (*hĕl-vē'shănz*). An ancient Celtic people who, in the 1st century B. C., lived in the country between the Rhone and Rhine, and between the Jura mountains and the Rhætian Alps. Their territory was somewhat smaller than modern Switzerland. Cæsar opposed their migration into Gaul and drove them back into their mountains, with great slaughter. In the reign of Vitellius they were again mercilessly attacked. After this they disappeared from history.

Hindus (*hĭn'do͞oz*). This name is commonly applied to all the inhabitants of India, but it properly names only the Aryan people of the north central portion of the peninsula. At a very early period, this people descended into India from the northwest and crowded the inhabitants, known as the Tamils, toward the south. The religion of the Hindus is the ancient Brahmanism, which dates from the period of the *Vedas.* See *India.*

Hottentots (*hŏt''n-tŏts*). The aboriginal race of South Africa. They are thought to be an ancient mixture of the

Bantus and the Bushmen. When the Dutch first settled at the Cape of Good Hope, the Hottentots occupied a large territory and had large herds of cattle. This race has now become much degenerated. The people are of low stature, with yellow wrinkled skin, small broad noses, high cheek bones, and tufty hair. When past their youth they become more repulsive in appearance by reason of curvature of the spine. They are fairly gifted intellectually and in disposition are said to be cheerful and happy-go-lucky.

Huns. A people, probably of Mongolian origin, who are first noticed in history about 375 A. D., when they moved westward into the Danube valley. A half century later they became the terror of Europe. Under their vigorous leader, Attila, whose boast it was that grass never grew again where his horse's hoofs had trod, they swept across the Rhine, burning and devastating. Their host included conquered Ostrogoths and many other tribes. The Romans and their allies, the Visigoths, Burgundians, and Franks, met and defeated the Huns at the battle of Châlons in 451. Within a few years they withdrew to Asia or mixed with their conquered tribes, leaving only their name as the synonym for barbarous cruelty.

Incas (*ĭng'kȧz*). A civilized people formerly inhabiting the country which now is Peru. They were subjugated and almost exterminated by the Spaniards in the 16th century. Our knowledge of the people is derived mainly from accounts left by their conquerors and from buildings and monuments which the Incas constructed.

Their buildings were often of immense size, and showed that the builders possessed a rare skill in the cutting and fitting of stone. The Incas were superior to their European conquerors in engineering and in agriculture. A literature had been developed, by which the native history and traditions were preserved. Dramas, also, were acted before the royal court.

Indians. See *American Indians.*

Iranians (*ī-rā'nĭ-ănz*). A branch of the Aryan peoples. They are represented now principally by the Persians, by the Kurds, and by part of the inhabitants of Afghanistan and of Turkestan.

Irish. The name applied generally to the people of Ireland. In the population of the island, however, are included three physical types: (1) a short, dark-haired type, representing the primitive race; (2) a taller, blond type, representing the Tuatha De Danaan (tribe of the goddess Danu) of Irish tradition; (3) the Celtic, which is the dominating Irish type of the present day, representing that of a people who conquered the island probably within historic times. Included also in the term Irish is the large population in the East and North of Ireland, made up of descendants of English and Scotch settlers. Large numbers of Irish have emigrated to all parts of the world, particularly to Canada and the United States. See *Celts, Ireland.*

Japanese. The modern Japanese people are a mingled race of at least three strains which appear quite distinctly in various groups of the population. The Ainus are usually regarded as the aborigines of Japan. They are of short, thickset build and have much hair on the face and body. This type is most frequent in the northern part of the empire. A Malayan element is present also, most noticeably in central and eastern Japan. The dominant type, however, is Korean-Manchu, of Mongolian origin, characterized by more slender build and greater height.

Physically, the Japanese are capable of great endurance, a quality which has been developed through the hard conditions of life among great numbers of the people. In character, the Japanese are frugal, obedient to authority, and altruistic. They are intellectually quick and eager, and possess marked powers of imitation.

Kafirs (*kä'fẽrz*). The word is Arabic, meaning "unbeliever." The Kafirs are the principal native race of South Africa. They are a branch of the Bantus and include the Zulus. In stature and shape of head they are more like Europeans than like Negroes. Their chief occupation is cattle raising. They are of peaceful character, and some of them have become somewhat civilized.

Kalmucks (*kăl'mŭks*). A nomadic Mongol race of fearless horsemen and soldiers, Buddhists in religion, who inhabit parts of China, Siberia, and Russia. Although of small stature, for centuries they have been notorious as quarrelsome warriors.

Kirghiz (*kĭr-gēz'*). A nomadic Turkish-Tatar people who inhabit the steppes, or vast tracts of land, between the lower Volga and the Caspian Sea on the west and the Altai mountains on the east. They are divided into hordes, the Great Horde, the Middle Horde, and the Little Horde. Their food is chiefly mutton and horseflesh, with kumiss, or fermented mare's milk. They live in hemispherical tents made of felt stretched over a frame of boughs, and manufacture woolen cloth, carpets, and leather goods, which they trade for cutlery and silks.

Kurds (*kōōrdz*). A people of Iranian race who occupy Kurdistan, partly in Asiatic Turkey and partly in Persia. They are a brave, freedom-loving folk, but are not inclined to industry. The nomad Kurds live in tents of black skins, while the settled communities use low houses with flat wooden roofs. The Kurdish women have more freedom than most Oriental women; the girls are married, upon payment of a dower, at ten or twelve years of age. The men shave their heads and faces, leaving only a mustache, though old men wear full beards. They have been known in history since the time of ancient Assyria. In religion they are mostly Mohammedans.

Lapps (*lăps*). The non-Aryan people, of Asiatic origin, who inhabit the forbidding arctic shores of Europe from Norway to the White Sea. They are the shortest people of Europe, ranging from four to five feet in height. Though not very muscular they are capable of bearing great fatigue. Their only source of wealth is their herds of reindeer, which give them food, clothing, and means of travel. They profess Christianity but preserve many old pagan superstitions.

Lithuanians (*lĭth'ū-ā'nĭ-ănz*) and **Letts.** Two related groups of Aryan people, neither Slav nor German, inhabiting a small territory bordering the Baltic Sea and the Gulf of Riga, formerly included in Russia and East Prussia. The date of their migration to their present home is not known. In the 13th and the 14th century the Lithuanians built up a large independent state, and for several centuries these two peoples have maintained their ancient customs and language against tyrannical pressure from Slavs and Germans. Many of both peoples have emigrated to the United States. Until the 18th century they had no native written literature, but they possessed many songs, celebrating every phase of life except war. Recently, a modest beginning in literature has been made. The Lithuanian language is reckoned by scholars the oldest of living tongues. It closely resembles Sanskrit and has remarkable likenesses to Greek and Latin. Lettish is in some points more primitive than Lithuanian. See *Lithuania.*

Lombards (*lŏm'bȧrdz*) or **Longobardi** (*lŏng'gō-bär'dī*). A Germanic people, originally from the region of the lower Elbe river, not very numerous, but of distinguished valor, who played an important part in the early history of Europe. The name may have been given with reference to their long beards. About the 2d century they seem to have begun to leave their original district and to have fought their way south and east till they came in close contact with the Eastern Roman Empire on the Danube and adopted an Arian form of Christianity. After having been for some time tributary to the Heruli, they raised themselves upon the ruins of their power and of that of the Gepidæ, shortly after the middle of the 6th century, to the position of masters of Pannonia and became one of the most wealthy and powerful nations in that part of the world. Under their king, Alboin, they invaded and conquered the northern and central parts of Italy (568–572). The conversion of the Arian Lombards to the orthodox faith was brought about by the policy of Gregory the Great and the zeal of Theodolinda, wife of Authari and subsequently of his successor, Agilulf (590–615). Charlemagne put an end to the Lombard kingdom in 774. The name remains in modern Lombardy. See *Italy.*

Magyars (*mŏd'yŏrz*). This remarkable people are compactly settled in the central part of Hungary, which they invaded at the close of the 9th century. They are strikingly handsome and well developed, their beauty being of an Oriental type with somewhat prominent semi-Tatar cheek bones. Their language, known as Finno-Turki or Finno-Ugric, they have preserved intact for over a thousand years. It is written in Roman letters, with certain distinguishing signs, and is noted for its harmonious vowel sounds. The Magyars are of Tatar descent and are renowned for their passionate patriotism. See *Hungary.*

Malays (*mȧ-lāz'*). A brown-skinned race resembling physically the Mongolians of eastern Asia, but differing from them in language, and now found in the Malay peninsula, the East Indies, the Philippines, and other Pacific islands. Their original home was probably Sumatra. They are of a spirited and warlike disposition, and in the 13th century they controlled an empire with its capital on the Malay peninsula. Europeans and Americans have forced them to give up piracy, and they are now separate tribes with little unity. The Malays of the forests are superior craftsmen, and they are notable for their sense of loyalty and honor.

Manchus (*măn-chōōz'*). The Tatar people who overran China in the 12th century and again in the 17th, establishing the dynasty which ruled the country until the establishment of the republic in 1912. The queue was formerly a symbol of the subjection of the Chinese to the Manchus. They are now a small minority in China. See *China, Chinese.*

Maoris (*mä'ô-rĭz*). The natives of New Zealand, who probably displaced a still earlier people when they migrated from their own early home, which their tradition says was Hawaiki, perhaps Hawaii or Samoa. They are tall of stature, vigorous, and athletic, and are ranked among the bravest and most warlike peoples of the earth. They are noted for their marvelous wood carving, their elaborate tattooing, and their poetic nature lore. Their religious hymns of great beauty and antiquity have been translated by many eminent anthologists. Most of the Maoris now profess the Christian religion, but they have always resisted British rule over them. Numbers of them fought side by side with the Allies in the great World War. See *New Zealand, Polynesians.*

Mayas (*mä'yäz*). A group of tribes living in Mexico. They developed a high stage of civilization, which was already in its decline at the time of the invasion of the Spaniards.

They built large cities and durable buildings, including temples, market places, palaces, and ball courts. They also constructed paved highways and artificial reservoirs to conserve water for use during the dry season. The structure of their language was simple, and their speech has shown great vitality in competition with European languages. They had a system of writing which is the only known example of that stage of language development in which signs for objects or for ideas are being replaced by signs to represent sounds. It was in use long before the beginning of the Christian era. These remarkable people had devised a system of chronology so accurate that no one day could be confused with another over a period of 370,000 years. Their calendar was perfected on December 10, 580 B. C. on the basis of records begun on August 6, 613 B. C. It assigned 3373 B. C. as the zero year, that is, as the beginning of the world's past. It was used for 2000 years up to the time of the Spanish conquest of Central America.

Medes (*mēdz*). See *Persia.*

Mongolians (*mŏng-gō'lĭ-ănz*). The name applied to the inhabitants of eastern and northern Asia. This race includes the Mongols, natives of Mongolia, and the Chinese, Japanese, Burmese, Tatars, and Turks. Closely related to these are the Magyars, Finns, and Lapps of Europe.

Mongols (*mŏng'gōlz*). The natives of Mongolia, a country of Asia, since the 17th century tributary to China, lying between that country and Siberia and extending from eastern Turkestan to Manchuria. Cattle raising and transportation of goods are their chief occupations. The most important tribe is that of the Khalkhas in northern Mongolia. Within the limits of the districts into which their country is divided, they are nomads, moving about in search of pastures for their herds, and living in *yourtes*, or circular tents of felt laid over a light framework. Among their marriage customs, the primitive capturing of the wife still persists. In history, the one great performance of the Mongols was the conquering of an empire, in the 13th century, which reached from northern China into Russia. Their leader was Jenghis Khan, "the most powerful prince." About 1259 Kublai Khan made Peking his capital. Marco Polo, the celebrated Venetian traveler, when but a boy of 17, was received into favor by the emperor and was employed by him (1275–92) on important missions throughout various parts of the empire. See *China.*

Moors (*mo͞orz*). The people of Morocco, where the Arab conquerors of the 7th century mixed with the natives of the Roman province of Mauretania. The Spaniards called the invaders of Spain in the 8th century, Moors, and the term was loosely extended to all Mohammedans of northern Africa. See *Morocco, Spain.*

Moravians (*mô-rā'vĭ-ănz*). A Slavic people who in the 6th century displaced Germanic tribes in the valley of the Morava river, south of Silesia. In the mild climate of their district, they have a wide variety of agricultural products, and their flocks produce a fine quality of wool. In religion they are mostly Roman Catholic. After the World War they were included in the republic of Czechoslovakia. See *Moravia, Hussites.*

Negritos (*nē-grē'tōz*). The name means "little negroes." It was given by the Spaniards to the pygmy negroid race of the Philippines. They are probably the aboriginal people of these islands. Other groups of them are found in the Andaman islands and on the Malay peninsula. They are usually about 4 feet, 6 inches in height, their skin is a very dark, coppery brown, and their hair thick and bushy. They wear only a girdle about the waist. Their intelligence is of a very low grade, and their habits are those of nomad savages. See *Filipinos.*

Negroes. The name generally applied to the variety of the human race characterized by dark skin and woolly hair. In the United States, the term includes all persons with any trace of Negro blood. These people are most numerous in Africa, but are also widely dispersed over the world. The wide distribution of Negroes throughout the world is due chiefly to the prevalence of the slave trade in both ancient and modern times.

The transportation of Negro slaves to America began with the early voyages of Spanish explorers. The greater number of these slaves were brought from all parts of Africa, although some were trained artisans and agriculturists from Spain. Negroes accompanied the Spanish expeditions into western America, and it is said that one, Estevancio, led the first party of Spaniards into the district now included in the state of Arizona. There is a substantial percentage of Negro blood in the population of Brazil.

In the population of the independent state of Ethiopia there is a strong Negro element, but the only African state ruled by Negroes is Liberia. In the New World is the Negro republic of Haiti. The most highly civilized and progressive group of Negroes are those of the United States. With few exceptions, they are the descendants of slaves held in the various states before the Civil War.

The first Negroes were brought to Virginia in 1619. By gradual steps, in the course of the 17th century, Negro slavery became a recognized institution in the American colonies. In 1710, there were in the United States about 750,000 Negroes, of whom 60,000 were free; in 1860, about 4,400,000, of whom about 490,000 were free; in 1940, 12,865,518, an increase of 8.2 per cent from 1930.

The notable progress of the American Negroes since the Civil War may be judged by the development of means and methods of education among them and by their economic advance. Before the war, some public and private schools for Negroes had been established. In 1861, the foundations of the great Hampton Institute were laid by the American Missionary Association. Emancipation, however, precipitated a crisis, which was rendered yet more serious by the constitutional amendments which gave citizenship and suffrage to the Negro. Soon after the close of the war, various individuals, churches, and other agencies, directed and financed by whites, attacked the problem.

The greatest service of the schools thus established was to start the Negro upon the way to self-help by preparing Negro teachers and other leaders. At the present time, with the aid of various educational foundations for the support of both public and private schools, Negroes and whites are co-operating in an increasing number of enterprises to meet the diverse needs of the colored people. The greatest leader who has yet arisen among the Negroes themselves was Booker T. Washington.

In business and industry, progress has been equally substantial. Negroes engaged in business have increased from about 4000 at the close of the Civil War to upwards of 70,000, doing an annual business of 1½ billion dollars. Some 50 Negro banks have aggregate resources exceeding 20 million dollars. Property owned by Negroes is estimated at more than 2 billion dollars. The largest predominantly Negro communities in the United States include the Negro section of Chicago and Harlem in New York City.

Negroes have entered all the professions. More than 150 hospitals and training schools for nurses are operated for colored people, mostly controlled and directed by Negroes. Some 400 periodicals are published by and for the colored race in the United States. During World War II, discrimination in employment and industrial training on account of color was forbidden by order of President Roosevelt.

The American Negro has made distinct contributions to modern art, most noticeably in music. The Spiritual in sacred music and the so-called ragtime, blues, and jazz, in secular music, trace their origin to the colored race. In poetry also, as well as in sculpture, drama, painting, and general literature, Negro artists of distinction have arisen.

Normans, Northmen, or **Norsemen.** The sea rovers from Scandinavia who, in the early middle ages, ravaged the coasts of England, Germany, and France and established themselves in various parts of western Europe and Russia. They were called Danes in England, where they gained a foothold in the 9th century, after having made settlements in Ireland. In the 11th century, Canute and two successors ruled England for about 25 years.

Meanwhile, other bands had settled in northern France and compelled the French king to give his daughter in marriage to Rollo, their chieftain. Rollo embraced Christianity and became Robert, first duke of Normandy. The name Normans is usually restricted to these settlers in France, who assimilated the culture, language, religion, and manners of the Frankish kingdom. William, duke of Normandy, led the Normans into England in 1066. Mention should be made also of the expeditions of Leif and other Norsemen to the American coast early in the 11th century.

In 1059 Robert Guiscard, a Norman noble, became duke of Apulia and Calabria in Italy, and his brother Roger conquered Sicily. In the 12th century the Norman kingdom of Sicily attained great importance, especially in connection with the Crusades.

The vikings of the West seem to have been mostly Danes and Norwegians. The Swedish Norsemen directed their energies toward the eastern Baltic lands. Rurik founded a kingdom at Novgorod about 862, and bodies of Norsemen, united with their Slavic subjects, even penetrated Persia. They frequently menaced the Byzantine capital, Constantinople. Other bands of these Scandinavian warriors are said to have served in the bodyguard of Byzantine emperors from the 9th to the 12th century. See *England*, page 430a; *Normandy*, page 571; *Russia*, page 504c.

Parsis, or **Parsees** (*pär'sēz*). The modern followers of Zoroastrianism, which was the ancient religion of Persia. They are popularly called "fire worshipers," but to this designation they strongly object, since the fire to them is simply one of the emblems of the power of Ormuzd. Their beliefs have changed somewhat since ancient times, but they are still scrupulously careful about purification. The elements, earth, fire, water, must not be defiled by dead matter. Hence they expose their dead on *dakhmas*, or "towers of silence," to be devoured by vultures. They are believers in one god and in a life after death.

After the Mohammedan invasion of Persia in the 7th century, several bands of Zoroastrians emigrated to India, and from these have sprung the Parsi communities of present day India. They are most numerous in the vicinity of Bombay. Almost all are well to do. They are leaders among Oriental peoples in education, and their community life is notable for its high moral character.

Philistines (*fĭ-lĭs'tĭnz*). A non-Semitic people who are believed to have come originally from Crete. They settled in Palestine and waged more or less continuous warfare with the Israelites for several centuries.

Picts. The early inhabitants of the northern part of Great Britain. They were called Caledonians by the Romans, the name Picts being given later because of their custom of painting the skin. The origin of this people is uncertain. They carried on continual warfare with the Romans, who built long walls to keep them out of the southern provinces. In the 7th century the Saxons came into conflict with them. After their conversion to Christianity, their king, Angus MacFergus, ruled all Scotland for a period in the early part of the 8th century. About the beginning of the 9th century, they disappeared as a separate people, leaving no literature and but scanty traces of their language.

Polynesians. The name applied to the brown race whose principal habitat includes the most easterly of the three groups of Pacific islands. Their physical characteristics, as well as their language, distinctly mark them off from the Malays and other races of the southern Pacific region. In stature they are reckoned by many authorities as the tallest people in the world, with an average height of 5 feet, 10 inches. They are well proportioned; their features are regular and often of a distinct beauty; their eyes are invariably black their hair, black or dark brown and either smooth or curly. In personal habits they are cleanly, neat, and orderly. Where they have not adopted European dress, the men wear a loin cloth, while the women's dress consists of a petticoat of leaves and, sometimes, a covering for the shoulders.

The temperament of the Polynesians varies from apathetic, under the enervating conditions of climate in most of the islands, to a more energetic type in regions where harder conditions prevail. Essentially they are a remarkably cheerful race. They possess a well developed body of historic legends of which their orators make lavish and impressive use.

Ethnologists now believe that the earliest home of this race was in some part of southern Asia, whence they migrated to the East Indian islands. They were skillful shipbuilders and navigators, and, when hard pressed by a Malay migration, they sought new homes farther to the west. Some scholars suggest that they are of Aryan stock, but this point is still in dispute. Polynesian traditions indicate that the migration to the Pacific islands took place about the beginning of the Christian era, and suggest that the Polynesians made their home first in Samoa.

Since their first contact with Europeans, a variety of causes has brought about a great decrease in their numbers. Of late years, however, this decimation seems to have been checked, and it appears not improbable that many groups of the Polynesians will make marked progress in civilization. See *Hawaii*, *Maoris*, *Samoans*.

Pygmies (*pĭg'mĭz*). Human tribes among whom the average height of males is regularly not more than 4 feet, 11 inches are called pygmies. The existence of such tribes was alluded to by Homer and affirmed by Herodotus, but was treated for many centuries as a myth. Du Chaillu, the French explorer, early in the 18th century, reported finding them on the west coast of Africa, and Stanley encountered them on his journey in 1887–89. He reported at least two distinct physical types, one more highly developed in the human scale than the other. A pygmy boy and girl joined his expedition as servants. Later explorers, engineers, and traders in Central Africa have found these little people in the jungles. Those that have been most closely observed are a woolly-haired people of Negro features and a dark olive skin. They are well proportioned and have remarkable muscular development. The women average about 3 feet, 11 inches in height, and the men range from 3 to 6 inches taller. They are a very shy folk, living in small, leaf-covered huts in the jungles around the villages of the larger Bantu Negroes. Their weapons are bows and arrows. When they hunt, they tip these arrows with a paralyzing poison, so that the small birds and animals which they shoot may be captured. This game they trade to the larger tribes for vegetables and fruit.

Other so-called pygmy tribes are found in the Malay peninsula and the East Indies, the Philippines, and India, but most of these are of mixed breeds and vary greatly in height.

Rumanians (*rōō-mā'nĭ-ănz*). A people of mixed race who, since the 12th century, have occupied the territory north of the lower Danube and the slopes of the Transylvanian Alps. Most of them now live in the kingdom of Rumania, although there are scattered communities throughout the Balkans. They speak a Romance language which closely resembles the Latin. Scholars now believe that the Roman colonists of the Province of Dacia, established along the lower Danube by Trajan, withdrew to the Illyrian coast before the inroads of barbarians, but later re-entered the Danube country, preserving their Latin speech in spite of mingling with Slavic, Greek, and Turkish peoples. See *Rumania*.

Ruthenians (*rōō-thē'nĭ-ănz*). A group of Slavic tribes inhabiting eastern Galicia and Bukowina on the eastern slope of the Carpathian mountains. They belong by race to the "Little Russians" of the Ukraine. Their name is a German form of Ukrainians. For centuries they were the victims of Russian, Polish, and Austrian oppression, the peasants being reduced to a wretched state of serfdom.

Samoans (*sȧ-mō'ănz*). The Polynesian inhabitants of the Samoan Islands in the South Pacific. They are recognized as the best representatives of the remarkable and interesting Polynesian race, and their traditions hold that these islands were the center from which the race spread to other Pacific islands. The Samoans have long been famous as sailors and boat builders, and they have many legends and tales of great beauty and interest. They are a folk of splendid physical build, showing marked likenesses to the Caucasian type. Practically all are now Christians, and they have shown keen appreciation of the education offered by the mission schools. See *Polynesians*.

Saracens (*săr'ȧ-sĕnz*). A name derived from an Arabic word meaning "rise." It was applied in the 1st century A. D. to a tribe in northwestern Arabia. Later, the name was used by medieval writers to designate all Mohammedans.

Saxons. A Germanic people first heard of in the 2d century as inhabiting what is now southern Denmark. They migrated southward, subdued all northwestern Germany, and invaded the Roman Empire. In the 5th century they invaded Normandy, and, in that and the next century, many settled in England. The Saxon strain is very prominent in the modern population both of Germany and of England.

Scots or **Scotch.** Scotland takes its name from a group of Gaelic invaders, called Scots or Dalriads, who came from Ireland in the 3d or the 4th century A. D. The strongest of the earlier inhabitants were the Picts, also a Celtic people. The Angles, or English, early established a kingdom in southern Scotland, and Scandinavian immigrants were mingled with these people of the Lowlands as well as with the Highlanders. In many parts of North and West Scotland, known as the Highlands, a Gaelic tongue is spoken; the dialect of the South and East Lowlands is a mixture of English and Scandinavian speech. See *Picts*; also *Scotland*, page 438c.

Scythians (*sĭth'ĭ-ănz*). An ancient nomadic warrior people, famous as horsemen and bowmen, who inhabited what is now southwestern Russia. Herodotus and other Greek writers describe this wandering tribe and their life in tent-covered wagons. They were conquered by neighboring tribes, and disappeared from European history in the 2d century B. C. The name Scythian was later used loosely for any northern and central Asiatic tribes.

Semites (*sĕm'īts*). A dark-skinned branch of the Caucasian race. It includes the Jews and the Arabians among modern peoples and, among ancient nations, the Assyrians and the Phœnicians. The name is so applied because of the traditional belief, without historical foundation, that this race was descended from Noah's son Shem.

Serbians, or **Serbs.** The group of southern Slavic peoples who occupy the former kingdom of Serbia and neighboring lands of Croatia, Bosnia, and Dalmatia. They joined with the Croats and Slovenes in 1918 to from the

Kingdom of the Serbs, Croats, and Slovenes (Yugoslavia). The term Serbo-Croatian is frequently used to include the Serbs and Croats, who differ only slightly in language. The Croats are Roman Catholics, while the Serbs are mostly of the Greek Catholic faith. An interesting national characteristic of the Serbs is the love of all classes for their legends, ballads, and romances about old national heroes. See *Croatians, Jugoslavia.*

Serbo-Croatian (*sẽr'bô-krô-ā'shăn*). The name applied to the Slavic language which, with slight variations, is common to the Serbs and Croats. The Croats use the Latin alphabet, while the Serbs use the Cyrillic, a modified and enlarged form of the Greek, adapted to sounds of the Slavic speech. The term is used also to designate the two peoples, who are of the same stock, although they were separated politically for centuries until united in 1918 in the Slavic state of Jugoslavia, known officially until 1929 as the Kingdom of the Serbs, Croats, and Slovenes.

Sicilians (*sĭ-sĭl'ĭ-ănz*). The earliest known inhabitants of Sicily were the Siculi, who gave their name to the island. In historic times, Phœnicians, Greeks, Romans, Saracens, Normans, Germans, French, and Italians have at different times ruled and colonized Sicily. The Sicilians have long had an unenviable reputation for turbulence and violence, a temper probably the result of centuries of backward economic and social conditions due to the repeated struggles of many nations for possession of the island.

Singhalese, Cingalese (*sĭng'gȧ-lēz'*) or **Ceylonese** (*sē'lŏn-ēz'*). Descendants of immigrants to Ceylon, in the 6th century B. C., from Hindustan, now represented in the island by two groups. The Singhalese of the coast are a mild-mannered race. In stature they are below middle size, their features are rather finely molded, and their skin is of a light or dark bronze hue. The men wear their long, black hair fastened on top of the head with a shell comb. The Singhalese of the interior are a more handsome, manly race of higher intelligence. The classical writings of the Singhalese are in Pali or Sanskrit; their colloquial language is Aryan, closely related to Pali, but mixed with many foreign words. In religion, they are divided between Buddhism, Brahmanism, and Christianity.

Slavs (*slävz*). The name of the group of Aryan peoples to be found in eastern and central Europe. Their early home seems to have been along the Baltic, northeast of the Carpathian mountains. From this district, two principal migrations took place. One movement toward the south and west, beginning in the 4th century, carried the Slavs into Bohemia and western Hungary, across the Danube, and as far as the shores of the Adriatic. A little later, other tribes moved in a northeasterly direction, and they became the nucleus of the Russian people. The group of Slavic peoples now includes the Russians, Bulgarians, Serbians, Croatians, Slovenians, Czechs (Bohemians and Moravians), Slovaks, and Poles. The origin of the name Slav is not known. The word slave is said to have come into use when the Germans sold Slavonic captives in the markets. Of the primitive culture of the Slavs, we have but scanty information. Christianity made rapid progress among them, and traces of their pagan religion were all but obliterated. Their mythology of lesser deities and spirits was, however, very full and rich. The social organization of the early Slavs, who were a peaceful, agricultural people, was patriarchal. This system later merged into a type of communal government.

Slovaks (*slô-văks'*). The Slavic people who for several centuries maintained an independent kingdom on the south side of the Carpathians and in the 9th century formed the basis of the Moravian state. Conquered by the Magyars, many of them became scattered over Hungary. After the World War they united with the Czechs in the republic of Czechoslovakia. The Slovak dialect possesses numerous very beautiful popular songs, many of which have been collected and published. See *Czechs, Czechoslovakia.*

Slovenians (*slô-vē'nĭ-ănz*) or **Slovenes** (*slô-vēnz'*). The Slavic people who, from the 6th century, have lived in the southern districts of the former Austrian empire, reaching to the Adriatic. Most of them have been included in the new state of Jugoslavia. They possess in their language some of the earliest Slavic writings. Their name is a survival of the ancient name for Slavs, and probably means "speaking," or "those who speak," as the ancient Slavs called foreigners "the dumb," that is, those not speaking the Slavic language.

Sumerians (*sû-mē'rĭ-ănz*). The earliest known occupants of the lower Mesopotamian valley. They were a non-Semitic people who probably came from the north; they developed a high civilization and used the cuneiform system of writing. They were later absorbed by the Semitic peoples who founded the Babylonian state. The word Sumerian is thought to refer to the marshy, "reedy" landscape of the country, which is called Shinar in the Bible.

Syrians (*sĭr'ĭ-ănz*). The people of ancient Syria were mainly of the Semitic race, the Semite stock having succeeded in absorbing those stocks which preceded or came later among them, such as the Philistines and the Hittites. The modern Syrians are, for the most part, descendants of the ancient Syrians, Arabs, Turks, Greeks, and Jews, with an admixture of Romans and Christian crusaders. They are generally an intelligent people with a marked power of appropriating foreign ideas. The old enterprising Phœnician spirit is strong among the people of the north Syrian coast. Many Syrian merchants, settled in the cities of Europe and America, are zealous in promoting the trade and industry of their native land.

Tatars (*tä'tȧrz*) or **Tartars** (*tär'tȧrz*). The true Tatars appear to have been a tribe of Mongols who lived in the 9th century along the upper Amur river in Asia. They later formed part of the horde led by Jenghis Khan, and the name came to be applied to all Mongols. Their fierceness is said to have given rise to the notion that they came from Tartarus, or hell; hence the familiar name for them, Tartars. See *China*, page 466d; *Russia*, page 504d.

Toltecs (*tŏl'tĕks*). An Indian tribe that is believed to have occupied parts of central Mexico before the coming of the Aztecs, or from the 7th to the 11th century. Probably they came from the country farther north, and after being driven from Mexico some of them may have settled in Guatemala. Their history is legendary, some ethnologists denying that they ever existed. Archeologists apply the term more generally to the race whose civilization preceded the Mayas. See *Mexico*, page 458d; *Mayas*, page 520.

Vandals (*văn'dălz*). A people closely related to the Goths, who, during the first four Christian centuries, moved southward from their early home along the southern shore of the Baltic Sea, then westward into Gaul. They swept through Spain in the 5th century and established a kingdom in northern Africa, thence invading Italy. They were overthrown in 534 by the troops of Justinian, under Belisarius. Later, they were converted from Arianism to the orthodox Catholic faith. Their reputed cruelty and destructive methods in warfare gave us the word vandal. See *Rome*, page 503a.

Visigoths (*vĭz'ĭ-gŏths*). The West Goths, who, at the first approach of the Huns in the Danube valley in the 4th century, were allowed by the Romans to settle in Roman territory south of the Danube. Having learned their power in battle with the Roman legions, they moved westward through Greece to the valley of the Po. In 410 they conquered and plundered the city of Rome, sparing the churches at the command of Alaric, their young leader. After his death in southern Italy, they moved into Gaul and northern Spain, founding a Visigothic kingdom with its capital at Toulouse. Under their great king Theodoric, they aided in defeating Attila and the Huns in 451. But the Franks drove them from Gaul in 507. They re-established themselves in Spain, with a capital at Toledo. When the Arabs invaded and seized the greater part of Spain in the 8th century, the Visigoths retired to the mountains in Asturia and Galicia, whence their descendants issued to drive out the Arabs and to found the modern states of Spain and Portugal. See *Rome, Spain.*

Walloons (*wŏ-lōōnz'*). The modern descendants of the ancient Belgæ mentioned by Cæsar, occupying the southern part of Belgium and some districts in France. Their mother tongue is a French dialect. The name Walloons, which means "strangers," was given them by the Dutch, when in 1567 large numbers of the Protestant population fled to Holland. From there, a company of them emigrated to America in 1624, settling on the Hudson, near Albany, and on the Delaware, near Gloucester, N. J., the first white people to till the soil of New Netherlands. The Walloons resemble the French in physical type; they are more vivacious and industrious than their northern neighbors, the Flemish, but not so conspicuous for artistic works. See *Belgians, Belgium.*

Welsh. The Celtic people of Wales. They are the descendants of the Brythonic Celts who occupied Britain when the Anglo-Saxons entered the island. They are most closely related to the Celtic people of Brittany. See *Bretons, Wales.*

Zulus (*zōō'lōōz*). The remarkable Kafir tribes who now occupy a district in the northeast part of Natal, South Africa. They are chiefly herdsmen, but they also raise crops of millet, corn, sweet potatoes, and tobacco. They are of fine physical build and are formidable soldiers. Their dwellings are thatched and plastered huts of beehive form, which they arrange in a circular group, or kraal, with their cattle in the center. At the beginning of the 19th century, they controlled, by a splendid military organization, a large part of southeast Africa, and they maintained their independence until after their conflicts with the British in 1883-84. In 1887 the British annexed all their territory.

WORLD WAR I

The immediate occasion of the World War of 1914–18 was the assassination of a Habsburg prince in a remote city of Austria-Hungary, but the real causes lay far deeper, and reached far back into the past. The century-long rivalry of French and Germans, the aspirations of united Germany for a position as a world power, her fear of the pressure of the Russian glacier, ever crowding west and south, the commercial rivalry of Great Britain and Germany, the unrest of the smaller states and of racial minorities,—all had contributed to set up stresses and strains which were sure to fracture the thin crust of international peace when the occasion arose.

There had been other world wars, such as the Seven Years' war of 1756–63, or the Napoleonic wars, but in sheer magnitude the war of 1914–18 dwarfed all that had gone before. In the end it embattled twenty-eight nations, embracing more than nine-tenths of the entire population of the globe.

German Pre-War Policy. Racial rivalry was one of the causes of the war, and in its earliest phase the conflict was a clash of Pan-German and Pan-Slavic aspirations in the region of the Balkans. But the World War was more than a conflict of Teuton and Slav. Germany, united under the house of Hohenzollern and allied to the Habsburg empire of Austria-Hungary, controlled Central Europe. The Germans had gained that position by war, and it was natural that they should think that war was a paying business. Yet, mighty as was Germany's power, the Germans were not content with their position in the world. To spread German "kultur" and German rule became the ardent desire of millions of Germans. Many writers emphasized Germany's need for expansion to furnish an outlet for German population and energies. Not a few openly proclaimed that this expansion must be obtained by conquest. Great efforts even were made to prevent German emigrants to other countries forgetting their loyalty to their Fatherland.

Alliances with other powers were builded to strengthen the German position. The Dual Alliance of 1879 with Austria-Hungary was broadened in 1882 into the Triple Alliance by the inclusion of Italy. Unfortunately Bismarck's policy of a good understanding with Russia was neglected. Much attention was paid to cultivating friendly relations with Turkey, and this policy proved fruitful. Geographical factors counted here. Germany in a general war would be exposed to attack from both east and west. Whether for attack or for defense, she must be ready to strike hard and swiftly in either direction. For this reason the German army must be made—and was made—the strongest in Europe.

French and German Antagonism. It had been a principle of French policy since Louis XIV to keep Germany disunited and helpless; and German particularism and rivalries had helped her opponents. In the Franco-Prussian war of 1870–71 Germany had become united and had inflicted a humiliating defeat on France. Ever since that conflict her people had dreamed of revenge and of regaining their lost provinces of Alsace-Lorraine. The increasing population of Germany and the static population of France was also making Germany increasingly dangerous should she, as some Germans wished, attack France again. France needed allies; hence the Dual Alliance.

Germany and Great Britain. In the last analysis, the rivalry that had developed between these two peoples arose out of the fact that one was already what the other wished to become. The British had entered early into the work of Empire building, and had arrived. The Germans entered the race very late. Having already acquired all that she desired, Great Britain coveted nothing that Germany possessed, but in course of time she came to have an uneasy feeling that Germany was becoming a menace to her position in the world. The development of German industry was cutting into British markets; the increase of her commerce and merchant marine was making her a dangerous rival in world trade. The open declarations of hostility by some Germans tended to deepen British distrust. Worst of all was the increase in the German navy. For Great Britain, control of the sea-routes by her own navy was vital; Germany, Great Britain thought, was under no such necessity. Great Britain increased her navy accordingly.

Fear of Germany had already brought about an important diplomatic revolution. For centuries Great Britain and France had been rivals, but common dread of Germany led, about 1904, to the forming of the *Entente Cordiale* between the two nations. In 1891, as a makeweight against the Triple Alliance, France and Russia had formed the Dual Alliance. Differences between Great Britain and Russia were now composed, for Germany seemed to have become a greater danger to the Empire than Russia, and the *Entente Cordiale* was broadened into the Triple Entente. The Entente powers said their purpose was purely defensive; the Germans called it an "encirclement" and grew restive. These alliances meant a balance of power, and to that extent made for peace; on the other hand they made it inevitable that, if war ever began, all would be drawn in.

The Balkan Problem. In 1909, Austria-Hungary, without consulting the other interested powers, annexed Bosnia and Herzegovina, former Turkish provinces over which she had held a protectorate since 1878. These provinces were largely Serb in population, so Austria-Hungary's action was a blow to the desires of the Serbians for national unity. In 1912 and 1913 came the Balkan wars. The result was a great increase in the territory and strength of Serbia, although the creation of Albania cut her off from the Adriatic. Serbia had the sympathy and support of Russia, who had never lost sight of her old desire to control Constantinople (Istanbul) and the Straits. A general European war was narrowly averted by the efforts of Great Britain and Germany, but Teutonic prestige in the Balkans suffered, and the hostility of Austria-Hungary and Serbia increased.

The Immediate Occasion of the War. On June 28, 1914, Archduke Francis Ferdinand, heir apparent to the Habsburg monarchy, and his morganatic wife, were assassinated while on a visit to Sarajevo, the capital of Bosnia. The murderers were Habsburg subjects of Serbian blood. Later investigations showed that the plot had been formed in Serbia by a powerful Pan-Serbian secret society, the Narodna Odbrana, and included some Serbians, one a member of the Serbian general staff. Count Berchtold, the Austrian premier, thought he saw the opportunity to settle scores with Serbia once and for all. The German government rashly promised to support Austria-Hungary, unfortunately without knowing the details or full extent of Berchtold's plans. On July 28 the Austrian government dispatched to Serbia an ultimatum demanding reparation and suppression of the Pan-Serbian movement in a form which meant Austrian intervention in Serbian domestic affairs. An answer was demanded within forty-eight hours.

From the outset the dangerous possibilities of the situation were apparent in the European chancelleries, and the Great Powers, especially England, were at work to prevent war, or at least to localize it. Germany, whose influence at Vienna was the greatest, was hampered by the "blank check" she had already given, and her efforts to restrain Austria came too late. The Serbian reply conceded almost everything, in form, but it made no difference. Austria-Hungary rejected her answer, broke off diplomatic relations, and on the 28th declared war.

THE WORLD WAR IN OUTLINE

Remote Causes: Racial rivalry between Slav and Teuton in Balkans; German ambition for world aggrandizement; interlocking of national interests. Immediate Causes: Extreme Austrian demands on Serbia arising from murder of Archduke Ferdinand; Russian support of Serbia; German support of Austria; French alliance with Russia; German invasion of Belgium; British support of Belgium and France; Japanese alliance with Britain; Turkish, Bulgarian, Italian, and Rumanian hope of advantage; American defense of rights at sea.

	Western Front	Eastern Front	Italy and Balkans	Turkey; Other Regions	High Seas
1914 July			Austrians invade Serbia; defeated.		
Aug.	Germans invade Belgium; Defeat French at Charleroi; British retreat from Mons.	Russians invade Austria, E. Prussia; routed at Tannenberg.		British seize German island colonies; also Togoland.	Brit. victory at Helgoland Bight.
Sept.	First Battle of Marne; Germans retreat to Aisne R.; capture Maubeuge	Russians capture Lemberg; besiege Przemysl; defeated at Masurian Lakes.	Serbs invade Austria; are forced back.	Japanese capture Shantung from Germany.	German submarines sink three British cruisers; one dreadnought.
Oct.	and Antwerp. Battle of Yser. First Battle of Ypres.				
Nov.	Trench warfare begins on Western Front.	Przemysl relieved; again besieged.	Austrians invade Serbia.	Turkey joins Central Powers.	German victory off Coronel, Chile.
Dec.			Austrians capture Belgrade. Austrians expelled from Serbia.	British take S. W. Africa and Cameroons.	British victory at Falkland Islands.
1915 Jan.					British victory at Dogger Bank.
Feb.		Russ. defeated at Masurian Lakes.		Turks routed at Suez.	
Mar.	Battle of Neuve Chapelle.	Russ. take Przemysl.			
Apr.	Second Battle of Ypres; Germans use poison gas.			Allied troops land at Gallipoli.	
May	Zeppelins bomb London.	Battle of Dunajec; Russ. lose 750,000 prisoners.	Italy joins Allies.		*Lusitania* torpedoed by German submarine.
June		Germans take Lemberg, Przemysl, Warsaw, Kovno, Grodno, Vilna.	Battle of Isonzo 1.	British take Imara and An Nasiriya.	
July			Battle of Isonzo 2.		
Aug.				Allied defeat at Gallipoli.	
Sept.	Battles of Loos, Champagne; local Allied gains.				
Oct.			Battle of Isonzo 3. Bulgaria enters war.	British capture Kut-el-Amara.	
Nov.			Battle of Isonzo 4. Serb army routed.	British defeated at Ctesiphon; Allies abandon Gallipoli.	
Dec.					
1916 Jan.				British clear Sinai desert of Turks.	
Feb.	Battle of Verdun begins.			Russ. take Erzerum.	
Mar.		Russians repulsed at Lake Naroch.	Battle of Isonzo 5.	British lose Kut.	
Apr.				Russ. take Trebizond.	
May			Battle of Asiago; Austrians capture 45,000 Italians.		Battle of Jutland; German fleet escapes.
June		Battle of Lutzk; Russ. take 400,000 prisoners.			
July	Battle of Somme begins; British gain ground.		Battle of Isonzo 6. Allies retake Monastir.		
Aug.		Rumania joins Allies; invades Austria.	Ital. take Gorizia.		
Sept.	British use tanks.	Rumania invaded; army routed.	Battle of Isonzo 7.		
Oct.	Battle of Verdun ends; French regain lost ground.		Battle of Isonzo 8.		
Nov.		Germans capture Bucharest.	Battle of Isonzo 9.		
1917 Jan.					
Feb.				British retake Kut.	Germans begin unrestricted submarine warfare; U. S. enters war; huge shipping losses by Allies, exceeding 500,000 tons per month.
Mar.	Germans withdraw to Hindenburg line.	Russian Revolution; army weakens.		British capture Bagdad.	
Apr.	Canadians take Vimy Ridge;				
May	French gains in Champagne.		Battle of Isonzo 10.		
June	Battle of Messines.		Greece joins Allies.		
July	3d Battle of Ypres begins. First American troops reach Paris.	"Kerensky off'sive" Russ. line crumbles.			
Aug.		Battle of Marasesti; Rumanians defend positions.			
Sept.			Battle of Isonzo 11.		
Oct.					
Nov.	3d Battle of Ypres ends with British gains. Battle of Cambrai; local British gains.	Russia and Rumania forced to make peace with Central Powers.	Ital. defeated at Caporetto; lose 260,000 prisoners; retreat to Piave R.	British capture Beersheba; Allies take German E. Africa.	
Dec.				Brit. take Jerusalem.	
1918 Jan.	Germans transfer troops from Eastern to Western Front.				Scotland, Norway linked by mine barrage laid by Amer. Navy.
Feb.					
Mar.	Battle of St. Quentin; Germ. take 90,000 prisoners; penetrate Allied lines 38 miles deep.				
Apr.	Battle of Lys; Germans take 30,000 prisoners.				Brit. block sub. bases, Ostend, Zeebrugge.
May	Americans capture Cantigny.				
June	Battle of Soissons-Reims. German drive toward Paris halted near Chateau-Thierry.		Austr. drive over Piave R. checked.		
July	Second Battle of Marne; Allies check Germ. in Champagne; attack; take 30,000 prisoners.				Over 300,000 American troops transported to France in month; over 2,000,000 during War.
Aug.	Battle of Amiens; Allies take 40,000 prisoners. Battle of Bapaume-Peronne; Allies take 35,000 prisoners.				
Sept.	Brit. break Hindenburg line; take 36,000 pris. Amer. take St. Mihiel, 16,000 prisoners. Battle of Meuse-Argonne; Amer. break Germ. line.		Allies rout Bulgarian army.	Brit. destroy Turkish armies in Palestine, Mesopotamia; capture Damascus, Mosul.	
Oct.	French offensive on whole front; Belgians recover large territory; take 20,000 prisoners.		Battle of Vittorio Veneto; Ital. rout Austrians; capture over 300,000.		
Nov.	General Allied advance; Americans enter Sedan. Armistice signed, November 11.				German fleet surrenders.

Now the effect of the alliances began to appear. Along with it came the influence of the general staffs in Russia, Germany, and France, none of whom wished to lose the advantage of speedy mobilization. But mobilization meant war. Russian interests could not allow Serbia to be crushed. On July 26 she began premobilization measures; on July 29 she mobilized against Austria-Hungary. Germany could not allow Austria-Hungary to be defeated. On July 31, she demanded that Russia cease her war preparations and peremptorily asked France to state her position. On August 1, Germany declared war against Russia, and France ordered mobilization. On August 3 Germany declared war against France. On August 2 Sir Edward Grey assured France of the assistance of the British fleet in the North Sea and the Channel.

British doubts were resolved by the German invasion of Belgium. German military strategy had long planned, in the event of a war on two fronts, an overwhelming attack upon France before Russia could mobilize. But the Franco-German frontier was strongly protected by nature and art, and military opinion had long foreshadowed a movement through Belgium by one side or the other. Belgium's neutrality had been guaranteed by treaties, but the German government pleaded a "state of necessity." On August 2 they demanded the right to cross Belgium, alleging that France intended to march through the country, and offering guarantees and indemnity. Belgium replied (August 3) that she would defend her neutrality, and King Albert appealed for aid to Great Britain.

On August 4 Sir Edward Grey sent an ultimatum to Berlin demanding that Germany should immediately promise to respect the neutrality of Belgium. The German chancellor Bethman-Hollweg expressed regret that Great Britain should go to war "just for a word . . . just for a scrap of paper," but he refused to give the promise.

Comparison of the Combatants. In area the Entente Powers were very much superior to the Central Powers; in population and wealth about double. On land, Germany had an army of 5,400,000, war strength, splendidly organized; the Russian army was about equal, but poorly organized; the French, somewhat less but on a par with Germany. Austria-Hungary's army of 3,600,000 was much less efficient than Germany's. The armies of the smaller powers were insignificant in comparison. Great Britain's regular army amounted to 137,000 men, besides territorials and colonial forces. The Central Powers possessed an immense military advantage because their position, while it exposed them to attack on two sides, enabled them to fight on interior lines.

The German navy was greatly superior to the combined forces of France and Russia, but Great Britain brought into the conflict the mightiest fleet ever built up to that time. For many years it had been her policy to maintain a navy superior to that which any two powers combined could bring against her. Furthermore the combined fleets of France and Russia were much superior to that of Austria-Hungary, but the Russian fleets were bottled up in the Baltic and Black Sea.

The Invasion of Belgium and France. The best chance for the Central Powers to win was to make the war a short one, getting a decision before the superior naval strength of the Allies and the inevitable blockade could do their work. The German high command, therefore, planned to throw an immense army against France through Belgium and Luxemburg, the latter also a neutral state, and crush her before Russia could be ready. To the Austro-Hungarian forces and to a few German army corps was left the task of holding the eastern front.

The first German troops to enter Belgium crossed the frontier on August 3. Their objective was the city of Liége, whose forts commanded the railway lines that must be used in any invasion of France from the northeast. The German heavy artillery broke the ring of forts, and Liége fell on the 7th. The Germans pushed on to the heart of Belgium. Brussels was captured on the 20th and the main Belgian army moved north to defend Antwerp. Detaching a small force to keep the Belgians in check, the main German army moved south to the French frontier.

The French meanwhile had attempted a generally unsuccessful invasion of Alsace and Lorraine. The strength of the movement through Belgium had been underestimated by General Joffre, the French commander in chief, and the forces along the Belgian border were inadequate, though reinforced by two British army corps under the command of Field Marshall Sir John French. The defenses of Namur were crushed by the German 42-centimeter howitzers, and by the 23d of August the invaders had won control of the passages over the Meuse and Sambre.

The French around Charleroi were forced back. The little British army around Mons held back the German right wing under General von Kluck until the 24th. Then, outnumbered and outflanked, the corps commanders, Generals Haig and Smith-Dorrien, began a stubborn retreat. The Germans pursued with unprecedented rapidity, making use of motor transport.

On August 27 it was announced that the French government had been reconstituted on a war basis. General Galliéni was appointed governor of Paris, and preparations for a siege were hurriedly made. On the 30th a German airplane dropped bombs upon the city. The government was hastily removed to Bordeaux, and a large part of the civil population fled, but French morale continued good.

Meanwhile the French and British armies on the northern front fell back southward, pivoting on the great fortress of Verdun—swinging back upon Paris like a door. On the 17th the German right was within 17 miles of Paris, but, instead of stopping to besiege the city, the Germans turned southeastward after their true objective, the retreating Allied armies.

First Battle of the Marne. The French retreat had been calculated strategy on the part of General Joffre, who was determined to fight the decisive battle on ground of his own choosing. Von Kluck's movement to the southeast (ordered by von Moltke, the commander in chief) had exposed his right flank to an attack from Paris. Urged by Galliéni, Joffre now halted his retreat, and, on September 5, the Allied armies, on a front of 180 miles from Paris to Verdun, turned upon the invaders and began the battle of the Marne. The French efforts were directed to defeating and rolling up the German right wing under von Kluck, which was now over-extended, and had been weakened by the withdrawal of troops for the eastern front; that of the Germans, to breaking through the French center. In defending his exposed flank against Galliéni's attack (at a critical moment, that general commandeered all the taxicabs in Paris to bring out his reserve) von Kluck opened a gap between the First and Second armies. The French broke through, and the Germans were forced to retreat. The battle of the Marne stopped the first German drive, and, as the event proved, decided the war. The German retreat was skillfully conducted, with small losses, and their army now took position behind the river Aisne.

The fighting now moved north. The Germans had already taken Maubeuge; they now attacked Antwerp. The "Big Bertha's" (42-centimeter howitzers) smashed through the defenses, and on October 9 the city surrendered. Their next move was toward Dunkirk and Calais. They were opposed by a mixed force of British and colonial troops, the remains of the Belgian army under King Albert, and French reinforcements, the whole commanded by General Ferdinand Foch. The Allies won this "race to the sea" by a narrow margin. When, after six weeks of desperate fighting the battle died down, they still held a small corner of southwestern Belgium.

The battle in the west now resolved itself into a warfare of trenches, each side holding a front of more than 400 miles from Switzerland to the North Sea. Until almost the end of the war, this condition of stalemate was to continue.

First Battles on the Eastern Fronts. Meanwhile, great events had been taking place on the eastern front. Although the main Teutonic effort had been in the west, the Austro-Hungarians massed about a million men in Galicia and undertook an invasion of Poland from the southwest.

But the Russians managed to mobilize their forces more rapidly than had generally been considered possible. Under the skilled generalship of the Russian commander in chief, the grand duke Nicholas, immense forces were hurled against the Austrians in Galicia, while by way of diversion in favor of hard-pressed France, two armies totaling about 250,000 men undertook an invasion of East Prussia.

For a time the Russians carried all before them. The Germans were defeated at Gumbinnen, and the Russians ravaged the country. To hold the Russians in check, several army corps were hastily detached from the western front and were hurried to meet the Muscovites. This was a serious military blunder, since the presence of these troops on the Marne might have changed the result.

To command the German forces in East Prussia a new general was selected, General Paul von Hindenburg, a veteran of the wars of 1866 and 1870. The new leader had made a careful study of the country which he was now called upon to defend, and he enjoyed the assistance of a capable chief of staff, General von Ludendorff. On August 26 began what is generally known as the battle of Tannenberg. Von Hindenburg's plan was masterly, resembling that of Hannibal at Cannæ. After four days of fighting, the Russians attempted to retreat, but they were hopelessly involved in a labyrinth of lakes and swamps, and their army was almost annihilated.

Meanwhile a vast and complicated conflict was being fought out in southern Poland and Galicia. Here the outnumbered Austro-Hungarians were badly defeated. Lemberg was captured; by September 16 the Russians claimed to have taken 250,000 prisoners, besides immense quantities of supplies and cannon. Siege was laid to Przemysl, and Hungary was in danger.

The blow dealt Austria-Hungary at this time was a staggering one and might have proved fatal had not the Germans rendered aid. Von Hindenburg advanced through Silesia into Poland, while the Austrians moving forward from Krakow succeeded in raising the siege of Przemysl. By a sudden dash the Germans almost captured Warsaw. Again assuming the offensive, the Russians drove von Hindenburg back toward Silesia and the Austrians to Krakow and again laid siege to Przemysl. To effect a diversion in behalf of their western allies, the Russians also attempted a new invasion of East Prussia. In November another German attempt to take Warsaw failed, and another attempt to relieve Przemysl was foiled. In February 1915 von Hindenburg concentrated about 200,000 men in East Prussia and fell like a thunderbolt upon the inferior Russian army. In this conflict, known as the battle of the Masurian Lakes, the Russians were almost annihilated and suffered losses almost equal to those at Tannenberg. He followed up this victory by an invasion of Poland from the north, but after bitter fighting was repulsed.

Meanwhile the Russians had continued to besiege the great fortress camp of Przemysl in Galicia. Repeated Austrian efforts to relieve the fortress were foiled. On March 22 the fortress surrendered. The prisoners taken numbered over 119,000, the greatest number that had ever surrendered at one time in warfare. The grand duke Nicholas followed up this great victory by a drive designed to capture the passes of the Carpathians.

On the Seas. As was generally expected by naval experts, the control of the high seas was immediately seized by the Entente Allies. German and Austrian merchant ships either sought safety in home ports or in those of neutral powers or were captured by the enemy. In the Mediterranean the Austrian navy took refuge in home ports on the Adriatic, while the German protected cruiser *Breslau* and the giant battle cruiser *Goeben* managed to evade French and British pursuers and steamed up the Dardanelles and through the Sea of Marmora to Istanbul, where they played an important part in bringing Turkey into the war on the Teutonic side.

Just before the war began, the main British battle fleet had assembled at Spithead for maneuvers. The admiralty had held them there and had them ready at the critical moment. The German fleet retired behind the fortified island of Helgoland, and there, protected by mine fields and heavy guns of their land forts, they were safe from attack.

At the outbreak of the war, German naval vessels scattered in various parts of the world at once began to prey upon Allied commerce. The most famous of these, the *Emden*, in three months captured over a score of merchant ships. On November 9, 1914, while attempting to destroy a wireless station on one of the Cocos islands, she was destroyed by a much more powerful Australian cruiser, the *Sydney*.

The largest German fleet outside of European waters was the Pacific squadron, commanded by Admiral von Spee. It consisted of the armored cruisers *Scharnhorst* and *Gneisenau*, the light cruisers *Dresden*, *Nürnberg*, and *Leipzig*, and an armed liner. After destroying a number of allied vessels, they met, off Coronel, Chile, on November 1, a British squadron of two armored cruisers and two lighter ships. The British commander, Vice Admiral Sir Christopher Cradock, decided to give battle. The two British cruisers, the *Good Hope* and *Monmouth*, were sunk; the other two vessels escaped in the darkness. The British admiralty hurriedly sent a powerful British squadron southward, under the command of Vice Admiral Sturdee. This squadron, two battle cruisers, two armored cruisers, and some lighter cruisers, met the German squadron off Port Stanley, in the Falkland islands. Only the *Dresden* escaped; she was destroyed later in neutral waters near the island of Juan Fernandez.

Events in the North Sea. The British grand fleet was based on Scapa Flow, in the Orkneys; the German, as has been said, on Helgoland. Each wisely refused to attack the other in its fortified base. It was the British policy to keep the German fleet off the high seas, meantime preserving their own fleet for the defense of Great Britain; it was the German policy to whittle down the superior British fleet, if possible, by floating mines, Zeppelins, and U-boat attacks until they could risk a fleet action.

This policy of attrition at first had some success. The Germans sowed floating mines, illegal by international law, but later the Allies adopted the same practice. One British dreadnaught, the *Audacious*, (October 27, 1914), some smaller warcraft, and many merchant vessels were sunk in this way. The Zeppelins were practically useless. But the submarines were more effective. Their greatest success was on September 22, 1914, when three British cruisers, the *Aboukir*, *Cressy*, and *Hogue*, were sunk by one submarine, the *U-29*, commanded by Captain Lieutenant Otto Weddingen.

The first important naval battle of the war took place on August 28, 1914, in Helgoland Bight, the German losses amounting to three light cruisers and a destroyer.

In November and December the Germans raided the English coast without material results. In January a German raiding squadron met a superior British force and lost the armored cruiser *Blücher*. It soon became evident that the policy of whittling down would not succeed. British dockyards were building ships faster than the Germans could sink them.

The Allied Blockade. Meantime the Allies sought to make use of their sea power to cut off the communications of the Central Powers with the rest of the world. The right of blockade was well established under international law, provided a real and not a "paper" blockade was maintained. But with their own ports closed the Central Powers were still able to carry on trade with Switzerland, Holland, and Denmark, and with Norway and Sweden across the Baltic. The quantity of goods directly obtainable in this way was comparatively small, but an effort quicky developed to use the neighboring neutral states for transshipment from other countries.

At first the Entente powers did not attempt to exclude all goods, but limited their efforts to certain "contraband" articles of distinctly warlike nature. Early in the war, however, they began to extend the list of contraband articles, and to seize them even when consigned to a neutral port. International law on this point was not so clear, but they could cite the practice of the United States during the Civil War.

Food, by international law, was only "conditionally" contraband, that is, if destined for the armed forces. With that excuse a German raider sank an American sailing ship, the *William P. Frye*, carrying a cargo of grain consigned "to order" at British ports which were fortified naval bases. Late in January 1915, the German government took all supplies of grain and flour under government control and established a rationing system. This gave their enemies a pretext for declaring all food contraband.

On October 2, 1914, Great Britain announced that she would lay mines in designated areas in the North Sea. A month later she declared the whole sea a military area, and warned neutral vessels against entering it without stopping at a British port for sailing directions.

On February 4, the German Government announced that, by way of retaliation against the English policy, all waters around the British Isles would be treated as within the "zone of war," and that "all enemy merchant vessels encountered in these waters will be destroyed, even if it will not always be possible to save their crews and passengers."

Neutrals protested against this decree, but the Germans persisted in their course, and sank several vessels, including the *Lusitania.* An extended controversy followed, and Germany for a while modified her policy, but without yielding on the principle.

On March 11, 1915, by way of retaliation for the German submarine decree, the British government issued an order in council establishing a virtual blockage of Germany, though the word "blockade" was not used. Thenceforth all goods of every kind were to be kept out of Germany, and neutral goods destined for Germany, if not contraband, were, when seized, to be purchased by the captors instead of confiscated. All German goods, wherever found, were to be confiscated.

Their control of the high seas enabled the Allies, to conquer the German colonies. Japan declared war on Germany on August 23, 1914, and a Japanese expedition, aided by a small British contingent landed in Shantung and captured the German fortress of Tsing-Tao (November 7, 1914). Japanese warships also captured the Caroline Islands and other German possessions in that region, while Australasian forces took German Samoa, New Guinea, and other islands in that part of the world. In Africa the French and British speedily overran Togoland and, by February 1916, completed the conquest of Kamerun. In South Africa dissatisfied Boers attempted a revolt against British rule but were soon put down. An expedition from South Africa, led by Premier Botha, with General Jan C. Smuts as second in command, invaded German Southwest Africa and conquered it. In German East Africa more resistance was encountered, and a small German force managed to hold out until the end of the war.

Turkey Enters the War. As a part of the "Drang nach Osten," the eastward movement exemplified by the Baghdad railway, German diplomatic influence had been steadily increasing at Istanbul. The German cruisers *Breslau* and *Goeben* had been allowed to take refuge there under the special permission required by the treaties of 1856 and 1879. Instead of expelling or interning them the Turkish government "purchased" them, against the protest of the Entente powers. The German officers and crew continued to man the ships. Many of the Turks and some members of the cabinet desired to remain neutral, but they were overborne by the pro-German party, headed by Envar Pasha, the minister of war. When, in October, the *Breslau* and *Goeben* raided the Russian ports on the Black Sea, the Entente powers announced a state of war with Turkey. Five months later, Great Britain and France agreed to Russian control of Istanbul and the straits at the end of the war.

Warfare with Russia in the Transcaucasus region began immediately and continued with varying fortunes. Early in February 1915 a Turkish attack on the Suez canal was defeated but the canal continued to be in some danger for two years longer.

The Gallipoli Campaign. The importance of opening the Dardanelles and Bosporus and reestablishing communication with southern Russia was obvious to good strategists everywhere, but the Allies delayed fatally. They blockaded the Dardanelles, but Earl Kitchener, with his eyes on the western front, underestimated the importance of sending the necessary land forces. The navy destroyed the forts at the mouth of the Dardanelles on February 19, but an attack on the main defenses at the Narrows, a month later, cost the British three ships.

At last the Allies decided to send a land force, after further delays had given the Turks and Germans time to strengthen their defenses. Hoped-for aid from Russia and Greece was prevented by the German drive against Russia and the refusal of the pro-German King Constantine to bring Greece into the war. Not until April 25 was the first landing attempted, and then the 45,000 troops used, mostly "Anzacs" (Australian-New Zealand Army Corps) could do little more than seize and hold positions near the tip of Gallipoli peninsula. When in May a German submarine sank two battleships, the navy became of less assistance. After further delays more troops were sent, but no important gains resulted. For many weeks the troops held on, suffering from disease and the enemy fire. A last effort in August, after heavy reinforcements had arrived, failed to reach the key positions. A new landing at Suvla Bay resulted only in immense losses, with no material gains.

The Allies held their positions for months longer, until the conquest of Serbia and the entrance of Bulgaria on the German side, gave the Central Powers a clear road to Istanbul and no hope of opening the straits remained. At the end of 1915 the Allied positions were abandoned. This campaign cost the Allies more than 230,000 men.

Italy Declares War. Italy had refused to join her partners in the Triple Alliance in 1914, alleging that Germany and Austria-Hungary were the aggressors. The old hatred of Austria still persisted and with it the desire to "redeem" the Italian-speaking regions of the Dual Monarchy. Both sides bid for Italian support, and the Allies bid higher. In April the secret Treaty of London with the Entente powers promised to Italy the Trentino, Trieste, South Tyrol, and other territory and concessions, and the next month Italy declared war. Italy brought to the Entente a navy more powerful than Austria's and an army of 1,200,000 trained men with considerable reserves. In their attack upon Austria the mountainous character of the frontier country was against them. Their main movement against Trieste was checked at the Isonzo river, and they made no great progress in the next two years.

The Great Drive against Russia. In the campaign of 1915, the Teutonic leaders, accepting the defensive in the west, launched a great offensive in the east, designed to free Austrian Galicia, to conquer Russian Poland, to destroy the Russian army, and thus to eliminate Russia from the war.

On May 2 General von Mackensen broke through the Russian lines on the Dunajec river in Galicia. Far inferior in artillery, the Russians were unable to check him. In a few weeks von Mackensen retook Przemysl and Lemberg and practically all of Austrian Galicia, together with immense quantities of booty and hundreds of thousands of prisoners.

Meanwhile, in the north, von Hindenburg had taken Libau and had overrun a large part of Courland. Poland was now like a nut in the grasp of a giant nutcracker. Russians were aided by great fortresses such as Ossowetz, Novo Georgievsk, and Ivangorod; but they were handicapped by their lack of artillery, shells, and other munitions. The war had already shown that infantry, no matter how brave, was practically helpless against an enemy that enjoyed a great superiority in artillery. After suffering enormous losses, Grand Duke Nicholas, in order to save his whole army from capture, was forced to evacuate Poland. Warsaw was occupied by the victors on August 5, and the fortress of Novo Georgievsk fell on August 20. After an unsuccessful attempt to make a stand on a line running through Brest-Litovsk, Osowiec, and Kovno, the great retreat had to continue. Grand Duke Nicholas was transferred to the Caucasus, where he was successful against the Turks, and the czar himself assumed nominal command, the real direction, however, being exercised by General Alexieff. The Teutons took Vilna, but their efforts to capture Dvinsk and Riga were foiled by stiffening Russian resistance. The Russians even launched an offensive in Galicia and checked the Germans in that quarter.

The Conquest of Serbia and Montenegro. The Teutonic victories over Russia made a profound impression, particularly in the Near East. In October 1915 Bulgaria threw in her lot with the Central Powers and attacked Serbia from the rear. Greece remained neutral. A strong army under General von Mackensen invaded Serbia from the north, recaptured Belgrade, and drove the Serbians southward. The allies of Serbia procrastinated as usual, and, too late, landed an army at Saloniki. Late in October the Bulgarian and Teutonic armies joined hands in eastern Serbia, and both Serbia and Montenegro were speedily conquered.

Through the conquest of Serbia the Teutons opened a way by which to aid hard-pressed Turkey, and trains loaded with munitions were soon running to Istanbul. With Istanbul under their control, the Teutons hoped to break through to Suez and the Persian Gulf, but that hope was never realized.

On the western front the deadlock that had begun after the repulse of the Germans in Flanders continued throughout 1915. In the second week of March, an attack on Neuve Chapelle, preceded by a heavy bombardment, in which more shells were fired than in the whole of the Boer war, resulted in slight success, and the loss of almost 13,000 men.

Poison Gas and Air Warfare. In an offensive against the British lines near Ypres, April 22, 1915, the Germans for the first time made use of poison gas. It had a momentary success, but the Germans failed to make the most of their advantage, partly by not fully understanding how much the gas had done, partly because of the gallant resistance of a Canadian division. The use of poison gas was denounced as illegal, but the Allies soon adopted it; improvements in technique were made by both sides, and it became an accepted feature of the war.

Aerial warfare also began. The German Zeppelins, or dirigible balloons, made raids on the English coast towns and finally, on the last night of May, reached London and dropped nearly a hundred incendiary bombs. The Germans claimed substantial damage to military objectives from these raids; the British said that only civilian lives and property suffered.

The use of airplanes expanded with astounding rapidity. New types were developed. Within a few months there were fighting planes, bombing planes, observation planes, —a type for each kind of work. By far the most important use to which planes were put was observation, spying out the enemy's movements and directing artillery fire. Later the planes were armed, and real battles were fought in mid-air.

The Deadlock on the Western Front. During the greater part of the campaign of 1915 the French and British attempted no great offensives but confined their efforts to what Marshal Joffre called "nibbling." In April the French failed at the St. Mihiel salient, south of Verdun. In May they had more success at "The Labyrinth," near Arras, but the method was costly out of proportion to results. One reason for this comparative inaction was the scarcity of munitions, particularly high explosive shells. The new technique of intensive artillery preparation before an attack, introduced by the Germans, entailed an expenditure of ammunition undreamed of in the past and not fully appreciated by the Germans themselves, much less by their opponents.

Late in September the British and French began the most serious offensive they had yet undertaken. They attacked a sector in Champagne, a second in Artois, and a third near Ypres after a fierce cannonade, or "drum fire," in places continued for 72 hours. Gas was also used. On the morning of September 25 the Allies delivered assaults in great force in each sector, and for days a bloody confusion of attack and counter-attack followed. Ultimately a little ground was gained but the main German lines held. The total German losses were estimated by the French at 120,000; the Allied losses probably exceeded those of the Germans.

The Drive against Verdun. At the beginning of the campaign of 1916 the Germans again turned their main attention to the western front. With the purpose of "bleeding France white," by drawing the French reserves to one point and destroying them, they launched late in February a tremendous offensive against the great armed camp of Verdun. Their first attacks made substantial gains, but General Joffre and his advisers decided to hold the place at any cost, partly because to lose it would have a depressing effect upon Allied morale.

For months thereafter the bitter battle continued. Hundreds of thousands fell on each side; week after week the Germans forged slowly forward against the bitterest resistance of the French, whose watchword was "They shall not pass." Early in July, the Germans got within a thousand yards of Fort Souville, the key to the French position, only three miles from Verdun. But the British advance on the Somme forced them to withdraw many troops and the fighting gradually diminished. In the following October and December, General Nivelle recaptured almost all the ground that had been lost.

The Battle of Jutland. On the last day of May the main fleets of Great Britain and Germany at last met in battle. On that day, both fleets were in the North Sea to the west of Jutland, neither knowing of the other. Shortly after two o'clock the advance squadron of the German fleet under Vice Admiral von Hipper met a heavier British squadron under Admiral Beatty, and turned back to the main fleet, sixty miles to the south. Beatty pursued, signalling to his main body, seventy miles to the north. In the running fight which followed, the British lost two battle cruisers, the *Indefatigable* and *Queen Mary*. On sighting the German fleet, Beatty turned back north to draw the Germans into conflict with the grand fleet under Admiral Jellicoe, which was hastening to his support. The Germans lost a battle cruiser, the *Luetzow*, in the pursuit. About 6 P. M. the main British fleet came up. Another British battle cruiser was sunk in the first clash but von Scheer saw he was outmatched. By skillful maneuvering he mystified the British admiral and, before the enemy could close in upon him, escaped in the darkness.

Both sides claimed the victory. The Germans had inflicted heavier losses on a superior fleet, six British capital ships against two of their own,—but the British could better afford it. On the other hand, the British retained command of the sea, and the Germans never ventured another battle.

Only seven days after the battle of Jutland, the British armored cruiser *Hampshire*, which was carrying Secretary of War Kitchener to Russia, struck a German mine off the coast of one of the Orkney islands, and all on board except eleven men perished. Kitchener's tragic death created a great impression.

The Italian and Russian Fronts in 1916. In the middle of May 1916, the Austro-Hungarians launched in the Trentino a great offensive which they hoped would result in their breaking through into the Lombard plain, Milan, and taking Venice and enveloping of the Italian main army along the Isonzo front. Their first attack, on May 15, was very successful and was so competently followed up that by the end of May they had taken two or three hundred cannon and over 30,000 prisoners, and the whole Italian army was in peril.

Once more, however, the Russians made an effective diversion in favor of their hard-pressed western allies. Under the leadership of General Brussilov, the Russians on June 2 attacked along the southern half of the eastern front. They broke Austrian lines and took the great fortress of Lutzk and Dubno. The whole Austrian line in the east crumbled, Bukowina was overrun, and 100,000 prisoners were captured. The Dual Monarchy had to suspend its drive against Italy and withdraw troops from that front to meet the victorious Muscovites. Germany also had to slacken her own offensive against Verdun. The Russians were held in check before Lemberg and Kovel after enormous losses on both sides.

Thanks to this opportune Russian diversion, the Italians were able to regain most of the ground they had lost. Early in August they captured Gorizia, but there their success ended, and the virtual deadlock along the Isonzo continued.

The Battle of the Somme. The British army in France had now grown to over seventy divisions, well-trained, fully equipped, and organized. Under the command of General Sir Douglas Haig, it was now ready for an offensive movement. On June 24 the British artillery began a terrific bombardment of the German lines and continued it until the morning of July 1, when British and French infantry attacked on a front of over twenty miles in the region of the Somme river. The British objective was Bapaume; the French, Peronne. Both were successful in taking the first lines, but resistance stiffened as they advanced. On the first day of the attack the British lost 60,000 men, and advanced half a mile.

To pound unceasingly was the Allied policy; the Germans brought up thousands of reserves for resistance and counterattack. Aloft, the opposing aircraft fought for the control of the air, a necessity in so flat a country for directing artillery fire. The surface for miles was transformed into a barren wilderness of shell craters. In an attack on September 15 the British for the first time made use of "tanks,"—armored cars mounted on caterpillar tractors. The smaller tanks were armed only with machine guns; the larger ones, with small pieces of artillery also. The tanks proved able to move through barbed wire entanglements, to cross trenches, to push down walls and even trees, and were especially helpful in destroying machine gun "nests." They proved, on the whole, successful, and assumed greater and greater importance as the war progressed.

Late in November the coming of wet, wintry weather brought the battle to a close. The Allies had gained something less than seven miles on a twelve mile front; they had not gained the break-through for which they had hoped. This gain had cost the British 420,000 men; the French, nearly 200,000. The German loss may have been as great.

The Defeat of Rumania. Meanwhile Rumania had entered the war on the side of the Entente. She was promised the Banat, Transylvania, and other territory, in much of which the population was largely Rumanian. On August 28, 1916, she declared war on Austria-Hungary, and hostilities with the other Central Powers soon followed. After some initial Rumanian successes, the armies of the Central Powers, led by Generals von Mackensen and von Falkenhayn, attacked Rumania from the north, west, and south, captured the capital, and overran two-thirds of the country, while an Allied force remained immovable at Saloniki. Russian reinforcements finally checked the invaders, at a line running along the lower Sereth river, and thence northeastward to the Carpathians.

The Rumanian fiasco created much dissatisfaction in Allied countries, and was instrumental in bringing about cabinet changes in both France and Great Britain. In the latter country the Liberal cabinet under Asquith had declared the war. The Conservatives had supported them, but early in 1915 had demanded a share in power as well as in responsibility, and a coalition cabinet had been formed. Now the feeling grew that Asquith was too careful of the rights of the citizen and lacked the energy necessary for a war premier. He retired and was succeeded by David Lloyd George. In France similar conditions brought about, after some friction, the appointment of "the Tiger," Georges Clemenceau, as a premier in November 1917. In the field Joffre retired at the end of the year; he was succeeded by General Nivelle, the defender of Verdun.

Peace Discussions. Toward the end of 1916 proposals for peace came forward from two quarters. On December 12 the German government announced its willingness to enter into peace negotiations. On December 18, President Wilson, in a note framed before the German proposal appeared, asked the belligerents to state the terms on which peace might be concluded. The replies to both propositions showed that no agreement was yet possible. On January 22, President Wilson explained his position to the Senate, saying that there must be a "peace without victory," since "only a peace between equals can last"; and favoring a League of Peace to secure the fulfillment of such a treaty.

The United States Enters the War. In the United States, especially in the northeast, popular sympathy had been generally with the Allies from the beginning. German policies toward the United States, even before the war, had been irritating; the old feeling against England was weakening; and France had been our traditional ally. At the outset of the war President Wilson, following our accepted policy, had issued a neutrality proclamation and had repeatedly protested against both British and German violations of international law. American feeling, however, especially in the West and Middle West, was against any participation in a European war, and Wilson was re-elected in 1916 under the campaign cry, "He kept us out of war."

The submarines brought matters to a crisis. Wilson had protested against the German war zone of February 1915. After the sinking of the *Lusitania* and later the *Sussex*, with the loss of American lives, his position held such prospects of vigorous action that, in May 1916, the German government agreed not to sink merchant vessels without warning, provided the United States held Great Britain also to "strict accountability." On January 31, 1917, the German high command suddenly announced that it would resume unrestricted submarine warfare against any merchant ships found in "barred zones" around the British Isles, along the Atlantic coast of France, and in the Mediterranean. The United States was permitted, under certain restrictions, to send one ship a week to Falmouth in southern England. President Wilson's answer was the breaking off of diplomatic relations with Germany, on February 3.

The unrestricted submarine warfare continued. On February 26, President Wilson announced that he deemed it desirable for the United States to adopt an attitude of "armed neutrality," and asked for authority to arm American merchant ships. This was obviously a step toward war. The same day word reached Washington of the loss of three Americans on the British ship *Laconia.* A few days later an intercepted dispatch was published which showed that Zimmerman, the German foreign minister, was seeking to stir up Mexico and Japan against the United States in the event of war with Germany. A bill empowering the president to arm merchantmen, and making appropriations for that purpose, passed the House by 403 to 13, but Senator La Follette and other opponents of war defeated it by a filibuster in the Senate. The president then found authority, under an act of 1797, for placing naval guns and crews on merchant ships. Congress was called to meet in special session on April 16, a date later advanced to April 2.

Meantime the submarines had been working great havoc. In February the Germans claimed the sinking of 781,000 tons of shipping; the British admitted 490,000. The peak was reached in April, with the loss of nearly a million tons. Then, with the adoption of the convoy system, due largely to Lloyd George, the Allies began to get the upper hand. American ships were among those lost.

On April 2, President Wilson appeared before Congress and delivered a war message. He stated that the recent course of the German government constituted a "warfare against mankind." Armed neutrality had proved ineffectual, and he asked Congress to recognize that war had been thrust upon the United States by the acts of the German government. He requested the necessary steps to force the German government to terms and end the conflict. Resolutions to that effect passed the Senate on the night of the 4-5th of April by a vote of 82 to 6 and the House on the early morning of the 6th by a vote of 373 to 50. The same day, the president signed the resolutions, and America and Germany were formally at war.

Relations with Austria-Hungary had long been strained, and in September 1915 the United States had demanded and secured the recall of Constantine Dumba, the Austro-Hungarian ambassador, for attempting to stir up strikes in American munition factories. Diplomatic relations were severed by the dual monarchy on April 8, but war was not formally declared until the 7th of the following December, the declaration being made by the United States. Turkey severed relations on April 17, but a state of war was never declared. Diplomatic relations between the United States and Bulgaria were continued throughout the conflict.

American Preparations. America's entry into the conflict greatly heartened the Entente Powers. Furthermore, it encouraged several other nations, such as China, Brazil, Panama, Cuba, and Bolivia, to break relations with Germany or to declare war against her.

Within less than three weeks after the declaration of war Congress appropriated seven billion dollars for war purposes. Subsequently other immense appropriations were made. A policy of advancing loans to our Allies was at once adopted, and by the close of hostilities about eight billion dollars had been so advanced. In May, Congress passed and the president signed a Selective Service bill, and under this and subsequent extensions all male persons not alien enemies, between the ages of 21 and 45, were required to register. After exemptions, about 3,000,000 soldiers and sailors were obtained. Some hundreds of thousands, also, volunteered.

To obtain money with which to conduct the war, Congress enacted special tax legislation and authorized the issuance of certificates of indebtedness, war savings certificates, better known as thrift stamps, and government bonds. By far the largest sum was realized from the sale of bonds, of which five great issues were floated, the first on May 14, 1917. The four liberty loans aggregated $14,000,000,000, at rates varying from 3½ to 4¼ per cent. A fifth, called the victory loan, for $4,500,000,000, was floated soon after the armistice. All were oversubscribed.

The country now had to prepare for war. Between April 5, 1917, and June 30, 1919, 35 billion dollars were expended, which was several billions more than had been spent for all purposes from the beginning of the Revolution down to 1917. Of this sum, however, nine billions were advanced to our allies in the conflict.

Work of the American Navy. Shortly before the United States entered the war, Vice Admiral William S. Sims was sent to England to arrange cooperation of American naval forces with those of the Allies. On his arrival in London he found the British much depressed over the submarine situation. The American navy took over the work of patrolling a large part of the Atlantic, thus freeing British ships for use in home waters, and from May on destroyers and other craft were sent abroad. In December 1917 a squadron of four dreadnoughts (a fifth was later added) was sent over under command of Rear Admiral Hugh Rodman and joined the British Grand Fleet. Two other battleships in the early summer of 1918 began operations from a base in Ireland. An immense amount of work was done in convoying ships across the Atlantic and through the war zone.

The greatest loss suffered by the American navy during the war was the sinking of the armored cruiser *San Diego*, which struck (July 1918) a German mine laid by a submarine off Long Island. One destroyer, the *Jacob Jones*, was sunk (December 6, 1917) by a submarine in European waters. Other destroyers and smaller vessels were sunk or damaged, and a large number of armed merchant vessels and transports were lost. In return we captured one submarine and probably sank others.

American Troops sent to France. The American regular army, on April 1, 1917, numbered only 128,000 men. The French government, however, urged that at least a few American troops should be sent to France as speedily as possible, for the sake of the effect on Allied morale. To command the overseas force the president selected Major General John J. Pershing. General Pershing and his staff sailed from New York late in May. Late in June the first contingent of troops landed at St. Nazaire, whence they were transferred to training bases in Lorraine.

The Western Front in 1917. During the first two months of 1917 the French and British made preparations for a grand offensive. General von Hindenburg who in the previous summer had succeeded von Falkenhayn, forestalled them by withdrawing to a shorter and stronger zone of defense, the Hindenburg line, laying waste the country behind him. Although the conditions had changed, the offensive was not given up. On April 9 the English launched a great attack about Lens and Arras. Canadian troops carried the important Vimy Ridge, and more gains were made at less cost than in the battle of the Somme; but the German lines still held. On April 16, the French, under Nivelle, attacked in front of Reims. They gained some initial successes, but their losses were severe, even resulting in mutinies among the French troops. General Nivelle was succeeded by General Pétain, with General Foch as his chief of staff.

Again in June the British launched another attack in Flanders. They took Messines Ridge, after the explosion of a gigantic mine, and bitter fighting continued through the summer. In the fall British operations in the low ground about Passchendaele literally bogged down in the swampy terrain, though a part of Passchendaele Ridge was taken. The French meanwhile had recovered sufficiently to make another drive with some success, near Soissons, and drove the Germans from the Chemin des Dames.

The Russian Revolution. Unintelligent despotism, universal corruption, and radical intrigue were doing their work in Russia. In March a revolution broke out, which resulted in the deposition of the czar and the establishment of a republic. Moderate revolutionists who favored continuing the war at first managed to control, but the Soviets, or councils of workmen's and soldier's delegates, who desired more radical measures and a speedy peace, constantly increased in power. German secret agents took advantage of the situation. The republican government, headed by Kerensky, inspired the army to a last effort. In July an offensive was launched in Galicia; successful at first, it turned into a disgraceful rout. The Germans occupied Riga and Odessa. For a time Kerensky held power as a virtual dictator, but in November the radical revolutionists, or Bolsheviki, under Lenin and Trotzky, seized control. They not only carried through a complete economic and social revolution but, on December 15, 1917, signed an armistice, and, in the following March, the humiliating treaty of Brest-Litovsk.

The breakdown of Russia enabled the Germans, even in 1917, to concentrate most of their forces on the Western front. Large forces of men and guns were transferred to Flanders to hold the British in check and a grand drive was prepared against Italy.

The Italian Disaster. During the spring, summer, and early fall the Italians had continued to make slow progress on the Isonzo. On October 24 the Austro-Hungarians and some German divisions launched a sudden offensive. German shock troops broke through the Italian lines in the region of Caporetto and drove them westward in disastrous rout. Venice and Milan were in grave danger; the whole of the Lombard plain was threatened. General Diaz, who succeeded General Cadorna, rallied the Italians behind the Piave river, and the arrival of French and British reinforcements helped to save the situation. A German attack from the Trentino, to turn the Piave line, was finally checked.

The Italian defeat had, however, been a major disaster; northeastern Italy was overrun; and the enemy had taken a quarter of a million prisoners, about 2500 guns, and vast stores of munitions. The Italian situation continued to be grave until near the end of the war.

Partly to prevent the Germans from sending any more troops against the Italians, the British Third Army under General Byng, on November 20, launched a sudden attack on the German lines in front of Cambrai. A great number of tanks were used to break through the barbed wire entanglements and destroy machine gun nests. The British got within three miles of Cambrai, but had not sufficient reserves with which to follow up the success. On November 30 the Germans restored their lines by a powerful counterattack and recovered about a third of the ground lost. The main importance of the battle was that it demonstrated the possibilities of tanks.

Campaign in Mesopotamia (Iraq) and Palestine. The Allied hope of victory in 1917 had not been realized. In some important fields of action their arms had met with disaster, and only in Iraq and Palestine could they point to really notable successes. Late in 1914 an expedition, composed mainly of troops from India, had landed at the head of the Persian gulf, and managed to fight its way in November 1915 almost to Baghdad. At Ctesiphon, however, it met superior forces and had to retreat down the Tigris river to Kut-el-Amara, where, despite the efforts of a relieving army, it was forced to surrender (April 29, 1916). In the following December the relieving army, commanded by General Maude and increased to over a hundred thousand men, again assumed the offensive in Iraq, recaptured Kut-el-Amara, and after decisive victories entered the city of Baghdad, March 11, 1917.

Meanwhile the British had encouraged the Arabs in Arabia to revolt against the Turks. Thomas Edward Lawrence, a young British archeologist, organized and led the Arab tribes. Utilizing their methods of desert warfare, he made them an invaluable auxiliary force.

In March 1917 a British army pushing northward from the Isthmus of Suez defeated a Turkish force near the ancient city of Gaza. In October General Sir Edmund Allenby took command and began an active campaign, and in December, for the first time since the Crusades, the flag of a Christian nation floated over Jerusalem.

In Greece, also, affairs had taken a turn more favorable to the Allies. Former Premier Venizelos and Admiral Condouriotis began a revolutionary movement in Crete and established a provisional government, which won over other islands and most of the Greek fleet, and entered the war on the side of the Entente. In June 1917, the Allies compelled King Constantine to resign in favor of his second son, Prince Alexander. Venizelos became premier, and Greece was brought into the war.

The Great German Offensive of 1918. During the winter of 1917-18 both Teutonic and Allied leaders made pronouncements with regard to peace, but their views as to terms differed so widely that it was clear that the war must go on. Meanwhile the Germans made preparations to launch a stupendous blow which they hoped would bring them victory before America could take a real part in the war. With forces released by the collapse of Russia, they were now equal to the Allies on the Western front. The place selected for the offensive was in the region between Arras and La Fere, at the point of junction of the French and British lines. At five o'clock on the morning of March 21 the Germans began a terrific bombardment on a front of about sixty miles.

After four hours the infantry moved forward to the attack. The British, outnumbered five to one at the point of attack, were unable to withstand the blow. The Fifth British Army was practically cut to pieces. In a few days the Germans had regained practically all the territory they had lost. At one time it seemed probable that the Germans would be able to separate the British from the French and to defeat each in detail. France was in greater danger than at any time since the battle of the Marne. Paris was subjected to repeated air raids and was bombarded by super-guns concealed in the forest of St. Gobain at the unheard-of distance of 74 miles.

But the British Third Army under Byng held like a wall before Arras, containing the flood on the north, while hastily gathered French forces, after bloody fighting, dammed it on the south. The French and British joined hands once more, and the Germans, worn out by their gigantic efforts, failed to reach the vitally important town of Amiens.

On April 9, Ludendorff and Hindenburg delivered another great blow against the British lines in Flanders. The Germans broke through a portion of the line held by a Portuguese division, took the Passchendaele and Messines ridges, Armentieres, and Kemmel Hill, and threatened Ypres. There was grave danger that the whole British army might be hurled back in irretrievable disaster upon the Channel, but British fighting qualities and French reenforcements once more brought the assailants to a pause.

Foch Becomes Commander in Chief. From the Allied point of view the German offensive had been productive of at least one good result. Hitherto in the war their activities had been greatly hampered by lack of united command. A Supreme War Council had been created. But this was not enough. On March 27, in the midst of the first German offensive, British and French representatives met and gave the supreme command to Ferdinand Foch. On the next day General Pershing tendered his forces to Foch, and ultimately the great Frenchman became generalissimo of all the Allied armies on all fronts.

At the time Pershing made his tender there were less than 370,000 American troops in Europe, of whom about half were noncombatants. American participation in the fighting had been almost wholly confined to meeting petty German raids. The First Division was now sent to the active front near Montdidier, and, at the urgent request of the French and British leaders, great efforts were concentrated upon bringing more American troops over. During the war only 396 American soldiers were lost as a result of submarine activities.

The Final German Efforts. On May 27 the Germans launched a new offensive on a thirty-mile front between Reims and Soissons. The Allies were taken by surprise, and with comparatively slight losses the Teutons recaptured the Chemin des Dames Ridge and drove a deep salient to the river Marne, taking great numbers of prisoners and guns.

On the day after the Germans launched this offensive, the American First Division under Major General Bullard captured the town of Cantigny near the apex of the Amiens salient. This was the first considerable operation in which American troops were engaged, but the Second and Third divisions were now sent to the Marne front in the Chateau-Thierry region and helped to bring the German drive to a pause. In fighting for Belleau Wood a brigade of marines won great distinction. Meanwhile, French troops in the region of Compiegne had defeated with great slaughter a German effort to connect the Marne salient with that driven toward Amiens.

By July 1 the Germans claimed to have captured, since the launching of their March offensive, 191,454 unwounded prisoners and over 2000 cannon, but they had failed to obtain the decisive victory they had hoped to win. Owing to the rapid arrival of American troops, the "rifle strength" of the Allies on the western front had passed that of the Germans.

The scene of the last German attack was the Reims salient, on a great front from Chateau-Thierry almost to the Argonne Forest. But the Allied leaders divined the German plan and concentrated great numbers of troops and guns to meet it. When the attack came on the morning of July 15, the Allies, by using a "yielding defense," stopped the German drive in most places after inflicting great losses. Some German divisions forced their way over the river Marne, but on the sector held by the American Third and Twenty-eighth divisions determined counter-attacks speedily hurled the assailants back across the river. By the end of the third day of battle it was evident that the drive was doomed to failure.

The Allies Assume the Offensive. The time had come for which Foch had long been waiting. At dawn of the 18th he attacked the western side of the Marne salient. The American First and Second divisions participated in the initial attack, and others were soon thrown into the fight. There was no preliminary artillery preparation, but the troops charged behind a rolling barrage and were aided by many tanks. The surprise was complete. The Allies advanced eight miles. The salient was no longer tenable, and the Germans retreated over the Vesle river, with heavy losses.

On August 8 a new offensive was launched against the salient projecting toward Amiens. The Canadian army formed the center of this attack and made a greater advance on the first day than was accomplished by any other army on the western front in the campaign of 1918.

"To make war is to attack" had long been General Foch's maxim. He followed up these initial successes and by the middle of September the Germans had been driven back virtually to the old Hindenburg Line, from which they had launched their offensive in the spring.

In these operations American troops fighting with the French and British armies played a glorious part, and General Pershing with a newly organized army performed a notable exploit by taking the St. Mihiel salient northeast of Verdun. Careful preparations were made, and an army of about 600,000, including some French troops, was concentrated for the purpose. The attack was made on September 12. The Germans, already withdrawing, were caught in the act; they lost 16,000 prisoners and the salient was wiped out. In the two months since the middle of July the Germans had lost nearly half a million men. In the words of Pershing: "The Allies found they had a formidable army to aid them, and the enemy learned finally that he had one to reckon with."

Bulgaria and Turkey Beaten. In late September the Allied army in the Balkans began a sudden offensive northward from Saloniki. In a few days the lines of the enemy were broken, and Bulgaria, threatened with annihilation, signed (September 30) an armistice which was practically an unconditional surrender. Bulgaria's withdrawal from the war isolated Turkey. The dual monarchy was attacked from the south.

On September 19, General Allenby launched a blow at the Turkish army in Palestine and in a few days practically annihilated it, taking 75,000 prisoners and 360 cannon. The victors took Damascus, and in the middle of October they reached Aleppo and cut the Berlin to Baghdad railway, thereby isolating the Turkish army in Iraq, which on October 30 surrendered to the British army under General Marshall. On the same day the Turkish government bowed to the inevitable and withdrew from the war.

The Battle of the Hindenburg Line. In the last days of September the Allies on the western front began an epic assault on the Hindenburg Line. Belgian, British, and French troops under King Albert took the offensive in Flanders, British and French armies thundered against the zone of defenses in front of St. Quentin and Laon, and a great American army, aided by French troops on their left, began a drive down the valley of the Meuse river. The German lines were broken; Dixmude, Lens, Armentieres, and the great city of Lille were taken; and in the middle of October the Germans evacuated the Belgian coast.

Meanwhile, British, Canadian, and Australian troops, aided by the 30th and 27th divisions of Americans, steadily battered their way through the immensely strong zone of defenses in front of Cambrai and St. Quentin. Tanks and artillery were used in great profusion, and defensive works were taken that had once been considered impregnable. In the second week of October, Haig's forces finally burst through the German system of defenses and took Cambrai and St. Quentin.

In front of the Americans and French in the region of the Meuse lay the rugged Argonne Forest and three German zones of defense. The Germans were not expecting an offensive in this quarter, and at first their lines were lightly held. An initial attack was made on September 26. The French forces, operating on the west side of the Argonne Forest, made good progress the first day; on the east side the Americans advanced in places for six or seven miles, but strong resistance encountered at Montfaucon and elsewhere prevented them from breaking completely through the first zone of defense, and assaulting the second, before the Germans could bring up reserves. The attack was continued the next two days against increasingly strong resistance, due to the arrival of German re-enforcements; Montfaucon and other strong points were taken, and in the three days about 10,000 Germans were captured.

Thus began the bloodiest battle in American history, a conflict comparable to that in the Wilderness in Civil War days, but on a larger scale and much more prolonged. Both sides constantly threw fresh divisions into the fray, and every day bitter but confused fighting took place. German machine-gunners fought for every foot of ground and exacted a heavy toll from the Americans, most of whom were taking part in their first great battle. The American losses were enormous, but the troops from beyond the seas fought with a dogged determination to win through at any cost. By October 10, with French assistance, they had cleared the Argonne Forest of the enemy. The great obstacle before them now was the powerful German line known as the Kriemhilde Stellung.

By the end of October the Americans were through the Kriemhilde zone of defense, and on November 1 the final advance was begun. The third German line, the so-called Freya Stellung, was incomplete, and it was mastered with comparative ease. On November 6 the Rainbow Division reached a point on the Meuse opposite Sedan. The Americans had now attained their objective—the railways running through Sedan and Mezieres. In the words of General Pershing: "The strategical goal which was our highest hope was gained. We had cut the enemy's main line of communications, and nothing but surrender or an armistice could save his army from complete disaster."

The total number of Americans engaged in the Meuse-Argonne offensive has been estimated at 631,000, the French at 138,000, making a total of 769,000. The Germans had less than 400,000. In the battle the Americans had taken 16,059 prisoners and 468 guns; their own losses in killed, wounded, and missing exceeded 100,000. During the whole campaign the Americans captured about 44,000 prisoners and 1400 guns. In all, 2,034,000 American soldiers reached France, and of these 1,390,000 saw more or less active service at the front. In all, 29 divisions took part in active combat service.

The Americans were undoubtedly the decisive factor in winning victory; without their aid the war might have been lost. It should be remembered, however, that they came in at the end, when the enemy had been worn down. Even in the campaign of 1918 the French and British losses were much heavier than those of the Americans, and each of them captured more prisoners and guns.

Great credit is also due to the Canadians. Their troops performed some of the most brilliant exploits of the whole war, and no other soldiers were more dreaded by the Germans.

They broke through the Hindenburg Line between Queant and Drocourt. In this victory and the one near Amiens mentioned above their casualties were numerous but were exceeded by the number of prisoners which they captured. On Oct. 9 they took Cambrai and on Nov. 2, Valenciennes. A few hours before the armistice became effective, Canadian troops entered Mons, from which the British expeditionary force had begun its retreat before the on-pouring flood of Germans in the last week of August 1914.

In the whole war nearly 600,000 Canadians, 7 per cent of the population, served in the army, nearly all by voluntary enlistment. The financial cost was met largely by internal popular loans, amounting in all to $2,202,762,250 and subscribed for by well over a million persons. At the same time, special taxes were imposed calculated to retire these extraordinary loans and maintain the country's credit. Nearly 1000 ships were built during the war in Canadian shipyards for Canada or her allies. The losses in men during the war were approximately equal to those of the United States. The Canadian army captured 45,000 prisoners and retook 130 towns. A Canadian aviator, Colonel William Avery Bishop, of Ontario, was credited with 72 official victories, a record exceeded by only one German and one French aviator.

On October 24 General Diaz's army assumed the offensive in the Trentino and along the Piave river against the Austro-Hungarians. The Austrian army was broken and demoralized; three hundred thousand prisoners were taken. Revolutions broke out in Hungary and Austria, and the emperor Charles, the last of the Habsburgs, was forced to abdicate. On November 3, military representatives of the falling dual monarchy signed in the field an armistice that amounted practically to a complete capitulation.

The War Ended. With her last ally gone, Germany stood alone, facing a world of determined enemies. Before the end of September the German high command had realized that peace must be made, and, on October 4, Prince Maximilian of Baden, who had recently become imperial chancellor, sent to President Wilson a request for an armistice. Exchange of notes continued for more than a month; meanwhile the German armies were driven back, and the allies of Germany retired from the conflict. On the last day of October a mutiny began in the German fleet. In a few days uprisings took place in Berlin and elsewhere. Emperor William and the crown prince fled to Holland. On November 8 German representatives met Marshal Foch and other Allied representatives in a railway car near Rethondes, and, at five o'clock on the morning of the 11th, signed an armistice to take effect six hours later.

In the negotiations leading up to the armistice, the Germans had agreed to accept as a basis for peace the program set forth by President Wilson in an address to Congress on January 8, 1918, and in later pronouncements, particularly in a speech of September 27. In his address of January 8 the president had stated fourteen points which he considered essentials. These included "open covenants of peace openly arrived at" and no secret diplomacy in the future; freedom of the seas in both peace and war; reduction of armaments; evacuation of all territory conquered by the Central Powers, with reparation and restoration of Belgium, Serbia, etc.; Alsace and Lorraine to be returned to France; readjustment of the frontiers of Italy along lines of nationality; an independent Poland; and the formation of an association of nations to safeguard the independence and territorial integrity of both great and small states. The European allies of the United States had, however, reserved complete freedom of action on the matter of "the freedom of the seas" and had insisted that the sweeping stipulation that "invaded territories must be restored as well as evacuated" must be interpreted to mean "that compensation will be made by Germany for all damage done to the civilian population of the Allies and their property by the aggression of Germany by land, by sea, and by the air." In addition to these terms, the Germans were required by the armistice to surrender 5000 cannon, 25,000 machine guns, 1700 airplanes, all the German submarines, and practically all their above-water navy. All of Germany west of the Rhine was to be occupied by Allied troops, a neutral zone ten kilometers wide was to be drawn on the east bank, and the Allies were to have bridgeheads east of the river at Mayence, Coblenz, and Cologne.

Treaty Negotiations. The opening session of the Peace Conference was held at Versailles, near Paris, on January 18, 1919. Representatives of all the Allied nations were present, but the decisions were made by the leaders of the five chief powers.

The document containing the terms fixed upon for Germany was delivered to the German delegates on May 7. In Germany it was considered a "monstrous document," but the victors would consent to only a few modifications, and the vanquished, being powerless to resist, were obliged to accept it, the actual signing taking place on June 28, the fifth anniversary of the assassination of the archduke Francis Ferdinand. Under it Germany gave up all her colonies, ceded Alsace and Lorraine to France and a small strip of territory to Belgium, and consented that the Sarre (Saar) Basin, with its rich iron and coal mines, should be internationalized for fifteen years, after which the inhabitants were to be given the right to decide as to their future. Plebiscites were to be held in Schleswig, Silesia, and parts of East Prussia to determine the future political affiliation of these regions, and the port of Danzig was to be internationalized. The German army was to be reduced to 100,000 men; the German navy, to six battleships, six light cruisers, and some smaller vessels. The fortifications of Helgoland were to be destroyed, and the Kiel canal must be opened to all nations. Germany accepted responsibility for all damages done to the Allies and their peoples and agreed to reimburse civilians for their losses and to restore the devastated regions in Belgium, France, and elsewhere. She also agreed to the trial of the kaiser and other Germans accused of offenses against international morality and the laws of war.

Subsequently it was found difficult to enforce all the provisions of the treaty, and some modifications were made. The claims for reparations were scaled down, and comparatively little was collected. Holland refused to give up Wilhelm II and but few of the others accused were ever brought to trial.

Treaties were later concluded with Bulgaria, Austria, and Turkey. Bulgaria was compelled to surrender territory and to pay an indemnity. Parts of the old dual monarchy were ceded to Italy, Rumania, and Poland; Hungary and Czechoslovakia were recognized as independent republics; the regions chiefly inhabited by Yugoslavs were united with Serbia and Montenegro into a greater Serbia, — the Kingdom of the Serbs, Croats, and Slovenes. Of Austria proper there remained only about 32,000 square miles, with a population of 6,000,000 or 7,000,000, chiefly of German blood. A republican form of government was adopted.

The Turkish treaty reduced the domains of the sultan to Istanbul and a small region round about it and to part of Asia Minor. An international force was to be maintained at Istanbul, and the Dardanelles and the Bosporus were neutralized. Arabia was to be independent; Iraq and Palestine were to be under British control; Thrace and the region about Smyrna, under that of Greece; and France and Italy were given spheres of influence in Syria and Anatolia respectively. The mandate over Armenia was offered to the United States, but Congress declined it.

Russian and Turkish Affairs. Unfortunately the conference was unable to bring peace everywhere to a distracted world. At the time of the signing of the German treaty a score of other wars, or conflicts amounting to a state of war, were still raging. For example, Poland was fighting the Ruthenians, the Ukrainians, the Germans, the Yugoslavs, and the Russian Bolshevists.

In Russia the Allies lent assistance to the opponents of the Bolshevists, but all counter-revolutionary movements ultimately failed. The Bolshevist regime, dedicated to an experiment in communism on a scale never before witnessed, consolidated its position as a class dictatorship by means of a Revolutionary court and the army. It survived widespread famine and acute industrial disorganization.

Turkish Nationalists refused to accept the terms imposed upon their country, and one of their leaders, Mustapha Kemal, assembled a large army in Asia Minor. Allied jealousies also complicated the Turkish situation. The main burden of opposing the Nationalists was assumed by the Greeks, who overran Thrace in the summer of 1920, and in 1921 conducted a successful offensive against the Nationalists in Asia Minor, but in 1922 the Greeks were defeated and driven out of Asia Minor. The Turks subsequently, by the Treaty of Lausanne (July 1923), obtained much more favorable terms.

America Rejects the League of Nations. In the United States a bitter political struggle developed over the peace treaty. To be ratified, the treaty had to receive a two-thirds majority in the Senate. A majority of the Senate were Republicans, and in that body, as well as among the people at large, there existed a great deal of hostility toward President Wilson. Special objection was made to Article X of the Covenant, which bound members of the League "to respect and preserve as against external aggression the territorial integrity and existing political independence of all members of the League." In an effort to win popular support for the treaty and the League, President Wilson set out (September 1919) on a tour of the country, but on the way back from the Pacific coast he had an apoplectic stroke and was forced to return to Washington, where for months he was confined to the White House unable to attend to any but the most urgent public business. Meanwhile the Senate adopted a number of reservations to the Covenant, including one which provided that the United States assumed no obligation to use its military or naval forces or otherwise aid to enforce Article X unless Congress should by act or joint resolution so direct. In defense of this reservation its supporters pointed to the constitutional clause that provides that only Congress can declare war. All attempts to secure ratification of the treaty, with or without reservations, failed (November 1919, March 1920). The Senate also refused to ratify an agreement by which the United States and Great Britain bound themselves to go to the assistance of France in case of unprovoked attack by Germany. A joint resolution declaring the war at an end was passed by both houses, but the president vetoed it (May 27, 1920). Under Harding's administration a treaty embodying many of the terms of the Versailles Treaty but omitting the League of Nations Covenant was negotiated with Germany and was ratified by the Senate. On November 11, 1921, exactly three years after the close of hostilities, the two governments exchanged ratifications.

Results of the War. Three famous royal houses, the Romanovs, the Habsburgs, and the Hohenzollerns, were swept from their thrones. King Ferdinand of Bulgaria and King Constantine of Greece also lost their crowns. Monarchy, as a system of government, disappeared in Germany; the various states set up republican forms, which united into a new German republic, with Socialist tendencies, but keeping the old name of the Reich.

The Habsburg dominions were broken into fragments. Three republics—Hungary (later declared a monarchy), Austria, and Czechoslovakia—arose from the ruins, while portions were incorporated with Italy, Rumania, Poland, and Yugoslavia. Germany lost Alsace-Lorraine to France, a small district to Belgium, part of Schleswig to Denmark, large territories in the east to Poland, and all of her colonies, amounting to more than a million square miles. Bulgaria lost territory, and of the once vast dominions of the sultan nothing remained save a small tract of land about Istanbul and part of Asia Minor. Heavy indemnities were saddled upon all the vanquished peoples.

Russia, which entered the war on the side of the Entente but withdrew from the conflict before victory was won, underwent a social and economic revolution, which set off a train of events destined to lead to a still more terrible war of worldwide extent 20 years later. On her western border new states were created or old ones were restored: Finland, Estonia, Lithuania, and Poland—all republics.

The victors enlarged their territorial domains, but the condition of many of them was little better than that of the vanquished. All that took a real part in the conflict emerged from it bearing immense burdens of debt. Russia and Germany found it necessary to repudiate their national currencies. Hungary and Austria were in scarcely less difficult situations. Even France and Italy failed to stabilize their currencies until these had dwindled to a mere fraction of their pre-War values. Great Britain was least affected financially, but her economic recovery was slow and halting.

The net result of the disorganization and economic losses of the chief belligerents was a shift in balance of strength from Europe to America. The United States became a creditor nation instead of a debtor nation. Governmental debts alone due from European nations to the United States totaled approximately 10 billion dollars. According to agreements negotiated with the individual debtor governments, these amounts were to be paid off in a period of about 60 years. The Allied powers expected to obtain the funds for payment from the indemnity imposed on Germany. Only a small fraction was ever paid.

LEAGUE OF NATIONS

During World War I, the necessity for an association of nations, to settle controversies threatening the peace of the world, was voiced at frequent intervals. Premier Asquith of Great Britain made one of the first official utterances to this effect. President Wilson, in Number 14 of his famous "Points," appealed for a "league of nations." Thus, the delegates to the Peace Conference at Paris in 1919 were generally receptive to such a plan, and several brought concrete suggestions.

Organization. The Covenant of the League of Nations was adopted by the conference April 28, and became binding, upon the powers ratifying the treaty with Germany, on January 10, 1920. The Covenant provides an organization designed to embrace eventually all independent states and self-governing dominions. The organization consists of three parts: a Council; an Assembly; and a permanent secretariat.

The Council. The Council is composed of representatives of the British Empire, Russia, France, Italy, and nine (originally four) other member nations, elected by the Assembly for three-year periods, three being chosen each year. The Covenant provided places for the United States, Germany, and Japan as permanent members of the Council. Germany and Japan resigned from the League and the United States never joined. The Council meets at least annually and may deal with any matter affecting the peace of the world. Its first meeting was held January 16, 1920.

The Assembly. The Assembly is made up of representatives of nations which are members of the League. It has power to deal with any matter within the sphere of action of the League, or affecting the peace of the world. Each power is entitled to at most three delegates but to only one vote. Seven members of the British Commonwealth of Nations are regarded as distinct powers, each with one vote in the Assembly. At the seat of the League, in Geneva, Switzerland, the Assembly holds annual meetings, opening on the first Monday of September.

The Secretariat. The secretariat of the League is established at the headquarters of the League in the city of Geneva. It consists of the secretary general and the necessary staff of secretaries and advisers.

Program of the League. The nations which are members of the League agree to respect and preserve, as against external aggression, the territorial integrity and existing political independence of all members. They are further pledged to submit, either to arbitration or to inquiry by the League, any disputes likely to lead to a rupture of friendly relations.

The Covenant also provides for the registration, with the permanent secretariat, of all treaties between states; for issuing commissions to administer territory under mandate; and for the taking over by the League of all international bureaus, with the consent of the states establishing them. The Covenant provided also for the establishment of the Permanent Court of International Justice at The Hague. Amendments to the Covenant can take effect only when ratified by all members of the League represented in the Council and by a majority of the members whose representatives compose the Assembly.

Member Nations. At the first meeting of the Assembly, November 15, 1920, 42 states were members of the League. Its largest membership was 57, in 1934; first and last 63 nations have been members. At the beginning of 1942, the League nominally included 45 nations: Afghanistan, Argentina, Australia, Belgium, Bolivia, Bulgaria, Canada, China, Colombia, Cuba, Czechoslovakia, Denmark, Dominican Republic, Ecuador, Egypt, Eire, Estonia, Ethiopia, Finland, France, Great Britain, Haiti, Greece, India, Iran, Iraq, Latvia, Liberia, Lithuania, Luxemburg, Mexico, Netherlands, New Zealand, Norway, Panama, Poland, Portugal, Rumania, South Africa, Sweden, Switzerland, Thäi, Turkey, Uruguay, and Yugoslavia. Of these Denmark, Finland, France, and Rumania had given notice of withdrawal; Belgium, Luxemburg, Netherlands, Norway, Greece, Czechoslovakia, and Yugoslavia were under the military control of the Axis powers; Estonia, Latvia, and Lithuania were absorbed in Russia, and Poland was divided between Russia and Germany. Ethiopia had been conquered by Italy and reconquered by Great Britain.

CASUALTIES IN THE UNITED STATES ARMY AND NAVY DURING WORLD WAR I

Cause of Death	Foreign			Domestic			Grand Total		
	Officers	Enlisted Men	Total	Officers	Enlisted Men	Total	Officers	Enlisted Men	Aggregate
Killed in action	1,618	35,193	36,811	....	5	5	1,618	35,198	36,816
Died of wounds received in action	603	13,108	13,711	1	44	45	604	13,152	13,756
Died of disease	609	23,091	23,700	1,037	37,369	38,406	1,646	60,460	62,106
Died of accident	355	2,203	2,558	357	1,535	1,892	712	3,738	4,450
Drowned	17	308	325	13	372	385	30	680	710
Suicide	60	237	297	75	598	673	135	835	970
Murder or homicide	6	152	158	13	146	159	19	298	317
Executed	.....	11	11	....	24	24	.....	35	35
Other causes	1	120	121	2	154	156	3	274	277
Totals	3,269	74,423	77,692	1,498	40,247	41,745	4,767	114,670	119,437
Total wounded	7,292	190,657	197,949	....	.....	.....	7,292	190,657	197,949
Grand total died and wounded *	10,561	265,080	275,641	1,498	40,247	41,745	12,059	305,327	317,386

Casualties in the Navy and Marine Corps: Killed in action, 3129; Died of disease, 6600; Wounded in action, 10,789. The Marine Corps lost 2707 killed in action; the Navy, 422.

* Note.—The figures given in the above table represent the latest available government statistics. As in the case of casualty statistics of other wars, however, they are subject to correction in detail.

Sixteen former members have withdrawn: Albania, Brazil, Costa Rica, Chile, Germany, Guatemala, Honduras, Hungary, Italy, Japan, Nicaragua, Paraguay, Peru, Salvador, Spain, and Venezuela. Russia was expelled, December 1939. Austria was annexed to Germany. The United States and Saudi Arabia have never been members.

The United States and the League. President Wilson, who represented the United States at the Peace Conference, was an active promoter of the League, and, by his insistence, the Covenant was made an integral part of the Treaty of Versailles, fixing the conditions of peace with Germany. Upon his presentation of this treaty to the Senate for ratification, serious objections were raised. The most important of these were: (1) the impairment of the fundamental principle of American foreign policy known as the Monroe Doctrine; (2) the guarantee to respect and preserve against external aggression the territorial integrity and existing political independence of all members of the League. This provision, embraced in Article X, was declared by President Wilson to be the "heart of the Covenant" and incapable of amendment without destroying the purpose of the instrument. Reservations embracing these and some minor points were framed by the Senate, and the ensuing deadlock between the president and the Senate led to the rejection of the entire treaty.

The Work of the League. Among the political undertakings of the League were the government of the Saar basin through an international commission, the protection of Danzig, the regulation of traffic on the Danube, the supervision of a corridor giving Bulgaria access to the Ægean Sea at Kavala, Greece, and the settlement of a number of geopolitical problems.

Conspicuous failures of the League to prevent conflicts include Japan's refusal to desist from "aggressive" action against China in 1931 and Italy's defiance of economic sanctions invoked after an "aggressive" warfare against Ethiopia in 1935-36. The League was helpless in the face of Germany's seizure of Austria in 1937, of Czechoslovakia in 1938, and of Danzig and Poland in 1939.

Dissolution. The League ended with World War II. A meeting at Geneva in September 1939 delegated authority for League activities for the duration of the war to a Supervisory Committee. A small part of the Secretariat remained at Geneva, while important nonpolitical branches were moved to Princeton university, Montreal, and Washington. On April 8, 1945 the last Assembly met at Geneva. Ten days later the League voted its dissolution, transferring its material property to the United Nations.

MANDATES

Politically, the term "mandate" was devised by the Peace Conference of 1919, as a system of trusteeship for the government and development of dependent peoples wrested from the possession of Germany and from the Ottoman empire.

On May 16, 1919, the Paris Conference agreed to allot to Great Britain, German East Africa; to the Union of South Africa, German Southwest Africa; to New Zealand, German Samoa; to Australia, German New Guinea, the Bismarck archipelago and adjoining islands; and to Japan, the former German islands north of the equator, with the exception of the Island of Nauru, which was allotted to Great Britain. At this same meeting, Great Britain and France agreed to divide the German colonies of Togoland and Cameroon between them. This was accomplished, July 10, 1919.

An allocation of territories of the Ottoman empire was accomplished at the conference of San Remo, April 18 to 25, 1919, where the representatives of Great Britain and France agreed that the former power should receive Iraq and Palestine, and the latter, Syria and Lebanon. A subsequent agreement, at Paris, December 23, 1920, transferred a portion of Syria to the British mandate of Palestine, and France received, as a consideration, a share in oil land concessions in Iraq, and other advantages.

PERMANENT COURT OF INTERNATIONAL JUSTICE (WORLD COURT)

The establishment of an international court for the adjudication of disputes between nations was provided for by the Peace Conference of 1919. Such a tribunal had already been proposed by Elihu Root in 1907. An arrangement in 1910 to which the United States, France, Germany, and Great Britain were parties was stopped by the World War. Pursuant to Article XIV of the Covenant, the Council of the League, early in 1920, appointed a committee of jurists to formulate a plan or organization. With some modifications, this plan was adopted by the Assembly of the League of Nations, December 13, 1920.

Organization. The Court consists of 15 members, elected for terms of nine years by the Assembly and Council of the League of Nations from a list of names nominated by the panels of jurists from which members are appointed to the Permanent Court of Arbitration at The Hague.

Jurisdiction. For trial of international disputes, the court is open to members of the League and to states mentioned in the annex to the Covenant of the League. States ratifying its constitution may recognize as compulsory the jurisdiction of the court in any or all of the following classes of legal disputes: (a) the interpretation of treaties; (b) questions of international law; (c) the existence of any fact which, if established, constitutes a breach of international obligations; (d) reparation for such a breach. Over 45 nations, including Great Britain, France, Italy, and Japan, accepted this compulsory feature.

The court, in making its awards, was to apply the principles of international conventions, international law, general principles of law recognized by civilized nations, and, as a subsidiary means of determining the rules of international law, the teachings of the most highly qualified publicists of various nations. A majority of the court might render a decision. The court was empowered to render advisory opinions.

The Permanent Court of International Justice was dissolved by the last Assembly of the League of Nations. It was replaced, and its work continued by the International Court of Justice, organized at the Hague, April 18, 1946, under the charter of the United Nations.

REPARATIONS

Under the Treaty of Versailles a commission was set up to fix the amount of the reparation payments to be made by Germany and to determine its division among the recipients. A definite assessment was finally made on April 21, 1921, at London. It amounted to about 32 billion dollars.

The first plan for collection proved impossible. Under the Dawes plan of 1924 and the Young plan of 1929, the total was finally scaled down to 8.806 billion dollars, as of September 1, 1929. Payments were to be spread over 59 years. In July 1931 a one-year moritorium was granted; no payments were made thereafter. The amount actually paid under all the plans was about $4,470,300,000.

BANK FOR INTERNATIONAL SETTLEMENTS

This bank was created under the Young plan to handle the reparation funds. It was in addition to provide facilities for international financial operations. It was organized in May 1930 with headquarters at Basel, Switzerland. Its directors are named by the central banks of the leading countries. It cannot issue currency or make loans to governments. It may, however, hold gold reserves for central banks, thus reducing the need for shipments and acting as a clearing house.

WORLD WAR II

As compared with World War I, World War II was more nearly a universal war. It was also much more complex. Many of its issues grew out of World War I but many others did not. Both wars might be regarded as phases of a continuing struggle to determine by whom the world should be controlled.

Such struggles had been going on from the beginning of history, but the advances of the last century in the means of transportation and communication and in the mechanization of production made it possible to correlate activities of armed forces on a global scale. They also made war potentially more decisive, for the victor would control the means necessary for any resistance, present or future, and the vanquished would be powerless. The rapidly increasing population of the world added an element of urgency.

Comparison between the Two Wars: The Line-Up. In both wars Germany was the leading antagonist against an alliance of other powers. She had as allies in World War I Austria-Hungary and later Bulgaria and Turkey. In World War II, Germany, enlarged by portions of the old Austria-Hungary, was joined by Italy and Japan. She also had the more or less reluctant assistance of four satellite states—Finland, Hungary, Rumania, and Bulgaria. Early conquests gave her control of the resources, human and material, of Norway, Denmark, France, Belgium, The Netherlands, Poland, Yugoslavia, Greece, and part of Russia.

Great Britain and France were leading powers against Germany at the opening of both wars. In World War I Russia was an ally from the first, but she did not enter World War II until attacked in mid-1941. As the war enlarged, however, the alliance against Germany embraced also the United States, China, the nations originally non-belligerent which Germany had conquered, and a number of countries of Latin America, the most active of which was Brazil.

Geography of the War. World War I was waged almost exclusively in Europe, though operations were carried on to some extent also in Africa, in southwestern Asia, and on the high seas. With World War II, besides the primary conflict in Europe, eastern Asia and the Pacific became a major theater of warfare; Africa was involved from the equatorial lakes to the Mediterranean; Australia was attacked; even the Americas found their outlying shores and islands within the zone of conflict. Air power made war on the oceans more widespread and intense.

Weapons and Methods. These and other contrasts were due to radical developments in weapons and methods of their use, particularly the airplane, the tank, and electrical devices.

Airplanes.—Airplanes during World War I had been used chiefly as the "eyes" of the land forces; combat had been incidental to their major use, and bombing raids were few. During World War II, they constituted a fighting force without which no army or navy could achieve victory. The airplane and glider were also developed for the transport of troops to hostile islands or behind enemy lines.

Still more revolutionary was the use of airplanes to destroy entire cities, wiping out large sections of a nation's production and transport facilities. The airplane above all other weapons brought civilians into the center of warfare, for in such raids little discrimination of "military objectives" could be made.

The airplane also greatly altered the form of naval warfare. By means of aircraft transported on carriers battle fleets were enabled to concentrate striking power against opponents long before ships came within range of each other.

Tanks.—The caterpillar tractor, already used in agriculture and industry, was applied to armored motor vehicles in World War I. Such bullet-proof tanks broke down the advantage which the machine gun had given to the defense. In World War II the tank was given heavier armor and heavier guns, which made it extremely formidable despite development of anti-tank guns. Above all, its speed was increased. Tanks moving at forty miles an hour were fortress and cavalry combined. Land and amphibious truck transportation and the equipping of ordnance with self-propulsion vastly increased mobility.

This superior mobility made World War II predominantly a war of movement. Conflicts of tank divisions became a feature of most battles. Add to this the immense numbers of troops employed, and a single battle might cover a terrain hundreds of miles in extent. Whereas in 1815 the battle of Waterloo, fought within an area less than three miles square, decided the fate of Europe, in 1940 the battle of Flanders, with a battle line a hundred miles long, was merely one phase of an operation extending from the North Sea to the Pyrenees.

Electrical Devices.—Radio communication, in its infancy in World War I, was a necessity of World War II. Only by means of radio signals could the movements of airplanes, tanks, and motorized troops be co-ordinated. Radio beams directed air raids. "Radar," a newly developed electrical instrument, permitted detection with amazing accuracy. Electrical sighting devices were used for bombing and anti-aircraft guns, for naval guns, and torpedoes.

Importance of Productive Facilities. World War I marked a real departure from previous wars in the extent to which the decision turned on the manufacturing ability of the participants and of the nations which could be counted on to supply them. The greater ascendancy of machinery in World War II made the ability to produce and supply such machinery an indispensable element of success. This brought the factory into the battle line, for the destruction of the factory and its civilian worker became as necessary and almost as desirable as the destruction of a field force. In the airplane was found an ideal weapon for that purpose. Protection against an air raid is difficult, retaliation is much easier. But the airplane can only strike and destroy, it cannot capture and carry away. So sheer destruction became more than ever before a dominant feature of war. The phrase "total war" began to be used, implying that every element of a nation's life and energies must be employed for victory. The civilian at home was a participant as truly as the soldier in the field—and therefore equally open to attack.

Psychology and Economics. On both sides psychological weapons were used with new skill. "Wars of nerves" played on the popular fears and uncertainty by radio, leaflets, and press reports. Economic threats and trade agreements were used to bring under control smaller countries, especially those with useful natural resources.

Causes of the War: The Heritage of World War I. Two main groups of causes combined to bring about World War II. First were questions inherited from World War I: the desire of Germany to regain her lost territory and prestige; the desire of the winning powers to hold their gains; the dissatisfaction of some of them with their share of the spoils; and the fear by the new national governments created after the war of losing their independence, particularly in view of the frequent existence of dissatisfied minorities within their borders.

Causes of the War: The Conflict of Idealogies. Before the war and in its early stages, an idealogical conflict, cutting across national lines, appeared as a prominent factor. As the war went on, this element was pushed into the background by rising national feeling and power politics. With the end of the war, the idealogical conflict showed signs of revival, but on different lines: a leftward tendency within the western European democracies, and signs of divergence between them and communist Russia.

Communism. The Russian revolution represented the first large scale application of Marxian socialism. The absolute control of the individual it involved was the antithesis of the individual freedom which was the ideal of democratic nations. A government based on control from the top and by the Communist party professed to attend a future return to individual freedom, but that future was distant. One reason was the belief of the leaders in a future struggle with capitalistic countries. To prepare for the struggle they worked for the extension of the party to other countries, enlisting party members abroad, and training them, for action in the party interest, even against their own country.

Anti-Communism. The natural result was agitation and organization against Communism. This feeling helped Mussolini and Hitler. Hitler was aided also by the economic depression, a powerful factor in bringing about other dictatorships after 1930. The peoples were willing to follow any leader who promised to help them. This internal social conflict helped also to paralyze the resistance of small countries to the possible danger from Fascism. Pacificism also played a part. But the German leaders were not pacifists. See *Germany*, *Hitler*, *Adolf*, *Anti-Semitism*.

The Axis and the Anti-Comintern Pact. In 1935 and 1936 Germany and Italy developed a common policy based on opposition to communism as embodied in the Russian-controlled Third Communist International (Comintern) and also to democratic governments and their principles. Both nations, moreover, asserted their need of expansion to relieve their growing populations. This understanding, popularly referred to as the Rome-Berlin Axis, met a sympathetic response from Japan.

On November 25, 1936, Japan and Germany signed the Anti-Comintern pact, ostensibly providing for consultation and cooperation against the Communist International but directed also against the democratic governments. Other powers which might feel themselves threatened were invited to join. Italy joined the next year and was followed two years later by Manchukuo, Hungary, and Spain. The agreement was to last for five years. On its expiration in 1941, it was renewed at Berlin, and seven other governments adhered: Bulgaria, Croatia, Denmark, Finland, Rumania, Slovakia, and the Nanking government of China, while the Vichy government of France endorsed its principles.

Beginnings of the War. It is part of the complexities of World War II that no one date can be confidently fixed on for its outbreak. There is rather a series of dates on which different stages of the war began.

Of the dates which might be selected, the most important are:

September 1, 1939, when Germany invaded Poland, thus bringing France and Great Britain into the war;

June 22, 1941, when Germany attacked Russia;

December 7, 1941, when Japan attacked the United States.

There are, however, several earlier dates, marking the stages of its approach, when hostilities were begun which preluded or merged into the general war. These dates are:

September 18, 1931, when Japan occupied Mukden and began the conquest of Manchuria, which it erected into the puppet state of Manchukuo;

July 7, 1937, when Japan attacked China proper, thus beginning a war which later became an integral part of the larger global war after Japan had attacked the United States and Great Britain;

October 1935, when Italy began the conquest of Ethiopia in an attempt to build up her African empire;

July 17, 1936, when a conservative party rebellion against the left-wing government of Spain provided an opportunity for the Fascist powers to set up a government favorable to their cause;

March 12, 1938, when Germany occupied Austria;

October 1, 1938, when Germany took over the Sudetenland from Czechoslovakia.

Expansion by Italy and Japan. Beginning with 1935, the axis powers, either by war or other politico-military techniques, expanded their territories. Italy conquered Ethiopia in 1935–36. When the League of Nations attempted to enforce sanctions Italy resigned, as Germany and Japan had done the year before. In April 1939, Italy overran Albania, which was erected into a separate kingdom under the king of Italy.

Japan had seized Manchuria in 1931 and the northern provinces of China in 1935. In 1937, she entered upon an undeclared war with China. By 1939 she was in control of the coastal regions and of most of the large cities, and had set up a puppet government at Nanking. But the Chinese under Chiang Kai-shek still held out in the interior.

The Spanish Civil War. As the Balkan Wars had been a prelude to the First World War, so the Spanish Civil War preceded the second. It had started in appearance as a revolt of the conservative army leaders, representing the monarchical and clerical tradition of old Spain, against the Republican government. The communist wing of the Republicans gained control and was supported by Russia to the end, while the Insurgents, quickly assuming Fascist forms and principles, received men and munitions from Germany and Italy. Great Britain, France, and the United States pursued a policy of non-intervention which operated decisively against the Government. The war ended in 1939 with the triumph of the Insurgents under General Franco and the establishment of a totalitarian government bound by close ties to the Axis.

German Expansion. In 1935 a plebescite in the Saar District, in accordance with the Treaty of Versailles, resulted in a ten-to-one vote in favor of reunion with Germany. Germany was now showing her intention of disregarding all the restrictive clauses of the treaty. In 1936 she reintroduced conscription and began to rearm. The Rhineland was again occupied by German troops and fortified while France and Britain looked on. They remained silent. Hitler then turned to Austria. The government of that country was now a practical dictatorship under Chancellor Schuschnigg after the Socialist party had been suppressed. Schuschnigg made a gesture of resistance by calling for a plebescite, whereupon Hitler, on March 12, 1938, moved German troops into Austria and occupied the country. A vote taken under German auspices showed a heavy majority for union. Austria became the *Ostmark*.

The Munich Pact. Czechoslovakia came next. The Versailles treaty had included in that country border districts largely populated by Germans—the Sudeten lands. These claimed to be treated unfairly by the Czechs, appealed to Hitler for aid, and threatened revolt. The Czech government appealed to France, England, and Russia for assistance. A crisis threatened which might result in a European war.

Premier Chamberlain averted the immediate danger by flying to a conference with Hitler at Berchtesgaden. England and France advised Czechoslovakia to submit, and with Mussolini's help, persuaded Hitler not to use force. The final adjustment was made at Munich, September 29-30. The parties were, in addition to Hitler and Mussolini, Neville Chamberlain and Edouard Daladier, premier of France. Russia was ignored. Czech territory with more than fifty per cent of German population was taken over by the Reich. Final determination of the boundary was to be made by a commission of the four powers and Czechoslovakia.

The Fruits of "Appeasement." Chamberlain's action was generally approved in England. Hitler had promised at the time of the Munich pact, to respect the independence of Czechoslovakia, and had said that Germany had no further territorial claims in Europe, but he made no opposition when Hungary and Poland took parts of the weakened state and when Slovakia demanded autonomy. In March 1939, on the occasion of trouble in Slovakia, Hitler moved troops into Bohemia and Moravia, and declared them a protectorate of the Reich. Slovakia became independent, but under German control. Great Britain, France, Russia, and the United States, refused to recognize the new status. In March 1939 also, Memel, with a large German population, was yielded by Lithuania. All these additions to the Reich were justified by the Germans as reclamations of territory unjustly taken from them in World War I.

Germany, Poland, and Russia. Hitler now turned to Danzig and the Polish corridor. The corridor, cutting off East Prussia from the rest of Germany, had been created to give Poland an outlet to the sea; a large part of its population was German. Danzig, German from its foundation, had been made a free city under the League of Nations with guarantees for German and Polish commercial rights. Near it, the Poles had built their own seaport of Gdynia. Hitler was now demanding that Danzig be returned to the Reich with guarantees for Polish commercial rights and that Germany be given an extraterritorial corridor across the corridor. Poland refused, and the deadlock continued for several months.

One reason for the delay was the position of Russia. Great Britain had already declared, on March 31, that she would support the Poles against any action which threatened their independence. France was committed to the same policy. But Russia was the only power which could give Poland real military assistance against a German attack.

Russia had formerly cooperated with Great Britain and France, fearing Nazi policies. The western powers had ignored her in the Munich agreement. Now Britain and France asked her support for Poland. Stalin, now the real ruler of Russia, negotiated with both sides. At last, on August 20, 1939, he signed a trade treaty with Germany and, four days later, a ten-year non-aggression pact.

Stalin gained by this treaty the time which Russia needed to strengthen her army and defenses against a possible German attack. He also divided the western powers, setting Great Britain and France against Germany. The price he received was a free hand with the Baltic states and Poland. The immediate effect was to free Germany from any fear of an attack from the east, and to cut off Poland from any effective military assistance.

The news of the German-Russian alliance burst upon the world like a thunderbolt. But if Hitler expected it to deter the British and French from going to war, he was disappointed. Neville Henderson, the British ambassador, made it clear that Great Britain would fight if Poland was attacked.

At the last moment Germany put forward proposals for a peaceful settlement, but the Poles were given no opportunity to consider or hardly to understand them. On September 1, the German armies invaded Poland. For two days longer the British and French governments, without success, continued to urge withdrawal of the troops and a conference. On September 3, at 11 A.M., Great Britain declared war; six hours later France followed her example.

Great Britain was followed in its declaration of war by most of the British dominions. Australia and New Zealand declared war simultaneously; Canada settled a constitutional question without raising it by delaying her declaration of war until her parliament had acted on September 10. South Africa, after some deliberation and a change of ministry from General Herzog to General Smuts, severed diplomatic relations on September 5. Eire, refusing to follow the other dominions, remained neutral.

The Polish War. Poland had no natural frontier defense. The surface of the country was generally level, dry at that time of year, ideal terrain for mechanized armies. The industrial district was near the German border. To defend this open country the Poles had about 600,000 men and 900 planes.

The Poles hoped to delay the Germans in western Poland, and on the line of the Vistula, until the fall rains and the English and French armies in the west could come to their relief. The German plan was a double "pincers" movement. Two armies converged on Warsaw from East Prussia and Pomerania; two others, cutting off the industrial district, and outflanking the Vistula line, converged upon Warsaw from the south and southwest. Germany used most of her first line troops, almost a million men. General von Brauchitsch was commander in chief, General von Bock led the northern army, and General von Rundstedt, the southern.

It was the German plan which succeeded. The Poles were driven back in the north and west and were outflanked in the south. The rains did not come. The Germans made abundant use of mechanized troops, but a great part of their success was due to air power. Their overwhelming air force crushed the Polish air defense at the first onslaught, broke up the mobilization by attacking concentration points, especially in eastern Poland, bombed Warsaw and other cities, and kept the Germans fully informed of Polish troop movements. On September 5 the Germans were within 40 miles of Warsaw, on the 6th the southern army entered Krakow, by the 14th the Germans were closing in on Warsaw itself. The western army was cut off; the only hope of the eastern army was to make a last stand in the marshes on the eastern border.

Poland's deathblow came from Russia. On September 17 Russian troops, "to protect Russian interests and the White Russian and Ukrainian minorities," entered Poland and occupied the eastern half, as far as Brest-Litovsk and Lemberg (Lvov), with little resistance. Half a million Polish troops were captured. Warsaw held out until the 27th.

Danzig, the occasion of the trouble, had, meantime, announced its union with the Reich.

President Moscicki and the Polish government fled to Rumania, thence to France, and ultimately to London. They organized a government which Great Britain, France, and the United States continued to recognize as the legitimate Polish government.

Germany and Russia now divided Poland—its fourth partition—on the general lines of the Bug and San rivers, the "Curzon line." Russia received the larger territory, but the smaller population. Her share was mostly annexed to the Soviet Republics of White Russia and the Ukraine, with which its population was racially connected. Germany left the part around Warsaw for the Poles, and prepared the rest for German occupation. The price the Germans paid was 43,000 casualties, 10,000 killed.

Defensive Attitude of Allies. France and Britain had declared war, but in neither country was the mental attitude propitious for victory. England was trusting to her seapower and her blockade; France, to her fortifications. In England Chamberlain, a competent peace minister, was not the man to conduct a war. In France, the administration was weakened by personal rivalry and party politics. In both countries pacifist feeling was strong. Both countries were thinking first of defense. Germany, schooled by her years of adversity under the Versailles treaty, and forced by her disarmament to start from scratch, could take advantage of changes in technique to develop a new army and a new type of war, the *Blitzkrieg*. See *Blitzkrieg*.

British and French Preparation. Great Britain had introduced compulsory military service in May 1939; now the draft was extended to men twenty to forty-one. The "territorials" (militia) were increased. Air raid precautions were taken and a rationing system was set up. France was more advanced in preparations. The Chamber in May had given Daladier "full powers" for national defense. Very early in the war a joint war council was established to co-ordinate operations.

Strength of the Opposing Forces. On paper the armies were not very unequal. Germany had potentially six million men, 160 divisions. Against these England could bring about four million men, 600,000 being in the regular army. France had 765,000 regulars, with 4,250,000 reserves. The German army, however, was at home, and could be used there. The British and French armies had the areas of their empires to cover.

In naval strength, especially in capital ships, the Allies had an overwhelming advantage, but the Germans were strong in submarines. In the air the Germans had 11,000 planes against the Allies' 8,000, and superior facilities for replacement.

Maginot and Siegfried Lines. In the hope of preventing such an invasion as they had suffered in 1914, the French had constructed their great Maginot line, so called from the war minister who had initiated its construction. This was a continuous fortification from Switzerland to the Belgian border. It cost $150,000,000, and was believed impregnable against assault or siege. Unfortunately, it was not continued along the Belgian border. Over against it, the Germans were hastily building the Siegfried line, or Westwall, a zone of disconnected but supporting redoubts, 30 miles wide.

When Poland was attacked, the French manned the Maginot line, but failed to use their time to strengthen the defenses on the Belgian border. They made only futile demonstrations against the German reserves in the Siegfried line. A British expeditionary force of 350,000 men, under General Viscount Gort, took over a sector near Luxemburg in December. General Maurice Gamelin, commanding the French army, was made commander in chief of the Allied armies. The British Admiralty directed the navies.

First Stages of the War at Sea. Naval warfare was begun at once by Britain on the lines of World War I. The battle fleet was concentrated at Scapa Flow and in the Firth of Forth. A strict blockade was established. Control ports were set up at strategic points, and the usual friction with neutral powers began.

The Germans at once began a counter-blockade. They had about 50 submarines and were building more. They sent them out to prey upon enemy commerce and sank 785,000 tons of shipping, neutral as well as allied, in the first four months. The British met the attack with some success by using the convoy system. Both sides laid mines.

German submarines sank two British capital ships but only one real ship action occurred, the sinking of the *Graf Spee*. She was driven into Montevideo, Uruguay, by three British cruisers, and scuttled in the River La Plata.

Russia Moves on the Baltic. As soon as the treaty with Germany was signed, Russia began to move on the Baltic with German approval. Her aim was to regain control of the Baltic states—Finland, Estonia, Latvia, and Lithuania, which had become independent in 1919. In September and October 1939 she obtained treaties of "mutual assistance" which gave her military control of the eastern end of the Baltic. Then the Communist parties within the states acted, and in July 1940 Latvia, Estonia, and Lithuania were admitted to the Soviet Union.

The Finnish War. Finland, however, was stronger and less complaisant. She refused Moscow's demands for a cession of territory at the head of the Gulf of Finland. On November 30, Russia invaded the country, alleging the necessity of defending Leningrad from attacks by or through Finland.

The key to the Finnish defense was the Mannerheim line, across the Karelian isthmus, from Viborg (Viipuri) on the Gulf to Lake Ladoga. To defend these works and the long eastern boundary General Mannerheim had 225,000 trained troops and a militia force of about 100,000.

For two months the Finns repulsed the Russians from the Mannerheim line and threw back attacks around Lake Ladoga and along their eastern frontier, though the Russians took Petsamo in the north. The weather, exceptionally severe, was on their side, and the Russian troops were second-rate and poorly led. In February the Russians sent better commanders with more troops, bringing their force up to 800,000, and broke through the Mannerheim line.

The Scandinavian countries, though traditionally suspicious of Russia, gave Finland no open assistance. Fearing German reprisals, they refused passage to British and French troops.

On March 12, a treaty was signed at Moscow by which Finland gave up Viborg and the Karelian isthmus, leaving her defenseless in that quarter. The cession of Hango and its islands completed Russian control of the Gulf of Finland.

The Norwegian War. Norway, Sweden, and Denmark had hoped to maintain their neutrality in this war, as in the last. Sweden alone succeeded.

Norway lay between the two belligerents. The Germans alleged that her neutrality had been invaded by the British seizure of a German prisonship in Norwegian waters, and by British mine-laying in the route of ships bringing iron ore from Narvik. Under pretext of protecting Norway and Denmark from Allied invasion, the Germans themselves invaded these countries on the night of April 9, 1940. They promised the territorial integrity of both countries in the future.

Denmark could not resist, and King Christian advised his people to make no opposition. But outside the continent, Iceland declared its independence, and received a British garrison; Greenland turned to the United States for support; and the British occupied the Faroe Islands.

In Norway the German attack was directed against Oslo, and the western ports of Bergen, Trondheim, Narvik, and Stavanger. The attacking force numbered about 25,000, later increased fourfold. Norway had about 15,000 trained soldiers, and no air force to speak of. Oslo was taken, but the king, ministry, and parliament escaped.

Most of Norway's wealth, population, and resources are concentrated south of Trondheim, in the coast towns, and the two river valleys, Ostendal and the Godbrandsdal. The Germans had already seized the coast towns. They now fanned out from Oslo up the river valleys, meeting brave but inadequate resistance. The Allied troops sent to assist Norway were too few and came too late. By early June the Norwegian army had surrendered and the Allies were forced to withdraw.

By this success the Germans had made secure their ore supplies from the Swedish mines, clinched their hold on Sweden, blocked any chance of attack from the north, and secured bases for sea and air operations against Britain.

King Haakon, his family and ministers escaped to England. Since the Storting had authorized him to act from outside Norway, his continued to be the only legal government. The gold reserve had been sent to England, and the Norwegian merchant marine obeyed his orders. The Germans set up a government of Nazi sympathizers, headed by Vidkun Quisling, which met determined resistance, active and passive. See *Quisling*.

The Norwegian fiasco brought about the fall of the British cabinet headed by Chamberlain. He was succeeded by Winston Churchill, who told the Commons, quoting Garibaldi, "I have nothing to offer you but blood, toil, tears, and sweat."

The Invasion of the Netherlands. Scarcely had Winston Churchill taken office when he had to meet a new German attack on the Continent. On the morning of May 10 the Germans, without a formal declaration of war, poured over the borders of the Netherlands and Belgium.

Unlike Norway, both countries were ready for and expecting an attack. Both had counted on holding their defense lines until help should come from Great Britain and France. Both countries had insisted on their neutrality to the last, and no Allied troops were in either country when the invasion came.

The Germans crushed the Dutch resistance in the north of Holland and cut off relief from the south. Air power, with the use of parachute troops, and the fifth column, partly of pro-German Netherlanders, wrecked the Dutch resistance. Airfields were seized, Rotterdam was bombed, the Dutch army, under General Winkleman, fought bravely, but was forced to surrender May 14.

On May 13th Queen Wilhelmina with her ministers left the Hague for England on a British cruiser and she continued to govern the Dutch colonial empire from London. They had brought with them the Dutch gold reserve and control over the great Dutch merchant marine, which was largely still at sea. The Germans organized in Holland, as in Norway, a government of Dutch Nazis.

The Battle of Flanders. This name is given to the fighting in Belgium and northern France between the German frontier and the Channel ports. On the morning of May 10 the German army swept into Belgium.

In this quarter Belgium was defended by Liège and its forts, the fortified line of the Albert canal, and the supposedly impassable ground of the Ardennes Forest. To defend these the Belgians had mobilized perhaps 800,000 men. General Gamelin had assumed that this line would delay the Germans for four or five days, giving the Allied forces time to establish themselves on the line of Antwerp-Louvain-Namur for defense or counterattack. Accordingly, on the first news of the German invasion, the British expeditionary force and three French armies left their defensive positions in northern France and moved north into Belgium.

But the Germans moved too rapidly. They attacked Fort Eben Emael, north of Liège, and crossed the Albert canal on the first day of their advance. On the second day they had taken or destroyed the defenses of Liège. The Albert canal defenses gave way entirely, perhaps through treachery, and the invaders were passing the Ardennes, threatening the right flank of the Allies moving north.

The French Ninth Army under General Corap was to occupy the defenses along the Belgian border, but the Germans struck it before it got fairly into position. The Ninth Army disintegrated. Sedan was taken, and with it the bridge over the Meuse, which, for reasons never fully explained, had not been destroyed. The rout of Corap's army opened a gap fifty miles wide in the French line, and through it the invaders poured, heading westward to the sea.

The Allied forces in Belgium now met the main German advance in a confused struggle. In a tank battle near Gembloux the French fought creditably, but were outnumbered. Meanwhile the German air force operated in the rear of the Allied army, bombing the advancing reserves, the railways, and concentration points. The Allies found their movements handicapped by the crowds of fleeing civilians, panic-stricken by the planes which swept over them and machine-gunned them as well as troops. On the 17th Brussels, whence the Belgian government had already removed to Ostend, was occupied by the Germans, and Namur was taken. On the 18th the Germans entered Antwerp. The plan for a second line of defense had broken down.

Meantime the Nazi southern column was driving west across northern France. It passed the Aisne and Oise rivers and swept down the Somme valley. On the 20th it had reached Cambrai, the scene of the Battle of the Somme in 1916. On the 21st the Germans entered Amiens, which they had just failed to reach in 1918. The same day they reached Abbeville, at the mouth of the Somme.

It was now evident that the French high command had made a terrible mistake in the movement north. The Belgian army, the British Expeditionary Force, and the remnants of three French armies, the First, Seventh, and Ninth, were pressed by the Germans from the north and east, the advance of the southern column had cut them off from the main French army. Their only source of supply was the Channel ports, which were being bombed by the German air force, while the German mechanized columns, having turned north, were attacking from Arras and driving along the coast. Boulogne was taken on the 28th, and fierce fighting began near Calais. The Allies were now pressed back into a rough crescent around Dunkirk, with the Belgian army forming the north wing.

There was still hope if they could break through to the south, and such a movement, co-ordinated with a French attack from that quarter, would put the long, thin German salient in grave peril. General Weygand, who had replaced Gamelin in command of the French army, began to mass troops near Amiens for such a movement.

Any chance for the forces cornered in Belgium vanished when, on the morning of May 28, the Belgian army was surrendered by King Leopold, who declared that his army was starving and out of ammunition. The Belgian surrender exposed the right flank of the British. They could do nothing but fall back upon Dunkirk, the only port left in their hands. With them were a few Dutch troops and the remains of the French armies, about 400,000 men in all.

Dunkirk. The evacuation of the British army from Dunkirk was the one bright spot in the gloomy picture of disaster. The nearly 400,000 men in the town and its environs were crowded into an ever narrowing space by unceasing attacks, under fire from the German batteries, and bombed at times by the German airplanes. Military experts estimated that possibly 25 per cent of them could be rescued. British cruisers and destroyers fought off German submarines in the Channel. British and French aircraft, helped by cloudy weather, struggled with enemy planes above the town, and for a few days kept qualified control of the air. The British garrison in Calais fought to the last man to gain time.

Meantime every available craft on the opposite coast, merchant ships, tugboats, ferryboats, fishing boats, pleasure craft, river steamers, was called into service to assist the navy and the army transports in bringing the cornered troops to safety.

While the rearguard fought desperately on the hills around the town, this nondescript transport fleet took off the soldiers, dropping from the ruins of the shattered piers or wading out in long lines into the shoal waters from the beaches. Loaded to the gunwale, they steamed off for the English coast—and came back for more. The Admiralty estimated that 222 naval vessels and 665 other craft, besides French naval and private vessels took part in the embarkation. For three days and nights the evacuation went on. When the Germans finally forced their way through the town, 335,000 men, more than three-fourths of the Allied force were in England. All their heavy arms and equipment were lost.

The Germans now held all the Netherlands and Belgium, with a strip of northern France, including the Channel ports. The Dutch and Belgian armies were non-existent. The British Expeditionary Force had been driven off the Continent, and three French armies had been cut to pieces. In all the Allies had lost not far from a million men, including the larger part of their mechanized forces. The price the Germans paid, according to their own statements, was 10,252 dead, 42,523 wounded, and 9,463 missing.

The Collapse of France. The German army now turned southward. General Weygand was attempting to form a new line on the Aisne and Somme, but his troops had lost confidence in their commanders. Nevertheless, the Germans admitted losses of 17,000 killed and 68,000 wounded before the armistice.

The Germans now threatened Paris from two directions—from Rouen on the west and from the Marne on the east. The French government retired to Tours and later to Bordeaux. On June 13, Paris was proclaimed an "open city" and evacuated; the Germans entered it the next day without resistance. Verdun fell on the 15th, and the impregnable Maginot line lost its significance; Weygand withdrew a part of its garrison to a new line he was attempting to form on the Loire; the rest surrendered.

Italy, thinking the end was in sight, declared war on June 10, 1940. She made some slight advances in the Alps and on the southern coast, but her action made very little difference.

On June 16 defeatist elements in the French cabinet forced out Premier Reynaud. He was succeeded by Marshal Pétain, now controlled by a fascist group. The new government ignored its promise to make no separate peace, gave up its opportunity to retreat to Africa and carry on the war from there, and on June 17, asked for an armistice. It was signed on June 22; fighting ceased on June 25. The Germans staged the signing in the same railroad car, and at the same spot, Rethondes, where Germany had received the armistice terms of 1918.

Under the armistice the Germans occupied Paris, the northern industrial districts, and the west coast. The Italian border, the Mediterranean naval bases, and certain African districts were to be demilitarized. The French navy was concentrated and disarmed; the army demobilized; German and Italian prisoners were released. French communications and trade passed under German control. Pétain set up his government for unoccupied France at Vichy.

Control of Colonies. All five of the conquered countries had dependencies which remained out of German control. On Spitsbergen, Norway's arctic coal-mining settlement was destroyed by an Anglo-Norwegian expedition in September 1941, and the population was removed. A later German attempt to occupy the islands was destroyed. The action of the Danish colonies has been described. The Dutch colonies obeyed the queen and her government in London; Belgian Congo, the ministers of the captive King Leopold.

The French colonial empire was divided. Indo-China passed into the hands of a watchful and aggressive Japan. North Africa and West Africa, with Madagascar, obeyed the Vichy French government, as did the West Indies. One of the younger French generals, Charles de Gaulle, fled to London at the armistice and organized there the French National Committee, the "Free French" government, which was recognized by Britain. This government was recognized by French Equatorial Africa, French Cameroon, and some of the Pacific dependencies. In September 1940, with British assistance, he made an unsuccessful attempt to take Dakar, in French West Africa. In May and June 1941, Syria and Lebanon were forcibly occupied by British and Free French troops.

The Siege of Britain. After the fall of France Britain alone seemed to stand between Hitler and complete victory. There is some evidence that he expected her to yield and delayed his attack. But Britain had in Winston Churchill a leader who refused to acknowledge defeat. The British set to work with feverish haste to transform their country into an armed camp. The government was given absolute power over persons and property. Potential "fifth columnists" were imprisoned.

Whether an invasion was actually attempted was never made known, but there is considerable evidence that a large scale rehearsal met with disaster. At any rate, the German attempts to "soften" Britain by air attack definitely failed.

After a period of comparative quiet following the French armistice, German air attacks became more intense and frequent. They culminated on August 15, when wave after wave of planes swept over England, ranging as far north as Scotland. The British claimed to have brought down 180 planes on this occasion and 185 during a raid on London on September 15. No raid at this time was participated in by as many as 500 planes. Losses of this proportion appeared ruinous, although the British air strength, technically superior but much inferior numerically, had been whittled down to dangerously low levels. At any rate, daylight raids were abandoned.

The Germans then turned to night raids and, for 13 consecutive nights in September, did terrible damage to London, striking Buckingham Palace, the British Museum, and the Houses of Parliament. Outlying cities like Birmingham and Coventry, harbors like Southampton and Bristol were attacked. At Coventry, on the night of November 14, an intensive raid showered bombs on the city for ten and a half hours. At the end of the year, official figures showed 23,081 killed and 32,296 wounded as a result of the raids.

The Royal Air Force retaliated with raids upon German cities. The striking force of their air power steadily grew until the blows they struck dwarfed anything the Germans had attempted.

At sea the British blockade still made itself felt in the Axis countries, though severely handicapped. The German counter-blockade at sea became more effective and caused serious losses in 1941 and 1942.

Two incidents of naval warfare may be mentioned in this connection. While the French armistice only provided for its internment, the British had always feared the acquisition of the French fleet by Germany. On the refusal of the squadron at Oran, in Algeria, to surrender or proceed to the West Indies, the British attacked it and destroyed its most important ships, July 3, 1940. In May 1941, the new German battleship *Bismarck* sank the *Hood*, the largest of the British battle fleet, in an encounter near Greenland. A few days later, other units of the British navy, assisted by aircraft, sank the *Bismarck*.

Italy in the War. The entry of Italy into the war at a time calculated to bring her "in on the kill" greatly broadened the area of the war. Italy's African territory was extensive—Libya in Africa and Italian East Africa, consisting of Eritrea, Italian Somaliland, and Ethiopia. Across the Adriatic was her subject kingdom of Albania. Between them lay the Mediterranean, where Italy menaced also the "lifeline" of the British Empire, the route by Suez to India. Italy hoped to make the Mediterranean an "Italian lake" and to increase her African possessions at the expense of the British and the French.

Italy brought to the Axis battle line an army of perhaps 1,500,000, including native troops, and varying greatly in quality. She had about 3000 available planes. Her navy was weak in capital ships but strong in smaller craft. Her natural resources were limited.

Italy gained some initial successes in Somaliland but the British soon came back. An imperial force, partly South African, took the coast colonies and brought back Haile Selassie to Ethiopia. The main Italian army surrendered on May 19, 1941; the last remaining force, in November.

The war in North Africa showed a series of alternations of fortune. In September 1940, Marshal Graziani with 280,000 troops pushed 70 miles into Egypt. Egypt did not declare war, leaving its defense to the British. In December, the British general, Sir Archibald Wavell, attacked the Italians with 100,000 men, mainly Australians and New Zealanders, and by February 1941 had taken over 100,000 prisoners, occupied all Cyrenaica, and completely destroyed the Italian army as a fighting force.

A large part of the British force was now withdrawn to aid in the defense of Greece. In consequence the British were forced back to their Egyptian bases by the German General Rommel, Graziani's successor, but they still held the fortified port of Tobruk. Receiving reinforcements, the British again advanced in November and drove the Italians, now strengthened by German tank troops, to the borders of Tripoli. After desultory fighting, Rommel, with some reinforcements, advanced again in May 1942, and by the middle of July had recaptured Tobruk, invaded Egypt, and was threatening the British base at Alexandria and the Suez canal. In this fighting, tanks, some of them American, played a great part, being well adapted to deal with the distances and the desert terrain.

In the Mediterranean the Italians for a time closed the Suez canal route to India, and bombed Malta, unsuccessfully. On the other hand the British severely damaged the Italian navy in engagements at Tarano and off Cape Matapan.

The Balkan War. On October 28, 1940, Italy suddenly attacked Greece, striking from Albania. To everyone's surprise the small Greek army, of 150,000 men, not only repulsed the Italians, but advanced into Albania.

In the spring of 1941 Germany turned her military power toward the Balkans. Her diplomacy already had prepared the way. Hungary and Rumania were now under German control, and Rumania had been forced to return much of her gains of 1919 to Hungary, Bulgaria, and Russia. King Carol had abdicated in September 1940, and a Fascist government took his place. On November 23, 1940, Rumania signed the Axis pact. Bulgaria did the same. Turkey remained neutral, signed non-aggression treaties with both sides, and refused to be drawn in by either. In Yugoslavia the pro-German regent, Prince Paul, on March 20, accepted the German "new order." On the 27th the Serbian party staged a revolution which put his nephew, King Peter, on the throne, and repudiated the treaty.

Yugoslavia had about 550,000 men, poorly organized and equipped. They were assisted by the Greeks, and by an English contingent of 60,000 from Africa. The German army of 550,000, massed in Bulgaria, struck east and south. On April 9, Saloniki was taken. On April 17, the main Yugoslav army, attacked from the east and north, surrendered. Belgrade was taken.

The Germans now advanced on the Anglo-Greek army defending the Greek peninsula. On the 24th the Greek army in the west, about 220,000 men, capitulated. From the 11th to the 24th Australians and New Zealanders successively defended positions on the lines of Mt. Olympus and Thermopylae, but the increasing German pressure made further resistance impossible. About 45,000 of the British forces were evacuated from Megara and other ports, abandoning large amounts of equipment. By May 1 the Germans had conquered Yugoslavia and Greece. In the last days of May, a German attack, conducted almost entirely by air-borne troops, conquered Crete. The British lost six naval vessels from air attacks while defending it and about half of their garrison of 27,000 men.

The Axis powers now controlled the Balkan peninsula, with the important exception of Turkey. They controlled also most of the islands and had secured a base for operations in the Middle East. Yugoslavia fell apart into its original elements, while Italy and Hungary took large areas. Bulgaria took parts of Macedonia and Thrace from Greece, Serbia received a puppet government at Belgrade, but many of the Serbs continued a resistance in the mountains which took on the character of organized warfare. This resistance increased in importance as the war went on.

It was at this time that the British and Free French seized Syria and Lebanon to forestall a German march to India. German intrigue in Iraq brought prompt repressive action by Britain. A year later, a similar situation in Iran led to joint Russian and British occupation of Teheran.

The position of Italy was unenviable. Germany had saved her in North Africa and in the Balkans, and her price was entire subordination. German troops and officials in large numbers moved in.

The Atlantic Charter. The triumph of German arms in southeastern Europe was followed by a pause in which the anti-Axis world breathlessly awaited hints of the direction in which new blows would fall. At this point the leaders of the two great English-speaking nations met to provide a statement of the principles about which all nations opposed to the "New Order" of the Axis might rally.

Framed by President Roosevelt and Premier Churchill at a meeting on naval vessels "somewhere in the Atlantic" in August 1941, the statement was given the name of the Atlantic Charter. It was a statement of post-war aims despite the fact that the United States was not formally at war.

The Charter contained eight points: (1) The United States and Great Britain seek no aggrandizement, territorial or other; (2) they desire no territorial changes except with the approval of the peoples concerned; (3) they pledge themselves to further self-determination and the restoration of self-government; (4) to secure to all, victors and vanquished, access on equal terms to trade and raw materials; (5) the fullest collaboration of all nations in the economic field; (6) after the destruction of "Nazi tyranny," a secure and lasting peace, with freedom from fear and want; (7) enabling all men to traverse the seas without hindrance; (8) to secure the abandonment of force, for which, pending the establishment of a wider system of general security, "the disarmament of aggressor nations is essential." At an Inter-Allied Conference in London, September 24, twelve governments pledged adherence to the Charter. The term United Nations was applied to the signatories.

The Russian War. The war took a new turn on June 22, 1941, when Hitler suddenly hurled the full force of his armies against Russia. Hitler alleged that Russia was treacherously preparing to attack him when engaged elsewhere.

Military experts gave Russia six weeks to last. Expert opinion, however, both German and other, has seldom so completely underestimated the power of a nation. Russia had used the two-year respite secured by the German treaty to speed the construction of a war machine comparable technically with that of Germany. She alone among German foes had a first-class tank and air force. The industrial development required to support a large-scale war had been speeded with an astonishing energy. The world assumed that Russia under a communistic government lacked efficiency; an earlier "purge" extending throughout the army had raised doubts as to the loyalty of the people to their rulers. When the cloud of secrecy partly lifted, it was found that the "fifth column" in Russia had been completely eliminated; not only the army but the civilian population was trained and keyed to fight with a tenacity which for the first time was to halt the German legions.

Germany put into the field against Russia an army of 160 divisions, perhaps 2,400,000 men, increased as the war went on. Besides these Hitler had, like Napoleon, contingents from his subject nations, Italians, Slovakians, Rumanians, and Magyars; and the Finnish army in the north. Russia, though not fully mobilized, could put 2,000,000 men into the field, later increased to 4,000,000.

The plan of the war was simple. An advance on a 2,000 mile front, from the Baltic to the Black Sea, with all the German military technique, met by a "defense in depth" along the same line, withdrawing as necessary to preserve their fighting forces, and leaving "scorched earth" behind them. The German objectives were Leningrad in the north, Kiev and Odessa in the south, and Moscow in the center.

On the outbreak of the war, Winston Churchill forestalled any attempt by Hitler to assume leadership of an anti-communist crusade by accepting Russia immediately as a full ally. President Roosevelt pledged all possible aid. On July 13 a formal treaty of alliance was concluded between Great Britain and Russia, succeeded a year later by a 20-year pact for military and economic cooperation, within the framework of the Atlantic Charter.

The Anglo-Russian treaty of 1942 was signed on May 28. It consisted of two parts, one relating to the war and the other to post-war relations.

Under Part I, each nation pledged full military aid to each other and promised to refuse to enter negotiations for a separate peace with Germany or any of her satellites in Europe.

Under Part II, both parties accepted the principles of the Atlantic Charter. Specifically they renounced territorial aggrandizement. They also promised non-interference with the internal affairs of other states and co-operation in seeking the security and economic advancement of the two nations.

In the north the Germans attacked Leningrad from the south and west. The Finns, under General Mannerheim, retook Viborg and Karelia and threatened the city from the north. The siege of Leningrad, thus begun, lasted for 30 months.

The central armies under Marshal von Bock met with stubborn resistance from Marshal Timoshenko's forces. They took Smolensk July 16, and stopped there for a time.

In the South General Rundstedt's armies, with Magyar and Rumanian contingents, overran Bessarabia and Galicia; while one army group pressed along the Black Sea, another turned north toward Kiev. Odessa was passed by and left to the Rumanians; it fell on October 16. By the middle of August, the Russians were forced across the Dnieper, where they blew up the famous Dnepropetrovsk dam. Kiev fell in the last weeks of September. The southern German columns pressed on to the Crimea and the industrial region of the Donets basin, taking Kharkov on October 24 and Rostov on November 22. The Russians were "trading space for time." In spite of heavy losses, they kept their armies largely intact.

Meantime the struggle for Moscow, under Hitler's personal supervision, was renewed in the central sector. In October the Germans were within a hundred miles of the city on the north and south, and Stalin sent the government offices to Kuibeshev (Samara) on the Volga. Some German units approached within 37 miles of the city. Against the advice of his generals, Hitler ordered Moscow taken at any cost. A final assault was made in mid-November. It failed.

The Russian winter closed down. Unexpectedly the Russians attacked in the south, retaking Rostov and Kerch. The Russian armies advanced farther north also but were unable to take any of the numerous fortified "hedgehog" points on which the German army relied for defense.

Russia in 1942; Stalingrad. In the spring of 1942, the Germans, paying less attention to Leningrad and Moscow, concentrated their forces in the south. Their general aim was to gain the manufacturing and food-producing districts of southern Russia and to destroy the Russian armies. Their specific objective was threefold: to reach the Volga and cut the north and south lines of communication by rail and river; to acquire the oil wells of the Caucasus; and by holding the northern Caucasus to cut off the supplies which were reaching the Russians by the Persian Gulf.

With about two million men at his disposal, Marshal von Bock moved into the lower Don valley. He occupied the Donetz basin, but the Russians under Timoschenko avoided encirclement. Rostov was retaken on July 24, and the way was open southwest to the Caucasus and northwest to the Volga. The advance into the Caucasus reached the seaport of Novorossisk and the Maikop oil fields. Driving through the northern foothills of the Caucasus, the Germans reached Mozdok on August 24. But the Russians held them back from the more important Grozny and Baku oil fields, and winter stopped further advance.

The northern drive reached Stalingrad, a leading industrial city on the west bank of the Volga, and began its attack on August 31. For four months the siege continued. Stalingrad was bombed by planes and heavy artillery into a rubbish heap, in which Germans and Russians fought from ruined house to ruined house. It was estimated that the Russians lost 6000 men each day but they took 2000 Germans with them. Reinforcements from the eastern provinces crossed the Volga under fire.

In late November, the Russians struck back and inflicted on Germany a major disaster which marked the turning point of the Russian war. Two flanking movements across the Volga to north and south cut the German supply lines. The Germans were forced to abandon the army besieging Stalingrad. In January 1943, the Russians claimed the destruction or capture of 22 divisions, 330,000 troops, with their commanding generals.

Japan and the Far East. When the war broke out in 1939, Japan had for two years been engaged in an undeclared war with China. She was meeting stubborn resistance from General Chiang Kai-shek's forces in western China and from guerilla bands in the east. Great Britain and the United States were unofficially supporting General Chiang Kai-shek and the Chungking government, whose chief line of supply was the Burma Road from Rangoon.

In the European war, Japan, ruled by its military class, was in natural sympathy with the Axis powers. On September 27, 1940, she signed a defensive treaty with Germany and Italy, under which each of these powers would come to the assistance of any one of their number attacked by a third power not already at war with it. It was obviously aimed at the United States.

With the fall of France Japan seized her opportunity to get control of French Indo-China. She was now in position to menace the American Philippines and the British possessions in Malaya, as well as the Netherlands Indies to the south. Her move fitted into a policy pursued since 1930, when Manchuria was invaded, the ultimate objectives of which involved establishment of a "New Order" in Eastern Asia.

With Great Britain in a death-grapple in Europe, opposition to Japan fell to the United States. Both sides professed a desire for peace and continued negotiations up to and beyond the moment when war began. But peace could endure only if one or the other side abandoned its objective—the "New Order" on the side of Japan and an "open door" economic policy for other nations on the part of the United States.

On November 26, 1941, Secretary of State Hull gave Japan a final and definite statement of the American position. Hull proposed: a multilateral pact guaranteeing non-aggression in eastern Asia; that Japan should withdraw her troops from French Indo-China; that she should cease her opposition to the Chungking government in China. In return he offered a reciprocal trade agreement and the removal of the "freezing" restrictions on Japanese credit. On Sunday afternoon, December 7, the Japanese envoys handed to Secretary Hull a memorandum charging the United States and Great Britain with "imperialistic exploitation" in that region and with maliciously opposing Japan's efforts for peace and order. The memorandum proposed that the United States, in agreement with Japan, should send no more forces into the western Pacific, restore commercial relations as before the "freezing," supply Japan with oil, and cease support of China. When these things were done, Japan agreed to withdraw its forces from Indo-China.

As the Japanese envoys were presenting the memorandum, news arrived that a Japanese air force, which must have taken weeks in preparation, had attacked the American naval base at Pearl Harbor.

America at War. Up to this point, American opinion on entering the war had been divided. The attack on Pearl Harbor instantly brought about the closing of ranks in preparation for what was recognized as a life-and-death struggle.

On President Roosevelt's recommendation, Congress declared war on Japan the next day, December 8. Japan's Axis partners, Germany and Italy, declared war on the United States December 11, and Congress at once reciprocated. At a Congress which met at Rio de Janeiro January 15, 1942, all Latin-American nations suspended diplomatic relations with the Axis powers except Argentina and Chile. Nine countries, the Central American and island republics, had already declared war. Hungary and Bulgaria declared war on the United States, December 13; in July 1942, the United States declared war on Hungary, Bulgaria, and Rumania.

Premier Churchill promised that, in the event of an American declaration, Britain would follow. Her declaration slightly preceded that by the United States.

Britain had sufficient reason, for Japan had simultaneously attacked Hong Kong and moved into Thai. Thai capitulated at once, and the Japanese entered Malaya. At the same moment Japan struck at the Philippines, where for six years General Douglas MacArthur had been training the Filipino army. With command of the sea and air and superior equipment, the trained Japanese forces landed on Luzon and pushed toward Manila, resisted but not stopped by the island forces. MacArthur abandoned Manila December 27 and declared it an open city, concentrating his troops in Bataan peninsula, across Manila Bay. The Japanese nevertheless bombed Manila. MacArthur's Americans and Filipinos held out in Bataan, keeping Japanese forces estimated at 300,000 fully occupied, until April 8, 1942, when what were left of Bataan's 36,000 defenders surrendered. Corregidor fortress was taken May 5, and Japan held the Philippines. Before the surrender of Bataan, General MacArthur had been ordered to Australia to take command in the western Pacific. General Jonathan M. Wainwright succeeded him, and conducted the defense until he was forced to surrender.

The attack on Pearl Harbor gave the Japanese temporary control of the Pacific. Five American battleships were sunk or put out of action, 3 battleships, 3 cruisers, and 8 other vessels were damaged, and 240 planes were destroyed; airfields were wrecked; about 3000 were killed and wounded. For the moment it was impossible to maintain American outposts against the Japanese; Guam was taken at once; Wake three weeks later, after considerable damage to the attacking fleet; Midway held out. Japanese submarines appeared on the west coast, but did no serious damage. On February 1, an American task force inflicted heavy damage on the Japanese bases in the Gilbert and Marshall islands.

Meanwhile the Japanese armies had been victorious on the Asiatic mainland. Hong Kong fell on Christmas Day. The Japanese were already attacking Malaya, and the British slowly retreated southward toward Singapore. The battleship *Prince of Wales* and the battle cruiser *Repulse,* recently sent to aid in its defense, were sunk December 10 by Japanese torpedo bombers. Singapore had been made impregnable from the sea, but not from the land side. It fell February 17.

The conquest of the Malay peninsula gave the Japanese the world's chief source of tin, one of the two chief sources of rubber, and the greatest British naval base in the Far East, on which all Allied plans for Pacific warfare had centered.

Already Japanese sea and air forces had been raiding the East Indies. Before the fall of Singapore, they had occupied Sarawak, in Borneo, had a footing in Celebes, had taken the Amboina naval base, and were attacking Sumatra. The small Dutch army and navy with the American Asiatic squadron and a few British ships resisted bravely. In a week of fighting in Macassar Strait at the end of January Dutch and American sea and air forces sank nearly half of a large Japanese fleet, but Java was occupied three weeks after the fall of Singapore, and the American-Dutch fleet was destroyed in a battle in the Java sea.

With the Dutch East Indies in their hands, the Japanese now controlled the second major source of rubber. By occupying the oil fields they cut off the Allies from their nearest supply of oil.

Australia was now faced with the danger which had been its nightmare for 60 years. The Commonwealth had already made preparations, but the arrival of an American expeditionary force was welcome. The Japanese had taken Rabaul in New Britain in January and had occupied positions in the Solomon islands. They had made landings in New Guinea and were bombing Port Moresby in that island and Darwin in Australia. In April they began concentrations at their bases. On May 4 their fleet, moving south in the Coral Sea, met the American fleet, which had been watching them. The battle which followed set a precedent in naval warfare in that the contending ships never saw nor fired on one another; it was a battle of aircraft. In the next four days the Japanese lost 2 aircraft carriers, 7 cruisers, and 5 destroyers, sunk or damaged, with other vessels, 23 in all. The Americans lost the carrier *Lexington* and two smaller ships.

The Japanese had turned north upon Burma, not only to occupy it, but to cut the Burma Road, the supply line of China. In spite of desperate British resistance, they reached Lashio, its southern terminus, at the beginning of May. By early June, when the rains stopped further progress, they were threatening Assam. Beyond Assam lay India, where the demands of Gandhi and the Indian Native Congress for immediate independence were hampering British defense.

The Japanese check in the Coral Sea may have contributed to greater activity in the North Pacific. On April 17 American carrier-based aircraft—from "Shangri-La," President Roosevelt explained,—dropped bombs on Tokyo and Yokohama. Admiral Nimitz, expecting some Japanese attack, had centered his defense on Midway Island. On June 3 patrol planes picked up a Japanese force of about 80 vessels, including transports, heading toward the island. Their purpose appeared to be an attack on Midway or possibly on Pearl Harbor itself. An American carrier force farther north was notified and hastened to the scene. Meantime the land based airplanes from Midway attacked and inflicted considerable damage. Carrier-based planes from the Jap fleet bombed Midway, but the damage, though serious, was not disabling. As the Japanese turned to retreat the next morning, the American carrier fleet came up and pursued them. In a three-days running fight, again entirely by airplanes, four Japanese carriers and two heavy cruisers were sunk; three battleships and ten other vessels were sunk or damaged. The American carrier *Yorktown,* and one American destroyer were sunk, the latter by a submarine. The American loss was 92 officers and 215 men. Japanese casualties were estimated at 4800.

The battle of Midway Island was the turning point in the Pacific war. Thereafter the initiative was in the hands of the United Nations.

The Invasion of Africa. The late summer of 1942 marked the height of Axis success. The Germans had driven the Russians back to the Volga and entered the Caucasus; in Africa, Rommel was threatening the British hold on Egypt; Japanese conquests had reached Burma and New Guinea and threatened India and Australia. Against this could only be set the damage by Allied air raids, the improvement in the submarine situation, and the growth of production in the United States. With the autumn of 1942 the scales began to tip in favor of the Allies.

Toward midnight on November 7, radios announced that American and British forces had successfully invaded northwest Africa. A fleet of 850 ships under British naval escort at 1 A.M. on November 8 had landed American and British battalions near Oran and Algiers; a few hours later other American forces, moving directly across the Atlantic, reached Casablanca, in Morocco. At dawn, parachute troops flown directly from England landed and siezed the airfields. There was little resistance, most vigorous at Casablanca. Algiers surrendered on the evening of the 8th, Oran the next day, and Casablanca on the 11th. The Americans had less than 2000 casualties. Sixteen ships were sunk, including five transports, but most of the men were rescued. The expedition was directed by Lieutenant-General Dwight B. Eisenhower.

In four days the Allies had gained possession of all French North Africa except Tunisia. The operation presented a political as well as a military problem. It happened that Admiral Jean Francois Darlan, commander of all French forces and Pétain's designated successor in the Vichy government of France, was in Algiers at the time of the invasion. Darlan, after negotiations with General Eisenhower, on November 11 ordered the French troops to cease firing and proclaimed a provisional government for North Africa aligned with the United Nations with himself as chief of state. French West Africa, including the important port of Dakar, accepted the new regime. The recognition of Darlan, whom the Free French regarded as dyed in the treasonable colors of Vichy, excited alarm among those who feared compromise with the Nazis. The plan was said to be temporary and was adopted to save lives and time.

The problem was somewhat simplified when, on Christmas eve, Darlan was assassinated by a young French national. Darlan's recently organized imperial council chose General Henri Giraud, who had made good his escape from France with American aid, as high commissioner and commander in chief.

De Gaulle controlled most of the rest of the French empire. To achieve a measure of unity, he was accepted as co-chairman with Giraud in a committee of national liberation, which superseded the imperial council. Soon eclipsing Giraud, De Gaulle purged the administration of pro-Vichy elements and became the recognized French leader.

Repercussions in France. The Allied seizure of North Africa was answered by Hitler's cancellation of the armistice with France and the sending of German troops into the unoccupied section. Pétain disavowed Darlan's action and removed him from office. On November 17, he transferred his powers to Hitler's tool, Laval.

Meanwhile most of the French fleet lay at the great naval base of Toulon, immobilized under the armistice. On the morning of November 27, the Germans sent troops to seize them. The commanders, under orders of their admiral, at once proceeded to scuttle the ships while French troops on guard kept off the Germans. About nine-tenths of the fleet was destroyed. A few submarines escaped to Africa.

With Morocco and Algeria secured, a race began for Tunisia. This race the Allies lost. In spite of the efforts of sea and air forces, the Germans under General von Arnim poured men and munitions across the narrow straits from Sicily into Tunis and the naval base of Bizerta, overwhelmed the French garrisons there, and occupied the coastal plain behind the ports of Sfax and Gabes.

Montgomery and Rommel. Meantime, at the other corner of the Mediterranean, the British Eighth army, now commanded by General Sir Bernard Montgomery, faced Rommel's Germans and Italians at El Alamein between the sea and the soft sands of the Qattara depression. Montgomery had been reinforced to 200,000 men, with 1000 tanks and other munitions. Rommel also received reinforcements and had about 140,000 men and 500 tanks.

Montgomery moved first. On October 22, the British artillery began blasting a way through the opposing lines. Two weeks later Rommel's forces were in full retreat. Tanks were half the battle in this desert warfare, and Rommel lost half of his, besides 600 planes and 9000 prisoners. The mechanized German force retreated along the coast road, abandoning several divisions of Italian troops, who surrendered gladly. Tobruk was retaken on November 13. On the 20th, Rommel gave up Benghazi. He had now lost 75,000 men. With the German Afrika Corps, he made a stand at El Agheila, 560 miles west of his initial position.

El Agheila, on the border of Tripolitania, had been the limit of previous British advances. For three weeks Montgomery reorganized his transport and brought up supplies. Then, on December 13, he struck again, and two days later Rommel was again in retreat. Tripoli was abandoned January 23. Rommel, with about half his original force, made his final stand on the Mareth line, the border fortifications of Tunisia. He had conducted a masterly retreat of 1500 miles from his position in Egypt. He had left about half of his original force. His purpose was now to support General von Arnim's forces in Tunisia.

Tunisia. Tunisia is an irregular quadrilateral, washed on the north and east by the Mediterranean. The northwestern part is mountainous, one ridge running out into the promontory of Cape Bon. In the southeast is a broad coastal plain. The important military objectives were Tunis and Bizerta on the north coast, held by the Germans, who held also the coastal plains and the coast towns.

The Allied forces held a generally north and south line in western Tunisia. On February 24 the Germans struck in the south at the Americans holding the Kasserine Pass. Inexperienced and outnumbered, the Americans were driven back about 28 miles but recovered the lost ground by the beginning of March. On March 20, the Eighth army launched an attack on the Mareth line, while the Americans and British to the north increased their pressure. A New Zealand corps under Montgomery's command outflanked the Mareth line. On April 7 American patrols made contact with units of the Eighth army. Under the combined attack Rommel was forced to retreat north nearly to Cape Bon.

From the beginning of the movement the sea and air forces of the Allies had been watching and attacking the Axis transport. On April 5 a smashing attack on the aerodromes of Sicily and Italy crippled the Axis air force, and continuous bombing cut their communications with Sicily. A combined assault by the ground forces followed. The Axis line was broken by a tank attack. On the 7th the Americans entered Bizerta, and the British entered Tunis at almost the same time. A part of the enemy, trapped between them, surrendered on May 9. The remainder were driven into the Cape Bon peninsula and surrendered the next day. The captured troops numbered some 252,000, besides large quantities of equipment. They included General von Arnim but not General Rommel, who had been previously ordered to Italy to direct the defense there.

By this campaign the German plan to join forces with Japan by taking the Suez canal was ruined. In its place, a line of attack on southern Europe was opened up for the Allies. The route to the Japanese war by the Suez canal was now open to the Allies.

The Collapse of Italy. The Allied army was now poised on the tip of Africa, ready to strike at "Fortress Europe." The air forces began the work by bombarding the fortified islands between Africa and Italy and the supply bases in Italy itself. On the morning of July 10 a fleet of 2000 vessels of all sizes landed 150,000 British, Americans, and Canadians on the south and east coasts of Sicily. There was very little resistance, for the enemy had expected them in the west of the island, and clouds of parachute troops the night before had seized the principal airfields.

Sicily is, for the most part, a mass of mountains culminating in Mt. Etna at the northeast corner. There the narrow strait of Messina separates it from Italy. The British Eighth army moved up the east coast, took Syracuse, and, on the 19th, was stopped at Catania just south of Mt. Etna by stiff German resistance. The Canadians moved forward in the center. The American Seventh army, under command of General George Patton, was nearer the region where the defenders were prepared and met more opposition at first. From Agrigento (Girgenti) it advanced inland. Americans and Canadians reached Enna, in the center of the island, on the 21st, and resistance in the west practically ceased. The Americans pushed through to the north coast, taking 100,000 prisoners and much undamaged war material. They had throughout overwhelming air support. The Germans fought stubbornly, but the Italians were more willing to surrender. From Palermo the Americans turned east to outflank the German position at Catania. By the end of the month the whole enemy force was crowded into the northeastern corner of the island between Mt. Etna and the sea. On August 5 the British took Catania, on the 17th resistance ceased in Messina, and Sicily was conquered. Some of the garrison escaped, but about 200,000 were captured.

The losses in Sicily brought about a revolution at Rome. On July 25 King Victor Emmanuel requested Mussolini's resignation and appointed Marshal Badoglio premier. The new government soon began secret negotiations with the Allies. After an attempt to make terms, the Badoglio government surrendered unconditionally September 8, handing over most of the fleet. About the same time, Mussolini, who had been taken into custody by the new government but rescued by a daring German raid and taken to northern Italy, was set up by the Germans as a puppet ruler. Italian liberals, meanwhile, led by Count Carlo Sforza and Benedetto Croce, demanded that the king abdicate in favor of his young grandson. The Allies recognized the Badoglio government, which declared war on Germany October 13. The king and Badoglio were safe behind the Allied lines.

Mussolini's retirement had taken everyone by surprise—including the Allies. The Germans rushed 19 divisions into northern Italy and proceeded to strengthen their position there and at Rome despite Italian opposition. They had two powerful advantages: Most of the Italian army was in garrisons under control of the Germans; and 200,000 Italians, laboring in Germany, were hostages. As the king and Badoglio played for time, the Allies acted. On September 3, the British Eighth Army landed in Calabria and advanced with little opposition. On the 8th, the American Fifth Army under Lieutenant General Mark Clark landed near Naples. It was vigorously opposed by German forces in readiness to meet the landing and escaped disaster at the Salerno beachhead only by concentration of all available air and sea support. Meantime the British took Bari and the important airfields of Foggia. Their left made contact with the Americans on the 17th, and the advance up the peninsula continued. On the 30th the Americans entered Naples.

The Germans were now in complete control of northern and central Italy, and the beginning of 1944 found them struggling fiercely with the Allies on the so-called Gustav line extending across the peninsula from Piscara to Cassino. On January 22 a surprise landing by the Fifth Army within a few miles of Rome threatened the entire German army south of that point. Skilful German defense in a rugged terrain, however, delayed the fall of Rome for nearly six months.

The Gustav line was finally broken and on June 5 the Allies entered Rome. A repetition of the German tactics of delay, taking every advantage of favorable terrain, slowed down the Allied advance again. By the end of the year, the Allies, reinforced by French and Brazilian contingents, had taken Florence and Pisa, but were still struggling on the southern edge of the Po valley. Italy was now becoming, however, a secondary theater, mainly important for its effect on greater operations elsewhere.

Russian Victories of 1943. In the campaign of 1943, the Russians drove the German army from the Volga to the former Russian boundary, recovering over 300,000 square miles of territory.

Russian successes began with the encirclement and destruction of the German armies besieging Stalingrad. This success was followed by new offensives which retook Rostov and Kharkov in February. The Germans saved their men, however, and a month later retook Kharkov. The Germans in the Caucasus were cut off.

To the west of Moscow the Russians had taken Velikye Luki in December, and were breaking into a German salient at Rzhev. Farther north they partially relieved Leningrad in January, but the Germans still clung to their positions within artillery range of the city. The Russians claimed that the Germans, in the winter campaign, had lost 850,000 men killed and wounded, and 344,000 prisoners.

The Germans started their last offensive in July. It was soon stopped, and they began a slow withdrawal, closely followed by the Russians, but the skill of the German "strategic retirement" prevented heavy losses. The Russians now retook Kharkov—its fourth change of hands—and recovered the Donets basin. By October they had retaken the Caucasus, and were entering the Crimea.

The Germans may have expected to hold the line of the Dnieper, but did not succeed. The Dnepropetrovsk dam was recovered. Kiev was taken November 7. Before the end of the year the Russians were across the Dnieper in many places, aiming for the vital Odessa-Warsaw railway.

In the center, advancing from Moscow, they took Smolensk, and had reached the old Polish border in January. In the north Leningrad was completely freed and Novgorod retaken.

While carrying out this sustained and gigantic offensive, Stalin planned sagaciously for the future. A 20-year treaty was signed with the friendly government-in-exile of Czechoslovakia. Grounds for suspicion in the West were weakened by dissolution of the Comintern and by recognition of the Greek Orthodox Church. Stalin, however, refused to recognize the unfriendly Polish government-in-exile located at London and made clear Russia's intention to keep territory which Poland took from Russia in 1920.

The Ukraine Recovered. The Russian activity now centered in the Ukraine. The Germans on the lower Dnieper were encircled, and some ten divisions, over 100,000 men were taken. Kherson, on the Black Sea, surrendered. The Russians passed the Dniester, and the boundary river Pruth. By the end of March they were attacking Czernowitz (Cernauti) in Rumania. Odessa was retaken on April 10, and Sevastopol a month later. The Russians announced that in the spring campaign the Red army had liberated 16,000 square miles of territory, and had killed or captured 500,000 of the enemy.

Poland and the Satellites. As the ground dried and military operations became possible, the Russians were again in motion. By July the Germans were pushed back to Minsk and the Polish border. In central Poland the Red army reached the Vistula in mid-July and attacked Warsaw, but there the advance was halted. In August an insurrection of the Polish underground broke out in Warsaw and held a part of the city for several weeks, but the Russians gave no assistance, and the Poles were forced to surrender. The Russians asserted that the uprising was premature and uncoordinated with Russian plans; the Poles charged betrayal.

For the time the main Russian effort was directed to the south. Lwow (Lemberg) was taken on August 17. On August 22 the Russians took Jassy, and the next day Rumania asked for an armistice, surrendered, and two days later declared war on Germany. The Russians nevertheless advanced across Rumania, occupied Bucharest, the Ploesti oil fields, and Constanta and the Black Sea coast. It was now Bulgaria's turn. Bulgaria had maintained a formal peace with Russia, but now Russia declared war on Bulgaria, entered the country on September 8, and occupied Sofia five days later. Bulgaria made peace with Russia, and declared war on Germany, opening the way to Yugoslavia and Greece. The German forces in these countries withdrew as best they could. Marshal Tito and the Partisans in Yugoslavia joined forces with the Red army. They entered Belgrade on October 14. Greece was liberated by the British, who had been landing forces since September and had pushed north with almost no resistance. By November Greece was free.

Red armies were already pressing forward in other quarters. They passed the prewar boundary of Hungary early in October. Admiral Horthy asked for an armistice, and the Germans took possession of the country. The Russian advance drove the Germans back beyond the Tisza and Lake Balaton and began the siege of Budapest, which fell in early 1945, while other Russian forces were entering Slovakia. In the north, the Baltic provinces were also falling. In July and August Lithuania had been conquered. By the end of September Estonia was cleared, and the Russians were in Riga and attacking East Prussia. Finland was forced to agree to terms, returning to the boundaries of 1940. The Germans in Finland retired to northern Norway. The Red army followed and the Germans gave up Finnmark, laying waste the country as they retreated.

The Invasion of France. The part taken by Russia in the war led to repeated intimations from Russia and demands in Britain and the United States for the opening of a "second front" in order to deliver the decisive blow of the war. At the beginning of 1944, preparations were in progress for such an invasion, the nature and magnitude of which were unprecedented in the history of warfare.

Meanwhile the aerial offensive from British bases against Germany and the occupied countries rose to a terrible crescendo. The Ruhr valley was wrecked. A raid on Cologne in May 1942 in which 1130 planes took part was called the greatest air raid in history, but it was surpassed by later attacks which demolished Hamburg, a large part of Berlin, and numerous other cities. The Rumanian oil fields and Sofia, in Bulgaria, were likewise visited. Skilfully directed air assault on German aircraft factories in February 1944 was credited with so crippling German airpower that Allied supremacy in the skies was never seriously challenged thereafter.

Among pre-invasion devices experimented with was the commando raid, undertaken by small parties which did the greatest possible damage to a definite objective and retreated with what information they could acquire about defenses. The most elaborate of these was the raid on Dieppe, August 19, 1942. It was carried out by 5000 Canadians with British, American, and French contingents, 10,000 in all, and with tanks and air support. The Canadians lost 67 per cent of their men. The experiment was not repeated.

The most serious obstacle to invasion at first was the submarine, but by mid-1943 it was definitely eliminated as a factor. In 1942, about 7,000,000 tons of Allied shipping were sunk. In late 1943 almost as many German submarines as Allied ships were sent to the bottom. Moreover, Allied shipping was growing at the rate of more than half a dozen ships a day.

In preparation for the attack on "Fortress Europe," General Dwight D. Eisenhower was appointed Supreme Allied Commander in Western Europe. General Sir Bernard L. Montgomery commanded the British ground forces; Lieutenant General Omar P. Bradley, the American; Admiral Sir Bertram Ramsay was naval commander. To oppose them the Germans had assigned command to Field Marshal Rommel and General Von Kluge.

Meanwhile the Germans on their side were preparing new secret weapons, the most formidable of which was the robot bomb, propelled from a ramp to travel great distances and fall with terrific explosive force. In the months immediately after the invasion of Europe began, London suffered damage or destruction of a large proportion of its buildings through this weapon.

On "D-Day," June 6, 1944, the Anglo-American expeditionary force struck the French coast in the most gigantic amphibious operations ever undertaken. Supporting 3200 transports and landing craft were 800 fighting ships. Some 8000 Allied planes held control of the air. Three divisions of airborne troops preceded the landing craft and held off the enemy; the warships shelled the shore fortifications. The Americans landed at the foot of the Cotentin peninsula, while the British struck farther west toward Caen, holding between them some 30 miles of the Normandy beaches. Initial losses were heavy enough, but less than had been expected. Within a week the beachheads were secure against counterattack. Then the Americans turned against Cherbourg, while the British around Caen protected their flank. Cherbourg was taken by the end of June, and its port facilities were soon available. The safety of the Allied position was assured.

Three weeks of "hedgerow war" followed; the British holding off the Germans around Caen, the Americans struggling inland, until the capture of St. Lo on July 18 placed them in position for a breakthrough. Another American army, the Third, commanded by Lieutenant General George S. Patton, was now in operation. Its armor overran Brittany, then, turning, swept east across France through Tours and Orleans. Paris was entered on August 25. The German Seventh Army attempted a counterattack but was driven, wholly disorganized, across the Seine. The British and Canadians followed them eastward along the coast. In the first days of September they crossed Belgium and entered the Netherlands, taking Antwerp and Breda. The Americans swung north to western Belgium and Luxembourg. In late September a daring attempt by parachute troops to secure a position at Arnheim, beyond the lower Rhine, was unsuccessful, but the Americans took Aachen in October against desperate resistance.

Meantime another American force had made a landing, August 15, on the southern coast of France between Nice and Cannes. Taking Marseilles and Toulon, they pushed up the Rhone valley, meeting little resistance. The French "Forces of the Interior," whose time had now come, rose all over France. A part of the German army of occupation escaped through the Gap of Belfort; more surrendered. The American and French armies, crossing the Vosges mountains at Belfort, joined the northern armies on the Rhine. By the end of October France and Belgium were liberated. The Germans had suffered a terrible but not yet fatal disaster. Over 800,000 of their troops had passed into Allied prison camps. Their enemies faced them across the Siegfried line.

Anglo-American Assault on Germany. Steady Allied advances into the deep defenses of the Siegfried line were interrupted in December 1944 by a strong German counterattack into Belgium and Luxembourg. Massing three armies in this area and favored by weather conditions which kept down the stronger American air force, the Germans drove through the Ardennes 50 miles into Belgium, their objectives probably Liege, Numur, and perhaps Antwerp. General Eisenhower concentrated his defenses at the northern and southern flanks. The heroic resistance of an American division at Bastogne and prompt counterattacks from north and south brought the Germans to a halt. They were forced back to their original lines and beyond. The "Battle of the Bulge," while costing the Allies 40,000 casualties, was estimated to have brought the Germans losses of several times this number.

The Allied pressure against the German lines culminated in several breakthroughs in late February 1945, and the German army was soon in full retreat beyond the Rhine, destroying bridges as they retired. The Americans entered Cologne on March 7; the next day, seizing a bridge at Remagen before it could be destroyed, they began to pour troops across the river for an advance into central Germany.

The War in the Pacific. The Japanese drive in the summer of 1942 had carried them to the Solomon Islands and New Guinea. Both positions threatened Australia. In the easternmost islands of the Solomon group, the fine harbor of Tulagi, with an airfield on the neighboring island of Guadalcanal, offered a base for attacks on New Caledonia and the supply line from the United States. Behind and supporting both was the air and naval base under construction at Rabaul on New Britain. One thousand miles to the north was Japan's "Pearl Harbor," Truk.

The first Japanese attack was on Port Moresby in southern New Guinea. In July, the Japs made a landing at Buna, farther down the coast. Two attempts to take Port Moresby failed.

In August the American and Australian navies took the offensive and attacked the Japanese positions in the eastern Solomons. Tulagi was taken and held. American marines landed on Guadalcanal August 7 and seized the almost completed airfield.

Around this airfield, renamed Henderson Field, American and Japanese were locked for months in the most crucial struggle of the campaign, the final outcome of which was destined to be decided by the naval and aerial conflict.

On the night of August 8, a Japanese air force attacked the Allied fleet and sank four heavy cruisers—the American *Quincy, Astoria,* and *Vincennes,* and the Australian *Canberra,* but did not reach the transports. In October, November, and December, the Japanese renewed their attacks, first to reinforce their men and, as the great battle gradually turned against them, to evacuate their troops. In October, Vice Admiral William F. Halsey was placed in command of the operations. In a final Japanese assault in November, officially called the battle of Guadalcanal, the Japanese lost two battleships, four cruisers, six destroyers, and eight transports with other vessels, 28 in all, and an estimated 40,000 men. Allied losses were two cruisers and seven destroyers. By January 1943, the fighting around Guadalcanal was practically over. The Americans renewed their offensive, slowly drove the Japanese from the middle Solomons, and at the beginning of 1944 had made lodgments on New Britain and were closing in on the principal base at Rabaul.

On January 31, 1944, with perhaps the largest fleet ever assembled up to that time, the Americans struck Japan's Marshall islands. Within a few days this outpost of the Japanese Empire was taken. The Gilbert islands had already been occupied in November 1943 in a swift but costly three-day assault.

Meantime General MacArthur was taking personal charge of the offensive on the northern coast of New Guinea. Buna and Gona were taken in December 1942. In March 1943, a Japanese transport fleet attempting to reinforce Lae, was caught by land-based aircraft in the Bismarck sea. All twelve transports and their escort were sunk, with an estimated loss of 40,000 men. In September Salamaua and Lae were captured, and the Japanese were driven from eastern New Guinea.

In the Aleutians, the Japanese had made lodgments on Attu and Kiska islands after the battle of Midway. Weather conditions made fighting extremely difficult, but in May Attu was taken. Kiska was later evacuated, and the Aleutians were clear.

"Island Hopping" Stage. With the Gilbert and Marshall islands and eastern New Guinea in their hands, the American forces in the Pacific moved westward on two lines, converging on the Philippines. General MacArthur's Southwest Pacific command worked along the coast of New Guinea. Admiral Nimitz and the fleet continued their conquest of Micronesia. Sea, land, and air forces co-operated. The method called first for a preliminary bombardment by carrier planes or, if possible, by land-based planes. When the position had been sufficiently "softened," landing and occupation followed, or, if it seemed preferable, the position might be by-passed and left to "wither on the vine," cut off from supplies and assistance from the homeland.

By such means the American and Australian forces, with assistance from the fleet, took Hollandia and later Biak island in New Guinea. By August, MacArthur was at the tip of the island, and the Japanese left behind were negligible. In September he occupied Morotai and neutralized Halmahira in the sea between New Guinea and the Philippines.

Meanwhile the fleet had been moving westward. The Carolines, with the fabulously strong base at Truk, was the next objective. Truk was repeatedly bombed until it was temporarily harmless. Halsey's Third fleet assisted MacArthur's advance and carried out carrier-based bombing raids as far as Luzon.

On June 14, 1944, marines were put ashore at Tinian and in the Marianas within range of Japan itself. The danger brought out a Japanese naval force, which was defeated with heavy loss by Admiral Spruance. Saipan resisted for several weeks; in August the recapture of near-by Guam was announced. The Palau islands were taken in September. Admiral Halsey extended his activities to Formosa and the Ryukyu islands, but the Japanese fleet avoided an action.

Return to the Philippines. The way was now clear for the invasion of the Philippines. General MacArthur, with 600 ships and 250,000 men, landed on Leyte island, in the middle of the group, on October 17. The initial resistance was slight, but apparently the Japanese determined to make their fight for the Philippines there, for reinforcements were sent—not all of them arrived—and three Japanese task forces converged on Leyte October 25 to destroy the American transports. The Third and Seventh fleets met them off the eastern coast in the Second Battle of the Philippine Sea. One task force was destroyed, the others were driven off with 24 vessels sunk, including at least three battleships and four carriers, and 33 others damaged. The American loss was one carrier and five smaller ships. Fighting in Leyte continued into December. Meanwhile the Americans occupied near-by Samar and Mindoro.

The occupation of Mindoro cleared the way to Luzon. In early January 1945, a fleet of 800 ships steamed through the Sulu sea and landed at the head of Lingayen Gulf, where the Japanese had landed three years before. A series of air raids upon Formosa prevented opposition from that quarter. The Japanese resistance was surprisingly light; on February 6 MacArthur entered Manila. Although groups of Japanese held out stubbornly at Corregidor and in the old walled city, by early March all resistance was wiped out. A part of the Japanese forces, however, retreated into northern Luzon, and some units maintained themselves there, and at other points, until the general surrender.

On the mainland the Japanese had better fortune. By occupying the line of the Peiping-Hankow railway, they cut Free China in two. On the other hand they lost ground in Burma, where the British entered Mandalay on March 8, 1945. About the same time a Chinese army took Lashio, the old terminus of the Burma road.

Earlier Conferences. As it became apparent that the unexpected power of Russian arms and the potentially crushing weight of American materials and forces spelled doom to Germany in a military sense, hope of escape turned to dividing the Allies. This hope was effectively cut off by inter-Allied conferences and agreements. January 14-24, 1943; Roosevelt and Churchill with their military advisers met at Casablanca, Morocco. "Complete agreement" was reached for the "intensive prosecution of the war in 1943."

Another conference, at Quebec, between Roosevelt, Churchill, and King, prime minister of Canada, August 20-24, was preceded by meetings of British and Canadian officials and followed by a visit of Churchill to Washington. T. V. Soong, Chinese foreign minister, also attended. Decisions were reached on military movements and the political issues.

Decisions of the highest importance were made by the Moscow conference, October 18-30, between the three secretaries, Hull, Eden, and Molotov.

Its communiqué recognized the importance of collaboration for carrying on the war, making peace after it, and determining the treatment of "Hitlerite Germany." As machinery for these purposes, a European Advisory Council was to be established in London; also an Advisory Council for Italy. A joint four-nation declaration pledged joint prosecution of the war until the "unconditional surrender" of the Axis powers and continued cooperation for peace. It recognized the necessity of a "general international organization, based on the principle of the sovereign equality of all peace-loving states"; and hoped to bring about a regulation of armaments. The powers agreed not to use their military forces within the territories of other states except, after consultation, for the purposes of this declaration.

Supplementary declarations by Britain, the United States, and Russia dealt with the reorganization of Italy and promised to "liberate" Austria. A final statement signed by the three rulers demanded that punishment of those guilty of "atrocities" should be in the countries where their offenses were committed.

Russia naturally could not participate in conferences regarding the war with Japan. For this purpose President Roosevelt, Premier Churchill, and Generalissimo Chiang Kai-shek met at Cairo (November 22-26). They committed their nations to the restoration of all Japanese conquests, including Formosa and Manchuria, and proposed the future independence of Korea.

The fifth of these conferences followed almost immediately. It was signalized by the presence of Marshal Stalin, who at last met President Roosevelt and Premier Churchill at Tehran, Iran, November 28-December 1, 1943. Their declaration stated that they had "concerted their plans for the destruction of the German forces," and "no power on earth could prevent" Germany's overthrow. In a supplementary statement they recognized the assistance given by Iran; pledged her economic assistance in postwar problems; and expressed their desire for "maintenance of the independence, sovereignty, and territorial integrity of Iran."

Later Conferences and Postwar Plans. President Roosevelt and Premier Churchill met in a second conference at Quebec, September 11-16, 1944, dealing chiefly with questions relating to the war in the Pacific. A more important conference was held at Yalta, in the Crimea, February 4-11, 1945, where Marshal Stalin met the two Western leaders. At this conference, plans for the defeat, occupation, and control of Germany were settled. Russia largely had her way in the Polish dispute, taking the eastern provinces and promising compensation at German expense. Preliminary plans were made for a world peace organization to be further considered by an assembly of the United Nations, called for April 25, 1945, at San Francisco.

Another class of conferences, of larger membership and limited scope, dealt with postwar problems. The International Monetary Conference, held at Bretton Woods, N. H., July 1-23, 1944, proposed the establishment of an international monetary fund and of an International Bank of Reconstruction and Development to stabilize currency, prevent inflation, and promote reconstruction after the war. The International Security Conference, at Dumbarton Oaks, Washington, D. C., June 21-October 7, 1944, participated in by representatives of the United States, Great Britain, and Russia, and later China, formulated a plan for a world organization to preserve peace. The Pan-American Conference at Mexico City in March 1945 put forward a similar plan for the Americas, the Act of Chapultepec. An International Aviation Conference at Chicago January 1-5, 1945, agreed upon some features of the control of civil international aviation.

The Western Front. The American crossing of the Rhine at Remagen was inadequate, and led into a terrain where an advance could easily be contested. A successful advance could only be made over the Baltic plain. This was soon remedied. While General Hodges' First Army enlarged its bridgehead and threatened the Ruhr district, General Patton's Third Army drove down the Moselle valley to Coblenz; reaching it March 17, they trapped the German armies still east of the Rhine. Farther south the Seventh Army advanced toward Karlsruhe, pocketing the Germans in the Saar basin. In the north, Marshal Montgomery's British and Canadian armies forced a passage at Wesel on March 23, and drove north and northeast, the British toward Bremen and Hanover, the Canadians along the Dutch border, trapping the enemy forces who remained in Holland. The Germans were unable to hold the line of the Wesel against the British and American armies. Bremen and Hamburg were taken, the Allies pressed on to the Elbe, and by mid-April their advance had passed it, but was held back to avoid possible collision with the Russians. The Germans pocketed behind them in the Ruhr valley, upwards of 300,000, surrendered on April 19th.

While the British were overrunning the northern plain the American Third Army had reached the Main valley and entered Frankfort. The Seventh Army, crossing near Karlsruhe, approached Nuremberg, and the First French army entered Germany farther south. It was the part of the Third Army, noted for its rapidity of movement, to cut off southern Germany, and forestall the rumored intention of the Nazi leaders to retire into the mountains of Bavaria for a final stand. This was done by mid-April. The Third Army took Leipzig on the 19th, and pressed on into Czechoslovakia. Farther south the Seventh Army, with the French on their right flank, occupied the Bavarian cities, Nuremberg, Augsburg, and Munich (April 30). The German line was now completely fragmented, and resistance, though sometimes vigorous, was local and without co-operation. On April 26 Russian and American forces met at Torgau in Saxony.

Meantime the air forces were in constant action, assisting the ground forces and bombing industrial centers and communication lines. Berlin was continually under fire. The Germans retaliated with a new secret weapon, the V-2 rocket bomb, causing great damage in London and southern England.

The Final Russian Victory. On January 12, 1945, Stalin ordered a grand offensive, designed to destroy the German armies in the east. Beginning with a drive upon Krakow, it extended to East Prussia on the north, and Silesia on the south. Warsaw was taken in passing, and Poland overrun, as the Germans drew back to the Oder, their last line of defense. The southern column, crossing the Oder, attacked and surrounded Breslau, and deprived Germany of its industrial district of Silesia. The central column, under General Zhukov, drove through Poland toward Berlin. The Oder was crossed in force near Berlin, but before delivering its principal blow at the German capital, the Russian army secured its northern flank. By the beginning of March, the Russians had sliced up northeastern Germany, and were taking it piecemeal. Konigsberg and Danzig resisted until April; Stettin, the seaport of Berlin, until April 27; and the Russians moved down the Baltic coast as far as Rostock.

In the south, the Red army, by the end of March, had cleared Hungary of the Germans, taken Bratislava in Slovakia, and were entering Austria. Vienna was attacked on April 6, and surrendered on the 13th. Farther north another army, passing around besieged Breslau, was entering Saxony to meet the Americans at Torgau.

Thus the stage was set for the climacteric attack on the brain and nerve center of the German Empire —Berlin itself. On April 15 the final drive began. The city had already been devastated by incessant air attacks from east and west. The Soviet armies converged upon it from three sides. On the 25th, Berlin was completely surrounded. Foot by foot, Russian tanks and infantry fought their way into the doomed city, while from the housetops to the subways the garrison and armed citizens contested their advance. On May 2, at three P. M., the last resistance ended, and the Soviet flag floated over the heap of rubble which had been Berlin.

The End of Adolf Hitler. Contrary to many predictions, and, it would seem, to the advice of his associates, Adolf Hitler remained in Berlin to the last. On May 1, Grand Admiral Karl Doenitz announced over the Hamburg radio that the Fuehrer had fallen that afternoon at his operational headquarters in the Reichschancellery. The exact circumstances of his death were not stated and later stories were conflicting but it is probable he committed suicide. Dr. Goebbels, propaganda minister, committed suicide at about the same time. Of the other Nazi leaders, Marshals Goring and Von Rundstedt were captured earlier by the Americans. Himmler, the hated chief of the police, was captured and committed suicide. Ribbentrop was arrested later. Admiral Doenitz announced that Hitler, a few days before, had designated him as his successor.

The Surrender of Germany. For the new Fuehrer nothing was left but surrender. While the German field armies continued to fight fiercely against the Russians, they seemed quite willing to surrender to the Anglo-American forces in the west. The army in Italy had signed articles of surrender on April 29. On May 4, Marshal Montgomery received the surrender of the German forces in the Netherlands, Denmark, and Northwest Germany. The next day, two German armies in Austria surrendered to General Devers. Admiral Doenitz accepted the situation. On May 7 his representatives surrendered to General Eisenhower, at his headquarters at Reims, the entire armed forces of the Reich. The German garrisons still holding out in the French seaports, La Rochelle, Lorient, St. Nazaire, and Dunkirk, and in the English Channel islands, were included. The surrender was formally announced on the morning of the 8th by President Truman and Premier Churchill. A few hours later the final articles of surrender to Russia were signed at Berlin by Marshal Zhukov and Marshal Keitel. So the European war officially ended, five years, eight months, and six days after the invasion of Poland.

The End in Italy. On April 10, the Allied armies, long stalled on the edge of the Po valley, launched their final offensive. German resistance was vigorous at first, more so against the British Eighth Army in the east than against the American Fifth in the west. Bologna, the primary objective, fell on the 21st, and resistance began to weaken as the Allies pushed northward. The Italian partisans rose as the German retreat became more disorderly. Genoa and Milan fell to the Americans on the 29th, and Venice to the British. Realizing that the American advance in Germany left them no refuge there, and threatened by a flank attack from France, the German commanders opened negotiations for a surrender. The capitulation was signed at Naples on the 29th, becoming effective on May 2d, and northern Italy, with the adjacent Austrian territory, passed to the Allies.

Even before the surrender the end had come for Benito Mussolini, Duce and dictator. Attempting to escape to Switzerland, he was arrested by Italian partisans, given a "trial," and shot, at a village near Lake Como. With him died his mistress, and a number of leaders in his puppet government. Their bodies were brought to Milan and exposed in a public square.

The Occupation of Germany. The Third Reich came to an end on May 23, when Admiral Doenitz and his officers, who had been carrying on an administration, under Allied supervision, were put under arrest. Germany was now without a government. In its place was military control by the Allies.

In persuance of the arrangements made at Yalta, Germany was to be divided into four zones of military occupation. The Russians took charge of most of Germany beyond the Elbe. The Americans were to occupy southern Germany, with lines of communication through the British zone in the northwest and along the North Sea. France occupied the regions adjoining the upper Rhine. A central council, with its seat at jointly-occupied Berlin, was to co-ordinate the administration of the four zones.

The Potsdam Conference. The further disposition of the conquered Reich was decided at a conference held at the old royal Prussian palace of Potsdam, July 17 to August 2, 1945, between President Truman, Premiers Churchill and Attlee and Marshal Stalin. It was announced that German life was to be reorganized. Army and navy were to be abolished and war production, actual or potential, to be eliminated. Reparations in kind were divided on a basis which gave the largest share to Russia. Eastern Germany was divided between Russia and Poland. Poland's western boundary was not fixed, but the country west of the Oder was placed under Polish administration. The conference also created a Council of Foreign Ministers, to meet at the respective capitals.

For the trial and execution of the war criminals, among whom were included the surviving Nazi leaders, an International Military Tribunal was set up at Nuremberg, September 1945. On October 1, 1946, the verdicts were pronounced. Goring, Keitel, Jodl, Von Ribbentrop, and eight others were sentenced to death; seven others to terms of imprisonment. The other liberated countries were already dealing with their own "collaborators." France imprisoned Petain, and executed Laval and others. Norway executed Quisling. The Netherlands and Belgium took similar action.

The Fall of Japan. In the United States rejoicing at the end of the war with Germany was tempered by the realization that another war was still to be won. The bulk of our troops in Europe had now to be transferred to the Pacific.

With the reconquest of the Philippines and the occupation of the Marianas islands, Japan's outer ring of defenses had fallen. The next attack was made on the inner line. It began at the little island of Iwo (Iwojima) in the Volcano group. After repeated bombings from air and sea, the first landing was made on February 18, but so stubborn was the resistance from strongly fortified positions that the island was not completely occupied until March 18, at a cost of 20,000 casualties, including 4000 dead.

The next point of attack was Okinawa, in the long chain of the Ryukyu (Nansei) islands, between Formosa and Japan. On April 1 a fleet of more than 1400 vessels landed the Tenth army, under General S. B. Buckner. The landing was made and the northern portion of the island occupied with little resistance, but on the hilly and strongly fortified southern tip the Japanese garrison of over 100,000 made a desperate resistance. Marines and infantry advanced foot by foot over rugged hills in the hardest fighting yet seen in the Pacific. Repeated attempts to relieve the island were beaten off. Constant "suicide" attacks on the American fleet sunk or damaged nearly 100 vessels. Okinawa fell on June 22. Its capture cost the Americans 39,000 casualties. The 11,000 dead, included General Buckner killed in the last days of the attack, but they now had a base only 800 miles from Tokyo.

The war now came home to Japan. Large sections of Tokyo, Osaka, and Nagoya had already been destroyed by long range bombers from Saipan. The Japanese navy had been driven from the sea, and a sea and air blockade was cutting off supplies from the Japanese conquests in the south. Now mines, sown from the air, blocked the Japanese ports. What was left of the fleet was destroyed in its harbors. The navy came into action, assisted by a British squadron, and through July the Third fleet ravaged the coasts with carrier-based planes, and even naval gunfire. City after city was reduced to ruins, industrial centers were destroyed and transportation wrecked. The Japanese air force, now suffering from a scarcity of gasoline, had lost many of its best pilots, and their successors were less efficiently trained. Then, on August 6, the first atomic bomb fell.

For some years the problem of the "splitting of the atom," and the release of atomic energy for man's use had occupied the minds of physicists. Before the war some progress had been made, but the theoretical and technical difficulties were enormous, as was the expense involved. For three years American, British, and Canadian scientists, with some assistance from European exiles, had been working on a mysterious "Manhattan Defense Project." Its reported cost was two billion dollars, but the result was the splitting of the uranium atom (already accomplished) in such a way that its force could be controlled and used as an explosive. On July 16 the first successful experiment was made near Alamogordo, N. M. The first atomic bomb used in warfare was dropped upon the city of Hiroshima, and an area of 4½ square miles, 60 per cent of the city, was wiped out of existence. Two days later another bomb was dropped upon the seaport of Nagasaki.

In January 1945, Russia had given the required twelve months notice of the end of her non-aggression treaty with Japan. At Potsdam the Russians had promised to engage in the Asiatic war within three months after the surrender of Germany. On August 8 Russia declared war, and her armies swept into Manchuria and Korea. Meantime in the south Japan was losing. The British capture of Rangoon on May 4 completed their conquest of Burma. The Burma road was again open. The Chinese, with American assistance, were taking the offensive.

Already at Potsdam the Japanese had put out peace feelers through Russia, then a neutral, and had received a very definite choice between unconditional surrender and "total destruction." The atomic bomb gave meaning to the second alternative. With the Russian entry, it also gave opportunity for the "saving of face" so dear to the oriental mind. On August 10, the Japanese emperor made, through Switzerland as an intermediary, a qualified proposal of surrender, "ever anxious," as he later explained, "to advance the cause of world peace, and with a view to saving mankind the calamities to be imposed by further continuance of the war." For four days questions and answers, dealing mainly with the emperor's status, went back and forth through the Swiss legation. At last, at 7 P. M. August 14, President Truman announced to the country that Japan had surrendered unconditionally.

End of World War II. On September 1 (September 2, by Tokyo time) on the U. S. battleship Missouri, in the harbor of Tokyo, General MacArthur, as Supreme Allied commander, accompanied by representatives of the Allied powers, received the formal surrender of Japan.

So the war ended, six years to a day after the German invasion of Poland; 3 years, 8 months, and 25 days after the Japanese attack on Pearl Harbor. America had paid for its victory with 1,058,000 casualties; 248,000 killed. Another million casualties might well have been added had we been forced to invade Japan. Canada lost 36,000 killed, out of 101,000 casualties. Great Britain and the other dominions, 300,000 killed, with total casualties of 1,132,000. The one redeeming feature was the high percentage of wounded who recovered and could be rehabilitated, due to the efficient provision for first aid, and the progress, under pressure, of military surgery and medicine.

The San Francisco Conference. In pursuance of the recommendations of the Dumbarton Oaks and Yalta conferences, delegates from 51 nations met at San Francisco, April 25, 1945, to frame a "charter" for an organization of nations to maintain peace. The nations represented were: China, Soviet Russia, Great Britain, the United States, France, Argentina, Australia, Belgium, Bolivia, Brazil, Byelo-Russian Soviet Socialist Republic, Canada, Chile, Colombia, Costa Rica, Cuba, Czechoslovakia, Denmark, Dominican Republic, Ecuador, Egypt, El Salvador, Ethiopia, Greece, Guatemala, Haiti, Honduras, Iceland, Iraq, Iran, Lebanon, Liberia, Luxemburg, Mexico, the Netherlands, New Zealand, Nicaragua, Norway, Panama, Paraguay, Peru, Philippine Commonwealth, Poland, Saudi Arabia, Syria, Turkey, Ukrainian Soviet Socialist Republic, Union of South Africa, Uruguay, Venezuela, and Yugoslavia. These included the nations which had fought through the war, with several such as Turkey and Argentina, which had broken with the Axis powers at the last moment. Denmark was admitted during conference, and Poland, owing to a dispute about which government should receive recognition, did not take part in the conference, but signed the charter later.

The United States was represented by Secretary of State Stettinius and his predecessor Cordell Hull, Senators Connally and Vandenberg, Representatives Bloom and Eaton, Commander Harold Stassen, and Dean Virginia Gildersleeve. Other countries were represented by their foreign secretaries.

Differences of opinion appeared. The questions of the control of the reconquered colonies, of the voting power in the Council, and of the relation to the new league of regional associations, like that formed by the Declaration of Chapultepec, were debated and adjusted. But beneath the ruffled surface the business of the conference moved steadily along.

The charter was framed and adopted June 26, 1945, and submitted for ratification to the member nations. The United Nations came into being October 24, 1945, when Soviet Russia deposited with the United States Department of State the twenty-ninth instrument of ratification.

The United Nations (UN). Its avowed purpose is "to maintain peace and security," and to prevent acts of aggression; and to encourage respect for human rights and fundamental freedoms for all. It is to ensure that states not members act in accordance with these principles. New members may be admitted, and members may be expelled.

The organs of UN are the General Assembly and the Security Council. The General Assembly is made up of delegates from all the member nations. Each nation has one vote. Important questions require a two-thirds majority. It meets annually, and special sessions may be called by the Secretary-General.

The Security Council is made up of five permanent members: The United States, Great Britain, Russia, China, and France; and six non-permanent members, to be chosen for two years by the General Assembly. With the Security Council rests primary responsibility for action. Decisions require a vote of seven members, including all the permanent members. Herein lies the so-called veto, as any one of these may block action by a negative vote. The Council may intervene in any dispute, "or any situation," which may endanger international peace. All members are pledged to assist UN in the peaceful settlement of disputes, and for this purpose to furnish such armed forces as may be later agreed upon. A military staff committee is to advise the council in taking such action. The right of self-defense is reserved. Other organs are the United Nations Economic and Social Council (UNESCO) to promote higher standards of living and better social conditions; the Trusteeship Council, with supervision over colonial areas assigned to member nations. The International Court of Justice is its principal judicial organ. Other related organizations are the United Nations Relief and Rehabilitation Administration (UNRRA) established in 1943, which did much to relieve the famine conditions in 1945–46; and the International (World) Bank.

The first part of the first session of the United Nations was held in London, Jan. 9–Feb. 14, 1946. It effected organization, choosing the Belgian Foreign Minister, Paul Henri Spaak, as president, and Trygve Lie, of Norway, as Secretary-General. The second part of the session, held at New York, October 23–December 16, 1946, passed resolutions on limitation of armaments; admitted Afghanistan, Iceland, Siam, and Sweden as members; and accepted from John D. Rockefeller, Jr., the gift of a site on Manhattan island for its permanent location.

The Security Council was completed at the first session by the election of Brazil, Poland, Australia, Mexico, Egypt, and the Netherlands as non-permanent members. It organized January 17 and remains in continuous session. An ominous feature of its transactions has been the chronic difference of opinion between Russia and the Western democracies. Meantime a Peace Conference at Paris (July 29–October 15) approved in principle treaties of peace with Italy, Bulgaria, Rumania, Hungary, and Finland. These were revised by the Council of Foreign Ministers, and signed February 10–15, 1947.

DICTIONARY OF WORLD HISTORY

The following section deals with topics of world history which do not specifically concern the United States. These topics as a rule have respect to countries whose histories are to be found in the preceding sections. The topics are of such a nature, however, that they can be dealt with more satisfactorily in separate articles. In some cases, this situation is due to the fact that the topic concerns several countries; in other cases, an adequate treatment of a certain phase of a national history would be impossible without unduly interrupting the connected narrative of the country's development. Such topics have therefore received special treatment in accordance with their interest and importance.

Abbassides, The (*ă-băs′ĭ-dēz*). The most famous dynasty of Mohammedan caliphs, taking its name from Abbas, the uncle of Mohammed. This family reigned in Bagdad from 750 until 1058, when the temporal power as monarchs was taken from it, though for 200 years following this date the caliphs were recognized as the spiritual heads of Islam. The greatest glory of the dynasty was the reign of Haroun-al-Raschid, 786–809, the contemporary and admirer of Charlemagne. The wealth and luxury of this period are celebrated in many stories of the *Arabian Nights*. Haroun-al-Raschid became a prince of romance, and Bagdad a synonym for courtly splendor. In the following reign, science and philosophy which enriched Europe were cultivated. But underneath the splendid surface were poverty and injustice which weakened the state and made it an easy prey to the invader. In 1258 the Abbassides were driven out of Bagdad by the Mongols, who burned the city. From 1258 to 1517 the Abbassides maintained a limited power in Egypt, when the last of the line was taken captive by the Turkish sultan, Selim I. See *Egypt*.

A. B. C. Powers. An expression which came into general use about 1914-15, to designate the group of three principal South American powers, Argentina, Brazil, and Chile. In the former year, these powers joined in a diplomatic effort to mediate in the difficulties between Mexico and the United States. In 1915, they concluded among themselves a group of treaties of peace and arbitration. See *Argentina, Brazil, Chile*.

Abdication. The renunciation of an office. Strictly this term is applied to the giving up of crown and authority by sovereign rulers of states, or by occupants of the papal throne. Various influences have prompted historic abdications. Sometimes the only motive has been the desire of the monarch to escape the cares of state; more often, however, compulsion, rebellion, or conquest has rendered such an act imperative. It is worthy of note that, though despotic or absolute monarchs are free to hand over the cares of state to another at any time they will, the situation is different in a limited monarchy. The king of England, for example, cannot lawfully abdicate without the consent of Parliament, the government of that country being in the nature of a constitutional contract between king and people.

In the following list are enumerated most of the important abdications recorded in history, including those which have resulted from the universal cataclysm due to the World Wars.

Diocletian	305
Maximian	305
Richard II of England	1399
Amadeus VIII of Savoy	1449
Charles V of the Holy Roman Empire	1556
Christina of Sweden	1654
Augustus of Poland	1706
Philip V of Spain	1724
Victor Amadeus II of Sardinia	1730
Stanislaus Leszczynski (of Poland)	1735
Poniatowski Leszczynski (of Poland)	1795
Charles Emmanuel II of Sardinia	1802
Charles IV of Spain	1808
Louis Bonaparte of Holland	1810
Napoleon	1814 and 1815
Victor Emmanuel I of Sardinia	1821
Charles X of France	1830
William I of the Netherlands	1840
Ferdinand of Austria	1848
Ludwig of Bavaria	1848
Louis Philippe of France	1848
Charles Albert of Sardinia	1849
Amadeus of Spain	1873
Alexander of Bulgaria	1886
Milan I of Serbia	1889
Dom Pedro of Brazil	1889
Hsuan-Tung, emperor of China	1912
Nicholas II of Russia	1917
William II, emperor of Germany	1918
King of Württemberg	November 10, 1918
King of Saxony	November 11, 1918
Grand Duke of Oldenburg	November 11, 1918
Charles, emperor of Austria	November 12, 1918
Prince of Reuss	November 12, 1918
Grand Duke of Saxe-Weimar	November 13, 1918
Prince of Waldeck-Pyrmont	November 14, 1918
Duke of Anhalt	November 14, 1918
King of Bavaria	November 16, 1918
Grand Duke of Baden	November 17, 1918
Duke of Saxe-Coburg	November 17, 1918
Grand Duke of Mecklenburg-Schwerin	November 17, 1918
Constantine of Greece,	June 12, 1917, and Sept. 27, 1922
Alfonso XIII of Spain	April 14, 1931
Prajadhipok of Siam	March 2, 1935
Edward VIII of Great Britain	December 10, 1936
Victor Emmanuel III	May 9, 1946
Wilhelmina of the Netherlands	Sept. 4, 1948

Popes who have abdicated:

Marcellinus	308
Liberius	366
Benedict IX	1044
Gregory VI	1046
St. Celestine V	1294
Gregory XII	1415

Abencerrages (*ȧ-bĕn′sĕ-rā′jĕz*). This celebrated family of Moors held pride of place among Oriental races as being of pure Arab descent. They were famous in Granada in the 15th century and figured prominently in Spanish romance, especially in the many accounts given of their massacre by the Zegris, inveterate rivals of that period. Accused by the latter of an intrigue against Abdallah, king of Granada, the Abencerrages were decoyed into the Alhambra, where 36 of their number were slain.

Achæan (*ȧ-kē′ăn*) **League, The.** This confederacy of Greek city-states of the Peloponnesus has been called "the most remarkable federal union in history before the founding of the United States of America." About 280 B. C. four little towns on the south shore of the Gulf of Corinth revived an ancient confederacy that had been destroyed by the Macedonian conquerors. Soon other towns joined in driving out the Macedonian tyrants. Within a few years the league included most of the cities of the Peloponnesus in its federal assembly, in which all citizens of the cities who chose to attend had a voice and a vote. For a hundred years, in spite of the narrow aristocratic power allowed by the character of the assembly, the league gave good government to its citizens. It was finally dissolved after the capture and destruction of Corinth by the Romans in 146 B. C. See *Greece*.

Adscriptus Glebæ (*ăd′skrĭp′tŭs glē′bē*). This Latin phrase means "bound" or "attached to the soil." An adscript was, in feudal times, a serf. He was regarded as an implement or chattel on his master's estate and in this sense belonged, or was attached to, the land. So true was this, that, on the transfer of an estate from one ownership to another, the new owner claimed as a right the serfs who were working on the estate at the time of purchase or transfer.

Afrikander. The Dutch name for African. Commonly used of native whites of Dutch or Huguenot ancestry in South Africa.

Albigenses (*ăl'bĭ-jĕn'sēz*). A name given to a sect also called Catharists, or "the pure," which taught a Manichean dualism, the conflict of two principles, good and evil. Triumph of the "good" was sought through extreme asceticism. The center of the heresy was in Languedoc, and it took its name from the city of Albi. In an endeavor to suppress the heresy, Innocent III sent legates in 1203 to southern France. One of them was assassinated, and the pope organized a crusade against the Albigenses. Its leader was Simon de Montfort, and he and his followers seemed chiefly anxious to conquer rich estates in the South. The final result was to bring southern France under royal control.

Algeciras Conference. Prior to 1905, France carried on a policy of "peaceful penetration" in Morocco. In that year Wilhelm II of Germany visited Tangier and promised to uphold Moroccan independence. Peace being threatened, a conference of leading European powers was called at Algeciras in 1906. Aided by British influence, France's claims were upheld, and a mixed French and Spanish police force was set up.

When native disturbances occasioned the French seizure of Fez in 1911, the Germans protested and sent the warship *Panther*. This was known as the Agadir affair. In subsequent negotiations, France won from Germany recognition of her Morocco claims, ceding in return extensive territories in the Congo. Germany nevertheless considered herself humiliated and increased her army, thereby augmenting the suspicions which culminated in the World War.

Allied Debts. The World War and the readjustments immediately ensuing left the various Allied countries in debt to the United States to the amount of about 10.338 billion dollars, of which Great Britain owed 4.277 billion and France, 3.405 billion. Great Britain was a creditor to other Allies to the extent of about 7.270 billion dollars, and France had advanced to others about 2.775 billion dollars. The United States was thus the largest creditor; Great Britain was second, being owed about 3 billion more than her debt to the United States. On August 1, 1922, the British government announced that it would cancel all debts to it and reparation claims over and above what were required to meet its payments to the United States. The American government refused to admit any connection between reparations and Allied debts.

The British debt to the United States was funded in 1923, payments to be made over a period of 62 years. Most of the other debtor countries followed, the interest charges and installments being adjusted to their estimated capacity to pay. Payments were made regularly until 1931, when a world-wide financial crisis led President Hoover to propose a moratorium, subsequently ratified, on all Allied debts and German reparations. No more reparations were paid. After the moratorium most debtor countries defaulted immediately. Great Britain made one complete payment and two "token" payments. Finland alone continued to make her small payments due.

Amphictyonic (*ăm-fĭk'tĭ-ŏn'ĭk*) **League, The.** This name means "league of neighbors." In ancient Greece, before 500 B. C., there were several such leagues formed for the protection of various shrines and temples. The chief of these was the Delphic Amphictyony, or "The Amphictyonic League," which included in its council delegates from all the important states and represented a religious union of the Greek people. Its original purpose was the care of the temple at Delphi; but its council also laid down rules for more humane warfare, for instance, forbidding the cutting off of a town's water supply in war or peace. This was a first step in international law. The Amphictyonic League continued to exercise great religious and political sway as late as the 3d century A. D. See *Greece*.

Annus Mirabilis, "Wonderful Year." A phrase applied to various noted years in history. It gave the title to Dryden's poem, in which are commemorated the two English victories over the Dutch in 1666 and the Great Fire of London in the same year.

Armada, The. A Spanish word, meaning "armed force," but applied especially to the great naval expedition sent against England by Philip of Spain in 1588 and decisively defeated by the English fleet and the storms of the North Sea. Philip's purpose was three-fold: to suppress English Protestantism, to stop English piracy in Spanish America, and to prevent English aid from reaching the rebellious Netherlanders. When, after long delays in storms, the vast Spanish fleet appeared in the English channel, it numbered 120 ships, carrying 20,000 soldiers and 8000 sailors, besides the galley slaves. But Philip, whose policy suppressed invention in his own dominions, had failed to reckon with the superior intelligence of the Englishmen and also with their patriotism. Catholic and Protestant had united in a supreme effort to build up the depleted English navy. The Spanish ships, built after an old, high, unwieldy type, to carry many soldiers for fighting at close quarters, were no match for the new English vessels, built to sail swiftly and to carry heavier guns. The English commanders, Lord Howard, Drake, Hawkins, and Frobisher, allowed the *Armada* to pass Plymouth, July 21, 1588. Then, with a favoring southwest wind, they followed, and, in a series of sharp attacks at long and short range, so harried and crippled the Spaniards that on the 27th of July they anchored off Calais. Here eight fire ships were sent into the midst of the unwieldy floating castles, and they were compelled to put to sea. On the following day, off Gravelines, the helpless *Armada* was riddled by English shot. The wind rose to a storm which drove pursuers and pursued northward past the coasts of Holland, where the waiting prince of Parma saw his hope of transporting his army to England vanish. The Spanish admiral, the duke of Sidonia, himself utterly unpracticed in seafaring, saw his only chance of escape around the north of Scotland. Storm and wreck followed him into the Atlantic. Of the "invincible *Armada*" but 54 battered hulks were finally anchored in Santander bay. See *England*.

Armenian Massacres. By the Treaty of Berlin in 1878, the sultan of Turkey promised reforms in the government of Armenia; but these promises were not kept, and revolutionary movements arose among the oppressed people. In 1895 the Kurds, called in to police the country, carried on brutal massacres. Protests by England, France, and Russia were ignored. In 1909 at Adana and in Cilicia and northern Syria 30,000 Armenians were killed. It is estimated that, between April 1915 and January 1922, through a Turkish policy of extermination, nearly a million Armenians were massacred. See *Turkey, World War*.

Assassins or **Hashisheens.** A fanatical military order instituted in Persia about 1090 by Hassan ben Sabah. They migrated to Syria and settled in the mountains of Lebanon, whence the name of their chief, who was known as "the Old Man of the Mountain." The secret murders they committed, in obedience to this chief, made them notorious. Their religion was a mixture of Mohammedanism, Judaism, and Christianity. They believed the Holy Spirit dwelt in their leader, and so they obeyed his orders as coming direct from God. For two centuries they were the terror of the surrounding nations. They fought, 50,000 strong, against the crusaders and became a formidable obstacle to the success of the Christian armies. They were at length overcome by the sultan Bibars in 1272.

Austrian Succession, War of. In 1740 Charles VI, Habsburg emperor, died without male heirs. Frederick II (the Great) seized Silesia. Other countries hastened to help divide the Austrian realms. Maria Theresa, daughter of Charles, loyally supported by her subjects and later aided by England and Holland, succeeded in preventing any losses of territory besides Silesia. Out of this war, ended by the Peace of Aix-la-Chapelle in 1748, grew the rivalry of Prussia and Austria in Germany and that of England and France in America. See *Hungary*, page 488b; *Pragmatic Sanction*, page 574.

Avignon (*ȧ'vē'nyôɴ'*) **Captivity.** The period of 70 years during which the popes were forced to reside at Avignon, on the southeastern border of medieval France. The influence of the French kings in the affairs of the papacy seemed so predominant that, when the Hundred Years' war broke out, England distrusted the popes as tools of the enemy. This humiliating sojourn lasted from the papacy of Clement V, 1309, until that of Gregory XI, 1377. It is known also as the Babylonian Captivity, the period of exile approximating to that of the Jews in the time of Nebuchadnezzar.

Babington Plot. A plot set on foot in 1585 by a number of young Catholic noblemen at court, acting, it is alleged, under the instructions of a Jesuit named Ballard. Letters secured by Walsingham, secretary of state and head of the secret service, were said to have proved Mary Stuart's complicity in the plot. Babington and his companions were condemned to death, Mary also being subsequently tried and executed for her part in this conspiracy.

Baghdad Railway. Before the World War, the plans of the German government involved extension of control over territory and trade in the Near East. One of the chief means of maintaining German predominance in this territory was the project of a German controlled railway from the Ægean Sea to the Persian gulf. Together with the railway lines from Berlin to Istanbul, this formed the famous Berlin to Baghdad route. The first concessions were obtained by Baron Marschall von Bieberstein in 1888. Work on various sections of the route was carried forward until 1914, when negotiations for the last portion, from Baghdad to Basra on the Persian gulf, were interrupted by the World War. This stretch was completed by the British during the war. Since the Armistice the remaining 325 miles of road has been completed. Control, however, is no longer in German hands.

Balaklava (*bȧ'lȧ-klä'vȧ*). The name of this little Russian seaport in the Crimea is famous because of two exploits of British troops in the battle of Balaklava, Oct. 25, 1854. A brigade of heavy cavalry, in a brilliant charge, repulsed a huge mass of Russian horsemen. More famous is the charge of the brigade of light cavalry, "the light brigade." A vague order to retake some guns was misunderstood, and the brigade, under Lord Cardigan, rode against the very center of the Russian army. Few escaped from the ensuing slaughter. "It is magnificent," said a French officer, "but it is not war."

Balance of Power. The name at first given to that relation of European states in which no one country is strong enough to threaten the safety of its neighbors. From the close of the religious struggle of the Thirty Years' war in 1648 to the World War, 1914–18, the chief concern of European diplomacy was the maintaining of the "balance of power." The advocacy of disarmament aims at bringing about an adjustment of power, not only among the sovereign states of Europe, but also among those throughout the rest of the civilized world, so that no one state can be in a position to menace or dominate another. See *Disarmament*.

Balkan League, The. An alliance formed in 1912 by Bulgaria, Serbia, Greece, and Montenegro for the purpose of action against Turkey. It lasted barely a year, being broken in the bloody dispute which arose among the allies after their complete defeat of the Turk in 1913. See *Greece*, *Turkey*.

Barmecides. A wealthy Persian family who furnished viziers to Haroun-al-Raschid and to former caliphs of Baghdad; so called from their founder Barmek. Jaffar became the favorite vizier of the caliph, and, by his magnificent services and patronage of the arts, reflected great glory on his master's reign. Through jealousy or suspicion or both, Jaffar fell into disgrace with Haroun-al-Raschid, who without apparent reason put him to death in 802, together with nearly all of the Barmecide family.

Bashi-Bazouks (*băsh'ĭ-bȧ-zo͝oks'*). Irregular troops or volunteers attached to the Turkish army and noted for their wildness and cruelty. As a rule, they are mounted and serve for their maintenance without pay; this deficiency, however, they rectify by acts of pillage. Their services are also used by the municipal authorities, who often detail them to escort travelers wishing to explore the country. Such services are by no means inexpensive, as the Bashi-Bazouks expect not only to be fed well, but to be rewarded generously. Their uniform being that of tatterdemalions, they are called *Bashi-Bazouks*, which signifies "disorderly appearance."

Bastille (*bȧs-tēl'*), **Destruction of the.** The famous fortress of the Bastille once flanked the city gate of St. Antoine, Paris. Its construction was begun, under Charles V, by the provost Hugh Aubriot in 1370 and was completed in 1382. It became in a short time a prison of state and held within its walls, among other illustrious victims, such men as Jacques d'Armagnac, "The Man with the Iron Mask," Voltaire, and Lally-Tollendal. Its terrors reached their climax during the ministry of Richelieu, 1624–42. In the reign of Louis XI, cages of iron had been built, and the vaults beneath the towers, being on a level with the water in the moat, were the object of especial dread. For the populace, the Bastille stood as the symbol of royal despotism.

Louis XVI, June 23, 1789, had declared certain recent acts of the third estate of the National Assembly to be unconstitutional. He sent Brézé, his master of ceremonies, to bid the members withdraw from the hall of the Convention. Mirabeau, a French noble who had been chosen a deputy by the third estate, exclaimed with passion, "Go tell your master we are here by the will of the people and shall leave only at the point of the bayonet!" A few days later foreign mercenaries appeared in Paris. The Assembly sent to the king, demanding their removal. Louis replied by dismissing Necker, a minister favorable to reform and trusted by the people. Camille Desmoulins, a young journalist, announced the news in public on July 12. Paris was all aflame. Two days later, July 14, the populace, re-enforced by companies of French Guards, attacked the ancient monument of tyranny. De Launay, the commander, offered to surrender. When the doors of the fortress were thrown open, the mob seized him and a few of the Swiss Guards and murdered them. The heads of De Launay and Major de Losme of the Swiss were mounted on pikes and carried about the city. The walls of the grim fortress were later pulled down, so that not "one stone was left upon another." The fall of the Bastille is one of the most dramatic events in modern history. Its anniversary is celebrated in France as the chief national holiday and as the day when a new era of liberty dawned for the people and an end was put to the *ancien régime*. It is interesting to note that Lafayette sent the key of the fortress to George Washington "because the principles of America it was that opened the Bastille." This relic may still be seen at Mt. Vernon.

Bath, Order of the. An order of knighthood, founded by Henry IV in 1399. From the time of Charles I it lapsed, until revived by George I in 1725 as a military order, which it remained until 1845. It was then established on its present basis with a military and a civil division.

BATTLES OF THE WORLD, DECISIVE

1. Marathon, Sept., 490 B. C. A small Greek army, commanded by Miltiades, defeated a much larger Persian force. The Persians were compelled to retreat into Asia.

2. Syracuse, 413 B. C. The besieged Syracusans turned upon and almost completely destroyed the invading Athenian forces.

3. Arbela, Oct. 1, 331 B. C. The Greeks, led by Alexander the Great, defeated the Persian armies of Darius and overthrew the Persian power.

4. Metaurus, 207 B. C. The Carthaginians, led by Hasdrubal, the brother of Hannibal, were defeated by the Romans under the command of Marcus Livius and Claudius Nero.

5. Teutoburg, 9 (?) A. D. The Roman legions, led by Varus, were defeated by the Germans under Arminius. This victory freed Germany permanently from the Roman power.

6. Châlons, 451 A. D. The Romans and their allies, the Visigoths, led by Aëtius, defeated the Huns and their Ostrogoth and other allies, led by Attila, compelling them to retire into Pannonia.

7. Tours, 732 A. D. The Franks under Charles Martel, won a great victory over the invading hosts of the Saracens, led by Abderrahman. This conflict, which checked the Mohammedan invasion of western Europe, is known also as the battle of Poitiers.

8. Hastings, October 14, 1066. The Norman invaders defeated the Saxons. King Harold of England lost his life, and the kingdom passed to William, duke of Normandy.

9. Orleans, May 8, 1429. The siege of Orleans by the English was raised by the French, led by Joan of Arc. This victory insured the final defeat of the English invaders of France.

10. Defeat of the Spanish Armada, July 20–29, 1588. The Spanish fleet was almost completely destroyed by the British fleet and by severe storms.

11. Blenheim, Aug. 13, 1704. The French and Bavarians were defeated by the English under the duke of Marlborough, aided by their allies led by Prince Eugene.

12. Pultowa, July 8, 1709. Charles XII of Sweden was completely defeated by the Russians under Czar Peter the Great.

13. Quebec, Fall of, Sept. 17, 1759. After an extended siege and after the battle on the Heights of Abraham, where the English under Wolfe defeated the French under Montcalm, the French surrendered the city.

14. Saratoga, Oct. 7, 1777. The British army under General Burgoyne was utterly defeated by the Americans. The entire force was surrendered on Oct. 17 to the American commander, General Gates.

15. Valmy, Sept. 20, 1792. The French forces, commanded by Kellermann, defeated the Prussians, commanded by the duke of Brunswick.

16. Waterloo, June 18, 1815. Napoleon and his French forces were finally defeated by the British and their allies under the duke of Wellington.

17. Gettysburg, July 1–3, 1863. The Confederate troops under Lee were defeated by the Federals under Meade. Confederate invasion of the North was proved impossible.

18. Vicksburg, The Fall of, July 4, 1863. The capture of this stronghold by Grant, in command of the Federal army, gave command of the Mississippi to the North and cut the Confederacy in two. The Confederate general, Pemberton, surrendered after a long siege.

19. Sedan, Sept. 1, 1870. Defeat of the French forces by the Germans compelled the surrender of the French army in Sedan and of Emperor Napoleon III.

20. Tsushima, or **The Sea of Japan,** May 27–28, 1905. The Japanese, under Admiral Togo, destroyed Rojestvensky's Russian fleet, establishing Japanese sea-power.

21. The Marne, First Battle of, Sept. 6–9, 1914. The British and French armies checked the German advance, and with it the German hope for a speedy victory.

22. Jutland, May 31, 1916. The defeat of the German fleet confirmed British control of the sea.

23. Stalingrad, Aug. 1942–Jan. 1943. The Russian resistance at Stalingrad on the Volga, and the destruction of the German army besieging it, was the turning-point on the eastern front.

24. Normandy, June 6–July 18, 1944. The landing and establishment of the Anglo-American armies on the Norman coast made possible the liberation of France and the invasion of Germany.

25. Philippine Sea, Second Battle of, Sept. 25, 1944. The defeat of the Japanese fleet off Leyte ruined Japan's sea-power, and left her open to invasion.

Bayonne (*bȧ'yôn'*) **Decree.** Napoleon's decree of 1808, ordering the seizure of all vessels under the American flag found in French ports, claiming that since all American vessels were held at home by the Embargo Act, these were English vessels in disguise.

Belgian Congo. Formerly Congo Free State. This owed its existence largely to Leopold II, king of the Belgians. In 1876, Leopold, in co-operation with several European governments, formed the International African Association, to promote the exploration and colonization of Africa. He employed Henry M. Stanley to explore the Congo region, and Stanley was active in founding stations, and making treaties with the native chiefs. After several powers, including the United States, had recognized the independent Congo Free State, the Berlin Conference of 1885 declared it neutral, and open to the trade of all nations, with Leopold as its personal sovereign. Governmental abuses, which arose under this régime, aroused international protest. In 1908 the country was annexed by Belgium, and since that time it has been governed as a colony under the title of Belgian Congo.

Belgian Neutrality Treaty. The Treaty of London, 1839, signed by Austria, Belgium, France, Great Britain, Prussia, and Russia, guaranteed the perpetual neutrality of Belgium. This neutrality being threatened by the Franco-Prussian war in 1870, the belligerents signed special agreements with Great Britain to respect Belgian neutrality. In 1914 Germany was charged with violating the treaty obligation. The agreement was abrogated by the Treaty of Versailles in 1919.

Benelux. A term applied to an economic agreement made in 1947 between Belgium, the Netherlands, and Luxembourg. Its aims are a uniform tariff for all three countries, uniform excise and sales tax, and full economic and monetary union, possibly by 1952.

BISHOPS AND POPES OF ROME

The word pope is derived from an ecclesiastical Latin word *papa*, meaning "father," applied in the early Christian centuries as a term of respect to clergy of high rank, especially bishops. By the 5th century, the title had come to be applied almost altogether to the bishop of Rome, and from the 11th century it has been claimed exclusively for him as the sovereign pontiff of the Roman Catholic Church.

Primarily the pope, as the successor of Saint Peter, is the bishop of Rome. The actual predominance of Rome over other episcopal sees was, as early as the 1st century, acknowledged by the then universal church. This supremacy, through a gradual process extending over several centuries, grew and expanded with the natural development of the Christian Church. The council of Chalcedon in 451 accepted as authoritative the profession of faith proposed by Leo I. The pontificates of Gregory the Great (590–604), Gregory VII (1073–85), and Innocent III (1198–1216) mark important stages in the growth of the papal power.

Electors. Early accounts of elections indicate that for several centuries the right of choosing bishops and the early popes was shared by both the clerical and the lay members of the Christian community of Rome and of its neighboring territory. After the election had come to be a concern of the entire Church, the possession of the right was restricted, until at length, in the 12th century, it came to be confined to the college of cardinals. The pope is now elected by a body known as the conclave, which includes all cardinals of the world.

The Conclave. The word conclave formerly signified a room which might be locked, and is often applied to the apartments in which the papal electoral body meets, as well as to the assemblage itself. The cardinals are required to live in entire seclusion from the outside world during the period necessary to secure the election of a new pope. For this purpose, after the death of a pope, a portion of the Vatican adjoining the Sistine Chapel is walled off and divided into apartments of three or four rooms each. In these live the cardinals, each of whom may be accompanied by a secretary and a servant, who are called conclavists.

Method of Election. The conclave opens officially the evening of the fifteenth day after the pontiff's death. On the morning of the sixteenth day, the cardinals assemble for the actual balloting in the Sistine Chapel. The voting is by secret ballot, and for an election a two-thirds vote is required.

Two ballots are taken each day, in the morning and in the evening, until an election is secured. After each ballot, the votes are burned. If no election has taken place, damp straw is mixed with the paper, and the resulting dark smoke, the famous *sfumata*, from the chimney, informs the people waiting outside that a new pope has not yet been chosen. When the new pope has been chosen, the paper ballots alone are burned without the straw and a white almost invisible smoke from the chimney notifies the populace that the pope at last has been elected.

Installation. When a candidate has received the necessary two-thirds vote, the doors of the chapel are opened. Upon formal inquiry by the presiding dean as to whether the newly chosen pontiff is willing to accept the burden of the papacy, the pope-elect duly declares his assent and announces the name by which he desires to be known. He is then clothed in the papal vestments, and receives the first homage of the cardinals. Following this ceremony occurs the public announcement of the election. On the election of Pius XI in 1922, this proclamation, for the first time since 1870, was made from the gallery of Saint Peter's. The pope's jurisdiction begins with his election, but he dates his pontificate from the following Sunday or holyday upon which the formal coronation takes place.

The following list contains the names, with the dates of their pontificates, of the pontiffs who have occupied the chair of Saint Peter. The list will be found especially valuable for reference in connection with the study of the various periods of European history.

Pontiff	Pontificate	
	First Century	
	A. D.	A. D.
1 Saint Peter		67(?)
2 Saint Linus	67	79(?)
3 Saint Anacletus	79	90(?)
4 Saint Clement I	90	99(?)
	Second Century	
5 Saint Evaristus	99	107(?)
6 Saint Alexander I	107	116(?)
7 Saint Sixtus I	116	125(?)
8 Saint Telesphorus	125	136(?)
9 Saint Hyginus	136	140(?)
10 Saint Pius I	140	154(?)
11 Saint Anicetus	154	165(?)
12 Saint Soter	165	174
13 Saint Eleutherius	174	189
14 Saint Victor I	189	198
15 Saint Zephyrinus	198	217
	Third Century	
16 Calixtus I	217	222
17 Urban I	222	230
18 Saint Pontian	230	235
19 Saint Anterus	235	236
20 Saint Fabian	236	250
21 Cornelius	251	253
22 Saint Lucius I	253	254
23 Saint Stephen I	254	257
24 Saint Sixtus II	257	258
25 Saint Dionysius	259	268
26 Saint Felix I	269	274
27 Saint Eutychianus	275	283
28 Saint Caius	283	296
	Fourth Century	
29 Saint Marcellinus	296	304
30 Saint Marcellus I	308	309
31 Saint Eusebius	309 (310)	
32 Saint Miltiades	311	314
33 Saint Silvester I	314	335
34 Saint Mark	336	
35 Saint Julius I	337	352
36 Liberius	352	366
37 Saint Damasus I	366	384
38 Saint Siricius	384	398
39 Saint Anastasius I	398	401

Pontiff	Pontificate	
	Fifth Century	
	A. D.	A. D.
40 Innocent I	402	417
41 Saint Zosimus	417	418
42 Saint Boniface I	418	422
43 Saint Celestine I	422	432
44 Saint Sixtus III	432	440
45 Saint Leo I, "The Great"	440	461
46 Saint Hilarius	461	468
47 Saint Simplicius	468	483
48 Saint Felix III	483	492
49 Saint Gelasius I	492	496
50 Anastasius II	496	498
	Sixth Century	
51 Saint Symmachus	498	514
52 Saint Hormisdas	514	523
53 Saint John I	523	526
54 Felix IV	526	530
55 Boniface II	530	532
56 John II	533	535
57 Saint Agapetus I	535	536
58 Saint Silverius	536	538(?)
59 Vigilius	538(?)	555
60 Pelagius I	556	561
61 John III	561	574
62 Benedict I	575	579
63 Pelagius II	579	590
	Seventh Century	
64 Saint Gregory I, "The Great"	590	604
65 Sabinianus	604	606
66 Boniface III	607	
67 Saint Boniface IV	608	615
68 Saint Deusdedit	615	618
69 Boniface V	619	625
70 Honorius I	625	638
71 Severinus	638	640
72 John IV	640	642
73 Theodore I	642	649
74 Saint Martin I	649	655
75 Saint Eugenius I	654	657
76 Saint Vitalianus	657	672
77 Saint Adeodatus	672	676
78 Donus	676	678
79 Saint Agatho	678	681
80 Saint Leo II	682	683
81 Saint Benedict II	684	685
82 John V	685	686
83 Conon	686	687
	Eighth Century	
84 Saint Sergius I	687	701
85 John VI	701	705
86 John VII	705	707
87 Sisinnius	708	
88 Constantine	708	715
89 Saint Gregory II	715	731
90 Saint Gregory III	731	741
91 Saint Zacharias	741	752
92 Stephen III	752	757
93 Paul I	757	767
94 Stephen IV	768	772
95 Adrian I	772	795
	Ninth Century	
96 Saint Leo III	795	816
97 Stephen V	816	817
98 Paschal I	817	824
99 Eugenius II	824	827
100 Valentine	827	
101 Gregory IV	827	844
102 Sergius II	844	847
103 Saint Leo IV	847	855
104 Benedict III	855	858
105 Saint Nicholas I	858	867
106 Adrian II	867	872
107 John VIII	872	882
108 Marinus I	882	884
109 Saint Adrian III	884	885
110 Stephen VI	885	891
111 Formosus	891	896
112 Boniface VI	896	
113 Stephen VII	896	897
114 Romanus	897	
115 Theodore II	897	
116 John IX	898	900
	Tenth Century	
117 Benedict IV	900	903
118 Leo V	903	
119 Christopher	903	904
120 Sergius III	904	911

Pontiff	Pontificate	
	Tenth Century—Con.	
	A. D.	A. D.
121 Anastasius III	911	913
122 Lando	913	914
123 John X	914	928
124 Leo VI	928	
125 Stephen VIII	928	931
126 John XI	931	936
127 Leo VII	936	939
128 Stephen IX	939	942
129 Marinus II	942	946
130 Agapetus II	946	955
131 John XII	955	964
132 Leo VIII	963	965
133 Benedict V	964	
134 John XIII	965	972
135 Benedict VI	973	974
136 Benedict VII	974	983
137 John XIV	983	984
138 Boniface VII	984	985
139 John XV	985	996
140 Gregory V	996	999
	Eleventh Century	
141 Silvester II	999	1003
142 John XVII	1003	
143 John XVIII	1003	1009
144 Sergius IV	1009	1012
145 Benedict VIII	1012	1024
146 John XIX	1024	1032
147 Benedict IX	1032	1045
148 Gregory VI	1045	1046
149 Clement II	1046	1047
150 Damasus II	1048	
151 Saint Leo IX	1049	1054
152 Victor II	1055	1057
153 Stephen X	1057	1058
154 Benedict X	1058	1059
155 Nicholas II	1059	1061
156 Alexander II	1061	1073
157 Saint Gregory VII	1073	1085
158 Victor III, Blessed	1087	1087
159 Urban II, Blessed	1088	1099
	Twelfth Century	
160 Paschal II	1099	1118
161 Gelasius II	1118	1119
162 Calixtus II	1119	1124
163 Honorius II	1124	1130
164 Innocent II	1130	1143
165 Celestine II	1143	1144
166 Lucius II	1144	1145
167 Eugenius III, Blessed	1145	1153
168 Anastasius IV	1153	1154
169 Adrian IV	1154	1159
170 Alexander III	1159	1181
171 Lucius III	1181	1185
172 Urban III	1185	1187
173 Gregory VIII	1187	
174 Clement III	1187	1191
175 Celestine III	1191	1198
	Thirteenth Century	
176 Innocent III	1198	1216
177 Honorius III	1216	1227
178 Gregory IX	1227	1241
179 Celestine IV	1241	
180 Innocent IV	1243	1254
181 Alexander IV	1254	1261
182 Urban IV	1261	1264
183 Clement IV	1265	1268
184 Gregory X	1271	1276
185 Innocent V, Blessed	1276	
186 Adrian V	1276	
187 John XXI	1276	1277
188 Nicholas III	1277	1280
189 Martin IV	1281	1285
190 Honorius IV	1285	1287
191 Nicholas IV	1288	1292
192 Saint Celestine V	1294	
193 Boniface VIII	1294	1303
	Fourteenth Century	
194 Benedict XI	1303	1304
195 Clement V	1305	1314
196 John XXII	1316	1334
197 Benedict XII	1334	1342
198 Clement VI	1342	1352
199 Innocent VI	1352	1362
200 Urban V, Blessed	1362	1370
201 Gregory XI	1370	1378
202 Urban VI	1378	1389
203 Boniface IX	1389	1404

Pontiff	Pontificate	
	Fifteenth Century	
	A. D.	A. D.
204 Innocent VII	1404	1406
205 Gregory XII	1406	1415
206 Alexander V	1409	1410
207 John XXIII	1410	1415
208 Martin V	1417	1431
209 Eugenius IV	1431	1447
210 Nicholas V	1447	1455
211 Calixtus III	1455	1458
212 Pius II	1458	1464
213 Paul II	1464	1471
214 Sixtus IV	1471	1484
215 Innocent VIII	1484	1492
216 Alexander VI	1492	1503
	Sixteenth Century	
217 Pius III	1503	
218 Julius II	1503	1513
219 Leo X	1513	1521
220 Adrian VI	1522	1523
221 Clement VII	1523	1534
222 Paul III	1534	1549
223 Julius III	1550	1555
224 Marcellus II	1555	
225 Paul IV	1555	1559
226 Pius IV	1559	1565
227 Saint Pius V	1566	1572
228 Gregory XIII	1572	1585
229 Sixtus V	1585	1590
230 Urban VII	1590	
231 Gregory XIV	1590	1591
232 Innocent IX	1591	
233 Clement VIII	1592	1605
	Seventeenth Century	
234 Leo XI	1605	
235 Paul V	1605	1621
236 Gregory XV	1621	1623
237 Urban VIII	1623	1644
238 Innocent X	1644	1655
239 Alexander VII	1655	1667
240 Clement IX	1667	1669
241 Clement X	1670	1676
242 Innocent XI	1676	1689
243 Alexander VIII	1689	1691
244 Innocent XII	1691	1700
	Eighteenth Century	
245 Clement XI	1700	1721
246 Innocent XIII	1721	1724
247 Benedict XIII	1724	1730
248 Clement XII	1730	1740
249 Benedict XIV	1740	1758
250 Clement XIII	1758	1769
251 Clement XIV	1769	1774
252 Pius VI	1775	1799
	Nineteenth Century	
253 Pius VII	1800	1823
254 Leo XII	1823	1829
255 Pius VIII	1829	1830
256 Gregory XVI	1831	1846
257 Pius IX	1846	1878
258 Leo XIII	1878	1903
	Twentieth Century	
259 Pius X	1903	1914
260 Benedict XV	1914	1922
261 Pius XI	1922	1939
262 Pius XII	1939	

Black Death. One of the most famous and most destructive plagues of history. Spreading westward from Asia, it swept away from one-third to one-half the population of Europe in the years 1347–50. The disease was named from the black spots that appeared on the bodies of those afflicted. It may have been similar to what is now called "bubonic plague."

Black Hole of Calcutta. A small cell, intended for two or three men, in the East India Company's citadel, Fort William. The story told by the commandant, J. Z. Holwell, is that the subahdar of Bengal, who stormed the fort, June 20, 1756, had his guards drive all the white inmates of the fort, 146 in number, into this almost airless room where they were left overnight to die of suffocation. Only 23 were alive in the morning. Recent studies have seriously discredited this story. Some authorities maintain that only nine men, East India Company officers, were imprisoned, two dying of wounds.

Black Shirts. A name applied to the members of the Fascist party in Italy, by whom the black shirt is worn as a party badge.

Boers (*bōōrz*). The Dutch colonists in South Africa. Boer is a Dutch word meaning peasant or farmer. The Boers first settled in Cape Colony in 1652. Through a century and a half of pioneer life, these people maintained a stern type of Calvinistic faith which intensified their severe exclusiveness. Besides, they firmly believed in their right to enslave the native peoples. When the colony was finally ceded to Great Britain in 1815, the policies of the new government in respect to the natives roused the opposition of the Boers. In 1835 they started the Great Trek, or migration, to the Orange River district, where they settled in the Orange Free State. Later, a large body moved beyond the Vaal, where they organized the Transvaal Republic. Here, under the presidency of Paul Kruger, elected in 1883, they maintained a stubborn independence until the victory of the British in the Boer war. Since that time, through the statesmanship of such men as Lord Milner, General Botha, and General Smuts, the reconciliation of Boers and English has progressed rapidly inside the Union of South Africa.

Bolsheviki (*bôl′shĕ-vē-kē′; bŏl′shĕ-vē′kē*). The name applied to the majority party at the second congress of the Russian Socialist party in 1903, as opposed to the Mensheviki, or minority. The name is derived from the Russian word for majority. The party stood for an application of communism and its program called for the capture of the means of production by the proletariat, by force if necessary, the proletariat continuing to exercise a dictatorship over society.

With the revolution of November 1917, this party, under the leadership of Lenin, came into power and speedily suppressed all other political groups. It became a synonym for the Russian government, the various organs of which it controlled absolutely. Joseph Stalin succeeded Lenin as party leader about 1924. The total membership of the party, which is kept loyal by periodic "purgings," was about 2,500,000 in 1933. See *Russia*.

Botany Bay. A small inlet on the coast of New South Wales, where the first convict establishment was formed in 1788. Later in the same year the penal settlement was removed to Port Jackson, but the name Botany bay was constantly used, generically, for the convict settlements in Australia. Captain Cook, in 1770, gave the bay its present name on account of the many strange plants he found there.

Bourbon Family. Members of this royal line have governed France, Spain, the Two Sicilies, Lucca, and Parma. The family is traced to Robert of Clermont, youngest son of Louis IX, but the name comes from Louis, duke of Bourbon, who died in 1341. French kings of this house were Henry IV, Louis XIII, XIV, XV, XVI, XVII, XVIII, and Charles X.

Boxer Uprising. The patriotic, antiforeign demonstration in China in 1900 led by the Chinese secret society called "The Fist of Righteous Harmony" or, popularly, "Boxers." The outbreak was precipitated by the foreign occupation of Chinese ports,—Kiaochow by Germany, Port Arthur by Russia, Weihaiwei by England, and Kwang-chow by France. The government failed to control the insurgents, and the warships of the powers, except the United States, intensified the antiforeign feeling of the Chinese by bombarding the forts at Taku. The foreign legations at Peking were besieged, and finally a relief force of Japanese, Russian, British, French, German, and American troops, commanded by Count Waldersee, advanced on the capital and relieved the legations on August 14. The 9th regiment, United States army, suffered heavy losses, including its colonel and several other officers. Military operations continued until the spring of 1901. An indemnity of $333,000,000 was imposed on China by the allied powers, the United States and various other countries later resigning claim to their shares. See *China*.

Boycotting. A system of reprisals organized in 1880 by the Land League in Ireland in return for the harsh treatment of tenants by landowners and their agents. It took its name from one Captain James Boycott, a landlord of Mayo. The victim of boycotting was cut off from the social and commercial life of the community, being permitted neither to buy nor to sell, and those attempting to deal with him were treated in like manner. The weapon has been put to frequent use in labor disputes.

Brest-Litovsk (*brĕst′lyĕ-tôfsk′*), **Treaty of.** The treaty of peace concluded March 3, 1918, between Germany and the Bolsheviki, by which Germany was to gain control of Finland, the Baltic provinces, Lithuania, Poland, and the Ukraine, and direction of Russian industry. Although never enforced, it enabled the Germans to transfer troops to the western front at a critical moment of the World War. See *World War*, page 539c.

British Commonwealth of Nations. This term was used officially for the first time in the text of the Irish Free State treaty of 1921. It relates to the self-governing dominions within the British Empire. These comprise Canada, Australia, Irish Free State, South Africa, New Zealand, and Newfoundland. In accordance with recommendations made by the Imperial Conferences of 1926 and 1930, the British Parliament passed in 1931 the statute of Westminster. This statute formally terminated the theoretical right of the British government to pass legislation valid in the Dominions and empowered the Dominions to make laws having extra-territorial operation. United by allegiance to a common sovereign, the Dominions and Great Britain were thus placed largely on a footing of equality, each having the right to appoint its own diplomatic representatives. Nevertheless, the written constitution of each dominion is still in form an act of the British Parliament, which can be altered only by an amending act through the same authority, and the court of final appeal for each dominion remains the judicial committee of the British Privy Council. See pages 440-441.

Buccaneers. An association of sea rovers formed about 1525, to harry the Spanish possessions in South America and prey upon their commerce. They were of various nationalities, but chiefly English and French, their most famous leaders being Montbars, known as the Exterminator, and Henry Morgan, afterwards Sir Henry and deputy-governor of Jamaica. Under the latter leader they crossed the isthmus and sacked the city of Panama in 1671, and for years they paralyzed the Spanish trade, both in the Caribbean Sea and in the Pacific. They ceased to exist as an association early in the 18th century, but some of them continued careers of indiscriminate piracy for many years longer. The name is said to be derived from *buccan*, which in the Caribbean islands meant to dry meat on a frame, or *buccan*, over smoke. The early French adventurers adopted this custom.

Bulgarian Atrocities. A rising of the Mohammedan inhabitants of Bulgaria, assisted by the Bashi-Bazouks, or Turkish Irregulars, against the Christians in 1876. Thousands of Christians were massacred and horrible cruelties were perpetrated, though it is held by some authorities that the stories told were grossly exaggerated. Turkey refused redress, and Russia consequently declared war in the following year.

Burgundy. The name is derived from the Burgundians, a Teutonic people who settled in eastern Gaul in the 5th century. In 1361 the duchy of Burgundy, of which the chief town was Dijon, became a possession of the French crown. It was conferred upon Philip the Bold. He and his vigorous descendants enlarged their territories until, in the

15th century, Burgundy was one of the most important European states, controlling the rich territories and cities of the Low Countries, now Holland and Belgium. Duke Charles the Bold successfully maintained his position against the scheming Louis XI, until he was slain at the battle of Nancy in 1477. The Burgundian realms were then divided between France and Austria, since the Habsburg Maximilian had married Mary, daughter and sole heir of Charles.

Cahiers de Doléances (*kȧ'yā' dĕ dȯ'lā'ȧɴs'*). "Documents of Grievances." These documents contained representations of grievances and demands made by the people. They were signed and laid before the king of France in 1789 by the deputies of the States-General. The principal demands were: suppression of the sale of public offices; the abrogation of judicial power claimed by the owners of certain hereditary estates, who acted as resident magistrates; the repeal of the gabelle, an iniquitous tax on salt; the abolition of the corvée, which exacted free labor from the peasant on the part of the landowner; the suppression of the militia ballot; religious toleration; and better conditions for the clergy.

Caliphate of Cordova. The powerful western dynasty of caliphs. After the decisive battle of Tours in 732, Cordova became the capital of Moorish Spain. Abderrahman, one of the family of Ommiad caliphs of Damascus, who had escaped the massacre inflicted on his house by the rival Abbassides, founded there a new caliphate. Under this powerful dynasty, the caliphate of Cordova became, in culture, wealth, and splendor, the formidable rival of the Abbasside caliphate at Baghdad. This division in the world of Islam relieved Europe from the threat of Mohammedan conquest. See *Abbassides, Arabs, Moors, Spain.*

Canossa. The castle of Matilda of Tuscany, where Gregory VII was staying when the emperor Henry IV made a pilgrimage to Italy, in 1077, to make his submission to the pope, who had excommunicated him. He was treated in the most humiliating fashion by Gregory, who left him for three days in the snow in the courtyard of the castle before consenting to receive him. Hence arose the proverbial expression "Go to Canossa," meaning surrender to the claims of the Church. See *Germany.*

Capetian Dynasty. The remarkable line of kings who ruled France from the election of Hugh Capet in 987 to the fall of Louis Philippe in 1848. The real father of the line was Robert the Strong, said to have been the son of a butcher in Paris. He and his son Odo held the Northmen back from Paris and central France. Odo was chosen king in 887, and in 987 his grandnephew Hugh was made king when the Carolingian line had died out. The name *Capet* comes from Hugh's custom of wearing an abbot's *cape.* The first break in the direct line of descent came with the accession of Philip VI (of Valois) in 1328. The houses of Valois, Bourbon, and Orleans were branches of the Capetian family. See *France.*

Carolingian or **Carlovingian Dynasty.** The second dynasty of the Frankish kings. The name is derived from the Latin *Carolus* (Charles), the name of Charles Martel or of Charles the Great. The first king of the line was Pepin the Short, son of Charles Martel, who deposed the Merovingian king in 751. Charles the Great, or Charlemagne, the greatest of the family, reigned from 768 to 814. The line died out with Louis V in 987. See *France.*

Catacombs. Underground galleries of intricate pattern used, particularly by the early Christians in Rome, as places of burial, of religious worship, and of refuge during persecutions. Catacombs had been employed as burial places by the Etruscans some eight centuries before the Christian era. Roman noble families and Jews in Rome also made use of them. Their greatest development, however, was due to the Christians.

These labyrinthine passages, often one above the other, with many interconnecting branches and blind alleys, are from 30 to 50 feet underground, descent being provided by stairways. In width about three to four feet and twelve feet in height, they honey-comb the environs of Rome, encircling the city at a distance of a mile or two outside the city walls. Their total length is estimated to exceed 750 miles in some 75 separate units. Chambers or chapels were constructed at intervals, their walls being frequently ornamented with paintings of sacred subjects. The dead were placed in recesses excavated in the side walls of the passages and were closed in with slabs sealed with cement. Some two million corpses are estimated to have been so interred. Burial in the catacombs ceased with the sack of Rome by the Goths in 410 A. D. Their existence was forgotten from the 12th century until their accidental rediscovery in 1578. Catacombs have been discovered also in Syracuse, Alexandria, and other communities of the Mediterranean region.

Cavaliers. Royalist sympathizers in England and in the American Colonies during the reigns of Charles I and Charles II. See *Roundheads.*

Cawnpore or **Cawnpur, Massacre of.** The massacre by Nana Sahib of the English garrison in Cawnpore, during the Indian mutiny of 1857. The garrison had surrendered under a pledge of being permitted to retire unharmed. Of those massacred, 560 were women and children. See *Sepoy Mutiny.*

Chaldea (*kăl-dē'ȧ*). The most ancient name of the territory in the lower Tigris and Euphrates valley, practically identical with Babylonia. About 2800 B. C. it became the center of an empire under Sargon, king of Accad. His power extended into the northern Mesopotamian valley and westward to the Mediterranean, but after his death this empire broke up. New Arabian invaders entered Chaldea and made Babylon their capital. They continued to spread Chaldean culture, traditions, and the cuneiform (wedge-shape) system of writing over all western Asia.

Chartist Movement, The, or **Chartism.** A radical reform movement in England in the period from 1838 to 1848. The name arose from the National or People's Charter drawn up by a group of members of Parliament and workingmen, which demanded universal suffrage and salaries for members of Parliament. The causes of the movement were the failure of the Reform bill of 1832 to include the working classes in its benefits and the terrible misery and want among these classes. The movement continued, with various attempts to secure Parliamentary action and with frequent riots, until 1848, when some improvements in working conditions and a period of cheaper food following the repeal of the corn laws robbed it of its strength. See *England.*

Children's Crusade. This tragic incident of the period of the Crusades has been the theme of sober history and of legend. The facts are established that thousands of children and youths—their numbers being estimated at from 50,000 to 90,000—inspired apparently by the crusading spirit of the times, left their homes in the year 1212 and marched in many bands toward the Mediterranean ports of embarkation for the Holy Land. The leaders in France and Germany were two peasant boys. Some of the bands were accompanied by a few older persons, who in most cases appear to have preyed upon the children rather than to have protected them. The fate of the young crusaders is obscure. Some returned sadly to their homes, but many lost their lives. Some are said to have been lost at sea; others, sold into slavery.

Cinque (*sĭngk*) **Ports.** The ancient name of five English Channel ports, Sandwich, Dover, Hythe, Romney, and Hastings, to which later two more,

Winchelsea and Rye, were added. *Cinque* is the Old French word for "five." These towns were granted certain independent privileges by the early Norman kings, in return for which their chief service was to furnish ships and sailors to the king, England having no regular navy before the reign of Henry VII (1485–1509). The ancient privileges have been abolished; but the office of warden, or governor, of the Cinque Ports still remains, a sinecure with a salary of £3000 a year.

Clan-na-Gael (*klăn'nȧ-gāl'*). An Irish secret society, an offshoot of the Fenians, formed in 1881. It was composed of the extreme physical force men among the Fenians and was known also as the United Brotherhood. See *England, Fenians, Ireland.*

Cockpit of Europe. The name given to Belgium on account of the numerous important battles which have been fought there. See *Belgium.*

Code Napoleon. The code of law issued by Napoleon in 1804. It was based on the old French law, with such alterations as had been rendered necessary by the Revolution, and on certain new provisions, introduced by Napoleon, notably those relating to the law of succession and to the marriage law. For the purpose of this codification, which remains the law of France, he called to his councils the most eminent French lawyers, irrespective of party,—among others Tronchet, Cambacérès, Portalis, and Roederer.

Code of Justinian. The systematic body or code of Roman law prepared by a commission of lawyers appointed by the emperor Justinian (527–565). This code, called the *Corpus Juris Civilis*, or "Body of Civil Law," became the basis of nearly all modern European legal systems. Its principles influenced the common law of England, which has prevailed also in the United States. See *Rome.*

Commune, Paris. An outbreak of the extreme revolutionary party in Paris in 1871 (March 18–May 27), after the National Assembly, which met at Bordeaux, had agreed to peace with the victorious Germans, ceding Alsace and Lorraine, and had decided to transfer its sittings to Versailles rather than to Paris. The radical Parisians accused the Assembly of being monarchist and of the design of overthrowing the republic constituted the September previous. Among the revolutionaries were leading socialists and representatives of the *Internationale*. One of the leading projects was to grant autonomy to the communes, or city governments, uniting them by a loose tie to the central government. Among their leaders were Delescluze, Félix Pyat, Paschal Grousset, Raoul Rigault, and General Cluseret. Thiers, who had been chosen head of the executive in the new government, reorganized the army and prepared to capture Paris. The Germans still occupied the forts on the northern side of the city, for the Peace of Frankfort was not signed until May 18. In the struggle that followed, neither side gave quarter. The *Communards* even put to death the hostages they had seized, including the archbishop of Paris. In the final week, when Paris was attacked street by street, they burned many great public buildings, including the palace of the Tuileries and the Hôtel de Ville. Thousands of those who were captured by the national troops were shot without a trial. Others were tried and executed, and still others were exiled. For years the socialist party remained without leaders.

Concert of Europe. A diplomatic term long applied to the idea of European powers acting as a unit. Such a concert of princes was set up after the Congress of Vienna in 1815. This broke down before the rise of national ambitions. The ideal expressed in the phrase is a vague foreshadowing of a league of nations. See *Congress of Vienna*; *France*; also *Concert of Powers*, under department of Government.

Concordat (*kŏn-kôr'dăt*), **French.** An agreement entered into in 1801, but abrogated in 1905, between Napoleon and the pope, providing for the re-establishment of the French Catholic Church, which had been disrupted during the Revolution. Roman Catholicism was declared to be the religion of the majority of the French nation. It was agreed, among other provisions, that bishops were to be nominated by the government, but consecrated by the pope. The nomination of parish priests was vested in the bishops, the government having a right of veto. The state undertook to see that adequate stipends were provided for the clergy, to replace the ancient revenues which had been confiscated during the Revolution. See *France.*

Concordat of Worms. The agreement reached in 1122 between the German emperor, Henry V, and the pope upon the old dispute over the appointment and investiture of bishops. It provided that bishops should be elected by the clergy and consecrated by the pope, but that the emperor might veto any election, since he was to invest the bishop with the episcopal lands. See *Germany.*

Condottieri (*kôn'dôt-tyâr'ē*). Soldiers of fortune who hired themselves out to the various petty states of Italy during the wars of the 14th and the 15th century. Their contests came to be bloodless, because each side wanted only to take prisoners for the sake of ransom money to be exacted.

Confederation of the Rhine. A league of German states, at first chiefly southern but finally including all, save Prussia and Austria, with Napoleon as "protector," formed in 1806. These states were permitted to absorb many of their smaller neighbors by a process known as "mediatization." They withdrew from the Holy Roman Empire, which then came to an end. Together with the "secularizations" in 1803, which destroyed the independence of 112 ecclesiastical, city, and other small states, the annexations of 1806 marked the beginning of unification in Germany. The Confederation was broken up in 1813 by the defeat of Napoleon at Leipzig. See *France, Germany.*

Congress of Berlin. A congress held at Berlin in 1878, after the conclusion of the Russo-Turkish war. The outcome of the congress was a treaty which modified the terms of the Treaty of San Stefano. Rumania, Serbia, and Montenegro were made independent states, Montenegro also obtaining a port on the Adriatic. The northern portion of Bulgaria was made a self-governing state, under the suzerainty of the Porte, and the southern portion, known as Eastern Rumelia, remained Turkish territory, but under a Christian governor. Austria was to administer Bosnia and Herzegovina; Rumania returned a portion of Bessarabia to Russia, while, in Asia, Turkey ceded Ardalian, Kars, and Batum to Russia. The action of the congress prevented the formation of a strong Slav state in the Balkans and kept Russia out of the Mediterranean. It is of this treaty that Lord Beaconsfield used the famous phrase "We have brought back peace with honor." In 1909 Great Britain, Germany, France, and Russia consented to Austria's annexation of Bosnia and Herzegovina. See *World War.*

Congress of Vienna, The. The congress of all the sovereigns of Europe, called after the fall of Napoleon by the four powers allied against him. It met in Vienna in November 1814, and completed its work in June 1815, after the final defeat of Napoleon at Waterloo. The general purpose of the congress was to restore all "legitimate" princes and kings, as nearly as possible, to the power they enjoyed before the French Revolution. The interests and desires of nations and peoples had no place in the plans of this great reactionary congress. All republics, old and new, except Switzerland, were given to monarchs. The 12 states of Italy and the 38 of Germany were restored to their old ruling families. Holland, with Belgium unwillingly added, was made the Kingdom of the Netherlands. Territory west of the Rhine, taken from France, was divided between Bavaria and Prussia. To Austria went Venice in exchange for Belgium. Russia took the kingdom of Poland and also secured Finland from Sweden, which as compensation received Norway (formerly Danish). Prussia, with half of Saxony and land west of the Rhine as her share of the spoils, was set on the road to German leadership. England obtained some colonial territory, including Cape Colony and Ceylon.

But the congress did some constructive work. At the suggestion of England, it declared against the slave trade. It also declared that navigable rivers flowing through or between different countries should be open to all commerce, and it guaranteed the neutrality of Switzerland.

Conservatives, English. One of the two great political parties of Great Britain. This party has usually been regarded as opposed to radical change or innovation of any character in government, and particularly to the liberal, socializing movements which seek to increase the political power of the masses, to ameliorate their conditions, and to mitigate the effects of the uneven distribution of wealth. The party has in the past drawn most of its strength from the so-called "landed aristocracy," and other landed interests of England. It is the direct successor to the Tory party of the 18th and early 19th centuries, the name Conservative having been substituted for the older name Tory soon after the Reform act of 1832. Although the Conservative has traditionally been regarded as the party of reaction, yet under the leadership of Disraeli in 1867, and of Salisbury in 1884, this party was responsible for the extension of the franchise to the great mass of the English people. In recent years, the Conservative party has been regarded as the party of Imperialism, standing for the extension and strengthening of the British Empire.

Constitutions of Clarendon. A body of 16 regulations drawn up at the Great Council summoned by Henry II of England to meet at Clarendon in 1164. These regulations were intended to settle points in dispute between king and clergy. They specified, among other things, that clergy accused of civil crime should be turned over to the civil courts for punishment. Archbishop Thomas Becket refused to sign the document. After Becket's murder, Henry, in 1172, seeking reconciliation with the pope, renounced the Constitutions. But some of their provisions remained in force as permanent gains to the civil power in England. See *England*.

Corn Laws. English laws regulating grain imports. In 1815, in the midst of agricultural and industrial depression following the end of the Napoleonic wars, a Parliament made up of landowners passed a law forbidding the importation of corn (wheat) unless the price should rise to 80 shillings a quarter. The price, however, went down. This law was amended from time to time, to provide heavy import duties whenever the English harvest was good, in order to keep prices up. In 1838 an Anti-Corn-Law League was organized, which worked for the repeal of the corn laws. No action was secured until, under the stimulus of the Irish famine in 1845-46, a repeal bill introduced by the prime minister, Sir Robert Peel, was passed in 1846. This act is an important incident in the long controversy between protectionists and free traders. See *Chartist Movement, England, Ireland*.

Corvée (*kôr′vā′*). Enforced labor on the roads and other public works, exacted from the French peasants before the Revolution. Distinction should be made between the "royal" corvée, which exacted from 8 to 40 days of labor on the high roads, and the "seigniorial" corvée, or services claimed by the lords. The latter had nearly disappeared by the 18th century. The same system prevailed in Egypt prior to the English occupation.

Coup d'Etat (*kōō dā′tà′*). There is no English equivalent for this term. It means the sudden overthrow of government by force and the consequent seizure of state and power. (1) The most remarkable example of this in history is the *coup d'état* of Napoleon I. The government of France from 1795 to 1799 was known as the Directory. It had proved corrupt and incompetent. Napoleon, now the idol of France by reason of his successful campaigns, saw his opportunity. With the aid of Abbé Sieyès, a statesman who planned a change in the constitution, Napoleon overthrew the Directory on the 18th of Brumaire (November 9, 1799). The plan of Sieyès was adopted but with drastic amendments dictated by Napoleon. Napoleon was chosen first consul and given the substance of power, his two colleagues being merely consultative. In 1802 he was made consul for life and on May 18, 1804, was proclaimed emperor of the French.

(2) Half a century later a similar *coup d'état* was made by Louis Napoleon Bonaparte, nephew of Napoleon I. Louis conceived the idea that he had a right to rule over France. The revolution of 1848 gave him the opportunity of offering his services to that country. He knew the name he bore was one to conjure with. He became a candidate for the presidency and was elected with an overwhelming majority in December of the same year. He had taken an oath to uphold the Republic. On Dec. 2, 1851, he broke this oath. In the early hours of the morning he had the civil and military leaders who might prove obstacles to his plans arrested. These were afterwards imprisoned or exiled. He next proclaimed martial law throughout France and instituted a plebiscite. The French people were to register their vote on the question of the re-establishment of the imperial dignity. The people proved willing to make the experiment, and on Dec. 2, 1852, Louis Napoleon Bonaparte, having skillfully maneuvered his *coup d'état*, was proclaimed emperor of France under the name of Napoleon III.

Curfew. From *couvre feu*, meaning "cover fire." The famous enactment of William the Conqueror, ordering all persons in the country districts to be in their houses, with all lights extinguished, by eight o'clock in winter and by sunset in summer. It was presumably designed to prevent secret meetings and conspiracies directed against the king among the Saxon element of the population.

D-Day. The opening day of a military operation, from which other days are reckoned,—D-day+1, D-day+2, etc. Notably, the day of the Allied invasion of Normandy, June 6, 1944.

Declaration of London. A set of rules formulated by an international conference at London in 1909, designed to govern the naval prize court established at The Hague in 1907. The Declaration was never accepted by a sufficient number of nations to put it in force. At the outbreak of World War I, Great Britain announced that the Declaration would be adhered to by the Allies. But under the stress of actual war conditions the provisions of the Declaration were disregarded.

Declaration of Paris. A formal statement of rules governing naval warfare, drawn up by the powers that signed the Treaty of Paris in 1856 after the close of the Crimean war. These rules abolished privateering; established the protection of enemy goods, except contraband, by a neutral flag, the protection of neutral goods, except contraband, by an enemy flag; and declared that blockades, to be binding, must actually be effectively maintained by naval force. The United States, not having a strong navy, maintained that in war she would be dependent upon privateers, and therefore did not adopt the Declaration.

Disarmament. The abandonment of huge naval and military establishments or the radical reduction of them by international agreement was discussed at the Congress of Vienna in 1815. But the state of European affairs in the later 19th century, especially after 1859, brought about compulsory military service and increase of armaments. The Hague Conference of 1899 failed to make any progress in the matter, chiefly because of the opposition of Germany. The Hague Conference of 1907 recommended "serious examination of this question." After the close of the World War, the enormous economic burden of war debts and of increasing expenditures for naval and military establishments forced the great nations to consider means of reducing armaments. See *Washington Conference.*

Divine Right. The patriarchal theory or doctrine that neither kings nor their heirs for any reason whatsoever can forfeit their right to the throne and to the obedience of their people. Under this theory, the king is the direct representative of God and can do no wrong. This doctrine was promulgated and reached its climax in England in the Stuart times, but it was set aside at the accession of William III as king of Great Britain and Ireland in 1688.

Domesday Book. A book containing a written synopsis in Latin of the census of the population, lands, and live stock of England, compiled under the direction of William the Conqueror and completed in 1086. The work forms the most valuable existing source of facts about early English history.

Draco, Laws of. In the latter part of the 7th century B. C., the people of Athens, suffering under the unjust administration of justice by the ruling class of nobles, demanded a written code. An Athenian named Draco was employed to draw up such a body of laws. The severity of these laws, under which the penalty for most offenses was death, gave rise to the saying that the Draconian code was written, "not in ink, but in blood."

Drang nach Osten. A German phrase meaning "push toward the East." It was originally applied to the eastward extension of German power over Slavic and Baltic territory. Its most important meaning, however, is that steady extension of German and Austrian influence in the Balkans and in Asia Minor which brought on the World War.

Dreyfus (*drā′fŭs′*) **Affair.** The imprisonment and persecution of Alfred Dreyfus, member of a wealthy Jewish family and an officer on the general staff of the French army. He was charged in 1894 with revealing military secrets to a foreign government, condemned, and sent to Devil's island for life. New evidence was discovered in 1896, pointing to another officer, Esterhazy, as the real traitor. A new court-martial in 1899 again condemned Dreyfus, but this time to only ten years' imprisonment. President Loubet gave him a full pardon. The Court of Cassation reviewed the case in 1906, declared the court-martial verdict in error, and Dreyfus was restored to the army and promoted. The affair was inspired by anti-Semitism.

Druids (*drōō′ĭdz*). The powerful order of priests and judges who ruled the Celtic peoples of Gaul, Britain, and Ireland. The institution of druidism was probably common to all the Celts, but the best description of it is that given by Cæsar, who observed it in Gaul. The druids gathered youths about them for oral instruction, as they never committed their secret lore to writing. The oak and the mistletoe were sacred among the druids, and their ceremonies were frequently performed in oak groves. They used their influence against the Romans, but they were finally driven to the island of Anglesey and subdued in 78 A. D.

Dual Monarchy. The name used to describe the organization of the empire of Austria-Hungary from 1867 to 1918. The two states stood on a plane of complete equality, the emperor of Austria being king of Hungary. Although each had its own Parliament, there was a joint ministry of three departments—foreign affairs, war, and finance.

Dukhobors (*dōō-kō-bôrz′*). A Russian religious sect, founded about the middle of the 18th century at Kharkov. Their principal tenet is that Christ was only human, not divine, and that at certain periods He reappears in mortals. They reject the need of rulers, priests, or churches, and have no confession, images (*icons*), or marriage ceremonies. They are opposed to all violence and refuse to make use of the labor of animals. Driven out of Russia, many of the Dukhobors emigrated to western Canada. Conflict with authorities, chiefly over educational regulations, led part of this group in 1926 to sell 50,000 acres they had acquired, in order to migrate to Paraguay.

Eastern Question. A name given to the political problems raised by the gradual dissolution of the Turkish Empire in Europe from about 1822 to 1922. Russia aimed to secure Constantinople (Istanbul). She fought two wars for it. In the first (Crimean, 1853-56), she was defeated by France and England. After the second (Russo-Turkish, 1877-78), while victorious, she was balked by the other powers. German ascendancy in Turkey began in 1889 and ended when the two nations suffered defeat in the World War. The prize of Istanbul went to none of the great powers. It remained Turkish, but was placed under control of an international commission. This commission's control ceased by agreement in 1936.

East India Company, British. "The Governor and Company of merchants trading to the East Indies," chartered in 1600, became in time incorporated with several other important companies and in 1660 was known as "The United Company of Merchants Trading to the East Indies." It is usually referred to as the British East India Company.

In 1612 it obtained from the rajah of Delhi the privilege of establishing a factory at Surat, which was regarded as the chief British station in India until a later organization at Bombay. By a charter of Charles II in 1661, it was empowered to sign treaties, make peace or war with infidels, erect fortifications, acquire territory, and exercise civil jurisdiction. In 1668 it secured a grant of the Island of Bombay, and in 1675 established a factory in Bengal which paved the way to the foundation of Calcutta. A dispute with the rajah of Tanjore in 1749 resulted in a series of territorial acquisitions which became the nucleus of the British Empire in India. A board of control was eventually set up by Parliament in 1784, and in 1858 the company gave over the reins of government to the British crown. See *England, India.*

East India Company, Dutch. A company formed by the union of several small trading companies, March 20, 1602. The government granted it a charter, by which it was given the monopoly of trade on the farther side of the Strait of Magellan and of the Cape of Good Hope. It was also given the right to establish factories, build fortresses, employ soldiers, and make alliances in the name of the States-General. In 1619 it established the colony of Batavia in Java; within less than half a century it became the principal trading power in Ceylon, Sumatra, and Borneo, and possessed flourishing colonies in South Africa. In 1795 the company became insolvent, and its territories were handed over to the state.

Elamites (*ē′lăm-īts*). The ancient people who inhabited the plateau and plain east of the lower Tigris and north of the Persian gulf. The name is derived from the Assyrian word for "highlands." The race to which they belonged is not known. They maintained a long struggle against the Babylonians and Assyrians. The latter finally subdued the Elamite state in 642 B. C. Later references to Elam are uncertain, the word sometimes meaning Persia.

Electors. In the Holy Roman Empire, a body of German princes, originally seven in number, with whom, from the 13th to the beginning of the 19th century, rested the election of the emperor.

Emancipation Act. For many years the English courts of law strongly held that slavery should not be allowed to exist in any part of the British dominions and that in tolerating it the prestige of England suffered. Two of the greatest pleaders in the cause of the slave were Sir Thomas Buxton and Zachary Macaulay, father of the historian. In 1833, Colonial Secretary Stanley came into office. A man of great ability and ardent temperament, he set to work to master the details of this crying injustice. In the space of three weeks he introduced into Parliament a bill for the complete abolition of slavery, which was immediately passed. All children under six and those born after the passing of the act thenceforward were free. All others ceased to be slaves, but were to remain as apprentices to their masters for a period of twelve years. The slave owners were indemnified for their loss in the sum of $100,000,000. Though they showed dissatisfaction with this amount, they were forced to accept it. The system of apprenticeship proved, after four years, to be unsatisfactory and so was abandoned. See *Slavery*, page 578.

Emigrés (*ā'mē'grā'*). The name given to the French aristocracy, or, more accurately, to the partisans of the *ancien régime*, or royalists, who were forced to fly from France during the French Revolution. The émigrés, in order to crush the Revolution, appealed to other European powers to send armies into France. For this, the Legislative Assembly and the Convention passed measures of reprisal against the émigrés, whereby their lands and estates became forfeit to the Republic. The term has been applied also to those who fled the Russian and other revolutions in the 20th century, particularly if they belonged to the aristocracy.

Entente Powers or **Triple Entente** (*äN'täNt'*). England, France, and Russia, who, before the opening of the World War, had concluded an *entente* or "understanding" among themselves with respect to a common defensive attitude toward the Triple Alliance,—Germany, Italy, and Austria. This Triple Entente was not an alliance. It was composed of two "ententes." The first was negotiated in 1904 between England and France, in order to bring to an end controversies chiefly in relation to Egypt and Morocco. The second was between England and Russia, in 1907, and centered in Asiatic questions, marking out for the two powers spheres of interest in Persia. France was already bound to Russia by a military alliance. For this reason, when Germany declared war against Russia in 1914, France was necessarily involved. The obligations of England, on the other hand, were principally moral. See *Triple Alliance, World War*.

Fabian Society of Socialists. One of the most important socialistic societies in England, organized in London in 1884. It derives its name from Fabius, the Roman general, who hoped to conquer "by delaying," and supports meliorative tendencies rather than revolution.

Fascism (*făsh'ĭz'm*). A political party and governmental régime of contemporary Italy. Founded by Benito Mussolini at Milan in 1919, the movement was inspired by an exalted patriotism. Its members banded themselves together to crush communistic outbreaks and other disruptive factors in Italian life. Its expanding influence enabled Mussolini, at the head of his armed followers, to take control of the Italian parliament on October 28, 1922. The party's control of the government was maintained by drastic action. The term has been generalized to describe movements seeking to safeguard the capitalistic system by establishment of a corporate state. In purpose it contrasts with communism; in method, with democracy.

Fashoda (*fä-shō'dä*) **Question.** Commercial and colonial jealousies between France and England in 1898 led to a French general's hoisting of the French ensign over Fashoda, which Great Britain regarded as within her particular zone of influence. English armies had for two years been engaged in a campaign against the Khalifa for the recovery of the Sudan. Their commander, General Kitchener, invited Marchand to withdraw. Marchand refusing, the matter was referred to London and Paris. France acquiesced in the wishes of England. On April 8, 1904, an agreement was signed between the two countries, each acknowledging the other's rights in Morocco and in Egypt. This friendly understanding came to be known as the *Entente Cordiale*. See *Entente Powers*.

Fenians. The members of an Irish revolutionary society, started in Paris in 1848. Their avowed object was the fomenting of disturbances in Ireland, to make the government of that country by England impossible. The leader was James Stephens. The Fenians in the United States attempted raids into Canada in 1866, 1870, and 1871. In 1867 a general rising in Ireland was planned. These projects were all anticipated or promptly suppressed.

Feudalism. The system of land tenure and personal relationships prevailing throughout Europe especially from the 9th to the 13th century. Its activating cause was the need of protection, which could no longer be secured by governmental authority. The base of the structure was the fief, a body of land which a tenant held from his lord who protected him in return for certain feudal services, such as aid in war. The tenant was thus also a vassal. The lord exercised judicial and many other rights over his tenants, who often became virtually his subjects. The tenant might also, if holding a large tract of land, grant parts of it to others, who would be his tenants and vassals and to whom he stood in the relation of lord.

Field of the Cloth of Gold. The meeting place of Henry VIII and Francis I in the valley of Ardres on the border of the territory of Calais. This meeting in 1520 was arranged by Francis to detach Henry from his Spanish alliance. The name arose from the magnificance of the display on both sides. No political result followed.

Fifth Column. A term used to describe persons ready to cooperate with an aggressor against the country of which they are citizens or residents. It obtained currency from a remark of General Franco, Spanish insurgent leader, as he was advancing in 1939 on Madrid with four converging columns in the final action of the Spanish civil war. He declared that he was attacking with four columns outside the city and with a "fifth column" within the city.

Flagellants (*flăj'ĕ-lănts*). A sect which appeared in Europe during the middle ages, notably in Italy in 1360, and in Hungary and other countries during the terror occasioned by the Black Death in 1348. They looked upon scourging as the only means of avoiding divine punishment for sin. See *Black Death*.

Flodden Field. Name of a battle fought near the hamlet of Flodden in Northumberland, Sept. 9, 1513, between the Scots and the English, in which the Scottish king, James IV, was defeated and slain by the earl of Surrey.

Franco-Prussian War. The conflict between France and Prussia in 1870-71. The immediate occasion of the war was the election of a Hohenzollern prince to the throne of Spain. The chief military events were the siege of Metz and the siege of Strasbourg, in August and September 1870; the fall of Sedan on September 1, 1870; and the siege of Paris, September 19, 1870 to January 28, 1871. After the fall of Sedan, a republic was proclaimed at Paris, and a provisional government undertook the defense of the city. The close of the war saw the founding of the new German Empire. See *Alsace-Lorraine, France, Germany*.

Francs-Tireurs (*frän'tē'rûr'*). As the name implies, an independent band of "free-shooters," composed of French peasants who at first fought alone a guerrilla warfare against the Germans in the Franco-Prussian war of 1870. When captured, they were usually shot by the enemy as brigands. Later in the campaign they were organized by the French military authorities and used as a corps of detached light troops engaged in forays, skirmishes, and such minor actions. Thenceforward they were recognized by the Germans as lawful belligerents. See *Franco-Prussian War*.

Freedom of the Seas. This phrase means, in general, the right of the ships of any nation to free use of the highways of the sea. In particular it has come to mean: (1) that the jurisdiction of a government extends to a distance of three nautical miles beyond its coast line and no farther; (2) that neutral ships are not liable to capture on the high seas by belligerents in time of war; (3) that, in time of war, private property, unless contraband or destined for a blockaded port, is not liable to seizure. See *World War*.

Free Imperial Cities. Certain towns in Germany that owed allegiance to no sovereign prince except the emperor. They exercised sovereign powers within their own limits and sent representatives to the Imperial Diet. In 1790 they were 51 in number. Until the dismemberment of the German Empire at the close of the World War, Lübeck, Bremen, and Hamburg still retained the privilege of sending representatives to the Reichstag and the Bundesrath. Each is now a "free state and city" within the German Republic. See *Germany*.

Fronde (*frônd*). The name given to the civil war which broke out in France, 1648–53, between the party of the court (Anne of Austria and Mazarin) and the parlement of Paris. The Fronde originated in the deplorable financial policy of Mazarin and passed through two phases. The first was known as the Old Fronde, in which the parlement, allied to Condé and Cardinal de Retz, played the principal rôle. The most notable incidents under its short régime were the arrest of Counselor Broussel, the setting up of barricades by the people of Paris, and the withdrawal of the court to Saint Germain. During the second phase, with the title of the Young Fronde or Fronde des Princes, Condé, Beaufort, and Madame de Longueville, with the secret support of Spain, gave battle to the royal troops under Turenne at Bléneau and Porte St. Antoine. Turenne proved superior on both occasions, and the revolt was crushed in 1653. The Old Fronde lasted from 1648 to 1649; the Young Fronde, from 1649 to 1653. The word *fronde* means a "sling," used sometimes by the small boys of Paris against the police. The adversaries of Mazarin had been called *frondeurs*, or "slingers," by a French humorist; hence the application.

Geneva Convention. An agreement made by the representatives of the great European powers at Geneva in 1864, by which were established more humane regulations regarding the sick and the wounded in war and also the status of those who attend them. Ambulances and military hospitals are regarded as neutral, as are physicians, chaplains, nurses, and the ambulance corps. In 1868, a second conference at Geneva supplemented the former one and partly applied its principles to naval warfare. The agreement received the sanction of all the European powers at the time, also that of the United States and of many other countries.

Germany, Unification of. The North German Confederation, which embraced the 22 states north of the river Main, was the work of Bismarck. The inclusion of the south German states was yet necessary to the perfect unification of Germany. Since Napoleon III was known to be averse to this plan, Bismarck deemed a war with France a necessary contingency. In this instance, it would seem "the wish was father to the thought," for on July 5, 1870, the rest of Europe woke to the fact that France and Prussia were at war. Germany emerged as victor from the series of campaigns. While the war was being waged, negotiations had been carried on between Prussia and the south German states. Accordingly, treaties were signed and the confederation widened so as to include all the German states. Thus was brought about the complete unification of Germany, and Bismarck's lifelong dream was realized. Berlin became the capital of a federal empire, and on Jan. 18, 1871, in the royal palace of Versailles, William I was proclaimed emperor of Germany.

Golconda. A ruined city in the Nizam's dominions, seven miles northwest of Hyderabad. It is celebrated for its fortress and for the mausoleums of its ancient kings. The diamonds cut and polished in Golconda were once world renowned. From 1512 it was the seat of a powerful government until it was taken by Aurungzebe in 1687 and made a Mogul province. See *Moguls*.

Golden Bull (Germany). So called from the golden seal with which it was stamped. The Golden Bull was an imperial edict issued in 1356 by the emperor Charles IV, which fixed the form and places of the imperial election and coronation. It also determined the privileges and duties of the electors. This electoral constitution continued unaltered until the extinction of the Holy Roman Empire in 1806.

Good Parliament. A Parliament of Edward III which met in 1376. The Commons refused to grant supply till an account of receipts and expenditures had been placed before them. Edward's brother Lancaster sought to intimidate the Parliament but failed. The Commons secured a new Council, from which Lancaster was debarred and in which William of Wykeham was included. They then proceeded to impeach, before the House of Lords, Lyons and Latimer on the charge of embezzlement of the king's revenue. Both were sentenced to imprisonment on the charge. These two cases form the first instance of the accusation of political offenders by the Commons before the House of Lords. See *England*.

Guelphs (*gwĕlfs*) and **Ghibellines** (*gĭb'ĕl-ĭnz*). The names of two celebrated political factions in the middle ages. The Guelphs were the popular party in Italy, and ranged on the side of the pope. The Ghibellines formed the imperial and aristocratic party, and were opposed to the Guelphs. In 1140 the two factions engaged in civil war. The imperialists besieged the town of Weinsberg, and the papal party under Welf VI endeavored to beat them back. In the course of the battle the family names of "Welf" and "Waiblingen" became the respective rallying cries of the contestants. The Guelphs were defeated in the battle of Weinsberg, and, though the quarrel between the two parties ceased in Germany, it was continued for other reasons in Italy, and the two names were used until the beginning of the 16th century to designate the two antagonistic factions. The usual writing of the names is the Italianized form. See *Italy*.

Gunpowder Plot. This was a plot engineered by a Catholic named Robert Catesby, in 1604, to blow up king, lords, and commons at the opening of Parliament. Both the Catholics and the Puritans of the time had appealed to James I for better treatment. They were being fined for recusancy, that is, for refusing to attend the services of the established form of worship. James remitted the fines for recusancy, but banished the Catholic priests from London. Thereupon, Catesby determined upon destroying the powers that dealt so harshly with his coreligionists. He communicated his plans to Guy Fawkes, a cool and intrepid soldier in Flanders. Fawkes favored them and came to England. By accident, the conspirators found that a cellar ran beneath both houses of Parliament. Into this they managed to convey barrels of gunpowder, and the mine was laid for the second session of Parliament on Nov. 5, 1605. However, the plot was doomed to failure. One of the conspirators in fear betrayed the secret, and Fawkes was seized in the very act of setting the fuse to the powder. He, with those of his companions who were captured, was forthwith executed, and the persecution of the Catholics waxed stronger than before. See *England.*

Habeas Corpus Act. The Latin term is an injunction, meaning "Have thou the body" (in court). The act was passed by the Parliament of England during the reign of Charles II, 1679. The "habeas corpus" is a common law writ, or mandate, issued by a judge on the petition of some friend of an accused person detained in prison or in any other way deprived of liberty. It calls upon the jailer to bring such a person actually into court at a specified time, in order that his case may be examined and judgment passed. Moreover, any accused person held in prison too long without a hearing can claim a writ of habeas corpus to be issued in his behalf, in order to force his accusers to show cause why he should be detained longer in custody. The habeas corpus acts of the United States and of Canada follow lines similar to those of the English statute.

Hague Peace Conferences. Meetings of representatives of leading nations of the world, to consider means for arresting the danger of war and for mitigating the burdens of armaments. Two conferences have been held at The Hague in Holland. The first was convened, at the suggestion of Czar Nicholas of Russia, in 1899. It formulated regulations for more humane conduct of warfare and established an international tribunal to which nations might submit their disputes for arbitration. The second Hague Conference met in 1907, at the suggestion of the United States. This Conference enlarged somewhat the work of the first Conference. But neither body was able to adopt any resolution either for disarmament or for limiting of armaments.

Hanseatic League. A federation of northern German cities, formed in the 13th century for mutual protection and assistance, particularly in trade. The immediate cause of this famous and powerful organization was the insecurity of trade routes. The princes and states of the time were unable to afford protection against the pirates and robbers on sea and land. The alliance of the towns of Hamburg and Lübeck, about the middle of the 13th century, is regarded as the beginning of the confederacy, to which the name *Hansa,* meaning "league," was later applied. The organization at the height of its prosperity, in the 14th and 15th centuries, included about ninety cities and towns. It passed out of existence about the middle of the 17th century. See *Venice and the Hanse,* page 1200b.

Hearth Money. A tax laid in England on hearths. It was first levied in 1663. Each hearth in every house that paid church and poor rates was taxed at the rate of two shillings. This tax, known also as chimney money, was repealed in the reign of William and Mary, 1689.

Hegira or **Hejira** (*hĕj'ĭ-rȧ*). An Arabic word meaning "departure." It is used to designate the flight of Mohammed from Mecca to Medina in 622. Mohammed sought to persuade his countrymen to forsake idolatry. They rose in anger against him, and he was forced to flee for his life to Medina. The Mohammedan calendar is dated from this flight, as that of the Christians is dated from the birth of Christ. See *Arabia, Arabians.*

Heptarchy. A government of seven rulers; a union of seven territories. In Saxon times in England seven small kingdoms or principalities were established, known as Northumbria, East Anglia, Mercia, Kent, Sussex, Essex, and Wessex. The number of these tribal divisions was not constant. Feuds and struggles between rival princes at times merged one principality into another. Egbert, who was king of the West Saxons, 802–839, is said to have made himself Bretwalda or overlord of the British. It was this, no doubt, that gave the 16th century historians the idea that the seven Angle and Saxon kingdoms were really a monarchy ruled by one supreme king; hence they introduced the word *heptarchy* into their writings to convey this conception. Though the designation is questionable, it seems to have been preserved as a matter of convenience. See *England.*

Hindenburg Line. A system of elaborate entrenchments on the western front in the World War. It was established by Hindenburg, commander in chief of the German field forces, after the fighting on the Somme in 1916. These entrenchments took approximately the shape of a crescent whose arc swept from the North Sea, between Nieuport and Westende, until it reached the banks of the Aisne river on the south. At the northern horn of the crescent stood what was known as the "*Wotan*" *line,* the middle of the crescent was occupied by the "*Siegfried*" *line,* and at the southern horn was placed the "*Albrecht*" *line.*

The Allied front opposed to the Hindenburg line was divided into three sections: a British front from the North Sea to the Oise river, a distance of 125 miles; a French front from the Oise to Verdun, about 150 miles; and an American front from Verdun to the Swiss frontier—the latter known as the Lorraine front. The supposedly impregnable German defense was first penetrated by Australian troops, May 3, 1917. On September 29, 1918, the Siegfried line was broken at the famous tunnel sector, near Cambrai, by American troops acting with British and Australian forces. See *World War.*

Hinterland Doctrine. After the explorations of Livingstone and Stanley, Africa no longer remained an "unknown land." Upon various pretexts, European powers appropriated large areas to themselves. Germany, to make secure and to enlarge her new acquisitions, enunciated in 1883 a doctrine by which the possession of a stretch of coast line carried with it the right to the territory lying inland. This doctrine maintained that no other country could annex such territory.

Hittites. A people primarily of Indo-European stock. Their original home was in central Asia Minor, whence they gradually pushed southward, invading Babylonia about 2000 B. C. and conquering northern Mesopotamia, Syria, and Palestine. In the 14th century B. C., they were driven from Palestine by the Egyptians, with whom, after an indecisive battle at Kadesh in Syria, they concluded a treaty, the oldest written treaty in history. Hittite dominion over Syria lasted until the 8th century B. C., when this country too was conquered by Assyria. A century later they had disappeared from history. Little was known about the Hittites until quite recently. Excavations, begun by Winckler, a German scholar, in 1905, at Boghaz-Köi on the Halys river, the site of the ancient Hittite capital, yielded about 10,000 baked clay tablets, with writing practically identical with Babylonian cuneiform, but in an unknown language. The key to this was discovered by Hrozný, a Czechoslovakian Assyriologist, in 1915.

Hohenstaufen Dynasty. The line of emperors who ruled Germany from 1138 to 1254. They were distinguished for patronage of commerce and the arts. The greatest of the family were Frederick Barbarossa (1152–90) and Frederick II (1215–50).

Hohenzollern Family. A family of German princes tracing descent from Thassilo, count of Zollern, who, in the 8th century, founded a castle on the Zollern hill in the Swabian Alps. In 1415 Frederick VI of the younger line of Hohenzollern was made elector of Brandenburg. He thus became the founder of the former royal house of Prussia. See *Germany, World War*.

Holy Alliance. An alliance formed between Russia, Austria, and Prussia in September 1815, by which the three sovereigns undertook that for the future their policy, both domestic and foreign, should be guided solely by the precepts of the Christian religion. In reality, it was regarded by those powers who were asked for their approval as a huge farce and one of dubious taste. But the name was too good to be ignored; and Russia, Austria, and Prussia came to be known as the "holy allies." The alliance aimed at stemming the tide of political liberty, set flowing by the French Revolution. The threatened interference of this alliance in the quarrel between Spain and her American colonies provoked the enunciation of the Monroe Doctrine in 1823. See *Monroe Doctrine*.

Holy Sepulcher, Knights of the. The Turks had secured dominion over the Holy Land. Pilgrims to the holy places had been tortured and put to death by these fierce Mohammedan warriors. Under Pope Urban II, a military order, Knights of the Holy Sepulcher, was instituted by Godfrey de Bouillon in 1099 to watch the sepulcher of Christ and protect the pilgrims. The knights fought their way through Asia Minor and took the Holy City by storm. Godfrey was made its king but refused to be crowned. "Why wear a crown of gold," he said, "when my Savior wore one of thorns?"

Hudson's Bay Company. A British joint-stock association chartered in 1670 by Charles II. It was given vast tracts of territory and exclusive trade rights throughout what is now Canada. It engaged exclusively in the skin and fur trade with the North American Indians. The company spread a chain of forts and trading posts from the Atlantic to the Pacific and exercised complete legislative and executive power within these precincts. By the Indians it was looked upon as more powerful than any nation. It played a prominent part in the disputes between the United States and Great Britain over the northwest boundary. In 1869 it sold its territorial rights to the Dominion of Canada, but it still operates as a trading company. See *Canada*.

Huguenots (*hū'gĕ-nŏts*). The name given to the French Protestants in the 16th and the 17th century. Huguenot is said to be derived from the German word *Eidgenoss*, a "confederate by oath," or perhaps from the name of Hugues, one of their leaders. Under Francis I and his successors, the Huguenots were welded together in a kind of politico-religious unity. Under Condé and Admiral Coligny they fought several wars against the Catholics. When, by the revocation of the Edict of Nantes, they were deprived of religious liberty, they left France in vast numbers. Thousands of them emigrated to England, Holland, and other Protestant countries. Many settled in America, especially in South Carolina.

Hundred Years' War. The name given to the series of wars between England and France from 1337 to 1453, due in part to the claim of the English kings to the French throne. The English won three great battles,—Crécy, 1346, Poitiers, 1356, and Agincourt, 1415,—but finally lost all their French possessions except Calais, which they retained till 1558.

Hussites. The followers of John Huss, a native of Bohemia and rector of the University of Prague, 1402-03. The writings of Wiclif had attracted him, and he spread the Wiclifite doctrine among the people. He attacked the abuses of the clergy and expressed opposition to the pope's supremacy. Alexander V excommunicated him, but this sentence failed to quench his ardor. He was finally cited before the Council of Constance, which condemned him as a heretic in 1415. The emperor Sigismund, who had granted Huss safe-conduct, violated his word and allowed him to be burned at the stake. The flames that burned Huss set all Bohemia on fire. The Hussites looked upon him as a national hero and made his martyrdom the signal for rebellion against the Holy Roman Empire. Under the leadership of John Ziska, they began a long series of wars against Sigismund and his successors, which came to an end only in the year 1471. A part of the Hussites returned at length to the Catholic faith. From those who remained Protestants the groups of Bohemian Brethren and Moravian Brethren later developed.

Hustings. The name of a court of limited jurisdiction which at one time sat in London. Before the English Ballot act of 1872, this court was the place where members of Parliament were usually nominated, the method of nomination being by a speech made from the platform of the court. From this custom, the term "hustings" came to be applied to any stump speech or organized canvassing for votes in a political campaign.

Imperial Federation. The policy within the British Empire of closely uniting the mother country and the colonies for defense and trade, while at the same time maintaining the self-governing character of each colony. The Imperial Federation League was formed in 1884, and in 1897 the practice of holding conferences of prime ministers and delegates from the colonies in London was begun. The united action of the colonies at the outbreak of war in 1914 is pointed out as a result of this policy, one recent phase of which has been economic co-operation.

Inquisition. Tribunals established in the middle ages and in still later times, for the seeking out and for the punishment of heretics, were designated by this name. The condemnation of heretics was entrusted to the Lombard bishops in 1183 by the Council of Verona, which may be said to have laid the foundation of the Inquisition. If a heretic refused to renounce his heresy, the ecclesiastical authorities handed him over to the civil authorities to be dealt with. This institution was first put into effect in Languedoc against the Albigenses. It then spread, little by little, over the Christian world. In France, however, it played a small part. Spain and Italy were the countries in which the majority of cases were brought before the papal inquisitors. Used during its earlier stages against secret Judaism and secret Mohammedanism, it served also to repress all those who dissented from Catholic doctrine.

Viewed in the eyes of the 20th century, the Inquisition was the most intolerant, biased, and unjust institution in history. In view of the intimate union of Church and State, however, which formerly existed, heresy was naturally regarded as a crime punishable by the State and with the severe penalties then customarily inflicted on criminals of every type. The number of those who were put to death by the inquisitorial courts has frequently been exaggerated. The sentences passed by the courts tended in later centuries to take the form of excommunication.

Irish Nationalists. Irish members of the House of Commons who formed an independent group for the purpose of using their strength in Parliament to further the cause of home rule for Ireland.

Italia Irredenta (*ē-täl'yä ĕr'rā-dĕn'tä*). A name meaning "unredeemed Italy." It was applied after 1870 to Trieste and the Trentino, territories mainly Italian in population but under Austrian rule. The peace treaty of 1919 gave these territories to Italy.

Italy, Unification of. Italy was being torn to pieces by conflicting political parties, each of which sought to bring about her unification in its own especial way. In 1849 Victor Emmanuel succeeded to the throne of Sardinia. The unification of Italy was also his dream. He chose Cavour, one of the most distinguished statesmen of Europe, to be his prime minister. Cavour set to work to bring about the realization of his master's vision. In 1854 the Crimean war broke out, and at once Cavour signed an alliance with France and England and sent troops to their aid. In 1859 Victor Emmanuel managed to bring about a war with Austria. France came to his aid and helped to defeat the Austrians at Magenta. Lombardy was then ceded to Victor Emmanuel by Austria. In 1860 Parma, Modena, and Tuscany declared for the expulsion of their respective rulers and for annexation to the kingdom of Sardinia, which accordingly was brought about. The Romagna repudiated the temporal rule of the pope and in due course was joined to Sardinia. The Two Sicilies, the Marches, and Umbria next followed. In 1861 Victor Emmanuel declared himself king of Italy. In 1866 he joined Prussia in a new war against Austria and secured Venetia. In 1870 the complete union of Italy was effected by the taking of Rome, the last of the papal territories. See *Italy*.

Jacobins (*jăk'ô-bĭnz*). The most famous of the political clubs of the French Revolution, so called because originally its members met in a Jacobin monastery. They were the most radical of all the revolutionists. The political party of which the Jacobins were members was the Mountain. From its use at this period, the name Jacobin has come to denote any extreme radical wing of politics.

Jacobites (*jăk'ô-bīts*). A name given to the adherents of James II after his forced abdication, and in general to the supporters of the claim of the Stuarts after the revolution of 1688. See *England*.

Jameson Raid. Various causes led up to this notorious raid. The uitlanders, or foreigners, at work in the gold mines of the South African Republic, sought equal rights of citizenship with the Boers. The Boers, in turn, suspected British control, north and west of the Transvaal, and likewise rejected the British claim of suzerainty. Rhodes, premier of Cape Colony, planned to place the Dutch states under British rule, and connived at a conspiracy of the uitlanders to raid Johannesburg. To this end he sent troops under Jameson to take that city. The Boers routed the invaders, captured Jameson, and handed him over to the British authorities, who, disclaiming the raid, sentenced Jameson to six months' imprisonment. See *Boers, Transvaal, Union of South Africa*.

Janizaries (*jăn'ĭ-zâ-rĭz*). A military force established in the 14th century by the Turkish sultan Orkhan and further developed by Amurath I. They were recruited from Christian youths captured in war, who were brought up in Mohammedan faith and trained to arms. It was their boast that they had never fled in battle. They finally became ungovernable, and, after a revolt, the corps was abolished in 1826. The name means "new troops."

Jingoes. The nickname given in England to the supporters and enthusiasts of Lord Beaconsfield, who sent a fleet to Turkish waters to oppose Russia's advance on Constantinople in 1878. Originally a jocular oath, "By Jingo" came into popular vogue when used by "The Great Macdermott" in a famous music hall song.

Junius, Letters of. This remarkable series of political letters, to the number of 69, were written under the mysterious pen name of "Junius," and appeared at intervals between Jan. 21, 1769, and Jan. 21, 1772, in the pages of the *Public Advertiser*, the most popular newspaper in Great Britain at the time. Masterly in style, they attacked all the leading characters of the government, not excepting royalty itself. The authorship of the "Letters of Junius" has been attributed to no fewer than 50 different persons, but it is now generally accepted that they were written by Sir Philip Francis.

Junkers (*yŏŏng'kĕrz*). The name applied to the arrogant, reactionary class of Prussian landowning nobility. From their feudal spirit and ideals the Prussian army officer took his peculiar haughty air of superiority.

Jutland, The Battle of. The decisive naval engagement of the World War, fought in the North Sea on the night of May 31–June 1, 1916. The English losses were 6014 killed and drowned and 674 wounded. The German losses were reported to be 3076, of which number 2000 were drowned. But the German navy undertook no further action during the war chiefly because of the destruction of morale resulting from this battle. See page 528.

Kenya. A British crown colony of central east Africa. Prior to 1920, the territory was a protectorate under the name of British East Africa. Although traversed by the equator, the country has, in part, an altitude sufficiently great to make its climate suitable for white settlers.

The district was subject to Arab control from the 8th century. In 1887, it came within the British sphere of influence and, in 1903, was opened for European settlement. A civilized community rapidly grew up, the citizens of which, in 1916-17, took an active part in the conquest of German East Africa. In 1920, the protectorate became a colony. The administration, being in the hands of European settlers, discriminated against settlers from India, who numbered about 40,000 in comparison with some 10,000 of the white race. The resulting dispute led to the adoption of a new constitution in 1925, by which the non-European population was given representation but not control.

Ket's Rebellion. During the reign of Edward VI, the gentry had enriched themselves at the expense of both the clergy and the poor, whose claims had been contemptuously set aside. A tanner named Ket raised the standard of rebellion on Mousehold hill near Norwich, and commanded his followers to pull down the enclosures on all estates. The earl of Warwick, supported by German and Italian mercenaries, quelled the rising with great slaughter. Ket, with several other leaders, was captured and hanged.

Knights Templars. A military and religious order founded at Jerusalem in 1118 for the protection of pilgrims and for the protection of the Holy Sepulcher. It was confirmed by Honorius II in 1128. The members took their name from the site of Solomon's temple, on which their headquarters were located. They were bound by vows of chastity and poverty. After the conquest of Palestine by the Saracens, the Knights Templars spread over Europe and received donations in wealth and lands. They soon became a great political power; consequently, their enemies accused them of heresy and other crimes. Finally the order was proscribed by Clement V in 1312, and its property was confiscated. For Masonic order of Knights Templars, see *Masons, Free and Accepted*, page 2051.

Kulturkampf (*kŏŏl-tŏŏr'kämpf'*). "Battle for civilization." The name given by Virchow to the struggle between the German government and the Catholic Church which arose about 1870. Bismarck regarded the Catholic Church and its Center party as an anti-national influence, and the contest within the Church over papal infallibility embittered the feeling. The Jesuits were expelled, and the so-called Falk or May laws, 1873–75, resulted in the suppression of religious orders. Most of these laws were repealed in 1878–87, when Bismarck wished the support of the Catholics against socialism.

Labor Party, British. This party was organized in 1906. In 1923, with passive support from the Liberals, it took over the government, under J. Ramsay MacDonald as premier, but fell when Liberal support was withdrawn the next year. The weakness of the Liberals made it the leading opposition party. It returned to power again in 1929, but a financial crisis forced it to yield to a National ministry, mainly Conservative, in 1931. Its leaders entered Winston Churchill's war ministry in 1940. At the general election of 1945 it returned, with a heavy majority, under Clement Attlee, and carried out policies of a definitely socialistic character.

Laissez Faire (*lĕ'sā' fâr'*). A phrase used in economics to deprecate any sort of governmental interference in trade, commerce, or manufactures. The expression in full, *Laissez faire, laissez aller*, means that anyone should be allowed to make what he likes and as he likes, without minute government regulations. Historically, it was opposed to the restrictions on trade imposed by feudal regulations. Today it is the rallying cry of those opposed to economic planning and the governmental controls which this entails.

Land League. This Irish organization was founded in 1879 by Michael Davitt, a member of the British Parliament and a bitter opponent of English rule in Ireland. In October of the same year, Parnell was elected its president. The League became a powerful weapon aimed at the rack-renters as the landlords of that period were called. Its main objects were the reduction of the rents of small farmers and tenant-laborers. It was met by truculent and stubborn opposition on the part of the landlords. Agrarian crimes followed, and the league was suppressed in 1881. By the Wyndham act of 1903 most of the claims insisted on by the Land League were granted. See *England*, *Ireland*.

Last Battle. The battle of Culloden, 1746, between Charles Edward, the Young Pretender, and the duke of Cumberland; so called by reason of its being the last battle fought on British soil.

Legitimists. The supporters of the claims of the elder branch of the Bourbon dynasty to the throne of France. As partisans of Charles X, king of France (1824–30), and of his family, they were known as Carlists. On the death of the Comte de Chambord, last of the French Bourbons, most of the Legitimists gave their adhesion to the Orleans branch, a few only, who were called *Blancs d'Espagne*, choosing to transfer their allegiance to the Spanish claimants represented by the family of General de Bourbon. See *Spain*.

Letters of Marque. A license or commission granted by a government to a private individual, to fit out an armed vessel for the purpose of cruising at sea as a privateer and capturing the enemy's ships and merchandise. Such acts were formerly not regarded as piracy. Letters of marque were condemned and abolished by the powers that signed the Treaty of Paris in 1856, and they are no longer recognized by civilized powers. See *Declaration of Paris*.

Lettres de Cachet (*lĕt'r' dĕ kă'shĕ'*). Letters, or warrants, bearing the royal seal. Before the French Revolution, French monarchs often issued such letters, containing arbitrary orders for the imprisonment, without trial, of certain persons who might be regarded as obnoxious to the court. These warrants were used also to protect family honor or to discipline unruly sons like the Comte de Mirabeau.

Liberals, British. With the transformation of English political parties and political institutions that accompanied the important political and industrial reforms of 1832 and the period that followed, the Whigs, the more progressive English party, gradually assumed the name Liberals, and the Tories, the name Conservatives. The Liberals have traditionally been the party of peace, anti-imperialism, free trade, and social reforms. See *Whigs*, *Conservatives*.

Liberal Unionists. Faction of the Liberal party in England, which, under the leadership of Joseph Chamberlain, refused to support Gladstone's Irish Home Rule bill in 1886 and formed an independent group which finally merged into the Conservative party.

Liberum Veto (*lĭb'ĕ-rŭm vē'tō*). In the ancient diet, or state assembly, of Poland, before any measure of legislation could be passed, complete unanimity among the members was required. Any one member could veto any proposition under discussion and so prevent its passage into law. This extraordinary right was called the *liberum veto*.

Little Entente. A name applied to the series of agreements among Czechoslovakia, Yugoslavia, Rumania, and Poland, which followed the convention signed on August 13, 1920, between the first two of these powers. Edward Benes, foreign minister of Czechoslovakia, was the leading spirit of the Entente. Its purpose was mutual protection and it served powerfully to support the interests of France against those of Germany. It opposed consistently the union of Austria with Germany. Its power was broken when Germany occupied Austria and later Czechoslovakia without France coming to its assistance.

Locarno Treaties. At Locarno, Italy, on October 5, 1925, representatives of Great Britain, France, Italy, Belgium, Germany, Poland, and Czechoslovakia met for the purpose of insuring mutual security from war. As a result, the Rhine Security Pact was agreed to by Germany, Great Britain, France, Italy, and Belgium. It bound the signatories to accept the existing frontiers established by the Versailles treaty and to the demilitarization of the Rhineland, a provision subsequently repudiated by Germany. Germany and France, and Germany and Belgium undertook not to attack each other, but to submit possible disputes to conciliatory bodies.

Lollards. A nickname given to the followers of Wiclif about the year 1381. Calling themselves "poor preachers," they attacked the abuses of the wealthy religious orders and some of the most vital teachings of the Church. In the reign of Henry V, 1414, a plot against the life of the king was traced to some of the Lollards, and as a consequence many of them were hanged or sent to the stake. Those who escaped were forced to live in the larger cities, where they are reputed to have paved the way for the reformed doctrines in the reign of Henry VIII.

Long Parliament. The fifth parliament of Charles I, which assembled Nov. 5, 1640. In 1653, reduced to 60 members, the Rump, it was turned out by Cromwell. It was recalled in December 1659, and dissolved itself March 16, 1660. See *England*, page 433 b.

Mad Parliament. The Parliament held in 1258 to settle the differences between Henry III and his barons, and so called, in derision, by the adherents of the king. It drew up the Provisions of Oxford, by which an advisory council of fifteen was to meet twelve representatives of the barons thrice a year for consultation. This plan operated until the rising of the barons in 1263, under Simon de Montfort.

Madras (*mȧ-dräs'*) **Mutiny.** This mutiny, among the officers in the Madras army of the East India Company, arose from the action of the directors, who sought to deprive the officers of certain perquisites which had been looked upon as rights. Sir George Barlow made an appeal to the sepoys, who took the side of the authorities, so that the officers were forced to submit. Twenty-one of the ringleaders were punished, the rest of the mutineers being allowed to resume their duties.

Maffia (*mäf'fē-ä*). An Italian secret society which attains its ends by assassination and murder. The murder of Notarbartolo, deputy of Palermo, in 1899, forced the Italian government to institute a close investigation, which led to the temporary suppression of the maffia in Italy. Many atrocities in the United States, notably in New Orleans in 1890, have been traced to the activities of this ruthless gang. Its strength is said to have been broken through the conviction, in 1928, of 214 members of the organization in Italy.

Magdeburg, Sack of. The Thirty Years' war (1618–48) began in Germany with the rising of the Protestant nobility against the emperor Matthias, a Catholic. Henceforward, it might be said, religion was made a pretext in Europe for incessant warfare, in which neither side gave quarter to the other. An instance of this ruthless fighting was the sack of Magdeburg in 1629, when nearly the entire population of this Protestant town was put to the sword by the troops under the Austrian general Tilly.

Magna Charta (*măg'nȧ kär'tȧ*). The great charter which the English barons forced King John to grant at Runnymede, June 15, 1215. It was an amplification of a previous charter granted by Henry I a century before, and included certain rights and privileges, which in the course of time had come into existence. It was the foundation of the personal liberty of the English people. It limited the feudal obligations of the barons and others toward the crown, restricted the powers of sheriffs and other legal officers, and gave an accused person the right to be tried by his peers. See *England.*

Mahdi. The last *imam,* or spiritual leader of the faithful, expected by the Mohammedans. This title has been taken by several leaders of Moslem sects, notably by Mohammed Ahmed, who in 1885 captured Khartum and put to death General Gordon, who was then Egyptian governor of that region. See *England.*

Majuba Hill. Gladstone, in 1880, had denounced the annexation of the Transvaal by the English government under Disraeli. But, before he could alter the government's policy, the Boers rose in revolt and defeated a detachment of British troops at Majuba hill, Feb. 7, 1881. The name became a battle cry of the English, during the Boer war of 1899–1902. The disgrace of Majuba hill was wiped out, in some degree, by the surrender of the Boers at Paardeburg in 1900.

Malta. The island of Malta has been recognized since very ancient times as an important strategic base in the Mediterranean. Architectural remains bear testimony to the presence of civilized peoples in Malta in the third millennium B. C. The Phœnicians, who long occupied the island, were displaced by the Greeks in the 8th century B. C. Malta was later a stronghold of the Carthaginians and of the Romans. It was on this island that the apostle Paul, on his journey from Cæsarea to Rome, suffered shipwreck. The Arabs were in possession from about 870 to 1190. From 1530 until 1798, Malta was controlled by the Knights of Saint John, who waged war against the Turks and the Barbary pirates. The knights surrendered to Napoleon in 1798. Since 1814, Malta has been a British possession.

Mamelukes. A corps of Turko-Egyptian cavalry formed originally from slaves who had been sold by Jenghis Khan to the Egyptian sultan in the 13th century. Becoming powerful, they established their own government by appointing one of their leaders sultan in 1251. This government was overthrown by Selim I of Turkey, who took Cairo, their capital, by storm in 1517. The Mamelukes, however, remained attached to the Egyptian army until 1811. They were defeated by Bonaparte at the battle of the Pyramids in 1798. See *Egypt.*

Manchukuo (*măn'cho͞o'kō'*). A state erected under Japanese suzerainty in 1932 out of the Chinese territory formerly known as Manchuria. Ex-emperor Hsuantung of China was made regent as Henry Pu-Yi. Ostensibly to protect Japanese investments and rights under various "secret treaties," the Japanese army seized this territory in 1931, the population of which is over 90 per cent Chinese. Active economic development of the country began at once with Japanese capital. In 1934 Pu-Yi was made Emperor Kang Teh.

Mandarins. The term is properly applied only to officials called *kwan* by the Chinese. There are nine grades of kwan, and a distinguishing colored button or stone set in the hat is worn by each to denote the particular grade to which the wearer belongs. The word probably comes from the Sanskrit and signifies "a counselor."

Mestizos (*mĕs-tē'zōz*). In Spanish America and in the Philippines, this name is applied to persons of mixed blood; especially the offspring of a European or person of European stock and an East Indian, a Negro, a Malay, or other person of dark non-European stock. Often in the Philippine Islands, the term is applied to those of Chinese and native blood.

Métayage (*mĕ-tā'yȧj*). The system of cultivating land for a share of its yield, carried out in France before the days of the Revolution. The tenant was supplied with stock, seed, and implements, receiving in return for his labor one-half of the produce. This system was once common in England, and it is still found in Italy and in certain districts of the United States.

Mississippi Bubble. A speculative scheme projected by John Law in Paris about 1717. Well known in the financial world as an ardent advocate of paper money, Law in 1716 founded the Banque Générale and began to carry out his views regarding this form of currency. So successful was he, at first, that the French government granted him control of the trade with Canada and the Mississippi country. For a while his "system" prospered and large fortunes were made. But the overissue of paper money proved his undoing; this, together with government hostility, brought about the inevitable collapse, which left France on the verge of bankruptcy and thousands of families in financial ruin.

Mogul. The word is the same as *Mongol.* The moguls, or "great moguls," were the descendants and successors of the Mongol conqueror, Timur, or Tamerlane. They ruled India from 1526 to 1765, when their power was subordinated to English authority. See *India.*

Molly Maguires. Members of a secret society in Ireland, formed in 1843 to intimidate law officers and prevent the service of writs. Their name came from an Irish rebel leader in 1641, and from the fact that they wore women's attire as a disguise. A similar Irish association was organized in the coal districts of Pennsylvania against the mine owners in 1854, which, after a series of many crimes, was at length vigorously suppressed in 1877.

Moros (*mō'rōz*). A group of Mohammedan Malays inhabiting the southwestern part of the Philippines, chiefly the Sulu archipelago and the islands of Palawan and Mindanao. Their social and legal customs are interpretations of the *Koran.* Polygamy and slavery were formerly established customs among them, and their piracy was long a source of trouble. Since the United States took over the islands, a Moro province has been organized, education has been introduced, slavery has been abolished, and the natives have been disarmed.

Mountain (**La Montagne**). A name given to the extreme revolutionary faction in the National Convention during the French Revolution. It was so called because the Jacobins, with Robespierre and Danton at their head, occupied the upper tiers of seats at the left in the Convention. The "mountain" came to an end soon after the fall of Robespierre in 1794.

Nantes, Edict of. This name designates the law of Henry IV in France which, in 1598, gave a measure of religious freedom to the French Protestants, or Huguenots. They received liberty of conscience, full civil rights, permission to meet for worship in certain places, and provision by the government of 100 places of safety. The privileges enjoyed by the Huguenots under the Edict of Nantes were under constant attack by the Catholic majority. Churches built in places not specified in the Edict were destroyed. At length, in 1685, Louis XIV revoked the law, and all civil rights and religious liberties were withdrawn from the Huguenots. Approximately 400,000 migrated to other countries. French

Protestantism was again accorded tolerance at the time of the Revolution.

Nations, Battle of the. The battle of Leipzig, Oct. 16, 17, 18, 1813. Five nations were represented. The armies of France met the combined forces of Prussia, Russia, Austria, and Sweden. The battle was followed by the retreat of the French, under Napoleon. See *France.*

Naval Limitation. On July 11, 1921, the Congress of the United States, by an amendment to the naval appropriations bill, authorized President Harding to arrange for an international conference upon limitation of armaments. The president, on August 11, 1921, issued formal invitations to Great Britain, France, Italy, Japan, and China; later, to Belgium, the Netherlands, and Portugal. The conference assembled in Washington on November 12, 1921, and terminated its deliberations on February 6, 1922.

Agreement upon any limitation of military armaments proved impossible, and restriction of naval forces was virtually confined to placing limitations upon the building of capital ships. Seven treaties embodied the results of the work of the conference. Of these the most important were:

1. A *Five-Power Naval Treaty,* by which the capital ship strength of the United States and Great Britain was fixed at 525,000 tons each, that of Japan at 315,000 tons, that of France and Italy at 175,000 tons each.
2. A *Nine-Power Treaty,* with reference to Chinese affairs. This treaty was signed by representatives of the United States, Great Britain, Japan, France, Italy, Belgium, the Netherlands, Portugal, and China. It provided essentially for recognition of the territorial integrity of China and for an open-door policy in respect to economic rights and privileges.

The Washington Conference set a precedent in naval limitation by agreement. This precedent was followed in the London naval arms conference of 1930, where the battleship tonnage of the United States and that of Great Britain were further reduced to about 460,000 and Japan's to 290,000. Limitation agreements were extended also to cruisers and other classes of ships.

By 1937, the results of the Washington conference had largely been erased. The territorial integrity of China was ignored in Japanese aggression that resulted, among other gains, in erecting the puppet state of Manchukuo in 1932. The Japanese refused to renew the London agreement on any terms short of naval parity with the United States and Great Britain, and these powers refused to accede to terms demanded. The United States, Great Britain, and France agreed to a conditional limitation of the caliber of guns used on certain types of ships. The essential failure of agreement in any large sense, however, ushered in a period of rearmament that cast its shadow over the entire international horizon.

Nihilists. Members of a great revolutionary party organized in Russia as early as 1818, to whom the term "nihilists" was first applied in 1860 by Turgenev, the Russian novelist. Their aim was the emancipation of the serfs and the setting up of constitutional government in place of despotic rule. In 1870 the nihilists advocated socialistic propaganda. They held that social conditions were so bad that they could not be remedied and therefore must be destroyed.

The Russian government sought to crush the movement with an iron hand, many persons being imprisoned or exiled to Siberia. Reprisals on the part of the nihilists followed, culminating in the assassination of Alexander II in 1881. For many years after this event, nihilism appeared to lie dormant and inactive, but in 1917 it was discovered that its spirit had spread throughout Russia, not only among the working classes, but also among members of the aristocracy and of the army. The recent revolutions in Russia have resulted in freeing the nihilists from the dread of former oppression. Indeed it would seem that their mantle has fallen on the shoulders of the Bolsheviki, who have willingly imbibed their doctrines. See *Bolsheviki, Russia.*

Nîmes (*nēm*), **Pacification of.** The proclamation of an edict at Nîmes in 1629, confirming the religious freedom of the Huguenots who had been defeated the previous year at the siege of La Rochelle. While it endorsed the Edict of Nantes, it left the Huguenots a powerless and unarmed political party, without rights or privileges as citizens. As a result, the Huguenot League in a short time was disbanded.

"No Bishop, No King." Utterance credited to James I, in criticism of the self-governing organization of the Presbyterian and Independent churches. The phrase involves recognition of the kinship between revolt against the authority of an established head of the church and revolt against the authority of a single monarch in the state. Events proved the truth of James's prophesy. The democratic organization of Presbyterian and Independent churches gave substance and currency to the principle of self-government, which, carried over into the organization of the state, resulted in the English Revolution of 1649, the decapitation of Charles I, and the founding of the English Commonwealth. The later Revolution of 1688 and the American Revolution were likewise, in no inconsiderable degree, the product of the democratic spirit fostered by the self-governing organization of the Independent churches.

Noche Triste (*nō'chā trēs'tā*). The "mournful" or "disastrous night" of June 30, 1520, when the Spanish conquerors of Mexico were well-nigh annihilated. On the death of the friendly disposed chieftain Montezuma, Cortés, fearing violence from the natives, decided to withdraw secretly from Mexico City. His intentions, however, had been anticipated; for he and his troops were met by the natives at the pass of Tlacopan. A terrible slaughter followed, in which the Spaniards lost 450 of their own men together with 4000 Indians who fought with them as allies. Most of the rich plunder they had secured and the costly treasures given them by Montezuma were sunk in the lake and never after recovered. See *Mexico.*

Normandy. The district of northern France, bordering on the English channel, and now included in the departments of Seine-Infèrieure, Eure, Orne, Calvados, and Manche. The name Normandy comes from the Normans, or Northmen, who conquered the territory in the 10th century. In 1066 William II, duke of Normandy, became William I of England and united the two realms. The French regained Normandy in 1204 and held it until 1417. Then the English recovered it and maintained their authority until 1450, when Charles VII finally seized it for the French. Small remnants of the old province, the Channel islands, still belong to England. In them much of the old customary law of Normandy is in force, and many of the people continue to speak the old Norman French tongue. See *England, Normans.*

North German Confederation, The. This union of all the German states north of the river Main was formed in 1867, after the close of the Austro-Prussian, or Seven Weeks', war. It was Bismarck's creation. A legislature of two houses, the Bundesrath and the Reichstag, was provided for. The members of the Bundesrath were appointed by the sovereigns of the states, and Prussia had 17 out of the total of 43 votes. The members of the Reichstag were elected by the people. The Confederation gave way, in 1871, to the German Empire. See *Germany.*

Olympiad (*ô-lĭm'pĭ-ăd*). In ancient Greece, the interval of four years between successive celebrations of the Olympic games. Said to have been used first by the historian Timæus as a unit for computing time. The year 776 B. C., when Corœbus won the foot race, was taken as the first year of the first Olympiad. The use of this system ceased with the abolition of the Olympic games in 394 A. D.

Open-Door Policy. The arrangement with respect to Chinese commerce, supported by general consent rather than by special treaties of the nations, under which all nations shall be allowed to trade in China upon equal terms. The policy is opposed to that of special "spheres of influence." The policy has gained larger importance since the close of the World War, through the question of applying it to the various "mandatories" or protectorates created by the League of Nations. See *China, Washington Conference*.

Opium War. This war (1840–42) between Great Britain and China was precipitated by the attempt of the Chinese government to stop the importation of opium, which was being smuggled into China by British merchants. It ended in the Treaty of Nanking, by which Hongkong was ceded to Great Britain, while Canton, Amoy, Foochow, Nangpo, and Shanghai were opened as treaty ports, thus giving a free hand to the opium merchants for their illegal traffic. See *China*.

Orangemen. A secret politico-religious society founded by Ulster Protestants in 1795 to uphold Protestant ascendancy against Catholic influence in the government of Ireland. Lodges or branches of this society are to be found throughout the British Empire and in many parts of the United States. The name was given them by the Catholics of Ireland on account of the Protestant support of the cause of William III, prince of Orange, in the revolution of 1688.

Ordeal, Trial by. This ancient method of determining the guilt or innocence of a person by putting him to painful or dangerous tests was supposed to be under divine control and intervention. It formed a part of judicial procedure in Europe as late as the 13th century. One of the severest of these tests was that by which the accused person was forced to walk blindfolded over red-hot plowshares. If he escaped injury, he was adjudged innocent. Other kinds of trial by ordeal were those by battle, by water, and by the drawing of lots. Such trials were condemned by the Church in 1215 and were abolished in England in the same year, with the exception of the ordeal by battle.

Orders in Council, 1807. These were specific orders made in Council and promulgated by the British government, as a reply to Napoleon's Berlin Decree, establishing a blockade on the continent. They prohibited any neutral from trading directly with France or with her allies. All goods were to be landed in England for the payment of duty and were then to be re-exported according to English regulations. These orders had an especially serious effect on American commerce, and the irritation they caused was, without doubt, one of the chief causes of the War of 1812. See *Berlin Decree*.

Organizer of Victory. The popular title of Lazare Nicolas Marguerite Carnot, noted French statesman, strategist, and scientist, whose services as war minister (1793–95) were marked with great distinction and success. He became governor of Antwerp in 1814 and was minister of the interior under Napoleon in 1815. He was born at Nolay, Burgundy, France, May 13, 1753, and died at Magdeburg, Prussia, Aug. 2, 1823.

Outlawry. In early days, outlawry was a declaration of hostility by the community against one who defied its constituted authority. The goods of such a person were forfeit, and he was liable to be killed at sight. Later, it became a mere process by which the criminal was brought within the jurisdiction of the courts. After the 13th century the wanton killing of the outlaw was forbidden. Outlawry in this sense is now practically abolished in England and is completely obsolete in the United States. The term is also used to express the process of making a particular act or course of conduct unlawful, either by legislation, by judicial interpretation, or, in the case of nations, by treaty.

Oxford Group. A semi-religious but informal movement founded by Frank N. D. Buchman while an undergraduate at Oxford University in 1921. The name was first applied by the press of South Africa in 1928. The professed purpose of the movement is "to solve personal, national, and international problems by bringing men and women everywhere back to the basic principles of the Christian faith, enhancing all their primary loyalties."

Without organization, membership, subscriptions, or definite creed, the movement rapidly obtained adherents in nearly all countries of the world, particularly among the middle and upper classes, and was accorded recognition by leading figures in many governments. Adopting the slogan of "moral rearmament" in 1938, the leaders of the movement sought by spread of its principles to stem the rising tide of national hostilities. Buchman was born at Pennsburg, Pa., in 1878.

Oxford Movement. This was a movement to counteract the liberalism and rationalism toward which the clergy of the Church of England, at the time, were tending. It originated at Oxford university in 1833 in an endeavor to bring the Anglican Church back to the principles of the early Christianity of the Fathers. Its fundamental principles were laid down in a series of ninety pamphlets known as "Tracts for the Times." These tracts, contributed mainly by Newman, Pusey, Froude, and Isaac Williams, set forth the necessity of a visible church with sacraments and theological dogmas, and they supported the contention that this church is based upon unbroken apostolic succession and includes the Anglican Church. Tract No. 90, written by Newman, declared that the Thirty-nine Articles might be so interpreted as to be consistent with the doctrines of the Council of Trent. It caused a great sensation among the Anglican bishops and was condemned by them in 1841. Newman, with several other leading tractarians, thereupon entered the Church of Rome.

Panama Scandal. The estimate for the building of the Panama canal was given by De Lesseps, the French engineer, as $169,000,000. The French Panama Company was accordingly formed, shares were taken rapidly throughout France and elsewhere, and the work was begun in 1881. In 1889 the company declared itself bankrupt, and an investigation followed. It was found that of the 54 miles only 12 had been finished, and that no less than $260,000,000 had been expended. The directors of the company, including De Lesseps and his son, were tried and found guilty,—some of bribery, others of misuse of the company's funds. This great scandal was called by the Parisians *La Lessive du Panama*—"the Panama dirty linen." In 1904, the United States acquired by purchase the rights of the French company and undertook to build the canal. See *Colombia, Panama Canal*.

Pan-Germanism. A movement in Germany which developed in 1894 into the Pan-German League. The purposes of the league were stated in 1903 as (1) the strengthening of German national self-consciousness, (2) the education of German youth in German ideals, (3) the uniting of all Germans wherever they resided, (4) the furthering of German colonization.

Pan-Slavism. A Russian movement having for its ideal the confederation of all the Slavic nations under the leadership of Russia. The natural conflict of this policy with the designs of Turkey and those of Germany had much to do with precipitating the World War.

Paris Pact. This treaty, known also as the Briand-Kellogg peace treaty, grew out of an original proposal of April 1927 by Aristide Briand, foreign minister of France, that France and the United States should agree mutually to outlaw war as a means of settling their disputes. Secretary of State Frank B. Kellogg proposed that the treaty be multilateral. This proposal was accepted. The pact was signed in Paris on August 27, 1928, by representatives of the following fifteen nations: United States, France, Great Britain, Germany, Italy, Japan, Irish Free State, Canada, Australia, New Zealand, South Africa, India, Belgium, Czechoslovakia, and Poland. All other nations were invited to be adherents.

By this pact, the contracting parties condemn recourse to war for the solution of international controversies and renounce it as an instrument of national policy in their relations with one another. They further agree that the settlement of all disputes arising among them shall never be sought except by pacific means. An important effect of this agreement is to confer on all signatory governments the legal right to express an opinion on any incident which threatens war. The exercise of this right involves consultation. In general, aggressive wars thereafter were carried on without official declaration.

Partition of New World, Papal. Pope Alexander VI, in order to prevent disputes between the Spaniards and the Portuguese in regard to their discoveries in the East Indies and the West Indies, established, in 1493, a line of demarcation which was to serve as a permanent division between the claims of the two rival powers. The pope had already confirmed Portugal in her claims to the islands and countries of Africa which she had discovered. Spain asked for a similar confirmation of her claims in the West. Accordingly, the pope drew upon the map a line from the north to the south pole, at a distance 100 leagues west of the Azores, and decreed that the newly discovered lands west of that line should belong to the Spaniards, and those east of it to the Portuguese. Portugal, however, proved dissatisfied with this arrangement, and, by the Treaty of Tordesillas in 1494, another line 370 leagues west of the Cape Verde islands was substituted. By the new adjustment, Portugal eventually obtained possession of Brazil.

The authority claimed for the partition was a document which later was found to be a forgery but at the time was generally regarded as authentic. This was the so-called Donation of Constantine, purporting to be a grant by the Emperor Constantine (324-337 A. D.) to the Pope of temporal dominion over Rome and the states of the West. The document was proved to have been fabricated in Rome in the 8th century.

Patricians and Plebeians. The two classes of citizens in ancient Rome. The struggles of the plebeians to gain social and political rights mark the early history of the republic. The patricians were the descendants or adopted members of the original ruling *gentes* or "clans." The heads of these clans were called *patres*, or "fathers," hence the word "patricians." The plebeians, from *plebs*, or "multitude," were mostly small landowners of the country near Rome. See *Rome*.

Peace of Portsmouth. The peace treaty which closed the Russo-Japanese war was signed at Portsmouth, N. H., September 5, 1905. The envoys of Japan and Russia had been brought together through the mediation of President Theodore Roosevelt. The treaty provided for (1) a Japanese guardianship of Korea, (2) evacuation of Manchuria by both powers, (3) transfer of Russian rights at Port Arthur to Japan, (4) division of the Manchurian railway between Japan and Russia.

Peasant War, The Great. The most important of a series of peasant uprisings in the 16th century. This revolt spread, in 1525, from the southern Black Forest through Austria, Alsace, and the lower Rhine. At first, the peasants were under the leadership of Götz von Berlichingen, who finally deserted them. He was succeeded by an Anabaptist fanatic named Münzer, who, with vast numbers of his admirers, played the leading part in this most bloody insurrection. After issuing a manifesto, in which they set forth their demands, they finally proclaimed a community of goods. None of their demands was granted. Münzer was captured at Frankenhausen and was executed. The rebellion, quelled with unheard-of cruelty, left the peasants in a worse condition than they were in before.

Peking, Treaty of. This treaty, signed Oct. 24, 1860, by China, Great Britain, and France, ratified that of Tientsin, made two years previous. It also imposed upon the Chinese the payment of a large indemnity for insults offered to the plenipotentiaries on their way to Peking. Moreover, it stipulated that Christianity was to be tolerated, that the Chinese tariff should be revised, and that, in the future, ambassadors should reside in Peking.

Peninsular War, The. Sometimes called the War of Spanish Independence. A series of campaigns conducted from 1808 to 1814 by the English, Spanish, and Portuguese against the French forces in Spain. The English general, Wellington, had succeeded in driving the French from Spain at the time of Napoleon's abdication, April 6, 1814. See *England, France, Spain.*

Pericles (*pĕr'ĭ-klēz*), **The Age of.** The period in the 5th century B. C. in which Athens reached its highest point of achievement in democratic government, in literature, and in art. The era takes its name from Pericles, who from about 461 to 429 was the most influential leader in Athens. Some historians reckon this entire period as the age of Pericles; others restrict the term to the fifteen years, 445–431, when Pericles was sole ruler of the Athenian democracy. During this latter period Pericles brought about the adornment of Athens with statues and public buildings, including the Parthenon and other structures on the Acropolis, which reflect the greatest glory upon his age. See *Greece.*

Personal Union. Where two countries are united, not organically or politically, but through the person of their common ruler, their relation is a personal union. Such was the union of England and Scotland from 1603 to 1707. Other instances are the following: From 1815 until 1831 the czar of Russia was king of Poland; the king of the Netherlands was also grand duke of Luxemburg (1814–90); the king of Denmark was, for several centuries, duke of Schleswig and Holstein (see *Seven Weeks' War*); in 1920, Iceland ceased to be a Danish possession, and assumed the status of a personal union by electing the king of Denmark as her king.

Peter's Pence. Voluntary contributions sent from all over the world by members of the Catholic Church, for the use of the pope. It serves not only as maintenance of the papal household, but also for the multitudinous expenses of the Vatican, a great portion of these funds going to the support of Catholic missions abroad. It is said that the largest donations come from the United States, France, and Ireland. Peter's pence dates its origin to Offa, king of Mercia, in the 8th century, and had then for its object the establishment and the upkeep of a Saxon college in Rome.

Physiocrat. A follower of the 18th century school of economic thought which maintained that land is the sole source of national prosperity, and that wealth itself consisted of nothing more than raw materials and other products of the soil. The farmer, under the physiocratic doctrine, was the only productive worker in the state; the merchant, capitalist, and town laborer were in large measure looked upon as parasites who added nothing at all to the total production of the state. The founder of this school of thought was a Frenchman, Francois Quesnay.

A corollary of the central principle of the physiocratic theory was that all revenues required by the state should be derived from a single, direct tax upon the land—that being the only true resource of the nation. Likewise, the *laissez-faire* doctrine was approved, according to which the state should not interfere with the natural economic and social evolution of the community.

Plantagenets (*plăn-tăj'ē-nĕts*). The ruling house in England from the accession of Henry II in 1154 to the accession of Henry VII in 1485. Matilda, daughter of Henry I, married Geoffrey, count of Anjou, and Henry II was the child of this marriage. Geoffrey, it is said, usually wore in his cap a sprig of broom, or *plante de genêt*, whence arose the family name.

Plebiscite (*plĕb'ĭ-sĭt*). An expression of the will of the whole people, sought in ratification or disapproval of a particular measure, already decided upon, but regarding which their elected representatives hesitate to act. It is of French usage and was adopted by Napoleon III in 1851, when he referred to the French people the question of his assuming the imperial dignity. In recent times an appeal to this method has been frequently advocated. The Treaty of Versailles, 1919, provided for plebiscites to determine finally the control of certain districts formerly under German rule. See *Poland, Schleswig-Holstein Question, Silesia, World War.*

Poland, First Partition of. By a mutual arrangement in 1772, between Catherine of Russia, Maria Theresa of Austria, and Frederick of Prussia, the following division of Poland was made: Russia received the eastern part of Lithuania; Austria, East Galicia and Lodomeria; Prussia, Polish Prussia (except Danzig, Thorn, and Ermeland) and the Netze district. The exertions of these powers to preserve the Polish constitution, after such high-handed confiscation, ended in anarchy and fostered rebellion. See *Poland.*

Poland, Second Partition of. At the close of the Polish civil war in 1793, Russia and Prussia invaded Poland and extorted new cessions. Russia took the remaining part of Lithuania, together with Volhynia and Podolia; Prussia took Danzig, Thorn, and the whole of Great Poland. In addition to this, Russia forced the Poles to a *treaty of union,* by which the former received: (1) free entry for her troops into Poland; (2) the conduct of all future wars; (3) the right of confirming all foreign treaties made by Poland. All this ruthless treatment and appropriation led to the famous revolution in Poland the following year, under the leadership of Kosciusko. See *Lithuania, Poland.*

Poland, Third Partition of. The remaining territories of Poland were divided between Prussia, Austria, and Russia in 1795, after the defeat of Kosciusko. By the three partitions, the following increase of territory had been acquired:

Russia, 181,000 sq. mi., 6,000,000 inhabitants
Austria, 45,000 sq. mi., 3,700,000 inhabitants
Prussia, 57,000 sq. mi., 2,500,000 inhabitants.

Popes. See *Bishops and Popes of Rome.*

Popish Plot. In August 1678, there appeared in England an adventurer of the name of Titus Oates, who sought to make profit out of the prevailing distrust of the English people for Charles II. Oates had adopted various religions and had actually been a Jesuit lay brother in Spain, where he had been expelled by that society for drunkenness and worse. He announced the existence of a great "popish plot," which proved to be a tissue of lies and absurdities. Nevertheless, the populace was more than inclined to believe him. Shortly after his "revelations," Sir Edmund Berry Godfrey, before whom Oates had made his depositions, was murdered. All London became inflamed, and the Catholics were at once accused of the crime. A new test act was hurriedly passed, excluding all Catholics from Parliament, and five Catholic peers were sent to the Tower. Coleman, secretary to the duchess of York, was tried for treason and was executed.

Pragmatic (*prăg-măt'ĭk*) **Sanction.** An edict upon important state business, issued by the head of the state and formerly regarded as an unchangeable part of the fundamental law of a country. The most important of such papers in European history is that published in 1713 by the Holy Roman emperor, Charles VI. Having no son, Charles VI, by this instrument, settled his dominions on his daughter Maria Theresa. He induced most of the European sovereigns to guarantee it; but Charles Albert, elector of Bavaria, the next heir to his dominions, refused. This caused the War of the Austrian Succession after the death of the emperor in 1740. Bavaria finally acknowledged the pragmatic sanction in the Peace of Füssen (1745). See *Austrian Succession, War of; Hungary.*

Prague, Peace of. The name applied to two important treaties. (1) A treaty signed in 1635, to which the various sovereign states of Germany were parties. By it the following provisions were made: The elector of Saxony was to receive Lusatia, and his son August, the archbishopric of Magdeburg for life. The hereditary right of Austria to Bohemia was to be recognized and Pomerania given to the elector of Brandenburg. Certain ecclesiastical estates, confiscated before the Convention of Passau and now at the disposal of the emperor, were to be retained by the present possessor forever. Common cause was to be made in driving out the Swedes from Germany, and religious freedom was to be allowed to Lutherans alone. (2) The treaty between Prussia and Austria, Aug. 23, 1866. It closed the Seven Weeks' war. Austria recognized the dissolution of the German Confederation, the reorganization of Germany to the exclusion of Austria herself, and the annexations contemplated by Prussia. See *Germany.*

Pride's Purge. The name given to the act of Colonel Pride and his troopers, who forcibly ejected from the House of Parliament, in 1648, the Presbyterian majority of the Long Parliament, who favored reconciliation with the king, Charles I. The remaining sixty members, army sympathizers, came to be known as the Rump Parliament. See *Rump Parliament.*

Primogeniture (*prī'mô-jĕn'ĭ-tûr*). The law or custom, still in force in Great Britain, by which all real estate descends to the oldest son. The custom derives historical importance from its effect upon succession to the throne or to titles of nobility.

Quietists. A body or sect of religious mystics, whose system was based on the withdrawal of the mind from all worldly matters and its constant employment in the passive contemplation of God and His attributes. This system was first set forth by Miguel de Molinos, a Spanish priest living in Rome. His views were opposed by the Jesuits, and he was condemned by the inquisition. About 1680 Quietism came into vogue among certain devotees in France, under the guidance of Madame Guyon.

Quisling. Term used in World War II to characterize those who, in the countries conquered by Germany, aided the invaders, and took part in governments formed by them on Nazist principles. It derived from Major Vidkun Quisling, an officer in the Norwegian army, who used his position to aid the invasion, and was placed at the head of a German-controlled government.

Reconcentrados. The noncombatants of the rural districts of Cuba during the rebellion of 1895–98. General Weyler forced them to leave their homes and concentrated them in camps, where many died as a result of government neglect.

Red River Rebellion. A rising, in 1869, of the half-breed settlers in the valley of the Red River of the North, as a protest against the transfer of this settlement to the new province of Manitoba. The rebels, led by Riel, became a serious menace. Sir Garnet Wolseley was sent against them the following year and succeeded in quelling the insurrection. Riel escaped, but, leading a later rebellion in 1885, he was captured and executed. See *Canada, Riel's Rebellion.*

Reformation, The. The name applied to the religious movement in the 16th century, to which the Protestant Church traces its origin. As a result of this revolution, several European states renounced their adherence to the Roman Catholic Church and adopted some form of Protestant belief and organization. John Huss of Bohemia and John Wiclif in England, who belong to the 14th century, are regarded as forerunners of the Reformation, but Germany was the scene of the first decisive action. Here the movement began in 1517 with Martin Luther's attack on what he called the sale of indulgences. He was excommunicated and in 1521 placed by the Diet of Worms under imperial ban. Other leaders of the revolt on the continent were Zwingli in Zurich and Calvin in Geneva. In England, the direct separation from the Roman Church was brought about by Henry VIII. In its main phases, the Reformation movement was virtually completed by the end of the 16th century. See *Germany, Thirty Years' War.*

Reform Bills, English. The Reform bill of 1832 provided for more equitable representation of boroughs and towns in Parliament and extended the suffrage. Its provisions as to redistribution and the franchise, however, still left the larger share of political power in the hands of the landowning classes. The Reform bill of 1867, introduced by Disraeli, provided further extension of suffrage, so that workingmen in large towns were given the ballot. The third Reform act of 1884 gave suffrage to counties on the terms given to boroughs in 1867, and so divided constituencies that, with few exceptions, but one member of Parliament is now elected by each constituency. See *England.*

Regicides. The name given by the supporters of Charles I to the members of the high court of justice, before whom the king was arraigned on the charge of treason and by whom he was found guilty and was sentenced to death in 1649. See *England.*

Renaissance or **Renascence, The.** The name signifies the period of transition, in western Europe, from the middle ages to modern times. With the meaning "re-birth," it is associated with the brilliancy of Petrarch and that of the classic scholars of the 14th century in Italy, where it led to great advances in expressional painting and sculpture and to a return to classical design and form in architecture. The glorious works of such men as Michelangelo, Brunelleschi, Leonardo da Vinci, Raphael, Correggio, Titian, and others testify to what heights this movement rose toward the end of the 15th and early in the 16th century.

The renewal of relations between Italy and Constantinople, due to the menace of Turkish advance at the close of the 14th century, brought the Byzantine scholars, with the literature of Greece, into Italy, and further stimulated the free spirit of the Renaissance in the culture of art and letters, which spread rapidly throughout the rest of Europe. Such momentous events, too, as the invention of printing, the discovery of America and of the sea route around Africa, added a new impetus to this great revival and conduced to wonderful expansion in every branch of trade, industry, and commerce.

Reptile Fund. A name given in Germany to a Prussian fund, held as indemnity for the deposed king of Hanover, the interest on which fund was payable to the king for the loss of his sovereign rights. A part of this fund, it was said, was diverted by Bismarck to subsidize certain journals in the interest of the government.

Revolution of February 1848. The French Revolution which overthrew the government of Louis Philippe, drove him into exile, and established the Second Republic. Its effects were felt in other countries in Europe; for risings followed quickly in Germany, Italy, Belgium, and elsewhere.

Rhodesia (*rō-dē'zhĭ-ȧ*), **Northern.** The African territory under British control, lying between the Belgian Congo and the Zambezi river. Governed by the British South Africa Company from 1889, it was taken over by the British government in 1924. Its affairs are administered by a governor and an executive council.

Rhodesia, Southern. The colony which includes the British territory between the Zambezi river and the Transvaal province. Formerly under the government of the British South Africa Company, the colony was granted responsible government under the British crown in 1923.

Riel's Rebellion. This was a rising of Indian half-breeds in Saskatchewan, Canada, in 1885. They were led by Louis Riel, who had been at the head of a similar rebellion, which took place in the valley of the Red River of the North in 1869. It was suppressed by the Canadian militia under Middlelow, Riel being captured and executed. See *Red River Rebellion*; also *Canada*, page 445a.

Riff. This mountainous district adjacent to Spanish Morocco in northwestern Africa was the scene of repeated attacks by natives under Raisuli against Spanish outposts prior to 1921. In that and the following year, Abd-el-Krim led the native troops to further victories, threatening Spain's hold over the protectorate. In 1925 Abd-el-Krim attacked French Morocco, but after initial successes was driven into the Spanish zone. As a result of concerted attacks of French and Spanish troops in 1926, the native forces took refuge in the Atlas mountains, and Abd-el-Krim surrendered to the French.

Romanovs (*rō-mä'nŏfs*). The reigning family in Russia from the accession of Michael Feodorovich Romanov, founder of the family, in 1613, to the deposition of Nicholas II in 1917. Through the grandmother of Michael, the family is connected with the line of Rurik, the Scandinavian ruler of Novgorod in the 9th century.

Roundheads. Nickname given to the Anti-Royalist party in England during the period of the Civil War and the Commonwealth, so-called because of their Puritan custom of wearing the hair closely cut, as distinguished from the Cavalier habit of wearing the hair in long flowing locks. The Roundheads were the immediate precursors of the Whigs, as the liberal party in English politics. The term was also sometimes applied to members of the Whig party by their opponents.

Rump Parliament. The name given to the 60 members of the Long Parliament left sitting after "Pride's purge." Having been expelled by Cromwell in 1653, they were recalled to the House in May 1659, their number now reduced to 42, and again turned out in October. Recalled two months later, they were forced by Monk, in the succeeding year to receive the excluded members, and the Rump, as such, came to an end. See *Pride's Purge.*

Rye House Plot. A plot hatched in 1683 by the Whigs to kill Charles II and the duke of York. It owed its name to a farmhouse in Hertfordshire, the supposed meeting place of the conspirators. Lord Russell and Algernon Sidney, said to be the ringleaders, were tried and executed.

Ryswick, Treaty of. A treaty signed at a village of this name near The Hague, Sept. 21, 1697, between France on the one side and England, Holland, and Spain on the other. Its chief provisions were: (1) France acknowledged William III as king of England and Anne his lawful successor, thus abandoning the cause of James. All conquests in Catalonia were restored to Spain as well as those in the Spanish Netherlands, with the exception of 82 places. (2) The Dutch restored Pondicherry in India to the French, receiving commercial privileges in return. (3) England and France mutually restored conquests in America. The treaty was ratified a month later by the emperor Leopold, when France ceded all the annexed territories except Alsace and restored to the duke of Lorraine most of his dominions. See *England.*

Salic Law. A code of laws relating to crimes, civil injuries, and inheritance of estates among the Salian or Merovingian Franks. It was compiled, probably, toward the end of the 5th century. By the Salic law, "no portion of Salic land shall come to a woman; but the whole inheritance of the land shall come to the male sex." The reason for this exclusion was, it is said, that certain military duties attached to the possession of land at that time. By the arbitrary application of this law to the succession to the crown, women were excluded from the throne of France in the 14th century; and it is in this sense that the term "Salic law" is commonly used. In medieval France great fiefs were held by women, and the "law" would have had no application to the royal domain and the crown, save for intrigues which followed the death of the sons of Philip IV without male issue. The same principle was successfully used by Philip of Valois, who became Philip VI. It was partly involved in his conflict with Edward III of England and in similar conflicts in Spain from 1714 to 1830. See *England, France, Hundred Years' War.*

Sanctions. A term applied to penalties that may be imposed under terms of the League of Nations Covenant against a nation officially declared an aggressor. They may be economic, involving partial or complete trade boycotts, or military, involving armed force. Economic sanctions were applied ineffectively against Italy in 1935-36 as penalty for an aggressive war against Ethiopia.

Sanctuary. The protection afforded to criminals, debtors, and others, from the ordinary operation of the law, by reason of the sacred character of the place to which they fled, such as a church or abbey. From the days of Constantine, in many Catholic countries, certain churches were set aside and privileged as asylums for those escaping from the hands of justice. In England down to the Reformation, any person who sought refuge in such a place was immune from the law—except in the case of sacrilege or treason—if, within forty days, he showed signs of repentance and expressed his willingness to go into exile. Sanctuary for crime was abolished by James I; but sanctuaries for debtors continued to exist in and around London till 1697, the most noted of these being that of Whitefriars, near the Temple, which claimed this privilege to a much later date. The Abbey of Holyrood in Scotland still retains the right of giving sanctuary; but, since the abolition of imprisonment for debt, the need for seeking it no longer exists.

San Salvador. A little island of the Bahama group, West Indies, known also as Watling's island. This probably is the island upon which Columbus made his first landing in the New World, October 12, 1492, and to which he gave the name of San Salvador.

Sans-Culottes (*sănz'kū-lŏts'*). Literally, "without breeches." An opprobrious name given by the aristocrats during the French Revolution to the advanced republicans and to the Paris mob in general, who stormed the Bastille. It appears to have been a name willingly assumed, as many of the revolutionaries had, in contempt, discarded the knee breeches affected by the royalists and now wore trousers as a mark of differentiation.

Saragossa (*sä'rȧ-gŏs'ȧ*). A city of northeastern Spain, situated on the Ebro river. It rises picturesquely on a fertile plain, a cluster of castles and palaces. Saragossa was one of the first Spanish cities to adopt Christianity. In 1808-09 the French besieged the city, which resolutely resisted, the siege costing 60,000 lives. The citadel was formerly the palace of the kings of Aragon and the headquarters of the Inquisition.

Sardinia, Kingdom of. An old-time dynasty, restored in 1720, when Austria ceded Sardinia to the duchy of Savoy. It comprised principally Savoy, Piedmont, and the island of Sardinia, and became the nucleus of the present kingdom of Italy. King Charles Albert, being defeated in a war with Austria in 1848-49, abdicated in favor of Victor Emmanuel. Cavour was then appointed premier. He sought for and achieved the unification of Italy. Emilia, Tuscany, the papal states, and Naples were, in turn, annexed in 1860, and in the following year Victor Emmanuel assumed the title of king of Italy. See *Italy.*

Sassanidæ (*să-săn'ĭ-dē*) or **Sassanids** (*săs'ȧ-nĭdz*). A strong Persian dynasty named from Sassan, the grandfather of Ardeshir, or Artaxerxes, the founder of the dynasty. In 226 Ardeshir overthrew the Parthian rule. He revived the Zoroastrian religion, and began the extension and strengthening of his realm which was continued by his successors. The last of the line, Isdegerd III, was defeated by the caliph Omar in 641 at the battle of Nehavend, and in 651 was murdered. The caliphs thereafter ruled Persia. See *Parthia, Persia.*

Scapa Flow. An enclosed water area in the Orkneys, off the north coast of Scotland, between the islands of Mainland and Hoy. Scapa Flow became of note during the World War of 1914–18 as the base of the British fleet. In 1919, it was the scene of the scuttling of the German fleet, which lay anchored there after its surrender to the Allies.

Schism (*sĭz'm*) **of the East, The Great.** Called also the Eastern Schism. The severance of the Greek from the Roman Church in the 9th century. It began by a dispute over what is known as the *Filioque* clause, inserted in the Nicene Creed in 589, affirming that the Holy Ghost proceeds from the Father *and the Son.* The Greek theologians raised doctrinal difficulties on this point and denied such procession of the Holy Ghost. In this way a bitter and endless controversy arose between the two great churches. To this dispute was added the high-handed action of the emperor Michael III in 857, who intruded Photius into the see of Constantinople in place of Ignatius, the rightful patriarch, thereby overriding the papal jurisdiction. Still further differences arising between Pope Leo IX and Patriarch Michael Cerularius in 1054, the Greeks were at length cut off from communion with the Church of Rome.

Schism of the West, The Great. After the return of the papal court from Avignon to Rome and the death of Gregory XI (1378), an Italian was elected his successor as Urban VI. The French cardinals refused to acknowledge him and named Clement VII as their choice. This scandal of two rival popes lasted nearly forty years. It was finally quelled in 1417 by the deposition of no less than three phantom popes and the election of Martin V. It is known as the Great Schism of the West.

Schleswig-Holstein Question. From 1386, when the two duchies, Schleswig and Holstein, came under one government, to 1850, their political relations formed a vexed question. Schleswig was mostly Danish in population; Holstein, mostly German. Holstein was a member of the German Confederation, Schleswig was not. The Germans in Schleswig sought to induce the Danes to enter the

Confederation; but the latter resented such attempts and in 1863 declared Schleswig incorporated in Denmark. In the quarrel that ensued, Bismarck saw the means of possible aggrandizement for Prussia and for later differences with Austria. He invited Austria to co-operate with him in settling the Schleswig-Holstein entanglement. War was declared by the two powers against Denmark, which, being defeated, was forced to cede the two duchies to her joint conquerors. These, in turn, now disputed as to the disposition of their spoils. This was the opportunity for which Bismarck had planned. Accordingly, in 1866, he forced Austria into war. It took but seven weeks for Prussia to overthrow her unyielding rival; as a result the duchies of Schleswig and Holstein were annexed and incorporated in the Prussian kingdom. After the World War, a plebiscite provided for by the peace treaty gave North Schleswig to Denmark, South Schleswig and Holstein to Germany. See *Denmark, Plebiscite, World War.*

Scutage, "Shield Money." This was a tax first levied by Henry II in 1159. The owner of every knight's fee or shield (*scutum*) was obliged to pay a sum of money known as scutage, or escuage, in lieu of personal service. The feudal vassals were bound to but forty days' foreign service, whereas Henry needed a standing army in Europe to defend his continental possessions against the king of France. By this levy, he was enabled to hire mercenaries abroad, and the vassals were saved from taking part in quarrels in which they took no interest.

Seleucidæ (*sē-lū'sĭ-dē*). The dynasty of kings descended from Seleucus who, after the death of Alexander, came into possession of the satrapy of Babylon in 323 B. C. He assumed the kingship of territory reaching from the Euphrates to the Indus and later conquered Syria and Asia Minor. The later kings of the dynasty gradually lost power and territory until the last, Asiaticus, was conquered by Pompey in 64 B. C.

Sepoy Mutiny, The. In the history of India in modern times no episode has attracted so much attention, or has been so long remembered, as the sepoy mutiny of 1857. It was popularly believed to have been caused by the refusal of sepoys, or native soldiers, to use cartridges that were greased with pork or beef fat, the muzzle-loading rifles requiring the soldier to bite off the end of the cartridge. But this was only incidental. There was evidently a carefully laid plot, with powerful influence behind it. The revolt spread through the greater part of India, the principal leader being Nana Sahib, rajah of Bithoor. His grievance was that the East India Company, which virtually ruled India, had stopped the pension that was granted to his family and had refused to let him, an adopted son, inherit lands. Among the other leaders was the ranee, or princess, of Jhansi, who appeared in the field at the head of two mutinous regiments. She fought ferociously and was killed at Gwalior in the last great battle. There were sieges at Lucknow, Bithoor, Cawnpore, Gwalior, Delhi, and at other towns; and there were fearful massacres by the natives, with terrible vengeance by the British. Two generals, Lawrence and Havelock, died in the war. Sir Colin Campbell, general in chief, defeated Nana Sahib at Cawnpore and then, with increased forces, conquered the other bands of mutineers, destroyed many forts, and disarmed the people. More than 1,300,000 arms were surrendered. Hindu astrologers had predicted that the rule of the East India Company would end on the centenary of the battle of Plassy, which was fought in June, 1757. See *East India Company, British; India.*

Serfs, Russian. Formerly, nine-tenths of the agricultural land of Russia was owned by the imperial family and by the Russian nobility. It was tilled by the millions of people known as serfs, whose condition was little better than that of slaves. They were attached to the soil by what was known as seigniorial prescriptive right, that is to say, they were bound to cultivate the land for the owner, from the fact that they were born or lived on the estate.

Alexander II began in 1859 to free the crown serfs. In 1861 he issued an edict of emancipation which abolished serfdom throughout the empire and won for him the title of "Czar Liberator." But it brought neither peace nor prosperity. The peasants found that they were worse off than in pre-emancipation days and were paying the landlords, through the state, more than the land given them was worth. The following fifty years saw the steady growth of unrest and dissatisfaction, ending in the most appalling tragedies that modern times have ever witnessed. See *Russia.*

Sevastopol (*sē-vȧs'tô-pôl*). A seaport in southern Russia, on the Black Sea. The town submitted to a memorable siege in the Crimean war of 1854-55, being beleaguered by the British, French, and Turks for eleven months, the Russians finally yielding. Sevastopol was virtually created anew after the ruin wrought by the conflict. In World War I it was a Russian naval base, and its occupation by the Bolsheviki marked the end of the Czarist resistance. In World War II it was taken by the Germans, after a long and heroic defense, in July 1942; and retaken by the Russians in May 1944.

Seven Years' War. One of the most important wars, in its far-reaching effects, of the 18th century. It was waged (1756–63) between Frederick the Great of Prussia and the allied forces of Austria, France, Russia, Saxony, and Sweden. Frederick received naval and financial aid from England and had the support of Hanoverian troops. It is referred to, also, as the third Silesian war. In 1762 Peter III of Russia made alliance with Frederick and supported him until the end of the struggle. In close conjunction with the Seven Years' war was the conflict between France and England, 1754–63, ending in the Peace of Paris and leaving the British triumphant in North America and in India. Through this series of conflicts, Prussia was raised to the rank of a first-class power, and England expanded her colonial empire. See *American History, Canada, England.*

Shantung (*shăn'tŏŏng'*). This historic province of China embraces an area of about 56,000 square miles in the peninsula lying between the Gulf of Chihli and the Yellow Sea. Here live approximately 26 million people in one of the most densely populated districts of the world. Shantung is famous as the birthplace of the Chinese sages, Mencius and Confucius. The loftiest mountain in the province, Tai-shan, near the western boundary, has for centuries been a sacred place of pilgrimage.

The Boxer rebellion centered in Shantung. In 1897-98, Germany secured a lease of the port of Kiaochow, with some inland territory and valuable mining concessions in this province, as indemnity for the killing of German missionaries. Early in the World War, Japan seized Kiaochow, and by the Treaty of Versailles she was confirmed in the possession of all rights and concessions which Germany had held. To this arrangement China refused to subscribe, and, by a treaty negotiated at Washington in 1922, Japan agreed to surrender these privileges to China. Japanese forces were withdrawn from Shantung in December 1922. See *China, World War.*

Shimonoseki (*shē'mô-nō-sâ'kē*), **Treaty of.** The Chinese, defeated by Japan in the Chinese-Japanese war and alarmed for the safety of Peking, agreed to make peace and signed the Treaty of Shimonoseki, April 17, 1895. By the terms of this treaty, China ceded Port Arthur, the Liaotung peninsula, the island of Formosa, and the Pescadores islands to Japan, agreeing to pay also an indemnity of about

$300,000,000. Moreover, China recognized the independence of Korea. But Japan was, in the end, deprived of the most coveted fruits of her victory. She was forced, by Russia, France, and Germany, to surrender the Liaotung peninsula on the ground that Japanese possession of Port Arthur would be a menace to the peace of the Far East. See *China, Japan, Russia.*

Sicilian Vespers. A name given to the great massacre of the French in Sicily, which began at Palermo on Easter Sunday (1282) at the hour of vespers. The Sicilians were driven to this act of vengeance by the unspeakable cruelties of the French, under Charles of Anjou. The result was the expulsion of Charles and the introduction of Spanish rule in the island.

Sikhs (*sēks*). A religious sect constituting the greater part of the population of the Punjab in India. The sect, founded about 1500 by Nanak Shah, profess belief in the unity of the Godhead and in human brotherhood. The name *sikhs* means "disciples." They were organized into a military force by Guru Govind in the latter part of the 17th century, for defense against the Mohammedans and various other religious groups. This force was called the *khalsa*, and every member received the title of *singh*, meaning "lion," hence "noble." Overcome by the Mohammedans after the death of Guru Govind (1708), the sikhs lived in separate communities until they were united under Ranjit Singh in 1792. As a military organization they were crushed by the British in 1849, but they have since proved a valuable asset to the British army in India. They number about 3,000,000 and are chiefly an agricultural people.

Silesia (*sĭ-lē'shĭ-ȧ*). This coveted industrial territory of central Europe has never enjoyed more than a temporary independence, but it has played an important part in the history of Austria, Germany, and Poland. In the 10th century, it first appears in history, occupied by Slavonic clans. One of these tribes took its name from the Zlenz mountain, and from this source the modern name Silesia is derived.

About the year 1000, the Silesian lands were incorporated into the kingdom of Poland, but through various partitions the country had, by 1201, become entirely separate from Polish dominions. It was in the middle of the 12th century that the practical division of the district into Upper Silesia and Lower Silesia was brought about. After 1163, the dukes of these two territories began to invite German colonists to settle in their domains. As a result of this policy, both Upper and Lower Silesia, by the end of the 13th century, had become virtually German lands. This period is notable for the rise of the great Silesian industries of mining and weaving. The strength of these realms is indicated also by the fact that Henry II, duke of Lower Silesia, was able to turn back the Mongol invasion at the battle of Liegnitz (Wahlstatt) in 1241.

The Silesian nobility, however, followed a practice of dividing their lands among their heirs, a policy which resulted in so weakening the political power of each prince that all were glad to seek the protection of the kings of Bohemia. For a short period in the 15th century, the Silesians enjoyed virtual autonomy under Bohemian rule, but, with the rise of a more vigorous policy in the Bohemian state, Silesian administration passed finally into foreign hands, soon falling to the control of the Habsburgs.

During the Thirty Years' war, Silesia shared the fate of Bohemia, in devastation, in ruin of industries, and in decimated population. In 1741, Maria Theresa of Austria was forced to cede Lower Silesia to Frederick of Prussia. In 1742, Frederick wrested from her control Upper Silesia also, except a small group of provinces, known down to the World War as Austrian Silesia.

At the close of the World War, Austrian Silesia was incorporated in the republic of Czechoslovakia. The new state of Poland laid claim to Upper Silesia, which had been a part of the German empire. The Treaty of Versailles provided for a plebiscite to determine the question. The plebiscite was held in March 1920, and, upon the general basis of the distribution of German and Polish majorities, a commission of the League of Nations, in 1921, divided Upper Silesia between Germany and Poland.

Slavery. The system of holding certain persons as the property of other persons to whose will they are wholly bound. Slavery was practiced among all ancient peoples, and in Christian Europe the slave trade did not begin to decline until the 13th century. In the 16th, 17th, and 18th centuries, both Christians and Mohammedans engaged in the African negro slave trade. The Portuguese landed the first shipment of negro slaves to the New World in Santo Domingo in 1503. The first shipload of slaves brought into the British American colonies arrived at Jamestown in 1619.

Great Britain abolished slavery in her colonies in 1833, Sweden took similar action in 1846, France in 1848, Holland in 1859, the United States in 1863, Brazil in 1871, Puerto Rico in 1873, and Cuba in 1880. Slaveholding, though officially prohibited, still exists in many Mohammedan countries and in some Portuguese colonies. See ***American History, Emancipation Act, England.***

Solon, Laws of. In 594 and 593 B. C. Solon, already famous as poet, philosopher, and general, was made archon of the city of Athens, with power to make new laws and to remodel the government. In the first year of his archonship, Solon made several changes in the laws relating to property: (1) Tenants were given full ownership of land which they had tilled for nobles; (2) All debts were canceled; (3) Athenians enslaved in Attica were freed; (4) Enslavement of Athenians was made illegal; (5) The amount of land to be owned by any one person was limited. In his second year Solon created a senate, enlarged the assembly, introduced coinage, required each father to teach his son a trade, and restricted the public appearance of women. See *Greece.*

South Sea Bubble. A financial scheme which was launched in 1711 and which collapsed in 1720. The national debt of England had been causing anxiety to politicians. Accordingly, a bill was passed, enabling those to whom the nation owed money to take shares in the South Sea Company, in place of their claims upon the nation. All classes were under the delusion that the wealth of Spanish America, with which the company proposed to trade, was so enormous that they would be enriched beyond expectation. The madness of speculation spread like an epidemic. Landlords, clergymen, and widows hastened to invest their savings in the South Sea Company. But Spain's refusal to enter into commercial relations with England had rendered the privileges of the company worthless. The result was disaster, which brought appalling distress to thousands of impoverished families in England. See *England.*

Spanish Succession, War of the. A war (1702–14) arising out of disputes regarding succession to the Spanish crown. Charles II of Spain, dying childless, left by will the whole of his dominions to Philip of Anjou, the grandson of Louis XIV of France. Louis, setting aside the Treaty of Partition, which he had made with William III, chose to follow out the will and proceeded to support the claims of his grandson. The Grand Alliance of England, Holland, and the Holy Roman Empire was thereupon formed to oppose his designs. A series of bloody campaigns ensued, lasting nearly ten years. Marlborough fought in Flanders, while Archduke Charles overran Spain. The war came to an end with the Treaty of Rastatt and Baden in 1714, by which Philip was recognized as king of Spain, under the title of Philip V.

Sphere of Influence. A region in which some foreign state claims superior rights as against all other outside powers, hoping eventually to convert this right into supreme control. Morocco was a French sphere of influence before it became in large part a French protectorate. Manchuria is generally regarded as a Japanese sphere of influence. But the term is also more loosely used. The Caribbean, for example, is sometimes spoken of as a "sphere of influence" of the United States.

Star Chamber, Court of. So called, either from the decorations of the roof, or because it had been the safe-room where formerly Jewish bonds, or "starres," were kept. It was established by Henry VII to put an end to the tyrannous power of the feudal nobles. Its results were excellent. Wealthy landowners—the terror of their neighbors—who frequently bribed juries and sent retainers to punish those who had displeased them, were brought to Westminster before a court, which meted out strict justice. The greatest merit of this court was that it acted independently of juries, which in those days dared not give verdicts according to conscience. Later, in the time of Charles I, the power of the Star Chamber became a mere instrument of vindictive suppression and the court was at last abolished in 1641.

States-General (France). The name given to the legislative assembly in France, before the Revolution, consisting of the nobles, clergy, and commons. It is said to have been first summoned in 1302 by Philip the Fair. Sessions were rare, and none were summoned between 1614 and 1789.

Sublime Porte. The name adopted by Western nations to designate the Turkish government at Constantinople. In allusion to the ancient Eastern custom of administering justice at a gate of a city or of a palace, the Ottoman rulers referred to their court as "the lofty gate." The equivalent Turkish phrase was translated into French, the language of diplomacy, and hence into English as Sublime Porte.

Submarine Warfare. The indiscriminate and inhumane use of the submarine, or U-boat, as an instrument of warfare by Germany was a main cause of America's entering the World War. After various experiments with the submarine in attacking British warships, the German navy under von Tirpitz began, January 31, 1915, to destroy without warning British merchant and cargo ships. This policy was followed by the war zone decree of February 4, 1915, and reached its full development on May 7, 1915, when the passenger vessel *Lusitania* was sunk with a loss of 114 American lives. Owing to the protests of the United States, Germany later made some pretense of curbing the activities of the U-boats, but on February 1, 1917, the German government inaugurated a new policy of sinking all ships found within the waters around the Allied countries.

In World War II, the scope of submarine warfare was greatly expanded. Larger submarines with much greater cruising ranges were built. Germany relied heavily on this arm for victory after the United States entered the war, and in 1942 it was estimated that over 7,000,000 tons of Allied shipping was lost through the U-boats.

In the following year, however, the submarine menace to the Allies was practically eliminated by a combination of moves, including provision of "air umbrellas" over convoys, improved methods of detection, and use of special types of boats to track down submarines and destroy them by depth bombs. The Japanese failed to perfect like weapons and continued to suffer extremely heavy shipping losses from American submarines. Submarines also played a large part in preventing the Axis powers from supporting their forces in the African campaigns of 1940-42.

Suttee (*sŭ-tē'*). A Hindu woman who cremates herself on the funeral pile of her husband; also the act of cremation itself. This dread custom is now practically obsolete in India, having been made illegal by the British government in 1829, under Lord William Bentinck.

Taiping (*tī'pĭng'*) **Rebellion.** A rebellion instigated in southern China, in 1850, by Hung-siu-tsuen, who pretended he was divinely inspired to overthrow the Manchu dynasty and to set up in its place the *Taiping Chao*, or "Great-Peace" dynasty. He promulgated a vague form of Christianity, in which God was called the "Heavenly Father," and Christ, the "Heavenly Elder Brother." Discarding the queue, the insurrectionists went with unshaven heads and flowing locks and were known as the "long-haired rebels." They made many daring attacks on different cities, but were at length overcome in 1864 by forces under the command of Charles George Gordon, known afterwards as Chinese Gordon. See *China*.

Tatar or **Tartar Invasion.** Russia, located on the borders of Asia, fell an easy prey to the Tatars, or Mongols, of the East. In 1237 the successors of Jenghis Khan swept resistlessly over the Russian lands. In a short time the greater part of the country was in their hands, and, after subjugating the people, they obliged them to pay tribute and to furnish soldiers for the Tatar armies. For 250 years the Tatars ruled Russia and to some extent "orientalized" it; but they did not interfere with the religion, laws, and customs of her people. Toward the end of this period, in 1462, Russia under Ivan the Great found herself strong enough to throw off the Mongol yoke. See *Mongols, Russia.*

Terror, Reign of. That period of the French Revolution, between September 1793 and July 1794, when fear was an instrument of government. France was then battling a coalition of all Europe and was at the same time torn by bitter civil strife. The dominant party, of which Robespierre is the best-known member, believed itself justified in obtaining unity of action by literally destroying the opposition. The revolutionary tribunal and the guillotine were the instruments. The government was, however, not responsible for all the atrocities which characterized the time. The deeds of a Carrier at Nantes or of a Fouché at Lyons shocked even Robespierre himself. In Paris about 3000 persons were executed, and no fewer than 15,000 perished in other parts of France. See *France, French Revolution.*

Terrorists. The extreme revolutionary mob of Paris in 1848. Imbued with advanced socialistic ideas, they sought to end their real and imaginary wrongs by the spoliation of the rich. They refused to work and proceeded to set up a revolutionary government at the Hôtel de Ville, but they were overpowered by the garde mobile.

Teutonic Knights. A military and religious order, similar to that of the Templars, established at Acre in 1190 as a brotherhood of German crusaders. It became a political rival of the Knights Templars and Hospitalers, excelling them in lands and riches and winning great prestige in its conquest of the heathen Prussians. The order was dissolved by Napoleon in 1809, but up to a recent period a branch of it existed in Austria, as a semireligious knighthood, devoted especially to ambulance service. See *Germany.*

Thirty Years' War. This religious and political war began in 1618 with the rising of the Protestant nobility of Bohemia against Matthias, their king, who was also emperor. Matthias having died, the following year the nobles sought to depose Ferdinand, his successor, and elected Frederick, the Calvinist son-in-law of James II, to the imperial throne, taking up arms in his support. In 1620 Frederick was defeated at the battle of the White

Mountain near Prague, and driven from Bohemia. France, Spain, Sweden, and England became involved in this prolonged war, which was brought to an end in 1648 by the Peace of Westphalia. See *Germany*.

Thugs. A fraternity of religious fanatics in India, who worshiped the terrible goddess Kali, to whom it had long been the custom to make bloody sacrifices. From plunder of the property of their victims, murdered by strangling, the thugs derived their support. They were suppressed by the British government, 1830–40, though occasional instances of their peculiar methods serve to show that the thugs are not yet quite extinct.

Tiers Etat (*tyâr' zā'tä'*). In France, the "third estate," or that portion of the nation which was not included in the nobility nor in the clergy. It included the landholding peasantry. In the last States-General (1789) they struggled fiercely for power equal to that of the two privileged classes of nobles and clergy. The "third estate" succeeded at length in reorganizing all the deputies of the three orders as a single National Assembly. They had 600 deputies, equal to the number for the other two orders together, so that with the aid of the minor clergy and the liberal nobles they now took the lead. See *France*.

Tilsit, Treaty of. A treaty between France on the one side and Russia and Prussia on the other. Napoleon and Alexander met on a raft on the river Memel, June 25, 1807. Napoleon dictated the terms, according to which (1) the grand duchy of Warsaw was created out of parts of Prussia; (2) a part of Prussia was ceded to Russia; (3) Danzig was made free; (4) the region on the left bank of the Elbe was ceded to Napoleon; (5) the Confederation of the Rhine was recognized, and Joseph, Louis, and Jerome Bonaparte were acknowledged as kings of Naples, Holland, and Westphalia respectively; (6) Prussian harbors were closed to the British, the Prussian army was reduced to 42,000, and Prussia was to pay large indemnities and be reduced to a second-rate power. See *France, Russia*.

Toleration Act. An act passed in 1689, during the reign of William and Mary, by which Protestant dissenters from the Church of England were given the legal right to worship publicly in their own chapels. They were, however, bound to take the oaths of supremacy and allegiance and to repudiate the doctrine of transubstantiation. See *England*.

Tories, British. After the English revolution of 1688-89, two distinct parties with opposite political views came into existence—the Whigs and the Tories. The Whigs stood for the supremacy of Parliament as against the authority of the king, and for a more liberal, more democratic view of social, economic, and public questions. The Tories, on the other hand, stood for the continuance of the broad royal powers of the Stuart monarchs. When, after a long period of Whig supremacy, George III placed Lord North in power in 1770, the Tory principle of the supremacy of the king in the choice of ministers was put into effect. The period from 1783 to 1794 saw the Tories in power, led by Pitt, and opposed to the landholding group of Whigs. From 1794 until 1830, the Tories and the great Whig landowners were generally united in opposition to popular reform. In 1830, the name Conservative was suggested as a substitute for Tory and was generally used after 1832.

Torres Vedras (*tōr'rĕsh vä'dräsh*), **Lines of.** The fortifications which extended from near the old town of Torres Vedras to the banks of the Tagus. The Anglo-Portuguese armies under Wellington defended these lines against the French led by Masséna, during the winter of 1810-11, and checked their advance toward Lisbon. The longest of the three lines of defense, protecting 500 square miles of territory, measured 29 miles.

Treaties. Treaties are formal written agreements between independent states, with reference to political, commercial, or territorial relations, or other matters of common concern. The constitution and laws of each state determine what authorities shall negotiate treaties. The following are the most important treaties recorded in medieval and modern times. See *Treaties of United States*.

843 Treaty of Verdun. Between Lothair, Louis, and Charles the Bald. It divided Charlemagne's empire among these three grandsons of Charlemagne. To Louis was given the land east of the Rhine; to Charles, the country west of the Rhone and the Meuse; to Lothair, the strip between, including most of Italy.

911 (?) Treaty of St. Clair-sur-Epte. Between Rollo the Northman and Charles the Simple of France. The Northmen were granted a permanent possession of territory along the Seine, later known as Normandy, and feudal sovereignty over Brittany.

1122 Concordat of Worms. Between the emperor (Henry V) and the pope (Calixtus II). It settled by compromise the dispute over investitures.

1183 Peace of Constance. Between Frederick Barbarossa and the Lombard cities. The emperor renounced all royal privileges and rights in the cities, and acknowledged their right to raise armies and to manage their own local affairs. The cities recognized the overlordship of the emperor by an annual money payment.

1360 Brétigny. Between England and France. Closed first period of Hundred Years' war. Edward III renounced claim to French crown, and received sovereignty over Aquitaine, Ponthieu, Guisnes, and Calais.

1397 Union of Calmar. Between Denmark, Sweden, and Norway. United the three kingdoms under Queen Margaret of Denmark.

1420 Peace of Troyes. Between England, France, and Burgundy. Henry V of England married Katherine, daughter of Charles VI of France, and became regent and heir to the French throne.

1466 Second Peace of Thorn. Between Poland and Teutonic Knights. West Prussia and Ermeland were ceded to Poland. The Knights retained East Prussia as a Polish fief.

1508 League of Cambrai. Between Pope Julius II, Emperor Maximilian, Louis XII of France, and Ferdinand of Spain, against Venice.

1529 Peace of Cambrai. Between Francis I and Charles V. Called *Paix des Dames* because negotiated by Margaret of Austria and Louise of Savoy. Francis paid two million crowns and gave up claim to Italy, Artois, and Flanders. Charles temporarily gave up claim to Burgundy and released the French princes, held as hostages since 1526 (Peace of Madrid).

1552 Convention of Passau. Provided for free exercise of religion by adherents of the Confession of Augsburg until the next diet.

1555 Peace of Augsburg. Granted to the territorial princes and the free cities, adhering to Augsburg Confession, freedom of worship and right to introduce the Reformation in their territories.

1576 Pacification of Ghent. Treaty between the provinces of the Netherlands, whereby they united to drive the Spaniards from the country.

1579 Union of Utrecht. The seven northern Netherlands provinces united and declared their independence of Spain.

1632 Treaty of St. Germain. Between France and England. Canada, Acadia, and New France were ceded to France.

1648 Peace of Westphalia. Between France, Sweden, and the Estates of the Empire. Closed the Thirty Years' war.

1659 Peace of the Pyrenees. Between France and Spain. France received some territory. Louis XIV married Maria Theresa, eldest daughter of Philip IV of Spain. She renounced all claim upon her Spanish inheritance, in consideration of a dowry of 500,000 crowns to be paid by Spain. England received the town of Dunkirk by this peace.

1660 Peace of Copenhagen. Between Denmark and Sweden. Denmark surrendered the southern part of the Scandinavian peninsula.

1667 Treaties of Breda. Between England, Holland, France, and Denmark. France was given Acadia; England received Antigua, Montserrat, and English St. Christopher's; Holland retained Surinam; England, New Amsterdam. The treaty provided that goods brought down the Rhine could be shipped to England in Dutch vessels.

1668 Peace of Aix-la-Chapelle. The formation of the Triple Alliance forced Louis XIV to sign this peace, thereby ending his war with Spain. Burgundy was restored to Spain by Louis in return for 12 fortified frontier towns.

1678-79 Peace of Nimwegen. A series of treaties: between Holland and France; Spain and France; the emperor (Holy Roman Empire), France, and Sweden; Holland and Sweden; France and Denmark; Denmark and Sweden. Holland received its entire territory back on condition of neutrality. Spain and France exchanged large cessions of territory.

1679 Peace of Saint-Germain-en-Laye. Between Louis XIV and the elector of Brandenburg. The elector surrendered his Pomeranian conquests to Sweden.

1686 League of Augsburg. Signed by the emperor, the kings of Spain and Sweden, the electors of Bavaria, Saxony, and the Palatinate. Directed against Louis XIV of France.

1697 Peace of Ryswick. Between France and the allied powers,—England, Spain, Holland, and the Holy Roman Empire. Two treaties, providing, among other things, for general restoration of conquests, recognition of William III as king of England and of Anne as his successor. France was given permanent possession of Alsace.

1699 Peace of Karlowitz. Between Turkey and the allies,—Austria, Poland, and Venice. Turkey and Austria divided the territory of Hungary and Transylvania. Venice received Morea (the Peloponnesus).

1713 Peace of Utrecht. Between France and the allies,—England, Holland, Savoy, Prussia, and Portugal. Ended the War of the Spanish Succession. The separate treaties recognized the Protestant succession in England and provided for separation of the crowns of France and Spain. England received Gibraltar, and Sicily was given to Savoy.

1714 Peace of Rastatt and Baden. Between France and the emperor and the Holy Roman Empire. A separate peace by which Austria received the Spanish Netherlands.

1718-19 Quadruple Alliance. Between Great Britain, France, the emperor, and Holland. Designed to maintain the Peace of Utrecht. Spain was forced out of Sicily and Sardinia; Savoy exchanged Sicily for Sardinia.

1721 Peace of Nystad. Between Sweden and Russia. Cession of some territory on the part of Sweden. Russia restored Finland and paid indemnity.

1738 Peace of Vienna. Between France and Austria. Ended the War of the Polish Succession. Provided for French possession of Lorraine; for cession of Naples and Sicily from Austria to Spain; for French guarantee of the Pragmatic Sanction.

1742 Peace of Breslau. Between Maria Theresa of Austria and Frederick II of Prussia. Closed First Silesian war. Frederick withdrew from alliance against Maria Theresa; he received Upper and Lower Silesia from Austria.

1748 Peace of Aix-la-Chapelle. Between Austria, supported by Holland and England, and Prussia, associated with France and Spain. Silesia was confirmed to Prussia; the Pragmatic Sanction was sustained in Austria.

1763 Peace of Paris. Between Great Britain, France, Spain, and Portugal. Canada was ceded to Great Britain by France; Florida to England by Spain; Louisiana to Spain by France (treaty of 1762). This peace, with the Treaty of Hubertusburg, closed Seven Years' war.

1763 Treaty of Hubertusburg. Between Austria and Prussia. Ratified Treaty of Breslau.

1774 Treaty of Kutchuk-Kainardji. Between Turkey and Russia. Brought Tatars under Russian influence; gave Russia a powerful position on the Black Sea.

1783 Treaty of Versailles. Between Great Britain, France, and Spain. Great Britain ceded Tobago to France and Florida to Spain.

1795 Peace of Basel. Between France and Prussia and between France and Spain. France was given temporary possession of the left bank of the Rhine, which Prussia, in secret treaty, agreed should be permanent.

1797 Treaty of Tolentino. Between the pope and the French Republic. The pope ceded the Romagna, Bologna, and Ferrara.

1797 Treaty of Campoformio. Between France and Austria. Provided for convening of Congress of Rastatt. Gave France the Austrian Belgian provinces and most of the left bank of the Rhine. Austria received Venice and other territory.

1797-99 Congress of Rastatt. Between France and the Holy Roman Empire. Fruitless negotiations.

1801 Concordat. Between Napoleon I and Pius VII. Provided that French bishops and archbishops should be appointed and supported by the government and confirmed by the pope.

1801 Peace of Lunéville. Between France, Austria, Spain, and the Holy Roman Empire. The Empire virtually abolished. Treaty of Campoformio confirmed. Left bank of Rhine given to France. Louisiana ceded to France by Spain.

1802 Treaty of Amiens. Between Great Britain, Holland (the Batavian Republic), France, and Spain. England surrendered all conquests to France; Spain ceded Trinidad to England; Holland ceded Ceylon to England.

1805 Treaty of Pressburg. Between France and Austria. Austria made large cessions to France and to the kingdom of Italy, recognizing Napoleon as king of Italy. Bavaria and Württemberg recognized as kingdoms.

1805 Treaty of Schönbrunn. Between Napoleon and Prussia. Prussia ceded Cleves, Ansbach, and Neuchâtel to France, on the promise of receiving Hanover in exchange.

1807 Peace of Tilsit. Treaties between France and Russia, and between France and Prussia. Provided large cessions of territory and payment of indemnities by Prussia, and for alliance between France and Russia.

1809 Peace of Vienna. Between Napoleon and Francis I of Austria. Signed at Schönbrunn. Austria ceded 32,000 square miles of territory.

1814 Peace of Kiel. Between Denmark, Sweden, and England. Denmark surrendered Norway. Sweden ceded western Pomerania and Rügen to Denmark. England retained Helgoland.

1814-15 Peace of Paris. Between France and the Coalition. By the treaty of 1814 France retained her general boundaries of 1792, paid no indemnities, and retained captured art treasures. By the treaty of 1815, she was reduced to her boundaries of 1790, an indemnity of 700 million francs was exacted, and art treasures were reclaimed. Louis XVIII made king.

1829 Peace of Adrianople. Between Russia and Turkey. Russian conquests in Turkey surrendered. Recognition by Turkey of the independence of Greece.

1839 Treaty of London. Between Great Britain, Austria, France, Prussia, Russia, and the Netherlands. Regulated position of Belgium (neutralized) in international law.

1842 Treaty of Nanking. Between Great Britain and China. Closed the Opium war. Hongkong ceded to England. Several treaty ports opened.

1856 Treaty of Paris. Between Russia, Turkey, England, France, Sardinia, Austria, and Prussia. Ended the Crimean war. Declaration signed with respect to privateering, blockades, and contraband.

1859 Treaty of Zürich. Between Austria and France and Sardinia. Sardinia received the greater part of Lombardy. Italy was to be a confederation under the honorary presidency of the pope. Treaty provisions soon overridden.

1860 Peace of Peking. Between China and the Western Powers. Ratified the Treaty of Tientsin (1858) and imposed indemnity on China.

1865 Convention of Gastein. Between Prussia and Austria. Provided for control of the duchies of Schleswig and Holstein.

1866 Peace of Prague. Between Prussia and Austria. Closed the Austro-Prussian (Seven Weeks') war. Austria separated from reorganized Germany. Prussian territory largely increased. Venice ceded to Italy.

1871 Convention and Preliminary Treaty of Versailles. Between France and Germany. Provided for cession of Alsace and German Lorraine to Germany and for payment of large indemnity by France.

1871 Peace of Frankfort-on-Main. Final settlement which ended the Franco-Prussian war.

1878 Treaty of San Stefano. Between Russia and Turkey. Closed Russo-Turkish war. Provided for large cessions of Turkish territory to Montenegro, Serbia, Rumania, Bulgaria, and Russia.

1878 Treaty of Berlin. Between Great Britain, Germany, France, Austria, Russia, Turkey. Called to consider Eastern Question. Declared inoperative most of the terms of San Stefano.

1882 Triple Alliance. Between Austria, Germany, and Italy.

1891 Dual Alliance. Between Russia and France. Served to counterbalance the Triple Alliance, formed by Germany, Austria, and Italy.

1895 Treaty of Shimonoseki. Between Japan and China. China acknowledged independence of Korea and ceded Formosa, the Pescadores, and Liaotung peninsula to Japan, besides paying a large indemnity. Cession of Liaotung later exchanged for larger indemnity.

1902 Anglo-Japanese Treaty. A defensive alliance between Japan and Great Britain. Provided mutual aid in case of attack by more than one outside power.

1905 Treaty of Portsmouth. Between Japan and Russia. Russia acknowledged Japan's paramount interest in Korea; transferred lease of Port Arthur to Japan. Both powers were to evacuate Manchuria and restore it to China.

1907 Triple Entente. Treaty between England and France in 1904; between England and Russia in 1907. A diplomatic understanding which developed into the alliance of 1914.

1912 Treaty of Lausanne. Between Italy and Turkey. Closed Turco-Italian war. Tripoli was ceded to Italy.

1913 Treaty of London. Between Balkan states and Turkey. Provided for restriction of Turkey to Constantinople and small adjoining territory. Redistributed conquered Balkan territory.

1913 Treaty of Bucharest. Between Balkan states. Ended second Balkan war. Serbia, Greece, Rumania, and Turkey enlarged at expense of Bulgaria.

1918 Treaty of Brest-Litovsk. Between Germany and Russia. Ended hostilities between the two countries.

1919 Paris-Versailles Treaty. Between the Entente Allies and Germany. Marked the close of the World War. Provided for cession of Alsace and Lorraine to France. Indemnity imposed on Germany.

1919 Treaty of St. Germain. Between Entente Allies and Austria. Provided for greatly reduced Austrian boundaries.

1921 Four-Power Pacific Treaty. Between the United States, Japan, Great Britain, and France.

1922 Five-Power Treaties. Between the United States, Great Britain, France, Japan, and Italy, providing for the limitation of naval armaments. See *Washington Conference.*

1922 Nine-Power Treaties. Between the United States, Great Britain, France, Japan, Italy, Holland, Belgium, China, and Portugal, providing for adjustment of Chinese tariffs and for the open-door policy in China. See *Washington Conference.*

1923 Treaty of Lausanne. Between Turkey and Greece, Great Britain, France, Italy, and Rumania, defining limits of Turkish territory.

1925 Locarno Treaties. Between France, Germany, Great Britain, Belgium, and Italy, demilitarizing the Rhineland and providing for peaceful settlement of disputes; between Germany, Czechoslovakia, and Poland providing for peaceful settlement of disputes.

1928 Pact of Paris. Between 15 leading nations as original signatories, most other nations later adhering. Renounced war as an instrument of national policy in dealing with parties to the treaty.

1945 United Nations Treaty. The United States and fifty other nations accepted the charter of the United Nations Organization.

1949 North Atlantic Treaty. Alarmed by Russia's use of the veto to obstruct United Nations action and by her expansionist moves in eastern Europe, the countries of the North Atlantic region decided to formulate a security pact for their common defense. This document, "The North Atlantic Treaty," was published on March 18, subject to final ratification. Countries negotiating the pact were the United States, Canada, Britain, France, Belgium, the Netherlands, Luxembourg, and Norway. Others invited to join were Italy, Portugal, Denmark, and Iceland.

Triple Alliance. In 1879 Germany and Austria formed an alliance by which they bound themselves "to lend each other reciprocal aid with their whole military force and to conclude no peace, except conjointly and in agreement." It was aimed particularly against Russia and, in a lesser degree, against France. In 1882 Italy became a party to this alliance, which then became known as the Triple Alliance. It was several times renewed, the last occasion being in 1912. In 1915 Italy declared the alliance dissolved, holding Germany and Austria to be aggressors in the hostilities of 1914.

Trojan War. A conflict between the ancient Greeks and the people of the city-state of Troy, on the coast of Asia Minor. Concerning this war, only the vague traditions and hero tales found in the Homeric poems have survived. Modern excavations on the site have disclosed a ruined city of the 12th century B. C., which is generally presumed to be the city to which Homer's *Iliad* refers.

The city is said to have been captured by the strategem of the "Trojan horse." This was a huge wooden horse in which a company of Greeks belonging to the besieging army was concealed. The main Greek army pretended to withdraw. The Trojans took the horse inside the city walls. The troops concealed in the horse, emerging at night, opened the gates to the Greek army and the city was sacked.

This term was applied to a device by which Adolf Hitler seized Austria in 1938. After the Austrian Chancellor, Schuschnigg, had suppressed a Nazi uprising intended as a means of adding Austria to Germany, Hitler insisted that Schuschnigg accept in his cabinet Dr. Arthur Seyss-Inquart, a Nazi sympathizer who soon acquired control of the police and cooperated in the subsequent annexation of Austria to Germany. The term was later widened to include all persons ready to further the German conquest of their own countries.

Tyrol or **Tirol** (*tĭr'ŏl*). An Alpine district which was formerly a crownland of Austria. By the peace treaty of 1919 the northern part of the district was included in Austria as North Tyrol, while the southern part was given to Italy.

Ukase (*ū-kās'*). In Russia, under the monarchy, the public proclamation, or edict, of the czar, bearing the imperial seal and having the force of law. The whole system of Russian government was based on such absolutism.

Ulster Massacre. Repressive measures against the Catholics and the influx of fresh colonists from England, to oust the Irish more completely from the land, led to this fateful massacre in 1641. The Irish, impatient of promised amelioration, attempted to seize Dublin. This plot being frustrated, they turned savagely on the English and Scottish colony in Ulster and put to death, indiscriminately, many thousands of the inhabitants. See *Ireland.*

Ultramontanes. Formerly this term applied to the members of a schismatic body, for instance, those of the Gallican Church who were opposed to papal supremacy. It is now used to designate any party that upholds the papal claim to temporal power, such as the Catholic party in Germany under Doctor Windthorst during the Kulturkampf. See *Kulturkampf.*

Union Jack. The national ensign of Great Britain and Ireland. The flag is composed of the red cross of St. George on a white field (England), the white X-shaped cross of St. Andrew on a blue field (Scotland), and the red X-shaped cross of St. Patrick on a white field (Ireland). The application of the term "Union Jack" to the national ensign, or Union flag, is an extension of its use by sailors to signify a small flag of like design used as a signal flag, and also flown at the bowsprits of men-of-war and from the mainmast by an admiral of the fleet. Usage, however, seems to have sanctioned the misnomer.

Utrecht, Treaty of. A treaty signed in 1713 between Louis XIV and the allies, England and Holland, at the close of the War of the Spanish Succession. By its terms, Spain and the Indies were to remain under Philip V, who renounced all claim to the throne of France. Sicily was to go to the duke of Savoy, who was to be known as king of Sicily; Naples, Milan, and the Netherlands were to be given to Charles VI; the Dutch were allowed to garrison the southern frontier of the late Spanish Netherlands; France recognized Anne and the Protestant succession in England. The greatest beneficiary of the treaty was England. She retained Gibraltar, Minorca, and in America acquired Hudson Bay territory, Nova Scotia, Newfoundland, and the French part of St. Christopher in the West Indies. Spain also granted her the right of importing slaves into the Spanish colonies and of sending goods to Panama for the Spanish colonists. See *England*.

Vassalage. In the middle ages, the tie between the tenant and the lord from whom he held his land or estate was known as vassalage. Every holder of land was the vassal of some lord. The vassal owed to his lord civil and sometimes military services, also payments of money. In return for such services the lord was bound to protect the life and property of his vassals—in those days no trivial undertaking. All below the king, down to the lesser knights, were regarded as vassals and owed fealty to their immediate superiors.

Vendée, Wars of the. At the period of the French Revolution, the western district of France called La Vendée, with neighboring territories, was inhabited chiefly by a peasant population, among whom the ideas of the Revolution found little acceptance. When, in 1793, a conscription was decreed throughout France, the Vendéan peasants, fond of their old institutions, rose in revolt. Some of the émigrés took advantage of the ensuing conflict to land in France. By the end of the year 1793, however, the republican armies had suppressed the revolt. A policy of conciliation was then followed until the last remnants of the uprising were quelled in 1796. See *Emigrés*, *France*.

Vikings (*vī'kĭngz*). The name applied to members of the bands of Norse sea rovers who harried the northern coasts of Europe from the 8th to the 10th century. The word means "those who lurk in bays and come out for plunder," *vik* being an Icelandic word for "bay." The period of two centuries during which the Norsemen were most active on the sea is commonly known as the Viking age. In the earlier part of this period, they appear as occasional marauders on the coasts of England and France, their first recorded expedition being one to the coast of Dorsetshire in 789. Their usual method was to make sudden attacks upon a coast in the summer months. After a few seasons, they would prepare for more permanent conquest of a district by "wintering" in it. Then, upon a period of strife, amalgamation with the native people usually ensued. See *Normans*.

Villafranca, Armistice of. After the defeat of Austria by Piedmont and France at Solferino and Magenta, Napoleon III, without consulting his ally, concluded a truce with Austria. By the terms it was agreed: that Lombardy should be ceded to Piedmont; that Austria was to retain Venetia; that the Italian states were to form a federation; and that the rulers of Tuscany and Modena were to be returned to their duchies. The disloyalty of Napoleon toward his ally, as it appeared in this action, caused the indignant resignation of Cavour. The terms of the armistice were never enforced. Nor indeed were the people of Italy prepared to observe them, as they were determined that nothing should prevent them from reaching their goal, which was the unification of Italy. See *Italy*.

Waldenses. The followers of Peter Waldo, who was a Lyons merchant about 1160. Though they did not seek to set up a new religion, they objected to certain doctrines of the Church, such as the Mass and the praying to saints. They advocated the charity and the poverty of the Apostles and held that the Bible was the only guide to the religious life. They spread from France through many countries in Europe, but exerted no great influence as reformers. They survived much persecution and are still to be found as a Protestant sect in Italy and in other parts of Europe.

Wergild (*wûr'gĭld'*). Among the Anglo-Saxons and other Teutonic races, the money compensation that had to be paid by a murderer to the relatives of his victim in order to avoid a blood feud, or vendetta. Acceptance of the wergild was at first optional, then it became compulsory. Later, it could not be demanded, nor the feud waged, the slayer being left to public justice.

Westminster Confession. The confession of faith framed by Presbyterian and Calvinistic divines at the Westminster Assembly, whose sessions lasted from 1643 to 1649. The confession was mainly an exposition of the Calvinistic doctrine.

Westphalia, Treaty of. This treaty, signed in 1648 by France, Sweden, and Germany, put an end to the Thirty Years' war. It provided that each reigning prince should be free to choose Catholicism, Lutheranism, or Calvinism as the religion of his subjects. In Germany, Protestantism was recognized as the state religion, but provision was made for equal representation of Catholicism in the German diet. The independence of Holland and Switzerland was acknowledged; France acquired Alsace; Sweden secured Bremen, North Pomerania, and Stettin. With this treaty the period of religious wars in Europe ceased.

Whigs, English. One of the two great English parties from the English Revolution of 1688 until about 1835, when the name Liberals gradually replaced the name Whigs. The Whigs were the anti-Court, anti-Clerical party as distinguished from the Tories who tended to support the old privileges of the king and clergy. From 1714 to 1761, the Whigs were continuously in power, and it was during this period that the cabinet system of England developed into its present form. The Whigs displaced the Tories in 1830 and carried through the reform measures of that period. See *Tories*.

Witenagemot (*wĭt'ĕ-nȧ-gĕ-mōt'*). In Anglo-Saxon times, the king sought the advice and consent of a body of thegns, nobles, bishops, and abbots, which was known as the *Witenagemot*, or "Assembly of Wise Men." This assembly served as a court of appeal, and, within certain limitations, it could elect or depose a monarch. After the Norman Conquest it still continued to meet under the name of the Great Council, and in the reign of Henry III became transformed into a national parliament representing the people.

Worms, Diet of. An assembly held at the city of Worms in 1521, before which Luther was summoned to answer the accusation of heresy made against him. He refused to retract any of his writings or teachings and was ordered to return to Wittenberg to await the imperial edict. The elector of Saxony, who feared for Luther the fate of Huss, had him conducted in secret to the castle of Wartburg, where he spent a year in translating the New Testament. He then returned to Wittenberg, where he died 24 years later.

Young Italy. A society of enthusiastic Italian republicans led by Giuseppe Mazzini. Formed in 1831, the organization reached the climax of its activity in the unsuccessful invasion of Savoy, under Mazzini, in 1834. This society served, not only to inspire Italian patriotism, but also to arouse the youth of other European nations to progressive political ideals.

Zollverein (*tsôl'fĕr-īn'*). A union of German states for the purpose of establishing and maintaining uniform rates of duty on imports from foreign countries and of free trade among themselves. It was inaugurated under the auspices of Prussia in 1834. The growth and success of this economic system contributed much to the political unification of Germany.

PERIODS, EVENTS, AND MOVEMENTS OF WORLD HISTORY

In the preceding pages, the stories of the rise and progress of the states and nations of the world are recounted at some length. Moreover, many special topics, including notable movements, parties, periods, and events of international importance, are treated succinctly in the Dictionary of World History. To complete this plan, and still further to unify the treatment of the subject, the entire course of world history is graphically presented in the following comparative summary of outstanding facts in the story of mankind. The chronological outline histories of the nations are arranged in parallel columns in order to facilitate the attainment of *comparative view* that is so important in the study of history.

Progress in civilization and in political and social development has not been uniform among the nations. In a comparative chart, the occasional long blank spaces in a column, parallel with other quite crowded columns, are instructive. They frequently mark the shallows and the backwaters in the stream of history, telling a story of the persistence of primitive culture, of political stagnation, or of subordination to foreign invaders.

Besides being a convenient source of information, this chart furnishes a study plan for fixing in the memory *related* events and dates, thus supplementing the preceding historical narratives. In this connection, two features especially distinguish this plan: (1) The entries in the column of Arts of Civilization summarize, in its varied phases, the advance of human culture; (2) the distinctive character of modern history since 1815 finds emphasis in the column of International Affairs.

A similar chart, covering the history of the United States and the other American nations, will be found at the close of the section devoted to American history.

	PREHISTORIC MAN IN EUROPE		
About 50,000 years ago EARLY STONE AGE	Beginning of 3d warm period. Climate grows warm.	Men are hunters. They know the use of fire.	First stone tools. Use of the first hatchet. Flint chipped by pounding.
MIDDLE STONE AGE	Beginning of 4th glacial period. Climate grows cold. Reindeer are plentiful.	Men are still hunters. They begin to live in caves. Clothing of skin sewed with bone needles. Cave walls decorated with drawings. Dead buried under family hearth.	Flint tools sharpened by pressing along edge with hard bone. Ivory tools. Weapons of bone, wood, and flint. Bone whistles.
LATE STONE AGE About 10,000 B. C. Period Begins	Beginning of 4th warm period (which includes present time).	Men hunt; women learn to plant seed and to harvest. Wooden dwellings along streams. Pile dwellings in Swiss lakes. Agriculture leads to permanent settlements. Towns. Primitive commerce. Wars among communities. Rise of nomad tribes, herdsmen, in country east of the Danube.	Polished flint and stone tools. Tools ground on whetstones. Earliest use of the plow. Pottery made.
Period closes about 3000 B. C.	Metals (copper) discovered, probably in peninsula of Sinai, as early as 4000 B. C.; introduced in southeastern Europe about 3000 B. C.; in Britain about 2000 B. C. Bronze age begins.		

B. C.	FROM EARLIEST RECORDS TO THE EIGHTH CENTURY B. C.		
	ASIA	EUROPE	EGYPT
			4241. Solar calendar adopted; earliest dated event in history.
4000	Sumerians in Babylonia. Cuneiform writing in use.		4000. By this date copper tools and hieroglyphic writing were in use. Before 3500, Egyptians had an alphabet of 24 letters. 3400. Two kingdoms of Upper and Lower Egypt united. 3400–2400. "Old Kingdom" period; capital at Memphis. 3050 (about). Earliest stone masonry.
3000	By this time, the Sumerians had built a civilized state in Babylonia.	3000 (about). Ægeans use metal tools and weapons. Rise of Cretan civilization.	3000–2500. Age of pyramid building. 3000. Book of the Dead already venerable. Egyptians have seagoing ships. Great progress in woodworking, paper making, weaving, glassmaking, metal working, pottery, and painting. Portrait sculpture.
3000 (about)	Canaanites settling in Palestine. Nineveh a trading city.		
3050–2750 (about)	Age of Sumerian city-states in Babylonia.		
2800 (about)	Sargon I builds a strong Babylonian kingdom (Akkad).		
2500	Parent people of Indo-Europeans living on steppes east of Caspian Sea. They have the horse, domestic oxen, and wheeled carts.	2200. Egyptian influence in Crete.	
2150 (about)	Hammurabi makes Babylon the center of a powerful state.		
2000 (about)	Hittites (in Asia Minor) use hieroglyphic writing. Light-skinned Indo-Europeans settle in the Punjab. Establishment of Vedic culture.	2000 (about). Indo-Europeans in the Balkan peninsula. Bronze and copper in use in Norse countries.	2000. Egyptian mathematics well developed. 2000–1500 (about). Feudal Age in Egypt. 1800 (about). The Hyksos gain control of Egypt.
	Barbarian Kassites from the East conquer Babylonia. They introduce the horse, the training of which they learned from Indo-European tribes of the North.	1700. Cretan influence in Greece.	1700 (about). Horse introduced. Cliff tombs. Oldest libraries found in tombs of nobles.

B. C.	From Earliest Records to the Eighth Century B. C.—Con.		
	Asia	**Europe**	**Egypt**
			Development of literature and government, religion, and ideas of social justice and kindness.
1600 (about)	Feudal system extended throughout China.	1600–1100. Cretan (Ægean) civilization at its height.	1580–1150. Egypt a world power. Period of the New Kingdom. Development of monotheism in religion.
1400 (?)	Hindu kingdoms established on the Ganges.		
1400 (about)	Hebrews and Arameans settle in Syria and Palestine.		
1200 (about)	Exodus of Hebrews from Egypt, led by Moses.	1200. Rise of Mycenæ and Tiryns in Greece. 1193–1184. Conquest and destruction of Troy.	
1140–1040 (about)	Era of the Judges in Israel.	1100–750 (about). Homeric Age in Greece, Asia Minor, Ægean islands.	1180–1050. Decline of the New Kingdom.
1025 (about)	Reign of Saul in Israel.		
1010–975	Reign of David; kingdom of Israel at its zenith.		
1000 (about)	Ionians settle in Asia Minor. Phœnicians become powerful.		
975–935 (about)	Reign of Solomon in Palestine.		
935	Israel divided into northern kingdom (Israel) and southern kingdom (Judah).		926. Shishak, king of Egypt, invades Palestine.
10th Century	Alphabet, without vowel signs, in use by Phœnicians.	900–700. Greek epic poetry is at its zenith. Age of Homer.	
860–825	Shalmaneser II, a great warrior, reigns in Assyria and makes conquests in western Asia. He defeats Ahab, king of Israel, and his allies in battle of Karkar (854).	820 (?). Lycurgus introduces many reforms in Sparta.	814 (?). Carthage founded.

B. C.	From the Eighth Century B. C. to the Greco-Persian Wars, About 490 B. C.				
	Arts of Civilization	**Judah**	**Israel**	**Asia and Africa**	**Europe**
8th Cent.	Coinage in Lydia. Period of the great writing prophets in Judah and Israel.		782–741. Reign of Jeroboam II. Period of Amos and Hosea.		
776	Olympic games. Beginning of first Olympiad.				
763	A solar eclipse recorded in this year; it determines dates in Assyrian chronology.	740–701. Period of the ministry of Isaiah.	734–732. Pekah, king of Israel, is deposed and slain. Hoshea appointed in his place.	745. Pul, or Tiglath-Pileser II, seizes the throne of Assyria. 732. Damascus taken by Tiglath-Pileser.	753. Building of Rome (legend). 734. Syracuse and Corcyra are founded by the Corinthians.
		728–697. Hezekiah, king; abolishes idolatry; makes alliance with Egypt.	722. Samaria taken by the Assyrians. End of the kingdom of Israel.	722. Sargon II, king of Assyria, takes Samaria and carries the Ten Tribes into captivity.	721. Sybaris founded in Magna Græcia by Achæans.
700 (about)	Writing common among the Greeks.	Sennacherib invades Judah. His army destroyed by pestilence.	705. Sennacherib, king of Nineveh.		
700–460	Lyric poetry flourishes in Greece.	697–642. Manasseh, king; carried to Babylon; afterward restored to throne.	681. Babylon and Nineveh are united under Esarhaddon.		678. Argæus, first king of Macedon. 665. First naval battle recorded in history, between the Corinthians and Corcyræans.
	Spherical form of the earth and true cause of lunar eclipses taught by Thales, who also discovered the electricity of amber.		660. First mikado of Japan, named Jimmu Tenno. 657. Byzantium founded.	**Egypt** 660 (about). Psammetichus, king of Egypt. Memphis becomes the capital.	645. Second Messenian war in Greece. 629. Periander rules Corinth.
		622 (about). Religious reform. Prophet Jeremiah.	624. Greeks from Thera found a new colony in Libya, named Cyrene.		
621	Draconian code formulated.	621. Book of Deuteronomy discovered at Jerusalem.			

B. C.	From the Eighth Century B. C. to the Greco-Persian Wars, About 490 B. C.—Con.				
	Arts of Civilization	**Judah**	**Babylonia**	**Egypt**	**Europe**
610	Pharaoh Necho begins a canal between the Mediterranean and Red Sea. Many lives lost in the attempt. He also sent out a Phœnician fleet which circumnavigated Africa.	609. Battle of Megiddo. Judah subject to Egypt. 605. Battle of Carchemish; Judah subject to Babylon.	606. Nineveh a second time destroyed. 605. Nebuchadnezzar defeats Necho of Egypt; invades Judea. Battle of Carchemish.	609. Pharaoh Necho, king of Egypt.	
6th Cent.	Taoism, a system of philosophy, founded in China by Lao Tzu. Written laws in existence in Crete.				600 (about). Foundation of Massilia (Marseille).
594	Solon's code supersedes that of Draco in Athens.			589 (about). Pharaoh-Hophra, king of Egypt.	594. Solon, archon of Athens.
586?	Pythian games established at Delphi.	586. Captivity of Judah completed. Jerusalem destroyed. Jews carried to Babylon. Prophet Ezekiel.			
582?	Establishment of Nemean games in Greece.				
578	Money coined at Rome by Servius Tullius. (Legend)		573. Nebuchadnezzar takes Tyre.	569. Amasis, king of Egypt, makes alliance with Greece.	578. Servius Tullius, king of Rome. (Legend)
		Persia			
		558. Persian Empire founded by Cyrus.	562. Crœsus, king of Lydia, subjects Asia Minor.	568. Egypt invaded by Nebuchadnezzar.	600–500 (about). Etruscans supreme in Italy.
557	Gautama Buddha is born.		556–539. Nabonidus rules in Babylon.		
551 (about)	Era of Confucian philosophy in China.	546. Cyrus conquers Lydia. 539. Cyrus takes Babylon. 537. Jews returned to Palestine; Zerubbabel, leader.			
					Rome, Etc.
		529. Death of Cyrus; Cambyses, king of Persia.			534–510. Tarquin the Proud, king. 530. Cadiz built by the Carthaginians.
			Greece		
			527. Pisistratus dies.		
525–456	Æschylus, greatest of the Greek tragic poets; won thirteen contests; defeated in 468 by Sophocles.	525. Cambyses conquers Egypt and makes it a Persian province. Psammetichus, last king of Egypt. 522–486. Darius I, king of Persia.		525. Egypt becomes a Persian province.	
				Macedonia	
		516. Second temple at Jerusalem completed. 508 (about). Darius conquers the Punjab.	510. Followers of Pisistratus expelled; democracy established at Athens.		509 (about). The Tarquins expelled from Rome. Patrician commonwealth established. Brutus and Collatinus, first consuls. Roman treaty with Carthage.
500 (about)	Voyage of Hanno, a Carthaginian, down west coast of Africa.				
500–406	Tragedy flourishes at Athens.				
5th Cent.	Use of water clock in Greece. Hippocrates begins development of medical science.	499 (about). The Ionians revolt and burn Sardis. 494. The Persians destroy Miletus.		498. Alexander I rules in Macedonia.	496. Romans win battle at Lake Regillus. 494. Tribunes of the people chosen. 491. Coriolanus banished.

B. C.	From the Battle of Marathon to the Death of Alexander the Great—B. C. 490–323				
	Arts of Civilization	Persia	Greece	Macedonia	Rome, Etc
		490. Darius sends an army into Greece. 486. Xerxes, king of Persia. 481. Expedition of Xerxes into Greece; destroys Athens.	490. Battle of Marathon. Persians under Datis defeated (Sept. 12). 483. Aristides banished. 480. Battle of Thermopylæ. Battle of Salamis and defeat of Persians. 479. Battle of Platæa; Persian fleet destroyed at Mycale. 478–477. Themistocles rebuilds Athens.		486. Agrarian riots at Rome; the patricians kill Spurius Cassius. 480. Carthaginians defeated. Hamilcar killed in battle.
477	Death of Buddha; first Buddhistic council held at Rajagriha.		477. Sparta assumes conduct of war.		
469	Socrates born.				
		465. Xerxes assassinated. Artaxerxes I, king. 458. Ezra arrives at Jerusalem.	461. Pericles impresses himself upon Greek affairs. 457–455. Sparta wars on Athens.		460 (about). Cincinnatus, consul. 458 (about). Cincinnatus, dictator.
456	Æschylus dies at Gela in Sicily. The Secular games instituted at Rome.		456. Long walls of Athens completed.	454. Perdiccas II reigns in Macedonia.	450 (about). Laws of the 12 tables.
446	Herodotus, the historian, in Athens.	445. Nehemiah comes on a mission to Jerusalem. Walls of Jerusalem rebuilt by Nehemiah.	446. First Peloponnesian war ended.		
438	The Parthenon completed at Athens.		431. Second Peloponnesian war begun.		
429	Birth of Plato.		429. Death of Pericles.		
427	Aristophanes produces first comedy at Athens.		415. Expedition against Syracuse. 413. Expedition ends in failure. 411. Athens governed by the "400." Alliance of Sparta with Persia. 409. Capture of Byzantium by Athenians. 404. Surrender of Athens and end of war.	413. Archelaus, patron of learning, seizes the throne and kills Perdiccas.	413. Egypt regains independence.
399	Death of Socrates.	401. Cyrus the Younger defeated. Retreat of the 10,000 under Xenophon.		399. Archelaus murdered. The Illyrians invade Macedonia. 394–370. Reign of Amyntas.	
390	Inauguration of Capitoline games at Rome.	387. Greek cities of Asia made tributary to Persia.			390. Rome destroyed by the Gauls.
383	Birth of Demosthenes.				
377	Second Buddhistic council assembles at Vesali.		371. Battle of Leuctra. Predominance of Thebes. 362. Battle of Mantinea; death of Epaminondas; end of Theban power. Decline of Greek city-states.	359. Philip II, king; institutes the Macedonian phalanx; defeats the Athenians.	376. War between patricians and plebeians. Lucius Sextus, first plebeian consul. 371. Curule magistrates appointed. 367. Licinian laws passed after ten-year struggle; patricians and plebeians are granted equal rights.
354	Demosthenes makes his first appearance in public in an affair of state.			356. Philip II conquers Thrace and Illyria. Birth of Alexander the Great.	

B. C.	From the Battle of Marathon to the Death of Alexander the Great—B. C. 490–323—Con.				
	Arts of Civilization	Persia	Greece	Macedonia	Rome, Etc.
351	Demosthenes delivers the first of his orations, known afterward as "Philippics."				348. Commercial treaty between Rome and Carthage.
347	Plato dies.				
344 (about)	The philosophers, Zeno and Epicurus, flourish.	344. Aristotle visits Mytilene.		341. War against the Athenians.	343. Samnian war; continued fifty-three years. 340. War with the Latins. They obtain rights of Roman citizens.
			339. War with Macedonia.	338. Athenians and Thebans defeated at Chæronea.	337. First plebeian prætor.
		336. Darius III, king.	336. Philip slain. Thebes destroyed.	336. Alexander the Great succeeds to the throne.	
			335. Greeks conquered by Alexander the Great.	335. Alexander the Great conquers Greeks and leads army against Persians.	
		334. Alexander the Great invades Persia.		334. Alexander the Great invades Persia; defeats Darius at the Granicus. 333. Battle of Issus. 332. Egypt conquered by Alexander; Alexandria built.	332. Roman treaty with Alexander of Epirus.
		331. Battle of Arbela. 330. Darius III murdered. Alexander founds the Grecian, or Macedonian, monarchy.	330. Æschines, the orator, banished. 324. Demosthenes banished.	327. Alexander invades India.	
323	Aristotle founds Lyceum in Athens.			323. Ptolemy I restores the independence of Egypt. Alexander the Great dies in Babylonia.	

B. C.	From the Death of Alexander the Great to the Roman Conquest of Carthage and Corinth—B. C. 323–146					
	Arts of Civilization	Rome, Etc.	Macedonia	Greece	Asia Minor, Syria, Judea, India, China	Egypt, Carthage
322	Demosthenes dies at Calauria; Aristotle dies at Chalcis.	321. Roman army surrenders to the Samnites.			320 (about). Founding of empire of Magadha in India.	320 (about). Ptolemy I, called Soter, makes a military expedition into Palestine; takes Jerusalem.
		319. Samnites defeated at Luceria.	319. Cassander assumes the throne of Macedon.	319. Polyperchon succeeds Antipater. 318 (about). Birth of Pyrrhus II, greatest hero of his time. 317. Demetrius Phalereus governs Athens. 315. Cassander rebuilds Thebes.	315 (about). Maurya dynasty founded in India by Chandragupta.	317–275. Wars between the Sicilian Greeks and the Carthaginians.
312	Appian Way begun by Appius Claudius.	312. War with the Etruscans.			312. Seleucus I retakes Babylon and restores its independence. 301. Battle of Ipsus, Alexander's empire divided anew into four parts: Syria, Macedon, Greece, Egypt.	
300 (about)	Euclid, the celebrated mathematician, writes on geometry. The Indian epic *Ramayana* composed.	287. Law of Hortensius, by which the decrees of the people had the force of those of the senate.	288. Lysimachus, king of Thrace, subdues Macedonia.	294. Demetrius murders King Alexander and seizes throne of Macedon.		

B. C.	From the Death of Alexander the Great to the Roman Conquest of Carthage and Corinth—B. C. 323–146—Con.					
	Arts of Civilization	Rome, Etc.	Macedonia	Greece	Asia Minor, Syria, Judea, India, China	Egypt, Carthage
285 (about)	Science and literature flourish at the Museum of Alexandria. The work of translating the Hebrew Scriptures into Greek for the Jews at Alexandria is begun. Era of bucolic poetry. Theocritus writes his famous idyls.	280. Pyrrhus in Italy. 280–275. The Tarentine war. 275. Pyrrhus defeated by the Romans at Beneventum; date of Rome's supremacy.	281. Pyrrhus of Epirus aids Tarentum in Italy. 274. Pyrrhus invades Macedonia, defeats Antigonus, and is proclaimed king. 272. Antigonus restored.	280. The Achæan League formed. 278. Invasion by the Gauls, who are routed by the Greeks at Delphi.	285. The Scythians invade Bosporus. 281. Antiochus Soter succeeds Seleucus in Syria. 278. Settlement of Gauls in Asia Minor. Later they became the Galatians.	285. Ptolemy Philadelphus, king of Egypt. 283. Death of Ptolemy Soter. 276. A Carthaginian fleet defeats Pyrrhus of Epirus.
270	Epicurus, the philosopher, dies.					
269 (about)	Silver money first coined at Rome.	266. Rome mistress of all Italy. 264. First Punic war begun.	268. Second incursion of the Gauls.	268. Athens taken by Antigonus.		
263	Aristarchus teaches that the earth moves around the sun.		250. Parthia revolts from Macedon.	255. Athens joins the Achæan League.	260. Asoka, the king of Magadha, brings northern India beneath his rule.	
246 (?)	The building of the Great Wall of China begun under the emperor Chi Hwang-ti.	241. End of first Punic war.			246 (?). Chi Hwang-ti first autocratic emperor of China; destroys feudalism and extends empire to its modern limit. 246. Death of Antiochus II. 226. Seleucus III, king of Syria.	246. Ptolemy Euergetes subdues Syria.
224 (about)	Archimedes makes known his discoveries in mechanics.	225. The Gauls repulsed in Italy. 219. Hannibal takes Saguntum and crosses the Alps. 218. Second Punic war. Hannibal defeats the Romans at the Ticinus and the Trebia. 216. Varro at Cannæ totally defeated by Hannibal. 214. First Macedonian war.	220. Philip V assists the Achæans against the Ætolians. 217. Philip V makes peace with the Ætolians at Naupactus. 214. Alliance of Philip and Hannibal.	220. The Social war begins, between Achæan and Ætolian leagues.	223. Death of Asoka, king of Magadha. 222. Antiochus the Great, king of Syria. 219. War between Antiochus and Ptolemy. 217. Ptolemy defeats Antiochus at Raphia.	221. Ptolemy Philopator, king.
213	Burning of the books by Chi Hwang-ti, the Chinese emperor.					
206	Revival of classics and general learning in China.	206. Carthaginians driven out of Spain.		206. Spartans defeated at Mantinea.	206. Founding of Han dynasty of China.	205. Ptolemy Epiphanes, king.
204	Death of Livius Andronicus who translated the *Odyssey*; first of Latin dramatic writers.	202. Hannibal defeated by Scipio at Zama in Africa. End of war.				

From the Death of Alexander the Great to the Roman Conquest of Carthage and Corinth—B. C. 323–146—Con.

B. C.	Arts of Civilization	Rome, Etc.	Macedonia	Greece	Asia Minor, Syria, Judea, India, China		Egypt, Carthage
204—con.	The Great Wall of China completed.	201. Second Macedonian war. 190. Rome shatters power of Syria.	201. Second war with Rome. 197. Philip V defeated at Cynoscephalæ.	198. Achæan League makes first treaty with Rome. Achæans and Spartans join the Romans against Macedon.	198. Jews assist Antiochus in expelling the Egyptian troops from Jerusalem. 190. Scipio Africanus defeats Antiochus at Magnesia. 187. Antiochus killed. Syria becomes temporarily a Roman province.		198. Egypt loses her Syrian possessions.
					Syria	Judea	
					187. Seleucus IV, king.		
184	Death of Plautus, foremost among the early Roman writers of comedy.		179. Reign of Perseus. 171. Third war with Rome.		175. Antiochus IV, king.	170. Jerusalem plundered by Antiochus Epiphanes.	182. Ptolemy Philometor, king. 175. Cato's embassy to Carthage.
169	Death of Ennius, first of the great Roman epic poets.		168. Perseus defeated at Pydna.	167. Romans enter Achæa.		168. Jews persecuted by Antiochus; the temple of Jerusalem defiled.	
166	Book of Daniel probably written in this year.					165. Judas Maccabeus expels the Syrians. 161. Treaty with Romans.	
156 (about)	Paper made in China.						
149	Death of Cato the Censor, historian and economist.	149. Third Punic war begins. 146. Conquest of Carthage and Corinth. Greece annexed to the Roman Empire.	146. Macedonia becomes a Roman province.	146. Corinth destroyed by the Romans. Greece becomes a Roman province under the name Achæa.			150. Massinissa defeats the Carthaginians. 146. Carthage destroyed by the Romans. Ptolemy Physcon becomes sole king of Egypt.

From the Roman Conquest of Carthage and Corinth to the Birth of Christ—B. C. 146–4

B. C.	Arts of Civilization	Rome, Etc.	Syria	Judea	Egypt, Carthage
		133. Spain becomes a Roman province. 123. Caius Gracchus, tribune, endeavors to follow out constitutional reforms advocated by his brother; is killed. 113. First great migration of the German nations.	139–129. Antiochus VII, king.	135–105. John Hyrcanus reigns as prince and high priest in Jerusalem.	130. Physcon driven from his throne for cruelty. 107. Alexander I, king of Egypt.
104	A new calendar is adopted in China on the calculations of Ssu-ma Ch'ien; the Chinese date their chronology from this epoch.	102. Battle of Aquæ Sextiæ. Marius defeats Teutones. 101. Battle of Vercellæ. Marius defeats the Cimbri. 100. Birth of Julius Cæsar.		104. War with Egypt.	
91	First comprehensive history of China written by Ssu-ma Ch'ien.	91–88. Social war in Italy.			

From the Roman Conquest of Carthage and Corinth to the Birth of Christ—B. C. 146–4—Con.

B. C.	Arts of Civilization	Rome, Etc.	Syria	Judea	Egypt, Carthage
88	Texts of Buddha transferred to Pali writing in Ceylon.	88. War with Pontus. 82. Sulla defeats Marius and is created dictator.			81. Alexander II, king of Egypt. 80. Ptolemy Auletes, king.
			66. Mithridates, the Parthian emperor, defeated by Pompey.		
		64. Syria becomes a Roman province. 63. Cicero, consul. Catiline's conspiracy detected and suppressed by Cicero. 60. First triumvirate,—Pompey, Crassus, and Cæsar. 59. Cæsar, consul.	64. Syria passes under Rome.	63. Judea a Roman province.	
55	Death of Lucretius Carus, poet and philosopher.	55. Cæsar passes the Rhine, defeats the Germans and Gauls, and invades Britain. 53. Crassus defeated and killed in Parthia. 51. Cæsar completes conquest of Gaul, which becomes a Roman province. 49. Civil war between Cæsar and Pompey. Pompey defeated; Cæsar, dictator. 48. Battle of Pharsalus—Pompey defeated by Cæsar. Death of Pompey in Egypt.			55. Auletes restored. 51. Cleopatra driven from throne of Egypt.
47	Library at Alexandria said to have been destroyed.	47. Cæsar takes Alexandria and conquers Egypt.			47. Cleopatra, with her brother, Ptolemy XV, on throne of Egypt. 46. The African war.
45	Cæsar reforms the calendar by introducing the solar for the lunar year.	44. Cæsar assassinated. Antony, master of Rome. 43. Second triumvirate,—Octavius Cæsar, Mark Antony, and Lepidus. 42. Battle of Philippi; defeat and death of Brutus and Cassius.			
39 (?)	Pollio founds first public library at Rome.	31. Battle of Actium. Antony defeated. Octavius, master of Roman world. 27. Titles of Augustus and Emperor conferred on Octavius for ten years.			31. Defeat at Actium. 30. Suicide of Antony and Cleopatra. Egypt passes to Rome.
		19. Conquest of Spain completed. Death of Virgil. 15. Austria and other territory conquered by Drusus is added to the Empire.			
8	Calendar corrected by Augustus.	4 or 6 (about). Birth of Christ.			

From the Birth of Christ to the Fall of Rome—B. C. 4–A. D. 476

A. D.	Arts of Civilization	Development of Christianity	The Roman Empire
			6. Romans abandon Germany. 14. Augustus dies at Nola; is succeeded by Tiberius as emperor.
		29. Crucifixion of Jesus.	29. Agrippina banished. 37. Tiberius succeeded by Caligula, noted for his profligacy. 41. Claudius, emperor.
46	Birth of Plutarch, Greek biographer and moralist.	44–66. Judea under the Roman procurators. 47–48. Paul's first missionary tour; into Asia Minor.	46. Thrace becomes a Roman province. 47. The Romans subjugate southern Britain. 48. Claudius orders a census to be taken.
50 (about)	Development of realistic sculpture in Rome.	49–52. Paul's second missionary tour; reaches Athens and Corinth. 52–56. Paul's third missionary tour; long residence at Ephesus. 59 or 60. Paul a prisoner in Rome.	49. He expels the Jews from Rome. Builds a camp on the site of London. 51. Caractacus, king of the Britons, is brought to Rome in chains. 54. Nero, emperor; a profligate and tyrant.
		64 or 65. Martyrdom of Paul and Peter.	61. Revolt of the Britons under Queen Boadicea. 64. Nero sets fire to Rome; accuses Christians. 68. Galba, emperor. 69. Otho, emperor. Vitellius defeats Otho. Vespasian defeats Vitellius.
		70. Destruction of Jerusalem by Titus.	70. Vespasian, emperor.

A. D.	From the Birth of Christ to the Fall of Rome—B. C. 4–A. D. 476—Con.			
	Arts of Civilization	Development of Christianity	The Roman Empire	
75	Vespasian undertakes the building of the Colosseum.			
78	Era of Shalivahana, or Shaka, in India.		78. Agricola, governor of Britain; completes conquest as far north as Scottish Highlands. 79. Titus, emperor. Pompeii and Herculaneum destroyed by Vesuvius.	
	Jurisprudence flourishes.		81. Domitian, emperor.	
	Forum built. Pillar of Trajan, and Baths.	95. Persecution of the Christians by Domitian.	96. Nerva, emperor. 98. Trajan, emperor; Roman Empire at its greatest extent.	
	Bridge built over the Danube. Silver Age of Roman literature.	107. Persecution by Trajan. 118. Persecution by Hadrian.	117. Hadrian, emperor; makes a journey through the provinces; visits Britain and builds there a wall from the Tyne to Solway Firth; builds a wall from the Rhine to the Danube.	
130 (about)	Great buildings of Palmyra. The Pantheon built at Rome.	134. Heresy of Marcion.	138. Antoninus, emperor.	
		150. Canon of Scriptures fixed about this time.	145–152. Antoninus defeats the Moors, Jews, and Brigantes. Antoninus partly stops the persecution of the Christians. 161. Marcus Aurelius, emperor.	
166 (?)	Apuleius writes the *Golden Ass*, one of the earliest romances.		166. Very destructive Asiatic plague in the empire. 191. Rome nearly destroyed by fire. 193. Septimius Severus, emperor. A vigorous ruler. Emperors (to 284) appointed by the army. 194. Septimius Severus besieges Byzantium.	
		202. Persecution under Severus.	208. Severus builds the wall of Severus in Britain. 226. Artaxerxes begins the new kingdom of Persia. 232. Persian war.	
		235. Persecution under Maximinus.	240 (about). The Franks appear in history. 248. Celebration of 1000th anniversary of the founding of Rome.	
		250. Persecution of the Christians.	253–268. Goths invade Asia Minor and Greece. 261. Sapor, the Persian, takes Antioch.	
		262. Paul, bishop of Samosata, denies the divinity of Jesus Christ.	264. Alliance with Odenathus, king of Palmyra, who is succeeded by his wife Zenobia, who reigns with the titles of "Augusta" and "Queen of the East." 270. Aurelian, a great warrior, becomes emperor. 271. Aurelian defeats the Alemanni.	
		272. Persecution of Christians under Aurelian.	272. Zenobia conquers Egypt. 273. Aurelian reduces Palmyra and takes Queen Zenobia prisoner. 274. Franks, Spain, and Britain reduced to obedience. 275. Aurelian killed near Byzantium. 276. Great wall around Rome completed.	
		277. The emperor Probus expels the Germans from Gaul. 283 (about). Religious ceremonies multiplied. Pagan rites imitated by the Christians.	284. Diocletian, emperor.	
		296. Monks in Spain and Egypt. 303. Persecution under Diocletian.	296. Diocletian divides the empire among four assistant rulers.	
305 (about)	Constantine's Basilica built at Rome.	311. Galerius recognizes Christianity.	305. Diocletian and Maximian resign the empire to Constantius and Galerius.	
		313. Edict of Milan proclaims religious toleration. 325. Council of Nicæa.	324. Constantine the Great, first Christian emperor. 330. Founding of Constantinople. 337. Death of Constantine; accession of his three sons to the empire.	
		339. Persecution of Christians in Persia.	364. Death of Jovian; accession of Valentinian and Valens, under whom the empire is divided.	
			Western Empire	Eastern Empire
			364. Valentinian, emperor. 368. The Picts and Scots invade Britain, but are defeated by Theodosius.	364. Valens, emperor.
		373. Bible translated into Gothic language. Death of Athanasius.	375. Valentinian gains victory over the Germans.	376. Hungary, ancient Pannonia, invaded by the Huns, from whom it is named.
		379. Prerogatives of the Roman See much enlarged.		379. Theodosius the Great becomes emperor; a zealous supporter of Christianity.

A. D.	From the Birth of Christ to the Fall of Rome—B. C. 4–A. D. 476—Con.			
	Arts of Civilization	**Development of Christianity**	**Western Empire**	**Eastern Empire**
382	St. Jerome revises the Latin version of the New Testament at Rome.	381. Second general Council of Constantinople. 384. Symmachus pleads in the Roman Senate for paganism against St. Ambrose. 392. St. Chrysostom, patriarch of Constantinople.	388. St. Patrick taken captive to Ireland by Niall of the Nine Hostages. 392. Theodosius becomes sole emperor of the East and West.	388. Theodosius defeats Maximus, the tyrant of the Western Empire.
394	Olympian games abolished.		394. Final division of empire between the sons of Theodosius. 401. Europe overrun by the Visigoths. 406–409. Vandals allowed to settle in Spain and Gaul. 410. The Goths under Alaric sack and burn Rome. 412. Rise of the Vandal power in Spain. 413. Burgundian kingdom begun near the Rhine.	408. Theodosius II, a child, emperor. 410. Honorius abdicates his kingship of Britain.
420	St. Jerome dies, after completing translation of the Bible (Vulgate).	416. The Pelagian heresy condemned.	420. The Franks form a kingdom, under Pharamond, on the lower Rhine. 425. Valentinian III, emperor.	414. Regency of the emperor's sister, Pulcheria. 420. Persian war. 425. University of Constantinople organized.
426	St. Augustine of Hippo publishes his famous work *De Civitate Dei*, "The City of God."	431. Third general Council at Ephesus. 432. St. Patrick preaches the Gospel in Ireland. 435. Nestorianism prevails in the East. 443. The Manichean books burned in Rome.	439. The Vandals, under Genseric, form Kingdom of Africa, take Carthage, and plunder Italy.	442. Thrace invaded by Attila.
450	Establishment of Buddhism in Burma.	447. Eutyches asserts the existence of only one nature in Jesus Christ. 451. Fourth general Council at Chalcedon.	449–455. Arrival of Saxons in Britain. 451. Battle of Châlons. Attila driven back east of Rhine. 452. City of Venice founded. 455. Rome plundered by Vandals. 458. Franks, under Childeric I, conquer as far as the Loire and take Paris.	450. Marcian, emperor. 457–461. War with the Goths. 457–484. Peroz rules in Persia.
473	Topography of Japan written for the first time by Ki no Tsuno no Sukune.	465–476. Oligarchy of the bishops of Rome, Constantinople, Alexandria, Antioch, and Jerusalem. The Church now begins to assume a political aspect.	466–483. The Visigoths under Eric establish their kingdom in Spain. 476. Odoacer, king of the Heruli, takes Rome and founds a short-lived kingdom lasting fourteen years. With him ends the Roman Empire and ancient history in Europe.	474. Zeno, emperor; a turbulent reign marked by debauchery and conspiracies.

A. D.	From the Fall of Rome to the Division of the Western Empire—A. D. 476–843				
	Arts of Civilization	**The Eastern Empire**	**Great Britain and Ireland**	**Italy and the Church**	**France**
	Fifth Century				
		477. A rising in Constantinople.	477. Saxons win foothold in Sussex. Followed by other Saxons (Wessex and Essex) and by Angles.	482. Christians persecuted by the Vandals.	481. Clovis I, founder of the French monarchy. 486. Battle of Soissons gained by Clovis.
493	Theodoric gives new impetus to architecture in Italy. Beautiful buildings at Ravenna.	488. Theodoric, chief of the Ostrogoths, invades Italy.	491. Capture of Anderida by Ella, king of the South Saxons.	493. Italy conquered by Theodoric, chief of the Ostrogoths.	

From the Fall of Rome to the Division of the Western Empire—A. D. 476–843—Con.

A. D.	Arts of Civilization	The Eastern Empire	Great Britain and Ireland	Italy and the Church	France
			495. Beginning of the kingdom of Wessex, under Cerdic and Cymric.		496. Clovis baptized. Christianity introduced into France.
	Sixth Century				
	Cassiodorus (490–580), in his library and monastery, encourages learning.	503–505. War with Persia.		510. Boethius becomes consul at Rome.	510. Clovis makes Paris his capital.
524 (about)	*Consolations of Philosophy* by Boethius.		520. Battle of Mt. Badon. West Saxons defeated by Britons.	524. Boethius put to death by Theodoric. 526. Death of Theodoric.	
		527. Justinian I begins a brilliant reign over the Eastern, or Byzantine, Empire. 528. Belisarius, the famous general, defeats the Persians.		529. Order of the Benedictine monks instituted at Monte Cassino, near Naples.	
531	Khosru I, king of Persia, great patron of learning.				
532	The Christian era proposed and introduced by Dionysius, a monk.	533. Belisarius defeats the Vandals in Africa.			
	Completion of Justinian's code.	534. Belisarius takes possession of Africa, Sardinia, and Balearic Isles.			534. Burgundy conquered by the Franks.
	Manufacture of silk introduced from China into Europe by monks.	535. Belisarius subdues Sicily. 536. Belisarius takes Naples and Rome.		536. Italy conquered by Belisarius, for Justinian.	536. Ostrogoths surrender their possessions in Gaul to the Franks.
537	Church of Santa Sophia at Constantinople completed.			539. Milan ravaged by the Goths.	
	Alexander of Tralles, a noted physician, teaches prevention of disease as important part of physician's work.	548–553. Italy governed by Greek Exarchs. 552. Narses overthrows Totila. End of Ostrogothic kingdom. 558. A plague extends over Europe and Asia and lasts about fifty years.	547. Ida, king of Bernicia. 552. Cymric, king of West Saxons, captures Sorbiodunum. Master of Salisbury plain.		557. Church of St. Germain des Prés built at Paris. 558. Clothaire I, king; unites Franks into a kingdom.
	St. Benedict establishes his "rule," enjoining both labor and prayer. The Benedictines begin important work in agriculture and industry.	570. Birth of Mohammed.	Union of Celtic tribes, under name of Cymry, or Comrades. 593. Ethelbert, king of Kent, gains the ascendancy.	568. Italy conquered by the Lombards. 590. Gregory the Great, bishop of Rome. Beginning of the papacy. 597. St. Augustine, goes as missionary to Britain; made first archbishop of Canterbury.	561. Clothaire dies; kingdom again broken up into petty states.
	Seventh Century				
600	First code of English laws drawn up by Ethelbert.	602. Invasion of the Persians.	600 (about). St. Paul's church founded by Ethelbert of Kent.	608 (about). The Pantheon of Rome dedicated to Christianity.	
	Literature and learning fostered in English abbeys of Whitby and Glastonbury.	610. Heraclius takes Constantinople, kills Phocas, the emperor, and makes himself king.			613. Clothaire II, king. Franks again united under one king.
	Rise of Mohammedanism.	614. Jerusalem taken by the Persians.	St. Peter's (1050, Westminster Abbey) founded by Sebert of Essex.		
	Islamism and the power of the caliphs established in the East. In the caliphs were united the highest spiritual and regal authority.	622. The Hegira, or Mohammed's flight, from Mecca to Medina. 632. Death of Mohammed.	626. Edwin of Northumbria, overlord of English kingdoms.	625–640. Churches of Jerusalem, Antioch, and Alexandria lost to the Christian world by the sweep of Mohammedanism.	630 (about). Dagobert I builds the church of St. Denis, the sepulture of the French kings.
633 (about)	Isidore of Seville encourages learning in the West.	636. Omar, caliph, takes Jerusalem.	664. Synod of Whitby; triumph of Roman over Celtic Church.		

A. D.	From the Fall of Rome to the Division of the Western Empire—A. D. 476–843—Con.				
	Arts of Civilization	The Eastern Empire	Great Britain and Ireland	Italy and the Church	France
633 (about)–con.	Arts and crafts encouraged by Dagobert I, Frankish king.	673. Siege of Constantinople by the Saracens, whose fleet is destroyed by the Greek fire of Callinicus.	673. First English church council at Hertford.		
	Appreciation of art and literature preserved in Ravenna.	680. First kingdom of Bulgaria founded. 698. Carthage destroyed by the Saracens, and the north coast of Africa subjugated.	688–726. Ine, king of Wessex.	680. The sixth general Council called at Constantinople.	687. Pepin d'Heristal, mayor of the palace.
	EIGHTH CENTURY	709. North Africa subdued by the Saracens.			
	Charlemagne's schools provide for women as well as men.	711. Saracens cross over to Spain. 717. Leo III, emperor.			714. Charles Martel, mayor of the palace.
	Charlemagne founds hospitals.	718. The Saracens invest Constantinople, by land and sea. City saved by Greek fire.		726. The emperor Leo forbids image worship.	725. Charles Martel subdues Bavaria. 732. Charles Martel defeats the Saracens at battle of Tours.
	Three great scholars of the 8th century: Bede, John of Damascus, Vergilius of Salzburg.	746–747. A plague in Constantinople.	735. Death of the Venerable Bede.	751. The pope dethrones Childeric, king of France, by a papal decree. 754. Pepin aids Pope Stephen III against the Lombards.	751. End of Merovingian line of French kings. Pepin the Short, first of the Carolingian line.
	Golden period of learning in Arabia under Caliph Haroun-al-Raschid and Caliph Al-Mamun.	755–775. Constantine V wars with the Bulgarians. 762 (about). Caliph Al-Mansur builds Bagdad and makes it his capital.	757. Offa of Mercia begins his reign.	756. Donation of Pepin. Foundation of Papal States.	771. Charlemagne becomes sole ruler of Franks.
	Foundation of schools in monasteries and cathedrals by Charlemagne.	783. The Empire makes peace with the Arabs.	787. First recorded invasion of the Danes—the sea kings and vikings.	787. Seventh general Council of Nicæa.	
	NINTH CENTURY				
	Agriculture and horticulture encouraged by Charlemagne; both flourish in Spain under the caliphs.			800. Charlemagne reforms the Church. Many bishoprics founded.	800. Charlemagne founds the new Western Empire and is crowned at Rome, emperor of the Romans. 801. Charlemagne receives an embassy from Haroun-al-Raschid.
	Rapid growth of feudal system.	812. Peace between Michael I and Charlemagne.			814. Death of Charlemagne. His son, Louis the Pious, succeeds him.
		816. A council condemns the worship of images.	815–823. Egbert, king of Wessex, conquers the Britons in Cornwall.		
827 (about)	Arabian geographers calculate size of earth.	827. Arabia begins conquest of Sicily. 829. Theophilus, emperor.	827. The Anglo-Saxon kingdoms acknowledge Egbert, king of Wessex, as suzerain or overlord.	827–865. Christianity carried to Denmark and Sweden.	
	John Scotus Erigena, great scholar of the century.		839. Death of Egbert, king of the West Saxons, who had become overlord of the other kingdoms. Ethelwulf, king.		840. Louis the Debonair dies; his three sons fight for the possession of the kingdom.
		842. Theodora restores image worship.	About this time, Kenneth MacAlpin unites Picts and Scots in one kingdom.		841–844. The Northmen take Rouen and Nantes and advance to Toulouse. 843. Treaty of Verdun.
	Venetians become a great merchant people. Architecture encouraged in Venice. St. Mark's cathedral built.				Charles I, king of France. Louis I, king of Germany. Lothair, king of Italy.

A. D.	From the Division of the Western Empire to the Norman Conquest of England—A. D. 843–1066			
	Arts of Civilization	Italy and the Church	Eastern Empire	The British Isles
		844. Ignatius, patriarch of Constantinople. 846. The Saracens destroy the Venetian fleet and besiege Rome. 850. Persecution of the Christians in Spain.	844 (about). Decline of the caliphate begins. Frequent wars between the Greeks and the Saracens.	851. Danes capture and sack Canterbury and London. 855. Danes begin to settle in England.
		860. The False Decretals brought to Rome.		
866 (about)	Bible translated into Slavonian.	866. Schism of the Greeks begins.	866. Synod of Constantinople. Break between Eastern and Western Church. 867. Basil inaugurates the Macedonian dynasty.	866–870. Danish conquest of Northumbria.
	Alfred gives great encouragement to literature and learning in England; founds schools; codifies English law.	869. Eighth Council at Constantinople.		871. Alfred the Great becomes king of Wessex.
		877. Arabs take Syracuse.		878. Alfred defeats the Danes. Treaty of Chippenham. Danes retain eastern and northern England.
882	First mention of episcopal school at Paris,—later became university.		886. Leo VI, emperor.	886. Danes surrender London to Alfred.
	The Moors in Spain promote architecture and adorn their cities with rich buildings.		890. Southern Italy subject to the Greek Empire. Seat of power at Bari.	
	Cordova, in Spain, becomes famous as a center of science, learning, industry, and commerce.	911 (about). The Normans in France embrace Christianity.	907. Russian expedition under Oleg against Constantinople.	899 (?). Edward the Elder succeeds Alfred. At his death in 925 he was overlord of all the kingdoms.
	The figures of arithmetic brought into Europe by the Saracens.	921 (about). The Bohemians adopt Christianity.	919. Romanus, general of the fleet, usurps the empire and rules with his three sons.	
	Linens and woolens manufactured in Flanders.			925. Athelstan, king.
932	Printing in use in China. Confucian Canon printed.			
	Hroswitha, the nun at Gandersheim, writes comedies to counteract evil influence of classical plays.		941. Romanus gains a naval victory over the Russians.	937. Athelstan defeats the northern king at Brunanburh. 943. Malcolm I, king of Scotland.
		955. Baptism of Olga; conversion of Russia to Christianity. 959. St. Dunstan, archbishop of Canterbury, attempts to reform the Church. 962. Otto crowned emperor of the Romans by Pope John XII. Holy Roman Empire of the German Nation.	959. Emperor Romanus II. 966. Miecislas, king of Poland, becomes a Christian. 969. The Fatimites subjugate Egypt.	955. Dunstan, abbot of Glastonbury, rises to great power.
980	Birth of Avicenna, Arabic writer on medicine.			984. Renewed Danish invasions.

A. D.	From the Division of the Western Empire to the Norman Conquest of England—A. D. 843–1066				
	France	**Germany**	**Spain**	**Russia**	**Lesser Countries**
		843. Louis I, king.			
845	Northmen take Rouen and sack Paris.				
847	Defense against the inroads of the Northmen occasions the Edict of Mersen, which required every man to have a feudal lord.	847. Raid of the Northmen up the Elbe as far as Hamburg. 855. Louis II becomes king.	850 (about). Under Abderrahman II and his successors, caliphate of Cordova enters period of weakness.		
857	Charles the Bald and Lothair II unite against the Northmen.				
858	Louis of Germany makes war on Charles and Lothair, and is defeated.	860. Peace between Louis and Charles of France.		860. Russian campaign against Constantinople. 862. Rurik the Northman, grand duke of Novgorod.	860. Gorm unites Jutland and the Danish Isles and becomes king of Denmark. 861 (about). Iceland discovered.
			866. Alfonso the Great becomes king of Asturia, the Christian monarchy in Spain, afterward called León.		
870	Lorraine divided between France and Germany by Treaty of Mersen.		873. Sancho Iñigo, count of Navarre.		872. Harold, first king of Norway. 874. Northmen colonize Iceland.
876	First settlement of Northmen in France.	876. Charles the Fat, emperor 880–888.			
879	Louis III and Carloman reign jointly.	881. Treaty of Elslan with the invading Danes.			
885	Paris besieged by Northmen; city defended by Count Odo; Charles the Fat buys off the besiegers.	887. Arnulf, emperor.			889 (about). Arpád lays the foundation of Hungary.
898	Charles III, sole king.	899. Invasion by the Hungarians.	905. Kingdom of Navarre founded. 910. Kingdom of León founded by Garcia.	907. Oleg invades the Greek Empire.	
911	The Northmen, under Rollo, establish themselves in Normandy.	911. Conrad I, king. Carolingian dynasty becomes extinct. 919. Henry the Fowler, king.	912. Abderrahman III begins to reign in Cordova, introducing the golden age of Arabian power in Spain.		
923	Civil wars.				
					933. The union of the two Burgundies, forming the kingdom of Arles, which lasted a century.
936	Louis IV, son of Charles the Simple, king.	936. Otto the Great becomes king. 950. Bohemia annexed.	939. Ramiro, king of León, defeats the Moors at Simancas.		
954	Louis confers the dukedoms of Burgundy and Aquitaine on Hugh the Great.		955. Sancho I, king of León.	957. Swatoslav, king of Russia.	951. Decay of Saracen power begins. 955. Otto overcomes the Hungarians on the Lech.
		962. Beginning of the Holy Roman Empire. Crowning of Otto. 978. Otto at war with Lothair.	976. Hisham II, caliph of Cordova.	980. Vladimir the Great, the first Christian ruler.	
986	Louis V, last of the Carolingians.				

A. D.	FROM THE DIVISION OF THE WESTERN EMPIRE TO THE NORMAN CONQUEST OF ENGLAND—A. D. 843–1066—CON.			
	ARTS OF CIVILIZATION	ITALY AND THE CHURCH	EASTERN EMPIRE	THE BRITISH ISLES
		989. Greek Christianity propagated in Russia by Vladimir. 993. First canonization of saints.		
997	Venice under the doges dominates the Mediterranean and with Genoa rises to great importance in commerce.	999. Hungary becomes a fief of the Church.	996. War with Bulgaria.	994. Olaf Trygvasson and Svend attack London.
	ELEVENTH CENTURY			
	Firdousi, the Persian Homer, flourishes (940?–1020).		1001. Invasion of India by Mahmud of Ghazni.	1002. Massacre of the Danes in England. 1002–14. Brian Boroihme, sole ruler of Ireland. 1005. Scotland ruled by Malcolm II. 1013. Danes, under Svend, become masters of England.
	Great activity in the repairing and rebuilding of churches. Rise of the Romanesque style of architecture.			
	Foundation of University of Salerno; a famous medical school was chief department. Teachers in this school, famous surgeons. Both women and men admitted.	1024. John XIX, pope.	1018. Bulgaria reduced to a Grecian province.	1016. Edmund Ironside fights six battles with Canute, king of the Danes, with whom he divides the kingdom. Edmund dies, leaving Canute sole ruler.
	Truce of God, forbidding warfare on certain days and at certain seasons, an effort toward peace in this disturbed century.			1034. Duncan, king of Scotland.
	Lanfranc and Queen Matilda famous for their establishment of hospitals.	1041. Normans establish power in Apulia.	1042. First invasion of the Seljuk Turks. 1043. The Russians invade Thrace with 100,000 men and are repulsed by the Greeks.	1040. Macbeth murders Duncan and usurps the throne. 1042. The Saxon line restored under Edward the Confessor.
	Anselm, great scholar of this century.	1049. Leo IX, the first pope to keep an army. 1054. Excommunication of the patriarch of Constantinople and the Greeks. 1059. Quarrel between the popes and the German emperors. Robert Guiscard, duke of Apulia.	1054. Theodora, last of the Macedonian dynasty. 1058. Supremacy of the Seljuk Turks.	1051. William, duke of Normandy, visits England. 1066. Harold II, king, killed at the battle of Hastings. William the Conqueror, king. End of the Anglo-Saxon line.

A. D.	FROM THE NORMAN CONQUEST OF ENGLAND TO THE FALL OF THE EASTERN EMPIRE—A. D. 1066–1453			
	ARTS OF CIVILIZATION	ITALY AND THE CHURCH	EASTERN EMPIRE	THE BRITISH ISLES
	Margaret of Scotland, wife of Malcolm III, does much to refine manners and secure justice for the poor.	The papacy at the height of its power. College of Cardinals founded by Nicholas II for the election of the popes. 1073. Quarrel of Pope Gregory VII (Hildebrand) with the emperor Henry IV.	1071. Emperor Romanus IV defeated and taken prisoner by the Turks. Turks seize Asia Minor; Normans take Bari, last Greek possession in Italy.	1070. Lanfranc, archbishop of Canterbury. 1071 (about). Feudal system introduced.
		1074. Celibacy of the clergy decreed at a council summoned by Pope Gregory VII. 1075. The pope sends legates to the various courts of Europe. 1077. Submission of Henry IV to the pope at Canossa.	1074. Syria and Palestine subdued by Melek Shah.	1075. Rebellion of the Norman earls against William.

A. D.	From the Division of the Western Empire to the Norman Conquest of England—A. D. 843–1066—Con.				
	France	Germany	Spain	Russia	Lesser Countries
987	Hugh Capet, king, and founder of the Capetian line of French kings.				
996	Robert II succeeds his father on the throne.		999. Alfonso V, king of León.		994. Svend I of Denmark invades England.
1000	The end of the world expected; consequent religious excitement.	1002. Henry II, emperor.			1000 (about). Hungary a kingdom under its first hereditary king, St. Stephen.
				1015. Death of Vladimir.	1014. Canute II, king of Denmark. 1017. Canute supreme in England.
		1024. Conrad II, first of the Franconian line.	1020 (about). Rise of burgher class.	1019. Yaroslav rules Russia.	1028. Norway conquered by Canute. Danish ascendancy.
1031	Henry I, king.		1031. Ommiad dynasty ends with death of Hisham III of Cordova.		
1034	Burgundy annexed.		1033. Sancho the Great of Navarre constitutes Castile a kingdom. 1035. Ramiro I, king of Aragon.		
		1039. Henry III becomes emperor. 1041. Henry III defeats the Bohemians and Hungarians. Truce of God proclaimed.			
1066	William, duke of Normandy, claims the crown of England and wars on Harold to obtain it.	1054. Henry III causes his son, Henry, to be proclaimed king of the Romans. This title was applied for several centuries to the emperor's eldest son		1054. Russia violently dismembered. Civil wars and great distress.	1055. The Turks reduce Bagdad and overturn the empire of the caliphs.

A. D.	From the Norman Conquest of England to the Fall of the Eastern Empire—A. D. 1066–1453				
	France	Germany	Spain	Russia	Lesser Countries
					1067. Polish conquests in Russia. 1069. Olaf III, king of Norway. 1070. Bergen, Norway, built.
1073	Maine conquered by William, king of England.	1073. Revolt of the Saxons.	1072. Alfonso VI, king of Castile and León.		
			1074–99. Time of Rodrigo Díaz, "the Cid."		
1079	Birth of Abélard.	1077–80. Civil war in Germany.			

A. D.	From the Norman Conquest of England to the Fall of the Eastern Empire—A. D. 1066–1453—Con.			
	Arts of Civilization	**Italy and the Church**	**Eastern Empire**	**The British Isles**
			1081. Alexius I (Comnenus), emperor. 1082. Robert Guiscard invades the empire and defeats Alexius.	
	Omar Khayyam, poet-astronomer of Persia, corrects the calendar.	1084. Triumph of Henry IV over Gregory. The order of the Carthusians instituted by Bruno.	1084. After the capture of Jerusalem by the Turks, the Christian pilgrims are insulted and oppressed, which gives rise to the Crusades.	1087. William invades France and is killed at Mantes. 1093. Malcolm III of Scotland invades England and is slain near Alnwick castle.
		1095. Peter the Hermit preaches against the Turks. 1096. The First Crusade.		
			1099. Jerusalem taken by Godfrey. Battle of Ascalon and defeat of the Turks. 1104. Battle of Acre. 1109. Tripoli taken by crusaders.	1100. Henry I, king of England, unites the Normans and Saxons. 1107. Henry's quarrel with Anselm ended.
1118	Knights Templars instituted. Scholastic philosophy reaches a high point under Abélard.	1123. First Lateran, or ninth general, Council. 1127. Pope Honorius II makes war against Roger, king of Sicily.	1118. John Comnenus reforms the manners of his people. 1124. Tyre taken by crusaders.	1124. David I promotes civilization in Scotland.
		1139. Second Lateran, or tenth general, Council. Senate revived in Rome.	1143. Manuel Comnenus, emperor.	
	Age of cathedral building. Rise of the Gothic style.	1147. The Second Crusade.		
	Colleges of theology, philosophy, and law at Paris. Woolen manufactories established in England.	1154. Pope Adrian IV, an Englishman.		1154. Henry II, king of England; also possessed more than half of France. 1155–64. Ascendancy of Thomas Becket, archbishop of Canterbury.
		1167. Rome taken by Frederick Barbarossa. League of Lombard cities formed.		1170. Becket assassinated at the instigation of Henry II.
		1172. Grand Council of Venice formed.	1171–74. War between Venice and the Eastern Empire. Venetians keep their commercial privileges. 1175. Saladin founds the Sultanate of Egypt.	1171. Henry invades Ireland.
		1178. Renewed activity of the Waldenses, forerunners of Protestantism. 1179. Third Lateran, or eleventh general, Council. Waldensian teaching forbidden.	1185. Dynasty of the Comneni overthrown.	
		1189. The Third Crusade.		1188. Collection of the Saladin Tithe. Beginning of taxation on movable goods. 1189. Richard I engages in the Third Crusade. 1193. John attempts to seize the crown in the absence of Richard.

From the Norman Conquest of England to the Fall of the Eastern Empire—A. D. 1066–1453—Con.

A. D.	France	Germany	Spain	Russia	Lesser Countries
		1080. Henry degrades the pope and triumphs.			
			1085. Toledo taken from the Moors by Alfonso.		1084. Bohemia made a kingdom by Henry IV of Germany.
		1090–1100. The popes continue their struggle against the Empire.			1090. Sicily taken from the Saracens by Roger the Norman.
			1094. Pedro I, king of Navarre and Aragon.		
			1095. Conquest of Valencia by the Cid.		
1096	Many French noblemen take part in the First Crusade.				
1100 (about)	Rise of the troubadours in Provence.			1100 (about). Many ephemeral principalities contend for supremacy in Russia.	
			1104. Alfonso I, king of Navarre and Aragon.		
1108	Abbé Suger, minister to Louis VI of France.				
		1111. Henry V enters Italy and compels the pope, who is his prisoner, to crown him.			
		1114. Henry V marries Matilda of England.	1118. Alfonso captures Saragossa.		
					1119. Charles the Good becomes count of Flanders.
		1125. Lothair II opposed by Conrad and Frederick, duke of Swabia.			
		1138. Dissensions of the Guelphs and Ghibellines break out.	1139. Battle of Ourique. Alfonso, duke of Portugal, defeats Saracens and Moors and becomes first king of Portugal.		1139. Pope Innocent compelled to recognize the kingdom of Sicily and southern Italy, under Roger.
1147	Louis VII joins the Second Crusade.			1147. Moscow founded.	
					1150–1162. Erik the Saint, king of Sweden; Christianity introduced.
		1152. Frederick Barbarossa, emperor of Germany and Italy.			
			1157. Castile and León divided.	1158. Riga on the Baltic founded.	
1159	War with the English.				
					1167. League of the Italian cities.
1170	Rise of the Waldenses.	1169. Frederick's son, Henry, crowned king of the Romans. This title afterward implied the right to the imperial throne.	1169. Towns send representatives to the Cortes of Castile.	1169. Final overthrow of Kiev.	
					1171. Saladin, sultan of Egypt, extends his dominions; conquers Syria, Assyria, and Arabia.
		1174. Frederick's fifth expedition into Italy.			
		1176. Frederick defeated at the battle of Legnano.			
		1183. The Peace of Constance reestablishes the independence of the Italian republics.	1188. Alfonso IX, king of León.		1187. Saladin directs all his efforts against the crusaders; takes Jerusalem.
1190	Philip Augustus, one of the leaders of the Third Crusade.	1190. Henry VI, emperor, and king of Italy.			1191. Battle of Ascalon. Saladin defeated.
					1193. Death of Saladin.

A. D.	From the Norman Conquest of England to the Fall of the Eastern Empire—A. D. 1066–1453—Con.			
	Arts of Civilization	Italy and the Church	Eastern Empire	The British Isles
				1199. John, king of England.
		1202. The Fourth Crusade. Constantinople taken.	1204. The crusaders plunder Constantinople.	
	Period of the troubadours in France; the minstrels in England; minnesingers in Germany.			
		1215. Fourth Lateran Council, against the Albigenses. 1217. The Crusade of Andrew II of Hungary.		1215. Magna Charta signed at Runnymede. 1216. Henry III, king.
1222	University of Padua founded.			
	Architecture, and arts and crafts flourish in western Europe.	1226. The Lombard League renewed to resist Frederick. 1228–1270. Fifth, Sixth, and Seventh crusades.		
1229	University of Cambridge, England, founded. Rise of strong guilds of artisans.	1229. Papal troops defeat Frederick's army and occupy the mainland part of the Kingdom of the Two Sicilies.	1229. Frederick II occupies Jerusalem, which is ceded to the Christians by the sultan of Egypt.	1236. Henry marries Eleanor of Provence.
1239 (about)	Coal mining begun at Newcastle-upon-Tyne.	1243. Struggle of Pope Innocent IV with Emperor Frederick.		
1250 (about)	Roger Bacon describes principle of the telescope.			1254. Knights of the shires in Parliament. 1258. Famous "mad" Parliament at Oxford.
			1261. Emperor Michael Palæologus recovers Constantinople.	1265. First regular Parliament. Civil war.
		1267. Dominion of Italy passes to the pope.		
	Literature and science flourish in Spain under Alfonso the Learned.			1272–1307. Reign of Edward I.
		1274. Fourteenth general Council at Lyons.		1276. War between England and Wales.
1280	Institution of the three great courts of law in England.			1283. England and Wales united.
			1288 (about). Osman establishes an independent rule in the north of Asia Minor.	1291-92. Robert Bruce and John Balliol contend for the crown of Scotland.
	Cimabue, the first of modern painters at Florence.	1296. Struggle of the Church with France. Bull *Clericis Laicos* forbids ecclesiastics to pay taxes to the civil power.		1296. Scotland submits to England. 1297. Scotland rebels. War between England and Scotland follows.
	Roger Bacon makes many scientific discoveries.		1299 (about). Osman invades Nicomedia; establishes the Ottoman empire.	
	Fourteenth Century			
1300 (about)	Beginning of the Renaissance or revival of learning. Indian spinning wheel introduced into Europe. Knives made in England at Sheffield.			
1301	Duns Scotus becomes professor of theology at Oxford.	1303. Papal power declines.	Genoese control trade of Black Sea.	
				1304. Scotland conquered by Edward I. 1306. Robert Bruce proclaimed king of Scotland. War with England continued.
		1309. Seat of the popes transferred to Avignon. 1311. General Council at Vienna. 1312. Knights Templars condemned by the Council of Vienna.		1314. Bruce defeats the English at Bannockburn, June 24.

A. D.	From the Norman Conquest of England to the Fall of the Eastern Empire—A. D. 1066–1453—Con.				
	France	**Germany**	**Spain**	**Russia**	**Lesser Countries**
1204	Normandy reunited to France.				
1207	Albigensian crusade begun.				1206 (about). Jenghis Khan subdues the north of China.
		1215. Frederick II, crowned emperor.	1212. The Christians gain the battle of Las Navas de Tolosa. 1217. Ferdinand, king of Castile.		1216 (about). Tartary overrun by Jenghis Khan. 1222. Hungarian liberty assured by charter of Andrew II.
1223	Louis VIII conducts crusade against the Albigenses.			1224. Mongolian invasion, known as the "Golden Horde."	
1226	Louis IX, king.	1226. Frederick grants Prussian territory to Teutonic Knights.			
		1230. Teutonic Knights begin to settle in Prussia.	1230. Castile and León united by Ferdinand III, who takes large territory from the Moors.	1237. Second Mongolian invasion. Moscow burned. 1238. Russian independence overthrown by the Tatars. Khan of Kiptchak, grand duke.	1241. Mongolian invasion of Europe under Batu Khan.
1248	Louis IX leads the Sixth Crusade.	1250. Conrad IV, emperor.	1250–1282. Alfonso the Learned, king of León and Castile.		1258. Mongols overthrow caliphate of Bagdad.
1270	Louis IX sets out on the Last Crusade.				1267 (about). Kublai Khan builds Peking and makes it his capital.
1276	France at war with Castile.	1273. Rudolf, emperor, founds house of Habsburg.	1274. Crown of Navarre passes to France.	Khan of Kiptchak wields strong rule in Russia.	
1294	English fiefs in France declared forfeited.	1291. League of Swiss cantons formed.	1291. James II, king of Aragon.		1290. Wenceslas, king of Bohemia, takes Cracow.
1297	Invasion of Flanders.	1298. Adolphus, emperor, deposed and Albert I enthroned.	1296. Ferdinand IV, king of Castile. Period of anarchy.		1299 (about). Foundation of the Ottoman empire.
				1300. Kremlin built.	
1302	First convocation of the States-General in France.				
1304	War with Flanders.				1307. Swiss republic founded.
		1308. Henry of Luxemburg, emperor. 1309. Swiss Confederacy recognized by the emperor.	1312. Alfonso XI, king of Castile and León.		
1315	Edict for the enfranchisement of slaves.	1314. Louis of Bavaria and Frederick of Austria contend for the crown.			

A. D.	From the Norman Conquest of England to the Fall of the Eastern Empire—A. D. 1066–1453—Con.			
	Arts of Civilization	Italy and the Church	Eastern Empire	The British Isles
1318	Dante completes *Divina Commedia*; dies 1321.			
			1321. Civil war in the Eastern Empire between the emperor and his grandson.	
			1326. Orkhan, sultan of the Turks, makes Brusa his capital.	1328. Peace. Independence of Scotland.
1340	Chaucer, father of English poetry, born in London.	Struggle in Rome between the Colonna and the Orsini.		1337. Struggle for the French crown begins.
1340 (?)	Coal used in iron smelting in Belgium.			1346. Battle of Crécy.
1347	First recorded importation of wheat into England.	1347. Democracy in Rome under Rienzi, last of the tribunes.		1348. The plague of the Black Death sweeps over Europe, lasting four years.
1352	Library of St. Mark's in Venice, founded by gifts from Petrarch.	1354. Rienzi killed; papal dominion restored.	1355. John Palæologus, emperor.	1356. Edward, the Black Prince, wins the battle of Poitiers.
			1373. Treaty with Amurath, the Ottoman emperor.	1376. Death of the Black Prince.
		1377. Papal court reestablished at Rome; end of the "Babylonian Captivity."		
		1378. Schism of the West; Pope Urban VI acknowledged in England; Clement VII in France, Spain, and Scotland.		1381. Peasants' Revolt.
				1385. The Scots, assisted by France, invade England.
			1389. Bajazet, sultan of the Turks.	
1400 (about)	Wood engraving.			1399. Henry IV, king. House of Lancaster begins.
1400	Chaucer dies.			
1401	Bank of Barcelona (earliest existing) founded.			
		1409. The Council of Pisa.	1402. Bajazet defeated and made prisoner by Timur at the battle of Angora.	1406. James I, king of Scotland.
		1414. Council of Constance. 1415-16. Huss and Jerome burned for heresy.		1414. Henry V claims the French crown. 1415. Henry V gains the battle of Agincourt.
		1417. Schism of the West ended by election of Pope Martin V.	1419. The Portuguese explore the Madeira Islands under the patronage of Henry the Navigator.	1422. Death of Henry V. Accession of Henry VI. War with France.
			1425. Emperor John VII visits Italy to obtain help against the Turks.	
1436	First public library in Italy, at Florence; gift of Niccolo Niccoli.			
			1444. Vladislas, king of Poland, defeated and killed by the Turks.	1444. Truce with France. 1445. Marriage of Henry to Margaret of Anjou.
1447	Vatican library founded.	1447. Congress by which the liberties of the German Church are compromised.	1448. Constantine XI, last of the Greek emperors.	
1450 (about)	Gutenberg invents printing with metal types.			
1450	The Renaissance, at first a literary revival, now extends to art in general, particularly architecture, which is influenced throughout central and western Europe.		1453. Siege and capture of Constantinople by the Turks, ending the Eastern Empire.	1450. Insurrection of Jack Cade. Richard, duke of York, claims the throne.

A. D.	From the Norman Conquest of England to the Fall of the Eastern Empire—A. D. 1066–1453—Con.				
	France	Germany	Spain	Russia	Lesser Countries
1316	Philip V succeeds by virtue of the Salic law, now first established.			1318. Finland invaded by Russians.	1319. The oligarchy of Venice established.
		1322. Frederick of Austria defeated.			
1337	War with England.				1336. Timur (Tamerlane) born at Kesh, Tartary.
			1340. Moors defeated near Tarifa.		
				1346. Novgorod at height of its commercial importance.	
1356	King John defeated and taken prisoner at Poitiers.	1356. Promulgation of the Golden Bull.			1355. Establishment of the Ottomans in Europe.
1360	John regains his liberty; cedes much territory to England.		1365. War between Navarre and France.		1369. Timur makes Samarkand the capital of his new empire.
1380	Charles VI, king.	1378. Wenceslas, king of Bohemia, emperor.		1380. Tatar war. Dimitri Ivanovitch checks Tatars at the Don.	
1382	Defeat of the Flemings at Roosebec. Victory of nobles over the cities.			1382. Moscow burned.	
1386	Fruitless attempt to invade England.				
		1394. The emperor imprisoned at Prague.		1395. Timur invades Russia. Russia under the Mongol Tatars until 1480.	1389. Swiss force the Habsburgs to make a truce. 1398. Invasion of India by Timur.
		1400. Rupert, Count Palatine, emperor.			
			1406. John II, king of Castile.		
1410	Civil war between Orleans and Burgundy.	1411. Sigismund, king of Hungary, emperor.		1410. Battle of Tannenberg. Poles and Lithuanians defeat Teutonic Knights.	
1415	French defeated by the English at Agincourt.		1416. Alfonso V, king of Aragon and Sicily.		
1422	Henry VI, proclaimed at Paris, king of France and England.				1419–27. The Hussite war in Bohemia.
1429	Orleans saved by Joan of Arc. Charles VII crowned at Reims.			1429. Founding of Solovetski monastery on White Sea.	
1431	Joan of Arc burned.				
		1438. Albert II, first emperor of the house of Habsburg.			1437–38. Rise of Portugal.
1453	End of the Hundred Years' War.	1453. Austria made a hereditary duchy by Emperor Frederick III.			

A. D.	From the Fall of the Eastern Empire to the Close of the Thirty Years' War—A. D. 1453–1648				
	Arts of Civilization	Italy and the Church	Great Britain	Germany	Spain and Portugal
					1454. Henry IV, king of Castile.
			1455. Wars of the Roses begin.		
		1458. The French rule in Genoa.			
1460 (about)	Copperplate engraving.		1461. Edward IV, king. House of York.	1462. Civil war in Germany.	
		1463. War of Venice with the Turks.			
		1469. Lorenzo de' Medici succeeds Piero at Florence. 1471. Sixtus IV, pope.	1470. Henry VI restored by Warwick; dies 1471.		1469. Marriage of Ferdinand of Aragon with Isabella of Castile.
1474	First book printed in England by Caxton.				
			1475. Edward IV invades France; signs seven year truce with Louis XI.		
1477	Watches made at Nuremberg.			1477. Marriage of Maximilian and Mary of Burgundy.	1479. Union of Castile and Aragon.
			1483–1485. Richard III, king.		
1488	Bartholomew Diaz, a Portuguese, discovers the Cape of Good Hope.				
					1491. Conquest of Granada by Spaniards.
1492	Discovery of America by Columbus begins era of discovery.	1492. Alexander VI, pope.	1492. Henry VII invades France.	1493. Maximilian I, emperor.	1492. The Jews are expelled from Spain. 1498. Vasco da Gama reaches India via Cape of Good Hope.
1500 (about)	Clocks first used in astronomy.	1504. Naples annexed to the Spanish crown. Julius II, pope.			
1506	First stone laid for St. Peter's church at Rome.		1509. Henry VIII, king.		
		1513. Pope Leo X, patron of literature and the arts.	1512. War with France. 1513. Battle of Flodden; James IV of Scotland killed. 1515. Wolsey, chancellor and cardinal.	1512. Maximilian divides the empire into 10 administrative circles.	
1516	Juan Diaz de Solis discovers the river La Plata; declares the country Spanish possession.			1517. Beginning of the Reformation; Luther's theses at Wittenberg. 1519. Charles V, emperor.	1516. Charles, king of all Spain and the Netherlands. (As emperor, Charles V.)
1520	Fernando Magellan navigates the straits between Tierra del Fuego and Patagonia.	1520. Pope Leo X excommunicates Luther. 1525. Spanish ascendancy by the victory of Pavia.	1520. Francis I of France and Henry VIII meet on the Field of the Cloth of Gold near Guînes.	1521. Diet of Worms. 1525. German Peasants' war. 1529. Turks invade Germany; besiege Vienna.	1525. Charles V defeats French and Italians at Pavia.
1530 (about)	"Saxony" flax wheel in Nuremberg.		1531. The English clergy acknowledge Henry as head of the Church. 1534. Henry excommunicated by the pope.		
1533	Flax growing ordered by law in England.				
		1540. Order of Jesuits founded by Loyola. 1545. Council of Trent.	1544. Invasion of France.	1542–54. War with France.	1540. Lisbon, the market of the world.
1547	First China orange tree brought to Europe by Portuguese. Rude carriages used in France.	1550. Julius III, pope.	1547. Formal establishment of Protestantism. Edward VI, king.	1552. Treaty of Passau secures religious liberty to the Protestants.	
			1553. Mary, queen of England. 1554. Lady Jane Grey executed. 1555. Persecution of the Protestants. 1558. Elizabeth, queen. Rise of the Puritans.	1553. Michael Servetus, Spanish philosopher, burned at Geneva. 1556. Charles V abdicates.	

A. D.	From the Fall of the Eastern Empire to the Close of the Thirty Years' War—A. D. 1453–1648				
	France	Russia	Scandinavia	Ottoman Empire	Lesser Countries
					1454. Poland's independence confirmed by diet of Petrekin.
				1456. War with Hungary.	1458. Hungary vigorous under Matthias Corvinus.
				1460. Greece subjected to the Turks.	
1461	Louis XI, king.				
		1462. Ivan III founds czardom of Muscovy.			
					1466. Prussia a fief of Poland.
					1468. Uzun Hassan, master of Persia.
			1470. Sten Sture, regent of Sweden.		
		1472. Ivan marries Sophia, niece of the Greek emperor.			
1474	War between France and Burgundy.				
1477	Artois and Burgundy united to France.	1479. Great invasion of the Tatars.			
		1480. Power of the Tatars overthrown.		1480. Otranto taken.	
			1481. Hans, king of Denmark, partially acknowledged in Sweden.	1481. Bajazet II, sultan.	
					1485. Matthias of Hungary takes Vienna.
1491	Brittany united to the crown.				
1498	Louis XII, king.				
1499	Conquest of Milan.				1499. Swiss independence acknowledged by the Empire.
					1506. Poland under Sigismund the Great.
1510	Council of Tours.				
			1513. Christian II, king of Norway and Denmark.	1512. Accession of Selim I.	
				1514. Persians defeated; Kurdistan added to the empire.	
1515	Francis I invades Italy.				
				1517. Selim conquers Egypt.	
					1519–21. Spaniards, under Cortés, conquer Mexico.
			1520. Christian, king of Sweden.	1520. Solyman the Magnificent, sultan.	
1521	Long conflict with the Habsburgs begins.		1523. Gustavus Vasa, king of Sweden. Union of Calmar dissolved.		
1525	Francis defeated and taken prisoner at Pavia.			1526. Invasion of Hungary.	
				1529. Invasion of Germany. Siege of Vienna.	
		1533. Accession of Ivan the Terrible.			1533. Pizarro conquers Peru.
					1545. Mines at Potosi discovered.
1547	Henry II, king; Catherine de' Medici, queen.	1547. Ivan the Terrible takes the title of Czar.			
				1551. Tripoli taken.	
					1556. Akbar raises the Indian empire to its greatest splendor.

A. D.	FROM THE FALL OF THE EASTERN EMPIRE TO THE CLOSE OF THE THIRTY YEARS' WAR—A. D. 1453–1648—CON.				
	ARTS OF CIVILIZATION	ITALY AND THE CHURCH	GREAT BRITAIN	GERMANY	SPAIN AND PORTUGAL
		1559. Termination of French wars in Italy.			
1562	Tusser's *Five Hundred Points of Husbandry.*			1564. Maximilian II, emperor.	1564. Settlement of the Philippines. 1567. Duke of Alva, governor of the Netherlands.
		1569. Florence becomes capital of grand duchy of Tuscany. 1570. The Catholics and Huguenots sign a treaty of peace at St. Germain.	1568. Mary Queen of Scots takes refuge in England and is made captive by Elizabeth.		1571. Battle of Lepanto. Turks defeated by the Holy League under John of Austria. 1572. Crown of Poland becomes elective.
1576	Martin Frobisher, an Englishman, sets out to explore a northwest passage to India.			1576. Rudolf II, king of Bohemia and Hungary, emperor.	
1580	Coarse white paper made in England.				1580. Portugal passes under Spanish dominion.
1582	Pope Gregory XIII reforms the calendar, changing Oct. 5 to Oct. 15.	1585. Pope Sixtus V restores the Vatican library.	1587. Execution of Mary Queen of Scots. 1588. Spanish *Armada* destroyed.		
1588	First English work on shorthand published by Doctor Timothy Bright.				
1600	Gilbert generates electricity by rubbing substances other than amber.		1600. British East India Company chartered. 1603. Union of England and Scotland under James I. Tudor dynasty in England ends. 1605. Guy Fawkes's plot to blow up Parliament.		
1608	Telescopes manufactured in Holland.			1608. Protestant union under Frederick the Elector.	1609. Expulsion of the Moors.
1609–18	Kepler announces laws of planetary motions.				
1614	Lord John Napier invents system of logarithms.				
1616	William Harvey, famous physician, demonstrates the circulation of the blood. Death of Shakspere, April 23.		1618. Sir Francis Bacon, lord chancellor. 1620. Pilgrims sail in *Mayflower*.	1618. Thirty Years' War begins. 1620. Battle of Prague.	1621. Dutch war.
		1626. St. Peter's dedicated.	1625. Charles I, king. 1627. War with France.	1628. Victories of Wallenstein. 1632. Battle of Lützen.	1625. Naval war with England.
1635	French Academy of Arts and Sciences founded at Paris. First Irish theater opened at Dublin.		1638. Abolition of the episcopacy in Scotland; publication of the National Covenant.		
1639	Transit of Venus first recorded by Horrocks.				
1641	Descartes enunciates his system of philosophy.	1641. War between Pope Urban VIII and the Italian princes.	1640. Short Parliament. Long Parliament.		1640. Portugal regains independence.
1642	Van Diemen's Land and New Zealand discovered by Tasman, a Dutchman.		1642. Civil war and revolution.		

A. D.	From the Fall of the Eastern Empire to the Close of the Thirty Years' War—A. D. 1453–1648—Con.				
	France	**Russia**	**Scandinavia**	**Ottoman Empire**	**Lesser Countries**
			1560. Eric XIV, king of Sweden. 1563. Seven Years' War between Sweden and Denmark begins.	Military power of the Turks at its greatest height under Solyman.	
1562	Religious liberty granted to the Huguenots. Huguenot wars.			1566. Selim II, emperor.	1566. The Compromise, a league of nobles against the Inquisition in the Netherlands.
		1571. Russia devastated by the Tatars and Moscow burned.	1570. Peace of Stettin.	1571. Turks defeated at battle of Lepanto.	
1572	Massacre of St. Bartholomew.				
1574	Henry III, king.			1574. Amurath III, emperor	
1576	The Catholic League.	1578. Alliance of Sweden and Poland against Russia.			1579. Beginning of the republic in Holland.
					1585. Persia acquires great power under Abbas the Great.
1588	Revolt of Paris.		1588. Christian IV, king of Denmark.		
1589	House of Bourbon begins with Henry IV.			1589. Revolt of the Janizaries.	
1590	Siege of Paris raised by the Spaniards.			1595. Power in Hungary declines; revolt of Wallachia.	
1598	Edict of Nantes—toleration granted to the Protestants.	1598. Boris Godounov begins a new dynasty.			1601 Portuguese expedition reaches Australia.
					1605. Jehangir, Mogul emperor of India.
1610	Assassination of Henry IV. Louis XIII, king.		1611. Gustavus Adolphus, king of Sweden.		1609. First envoy of the British East India Company sent to India.
1614	Last assembly of the States-General before French Revolution.	1613. Michael Feodorovich, czar, founds the house of Romanov.	War between Sweden and Denmark. 1617. Sweden dominates the North.		
				1620. War with Poland.	
1624	Ministry of Cardinal Richelieu begins.				
1627	War with England over the Huguenots.				
		1632. War with Poland.	1632. Christina, queen of Sweden; Oxenstierna, regent.		
1638	Invasion of Spain.			1638. Final and greatest expedition against Persia.	
					1639. Great naval victory of the Dutch admiral, Van Tromp, over the Spanish fleet in the Downs.
1640	Turin taken by the French.				1640. Madras, India, founded.
1642	Death of Richelieu.				

A. D.	From the Fall of the Eastern Empire to the Close of the Thirty Years' War—A. D. 1453–1648—Con.			
	Arts of Civilization	**Italy and the Church**	**Great Britain**	**Germany**	**Spain and Portugal**
1643	The barometer invented by Torricelli.				1643. The colonies of New England form a union.
1647	Society of Friends founded by George Fox.	1647. Revolt of Naples under Masaniello.	1648. Second civil war.	1648. Peace of Westphalia. End of Thirty Years' War. The balance of power in Europe practically established by this treaty.	

A. D.	From the Close of the Thirty Years' War to the Beginning of the French Revolution—A. D. 1648–1789				
	Arts of Civilization	**Italy and the Church**	**Great Britain**	**Germany**	**Spain and Portugal**
1650	First coffeehouse in England.		1649. Commonwealth under Cromwell. 1652. War with Holland. 1653. Cromwell, lord protector.		1654. Brazil recovered from the Dutch.
			1660. Charles II, king. Restoration of Stuarts.	1658. Leopold I, emperor.	1660. Portugal makes alliance with England.
1662	Coffee introduced into France.				
1663	First newspaper in England, *Public Intelligence*.				
1667	First designs drawn for Gobelin tapestry.		1666. Great fire in London. St. Paul's rebuilt by Sir Christopher Wren.		
1669	British East India Company first import tea.		1668. Triple Alliance of England, Sweden, and Holland against France.		
		1676. Messina revolts in favor of the French; blockaded by the Dutch and Spanish fleets.	1678 (about). Rise of the Whigs and Tories. 1679. Habeas corpus act passed.	1674. War of Austria and France.	1673. War with France to protect Holland.
1681	Canal of Languedoc completed.			1680. Part of Alsace seized by France.	
1684	Newton announces theory of gravitation.		1685. James II, king. 1688. Revolution.	1683. Siege of Vienna by the Turks and Hungarians. 1687. Joseph I, king of Hungary.	
		1689. Alexander VIII, pope.	1689. William III, king, and Mary II, queen.		1689. Revolt in Catalonia in favor of France.
1690	Manufacture of paper for writing and printing encouraged by law in England.	1693. Battle of Marsaglia.	1690. Battle of the Boyne. James defeated. 1694. Bank of England chartered.	1690. Joseph I elected king of the Romans.	1691. Incursion of the French into Aragon.
1696	Hoste writes on science of shipbuilding.		1697. Peace of Ryswick.	1697. Victory of Prince Eugene over Sultan Mustapha at Zenta.	
1698	Linen manufacture established in northern Ireland.				1700. Philip V, king of Spain.
		1702. Battle of Luzzara between French under Vendôme and the Imperialists.	1702. Queen Anne. War against France and Spain. 1704. Gibraltar taken by English.	1701. Prussia made a kingdom. Hohenzollern dynasty established.	
		1706. French driven from Italy by Prince Eugene.			1705. Barcelona taken by the allies.

A. D.	From the Fall of the Eastern Empire to the Close of the Thirty Years' War—A. D. 1453–1648—Con.				
	France	Russia	Scandinavia	Ottoman Empire	Lesser Countries
1643	Louis XIV, king.	1645. Era of progress begins with reign of Czar Alexis.	1645. Peace between Sweden and Denmark.	1645. War with Venice.	
1648	Wars of the Fronde.				1648. Independence of the Republic of the United Provinces.

A. D.	From the Close of the Thirty Years' War to the Beginning of the French Revolution—A. D. 1648–1789				
	France	Russia	Scandinavia	Ottoman Empire	Lesser Countries
1649	Siege of Paris.				
1653	Mazarin enters Paris in triumph.	1654. Russian victories in Poland.	1657. War between Denmark and Sweden. 1660. Peace of Copenhagen and Oliva.	1657. Leopold I of Germany becomes king of Hungary. 1661. War with Austria.	1653. John de Witt, grand pensionary of Holland.
1659	Peace of the Pyrenees.				1661. Bombay ceded to England.
				1663. Invasion of Hungary. 1664. Germans win the battle of St. Gotthard.	
1667	War with Spain over possession of the Spanish Netherlands.				
1672	War with Holland.	1671. The Cossacks subjugated.		1672. Invasion of Poland.	1674. Sobieski, king of Poland.
1678	Peace with Holland and Spain restores tranquillity to Europe. France the most formidable power in Europe.	1682. Ivan and Peter, czars.	1680. Diet of Stockholm.	1678. First war with Russia. 1682. War with Austria. 1683. Defeat at Vienna.	
1685	Revocation of the Edict of Nantes.				
1688	Louis declares war against the Empire and the United Provinces.	1689. Peter the Great, czar.		1687. Revolution in Constantinople, Soliman II, sultan. 1689. Recovery of Belgrade from the Austrians.	1689 (about). Mogul power at its height in India.
1697	General Peace of Ryswick between France and the Allies.		1693. The king of Sweden declared absolute. 1697. Charles XII begins to reign.		1695. Brussels bombarded by the French.
1702	Invasion of Holland. Revolt of the Camisards (Protestants).	1700. Peter the Great wars with the northern powers. 1703. Petrograd founded.	1700. Defeat of the Russians at Narva. 1702–08. Charles XII sweeps Poland and Russia.	1699. Peace of Karlowitz. The Ottoman power broken. 1703. Mustapha II deposed by the Janizaries.	
1704	Defeat at Blenheim.		1705. Denmark joins Russo-Polish alliance.		1704. Stanislas I, king of Poland.

A. D.	From the Close of the Thirty Years' War to the Beginning of the French Revolution—A. D. 1648–1789—Con.				
	Arts of Civilization	Italy and the Church	Great Britain	Germany	Spain and Portugal
		1707. All Spanish possessions in Italy abandoned.	1707. Act of union of England and Scotland. First united Parliament of Great Britain meets.		
1710	First "self-acting steam engine" patented by Thomas Newcomen.		1713. Peace of Utrecht. England acquires large American possessions.	1711. Charles VI, emperor.	
			1714. Accession of George I. Beginning of the house of Hanover.		
		1718. Sicily invaded by the Spanish.	1720. South Sea Bubble.	1718. Quadruple Alliance against Spain.	
1721	Inoculation for smallpox introduced into England.				
				1725. Alliance of Spain and Austria.	1725. Alliance with Austria.
		1730. Clement XII, pope.	1727. George II, king of England.		
1731	An early book on farming: Tull's *Horse-Hoeing Husbandry*.			1733. War of the Polish Succession.	1734. Conquest of Sicily and Naples by Don Carlos.
1735	Linnæus publishes his *Systema Naturæ*.		1739. War with Spain.	1740. War of the Austrian Succession. Maria Theresa succeeds to the hereditary states.	
		1744. Italy invaded by the French and Spaniards.			
			1745. The Young Pretender in Scotland.	1745. Francis I, husband of Maria Theresa, emperor.	
1747	Franklin announces single fluid theory of electricity.	1746. French and Spaniards driven from Lombardy.			1746. Ferdinand VI, king of Spain.
1752	Franklin demonstrates identity of electricity and lightning.		1760. Accession of George III. 1763. Peace of Paris.	1756. Seven Years' War—Austria and France against Prussia and England.	
1767	Hargreaves builds a spinning jenny.				1767. Jesuits expelled from Spain.
1769	Arkwright builds a spinning mill.				
1773	First regular academy for deaf-mutes (in Great Britain) opened in Edinburgh.	1773. Jesuit order suppressed.			
			1775. War with the American colonies. 1776. British army takes possession of New York. Hessians hired for service in America. City of London remonstrates against American war.		
1780	Sunday schools organized at Gloucester, England, by Robert Raikes.			1778. War of the Bavarian Succession. Bavaria seized by Germany.	
1781	Watt first patents a double steam engine.		1781. Surrender of Cornwallis at Yorktown.		
1782	Montgolfier successfully uses heated air balloons.		1783. Treaty of Versailles with United States.		
1787	Society for the Suppression of the Slave Trade founded.		1786. Impeachment of Warren Hastings.		1788. Charles IV, king of Spain.

A. D.	From the Close of the Thirty Years' War to the Beginning of the French Revolution—A. D. 1648–1789—Con.				
	France	**Russia**	**Scandinavia**	**Ottoman Empire**	**Lesser Countries**
		1708. Revolt of the Cossack Mazeppa. Charles XII of Sweden invades Russia.			
		1709. Charles is defeated at Pultowa.		1710. The sultan declares war on Russia.	
1713	Peace of Utrecht—perpetual separation of the crowns of France and Spain.		1714. Charles returns to Sweden.		
1715	Louis XV, king (Regency till 1723).	1716. Finland conquered.		1717. Turks lose Belgrade.	1715. Treaty of Antwerp with Austria. "Barrier Treaty."
1718	The Quadruple Alliance against Spain.	1720. Treaty of Stockholm between Sweden and Russia.	1718. Charles invades Norway and is killed at the siege of Frederikshald.		
		1721. Peter assumes the title "Emperor of all the Russians."	1721. Peace of Nystadt between Sweden and Russia.	1723. Turks and Russians attempt to dismember Persia.	
1724	Congress of Cambrai.	1725. Catherine I, empress.			1724–32. Jesuits expelled from China.
		1726. Alliance with Austria.			
		1730. Death of Peter II, last of the male line of Romanovs.	1730. Christian VI, king of Denmark.		
1733	The Polish succession involves France in war.			1734. Turks driven from Persia by Nadir Shah.	1733. Frederick Augustus II, king of Poland.
					1739. India invaded by Nadir, shah of Persia, who takes Delhi.
1744	War with England and Austria.		1742. Swedes driven out of Finland.		
				1745. Defeat of the Turks at Kars.	
1747	War with Holland.				1746–49. Hostilities between the French and English in India.
					1756. Calcutta taken by the nabob of Bengal.
1760	Loss of all Canada.	1762. Catherine II reigns.			
1764	Dissolution of Jesuit order.				1765. Establishment of the English in India.
					1766. Power of the Mamelukes revived in Egypt under Ali Bey.
		1768. War with the Ottoman empire.			
1770	Marriage of the Dauphin to Marie Antoinette.	1772. First partition of Poland.	1772. Despotism reestablished in Sweden by Gustavus III.		
		1773. Revolts of the Cossacks.			
1774	Louis XVI, king.				1774. Warren Hastings, first governor-general of India.
1776	Franklin in Paris.				
1778	Alliance with America.				
				1783. The Crimea annexed to Russia.	
		1787. War with the Turks.		1787. Disastrous war with Austria and Russia.	
1789	The States-General meets at Versailles.				

From the Beginning of the French Revolution to the World War—A. D. 1789–1914

A. D.	Arts of Civilization	Italy and the Church	Great Britain	Germany	Spain and Portugal
1792	First use of gas for illuminating.			1792. War with France.	
			1793. First coalition against France.		
		1796–97. Napoleon's Italian campaign.		1797. Napoleon's Austrian campaign.	
1798	Invention of lithography.	1798. Roman Republic proclaimed by the French.	1798. Nelson destroys French fleet at battle of the Nile.		
			1799. Second coalition against France. 1801. Union of England and Ireland.		
1802	Wedgwood's photographic experiments.	1802. Napoleon, president of the Italian Republic.			
1803	Fulton's steamboat *Clermont* operated on the Seine.		1803. Successful war in India.		
		1805. Napoleon crowned king of Italy.	1805. Napoleon defeated at Trafalgar.	1805. Battle of Austerlitz.	1805. Battle of Trafalgar.
				1806. Confederation of Rhine. End of Holy Roman Empire.	
		1808. Rome annexed by Napoleon to the Kingdom of Italy.		1809. Peace of Vienna.	1808. Madrid taken by the French. Joseph Bonaparte, king.
			1812. War with the United States.	1812. Austria in alliance with France against Russia.	1812. Battle of Salamanca. 1814. Ferdinand VII restored.
1814	Steam cylinder printing press first used for *London Times*.	1814. Fall of Napoleon. Kingdom ceases.			
			1815. British defeated at New Orleans. Wellington victorious at Waterloo.	1815. Congress of Vienna.	

A. D.	Arts of Civilization	International Affairs	Great Britain	Prussia	Austria
		1815. Congress of Vienna. Holy Alliance. Abolition of slave trade. 1818. Great Lakes Anglo-American naval agreement.	1816. Bombardment of Algiers. The Dey compelled to abolish slavery.	1818. The Zollverein policy initiated.	
1819	S. S. *Savannah* makes the first trip across Atlantic. Electromagnetism discovered.		1820. Accession of George IV.		
1822	Hieroglyphics deciphered by Champollion.	1821. Conference of monarchs at Laibach.			
1824	Inland navigation stimulated in the United States.	1823. Proclamation of Monroe Doctrine.	1823. Catholic Association formed in Ireland.		
1825	Steam navigation on the Rhine. Vast increase in periodical literature. First passenger railway, Stockton to Darlington, England.		1826. England and Russia sign agreement for settlement of Greek question.	1826. Austria and Prussia oppose English-Russian mediation in Greece.	
1827	Improved cylinder printing press, *London Times*, 5000 impressions per hour.	1827. Treaty of nations with respect to Greece. 1828. Independence of Uruguay.	1828. Wellington ministry. Irish disturbances. 1830. William IV, king.		
1831	Reaper invented. Dynamo electric machine.	1831. Belgian independence and neutrality agreed to by the powers.	1832. Reform bills passed. 1834. Difficulties with China. Robert Peel, premier.	1834. Zollverein includes most of the German states.	1831. Austria interferes in Italian affairs. 1835. Ferdinand I, emperor.

From the Beginning of the French Revolution to the World War—A. D. 1789–1914

A. D.	France	Russia	Scandinavia	Ottoman Empire	Lesser Countries
1789	National Assembly adopts Declaration of the Rights of Man.				
1792	War with Germany. France declared a republic.		1792. Gustavus III assassinated. Gustavus IV, king.		
1793	Reign of Terror.	1793. Second partition of Poland.			1794. Polish revolt at Cracow.
1795	Napoleon Bonaparte commands army.	1795. Final partition of Poland.			
1796	War in Italy.	1796. Unsuccessful war with Persia.			
1797	Napoleon in Austria.				
1798	Expedition to Egypt.			1798. Turkey joins coalition against France.	1798. Swiss revolution. Helvetian Republic declared.
1799	Swiss campaign.				
1800	Battle of Marengo.				
1802	Napoleon made consul.	1801. Alexander, czar.	1801. Denmark and Sweden accede to the alliance between England and Russia.		
1803	War with England.			1803. Insurrection of Mamelukes at Cairo.	
1804	Napoleon I, emperor of the French.				
1805	Battle of Austerlitz.	1805. Russia joins the coalition against France.			1806. Louis Napoleon, king of Holland.
1807	War with Russia. Invasion of Portugal.	1807. Treaty of Tilsit.	1808. Finland invaded by the Russians.		1807. Duchy of Warsaw formed.
1809	Battle of Wagram.		1809. Charles XIII, king of Sweden.	1809. Russians defeated at Silistria.	
1810	Continental peace except with Spain.				
1812	Russian campaign.	1812. Invasion by Napoleon. Moscow burned.		1809–12. War with Russia.	1812. American war with England.
1814	Allies enter Paris. House of Bourbon restored; Louis XVIII, king.		1814. Union of Sweden and Norway as two kingdoms under one monarch.	1814. Malta falls to England.	
1815	Napoleon defeated at Waterloo; abdicates; banished to St. Helena.	1815. The Holy Alliance formed.			1815. William I, king of the Netherlands.

A. D.	France	Spain and Portugal	Italy and Greece	Russia	Lesser Countries
		1816. Union of Portugal and Brazil.	1816 Kingdom of Two Sicilies restored.	1815. Poland united to Russia.	1816. Lord Amherst's unsuccessful mission to China.
		1817. Slave trade abolished.			
1818	France joins the Holy Alliance.				1818. The Mahratta power completely overthrown in India by the British.
			1821. Austrian invasion of Italy. 1822. Greek revolution. Declaration of Independence.		
1824	Charles X, king.	1823. Constitutional movement in Spain crushed.			
			1825. Death of Ferdinand IV of Naples, after reign of 66 years.	1826. Nicholas I crowned at Moscow. War against Persia.	1826. Missolonghi taken by the Turks. Athens taken by the Turks.
1830	Revolution and abdication of Charles X. Louis Philippe, king. Algiers taken by the French.			1830-31. Polish insurrections.	1830. Polish struggles for nationality begin.
1831	Abolition of hereditary peerage in France.	1833. Isabella II, queen of Spain. 1834. The Carlist war.	1832. Kingdom of Greece founded.	1832. Poland made part of empire.	1831. Leopold I, king of the Belgians. 1833. Portugal, a constitutional monarchy.

A. D.	From the Beginning of the French Revolution to the World War—A. D. 1789–1914—Con.				
	Arts of Civilization	International Affairs	Great Britain	Prussia	Austria
1837	Morse patents his telegraph. Wheatstone's telegraph patented in England.	1839. Dutch and Belgian boundary dispute settled.	1837. Difficulties in Canada. Victoria, queen. 1840–42. War with China over the opium trade.	1840. Frederick William IV, king.	1838. Commercial treaty with England.
1842	Ether as an anesthetic.				
1844	First telegraphic message, Washington, Baltimore.				
1845	Gutta-percha used.				
1846	Howe's sewing machine patented.	1846. Oregon boundary treaty.	1846. Repeal of the corn laws.		1846. Austria takes possession of Kracow.
1847	Great canal from Durance to Marseille completed.		1846-47. Severe famine in Ireland.		
1848	Girard College opened.	1848. Treaty of Guadalupe Hidalgo between Mexico and United States. Revolutionary disturbance in Europe.	1848. Civil war in Ireland. Habeas corpus act suspended.	1848. Insurrection in Berlin.	1848. Revolution in Hungary and Austria. Francis Joseph, emperor.
1849	Magnetic clock invented by Doctor Locke of Cincinnati.		1849. Punjab annexed to England.	1849. The king declines the imperial crown.	1849. New constitution promulgated.
1850	Tubular bridge in Anglesey, England. Woman's Rights convention at Worcester, Mass.		1850. The war in Lahore ended.	1850. Treaty of peace with Denmark. New constitution for Prussia.	
1851	Railway between Moscow and Leningrad opened. Cable across the English Channel.	1851. International exhibition at London.			1851. Louis Kossuth sentenced to death at Pest.
1853	First Norwegian railway opened.				
1854	First railway in Brazil.	1854. Commercial treaty between the United States and Japan. France, England, Sardinia, Russia, Turkey in Crimean War.	1854. Crimean War. Treaty of alliance with France.	1854. Treaty with Austria, offensive and defensive.	1854. Alliance with England and France.
1855	Panama railway completed. Bessemer's steel process patented.				
1856	Submarine telegraph laid from Cape Breton to Newfoundland.	1856. Close of Crimean War. Treaty of Paris.	1856. British fleet bombards and partially destroys Canton, China.		1856. Hungarians granted amnesty.
1857	Peabody Institute founded at Baltimore.		1857. Rebellion in India begins. King of Delhi proclaimed sovereign of India.		
1858	*Great Eastern* launched. Boston Public Library opened.	1858. Laying of Atlantic cable.			
1859	Storage, or secondary, battery.	1859. India and England connected by telegraph.			1859. War with France and Sardinia. Peace after battle of Solferino.
1860	Ammonia absorption ice machine.				
1861	Passenger elevator.		1861. Death of Prince Albert.	1861. William I, king. 1862. Bismarck, premier.	1861. New constitution for the Austrian monarchy.
1863	Abolition of slavery in the U. S. Pneumatic pianoforte player (first to strike keys by pneumatic pockets).	1864. Convention (International) for telegraph to U. S. Geneva convention (Red Cross).		1864. War with Denmark.	1864. Alliance with Prussia against Denmark.
1865	Antiseptic surgery.		1865. Fenian outbreaks in Ireland.		
1866	Open-hearth steel process.	1866. Atlantic telegraph completed. Latin union begun.		1866. Prussia wars on Austria; annexes Hanover.	1866. War with Prussia and Italy.

A. D.	FROM THE BEGINNING OF THE FRENCH REVOLUTION TO THE WORLD WAR—A. D. 1789–1914—CON.				
	FRANCE	SPAIN AND PORTUGAL	ITALY AND GREECE	RUSSIA	LESSER COUNTRIES
1836	Insurrection attempted by Louis Napoleon at Strasbourg.	1836. The monasteries in Spain dissolved.			
1838	Death of Talleyrand.				1839. Turkey at war with Egypt. 1840. William I abdicates as king of Holland.
		1841–42. Insurrection in Barcelona.	1843. King Otto of Greece compelled to accept a constitution.		1842. Insurrection in India.
1844	War with Morocco.			1844. Emperor visits England.	
		1846. Marriage of Isabella to the Duke of Cadiz. Civil war in Portugal.			1847. Soulouque, president of Haiti.
1848	Abdication of Louis Philippe, and a republic proclaimed. Louis Napoleon, president. Bloody insurrection in Paris.		1848. Rising of the great Italian cities in revolution. Roman republic proclaimed. 1849. Victor Emmanuel, king of Sardinia.	1849. Russia aids Austria in subduing Hungary.	1848. Holland receives a new constitution. Hungary given an independent ministry.
1850	Jerome Bonaparte, marshal of France. Death of Louis Philippe.			1850. Harbor of Sebastopol completed.	1850. Death of Emperor Tau-Kwang of China. Battle of Idstedt, Denmark. Outbreak of Taiping rebellion.
1851	Louis Napoleon elected president for ten years (*coup d'état*).	1851. Death of Godoy, "prince of peace."			1851. Discovery of gold in Australia.
1852	Louis Napoleon declared emperor as Napoleon III.			1853. War begins with Turkey.	1852. Buenos Aires taken by the liberating army.
1854	Crimean War. Allies victorious at Inkerman.	1854. Military insurrection under O'Donnell.	1854. Sardinia takes part in the Crimean War.	1854. War with France and England. Siege of Sebastopol. Battle of Balaklava. 1855. Alexander II, emperor.	War between Turkey and Montenegro. 1855. Santa Anna abdicates the presidency of Mexico.
1856	Peace with Russia.			1856. Evacuation of the Crimea.	1857. Mexican constitution promulgated.
				1858. Partial emancipation of the serfs.	1858. Massacre of Christians in Turkey. Suez railroad completed.
1859	War of France and Sardinia against Austria.	1859. War with Morocco.	1859. War between Austria and Italy.		
1860	Commercial treaty with England. Savoy and Nice surrendered to France by Sardinia. Colonial expansion in West Africa.	1860. Defeat of the Moors.	1860. Sicily and Naples annexed to Sardinia. 1861. Victor Emmanuel, king of Italy. Death of Cavour.	1861. Emancipation of serfs completed.	1861. Canton restored to the Chinese by the French and English.
1863	The French occupy Mexico.		1862. Insurrection in Greece.		
1864	Maximilian proclaimed emperor of Mexico.	1864. Rupture with Peru.	1864. Ionian Isles made over to Greece.	1864. Emigration of Caucasian tribes into Turkey.	1864. Nanking, China, taken by Gordon for the Imperialists. End of Taiping rebellion.
1865	Death of Proudhon. Bismarck visits Napoleon.	1865. Dispute with Chile. 1866. Military revolt led by General Prim.	1865. Florence made capital of Italy. 1866. Austrian war. Venetia made part of Italy.	1866. Inauguration of trial by jury.	1866. Valparaiso bombarded by Spanish fleet.

A. D.	From the Beginning of the French Revolution to the World War—A. D. 1789–1914—Con.				
	Arts of Civilization	International Affairs	Great Britain	Prussia	Austria
		1867. International exposition at Paris.	1867. Passage of Reform bill.	1867. First parliament of the North German Confederation.	1867. Autonomy for Hungary announced. Emperor crowned king of Hungary.
1868	First practical typewriting machine.	1868. Burlingame Treaty (United States and China).			
1869	French Atlantic telegraph completed.	Suez canal formally opened.			
1870	Railway from Calcutta to Bombay. Mount Cenis tunnel boring completed.		1870. Irish Land act passed.	1870. War with France.	1870. Concordat with Rome suspended.
				Germany	
		1871. Treaty of Washington between United States and Great Britain.		1871. William I, of Prussia, emperor.	1871. New German Empire recognized.
1873	Japan adopts European calendar.			1874. Kulturkampf laws against Catholics.	
		1875. Formation of International Bureau of Weights and Measures.	1875. Purchase of Suez Canal shares from khedive of Egypt.		
1876	Exposition at Philadelphia. Telephone invented by Bell.				
1877	Four cycle gas engine invented.		1877. Queen Victoria proclaimed empress of India.		
		1878. Congress of Berlin.			1878. Occupation of Bosnia and Herzegovina.
1879	Edison's incandescent electric lamp.				
1882	Tuberculosis bacillus isolated. Hydrophobia bacillus isolated.	1882. Triple Alliance formed. 1883. International society founded for protection of industrial property.	1882. Control of Egypt secured.	1882. German Colonial Society founded.	
1884	Rotary steam turbine.				
1885	Linotype machine. Revised version of the Old Testament published.	1885. International exhibition at Antwerp.	1885. Khartum captured by the Mahdi. Death of Gordon.		
		1887. Convention of Bern.	1887. Queen's jubilee.		
1888	Pasteur discovers cure for hydrophobia.	International copyright agreement.	1889. Great labor strikes.	1888. Frederick III, William II, emperors.	
		1890. Anti-slave trade agreement.	1890. Stanley returns from Africa.	1890 Bismarck dismissed.	
1891	Carborundum.	1891. Renewal of Triple Alliance.			
1892	Color photography.		1892. Gladstone's fourth premiership.		
1893	Electrical measurements established.	1893. Exposition at Chicago.	1893. Bering Sea arbitration.	1893. Anti-Jesuit law repealed.	
		1894. War between China and Japan.	1894. Manchester ship canal opened.		1894. Commercial treaty with Russia.
1895	Lick refracting telescope made by Clark. Discovery of X-rays.			1896. New civil code completed.	1896. Archduke Karl Ludwig, heir to the throne, dies.
		1897. Universal postal congress.	1897. Queen's diamond jubilee celebrated.		
1898	Reform edict issued in China. Discovery of radium.	1898. Pope offers mediation in Cuba.	1898. Irish local government bill passed. Death of Gladstone.	1898. Emperor visits Jerusalem.	1898. Assassination of the empress.
		1899. First Hague conference.	1899. The Boer war in South Africa begins.		
1900	Opening of the Elbe and Trave canal, Germany.	"Open door" policy for China declared by U. S.	1901. Death of Victoria; Edward VII king.	1900. Abolition of Roman law. New civil code goes into effect.	1900. Marriage of Francis Ferdinand.
1902	First wireless message across the Atlantic.	1902. Venezuelan claims of European powers arbitrated.	1902. Japanese alliance. End of Boer war.		1902. Triple Alliance renewed.
1903	Completion of the Pacific cable.	1903. Canal treaty with Panama.	1903. King visits Italy, Portugal, and France.		
1904	New York subway opened.		1904. Younghusband enters Tibet.		
1905	Power plants erected at Niagara Falls. Simplon tunnel.	1905. Norway and Sweden separate. 906. Algeciras conference.	1906. Militant agitation for woman suffrage begun.	1905. Moroccan intervention.	1905. Treaty with Germany.
1907	*Lusitania*'s first voyage.	1907. Second Hague conference.		1907. William II in London.	1907. Universal suffrage bill.
			1908. Asquith, prime minister. Old Age Pension act passed.		1908. Bosnia and Herzegovina acquired.
1909	Discovery of north pole announced.				
1910	Woman's suffrage movement grows.				
1911	Amundsen discovers south pole.	1911. Atlantic fisheries dispute between U. S. and Great Britain settled by Hague Tribunal. Agadir affair.	1911. Coronation of George V.	1911. Moroccan disagreement.	1911. Austria increases army.
1912	*Titanic* disaster. Scott at south pole.		1912. Minimum wage bill.		
1913	Wireless messages across Atlantic.				

From the Beginning of the French Revolution to the World War—A. D. 1789–1914—Con.

A. D.	France	Spain and Portugal	Italy and Greece	Russia	Lesser Countries
		1867. Death of Marshal O'Donnell. 1868. Queen deposed.	1867. Garibaldi and the Papal States. Second attempt to take Rome.	1867. Russian America (Alaska) sold to the United States.	1867. City of Mexico evacuated by French. Execution of Maximilian in Mexico. Egypt declared by the sultan to be a separate sovereignty.
1870	New liberal constitution approved by a plebiscite. War with Prussia.	1870. Amadeus, king of Spain.			
1871	Capitulation of Paris. Peace ratified.	1871. Sagasta, minister.	1871. Rome made capital of Italy.	1871. Telegraph between Russia and Japan.	1871. Abolition of Feudalism in Japan.
1874	Endeavor to establish monarchy.	1874. Alfonso XII, king. 1875. Civil war.			
1876	Large republican gains in elections.				
				1877. War against Turkey.	
			1878. Humbert, king. Leo XIII, pope.	1878. Spread of nihilism.	1878. Montenegro, Serbia, and Rumania, independent.
1879	Jules Grévy, president.				
1881	Protectorate over Tunis.	1881. Sagasta, minister.		1881. Alexander III, czar.	1882. Beginning of Pan-Islam movement in Turkey.
1883	Madagascar occupied.				
1884	War with China.				
1885	Death of Victor Hugo.		1885. War with Abyssinia.	1885. Kronstadt canal opened.	
1887	Boulanger incident. Military scandals.		1887. Failure of Abyssinian expedition.	1887. Czar forbids real estate holding by foreigners.	
1890	War with Dahomey.	1890. Castillo, premier.		1890–92. Famine throughout the country.	1890. First Japanese parliament opened.
1892	Panama scandals.				
		1893. War with Morocco.	1893. Pope's jubilee (Leo XIII).		
1894	Casimir-Périer, president. Dreyfus tried; imprisoned.		1896. Peace with Abyssinia.	1894. Nicholas II, czar.	1895. Federation act of Australia approved. 1896. Jameson raid in South Africa.
1897	Fashoda Incident.	1897. Assassination of Castillo.			1897. Turko-Grecian war.
1898	Review of Dreyfus case.	1898. Spanish-American war.		1898. Port Arthur leased from China.	1898. Hawaii annexed to U. S. Wilhelmina, queen of Holland.
1899	Loubet, president.				
		1902. Alfonso XIII, king.	1900. Victor Emmanuel III, king.	1901. Tolstóy excommunicated.	1900. Outbreak of the Boxers in China. 1901. Submission of China to the allied powers.
1903	Dreyfus declared innocent.		1903. Accession of Pope Pius X. 1904. General strike in Italy.	1904. War with Japan. 1905. Constitution granted. 1906. First Russian Duma opens.	1903. Peter I, king of Serbia.
1907	French occupation of Morocco.	1908. Manuel II, king of Portugal.	1907. Italo-Argentine treaty.		
					1909. Abdication of Abdul Hamid II.
1910	Railway strike suppressed.	1910. Portugal a republic.	1910. New Greek constitution. 1911. Italo-Turkish war.	1910. Cholera epidemic. 1911. Treaty of 1832 abrogated by U. S.	1910. Japan annexes Korea. 1911. Diaz overthrown in Mexico.
1912	Morocco made a protectorate.	1912. Franco-Spanish treaty.	1912. Balkan war.	1912. Russia increases navy.	1912. China a republic. War in the Balkans.
1913	M. Poincaré, president.		1913. Constantine, king of Greece.	1913. Serf class abolished.	1913. Balkan war closes.

A. D.	From the Beginning of the World War, 1914, to the Present Time				
	Arts of Civilization	International Affairs	Great Britain	Germany	Austria
1914	First important use of airplanes in warfare.	1914. World War. Panama canal opened.	1914. Irish home rule bill passed. War with Germany.	1914. War with Russia, France, Belgium, England, Serbia.	1914. Assassination of Francis Ferdinand and wife.
1915	Voice transmitted by wireless telephone from Arlington, Va., to Honolulu, 4900 miles.	1915. Belgian relief under commission directed by Herbert Hoover.	1915. War continues. New coalition ministry.	1915. Germany declares waters around British Isles war zone. War with Italy.	1915. Przemysl taken by Russians. Italy wars on Austria-Hungary.
1916	Marseille-Rhone canal completed. Alaskan railway building.	1916. United States sends peace note to warring nations.	1916. Compulsory military service bill. Lloyd George, prime minister.	1916. Siege of Verdun fails. Rumania conquered.	1916. Charles I succeeds Francis Joseph.
1917	Food production increased in belligerent countries by public instruction and control.	1917. United States enters World War. 1918. Central Powers collapse; Armistice.	1917. Imperial war cabinet. 1918. Suffrage granted to women.	1917. Use of submarines increased. 1918. Treaty of Brest-Litovsk with Russia.	1917. German-Slav dissension. 1918. Breakdown of the dual monarchy.
1919	Airplane flight across Atlantic.	1919. Paris Peace Conference.		1919. Ebert elected president.	1919. Treaty of Saint Germain.
1920	Notable progress in flood protection projects in United States.	1920. Versailles Peace Treaty in effect. League of Nations holds first meetings.	1920. Continued industrial disturbances. Rebellion in Ireland.	1920. Industrial unrest. Communist uprising.	1920. Czechoslovakia in defensive alliance with Jugoslavia forms nucleus of Little Entente.
1921	Great extension in use of radio. Second Simplon tunnel completed. Michelson measures diameter of two stars.	1921. Continued difficulties over reparations payments. Arms conference meets at Washington.	1921. Imperial Conference of Premiers at London. Establishment of Irish Free State approved by Parliament.	1921. Ludendorff conducts reactionary militarist campaign.	1921. Rumania joins Little Entente, which prevents ex-Emperor Charles from regaining throne of Hungary.
1922	Radio broadcasting daily feature in many cities. Einstein relativity theory confirmed by solar eclipse observations in Australia.	1922. Washington Conference adopts several treaties. First meeting of World Court. Peace treaties between U. S. and Germany and Hungary.	1922. Gandhi, in India, imprisoned for sedition. Irish Free State established. Independence of Egypt recognized. Premier Lloyd George resigns.	1922. Treaty of Rapallo with Russia. Foreign minister Rathenau assassinated. Germany in default of reparations payments.	1922. Swiss reject capital levy. Anthony Svehla, an Agrarian, becomes premier in Czechoslovakia. Hungary abolishes secret voting.
1923	Holland-Java wireless service, 7500 miles. First transcontinental air mail service inaugurated by United States. Insulin treatment for diabetes.	1923. Treaty between Yugoslavia and Italy over Dalmatia. Turkish-Allied Treaty of Lausanne. Naval Limitation treaties ratified.	1923. Bonar Law succeeded by Stanley Baldwin as premier. War debt to United States funded. Development of great naval base at Singapore announced.	1923. Part of Rhineland occupied by France. Chancellor Cuno succeeded by Streseman. The mark continues to fall in value.	1923. Czechoslovakia and Rumania sign a defensive military treaty. Legitimists plot to restore Habsburgs to Hungarian throne.
1924	U. S. navy fliers encircle globe.	1924. Dawes Reparations Plan accepted by the powers concerned.	1924. Labor government in power; after defeat, is succeeded by Conservative government under Baldwin.	1924. Evacuation of Ruhr by French. Currency stabilized.	1924. Czechoslovakia concludes treaties of amity with Italy and France.
1925	Discovery by Millikan of cosmic rays. Body of Tutankhamen disinterred. Discovery of phototelegraphy.	1925. Locarno treaties for replacement of war by arbitration among European powers ratified.	1925. Government restores gold standard of currency. Coal mine operators subsidized to avoid strike over wage cut.	1925. President Ebert's death followed by election of Hindenburg.	1925. Deportation of Germans from Polish Upper Silesia and of Poles from German portion.
1926	North Pole reached by airplane and dirigible. Production of "Coolidge" rays.	1926. Arms traffic treaty signed by 32 nations at Geneva.	1926. General strike called to support miners, who struck on withdrawal of government subsidy to coal mines.	1926. Germany admitted to League of Nations. Neutrality Treaty with Russia.	1926. General Pilsudski overthrows Polish government with the help of the army; makes himself dictator.
1927	Transatlantic radio-telephone service. Television demonstrated. First solo transatlantic flight, by Lindbergh.	1927. Poland-Lithuania break averted through League of Nations. 1928. Signing of Paris Pact for outlawing war.	1927. Rupture of trade relations with Russia. Britain recognizes independence of Iraq.	1927. Continued progress in industrial expansion; leads in forming international trusts.	1927. Serious labor riots in Vienna suppressed. Treaty between Yugoslavia and France.
1928	Turkey adopts Latin alphabet. Louvain library dedicated. Invention of teletypesetter.	Bolivia - Paraguay war postponed through League and Pan-Amer. Conference.	1928. Continued depression in Coal mining industry. Simon Commission on Indian home rule.	1928. Government upheld in general election; chancellor advocates union with Austria.	1928. Polish elections strengthen Pilsudski. Peasant party wins power in Rumania.
1929	Byrd leads Antarctic expedition; flies over South Pole. *Graf Zeppelin* flies around world.	1929. Young Plan supersedes Dawes Plan for final settlement of reparations problem.	1929. First election under universal adult suffrage. Labor party wins plurality. MacDonald premier.	1929. Serious Communist riots in Berlin suppressed by police.	1929. King of Yugoslavia becomes dictator.

A. D.	From the Beginning of the World War, 1914, to the Present Time				
	France	Spain and Portugal	Italy and Greece	Russia	Lesser Countries
1914	War with Germany, Austria, Turkey. Battle of the Marne. Battle of the Aisne.	1914. Spain and Portugal neutral in European war.	1914. Italy proclaims her neutrality.	1914. War with Germany, Austria, Turkey.	1914. Chinese parliament dissolved. Japan seizes Kiaochow.
1915	War continues. War with Bulgaria.	1915. Revolution in Portugal. Spanish cabinet resigns.	1915. Italy at war with Austria, Germany, Turkey, Bulgaria.	1915. Evacuation of Warsaw. War with Bulgaria.	1915. Allies attack Dardanelles. Massacre of 800,000 Armenians. Bulgaria makes war on Serbia.
1916	$15,000,000 loan from New York financiers. Siege of Verdun successfully resisted. Battle of the Somme.	1916. Portugal seizes Austrian and German vessels. War on Portugal declared by Germany.	1916. Italians capture Gorizia. Provisional government in Greece. 1917. King Constantine of Greece abdicates.	1916. Russians capture Erzerum; Brusilov advances. 1917. Monarchy ended. Soviet Republic established.	1916. Allies withdraw from Dardanelles. Rumania at war with Teutonic powers. China again a republic. Denmark ratifies sale of Danish West Indies to the United States.
1918	Foch, generalissimo.				
1919	Electoral reform act.	1919. Spain joins League of Nations.	1919. D'Annunzio enters Fiume.	1919. Bolshevists defeat all invaders.	1919. Paderewski ministry in Poland.
1920	Serious railroad strike. Fiftieth anniversary of Republic. Millerand elected president.	1920. In Portugal, former king, Manuel II, renounces claim to the throne.	1920. *Greece:* Constantine recalled by plebiscite. *Italy:* Strong agrarian and socialist movements.	1920. Bolsheviki defeat General Wrangel. Attempted invasion of Poland repelled.	1920. *Turkey:* Treaty of Sèvres signed. Nationalist movement in Asia Minor.
1921	Briand, prime minister, succeeding Leygues. France supports Turkey against Greece in the Near East.	1921. Spanish troops defeated in Morocco. Premier Dato assassinated.	1921. *Italy:* Fascisti movement against the socialists. *Greece:* King Constantine leads Greek army against Turks in Asia Minor.	1921. Breakdown of Bolshevist industrial scheme. Famine conditions widespread.	1921. Non-co-operation movement under Gandhi in India. Mining and oil rights exempted from government appropriation in Mexico. Famine in China.
1922	Poincaré succeeds Briand as premier. Stinnes-Lubersac agreement for handling reparations payments in materials.	1922. Moors on the Riff coast resist Spanish troops successfully. Portugal has nine ministries within the year.	1922. Greeks defeated. Fascisti under Mussolini seize government in Italy. Pope Benedict XV succeeded by Pius XI.	1922. Commercial treaties with Germany and Italy. Conflict between the government and the Church.	1922. Civil war in China. Japan completes evacuation of Shantung province. Turkish National Assembly at Angora deposes the sultan. Poland takes Vilna from Lithuania.
1923	French and Belgian troops occupy the Ruhr valley. Pacific and Naval Limitation treaties ratified.	1923. Spanish campaigns in Morocco. Rivera becomes dictator of Spain.	1923. Violent eruption of Mt. Etna. Fascist reorganization of army, under General Diaz.	1923. American relief commission terminates work. Diplomatic differences with Great Britain adjusted.	1923. Memel assigned to Lithuania by council of ambassadors. Li Yuan Hung, president of China, compelled to resign.
1924	Poincaré defeated. Succeeded by Herriot, who adopts more conciliatory tone in international relations.	1924. Continued hostilities in Spanish Morocco.	1924. Greece made a republic. Fiume annexed to Italy by agreement with Yugoslavia.	1924. Lenin dies and is succeeded by Stalin. Trotzky loses power in government.	1924. Turkish government abolishes the caliphate and declares for a republic. Disastrous earthquake in Japan.
1925	France wars with native tribes in Morocco and Syria. Financial difficulties occasion several ministerial crises.	1925. General Rivera assumes title of premier, relinquishing that of dictator. General growth of prosperity.	1925. Pangalos seizes Greek premiership. Marked economic recovery of Italy under Fascist direction.	1925. Treaty with Japan, by which Japan withdrew troops from northern Sakhalin.	1925. Chinese tariff autonomy granted. Tacna-Arica plebiscite commission headed by General Pershing.
1926	French victorious over Riff tribesmen. Poincaré forms national government; balances the budget.	1926. Rivera proclaims end of parliamentarianism. Republican régime in Portugal overthrown.	1926. Attempted assassination of Mussolini. Greece returns to constitutional government.	1926. Communistic practices greatly modified to secure co-operation of peasants.	1926. General Chang in China seizes Peiping. Poland and Rumania sign 5-year mutual guarantee treaty.
1927	Trade treaty with Germany. Treaties of arbitration with Yugoslavia and Rumania.	1927. Rivera summons national assembly; it acts in advisory capacity only.	1927. Italian treaty with Albania. Italian electoral laws increase power of Mussolini.	1927. Defeat of revolutionary efforts in Europe and China.	1927. Continued civil war in China. Financial panic in Japan; Hirohito crowned emperor.
1928	Poincaré returned to power by large majority. France on gold standard.	1928. American and British loans for stabilizing exchange.	1928. Italian parliament replaced by Fascist controlled chamber. Venizelos again premier of Greece. Italo-Greek treaty of friendship.	1928. Stalin succeeds in banishing opponents; Five-year plan for economic progress begun.	1928. Albania becomes kingdom. Famine in China; Chiang Kai-shek becomes president.
1929	Death of Marshal Foch. Tardieu becomes premier.	1929. Attempted revolution suppressed.	1929. Temporal power of Pope restored by Mussolini.	1929. Trotzky exiled. War with China averted.	1929. China enacts first national tariff. Tacna-Arica dispute settled.

A. D.	From the Beginning of World War I, 1914, to the Present Time—Con.				
	Arts of Civilization	International Affairs	Great Britain	Germany	Central Europe
1930	International bank begins operations.	1930. Naval disarmament conference in London.	1930. "Civil disobedience" riots in India. Unrest in Egypt.	1930. Occupation of German territory by Allies terminated.	1930. Monarchists and Socialists in Hungary endanger public peace. Carol seizes throne of Rumania.
1931	Rapid progress in discovering the nature of atoms and of celestial bodies.	1931. Year's moratorium on German reparations and Allied debts granted.	1931. Gold standard suspended. Coalition government under MacDonald introduces tariff.	1931. Plans for customs union with Austria abandoned under pressure. Bruening chancellor.	1931. Yugoslavia adopts new constitution.
1932	Zuider Zee reclamation dike in Holland completed. Pontine marshes in Italy reclaimed.	1932. Lausanne conference puts virtual end to German reparation payments.	1932. Imperial Economic Conference at Ottawa promotes economic cohesion of Empire. Irish Free State in tariff war with Great Britain.	1932. Hindenburg re-elected president. Hitlerites gain in power.	1932. Hungary and other countries default on foreign debt payments.
1933	Century of Progress Exposition, Chicago. Lindberghs fly 30,000 miles visiting 21 countries.	1933. World Economic Conference at London meets; disbands without results.	1933. De Valera president of Irish Free State; abolishes oath of allegiance. Constitution for India announced.	1933. Hitler made dictator; Nazi rule. Withdrawal from League of Nations.	1933. Austria, under Dolfuss, resists German attacks; Socialist party crushed. Union of Little Entent—Czechoslovakia, Yugoslavia, Rumania.
1934	U. S. naval squadron flies from west coast to Hawaii.	1934. Japan ends naval limitation agreement.	1934. Progress in economic recovery.	1934. Hindenburg dies. Anti-Jew decrees. Party purged by assassinations.	1934. Dolfuss assassinated by Nazis. Schussnigg chancellor of Austria.
1935	Trans-Pacific air service begun — San Francisco to Manila.	1935. England, France, and Italy meet in conference at Stresa to discuss peace problems.	1935. Stanley Baldwin, prime minister. Silver Jubilee of King George V. Conciliatory policy toward Italy reversed through popular pressure.	1935. Saar returns to Germany. Naval Treaty with Britain.	1935. Death of Pilsudski. Polish treaties with Russia and Germany.
1936	Hoover dam completed. Launching of the *Queen Mary*. Zeppelin inaugurates trans-Atlantic service. Great Lakes Exposition, Cleveland, Ohio.	1936. Sanction policy against Italy fails. Fascist and Communist powers clash in Spain. League declares Italy aggressor in Ethiopian war.	1936. Deaths of King George V and Rudyard Kipling. Edward VIII king; abdicates. George VI succeeds. Eire abolishes Governor Generalship. Egypt independent.	1936. Aids Spanish rebels. Alliance with Japan. Sends troops into demilitarized Rhine zone.	1936. Economic penetration by Germany. Continued friction in Austria with Nazi Partisans.
1937	Automatic landing device for airplanes introduced. Paris Exposition. Construction of solar heat collector for power. Two longest span bridges in the world opened at San Francisco.	1937. Unrestricted armaments race. Belgium returns to status of neutral state, cutting tie with France and England. Patrol of Spanish coast by ships of 27 nations to prevent outside aid to either party.	1937. Tariff reductions within empire. Chamberlain succeeds as prime minister. Coal mines nationalized, effective in 1942. Federal constitution for India effective. New constitution adopted by Irish Free State (Ireland)	1937. Rapprochement with Italy and enlargement of influence among central European nations.	1937. Balkans in move to curb outside intrigue. Yugoslavia signs 5-year treaty of friendship with Italy.
1938	Production of practical lightweight Diesel engine announced.	1938. Munich conference: Britain and France abandon Czechoslovakia to Germany.	1938. Parleys with Ireland for settlement of pending controversies.	1938. Austria and Czechoslovakia taken.	1938. Czechoslovakia seized by Germany.
1939	New York and San Francisco expositions. First year of commercial air traffic in U. S. without fatal accident.	1939. Political influence of League of Nations in eclipse. World War II begins.	1939. Declaration of war against Germany.	1939. Danzig taken. Poland conquered and divided with Russia. Alliance with Russia.	1939. Poland conquered by Germany and Russia.
1940	Laboratory method devised for release of atomic energy.	1940. Tokyo joins Rome-Berlin axis. International Labor office removed to Montreal.	1940. Churchill premier. Army driven from France; German invasion threatened; Terrific aerial raids. Conquest of Italian East Africa.	1940. Conquest of Norway, Lowlands, France.	1940. Germany takes control of Hungary, Bulgaria, Rumania; gains access to Black Sea.
1941	Grand Coulee dam completed; largest in world. War needs cause improvement in aircraft.	1941. Atlantic Charter promulgated by Roosevelt and Churchill.	1941. Reverses in Greece; huge shipping losses; alliance with Russia; war against Japan.	1941. Conquest of Yugoslavia and Greece. War declared on Russia and U. S.	1941. German domination complete.
1942	Announcement of radar detection device.		1942. Loss of Malaya, Singapore, Burma.	1942. Advance into Russia to Don; in N. Africa to Egypt.	
1943	Use of penicillin.	1943. Conferences at Casablanca, Quebec, Moscow, Cairo, Tehran.	1943. Victories in N. Africa and Italy; submarines beaten.	1943. Driven from N. Africa; defeat in Russia; cities ruined from air; submarines fail.	1943. Yugoslav patriots battle Germans.

A. D.	From the Beginning of World War I, 1914, to the Present Time—Con.				
	France	Spain and Portugal	Italy and Greece	Russia	Other Countries
1930	Briand urges formation of United States of Europe.	1930. Spanish dictator, Rivera, resigns. Berenguer becomes premier.	1930. Italian naval rivalry with France. Turco-Greek treaty of friendship.	1930. Rapid progress in economic plan and extension of "collective" farms.	1930. Renewed civil war in China.
1931	Doumer president. Death of Briand. Laval premier; visits President Hoover.	1931. Republic in Spain; Alfonso XIII flees; church and state separated.	1931. Controversy between Italy and Vatican; temporary suppression of Catholic organizations in Italy.	1931. Rapid industrialization during five-year plan. Socialization of agriculture.	1931. Japan seizes Manchuria.
1932	Tardieu premier. Herriot premier, defeated on issue of war debt payments to U. S.	1932. Catalonia made autonomous within Spain. Jesuits expelled from Spain.	1932. Amnesty for political prisoners in Italy. Greece defaults on foreign debt payments.	1932. Non-aggression treaties with France and Poland. Food crisis with widespread distress.	1932. Japan takes and relinquishes Shanghai; establishes Manchukuo.
1933	Several premiers defeated on budget proposals for meeting deficit.	1933. Portugal ends dictatorship; resumes constitutional government.	1933. Italy negotiates 4-power pact with Britain, France, Germany on arms, economic interests.	1933. Non-aggression treaties with nine countries. Relations with U. S. resumed.	1933. Japan resigns from League of Nations.
1934	Financial scandal compromises officials.	1934. Conservatives gain in Spanish Cortes.	1934. Italy plans abolition of Chamber.	1934. Communist control legalized.	1934. Japan moderates militant attitude.
1935	Laval premier. Deflation by decree as depression makes itself felt.	1935. Political crisis in Spain.	1935. Civil war in Greece. Italy invades Ethiopia.	1935. Closer relations with Great Britain.	1935. Threatened Chino-Japanese conflict in North China; Japs seize Chahar.
1936	Blum premier. Popular front government. Alliance with Russia. Munitions manufacture nationalized. Autonomy granted to Syria, a mandated territory.	1936. Liberals win. Conservatives rebel, supported by Fascist powers, Italy and Germany.	1936. Italy conquers Ethiopia; aids Spanish rebels. New Roman Empire proclaimed. Greece goes Fascist, a dictatorship being set up under Gen. Metaxas.	1936. Adopts constitution democratic in form. Alliance with France. Stalin removes opponents by treason trials.	1936. Chinese resistance to Japan hardens. Japanese pro-army cabinet defeated; refuses to resign. Turkey remilitarizes the Dardanelles.
1937	Checks German penetration of Morocco. Blum resigns after having been refused extraordinary fiscal powers. Chautemps succeeds as premier.	1937. Civil war continues. Portugal aids rebels.	1937. Italo-British treaty on Mediterranean fleet. Italy joins pact with Germany and Japan to combat Communism.	1937. Treason purge extends to army command and throughout every department of life. First popular election held for legislators.	1937. Chinese Communists grow in power. Japan seizes Peiping, Shanghai, Nanking.
1938	Enlarged armament program. Daladier premier. Policy of appeasement toward Germany.	1938. Government and rebel forces struggle, success varying.	1938. Closer relations with England and Germany enhance power of Italy in Mediterranean.	1938. First meeting of national legislature.	1938. Chinese resist Jap invasion, using Guerilla warfare.
1939	War against Germany in aid of Poland.	1939. Spanish government forces conquered. Franco dictator.	1939. Italy declares neutrality in War of 1939.	1939. Alliance with Germany; bases obtained from Baltic states. Poland divided with Germany. War on Finland.	1939. Japan exerts pressure to drive nationals of other countries from captured Chinese cities.
1940	Defeat by Germany; two-thirds of country occupied; Pétain chief of state.	1940. Spain hovers between neutrality and affiliation with axis powers.	1940. Italy declares war on France; attacks Greece and British Africa; disastrous defeats.	1940. Finland cedes territory; three Baltic states incorporated.	1940. Stalemate in China; United States obtains 8 bases in British America.
1941	German pressure to force cooperation. "Free French" in Africa and Syria.	1941. Germany seeks passage to Gibraltar.	1941. Greece conquered by Germany. Italy under German control.	1941. Germany declares war; takes Odessa and Kiev; fails at Moscow and Leningrad.	1941. Japan attacks United States.
1942	Laval in power.		1942. Allies take Libya.	1942. Germans reach Don.	1942. Japan takes Philippines, Singapore, Burma, East Indies; defeated at Coral Sea, Midway.
1943	Germany completes occupation; fleet scuttled; DeGaulle rises in power abroad.	1943. Portugal permits British bases in Azores.	1943. Allies invade Italy; Fascism abolished; peace with Allies, war with Germany.	1943. Germans retreat to Dnieper.	1943. Japan defeated in Solomons, New Guinea.

A. D.	From the Beginning of World War I, 1914, to the Present Time—Con.				
	Arts of Civilization	International Affairs	Great Britain	Germany	Central Europe
1944	Development of rocket planes.	1944. Dumbarton Oaks agreement on draft of international charter. Benelux agreement.	1944. Invasion of Normandy. British in northern France and Belgium. V-bomb attack on England.	1944. Germans defeated in Italy, driven from France and Poland. Americans cross Rhine. Hitler injured in assassination plot.	1944. Rumania and Bulgaria desert Germany. Yugoslavia and Greece freed. Polish rising crushed by Russian inaction.
1945	Atomic bomb tested successfully at Los Alamos; used at Hiroshima. First use of atomic energy. U. S., Great Britain, Canada, decide to keep atomic bomb secrets until U. N. can take over.	1945. Crimean Conference at Yalta. Act of Chapultepec. Potsdam Conference: Churchill (Attlee), Truman, Stalin. San Francisco Conference. Charter of United Nations framed by 51 nations.	1945. British in northern Germany. Germany surrenders. General election. Attlee (Labor) succeeds Churchill.	1945. Berlin taken by Russians. German armies surrendered. Germany occupied by Allies.	1945. Poland and Czechoslovakia liberated. Austria and Hungary occupied.
1946	Radar signals reflected from moon. Bikini tests of atom bomb.	1946. League of Nations dissolved. First General Assembly of U. N. at London and New York. Trygve Lie secretary general of U. N. U. N. accepts Rockefeller gift of New York site for permanent headquarters. Secret agreements at Yalta made public. Paris Conference on peace treaties with Axis satellites.	1946. Bank of England nationalized. Churchill's "Iron Curtain" speech.	1946. Scarcity and food riots. Skilled workmen deported to Russia. Nuremburg trials of war criminals. Amnesty for minor Nazis. Russia blocks economic union; American and British zones become one (Bizonia).	1946. Readjustment in Poland; pro-Russian party in power. Austria under 4-power military rule.
1947	Baruch (U. S.) plan for atomic control fails through Russian opposition. U. S. expedition under Byrd in Antarctica. U. S. offers radioactive isotopes for medical research. Automatic plane flies from Newfoundland to England.	1947. Treaties with satellites made. U. N. admits Thai, Yemen, Pakistan. U. N. establishes permanent interim committee (Little Assembly). Marshall plan for European rehabilitation proposed.	1947. Coal industry nationalized. Coal famine causes power shortage. India given dominion status as India and Pakistan. Ceylon given dominion status. Severe food shortage. Cripps economic dictator. Railways and electrical industries nationalized.	1947. Moscow conference on German and Austrian treaties fails. London Conference on German and Austrian treaties fails. Hunger strikes. Helgoland naval base destroyed.	1947. Peace treaties with Hungary, Bulgaria, and Rumania. Communists seize governments in Bulgaria and Hungary. Mikolajczyk, anti-Communist leader, flees Poland.
1948	Jet planes developed to exceed speed of sound. Hale 200-inch reflecting telescope dedicated at California Tech observatory, Mt. Palomar, Cal. Virus of common cold isolated. Increasing use of television.	1948 U. N. admits Burma. Brussels conference and agreement of Britain, France, and Benelux nations for defense. Danube conference controlled by Russia. Tension between East and West increases.	1948. National Health Service act goes into effect. National unemployment benefits and old age pensions extended. Burma becomes independent. Proposed nationalization of iron and steel.	1948. Economic parliament of Bizonia begins operations. Four-party gov't of Berlin ceases. Russians blockade Berlin by land. "Airlift" supplies city's Western sectors. Provisional assembly forming gov't for western Germany.	1948. Communist coup gains control of Czechoslovakia. Cominform denounces Tito for nationalist practices.
1949	U. S. bomber circles globe in 94 hours in first non-stop flight.	1949. U. N. mediates truce between Palestine and Egypt. International wheat agreement for production and marketing adopted by 42 nations.	1949. Northern Ireland votes to stay in United Kingdom. Clothes rationing ended. Britain, United States, Canada, France, Belgium, the Netherlands, Luxembourg, Norway, negotiate North Atlantic pact initiated by Winston Churchill.	1949. Marshall Plan production goals in Western Germany retarded by lack of long-term investment capital.	1949. Hungarian Communist court convicts Cardinal Mindszenty of treason. Protests from Vatican and Western powers. Bulgaria attacks Protestant clergy.

A. D.	From the Beginning of World War I, 1914, to the Present Time—Con.				
	France	**Spain and Portugal**	**Italy and Greece**	**Russia**	**Other Countries**
1944	Liberation from Germany. DeGaulle assumes leadership.	1944. Franco isolated by German reverses, but maintains power.	1944. Rome taken. Germans driven into north Italy, where Mussolini sets up puppet government. Greece freed by English.	1944. Germans driven from Russia. Balkans and Finland make peace.	1944. Japan gains in China; defeated in Burma; loses Guam, Saipan. Fleet ruined at Leyte.
1945	Constituent assembly meets. Petain, Laval, and other collaborators prosecuted.		1945. Germans in northern Italy surrender. Mussolini killed.	1945. Russia liberates Poland; occupies Berlin and eastern Germany, Hungary, Austria. At Yalta, Russia is promised the Kuriles and Sakhalin. Russia enters war against Japan.	1945. Japan loses Iwo Jima and Okinawa, trade cut off, main islands bombed. Atomic bomb at Hiroshima. Japan surrenders. Chinese Nationalists occupy southern Chinese cities.
1946	DeGaulle resigns. Felix Gouin succeeds. First proposed constitution rejected; second, adopted. Blum interim ministry.	1946. U. N. recommends that its members withdraw diplomats from Madrid.	1946. Peace treaty signed. Victor Emmanuel III abdicates. Italy votes for a republic. Humbert II and the House of Savoy leave Italy. Trieste neutralized. DeGasperi expels Communists from cabinet. King George II returns to Greece. Civil conflict.	1946. Disputes with Iran over Azerbaijan. New 5-year plan. Attempt to get control of Dardanelles opposed by Turkey.	1946. Japan under control of Allied Supreme command, adopts new constitution. War criminals executed. Civil war in China; Nationalists adopt permanent constitution. Philippines become independent. Race war and terrorism in Palestine.
1947	Fourth Republic inaugurated: president, Vincent Auriol; premier, Paul Remadier. Remadier ejects Communists from cabinet. DeGaullists win local elections. Remadier resigns; Schuman succeeds. Communist-led political strikes.	1947. Franco gets overwhelming majority in plebiscite.	1947. King George II dies; his brother Paul succeeds. Guerilla warfare continues. U. S. gives to Greece and Turkey $400,000,000 for defense against Communist aggression.	1947. Russia in general opposition to Western powers. Liberal use of veto. Revival of Comintern as Communist Information Bureau (Cominform).	1947. U. S. gives up attempt to mediate in China. Civil war continues with Communist gains. Palestine: illegal immigration and terrorism continue. U. N. recommends partition.
1948	Queille succeeds Schuman as premier. Political strikes continue, directed now against Marshall plan.		1948. Political strikes against DeGasperi gov't. DeGasperi (Christian Democrat) and gov't parties carry elections against Communists.	1948. Russian blockade of Berlin met by airlift. Negotiations fruitless. Tightening of control over Communist parties without Russia.	1948. Communists extend control to Yangtze. In Korea two gov'ts are set up in north and south. Palestine: state of Israel set up by Jews.
1949	"Merci" train of 49 cars, one for each state, sent to United States as an expression of gratitude for the Friendship Train that was sent to France in 1948. Death of General Henri Giraud.		1949. Italy and France sign plan to seek customs union and other economic accords. Italy signs North Atlantic pact.	1949. Russia forms Council for Mutual Aid in opposition to Marshall Plan. Andrei Vichinsky succeeds Vyacheslav Molotov as foreign minister and M. A. Menshikov succeeds Anastas Mikoyan as minister of foreign trade.	1949. Nationalist government under rule of Chiang Kai-shek overthrown by Communists. Li Tsung-jen named acting president and Ho Ying-chin premier of Nanking Government. Chaim Weizmann first president of Israel.

IMPORTANT WARS OF HISTORY

Time	Name and Results	Leading Battles	Chief Leaders
B. C. 2750	Triumph of Semitic invaders over people of the Mesopotamian valley.	. . . .	Sargon of Accad.
2200	Amorite kings conquer Babylon, Sumer, and Accad.		
1600	Egyptians make conquest of western Asia.		
14th to 12th century	Hittites and Hebrews conquer and occupy the Asiatic realms of the Egyptians.		
1300–1000	Greeks conquer the Ægean lands.	Siege of Troy.	
13th century	Hittite empire overthrown by Indo-European invaders.		
750–700	Assyrian kings become masters of western Asia.	. . . .	Sargon II.
606	Assyrian empire overthrown by the Chaldeans.		
550–525	Persian Conquests. Persia supreme in western Asia and in Egypt.	. . . .	Cyrus; Cambyses.
500–479	Greco-Persian Wars. Greece successfully resists Persian invasion.	Marathon; Thermopylæ; Salamis; Platæa; Mycale.	Miltiades; Leonidas; Themistocles; Pausanius; Xerxes; Darius.
431–404	Peloponnesian War. Athens conquered by Sparta.	Mytilene; Platæa; Sphacteria; Amphipolis.	Pericles; Alcibiades; Lysander.
343–290	Samnite Wars. Romans conquer Samnites.	Caudine Forks; Sentinum.	Fabius Maximus; Gaius Pontius.
334–323	Wars of Alexander the Great. Greek forces conquer Persia and Egypt.	Granicus; Issus; Arbela.	Alexander the Great; Darius.
264–146	Punic Wars. Romans destroy Carthage.	Ticinus; Trebia; Thrasymenus; Cannæ; Metaurus; Zama.	Fabius; Scipio; Hannibal.
200–146	Greco-Roman War. Greece subdued by Rome.	Cynoscephalæ; Pydna.	Flaminius; Æmilius Paulus; Mummius; Perseus.
112–106	Jugurthine War. Romans conquer Numidia.	Muthul; Cirta.	Jugurtha; Metellus; Marius.
90–88	Roman Social War. Right of Roman citizenship granted the Italian allies.	. . . .	Sulla.
88–65	Mithridatic Wars. Mithridates, king of Pontus, defeated.	Chæronea; Orchomenus.	Lucullus; Pompey; Sulla; Mithridates; Archelaus.
73–71	Gladiatorial War. Gladiators defeated.	Petelia.	Spartacus; Crassus.
58–51	Gallic War. Gauls conquered by Cæsar.	Bibracte (Autun); Alesia (Alise Sainte-Reine).	Cæsar; Ariovistus; Vercingetorix.
50–31	Roman Civil War. Roman Empire established.	Pharsalus; Thapsus; Munda; Philippi; Actium.	Cæsar; Pompey; Brutus; Cassius; Antony; Augustus.
A. D. 70	Jewish-Roman War. Jerusalem taken; temple destroyed.	Siege of Jerusalem.	Titus.
101–106	Dacian War. Country beyond Danube conquered.	. . . .	Trajan; Decebalus.
400–493	Barbarian Wars. Teutonic hordes capture Rome, ravage Italy, and displace Roman emperors.	Sack of Rome; East Gothic kingdom set up.	Alaric; Genseric; Attila; Theodoric.
709–1492	Saracen Conquests. The Saracens occupy northern Africa and Spain; defeated in France; driven from Spain.	Xerez; Tours; Tarifa; Granada.	Musa; Tarik; Charles Martel; Cid Campeador.
1095–1291	The Crusades. Christians capture Palestine and set up the feudal kingdom of Jerusalem, but are finally repulsed.	Siege of Jerusalem; Acre.	Godfrey of Bouillon; Conrad III; Louis VII; Frederick II; Philip Augustus; Richard the Lion-Hearted; Louis IX; Edward I; Saladin.
13th century	Mongol Conquests, from southern Russia eastward to China.	Wahlstatt.	Batu; Henry the Pious.
1337–1453	Hundred Years' War. England lost all her possessions in France except Calais.	Crécy; Calais; Poitiers; Agincourt.	Edward III of England; Edward the Black Prince; Henry V of England; Joan of Arc.
1386–1388	Austro-Swiss War. Independence of Switzerland.	Sempach; Näfels.	Arnold von Winkelried; Leopold of Austria.
1419–1436	Hussite War. Religious toleration secured.	Deutsch-Brod; Böhmisch-Brod.	John Ziska; Sigismund.
1455–1485	Wars of the Roses. House of York supplants that of Lancaster on English throne.	St. Albans; Bloreheath; Wakefield; Towton; Barnet; Tewksbury.	Richard, duke of York; Edward, duke of York; Earl of Warwick; Queen Margaret; Henry VI.
1526–1565	Mogul Conquest of India.	Panipat; Talikota; Sikri.	Baber; Akbar; Vijayanagar.
1562–1598	French Civil Wars. Edict of Nantes, Protestant toleration.	Dreux; St.-Denis; Jarnac; Moncontour; Ivry.	Duke of Anjou; Henry III; Henry IV; Prince de Condé.
1567–1609	Spanish-Netherlands War. Independence of the Netherlands achieved.	Zutphen; Nieuport; various sieges and naval conflicts.	William of Orange; Maurice of Nassau; Duke of Alva; Alexander Farnese, duke of Parma.
1616	Invasion of China by Manchu Tatars.		
1618–1648	Thirty Years' War. Religious freedom secured in Germany.	Dessau; Leipzig; Lech; Lützen; Nördlingen.	Gustavus Adolphus; Wallenstein; Tilly; Turenne.

IMPORTANT WARS OF HISTORY—Con.

Time	Name and Results	Leading Battles	Chief Leaders
A. D.			
1642–1653	English Civil War. English Commonwealth established.	Edgehill; Marston Moor; Naseby; Worcester.	Prince Rupert; Fairfax; Charles I; Cromwell.
1700–1709	Swedish-Russian War. Defeat of Charles XII.	Narva; Pultowa (Poltava).	Charles XII of Sweden; Peter the Great.
1701–1714	Spanish Succession. French and Spanish crowns disunited. Protestant succession in England recognized.	Blenheim; Ramillies; Turin; Oudenarde; Malplaquet.	Duke of Marlborough; Prince Eugene; Marshals Tallard and Villars.
1740–1748	Austrian Succession. Many previous treaties affirmed; Maria Theresa, empress of Austria.	Dettingen; Fontenoy; Piacenza.	Marshal Saxe; George II of England; Duke of Cumberland.
1756–1763	Seven Years' War. Prussia gains high rank as military state.	Prague; Kolin; Rossbach; Minden; Torgau; Freiberg; Kunersdorf.	Marshal Daun; Frederick the Great.
1775–1783	American Revolutionary War. The United States achieve their independence.	Bunker Hill; Saratoga; Monmouth; Yorktown.	Washington; Greene; Burgoyne; Cornwallis; Clinton; Howe; Lafayette; Gates.
1789–1799	French Revolution. Bourbons defeated. Republic established, followed by *coup d'état* of Bonaparte.	Valmy; Jemappes; Wattignies; Lodi; Arcole.	Kellerman; Dumouriez; Jourdan; Moreau; Bonaparte.
1800–1815	Napoleonic Wars. France advances to the first place in Europe, and falls with Napoleon.	Marengo; Trafalgar; Austerlitz; Jena; Eylau; Friedland; Wagram; Borodino; Leipzig; Waterloo.	Napoleon; Wellington; Nelson; Blücher; Alexander I; Francis I; Frederick William III; Ney.
1812–1815	War of 1812. The United States entirely independent of Great Britain.	Lake Erie; New Orleans.	Perry; Cockburn; Ross; Jackson; McDonough.
1821–1829	War for Greek Independence. Greece independent of Turkey.	Missolonghi; Navarino.	Kanaris; Byron; Ibrahim Pasha; Marco Bozzaris; Prince Ypsilanti.
1846–1848	Mexican War. Boundary between the United States and Mexico fixed.	Buena Vista; Cerro Gordo; Capture of Mexico City.	Taylor; Scott; Santa Anna.
1854–1856	Crimean War. Independence of Turkey guaranteed. Peace of Paris.	Alma; Balaklava; Inkerman; Malakov.	Lord Raglan; St.-Arnaud; Prince Menshikov; Canrobert.
1859–1861	Italian War. Victor Emmanuel becomes king of united Italy.	Magenta; Solferino; Castelfidardo; Gaëta.	Napoleon III; Victor Emmanuel; Francis Joseph; Garibaldi.
1861–1865	American Civil War. Abolition of slavery; preservation of the Union.	Bull Run; Shiloh; Seven Days; Antietam; Murfreesboro; Chancellorsville; Vicksburg; Gettysburg; Chickamauga; Chattanooga; Atlanta; Wilderness.	McClellan; Grant; Sherman; Sheridan; Jackson; Thomas; Lee; J. E. Johnston; Meade.
1866	Seven Weeks' War. Prussia defeats Austria and unifies Germany.	Langensalza; Königgrätz (Sadowa).	Benedek; William I; von Moltke.
1870–1871	Franco-Prussian War. Paris taken and Alsace and Lorraine added to German Empire.	Wörth; Gravelotte; Sedan; Metz; Capture of Paris.	William I; von Moltke; Frederick; Frederick Charles; Napoleon III; MacMahon; Bazaine.
1877–1878	Russo-Turkish War. Rumania, Serbia, and Montenegro become independent of Turkey. Treaty of Berlin.	Shipka Pass; Kars; Plevna.	Grand Duke Nicholas; Gurko; Skobelev; Totleben; Osman Pasha; Mukhtar Pasha.
1894–1895	Chinese-Japanese War. Indemnity to Japan; independence of Korea.	Occupation of Korea by Japanese; Port Arthur; Weihaiwei; Niuchuang.	Prince Oyama; Prince Arisugawa; Prince Komatsu.
1898	Spanish-American War. End of Spanish rule in America; Cuba independent; U. S. takes Puerto Rico and Philippines.	Manila Bay; Santiago; San Juan; El Caney.	Dewey; Schley; Sampson; Montojo; Cervera; Shafter; Toral.
1899–1902	South African War. Annexation of Transvaal and Orange River colony to British Empire.	Kimberley; Ladysmith; Mafeking; Pretoria.	Joubert; De Wet; Botha; De la Rey; French; White; Buller; Kitchener; Roberts.
1904–1905	Russo-Japanese War. Mutual concessions, confirmed by Treaty of Portsmouth.	Yalu; Liaoyang; Shaho; Siege of Port Arthur; Mukden; Battle of the Japan Sea.	Kuropatkin; Linevitch; Prince Oyama; Kuroki; Togo; Rojestvensky; Nogi; Oku.
1911–1912	Turco-Italian War. Tripoli ceded to Italy.	Bengazi; Derna; Tobruk; Hodeida.	Aubry; Enver Bey; Farrabelli.
1912–1913	Balkan Wars. Turkey loses much territory in Europe.	Scutari; Saloniki; Lule-Burgas; Monastir; Adrianople.	Putnik; Savov; Kleomenes; Hassan Tahsi; Enver Bey.
1914–1918	World War I. Downfall of the Romanov, Hohenzollern, and Habsburg dynasties. Establishment of several new republics. Defeat of Central Powers.	Liege; Marne; Tannenberg; Ypres; Gallipoli; Verdun; Jutland; Somme; Vimy Ridge; Caporetto; Erzerum; Chateau-Thierry; St. Mihiel; Argonne; Samaria.	Foch; Joffre; Pétain; French; Haig; Jellicoe; Allenby; Pershing; Cadorna; Brusilov; Hindenberg; Ludendorff; Mackenson.
1937–1945	Chinese-Japanese war. Japanese driven from China.	Japanese invasion and occupation of eastern China.	Chiang Kai-shek; Noboyuki Abe.
1939–1945	World War II. Defeat of Axis powers.	Poland; Finland; Norway; Flanders; France; North Africa; Coral Sea; Midway; Stalingrad; the Solomons; Italy; Normandy; the Ardennes; Germany.	Pétain; Alexander; Wavell; Montgomery; Göring; von Runstedt; Rommel; Marshall; MacArthur; Nimitz; Eisenhower; Patton; Zhukov; Vatutin.

BIBLIOGRAPHY

The following titles of books have been chosen from lists prepared for the use of students and schools by leading authorities upon the teaching of history. While not forming in any sense an exhaustive catalogue of history readings, this bibliography represents a selected library of authoritative and readable works upon American history, upon the special histories of the other great nations, and upon the generally recognized periods of world history. For perspective on the entire field of human history, the reader is referred to Arnold J. Toynbee's *A Study of History* (available in abridged form) and to *The Outline of History* by H. G. Wells. Books which furnish background for an understanding of history are listed under fiction, biography, geography and other classifications.

AMERICAN HISTORY

Adams, Henry—History of the United States under Jefferson and Madison . . . *Houghton Mifflin*
Adams, James Truslow—The Epic of America. *Little, Brown & Co.*
American Commonwealths (histories of the individual states) . . . . *Houghton Mifflin*
Bancroft, George—History of the United States. *Appleton*
Bassett, J. S.—A Short History of the United States. *Macmillan*
Beard, Charles and Mary—The Rise of American Civilization . . . . *Macmillan*
Channing, Edward—A History of the United States. *Macmillan*
Hart, A. B. (Ed.)—The American Nation Series. *Harper*
Haworth, Paul L.—The United States in Our Own Times. . . . . *Scribner*
McGrane, R. C.—The Economic Development of the American Nation . . . . *Ginn*
McMaster, J. B.—History of the People of the United States . . . . *Appleton*
Muzzey, D. S.—The United States of America. *Ginn*
Parkman, Francis—A Half Century of Conflict. *Little, Brown & Co.*
Rippy, J. F.—The United States and Mexico. *Knopf*
Roosevelt, Theodore—The Winning of the West. *Putnam*
Thwaites, R. G.—France in America. . . *Harper* (One of the 28 vols. in the American Nation Series.)
Wilson, Woodrow—A History of the American People. . . . . *Harper*

ANCIENT HISTORY

Botsford, G. W. and Robinson, C. A.—Hellenic History . . . . *Macmillan*
Breasted, J. H.—History of Egypt . . . *Scribner*
Bury, J. B.—History of Greece to the Death of Alexander . . . . *Macmillan*
Cary, Max—A History of Rome down to the Reign of Constantine . . . . *Macmillan*
Cumont, Franz—Oriental Religions in Roman Paganism . . . . *Open Court Pub. Co.*
Ferrero, G.—The Greatness and Decline of Rome. *Putnam*
Grote, George—History of Greece . . . . *Dutton*
Hall, H. R. H.—The Ancient History of the Near East . . . . *Methuen*
Hawes, C. H. and H. B.—Crete the Forerunner of Greece . . . . *Harper*
Jastrow, M.—The Civilization of Babylonia and Assyria . . . . *Lippincott*
Mommsen, Theodor—The History of Rome. *Dutton*
Osborn, H. F.—Men of the Old Stone Age. *Scribner*
Rogers, R. W.—A History of Ancient Persia. *Scribner*
Smith, G. A.—The Historical Geography of the Holy Land . . . . *Long & Smith*
Tucker, T. G.—Life in the Roman World of Nero and St. Paul . . . . *Macmillan*

MEDIEVAL AND MODERN HISTORY

Adams, G. B.—Growth of the French Nation. *Macmillan*
Beazley, C. R., Forbes, N. and Birkett, G. A.—Russia from the Varangians to the Bolsheviks. *Oxford*
Bertrand, L.—The History of Spain . . *Appleton*
Bradley, A. G.—The Making of Canada. *Dutton*
Bryce, James—The Holy Roman Empire. *Macmillan*
Buchan, John—A History of the Great War. *Houghton Mifflin*
Carlyle, Thomas—The French Revolution. *Harper*
Chapman, Charles E.—Colonial Hispanic America. *Macmillan*
—Republican Hispanic America . . *Macmillan*
Creasy, E. S.—Fifteen Decisive Battles (revised to World War I) . . . . *Oxford*
Creighton, D. G.—Dominion of the North; a History of Canada . . . . . . *Houghton Mifflin*
Davis, W. S.—Europe since Waterloo. . . *Century*
Denis, Pierre—The Argentine Republic . . *Unwin*
—Brazil . . . . *Scribner*
Duruy, Victor—A Short History of France. *Dutton*
Dyboski, Roman—Outlines of Polish History. *Allen*
Emerton, E.—An Introduction to the Study of the Middle Ages . . . . *Ginn*
Fisher, H. A. L.—A History of Europe. *Houghton Mifflin*
Grant, Arthur J.—Europe in the Nineteenth and Twentieth Centuries . . . . . *Longmans Green*
Green, John Richard—A Short History of the English People . . . . *Dutton*
Griffis, W. E.—The Mikado's Empire . . *Harper*
Hayes, C. J. H.—A Political and Cultural History of Modern Europe. . . . . *Macmillan*
Hazen, C. D.—Europe since 1815 . . . . . *Holt*
Henderson, E. F.—A Short History of Germany. *Macmillan*
Hitti, Philip—History of the Arabs . *Macmillan*
Hunter, W. W.—A brief History of the Indian Peoples . . . . *Oxford*
Johnston, H. H.—A History of the Colonization of Africa by Alien Races . . . . . . *Macmillan*
Kornilov, Alex.—Modern Russian History. *Knopf*
Latourette, Kenneth S.—The Development of China. *Houghton Mifflin*
—The Development of Japan . . . *Macmillan*
Lucas, H. S.—The Renaissance and the Reformation . . . . *Harper*
Madelin, Louis—The French Revolution. *Putnam*
Mahan, Alfred T.—The Influence of Sea Power upon History . . . . . . *Little, Brown & Co.*
Mirsky, Dmitry—Russia, a Social History. *Cresset*
Morison, S. E. and Commager, H. S.—The Growth of the American Republic . . . . *Oxford*
Motley, J. L.—The Rise of the Dutch Republic. *Dutton*
Pares, Sir Bernard—A History of Russia. . *Knopf*
Robertson, Wm. S.—A History of the Latin-American Nations . . . . *Appleton*
Robinson, Howard—The Development of the British Empire . . . . *Houghton Mifflin*
Robinson, J. H. and Beard, C.—The Development of Modern Europe. . . . . *Ginn*
Sansom, G. B.—Japan: A Short Cultural History. *Appleton-Century*
Seignobos, Charles—The Rise of European Civilization . . . . *Knopf*
Smith, V. A.—The Oxford History of India. *Oxford*
Stromberg, A. A.—A History of Sweden. *Macmillan*
Symonds, J. A.—A Short History of the Renaissance in Italy . . . . *Holt*
Thompson, J. W.—An Introduction to Medieval Europe . . . . *Norton*
Thorndike, Lynn—A Short History of Civilization. *Crofts*
Trevelyan, G. M.—Garibaldi and the Making of Italy . . . . *Longmans Green*
Vinacke, H. M.—A History of the Far East in Modern Times . . . . *Crofts*

TEST QUESTIONS

State two common meanings of the word history. What kinds of records may the historian use? 353

Give three reasons why every one should read and study history 353

Analyze the task of the historian. Name two ancient historians and characterize their work. Describe the modern methods of writing history 353

How do we derive our knowledge of the life of primitive man? 353

Name the three common divisions of history. 354

Outline the particularly notable characteristics of the history of the Hebrew people; of the Greeks; of the Romans 354

AMERICAN HISTORY

Why is a study of the European background of American history important? 355

What nation initiated the voyages of discovery and exploration in the 15th century? 355

Describe the equipment and the preparations of Columbus for his first voyage to the west. Name three other great discoverers of this period 355

To what country did leadership in early 16th century exploration fall? What American territory did its explorers visit in this period? 355

In what year did Jacques Cartier first sail up the Saint Lawrence river? 356

Describe the career of Sir Francis Drake. . . 356

Recount the efforts of Gilbert and Raleigh to colonize North America 356

Who first led the French into the interior of the North American continent? What source of wealth attracted French enterprise in the North? State two weaknesses of French colonization policies in America. 356

By what circumstances was Spanish control limited to the southern part of the North American continent? 356

Summarize the history of Dutch exploration and colonization in North America 356

Colonial Period

Account for the English Puritan and Cavalier migrations to America 356–357

What motives prompted English colonization in the 16th and 17th centuries 357

Describe the first organization and management of the Virginia colony. Recount the events which led up to the assembling of the first House of Burgesses 357

What was the most notable feature of the Maryland charter? 357

Describe the early activities of the Plymouth Company in New England. What was the policy of the Council for New England? . . 357

Recount the conditions under which the Pilgrims settled at Plymouth in 1620. What is the Mayflower Compact? 357–358

What was the Cambridge Agreement? 358

How many colonists came to New England in the Puritan migration? Who was the leader of this movement? 358

Explain how representative government and the ballot were introduced in New England . . 358

Account for the rise of the town meeting in New England and for the prevalence of the county form of government in Virginia 358–359

Under what circumstances and with what purpose did Roger Williams found Rhode Island? 359

Give the title of the "first written constitution" in America. 359

What was the purpose of the New England Confederation? Name the colonies included in it. 359

State the purpose of the Navigation acts. Cite two notable results 359

Describe the consolidation of the colonies under Andros. What event in England brought the end of this policy? 359

State three important provisions contained in the first charter of Pennsylvania. How did this colony differ from the others? 360

Discuss the growth of population in America from 1690 to 1760. From what countries did immigrants come? 360

Summarize the story of the struggle between the French and the English for control of the North American continent 360–361

State two restrictions placed by England upon colonial industry 361

What important change in the form of colonial governments in America was made during the 18th century? 361

Describe Virginia plantation life in the 18th century. What were the industries of the middle colonies? of New England? . . 361–362

Revolutionary Period

Account for the efforts of England to impose taxes on the colonies after 1763 362

What was the purpose of the sugar act of 1764? Why did New England oppose the sugar act? Upon what basis was opposition to the stamp tax founded? 362

Describe the Townshend acts; the results of the treason act of 1769 362–363

Why was the tea tax retained by Parliament when the Townshend acts were repealed? . . 363

Show the connection between the Boston Port bill and the First Continental Congress. What was the most important act of this Congress? 363

For what purposes did General Howe send troops to Lexington on April 18, 1775? Describe the conflict of April 19. To what proceedings did this day's events encourage the colonies? 363

Why may the battle of Bunker Hill be called an American victory? 363

What pamphlet issued in the spring of 1776 crystallized sentiment for independence? Who moved in Congress on June 7, 1776 that the united colonies should be independent? . 365

What advice did the Second Continental Congress give as to state governments? Describe the most notable feature of the Virginia constitution. What qualifications for voters prevailed in the new states? 365

Recount the chief military events of 1776. What notable service did Robert Morris render to the American cause? 365–366

Explain the importance of the surrender of Burgoyne at Saratoga in 1777. Who secured the treaty of alliance with France in 1778? . . 366

When did efforts to form a union of the colonies begin? When were the Articles of Confederation finally ratified? What was the chief cause of delay in ratification of the Articles? 366

State the immediate results of Daniel Boone's pioneering in Kentucky; of George Rogers Clark's expedition into the Illinois country . 366

Name seven leaders in the Constitutional Convention. What were the three chief difficulties met by the delegates? Who were the authors of the "Federalist"? 367

From 1789 to 1861

Analyze the composition and the distribution of population in the colonies in 1790. Cite two facts which illustrate the development of American manufacturing from 1800 to 1814. 367

In what foreign commerce were many New Englanders engaged about 1800? How were means of communication within the colonies improved? 367

When and where was the first Congress of the United States under the Constitution organ-

From the Civil War to the Present Day

DICTIONARY OF SUPPLEMENTAL TOPICS IN AMERICAN HISTORY

Out of what movements did the American party of the 1850's grow? What were its characteristic principles? 394
Explain the use of the phrase, American System, about the year 1830. What statesman's name is connected with it? 394
How did the feudal patroon system of the Dutch settlements give rise to the Antirent riots in New York? 394–395
When was the Military Academy established at West Point? How were United States troops raised in the Civil War? in the World wars? What changes were made in the Army of the United States in World War II? . . 395
Tell briefly the story of Bacon's rebellion 395–396
Recount the history of the Bering Sea controversy. State the sealing regulations put into effect in 1911 396
Name an English precedent for the Bill of Rights embodied in the first ten amendments to the American Constitution 396
Whence is the name Black Hawk war derived? What famous American served in this conflict? 396
Explain the designation Black Republicans. Outline the story of the *Black Warrior* case . 396
Define the phrase "blue laws." Account for the use of blue in this connection. Is there any justification for the phrase "blue laws of Connecticut"? 396
Tell the story of Booth's conspiracy . . . 396–397
When did the Boston Massacre occur? What two patriots volunteered to defend the soldiers at their trial? 397
What was the purpose of the Boston Port bill? How was its effect largely nullified? To what action is the name Boston Tea Party applied? 397
Where and when did the engagement known as Braddock's defeat take place? 397
Explain the application of the following political nicknames: Bucktails; Bull Moose; Burrites; Butternuts 397
Outline the history of the Canadian Fisheries question. What is meant by carpetbaggers? 397
Cite the five provisions of the Compromise of 1850 398
When and at what place did the First Continental Congress meet? How long did the Second Continental Congress continue as the national government? When and where did the first Congress under the Constitution meet? Upon what date was the first session of Congress in Washington opened? 398
Account for the use of the nickname Copperheads during the Civil War. Who were the Cotton Whigs? 398
Characterize the Credit Mobilier as to its origin and purpose 398
What is meant by Crime of '73? 398
Recount the story of Custer's last fight . 398–399
Explain the political expression, "dark horse." 399
State the main points of the decision of the supreme court in the Dartmouth College case. 399
By whom was the State of Deseret organized? 399
Explain the occasion of the draft riots in New York City in 1863 399
Recount the history of the Dred Scott case. Indicate the effect of the supreme court's decision upon Northern sentiment 399
In what year did Nast originate the Republican Elephant symbol? 400
State the purpose of the Embargo act of 1807. 400
What was the Era of Good Feeling? 400
Whence is the name of Faneuil Hall derived? Why is it historically important? 400
Outline the history of the Farmers' Alliance . 400
Describe the rise of the Federalist party. Who were its chief leaders? 400
Who were the Federal Republicans? 400
Indicate the significance of the slogan Fifty-Four Forty or Fight 400
Who were called Finality Men? Who were the so-called Fire Eaters? 400
What were the Five Nations? 400
Explain the historical interest attaching to Fort Sumter 401
What are the Four Freedoms? 401
State the so-called Freeport Doctrine 401
Explain the term Free Silver movement . . . 401
Outline the leading facts with respect to the composition, the platform, and the history of the Free-Soil party 401
Give the dates of passage of three fugitive slave laws. State some of the provisions of the last of these acts; the effects of attempted enforcement of these provisions. When was this law repealed? 401
Outline the main features of the Geneva award. Indicate the importance of this decision in general international relations 401
To whom was the nickname Goldbugs applied? Explain the party name Gold Democrats. Who were their candidates in 1896? 402
What were the Grandfather Clauses? 402
To what doctrine is the name Greenbackism applied? 402
Who were the Green Mountain Boys? What dispute occasioned their organization? . . . 402
To what political groups was the term Half-Breeds applied? 402
Why was the Hampton Roads Conference held? 402
Who were the members of the Hartford Convention? What did this meeting propose? . 402
Quote from Wm. H. Seward's speech of 1850 the "higher law" passage 402
When was the first Homestead act passed by Congress? In what year were settlement rights withdrawn? 402–403
To what political group was the nickname Hunkers applied? 403
State the reason for the impeachment of President Johnson; the result of the proceedings. 403
Define the terms "impressment" and "search." 403
What were the Intolerable acts? 403
When was the so-called ironclad oath established? State the purpose of its application. 403
Account for the political use of such phrases as Jackson men and Adams men from 1822 to 1828 403
Distinguish between Jeffersonian democracy and Jacksonian democracy 403
Explain the meaning of Jeffersonian Republican. 404
Tell the story of John Brown's raid on Harpers Ferry. Estimate the effect of the raid. . 403–404
State the relation between the Kansas-Nebraska bill and border warfare in Kansas. What part did President Pierce play in this conflict? . 404
What events precipitated King Philip's war? . 404
What was the character of the order known as Knights of the Golden Circle? 404
Outline the history of the Know-Nothing movement 404
Recount the history of the Ku-Klux Klan. Whence is the name derived? 404
Outline the history of the first national American labor party 404
State one of the most important results of the Lewis and Clark expedition. What part did Jefferson play in the enterprise? 404
Tell the story of the Liberty Bell 405
Explain the origin of the political nickname Locofocos 405
State the general extent of the Louisiana Purchase. What price was paid for this domain? 405
When was the McKinley tariff act passed? What novel feature was embodied in it? . . 405
Explain the origin of the name Mason and Dixon's Line. What historical interest attaches to this boundary? 405
Narrate the leading facts about the historic voyage of the *Mayflower* in 1620. How many persons arrived at Plymouth on this vessel? 405

ENGLAND

SCOTLAND AND WALES

CANADA

IRELAND

AUSTRALIA AND NEW ZEALAND

INDIA AND UNION OF SOUTH AFRICA

LATIN AMERICA

ABYSSINIA AND AFGHANISTAN

ANATOLIA, ANDORRA, ARABIA, AND ARMENIA

BELGIUM

BULGARIA

CHINA

CORSICA, CRETE, CZECHOSLOVAKIA

What great European ruler was born in Corsica? Enumerate the peoples who held this island before its occupation by the Romans . . . 468
What was the Terra di Comune? When did the vendetta arise in Corsica? Name an 18th century hero of Corsican freedom 468
Explain the application of the term Minoan to early Cretan history. Indicate the ancient commercial and naval importance of Crete . 468
By what peoples has Crete been governed within historic times? 468
When was the republic of Czechoslovakia founded? What countries were included in it? 468
Explain the meaning of the name Bohemia. At what period was Bohemia a powerful, independent state? 468–469
Explain the rise of the Czech movement for independence in the 19th century. Discuss the treatment of the Czechs by Hitler. Discuss Communism in Czechoslovakia 469

DENMARK

With what century does reliable history of Denmark begin? When was the country converted to Christianity? 469
By what means did the first monarch of the Oldenburg line come to the Danish throne? 469
Explain the reason for the rising of the people against the nobles in 1660. 470
Outline the constitution of 1849. 470

EASTERN EMPIRE AND EGYPT

When was the Roman Empire permanently divided into East and West? 470
Who was the greatest Eastern emperor? What was his most notable work? Indicate the extent of his realm 470
Describe the effect of the Fourth Crusade upon the Eastern Empire 470
In what year did the surrender of Constantinople to the Turks take place? 470
At about what date was the Great Pyramid erected? by what monarch? Characterize the civilization of the Middle Kingdom . . 470
What great services did Psammetichus render to Egypt and to the Western world? . . . 471
Characterize the rule of the Ptolemies in Egypt. Name two great Christian teachers of Alexandria; two neoplatonic philosophers. 471
When, and under what leader, did the Saracens conquer Egypt? At what period did the French hold the country? 471

FRANCE

What is the principal racial element of the French nation? 472
In what century, and under what dynasty, did the kingdom of France "in the narrower sense" begin? What was the task of the French kings, down to the time of Charles VIII? 472
Describe the membership of the States-General summoned in 1302 472
Out of what disputed succession to the French throne did the Hundred Years' war arise? Enumerate the battles that rendered this war illustrious 473
Characterize the work of Cardinal Richelieu and Cardinal Mazarin. What kind of government was wielded by Louis XIV? 473
Who were the finance ministers of Louis XVI? 473–474
Enumerate the reforms effected by the National (Constituent) Assembly 474
Describe the career of the Revolutionary Commune 474
Characterize the Convention. What was its first act? How did the Convention meet its foreign and domestic difficulties? . . . 474–475
Outline the peaceful achievements of the Convention 475
Describe the circumstances that brought Napoleon Bonaparte to the front. Why was the time auspicious for him? By what steps did Napoleon become emperor? 475
Summarize the military successes of Napoleon from 1805 to 1807. Name the two military disasters that overtook him in 1812 and 1813. What was his last battle? 475–476
Tell the story of the fall of Napoleon III 476
Recount the history of the Commune of Paris 476
What disasters befell France in World War II? 477

GERMANY

With what event does the history of Germany properly begin? 479
Name two great Hohenstaufen kings 479
Characterize the reign of Frederick III as to its effect upon Germany. What dispute occasioned the Thirty Years' war? 479–480
What acquisition of territory formed the basis of Hohenzollern power? Name the two 18th century rulers who made Prussia powerful . 480
Describe the social changes that took place in Germany after 1871 480
How was German foreign policy shaped under William II? 480
Discuss the expansion and fall of Germany under Hitler. 481

GREECE

Point out the most important contributions that Greek states made to civilization . . . 483
Describe the conquest of Greece by the Hellenes. Name the four historic groups of this people 483
What caused early Greek colonization? . . . 483
Through what three stages did city-state government in Athens pass before the end of the 6th century B. C.? 484
Compare the Spartan with the Athenian government 484
Who was the pioneer of Greek philosophy? . . 485
Explain the occasion of the Persian wars. For what exploits are the following places famous: Marathon? Thermopylæ? Salamis? Platæa? 485
Describe the Confederacy of Delos. For what is the Periclean age famous? 485
Tell the story of the downfall of Athens, 431–405 B. C. 485–486
Narrate the story of Pelopidas and Epaminondas 486
By what power was Greece finally unified politically? 486
When did Greece become independent of Turkey? What part did Greece take in the Balkan wars? in the World wars? 487

GREENLAND, HUNGARY, AND ICELAND

Summarize the early history of settlements in Greenland. Characterize the Danish administration of the country 487
State the circumstances that brought about the dual monarchy organization in 1867. How did the World wars affect Hungary? . 488
Recount the story of the discovery and colonization of Iceland. What was the form of the country's early government? Discuss the recent political progress of Iceland 489

ITALY

Who established the Ostrogothic kingdom in Italy? By whom were the Goths driven out of Italy? 489
Discuss the origin and the character of the Lombards. How long did their kingdom endure? 489

JAPAN

THE JEWS

THE NETHERLANDS AND NORWAY

PERSIA, POLAND, AND PORTUGAL

ROME

RUMANIA AND RUSSIA

SPAIN, SWEDEN, AND SWITZERLAND

TURKEY AND YUGOSLAVIA

ANCIENT CITIES

For what famous citizens is Thebes (Greece) most interesting? 512
Outline the facts that archeological excavation has revealed about the history of the sites of Troy and Ur 512

RACES AND PEOPLES

Of what use are *kitchen middens* or *shell heaps* to the archeologist? In what age is the earliest type of human being believed to have arisen? 513
Describe the evidences of the artistic ability of Cro-Magnon men 513
Who were the Mound Builders? What is believed to have been their relation to the Indians? 513
Describe the skeleton remains of Neanderthal Man 513
To what grades of culture had the native American peoples attained at the time of Columbus? 514
Who were the so-called Cliff Dwellers? . . . 515
Review the United States government methods of dealing with the Indians 515
Outline the Canadian government's policy toward Indians 515
Summarize the chief services of the Arabians to civilization 516
To what peoples is the family name Aryan applied? 516
Characterize the Aztec civilization. 516
Who are the so-called Caucasian peoples? . . 517
Explain the application of the term Celts. Indicate the wide distribution of the Celts . 517
What is the chief racial element in the Chinese people? 517
Who were the Dorians? 518
What is the meaning of the name Eskimo? What is the Eskimos' native name? 518
Who were the Etruscans? 518
Outline the probable Malay migrations into the Philippine Islands. Who are the mestizos? 518
To what peoples are the Finns racially related? 518
State the probable origin of the gypsies . . . 518
Describe the three physical types found in the population of Ireland 519
Who are the Lithuanians and the Letts? Characterize the Lithuanian language . . . 519
Where are the Malay peoples now found? Who are the Manchus? 519
For what abilities and achievements are the Maoris notable? 520
Point out evidence of the high state of civilization once developed by the Mayas 520
To what cause is the wide distribution of the Negroes to be ascribed? 520
Outline the scope of the widespread migrations of the Northmen 520–521
Explain the belief of the Parsis about fire and their practice of exposing the dead 521
Describe the physical characteristics of the Polynesians 521
Describe the pygmies of Central Africa . . . 521
What peoples are included under the name Semitic? 521
To what peoples is the general term Slav applied? Who were the Sumerians? What people are called Walloons? 522

WORLD WAR I

What were the causes, immediate and more remote, of World War I? 523
State the pre-war relations of Austria, Italy, and Turkey with Germany 523
Explain the nature of the French and German antagonism 523
Account for the strained relations of Great Britain and Germany before the war . . . 523
Explain the hostility of Austria and Serbia . . 523
Outline the events that led directly to war; why did Great Britain enter? 523–525
Compare the strength of the combatants at the opening of the war 525
In what respects was the battle of the Marne among the decisive battles of the world? . . 525
How did the type of warfare then change? . . 526
How did von Hindenburg become a national hero? 526
What were the British and German naval policies at the beginning of the war? 526
Describe the battles of Coronel and the Falkland Islands 526
Tell the story of the Breslau and Goeben affair and its consequences 527
Outline the Gallipoli campaign 527
In what respect did the German war plans of 1915 differ from those of 1914? 528
How was poison gas introduced? how did airplanes develop? 528
Account for the inaction on the western front in 1915 528
Tell the story of the German drive against Verdun 528
State the result of the battle of Jutland . 528–529
What new fighting machine was used in the battle of the Somme? 529
Why did Rumania enter the war? with what result? 529
Summarize the peace discussions of 1916 . . 529
How and why did the United States enter the war? 529–530
When did the first American troops arrive in France? 530
In what kinds of service did the American navy engage during the war? 530
What gains did the French and British make in 1917? 530–531
What was the effect on the war of the Russian Revolution? 531
Discuss the Italian disaster in 1917 531
Describe the method and the results of the German offensive of 1918 531
What victories in Mesopotamia and Palestine restored British prestige in the Orient? . . 531
By what tactics did Foch drive the Germans back to the Hindenburg line? 532
What part was played by American and Canadian troops in the assault on the Hindenburg line? 532–533
With what American Civil War campaign is that of the Argonne compared? 533
What defeat compelled the Austrians to sign an armistice? 533
When and where was the armistice with Germany signed? 533
Summarize the provisions of the treaty signed June 28, 1919 by the Allies and Germany. 533–534
State several governmental and territorial changes in Europe, resulting from the war. 534–535
Outline the organization of the League of Nations 535
State the program of the League of Nations . 535
Why did the United States reject the treaty and the League? 536
Summarize the most notable activities of the League 536
Define the term mandate 536
Describe the organization of the Permanent Court of International Justice. Indicate the extent of the court's jurisdiction 536
How much did Germany pay in reparations? . 536

WORLD WAR II

Compare the two World Wars as to extent, weapons, and method 537
What part was played by communism? . . . 537
When did World War II begin? 538
What were the Axis powers? what advances did they make before 1939? 538

DICTIONARY OF WORLD HISTORY

IV

Geography and Travel

SUBJECT GUIDE

LINCOLN LIBRARY INDEXES

• • •

GEOGRAPHY AND TRAVEL

DIAMOND HEAD - HAWAII

ST. MORITZ - SWITZERLAND

GOLDEN GATE BRIDGE - SAN FRANCISCO

RIO DE JANEIRO - BRAZIL

TAJ MAHAL - INDIA

HOOVER DAM - ARIZONA - NEVADA

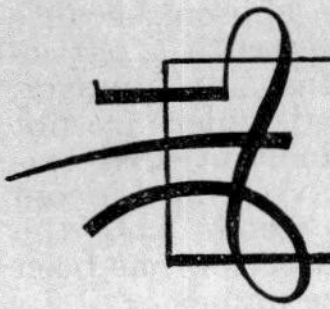

GEOGRAPHY AND TRAVEL

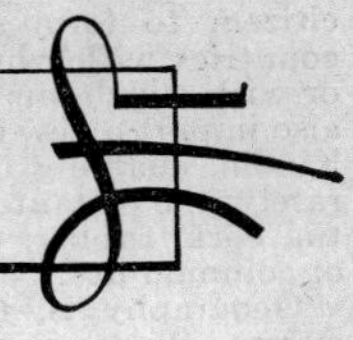

INTRODUCTORY

THE word geography comes from *ge* and *grapho*, two Greek words which, in combination, mean a description of the earth. Geography differs from geology and other sciences of the earth in the fact that geography studies the earth as the abode of mankind. It is closely related, in certain of its aspects, to the sciences of economics, history, astronomy, botany, zoology, and meteorology.

Divisions. Geography is usually classified, on the basis of its subject matter, into mathematical geography, physical geography, or physiography, and biological geography. Mathematical geography concerns the size, shape, and movements of the earth; physical geography deals with the layers of the earth's surface—land, sea, and air; and biological geography studies the life conditions of plants and animals, on the one hand, and of man on the other.

The geography of man discusses the races of mankind and their distribution throughout the earth; it discusses also density of population and the various types of human occupation—fishing, hunting, pasturing, agriculture, mining, manufacture, and commerce. That part of human geography which is concerned with man's industries is classified as economic, or commercial, geography. The study of mankind by countries is known as political geography.

Development of Geography. Nearly all parts of the world have been inhabited by men from very early times and, consequently, have been known in a certain sense. Such knowledge, however, does not constitute geography. The science of geography begins only when people attempt to describe by word or chart the relations of one part of the earth's surface to other parts.

Advance in geographical knowledge has been due mainly to the enterprise of the white race. The rate of advance, however, has been highly irregular. Three chief periods of progress may be roughly distinguished: first, that of ancient Greece, when the first serious attempts were made to describe and to explain scientifically the varied conditions of different localities; secondly, the age of discovery, from the 15th to the 19th century, when the main features of the earth were finally learned; and, lastly, the modern scientific period, more or less overlapping the second in time and continuing to the present, when the utmost resources of science have been systematically utilized to chart and to describe every part of the earth's surface.

As a descriptive and systematic science, geography is of comparatively recent origin. Its foundation is due in large part to Alexander von Humboldt, a German scholar who was born in 1769. He developed and supported with observed facts the concept of the earth in evolution, which had been previously set forth in outline by the philosopher Kant. Advancing from this fundamental conception, recent geographers have devoted much of their attention to studies of the effect of geographical environment on human settlement and ways of life.

The Earth and Mankind. The degree of man's dependence on the earth is apt to be obscured in a highly developed society. In point of fact, both in the state of savagery and of civilization, his activities and very life rest solely on the bounty of the earth. A sudden rise or fall of 100° in the mean temperature of the earth's surface would wipe out civilization and probably exterminate the human race.

Climate not only determines what plants and animals can thrive so as to enable any people to subsist, but it exerts decisive effects on their appearance, their stature, their vigor, and their health. The tropics, while bountiful, discourage activity. The polar regions restrict all manner of life. But the seasonal changes of the temperate zones not only predispose populations to activity but force them to make use of their resources to provide against the winters. Hence it is from these regions that practically all the advances in civilization have come.

Mountains and coasts have served to restrict settlements; rivers and plains, to extend them. Each of these natural features has placed a characteristic imprint on the society which it dominated, largely fashioning its mode of life, its customs, morals, and temperament.

With the growth of inventions, however, the range of the earth's gifts to man has multiplied and has tended to free him from the effects of a restricted environment. Minerals and waterfalls, once useless, now provide shelter, heat, light, power, and transportation in extraordinary abundance. These developments, together with the world-wide exchange of commodities, processes, and ideas, multiply the bonds of man to the earth but also make these bonds much more elastic. To an ever greater degree the earth itself, rather than any particular locality, is becoming the environment of each person. One result is a tendency toward uniformity. Another is an extremely rapid increase of population, the growing pressure of which, in the opinion of many observers, is full of portent for human institutions and customs.

Geography in Schools. The first modern geography in English which was written explicitly for use in schools appeared in 1746 It was called *Introduction to Geography* and was published in England by J. Cowley, "geographer to his Majesty." The first professor of geography in an American university was Arnold Henry Guyot, appointed by Princeton university in 1854.

The study of geography has long held an important place in the public schools of America. The manner of teaching the subject, however, has changed considerably in the past 70 years. The major emphasis was first placed on the facts of political geography. More especially in the years following 1890, physical geography received greater attention. In the past two decades, the study of "home geography" has been favored, chiefly as a means of making pupils familiar with geographical causes operating in their own neighborhood; this familiarity in turn has enabled them to see how larger regions of the earth are affected by the same causes. Finally, with the development of human geography, regional studies are encouraged in order to determine the factors of all kinds which have affected human habitation in a particular region or may be expected to do so in the future.

Value of the Study. A knowledge of geography is necessary for the intelligent reading of newspapers and of books. Such knowledge enables one, as a citizen, to form sounder opinions of the foreign countries with which our government has relations or with which our merchants deal. The study may also impart a new interest to the materials which we handle, enabling us to picture, more or less accurately, the distant scenes from which have come our tin, cork, rubber, tea, chocolate, and other articles of common use.

Geography is, to a large extent, the study of causes. To learn many facts, more or less isolated, about countries, rivers, cities, and peoples has its value. It is more enlightening, however, to understand the *causes* behind the facts; to know, for example, *why* Arizona is dry, *why* northern Europe is warmer than Labrador, and *why* Chicago has grown up where it is. Familiarity with the reasons lying behind such facts gives us a new interest also in the conditions of our own locality.

Travel. Improved means of transportation within the past century have made it possible for hundreds now to travel for each one that did so in earlier times. Travel has become a new form of enjoyment and a new means of instruction. The novelty of unfamiliar scenes, the glamor of places famous in history, the fascination of nature in its most charming or its most desolate aspects, engage the mind and bring home to it the varied panorama of the great world in which we live.

Geography a Substitute for Travel. Many people, however, lack the financial means and the leisure necessary for extensive travel. For such people, geography provides the nearest equivalent of travel. By the printed word and by picture, one may visit the most interesting and the most remote parts of the world. He may see the head-hunters of Borneo, the crowded cities of China, the treeless steppes of central Asia, or the jungles of the Amazon, inhabited by naked savages. Under the guidance of what he reads, he may take a trip to the "land of the midnight sun," and he may enjoy the beauties of Yellowstone park or of Paris.

Plan of Department of Geography. In the following pages, the geography of the world is treated by continents. This plan has at least two distinct advantages over an alphabetic arrangement of geographical topics. In the first place, it is possible in this way to bring into strong relief the contrast between the continents. Secondly, the reader is enabled to obtain a single view of each continent as a whole. There are certain aspects of geography which cannot be classified under continents. Such, for example, are the oceans, the zones, and the movements of the earth. A treatment of these general facts concerning the earth precedes the description of the continents.

Treatment of Countries. Following the general account of each continent, the countries and other political divisions within it are described in more detail. For the United States, the treatment has been made regional, each subdivision consisting of a group of states having a common geographic character. Moreover, information regarding the individual states has been grouped in several tables, carefully prepared with a view to conciseness, ease of visualization, and facility for comparison.

Cities and Other Points of Interest. The description of countries or other divisions is followed by sections in which, under alphabetic arrangement, the cities, towns, and other places of interest are each accorded a special treatment. In the selection of such places, the guiding principle has been the importance of the place and its interest to the general reader. The lists contain the capitals of all countries as well as those of the American states and of the Canadian provinces. They contain also the important cities in all parts of the world. In the United States, all cities above 50,000 are specially described; in Canada, all above 25,000. A very large number of other places are included. Some of these are notable for historic reasons, such as Yorktown or Ypres. Others are chosen because their names have become associated with a particular industry, such as Waltham, Mass., or Limoges, France. Many places are described which are not incorporated settlements. These include such features as Pikes peak, Mammoth cave, and Lincoln highway in America or Belleau woods and the Riviera in Europe. An instructive section has been added also on the meanings of place names.

Scope. In mere extent of text, this department far exceeds the volume of the average school geography, being more thorough in treating each subject and more inclusive in the selection of topics, especially topics that have recently become important. The point of especial distinction, however, is the addition of material having a travel interest. The study of geography is thereby made more entertaining and far more helpful to the student.

Purposes. The department of geography is not intended to be used as a textbook for the schoolroom. It is too complete for that purpose. On the other hand, it does not purport to describe every place, without exception, which appears on the map. In other words, it is not an atlas or a gazetteer. Consequently, it is neither dry nor mechanical. It is much more than a textbook or an atlas.

This treatment of geography has three principal purposes. In the first place, it contains a rich store of supplementary material both for the student and for the teacher of geography. Secondly, when used in connection with the test questions, it provides an extremely valuable aid for any person desiring systematically to study geography by himself. Lastly, it is an excellent source of general information for all ages and all classes of people.

Statistics. The figures published in this department have been prepared with unusual care. Those representing factors which constantly change, such as population and trade, are based, in all cases, on the latest official bulletins.

It is a fact that even in statistics representing such constant factors as the length of coast lines and areas of districts adjoining the sea, a considerable divergence often appears among geographical authorities. Such differences are frequently due to methods of measurement. A coast line, for example, may be surveyed from headland to headland, and the result obtained may be much less than the total arrived at by including all the insignificant inlets. Somewhat similar difficulties arise in statistics regarding lengths of rivers, heights of mountains, and many other such measurements.

These difficulties, however, detract nothing from the real value of statistics, which is to enable the reader to make comparisons. For ordinary purposes, it is of no significance whether Mount Everest is 29,140 or 29,141 feet high or whether Mount McKinley is exactly 20,300 feet in altitude. The essential value of the figures is in showing that Mount Everest is about 9000 feet higher than Mount McKinley. In spite of such considerations, however, the statistics in this department represent the most painstaking efforts to reconcile authorities where they differ and to attain a degree of accuracy that is not to be found in any similar material in print.

Maps. Geographical position has been indicated throughout the text with a view to enabling the reader, by consulting the pertinent maps, to see at a glance the location of the principal places. The maps have been recently revised and take into account the numerous changes that have occurred during and since World War II.

Spelling of Names. The form of the names in the text has been made, in most instances, to conform with the spelling adopted by the United States Geographic Board. Those names which have not been made the subject of decisions by this board follow the spelling of the National Geographic Society, or, failing authority from either source, they conform to Webster's *Gazetteer*.

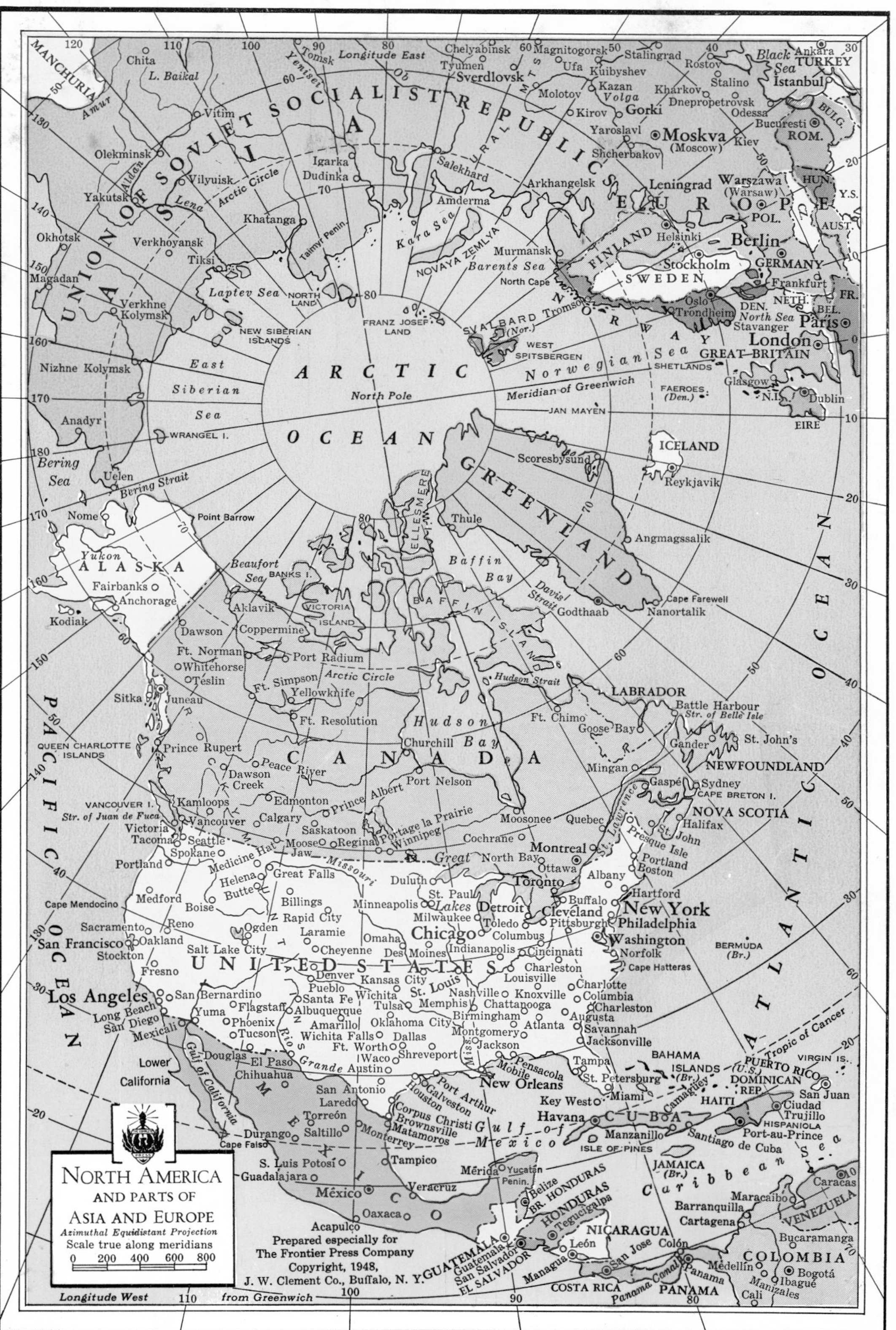

NORTH AMERICA
AND PARTS OF
ASIA AND EUROPE
Azimuthal Equidistant Projection
Scale true along meridians
0 200 400 600 800
Prepared especially for
The Frontier Press Company
Copyright, 1948,
J. W. Clement Co., Buffalo, N. Y.
Longitude East
Longitude West
from Greenwich
UNION OF SOVIET SOCIALIST REPUBLICS
ASIA
EUROPE
ARCTIC OCEAN
North Pole
Arctic Circle
Meridian of Greenwich
GREENLAND
CANADA
ALASKA
UNITED STATES
MEXICO
PACIFIC OCEAN
ATLANTIC OCEAN
Tropic of Cancer
MANCHURIA
Amur
Chita
L. Baikal
Vitim
Olekminsk
Aldan
Yakutsk
Vilyuisk
Lena
Okhotsk
Magadan
Verkhoyansk
Tiksi
Khatanga
Taimyr Penin.
Igarka
Dudinka
Tomsk
Yenisei
Ob
Chelyabinsk
Tyumen
Sverdlovsk
Magnitogorsk
Ufa
Molotov
URAL MTS.
Salekhard
Amderma
Kara Sea
NOVAYA ZEMLYA
Barents Sea
Murmansk
North Cape
Arkhangelsk
Kirov
Gorki
Kazan
Volga
Kuibyshev
Stalingrad
Rostov
Stalino
Kharkov
Dnepropetrovsk
Odessa
Kiev
Moskva
(Moscow)
Yaroslavl
Shcherbakov
Leningrad
Black Sea
Ankara
TURKEY
Istanbul
BULG.
Bucuresti
ROM.
HUN.
Y.S.
AUST.
Warszawa
(Warsaw)
POL.
Berlin
GERMANY
Frankfurt
FR.
Paris
NETH.
BEL.
DEN.
North Sea
London
GREAT BRITAIN
Glasgow
N.I.
Dublin
EIRE
SHETLANDS
FAEROES
(Den.)
JAN MAYEN
ICELAND
Reykjavik
FINLAND
Helsinki
SWEDEN
Stockholm
NORWAY
Oslo
Trondheim
Stavanger
Tromsø
SVALBARD
(Nor.)
WEST SPITSBERGEN
Norwegian Sea
FRANZ JOSEF LAND
NORTH LAND
Laptev Sea
NEW SIBERIAN ISLANDS
Verkhne Kolymsk
Nizhne Kolymsk
East Siberian Sea
Anadyr
WRANGEL I.
Bering Sea
Uelen
Bering Strait
Nome
Point Barrow
Yukon
Fairbanks
Anchorage
Kodiak
Beaufort Sea
BANKS I.
VICTORIA ISLAND
ELLESMERE
Thule
Scoresbysund
Angmagssalik
Baffin Bay
BAFFIN ISLAND
Davis Strait
Godthaab
Cape Farewell
Nanortalik
Hudson Strait
Aklavik
Dawson
Coppermine
Ft. Norman
Port Radium
Whitehorse
Teslin
Ft. Simpson
Yellowknife
Sitka
Juneau
Ft. Resolution
Hudson Bay
Churchill
Ft. Chimo
LABRADOR
Goose Bay
Battle Harbour
Str. of Belle Isle
Gander
St. John's
NEWFOUNDLAND
QUEEN CHARLOTTE ISLANDS
Prince Rupert
Peace River
Dawson Creek
Edmonton
Prince Albert
Port Nelson
Kamloops
Calgary
Saskatoon
Vancouver
VANCOUVER I.
Str. of Juan de Fuca
Victoria
Tacoma
Seattle
Spokane
Medicine Hat
Moose Jaw
Regina
Portage la Prairie
Winnipeg
Moosonee
Cochrane
Quebec
St. Lawrence
Mingan
Gaspé
Sydney
CAPE BRETON I.
NOVA SCOTIA
Halifax
St. John
Presque Isle
Portland
Boston
Montreal
Ottawa
North Bay
Great Lakes
Toronto
Albany
Hartford
New York
Philadelphia
Washington
Norfolk
Cape Hatteras
BERMUDA
(Br.)
Missouri
Portland
Helena
Butte
Great Falls
Duluth
St. Paul
Minneapolis
Billings
Rapid City
Medford
Boise
Cape Mendocino
Sacramento
Reno
Ogden
Laramie
Milwaukee
Detroit
Toledo
Cleveland
Buffalo
Pittsburgh
Chicago
Columbus
Omaha
Des Moines
Indianapolis
Cincinnati
San Francisco
Oakland
Stockton
Salt Lake City
Cheyenne
Denver
Kansas City
St. Louis
Charleston
Louisville
Charlotte
Fresno
Pueblo
Santa Fe
Wichita
Nashville
Knoxville
Columbia
Los Angeles
San Bernardino
Long Beach
San Diego
Yuma
Flagstaff
Albuquerque
Tulsa
Memphis
Chattanooga
Charleston
Phoenix
Amarillo
Oklahoma City
Birmingham
Atlanta
Augusta
Savannah
Mexicali
Tucson
Wichita Falls
Dallas
Ft. Worth
Montgomery
Jackson
Jacksonville
Lower California
Gulf of California
Douglas
El Paso
Rio Grande
Waco
Shreveport
Miss.
Austin
Mobile
Pensacola
New Orleans
Tampa
St. Petersburg
Miami
Key West
Chihuahua
San Antonio
Laredo
Port Arthur
Galveston
Houston
Corpus Christi
Brownsville
Matamoros
Torreón
Saltillo
Monterrey
Durango
Cape Falso
S. Luis Potosí
Tampico
Guadalajara
Gulf of Mexico
Mérida
Yucatan Penin.
México
Veracruz
Oaxaca
Acapulco
Belize
BR. HONDURAS
HONDURAS
Tegucigalpa
GUATEMALA
Guatemala
San Salvador
EL SALVADOR
NICARAGUA
León
Managua
San Jose
COSTA RICA
Colón
Panama
Panama Canal
PANAMA
BAHAMA ISLANDS
(Br.)
Havana
CUBA
Camagüey
Manzanillo
Santiago de Cuba
ISLE OF PINES
JAMAICA
(Br.)
HAITI
DOMINICAN REP.
Port-au-Prince
HISPANIOLA
Ciudad Trujillo
PUERTO RICO
(U.S.)
San Juan
VIRGIN IS.
Caribbean Sea
Barranquilla
Cartagena
Maracaibo
Caracas
VENEZUELA
Bucaramanga
COLOMBIA
Medellin
Bogotá
Ibagué
Manizales
Cali

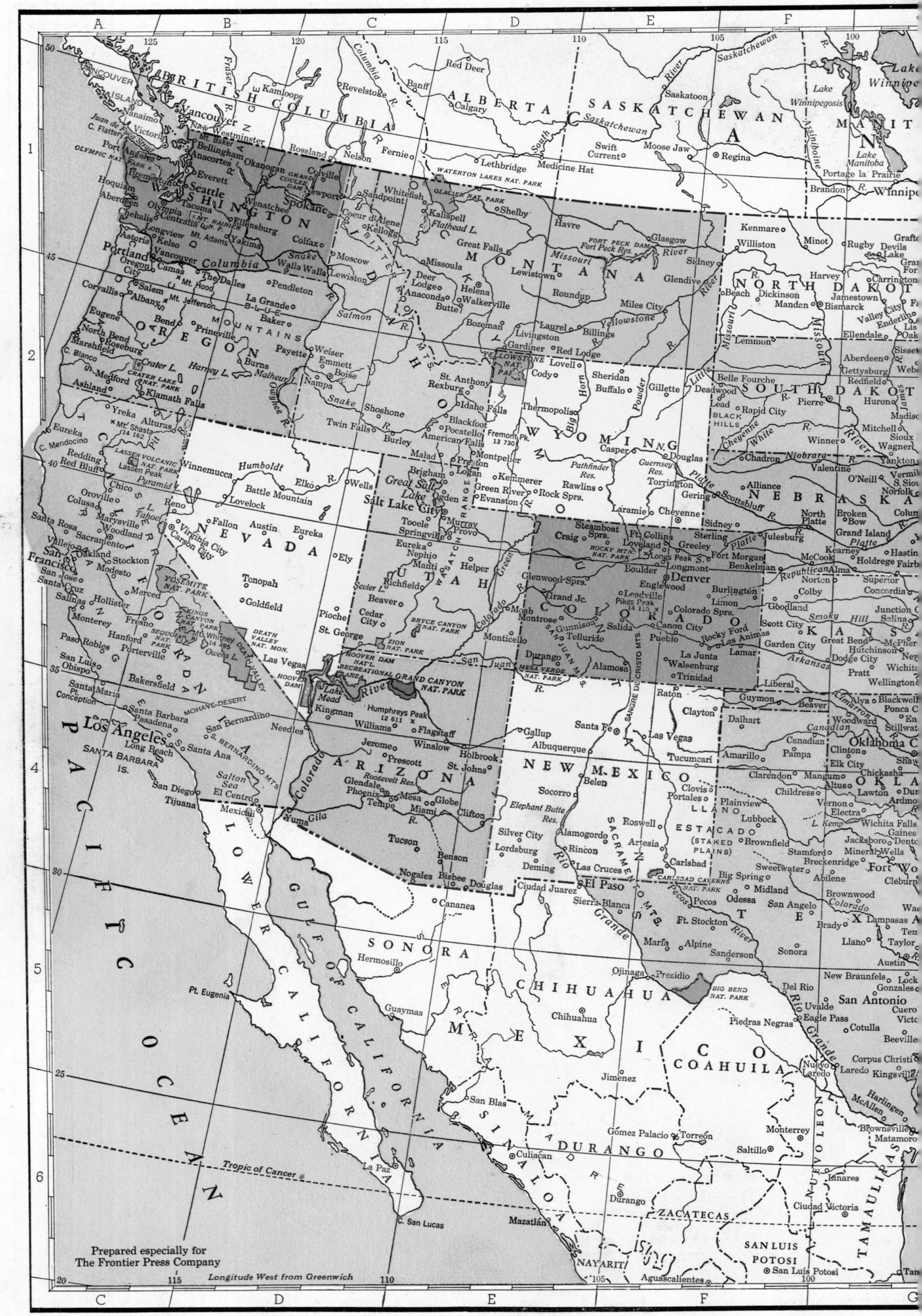
BRITISH COLUMBIA
ALBERTA
SASKATCHEWAN
CANADA
MANITOBA
WASHINGTON
OREGON
IDAHO
MONTANA
WYOMING
NORTH DAKOTA
SOUTH DAKOTA
NEBRASKA
KANSAS
CALIFORNIA
NEVADA
UTAH
COLORADO
ARIZONA
NEW MEXICO
TEXAS
OKLAHOMA
MEXICO
SONORA
CHIHUAHUA
COAHUILA
DURANGO
SINALOA
ZACATECAS
NAYARIT
SAN LUIS POTOSI
NUEVO LEON
TAMAULIPAS
LOWER CALIFORNIA
GULF OF CALIFORNIA
PACIFIC OCEAN
Tropic of Cancer
VANCOUVER ISLAND
Vancouver
Victoria
Nanaimo
New Westminster
Kamloops
Revelstoke
Nelson
Rossland
Fernie
Banff
Calgary
Red Deer
Lethbridge
Medicine Hat
Swift Current
Moose Jaw
Regina
Saskatoon
Brandon
Portage la Prairie
Winnipeg
Lake Winnipeg
Lake Winnipegosis
Lake Manitoba
Seattle
Tacoma
Olympia
Everett
Bellingham
Anacortes
Bremerton
Port Angeles
Aberdeen
Hoquiam
Chehalis
Centralia
Longview
Kelso
Vancouver
Spokane
Wenatchee
Ellensburg
Yakima
Walla Walla
Colfax
Okanogan
Colville
Newport
GRAND COULEE DAM
OLYMPIC NAT. PARK
MT. RAINIER NAT. PARK
Mt. Baker
Mt. Adams
Portland
Oregon City
Salem
Albany
Corvallis
Eugene
The Dalles
Pendleton
La Grande
Baker
Bend
Prineville
North Bend
Marshfield
Roseburg
Medford
Ashland
Klamath Falls
Burns
Crater L.
CRATER LAKE NAT. PARK
Harney L.
Mt. Hood
Mt. Jefferson
BLUE MOUNTAINS
C. Blanco
Boise
Nampa
Weiser
Emmett
Payette
Moscow
Lewiston
Coeur d'Alene
Kellogg
Sandpoint
Twin Falls
Burley
Shoshone
Pocatello
Blackfoot
Idaho Falls
Rexburg
St. Anthony
American Falls
Malad
Preston
Montpelier
BITTER ROOT MTS.
Salmon
Snake
Missoula
Kalispell
Whitefish
Flathead L.
GLACIER NAT. PARK
WATERTON LAKES NAT. PARK
Shelby
Havre
Great Falls
Lewistown
Helena
Butte
Anaconda
Deer Lodge
Walkerville
Bozeman
Livingston
Billings
Laurel
Red Lodge
Gardiner
Roundup
Miles City
Glendive
Sidney
Glasgow
FORT PECK DAM
Fort Peck Res.
Missouri
Yellowstone
YELLOWSTONE NAT. PARK
Cody
Lovell
Sheridan
Buffalo
Gillette
Thermopolis
Casper
Douglas
Rawlins
Rock Sprs.
Green River
Kemmerer
Evanston
Laramie
Cheyenne
Torrington
Fremont Pk. 13 730
Pathfinder Res.
Guernsey Res.
Kenmare
Williston
Minot
Rugby
Devils Lake
Harvey
Carrington
Jamestown
Bismarck
Mandan
Dickinson
Beach
Valley City
Enderlin
Ellendale
Lemmon
Belle Fourche
Deadwood
Lead
Rapid City
BLACK HILLS
Pierre
Huron
Aberdeen
Gettysburg
Mitchell
Winner
Yankton
Chadron
Alliance
Gering
Scottsbluff
Valentine
O'Neill
Norfolk
North Platte
Broken Bow
Grand Island
Kearney
Holdrege
McCook
Benkelman
Sidney
Julesburg
Niobrara
Platte
Eureka
C. Mendocino
Yreka
Mt. Shasta 14 162
Alturas
Redding
Red Bluff
LASSEN VOLCANIC NAT. PARK
Lassen Peak
Chico
Oroville
Colusa
Marysville
Woodland
Sacramento
Santa Rosa
Vallejo
San Francisco
Oakland
Stockton
Modesto
San Jose
Santa Cruz
Salinas
Monterey
Hollister
Merced
Fresno
Hanford
Porterville
Paso Robles
San Luis Obispo
Bakersfield
Santa Maria
Pt. Conception
Santa Barbara
Pasadena
Los Angeles
Long Beach
Santa Ana
San Bernardino
San Diego
Tijuana
El Centro
Mexicali
Salton Sea
Needles
SANTA BARBARA IS.
MOHAVE DESERT
YOSEMITE NAT. PARK
KINGS CANYON NAT. PARK
SEQUOIA NAT. PARK
Mt. Whitney 14 495
Owens L.
DEATH VALLEY NAT. MON.
SAN BERNARDINO MTS.
Pyramid L.
L. Tahoe
Reno
Virginia City
Carson City
Winnemucca
Lovelock
Battle Mountain
Elko
Wells
Fallon
Austin
Eureka
Ely
Tonopah
Goldfield
Pioche
Las Vegas
Humboldt
Salt Lake City
Great Salt Lake
Ogden
Brigham
Logan
Tooele
Murray
Provo
Springville
Eureka
Nephi
Manti
Richfield
Helper
Beaver
Cedar City
St. George
Moab
Monticello
Sevier L.
WASATCH RANGE
BRYCE CANYON NAT. PARK
ZION NAT. PARK
HOOVER DAM
HOOVER DAM NAT'L RECREATIONAL AREA
Lake Mead
GRAND CANYON NAT. PARK
Kingman
Williams
Flagstaff
Humphreys Peak 12 611
Winslow
Holbrook
St. Johns
Jerome
Prescott
Glendale
Phoenix
Tempe
Mesa
Miami
Globe
Clifton
Roosevelt Res.
Yuma
Tucson
Benson
Nogales
Bisbee
Douglas
Gila
Colorado
Steamboat Sprs.
Craig
Ft. Collins
Loveland
Greeley
Sterling
Fort Morgan
Longs Peak
ROCKY MTN. NAT. PARK
Boulder
Longmont
Denver
Englewood
Glenwood Sprs.
Grand Jc.
Leadville
Pikes Peak 14 110
Colorado Sprs.
Burlington
Limon
Montrose
Gunnison
Salida
Canon City
Pueblo
Rocky Ford
Las Animas
Lamar
La Junta
Walsenburg
Trinidad
Telluride
Durango
Alamosa
MESA VERDE NAT. PARK
SAN JUAN MTS.
SANGRE DE CRISTO MTS.
Raton
Clayton
Santa Fe
Las Vegas
Gallup
Albuquerque
Tucumcari
Belen
Socorro
Clovis
Portales
Roswell
Artesia
Carlsbad
CARLSBAD CAVERNS NAT. PARK
Silver City
Lordsburg
Deming
Alamogordo
Rincon
Las Cruces
Elephant Butte Res.
SACRAMENTO MTS.
LLANO ESTACADO (STAKED PLAINS)
El Paso
Ciudad Juarez
Sierra Blanca
Pecos
Ft. Stockton
Marfa
Alpine
Sanderson
Presidio
Ojinaga
BIG BEND NAT. PARK
Dalhart
Amarillo
Pampa
Canadian
Clarendon
Childress
Plainview
Lubbock
Big Spring
Midland
Odessa
San Angelo
Sweetwater
Abilene
Brownwood
Del Rio
Uvalde
Eagle Pass
San Antonio
New Braunfels
Cotulla
Laredo
Corpus Christi
Harlingen
McAllen
Brownsville
Matamoros
Piedras Negras
Nuevo Laredo
Monterrey
Saltillo
Torreon
Gomez Palacio
Chihuahua
Jimenez
Durango
Culiacan
Mazatlan
San Blas
Hermosillo
Guaymas
Cananea
Pt. Eugenia
La Paz
C. San Lucas
Linares
Ciudad Victoria
San Luis Potosi
Aguascalientes
Liberal
Guymon
Beaver
Garden City
Dodge City
Great Bend
Hutchinson
Pratt
Wichita
Wellington
Goodland
Colby
Scott City
Norton
Junction City
Salina
Oklahoma City
Clinton
Elk City
Chickasha
Lawton
Altus
Mangum
Vernon
Electra
Wichita Falls
Prepared especially for
The Frontier Press Company
Longitude West from Greenwich

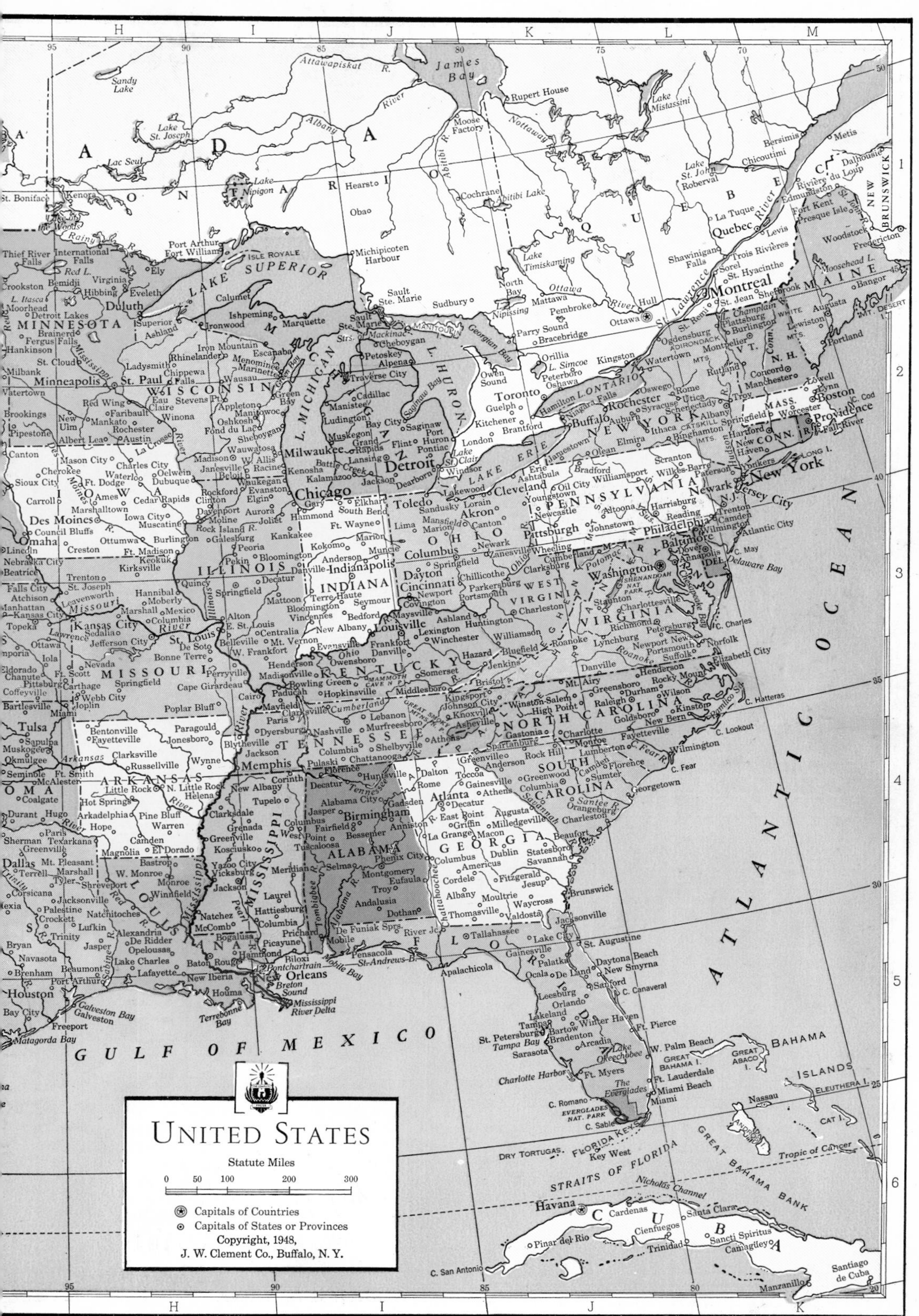
UNITED STATES
Statute Miles
0 50 100 200 300
Capitals of Countries
Capitals of States or Provinces
Copyright, 1948,
J. W. Clement Co., Buffalo, N. Y.
CANADA
ONTARIO
QUEBEC
NEW BRUNSWICK
James Bay
LAKE SUPERIOR
L. MICHIGAN
L. HURON
L. ONTARIO
LAKE ERIE
ATLANTIC OCEAN
GULF OF MEXICO
STRAITS OF FLORIDA
BAHAMA ISLANDS
GREAT BAHAMA BANK
Tropic of Cancer
CUBA
MINNESOTA
WISCONSIN
IOWA
ILLINOIS
INDIANA
OHIO
PENNSYLVANIA
NEW YORK
MAINE
VT.
N. H.
MASS.
CONN.
R. I.
N. J.
DEL.
MARYLAND
WEST VIRGINIA
VIRGINIA
KENTUCKY
TENNESSEE
NORTH CAROLINA
SOUTH CAROLINA
GEORGIA
ALABAMA
MISSISSIPPI
LOUISIANA
ARKANSAS
MISSOURI
FLORIDA
Montreal
Quebec
Ottawa
Toronto
Detroit
Chicago
Milwaukee
Cleveland
Pittsburgh
Buffalo
New York
Boston
Philadelphia
Baltimore
Washington
Richmond
Indianapolis
Cincinnati
Columbus
Louisville
St. Louis
Kansas City
Minneapolis
St. Paul
Duluth
Des Moines
Omaha
Memphis
Nashville
Atlanta
Birmingham
New Orleans
Houston
Dallas
Tulsa
Jacksonville
Tampa
Miami
Key West
Havana
Charleston
Savannah
Norfolk
Providence
C. Hatteras
C. Lookout
C. Fear
C. Cod
C. May
C. Charles
C. Sable
C. Canaveral
C. San Antonio
Florida Keys
Dry Tortugas
The Everglades
L. Okeechobee
Nassau
Santiago de Cuba

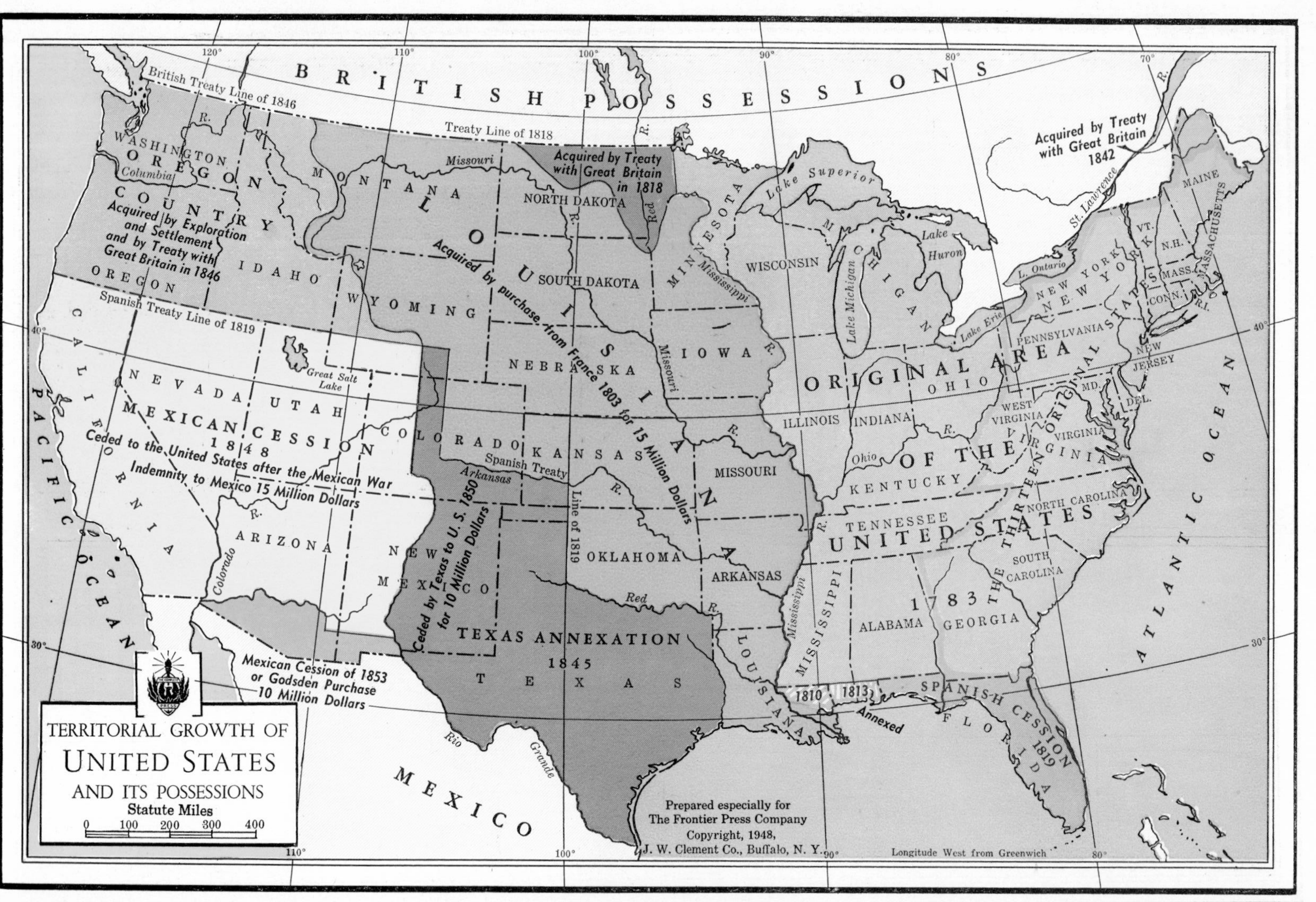
BRITISH POSSESSIONS
British Treaty Line of 1846
Treaty Line of 1818
Acquired by Treaty
with Great Britain
in 1818
Acquired by Treaty
with Great Britain
1842
St. Lawrence R.
OREGON COUNTRY
Acquired by Exploration
and Settlement
and by Treaty with
Great Britain in 1846
Spanish Treaty Line of 1819
LOUISIANA
Acquired by purchase from France 1803 for 15 Million Dollars
MEXICAN CESSION
1848
Ceded to the United States after the Mexican War
Indemnity to Mexico 15 Million Dollars
Spanish Treaty
Line of 1819
Ceded by Texas to U. S. 1850
for 10 Million Dollars
TEXAS ANNEXATION
1845
TEXAS
Mexican Cession of 1853
or Godsden Purchase
10 Million Dollars
ORIGINAL AREA
OF THE
UNITED STATES
1783
THE THIRTEEN ORIGINAL STATES
1810
1813
Annexed
SPANISH CESSION
1819
FLORIDA
WASHINGTON
OREGON
IDAHO
MONTANA
WYOMING
NORTH DAKOTA
SOUTH DAKOTA
NEBRASKA
KANSAS
COLORADO
UTAH
NEVADA
CALIFORNIA
ARIZONA
NEW MEXICO
OKLAHOMA
MINNESOTA
IOWA
MISSOURI
ARKANSAS
LOUISIANA
WISCONSIN
MICHIGAN
ILLINOIS
INDIANA
OHIO
KENTUCKY
TENNESSEE
MISSISSIPPI
ALABAMA
GEORGIA
SOUTH CAROLINA
NORTH CAROLINA
VIRGINIA
WEST VIRGINIA
PENNSYLVANIA
NEW YORK
NEW JERSEY
MD.
DEL.
CONN.
R.I.
MASS.
N.H.
VT.
MAINE
MASSACHUSETTS
Columbia
Missouri
Red
Mississippi
Great Salt Lake
Colorado
Arkansas
Rio Grande
Ohio
Lake Superior
Lake Michigan
Lake Huron
Lake Erie
L. Ontario
PACIFIC OCEAN
ATLANTIC OCEAN
MEXICO
TERRITORIAL GROWTH OF
UNITED STATES
AND ITS POSSESSIONS
Statute Miles
0 100 200 300 400
Prepared especially for
The Frontier Press Company
Copyright, 1948,
J. W. Clement Co., Buffalo, N. Y.
Longitude West from Greenwich

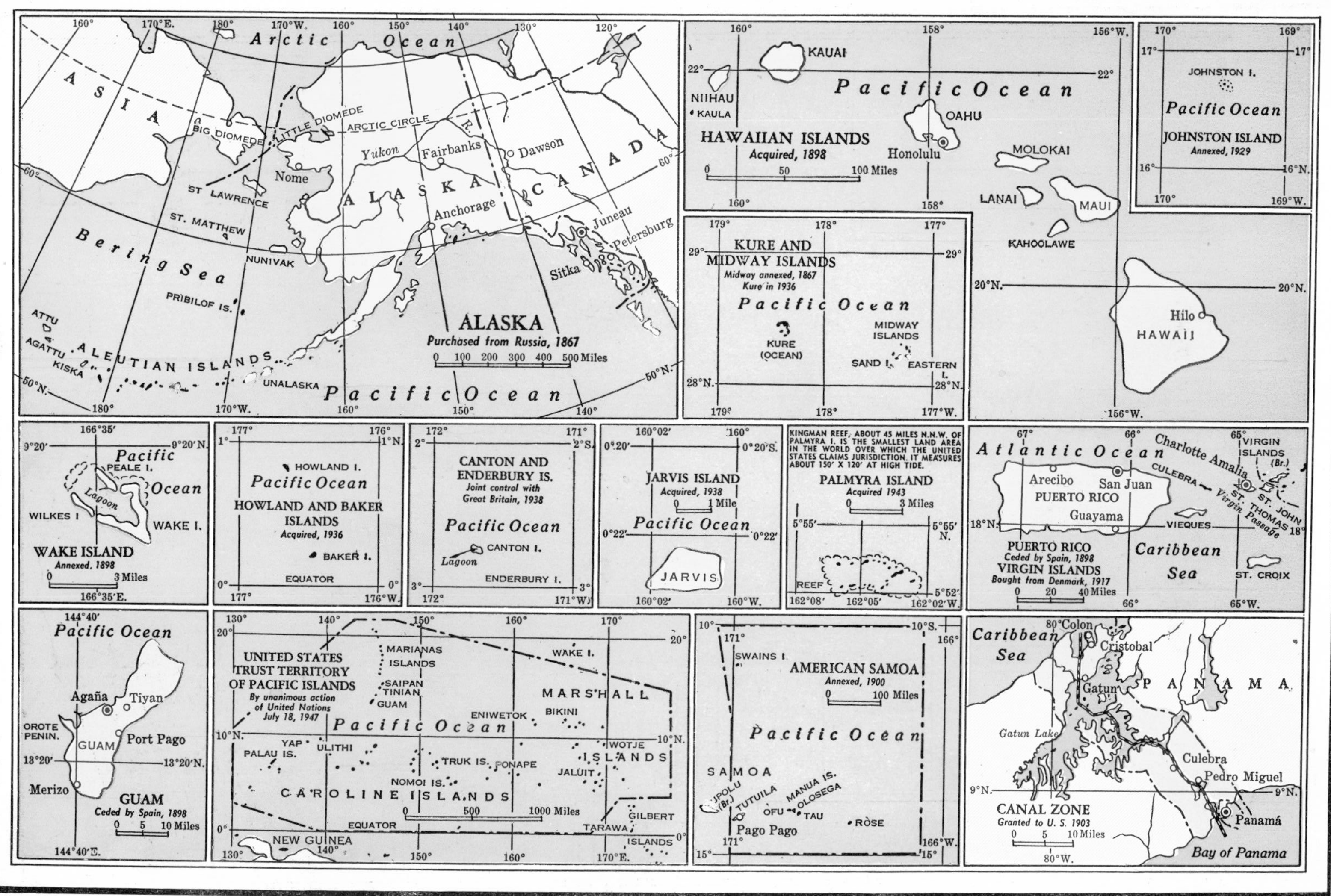
ALASKA
Purchased from Russia, 1867
0 100 200 300 400 500 Miles
Arctic Ocean
Bering Sea
Pacific Ocean
ASIA
CANADA
ALASKA
ARCTIC CIRCLE
BIG DIOMEDE
LITTLE DIOMEDE
Nome
Yukon
Fairbanks
Dawson
Anchorage
Juneau
Petersburg
Sitka
ST LAWRENCE
ST. MATTHEW
NUNIVAK
PRIBILOF IS.
ATTU
AGATTU
KISKA
ALEUTIAN ISLANDS
UNALASKA
HAWAIIAN ISLANDS
Acquired, 1898
100 Miles
Pacific Ocean
KAUAI
NIIHAU
KAULA
OAHU
Honolulu
MOLOKAI
LANAI
MAUI
KAHOOLAWE
HAWAII
Hilo
JOHNSTON I.
Pacific Ocean
JOHNSTON ISLAND
Annexed, 1929
KURE AND MIDWAY ISLANDS
Midway annexed, 1867
Kure in 1936
Pacific Ocean
KURE (OCEAN)
MIDWAY ISLANDS
SAND I.
EASTERN I.
WAKE ISLAND
Annexed, 1898
3 Miles
Pacific Ocean
PEALE I.
Lagoon
WILKES I
WAKE I.
HOWLAND I.
Pacific Ocean
HOWLAND AND BAKER ISLANDS
Acquired, 1936
BAKER I.
EQUATOR
CANTON AND ENDERBURY IS.
Joint control with Great Britain, 1938
Pacific Ocean
CANTON I.
Lagoon
ENDERBURY I.
JARVIS ISLAND
Acquired, 1938
1 Mile
Pacific Ocean
JARVIS
KINGMAN REEF, ABOUT 45 MILES N.N.W. OF PALMYRA I. IS THE SMALLEST LAND AREA IN THE WORLD OVER WHICH THE UNITED STATES CLAIMS JURISDICTION. IT MEASURES ABOUT 150' X 120' AT HIGH TIDE.
PALMYRA ISLAND
Acquired 1943
3 Miles
REEF
Atlantic Ocean
Caribbean Sea
Arecibo
San Juan
PUERTO RICO
Guayama
Charlotte Amalia
CULEBRA
VIRGIN ISLANDS (Br.)
ST. JOHN
ST. THOMAS
Virgin Passage
VIEQUES
ST. CROIX
PUERTO RICO
Ceded by Spain, 1898
VIRGIN ISLANDS
Bought from Denmark, 1917
40 Miles
GUAM
Ceded by Spain, 1898
10 Miles
Pacific Ocean
Agaña
Tiyan
OROTE PENIN.
Port Pago
Merizo
UNITED STATES TRUST TERRITORY OF PACIFIC ISLANDS
By unanimous action of United Nations July 18, 1947
Pacific Ocean
MARIANAS ISLANDS
SAIPAN
TINIAN
GUAM
WAKE I.
MARSHALL ISLANDS
ENIWETOK
BIKINI
WOTJE
JALUIT
YAP
ULITHI
PALAU IS.
TRUK IS.
PONAPE
NOMOI IS.
CAROLINE ISLANDS
EQUATOR
NEW GUINEA
GILBERT ISLANDS
TARAWA
1000 Miles
AMERICAN SAMOA
Annexed, 1900
100 Miles
Pacific Ocean
SWAINS I
SAMOA
UPOLU (Br.)
TUTUILA
MANUA IS.
OFU
OLOSEGA
TAU
ROSE
Pago Pago
CANAL ZONE
Granted to U. S. 1903
10 Miles
Caribbean Sea
Colon
Cristobal
Gatun
Gatun Lake
PANAMA
Culebra
Pedro Miguel
Panamá
Bay of Panama

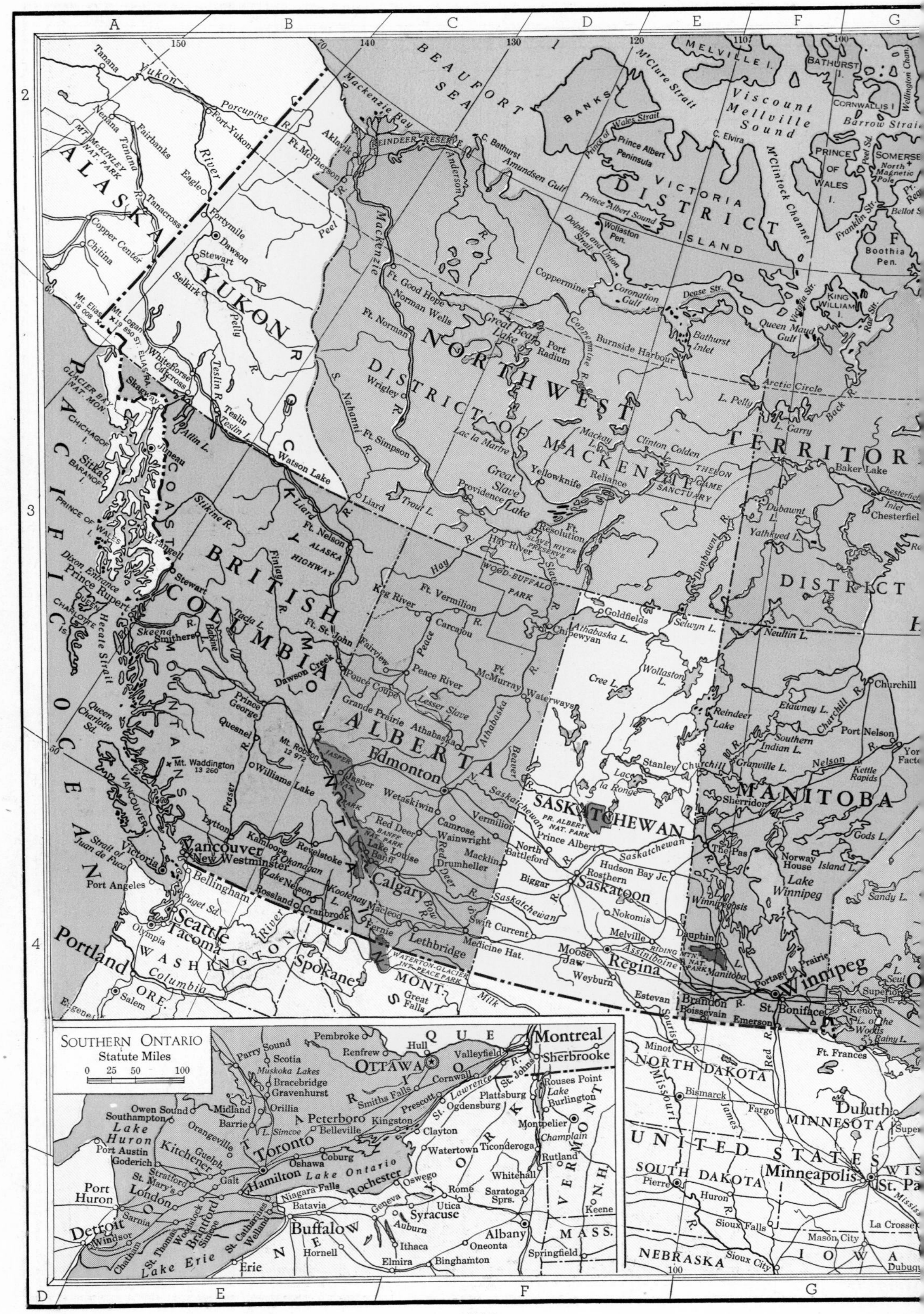

SOUTHERN ONTARIO
Statute Miles
0 25 50 100
ALASKA
YUKON
BRITISH COLUMBIA
ALBERTA
SASKATCHEWAN
MANITOBA
NORTHWEST TERRITORIES
DISTRICT OF MACKENZIE
DISTRICT OF FRANKLIN
DISTRICT OF KEEWATIN
BEAUFORT SEA
PACIFIC OCEAN
UNITED STATES
WASHINGTON
NORTH DAKOTA
SOUTH DAKOTA
MINNESOTA
Edmonton
Calgary
Vancouver
Victoria
Regina
Saskatoon
Winnipeg
Seattle
Tacoma
Portland
Spokane
Ottawa
Montreal
Toronto
Hamilton
Buffalo
Detroit
Rochester
Syracuse
Albany
Minneapolis
St. Paul
Duluth

CANADA
Statute Miles
0 50 100 200 300 400
Capital of Dominion
Capitals of Provinces and States
Size of type indicates relative importance of places
Copyright, 1948,
J. W. Clement Co., Buffalo, N. Y.
GREENLAND
(Denmark)
BAFFIN BAY
FRANKLIN
BAFFIN ISLAND
FOXE BASIN
Davis Strait
Hudson Strait
Ungava Bay
LABRADOR
QUEBEC
ONTARIO
NEWFOUNDLAND
NOVA SCOTIA
NEW BRUNSWICK
Gulf of St. Lawrence
ATLANTIC OCEAN
James Bay
Montreal
Quebec
Ottawa
Toronto
Halifax
Boston
New York
Prepared especially for
The Frontier Press Company
Longitude West from Greenwich

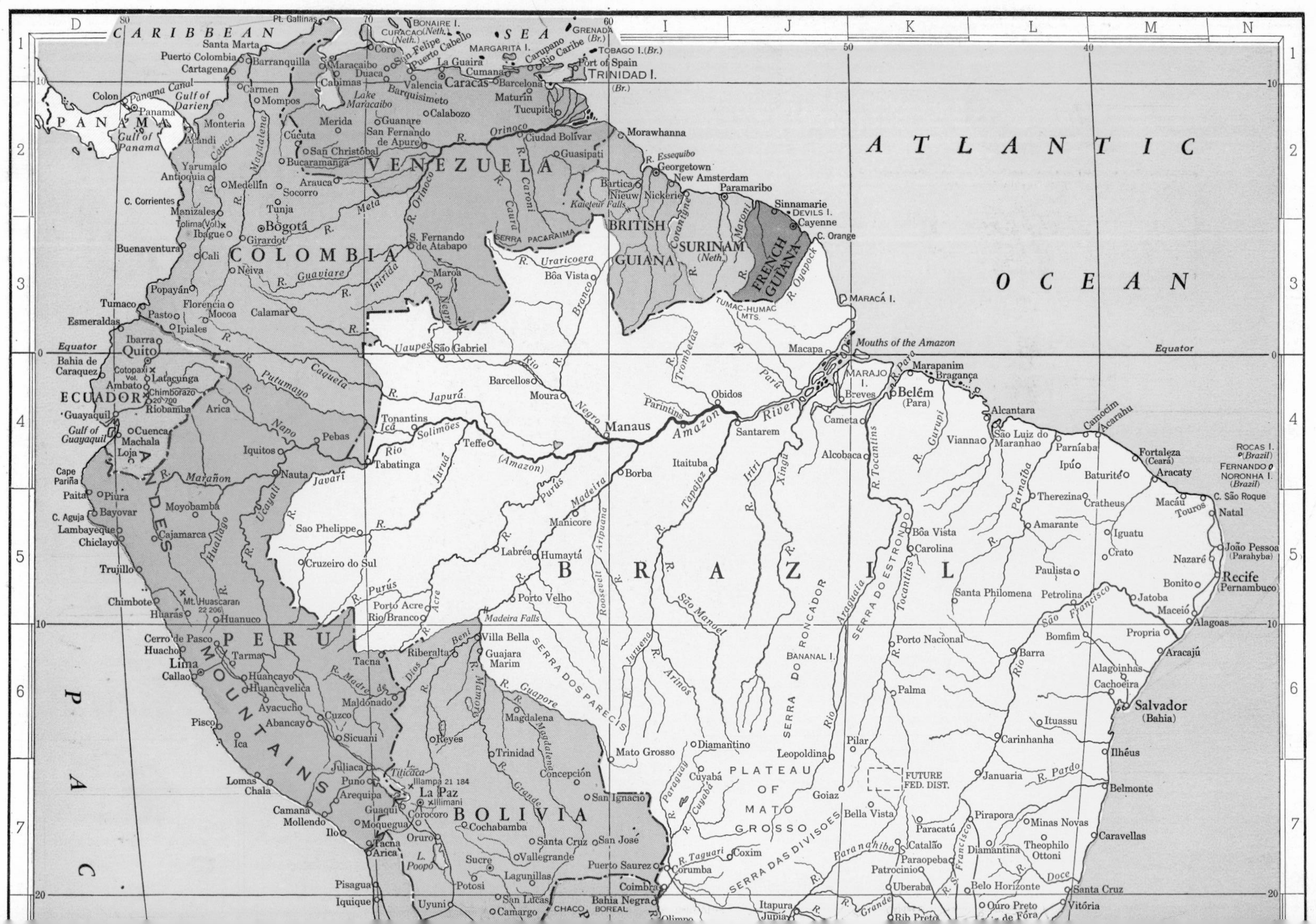

C A R I B B E A N
S E A
A T L A N T I C
O C E A N
P A C
Equator
PANAMA
VENEZUELA
COLOMBIA
ECUADOR
PERU
BOLIVIA
BRAZIL
BRITISH GUIANA
SURINAM (Neth.)
FRENCH GUIANA
ANDES MOUNTAINS
PLATEAU OF MATO GROSSO
SERRA DO RONCADOR
SERRA DO ESTRONDO
SERRA DOS PARECIS
SERRA DAS DIVISOES
Mouths of the Amazon
Amazon River
Caracas
Bogotá
Quito
Lima
La Paz
Manaus
Belém (Para)
Recife (Pernambuco)
Salvador (Bahia)
Georgetown
Paramaribo
Cayenne
TRINIDAD I.
FUTURE FED. DIST.

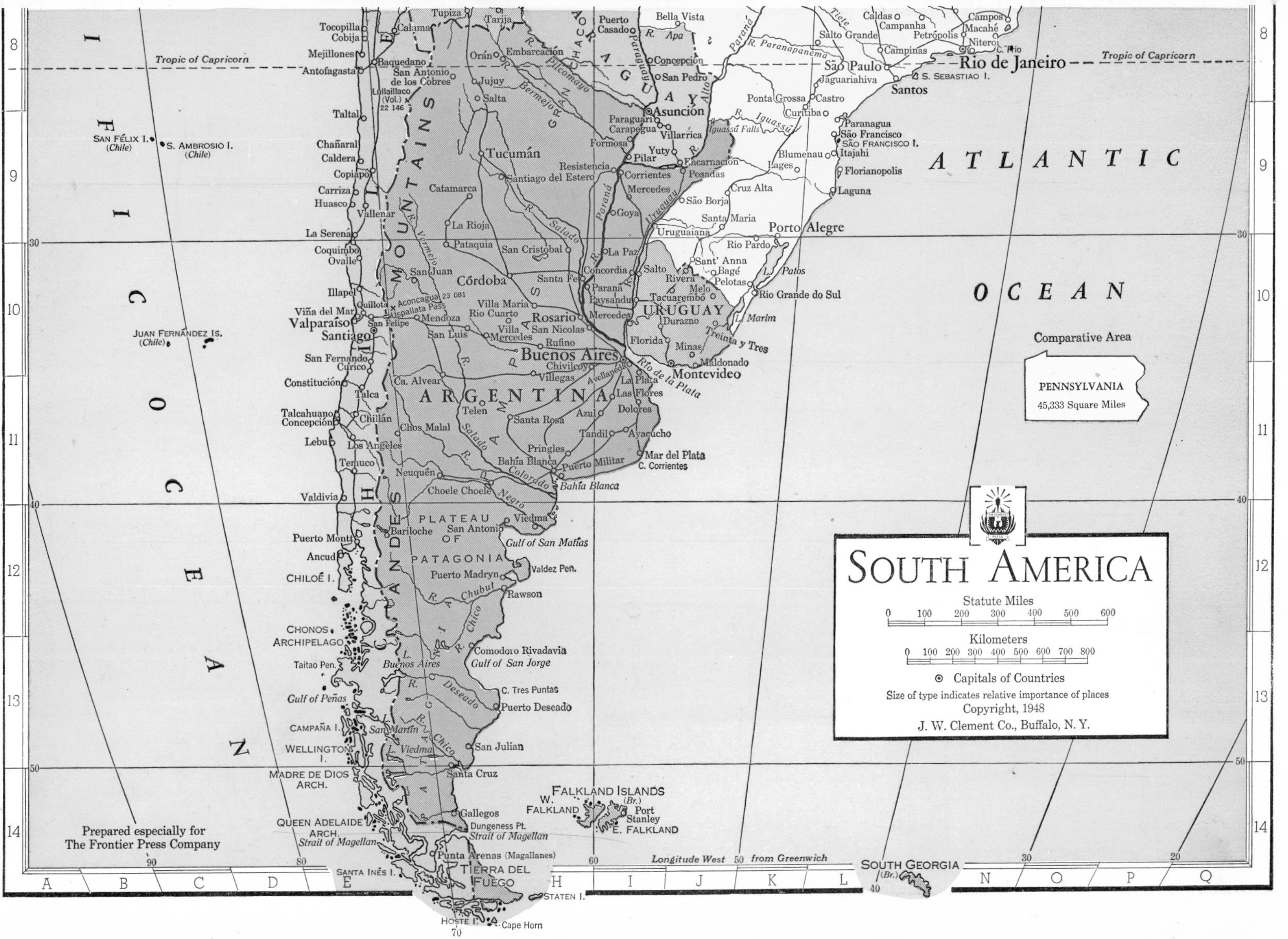
SOUTH AMERICA
Statute Miles
0 100 200 300 400 500 600
Kilometers
0 100 200 300 400 500 600 700 800
⊙ Capitals of Countries
Size of type indicates relative importance of places
Copyright, 1948
J. W. Clement Co., Buffalo, N. Y.
Comparative Area
PENNSYLVANIA
45,333 Square Miles
ATLANTIC OCEAN
PACIFIC OCEAN
Tropic of Capricorn
Longitude West from Greenwich
Rio de Janeiro
São Paulo
Santos
Porto Alegre
Rio Grande do Sul
Montevideo
URUGUAY
PARAGUAY
Asunción
Buenos Aires
Rosario
Córdoba
Tucumán
ARGENTINA
Mendoza
Santiago
Valparaiso
ANDES MOUNTAINS
PLATEAU OF PATAGONIA
Bahía Blanca
Mar del Plata
Gulf of San Matías
Gulf of San Jorge
FALKLAND ISLANDS (Br.)
Port Stanley
SOUTH GEORGIA (Br.)
TIERRA DEL FUEGO
Punta Arenas (Magallanes)
Strait of Magellan
STATEN I.
HOSTE I.
Cape Horn
JUAN FERNÁNDEZ IS. (Chile)
SAN FÉLIX I. (Chile)
S. AMBROSIO I. (Chile)
CHILOÉ I.
CHONOS ARCHIPELAGO
Gulf of Peñas
WELLINGTON I.
MADRE DE DIOS ARCH.
QUEEN ADELAIDE ARCH.
Prepared especially for
The Frontier Press Company

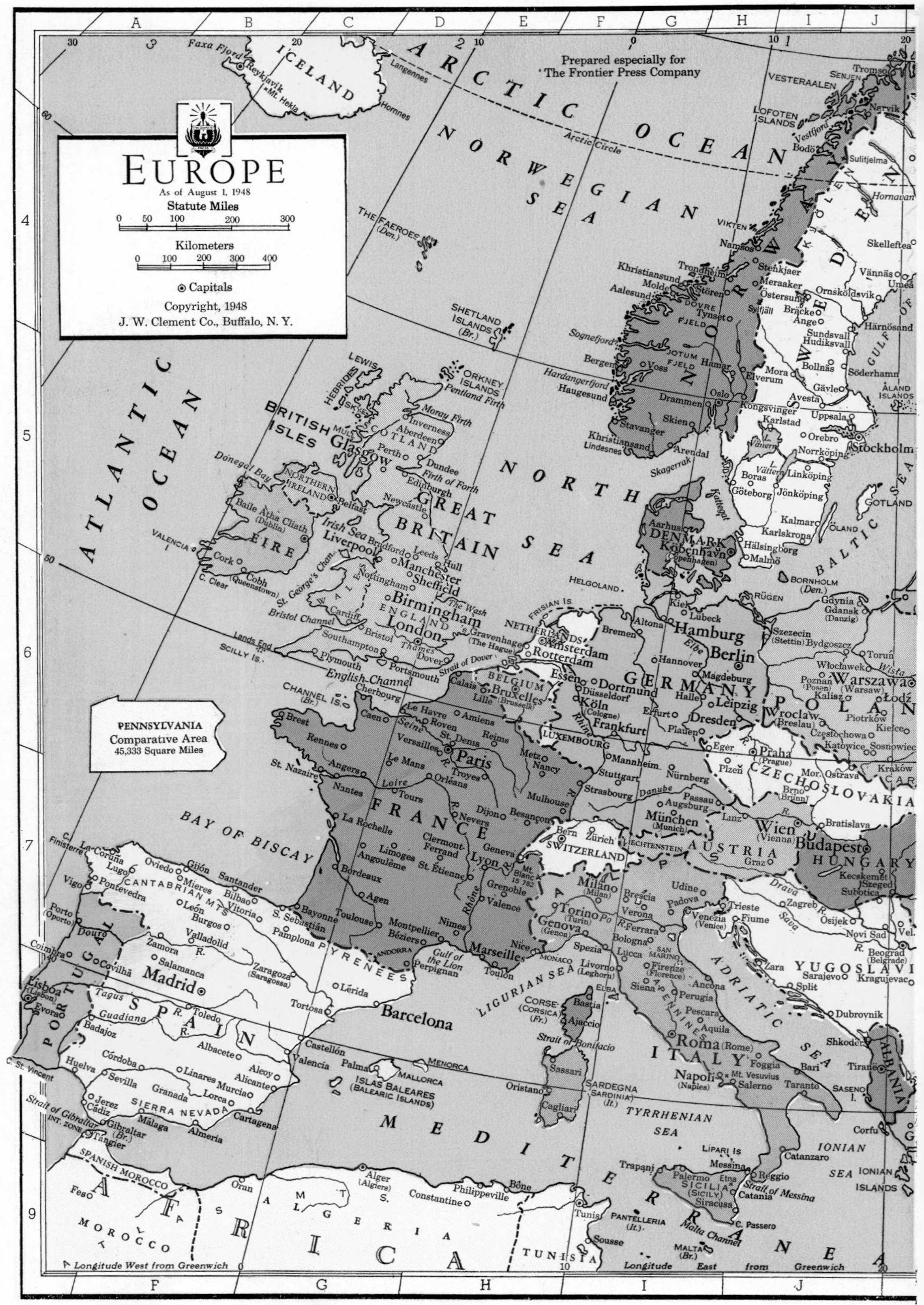
EUROPE
As of August 1, 1948
Statute Miles
0 50 100 200 300
Kilometers
0 100 200 300 400
Capitals
Copyright, 1948
J. W. Clement Co., Buffalo, N. Y.
Prepared especially for
The Frontier Press Company
PENNSYLVANIA
Comparative Area
45,333 Square Miles
ARCTIC OCEAN
NORWEGIAN SEA
ATLANTIC OCEAN
NORTH SEA
BAY OF BISCAY
MEDITERRANEAN
TYRRHENIAN SEA
LIGURIAN SEA
ADRIATIC SEA
IONIAN SEA
BALTIC SEA
ICELAND
Reykjavik
Mt. Hekla
Faxa Fjord
Langennes
Hornnes
Arctic Circle
THE FAEROES (Den.)
SHETLAND ISLANDS (Br.)
ORKNEY ISLANDS
Pentland Firth
Moray Firth
LEWIS
HEBRIDES
BRITISH ISLES
SCOTLAND
Inverness
Aberdeen
Perth
Dundee
Firth of Forth
Edinburgh
Glasgow
Newcastle
GREAT BRITAIN
NORTHERN IRELAND
Belfast
Donegal Bay
EIRE
Baile Átha Cliath (Dublin)
Cork
Cobh (Queenstown)
C. Clear
VALENCIA
Irish Sea
Liverpool
Bradford
Leeds
Hull
Manchester
Sheffield
Nottingham
WALES
St. George's Chan.
Cardiff
Bristol Channel
Bristol
Birmingham
ENGLAND
The Wash
London
Thames
Dover
Southampton
Plymouth
Portsmouth
Lands End
SCILLY IS.
English Channel
Strait of Dover
CHANNEL IS. (Br.)
NORWAY
Tromsø
SENJEN
VESTERAALEN
LOFOTEN ISLANDS
Vestfjord
Narvik
Bodø
Sulitjelma
VIKTEN
Namsos
Trondheim
Christiansund
Molde
Aalesund
Støren
DOVRE FJELD
Tynset
Sognefjord
Bergen
Voss
JOTUM FJELD
Hamar
Hardangerfjord
Haugesund
Elverum
Oslo
Drammen
Kongsvinger
Skien
Stavanger
Christiansand
Lindesnes
Arendal
Skagerrak
Kattegat
SWEDEN
Hornavan
Skellefteå
Vännäs
Umeå
Steinkjaer
Meraaker
Östersund
Sylfjäll
Bräcke
Örnsköldsvik
Ange
Härnösand
Sundsvall
Hudiksvall
GULF OF BOTHNIA
Bollnäs
Mora
Söderhamn
Gävle
ÅLAND ISLANDS
Avesta
Uppsala
Karlstad
Vänern
Orebro
Stockholm
Norrköping
Vättern
Linköping
Boras
Göteborg
Jönköping
GOTLAND
Kalmar
ÖLAND
Karlskrona
Hälsingborg
Malmö
BORNHOLM (Den.)
DENMARK
Aarhus
København (Copenhagen)
HELGOLAND
Kiel
Lübeck
RÜGEN
Gdynia
Gdansk (Danzig)
FRISIAN IS.
NETHERLANDS
Amsterdam
's Gravenhage (The Hague)
Rotterdam
Bremen
Altona
Hamburg
Elbe
Szczecin (Stettin)
Bydgoszcz
Toruń
Hannover
Berlin
GERMANY
Magdeburg
Essen
Dortmund
Düsseldorf
Köln (Cologne)
Halle
Leipzig
Dresden
Erfurt
Plauen
Frankfurt
Rhine
Włocławek
Wisła
Poznań (Posen)
Kalisz
Warszawa (Warsaw)
Łodź
POLAND
Wrocław (Breslau)
Piotrków
Kielce
Częstochowa
Katowice
Sosnowiec
Kraków
BELGIUM
Bruxelles (Brussels)
Calais
Lille
LUXEMBOURG
Eger
Praha (Prague)
Plzeň
CZECHOSLOVAKIA
Mor. Ostrava
Brno (Brünn)
Mannheim
Stuttgart
Nürnberg
Danube
Passau
Augsburg
München (Munich)
Strasbourg
Linz
Wien (Vienna)
Bratislava
Budapest
HUNGARY
Kecskemét
Szeged
Subotica
FRANCE
Cherbourg
Le Havre
Rouen
Amiens
Caen
Seine
St. Denis
Reims
Brest
Rennes
Versailles
Paris
Metz
Nancy
Le Mans
Troyes
Angers
St. Nazaire
Nantes
Loire
Orléans
Tours
Dijon
Mulhouse
Besançon
La Rochelle
Nevers
Clermont-Ferrand
Limoges
Angoulême
Lyon
St. Étienne
Geneva
Bordeaux
Grenoble
Valence
Agen
Rhône
Bayonne
Toulouse
Montpellier
Béziers
Nîmes
Marseilles
Nice
Toulon
Perpignan
Gulf of the Lion
MONACO
ANDORRA
SWITZERLAND
Bern
Zürich
LIECHTENSTEIN
Mt. Blanc 15 782
AUSTRIA
Graz
ITALY
Milano (Milan)
Brescia
Verona
Udine
Padova
Venezia (Venice)
Trieste
Fiume
Torino (Turin)
Po
Ferrara
Genova (Genoa)
Bologna
SAN MARINO
Spezia
Lucca
Livorno (Leghorn)
Firenze (Florence)
Siena
Ancona
Perugia
Pescara
Aquila
ELBA
APENNINES
Roma (Rome)
Foggia
Bari
Napoli (Naples)
Mt. Vesuvius
Salerno
Taranto
CORSE (CORSICA) (Fr.)
Bastia
Ajaccio
Strait of Bonifacio
SARDEGNA (SARDINIA) (It.)
Sassari
Oristano
Cagliari
LIPARI IS.
Messina
Reggio
Strait of Messina
Trapani
Palermo
Etna
SICILIA (SICILY)
Catania
Siracusa
C. Passero
PANTELLERIA (It.)
Malta Channel
MALTA (Br.)
Catanzaro
YUGOSLAVIA
Zagreb
Drava
Sava
Osijek
Novi Sad
Beograd (Belgrade)
Kragujevac
Sarajevo
Zara
Split
Dubrovnik
Shkodër
Tiranë
ALBANIA
SASENO I.
Corfu
IONIAN ISLANDS
SPAIN
C. Finisterre
La Coruña
Lugo
Oviedo
Gijón
Santander
Bilbao
Vitoria
Mieres
CANTABRIAN MTS.
Vigo
Pontevedra
León
Burgos
S. Sebastián
Pamplona
PYRENEES
Valladolid
Zamora
Salamanca
Zaragoza (Saragossa)
Madrid
Lérida
Tortosa
Barcelona
Tagus
Toledo
Guadiana
Badajoz
Albacete
Castellón
Valencia
Palma
MENORCA
MALLORCA
ISLAS BALEARES (BALEARIC ISLANDS)
Córdoba
Linares
Alcoy
Alicante
Murcia
Huelva
Sevilla
Granada
Lorca
Jerez
Cádiz
SIERRA NEVADA
Málaga
Almería
Cartagena
PORTUGAL
Porto (Oporto)
Douro
Coimbra
Covilhã
Lisboa (Lisbon)
Évora
C. St. Vincent
Strait of Gibraltar
Gibraltar (Br.)
INT. ZONE
Tangier
SPANISH MOROCCO
Fes
MOROCCO
AFRICA
Oran
Alger (Algiers)
ALGERIA
ATLAS MTS.
Constantine
Philippeville
Bône
Tunis
Sousse
TUNISIA
Longitude West from Greenwich
Longitude East from Greenwich
A B C D E F G H I J

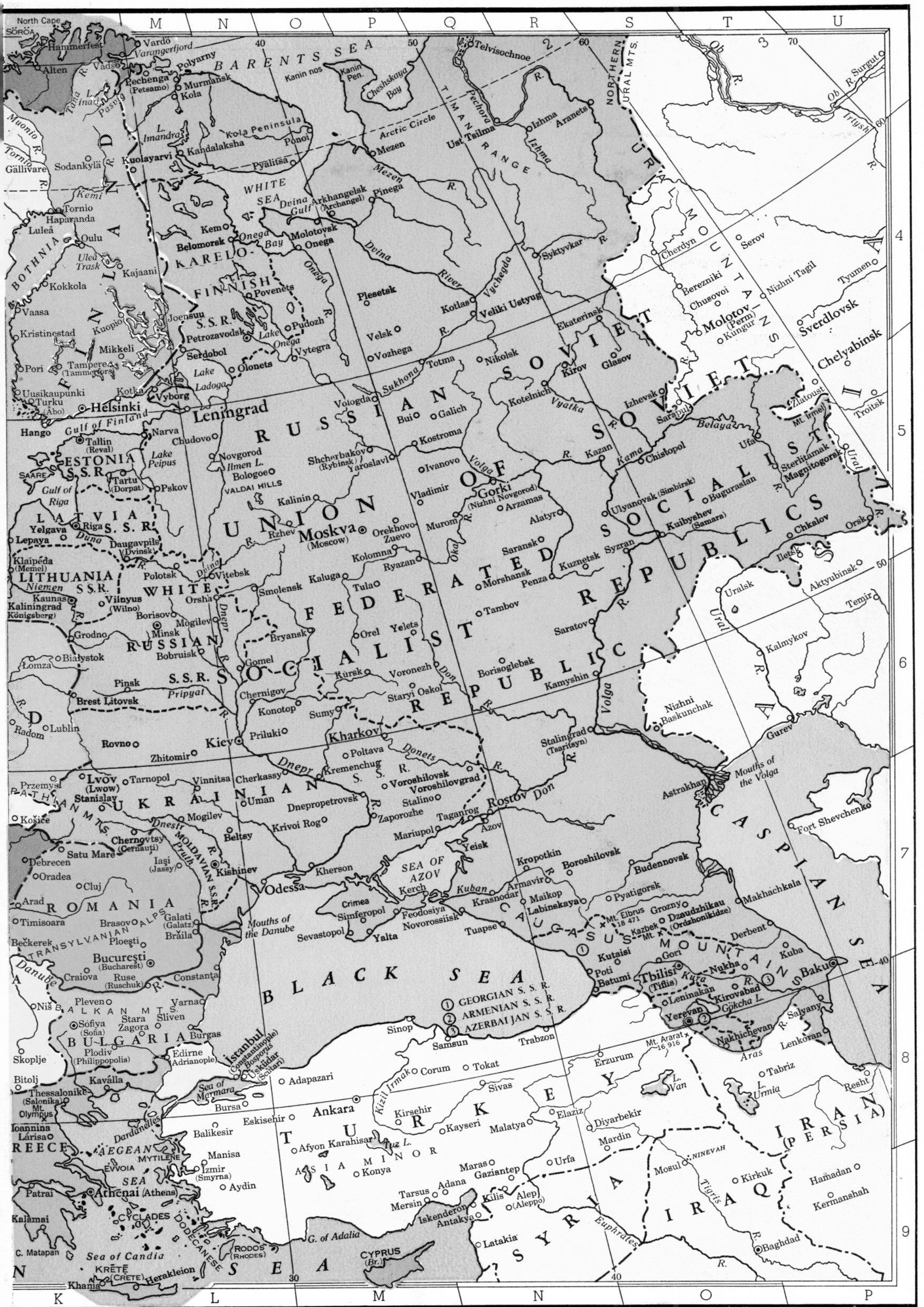

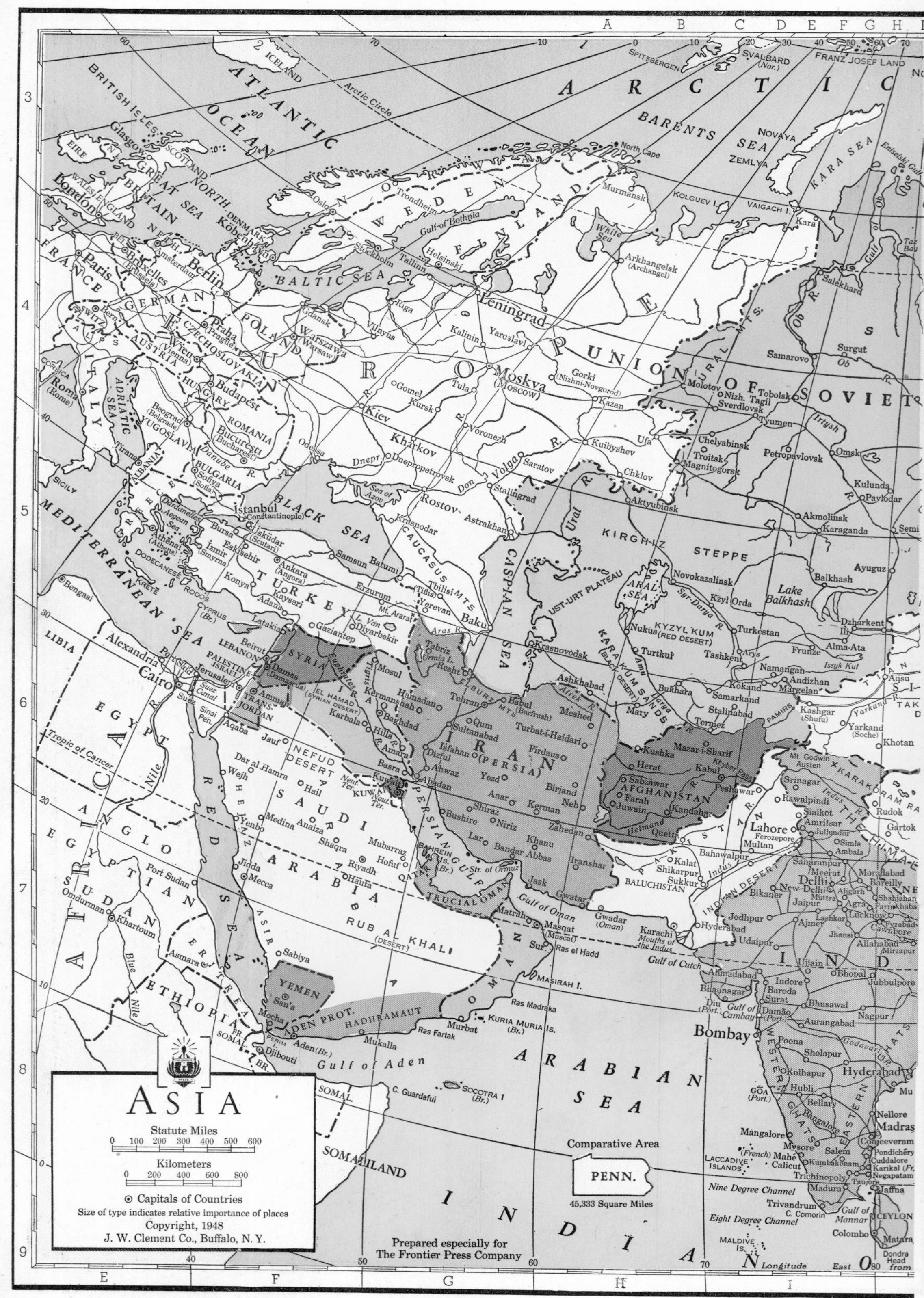
ASIA
Statute Miles
0 100 200 300 400 500 600
Kilometers
0 200 400 600 800
⊙ Capitals of Countries
Size of type indicates relative importance of places
Copyright, 1948
J. W. Clement Co., Buffalo, N. Y.
Prepared especially for
The Frontier Press Company
Comparative Area
PENN.
45,333 Square Miles
ARCTIC
ATLANTIC OCEAN
BARENTS SEA
NOVAYA ZEMLYA
KARA SEA
FRANZ JOSEF LAND
SPITSBERGEN
SVALBARD (Nor.)
ICELAND
BRITISH ISLES
EIRE
SCOTLAND
GREAT BRITAIN
NORTH SEA
London
Glasgow
Paris
FRANCE
Bruxelles (Brussels)
Amsterdam
Berlin
GERMANY
København
DENMARK
Oslo
NORWAY
SWEDEN
Stockholm
FINLAND
Helsinki
Gulf of Bothnia
BALTIC SEA
Tallinn
Riga
Vilnyus
Gdansk
POLAND
Warszawa (Warsaw)
Praha (Prague)
CZECHOSLOVAKIA
Wien (Vienna)
AUSTRIA
SWITZ.
Bern
HUNGARY
Budapest
ROMANIA
Bucuresti (Bucharest)
YUGOSLAVIA
Beograd (Belgrade)
BULGARIA
Sofiya (Sofia)
ALBANIA
Tiranë
ITALY
Roma (Rome)
CORSICA
SICILY
ADRIATIC SEA
GREECE
Athénai (Athens)
Aegean Sea
Dardanelles
DODECANESE
KRETE
RODOS
MEDITERRANEAN SEA
EUROPE
Murmansk
North Cape
White Sea
Arkhangelsk (Archangel)
Leningrad
Trondheim
KOLGUEV I.
VAIGACH I.
Kara
Salekhard
Kalinin
Yaroslavl
Moskva (Moscow)
Gorki (Nizhni-Novgorod)
Tula
Kursk
Gomel
Kiev
Kharkov
Voronezh
Odessa
Dnepr
Dnepropetrovsk
Sea of Azov
Rostov
Don
Volga
Saratov
Stalingrad
Astrakhan
Kuibyshev
Kazan
Molotov
Ufa
Chkalov
Magnitogorsk
Troitsk
Chelyabinsk
Sverdlovsk
Nizh. Tagil
Tobolsk
Tyumen
Omsk
Petropavlovsk
Irtysh
Samarovo
Surgut
Ob R.
URAL MTS.
UNION OF SOVIET
Kulunda
Pavlodar
Akmolinsk
Karaganda
Aktyubinsk
Ural R.
KIRGHIZ STEPPE
UST-URT PLATEAU
ARAL SEA
Novokazalinsk
Kzyl Orda
Syr-Darya
Lake Balkhash
Balkhash
Ayuguz
Dzharkent
Alma-Ata
Frunze
Issyk Kul
Turkestan
Tashkent
Arys
Namangan
Andizhan
Kokand
Margelan
Samarkand
Bukhara
Stalinabad
Termez
KYZYL KUM (RED DESERT)
KARA KUM SANDS
Nukus
Turtkul
Amu Darya
Krasnovodsk
Ashkhabad
Mary
PAMIRS
Kashgar (Shufu)
Yarkand (Soche)
Khotan
BLACK SEA
Istanbul (Constantinople)
Üsküdar (Scutari)
Bursa
Eskişehir
Izmir (Smyrna)
Ankara (Angora)
Konya
Adana
Kayseri
Samsun
Batumi
TURKEY
Erzurum
Mt. Ararat
Tbilisi (Tiflis)
CAUCASUS MTS
Krasnodar
Yerevan
Baku
CASPIAN SEA
L. Van
Diyarbekir
Gaziantep
Aras R.
Latakia
CYPRUS (Br.)
Beirut
LEBANON
SYRIA
Damas (Damascus)
PALESTINE-ISRAEL
Jerusalem
TRANS-JORDAN
Amman
Mosul
Tigris R.
Euphrates R.
IRAQ
EL HAMAD (SYRIAN DESERT)
Kermanshah
Baghdad
Karbala
Hilla
Amara
Basra
Kuwait
KUWAIT
Neut. Ter.
Tabriz
Urmia L.
Resht
ELBURZ MTS.
Tehran
Babul (Barfrush)
Meshed
Hamadan
Qum
Sultanabad
Isfahan
Dizful
Ahwaz
Abadan
IRAN (PERSIA)
Turbat-i-Haidari
Firdaus
Yezd
Birjand
Neh
Anar
Kerman
Shiraz
Niriz
Bushire
Lar
Bandar Abbas
Khanu
Zahedan
Iranshar
Jask
Gwatar
Str. of Ormuz
PERSIAN GULF
BAHREIN Is. (Br.)
QATAR
TRUCIAL OMAN
Kushka
Mazar-i-Sharif
Herat
Kabul
Khyber Pass
Sabzawar
AFGHANISTAN
Farah
Juwain
Kandahar
Helmand
Peshawar
Quetta
PAKISTAN
Kalat
Shikarpur
Sukkur
BALUCHISTAN
Bahawalpur
Indus R.
INDIAN DESERT
Karachi
Mouths of the Indus
Gwadar (Oman)
Gulf of Oman
Matrah
Masqat (Muscat)
Sur
Ras el Hadd
OMAN
MASIRAH I.
Ras Madraka
KURIA MURIA IS. (Br.)
Murbat
Ras Fartak
HADHRAMAUT
ADEN PROT.
Mukalla
Aden (Br.)
Gulf of Aden
SOCOTRA I (Br.)
C. Guardafui
Sabiya
YEMEN
San'a
Mocha
RUB AL KHALI (DESERT)
ASIR
SAUDI ARABIA
NEFUD DESERT
Jauf
Dar al Hamra
Wejh
Hail
HEJAZ
Medina
Anaiza
Shaqra
Mubarraz
Hofuf
Riyadh
Hauta
Yenbo
Jidda
Mecca
RED SEA
Aqaba
Sinai Pen.
Suez Canal
Suez
Port Said
Alexandria
Cairo
EGYPT
Nile R.
Tropic of Cancer
LIBIA
Bengasi
AFRICA
ANGLO EGYPTIAN SUDAN
Port Sudan
Omdurman
Khartoum
Blue Nile
ERITREA
Asmara
ETHIOPIA
FR. SOMAL.
PERIM
Djibouti
BR. SOMAL.
SOMAL.
SOMALILAND
ARABIAN SEA
INDIAN OCEAN
Srinagar
Mt. Godwin Austen
KARAKORAM RA.
Rawalpindi
Sialkot
Lahore
Amritsar
Ferozepore
Jullundur
Multan
Simla
Ambala
Saharanpur
Meerut
Moradabad
Bareilly
Delhi
New Delhi
Aligarh
Muttra
Agra
Shahjahanpur
Farrukhabad
Lucknow
Cawnpore
Fyzabad
Bikaner
Jaipur
Jodhpur
Ajmer
Lashkar
Jhansi
Allahabad
Mirzapur
Udaipur
Hyderabad
Gulf of Cutch
Ujjain
Bhopal
Jubbulpore
Ahmadabad
Indore
Baroda
Surat
Bhaunagar
Diu (Port.)
Gulf of Cambay
Damão (Port.)
Bhusawal
Nagpur
Aurangabad
Bombay
Poona
Sholapur
Godavari R.
Hyderabad
Kolhapur
WESTERN GHATS
EASTERN GHATS
Hubli
Bellary
GOA (Port.)
Nellore
Madras
Bangalore
Mangalore
Mysore
Conjeeveram
Pondichéry
(French) Mahé
Calicut
Salem
Cuddalore
Kumbakonam
Karikal (Fr.)
Negapatam
Tanjore
Trichinopoly
Madura
Jaffna
LACCADIVE ISLANDS
Nine Degree Channel
Trivandrum
C. Comorin
Gulf of Mannar
Eight Degree Channel
CEYLON
Colombo
Matara
Dondra Head
MALDIVE IS.
INDIA
Longitude East from
A B C D E F G H I
E F G H I
3 4 5 6 7 8 9

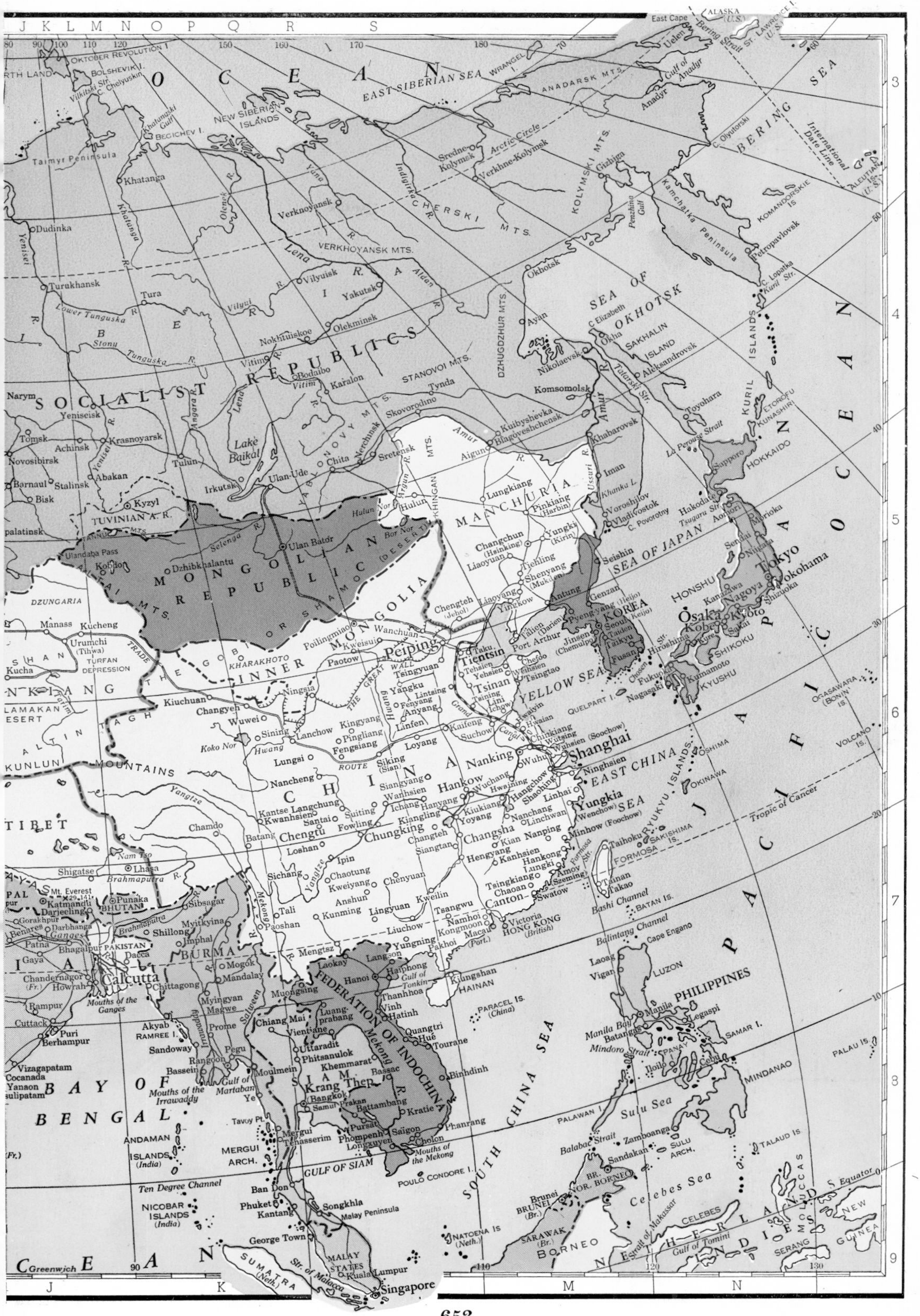

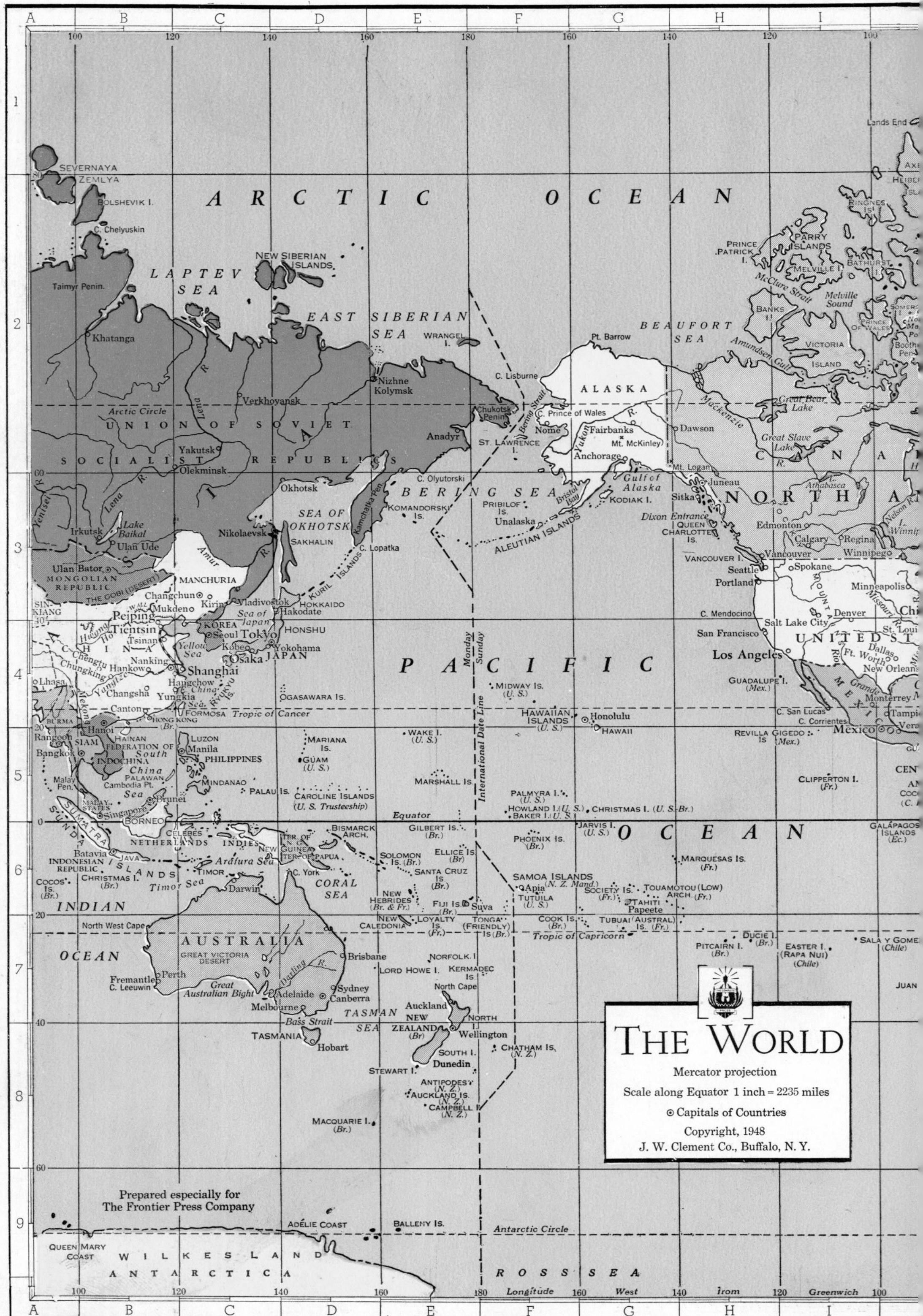
THE WORLD
Mercator projection
Scale along Equator 1 inch = 2235 miles
⊙ Capitals of Countries
Copyright, 1948
J. W. Clement Co., Buffalo, N. Y.
Prepared especially for
The Frontier Press Company
ARCTIC OCEAN
PACIFIC OCEAN
INDIAN OCEAN
LAPTEV SEA
EAST SIBERIAN SEA
BEAUFORT SEA
BERING SEA
SEA OF OKHOTSK
Sea of Japan
Yellow Sea
East China Sea
South China Sea
Celebes Sea
Arafura Sea
Timor Sea
CORAL SEA
TASMAN SEA
ROSS SEA
UNION OF SOVIET SOCIALIST REPUBLICS
MONGOLIAN REPUBLIC
MANCHURIA
CHINA
KOREA
JAPAN
HONSHU
HOKKAIDO
SIAM
BURMA
FEDERATION OF INDOCHINA
PHILIPPINES
NETHERLANDS INDIES
INDONESIAN REPUBLIC
BORNEO
SUMATRA
JAVA
AUSTRALIA
GREAT VICTORIA DESERT
TASMANIA
NEW ZEALAND (Br)
NORTH I.
SOUTH I.
ALASKA
CANADA
NORTH AMERICA
UNITED STATES
MEXICO
ANTARCTICA
WILKES LAND
QUEEN MARY COAST
ADÉLIE COAST
BALLENY IS.
Antarctic Circle
Arctic Circle
Tropic of Cancer
Tropic of Capricorn
Equator
International Date Line
Monday
Sunday
Longitude 160 West 140 from 120 Greenwich 100
SEVERNAYA ZEMLYA
BOLSHEVIK I.
C. Chelyuskin
Taimyr Penin.
Khatanga
NEW SIBERIAN ISLANDS
WRANGEL I.
Nizhne Kolymsk
Verkhoyansk
Yakutsk
Olekminsk
Okhotsk
Nikolaevsk
SAKHALIN
Kamchatka Pen.
C. Lopatka
KOMANDORSKI IS.
C. Olyutorski
Anadyr
Chukotsk Penin.
C. Lisburne
Bering Strait
C. Prince of Wales
Nome
ST. LAWRENCE I.
PRIBILOF IS.
Unalaska
ALEUTIAN ISLANDS
KURIL ISLANDS
Irkutsk
Lake Baikal
Ulan Ude
Ulan Bator
THE GOBI (DESERT)
Changchun
Mukden
Kirin
Vladivostok
Hakodate
Peiping
Tientsin
Tsinan
Seoul
Tokyo
Kobe
Osaka
Yokohama
Nanking
Shanghai
Hankow
Chengtu
Chungking
Changsha
Hangchow
Yungkia
Lhasa
Canton
HONG KONG (Br.)
FORMOSA
Hanoi
HAINAN
Rangoon
Bangkok
Malay Pen.
Cambodia Pt.
Singapore
Brunei
LUZON
Manila
PALAWAN
MINDANAO
CELEBES
Batavia
TIMOR
CHRISTMAS I. (Br.)
COCOS IS. (Br.)
Darwin
C. York
North West Cape
Perth
Fremantle
C. Leeuwin
Great Australian Bight
Adelaide
Melbourne
Bass Strait
Hobart
Sydney
Canberra
Brisbane
Auckland
Wellington
North Cape
Dunedin
STEWART I.
CHATHAM IS. (N. Z.)
ANTIPODES (N. Z.)
AUCKLAND IS. (N. Z.)
CAMPBELL I. (N. Z.)
MACQUARIE I. (Br.)
LORD HOWE I.
NORFOLK I.
KERMADEC IS.
NEW CALEDONIA
LOYALTY IS. (Fr.)
NEW HEBRIDES (Br. & Fr.)
FIJI IS. (Br.)
Suva
TONGA (FRIENDLY) IS (Br.)
SANTA CRUZ IS (Br.)
SOLOMON IS. (Br.)
ELLICE IS (Br)
GILBERT IS. (Br.)
BISMARCK ARCH.
TER. OF NEW GUINEA
TER. OF PAPUA
OGASAWARA IS.
MARIANA IS.
GUAM (U. S.)
PALAU IS.
CAROLINE ISLANDS (U. S. Trusteeship)
MARSHALL IS.
WAKE I. (U. S.)
MIDWAY IS. (U. S.)
HAWAIIAN ISLANDS (U. S.)
Honolulu
HAWAII
PALMYRA I. (U. S.)
HOWLAND I. (U. S.)
BAKER I. (U. S.)
CHRISTMAS I. (U. S.-Br.)
JARVIS I. (U. S.)
PHOENIX IS. (Br.)
SAMOA ISLANDS (N. Z. Mand.)
Apia
TUTUILA (U. S.)
COOK IS. (Br.)
SOCIETY IS. (Fr.)
TAHITI
Papeete
TUBUAI (AUSTRAL) IS. (Fr.)
TOUAMOTOU (LOW) ARCH. (Fr.)
MARQUESAS IS. (Fr.)
PITCAIRN I. (Br.)
DUCIE I. (Br.)
EASTER I. (RAPA NUI) (Chile)
SALA Y GOMEZ (Chile)
CLIPPERTON I. (Fr.)
REVILLA GIGEDO IS (Mex.)
GUADALUPE I. (Mex.)
GALÁPAGOS ISLANDS (Ec.)
Pt. Barrow
Fairbanks
Mt. McKinley
Anchorage
Yukon R.
Gulf of Alaska
KODIAK I.
Bristol Bay
Dawson
Mt. Logan
Juneau
Sitka
Dixon Entrance
QUEEN CHARLOTTE IS.
VANCOUVER I.
Vancouver
Seattle
Portland
Spokane
C. Mendocino
San Francisco
Los Angeles
Salt Lake City
Denver
Minneapolis
Dallas
Ft. Worth
New Orleans
Rio Grande
Monterrey
Mexico
C. San Lucas
C. Corrientes
Edmonton
Calgary
Regina
Winnipeg
Mackenzie R.
Great Bear Lake
Great Slave Lake
L. Athabasca
Amundsen Gulf
McClure Strait
Melville Sound
PRINCE PATRICK I.
PARRY ISLANDS
MELVILLE I.
BATHURST I.
BANKS I.
VICTORIA ISLAND
PRINCE OF WALES I.
RINGNES IS.
Lands End

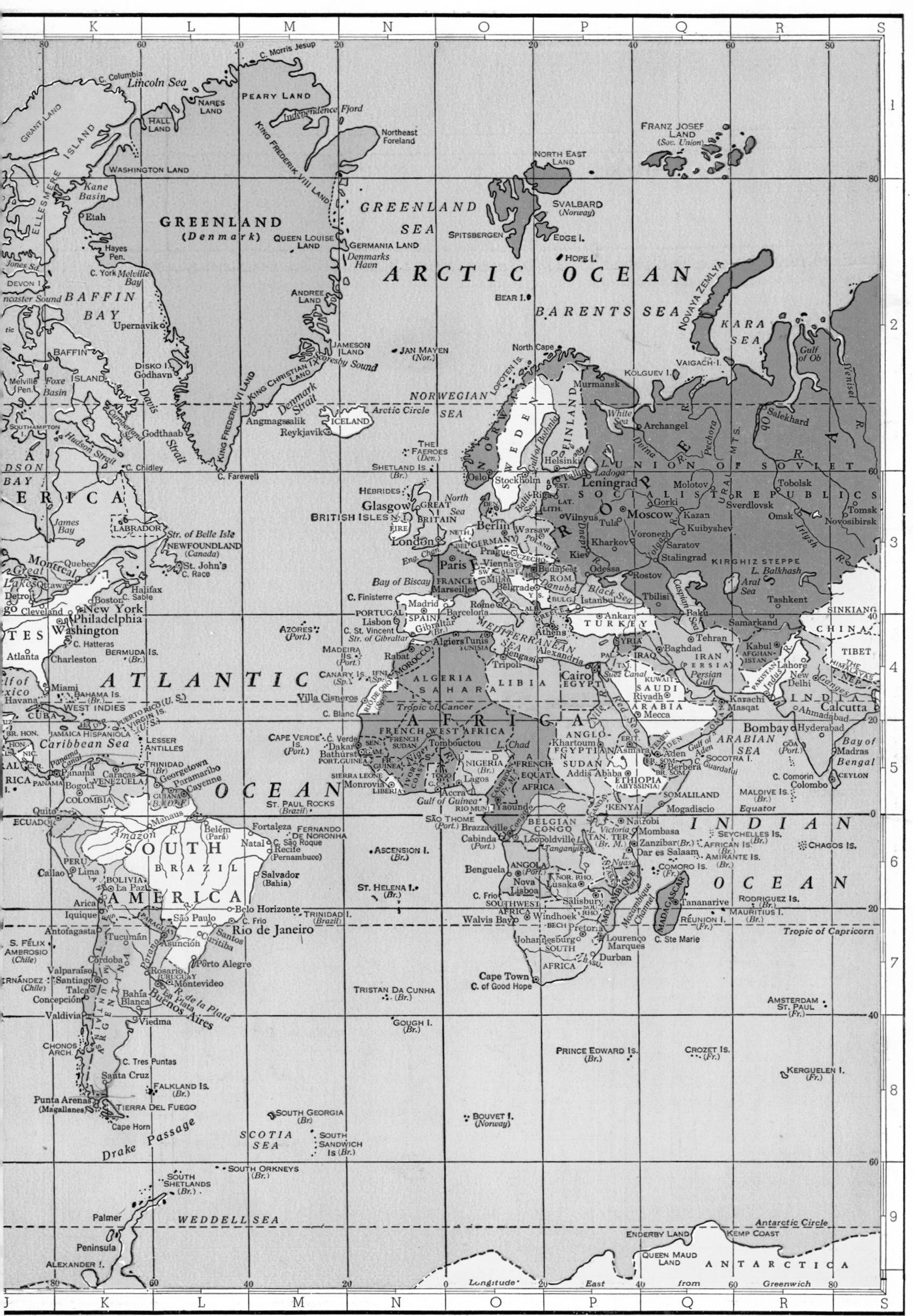

K L M N O P Q R S
Lincoln Sea
C. Columbia
C. Morris Jesup
PEARY LAND
NARES LAND
HALL LAND
GRANT LAND
Independence Fjord
Northeast Foreland
KING FREDERIK VIII LAND
WASHINGTON LAND
ELLESMERE ISLAND
Kane Basin
Etah
GREENLAND
(Denmark)
QUEEN LOUISE LAND
GERMANIA LAND
Denmarks Havn
GREENLAND SEA
Hayes Pen.
C. York
Melville Bay
Jones Sd.
DEVON I.
BAFFIN BAY
ANDREE LAND
Upernavik
JAMESON LAND
Scoresby Sound
KING CHRISTIAN IX LAND
KING FREDERIK VI LAND
Disko I.
Godhavn
BAFFIN ISLAND
Foxe Basin
Melville Pen.
Davis Strait
Cumberland Sd.
SOUTHAMPTON I.
Hudson Strait
Godthaab
C. Chidley
C. Farewell
Denmark Strait
Angmagssalik
Reykjavik
ICELAND
Arctic Circle
FRANZ JOSEF LAND
(Sov. Union)
NORTH EAST LAND
SVALBARD
(Norway)
SPITSBERGEN
EDGE I.
HOPE I.
BEAR I.
ARCTIC OCEAN
BARENTS SEA
NOVAYA ZEMLYA
KARA SEA
Gulf of Ob
Yenisei R.
VAIGACH I.
KOLGUEV I.
North Cape
JAN MAYEN
(Nor.)
NORWEGIAN SEA
LOFOTEN IS.
Murmansk
White Sea
Archangel
Salekhard
THE FAEROES
(Den.)
SHETLAND IS.
(Br.)
HEBRIDES
Glasgow
GREAT BRITAIN
BRITISH ISLES
EIRE
London
North Sea
NORWAY
SWEDEN
FINLAND
Gulf of Bothnia
Helsinki
Oslo
Stockholm
Leningrad
Ladoga
UNION OF SOVIET SOCIALIST REPUBLICS
EUROPE
URAL MTS.
Molotov
Gorki
Sverdlovsk
Tobolsk
Omsk
Tomsk
Novosibirsk
Irtysh R.
Moscow
Kazan
Kuibyshev
Vilnyus
Tula
Riga
Baltic Sea
Berlin
Warsaw
GERMANY
POLAND
NETH.
BEL.
Eng. Chan.
Paris
FRANCE
Prague
CZECH.
Vienna
AUST.
SW.
HUNG.
Budapest
Kiev
Kharkov
Voronezh
Saratov
Stalingrad
Volga R.
Dnepr R.
Odessa
Rostov
KIRGHIZ STEPPE
L. Balkhash
Aral Sea
Tashkent
Caspian Sea
Tbilisi
Baku
Black Sea
ROM.
Danube
Belgrade
Milan
ITALY
Rome
BULG.
Istanbul
Ankara
TURKEY
Samarkand
SINKIANG
CHINA
TIBET
Bay of Biscay
Marseilles
C. Finisterre
Madrid
SPAIN
PORTUGAL
Lisbon
Barcelona
C. St. Vincent
Str. of Gibraltar
Gibraltar
AZORES
(Port.)
MADEIRA IS.
(Port.)
MEDITERRANEAN SEA
Algiers
Tunis
TUNISIA
Rabat
MOROCCO
Bengasi
Tripoli
Athens
GREECE
SYRIA
IRAQ
Baghdad
Tehran
IRAN
(PERSIA)
Kabul
AFGHANISTAN
PAKISTAN
Lahore
New Delhi
THE HIMALAYAS
NEP.
Ganges R.
Indus R.
Alexandria
Cairo
EGYPT
Suez Canal
KUWAIT
SAUDI ARABIA
Riyadh
Mecca
Persian Gulf
Karachi
Masqat
INDIA
Ahmadabad
Calcutta
CANARY IS.
(Sp.)
IFNI
RIO DE ORO
Villa Cisneros
ALGERIA
SAHARA
LIBIA
Tropic of Cancer
C. Blanc
AFRICA
FRENCH WEST AFRICA
FRENCH SUDAN
Tombouctou
L. Chad
ANGLO-EGYPTIAN SUDAN
Khartoum
Red Sea
ERIT.
YEMEN
ADEN
Gulf of Aden
Aden
ARABIAN SEA
Bombay
Hyderabad
GOA
(Port.)
Bay of Bengal
Madras
CAPE VERDE IS.
(Port.)
C. Verde
Dakar
SEN.
Bathurst
PORT. GUINEA
FR. GUINEA
Niger R.
SIERRA LEONE
Monrovia
LIBERIA
IVORY COAST
G.C.
TOGO
NIGERIA
(Br.)
Lagos
Accra
Gulf of Guinea
RIO MUNI
CAMEROON
FRENCH EQUAT. AFRICA
Yaounde
SUDAN
Addis Ababa
ETHIOPIA
(ABYSSINIA)
FR. SOM.
Berbera
BR. SOM.
SOCOTRA I.
C. Guardafui
SOMALILAND
Mogadiscio
C. Comorin
Colombo
CEYLON
MALDIVE IS.
(Br.)
Equator
ST. PAUL ROCKS
(Brazil)
SÃO THOMÉ
(Port.)
Brazzaville
Congo R.
BELGIAN CONGO
Léopoldville
Cabinda
(Port.)
KENYA
Nairobi
Mombasa
L. Victoria
TAN. TER.
(Br. M.)
Zanzibar (Br.)
Dar es Salaam
L. Tanganyika
SEYCHELLES IS.
(Br.)
AFRICAN IS.
(Br.)
AMIRANTE IS.
(Br.)
CHAGOS IS.
INDIAN OCEAN
ASCENSION I.
(Br.)
Benguela
ANGOLA
(Port.)
Nova Lisboa
NOR. RHO.
Lusaka
L. Nyasa
MOZAMBIQUE
(Port.)
Mozambique Channel
COMORO IS.
(Fr.)
MADAGASCAR
Tananarive
RODRIGUEZ IS.
(Br.)
MAURITIUS I.
(Br.)
RÉUNION I.
(Fr.)
ST. HELENA I.
(Br.)
C. Frio
SOUTHWEST AFRICA
Walvis Bay
Windhoek
BECH.
Salisbury
SOU. RHO.
Pretoria
Johannesburg
SOUTH AFRICA
Lourenço Marques
Durban
SWA.
BASU.
C. Ste Marie
Tropic of Capricorn
Cape Town
C. of Good Hope
TRISTAN DA CUNHA
(Br.)
AMSTERDAM
ST. PAUL
(Fr.)
GOUGH I.
(Br.)
PRINCE EDWARD IS.
(Br.)
CROZET IS.
(Fr.)
KERGUELEN I.
(Fr.)
BOUVET I.
(Norway)
SOUTH GEORGIA
(Br.)
SOUTH SANDWICH IS. (Br.)
SCOTIA SEA
SOUTH ORKNEYS
(Br.)
SOUTH SHETLANDS
(Br.)
WEDDELL SEA
Antarctic Circle
ENDERBY LAND
KEMP COAST
QUEEN MAUD LAND
ANTARCTICA
Palmer Peninsula
ALEXANDER I.
Drake Passage
Longitude East from Greenwich
HUDSON BAY
AMERICA
James Bay
LABRADOR
Str. of Belle Isle
NEWFOUNDLAND
(Canada)
St. John's
C. Race
Quebec
Montreal
Great Lakes
Ottawa
Halifax
C. Sable
Detroit
Boston
New York
Philadelphia
Cleveland
Washington
UNITED STATES
C. Hatteras
BERMUDA IS.
(Br.)
Atlanta
Charleston
ATLANTIC OCEAN
Gulf of Mexico
Miami
BAHAMA IS.
(Br.)
Havana
CUBA
WEST INDIES
PUERTO RICO (U.S.)
VIRGIN IS.
(U.S.)
JAMAICA
HISPANIOLA
BR. HON.
HON.
NIC.
C.R.
Caribbean Sea
LESSER ANTILLES
Panama Canal
Panama
TRINIDAD
(Br.)
Caracas
VENEZUELA
Georgetown
Paramaribo
Cayenne
BR. GU.
SUR.
FR. GU.
Bogotá
COLOMBIA
Quito
ECUADOR
Manaus
Amazon R.
Belém
(Pará)
Fortaleza
FERNANDO DE NORONHA
Natal
C. São Roque
Recife
(Pernambuco)
SOUTH AMERICA
BRAZIL
PERU
Callao
Lima
BOLIVIA
La Paz
Salvador
(Bahia)
Arica
Iquique
Belo Horizonte
TRINIDAD I.
(Brazil)
PARAGUAY
São Paulo
C. Frio
Rio de Janeiro
Santos
Antofagasta
Tucumán
Asunción
Curitiba
S. FÉLIX
AMBROSIO
(Chile)
Córdoba
Pôrto Alegre
Rosario
URUGUAY
Montevideo
Valparaíso
Santiago
J. FERNÁNDEZ
(Chile)
Talca
Concepción
Bahía Blanca
Buenos Aires
R. de la Plata
Valdivia
ARGENTINA
CHILE
Viedma
CHONOS ARCH.
C. Tres Puntas
Santa Cruz
FALKLAND IS.
(Br.)
Punta Arenas
(Magallanes)
TIERRA DEL FUEGO
Cape Horn

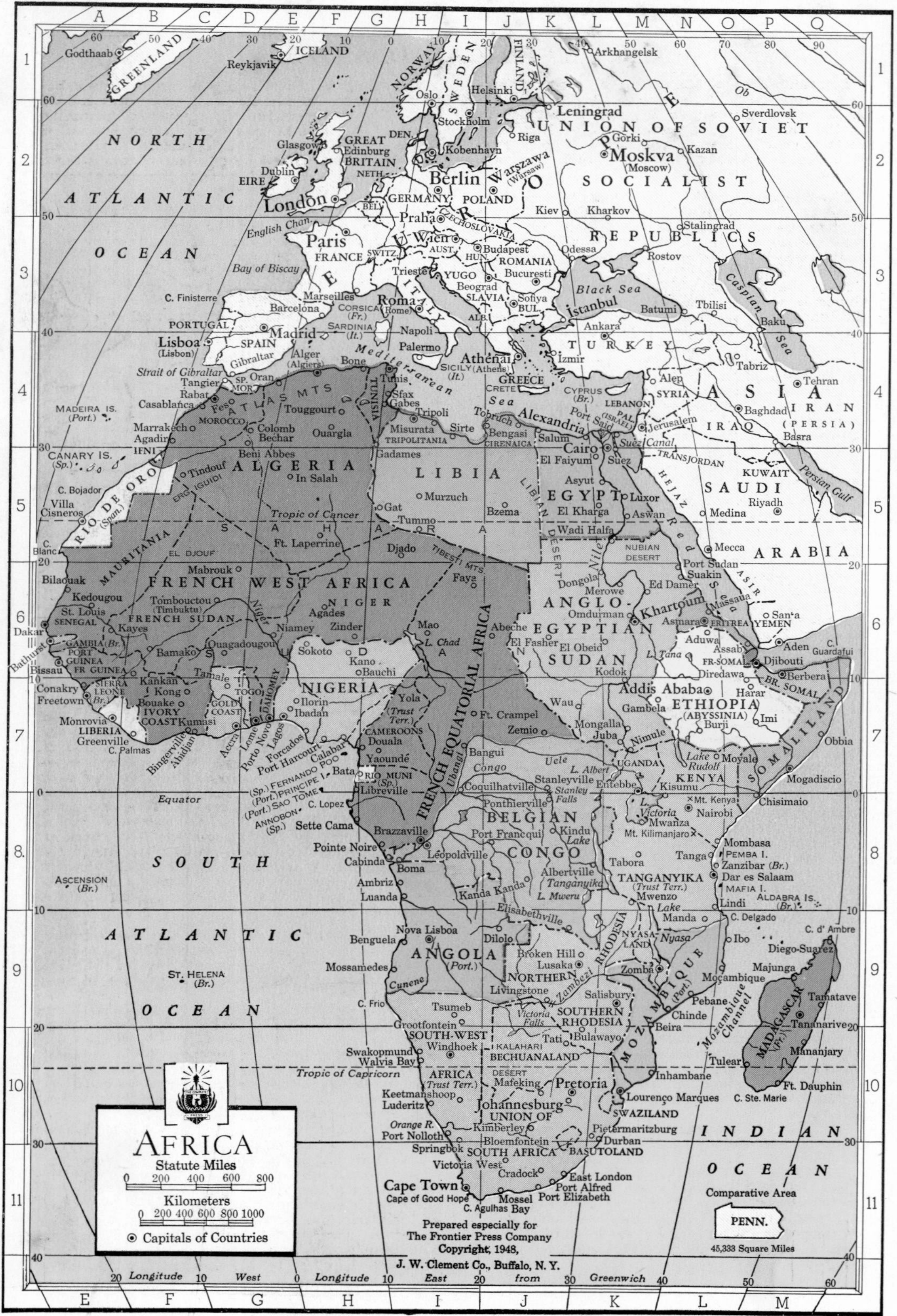
AFRICA
Statute Miles
0 200 400 600 800
Kilometers
0 200 400 600 800 1000
Capitals of Countries
Comparative Area
PENN.
45,333 Square Miles
Prepared especially for
The Frontier Press Company
Copyright, 1948,
J. W. Clement Co., Buffalo, N. Y.
Longitude West Longitude East from Greenwich
Tropic of Cancer
Equator
Tropic of Capricorn
NORTH ATLANTIC OCEAN
SOUTH ATLANTIC OCEAN
INDIAN OCEAN
GREENLAND
ICELAND
Godthaab
Reykjavik
NORWAY
SWEDEN
FINLAND
Oslo
Stockholm
Helsinki
Leningrad
Arkhangelsk
Sverdlovsk
Ob
UNION OF SOVIET SOCIALIST REPUBLICS
EUROPE
Riga
Gorki
Kazan
Moskva
(Moscow)
Kiev
Kharkov
Stalingrad
Odessa
Rostov
Glasgow
Edinburg
GREAT BRITAIN
Dublin
EIRE
London
DEN.
Kobenhavn
NETH.
Berlin
Warszawa
(Warsaw)
GERMANY
POLAND
BELG.
Praha
CZECHOSLOVAKIA
English Chan.
Paris
FRANCE
SWITZ.
Wien
AUST.
HUN.
Budapest
ROMANIA
Bucuresti
Bay of Biscay
Trieste
YUGOSLAVIA
Beograd
Sofiya
BUL.
ALB.
ITALY
Marseilles
C. Finisterre
Barcelona
CORSICA
(Fr.)
Roma
(Rome)
SARDINIA
(It.)
Napoli
Palermo
SICILY
(It.)
PORTUGAL
Madrid
SPAIN
Lisboa
(Lisbon)
Gibraltar
Strait of Gibraltar
Black Sea
Istanbul
Batumi
Tbilisi
Caspian Sea
Baku
Ankara
TURKEY
Izmir
Athenai
(Athens)
GREECE
CRETE
Mediterranean Sea
CYPRUS
(Br.)
LEBANON
SYRIA
Alep
Tabriz
Tehran
ASIA
IRAN
(PERSIA)
Baghdad
IRAQ
Basra
PAL.
(ISRAEL)
Jerusalem
TRANSJORDAN
KUWAIT
Persian Gulf
SAUDI ARABIA
Riyadh
Medina
Mecca
HEJAZ
ASIR
Red Sea
YEMEN
San'a
Aden
Alger
(Algiers)
Bone
Tunis
Sfax
Gabes
TUNISIA
Oran
Tangier
SP. MOR.
Rabat
Fes
Casablanca
ATLAS MTS.
MOROCCO
Marrakech
Agadir
IFNI
MADEIRA IS.
(Port.)
CANARY IS.
(Sp.)
Touggourt
Colomb Bechar
Ouargla
Beni Abbes
Tindouf
ALGERIA
In Salah
ERG IGUIDI
RIO DE ORO
(Span.)
C. Bojador
Villa Cisneros
C. Blanc
SAHARA
Tripoli
Misurata
TRIPOLITANIA
Sirte
Bengasi
CIRENAICA
Tobruch
Gadames
LIBIA
Murzuch
Gat
Tummo
Bzema
LIBIAN DESERT
Alexandria
Port Said
Salum
Cairo
El Faiyum
Suez
Suez Canal
Asyut
EGYPT
Luxor
El Kharga
Aswan
Wadi Halfa
NUBIAN DESERT
Nile
Port Sudan
Suakin
Dongola
Merowe
Ed Damer
Khartoum
Omdurman
Massaua
Asmara
ERITREA
ANGLO-EGYPTIAN SUDAN
El Fasher
El Obeid
Kodok
Aduwa
Assab
FR.-SOMAL.
Djibouti
Berbera
C. Guardafui
BR. SOMAL.
Diredawa
Harar
L. Tana
Addis Ababa
ETHIOPIA
(ABYSSINIA)
Gambela
Burji
Imi
Obbia
ITALIAN SOMALILAND
Mogadiscio
Chisimaio
Moyale
L. Rudolf
MAURITANIA
EL DJOUF
Mabrouk
FRENCH WEST AFRICA
Bilaouak
Kedougou
St. Louis
SENEGAL
Dakar
Tombouctou
(Timbuktu)
FRENCH SUDAN
Kayes
Niger
Agades
NIGER
Zinder
Niamey
GAMBIA (Br.)
Bathurst
PORT. GUINEA
Bissau
FR. GUINEA
Bamako
Ouagadougou
Conakry
SIERRA LEONE
(Br.)
Freetown
Kankan
Kong
Bouake
IVORY COAST
Kumasi
Tamale
TOGO
DAHOMEY
GOLD COAST
Monrovia
LIBERIA
Greenville
C. Palmas
Bingerville
Abidjan
Accra
Lome
Porto Novo
Lagos
Forcados
Port Harcourt
Calabar
Sokoto
Kano
Bauchi
NIGERIA
Ilorin
Ibadan
Yola
(Trust Terr.)
CAMEROONS
Douala
Yaoundé
Tibesti Mts.
Djado
Faya
Mao
L. Chad
Abeche
FRENCH EQUATORIAL AFRICA
Ft. Crampel
Zemio
Wau
Mongalla
Juba
Nimule
UGANDA
L. Albert
Entebbe
KENYA
Kisumu
Mt. Kenya
Nairobi
(Sp.) FERNANDO POO
(Port.) PRINCIPE I.
(Port.) SAO TOME I.
ANNOBON
(Sp.)
Bata
RIO MUNI
(Sp.)
Libreville
C. Lopez
Sette Cama
Bangui
Congo
Ubangi
Uele
Coquilhatville
Stanleyville
Stanley Falls
Ponthierville
BELGIAN CONGO
Port Francqui
Kindu
Lake
Pointe Noire
Brazzaville
Leopoldville
Cabinda
Boma
Kanda Kanda
Albertville
Tanganyika
L. Mweru
L. Victoria
Mwanza
Mt. Kilimanjaro
Tabora
TANGANYIKA
(Trust Terr.)
Mwenzo
Tanga
Mombasa
PEMBA I.
Zanzibar (Br.)
Dar es Salaam
MAFIA I.
Lindi
ALDABRA IS.
(Br.)
ASCENSION
(Br.)
Ambriz
Luanda
Elisabethville
Nova Lisboa
Benguela
Dilolo
ANGOLA
(Port.)
Mossamedes
Cunene
ST. HELENA
(Br.)
Broken Hill
Lusaka
NORTHERN RHODESIA
Zambezi
NYASALAND
Nyasa
Manda
Zomba
C. Delgado
Ibo
Moçambique
C. d' Ambre
Diego-Suarez
Majunga
Tamatave
MADAGASCAR
(Fr.)
Tananarive
Mananjary
Ft. Dauphin
C. Ste. Marie
Tulear
Mozambique Channel
MOZAMBIQUE
(Port.)
Pebane
Chinde
Beira
Inhambane
Livingstone
Victoria Falls
Salisbury
SOUTHERN RHODESIA
C. Frio
Tsumeb
Grootfontein
SOUTH-WEST AFRICA
(Trust Terr.)
Windhoek
Swakopmund
Walvis Bay
KALAHARI DESERT
BECHUANALAND
Tati
Bulawayo
Mafeking
Pretoria
Johannesburg
Lourenço Marques
SWAZILAND
Keetmanshoop
Luderitz
Orange R.
Port Nolloth
Springbok
Kimberley
Bloemfontein
UNION OF SOUTH AFRICA
Pietermaritzburg
Durban
BASUTOLAND
Victoria West
Cradock
East London
Port Alfred
Port Elizabeth
Cape Town
Cape of Good Hope
C. Agulhas
Mossel Bay

GEOGRAPHICAL DISCOVERY

Ancient ideas of the earth were vastly different from those of the present day. One of the earliest concepts of the earth is that revealed by the Homeric poems, written about 1000 B. C. In these poems, the earth is supposed to be a circular disk surrounded by a river, which was called Ocean.

Phœnicians. Such early views were probably based on the reports of the Phœnicians, who were the earliest navigators known to history. From these people, too, in all likelihood, came the information which the Hebrews had regarding such distant points as those called, in Hebrew literature, Gomer, Sinim, Cush, Sheba, Ophir, and Tarshish. Gomer is believed to mean the northern shores of the Black Sea; Sinim is conjectured to be southern Egypt; Cush is identified with Abyssinia; Sheba, with Yemen in southwestern Arabia; Ophir is placed in southeastern Africa; and Tarshish, in southeastern Spain.

Africa was circumnavigated as early as 600 B. C. by a Phœnician expedition. This expedition was dispatched by Necho, king of Egypt, with orders to sail through the Red Sea into the Indian Ocean and around Africa. After three years, the ships returned by way of the Strait of Gibraltar and the Mediterranean Sea.

Greeks. The earlier Greek geographers, Hecatæus and Herodotus, both of the 5th century B. C., did not advance beyond the idea of the earth conceived of as a disk. Hecatæus in his *Periodos*, "Trip around the World," and Herodotus in his *Histories*, added immensely to the available knowledge of different lands and peoples, each writer having traveled over most of the world as then known.

Aristotle, living in the 4th century B. C., has the honor of being the first to demonstrate that the world is a sphere. He based his proof on two facts which could be tested by observation: first, that the shadow of the earth thrown on the moon during an eclipse is always circular; and, secondly, that the horizon always retreats as the observer advances. To Aristotle also is due the division of the earth into a torrid zone bounded by two temperate zones with a frigid zone surrounding each pole.

It was in this period that maps of the world first showed the land surface of the earth surrounded by a wide expanse of sea instead of by a river. The name Ocean, which formerly designated the river, was applied to this sea. The sea was believed to extend around the globe, bathing on every side the great land mass in the eastern hemisphere. Our modern sense of ocean, as one of the major divisions of the water surface of the earth, arose since the 15th century, when it was learned that the universal sea was divided into parts by the continent of America and by other land areas previously unknown.

The inclination of the earth to the plane of its orbit was first measured by Eratosthenes, who lived in the 3d century B. C. His result was correct within 23 minutes of the angle as determined by the most accurate modern instruments. Eratosthenes also calculated the size of the earth and devised a system of indicating geographical position by drawing two lines of reference, one from east to west and the other from north to south. The location of any place could thus be indicated by giving its distance north or south of the one line and east or west of the other line.

The lines of reference drawn on the earth by Eratosthenes suggested to Hipparchus of Nicæa, in the 2d century B. C., the idea of drawing a series of circles of latitude and longitude. One circle was drawn for each degree on the earth's surface. In the 2d century A. D., Ptolemy, a Greek of Alexandria, compiled a work on geography which embraced all that was known of the earth until his day. This work formed the starting point of modern geography.

According to Ptolemy's geography, Africa extended southward and eastward, eventually joining Asia. The two continents thus enclosed the Indian Ocean. The farthest land to the north was called Thule, probably the Shetland islands. Something also was known of the Baltic Sea, western Russia, the great plains of Asia, and even the distant countries of China and Japan.

Romans. The Romans did little in the field of scientific geography. For the purpose of conquest and organization, however, surveys were made of practically all the territory surrounding the Mediterranean Sea, as well as of France, part of Britain, and Asia Minor. Nero dispatched an expedition in search of the source of the Nile river about 60 A. D. In the 6th century A. D., Justinian sent two monks to China, who returned with eggs of the silkworm concealed in a hollow cane. The culture of the silkworm was thus introduced into Europe.

Middle Ages. With the general decline of learning after the downfall of Rome, Ptolemy's work was forgotten in Europe, and people reverted to a primitive conception of the earth, believing it to be flat. Maps of this period frequently show Jerusalem as the center of the terrestrial disk.

The Arabs, however, translated Ptolemy's work into their own language, keeping alive a knowledge of geography as it had been developed. Arab astronomers measured a degree of latitude on the plains of Mesopotamia, deducing from it the approximate size of the earth. Prominent among Arabian books of travel was the *Meadows of Gold*, written by Masudi about 950 A. D. It contained geographical observations collected by its author, who, with this purpose in view, traversed all the countries lying between China and Spain. Ptolemy's geography became known to Europe by translation into Latin from the Arabic and later from the original Greek text.

Earliest Modern Discoveries. Before the period of the Renaissance, a number of notable voyages and discoveries were recorded. Greenland was sighted by Northmen in the 9th century, and, in the following century, men of the same race landed on the coast of North America. Little geographic interest, however, was aroused by these discoveries or by the trips of monks to remote parts of Asia and of Africa in search of a mythical Christian kingdom, ruled over by Prester John. The travels of Marco Polo, however, in the 14th century, did much to stimulate interest in distant lands. He visited the Far East, where he ruled a province of China for three years. A golden statue of him in a great temple at Soochow, China, still bears witness to his former influence in the Orient.

Age of Discovery. The 15th and the 16th century were distinguished by extraordinary activity in exploration. The previous invention of the mariner's compass did much to facilitate the sea voyages of the period.

Portuguese sailors discovered the Madeira islands and, by 1482, had sailed south as far as the Congo river. In 1486, a Portuguese ship sighted the Cape of Good Hope, and, 11 years later, Vasco da Gama doubled the cape and finally reached India.

In 1492, Columbus, sailing west, discovered the New World and thereby revolutionized the prevailing conception of the earth. Within 30 years from his historic landing on San Salvador island, the whole east coast of America from Greenland to Cape Horn had been explored, and the globe had been circumnavigated. Before the middle of the 16th century, America's west coast had been explored as far north as San Francisco bay, and Spanish colonists had settled in various parts of South America. On the other side of the world, progress had been made in knowledge of countries whose coasts were bathed by the Indian Ocean, including

Arabia, East Africa, India, and the great Malay archipelago. Apart from the Portuguese and the Spaniards, the nations most active in discovery at this period were the English, the Dutch, and the French.

The 17th and the 18th century witnessed the discovery of Australia, Tasmania, and New Zealand. Captain Cook, an English navigator, in the last quarter of the 18th century, explored widely in the Pacific Ocean, adding Hawaii and numerous other islands to the known world.

The task of geographical discovery was completed in the 19th and the 20th century. The chief accomplishments in this period were the exploration of Africa; the forcing of a passage by water northwest of America and of a passage through the ice-bound seas northeast of Asia; and, finally, the discovery of the north and south poles. The exploration of Africa is described in the section devoted to that continent.

Polar Exploration. Repeated efforts were made, from the 16th century on, to sail around North America's northern boundary. It was thought for many years that North America terminated in a northern cape, just as South America tapers to a cape at its southern extremity. As no such cape was found in the north, many later geographers believed that North America extended in an unbroken land mass to the north pole. The overland journeys of Hearne and Mackenzie, however, refuted that error and proved that an ocean washed the northern limits of the western continent.

Among the navigators who tried to effect this northwest passage from the Atlantic to the Pacific Ocean were Davis, Hudson, Baffin, Scoresby, Parry, Ross, and Franklin. Finally, in 1851-53, McClure entering from Bering strait, was forced to abandon his ship on Banks Land, but he and his crew were brought out to Baffins bay by another expedition, thus demonstrating the northwest passage. In 1903-06, Roald Amundsen sailed by a more southern route from Baffins bay to San Francisco. In 1878-79 Nordenskjöld sailed through the northwest passage from Sweden to Bering strait.

The quest for the north pole engaged many explorers during the latter half of the 19th century. These include Greely, Nansen, and the duke of Abruzzi. The goal was actually reached, however, by Peary, who, on April 7, 1909, raised the American flag over the north pole.

Land was first found in the south polar region by Captain Palmer, an American officer who landed there in 1820. This land was further explored by Bellingshausen, Biscoe, Weddell, Ross, Dumont d'Urville, and Borchgrevink. The pole was finally reached by the Norwegian explorer Amundsen, December 14, 1911.

Recent Geographical Research. The major explorations in recent years have been made in Antarctica, South America, Central America, Mexico, Africa, and the Arctic region. Commander Richard E. Byrd has made the most comprehensive explorations in Antarctica. Most of his work was carried out from the air. Vast areas of newly discovered terrain were photographed which revealed new archipelagoes, peninsulas, islands, and seas. Scientific data related to the earth's magnetic currents, meteorology, and plankton were collected.

The Carnegie Institution in Washington in cooperation with the United Fruit Company and the Mexican government have recently discovered some fine examples of Mayan jade and brightly colored Mayan wall paintings in Guatemala and Mexico. A group of Russian specialists from the USSR Academy of Sciences in the fall of 1946 discovered in the Gobi desert what they believed to be the richest deposits of bones of prehistoric animals in paleontological history. The first complete exploration of the Niger river of Africa was carried out in 1946-47, under the auspices of the French Ministry of Colonies.

DATES OF GEOGRAPHICAL DISCOVERIES*

	B. C.
Phœnicians circumnavigate Africa	600
Himilco, Carthaginian merchant, at Ierne (Ireland)	500
Hanno, Carthaginian navigator, off Sierra Leone, Africa	470
Alexander the Great in the Punjab, India	327
Nearchus, Greek general, in the Indian Ocean	325
Pytheas of Marseilles at Ultima Thule (Shetland Islands)	320
Megasthenes, Greek ambassador reaches Patna, India	300
Eudoxus, Greek sailor, crosses the Arabian Sea	118
Julius Cæsar in England	55
	A. D.
Cosmas Indicopleustes, Egyptian merchant, in India	550
Suleiman, Arab trader, voyages to China	850
Ottar, Norwegian explorer, rounds the North Cape, Europe	852
Sindbad the Sailor on the coast of India	9th c.
Al Masudi, Arab traveler, in China	920
Iceland colonized from Norway	930
Eric the Red colonizes Greenland	982
Bjarni Herjulfson, Icelander, visits Labrador	986
Benjamin of Tudela, Spanish traveler, visits India	1160–73
Friar John of Carpini, visits Karakorum, Asia	1246
Rubruquis, Flemish traveler, explores the Caspian Sea	1247
Marco Polo, the Venetian, at the Court of Kublai Khan, China	1270
Fr. Odoric, of Pordenone, Italian monk, enters Lhasa, Tibet	1320
Ibn Batuta, the Arab traveler, reaches Quiloa, E. Africa	1329
Ibn Batuta visits Timbuktu and the Niger River	1350
Clavijo, a Spanish knight, ambassador at Samarkand	1405
Zarco, Portuguese navigator, sights the Madeira Islands	1418
Conti, Italian traveler, explores southern China	1440
Cintra, Portuguese navigator, at Sierra Leone, Africa	1462
Cão, Portuguese navigator, discovers the Congo River, Africa	1484
Bartholomew Diaz, Portuguese navigator, doubles the Cape of Good Hope, South Africa	1488
Covilhão, Portuguese ambassador, penetrates into Abyssinia	1490
Columbus, Italian navigator, discovers San Salvador Islands, West Indies	1492
Vasco da Gama, Portuguese navigator, voyages to India by the Cape route	1497
John Cabot, Italian navigator in English service, lands on coast of North America	1497
Vespucci, Italian navigator, coasts along North American and South American shores†	1497–1503
Cabral, Portuguese explorer, discovers South America	1500
Pinzon, Spanish navigator, at the mouth of the Amazon, South America	1500
Columbus sights Central America	1502
Varthema, Italian traveler, visits the sacred city of Mecca	1503
Serrão, Portuguese sailor, reaches the Molucca Islands by way of India	1512
Balboa, Spanish explorer, discovers the Pacific Ocean	1513
Ponce de Leon, Spanish explorer, traverses Florida	1513
Solis, Spanish navigator, ascends the La Plata River, South America	1516
Grijalva, Spanish navigator, touches coast of Mexico	1518
Cortés, Spanish adventurer, in central Mexico	1518
Expedition of Magellan circumnavigates the globe	1521–22
Pizarro, Spanish adventurer, in Peru	1532
Cartier, French navigator, in the Gulf of St. Lawrence	1534
Coronado, Spanish explorer, marches from Mexico through Arizona and New Mexico to Kansas	1539–42
Alarcon, Spanish explorer, reaches the Colorado River, U. S.	1540
Cardenas, Spanish explorer, at the Grand Canyon, Arizona	1540
Valdivia, Spanish soldier, reaches Western Patagonia	1540

*Dates for ancient and medieval discoveries in various instances are only approximate.

†According to his narratives, the trustworthiness of which is disputed.

	A. D.
De Soto, Spanish explorer, discovers the Mississippi River	1541
Orellana, Spanish explorer, descends the Amazon	1541
Cabrillo, Portuguese navigator, on California coast	1542
St. Francis Xavier, Spanish Jesuit missionary, visits Japan	1549
Chancellor, English navigator, reaches the White Sea, Russia	1553
Willoughby, English navigator, sights Nova Zembla	1553
Gaetano, Spanish navigator, lands on the Hawaiian Islands	1555
Jenkinson, English traveler, reaches Persia	1561
Frobisher, English navigator, in Frobisher Bay, Arctic North America	1576
Davis, English navigator, in Davis Strait, Arctic North America	1587
Barentz, Dutch navigator, at Spitzbergen, Arctic Europe	1594
Western Australia sighted by Portuguese sailors	1601
Gosnold, English navigator, at Cape Cod, United States	1602
Göes, a native of the Azores, traverses Central Asia	1603–05
Champlain, French explorer, on Maine coast, United States	1604
Torres, Spanish navigator, in New Guinea	1606
Smith, English colonist, in Chesapeake Bay	1608
Hudson, English navigator, ascends Hudson River to present site of Albany	1609
Champlain, French colonizer, discovers Lake Champlain	1609
Hudson, English navigator, discovers Hudson Bay, Canada	1610
Baffin, English navigator, in Baffin Bay	1616
Hartog, Dutch navigator, on the Australian coast	1616
Schouten, Dutch navigator, discovers Cape Horn, South America	1616
Nicolet, French voyager, reaches Lake Michigan	1634
Tasman, Dutch navigator, at Tasmania	1642
Deshnev, Russian navigator, sights Bering Strait	1648
Fr. Menard, French missionary, reaches Lake Superior	1660
Marquette and Joliet, French explorers, reach the Arkansas River	1673
Fr. Hennepin, Flemish missionary, at Niagara Falls, Canada	1678
Fr. Hennepin, at St. Anthony Falls, U. S.	1680
La Salle, French explorer, descends the Mississippi	1682
Fr. Kino, Spanish Jesuit, discovers the Casa Grande ruins, U. S.	1694
Bering, Danish navigator, in Bering Strait	1728
Gwosdef, Russian sailor, lands on the Alaskan coast	1731
Verendrye, French explorer, reaches the Rocky Mountains	1740
Karstens Niebuhr, German traveler, explores Arabia	1761–67
Bruce, Scotch traveler, on the Blue Nile, Abyssinia	1768–73
Hearne, English traveler, discovers Great Slave Lake	1772
Cook, English navigator, first to cross the Antarctic circle	1773
Cook, English navigator, explores the Hawaiian Islands	1774–79
Peter Pond, Canadian explorer, reaches Lake Athabaska	1778
La Perouse, French navigator, explores eastern coast of Asia	1787
Mackenzie, Scotch explorer, discovers the Mackenzie River, Canada	1789
Gray, American navigator, ascends the Columbia River, U. S.	1792
Mungo Park on the Gambia river, West Africa	1795
Humboldt, German scientist, explores South America	1799
Lewis and Clark explore the northwestern United States	1804–06
Colter, American trapper, discovers Yellowstone Park, U. S.	1807
Hutchins, American pioneer hunter, discovers the Mammoth Cave, United States	1809
Bellingshausen, Russian navigator, on the Antarctic continent	1821
Clapperton and Denham, English travelers, cross the Sahara	1822
James Bridger, American explorer, discovers Great Salt Lake, United States	1824
Sturt, English explorer, traverses Australia	1828
Ross, English navigator, in Boothia Felix, Arctic North America	1831
Schoolcraft, American scientist, discovers Lake Itasca	1832
Wilkes, American navigator, on the Antarctic continent	1840
Abbé Huc travels in Tibet	1844
Krapf and Rebmann, German missionaries, at Mt. Kilimanjaro, East Africa	1848
McClure, Irish navigator, achieves the Northwest Passage, Arctic Ocean	1851
Boling, American soldier, visits the Yosemite	1851
Livingstone, Scottish missionary, discovers Zambesi River	1851–56
Kane, American explorer, on Grinnell Land, Arctic North America	1853
Livingstone, Scottish missionary, at Victoria Falls, Africa	1855
Barth, German traveler, explores the Sudan	1856
Burton and Speke, English explorers, discover Lake Tanganyika, Africa	1858
Speke, English explorer, discovers Victoria Nyanza, Africa	1858
Burke and Wills, Irish explorers, cross Australia from south to north	1860–61
Richthofen, German scientist, explores China	1868–72
Przhevalski, Russian traveler, crosses Mongolia	1871–73
Stanley, American explorer, traces the course of the Congo	1876–77
Nordenskjöld, Swedish explorer, accomplishes the Northeast Passage, Arctic Ocean	1878–79
Borchgrevink, Norwegian explorer, at the South Magnetic Pole, Antarctic continent	1899
Hedin, Swedish scientist, explores Central Asia.	1890–1908
Peary, American naval officer, proves the insular character of Greenland	1892
Roald Amundsen, Norwegian navigator, sails through Northwest Passage	1903–06
Peary discovers the North Pole	1909
Amundsen discovers the South Pole	1911

GENERAL FACTS ABOUT THE EARTH

The earth, or globe, is an oblate spheroid; that is, a sphere slightly flattened at two opposite points, called the poles. The two poles are the ends of the axis about which the globe rotates. The north pole is in the Arctic Ocean. The south pole is in the continent of Antarctica, which, directly at the pole, reaches an elevation of about 10,000 feet.

In order to make it possible to describe the exact location of any place on the earth, geographers have drawn around the globe certain circles, to which the position of any point may be referred. The equator is such a circle, encompassing the earth equidistant from the poles. Other circles are drawn parallel to the equator, dividing the distance between the equator and each pole into 90 equal parts. These circles are called parallels of latitude, and the distance between successive circles is called a degree. A degree (°) of latitude measures about 69 miles. Parallels of latitude are numbered from the equator north and south. Thus the north pole lies at 90° north latitude, and the south pole is at 90° south latitude. In passing from the north pole to the south pole, a traveler would traverse 180° of latitude and, in completing the circuit of the earth, he would pass through a total of 360° of latitude.

A second series of circles, 180 in number, is drawn about the earth, each circle passing through both poles. That half of each circle which extends from one pole to the other is called a meridian of longitude. Since each circle consists of 2 meridians, the 180 circles comprise a total of 360 meridians. Meridians are distant from each other about 69 miles at the equator. As one approaches the poles, however, the distance between two successive meridians decreases. Thus a degree of longitude is not constant, but varies from about 69 miles at the equator to zero at the poles. Meridians of longitude are numbered east and west from the meridian passing through Greenwich, England. The 180th meridian of east longitude coincides with the 180th meridian of west longitude, this meridian being the meridian in the western hemisphere corresponding to the Greenwich meridian in the eastern hemisphere.

The rotation of the earth takes place from west to east—the direction opposite to that in which the hands of a clock move. This movement of the earth causes the alternation of day and night.

A second movement of the globe is its revolution about the sun. The revolution takes place in an almost circular orbit. The earth's axis is not perpendicular to the plane of this orbit, but is inclined 23½° away from the perpendicular. To this inclination are due the varying lengths of day and night at different latitudes and in different seasons and also most of the seasonal variations in temperature. It provides the basis also for the division of the earth into zones, or "belts."

The boundaries of the zones are determined by the noonday inclination of the sun's rays to the surface of each zone. Thus the Torrid Zone comprises that part of the earth over which, at some time of the year, the sun is directly overhead. This zone extends for 23½° of latitude north and 23½° of latitude south of the equator, so that it has a total width of 47° of latitude. The North Frigid Zone and the South Frigid Zone, each of which extends 23½° of latitude from the poles toward the equator, comprise those parts of the earth in which, at some time in the year, the sun does not rise above the horizon at noon. Of the two remaining zones,—the North Temperate Zone and the South Temperate Zone,—each occupies 43° of latitude. In these zones, the sun never stands directly overhead and never remains for a whole day beneath the horizon. The variations of temperature between the different seasons are least in the Torrid Zone and are greatest in the two frigid zones.

The Torrid Zone is divided from the North Temperate Zone by the circle called the Tropic of Cancer and from the South Temperate Zone by the Tropic of Capricorn. The North Temperate Zone is separated from the North Frigid Zone by the Arctic circle. The corresponding line of division between the South Temperate Zone and the South Frigid Zone is called the Antarctic circle.

The following statistics regarding the earth are based on the latest research and are the nearest available approximations to the actual facts.

Equatorial diameter (miles)	7,926.6
Polar diameter (miles)	7,899.9
Circumference at the equator (miles)	24,901.7
Meridional circumference (miles)	24,859.4
Area of land surface approximately (square miles)	54,000,000
Area of water surface approximately (square miles)	143,000,000
Total area of the earth's surface approximately (square miles)	197,000,000
Volume of the earth (cubic miles)	259,900,000,000
Mean density of the earth	5.53
Density of water	1.00
Density of surface rock	2.72
Density at the earth's center	10.87
Pressure at earth's center (tons per square inch)	22,500
Weight of the earth (tons)	6,592,000,000,000,000,000,000

(Six sextillion five hundred ninety-two quintillion tons)

CONTINENTS, AREA AND POPULATION

The following table gives the area and the population of each of the continents, as estimated by the latest reliable authorities.

In the present state of geographical knowledge, it is impossible to obtain exact and strictly accurate statistics covering such large divisions of land as the continents. Even for North America, Europe, and Australia, all of which are inhabited by civilized peoples, no complete measurement of the area has been made. Only small parts of South America, Asia, and Africa have been surveyed. Consequently, it is impossible to obtain more than a careful estimate of the extent of land surface in each continent.

In arriving at the figures for population, somewhat similar difficulties have been encountered. It still remains impossible to obtain exact statistics for the number of inhabitants in large parts of Asia and of Africa. Official estimates have been utilized for these regions. In all places where regular censuses are taken, the figures here given are based on the latest returns except in a few instances, in which the most recent official estimates are used.

Name	Area Sq. Miles	Population
North America	8,500,000	180,000,000
South America	7,500,000	80,000,000
Europe	3,900,000	510,000,000
Asia	17,200,000	1,117,000,000
Africa	11,500,000	130,000,000
Australia (incl. N. Zealand)	3,000,000	9,500,000
Antarctica	2,400,000	none
Total	54,000,000	2,026,500,000

OCEANS, AREA AND DEPTH

Authorities differ widely in their estimates of the areas of oceans. This is owing in part to the absence of definite boundaries for separating the oceans. It is due also to the fact that, while some authorities include with the oceans various inland seas, such as the Mediterranean or Hudson bay, others exclude them.

Name	Estimated Area Sq. Miles	Greatest Depth Feet	Mean Depth Feet
Arctic	4,000,000	13,120	3,840
Atlantic	34,000,000	27,972	12,660
Indian	28,000,000	22,968	12,888
Pacific	71,000,000	35,401	13,440
Southern or Antarctic	6,000,000	13,932	

HIGHEST, LOWEST, AND MEAN ALTITUDES OF THE CONTINENTS

The following table gives the highest and the lowest point in each of the continents. It will be observed from the figures given that the highest part of the land surface of the earth is the peak of Mount Everest, 29,141 feet above the sea, and the lowest point is the shore of the Dead Sea, which is 1290 feet below the level of the ocean. The land elevation of the world, therefore, varies within the limit of 30,431 feet, or about 5.8 miles. The figures for the mean elevations of the continents are approximations, being the latest estimates published by the United States Geological Survey.

Continent	Mean Elevation * (feet)	Highest Point		Lowest Point	
		Name	Above Sea Level (feet)	Name	Below Sea Level (feet)
North America	2,000	Mount McKinley, Alaska	20,300	Death Valley, Cal.	276
South America	1,800	Mt. Aconcagua, Chile-Arg.	22,834	Sea level	....
Europe	980	Mt. Elbruz, Caucasus Mts.	18,465	Caspian Sea, Russia	86
Asia	3,000	Mt. Everest, India	29,141	Dead Sea, Palestine.	1,290
Africa	1,900	Kibo Peak, (Kilimanjaro) Tanganyika	19,710	Libyan Desert	440
Australia	1,000	Mt. Kosciusko, N. S. W.	7,328	Lake Eyre, South Aust.	38

* Approximate.

NORTH AMERICA

THE land mass of the western hemisphere with the adjacent islands is called America. The name was given in honor of Amerigo Vespucci, an Italian navigator who is said to have visited South America in 1499. It is often styled the New World because of its discovery and settlement in modern times by peoples from the eastern hemisphere, now commonly spoken of as the Old World.

Extent of America. The mainland extending from Alaska in the northwest and from Boothia Felix in the northeast to the south end of Patagonia is about 8700 miles long. This immense length is prolonged to about 9600 miles by the vast archipelago north of Hudson bay and by the island of Tierra del Fuego south of Patagonia. Cape Columbia in Grant Land and Cape Morris Jesup in Peary Land are within 450 miles of the north pole. Cape Horn, the southernmost point of Tierra del Fuego, is 2350 miles from the south pole. Greenland belongs to America, but Iceland, though partly in the western hemisphere, is associated with Europe. The area of America, including islands, is about 16 million square miles.

The Two Continents Compared. America comprises the two continents of North America and South America. These are connected by the narrow Isthmus of Panama. Each continent, like Africa, bears some resemblance to a triangle, the base, or shortest line, being along the northern border, and the apex, at the southern end. The climates, however, of the corresponding parts of the two continents are reversed. The northern part of North America is polar in character, while the northern part of South America is tropical. The physical features of America are displayed on a gigantic scale. There are great rivers, fresh-water lakes that are veritable inland seas, long, lofty ranges of mountains, and vast plains.

North America and South America alike have a chain of mountains extending from north to south along their western sides. Moreover, each continent has a broad central plain and a low eastern mountain range, and both continents have magnificent rivers affording access far into the interior. Vast, unbroken plains and immense forests are other characteristic features common to the two continents.

Extent of North America. The name, North America, is assumed by most geographers to mean all the continent, and all the outlying islands, north of the narrowest part of the Isthmus of Panama. Thus defined, North America includes Central America, Mexico, the West Indies, the United States, Canada, Alaska, and Greenland. For convenience of reference, Central America is often regarded as a separate section of the western hemisphere. The area of North America, including islands, is about 8.5 million square miles.

Oceans and Coasts. North America's shores are washed by the waters of three oceans—the Arctic on the north, the Atlantic on the east, and the Pacific on the west. On the south, the Gulf of Mexico and the Caribbean Sea are large bodies of water also associated with North America. Deep indentations mark the Atlantic coast and form many excellent harbors. The Pacific coast, for the most part, is without sheltered bays, and, in consequence, has fewer seaports.

Surface Features. Two mountain systems dominate the surface of the continent. On the east side is the Appalachian system. This is a series of worn-down mountains, very old geologically, which stretch from the coast plain of the Gulf of Mexico northeast to Labrador. On the west side of the continent rise the lofty ranges of the great Cordilleran system. These massive, rugged mountains are of relatively recent geological formation.

Cordilleran System. As a whole, this system extends in a northwest direction from Central America to the northern shores of Alaska. The most important ranges are the Sierra Madre of Mexico and the Rockies of the western United States, Canada, and Alaska. Between the Rocky mountains proper and the Pacific Ocean lie the Sierra Nevada of California, the Cascades of Oregon and Washington, the Selkirks of British Columbia, and the Coast ranges. Each of more than 30 peaks of the Rocky Mountain chain is over 14,000 feet high. Mt. Whitney, with an altitude of 14,496 feet, in California, is the highest peak in the continental United States. Mt. Logan, 19,850 feet high, in Yukon Territory, is the loftiest summit in Canada. Mt. McKinley, with a height of 20,300 feet, in Alaska, is the culminating point of North America.

Between the Appalachian system in the east and the Rocky Mountain system in the west lie the great medial plains. These occupy a central depression extending from the Arctic Ocean to the Gulf of Mexico. In this vast valley are situated Hudson bay, the Great Lakes, and the drainage basins of many large rivers.

Appalachian System. The Appalachian Mountain system, which trends generally northeast and southwest, consists of numerous ranges. Among these are the Great Smoky, the Allegheny, the Blue Ridge, the Catskill, the Adirondack, the Green, and the White mountains in the United States and the Notre Dame mountains in Quebec. The loftiest summit is Mt. Mitchell, 6684 feet high, in North Carolina.

Great Basin. A vast plateau, called the Great Basin, with an elevation of from 5000 to 7000 feet, lies between the lofty Wasatch range of eastern Utah and the still higher Sierra Nevada of eastern California. In this arid region, rivers disappear in sandy wastes or flow into saline marshes and salt lakes. North of the Great Basin is the less elevated and more fertile Columbia River plateau, situated between the Rockies and the Cascades. Between the Rocky mountains and the Coast ranges of Canada, a somewhat lower plateau, called the Northern Interior plateau, extends northwest to Alaska where it joins the Yukon plateau named for the great river which drains it.

Colorado Plateau. South of the Great Basin is an immense elevated tract called the Colorado plateau. This forms a plain that extends far into Mexico but attains its widest development in the southwestern United States. Much of this vast highland is from 7000 to 9000 feet above sea level. In it the Colorado river and its tributaries have carved the most stupendous examples of erosion in the world.

Mexican Plateau. This is the southeastern continuation of the great Colorado plateau. In shape, the Mexican plateau, called also the plain of Anahuac, resembles a broad wedge, with its widest portion adjoining the southwestern United States and with its narrowest portion extending to southern Mexico.

This interior plain is bordered both on the east and on the west by high ranges of the Sierra Madre, those on the west having an average elevation of 10,000 feet. On either side, the mountain slopes which face toward the sea are usually very steep and precipitous, while those which face inland toward the plateau are, for the most part, much more gentle.

The Mexican plateau increases in elevation southward, rising from about 3500 feet above sea level, opposite western Texas, to 9000 feet around the southern border. In the high southern portion lies the famous "valley of Mexico," containing Lake Tezcuco, on the shores of which were built the ancient Aztec capital and the present city of Mexico.

Medial Plains. Because of their immense extent in the northern part of the continent, the medial plains are sometimes called the Arctic valley. The width of this region, measured from the highlands of Labrador to the Rockies of northern Alberta, is fully 2000 miles. Between the Allegheny mountains of Pennsylvania and the Rocky mountains of Colorado, the plains region is about 1400 miles wide. This central depression extends south from the Arctic Ocean to the Gulf of Mexico, a distance of about 3000 miles. In this vast interior portion of the continent lie the drainage basins of large river systems. The most important of these are the Mississippi-Missouri draining into the Gulf of Mexico, the Saint Lawrence flowing into the Atlantic Ocean, the Nelson-Saskatchewan emptying into Hudson bay, and the Mackenzie-Athabaska with outlet to the Arctic Ocean. The total area drained by the four systems is about three million square miles.

Rivers. Numerous navigable rivers afford entrance to the interior of the continent. The Mackenzie and the Yukon, flowing into northern waters, are icebound during the greater part of the year. The Saint Lawrence, which flows into the Gulf of Saint Lawrence, is likewise frozen during the winter months. But portions of the Hudson, the Delaware, the mighty Mississippi with many important tributaries, are open practically all the year, as are also the navigable parts of the Rio Grande, the Colorado, the Sacramento, the Columbia, and numerous lesser streams. These provide transportation for much inland commerce and some furnish water for irrigation purposes.

Lakes. Besides the five Great Lakes in the east central part of the continent, there are several other large lakes. Of these, the most important are Great Bear lake, Great Slave lake, and lakes Winnipeg and Athabaska, situated in central and northwestern Canada. In the western United States is Great Salt lake. This is a relic of a former sea which, in geological times, occupied a large part of the Great Basin.

Glaciers. The most extensive remnants of the ice age on the mainland of North America are found in the coastal mountains of Alaska. Some of the great glaciers in the region bordering on the Gulf of Alaska are hundreds of square miles in extent. These continental glaciers, however, are very small when compared with the immense ice sheet that covers the greater part of Greenland. The higher mountains from Colorado and California northwestward to Alaska contain many glaciers.

Volcanoes. In North America, as in South America, there are extensive volcanic areas in the great mountain system bordering on the Pacific coast. Central America contains many active volcanoes, among the most noted of which are Coseguina, Izalco, Cerro Quemado, Santa Maria, Fuego, and Agua. On the Mexican plateau are situated some of the world's most gigantic volcanic mountains, as, for example, Orizaba, altitude 18,250 feet, and Popocatepetl, with an elevation of 17,876 feet. A short distance west of the plateau is Colima, a very active volcano, which rises to a height of about 13,000 feet. Another noted Mexican volcano is Jorullo.

In the United States, Lassen peak, in California, is the only active volcano. The Cascade range has many volcanic peaks but only a few display signs of volcanic activity. Mt. Saint Helens and Mt. Baker, both in the state of Washington, are said to have been in eruption between 1840 and 1850. Mt. Hood, in Oregon, exhales volcanic vapors. Of volcanic origin also are Mt. Shasta and Mt. Rainier, which rank among the grandest peaks of the continent. In the Rocky mountains, there are but few volcanic peaks, but evidence of volcanic activity is very marked in the geysers and in other wonderful features of Yellowstone national park.

Alaska contains numerous volcanoes, some of which are very active. These are found along the coast ranges of southern Alaska and in the Aleutian islands. Among the more noted of the active or the recently active volcanoes on the mainland are Mt. Fairweather, Mt. Wrangell, and Mt. Katmai. The Aleutian volcanic belt is a narrow chain of islands extending westward from the Alaskan peninsula for a distance of more than 1500 miles. Some 25 of these islands contain one or more volcanoes, either active or only recently extinct. On Unimak island, near the southern mainland, is Mt. Shishaldin, with a symmetrical cone rivaling that of Fuji, Japan, in graceful contour.

Climate. In so vast a continent, extending through 75 degrees of latitude, great variations of climate naturally occur. In the far north, arctic severity rules, while in southern Mexico and Central America the climate is tropical. Most of the central portion of the continent has a temperate climate. However, a marked difference exists between the temperatures of parts of the Atlantic and of the Pacific coast having the same latitude. The climate of Washington or of Oregon, on the Pacific coast, is much milder than the climate of Maine or of Massachusetts, which are Atlantic coast states situated in nearly the same latitudes.

In July, a great inland area in North America becomes much warmer than the waters on the east and west coasts. Compared with the weather then prevailing on the oceans, the summer heat of eastern North America is excessive. Moreover, the winter cold is severer than in European countries of the same latitude. For example, in January, Labrador is 40° F. colder than northern Germany.

As the great interior plain has no mountain ranges crossing it, cold winds from the north sometimes sweep unimpeded far to the south, suddenly causing a fall of many degrees in temperature. Occasionally, these winds destroy early plantings or belated harvests as far south as Texas. In the plains region east of the Rocky mountains, a drop of 110° F. within 48 hours has been recorded. Such great changes of temperature are unknown on the Pacific coast. In the eastern part of the continent, quick changes of temperature occur, especially in winter, but are much less extreme than in the Great Plains region.

Rainfall. Along the Gulf coast from 50 inches to 55 inches of rain fall every year. At some points near the Gulf of Mexico, the annual rainfall exceeds 60 inches. A rainfall of 80 inches in a year is not uncommon in the Puget Sound region, and in some localities on the northern Pacific coast the annual precipitation is more than 100 inches. From Manitoba and central Kansas eastward the annual rainfall averages about 35 inches. On the high plains immediately east of the Rocky mountains, the rainfall seldom exceeds 20 inches annually. In Wyoming west of the Rockies and in Nevada, the rainfall is rarely more than 10 inches. Arizona and southern California contain limited areas which are practically rainless.

Minerals. In mineral wealth, North America leads all the other continents. Gold, silver, iron, copper, lead, zinc, nickel, coal, and other minerals are produced in immense quantities. The continent is the world's chief source of petroleum. Large quantities of natural gas occur in many widely separated regions.

Flora. The flora of the temperate regions of North America is remarkable for the great number of species of trees which it contains. Forests, whose acreage totals hundreds of millions, yield enormous quantities of hard and of soft wood timber. The lowland flora of the North American countries which lie south of the United States is characterized by a profusion of tropical flowers, vines, and trees. Mexican and Central American forests produce mahogany, rosewood, ebony, and other fine cabinet woods. The plant life of the Pacific coast region differs in a marked degree from that of the eastern part of the continent. The pines, spruces, firs, and redwoods of the Pacific slope have no equals in size elsewhere in America. In bulk, the gigantic sequoias or "big trees" of California surpass all other known trees.

Fauna. Many of the animals native to North America closely resemble those found in the temperate parts of Europe and Asia. The bird fauna, for example, is strikingly similar. But the mocking bird, catbird, Baltimore oriole, wild turkey, turkey buzzard, bobolink, sage grouse, and various humming birds represent species found only in America. North America has various other distinctive animals which do not occur in the Old World. Among these are the American bison, popularly called buffalo, the grizzly bear, musk ox, bighorn sheep, Rocky Mountain goat, pronghorn, rattlesnake, Gila monster, and prairie dog.

GREENLAND

The largest island in the world, with the exception of Australia. The island lies northeast of Canada, from which it is separated by Baffin bay and Davis strait. It is almost wholly within the North Frigid Zone and stretches to a point within 450 miles of the north pole. Its estimated area is 825,000 square miles, and it has a maximum length north and south of 1400 miles, with a maximum width of 690 miles.

Physical Features. Greenland is bordered by a rocky shore rising abruptly several hundred feet above the water and cut by numerous deep fiords. The surface is a plateau having an average elevation of about 4500 feet but reaching, at a few points, an altitude of more than 10,000 feet. Spreading over about 85 per cent of the island's area is a covering of perpetual ice. This inland ice buries far below it all but the highest mountains, thereby affording an excellent example of such conditions as prevailed in the ice age. The ice constitutes a huge glacier flowing slowly toward the coasts. Each year it discharges into the ocean icebergs estimated to weigh in the aggregate more than one billion tons. The interior of Greenland contains one of the coldest areas on the globe, in which a temperature of 92° below zero has been recorded.

Area of Habitation. The southwest part of Greenland has a coastal strip which, in the summer, is covered with green lichens, trailing plants, and berries. The musk ox, white bear, wolf, arctic fox, and many varieties of birds subsist there.

This coastal strip has been settled by Danes and is a colony of Denmark. About 98 per cent of the 16,630 inhabitants are Eskimos, who, although professing Christianity, still adhere to many of their pagan customs. Apart from the mining of cryolite by an American firm, the only industries are fishing and hunting. Whale oil, seal oil, skins, and eider down are exported. The trade is a monopoly of the Danish government. Visitors may land only by special permission of the Danish government.

Greenland was so named by Eric the Red, a Norseman who voyaged along the coast about 982 A. D. It was colonized by Scandinavians in the same century. Between 1410 and 1721, however, the island was neglected, and the European settlers disappeared, probably by intermarriage with the Eskimos. The present colony was planted in the 18th century. The largest settlement is Sydproven, with a population of approximately 1000.

HUDSON BAY

A large inland sea, situated in northeastern North America, and connected with the Atlantic Ocean by Hudson strait. From Fox channel, at the north, to the southern end of James bay, at the south, Hudson bay is about 1300 miles in length. In its main body, it is about 600 miles wide. It lies wholly within the Dominion of Canada, in a region of rigorous climate.

Area and Depth. The area of Hudson bay, estimated at 475,000 square miles, is about three times that of the Baltic Sea, and approximately half that of the Mediterranean. In its main portion, the bay varies in depth from 400 to 600 feet. The southern extension, called James bay, is very shallow except in the center.

Tides and Currents. On the extreme north, Hudson bay communicates with the Arctic Ocean through Fury and Hecla strait and the Gulf of Boothia. From this passage Hudson bay receives much arctic ice. In Fox channel the tide rises 40 feet, producing a strong current by which thick ice floes are driven southward into Hudson strait, where they menace navigation.

Character of Shores. The eastern shore, called the East Main, and the western shore north of Churchill are, for the most part, rocky and fringed with numerous small islands. The western shore is called the West Main. From Churchill southward it is low and flat. A low divide separates the drainage basin of Hudson bay from the two other great drainage basins of Canada, namely, the Mackenzie and the Saint Lawrence.

Tributary Rivers. The most important river system tributary to Hudson bay is the Nelson-Saskatchewan. Within this great drainage system lie the chief wheat producing areas of Manitoba, Saskatchewan, and Alberta. The system includes also the Red River of the North, which drains parts of North Dakota, South Dakota, and Minnesota, in the United States. This river flows north into Lake Winnipeg, the outlet of which is the Nelson river. The Nelson river empties its waters into Hudson bay at Port Nelson on the southwest coast.

Second in importance among tributaries is the Churchill river, which enters the bay at Churchill, about 125 miles northwest of Port Nelson. Its deep, capacious mouth forms the best harbor on the entire coast of Hudson bay. Among other affluents are the Albany river, on the southwest, flowing into James bay, and the Big, the Moose, and the Rupert river entering from the east shore. The total area of the Hudson Bay drainage basin is estimated at 1,486,000 square miles, or about one-half of the entire mainland of Canada.

Fisheries and Fur Trade. Hudson bay contains extensive and valuable fisheries. American whaling vessels often winter at Marble island in the northwest part of the bay, and the cod fisheries extend into Hudson strait. The Hudson's Bay Company has several stations, called factories, at various points on the coast. Of these, York Factory, at the mouth of Hayes river, is the leading trading post. For more than 200 years a cargo of valuable furs has been shipped annually from York Factory to England.

East and west of the northern part of Hudson bay are the Barren Grounds. These are dreary wastes where only stunted forms of vegetable life exist. But this desolate region is the feeding ground of caribou and musk oxen, and of various smaller animals hunted for their fur.

Commercial Importance. From Montreal and from Port Nelson the sailing distance to Liverpool is practically the same. Much of the grain produced in the Canadian Northwest is shipped to Montreal by way of Winnipeg and the Great Lakes. The distance from Winnipeg to Liverpool, by way of Port Nelson or Churchill, is more than 500 miles shorter than by way of Montreal. From Edmonton to Liverpool, by way of Hudson Bay ports, the distance is more than 1000 miles less than by way of Winnipeg and Montreal.

Other conditions being equal, it would be cheaper to export grain to Europe by way of Hudson bay. Wheat exports were begun over this route after the completion in 1929 of a railroad to Churchill. While neither Hudson bay nor Hudson strait is ever entirely frozen over, there is great danger to navigation from floating ice during the greater part of the year. For sailing ships, the season for safe navigation is from about July 15 to October 1.

THE GREAT LAKES

A chain of large fresh-water lakes, situated in the east central part of North America. They include lakes Superior, Huron, Michigan, Erie, and Ontario, and form a part of the boundary between the United States and Canada. None lies entirely within the territory of either country except Lake Michigan, which is situated wholly within the United States.

Area and Drainage Basin. The combined area of these lakes is about 94,600 square miles and constitutes the largest body of fresh water in the world. The land area in their drainage basins exceeds 185,000 square miles. No large river arising in the land flows into any of the Great Lakes; but the Saint Lawrence, the stream through which the system finally drains into the Atlantic, is one of the great rivers of the continent. The depressions occupied by the Great Lakes system are separated by low ridges from two other large drainage systems. One of these, lying on the north, drains into Hudson bay; the other, lying on the south and the west, drains through the Mississippi River system into the Gulf of Mexico.

Outlets and Connections. Lake Superior, situated at the head of the great chain, is the largest and deepest of the series. It empties through the Saint Marys river, 55 miles long, into Lake Huron. At Saint Marys rapids, called also Sault Sainte Marie, and the Soo, the river falls about 20 feet. The Sault Sainte Marie canals and locks, built on both the Canadian and the American side, permit deep-water navigation around these rapids. They form one of the most important artificial waterways in the world.

The outlet of Lake Michigan is the Strait of Mackinac, which empties into Lake Huron at a point near the mouth of the Saint Marys river. Lake Huron drains into Lake Erie through the Saint Clair river, 42 miles long; Saint Clair lake, 29 miles long; and the Detroit river, 28 miles long. Lake Erie empties into Lake Ontario through the Niagara river, 26 miles long. In its course between the two lakes, the Niagara river makes a descent of 326 feet, half of which occurs in one sheer drop at Niagara falls, the most noted of the world's great cataracts.

In order to establish navigation between Lake Erie and Lake Ontario, the Welland canal, 26 miles long, with an elaborate system of locks, was completed in 1833. This connected Port Colborne, on Lake Erie, with Port Dalhousie on Lake Ontario. In 1912, enlargements were begun, which are designed to transform this early Canadian waterway into a modern ship canal.

Lake Ontario drains through the Saint Lawrence river, about 750 miles long, into the Atlantic Ocean. In various rapids between the outlet of Lake Ontario and Montreal, the Saint Lawrence river descends nearly to sea level. As Lake Superior, with an altitude of 602 feet, is only 30 feet higher than Lake Erie, it will be seen that most of the descent to sea level is made in the Niagara and Saint Lawrence rivers between Buffalo and Montreal. Despite the rapids, the Saint Lawrence is navigable for downstream boats, including passenger steamers, but a series of canals has been constructed on the Canadian side to permit of upstream navigation.

The total length of the Great Lakes-Saint Lawrence water system is about 2200 miles. From Duluth to Buffalo the sailing distance is 997 miles; from Chicago to Buffalo, 929 miles; from Duluth to Ogdensburg, 1235 miles; and from Duluth to Montreal, 1350 miles.

Commercial Importance. In the industrial and commercial development of the eastern United States and Canada, the Great Lakes have been a factor of immense importance. For the early explorers, these lakes, with their river connections, furnished easy routes to the unknown interior. They also afforded avenues through which settlers reached the productive lands adjoining their waters. Later, these inland waterways provided efficient transportation of farm, forest, and mineral products throughout a vast region rich in natural resources. Thus the Great Lakes have contributed in a marked degree to the industrial supremacy of the United States. For example, the rapid development of the immense iron ore resources of the Lake Superior region was made possible by cheap water transportation.

From the times of the French-Canadian fur traders, with their flotillas of birch-bark canoes, the Great Lakes have been a water highway between eastern and western Canada. Down this waterway float much of Canada's huge surplus of wheat for export and also flour, iron, and lumber in vast quantities. In the opposite direction go coal and those manufactured articles for which the West exchanges its products with the East.

At Buffalo, on Lake Erie, is the western terminus of the New York State Barge canal. This gives the Great Lakes a very important connection with the seaboard by way of the Mohawk and the Hudson river to New York harbor. With no increase in capacity, the barge canal is capable of transporting every year millions of tons of grain and other staple products from the lake region to tidewater.

Magnitude of Lake Traffic. The total population of the eight American states and of the Canadian province bordering on the Great Lakes exceeds 45 million. The three largest inland cities of the New World are situated on their shores. In volume, the lake traffic is enormous. The tonnage passing annually through the Detroit river exceeds that which enters and clears in the foreign trade of both the Atlantic and the Pacific ports of the United States. The yearly traffic through the Sault Sainte Marie canal around Saint Marys falls is greater in point of tonnage than that of any other artificial waterway.

THE GREAT LAKES

Item	Superior	Michigan	Huron	Erie	Ontario
Latitude, north	46° 30′ 49° 00′	41° 37′ 46° 06′	46° 00′ 43° 00′	41° 23′ 42° 53′	43° 10′ 44° 10′
Longitude, west	84° 30′ 92° 06′	84° 45′ 88° 00′	80° 00′ 84° 45′	78° 50′ 83° 30′	76° 10′ 79° 53′
Elevation above sea level in feet	602.3	581.2	581.2	572.5	246.2
Greatest length in miles	360	307	206	241	193
Greatest breadth in miles	160	118	101	57	53
Maximum depth in feet	1,012	870	750	210	738
Area in square miles	32,060	22,336	22,978	9,968	7,243
Length of coast line in miles	1,500	745	1,165	657	540
Drainage basin in square miles	44,074	43,463	49,300	24,605	25,737
United States shore line in miles (approx.)	735	1,200	470	350	230
Boundary line in miles	280	None	220	250	160
Outlet	St. Marys River	Str. of Mackinac	St. Clair River	Niagara River	St. Lawrence River
Discoverers or early explorers	Brulé	Nicolet	Brulé and Le Caron	Chaumonot and Brébeuf	Champlain
Date of exploration or discovery	1622	1634	1615	1640	1615
Largest port	Duluth	Chicago	Bay City	Cleveland	Toronto

THE UNITED STATES

The United States, a Federal republic, occupies the central part of North America, and extends from the Atlantic Ocean to the Pacific and from Canada to Mexico. The area of the continental United States, including Alaska, almost equals the area of Europe. Besides Alaska, the republic possesses various island dependencies. See *Territorial Growth of the United States.*

LENGTH OF U. S. COAST LINE BY CHIEF DIVISIONS

Division	Mainland	Islands	Total
Atlantic coast	5,565	6,114	11,679
Gulf coast	3,641	2,777	6,418
Pacific coast	2,730	1,035	3,765
Total	11,936	9,926	21,862

Character of Coasts. In the northeast, the Atlantic shore is rugged and has numerous inlets, but south of New York bay the coast belt is flat, sandy, and in only a few places rises more than 100 feet above the sea. Numerous lagoons, reefs, keys, and sandbars render the Gulf coast dangerous to navigation. Most of the Pacific shore is bold and rocky, San Francisco bay and Puget sound being the only important indentations. On the northern border are the Great Lakes—Superior, Huron, Michigan, Erie, and Ontario.

LENGTH OF COAST LINE OF THE UNITED STATES BY STATES

(Tidal Shore Line, Unit Measure 1 Statute Mile)

State	Mainland	Islands	Total
Alabama	174	117	291
California	1,264	291	1,555
Connecticut	126	18	144
Delaware	140	14	154
Florida—Atlantic	714	507	1,221
Florida—Gulf	1,273	1,257	2,530
Georgia	166	727	893
Louisiana	1,122	591	1,713
Maine	558	761	1,319
Maryland	770	275	1,045
Massachusetts	421	250	671
Mississippi	99	103	202
New Hampshire	15	5	20
New Jersey	392	368	760
New York	31	798	829
North Carolina	1,040	831	1,871
Oregon	429	60	489
Pennsylvania	13	...	13
Rhode Island	118	100	218
South Carolina	281	960	1,241
Texas	973	709	1,682
Virginia	780	500	1,280
Washington	1,037	684	1,721
Total	11,936	9,926	21,862

Surface Features. Dominant physical features of the republic are the Appalachian Mountain system along the Atlantic side with a lowland between the mountains and the ocean; the great Rocky Mountain system in the west, extending nearly north and south; and the vast valley between these highlands.

Other important physical features are the Sierra Nevada, the Cascade, and the Coast ranges, situated between the Rocky mountains and the Pacific Ocean; the vast desert area, called the Great Basin, lying between the Rockies and the Sierra Nevada; and the narrow fertile valleys, extending north and south, between the Sierra Nevada and the Coast ranges. Flanking the Great Basin on the east and the south are the lofty plateaus of Utah and Arizona. To the north of the Great Basin lies the less elevated Columbia River plateau.

Mountains and Plateaus. The high plateaus and mountain ranges of the western United States are a part of the great Cordilleran system which dominates the whole western side of North America. This system extends entirely across the United States from Mexico to Canada, through New Mexico, Colorado, Wyoming, and Montana, and throughout the region between these states and the Pacific Ocean. Measured from the eastern base of the Rockies, across Colorado, Utah, Nevada, and California, to the western base of the Coast ranges, the Cordilleran system is about 1000 miles in breadth.

The northern section of this western mountain region, particularly the Columbia River plateau, contains more extinct volcanoes than are found in any other equal area in the world. Here lavas, from ancient fissure eruptions, overspread an area of 200,000 square miles.

Scenery. The sublimity of the scenery of the western mountains is celebrated. The Yosemite falls of the Merced river in the Sierra Nevada are the highest in the world. In grandeur the Shoshone falls of the Snake river in southern Idaho rival Niagara. No Alpine lakes surpass Crater lake and Lake Tahoe in scenic beauty. The wonderlands of the globe, Yellowstone national park and Glacier park, are in the Rocky Mountain country. The Grand Canyon, nature's most marvelous example of erosion, traverses the high plateau of northwestern Arizona.

Mississippi Basin. The vast valley between the Rocky mountains and the Appalachians, called the Mississippi basin, is chiefly a grassy plain, mostly treeless, rising gently from the Gulf of Mexico toward Canada and also toward the highlands east and west. Through this basin the great Mississippi river, rising near the Canada border, flows southward into the Gulf of Mexico. In the south-central part of the valley is the only elevated section. This is the Ozark plateau, mostly from 800 feet to 1000 feet above the sea, but with summits in Arkansas which reach an elevation of 2800 feet.

About one-half the total area of the United States lies within the Mississippi basin. This basin, on account of the great fertility of its central and its eastern parts, is the most important agricultural region of the globe. Much of the western part, known as the Great Plains, with an elevation of 6000 feet in some places, has only a light rainfall. This region affords excellent natural pasturage, and, when irrigated, the soil is very productive.

Drainage Systems. The drainage waters of the United States find their way into the adjoining oceans chiefly through streams grouped in four general drainage systems, namely, the Atlantic, the Gulf, the Great Lakes, and the Pacific. Parts of North Dakota, South Dakota, and Minnesota, however, are drained by the Red River of the North, whose waters, joining those of the Nelson-Saskatchewan, flow into Hudson bay. Of the river systems, the Mississippi-Missouri, with numerous tributaries, is by far the largest. Other important large river systems are the Rio Grande, the Colorado, and the Columbia.

Climate and Rainfall. Situated within the Temperate Zone, but covering a vast area having lowlands and highlands, the United States has many varieties of climate. In general, however, the climate is that which normally prevails in temperate regions, though subject to greater extremes than those which occur in Europe. Intense heat prevails in the southwest deserts in summer. In the northwest, in winter, the mercury falls below −40° F. But the dryness of the air in these regions renders endurable extremes of both heat and cold. Within the same degrees of latitude, the Pacific coast is much warmer than the Atlantic coast. Over the central and eastern portions of the country, the climate is continental.

HIGHEST AND LOWEST POINTS AND AVERAGE ELEVATION

United States and Possessions

State or Possession	Highest Point			Lowest Point			Mean Elevation (feet)
	Name	County	Elevation (feet)	Name	County	Elevation (feet)	
Alabama	Cheaha Mt.	Clay-Talladega	2,407	Gulf of Mexico		S. l.*	500
Alaska	Mt. McKinley		20,300	Pacific Ocean		S. l.	
Arizona	San Francisco Pk.	Coconino	12,611	Colorado River	Yuma	100	4,100
Arkansas	Blue Mountain Magazine Mt.	Polk-Scott Logan	2,800 2,800	Ouachita River	Ashley-Union	55	650
California	Mount Whitney	Inyo-Tulare	14,496	Death Valley	Inyo	−276†	2,900
Canal Zone	Cerro Galera	S. W. part of Zone	1,207	Pacific Ocean		S. l.	100
Colorado	Mount Elbert	Lake	14,420	Arkansas River	Prowers	3,350	6,800
Connecticut	Bear Mountain	Litchfield	2,355	Long Is. Sound		S. l.	500
Delaware	Centerville	New Castle	440	Atlantic Ocean		S. l.	60
Dist. Columbia	Tenleytown	Northwest part	420	Potomac River		S. l.	150
Florida	Iron Mountain	Polk	325	Atlantic Ocean		S. l.	100
Georgia	Brasstown Bald	Towns-Union	4,768	Atlantic Ocean		S. l.	600
Guam	Mt. Lamlan		1,334	Pacific Ocean		S. l.	
Hawaii	Mauna Kea	Hawaii	13,784	Pacific Ocean		S. l.	
Idaho	Borah Peak	Custer	12,655	Snake River	Nez Percé	720	5,000
Illinois	Charles Mound	Jo Daviess	1,241	Mississippi R.	Alexander	279	600
Indiana	Greensfork Tp.	Randolph	1,240	Ohio River	Vanderburg	316	700
Iowa	West boundary	Osceola	1,675	Mississippi R.	Lee	477	1,100
Kansas	West boundary	Wallace	4,135	Verdigris R.	Montgomery	700	2,000
Kentucky	Big Black Mt.	Harlan	4,150	Mississippi R.	Fulton	257	750
Louisiana	N. W. part of Co.	Claiborne	400	Gulf of Mexico		S. l.	100
Maine	Mt. Katahdin	Piscataquis	5,267	Atlantic Ocean		S. l.	600
Maryland	Backbone Mt.	Garrett	3,340	Atlantic Ocean		S. l.	350
Massachusetts	Mount Greylock	Berkshire	3,505	Atlantic Ocean		S. l.	500
Michigan	Porcupine Mts.	Ontonagon	2,023	Lake Erie		572	900
Minnesota	Mesabi Range	St. Louis	1,920	Lake Superior		602	1,200
Mississippi	Near Iuka	Tishomingo	780	Gulf of Mexico		S. l.	300
Missouri	Taum Sauk Mt.	Iron	1,800	St. Francis R.	Dunklin	230	800
Montana	Granite Peak	Park	12,850	Kootenai River	Flathead	1,800	3,400
Nebraska	S. W. part of Co.	Banner	5,300	S. E. part of Co.	Richardson	825	2,600
Nevada	Boundary Peak	Esmeralda	13,145	Colorado River	Clark	470	5,500
New Hampshire	Mt. Washington	Coos	6,288	Atlantic Ocean		S. l.	1,000
New Jersey	High Point	Sussex	1,805	Atlantic Ocean		S. l.	250
New Mexico	N. Truchas Peak	Rio Arriba	13,306	Red Bluff	Eddy	2,876	5,700
New York	Mount Marcy	Essex	5,344	Atlantic Ocean		S. l.	1,000
North Carolina	Mount Mitchell	Yancey	6,684	Atlantic Ocean		S. l.	700
North Dakota	Black Butte	Slope	3,468	Pembina	Pembina	790	1,900
Ohio	Campbell Hill	Logan	1,550	Ohio River	Hamilton	425	850
Oklahoma	Black Mesa	Cimarron	4,978	Red River	McCurtain	300	1,300
Oregon	Mount Hood	Clackamas-Hood River	11,253	Pacific Ocean		S. l.	3,300
Pennsylvania	Negro Mountain	Somerset	3,213	Delaware River		S. l.	1,100
Puerto Rico	Luquillo Mts.	Humacao	3,532	Atlantic Ocean		S. l.	
Rhode Island	Durfee Hill	Providence	805	Atlantic Ocean		S. l.	200
Samoa	Lata	Tau Island	3,056	Pacific Ocean		S. l.	
South Carolina	Sassafras Mt.	Pickens	3,548	Atlantic Ocean		S. l.	350
South Dakota	Harney Peak	Pennington	7,242	Big Stone Lake	Roberts	962	2,200
Tennessee	Clingmans Dome	Sevier	6,642	Mississippi R.	Shelby	182	900
Texas	El Capitan	Culberson	8,700	Gulf of Mexico		S. l.	1,700
Utah	Kings Peaks	Duchesne	13,498	Beaverdam Crk.	Washington	2,000	6,100
Vermont	Mt. Mansfield	Lamoille	4,393	Lake Champlain	Franklin	95	1,000
Virginia	Mount Rogers	Crayson-Smyth	5,719	Atlantic Ocean		S. l.	950
Virgin Islands	Crown Hill	Is. of St. Thomas	1,550	Atlantic Ocean		S. l.	
Washington	Mt. Rainier	Pierce	14,408	Pacific Ocean		S. l.	1,700
West Virginia	Spruce Knob	Pendleton	4,860	Potomac River	Jefferson	240	1,500
Wisconsin	Rib Hill	Marathon	1,940	Lake Michigan		581	1,050
Wyoming	Gannett Peak	Fremont	13,785	Belle Fourche R.	Crook	3,100	6,700
United States ‡	Mount Whitney	Inyo-Tulare, Cal.	14,496	Death Valley	Inyo, Cal.	−276†	2,500

* Sea level. † Below sea level. ‡Exclusive of Alaska.

The rainfall varies greatly in different sections. The northwest Pacific coast and the Gulf coast have a heavy annual rainfall. In the central Mississippi valley the rainfall is ample for crop production. Around the Great Lakes the precipitation is moderate, but sufficient for agriculture. Tornadoes occur from the Great Plains eastward, but are most destructive in the lower Mississippi valley. Tropical hurricanes, sweeping northward from the Gulf of Mexico, sometimes cause serious damage along the coast from Texas to Florida.

Minerals. No other country in the world is so rich in minerals. Coal, iron ores, lead, zinc, silver, tungsten, gold, quicksilver, and copper are mined. Petroleum, natural gas, clays, cement, building stone, sulphur, lime, salt, slate, and other minerals are also produced in the United States. The mineral industry has developed with extraordinary rapidity. In 1870, the value of mineral products was about $200,000,000; in 1900, $1,109,000,000; and, in 1920, $6,981,000,000, a total not since equalled. See page 1322.

Vegetation. A wide range of climatic conditions, many different soils, and a surface diversified with mountains and valleys produce a varied vegetation. Plants characteristic of the North Temperate Zone are well represented, and there are also many species peculiar to the United States. Large forests are found in the extreme northwest and also in the southern, north central, and eastern states. It is estimated that there are at least 150 species of trees of industrial importance.

The central and eastern United States has many forests containing oaks, elms, maples, chestnuts, hickories, ashes, walnuts, and other well-known species. Characteristic trees of the South are palmettoes, magnolias, tulip trees, sour gums, and yellow pines. Cypresses are abundant in the southern swamps. In the Great Lakes region, firs, pines, spruces, and larches abound. Pines, spruces, and junipers are common in the Rocky Mountain region and yuccas and cactuses in the southwestern deserts.

Cone-bearing trees attain their greatest development in the Pacific Coast region. Gigantic sequoias, believed to be the largest and the oldest of living plants, form groves in the Sierra Nevada. These remarkable trees are unknown elsewhere on the globe. Douglas firs, true firs, and various pines, cedars, hemlocks, and spruces also attain immense size, the Douglas fir and the sugar pine ranking with the sequoias among the great trees of the continent. There are many species of native grasses suitable for fattening live stock. Numerous kinds of berries, various species of nut trees, and hundreds of varieties of wild flowers are also found.

The original forests of the United States covered about 820 million acres and contained, it is estimated, over five trillion board feet of lumber. There remain now about 470 million acres of forested land, containing more than two trillion board feet. The annual growth of forest timber is only about one-sixth of the amount removed. The United States Bureau of Forestry is endeavoring to conserve the country's valuable timber resources and to grow new forests in suitable regions.

Animal Life. With the exception of arctic and tropical species, practically all the larger animals native to North America are found in the United States. Among grazing mammals now occurring wild are the moose, the wapiti or American elk, the bighorn, the Rocky Mountain goat, the pronghorn or American antelope, and various species of deer. Among native flesh-eating mammals are the black and the grizzly bear, the timber wolf, coyote, fox, puma, lynx, wolverene, raccoon, and cacomistle. Other interesting mammals are the beaver, porcupine, opossum, muskrat, woodchuck, badger, prairie dog, peccary, armadillo, numerous rabbits, hares, and squirrels, and various small fur-bearers, such as the skunk, mink, and ermine. The manatee or sea cow is found in Florida waters, and sea lions occur on the Pacific coast.

The birds are represented by several hundred species. Among game birds, the more highly prized are the partridge, sage hen, prairie hen, and other species of grouse; the mallard, teal, canvasback, and other kinds of ducks; the wild turkey, bobwhite, plumed quail, woodcock, and various kinds of geese, rails, plover, and snipe. Typical song birds are the robin, mockingbird, brown thrasher, wood thrush, bluebird, cardinal, goldfinch, and catbird; also several species of orioles, grosbeaks, and wrens. The birds of prey include the bald eagle (the American national emblem), the golden eagle, and numerous hawks, buzzards, owls, and vultures. Among birds of prey, the huge California vulture ranks second in size only to the condor of the Andes.

Of the large reptiles, the alligator is the best-known, though a true crocodile occurs in Florida. Numerous sea turtles, fresh-water terrapins, and land tortoises are found. The so-called horned toad, the chuckwalla, and the Gila monster are peculiar kinds of lizards inhabiting southwestern deserts. There are numerous species of snakes, but only the rattlesnakes, the copperhead, the water moccasin, and a few other species are venomous.

Both the coastal and the inland waters abound in fish. Cod, halibut, mackerel, bluefish, tuna, and many other valuable food fishes are taken in large quantities by the fisheries. Many inland streams teem with salmon, trout, shad, catfish, and sturgeon. In the larger lakes, various food fishes, such as whitefish, lake trout, ciscoes, bass, pike, and perch, occur in immense numbers. Along the north Atlantic coast, oysters and lobsters abound, the annual catch being one of the most valuable of American fisheries.

Manufacturing. In manufacturing, the United States surpasses all other countries. Immense natural resources—minerals, timber, water power, hydroelectric power—and an ample supply of skilled labor enable the republic to produce, year after year, a vast, varied, and increasing output of manufactures. In 1860, the total value of manufactures was less than 2 billion dollars; in 1929, it exceeded 70 billion dollars.

Commerce. The rapid development of the three great industries, mining, agriculture, and manufacturing, produced an equally rapid increase in railroad construction and also gave rise to an enormous foreign trade. The commerce of the United States is sure to increase to still greater dimensions because, in addition to its immense trade with countries in the temperate zones, the imports from tropical or subtropical countries are increasing. Rubber, tea, coffee, cacao, sugar, raw cotton, raw silk, tin, hides, nitrates, and gums come from countries lying within the Torrid Zone or near it. In 1860, the total foreign commerce of the United States was valued at about 700 million; in 1920, at about 13 billion, a total not since exceeded.

GEOGRAPHICAL FACTS ABOUT THE UNITED STATES

The land area of the United States is 2,977,128 square miles.

The water area, exclusive of the Great Lakes, is 45,259 square miles.

The most northern point of the United States is in Minnesota, latitude 49° 23′ N. and longitude 95° 9′ W.

The most southern point of continental United States is Cape Sable, Florida, latitude 25° 7′ N. and longitude 81° 5′ W. Hence Cape Sable is 49 miles farther south than the extreme southern point of Texas.

The most eastern point of the United States is West Quoddy Head, a Maine cape which projects into the Atlantic Ocean. This headland is in longitude 66° 57′ W. and latitude 44° 49′ N.

The most western point is Cape Alva in Washington. This cape, which projects into the Pacific Ocean, is in longitude 124° 44′ W. and in latitude 48° 10′ N.

The longest distance in a straight line from north to south is measured from the boundary between Canada and the United States, the 49th parallel of latitude, to the southernmost point of Texas—1598 miles.

The shortest distance from the Atlantic to the Pacific is a straight line drawn from a point near Charleston, South Carolina, to a point near San Diego, California. This distance is 2152 miles.

The longest distance in a straight line from the Atlantic to the Pacific is measured from West Quoddy Head to a point near Yaquina Head, an Oregon cape projecting into the Pacific Ocean. These points are 2807 miles apart.

The length of the boundary of the United States, as given by the United States Coast and Geodetic Survey, is 10,748 miles, divided as follows: Atlantic Ocean, 1883; Gulf of Mexico, 1639; Pacific Ocean, 1316; Mexico, 2013; Canada, 3897.

In the continental United States the temperature has fallen as low as 60° below zero in northern Montana and has risen as high as 134° in the shade in Death valley, California.

The annual rainfall on the north shore of the Gulf of Mexico exceeds 60 inches. Around Puget sound it reaches 100 inches. In the vicinity of the Great Lakes it ranges between 30 and 35 inches. At the eastern base of the Rocky mountains it is about 15 inches. In the deserts of the Great Basin it is usually less than 10 inches. At Yuma, in southwestern Arizona, it is only 3 inches.

The average yearly rainfall over all the continental United States equals 1300 cubic miles. This quantity of rain water would weigh six trillion tons.

The geographic center of the United States is a point near Lebanon in Smith county, Kansas, latitude 39° 50′ N., longitude 98° 35′ W.

The center of population in the United States in 1940 was at a point two miles southeast by east of Carlisle, Sullivan county, Indiana, latitude 38° 56′ 54″ N., longitude 87° 22′ 35″ W. Thus the center of population was then about 595 miles to the east and 61 miles to the south of the geographic center.

The highest peak in the United States, including all territories, is the Alaskan mountain, Mt. McKinley, 20,300 feet.

The state having the lowest average elevation is Delaware. Its surface, if leveled, would be only 60 feet above the sea. Colorado has the highest average elevation, 6800 feet.

NATIONAL PARKS

Name	Location	Area Sq. Mi.	Established	Distinctive Characteristics
Acadia	Maine Coast	44.21	1919	Mountains and coastal area on Mount Desert island.
Big Bend	West Texas	1080.21	1944	Last great Texas wilderness, in bend of Rio Grande.
Bryce Canyon	Southwestern Utah	56.26	1928	Massive mountain uplift; magnificent forests; fantastically eroded pinnacles; extraordinary natural coloring.
Carlsbad Caverns	New Mexico	71.13	1930	Largest and deepest known cavern system.
Crater Lake	Southwestern Oregon	250.45	1902	Lake of extraordinary blue in crater of extinct volcano. No known inlet or outlet. Sidewalls 1500 to 2000 feet high.
Everglades	Southern Florida	423.	1947	Part of the only subtropical area in the United States; vast forests, prairies, and watercourses; abundant bird life.
Glacier	Northwestern Montana	1558.20	1910	Mountain region, 250 glacier-fed lakes of romantic beauty, 60 glaciers. Precipices thousands of feet high. Trout fishing. With the adjoining Waterton Lakes national park of Canada, dedicated in 1932 as an international peace park.
Grand Canyon	North central Arizona	1008.27	1919	Greatest example of erosion and most wonderful scenic spectacle in the world. The stupendous gorge has average depth of about 1 mile and is from 4 to 18 miles wide.
Grand Teton	Wyoming	148.27	1929	Picturesque mountains in a great "dude ranch" district.
Great Smoky Mountains	North Carolina and Tennessee	720.31	1930	Picturesque mountains, including about 40 peaks.
Hawaii	Hawaiian Islands	270.94	1916	Kilauea, Mauna Loa, largest active volcanoes in the world. Haleakala, 10,000 feet high; has gorgeous tropical forests, mahogany groves, and lava caves.
Hot Springs	Arkansas	1.59	1921	Forty-seven hot springs possessing curative properties.
Isle Royale	Lake Superior N. Michigan	209.12	1940	Extensive wilderness; habitat of one of the largest moose herds in America.
Kings Canyon	Middle eastern California	707.66	1940	Two canyons of the Kings river; mountain peaks to 14,000 feet; General Grant tree 40.3 feet in diameter.
Lassen Volcanic	Northern California	161.36	1916	Lassen Peak, 10,453 feet in altitude. Only recently active volcano in continental United States. Hot springs; mud geysers; ice caves; majestic canyons.
Mammoth Cave	S. W. Kentucky	79.04	1936	Large cavern including spectacular onyx cave formations.
Mesa Verde	S. W. Colorado	79.72	1906	Best preserved prehistoric cliff dwellings in United States.
Mount McKinley	South central Alaska	3030.19	1917	Highest mountain in North America (altitude 20,300 feet).
Mount Rainier	West central Washington	377.38	1899	Forty-eight square miles of glacier, 50 to 500 feet thick. Immense fields of wild flowers.
Olympic	N. W. Washington	1323.	1938	Finest remnant of the Pacific northwest forests; numerous glaciers; feeding ground for rare Roosevelt elk.
Platt	So. Oklahoma	1.42	1906	Numerous well-known medicinal springs.
Rocky Mountain	North middle Colorado	394.98	1915	Heart of the Rockies; snow-topped range; peaks 11,000 to 14,255 feet high; sublime scenery.
Sequoia	California	601.72	1890	The Big Tree National Park; 12,000 sequoia trees ranging from 10 to 36 feet in diameter; towering mountain ranges; startling precipices.
Shenandoah	N. W. Virginia	302.3	1935	Region of scenic grandeur in the Blue Ridge mountains.
Wind Cave	South Dakota	41.54	1903	Cavern having miles of galleries and numerous chambers containing many peculiar geological formations.
Yellowstone	Wyoming, Montana, and Idaho	3458.14	1872	More geysers than in all rest of world; boiling springs; mud volcanoes; petrified forests; Grand Canyon of the Yellowstone; waterfalls; vast wilderness inhabited by deer, elk, bison, bear, mountain sheep, and other wild animals.
Yosemite	California	1181.94	1890	Valley of world famed beauty; lofty cliffs; romantic vistas; waterfalls of extraordinary height; many snow-crowned peaks; good trout fishing.
Zion	Southwestern Utah	147.25	1919	Magnificent gorge (Zion canyon), depth from 1500 to 2500 feet, with precipitous walls of great beauty; picturesque scenery.

Parks and Monuments. The Federal government, most of the state governments, and many municipalities of the United States have set aside tracts of land reserved for public recreation and enjoyment. These aim to preserve areas of scenic, historic, or scientific interest, as well as to provide playgrounds for the people and, in some instances, to conserve forest growth and wild animal life. Practically all are easily accessible for automobiles.

The number of areas supervised by the National Park Service as reported June 30, 1948, was 174, with a total area of 21,630,133 acres. Of this number, 28 were national parks, 86 were national monuments, 11 were national military parks, 6 were battlefield sites, 5 were national historical parks, and the remainder were cemeteries and miscellaneous areas.

Besides national parks and monuments, there were, in 1946, 1774 state parks and related areas, with a total of 7,660,073 acres.

STATE PARKS AND RELATED AREAS

State	No.	Acres	State	No.	Acres	State	No.	Acres
Alabama	25	77,604	Maryland	17	123,634	Oklahoma	11	43,878
Arizona	3	10,140	Massachusetts	40	108,505	Oregon	169	451,369
Arkansas	9	20,199	Michigan	142	89,550	Pennsylvania	108	86,701
California	75	519,750	Minnesota	54	1,599,018	Rhode Island	48	15,904
Connecticut	64	15,642	Mississippi	12	11,009	South Carolina	18	37,260
Delaware	1	2	Missouri	28	145,158	South Dakota	1	128,000
Florida	20	32,255	Montana	1	2,777	Tennessee	17	118,100
Georgia	15	23,603	Nebraska	37	8,338	Texas	51	65,670
Idaho	4	58,193	Nevada	5	11,489	Utah	1	....
Illinois	79	38,578	New Hampshire	46	37,625	Vermont	28	52,822
Indiana	34	165,802	New Jersey	29	76,857	Virginia	13	26,451
Iowa	81	35,148	New Mexico	10	2,991	Washington	70	47,476
Kansas	25	39,533	New York	126	2,568,890	West Virginia	22	97,812
Kentucky	22	35,407	North Carolina	12	35,309	Wisconsin	29	272,111
Louisiana	8	10,636	North Dakota	45	3,514	Wyoming	4	57
Maine	21	131,347	Ohio	94	177,959	Total	1,774	7,660,073

Photos from Brown Bros., New York.

NATIONAL PARKS

1 The Three Patriarchs, Zion National Park. 2 Zion Canyon, Zion National Park. 3 Taylor Peak, Rocky Mountain National Park. 4 Bluebird Lake, Rocky Mountain National Park. 5 Granite Park, Glacier National Park. 6 Gould Mountain, Glacier National Park.

Photos from Brown Bros., New York.

NATIONAL PARKS

1 Summit of Mt. Rainier, Mt. Rainier National Park. 2 Mirror Lake, Mt. Rainier National Park. 3 On Evelyn's Mile, Acadia National Park. 4 Otter Cliffs, Acadia National Park. 5 Lookout Mt., Mesa Verde National Park. 6 Spruce Tree House, Mesa Verde National Park.

NATIONAL MONUMENTS AND ALLIED AREAS*

Name	Location	Area (Acres)	Estab-lished	Distinctive Characteristics
Abraham Lincoln (*h*)	Kentucky	116	1916	Contains log cabin where Abraham Lincoln was born.
Ackia Battleground (*m*)	Miss.	49	1938	Scene of battle, May 26, 1736, in French and Indian conflict.
Andrew Johnson (*m*)	Tennessee	17	1942	Andrew Johnson's home, tailor shop, and grave.
Appomattox House (*m*)	Virginia	968	1940	Scene of the surrender of the Confederate Army, April 9, 1865.
Antietam Battlefield (*b*)	Maryland	183	1890	Scene of one of the greatest battles of the Civil War.
Arches (*m*)	Utah	33,770	1929	Natural arches, windows, and other effects of wind erosion.
Aztec Ruins (*m*)	N. Mex.	27	1923	Pueblo ruins, one containing 500 rooms.
Badlands (*m*)	S. Dakota	122,972	1939	Spectacular exhibit of erosion—fantastic ridges, cliffs.
Bandelier (*m*)	N. Mex.	27,049	1916	Vast ruins of prehistoric cliff dwellings.
Big Hole Battlefield (*m*)	Montana	200	1910	Scene of victory, 1877, over force of Nez Perce Indians.
Black Canyon of the Gunnison (*m*)	Colorado	13,176	1933	10 miles of deepest and most scenic portion of Black Canyon.
Canyon de Chelly (*m*)	Arizona	83,840	1931	Deep canyon; Indian cliff dwellings; very ancient ruins.
Capitol Reef (*m*)	Utah	33,069	1937	Cliff dwellings, fossils, imprints of prehistoric animals.
Capulin Mountain (*m*)	N. Mex.	680	1916	Cinder cone of geologically recent formation.
Casa Grande (*m*)	Arizona	473	1889	Buildings of a prehistoric race. Ruins discovered in 1694.
Castillo de San Marcos (*m*)	Florida	19	1924	Oldest masonry fort in the United States; built 1672.
Cedar Breaks (*m*)	Utah	6,172	1933	Spectacular canyons and cliffs of vivid coloring.
Chaco Canyon	N. Mex.	18,039	1907	Numerous ruins of cliff dwellings, including communal houses.
Chalmette (*h*)	Louisiana	33	1907	Scene of battle of New Orleans, January 8, 1815.
Channel Islands (*m*)	S. Calif.	1,120	1938	Parts of Anacapa and Santa Barbara islands; fossil elephants.
Chickamauga and Chattanooga (*b*)	Ga.-Tenn.	8,149	1890	Beautiful scenic park, embracing battlefields of Chickamauga, Missionary Ridge, and other conflicts of the Civil War, 1863.
Chiricahua (*m*)	Arizona	10,530	1924	Natural rock formations.
Colonial (*h*)	Virginia	7,233	1936	Jamestown, Williamsburg, Yorktown, connected by parkway.
Colorado (*m*)	Colo.	18,121	1911	Many lofty monoliths; unusual scenic beauty.
Craters of the Moon (*m*)	Idaho	47,211	1924	Volcanic region with weird landscape effects.
Custer Battlefield (*m*)	Montana	765	1946	Site of Battle of the Little Bighorn River, June 25, 1876.
Death Valley (*m*)	Calif.-Nev.	†2,891	1933	Arid tract containing lowest point in the western hemisphere.
Devil Postpile (*m*)	Calif.	798	1911	Spectacular six-sided aggregation of basaltic columns.
Devils Tower (*m*)	Wyoming	1,194	1906	Natural rock tower of volcanic origin, 1200 feet high.
Dinosaur (*m*)	Utah-Col.	190,799	1915	Deposits of fossil animal remains of great scientific interest.
El Morro (*m*)	N. Mex.	240	1906	Rock containing inscriptions cut by early Spanish explorers.
Fort Donelson (*p*)	Tennessee	103	1928	Site of Civil War fort.
Fort Frederica (*m*)	Georgia	75	1945	Built (1736–54) by Gen. James E. Oglethorpe.
Fort Jefferson (*m*)	Florida	87	1935	Largest all-masonry fort in Western world, built 1846.
Fort Laramie (*m*)	Wyoming	214	1938	Center for migrants and explorers 1834–90.
Fort Matanzas (*m*)	Florida	228	1924	Early Spanish stronghold.
Fort McHenry (*m*)	Maryland	48	1925	Defense of this fort on Sept. 13–14, 1814 inspired the composition of the national anthem.
Fort Pulaski (*m*)	Georgia	5,427	1924	Brick fort built 1829–47, bombarded in Civil War.
Fossil Cycad (*m*)	S. Dakota	320	1922	Area rich in fossil plants.
Fredericksburg and Spotsylvania (*p*)	Virginia	2,421	1927	Six great battlefields of Civil War.
George Washington Birthplace (*m*)	Virginia	394	1930	Memorial mansion and gardens.
Gettysburg (*p*)	Penn.	2,463	1895	Beautiful natural park. Scene of great Civil War combat, 1863.
Gila Cliff Dwellings (*m*)	N. Mex.	160	1907	Highly interesting remains of cliff dwellings.
Glacier Bay (*m*)	Alaska	†3,590	1925	Tidewater glaciers of first rank.
Grand Canyon (*m*)	Arizona	196,051	1932	Adjoins Grand Canyon Nat. Park.
Gran Quivira (*m*)	N. Mex.	451	1909	Important relic of Spanish missions in the United States.
Great Sand Dunes (*m*)	Colorado	35,908	1932	Sand dune 1000 feet high in San Luis Valley.
Guilford Courthouse (*p*)	N. Car.	149	1917	Near Greensboro. Scene of great battle of the Revolution, 1781.
Holy Cross (*m*)	Colo.	1,392	1929	Figure of cross visible on mountain due to snow-filled crevices.
Homestead (*m*)	Nebraska	163	1939	Site of first homestead in the United States.
Hovenweep (*m*)	Utah-Col.	299	1923	Groups of prehistoric towers and pueblo ruins.
Jackson Hole (*m*)	Wyoming	173,065	1943	Part of Teton "black-fault"; potholes; other glacial phenomena.
Jewel Cave (*m*)	S. Dakota	1,275	1908	Vast limestone cavern of extraordinary beauty.
Joshua Tree (*m*)	Calif.	655,961	1936	The Joshua tree, a spectacular feature of western desert land.
Katmai (*m*)	Alaska	†4,215	1935	Volcanic phenomena; "Valley of Ten Thousand Smokes."
Kennesaw Mountain (*b*)	Georgia	3,094	1935	Scene of battle in Civil War, June 27, 1864.
King's Mountain (*p*)	S. Car.	4,012	1931	Site of American victory, Oct. 7, 1780, in Revolutionary War.
Lava Beds (*m*)	Calif.	46,028	1925	Volcanic formations; battleground Modoc Indian War, 1873.
Lehman Caves (*m*)	Nevada	640	1922	Limestone caverns of much beauty and scientific interest.
Meriwether Lewis (*m*)	Tennessee	300	1925	Contains grave of Lewis of Lewis and Clark expedition.
Montezuma Castle (*m*)	Arizona	783	1906	Prehistoric cliff-dwelling in the face of a high cliff.
Moores Creek (*p*)	N. Car.	30	1926	Scene of a memorable battle of the Revolutionary War.
Morristown (*h*)	N. Jersey	958	1933	Washington's headquarters in 1779–80.
Mound City Group (*m*)	Ohio	57	1923	Prehistoric mounds in Camp Sheridan military reservation.
Muir Woods (*m*)	Calif.	425	1908	Noted redwood grove; located 7 miles from San Francisco.
Natural Bridges (*m*)	Utah	2,650	1908	Three natural bridges, largest 223 feet high; span 261 feet.
Navajo (*m*)	Arizona	360	1909	Numerous ancient pueblos, or ruins of cliff dwellings.
Ocmulgee (*m*)	Georgia	684	1936	Indian mounds in and around Macon.
Old Kasaan (*m*)	Alaska	38	1916	Abandoned Indian village.
Oregon Caves (*m*)	Oregon	480	1909	Vast caves of dazzling whiteness called "Marble Halls."
Organ Pipe Cactus (*m*)	Arizona	328,162	1937	Unique forms of native plant and animal life.
Perry's Victory Mem'l (*m*)	Ohio	14	1936	Commemoration of victory over British fleet in 1813.
Petersburg (*p*)	Virginia	1,325	1926	Scene of Civil War conflicts.
Petrified Forest (*m*)	Arizona	85,304	1906	Petrified trees; colored rocks of Painted desert.
Pinnacles (*m*)	Calif.	12,818	1908	Many spirelike rock formations, 600 to 1000 feet high.
Pipe Spring (*m*)	Arizona	40	1923	Spring of pure water in desert region.
Pipestone (*m*)	Minnesota	116	1937	Source of material for Indian peace pipes.
Rainbow Bridge (*m*)	Utah	160	1910	Natural bridge 300 feet above water; span is 278 feet.
Richmond (*n*)	Virginia	684	1944	Scene of battles in defense of Richmond during Civil War.
Saguaro (*m*)	Arizona	53,669	1933	Giant cacti of unusual scientific interest.
Saratoga (*h*)	New York	1,865	1938	Scene of American victory over British, 1777.
Scotts Bluff (*m*)	Nebraska	2,196	1919	Landmark on Oregon trail.
Shiloh (*p*)	Tenn.	3,729	1894	Embraces the battlefield of Shiloh, near Pittsburg Landing.
Shoshone Cavern (*m*)	Wyoming	212	1909	Cavern of great extent; near Cody.
Sitka (*m*)	Alaska	57	1910	Park of great natural beauty, scene of massacre of Russians.

NATIONAL MONUMENTS AND ALLIED AREAS*—Continued

Name	Location	Area (Acres)	Established	Distinctive Characteristics
Statue of Liberty (*m*)	New York	10	1924	Bedloe's Island, containing famous statue.
Stones River (*p*)	Tennessee	324	1927	Scene of Civil War battle.
Sunset Crater (*m*)	Arizona	3,040	1930	Volcanic crater with lava flows and ice caves.
Timpanogos Cave (*m*)	Utah	250	1922	Limestone cavern almost 600 feet in length.
Tonto (*m*)	Arizona	1,120	1907	Cliff dwellings in an unusually good state of preservation.
Tumacacori (*m*)	Arizona	10	1908	Spanish Mission established in late 17th century.
Tuzigoot (*m*)	Arizona	43	1939	Ruins of ancient pueblo with valuable relics.
Verendrye (*m*)	N. Dakota	253	1917	Butte whence Verendrye first saw beyond Missouri river.
Vicksburg (*p*)	Miss.	1,324	1899	Scene of the siege and surrender of Vicksburg, 1863.
Walnut Canyon (*m*)	Arizona	1,642	1915	Cliff dwellings of much scientific and popular interest.
Wheeler (*m*)	Colo.	300	1908	Extinct volcano of great geological value. Strange erosion.
White Sands (*m*)	N. Mex.	140,247	1933	Sands resembling snow; interesting plant and animal life.
Whitman (*m*)	Wash.	46	1940	Site of first mission in Pacific Northwest.
Wupatki (*m*)	Arizona	34,853	1924	Prehistoric dwellings of ancestors of Hopi Indians.
Yucca House (*m*)	Colo.	10	1919	Mounds left by prehistoric people.
Zion (*m*)	Utah	33,921	1937	Hurricane cliffs; notable geologic formations.

*Exclusive of areas less than 5 acres. (*b*) national battlefield sites, (*h*) national historical parks, (*m*) national monuments, (*n*) national battlefield parks, and (*p*) national military parks. †Square miles.

NEW ENGLAND STATES

The New England states, comprising Maine, New Hampshire, Vermont, Massachusetts, Rhode Island, and Connecticut, are situated in the northeastern part of the United States. The total area of these six states, 66,608 square miles, is less than the area of Oklahoma, 69,919 square miles, while the total population, 8,437,284, is more than three times the population of that state, 2,336,434.

Surface. The principal upland regions of New England are the old, worn-down White mountains in New Hampshire, the Green mountains in Vermont, and the Berkshire Hills in Massachusetts. Numerous harbors, formed from submerged valleys, indent the coast. Northern New England has many small lakes noted for scenic beauty. The Rangeley lakes in Maine and lakes Sunapee and Winnepesaukee in New Hampshire are popular resorts.

Rivers. New England is well watered. Many of the rivers are broken by falls or rapids, and some of these furnish hydroelectric power. The Connecticut, Penobscot, Kennebec, Mystic, Charles, and Thames are navigable for steamers. In the days of the water wheel, the Merrimac was said to turn more factory wheels than any other stream in the world.

Climate. The climate is continental. Winter, a very cold season, is rendered more unpleasant by the humidity of the air. Northeast winds passing over the cold Labrador current flowing along the New England shore are chilled and, blowing inland, bring heavy snows in winter and cause fogs and cold rains in summer. The southeast winds are much milder, as they sweep over warm ocean currents from the Gulf of Mexico.

Minerals. New England has but little mineral wealth. Building stones, feldspars, and various clays are found. Granite, basalt, marble, and slate are the chief quarry products, and rank in importance in the order named. Among these states, Vermont stands first in total value of quarry products, with Massachusetts second, and New Hampshire third. Besides leading in the production of granite, Vermont quarries large quantities of slate and much beautiful marble. In each of the New England states, except Connecticut in which basalt leads, granite is the most valuable quarry product.

Fisheries. Fishing early became a prominent industry, the nearness of rich fishing grounds attracting a large class of workers. Cod, halibut, mackerel, swordfish, haddock, hake, herring, and pollock are the principal catches. Oysters, clams, crabs, lobsters, and shrimps form important items in the total annual value of the fisheries. Menhaden are taken in immense quantities for oil and fertilizing material. In amount and value of sea fish taken, Massachusetts leads all other states in the Union.

Forests. Forests still cover large tracts of land in this section, especially in Maine, New Hampshire, and Vermont. The pine is the most common tree. Spruce is cut in Maine for making paper and wood pulp, the principal manufactures of the state. Maine still ships considerable lumber.

Agriculture. Much of New England is stony and difficult to cultivate, and abandoned farms are not uncommon. The Connecticut valley, however, has very fertile soil, and there is also considerable good farm land in the valleys of several smaller rivers. Hay is the chief crop. Potatoes, rye, corn, and oats are also raised. Connecticut Valley tobacco ranks second only to Cuban tobacco. Dairying is an important occupation, especially in Vermont. Market gardening for the cities has become a profitable industry in recent years. Apples, pears, and cherries are the chief orchard fruits.

Manufacturing. In all these states, manufacturing is the principal occupation. Hundreds of different articles are made. Among the chief products are cottons, woolens, metal wares, boots and shoes, leather, paper, brass goods, machinery, electrical apparatus, clothing, rubber goods, barbed wire, carpets, and refined sugar. Every city in this division is a manufacturing center.

Many western states have counties each larger than southern New England. This section lacks coal, iron, copper, lead, zinc, timber, wool, cotton, hides—in short, all the basic materials of industrial work in mill, factory, or machine shop. Yet the intelligence, skill, energy, and inventiveness of its people have made southern New England the greatest center of diversified manufacturing in the Union. Massachusetts is a striking example. Forty-three states exceed it in area. It has a barren soil and an inhospitable climate. Yet in population it stands eighth among the states, and its enormous manufacturing output gives it still higher rank in commerce.

Commerce. The seaboard states have a large commerce, both domestic and foreign, and the harbors of their important ports are crowded with shipping at all times of the year. Manufactures constitute the bulk of the exports; the imports consist mainly of raw materials from various parts of the globe. The West India trade—a trade long associated with New England merchants—is very valuable. Numerous railroads link this section with the rest of the Union; and trolley lines and surfaced highways facilitate inland traffic. The principal ports are Boston, Mass., Portland, Me., Providence, R. I., Portsmouth, N. H., and New Haven, Conn.

MIDDLE ATLANTIC STATES

Because of their medial position with reference to the seaboard, and on account of a general similarity in surface features, the states of New York, New Jersey, Pennsylvania, Delaware, Maryland, Virginia, and West Virginia are generally grouped together. The first four have been called the "Middle" states and the last three have been placed with "South Atlantic" or "Southern" states. By some, the first three are styled "Middle Atlantic" while

GROWTH OF THE UNITED STATES IN POPULATION, 1850-1940

STATE	Population 1850	Population 1880	Population 1910	Population 1930	Population 1940	% of inc. 1930–40	Rank	Largest City
Alabama	771,623	1,262,505	2,138,093	2,646,248	2,832,961	7.1	17	Birmingham
Arizona	....	40,440	204,354	435,573	499,261	14.6	43	Phoenix
Arkansas	209,897	802,525	1,574,449	1,854,482	1,949,387	5.1	24	Little Rock
California	92,597	864,694	2,377,549	5,677,251	6,907,387	21.7	5	Los Angeles
Colorado	....	194,327	799,024	1,035,791	1,123,296	8.4	33	Denver
Connecticut	370,792	622,700	1,114,756	1,606,903	1,709,242	6.4	31	Hartford
Delaware	91,532	146,608	202,322	238,380	266,505	11.8	46	Wilmington
Dist. Columbia	51,687	177,624	331,069	486,869	663,091	36.2		Washington
Florida	87,445	269,493	752,619	1,468,211	1,897,414	29.2	27	Jacksonville
Georgia	906,185	1,542,180	2,609,121	2,908,506	3,123,723	7.4	14	Atlanta
Idaho	....	32,610	325,594	445,032	524,873	17.9	42	Boise
Illinois	851,470	3,077,871	5,638,591	7,630,654	7,897,241	3.5	3	Chicago
Indiana	988,416	1,978,301	2,700,876	3,238,503	3,427,796	5.8	12	Indianapolis
Iowa	192,214	1,624,615	2,224,771	2,470,939	2,538,268	2.7	20	Des Moines
Kansas	....	996,096	1,690,949	1,880,999	1,801,028	-4.3*	29	Kansas City
Kentucky	982,405	1,648,690	2,289,905	2,614,589	2,845,627	8.8	16	Louisville
Louisiana	517,762	939,946	1,656,388	2,101,593	2,363,880	12.5	21	New Orleans
Maine	583,169	648,936	742,371	797,423	847,226	6.2	35	Portland
Maryland	583,034	934,943	1,295,346	1,631,526	1,821,244	11.6	28	Baltimore
Massachusetts	994,514	1,783,085	3,366,416	4,249,614	4,316,721	1.6	8	Boston
Michigan	397,654	1,636,937	2,810,173	4,842,325	5,256,106	8.5	7	Detroit
Minnesota	6,077	780,773	2,075,708	2,563,953	2,792,300	8.9	18	Minneapolis
Mississippi	606,526	1,131,597	1,797,114	2,009,821	2,183,796	8.7	23	Jackson
Missouri	682,044	2,168,380	3,293,335	3,629,367	3,784,664	4.3	10	St. Louis
Montana	....	39,159	376,053	537,606	559,456	4.1	39	Butte
Nebraska	....	452,402	1,192,214	1,377,963	1,315,834	-4.5*	32	Omaha
Nevada	....	62,266	81,875	91,058	110,247	21.1	48	Reno
New Hampshire	317,976	346,991	430,572	465,293	491,524	5.6	44	Manchester
New Jersey	489,555	1,131,116	2,537,167	4,041,334	4,160,165	2.9	9	Newark
New Mexico	61,547	119,565	327,301	423,317	531,818	25.6	41	Albuquerque
New York	3,097,394	5,082,871	9,113,614	12,588,066	13,479,142	7.1	1	New York
North Carolina	869,039	1,399,750	2,206,287	3,170,276	3,571,623	12.7	11	Charlotte
North Dakota	....	....	577,056	680,845	641,935	-5.7*	38	Fargo
Ohio	1,980,329	3,198,062	4,767,121	6,646,697	6,907,612	3.9	4	Cleveland
Oklahoma	....	....	1,657,155	2,396,040	2,336,434	-2.5*	22	Oklahoma City
Oregon	13,294	174,768	672,765	953,786	1,089,684	14.2	34	Portland
Pennsylvania	2,311,786	4,282,891	7,665,111	9,631,350	9,900,180	2.8	2	Philadelphia
Rhode Island	147,545	276,531	542,610	687,497	713,346	3.8	36	Providence
South Carolina	668,507	995,577	1,515,400	1,738,765	1,899,804	9.3	26	Charleston
South Dakota	....	135,177	583,888	692,849	642,961	-7.2*	37	Sioux Falls
Tennessee	1,002,717	1,542,359	2,184,789	2,616,556	2,915,841	11.4	15	Memphis
Texas	212,592	1,591,749	3,896,542	5,824,715	6,414,824	10.1	6	Houston
Utah	11,380	143,963	373,351	507,847	550,310	8.4	40	Salt Lake City
Vermont	314,120	332,286	355,956	359,611	359,231	-0.1*	45	Burlington
Virginia	1,421,661	1,512,565	2,061,612	2,421,851	2,677,773	10.6	19	Richmond
Washington	....	75,116	1,141,990	1,563,396	1,736,191	11.1	30	Seattle
West Virginia	....	618,457	1,221,119	1,729,205	1,901,974	10.0	25	Huntington
Wisconsin	305,391	1,315,497	2,333,860	2,939,006	3,137,587	6.8	13	Milwaukee
Wyoming	....	20,789	145,965	225,565	250,742	11.2	47	Cheyenne
Total	23,191,876	50,155,783	91,972,266	122,775,046	131,669,275			New York

* Minus sign denotes decreases.

all the others are called "South Atlantic" states.

The total area of the states comprising this group is less than one-sixteenth of the entire area of the country. Yet these seven states have one-fourth of the population, own more than one-third of the manufacturing capital, and contain nearly two-fifths of the wage earners of the United States.

Surface. The Appalachian Mountain system extends across this group of states from northeast to southwest, and the coastal plain gradually widens southward. On the west side of the mountains is the Allegheny plateau. It is a rugged area, sloping toward the Mississippi, and is but thinly populated. Numerous bays and inlets indent the Atlantic coast, and several of them form excellent harbors.

The coastal plain is low and sandy, and much of it is bordered by swamps. Some of the rivers are navigable and add greatly to the transportation facilities of the region. Among the more important tidal streams are the Hudson, the Delaware, the Patapsco, and the James. The Ohio river on the west is a great artery of interstate trade. The shores of Chesapeake bay are dotted with ports actively engaged in coastwise traffic.

Climate. Between the northern and southern limits of this division the distance is nearly 600 miles. This distance, together with variations in surface features, causes marked differences in the climatic conditions of the northern and southern parts. In northern New York the mean winter temperature is 17° F.; in southern Virginia, 35° F. The summer temperature averages 60° F. along the northern boundary of this group of states and 75° F. along the southern. The fruit belt of western New York owes its favorable climate to the equalizing influence of Lake Erie and Lake Ontario. The Gulf Stream passes near the Virginia coast and moderates the winds blowing from the ocean. In all the states of this division the rainfall is amply sufficient for farming.

Mining. Iron is found in all the states except Delaware. Enormous quantities of coal are mined in Pennsylvania, West Virginia, Maryland, and Virginia. Petroleum, first discovered in Pennsylvania in 1859, is produced in that state, in New York, and in West Virginia. Natural gas, piped from the gas fields, is utilized for heating and lighting in many cities.

Their vast supplies of coal, iron, petroleum, and natural gas, the basic materials of industrial wealth, have enabled these states to lead the nation in various steel and iron manufactures.

Forests. Northern New York is well forested, and much forest land in the Adirondack region is under the protection of the state. In the Appalachians, the United States government has reserved extensive forested tracts. Hemlock is the principal timber cut in New York and Pennsylvania. Spruce for making wood pulp is obtained chiefly in New York and in West Virginia. Oak, maple, poplar, walnut, and other broad-leaved trees are common in all these states. Yellow pine is an important source of lumber in Virginia, and cypress and cedar are found in the coastal swamps. The hardwoods produced in this group of states come mostly from West Virginia.

Agriculture. In these states, agriculture has always been an important industry. There is much fertile soil, and large crops of grains, potatoes, apples, peaches, pears, grapes, and strawberries are grown. Virginia ranks as one of the leading tobacco states. Peanuts also form an important crop in that state. Buckwheat is grown extensively in Pennsylvania and in New York. Peas, corn, tomatoes, berries, and orchard fruits are canned in enormous quantities. Market gardening is a profitable occupation near the large centers of population. Much attention is paid to dairying, especially in New York. The annual output of butter and cheese is very large. Vast quantities of milk are supplied to the great cities in this section. Besides cattle, the other large farm animals most commonly reared are horses, sheep, and hogs. Poultry raising is an important industry.

Fisheries. Fishing is an occupation of great importance. Oysters form the most valuable single item. Shad, bluefish, and mackerel are taken in the bays and rivers. Lakes Erie and Ontario furnish large quantities of lake trout, pike, ciscoes, and other food fish.

Manufacturing. In this section, manufacturing is the foremost industry. New York, called the Empire State, ranks first in the Union in manufacturing as well as in population, wealth, and commerce. Of its long list of diversified manufactures, the most valuable single industrial product is wearing apparel. Other important manufactures of this division of states are iron and steel wares, foundry and machine shop products, chemicals, woolen goods, silk, glass, and leather goods. Oil refining is the leading industry in New Jersey.

Commerce. The commercial supremacy of this group of states arises from favoring geographic conditions and from abundant transportation facilities. Two-thirds of the foreign commerce of the United States passes through New York, Philadelphia, Baltimore, and other ports of this division. Unsurpassed facilities for collecting raw materials and for distributing manufactured goods account for the growth of the larger industrial cities. Equal facilities for gathering and for distributing exports have made several cities great seaports.

The Great Lakes aid the growth of the Middle Atlantic states by furnishing a waterway for transporting raw materials needed in many industries. Of high value also are the Hudson and Mohawk valleys. These furnish easy routes of rail, river, and canal communication between the Atlantic seaboard and the West. The New York State Barge canal connects the Hudson river with the Great Lakes. The Allegheny and Monongahela rivers, uniting to form the Ohio, afford water transportation between this group of states and the central and southern parts of the United States.

CENTRAL STATES

The large division of the Union called the Central states consists of Kentucky, Ohio, Indiana, Illinois, Michigan, Wisconsin, Missouri, Iowa, Minnesota, North Dakota, South Dakota, Nebraska, and Kansas.

Surface. Prairies occupy a large part of this division. They are level or gently rolling and for the most part are covered with a rich dark soil. On such plains modern farm machinery can be used to great advantage; hence the central and eastern parts have become the chief agricultural regions of the United States.

Along the western border there is considerable highland, including the Black Hills, noted for their gold mines. In the southwest corner of South Dakota are the famous Bad Lands. These consist of a maze of ridges and pinnacles of sandstone; the soil is mostly bare clay of different colors, and the whole region is very difficult of travel.

Rivers. Most of this division is drained by the Mississippi and its affluents. Six of the states, however, border on the Great Lakes and are in part in the Saint Lawrence basin. Some streams in Minnesota, North Dakota, and South Dakota flow into the Red River of the North. Hence the waters of the Central states find their way into the Atlantic through the Gulf of Mexico, the Saint Lawrence gulf, and Hudson bay. Besides the hundreds of streams that water this vast valley, there are thousands of small lakes that dot the surface, especially in Minnesota and in North Dakota. The principal rivers navigable by steamboats are the Mississippi, Missouri, Ohio, Wabash, Illinois, and Red River of the North.

Climate. In the north, the winter is long and extremely cold weather prevails, while the summers are short and hot. Along the southern border, in Kentucky, Missouri, and Kansas, the climate is milder. Snow seldom falls there and never stays on the ground long. The rainfall is sufficient for farming over all this division, except in the extreme western plains.

Minerals. This group of states is very rich in mineral wealth. Coal is mined extensively in Kentucky, Iowa, Indiana, Ohio, Kansas, and Illinois, the last ranking third among the coal producing states of the Union. Petroleum wells are in operation in Kentucky, Indiana, Kansas, and Illinois. Natural gas is produced in several states, notably in Illinois and Indiana. Gold, silver, lead, zinc, potter's clays, building stone, gypsum, asbestos, and graphite are obtained. Michigan has long been noted for its yield of copper and salt. In Minnesota and Michigan there are vast deposits of iron ore. Because of this supply, made available by cheap transportation, great centers of the iron industry have been developed on lakes Michigan and Erie.

Forests. Michigan, Wisconsin, and Minnesota, once leaders in the cutting of timber, are still important producers of lumber and pulp wood. Pine for lumber and spruce and hemlock for pulp wood are the principal items in the annual timber cut. Despite the destruction of the chief forests, large woodlands still exist in several of the states, and forest industries furnish employment for many workers.

Agriculture. Every crop known to the temperate zones can be grown in this division. Hundreds of millions of bushels of corn, oats, barley, rye, and wheat are raised annually. Hay, potatoes, vegetables, and orchard fruits are important crops. Tobacco is cultivated in the eastern part of this division. Kentucky is one of the leading states in the Union in tobacco production. Sugar beets are grown in ten states in this group; Nebraska, Michigan, and Minnesota lead in sugar beet production. Flax is grown in the northwest. No other section of equal area on the globe rivals the central Mississippi valley in agricultural productiveness. Even on the higher western plains, abundant harvests are reaped wherever the land is irrigated.

Live Stock. Cattle, horses, mules, and hogs (fattened on corn) are raised in immense numbers. Sheep are reared in every state, and the annual wool clip totals about one-third of that of the entire United States. Dairy interests, already very large, are becoming increasingly valuable. Butter, cheese, and condensed milk from this division now go to all parts of the civilized world. Poultry farming is a profitable occupation.

Manufacturing. The range in manufacturing is exceedingly extensive. In several states the manufactures surpass in value the farm products. More automobiles are made in this division than in all the rest of the world. Meat packing is so vast an industry that it influences prices in every city in the United States. Much of the world's supply of flour is milled in these states.

The iron and steel interests, concentrated in centers of industry in northern Ohio, Indiana, and Illinois, employ many thousands of workers. The yearly output of refined petroleum represents many millions of dollars. Glass, furniture, wearing apparel, foundry and machine shop products, pottery, lumber, agricultural implements, tobacco goods, chemicals, metal wares, farm machinery, boots and shoes, beet sugar, paints and varnishes are other products whose aggregate output is enormous.

Fisheries. The Great Lakes supply annually over 100 million pounds of fish. Whitefish, ciscoes or lake herring, and lake trout constitute the principal catch. The frozen fish industry has become extensive.

Commerce. The states in this division have excellent railway facilities. Within their borders are operated more than 100,000 miles of railways, or about two-fifths of the entire railway mileage of the United States. The Ohio river and the Mississippi river are important arteries of commerce. Fleets of steamers, handling an enormous tonnage, ply on the Great Lakes. In connection with the lake traffic, the New York State Barge canal is used to transport various raw materials to the Hudson river, which serves as the final link in an all-water connection with the seaboard. But by far the larger part of the foreign shipments reach the great eastern seaports, New York, Boston, Philadelphia, and Baltimore, by railroad.

SOUTHERN STATES

Alabama, Arkansas, Florida, Georgia, Louisiana, Mississippi, North Carolina, Oklahoma, South Carolina, Tennessee, and Texas comprise the Southern states.

This division of the Union is bounded on the north by the Middle Atlantic states and by the Central states; on the east by the Atlantic Ocean; on the south by the Gulf of Mexico and Mexico; and on the west by New Mexico. The shortest distance between the extreme eastern and western limits is about 1700 miles. The width from north to south varies from about 425 to 850 miles. The total area of these eleven states is 781,657 square miles, or more than one-fourth of the area of the continental United States. For convenience of reference this division is treated in two sections—an eastern section and a western.

EASTERN SECTION

North Carolina, South Carolina, Tennessee, Georgia, Florida, Alabama, and Mississippi constitute the eastern section of the Southern states.

Surface. The Appalachian Mountain system, occupying much of this section and broadening out in the north, reaches its highest point in Mt. Mitchell, 6684 feet high, in North Carolina. Southward the mountains diminish in height until, in Alabama, they become low hills. All Florida and Mississippi, and parts of North Carolina, South Carolina, Georgia, and Alabama, are in the coastal plain. The principal rivers, including the Mississippi, Savannah, Saint John's, and Cape Fear, are navigable for steamers.

Climate and Rainfall. Along the Gulf coast, a region of heavy rains, the temperature averages about 85° F. in summer and 50° F. in winter. On the Atlantic shore, the climate is almost as warm, though not so humid. The climate of the upland districts is cool and bracing. Flowers bloom the year round in the more southern section, and the mildness of the climate draws numerous visitors to the winter resorts along both the Atlantic and the Gulf coast. From 40 inches to 60 inches of rain a year falls in the seaboard districts.

Minerals. Coal and iron ore are mined in Tennessee and Alabama, and mica in North Carolina. Georgia and Tennessee produce excellent marble. Granite, limestone, and sandstone are abundant. Florida has large deposits of phosphate rock. In all these states there are numerous beds of potter's clay and other minor minerals.

Forests. Forests overspread thousands of square miles, the trees including yellow pine, cypress, hickory, ash, maple, and other hardwoods. In size and variety of species the forest trees of this section exceed those of all other parts of the Union, except the Pacific states. Lumbering is an important industry in many sections.

Agriculture. The chief occupation is farming. All the crops of the Temperate Zone can be grown in these states. Cotton is the most valuable single crop. Sea-island cotton is grown along the Atlantic coast. Millions of acres are devoted to corn and tobacco. Oats, white potatoes, peanuts, sweet potatoes, hay, wheat, and fruits are also widely cultivated. Rice is raised in the coast belt. Apples, plums, pears, watermelons, strawberries, peaches, and grapes grow in abundance. Southern Florida produces pineapples, figs, oranges, grapefruit, avocados, guavas, and other subtropical fruits. Garden vegetables are grown extensively for northern markets. Strawberries are shipped north every spring by fast-freight trains. Similarly, oranges, grapefruit, and various vegetables are sent in winter. Georgia leads in the production of pecans.

Fisheries. Oysters are obtained along the Atlantic shore. Bluefish, mullet, shad, mackerel, kingfish, tarpon, and other sea fish are caught. Valuable fisheries, including sponge fishing, are established on the Florida coast.

Stock Raising. Hogs, horses, mules, sheep, and cattle are raised in every state. Dairying has become an important industry. Milk, butter, and cheese are produced in large quantities.

Manufacturing. Manufacturing is developing rapidly in this section. Among the important industrial products are cotton textiles, cottonseed oil, cottonseed cake, lumber, iron and steel, tobacco goods, and naval stores. Cigars and cigarettes are made in great quantities in North Carolina and in Florida. Cotton goods form the leading industrial product. North Carolina leads all other states of the Union in cotton manufacturing. Flour milling and woodworking are valuable industrial interests. Iron and steel products are made in Tennessee and in Alabama. Aluminum is produced in Tennessee and North Carolina. The canning of fruits and vegetables is a growing industry in all these states. In this group, North Carolina, Georgia, and Tennessee lead in manufactures in the order named. Among important industrial centers are Atlanta, Ga., Birmingham, Ala., Winston-Salem, N. C., Memphis, Tenn., and Nashville, Tenn.

Commerce. Much merchandise for export is shipped down the Mississippi to New Orleans, where it is transferred to seagoing vessels. Portions of other rivers are utilized to some extent as inland waterways. Cotton is the largest export of this section. Pine lumber, phosphate rock, and naval stores are also sent abroad in large quantities. There are ample facilities for transportation by rail to all parts of the Union. The principal seaports serving these states are Wilmington, N. C., Charleston, S. C., Savannah, Ga., Jacksonville, Fla., Tampa, Fla., Pensacola, Fla., Mobile, Ala., and New Orleans, La.

WESTERN SECTION

Arkansas, Louisiana, Texas, and Oklahoma form the western section of the Southern states.

Surface. The northeastern part of this section is included in the Ozark plateau. This upland extends into the northern part of Arkansas and into the eastern part of Oklahoma. Louisiana and southeastern Texas lie in the coastal plain. The elevated western parts of Texas and Oklahoma form the southern extension of the Great Plains. The principal rivers are the Mississippi, Red, Brazos, Sabine, Trinity, and Colorado. All these drain into the Gulf of Mexico.

Climate and Rainfall. An abundant rainfall occurs over the eastern and southern parts of this section, while on the western side, which is mostly an elevated plain, the rainfall seldom exceeds 20 inches annually. The extreme southwest is dry. The summers are long and hot, but the Gulf winds lower the temperature, and winter is a pleasant season.

Agriculture. Agriculture is the chief source of wealth. Rich soil and favorable climate make it possible to grow in this section any crop of the Temperate Zone. Cotton is the principal crop. Other important products are rice, corn, potatoes, sweet potatoes, hay, wheat, tobacco, and numerous fruits. Vegetables are grown in enormous quantities for the northern markets. Louisiana is the leading state in sugar production. Texas is a large producer in several lines of agriculture. It is easily the first state in cotton. Texas also leads all the other states in value of crops produced. These frequently approximate a billion dollars in total value.

Lumbering. There are great forests of pine and cypress in the coastal plain and immense forests of hardwoods in high lands in the interior. This section is one of the chief timber regions of the country. Louisiana is the second state in the Union in lumber production.

Minerals. Sulphur mining is important in Louisiana and Texas. These states now furnish the world's chief supply of sulphur. Bauxite, the most valuable ore of aluminum, is obtained in Arkansas. In Oklahoma, Texas, and Louisiana, immense quantities of petroleum and natural gas are found. The Oklahoma oil field yields a very substantial proportion of the annual output of the petroleum of the United States. Beds of rock salt are worked in both Louisiana and Texas. Oklahoma is one of the leading states of the Union in zinc production and a considerable amount of lead also is obtained there. Manganese, potter's clay, quicksilver, coal, and copper are other valuable minerals obtained in this section. Building stone is abundant in all the states.

Stock Raising. The farm animals reared in this section bring enormous sums annually. Texas is the chief cattle raising state. Mules, horses, hogs, and sheep also are raised in great numbers. Texas ranks as one of the foremost wool producing states. The wool clip of Texas normally exceeds 25 million pounds annually.

Manufacturing. The principal manufactures of this section are petroleum products, lumber, refined sugar, packed meats, flour, cottonseed oil, and cottonseed cake. The manufacture of ice is a growing industry. Louisiana leads the group in the refining of cane sugar and in rice polishing, rice and sugar cane being distinctive crops of that state. Oklahoma ranks highest in the production of flour. Texas leads in manufactures, and is followed by Louisiana, Oklahoma, and Arkansas in the order named.

Commerce. The eastern part of the section has ample transportation facilities, and the thinly populated western section is crossed by numerous railways. Railroads connect all the commercial centers with the large cities east and north, and the rivers furnish hundreds of miles of waterways navigable for steamboats. The chief seaports are New Orleans, La., and Galveston, Houston, and Port Arthur, Texas. Important inland cities are Little Rock, Ark., Shreveport, La., Oklahoma City and Tulsa, Okla., Dallas, Fort Worth, San Antonio, and El Paso, Texas.

PLATEAU STATES

The Plateau states division of the Union is composed of Arizona, Colorado, Idaho, Montana, Nevada, New Mexico, Utah, and Wyoming. These states cover more than 850,000 square miles, or more than one-fourth of the total area of the United States. Idaho, the smallest state in the group, is larger than all the New England states combined.

Surface. This division embraces most of the region occupied by the Rocky Mountain system in the continental United States. The surface is mainly a series of plateaus surmounted by lofty ranges, which attain their greatest height in Colorado. The mean or average elevation of the Plateau states is approximately 5300 feet, or slightly more than one mile, above sea level. Colorado and Wyoming have the highest average elevation; Montana and Arizona, the lowest. In all of the states there are mountains which rise above 12,000 feet. Peaks more than 13,000 feet high are found in Nevada, New Mexico, Utah, and Wyoming. In Colorado, many summits rise above 14,000 feet.

In geological times, this vast upland was a scene of tremendous volcanic action. There are many extinct volcanoes, and ancient lava beds cover many thousand square miles. The great geysers of Yellowstone park are situated in a volcanic region.

Rivers. The Plateau states are drained chiefly by streams belonging to two great drainage systems, the Gulf and the Pacific. Important rivers whose waters reach the Gulf of Mexico are the Rio Grande, the Arkansas, the Platte, the Yellowstone, and the Missouri. The principal rivers whose waters finally flow into the Pacific are the Colorado, Green, Grand, Snake, and Clark Fork. The Green and the Grand are affluents of the Colorado; the Snake and Clark Fork are tributaries of the Columbia.

The streams of the Great Basin, a very dry region comprising much of western Utah and nearly all of Nevada, usually flow only during the brief rainy season. They either disappear in sandy valleys or discharge their scanty waters into alkaline lakes having no outlet. The Humboldt, the largest river in Nevada, flows nearly across the state from east to west. It empties into the Humboldt and the Carson sinks where its waters evaporate, leaving alkaline deposits. Similarly, the Sevier river, the longest stream in western Utah, flows into the salty Sevier lake. The Weber, the Bear, and the Jordan are small rivers which empty into Great Salt lake.

Climate. Because of a wide range in latitude, great variations in altitude, and marked diversity of surface features, the Plateau states have many varieties of climate. On the highest mountains, arctic conditions prevail. In the elevated plains at the base of the mountains there are severe extremes of heat and cold. In the far southwest are some of the hottest desert areas known.

The widest extremes of temperature are observed on the high plains of Montana, flanking the eastern base of the Rockies. Here temperatures ranging from about 60° below zero in winter to 108° above zero in summer have been noted. In southwestern Arizona, near the Mexican border, summer temperatures of 120° have been recorded, but in winter the thermometer rarely falls below freezing. The climate of the various interior parts of the Plateau states is similar, but with less pronounced extremes.

A noteworthy feature of the climate of the plateau region is the great daily variation in temperature which takes place, especially in summer. No matter how warm the days, the nights are almost invariably cool, even in the hottest deserts.

Strong winds, which prevail in many sections, often exercise a marked influence on the climate. A well-known example is the so-called chinook, a warm wind which, sweeping down the eastern slope of the Rockies and far out on the adjacent plains, sometimes melts heavy snowfalls within a few hours.

Notwithstanding severe extremes, the climate of the Plateau states is dry and invigorating, and, on the whole, unusually salubrious.

Rainfall. On one-fifth of the United States the rainfall is so light that agriculture cannot be successfully carried on without irrigation. Most of the dry area is in this division. Because of scanty rainfall, all these states have tracts of true desert. Thousands of square miles also are covered with alkali deposits. These dreary wastes have often no vegetation whatever. In other sections, the traveler may ride for hours over dusty plains, with yuccas, cactuses, greasewoods, or sagebrushes the only conspicuous plants in sight. These require but very little moisture.

Forests. In all of the Plateau states, forests are found on the slopes of the mountains. The trees are generally pines, spruces, firs, and other conifers. About one-sixth of the total area is more or less wooded. In each state there are large forested districts under government protection. These reserves, some 90 in all, are known as national forests. Their total area, about 140,000 square miles, is greater than that of any state in the group except Montana. Among the Plateau states, Idaho, with over 30,000 square miles of protected woodlands, has the greatest area in national forests. Montana ranks second, with Colorado, Arizona, Wyoming, New Mexico, and Utah following in the order named. Nevada, with reserves of 7780 square miles, ranks last. See *Forests, U. S. National*, page 1308.

Minerals. The Plateau states are exceedingly rich in mineral wealth. Among important mineral productions are gold, silver, copper, coal, petroleum, lead, tungsten, uranium, vanadium, gems, and precious stones. In gold production, Colorado, Utah, and Arizona rank highest in the group. Utah, Montana, and Idaho are the chief producers of silver in the United States. In copper production, Arizona stands first, while Utah and Montana also rank among the most important copper producing states of the Union. Colorado, Wyoming, Utah, and New Mexico have valuable coal deposits. Wyoming contains rich petroleum fields. Colorado is the world's chief source of molybdenum, and Nevada and Colorado stand first in the production of tungsten.

Agriculture. Dry farming is successfully practiced in some districts, but dependence is placed chiefly upon irrigated land. This will grow most of the standard crops of the temperate zones. Wheat, barley, oats, potatoes, and sugar beets are raised. Alfalfa is a highly profitable crop, several harvests being reaped in a year. Truck farm products, as Colorado and Arizona melons, bring high prices in eastern markets. Apple culture has become a valuable pursuit in Montana and Idaho. Peaches are grown in Colorado and Utah. In the southwest, the hot climate fosters the growth of dates, olives, figs, oranges, and other subtropical fruits. Egyptian or long-staple cotton has become a leading crop in Arizona.

Government irrigation work has already reclaimed millions of acres of arid land. Farms of irrigated soil are small, and intensive agriculture is practiced. Improved land in farms comprises about one-twentieth of the total area. Montana has the largest acreage of crop land, Colorado stands second, and Idaho is third.

Stock Raising. For many years, stock raising has been an important industry in this division, and much capital is invested in the rearing of cattle, sheep, and horses. These rank in value in the order named. The annual wool clip of these states amounts to about two-fifths of that of the entire United States. Native grasses afford excellent pasturage, and, in the southern and central parts, farm animals feed in the open all the year round. Large numbers of cattle are sent to Omaha, Kansas City, Chicago, and other meat packing centers, where they are slaughtered, the meat being packed and distributed largely in refrigerator cars.

Manufacturing. Copper, lead, refined ores, flour, beet sugar, butter, condensed milk, dressed meat, canned vegetables, railroad cars, foundry materials, and lumber are the principal industrial products of the Plateau states. Manufacturing to supply local needs is increasing. Immense water power is available for future development. Colorado stands first among these states in value of manufactures; Montana is second, Utah third, and Arizona fourth.

Commerce. Railroads afford ready transportation to all parts of the Union. Several transcontinental lines cross this section, and there are numerous local lines. Mine products, lumber, cattle, cotton, and fruits form the chief items of outgoing shipment. These are sent both to the East and to the West chiefly in exchange for manufactures and other staples which the plateau region does not as yet produce.

PACIFIC STATES

California, Oregon, and Washington constitute the Pacific states.

Surface. No other equal area in the continental United States displays such diversity in surface features as does this division. In its mountain ranges are found the highest peaks, and in its deserts occur the lowest depressions. The rivers plunge down from alpine valleys over the highest known waterfalls. Here also is the only active volcano in the country.

The Sierra Nevada range extends nearly north and south through eastern California and, under the name of the Cascade range, continues northward through Oregon and Washington. Near the Pacific shore, the Coast ranges traverse these states from north to south. Between the Sierra Nevada and the Coast ranges lies the great central valley of California. This is about 50 miles wide and 400 miles long and is remarkably fertile. In the southern part, irrigation is needed for successful farming. Farther north are the Columbia, Willamette, and Puget Sound valleys, all having soil of great fertility.

The extensive region lying east of the Sierra Nevada and the Cascades is mostly a barren desert. An exception is the fertile district situated between the Columbia and Snake rivers. A highland, largely of volcanic origin, known as the Columbia River plateau, occupies much of eastern Oregon and Washington. Parts of California adjacent to Nevada form the western rim of the Great Basin. East of the southernmost extensions of the Sierra Nevada and bordering on Arizona are the Mojave desert and the Colorado desert. On the Pacific side of the Sierra Madre, San Bernardino, and other ranges that form the western borders of these deserts, lies the valley of southern California, a coastal plain of remarkable productiveness under irrigation.

Rivers. The Columbia, which rises in Canada, is the only large navigable river in the Pacific states. Together with its tributaries, the most important of which are the Snake and the Willamette, the Columbia drains the greater part of Oregon and Washington. Next in importance are the Sacramento and the San Joaquin. The lower portions of each of these streams are navigable. These two rivers, with their affluents, drain the great central valley of California. There are numerous smaller streams, many of which are broken by rapids or falls. Some of these furnish hydroelectric power. Numerous streams supply water for mining and for irrigation purposes.

Climate. The great length of this division and its intersection by several mountain ranges result in many varieties of climate. These range from the very wet to the very dry, and from the arctic cold of high mountain tops to the torrid heat of California's southeastern deserts. Owing to the moderating influence of winds from the ocean, a mild climate prevails along the entire Pacific shore. This

RANK OF THE STATES* IN POPULATION, 1800-1940

State	1800	1810	1820	1830	1840	1850	1860	1870	1880	1890	1900	1910	1920	1930	1940
Alabama	..	..	19	15	12	12	13	16	17	17	18	18	18	15	17
Arizona	..	..	..	..	..	..	..	46	44	47	47	46	46	44	44
Arkansas	..	26	26	28	25	26	25	26	25	24	25	25	25	25	24
California	..	..	..	..	..	29	26	24	24	22	21	12	8	6	5
Colorado	..	..	..	..	..	..	38	41	35	31	32	32	33	33	33
Connecticut	8	9	14	16	20	21	24	25	28	29	29	31	29	29	31
Delaware	17	19	22	24	26	30	32	35	38	43	45	47	47	47	47
District of Columbia	19	22	25	25	28	33	35	34	36	40	41	43	42	41	37
Florida	..	..	..	26	27	31	31	33	34	32	33	33	32	31	27
Georgia	12	11	11	10	9	9	11	12	13	12	11	10	12	14	14
Idaho	..	..	..	..	..	..	..	44	46	46	46	45	43	43	43
Illinois	..	24	24	20	14	11	4	4	4	3	3	3	3	3	3
Indiana	21	21	18	13	10	7	6	6	6	8	8	9	11	11	12
Iowa	..	..	..	..	29	27	20	11	10	10	10	15	16	19	20
Kansas	..	..	..	..	..	..	33	29	20	19	22	22	24	24	29
Kentucky	9	7	6	6	6	8	9	8	8	11	12	14	15	17	16
Louisiana	..	18	17	19	19	18	17	21	22	25	23	24	22	22	21
Maine	14	14	12	12	13	16	22	23	27	30	31	34	35	35	35
Maryland	7	8	10	11	15	17	19	20	23	27	26	27	28	28	28
Massachusetts	5	5	7	8	8	6	7	7	7	6	7	6	6	8	8
Michigan	..	25	27	27	23	20	16	13	9	9	9	8	7	7	7
Minnesota	..	..	..	..	..	36	30	28	26	20	19	19	17	18	18
Mississippi	20	20	21	22	17	15	14	18	18	21	20	21	23	23	23
Missouri	..	23	23	21	16	13	8	5	5	5	5	7	9	10	10
Montana	..	..	..	..	..	..	..	43	45	45	43	40	39	39	40
Nebraska	..	..	..	..	..	..	39	36	30	26	27	29	31	32	32
Nevada	..	..	..	..	..	..	41	40	43	49	49	49	49	49	49
New Hampshire	11	16	15	18	22	22	27	31	31	33	37	39	41	42	45
New Jersey	10	12	13	14	18	19	21	17	19	18	16	11	10	9	9
New Mexico	..	..	..	..	..	32	34	37	41	44	44	44	44	45	42
New York	3	2	1	1	1	1	1	1	1	1	1	1	1	1	1
North Carolina	4	4	4	5	7	10	12	14	15	16	15	16	14	12	11
North Dakota	..	..	..	..	..	..	42	45	40	42	40	37	36	38	39
Ohio	18	13	5	4	3	3	3	3	3	4	4	4	4	4	4
Oklahoma	..	..	..	..	..	..	..	..	..	39	30	23	21	21	22
Oregon	..	..	..	..	..	34	36	38	37	38	36	35	34	34	34
Pennsylvania	2	3	3	2	2	2	2	2	2	2	2	2	2	2	2
Rhode Island	16	17	20	23	24	28	29	32	33	36	35	38	38	37	36
South Carolina	6	6	8	9	11	14	18	22	21	23	24	26	26	26	26
South Dakota	..	..	..	..	..	..	..	..	..	35	38	36	37	36	38
Tennessee	15	10	9	7	5	5	10	9	12	13	14	17	19	16	15
Texas	..	..	..	..	..	25	23	19	11	7	6	5	5	5	6
Utah	..	..	..	..	..	35	37	39	39	41	42	41	40	40	41
Vermont	13	15	16	17	21	23	28	30	32	37	39	42	45	46	46
Virginia	1	1	2	3	4	4	5	10	14	15	17	20	20	20	19
Washington	..	..	..	..	..	..	40	42	42	34	34	30	30	30	30
West Virginia	..	..	..	..	..	..	..	27	29	28	28	28	27	27	25
Wisconsin	..	..	..	..	30	24	15	15	16	14	13	13	13	13	13
Wyoming	..	..	..	..	..	..	..	47	47	48	48	48	48	48	48

* Including District of Columbia.

coastal climate ranges from subtropical and dry in southern California to temperate and moist in the Puget Sound region.

Rainfall. In western Washington, the rainfall over the valleys averages 65 inches a year and, in the mountain districts, reaches 100 inches. Western Oregon also has a heavy rainfall. But in the eastern sections of both states less than 20 inches of rain falls annually. In parts of the Colorado desert near the Arizona boundary, the average yearly rainfall is less than three inches.

Summer is a dry season in this division, and the winters are wet. In summer, trays of fruits are left outdoors, day and night, to dry, the drying period often lasting several weeks. Abundant rain falls in northern California, but, in the southern part of the state, irrigation is essential for crop raising.

Minerals. Gold was discovered in California in 1848, and since then the state has yielded every year millions of dollars' worth of this precious metal. Though gold is now mined in several other states, California still leads in gold production.

At least 50 other minerals of high commercial value are found in this division. Among them are silver, lead, copper, bismuth, manganese, quicksilver, tungsten, chromium, zinc, magnesite, lithium, and arsenic. The southeastern deserts of California contain immense deposits of borax. Coal of good quality is mined in Washington. Building stone is quarried in all the states. But the most important product is petroleum. California's output of petroleum exceeds in value the yield of all her mines.

Forests. The coniferous forests of the Pacific states are the noblest in the world. In variety of species, in yield of merchantable timber, and in size, age, and beauty of trees, they are unsurpassed. Oregon and western Washington constitute the most important lumber region in the United States.

The heavy rainfall of the coast districts promotes forest growth. West of the Cascades the Douglas fir attains immense size. In dense, nearly pure forests, this tree covers large areas, and furnishes more than half of the available timber. Large spruces, cedars, and hemlocks also abound. East of the Cascades, western yellow pine and sugar pine are valuable timber trees, the former ranking second in importance to the Douglas fir.

The redwood, a magnificent conifer of the northern California coast, supplies excellent building material. Along the western slopes of the Sierra Nevada there are groves of giant sequoias, the most ancient and massive trees known. Many species of broad-leaved or deciduous trees are found, but native hard woods are of minor importance. In the plains districts of California, various species of eucalyptus provide quick timber and shade.

Agriculture and Horticulture. Farming is the chief industry in the Pacific states. Because of wide diversity in soil and climate, a greater variety of agricultural products is grown than in any other equal area in the United States.

In most of the large valleys of Washington, western Oregon, and north central California, sufficient rain falls to insure good harvests. In southern California and in the more arid parts of Oregon and

Washington, irrigation is necessary. Among the principal crops are wheat, barley, oats, hay, alfalfa, potatoes, sugar beets, cotton, rice, beans, corn, and numerous fruits and vegetables. In total value the fruits outrank all the other agricultural products of this division. Next to fruits, wheat is the most important single crop, ranking first in value of all crops in Washington, second in Oregon, and third in California. Among hay and fodder crops, alfalfa leads. Although unsuited to the climate, corn, the great staple of the Central states, is grown to a limited extent.

California's great wheat ranches are disappearing, but intensive agriculture, especially fruit growing in connection with irrigation, is making notable progress. All of the Pacific states are famous for their fruits. Apples grown in the Hood River valley in Oregon and in the Yakima district in Washington command high prices in eastern markets. Along the Willamette river thousands of acres are planted with apple, peach, pear, and plum trees. In western Oregon, loganberry culture is an extensive industry.

California ranks as the foremost fruit producing state in the Union. Contrary to general opinion in the eastern states, most of this state's great fruit harvest consists of the orchard and vineyard fruits of temperate latitudes,—apples, apricots, cherries, grapes, peaches, pears, plums, and prunes. The best varieties of the European grape flourish, and large quantities of grape juice and raisins are produced. The growing of citrous fruits is a large industry in southern California. From its extensive groves thousands of carloads of oranges, lemons, and grapefruit are shipped to the eastern states every year. Almonds, figs, olives, English walnuts, and melons are grown in large quantities. Among less common fruits whose cultivation has been established in California are the avocado, cherimoya, date, and feijoa.

Irrigation. By irrigation many arid areas in the Pacific states have been turned into highly productive lands. A half century ago southern California was mostly a dreary waste. Much that was then desert is now covered with groves of oranges and other fruits, or with fields of grain, alfalfa, melons, or cotton. In no other part of the United States is irrigation so extensively established or devoted to the production of such an immense variety of crops. California leads all the states of the Union in acreage under irrigation and in value of crops produced on irrigated land.

Animal Industry. Large areas in the drier sections are devoted to the raising of cattle and sheep. About one-sixth of the entire wool clip of the United States is produced in the Pacific states. Dairying is a profitable industry. Poultry raising is important, and in some localities, as at Petaluma, California, it has become highly specialized. In the production of honey California usually leads all the other states.

Fisheries. Salmon is the most valuable fish. Puget sound and the Columbia river are the principal salmon fishing grounds. Millions of pounds of salmon are canned every year and exported to all parts of the world. Fresh salmon are also shipped in refrigerator cars to all the large cities of the Union. Halibut, tuna, herring, and other valuable food fish are taken along the Pacific coast.

Manufacturing. In the Pacific states, manufacturing ranks second only to agriculture in importance. Among the chief manufactures are lumber, canned fruits, refined petroleum, flour, packed meats, and dairy products. Other important products of manufacture are refined sugar, canned fish, and mining machinery.

Manufacturing has been greatly stimulated by the extensive development of hydroelectric power, especially in California and Washington. Particularly since 1910, this factor has been one of rapidly increasing importance in the industry of the Pacific Coast. In southern California many factories use crude petroleum for fuel. Lumber, flour, slaughtering and meat packing, and paper and wood pulp are the leading products of manufacture in Washington; lumber and flour lead in Oregon; and petroleum products, canned fruits, and meat products rank in the order named in California. In total value of manufactures, California stands ninth among the states of the Union.

Commerce. The Pacific states occupy a geographical position of great commercial advantage. They have fine harbors on the Pacific Ocean and an immense hinterland whose products of farm, forest, and mine are increasing every year. A great trade is carried on through Puget Sound ports. The Panama canal has brought Europe and the Atlantic states much nearer to this division and thereby stimulated its commerce with those older manufacturing parts of the world. Since 1910 the trade of the Pacific states with China, Japan, the Philippines, Hawaii, New Zealand, Australia, and South America has made a marked gain.

TWENTY-FIVE LARGEST CITIES OF THE UNITED STATES

With Statistics Showing Growth 1840-1940

City and Rank	Population 1840	Population 1860	Population 1880	Population 1900	Population 1910	Population 1920	Population 1930	Population 1940
1. New York, N. Y.*	391,114	1,174,779	1,911,698	3,437,202	4,766,883	5,620,048	6,930,446	7,454,995
2. Chicago, Ill.	4,470	109,260	503,185	1,698,575	2,185,283	2,701,705	3,376,438	3,396,808
3. Philadelphia, Pa.	93,665	565,529	847,170	1,293,697	1,549,008	1,823,779	1,950,961	1,931,334
4. Detroit, Mich.	9,102	45,619	116,340	285,704	465,766	993,678	1,568,662	1,623,452
5. Los Angeles, Cal.	....	4,385	11,183	102,479	319,198	576,673	1,238,048	1,504,277
6. Cleveland, Ohio	6,071	43,417	160,146	381,768	560,663	796,841	900,429	878,336
7. Baltimore, Md.	102,313	212,418	332,313	508,957	558,485	733,826	804,874	859,100
8. St. Louis, Mo.	16,469	160,773	350,518	575,238	687,029	772,897	821,960	816,048
9. Boston, Mass.	93,383	177,840	362,839	560,892	670,585	748,060	781,188	770,816
10. Pittsburgh, Pa.	31,204	77,923	235,071	451,512	533,905	588,343	669,817	671,659
11. Washington, D. C.	23,364	61,122	177,624	278,718	331,069	437,571	486,869	663,091
12. San Francisco, Cal.	....	56,802	233,959	342,782	416,912	506,676	634,394	634,536
13. Milwaukee, Wis.	1,712	45,246	115,587	285,315	373,857	457,147	578,249	587,472
14. Buffalo, N. Y.	18,213	81,129	155,134	352,387	423,715	506,775	573,076	575,901
15. New Orleans, La.	102,193	168,675	216,090	287,104	339,075	387,219	458,762	494,537
16. Minneapolis, Minn.	....	2,564	46,887	202,718	301,408	380,582	464,356	492,370
17. Cincinnati, Ohio	46,338	161,044	255,139	325,902	363,591	401,247	451,160	455,610
18. Newark, N. J.	17,290	71,941	136,508	246,070	347,469	414,524	442,337	429,760
19. Kansas City, Mo.	....	4,418	55,785	163,752	248,381	324,410	399,746	399,178
20. Indianapolis, Ind.	2,692	18,611	75,056	169,164	233,650	314,194	364,161	386,972
21. Houston, Texas	....	4,845	16,513	44,633	78,800	138,276	292,352	384,514
22. Seattle, Wash.	....	....	3,533	80,671	237,194	315,312	365,583	368,302
23. Rochester, N. Y.	20,191	48,204	89,366	162,608	218,149	295,750	328,132	324,975
24. Denver, Colo.	....	....	35,629	133,859	213,381	256,491	287,861	322,412
25. Louisville, Ky.	....	68,033	123,758	204,731	223,928	234,891	307,745	319,077

*Population of the city as now constituted.

GROWTH OF THE

In Area, Population, Wealth, Agriculture, Com-

Item	1840	1850	1860	1870	1880
Area, Population, Wealth, and Debt:					
Area . . . . Sq. mi.	1,792,223	2,997,119	3,026,789	3,026,789	3,026,789
Population	17,069,453	23,191,876	31,443,321	38,558,371	50,155,783
Wealth . . . . $	....	7,135,780,000	16,159,616,000	30,068,518,000	43,642,000,000
Wealth per capita . . . . $	....	307.69	513.93	779.83	870.20
Debt, national . . . . $	3,573,343	63,452,773	59,964,402	2,331,169,956	1,919,326,747
Debt, per capita . . . . $	.21	2.74	1.91	60.46	38.27
Interest on debt . . . . $	174,598	3,782,393	3,443,687	118,784,960	79,633,981
Agriculture:					
Farms, number of	....	1,449,073	2,044,077	2,659,985	4,008,907
Persons engaged in agriculture . . . No.	....	....	....	5,922,471	7,713,875
Value farms and farm property . . . . $	....	3,967,343,580	7,980,493,063	8,944,857,749	12,180,501,538
Value farm products . . . . $	....	....	....	1,958,030,927	2,212,540,927
Wheat produced . . . . bu.	84,823,272	100,485,943	173,104,924	235,884,700	498,549,868
Corn produced . . . . bu.	377,531,875	592,071,104	838,792,740	1,094,255,000	1,717,434,543
Cotton produced . . . . . . 500 lb. bales	1,347,640	2,136,083	3,841,416	4,024,527	6,356,998
Sugar (cane) produced . . . . lbs.	120,851,074	247,577,000	230,982,000	87,043,000	178,872,000
Sugar (beet) produced . . . . lbs.				806,000	2,688,000
Farm animals, value . . . . $	....	544,180,516	1,089,329,915	1,518,465,000	1,576,917,556
Wool produced . . . . lbs.	35,802,114	52,516,959	60,264,913	162,000,000	232,500,000
Mineral Production:					
Gold, value of . . . . $	11,697,829	50,000,000	46,000,000	50,000,000	36,000,000
Silver, value of . . . . $	252,300	50,900	156,800	16,434,000	34,717,000
Coal . . . . tons	1,848,249	6,266,233	13,044,680	29,496,054	63,822,830
Petroleum . . . . gals.			21,000,000	220,951,290	1,104,017,166
Iron ore . . . . tons	....	....	....	3,031,891	7,120,362
Pig iron . . . . tons	286,903	563,755	821,223	1,665,179	3,835,191
Steel . . . . tons	....	....	....	68,750	1,247,335
Copper . . . . tons	100	650	7,200	12,600	27,000
Total minerals . . . . $	....	....	....	218,598,994	364,928,298
Manufactures:					
Establishments . . . . No.	....	123,025	140,433		253,852
Officials, clerks . . . . No.	....	....	....	....	....
Salaries paid . . . . $	....	....	....	....	....
Wage earners . . . . No.	....	957,059	1,311,246	....	2,732,595
Wages paid . . . . $	....	236,755,464	378,878,966	....	947,953,795
Cost of materials . . . . $	....	555,123,822	1,031,605,092	....	3,396,823,549
Products, value of . . . . $	....	1,019,106,616	1,885,861,676	....	5,369,579,191
Iron and steel manufactures . . . . . . $	....	....	....	....	296,557,685
Cotton manufactures . . . . $	46,350,453	61,869,184	115,681,774	....	192,090,110
Wool manufactures . . . . $	....	48,608,779	73,454,000	....	238,085,686
Electricity generated 1000 kilowatt hours					
Radios manufactured, value . . . . . . $					
Rayon manufactured, value . . . . . . $					
Transportation:					
Vessels built . . . . tons	121,203	279,255	214,797	276,953	157,409
Vessels, foreign trade . . . . tons	899,765	1,585,711	2,546,237	1,516,800	1,352,810
Vessels, coastwise trade . . . . . . tons	1,280,999	1,949,743	2,807,631	2,729,707	2,715,224
Vessels, Great Lakes trade . . . . . tons	54,199	198,266	467,774	684,704	605,102
Railways . . . . miles	2,818	9,021	30,626	52,922	93,262
Electric railways . . . . miles					

* The information herein given has been derived from the Statistical Abstract of the United States and other authoritative sources. For various items satisfactory statistics covering some dates are unavailable. In such cases the spaces are marked with leaders, thus..... In other cases, such as petroleum, the telephone, or beet sugar, in which the subject in question had not yet been discovered, invented, or brought to substantial production or use, the space corresponding to the date is left blank. The statistics of manufactures from 1880 to 1940, inclusive, are those of the Federal census, but, in each case, the figures are those of the preceding year, 1879, 1889, 1899, 1909, 1919, 1929, and 1939. The same applies to agricultural production.

UNITED STATES, 1840-1940

merce, Industry, and Important Productions*

1890	1900	1910	1920	1930	1940
3,026,789	3,026,789	3,026,789	3,026,789	3,026,789	3,022,387
62,947,714	75,994,575	91,972,266	105,710,620	122,775,046	131.669.275
65,037,091,000	88,517,307,000	187,739,071,090 (*a*)	290,000,000,000 (*b*)	320,840,000,000 (*j*)	365,000,000,000(*o*)
1,035.57	1,164.79	1,965.00 (*a*)	2,689.34 (*b*)	2,919 (*j*)	2,862(*o*)
890,784,370	1,107,711,257	1,046,449,185	24,330,889,731	16,185,310,000	42,967,513,037
14.13	14.55	11.34	228.64	131.83	325.19
29,417,603	33,545,130	21,275,602	1,016,592,219	659,347,613	1,040,935,697
4,564,641	5,737,372	6,361,502	6,448,343	6,288,648	6,096,799
8,565,926	10,381,765	12,659,203	10,661,410	10,482,323	9,162,547
16,082,267,689	20,439,901,164	40,991,449,090	77,924,100,338	57,245,544,269	33,641,738,726
2,460,107,454	4,717,069,973	8,498,311,413	21,425,623,614	11,387,396,953	9,583,000,000
399,262,000	522,229,505	635,121,000	833,027,000	806,648,955	816,698,000
1,489,970,000	2,105,102,516	2,886,260,000	3,208,584,000	2,130,751,782	2,449,200,000
8,562,089	10,123,027	11,608,616	13,439,603	14,574,405	12,686,000
301,284,395	322,549,011	750,400,000	241,998,400	399,218,000	1,008,000,000
4,934,720	163,458,075	1,024,938,000	1,452,902,000	2,036,000,000	3,516,000,000
2,418,766,028	2,228,123,134	5,138,486,000	8,165,194,000	6,064,051,430	5,181,951,000
276,000,000	288,636,621	321,362,750	277,905,000	336,007,000	449,800,000
32,845,000	79,171,000	96,269,100	51,186,900	47,247,600	210,108,700
57,242,100	35,741,100	30,854,500	60,801,955	19,538,029	49,483,000
140,866,931	240,789,310	447,853,909	587,331,190	536,911,136	504,729,640
1,924,590,024	2,672,062,218	8,801,404,416	18,622,884,000	37,643,130,000	56,777,574,000
16,036,043	27,553,161	56,889,734	69,558,000	58,408,664	75,198,084
9,202,703	13,789,242	27,303,567	36,925,987	31,752,169	41,927,645
4,277,071	10,188,329	26,094,919	42,132,934	40,699,483	66,983,000
115,966	270,588	482,214	539,759	697,195	909,084
606,476,380	1,107,031,392	1,991,216,220	6,707,000,000	4,764,800,000	5,582,500,000
355,405	207,514	268,491	290,105	210,710	184,230
461,001	364,120	790,267	1,447,227	1,377,760	1,048,607
391,984,660	380,771,321	938,574,967	2,892,371,494	3,579,624,574	2,540,357,370
4,251,535	4,712,763	6,615,046	9,096,372	8,807,536	7,886,567
1,891,209,696	2,008,361,119	3,427,037,884	10,533,600,340	11,649,536,855	9,089,940,916
5,162,013,878	6,575,851,491	12,142,790,878	37,376,380,283	38,293,533,500	32,160,106,681
9,372,378,843	11,406,926,701	20,672,051,870	62,418,078,773	70,137,459,352	56,843,024,800
478,687,519	803,968,273	1,377,151,817	3,623,368,934	7,138,007,000	4,779,866,341
267,981,724	339,200,320	628,391,813	2,195,565,881	1,524,177,000	1,168,171,469
270,527,511	296,990,484	507,166,710	1,234,657,092	827,006,000	711,580,350
	4,768,000(*c*)	17,572,000 (*d*)	43,555,900	95,936,000	144,984,565
				411,637,000	275,870,165
				149,546,000 (*l*)	247,065,556
294,122	393,790	342,068	3,880,639	254,296	449,221
946,695	826,694	791,825	9,928,595	6,303,000	3,047,000
3,477,802	4,338,145	6,716,257	6,395,429	9,765,000	10,654,000
1,063,063	1,565,587	2,895,102	3,138,690	2,758,000	1,641,000
163,597	193,346	240,293	252,845	249,052	233,670
5,783	16,645	30,437	47,555	40,722(*k*)	23,770(*n*)

(*a*) 1912. (*b*) Estimate of Prof. David Friday. (*c*) 1902. (*d*) 1912. (*e*) Exclusive of rural delivery routes. (*f*) Includes food animals. (*g*) Includes foodstuffs partly, as well as wholly, manufactured. (*h*) Includes manufactures ready for consumption and manufactures for further use in manufacturing. (*i*) Ordinary disbursements which include disbursements for war, navy, Indians, pensions, payment for interest, and "civil and miscellaneous," but do not include payments for Panama canal, public debt, special purposes, or postal service. (*j*) 1926. (*k*) 1927. (*l*) Includes "allied products," such as cellophane. (*n*) 1937. (*o*) 1938; estimate by National resources planning board.

GROWTH OF THE

In Area, Population, Wealth, Agriculture, Com-

Item	1840	1850	1860	1870	1880
Transportation—Con.					
Automobiles manufactured . . . . . No.					
Automobiles in use . . . . No.					
Aircraft manufactured, value . . . . $					
Communication:					
Post Offices . . . . No.	13,468	18,417	28,498	28,492	42,989
Post Routes (*e*) . . . . miles	155,739	178,672	240,594	231,232	343,888
Air Mail Routes . . . . miles					
Telegraphs . . . . miles of line		....	....	....	85,645
Telephones . . . . No. stations					47,880
Commerce:					
Imports, merchandise, total . . . . . . $	98,258,706	173,509,526	353,616,119	435,958,408	667,954,746
Imports, free . . . . $	48,313,391	18,081,590	73,741,479	20,140,786	208,301,863
Imports, dutiable . . . . $	49,945,315	155,427,936	279,874,640	415,817,622	459,652,883
Imports, per cent free	49.17	10.42	20.85	4.62	31.19
Imports, per capita . . . . $	5.76	7.48	11.25	11.06	12.51
Imports, agricultural . . . . $	....	....	129,816,165	191,559,361	314,617,480
Imports, foodstuffs (crude) (*f*) . . . . . $	15,273,321	18,011,659	45,743,826	54,081,091	100,297,040
Imports, foodstuffs (manufactured) (*g*) . $	15,188,845	21,465,776	59,837,674	96,081,635	118,125,216
Imports, raw material for manufacturing. $	11,510,245	11,711,266	39,691,797	55,615,202	131,861,617
Imports, manufactures (*h*) . . . . $	55,659,201	121,475,651	207,028,294	229,183,959	307,366,921
Imports, sugar . . . . lbs.	120,940,747	218,430,764	694,838,197	1,196,773,569	1,829,291,684
Imports, coffee . . . . lbs.	94,996,095	145,272,687	202,144,733	235,256,574	446,850,727
Imports, tea . . . . lbs.	20,006,595	29,872,654	31,696,657	47,408,481	72,162,936
Imports, wool (raw) . . . . lbs.	9,898,740	18,695,294	26,282,955	49,230,199	128,131,747
Imports, cotton (raw) . . . . lbs.	2,774,722	269,114	2,005,529	1,698,133	3,547,792
Imports, raw silk . . . . lbs.				583,589	2,562,236
Imports, rubber (crude) . . . . lbs.				9,624,098	16,826,099
Exports, domestic, total . . . . $	111,660,561	134,900,233	316,242,423	376,616,473	823,946,353
Exports, agricultural . . . . $	....	....	260,280,413	296,962,357	694,315,497
Exports, foodstuffs (crude) (*f*) . . . . . $	4,564,532	7,535,764	12,166,447	41,852,630	266,108,950
Exports, foodstuffs (manufactured) (*g*) . $	15,936,108	20,017,162	38,624,949	50,919,666	193,352,723
Exports, raw materials for manufacturing $	75,488,421	83,984,707	216,009,648	213,439,991	238,787,934
Exports, manufactures (*h*) . . . . . . $	15,425,180	23,223,106	48,453,008	70,040,845	121,818,298
Exports, iron and steel manufactures . . $	1,127,877	1,953,702	5,870,114	13,483,163	14,716,524
Exports, automobiles . . . . $					
Exports, meat and meat products . . . $	....	....	14,224,412	21,396,050	113,769,604
Exports, wheat . . . . $	1,635,483	643,745	4,076,704	47,171,229	190,546,305
Exports, wheat flour . . . . $	10,143,615	7,098,570	15,448,507	21,169,593	35,333,197
Exports, cotton, quantity . . . . . . lbs.	743,941,061	635,381,604	1,767,686,338	958,558,523	1,822,061,114
Exports, cotton, value . . . . $	63,870,307	71,984,616	191,806,555	227,027,624	211,535,905
Finance:					
Money in circulation . . . . $	186,305,488	278,761,982	435,407,252	676,284,427	973,382,228
Circulation per capita . . . . $	10.91	12.02	13.85	17.51	19.41
Government receipts . . . . $	19,480,115	43,592,889	56,054,600	395,959,834	333,526,501
Receipts per capita . . . . $	1.14	1.88	1.78	10.26	6.65
Customs . . . . $	13,499,502	39,668,686	53,187,512	194,538,374	186,522,065
Internal Revenue . . . . $	1,682			184,899,756	124,009,374
Government disbursements (*i*) . . . . . $	24,314,518	40,948,383	63,200,876	293,657,005	264,847,637
Disbursements per capita . . . . $	1.42	1.77	2.01	7.61	5.28
Disbursements, war . . . . $	7,095,267	9,687,025	16,472,203	57,655,675	38,116,916
Disbursements, navy . . . . $	6,113,897	7,904,725	11,514,650	21,780,230	13,536,985
Pensions paid . . . . $	2,603,562	1,866,886	1,100,802	28,340,202	56,777,174
Pensioners . . . . No.				198,686	250,802

* The information herein given has been derived from the Statistical Abstract of the United States and other authoritative sources. For various items satisfactory statistics covering some dates are unavailable. In such cases the spaces are marked with leaders, thus. . . . . In other cases, such as petroleum, the telephone, or beet sugar, in which the subject in question had not yet been discovered, invented, or brought to substantial production or use, the space corresponding to the date is left blank. The statistics of manufactures from 1880 to 1940, inclusive, are those of the Federal census, but, in each case, the figures are those of the preceding year, 1879, 1889, 1899, 1909, 1919, 1929. The same applies to agricultural production.

UNITED STATES, 1840-1940—Con.

merce, Industry, and Important Productions*

1890	1900	1910	1920	1930	1940
	3,700 (c)	127,731 (d)	1,974,016	4,587,400	3,692,328
	5,000	501,000	9,231,941	23,121,589	32,025,365
				72,019,000	550,000,000
62,401	76,688	59,580	52,638	49,063	44,095
427,990	500,990	447,998	435,342	503,918	541,514
			3,094	14,907	37,943
183,917	192,705	214,360	246,214	256,809(k)	250,880(n)
227,857	1,355,911	7,635,367	13,329,379	20,201,576	20,830,950
789,310,409	849,941,184	1,556,947,430	5,238,352,114	3,060,908,000	2,625,445,000
265,668,629	367,236,866	755,311,396	3,405,233,003	2,051,110,000	1,648,285,000
523,641,780	482,704,318	801,636,034	1,833,119,111	1,009,798,000	892,004,000
33.66	43.21	48.51	65.01	67.0	65
12.14	10.91	16.52	47.22	24.90	19.93
384,100,435	420,139,288	87,509,115	3,011,368,157	1,899,521,000	1,285,300,000
128,480,142	97,916,293	144,776,636	577,626,948	400,125,000	285,112,000
133,332,031	133,027,374	181,566,572	1,238,138,941	293,448,000	277,444,000
170,637,250	276,241,152	566,270,770	1,751,893,014	1,002,161,000	1,010,394,000
347,609,661	337,348,386	652,861,740	1,679,228,466	1,365,175,000	967,339,000
2,934,011,560	4,018,086,530	4,094,545,936	8,073,759,849	6,989,319,000	5,829,080,000
499,159,120	787,991,911	873,983,689	1,417,063,513	1,599,317,000	2,055,065,000
83,886,829	84,845,107	85,626,370	97,826,106	84,926,000	98,963,000
105,431,285	155,928,455	263,928,232	259,617,641	163,734,000	360,637,000
8,606,049	67,398,521	86,037,691	299,994,378	128,373,000	131,780,000
7,510,440	13,073,718	23,457,223	30,058,374	81,993,000	47,600,000
33,842,374	49,377,138	101,044,681	566,546,136	1,089,830,000	1,824,722,000
845,293,828	1,370,763,571	1,710,083,998	8,080,480,821	3,843,181,000	4,021,564,000
634,855,869	844,616,530	871,158,425	3,466,619,819	1,495,823,000	516,856,000
132,073,183	225,906,246	109,828,320	917,990,828	178,533,000	74,019,000
224,756,580	319,696,334	259,259,654	1,116,605,173	362,650,000	166,881,000
304,566,922	325,244,296	565,934,957	1,870,767,054	829,098,000	456,078,000
178,982,042	485,022,156	766,981,245	4,163,354,637	1,898,089,000	3,237,687,000
25,542,208	121,913,548	179,133,186	1,112,835,237	1,186,827,000	515,595,000
				314,536,000	254,322,000
123,880,422	175,226,535	128,382,362	463,256,758	186,563,000	35,900,000
45,275,906	73,237,080	47,806,598	596,975,396	88,093,000	11,209,000
57,036,168	67,760,886	47,621,467	224,472,448	69,401,000	20,400,000
2,471,799,853	3,100,583,188	3,206,708,226	3,179,313,336	3,492,234,000	2,046,310,000
250,968,792	241,832,737	450,447,243	1,136,408,916	496,798,000	213,400,000
1,429,251,270	2,055,150,997	3,102,355,605	5,467,600,000	4,521,987,962	7,847,500,588
22.82	26.93	34.33	51.32	36.71	59.39
403,080,983	567,240,852	675,511,715	6,704,414,438	4,177,941,702	5,924,836,402
6.43	7.43	7.48	63.00	34.47	44.09
229,668,585	233,164,871	333,683,445	323,536,559	587,000,903	348,590,635
142,606,706	295,327,927	289,933,519	5,399,149,245	3,039,295,013	5,340,452,346
297,736,487	487,713,792	659,705,391	6,141,745,240	3,994,152,487	9,666,085,539
4.75	6.39	7.30	57.72	32.96	73.16
44,582,838	134,774,768	155,911,706	1,094,834,202	453,524,973	667,100,000
22,006,206	55,953,078	123,173,717	629,893,116	374,165,639	891,600,000
106,936,855	140,877,316	160,696,416	213,344,204	418,433,000	556,700,000
537,944	993,529	921,083	592,190	451,433	600,848

(a) 1912. (b) Estimate of Prof. David Friday. (c) 1902. (d) 1912. (e) Exclusive of rural delivery routes. (f) Includes food animals. (g) Includes foodstuffs partly, as well as wholly, manufactured. (h) Includes manufactures ready for consumption and manufactures for further use in manufacturing. (i) Ordinary disbursements which include disbursements for war, navy, Indians, pensions, payment for interest, and "civil and miscellaneous," but do not include payments for Panama canal, public debt, special purposes, or postal service. (j) 1926. (k) 1927. (l) Includes "allied products," such as cellophane. (n) 1937.

TRAVEL DISTANCES BETWEEN IMPORTANT CENTERS IN THE UNITED STATES

	Atlanta, Ga.	Baltimore, Md.	Boston, Mass.	Buffalo, N. Y.	Chicago, Ill.	Cincinnati, O.	Cleveland, O.	Denver, Colo.	Detroit, Mich.	Galveston, Tex.	*Havana, Cuba via Tampa	*Honolulu, H. I. via San Francisco	Indianapolis, Ind.	Jacksonville, Fla.	Kansas City, Mo.	Little Rock, Ark.	Los Angeles, Cal.	*Manila, Ph. Is. via San Fran. and Honolulu	Minneapolis, Minn.	Nashville, Tenn.	New Orleans, La.	New York, N. Y.	Omaha, Neb.	Philadelphia, Pa.	Pittsburgh, Pa.	Portland, Me.	Portland, Ore.	Saint Louis, Mo.	*Salt Lake City, Utah	San Francisco, Cal.	*San Juan, P. R. via New York or Tampa	Seattle, Wash.	*Sitka, Alaska via Seattle	Washington, D. C.
Atlanta, Ga.		689	1108	933	733	488	750	1529	748	912	921	4846	598	331	889	551	2496	10786	1141	288	493	876	1025	784	799	1217	2810	611	2052	2808	2275	2939	4057	649
Baltimore, Md.	689		419	396	797	593	446	1831	617	1577	1610	5134	703	795	1210	1104	2990	9901	1205	811	1158	187	1285	95	314	528	3050	932	2297	3068	1586	2995	4345	40
Boston, Mass.	1108	419		498	1033	943	681	2067	750	1996	1800	5363	965	1214	1484	1566	3264	11281	1441	1243	1577	232	1521	324	673	109	3286	1217	2526	3304	1628	3231	4129	459
Buffalo, N. Y.	933	396	498		525	445	183	1559	252	1583	1802	4865	467	1191	969	1068	2749	10783	933	745	1281	396	1013	416	272	607	2778	719	2028	2796	1795	2723	3631	436
Chicago, Ill.	733	797	1033	525		285	357	1034	272	1148	1621	4352	184	1088	451	633	2231	10258	408	445	930	909	488	817	468	1142	2253	284	1515	2271	2208	2198	3118	787
Cincinnati, O.	488	593	943	445	285		262	1257	260	1157	1408	4582	110	822	617	627	2397	10473	693	300	836	751	773	660	311	1052	2538	339	1745	2556	2149	2483	3402	553
Cleveland, O.	750	446	681	183	357	262		1391	171	1400	1671	4691	284	1084	757	885	2537	10592	765	562	1098	579	845	487	135	790	2610	536	1854	2628	1970	2555	3457	437
Denver, Colo.	1529	1831	2067	1559	1034	1257	1391		1306	1146	2447	3531	1159	1869	636	1094	1422	8298	919	1241	1349	1943	538	1851	1502	2176	1376	918	620	1374	3334	1559	2399	1810
Detroit, Mich.	748	617	750	252	272	260	171	1306		1352	1680	4624	276	1082	715	837	2495	10525	680	560	1096	648	760	668	318	859	2525	488	1787	2543	2036	2470	3390	608
Galveston, Tex.	912	1577	1996	1583	1148	1157	1400	1146	1352		1104	4255	1105	1031	806	515	1698	9022	1306	895	419	1764	1000	1672	1476	2105	2522	864	1743	2173	3127	2827	3522	1537
*Havana, Cuba via Tampa	921	1610	1800	1802	1621	1408	1671	2447	1680	1104		5319	1469	561	1704	1347	2693	10023	2102	1209	692	1567	2000	1475	1642	1729	3775	1532	2545	3887	978	3611	4043	1340
*Honolulu, H. I. via San Francisco	4846	5134	5363	4865	4352	4582	4691	3531	4624	4255	5319		4471	5179	4060	4328	2564	4767	4221	4713	4564	5261	3864	5169	4820	5501	2863	4278	2911	2418	8751	3050	3982	5122
Indianapolis, Ind.	598	703	965	467	184	110	284	1159	276	1105	1469	4471		932	519	590	2299	10359	592	298	899	812	672	720	371	1074	2437	241	1698	2455	2226	2382	3310	663
Jacksonville, Fla.	331	795	1214	1191	1088	822	1084	1869	1082	1031	561	5179	932		1233	882	2615	9946	1496	643	612	982	1380	890	1057	1323	3165	966	2376	3058	1151	3294	4148	755
Kansas City, Mo.	889	1210	1484	969	451	617	757	636	715	806	1704	4060	519	1233		527	1780	9956	500	601	868	1331	194	1239	890	1593	1979	278	1260	1977	2759	2050	2995	1170
Little Rock, Ark.	551	1104	1566	1068	633	627	885	1094	837	515	1347	4328	590	882	527		1818	10216	937	365	471	1291	721	1199	961	1675	2506	349	1700	2293	2690	2577	3480	1064
Los Angeles, Cal.	2496	2990	3264	2749	2231	2397	2537	1422	2495	1698	2693	2564	2299	2615	1780	1818		7331	2202	2198	2003	3111	1821	3019	2670	3373	1129	2058	784	475	4463	1312	2273	2950
*Manila, Ph. Is. via San Fran. & Honolulu	10786	9901	11281	10783	10258	10473	10592	8298	10525	9022	10023	4767	10359	9946	9956	10216	7331		10076	10601	10465	11073	8631	11075	10726	11389	7630	9045	8799	7893	12565	8936	8160	10951
Minneapolis, Minn.	1141	1205	1441	933	408	693	765	919	680	1306	2102	4221	592	1496	500	937	2202	10076		853	1306	1317	381	1225	876	1550	1815	588	1384	2164	2729	1774	2697	1195
Nashville, Tenn.	288	811	1243	745	445	300	562	1241	560	895	1209	4713	298	643	601	365	2198	10601	853		623	998	737	906	611	1352	2522	323	2065	2520	2349	2651	3583	771
New Orleans, La.	493	1158	1577	1281	930	836	1098	1349	1096	419	692	4564	899	612	868	471	2003	10465	1306	623		1345	1062	1253	1147	1686	2725	718	1950	2446	1566	2918	3729	1118
New York, N. Y.	876	187	232	396	909	751	579	1943	648	1764	1567	5261	812	982	1331	1291	3111	11073	1317	998	1345		1397	92	441	341	3162	1053	2434	3180	1559	3107	4027	227
Omaha, Neb.	1025	1285	1521	1013	488	773	845	538	760	1000	2000	3864	672	1380	194	721	1821	8631	381	737	1062	1397		1305	956	1630	1785	414	1027	1783	2796	1909	2799	1275
Philadelphia, Pa.	784	95	324	416	817	660	487	1851	668	1672	1475	5169	720	890	1239	1199	3019	11075	1225	906	1253	92	1305		349	433	3070	961	2332	3088	1490	3015	3935	135
Pittsburgh, Pa.	799	314	673	272	468	311	135	1502	318	1476	1642	4820	371	1057	890	961	2670	10726	876	611	1147	441	956	349		782	2721	612	1983	2739	1839	2666	3586	302
Portland, Me.	1217	528	109	607	1142	1052	790	2176	859	2105	1729	5501	1074	1323	1593	1675	3373	11389	1550	1352	1686	341	1630	433	782		3395	1326	2765	3413	1740	3340	4257	568
Portland, Ore.	2810	3050	3286	2778	2253	2538	2610	1376	2525	2522	3775	2863	2437	3165	1979	2506	1129	7630	1815	2522	2725	3162	1785	3070	2721	3395		2199	887	772	4571	183	1119	3040
Saint Louis, Mo.	611	932	1217	719	284	339	536	918	488	864	1532	4278	241	966	278	349	2058	9045	588	323	718	1053	414	961	612	1326	2199		1441	2197	2458	2328	3213	892
*Salt Lake City, Utah	2052	2297	2526	2028	1515	1745	1854	620	1787	1743	2545	2911	1698	2376	1260	1700	784	8799	1384	2065	1950	2434	1027	2332	1983	2765	887	1441		820	3823	980	1912	2312
San Francisco, Cal.	2808	3068	3304	2796	2271	2556	2628	1374	2543	2173	3887	2418	2455	3058	1977	2293	475	7893	2164	2520	2446	3180	1783	3088	2739	3413	772	2197	820		6660	955	1302	3058
*San Juan, P. R. via New York or Tampa	2275	1586	1628	1795	2208	2149	1970	3334	2036	3127	978	8751	2226	1151	2759	2690	4463	12565	2729	2349	1566	1559	2796	1490	1839	1740	4571	2458	3823	6660		4494	5426	1626
Seattle, Wash.	2939	2995	3231	2723	2198	2483	2555	1559	2470	2827	3611	3050	2382	3294	2050	2577	1312	8936	1774	2651	2918	3107	1909	3015	2666	3340	183	2328	980	955	4494		932	2985
*Sitka, Alaska via Seattle	4057	4345	4129	3631	3118	3402	3457	2399	3390	3522	4043	3982	3310	4148	2995	3480	2273	8160	2697	3583	3729	4027	2799	3935	3586	4257	1119	3213	1912	1302	5426	932		3888
Washington, D. C.	649	40	459	436	787	553	437	1810	608	1537	1340	5122	663	755	1170	1064	2950	10951	1195	771	1118	227	1275	135	302	568	3040	892	2312	3058	1626	2985	3888	

The figures in this table are taken from "Official Table of Distances" used by the War Department of the U. S. Government, except the distance to cities marked with an asterisk (*), which are computed along the best routes of travel. All distances are in STATUTE MILES.

UNITED STATES DEPENDENCIES

Beginning with the purchase of Alaska in 1867, the United States has come into control of a considerable number of dependencies. Named in the order of their acquisition, they are as follows: Alaska, Midway islands, Hawaiian islands, Guam, Palmyra, Puerto Rico, Philippine Islands, American Samoa, the Canal Zone, and Virgin islands. Midway islands and Palmyra have been incorporated with the Hawaiian islands to form the territory of Hawaii. The official designation of "territory" has been given also to Alaska. The Canal Zone will be found treated under *Panama Canal Zone.*

In 1946 the Philippine Islands were given their independence, thus reducing the dependencies by 114,400 square miles to 601,600 square miles and by 10,350,730 population to about 1,600,000 population. However, many small Pacific islands formerly held by Japan are now being held by the United States in trust as a result of World War II pending official action of the United Nations.

The American dependencies all lie in or near the tropics, with the exception of Alaska, a large part of which falls within the Arctic circle. The total area of these dependencies is about 716,000 square miles, and the total population is nearly 12 million. For historical data, see *Historical Growth of the United States*, page 372.

LENGTH OF COAST LINE OF UNITED STATES DEPENDENCIES

DEPENDENCY	Mainland	Islands	Total
Alaska	6,542 *	8,590 *	15,132 *
Guam	...	...	84 *
Hawaiian Islands .	...	...	810 *
Panama Canal Zone	29	4	33
Puerto Rico . . .	...	...	362
U. S. Samoan Islands	...	...	91 *
Virgin Islands . .	...	...	163 *
Total	6,571	8,594	16,675

* Tidal shore line, unit measure 3 statute miles.

ALASKA

The largest territorial possession of the United States, situated in the extreme northwestern part of North America. All of Alaska lies to the north and to the west of the United States. Its northernmost point is about 1450 miles farther north than its southernmost point. From its easternmost point to its westernmost point, Alaska extends through a distance greater than that from New York to San Francisco.

Area and Location. Alaska embraces three distinct regions—the main territory, the panhandle, or southeastern Alaska, and the Aleutian islands.

The main territory comprises all of continental North America lying west of the 141st meridian of west longitude. It is bounded on the east by Canada, on the north by the Arctic Ocean, on the west by the Arctic Ocean, Bering strait, and Bering Sea, and on the south by the Pacific Ocean and the Gulf of Alaska. The panhandle of southeastern Alaska consists of a narrow fringe of mainland and various islands along the coast, between British Columbia and the Pacific Ocean, extending from Cape Muzon and the Portland canal, at the extreme south, northward to Mount Saint Elias, where the panhandle joins the main territory.

The Aleutian islands extend westward from the southwestern part of the main territory, as far as, and including, Attu, off the coast of Asia. Various islands in Bering Sea near the American mainland, including the Pribilof and the Saint Lawrence islands, also belong to Alaska.

The area of Alaska, about 590,000 square miles, is nearly one-fifth that of the continental United States, or about one-third larger than all of the Atlantic states from Maine to Florida.

Surface. There are four distinct natural surface divisions in the mainland of Alaska. From south to north, these are the Pacific Mountain system, the Central Plateau region, the Rocky Mountain system, and the Arctic Slope region.

The Pacific Mountain system comprises the Coast, the Mount Saint Elias, the Aleutian, and the Alaska ranges. These form great barrier walls along and near the southern shores. This rugged highland contains the loftiest mountains of the continent, culminating in Mount McKinley, in the Alaska range, the highest peak in North America.

East and north of these majestic ranges is the great central plateau, drained chiefly by the Yukon river. This plateau extends entirely across Alaska from east to west. North of it, the Rocky Mountain system, locally called the Brooks Range, which crosses the international boundary about 100 miles north of the Arctic circle, extends westerly across Alaska nearly to the Arctic Ocean. North of the Rockies is the Arctic Slope, a barren, featureless, coastal plain.

For about 1000 miles southwestward from the Alaska peninsula extends the Aleutian archipelago which consists of about 70 treeless islands and numerous islets, mostly uninhabited.

Volcanoes. The Aleutian range, in the Alaska peninsula, contains a group of active volcanoes, which, in some respects, are the most remarkable in the world. The eruption of Katmai in this group, in 1912, was one of the most violent volcanic outbursts recorded in modern times. Katmai and its vicinity, including the famous "Valley of Ten Thousand Smokes," have been made a national monument. Aniakchak and Veniamin, with craters 21 and 20 miles in circumference respectively, rank first among active volcanoes in size of their vents.

Glaciers. The mountains bordering on the Gulf of Alaska are covered with perpetual snow. From their slopes, immense glaciers, which increase in size from Glacier bay northward, extend down to the sea. On the shores between Glacier bay and Kenai peninsula are found nine-tenths of the permanent ice fields on the mainland of the continent. Here are some 25 active glaciers which discharge their slowly flowing ice into the sea. Among the most noted is the Muir glacier, which has a seaward face 3 miles wide and 300 feet high. The greatest example of all is the Malaspina glacier, 1200 square miles in extent, which rests on the southern slope of Mount Saint Elias and reaches the ocean at Icy cape.

The Muir glacier has recently attracted much scientific attention because of its rapid recession due to melting. This has aroused speculation as to whether the world's climate is gradually becoming warmer.

This great glacier was first visited by John Muir in 1880 and has been named in honor of him. Net recession since then has been almost two miles with parts of the ice mass which melted having been nearly one-half mile thick. The formerly great central ice stream is all melted leaving now 12 separate glacial streams. This is reputed to be the best area in the world for study of glacial phenomena.

Rivers. The chief river in Alaska is the Yukon, the largest American river emptying into the Pacific Ocean. This magnificent river, some 2300 miles long, is formed by the confluence of streams having their headwaters in British Columbia. It flows northward in Yukon territory, and, about midway on the international boundary, enters Alaska. At the northernmost point in its bow-shaped course of about 1500 miles from the Canada boundary to Bering Sea, the Yukon swings slightly north of the Arctic circle. Its chief tributaries are the Tanana, the Porcupine, and the Koyukuk. Other important

Alaskan rivers are the Kuskokwim, the Copper, Matanuska, Kenai, Nushagak, Kobuk, Noatak, Colville, Stikine, Taku, and the Susitna.

Scenery. Alaska, with its great mountains, volcanoes, glaciers, and rivers, is noted for the magnificence of its scenery. The Portland canal, Chatham strait, and the Lynn canal, in southeastern Alaska, surrounded by snow-capped mountains rising above immense forests, rank among the finest scenic waterways in the world. Around the Gulf of Alaska, the coast is indented with deep bays resembling the noted fiords of Norway and which likewise include magnificent glaciers. The Taku glacier is only a few miles from the steamer track of the famous inside passage and can be seen from the largest ocean steamers that ply Alaskan waters. Mount McKinley national park, which includes the great mountain, affords some of the grandest mountain views on the continent.

Climate. Climatically, Alaska is naturally divided into three areas—(1) southeastern and southern, which includes the panhandle and the Aleutians; (2) central plateau and valley; and (3) western and northern. The panhandle region, lying between British Columbia and the Pacific Ocean, has a mild climate, with heavy rainfall, similar to that of the northwest coast of the United States. The rainfall varies from 80 to 150 inches and the temperature rarely falls below zero or rises above 75° F. Ketchikan has a January average of 32.6° F. and has reported a maximum temperature of 96° F. and a minimum of −8° F. Average rainfall here is 150.9 inches annually. The coast region northward in the vicinity of Cook inlet and Kodiak island is slightly colder, with somewhat less rainfall.

Anchorage, near the Matanuska valley farming area, has a January average of 11.2° F., about like Minneapolis, Minnesota, and a July average of 57° F., about like April and May in central and northern United States. Maximum temperature reported is 92° F. and minimum −36° F. This latter temperature occurs every year in such states as North Dakota and Minnesota. Precipitation at Anchorage is 14.32 inches annually. The low rate of evaporation makes the low rainfall adequate. The growing season is 110 days. On the Aleutians, Dutch Harbor has a January average of 32.2° F., July 51.3° F., maximum 80° F. and minimum 8° F. Precipitation here is 56.77 inches annually. This Pacific area, especially the Aleutians, is one of the cloudiest and foggiest of the world. The average is 200 cloudy days a year with the Aleutians 15 to 25 per cent of the days foggy in winter. Eight feet of snow falls in 8 winter months on sea-facing slopes.

In the great interior valley of the Yukon, the climate is semiarid, with great extremes of heat and cold. Fairbanks has a January average of 11.6° F. (lowest U. S. places −2° F.) and July 60° F. with highest 99° F. and lowest 66° F. Within this central region a high of 100° F. is officially reported from Fort Yukon and a low of −78° F. from the same station. Precipitation at Fairbanks totals 11.87 inches annually with 3 to 5 feet of snow falling over a ten month period. The growing season is 89 days—May 29 to August 26. The long summer days is a big factor here in plant growth.

The Arctic coast has a frigid climate, with low average temperature and scant rainfall. Barrow, well within the Frigid zone at 71° North latitude, has a January average of −18° F. and a July average of 40.2° F. Maximum reported 78° F. and minimum −56° F. This minimum, higher than at Fairbanks and points inland, is due to its open coastal location. Precipitation is very light at 4.34 inches annually with at least some snow every month of the year. Winter snow is not heavy and usually is under 3 feet. Much of the tundra is so lightly covered as to permit year round reindeer grazing. The growing season is 17 days long—July 4 to July 21. This is the most northerly Alaskan town and the sun circles the sky without setting for about 2 months in summer and the Arctic night is also about 2 months in length.

Vegetation. The southern coastal region is heavily forested and contains much valuable timber, chiefly Sitka spruce and hemlock. The Tongass national forest comprises southeastern Alaska, and the Chugatch national forest extends from Controller bay to Cook inlet. Extensive forests of spruce and tamarack, interspersed with poplar, aspen, white birch, and alder, occur along numerous watercourses in the Yukon valley. These forests total nearly 21 million acres with practically all under National Forest Service Administration. In the remaining portions of Alaska, there are but few trees. The Alaska peninsula and the Aleutian islands are grasslands. These grasslands are composed of highly nutritious grasses and are available as pasturage the year round. Cattle and horses released on these areas have grown fat and sleek without attention from man.

The coastal region of Bering Sea and the Arctic Ocean is covered with tundra. The tundra furnishes very desirable pasturage for caribou, reindeer, and musk ox.

Animal Life. Alaska is rich in animal life, especially in game animals, fur bearing animals, and in food fishes. Among the larger land animals are moose, caribou, deer, bighorn, and mountain goat. There are also several species of bear, including the polar bear, the rare glacial bear, and the great Kodiak bear. The reindeer, introduced from Siberia to provide food for the native Indians and Eskimos, now abounds in great herds. Estimates vary from 200,000 to 1,000,000 head. It is reared like cattle, and reindeer meat is an article of export to the United States. In the coastal waters are found the walrus, the hair seal, and various whales. The fur bearing animals include the fur seal, sea otter, beaver, ermine, mink, marten, and wolverine. Salmon, cod, halibut, and herring are immensely abundant in Alaskan waters.

Minerals. Alaska possesses vast mineral resources, most of which are undeveloped. The most important mineral products are gold, copper, and coal. Many other valuable metals and minerals are found, among which are silver, lead, antimony, tin, tungsten, platinum, quicksilver, and marble.

Gold has been found chiefly in the Juneau district, the Copper River district, the Yukon valley, and in the Seward peninsula, or Nome region. Rich deposits of copper occur in the coast region from Mount Saint Elias to Cook inlet. Extensive coal fields are found in widely separated districts from southern Alaska to the Arctic coast. It is estimated that more than 12,000 square miles are underlaid with coal deposits ranging in quality from anthracite to lignite. Petroleum fields have been discovered near Controller bay and also on the Alaska peninsula. Recently numerous seepages indicate very large sources in the vicinity of Point Barrow.

Transportation. The development of Alaska's immense resources depends upon the establishment of quick and cheap transportation. The coasts have many good harbors, and the Yukon and other rivers provide some 3000 miles of inland waterways. But the water routes are long, are open only in summer, and do not reach some of the most important districts. Short railways have been built in connection with mining enterprises, but they were not constructed as correlated parts of a railway system designed to serve the needs of the whole territory.

The United States government has, however, completed a railway, some 470 miles long, from Seward, on the Gulf of Alaska, to Fairbanks, at the head of deep water navigation on the Tanana river, chief tributary of the Yukon. This connects the southern coast with the interior valley. Construction of a motor highway through Canada to Alaska was begun in 1942.

This highway has now been completed and tourist services are available along its entire length. Lodging and meal service are good and moderate in cost. Gasoline is available but as yet relatively costly. Autos may now make the round trip overland to Fairbanks; but a tourist seeking variety may drive from Fairbanks to Anchorage or Seward and take a boat over the attractive ocean route to Seattle. The Alaska Highway is now all-weather, but all-macadam will not be completed before 1950. The present surface is very wearing on tires and cars.

Numerous airports have facilitated rapid transit to otherwise inaccessible points. There are 15 certified carriers and 50 or more irregular carriers. There are also 153 territorial fields. Outposts such as Nome are finding the quick connection by planes much more dependable and desirable than dog teams, which are costly to maintain, requiring constant feed and care.

Several Federal Airports are maintained and a regular biweekly weather run is made over the North Pole from Barrow. In the year ending June 20, 1948, Alaskan air carriers flew 7,756,869 miles and carried 129,616 passengers, 18,758,495 pounds of freight, and 1,994,091 pieces of mail. Carriers between Alaska and United States flew 4,236,357 miles and carried 48,270 passengers, 9,441,511 pounds of freight, and 588,417 pieces of mail.

Commerce and Industry. The industries of Alaska are chiefly in connection with mining, fisheries, and the fur trade, with a limited amount of lumbering. The dominant tree of the commercial timber type is western hemlock, with Sitka spruce a close second. Western red cedar and Alaska yellow cedar are produced to some extent. Local uses of forests are fuel, log cabins, mines, docks, salmon packing cases, etc. During World War II Sitka spruce provided airplane construction material. A future for pulp mills is indicated. The principal exports are canned salmon, copper ore, gold, and furs. Among the most important imports are foodstuffs, clothing, and machinery. The notable growth of Alaskan commerce is shown in the accompanying table.

Fisheries. The salmon fisheries of Alaska are the most valuable in the world. Next in importance to salmon are herring, halibut, clams, and shrimps. The value of fishery products shipped to the United States from Alaska is normally from three to five times that of the copper and of the gold combined.

The total Alaskan catch in 1941 was 383,332,387 pounds, with a value of $61,076,073. This represents the maximum that should be taken of the species now generally utilized, but others that could supply large quantities are as yet untouched. In addition, meals and oils totaling 47,793,133 pounds, with a value of $2,401,222 were produced from offal and fish not utilized for food. Salmon oil, when properly prepared, is rich in vitamins A and D. The annual value of these products to Alaskan fishermen is over 20 million dollars. The 1945 catch was one of the largest, nearly 600 million pounds, giving the fishermen over 22 million dollars. Eight thousand fishermen are employed using 1000 vessels and about 3000 boats.

Gold and Other Minerals. Of all the products of Alaska, gold has undoubtedly attracted the greatest attention. The earliest discovery of this metal in Alaska dates from 1861, but the so-called gold rush did not begin until 1883, when news of more substantial discoveries spread. The height of this boom occurred about 1887, which was followed by a still greater rush when a gold claim was located in the Klondike, Canada, in 1896.

Gold mined in Alaska from 1880 until 1930 is valued at approximately 380 million dollars. Annual production is in the neighborhood of 7 million dollars, slightly over one-third that mined in 1910. Juneau is the center of the gold mining industry.

The decline in gold production has been accompanied by a rise in the mining of copper, which, beginning in 1901, soon surpassed in value the output of gold, and from 1918 exceeded in value all other mineral production in the territory. Silver, lead, lignite coal, and petroleum are also produced in significant quantities. Practically all the tin mined in North America comes from Alaska. Other im-

GROWTH OF ALASKAN COMMERCE

Imports and Exports of Merchandise, 1880–1938

Year Ended	Imports*: From United States	Imports*: From Other Countries	Imports*: Total	Exports: To United States	Exports: To Other Countries	Exports: Total
	Dollars	Dollars	Dollars	Dollars	Dollars	Dollars
June 30:						
1880	463,000	3,032	466,032	....	31,543	....
1885	853,000	8,944	861,944	....	24,468	....
1890	1,897,000	24,577	1,921,577	....	4,682	....
1895	3,017,000	55,850	3,072,850	....	11,520	....
1900	18,463,000	385,317	18,848,317	....	566,347	....
1905	11,504,255	1,450,910	12,955,165	10,801,446	1,088,165	11,889,611
1910	18,670,339	619,348	19,289,687	12,440,380	1,168,014	13,608,394
1915	21,260,042	640,886	21,900,928	27,442,335	1,001,389	28,443,724
Dec. 31:						
1920	36,876,855	1,512,118	38,388,973	60,939,061	1,530,035	62,469,096
1922	26,777,806	870,927	27,648,733	51,082,995	1,371,490	52,454,485
1923	30,631,366	514,466	31,145,832	53,761,494	1,325,773	55,087,267
1924	32,046,273	529,618	32,575,891	54,974,168	1,351,380	56,325,548
1925	32,352,530	846,981	33,199,511	55,434,210	901,543	56,335,753
1926	31,587,337	543,683	32,131,020	73,300,506	521,881	73,822,387
1927	35,604,108	766,302	36,370,410	51,348,688	483,679	51,832,367
1928	32,058,976	559,262	32,618,238	67,587,207	619,065	68,206,272
1929	33,220,584	954,273	34,174,857	63,567,677	607,017	64,174,694
1930	31,303,291	1,709,636	33,012,927	48,996,962	347,191	49,344,153
1931	22,489,895	546,598	23,036,493	43,276,364	314,908	43,591,272
1932	19,573,105	302,451	19,875,554	30,183,355	235,528	30,418,883
1933	20,685,622	131,245	20,816,867	33,131,461	166,281	33,297,742
1934	29,998,840	270,768	30,269,608	45,058,950	322,512	45,381,462
1935	32,007,856	253,976	32,261,832	36,868,697	262,135	37,130,832
1936	39,060,577	265,148	39,325,725	60,807,603	452,204	61,259,807
1937	42,860,774	223,221	43,083,995	62,363,327	400,117	62,763,444
1938	42,676,622	175,025	42,851,647	56,044,728	605,300	56,650,028

* From 1880 to 1900, unofficial estimates of the value of merchandise shipped from Pacific Coast ports to Alaska; from 1905, official figures of shipments to Alaska. Where figures are omitted for imports or exports, statistics are not available.

portant mineral products include platinum, mercury, and marble.

While the value of Alaskan minerals was still just over ten million dollars in 1945, the industry suffered a severe decline during the war period, as the output in 1939 was well over 25 million dollars. Gold and especially copper declined sharply.

Furs and Game. Next in value below fishery and mineral products are furs. The most important land furs include red fox, white fox, blue fox, ermine, lynx, marten, mink, muskrat, and land otter. Fur farming, especially with foxes, is carried on extensively. The fur seal herds, on the Pribilof islands, increased, under government supervision, from 215,000 animals in 1912 to about nine times that number in the 30 years following.

The 1940 seal population of these islands was 2,185,136. Sealskins taken in 1941 were 95,013. The handling of this fur seal herd has been one of the most successful in wildlife administration. The total value of furs shipped from Alaska annually frequently exceeds 4.5 million dollars.

Fine and useful game animals are caribou; reindeer; moose; Dall mountain sheep; mountain goats; brown, grizzly, polar, and black bears; elk; deer; and, at present, a herd of musk oxen are being developed on Nunivak island and a herd of bison near Fairbanks. Immense numbers of ducks, geese, and swans of several species breed abundantly throughout practically the entire territory. Other aquatic fowl form almost continuous coastal rookeries—auklets, murres, guillemots, puffins, cormorants, sheerwaters, gulls, and kittiwakes. Eagles, owls, hawks, gyrfalcons are included among the land birds.

Agriculture. Owing chiefly to the shortness of the growing season, agriculture is successful only in limited areas and to a moderate degree. Vegetables are the most important products. These are grown in favored ground in the valleys of the Susitna, the Matanuska, the Kenai, the Koyukuk, the Copper, and the Tanana rivers. Hay, barley, and hardy fruits are also produced. Grazing and dairying are carried on in Kodiak island and other grassland districts. Reindeer thrive in moss covered and lichen covered areas. The government maintains four agricultural experimental stations,—a nursery at Sitka, a grain farm at Rampart, a dairy at Kodiak, and a demonstration farm at Fairbanks.

It is estimated that 65,000 square miles is potential farm land and 35,000 square miles is potential grazing land, not including the reindeer range which is very extensive. However, only 3000 square miles are now in farms with 12 square miles actually cropped. The last census placed the number of farms at 623 with a considerable variety of crops and livestock. Livestock included: Cattle, 3749, of which 1217 were dairy cows; sheep, 17,076; goats, 280; swine, 959; chickens, 18,374; fur animals on farms, 34,433; and the reindeer herds at 312,854. The reindeer industry shows a great decline from the 712,500 in 1929. Crops were: Barley (in bushels), 13,219; oats, 13,661; potatoes, 41,887; and wheat, 9479. Curing hay appears to be a problem and none is reported as a crop. Fruits and vegetables reported in quantity are: currants, raspberries, gooseberries, radishes, lettuce, mustard, cabbage, turnips, rutabagas, kale, brussels sprouts, broccoli, cauliflower, carrots, beets, and peas.

Since imported foods from the United States are over five million dollars in value, and since the Alaskan farm produce supplies only one-fourth this amount, considerable opportunity for local expansion appears possible.

In 1945, the population of the territory was 81,441, of whom approximately half were whites and the remainder were Indians, with a few Negroes and Japanese.

The Indians of Alaska belong mainly to four great stocks—the Eskimos, the Aleuts, the Athapascans, and the Tlingits. The Eskimos, 15,576 in number, live near the seashore and on islands, chiefly along Bering Sea and the Arctic Ocean. The Pacific Eskimos live on the south coast around Kodiak island, Controller bay, and Prince William sound. The Aleutian Eskimos occupy areas about the Alaskan Peninsula and extending along the Aleutian islands. Asiatic Eskimos live on St. Lawrence island which is part of the Alaskan Territory. The Bering Sea Eskimos live on Nunivak island and the opposite mainland including the lower Yukon. The Colville Eskimos occupy the Arctic coast near Wainright Inlet, Cape Smyth, and Point Barrow. The Eskimos have proven good workers and are employed at such summer tasks as longshoremen in loading and unloading supply ships. Able bodied Eskimos were drafted for war service in Alaska in World War II.

Juneau, the capital and largest town, had, in 1939, a population of 5729. Other important towns are Ketchikan, Fairbanks, Sitka, Anchorage, Seward, Nome, Matanuska, and Barrow. Many of these towns have increased considerably in population. It is reported that Anchorage has over 11,000 inhabitants at present.

History. In 1741, Bering, a Russian navigator, explored the coast of Alaska. Kodiak island was discovered in 1761 by the Russians, who made a settlement there in 1783. Captain James Cook, in 1778, and Vancouver, in 1793-94, made extensive coastal surveys. Sitka, founded in 1804, became the capital of the Russian territory. The Russians, who were engaged chiefly in fur sealing, did not extensively explore the interior.

In 1867, the United States purchased Alaska from Russia for the sum of $7,200,000—about $12 per square mile, or less than 2 cents an acre.

Preceding the discovery of the gold fields, there was little development, except in connection with the fur trade. Important events in the recent history of Alaska were the fur seal arbitration of 1893, the great gold rush of 1898, the settlement of the Alaska-Canada boundary dispute in 1904, and the construction of the government railway from Seward to Fairbanks, 1916–23.

During the World War, the white population of Alaska declined, but, following the completion of important portions of the government railway and the return of stable conditions, development was again stimulated. Growth of air travel provided an impetus. Point Barrow and Nome were used as points of landing or departure for air exploration in the Arctic, including Amundsen's and Byrd's flights over the north pole in 1926. Beginning in 1939, several army and naval air bases were established in Alaska.

AMERICAN SAMOA

A group of four inhabited and several uninhabited islands in the south Pacific Ocean, about 4200 miles southwest of San Francisco and about 2000 miles east of Australia. The inhabited islands are Tutuila, Tau, and those of the Manua group—Ofu and Olosega. The total area of the group is 58 square miles.

The islands are largely mountainous in character, but much of the soil is extremely fertile. The moist tropical climate of the islands fosters a luxuriant vegetation. Agriculture is the principal occupation and is carried on mainly by family groups, each of which is directed and ruled by a patriarch, or *matai*. The chief products include copra, taro, breadfruit, yams, pineapples, oranges, and bananas. Copra is the only article exported.

The only large port of American Samoa is Pagopago. It is a United States naval station under a commandant, who acts also as governor of the islands. The population in 1940 was 12,908. Schools were established in Samoan villages by Christian missionaries as early as 1830. Elementary education in English is available for all in schools supported by the government.

This group of islands came under American sovereignty in 1899 as the result of a treaty with Great

Britain and Germany. Since the establishment of American control, the islands have made substantial gains in population and in social welfare.

GUAM

The largest and most southerly of the Marianas islands, which are known also as the Ladrone islands. It is situated in the Pacific Ocean about 1700 miles east of Manila and some 3800 miles west by south of Honolulu.

The island of Guam is about 30 miles long, and varies in breadth from 4 to 8½ miles, its estimated area being 210 square miles. It is mountainous in the south but plateau-like in the north and is crossed near the central line by a low ridge of hills. Broken coral reefs fringe the shore.

There are only two seasons—a wet season and a dry one. Though the temperature averages 81° F. the year round, the climate is healthful. The soil is fertile, well watered, and yields abundant crops of copra, the chief export, and cacao, coffee, corn, rice, and tobacco. Agana, the capital, is the chief city. Piti, near the harbor of Apra, is the port of entry.

As the island is under the jurisdiction of the United States navy department, the governor is a naval officer. He has full executive, legislative, and judicial powers. The natives are of a mixed race, called Chamorros, with the Malayan strain predominating. Chamorro, the native language, and also Spanish and English are spoken.

Guam was discovered in 1521 by Magellan. In 1565, the Spanish took possession of the island. It remained under Spanish rule until 1898, when, as a result of the Spanish American war, it was ceded to the United States. Because of its location, Guam is an important naval station for vessels sailing to and from the Philippines. Population, 1940, 22,290.

HAWAII

A territory of the United States consisting of a chain of nine inhabited and several uninhabited islands in the mid-Pacific Ocean. The chief islands are about 2100 miles southwest of San Francisco and approximately 3400 miles southeast of Yokohama, Japan. Their central position in relation to Pacific ports has won for Hawaii the sobriquet "crossroads of the Pacific," and, with the independence of the Philippines, our most important possession among the Pacific islands.

Palmyra island, 1½ miles in area, lying about 700 miles south of the main group, is officially included in the territory. The extreme northwestern islets of the group are called the Midway islands or Ocean Midway, being about halfway between Asia and North America. They are protected by outlying coral reefs and are inhabited only by the employees of a United States cable station there.

The following table gives the area and the population, for 1940, of the chief islands and of the whole group:

Island	Area	Population
Hawaii	4,016	73,276
Maui	728	46,919
Oahu	598	257,664
Kauai	547	35,636
Molokai	261	5,340
Lanai	139	3,720
Others	160	775
Total	6,449	423,330

The islands of Hawaii are of volcanic origin. Their surface is mountainous, reaching, in Mauna Kea, "White Mountain," a maximum altitude of 13,784 feet. If measured from the deep ocean floor, on which it stands, this volcanic giant is several hundred feet higher than Mt. Everest, the world's highest inland mountain. This peak and Mauna Loa (13,675 feet), both in the island of Hawaii, are higher than any other mountain in the islands of the Pacific Ocean. Mauna Loa, "Long Mountain," shares with the near-by mountain of Kilauea the distinction of having active craters which rank among the largest in the world. That of Kilauea is about 8 miles in circumference and is the seat of unceasing volcanic activity.

Haleakala, on the island of Maui, has one of the largest of all extinct craters. This crater is 20 miles around and is 2720 feet deep. The island of Molokai is notable for its famous leper settlement. Lanai is owned by a pineapple company which constructed a harbor and a model city. Pearl harbor, on the island of Oahu, is a United States naval base. It is landlocked, with an area of 10 square miles. The Hawaii national park includes Kilauea and Mauna Loa on Hawaii island and Haleakala on Maui.

The climate of the Hawaiian islands is delightfully equable and invigorating considering its tropical position. Sea level temperatures average between 68.7° F. and 75.8° F. for the Territory. At Honolulu, the maximum recorded temperature is 90° F. and the minimum, 52° F. However, it is a rare summer day in which temperatures rise over 85° F. and a rare winter night when the low is 60° F. Especially noteworthy is the fact that damaging storms, such as hail, tornadoes, hurricanes, and typhoons, are practically nonexistent. Northeast trade winds blow prevailingly for about 10 months in the year. On account of the mountainous character of the islands, much of the moisture in the winds is precipitated, falling mainly on the northeastern side of each island. As a result, the opposite side has insufficient rainfall and frequently suffers from drought. This rainfall variation is one of the

GROWTH OF HAWAIIAN COMMERCE

Imports and Exports of Merchandise, 1901–1938

Year Ended	Imports* From United States	Imports* From Other Countries	Imports* Total	Exports To United States	Exports To Other Countries	Exports Total
June 30:	Dollars	Dollars	Dollars	Dollars	Dollars	Dollars
1901	....	2,835,278	....	27,903,058	120,211	28,023,269
1905	11,753,180	3,014,964	14,768,144	36,112,055	59,541	36,171,596
1910	20,560,101	4,606,334	25,166,435	46,183,265	306,763	46,490,028
1915	25,004,764	5,716,023	30,720,787	62,087,250	377,509	62,464,759
Dec. 31:						
1920	74,052,453	12,284,592	86,337,045	192,383,185	3,437,699	195,820,884
1925	72,952,949	10,829,509	83,782,458	102,780,509	1,844.782	104,625,291
1930	81,726,404	9,399,645	91,126,049	98,923,737	1,992,046	100,915,783
1933	57,894,488	5,233,481	63,127,969	92,276,992	675,809	92,952,801
1934	63,472,395	5,761,288	69,233,683	94,513,699	1,316,360	95,830,059
1935	78,924,776	5,628,108	84,552,884	98,695,969	1,338,027	100,033,996
1936	85,743,998	6,699,913	92,443,911	125,537,355	1,639,450	127,176.805
1937	104,302,531	9,672,928	113,975,459	130,138,166	2,101,648	132,239,814
1938	101,227,151	8,432,570	109,659,721	96,556,679	1,529,442	98,086,121

* Statistics of imports from the United States for 1901 not available.

largest in the world. Many rain-drenched windward towns officially report well over 200 inches a year. Eke on the island of Maui is one of the world's wettest places, averaging 249.2 inches a year, with some years well over 300 inches. On the leeward side, averages of 20 to 30 inches are common (Honolulu, 25.8 in.) and are often inadequate for crops and water supply. Rain falls every month of the year, but the summer months are markedly drier. The prevailing sunniness of such lee locations as Honolulu is a notable attraction.

Another significant mountain influence is the change of temperature with altitude. In the land below 2500 feet (Tierra Caliente) frost never occurs and rarely forms even up to 4000 feet. Above 4000 feet (Tierra Templada) frost may occur, and at elevations of 6500 feet snow is occasionally reported. Above 9000 feet (Tierra Fria) both frost and snow occur regularly and the higher peaks are frequently snow covered. Altogether the Hawaiian Islands are climatically among the most varied in the world.

Plant life is highly varied from tropical jungle to tropical steppe and desert. Only about 10 per cent is grazing land. Approximately four-fifths of the area is unused desert, semidesert, and volcanic waste with dense tropical jungle in favored spots. In the National Park area of the island Hawaii, locally called Big Island, is the world famous "Fern Forest" with some ferns attaining the height of 50 feet. Plant life in the inhabited areas is highly colorful and ornamental providing a major attraction. Among the most noted are royal palms, coconut palms, banyan trees, monkeypod trees, flame trees, bougainvillia, orchid, cacti, hibiscus, poinsettia, plumerias, and ilima. Many of these blooms are made into welcoming leis, a world famous Hawaiian custom with considerable commercial significance.

The soil along the coastal lowlands and in many valleys is very fertile and supports a flourishing agriculture of a tropical type. Since the soils are of volcanic origin they are deep rich clays high in mineral content and capable of sustained yields under cultivation. The staple crops are pineapples and sugar cane. Large quantities of cane sugar and of pineapples are shipped, principally to the United States. Other products exported include coffee, honey, hides, sisal hemp, bananas, rice, wool, tobacco, and cotton. Over half of the total area is in farms and ranches (2.5 million acres), yet only 10 per cent of the total area is cropped.

About 250,000 acres is kept in sugar cane, the major crop, using five times as much land as pineapples. Since the cane is allowed to grow 18 to 20 months before harvesting, the yield per acre is three times that of the annually harvested cane of the United States. Hawaiians annually cut just over half of the acreage in cane. Annual production varies from 700,000 to 1,000,000 tons, about equaling Puerto Rico and the Philippines, or half of the total sugar production (cane and beet) of Continental United States. Fifty million dollars' worth of sugar and molasses are annually exported to the United States, half of the islands' income.

Eighty to ninety per cent of the pineapple products of world trade originate in the Hawaiian Islands, making them world famous. This fame is justly merited, not only in quantity domination over all competitors, but also in leadership in methods of production and processing. Eight corporations dominate the field, led by the Hawaiian Pineapple Corporation founded by James D. Dole, 1922. Confronted by labor shortage, limited water supply, aridity, blowing soil erosion, soil and plant infestations and certain plant food deficiencies, these companies inaugurated far reaching conservation practices. Slopes are contoured; paper covers the soil, conserving moisture, preventing blowing and washing, checking weed growth, thus saving costly weeding; soils are fumigated with DDT, destroying infestation and multiplying yields; needed plant foods are both sprayed on the plants and added to the soil; spray also controls foliage parasites; plant hormones are also sprayed on to achieve uniform ripening and to extend the harvest period by accelerating growth and ripening; water supply is obtained by wells, local galvanized roofs, and acres of galvanized sheds on the wetter upper slopes, from which the water can be channelled down as needed machinery cultivates, plants, harvests, and transports the fruit to the processing factories where all of the pineapple is reduced to valuable products as canned fruit, juice, and citric acid. Cost of services in sanitation, health, and public utilities, formerly provided, must now be borne by the worker. Over $25,000,000 in pineapple products are sold to the United States.

Land tenure is a problem with 60 per cent of the land owned either by the Territory or by large estates. The famous Bishop Estate owns 10 per cent and endows philanthropic enterprises such as the Kamehameha schools with the million dollar income. The Federal Government owns 429,076 acres, of which 373,384 is in National Parks and 55,559 is under the Navy.

The tourist industry ranks third after sugar and pineapples as an industry. Superior natural attractions are enhanced by luxurious accommodations to make this a world prominent resort. The Pan American Airways and United Air Lines contact the islands from San Francisco in a breakfast-to-dinner run. Limited steamship accommodations are available on the Maston and Presidential lines. The Moana and Royal hotels on Waikiki beach are widely known. Pre-war tourist expenditures reached 12 million dollars annually from 65,000 tourists.

Honolulu, on Oahu island, is the capital and chief port of Hawaii. The population of the territory has a mixed character. More than half are Japanese and Chinese. White inhabitants number less than one-fourth of the total. The aborigines constitute a still smaller proportion. A similar complexity characterizes the language and the religion of the territory. The aborigines are mainly Protestant Christians, although some of their pagan beliefs and customs survive. The Hawaiian natives belong to the Malayan race. When discovered, they had a well developed political system and a literature. Niihau is still maintained as a pure native asylum by the exclusive Robinson family.

The Hawaiian islands were first made known to the world by Captain James Cook, who discovered them in 1778. He called them Sandwich islands after the earl of Sandwich. At that time, each island had its king, who exercised authority by a species of feudal organization. In 1790, Kamehameha, one of the kings, extended his sway over the entire group of islands. His successor, being opposed by those who upheld the native worship, abolished the old religion. Christianity was introduced as early as 1820. A system of universal, compulsory education is now established there.

In 1842, the kingdom of Hawaii was recognized by the United States. An internal struggle for constitutional rights arose and lasted, with interruptions, until 1893, when the reigning queen, Liliuokalani, was deposed. An appeal for annexation to the United States was made, but it was rejected by President Cleveland. A second appeal, made to President McKinley, resulted in the approval by Congress, July 7, 1898, of a treaty of annexation. In 1900, the islands were formally organized into the territory of Hawaii, and a territorial governor was appointed by the president. The question of admitting the Territory to the Union as the 49th state is now being considered.

On Kealakekua bay, Hawaii island, stands an obelisk commemorating Captain Cook, who was slain near that point by natives in 1779. In 1928, a bronze tablet was dedicated in his honor and placed just below the surface of the water to mark the exact spot where he fell. The adjacent region, known as Kaawaloa, was made into a public park.

tianized the inhabitants, who constitute the only large body of Asiatic people permanently converted to Christianity in modern times.

The islands remained under Spanish rule until 1898, when, as a result of the Spanish American war, they were ceded to the United States. In 1899, an extensive insurrection of the Filipinos broke out. Aguinaldo, the leader of the rebellion, was captured in 1901, and, in 1902, the insurrection was formally proclaimed at an end. A ten-year period of semi-independence began in 1935, when a constitution was adopted in accordance with an enabling law of the United States Congress in 1933. After 1945, the tie with the United States is to be chiefly for defense.

PUERTO RICO

A West India island lying about 70 miles east of Haiti and 1425 miles southeast of New York. The island is about 100 miles long and from 30 to 40 miles wide, and has about three times the area of the state of Rhode Island.

The climate of Puerto Rico is regarded as the most healthful in the tropics of the western hemisphere. Through the middle of the island, a broken range of mountains extends from east to west, their altitude varying from about 2000 feet to that of the culminating peak of El Yunque, 3532 feet high. These mountains are clothed to their summits with luxuriant vegetation. The coast belt is a broad, level alluvial plain. The soil is exceedingly fertile and, as the population is dense, most of the arable land is under cultivation.

On the eastern and on the northern slopes of the mountains there is abundant rainfall, the average yearly precipitation being 65 inches. But, in the southern part of the island, irrigation is required in some districts, as the mountains intercept much of the moisture in the trade winds. Puerto Rico is noted for its fine forest trees. Palms, Spanish cedar, ebony, mahogany, ausubo, laurel, sandalwood, and dyewoods abound.

The mineral resources of Puerto Rico, so far as developed, consist chiefly of limestone and volcanic bowlders, used in building; various clays, used in making brick and pottery; and gypsum, used for stucco, plaster, and fertilizer. Deposits of marble and lignite occur, and along the south coast there are extensive phosphate beds. Gold, copper ore, iron ore, and the ores of various other metals have been found in small quantities but, as yet, the character and extent of the island's metallic resources are largely unknown.

Agriculture is the chief industry. Among the island's principal products are sugar, tobacco, coffee, grapefruit, oranges, pineapples, and other tropical fruits. Sugar is the chief export, and tobacco and coffee are also important. In 1939, the island sent abroad nearly 950,000 tons of sugar, valued at $53,000,000. This one product amounted to 62 per cent of all the exports. In 1899, before the introduction of modern methods of sugar growing, the total quantity of sugar produced was only 35,000 tons. Exports of tobacco and tobacco products amount to more than 8 million dollars; of fresh pineapples, usually to more than one million dollars. Manufacturing is limited, tobacco goods forming the chief product. Less important are coffee cleaning and the manufacture of clothing.

The principal cities and seaports are San Juan, the capital, on the north coast, Ponce, on the south coast; and Mayaguez, on the west coast. The harbor at San Juan, which has been extensively improved by the United States government, is one of the best in the West Indies. A railroad, built near the coast, almost completely encircles the island, and there are branches into the interior. Surfaced highways, of which more than 1400 miles have been constructed, facilitate transportation in various parts of the island.

Under the school system, education is free and compulsory. There are upwards of 2300 school buildings, with more than 280,000 pupils enrolled. There is also a well distributed system of night schools and kindergartens. The University of Puerto Rico, at Rio Piedras, is open to both men and women. The percentage of illiteracy, which, in 1899, was 83 per cent, had decreased in the following 40 years to 30 per cent. The white population is increasing and the mulatto population, now about 23 per cent of the whole, is decreasing.

Puerto Rico was discovered in 1493 by Columbus. The first settlement was made at Pueblo Viejo in 1508 by Ponce de Leon, who, in 1509, was appointed governor by King Ferdinand of Spain. Although attacked at various times by the English and the Dutch, Puerto Rico remained in the possession of Spain until 1898, when, at the close of the Spanish American war, it was ceded to the United States. Since the establishment of American methods of agriculture, American public schools, improved highways and railways, and various civic improvements, Puerto Rico has made remarkable progress. Population, 1945, 2,087,112.

GROWTH OF PUERTO RICAN COMMERCE

Imports and Exports of Merchandise, 1900–1938

Year Ended	Imports			Exports		
	From United States	From Other Countries	Total	To United States	To Other Countries	Total
June 30:	Dollars	Dollars	Dollars	Dollars	Dollars	Dollars
1900	3,286,168	1,965,289	5,251,457	2,477,480	1,833,796	4,311,276
1905	13,974,070	2.562,189	16,536,259	15,633,145	3,076,420	18,709,565
1910	27,097,654	3,537,201	30,634,855	32,095,897	5,864,617	37,960,514
1915	30,929,831	2,954,465	33,884,296	42,311,920	7,044,987	49,356,907
Dec. 31:						
1920	121,561,574	7,512,404	129,073,978	158,322,083	16,346,697	174,668,780
1923	76,919,616	7,547,504	84,467,120	80,303,272	5,768,723	86,071,995
1924	78 412,003	9,337,444	87,749,447	77,330,748	7,397,792	84,728,540
1925	78,078,579	11,620,875	89,699,454	92,679,754	7,053,295	99,733,049
1926	84,737,537	12,664,064	97,401,601	90,166,856	7,579,594	97,746,450
1927	86,326,546	11,264,383	97,590,929	96,902,024	7,557,741	104,459,765
1928	81,981,460	13,325,628	95,307,088	97,268,763	6,338,039	103,606,802
1929	75,979,914	11,728,596	87,708,510	78,126,574	5,117,801	83,244,375
1930	74,219,219	10,318,649	84,537,868	99,880,061	4,068,810	103,948,871
1931	60,636,751	7,874,291	68,511,042	87,911,706	3,172,479	91,084,185
1932	48,780,141	7,256,335	56,036,476	74,290,250	2,127,827	76,418,077
1933	51,696,988	6,146,587	57,843,575	76,211,940	2,449,143	78,661,083
1934	59,477,288	6,762,041	66,239,329	81,184,396	2,723,351	83,907,747
1935	70,053,010	6,595,277	76,648,287	87,726,308	1,915,113	89,641,421
1936	86,351,952	6,807,353	93,159,305	103,951,645	1,949,289	105,900,934
1937	90,043,856	9,144,454	99,188,310	102,859,041	2,646,200	105,505,241
1938	80,746,030	7,937,736	88,683,766	84,663,860	1,867,278	86,531,138

VIRGIN ISLANDS

A group of some 50 tropical islands and islets formerly called the Danish West Indies. They lie about 40 miles due east of Puerto Rico. The total area of the group is about 149 square miles, of which 132 is comprised in the three largest islands—Saint Thomas, Saint John, and Saint Croix (Santa Cruz). Almost all the inhabitants are Negroes or mulattoes.

Saint Thomas is the best known of the islands because its principal town, Charlotte Amalie, population 9801, is located on one of the finest harbors in the West Indies. The surface of the island is rugged and elevated, and the soil is poor. The exports are principally rum and hides. Most of the imports are foodstuffs and wearing apparel. The area of the island is about 28 square miles. Population, 1940, 11,265.

Saint Croix, the largest, wealthiest, and most thickly populated of the islands, lies about 40 miles southeast of Saint Thomas, and has two well-known towns, Frederiksted (Westend), with a population of 2698, and Christiansted (Bassin), having a population of 3767. The latter was the capital of the islands under Danish rule. Sugar cane is the chief crop. Long-staple cotton is grown, and cattle are raised. The area of the island is about 84 square miles; population, 1940, 12,902.

Saint John, the smallest of the three main islands, grows bay leaves for the distillation of bay oil and also has a considerable acreage devoted to cotton, sugar cane, and tobacco. The entire population is considered rural. The area of Saint John is about 20 square miles; population, 1940, 722.

The Virgin islands were discovered in 1493 by Columbus. Saint Thomas was first colonized in 1672 by the Danes. Saint Croix, first occupied in 1625 by Dutch and English settlers, came into the possession of Denmark in 1733. With the exception of two periods—1801-02 and 1807-15—during the Napoleonic wars, when they were seized and held by the English, most of the islands were under the Danish flag for a period of 245 years. In 1917, upon payment of $25,000,000, they came into the possession of the United States by purchase.

During the days of sailing ships, especially about 1820, Saint Thomas was a supply point of great importance in the West Indian trade. Before the abolition of slavery, in 1848, in the islands, sugar growing was a substantial industry. With the decline of the sugar industry, the population decreased, falling gradually from about 40,000 in 1850 to about 26,000 when the United States took possession in 1917.

The value of the Virgin islands now lies chiefly in their geographic location and their exceptionally fine harbor facilities. Their situation with reference to the Panama canal makes Saint Thomas of great strategic importance as a naval base and as a coaling station.

GROWTH OF THE AMERICAN DEPENDENCIES

With the exception of Alaska, all of the most important dependencies of the United States came under its control at about the beginning of the present century. The Philippines (now independent), Puerto Rico, and Guam were acquired at the close of the Spanish American war in 1898. American Samoa was secured by treaty in 1899, and Hawaii was annexed in 1900. Although acquired by purchase some 30 years earlier, Alaska remained largely an unexplored wilderness until after the gold rush in 1898. Its period of development, therefore, began practically at the same time as that of the other large dependencies.

From the beginning, the chief aims pursued in the administration of these dependencies have been the maintenance of stable government and the continuous improvement of social and economic conditions. The latter aim has included the building of railroads, highways, and waterways, the construction of harbor facilities, the introduction of modern methods of agriculture, and the founding of various manufactures. Most important of all, it has included also the extension of American education as rapidly as possible to all classes of the people by means of free public schools.

The Philippines made rapid economic, commercial, and educational progress during the half-century they were under the control of the United States. Exports and imports increased manyfold. The enrollment of public school pupils rose from about 150,000 to more than 1,800,000 in the first four decades of the century. The rapid strides made in public education was a great factor in the preparation of the Philippines for self-government.

The substantial economic progress made during the period of American control is indicated in the foregoing tables giving the growth of Alaskan, Hawaiian, and Puerto Rican commerce since 1900. These tables show that the products exported from Alaska rose in value from about 12 million dollars in 1905 to about 70 million dollars in the succeeding 25 years, an increase of nearly 500 per cent. The growth of Hawaiian commerce for this period is likewise impressive. In 1905, Hawaii exported products valued at 36 millions and imported merchandise valued at about 15 millions. A quarter century later the exports had risen to approximately 120 millions and the imports to nearly 90 millions, a gain for exports and imports combined of over 300 per cent.

Puerto Rico made the most striking advance. During 30 years of progress under American methods, the value of products of the island sold abroad increased 24-fold and the value of goods brought into the country, chiefly from the United States, increased 19-fold.

During the period of American control, each of the more populous dependencies—Hawaii and Puerto Rico—has made substantial gains in population. Guam and American Samoa, among the lesser dependencies, likewise showed a marked growth. Important factors contributing to this increase were a more ample and uniform food supply, and also improved sanitary conditions, resulting from the adoption of modern methods of combating disease.

This great gain in material and physical welfare in the various dependencies is attributable, in very large measure, to the remarkable advances made in education. In Puerto Rico, more than 12 times as many pupils were attending public schools in 1940 as in 1899. In Hawaii, the attendance at public schools quadrupled between 1910 and 1940. Moreover, in each of the larger dependencies, institutions for higher education have been established.

An instructive illustration of the American policy is seen in results attained in Alaska. In 1885, the direction of the education and welfare of the Indians in the territory was assigned to the United States bureau of education. This involved far more than academic instruction in the schoolroom. The first task was to teach the fundamentals of sanitary living. The Alaskan natives, especially the Eskimos, lived largely by hunting and fishing. Because of their migratory habits, it was difficult to carry to them effective means of civilization.

It was therefore proposed, in 1889, to import domestic reindeer from Siberia and to establish reindeer raising as an industry among the Alaskan natives. This would provide them an assured means of support, and, in time, would change them from a nomadic to a pastoral people. Between 1892 and 1902, some 1300 reindeer were imported. Young Eskimos, after being taught how to care for the animals, were permitted to establish herds. As a result, there were, in 1940, at least 600,000 reindeer in Alaska, and, of these, two-thirds were owned by natives. In the meantime, schools, largely industrial in character, were established, hospitals and other medical relief were provided, and more sanitary means of living were maintained. In 1940, there were some 100 schools in operation, with a total enrollment of more than 6000.

DICTIONARY OF AMERICAN GEOGRAPHY

In the selection of topics for this section of American geography, the following considerations have governed:

Capital Cities. All capitals of states, territories, and dependencies, of the United States are given an item because of their political importance.

Largest Cities. All cities of the United States and dependencies, including the Philippine Islands, having, in 1940, a population of 50,000 and upwards, are arbitrarily included on account of size.

Smaller Cities and Places. Various cities and towns with a population of less than 50,000 have been included for specific reasons. Among these are Gettysburg, Plymouth, and Ticonderoga, which were selected because of historical interest. Certain cities and towns were selected because of some feature of travel interest at or near the place; for example, Adamana and Grand Junction.

Other cities, such as Butte, Cohoes, Hibbing, Riverside, and Anaconda, are included because they are leading centers in some important economic enterprise. Still others have been selected primarily because they are seats of universities, colleges, or other important educational institutions. Examples of this kind are Ann Arbor, Ithaca, Oberlin, and Princeton.

Again, the more important Indian towns of the Southwest have been given brief treatment. Among these are the pueblos of Isleta, Laguna, Walpi, and Zuni. Selections of summer, winter, and health resorts have been made, including such places as Lake Placid, Manitou Springs, Palm Beach, Santa Barbara, Hot Springs, and Mount Clemens. Of the less populous states, the largest and, usually, the second and the third largest cities have been included; as, for example, Albuquerque and Reno.

In the United States, there are more than 1500 cities and towns which have a population of from 5000 to 50,000. Moreover, there are upwards of 1500 towns of from 2500 to 5000 inhabitants. It is manifestly impossible, in a section of this kind, to give descriptions of *all* of these places. Those selected, however, are the most noted and the most interesting of this great group of towns and cities.

Cities of continental United States whose population in 1940 exceeded a half million have been given special topical treatment. The descriptive matter is divided into topics and the topics are given separate subheadings. The treatment follows a simple, uniform plan, beginning with a description of the site of the city, then describing streets, parks, buildings, educational institutions, industries, and other leading features, and ending with important points concerning its history.

Scenic and Travel Interest. Among topics of scenic and travel interest will be found descriptions of some of the most noted features of the continent, including mountains, lakes, deserts, islands, waterfalls, gorges, cliffs, and caves. Examples of the mountains are Mount Rainier, Mount Shasta, Lassen peak, and Mount Washington. The lakes include Lake Champlain, Lake George, Itasca lake, and Lake Tahoe. Among the deserts described are Death Valley, the Mojave, the Colorado, and the Painted desert. Representative of the other scenic features mentioned above are Niagara falls, Luray Cavern, Mammoth Cave, and the Palisades.

Numerous features, combining both scenic and historic interest, include Harpers Ferry, Lookout Mountain, Stone Mountain, and Starved Rock. Various special regions, such as the Cotton Belt, the Corn Belt, the Wheat Belt, the Citrus Belt, the Blue-Grass Region, and the Inland Empire, are also described. Although the numerous national parks and national monuments are given tabular treatment elsewhere, some of the most noted are described in greater detail in this section; as, for example, Yellowstone park and the Grand Canyon.

Aberdeen (*ăb'ẽr-dēn'*). The second largest city of South Dakota, situated in the northern part of the state, about 170 miles northeast of Pierre. Aberdeen is the commercial center of a rich agricultural district, producing large crops of wheat, flax, hay, and potatoes. Its industries include meat packing, flour milling, and the manufacture of machinery. The city is the seat of Northern State teachers college, which has a large open-air theater. Aberdeen was incorporated as a city in 1882. Population, 1940, 17,015.

Aberdeen. A city of western Washington, on Grays harbor, 50 miles west of Olympia. Aberdeen is a timber, dairy, and agricultural center, with lumber and plywood mills, fish-curing houses, canning establishments, and excellent port facilities. It adjoins Hoquiam on the west and Cosmopolis on the east. Its inhabitants have a large Scandinavian element. Population, 1940, 18,846.

Acoma (*ä'kô-mä*). An Indian pueblo situated on a rocky mesa 350 feet high, about 70 miles west of Albuquerque, New Mexico. Visited in 1540 by members of Coronado's exploring party, Acoma is believed to be, after Oraibi, the oldest continuously occupied town in the United States. Franciscan missionaries labored in Acoma as early as 1629 and later established San Estevan mission. The inhabitants speak the Keresan language. Population, about 1000.

Adamana (*ä'dä-mä'nä*). A small village on the Santa Fe railway in eastern Arizona. Near it are located the celebrated "petrified forests." Of the three forests which together constitute the Petrified Forest national monument, two lie at distances of from 6 to 9 miles south of Adamana. Here some thousands of acres are covered with fragments of petrified wood and with wonderfully preserved fossil tree trunks, many of which are 4 feet in diameter. One of these large mineralized trunks, by spanning a ravine 45 feet wide, forms a natural bridge.

The third forest, usually called "Rainbow Forest," is more readily reached by automobile road from Holbrook, a railway town 20 miles west of Adamana. In this petrified forest there are several hundred whole trees, some of which are more than 200 feet long and 6 feet in diameter, all partially embedded in the ground. These are the remains of great cone-bearing trees that grew in geological times. They are of many kinds, most of them closely related to the araucaria or Norfolk Island pine, now widely grown as an ornamental tree.

While the remains of fossilized trees near Adamana are among the most extensive known, there are other noteworthy petrified forests in various parts of the West. The fossil forest in the vicinity of Napa, California, is noted for its immense tree trunks. The Bad Lands of the upper Missouri River region abound in petrified trees, and in Yellowstone park there are numerous fossil tree trunks, some of which stand erect. See *Yellowstone Park*, *Bad Lands*.

Agana (*ä-gän'yä*). The capital and chief town of Guam, situated on the west coast of the island. It is the seat of a United States naval station and contains the government house on a large open, green square; also an arsenal, a public market, and various churches and schools. The people are engaged principally in simple trades and in local agriculture. Nine-tenths of the inhabitants are natives of mixed Malayan stock, called Chamorros. Population, 1940, 10,004.

Akron. A rubber manufacturing city of Ohio, so named because it was believed to occupy the highest point of land in the state. The name is a Greek word, meaning "summit." Akron lies 35 miles southeast of Cleveland, with a grain producing country to the south and a rich dairy country to the north.

Akron has long been noted for its clay products and cereal mills. With the rise of the automobile industry, the city became the center of the world's most extensive manufacture of automobile tires and of rubber goods in general. It produces also synthetic rubber, fishing tackle, zinc oxide, machine shop products, sulphur, salt, and children's books and is the principal center for the manufacture of airships. A colossal hangar, covering 9 acres, was opened for use in 1930.

Within the city there are 26 beautiful parks; these cover a total area of 2200 acres. The Portage Lakes, a 2250-acre state park, lies just south of the city. It contains about 300 acres of connecting lakes and channels. A concrete bridge, 190 feet high, spans the Cuyahoga river within the city, and the North Hill viaduct, 135 feet high and 2810 feet in length, provides the main approach from the north and east. The chief educational institution is the University of Akron, maintained as part of the free public school system of the city. A municipal stadium the "Rubber Bowl," has a seating capacity of 36,000. Population, 1940, 244,791.

Alameda (*ăl'ȧ-mā'dȧ; -mē'dȧ*). A city of California, occupying a narrow island on the east side of San Francisco bay, opposite San Francisco and directly south of Oakland, with which it is connected by three bridges across an estuary and by the Posey Tube. Alameda is a beautiful residential city, with numerous fine streets and homes. It also maintains substantial industries, among which are potteries, shipbuilding, and the manufacture of motors, pumps, engines, airplanes and lumber. A large naval air station is located there. Alameda's seven miles of municipal beaches, including Neptune beach, and its seven parks provide recreational facilities. Population, 1940, 36,256.

Albany. The capital of New York State, picturesquely situated on the west bank of the Hudson river, near the head of tidewater, 145 miles north of New York City.

Albany is the connecting link between the state's barge canal system and ocean navigation via the Hudson river, which is deepened to 27 feet as far as Albany. A feature of its terminal facilities is a grain elevator covering eight acres. Because of its very extensive railway connections, the city is one of the leading transfer points in the United States for passenger, express, and mail traffic. Near-by is a vast terminal classification yard with capacity for nearly 20,000 cars. Albany is said to have been the first American city to have a municipal airport, having provided one in 1917. The city's manufactures are extensive and varied. Among the chief products are car heaters and other metal wares, clothing, knit goods, paper products, flour, printing, railway car repairing, meat packing products, and felts.

The city occupies a commanding site, affording superb views of the Hudson River valley. There are many fine streets, among which are Broadway, Pearl, and State streets. Washington park, the largest of the 20 units in the city's park system, is noted for its natural beauty.

The most imposing building is the State capitol, which cost over 29 million dollars. This magnificent structure, 400 feet long and 300 feet wide, is built of Maine granite in the Renaissance style. The State Office Building, 34 stories high, is the city's tallest structure. Among other noteworthy buildings are: the State Education building; the Delaware & Hudson building; the Albany Institute of History and Art; the old Schuyler Mansion, dedicated in 1917 as a historical monument; and Saint Peter's church.

Albany is said to be the second oldest permanent settlement within the limits of the thirteen colonies, the first settlers being mainly Dutch. Its charter, granted in 1686, is said to be the oldest in the United States. The city was Burgoyne's objective before the battle of Saratoga and was the scene of Antirent riots in 1839. Population, 1940, 130,577.

Albuquerque (*ăl'bū-kûr'kē*). The largest city of New Mexico, on the Rio Grande river, slightly northwest of the center of the state. It lies at an elevation of 5000 feet, in a bracing, sunshiny climate, and is a noted health resort. The old town, founded in 1705 by the Spanish, remains as a division of the modern city, which dates from 1879.

Albuquerque is the trade center of a rich timber, livestock, and irrigation farming district. A leading occupation is the entertainment of tourists. The University of New Mexico is located here. The more notable structures include a Federal building and the Harvey Indian Museum. Features of interest in the vicinity are the ancient church of San Felipe de Neri, built in 1735, and the Isleta Indian pueblo. Population, 1940, 35,449.

Alcatraz. An island in San Francisco bay, about a mile from the mainland. Its shores rise precipitously from the sea. It had been fortified by the Spaniards. From 1858, it was used by the United States government to intern military prisoners. Beginning in 1933, it was used to incarcerate prisoners convicted of kidnapping, murder, and other serious charges, mostly involving life sentences. It was chosen for the purpose as being practically escape-proof and was designed for punishment rather than reformation.

Alexandria. A historic city of northern Virginia on the west bank of the Potomac river, six miles below Washington, D. C. Among its many quaint old buildings are Old Christ church, which George Washington and Robert E. Lee attended; Carlyle house, where Braddock, in 1755, organized his expedition against Fort Duquesne; and the home of Robert E. Lee. The George Washington National Masonic memorial, erected at a cost of $5,000,000, is the most imposing modern building. Alexandria's freight classification yard is one of the largest in the country. Refrigerator cars are made in the city. Population, 1940, 33,523.

Allentown. A manufacturing city of Pennsylvania, 55 miles north of Philadelphia. Besides its huge cement mills and its steel factories, Allentown has important silk, textile, tobacco, iron, furniture, and dyeing industries. The city is the seat of the famous "Allentown Fair." During the Revolutionary War, the Liberty Bell was concealed in one of the city's churches to prevent its capture by the British. The educational institutions include Muhlenberg college and Cedar Crest college, the latter for women. Population, 1940, 96,904.

Altoona. A railroad city of central Pennsylvania, picturesquely situated in a mountainous district about 100 miles east of Pittsburgh. The major industry is railway shop construction and repairs, enormous car shops of the Pennsylvania railroad being located in the city. Other products are textiles and clothing. Population, 1940, 80,214.

Amarillo. The chief commercial and industrial center of the northwestern arm of Texas, known as the "Panhandle." It is a focal point by rail, air, and highway for a region known as one of the richest gas and oil regions in the United States. Natural gas and oil are piped direct as far as the northern states. Helium-bearing sands are found near by, and the city is the chief producer of this gas for airships. Other industries include oil refining, zinc smelting, meat packing, and flour and cottonseed oil milling. Educational institutions include Amarillo college. Population, 1940, 51,686.

Anaconda. A mining city of southwestern Montana, 26 miles northwest of Butte. Anaconda was founded in 1884 by the Anaconda Copper Mining Company, which has there one of the world's largest non-ferrous reduction plants. It is often called the smelting city and is said to have the tallest smokestack in the world. Population, 1940, 11,004.

Annapolis. The capital of Maryland, situated on the right bank of the Severn river, near the center of the western coast of Chesapeake bay. The city was first settled in 1649, and was called Providence. In 1694, it was named after Queen Anne and was made the capital of the colony of Maryland. The first Federal Constitutional Convention met in Annapolis in 1786. The city is the seat of the United States Naval Academy, on a beautiful site of 200 acres, organized in 1845, and of Saint John's college, founded in 1696. The industries include an oyster packing plant. Population, 1940, 13,069.

Ann Arbor. A city of southeastern Michigan, on the Huron river, 37 miles west of Detroit. While Ann Arbor is the trade center of a rich farming district and has substantial local industries, it is most widely known as the seat of the University of Michigan, one of the leading state universities. The city was founded in 1824, and the university was opened in 1837. Population, 1940, 29,815.

Appalachian Trail. A wilderness foot trail extending 2050 miles from Mount Katahdin, Me., to Mount Oglethorpe, Ga. The longest marked foot path in the world, it follows in general the ridge of the Appalachian mountains, traversing parts of New Hampshire, Massachusetts, Connecticut, New York, Pennsylvania, Maryland, West Virginia, Virginia, Tennessee, and North Carolina.

The project was begun in 1921, largely through the initiative of Benton MacKaye (1879–), forester and specialist in regional planning. It was substantially completed by 1938 through the efforts of regional Appalachian Trail clubs and, where it passes through the Great Smoky and Shenandoah national parks, by the National park service. Campsites, open shelters, and permanent camps are provided at intervals for the accommodation of hikers. The purpose of the clubs which maintain and foster the use of the trail is to provide educational recreation, to foster a spirit of appreciation of nature, and to add to the fund of regional and scientific knowledge regarding the territory through which the trail passes.

Asbury Park. A city of New Jersey, on the Atlantic Ocean, about 35 miles south of New York City. Asbury Park is noted chiefly as a seaside resort and residential city. It has, however, various small industries, including the manufacture of silk, women's apparel, and leather clothing. Population, 1940, 14,617.

Asheville. A mountain resort and city of North Carolina, picturesquely situated in "The Land of the Sky," a plateau of the southern Appalachian mountains, 2300 feet above sea level, at the western extremity of the state. It is near Great Smoky Mountains national park, Mount Mitchell, and numerous other points of scenic interest, which are reached by beautiful highways, one of which penetrates Beaucatcher mountain by means of a 2000-foot tunnel. Near Biltmore Forest, a suburb, is situated the magnificent estate of George W. Vanderbilt, which is open to the public. Other features of the city include Pack Memorial library, Grove Arcade, covering an entire block, and the civic center on Pack square, where rise the impressive city hall and court house built in a modern style. Craggy Rhododendron gardens, 600 acres of royal purple rhododendrons 15 miles from the city, is one of the finest natural gardens in the world.

Asheville provides a market for near-by producers of fruit and is an important distribution center. Manufactured products include furniture, leather, mica, rayon, cotton textiles, and blankets. The city was incorporated in 1797. Population, 1940, 51,310.

Astoria. A port of northwestern Oregon, located on the Columbia river, about 10 miles from its mouth. It is noted chiefly for the catching and canning of salmon on an immense scale. Tuna also is caught and packed there. Other industries include lumber mills, flour mills, and creameries. Astoria has river, rail, and bus transportation to Portland, 105 miles distant, and also considerable ocean commerce, with exports of lumber, grain, fish, and flour. It has also a large tourist traffic. Astoria was named for John Jacob Astor, who founded it in 1811. It was largely destroyed by fire in 1922 and has since been rebuilt in a more modern style. Population, 1940, 10,389.

Athens. A city of northern Georgia, on the Oconee river, some 70 miles northeast of Atlanta. Its industries include cotton, textile, and lumber mills, marble and granite works, and fertilizer and bed-spring factories. Athens is a noted educational center and is sometimes styled the "classic city of the South." Its leading institutions include the University of Georgia, the State teachers college, the State agricultural college, the Lucy Cobb institute, the Knox institute, and Jeruel academy. Population, 1940, 20,650.

Atlanta. The capital and largest city of Georgia, situated in the north central part of the state, about 290 miles by rail northwest of Savannah.

The ridge on which the city is built is a part of a watershed dividing streams that flow into the Atlantic from those that flow into the Gulf of Mexico. The city lies about 1050 feet above sea level, an elevation higher than that of any city of equal or greater size east of Denver. The Chattahoochee river, flowing within 8 miles of the city, is the source of its water supply.

Atlanta is admirably, though somewhat irregularly, laid out, and contains many beautiful avenues and streets. Peachtree and West Peachtree streets, Pace's Ferry road, and Ponce de Leon avenue are fine residence streets, and Druid Hills and Ansley park are beautiful residence sections. The city covers about 34 square miles, and includes a park system embracing a total area of more than 1200 acres and containing 75 parks, squares, and open spaces. In Grant park there is a great cycloramic painting of the battle of Atlanta. About 15 miles to the east of Atlanta is situated Stone Mountain, on the face of which is a huge sculptured memorial to the valor of the Confederate soldiers. The commercial district contains many notable buildings, giving the city a metropolitan aspect. Among these are the State capitol, the Federal building, the Terminal station, the Federal Reserve bank, and numerous imposing office buildings.

Atlanta is a prominent educational center and contains many widely known institutions of learning. Among the leading institutions of higher learning are the Georgia institute of technology, Emory university, Oglethorpe university, and Columbia theological seminary. The institutions for women include Agnes Scott college, located in the adjoining suburb of Decatur. Among the institutions for Negroes are Atlanta, Clark, and Morris Brown universities, Morehouse college, and Gammon theological seminary. There are excellent libraries, and the city is one of the chief centers of printing and publishing in the South.

Because of its advantageous situation and excellent railway facilities, Atlanta has become the chief inland commercial city of the southeastern states. It is the distributing center for a large region and has developed extensive industries, ranking first in the state in manufactures. The leading products include cotton mill products, confectionery and ice cream, Coca-Cola, furniture, mattresses and bed springs, lumber, clothing, and fertilizers. The city is a leading mule market and conducts a large merchandising trade.

The growth of Atlanta dates from the building of the first railroads in northern Georgia. The site was settled about 1839. In 1843 it was incorporated as Marthasville. This name was changed to Atlanta in 1845, and in 1847 a city charter was granted. Because of its location, it was one of the most important cities of the Confederacy, and in 1864 was the objective of General Sherman's campaign from Chattanooga. The battle of Atlanta and other severe engagements were fought near the city, which was finally taken by the Union forces and largely destroyed. It was quickly rebuilt after the war and grew rapidly. In 1878, it was made the capital of the state. During 1895-96, the Cotton States and International exposition was held at Atlanta. Population, 1940, 302,288.

Atlantic City. An all-year seaside resort on Absecon Beach, a sandy island five miles off the southeastern mainland of New Jersey, about 55 miles southeast of Philadelphia. There are about 1200 hotels for the accommodation of visitors, the number of which often exceeds 15 million annually. The attractions include many miles of beaches, six large recreation piers, a 15-million dollar convention hall covering 7 acres and seating 41,000 people in its auditorium, and the "Board Walk," a magnificent promenade, 60 feet wide, extending along the ocean front for a distance of eight miles. Permanent population, 1940, 64,094.

Augusta. A commercial and manufacturing city of eastern Georgia, located at the head of navigation on the Savannah river, about 132 miles northwest of Savannah. Augusta is the trade center of a rich agricultural district and one of the leading cotton markets in the United States. Water power and hydroelectric power are extensively used in the city's substantial industries, the chief of which are the manufacture of cotton goods and cottonseed products. Other manufactures include brick, lumber, and fertilizers. A United States arsenal is located there. Augusta was established in 1735, and for a time during and after the Revolutionary War was the capital of Georgia. Population, 1940, 65,919.

Augusta. The capital of Maine, situated on both banks of the Kennebec river, about 40 miles from its mouth. The State capitol is a handsome structure, built of granite quarried locally. The Maine Insane hospital is situated in Augusta and a Veterans Administration facility is located five miles from the city. Excellent water and rail transportation facilities have made the city the trade center of a large district. It is also one of the chief air travel centers of the Northeast. Local industries include cotton, paper, and lumber mills. Population, 1940, 19,360.

Aurora. A city of northeastern Illinois, occupying a beautiful site on the Fox river, 38 miles west of Chicago. It is an important manufacturing and railroad center, producing road-building machinery, pumps, drills, and other metal products; also toilet articles and animal serums. Its educational institutions include Aurora college. Aurora was settled in 1834 and chartered as a city in 1857. Population, 1940, 47,170.

Ausable (*ô-sā'b'l*) **Chasm.** A narrow gorge of great scenic attractiveness, situated in northeastern New York, about midway between the Adirondacks and Lake Champlain. The rocks forming the walls are of hard Potsdam sandstone, traversed by numerous fault lines or displacements. Through these the Ausable river has worn a zigzag course about 2 miles long and, in places, 175 feet deep.

Austin. The capital of Texas, picturesquely located on the north side of the Colorado river, in the south central part of the state. The state capitol, situated in the ten-acre Capitol square, is one of the largest in the country. Austin is the seat of the University of Texas.

Within a radius of 60 miles of the city are five lakes created by dams as part of a system of flood control, irrigation, power development, and provision for recreation. The largest is Lake Austin, about 22 miles long. The industries include the manufacture of lumber, furniture, truck bodies, oil engines, cottonseed oil, food products, finished stone, and leather goods. The city is the center of a considerable wholesale and shipping business, and carries on an extensive trade in agricultural products, wool, and live stock. Austin was incorporated in 1839 and named for S. F. Austin, the "Father of Texas." The site had been selected in 1837 by a state commission instructed to find the most attractive spot for the capital. Population, 1940, 87,930.

BALTIMORE. The principal city of Maryland, the seventh in population in the United States, and the largest on the Atlantic seaboard south of Philadelphia. It is situated on the estuary of the Patapsco river, 12.5 miles from Chesapeake bay and about 170 miles by water from the Virginia capes on the Atlantic. Washington, D. C., lies about 40 miles southwest, and Philadelphia, 97 miles to the northeast. The area of Baltimore is about 79 square miles.

Streets and Buildings. The principal thoroughfares are Baltimore, Fayette, Pratt, and Lexington streets running east and west, and Charles, Saint Paul, Calvert, Gay, and Howard streets extending north and south. Many of the public buildings are noted for size and architectural beauty. Among these are the Peabody institute, the Roman Catholic cathedral, said to be the oldest in the United States, the First Presbyterian church, the Enoch Pratt free library, the Walters art gallery, the Baltimore museum of art, the city hall, the Federal building, and the Masonic temple. The Baltimore Trust Company building, 509 feet high, affords a landmark of conspicuous beauty.

Parks and Monuments. Many fine parks are scattered throughout the city. Of these, Druid Hill park is the largest and finest. Other noteworthy parks are Clifton, Patterson, Carroll, Herring Run, and Gwynn's Falls. A statue of Columbus, unveiled in 1792, the first in any American city to be dedicated to the great discoverer, stands on the grounds of the old Ready school. Mount Vernon Place, the nominal center of the city, is the site of the Washington Monument, a stately column of marble 210 feet high. This monument, the corner stone of which was laid July 4, 1815, was the first erected by any city in memory of George Washington, and gave to Baltimore her designation as the "monumental city." In Westminster cemetery, one of the oldest and smallest in Baltimore, is buried Edgar Allan Poe.

Educational Institutions. Baltimore is the seat of Johns Hopkins university, a leading institution of higher learning. Connected with it is the widely known Johns Hopkins hospital and the Johns Hopkins medical school. Among other important educational establishments are the University of Maryland, Goucher college for women, Loyola college, Morgan college, St. Mary's seminary, and Notre Dame academy. The Peabody institute contains a valuable historical library.

Transportation. In its magnificent system of railroads, its excellent harbor, and its extensive docks, Baltimore has every facility for railway and overseas transportation. Baltimore harbor, one of the largest on the continent with a minimum depth of 35 feet, is capable of accommodating large ocean steamers. Ocean steamers load and unload directly from and into railroad cars at the piers.

Commerce. Baltimore is the chief mercantile and jobbing city of the south Atlantic states and ranks as one of the leading export and import centers of the country. It exports large quantities of corn, wheat, and other grains, iron, steel, and copper products, fertilizers, and chemicals. Among the articles of import are sugar, petroleum, iron ore, manganese, bananas, tin, potash, rubber, and coffee. There is also an extensive coastwise and intercoastal trade.

Manufactures. Baltimore ranks among the leading cities of the United States in total value of manufactures produced. The principal industries are the making of iron and steel products (the largest single group), shipbuilding, copper, petroleum and sugar refining, and the manufacture of clothing, aircraft, malt and distilled beverages, tin plate, fertilizers, chemicals, and copper products. There are also large establishments for canning fruits and for packing meats and oysters.

Baltimore owes its commanding position as regards manufactures to its easy access to domestic and foreign raw materials and to principal American and world markets.

History. The first settlement within the present limits of the city was made in 1662. The city was founded in 1729 and was incorporated in 1796. At the time of the American Revolution and especially during the Napoleonic wars, Baltimore attained prominence as a seaport. Its fame was spread throughout the world by its fast-sailing ships called "Baltimore clippers." During an unsuccessful attack by the British on Ft. McHenry, which guarded the city, Francis Scott Key, in 1814, wrote the "Star-spangled Banner."

Baltimore was the first American city to be lighted by gas (1821). The first gas company in America was established there in 1816. The construction of the first important line of railway in the United States, the Baltimore and Ohio railroad, was begun in Baltimore in 1828. Here, also, the first iron steamship was built. In 1844, the first electric telegraph line ever operated was strung between Baltimore and Washington. The first complete, practical electric street railway in the world was installed in Baltimore in 1888.

In 1904, the whole business section was ravaged by fire, with a property loss exceeding $125,000,000. The destroyed area was soon rebuilt with wider streets and finer structures. The waters impounded by the Loch Raven and Pretty Bay dams, provide the city's water supply. Population, 1940, 859,100.

Bar Harbor. A summer resort in Maine, on the east shore of Mount Desert island, which lies near the center of the state's coast line. Bar Harbor is partially within Acadia national park. The scenery in the vicinity is enriched by mountains, by numerous small inlets on the coast, and by many picturesque lakes. Population, 1940, 4378.

Baton Rouge (*băt'ŭn ro͞ozh'*). The capital of Louisiana, located on the east bank of the Mississippi river, about 85 miles northwest of New Orleans. The river is spanned at this point by a 10-million dollar bridge. The city occupies a picturesque site on the river bluff, and receives additional charm from its sub-tropical foliage trees and old houses in the Spanish style. The imposing capitol, dedicated in 1932, has a 33-story tower. South of the city on a 3100-acre campus is the State university. By reason of its fine harbor, Baton Rouge carries on an extensive shipping trade. Its manufacturing interests include sugar and rice mills, chemical and wood-working factories, and a large oil refinery. Population, 1940, 34,719.

Battle Creek. A city of south central Michigan, situated about midway between Detroit and Chicago. The city lies in the center of a rich agricultural region and has become noted for its manufacture of cereals, dietetic foods, and therapeutic appliances. The Battle Creek sanitarium is visited by thousands of persons yearly. Population, 1940, 43,453.

Bay City. A city of eastern Michigan, on the Saginaw river, some 4 miles from Saginaw bay, an arm of Lake Huron, and about 100 miles northwest of Detroit. Bay City has excellent transportation facilities, both by rail and by water, the river being navigable for the largest lake vessels. The surrounding farming district produces large crops of sugar beets. Among the principal industries are automobile parts, electrical and other machinery, fabricated houses, cement, and beet sugar. First settled in 1837, Bay City was incorporated in 1859 and received its charter in 1865. Population, 1940, 47,956.

Bayonne (*bā'yōn'*). An industrial city of New Jersey, situated on New York harbor 7 miles southwest of New York City. Bayonne is one of the world's most important centers for the refining of petroleum. It is the terminal of oil pipe lines leading to New York and other eastern cities. The Bayonne Port terminal offers docking facilities among the finest in the New York area. Population, 1940, 79,198.

Beaumont (*bō'mŏnt*). A deep-water port of southeastern Texas, on the Neches river, about 84 miles northeast of Houston. Beaumont is the center of an important rice growing district, and there are great oil fields and large pine and cypress forests in the vicinity. The chief industries are oil refining, lumbering, shipbuilding, and the cleaning and the marketing of rice. Population, 1940, 59,061.

Bellingham. A port of northwestern Washington, located on a natural harbor on Bellingham bay. It is the commercial center of an extensive agricultural, poultry, and lumbering region. Salmon fishing is an important industry. The leading manufacturing establishments include lumber, pulp, and paper mills, salmon and fruit canneries, and cement and sugar beet factories. The city is the seat of the Western Washington college of education. Population, 1940, 29,314.

Berkeley (*bûrk'lĭ*). A city of California, situated on San Francisco bay opposite the Golden Gate and adjoining Oakland, which lies to the south. Berkeley's beautiful site overlooking the bay and the equable climate unite to make the city highly attractive from a residential point of view.

Berkeley is the seat of the University of California, the largest in the world. Excellent transportation facilities and low priced electrical power have favored the development of various industries. The manufactures include soap, printers ink, gasoline engines, pumps, fertilizers, food products, steel tanks, leather, and serums.

Berkeley was first settled in 1868, and was incorporated as a town in 1878. It was named after Bishop Berkeley, the noted British philosopher and author of the saying, "Westward the course of empire takes its way." Population, 1940, 85,547.

Bethlehem (*bĕth'lē-hĕm; -lē-ĕm*). A manufacturing city of eastern Pennsylvania, 52 miles northwest of Philadelphia. It is built on two hills separated by the Lehigh river, which is here spanned by three bridges, including a hill-to-hill bridge erected at a cost of $3,500,000. The leading industries are steel, foundry and machine products, and silk. Other industrial products include flour, knit goods, radios, cigars, electrical equipment, and furniture. Founded in 1741 by Moravians, Bethlehem is the center of the Moravian sect in America and contains two Moravian colleges. The city celebrates an annual musical festival which is sometimes styled the American Bayreuth. Bethlehem is also the seat of Lehigh university. Population, 1940, 58,490.

Binghamton. A manufacturing city of south central New York, about 125 miles southwest of Albany. Binghamton is picturesquely situated at the junction of the Susquehanna and Chenango rivers, which are here crossed by various bridges, Memorial and Clinton Street spans being particularly noteworthy. The city is made attractive by fine parks, the larger of which are Ross, Ely, Southside, and Recreation parks, and by beautiful drives. The city's industries are extensive and varied, the more prominent ones including the manufacture of shoes, photographic equipment, furniture, and business machines. The first settlement on the site of the city, made in 1787, was known as Chenango Point. In 1800 this was renamed Binghamton, which was incorporated as a village in 1834 and became a city in 1867. Population, 1940, 78,309.

Birmingham. The largest city of Alabama, slightly north of the center of the state. The city was named after Birmingham, England, in allusion to the proximity of rich deposits of iron. Being situated in the midst of immense coal deposits also, Birmingham has risen to high rank among the iron and steel producing centers of the country. Steel and steel products and coke account for a high percentage of the city's extensive output of manufactures, although in recent years the industries of Birmingham have become considerably diversified. The tonnage of its freight is said to be greater than that of all the rest of the South combined. Birmingham is also the trade center of a large and highly productive agricultural district.

The city is substantially and handsomely built, and has many fine streets, beautiful residences, and imposing public buildings, and also numerous commercial structures of the skyscraper type. The municipal park system contains upwards of 39 public parks. Among the most prominent of these are Wilson, North Birmingham, East Lake, Lake View, and Highland parks.

Birmingham is a notable product of the industrial transformation that has taken place in the South since the Civil War. In 1870, the site of the city was a cotton field. In 1871, following the discovery of valuable coal and iron ore deposits in the vicinity, a land company founded Birmingham. Growth at first was slow, but the population rose from about 3000 in 1880 to more than 26,000 in 1890. Since the latter date, Birmingham has enjoyed remarkable growth. Population, 1940, 267,583.

Bismarck (*bĭz'märk*). The capital of North Dakota, situated on the east bank of the Missouri river, slightly southwest of the center of the state. The most notable buildings include the State capitol and the World War Memorial Building. The Missouri river is spanned here by a vehicular bridge. Creameries and nurseries are representative of the city's industries. Population, 1940, 15,496.

Black Hills. A picturesque, mountainous region in South Dakota and northeastern Wyoming. Its 6000 square miles are rich in minerals, particularly gold, and embrace the Black Hills national forest (970 square miles) and Custer state park (168 square miles). The highest point is Harney peak (7216 feet). On Mount Rushmore was begun in 1927 a huge memorial depicting in colossal sculpture the figures of Washington, Jefferson, Lincoln, and Theodore Roosevelt.

Black Rock Desert. A dreary waste fully 70 miles long and in some places 20 miles wide, extending northeast from Pyramid lake in northwestern Nevada. This area, which embraces nearly 1000 square miles, is an alkaline flat or sink, practically devoid of vegetation. In summer, it is a barren plain covered with dun-colored, alkaline dust which is blown into vast clouds by the wind. During winter, portions are covered with shallow water, whence the name "mud lake," sometimes applied to the region.

Blue-Grass Region. A district in central Kentucky, lying between the low plains of the west and the mountains on the east. This region is devoted largely to stock raising and is famous for its thoroughbred horses. It is so named because of the prevalence and fine quality of its blue-grass pastures, which are a common feature of the landscape.

Boise (*boi'sĭ*). The capital of Idaho, located on the Boise river in the southwestern quarter of the state. The surrounding country is rich in minerals and in agricultural products, and the city is an important inland wool market. The varied industries utilize hydroelectric power from the celebrated Arrowrock dam, constructed 22 miles east of the city and having a height of 349 feet. Boise is unique among cities in possessing a natural supply of hot water from a flowing well. This is used for heating houses and for supplying the city's large outdoor swimming pool at White City park. Population, 1940, 26,130.

BOSTON (*bŏs'tŭn*). The capital of Massachusetts, the chief city of New England, and the ninth in population in the United States, is situated on Boston bay, at the mouth of the Charles and the Mystic river, about 230 miles northeast of New York City.

Site. The original site of Boston was a peninsula marked by three historic hills, Beacon hill, Copp's hill, and Fort hill, and contained about 780 acres. By leveling portions of the hills and by filling in various inlets and tidal marshes, this original area was gradually expanded to 1800 acres. To this, various adjoining districts have been added, including Dorchester, Charlestown, West Roxbury, Brighton, and Hyde Park, until the city now contains an area of more than 30,000 acres, or about 50 square miles.

Metropolitan District. Modern Boston consists of the city proper and of the populous metropolitan district of which it is the center. The cities of Somerville and Cambridge extend almost to the heart of Boston, and the fine suburb of Brookline lies almost wholly within the city. These are closely surrounded by other large suburban communities. The population of the metropolitan district, lying within 20 miles of the center of Boston, exceeds 2,400,000. The center of population in the state of Massachusetts lies within the metropolitan district.

Streets. The narrow, irregular streets, characteristic of the old town, now form but a small section of the North End, mainly an Italian center. The modern city contains about 700 miles of paved streets, which, in the newer districts, are handsomely laid out. Beacon street, rich in historic associations, and Commonwealth avenue, one of the finest boulevards in America, are representative of Boston's finest residential avenues. Washington, Tremont, and Boylston streets constitute the center of retail trade, and State street is the financial center.

Parks. Boston ranks high among American cities in the development of parks and playgrounds. This has two distinct phases, municipal and metropolitan. The municipal park system covers 3500 acres, or more than one-tenth of the city's total area. It embraces the historic Common, 48 acres in extent, set aside in 1634, now in the heart of the city, and includes a chain of parks in various other sections, connected by beautiful parkways. These almost encircle the city, beginning with the Charles River esplanade and continuing to Marine park in South Boston. Among them are Olmstead park, Jamaica pond, the Arnold arboretum, and Franklin park with a large zoological garden.

The Metropolitan parks district includes, with Boston, about 40 municipalities. These are administered by a state commission. The Metropolitan parks plan includes such reservations as the Middlesex Fells, 1900 acres; the Blue Hills, 4900 acres; Stony Brook Woods, 460 acres; and Lynn Woods, 2000 acres. With these are grouped also Revere beach, Nantasket beach, and improvements along the Charles, Mystic, and Neponset rivers. The scheme embraces reservations with connecting parkways covering upwards of 10,000 acres.

Monuments. Boston is noted for its monuments and statues, embracing some of the finest sculptural work in America. The most striking is Bunker Hill monument, a granite obelisk, about 220 feet high, in Charlestown. In the Common is the great army and navy memorial, by Milmore, and the monument commemorating the Boston Massacre, by Kraus. In the Public Gardens is an equestrian statue of Washington, by Ball; and the Ether monument, commemorating Dr. W. T. G. Morton's discovery, by J. Q. A. Ward. Facing the capitol is the impressive Shaw memorial by Saint Gaudens. At Trinity church there is a statue of Philips Brooks, also by Saint Gaudens. In the Fenway is the John Boyle O'Reilly memorial, by D. C. French. Cyrus Dallin, a Boston sculptor, is represented by "Appeal to the Great Spirit," before the Fine Arts Building, and by other works.

Buildings. The newer portions of Boston contain some of the finest examples of modern architecture in the United States. Among many notable buildings may be mentioned the capitol, the public library, Federal Building, Trinity church, Holy Cross cathedral, the First Church of Christ Scientist, and the museum of fine arts. The customhouse, with a tower 505 feet high, is one of the landmarks of the city.

Educational Institutions. Boston is unsurpassed as an educational center. Among its leading institutions are Boston university, Boston college, Simmons college, the New England conservatory of music, the Harvard medical and dental schools, Northeastern university, and the art school in connection with the museum of fine arts. Harvard university, Radcliffe college, and the Massachusetts institute of technology are located across the Charles river in Cambridge. Tufts college, Wellesley college, and other noted institutions are in near-by suburbs. Boston is the home of many important historic, scientific, literary, and musical societies. The Boston Symphony Orchestra is one of the leading organizations of its kind.

Transportation. In large measure, Boston owes its commercial prominence to excellent transportation facilities. It is the chief railway center of New England, and its harbor is one of the finest and best equipped on the continent. It has 8 miles of wharfage, giving 40 miles of berthing space. Local transportation includes both elevated railways and subways and an immense system of street railways with extensive suburban connections.

Commerce. Boston is the chief seaport of New England and one of the foremost in the United States. The exports are chiefly provisions and manufactures of cotton, wool, leather, iron and steel, and rubber. Among the principal imports are wool, cotton, fibers, sugar, hides, tea, tin, wood products, and chinaware. There is an extensive coastwise trade, and the city has become the leading fish market in the United States. Among the world's wool markets, Boston ranks second only to London. As a chief distributing point for New England, Boston conducts an enormous wholesale trade. The city is also the center of immense mining, railway, and insurance interests.

Manufactures. As a manufacturing center, the Boston area ranks about tenth among the industrial regions of the United States. While no single industry predominates, the city is a leading center for the manufacture of boots and shoes, clothing, confectionery, cocoa products, books, textile and electrical machinery, edge tools, shipbuilding, and numerous specialties.

Points of Interest. Boston, with its environs, offers the traveler an immense number of points of historic and literary interest. Many of the more famous of the earlier buildings have been carefully preserved. Among these are Christ church (Old North), dating from 1723, Faneuil hall, the old statehouse, King's chapel, and the Old South meetinghouse. Bunker Hill monument and the navy yard are within the city. In the environs to the northwest are Concord and Lexington, and farther away to the southeast are Plymouth and Plymouth rock.

Many great writers and scientists lived in or near Boston, including Longfellow, Lowell, Emerson, Holmes, Hawthorne, Thoreau, Dana, Aldrich, Parkman, Prescott, Motley, and Agassiz. Numerous homes and other places of interest connected with the lives of these men are readily accessible.

History. In a large sense, the history of Boston is the history of New England. Founded in 1630 by Puritans under the leadership of Governor John Winthrop, it was made the capital of the Massachusetts Bay Colony, and has since remained the dominant center of New England. In 1704 the *Boston News Letter*, the first regular newspaper printed in America, began publication. In 1765 began the resistance to the Stamp act, which culminated in the Revolution. In 1770 occurred the "Boston Massacre," and, in 1773, the famous "Boston Tea Party." At the beginning of the Revolution, Boston was occupied by British troops who defeated the colonists at the battle of Bunker Hill, 1775, but early in 1776 Washington forced the British to evacuate the town. Boston received its charter as a city in 1822. About 1830 the city became the center of the Abolitionist movement. During the greater part of the 19th century, Boston was regarded as the literary center of America. Population, 1940, 770,816.

Boulder. A city of northern Colorado, 30 miles northwest of Denver, at the foot of the Rocky mountains. It is the center of a farming, stock raising, and mining region, and its industrial establishments include flour mills, lumber mills, ore sampling works, and manufactories of clay and kaolin products. The city owns 6000 acres of mountain park land, including Arapahoe glacier, from which the municipal water supply is obtained. Boulder canyon near by possesses great scenic interest. The city is a noted summer and health resort, and is the seat of the University of Colorado. Population, 1940, 12,958.

Bridgeport. The chief manufacturing city of Connecticut, situated in the southwestern part of the state on a natural harbor of Long Island sound. The city is noted for the great diversity of its manufactures, which include electrical machinery, sewing machines, corsets, phonographs, plated ware, firearms, ordnance, ammunition, clothing, airplanes, brass products, machine tools, drugs, typewriters, and numerous other products. Bridgeport first attained importance as the seat of the manufacture of sewing machines and as the headquarters of Barnum's circus. The park system includes the beautiful Seaside park with its two-mile boulevard along the sea wall. Population, 1940, 147,121.

Brockton. A manufacturing city of eastern Massachusetts, about 20 miles south of Boston. Brockton is one of the largest shoe manufacturing centers in the United States. Other industries include the manufacture of elastic goods, shoe machinery, shoe blacking, nails, and tools. Brockton was settled in 1700, became a town in 1821, and a city in 1881. Population, 1940, 62,343.

Brookline. A town of eastern Massachusetts, on the Charles river, about 3 miles west of Boston. Brookline is chiefly a residential place and ranks among the most beautiful and wealthy suburban towns in America. It produces some manufactures, among which may be mentioned scientific instruments and automobile bodies. Population, 1940, 49,786.

Brooklyn. See *New York.*

BUFFALO (*bŭf'ȧ-lō*). The second largest city of New York, situated at the eastern end of Lake Erie, about 22 miles south of Niagara Falls. Buffalo occupies a commanding site facing westward on Lake Erie and the Niagara river, and southward to the valley of Buffalo creek.

Streets and Buildings. The city is regularly laid out, with mostly broad streets crossing each other usually at right angles. There are, however, several great diagonal thoroughfares radiating from the commercial center. Main street, the chief business thoroughfare, extends northeasterly from its foot at the lake front. From Main street, Broadway, Seneca street, Genesee street, and other important thoroughfares reach into the densely populated district of the east side. Similarly, Niagara street extends from Main street northwesterly along the lake and river.

The fine residential sections, which are among the most beautiful in America, lie in the northwestern and in the northern parts of the city. Delaware avenue, with its handsome mansions, ranks high among the residential streets of the country. Other noteworthy residential streets are Linwood and Richmond avenues, lined with magnificent elms; Summer and West Ferry streets; Lincoln parkway; and Depew avenue in the Central Park district.

Buffalo is substantially built and contains many fine edifices. Among these are the Federal building, an impressive granite structure in the French Romanesque style; the county courthouse, also of granite; and surmounted by a tower 245 feet high; the 32-story city hall costing $7,000,000 and New York State building, both in the civic center; the Liberty Bank and Rand buildings; the impressive Union station; the State teachers college; the 174th Infantry and the 106th Field Artillery armories; the museum of natural history and science, the Buffalo Historical Society building; the Albright art gallery, an excellent example of refined classical architecture; the modernistic Kleinhans music hall, partly surrounded by a reflecting pool; a $2,700,000 memorial auditorium; and Saint Joseph's cathedral. In the adjoining suburb of Lackawanna is the beautiful Basilica of Our Lady of Victory, a national shrine of the Roman Catholic Church.

Parks and Monuments. The municipal park system consists of a chain of parks and parkways which nearly encircle the city, covering in all an area of more than 1250 acres. In these are golf links, lakes and ponds, and numerous other facilities for recreation. Delaware park, 365 acres, with an artistic blending of lake, field, and natural forest, ranks scenically among the leading American parks. The Front, 45 acres, and Centennial park, 66 acres, two beautifully landscaped tracts, overlook the outlet of Lake Erie into the Niagara river. Other recreational areas are Humboldt, South, and Cazenovia parks.

The principal public memorials are the McKinley monument in Niagara square and the Soldiers' and Sailors' monument in Lafayette square. In Forest Lawn cemetery, there are monuments in memory of the Indian-chief Red Jacket and of President Fillmore.

Educational Institutions. The chief educational institutions are the University of Buffalo, Canisius college, D'Youville college, the Buffalo Seminary, a State teachers college, and the Fine Arts academy connected with the Albright art gallery.

Transportation. Buffalo's unique situation on the Great Lakes, combined with highly developed transportation facilities, gives the city its rank as a world port. The harbor, protected by an immense breakwater, is one of the best on the Great Lakes. The New York State barge canal forms a continuous water route to the Hudson river. The Welland canal, 20 miles northwest of Buffalo, gives water connection with Lake Ontario and the Saint Lawrence river. Ferry service, a railroad bridge, and the Peace bridge for general traffic connect the city with Canada. Moreover, Buffalo is one of the most important railway centers east of Chicago, being served by 11 major railroads. Thus, by rail as well as by water, Buffalo is on the direct line of communication between the lake ports and the Atlantic seaboard.

Commerce. In tonnage and in extent of traffic, Buffalo ranks with the leading American and European ports. The water-borne traffic from the West consists principally of grain, iron ore, flour, and general merchandise. Wheat is the chief commodity received, with iron ore second, the two constituting more than half of the total. The water-borne traffic to the West is comprised mostly of manufactured goods, sugar, and anthracite. The total value of goods entering and leaving the port exceeds a half billion dollars annually. Besides this large lake and barge canal traffic, immense quantities of merchandise are received and distributed by rail. The city is an important center for the transshipment of grain, its grain elevators having a capacity of about 30 million bushels. Buffalo is also the general trade and wholesale distributing center of a large and highly populous region.

Manufactures. In manufactures, Buffalo usually ranks eighth among the cities of the United States. The city's industries are extensive and varied and their growth has been substantial and enduring. The production of iron and steel and various iron and steel products constitutes the chief industry, with flour milling and meat packing next in importance. It is, with Minneapolis, one of the two largest centers of flour milling in the country. Among other noteworthy manufactures are automobiles, rubber tires, rayon and other chemicals, airplanes, food preparations, books, linseed oil, and furniture. Buffalo owes its eminence in manufactures to hydroelectric power, derived from Niagara falls; to large supplies of natural gas, and other readily available fuel; and to unexcelled transportation advantages for the distribution of its products.

Points of Interest. The pre-eminent feature of scenic interest in the vicinity of Buffalo is Niagara falls. This great cataract is most conveniently reached from Buffalo and is visited annually by scores of thousands. There are also many points of historical interest in connection with the early settlement of the Niagara frontier and of the conflict with the British and Indians in the war of 1812–15.

History. La Salle visited the site of Buffalo as early as 1679. The first white settlement was made about 1788 by Indian traders. In 1801–02, a village called New Amsterdam was laid out at the mouth of Buffalo creek. This village was incorporated and renamed Buffalo in 1810. Three years later it was captured and practically destroyed by the British. It was rebuilt but grew slowly until the completion of the Erie canal in 1825. Since that date,

Buffalo's progress has been continuous and substantial. In 1832, Buffalo received its charter as a city. The first grain elevator in the world was built in Buffalo in 1843. The city has given to the United States two presidents, Millard Fillmore and Grover Cleveland. In 1901, the Pan-American exposition was held at Buffalo. Population, 1940, 575,901.

Burlington. The largest city of Vermont, located at the approximate center of the east shore of Lake Champlain. Burlington had formerly a large import trade in lumber from Canada. Among its manufactures are textiles, cereals, dyes, and apparel. In the vicinity are large quarries of marble and limestone. The city is the seat of the University of Vermont, chartered in 1791, and Trinity college for women. It is headquarters of the Champlain Transportation Company, reputedly the oldest steamship corporation in the world. Greenmount cemetery contains the grave of Colonel Ethan Allen. Population, 1940, 27,686.

Butte (*būt*). The largest city of southwestern Montana, situated in a mountainous region at an elevation of 5800 feet above sea level. Incorporated in 1879, Butte is the center of an extremely rich copper mining region. Recognition of the city's indebtedness to Marcus Daly, discoverer of the rich copper veins, is expressed in the form of a statue by St. Gaudens, funds for which were raised by public subscription. The famous Anaconda mine, said to be the largest copper mine in the world, and many other valuable mining properties are located within a radius of a few miles. Besides copper, the principal product, manganese, gold, silver, lead, and zinc are obtained. The total value of the mineral output to date is approximately 2 billion dollars. The city supports various minor industries, has an extensive local trade, entertains numerous tourists, and is the seat of the Montana School of Mines. Population, 1940, 37,081.

Cambridge. A city of Massachusetts, situated on the Charles river opposite Boston. Cambridge is exceedingly rich in historical, literary, and educational associations.

The Washington elm, under which Washington took command of the American army, stood in Cambridge until 1923, when it was blown down. Elmwood park commemorates the home of James Russell Lowell. Craigie House, once the headquarters of General Washington, became the home of Henry Wadsworth Longfellow. Because of its historic association and its distinguished architecture, this building has long been one of the most famous points of interest in Cambridge. Among the illustrious figures once resident in Cambridge were Oliver Wendell Holmes, Louis Agassiz, and John Fiske. The city is the seat of Harvard university, the oldest university in the United States, of Radcliffe college, of the Massachusetts institute of technology, and of the Andover theological seminary. A beautiful system of parks includes nearly the entire river front and extends around the manufacturing district.

The city has numerous important industries, among which are printing and publishing, and the manufacture of electrical machinery, rubber goods, structural ironwork, chemicals, soap, candy, and bakery products.

Cambridge was settled in 1630 by Governor Winthrop and others as Newe Towne. In 1638, Newe Towne was renamed Cambridge; in the same year, Harvard college (founded in 1636) was opened. In 1639, the first printing press in English-speaking North America was set up in Cambridge. The first book printed here was "The Bay Psalm Book," which appeared in 1640. The city's population in 1940 was 110,879.

Camden. A city of southwestern New Jersey, located on the east bank of the Delaware river, opposite Philadelphia. The city occupies a level site, covering an area of about 10 square miles. The park system contains Forest Hill park and about 40 other parks or playgrounds. Among the leading industries are shipbuilding and the manufacture of radios, phonographs, canned soups, and worsted goods. Other important manufactures include iron and steel forgings, foundry products, linoleum, chemicals, and pens. In the suburbs are immense market gardens. The city is connected with Philadelphia by steam ferries and by a bridge which, on its completion in 1926, was the greatest suspension bridge in the world. First settled by Quakers, Camden was organized and named in 1773 and became a city in 1828. Population, 1940, 117,536.

Canton. An industrial and manufacturing city of northeastern Ohio, situated in a rich agricultural district. The manufacture of iron and steel products constitutes the leading group of industries, the second most important being the production of brick and tile. Canton was the home and burial place of President McKinley, in honor of whom a beautiful national memorial has been erected in West Lawn Cemetery. Population, 1940, 108,401.

Carlsbad Cave. A cavern in southeastern New Mexico, believed to be the largest and deepest in the world. It is entered at the foot of a cliff in the Guadalupe mountains about 20 miles south of Carlsbad, New Mexico, and 130 miles east of El Paso, Texas.

The cave was formed by water filtering through overlaid rocks and slowly dissolving out beds of rock salt, limestone, and gypsum. The dripping water carrying dissolved minerals has formed stalagmites and stalactites of unrivaled beauty. In the so-called "King's Room," stalactites hang like the iridescent folds, pleats, and ruffles of a canopy. One of the most impressive portions is the "Big Room," about 4000 feet long with a maximum width of 625 feet. At one point the ceiling is 300 feet high. No less spectacular is a room known as "Hell's Half Acre," lavishly studded with stalactites, pools of water, and a fountain. The "Giant Dome" resembles the leaning tower of Pisa. It is estimated to be 60 million years old. The lowest known point in the cave is some 1350 feet below the earth's surface.

The cave is known to extend at least 25 miles, approximately a third being accessible to the public over carefully marked trails. Artistically concealed electric flood lights emphasize the natural beauty of the cavern. The temperature is constant throughout the year at 56°F.

The most interesting feature of animal life within the cave is a huge colony of bats, estimated to number 3 million, which issues forth from the entrance each evening of summer like a thick cloud. It was this cloud of bats which led to the discovery of the cave in 1901 by Jim White, a cowboy. Milk-white crickets have been found in the cave.

In 1923, an area of about 719 acres surrounding the mouth of the cavern was set aside as a national monument. This was made into a national park in 1930, an additional 193 square miles being authorized for inclusion later.

Carson City. The capital of Nevada, picturesquely located near the foot of the Sierra Nevada, about 12 miles from Lake Tahoe. It contains the capitol, a Federal building, a branch of the United States mint, and a museum containing a series of mastodon skeletons discovered near by. In the vicinity are the state penitentiary and a government Indian school. Population, 1940, 2478.

Casa Grande (*kä'sä grän'dā*). The remains of a prehistoric building, situated near the south bank of the Gila river, about 12 miles west of Florence, Arizona, and at a somewhat greater distance from Casa Grande railway station. The first known white man to visit this impressive structure was Father Kino, a Jesuit missionary. In 1694, he said Mass in one of its rooms. It was made a national monument in 1892.

The principal edifice is about 45 by 60 feet in extent. The height of the walls indicates that there were at least three stories, each having various rooms. Above the third story was a smaller room, apparently a watch tower. This structure is only one of many blocks of buildings whose former existence near by is marked by mounds of debris.

Casa Grande stood within a walled enclosure with similar "compounds" around it. The walls of the building are of a fawn color, slightly tinged with red. Externally they are rough and very much eroded. The interior walls, however, are smoothly plastered. The structure is built of a natural cement, called *caliche* by the Mexicans, composed of lime, earth, and pebbles. This was made into blocks laid in courses.

Casa Grande was probably built about 1350 by the Salado Indians and was occupied by them and the Hohokams for nearly a century. It was then abandoned for reasons unknown.

Casper. A city of Wyoming, in the east central part of the state, on the North Platte river, 150 miles northwest of Cheyenne. It is the site of Fort Caspar, and has extensive commercial interest in the cattle, sheep, wool, and petroleum produced in the surrounding districts. The refinement of petroleum is the chief industry. Casper owns a 440-acre mountain park 5 miles south of the city. Population, 1940, 17,964.

Castle Gate. The entrance to Price River canyon in central Utah, about 115 miles southeast of Salt Lake City. This gatelike passage is formed by two immense pinnacles of sandstone, 450 to 500 feet in height. These pinnacles, strikingly colored, rise sheer from the narrow canyon bed, barely leaving room for the railway and the river to pass.

Catskill Mountains. A group of mountains in the southeastern portion of New York State about 100 miles north of New York City. The system is about 50 miles long, north and south, and has a breadth of some 30 miles. The highest peak is Slide mountain, 4204 feet in elevation. In order to supply New York City with water, two creeks on the southern slopes of the Catskills have been impounded: the Esopus by the Ashokan dam and the Scholarie by the Gilboa dam. From the resulting reservoirs, which communicate by the 18-mile Shandaken tunnel, water is conveyed to New York City by the Catskill aqueduct, which includes a 17-mile tunnel.

Cedar Rapids. A manufacturing city and railway center of east central Iowa, situated on the Cedar river, 220 miles west of Chicago. Among the chief industries are meat packing, cereals, corn products, machinery, and radio equipment. In total value of manufactures, Cedar Rapids ranks first among the cities of the state. The city is the mercantile center for a rich agricultural region, and enjoys an extensive wholesale trade. The first settlement was made in 1838 at the rapids of the Cedar river. These furnish the water power which has been an important factor in the city's growth. Cedar Rapids is the seat of Coe college. Population, 1940, 62,120.

Champlain, Lake. An important lake, lying between New York and Vermont, draining through the Richelieu river into the Saint Lawrence. Lake Champlain is about 110 miles long and, at its broadest northern portion, about 13 miles wide. It has a total area of about 600 square miles, two-thirds of which is in Vermont. Its greatest depth is about 300 feet, and it is navigable for the largest vessels.

Lake Champlain is connected with the Hudson river by a canal from Whitehall and serves as a link in New York's extensive system of inland waterways. Among the towns along its shores are Rouses Point, Plattsburg, Port Henry, Crown Point, and Whitehall in New York, and Burlington in Vermont.

Discovered by Champlain in 1609, the lake and its environs became the scene of many stirring events in the French and Indian war and in the Revolutionary War. The decisive naval battle of Lake Champlain was fought off Plattsburg in 1814.

Charleston. The chief city and seaport of South Carolina, situated 7 miles from the ocean on a peninsula between the Ashley and Cooper rivers. The estuary of these rivers forms a fine landlocked harbor—one of the deepest and most spacious on the Atlantic coast.

The attractive appearance of the city is enhanced by such features as Washington park, with its pre-Revolutionary statue of William Pitt; Hampton park; the customhouse, built of white marble at a cost of $3,400,000; White Point Gardens; and the Esplanade, comprised of the broad, beautiful promenade of the Battery seawall drive.

The chief industries of Charleston include the manufacture of fertilizers, lumber, and paper. There are large oil refineries and storage tank farms. In recent years the city has made scientific efforts to realize the possibilities arising from the natural advantages of Charleston as a seaport. It has repurchased a large part of its waterfront and established a port utilities commission. Leading articles of export are cotton, lumber, coal, tobacco, vegetables, metals, and manufactures. From Charleston, in 1784, was sent the first bale of cotton exported from the United States to Europe. Although possessing an excellent harbor, the sea-borne commerce of Charleston developed slowly until about 1920. Since that date, it has made notable growth.

The vicinity of Charleston was the scene of the earliest attempts at colonization in South Carolina. A temporary settlement was made by the French in 1562. The first settlement on the present site of the city was made by English colonists in 1670, who were joined in 1686 by groups of Huguenot refugees. In 1755, a colony of 2000 deported Acadians settled in Charleston.

During the American Revolution, Charleston was captured by the British. The city suffered immense damage in the final campaign of the Civil War in 1865. On August 31, 1886, a heavy earthquake caused great destruction of life and property. After each period of devastation, the city was rebuilt more substantially than before.

Charleston has preserved, to a remarkable degree, her interesting historic places and features. These include, not only the famous gardens, much visited in azalea season, but also many points illustrating the periods of American life from 1700 to the present day. Charleston's individuality has often been noted by travelers. Her historic and architectural charm has been described as a "lingering fragrance."

Possessing a well equipped navy yard, Charleston is a naval base of great strategic importance. The system of harbor defenses includes Fort Sumter, whose bombardment in 1861 was the beginning of the Civil War.

Among the city's leading educational institutions are the College of Charleston, the Medical College of South Carolina, and the Citadel, or State military college. Population, 1940, 71,275.

Charleston. The capital of West Virginia, built at the confluence of the Elk and the Kanawha river toward the western end of the state. Charleston is a distributing point for coal, salt, and hardwood. The city has numerous industries, the more important establishments being chemical and sheet glass plants and an ax factory which ranks among the largest in the world. In the vicinity are extensive deposits of coal, oil, salt and natural gas. The principal buildings include the magnificent State capitol, dedicated in 1932, near which is a fine monument erected to the memory of "Stonewall" Jackson. Charleston was incorporated in 1794, and became the capital of the state in 1870. Population, 1940, 67,914.

Charlotte (*shär'lŏt*). A cotton manufacturing city of North Carolina, located in the rich cotton growing district of the southwestern part of the state. It is at the heart of the hydroelectrical development in the state, and, besides cotton textile mills, has dye and engineering works, flour mills, and automobile assembly plants. The city has a monument erected to the memory of those who, at Charlotte in 1775, signed the Mecklenburg Declaration of Independence. The leading educational institution is Queen's college. Charlotte is the birthplace of President Polk. Population, 1940, 100,899.

Charlotte Amalie. The capital of the Virgin Islands, on the southern side of the island of Saint Thomas, about 40 miles east of Puerto Rico and 1440 miles southeast of New York. Situated on Saint Thomas harbor, one of the finest in the Antilles, it commands strategically the important Virgin Passage. It has a large coaling and fuel oil station. Population, 1940, 9801.

Charlottesville (*shär'lŏts-vĭl*). A city of central Virginia, built on the Rivanna river, about 70 miles northwest of Richmond. Charlottesville is the seat of the University of Virginia. This was founded by Thomas Jefferson, whose home at Monticello is only 3 miles distant. The city is beautifully located in a rich agricultural and fruit growing region. It was settled in 1744, and the vicinity abounds in historical associations connected with the Revolutionary War. Population, 1940, 19,400. See *Monticello*.

Chattanooga (*chăt'ȧ-nōō'gȧ*). A railroad center and manufacturing city of southeastern Tennessee, situated on the south bank of the Tennessee river. Near-by deposits of coal and iron together with abundant hydroelectric power, marketed at low cost by the Tennessee Valley Authority, facilitate the operation of many industries. Of these, the most important are the manufacture of steel, steel products, and cotton goods. Near the city stands Lookout mountain, from whose summit seven states can be seen. Several important battles of the Civil War were fought in the vicinity of Chattanooga. The educational institutions include the University of Chattanooga and the Chattanooga college of law. Population, 1940, 128,163.

Chautauqua (*shȧ-tô'kwȧ*) **Lake.** A small lake in the extreme southwestern part of New York. It is about 18 miles long and 2 miles wide, and drains through Conewango creek into the Allegheny river. It lies about 1300 feet above sea level, and 730 feet above Lake Erie, which is only a few miles distant but separated by a range of hills. Chautauqua lake is noted for its beautiful surroundings and for the widely known Chautauqua summer school located on its banks.

Chelsea (*chĕl'sē*). A city of eastern Massachusetts, situated on the Mystic river, about 3 miles northeast of Boston. Chelsea has substantial industries. These include the manufacture of lithographs, shoes, car wheels, and rubber products. First settled in 1642, as Winnisimmet, Chelsea was incorporated under its present name in 1739. In 1908, a great fire destroyed a large portion of the city. The devastated area, however, was rapidly rebuilt. Population, 1940, 41,259.

Chester. A manufacturing city of southeastern Pennsylvania, located on the Delaware river, about 13 miles southwest of Philadelphia. The chief industrial interests include steel products, munitions, locomotives, automobiles, chemicals, paper, petroleum, machinery, and textiles. It has also one of the largest shipbuilding yards in the country. The city has three parks, also the Deshong Memorial grounds. It is the seat of Pennsylvania military college. Chester was first settled about 1640 by Swedes. Of historic interest are the city hall, built in 1724, and the house of William Penn. Population, 1940, 59,285.

Cheyenne (*shī-ĕn'*). The capital and largest city of Wyoming, situated in the southeast part of the state, 106 miles north of Denver. The city was founded in 1867 by engineers of the Union Pacific railroad, which has since maintained work and repair shops in Cheyenne. Because of its central location in an extensive stock growing section, the city is an important shipping point for beef cattle and for sheep. Among the chief buildings are the State capitol, the Federal building, and the governor's mansion. A three-mile boulevard extends from the city to Fort Francis E. Warren, an important government military post. There are many attractive streets and parks, the latter covering 800 acres. Population, 1940, 22,474.

CHICAGO. The chief city of Illinois, the metropolis of the Middle Western states, and the second most populous city in the western hemisphere. It is situated on the southwestern shore of Lake Michigan and on the Indiana boundary, about 185 miles northeast of Springfield, the capital of the state.

SITE. Chicago occupies a remarkably level site, extending along the lake shore for 24½ miles. The city extends inland, at its widest point, for a distance of about 10 miles and embraces a total area of some 212 square miles.

By the Chicago river, a small stream, and by its two branches, the city is divided into three principal districts. The branches of the river unite about a mile west of the lake and approximately midway between the north and the south boundaries of the city. The district lying north of the river and the north branch is called the North Side; that lying south of the river and the south branch is called the South Side; and the much larger district lying west of the two branches is known as the West Side.

STREETS. With few exceptions, Chicago's streets cross at right angles and in east-and-west and in north-and-south directions. Chicago is noted for its exceedingly long and straight streets. Many continue in a direct line for from 5 to 10 or more miles. Some, as, for example, Western avenue and Halstead street, extend without deviation for practically the entire length of the city, a distance of 25 miles.

The chief commercial and mercantile center lies south of the river between its south branch and the lake. Here, in an area approximately a mile square, are found most of Chicago's great public edifices, office buildings, and department stores. Many of these are grouped within the so-called "loop," a section surrounded by elevated railroads. On the north it is bounded by the two-level Wacker drive. State street contains the great department stores, and, with Wabash and Michigan avenues, constitutes the chief shopping district. LaSalle street, the center of the financial district, is sometimes styled the "Wall Street" of Chicago. Franklin and Market streets are the principal center of the wholesale trade. The most notable street of the commercial district is Michigan avenue. For more than a mile this overlooks Grant park, and its massive buildings, when viewed from Lake Michigan, dominate the city's sky line. Extending northward over the Link bridge, which spans the Chicago river, it becomes the beautiful Lake Shore drive. On the west side are the city's famous stockyards and a 17 million dollar produce terminal.

From the loop district or near it, several great thoroughfares, each several miles long, run diagonally to various quarters of the city. Among these are Cottage Grove, Archer, and Milwaukee avenues, extending southeast, southwest, and northwest, respectively. Various boulevards, connecting the parks, serve also as thoroughfares, and, along these, in each side of the city, are fine residence sections. Among important residential streets, containing numerous palatial homes, are Lake Shore drive, Sheridan road, and South Shore drive.

BUILDINGS. Near the center of the business district is the magnificent county courthouse and city hall. This is a twin structure of limestone and granite, built in the French Renaissance style. The United States courthouse, one of the largest structures erected by the United States government outside of Washington, covers an entire city square, about 320 by 400 feet. It is built of granite, 16 stories high, and is surmounted by a massive dome nearly 300 feet high. The Field museum, on the lake front, erected at a cost of $8,000,000, ranks among the finest museum buildings of the world. Near by, on an artificial island, is the Adler planetarium, the first to be erected in America (1930). Among other notable structures are the public library, the great stadium, on West Madison street, the Municipal pier, the Wrigley building, the Tribune tower, the Pure Oil building, the Board of Trade building, the Field building, the Morrison Hotel, the Stevens Hotel, the Merchandise Mart, and a 21 million dollar post office.

PARKS AND MONUMENTS. Chicago has a magnificent park system embracing about 208 large and small parks, with a total area of more than 7300 acres. The major parks are connected by a system of boulevards and parkways, aggregating 162 miles in length. The circuit through the park system affords one of the finest drives in America. The larger units of the system are Lincoln, Humboldt, Garfield, Douglas, Marquette, Washington, Jackson, Burnham and Grant parks. Among the parkways and drives which link these units into one organic whole are Lake Shore drive, Sheridan road, the Outer drive, and Diversey avenue on the North Side; Humboldt, Jackson, and Washington boulevards on the West Side; and Eriksen drive, Michigan avenue, Grand, Drexel, South Shore drive, and Garfield boulevard on the South Side.

Grant park, on the lake, in front of the business district, contains the Art institute and the beautiful Buckingham fountain. Lincoln park contains a large conservatory and zoological garden and notable statues of Grant and Lincoln, the latter an impressive work by Saint Gaudens.

Jackson park, the largest of all, overlooks the lake on the South Side. Along the Midway plaisance, connecting Jackson and Washington parks, are the buildings of the University of Chicago. In this plaisance is the impressive sculptural group "Fountain of Time," by Lorado Taft.

Besides the extensive recreation grounds within the city, a metropolitan park district has been created outside of the city. For the purpose of establishing an outer ring of parks, several large forested areas, aggregating more than 37,800 acres, have been purchased.

EDUCATIONAL INSTITUTIONS. Chicago is one of the important educational centers of the country. It is the seat of the University of Chicago, noted for its large post-graduate school. Northwestern university, in the adjoining suburb of Evanston, has most of its professional departments in the city. Other important institutions are Loyola university, De Paul university, the Armour institute of technology, the Lewis institute, and the art school in connection with the Art institute.

TRANSPORTATION. Chicago is the chief railway center of America, being the terminus of railway systems embracing about half the total railway mileage of the country. No railroad runs through Chicago, for all of the 22 trunk lines, radiating to all parts of the United States, have terminals in the city. The business district is surrounded by a ring of great passenger stations, the largest of which cost 75 million dollars to construct. Outside of these are immense freight depots. A series of belt lines around the city connects the different railroads, forming a complete transfer system. Chicago's 640-acre airport is the terminus of numerous converging airplane routes.

Chicago has also the advantage of inland water transportation, and ranks as one of the chief ports on the Great Lakes. There is a well protected harbor, with docking facilities furnished by the Municipal pier, which extends 3000 feet into the lake. The river and its branches have been deepened so that an immense tonnage, greater than that passing through the Panama canal, is handled at wharves within the city. By the construction of the Chicago drainage canal, whereby the waters of the river are made to flow outward from the lake into the Des Plaines river, an all-water route to the Mississippi and to the Gulf of Mexico has been made possible.

Local transportation is served by an extensive system of elevated electric railways and by an immense network of surface trolley lines. The elevated railways radiate from the central loop in the commercial district to all sides of the city. In addition, there is an extensive system of motor bus transportation. Chicago is served also by a large number of suburban electric lines. A unique feature of local transportation is a large system of freight tunnels, or subways, aggregating 60 miles in length, constructed beneath the business district.

COMMERCE. Chicago owes its supreme position in American inland commerce to superior advantages of location and to marvelously developed facilities for transportation. It is situated at the crossroads between the populous industrial sections of the northeastern states and the rich agricultural districts of the Mississippi valley and the great Northwest. The city is the center of shipment of western produce to the East and of eastern manufactures to the West. It is the greatest distributing point in the United States for dry goods, foodstuffs, clothing, household articles, and general merchandise. Chicago is the world's greatest live stock market and ranks among the leading markets of the globe for grain, hides, and lumber. In Chicago was developed the now extensive business of mail order merchandising.

MANUFACTURERS. Chicago is the industrial as well as the commercial metropolis of the Mississippi Valley region. Among American cities, it stands second only to New York in value of manufactures. Chicago's manufactures normally exceed 3½ billion dollars in value, or more than two-thirds that of New York's manufactures. Chicago is the world's greatest meat packing center, and leads the country in the manufacture of farm implements, farm machinery, and railroad cars. Its other industries are extensive and exceedingly varied.

HISTORY. In 1803, John Kinzie, the first American settler, built a house on the north bank of the river. In 1804, Fort Dearborn was erected. During the War of 1812, this fort was captured and the settlers massacred by the Indians. Fort Dearborn was reconstructed in 1816, but the village around it grew very slowly until the building of the Illinois and Michigan canal in 1830.

Made a town in 1833, Chicago was incorporated as a city in 1837 with a population of 4170. In 1852, the first railway from the East reached Chicago. Following this event the city's growth was rapid, rising from 28,000 in 1850 to 109,000 in 1860, and to 298,000 in 1870. Since 1870, Chicago has increased in population at the rate of more than a half million in each decade.

In 1871 occurred the "great fire," the most appalling disaster that as yet had befallen an American city. Within a few years the devasted areas were rebuilt and made more substantial than before. In 1893 was held the World's Columbian exposition, erected at a cost of about 43 million dollars. The centennial of Chicago's incorporation as a town was celebrated by the Century of Progress exposition in 1933. Population, 1940, 3,396,808.

Chicopee. A manufacturing city of southwestern Massachusetts, located on the Connecticut river, at the mouth of the Chicopee, about 4 miles north of Springfield. Abundant water power is furnished by the Chicopee river for the city's varied and extensive industries. These include the manufacture of firearms, cotton and knit goods, bronze statuary, knitting machines, rubber goods, athletic goods, regalia, swords, and many other articles. Near by is a large army air base. Population, 1940, 41,664.

Cicero. A town of Illinois, partially surrounded by Chicago, of which it is an industrial suburb, being about 7 miles west of Chicago's "loop." Manufactures comprise chiefly electrical equipment, pumps, engines, iron castings, and enamel ware. Population, 1940, 64,712.

Cincinnati (*sĭn'sĭ-năt'ĭ*). The second largest city in Ohio, situated on the north bank of the Ohio river, 120 miles southwest of Columbus and 270 miles southeast of Chicago.

Cincinnati is environed by a semicircular range of high hills. From the river bank, it rises in two great terraces or steps, finally reaching a height of 450 feet above the river. Several fine bridges connect the city with Covington, Newport, Ludlow, and other towns on the Kentucky side. Through the center, of the city passes Central parkway, a 4½-mile boulevard on the site of the old Miami and Erie canal. Part of this canalway was used also for a rapid transit subway system. The picturesque residence sections of Mount Auburn, Mount Adams, Fairview, Avondale, Hyde Park, College Hill, and Clifton are reached by electric railway lines and by splendid highways.

Among the more notable buildings are the post office, the public library, the music hall, the county courthouse, Carew Tower (48 stories, 574 feet high), the Union Central Life building (34 stories, 495 feet high), Saint Peter's Cathedral, and a magnificent terminal station costing about 42 million dollars. Of public monuments, the most artistic are the Tyler-Davidson Fountain, in Fountain square, and the Lincoln statue, in Lytle park. The extensive park system, embracing over 2800 acres, includes Mount Airy Forest, Eden park, Burnet Woods, Ault, Mount Echo, and various smaller parks.

The city has been long known as an educational, art, and musical center. Among the principal institutions are the University of Cincinnati, a leading municipal university in the United States; the Ohio Mechanics' institute; the Art School and Art Museum, in Eden park; Saint Xavier university; and Hebrew Union college. For many years the May Musical Festivals, held biennially, have been an indispensable feature of the city's cultural life. The widely known Cincinnati Symphony Orchestra is a well-endowed, permanent organization.

Cincinnati ranks high as a manufacturing city, and owes much of its success as such to its advantageous location midway on the great Ohio river. In addition, the city has the service of seven trunk lines of railway, one of which, the Cincinnati Southern, 338 miles long, is owned by the municipality itself. It is an important air-route center and has an airport nearly 1000 acres in area. The total output of manufactures normally amounts to about 800 million dollars. The more important products include machine tools, paper, automobile parts, clothing, boots and shoes, meat products, machinery, engines, safes, soaps, printing, paints, furniture, radios, watches, jewelry, and pottery. For many years the city has been celebrated for the fine wares produced at the Rookwood Pottery Works. It is an outlet for the bituminous coal fields of Kentucky and West Virginia and for fruits and vegetables grown in the South.

In 1788, a village called Losantiville was laid out on the present site of the city. The name of this village was changed in 1790 to Cincinnati, which, in 1802, became incorporated as a town. Its steady growth and development dates from 1816, when steam navigation was inaugurated on the Ohio river. Cincinnati was incorporated as a city in 1819. Few large cities in the United States have a larger proportion of native-born inhabitants. Population, 1940, 455,610.

Citrus (*sĭt'rŭs*) **Belt.** The name applied to those parts of the states of California and Florida in which the leading citrus fruits—oranges, lemons, and grapefruit—are chiefly produced. Many counties in various parts of California grow oranges on a small scale, but by far the largest part of the state's commercial crop of all citrus fruits is grown in seven counties in the southern part of the state. These are Los Angeles, San Bernardino, Orange, Tulare, Riverside, Ventura, and San Diego counties. Santa Barbara County is an important producer of lemons, and, farther north in the state, Fresno, Sacramento, Butte, Tehama, and Glenn counties market substantial quantities of oranges.

The citrus belt of Florida comprises about 15 counties in the central part of the peninsular portion. It extends across the state from the Gulf of Mexico to the Atlantic Ocean, its center lying a short distance north of Tampa. In this belt the chief citrus fruits produced are oranges and grapefruit. The leading counties in the production of oranges are Polk, Orange, DeSoto, Brevard, Lake, Hillsborough, Volusia, and Pinellas. These counties produce about two-thirds of the total orange crop of the state. The counties leading in the production of grapefruit are Polk, Manatee, Pinellas, Lee, DeSoto, and Saint Lucie. These five counties produce about two-thirds of Florida's total yield of grapefruit.

California produces practically all of the lemons, about 70 per cent of the oranges, and some 13 per cent of the grapefruit grown in the United States. Florida grows about 60 per cent of the grapefruit and about 28 per cent of the oranges produced in the country. Texas and Arizona also rank high in the production of grapefruit, each growing between 10 and 20 per cent of the nation's crop.

Clarksburg. A manufacturing city and trade center in the north central part of West Virginia. It is situated in the midst of rich gas, coal, and oil fields. Clarksburg was founded in 1782 and is the birthplace of "Stonewall" Jackson, after whom one of the city's leading hotels is named. Population, 1940, 30,579.

CLEVELAND. The chief city of Ohio and the sixth largest in the United States, situated on Lake Erie at the mouth of the Cuyahoga river. It is located in the northeastern part of the state, about 625 miles by rail northwest of New York, and some 360 miles east of Chicago.

Site. Cleveland occupies a beautiful site on elevated ground sloping gently toward the lake, along which it has a frontage of 14 miles. The city is divided unequally by the windings of the Cuyahoga river into a larger portion on the east side and a smaller portion on the west side. The highest point reaches an elevation of about 300 feet above the level of the lake; the lowest points are in the valley of the river and along the lake shore. Immense viaducts, spanning the deep valley of the river, connect the eastern and the western sections. Among the most notable of these are the High Level and Main Avenue bridges and the Abbey Street, Clark Avenue, Lorain-Central and Harvard-Denison viaducts.

Streets and Buildings. Cleveland is well laid out with many broad, well shaded streets and handsome boulevards. At the intersection of Superior avenue and Ontario street, in the heart of the city, is the Public square. From this and from Ontario street, which extends north and south, all the principal east side streets diverge. There are also streets connecting with the great viaducts leading to the west side of the city. From the southeast corner of the Public square extends Euclid avenue, once one of the most famous residential streets in America, but now largely absorbed in the ever-expanding business district.

The chief business section extends from the lower part of the river eastward along Superior avenue and along Euclid avenue to the vicinity of 22nd street. The manufacturing districts are mostly along the lake front, in the low flat valley of the river, and along various lines of railway. Among the fine residential streets are Bellflower road, Clifton, East, and Lake Shore boulevards, Magnolia and Juniper drives, East 115th street, and the beautiful boulevards of Cleveland Heights and Shaker Heights.

A notable architectural feature in the heart of the city is the array of buildings forming the "Municipal Group," or civic center. The project, designed by leading American architects, includes the erection of structures of beautiful and harmonious architecture on a T-shaped tract of land, known as the Mall. The buildings include the county courthouse, the city hall, the Federal building, the auditorium, the Board of Education building, and the public library. The city is noted for its superb office buildings. Among noteworthy structures are the museum of art, the auditorium, the Keith building, Federal Reserve bank, and, adjoining Public square, the Union station with its associated buildings, including the 708-foot Terminal Tower building, the Medical Arts building, and the Builders Exchange.

Parks and Monuments. Cleveland's public park system covers a total area of about 3000 acres and includes upwards of 40 miles of connecting boulevards. Important units in the park system are Gordon, Edgewater, Brookside, Garfield, Monumental, Washington, Rockefeller, Wade, and Woodland Hills parks. Among attractive drives are Euclid avenue, Fairmont and Shaker boulevards on the east side and, on the west side, Lake avenue and Clifton boulevard. Several of the parks contain notable monuments or are adorned with fine pieces of sculpture. Gordon park, on the lake front, contains a statue of Commodore Perry. In Wade park are located the Goethe-Schiller monument and the art museum. The most notable monument in the city is the impressive Garfield memorial, situated on a commanding eminence in Lake View cemetery. About the three landward sides of the city extends a belt of boulevards and natural park lands, known as Metropolitan park.

Educational Institutions. Cleveland is the seat of Western Reserve university, with which is affiliated Cleveland college. Prominent among the city's other educational institutions are the Case School of Applied Science, John Carroll university, Fenn college, the museum of art, and the museum of natural history.

Transportation. The harbor, which is protected by an immense breakwater, nearly 6 miles long, is one of the most spacious on the Great Lakes. There is a total lake dock frontage of more than 13 miles, and the Cuyahoga river is also lined with docks. These are equipped with unexcelled facilities for handling iron ore, coal, and lumber, and there is ample dockage at special piers for the extensive passenger service. Cleveland is also one of the great railway centers of the country, with direct lines to most of the leading cities of the United States.

Commerce. Cleveland owes its commanding position in commerce and industry to superior advantages of location. It is situated at the economic focus for the assembly of the raw materials of iron and steel. It is said to be the largest ore market in the world. Within a short distance to the southeast lie iron mines, limestone quarries, and immense coal fields. From the northwest, by cheap all-water transportation, are received enormous supplies of Lake Superior iron ore. In consequence, the city's railways and lake steamer lines handle an immense tonnage of raw materials and distribute manufactured products valued at hundreds of millions of dollars. It is estimated that the total shipments handled at Cleveland aggregate in value more than a billion dollars annually.

Manufactures. Cleveland is one of the great manufacturing centers of America. It ranks fifth among the cities of the United States, being surpassed only by New York, Chicago, Philadelphia, and Detroit. While there is an immense diversity of manufactures, the chief industries are concerned with the manufacture of iron and steel and their products. Other important manufactures are automobile parts, machine tools, household appliances, packed meats, clothing, electrical machinery, and refined petroleum. The Standard Oil Company, which began its operations in Cleveland, has immense refineries in the city. Cleveland is one of the greatest wire and bolt manufacturing centers in the world.

History. Cleveland was laid out in 1796 and was incorporated in 1814. In 1818, the first newspaper began publication. The Ohio canal was opened to Akron in 1827, and in 1832 was completed to the Ohio river. This stimulated the growth of Cleveland, which received its city charter in 1836. Since the discovery of iron ore in the Lake Superior region and the construction of the first railroads, 1850–60, Cleveland's growth has been rapid and continuous. The centennial of its status as a city was celebrated by the Great Lakes Exposition in 1936. Population, 1940, 878,336.

Cleveland Heights. A city of northeastern Ohio, being a residential suburb of Cleveland, which it adjoins at Cleveland's eastern boundary. Between 1920 and 1930 it increased in population from 15,236 to 50,945. Population, 1940, 54,992.

Cohoes (*kô-hōz'*). A manufacturing city of eastern New York, located on the Hudson river and the State barge canal, at the mouth of the Mohawk river, about 9 miles north of Albany. Abundant water power and hydroelectric power have led to the development of extensive industries. Cohoes leads all other cities of the United States in the manufacture of knit underwear. Other industries include the manufacture of paper products, shirts and collars, machinery, and building materials. Population, 1940, 21,955.

Colorado Desert. An arid region in southeastern California. It is separated from the Mojave desert, which lies to the north, by the San Bernardino and the Chocolate ranges, and is bounded on the south by the San Jacinto, the Santa Rosa, and the Superstition mountains.

From the eastern entrance of San Gorgonio pass, the desert extends to the Colorado river, from which it takes its name. It is more than 100 miles long, in some places more than 20 miles wide, and covers an area of about 2000 square miles. Much of this region lies below the sea level. The lowest portion is known as the Salton Sink. In this lies the salt lake, called the Salton Sea, the surface of which is about 280 feet lower than that of the Gulf of California. Parts of the desert show traces of volcanic activity, and there are mud volcanoes and numerous thermal springs.

As in the case of the Mojave desert and Death valley, lofty mountain ranges on the west cut off the vapor-laden breezes from the Pacific. Consequently, the Colorado desert is a region of extreme aridity,—in fact, one of the driest and hottest in the world. The normal rainfall ranges from 3 to 4 inches, and summer temperatures as high as 130° have been recorded.

The scanty vegetation is typical of southwestern deserts. It includes the creosote bush, mesquite, cat's-claw, smoke tree, paloverde, and numerous kinds of cactus. In the spring the desert wild flowers present a scene of surpassing beauty. In a few canyons at the western end of this desert are the only known groves of the native American fan palm, or Washington palm, now cultivated as an ornamental tree on the Pacific coast. Among characteristic desert animals are the chuckwalla lizard and the sidewinder, or horned rattlesnake.

Wherever irrigation is practicable, much of this seemingly worthless desert will produce immense crops of fruits, alfalfa, cotton, and grains. In consequence, prosperous towns and agricultural communities grew up in various parts, most notably the now rich and populous Imperial valley. In many points this California desert resembles Arabia or Egypt. Here, as in those ancient countries, the date palm, long-fibre cotton, and alfalfa flourish. The Colorado desert is traversed from end to end by the Southern Pacific railway, and by the Los Angeles-Yuma and other automobile highways. See *Mojave Desert, Palm Canyon, Salton Sea.*

Colorado Springs. A city of central Colorado, situated near the eastern base of Pikes peak at an elevation of 6000 feet above the sea. The city is a noted health and pleasure resort and has a beautiful system of parks, covering some 3000 acres. Among places of historic and scenic interest in the vicinity are Pikes peak, Ute Pass highway, the Garden of the Gods, Glen Eyrie, Cave of the Winds, Manitou springs, Phantom Cliff canyon, and Will Rogers shrine, half way up Cheyenne mountain. The city is the seat of Colorado college with its widely known art center. The industries are largely confined to the manufacture of pottery and beet sugar and the reduction of ores, chiefly gold. Population, 1940, 36,789.

Columbia. The capital of South Carolina, situated near the center of the state on the high eastern bank of the Congaree river. The State capitol, built of granite at a cost of $6,000,000, is modeled after the national Capitol. Radiating from the capitol are four wide, well shaded avenues. The most important industry is the manufacture of cotton. Electricity is provided by large hydroelectric developments in the vicinity, including the huge Saluda dam. The city is the seat of the University of South Carolina and five colleges. The site of Columbia was settled about 1700; it was chosen for the capital, and the town was laid out in 1786. The legislature first met there in 1790. Population, 1940, 62,396.

Columbia River Highway. An important scenic highway constructed along the south side of the Columbia river in Oregon. It extends west from Portland through Astoria to Seaside on the Pacific Ocean, and east from Portland to Hood River, northeast of Mount Hood, a total distance of about 150 miles. This magnificent highway, 18 feet wide with no grades exceeding 5 per cent, skirts the Columbia river by running around mountains, over hills, through tunnels, across viaducts, and along embankments.

At some points the highway reaches a height of 700 feet above the river, affording magnificent views. The highway passes near many beautiful cataracts, running immediately beside the celebrated Multnomah falls, 607 feet high, and so close to Horse Tail falls that the spray keeps the roadway moist. A feature of the highway is its numerous concrete bridges of pleasing architectural design. Some of these are more than 300 feet long and one viaduct exceeds 800 feet in length.

Columbus. A city of Georgia, situated on the Chattahoochee river, on the western border of the state, about 95 miles southwest of Atlanta. Columbus is the trade center of a large agricultural district devoted to growing live stock, cotton, corn, wheat, and peanuts. The city has extensive manufacturing industries, which include cotton mills, iron and steel mills, cottonseed oil mills, fertilizer factories, peanut factories, carbonated beverage plants, and agricultural implement works. Population, 1940, 53,280.

Columbus. The capital and third largest city of Ohio, located in the central part of the state, about 135 miles southwest of Cleveland. Surrounded by a productive agricultural region and by rich coal, iron, and natural gas fields, the city has developed into an important industrial and commercial center. The leading manufactures include agricultural, electrical, mill, and mining machinery, steel and steel products, boots and shoes, drugs, caskets, meat and other food products. The city is served by five trunk line railroads.

Columbus is laid out in a form somewhat resembling a Maltese cross. Parks and public grounds cover more than 1100 acres. Columbus is the seat of Ohio State university, which has an exceptionally beautiful campus and a stadium capable of seating nearly 100,000 persons. Other educational institutions are the Capital university, Saint Mary of the Springs, the Josephinum college, and the Columbus art school. The State capitol, built in the Doric type of architecture, is the most impressive of many fine buildings throughout the city. Near the capitol stands a group of statues representing distinguished Americans, the group being known as "My Jewels." Bordering the beautiful civic center is the Le Veque Lincoln Tower, an imposing office building 555 feet in height. Civic center buildings include the city hall, state and federal government buildings, Central high school and Columbus auditorium.

The first permanent settlement on the present site of the city was made in 1797. Columbus was laid out and was made the capital of the state in 1812. In 1816, the legislature first met in Columbus. Population, 1940, 306,087.

Concord (*kŏng'kŏrd*). A town of Massachusetts, rich in historical and literary interest, situated some 20 miles northwest of Boston. Concord was founded in 1635. It was the British objective in the battle of Lexington, and became the scene of the first armed conflict of the Revolution. The battle of Concord began at the Old North bridge. Here, April 19, 1775, the "embattled farmers fired the shot heard round the world." The town contains various memorials of the struggle, the most notable of which is the statue of "The Minute Man." Concord is celebrated also as the home of a number of distinguished figures in American literature, including Emerson, Hawthorne, Thoreau, and Louisa M. Alcott. Antiquarian house contains many mementos of the city's rich history. Population, 1940, 7972.

Concord. The capital of New Hampshire, built on the banks of the Merrimac river, about 75 miles northwest of Boston. Having an abundance of water power, Concord has developed important manufactories of leather goods, silverware, machine shop products, smoking pipes, and insulated wire. In the vicinity are extensive quarries of the fine-grained white granite from which the impressive State capitol is built. The site was settled in 1725 by whites who called their village Pennacock. In 1733, the village was incorporated as the town of Rumford. This later was named Concord, which became a city in 1853. It was the home of Mary Baker Eddy, founder of Christian Science. Population, 1940, 27,171.

Coney Island. A narrow island five miles in length, situated at the southwestern point of Long Island, near the entrance to New York harbor. The island is the most popular seashore resort in the United States. Coney Island is divided into four well-defined districts: West Brighton, which is provided with numerous popular means of amusement; Brighton Beach, containing a race track; Manhattan Beach, which is partly residential; and Sea Gate, the home station of the Atlantic Yacht Club.

Continental Divide. The crest or height of land in the United States which separates the waters draining into the Atlantic Ocean from those draining into the Pacific, is called the Continental Divide. This extends from the Mexican boundary northward across western New Mexico and then somewhat eastward to Rocky Mountain national park in north central Colorado, its easternmost point. Thence the "great divide" trends northwest through northern Colorado and western Wyoming to Yellowstone national park. Continuing westward and northward across Montana, it passes through Glacier national park to the Canadian boundary. In some parts of its course, the Continental Divide is at the crest of the loftiest ranges; in others, it is on gently rolling uplands at the summit of high plateaus, usually 7000 feet or more above sea level.

Corn Belt. The fertile region in the east central United States which is largely devoted to the growing of corn. The most productive area embraces western Ohio, Indiana, Illinois, Iowa, Missouri, eastern Nebraska, eastern Kansas, and southeastern South Dakota. Adjoining parts of Kentucky, northern Oklahoma, and southern Minnesota, which produce large yields of corn, are usually considered as belonging to the Corn Belt. More than half of the corn crop of the United States is grown in this central zone. The two most productive states, Iowa and Illinois, usually contribute about one-fourth of the nation's total yield of corn. No other corn-growing region approaches the Corn Belt in productiveness.

Corpus Christi. A city and seaport of southern Texas, situated at the mouth of the Neuces river on Corpus Christi bay. A deep water channel to the Gulf of Mexico gives access for ocean ships to the city's well-equipped port facilities, opened in 1926. Its industries and its exports are based largely on the resources of the surrounding territory, which include cotton, petroleum, and seafoods. Corpus Christi was chartered as a city in 1876. After the opening of the port, it grew rapidly, almost doubling its inhabitants in the decade of 1930-40. Population, 1940, 57,301.

Cotton Belt. The extensive region in the southern United States in which the immense cotton crop is produced. This includes a broad, exceedingly fertile belt, extending from eastern North Carolina to west central Texas.

The northern boundary is approximately the line of 77° mean summer temperature, along which there is an average growing season, free from frost, of about 200 days. The southern boundary is determined largely by the amount of autumn rainfall. As wet weather interferes with picking and damages the lint, cotton is not extensively grown in the districts bordering on the Atlantic Ocean and the Gulf of Mexico where the autumn rainfall exceeds 11 inches. The southern boundary, however, is moving northward, for the reason that the milder winter and longer growing season near the Gulf permit increased injury by the boll weevil.

The zone of greatest productivity embraces eastern North Carolina, most of South Carolina, Georgia, Alabama, and Mississippi, parts of Arkansas, western Tennessee, northern Louisiana, and southern Oklahoma, and much of the northeastern half of Texas. Texas, Mississippi, and Arkansas are the leading states. The Cotton Belt produces about three-fifths of the world's supply of cotton.

Council Bluffs. A railroad, manufacturing, and commercial city of southwestern Iowa, located on the Missouri river opposite Omaha, Nebraska. For the most part, the city, which is well laid out, lies upon a plain largely surrounded by lofty bluffs. There are several parks, of which the chief one is Fairmount. Railroads, and vehicle bridges over the Missouri river, and also electric lines, connect the city with Omaha. Served by 8 major railroads, the city is a leading grain marketing center and has varied industrial interests, including the manufacture of truck bodies, farm implements, freight car wheels, bee supplies and cereals. The name Council Bluffs is said to have been given because of the council held at this point in 1804 between the Indians and the explorers Lewis and Clark. Population, 1940, 41,439.

Covington. The second largest city of Kentucky, situated on the Ohio river, opposite Cincinnati. Covington occupies a beautiful site, partly surrounded by lofty hills, and contains many fine streets and homes. It has excellent transportation facilities by rail and by river, and is connected with Cincinnati by a handsome suspension bridge. While largely residential, Covington has substantial industries. These include meat packing and the manufacture of X-ray machines, machine tools, canvas goods, hardware, and structural iron. Devon park, 550 acres, on the outskirts, has a natural amphitheater which will accommodate 25,000 persons. St. Mary's cathedral, patterned after Notre Dame in Paris, has one of the largest stained-glass windows in the world. Covington was settled in 1812, and became a city in 1834. Population, 1940, 62,018.

Crater Mound. A remarkable geological formation in central Arizona, about 40 miles southeast of Flagstaff. First known as Coon butte and later as Meteorite mountain, Crater mound ranks as one of the most remarkable geological features of the West.

Viewed from the Santa Fe railway, which passes some miles to the north, it appears as a low ridge. Upon close approach, this ridge is found to be circular in form and to enclose an immense crater-like hole or depression 4000 feet in diameter and 600 feet deep. The encircling ridge, 100 to 150 feet in height, is composed of fragments of rock and sand blown up from the hole. The beds of rocks in the walls of the hole are limestone above and sandstone below, both more or less upturned near the hole and in part considerably shattered.

The cause of this great hole was long a mystery. The occurrence of many small masses of meteoric iron in the vicinity suggested that it was made by the impact of a meteorite. All efforts to locate the main body of such a meteorite failed until 1932, when with the aid of electrical instruments, geophysicists located the metallic mass at a depth of 680 feet.

Crawford Notch. A picturesque gorge between Mount Webster and Mount Willey, in the White mountains of New Hampshire. In a narrow passage, at an elevation of about 1900 feet, the Saco river traverses the Notch, which is notable for its fine rock scenery.

Cumberland. A city of western Maryland, situated on the Potomac river, about 155 miles northwest of Baltimore. Cumberland is located in a mountainous region near important coal fields. It ships immense quantities of semi-bituminous coal, highly valued for steaming purposes, and has other extensive industries. The principal manufacturing establishments are railway repair shops, rubber tire, cellulose, glass, and tin plate factories, brick and dye works, and silk, flour, and lumber mills. Population, 1940, 39,483.

Currecanti Needle. One of the striking scenic features of the Black Canyon or Grand Gorge of the Gunnison river, in southwestern Colorado. It is a massive pinnacle of highly colored rock, hundreds of feet in height, and tapering at the top to a somewhat pointed spire, whence the name "needle."

Dallas. The second largest city of Texas, located on Trinity river, in the northeastern part of the state, about 185 miles northeast of Austin. Dallas is located in an exceedingly fertile agricultural region, the chief cotton growing district of the state. The city is in the center of the world's largest oil field. It is the largest inland cotton market in the United States, and the leading wholesale and jobbing center southwest of Saint Louis. Dallas is the chief distributing point in the Southwest for farm implements and automobiles. In manufactures, Dallas ranks first among the cities of the state. The principal industries include oil refining, meat packing, printing and publishing, the manufacture of oil well and cotton ginning machinery, cottonseed oil, saddlery, harnesses, and cotton goods. Its fine commercial structures include the 28-story Magnolia building and the twin 20-story Medical Arts building.

The city's parks embrace an area of more than 4000 acres, and there are extensive boulevards and drives. The state fair, held annually in the city, sometimes attracts more than a million visitors. The city is the seat of the Southern Methodist university, Baylor medical and dental colleges, Dallas art institute, and museums of fine arts and natural history. Dallas was settled in 1841 and chartered as a city in 1856. The Texas Centennial Exposition was held here in 1936. Population, 1940, 294,734.

Davenport. A commercial and manufacturing city of eastern Iowa, beautifully situated on the slope of a steep bluff of the Mississippi river, opposite Rock Island, Illinois. The chief industries include flour milling and the manufacture of freight cars, foundry products, and ready-cut houses. An extensive business is carried on in flour and grain, by river as well as by rail transportation. The river at Davenport is spanned by three fine bridges, the cost of which aggregated about $4,000,000. The city has a municipal art gallery and a public museum. It is the seat of the Palmer School of Chiropractic. Founded in 1835, Davenport was incorporated as a town in 1838, and received its charter as a city in 1851. Population, 1940, 66,039.

Dayton. A manufacturing city of southwestern Ohio, situated on both banks of the Miami river, about 50 miles northeast of Cincinnati. Among the leading manufactured products are cash registers, computing scales, envelopes, electric motors, airplanes, electrical refrigeration machinery, and automobile accessories. A great contribution to the city's prestige has been made by the airplane industry, founded by the Wright brothers, to whose memory a beautiful monument has been erected in the city. Other structures of note include the art institute and museum and the Deeds' carillon tower with 32 bells. Wright field accommodates the experimental laboratories of the United States air corps.

Dayton was settled in 1796, was incorporated in 1805, and received its charter as a city in 1841. In 1913 a disastrous flood caused great destruction of property and loss of life. The devasted sections were rebuilt, and a system of five reservoirs, costing $32,000,000, was constructed to prevent a repetition of the disaster. Population, 1940, 210,718.

Dearborn. A city of southeastern Michigan, ten miles west of Detroit, of which it is a residential suburb. Henry Ford has his home there, his birthplace being on a farm in the vicinity. This farm he restored to its early appearance and he built there a village museum, "Greenfield village," consisting of old buildings collected from all parts of the United States and from England. Population, 1940, 63,584.

Death Valley. An extremely arid desert in eastern California, near the Nevada boundary, containing the lowest point of dry land in the United States. The name was given by a survivor of a party of 30 "forty-niners," most of whom perished of thirst in its sands. It lies in a north-and-south direction, is about 150 miles long, and varies in width from less than 10 miles to about 20 miles. On the west it is bordered by the high Panamint range; on the east it is flanked by the Funeral, the Black, and the Grapevine mountains. The lowest point in Death valley is 276 feet below sea level. In a direct line, this lowest point is about 86 miles east of Mt. Whitney, 14,496 feet high, the loftiest peak in the United States.

The valley is in the sink of the Amargosa river, a stream that is dry for the greater part of the year throughout much of its course. The eastern side of the valley was formerly the bed of a salt lake. In the entire area, drinkable water can be obtained in only a few places. The salty bottom of the valley is destitute of vegetation, but the bordering slopes have a sparse growth of desert shrubs. The annual rainfall is about 4 or 5 inches; the average humidity is very low,—no dew ever forming, and the summer temperatures, reaching 134°, being the hottest authentically recorded in America. See *Colorado Desert, Mohave Desert.*

Decatur (*dē-kā'tŭr*). A city of central Illinois, located near the Sangamon river, about 40 miles east of Springfield. Decatur lies in a highly productive corn and soy bean belt and carries on a large trade in grain, live stock, coal, and manufactured goods. The city's chief industrial establishments include railway shops, metal and woodworking plants, and factories for making corn and soy bean products, cotton garments, drugs, and gas and plumbing fixtures. Decatur is the seat of James Millikin university. Recreation is afforded at Lake Decatur, 12 miles long, formed by a dam across Sangamon river, and in the city's 960-acre park system. Population, 1940, 59,305.

Delaware Water Gap. A picturesque gap and narrow gorge in the Kittatinny range, near Stroudsburg, Pa., on the borders of Pennsylvania and New Jersey. The steep sides of the mountain here rise to an elevation of 1400 feet above the Delaware river, which flows through the gap.

Denver. The capital and largest city of Colorado. It is situated at the junction of Cherry creek and South Platte river. The site, which has an altitude of one mile above the level of the sea, slopes back from both banks of the river and commands a magnificent view of the Rocky mountains. Denver is the largest city between the Missouri river and the Pacific coast. It is also one of the most important railway centers of the West, to which fact, in great measure, it owes its growth and prosperity.

The city is handsomely planned and contains many fine public buildings and substantial private residences. Among the former may be noted the State capitol, the auditorium, the United States mint, and the civic center, whose 5 million-dollar City and County building is said to have the largest bronze doors in the world. The Fitzsimons general hospital for army tubercular patients, is one of the largest buildings in Colorado. Some of the principal educational institutions are the University of Denver, Regis college, Westminister college, and Colorado Woman's college. The City park, which covers 408 acres, has a zoological garden, a lake, a museum, aviary, and speedway. The park system, including about 40 parks in all, is one of the finest in the United States and is supplemented by a system of 38 municipal mountain parks in the vicinity.

Denver is the principal center of mercantile supply for the agricultural, stock raising, and mining districts of Colorado and New Mexico. It has extensive mining interests. The chief industries include meat packing, flour milling, railway car construction, printing and publishing, and the manufacture of iron and steel products, structural iron, clothing, paints, automobile accessories, and chemicals. Population, 1940, 322,412.

Des Moines (*dĕ moin'*). The capital and largest city of Iowa, built on both banks of the Des Moines river, in the central part of the state. Des Moines is the commercial center of an exceedingly fertile farming region, with which it carries on an extensive marketing and wholesale trade. Surrounded by rich coal beds, the city has developed numerous and varied industries prominent among which is the production of machinery, food products, and clothing. Many important farm journals and other publications are printed in Des Moines, which is also the center of large insurance interests.

Chief among many imposing public buildings is the capitol, built on a slight eminence, and approached by Capitol Extension park. Adjoining this park is the fine State Historical building. The city's park system includes 45 parks and covers 1400 acres. To this total may be added the 600 acres comprising the State fairgrounds. Des Moines is the seat of Drake university.

By reason of its central location, together with ample hotel and auditorium facilities, Des Moines is a favorite meeting place for conventions, its accommodations including a large coliseum adjoining the city's unique civic center. This consists of a landscaped area taking in the opposite banks of the river. In the group opposite the coliseum, post office, and library stand the city hall, federal court building, and municipal armory.

Around Fort Des Moines, which was established in 1843, settlers, in 1846, built a village. This village was incorporated in 1851 as the town of Fort Des Moines. In 1856, the town was made the capital of the state. In the following year, it was chartered as the city of Des Moines. Population, 1940, 159,819.

DETROIT. The chief city of Michigan and the fourth most populous in the United States, situated on the Detroit river, 18 miles from Lake Erie. It lies some 90 miles southeast of Lansing, the capital of the state, and is about 250 miles west of Buffalo and 285 miles east of Chicago. The city occupies a nearly level but gently rising site, extending some 12 miles along the river front, and containing an area of about 138 square miles.

Streets and Buildings. The city is regularly laid out, with wide streets, most of which cross at right angles on the checkerboard plan. There are, however, several broad avenues, 100 to 200 feet wide, which radiate from the Campus Martius and the Grand Circus in the heart of the city. Woodward avenue, one of the most important commercial and residential streets, passes through both the Campus Martius and the Grand Circus, and divides the city into two nearly equal parts. Important thoroughfares extending diagonally are Michigan, Grand River, and Gratiot avenues.

The commercial district is located mainly around and near the Grand Circus and the Campus Martius. The former is a small, semicircular park, and the latter is a large plaza. These are situated near each other and give an air of openness and spaciousness to the business center of the city. Griswold street, lined with great office buildings and banking houses is the "Wall Street" of Detroit.

The outer portions of the great radiating avenues, especially Woodward avenue toward Palmer park, and also Lafayette avenue and Fort street, extend through fine residence sections.

The chief public buildings are located on or near the Campus Martius. Within it is the Michigan Soldiers' and Sailors' monument, facing the city hall. Near by is the county courthouse, the largest public building in the city. Numerous great office buildings, of the finest modern type, are built around portions of the Grand Circus. Among many notable buildings may be mentioned the General Motors building, the Fisher building, the Federal building, the Board of Commerce, the Michigan Central station, the Masonic temple, the Ford, Penobscot, Stroh, First National Bank, Dime Bank, and Majestic buildings, the public library, and the Detroit institute of art.

Parks and Boulevards. The municipal system contains upwards of 242 parks, embracing an area of about 3600 acres. The most notable of these is the island park, Belle Isle, with an area of 1000 acres, where is situated one of the country's best zoological gardens. This lies opposite the eastern part of the city, with which it is connected by a bridge. River Rouge park is the largest, 1204 acres in area. In addition to the numerous small parks, many triangles at diagonal street intersections have been improved and ornamented, and there are numerous boulevards. Grand boulevard, a parkway 150 feet wide and 12 miles long, encircles the heart of the city from the Belle Isle bridge on the east to the foot of Twenty-second street on the west.

Educational Institutions. Detroit is the seat of Detroit university, Wayne university, the Detroit college of law, the Michigan college of medicine, the Michigan State auto school, and various other educational institutions. The University of Michigan is situated at Ann Arbor, only a short distance west, and there is a State normal school at Ypsilanti, still nearer the city.

Transportation. The city owes its greatness, in a large part, to unique advantages in transportation both by lake and by rail. It is situated midway on the inland waterway system of the Great Lakes. The deep Detroit river, sometimes called the "Dardanelles of America," affords a spacious harbor, accommodating the largest lake vessels. There is a numerous passenger fleet, and the city is a port of call for all steamers from Buffalo to the upper lakes. The tonnage passing through the Detroit river is more than double that passing through the Suez canal, and is immensely greater than the tonnage arriving at and leaving any other inland seaport in the world.

Local transportation is effected by a comprehensive system of municipally owned street railways and bus lines. The city is connected with Windsor, Canada, by a tunnel and the great Ambassador suspension bridge.

Commerce. Enormous quantities of iron ore, copper products, grain, and coal are handled by the lake traffic. There is a large export trade to Canada and Europe, chiefly foodstuffs, automobiles, and steel products. The city is the commercial center of a great interior district with which it carries on an immense distributing trade. In addition, it ships the products of its vast industries to all parts of the country.

Manufactures. Detroit is the greatest automobile manufacturing center in the world. Its phenomenal growth in the early 20th century corresponded with the vast development of the automobile industry. In value of manufactures, Detroit stands fourth among the cities of the United States. The greater part of this production is automobiles and automobile accessories and parts. There are numerous other substantial industries. Detroit is a leading center for the manufacture of aircraft, brass and bronze products, adding machines, stoves and furnaces, malleable iron, and aluminum castings. Other important manufactures include railway cars, machine tools, electrical apparatus, drugs, chemicals, engines, paint, tobacco, and rubber goods.

History. The first settlement at Detroit was made in 1701 by Cadillac, the French governor of Michillimackinac, who built Fort Pontchartrain. During the French and Indian war, this was captured, 1760, by the British. The first act of Pontiac's conspiracy, 1763, was an unsuccessful attempt to seize this important fort. Detroit was incorporated in 1802 and became the capital of Michigan territory in 1805. In 1812, William Hull surrendered the town to the British, who evacuated it the following year.

Detroit was chartered as a city in 1824, continued as the capital of the territory until 1835, and was the capital of the state, 1835–47. Its growth until 1910 was continuous and substantial. In the decade 1910-20, the city more than doubled in population and more than quadrupled in value of manufactures. Population, 1940, 1,623,452.

Diablo (*dē-ä'blō; dĭ-ăb'lō*), **Mount.** A mountain of west central California, situated on the edge of the great interior valley, about 30 miles air-line distance nearly due east of San Francisco. Its general domelike outline and isolated position have given the erroneous impression that Mount Diablo is an old volcano. It is, in fact, the higher portion of a great overturned arch of sedimentary rocks.

Because of its visibility for long distances in many directions, Mount Diablo has been a noted landmark since the days of the "forty-niners." Through it run the meridian and the base line from which the land surveys of a large part of California are reckoned. While of moderate height, the elevation being 3849 feet, its unique situation makes it one of the finest scenic viewpoints in the state. From its top, on a clear morning, the summits of the Sierra Nevada can be traced for 200 miles.

Dismal Swamp, Great. A tract of marshy land in southeastern Virginia and northeastern North Carolina. It begins a short distance south of Norfolk, Virginia, extends southward for about 30 miles, and embraces a total area of some 750 square miles. Near its center is Lake Drummond, about 2 miles in diameter and very shallow. The remainder of the swamp is covered, for the most part, with heavy timber and a thick tangled undergrowth. The swamp originally contained an area of about 2200 square miles, but much of its has been reclaimed and placed under cultivation.

Dobbs Ferry. A village of New York State, on the Hudson river 20 miles north of New York City. In the Livingston manor here Washington and Rochambeau planned the Yorktown campaign. Opposite this village the American flag was saluted for the first time by a British sloop of war. Population, 1940, 5883.

Dover. The capital of Delaware, located slightly north of the center of the state. Dover is surrounded by a rich fruit growing country, the chief crops being apples, grapes, melons, and peaches. The principal industry is the canning of plum pudding, poultry, and other foods. There is an impressive State capitol and a handsome monument erected to the memory of Cæsar Rodney, one of the signers of the Declaration of Independence. The Archives building houses Delaware's earliest records. Silver Lake park and Dover Green are other features of interest. Dover was laid out in 1717 and became the capital of Delaware in 1777. It became a town in 1829; a city in 1925. Population, 1940, 5517.

Dubuque (*dōō-būk'*). A city of northeastern Iowa, built on the west bank of the Mississippi river, about 200 miles northeast of Des Moines. Dubuque lies in a fertile farming district and the surrounding region is rich in lead and zinc deposits. Dubuque has substantial manufacturing industries, and is the center of a large marketing and distributing trade by river and by rail. The city is situated partly on a terrace 20 feet above the river and partly on a hill, which rises to a height of 200 feet.

Among the notable features are Eagle Point park which has a very large ledge garden and a monument of Julien Dubuque, who settled on the site of the city in 1788. The first permanent settlement dates from 1833. The village was incorporated as a town in 1837, and, in 1840, was chartered as a city. The educational institutions include Loras and Clarke colleges and the University of Dubuque. Population, 1940, 43,892.

Duluth. An important lake port and the third largest city of Minnesota. It is built on steep and picturesque slopes overlooking a fine natural harbor at the western end of Lake Superior. Drawing on the rich agricultural and iron mining regions of the Northwest, and enjoying the advantages of exceptional railroad and port facilities, Duluth handles an annual tonnage of grain and iron ore of stupendous proportions. The city is also a great coal distributing point. Hydroelectric power, available in abundance, contributes to a large industrial activity, which includes the manufacture of steel, wood products, clothing, matches, cement, and flour.

The city's natural beauty is enhanced by 106 miles of scenic drives, by 3,216 acres of parks, 74 in all, including Minnesota point, which extends 7 miles into the lake, and by facilities for summer and for winter sports. The chief public buildings cluster about the attractively designed civic center. Population, 1940, 101,065.

Durham. A city of central North Carolina, 25 miles northwest of Raleigh. It is one of the leading tobacco centers of the country, both for marketing and manufacturing. Cotton and hosiery mills constitute a second industry of large proportions. Durham is the seat of Duke university, developed from Trinity college and richly endowed by James B. Duke, a large tobacco manufacturer and developer of hydroelectric power. The city contains also North Carolina college for Negroes and is the headquarters of the country's leading life insurance company for Negroes. General Johnston surrendered to Sherman at Durham in 1865. Population, 1940, 60,195.

SCENIC LAKES OF NORTH AMERICA

1 Lake McDermott, Glacier National Park; *copyright by Ewing Galloway.* 2 Emerald Bay, Lake Tahoe, California; *copyright by Ewing Galloway.* 3 Lake Ellen Wilson, Glacier National Park; *copyright by R. E. Marble.* 4 Crater Lake, Oregon; *photo from Brown Bros.* 5 Lake Louise, Canadian Rockies; *copyright by Ewing Galloway.* 6 Mirror Lake, New York; *copyright by Ewing Galloway.*

Photos copyright by Harris & Ewing.

NOTED BUILDINGS IN WASHINGTON

1 National American Red Cross. 2 Scottish Rite Temple. 3 White House. 4 Continental Memorial Hall, D. A. R. 5 East Room, White House. 6 Congressional Library. 7 Pan-American Building. 8 Smithsonian Institution.

East Chicago. A city of northwestern Indiana on Lake Michigan. It adjoins Hammond and Whiting and is 20 miles southeast of the center of Chicago, of which it is an industrial suburb. The part of the city along the lake is known as Indiana harbor, and handles a large traffic of incoming coal, iron ore, and limestone with shipments of gasoline and steel products. The chief industries are steel manufacture and oil refining. East Chicago was founded in 1888 and incorporated as a city five years later. Population, 1940, 54,637.

East Orange. A city of northeastern New Jersey, adjoining Newark, and about 11 miles west of New York City. East Orange is mainly residential, being populated largely by persons doing business in New York and Newark. The city has wide, well shaded streets, and contains many attractive homes and public buildings. There are substantial industries and the chief manufactures include electrical machinery, valves, tools, sewer pipe, and knit goods. East Orange was separated from Orange in 1863 and became a city in 1899. Population, 1940, 68,945.

East St. Louis (*lōō'ĭs; lōō'ĭ*). A city of southwestern Illinois, built on the east bank of the Mississippi river, opposite Saint Louis. The city is an important railway and manufacturing center. It is also a leading market and distributing point for live stock, especially horses, mules, and hogs. The leading industries include meat packing, flour milling, and the manufacture of iron and steel products, aluminum, baking powder, glass, paints, chemicals, and refined petroleum. East Saint Louis was incorporated in 1861 and became a city in 1865. Population, 1940, 75,609.

Elgin. A city of northeastern Illinois, located on the Fox river, about 35 miles west of Chicago. Elgin's two outstanding industries, for which the city is widely noted, are the manufacture of watches and of butter tubs. Other manufacturers include meat products, electrical appliances, pianos, and automobile parts. Home ownership exceeds 75 per cent. The city is the seat of Elgin Academy. Population, 1940, 38,333.

Elizabeth. A manufacturing and suburban residential city of New Jersey, lying 12 miles southwest of New York City. It is connected with Staten island by Goethals bridge, opened in 1928. Among important industries are oil refining, shipbuilding, and the manufacture of sewing machines, chemicals, and electrical machinery. Elizabeth was settled in 1664 and still preserves many examples of colonial architecture. From 1755 to 1757 the city was the capital of New Jersey. Population, 1940, 109,912.

Ellis Island. A small island in New York bay one mile southwest of the southern tip of Manhattan island. It is notable as the point where prospective immigrants held for investigation are detained until admitted into the country or deported.

Sold by New York State to the Federal government in 1808, it was used first as a powder magazine. It was made into an immigrant station in 1891.

Elmira. A city of south central New York, built on both banks of the Chemung river, about 150 miles southeast of Buffalo. Elmira is well built and contains many fine streets, residences, and public buildings. It is the trade center of a large farming and dairying district and has extensive manufacturing interests. The more important products include steel bridges, valves, fire engines, silk and knit goods, automobile parts, milk bottles, and coaster brakes. The city is the seat of Elmira college. Mark Twain's grave is in Woodlawn cemetery. A glider contest is held annually on Harris hill nearby. Population, 1940, 45,106.

El Paso (*ĕl păs'ō*). An important railway center and manufacturing and commercial city of western Texas, about 1200 miles by rail from New Orleans and 800 miles from Los Angeles. El Paso is situated on the Rio Grande river opposite Ciudad Juarez, and is the largest city on the Mexican border.

The chief industries include smelting, flour milling, railway car repairing, box making, meat packing, cotton milling, and the manufacture of cement. The city has extensive wholesale and jobbing establishments, and carries on a substantial trade in copper, silver, lead, wool, hides, and live stock. Trade with Mexico amounts to many millions of dollars annually.

Located at an elevation of about 3800 feet in a region of almost perennial sunshine, El Paso has become a noted health resort. Buildings show a pronounced Mexican influence. Much of the surrounding district is irrigated by the great Elephant Butte dam, and produces large crops of grains, fruits, vegetables, and cotton, which are marketed chiefly through El Paso. El Paso is the seat of Texas college of mines and metallurgy.

The first settlement was made in 1829, the town was incorporated in 1869. Population, 1940, 96,810.

Enchanted Mesa (*mā'sä*). A remarkable castle-like rock or, more accurately speaking, a butte, situated near the Indian pueblo of Acoma in west central New Mexico. It is an immense mass of buff sandstone, with perpendicular sides, rising boldly from an arid plain. In shape it is elongated, the length measuring about 2000 feet and the width from 100 to 350 feet. At the base there is a sloping heap of rock débris. 100 to 200 feet high, above which towers the vertical wall to an elevation of 430 feet above the plain. The nearly level summit consists of a layer of hard rock on which grow a few stunted junipers.

The neighboring Indians, who call it Katzimo, regard this rock with superstitious awe. The evidences of former human occupation are very slight, but, according to traditions current among the Acoma Indians, their remote ancestors inhabited a pueblo built upon the flat-topped summit.

Endless Caverns. A large cave two miles south of New Market, Virginia. Its name indicates that its farthest reaches are unknown.

The cave was discovered by two boys on October 1, 1879. After a period of popularity, the cave was unvisited for over 30 years prior to 1919 when it was opened up, made safe for visitors, and illuminated by electric floodlights. Among the marvelous formations within the cave are "Skyland," recalling by its coloring the play of sun and cloud in the sky, "Alpine Pass," the "Arctic circle," "Diamond lake," and "Oriental palace."

Erie. A manufacturing city of northwestern Pennsylvania, situated on a large natural harbor on Lake Erie. The harbor is protected by Presque Isle, a peninsula about 11 miles long and a mile wide, on which there is a 7700-acre forested state park. There is considerable lake commerce; the leading articles of shipment include pulpwood, sand and gravel, coal, iron ore, petroleum, fresh-water fish, and manufactured goods. Among the city's varied manufactures are foundry and machine shop products, engines, excavating machinery, and paper. Erie has 19 parks, one of which, Presque Isle State park, near the harbor entrance, is the site of an old French fort, erected in 1753. The original site is now occupied by a blockhouse, built by the state in order to commemorate Anthony Wayne, who died at the old fort in 1796. In the War of 1812, Erie was Commodore Perry's headquarters. Population, 1940, 116,955.

Eugene (*ū-jēn'*). A city of western Oregon, located at the head of navigation on the Willamette river, about 70 miles south of Salem. It is the commercial center of an extensive farming and stock raising region, and its industrial products include lumber and woolen products and canned fruit and vegetables. Eugene was first settled in 1864 and is the seat of the University of Oregon. It is at the head of the Willamette flood control basin. Population, 1940, 20,838.

Evanston. A city of northeastern Illinois, situated on Lake Michigan at the northern boundary of Chicago, of which it is a residential suburb. Evanston is the seat of Northwestern university, including a large technological institute. It is also the national headquarters of the Women's Christian Temperance Union. Manufactures include steel tubing, toys, and radios. Population, 1940, 65,389.

Evansville. A manufacturing and commercial city of southwestern Indiana on the Ohio river, about 180 miles southwest of Indianapolis. The city is situated on a high bank of the river and has many fine parks, streets, and drives. It is surrounded by a rich agricultural district, and within the vicinity of the city are numerous coal mines. The chief industries include the manufacture of motor vehicles, and bodies, refrigerators, steam shovels, lacquers, and grain products. Founded in 1816 by General R. M. Evans, Evansville became a city in 1847. Population, 1940, 97,062.

Everett. A city of eastern Massachusetts, located on the Mystic river, about 3 miles north of Boston. While mainly a residential suburb, containing many fine streets and homes, Everett is also the seat of important industries. Among these are the manufacture of coke and petroleum products. Everett was settled in 1643, but until 1873 was known as South Malden. In 1892, it was chartered as a city. Population, 1940, 46,784.

Everett. A city of northwestern Washington, with a good harbor on Puget sound, about 28 miles north of Seattle. The surrounding region is heavily timbered, and there are extensive agricultural, mining, sporting and fishing interests. With these, the various enterprises of the city are chiefly connected. Among leading industrial products are the manufacture of shingles, lumber, pulpwood, paper, stoves, and machinery. Population, 1940, 30,224.

Everglades. An immense marshy tract in southern Florida, covering an area about 140 miles long and 50 miles wide. Drainage canals have been cut through various parts of the swamp, and some of the higher portions have been rendered suitable for agriculture. It is estimated that some 5000 square miles may eventually be reclaimed.

Fairbanks. A city of Alaska located on the Tanana river, practically at the head of navigation. It is the terminus of the government railway from the coast, has a large airport, and is the commercial center of an extensive gold mining district. Population, 1940, 3455.

Fall River. A manufacturing city and seaport of southeastern Massachusetts. It is built on the shore of Mount Hope bay, at the mouth of Taunton river, about 50 miles south of Boston. Abundant hydroelectric power for the city's extensive industries is furnished by the Fall river, which here makes a descent of about 130 feet in half a mile.

Fall River is one of the chief centers in the United States for the manufacture of cotton goods. Other important industries include the dyeing and finishing of textiles, oil refining, and the manufacture of men's hats, rubber, and silk.

The city is well laid out and substantially built. Many of the buildings are constructed of fine red granite quarried in the vicinity. There are several parks, with beautiful drives to the suburbs. The Bradford Durfee textile school, supported by the state, furnishes instruction pertaining to the textile industry. Population, 1940, 115,428.

Fargo. The largest city of North Dakota, situated on the Red river, somewhat south of the center of the state near the Minnesota boundary. Fargo is the commercial center of a large wheat growing and mixed farming region, and is a leading distributing point for farm implements. Industries include meat packing and manufacture of steel products. It is the seat of the State agricultural college and other educational institutions. There are a number of fine parks totaling 480 acres in area and several beautiful drives. Population, 1940, 32,580.

Finger Lakes. The name given to a group of beautiful lakes in west central New York. These lakes, which are long, narrow, and somewhat finger-like in shape, were formed by the blocking up of deep river valleys with glacial materials. They lie somewhat parallel to each other, extend in a general north and south direction, and give a distinctive character to a fine scenic region.

The largest are lakes Seneca and Cayuga, each of which is about 40 miles long and from 2 to 3 miles wide. Others of the group are lakes Canandaigua, Owasco, Skaneateles, and Otisco. Oneida lake, northeast of Syracuse, and Lake George, in eastern New York, are of similar formation.

Fitchburg. A manufacturing city of northeastern Massachusetts, built on a branch of the Nashua river, about 48 miles northwest of Boston. Fitchburg is attractively located and has many fine homes, public buildings, and parks. The citys' extensive manufactures include cotton and woolen goods, paper, saws, bicycles, hardware, and shoes. The city is the seat of a State teachers college. Fitchburg was settled in 1719, was incorporated in 1764, and became a city in 1872. Population, 1940, 41,824.

Flagstaff. A town of north central Arizona, picturesquely located at an altitude of 6907 feet, near the southern base of the San Francisco mountains. It is the commercial center of a lumbering, mining, and stock raising district, has large lumber mills, and carries on a trade in Indian curios and blankets.

By reason of its fine climate and varied scenic attractions, Flagstaff is also a tourists' resort. Ten miles north is San Francisco mountain, 12,611 feet high, the loftiest peak in the state. This great mountain, itself an extinct volcano, is the center of an extensive region of ancient lavas and interspersed with numerous cinder cones. One of the most conspicuous of the latter is Sunset peak, a large cone tipped with bright red cinders which give it the appearance of being illumined by the setting sun.

About 8 miles east of Flagstaff are the remarkable sink holes in the Kaibab limestone known as the "Bottomless Pits." In the near vicinity also is the Walnut Canyon national monument containing prehistoric cliff dwellings.

Flagstaff is the seat of Arizona State teachers college; and Lowell observatory is situated on a high mesa near the town. Population, 1940, 5080.

Flint. A manufacturing city of southeastern Michigan, situated on the river of the same name, about 70 miles northwest of Detroit. Flint is, after Detroit, the world's largest center of automobile manufacture. Its industries center around various subsidiaries of the General Motors Corporation, including the Chevrolet, Buick, and Fisher Body divisions. The 42 public parks of the city have a total area of 1275 acres. Population, 1940, 151,543.

Fort Knox. A United States fort in eastern Kentucky directly south of Louisville and 600 miles west of New York City. It is noted as the repository of the greater part of the monetary gold stock of the United States, its location west of the Allegheny mountains making it comparatively secure from a hypothetical invader from the East. The gold storage building is constructed with walls of solid granite two feet thick behind which are fabricated coils of steel set in concrete. The building, having a floor area of 10,000 square feet, is two stories high, the second set back so as to leave a parapet at each corner of which machine guns are mounted. The gold vault is 60 feet long, 40 feet wide, and two stories high. All parts of the vault's exterior are visible to guards from all angles by means of mirrors. Microphones and automatic alarms communicate with the guard room, from which messages may be sent to a motorized unit of the army in the adjacent fort. The first shipment of gold was taken to Fort Knox in 1937. The gold is stored in the form of bars, each weighing about 400 ounces and worth $14,000.

Fort Wayne. A railroad center and manufacturing city of northeastern Indiana. It is built at the confluence of the St. Joseph and the St. Mary's river, which here join to form the Maumee river. Car shops, car wheel works, foundries, hosiery mills, clothing, motor truck, copper, and enamelled wire factories, electrical machinery works, and oil tank shops are among the chief industrial interests. Among the largest buildings is the office of the Lincoln National Life Insurance Company, occupying an entire block. The city encloses the site of a fort built in 1794 by Anthony Wayne, to whom a monument has been erected. Population, 1940, 118,410.

Fort Worth. An important commercial city and railway center of northeastern Texas, situated in the midst of a rich agricultural and oil producing territory. The city is one of the great cattle and grain markets of the United States and one of the world's greatest petroleum pipe-line centers. Seventeen railways enter the city. Industries include oil refining, meat packing and the manufacture of flour, textiles, cement, and cottonseed products.

The city has numerous parks, covering 10,342 acres. The educational institutions include the Texas Christian university and the Texas Wesleyan college. A Centennial Exposition was held here in 1936. Population, 1940, 177,662.

Franconia Notch. A narrow picturesque passage in the Franconia range of the White mountains in New Hampshire, through which the Pemigewasset river flows. Entering the notch from the east is a narrow passage excavated in the rock, called the "flume." Near by is the "great stone face" celebrated by Hawthorne. The territory is embraced in a 6000-acre state park.

Frankfort. The capital of Kentucky, situated on the Kentucky river, in the rich "Blue-Grass region" somewhat northwest of the center of the state. The city numbers among its industries the manufacture of lumber, shoes, and concrete pipe. Many thoroughbred trotting horses are raised in the vicinity. The various state buildings include the capitol, a State arsenal, and a State normal school (colored).

Frankfort was founded in 1786, and, in 1792, when it had a population of less than 500, was made the capital of the state. The city contains the grave of Daniel Boone and is rich in historical associations. Population, 1940, 11,492.

Fresno. (*frĕz'nō*). A city of south central California, situated in the irrigated portion of the fertile San Joaquin valley, about 200 miles southeast of San Francisco. Fresno county, of which the city is the commercial center, is one of the most highly productive fruit growing districts of the continent.

This county is normally the leading peach growing, grape growing, and raisin producing county in America. Its grape yield is nearly half the entire crop of the state and more than twice that of the whole United States, exclusive of California. The peach crop of Fresno county, about one-third that of all California, exceeds that of any other single state in the Union. The county stands second in the state in the production of hay and alfalfa. Besides these leading crops cotton, flax, sugar beets, grain, and many subtropical fruits and various vegetables are grown.

The industrial and commercial activities of the city, are centered chiefly upon handling and marketing the county's staple productions. Places of interest in the vicinity are King's River canyon, Roeding park, and Kearney park, the last an irrigated experimental farm belonging to the University of California. Population, 1940, 60,685.

Galveston. The world's largest cotton and sulphur port, situated in southeastern Texas. It is built on the east end of Galveston island between Galveston bay on the north and the Gulf of Mexico on the south.

The excellent natural harbor facilities have been further improved at vast expense, and the port has been fortified by modern coast defensive works. Manufactures include flour, ships, and steel wire. Since a disastrous flood, caused by a hurricane in 1900, the level of the city has been raised, a sea wall has been built along the shore facing the Gulf, and 2 two-mile causeways have been constructed joining the city with the mainland. The city has four public parks. A hard, level beach provides a 38-mile natural speedway, on which automobile races are held. The medical school of the University of Texas is situated in the city. In 1901, Galveston adopted the commission form of government, which has since been widely adopted by other American cities. Population, 1940, 60,862.

Garden of the Gods. A small region of about 500 acres, near Colorado Springs, Colorado, noted for its curiously shaped rock formations and for its magnificent views of Pikes peak. By the action of wind and water, the red and the white sandstone strata have here been worn into many grotesque shapes. To these, various fanciful names have been given, such as "Cathedral Spires," "Balanced Rock," "Siamese Twins," and the "Seal and the Bear." The gateway to these interesting examples of erosion consists of two massive pinnacles of red rock, 300 feet high, which, at their bases, leave barely room for a vehicle to pass between them.

Gary (*gā'rĭ*). A steel manufacturing city of northwestern Indiana, at the southern end of Lake Michigan, about 30 miles southeast of Chicago. The city was founded in 1906 and is virtually the creation of the United States Steel Corporation. It contains immense steel works, tin and rail mills, and a cement plant, which are among the largest of their kind. The city is well planned with broad boulevards, giving an air of spaciousness. Its 12 parks cover 544 acres, Marquette park being particularly attractive. A civic gateway flanked by twin-designed courthouse and city hall, leads to the great steel mills over an area traversed by trunk-line railroads. Near by is the Indiana Dunes state park. The so-called Gary plan of elementary education originated in the public schools of the city. Population, 1940, 111,719.

Gettysburg. A town of southern Pennsylvania, located about 35 miles southwest of Harrisburg. Gettysburg occupies a picturesque site in a hilly but fertile farming country. Its population in 1940 was 5916.

In the vicinity was fought, July 1-3, 1863, one of the most decisive battles of the Civil War. Here the Union army under General Meade defeated the Confederate forces under General Lee. The entire battlefield, comprising 2392 acres, has been converted into a national monument, in which memorial structures mark the sites of particular actions which took place during the conflict. On Cemetery hill is the National cemetery, dedicated by Lincoln in his famous Gettysburg address. An eternal light peace memorial was dedicated on the battlefield by President Roosevelt in 1938.

Glendale. A city of southern California, adjoining Los Angeles on the north. Its elevation varies from 400 feet to 1200 feet. It is a popular residential suburb, but with rapidly expanding industrial interests, which include pottery, airplanes, and drugs. A feature of particular interest is Forest Lawn memorial park, the court of which has a stained glass window design copied from Da Vinci's "Last Supper." Glendale was incorporated in 1906. Population, 1940, 82,582.

Gloucester (*glŏs'tẽr*). A seaport of northeastern Massachusetts, built on the south side of the Cape Ann peninsula, about 28 miles northeast of Boston. The city is an important fishing port, with a large fleet engaged in taking cod, haddock, halibut, redfish, and mackerel. There are various other industries, largely connected with the fisheries. By reason of its picturesque location, quaint, old-fashioned streets, and interesting historic associations, the city is a favorite travel and summer resort, especially for artists. Gloucester was founded in 1623, was incorporated in 1642, and became a city in 1874. Population, 1940, 24,046.

Gloversville. A city of east central New York, noted as the chief glove manufacturing center in the United States. Its factories, together with those of the neighboring town of Johnstown, produce a substantial percentage of the gloves made in the country. The leather glove industry is said to have been first introduced into the United States by Sir William Johnson, who, in 1760, settled several families of Scotch glove makers on his lands near the site of Gloversville. Other manufactured products include silk and knitted goods, leather, and lumber. Population, 1940, 23,329.

Grand Canyon of the Colorado. The most magnificent scenic spectacle of its kind in the world. This immense gorge, the greatest example of stream erosion known, has been cut by the Colorado river in the high plateau of northern Arizona. The deeper portion is more than 200 miles long; its vast chasms range from 4000 to 6000 feet in depth from the uppermost rim to the river; and its width from rim to rim varies from 4 to 18 miles.

The canyon consists of two distinct parts: the broad, outer, upper portion, which has been eroded through stratified rocks; and the narrow, inner, lower portion, which has been worn down through unstratified rocks. The outer or upper walls are carved in alternating layers of limestones, sandstones, and shales. These descend in successive benches or escarpments, displaying a multitude of beautifully castellated, temple-like forms, banded in splendid colors, and finally reach the top of the gloomy inner gorge. This is irregularly cut in tough dark granite, and, at its bottom, extending usually from wall to wall, flows the foaming, torrential river.

The descent throughout the entire length of the canyon is so great that the river is broken into many rapids and semirapids. These, rushing between almost vertical walls of rock, make navigation, even for the staunchest boats, exceedingly dangerous. The current rolls great bowlders along the bottom of the narrow channel, and, at some points, the noise of their grinding in the rocky river bed can be heard above the roaring of the waters.

The most impressive portion of the canyon is included in Grand Canyon national park. Its area, 1008 square miles, embraces 56 miles of the Grand Canyon, stretching from east to west from its beginning at the mouth of the Little Colorado river. From rim to rim this part of the canyon is from 8 to 15 miles wide; it is more than a mile deep measured from the north rim, which averages nearly 1000 feet higher than the south rim. The eastern boundary includes the lofty, richly colored walls east of which lies the Painted desert. The western boundary of the park includes the broad Cataract canyon, entering from the south. In this tributary canyon is the Havasupai Indian reservation and a group of five waterfalls.

The south rim of the canyon is accessible by a branch railway which runs 64 miles north from Williams, Arizona. The station at the rim is about 6850 feet above sea level. There are also automobile roads from Williams and Flagstaff. At this point on the rim the canyon may be visited every day in the year, and there are excellent accommodations for travelers. Many fine views on the rim are reached by motor roads, including Grandview, the most famous of all, and Desert View, looking eastward over the Painted desert. There are two well-constructed trails for making on muleback the interesting descent from the rim to the river: Bright Angel trail starts from El Tovar hotel; Hermit trail, longer and more beautiful, descends Hermit canyon, about 7 miles west of El Tovar.

The north rim is reached by motor roads from various railway points in Utah. Special tours by auto stages are arranged so as to include visits to Bryce canyon and Zion national park. Camps are maintained for tourists. At Bright Angel point, opposite El Tovar, the north rim is about 8150 feet above sea level.

The first white man to see the Grand Canyon was Cardenas, a member of Coronado's party, who, in 1540, visited the south rim. The first successful passage of the Grand Canyon by boat was made in 1869 by Major John Wesley Powell. An isolated plateau known as Shiva's Temple, believed to have been cut off in the glacial age 12,000 to 35,000 years ago, was explored for the first time in 1937 by Dr. Harold E. Anthony. Ascending the precipitous edge, he conducted an investigation into the effects produced on animal life there by its long separation from outside influences.

Grand Coulee Dam. The largest dam in the world, backing up the Columbia river in Washington into a lake that extends 151 miles to the Canadian border. The height of the dam is 553 feet and its length is 4200 feet. Into its construction went 11.5 million cubic yards of concrete, an amount of construction unmatched by any other engineering work. The dam is designed to produce 1,974,000 kilowatts of electricity and to irrigate 1,250,000 acres of land. The cost of the dam and power plant, opened in 1941, was 181 million dollars. An additional 209 million dollars was allocated to irrigation canals.

A peculiarity of the dam is that, to be useful for irrigation, a reservoir of water must be created 280 feet above the level to which the dam raises the river. Power developed at the dam is used to pump water into such a reservoir, which, when full, is 23 miles long and covers 2300 acres.

Grand Junction. A city of southwestern Colorado, 255 miles southwest of Denver, at the junction of the Colorado and the Gunnison river. It is the commercial center of a fertile farming and fruit growing district, watered by a large irrigation canal. The city lies 4600 feet above sea level, and is surrounded by some of the most noted scenic points in Colorado, notably Colorado national monument and Grand Mesa. Population, 1940, 12,479.

Grand Rapids. A city of Michigan, built on both banks of the Grand river, about 150 miles northwest of Detroit. The city takes its name from the rapids of the river, which here descends 18 feet in about a mile, furnishing extensive water power. While maintaining numerous important industries, Grand Rapids is noted chiefly as a center for the manufacture of furniture. Although exceeded in volume by New York and Chicago, Grand Rapids is distinguished for the design, quality, and finish of its product. In the heart of the city there are large exposition buildings for the display of samples of furniture for wholesale buyers. A furniture museum was opened in 1938.

Among other leading manufactures are automobile parts, carpet sweepers, knit goods, house furnishings, chemicals, textiles, and gypsum plasters. The city is well laid out, and has numerous fine streets, residences, and public buildings. Public parks cover over 1245 acres.

Grand Rapids was settled in 1833, became a village in 1838, and a city in 1850. Population, 1940, 164,292.

Great Falls. The leading manufacturing city of Montana, picturesquely situated at the Great Falls of the Missouri river, about 100 miles north of Helena. The development of immense hydroelectric power in the center of a rich mining and agricultural region has been the chief factor in the growth of the city's manufactures.

Among the leading industrial establishments are copper reduction works, smelting and refining works, flour and cereal mills, and factories for making beet sugar. A notable feature in connection with the smelting industry is a smokestack 500 feet high, a structure exceeded in height by comparatively few buildings in the United States. The city is also an important market for wool, shipping several million pounds annually. The municipal park system embraces 7 parks with a total area of 640 acres. Population, 1940, 29,928.

Great Salt Lake. A salt-water lake in northwestern Utah. Situated at an altitude of 4218 feet above sea level, it has an area of about 1750 square miles with a maximum length of 75 miles and a width of from 30 to 50 miles. Its mean depth is about 20 feet with a maximum of 40 feet. The lake has no outlet, but is fed by the Jordan, Weber, and Bear rivers. Variations in rainfall have a very pronounced effect on its size and on its salinity, the latter fluctuating from 12 to 23 per cent according as the water is high or low. Since the salinity of the ocean is about 3.44 per cent, Great Salt lake is from four to six times as salty as the ocean. Common salt is the chief mineral constituent of the water, and its recovery is the basis of an active industry. Sodium sulphate and gypsum are also obtained. It is impossible for a bather to sink in the water of the lake.

Great Salt lake was first accurately described by John C. Frémont in 1845. Geological observations indicate that the lake is the shrunken remnant of an inland sea, Lake Bonneville, which, centuries ago, covered some 19,000 square miles. Great Salt lake contains nine islands, the longest being 16 miles in length. It is crossed by the Southern Pacific railroad over the Lucin cutoff, a trestle and gravel fill about 27 miles long.

Greeley. A city of northern Colorado, 50 miles north of Denver, on the Cache la Poudre river. It is situated in a fertile agricultural district, and its industries are chiefly based on agriculture. They include sugar refining, flour milling, cold storage warehousing, and canning. The place was settled in 1870 by the "Greeley Colony," named after Horace Greeley, and composed mainly of New England people. By establishing irrigation, these pioneers transformed an almost barren wilderness into a highly productive region. Greeley is the seat of Colorado State college of education. Population, 1940, 15,995.

Green Bay. A city of eastern Wisconsin on high level ground on both sides of the Fox river where it empties into Green bay, an arm of Lake Michigan. Dating from 1745, it is the oldest settlement in Wisconsin, and Tank cottage, in Washington park, is said to be the oldest house in the state. Paper manufacture is prominent among the varied industries. The city is a busy port, shipping chiefly cheese, grain, and fish, and receiving coal, sulphur, steel, and motor cars. Green Bay became a city in 1854. Population, 1940, 46,235.

Greensboro. A cotton manufacturing city in the north central part of North Carolina. The chief textile products are blue denim, rayon cloth, and apparel. The city is spacious and open with 425 acres of beautiful parks. It is the seat of Guilford college and two colleges for women—Greensboro and North Carolina. Greensboro was founded in 1809 and named for General Nathanael Greene, the hero of the battle of Guilford Court House, which is memorialized by a national military park six miles to the northwest. Population, 1940, 59,319.

Greenville. A city of northwestern South Carolina, built on the banks of the Reedy river, about 110 miles northwest of Columbia. Greenville is an important textile manufacturing center and contains many large cotton mills. Other industrial establishments include foundries, dye works, and garment, textile machinery, and furniture factories. Greenville is the seat of Furman university. Population, 1940, 34,734.

Greylock, Mount. The highest summit in Massachusetts, situated in the Berkshire hills, on the western border of the state, about 5 miles southwest of North Adams. The broad, flat top, which rises to an elevation of 3500 feet, is accessible by highway and by many beautiful trails. A tract of about 8600 acres on the upper part of the mountain has been purchased by the state for a permanent park.

Gulfport. A port, city, and pleasure resort of southeastern Mississippi, on Mississippi sound, an arm of the Gulf of Mexico. It is about midway between New Orleans and Mobile. The shore is protected by a 24-mile concrete sea wall surmounted by a four-lane scenic driveway. Gulfport has a relatively large foreign trade, shipping, among other commodities, lumber and cottonseed products and receiving fertilizers and sugar. Population, 1940, 15,195.

Hagerstown. A city of western Maryland, built on Antietam creek, about 72 miles northwest of Baltimore. Hagerstown is the trade center for a large agricultural district and has extensive and varied industries. The city's industrial products include silk and knit goods, shoes, aircraft, cement, fertilizers, and sheet metal. In the vicinity are Fort Frederick and the battlefields of Antietam and Gettysburg. Population, 1940, 32,491.

Hamilton. A manufacturing city of southwestern Ohio, built on both banks of the Miami river, about 25 miles north of Cincinnati. Machinery, machine tools, office fixtures, safes and bank vaults, paper, woolen goods, and engines are among the products extensively manufactured. The city is said to have been the first in the country to own its waterworks, gas plant, and electric light plant. Population, 1940, 50,592.

Hammond. A city of northwestern Indiana, on Lake Michigan, about 18 miles southeast of the center of Chicago, of which it is an industrial suburb. It adjoins the cities of Whiting, East Chicago, and Calumet City. Hammond arose as a packing center, George Hammond having established a plant there in 1868. After 1900, steel and railroad car manufacture became of chief importance, and immense oil refineries were built. Other industries include printing, bookbinding, and the making of railroad equipment and chemicals. Population, 1940, 70,184.

Hamtramck (*hăm-trăm'ĭk*). A city of southeastern Michigan, existing as an island municipality within the city of Detroit. It was incorporated as a city in 1922. Hamtramck owes its rapid growth to the immense development of automobile industries. The city has extensive manufactures of automobile accessories, iron and aluminum castings, wheels, radiators, brass goods, and paints. Population, 1940, 49,839.

Hannibal. A city of northeastern Missouri, situated on the Mississippi river, about 120 miles above Saint Louis. It is the trade center of an agricultural district, and there are coal mines in the vicinity. The chief manufactures include shoes, Portland cement, lime, structural steel, and foundry products. Hannibal was settled in 1819 and became incorporated in 1839. During boyhood, Mark Twain lived in Hannibal, and his early home is the property of the city. A statue of him stands in the 200-acre Riverview park. The Mark Twain memorial bridge spans the Mississippi at Hannibal. Population, 1940, 20,865.

Harpers Ferry. A historic town on the extreme eastern border of West Virginia, about 55 miles northwest of Washington. It occupies a site of remarkable scenic beauty at the junction of the Shenandoah and Potomac rivers, at the point where the latter stream flows through a gap in the Blue Ridge mountains. Here, in 1859, John Brown attempted his famous raid. During the Civil War, the town was alternately in the possession of the Union and of the Confederate forces. Population, 1940, 665.

Harrisburg. The capital of Pennsylvania, situated on the Susquehanna river, in the southeastern part of the state. The city is noted for its diversified manufactures, chiefly of steel and of steel products, and for the extensive railway roundhouses, repair shops, and freight yards, which have made Harrisburg a great distribution center.

The most beautiful of the city's fine buildings is the State capitol. This impressive edifice, constructed of steel and faced with granite and marble, and decorated with elaborate sculptures, was erected at a cost of $13,000,000. East of it lies Memorial park, where there are four monumental-type office buildings and a half-mile viaduct in memory of Pennsylvanians who served in the World War. Since 1900, extensive civic improvements have won for Harrisburg the sobriquet of the "Model City." The park system covers 1100 acres, of which 666 acres are included in the picturesque Wildwood park. A beautiful riverside park and boulevard borders on the Susquehanna.

Harrisburg was named for John Harris, an English trader, who settled on its site in 1719. It was incorporated in 1791, and in 1812 became the capital of the state. Population, 1940, 83,893.

Hartford. The capital of Connecticut, built on the west bank of the Connecticut river, in the north central part of the state. The city occupies a commanding site on rolling ground, affording fine views of the Connecticut valley.

Hartford is laid out with wide, well shaded streets and beautiful boulevards. Its 27 parks embrace 2700 acres. The city is noted for its artistic homes and for its excellent public buildings, which, architecturally, rank among the finest in New England. The most notable structure is the State capitol, in Bushnell park, to which an impressive approach is provided by the Soldiers' and Sailors' Memorial bridge and arch. The Bulkeley memorial bridge, over the Connecticut river, ranks as one of the finest in the country.

In value of manufactures, Hartford normally ranks second among the cities of the state. Its important industries include the manufacture of firearms, typewriters, brushes, precision tools, oil burners, and counting devices. For a long period, Hartford has been one of the leading insurance centers of the country, containing the home offices of nearly 50 companies. The Travelers Insurance Company tower is 527 feet in height. Hartford is the seat of Trinity college and the J. Pierpont Morgan museum. It has a famous municipal rose garden and celebrates a rose festival annually.

The first white settlement on the site of Hartford was made in 1633. At Hartford, in 1639, were drawn up and adopted the "Fundamental Orders of Connecticut," said to be the first written constitution of modern times. In 1687 occurred the attempt of Governor Andros to seize the charter of the colony, and its alleged concealment in the famous "Charter Oak." Hartford was the capital of Connecticut colony until 1701, when it was made joint capital with New Haven. In 1873, Hartford became the sole capital of the state. Population, 1940, 166,267.

Haverhill (*hā'vẽr-ĭl*). A manufacturing city of northeastern Massachusetts, built on both banks of the Merrimac river, about 30 miles north of Boston. Haverhill is one of the chief centers in the United States for the manufacture of boots and shoes. About seven-eighths of the city's extensive manufactures consist of products connected with this industry. The city was settled in 1640–41 and almost since its founding has been noted for the manufacture of shoes. It now makes about-one-sixth of all the women's shoes produced in the United States. The city contains many fine parks, lakes, and drives; also many handsome residences and public buildings. It is the birthplace of John Greenleaf Whittier. Population, 1940, 46,752.

Helena (*hĕl'ê-nȧ*). The capital of Montana, situated in the west central part of the state. The city overlooks an arable valley, the scene of extensive cattle raising, and is surrounded by a mountainous region, rich in gold and other valuable metals. Helena was founded by mining prospectors in 1864 on Last Chance gulch and was incorporated in 1881. From this gulch gold was extracted to the value of 40 million dollars. The industries include lead and zinc smelting.

The per capita wealth of the inhabitants is very high and is reflected in the many fine residences of the city. Among the chief buildings are the State capitol, the Federal building, Consistory temple, Civic Center and Saint Helena cathedral. Many points of scenic interest exist in the neighborhood, notably the "Gates of the Mountains," named by Lewis and Clark in 1805. The educational institutions include Carroll college. Population, 1940, 15,056.

Hibbing. A mining village of northeastern Minnesota, located near the Mesaba Iron Ore range, about 75 miles northwest of Duluth. From the vicinity of Hibbing comes a large proportion of all the iron ore produced in the United States. The largest open-pit iron ore mine in the world is within the village. There is a 4-million dollar public school housing all grades up to junior college. Population, 1940, 16,385.

Highland Park. A city of southeastern Michigan adjoining Detroit on the north, of which it is an industrial suburb. Highland Park was at one time the headquarters of the Ford Motor Company and owes its growth largely to the automobile industry. In 1900, it was a village of 427 inhabitants. Population, 1940, 50,810.

High Point. A manufacturing city of central North Carolina, 99 miles northwest of Raleigh. It is the chief southern center for the manufacture of furniture. The Southern furniture exposition is held there twice annually, and is visited by buyers from all parts of the United States. Other important industrial products include textiles, tile, and tobacco. Population, 1940, 38,495.

Hoboken. (*hō'bō-kĕn*). A manufacturing city of northeastern New Jersey. It is situated on the Hudson river opposite New York, with which the city is connected by passenger tubes, ferries, and the Holland and Lincoln vehicular tunnels. Hoboken is a large seaport, and is the terminus of several important transatlantic steamship lines. Its industrial output includes lead pencils, foundry products, measuring instruments, electric equipment, and ships. The city is the seat of the Stevens institute of technology, which stands opposite Hudson park. The first steam-propelled ferryboat was invented and put in operation at Hoboken. Population, 1940, 50,115.

Hodgenville. A town of central Kentucky, the county seat of Larue county. It is situated about 50 miles almost due south of Louisville in a fertile region devoted to growing grain, tobacco, and live stock. The town is noted as the birthplace of Abraham Lincoln. On Lincoln farm, about 3 miles distant, there is a beautiful memorial building. In this is preserved the log cabin in which the great emancipator was born. Population, 1940, 1348.

Holy Cross, Mountain of the. A high peak of the Rockies, 30 miles northwest of Leadville, Colorado. The emblem from which this mountain takes its name appears about midsummer. At that time the snow has melted from the higher slopes and ridges and is retained only in two deep canyons, which, by their intersection, form an immense cross high up on the side of the mountain. This white cross remains in view until late autumn, when the entire crest is again covered with snow. This noted mountain is one of more than 30 peaks in Colorado which exceed an elevation of 14,000 feet.

Holyoke (*hōl'yōk*). A manufacturing city of southwestern Massachusetts, built on the west bank of the Connecticut river, about 75 miles southwest of Boston. Immense water power, derived from falls in the river, promoted the rise of the city's extensive industries. These are concerned chiefly with the manufacture of paper, paper products, and textiles. Holyoke is one of the largest producers of fine writing papers and envelopes in the United States. Because of the number and size of its mills, it has long been styled the "Paper City."

The total value of the city's paper products is, however, exceeded by that of its textile products. These include cotton and woolen goods, thread, knit goods, alpaca, and silk. Among other important manufactures are machinery, blank books, and school supplies. Mount Tom and Mount Holyoke are among the many points of interest in the vicinity. Population, 1940, 53,750.

Homestead. A manufacturing city of western Pennsylvania, located on the Monongahela river, about 7 miles southeast of Pittsburgh. Its chief manufacture is steel, and its vast steel plants rank among the largest in the country. Among the "Homestead steel mills," in and around Homestead, is the Carnegie-Illinois strip steel mill, costing 60 million dollars, one of the largest of its kind in the world. Homestead was settled in 1871 and in 1880 was incorporated. Population, 1940, 19,041.

Honolulu (*hō'nō-lōō'lōō*). The capital and chief commercial center of the Hawaiian islands, situated on a good harbor on the south coast of Oahu. Honolulu is noted for its delightful climate and for its luxuriant tropical gardens. It possesses fine clean streets, spacious open squares, and many handsome public buildings. These include colleges, schools, hospitals, banks, and a public library.

Among the city's representative industries are pineapple canneries, sugar factories, iron foundries, artificial ice plants, and rice mills. The native population is industrious and self-supporting. Honolulu occupies a vantage ground of immense importance on the trade routes of the Pacific, and, from a strategic point of view, is of great value as a naval station of the United States. Honolulu harbor was discovered in 1794. The modern town was founded in 1816, and in 1820 it was made the capital of the islands. The population is composed of a mixture of various races, among which predominate Hawaiians, Japanese, Chinese, and Portuguese. Population, 1940, 179,358.

Hood, Mount. A peak of the Cascade range in northern Oregon, about 50 miles east of Portland. It is of volcanic origin and rises symmetrically to a height of 11,225 feet, the loftiest elevation in the state. The lower slopes are forested but the peak is snow capped and there are glaciers on the upper slopes. An automobile road leads from the railway station at Hood River to Cloud Cap Inn, near the snow line. From this point the glaciers are readily accessible. The summit, which may be ascended without serious difficulty, commands magnificent views of the Columbia River valley and also of many great peaks of the Cascades, including mounts Rainier, Adams, and Jefferson.

Hood River. A town of northern Oregon on the Columbia river, 67 miles east of Portland. It is the trade center and shipping point of the Hood River valley, which extends southward 25 miles to Mt. Hood. This valley, protected by Cascade ranges and provided with a constant flow of gravity-irrigation water, is excellently adapted to fruit growing. Hood River apples and pears are famed throughout the continent and command maximum prices. The Bonneville dam, 24 miles down the Columbia river, backs the water up to Hood river, thus forming a pool for water sports and recreation. Population, 1940, 3280.

Hoquiam (*hō'kwĭ-ăm*). A city of western Washington, situated on Gray's harbor, about 90 miles by rail southwest of Tacoma. It adjoins Aberdeen, with which it shares the distinction of being one of the greatest seaports of the world for shipment of forest products. The industries include lumber mills, wood product factories, and fisheries. Population, 1940, 10,835.

Hot Springs. A health and travel resort, located in western Arkansas 58 miles southwest of Little Rock. The city is picturesquely situated in a narrow valley sheltered by two ridges of the Ouachita mountains. It lies adjacent to Hot Springs national park, celebrated for its numerous hot springs having valuable medicinal properties. There are numerous large hotels, sanitariums, and sumptuous bathhouses. Hot Springs medical center is one of the tallest buildings in Arkansas. The resort is nearly surrounded by Lakes Catherine and Hamilton, created by power dams in the Ouachita river. Population, 1940, 21,370.

Houston (*hūs'tŭn*). The largest city of Texas, situated in the southeastern part of the state. It is about 50 miles northwest of Galveston, on a sluggish stream formerly known as Buffalo bayou. This has been widened and deepened into a canal called the Houston ship channel, which permits large ocean steamers to reach the city's wharves.

Houston is the commercial center of a rich agricultural and lumbering region and is one of the world's richest oil producing territories. The city is one of the greatest cotton markets and ports in the South. In manufactures Houston ranks first among the cities of the state. Its varied industries include petroleum refining, sugar, rice and flour milling, and the manufacture of fertilizers, cement, and chemicals.

The city is laid out with wide, shaded streets, beautiful parks, handsome residences, and imposing public and commercial buildings. The Esperon and Gulf buildings are among the tallest in the South. Houston is the seat of Rice institute and University of Houston, and has a magnificent museum of fine arts. Houston was settled after the battle of San Jacinto, which was fought near its site in 1836. It was incorporated in 1837, and in 1840 became the capital of the former republic of Texas. Population, 1940, 384,514.

Huntington. A commercial and industrial city situated on the Ohio river, in a rich natural gas and coal region at the extreme western part of West Virginia. Among its leading industrial establishments are railway car shops, a nickel refinery, foundry and machine shops, clay works, lumber and textile mills, and glass factories. The city is the seat of Marshall college. Population, 1940, 78,836.

Imperial Valley. A former desert area in southeastern California, which has been made remarkably productive by irrigation. It lies east and south of the Salton Sea and extends southward to the Mexican border. The improved district is about 40 miles long, with a maximum breadth of 30 miles, and embraces a total area of about 500,000 acres. Previously to 1900, it was a part of the Colorado desert—a hot, arid, barren waste in which neither man nor beast could live. The average annual rainfall is from 3 to 4 inches, and, in the summer, temperatures range from 100° to 120°, rarely falling below 70°. The unusual dryness of the air makes these extremes of heat endurable, and sunstroke is practically unknown.

Water for irrigation is taken from the Colorado river near Yuma, and conducted to the south end of the valley. Thence it is distributed in a network of waterways covering the district. The soil is largely composed of the silts of an ancient delta of the Colorado river. It is of unmatched and seemingly of inexhaustible fertility. Owing to the warm climate and almost continuous sunshine, the growing season is not only very long but also very rapid. By rotation, two or more crops a year are often produced from the same field.

The Imperial valley has become widely noted for the production of long-staple cotton of unexcelled quality. The district produces also immense quantities of melons, lettuce, asparagus, onions, grapes, oranges, and various other vegetables and fruits. Date culture on a commercial scale is becoming established.

In 1910, the district under irrigation contained fully 10,000 inhabitants and included 6 newly incorporated towns. With its water system effectively established, the valley developed with still greater rapidity. In 1940, the population was about 60,000.

Independence. A city in the western part of Missouri, located in an agricultural district adjacent to Kansas City. Recently, it has become well known as the home of President Harry S. Truman and the site of the "temporary" White House during his visits to his native state. In an earlier period it was important as a supply point for caravans of pioneers who were going west over the Oregon Trail or the Santa Fe Trail. Its population in 1940 was 16,066.

Indianapolis. The capital and largest city of Indiana, situated on the White river, near the center of the state, about 185 miles southeast of Chicago. In population, transportation facilities, and volume of business transacted, Indianapolis is the largest inland city of the United States not located on a navigable body of water.

The city occupies a nearly level site, is regularly laid out, for the most part with broad streets, and is substantially and handsomely built. Indianapolis, preeminently a city of homes, is widely noted for its advantages as a residential city. The principal business streets are Ohio, Market, Washington, Maryland, and Georgia, all running east and west, and Capitol, Illinois, Meridian, Pennsylvania, and Delaware streets, running north and south. In addition to these, radiating from the circular Monument place in the heart of the city, there are four diagonal avenues—Massachusetts, Indiana, Virginia, and Kentucky—extending to the four corners of the city.

The park system, which embraces a total area of more than 3230 acres, contains 32 parks. Of these, Riverside park, the largest, covering some 936 acres, extends along both banks of the White river for a distance of about 5 miles. The Soldiers' and Sailors' monument, in Monument place, a lofty shaft of stone and bronze, 285 feet high and richly decorated with sculptures, is one of the notable military memorials in America. Among numerous fine buildings are the capitol, the Federal building, the Riley public library, Christ church, the Herron art institute, the Scottish Rite cathedral, and Indiana State library. A 15-million dollar World War memorial plaza occupies five blocks in the downtown district of the city. The principal structure is the magnificent Shrine building. A cenotaph stands in the north square at the head of a mall two blocks long. In the northeast corner is a four-story building of Greek architecture which houses the national headquarters of the American Legion. The city's educational institutions include Butler university, Indiana Central college, and several professional schools of the University of Indiana.

Indianapolis owes its prominence largely to three important advantages. First, it is the center of a large and highly productive agricultural region; second, it lies near immense supplies of coal, insuring cheap fuel, and third, it possesses unusually excellent transportation facilities. The city is served by numerous railways radiating in all directions and by very extensive truck and bus systems. A feature for which the city is widely noted is the Indianapolis motor speedway. Among the chief industries are meat packing and the manufacture of drugs, motor vehicle engines and parts, aircraft engines, refrigerators, electrical equipment, apparel, furniture, and inner tubes for tires.

The site on which the city is located was selected for the state capital and named Indianapolis in 1821. The legislature first met there in 1825. Population, 1940, 386,972.

Inland Empire. A name popularly given to a rich agricultural, stock raising, and mining region of the northwestern United States, lying between the Rocky and the Cascade mountains. It embraces a considerable part of the Columbia River plateau, including eastern Washington, northeastern Oregon, the northern part or "panhandle" of Idaho, and the extreme western part of Montana. The chief railway and commercial center in this large region is Spokane. Other important cities and towns are Walla Walla, Washington; Pendleton, Oregon; Lewiston and Coeur d'Alene, Idaho; and Missoula and Kalispell, Montana.

Irvington. A town of northeastern New Jersey. It is a residential suburb of New York and Newark, and adjoins the latter on the southwest. It has also various industries, including the refining of metals and the manufacture of chemicals, metal products, and lumber. Settled in 1692, it was called Camptown until 1852 and was then renamed in honor of Washington Irving. Its incorporation as a village dates from 1835 and, as a town, from 1898. Population, 1940, 55,328.

Isleta (*ēs-lā'tä*). An Indian town situated on the west bank of the Rio Grande river, about 10 miles south of Albuquerque, New Mexico. The present town was founded early in the 18th century.The inhabitants, who are of Tanoan Indian stock, retain much of their aboriginal social organization. By primitive means of irrigation, they produce from an arid soil excellent crops of corn, fruits, and vegetables. Population, about 1100.

Itasca (*ī-tăs'kȧ*), **Lake.** A small lake in north central Minnesota. It consists of three long narrow arms, from the northern one of which emerges the Mississippi river. The region immediately surrounding the lake, embracing an area of about 35,000 acres, has been made a state park. Its waters abound in many kinds of fish, beavers are abundant, and a band of elks has been established in the park.

Ithaca. A city of west central New York, located at the south end of Cayuga lake, about 40 miles south of Syracuse. While the city conducts a substantial trade and maintains various local industries, it is noted chiefly as the seat of Cornell university, with which is connected the New York State agricultural college. This important educational institution occupies a magnificent campus on East Hill, an eminence rising about 400 feet above the lake and lower city, and commanding unexcelled views of a highly picturesque region. Ithaca was founded in 1789, and was chartered as a city in 1888. Population, 1940, 19,730.

Jackson. A city of southern Michigan, built on both banks of the Grand river, about 70 miles west of Detroit. Jackson is an important railway center, and is situated in the midst of a rich agricultural region. It carries on an extensive trade in grain, fruit, and vegetables, and has substantial industries. The city's manufactures include automobile parts, tires, machine tools, machinery, airplane wheels, and food products. Near by is a cascade 500 feet long and 64 feet high which is illuminated each night in summer. Jackson was settled in 1829, became a village in 1843, and a city in 1857. The Republican party was organized and named at Jackson in 1854. Population, 1940, 49,656.

Jackson. The capital of Mississippi, located on the Pearl river, about 40 miles east of Vicksburg. Possessing both railway and water transportation, Jackson has become a commercial center for agricultural and manufactured products, with an extensive trade in cotton. The chief local industries include cottonseed oil mills, foundries, lumber mills, and woodworking shops. Among the prominent public buildings are the capitol and the Carnegie library. Jackson is the seat of Millsaps college, Bellhaven college, and the James observatory.

The site of Jackson was chosen for the state capital in 1821. During the Civil War, Jackson was the scene of many conflicts, and in 1864 was largely destroyed by General Sherman. Population, 1940, 62,107.

Jackson. A city of western Tennessee, about 80 miles northeast of Memphis. Jackson is the trade center of a rich farming and fruit growing district, is an important cotton and fruit market, and has substantial local industries. Among the city's manufactures are cotton goods, cottonseed oil, lumber, and furniture. Jackson is the seat of Union university and of Lambuth and Lane colleges. Population, 1940, 24,332.

Jacksonville. The largest city and chief commercial center of Florida, situated on Saint Johns river, about 27 miles from its mouth. It has an excellent harbor, with a 30-foot channel to the ocean, and carries on an extensive coastwise and foreign trade in lumber, cotton, phosphates, fruits, and vegetables. The leading industries include shipbuilding and the manufacture of fertilizers, lumber, cigars, chemicals, and naval stores; also fruit packing, crab meat packing, and spice milling.

The city's streets, parks, and private residences are rendered attractive by the luxuriance of semi-tropical vegetation. By reason of its mild climate and near-by ocean beaches, Jacksonville is a favorite winter resort. An air defense base of 3200 acres is situated 7 miles to the south at Black and Piney points. Population, 1940, 173,065.

Jamestown. A manufacturing city of western New York, about 75 miles southwest of Buffalo. Jamestown occupies a picturesque, hilly site on the outlet of Chautauqua lake, with abundant water power. It is one of the leading centers for the manufacture of furniture. Other important industries include woolen and silk mills, lumber and woodworking mills, metal furniture shops, and factories for making automobile parts. The city is also an important dairy center. Population, 1940, 42,638.

Jamestown. The first permanent English settlement in the United States. It was founded in 1607 on the banks of the James river, in Virginia, about 32 miles above its mouth, and nearly opposite the present town of Williamsburg. The first legislative assembly held in America met at Jamestown in 1619, and here, in the same year, slaves were first introduced into the colonial territory.

During Bacon's rebellion, 1676, Jamestown was burned to the ground. It was rebuilt and remained the capital of Virginia until 1698, when it was again destroyed by fire and was never reconstructed. The site of the settlement, originally a peninsula, later became an island. Of the former town, there remain only the ruins of one dwelling and of a church built about 1680. Near these is the site of the Jamestown Tercentennial exposition, held in 1907. Jamestown now forms part of the Colonial national monument, established in 1930.

Jefferson City. The capital of Missouri, situated on the south bank of the Missouri river, about 110 miles west of Saint Louis. The city is a trade and commercial center of a rich farming district and contains large railway shops. The chief manufacturing interests include shoe factories, flour mills, machine shops, and foundries. A fine steel bridge spans the Missouri at Jefferson City. Among prominent buildings are the State capitol, erected at a cost of $4,215,000, the State supreme courthouse, and the state office building. The site was chosen for the state capital in 1821, the town was laid out in 1822, and the legislature first met here in 1826. Population, 1940, 24,268.

Jersey City. The second largest city of New Jersey, built on the west bank of the Hudson river. It occupies an area of 20.2 square miles and lies directly opposite the lower end of New York City, with which it is connected by four tubes under the Hudson, the Holland vehicular tunnel, and numerous ferries.

Jersey City is the terminus of a large number of railroads, which link it with the South and West. As a shipping and receiving port it is probably second in importance only to New York. Among the chief of its numerous and varied manufactures are electrical and scientific apparatus, railway locomotives and cars, electrical machinery, crucibles, jewelry, musical instruments, soap, radios, and tobacco. It contains immense grain elevators and meat packing establishments.

The city has many notable public buildings and several parks. The Hudson boulevard, a magnificent promenade 19 miles long and 100 feet wide, follows the crest of Bergon hill, extends past West Side park, and gives a splendid view of the river and upper New York. Population, 1940, 301,173.

Johnstown. A manufacturing city in southwestern Pennsylvania, about 75 miles east of Pittsburgh. Johnstown is located in a picturesque valley at the foot of the Allegheny mountains, in a rich coal mining and iron producing region.

The city is one of the leading centers in the state for the manufacture of steel and steel products. Other manufactures include silk, radios, radiators, and paint. Johnstown has a municipal stadium seating 17,000 people; also 230 acres in 14 public parks. On May 31, 1889, as a result of a flood caused by the bursting of a dam on the south fork of the Conemaugh river, Johnstown was largely destroyed and 2000 lives were lost. Prompt outside aid was extended, and the city was soon rebuilt and its industries re-established. Population, 1940, 66,668.

Joliet (*jō'lĭ-ĕt*). A manufacturing city of northeastern Illinois, situated on the Des Plaines river, about 40 miles southwest of Chicago. The manufacture of steel products, chiefly rods and wire, and of wall paper are major industries. Other products include refined oil, chemicals, and stoves. The American institute of laundering is located there. Joliet is also noted for its quarries of fine building stone, known as Joliet limestone. Population, 1940, 42,365.

Juneau (*jōō'nō*). The territorial capital of Alaska, and the supply center of mining, fishing, and lumbering camps. It is situated on a good harbor on the Gastineau channel, in the "panhandle" portion of southeastern Alaska. Huge quantities of salmon, halibut, and other fish are shipped, mainly to the United States. A decline in gold mining has been accompanied by a growth of the pulp and lumber industry and fur farming. Population, 1939, 5729.

Kalamazoo. A railway and manufacturing center of southwestern Michigan, situated in a rich agricultural district. The principal industries include celery, grape, and peppermint growing, and the manufacture of paper, paper boxes, machinery, stoves, drugs, and printing machinery. The city is the seat of Kalamazoo college and Western State teachers college. Population, 1940, 54,097.

Kansas City. The largest city of Kansas, built on both banks of the Kansas river at its junction with the Missouri. It lies adjacent to Kansas City, Missouri, with which communication is facilitated by a two-mile intercity viaduct connecting the higher levels of the cities. It is the second greatest live stock market and meat packing center in the United States. Its stockyards handle several million head of live stock yearly and there are immense meat packing establishments. Flour milling is second in importance among the city's extensive industries, which include petroleum refining, soap making, car repairing, and the manufacture of structural ironwork, boxes, chemicals, cooperage, and fertilizers. A feature of the city is a 5-million dollar food terminal. Parks cover 330 acres, and near by is Wyandotte County park of 1400 acres with a 333-acre lake created by an earthen dam. Population, 1940, 121,458.

Kansas City. The second largest city of Missouri, situated on the western border of the state, about 280 miles west of Saint Louis. It occupies a commanding site on the south bank of the Missouri river, at its junction with the Kansas river. Kansas City, Missouri, and Kansas City, Kansas, though separate in municipal government, form a continuous settlement, which, industrially and commercially, is a single city. The state boundary line passes through this densely populated district, leaving the seat of the two major industries—meat packing and flour milling—largely in the state of Kansas, but the greater part of the population in Missouri.

Kansas City owes its commercial importance to its situation in the midst of an extremely rich agricultural country, in a position favorable for the distribution of manufactured goods. The city is especially noted as a market and wholesaling center, standing first in America as a distributing point for agricultural implements, hay, and lumber. The city ranks second only to Chicago as a railroad center. It is also the second largest horse and mule market in the country. In addition to its meat packing and flour milling interests, Kansas City has important industries, including oil refining and the manufacture of structural steel, automobiles, paints, and clothing.

The city is built on three different levels, in a landscape made picturesque by high bluffs. Parks totaling 3678 acres are connected by about 114 miles of boulevards. Across a plaza to the south of the magnificent Union station is the shaft of the Liberty memorial, 385 feet high, designed to show a pillar of cloud by day and a pillar of fire by night. Among the city's more prominent buildings are a municipal auditorium, the city hall, the Federal building, and the magnificent Nelson gallery of art. The city has also an art institute, conservatory of music, and the University of Kansas City. Population, 1940, 399,178.

Katahdin (*kȧ-tä'dĭn*), **Mount.** The highest mountain in Maine, located in Piscataquis county, slightly northeast of the center of the state. It rises to an elevation of about 5200 feet, with precipitous slopes and massive cliffs of richly colored granite. The bare summit furnishes a grand view of forests, rivers, lakes, and mountains.

Kenosha (*kē-nō'shȧ*). A manufacturing city of southeastern Wisconsin, overlooking a fine harbor on Lake Michigan, 34 miles south of Milwaukee. The city's extensive industries include large establishments for the manufacture of automobiles, iron beds, stockings, underwear, and furniture. Population, 1940, 48,765.

Key West. The southernmost city of the United States, situated on Key West island, one of the Florida Keys. This small coral island lies in the Gulf of Mexico, about 50 miles southwest of Cape Sable, Florida. It is connected with the mainland by an oversea highway built, in part, upon the chain of low islands, of which Key West is the terminal, and, in part, upon huge concrete causeways connecting the islands. There is a fine harbor, with regular steamer service; also a ferry service for transporting railroad cars to Habana.

Key West has many fine residences, set in luxuriant tropical vegetation, and is a popular tourist resort. There are large shipping interests and important fisheries. Cigar manufacture, long the predominant industry, declined through competition with the machine made product. Key West reached its peak of population in 1910, with 19,945. Population, 1940, 12,927.

Kings Mountain. A ridge 100 feet high and a mile long in South Carolina, about 30 miles southwest of Charlotte, N. C. Here on October 7, 1780, a British force of 1100 troops was defeated and captured by less than 1000 mountaineers, who thereby spoiled the strategy of Cornwallis and prepared the way for victory at Yorktown.

Knoxville. An industrial and educational center in eastern Tennessee, built on the north bank of the Tennessee river, about 160 miles east of Nashville. It lies between the Cumberland and Great Smoky mountain ranges in a rich coal mining, iron producing, and marble quarrying region, with which it conducts an extensive trade. Knoxville ranks fourth among the cities of the state in manufactures. Its leading industrial products include textiles and clothing, iron and steel products, furniture, plastics, and marble. The city is the seat of the University of Tennessee and Knoxville college for Negroes. It is headquarters of the Tennessee Valley Authority. Population, 1940, 111,580.

La Crosse. A city of western Wisconsin, on the Mississippi river at the mouth of the La Crosse and Black rivers. Its site is on level ground extending about 2½ miles back from the Mississippi to bluffs which command fine views. Lumber manufacture, formerly the leading industry, has been replaced by a great variety of new industries including the manufacture of motor car instruments and farm machinery. It is the trade center for a rich dairying district. The numerous lakes, picturesque crags, and winding valleys near by make La Crosse a popular center for tourist travel. Population, 1940, 42,707.

Laguna (*lä-gōō'nä*). The second largest Indian pueblo in New Mexico, located near the San Jose river, in an arid desert, 67 miles west of Albuquerque. The inhabitants, who are of Keresan stock, are industrious and self-supporting. By primitive methods of irrigation, they produce crops sufficient for their needs. Wool growing is carried on to some extent. Population, about 2150.

Lake Geneva. A summer resort town of southern Wisconsin, situated on a lake of the same name, about 40 miles southwest of Milwaukee. The lake is a fine body of water, 9 miles long and from 1 to 3 miles wide. Many residents of Chicago have villas on its shores. The town is the seat of a large sanitarium and a military school. Near by is Yerkes observatory, containing the great Yerkes 40-inch refracting telescope. Population, 1940, 3238.

Lake George. A small lake in eastern New York, one of the most picturesquely beautiful in America. It is fed chiefly by cold springs, and its waters flow into Lake Champlain through a series of cascades, with one abrupt fall of 30 feet at Ticonderoga. The lake, which is about 30 miles long, contains about 200 miniature islands. In Colonial and Revolutionary days, the immediate region was the scene of many events of great importance and abounds in historic landmarks and associations.

Lake Mohonk (*mō-hŏngk'*). A popular summer resort, charmingly situated on a small lake of the same name in the Catskill mountains, of Ulster county, about 75 miles north of New York City. Lake Mohonk is noted also as the seat of a long series of annual conferences on international arbitration, the first of which was held in 1895.

Lake Placid. A beautiful small lake in the Adirondacks of northeastern New York. It is situated at the foot of Whiteface mountain, some 10 miles northeast of Mount Marcy. The lake lies at an altitude of about 2000 feet in one of the most charming scenic regions in the eastern United States. The town of Lake Placid, located on its banks, is a noted summer resort and a famed center for winter sports. Population of town, 1940, 3136.

Lakewood. A city of northern Ohio on Lake Erie and adjoining the western limits of Cleveland, of which it is a residential suburb. Lakewood was incorporated in 1911. Population, 1940, 69,160.

Lancaster. A city of southeastern Pennsylvania, about 65 miles west of Philadelphia. Lancaster is the trade center of one of the most productive tobacco and grain growing counties in the United States, and has varied and extensive industries. It is noted for its output of watches, umbrellas, locks, linoleum, cork, silk goods, cotton goods, and leather. Franklin and Marshall college and the Theological seminary of the Reformed Church are located here. At Millersville, in the near vicinity, there is a large state teachers college. Lancaster was first settled about 1718 and became a city in 1818. It was the home of James Buchanan, the 15th president of the United States. Population, 1940, 61,345.

Lansing. The capital of Michigan, built at the junction of the Grand and Cedar rivers, about 85 miles northwest of Detroit. Power developed from these streams is utilized in the city's extensive industries. In the value of manufactures, Lansing stands fourth among the cities of the state. Of its industries, the manufacture of automobiles is by far the most important. Other manufactures are gas and steam engines, lumber products, machine shop products, flour, and beet sugar. Among important public buildings are the capitol, the State library, and various state institutions. Parks cover 825 acres. East Lansing is the seat of the State college of agriculture and applied science, said to be the oldest land grant college. Lansing was settled in 1837, was laid out for the capital in 1847, and became a city in 1869. Population, 1940, 78,753.

Lassen Peak. A volcanic mountain in northern California, situated at the north end of the Sierra Nevada range, about 135 miles north of Sacramento. It stands at the extreme southwestern border of the great ancient lava beds which cover more than 200,000 square miles in the Columbia River plateau. Lavas from its own prehistoric eruptions are abundant. The peak, in which there is an extensive crater, rises to an elevation of about 10,500 feet.

Long inactive and regarded as extinct, Lassen peak in 1914 suddenly began to emit immense clouds of steam and smoke. Since that outburst, there have been hundreds of eruptions, mostly of a moderate character. Some, however, have been accompanied by the ejection of mud lavas and hot gases, causing extensive destruction in adjacent forests. An area of 163 square miles surrounding and including Lassen peak has been created a national volcanic park. In this are smaller volcanoes, lava fields, cinder cones, fumaroles, hot springs, solfataras, boiling lakes, and other features characteristic of a volcanic region.

Lawrence. A city in eastern Kansas, on both banks of the Kansas river, about 40 miles west of Kansas City. Lawrence is the trade center of a rich agricultural region and has various local industries, including flour mills, pipe organ and box factories, nurseries, and canning works. It is the seat of the University of Kansas, and the Haskell institute for Indians is also located here. Founded in 1854 by settlers from New England, Lawrence was the first of the Kansas Free State towns, and became an antislavery stronghold. It was sacked by a band of bush rangers from Missouri in 1856. In 1863, Quantrell, the Confederate raider, attacked the town, killing more than 100 of its citizens. Population, 1940, 14,390.

Lawrence. A manufacturing city of northeastern Massachusetts, built on both sides of the Merrimac river, about 26 miles north of Boston. The Merrimac falls of the river at this point originally played an important part in building up the city's industries. In the production of worsted cloth, Lawrence leads all other cities of the United States. Here are located the huge mills of the American Woolen company as well as the Pacific and Arlington mills. Other manufactures include foundry and machine shop products, shoes, and paper. Population, 1940, 84,323.

Leadville. A mining city of central Colorado, located near the Continental Divide, at an elevation of 10,200 feet. First settled by gold prospectors in 1860, it was a prosperous gold mining center for a few years until the deposits at that time known were exhausted. Thereupon the place was practically abandoned. In 1877, exceedingly rich lead and silver ore bodies were discovered. As a result, the population, which had declined to about 300, increased to more than 6000 in 1878, and to about 35,000 in 1879. For a time thereafter, Leadville held first place in the United States in lead and silver production. During the period

1879–1940, the total value of its mineral output exceeded $550,000,000. Mineral production has declined to a small fraction of its former value. Near by is a mine producing most of the world's molybdenum. Population, 1940, 4774.

Lewiston. A leading manufacturing city of Maine, built on the east bank of the Androscoggin river opposite the city of Auburn, about 35 miles north of Portland. The river here falls 60 feet; at the five million dollar Gulf Island dam it furnishes immense hydroelectric power which is utilized in the city's extensive industries. The chief manufacturing establishments are cotton and woolen mills, shoe factories, dye works, and bleacheries. The city is the seat of Bates college. Population, 1940, 38,598.

Lexington. The chief city of the "Blue-Grass region," situated about 80 miles southeast of Louisville, Kentucky. It is located in a highly productive agricultural and stock raising district, with which it carries on an extensive trade. It is an important market for grain, loose leaf tobacco, and live stock, especially horses. The manufactures include saddlery, harnesses, flour, canned goods, lumber, and whiskey. The production of blue grass seed is an important industry. Lexington is the seat of Kentucky university, Transylvania university, and other educational institutions. Henry Clay lived in Lexington from 1797 until his death in 1852. His estate, Ashland, is in the vicinity. Population, 1940, 49,304.

Lexington. A town of northeastern Massachusetts, situated about 12 miles northwest of Boston. The town embraces an agricultural district in which are located the villages of Lexington, East Lexington, and North Lexington. Lexington village, now chiefly residential, is noted as the scene of the first conflict between the colonists and the British in the Revolutionary War. In the village and its vicinity are many points of great historic interest. Among these are the first battle ground of the Revolution; numerous houses, taverns, and other buildings associated with the conflict; and various monuments in commemoration of the men and of the events that made Lexington famous.

Lexington was settled about 1642 and for some 50 years was known as Cambridge Farms. In 1839, the first normal school in the United States was opened in Lexington. Population, 1940, 13,187.

Lima. A city of western Ohio, located on the Ottawa river, 79 miles south of Toledo. Among the chief industrial products are cigars, locomotives, power shovels, electric motors, diesel engines, bus bodies, and steel castings. Population, 1940, 44,711.

Lincoln. The capital and second largest city of Nebraska, situated on a gently sloping site, about 55 miles southwest of Omaha. It is the center of a highly productive agricultural and stock raising section, with which it carries on an extensive trade. The industrial products include food, textile, forest, and clay products, chemicals, and machinery. The city is regularly laid out, with wide streets, and contains many important public buildings, one of which, the capitol, is among the greatest architectural achievements of America. Parks, numbering 13, cover 1338 acres.

Lincoln is the seat of the State university and agricultural college, Nebraska Wesleyan university, and Union college. Fairview, the estate of William Jennings Bryan, a former resident, is used as a hospital. The first permanent settlement on the site of the city was made in 1856, and in 1864 a village was laid out, called Lancaster. This, in 1867, was selected for the state capital and renamed Lincoln. Population, 1940, 81,984.

Lincoln Highway. A road extending entirely across the northern United States and named in honor of Abraham Lincoln. It was laid out in 1913 with the purpose of establishing a modern vehicular highway, national in character and free to the public at all points, connecting New York and San Francisco.

The route, 3,384 miles long, crosses 11 states. Cities served by it include Jersey City, Philadelphia, Pittsburgh, Canton, South Bend, Chicago Heights, Cedar Rapids, Omaha, Cheyenne, Salt Lake City, Reno, Oakland.

The Lincoln highway is distinctively marked with a red, white, and blue marker bearing a blue letter "L" on a white field. Throughout its entire length the highest types of roadway construction are represented, including concrete, brick, bituminous, macadam, and graded gravel.

Little Rock. The capital and largest city of Arkansas, on the south side of the Arkansas river, near the center of the state. The name has reference to a bold cliff rising 50 feet above the river at this point. The city is situated near the foothills of the Ozark mountains in a rich lumbering and cotton growing district, of which it is the commercial center. The chief industries include the manufacture of cottonseed oil and of lumber products.

There are many fine public buildings, among which is the new capitol, built of native Arkansas marble. The park system covers 400 acres. Because of the profusion of roses in its well kept gardens, Little Rock is called the "City of Roses." Big Rock, an eminence 500 feet high, 8 miles distant, was formerly the site of an army post. The city is the seat of Little Rock college and of the medical department of the University of Arkansas. Population, 1940, 88,039.

Lockport. A city of western New York, situated on the State Barge canal, 26 miles northeast of Buffalo and in the center of the highly productive Niagara fruit belt. It occupies a commanding though somewhat uneven site, part of the city being built on a sloping terrace known as "Mountain Ridge." At this point the canal drops some 66 feet, from the level of Lake Erie to that of the Genesee river, by massive locks of masonry, and is crossed by one of the widest bridges in the world. The varied industries include numerous manufactures, notably automobile parts and pulpwood products, textiles, chemicals, and high-grade steel. There is a large trade in fruit and grain. Lockport was chartered as a city in 1865. Population, 1940, 24,379.

Logan. A city of northern Utah, on Logan river, about 70 miles north of Salt Lake City. Logan is the commercial center of the Cache valley, a rich agricultural district, with some mineral deposits. Its industrial establishments include flour mills, condensed milk plants, and beet sugar and knitting factories. The state agricultural college is located there, and a Mormon temple with grounds of great beauty overlooks the city from a hilltop. Population, 1940, 11,868.

Long Beach. A tourist resort and city on the southern coast of California, 22 miles south of Los Angeles. It is beautifully located, looking out on the harbor of San Pedro, while the beach from which it takes its name is one of the finest along the Pacific coast. Its harbor, elaborately improved, is the base of the Pacific battle fleet. It accommodates a large trade in fruit, canned fish, petroleum, and lumber, the last two being the chief products of the city's industry. Petroleum is extensively produced within the city limits and is used as fuel for an electric generating plant, one of the largest on the continent. Population, 1940, 164,271.

Lookout Mountain. A steep ridge which rises to an elevation of 2100 feet, overlooking the city of Chattanooga, Tennessee. This rocky height was the scene of the famous battle of the Civil War, sometimes called the "Battle above the Clouds." The summit commands a superb view of the Tennessee river and its valley, the city of Chattanooga, and the surrounding mountainous region.

LOS ANGELES (*lŏs ăng' gĕl-ĕs; lŏs ăn'jĕl-ĕs*). The chief commercial center of southern California and the fifth most populous city in the United States, Los Angeles is situated on the Pacific coast, about 475 miles southeast of San Francisco and about 10 miles south of the Sierra Madre mountains. Through it passes the Los Angeles river, a dry bed in summer but a considerable stream in winter.

Site. The city lies, for the most part, in a gently sloping plain, with an average elevation of about 270 feet. The site is fairly level, though there are a few steep eminences, and the northern suburbs extend into the foothills. Including extensions to the ocean and taking in San Pedro harbor, the total area of the city exceeds 441 square miles.

Streets and Buildings. The city is regularly laid out, with wide, straight streets, and an extensive system of boulevards and drives. Main, Spring, Broadway, and Hill are important thoroughfares in the commercial section, which is dominated by immense office buildings and department stores. About the old Plaza is a civic center, which includes the 10-million dollar city hall with a 452-foot tower surmounted by the Lindbergh beacon. Near the plaza is the union station, an 11-million dollar structure. The railway terminals and manufacturing districts lie chiefly to the east and south of the business center, while the large and handsomely built residence sections flank it on the west and north. White is the prevailing color of all buildings and preserves its freshness because there is but little smoke. Los Angeles is preeminently a city of beautiful homes, with the Mission style of architecture, adopted from the Spanish, and the bungalow as characteristic types. The broad avenues and spacious grounds are luxuriant with evergreen foliage and a profusion of flowers which bloom throughout the year.

Parks and Boulevards. There are 87 public parks embracing a total area of more than 5486 acres. Among the more noteworthy of these are Griffith, Elysian, Westlake, Lincoln, Echo, Hollenbeck, Exposition, Central, and Plaza parks. Griffith park, a hilly, wooded tract of 3751 acres, is one of the largest municipally-owned parks in the United States. Many handsome boulevards and driveways connect the parks with various parts of the city and with fine scenic roads to the ocean, fruitful valleys, and mountain wildernesses.

Educational Institutions. Los Angeles is the seat of the University of Southern California, the University of

California at Los Angeles, Occidental college, Loyola university, and Los Angeles City college. The museum of history, science, and art, in Exposition park, has a large display of skeletons of extinct animals. The Southwest museum exhibits relics of ancient North and Central American civilizations.

Transportation. Los Angeles owes its great growth in part to unusually complete transportation facilities. The city contains terminals of three transcontinental railways which enter the magnificent union station, completed in 1939 at a cost of 11 million dollars. There is also a capacious harbor for coastwise and foreign shipping in its municipally-owned wharves at San Pedro. It is connected with the surrounding country by a large system of electric interurban railway lines, some of which have four tracks and reach towns 60 miles distant. Well paved public highways form a huge network over country districts in all directions. One of the finest is the Arroyo Seco parkway. These serve as thoroughfares for extensive regularly operated systems of autobuses and autotrucks.

Commerce. Los Angeles is the commercial center of the far Southwest and has extensive fruit growing, petroleum producing, manufacturing, and shipping interests. Its foreign and intercoastal shipping vies with that of New York City. The chief imports are lumber and raw materials such as rubber, silk, coffee, and cacao. Exports are largely petroleum and other minerals, food products, and factory goods. The city is a general market for one of the most productive horticultural and agricultural sections of the country. Among leading products handled are oranges, lemons, walnuts, olives, vegetables, beet sugar, beans, cereals, and cotton. Citrous fruits and petroleum are the chief products of the immediate district.

Manufactures. By reason of cheap fuel, in the form of crude petroleum, and abundant hydroelectric power derived from streams in the mountains, Los Angeles has grown at a prodigious rate as a manufacturing city. The motion picture industry is the best known. Hollywood, the chief center of this industry, is famous throughout the world. The Los Angeles area leads the country in aircraft manufacture. Other important manufactures include petroleum and metal products, lumber, packed meats and other food products, and furniture. The outdoor life and the importance of the motion picture industry have made Los Angeles a style center for sports and other clothes, and the manufacture of women's clothing has become a large industry. Important too is the entertainment of tourists, both in summer and in winter.

Features of Interest. With its picturesque setting between the mountains and the sea, its numerous historic associations, and its many attractive suburbs, Los Angeles presents an immense number of points of interest. Among those within the city are the Old Plaza church, China city and Chinatown, Griffith observatory and planetarium, the Los Angeles coliseum, with a seating capacity of 100,000, and the Hollywood bowl, seating 25,000, the Pilgrimage play, Radio center, and Le Brea pits in Hancock park. In the near vicinity are San Gabriel Mission with its Mission Play theater, Mount Lowe, and Mount Wilson observatory, Huntington library and art gallery, and Palos Verdes hills. Attractive beach resorts include Santa Monica, Venice, Redondo Beach, Long Beach, and Santa Catalina island. Interesting suburban cities include Pasadena, Riverside, Alhambra, Universal City, Glendale, Orange, Pomona, and San Bernardino.

History. In 1781, Los Angeles was settled by Spanish colonists from Mexico who named it *Pueblo de Nuestra Senora la Reina de Los Angeles* (City of Our Lady the Queen of the Angels). Until its final capture in 1847 by United States troops under General Philip Kearny, it served alternately with Monterey as capital of the Mexican province of California.

Los Angeles was chartered as a city in 1850, and attained its first railway connection with San Francisco in 1876. Following the completion, in 1885, of the Santa Fe railway, giving direct access to the East, the growth of Los Angeles was rapid, and, since 1900, it has been remarkable.

The genial climate, the great fertility of the surrounding region under irrigation, and large local supplies of natural gas and petroleum have been influential factors in this development. Two important municipal achievements have also contributed substantially to its rise as a great city. The first was the extension, in 1909, of the city to the ocean at San Pedro, making possible the establishment of a commodious, municipally controlled harbor. The second was the completion, in 1913, at a cost of $25,000,000, of a great aqueduct from the slopes of Mount Whitney in the Sierra Nevada, across the Mojave desert, and through the Sierra Madre range, by tunnel, to the city. In the 1930's, water from the Colorado river was made available through a 250-mile aqueduct, 108 miles of which was tunneled through the rock, the total cost being 220 million dollars. A third source of supply was secured with the completion of the Mono Basin project in 1940 at a cost of $20,000,000. Population, 1940, 1,504,277.

Louisville (*lo͞o'ĭs-vĭl; lo͞o'ĭ-vĭl*). The chief city of Kentucky, located on the south bank of the Ohio river, about 65 miles west of Frankfort. Louisville occupies a commanding site opposite the rapids or "falls" of the river, which here descends 26 feet in 2 miles.

The city's park system, covering some 2177 acres, includes Shawnee park on the west, Cherokee and Seneca parks on the east, Iroquois park on the south, and various smaller parks. Cherokee park, 409 acres, is cut into picturesque ravines by Beargrass creek. Iroquois park, the largest, 676 acres, rises to eminences of nearly 300 feet, affording superb views of the city and of the river.

Louisville has excellent transportation facilities, both by rail and the canalized Ohio river, and is the commercial center of a large and highly productive agricultural region. Its leading manufactures include tobacco, packed meats, whiskey, railroad cars, sanitary plumbing supplies, and gasoline. It leads the country in the production of bathtubs, baseball bats, hickory handles, and wagons. The city is the seat of the University of Louisville, a municipal university, of the Jefferson law school, and of various other educational institutions.

The first settlement at Louisville was made in 1778, a town was laid out and named in 1779, and in 1828 became a city. Louisville's early growth was greatly stimulated by the establishment, in 1811, of steam navigation on the Ohio river, and especially by the completion, in 1830, of the Louisville and Portland canal around the rapids. The first railway, connecting the city with the interior of the state, was finished in 1851. Near the city is the old home and the grave of Zachary Taylor. Population, 1940, 319,077.

Lowe, Mount. A peak of the Sierra Madre in southern California. It is situated some 15 miles in direct line northeast of Los Angeles and rises to an elevation of 5650 feet above sea level. An electric scenic railway ascends almost to the summit, which affords superb views of the surrounding region.

Lowell. A manufacturing city of northeastern Massachusetts, situated at the junction of the Merrimac and Concord rivers, about 25 miles northwest of Boston. Immense power from falls in the rivers is developed for use in its extensive industries, the chief of which is the manufacture of textiles. Other important industrial products include hosiery, machinery, woolen goods, and shoes. The city is the seat of a State teachers college and the Lowell textile institute. It is the birthplace of James McNeill Whistler, whose home is now a museum. The beautiful Memorial auditorium is among the most noteworthy buildings. Population, 1940, 101,389.

Luray Cavern. A remarkable cave, situated near the town of Luray, Virginia, about 90 miles northwest of Richmond. It underlies an area of more than 100 acres in the foothills of the Blue Ridge mountains. In this vast cavern there are numerous galleries, rising above one another in tiers to a height of nearly 300 feet. In some of these, streams and small bodies of water are found; others contain stalactites and stalagmites of great size and unusual beauty of coloration. The cavern, which was discovered in 1878, is lighted by electricity and traversed by paths making its exploration easy for visitors.

Lynchburg. A city of central Virginia, on the James river, 112 miles west of Richmond. The city is picturesquely located, sloping in steep terraces upward from the river, with the Blue Ridge and the Peaks of Otter as background. It is situated in a tobacco producing district, of which it is the trade center. Power developed from the river is utilized in various local industries, among the chief of which is the manufacture of shoes and clothing. Educational institutions include Randolph-Macon woman's college and Lynchburg college. During the Civil War, Lynchburg was used as a base of supplies for the Confederate army. Population, 1940, 44,541.

Lynn. A manufacturing city of eastern Massachusetts, located about 10 miles northeast of Boston. The city is beautifully situated and admirably laid out. The commercial and industrial districts extend for about 3 miles along Massachusetts bay, on which the city has a well-developed harbor, while the residential sections occupy the higher portions overlooking the harbor. There is a fine boulevard along the ocean front and a superb park, called Lynn Woods, containing 2000 acres.

Lynn is one of the chief centers in the United States for the manufacture of women's and children's shoes. The city has other important industries, chiefly the manufacture of electrical machinery, finished leather, adhesives, boxes, and proprietary medicines. Lynn was settled in 1629 but was known as Saugus until 1637, when it was given its present name. Its great shoe industry had its beginnings about 1750. Population, 1940, 98,123.

McKeesport. A manufacturing city of Pennsylvania, on the Monongahela river, 14 miles southeast of Pittsburgh. Advantageously situated in a region rich in bituminous coal, iron, and natural gas, the city has become a leading center for the manufacture of iron and steel. It possesses one of the greatest steel tube and iron pipe works in the world, which has earned for it the name of the "Tube City." Among other industrial products are chromium sheet, tools, and other steel products. Population, 1940, 55,355.

Macon (*mā'kŏn*). A city of central Georgia, built at the head of navigation on the Ocmulgee river, about 80 miles southeast of Atlanta. Macon is the commercial center of a highly productive farming and fruit district, and is a leading market for peanuts, pecans, and peaches. Hydroelectric power, derived from the river, is utilized in the city's extensive industries, which include the manufacture of cotton and knit goods, cottonseed oil and cottonseed cake, brick, tile, lumber, flour, fertilizers, foundry and machine shop products, and packed meats. Macon has a municipal auditorium with a huge copper dome.

The city is the seat of Macon and Mercer universities and Wesleyan college. Macon was first settled in 1822 and was incorporated as a city in 1832. Population, 1940, 57,865.

Madison. The capital of Wisconsin, situated in the south central part of the state. The city occupies a picturesque site between lakes Mendota and Monona, in the so-called "Four-Lakes region." It is surrounded by a rich agricultural district, of which it is the trade and industrial center. Madison is noted for its beautiful parks, wide, heavily shaded streets, and scenic lake shore drives. Its industrial output includes meat and dairy products, dry cell batteries, and machine tools. There are many fine public buildings, the most imposing of which is the capitol, built of granite in the Renaissance style.

The city is the seat of the University of Wisconsin, which occupies a magnificent campus, more than a mile in length, bordering on Lake Mendota. Madison has a United States forest products laboratory, opened in 1910, the first in the world. The site of Madison was chosen for the state capital in 1836, and the first buildings were erected on it in 1837. Population, 1940, 67,447.

Malden. A city of eastern Massachusetts, built on the Malden river, 5 miles north of Boston. Malden is noted for its extensive manufactures of rubber boots and shoes, and contains some of the largest rubber shoe factories in the United States. Among numerous other manufactures may be mentioned knitted goods, soap, paints, chinaware, and precision instruments. Malden was first settled in 1641, was incorporated in 1649, and was chartered as a city in 1881. Population, 1940, 58,010.

Mammoth Cave. The second largest known cavern in the world, being exceeded in size only by Carlsbad cave in New Mexico. Situated near the Green river, about 100 miles south of Louisville, Kentucky, it is located in a region which abounds in large caverns and whose surface is marked by thousands of sink holes. Through these depressions, drainage waters find their way to underground streams whose solvent and erosive action has largely produced the caves.

To the geologist, the cave is a laboratory and museum inexhaustibly rich in materials for the study of rock formations and the effects of erosion. For the tourist, the processes of geologic change have created a picturesque setting unlimited in interest and variety. In the St. Louis limestone, a layer of soluble rock capped by sandstone and sometimes reaching a thickness of 300 feet, underground waters have carved a series of pools and streams that are bordered by cathedral-like rooms and ornamental passageways. The walls are lined, not only with the usual rows of stalactites and stalagmites, but also with a panorama of symmetrical statues and grotesque gargoyles.

Four separate tours covering different parts of the cave have been charted. Some notion of the variety that Nature has provided is suggested in the names of points and objects of interest mentioned in the outlines of the tours. Some of these are found in the description given below. Others include such imaginative names as Bridal Altar, Pillars of Hercules, Giant's Coffin, Albert's Stairway, Proctor's Arcade, Wright's Rotunda, Diamond Grotto, and Valley of Flowers. They offer unlimited range of imagery and association.

In more matter-of-fact terms, Mammoth Cave may be described as a complex series of caverns, including more than 200 so-called rooms, chambers, domes, pits, abysses, grottoes, avenues, and galleries, which extend for 9 miles underground. In the lower portions, there are rivers, waterfalls, and small lakes. Among the most interesting features are the vast pits or domes, which are caverns of unusual height. The largest of these, called the Chief City, is 450 feet long and 130 feet wide. Stella, Mammoth, and Gorin domes are each about 250 feet high.

Cleveland avenue, which extends for fully 2 miles, presents wonderful displays of crystals and incrustations. Stalactites and stalagmites in a great variety of grotesque shapes, many of which resemble architectural forms, contribute also to the unusual scenery of the cavern. An example is a "mushroom" 15 feet in height. When the incrustations are covered with crystals, as in Star Chamber, their sparkling effect when the cavern is lighted is impressive. Among the larger bodies of water within the cavern are the so-called Dead Sea, the Styx, Lethe lake, Roaring river, and Echo river. The latter stream is three-fourths of a mile long, and has an underground connection with Green river.

In the waters of the cave are 2 species of blind fish. These, together with crayfish and a few insects, make up the animal life. The temperature remains almost constant at about 54°. The cavern was discovered in 1809 by a hunter named Hutchins. A tract of 63 square miles including the site of the cave was created Mammoth Cave national park in 1936.

Manchester. The largest city of New Hampshire, built on the Merrimac river, 18 miles south of Concord. A fall of some 50 feet in the river, formerly used as direct water power, now provides one of the units in a super-power system. The city's extensive industrial output includes cotton textiles, worsted dress goods, rayon mixtures, shoes, brushes, and cigars. The city has many fine parks, municipal buildings, and educational institutions, including the Manchester institute of arts and sciences and the Currier gallery of art. Population, 1940, 77,685.

Manitou (*măn'ĭ-too͞*) **Springs.** A health and pleasure resort, located at the foot of Pikes Peak, 6 miles northwest of Colorado Springs, Colorado. The town lies at an elevation of about 6300 feet in a region noted for picturesque scenery. The numerous features of interest in the locality include Pikes Peak, the Cave of the Winds, Soda Springs park, the Garden of the Gods, and various canyons, Cliff Dwellers' ruins, waterfalls, and scenic drives. The famous radioactive mineral springs flow at the rate of a quarter million gallons daily. The summer population is estimated at 25,000. Resident population, 1940, 1462.

Marcy, Mount. The loftiest summit of the Adirondack mountains and the highest peak in the state of New York. It is situated about 10 miles south of Lake Placid, and 30 miles southwest of Lake Champlain. It is a dome-shaped mountain rising to an elevation of 5344 feet. The slopes, except near the summit, are generally wooded. The summit and a portion of the upper northern slope are above timber line. The vegetation above the zone of trees consists of dwarfed and stunted heaths and willows and other plants peculiar to an arctic-alpine vegetation.

From the crest of Mount Marcy, panoramic views of the entire Adirondack region may be obtained. Lake Tear of the Clouds, usually regarded as the main source of the Hudson river, lies at an elevation of 4300 feet, immediately southwest of the mountain. Theodore Roosevelt was in camp at the summit of Mount Marcy when summoned to take the oath of office as president in 1901.

Marion. A city of central Ohio, situated 44 miles north of Columbus, in a rich agricultural and quarrying region. The city's extensive industries include the manufacture of power shovels, steel products, road rollers, and electric refrigerators. There are several large limestone quarries in the vicinity. Marion has many fine streets and buildings. The city was the home of President Warren G. Harding, whose tomb stands near the city within a circular colonnade surrounded by a beautifully landscaped tract of 100 acres. Population, 1940, 30,817.

Medford. A city of eastern Massachusetts, five miles northwest of Boston, of which it is a residential and manufacturing suburb. It has some of the oldest examples of colonial architecture, including Wellington house, dating from 1657, and the Cradock house, built 1677-80. Medford is the seat of Tufts college, which has a campus of 80 acres. Population, 1940, 63,083.

Memphis. The chief city of Tennessee, built on the east bank of the Mississippi river, about 210 miles southwest of Nashville. The city occupies an undulating site, on Chickasaw bluff, about 450 miles by river south of Saint Louis and 740 miles by river north of New Orleans.

At Memphis, the river is spanned by two immense cantilever bridges, and railways radiate from the city in all directions. Because of its advantageous situation on the Mississippi river, in a rich agricultural and lumbering region, Memphis has become an important marketing, manufacturing, and distributing center. It is the chief center of hardwood lumber production in the United States, and is one of the principal inland cotton markets of the South. It also ranks as one of the leading horse and mule markets in the country. The city's varied and extensive industries include the manufacture of cottonseed oil and cake, food preparations, lumber, cooperage, window screens, flavoring extracts, drugs, and automobile bodies and tires. The city owns its electric distribution system, purchasing current from the T.V.A.

Memphis is regularly laid out, with wide, well shaded streets and handsome residences, and contains many excellent public and commercial buildings. The city's park system, connected by a boulevard 11 miles long, is one of the finest in the South. This system covers a total area of 1412 acres. Important units are Riverside park, 427 acres, and Overton park, 335 acres, the latter containing an art gallery and a large zoological garden.

The city is the seat of the medical and law schools of the University of Tennessee. a State normal school, and Southwestern college. Memphis was laid out in 1818 by General Andrew Jackson and associates. It was incorporated in 1826, and, in 1849, received its charter as a city. Population, 1940, 292,942.

Meridian. The second largest city of Mississippi, in the east central part of the state. It is surrounded by a rich cotton and vegetable growing district, of which it is the market center. The principal industries include the manufacture of cottonseed oil, cotton gins, lumber, bricks, and knitted goods. Population, 1940, 35,481.

Miami (*mī-ăm'ĭ*). A commercial city and winter resort of southeastern Florida, located at the mouth of the Miami river on the Atlantic coast, about 365 miles south of Jacksonville.

The city lies only about 150 miles north of the tropics, in a region of luxuriant vegetation, producing grapefruit, oranges, limes, guavas, pineapples, avocadoes, coconuts, and other subtropical fruits. There are large sugar mills, extensive fisheries, and various other industries. Miami has steamer connections with Habana, Nassau, and San Juan, and it is an important shipping center for fruit and winter vegetables to northern markets.

In 1896, Miami was made the terminus of the Florida East Coast railway, which was later extended southward. Since that date, and particularly in the "boom" period of 1922 to 1926, the growth of Miami was rapid. Miami is celebrated for its fine hotels and varied pleasure attractions and for its many delightful boulevards and drives, including a 100-foot boulevard along the water front. Its 27-story city hall is one of the tallest buildings in the South. Population, 1940, 172,172.

MILWAUKEE. The chief city of Wisconsin. It is situated on Lake Michigan about 85 miles north of Chicago. Its area is 44 square miles.

Site. Milwaukee occupies a commanding site overlooking beautiful Milwaukee bay. Within the city three small rivers join before emptying into the lake—the Milwaukee from the north, the Kinnickinnic from the south, and the Menominee from the west. These rivers divide the city into parts known locally as the east, west, and south sides.

Streets and Squares. Noteworthy streets include Lincoln memorial drive on the shore of Lake Michigan and Wisconsin avenue, the leading business thoroughfare, along which for three blocks extends the Court of Honor, a broad parked space dedicated to those who took part in the wars of America. The finest residential section occupies the bluffs, 150 feet high, overlooking the lower city and the lake.

Buildings. Prominent among the city's imposing edifices is the municipal auditorium, comprising eight halls and covering an entire city block. Other impressive buildings include the city hall, the courthouse, Safety building, the Federal building, the public library, the art gallery, the Gas Company building, Northwestern Mutual Life Insurance building, and St. Josaphat's basilica.

Parks. The park system of Milwaukee covers about 1600 acres. Among its 34 units are Mitchell park, noted for its floral displays; Washington park, containing a fine zoological garden; and Gordon park, with recreational facilities.

Commerce. The city's harbor is protected by a long breakwater. The deepened channels of its rivers, together with various canals, provide access for lake ships into the heart of the city. Shipping trade is very extensive and embraces an immense tonnage of coal, grain, and manufactured products. The transportation facilities include several railroad, steamship, bus, and airplane lines, and also a daily car ferry service which transports railroad trains to the east shore of Lake Michigan.

Industry. Milwaukee is one of the leading industrial centers of the country, ranking among the first ten cities of the United States in value of manufactures. These include silk hosiery, electrical control apparatus, power shovels, electric generators, automobile frames, packed meats, railway cars, engines, shoes, and knit goods.

Educational Institutions. Milwaukee has many educational institutions, including Marquette university, Milwaukee-Downer college, Milwaukee State teachers college, and Mount Mary college.

History. The site of Milwaukee was visited in 1673 by Fathers Marquette and Joliet. The first permanent settlement dates from 1818. The village was organized in 1837, and, in 1845, it became a city. Although Germans predominated in the population during its earlier years, they were later far outnumbered by people from other countries. Population, 1940, 587,472.

Minneapolis. The chief city of Minnesota, built on both banks of the Mississippi river, at Saint Anthony's falls. Immediately below lies Saint Paul, which adjoins Minneapolis.

Minneapolis attained industrial and commercial importance primarily by reason of the immense water power derived from the falls. This was first utilized principally in sawmills and flour mills. Until about 1870, lumber was the leading product, but since that date the milling of grain has become a pre-eminent industry. The value of its flour and gristmill products entitled Minneapolis to first rank among flour producing cities. One of the great mills situated around Saint Anthony falls is the largest single flour mill in the world. Other important manufactures are linseed oil, cereal foods, agricultural implements, machinery, knit goods, and dairy products.

The city is served by 29 railroads, 10 of which are trunk lines, and stands at the head of navigation on the Mississippi river. By reason of its extensive transportation facilities, Minneapolis has become the wholesale distributing center for the Northwest. It is also one of the chief primary wheat markets of the country, with elevator capacity in excess of 50 million bushels.

Minneapolis is predominantly a city of homes, with wide, well shaded streets, handsome residences, charming parks, and beautiful drives. The park system, containing 141 parks, covers 5336 acres. It includes Lake Calhoun, Lake Harriet, and several smaller lakes. By means of canals connecting several lakes, a scenic waterway 9 miles long has been made available for canoes and launches. Minnehaha park contains the beautiful Minnehaha ("falling water") falls, immortalized by Longfellow. Here Minnehaha creek, the outlet of Lake Minnetonka, plunges over a 50-foot cliff just before joining the Mississippi.

There are many notable buildings, among them the public library, the city hall, the art institute, the Pro-cathedral, Saint Mark's church, Hennepin Avenue Methodist church, the Federal Reserve Bank, the 32-story Forshay tower, the 4-million dollar post office, the Telephone building, and the Minneapolis auditorium. A feature of the city is the large number of handsome bridges across the Mississippi river. The city is the seat of the University of Minnesota, Minnesota college, De La Salle institute, Dunwoody institute, Augsburg seminary, and the MacPhail and Minneapolis schools of music. The Minneapolis Symphony Orchestra is one of the greatest organizations of its kind.

Father Hennepin, a French missionary, discovered and named the Falls of Saint Anthony in 1680. In 1766, the site of the city was visited by Jonathan Carver, an American traveler, and, in 1805, by Lieutenant Z. M. Pike, who purchased the site of Fort Pike from the Indians. Fort Saint Anthony, later called Fort Snelling, was established in 1819. The first sawmill at the falls was erected in 1822 to provide lumber for the fort. The village of Saint Anthony, on the east side of the river, was incorporated in 1855, and Minneapolis, on the west side, in 1856. In 1872, the two places were united. Population, 1940, 492,370.

Missoula (*mĭ-zōō'lȧ*). A city of western Montana, on the Clark Fork river, about 125 miles by rail northwest of Helena. It is the distributing center for a large farming and fruit growing, lumbering, and mining region, and is the seat of the University of Montana. The extensive Flathead Indian reservation lies to the north of the city. Population, 1940, 18,449.

Mitchell, Mount. The highest point in the state of North Carolina, and the loftiest summit of the eastern United States. It is a massive, dome-shaped mountain, sometimes called Black Dome, rising to an elevation of 6684 feet, with many high cliffs and precipitous slopes. It is named for Elisha Mitchell, a distinguished scientist who lost his life while attempting, in 1857, to scale the mountain. His remains are buried at the top of the mountain. A large tract of land, including the summit and surrounding spruce forests, has been created a state park, which provides accommodations for travelers.

Mobile. The second largest city and only seaport in Alabama, located on Mobile bay, about 26 miles north of the Gulf of Mexico. It is a leading cotton market and has varied industries, among them shipbuilding, cotton, lumber, and paper mills, chemical and steel factories, oil refineries, and seafood canneries. The harbor has been elaborately improved, and the bay is spanned by the Cochrane bridge. The Bankhead tunnel beneath the Mobile river accommodates vehicular traffic. The chief exports include logs, hewn timber, pine lumber, rosin, cotton, paper, metals, machinery, and coal; the leading imports are bananas, ores, sugar, and chemicals. There is also an extensive local trade in vegetables, fish, and oysters.

The city has broad, regular streets, shaded with live oaks and magnolias and lined with beautiful residences, many of which are in the colonial style. Azaleas blooming profusely in the early spring provide a feature of unusual attractiveness. Mobile was founded in 1702 by the French. Later, it was in the possession of the English, the Spanish, and again of the French. It became a part of the United States by the Louisiana Purchase in 1803. Population, 1940, 78,720.

Mojave (*mō-hä'vä*) **Desert.** A desert of southeastern California, situated chiefly within the boundaries of San Bernardino county and embracing an area of about 15,000 square miles. It lies south and east of the Tehachapi mountains and north of the Sierra Madre and the San Bernardino mountains. These high ranges intercept the moisture-laden winds from the Pacific, and, in consequence, the Mojave is an exceedingly arid region. The average annual rainfall is only 5 or 6 inches, and the temperature in summer sometimes reaches 120°.

The surface is that of a more or less elevated plateau, broken by numerous small mountains, with intervening valleys and plains. From an elevation of about 4000 feet on the west, this plateau slopes down to 1500 feet elevation or less toward its eastern border. Much of the southwestern portion drains into the Mojave river, which, after flowing in a definite channel for some 50 miles, entirely disappears in valley sands to the eastward.

For the most part, the Mojave desert presents an aspect of extreme barrenness and desolation. The smaller mountains are mostly jagged masses of naked rock. Many plains are interspersed with saline sinks and dried-up lakes. Some of the valleys are covered with dark-colored sheets of anciently erupted lavas. These volcanic areas also contain numerous cinder cones and small craters.

Vegetation is everywhere scant, and many alkaline and rocky wastes are practically devoid of plant life. In the low plains, the creosote bush is a characteristic shrub, while in the higher portions the weirdly-branching Joshua tree, a kind of yucca, is a striking object in the landscape. Many species of cactus and various other desert plants are found, such as the mesquite, cat's-claw, and paloverde. For a few weeks following the brief winter rains, millions of acres in the Mojave fairly blaze with the brilliant hues of desert annuals. These bloom in indescribable profusion but wither and disappear soon after the rains cease.

There are valuable mineral deposits, and, where water for irrigation is available, a few small areas yield good crops. The Santa Fe and the Salt Lake railway cross this desert, as do several well constructed automobile highways. See *Colorado Desert.*

Moline. A city of western Illinois, situated at the junction of the Rock and Mississippi rivers, about 180 miles southwest of Chicago. The city of Rock Island adjoins Moline on the west, and across the Mississippi river from Rock Island is Davenport, Iowa. These three cities constitute a metropolitan area with a population of over 150,000 people. Moline is known as the "Plow City," because it has one of the largest steel plow plants in the country. Manufacture of agricultural implements is Moline's chief industry. A feature of interest in the vicinity is the United States arsenal on Rock island. Between this island and Moline is a large roller dam for flood control. Population, 1940, 34,608.

Monadnock, Mount. A noted mountain of southwestern New Hampshire, situated about 10 miles southeast of Keene. It is a bold granitic peak with precipitous walls and extremely rugged contour, rising to an elevation of 3186 feet. Because of its isolated position and unusual form, it is one of the most impressive mountains in New England. It has given its name to a type of mountain rising conspicuously in isolation from other peaks.

Monterey (*mŏn'tĕ-rā'*). A seaside resort of the California coast, about 125 miles south of San Francisco. Monterey occupies a charming site on a fine harbor, facing the beautiful bay of Monterey, and, in addition to its scenic and climatic attractions, possesses features of great historic interest. Six miles from its site, in 1770, Father Junipero Serra, Spanish missionary to the Indians, established the mission of San Carlos Borromeo. After more than 75 years of Spanish and Mexican occupation, the American flag was run up at Monterey in 1846, and, in 1847, it became the capital of the military government of California. The chief industries are fishing and sardine packing.

Among numerous features of interest are the Presidio church, the Carmel mission, the old customhouse, and the old capitol building. Other points worthy of mention are the former home of Robert Louis Stevenson, the artist colony and resort at Carmel-by-the-Sea, and the grove of ancient trees, of a species not known to occur native elsewhere in the world, now confined to a small area on Cypress point. Population, 1940, 10,084.

Montgomery. The capital of Alabama, on the Alabama river, slightly southeast of the geographical center of the state. It is surrounded by a highly productive grain, fruit, vegetable, livestock, and cotton growing region, for which it is the central market. Hydroelectric power is available for the city's growing industries, which include car shops, foundries, cottonseed oil factories, and fertilizer plants. The city is one of the leading wholesale grocery, livestock, and hard wood markets in the South.

There are many fine public buildings, including the city hall and the capitol, the rotunda of which is decorated with scenes from the state's history. The city is the seat of a State normal school and of Huntingdon college. Montgomery was founded in 1817, and, in 1846, was made the state capital. In 1861, the government of the Southern Confederacy was organized at Montgomery, which was made its first capital. The house occupied by Jefferson Davis, "the first White House of the Confederacy," is now a museum. Population, 1940, 78,084.

Monticello. The residence and estate of Thomas Jefferson, situated in Albemarle county, Virginia, about 3 miles east of Charlottesville. Standing on the summit of a hill (whence the name Monticello, "little mountain"), it commands an extensive view of the surrounding country and, for a long period, was regarded as one of the most elegant and picturesque residences in the South. It was constructed from designs made by Jefferson himself, was first occupied in 1770, and remained his home for 56 years. In 1926, it was purchased by patriotic admirers of Jefferson for $500,000 and presented to the nation.

Montpelier (*mŏnt-pēl'yẽr*). The capital of Vermont, located in the north central part of the state. It is the center of an agricultural district and there are many valuable granite quarries in the vicinity. The insurance business is a leading interest. The finest building is the capitol, a granite structure surmounted by a handsome dome. Among its notable institutions are the State library and the Wood art gallery. The town was first settled in 1787, and, in 1805, was selected as the capital of the state. It was made a city in 1895. Population, 1940, 8006.

Moundsville. A city of West Virginia, on the Ohio river about 11 miles south of Wheeling. It is the center of an important agricultural, coal mining, and oil producing district and has varied local industries, including aircraft factories. Langin field, one-half mile west, is a landing ground of the Army air corps. Moundsville is noted for a huge, prehistoric mound, a famous relic of the Mound Builders, after which the city is named. Population, 1940, 14,168.

Mount Clemens. A city and health resort situated on the Clinton river, about 20 miles northeast of Detroit, Michigan. It has numerous medicinal springs, which attract thousands of persons suffering from chronic ailments, especially rheumatism. There are extensive greenhouses. Its parks, drives, and well shaded streets, together with fine churches and schools, increase the city's attractiveness. Selfridge aviation field lies immediately to the east. Population, 1940, 14,389.

Mount Rubidoux. A bold rocky summit rising abruptly from the Santa Ana valley at Riverside, California. At its crest is a cross dedicated to the memory of Father Junipero Serra, the heroic Franciscan missionary to the Indians. A feature of special interest connected with this small mountain is the impressive service which is held on its summit each Easter Sunday at sunrise.

Mount Tom. A small mountain in Massachusetts which rises precipitously in the Connecticut valley, opposite Mount Holyoke and about 4 miles south of Northampton. The summit, 1200 feet high, is reached by highway and an incline railroad and affords exceptionally fine views of the surrounding region. A tract of 1700 acres on the mountain has been created a state park.

Mount Vernon. A residential city bordering on the Bronx river and adjoining the northeast section of New York City. Mount Vernon occupies an attractive site, and has wide, well shaded streets and handsome lawns and gardens. While a large portion of the city is restricted to residential purposes, there are several important industrial establishments and a considerable local trade. Its educational institutions include the Industrial Arts and Concordia colleges. Population, 1940, 67,362.

Mount Vernon. The home and burial place of George Washington, situated on the right bank of the Potomac river, in Fairfax county, Virginia, 15 miles south of the national capital. Located on an eminence 200 feet high, the mansion house commands a beautiful view of the river. It is constructed of wood, 2 stories high, 96 feet long, and 30 feet deep, with a high piazza along the front, and is painted white to resemble stone. The main part was built in 1743 by Lawrence Washington, Washington's elder brother, who named it in honor of Admiral Vernon of the British navy. Upon the death of his brother Lawrence, in

1752, the estate came into the hands of George Washington, who added the wings to the house.

In 1858, a tract of 200 acres of the original estate, including the mansion and the brick tomb containing the remains of George and Martha Washington, came into the possession of an association of Southern women which holds it in trust as a shrine of national interest. The six rooms on the ground floor contain many objects of historic value, including the key to the French Bastille, and various pieces of furniture used by the family.

Muscle Shoals. A series of shallow rapids in the Tennessee river where the stream has a fall of about 134 feet within 37 miles. The shoals terminate just above Florence, in northwestern Alabama. They form the one interruption to navigation of the river within the state.

A canal around the rapids was opened in 1890. In 1918, further development was undertaken by the Federal government for the purpose of improving navigation, generating electric power, and manufacturing a part of the nitrates needed for explosives during the World War.

The complete project called for the construction of three dams and a cyanamid process nitrate plant capable of an annual production of 110,000 tons of ammonium nitrate.

During the war, and for some time afterwards, construction went forward rapidly. The nitrate plant was practically ready to begin production.

In the spring of 1921, when the hydroelectric power project had been about one-third completed, at a cost of more than 15 million dollars, Congress refused further appropriations. Construction therefore came to a halt. Somewhat later, funds were made available to the war department so that work was resumed on the great Wilson dam, which, in volume, is one of the largest in the world. It was completed in 1925.

Except for sale of current from this dam, the costly property remained idle until 1933. By that time the process for which the nitrate factories had been equipped had become obsolete.

The Tennessee Valley Authority was established in that year to take over the properties and to use them in a demonstration of regional planning for the Tennessee River watershed. Other dams were built, making possible a regulated flow the year round, and the nitrate factories were adapted to development of phosphate fertilizers of a superior type. See *Ammonia, Cyanamid, Fertilizers, Tennessee Valley Authority*.

Muskogee (*mŭs-kō'gē*). A city of eastern Oklahoma, situated in the valley of the Arkansas river, about 130 miles east of Oklahoma City. Muskogee is the trade center of a rich agricultural region devoted to the production of cotton, wheat, fruits, and vegetables, and to cattle raising. It has, in addition, large supplies of petroleum and natural gas. Its manufactured products include cottonseed oil, oil well supplies, and refined petroleum. There are many fine public buildings and several educational institutions. Population, 1940, 32,332.

Nashville. The capital and second largest city of Tennessee, built on both banks of the Cumberland river, in the north central part of the state. Nashville is situated in a productive agricultural and lumbering region, near extensive coal fields. These advantages have contributed to make it an important commercial and manufacturing city. It carries on an extensive wholesaling trade. Its leading industries include flour milling, lumber milling, printing and publishing, meat packing, and the manufacture of food products, cotton goods, clothing, fertilizers, stoves, tobacco, and furniture. Rayon and cellophane are extensively manufactured in the suburb Old Hickory.

Nashville occupies a hilly site, with eminences commanding fine views. On the most lofty hill, stands, like the Acropolis at Athens, the imposing State capitol. The streets are wide and well shaded. The city has 27 parks and playgrounds covering 3583 acres. They include Centennial park, where stands an exact replica of the famous Parthenon in Athens, Greece.

The city is one of the most important educational centers in the South. It is the seat of Vanderbilt university, Ward-Belmont college, the George Peabody college for teachers, and various other educational institutions for white students. Negro institutions include Fisk university and Meharry college.

The first settlement on the site of Nashville was made in 1780, and, in 1806, the city received its municipal charter. During 1812-15, it was the seat of the state legislature. In 1843, it was made the permanent capital of the state. In the park surrounding the State capitol is the tomb of James K. Polk. The Hermitage, the former home of Andrew Jackson, is about 10 miles east of the city. In 1864, one of the great battles of the Civil War was fought in the environs of Nashville. Population, 1940, 167,402.

Natural Bridge. A bridge of natural rock spanning Cedar Creek about 16 miles southeast of Lexington, Va. It is 90 feet long, 50 to 150 feet wide, and about 215 feet above the creek bed. It consists of horizontal limestone strata, which are the remains of the roof of an underground tunnel or a cave through which the creek once flowed. The bridge is crossed by a public road.

Newark (*nū'ẽrk*). The largest city of New Jersey, situated on the Passaic river and Newark bay, about 8 miles west of New York City, with which it is connected by several railways, an electric high speed line, and the Holland and Lincoln vehicular tunnels.

The city extends some 3 miles along the west shore of Newark bay and about 7 miles up the west bank of the Passaic river, from its mouth in Newark bay to the suburb of Belleville. The site of the city occupies an area of about 24 square miles. For a mile inland from the water front, the surface is fairly level and it then rises gently in a series of plateaus.

Immediately adjoining the city on the north, west, and southwest is a group of smaller municipalities, including Belleville, Bloomfield, East Orange, Orange, West Orange, South Orange, and Irvington. Opposite Newark, on the east bank of the Passaic, are East Newark, Harrison, and Kearny.These and other suburbs are intimately connected with the city and, with it, form a greater Newark whose total population exceeds 1,000,000.

The port of Newark is a deep water harbor 700 feet wide, extending 7000 feet inland. Because of favorable location and fine transportation facilities, including a subway, Newark has become a great manufacturing center, sometimes styled the "Birmingham of America." Its industries are numerous and varied. Among important products are jewelry, electrical machinery, chemicals, paints, varnishes, malt liquors, ships, and meat products. The city is the headquarters of some of the largest life insurance and fire insurance companies.

Newark is a city of fine buildings, wide streets, and spacious parks. Military park contains Borglum's colossal sculptural group in bronze known as "The Wars of America." Among Newark's more noted buildings are the public library, the county courthouse, city hall, Federal building, the University of Newark, and the Roman Catholic cathedral. Newark was settled in 1666 by Puritans from Connecticut. It was first called Milford but was soon after given its present name. In 1836, it was chartered as a city. Population, 1940, 429,760.

New Bedford. A seaport and manufacturing city of Massachusetts, situated on the Acushnet river, at its mouth in Buzzards bay, about 55 miles south of Boston. New Bedford was formerly the principal whaling port in the world. This stage of its history is memorialized by the Bourne whaling museum and by a rich collection of whaling material in the public library, one of the first free libraries established in the country. After the decline of the whaling industry, it became the leading city in the United States in the manufacture of cotton yarn and cotton cloth. Less important industries include the manufacture of silk goods, fine tools, sperm and whale oil, rayon, shoes, rope cordage, toys, and rubber and paper goods. New Bedford was settled in 1652, on land purchased from Massasoit by a company from Plymouth. Population, 1940, 110,341.

New Britain. A manufacturing city of Connecticut, situated in the central part of the state, about 10 miles southwest of Hartford. Because of its extensive production of cutlery, edged tools, and other kinds of hardware, New Britain is sometimes styled the "Hardware City." Other important manufactures include electrical appliances, knit goods, and machine shop products. The city is the seat of a State teachers college and has a unique World War memorial. New Britain was settled in 1687 but remained a part of Berlin until 1850, when it was incorporated as a town. In 1871, New Britain received its charter as a city. Population, 1940, 68,685.

New Castle. A manufacturing city of western Pennsylvania, built at the junction of the Shenango and the Neshannock rivers, about 50 miles northeast of Pittsburgh. The city's industrial products include chinaware, bronze bearings, strip steel, tin plate, and clothing. New Castle is situated in a fertile agricultural district, rich in coal, limestone, and other mineral deposits. Population, 1940, 47,638.

New Haven. The second largest city of Connecticut, on an inlet of Long Island sound, some 70 miles northeast of New York City. It occupies a level site partly enclosed by a range of precipitous hills, from 300 to 400 feet high. While a commercial city with extensive shipping interests, the leading industry is manufacturing. In its exceedingly varied industries, there are more than 600 separate manufacturing establishments. Among important manufactures are firearms, clocks, rubber goods, electrical machinery, and an immense variety of iron and steel goods.

The city is well laid out with many imposing public buildings, beautiful parks, and broad, shaded streets. Because of the great number of elms formerly planted in the older sections, New Haven has been called the "City of Elms." It is the seat of Yale university, founded at Saybrook in 1701 and removed to New Haven in 1716. The Harkness memorial tower at Yale is one of the finest Gothic towers erected in modern times. The Yale Bowl seats 70,896 people. The first settlement, made by a company of Puritans in 1638, was known as Quinnipiac, but in 1640 it was renamed New Haven. The city is the burial place of S. F. B. Morse, Eli Whitney, Noah Webster, and other noted men. Population, 1940, 160,605.

New Orleans (*ôr'lē-ănz*). The chief city of Louisiana, the commercial metropolis of the Gulf states, and, after New York City, one of the greatest centers of domestic and foreign trade in the United States. It is situated on the Mississippi river 107 miles above its mouth in the Gulf of Mexico.

The city originally was built along the bend of the river in a semicircular curve and became known as the "Crescent City"; later, its growth up the river followed a backward curve toward Lake Borgne and Lake Pontchartrain, which is spanned by two concrete highway bridges, each about 5 miles in length.

New Orleans is connected with nearly all the important ports of the world by direct steamship lines, the markets of Asia and western South America being accessible through the Panama canal. The city forms the gateway to the Mississippi valley, the greatest agricultural region in the world. It has one of the safest harbors in existence, with a deep water canal from the river through the city to Lake Pontchartrain. More than 100 steamers from 400 to 500 feet in length can be berthed along seven miles of steel docks. Besides public wharves, grain elevators, and coal tipples, the port facilities include also a municipally owned and operated belt line railway.

New Orleans is a leading market for cotton, sugar, molasses, coffee, rice, burlaps, cigars, nitrate, sulphur, timber, and cereals, these products being its principal exports. It is, moreover, one of the principal manufacturing cities in the South. It makes over three-fourths of the men's wash clothing worn in the United States.

The extensive park system of New Orleans includes the 234-acre Audubon park, City park, covering 1426 acres, and a 1400-acre "made" area of boulevards, parks, and bathing beaches on the southeast shore of Lake Pontchartrain. The parks are extensively ornamented with palms, live oaks, magnolias, and a profusion of subtropical shrubs and flowers. The newer residential districts have broad streets, spacious grounds, handsome gardens, and pretentious houses. The old French quarter is a city by itself, with narrow streets lined with rows of quaint old dwellings, built over a hundred years ago in the style of the houses of southern Europe. The famous Mardi Gras carnival, held yearly, is another heritage of the Latin Old World.

Among the buildings of historic interest are the Cabildo, the old archbishop's palace, and the Saint Louis Cathedral, one of the best-known churches in the United States. The principal educational institutions are Tulane and Loyola universities and Newcomb Memorial college for women.

New Orleans was founded by the French in 1718, and came into the possession of the United States with the Louisiana Purchase of 1803, of which territory it was the capital. It remained the capital of the state of Louisiana until 1849. Population, 1940, 494,537.

Newport. A city and seaside resort of Rhode Island. It has a fine harbor which serves as a naval base for the United States Atlantic fleet. Its palatial private residences, public buildings, parks, fountains, and old-time historic structures render it one of the most attractive cities in the country. In Touro park is the old Stone Mill, or "Round Tower," mentioned by Longfellow in his "Skeleton in Armor." Other features of interest include a Jewish synagogue dating from 1763. There are various local industries, including manufactures of furniture and brass goods, and extensive fisheries. Population, 1940, 30,532.

Newport News. A city in Virginia, situated on the north side of Hampton Roads near the mouth of the James river, about 12 miles northwest of Norfolk. Newport News is one of the leading ports of the Southern states and an important coaling station. It has enormous shipbuilding yards, drydocks, and ironworks, and is the center of much agricultural and fishing trade. Points of interest include Fort Monroe, Langley air field, one of the greatest in the United States, and the Huntington mariners museum. Hampton Roads off Newport News was the scene of the battle between the *Monitor* and the *Merrimac* in 1862. Population, 1940, 37,067.

New Rochelle. A city of southern New York on Long Island sound 16 miles northeast of Grand Central station in New York City, of which it is a residential suburb. The city consists characteristically of modern residential districts of beautiful parklike contour. Westchester county owns 385 acres of parks and bathing beaches within the city limits. New Rochelle is named for the French city of La Rochelle, the home of Huguenots who settled on the site in 1688. Population, 1940, 58,408.

Newton (*nū'tŭn*). A city of eastern Massachusetts, built on the Charles river, 8 miles west of Boston. Newton is chiefly a residential city but maintains substantial industries. The city is admirably laid out, with fine streets, parks, and drives, and contains many beautiful homes. Among the city's manufacturing establishments are silk mills, printing works, worsted mills, curtain factories, and rubber works. The city is the seat of Boston college, Newton theological seminary, and other educational institutions. Newton was settled in 1630 as a part of Cambridge. In 1688, it was made a separate town, called New Cambridge, but, in 1692, it received its present name. In 1873, Newton became a city. Population, 1940, 69,873.

NEW YORK. The chief city of the state of New York, the commercial metropolis of the United States, and the most populous city in the western hemisphere. It is situated on New York bay at the mouth of the Hudson river, about 205 miles in direct line northeast of the national capital at Washington.

Site. No metropolis in the world is more strikingly or more beautifully situated than is the city of New York. It is built on three islands, Manhattan, Staten, and Long Island, with a portion on the adjacent mainland, the Bronx.

The Hudson river, here nearly a mile wide, sweeps majestically down the western side of Manhattan and pours its vast waters into the landlocked harbor of New York bay at the south end of the island. The bay is connected with the ocean by a mile-wide channel running between Long Island on the east and Staten on the west. Between the Bronx and Manhattan is the Harlem river which is connected with the Hudson by Spuyten Duyvil creek. Separating Manhattan and the Bronx from Long Island is East river, properly an arm of Long Island sound.

On the west bank of the Hudson, opposite the upper part of the city, the picturesque Palisades tower to a height of from 300 to 400 feet. The surface of the various divisions of the city is fairly level but rises in some parts, as in upper Manhattan, to commanding elevations affording magnificent views of the city and the harbor.

Main Divisions. Originally, the city was confined to Manhattan island. This is 13½ miles long, with a maximum width of 2¼ miles and an area of about 22 square miles. In addition to Manhattan, Greater New York, by consolidation, has since come to embrace Staten island, called Richmond, with an area of about 60 square miles; the western end of Long Island, known as Brooklyn, 80 square miles; an adjoining part of Long Island, known as Queens, 120 square miles; and the portion of the mainland known as the Bronx, 40 square miles. Each of these divisions includes several small adjacent islands. Officially, New York consists of five boroughs, Manhattan, Brooklyn, Queens, Richmond, and the Bronx, and contains a total area of some 325 square miles.

Manhattan is the heart of New York and contains its great commercial, financial, and mercantile institutions, and also its famous museums, libraries, cathedrals, railway stations, and imposing residences. Brooklyn is a residential district with a large number of industrial establishments. Staten island is mainly residential, with an increasing number of industries; the Bronx is also chiefly residential, while Queens, containing more than a third of the total area of Greater New York, is the "home" borough. Long Island City, in Queens borough, is its industrial center, while the remainder of the borough is principally a district of suburban homes.

Streets and Avenues. In the older portions of various divisions of the city there are narrow, short, irregular streets. The newer sections, however, have been admirably planned, and contain many magnificent thoroughfares.

At the south end of Manhattan, the streets are cramped and irregular, but, north of Washington square, they cross at right angles. The great, long north-and-south streets, usually 100 feet wide, running lengthwise of the island, are called avenues. The shorter east-and-west thoroughfares, mostly 60 feet wide, are called streets. Differing from the plan of most American cities, the blocks are solid, having practically no alleys.

An exception to this regular street plan is Broadway, the "greatest street in the world." This noted thoroughfare runs diagonally through the city, in a northwesterly direction, from the Battery, at the sea front, to the extreme northern boundary, a distance of about 16 miles. It traverses the entire length of Manhattan island and continues through the Bronx into Yonkers, completely changing its character in the different portions of the city through which it passes.

Equally famous with Broadway is Fifth avenue, the most beautiful thoroughfare in the city, and one of the finest streets in the world. It begins at Washington arch, about a quarter of a mile west of Broadway, and extends northward for 6 miles, crossing to the east of Broadway at 23d street. It is lined with fashionable shops, beautiful churches, elegant clubs, immense hotels, and palatial residences. Above 59th street, it is restricted to residences by a zoning ordinance.

Other beautiful streets are Morningside drive, which passes Saint John's cathedral; and Riverside drive along the Hudson, passing Grant's tomb and commanding excellent views of the Palisades. A considerable portion of this drive accommodates two levels of traffic.

Beginning at Trinity church on Broadway and extending eastward to East river is Wall Street, long the money center of America and, since the World War, the chief financial center of the world. In Brooklyn, Ocean parkway and Flatbush avenue are magnificent drives; Northern boulevard, Queens boulevard, and Hillside avenue, in Queens, are noteworthy thoroughfares.

Parks. Lying in the center of Manhattan island is Central park, one of the most beautiful pleasure grounds in the world. On its eastern border is the magnificent Metropolitan museum of art, and on the west side is the great American museum of natural history. This park embraces 840 acres, is largely forested, and contains a reservoir, small lakes, and scores of miles of charming drives, roadways, and footpaths. In it are located the Obelisk, or Cleopatra's Needle, and many fine works of sculpture.

Other important parks are Prospect park, Brooklyn, with an area of 526 acres, noted for the natural beauty of its wooded hills and broad meadows; Bronx park, 719 acres, containing superb zoological and botanical gardens; Van Cortlandt park, embracing 1132 acres and containing immense recreation grounds; Pelham Bay park, containing 1788 acres, with a shoreline of 9 miles; Marine park, covering 1522 acres; and the 1200-acre Flushing Meadow park, where the world's fair of 1939-40 was held.

Monuments. In New York are many of the most noted monuments, memorials, and other fine sculptural works of America. The famous Statue of Liberty, designed by Bartholdi and presented to the American people by the French nation, stands on Bedloe's or Liberty island in New York bay. Grant's tomb, a mausoleum of great dignity, overlooks the Hudson from Riverside park, as does the beautiful Soldiers' and Sailors' monument from Riverside drive. At the entrance to Prospect park, Brooklyn, there is an imposing memorial arch, surmounted by a large quadriga by Macmonnies, erected in honor of the soldiers and sailors of the Civil War.

On the Plaza, at the southeast corner of Central park, stand an impressive equestrian statue of General Sherman by Saint-Gaudens. By the same noted sculptor is the fine statue of Peter Cooper, at Cooper Union, and the noble monument to David Farragut, in Madison square.

Buildings. New York excels all other cities in the size, height, elegance, and costliness of its buildings. These include immense commercial structures, towering temples of finance, imposing public edifices, monumental railway stations, beautiful cathedrals and churches, magnificent apartment houses, and palatial residences. There is a greater number of large and costly buildings on Manhattan island than upon any other equal area on the globe. For miles, the buildings contain from 12 to 30 or more stories, rising from 200 to 500 feet in height, with some towering higher than the pyramids or the loftiest cathedrals.

Among the large number of great commercial structures may be mentioned the Metropolitan building, 50 stories and 700 feet high; the Woolworth building, 55 stories, more than 792 feet high; R. C. A. building at Rockefeller center, the largest office building in the world, 69 stories, 853 feet high; Bank of the Manhattan building, 70 stories, 927 feet high; Sixty Wall Tower (Cities Service Building), 67 stories, 950 feet high; the Chrysler building, 77 stories, 1046 feet high; and the Empire State building, 102 stories, 1248 feet high.

Prominent among public edifices is the Municipal building 41 stories high, covering two city blocks and surmounted by a tower and statue which rise to a height of 580 feet. Among structures noted for their architecture are the marble Stock Exchange, the New York Clearing House, the granite and marble Chamber of Commerce, the Hall of Records, Madison Square Garden, the Tiffany building, and the New York Public library.

The Grand Central station and the Pennsylvania station are each great achievements of architectural and engineering skill. Other notable buildings include the Metropolitan museum of art, the American museum of natural history, the Columbia University library, and the Eighth Regiment armory. A unique architectural unit is Rockefeller center, or "Radio City," covering three city blocks. Its ten building units, ornamented with hanging gardens and artificial waterfalls, house elaborate broadcasting and theatrical facilities and magnificent stores and offices.

Among hundreds of beautiful churches may be mentioned Saint Patrick's cathedral built of white marble with spires rising 332 feet. This ranks among the finest Gothic structures in America. Other noteworthy churches are the partially completed cathedral of Saint John the Divine, Saint Thomas's church, Saint Bartholomew's church, the Temple Emanu-El, the great church of Saint Paul the Apostle, and the Riverside church, containing one of the finest carillons of bells in the western hemisphere.

Intercommunication. East river is spanned by six monumental bridges, ranking among the largest in the world. Four of these—Brooklyn bridge, Manhattan bridge, and Williamsburg bridge—connecting New York and Brooklyn,—and Triborough bridge, joining Queens with the Bronx and sending out an arm to 125th street, Manhattan, are suspension bridges. The Queensboro bridge, connecting New York and Queens, is a massive cantilever structure. Hell Gate bridge, an immense steel arch, connects the Bronx with Queens and provides direct rail connection between New England and the West. Staten island is connected with New Jersey by three immense bridges, Kill van Kull at Bayonne, Goethals at Elizabeth, and Outerbridge Crossing at Perth Amboy.

The greatest of all New York bridges, and one of the greatest in the world, is the Washington Memorial bridge over the Hudson river. It connects 178th street with the New Jersey shore by a single span 3500 feet in length.

An extensive ferry service and two pairs of subway tunnels for electric cars connect Manhattan with Brooklyn, and two pairs also connect Manhattan with Queens. The Holland and Lincoln vehicular tunnels, under the Hudson river, connect New York City with Jersey City, and a 3½-mile viaduct connects it with Elizabeth, New Jersey.

Most of New York's local transportation system is municipally owned. The city operates 250 route miles of rapid transit subway lines, 212 route miles of trolley lines, and 80 miles of bus routes. Running north and south in the narrow island of Manhattan, there are two 4-track subway lines, both of which continue under the East river to Brooklyn where they connect with steam and electric rapid transit to all parts of Long Island. The Long Island railroad transports more commuting passengers than any other railroad in the world.

Educational Institutions. New York is the seat of two great universities, Columbia university, on Cathedral Heights, and New York university in the Bronx, overlooking the Harlem river. With the former is affiliated Barnard college, the Teachers' college, and the Horace Mann school. Connected with New York university is the Hall of Fame for noted Americans.

Among many other prominent educational institutions are the College of the City of New York, Hunter college, Manhattan college, Brooklyn college, Fordham university, the College of Saint Francis Xavier, Cooper Union, the College of Physicians and Surgeons, and the Rockefeller institute for medical research. Of great influence in the educational life of the city are the public library, with more than 40 branches, the Metropolitan museum of art, the American museum of natural history, the planetarium and the Brooklyn institute of arts and sciences. The medical center on Washington heights, overlooking the Hudson river, takes the first place among institutions of the kind throughout the world.

Transportation. New York bay, nearly enclosed by islands, forms one of the finest harbors in the world. The city of New York, built around it, has a total water front of some 771 miles, of which more than 345 miles are developed with port facilities. About 100 ocean steamship lines, affording service to all parts of the world, have headquarters in New York. Some 40 lines of river and coastwise steamers likewise operate from the port. New York has water connections to the Great Lakes through the Hudson river and the State barge canal. The great railway systems of the New England and the Middle Atlantic states, and also various western railroads, have terminals, either within the city or across the Hudson on the New Jersey shore. The Pennsylvania railway is connected with New York City by tunnels under the Hudson river.

Commerce. New York's commercial supremacy is owing to its magnificent harbor facilities and to its geographical location. The largest ships are accommodated at its wharves, and railway and inland water routes afford quick collection and distribution of goods throughout the richest and most populous region in America. The commerce of New York is several times greater than that of any other port in the New World, and, in value, usually embraces about one-half the total imports and exports of the United States. The volume of the coastwise trade usually greatly exceeds that of the foreign trade. The wholesale and jobbing trade is enormous, as is also the distribution of the city's immense manufactures. In 1936, a zone in Staten island was made a free port.

Finance. Since the World War, New York has become the dominant money center of the world, with annual banking transactions aggregating some 300 billion dollars. Here are located the greatest financial institutions of the country, including powerful banks, trust companies, and insurance companies, the New York clearing house, the stock exchange, the cotton exchange, and casualty, credit, fidelity, and surety companies.

Manufactures. In value, the manufactures of the metropolis exceed those of any other manufacturing center in America. Usually about one-tenth of the total manufactures of the United States is produced in New York City. This supremacy is owing to an immense volume of light manufacturing, for the most part carried on in small factories. The industries are exceedingly diversified, including some 30,000 establishments and representing about 90 per cent of all the industries listed in the country. The largest single product is clothing; more than half of the clothing worn in the United States is made in the city. The second largest industry is the printing and publishing of newspapers, magazines, periodicals, and books. Other important industries are meat packing, sugar refining, petroleum refining, and the manufacture of millinery, lace, fur goods, jewelry, tobacco, drugs, shoes, and machinery.

History. In 1609, Henry Hudson, employed by the Dutch, sailed up the river which bears his name. Dutch fur traders began operations along the Hudson in 1613 and soon after built a fort, near which the first white settlement developed. The first permanent colonists, mostly Walloons, arrived in 1624. Peter Minuit, in 1626, bought Manhattan island from its Indian owners for $24, and named the settlement New Amsterdam. There were difficulties with the Indians, but, under the rule of Peter Stuyvesant, 1647-64, the settlement grew to a village of 1000 inhabitants.

In 1664, New Amsterdam was captured by the English, who renamed it New York. Despite political conflicts, the town in 1700 had increased to 5000 inhabitants, about half Dutch and half English. During the Revolutionary War, British armies occupied the town for 7 years, 1776–83. In this unfortunate period, New York lost about half its inhabitants and was largely destroyed by fire. Within 8 years, however, the population trebled, commerce revived, and for a year and a half, 1789–90, New York was the capital of the Federal government. Washington, the first president of the United States, was inaugurated, April 30, 1789, in Federal hall in Wall street.

The completion of the Erie canal in 1825, furnishing a waterway from the Hudson to the Great Lakes, made New York the gateway for the commerce of the rapidly developing nation. This so accelerated the city's growth that, in 1835, New York numbered 200,000 inhabitants. The first railway to the Great Lakes was completed in 1851, and thenceforward the history of New York is a record of continuous and monumental growth.

More recent achievements were the consolidation of the five boroughs into Greater New York, the construction of the subway system with tunnels under East river and the Hudson, and the completion of the gigantic Catskill aqueduct, insuring an adequate water supply to the expanding metropolis. Population, 1940, 7,454,995.

Niagara Falls. The grandest cataract in America and the second largest in the world, being exceeded in combined height and volume only by Victoria falls in South Africa. It is situated about 22 miles north of Buffalo, New York. The Niagara river in its northerly course of over 26 miles descends 326 feet from the level of Lake Erie to that of Lake Ontario. By far the greater part of this descent occurs at the falls and at the rapids immediately above and below them. For the first 2 miles after leaving Lake Erie the river is troubled and rapid. It then expands into a broad, placid stream, from 1 to 2 miles wide, and encircles several islands.

After flowing nearly 20 miles and descending only about 20 feet, the river suddenly narrows and enters a series of beautiful rapids. In about a half mile the river descends 52 feet, in seething, boiling torrents and eddies in which the whole surface is torn and tossed into white spray. The waters then reach the edge of an abrupt declivity, the Niagara escarpment, and make a sudden plunge to the bottom of an immense gorge. A short distance above the brink of the falls, Goat island separates the river into two unequal streams. The narrow, shallower one, on the American side, discharges over the American fall, 167 feet in height and 1060 feet wide. The main part of the river swings to the west of Goat island and discharges over the Canadian or Horseshoe fall, 158 feet high, with a deep retreating curve in the center and measuring about 2500 feet along the crest. A feature of unique interest is the illumination of the cataract each evening by shifting lights of rich and varied color. This is accomplished by a battery of 24 gigantic searchlights developing a total of 1.44 billion candle power, set in Queen Victoria park on the Canadian side of the river.

The water flowing over the American fall is from 1 to 4 feet deep, but that plunging over the Horseshoe fall is estimated at about 20 feet in depth. The main cataract carries over fully 90 per cent of the water, while the American fall discharges less than 10 per cent. The volume of flow does not vary greatly and is normally about 500,000 tons of water a minute.

The edge of the American fall is receding at a rate estimated at from 2 to 7 inches a year. Measurements by the United States Geological Survey indicate that the Horseshoe fall has been receding at the rate of about 5 feet a year for nearly a century. Since the Civil War, the main fall has worn back about 400 feet.

For about 7 miles below the foot of the falls, the river descends between nearly perpendicular cliffs, 200 to 300 feet high, through a series of magnificent rapids. This is the famous Niagara gorge, which is second in grandeur and scenic interest only to the majestic cataract itself. In width, the gorge varies from 1700 feet, opposite the American fall, to 700 feet, opposite the Whirlpool. The river at the bottom of the gorge is considerably narrower, with depths believed to range from 100 to 500 feet, and with a speed through the greater rapids estimated at 30 miles an hour.

About 3 miles below the falls the river rushes into the Whirlpool. This is a huge circular indentation worn into the Canadian side of the river and surrounded by walls 300 feet high. The river plunges into this great excavation in a northwesterly direction and is forced to leave it in a northeasterly direction, forming one of the most impressive maelstroms in the world.

At the end of the gorge, near Lewiston, the river again widens and flows tranquilly for about 7 miles to its mouth in Lake Ontario.

Niagara falls is the most accessible to the traveler of any of the great cataracts. Fine parks, with many conveniences for the public, have been established on both sides of the river. There is a bridge to Goat island. An aerial cable tramway spans the chasm over the Whirlpool, giving a unique view of this natural wonder.

While several early French missionaries, visiting the Niagara region, wrote accounts of the falls received from the Indians, the first white man to describe and depict the great cataract was Father Hennepin, who accompanied La Salle to the Niagara frontier in 1678. French domination of the region continued until 1759, when Fort Niagara was surrendered to the British. The region was controlled by the British until 1796—13 years after the close of the Revolution—and was the scene of many conflicts during the War of 1812.

Niagara Falls. A manufacturing city of western New York, situated on the Niagara river at the falls from which it takes its name. By utilizing immense power generated at the cataract, the city has developed extensive manufactories and has become an important center of electrochemical industry. Among the leading manufactures are chemicals, electrical machinery, aluminum ware, carborundum, paper and wood pulp, flour, shredded wheat biscuit, roofing materials, and metallurgical products.

By means of tunnels, water is conveyed from the river above the upper rapids to hydroelectric generators placed near the level of the river below the cataract. After passing through the turbines connected with the generators, the water is then discharged into the gorge below the falls. By thus diverting a small fraction of the great volume of water in the river and utilizing the power developed by a drop of about 200 feet, electricity in immense quantities is developed. This is used, not only in many local manufactories, but is also extensively distributed for industrial purposes to Buffalo, Rochester, Syracuse, and many other cities.

On account of the falls, which rank among the world's greatest scenic wonders, the city is visited yearly by tens of thousands of travelers. Niagara Falls and Suspension Bridge, formerly two villages, were, in 1892, united as the city of Niagara Falls. The adjacent village of La Salle was added in 1927. Population, 1940, 78,029.

Nogales (*nō-gä'lĕs*). A city on the southern boundary of Arizona, 65 miles south of Tucson. A fence, with gates always open, separates it from the Mexican city of the same name. Nogales is the trade center of a mining and grazing district and is an inland gateway to the western coast of Mexico. A feature of historical interest in the vicinity is the ruin of the Tumacacori Mission. This was founded in 1691 by Father Kino, a Jesuit missionary, was taken charge of by Franciscan fathers in 1769, and is now a national monument. Population, 1940, 5135.

Norfolk. The principal seaport and second largest city of Virginia, with about 50 miles of waterfront on the Elizabeth river, Hampton Roads, and Chesapeake bay. It has regular communication with European and American ports, and inland water connections by means of the Dismal Swamp and the Albemarle and Chesapeake canals.

Norfolk, together with Portsmouth, forms the largest naval station in the Union. It is the base for the Atlantic fleet. The harbor is capable of giving anchorage to the largest class of vessels. Its defenses are Fort Monroe, Fort Wool, and Fort Story. It is, moreover, one of the largest coaling stations in the world.

The port carries an extensive shipping trade in cotton, tobacco, lumber, corn, cattle, horses, fish, oysters, fruits, vegetables, and peanuts. The principal manufactures include ships, airplane parts, fertilizers, agricultural implements, lumber, cotton goods, flour, and roasted peanuts.

Among the public buildings may be noted the customhouse, the city hall, and the cotton exchange. The educational establishments include a branch of William and Mary college and Virginia polytechnic institute. Popular seaside resorts nearby include Virginia and Ocean View beaches. Norfolk was first settled in 1682, incorporated as a borough in 1736, and chartered as a city in 1835. Population, 1940, 144,332.

Oakland. The third largest city of California, situated on the mainland shore of San Francisco bay and connected with San Francisco by the 75-million dollar San Francisco-Oakland Bay bridge. Oakland occupies a site of great natural beauty, somewhat in the form of an amphitheater with its lower level portion adjoining the bay.

The city is served by three transcontinental railroads and has a spacious harbor for ocean-going vessels, with 27 miles of deep water frontage. It is connected with Alameda to the south by two bridges over an estuary and one large tunnel, known as the Posey Tube. Its 825-acre airport is the western terminus of the transcontinental air mail service. It is the natural outlet for the great agricultural and fruit growing valleys of California—the Sacramento and San Joaquin. The city is located near the terminals of pipe lines from vast oil fields, and readily secures low-priced fuel for its thriving industries. It is one of the largest automobile manufacturing centers and one of the greatest distributing centers for hydroelectric power in the West. Other important industries are canning, growing of flowers for cutting, and the manufacture of machinery, ships, and chemicals.

Oakland possesses many fine buildings, among which are the city hall and the municipal auditorium. It is the seat of Mills college. Features of interest include Lakeside park, Lake Merritt, Foothill boulevard, Skyline boulevard, and the Dimond Canyon road leading to the home of Joaquin Miller. The Pacific Coast terminus of the Lincoln highway is at Oakland. First settled in 1820, Oakland was incorporated in 1852 and in 1854 became a city. Population, 1940, 302,163.

Oak Park. A village of northeastern Illinois, about nine miles west of the center of Chicago, of which it is a residential suburb. Oak Park was incorporated in 1901. It is the largest village in the United States. Population, 1940, 66,015.

Oberlin. A town of northeastern Ohio, situated about 35 miles southwest of Cleveland. While it conducts a substantial trade with the surrounding agricultural districts and has local industries, it is chiefly noted as the seat of Oberlin college, the first American college to adopt coeducation. The town is well laid out, with broad, shady streets and fine residences. Population, 1940, 4305.

Ogden. The second largest city of Utah, situated at the junction of the Ogden and Weber rivers, at the foot of the Wasatch mountains, about 35 miles north of Salt Lake City. It is noted for its picturesque scenery. A boulevard passes through the scenic Ogden canyon a distance of 10 miles to Artesian park, the source of the city's water supply. Ogden is the distributing center of a productive agricultural, fruit growing, and stock raising district. Electricity for light, heat, and industrial purposes is supplied to the city by the waterfalls from surrounding canyons. Meat packing, fruit and vegetable canning, oil refining, and the manufacture of beet sugar and flour are among the chief industries. Ogden was founded in 1848 and in 1850, under the direction of Brigham Young, was laid out as a city. Population, 1940, 43,688.

Oklahoma City. The capital of Oklahoma, situated on the north branch of the Canadian river in the central part of the state. Lying in the midst of a rich oil producing, agricultural, and stock raising country, the city has developed important wholesale and distributing interests. It is the financial and commercial center of the state. Among the leading industries are oil refining, cotton and flour milling, and meat packing. The city's 71 parks and playgrounds cover 2900 acres. Architecturally outstanding is the municipal auditorium, one of four buildings in the 10-million dollar civic center. It was granted its charter in 1891 and was chosen as capital of Oklahoma in 1910. The capitol is a beautiful structure, built in the Ionic style of architecture. Population, 1940, 204,424.

Old Point Comfort. A favorite watering place in Virginia, situated on a neck of land where Hampton Roads at the mouth of the James river joins Chesapeake bay. The climate is delightful, and the excellent facilities for bathing, boating, and fishing, together with the attractions of picturesque scenery, have won for Old Point Comfort high rank among health and pleasure resorts.

Olympia. The capital of the state of Washington, situated on the southernmost inlet of Puget sound. The city is the port for a district rich in lumber and in agricultural products. Large quantities of fruit, fish, clams, and oysters are shipped. Manufacturing interests are promoted by the abundant hydroelectric power available, the chief industry being the production of lumber. The noteworthy buildings include the capitol, the Federal building, and four other governmental buildings costing in all $15,000,000. The first settlement was made at Olympia in 1845. The town was laid out in 1851, and became the territorial capital in 1853. Population, 1940, 13,254.

Omaha. The chief city of Nebraska, situated on a commanding site on the west bank of the Missouri river, opposite Council Bluffs, Iowa.

Omaha owes its position as the commercial and manufacturing metropolis of the state to the fact that it is one of the greatest gateways of the West, having the facilities afforded by several great railroad systems and the deepened channel of the Missouri river. The industries of the city, especially those based on agricultural products, are enormous. Its live stock market is the second in the world, while its creameries and macaroni factories are among the largest in the country. It is one of the greatest meat packing centers in the United States. Other industries and manufactures include ore smelting and refining, railway car repairing, flour, steam engines, machinery, and dairy equipment.

Omaha has some 2100 acres of parks and many fine public buildings. Among the city's numerous educational institutions may be mentioned the University of Omaha, Creighton university, and the Jocelyn memorial art museum. From 1854, the date of the first permanent settlement, to 1867, Omaha was the capital of Nebraska. Population, 1940, 223,844.

Oraibi (*ō-rī'bĭ*). A village of the Hopi Indians in northeastern Arizona, believed to be the oldest continuously inhabited community in the United States. It lies about 100 miles north of Winslow. The community existed as early as 1370, this fact being inferred from a study of the annual growth rings of timbers in the ruins. Population about 100.

Orlando. A city and winter resort of Florida, charmingly situated amidst numerous small lakes about 40 miles inland from the approximate center of the state's Atlantic coastline. There are 33 lakes within the corporate limits. Palms, magnolias, and laurels impart to the drives, lake shores, and 32 parks a subtropical beauty which vies with the delightful climate in attracting winter visitors.

Orlando lies in the center of a rich citrus fruit country, which produces also lettuce, cabbages, and pineapples. Industrial establishments include foundries, planing mills, and locomotive repair shops. Rollins college is located in the vicinity. Population, 1940, 36,736.

Oshkosh. A city of eastern Wisconsin, situated on the western shore of Lake Winnebago at Fox river, about 75 miles north of Milwaukee. It is located in a once densely wooded region, and the woodworking industry is still a leading commercial interest of the city. Other industries include the manufacture of matches, furniture, travel goods, overalls, and trucks. Oshkosh is a well-known pleasure resort. Lake Winnebago is noted for its game fishing; yachting in the summer and ice boating in the winter are favorite sports. Population, 1940, 39,089.

Pagopago (*päng'ō-päng'ō*). A fine natural harbor on the south coast of the island of Tutuila, American Samoa. On this harbor are situated the village of Pagopago and the American naval station, through which American Samoa is governed. Pagopago is populated almost entirely by native Polynesians. The chief commercial product of the island is copra. This is exported, and sold by the United States government for the benefit of the natives. Population of village of Pagopago, 1940, 934.

Painted Desert. An area of plateaus and low mesas in north central Arizona. It extends from the top of the Marble canyon of the Colorado river southeastward along the east side of the valley of the Little Colorado for about 100 miles, varying in width from 15 to 40 miles. At the south, it ends near the Santa Fe railway, which crosses it between Holbrook and Winslow. This desert lies at an altitude of about 5000 feet and has an exceedingly arid climate. In consequence, vegetation is so scant that vast areas of rocks are bare or very nearly so. These rocks, mostly Triassic shales and sandstones, exhibit a great variety of colors, including red, pink, purple, chocolate, lavender, pale green, and gray, whence the name "painted."

Situated on the margin of this desert, about 60 miles north of Winslow, are the seven villages of the Hopi Indians, the best known of which are Walpi and Oraibi. These pueblos are picturesquely built on cliffs which project from a high plateau of sandstone. See *Walpi*.

Palisades, The. The name given to a series of massive cliffs on the west bank of the Hudson river. From near Haverstraw, New York, these extend south to Weehawken, New Jersey, a distance of about 30 miles. For the most part, these precipitous cliffs rise almost directly from the water's edge, varying in height from 200 to 550 feet. They consist of basaltic trap rock or diabase, which exhibits marked columnar effects, forming a striking feature in the beautiful scenery of the lower Hudson. The Palisades Interstate park, a tract covering more than 48,000 acres in New York and New Jersey, embraces some of the finest portions of the Palisades.

Palm Beach. A noted winter resort on the southeast coast of Florida, about 300 miles south of Jacksonville. It is situated on Lake Worth, opposite West Palm Beach, the nearest railway town. Its delightful climate, together with its bathing, boating, and fishing facilities, makes Palm Beach one of the most desirable of pleasure haunts. Palatial hotels, spacious parks, and golf links attract thousands of visitors. Permanent population, 1940, 3747, winter population, about 22,000.

Palm Canyon. A narrow, rocky gorge opening upon the extreme western end of the Colorado desert, at the southeastern base of San Jacinto mountain, about 7 miles south of Palm Springs, California. Near the mouth of this canyon, growing along the small watercourse at its bottom, is one of the largest existing groves of the stately Washington palm, many trees being from 40 to 60 feet high. Their brilliant green foliage makes a striking contrast with the arid, barren rocks forming the canyon walls.

This handsome fan palm, now widely cultivated for ornament, is found native in only a few desert localities in southern California and adjacent Mexico. Most of these places are inaccessible for the ordinary traveler. Palm canyon, however, is easily reached by automobile from Whitewater railway station or from Palm Springs which is on the desert highway between San Gorgonio pass and the Imperial valley.

Palm canyon lies in the Aguas Calientes Indian reservation, but Congress, in 1922, authorized the purchase, under certain conditions, of 1600 acres in Palm canyon and in two near-by canyons. When these conditions are met, this area, containing the main grove and other fine specimens of these magnificent trees, will be preserved as a national monument. See *Colorado Desert, Palm.*

Pasadena. A residential city and widely known winter resort of southern California, northeast of Los Angeles and touching its boundaries at several points. It occupies a beautiful site in the foothills of the Sierra Madre mountains, in a region luxuriant with palms, orange groves, eucalyptus, and other subtropical vegetation. The city is noted for its spacious avenues, fine public buildings, and handsome residences, and is the seat of many educational institutions, including the California institute of technology.

Among the many features of interest within or near the city are the Huntington library and art gallery, the Rose Bowl, Mount Wilson observatory, a beautiful public library with out-door reading rooms, Mount Lowe, San Gabriel mission, and a mile-long avenue of deodars known as "the street of the Christmas trees." Its 13 parks cover 500 acres, the largest, Brookside, being within a great natural gorge, the Arroyo Seco, which is spanned at Colorado street by one of the country's most beautiful bridges. The city is widely known for its annual festival, called the "Tournament of Roses," celebrated on New Year's Day. In 1874, a colony from Indianapolis, Ind., settled on the site of Pasadena and began raising fruit; in 1886, Pasadena received its charter as a city. Population, 1940, 81,864.

Passaic (*pă-sā'ĭk*). A manufacturing city of New Jersey, situated on the Passaic river, about 12 miles northwest of New York City. The chief industry is the manufacture of woolen and worsted goods. Passaic is said to make one-third of the handkerchiefs produced in the United States. Other important industrial establishments include cigar factories, rubber, metal, and dye works. Population, 1940, 61,394.

Paterson. The third largest city of New Jersey, located on the Passaic river, about 16 miles northwest of New York City. Immense power, developed from Passaic falls, 50 feet in height, is utilized in the city's numerous industries. Paterson is the leading producer of silk fabrics in the United States. It has also cotton and woolen mills, dyeing and finishing establishments, airplane engine factories, and machine shops.

Paterson owes the beginnings of its great industrial growth to the "Society for Establishing Useful Manufactures," promoted largely through the efforts of Alexander Hamilton, in 1791, when he was secretary of the treasury. In 1792, the site, "by the Great Falls of the Passaic," was chosen for the location of the mills which were to be used in bringing about the commercial independence of the United States from Europe. At first, cotton and paper mills were established, but later these were largely superseded by silk works and other factories. Population, 1940, 139,656.

Pawtucket. The second largest city of Rhode Island, built on both banks of the Pawtucket river, about 4 miles northeast of Providence. Pawtucket falls, 50 feet high, provide abundant power, which is utilized in the city's varied industries. The city was the birthplace of the cotton goods industry of the United States. The original mill, founded by Samuel Slater in 1790, is now a museum.

Pawtucket is a leading producer of cotton goods. Its other manufactures include silk, woolen cloth, tire fabric, lace, auto accessories, knitted underwear, and electric refrigerators. There are also large dyeing and bleaching works and iron and steel shops. Fine parks and public squares, together with imposing bridges across the river serve to make Pawtucket an attractive city. Population, 1940, 75,797.

Pendleton. A city of northeastern Oregon, on the Umatilla river, 225 miles east of Portland. Pendleton is the supply center for the Umatilla irrigation district and has an extensive trade in grain, fruit, and live stock. Pendleton has become widely known through its annual exhibition festival "The Round-Up." Population, 1940, 8847.

Pensacola. A seaport of Florida, situated on Pensacola bay, 10 miles north of the Gulf of Mexico. It has a fine landlocked harbor and conducts an extensive domestic trade. Industrial products include paper, fertilizers, wood products, cottonseed oil, and naval stores. A huge navy aviation school is located there. The city was settled by Spaniards in 1696, and passed into the possession of the United States in 1821. Population, 1940, 37,449.

Peoria (*pē-ō'rĭ-ȧ*). A manufacturing city of Illinois built on the west bank of the Illinois river, 160 miles southwest of Chicago. Peoria is the commercial center of a rich agricultural district, in close proximity to large coal fields. The manufactures include agricultural implements, packed meats, paper goods, stoves, barrels, woven wire fence, cordage, washing machines, stock foods, and chemicals. Peoria has one of the largest truck-in stockyards in the country. Parks cover about 1640 acres. Lake Peoria and other natural features of the city's environment provide beautiful scenery within and around it. The city is the seat of Bradley polytechnic institute. Population, 1940, 105,087.

Pepin (*pē'pĭn*), **Lake.** An expansion of the upper Mississippi river, situated in a fine scenic region, about 30 miles south of Saint Paul, Minnesota. The lake is about 30 miles long and from 1 to 2 miles wide. It is surrounded by imposing bluffs of limestone, rising about 400 feet above the water and carved by erosion into many remarkable shapes. The town of Red Wing is situated at its northern end.

Perth Amboy. A city of eastern New Jersey, located on Raritan bay, about 20 miles southwest of New York City. Perth Amboy, by reason of its good harbor, has extensive shipping interests, and is an important commercial and industrial center. Among the chief industries are chemical works, copper and silver refineries, and the manufacture of clothing and hats. The city is connected with South Amboy by the Victory bridge, costing 10 million dollars, and with Staten island by a bridge completed in 1928 at a cost of 16 million dollars. Perth Amboy was settled in 1683, and, for a long period, was the capital of New Jersey province. It became a city in 1718. Population, 1940, 41,242.

Petersburg. A city of southeastern Virginia, situated on the south bank of the Appomattox river, 23 miles south of Richmond. Its chief industries consist of the manufacture of tobacco products, trunks, optical lenses and cotton clothing. The city is located in an extensive tobacco growing region at the northern end of the peanut belt, and carries on a substantial trade in these products. In the campaign about Petersburg in 1864-65, General Robert E. Lee was forced to surrender. Population, 1940, 30,631.

Petrified Forests. See *Adamana.*

PHILADELPHIA. The chief city of Pennsylvania, and the third most populous in the United States. It is situated at the junction of the Schuylkill and the Delaware river, some 50 miles from the mouth of the Delaware in Delaware bay and nearly 100 miles by water from the Atlantic Ocean.

SITE. From the confluence of the rivers, Philadelphia extends northerly along the Schuylkill for more than 20 miles and northeasterly along the Delaware for nearly the same distance, and has an irregular northern boundary. The site embraces a total area of about 130 square miles. At the south, between the two rivers, the surface is low and flat. The old city was laid out on this level peninsula. This section is now the business center.

To the north, the surface rises, culminating in Chestnut hill, 430 feet high, and other similar eminences. The factory districts were developed in this northern area, with Germantown, now within the city limits, occupying the heights above them. West of the Schuylkill, the surface is rolling, rising to elevations of 100 feet in the residential districts, and to 200 feet in Fairmount park. This part of the city began as a suburb and remains chiefly a residential district. The principal sections of the city are Overbrook, Roxborough, Germantown, Manayunk, Tioga, Frankford, Kensington, Torrisdale, Haddington, and Tacony.

Streets. Philadelphia was the first modern city to be laid out on the gridiron plan, with broad, long, straight streets, intersecting at right angles, and with small parks and squares located at suitable intervals. This general rectangular plan was followed in the layout for upper Manhattan in New York City, and has since largely guided American city planning.

Market street, extending east and west, is a leading commercial thoroughfare. On this street are the city hall, the Pennsylvania station, the Reading station, and the post office. Chestnut street, also an important business thoroughfare, parallels Market street, immediately to the south. Other noteworthy east-and-west streets are Walnut, Locust, Spruce, Pine, Arch, and Race.

Broad street, one of the greatest streets of America, bisects the city from north to south. From League Island park, at the southern boundary of the city, Broad street, 113 feet wide, extends due north, for about 12 miles, to the northern boundary. It crosses Market street at Penn square and the city hall. Most of the north-and-south streets are named by numbers beginning at the Delaware river. The diagonal streets, which are few in number, are usually called avenues. Besides Penn square and Independence square, the most centrally located squares are Washington, Franklin, Rittenhouse, and Logan. The last named encircles a beautiful fountain and is faced by the public library.

Parks and Monuments. The city park system, including 140 parks, squares, and parkways, embraces an area of about 7000 acres. The finest unit is Fairmount park, containing some 3600 acres along the Schuylkill river, and connected with the city hall by the magnificent Benjamin Franklin parkway. Wissahickon drive, 6 miles in length, along Wissahickon creek in Fairmount park is regarded as one of the finest scenic drives within the limits of an American city. Among other important parks are League Island park, 300 acres; Pennypack park, 726 acres; Tacony park, 250 acres; Cobb's Creek park, 288 acres; Hunting park, 86 acres; Burkolme park, 69 acres; Whitehall commons, 35 acres; Bartram's garden, 27 acres; and the Cope arboretum, 22 acres. Roosevelt boulevard, 300 feet wide, is a part of the Lincoln highway.

Important monuments are the Soldiers' and Sailors' memorial in Fairmount park, the imposing Washington monument at the main entrance to the park, and the World War memorial on the Parkway. Noted statues within the commercial district are: of Washington, in front of Independence hall; of Franklin, at the post office; and of Girard, Muhlenberg, Leidy, and McClellan, on the city hall plaza. On the plaza stands also Saint-Gaudens's statue of "The Pilgrim." Other noteworthy sculptural works in various parts of the city are Thorn's "Tam o'Shanter," Wolff's "Wounded Lioness," Remington's "Cowboy," and statues of Lincoln, Grant, Meade, Garfield, Columbus, Goethe, Schiller, Humboldt, and Joan of Arc.

Buildings. The monumental city hall, an immense marble structure, is about 470 feet square, and covers 4½ acres. The tower, some 548 feet high, is surmounted by a colossal statue of William Penn.

Among the older buildings, Christ church and Independence hall exemplify the Colonial style of architecture, the buildings of Girard college illustrate the Neo-Greek style, and Saint Mark's church is an example of the Gothic.

United States government buildings include the Federal building; the United States mint, one of the greatest in the world; the post office; and the customhouse. Other noteworthy structures include the Reading and the Baltimore and Ohio depots, the immense Pennsylvania railroad station, costing over 100 million dollars, the 16-million dollar Municipal art gallery on an eminence at the end of the Parkway, Convention hall, and Medical towers. Among numerous fine commercial buildings may be mentioned the Girard Trust, Market Street National Bank, the Curtis, the Bell Telephone, the Arcade, the Atlantic, the Morris, the Fidelity-Philadelphia Trust, and the North American buildings, the 35-story Lewis tower, and the Wanamaker, the Gimbel Brothers and the Strawbridge and Clothier stores. A stadium, seating 100,000 people, is a legacy of the Sesquicentennial exposition, held in 1926 in south Philadelphia.

Historic Structures. No city in the United States, except Boston, has preserved a larger number of important buildings associated with the early history of the nation. Chief among these is Independence hall, built 1729-34, America's most famous landmark. In this notable building, the second and the third Continental Congress met; here Washington was chosen commander in chief; in it the Declaration of Independence was signed; and from its tower the Liberty bell, still preserved in the building, pealed forth its message of freedom.

To the west of Independence hall is Congress hall, where the United States Congress met from 1790 to 1800, and where George Washington, in 1793, and John Adams, in 1797, were inaugurated. East of Independence hall is the old city hall, first occupied in 1791, now used as a historical museum. The three buildings—Independence hall, Congress hall, and the old city hall—form what is known as the State House group in Independence square. This famous square is situated on Chestnut street between Fifth street and Sixth street.

In the same vicinity is Carpenter's hall, where, in 1774, the first Continental Congress met, and where, in 1787, the Constitutional convention framed the Constitution of the United States. In Arch street stands the home of Betsy Ross, who is said to have made the first American flag.

Among historic churches are Old Swedes' church, built 1698–1700; Christ church, begun in 1727; Old Saint Joseph's church, dating from 1729; and Saint Mary's church, built in 1762.

The Penn mansion, built in 1682, was the first brick house erected in Philadelphia. It originally stood between Market and Chestnut streets, in the heart of the city. With the encroachment of great business structures, it was taken down and carefully re-erected in Fairmount park.

Educational Institutions. Philadelphia is the seat of the University of Pennsylvania. It is also a noted center of medical and dental education. Among its prominent medical schools are the Jefferson, the Hahnemann, the Woman's medical college, and the medical departments of Temple and Pennsylvania universities, which also have important dental schools. Other noteworthy institutions are the planetarium, the Drexel institute, the schools of the Pennsylvania academy of fine arts, the Franklin institute, the Curtis institute of music, the Spring Garden institute, Temple university, the public library, Rodin museum, the Franklin Memorial museum of graphic arts, Girard college, La Salle college, Saint Joseph's college, the William Penn Charter school, founded in 1701, and the Germantown academy. In near-by suburbs are Bryn Mawr, Haverford, Villanova and Swarthmore colleges, Ogontz school, and Overbrook seminary.

Transportation. Although ships from its wharves sail nearly 100 miles before entering the ocean, Philadelphia is an important seaport. It has more than 35 miles of water front on the Delaware river, which admits the passage of ocean-going ships. The Schuylkill is also navigable.

Philadelphia is also a great railroad center, with a huge network of lines extending, not only into the near-by coal and iron districts, but also into the Ohio and the Mississippi valley and into the South. The city is served chiefly by the Pennsylvania, the Reading, and the Baltimore and Ohio systems, and has the most direct connections with the Middle West of any great Atlantic port.

Local transportation consists of an immense system of surface electric railways, supplemented by both subway and elevated high-speed lines, together with an extensive steam and electric suburban service. Subways beneath Broad street, Ridge avenue, Eighth and Locust streets were constructed at a cost in excess of 140 million dollars.

Of numerous fine bridges, the most noteworthy are the Fairmount Avenue bridge, a double-deck truss structure completed in 1895, and the great Philadelphia-Camden bridge, over the Delaware river, which was completed in 1926 at a cost of nearly 25 million dollars.

Commerce. Philadelphia's high rank as a commercial city is primarily owing to its importance as a port; and its favorable location near vast supplies of raw materials has led to the development of immense industries. The city ranks among the leading ports of the United States in the value of its foreign commerce, and conducts a large coastwise trade, especially in oil and coal. Hog island was purchased from the Federal government by the city in 1930 to be made into a huge sea, rail, and air terminal.

Manufactures. Three factors have made Philadelphia a great manufacturing center—nearness to the sources of raw materials, its advantageous situation as the natural outlet of great coal and iron fields, and excellent transportation facilities. In total value of manufactured products, Philadelphia is surpassed only by New York and Chicago among American cities.

The city has the largest shipbuilding plant and, in the suburb of Eddystone, the largest locomotive works in the United States. The city leads in the quantity of rolling mill, foundry, and machine shop products, and in the manufacture of hats, carpets, and hosiery. In the production of woolen and worsted goods, leather goods, and saws, in the printing and publishing of books, newspapers, and periodicals, and in sugar refining, Philadelphia ranks among the chief manufacturing centers of the country. The League Island navy yard plant is valued at more than 100 million dollars and it includes one of the country's largest aircraft factories.

History. The earliest settlement within the limits of Philadelphia was made in 1636 by a company of Swedes. Late in 1681, William Markham, deputy governor for William Penn, organized an English settlement, and, in 1682, under Penn's supervision, the city was laid out and named. In 1683, a colony of Germans, invited by Penn, settled at Germantown, now a part of the city. In 1723, Benjamin Franklin came to Philadelphia, and in 1729 began the publication of the *Pennsylvania Gazette.* Philadelphia took a leading part in resisting British aggression, and the most important official events of the Revolutionary War occurred in the city. The battle of Germantown was fought in 1777. Philadelphia was occupied by British armies, 1777–78, while Washington's army was at Valley Forge.

Philadelphia was the capital of Pennsylvania from 1683 to 1799, was the seat of the Federal government, 1790–1800, and was the financial center of the country until 1836. The first daily newspaper in the United States, the *Pennsylvania Packet*, appeared in Philadelphia in 1784. The Centennial exposition, celebrating the centenary of American independence, was held in Fairmount park in 1876. Philadelphia is called the "Quaker City" and also the "City of Brotherly Love," the latter being the meaning of its name, which is Greek. A popular New Year festivity in Philadelphia is the Mummers parade, a survival from an Old-World custom with modifications coming from American pioneer life. Population, 1940, 1,931,334.

Phoenix. The capital and largest city of Arizona, in the south central part of the state, about 400 miles east of Los Angeles. Phoenix is the commercial center of the Salt River valley, the most productive agricultural region in the state. After the immense extension of irrigation following the construction of the Roosevelt dam in 1911, the city grew rapidly. Among the crops are Egyptian cotton, alfalfa, cereals, oranges, grapefruit, figs, olives, cantaloupes, strawberries, and winter head lettuce. The total value of the crops produced in Maricopa county, of which Phoenix is the county seat, far exceeds that of all the remainder of the state.

The city lies in a wide, irrigated plain surrounded by mountains. It has a mountain park of 14,000 acres 6 miles to the south. Its broad streets are ornamented with palms and other subtropical plants. Prominent public buildings are the capitol and the Carnegie library. By reason of its dry, salubrious climate, Phoenix is an important winter resort. In the vicinity are numerous points of interest, including Cactus park, petroglyphics, and the ruins of Aztec community houses. Phoenix was settled in 1870 and became the capital of the territory in 1889. Population, 1940, 65,414.

Piedmont. The name used in the United States to designate that part of the Atlantic plain which lies between the low, flat coastal plain and the true Appalachian highland. It consists chiefly of rolling, rugged lands with deeply eroded valleys. The rocks are a harder formation than those underlying the coastal plain. In consequence, there is a definite line of escarpments, over which most of the rivers descend in rapids or cataracts. This is known as the "fall line." The piedmont plain reaches its greatest extent in Virginia, South Carolina, and North Carolina, being about 300 miles wide in the latter state. The whole area is a rich agricultural and manufacturing district.

Pierre (*pēr*). The capital of South Dakota, situated on the Missouri river in the central part of the state. It is located in an agricultural and stock raising district and is an important cattle shipping center. Besides the capitol, Pierre has the State library, a Federal school for Indians, and a fine Federal building. The city's parks include the 1500-acre Farm island in the Missouri river. Fort Pierre, established in 1832, was for many years the chief fur trading post of the Upper Missouri River country. Pierre was laid out in 1880 and was incorporated in 1883. Population, 1940, 4322.

Pikes Peak. A mountain in Colorado, 14,108 feet high, situated in the easternmost range of the Rockies immediately west of Colorado Springs. It was discovered in 1806 by General Zebulon M. Pike of the United States army, and was first successfully ascended in 1819 by Major S. H. Long. In 1891, a cogwheel railway was completed to the summit, which is now reached also by a well constructed automobile road.

While not the highest mountain in Colorado, Pikes peak is one of the most majestic and imposing. Pine and spruce forests cover the slopes to an elevation of about 11,700 feet, above which there is a fringe of beautiful alpine flowering plants bordering the snow. The summit consists of bare granite rocks. The view from the top is one of unusual magnificence, including rugged mountains, vast plains, and numerous lakes and rivers in a landscape which extends 100 miles in all directions.

Pinehurst. A noted winter resort of southern North Carolina, about 60 miles southwest of Raleigh. It is 125 miles from the seacoast and 13½ hours ride by rail from New York City, and possesses a mild and equable climate. It was founded as a winter resort in 1895 by James W. Tufts, of Boston, and is famous for the beauty and excellence of its parks, bridle paths, polo grounds, golf links, tennis courts, and other facilities for recreation. The permanent residential population is about 1500, but the winter visitors number 10,000 or more annually.

PITTSBURGH. The second largest city of Pennsylvania and the tenth largest in the United States. It is situated at the junction of the Monongahela and Allegheny rivers, which here unite to form the Ohio. Pittsburgh lies in the southwestern part of the state, about 340 miles west of Philadelphia, and 430 miles west of New York.

Site. Pittsburgh occupies the most irregular and uneven site of any on which a great American city is built. The three rivers flow through deep narrow valleys and the highlands bordering upon them are broken into a large number of hills. These rise to heights of from 500 to 750 feet above the rivers and are separated by great ravines.

The Monongahela river, from the southeast, is joined by the Allegheny, from the northeast, and the Ohio river, formed by their union, flows northwesterly to the city limits. The chief business district and the greater part of the city lies between the Monongahela and the Allegheny. West of the Allegheny and north of the Ohio is the section which, before annexation, constituted the city of Allegheny. South of the Monongahela and the Ohio are the districts known as the South Side, Allentown, Mount Washington, Duquesne Heights, and the West End.

By annexation, there have been absorbed into the city more than 40 boroughs and townships. The names of many of these are still in common use locally, as, for example, Esplen, Beltzhoover, Sheraden, and Spring Garden.

Streets and Buildings. The narrow streets of the older districts still remain, but, in the newer and much larger sections, Pittsburgh is a distinctly modern city. Fifth and Sixth avenues, and Wood, Market, Federal, and Smithfield streets are important thoroughfares. Diamond street and Oliver avenue are new thoroughfares. The Boulevard of the Allies, a magnificent driveway overlooking the Monongahela, sweeps along the precipitous face of a cliff eastward from the business district to Forbes street, which leads to Schenley park. Penn avenue and lower Liberty avenue contain important retail stores, and Fourth avenue is the "Wall Street" of Pittsburgh. The most costly residences are found chiefly in the Bellefield, Shadyside, East Liberty, Homewood, and Squirrel Hill districts.

By reason of its extremely hilly site, Pittsburgh has perhaps more bridges and viaducts than any other city in the world. The city owns and maintains over 125, including the Liberty bridge, which connects the business section with the South Hills district via the Liberty tubes. These are twin tubes 5714 feet long and cost nearly $6,000,000 to construct. The Bloomfield bridge, spanning a deep valley between Herron Hill and the Bloomfield district, is nearly a mile long. The Larimer Avenue viaduct and the George Westinghouse bridge in East Pittsburgh have concrete arches ranking among the longest in America. Many inclined planes have been built to carry passengers and vehicles to higher levels. The Mount Washington incline lifts passengers 400 feet above the level of the old city to newer portions on the heights.

The commercial district, largely concentrated in "The Point," where the Monongahela and Allegheny rivers converge, is noted for its many fine office buildings of the skyscraper type, including the Grant, Koppers, and Gulf buildings. Other imposing structures are the courthouse, the Federal Building, Saint Paul's cathedral, and Trinity church.

Parks. The municipal park system includes 24 parks, covering a total area of more than 6000 acres. Of these, the finest is Schenley park containing, within its 422 acres, the Carnegie institute and library, and the Phipps conservatory. Highland park, covering 366 acres, commands a superb panoramic view of the Allegheny valley. In this park, which contains a large zoological garden, there is a memorial building to Stephen C. Foster, author of "Old Folks at Home," who was born and lived in Pittsburgh. At the entrance of Riverview park is the Allegheny observatory. Other noteworthy parks are McKinley, Grandview, and Allegheny. Highland and Schenley parks are connected by Washington boulevard.

Public Institutions. Foremost among the public institutions of Pittsburgh are the magnificent buildings of the Carnegie Institute, which includes library, museum, art gallery, and music hall. This beautiful structure, which covers nearly 6 acres, is built in the Italian Renaissance style. Memorial hall, containing a war museum and a large auditorium, is a notable structure. The Cathedral of Learning, a 40-story building 523 feet high and costing 6 million dollars, houses the University of Pittsburgh. The Phipps conservatory is one of the largest in America. All the above and many other buildings constitute a civic educational and social center at the entrance to Schenley park.

Education. The chief educational institutions of the city are the University of Pittsburgh, the Carnegie institute of technology, Duquesne university, the Pennsylvania college for women, the Mellon institute of industrial research, the Allegheny observatory, and the Buhl planetarium and institute of popular science, established in 1937.

Transportation. Transportation, provided by the rivers and by railroads, and abundant fuel, in the form of coal, petroleum, and natural gas from near-by fields, are some of the factors which have made the city of Pittsburgh one of the great "work shops of the world." The rivers afford connections with an immense system of inland waterways, including, not only those of the state, but also those of the Middle West and South. There is an extensive river traffic between Pittsburgh and Cincinnati, Saint Louis, and New Orleans. The city is served by five railways, and is within a night's railway ride of half of the population of the United States. Owing to the character of the commodities handled, largely coal, ores, and iron and steel products, the tonnage handled at Pittsburgh greatly exceeds that of any other city in the world.

Manufactures. Pittsburgh, long known as the "Steel City," is one of the leading centers of the world for the manufacture of iron and steel. About one-fifth of the pig iron and one-fourth of all the steel made in the western hemisphere are produced in the Pittsburgh district. Pittsburgh leads all other cities in the manufacture of steel rails, aluminum, pressed steel cars, iron pipe and tubing, and pressed steel plates for shipbuilding. The city is also the chief center in the country for the manufacture of coke, plate glass, window glass, and bottles, and produces a high quality of optical glass. Other important manufactures include aluminum wares, corks and cork products, pickles, bronze and copper wares, and refined petroleum.

History. In colonial times, the vicinity of Pittsburgh was the scene of many struggles with the French and Indians. In 1753, the site of Pittsburgh was visited by George Washington who regarded it "extremely well situated for a fort." The French and Indians, however, drove off the Virginians, and built Fort Duquesne. Endeavoring, in 1755, to capture it, Braddock, with a strong British force, met disastrous defeat. In 1758, General Forbes, marching from Philadelphia, took the fort, and, at Washington's suggestion, renamed it in honor of William Pitt. The Block House, built in 1759, the oldest building in the city, is preserved as a relic of colonial days. Pittsburgh was laid out in 1784, was incorporated in 1794, and became a city in 1816. Population, 1940, 671,659.

Pittsfield. A city of western Massachusetts, situated in the Berkshire valley, near Pontoosuc lake, with a background of fine mountain scenery. It is the largest city in the Berkshire Hills region, and is particularly noted for its wide, shaded streets, fine public buildings, and historic tradition. Its museum of natural history and fine arts contains the "one hoss shay," made famous by Oliver Wendell Holmes's poem. Holmes and Longfellow resided for a time at Pittsfield, and H. W. Shaw ("Josh Billings") lived near by. The city's industries produce plastics, transformers, bank note paper, textiles, machine tools, and silk. Population, 1940, 49,684.

Plymouth. A town on Plymouth harbor, Massachusetts, about 37 miles southeast of Boston. Founded by the Pilgrim Fathers in 1620, it is the oldest town in New England. Plymouth Rock, on which the Pilgrims are said to have landed, is preserved under a beautiful portico. Pilgrim hall contains many interesting relics and historical paintings. The city is a port of entry, has varied local manufactures, including one of the largest cordage factories in the world, and ships large quantities of cranberries grown in the vicinity. Population, 1940, 13,100.

Pocatello (*pō'kȧ-tĕl'ō*). A city of southeastern Idaho, about 170 miles north of Salt Lake City, Utah. Pocatello is situated in a region largely arid and volcanic but highly productive by reason of irrigation. The city's industries consist largely of processing farm and dairy products. Pocatello is the seat of the University of Idaho Southern. Population, 1940, 18,133.

Pontiac. A city of southeastern Michigan, on the Clinton river, about 25 miles northwest of Detroit. Pontiac is the trade center of a rich farming and dairying region, and has developed extensive industries. The chief manufactures include automobiles, automobile accessories and parts, trucks, buses, paints and varnishes, drop forgings, tools, and machine shop products. Pontiac was settled in 1818, was incorporated in 1837, and, in 1861, was chartered as a city. It was named after the Indian chief. Population, 1940, 66,626.

Port Arthur. A seaport of southeastern Texas, situated on Sabine lake, 12 miles from the Gulf of Mexico. Port Arthur is one of the largest oil refining centers in the United States. Since the completion of the Port Arthur ship canal, affording passage for large ocean vessels to its fine landlocked harbor, Port Arthur has become a leading port. The Neches river is spanned there by the Port Arthur-Orange bridge, costing $3,000,000. The city is the seat of Port Arthur college. Population, 1940, 46,140.

Portland. The commercial metropolis of Maine, located on Casco bay, 108 miles northeast of Boston. It is built on two peninsulas, some encircling territory on the mainland, and islands totaling 2585 acres. Portland is an important seaport and possesses one of the finest harbors on the Atlantic coast. It occupies a picturesque site, with handsome buildings and streets closely bordered with trees. Its industries are extensive and varied, including iron forging, shoe manufacturing, cod and mackerel fishing, the canning of fish and vegetables, and lumber milling. Longfellow was born here. Population, 1940, 73,643.

Portland. The chief city of Oregon, situated on the Willamette river, about 12 miles from its junction with the Columbia, and approximately 100 miles by water from the Pacific Ocean. It occupies a commanding site on the sloping banks of the river, with the snow-capped peaks of Mount Hood, Saint Helens, and Mount Adams in the background to the eastward.

Portland owes its growth and importance to great natural advantages of situation. It is surrounded by highly fertile valleys and heavily timbered mountains, and has an excellent fresh-water harbor with 27 miles of deep water frontage. The exports consist mainly of grain, flour, lumber, and salmon.

In manufactures, Portland ranks among the leading cities of the Pacific states, its favorable situation enabling it to utilize vast resources of hydroelectric power, as well as natural gas. Among important manufactures are lumber, pulp, paper, clothing, automobile tires, and flour. The city's industries include also fruit canning and meat packing.

The city contains many imposing public buildings, including an auditorium seating 5500 and a stadium to seat 25,000, and is noted for its fine residences. It is the seat of Reed college and several schools of the University of Oregon besides various other educational institutions. Among features of interest are Council Crest, affording a panoramic view of the city and its surroundings; Terwilliger boulevard on the west side of the city; Willamette boulevard on the east side; and Washington park, containing famous rose gardens and a fine statue of Sacagawea, a Shoshone Indian woman who guided the Lewis and Clark expedition. The environs of the city are reached by numerous scenic roads, including the famous Columbia River Highway, which extends 120 miles east, and 110 miles west to the sea. Portland is called the "Rose City." Its Rose Festival is a beautiful annual pageant.

Settlers from New England founded the city in 1844, naming it after Portland, Maine. Population, 1940, 305,-394.

Portsmouth (*pōrts'mŭth*). The only seaport of New Hampshire, built near the mouth of the Piscataqua river, opposite the Maine boundary, about 60 miles north of Boston. The city carries on a substantial coastwise trade, especially in coal, and has various local manufactures. Portsmouth was settled in 1623, and incorporated in 1849. It is a quiet city with a quaint, old-fashioned appearance, and contains many fine colonial houses rich in historic and literary interest. The Portsmouth navy yard, on an island in the river, is situated within the boundaries of Maine. In 1905, the Treaty of Portsmouth, ending the Russo-Japanese war, was signed in the "Peace Building" on Leavey's island. Population, 1940, 14,821.

Portsmouth. A city of southern Ohio, built on the north bank of the Ohio river, at the mouth of the Scioto river, about 80 miles south of Columbus. It is protected from floods by a concrete wall 62 feet above normal water stage. The city is located in an agricultural and mining region, of which it is the commercial center. In the vicinity are valuable deposits of fire clay, which is extensively manufactured into brick. Other important manufactures are steel and lumber products, shoes, airplanes, and furniture. Portsmouth was founded in 1803 and became a city in 1814. In the Scioto valley, north of the city, are interesting remains of the ancient Mound Builders. Population, 1940, 40,466.

Portsmouth. A seaport of southeastern Virginia, occupying the mainland side of the important harbor of Norfolk-Portsmouth. Here the larger railway systems of the South have deep-water terminals and are connected with Norfolk, just across the harbor, by passenger and railroad car ferries. An immense tonnage, both foreign and domestic, passes through the port of Norfolk-Portsmouth. This consists chiefly of cotton, coal, lumber, fruits, vegetables, oysters, fertilizers, grain, coffee, and peanuts. This port is the greatest peanut market in the world. There are extensive industries, including railroad shops, fertilizer works, barrel factories, cottonseed oil mills, and lumber mills.

A few blocks south of the center of Portsmouth is the navy yard, officially known as the Norfolk navy yard. This occupies 350 acres, contains immense dry docks, and is the most important naval establishment in the United States. Population, 1940, 50,745.

Poughkeepsie (*pō-kĭp'sĭ*). A city in New York State on the east bank of the Hudson river, about 75 miles north of New York City. It is picturesquely situated on high ground commanding a fine view of the Hudson river, which is here crossed by two magnificent bridges. The city conducts an extensive local trade. The chief manufactures include farm machinery, ball bearing, cough drops, and cigars. Poughkeepsie is the seat of Vassar college. Population, 1940, 40,478.

Princeton. A university town of central New Jersey, about 50 miles southwest of New York City. Founded in 1696, Princeton remained a straggling village until the College of New Jersey, now Princeton university, was removed, in 1756, from Newark to Princeton. It soon became a center of higher education and has remained distinctly a university town. Early in 1777, the battle of Princeton was fought in the vicinity. From June to November, 1783, Congress sat in Princeton. The town is built on an elevated site, commanding fine views of the surrounding country. It has broad, well shaded streets, and the architecture of its colonial period has been largely preserved. Besides the university, Princeton is also the seat of Princeton theological seminary, the Institute for Advanced Study, and the Rockefeller institute for medical research. The newer business section is built around Palmer square. Population, 1940, 7719.

Providence. The capital of Rhode Island, and the second largest city of New England. It is situated on Narragansett bay, about 45 miles southwest of Boston. The city has excellent railway facilities and a fine harbor.

While maintaining a substantial coastwise shipping trade, Providence is pre-eminently an industrial city, with extensive and varied manufactures. It is a leading center for the manufacture of jewelry, and for similar articles requiring a high degree of artistic skill. Among other important industrial products are abrasives, chemicals, precision tools, plastics, knit goods, pens, pencils, textiles, and textile machinery.

The city is substantially built, and contains many fine parks and public buildings, including an imposing civic center and the beautiful Roger Williams park. Brown university, chartered in 1764, and other important institutions are located in the city. Providence was founded and named in 1636 by Roger Williams, and here, in 1639, he organized the first Baptist church in America. Population, 1940, 253,504.

Provincetown. A small town in Massachusetts, at the extreme outer edge of Cape Cod Bay, known to history as the first landing point to which the Pilgrims came in November of 1620, and the place where the Mayflower Compact was signed before the settlers sailed on to Plymouth. Once a thriving center of the whaling trade, the town is still engaged mainly in fishing industries, particularly in the marketing of cod and mackerel. In recent years, Provincetown has become well known as a gathering place for various artist groups, who make up a considerable part of its summer population. Some years ago, through the Provincetown Players, it gained fame as a proving ground for budding playwrights, of whom probably the best known were Susan Glaspell and Eugene O'Neill.

Provo. A city of north central Utah, picturesquely situated in a fertile valley at the foot of the Wasatch mountains, 44 miles south of Salt Lake City. Provo is the trade center of a rich irrigated district devoted to agriculture, fruit growing, and stock raising, and is the seat of Brigham Young university. Population, 1940, 18,071.

Pueblo (*pwĕb'lō*). The second largest commercial and industrial city in Colorado, located on the Arkansas river, about 120 miles south of Denver. Pueblo has immense iron and steel works, and is conveniently near a region rich in coal and oil. The city has also various other manufactories and extensive stockyards. There are many fine public buildings, including the State mineral palace. Population, 1940, 52,162.

Quincy (*kwĭn'sĭ*). A manufacturing city of western Illinois, on the Mississippi river, about 110 miles northwest of Saint Louis. Built on the sides of a limestone bluff, Quincy overlooks an enchanting panorama of river, valley, and surrounding hills. The city is the commercial center of a rich agricultural region, and its chief industries include flour mills, machine shops, foundries, and the manufacture of agricultural implements, power pumps, incubators, and elevators. There are numerous fine parks, boulevards, and public buildings. The Mississippi is spanned here by a great bridge. Population, 1940, 40,469.

Quincy (*kwĭn'zĭ*). A city of eastern Massachusetts, situated on Quincy bay, about 8 miles south of Boston. While essentially a residential suburb of Boston, Quincy has a large granite quarrying industry, and also huge shipyards, engine works, brass and iron works, rivet mills, and soap and aluminum factories. The city contains many fine streets and homes, and the park system covers 2614 acres.

Settled in 1625 as Mount Wollaston, Quincy ranks among the oldest permanent settlements in New England. Until 1792, when the community was incorporated under its present name, it was a part of Braintree. The first railway in America was constructed here 1826–27 to transport granite used in building Bunker Hill monument. Quincy enjoys the distinction of being the birthplace of two presidents, John Adams and John Quincy Adams, and also of John Hancock. Population, 1940, 75,810.

Racine. A manufacturing city of southeastern Wisconsin, located on a fine harbor on Lake Michigan, 65 miles north of Chicago. In value of its manufactures, Racine ranks second only to Milwaukee among the cities of the state, and is noted especially for the manufacture of threshing machines and farm implements. Other important manufactures include automobiles, machine shop products, furniture, hardware, and electrical equipment. Washington park, the largest in the city's system of 635 acres, contains a $300,000 swimming pool. Population, 1940, 67,195.

Rainier (*rā-nēr'*), **Mount.** The loftiest peak in the Cascade range, situated in southwestern Washington about 50 miles southeast of Tacoma. It rises to an elevation of 14,408 feet, overtopping all other summits in the Pacific states except Mount Whitney in California.

Like Fuji in Japan, Mount Rainier rises majestically in graceful lines that proclaim its volcanic origin. Its summit lies in perpetual snow and on its upper slopes there are numerous glaciers. These are from 50 to 500 feet thick and cover a total area of about 50 square miles, the largest expanse of ice fields around any single mountain in the country. Some of these glaciers are from 4 to 6 miles long, and in size and beauty rival those of the Alps.

The lower slopes of the mountain are clothed with luxuriant forests, containing trees of unusual size. Above the forests, which extend to an elevation of about 7000 feet, are many picturesque mountain meadows. In summer, these bear a profusion of beautiful alpine flowers that follow the retreating snow banks almost up to the line of perpetual frost. The summit rises about 8000 feet above the general level of the Cascades and affords excellent views of the Puget Sound region. In order to preserve its fine scenic features and make them readily accessible to the traveler, Mount Rainier, in 1899, was created a national park.

Raleigh (*rô'lĭ*). The capital of North Carolina, situated in the central part of the state. Raleigh is a large cotton and tobacco market and has varied industries, the manufacture of textiles, fertilizers, and cottonseed oil being among the more important. The city contains some 13 park areas, including Pullen park, a 74-acre semiforest tract of exceptional beauty. Near by, on the campus of State college, is the house in which Andrew Johnson was born. The city's streets are wide and, for the most part, lined with beautiful shade trees. Among the more notable buildings are the state capitol on grounds covering four acres, the Federal Post Office and Court building, the state agricultural building, Sir Walter hotel, Christ church, and the municipal auditorium. Raleigh is the seat of North Carolina college of agriculture and engineering. The site of the city was selected for the state capital in 1792, and the city was founded in the same year. Population, 1940, 46,897.

Reading (*rĕd'ĭng*). A city of southeastern Pennsylvania, on the Schuylkill river, 58 miles northwest of Philadelphia. Situated in a rich agricultural region and near large fields of anthracite coal and iron ore, Reading possesses unusual commercial and industrial advantages. The chief industry is the manufacture of textile products, especially full-fashioned hosiery. Iron and steel manufacture comes second, followed by the making of food and tobacco products, paint, shoes, and other commodities. Other industries include railway car shops, machine shops, and the manufacture of shoes, tobacco, automobile parts, paints, and confectionery.

Reading occupies a picturesque site between the base of Mount Penn and the Schuylkill river. The many fine parks and public buildings include a public museum and art gallery maintained by the public school system. The summits of Mount Penn, to the east, and Neversink mountain, to the south, both rise to elevations of about 800 feet and command magnificent views. The city was laid out in 1748 in accordance with the plans of Thomas and Richard Penn, sons of William Penn. The early inhabitants were mostly German, the influence of whom is seen in choral societies and a symphony orchestra. Population, 1940, 110,568.

Redlands. A city of southern California, picturesquely situated in the foothills of the San Bernardino mountains, about 65 miles east of Los Angeles. Redlands is a noted residential city, health resort, and educational center, in the heart of an immensely productive orange growing district. Smiley Heights, one of the city's numerous parks, affords a magnificent view of the surrounding region, embracing orange and lemon groves, grain fields, forests, and snow-capped mountains. The city is the seat of the University of Redlands. Population, 1940, 14,324.

Reno. The chief commercial and industrial city of Nevada, located near the western boundary of the state, about 30 miles northwest of Carson City. Reno lies in a sheltered valley near the eastern base of the Sierra Nevada at an elevation of 4500 feet. It is on the Truckee river, which feeds the Truckee-Carson canal, a government irrigation project which waters more than 100,000 acres. The city is the distributing center of an extensive region devoted to mining, farming, and stock raising. Among the industrial establishments are ore reduction works, flour mills, lumber mills, and large railway shops. The University of Nevada and the Mackay school of mines are located here. Population, 1940, 21,317.

Richmond. The capital and largest city of Virginia, located at the head of navigation on the James river, about 100 miles almost directly south of Washington. Richmond is an important railway center, and has direct steamer connections with Atlantic coast ports. It is a leading tobacco market and one of the chief manufacturing centers of the South. The foremost industry is the manufacture of tobacco in various forms. Others include the manufacture of iron and steel, agricultural implements, and machine shop products.

The city occupies a commanding site, covering seven hills, and is sometimes styled the "Modern Rome." It is regularly laid out, rising in terraces from the river. There are many beautiful parks and imposing public buildings. Among the most noteworthy of the latter is the capitol, designed after the Maison Carrée at Nimes, France, and built 1785–92. The city possesses many fine monumental and sculptural works, including the equestrian statue of Washington at Capitol square.

Richmond is exceedingly rich in historic associations, and in colonial days, like Boston in New England, it played a prominent part in shaping the destinies of the country. In Saint John's Episcopal church, in March 1775, Patrick Henry made his noted speech containing the famous exclamation, "Give me liberty or give me death!" From May 8, 1861, to April 2, 1865, it was the capital of the Confederate states. The executive mansion, occupied by Jefferson Davis, 1862–65, has been transformed into a Confederate museum. The former residence of John Marshall, built in 1795, still stands, and the Lee mansion, occupied by General R. E. Lee's family during the Civil War, is occupied by the Virginia Historical Society. Richmond was established as a town in 1733, and chartered as a city in 1782. Population, 1940, 193,042.

Riverside. An important orange growing and poultry center of southern California, situated on the Santa Ana river, 53 miles east of Los Angeles. Riverside occupies a gently sloping site and is noted for its wide streets lined with palms, eucalypti, and roses and lighted with distinctive "Indian rain cross" lights. Many handsome avenues and driveways lead into the surrounding orange groves, alfalfa fields, and fig orchards. The city conducts a substantial local trade, has large Portland cement works, and ships annually from its warehouses many thousand carloads of oranges. Riverside is widely known for its unique hotel, the Mission inn. This contains a treasure house of interesting exhibits of historic value connected with the early Mission days of California. Riverside is the seat of Sherman institute, a United States Indian school. Population, 1940, 34,696.

Roanoke. An industrial city of southwestern Virginia on the Roanoke river, about 140 miles west of Richmond. The city is located in a picturesque valley between the Blue Ridge and the Allegheny mountains. As a center for the distribution of electric power, it affords ample facilities for the development of the city's extensive industries, which include rayon mills and car shops. In the vicinity are mineral springs of high medicinal value. The city with its environs is widely known as a health resort. It is the seat of Roanoke college. Population, 1940, 69,287.

Rochester. A city of southeastern Minnesota, on the Zumbro river, about 80 miles southeast of Saint Paul. It is the trade center of a rich agricultural district and has substantial industries. The city is the seat of Saint Mary's hospital and of the Mayo clinic, founded by the distinguished surgeons, Charles and William Mayo. The 19-story building which houses this clinic has, in its tower, a 23-bell carillon as a memorial "To the American Soldier." Population, 1940, 26,312.

Rochester. A city of west central New York, built on both banks of the Genesee river, at the Genesee falls, and extending to Lake Ontario. Rochester ranks third in population, and third also in manufactures, among the cities of the state. Factors which have contributed to its eminence as an industrial center are abundant power, derived from the falls of the river, and excellent transportation facilities afforded by Lake Ontario, the State barge canal, numerous steam railways, and electric and bus interurban lines. It has a port on Lake Ontario and a subway utilizing the abandoned bed of a canal.

The city's extensive manufactures embrace more than 350 different commodities. These are produced in upwards of 1700 factories and consist largely of articles requiring the employment of a high degree of mechanical skill. Rochester leads the world in the production of cameras and photographic supplies. Among other important manufactures are men's clothing, boots and shoes, cutlery, machine tools, electrical machinery, optical instruments, thermometers, flour, canned fruits, furniture, and refined petroleum. Rochester stands first among the cities of the United States as a nursery-garden and seed-distributing center.

Rochester occupies a nearly level site and is divided into two almost equal parts by the Genesee river, which is spanned by 12 bridges, some of which are 200 feet high. In the center of the city is the Upper falls, 96 feet in height; below them the river flows in a deep gorge to the Lower falls, 80 feet high. There are many fine streets and avenues, and the residential sections are especially attractive. The park system, covering nearly 2000 acres in 12 units, is one of the most beautiful in America. It includes a 4-mile frontage on Lake Ontario and some of the most picturesque stretches of the Genesee river.

The city is the seat of the University of Rochester, Saint Bernard's seminary, the Mechanic's institute, and other important educational institutions, and affords exceptional advantages for the study and enjoyment of art and music, particularly at the Eastman school of music and the beautiful Eastman theater.

First permanently settled in 1812, Rochester was incorporated as a village in 1817 and chartered as a city in 1834. The completion, in 1825, of the Erie canal greatly stimulated the city's growth. During the early period, when the Genesee valley was the chief wheat belt of the country, Rochester was known as the "Flour City." With the decline of milling and the rise of the nursery industry this sobriquet was changed to the "Flower City." Since the development of its great camera and photographic supply business, it has been styled the "Kodak City." Population, 1940, 324,975.

Rockford. A manufacturing city of Illinois, on the Rock river, about 90 miles northwest of Chicago. Abundant power, furnished by a great dam in the river, is utilized in its large and varied industries. Among these are the manufacture of machine tools, farm implements, furniture, hosiery, and hardware. The city is the seat of Rockford college. A park in the center of the city contains the Turtle Indian mound. First settled in 1834, Rockford was chartered as a city in 1852. Population, 1940, 84,637.

Rock Island. A city of western Illinois, on the Mississippi river, adjoining Moline, and opposite Davenport, Iowa, with which it is connected by bridges including the four-lane Centennial bridge. These three cities with East Moline are called the Quad-City area. The city takes its name from an island in the river opposite the upper section of the town. Abundant hydroelectric power, provided by a government dam, has aided in the development of the city's substantial industries, which include the manufacture of agricultural implements, rubber footwear, paint, and plumbing supplies. An immense government arsenal, the most extensive in the United States, is located on the island. Rock Island was chartered as a city in 1841. Population, 1940, 42,775.

ROCKY MOUNTAIN PARK. An area of about 405 square miles in the heart of the Rocky mountains, reserved as a national park in 1915. It is in north central Colorado about 50 miles northwest of Denver. It is traversed by the continental divide, which here rises to a height of over 14,000 feet and provides scenery of unsurpassed grandeur.

SIZE AND SURFACE. The park extends about 25 miles north and south, and from 12 to 20 miles from east to west. Altitudes within it range from 8000 to 14,255 feet above sea level, the highest point being Longs peak, in the southeastern portion of the park, a mountain of the Snowy range. This range follows a general north and south direction. On its west side this mountain chain slopes gently down in a lovely region diversified by streams and charming lakes, the largest and deepest being Grand lake. The eastern slope, however, is precipitous and awe-inspiring, bold summits standing out in daring relief separated by gorges with walls often 1000 to 2000 feet high. In the northern portion of the park are several peaks over 13,000 feet in height, including Hagues peak and Mummy and Ypsilon mountains. Mount Copeland at the extreme south also exceeds 13,000 feet in altitude.

GLACIERS. There are few places in the earth where the effects of glacial erosion can be seen and understood so easily as in Rocky Mountain park. Andrews glacier is the largest of those which still exist, but numerous huge moraines attest the stupendous force of these mountain-carving agents in past ages, when they were vastly more extensive. At Moraine park is a ridge 800 feet high marking the lower edge of an ice-age glacier which crept down from Forest canyon. The Mills moraine, at the foot of Longs Peak precipice, is 1000 feet high and four miles long. Glaciers still active seldom extend below an altitude of 12,000 feet. The timber line is reached about 11,000 feet above sea level.

TRAVEL FACILITIES. There are four principal approaches to Rocky Mountain park, three from the east converging at the hotel village of Estes park, and one western approach known as the Grand Lake route. The eastern approaches are from the railroad points Loveland, Lyons, and Ward, at which railroad tourists may transfer to motor coaches. Motor highways also give access to the park from Denver, Boulder, and Grand Junction over these same approaches.

The park has nearly 200 miles of trails, but the principal scenic road is the Fall River highway, which connects the western approach *via* Grand Lake with Estes park. Following the crest of the continental divide for about three miles at an altitude of 11,800 feet, it is one of the highest roads in North America. It commands superb views of mountain peaks, chasms, waterfalls, glaciers, and mountain lakes.

ANIMALS. Rocky Mountain park contains many bighorns, which particularly frequent Bighorn mountain, descending daily to drink from Sheep lake in Horseshoe park. Beavers are numerous, and much land on valley floors is marshy by reason of dams built by these animals. Deer abound and there are a number of bears. The streams and lakes are stocked with fish from a hatchery in Estes park.

Royal Gorge. The deepest part of the Grand Canyon of the Arkansas river. It is situated in central Colorado, 45 miles west of Pueblo. The entire canyon, about 8 miles long, has precipitous walls of eroded granite which rise to an immense height. In the portion a mile and a half long called the Royal Gorge, these titanic walls tower almost perpendicularly 2600 feet above the foaming torrent of the river. At the narrowest part, the stream fills the canyon nearly from wall to wall, and the railway passes through it over a bridge hung from transverse girders mortised into the rocks of both sides of the canyon. This picturesque passage is the gateway to western Colorado.

Sacramento. The capital of California, located on the Sacramento river 90 miles northeast of San Francisco. Sacramento lies in the midst of a very rich farming and fruit growing region, and the most important of the city's varied industries is the canning of fruit. Among the other establishments are large railroad shops; flour, rice, and lumber mills; meat packing houses; and a huge air corps supply depot of the army. The city is built on the site of Sutter's Fort, the first settlement in California reached by the gold seekers of 1849 and 1850. The fort, rebuilt, houses relics of the pioneer days.

The handsome capitol, completed in 1869, and two recent state buildings form a striking 8-million dollar group in a beautiful 38-acre park in the center of the city. The park system covers about 1200 acres, the largest unit being Del Paso park of 828 acres. Sacramento was incorporated in 1849 and became the state capital in 1854. Population, 1940, 105,958.

Sagamore Hill. The country estate and residence of Theodore Roosevelt, situated near the town of Oyster Bay, on the northern shore of Long Island, about 30 miles northeast of New York City. The substantial but unostentatious house stands on high ground and commands a charming view. For many years it was the cherished home of the great champion of the strenuous life and the Mecca of his admiring friends. Following his death in 1919, it became the residence of his son, Theodore Roosevelt. Young's Memorial cemetery, which contains the grave of the former president, is also situated at the town of Oyster Bay.

Saginaw. A city of southeastern Michigan, built at the head of navigation on the Saginaw river, 85 miles northwest of Detroit. The city lies in rich coal and oil fields and has immense supplies of hydroelectric power. There are many salt wells in the vicinity. Its industries produce, among other commodities, automobiles and parts, foundry and machine shop products, furniture, phonographs, coal, beet sugar, and oil. Saginaw has extensive car shops. There are several fine parks, and many handsome public buildings, including hospitals and educational institutions. Population, 1940, 82,794.

Saint Augustine (*ô'gŭs-tēn'*). The oldest city in the United States, situated on the east coast of Florida, about 30 miles southeast of Jacksonville. Saint Augustine was founded in 1565 by the Spanish under Pedro Menendez de Aviles, sent by Philip II of Spain. With the exception of 20 years, 1763–83, when it was in the hands of the British, Saint Augustine remained a Spanish city until 1821, when the United States acquired Florida. In the old part of the town, the quaint, narrow streets are lined with ancient houses built of the shell material known as coquina. Many of these houses have overhanging balconies and are set amid gardens luxuriant with semitropical vegetation.

Among the many historic buildings are Fort Marion, the oldest fort in the United States, begun in 1656; the remodeled governor's palace; and the famous city gates. Saint Augustine is a noted winter resort and contains many fine hotels. Among these are the Alcazar and the palatial Ponce de Leon hotel, built in the Spanish Renaissance style. Population, 1940, 12,090.

Saint Joseph. The third largest city of Missouri, built on the east bank of the Missouri river, about 60 miles north of Kansas City. The city lies picturesquely along the bluffs of the river. It is the center of a rich agricultural region with which it carries on a large merchandising and marketing trade. Saint Joseph is one of the leading live stock markets of the country, and contains several meat packing establishments. Its chief manufactures are packing-house products and flour products, including pancake flour. Other important manufactures include clothing, candy, harness, and cereals. Parks occupy about 1350 acres. A park about the civic center has a pony express monument, commemorating this service which began in 1860 between St. Joseph and Sacramento, Cal. Saint Joseph was first settled in 1826 by Joseph Robidoux, a French fur trader; it was incorporated in 1845 and became a city in 1851. Population, 1940, 75,711.

SAINT LOUIS (*lōō'ĭs*). The chief city of Missouri, and the eighth largest in the United States, situated on the Mississippi river, about 20 miles below the mouth of the Missouri. Chicago lies about 280 miles to the northeast, Kansas City about 260 miles west, Minneapolis about 600 miles north, and New Orleans about 700 miles south, of the city.

SITE. Saint Louis occupies a commanding site, rising in a succession of gently sloping hills and depressions, each ridge toward the west ascending higher and finally reaching, at the western limits, an elevation of some 300 feet above the river. The boundaries are two curved lines, the crescent-like bend of the Mississippi on the east and an arbitrary boundary on the west. The total frontage on the river is more than 19 miles, the length of the western boundary is about 21 miles, and the maximum width is nearly 7 miles. The total area slightly exceeds 61 square miles.

STREETS AND BUILDINGS. In the small, older portion of the city, the streets are narrow and more or less irregular. The modern parts of the city have been laid out, wherever possible, with wide streets, crossing at right angles, and in north-and-south and east-and-west directions.

Important east-and-west thoroughfares are Washington avenue, Locust street, and Olive street, with Easton avenue to the north. Lindell boulevard, diverging from Olive street near Grand boulevard, is the chief east-and-west boulevard. Chouteau avenue runs also east-and-west through the city to Forest park. Broadway follows the curve of the Mississippi from the extreme south to the northern limit of the city. Grand and Kings highway boulevards are important north-and-south boulevards, extending also the full length of the city. The Union boulevard route forms another extensive north-and-south boulevard, as does the Skinker and McCausland-River des Peres drive, skirting the western limits of the city. A depressed high-speed motor way extends three miles from the city's center to its outskirts.

Diagonal thoroughfares from the business center to the city boundaries are provided for over Twelfth street and Gravois avenue to the southwest, and over Twelfth street and Natural Bridge avenue to the northwest.

The Old cathedral on Walnut street is the most noteworthy example of the French period in the history of Saint Louis. Among the many notable modern buildings are the city hall, which resembles an old French hôtel de ville; the Union station, in Renaissance style; the buildings of Washington university, in Tudor Gothic style; the public library, built of Maine granite in the early Italian Renaissance style, and the art museum and the Jefferson memorial, in the classic style. Other noteworthy structures are the immense Saint Louis cathedral, distinctly Romanesque; the Protestant Episcopal cathedral, in modified Gothic; and the impressive Shaare Emeth synagogue. A group of imposing buildings on Lindell boulevard includes the Masonic temple, the Shriners' Moolah temple, and the Scottish Rite cathedral. The tallest buildings include the civil courts building and the 31-story Southwestern Bell Telephone building.

No city in America excels Saint Louis in the beauty of its exclusive residential districts, called "places." In these are magnificent homes with spacious grounds reflecting the highest skill of the architect and the landscape gardener. Washington Terrace, Westmoreland, Kingsbury, and Portland rank among the most noted of the places. Other fine residence sections are found in Compton Heights, Hortense place, Parkview, and in Hillcrest, and also along Forsythe and Lindell boulevards.

Saint Louis is distinctively a city of brick, and, with few exceptions, even the most elaborate mansions are built of this material. Owing to comparative cheapness of local building materials, especially brick and limestone, a very large percentage of the inhabitants of the city live in separate homes.

Civic Improvements. A unique recreation facility is the Open Air Municipal theater, with a seating capacity of 10,000, located in Forest park. A civic center on a memorial plaza, occupying 9 city blocks in the downtown section, accommodates an auditorium and other municipal buildings. A 37-block river front area was cleared for a great memorial to Thomas Jefferson and the Louisiana Purchase.

Parks. The city has 68 parks, covering an area of more than 3000 acres. Forest park, the largest, containing 1381 acres, lies almost directly west of the business center. Other important recreation grounds are the Missouri botanical garden, Tower Grove, O'Fallon, Carondelet, and Lafayette parks. Several of the parks are ornamented with noteworthy works of sculpture. There are fine statues of Shakspere, Columbus, Humboldt, Schiller, Thomas Jefferson, and of Saint Louis, the crusader king of France, for whom the city was named.

Educational Institutions. Among the leading educational institutions are Washington university, Saint Louis university, Christian Brothers college and Concordia and Eden seminaries. The Missouri botanical garden, founded by Henry Shaw and usually called Shaw's garden, is now maintained for the public. It contains a fine arboretum and a collection of native and foreign plants, especially orchids, rivaling in number and variety those of the Kew gardens in London.

Transportation. Two great advantages have made Saint Louis pre-eminent as a commercial and industrial center. The first is its location in the heart of the great Mississippi valley, the most fertile agricultural region in the world. The second lies in its unsurpassed facilities for transportation. Barge lines handle an immense tonnage passing between Saint Paul and Minneapolis on the north and New Orleans on the south, and a great network of railways radiates from Saint Louis throughout an immensely productive region.

Commerce. Saint Louis is the most important distributing center of the Mississippi valley, handling products representing the entire country. It is a great grain, live stock, horse, tobacco, and wool market and conducts an immense wholesaling trade, especially in dry goods, hardware, boots and shoes, lumber, drugs, and electrical machinery.

Manufactures. In value of manufactures, Saint Louis ranks among the nine leading cities of the United States. Its extensive industries embrace the manufacture of an exceedingly wide range of products. It is one of the greatest shoe and tobacco manufacturing centers of the United States. Other important manufactures include packed meats, coke, blast furnace, foundry, machine shop, and rolling mill products, refined petroleum, clothing, chemicals, medicinal compounds, locomotive parts, railway supplies, railway and street cars, jute goods, hot-air furnaces, stoves, clay products, automobiles, dresses, and furniture.

History. Saint Louis was established in 1764 as a fur trading station by Pierre Laclède Liguest, assisted by Auguste Chouteau. Though under the control of Spain from 1770 to 1804, the place remained essentially French. In 1804, Saint Louis came into the possession of the United States by the Louisiana Purchase. The first newspaper was published in 1808, and, with the arrival of the first steamboat in 1815, a new era in the history of Saint Louis was opened. From 1840 to 1880, it passed 38 other American cities in population, and was passed by only one—Chicago. In 1904, the Louisiana Purchase exposition was held in the city, and, in 1914, a great historic pageant and masque was presented in Forest park. A feature of interest is the annual festival of the Veiled Prophet, somewhat similar to the Mardi Gras of New Orleans. Population, 1940, 816,048.

Saint Paul. The capital and second largest city of Minnesota, built on both banks of the Mississippi river, immediately below Minneapolis. A part of the western boundary of Saint Paul is contiguous with the eastern limits of Minneapolis, but the commercial centers of these "Twin Cities" are about 10 miles apart.

The city is built chiefly on the left or east bank of the Mississippi, and occupies three terraces, rising in all from 100 to 200 feet above the river. The lowest section contains railway yards, stock yards, wholesale houses, and factories. Lying above this, on the middle terrace, is the commercial district and a part of the residential section. On the uppermost terrace, crowning the highest bluffs, is the fine residence section; Summit Avenue boulevard, 200 feet wide and extending along the heights for 2½ miles, is a noted residential street.

Saint Paul is admirably laid out, with many handsome streets, among the most scenic of which are Kellogg boulevard and Summit drive. The various parks, playgrounds, and connecting boulevards cover a total area of more than 2240 acres. In Como and Phalen parks there are picturesque lakes. Indian Mound park affords unsurpassed views of the Mississippi river.

Foremost among the city's notable buildings is the beautiful State capitol, constructed of marble and granite and containing many fine sculptural and mural decorations. Other fine structures are the Roman Catholic cathedral, the Hill Memorial library, the Minnesota Historical building, and the Union railway station, completed in 1926 at a cost of 15 million dollars. The beautiful buildings and grounds of the Minnesota Agricultural Society are at the northern end of the city. The annual state fair held here is one of the largest in the United States.

Within the city are several important educational institutions, including Hamline university, Macalester college, Concordia college, Saint Thomas college, and the Saint Paul college of law.

Saint Paul enjoys exceptional transportation facilities, both by rail and by river. On the completion of extensive canalization work in the Mississippi river, a barge service was opened in 1928. For a long period prior to this the river had scarcely been used for freight transfer although it had earlier been the main artery of commerce.

The city is one of the great wholesale and jobbing centers of the country, with a total annual trade exceeding 500 million dollars. The city is also an important market for live stock and, in manufactures, ranks second among the cities of the state. Prominent among the city's manufactures are railway cars, boots and shoes, fur goods, refrigerators, cordage and twine, law books, automobiles, glass, butter, and packed meats.

Settled in 1839, Saint Paul was made the territorial capital in 1849, and, upon the admission of Minnesota into the Union in 1858, was made the capital of the state. From about 1870, following the extensive building of railways and the settlement of the Northwest, the city grew rapidly. Population, 1940, 287,736.

Saint Petersburg. A summer and winter resort of western Florida, about 20 miles southwest of Tampa. The city is charmingly situated on Pinellas peninsula with the Gulf of Mexico on the west and, on the south and east, Tampa bay, which is here spanned by the 6-mile Gandy highway bridge. Extending 2400 feet into the bay is a million-dollar recreation pier. The city has 33 miles of water front. The post office is an open-air building, appropriate for the equable, sunny, subtropical climate which attracts an immense number of winter residents, pleasure seekers, and health seekers. Thousands of green benches on Central avenue are a feature of the city. Population, 1940, 60,812.

Salem. A city of eastern Massachusetts, built on a peninsula between two inlets of the Atlantic Ocean, about 14 miles northeast of Boston. Though irregularly laid out, Salem occupies an attractive site, with a fine drive along the north shore, and contains several beautiful parks. There are several very early colonial houses, numerous old mansions, dating from the period of the city's commercial supremacy, and many fine modern homes.

From early colonial years until about 1860, Salem was an important trading port. With the advent of steam navigation, its foreign commerce was largely transferred to Boston. The city still maintains an extensive coastwise trade, especially in coal. The substantial manufactures include cotton goods, games, radio tubes, leather, and shoes.

Salem is the seat of the Essex institute, Peabody museum, and a State teachers college. Founded in 1626, Salem is one of the oldest cities of New England, and is rich in historical associations. In 1692, it was the scene of the Salem witchcraft delusion. Many early dwellings are well preserved, as, for example, Hawthorne's birthplace, the House of Seven Gables, and the witch jail, built in 1684. Population, 1940, 41,213.

Salem. The capital of Oregon, situated on the Willamette river in the northwestern portion of the state. Salem is the trade center of a fertile agricultural region; the industrial interest center about hop products, peppermint oil, linen, fruit and meat packing, and wood products. Wide streets and two public parks enhance the appearance of the city. Among the principal buildings are the capitol, the Federal building, and the Supreme Court building. The city is the seat of Willamette university and of various state institutions. Salem was settled in 1840, was incorporated in 1853, and became the state capital in 1860. Population, 1940, 30,908.

Salt Lake City. The capital of Utah, the chief commercial city between Denver and San Francisco. The city is magnificently situated at the western base of the Wasatch mountains, at an elevation of about 4300 feet above the sea, some 12 miles southeast of Great Salt lake. It occupies a gently sloping site at the edge of a wide plain made highly fertile by irrigation. A noteworthy feature of the city is its unusually wide streets, at the sides of many of which run conduits bringing water from the mountains for freshening the vegetation of parks, lawns, and gardens. It has 6890 acres set aside as public parks.

Salt Lake City is the distributing center for a vast and rich region devoted to mining, stock raising, and agriculture. There are important mining interests, with large smelters and mineral mills in the city and vicinity. The city's industrial output includes also petroleum and steel products, woolens, beet sugar, shoes, cereals, candy, and salt.

In the heart of the city is Temple square, containing the famous Mormon tabernacle, a huge oval building capable of seating 8000 people; the impressive granite temple which took 40 years to erect (1853–93); and the large assembly hall built to accommodate 3000 persons. Among other fine buildings are the State capitol, city and county building and Saint Mary's of the Wasatch. Memory park, east of the capitol, commemorates local veterans of the World War. The city is the seat of the University of Utah, a state normal school, and several other educational institutions.

Among points of interest are Fort Douglas, which overlooks the city from an eminence on the east, Saltair beach on the shore of the lake, and the great Bingham copper mine to the southwest, reached by a scenic railway.

Salt Lake City was founded by Brigham Young, the leader of a party of Mormons who arrived in the valley in 1847, and it has since been the headquarters of the Church of Jesus Christ of Latter-Day Saints. About 40 per cent of the people now living in the city are Latter-Day Saints, who have more than 54 places of worship in the city. Population, 1940, 149,934.

Salton Sea. A brackish lake in the central depression of the Colorado desert in southeastern California. Prior to 1905, this was a salt marsh interspersed with shallow saline ponds and lakes, covering an area about 30 miles long and 12 miles wide, with the surface lying about 280 feet below sea level. During the spring rains, however, the lake usually expanded into a body of water occupying an area of some 60 or 70 square miles, which, with the coming of the dry season, rapidly receded.

In 1905 and 1906, by an accidental inflow of water from the Colorado river, through defective irrigation canals, this watery marsh expanded into a lake 40 miles long, from 10 to 16 miles wide, and 90 feet deep, covering in all some 515 square miles. At its greatest height, the surface of the lake was only 194 feet below sea level. The rising waters overwhelmed villages, farms, factories, and railways.

After the inflow of water from the Colorado river was stopped in 1907, the lake receded as a result of evaporation until, by 1920, it covered only 265 square miles. Its surface was then approximately 250 feet below sea level. Since that time it has remained fairly stable, due to the inflow of natural drainage and a large volume of seepage and waste water from the irrigated lands in the Imperial valley.

San Antonio. The oldest city of Texas, situated on a river of the same name, 80 miles southwest of Austin. San Antonio is noted for its delightful and healthful climate and is the pleasure resort of thousands of visitors. On all sides are spacious grounds, luxuriant gardens, and an abundance of subtropical foliage and flowers. The 56 public parks and plazas cover 2200 acres. Fort Sam Houston is one of the largest army posts in the United States. San Pedro park, with its picturesque live oaks and its famous springs, is the original site of the Indian settlement of San Antonio. Many of the old buildings, especially the Alamo and San Fernando cathedral, are full of historical interest. The cupola of the latter is exactly in the center of the city.

San Antonio is the commercial center of a large oil producing, agricultural and stock raising region, and is an important cattle, horse, and mule market. Its industrial establishments include oil refineries, flour mills, foundries, packing houses, and cement works.

The first permanent settlement was established in 1718 with the founding of the mission of San Antonio de Valero and the presidio of San Antonio de Bexar. In 1809 this settlement became a city. San Antonio was the scene of stirring events in the early history of Texas. Population, 1940, 253,854.

San Bernardino (*săn bûr'när-dē'nō*). A commercial and industrial city of southern California, about 60 miles east of Los Angeles. San Bernardino is situated in a beautiful valley surrounded by snow-capped mountains, near the entrance of the Cajon pass into the Mojave desert. It is the trade center of a rich irrigated district devoted chiefly to growing citrus fruits, grapes, and orchard crops. A national orange show is celebrated there annually. Its industrial establishments include large railroad shops, foundries, machine shops, and planing mills. First settled by Mormons in 1852, San Bernardino was incorporated as a town in 1868 and, in 1886, was chartered as a city. Population, 1940, 43,646. See *Citrus Belt.*

San Diego (*dē-ā'gō*). A city and port of southern California with an excellent harbor on San Diego bay, about 125 miles southeast of Los Angeles. The climate is mild and remarkably equable. Subtropical fruits, especially the lemon, orange, olive, and fig, flourish in the surrounding district. Among the leading industries are fish canning, meat packing, and the handling of fruits and fruit products. The manufactures include also aircraft, confectionery, paint, macaroni, and onyx products. The chief exports include fruits, honey, and citrus products.

San Diego is a United States naval base and one of the greatest naval aviation bases in America. It is also an important commercial aeronautical center, the airport, Lindbergh field, being within five minutes' drive of the central business district. San Diego possesses many fine parks, Balboa park alone having an area of 1400 acres. In it are located several notable museums. Among the city's more elaborate structures are the San Diego Trust and Savings Bank building, the Bank of America building, and the City-County building. By reason of its climate and location, San Diego is a prominent health and travel resort. Among local points of interest are Coronado Beach, Fort Rosecrans, Point Loma, and La Jolla caves. Population, 1940, 203, 341.

SAN FRANCISCO. The principal seaport and manufacturing city of the Pacific coast of America, and second only to Los Angeles in population among the cities of the Pacific states. San Francisco is situated about 600 miles northwest of San Diego and approximately 900 miles south of Seattle.

Site. San Francisco occupies a magnificent site overlooking one of the finest natural harbors in the world. The city is built on the northern end of a semimountainous peninsula lying between the ocean on the west and San Francisco bay on the east. The site, though generally sloping toward the east, is irregular, and embraces many bold hills, of which the highest, Twin Peaks, 925 feet high, separate the business district from the newer residential sections. The entrance from the ocean to the bay is through the Golden Gate, a narrow, rock-bound waterway whose attractive setting recalls Istanbul and Gibraltar. The city is connected with the north and east shores of the bay by the two greatest suspension bridges in the world—Golden Gate and San Francisco-Oakland Bay.

Streets and Buildings. In general, the streets of the city are broad and straight, in some cases leading directly up steep hills. The chief commercial thoroughfare is Market street, 120 feet wide and 3½ miles long, extending southwest from Union Ferry station on the bay. The next most noted thoroughfare is Van Ness avenue, which runs north from Market street near the Civic Center. Among other important streets are Kearney, Geary, Sutter, Post, and Stockton. The district bounded approximately by Kearney and Stockton streets and by California and Pacific avenues, in the heart of the commercial section, is Chinatown, long a picturesque feature of the city. The level section south of Market street contains the manufacturing district. Along the steep thoroughfares north of Market street are great office buildings and department stores, and to the west on the higher hills are the finest residential parts of the city.

Of many imposing public buildings, the most important are those of the group forming the Civic Center, including the city hall, the public library, and the auditorium. Other notable buildings are the post office, the United States mint, and the Union Ferry building. Among the larger office buildings are the Southern Pacific building, the Federal Reserve bank, the Russ building, 30 stories high, the Standard Oil building, 22 stories high, the Hobart building, 21 stories high, and the Claus Spreckles building, 19 stories high, which withstood the ravages of the great fire of 1906.

Parks and Boulevards. The municipal park system includes more than 46 parks, with a total area of about 3000 acres. The chief of these, Golden Gate park, covering 1013 acres, extends from near the center of the city west to the ocean. The principal points of scenic and historic interest are reached by an extensive system of boulevards and driveways. Those passing through the Presidio and Lincoln park give fine views of the Golden Gate. These lead also past Sutro baths and the Cliff House to the Great highway which runs close to the ocean for 3 miles. The historic Mission road, the city's oldest thoroughfare, has been modernized. A boulevard extends to the top of Twin Peaks, whose lofty crest affords a splendid panoramic view of the city and its surroundings.

Educational Institutions. Among the important educational and scientific institutions are the Memorial museum, the California school of fine arts, the Mechanics institute, the School of mechanical arts, the Cogswell polytechnic institute, and the Lux school of industry. The University of California is at Berkeley, across the bay; in San Francisco are located the affiliated colleges, which include the departments of medicine, dentistry, and pharmacy. Leland Stanford university is at Palo Alto, 33 miles distant.

Transportation. The harbor of San Francisco, completely sheltered from the sea by coastal hills, is one of the largest and safest on the globe. It has extensive docks, and is equipped with dry docks and other facilities for the care of vessels. The city is connected, by regular lines of steamships, with all ports on the Pacific coast of North and South America, with Atlantic seaports by way of the Panama canal, and with Hawaii, the Philippines, Australia, China, and Japan.

San Francisco is the terminus of the Southern Pacific railway from New Orleans. Oakland, on the eastern side of the bay, is the terminus of three transcontinental systems, and connection with San Francisco across the bay is afforded by ferry and bridge services. Two systems of street railways and buses, one municipally owned and operated, provide local transportation.

COMMERCE. In foreign commerce, San Francisco ranks among the chief seaports of the country. The leading articles of export usually include canned fruits, canned salmon, raw cotton, iron and steel manufactures, grain, and oils. Among the principal imports are sugar, coffee, copra, burlap, tea, rubber, silk, and tin. The city also conducts an extensive coastwise commerce with other ports of the United States, and much Western produce is collected at San Francisco for distribution by rail.

FINANCE. San Francisco is the financial center of the Pacific coast. It is noted for the size and strength of its banking institutions, and is the headquarters of two of the largest banking organizations in America.

MANUFACTURES. San Francisco is, after Los Angeles, the leading city of the western United States in the total value of manufactured products. Crude petroleum, piped from vast oil fields, is extensively used for fuel. Among important industries are printing and publishing, meat packing, shipbuilding, coffee roasting, fruit canning, and the manufacture of paper products, furniture, confectionery, and paint.

FEATURES OF INTEREST. Among many noteworthy places of interest within the city and its environs are the Presidio, a large military reservation; Telegraph hill, Russian hill, and Twin Peaks, affording excellent views; Chinatown, with its Oriental character and aspect; the ocean shore at Cliff House; the celebrated Seal rocks, Mission Dolores, Mount Tamalpais and Muir Woods, north of the Golden Gate; and Angel and Alcatraz islands, the latter a Federal prison island.

HISTORY. The site of San Francisco was visited in 1769 by Spaniards who called the place Yerba Buena. The first settlement began in 1776 with the establishment of Mission Dolores. In 1846, the United States took possession of California, and, in 1847, the name of the town was changed to San Francisco. Following the discovery of gold in California in 1848, the development of the town was spectacular, and, in 1850, it became a city. In 1862, telegraphic communication with the East was established, and, in 1869, the first transcontinental railway was completed. The most momentous event in the history of San Francisco was the earthquake of April 18, 1906, followed by a tremendous conflagration which almost totally destroyed the buildings on an area of more than 4 square miles, including the chief commercial and residential districts. Notwithstanding this enormous loss, the devastated area was rapidly rebuilt, and the city reconstructed on a grander and more substantial scale. Population, 1940, 634,536.

San Jose (*săn hō-sā'*). A city of west central California, situated in the beautiful and fertile Santa Clara valley, 50 miles southeast of San Francisco. It is in the midst of an important fruit growing region, and its principal commercial and industrial interests are connected with the cultivation of desiduous fruits. Santa Clara county, of which San Jose is the commercial center, produces about two-fifths of the total prune crop of California. San Jose is noted for its salubrious climate and delightful gardens. Alum Rock park, 716 acres in area, has 22 mineral springs, each with a grotto. San Jose possesses many fine buildings, including the San Jose State college and the University of Santa Clara. Lick observatory, situated on Mount Hamilton, about 25 miles east of the city, attracts many visitors. The Ames aeronautical research laboratory is 9 miles north of the city. Population, 1940, 68,457.

San Juan (*săn hwän'*). The capital city and chief seaport of Puerto Rico. It is built on two small islands, San Juan and Santurce, connected by five modern bridges. Santurce communicates with the mainland by the bridge of Martin Peña. It possesses an excellent harbor and several fine plazas and gardens. The capitol is a beautiful building of white marble in the classic style. The chief industry is the manufacture of tobacco and the handling of sugar, grapefruit, pineapples, and other fruits.

San Juan was founded about 1519 by Ponce de Leon. The main part of the city is surrounded by medieval ramparts. Morro Castle, built in 1584, as a part of the city's defenses, stands on a promontory to the west. San Juan came into the possession of the United States by cession at the close of the Spanish American war. Population, 1940, 169,247.

Santa Barbara (*săn'tȧ bär'bȧ-rȧ*). A city of southern California, situated on Santa Barbara channel, about 90 miles northwest of Los Angeles. Santa Barbara lies in a beautiful valley opening southward to the sea, but encircled on the north and east by the Santa Ynez mountains. Closely paralleling the shore, the high coast range extends for many miles in an east-and-west direction, resulting in a remarkably mild and salubrious climate. The city is in the midst of an important farming, lemon growing, walnut growing, and stock raising region. A large proportion of the lima beans grown for market in the United States are produced in this district.

The Santa Barbara mission, founded in 1786, stands in the northern part of the city, and is still occupied by Franciscan monks. Santa Barbara is widely known for its attractive buildings in Spanish architecture. An "Old Spanish Days" fiesta is held each August at the full of the moon. Santa Barbara is a noted all-year resort. Excellent roads in the vicinity afford fine views of the city, the channel, and the outlying islands. Population, 1940, 34,958.

Santa Catalina (*kăt'ȧ-lē'nȧ*). An island of southern California, separated from the mainland of Los Angeles county by San Pedro channel, some 20 miles wide. Santa Catalina is about 25 miles long and the average width is about 4 miles. The surface is semimountainous with bold, rocky coasts and numerous, more or less wooded, gorges. Many interesting trees, shrubs, and other plants grow on the island, some of which do not occur elsewhere. The clear waters, remarkable for the beauty and variety of their marine life, are famous game-fishing grounds. Sea lions inhabit the south coast; flying fish are numerous in the channel, and whales are sometimes seen. The only town, Avalon, population in 1940, 1637, is a noted resort.

Santa Fe (*săn'tȧ fā'*). The capital of New Mexico, situated in the north central part of the state. First established in 1610, Santa Fe has ever since been the capital of New Mexico. The city was taken from Mexico by the United States in 1846. Stock raising is the main industry of the surrounding district. Indian pottery in large quantities is made by the Pueblo Indians.

The older part of the city has narrow, crooked streets with houses made of adobe or sun-dried brick. There are many buildings of historic interest: the Palace, beside a central plaza, where the Mexican governors resided; San Miguel church; the capitol; the National Park Service building; Christo Rey church; Scottish Rite temple; and the State art museum, built in a mission style of architecture. In the vicinity are many remains of the cave and cliff dwellings of the Pueblo Indians. Population, 1940, 20,325.

Santa Monica. A city of southern California, on the Pacific Ocean, 16 miles west of downtown Los Angeles. By reason of its excellent climate, bathing beaches, and boating facilities, Santa Monica is a popular year-round seaside resort. Other features include the Palisades park and various amusement piers. Its industries include the manufacture of aircraft, cosmetics, ceramics, and soap. Population, 1940, 53,500.

Saratoga Springs. A city and famous watering place of eastern New York, situated about 30 miles almost directly north of Albany. It is noted for its numerous medicinal springs which have made it one of the most attractive health resorts in America. There are commodious hotels and bathhouses, polo grounds, race tracks, golf links, and many other facilities for recreation.

In 1909, the state of New York established a reservation, which covers 2700 acres and includes 122 natural springs, for the purpose of ensuring a continuous flow of these curative waters for the benefit of the public. Thousands of persons visit the city each year to use the waters and baths. These waters are bottled and shipped to various parts of the world. The city is the seat of Skidmore college for women. In a 30-acre park is the curious geological display known as the Petrified Sea Garden.

Saratoga Springs was founded in 1789. The Saratoga battlefield, the scene of Burgoyne's surrender, is located 12 miles east of the city. Population, 1940, 13,705.

Sault Sainte Marie (*sōō' sânt mä-rē'*). A city of northern Michigan, on the Saint Mary's river, and opposite a town of the same name in Ontario. At this point are the famous rapids (the *Sault* or "rapids" of Saint Mary), which make navigation impossible for lake vessels. However, between Lake Superior and Lake Huron, navigation has been made possible for ships of the heaviest tonnage by an extensive system of canals and locks. Some 25,000 ships, carrying about 100 million tons of freight, pass through this waterway every year. Immense hydroelectric power, generated at the rapids, is utilized in the city's growing industries, the chief of which are the manufacture of calcium carbide and leather. Other manufactories include planing, paper, and woolen mills, and machine shops. Sault Sainte Marie is the oldest settlement in Michigan. Population, 1940, 15,847.

Savannah. The second largest city of Georgia, situated on the Savannah river, about 18 miles from the sea. It occupies a fine level site and has an excellent harbor. Savannah is the chief cotton port on the Atlantic coast of the United States, and has also large exports of lumber, fertilizers, tobacco, and naval stores. It has extensive industries, which include the manufacture of cottonseed oils, fertilizers, resin, turpentine, refined sugar, foundry and machine shop products, paper, cloth and paper bags, and furniture. Savannah is noted for its well shaded streets and for its beautiful parks and gardens luxuriant with subtropical vegetation. The city was founded in 1733 and received its municipal charter in 1789. During the Revolutionary War it was captured by the British, and in the Civil War it was the objective of Sherman's march to the sea. Population, 1940, 95,996.

Schenectady. A city of eastern New York, located on the Mohawk river and the State barge canal, about 16 miles northwest of Albany. The older parts of the city are built along the river, but the more modern sections occupy the surrounding hills. Schenectady is unique among American cities of its size in that about 90 per cent of the persons employed in the city are engaged in the two leading industries, the building of locomotives and the manufacture of electrical machinery, apparatus, and supplies. A favorite local slogan is "Schenectady hauls and lights the world." It contains the laboratories and headquarters of the General Electric Company and the chief factory of the American Locomotive Company. The home of Steinmetz, famous inventor for the General Electric Company, was acquired by the state for a museum.

Schenectady was settled in 1661 and chartered as a town in 1798. In 1690, an attacking force of French and Indians massacred most of the inhabitants. The city is the seat of Union college, the second college incorporated in the state. Population, 1940, 87,549.

Scranton. The third largest city of Pennsylvania, situated on the Lackawanna river, about 105 miles northwest of Philadelphia. Scranton occupies an undulating site surrounded by low mountains. It is the richest coal mining city in the world, being the center of the chief anthracite producing region of the United States.

Scranton is also a leading silk manufacturing center, and its other noteworthy industries include the manufacture of locomotives, iron and steel goods, knit goods, cotton lace, women's clothing, and tobacco products. The fine parks and the lake resorts in the near-by mountains make the city and its environs attractive. Scranton was founded in 1840, incorporated as a borough in 1854, and was chartered as a city in 1866. Population, 1940, 140,404.

Seattle. The chief city of Washington, and the second largest seaport of the Pacific states. It is built on the hilly eastern shore of Puget sound, 933 miles by water north of San Francisco. The city occupies a commanding site between the Cascade and the Olympic range, with Puget sound forming its western front, and Lake Washington lying on its eastern border.

Surrounded by a tributary region rich in timber, fisheries, minerals, and agricultural resources, and possessing exceptional facilities for transportation, Seattle has become one of the foremost commercial centers of the Pacific coast. It is the terminal point of several transcontinental railroads and has regular steamship connections with all parts of the world by way of the Panama canal and the transpacific routes. In addition to other fine harbor facilities, a ship canal, 8½ miles long, situated wholly within the city, connects Puget sound with Lake Union and Lake Washington. The latter lake is spanned by a 6½-mile pontoon bridge. The leading exports of the port are wheat, flour, lumber, refined copper, automobiles, machinery, and fish; the imports are chiefly silk, rice, tea, coffee, sugar, copper ore, furs, and various Oriental products.

Seattle has one of the largest municipally owned hydroelectric power systems in the world. The leading industries include flour milling, shipbuilding, meat packing, and the manufacture of lumber and wood products, airplanes, iron and steel products, and machinery. The fishery interests of Alaska and Puget sound are largely centralized in Seattle which handles enormous quantities of canned salmon and other preserved fish. Gold from Alaska enters the country chiefly by way of this port.

Seattle contains many noteworthy buildings, among which are the Cathedral of Saint James, the public library, art museum, Northern Life tower, and the Smith tower, 42 stories high. The park and boulevard system embraces more than 1800 acres and includes upwards of 25 miles of scenic boulevards. The latter afford magnificent views of Mount Rainier and other snow-capped peaks of the Cascades. The campus of the University of Washington, covering 582 acres and situated between lakes Union and Washington, lies entirely within the city.

Seattle, named for a local Indian chief, was first settled in 1851. It was incorporated in 1865, and, in 1869, was chartered as a city. Population, 1940, 368,302.

Shasta, Mount. A majestic peak in the Sierra Nevada mountains of northern California, situated about 40 miles south of the Oregon boundary. This great mountain, one of the most imposing on the continent, is an extinct volcanic cone which rises to an elevation of 14,380 feet. The summit is continuously covered with snow, and on the north slope there are several glaciers. About 1400 feet below the summit there is a crater nearly 4000 feet in diameter and about 2500 feet deep.

Although regarded as extinct, Mount Shasta still shows vestiges of volcanic activity. At the summit there is a sulphurous fumarole which emits hot gases, and on the north slope there is another similar opening. During one of the prehistoric eruptions of Mount Shasta, a stream of lava flowed down its southern slope, entered the channel of the Sacramento river, and followed the bed of that stream for a distance of 50 miles.

The influence of temperature and moisture upon the distribution of plant life is well illustrated in the strong contrast between the vegetation of Mount Shasta and that of Shasta valley. The summit of the mountain is devoid of vegetation because of cold; the Shasta valley, 10 miles distant, is treeless because of a lack of moisture. Between these extremes lies the great forest belt of Mount Shasta. In this heavily forested area the different species of trees are arranged in zones, according to the requirements of each species as regards temperature and moisture. For example, yellow pine and sugar pine predominate in the Transition zone at the foot of the mountain; Shasta fir in the Canadian zone midway on the slope; and whitebark pine in the Hudsonian zone, immediately below the upper limit of trees, at about 9500 feet altitude. Small alpine plants are found as high as 13,000 feet.

Mount Shasta may be ascended with little difficulty. From Sisson railway station, a good trail, about 6 miles in length, leads to Timberline camp. From this camp, the summit may be reached and the return journey made to Sisson in a single day.

While the glaciers of Mount Shasta are smaller than those of Mount Rainier, and the charming mountain meadows found on the latter peak are wanting, the view from the summit of Mount Shasta is unsurpassed by that from any peak in the Cascade range.

Sheboygan (*shê-boi'găn*). A city of eastern Wisconsin, situated on Lake Michigan, 52 miles north of Milwaukee. The city is the trade center of a farming and dairying region and is noted for the extensive manufacture of chairs and other furniture. Other industries include the manufacture of enamelware, machinery, shoes, mattresses, and clothing. There are fishing interests, and a state fish hatchery is located here. Population, 1940, 40,638.

Sheridan. A mining and trade center of northern Wyoming. It is an important shipping point for farm products and live stock, and also for coal, which is mined extensively in the neighborhood. The Indian battles of Wolf Creek, Massacre Hill, and Great Wagon Box were fought in the vicinity, 1865–67. Population, 1940, 10,529.

Shoshone (*shô-shō'nê*) **Falls.** A great cataract of the Snake river, in southern Idaho, about 120 miles southeast of Boise. This magnificent waterfall is exceeded in grandeur, in the United States, only by Niagara and by the falls in the Yosemite valley. After coursing through a rocky canyon, some 1200 feet in depth, the deep river, here nearly 800 feet wide, first descends about 30 feet through several rocky channels. The waters then unite and the full volume of the river, in a single sheet, plunges over a precipice about 200 feet high, into the bottom of a narrow gorge. The cataract is easily reached from Twin Falls, about 5 miles distant.

Shreveport. The second largest city of Louisiana, on the Red river, in the northwestern part of the state, about 300 miles from New Orleans. The city has excellent railway facilities and is the commercial center of a large region, rich in oil, gas, lumber, and agricultural products. There is an extensive trade in cotton, corn, peanuts, pecans, fruit, truck crops, and live stock. The local industries include oil refineries, lumber, cotton, and cottonseed oil mills, glassworks, foundries, machine shops, and fertilizer factories. Industrial output includes also sulphur, salt, and glass. The Cado parish court house is an 8-story building of unusual beauty, having a jail on the two top stories. The 17-story Commercial National Bank building is a conspicuous landmark. Population, 1940, 98,167.

Sioux (*sōō*) **City.** The second largest city of Iowa, located on the Missouri river, 200 miles northwest of Des Moines. Sioux City occupies a commanding site embracing parts of the river valley and the encircling bluffs. It is the commercial center of a highly productive agricultural region and has extensive wholesaling and shipping interests. It stands at the head of navigation in the Mississippi river. The city is one of the important live stock markets of the country and has large meat packing establishments, creameries, and numerous other substantial industries. In total value of manufactured products, Sioux City ranks first among the cities of the state. There are many fine streets and public buildings, and the municipal park system covers an area of 1519 acres. The largest unit is Stone park, an 801-acre natural wooded tract on the northwestern edge of the city. Grand View park contains a music pavilion in a natural amphitheater.

Sioux City was founded in 1849 as an outfitting station for expeditions to the Black Hills, and received its municipal charter in 1857. It is the seat of Morningside college and of Trinity college. Population, 1940, 82,364.

Sioux Falls. The largest city of South Dakota, on the Big Sioux river, about 320 miles southwest of Minneapolis. The river here falls nearly 100 feet, furnishing abundant hydroelectric power for various industries. In the vicinity there are extensive beds of quartzite, usually called jasper or red granite. Many buildings, both public and private, are built of this native pink stone, which renders the appearance of the city remarkably attractive. Meat packing, stone quarrying, flour milling, and the manufacture of crackers are among the chief industries. Population, 1940, 40,832.

Sitka. A city and United States naval station of southeastern Alaska, on the west coast of Baranof island. The chief industry is the processing and packing of salmon. Though located in a high northern latitude, the winters are not severe, and the general climate is healthful. Across the channel is a large naval air base. Near by is the Sitka national monument, a 57-acre park of great natural beauty and the scene of a massacre of Russians by Indians in 1802. Sitka was founded by the Russians in 1799 under the name of New Archangel, and later became the capital of the Russian territory of Alaska. From 1867 until 1906, Sitka was the capital of the United States territory of Alaska. Population, 1939, 1987.

Somerville. A residential city of eastern Massachusetts, on the Mystic river, two miles northwest of Boston. It is built on a series of hills and has many historic associations connected with the War of Independence. Paul Revere on his memorable ride passed through Somerville along a road now known as Broadway. Prospect Hill is said to be the scene of the first unfurling of the American flag. Meat packing, railway car repairing, furniture making, and the manufacture of paper bags are among the city's leading industries. Population, 1940, 102,177.

South Bend. A city of northern Indiana, built at the south bend of the Saint Joseph river, about 85 miles east of Chicago. South Bend has excellent railway facilities, is the commercial center of a rich agricultural and peppermint growing district, and has developed extensive manufacturing industries. The city contains large factories making automobiles, airplanes, and agricultural implements. Other important manufactures include lathes, knit goods, roofing, men's clothing, sewing machine parts, stoves, watches, and washing machines. There are 34 parks covering 623 acres. South Bend was laid out in 1831 and, in 1835, was incorporated. The University of Notre Dame is situated in the environs of the city. Population, 1940, 101,268.

Southern Pines. A noted winter resort of North Carolina, situated some 70 miles south of Raleigh. It is located in a fruit growing region, producing berries, peaches, and grapes. By reason of its mild and equable climate, it is a favorite place of winter residence for people from the Northern states. Population, 1940, 3225.

Spartanburg. An industrial city of South Carolina, about 100 miles northwest of Columbia. It is located in a rich cotton growing section, and has large cotton and textile mills, car repair shops, bleaching and creosoting plants, and fertilizer works. Peaches and other fruits are grown near by in large quantities. It is the seat of Wofford college for men and Converse college for women. The site of Camp Wadsworth, established by the Federal government during the World War, has been utilized for suburban and industrial development. Population, 1940, 32,249.

Spokane (*spō'kăn'*). The second largest city of Washington, located near the eastern border of the state. It occupies a picturesque site at the falls of the Spokane river, which, with other falls in the district, provide immense hydroelectric power for manufacturing purposes. Served by five transcontinental railroads, Spokane has become the chief industrial city of the rich mining, lumbering, stock raising, and agricultural region known as the "Inland Empire." Among important manufactures are flour, lumber and timber products, wooden boxes, packed meats, and structural ironwork. The city has a system of beautiful parks embracing an area of more than 2700 acres and is the seat of several educational institutions. Fort Wright, a government military post, is located in the immediate vicinity. The first settlement at Spokane was made in 1872 and, in 1881, the city was incorporated. Population, 1940, 122,001. See *Inland Empire*.

Springfield. The capital of Illinois, situated in the south central part of the state, 185 miles south of Chicago. The city is the center of a highly productive agricultural and coal mining district and has extensive manufacturing interests. Its industries include flour milling and textiles and the manufacture of electrical apparatus, agricultural implements, shoes, tractors, garage equipment, and road grading machinery. The capitol, erected at a cost of $4,500,000, is built in the neoclassic style of architecture and surmounted by a lofty dome.

Among the points of historic interest are the former residence of President Lincoln and the Lincoln national monument. The mausoleum in the latter contains the remains of the president. Springfield was first settled in 1818 and was made the capital of Illinois in 1837. Population, 1940, 75,503.

Springfield. A city of southwestern Massachusetts, built on the Connecticut river, about 100 miles southwest of Boston. In appearance, Springfield is one of the most attractive cities in New England. It occupies a site of great natural beauty on the east bank of the river, and possesses many fine public buildings. Among the most impressive of these is the municipal group, including the administration building, the auditorium, and the campanile. The top of the campanile, 300 feet high, affords a magnificent view of the Connecticut valley. Other noteworthy structures are the public library, the art museum, the science museum, the United States armory, and Trinity church with a carillon of 61 bells.

Of the city's park system, embracing 1268 acres, the largest unit is the 757-acre Forest park with a zoological garden. In Merrick park stands the famous statue of "The Puritan" by Saint Gaudens. An interesting feature is a magnificent bridge spanning the Connecticut river, completed in 1922. Springfield is the seat of the American International college and the Springfield Y. M. C. A. training college.

The industries of the city are extensive and varied. Among the principal manufactures are firearms, bicycles and motor cycles, chemicals, envelopes, electrical machinery, toys, and automobile tires.

Springfield was first settled in 1636 and was called Agawam. It assumed its present name in 1640 and, in 1852, was chartered as a city. The city was the center of hostilities in King Philip's war, 1675, and was the scene of various conflicts which took place during Shays's rebellion, 1786–87. Population, 1940, 149,554.

Springfield. A city of southwestern Missouri, located on a plateau in the Ozark mountains, about 230 miles southwest of Saint Louis. The city is the commercial center of a large farming, fruit growing, dairy, and poultry region, with which it carries on an extensive trade. It has large interests connected with the mining and marketing of lead and zinc. The leading industrial establishments include railway shops, creameries, and furniture factories.

The city is picturesquely situated, has many handsome parks, streets, and buildings, and is the seat of Drury college. Springfield was laid out in 1843 and, in 1847, was chartered as a city. Population, 1940, 61,238.

Springfield. A city of southwestern Ohio, on the Mad river, 45 miles west of Columbus. It is the trade center of a rich agricultural region but is primarily an industrial city. Among its chief manufactures are agricultural implements, metallic caskets, motor trucks, gas and steam engines, musical instruments, and electrical machinery. There are many noteworthy public buildings, and the city is enriched with numerous parks and recreation grounds. Springfield is the seat of Wittenberg college. The first settlement in the vicinity was made in 1799; the town of Springfield was incorporated in 1827 and, in 1850, was chartered as a city. Population, 1940, 70,662.

Stamford. A manufacturing and residential city of southwestern Connecticut, situated on Long Island sound, 33 miles from New York City. Stamford is noted especially for the manufacture of locks and hardware. Other important products are automobile parts, electric motors, furniture, oil burners, engines, and chemicals. The city was first settled in 1641 by a colony from New Haven, became a borough in 1830, and, in 1894, was chartered as a city. Population, 1940, 47,938.

Starved Rock. A perpendicular cliff of white sandstone, on the south bank of the Illinois river, near the town of Utica, about 90 miles southwest of Chicago. This cliff overhangs the water's edge and rises sheer to a height of about 160 feet. The walls of the fortress-like rock slope precipitously in all directions, and the top is reached by a single narrow rocky stairway. The flat summit, about half an acre, commands an excellent view of the fertile river valley, bordered by wooded hills and grassy slopes.

This almost inaccessible rock was the scene of many interesting events in the early history of Illinois. In 1673, Father Marquette and Joliet spent many weeks at Kaskaskia, the great village of the Illini Indians, in the valley near the rock. In 1681, La Salle and Tonti built a palisaded stronghold on the top of the rock, which they named Fort Saint Louis.

About 1770 occurred the tragic events which gave the cliff its present name. Here perished by starvation the last remnant of the once powerful Illini tribe. At a council at Cahokia, Pontiac, the famous chief of the Ottawas, was stabbed to death by an Illini warrior. Pontiac's followers swore a war of extinction against the Illini, finally entrapping the last survivors of the tribe in this natural fortress. An area of more than 800 acres, including Starved Rock and other historic points, is a state park.

Stockton. An industrial and commercial city of central California, situated 78 miles east of San Francisco on the San Joaquin river, which is deepened so as to be accessible to ocean-going ships. Stockton has important fruit, grain, and live stock interests. Leading manufactures include canned and frozen foods, agricultural implements, and paper products. Stockton is the seat of the College of the Pacific. The settlement which became Stockton was founded in 1847 and was an outfitting point for miners during the gold rush. Population, 1940, 54,714.

Stone Mountain. A huge, dome-shaped hill of granite, located near the town of the same name, about 15 miles east of Atlanta, Georgia. It rises about 1000 feet above the surrounding country and covers an area of some 2 square miles. The surface is almost wholly naked rock.

At the base of the northern slope there is an almost vertical cliff, about 800 feet high and 5000 feet long. In 1926, work was begun on a project for transformation of this cliff into a Confederate memorial by chiseling in bold relief several hundred figures of Confederate soldiers, centered on colossal figures of Lee, Davis, and Jackson. The plan called for a vast memorial hall to be excavated from the rock and dedicated to the women of the Confederacy. Controversies and lack of funds delayed its completion.

Superior. A city of northwestern Wisconsin, situated on Lake Superior and lying adjacent to Duluth, Minnesota. Possessing a fine harbor and excellent railway facilities, Superior shares with Duluth the advantages of location at the head of navigation on the Great Lakes. The city ships large quantities of iron ore and grain by water and receives coal to be distributed by rail to inland districts. Among the chief industries are planing and flour mills, iron and steel works, and shipyards. Superior is the seat of a State teachers college.

The early explorers, Radisson and Groseilliers, are supposed to have made their headquarters on the site of Superior in 1661. The explorer Du L'Hut, after whom Duluth was named, established a trading post here about 1680. Superior was laid out as a town in 1853, and, in 1889, was chartered as a city. Population, 1940, 35,136.

Syracuse. The fourth largest city of New York State, located in the central part of the state, almost exactly midway between Albany and Buffalo, being about 150 miles from either of these cities. It occupies a fine, gently undulating site on Onondaga lake, 35 miles south of Lake Ontario.

Syracuse owes its prominence as a commercial and industrial city to its central location in a highly productive region and to its superior transportation facilities. It is served by numerous railways which radiate in all directions and by the State Barge Canal system, which affords water transportation north to Lake Ontario, west to Lake Erie, and east to the Hudson river. The city has extensive shipping interests and conducts a large wholesale trade.

Syracuse has upwards of 750 industrial establishments, producing a great variety of articles. Among important manufactures are typewriters, air conditioning equipment, soda ash, tool steel, candles, agricultural implements, chemicals, ceramics, and washing machines. The manufacture of salt, formerly the chief industry, is no longer carried on within the limits of the city.

The commercial district is substantially built, largely of brick and of the native Onondaga limestone, and contains many imposing buildings. The residential sections are noted for their broad, well shaded streets, and handsome residences and grounds. James street ranks among the most attractive residential avenues of the country. There are about 60 public parks, ranging in size from small plots at street intersections to spacious tracts, such as Burnet park, on the west, covering 120 acres. Lincoln park, on the east, affords a beautiful view of the city and its environs.

The city is the seat of Syracuse university, with which is connected the State college of forestry. Another institution, located permanently at Syracuse, is the State fair, managed by the State Fair commission.

The site of Syracuse originally belonged to the Onondaga Indians, whose survivors occupy a small reservation south of the city. The salt springs, long known to the Indians, became known to white settlers in 1789. The first settlement on the present site of the city was made about 1805. This was named Syracuse in 1819 and was chartered as a city in 1847. Population, 1940, 205,967.

Tacoma (*tȧ-kō'mȧ*). A city and port of western Washington, built on a fine harbor on Puget sound, about 30 miles south of Seattle. It occupies a commanding site, rising to an elevation of several hundred feet overlooking the sound, in a beautiful scenic region between the Olympic and the Cascade mountains. Mount Rainier lies about 56 miles southeast.

The city has a substantial wholesale trade, large manufacturing industries, and an extensive coastwise and foreign commerce. The leading manufactures include lumber, flour, furniture, and machine shop products. Tacoma contains many fine public buildings, has several picturesque parks, in all covering 1200 acres, and is the seat of numerous educational institutions. Old Tacoma, founded in 1868, and New Tacoma, founded in 1873, were united in 1883 to form Tacoma. Population, 1940, 109,408.

Tahoe (*tä'hō; tä'hō*), **Lake.** A beautiful lake, situated at the eastern base of the Sierra Nevada, at an elevation of about 6275 feet above sea level. The boundary line between California and Nevada passes through the lake, which lies about 85 miles (direct) northeast of Sacramento and 12 miles west of Carson City. It is about 20 miles long and from 8 to 12 miles wide, with an extreme depth exceeding 1650 feet. Its remarkably clear waters are discharged through the Truckee river, eastward into Pyramid lake, Nevada. Lake Tahoe is a favorite summer resort.

Tallahassee. The capital of Florida, located in the northwestern part of the state. It is the trade center of a rich dairying and poultry region, which grows corn, tobacco, cotton, vegetables, pecans, figs, grapes, and blueberries. The local industries include the manufacture of lumber and foundry, machine shop, and marble products. The city is located on a series of hills, with wide, well shaded streets. Among the principal buildings are the State capitol, the Federal building, and the county courthouse. When virtually uninhabited, Tallahassee, in 1824, was chosen by the United States government as the capital of the territory of Florida, and it remained the capital upon the admission of Florida as a state in 1845. Population, 1940, 16,240.

Tamalpais (*tăm'ăl-pīs'*), **Mount.** A mountain in the Coast range of California, situated on the Marin peninsula, about 15 miles in direct line northwest of San Francisco. The triple summit, about 2600 feet high, affords unsurpassed views of the surrounding region.

To the south are the Golden Gate, the city of San Francisco, and, far beyond them, Mount Hamilton, 4444 feet high, on which the Lick observatory is situated. To the east is San Francisco bay, with Oakland, Berkeley, and other cities on its eastern shore. Beyond these are the Contra Costa hills and Mount Diablo, the latter rising nearly 4000 feet high. Close by to the north is the reservoir called Lake Lagunitos, and in the distance are ridge after ridge of the Coast range. On the west is the ocean and the rocky Farallon islands, lying far out at sea. Within walking distance from West peak is Muir Woods, with its superb forest of sequoias, many of which are 300 feet high. Muir Woods is a national monument.

Tampa. A manufacturing city and winter resort of west central Florida, located at the head of Tampa bay, an inlet of the Gulf of Mexico. The city has a good harbor and is served by various steamer lines. A large part of the world's supply of Havana cigars is manufactured at Tampa. Other industrial products include cement, phosphate fertilizer, canned citrus fruit, and ships. Phosphate fertilizers, fruits, turpentine, rosin, and fish are exported in large quantities. Among the city's features are the semitropical Plant park, where Tampa university is situated, the Tampa dog racing track, the Gasparilla carnival, held each February, and the 19-story Floridan hotel. Davis island, a fine residential district, is a result of a great reclamation project. Population, 1940, 108,391.

Taos (*tä'ôs*). An Indian pueblo and village of northern New Mexico, built near the Rio Grande river, about 50 miles north of Santa Fe. The inhabitants are of Tanoan Indian stock. Like all pueblo dwellers, the people of Taos are industrious and self-supporting. Population, 1940, 965.

Tarrytown. A village of New York State on the Hudson river 25 miles north of New York City. It is noted as the scene of numerous skirmishes in the Revolutionary War. Major John André was captured in the vicinity. The village contains "Sunnyside," the home of Washington Irving, who made famous the near-by valley, Sleepy hollow. Its factories include an automobile assembly plant. Population, 1940, 6874.

Terre Haute (*tĕr'ē hōt'*). A railroad center and manufacturing city of west central Indiana, picturesquely situated on a high bank of the Wabash river, 73 miles southwest of Indianapolis. The city is the commercial center of a rich agricultural and coal mining district. Among the chief industries are railway car shops, paper mills, distilleries, foundries, and packing plants. Parks, 18 in number, cover 659 acres. The city has many fine public buildings and is the seat of the Rose polytechnic institute, Indiana State teachers college, and St. Mary of the Woods College for Women. Population, 1940, 62,693.

Thousand Islands. A numerous group of islands in the Saint Lawrence river, located immediately northeast of Lake Ontario. They are situated in an expansion of the river, 40 miles long and from 3 to 7 miles wide. Some of the islands are many acres in extent, but many are mere rocky islets. A large number belong to Canada, 14 of them forming part of the Saint Lawrence Islands national park, and others are a part of the State of New York. Their attractive scenic setting, together with their cool climate, make the Thousand islands an ideal place for summer recreation.

Ticonderoga. A village of northeastern New York situated on the creek connecting Lake George with Lake

Champlain, about 95 miles north of Albany. Paper and lumber are its chief industrial products. Because of its many associations with the French and Indian war and the Revolutionary War, Ticonderoga and its environs possess great historic interest. At this point, the French erected, in 1755, a fort which they called Fort Carillon. In 1757, this was heavily garrisoned by Montcalm, but, in 1759, it was taken by the English under General Amherst.

In the Revolutionary War, this stronghold, renamed Fort Ticonderoga, was captured from the English by Ethan Allen and his "Green Mountain Boys." Later, it was retaken by Burgoyne and held until his surrender. The fort fell into disuse but has since been restored and contains a valuable museum. Population, 1940, 3402.

Toledo. A city of Ohio, located on the northern border of the state, about 95 miles west of Cleveland. It occupies both banks of the Maumee river at its mouth in an inlet of Lake Erie. It is the fourth largest city in Ohio.

Toledo owes its commercial and industrial prominence to its advantageous location at the head of direct water transportation to the East and to its superior railway facilities. It is surrounded by a rich agricultural region, with which it maintains an extensive wholesale and marketing trade. It is one of the largest distributing points on the Great Lakes for soft coal, and handles also at its docks immense quantities of iron ore and lumber. It is an important primary market for winter wheat and stands first in the world as a market for clover seed.

Toledo ranks in manufactures among the leading cities of the state. There are more than 650 industrial establishments; their chief products include automobiles, iron and steel, refined petroleum, bottle making machines, plate and cut glass, tools, electrical machinery, ships, scales, tents and awnings, ducking and belting.

There are many notable public buildings, among which are the post office, the civic auditorium, the public library, and the museum of art. The park system, covering more than 1500 acres, includes several large parks and some 45 smaller parks, squares, and triangular spaces. The larger parks, charmingly situated on the banks of the river, are connected by boulevards. Among noteworthy educational institutions is the University of Toledo, maintained by the city. Toledo was founded in 1833 by the consolidation of two earlier settlements, and received its city charter in 1846. Population, 1940, 282,349.

Topeka. The capital and third largest city of Kansas, situated on Kansas river about 70 miles west of Kansas City. It is an important railroad center, being served by four railroad systems and having the extensive car shops of the Santa Fe railroad. An outstanding industry is the publication of farm journals which circulate widely throughout the Middle West. Meat packing, flour milling, and the manufacture of butter are other important industrial interests. The capitol stands in the center of a beautiful park area. Among other features of the city are a 9-acre rose and rock garden and the 572-acre Lake Shawnee park. Educational institutions include Washburn college and the Mulvane art museum.

Topeka was laid out in 1854 as one of the "free state" towns. In 1856 an antislavery convention there adopted the Topeka constitution, establishing a Topeka government, which was broken up by Federal troops. It became a city in 1857 and capital of the state in 1861. Population, 1940, 67,833.

Trenton. The capital of New Jersey, built on the eastern bank of the Delaware river, at the head of tidewater navigation, about 30 miles northeast of Philadelphia. Proximity to the coal fields of Pennsylvania and to the markets of New York and Philadelphia has contributed to its growth as an industrial center. Among its extensive and varied manufactures, the most noted is that of pottery, which ranks among the finest produced in the United States. Other important industries include the manufacture of wire cables, bridge sections, engines, electric lamps, rubber products, and linoleum.

The city is regularly laid out with many fine public buildings and residences. Among the more notable public buildings are the State capitol, the Federal building, the courthouse, the public library, and the State teachers college. A landmark of historic interest is Battle Monument surmounted by a colossal statue of Washington, which commemorates his command on the battlefield of Trenton. Trenton became a city in 1792. Population, 1940, 124,697.

Troy. A manufacturing city of east central New York. It is situated six miles north of Albany at the head of tidewater navigation on the Hudson river and at the point where the river is joined by the State barge canal. Troy is the chief center of the collar and cuff industry, manufacturing about nine-tenths of the collars and cuffs made in the United States. It is noted also for the manufacture of shirts, men's clothing, laundry machinery, valves, bells, engineering instruments, brushes, chains, and automobile parts. The chief educational institutions include the Rensselaer polytechnic institute and the Russell Sage college.

The vicinity of Troy was the scene of internecine struggles between the Mohawk and the Mohegan Indians, and during the Revolutionary War was the theater of stirring activities in resisting Burgoyne's invasion. Troy was incorporated as a village in 1794 and was chartered as a city in 1816. Population, 1940, 70,304.

Tucson (*tōō-sŏn'*). The second largest city of Arizona, situated in the southern part of the state, about 65 miles north of the Mexican border. It is the commercial center of a large district devoted to stock raising, mining, and farming. The local industries include ice factories, brickworks, and extensive railway shops. Tucson is the seat of the University of Arizona, the Desert botanical laboratory of the Carnegie institution, and other educational institutions. The warm, dry climate makes it a tourist and health center. A large desert sanatorium is located here. A replica of the walled city of Tucson as of 1859 stands 13 miles away, having been erected in making the motion picture *Arizona*. Population, 1940, 36,818.

Tulsa. One of the two largest cities of Oklahoma, on the Arkansas river, about 100 miles northeast of Oklahoma City. Tulsa is situated in one of the richest oil and natural gas fields in America. To the immense development of these resources, the city owes its remarkably rapid growth. More than 500 operating and refining oil companies are located in the city. The surrounding district also contains valuable deposits of coal.

The city is the trade center of a large outlying region devoted to farming, stock raising, and dairying, and, by reason of cheap and abundant fuel, has developed substantial industries. Among the chief of these are oil refining, flour and lumber milling, and the manufacture of aircraft, boilers, tools, stoves, and glass.

Tulsa occupies a fine, gently rolling site, and is well laid out, with many beautiful parks, boulevards, and handsome homes built by fortunes made in the oil fields. Mohawk park covers 2400 acres. The business district is noted for its impressive array of modern office buildings, including the 21-story Philtower building and the 27-story tower of the Exchange National Bank building. The city is the seat of Tulsa university and the Philbrook art center and Indian museum. Tulsa was founded in 1887 and was first chartered as a city in 1902. Population, 1940, 142,157.

Union City. A city of eastern New Jersey, adjoining Hoboken and Jersey City. It was formed in 1925 by a consolidation of the old towns of West Hoboken and Union. Weehawken, adjoining Union City on the east and fronting on the Hudson river, is the railroad terminal and port. Union City is a residential place for persons employed in New York City and Jersey City. It has also many local industries, their output including embroidery, silk, cement products, and rubber goods. Population, 1940, 56,173.

Utica. A city of central New York, situated on the Mohawk river and the State barge canal, about 95 miles west of Albany. Utica is the commercial center of a rich dairy-farming district. It is widely known for the excellence of its woolen, cotton, and knit goods and for a great variety of heating and ventilating apparatus. Other important manufactures are men's clothing, iron and steel forgings, iron beds and bed springs, air compressors, and rayon yarns. Dairy products are shipped in large quantities, and roses are extensively grown for the New York markets.

Utica is an important railway center and transfer point, and is often called the "Gateway to the Adirondacks." It occupies a beautiful site, is well laid out, and contains many fine public buildings and residences. Its parks cover 800 acres. Utica was incorporated in 1798. Population, 1940, 100,518.

Vallejo (*văl-yä'hō; vă-lā'ō*). A city of western California, located on an arm of San Pablo bay, opposite Mare island, about 25 miles northeast of San Francisco. Mare Island navy yard, contributes substantially to the commerce of the city. The city's industrial products include flour, lumber, and dairy products. Vallejo was founded in 1851 and was planned as the capital of the state. The legislature held sessions in Vallejo, 1851–53. Population, 1940, 20,072.

Valley Forge. A village on the Schuylkill river, in eastern Pennsylvania, about 24 miles west of Philadelphia. Valley Forge is famous as the place where Washington and the Colonial army of about 11,000 men endured terrible privations during the severe winter of 1777–78. The field with the trenches thrown up by the "ragged Continentals" remains substantially unchanged, and the old stone house where Washington made his headquarters still stands. An area of about 750 acres, including the old camp site, comprises Valley Forge Memorial park. This contains a carillon of bells, the complete number, 49, representing the individual states with one National Birthday bell.

Vancouver. A city of southwestern Washington, on the Columbia river, about 8 miles north of Portland, Oregon. The chief manufactures include lumber, aluminum, pulp and paper, canned fruit, metal castings, and machine shop products. A long interstate bridge over the Columbia river

SCENIC AMERICA. I—NATIONAL PARKS

Grand Canyon, Arizona, from Grand View Point
Grand Canyon, Arizona, from Hance's Point
Canyon of the Yellowstone
El Capitan, Yosemite
Lower Falls, Yellowstone
Glacier Point, Yosemite

Copyright by Detroit Photographic Co.

SCENIC AMERICA. II—EASTERN AND SOUTHERN SCENES

Bald Face Mountain, N. C.
Blue Mountain, Adirondacks
Ausable Chasm, N. Y.
Haines Falls, Catskills
Moccasin Bend, from Lookout Mt., Tenn.
Tomoka River, Florida

connects Vancouver with Oregon. Vancouver was established in 1825 by the Hudson's Bay Company and was incorporated in 1858. Population, 1940, 18,788.

Vicksburg. The third largest city of Mississippi, situated on the Mississippi river, about 45 miles west of Jackson. Vicksburg is attractively located on a high bluff and is an important river port with a large shipping trade in cotton. The chief manufacturing establishments include cottonseed oil mills, planing mills, foundries, and railway shops.

Vicksburg was incorporated in 1825 and came into great prominence during the Civil War. Its capture by the Union forces after a bitterly fought campaign was one of the decisive events of the great struggle between the North and the South. The Vicksburg National Military park, containing about 1300 acres and 30 miles of driveways with many monuments, restores the battle ground as it was in 1863. Population, 1940, 24,460.

Vincennes (*vĭn-sĕnz'*). A city of southwestern Indiana, on the Wabash river. It is the oldest settlement in the state, dating from 1727, when Sieur de Vincennes built a fortification there. A French trading post had been erected on the site as early as 1702. The city is in a rich agricultural region and has varied industrial interests, including structural steel, pearl buttons, glass, shoes, and flour.

Vincennes was under the French flag until 1777, was held by the British until 1779, and was taken by American troops in 1779 under George Rogers Clark, to whom is erected a $2,000,000 memorial on the river front. The house still stands where the first territorial legislature met in 1805, Vincennes having been capital of Indian territory from 1800 to 1813. Crossing of the Wabash river at this point by the Lincoln family in 1830 while migrating to Illinois is memorialized by a bridge, a marble shrine, and life-size bronze statue of Abraham Lincoln. Population, 1940, 18,228.

Waco. A city of east central Texas, on the Brazos river, about 105 miles northeast of Austin. Waco is the trade and shipping center of a rich agricultural region. The city is a leading cotton market for the interior of the state and has substantial industries. The principal manufactures are textiles, twine, woodwork, tents, awnings, camp furniture, clothing, and cement. Waco is the seat of Baylor university. The city was laid out in 1849 and was named for the Huaco Indians. Population, 1940, 55,982.

Walla Walla. A city of southeastern Washington, situated near the Oregon boundary. Walla Walla is the trade center of a fertile agricultural district with extensive dairy interests. The manufactures include farm machinery, flour, and lumber. The city is the seat of Whitman college and Walla Walla college. At Waiilatpu, six miles west, is a national monument park commemorating the first white family settling in the Pacific Northwest, that of Dr. Marcus Whitman, who founded a mission there in 1836. The settlers were massacred in 1847. Population, 1940, 18,109.

Walpi. A Hopi Indian village built on a lofty mesa, several hundred feet high, overlooking an arid desert in north central Arizona. The inhabitants are among the most interesting of the Pueblo tribes. These peaceful village dwellers steadfastly adhere to their aboriginal culture and ancient customs. Their houses are constructed of adobe or of stone set in clay mortar, with square rooms and flat roofs, through which trap doors provide entrances.

The elaborate ceremonials of the Hopi people include the celebrated snake dance, in which the performers carry living rattlesnakes. The Hopi are industrious farmers, and maintain abundant stores of corn, beans, and vegetables. They also weave excellent blankets and baskets and display great skill as potters and wood carvers. The village contains about 150 inhabitants.

Waltham (*wŏl'thăm*). A city of eastern Massachusetts, situated on the Charles river, about 10 miles west of Boston. Waltham is noted chiefly for the manufacture of watches. Here in 1854 was made the first successful attempt to manufacture watch movements, on an extensive scale, by machinery. These works now constitute one of the largest watch factories in the world. Other manufactures include emery wheels and furniture.

A point of interest is Norumbega tower, named in allusion to a fabulous city said by early explorers to be located in New England. Waltham was incorporated in 1738 and was chartered as a city in 1884. A mill established there in 1814 is said to have been the first complete power mill for the making of cotton cloth in America. Population, 1940, 40,020.

WASHINGTON (*wŏsh'ĭng-tŭn*). The capital of the United States, situated on the left bank of the Potomac river, about 100 miles from its mouth. Washington is coextensive with the District of Columbia. It is the administrative, legislative, and judicial center of the nation.

Site and Plan. The site was chosen by a commission headed by George Washington, and the city was planned by L'Enfant, a noted French engineer. Congress transferred its sittings from Philadelphia to the new capital in 1800. The city was captured and burned in 1814 by the British. At the time of the Civil War, it was fortified and made the headquarters of the Northern army. Following 1871, important improvements were made in the city, mainly in accordance with the original plan drawn up by L'Enfant. In the 1930's still greater improvements were made.

From 1802 until 1871, Washington's affairs were managed, under a charter, by its own citizens. In 1871, however, the charter was revoked, and the city was placed directly under the management of the Federal government. Residents have no voice either in civic or national government.

Area and Surface. The District of Columbia is about 70 square miles in area, including 8 square miles of water surface. The surface, on the whole, is gently undulating and the elevation of the land in the District varies within a range of approximately 400 feet.

Streets. The streets are laid out on a rectangular plan modified by a system of 26 avenues, which intersect the streets at different angles. A number of avenues converge on the two focal points of the city, namely, the Capitol and the executive mansion, or White House, the line of Pennsylvania avenue passing through both points of intersection. The streets and avenues are from 80 to 160 feet in width, many of them adorned on each side with a double row of trees.

Parks and Malls. In a central square stands a lofty monument erected to the memory of George Washington. Extending north, east, and west from this square are long, parklike areas, or malls. The north mall leads to the White House; the area to the east is the approach to the Capitol; and to the west of the monument along a reflecting pool stretches a vista terminating in the Lincoln memorial. Small parks and open squares or circles are found in various parts of the city and are usually dignified by the presence of statues or monuments. Potomac park consists of about 723 acres of land which has been largely reclaimed from the Potomac river. The "tidal basin," enclosed largely by reclaimed land, is partially surrounded by Japanese cherry trees. Rock Creek park, covering approximately 1600 acres, is a hilly tract of great natural beauty extending along both sides of the creek, which flows south, and widening at one point to form the picturesque National Zoological park, covering 170 acres.

Monuments. The monuments and buildings of Washington befit the dignity of the national capital. The Washington monument, already mentioned, is a majestic obelisk 555 feet in height. The stately Lincoln memorial takes the form of a Greek temple of the Doric order. It is surrounded by a peristyle of 36 columns, one for each of the states of the Union at the time of Lincoln's presidency. In the interior is a statue, heroic in size, of the martyred president. On the shore of the tidal basin rises the circular, dome-crowned memorial to Thomas Jefferson.

Buildings. The buildings of Washington, which are among the most beautiful in America, are characterized in general by the neoclassical type of architecture. The Capitol, a magnificent structure of the Corinthian order, having two immense wings and surmounted by a beautiful dome, occupies a commanding position on an eminence east of the Mall. The White House exhibits a pleasing and noble simplicity. The Library of Congress, containing one of the world's largest collections of books, is an imposing structure in the Renaissance style, near which stands the annex, modernistic in design. The Treasury, like the Supreme Court building, is an example of pure Greek architecture. One of the city's most exquisite structures is the Folger Shaksperian library.

The diverging lines of Constitution and Pennsylvania avenues form a triangular wedge of monumental buildings extending from the Apex building, nearest the Capitol, to the Department of Commerce building and the Treasury building, near the White House. This group includes the Archives and Internal Revenue buildings and structures housing the justice, post-office, labor and interior departments. South of this group are the Department of Agriculture building, the National Museum, and the Smithsonian Institution. Nearer to the Capitol is the National Gallery of art. West of the triangular wedge are the Federal Reserve building and the Interior Department building, one of the world's largest public office structures.

Other notable structures include the Corcoran Art Gallery, Continental Hall, the State, War, and Navy building, national Academy of Sciences, Pan-American, Red Cross, and Bureau of Engraving and Printing buildings.

The Naval Observatory is the source from which the official time is telegraphed to all parts of the country. Among Washington's many fine churches are the National Cathedral of Saint Peter and Paul, where President Wilson is buried, and the Franciscan monastery, which contains a replica of part of the Roman catacombs.

Commerce. The industries of Washington are devoted largely to the service of the government and to the supplying of local needs. The city's mercantile business, however, is very extensive. The city is entered by eight railroads and enjoys steamship service on the river. The street railway trolley wires are underground in the city proper.

Educational Institutions. The institutions of learning and research are numerous. They include George Washington university, Catholic University of America, American university, the Smithsonian Institution, the Carnegie Institution of Washington, Georgetown university, and Howard university. The Washington Academy of Sciences serves as "federal head" for many learned societies.

Points of Interest. The city and its environs are rich in historical associations. Mount Vernon, the home of Washington, lies on the right bank of the river, about 15 miles below the city. Across the Potomac from the Lincoln memorial, in Virginia, is Arlington national cemetery, containing a beautiful memorial amphitheater and the grave of the nation's Unknown Soldier. This cemetery is connected with Washington by the beautiful Arlington Memorial bridge. During the Civil War, Washington was encircled with a ring of 68 forts. These have since been unoccupied, except Fort Myer on Arlington Heights, opposite the city. Population, 1940, 663,091.

Washington, Mount. The highest peak in the White mountains of New Hampshire, and the loftiest summit in the northeastern United States. It rises from the massive Presidential range, in the central part of the White Mountain group, and reaches an elevation of 6288 feet. It lies east of Crawford Notch and is about 140 miles almost directly north of Boston.

The mountain is composed chiefly of granite. The east and north sides are gashed with deep gorges and the west slope is precipitous. The rocky summit, which rises many hundred feet above timber line, has a scant covering of alpine vegetation; the lower slopes are extensively forested. Trails, highways, and a rack-and-pinion railroad make it easy for travelers to reach the summit, on which are a government meteorological station and a commodious hotel.

Waterbury. A city of southwestern Connecticut, on the Naugatuck river, 32 miles southwest of Hartford. Abundant water power has contributed largely to the city's industrial prominence. Waterbury is the leading center for the manufacture of brass ware in the United States, and is often styled the "Brass City." It is noted also for the production of clocks and watches. In value of manufactures, Waterbury ranks among the first two or three cities of the state. The city occupies a hilly site and contains parks of great natural beauty. Population, 1940, 99,314.

Waterloo. A city of eastern Iowa on the Cedar river about 95 miles northeast of Des Moines. The surrounding country produces grain, cattle, and dairy products in great abundance, resulting in a large trade which centers in Waterloo. Industrial products include cream separators, tractors, automobiles, and agricultural implements. The Illinois Central railroad maintains car repair shops there. Waterloo is the headquarters for the Dairy Cattle Congress and the Belgian Horse Show. Population, 1940, 51,743.

Watkins Glen. A narrow gorge of unusual scenic beauty, situated near the village of Watkins Glen, New York, not far from the head of Seneca lake, and about 20 miles north of Elmira. Through this chasm, which, in places, is 300 feet deep, a narrow stream flows over a series of charming cascades and rapids. The rocks, which are Devonian shales, were worn into deep gorges by glacial ice.

West Point. A strong military post and noted military educational center in New York State. It occupies a picturesque site on the west bank of the Hudson river, about 50 miles north of New York City. The government reservation, including Constitution island, covers 3574 acres and is the seat of the United States Military Academy. It has a great repository for the storing of monetary silver. Among many fine buildings and monuments are Memorial Hall, containing trophies of war, and a handsome equestrian statue of George Washington. West Point was a position of great strategic importance in the Revolutionary War. Benedict Arnold plotted, while in command here, to betray it to the British, but this result was prevented by the timely discovery of the plot.

Wheat Belt. The name applied to the section of the United States in which more than two-thirds of the nation's wheat crop is grown. In reality, there are two wheat belts, the winter wheat belt and the spring wheat belt.

The winter wheat belt lies mostly south of the central corn belt, portions of which it overlaps. The chief producing area for winter wheat includes southern Nebraska, central Kansas, western Oklahoma, northern Texas, nearly all of Missouri, Illinois, Indiana, and Ohio, and a part of southern Pennsylvania.

The spring wheat belt lies almost entirely to the north of the corn belt, and is comprised chiefly in the states of North Dakota, South Dakota, and Minnesota. Outside of these three states, the most important district devoted to the production of spring wheat is eastern Washington.

Wheeling. The second largest city of West Virginia, on the Ohio river, in the northern "panhandle," about 65 miles southwest of Pittsburgh, Pennsylvania. Wheeling owes its industrial and commercial importance to large supplies of natural gas, to extensive near-by coal fields, and to abundant raw material, made available by excellent facilities for transportation, both by rail and by water. There are more than 200 manufacturing establishments in Wheeling, and the total value of its products is greater than that of any other city in the state. The leading manufactures include iron and steel products, pottery, glass, tobacco, tin plate, and aluminum ware. There are also print works, packing houses, tanneries, and large proprietary remedy works.

The city occupies an excellent site, rising gradually from the river, and contains many fine streets and public buildings. Among interesting features are the combined courthouse and city hall (formerly the State capitol), the government building, the Roman Catholic cathedral, the Market auditorium, and Wheeling park. Oglebay park, of 750 acres, is a country recreational center. Wheeling island, a beautiful residential section, is connected with the main part of the city by a historic suspension bridge. The West Virginia State fair is held at Wheeling.

The first settlement on the site of Wheeling was made in 1769 by Ebenezer Zane. Fort Henry, named for Patrick Henry, was built in 1774 and, during the Revolutionary War, was repeatedly, but unsuccessfully, attacked by the Indians and the British. Wheeling was incorporated in 1795 and was chartered as a city in 1836. From 1863 to 1870, and again from 1875 to 1885, Wheeling was the capital of the state. Population, 1940, 61,099.

White Sulphur Springs. A health and pleasure resort of southeastern West Virginia, situated in a picturesque mountain region not far from the Virginia border. The district is noted for its numerous mineral springs, and its fame as a watering place dates from the period of the Revolutionary War. Many thousands of tourists visit it annually. Permanent population, 1940, 2093.

Whitney, Mount. The highest peak in the United States, excluding Alaska. It is situated in the main range of the Sierra Nevada, in eastern California, and is surrounded by a region of unusual scenic magnificence. Its eastern slope rises precipitously nearly 11,000 feet above Owens valley, and the peak itself towers to an elevation of 14,496 feet above sea level. The lowest land in North America, Death valley, much of which is below sea level, lies only 86 miles east of this gigantic mountain.

While on its slopes there is extensive evidence of former glacial action, no glaciers now exist on Mount Whitney. Permanent snow and ice are confined to the upper northern slopes. The peak may be ascended with comparative ease, and extensive scientific observations have been carried on at its summit.

Wichita (*wĭch'ĭ-tô*). The second largest city of Kansas, situated on the Arkansas river, in the southern part of the state, about 160 miles southwest of Topeka. Wichita is located in the fertile Arkansas valley and is the commercial center of a region devoted to the production of wheat, corn, broom corn, sorghum, alfalfa, cattle, hogs, and poultry. It is also the supply depot for extensive oil fields in the vicinity.

The city has a large wholesale trade and is one of the chief distributing points in the Southwest. It is the leading broom corn market of the world and an important flour milling and meat packing center. A leading center of airplane manufacture, it numbers among its other industries railway car construction, publishing, and the manufacture of farm implements, rubber tires, stoves, and numerous other commodities.

The city occupies an excellent site, is regularly laid out, and there are many fine streets, parks, and public buildings. It has an airport one mile square. Wichita is the seat of the Friends university and the University of Wichita. Wichita is the name of a tribe of Indians. The city was settled in 1870 and incorporated in 1871. Population, 1940, 114,966.

Wichita Falls. A city of northern Texas, on the Wichita river, about 100 miles northwest of Fort Worth. Wichita Falls is the distributing center for a large agricultural and stock raising region, and is the metropolis of a rich petroleum oil and gas field. Its principal manufactures are window glass, auto trucks, flour, and oil well machinery. The refining of petroleum is one of the most important industries. Wichita Falls was settled in 1882 and was chartered as a city in 1884. Population, 1940, 45,112.

Wilkes-Barre (*wĭlks' băr'ĭ*). A city of northeastern Pennsylvania, on the Susquehanna river, about 100 miles northwest of Philadelphia. It is situated in the picturesque Wyoming valley and is in the center of one of the richest anthracite coal fields in the world. The value of its coal production is said to be greater than the annual production of gold, silver, lead, and aluminum in the United States.

Wilkes-Barre possesses some of the most extensive lace and silk mills in the country, and manufactures locomotives, boilers, airplanes, tobacco products, insulated wire, and wire rope. The city has handsome public buildings, and many fine streets, parks, and recreation grounds.

Wilkes-Barre was settled in 1769 by people from New England, and named in honor of John Wilkes and Isaac Barre, members of the British Parliament. It was the scene of desperate struggles with the British and Indians during the Revolutionary War, the Wyoming massacre taking place four miles from its site. The city is noted as the birthplace of the anthracite coal industry. Here "stone coal," as it was early called, was first used for domestic purposes. Population, 1940, 86,236.

Williamsburg. A historic city of eastern Virginia, 48 miles east by south of Richmond, in a peninsula between the James and York rivers. It was settled in 1632 and was known as Middle Plantation until 1699. From 1698 to 1799, it was the capital of Virginia. It is the seat of William and Mary college, opened in 1693, which, after Harvard, is the oldest college in the United States.

In 1927, under the active interest of John D. Rockefeller, Jr., the restoration of the colonial area of Williamsburg was undertaken. Among the many restored structures are the original college building, designed by Sir Christopher Wren, and the Raleigh tavern, where the Virginia assembly met when dissolved by royal governors. Recently erected business structures are made to conform with the earlier architectural style. Here in 1776 the Phi Beta Kappa society was organized. Population, 1940, 3942.

Wilmington. The chief city of Delaware, located on the Delaware river, at its junction with Christina river about 27 miles southwest of Philadelphia.

The favorable location, excellent transportation facilities, nearness to the great coal fields and to the sources of raw material, together with water power furnished by the Christina, have combined to make the city an important manufacturing center. It produces more than half of the industrial output of the state. The du Pont chemical industries center in Wilmington, which is the city of their origin. They began as a powder mill, established in 1802, the first in America. Other important industries are the manufacture of steam railway cars, paper, fiber products, machine shop products, and shipbuilding. Immense powder and dye mills, located across the river in New Jersey, contribute substantially to the city's trade. Public parks cover 907 acres.

The town was founded in 1638 by Swedes and was known by various names. It was incorporated in 1739, received the name of Wilmington in 1745, and, in 1832, was chartered as a city. Population, 1940, 112,504.

Wilmington. The chief port of North Carolina, situated on the Cape Fear river, 30 miles from its mouth. Wilmington has an excellent harbor, accommodating large seagoing vessels, and is an important commercial city with an extensive shipping trade, especially in tobacco, peanuts, and cotton. The city is located in a highly productive agricultural district, of which it is the mercantile center. The chief industries include the manufacture of ships, chemicals, fertilizers, lumber, petroleum and concrete products, cotton goods, and boxes.

Wilmington was first settled in 1730 and incorporated in 1739. Here, in 1765, was the first armed resistance to the British Stamp act. In 1781–82, the place was occupied by the British. During the Civil War, the port was the chief gateway between the South and foreign nations. It was the principal resort of the blockade runners. Population, 1940, 33,407.

Wilson, Mount. A peak in the Sierra Madre range of southern California, about 10 miles northeast of Pasadena. On its summit, which rises to an elevation of 5750 feet, is the Mount Wilson observatory, containing the famous Hooker 100-inch reflecting telescope and other powerful instruments for astronomical research. An automobile road leads from Pasadena to the summit, which affords excellent views of the surrounding region.

Winston-Salem. The second largest city of North Carolina, situated about 115 miles west of Raleigh. It is located in a region noted for tobacco growing, and has become the most important center for the manufacture of tobacco in the United States. Its immense factories are said to turn out more manufactured tobacco products than those of any other city in the world. In value of manufactures, Winston-Salem outranks practically all other cities of the South. Other products include hosiery, underwear, air conditioning machinery, and furniture.

The business and industrial establishments are, for the most part, centered in Winston, while Salem is chiefly residential and noted for its historic interest. The city is the seat of Salem college for young women and a State teachers college for Negroes. Salem was founded in 1766 by Moravians and long remained under the direct control of the Moravian church. Winston was founded in 1849 and received its municipal charter in 1899. The two communities were consolidated in 1913. Population, 1940, 79,815.

Woonsocket (*wōōn'sŏk'ĕt*). A city of Rhode Island, on the Blackstone river, about 16 miles northwest of Providence. Woonsocket is the seat of extensive manufactures, among the most important of which are cottons, woolens, worsteds, rubber boots and shoes, and wringing machines. It is the seat of Mount Saint Charles college, Saint Ann's academy, and the Harris Institute library. Woonsocket is a consolidation of several factory villages, and the first village called Woonsocket is not included within the present city, which received its charter of incorporation in 1888. Population, 1940, 49,303.

Worcester (*wŏŏs'tẽr*). The second largest city of Massachusetts, built on both banks of the Blackstone river, about 40 miles west of Boston. The city occupies a picturesque site covering the river valley and a number of the surrounding hills.

Worcester is pre-eminently a manufacturing city, and is one of the greatest machine tool centers in the world. Among noteworthy manufacturing establishments are immense rolling mills, wire factories, envelope factories, and loom works. Other important manufactures are carpets, leather goods, steam and electric cars, shoes, corsets, and firearms.

The city is admirably laid out, has many beautiful streets, parks, and public buildings, and ranks high among the cities of the state in general civic improvements. There are 17 public parks, covering a total area of 1254 acres, and the playgrounds occupy 74 acres. Among noteworthy buildings are the city hall, the Federal building, the courthouse, Mechanic's hall, Memorial auditorium, and the Masonic temple.

Worcester is the seat of Clark university, Holy Cross college, Assumption college, Worcester polytechnic institute, and a State teachers college. There is an excellent art museum, with an endowment of $4,000,000. The library of the American Antiquarian Society, founded in 1812, is rich in historical material, and the Worcester musical festival, held annually, is one of the most important institutions of its kind in the United States.

First settled in 1672, Worcester was twice abandoned because of the hostility of the Indians, especially during King Philip's war. It was incorporated in 1722 and was chartered as a city in 1848. Within the vicinity of Worcester were born Eli Whitney, inventor of the cotton gin; Erastus Bigelow, inventor of the carpet-weaving machine; Elias Howe, inventor of the sewing machine; Lucius Knowles, who perfected the modern power loom; and George Bancroft, the historian. Population, 1940, 193,694.

Wyandotte Cave. A natural formation in Crawford county, southern Indiana, five miles northeast of Leavenworth. It is third in size to Carlsbad cave and has a greater number and variety of stalactites and stalagmites than any other known cave in the United States. Besides the numerous chambers and galleries, the 23 miles of the cave that have been explored contain Monument "mountain," rising 175 feet from the floor, and the Pillar of the Constitution, a large stalagmite 30 feet high and 75 feet in circumference.

Yakima (*yăk'ĭ-mȧ*). A city of central Washington, situated about 160 miles southeast of Seattle. Yakima, formerly called North Yakima, is the commercial center of the Yakima valley. This valley contains one of the largest areas of irrigated land in the western United States and is widely noted for the excellent apples and other fine fruits which it produces. The city's chief industrial establishments include fruit canneries, fruit packing houses, flour mills, sugar, and lumber mills. Population, 1940, 27,221.

YELLOWSTONE PARK. The largest national park in the United States, situated mainly in northwestern Wyoming but encroaching slightly upon adjoining portions of Montana and Idaho. It is approximately 62 miles long and 54 miles wide, and covers an area of 3472 square miles. Of this area, 3200 square miles are in Wyoming, 236 square miles are in Montana, and 36 square miles are in Idaho.

Rivers and Lakes. Within the limits of the park are the headwaters of several large rivers, including the Yellowstone, the Snake, the Lewis, the Madison, and the Shoshone. The Continental Divide, passing through the park from southeast to northwest, marks the line of separation of the waters draining into the Atlantic from those flowing into the Pacific. There are also numerous lakes, the largest of which is Yellowstone lake, some 20 miles long and from about 5 to 15 miles wide. Below timber line, the less precipitous mountains, as well as the more level portions of the park, are beautifully forested with pine, spruce, and other evergreen trees.

Surface and Origin. The central part of the park is essentially a high plateau, lying at an average elevation of about 8000 feet above sea level. Except on its southwestern border, this plateau is surrounded by massive, snow-capped mountains, whose culminating peaks and ridges rise from 2000 to 4000 feet above the enclosed table-land.

In its origin, the whole region is volcanic. Not only the encircling mountains but also the interior plains are made up of volcanic ash and lava, ejected in some former geologic age from far below the surface. Striking evidences of this are seen in the black glass of Obsidian cliff, in the contorted lavas along the road near the summit of Mount Washburn, and in the fused, highly colored sands composing the walls of Yellowstone canyon.

Scenic Features. The entire park is a scenic wonderland. Its chief features are the geysers, which are the greatest in the world; the Grand Canyon of the Yellowstone, which, in beauty though not in size, rivals the Grand Canyon of the Colorado; Yellowstone falls, ranking among the finest of American cataracts; and the remarkable fossil forests along the Lamar river.

Geysers. There are five active geyser basins—the Norris, the Upper, the Lower, the Heart Lake, and the Shoshone—all lying in the west and south central parts of the park. The numerous geysers in these various fields differ greatly in size, character, and action. Some, as, for example, Old Faithful, spout at nearly regular intervals, longer or shorter, while others are exceedingly irregular. Some burst upward to a great height, displaying immense power; others shoot tiny streams or bubble and foam while in eruption.

Hot Springs. Besides the geysers, there are marvelously colored hot springs, mud volcanoes, and other strange and wonderful formations. At Mammoth Hot Springs, and also at Norris and at Thumb, the hot water has brought to the surface immense quantities of white mineral deposits. These have built up high terraces containing beautifully incrusted basins, over the edges of which the hot water pours. Microscopic plants, growing on the edges and on the sides of these basins, color them with brilliant hues of pink, red, and bluish gray. The surface of many hot springs appears brilliantly colored, and the deeper pools in the terraces are often intensely green.

Grand Canyon and Falls. Because of the vivid coloration of its walls, in some places 2000 feet high, the Grand Canyon of the Yellowstone is a scenic feature of the first order. The colors vary from pearly white and pale lemon to orange, pink, and crimson. With the deep green of the forest above, these give a beautiful setting to the Yellowstone falls, which are twice as high as Niagara. The view of the canyon and of the cataract is one of the most impressive in America.

Fossil Forests. The fossil forests along the Lamar river contain many petrified tree trunks which stand upright in the faces of nearly vertical cliffs that rise to a height of nearly 2000 feet above the valley floor. These petrified trunks are found at different depths, indicating a succession of forests, which, from time to time, have been overwhelmed, like Pompeii, with volcanic materials.

Animal Life. The park is a great wild-animal refuge or natural zoological garden. It contains protected herds of elk, moose, deer, antelope, and American bison. There are also numerous groups of brown, cinnamon, and grizzly bears, some of which have become remarkably tame and friendly. Yellowstone lake and the other waters of the park abound in trout.

Accessibility. Yellowstone park is reached by rail at Gardiner, Montana, on the north, and also at West Yellowstone, Montana, on the west. The eastern entrance to the park is reached by auto stage from Cody, Wyoming, 55 miles distant. The southern or Snake River entrance is reached by an auto road from the main north-and-south highway in Idaho. This turns eastward at Saint Anthony, crosses the famous Teton mountains and the Jackson Hole country, and thence proceeds northward to the park. The southern entrance may be reached also by various auto routes leading northward from the Lincoln highway in southern Wyoming.

Travel Facilities. Automobile roads and trails reach all the important features of the park. There are hotels, camps, stores, auto-transportation lines, and various other facilities and accommodations for travelers. The various park utilities are operated during the tourist season, which extends usually from June 20 to September 20.

Yonkers. A residential and manufacturing city of southeastern New York, on the Hudson river, 14 miles north of the center of New York City. It is magnificently situated along the east bank of the Hudson river, its site rising in a gradual slope to an elevation of 400 feet, from which may be obtained splendid views of the river and of the towering Palisades.

Of the many and varied industries of Yonkers, the principal are carpet weaving and the manufacture of machine shop products, elevators, drugs, clothing, auto trailers, and chemicals.

Yonkers was founded about 1646 and incorporated in 1788. The northern portion was chartered as a city in 1872; the southern portion was annexed to New York City in 1874. Population, 1940, 142,598.

York. A manufacturing and commercial center of southeastern Pennsylvania, 25 miles southeast of Harrisburg. York is situated in the midst of a highly productive agricultural district with which it conducts an extensive trade. Its chief industries are the manufacture of foundry and machine products and of cigars. Other manufactures include agricultural implements, safes and vaults, refrigeration machinery, artificial teeth, cigar boxes, silk goods, and hosiery.

York was first permanently settled in 1735 by a German colony. It was laid out in 1741 by the sons of William Penn, was incorporated in 1787, and received its city charter in 1887. In 1777–78, the Continental Congress held sessions in York while the British were occupying Philadelphia. Population, 1940, 56,712.

Yorktown. A village of southeastern Virginia, situated on an arm of Chesapeake bay, about 70 miles southeast of Richmond. Yorktown is famous as the scene of the surrender, October 19, 1781, of the British army, by Lord Cornwallis. This virtually ended the Revolutionary War, and there is an impressive monument commemorating the event. The Yorktown battlefield area, reconstructed with fortifications and marked with explanatory signs, forms part of the Colonial national historical park. In 1862, General G. B. McClellan, with a large Union army, besieged the place and compelled its evacuation by the Confederate forces under General J. E. Johnston. On the principal street of the village stands the oldest customhouse in the United States. Population, 1940, 521.

YOSEMITE (*yô-sĕm'ĭ-tê*) **PARK.** A national park, containing some of the most magnificent scenery in America. It lies immediately west of the summit of the Sierra Nevada, in central California, about 160 miles east of San Francisco.

Area and Surface. The park occupies a mountainous tract, some 50 miles long, north and south, with an extreme width, east and west, of about 35 miles, the whole embracing an area of 1176 square miles. This region, in general, slopes to the west, and is traversed by two main rivers, the Merced and the Tuolumne, and by their numerous tributaries.

The surface varies from deep valley floors on the west, which lie at an elevation of less than 4000 feet above the sea, to snow-capped peaks which tower to heights of 13,000 feet, along the eastern boundary. Extensive areas are covered with noble forests of immense evergreen trees. These are interspersed with charming mountain meadows and many beautiful lakes. There are innumerable canyons, gorges, and narrow valleys, with rushing streams, cascades, and cataracts, fed, in large part, from the glaciers and snow fields on the higher mountains.

The surface features that give to the park its most striking character were mainly formed by glacial action and by river erosion. These natural agencies, working through long periods of geological time, have produced the deepest valleys and the highest waterfalls on the continent.

Scenic Features. Like Yellowstone park, the Yosemite region presents a long succession of scenic wonders. The chief of these are included in the celebrated Yosemite valley, in the Tuolumne canyon with the Hetch Hetchy, and in the famous Mariposa grove of "big trees."

Yosemite Valley. This incomparable valley is about 7 miles long, with an average width of about a mile. Through the bottom of this valley, the Merced river flows. On either side, the valley is bordered with a succession of vast cliffs and lofty granite domes which rise almost vertically to immense heights. Among the most noted of these massive rock formations, with the heights of their summits above the valley floor, are: Cathedral Rocks, 2591 feet; El Capitan, 3604 feet; Sentinel Dome, 4157 feet; Half Dome, 4892 feet; and Clouds Rest, 5964 feet.

Waterfalls. Over the edges of towering precipices in the rock walls that enclose the Yosemite valley, plunge some of the most remarkable cataracts known. The Upper Yosemite falls drop 1430 feet in one sheer descent. Immediately below, the stream cascades through a drop of 620 feet, known as the Middle Yosemite falls, and then takes a drop of 320 feet over the Lower Yosemite falls. These three falls, which are parts of one great cataract, make a drop of 2370 feet, equal to 14 Niagaras, before their waters reach the Merced river. Bridal Veil falls has a drop of 620 feet; Vernal falls, 320 feet; Illouette falls, 370 feet; and Nevada falls, 594 feet. The Ribbon falls, the highest of all, drops 1612 feet sheer, a straight fall about ten times as great as that of Niagara. Nowhere else in the world is there such an array of stupendous waterfalls.

Tuolumne Valley. With the opening of roads and trails, making this region of the park accessible, the fine scenic features of the Tuolumne basin are also becoming celebrated. These include the beautiful Hetch Hetchy valley, the Grand Canyon of the Tuolumne, and the remarkable Waterwheel falls, in which enormous arcs of water are flung from 50 to 80 feet into the air.

Big Trees. The greatest grove of giant sequoias outside of Sequoia national park is the Mariposa grove on the southern border of Yosemite park. The monster tree of this grove is the Grizzly Giant, whose girth is 93 feet, whose diameter is 29½ feet, and whose height is 204 feet. In massiveness, this immense tree is exceeded only by the General Sherman tree, 36½ feet in diameter and 280 feet high, in Sequoia national park, and by the General Grant tree, 35 feet in diameter and 264 feet high, in General Grant national park. Other noted trees in the Mariposa grove are the Washington tree, slightly smaller than the Grizzly Giant; the Columbia tree, 294 feet high; and the Wawona tree, through the trunk of which runs an automobile road 26 feet wide. There are two minor sequoia groves in the park—the Merced and the Tuolumne.

Accessibility. Yosemite park is reached by rail to El Portal, near the western boundary of the park, and thence by automobile into the Yosemite valley. The park is reached also from Merced by auto stage to Mariposa and Wawona, thence to the Mariposa grove of "big trees," and into the Yosemite valley. It may be reached by auto roads from various other points, and the traveler usually has his choice of leaving by one of various routes other than the one by which he entered. The Tioga road, which crosses the park from east to west, forms a link in a fine scenic highway across the Sierras to Lake Tahoe. The Yosemite valley is the northern terminus of the John Muir trail, built southward along the crest of the Sierras.

Travel Facilities. Automobile roads and trails have been built to the chief places of interest. There are hotels, camps, stores, auto-transportation lines, saddle horses, camping and hiking equipment, and various other facilities and accommodations for travelers. Yosemite valley is always open and may be reached by way of El Portal throughout the year. The regular tourist season extends from May 1 to November 1, though the higher mountain roads usually are not open until midsummer. A feature of much interest is the presence of bears, usually eager to be fed by tourists.

Youngstown. A city of northeastern Ohio, on the Mahoning river, about 65 miles southeast of Cleveland. Youngstown owes its importance as a steel manufacturing center to its advantageous situation near necessary raw materials and to excellent transportation facilities. In the vicinity are coal mines and limestone quarries. Iron ore from Minnesota is available with a short haul from lake ports.

The city's chief industrial establishments are its immense blast furnaces, steel works, and rolling mills. Other manufactures include many subsidiary steel products, such as steel rails, steel pipes, and engine boilers; also tin plate, coke, rubber goods, and electrical machinery. The Youngstown steel district produces about one-sixth of all the pig iron and about one-eighth of all the steel made in the United States. The city has 1950 acres in public parks. Among the public buildings of especial note are the Stambaugh Memorial auditorium and the Butler art institute.

Youngstown was settled in 1796, was incorporated in 1848, and received its city charter in 1867. A blast furnace was built in 1805 and a rolling mill was erected in 1845. Population, 1940, 167,720.

Yuma. A city of southwestern Arizona, built on the east bank of the Colorado river, at the mouth of the Gila, about 7 miles from the Mexican boundary. The surrounding region is remarkable for its almost continuous sunshine and for the extreme dryness of its climate. The annual rainfall of 3.13 inches at Yuma is the lowest recorded at any station of the United States weather bureau. Summer temperatures of 110° to 120° in the shade are recorded. Yet, owing to the low humidity, sunstroke is practically unknown. Yuma was established in 1700 by Spanish missionaries. It is the trade center of a mining district in which large quantities of alfalfa seed and other field crops and fruits are produced through the development of irrigation. Population, 1940, 5325.

Zanesville. A city in Ohio, located on the Muskingum river at the mouth of the Licking, 58 miles east of Columbus. The Muskingum river is here spanned by a "Y" bridge, branches going to both sides of the Licking river. Zanesville occupies an attractive site, surrounded by lofty hills. It is well planned, with fine broad streets and several spacious parks. It is also well provided with educational institutions, including a Carnegie library. Its varied industries include the manufacture of pottery, glass, tiles, electrical transformers, steel, cement, shoes, and barrels. From its large pottery production it is sometimes known as the "Clay City."

Zanesville was founded in 1797 by Ebenezer Zane and others, and, during 1810–12, it was the capital of the state. It was incorporated in 1814 and was chartered as a city in 1850. Population, 1940, 37,500.

Zuñi (*zōō'nyê; sōō'-*). The largest of the Pueblo Indian villages, situated near the western boundary of New Mexico, about 40 miles south of Gallup. The inhabitants, who possess a distinct language, call themselves Ashiwi. They are descendants of the people of "Cibola," mentioned by the earliest Spanish explorers.

Like Pueblo Indians generally, the Zuñi people are peace loving, devoted chiefly to agriculture, and adhere with great tenacity to their ancient culture and customs. In the construction of their adobe and stone houses, in their methods of irrigation and agriculture, in weaving, in pottery making, and in other arts, as well as in their elaborate ceremonials, they closely resemble the other village-dwelling Indians of the Southwest.

The Spaniards first visited the Zuñi people in 1539 but were driven away. Later, Spanish missionaries gained considerable influence with them. Population, about 1900.

CITIES AND OTHER INCORPORATED* PLACES IN THE UNITED STATES HAVING A POPULATION OF 9000 AND UPWARD, 1940

City	Pop. 1940	Pop. 1930	City	Pop. 1940	Pop. 1930	City	Pop. 1940	Pop. 1930
Alabama:			**Arkansas—Con.:**			**California—Con.:**		
Anniston	25,523	22,345	El Dorado	15,858	16,421	Colton	9,686	8,014
Bessemer	22,826	20,721	Fort Smith	36,584	31,429	Compton	16,198	12,516
Birmingham	267,583	259,678	Hot Springs	21,370	20,238	Daly City	9,625	7,838
Decatur	16,604	15,593	Jonesboro	11,729	10,326	El Centro	10,017	8,434
Dothan	17,194	16,046	Little Rock	88,039	81,679	Eureka	17,055	15,752
Fairfield	11,703	11,059	North Little Rock	21,137	19,418	Fresno	60,685	52,513
Florence	15,043	11,729	Pine Bluff	21,290	20,760	Fullerton	10,442	10,860
Gadsden	36,975	24,042	Texarkana[1]	11,821	10,764	Glendale	82,582	62,736
Huntsville	13,050	11,554				Huntington Park	28,648	24,591
Mobile	78,720	68,202				Inglewood	30,114	19,480
Montgomery	78,084	66,079	**California:**			Lodi	11,079	6,788
Phenix City	15,351	13,862	Alameda	36,256	35,033	Long Beach	164,271	142,032
Selma	19,834	18,012	Albany	11,493	8,569	Los Angeles	1,504,277	1,238,048
Talladega	9,298	7,596	Alhambra	38,935	29,472	Lynwood	10,982	7,323
Tuscaloosa	27,493	20,659	Anaheim	11,031	10,995	Maywood	10,731	6,794
			Arcadia	9,122	5,216	Merced	10,135	7,066
			Bakersfield	29,252	26,015	Modesto	16,379	13,842
			Bell	11,264	7,884	Monrovia	12,807	10,890
Arizona:			Belvedere township†	37,192	33,023	Monterey	10,084	9,141
Phoenix	65,414	48,118	Berkeley	85,547	82,109	National City	10,344	7,301
Tucson	36,818	32,506	Beverly Hills	26,823	17,429	Oakland	302,163	284,063
			Brawley	11,718	10,439	Ontario	14,197	13,583
			Burbank	34,337	16,662	Palo Alto	16,774	13,652
Arkansas:			Burlingame	15,940	13,270	Pasadena	81,864	76,086
Blytheville	10,652	10,098	Chico	9,287	7,961	Piedmont	9,866	9,333

*Including unincorporated places which are classified as urban under a special rule by the Bureau of the Census. All such places are marked with a dagger(†).

†Classified as urban under a special rule of the Bureau of the Census.

CITIES AND OTHER INCORPORATED* PLACES IN THE UNITED STATES HAVING A POPULATION OF 9000 AND UPWARD, 1940—Con.

City	Pop. 1940	Pop. 1930
California—Con.:		
Pittsburg	9,520	9,610
Pomona	23,539	20,804
Redlands	14,324	14,177
Redondo Beach	13,092	9,347
Redwood City	12,453	8,962
Richmond	23,642	20,093
Riverside	34,696	29,696
Sacramento	105,958	93,750
Salinas	11,586	10,263
San Bernardino	43,646	37,481
San Buenaventura (Ventura)	13,264	11,603
San Diego	203,341	147,995
San Fernando	9,094	7,567
San Francisco	634,536	634,394
San Gabriel	11,867	7,224
San Jose	68,457	57,651
San Leandro	14,601	11,455
San Mateo	19,403	13,444
Santa Ana	31,921	30,322
Santa Barbara	34,958	33,613
Santa Cruz	16,896	14,395
Santa Monica	53,500	37,146
Santa Rosa	12,605	10,636
South Gate	26,945	19,632
South Pasadena	14,356	13,730
Stockton	54,714	47,963
Torrance	9,950	7,271
Vallejo	20,072	16,072
Whittier	16,115	14,822
Colorado:		
Boulder	12,958	11,223
Colorado Springs	36,789	33,237
Denver	322,412	287,861
Englewood	9,680	7,980
Fort Collins	12,251	11,489
Grand Junction	12,479	10,247
Greeley	15,995	12,203
Pueblo	52,162	50,096
Trinidad	13,223	11,732
Connecticut:		
Ansonia	19,210	19,898
Bridgeport	147,121	146,716
Bristol	30,167	28,451
Danbury	22,339	22,261
Derby	10,287	10,788
East Hartford town†	18,615	17,125
Hartford	166,267	164,072
Meriden	39,494	38,481
Middletown	26,495	24,554
Naugatuck	15,388	14,315
New Britain	68,685	68,128
New Haven	160,605	162,655
New London	30,456	29,640
Norwalk	39,849	36,019
Norwich	23,652	23,021
Shelton	10,971	10,113
Stamford	47,938	46,346
Stratford town†	22,580	19,212
Torrington	26,988	26,040
Wallingford	11,425	11,170
Waterbury	99,314	99,902
West Hartford town†	33,776	24,941
West Haven town†	30,021	25,808
Willimantic	12,101	12,102
Delaware:		
Wilmington	112,504	106,597
Dist. of Columbia:		
Washington	663,091	486,869
Florida:		
Clearwater	10,136	7,607
Daytona Beach	22,584	16,598
Fort Lauderdale	17,996	8,666
Fort Myers	10,604	9,082
Florida—Con.:		
Gainesville	13,757	10,465
Jacksonville[2]	173,065	129,549
Key West	12,927	12,831
Lakeland	22,068	18,554
Miami	172,172	110,637
Miami Beach	28,012	6,494
Orlando	36,736	27,330
Panama City	11,610	5,402
Pensacola	37,449	31,579
St. Augustine	12,090	12,111
St. Petersburg	60,812	40,425
Sanford	10,217	10,100
Sarasota	11,141	8,398
Tallahassee	16,240	10,700
Tampa	108,391	101,161
West Palm Beach	33,693	26,610
Georgia:		
Albany	19,055	14,507
Americus	9,281	8,760
Athens	20,650	18,192
Atlanta	302,288	270,366
Augusta	65,919	60,342
Brunswick	15,035	14,022
Cedartown	9,025	8,124
Columbus	53,280	43,131
Dalton	10,448	8,160
Decatur	16,561	13,276
District 1511, Center Hill†	12,155	8,460
East Point	12,403	9,512
Gainesville	10,243	8,624
Griffin	13,222	10,321
La Grange	21,983	20,131
Macon	57,865	53,829
Moultrie	10,147	8,027
Rome	26,282	21,843
Savannah	95,996	85,024
Thomasville	12,683	11,733
Valdosta	15,595	13,482
Waycross	16,763	15,510
Idaho:		
Boise City	26,130	21,544
Coeur d'Alene	10,049	8,297
Idaho Falls	15,024	9,429
Lewiston	10,548	9,403
Nampa	12,149	8,206
Pocatello	18,133	16,471
Twin Falls	11,851	8,787
Illinois:		
Alton	31,255	30,151
Aurora	47,170	46,589
Belleville	28,405	28,425
Berwyn	48,451	47,027
Bloomington	32,868	30,930
Blue Island	16,638	16,534
Brookfield	10,817	10,035
Cairo	14,407	13,532
Calumet City	13,241	12,298
Canton	11,577	11,718
Centralia	16,343	12,583
Champaign	23,302	20,348
Chicago	3,396,808	3,376,438
Chicago Heights	22,461	22,321
Cicero	64,712	66,602
Collinsville	9,767	9,235
Danville	36,919	36,765
Decatur	59,305	57,510
De Kalb	9,146	8,545
Des Plaines	9,518	8,798
Dixon	10,671	9,908
Downers Grove	9,526	8,977
East Moline	12,359	10,107
East St. Louis	75,609	74,347
Elgin	38,333	35,929
Elmhurst	15,458	14,055
Elmwood Park	13,689	11,270
Evanston	65,389	63,120
Illinois—Con.:		
Forest Park	14,840	14,555
Freeport	22,366	22,045
Galesburg	28,876	28,830
Granite City	22,974	25,130
Harrisburg	11,453	11,625
Harvey	17,878	16,374
Herrin	9,352	9,708
Highland Park	14,476	12,203
Jacksonville	19,844	17,747
Joliet	42,365	42,993
Kankakee	22,241	20,620
Kewanee	16,901	17,093
La Grange	10,479	10,103
La Salle	12,812	13,149
Lincoln	12,752	12,855
Marion	9,251	9,033
Mattoon	15,827	14,631
Maywood	26,648	25,829
Melrose Park	10,933	10,741
Moline	34,608	32,236
Monmouth	9,096	8,666
Mount Vernon	14,724	12,375
Oak Park	66,015	63,982
Ottawa	16,005	15,094
Paris	9,281	8,781
Park Ridge	12,063	10,417
Pekin	19,407	16,129
Peoria	105,087	104,969
Pontiac	9,585	8,272
Quincy	40,469	39,241
River Forest	9,487	8,829
Rockford	84,637	85,864
Rock Island	42,775	37,953
Springfield	75,503	71,864
Sterling	11,363	10,012
Streator	14,930	14,728
Urbana	14,064	13,060
Waukegan	34,241	33,499
West Frankfort	12,383	14,683
Wilmette	17,226	15,233
Winnetka	12,430	12,166
Indiana:		
Anderson	41,572	39,804
Bedford	12,514	13,208
Bloomington	20,870	18,227
Columbus	11,738	9,935
Connersville	12,898	12,795
Crawfordsville	11,089	10,355
East Chicago	54,637	54,784
Elkhart	33,434	32,949
Elwood	10,913	10,685
Evansville	97,062	102,249
Fort Wayne	118,410	114,946
Frankfort	13,706	12,196
Gary	111,719	100,426
Goshen	11,375	10,397
Hammond	70,184	64,560
Huntington	13,903	13,420
Indianapolis	386,972	364,161
Jeffersonville	11,493	11,946
Kokomo	33,795	32,843
Lafayette	28,798	26,240
La Porte	16,180	15,755
Logansport	20,177	18,508
Marion	26,767	24,496
Michigan City	26,476	26,735
Mishawaka	28,298	28,630
Muncie	49,720	46,548
New Albany	25,414	25,819
New Castle	16,620	14,067
Peru	12,432	12,730
Richmond	35,147	32,493
Shelbyville	10,791	10,618
South Bend	101,268	104,193
Terre Haute	62,693	62,810
Vincennes	18,228	17,564
Wabash	9,653	8,840
Washington	9,312	9,070
Whiting	10,307	10,880

*Including unincorporated places which are classified as urban under a special rule by the Bureau of the Census. All such places are marked with a dagger (†).

†Classified as urban under a special rule by the Bureau of the Census.

CITIES AND OTHER INCORPORATED* PLACES IN THE UNITED STATES HAVING A POPULATION OF 9000 AND UPWARD, 1940—Con.

City	Pop. 1940	Pop. 1930
Iowa:		
Ames	12,555	10,261
Boone	12,373	11,886
Burlington	25,832	26,755
Cedar Falls	9,349	7,362
Cedar Rapids	62,120	56,097
Clinton	26,270	25,726
Council Bluffs	41,439	42,048
Davenport	66,039	60,751
Des Moines	159,819	142,559
Dubuque	43,892	41,679
Fort Dodge	22,904	21,895
Fort Madison	14,063	13,779
Iowa City	17,182	15,340
Keokuk	15,076	15,106
Marshalltown	19,240	17,373
Mason City	27,080	23,304
Muscatine	18,286	16,778
Newton	10,462	11,560
Oskaloosa	11,024	10,123
Ottumwa	31,570	28,075
Sioux City	82,364	79,183
Waterloo	51,743	46,191
Kansas:		
Arkansas City	12,752	13,946
Atchison	12,648	13,024
Chanute	10,142	10,277
Coffeyville	17,355	16,198
El Dorado	10,045	10,311
Emporia	13,188	14,067
Fort Scott	10,557	10,763
Great Bend	9,044	5,548
Hutchinson	30,013	27,085
Independence	11,565	12,782
Kansas City	121,458	121,857
Lawrence	14,390	13,726
Leavenworth	19,220	17,466
Manhattan	11,659	10,136
Newton	11,048	11,034
Ottawa	10,193	9,563
Parsons	14,294	14,903
Pittsburg	17,571	18,145
Salina	21,073	20,155
Topeka	67,833	64,120
Wichita	114,966	111,110
Winfield	9,506	9,398
Kentucky:		
Ashland	29,537	29,074
Bowling Green	14,585	12,348
Covington	62,018	65,252
Fort Thomas	11,034	10,008
Frankfort	11,492	11,626
Henderson	13,160	11,668
Hopkinsville	11,724	10,746
Jenkins	9,428	8,465
Lexington	49,304	45,736
Louisville	319,077	307,745
Middlesborough	11,777	10,350
Newport	30,631	29,744
Owensboro	30,245	22,765
Paducah	33,765	33,541
Louisiana:		
Alexandria	27,066	23,025
Baton Rouge	34,719	30,729
Bogalusa	14,604	14,029
Crowley	9,523	7,656
Gretna	10,879	9,584
Houma	9,052	6,531
Lafayette	19,210	14,635
Lake Charles	21,207	15,791
Monroe	28,309	26,028
New Iberia	13,747	8,003
New Orleans	494,537	458,762
Shreveport	98,167	76,655
Maine:		
Auburn	19,817	18,571
Augusta	19,360	17,198
Maine—Con.:		
Bangor	29,822	28,749
Bath	10,235	9,110
Biddeford	19,790	17,633
Lewiston	38,598	34,948
Portland	73,643	70,810
South Portland	15,781	13,840
Waterville	16,688	15,454
Westbrook	11,087	10,807
Maryland:		
Annapolis	13,069	12,531
Baltimore	859,100	804,874
Cambridge	10,102	8,544
Cumberland	39,483	37,747
Frederick	15,802	14,434
Hagerstown	32,491	30,861
Salisbury	13,313	10,997
District 12 (Baltimore Co.)†	15,436	11,556
District 13 (Baltimore Co.)†	13,366	10,466
Massachusetts:		
Adams town†	12,608	12,697
Amesbury town†	10,862	11,899
Andover town†	11,122	9,969
Arlington town†	40,013	36,094
Athol town†	11,180	10,677
Attleboro	22,071	21,769
Belmont town†	26,867	21,748
Beverly	25,537	25,086
Boston	770,816	781,188
Braintree town†	16,378	15,712
Brockton	62,343	63,797
Brookline town†	49,786	47,490
Cambridge	110,879	113,643
Chelsea	41,259	45,816
Chicopee	41,664	43,930
Clinton town†	12,440	12,817
Danvers town	14,179	12,957
Dartmouth town†	9,011	8,778
Dedham town†	15,508	15,136
Easthampton town†	10,316	11,323
Everett	46,784	48,424
Fairhaven town†	10,938	10,951
Fall River	115,428	115,274
Fitchburg	41,824	40,692
Framingham town†	23,214	22,210
Gardner	20,206	19,399
Gloucester	24,046	24,204
Greenfield town†	15,672	15,500
Haverhill	46,752	48,710
Holyoke	53,750	56,537
Lawrence	84,323	85,068
Leominster	22,226	21,810
Lexington town†	13,187	9,467
Lowell	101,389	100,234
Lynn	98,123	102,320
Malden	58,010	58,036
Marblehead town†	10,856	8,668
Marlborough	15,154	15,587
Medford	63,083	59,714
Melrose	25,333	23,170
Methuen town†	21,880	21,069
Middleborough town†	9,032	8,608
Milford town†	15,388	14,741
Milton town†	18,708	16,434
Natick town†	13,851	13,589
Needham town†	12,445	10,845
New Bedford	110,341	112,597
Newburyport	13,916	15,084
Newton	69,873	65,276
North Adams	22,213	21,621
Northampton	24,794	24,381
North Attleborough town†	10,359	10,197
Northbridge town†	10,242	9,713
Norwood town†	15,383	15,049
Palmer town†	9,149	9,577
Peabody	21,711	21,345
Pittsfield	49,684	49,677
Massachusetts—Con.:		
Plymouth town†	13,100	13,042
Quincy	75,810	71,983
Reading town†	10,866	9,767
Revere	34,405	35,680
Salem	41,213	43,353
Saugus town†	14,825	14,700
Somerville	102,177	103,908
Southbridge town†	16,825	14,264
Springfield	149,554	149,900
Stoneham town†	10,765	10,060
Swampscott town†	10,761	10,346
Taunton	37,395	37,355
Wakefield town†	16,223	16,318
Waltham	40,020	39,247
Watertown town†	35,427	34,913
Webster town†	13,186	12,992
Wellesley town†	15,127	11,439
Westfield	18,793	19,775
West Springfield town†	17,135	16,684
Weymouth town†	23,868	20,882
Winchester town†	15,081	12,719
Winthrop town†	16,768	16,852
Woburn	19,751	19,434
Worcester	193,694	195,311
Michigan:		
Adrian	14,230	13,064
Alpena	12,808	12,166
Ann Arbor	29,815	26,944
Battle Creek	43,453	43,573
Bay City	47,956	47,355
Benton Harbor	16,668	15,434
Birmingham	11,196	9,539
Cadillac	9,855	9,570
Dearborn	63,584	50,358
Detroit	1,623,452	1,568,662
Ecorse	13,209	12,716
Escanaba	14,830	14,524
Ferndale	22,523	20,855
Flint	151,543	156,492
Grand Rapids	164,292	168,592
Grosse Pointe Park	12,646	11,174
Hamtramck	49,839	56,268
Highland Park	50,810	52,959
Holland	14,616	14,346
Iron Mountain	11,080	11,652
Ironwood	13,369	14,299
Ishpeming	9,491	9,238
Jackson	49,656	55,187
Kalamazoo	54,097	54,786
Lansing	78,753	78,397
Lincoln Park	15,236	12,336
Marquette	15,928	14,789
Menominee	10,230	10,320
Midland	10,329	8,038
Monroe	18,478	18,110
Mount Clemens	14,389	13,497
Muskegon	47,697	41,390
Muskegon Heights	16,047	15,584
Niles	11,328	11,326
Owosso	14,424	14,496
Pontiac	66,626	64,928
Port Huron	32,759	31,361
River Rouge	17,008	17,314
Roseville	9,023	6,836
Royal Oak	25,087	22,904
Saginaw	82,794	80,715
St. Clair Shores	10,405	6,745
Sault Ste. Marie	15,847	13,755
Traverse City	14,455	12,539
Wyandotte	30,618	28,368
Ypsilanti	12,121	10,143
Minnesota:		
Albert Lea	12,200	10,169
Austin	18,307	12,276
Bemidji	9,427	7,202
Brainerd	12,071	10,221
Duluth	101,065	101,463
Faribault	14,527	12,767

*Including unincorporated places which are classified as urban under a special rule by the Bureau of the Census. All such places are marked with a dagger (†).
†Classified as urban under a special rule by the Bureau of the Census.

CITIES AND OTHER INCORPORATED* PLACES IN THE UNITED STATES HAVING A POPULATION OF 9000 AND UPWARD, 1940—Con.

City	Pop. 1940	Pop. 1930
Minnesota—Con.:		
Fergus Falls	10,848	9,389
Hibbing	16,385	15,666
Mankato	15,654	14,038
Minneapolis	492,370	464,356
Moorhead	9,491	7,651
Red Wing	9,962	9,629
Rochester	26,312	20,621
St. Cloud	24,173	21,000
St. Paul	287,736	271,606
South St. Paul	11,844	10,009
Virginia	12,264	11,963
Winona	22,490	20,850
Mississippi:		
Biloxi	17,475	14,850
Clarksdale	12,168	10,043
Columbus	13,645	10,743
Greenville	20,892	14,807
Greenwood	14,767	11,123
Gulfport	15,195	12,547
Hattiesburg	21,026	18,601
Jackson	62,107	48,282
Laurel	20,598	18,017
McComb	9,898	10,057
Meridian	35,481	31,954
Natchez	15,296	13,422
Vicksburg	24,460	22,943
Missouri:		
Cape Girardeau	19,426	16,227
Carthage	10,585	9,736
Clayton	13,069	9,613
Columbia	18,399	14,967
Hannibal	20,865	22,761
Independence	16,066	15,296
Jefferson City	24,268	21,596
Joplin	37,144	33,454
Kansas City	399,178	399,746
Kirksville	10,080	8,293
Kirkwood	12,132	9,169
Maplewood	12,875	12,657
Mexico	9,053	8,290
Moberly	12,920	13,772
Poplar Bluff	11,163	7,551
Richmond Heights	12,802	9,150
St. Charles	10,803	10,491
St. Joseph	75,711	80,935
St. Louis	816,048	821,960
Sedalia	20,428	20,806
Springfield	61,238	57,527
University City	33,023	25,809
Webster Groves	18,394	16,487
Montana:		
Anaconda	11,004	12,494
Billings	23,261	16,380
Butte	37,081	39,532
Great Falls	29,928	28,822
Helena	15,056	11,803
Missoula	18,449	14,657
Nebraska:		
Beatrice	10,883	10,297
Fremont	11,862	11,407
Grand Island	19,130	18,041
Hastings	15,145	15,490
Kearney	9,643	8,575
Lincoln	81,984	75,933
Norfolk	10,490	10,717
North Platte	12,429	12,061
Omaha	223,844	214,006
Scottsbluff	12,057	8,465
Nevada:		
Reno	21,317	18,529
New Hampshire:		
Berlin	19,084	20,018
Claremont town†	12,144	12,377
Concord	27,171	25,228
Dover	14,990	13,573
Keene	13,832	13,794
Laconia	13,484	12,471
Manchester	77,685	76,834
New Hampshire—Con.:		
Nashua	32,927	31,463
Portsmouth	14,821	14,495
Rochester	12,012	10,209
New Jersey:		
Asbury Park	14,617	14,981
Atlantic City	64,094	66,198
Bayonne	79,198	88,979
Belleville	28,167	26,974
Bergenfield	10,275	8,816
Bloomfield	41,623	38,077
Bridgeton	15,992	15,699
Burlington	10,905	10,844
Camden	117,536	118,700
Carteret	11,976	13,339
Cliffside Park	16,892	15,267
Clifton	48,827	46,875
Collingswood	12,685	12,723
Cranford township	12,860	11,126
Dover	10,491	10,031
East Orange	68,945	68,020
Elizabeth	109,912	114,589
Englewood	18,966	17,805
Fair Lawn	9,017	5,990
Fort Lee	9,468	8,759
Garfield	28,044	29,739
Gloucester City	13,692	13,796
Hackensack	26,279	24,568
Haddonfield	9,742	8,857
Harrison	14,171	15,601
Hawthorne	12,610	11,868
Highland Park	9,002	8,691
Hillside township	18,556	17,601
Hoboken	50,115	59,261
Irvington	55,328	56,733
Jersey City	301,173	316,715
Kearny	39,467	40,716
Linden	24,115	21,206
Lodi	11,552	11,549
Long Branch	17,408	18,399
Lyndhurst township	17,454	17,362
Maplewood township	23,139	21,321
Millburn township	11,652	8,602
Millville	14,806	14,705
Montclair	39,807	42,017
Morristown	15,270	15,197
Neptune township	10,207	10,625
Newark	429,760	442,337
New Brunswick	33,180	34,555
North Arlington	9,904	8,263
North Bergen township	39,714	40,714
North Plainfield	10,586	9,760
Nutley	21,954	20,572
Orange	35,717	35,399
Passaic	61,394	62,959
Paterson	139,656	138,513
Pennsauken township	17,745	16,915
Perth Amboy	41,242	43,516
Phillipsburg	18,314	19,255
Plainfield	37,469	34,422
Pleasantville	11,050	11,580
Rahway	17,498	16,011
Red Bank	10,974	11,622
Ridgefield Park	11,277	10,764
Ridgewood	14,948	12,188
Roselle	13,597	13,021
Roselle Park	9,661	8,969
Rutherford	15,466	14,915
Secaucus	9,754	8,950
South Orange	13,742	13,630
South River	10,714	10,759
Summit	16,165	14,556
Teaneck township	25,275	16,513
Trenton	124,697	123,356
Union City	56,173	58,659
Union township	24,730	16,472
Weehawken township	14,363	14,807
Westfield	18,458	15,801
West New York	39,439	37,107
West Orange	25,662	24,327
Woodbridge township	27,191	25,266
New Mexico:		
Albuquerque	35,449	26,570
Clovis	10,065	8,027
Hobbs	10,619	598
Roswell	13,482	11,173
Santa Fe	20,325	11,176
New York:		
Albany	130,577	127,412
Amsterdam	33,329	34,817
Auburn	35,753	36,652
Batavia	17,267	17,375
Beacon	12,572	11,933
Binghamton	78,309	76,662
Buffalo	575,901	573,076
Cohoes	21,955	23,226
Corning	16,212	15,777
Cortland	15,881	15,043
Dunkirk	17,713	17,802
Elmira	45,106	47,397
Endicott	17,702	16,231
Floral Park	12,950	10,016
Freeport	20,410	15,467
Fulton	13,362	12,462
Garden City	11,223	7,180
Geneva	15,555	16,053
Glen Cove	12,415	11,430
Glens Falls	18,836	18,531
Gloversville	23,329	23,099
Hempstead	20,856	12,650
Herkimer	9,617	10,446
Hornell	15,649	16,250
Hudson	11,517	12,337
Irondequoit town†	23,376	18,024
Ithaca	19,730	20,708
Jamestown	42,638	45,155
Johnson City	18,039	13,567
Johnstown	10,666	10,801
Kenmore	18,612	16,482
Kingston	28,589	28,088
Lackawanna	24,058	23,948
Little Falls	10,163	11,105
Lockport	24,379	23,160
Long Beach	9,036	5,817
Lynbrook	14,557	11,993
Mamaroneck	13,034	11,766
Massena	11,328	10,637
Middletown	21,908	21,276
Mineola	10,064	8,155
Mount Vernon	67,362	61,499
Newark	9,646	7,649
Newburgh	31,883	31,275
New Rochelle	58,408	54,000
New York City	7,454,995	6,930,446
Bronx Borough	1,394,711	1,265,258
Brooklyn Borough	2,698,285	2,560,401
Manhattan Borough	1,889,924	1,867,312
Queens Borough	1,297,634	1,079,129
Richmond Borough	174,441	158,346
Niagara Falls	78,029	75,460
North Tonawanda	20,254	19,019
Ogdensburg	16,346	16,915
Olean	21,506	21,790
Oneida	10,291	10,558
Oneonta	11,731	12,536
Ossining	15,996	15,241
Oswego	22,062	22,652
Peekskill	17,311	17,125
Plattsburgh	16,351	13,349
Port Chester	23,073	22,662
Port Jervis	9,749	10,243
Poughkeepsie	40,478	40,288
Rensselaer	10,768	11,223
Rochester	324,975	328,132
Rockville Centre	18,613	13,718
Rome	34,214	32,338
Rye	9,865	8,712
Salamanca	9,011	9,577
Saratoga Springs	13,705	13,169
Scarsdale	12,966	9,690
Schenectady	87,549	95,692
Syracuse	205,967	209,326
Tonawanda	13,008	12,681

*Including unincorporated places which are classified as urban under a special rule by the Bureau of the Census. All such places are marked with a dagger (†).

†Classified as urban under a special rule by the Bureau of the Census.

CITIES AND OTHER INCORPORATED* PLACES IN THE UNITED STATES HAVING A POPULATION OF 9000 AND UPWARD, 1940—Con.

City	Pop. 1940	Pop. 1930
New York—Con.:		
Troy	70,304	72,763
Utica	100,518	101,740
Valley Stream	16,679	11,790
Watertown	33,385	32,205
Watervliet	16,114	16,083
White Plains	40,327	35,830
Yonkers	142,598	134,646
North Carolina:		
Asheville	51,310	50,193
Burlington	12,198	9,737
Charlotte	100,899	82,675
Concord	15,572	11,820
Durham	60,195	52,037
Elizabeth City	11,564	10,037
Fayetteville	17,428	13,049
Gastonia	21,313	17,093
Goldsboro	17,274	14,985
Greensboro	59,319	53,569
Greenville	12,674	9,194
Hickory	13,487	7,363
High Point	38,495	36,745
Kinston	15,388	11,362
Lexington	10,550	9,652
New Bern	11,815	11,981
Raleigh	46,897	37,379
Reidsville	10,387	6,851
Rocky Mount	25,568	21,412
Salisbury	19,037	16,951
Shelby	14,037	10,789
Statesville	11,440	10,490
Thomasville	11,041	10,090
Wilmington	33,407	32,270
Wilson	19,234	12,613
Winston-Salem	79,815	75,274
North Dakota:		
Bismarck	15,496	11,090
Fargo	32,580	28,619
Grand Forks	20,228	17,112
Minot	16,577	16,099
Ohio:		
Akron	244,791	255,040
Alliance	22,405	23,047
Ashland	12,453	11,141
Ashtabula	21,405	23,301
Barberton	24,028	23,934
Bellaire	13,799	13,327
Bellefontaine	9,808	9,543
Bucyrus	9,727	10,027
Cambridge	15,044	16,129
Campbell	13,785	14,673
Canton	108,401	104,906
Cheviot	9,043	8,046
Chillicothe	20,129	18,340
Cincinnati	455,610	451,160
Cleveland	878,336	900,429
Cleveland Heights	54,992	50,945
Columbus	306,087	290,564
Conneaut	9,355	9,691
Coshocton	11,509	10,908
Cuyahoga Falls	20,546	19,797
Dayton	210,718	200,982
Defiance	9,744	8,818
Dover	9,691	9,716
East Cleveland	39,495	39,667
East Liverpool	23,555	23,329
Elyria	25,120	25,633
Euclid	17,866	12,751
Findlay	20,228	19,363
Fostoria	13,453	12,790
Fremont	14,710	13,422
Garfield Heights	16,989	15,589
Girard	9,805	9,859
Hamilton	50,592	52,176
Ironton	15,851	16,621
Lakewood	69,160	70,509
Lancaster	21,940	18,716
Lima	44,711	42,287
Lorain	44,125	44,512
Mansfield	37,154	33,525
Marietta	14,543	14,285
Marion	30,817	31,084
Ohio—Con.:		
Martins Ferry	14,729	14,524
Massillon	26,644	26,400
Middletown	31,220	29,992
Mount Vernon	10,122	9,370
Newark	31,487	30,596
New Philadelphia	12,328	12,365
Niles	16,273	16,314
Norwood	34,010	33,411
Painesville	12,235	10,944
Parma	16,365	13,899
Piqua	16,049	16,009
Portsmouth	40,466	42,560
Salem	12,301	10,622
Sandusky	24,874	24,622
Shaker Heights	23,393	17,783
Sidney	9,790	9,301
Springfield	70,662	68,743
Steubenville	37,651	35,422
Struthers	11,739	11,249
Tiffin	16,102	16,428
Toledo	282,349	290,718
Troy	9,697	8,675
Van Wert	9,227	8,472
Warren	42,837	41,062
Washington Court House	9,402	8,426
Wooster	11,543	10,742
Xenia	10,633	10,507
Youngstown	167,720	170,002
Zanesville	37,500	36,440
Oklahoma:		
Ada	15,143	11,261
Ardmore	16,886	15,741
Bartlesville	16,267	14,763
Chickasha	14,111	14,099
Duncan	9,207	8,363
Durant	10,027	7,463
El Reno	10,078	9,384
Enid	28,081	26,399
Guthrie	10,018	9,582
Lawton	18,055	12,121
McAlester	12,401	11,804
Muskogee	32,332	32,026
Norman	11,429	9,603
Oklahoma City	204,424	185,389
Okmulgee	16,051	17,097
Ponca City	16,794	16,136
Sapulpa	12,249	10,533
Seminole	11,547	11,459
Shawnee	22,053	23,283
Stillwater	10,097	7,016
Tulsa	142,157	141,258
Wewoka	10,315	10,401
Oregon:		
Astoria	10,389	10,349
Baker	9,342	7,858
Bend	10,021	8,848
Eugene	20,838	18,901
Klamath Falls	16,497	16,093
Medford	11,281	11,007
Portland	305,394	301,815
Salem	30,908	26,266
Pennsylvania:		
Abington township†	20,857	18,648
Aliquippa	27,023	27,116
Allentown	96,904	92,563
Altoona	80,214	82,054
Ambridge	18,968	20,227
Arnold	10,898	10,575
Beaver Falls	17,098	17,147
Bellevue	10,488	10,252
Berwick	13,181	12,660
Bethlehem	58,490	57,892
Bloomsburg	9,799	9,093
Braddock	18,326	19,329
Bradford	17,691	19,306
Bristol	11,895	11,799
Butler	24,477	23,568
Canonsburg	12,599	12,558
Carbondale	19,371	20,061
Pennsylvania—Con.:		
Carlisle	13,984	12,596
Carnegie	12,663	12,497
Chambersburg	14,852	13,788
Charleroi	10,784	11,260
Cheltenham township†	19,082	15,731
Chester	59,285	59,164
Clairton	16,381	15,291
Clearfield	9,372	9,221
Coatesville	14,006	14,582
Columbia	11,547	11,349
Connellsville	13,608	13,290
Conshohocken	10,776	10,815
Coraopolis	11,086	10,724
Darby	10,334	9,899
Dickson City	11,548	12,395
Donora	13,180	13,905
Dormont	12,974	13,190
Du Bois	12,080	11,595
Dunmore	23,086	22,627
Duquesne	20,693	21,396
Easton	33,589	34,468
Ellwood City	12,329	12,323
Erie	116,955	115,967
Farrell	13,899	14,359
Franklin	9,948	10,254
Greensburg	16,743	16,508
Hanover	13,076	11,805
Hanover township†	16,439	17,770
Harrisburg	83,893	80,339
Harrison township†	13,161	12,387
Haverford township†	27,594	21,362
Hazleton	38,009	36,765
Homestead	19,041	20,141
Indiana	10,050	9,569
Jeannette	16,220	15,126
Johnstown	66,668	66,993
Kingston	20,679	21,600
Lancaster	61,345	59,949
Lansdale	9,316	8,379
Lansdowne	10,837	9,023
Latrobe	11,111	10,644
Lebanon	27,206	25,561
Lewistown	13,017	13,357
LockHaven	10,810	9,668
Lower Merion township†	39,566	35,166
McKeesport	55,355	54,632
McKees Rocks	17,021	18,116
Mahanoy City	13,442	14,784
Meadville	18,919	16,698
Monessen	20,257	20,268
Mount Carmel	17,780	17,967
Mount Lebanon township†	19,571	13,403
Munhall	13,900	12,995
Nanticoke	24,387	26,043
New Brighton	9,630	9,950
New Castle	47,638	48,674
New Kensington	24,055	16,762
Northampton	9,622	9,839
Norristown	38,181	35,853
North Braddock	15,679	16,782
Oil City	20,379	22,075
Old Forge	11,892	12,661
Olyphant	9,252	10,743
Philadelphia	1,931,334	1,950,961
Phoenixville	12,282	12,029
Pittsburgh	671,659	669,817
Pittston	17,828	18,246
Plains township†	15,621	16,044
Plymouth	15,507	16,543
Pottstown	20,194	19,430
Pottsville	24,530	24,300
Punxsutawney	9,482	9,266
Reading	110,568	111,171
Scranton	140,404	143,433
Shaler township†	11,185	9,573
Shamokin	18,810	20,274
Sharon	25,622	25,908
Shenandoah	19,790	21,782
Steelton	13,115	13,291
Stowe township†	12,577	13,368

*Including unincorporated places which are classified as urban under a special rule by the Bureau of the Census. All such places are marked with a dagger (†).

†Classified as urban under a special rule by the Bureau of the Census.

CITIES AND OTHER INCORPORATED* PLACES IN THE UNITED STATES HAVING A POPULATION OF 9000 AND UPWARD, 1940—Con.

City	Pop. 1940	Pop. 1930
Pennsylvania—Con.:		
Sunbury	15,462	15,626
Swissvale	15,919	16,029
Swoyerville	9,234	9,133
Tamaqua	12,486	12,936
Tarentum	9,846	9,551
Taylor	9,002	10,428
Turtle Creek	9,805	10,690
Uniontown	21,819	19,544
Upper Darby township	56,883	47,145
Vandergrift	10,725	11,479
Warren	14,891	14,863
Washington	26,166	24,545
Waynesboro	10,231	10,167
West Chester	13,289	12,325
Wilkes-Barre	86,236	86,626
Wilkinsburg	29,853	29,639
Williamsport	44,355	45,729
Windber	9,057	9,205
York	56,712	55,254
Rhode Island:		
Bristol town†	11,159	11,953
Central Falls	25,248	25,898
Cranston	47,085	42,911
Cumberland town†	10,625	10,304
East Providence town†	32,165	29,995
Johnston town†	10,672	9,357
Lincoln town†	10,577	10,421
Newport	30,532	27,612
North Providence town†	12,156	11,104
Pawtucket	75,797	77,149
Providence	253,504	252,981
Warwick	28,757	23,196
Westerly town†	11,199	10,997
West Warwick town†	18,188	17,696
Woonsocket	49,303	49,376
South Carolina:		
Anderson	19,424	14,383
Charleston	71,275	62,265
Columbia	62,396	51,581
Florence	16,054	14,774
Greenville	34,734	29,154
Greenwood	13,020	11,020
Orangeburg	10,521	8,776
Rock Hill	15,009	11,322
Spartanburg	32,249	28,723
Sumter	15,874	11,780
South Dakota:		
Aberdeen	17,015	16,465
Huron	10,843	10,946
Mitchell	10,633	10,942
Rapid City	13,844	10,404
Sioux Falls	40,832	33,362
Watertown	10,617	10,214
Tennessee:		
Bristol[3]	14,004	12,005
Chattanooga	128,163	119,798
Clarksville	11,831	9,242
Cleveland	11,351	9,136
Columbia	10,579	7,882
Dyersburg	10,034	8,733
Jackson	24,332	22,172
Johnson City	25,332	25,080
Kingsport	14,404	11,914
Knoxville	111,580	105,802
Memphis	292,942	253,143
Murfreesboro	9,495	7,993
Nashville	167,402	153,866
Texas:		
Abilene	26,612	23,175
Amarillo	51,686	43,132
Texas—Con.:		
Austin	87,930	53,120
Beaumont	59,061	57,732
Big Spring	12,604	13,735
Borger	10,018	6,532
Brownsville	22,083	22,021
Brownwood	13,398	12,789
Bryan	11,842	7,814
Cleburne	10,558	11,539
Corpus Christi	57,301	27,741
Corsicana	15,232	15,202
Dallas	294,734	260,475
Del Rio	13,343	11,693
Denison	15,581	13,850
Denton	11,192	9,587
El Paso	96,810	102,421
Fort Worth	177,662	163,447
Gainesville	9,651	8,915
Galveston	60,862	52,938
Greenville	13,995	12,407
Harlingen	13,306	12,124
Highland Park	10,288	8,422
Houston	384,514	292,352
Laredo	39,274	32,618
Longview	13,758	5,036
Lubbock	31,853	20,520
Lufkin	9,567	7,311
McAllen	11,877	9,074
Marshall	18,410	16,203
Midland	9,352	5,484
Odessa	9,573	2,407
Palestine	12,144	11,445
Pampa	12,895	10,470
Paris	18,678	15,649
Port Arthur	46,140	50,902
San Angelo	25,802	25,308
San Antonio	253,854	231,542
San Benito	9,501	10,753
Sherman	17,156	15,713
Sweetwater	10,367	10,848
Temple	15,344	15,345
Terrell	10,481	8,795
Texarkana, Tex.[4]	17,019	16,602
Tyler	28,279	17,113
University Park	14,458	4,200
Vernon	9,277	9,137
Victoria	11,566	7,421
Waco	55,982	52,848
West University Place	9,221	1,322
Wichita Falls	45,112	43,690
Utah:		
Logan	11,868	9,979
Ogden	43,688	40,272
Provo	18,071	14,766
Salt Lake City	149,934	140,267
Vermont:		
Barre	10,909	11,307
Brattleboro	9,622	8,709
Burlington	27,686	24,789
Rutland	17,082	17,315
Virginia:		
Alexandria	33,523	24,149
Arlington County†	57,040	26,615
Bristol[5]	9,768	8,840
Charlottesville	19,400	15,245
Danville	32,749	22,247
Fredericksburg	10,066	6,819
Lynchburg	44,541	40,661
Martinsville	10,080	7,705
Newport News	37,067	34,417
Norfolk	144,332	129,710
Petersburg	30,631	28,564
Portsmouth	50,745	45,704
Richmond	193,042	182,929
Roanoke	69,287	69,206
Staunton	13,337	11,990
Virginia—Con.:		
Suffolk	11,343	10,271
Winchester	12,095	10,855
State of Washington:		
Aberdeen	18,846	21,723
Bellingham	29,314	30,823
Bremerton	15,134	10,170
Everett	30,224	30,567
Hoquiam	10,835	12,766
Longview	12,385	10,652
Olympia	13,254	11,733
Port Angeles	9,409	10,188
Seattle	368,302	365,583
Spokane	122,001	115,514
Tacoma	109,408	106,817
Vancouver	18,788	15,766
Walla Walla	18,109	15,976
Wenatchee	11,620	11,627
Yakima	27,221	22,101
West Virginia:		
Beckley	12,852	9,357
Bluefield[6]	20,641	19,339
Charleston	67,914	60,408
Clarksburg	30,579	28,866
Fairmont	23,105	23,159
Huntington	78,836	75,572
Martinsburg	15,063	14,857
Morgantown	16,655	16,186
Moundsville	14,168	14,411
Parkersburg	30,103	29,623
South Charleston	10,377	5,904
Wheeling	61,099	61,659
Wisconsin:		
Antigo	9,495	8,610
Appleton	28,436	25,267
Ashland	11,101	10,622
Beaver Dam	10,356	9,867
Beloit	25,365	23,611
Chippewa Falls	10,368	9,539
Cudahy	10,561	10,631
Eau Claire	30,745	26,287
Fond du Lac	27,209	26,449
Green Bay	46,235	37,415
Janesville	22,992	21,628
Kenosha	48,765	50,262
La Crosse	42,707	39,614
Madison	67,447	57,899
Manitowoc	24,404	22,963
Marinette	14,183	13,734
Marshfield	10,359	8,778
Menasha	10,481	9,062
Milwaukee	587,472	578,249
Neenah	10,645	9,151
Oshkosh	39,089	40,108
Racine	67,195	67,542
Sheboygan	40,638	39,251
Shorewood	15,184	13,479
South Milwaukee	11,134	10,706
Stevens Point	15,777	13,623
Superior	35,136	36,113
Two Rivers	10,302	10,083
Watertown	11,301	10,613
Waukesha	19,242	17,176
Wausau	27,268	23,758
Wauwatosa	27,769	21,194
West Allis	36,364	34,671
Whitefish Bay	9,651	5,362
Wisconsin Rapids	11,416	8,726
Wyoming:		
Casper	17,964	16,619
Cheyenne	22,474	17,361
Laramie	10,627	8,609
Rock Springs	9,827	8,440
Sheridan	10,529	8,536

*Including unincorporated places which are classified as urban under a special rule by the Bureau of the Census. All such places are marked with a dagger (†).

†Classified as urban under a special rule by the Bureau of the Census.

[1]Population of Texarkana City, Tex., 17,019 in 1940; 16,602 in 1930.

[2]South Jacksonville with a 1930 population of 5,597, was annexed to Jacksonville in 1932.

[3]Population of Bristol, Va., 9,768 in 1940; 8,840 in 1930.

[4]Population of Texarkana, Ark., 11,821 in 1940; 10,764 in 1930.

[5]Population of Bristol, Tenn., 14,004 in 1940; 12,005 in 1930.

[6]Population of Bluefield town, Virginia, 3,921 in 1940; 3,906 in 1930.

SCENIC AMERICA. III—TRAVEL INTEREST SCENES

Fort Snelling, Minn.
Grand River Canyon, Colo.
Ruins of Ft Frederick, Crown Point, N.Y.

Harpers Ferry, W. Va.
Currecanti Needle, Colo.
Ft. Marion, St. Augustine, Fla.

SCENES IN CANADA

Cape Trinity, Saguenay River, Quebec
Twin Falls, Yoho Park, B. C.
Cascade Mt., Banff, Alta.

The Citadel, Quebec
Takakkaw Falls, Yoho Park, B. C.
Massive Range, Canadian Rockies

CANADA

The Dominion of Canada comprises all North America north of the United States, except Alaska, Newfoundland, Labrador, Greenland, and the islands of Saint Pierre and Miquelon. It is a self-governing British dominion.

Size. Canada, having an area of 3,849,923 square miles, covers a surface nearly as large as Europe and larger than the United States, excluding Alaska. The country measures from east to west at its widest extent more than 3000 miles and from north to south about 1600 miles. A number of islands, which are territory of the Dominion, lie off the northeastern coast. The most northerly island extends to a latitude of 85° N. A large inland sea, connected with the north Atlantic Ocean by Hudson strait, extends into the country from the northeast a distance of about 600 miles. Canada's southern boundary follows the 49th parallel of latitude from the western coast eastward to the Lake of the Woods. Inclining slightly southward to Lake Superior, it passes through the Great Lakes and part of the Saint Lawrence river, which it leaves at the 45th parallel. It then runs with an irregular course eastward to the Atlantic Ocean.

Topography. Canada may be divided into five natural divisions, based on the character of the land surface. These divisions are commonly called (1) the Acadian or Appalachian region, (2) the Canadian shield or Laurentian plateau, (3) the Saint Lawrence lowlands, (4) the great plains, and (5) the Cordilleran region.

1. The Acadian or Appalachian region embraces southeastern Quebec and the maritime provinces. This region is the extension into Canada of the Appalachian mountains of the United States.

2. The Canadian shield or Laurentian plateau is a huge V-shaped area of 2½ million square miles, which encloses Hudson bay at its center. It forms practically all of northern Canada, and comprises the area lying northeast of a line drawn from the Mackenzie River delta to the Lake of the Woods and northwest of a line which passes thence north of the Saint Lawrence River basin. Its southern and Atlantic borders are elevated and outwardly steep, forming the Laurentian mountains. From this outer rim its surface slopes gradually to its low center, Hudson bay. The western portion inclines similarly from an elevated rim toward Hudson bay and the Arctic Ocean. In detail, the surface of the plateau is often broken and rocky with innumerable lakes.

3. The Saint Lawrence lowlands, which run from Lake Huron down the Saint Lawrence valley between the Laurentian plateau and the Acadian highlands, are a northeasterly extension of the central plain of North America drained by the Mississippi valley.

4. The great plains form a northern extension of the topographical division which occupies all North America within the limits of the Appalachian mountains, the Canadian shield, and the Rocky mountains. At the international boundary line, this division has a width of 800 miles, but becomes narrower farther north. For 300 miles north of the boundary the region is prairie, but beyond this latitude it is forested. In the southern portion, traversed by the railway lines, three prairie steppes are clearly marked: an eastern steppe, the basin of the Red river, lying between the Canadian shield and the Manitoba escarpment and having an elevation of 800 feet above the sea; a central steppe, between this escarpment and the Missouri coteau, with an elevation of from 1600 feet in the east to about 2500 feet in the west; and a western steppe, rising to a height of 3000 or 4000 feet, which extends from the Missouri coteau to the Rockies.

5. The Cordilleran region, about 500 miles broad, is made up of a succession of mountain ranges running parallel to the Pacific coast and of the well marked longitudinal valleys which separate the ranges. In the south, where the mountains have been adequately explored, the district falls into three subdivisions: (1) an eastern group of mountain systems, consisting of the Rocky mountains, the Selkirk system, and the Columbian mountains, or Gold ranges; (2) the interior plateaus; (3) the coastal mountains, consisting of the Coast range and the Vancouver range, the latter being in places submerged. In the south the Rocky mountains are the highest, but in the north the coastal mountains far exceed them. Mount Logan, in the St. Elias range, Yukon, 19,850 feet elevation, is the highest point in Canada.

Climate. Canada covers so many degrees of latitude and possesses such vast areas of highland and lowland that it has many varieties of climate.

PRINCIPAL PRODUCTIONS OF CANADA

Showing Value in Dollars by Provinces, with Rank, 1940

Provinces	Field Crops	Livestock	Dairy Products	Fisheries	Mineral Products	Lumber*	Manufactures
Alberta	133,734,000	38,947,000	19,844,500	450,574	35,092,337	1,615,493	107,313,964
Rank	3	2	3	8	4	6	6
British Columbia	14,421,000	5,553,000	11,245,100	21,710,167	74,134,485	54,685,280	311,046,478
Rank	7	6	6	1	3	1	3
Manitoba	59,800,000	17,065,000	16,989,700	1,988,545	17,828,522	1,206,727	167,919,165
Rank	5	5	5	6	6	7	4
New Brunswick	18,446,000	3,656,000	5,457,500	4,965,618	3,435,916	5,626,273	89,281,908
Rank	6	7	8	3	9	4	7
Nova Scotia	13,347,000	3,265,000	7,588,500	9,843,456	33,318,587	2,954,498	113,814,650
Rank	8	8	7	2	5	5	5
Ontario	140,680,000	63,681,000	98,932,700	3,035,100	261,483,349	16,011,798	2,302,014,654
Rank	2	1	1	4	1	3	1
Prince Edward Is.	8,290,000	1,617,000	1,764,932	714,870	....	127,979	3,856,544
Rank	9	9	9	7		9	9
Quebec	89,531,000	34,941,000	59,471,500	2,002,053	86,313,491	17,129,042	1,357,375,776
Rank	4	3	2	5	2	2	2
Saskatchewan	172,979,000	26,188,000	19,646,000	403,510	11,505,858	775,507	76,284,332
Rank	1	4	4	9	7	8	8
Yukon and Northwest Territories	....	....	....	4,994	6,712,490†	....	266,745
Rank				10	8		10
	651,228,000	194,913,000	240,940,432	45,118,887	529,825,035	100,132,597	4,529,173,316

*Includes other sawmill products. †Exclusive of radium ore.

GROWTH OF CANADA, 1871-1941

Item		1871	1891	1911	1921	1931	1941
Population		3,485,761	4,833,239	7,206,643	8,787,949	10,353,778	11,506,655
Immigration		27,773	82,165	311,084	148,477	88,223	11,496
Agriculture:							
Wheat	bu.	16,723,873	42,212,811	215,851,300	300,858,100	298,000,000	540,190,000
Oats	bu.	42,489,453	83,428,202	348,187,600	426,232,900	331,243,000	346,154,000
Barley	bu.	11,496,038	17,209,989	40,641,000	59,709,100	67,972,000	116,659,000
Corn	bu.	3,802,830	10,711,380	18,772,700	14,904,000	5,643,000(5)	12,036,000(5)
Potatoes	bu.	47,330,187	53,490,857	66,023,000	107,346,000	91,815,000	65,206,000
Hay and Clover	tons	3,818,641	7,693,733	12,694,000	11,366,100	113,961,000	12,245,000
Horses	no.	836,743	1,470,572	2,266,400	3,813,921	3,129,058	2,881,400
Cattle	no.	2,624,290	4,120,586	7,086,600	10,206,205	7,990,947	8,797,800
Sheep	no.	3,155,509	2,563,781	2,389,300	3,675,860	3,608,340	3,550,500
Swine	no.	. . . . .	14,105,102	2,792,200	3,904,895	4,716,761	5,994,000
Cheese	lbs.	4,984,843	6,267,203	199,904,205	161,062,626	113,956,639	148,913,300
Butter	lbs.	74,190,584	111,577,210	64,489,398	122,776,580	225,955,246	286,109,500
Fisheries:							
Total value	$	7,573,199	18,977,878	29,965,433	34,931,935	30,517,306	62,258,997
Minerals:							
Total production	$	. . . . .	18,976,616	103,220,994	172,430,648	230,434,726	560,241,290
Gold	oz.	105,187	45,018	473,159	926,329	2,693,892	5,345,179
Silver	oz.	. . . . .	414,523	32,559,044	13,490,747	20,562,247	21,754,408
Copper	lbs.	. . . . .	9,529,401	55,648,011	47,620,820	292,304,390	608,825,570(6)
Lead	lbs.	. . . . .	88,665	23,784,969	66,679,592	267,342,482	388,569,550(6)
Nickel	lbs.	. . . . .	4,035,347	34,098,744	19,293,060	65,666,320	226,105,865(6)
Pig Iron	tons	. . . . .	23,891	917,535	665,676	420,038	1,364,336
Coal	tons	1,063,742(1)	3,577,749	11,323,388	15,057,495	12,243,211	18,225,961
Cement	bbl.	. . . . .	93,479	5,692,915	5,752,885	10,161,658	8,368,711
Manufactures:							
Capital	$	77,964,020	353,213,000	1,247,583,609	3,230,686,368(2)	3,705,701,893	4,095,716,836(7)
Employees	no.	187,942	272,033	515,203	682,434(2)	528,640	762,244(7)
Salaries and Wages	$	40,851,009	79,234,311	241,008,416	689,435,709(2)	587,566,990	920,872,865(7)
Products	$	221,617,773	368,696,723	1,165,975,639	3,520,731,589(2)	2,555,126,448	4,529,173,316(7)
Electric power	kwh.	. . . . .	. . . . .	793,162,316	1,400,231,340	16,330,867,000	33,445,000,000
Commerce:							
Exports	$	74,173,618	98,417,296	297,196,365	1,189,163,701	599,560,460	1,640,454,541
Imports	$	96,092,971	119,967,638	472,247,540	1,240,158,882	628,098,386	1,448,791,650
Exports, Domestic—							
Wheat	bu.	1,748,977	2,108,216	45,802,115	129,215,157	217,243,037	177,967,532
Wheat flour	bbl.	306,339	296,784	3,049,046	6,017,032	7,218,188	10,288,327
Oats	bu.	542,386	260,569	5,431,662	14,321,048	3,258,501	14,396,287(7)
Hay	tons	23,487	65,083	326,132	179,398	156,722	74,598(7)
Bacon	lbs.	10,344,400	7,150,756	56,068,607	98,233,800	12,177,000	345,604,200(7)
Butter	lbs.	15,439,266	3,768,101	3,142,682	9,739,414	1,162,900	1,337,600(7)
Cheese	lbs.	8,271,439	106,202,140	181,895,724	133,620,340	79,590,400	106,631,100(7)
Fisheries	$	3,994,275	9,715,401	15,675,544	33,662,751	28,894,983	31,650,889(7)
Forest products	$	24,459,877	24,282,015	45,439,057	105,325,375(3)	97,369,461	348,006,396(7)
Manufactures	$	2,432,750	6,296,249	35,283,118	403,132,161(3)	494,562,000	580,963,000(7)
Mineral products	$	2,841,124	5,784,143	42,787,561	62,316,304(3)	155,697,504	374,120,171(7)
Newsprint	tons	. . . . .	. . . . .	. . . . .	805,114	2,098,241	3,242,789(6)
Imports(4)—							
Agricultural	$	. . . . .	. . . . .	35,304,683	289,623,345	177,628,778	157,249,495(7)
Animal products	$	. . . . .	. . . . .	23,258,364	65,478,869	45,995,705	35,365,835(7)
Fisheries	$	. . . . .	. . . . .	1,995,091	3,947,608	2,885,203	3,503,450(7)
Forest products	$	. . . . .	. . . . .	12,873,875	19,024,778	46,042,029	40,688,785(7)
Manufactures	$	. . . . .	. . . . .	310,514,144	600,690,564	690,106,000	723,690,140(7)
Mineral products	$	. . . . .	. . . . .	44,020,074	161,393,718	408,090,364	560,156,309(7)
Transportation:							
Steam Railways	mi.	2,695	13,838	25,400	39,841	42,075	42,441
Electric Railways	mi.	. . . . .	. . . . .	1,224	1,687	1,386	1,040(7)
Shipping, seagoing, cleared	tons	5,116,033	10,695,196	22,297,186	24,916,729	26,535,387	34,865,229(7)
Communication:							
Telephones	no.	. . . . .	. . . . .	302,759	902,090	1,402,861	1,397,272
Telegraphs, government (8)	mi.	. . . . .	2,699	8,446	11,207	9,351	8,625(7)
Telegraphs, others(8)	mi.	. . . . .	27,866	33,905	41,621	43,473	43,771(7)
Postal revenue	$	803,637	2,515,823	9,146,952	26,331,119	30,416,106	40,383,366
Postal expenditure	$	994,876	3,161,676	7,954,223	24,661,262	36,292,603	38,699,674
Postal money orders issued	$	4,546,434	12,478,178	70,614,862	173,523,322	167,749,651	173,565,550
Finance:							
Revenue	$	19,335,561	38,579,311	117,780,410	434,386,537	349,587,299	872,169,645
Expenditures	$	15,623,082	36,343,568	87,774,198	361,118,145	440,057,336	1,249,641,446
Gross debt	$	115,492,683	289,899,229	474,941,487	2,902,482,117	2,610,265,698	5,011,399,120
Net debt	$	77,706,518	237,809,030	340,042,052	2,340,878,983	2,261,611,936	3,648,691,449
Bank deposits	$	66,623,400	198,779,226	1,073,298,505	2,362,324,319	2,568,683,245	3,464,781,844

(1) 1874. (2) 1919. (3) 1920. (4) Figures for 1921, 1931, and 1941 are not comparable with the earlier statistics, being based on a different classification of the items involved. (5) Exclusive of fodder corn. (6) 1939; military restrictions prevented publication of detailed figures for copper, lead, and nickel after 1939. (7) 1940. (8) Pole line mileage.

Over the larger part of the Dominion, especially over the great interior plain, a continental climate prevails, the temperature in Fort Simpson, for example, varying from a recorded minimum of 73° below zero to 101° above. In other sections, however, the extremes of heat and cold are modified by the presence of vast bodies of water, as the Atlantic Ocean, the Pacific Ocean, the Great Lakes, and Hudson bay.

In the maritime provinces, spring is retarded by the presence of the cold arctic current on the Atlantic coast. The summer climate, however, is equable and the autumn is long and open. British Columbia has one of the finest climates in North America. At New Westminster the mean temperature of the coldest month is 36° F. and that of the hottest is 58° F. The lowest recorded temperature of Vancouver is only 2° lower than that of San Antonio, Texas. The recorded rainfall reaches a higher figure on the Pacific coast than in any other part of Canada. The region of the Great Lakes has a temperate climate with a fairly high precipitation. The interior plains have a comparatively dry climate, but fortunately the precipitation occurs mainly in the summer, when it can be of value for agriculture.

Waterways. The rivers of Canada are of exceptional magnitude and number. They belong to four large drainage basins: (1) the Atlantic, including the Saint John, the Saint Lawrence and its tributaries, and the Hamilton; (2) the Hudson bay, including the Moose, the Albany, the Nelson and its tributary,—the Saskatchewan,—the Churchill, and many others; (3) the Arctic, including the Banks, the Coppermine, and the Mackenzie with its tributaries—the Liard, the Peace, and the Athabaska; (4) the Pacific, including the Columbia, the Fraser, the Skeena, the Stikine, and the Yukon, the last emptying into Bering Sea.

Rimming the outer border of the Laurentian plateau are the greatest lakes of the world, the lakes of the Saint Lawrence system—Lake Ontario, Lake Erie, Lake Huron, and Lake Superior. Other large lakes of Canada are Lake Winnipeg, Lake Athabaska, Great Slave lake, and Great Bear lake.

The Great Lakes system is the waterway of the most importance for transportation, although the Nelson-Saskatchewan river, flowing into Hudson bay, and the Mackenzie-Athabaska river, flowing into the Arctic Ocean, were well traveled water highways known to fur traders long before settlements had advanced as far west as Lake Ontario.

By means of enlarging the channel of the Saint Lawrence river, the Dominion government has made it possible for ocean steamers to reach Montreal, which is situated at a distance of 700 miles from the Atlantic Ocean. By the further construction of 117.2 miles of canals, an uninterrupted communication by water has been established from the head of Lake Superior to the Atlantic Ocean, an aggregate distance of 1594 miles.

Minerals. Canada is the world's chief source of nickel and ranks first also in the production of asbestos, second in cobalt and gold, third in silver, and fourth in lead, copper, and zinc.

The chief minerals of the maritime provinces are coal and iron, mined mostly in Nova Scotia. These provinces also produce gypsum in large amounts.

Canada's nickel, gold, and cobalt come mainly from northern Ontario, where platinum, copper, and silver also represent a large proportion of Ontario's annual output of minerals. Oil, natural gas, and salt are produced in southern Ontario. Quebec is one of the world's chief sources of asbestos. Other minerals produced in Quebec are mica, copper, gold, building stone, and clay for bricks.

The prairie provinces, particularly Alberta, have large coal deposits. Alberta also produces oil and natural gas in important quantities. From Manitoba come gold and copper.

The mineral output of British Columbia comprises chiefly copper, coal, gold, silver, lead, and zinc. Yukon territory has long been famous for its gold and silver mines. Important discoveries of silver, cobalt, and radium ore deposits were made in 1931 in the Northwest Territories, northeast of Great Bear lake, and the first shipments of radium ore were made in 1932 for reduction in Port Hope, Ont.

Flora. In Ontario and Quebec, south of a line running from Georgian bay to Montreal, the flora is of a southern forest type. North of this line to latitude 50°, from the Gulf of Saint Lawrence to Manitoba, a Temperate Zone forest type prevails. In Manitoba the forest disappears, giving place to the prairie grasses and herbage. Prairie vegetation spreads west as far as the foothills of the Rockies. Farther north, along a line drawn from latitude 55° on the Athabaska river to the south end of Lake Winnipeg, the prairie gradually gives place to the northern forest.

This northern forest belt extends from the Atlantic Ocean and the Gulf of Saint Lawrence to the Rockies. It covers all the country, extending from the temperate forest and the prairies northward as far as the Barren Grounds. In its southern half, this area is densely forested, but in the northern half the forest gradually becomes more open and the trees become smaller. The line between the forest and the Barren Grounds runs from Richards island in the Arctic Ocean to the general region of Churchill on Hudson bay, and from Richmond gulf on the east side of the bay to Ungava bay. In the Barren Grounds, the subsoil is permanently frozen.

In the Cordilleran belt, the flora varies according to climatic conditions. It is characterized by a tropical luxuriance on the coast and on the western slopes of the high ranges, but, in the dry areas east of the ranges, it takes on forms typical of the American desert.

Forests and Lumbering. Canada's forests cover 1,151,454 square miles, nearly one-third of the country's total surface. They are included more or less roughly in three areas: (1) the giant fir forest of the Rocky mountains and the Pacific coast; (2) the northern coniferous forest, lying between the prairies and the Barren Grounds; and (3) the deciduous, hardwood forest, extending from Lake Huron through southern Ontario and southern Quebec to New Brunswick and the Atlantic coast.

The chief timber trees of the Pacific coast area are Douglas fir, red cedar, Alaska pine, Sitka spruce, and Engelmann spruce. The dominant types of the northern forest include white spruce, balsam fir, tamarack, and black spruce. The more valuable trees of the southeastern forest area are yellow birch, white pine, red pine, eastern cedar, maple, elm, ash, oak, and hickory.

The forests of Canada are owned mainly by the provincial governments. Leases are extended to lumber or pulp companies to cut the timber, usually with the condition that the logs be sawed or manufactured into pulp in Canada.

The products of the forest which represent the largest value are pulp wood, lumber, and firewood. A large part of the lumber and pulp wood or paper manufactured from pulp wood is exported to the United States.

Fauna. The fauna of Canada resembles that of northern Europe. The carnivora are represented by several species of the weasel family, such as the ermine, the marten, and the mink. The lynx, bear, fox, wolf, and skunk are common at a distance from the settled districts. In the prairie provinces, small rodents, called gophers, are so numerous as to constitute a pest. The beaver is a characteristic Canadian animal and has been adopted, along with the maple leaf, as a national emblem. Otters and muskrats are numerous. Caribou range over the northern plains, which are also the habitat of the unique musk ox, an animal almost as large as the domesticated ox but having a close resemblance to the sheep. Moose and deer are found in the forested areas, and goats, sheep, and grizzly bears make the mountains their habitat. White bears, seals, and walruses are common along the northern coasts. Snakes are rare except in the extreme south.

Fur Bearing Animals. The animals which provide the largest aggregate value in pelts are the fox, muskrat, beaver, mink, ermine, and marten. Approximately one-fifth of all Canadian furs come from fur farms. The silver fox is the animal most successfully raised in captivity, but many fur farms are stocked with minks, raccoons, skunks, martens, coyotes, and badgers.

The fur trade constituted Canada's earliest commercial interest. It was formerly a monopoly of the Hudson's Bay Company, which controlled most of the northwest region until 1859. The company still has the largest share of Canada's fur trade, maintaining posts throughout the vast territory of the north.

Fisheries. Canada's sea fishing waters, including bays and inlets, total over 200,000 square miles. Conservation methods to protect the Dominion's immensely valuable fishing industry have been adopted both by the Federal government and by provincial governments. It is officially estimated that the government hatcheries plant annually in suitable waters about two billion fish fry.

Salmon are taken on the Pacific coast; lobsters are obtained from the shore waters of the maritime provinces and of Quebec. Herrings are caught both on the Atlantic coast and on the Pacific coast. Hake, pollock, mackerel, and paddock are products of Atlantic deep-sea fishing. Halibut were formerly plentiful in Atlantic waters, but they now come mostly from the Pacific coast. British Columbia and New Brunswick have developed sardine canning industries. In the Pacific Coast waters, are found the eulachon, or candlefish. Smelts are also abundant there as well as along the shores of the maritime provinces. Alaska black cod is highly prized but is not plentiful.

Prince Edward Island Malpeque oysters were formerly famous for size and quality, but the beds have been greatly depleted as a result of overfishing and of disease. Clams are found on the coasts of both oceans. Large quantities of fresh-water fishes are taken, such as perch, bass, pickerel, pike, tullibee, and whitefish, the last constituting the most valuable food fish obtained from the Great Lakes.

Agriculture. Agricultural land in Canada lies directly north of the American border in a strip extending east and west across the country with a width of several hundred miles. The fertile portion of this strip is interrupted by a large rocky territory in northern Ontario and by the mountains of British Columbia, where cultivation is confined mainly to the valleys. The total area of land under field crops is about 62,000,000 acres, although approximately six times this area is said to be of value for agriculture.

In the maritime provinces, fruit and potatoes are the most important cash crops, although hay, clover, and oats command the largest acreage. Farming in Quebec is mixed and largely self-contained; potatoes and buckwheat are the leading cash crops. Ontario supports dairy farming chiefly in the east; wheat, apples, tobacco, and sugar beets are the principal cash crops in the south; and the Niagara region specializes in the cultivation of peaches, grapes, cherries, and other fruits. The prairie provinces raise the bulk of Canada's wheat crop, which reached a high point of 567 million bushels in 1928. Canada leads the world in wheat exports, and its wheat production is exceeded only by those of Russia and the United States. British Columbia cultivates fruits intensively and raises poultry and cattle.

Live Stock. Stock raising is still an exclusive occupation in some parts of Alberta, Saskatchewan, and British Columbia, but elsewhere it is made a part of mixed farming. Specialization in stock raising, just as in grain growing, is being superseded by mixed farming. This change, however, has resulted in an increase rather than in a decrease of the number of live stock raised.

Dairying is an important industry, Canada being one of the largest exporters of cheese in the world. The factory system has been adopted in all the provinces. The production of creamery butter in 1929 was valued at more than 65 million dollars. Experimental farms distributed across the continent are maintained by the Dominion government.

Manufacturing. Industrial development has proceeded rapidly in Canada during recent years, partly as a result of the increased availability of cheap hydroelectric power. This expansion has been largely confined to the older provinces. Ontario ranks highest in manufacturing, Quebec comes next, and British Columbia takes the third place. Montreal heads the list of industrial cities with Toronto a close second, Hamilton, Windsor, and Vancouver following in the order named. The industrial output exhibits a wide variety of products, the most important of which is newsprint paper, in the production of which Canada leads the world. Flour manufacture, meat packing, sawmill operations, and automobile and textile manufacture follow. Canada is one of the largest manufacturers of rubber products in the world.

Water Power. The water power available in Canada is enormously extensive, the total available for electric generation being estimated at 33,113,200 horse power at ordinary 6 months flow. Over 80 per cent of all power used in Canada is in the form of electricity, and of this over 98 per cent is generated by water power. This situation is due chiefly to the fact that water power is available close to the centers of population. In the use of electricity Canada is exceeded only by the United States; in its use per capita, Canada leads the world.

Transportation. There are in Canada over 39,000 miles of railroad in operation, of which the government owns more than 20,000 miles. Two transcontinental systems span the country from east to west. These railroads serve to open up new territory for settlement and to bind together the provinces. By them, also, the route from Liverpool to the Orient is made 1000 miles shorter than the route via New York and San Francisco.

Roads and highways in Canada open to traffic in 1941 had a total mileage of 561,489, of which 120,971 miles were classified as improved highways. In ownership of motor vehicles, Canada ranks fourth among the nations of the world. Total registration stood at 1,572,784 in 1941.

Regular airplane routes connect the principal cities. Air mail service was inaugurated in 1927. Air transport is used extensively for patrolling the vast sparsely inhabited regions of Canada and for communication with the isolated settlements in the north.

Shipping. The principal seaports of Canada include Montreal, Vancouver, Victoria, Halifax, Saint John, Sydney, and Quebec. The countries with which Canada has the heaviest sea-borne commerce are the United States, Australia, and Great Britain. The shipping on the Great Lakes is heavy, traffic being mainly of grain, lumber, and ores passing east and of coal and manufactures going west.

Population and Language. More than one-half of the population of Canada is of British descent; about one-third is composed of the descendants of French colonists. In the prairie provinces large numbers of Americans have settled as well as a certain proportion of people from continental Europe. The majority of the latter, however, live in the industrial centers. There are more than 100,000 American Indians, mostly on reserves. The population in 1941 was 11,506,655.

French shares with English the status of an official language in Canada. Its use is confined mainly to

CANADA, GROWTH OF PROVINCES IN POPULATION, 1871-1941

Province	Population							
	1871	1881	1891	1901	1911	1921	1931	1941
Alberta	....	....	....	73,022	374,295	588,454	731,605	796,169
British Columbia	36,247	49,459	98,173	178,657	392,480	524,582	694,263	817,861
Manitoba	25,228	62,260	152,506	255,211	461,394	610,118	700,139	729,744
New Brunswick	285,594	321,233	321,263	331,120	351,889	387,876	408,219	457,401
Northwest Terr.*	48,000	56,446	98,967	20,129	6,507	7,988	7,133	12,028
Nova Scotia	387,800	440,572	450,396	459,574	492,338	523,837	512,846	577,962
Ontario	1,620,851	1,926,922	2,114,321	2,182,947	2,527,292	2,933,662	3,431,683	3,787,655
Prince Edward Is.	94,021	108,891	109,078	103,259	93,728	88,615	88,038	95,047
Quebec	1,191,516	1,359,027	1,488,535	1,648,898	2,005,776	2,361,199	2,874,255	3,331,882
Royal Can. Navy	....	....	....	....	....	485	....	....
Saskatchewan	....	....	....	91,279	492,432	757,510	921,785	895,992
Yukon Territory	....	....	....	27,219	8,512	4,157	4,230	4,914
Total	3,689,257	4,324,810	4,833,239	5,371,315	7,206,643	8,788,483	10,374,196	11,506,655

* The decrease shown in the population of the Northwest Territories after 1891 is due to the separation therefrom of vast areas to form Alberta, Saskatchewan, and the Yukon Territory, and to extend the boundaries of Quebec, Ontario, and Manitoba.

Quebec and to a few French settlements in other provinces.

Education. Instruction in elementary schools is free and compulsory, the requirements varying slightly in the different provinces. As a rule, the provinces provide for uniformity in the training of teachers, in the use of textbooks, and in the grading of pupils. In several provinces there are separate schools for Catholic and for Protestant children. Schools are maintained by funds from the province, the municipality, and the school district. There are 18 universities and about 135 other institutions providing higher education facilities. A National Research Council promotes industrial research.

PROVINCES

Canada is divided into nine organized provinces and four territories. The provinces, enumerated from east to west, are Nova Scotia, Prince Edward Island, New Brunswick, Quebec, Ontario, Manitoba, Saskatchewan, Alberta, and British Columbia. The territories are Franklin, Keewatin, Mackenzie, and the Yukon. Franklin, Keewatin, and Mackenzie are often referred to as the Northwest Territories.

Alberta. A province of Canada, situated between British Columbia on the west and Saskatchewan on the east and stretching from the American border about 750 miles north to the 60th parallel of north latitude. The southwestern border follows the summit of the Rocky mountains, thereby leaving in Alberta the western mountain slope and the foothills. From the foothills in the southern portion of the province, a plain slopes eastward, forming a part of the Saskatchewan River basin. The northern part of the province consists of a plain of northern drainage, belonging to the Mackenzie-Athabaska basin. A fringe on the extreme south drains into the Missouri river. The elevation varies from 12,294 feet on the top of Mount Columbia in the Rocky mountains to 568 feet at Slave river in the north. Except in the south, Alberta is well watered by numerous rivers, large and small. Lakes abound in the central and northern parts. The area of the province is 255,285 square miles.

The climate of Alberta is continental, involving great extremes of temperature. The air is dry and healthful. In southern Alberta the chinook winds, descending from the ridge of the Rocky mountains, often clear the ground rapidly of snow in the early spring, thus reviving the grasses which serve as sustenance for large herds of cattle.

A dark mold, mostly humus, overlying a clay subsoil, covers the surface of Alberta from six inches to several feet in depth. Such a soil, being exceedingly fertile and at the same time capable of retaining a large amount of moisture, supports a highly developed agricultural industry. Wheat and oats are the principal crops. Mixed farming has tended in recent years to replace specialized grain growing, with the result that potatoes, dairy products, flax, sheep, hogs, and poultry contribute a considerable amount to the total of the agricultural production.

In the southwest of the province, there is an area which requires irrigation in order to insure crops. Over 5400 miles of irrigation canals and ditches have been constructed.

The mineral resources of Alberta are of considerable importance. Immense areas of lignite and of a high grade bituminous coal have been discovered. Anthracite coal is also mined. The output of all kinds of coal amounts normally to over six million tons, a total exceeded by none of the other provinces. Petroleum and natural gas have been found both in the northern and in the southern part.

The capital and largest city of Alberta is Edmonton, in which is located the University of Alberta, supported by the province. The chief industries are those related to agriculture, such as meat packing. Population, 1941, 796,169.

British Columbia. The most western province of Canada, extending from the international boundary line to latitude 60°. The province is bounded on the east by Alberta; the western boundary is the Pacific Ocean, for a distance of 500 miles, and, for an additional 600 miles, the province borders on the coast strip of Alaska. British Columbia includes Vancouver island, the Queen Charlotte islands, and numerous other islands off the Pacific coast. The area is 366,255 square miles.

With the exception of a portion of the Peace River country in the northeast, the whole of British Columbia lies within the Cordilleran mountainous belt. The highest point is Mount Fairweather, 15,287 feet. Between the ranges, and occasionally cutting through them, are deep fertile valleys. Between the coastal mountains and the next important range to the east is an interior plateau having much agricultural or grazing land.

A submergence of the coast has resulted in an archipelago of innumerable islands, deep sounds, and fiords, many of them excellent harbors. As a result, the province has a coast line of 7000 miles. Of the rivers, the Fraser, 800 miles long, is the largest. The Columbia river rises in British Columbia and has a course of 500 miles before crossing the boundary line. Beautiful fiordlike lakes are a feature of many of the valleys. The islands and the coast region have a mild climate, rainy in winter but dry in summer. The interior plateaus are dry and subject to greater extremes of temperature.

British Columbia has one of the greatest forests of merchantable timber in North America, besides

CANADIAN NATIONAL PARKS AND RESERVES

Name	Location	Area Sq. Miles	Established	Distinctive Characteristics
Scenic and Recreational Parks:				
Banff	Alberta	2,585	1885	Ideal mountain playground containing the two famous resorts, Banff and Lake Louise.
Cape Breton Highlands	Nova Scotia	390	1936	Northern part of Cape Breton island; rugged coast line with mountain background.
Georgian Bay Islands	Ontario	5.37	1929	Thirty islands in Georgian bay, scene of bloody inter-tribal Indian war in 1649; includes Flowerpot Island reserve.
Glacier	British Columbia	521	1886	Summit of the Selkirks; Illecillewaet and Asulkan glaciers; Nakimu caves; Marion lake; Rogers and Baloo passes.
Jasper	Northern Alberta	4,200	1907	Immense mountain wilderness; unclimbed peaks, glaciers, snow fields, canyons, lakes; Mt. Edith Cavell, Miette Hot Springs, Mt. Robson.
Kootenay	British Columbia	587	1920	Mountain scenery, Briscoe range, Ice lake, Sinclair canyon, and Radium Hot Springs.
Mount Revelstoke	British Columbia	100	1914	Panoramic views of Columbia and Illecillewaet valleys, Clach-na-Coodin ice field.
Point Pelee	Lake Erie, Ontario	6	1918	Most southerly point in Canada; resting place of many migratory birds; recreational area; unique flora.
Prince Albert	Saskatchewan	1,869	1927	Recreational reserve and wild life sanctuary.
Prince Edward Island Shore	North Shore, P.E.I.	7	1936	Twenty-five mile strip of bathing beaches.
Riding Mountain	Western Manitoba	1,148	1929	Rolling wooded hills. Abundance of large game.
Saint Lawrence Islands	Ontario	185.6*	1904	Thirteen islands and one mainland reservation among the Thousand Islands.
Tar Sands Reservation	N. Alberta	3.2	1926	Four areas reserved for National Parks Branch to supply materials for road building.
Waterton Lakes	Southern Alberta	220	1895	With adjoining U. S. Glacier park forms international park. Mountains noted for beauty of coloring; lovely lakes, waterfalls, and snow peaks; excellent trout fishing; favorite camping resort.
Yoho	British Columbia	507	1886	Rugged scenery of west slope of Rockies; Yoho valley with falls over 1200 feet in height; natural bridge; Emerald lake.
Animal Parks and Reserves:				
Buffalo	Near Wainwright, Alberta	197.5	1908	Government's buffalo herd—over 3000 buffalo; also moose, elk, deer, yak, and catalo.
Elk Island	Near Lamont, Alberta	51	1911	Smaller fenced enclosure, containing about 2000 buffalo; also moose, elk, and deer.
Nemiskam antelope Reserve	Southern Alberta	8.5	1922	Fenced reserve containing about 300 prong-horned antelope.
Wood Buffalo	Alberta and N. W. T.	17,300	1922	Home of the wood buffalo.
Historic Parks:				
Fort Anne	Nova Scotia	31*	1917	Fort Annapolis Royal was the center of the struggle between France and England for the possession of the continent.
Fort Beauséjour	New Brunswick	59*	1926	Site of a fort built by the French in 1750-51.

* Acres.

millions of acres of pulp wood yet untouched. Douglas fir, cedar, spruce, western hemlock, larch, and pine attain an unusual diameter and height. Logs 30 feet in girth are not uncommon. In value of output lumbering ranks highest among the industries of the province, providing support for two-fifths of the population and entitling British Columbia to the first place among the lumber producing provinces of the Dominion.

In the fishing industry, British Columbia likewise ranks first among the provinces, supplying 47 per cent of the Canadian production. The salmon fisheries are the most important, and have given rise to a large salmon canning industry. Halibut, herring, and black cod form a considerable part of the annual catch.

The discovery of gold in 1858 in the Fraser River district was the occasion for the earliest settlements in British Columbia. The mineral production since that time has continued to be important, copper, gold, coal, and silver being among the more valuable products of the industry. Nearly all the lead produced in Canada comes from British Columbia, which has one of the greatest lead-zinc deposits in the world. The province mines about one-fourth of the Dominion's mineral output by value.

In recent years agriculture, fruit growing, stock raising, dairying, and poultry raising have made rapid advances. The chief fruits include apples, grapes, peaches, apricots, plums, strawberries, and cherries.

British Columbia has a native supply of coal and of iron, and the province is favorably situated for shipping goods to the markets of Australia, of South America, and of Asia. Mainly as a result of these facts, manufacturing has become important, entitling British Columbia to the third place in regard to industrial output among the provinces of the Dominion.

The public school system is nonsectarian. Instruction must be given in English. The provincial university, called the University of British Columbia, is situated at Vancouver, which is the largest city of the province. The capital is Victoria, on Vancouver Island. Population, 1941, 817,861.

Keewatin (*kē-wä′tĭn*), **Mackenzie, Franklin.** Three divisions, each known as a provisional district, formed on January 1, 1920, out of the vast Northwest Territories. The total area of these districts is 1,309,682 square miles, of which 1,258,217 square miles are land and 51,465 square miles are water. In 1941, the population numbered 12,028.

The land is a rolling plain. The principal lakes are Great Bear lake and Great Slave lake, both in Mackenzie; the largest river, the Mackenzie, flows for most of its course through that district, emptying into Mackenzie bay, an arm of the Arctic Ocean. Furs are obtained in all the districts, and minerals—radium, gold, copper, lead, petroleum, and coal—have been found.

Manitoba (*măn′ĭ-tō′bà*). A province of Canada, situated in the south central part of the Dominion between Ontario and Saskatchewan, stretching about 750 miles northward from the American border to 60° north latitude. The eastern boundary follows the 95th meridian about 275 miles northward, then cuts across at an angle of about 45° to Hudson bay, so that the northeastern part of the province has a coast line on the bay. In the southern part, the drainage is from the southeast and the west to Lake Manitoba and Lake Winnipeg and thence northeast by the Nelson river to Hudson bay. In the north, the Churchill River basin drains eastward into Hudson bay. Duck mountain, 2727 feet in altitude, is the highest point. The area of the province is 251,832 square miles.

A large part of the soil is alluvial, a vast lake having occupied the southern part of the province in geological times. This alluvium, a black loam of great fertility, has a very high content of potash, nitrogen, and phosphoric acid, and is, therefore, peculiarly well adapted to the growth of cereals. The southeastern part of the province is rocky and slopes rapidly from the highlands of northern Ontario. This fact has made possible the development, on the Winnipeg river, of extensive hydroelectric power.

The chief primary industry of Manitoba is agriculture. The growing season has a duration of from 85 to 105 days. This period, however, by reason of the long, bright summer days, is sufficient to ripen a hard type of spring wheat which holds a position in the world's markets second to none. Oats, barley, and potatoes are grown also in considerable quantities. The dairy products of Manitoba are important and a great deal of butter and cheese are shipped. Cattle and swine are raised.

Manufacturing in Manitoba has been promoted by the availability of cheap hydroelectric power. In the value of industrial output, the province normally ranks fourth in the Dominion.

The capital and largest city of Manitoba is Winnipeg, which is also the seat of the provincial university. The first permanent settlement was made in 1812 in the Red River district by a company of Scotch colonists. A unique feature of Manitoba's winter life is the annual dog derby, a race in which various dog teams compete on a course some 200 miles in length. Population, 1941, 729,744.

New Brunswick. A maritime province in the southeastern part of Canada, having an eastern coast line on the Gulf of Saint Lawrence and a southeastern coast line on the Bay of Fundy. Maine lies to the southwest of the province, and Quebec, to the northwest. The total coast line is 500 miles long and is indented with many fine harbors. Most of the surface is an undulating plain, lying between the low hills which, in the south, skirt the Bay of Fundy and the subdued mountains of the northwest. The highest point is Carleton mountain, which reaches an altitude of 2716 feet. The area is 27,985 square miles.

A number of navigable rivers traverse the province: the Saint John flows southward into the Bay of Fundy; the Mirimichi and Restigouche follow an eastward course into the Gulf of Saint Lawrence. At Grand Rapids the Saint John river, leaping over a precipice of 58 feet into a gorge, forms a waterfall of remarkable beauty. At the river's mouth in Saint John's harbor, occurs the famous "reversing falls."

New Brunswick's climate is subject to extremes. The thermometer has ranged from 95° F. in summer to −30° F. in winter.

Agriculture is the leading industry. The principal crops are hay, potatoes, oats, and turnips. Orcharding is important, apples forming the most valuable item. There are numerous cheese factories and creameries. Most of their products are exported to England. The province has much fertile land which has not yet been occupied.

Forests cover a large part of New Brunswick. Lumbering is an important industry, entitling the province to the fourth place in the Dominion in regard to lumber production. Spruce, pine, fir, maple, hemlock, birch, beech, ash, and elm are among the principal timber trees. At present, spruce is the principal commercial wood and is exported in large quantities.

The fisheries are very valuable, entitling New Brunswick to the third place among the provinces. Oysters, lobsters, herring, codfish, haddock, and smelts are caught. The canning of lobsters and oysters and the curing of codfish are important industries.

The principal manufactured products include lumber, woodenware, wood pulp, boots and shoes, paper, cottons and woolens, nails, mill machinery, and leather.

Saint John, the largest city, is an ice-free harbor at which two transcontinental railways reach tidewater. Population, 1941, 457,401.

Nova Scotia. A maritime province in the extreme southeast of Canada, consisting of a narrow peninsula and of the island of Cape Breton. The greatest length is 350 miles and the greatest breadth, 100 miles. The maximum elevation of 1500 feet is reached at North Cape plateau, Victoria county. The area of the province is 21,428 square miles.

The main peninsula is a long highland cut by transverse valleys. An important longitudinal valley, the Annapolis valley, runs parallel to the Bay of Fundy, being separated from it by a narrow ridge known as North mountain. The seacoast line is 1500 miles in length, and is indented by several inlets which form excellent harbors. The rivers are numerous but short.

Bras d'Or lake in Cape Breton is a magnificent landlocked body of salt water. It has become a popular resort for wealthy summer residents. Minas basin, the east arm of the Bay of Fundy, penetrates 60 miles inland. Here the tides, rising some 50 feet, rush in with great force, forming "bores."

Nova Scotia has a healthful climate, with a mean summer temperature of 65° F. and a mean winter temperature of 25° F. Winter weather is variable, and spring is late. The annual precipitation amounts to about 45 inches.

Agriculture is the chief occupation, hay, potatoes, turnips, and oats constituting the principal crops. Fruit growing, dairying, and stock raising are important. The Annapolis valley has been described as "Great Britain's apple orchard."

Coal is mined extensively in Cape Breton island and in the northern part of the mainland. Copper, tungsten, lead, gold, and manganese are found, and there are enormous beds of iron ore. Gypsum occurs in immense masses. Nova Scotia normally ranks fourth among the provinces of Canada in mineral output.

The fisheries of Nova Scotia are among the most productive in the world. The annual value is second only to that of British Columbia, among the Canadian provinces. Mackerel, cod, herring, haddock, and lobsters abound in the coast waters. Lobster canning has become a large industry.

Products manufactured in the province include iron and steel products, cotton and woolen goods, boots and shoes, machinery, farm implements, furniture, paper, sugar, condensed milk, and vehicles. Wood pulp is exported. Lumbering, formerly the chief industry, is still important.

The province is well supplied with railroads, chiefly lines of the Canadian National Railway. Shipping is important, especially in winter, when navigation on the Saint Lawrence is closed. There are three universities. The capital and largest city is Halifax. Population, 1941, 577,962.

Ontario. The most populous and most wealthy province of Canada. It is situated in the southeast of Canada, between Quebec and Manitoba and between the international boundary and Hudson bay. The province consists of a large northern area joined to a smaller but populous southern area by a narrow neck between Georgian bay and the Quebec border. The southern portion is part of the Saint Lawrence lowlands, belonging to the Saint Lawrence River basin. This basin is separated by a flat and ill marked watershed, called the height of land, from the Laurentian plateau, which is an area of southern drainage sloping toward Hudson bay. The bulk of the population is to be found in the lowlands, where the soil is adapted to agriculture. The northern country is rocky. Tiptop hill, 2120 feet high, in Thunder bay district, is the highest point in Ontario. The province is well watered by lakes and rivers. The area is 412,582 square miles.

Since Ontario extends from Hudson bay to Lake Erie, a distance of about 1000 miles, there is considerable climatic variation. Extreme cold in winter is experienced about the watershed. The southern part, however, has a much milder climate, while the climatic severity of the northern section is tempered by the lowness of its altitude.

In value of mineral production, Ontario leads all the other provinces. The chief products mined are gold, silver, nickel, copper, cobalt, platinum, lead, iron, and arsenic. Nickel and cobalt are distinctive of Ontario's mineral output. Nickel is produced in no other part of the world in similar quantities.

Farming is the most important primary industry. In value of field crops, Ontario usually ranks second among the provinces. The land under cultivation is almost entirely in the lowlands, although agriculture is practicable in parts of the Laurentian plateau, including the clay belt in northern Ontario, through which the Canadian National railway has been constructed. Oats, wheat, barley, and corn are the chief grains. Minor crops are peas, rye, sugar beets, tobacco, potatoes, and turnips. About half the fruit raised in Canada is produced by Ontario. Approximately one million barrels of apples of the high grade are annually shipped to Europe. Similarly, in the output of dairy products and in the number of live stock owned, the province holds the leading position.

In lumbering, Ontario yields the first place to British Columbia, and, in the production of pulp wood, the province ranks second to Quebec. Immense forests cover almost one-fourth of the area of the province. Spruce, pine, and poplar are the principal woods cut, although maple, birch, and elm are also found over considerable areas. Oak and hickory occur in the more southern parts.

The Great Lakes fisheries employ hundreds of vessels. Trout, whitefish, pickerel, and fresh-water herring form most of the catch, a part of which is canned for market.

Ontario is Canada's most highly developed industrial section, manufacturing industries supporting nearly one-half the population. Hydroelectric power is available in large quantities due mainly to the development of the water power of Niagara falls. The manufactures of the province include machinery, electrical equipment, automobiles, rubber products, farm implements, ironware, railroad rolling stock, metals and alloys, leather, furniture, paper, soap, boots and shoes, sewing machines, woodenware, and textiles. Milling, fruit canning, and meat packing employ many thousands of hands.

Ontario has seven universities, besides a number of church and technical colleges and agricultural schools. The province was formerly called Upper Canada. Its population was considerably augmented by the United Empire Loyalists. The capital and largest city is Toronto. The province also contains Ottawa, the capital of the Dominion. Population, 1941, 3,787,655.

Prince Edward Island. An island province of Canada, situated in the southern part of the Gulf of Saint Lawrence. Prince Edward Island is the smallest and most densely populated province of the Dominion. The island is about 145 miles long and varies in width from 5 miles to 34 miles. The coast line is a succession of bays and headlands. The surface is gently undulating, the greatest height being 306 feet, at Fredericton Station, Queens County. The area is 2184 square miles.

Due to the influence of the surrounding sea, the province is singularly free from extremes of heat and cold. Fogs are less frequent than on the mainland. The soil is fertile and produces, besides other crops, hay, potatoes, oats, and turnips.

The fisheries provide employment for a large part of the population. Lobsters and oysters of superior quality are canned for market. Cod, herring, hake, and mackerel are also taken.

Dairying receives much attention, and the island's creameries and cheese factories export large quantities of their products. Rivaling it in importance is the production of poultry and eggs. In recent years, silver fox farming has developed into a highly important industry.

Prince Edward Island attracts many summer residents by its pleasant summer climate and its facilities for surf bathing. Higher education is furnished by two colleges. Charlottetown, the capital, is the largest city. Population, 1941, 95,047.

Quebec. A province in eastern Canada, lying between the Gulf of Saint Lawrence on the east and Hudson bay and Ontario on the west and extending north about 1200 miles from the international boundary to Hudson strait and the Atlantic coastal strip known as Labrador. Quebec is the oldest as well as the largest province in the Dominion and was formerly known as Lower Canada. Its area is 594,434 square miles.

Except for a narrow strip along the Saint Lawrence river, the whole northern part of the province belongs to the Canadian shield with a drainage toward Hudson bay. To the south of the river rise the Notre Dame mountains, a continuation of the Appalachian system. Mount Jacques Cartier, on the Gaspe peninsula, is the highest point, in Quebec, with an altitude of 4230 feet.

The climate of Quebec is continental in severity, partly on account of the influence of cold arctic currents and of winds blowing above them and passing over the land. The air is dry, clear, and bracing.

The mining industry of Quebec is confined mainly to the eastern townships and to the district along the Ottawa river. Asbestos is a distinctive product, Quebec supplying over half of the world's market. Other products are copper, gold, chromic iron, cement, magnesite, mica, graphite, apatite, marble, serpentine, roofing slates, and building stone.

The lumber industry has always been of great importance in Quebec, which contains millions of acres covered with commercial timber. The lumber and the pulp industry yield approximately the same returns as in Ontario.

Agriculture and dairying form the chief occupations. The principal crops are hay, oats, and potatoes. Quebec is a close second to Ontario in the production of creamery butter and of factory cheese. Cattle are exported to Europe. The making of maple sirup and of maple sugar centers in this province.

The seacoast fisheries yield cod, mackerel, and lobsters as the principal items of the catch. Large amounts of salt fish are exported.

Quebec ranks second to Ontario as a manufacturing province. Wood pulp, timber products, machinery, cottons and woolens, aluminum, refined sugar, leather, and boots and shoes are included among the principal manufactures. Hydroelectric power installations exceed in horsepower those of any other province. Among the largest plants and ranking among the greatest in the world are those at Arvida near Lake St. John, at Gouin dam on the St. Maurice river, near Quebec, and at the Beauharnois dam, near Montreal.

Elementary instruction is free. Catholics and Protestants have separate schools. There are four universities in the province and several agricultural, technical, and trade schools. The capital is Quebec. The largest city is Montreal, which is also one of the largest wheat shipping ports of the world, in spite of the fact that it is icebound during the winter.

Most of the people are descendants of early French settlers, and in most of the rural districts French is the language in common use. Roman Catholicism is the predominant religion. Population, 1941, 3,331,882.

Saskatchewan (*săs-kăch'ĕ-wŏn*). A province of Canada, situated in the south central part of the country between Manitoba and Alberta and extending from the international boundary about 750 miles north to latitude 60° N. The southern half belongs to the great central plains region; the northern portion is part of the Laurentian plateau. South of the North Saskatchewan and of the Saskatchewan river, the surface is prairie, but north of these rivers the province is heavily forested with spruce, pine, tamarack, poplar, and birch. The eastern portion of the prairie belongs to the second prairie steppe; the western section forms a part of the third steppe, which angles across the province and stretches in rolling plains through Alberta to the Rocky mountains. On the plains, the soil is a rich loam. Excepting for the southwestern section, the province is well watered with rivers and lakes, which are especially numerous in the Laurentian area, in the northern and central parts. The surface covers 251,700 square miles.

On account of Saskatchewan's great length, there is a considerable diversity of climate and of temperature. The southern third has a moderate and changeable climate. The western portion of this section is dry, being subject to the warm chinook winds, and requires irrigation; the eastern part has more moisture and a steadier winter. The central third has a steady winter and a greater precipitation. The climate of the northern region is of a continental severity.

Agriculture is the great, almost the exclusive, industry of Saskatchewan. In point of wheat production in Canada, the province holds the first place. Its fields are free from rust and from insect pests which attack wheat. In the production of oats, Saskatchewan normally ranks first or near the first among the provinces. Mixed farming is increasing in the south. In the north, too, cattle raising is gradually giving place to mixed farming. Dairying is encouraged by the government, especially through the improvement of breeds of stock. Agricultural products are marketed by means of more than 6000 miles of railway, which have been constructed in the province. A government experimental farm, with headquarters at Indian Head, has performed valuable services in the agricultural development of Saskatchewan.

The capital and largest city is Regina. Other cities of importance include Moosejaw, Prince Albert, and Saskatoon, the last-mentioned city being the seat of the provincial university. Population, 1941, 895,992.

Yukon. A territory in the northwest of Canada between British Columbia and the Arctic Ocean. Ranges of the Rocky Mountain system traverse the northeastern portion of the territory, and are separated by the Yukon River basin from the Coast range and the Saint Elias range in the southwest. The Yukon River basin is a plateau country with a general slope toward the northwest. In the extreme southwest, Mt. Logan, the highest peak in Canada, reaches an elevation of 19,850 feet. The area of the territory is 207,076 square miles.

Mining is the principal occupation, gold and silver being the chief products. From 1895 to 1931 the value of the gold output was $211,000,000. The annual yield has greatly diminished, causing a decline in population from 27,219 in 1901 to 4157 in 1921. The development of a rich silver district later caused a fresh influx of settlers, but the inhabitants numbered only 4914 in 1941.

A railroad connects White Horse on the upper Yukon with Skagway in Alaska. Some of the hardier crops, as barley, oats, rye, potatoes, and turnips, are grown, and, in sheltered valleys, peas, cabbages, lettuce, and other garden vegetables thrive. Dawson, in the west central section, is the capital of the territory and is the center of the Klondike gold region.

TWENTY LARGEST CITIES OF CANADA

Showing Growth 1871–1941

City	Population							
	1871	1881	1891	1901	1911	1921	1931	1941
Montreal, Que.	115,000	155,238	219,616	328,172	490,504	618,506	818,577	903,007
Toronto, Ont.	59,000	96,196	181,215	209,892	381,833	521,893	631,207	667,457
Vancouver, B. C.	....	....	13,709	29,432	120,847	163,220	246,593	275,353
Winnipeg, Man.	241	7,985	25,639	42,340	136,035	179,087	218,785	221,960
Hamilton, Ont.	26,880	36,661	48,959	52,634	81,969	114,151	155,547	166,337
Ottawa, Ont.	24,141	31,307	44,154	59,928	87,062	107,843	126,872	154,951
Quebec, Que.	59,699	62,446	63,090	68,840	78,710	95,193	130,594	150,757
Windsor, Ont.	4,253	6,561	10,322	12,153	17,829	38,591	63,108	105,311
Edmonton, Alta.	....	....	....	4,176	31,064	58,821	79,197	93,817
Calgary, Alta.	....	....	3,876	4,392	43,704	63,305	83,761	88,904
London, Ont.	18,000	26,266	31,977	37,976	46,300	60,959	71,148	78,264
Halifax, N. S.	29,582	36,100	38,437	40,832	46,619	58,372	59,275	70,488
Verdun, Que.	....	278	296	1,898	11,629	25,001	60,745	67,349
Regina, Sask.	....	....	....	2,249	30,213	34,432	53,209	58,245
Saint John, N. B.	41,325	41,353	39,179	40,711	42,511	47,166	47,514	51,741
Victoria, B. C.	3,270	5,925	16,841	20,919	31,660	38,727	39,082	44,068
Saskatoon, Sask.	....	....	....	113	12,004	25,739	43,291	43,027
Three Rivers, Que.	7,570	8,670	8,334	9,981	13,691	22,367	35,450	42,007
Sherbrooke, Que.	4,432	7,227	10,110	11,765	16,405	23,515	28,933	35,965
Kitchener, Ont.	2,743	4,054	7,425	9,747	15,196	21,763	30,793	35,657

CITIES, TOWNS, AND OTHER POINTS OF INTEREST

The following section contains articles on all cities of Canada having a population for 1941 in excess of 25,000. It includes descriptions of the capital cities of the Dominion and of all the provinces. Since Canada is scenically one of the most attractive countries of the world and draws annually many hundreds of thousands of travelers, many of the places especially worth visiting are described. These include Banff in the Rocky mountains and Muskoka in Ontario. A number of other places are included for special interest attaching to them, such as the famous shrine center at Sainte Anne de Beaupré and Churchill, the sub-arctic port.

Banff. A health and pleasure resort of southwestern Alberta, picturesquely situated in Banff national park on the eastern mountain slope. It has a boiling sulphur spring and is the point of departure for numerous scenic features in the vicinity, including Bow falls, many rocks of unusual formation, and glacier fed lakes. The most beautiful of the lakes is Lake Louise, enclosed by gigantic pine-clad mountains. Lying about a thousand feet above Lake Louise are Lake Agnes and Mirror lake, often called the lakes above the clouds. Population, 1941, 2185.

Brandon. A commercial and railway city of southwestern Manitoba, the second largest city in the province. Industries include flour milling, brick manufacture, and creamery operations. The city has a college affiliated with McMaster university at Hamilton. A Dominion experimental farm and an Indian industrial school are located in the vicinity. Population, 1941, 17,383.

Brantford. A manufacturing city of southern Ontario, situated about 20 miles west of Lake Ontario's western extremity. One of the leading industries is the manufacture of agricultural implements. The provincial institute for the education of the blind is situated in the city. Brantford is named for a Mohawk chief, Joseph Brant, to whose memory a beautiful monument has been erected. Alexander Graham Bell, the inventor of the telephone, resided near Brantford in 1870 and 1871. Population, 1941, 31,948.

Calgary (*kăl'gȧ-rĭ*). A commercial and railroad city in the southern part of Alberta, picturesquely situated at the junction of the Bow river and the Elbow river. It is the gateway to Banff and the Canadian Rockies, the mountains, 80 miles distant, being visible on clear days.

Calgary is the trading center of a large agricultural and grazing region. Within 40 miles of it are the Turner Valley oil and gas fields. Oil refining is an important industry. Among the city's manufactures are flour and cereal foods, meat packing products, metal wares, leather goods, and farm implements. Shops of the Canadian Pacific railway, located in the city, provide employment for large numbers of workers. Manufacturing industries utilize electric power developed from the Bow river.

The more imposing buildings are constructed of sandstone quarried in the vicinity. The city has an institute of technology and art. Calgary was incorporated as a city in 1894. Population, 1941, 88,904.

Charlottetown. The capital of Prince Edward Island, occupying a high site at the head of Hillsborough bay at the junction of three tidal rivers. The city has an excellent harbor. The fisheries are extensive. Manufacturing interests include iron founding, pork packing, lobster and oyster canning, and the manufacture of brooms. Charlottetown has two colleges and several fine public buildings.

The city was founded in 1756 by French settlers but passed to Great Britain with the cession of Canada in 1763. Two American privateers raided the town in 1775; but the property seized was returned, and the prisoners were restored to their homes by order of General Washington. Population, 1941, 14,821.

Churchill. A port of northern Manitoba on Hudson bay. The first commercial shipments of wheat were made through this port in 1932. A railroad connects this point with Winnipeg, and large grain elevators and port facilities have been constructed. By using the route through Hudson bay during its open season of three or four months, shippers between Western Canadian points and Liverpool save 600 miles over the route via Montreal.

Cobalt. A mining town of Ontario, situated beside Lake Timiskaming on the upper Ottawa river. Cobalt is the center of one of the richest silver producing regions in the world. A large proportion of the world's supply of cobalt comes from the district. Nickel and arsenic are produced in large quantities. Population, 1941, 2376.

Dawson. The capital of Yukon territory, located in the west central part of the territory on the Yukon river just below the Klondike. At the height of the Klondike's gold-mining prosperity, Dawson had a population of over 20,000; but, when the rich claims in the district were worked out, the number of inhabitants decreased greatly. The name commemorates Dr. G. M. Dawson, the geologist, who first reported on the gold prospects of the district. Population, 1941, 1043.

Edmonton. The capital of Alberta, a commercial and railroad city in the central part of the province, occupying a picturesque site on the high banks of the North Saskatchewan river.

The city is served by thirteen lines of railway, and is a market and distributing point for a rich agricultural and grazing country in the vicinity and for the Peace River district to the north. Coal, found in abundance within the city and in the neighborhood, is utilized for manufacturing. The chief industries include meat packing, flour milling, and the manufacture of lumber, bricks, furniture, and clothing.

Edmonton is regularly laid out with wide streets crossing at right angles. The river is spanned by a bridge more than a mile long and 200 feet above the level of the water. The more imposing structures include the Parliament buildings, constructed of limestone quarried in the province, the Macdonald hotel, and the Arts and Medical buildings on the 250-acre campus of the University of Alberta. Population, 1941, 93,817.

Fort William. A transshipping point and flour milling city of northwestern Ontario, situated on Thunder bay in Lake Superior at the head of Canadian navigation in the Great Lakes. It is the Great Lakes terminal of Canada's transcontinental railway systems. The city has a storage capacity for more than 50 million bushels of grain. Along with Port Arthur, three miles distant, it is the most important grain shipping port in the world. It is also a large pulp and paper manufacturing center, being abundantly supplied with hydroelectric power. Population, 1941, 30,585.

Fredericton. The capital of New Brunswick, situated in the southwest part of the province at the head of navigation for large ships in the Saint John river, about 84 miles from its mouth. The leading industries include the manufacture of lumber, machine shop products, and boots and shoes. The chief edifices include the Parliament buildings, government house, and the legislative library. Fredericton is the seat of the University of New Brunswick. Population, 1941, 10,062.

Halifax. The capital of Nova Scotia, located on a natural harbor at the center of the southeast coast of the province. Halifax is an important naval base, an ice-free port, and the winter terminus of several steamship lines. The Canadian National railways also use the city as their eastern terminus. The steamship and railway terminal facilities are among the finest on the continent.

The chief interests of Halifax include transportation and shipping, fisheries, and manufacturing. The foreign trade of the port normally approximates 140 million dollars in value. Fish cured in the city are extensively exported to the West Indies and to South America. The leading industries are car shop production, sugar refining, and the manufacture of textiles, furniture, cordage, and foundry products.

The northwest arm of the harbor is used as a pleasure resort by citizens of Halifax. The educational institutions include Dalhousie university, Presbyterian college, Technical college, and Holy Heart theological college. On December 6, 1917, a collision between two vessels, one loaded with ammunition, caused an explosion that destroyed the north part of the city, killing 1158 persons and injuring 4000 others. Population, 1941, 70,488.

Hamilton. A manufacturing and railroad city and lake port of southern Ontario, the fifth largest city of Canada. It is situated on Burlington bay, a land locked harbor at the extreme western end of Lake Ontario. The Niagara escarpment, a height of land passing through the south of the city, imparts a picturesque effect which is further enhanced by the presence of numerous shade trees. The greater part of the city lies in the plain between the waterfront and the escarpment, known locally as the mountain.

Numerous railroads and highways enable the city to profit by its central location in the most populous region of Canada. Hydroelectric power from Niagara and Decew falls is abundant and cheap. Under these favoring circumstances, Hamilton has attracted numerous important industries, including many branch factories of American manufacturers. It ranks third in industrial output among the cities of Canada. The chief manufactures include iron and steel products, electrical equipment, glass, and textiles. It has the largest agricultural implement plant in the British Empire. Canning is also an important industry, Hamilton lying in one of the richest fruit growing regions on the continent.

The city has numerous parks, the finest being Dundurn, Gage, Victoria, and Gore. Hamilton, Burlington, and Grimsby beaches and many other summer resorts are located in the vicinity. A monument near the city commemorates the battle of Stony Creek, fought in 1813. Among the city's educational institutions are McMaster university, a normal school, and a technical school. Hamilton was incorporated in 1833. Population, 1941, 166,337.

Hull. A lumber and manufacturing city of southwestern Quebec, on the Ottawa river opposite the city of Ottawa, with which Hull is connected by three bridges. Pulp wood, matches, paper, and other wood products are among the chief items of manufacture, electric power being available in large quantities from the Chaudière falls near by. The city has a fine park. Population, 1941, 32,947.

Kingston. A city of Ontario, situated at the northeastern extremity of Lake Ontario, where the waters of the lake enter the Saint Lawrence river. The city's manufactures include locomotives, textiles, flour, and leather goods. A natural harbor and excellent railway facilities make Kingston an important point for the transshipping of grain. The Rideau canal connects the city with Ottawa.

Kingston is the seat of Queen's university and of the Royal Military college. The university buildings on a beautiful campus, the Roman Catholic and the Anglican cathedral, the streets adorned with numerous shade trees, and several parks make Kingston an attractive city. Numerous limestone buildings give a characteristic effect to the architecture. The historic associations of the city are emphasized by the elaborate fortifications, including the fort and martello towers, which command the harbor and the entrance to the canal.

Kingston was founded in 1673 by Frontenac and La Salle and formed one of the chief French centers of authority and trade with the West. It became the center of loyalist settlements in the West after the Revolutionary War. It was a British naval and military base, until the treaty by which the United States and Great Britain abolished naval establishments on the lakes. From 1841 to 1844 Kingston was the capital of the United Provinces of Upper and Lower Canada. Population, 1941, 30,126.

Kitchener. A prosperous manufacturing city in Waterloo county, southern Ontario. The chief manufactures include furniture, automobiles, shirts and collars, gloves, buttons, and rubber goods. The city is the seat of Saint Jerome college and has a large park. Kitchener was formerly called Berlin. Population, 1941, 35,657.

Klondike. A gold mining district in the Yukon Territory near the center of the Alaskan boundary. It covers an area of about 800 square miles. The principal settlement became notable for the discovery of gold there in 1896, since which time it has yielded about 211 million dollars worth of the metal.

London. A commercial, manufacturing, educational, and ecclesiastical center of southwestern Ontario. It is the tenth city of Canada in population. London is situated midway between Toronto and Detroit in a rich agricultural district. The chief industrial interests include petroleum refining, railway rolling stock, stoves, machinery, textiles, foodstuffs, electrical refrigerators, and household appliances. The city is the seat of the University of Western Ontario. London was founded in 1826. Population, 1941, 78,264.

Moncton. A manufacturing, railroad, and lumbering city of southeastern New Brunswick, standing at the head of navigation on the Petitcodiac river. Moncton is the headquarters for the Atlantic division of the Canadian National railways. It has a large lumber trade and manufactures stoves, engines, and boilers. The city has two parks. Population, 1941, 22,763.

Montreal. The largest city of Canada, situated in south central Quebec on Montreal island at the confluence of the Saint Lawrence and Ottawa rivers. The city lies mainly on the east and southern parts of the island and extends north and west to encircle Mount Royal, an eminence which reaches an altitude of 753 feet. It surrounds or is contiguous with the cities of Lachine, Outremont, Verdun, Westmount, and Mount Royal.

Montreal stands at the head of ocean navigation and at the foot of the Great Lakes navigation, which has access to the city by way of the Lachine canal. This canal was constructed to overcome the barrier of the Lachine rapids, which, together with several waterfalls in the vicinity, provide Montreal with an immense supply of hydroelectric power. The Victoria Jubilee Railway and South Shore vehicular bridges, spanning the Saint Lawrence, are among the greatest in the world. A cantilever railroad bridge also crosses the river.

In total tonnage entered and cleared and in the value of its foreign trade, Montreal ranks among the greatest ports of the world. Its grain shipments are exceeded by those of no other seaport. The city is the headquarters of the Canadian Pacific and Canadian National railways, which maintain enormous shops there. The Canadian National lines from the west enter the city by way of a tunnel cut through Mount Royal. Montreal is the leading financial center of Canada. It ranks first also in industrial production. The chief industries, in addition to car shop operations, include the refining of sugar and the manufacture of dairy products, flour, boots and shoes, tobacco goods, cement, iron and steel products, textiles, and furniture.

A small portion of Montreal still has narrow streets dating back to its early days, but the greater part is characterized by modern thoroughfares and broad boulevards, notably Sherbrooke street with its palatial residences and Saint Catherines street, a retail and theatrical thoroughfare. Mount Royal is laid out as a magnificent park, which commands a panoramic view of the city and its environs. The city has a number of public squares adorned with imposing monuments. Victoria square stands in the center of the city. Place d'Armes contains an imposing monument and statue of Maisonneuve, the founder of Montreal. It is surrounded by several fine buildings, including the head office of the Bank of Montreal and the parish church of Notre Dame, the latter being one of the largest churches in America. Bordering Dominion square is built the Catholic cathedral of Saint James, a modified reproduction of Saint Peter's at Rome and having a dome which is a conspicuous feature of the city.

Montreal is the seat of McGill university, Montreal university, and a number of colleges. A majority of the population is bilingual. About one-half the inhabitants are of French descent. The prevailing religion is Catholicism.

Montreal was founded in 1642 by Maisonneuve as a religious colony; but, as the outpost of civilization at the door of the Iroquois country, it became a military post, fur trading center, and base for explorations. It was taken by the British in 1760 and was held by the American Continental army in 1775-76. Population, 1941, 903,007.

Moose Jaw. A commercial and manufacturing city of south central Saskatchewan, the center of a rich mixed farming district. The city has large stockyards. The industries include meat packing, flour milling, foundry production, and the manufacture of agricultural implements. Population, 1941, 20,753.

Muskoka. A lake region of Ontario. It embraces about 4000 square miles lying east of Georgian bay and about 100 miles north of Toronto. Of its 800 to 1000 lakes, the chief are Muskoka, 19 miles long, Rosseau, 12 miles long, and Joseph, 14 miles long. These three lakes are connected and have regular steamship service in summer. The region has extensive forests. Its numerous rivers, lakes, and islands make it an extremely popular playground for summer residents and visitors. The eastern part of the territory is sometimes called the Lake of Bays region, after the largest lake in it. Farther to the northeast lies the Algonquin provincial park, an untamed region over 2000 square miles in area.

New Westminster. A lumber and fishing city of southwestern British Columbia, situated on the Fraser river about 17 miles from its mouth. The city is the center of the salmon fisheries, numerous large canneries being located in the vicinity. Ocean ships ascend the river to New Westminster for cargoes of lumber, which is very extensively manufactured in the city. Population, 1941, 21,967.

Niagara Falls. A city of Ontario on the Niagara river beside the cataract. Hydroelectric power developed at and near the city totals about 1,000,000 horse power, half of which is provided by the Chippewa Power canal, opened in 1922. The city commands a magnificent view of the Horseshoe falls and the American falls from the beautiful provincial park, named after Queen Victoria. Seven trunk lines of railway converge to enter the United States. Three large bridges connect it with Niagara Falls, N. Y. The chief manufactures include abrasives, cereals, insulators, and metal products. Population, 1941, 20,589.

Oshawa. A manufacturing city of Ontario, situated on Lake Ontario about 30 miles northeast of Toronto. It is the chief center in Canada for the manufacture of automobiles, particularly of those made by Canadian subsidiaries of the General Motors Corporation. Other industrial products include flour, woolens, farm implements, leather, foundry products, and canned goods. Its population more than tripled between 1911 and 1941, rising from 7436 to 26,813.

Ottawa. The capital and seventh largest city of Canada, lying in southeastern Ontario and picturesquely situated on the high southern bank of the Ottawa river about 120 miles above its mouth at Montreal. The river, following a winding course between wooded banks and dropping 40 feet at the magnificent Chaudière falls, presents a beautiful view from Parliament Hill, upon which stands the Parliament building. Rideau canal separates Ottawa into west and east parts, inhabited by French and English people respectively. These divisions are known as Upper Town and Lower Town.

The Parliament building, including the legislative halls and the library, is an imposing structure in the Italian-Gothic style of architecture. In the central tower is a carillon of 53 bells, one of the finest on the continent. Other notable buildings include the Cathedral of Notre Dame, Christ Church Cathedral, Rideau Hall, Victoria Museum, the Astronomical Observatory, and the Château Laurier. The educational institutions include the University of Ottawa and several colleges. The city has a number of fine parks connected by a driveway of more than 30 miles in length encircling the city.

Ottawa is one of the great lumbering centers of Canada. Hydroelectric power is provided in abundance by the Chaudière and Rideau falls and by other falls and rapids which, within a radius of 45 miles, serve to place over one million horse power at the disposal of the city's industries.

Ottawa was formerly called Bytown in honor of its founder, the engineer in charge of the construction of Rideau canal, which provides direct communication by water between the Ottawa river and Lake Ontario. The settlement was chartered as a city under the name of Ottawa in 1854 and was selected as the capital of Canada in 1858. Population, 1941, 154,951.

Outremont (*o͞o'tr'-môɴ'*). A city of Quebec on Montreal island, surrounded by the city of Montreal. It is almost entirely residential in character, having very few industries. Population, 1941, 30,751.

Prince Rupert. A seaport of west central British Columbia, situated on an island connected with the mainland by a steel bridge. It has a natural harbor formed by an inlet of the Pacific Ocean. Prince Rupert forms a western terminus of the Canadian National railways and ships great quantities of halibut and of grain. Population, 1941, 6714.

Quebec. The capital of the province of Quebec and sixth largest city of Canada. It is picturesquely situated on a bold promontory at the head of the Saint Lawrence estuary. The city was founded by Champlain in 1608 and was long the center of exploration and of government by the French in the northern part of the continent. In 1759, as a result of the battle of the Plains of Abraham, the city, along with the rest of French Canada, fell into the hands of the British. It was unsuccessfully attacked in 1775 by an American force under Montgomery.

The city's importance was due partly to its strong natural defenses and partly to its strategical position, which commanded the entrance to the river leading to the interior of the continent. Quebec is still the point of entry for immigrants from Europe and is the terminus of larger ocean liners. It has one of the largest dry docks in the world. The chief industrial interests include iron castings, pulp and paper, machinery, cutlery, steel, woolens, lumber, and rope. Hydroelectric power is available from the Montmorency and Shawinigan falls. The Saint Lawrence river is crossed at Quebec by a bridge which has one of the longest cantilever spans in the world.

The appearance of Quebec reflects the history of the city. The highest point, Cape Diamond, is 333 feet above the river and is crowned by a citadel within a walled enclosure covering 40 acres. On these defensive works over 30 million dollars were spent in the early decades of the 19th century. The upper town, containing the citadel, is used as a residential district and has many of the finer churches and public buildings. Dufferin terrace, a magnificent promenade, 1400 feet long, overlooks the Saint Lawrence, which lies 200 feet below. The upper town is reached from the other division of the city, called the lower town, by roads cut in the rock, by flights of steps, and by an elevator. The streets of the lower town are narrow and winding, and recall the appearance of certain provincial towns of France.

The city's most noteworthy edifices include the Parliament buildings; Château Frontenac; the church of Notre Dame des Victoires, built in 1688; the handsome Franciscan convent; the Ursuline convent, which contains the remains of Montcalm; the Anglican cathedral; and the Catholic cathedral built in 1647, which contained many valuable pictures and relics. The last-named building was burned in 1922 but has since been rebuilt on the original model. There are numerous statues and monuments of historic interest. In the governor's garden, stands a plain granite column erected to the memory of Wolfe and of Montcalm, both generals having fallen in action at the battle which decided the city's fate.

Quebec is the seat of Laval university, which was chartered by Queen Victoria and Pope Pius IX and is an outgrowth of the Grand Seminary founded in 1663. In the immediate vicinity are Battlefield park, Wolfe's cove, the Shrine of Sainte Anne de Beaupré, and many other points of interest. The city has a literary and historical society founded in 1824. The great majority of the population are of French descent, and the prevailing religion is Catholicism. Population, 1941, 150,757.

Regina. The capital and largest city of Saskatchewan, lying in the south central part of the province. Regina was formerly the capital of the Northwest Territories, and is still the headquarters of the Royal Canadian Mounted police.

Regina is the distributing point for a vast agricultural and stock raising territory and has an enormous trade in farming implements. Pork packing and oil refining are some of the city's industries. A district one mile long and one-half of a mile wide in the heart of the city has been reserved as an industrial zone for wholesale houses and for manufacturing concerns.

Regina is regularly laid out with streets intersecting at right angles. There are several parks and recreation grounds, and four colleges. The finest structure is the Parliament building, erected at a cost of more than $2,000,000. Regina was founded in 1883. Population, 1941, 58,245.

Sainte Anne de Beaupré (*săɴt än dĕ bô'prâ'*). A village and famous Catholic pilgrim resort 20 miles east of Quebec. A shrine was founded there about 1620 by Breton sailors in gratitude to Sainte Anne for their escape from imminent shipwreck. A chapel was built in 1658, on which occasion a devout inhabitant of Beaupré who suffered from rheumatism, after laying three stones on the foundation, found himself free from his affliction. This occurrence was the first of many instances of miraculous healing credited to the saint at the shrine. In 1676 the chapel was superseded by a church, which was replaced by a much larger one in 1876. In 1922 the building was destroyed by fire, but was replaced by a new church, which is one of the finest in Canada. The shrine is annually visited by pilgrims numbering upward of 150,000. Population, 1941, 1783.

Saint John. The largest city of New Brunswick, situated at the mouth of the Saint John river on the Bay of Fundy. In the vicinity is the noted "reversing falls," spanned by a steel arch bridge. Saint John is the Atlantic terminus of the Canadian Pacific and Canadian National railways. Its harbor, owned by the Canadian government, is ice free and ample for the accommodation of the largest ships. It has one of the greatest dry docks in the world and handles a large grain and miscellaneous commerce. The manufactures include pulp, sugar, lumber, brushes, brass valves, boxes, nails, pottery, and cotton goods.

The customhouse is a remarkably fine edifice. The parks and public gardens cover more than 500 acres. The city was founded by United Empire Loyalists, who left the United States in 1783. Two years later the city received its charter of incorporation, which is the oldest in Canada. Saint John was also the first city in the Dominion to adopt the commission form of government. Population, 1941, 51,741.

Saskatoon (*săs'kȧ-to͞on'*). The second largest city of Saskatchewan, situated on the Saskatchewan river about 200 miles south of the geographical center of the province. Saskatoon is the midwestern headquarters of the Canadian National railways. The industrial interests include flour, tractors, garments, and cereals. The city is the seat of the University of Saskatchewan, the Agricultural college, and the provincial experimental farm. Population, 1941, 43,027.

Sault Sainte Marie (*so͞o' sânt mä-rē'*). A manufacturing city of Ontario, situated on the Saint Mary's river and on the Sault Sainte Marie canal, which is the busiest ship highway in the world. The city is connected with Sault Sainte Marie, Michigan, by a bridge one mile in length and by a ferry service. A power canal makes water power available for the city's industries, which include pulp, steel, and chemical manufacturing, car shop operations, and lumber milling. Population, 1941, 25,794.

Sherbrooke. A manufacturing city of southeastern Quebec about 100 miles east of Montreal. Among the varied industries, the largest is the manufacture of woolens. Other products are cotton textiles, machinery, and lumber. Population, 1941, 35,965.

Sudbury. A mining city of Ontario about 60 miles north of the northern shore of Georgian bay. Here is mined the greater part of the world's output of nickel; also most of the copper produced in Ontario. The city has a government school of mines and a Jesuit college. Population, 1941, 32,203.

Sydney. A city in northeastern Nova Scotia, situated on a natural harbor to the east of Cape Breton island. Sydney is noted as a center for coal mining and for the manufacture of steel. It is also a well-known summer resort. Population, 1941, 28,305.

Thetford Mines. A mining town about 75 miles south of Quebec City, noted, along with Black lake in the vicinity, as a center of the district which produces a large proportion of the world's supply of commercial asbestos. Population, 1941, 12,716.

Three Rivers (Trois Rivières). A manufacturing city of Quebec, situated on the north bank of the Saint Lawrence river where the two mouths of the Saint Maurice river enter it. It is 78 miles southwest of the city of Quebec. Long the center of a large lumber, cattle, and grain trade, it began to grow rapidly with the development of hydroelectric power from near-by waterfalls. Paper and pulp manufacture became the leading industry. Three Rivers has a newsprint mill said to be the largest in the world. The city was founded by Champlain in 1634. Population, 1941, 42,007.

Toronto. The capital and largest city of Ontario and the second largest city in Canada, situated on the northwest shore of Lake Ontario. It has a natural harbor, which in recent years has been greatly enlarged and improved. Approximately 2000 acres at the water front, largely reclaimed land, is controlled by the city to provide for industrial sites, railroad sidings, waterways, and parks. The city is bounded on the west by the Humber river while the Don river flows through its eastern part.

As an industrial, railroad, financial, and commercial center, Toronto ranks second only to Montreal. The chief products of manufacture include lumber, agricultural implements, automobiles, car shop products, packed meats, rubber goods, food products, clothing, hosiery and knit goods, soap, iron castings, and musical instruments. The Toronto hydroelectric system is one of the largest municipal supply undertakings on the continent.

The city rises from the shore to an elevation of about 300 feet. This variation in level lends itself to the construction of many beautiful driveways and boulevards, connecting a large number of picturesque parks, the greatest of which is High park. Near this park at Sunnyside on the lake shore, the city has built an elaborate pleasure resort.

In Queen's park is situated the Parliament building, constructed of red sandstone in the Romanesque style of architecture. In the vicinity stand the numerous buildings of the University of Toronto, among which Hart House, built in the Norman style of architecture at a cost of about $1,500,000, is one of the finest university buildings on the continent. The city hall is a notable structure in the Renaissance style. Among numerous other beautiful buildings are University college, Osgoode Hall, Trinity college, an Anglican cathedral in the Early English style, a Catholic cathedral of the Gothic type, and the Timothy Eaton Memorial church. The Maple Leaf Gardens is Canada's largest auditorium. The Royal York hotel ranks among the finest in the country.

Toronto's educational institutions are numerous. The University of Toronto consists of a large number of colleges and professional schools. Other institutions of learning and of art include the Royal Ontario Museum of Archeology and an art gallery called the Grange. The main branch of the public library houses the valuable Robertson historical and ornithological collection. The city's zoological garden in Riverside park contains an exceptionally valuable collection of wild animals.

An annual institution of note is the Toronto exhibition, held in the Exhibition grounds, which are equipped for the purpose by many elaborate buildings. Annual attendance is normally over one million.

Toronto was founded in 1749 and, under the name of York, became the capital of Upper Canada in 1793. York was captured by the Americans in 1813. In 1834 the place was incorporated as a city under the name of Toronto, which is an Indian word for "place of meeting." Population, 1941, 667,457.

Vancouver. The largest city of British Columbia and third largest in Canada, situated at the southwest extremity of the mainland on Burrard inlet, a deep arm of the Strait of Georgia. The harbor is one of the finest on the globe and has helped to place Vancouver among the leading ports of the continent. The area of the harbor is 48 square miles, of which 28 is landlocked. One of the chief exports is wheat. Vancouver is equipped to handle Alberta's entire exportable wheat crop. The city is the western terminus of the Canadian Pacific railway and of the Canadian National railway. It is the commercial metropolis of British Columbia and the center of the great lumbering interests of the province. Other important industries include furniture making, sugar refining, fish and fruit canning, and jute and paper manufacturing. There are large shipbuilding yards, foundries, and machine shops.

Vancouver's places of recreation include a number of bathing beaches and the magnificent Stanley park, a partly cleared forest area of 1000 acres situated on a cape and surrounded by a 9-mile driveway along the shore. Among the more noteworthy structures are the general hospital, the courthouse, and the Vancouver and Georgia hotels. The city is the seat of the University of British Columbia. It has also a provincial art gallery, a museum, and technical, art, and normal schools.

Vancouver was named after Capt. George Vancouver, a British naval officer, and was incorporated in 1886 with a population of 600. The following year it was connected by railroad with eastern Canada, and a period of rapid growth began. Population, 1941, 275,353.

Verdun. A city of Quebec on Montreal island. It is a residential suburb of Montreal, the southern border of which it adjoins. Population, 1941, 67,349.

Victoria. The capital of British Columbia, occupying the extreme southeastern point of Vancouver island on the Strait of Juan de Fuca. Possessing a commodious harbor, and being advantageously located from a commercial standpoint, Victoria ranks as one of the four largest ports of Canada. Canadian Pacific steamers to Japan, China, and Australia make the city a port of call. Victoria's industrial establishments include lumber mills, furniture factories, iron foundries, shoe and clothing factories, soap factories, chemical works, and salmon canneries. There is a large shipbuilding yard. An extensive trade is carried on in coal, timber and canned salmon.

The city has fine streets with many beautiful residences, and its delightful climate and beautiful environment attract numerous summer visitors. Beacon Hill park is the city's chief recreation ground. The provincial Parliament buildings of gray stone are of high architectural merit. The Dominion astrophysical laboratory in the city has one of the world's largest telescopes. Adjoining Victoria is Esquimalt, the British naval base and dockyard now maintained by Canada.

Fort Victoria was erected on the present site of the city in 1843 as a trading post of the Hudson's Bay Company. The place was incorporated as Victoria in 1862 and became the capital of British Columbia in 1868. The inhabitants are predominantly of British birth or descent. Population, 1941, 44,068.

Windsor. The most southerly city of Canada, ranking eleventh in population. It lies in southern Ontario on the Detroit river, opposite Detroit, Michigan. The leading industrial products are automobiles, steel and iron, paints and varnishes, drugs, salt, and other chemicals. Windsor is connected with Detroit by a vehicular tunnel and by the Ambassador suspension bridge, which has a central span of 1850 feet. It is the seat of Assumption college. Contiguous with Windsor are the urban municipalities of East Windsor, Sandwich, Walkerville, and Riverside, which are frequently known as the Border cities. They constitute the chief center of automobile production in Canada. Windsor became a town in 1858 and was incorporated as a city in 1892. Population, 1941, 105,311.

Winnipeg. The capital of Manitoba and fourth largest city of Canada. It is located in the southern part of the province at the junction of the Red and the Assiniboine river. Winnipeg occupies, in respect to Canadian commerce, a strategic position, comparable to that of Chicago. All traffic passing between the eastern and the western part of Canada is routed through Winnipeg. The city is served by the Canadian transcontinental railways, by a number of American lines, and by many railroads radiating throughout the rich agricultural district in which it is situated. The car shops in the city are very extensive. The wholesale and mail order trade is enormous. The city is the largest cash grain market in the world. The live stock interests are also very important.

Winnipeg ranks among the leading manufacturing cities of Canada, partly by reason of the availability of cheap hydroelectric power, which is developed from the Winnipeg River rapids. Among the chief industrial products are flour, packed meats, agricultural implements, pulp, paper, and lumber.

The growth of Winnipeg has been very rapid. The city is well planned. Portage avenue, one of the chief business thoroughfares, is among the widest streets of the Dominion. There are several beautiful parks, of which the Fort Garry park has the greatest historic interest and City park, lying in a suburb and containing a zoological garden, is the largest. Winnipeg's water supply is brought by an aqueduct a distance of nearly 100 miles from a lake lying within the border of Ontario. Among a number of imposing buildings, including a fine Gothic cathedral, the outstanding structure is the provincial Parliament building, or capitol, which is constructed in the Greek style and surmounted by a beautiful dome.

The suburb of Saint Boniface, having a population in 1931 of 16,305, is the Roman Catholic headquarters of the West. It has a magnificent cathedral, the archbishop's palace, and the Catholic college of Saint Boniface. It is the birthplace and burial place of Louis Riel, leader of the Red River rebellion in 1869-70.

Winnipeg is the seat of the University of Manitoba and of four colleges affiliated with the university. The institutions of higher education include also a law school and a medical school.

In 1733, on the site now occupied by Winnipeg, the French explorer, Verandrye, built Fort Rouge, a name now used to designate a favorite residential section of the city. In 1821, the Hudson's Bay Company built Fort Garry. The population in 1870 was 250. In 1873 the place was incorporated and the name was changed from Fort Garry to Winnipeg. Population, exclusive of suburbs, 1941, 221,960.

CITIES AND TOWNS IN CANADA HAVING A POPULATION UPWARDS OF 8000, CENSUS OF 1941

City or Town	Pop. 1931	Pop. 1941
Amherst, N. S.	7,450	8,620
Barrie, Ont.	7,776	9,725
Belleville, Ont.	13,790	16,710
Brandon, Man.	17,082	17,383
Brantford, Ont.	30,107	31,948
Brockville, Ont.	9,736	11,342
Calgary, Alta.	83,761	88,904
Cap de la Madeleine, Que.	8,748	11,961
Charlottetown, P. E. I.	12,361	14,821
Chatham, Ont.	14,569	17,369
Chicoutimi, Que.	11,877	16,040
Cornwall, Ont.	11,126	14,117
Dartmouth, N. S.	9,100	10,847
Drummondville, Que.	6,609	10,555
Edmonton, Alta.	79,197	93,817
Forest Hill, Ont.	5,207	11,757
Fort William, Ont.	26,277	30,585
Fredericton, N. B.	8,830	10,062
Galt, Ont.	14,006	15,346
Glace Bay, N. S.	20,706	25,147
Granby, Que.	10,587	14,196
Grand' Mere, Que.	6,461	8,608
Guelph, Ont.	21,075	23,273
Halifax, N. S.	59,275	70,488
Hamilton, Ont.	155,547	166,337
Hull, Que.	29,433	32,947
Joliette, Que.	10,765	12,749
Jonquière, Que.	9,448	13,769
Kingston, Ont.	23,439	30,126
Kitchener, Ont.	30,793	35,657
Lachine, Que.	18,630	20,051
Lethbridge, Alta.	13,489	14,612

City or Town	Pop. 1931	Pop. 1941
Lévis, Que.	11,724	11,991
Lindsay, Ont.	7,505	8,403
London, Ont.	71,148	78,264
Magog, Que.	6,302	9 034
Medicine Hat, Alta.	10,300	10,571
Moncton, N. B.	20,689	22,763
Montreal, Que.	818,577	903,007
Moose Jaw, Sask.	21,299	20,753
New Glasgow, N. S.	8,858	9,210
New Toronto, Ont.	7,146	9,504
New Waterford, N. S.	7,745	9,302
New Westminster, B. C.	17,524	21,967
Niagara Falls, Ont.	19,046	20,589
North Bay, Ont.	15,528	15,599
North Vancouver, B. C.	8,510	8,914
Orillia, Ont.	8,183	9,798
Oshawa, Ont.	23,439	26,813
Ottawa, Ont.	126,872	154,951
Outremont, Que.	28,641	30,751
Owen Sound, Ont.	12,839	14,002
Pembroke, Ont.	9,368	11,159
Peterborough, Ont.	22,327	25,350
Port Arthur, Ont.	19,818	24,426
Prince Albert, Sask.	9,905	12,508
Quebec, Que.	130,594	150,757
Regina, Sask.	53,209	58,245
Rivière du Loup, Que.	8,499	8,713
Rouyn, Que.	3,225	8,808
St. Boniface, Man.	16,305	18,157
St. Catherines, Ont.	24,753	30,275
St. Hyacinthe, Que.	13,448	17,798

City or Town	Pop. 1931	Pop. 1941
St. Jean, Que.	11,256	13,646
St. Jérôme, Que.	8,967	11,329
St. John, N. B.	47,514	51,741
St. Thomas, Ont.	15,430	17,132
Sarnia, Ont.	18,191	18,734
Saskatoon, Sask.	43,291	43,027
Sault Ste. Marie, Ont.	23,082	25,794
Shawinigan Falls, Que.	15,345	20,345
Sherbrooke, Que.	28,933	35,965
Sorel, Que.	10,320	12,251
Stratford, Ont.	17,742	17,038
Sudbury, Ont.	18,518	32,203
Sydney, N. S.	23,089	28,305
Sydney Mines, N. S.	7,769	8,198
Thetford Mines, Que.	10,701	12,716
Three Rivers, Que.	35,450	42,007
Timmins, Ont.	14,200	28,790
Toronto, Ont.	631,207	667,457
Trail, B. C.	7,573	9,392
Truro, N. S.	7,901	10,272
Trenton, Ont.	6,276	8,323
Valleyfield, Que.	11,411	17,052
Vancouver, B. C.	246,593	273,353
Verdun, Que.	60,745	67,349
Victoria, B. C.	39,082	44,068
Victoriaville, Que.	6,213	8,516
Waterloo, Ont.	8,095	9,025
Welland, Ont.	10,709	12,500
Westmount, Que.	24,235	26,047
Windsor, Ont.	98,179	105,311
Winnipeg, Man.	218,785	221,960
Woodstock, Ont.	11,146	12,461

NEWFOUNDLAND

A former British dominion, consisting of the island of Newfoundland, lying across the mouth of the Gulf of Saint Lawrence, and a portion of the Labrador peninsula. Being situated 1640 miles west of Ireland, Newfoundland commands the shortest route from North America to Europe.

Contour. The island has an area of 42,734 square miles. In form it resembles a triangle with approximately equal sides of about 325 miles in length. The coasts are, in general, high and rocky, indented by innumerable fiords. Newfoundland's Labrador territory covers about 232,400 square miles, comprising the land draining into the Atlantic. Of this, 112,400 square miles came to Newfoundland in 1927 through the favorable outcome of a boundary dispute. Its value lies in the coast fisheries, in pulpwood, and in potential hydroelectric development.

Surface and Climate. The interior of Newfoundland is an undulating plain, interrupted by a few isolated peaks and rising on the northwest to a ridge of hills, called Long range. From this ridge eastward flows Exploits river, the country's longest stream. The Humber river has cut its way westward through Long range and flows into the Gulf of Saint Lawrence. The rivers are not navigable.

The climate is subject to less extreme variations of temperature than those occurring in any part of the interior of Canada. The mean temperature is lowered by the proximity of the arctic current, which brings melting icebergs from the north and occasions dense fogs along the coasts.

Flora and Fauna. Large portions of the island consist of marshes and of rocky soil supporting lichens and low shrubs of pine and of larch. The river valleys, however, contain large tracts of arable land and extensive areas heavily forested with conifers, birch, and red maple. The wild animals include the black bear, the wolf, the beaver, the deer, and the fox. The Newfoundland dog was developed by a cross between European species and a woolly-coated dog used by the Indians of Labrador.

Industries. Approximately one-fifth of Newfoundland's population is engaged in fishing and curing codfish. Nearly half the exports are codfish products. Herring, lobsters, salmon, and seals are also obtained.

The most important manufactures are pulp and paper. A very small fraction of the arable land is cultivated, in spite of the steps taken by the government to encourage agriculture. The chief crops are potatoes and turnips. Iron, zinc, and copper are mined. Silver, coal, and gypsum deposits, though largely undeveloped, form a promising source of future profits.

Inhabitants. The population of Newfoundland in the 1945 census was 320,101, concentrated mainly in the coast region of the southeast. This figure excludes 5,000 inhabitants of Labrador, mostly Indians. Nearly all the inhabitants are of British descent and Protestants. The schools and colleges are denominational. There is no university.

The government administered from St. John's has been undergoing changes since 1934, when the British government suspended the constitution and took over on account of internal financial difficulties. Union with Canada as a tenth province was carried by a small majority in a referendum conducted in Newfoundland July 1948, and was mutually agreed to in December of that year. Canadian and British parliaments and the Newfoundland government must ratify this union agreement to make it effective. The population of St. John's, the fishing, industrial, and educational center, in 1945 was 56,709.

MEXICO

A federal republic of North America, lying south of the United States and extending southeast to Guatemala. The outline of the country resembles a cornucopia modified by two irregularities,—the peninsula of Yucatan in the southeast and the peninsula of Lower California in the northwest. Its area is 767,198 square miles, about half of which is in the Torrid Zone. Its maximum length is over 1900 miles, and its width varies from 1833 miles, along the northern boundary, to 134 miles, at the Isthmus of Tehuantepec. The coast line on the Gulf of Mexico and the Caribbean Sea measures 1727 miles, while the coast line on the Pacific Ocean and on the Gulf of California has a total length of 4574 miles.

Surface and Drainage. The greater part of Mexico consists of a central plateau, called the *tierras templadas*, having an elevation of from 3000 to 8000 feet. It is flanked on the east by a high range of mountains called the Sierra Madre Oriental. At the Isthmus of Tehuantepec, this range converges with the Sierra Madre Occidental, which flanks the central plateau on the west. The mountains of the Isthmus of Tehuantepec belong to the Central American system. The lofty areas above an altitude of 8000 feet are known as the *tierras frias*. On each side of the country, lowlands, or *tierras calientes*, form a fringe between the coast and the mountain range. The peninsula of Yucatan is, for the most part, a low, sandy plain. Lower California is mountainous and consists of a southern extension of the Sierra Nevada range.

The central plateau is of volcanic origin and the sierras contain a large number of volcanoes. The highest, Orizaba, has not been active since the 16th century. Its elevation is 18,564 feet. Popocatepetl, "Smoky Mountain," and Iztaccihuatl, "White Woman," are extinct. Violent earthquakes are frequent. In 1920, in the Orizaba Volcano district, about 3000 people were killed by seismic disturbances and ten towns were partially or wholly destroyed.

The drainage system of Mexico is simple. The central plateau has a number of lakes but no large rivers. Several short streams flow from the mountain ranges into the sea. The Rio Grande, on the northern border, receives little water from the Mexican side. No river of Mexico is navigable throughout the year.

Climate and Flora. The *tierras calientes*, on the east, being subject to great heat and a heavy rainfall, are unhealthful. They support a luxuriant tropical vegetation. The banana, coconut, pineapple, pomegranate, vanilla, cacao, and ginger are produced in abundance. Sisal hemp is grown in Yucatan and is exported in large quantities to the United States to be used in the manufacture of rope. Mexico's forest areas, which are estimated to cover 44 million acres, are mainly in the lowlands. Mahogany, ebony, rosewood, and rubber are among the more valuable products of the tropical forests. The Pacific lowlands are arid in the north but have a more copious rainfall in the south.

The plateau has a temperate climate and is well adapted for the cultivation of cotton, tobacco, coffee, rice, sugar cane, corn, wheat, and potatoes. The rainfall in general is light but varies considerably in different parts. The north portion is dry; the cactus appears as a characteristic plant, and irrigation is necessary for successful agriculture. In some parts, however, two or three crops a year may be raised. The forest areas of the plateau contain oak, myrtle, fir, spruce, and pine. The higher mountain regions support an alpine flora.

Animal Life. The lowlands are the habitat of monkeys, pumas, jaguars, ocelots, sloths, armadillos, parrots, parrakeets, humming birds, alligators, venomous snakes, and many other animals characteristic of a tropical fauna. The wolf, coyote, otter, and deer are found in the central plateau.

Minerals and Mining. The mineral resources of Mexico make her potentially one of the richest countries in the world. Mining is the chief industry, and petroleum is the chief product, 193 million barrels having been obtained in 1921, a record not since equalled. It is estimated that Mexican mines have yielded over three billion dollars worth of silver. Mexico is also one of the world's greatest copper and lead producing countries. Gold, zinc, antimony, tungsten, molybdenum, mercury, and opals are also exported. Near the city of Durango is a large hill, the Cerro de Mercado, composed almost entirely of pure iron ore. Lack of transportation facilities and of adequate capital has retarded the exploitation of these vast mineral deposits.

Other Industries. The agricultural methods employed in Mexico are primitive. About two-thirds of the 30 million acres under cultivation require irrigation. The normal annual production of the largest crop, corn, is about 100 million bushels. The agave is cultivated for its fibers, used in rope making, and for its leaves, with which houses are thatched. Rice and coffee are grown. The area employed for grazing purposes is about four times that devoted to agriculture. Many tropical fruits are grown on plantations, including oranges, bananas, alligator pears, custard apples, and chichopoxtle, the last being a new fruit yielding a valuable lubricating oil. The chief manufactures are cotton textiles, tobacco products, and steel. The country has over 18,000 miles of railway. The chief ports are Vera Cruz and Tampico, both on the Gulf of Mexico.

Inhabitants. The population of Mexico in 1940 was 19,473,741. Of this number about half are mestizos and the rest are pure Indians and whites, the latter mainly of Spanish descent. The language is Spanish, and the prevailing religion is Roman Catholicism. Elementary education is free and compulsory. The chief cities, in addition to those described below, include Monterey (180,942), Merida (98,334), Leon (86,089), and Aguascalientes (81,124). The country is divided into 28 states, 2 territories, and 1 federal district.

Ruins in Yucatan. In Yucatan, the extreme eastern state of Mexico, are to be found the most impressive of the monuments left by the civilizations which flourished in America prior to its discovery by Europeans. Here was centered the New Mayan Empire, which was established by the Mayas after the fall of the Old Empire, the territory now known as Guatemala. The Old Empire flourished from the beginning of the Christian era until the 6th century A. D. The causes of its fall form one of the fascinating enigmas of early American history. Mayan settlers entered Yucatan as early as the 4th century A. D., but the New Mayan Empire was not definitely established until about 1100 A. D. It continued until the coming of the Spaniards in the early 16th century. The chief centers were the capital, Uxmal, and the cities of Mayapan and Chichen-Itza.

The buildings are of one story in height, but in nearly all cases are situated on terraces or pyramids constructed of earth. They are faced with stone and have masonry steps for ascent and descent. The Temple of the Magician at Uxmal crowns a majestic pyramid 80 feet high and 240 by 180 feet at the base. The exterior is richly ornamented with carvings and relief work. Such carving was executed by stone tools, the only metals known to the builders being gold, silver, and copper. Since the true arch was unknown, roofs of Mayan buildings were either flat or, more often, vaulted. The buildings are very narrow, and the walls are usually from three to nine feet thick.

In central Mexico also are numerous pyramids surmounted by stone temples or palaces built by the Toltecs and Aztecs. The roofs of these buildings are usually flat, being supported by beams.

Guadalajara (*gwä'thä-lä-hä'rä*). The second largest city of Mexico, situated about 150 miles inland from the center of the country's Pacific coast. The climate is agreeable, the range of the temperature being limited to a few degrees. Guadalajara is an important mining center. The large waterfall of Juanacatlan near by furnishes electric power for street railroads, city lighting, and manufacturing. Among the manufactures are cotton goods, art pottery, tiles, leather articles, and cordage.

The city is well built and has spacious streets and several large parks embellished with fountains and statues. The principal building, the cathedral, noted for its ornamentation and magnificent interior, contains one of Murillo's masterpieces. Aqueducts, eight miles long, bring water to the city. Population, 1940, 228,049.

Mexico. The capital and largest city of Mexico. It is situated somewhat southeast of the geographic center of the country at an elevation of 7415 feet. Majestic, snow-crowned mountains encircle the city, presenting a scene of surpassing grandeur. The climate is delightful; the air is dry, and the range of temperature seldom exceeds 15°.

Mexico City is the social, literary, financial, and industrial center of the country. Manufactures include textiles, chemicals, paper, boots and shoes, and foundry and tobacco products.

The city is regularly laid out with wide, well paved streets, shaded boulevards, numerous parks and driveways embellished with statues and monuments, and several ornate squares, the largest of which is the Plaza Mayor. Fronting this square is the great cathedral, a magnificent structure in the Spanish Renaissance type of architecture. Its foundations were laid in 1573 on the site of an Aztec temple. A splendid national museum contains numerous priceless relics of the Aztec civilization. Three miles outside the city is the executive mansion, Chapultepec castle, situated on a hill which has a monument commemorating those who, in 1848, gave their lives in its defense against the American army of invasion. Twelve miles south of the city stands San Cuicuilco, a lava hill from which was excavated a circular mound made by a prehistoric race. The mound, which is constructed of unhewn lava blocks, is estimated to be from 3000 to 7000 years old. It is 52 feet in height and has a diameter of 420 feet at the base.

The houses of Mexico City are, for the most part, of one story, being in an area liable to earthquake shocks. In 1629, 30,000 inhabitants of the city were drowned by a flood due to the overflow of Lake Tezcuco in the vicinity. To prevent a recurrence of the disaster, a tunnel six miles long was built to carry off the surplus water of the lake and discharge it into a 43-mile canal connecting with a river of the Gulf drainage system. Mexico City was founded by Cortés in 1521 on the site of the Aztec town Tenochtitlan, dating from 1325. Population, 1930, 960,905; 1940, 1,464,556. The increase was due partly to annexation of suburbs in 1931.

Puebla (*pwä'blä*). An important city of Mexico, situated in the vicinity of several of the highest mountains in the country about 60 miles southeast of Mexico City. The manufactures include textiles, soap, glass, straw hats, pottery, and leather goods. Onyx articles, made from the stone quarried near by, form an important article of export.

The city is well built and has all modern improvements. Besides several professional schools, there are three libraries, an imposing cathedral of Spanish architecture, an art gallery, a museum, an observatory, and many other institutions of note. A short distance from the city are the famous mineral springs of Tehuacan and the prehistoric pyramid of Cholula, 177 feet high and covering nearly 45 acres. The city was founded by the Franciscans in 1532. It was captured by the Americans in 1847 and was taken by the French in 1863. Population, 1940, 137,324.

Tampico (*täm-pē'kō*). The best equipped port of Mexico, on the Panuco river near its mouth in the Gulf of Mexico. Petroleum is produced in large quantities in the vicinity and forms the chief article of export. Ores, hides, wood, wool, and hemp are also exported; manufactured goods, mainly from the United States, are imported. Modern warehouses, offices, and municipal improvements give Tampico a thoroughly up-to-date appearance. Population, 1940, 81,334.

Vera Cruz. An important seaport of Mexico, situated on the Bay of Campeche, an arm of the Gulf of Mexico. An enervating climate and the prevalence of yellow fever once gave Vera Cruz the name of the City of the Dead. Modern sanitation measures, however, have completely transformed living conditions.

Twenty-five million dollars have been spent on the improvement of the harbor. On a reef near its entrance stands the fortress of San Jaun de Ulua. The exports consist chiefly of ore, chicle, dyewoods, and hides, and the imports include textiles, hardware, and other manufactured goods. Fishing is carried on extensively, and there is a considerable manufacturing industry. Population, 1940, 70,958.

CENTRAL AMERICA

A geographical term used to designate the neck of land which connects North America and South America. It stretches in a southeast and northwest direction, lies entirely within the Torrid Zone, and comprises the area between the Isthmus of Tehuantepec, in southern Mexico, on the north, and the Isthmus of Panama, immediately north of Colombia, in the south. Its area is approximately 200,000 square miles. Its width varies from about 30 miles at the Isthmus of Panama to 450 miles in southern Mexico.

Surface. The southwestern coast of Central America is skirted by a broken chain of mountains, which reach a maximum elevation of 13,000 feet. Their formation is distinct from that of the Rocky mountains and of the Andes range. Volcanic eruptions and violent earthquakes are very frequent. The largest interruption of the mountainous highlands is the basin of Lake Nicaragua, which has a water area in excess of 3500 square miles. The northeastern side of the isthmus slopes gradually toward the sea and has a fertile and well watered soil.

Climate and Flora. The climate varies, according to elevation, from a tropical heat to an arctic rigor. The lava areas are extremely fertile and, where the climate is favorable, produce coffee, sugar, corn, pineapple, bananas, and other products of tropical agriculture. The forests of the lowland are rich in dyewoods and valuable cabinet woods. The higher districts have a characteristic temperate-zone and alpine flora.

Inhabitants. The total population is estimated at more than 6,000,000, mostly of Indian and Spanish blood. The majority live on the southwestern coastal area. Agriculture is the chief occupation, although vast mineral and forest resources await development. Textiles and other manufactured goods are imported. More than 80 per cent of the trade is with the United States. Few good roads exist. There are in operation, however, three interoceanic railways. Furthermore, an intercontinental or Pan-American railway is projected, which would connect the United States with Colombia.

Politically, Central America comprises the countries lying between Mexico and Colombia. Apart from the Panama Canal Zone and the crown colony of British Honduras, they consist of six independent republics—Guatemala, Honduras, Salvador, Nicaragua, Costa Rica, and Panama. Roman Catholicism is the prevailing religion and Spanish is the common language. The general level of education is low, and the inhabitants are not characterized by the energy noticeable among most temperate-zone peoples.

British Honduras (*hŏn-dōō'ras*). A British crown colony in Central America, bordering on the Caribbean Sea, Mexico, and Guatemala. Its area is 8598 square miles. Most of the surface is covered with tropical forests yielding mahogany, chicle, and logwood. Bananas and coconuts are also exported in considerable quantities. The coast is low, marshy, and unhealthful. The population, 1946 census, was 59,149, of whom about 2 per cent were white, the remainder being chiefly of Negro and Indian blood. The capital is Belize. The control of the colony was long disputed by Spain and was not finally secured by Great Britain until 1836.

Costa Rica (*kŏs'tȧ rē'kȧ*). A country occupying the section of Central America between Nicaragua and Panama. The area is about 23,000 square miles, a large part of which is an irregular table-land in which some mountain peaks attain an altitude of more than 10,000 feet. Many mountains are volcanic and have caused a considerable loss of life.

Coffee is the staple product of the subtropical plateau, but cacao, tobacco, and sugar are also grown and exported. Costa Rica is one of the chief banana producing countries of the world. The fruit is grown extensively in the hot, tropical lowlands, from which also considerable amounts of hardwood and rubber are obtained. The industry second in importance is mining, the chief minerals being gold and silver. Live stock is raised in the elevated regions.

The population, 1945 census, was 746,535, of whom a large proportion were of Spanish origin. The people are industrious and claim to have more school teachers than soldiers. The capital is San José. The name of the country means rich coast and was given to the district in 1502 by Christopher Columbus.

Guatemala (*gwä'tâ-mä'lȧ*). The second largest and the most populous country of Central America, lying between Mexico and the republic of Honduras. Its area is 45,452 square miles. A mountain ridge, which includes a number of volcanoes, divides the long eastern slope from the narrower but more thickly populated Pacific drainage area. Lake Peten, in the northern part of the country, is noted for being the habitat of 30 species of fish not found elsewhere.

The hot lowlands in the north and east are unhealthful but produce large crops of cacao, sugar cane, and bananas. The dense forests of the valleys yield valuable hardwoods, chicle, and rubber. The staple export of the country, however, is coffee, grown principally on the rich, volcanic soil of the plateau and the western slope. Two annual crops of wheat and three of corn are raised in this district. At the higher altitudes, apples and potatoes are grown and many cattle are raised.

The population of Guatemala, 1946 est., is 3,706,205, more than half of whom are pure Indians. The owners of the coffee plantations are in large part Germans. Guatemala is the capital and lies on the interoceanic railway which connects Punto Barrios, the port on the Gulf of Honduras, with San José and other ports on the Pacific coast.

Honduras. A country of Central America, lying between Guatemala and Nicaragua, with a coast line of 400 miles on the Caribbean Sea. The southwestern boundary is Salvador and the Gulf of Fonseca, an inlet of the Pacific Ocean. The surface covers 44,275 square miles, the greater part of which is a plateau ranging in elevation from 5000 to 10,000 feet.

The hot, malarial coastal region produces the bulk of the country's staple export—bananas. Coconuts are grown there also, and, farther inland, large crops of sugar, tobacco, and coffee are produced. Corn is cultivated as the chief article of domestic consumption. Stock raising is one of the principal industries. The dense forests of the coast area and of the valleys yield rubber, dyewoods, and medicinal plants. Cigars and Panama hats are manufactured for export.

The mineral resources of the country are extensive but are little developed. Practically all the 1100 miles of railroad is owned or operated by fruit companies. The principal towns are connected by air service. The capital and largest city is Tegucigalpa.

The population of the country in 1940 was 1,105,504. A region in the eastern portion of the country, called La Mosquita, is still unexplored, and the uncivilized natives speak a language of their own.

Nicaragua (*nĭk'ȧ-rä'gwȧ*). The largest country of Central America, situated at the center of the intercontinental neck. Its surface is mountainous in the northern and western part, where there are several volcanoes. The eastern section is low, and, in the south, there is a depression forming the basin of Lake Nicaragua, Central America's largest inland body of water. The area of the country is 57,143 square miles.

Most of the population is found in the fertile, volcanic valleys of the uplands on the western side of the country, of which the chief agricultural products are coffee, cacao, sugar cane, and corn. Cattle are raised and the export of hides is important. Bananas are grown in large quantities in the eastern lowlands. Forest industries rank second in importance, timber, dyewoods, gums, oils, fibers, and rubber being obtained on both coasts of the country. Gold and silver are mined. The chief manufactures are Panama hats and cigars.

The population of Nicaragua in 1946 was estimated at 1,122,000, composed almost entirely of mestizos. The two principal cities are Managua and Leon, the former being the seat of the national government. The Pacific Coast ports of Corinto and San Juan del Sur handle most of the foreign trade. In 1916 the United States purchased from Nicaragua the right to build an interoceanic canal through the country.

Panama (*păn'ȧ-mä'*). The most eastern country of Central America, stretching from Costa Rica about 480 miles east to Colombia. It occupies the narrowest part of the intercontinental neck and is divided into two parts by the Panama Canal Zone, ten miles in width, which belongs to the United States. The area of the country is 28,576 square miles.

Panama is traversed by two broken mountain chains, which are overgrown with dense forests containing rubber trees and valuable hardwoods. Bananas and coconuts are produced in the hot lowlands, and sugar cane, coffee, cacao, and tobacco are grown at higher altitudes. A considerable number of cattle are raised, and hides form a valuable article of export.

The population of Panama, exclusive of the Canal Zone, was 622,576 in 1940. The city of Panama, which is the seat of government, is located in the Canal Zone, without, however, being politically a part of it.

Panama Canal Zone. A strip of land ten miles in width, through the center of which runs the Panama canal. The Canal Zone divides the Republic of Panama into two parts.

The zone was obtained in 1903 from the Republic of Panama for the sum of ten million dollars with an annual payment of $250,000, changed in 1936 to 430,000 balboas after the American dollar had been devalued in terms of gold. Its affairs are administered by a governor appointed by the United States government. A railroad connects the two terminals of the canal—Balboa, the Pacific port, and Cristobal, on the Caribbean sea. Population, 1940, 51,827. See *Panama Canal.*

Salvador. The smallest but, next to Guatemala, the most populous republic of Central America, situated southwest of Honduras with a coast line on the Pacific Ocean. Its area is 13,176 square miles.

There is a level coastal strip which rises, farther inland, to a mountainous plateau containing a number of active volcanoes. One of these, called the Izalco, or "lighthouse," began to rise from the plateau about a century ago and, by means of its own lava, has reached the height of a mile. San Salvador, the capital of the country, has been destroyed three times by eruptions of the volcanic mountain bearing the same name.

The volcanic area is extremely fertile and produces large crops of coffee, sugar, tobacco, and cacao. The chief export is coffee. Balsam and hardwoods are the principal forest products sent abroad. Cattle are raised extensively. The more important minerals obtained include gold and silver.

The population, 1946 census, was 2,018,895. The chief seaports, La Libertad and Acajutla, are connected with the capital by a section of the republic's 330 miles of railway.

Belize (*bĕ-lēz'*). The capital and chief seaport of British Honduras, situated at the mouth of the Belize river near the center of the colony's seacoast. The climate is hot but not unhealthful. The exports go mainly to the United States and consist chiefly of mahogany, logwood, coconuts, and bananas. Population, 1946 census, 26,757.

Guatemala. The capital of the country of the same name. Guatemala is an inland commercial city, situated in the southern part of the country about 85 miles from the Pacific coast on a plateau 5000 feet above the sea. A large part of its trade is in coffee. The city has various professional schools, a university, and a cathedral, which is the seat of the archbishop of all Central America, except Panama. Guatemala has been destroyed three times by earthquakes, most recently in 1917. Population, 1940, 176,780.

Leon (*lā-ōn'*). A metropolis of Nicaragua and formerly its capital, situated about 15 miles from the coast in the western portion of the country. It has an admirable cathedral built in the Renaissance style, and is the seat of a university. Population, 1946 est., 50,290.

Managua (*mä-nä'gwä*). The capital of Nicaragua, situated about 25 miles inland from the center of the state Pacific coast line. It is a commercial center for the marketing of coffee grown in the region. The city is the seat of the Central University of Nicaragua. Managua was almost entirely destroyed by earthquake in 1931, but rebuilding was begun at once. Population, 1946 est., 137,014.

Panama. The capital of the Republic of Panama, situated at the head of Panama bay near the southern terminus of the Panama canal. Geographically, Panama is located in the Panama Canal Zone, but politically it is a part of the Republic of Panama. The United States government, however, was authorized in 1903 to carry out improvements in sanitation.

Panama, founded by Pedro Arias in 1519, was one of the first European settlements in the western hemisphere. It was long the capital and Pacific metropolis of Spain's vast possessions in America. Population, 1940, 111,893.

San José (*sän hō-sā'*). The capital of Costa Rica situated in a rich coffee growing region. The city is regularly built and has broad streets, fronted for the most part by one-story brick houses. The principal buildings include the national palace, the university, and the national theater, the last erected in the style of the Library of Congress at a cost of about $1,000,000. Population, 1945 census, 79,613.

San Salvador. The capital and largest city of Salvador, situated in a fertile valley about 25 miles from the coast. It is about three miles from the volcano of San Salvador, which destroyed most of the city in 1919. The houses are surrounded by open ground and are built low in order to minimize the danger during possible earthquakes. The city carries on an active trade in tobacco, and other products of the region. It has a university, a national library, and a fine botanical garden. Salvador is one of the oldest settlements of the western hemisphere, being founded in 1528 by Alvarado. Population, 1946 census, 123,143.

Tegucigalpa (*tā-gōō'sē-gäl'pä*). The capital of Honduras, situated in the southern part of the country about 50 miles from San Lorenzo, its port on the Gulf of Fonseca. It has no railway communication with other cities. The agricultural and mining interests of the surrounding region center in the city, which is also the seat of a national university and of several colleges. Tegucigalpa was formerly an Aztec city. It was made the capital of Honduras in 1880. Population, 1945 census, 55,715.

THE WEST INDIES

A large group of islands lying between North America and South America and forming the barrier between the Atlantic Ocean and the Caribbean Sea. They stretch in a great curve from Florida east and south to the mouth of the Orinoco river in Venezuela. Their total area is about 92,000 square miles; their population, about 15,000,000. Most of the islands are rocky. They receive copious rain, brought principally in the summer by the northeast trade winds, which at times develop into destructive hurricanes.

The largest island is Cuba, which, like the two republics on the island of Haiti, is an independent country. Puerto Rico belongs to the United States. The other islands are dependencies of European countries. Most of them owe allegiance to Great Britain and are customarily described by the term British West Indies. The Netherlands and France control the remainder. Some distance to the north of the West Indies lie the Bermuda islands, which are possessions of Great Britain.

Cuba, Haiti, Jamaica, and Puerto Rico are sometimes referred to as the Greater Antilles, and the other West India islands, except the Bahamas, as the Lesser Antilles. Antilles is an Anglicized plural of Antilia, a name given on early maps to a mythical island in the Atlantic Ocean.

British West Indies. A term applied to the islands of the West Indies which are dependencies of Great Britain. For administrative purposes, they are divided into the following five groups: the Bahamas, Barbados, Jamaica and its dependencies, the Leeward islands, and the Windward islands. Trinidad and Tobago are sometimes added as a sixth group, but their proximity to South America makes it more natural to count them as insular parts of that continent. The total area of the islands is estimated at 12,000 square miles.

The chief occupation of the inhabitants is agriculture, although valuable hardwoods are to be found in the forested areas. English is the common language, and English currency is used. The population is 2,481,898, mostly of Negro blood.

Bahama Islands. A group of low islands in the British West Indies, extending from a point near the east coast of Florida, in a general direction parallel with the Cuban coast, to within 100 miles of the island of Haiti. While the group includes several hundred islands, only twenty have permanent settlements. These twenty cover an area of 4375 square miles. The population consists mainly of Negroes and, in 1943 was estimated at 80,640. The islands constitute a colony, with a capital at Nassau in New Providence island. The staple products of the colony are sponges and sisal hemp. Pineapples, both fresh and canned, oranges, and tomatoes are also exported. About one-half of the commerce is with the United States.

Barbados. The most easterly of the West India islands. The climate is healthful, fever being almost unknown. About two-thirds of its area of 166 square miles is under cultivation. The crop of paramount importance in Barbados is sugar, which is exported chiefly to Canada and the United States. About 1000 people are engaged in the fisheries.

The population, estimated in 1945 at 195,400, is denser than that of any other island of its size in the world; about 2 per cent are white. Washington's visit to Barbados in 1751 was the only foreign journey he ever made.

The capital and seaport is Bridgetown. Its houses are built of coral rock and of wood. Population, 13,486.

Jamaica. The largest island of the British West Indies, lying about 100 miles south of the eastern end of Cuba. Its area is 4411 square miles. To it are attached, for administrative purposes, a number of small islands, covering a total area of 224 square miles. Jamaica is traversed by low hills, which, at the eastern end, culminate in the Blue mountains with a maximum altitude of 7362 feet.

The chief exports of Jamaica are sugar, logwood and logwood extract, coconuts, cocoa, and rum. Textiles and flour are imported. The population is 1,237,063, of whom about 2 per cent are white. The prevailing religion is Protestantism.

The capital and chief port is Kingston, situated on a landlocked harbor on the southeast coast of the island. The city is well built. It has modern improvements and attractive suburbs. In one of its old parish churches stands the tomb of Admiral Benbow, an English seaman who distinguished himself in a battle with a French fleet in 1702. In 1907, Kingston was almost entirely destroyed by an earthquake. Its population is 1,314,430.

Leeward Islands. A group of West India islands forming a chain which begins to the east of Puerto Rico and curves southeast to the island of Saint Lucia. The majority of the islands are British. France, however, controls Guadeloupe, Martinique, Saint Bartholomew, and part of Saint Martin. The remainder of Saint Martin and the islands of Saint Eustatius and Saba belong to the Netherlands. The British dependencies are Antigua, Dominica, British Virgin islands, Saint Kitts, Montserrat, Barduda, Redonda, Sombrero, Nevis, and Anguilla. The British islands form one colony, having its seat of government at Saint John in the island of Antigua. The islands of the colony cover an approximate area of 412 square miles and support a population, principally Negroes, amounting to 108,850. The chief articles of export are cotton, sugar, molasses, cocoa, limes, and coconuts. The name was given in allusion to the fact that the islands are not swept by the northeast trade winds to so great a degree as are the Windward islands to the south.

Windward Islands. A group of British West India islands forming the eastern barrier of the Caribbean Sea. The chief islands are Grenada, Saint Vincent, and Saint Lucia, having a total area of 821 square miles and a population of 251,840. The three islands have separate administrative bodies. The products include excellent grades of cotton and of arrowroot; also sugar, cocoa, lime juice, and spices. Most of the trade is with Great Britain.

Bermuda Islands. A group of low coral islands belonging to Great Britain, about 880 miles due east of Charleston, South Carolina, and 699 miles from New York. Twenty of the 300 islands are inhabited. They supported in 1931, on an area of 19 square miles, a population of 27,789, of whom 11,353 were white. The chief exports are lilies and onions, sent almost entirely to the United States. Hamilton, situated on Bermuda island, is the capital and an important British naval base. The climate is genial and attracts numerous visitors from the United States and from Great Britain. The islands are named after the Spaniard, Bermudez, who discovered them in 1515. They were first settled in the 17th century by the Englishman, Somers, after whom they are sometimes called the Somers islands.

Cuba. The largest island of the West Indies, which, with the Isle of Pines and smaller adjacent islands, constitutes the independent republic of Cuba. Cuba is in the Torrid Zone and lies 92 miles south of Key West in Florida, the most southern town of the United States. The island has an average width of 50 miles and stretches about 730 miles in a general east and west direction. Its area is 44,206 square miles.

The surface of Cuba is in general low and undulating. Hills border the northern coast and in the southeast a short range of mountains, the Sierra Maestra, skirts the sea and reaches at one point an elevation of 8320 feet. The rivers are short. Many of them, however, are noted for disappearing throughout part of their courses. The Moa cascade in eastern Cuba is formed by a river which drops 300 feet into a cave. A number of springs of fresh water are found in the sea rising through the salt water. These springs are believed to be emerging rivers which disappeared inland.

The climate of Cuba is hot and moist. Recent improvements in sanitation have virtually banished yellow fever, which formerly afflicted the inhabitants as a yearly epidemic. The soil is rich and supports a luxuriant vegetation. Palms and valuable hardwood trees flourish in forests covering nearly half the island. Bananas and other tropical fruits provide food for the inhabitants and are exported in great quantities. The fauna includes the tarantula, chameleon, scorpion, vulture, scavenger buzzard, and, among the numerous species of snakes, a boa, which often attains a length of 18 feet. The rare insectivore, the almiqui, is indigenous to the island. Alligators infest the waters. Coral insects have produced coral reefs about the coasts in such number as to endanger navigation in many parts.

The chief industry of Cuba is the cultivation of sugar cane and of tobacco. Cuba is the chief source of America's sugar supply and leads the world in the production of sugar cane, the output in 1920 being valued at more than one billion dollars, a figure not since equalled. Live stock is raised, and mining is carried on to a limited degree. Manufacturing is almost entirely confined to the refining of sugar and the production of tobacco goods. Sponge fishing provides occupation for part of the inhabitants of the southwestern coast. The island has about 3057 miles of railroad, including 2640 miles belonging to sugar estates.

The population of Cuba, 1943 census, was 4,778,583, mostly of Negro origin. Spanish is the prevailing language, and the official religion is Roman Catholicism. Elementary education is free and obligatory. There are also normal schools, vocational schools, and a national university. The capital, largest city, and chief port is Havana.

Havana. The capital of Cuba, situated on an excellent natural harbor on the northern coast. The city lies directly south of Florida. Havana is the chief commercial city of the West Indies. It is the focus of Cuba's enormous trade in sugar and in tobacco, and has tobacco factories which are among the largest in the world.

The older section of the city, lying between the harbor and the sea, has narrow, irregular streets. The newer parts have wide, asphalt-paved streets and contain picturesque parks and promenades adorned with shade trees. The most attractive street is the Prado, which has in the center a parkway shaded by laurels and palms. Most of the public buildings are of limestone. They include the costly presidential palace, on the Prado; the Tacon theater, which is one of the largest playhouses in the western hemisphere; and the cathedral, said to have contained the remains of Columbus from 1796 to 1898. The city is a popular winter resort for Americans. The chief educational institutions include the University of Havana and the Jesuit College of Belen.

The harbor is equipped with three forts of obsolete construction. In 1898 the American battleship, the *Maine*, was blown up in the harbor. After the expulsion of the Spaniards in 1899, a program of improvements in sanitation was carried out which freed the city from the pestilential scourges to which it was formerly subject. Havana was founded in 1519. Population, 1943 census, 673,376.

Camagüey (*kä'mä-gwā'*). The largest inland city of Cuba, situated in the midst of rich savannas somewhat east of the center of the island. Its port, Nuevitas, located about 50 miles northeast on the Atlantic coast, is the outlet for the products of the live stock industry centering in the city. The sugar interests of Camagüey are also considerable.

Founded in 1516, the city retains an antiquated appearance with narrow, winding streets and poor houses. During the American occupation of Cuba, good water was provided by means of artesian wells and a drainage system was introduced. The city is sometimes known as Puerto Principe. Population, 1943 census, 155,827.

Cienfuegos (*syĕn-fwā'gōs*). A seaport of Cuba, situated on a landlocked harbor near the center of the island's southern coast. The commerce consists largely of sugar exports to the United States. Population, 1943 census, 94,810.

Matanzas (*mȧ-tăn'zȧs*). A city on the northern coast of Cuba, 55 miles east of Havana. It has tobacco factories, distilleries, and iron foundries, and ranks next to Havana in the export of sugar and tobacco. Population, 1943 census, 73,749.

Santiago de Cuba (*sän'tē-ä'gō dā kōō'bä*). A city of southeastern Cuba, situated on a deep, landlocked harbor on the Caribbean Sea. The port is the outlet for the tobacco raised in the district, for forest products, and for iron, manganese, and copper ores. The city was founded in 1514 by Diego Velasquez. In the Spanish American war, Spain's fleet under Cervera took refuge in Santiago harbor and was destroyed while attempting to escape. San Juan hill near by is a national park memorializing Theodore Roosevelt's assault in 1898. Population, 1943 census, 120,577.

Haiti (Hispaniola). The second largest island of the West Indies, a short distance southeast of Cuba. The island has an area of 29,536 square miles, with a maximum length of 405 miles and a maximum width of 165 miles. The surface is rugged and contains three mountain ranges running east and west. The highest peak is Loma Tina, which reaches an altitude of 10,300 feet. The southeast part of the island consists of flat grasslands, or llanos, which provide rich pasturage. Haiti has a large salt lake, called Enrequillo and a number of hot mineral springs.

The mountains are rich in undeveloped mineral deposits. An abundant rainfall fosters a luxuriant vegetation—valuable hardwood trees in the tropical forests and, in the cultivated areas, abundant crops of coffee, cacao, cotton, tobacco, and sugar. Coffee is the chief export.

The island is divided between two republics, Haiti and the Dominican Republic, which have a total population of over 5,500,000. It was called Espanola after its discovery on December 6, 1492.

Haiti. A Negro republic occupying the western third of the island of Haiti. Its area is 10,204 square miles. Most of the inhabitants live in the hot, unhealthful lowlands, and the death rate is high. The chief industry is the cultivation of coffee and other products of tropical agriculture. The mineral and forest wealth is little developed.

The population is estimated at 3,500,000, of whom about 90 per cent have no admixture of white blood. The spoken language is a corrupt dialect of French known as Creole French. The official religion is Roman Catholicism, although in many parts forms of African religion survive, as in the barbaric rites of Voodoo worship.

The capital and largest city is Port au Prince, situated at the head of the Bay of Haiti. The town is poorly built and has a low unhealthful location. It has a university, created in 1921. Port au Prince is sometimes called Port Républicain. Population, 1940 est., 170,000.

Dominican Republic. A republic of the West Indies, occupying the eastern two-thirds of the island of Haiti. Its surface, covering 19,332 square miles, rises in the interior to an elevation which culminates in Mount Loma Tina, the highest peak in the West Indies.

The chief industry is agriculture; sugar, cocoa, coffee, and tobacco are exported, mainly to the United States. Stock raising is an occupation of importance. The forest and mineral resources are extensive but are little developed.

The inhabitants are mostly of Negro origin. The common language is Spanish, and Roman Catholicism is the prevailing religion. Customs collections from 1907 and the general administration of the country from 1916 were in the hands of the United States until 1934. The American receivership was abolished in 1941. Population, 1947 est., 2,151,000.

The capital is Ciudad Trujillo, formerly Santo Domingo. The city is situated near the center of the republic's southern coast. The streets are regularly laid out but are unpaved. The city had a cathedral, in which the bones of Christopher Columbus were entombed from 1542 to 1796, and a statue of him stands in the public square. The settlement was founded in 1496 by the brother of the great discoverer, and, after Isabella on the northern coast, it is the oldest European settlement in the western hemisphere. Population, 1946 est., 139,090.

Curaçao (*kōō'rä-sä'ō*). A political name applied to a Dutch colony which comprises two groups of islands in the West Indies. Curaçao, the largest island, and two others lie about 40 miles off the northwestern coast of Venezuela, while the remaining three form part of the Leeward islands southeast of Puerto Rico. The total area of the colony is 403 square miles, and the population in 1947 amounted to 136,733. The chief industry is oil refining. These islands are sometimes included, along with Dutch Guiana, under the term Dutch West Indies.

STATISTICS OF LEADING COUNTRIES

COUNTRY	Area Sq. Miles	Population	Population per Square Mile	Capital	Largest City	Form of Gov't[1]
Afghanistan	250,000	12,000,000	48.0	Kabul	Kabul	C. M.
Argentina	1,079,965	16,107,870	14.9	Buenos Aires	Buenos Aires	Rep.
Australia	2,977,600	7,580,800	2.5	Canberra	Sydney	Dom.
Austria	32,369	7,000,000	216.2	Vienna	Vienna	Rep.(2)
Belgium	11,775	8,388,526	712.4	Brussels	Brussels	C. M.
Bolivia	419,470	3,722,700	8.8	La Paz (3)	La Paz	Rep.
Brazil	3,286,170	45,300,000	13.7	Rio de Janeiro	Rio de Janeiro	Rep.
Bulgaria	39,825	7,020,863	176.2	Sofia	Sofia	Rep.
Burma	261,757	16,823,798	64.3	Rangoon	Rangoon	Rep.
Canada	3,695,189	11,506,655	3.1	Ottawa	Montreal	Dom.
Chile	286,322	5,511,424	19.2	Santiago	Santiago	Rep.
China	3,924,668	461,006,285	117.4	Nanking	Shanghai	Rep.
Colombia	439,828	10,701,816	24.3	Bogota	Bogota	Rep.
Costa Rica	19,653	771,503	39.2	San José	San José	Rep.
Cuba	44,206	4,778,583	114.4	Havana	Havana	Rep.
Denmark	16,576	4,045,232	244.0	Copenhagen	Copenhagen	C. M.
Dominican Rep.	19,332	2,029,054	104.9	Ciudad Trujillo	Ciudad Trujillo	Rep.
Ecuador	104,000	3,200,000	30.7	Quito	Guayaquil	Rep.
Egypt	386,198	19,040,000	49.3	Cairo	Cairo	C. M.
Eire (Ireland)	26,959	2,953,452	111.0	Dublin	Dublin	Rep.
Finland	117,975	3,993,438	33.8	Helsinki	Helsinki	Rep.
France	212,659	40,517,923	190.5	Paris	Paris	Rep.
Germany (4)	137,640	66,410,999	482.5	Berlin	Berlin	Mil.
Great Britain (5)	94,278	51,889,513	508 0	London	London	C. M.
Greece	50,269	7,450,000	148.2	Athens	Athens	C. M.
Guatemala	42,042	3,706,205	88.1	Guatemala City	Guatemala City	Rep.
Honduras	59,159	1,200,542	20.3	Tegucigalpa	Tegucigalpa	Rep.
Hungary	35,875	9,106,252	253.8	Budapest	Budapest	Rep.
India, Union of	1,100,000	270,000,000	245.5	New Delhi	Calcutta	Dom.
Iran (Persia)	628,000	17,000,000	27.0	Tehran	Tehran	C. M.
Iraq	116,600	5,000,000	42.8	Baghdad	Baghdad	C. M.
Italy	116,332	46,000,000	395.4	Rome	Rome	Rep.
Japan	147,425	73,110,995	495.9	Tokyo	Tokyo	Mil.
Korea	85,246	24,326,327	285.3	Seoul (Keijo)	Seoul	Mil.(6)
Liberia	43,000	1,500,000	34.9	Monrovia	Monrovia	Rep.
Mexico	758,258	19,653,552	25.9	Mexico City	Mexico City	Rep.
Netherlands	13,440	9,630,000	716.5	The Hague (7)	Amsterdam	C. M.
New Zealand	103,935	1,802,840	16.3	Wellington	Auckland	Dom.
Nicaragua	57,143	1,082,439	18.9	Managua	Managua	Rep.
Norway	124,556	3,123,883	25.0	Oslo	Oslo	C. M.
Pakistan	300,000	90,000,000	300.0	Karachi	Lahore	Dom.
Palestine (Israel)	10,429	1,911,110	183.2	Sarona	Tel Aviv	P. G.
Panama	28,575	622,576	21.8	Panama	Panama	Rep.
Paraguay	149,807 (8)	1,108,040 (8)	7.4	Asunción	Asunción	Rep.
Peru	482,258	7,271,654	15.0	Lima City	Lima City	Rep.
Philippines	115,600	18,500,000	160.0	Manila	Manila	Rep.
Poland	121,131 (9)	23,622,334	112.4	Warsaw	Lodz	Rep.
Portugal	35,490	7,722,152	217.6	Lisbon	Lisbon	C. S.
Rumania	91,671	16,472,000	179.7	Bucharest	Bucharest	Rep.
Russia (USSR) (10)	8,708,900	191,888,500	22.0	Moscow	Moscow	S. R.
Salvador	13,176	2,018,895	153.2	San Salvador	San Salvador	Rep.
Siam (Thai)	200,148	17,256,825	86.2	Bangkok	Bangkok	C. M.
Spain	189,890	27,246,000	143.5	Madrid	Madrid	C. S.
Sweden	173,206	6,673,956	38.5	Stockholm	Stockholm	C. M.
Switzerland	15,950	4,265,703	267.4	Bern	Zurich	Rep.
Syria	74,000	3,400,000	45.9	Damascus	Alep	Rep.
Transjordan	34,740	500,000	14.4	Amman	Amman	C. M.
Turkey	296.107	18,860,222	63.7	Ankara	Istanbul	Rep.
United States	3,022,387	131,669,275	43.5	Washington	New York	Rep.
Uruguay	72,153	2,235,000	30.9	Montevideo	Montevideo	Rep.
Venezuela	352,143	4,299,638	12.2	Caracas	Caracas	Rep.
Yugoslavia	98,426	14,500,000	147.3	Belgrade	Belgrade	Rep.

1. Abbreviations: C. M.—Constitutional Monarchy; Com.—Commission; C. S.—Corporate State; Dom.—Dominion; Mil.—Military; P. G.—Provisional Government; Rep.—Republic; S. R.—Socialist Republic.
2. Republic—Subject to Allied Control Commission.
3. Actual seat of government; Sucre is the statutory capital.
4. Includes British, French, Soviet and United States occupation zones.
5. Includes Northern Ireland.
6. Since Sept. 1945 northern sector has been under Soviet Union and southern sector under U. S. Military Government.
7. Actual seat of government; Amsterdam is statutory capital.
8. Including Chaco.
9. Boundaries drafted at Yalta and Potsdam (1945).
10. Estimated area and population for 16 republics (1946).

SOUTH AMERICA

The southern continent of the western hemisphere, situated, for the most part, south of the equator. It lies east of a line drawn directly south from Florida and extends east to a point about 1000 miles west of Africa's most western meridian. South America is joined to North America by a narrow isthmus, called Central America. The continent extends north and south a distance of about 4550 miles and has a maximum width of approximately 3200 miles. The area is slightly less than that of North America, being commonly estimated at 7,500,000 square miles.

Contour. In outline, the continent has a general resemblance to a triangle. It is widest in the north and tapers in the south to a point several hundred miles farther south than any other large body of habitable land in the world. The coast line is simple, having no major indentations, such as Hudson bay in North America. There are, however, many small inlets, especially on the southwest coast of Chile, two large estuaries, that of the Amazon river and of the Plata river, and a number of bays and gulfs, of which the principal ones are: the Gulf of Guayaquil, Golfo Corcovado, and Golfo de Penas on the west; Bayia Grande, Gulf of Saint George, Golfo de San Matias, and Bahia Blanca, on the southeast; and on the north the Gulf of Paria and the Gulf of Maracaibo, the latter being connected with the inland sea, Lake Maracaibo.

Surface and Drainage. Along the western side of the continent extends a continuous mountain system, known as the Cordillera of the Andes. This system differs from the Rocky Mountain system of North America in being higher and in containing a large number of volcanoes. Numerous short rivers flow down the narrow west incline of the Andes into the Pacific Ocean. On the east, the mountains slope rapidly down to three great plains drained by three of the greatest rivers of the world. The most northerly plain is the basin of the Orinoco river, a level, grass-covered stretch called the llanos. Separated from it by the plateau of Guiana are the silvas, the vast forested plain of the Amazon valley. The llanos and the silvas drain to the east. The third great plain drains to the south. It is the basin of the Plata-Parana, consisting of undulating tracts, called pampas, adapted to pasturage.

The pampas are separated from the Amazon valley by a low plateau, which, extending westward, branches into a subdued mountain range skirting the Atlantic coast northeast almost to the Amazon and southwest to the mouth of the Plata. This range is cut in the north by a valley through which flows the Francisco river. South of the Plata-Parana river several streams drain into the Atlantic from the eastern slope of the Andes mountains. The largest of these are the Colorado river, the Rio Negro, and the Chubut river.

Islands. A number of islands are reckoned with the continent. In the southwest, numerous small islands are formed by the partially submerged Andes range. The group of islands at the extreme south is called the Archipelago of Tierra del Fuego and is separated from the continent by Magellan strait. Cape Horn is the most southerly of these islands and forms the most southerly point of the continent. The Galapagos islands lie about 600 miles off the Ecuador coast. The island of Trinidad is close to the delta of the Orinoco river. The Falkland islands are situated about 350 miles east of the continent at its southern extremity.

Climate. The greater part of South America lies within the tropics. Over this region the moist trade winds blow westward from the Atlantic, providing the country with a copious rainfall as far west as the Andes range. Impinging on the mountains, the winds rise and become cooled, thereby losing their moisture, which is precipitated as rain. They descend as hot, dry winds on the Pacific Coast region, in which, consequently, desert conditions prevail. The Atacama desert in northern Chile is said to be the driest area in the world. Farther south, moist winds blow from the Pacific, giving the western slope of the Andes mountains a heavy rainfall and rendering the pampas to the east a semidesert country.

South America does not experience such extremes of temperature as does North America, except on the mountains. The temperature in the moist Amazon valley is consistently high, varying little from about 80° F. The southwestern coast similarly has a fairly constant temperature, but the dry region of the western coast and that of the pampas show greater variation. The mean winter temperature in parts of the south falls to 35° F. The hottest mean midsummer temperature is 85° F. and is found in northern Argentina. The higher mountain peaks, however, are snow-capped even under an equatorial sun.

Flora. The hot, moist region at the extreme north of the continent has a characteristic tropical vegetation. Palms, bamboos, and tree ferns are predominant, giving place to conifers on the mountains and to tall grass in the Orinoco River basin. The silvas of the Amazon valley form the largest heavily forested area in the world. The pampas are luxuriantly grassed in their northern portions, but in the south the aridity occasions a stunted vegetable growth. The potato is indigenous to the continent, which is also the world's chief source of coffee. Rubber and quinine come from the tropical forests, and the Temperate Zone region is one of the world's principal wheat growing and stock raising areas.

Fauna. The animal life of South America includes a number of characteristic species. Among them are alpacas, vicuñas, llamas, condors, tapirs, and a number of toothless quadrupeds—sloths, anteaters, armadillos, and bloodsucking bats. Llamas are used as beasts of burden in the mountains, and alpacas provide a superior quality of wool. Birds of brilliant plumage abound in the tropical regions; many monkeys and reptiles and innumerable species of insects and of fish are found, especially in the Amazon basin. The electric eel and the caribe, a savage fish, are among the more noteworthy.

Minerals. The mineral resources of the continent, although great, have been very imperfectly developed, largely on account of difficulties of transportation and of climate. The Cordillera of the Andes contains the bulk of such minerals, although many are found in the Brazilian plateau. Silver and gold were produced extensively before Europeans came to South America. Brazil was long the chief source of diamonds, and Chile exports nitrates to all parts of the world. South America is also the chief source of monazite and of vanadium. Immense quantities of oil come from Venezuela, copper from Chile, and tin from Bolivia. Aluminum ore comes from the Guianas, and platinum and emeralds from Colombia.

Inhabitants. The population of South America is estimated at 95 million. The largest city is Buenos Aires, with a population of 3,000,371. The majority of the continent's inhabitants are mestizos, a mixture of white races with native Indians. Possibly one-fifth are pure Indians. Those of unmixed European origin are comparatively few, although they predominate in Argentina and comprise almost the whole of the population in Uruguay. Pure Indians predominate in Paraguay and Bolivia. Negroes and mulattoes are numerous in Brazil.

Most of the inhabitants speak Spanish, being descended from Spaniards, except in Brazil, where the European strain in the population is Portuguese and the Portuguese language is spoken. The Catholic religion prevails throughout the continent.

The upper classes in all the countries are well educated, having a culture akin to that of Spain and France. The level of education for the whole population, however, is considerably lower than that of North America.

The Andes Mountains. The system of mountains running north and south on South America's western border. This system, wide and high in the northern and central part, where it divides into three chains, becomes narrower toward the south and gradually sinks to the level of the sea at the continent's southern extremity. The highest peak is Aconcagua, in west central Argentina, which reaches a height of 22,834 feet. Mount Huascaran has an elevation of 22,051 feet. Several of the world's gigantic volcanoes belong to the Andes mountains, such as Chimborazo, Cotopaxi, Antisana, and Misti. Glaciers are found on the tall peaks, even those within the equatorial regions.

The continent's largest lake and one of the highest in the world, Lake Titicaca, lies among the Andes mountains at a level of about 12,500 feet above the sea. The lake, which has no outlet, has an area of 3200 square miles and a maximum depth of about 900 feet. Near its shores, there are many ruins of temples and other relics of a former civilization.

The Amazon River. The largest and one of the longest rivers of the world, draining a tropical basin in South America eastward from the Andes mountains and emptying into the Atlantic Ocean through an estuary which expands to a width of 150 miles. The river has several tributaries which are themselves among the major rivers of the world. The Rio Negro is the largest affluent on the north; on the south the chief tributaries are the Purus, the Tapajoz, the Xingu, the Araguaya, and the Madeira, the last of which has an affluent explored by Theodore Roosevelt and named, after him, the Roosevelt river.

The Amazon river is navigable for ocean steamers over a distance of 2300 miles, and 486 miles farther for smaller vessels. The river system affords navigable waterways of 27,000 miles.

Rising tides produce large tidal waves, or bores, which rush up the river with a loud roar and often endanger shipping. The effect of the river's current can be detected 200 miles out at sea. In the flood season the river rises 30 to 40 feet in some parts, inundating the banks for several months of the year.

Plata-Parana. The second largest river system of South America, consisting of the Parana river and the Uruguay river, which unite their streams in the Rio de la Plata, "Silver river," an estuary conducting the water of the system to the Atlantic Ocean, about 20° of latitude north of Cape Horn. The basin has a southern drainage, sloping from the Brazil plateau in the north. The estuary is 135 miles wide at its outlet. The Plata-Parana stream measures altogether about 2500 mtles, of which about 1200 miles are navigable. The chief tributary is the Paraguay river, which flows into the Parana.

Orinoco River. One of the three large rivers of South America, draining a tropical territory in the northern part of the continent. The river rises in the Parima mountains between Venezuela and Brazil. After traversing immense flat, treeless plains in a course running first west, then north, and finally east, the river winds through a dense tropical forest area and empties into the Atlantic Ocean through several mouths forming a delta south of the island of Trinidad. About 150 miles from its source the river discharges part of its water into the Rio Negro, an affluent of the Amazon river. The Orinoco river is navigable to a cataract 870 miles from its mouth. Its tributaries are very numerous, the chief navigable ones being the Guaviare, the Meta, and the Apure. The system has 4300 miles of navigable streams. See *Venezuela*.

POLITICAL DIVISIONS

The mainland of South America contains ten independent countries and three colonies. The independent countries are Argentina, Bolivia, Brazil, Chile, Colombia, Ecuador, Paraguay, Peru, Uruguay, and Venezuela. Each is a Federal republic. The country with the largest area is Brazil and the smallest is Uruguay. The colonies are called British Guiana, Surinam, and French Guiana. Among the islands, Trinidad and the Falkland islands are British dependencies. The Galapagos islands belong to Ecuador.

Argentina. The most highly developed country of South America and second largest in area, occupying the greater part of the southern portion of the continent. The country has an Atlantic seaboard of 1565 miles and a western land boundary of about 3000 miles, following the continental watershed formed by the Andes. Argentina measures about 2285 miles from north to south and has a maximum width of 930 miles, with an area of 1,079,965 square miles.

The country is drained in the north by the Plata-Parana river. In the south the surface slopes from the ridge of the Andes toward the Atlantic Ocean. The climate varies from the tropical warmth in the low plains of the north, where 120° F. has been recorded, to the more moderate conditions existing in the south, where 3° F. is the lowest temperature officially noted. The rainfall decreases from the eastern coast to the base of the Andes mountains.

The flora of Argentina shows variations following the differences in climate. In the partly unexplored tropical forests of the north, algaroba trees are especially numerous, and many medicinal shrubs and other plants abound, including the *yerba maté*, or Paraguay tea plant. The mountains are wooded, those around the Strait of Magellan and Tierra del Fuego being covered with immense forests of beech. The most valuable product of the forest is quebracho extract, a dye. The pampas are treeless but are covered with grass. Such tropical and subtropical fruits as oranges, lemons, grapes, and peaches are grown. The animals characteristic of Argentina include the viscacha and the hare of Patagonia.

The chief industries of Argentina are grazing and agriculture, for which the extensive pampas are admirably suited. Wheat and corn are the most valuable crops. Grain and meat form more than 75 per cent of the exports. Argentina is the world's largest exporter of beef, corn, and flaxseed. Lumbering and mining are carried on to some extent. Oil fields yielded 8,900,000 barrels of petroleum in 1930. There are more than 25,400 miles of railway, a greater mileage than that of any other South American country.

Argentina is divided into 14 provinces, 10 territories, and 1 federal district. The capital and largest city is Buenos Aires, which is also the largest city in South America. The country has received a great many European immigrants in recent decades, principally from Italy, Spain, and Germany. The Indian strain in the population is comparatively slight. The population, according to the 1947 census, was 16,107,870.

Bolivia. An inland country in the west central part of South America. The southwestern border follows the ridge of the western range of the Andean Cordillera, which in this section spreads out into the Bolivian plateau and occupies nearly half the surface of Bolivia. The average elevation of the plateau is 12,000 feet, but it contains some of the highest peaks of the continent, such as Illimani, Sorata, Cerro de Potosi, and Licancaur. In this plateau lies the lofty Lake Titicaca, with which is connected Lake Aullagas. East of the plateau, the surface slopes down in vast undulating plains toward the Amazon River valley in the north and, in the south, toward the llanos of the Parana River basin. The area of the country is estimated at 416,040 square miles.

Photos for 1, 4, and 6 from Brown Bros.; for 2 from Keystone View Co.; for 5 copyright by Underwood & Underwood; for 3, 7, 8 and 9 from Publishers' Photo Service.

SOUTH AMERICA

1 View in Rio de Janeiro. 2 Montevideo, Uruguay. 3 Art Museum, Buenos Aires. 4 Chamber of Deputies, Santiago, Chile. 5 The Christ of the Andes, Chile-Argentina. 6 Peace Monument, Rio de Janeiro. 7 Centenary Monument, Buenos Aires. 8 Straw Boats, Lake Titicaca, Bolivia. 9 Ancient Incan Fortress, Peru.

Photos for Nos. 1 and 5 from Brown Bros.; for Nos. 2, 3 and 4 from Keystone View Co.; for No. 7 from Publishers' Photo Service.

COFFEE INDUSTRY

1 Port of Santos, Brazil. 2 Coffee Plantation, Brazil. 3 Coffee Berries. 4 Gathering Coffee, Brazil. 5 Basins for Macerating Coffee Berries. 6 Drying Coffee; *copyright by Underwood & Underwood.* 7 Further Drying Coffee. 8 Heaps of Dried Coffee; *copyright by Keystone View Co.*

Bolivia is entirely in the Torrid Zone, but the climate of the upland is of an almost arctic severity. Parts of this plateau support grazing flocks of sheep, llamas, and alpacas, but it is for the most part arid and of value only for its minerals. The fertile eastern slope of the Cordillera, being warmer and well watered, produces wheat, corn, barley, peaches, grapes, and figs. The lowlands support a tropical vegetation. Coffee, cacao, rice, sugar cane, and medicinal plants are cultivated, and vast forests yield rosewood, mahogany, ebony, cedar, and rubber, the last being produced in quantities which entitle Bolivia to rank next to Brazil as a rubber exporting country.

Bolivia's principal industry is mining, and the principal mineral product is tin, in the export of which Bolivia ranks second among the countries of the world. Silver, gold, and copper are also mined in large quantities, and wolfram, vanadium, bismuth, lead, zinc, salt, and antimony are obtained in smaller amounts. Potosi, where the tin and silver mining interests center, is the highest city in the world, having an elevation of 14,350 feet. At such an altitude, operations can be carried on only by the natives. Its inhabitants numbered 40,000 in 1946.

Railroad transportation is limited by the natural obstacles in the way of construction. Some 1500 miles of track, however, are in operation. There is communication by airplane between the principal cities. Llamas are used for carrying light loads over mountainous districts.

The majority of the inhabitants live on the eastern slopes of the mountains. About one-half are pure Indians, and the white race forms about 12 per cent of an officially estimated (1947) 3,787,800. La Paz is the largest city and the seat of Congress, and Sucre is the statutory capital and seat of the supreme court. The country possesses many impressive remains of a vanished civilization. Bolivia was deprived of access to the sea by a disastrous war with Chile which ended in 1883.

Brazil. The largest country of South America, occupying the entire east central part of the continent and having a westward extension which reaches almost to the Andes mountains. The country's maximum extent north and south is 2660 miles and east and west it measures about 2700 miles, with a total area of 3,286,170 square miles, exceeding that of continental United States.

In the north the climate is moist and tropical in character, while toward the south it becomes more temperate and the rainfall is lighter. The northern region is drained by the Amazon river, south of which lies one of the world's largest unexplored forest areas. The eastern part of the country is a highland through which the river Francisco flows, and the southern district is drained by the Uruguay river and by the upper reaches of the Parana River system.

The mineral resources of Brazil are very great but are largely undeveloped. The production of gold and of diamonds was formerly of great importance. The Morro Velho gold mine, having a depth of 7000 feet, is one of the deepest mines in the world. The deposits of iron are very extensive. Brazil provides the greater part of the world's supply of monazite.

The tropical flora of Brazil includes trees producing an extraordinary variety of useful and of ornamental woods, 200 different kinds of timber having been shown at the national exhibition in Rio de Janeiro in 1922. These woods include mahogany, rosewood, brazilwood, and logwood. The rubber tree and the pine are among those of the greatest commercial value. The rank forests of the Amazon basin abound in brilliantly colored flowers and in countless monkeys, lizards, fish, gaudy butterflies, and other tropical animals. The portions of the country farther south are suitable for agriculture, and produce a large amount of coffee, sugar, cocoa, tobacco, and cotton. About three-fourths of the world's supply of coffee comes from Brazil. The country was formerly the world's chief source of rubber, and it still supplies a considerable amount to the world's trade. There are large areas of pasturage, on which immense numbers of live stock are raised.

Brazil exports mainly the products of the forest and farm, and imports manufactured goods. The textile industry, however, has received a considerable development in the country. There are also many mills for the manufacture of silk, woolen, and jute goods, and many tobacco factories and sugar refineries. About one-third of the foreign trade is with the United States. About 20,000 miles of railroad have been constructed.

The population of Brazil, according to the latest estimate is 45,300,000, making the country the most populous in the western hemisphere after the United States. Many Negroes and about 100,000 Indians live in the Amazon valley. In the south there are a number of settlements of Germans, of Spaniards, and of Italians. The majority of the inhabitants, however, are of Portuguese origin, and the language of the country is Portuguese.

Politically, the country consists of 20 loosely federated states, 1 federal district, and 1 territory. The most populous and most prosperous states are Bahia, Minas Geraes, and Sao Paulo, all bordering on the central part of the southeastern coast. These states produce the bulk of the minerals, coffee, sugar, cotton, and live stock. The most extensive state is Amazonas, occupying the upper Amazon valley. From it come most of the valuable woods. The capital and largest city of the country is Rio de Janeiro. The port Pernambuco, on the eastern coast, is nearer to Lisbon than to New York.

British Guiana. A British colony of continental South America, lying between Venezuela and Dutch Guiana near the center of the continent's northeastern coast line. Its area is 89,480 square miles. The interior is covered with dense forests as far as the highlands in the southwest. The rivers are not navigable, except for short distances, because of rapids and falls. In the Potaro river are the famous Kaieteur falls, having a drop of about 800 feet. The coast district, about 40 miles wide, is low, and part of it is protected by dikes. It is very fertile and produces large crops of sugar cane, rice, and coconuts. Gold and diamonds are mined in the highlands. Bauxite, the ore of aluminum, is exported.

The climate, being hot and moist, is unhealthful for Europeans, who compose about 4000 of the colony's total population of 375,819. About 130,000 are East Indians, who were brought in to work on the plantations. The capital is Georgetown. England's sovereignty over the colony was disputed by the Dutch and the French until 1815, when the territory finally passed into her possession The Venezuelan boundary was fixed after a dispute arbitrated in 1899 by jurists of Great Britain and of the United States.

Chile (*chē'lā*). A country of South America, lying on the western coast and extending, with an average width of about 87 miles, from the southern extremity of the continent northward about 2700 miles to Peru. The area is estimated at 286.322 square miles. The eastern boundary follows in general the ridge of the Andes mountains.

A high plateau rises abruptly from the sea along the greater part of the coast, leaving a lofty plain between the sea and the foot of the Andes. There is a gentle slope from the north to the south. The rivers are short and drain into the Pacific Ocean. A number of natural harbors are found among the fiordlike indentations and the numerous islands of the southern coast. The country is subject to severe earthquakes followed usually by destructive tidal waves. One of the most disastrous occurred in 1922. In 1751, the former city of Concepcion was sunk in the Pacific Ocean.

The climate of Chile is hot and extremely arid in the north, where a whole year often passes without rain. The central region, having a more moderate temperature and a greater precipitation, supports a flourishing agricultural industry and contains most of the population. In the south the increased rainfall permits the growth of forests of beech, cypress, and oak, the last of which has been introduced from abroad. In the extreme south the growth of the trees is stunted by the prevailing low temperatures.

The northern third of Chile is the world's chief source of natural nitrate of soda, which is used as a mineral fertilizer and in the production of explosives and of most of the world's supply of iodine. Chile is also one of the leading producers of copper. Other minerals mined in important quantities include iron ore, gold, silver, sulphur, borate, and salt. A large portion of the government's revenue is derived from the export of nitrate.

Agriculture provides employment for about half the population. The principal crops are grapes and wheat. Stock raising also is important. Most of the textiles and other manufactured goods consumed are imported. The United States and Great Britain receive most of the foreign trade.

Chile has a longitudinal railway system more than 2000 miles in length. The Trans-Andean railroad connects Valparaiso, on Chile's Pacific coast, with the Atlantic seaboard at Buenos Aires. Parts of it climb grades of a steepness nowhere else attempted by railroad engineers. The total length of railways is nearly 6000 miles. Air transportation is well developed.

The population of Chile in 1947 was 5,511,424, of whom about one-fourth were of Spanish descent. The influence of the Church is greater than in most other countries of the continent. Chile has a powerful fleet and is politically one of the three strongest countries of South America. The capital and largest city is Santiago. Valparaiso is the chief port.

Colombia. A country of South America, occupying the extreme northwestern part of the continent. Colombia borders on the Pacific Ocean for a distance of about 500 miles and on the Caribbean Sea for 700 miles. Its area is 439,828 square miles.

The country is traversed from northeast to southwest by the Cordillera of the Andes, which here consists of a western, a central, and an eastern range separated by fertile plateaus. The eastern slope of the Cordillera drains in the north into the basin of the Orinoco river and, farther south, into the basin of the Amazon river. The central plateaus drain northward by the Magdalena River system into the Caribbean Sea. The western slope of the Cordillera has a number of short rivers emptying into the Pacific Ocean. The Magdalena river is navigable for steamers to La Dorada, a point about 560 miles above its mouth.

The climate of Colombia varies from the intense tropical heat of the coast regions, the valleys, and the llanos, to the temperate conditions of the plateaus and the mountains. There are two wet seasons and two dry seasons over most of the country. The llanos, however, have two seasons only. The rainfall there is deficient and does not permit the growth of trees. The west coast, however, has a large rainfall. The mountain sides are covered with forests of a tropical character, containing, among many other varieties of plants, the wax palm, the rubber tree, and several species of cinchonas.

The mineral wealth of Colombia is great. Gold, platinum, copper, petroleum, and emeralds are exported, the last being produced in Colombia in greater quantities than in the rest of the world. The salt mines are a government monopoly and provide a considerable part of the national revenue.

The chief industries are agriculture and stock raising. Temperate zone cereals are grown on the plateaus, and coffee, sugar, bananas, and cocoa are produced in the valleys and the lower regions. Colombia provides most of the world's supply of mild coffee. Panama hats are produced extensively, although the industry is not centralized in factories. In addition to coffee, the chief exports are petroleum, bananas, gold, and platinum. The bulk of the foreign trade is with the United States. The mountainous surface of the country and the prevalence of tropical forests make transportation difficult except on the rivers and by air. Overhead ropeways are also a feature of Colombia's transportation facilities.

Colombia is divided into 14 departments, 3 intendancies, and 6 commissaries. The capital and largest city is Bogota. The population of the country in 1947 was 10,701,816.

Ecuador. A country in the northwest portion of South America, bordering on the Pacific Ocean and stretching south from Colombia to Peru. Its area is estimated at 104,000 square miles. Ecuador's coast line is broken by the Gulf of Guayaquil, the only large inlet on the south side of the continent.

The country is traversed from north to south by two ranges of the Andean Cordillera. Between the ranges lies a plateau, which has an average elevation of 9000 feet but in the south falls to a level of about 2000 feet. This plateau contains most of the cultivated land and has a delightful climate. The mountain ranges have many peaks of exceptional height, including Cotopaxi, the world's loftiest active volcano.

The coastal strip in Ecuador is not an arid waste, as in Peru and northern Chile, but is a stretch of tropical jungle with an excessive rainfall. Dense forests are found on the mountain slopes both on the west and on the east of the Cordillera. The east slope gives rise to several navigable rivers of the Amazon basin. One of the largest is the Napo, down which the explorer Orellana sailed in 1541 to the mouth of the Amazon river.

The immense virgin forests of Ecuador yield rubber, ivory nuts, dyewoods, cinchona bark, and many valuable kinds of cabinet wood. The distinctive products of the country, however, are cocoa and toquilla. The latter is the fabric from which Panama hats are made. It is shipped extensively to Colombia where the actual weaving is an important industry. Other products of the tropical agriculture pursued on the coastal strip are coffee, tobacco, and sugar. In the plateau, hay, cereal crops, and fruits and vegetables of a temperate zone character are cultivated, and cattle are raised in large numbers. Alligator skins are exported. Gold and petroleum are produced and silver, copper, iron, lead, coal, and sulphur are found. The production of salt is a government monopoly.

The population was estimated at 3,200,000, the great majority of whom are of Indian origin. The country is in a backward state of development, having few good roads and little more than 600 miles of railroad. The coinage of the country is minted in England and the United States. The country owns the Galapagos, or "turtle", islands, lying 750 miles to the west. The capital of Ecuador is Quito and the principal seaport and largest city is Guayaquil. The name of the country is the Spanish word for equator.

French Guiana and **Inini.** Prior to 1931, French Guiana comprised an area of about 34,740 square miles in northeastern South America bounded by the Atlantic Ocean, Brazil, and Dutch Guiana. In 1931, the name French Guiana was restricted to the coastal strip 25 miles deep, along with Devil's and other islands, used largely as a penal settlement. The hinterland, comprising about 30,000 square miles, was erected into a separate territory, known as Inini. This territory is rich in valuable hardwoods and has also considerable mineral wealth, including gold, silver, iron, and phosphates. The population of French Guiana in 1936 was 30,906, excluding penal and floating population. Most of the people live in the coastal strip, on which cacao, sugar, and spices are raised. The capital and chief port is Cayenne.

Paraguay. An inland country of central South America, bounded by Brazil, Argentina, and Bolivia.

Paraguay is a low-lying country situated between the Parana river and the Paraguay river, with the exception of a district to the northwest, the Gran Chaco. By arbitration with Bolivia in 1930, Paraguay received 91,800 square miles of the Gran Chaco, making her total area about 149,807 square miles.

Apart from the disputed territory, which is subject to alternate floods and droughts, the climate is delightful for the greater part of the year. During the three hottest months, however, the temperature not infrequently rises above 100° F. The rainfall is moderate, but sufficient to foster the growth of dense forests, and rich groves of tropical fruit, particularly oranges, bananas, and lemons. Fine cabinet timbers, dyewoods, drugs, gums, and oils are obtainable from the forests on the hills and in the valleys of the northeast part of the country. Occasional stretches of savannas afford rich pasturage, and flat marshes in the south are adapted to rice culture.

The chief cultivated plants are orange and other tropical fruit trees, corn, sugar cane, rice, tobacco, and cotton. Agricultural methods, however, are still primitive. *Yerba maté*, or Paraguay tea, found wild in great abundance and also cultivated to some extent, is exported to other parts of the continent. Stock raising is the second industry of the country. Iron, copper, manganese, and marble are to be found in the northeast of the country, but they are not mined extensively.

The transportation facilities of Paraguay are deficient. The roads are for the most part mere bullock tracks and the railroad mileage is small. The country has access to the sea only by river navigation through Argentina and by a railroad service to Buenos Aires. The chief exports are Paraquay tea, oranges, tobacco, beef, hides, quebracho logs and extract, and petit grain oil.

The population of Paraguay in 1944 was estimated at 1,108,040, a very small proportion of whom are white, these being mainly Italian and German immigrants. The settlements are largely confined to the vicinity of the Paraguay river. About one-seventh of the inhabitants are pure Indians, not yet civilized, and the native Guarani language is more widely used than Spanish. The percentage of illiteracy is high. The capital, chief port, and largest city is Asuncion.

Peru. A country of west central South America, bordering on the Pacific Ocean and stretching northward from Chile to Ecuador. Its area is 482,258 square miles.

Peru is traversed from north to south by the Cordillera of the Andes, which, under the name of the Sierra or uplands, constitutes one of the three physiographical divisions of the country. The uplands consist of three ranges, ill defined in parts, and of the intervening plateaus. There are several large volcanoes in this region and violent earthquakes are not uncommon. The rainfall is unevenly distributed.

Between the foothills of the Andes and the Pacific Ocean is a dry coastal strip averaging about 30 miles in width. This strip is cut by several rivers, which foster vegetation along their banks and afford means of irrigation. The civilization of the country centers about these rivers. Sloping eastward from the uplands is the Montana, a forest area with a heavy rainfall, in which the Amazon River system takes its rise.

Peru lies wholly within the Torrid Zone. The climate is not oppressively hot, however, except in the eastern valleys and lowlands. The greater part of the Sierra enjoys an equable temperature, and the heat of the coastal strip is moderated by the antarctic currents. Dense fogs frequently hang over the coast.

The eastern part of the Montana, being hot and well watered, supports a tropical vegetation. The cinchona tree is native to Peru and rubber trees grow in abundance but are comparatively inaccessible. Peru is the chief source of the coca shrub, from which cocaine is obtained.

The watered sections of the Sierra and of the coastal area produce sugar and cotton, the two principal exports of the country. Other agricultural products include coffee, grapes, palms, cocoa, corn, and wheat. A large number of sheep are raised in the Sierra, and wool, taken in part from sheep but to a great extent from llamas and alpacas, is exported in large quantities. The llama is the principal beast of burden. Mules are used extensively for traveling, the railway mileage being small on account of the mountainous character of the country. The various lines embrace about 2800 miles of track.

Mining ranks second to agriculture among the industries. The chief minerals are petroleum, copper, and silver, but over four-fifths of the world's supply of vanadium comes from Peru. The chief manufactures are sugar and cocaine, other necessary industrial products, such as textiles and lumber, being imported. Wheat and coal are also brought into the country. Most of the foreign trade is with the United States, Great Britain, and Chile.

Peru is the seat of the vanished civilization of the Incas, by whom Cuzco is said to have been founded in the 10th century. The population, according to the latest estimate, was 7,271,654, about 53 per cent being white and mestizos, and 46 per cent Indian.

The capital and largest city is Lima. The chief port is Callao on the Pacific Ocean. The steamship service between Peruvian and Bolivian ports on Lake Titicaca is unique in operating at an altitude unequalled on any other navigable body of water. Iquitos, on the upper reaches of the Amazon river, has steamer connections with the Atlantic Ocean, 2500 miles distant.

Surinam. A colony in continental South America belonging to the Netherlands, situated at the center of the continent's northeast coast between British Guiana and French Guiana. Its area is 54,291 square miles.

The cultivated area is confined to a coastal strip about 20 miles in width, the interior region being covered with a dense tropical forest as far as the highlands of the southeast. The chief agricultural products are bananas, sugar, cacao, coffee, and rice. Gold is exported also, much of it obtained from alluvium.

The estimated population in 1946 was 203,580, and consists largely of Negroes and people of East Indian origin, who were brought in to work on the plantations. The capital is Paramaribo. The name Surinam is a corruption of Surreyham, which was the original designation given in honor of the Earl of Surrey.

Uruguay. A country of South America, situated south of Brazil between the Atlantic Ocean and the Uruguay river. The southern coast line is on the Rio de la Plata. Having an area of 72,153 square miles, Uruguay is the smallest of the South American countries.

The surface is rolling and has several chains of hills reaching a maximum elevation of 2000 feet. The climate is equable in the south, but in the north it becomes continental, admitting of greater heat in the summer and of occasional frosts in the winter. The northern hills and valleys are covered with a subtropical forest, while the south and east form extensive fertile plains suited for agriculture and for stock raising. Deer, otters, wild hogs, and wildcats are indigenous. Rheas, or American ostriches, are found; and fur seals, protected by the government, inhabit Lobas island and Castillos island near the coast. There are also storks, swans, cranes, and wild turkeys.

Stock raising is the principal industry of Uruguay, animal products forming nearly nine-tenths of the exports. Wheat, oats, flaxseed, and grapes are also grown and exported. Less than 10 per cent of the country's area, however, is devoted to agriculture, in spite of the fact that the government encourages the industry by supporting agricultural schools. Hailstorms, destructive hurricanes, and occasional droughts occur as factors unfavorable to the raising of crops.

Gold mines are worked, and there are deposits of copper, iron, manganese, and lignite. Manufactures are very slightly developed, the population relying on importation for such industrial products as textiles and hardware. The United States and Great Britain have the largest share of the foreign trade. Transportation in Uruguay is facilitated by several hundred miles of navigable river streams and by more than 1700 miles of railway.

The population of Uruguay, according to the latest official estimate, was 2,235,000, of whom about nine-tenths are of European descent, mainly Spaniards and Italians. The earliest settlements were made by Spaniards in 1624 on the Rio Negro, a tributary of the Uruguay river. The capital, foreign port, and largest city is Montevideo.

Venezuela. The most northern country of South America, having a northern coast line of about 1700 miles on the Caribbean Sea and a land boundary separating the country from British Guiana, Brazil, and Colombia. Its area, including that of a large number of islands off the north coast, is 352,143 square miles.

Apart from the small basin of Lake Maracaibo in the northwest, Venezuela is drained by the Orinoco River system. This system flows eastward from the Andes mountains between the Guiana highlands to the south and a northeastern extension of the Andes mountains on the north, and enters the sea through a large estuary overgrown with a mangrove swamp. The upper portion of the river system traverses the llanos. The affluents of the Orinoco are numerous and, with the main stream, provide the country with about 4000 miles of navigable waterways.

The climate in the lower levels of Venezuela is tropical but becomes temperate in the highlands and frigid on the higher mountain peaks. The rainfall is copious in the east and in the northwestern parts near the mountains. On the llanos the comparative dryness during one season of the year prevents the growth of trees.

The flora of the eastern lowlands and of the better watered territory in the northwest consists of tropical forests similar to those of the Amazon valley. The forests include many plants from which are available such products as rubber, vanilla, brazil nuts, dyewoods, and drugs. Grasses form the characteristic vegetation of the llanos. The fauna of Venezuela is tropical and rich, and includes such species as the howling monkey, the spectacled bear, the vampire bat, the flamingo and other brilliantly colored but usually songless birds, the anaconda and other snakes, a frog with a voice resembling a human shout, the electric eel, and the caribe.

Venezuela is rich in minerals. It ranks among the world's largest producers of petroleum. Other minerals produced in quantity are confined to gold, salt, and asphalt, the last being found in lakes containing extensive remains of prehistoric animals. Pearl fishing is an industry on a number of islands off the north coast.

In the northern and western parts of Venezuela, where most of the population is concentrated, agriculture is carried on, the chief products being coffee, sugar, and cocoa. Grazing is the chief industry on the llanos. There are few manufactures. Most of the foreign trade is with the United States.

The name Venezuela is Italian, meaning Little Venice. It was given by early Italian explorers who found, on Lake Maracaibo, an Indian tribe inhabiting huts which were supported by piles driven into the bed of the lake. Reminded of Venice, they gave the region the name which is now applied to the country.

Venezuela is divided into 20 states, 2 territories, and a federal district. The capital and largest city is Caracas. The latest population figure is placed at 4,299,638, including 103,492 Indians. Pure whites number about 10 per cent of the total.

CHIEF CITIES AND OTHER PLACES OF INTEREST IN SOUTH AMERICA

The preceding articles on South America deal with the larger features of the continent. Other points of interest, including the principal cities, the national capitals, the trade centers, certain islands, and regions of especial note are covered in the section that follows.

Asuncion (*ä-so͞on'syōn'*). The capital and metropolis of Paraguay, situated on the east bank of the Paraguay river in the west central part of the country. The city is the port and trading center of Paraguay, and is connected by railroad with Buenos Aires. It has foundries, shipyards, and distilleries. The exports include Paraguay tea and lace, the latter a beautiful product of the industry of civilized Indian women. Population, 1945 est., 172,400.

Bahia (*bä-ē'ä*). A city of east central Brazil, picturesquely situated on a high peninsula which partly encloses an excellent natural harbor. Bahia, also called Sao Salvador, is a notable port, shipping coffee, sugar, rubber, cotton, and other products raised in the state. The manufactures are varied, the principal one being cotton cloth. Bahia was formerly the center of the world's largest diamond trade.

The lower part of the city, devoted to commerce, has narrow streets. The upper, or residential, part is accessible by elevators and is attractively built. The churches are very numerous. The cathedral of the archbishop of Brazil is situated in Bahia and is one of the finest basilicas in Brazil. The city is equipped with the principal modern improvements. It has a university, a medical college, and a museum. The culture of seedless oranges was introduced into the United States from Bahia.

The site of Bahia is said to have been visited in 1503 by Amerigo Vespucci. Founded in 1510 by Correa, a Portuguese navigator, the city was the capital of Brazil until 1763. Population, 1936 est., 363,726.

Barranquilla (*bär'rän-kēl'yä*). The chief port of Colombia, situated on the Magdalena river about 7½ miles from its mouth. The mouth of the river is not navigable. Traffic borne down the river to Barranquilla for export, therefore, is sent by rail to Puerto Colombia, a seaport on the Caribbean Sea. Population, 1947 est., 224,430.

Belem. A seaport of northeastern Brazil, situated on the Rio Para about 85 miles from the Atlantic Ocean. On the land side, it is flanked by dense forests. Belem is the headquarters for the navigation on the Amazon. Exports include cocoa, rice, cotton, rubber, and various forest products of the Amazon valley. Population, 1940 census, 166,662.

Bogota (*bō'gō-tä'*). The capital and largest city of Colombia, situated near the geographical center of the country on a fertile table-land at an elevation of about 8700 feet above the sea. There are many mountains in the vicinity and the mining interests of the city are considerable, the government's salt mines being a short distance north of the city. Coal, iron, and manganese mines lie to the north and east.

The more important edifices of Bogota include the government buildings and the cathedral, the latter being a structure in the Corinthian style of architecture. The city is the seat of the national university, of three endowed colleges, and of a museum containing many relics of the civilization of the Incas. The streets are narrow but well paved. Population, 1947, 482,480.

Buenos Aires (*bwā'nōs ī'rās; bō'nŭs ā'rĭz*). The capital of Argentina and the largest city in South America, situated on the south shore of the estuary of the Rio de la Plata about 170 miles from the Atlantic Ocean.

Buenos Aires handles the bulk of Argentina's foreign commerce and is one of the largest ports of the world, the harbor having been improved at a cost of about 50 million dollars. Near the wharves is the central fruit market, one of the largest warehouses in the world. The manufacturing industries produce mainly for home consumption. The city contains the residences of a large number of the country's wealthy owners of farming and grazing land.

The oldest part of Buenos Aires has narrow streets. The city is divided from east to west by the magnificent Avenida de Mayo, which is 100 feet wide and connects two beautiful squares. At the eastern end lies the Plaza de Mayo, having an area of more than four acres and fronted by several imposing buildings, including the executive palace and the cathedral. At the western end, the view terminates in the House of Congress, erected at a cost of $6,000,000. The office of the newspaper *La Prensa* is one of the most handsome buildings of the city.

Buenos Aires has a system of more than 100 parks, which cover a total area of over 3000 acres. Numerous monuments have been erected in the city, including a statue of George Washington set up in Palmero park by American residents of the city. The chief educational institution is the University of Buenos Aires.

Buenos Aires was founded by Pedro de Mendoza in 1535. It was destroyed by the Indians and was re-established in 1580 by Juan de Garay, the governor of Paraguay. The city has grown very rapidly in the past half century. Population, 1947, 3,000,371.

Callao (*käl-yä'ō*). The principal seaport of Peru, situated on an island-sheltered bay near the center of the country's Pacific coast line. The city is connected by steam and electric railroads with Lima, distant seven miles inland. The chief exports are sugar, cotton, cocaine, minerals, and wool. In 1746 the former city of Callao was submerged with all its inhabitants, and on calm days the ruins are still distinguishable under the water. Population, about 77,000.

Cape Horn. The most southerly point of South America. The name is applied to a small, rocky island and to the most southerly point of the island, a headland having a height of 600 feet. The cape was discovered by the Dutch navigator, Schouten, who named it after Hoorn, his native town in the Netherlands.

Caracas (*kä-rä'käs*). The capital and largest city of Venezuela, occupying a mountainous site 7 miles from La Guaira, a port near the center of the country's northern coast. The city is an important exporting center for cocoa, coffee, tobacco, and other products of the country. Its principal square contains a large statue of Bolivar. The capitol building covers an area of two acres. The city has all modern improvements. An earthquake in 1812 killed more than 12,000 inhabitants. Population, 1941, 369,030.

Cayenne (*kā-ĕn'; kī-ĕn'*). A fortified seaport, the capital of the colony of French Guiana. The town is built on a low island between the Cayenne river and the Mahury river. The harbor is insecure and shallow. The streets are well paved and regularly laid out, but the climate is hot and unhealthful. Sugar, gold, hides, woods, spices, and cacao are the principal exports. Thirty miles northwest is the Isle du Diable, "Devil's island," where Captain Dreyfus was imprisoned from 1894 to 1899. Population, 1946, 11,704.

Christ of the Andes. A bronze statue of Christ, by Mateo Alonzo, on the border of Chile and Argentina erected to commemorate the peaceful settlement in 1902 of a boundary dispute between the two countries. The statue, more than twice life-size, stands on a pedestal roughhewn from the natural rock near the summit of Uspallata pass in the Andes at an altitude of 12,796 feet. It was cast from bronze obtained by melting cannon.

Cordoba (*kôr'dō-bä*). A commercial city of central Argentina, situated on the Rio Primero, about 400 miles northwest of Buenos Aires. Live stock, wool, and hides are shipped from this city. Cordoba has a cathedral, a massive Jesuit church, a national observatory, two national colleges, and a university, the last founded in 1613. The city dates back to the year 1573. It was formerly the head of the Jesuit missions in South America. Population, 1943, 287,598.

Easter Island. An island possession of Chile, lying about 2000 miles to the west in the Pacific Ocean. It contains a number of colossal stone images made, apparently, many centuries ago by the ancestors of its present inhabitants. Its area is 45 square miles; population, about 250.

Falkland Islands. A group of about 100 small islands, forming a British crown colony situated in the south Atlantic Ocean, about 300 miles east of the Strait of Magellan. Only two of the islands are inhabited—East Falkland, with an area of 2580 square miles, and West Falkland, having 2038 square miles of surface.

The surface of the larger islands is treeless. Sheep farming was formerly the chief industry, but in recent years whaling has become more important. The climate is equable but cool and damp. South Georgia, the South Orkneys, the South Shetlands, the Sandwich group, and Graham's Land, all lying some hundreds of miles to the southeast, are regarded as dependencies of the Falkland islands. In 1944 the estimated population of the islands was 2361. The capital is Stanley, East Falkland. During Word War I, a British fleet defeated a German fleet near these islands.

Galapagos (*gä-lä'pä-gōs*) **Islands.** A group of small volcanic islands, sometimes called the Colon archipelago, lying about 600 miles west of the coast of Ecuador. They have an estimated area of 2868 square miles and a population of about 1000. Politically, they are a dependency of Ecuador. The United States has a naval base there.

The name means turtle islands, and was given because of the prevalence of large turtles described in 1858 by Darwin as capable of carrying several men on their backs. The flora and fauna are distinctive, about one-half of the species of plants being found nowhere else.

Georgetown. The capital and seaport of British Guiana, situated near the center of the colony's coast line. The city lies at the mouth of the Demarara river, which can be entered, however, by boats of light draft only. The chief exports are sugar, rice, coconuts, bauxite, gold, and diamonds. The streets cross each other at right angles. Some are 100 feet wide and have, in the center, canals leading to the roadways. Most of the better residences are surrounded by private groves of palms and other forest trees. Population, 1946 est., 77,585.

Guayaquil (*gwī'ä-kēl'*). The largest city and chief port of Ecuador, situated on the Guayas river about 30 miles from its mouth in the Gulf of Guayaquil. The principal export is cocoa. The climate is hot and unhealthful. Manufactures, including lumber, machine shop products, and artificial ice, are mainly for local consumption. Population, 1944, 181,893.

Juan Fernandez Island. An island possession of Chile in the Pacific Ocean, lying 400 miles west of Valparaiso. Alexander Selkirk lived here in solitude for four years. This fact is said to have suggested to Defoe the theme of *Robinson Crusoe*.

La Paz (*lä päs'*). The largest city of Bolivia and the seat of Congress, situated in the west central part of the country about 40 miles southeast of Lake Titicaca. The city has an elevation of 12,470 feet and is flanked by ranges of the Andes mountains. It is connected with the sea by two railroads, terminating at ports in Chile. The inhabitants are mostly Indians, and a large proportion of the houses are built of clay. The streets are narrow and irregular. There are, however, two fine public promenades, a university, and a museum containing a valuable collection of Inca antiquities. Population estimated in 1946 at 302,000.

Lima (*lē'mä*). The capital of Peru. It is situated in the west central part of the country on the Rimac river seven miles from Callao, its port, with which it is connected by two railroads, one on each side of the river. Lima is the western terminus of a transcontinental railroad which, at one point, is 15,000 feet above the sea. Earthquakes have several times destroyed large parts of the city.

There are several beautiful squares and promenades lined with trees and flowering plants and ornamented with statues and fountains. The University of San Marcos, founded here in 1551, is the oldest university in the western hemisphere. Of the numerous churches, the largest and finest one is the cathedral. It contains the tomb of Pizarro, the founder of the city. The manufactures include textiles, leather, furniture, cement, chemicals, and rubber, aluminum, tobacco, and petroleum products.

During the war between Chile and Peru, the Chileans held Lima from 1881 to 1883 and in that time destroyed the national library and many monuments, statues, and other works of art. This city was the home of Saint Rose of Lima, the first native inhabitant of the Americas to be canonized. Population, census of 1940, 522,826.

Magallanes (*mä'gäl-yä'näs*). The most southerly city in the world, a port in southern Chile on the Strait of Magellan. Formerly known as Punta Arenas, it is a coaling station for steamers passing through the strait and has a trade in wool, skins, and beef. Population, about 4000.

Manaos (*mä-nä'ōs*). A city of Brazil on the Rio Negro, 12 miles above its junction with the Amazon and about 1000 miles from the Atlantic. Manaos is the trading metropolis of the upper Amazon valley, upon which it draws for such articles of export as rubber, brazil nuts, and dyewoods. The city is well built and has a good harbor, accessible to ocean steamers. Manaos became the capital of the state of Amazonas in 1852. Population estimated in 1936 at 89,346.

Montevideo (*mŏn'tē-vĭd'ē-ō*). The capital and chief city of Uruguay, situated on a chain of hills overlooking a harbor on the north side of the Rio de la Plata. The harbor has been improved so that it will accommodate all but the largest ocean steamers.

The principal streets are wide and straight, and the city bears, in general, a European appearance, having all the modern municipal improvements and many fine residences. The Cagancha plaza and the Solis theater are among its more notable features. An equable climate makes possible an extensive cultivation of roses.

The city is cosmopolitan and handles all the foreign trade of the country. The chief industries are those connected with stock raising—the drying and packing of meats, and creamery and tannery operations. Montevideo is the seat of a military college and of the University of Uruguay. The name is a corruption of *montem video*, "I see the mountain," said in allusion to the Cerro, a picturesque mountain on the opposite side of the city's harbor. Population, estimated in 1941, 770,000.

Paramaribo (*păr'ā-măr'ĭ-bō*). The capital of Dutch Guiana, situated at the head of navigation on the Surinam river 16 miles from its mouth in the Atlantic Ocean. The climate is very hot, the mean yearly temperature being over 80° F. The town has regularly laid out streets, shaded by tamarind and orange trees and bordered by well built houses. A commodious harbor lined with wharves enables the town to handle the colony's commerce, most of which is with the Netherlands, Great Britain, and the United States. The chief exports are rice, sugar, rum, coffee, bananas, and gold. Population, 1944, 60,723.

Patagonia. A name formerly applied to the portion of South America stretching from the Strait of Magellan about 1200 miles north to the latitude of the Rio Negro. It was claimed both by Argentina and by Chile, and was divided between them in 1881 by a line of demarcation following the ridge of the Andes mountains. From that time the name has been restricted to southern Argentina, the part of the disputed territory sloping in terraces eastward from the mountains to the Atlantic Ocean.

Port of Spain. The capital of Trinidad and Tobago, situated in the northwest extremity of Trinidad. It has a fine harbor, and a large part of the products of the Orinoco basin are shipped from the port. The streets are wide and there are a number of fine residences and public buildings; also a university and a botanical garden. Population in 1945 estimated at 107,499.

Punta Arenas (*pōōn'tä ä-rā'näs*). See *Magallanes.*

Quito (*kē'tō*). The capital of Ecuador, situated in a mountainous plateau somewhat north of the country's geographical center and about 114 miles from the Pacific Ocean. The city is less than ten miles south of the equator, but its climate is rendered equable by its elevation of 9000 feet. It is built at the foot of a volcano and is traversed by two deep ravines. The streets are steep.

Quito was very difficult of access until the completion in 1903 of a railroad connecting the city with tidewater near Guayaquil. There is a university, an astronomical observatory, and a botanical garden which has the distinction of being the highest in the world. Quito was the central town of an ancient Indian nation until it was taken by the Incas in 1470. It was captured from the Incas by the Spaniards in 1534. Population, 1947 census, 211,174.

Recife (*râ-sē'fĕ*) (**Pernambuco**). A commercial city and port of Brazil, situated on the Atlantic coast at the extreme eastern point of the continent. The harbor is protected from the sea by a long reef and by a breakwater constructed at a cost of about 28 million dollars. Its distance from Lisbon is less than that between New York and Lisbon. The chief exports are sugar and cotton. The imports are mainly foodstuffs, textiles, and iron products.

The city consists of three parts, one built on a peninsula, one on an island, and a third, a pleasant residential section on the continent. Recife is therefore often called the Venice of South America. The climate is tropical.

The city has many fine churches and a celebrated law school. In population and wealth it ranks third among the cities of Brazil. The name Recife means "reef." The first settlement on the site was made in 1535 by Pereira, a Portuguese adventurer. Population, 1940 census, 327,753.

Rio de Janeiro (*rē'ō dä zhä-nā'rō*). The capital and largest city of Brazil, situated on a natural harbor near the center of the country's southeastern coast. Spurs from near-by mountains penetrate into the heart of the city, which spreads into the valleys and up the hillsides. Sugar-loaf peak rises abruptly above the city.

The interests of Rio de Janeiro are chiefly commercial. The leading export is coffee and the principal imports include cereals, coal, textiles, and machinery. Manufactures are confined mainly to textiles and flour.

Many of the streets in the older section of Rio de Janeiro are too narrow for wheeled vehicles. The newer portions, however, have wide, well paved avenues adorned with tall palm trees. Avenida Beira-Mar, a beautiful 20-mile boulevard, skirts the edge of the harbor. On the Avenida Presidente Wilson stands a colossal bronze figure representing Amicitia, "friendship," which was presented by the government of the United States. At the base of the pedestal are four statues representing Washington, Lincoln, Bonifacio, and Branco. On Corcovado mountain, above the city, stands a statue of Christ, 130 feet in height.

There are several fine parks and squares. The Praça 15 de Novembro is surrounded by imposing buildings, among which are the Senate house and the city hall. In the neighborhood is the former Imperial palace, occupied from 1808 to 1821 by the court of Portugal and now used as a national museum. Other institutions of education and research include the national library, the botanical garden, the historical and geographic institute, the observatory, and the University of Rio de Janeiro. The city was founded by Portuguese colonists in 1567 and became the capital of Brazil in 1762. Population, 1940 census, 1,563,787.

Rosario (*rô-sä'rē-ō*). A commercial city of Argentina, situated on the left bank of the Parana river, about 230 miles above Buenos Aires. Rosario is the trade center for northern Argentina, being served by six railroads which connect at the city with ocean steamers. The chief exports are wheat and animal products, and the imports consist mainly of manufactured goods, mostly textiles. The city has modern improvements and attractive residential districts. Population in 1944 estimated at 522,403.

Santiago (*sän'tē-ä'gō*). The capital and largest city of Chile, situated near the center of the country about 50 miles from the Pacific coast. The city lies at the northern edge of a rich agricultural district for which it is a distributing point and market.

Santiago's location is highly picturesque by reason of the surrounding mountains. A rock within the city, over 200 feet in height, once used as a citadel and a refuge from attacking Indians, is now a park, irrigated and supporting a luxuriant growth of vegetation. The city is traversed by a wide, ornate boulevard, the Avenida de las Delicias, which has a width of more than 300 feet.

Among the city's more impressive buildings are the exposition palace, the hall of Congress, the municipal theater, the cathedral, and the university building. At the head of the institutions of education and research stand the University of Chile and the agricultural school farm, an institution which embraces a zoological garden, a museum of natural history, and various schools for teaching different branches of rural industry. The city was founded in 1541 by Pedro de Valdivia. Population, 1940, 639,546.

Santos (*sän'tōōsh*). A large seaport of Brazil, situated on Santos bay on the Atlantic coast about 200 miles southwest of Rio de Janeiro. Santos is the world's largest coffee shipping port, being the outlet for the coffee collected at Sao Paulo. Population, 1940, 158,774.

Sao Paulo (*soun pou'lōō*). The capital of the state of Sao Paulo, Brazil, situated in the southeastern part of the state 25 miles inland from Santos, its port on the Atlantic Ocean. The city is the headquarters of the country's vast coffee industry. The coffee is transported from the plantations by a network of railroads leading to Saõ Paulo, whence it is sent on by rail to Santos.

Among the more imposing buildings are the cathedral, the government building, and the Ypiranga palace, erected to commemorate Brazil's declaration of independence. The city has a modern appearance, having grown very rapidly in the decades following 1900, when numerous immigrants were attracted to it. Population, 1940 census, 1,269,319.

Sucre (*sōō'krā*). The statutory capital of Bolivia and the seat of the supreme court, picturesquely situated on a wide plateau about 150 miles south of the country's geographical center. The city is a trade center for a rich agricultural and mining region and has rail connection with La Paz, and with Mollendo and Antofagasta on the Pacific coast. Sucre is the seat of an archbishop and has a normal school and an ancient university. Since 1898 Congress has met at La Paz. The city is 9328 feet above the level of the sea. Population estimated in 1944 at 30,000.

Tobago. An island situated 22 miles northwest of Trinidad and incorporated with it, for purposes of administration, to form the British colony of Trinidad and Tobago. Its area is 114 square miles and its population is 27,679. The chief products are cacao and coconuts. The island is frequently visited by tourists.

Trinidad. An island dependency of Great Britain, lying in the Atlantic Ocean, about ten miles off the northeast coast of Venezuela near the delta of the Orinoco river. Its area is 1862 square miles. The interior is a series of rolling, well watered plains, partly covered by magnificent forests of palms, breadfruits, tamarinds, and bamboo trees. The climate is malarious, except on the low mountain ranges, which parallel the north and the south coast.

The most valuable products include sugar, cocoa, petroleum, and asphalt. The asphalt comes partly from a reservoir of the mineral covering an area of 114 acres and known as Pitch lake. The island's trade is principally with Great Britain and the United States.

Negroes and people of East Indian origin make up the majority of the population, which, in 1946 was estimated at 540,940. The capital is Port of Spain. The island belonged to Spain from the time of its discovery by Columbus until 1802, when it was ceded to Great Britain. For administrative purposes it is combined with Tobago, an island to the northeast, to form the colony of Trinidad and Tobago.

Valparaiso (*väl'pä-rī'sō*). The chief seaport of Chile, situated on a bay at the approximate center of Chile's coast line. The port is strongly fortified. The chief imports are textiles and other manufactured goods. The leading articles of export include agricultural products and Chile saltpeter. Its trade increased considerably as a result of the opening of the Panama canal.

The city was one of the first in South America to introduce such modern improvements as the use of street cars, of gas, and of aqueducts for the water supply. There are a number of wide streets and a fine square adorned with many statues. Population, 1940, 215,614.

EUROPE

The continent consisting of the northwestern portion of the vast land surface in the eastern hemisphere. Europe may be regarded as a western peninsula of Asia, from which it is divided, more or less arbitrarily, by the Ural mountains, the Caspian Sea, the Caucasus mountains, the Black Sea, the Bosporus strait, the Sea of Marmora, the Dardanelles strait, and the Ægean Sea. To the south of Europe lies the Mediterranean Sea, which separates the continent from Africa. This inland sea communicates with the Atlantic Ocean by the Strait of Gibraltar, where Europe's most southern point, Cape Tarifa, is no more than nine miles from Africa's northern extremity. The continent is bounded by the Atlantic Ocean on the west and by the Arctic Ocean on the north. The continental part of Europe, as distinct from the islands, is often referred to as "the continent" by people in the British Isles and in America.

Size. With the exception of Australia, Europe is the smallest of the continents, covering about 3,900,000 square miles, or very little more than the area of the United States and Alaska. It includes, with all its outlying islands, little more than 7 per cent of the total land surface of the globe. Its greatest length from east to west is 3300 miles, and its maximum extent north and south is about 2400 miles.

Outline and Islands. Europe has a contour diversified by so many irregularities, great and small, that the coast line, winding about all the indentations of the mainland and of the chief islands, has a length of nearly 48,000 miles. The islands and peninsulas, occupying about one-third of the total area of the continent, partially enclose a number of large gulfs and inland seas. Thus, while the small inlets provide numerous harbors, the inland seas make all parts of the continent comparatively easy of access from the sea.

In the extreme northeast, the islands of Nova Zembla separate the Kara Sea from Barents Sea, the latter being shut off from the Arctic Ocean by the islands of Spitsbergen. From the southwest corner of Barents Sea, a strait, called the Gorlo, leads into the White Sea, a three-pronged gulf sheltered behind the Kola peninsula. The Kola peninsula is, itself, part of the huge Scandinavian peninsula, which encloses the Baltic Sea and its three major inlets, the Gulf of Bothnia, the Gulf of Finland, and the Gulf of Riga. The Scandinavian peninsula trends in a general southwestern direction and terminates in two diverging extensions, which open like jaws above the peninsula of Jutland and are separated from it by two straits, the Kattegat and the Skagerrack. The Jutland peninsula and part of the Scandinavian peninsula form the eastern shore of the North Sea, which, stretching westward to the British Isles, has a southwestern outlet through the English channel to the Atlantic Ocean. The British Isles consist of two principal islands, Great Britain and Ireland, separated by the Irish Sea. Dunmore Head on the southwestern coast of Ireland is the most westerly point of Europe. The Bay of Biscay is the only large western inlet.

The southern coast has three major peninsulas—the Iberian peninsula, Italy, and the Balkan peninsula. Between the Iberian peninsula and Italy, in the Mediterranean Sea, lie the Balearic islands, and the three islands—Corsica, Sardinia, and Sicily—which, with Italy, enclose the Tyrrhenian Sea. The Gulf of Taranto stretches inland between the toe and the heel of the bootlike peninsula of Italy, and the whole peninsula is separated by the Adriatic Sea from the Balkan peninsula, which, on its eastern side, is washed by the Ægean Sea, the Black Sea, and the smaller bodies of water connecting the two. The Ægean Sea is dotted with small islands, most of which cluster in archipelagoes known as the Cyclades and the Sporades.

At a distance from the continent, about 700 miles northwest of the Scandinavian peninsula, lies the large mountainous island of Iceland.

Surface. The average elevation of Europe is less than that of any other continent. The highest point is Mount Elbruz, in the Caucasus range, the peak of which reaches a height of 18,465 feet. Marked changes in land level at the coast have been observed within historical times. The land about the Gulf of Bothnia has risen, and the southern shore of the North Sea has subsided. On the eastern side of the Adriatic Sea near modern Rovigno, the island town of Cissa, which was flourishing in the 7th century, is now 85 feet below the sea.

Apart from the Ural and the Caucasus range, there are two chief systems of mountains in Europe—the Kiolen range, forming a longitudinal ridge in the Scandinavian peninsula, and an irregular group of ranges trending in a general east and west direction across southern Europe. This latter group consists of the Pyrenees range, which cuts across the neck of the peninsula of Spain; the Alps, forming a central highland north of Italy; the Apennines, extending to the southern extremity of Italy and finding a continuation in the mountainous regions of Sicily; the Carpathian mountains, extending northeast of the Alps for some distance and then turning southeast toward the Black Sea; the Pindus range, which forms the backbone of Greece; and the Balkan mountains passing eastward north of the Ægean Sea. Other mountainous regions are Iceland, Scotland, and Spain.

Volcanic activity is confined to Iceland and to the Mediterranean region and is most marked in southern Italy, Sicily, and the adjacent islands. Here are situated Mount Stromboli, Mount Etna, and Mount Vesuvius, the last being notable for the eruption which, in 79 A. D., buried the cities of Herculaneum and Pompeii. No part of the continent, however, is free of earthquakes except the great plains of Russia.

A large part of Europe's area consists of fertile plains. Western and northern France, northern Germany, and almost the whole of European Russia constitute what is sometimes called the Great Lowland Plain. Other plains are the Central Plain, occupying Ireland and England; the Plain of Lombardy, south of the Alps; the Hungarian Plain, hemmed in by the Carpathian mountains and by the highland extending from the Alps southeastward into Greece; and the Wallachian Plain, between the southern Carpathians and the Black Sea.

Drainage. Of the many rivers of Europe, only one, the Volga, is more than 2000 miles in length, and, of the others, only the Danube, the Dnieper, and the Don exceed a length of 1000 miles. With few exceptions, however, the rivers admit of navigation and contribute toward making the interior of the continent readily accessible from the coasts.

The chief rivers draining northward, named in order from east to west, are the Pechora, the Dvina, the Duna, the Vistula, the Oder, the Elbe, the Rhine, and the Seine. The Loire and the Gironde River system flow westward into the Bay of Biscay. The plateau of Spain is drained toward the Atlantic Ocean by the Douro, the Tagus, the Guadiana, and the Guadalquivir and, toward the Mediterranean Sea, by the Jucar and the Ebro river. Of the rivers of southern drainage, the Rhone flows into the Golfe du Lion, an inlet of the Mediterranean Sea; the Po, into the Adriatic Sea; the Danube, the Dniester, and the Dnieper, into the Black Sea; the Don, into the Sea of Azof, a northern inlet of the Black Sea; and the Volga, into the Caspian Sea.

Fresh-water lakes are particularly numerous in three regions—the highlands of the Alps, the British Isles, and the territory east and northwest of the Baltic Sea. The last-mentioned region contains by far the most lakes, including the two largest of the continent—Ladoga and Onega.

Climate. Europe lies almost entirely in the temperate zone, a small portion only projecting into the arctic region. The northern part, however, has a warmer climate than other regions of the same latitude on account of warm ocean currents which wash its shores. The southern limit of drift ice from the polar regions nowhere approaches within 50 miles of the Scandinavian peninsula. The northern interior plains, however, suffer much greater extremes of temperature than those occurring near the coast. The southern part of Europe has a subtropical climate.

Europe is the only continent which has no desert region. Warm, moisture-laden winds blow prevailingly from the southwest. In the absence of a mountain wall running north and south, these winds carry their moisture far inland, instead of being intercepted and losing it by precipitation near the coast.

Plant and Animal Life. There are three chief plant regions in Europe—the arctic, possessing scanty vegetation; the intermediate, comprising forest areas,—largely coniferous,—and level steppes which resemble the North American plains; and, lastly, the Mediterranean region in the south. The last is noted for the great variety and economic importance of its flora.

Next to Asia, Europe has contributed to the human race more cultivated plants than any other continent. The more important include, among the grains, oats and rye; among the vegetables, asparagus, beet, cabbage, carrot, endive, horseradish, lettuce, pea, and turnip; the forage plants, clover and timothy; and such fruits as the currant, gooseberry, and fig.

The fauna likewise is rich. It has a general similarity to that of North America. The characteristic mammals include the bear, lynx, badger, wolf, fox, otter, marten, ermine, polecat, squirrel, hedgehog, and rabbit. The desman and chamois are peculiar to the continent. In the south, the fallow deer, ibex, alpine marmot, and civet are found. Of the domesticated animals, Europe is the original home of the goose, pigeon, rabbit, reindeer, and swan.

Minerals. The geology of Europe reveals an immense wealth of mineral resources. Coal and iron are produced in the greatest aggregate value. The chief coal fields are those in Great Britain, in Upper Silesia, in the Ruhr district in Germany, in northeastern France, and in Russia. The Lorraine district in France, the Saar valley in Germany, and northern and central England are the most important iron producing regions. Spain and Upper Silesia produce the world's chief supply of zinc, as Russia does of platinum. Spain and Italy supply a large part of the world's market for quicksilver. Gold and asbestos are obtained from the Ural Mountain region in large quantities. Other mineral products of the continent include salt, sulphur, silver, lead, aluminum, tin, copper, and marble.

Industry. The industrial output of Europe exceeds that of any other continent. Industrial development, however, is concentrated largely in a few regions, chiefly those where coal and iron are found in close proximity. Among the principal industries are those making steel, fertilizers and other chemicals, glass, pottery, perfumes, and scientific instruments. There are also many highly specialized products exported, such as art objects, specially designed clothing, and time pieces.

Inhabitants. Human habitation in Europe is very ancient. In various districts, remains of prehistoric men have been found, the earliest going back probably 250,000 years to the second interglacial period. The inhabitants of Europe, now numbering over 500 million, are of the white race. With few exceptions, the languages of Europe belong to one family, called by philologists Indo-European. Peoples of Asia speaking related languages are believed to have migrated from Europe to Asia. Counter migrations from Asia brought some Oriental types into Europe, such as the Magyars and Huns.

POLITICAL DIVISIONS

Europe has more independent countries than any other continent. They comprise Albania, Andorra, Austria, Belgium, Bulgaria, Denmark, Estonia, Finland, France, Germany, Great Britain and Northern Ireland, Greece, Hungary, Iceland, Eire, Italy, Latvia, Liechtenstein, Lithuania, Luxemburg, Monaco, the Netherlands, Norway, Poland, Portugal, Rumania, Russia, San Marino, Spain, Sweden, Switzerland, Vatican City, and Yugoslavia.

Of these divisions, Eire is a self-governing dominion of the British Empire. Its geography, along with that of Northern Ireland, is treated under the head of Ireland. Vatican City is 109 acres of papal territory within the city of Rome. Andorra is a mountainous, pastoral country between France and Spain; Luxemburg is surrounded by France, Germany, and Belgium; and Liechtenstein is a small principality hemmed in by Austria and Switzerland. These countries, as well as San Marino, an ancient state surrounded by Italian territory in the northeastern part of the peninsula, will be found described from a geographical point of view in the departments of history and government.

In addition to the independent states, there is a territory north of the Sea of Marmora forming part of Turkey. Gibraltar, a bold promontory at the south of the Iberian peninsula, and the islands of Malta and Gozo, in the Mediterranean Sea south of Sicily, are dependencies of Great Britain.

Albania. A mountainous republic on the west of the Balkan peninsula with a coast line on the Adriatic Sea. It has an area of 10,629 square miles and a population, 1946 estimate, of 1,120,522. The people support themselves mainly by a primitive type of agriculture devoted chiefly to livestock. There are vast tracts of undeveloped forests and considerable unexploited mineral wealth, consisting largely of copper, salt, coal, and oil.

Tirana is the capital and largest city. Durazzo, the chief port is equipped with modern facilities. Work on Albania's first railroad, which is to connect Durazzo with Tirana and Elbasan, was reported begun in 1947.

Austria. An inland republic of central Europe, bounded on the north by Germany and Czechoslovakia and on the remaining sides by Hungary, Yugoslavia, Italy, and Switzerland. The western part, known as the Tyrol, is a mountainous region, widely celebrated for its bold, picturesque scenery. In the north, Austria is traversed by the Danube river, which provides a navigable waterway several hundred miles in length.

On an area of 32,369 square miles, Austria supports a population estimated in 1946 at 7,000,000. In spite of increased use of agricultural machinery, livestock and grain show a marked decline over prewar figures. The chief products are lumber, iron ore, cotton and woolen goods, glass, fruits, beet sugar, paper, furniture, chemicals, pianos, and automobiles. Coal is the largest single import.

Most of the inhabitants are Roman Catholic. There is a system of compulsory elementary education. The largest of the three state universities is situated in the capital, Vienna, a city which has for centuries been a center of learning and of art.

Belgium. A small kingdom of Europe with a coast line on the North Sea. The country is bounded by France, Luxemburg, Germany, and the Netherlands. Its area is 11,775 square miles, its population in 1946, 8,388,526. With 712 inhabitants to the square mile, Belgium ranks second in density of population. Only the Netherlands exceeds her.

Nearly all of the surface of Belgium is arable and is intensively cultivated. The country is also industrially one of the most highly developed in the world, being favored in this respect by the occurrence of coal and of iron deposits in close proximity to each other. The recovery of Belgium since its liberation in 1944 is extraordinary. Increases in the output of grains, potatoes, beet sugar, milk, meat, coal, chemicals, machinery, glass, paper, beer, textiles, and zinc are outstanding. Diamond cutting is an important industry. The electrification of the entire railroad system is well under way and airlines provide direct contact with Europe, America, and the Belgian Congo.

Two languages are spoken in Belgium—French in the south by the Walloons, a people of Celtic origin, and Flemish in the north by the Flemings, who are of the Teutonic race. The majority of the inhabitants professing a religion are Roman Catholics. Of the country's four universities, Louvain is the most celebrated. The capital and largest city is Brussels. Other cities of note are Antwerp, Ghent, Liège, and Ostend.

Bulgaria. A mountainous republic of southeastern Europe, with an eastern coast line on the Black Sea. Bulgaria lies between Rumania on the north and Greece on the south and stretches westward to the borders of Yugoslavia. Its area is 39,825 square miles.

The Balkan mountains divide southern Bulgaria from the northern zone, in which a cool climate and a fertile soil foster agriculture of a temperate zone type. The perfume attar of roses is a distinctively Bulgarian product. Apart from it the chief products are grains, tobacco, livestock, cotton, hemp, flax, silk, beans, sugar beets, fruits, rice, and various flowers. The manufacturing of textiles is the chief industry. The Danube river, which constitutes the northern border of Bulgaria, provides, with its affluents, important water highways for trade.

Agriculture of various kinds engages the activities of about four-fifths of Bulgaria's population, which the 1946 census listed as 7,020,863. The prevailing religion is Greek Catholicism. Elementary instruction is free and obligatory. There is one university, which is situated in Sofia, the capital and largest city of the country.

Czechoslovakia (*chĕk'ō-slō-vä'kĭ-ȧ*). An inland republic of central Europe, closely allied with the Soviet Union. The country is narrow and elongated, lying in a general east and west direction. It is bordered by Poland, Germany, Austria, Hungary, Rumania, and Russia. The area, 49,373 square miles, is about the size of the state of New York. The estimated population in 1947 was 13,047,000. Approximately three-fourths of the people are Czechs and Slovaks.

About one-third of its area is covered with valuable forests and by 1946 the pulp and paper industry had reached 80 per cent of prewar output. The soil is fertile and supports extensive and intensive agriculture; the chief crops are potatoes, sugar beets, wheat, barley, rye, oats, hops, tobacco, and various fruits and vegetables. The coal deposits are extensive and provide a surplus for export. Gold, silver, copper, lead, and rock salt are also found. The textile, porcelain, glass, furniture, sugar, chemical, and metal factories place Czechoslovakia among the more important manufacturing countries of Europe. By decrees of October 1945 all national resources, public utilities, and other important branches of industry and trade were nationalized. Transportation is provided by the Elbe and Danube rivers, and by more than 13,000 miles of railway and 60,000 miles of highway. In 1946 the estimated number of radios was 1,571,102.

Approximately seventy-five per cent of the inhabitants are Roman Catholics in spite of the fact that the provinces of Bohemia and Moravia constituted one of the earliest centers of Protestantism. The Moravian Church in America was founded by emigrants from this region. By 1945, universities and technical and special schools of university rank had a total attendance of 52,716. The capital and largest city is Prague.

Denmark. A small kingdom of northern Europe, consisting of the greater part of the Jutland peninsula and of several adjacent islands, the largest of which are Zealand and Funen. The Faroe islands, lying nearly midway between Scotland and Iceland, are administratively a part of Denmark. The total area of the country is 16,576 square miles. Greenland is a colony of Denmark. Iceland is an autonomous state under the Danish monarchy and is subject to Danish control in foreign affairs.

The surface of continental Denmark is a low rolling plain nowhere exceeding 570 feet in altitude. Sand dunes fringe much of the coast line, often extending five or six miles inland. Considerable areas of peat bog provide fuel for the inhabitants. Forests, mainly of beech trees, cover about 750 square miles. Apart from lumbering, the principal industries are agriculture, dairying, and fishing. The value of the annual catch of fish is considerably in excess of ten million dollars. There is no country in the world where mixed farming is carried on with more scientific skill than in Denmark. The farms are small. Butter, eggs, and bacon account for considerably more than half the exports. The farm produce is marketed largely by co-operative societies. Copenhagen porcelain is a distinctive product of the country's manufacturing industry.

The population of Denmark is 4,045,232, most of whom are Lutheran Protestants in religion. Illiteracy is virtually nonexistent, elementary education having been obligatory since 1814. The University of Copenhagen stands at the head of the educational system, which is of the most enlightened type and is well adapted to the agricultural interests of the people. The capital, Copenhagen, is situated on the island of Zealand. With a population of 927,404, it contains nearly one-fifth of the inhabitants of the country. Other cities are Aarhus (107,393), Odense (92,436), and Aalborg (60.680).

A territory known as Northern Schleswig was added to Denmark in 1920 as a result of the Treaty of Versailles. This territory had been wrested from the Danes by Germany in 1864.

Estonia (*ĕs-tō'nĭ-ȧ*). An agricultural country of northern Europe, republican in government, with a coast line on the Gulf of Finland in the north and on the Baltic Sea in the west. Estonia was formerly a province of Russia. Its area is 17,610 square miles, and the population in 1944 was estimated at 1,131,000.

Much of the surface is forested, and there are large areas of bog and of heath. The climate is severe. The chief crops are rye, barley, potatoes, and wheat. Dairy produce leads the articles of export, the other principal items being timber, textiles, paper, flax, and meat.

Estonia is a Protestant country, five-sixths of the total population being Lutherans. There are very few illiterate adults. Dorpat university, founded in 1632, is maintained by the government. The capital of Estonia is Tallinn, which has a population of 147,000. Tartu, or Dorpat, with 59,000 inhabitants, is the second largest city. Russia was granted in 1939 the right to use naval and military bases in Estonia. In the next year, the country was admitted into the Soviet Union.

Finland. One of the most northern countries of Europe, lying between the Gulf of Finland and the Gulf of Bothnia and extending northward almost entirely across the neck of the Scandinavian peninsula. The Aland islands off the southern coast are governed as part of Finland. About one-fourth of the country's 117,975 square miles of surface is within the Arctic circle. In the north, mountains rise to a height of 4000 feet, but the remainder of the country is, for the most part, a plateau having an average elevation of about 500 feet. The numerous lakes of glacial formation, which occupy 11 per cent of the area of the country, have won for Finland the name of "the land of the thousand lakes."

Although agriculture employs more workers, forest products, chiefly timber, pulp, and paper, account for almost the whole of the country's export trade. Nearly two-thirds of the country is covered with pine forests.

The population of Finland is 3,887,217. Lutheran Protestantism is the prevailing religion. The country has a well developed system of elementary, secondary, technical, and higher education, at the head of which stand three universities. The capital and largest city is Helsingfors, a city of 327,627 inhabitants, situated in the southern extremity of the country. Other important towns are Abo and Tammerfors.

The inhabitants of Finland are mostly of the Finnic race, which is believed to have occupied formerly the whole of northern Asia and northeastern Europe. They are, in general, tall with flaxen hair and blue eyes.

France. A republic of western Europe, bounded on the north by the English channel and on the west by the Bay of Biscay. On the south, France is separated from Spain by the Pyrenees mountains and has a southern coast line on the Mediterranean Sea. On the east and northeast, France adjoins Italy, Switzerland, Germany, Luxemburg, and Belgium. The island of Corsica in the Mediterranean Sea is politically a part of France. The coast line of the country is nearly 2000 miles in length, but, being either sandy or high and rocky, it affords few good harbors. The total area of the republic is 212,659 square miles.

Since World War II France has been successful in securing certain boundary changes and is seeking others. On the Italian border they acquired the pass and enclave of Tenda and Briga in 1947. France also secured minor border rectifications in the areas of Little St. Bernard Pass, Mt. Cenis Pass, and Mt. Thabor and Chaberton. Other eastern continental boundaries reflect the great zone of transition between western and central Europe. After both wars of this century the French were eager to have the Saar with its coal mines under their political, or at least economic, control. In the Rhineland the French have wanted to see an independent unit separate from Germany, and in the industrial Ruhr they have favored international control.

The most elevated part of France is in the southeast, where the Jura mountains and the Alps divide the country from Switzerland and Italy. Mont Blanc, an Alpine mountain within the French border, is the second highest peak in Europe, having an altitude of 15,781 feet. The lower, forest-clad Vosges ridge farther north separates Alsace from the rest of France. These mountain groups form the eastern side of the Rhone-Saone River valley, which is flanked on the west by the Cevennes mountains The Rhone, rising in Switzerland and being augmented by the Saone river, flows southward into the Mediterranean Sea. The Saone river is connected by a canal with the upper reaches of the Seine river, which, with its tributaries,—the Marne and the Oise,—drains northward into the English channel. The other chief rivers of France flow westward and empty into the Bay of Biscay. They are the Loire, to the north, and, farther south, the Garonne and the Dordogne, which mingle their waters in the broad estuary called the Gironde river.

The principal rivers are all more or less navigable and afford shelter for such seaports as Havre and Rouen on the Seine, Saint Nazaire and Nantes on the Loire, and Bordeaux on the Garonne. The rivers as highways of inland commerce are supplemented by numerous canals.

France has considerable deposits of coal centering around Valenciennes near the northeastern border. The mines of this region were wrecked by the Germans during World War I, and from 1920 to 1935 the French operated the German coal mines in the Saar basin. France controls more iron than does any other European country, the mines being located in Lorraine, from which about one-tenth of the world's supply of iron ore is obtained. Other minerals produced in important quantities include gold, antimony, salt, potash, manganese, and bauxite, the ore of aluminum.

Of the surface of France, about one-fifth is forested, and approximately three-quarters is devoted to agriculture and grazing. Wheat, oats, potatoes, rye, barley, corn, and sugar beets are the leading crops. The average farm covers about 17 acres of ground. In the south, the climate is subtropical and fosters the cultivation of olives, peaches, apricots, oranges, mandarins, lemons, walnuts, and almonds. Apples, pears, cherries, plums, and berries are also produced in important quantities. The abundance of grapes grown in France enables her to rank as the leading wine producing country of the world. The cultivation of silkworms is an important industry in the south.

The fisheries of France are among the more important in the world. Large fleets are sent each year to catch cod about Newfoundland and about Saint Pierre and Miquelon, which lie off the south shore of Newfoundland. These two small islands constitute the sole remaining part of France's former empire in North America. Sardines are caught on France's northwestern coast and anchovies and tunny fish are obtained from the Mediterranean Sea.

The textile industries of France are famous the world over. The city of Lyon is the greatest silk center in Europe. Rayon also is manufactured there in large quantities. Rouen, on the Seine river, is noted for its cotton cloth made mainly from cotton grown in the United States. A large wool industry flourishes in the northeast. Paris is the seat of manufacture for the most costly products, including tapestries, shawls, jewelry, watches, and scientific instruments. Other manufactured products include chemicals, iron and steel, automobiles, electrical equipment, fine leather goods, the exquisite porcelains of Sèvres and of Limoges, cut glass, pottery, perfumes, and similar articles requiring skill and taste for their production. France ranks third among European countries in extent of water power available for manufacturing.

The population of France is 40,830,028. The great majority of those professing a religion are Roman Catholics. Illiteracy is almost unknown. At the head of the educational system stand 17 universities, of which the University of Paris is the most notable. Apart from Paris, the capital, the great emporiums of trade include Lyon, Lille, Saint Etienne, Toulouse, Strasbourg, and Reims. The more attractive maritime ports are Marseille, Bordeaux, Le Havre, and Cette. The larger cities with their populations in 1946 are:

City	Population	City	Population
Paris	2,725,374	Strasbourg	175,515
Marseille	636,264	Toulon	125,742
Lyon	460,748	Nancy	113,477
Toulouse	264,411	Reims	110,794
Bordeaux	253,751	Clermont-Ferrand	108,090
Nice	211,165	Limoges	107,874
Nantes	200,265	Rouen	107,739
Lille	188,871	Le Havre	106,934
St. Etienne	177,966		

France controls a colonial empire second only to that of Great Britain. Its area, population, and dates of acquisition are shown in the table below. Practically all parts of this empire have a tropical climate, and France's trade with them embraces imports of such tropical products as palm and olive oil, fruit, rice, rubber, sugar, cotton, teakwood, gums, tea, and coffee. Phosphate is an important product of French Morocco. French colonial administration has been conspicuously successful in North Africa. Plans for a trans-Saharan railway have been officially approved. See *French Africa, French Dependencies* in Asia, *French Guiana.*

FRENCH COLONIAL DEPENDENCIES

Colony	Date Acquired	Area Sq. Miles	Population 1941-47
In Africa			
Algeria	1830-1902	847,552	8,000,000
Tunisia	1881	48,313	3,230,952
Morocco	1912	153,870	8,499,997
French West Africa			
Senegal and Dakar	1637-1889	77,790	1,895,000
French Sudan . .	1893	590,966	3,797,000
Guinea	1843	96,886	2,125,000
Ivory Coast . .	1843	184,174	4,056,000
Dahomey . . .	1893	43,232	1,458,000
Mauritania . .	1893	323,310	497,000
Niger	1912	499,410	2,168,000
Equatorial Africa .	1884	959.236	4,127,808
Cameroon (Mandate)	1919	166,489	2,816,000
Togo (Mandate) .	1919	21,893	781,000
Reunion	1649	970	220,955
Madagascar and dependencies . .	1643-1896	241,884	4,189,090
Somaliland	1864	9,071	44,776
Total in Africa . .		4,265,046	47,906,578
In Asia			
India (French) .	1679	196	323,295
Indo-China (French)			
Annam . . .	1884	56 974	6,200,000
Cambodia . .	1862	69,866	3,046,000
Cochin-China .	1861	24,974	5,200,000
Laos	1892	89,320	1,000,000
Tonkin	1884	44,660	9,600,000
Total in Asia . . .		285,990	25,327,895
In America			
St. Pierre and Miquelon . . .	1635	93	4,354
Guadeloupe . . .	1634	688	271.262
Martinique . . .	1635	385	261,595
Guiana (French) .	1636	34,740	28,537
Total in America .		35,906	565,748
In Oceania			
New Caledonia and	1854-1887	8,548	61,250
New Hebrides (1)		5,700	45,000
Oceania (French)	1841-1881	1,520	55,734
Total in Oceania .		15,768	161,984
Grand Total . . .		4,602.710	73,962.205

(1) Condominium with Great Britain.

Germany. A populous commercial and agricultural country occupying north central Europe with a short coast line on the North Sea and a longer one on the Baltic Sea. Germany's area in 1937 was 180,985 square miles. The census of May 1939 showed the area of the German Reich to be 137,640 square miles. The area of present-day Germany is somewhat different from that of the Third Reich, which crashed in defeat in May, 1945. The postwar country, according to the best estimates, will occupy about three-fourths of the area of Hitler's Germany. The major portion of the territory lost by Germany is in the east, where a radical boundary change places the new Polish border along the Oder and Neisse rivers. Among other things the westward shift of this boundary eliminated East Prussia and the detached German area east of the troublesome Polish Corridor. Elsewhere boundary changes will be less radical although prior to a final peace treaty the Rhineland will remain a critical issue. The ratios of postwar to prewar Germany are about—area, 76%; population, 86%; rural population, 80%; urban population, 90%; industrial population, 90%; industrial output, 93%; and steel production, 97%.

The northern portion of Germany forms part of the Great Northern Lowlands and is, for the most part, flat. Its soil is not very fertile, and forests alternate with heaths, morasses, and small, shallow lakes. Central Germany may be described as hilly; its soil is fertile and its scenery is often picturesque. Much of southern Germany is occupied by the plateau of Bavaria. This plateau rises about 1600 feet above the sea level and increases in elevation toward the west, where it forms the Black Forest range, which reaches a maximum altitude of 9725 feet in the Zug Spitze. The mountains of Germany as a rule are worn low and are clothed with beautiful forests, about two-thirds of which consist of coniferous trees. In the southeast of Germany the Alps rise to form the famous Tyrol region, celebrated for its bold, picturesque scenery. The eastern border is penetrated by the Carpathian mountains, which curve south and back eastward to encircle the Bohemian plain.

Apart from the South, which is traversed by the upper reaches of the Danube river flowing from west to east, Germany is drained northward by five rivers, all of which are navigable. The Rhine, lying farthest to the west, rises in the Swiss Alps. Most of its course is in Germany, but its several mouths are situated in the Netherlands. The other rivers are the Ems,—which receives an intermittent flow from the Rhine,—the Weser, the Elbe, and the Oder. The Rhine is connected by canals with the Danube and with the Rhone river.

The mineral deposits of Germany are among the richest in Europe. The coal mines are chiefly in the Saar valley adjoining Lorraine and in the Ruhr valley farther north. The Ruhr mines form the nucleus of Germany's richest industrial district. The remaining coal field of greatest value is in the Erzgebirge range in the east, where zinc and iron are also obtained. Silver and copper are mined in the Harz mountains, a low, isolated range in central Germany. Germany produces the bulk of the world's supply of potash. Other minerals which are obtained in exportable quantities include cobalt, arsenic, sulphur, saltpeter, alum, gypsum, bismuth, pumice stone, slate, ocher, emery, and vitriol. The Baltic shore of East Prussia is the world's chief source of amber.

Northern Germany is, agriculturally, the most productive part of the country, followed by the Bohemian plain in the south. Potatoes, which are a staple food of the people, form the leading crop, hay ranking second in value of production. Other crops are wheat, sugar beets, rye, oats, barley, tobacco, and flax. The valley of the Rhine produces large amounts of grapes, from which the famous Rhenish wine is made. Hops, grown in abundance, mainly in Bavaria, are used in the manufacture of beer. Permission to carry on lumbering operations involves the obligation to reforest the land, tree for tree. Although about one-fourth of Germany's surface is covered with forest, the consumption of lumber was so great before the World War that the commodity was imported in large quantities, chiefly from the countries bordering on the Baltic Sea.

Germany is one of the most highly industrialized countries in the world. The chief industries are the manufacture of iron and steel products, of cotton, woolen, and linen textiles, of glass, porcelain, chemicals, dyes, toys, earthenware, clocks, furniture, sugar, and liquor. German industry has shown an especial aptitude for the making of machinery and of toys. In no country except Russia has the centralization of industrial control been carried further. This has been accomplished through the creation of trusts or cartels.

The population of Germany in 1946 was 66,410,-999. The prevalent religion of northern Germany is Protestant; of southern Germany, Catholic. The German educational system has long been known as one of the most efficient in the world.

The capital and largest city of the country is Berlin. Leipzig is the seat of the supreme court. The leading cities in the American and British zones with their populations according to the census of 1946, are as follows:

City	Population	City	Population
Berlin	3,180,383	Stuttgart . . .	414,072
Hamburg . . .	1,384,106	Bremen	390.000
Munich	760.929	Duisburg-Hamborn . .	355,487
Essen	520,656	Hanover . . .	355,484
Cologne	488,039	Wuppertal	324,962
Dortmund . .	433,792	Nuremberg . .	322,043
Frankfort . . .	421,369	Gelsenkirchen .	271,101
Düsseldorf . .	419,589		

Gibraltar (*jĭ-brôl'tẽr*). A rocky promontory near the southern point of the Iberian peninsula and commanding the western entrance to the Mediterranean Sea. It is a colonial possession of Great Britain. It covers about two square miles and consists mainly of a fortified rock, 1439 feet high, at the foot of which is the town of Gibraltar with a population in 1946 of 21,233. The fortress was obtained by Great Britain from Spain in 1713. From 1779 to 1783, it withstood a siege of 3 years, 7 months, and 12 days at the hands of a Spanish fleet.

Great Britain. An island kingdom lying north and slightly west of France and separated from it by the English channel, which narrows from a maximum width of 150 miles near the west end to a neck in the east, 21 miles wide, called the Strait of Dover. Geographically, the term Great Britain has reference to the one large island divided, for historical reasons, into England and Wales in the south and Scotland in the north. As a political division, however, Great Britain, officially known as the Kingdom of Great Britain and Northern Ireland, includes also Northern Ireland, the Orkney islands, the Shetland islands, and the Hebrides,—three groups lying north of Scotland,—the Scilly islands and the Isle of Wight in the south, and nearly 800 smaller islands. The Isle of Man in the Irish Sea and the Channel islands,—Guernsey, Jersey, and their dependency, Sark island,—are not subject to British legislation unless specifically designated in particular enactments. The area and the population of Great Britain and of its principal divisions are given in the table of *The British Commonwealth.*

Since World War II, Great Britain finds her position increasingly precarious. She has never been self sufficient in the home islands in modern times and has become even less so. An estimate of her postwar trade as compared with prewar is:

	1936-38*	Postwar Estimate*
Excess of Imports over Exports	1,885	1,945
Invisible Exports	1,670	780
Debit	215	1,165

*Average in millions of dollars.

Moreover, Britain's carrying trade, with which she met a major part of her deficit, has been much reduced. In 1939 the British Merchant Marine was three times that of the United States. Following the war, it has been reduced to half ours with the likelihood of further reduction to one-third. Also Britain's empire is facing a growing decentralizing movement, with major dominions such as India already independent. The growing problems with Russia add a fourth hazard to British postwar problems. To counter these problems Britain is moving to strengthen her position in Africa; improve relations with her great dominions, Canada, Australia, and New Zealand; is intensely supporting the United Nations; is seeking constantly improved relations with the United States; and, finally, is making determined efforts to improve her home economy and social conditions.

The island of Great Britain is about 700 miles long from north to south, and its width varies from 280 miles in the extreme south to 30 miles in northern Scotland, where Dornoch Firth and Loch Broom penetrate deeply into the land from opposite sides of the island. The coast line is well in excess of 4000 miles, being deeply indented by the estuaries of tidal rivers and, especially in northern and western Scotland, by deep, rocky fiords. The chief of these inlets on the eastern side, named from south to north, are the estuary of the Thames, the Wash, the Humber River estuary, the Firth of Forth, the Firth of Tay, Moray firth, and Dornoch firth. On the western side, the principal inlets are Bristol channel, Cardigan bay, the Dee River and the Mersey River estuary, Morecambe bay, Solway firth, the Firth of Clyde, and the Firth of Lorne with its continuation known as Loch Linnhe.

The seas surrounding Great Britain are shallow, rarely exceeding 300 feet in depth. This circumstance has the effect of protecting the island from the cold arctic currents, so that the country enjoys a climate much milder than that in corresponding latitudes of America. The shallow waters provide a feeding ground for fish, thereby supporting fisheries of great value.

Great Britain has been the most active colonizing nation in Europe. As islanders, the British turned readily to seafaring and were among the first to explore the Americas, Australia, the Orient, Africa, and other regions. Seldom losing their identity by intermarriage with natives, the settlers succeeded in carrying their institutions to many distant parts of the world and thus laid the foundation for the present British Commonwealth of Nations and the system of dependencies which are found in every continent. The United States received its language and basic institutions from the same source.

ENGLAND. A division of Great Britain comprising most of the southern part of the island and divided from Scotland on the north by a low ridge, called the Cheviot hills. The maximum length of England is 425 miles, and the width varies from 280 miles to 62 miles. The surface is, in general, a rolling plain, rising in the north to the low mountains in Derbyshire, Yorkshire, Westmoreland, and Cumberland. In the northwest is the "lake district," where occur the largest lake and the highest mountain in England—Lake Windermere, 10½ miles long, and Sca Fell, 3210 feet high. The chief rivers flowing into the North Sea on the east are the Thames, the Humber, the Tees, and the Tyne. Those flowing west include the Severn, Dee, and Mersey.

England is the largest coal exporting country in the world. The richest coal fields are located in the region of Newcastle in northeastern England and in an area 100 to 150 miles farther south, where the proximity of large iron deposits has resulted in the growth of such huge manufacturing cities as Sheffield and Birmingham. In production of iron, England holds the fourth place, ranking next to the United States, France, and Germany. Her manufactures, however, require the importation of additional ore, which comes mainly from Spain and Sweden. The southwestern extremity of England has been the chief European source of tin since the days of the Phœnicians. Lead, silver, and zinc are mined in the northeast.

About 5 per cent of England is covered with forests, of which certain tracts, such as Epping forest near London, were formerly set aside as royal deer forests. Epping forest is now open to the public as a park. The greater part of the country's surface is fertile, and, being tilled according to the most advanced methods, it is highly productive. The well kept farmhouses and comfortable cottages, which everywhere meet the eye, give an air of neatness and beauty, distinctive of rural England. The live stock of England and of Great Britain generally is of a superior quality. No country has produced more standard breeds of domestic animals.

England was the first country in the world to become industrialized and still remains one of the greatest manufacturing nations. In the making of cutlery and other steel products and of cotton, woolen, and linen textiles, England is excelled by no other country. The shipbuilding industry of Great Britain, favored by the numerous harbors of the island, is likewise unsurpassed. British ships do a large part of the carrying trade of the world. The foreign trade of the country exceeds that of any other country of the world. The total length of canals is about 3700 miles, and of railways, nearly 20,000 miles.

The population of England is about 95 per cent Protestant, the majority belonging to the Anglican, or Protestant Episcopal, Church, which is the "established church" of the country. No civil disabilities, however, attach to any British subject on account of religion. The outstanding universities of England are Oxford, Cambridge, and the University of London. Illiteracy is almost unknown. By an act passed in 1918, part time attendance at free continuation schools is required of all people up to 16 years of age, and, when the necessary facilities are provided, the age limit is extended to 18 years.

London, the capital of Great Britain, is the second largest city in the world. The chief cities with their estimated populations in 1947 are as follows:

City	Population	City	Population
London (Greater)	8,244,370	Southampton .	170,360
Birmingham . .	1,097,900	Bolton	166,090
Liverpool . . .	769,170	Wolverhampton	158,610
Manchester . .	695,230	Brighton . . .	154,600
Sheffield . . .	514,290	Blackpool . .	152,470
Leeds	498,650	Southend . . .	147,410
Bristol	436,150	Middlesbrough	142,660
Nottingham . .	296,350	Stockport . .	142,540
Hull	294,730	Derby	142,280
Newcastle . . .	293,570	Bournemouth .	139,560
Bradford . . .	289,280	Birkenhead . .	135,820
Leicester . . .	280,170	Tottenham . .	130,990
Stoke-on-Trent	273,510	Huddersfield .	125,490
Coventry . . .	248,400	Walthamstow .	124,380
Croyden. . . .	247,340	East Ham . .	120,160
Portsmouth . .	216,030	Oldham . . .	119,400
Ealing	185,960	Preston . . .	118,040
Plymouth . . .	185,380	Norwich . . .	116,770
Ilford	182,080	Gateshead . .	114,940
Willesden . . .	180,770	Walsall . . .	111,010
Sunderland . .	180,130	Blackburn . .	109,300
Salford	176,600	St. Helens .	107,020
West Ham. . .	174,740	South Shields .	103,130

Wales. The roughly rectangular land projection west of England, which lies between the Irish Sea on the north and Bristol channel on the south. Its surface is more mountainous than that of England, the highest peak being Mount Snowdon, 3560 feet in altitude. Wales contains some of the most valuable coal beds in Great Britain, and its largest city, Cardiff, exports more coal than any other city of the world. The inhabitants are of Celtic origin rather than Germanic, and about 40 per cent of them can still speak the native Welsh language. In religion, most of the Welsh are nonconformists, principally Methodists and Presbyterians.

Scotland. The portion of Great Britain north of the Cheviot hills. It is, in general, a more mountainous country than England. The chief rivers flowing to the east are the Tweed, the Forth, and the Tay. The Clyde is the only important river draining westward. Scotland has many beautiful lakes, of which Loch Lomond, 24 miles long, is the largest. The country is divisible, by the nature of its surface, into the highlands of the north, the central lowlands, and the southern uplands.

The highlands of Scotland occupy nearly half the country. They are remarkable for their mountainous masses, which are especially rugged along the western coast. The region is cut into two parts by the Great Glen of Scotland, a depression in which lie the elongated lakes, Loch Ness and Loch Lochy. These have been connected and made part of the Caledonian canal, which provides a waterway from Moray firth in the east to the Firth of Lorne in the west. Southwest of the Great Glen are the Grampian hills, which culminate in Ben Nevis near the center of the western coast. This mountain, having an altitude of 4400 feet, is the highest peak in Great Britain.

The southern uplands constitute a region of low mountains, none exceeding 3000 feet in height. Between them and the highlands of the north lies a fertile plain, which supports a dense population and flourishing industries.

The minerals of Scotland include coal, iron, and oil shale. Of the last named, Scotland has about 80 per cent of the amount in the world known to be available. Agriculture in Scotland is often handicapped by an excessive rainfall. Of the chief crops,—oats, barley, turnips, and potatoes,—oats are grown in the most important quantities. The southern uplands are excellently adapted to grazing, and sheep are raised in large numbers. Cheviot sheep and the Ayrshire, Galloway, Polled Angus, and Jersey cattle were first bred in Scotland, while the Shetland breed of ponies originated in the Shetland islands lying to the northeast.

The industries of Scotland are similar to those of England, consisting chiefly of textiles, steel products, and shipbuilding. At Glasgow on the Clyde are located the world's largest shipbuilding yards. Most of the Cunard liners have been built in these yards. The country is noted also for its production of whisky and of preserved fruits.

Scotland is the original home of Presbyterianism, the form of Protestantism professed by the established church of Scotland. The Roman Catholic Church is relatively stronger than in England. There are four universities in the country—Edinburgh, Glasgow, Aberdeen, and Saint Andrews. Scotland enjoys the same system of continuation schools as that described under *England*. The county authorities are empowered to provide educational books for the use of the adult population. The Gaelic language is still spoken in parts of Scotland, those able to understand the language numbering about 4 per cent of the total population.

Three-quarters of Scotland's 5,139,000 inhabitants live in towns or cities. The largest urban center is Glasgow, population 1,106,000. Edinburgh, population 487,200, is the seat of the supreme court, Scotland having courts and a system of law differing from those of England and based on French models.

Greece. A maritime kingdom occupying the southern part of the Balkan peninsula and including about 500 near-by islands, of which Crete is the largest. The shores of the mainland are bold, rocky, and deeply indented. The Gulf of Ægina, stretching inland from the east, is connected by a canal with the Gulf of Corinth, which is an inland continuation of the Gulf of Patras on the west coast. The resulting peninsula, called the Peloponnese in ancient times, is now known as Morea. The total area of the country is about 50,269 square miles.

About four-fifths of the surface of the mainland is crumpled by a complex system of mountains, which divide the surface into a number of small plains. The chief range, running north and south, is called the Pindus. The highest peak is Mount Olympus, in northern Greece, which has an altitude of 9794 feet. Mount Parnassus, celebrated in literature as the home of the Muses, is 8070 feet high. It is situated just north of the Gulf of Corinth and is now known as Mount Liakura. The progressive deforestation which has taken place in Greece is believed to have made the country drier than it formerly was. The climate is otherwise marked by intensity of heat in the summers and occasionally by severe cold in the winters.

The small plains of Greece provide the major part of the arable land. Agriculture, though practicable on only one-fifth of the country's surface and though carried on by primitive methods, is nevertheless the leading industry of the country. By the draining of Lake Copais in central Greece, about 53,000 acres were reclaimed in 1894. The chief crops are olives, wheat, grapes, corn, currants, figs, tobacco, oranges, lemons, barley, and oats. Currants constitute a distinctive product. The English word currant is a corruption of Corinth, the name of a Greek city from which the fruit is exported. Other industries are the raising of sheep and of goats. Lignite, magnesite, iron, salt, lead, emery, and zinc are mined. Slag from the silver mines at Laurium is being worked over for lead that the ancient Athenians failed to extract.

The Greeks are a commercial people. Along with the manufacture of textiles, leather, and soap, shipbuilding ranks high among the industries. The Greek trader has for more than 2500 years been found everywhere throughout the Levant, as the countries washed by the eastern Mediterranean Sea are sometimes called. Seventy-five per cent of the Greek ocean-going ships were lost during World War II, the coastal fleet was ruined, and Greek ports were severely damaged. Railways and highways suffered similar losses.

Most of Greece's 7,450,000 inhabitants profess the Greek Catholic faith. The spoken language, known as Romaic, is related to ancient Greek much as Italian is related to Latin; the literary language, however, is much closer to classical Greek. Athens is the capital and largest city of Greece, its population in 1947 being about 1,000,000. Other notable cities are Salonika, Piræus, which is the port of Athens, and Patras. Elementary education is nominally obligatory, but the percentage of illiteracy is high. There are government commercial schools and two universities at Athens, where also schools of archeology are maintained by American, British, French, Italian, and German learned societies. The Greek ministry of education is charged with the duty of conserving, repairing, and excavating ancient monuments.

The most notable architectural monuments of Greece date back more than 2000 years. Many of the finest buildings have been seriously mutilated, but some remain almost complete and still retain the dignity of their former state. Apart from Athens, the places containing the more interesting ruins are Olympia, Delphi, and Mycenæ.

Hungary. An inland agricultural republic in the eastern part of central Europe, bounded by Austria, Czechoslovakia, Russia, Rumania, and Yugoslavia. In the past few decades, the rulers of Hungary have displayed a marked aptitude for choosing the losing side in the wars of Europe. As a result, her territory has been reduced from over 60,000 square miles to 35,875, and her population has declined from more than 13,000,000 to 9,106,252.

The chief crops raised in Hungary are corn, wheat, sugar beets, barley, rye, oats, grapes, and tobacco. Most of the industries are those based on agriculture, such as flour milling and sugar refining. There are also iron and steel works. Hard and soft coal and bauxite are mined. Forests cover about 6 per cent of the surface. Important quantities of fish are obtained from Lake Balaton, the largest lake in central Europe, and from the rivers.

The majority of the people are Roman Catholics. There is a well developed educational system with compulsory attendance between the ages of 6 and 14. There are six universities, supported by the government and 29 theological colleges. Budapest is the capital and largest city. Hungarians are sometimes called Magyars, in allusion to their origin as an Asiatic race which invaded Europe in the 9th century.

Iceland. An island state situated in the north Atlantic Ocean about 500 miles northwest of Scotland and 150 miles southeast of Greenland. The Arctic circle touches the most northern point of the island. The cold is not extreme, however, being moderated by the proximity of the ocean.

Almost the whole of Iceland's 39,709 square miles of surface is of volcanic origin, magnificent as scenery but unproductive. The ice-strewn plateaus, of which the island consists, average more than 2000 feet in altitude. The most celebrated of the island's 100 volcanoes is the Hecla, 5110 feet in height. The Great Geyser is 60 feet in diameter and, at intervals of several hours, projects immense quantities of hot water about 150 feet into the air. Boiling water from geysers is piped to the capital to heat buildings. About one-eighth of the island is covered by glaciers.

Nearly all the inhabitants of Iceland are dependent for their living on agriculture, stock raising, or fishing. Less than 1 per cent of the island is cultivated. The chief crops are hay, potatoes, and turnips. The exports consist almost entirely of live stock, mainly sheep and horses, and of fish and fish products. Trade is mainly with Great Britain, Russia, and the United States.

The population of Iceland is 108,644. The national church is Lutheran. There is a complete system of education culminating in a university situated at Reykjavik, the capital of the republic.

Ireland. The large island lying immediately west of Great Britain and separated from it by the Irish Sea, which is connected with the Atlantic Ocean by Saint George's channel and by North channel. In the narrowest part of North channel, Ireland is separated from Great Britain by 14 miles. The area of the island is about 32,000 square miles. It has a maximum length of 300 miles and a maximum width of 180 miles. Politically, the island is divided into two parts. Eire occupies the whole island except a comparatively small district in the north. This district, under the name of Northern Ireland, constitutes a division of the Kingdom of Great Britain and Northern Ireland. For the area and the population of Eire (Irish Free State) and of Northern Ireland, see the table of *The British Commonwealth.* Since 1850 nearly 4,500,000 Irish have emigrated to other countries, by far the greatest number having settled in the United States. The Irish are Celtic in race. The Irish language was spoken by about 13 per cent of the population in 1920, and since then its use has been actively fostered by the government of the Irish Free State. Along with English, it is the official language of that state.

About two-fifths of Ireland's surface consists of bog. Most of the remainder is fertile. The humidity of the climate and the equability of the temperature foster a verdant clothing of vegetation, which has earned for Ireland the name of the "emerald isle." The island is drained by the Shannon river, which, having a course of 250 miles, is the longest river in the British Isles. The enchanting and romantic scenery of the lakes of Killarney in the south attracts visitors from all parts of the world.

Eire. This portion of Ireland is predominantly agricultural in its interests, being Great Britain's most important single source of foodstuffs. Marketing is accomplished largely through co-operative societies. The chief crops are potatoes, oats, turnips, barley, and wheat. Dairying and stock raising form an important part of the farm operations. There are also valuable sea and fresh-water fisheries, the catches including salmon, mackerel, cod, and herring. The chief manufactures are food products, beer, ale, and tractors.

The population of Eire is predominantly Roman Catholic. At the head of the educational system stand two universities, both situated in Dublin, the capital and largest city of the country. Other cities of note include Cork and Limerick.

Northern Ireland. In addition to agriculture and fishing, the northern division of Ireland has a large manufacturing industry. This industry, which has been developed in spite of the lack of coal and of iron in the island, consists chiefly of shipbuilding, distilling, and the manufacture of linen and of other textiles.

The prevailing religion of Northern Ireland is Protestantism. The educational system is distinct from that of the other divisions of the United Kingdom. Belfast, the largest city, is the seat of a university and of the legislature and the judiciary of Northern Ireland. Londonderry is another important center of manufacture and of trade.

Italy. A kingdom occupying the large bootshaped peninsula of southern Europe. Italy includes also the islands of Sicily, Sardinia, Elba, and about 70 smaller islands in the surrounding seas. Its territory was increased by the acquisition of Albania in 1939. The land boundary at the north follows, in a roughly semicircular course, a mountain wall, which separates Italy from France, Switzerland, Germany, and Yugoslavia. To the east of the mainland lies the Adriatic Sea, at the head of which is the Gulf of Venice. The sea narrows toward the south to the Strait of Otranto, 45 miles wide at its narrowest point. Italy's western coast is washed by the Tyrrhenian Sea and by the Ligurian Sea, the latter having a broad northern inlet called the Gulf of Genoa. On the south, Italy is bounded by the Ionian Sea with its inlet, the Gulf of Taranto. The "toe" of Italy is separated from Sicily by the Strait of Messina, which has a minimum width of two miles. The mainland of Italy has an average width of about 100 miles and a maximum length of 780 miles. The total area of the country is 119,764 square miles, excluding 10,629 square miles in the Albanian protectorate.

Italy is mountainous and includes the only part of the European mainland which contains active volcanoes. Spurs of the Alps mountains, extending into Italy from the northern mountain wall, form the beautiful scenery of the celebrated Italian Tyrol. The range of the Apennines passes from the Gulf of Genoa to the southern extremity of the mainland. Vesuvius, a mountain of the latter range, Etna on Sicily, and Stromboli on one of the Lipari islands, north of Sicily, are volcanoes which are seldom quiescent. An earthquake at Calabria, southern Italy, in 1783, destroyed 100,000 lives, and another, about the Strait of Messina in 1908, resulted in the death of some 96,000 people.

The most important river of Italy is the Po, which drains the fertile, well watered plain of Lombardy in the north and discharges near the head of the Adriatic Sea. The Tiber, which empties into the sea near the center of the western coast, is richer in historical associations. The mineral resources of Italy are comparatively small. The chief products are sulphur, marble, quicksilver, copper, zinc, iron and manganese. The fisheries employ more than 150,000 workers.

The leading industry of Italy is agriculture. The climate, ranging from subarctic in the Alps to subtropical in the south, permits the cultivation of such varied crops as wheat, corn, potatoes, sugar beets, oats, grapes, olives, rice, beans, barley, and rye. Northern Italy is the most productive region, being cultivated by the most improved methods, while in the south the peasants are unprogressive and poor. Over 400,000 acres were reclaimed for agriculture in central Italy in the decade 1920-30. Silk culture is also a considerable industry. Wine, olive oil, and cheese are important exports of Italy. The chief manufacturing centers are in the north, where abundant hydroelectric power is available. The principal products include cotton and silk textiles, lace, straw hats, metal products, chemicals, sugar, rayon, leather goods, glass, pottery, perfumes, and paper. Shipbuilding is also an important industry. Among the distinctive products of Italian craftsmanship are cameos and marble statuettes.

The population of Italy proper is 42,993,602, while that of its Albanian protectorate is 1,003,124. The prevailing religion is Roman Catholicism. Elementary instruction is compulsory. Italy has 21 universities, many of them among the oldest in Europe. In addition, there are many technical colleges, art schools, and learned societies. Everywhere throughout Italy are to be found monuments, more or less ruined, which bear witness to the fact that Italy was the chief center of European civilization from the 2d century B. C. to the 16th century A. D.

Rome is the capital and largest city of Italy. The population of Italian cities is increased by the large number of people who merely reside in the city but obtain their livelihoods by cultivating land in the surrounding rural sections. The chief cities with their populations are given in the following table:

City	Population	City	Population
Rome	1,471,971	Bari	248,629
Milan	1,250,389	Messina	213,957
Naples	941,841	Verona	190,828
Turin	712,833	Taranto	180,852
Genoa	664,143	Padua	164,231
Palermo	445,132	Brescia	146,507
Florence	365,044	Reggio (Calabr.)	137,661
Bologna	332,989	Leghorn	137,226
Venice	292,813	Cagliari	133,962
Catania	272,824	Spezia	121,847

Albania is a mountainous area separated from the Italian mainland by the Strait of Otranto. A strip along the sea is cultivated. Many of the inhabitants, who are largely Moslems, live under a tribal organization. Durazzo on the coast is an improved port with modern facilities.

Latvia. A republic of northern Europe, having a coast line on the eastern side of the Baltic Sea and on the Gulf of Riga. Latvia lies between Estonia on the north and Lithuania on the south with an eastern limit bordering on Russia and on Poland. Its surface, 24,800 square miles in area, is level for the most part and is dotted with lakes. It is drained by the Duna river.

The chief industries of Latvia are agriculture, stock raising, lumbering, and fishing. Flax, butter, and timber were the main exports before the war. Pulp and paper, fats and vegetable oils, electric power, and furniture are produced. Most Latvian industry is socialized and small peasant and agricultural laborers have been allotted over 2,300,000 acres of land formerly belonging to large estates. Marketing cooperatives are encouraged and a network of state-owned machine and horse-hiring stations are available to farmers.

A majority of Latvia's 1,950,000 (1946 est.) inhabitants are Protestants, although there is a strong Catholic minority. The only university is situated at Riga, the capital, largest city, and fast becoming largest port in the Soviet Union. Riga and the two other ports, Libau and Windau, are served by the main lines of three Russian railways. After a plebiscite, Latvia was admitted into the Soviet Union in 1940.

Lithuania (*lĭth'ū-ā'nĭ-ȧ*). A republic of northern Europe, bounded by Latvia, Poland, Germany, and the Baltic Sea. The chief river is the Nieman. The country, with an estimated area of 31,600 square miles in 1946, has extensive forests.

Prior to 1940, when admitted into the Soviet Union, about three-fourths of her people were engaged in agriculture. Since then she has been considerably industrialized. The chief products are grains, potatoes, flax fiber, cotton fabrics, woolens, linens, silk, leather, meat, and dairy products. Most of the industry is nationalized and small peasant and agricultural laborers have been allotted 1,500,000 acres of land formerly belonging to large estates. Marketing cooperatives are encouraged and a network of state-owned tractor and horse-hiring depots are available to farmers.

The population, estimated in 1946 at 2,879,000, is predominantly Roman Catholic. A university was opened in 1922 at Kaunas.

Monaco (*mŏn'ȧ-kō*). One of the smallest states in Europe. Monaco is a constitutional monarchy, lying in southeastern France and bordering on the Mediterranean Sea. The surface, eight square miles in area, is mountainous and highly picturesque. The chief occupation of the 27,000 (1947 est.) inhabitants is to provide accommodation and entertainment for the visitors who, in numbers exceeding 1,500,000 each year, are attracted by this famous winter resort and gambling center. Despite popular misconception, the famous Monte Carlo gambling casino now furnishes less than 10 per cent of revenues. While tourist trade remains of chief importance, local industries include making electrical appliances, radios, pharmaceuticals, and cosmetics.

Netherlands, The. A kingdom of northwestern Europe, roughly triangular in shape, with a northwestern coast line on the North Sea. The country, sometimes called Holland after the name of two of its provinces, borders on Belgium to the south and Germany on the east. No point in it is more than 120 miles from the sea, which forms more than one-half the total of its boundary. Its seacoast is 465 miles in length.

The surface of the Netherlands, 13,440 square miles in area, is, in large part, too low for natural drainage, portions of it being from 16 to 20 feet below the level of the sea. An estimated population of 9,630,000 in 1946 averages 716.5 inhabitants to the square mile, which makes the Netherlands the most densely populated country on the earth. Belgium ranks second.

The former Zuider Zee, a large shallow gulf, formed by an inundation from the sea in the 13th century, was cut off from the sea by dikes in 1932, in order to be drained to one-third its former size, leaving a lake, Ijsselmeer. This reclamation project is the largest ever undertaken anywhere in the world. It adds 523,000 acres of arable land to the Netherlands, nearly one-tenth the previous land surface.

Part of the coast is bordered by sand dunes, which keep out the sea from the lowlands. In other parts, artificial embankments, or dikes, are erected for that purpose. In the interior of the country, also, such dikes are used to enclose swampy land, from which the water is pumped by windmills, leaving the soil of these so-called "polders" available for cultivation.

The Netherlands has a network of river mouths through which the Rhine, the Meuse, and the Scheldt rivers discharge their waters. These rivers are supplemented as trade highways by some 2000 miles of canals, which, both in mileage and in utility, vie in importance with the railroads. More than 50,000 people live on barges which ply along the waterways.

The distinctive products of the Netherlands are cheese, butter, margarine, and flower bulbs. More than one-half of the land is arable. It produces among other crops, rye, oats, potatoes, sugar beets, flax, and barley. Dairying is one of the leading occupations of the country. The Holstein breed of cattle, developed first in Holland, is one of the best milk producing varieties in the world. Herring and oysters are the chief products of the deep-sea fisheries, which formerly constituted the foundation of the country's wealth. The industries include shipbuilding, tobacco products, and pottery, and the refining of sugar, cocoa, and chocolate. Much of the raw materials for the industries is obtained from the country's rich possessions, which cover an area more than 50 times as great as that of the Netherlands. The fleet of the Dutch merchant marine ranks fourth after the United States, Great Britain, and Norway.

The majority of the inhabitants are Protestants, but there is a strong Catholic minority. Both Churches, as well as the Jewish religious bodies, receive grants from the government. Illiteracy is virtually unknown. The educational system provides widely different kinds of training. There are four state universities. Amsterdam was formerly the capital and is still the scene of the royal coronation. The seat of government, however, is The Hague. The following table gives the chief cities with their population in 1947.

City	Population	City	Population
Amsterdam . .	806,162	Utrecht. . . .	185,164
Rotterdam . .	644,076	Haarlem . . .	156,989
The Hague . .	532,239	Eindhoven . .	134,080

Norway. A kingdom of northern Europe, occupying that portion of the Scandinavian peninsula which lies west and north of the ridge of the Kiolen mountains. The country extends 300 miles within the Arctic circle to a latitude farther north than that of any other part of the European mainland. Norway possesses as a dependency the Spitsbergen islands, a coal producing archipelago which is situated some 600 miles north of the country's northern extremity and stretches to a point about 650 miles from the north pole. The area of the archipelago is estimated at 25,000 square miles.

The surface of Norway, 124,556 square miles in area, is mountainous and, for the most part, barren. About one-fifth is covered with forests, mainly of pine and fir. The arable portion comprises a scant 4 per cent of the total area. The coast line is cut by deep, picturesque fiords, and is fringed by some 150,000 islands, the larger ones being in the north.

The climate is moderated by the warm ocean currents which flow past the coast. The Arctic coast settlement, Hammerfest, which is the most northern town in the world, has a mean winter temperature higher than that of New York. Numerous summer tourists visit the country, attracted by Norway's scenic beauty and by the spectacle of the "midnight sun." In the north, the sun never sets between the middle of May and the last of July.

The chief occupations of Norway's inhabitants are lumbering and fishing. Herring, cod, mackerel, salmon, whale, walrus, seal, and lobsters form the most valuable part of the catch. Ships from Norway carry on most of the whaling in the Antarctic. The merchant marine of Norway ranks, in tonnage, among the great commercial fleets of the world. The manufacturing industries of the country are largely dependent on water power, which is available in great abundance. The most important industrial products are pulp, paper, and chemicals.

The population of Norway, amounting to 3,123,883, is almost entirely Protestant in religion. The Lutheran Church is endowed by the state. Education is obligatory and illiteracy is almost unknown. The one university is situated in Oslo (289,000), the capital and largest city. Other cities include Bergen (107,957), Nidaros, former Trondhjem, and Stavanger.

Poland. A republic of central Europe, which was divided up by Germany and Russia in 1939, a portion also being assigned to Lithuania. The partition, however, was not recognized by Great Britain and France, which countries made war on Germany to prevent the conquest of Poland.

Poland covers an area of 121,131 square miles between Russia on the east and the Russian Zone of Germany on the west. It adjoins Czechoslovakia on the south and the Baltic Sea on the north. Apart from the Carpathian foothills in the south with a maximum elevation of 2000 feet, the surface is a gently undulating plain, most of which is drained northward by the Vistula river and its tributaries.

Poland was primarily an agricultural country, about 30 per cent of its surface being cultivated. The chief crops in the area are rye, potatoes, oats, wheat, barley, sugar beets, hemp, hops, and tobacco. There is considerable mineral wealth. Poland was the third largest coal producer in Europe. Other mineral products are petroleum, zinc, iron, and salt. The manufacture of linen and other textiles, of steel, and of paper and paper bags are the leading industries.

The people of Poland have exerted great effort to restore production in agriculture and industry, and to rebuild cities, railways, highways, and waterways, badly damaged during World War II. The country suffered the severe loss of 22 per cent of her population and 38 per cent of her national wealth. About 5 million Poles expelled from the eastern provinces annexed by the Soviet Union have settled in the west.

The population of Poland in the 1946 census was 23,622,334. Roman Catholicism is the prevailing religion, but there are strong minorities of Greek

Catholics, Jews, and Protestants. Three of Poland's six universities were founded prior to 1700. There are also a number of technical schools and academies for science and fine arts. The capital is Warsaw. Other cities of note are Gdansk (Danzig), Lodz, Poznan, and Krakow.

Portugal. A republic occupying the most western part of the Iberian peninsula and washed on the south and on the west by the Atlantic Ocean. On the land side, to the north and the east, Portugal adjoins Spain. The area of Portugal is given as 35,490 square miles, little more than half of which is productive.

The country is traversed from east to west near its center by the Tagus river, the estuary of which forms one of the best harbors in the world. North of the river, the surface is a mountainous plateau, which is crossed by the deep, gorgelike bed of the Douro river. On the left of the Tagus river, a plain stretches southward to an irregular group of mountains in the southwestern extremity of the country. Between this group and a mountain ridge on the eastern border, the Guadiana river, rising in Spain, flows south to the Atlantic Ocean.

About 26 per cent of Portugal's surface is forested, mainly with pines, chestnuts, oaks, and cork trees. Cork is one of the chief sources of the national wealth. The acorns of the oak forests serve to fatten large herds of swine. The central part of the country produces enormous amounts of grapes, from which is made port wine, so called from Oporto, its point of export. In the south, olives, figs, oranges, lemons, and other tropical fruits are grown. Products of the fisheries—sardines and tunny fish—form, next to wines, the principal article of export. The mineral wealth is considerable but is inadequately developed. Wolfram, iron, copper, manganese, antimony, lead, tin, and gold are found. A characteristic industry is the manufacture of porcelain tiles. The chief manufactures are textile products.

The population of Portugal is 7,722,152. There is freedom of worship, but Roman Catholicism prevails almost to the exclusion of any other religion. Elementary education is compulsory and, since Portugal became a republic in 1910, has been rigorously enforced. There are three universities and several schools of technology and of art. The two principal cities are Lisbon—the capital—and Oporto. Portugal has a treaty of alliance with England, which, dating from 1703, is the oldest existing alliance in European history.

Rumania. A republic of southeastern Europe with an eastern coast line on the Black Sea. Russia is its immediate neighbor to the north; Hungary and Yugoslavia, to the west; and Bulgaria, to the south. The area of the country is 91,671 square miles.

Rumania is divided into an eastern and a western part by the Carpathian mountains, which, in Rumania, trend south and southwest. This ridge is often known as the Transylvanian Alps, and the western part of the country is known as Transylvania. The remainder of the country is a plain drained by the Danube. This river has 595 miles of its course in Rumania and along the southern border. After being joined by the Pruth, its great tributary from the north, the Danube empties through several mouths into the Black Sea. Navigation on the Danube according to the peace treaty of 1947 is free and open to all countries on an equal footing.

About four-fifths of the inhabitants of Rumania support themselves by stock raising and by agriculture of the usual temperate zone type, corn and wheat being the leading crops. Rumania is, next to Russia, the most important oil producing country of Europe. Other minerals obtained are lignite, coal, iron, copper, and salt, the mining of the last being a government monopoly. Flour milling, brewing, and distilling are the chief industrial interests. Apart from oil, the leading exports are grain, salt, coal, timber, and hides. In 1947 Rumania's transport services, oil, industry, and entire export-import trade were taken over by Soviet-controlled agencies.

The predominant religion of Rumania's 16,472,000 (1946 est.) people is Greek Catholic. More than half the population is illiterate. There are four universities in the country. Bucuresti (Bucharest) is the capital and largest city ot Rumania. Other cities of importance include Iasi (Jassy), Galati (Galatz), and Cluj.

Russia. The largest country in the world, occupying nearly half the total area of Europe and the whole northern portion of Asia. Including its Asiatic territory, Russia covers an area of 8,708,900 square miles, of which about 2,500,000 are in Europe. Officially known as the Union of Soviet Socialist Republics (U.S.S.R.) it is divided into the Russian Socialist Federated Soviet Republic (R.S.F.S.R.), which occupies about 78 per cent of the entire country, and fifteen other republics, of which seven are in Europe and eight in Asia.

The areas and population of the constituent republics as estimated in 1946 were as follows:

Republic	Area in sq. miles	Population
RSFSR*	6,609,000	109,279,000
Ukranian	225,200	38,500,000
White Russia (Byclorussia)	81,000	10,400,000
Karelo-Finnish	69,700	900,000
Moldavia	13,200	2,200,000
Estonia	17,600	1,120,000
Latvia	24,800	1,950,000
Lithuania	31,600	2,879,000
Azerbaijan	33,500	3,209,000
Georgia	37,500	3,542,000
Armenia	11,600	1,282,000
Turkoman	189,400	1,254,000
Uzbek	159,200	6,282,500
Tajik	55,700	1,485,000
Kazakh	1,072,000	6,146,000
Kirghiz	76,900	1,460,000
Total	8,708,900	191,888,500

*The first republic listed, the RSFSR, includes territory in Europe and Asia. The next 7 listed are in Europe. The last 8 are in Asia.

In 1939 and 1940 the U.S.S R. acquired territory from Finland, Poland, and Rumania and incorporated the three Baltic republics, with a total area of about 175,000 square miles and a population of 22,730,000.

The surface of European Russia is a vast rolling plain, which rises, in the Ural mountains on the east, to an altitude of about 8000 feet and, at Mount Elbruz in the Caucasus range, to a maximum height of 18,465 feet. Almost the whole surface, however, is less than 600 feet above the sea.

Extreme cold in winter and extreme heat in summer constitute a general characteristic of Russia's climate. The Valdai hills in the west central part of the country form the chief watershed and give rise to the Don, the Dnieper, and the Volga, all flowing southward. The Dvina, the Neva, and the Volkhof are the most important rivers of northern drainage. The Volga river is navigable for 1800 miles. Canals join the principal rivers, making a system of navigable waterways having a total length of about 60,000 miles. The northern region abounds in lakes of glacial formation. Lake Ladoga near the border of Finland, with an area of 7000 square miles, is the largest lake in Europe.

Until the last few years predominantly an agricultural country, Russia is now one of the leading nations of the world both in industry and in agriculture. Production is on a socialistic basis. That is to say, productive enterprises are publicly owned, although the prevailing pattern in agriculture is the large co-operative farm.

Russia is the world's largest producer of wheat, barley, rye, and flax, and one of the largest producers of oats. Other important crops are hemp, sugar beets, rice, cotton, tea, and tobacco. The richest soil lies in the so-called black earth belt, which extends from the Carpathian mountains through the Ukraine in southern Russia to the borders of China. This is by far the greatest single wheat growing land on the face of the globe. In production of farm animals, Russia vies with the United States for the first place.

Approximately 80 per cent of the country's output consists of industrial products. No country of the world has so rapidly become industrialized as the Soviet Union. New industries were created, involving many plants the largest of their kind in the world and often calling for the erection of entirely new cities.

Examples are Magnitogorsk for the manufacture of steel at Magnet mountain, one of the world's richest iron ore deposits; Dnieprostroy, where Europe's largest hydroelectric station is erected for supplying current to aluminum, ferroalloy, coke, and cement plants; and Azbest, where the world's largest asbestos mine is in operation. Production of tractors is centralized in Stalingrad and Chelyabinsk. Russia is one of the world's largest producers of petroleum, which comes mainly from the Baku district. Among the older centers of industry are Leningrad, which produces chemicals, matches, and rubber products; Kharkov, which, being close to the Donetz coal basin and large iron ore deposits, is a leading center of heavy industry; and Moscow, where the textile and publishing industries are located.

From the forests of the north come lumber, pulp, tar, turpentine, resin, and fur. Russia is the world's largest exporter of lumber. There are important fisheries in the Arctic Ocean and in the seas. The fisheries of the Volga river and of the Caspian Sea supply most of the sturgeon, whose eggs are salted and made into Russian caviar. From the Ural mountains come asbestos and platinum. Here, too, is produced gold, making Russia a rival of South Africa as the world's chief source of the yellow metal. One of the chief sources of manganese is southern Russia, where there are also very rich deposits of coal and of iron. Copper is mined in the north.

The population of Russia is 191,888,500. All forms of religion are permitted in Russia, but atheism is officially encouraged. Following the revolution in 1917, an ambitious and comprehensive system of education was inaugurated. Education is compulsory. It has a pronounced socialistic trend and is closely correlated with industrial needs. Marriage and divorce depend solely on the consent of the parties. A characteristic Russian utensil is the samovar, used for making tea. The capital and largest city of Russia is Moscow. Other large cities of European Russia are Leningrad, Kiev, Odessa, Kharkov, Rostov, Dnepropetrovsk, Saratov, and Gorki.

See also *Russia in Asia*.

Spain. A country in southwestern Europe, occupying about four-fifths of the Iberian peninsula. It is separated from France on the northeast by the Pyrenees mountains and, in the southwestern part of the peninsula, surrounds Portugal on the land side. Spain is otherwise bounded by the Atlantic Ocean and the Mediterranean Sea, which are connected, at the southern extremity of the country, by the Strait of Gibraltar. Spain has an area of 189,890 square miles. It extends north and south 540 miles and, east and west, about 620 miles.

Next to Switzerland, Spain has the most elevated surface in continental Europe. Most of the interior is a table-land varying from 2000 to 3000 feet above the sea level. It is divided irregularly by low mountain ranges, of which the Cantabrian mountains parallel the northern seacoast, the Sierra Nevada range skirts the Mediterranean coast, and the Sierra Morena trend east and west in the interior. Of Spain's rivers, the Douro, the Tagus, and the Guadiana have their mouths in Portugal. The Guadalquivir flows east and south into the Atlantic Ocean, while the Jucar and the Ebro empty into the Mediterranean Sea. The Guadalquivir and the Ebro are the only rivers which admit of navigation.

In the interior, the rainfall is light, and the climate is harsh, with cold winters and hot summers. The northern coast has the heaviest rainfall in Europe, and the southern coast has the warmest winter climate of any part of the continent. About one-sixth of the acreage is under forest, the more characteristic trees being the Spanish chestnut and the cork oak.

The leading occupations of the people are agriculture, grazing, fruit culture, mining, fishing, and manufacturing. Cereal crops are raised especially in the north and include, in order of importance, wheat, barley, rye, corn, and oats. Huge flocks of sheep and of goats graze on the dry, treeless plateau, where esparto grass is a characteristic type of vegetation. From this plant, rope and paper are made. In the southern part, which is known as Andalusia, grapes, oranges, olives, figs, peaches, dates, almonds, and other fruits and nuts are grown in abundance.

Spain is one of the chief wine producing countries of Europe. Mulberries are cultivated as a food for silkworms. Valencia in the south is the chief center of the Spanish silk industry. Raisins form a considerable item of export. Saffron and licorice are distinctive products of the region.

The mineral resources of Spain are among the richest in Europe, but are inadequately exploited. Iron ore is extensively exported. Spain is the chief European source of lead. Coal, copper, mercury, salt, zinc, tin, and potash are produced in important quantities. With the exception of steel and textiles, there are no important manufacturing industries. The country is deficient in petroleum. One of the chief products is cork, made from the bark of the cork oaks. The fisheries employ over 100,000, the chief catches being sardines, tunny fish, and cod. Oranges, olive oil, wines and cognacs, preserved fruits and fish, and almonds are among the chief exports.

The population of Spain is 27,246,000, practically all of whom are adherents of the Roman Catholic Church. The Basques, living near the head of the Bay of Biscay and numbering about 400,000, are believed to be descendants of a pre-Aryan people known to the Romans under the name of Iberians. Spain has also some 50,000 gypsies. Elementary education is compulsory. There are 12 universities. The capital and largest city is Madrid. Other important urban centers are Barcelona, Valencia, Seville, Malaga, Saragossa, Murcia, Bilbao, and Granada.

Spain was formerly one of the chief centers of Roman civilization. Bullfighting, the most popular national diversion, is a survival of the ancient Roman wild beast shows.

Sweden. A kingdom of northern Europe, occupying the eastern and larger part of the Scandinavian peninsula. The country is 950 miles long and tapers to a blunt point at the north and at the south. It is bounded on the west by Norway and the Kattegat, and, on the east, by the Baltic Sea, the Gulf of Bothnia, and Finland. Its average width is about 190 miles, and its surface covers 173,206 square miles. The country includes many adjacent islands, the largest being Gottland and Oland.

Sweden is mountainous in the west, but the remainder of the country is flat. Most of the rivers are fed by lakes at the base of the Kiolen mountains, which form the greater part of the Norwegian boundary. Toward the south, four large lakes occur, — Väner, Vätter, Mälar, and Hjälmar, — of which Lake Väner is the third largest in Europe. The first two are part of the Göta Canal system, which, giving access between the Baltic Sea and the Kattegat forms one of the chief arteries of Swedish commerce. The climate of Sweden is cold in winter and hot in summer, the other seasons being very short.

The most southern part of the country, known as Götaland, is the richest agricultural and industrial region and is the center of the shipping interests. North of Götaland lies Svealand, the center of the political and intellectual life of the country. Norrland, stretching to the northern extremity of Sweden, furnishes minerals and timber.

About one-half of the population of Sweden is supported by agriculture. Roots, hay, oats, and rye are the leading crops. Timber is one of the chief sources of Sweden's wealth, and the lumber and pulp wood manufactures hold the leading place among the industries. The iron of Sweden is of a particularly high grade. Rich gold mines at Boliden, in northern Sweden, began production about 1930. Manganese, lead, silver, copper, and zinc are also mined. The industries suffer from lack of coal, being compelled to utilize charcoal or hydro-electric power. The output of numerous manufactured goods has steadily increased.

The population of Sweden is 6,673,956. Lutheran Protestantism is the established form of religion. There is an excellent system of education, at the head of which are two universities. Illiteracy is almost unknown. The capital and largest city is Stockholm. Other cities of note are Göteborg and Malmö.

Switzerland. A mountainous inland republic of south central Europe, bounded on the north and east by Germany and Austria, on the west by France, and on the south by Italy. The surface of Switzerland, 15,940 square miles in area, has a greater average elevation than any other European country and contains the headwaters of four great European river systems,—the Rhine, the Rhone, the Po, and the Danube.

The northwestern half of the country is a rolling plateau hedged, near the northwestern border, by the Jura mountains. It drains northward toward the Rhine river and contains the lakes of Neuchatel, Bienne, Zurich, Lucerne, Thun, and Constance. The southeastern half is a region of picturesque mountains that has long been famous for its scenic beauty. The Southern Alps form much of the southern border of the country. Here are found the highest mountains, including Monte Rosa, 15,217 feet in height; Matterhorn, a towering pyramid of solid rock 14,782 feet high; Simplon, with an elevation of 11,117; Saint Bernard, 8110 feet high, near which the Saint Bernard breed of dogs was developed, the animals being used to help in the rescue of travelers lost in the snow. This range descends on the north to the valley in which the Rhone river rises and, flowing westward, broadens into Switzerland's largest body of water, the Lake of Geneva. At the southeastern border lies Lake Maggiore, which has a southern drainage into the Po river.

South of the Rhone valley rise the irregular Burnese Alps, the highest peak of which is the Jungfrau, "The Maiden," so called from the blush which suffuses its snowy peak at sundown. Its height is 13,670 feet.

The mountains of Switzerland are cut by some 40 passes, and over 1000 glaciers furrow the rocky slopes. The mountains are burrowed by several railroad tunnels, that at Mount Simplon, 12½ miles in length, being one of the longest in the world. A warm wind, known as the foehn, often, by rapidly melting the snow and ice, causes avalanches.

Partly as a protection against avalanches, the forests of the country, covering about one-sixth of the republic's area, are carefully guarded by the government. Maples, oaks, and chestnuts flourish at the lower levels. Higher up occur birches, and still higher, firs, pines, and larches. In this region, the characteristic alpine animals, the chamois and the ibex, may be seen. The edelweiss and certain other flowering plants grow almost as far up the mountain side as the summer snow line.

Switzerland is the third most highly industrialized country in Europe. Agriculture and dairying rank next as occupations of the inhabitants. Grapes, rye, barley, potatoes, oats, flax, hemp, and tobacco are grown in the valleys and on the plains, while the mountain sides provide abundant pasturage for cattle, goats, horses, and sheep. Swiss cheese forms, along with Swiss clocks, watches, and Swiss chocolate, one of the more distinctive products of the country. Machinery, textiles, clothing, chemicals, metals, and watches are the industries that employ the greatest number of people. The entertainment of tourists is one of the major industries.

The inhabitants of Switzerland, 4,265,703 in number, are a unit neither in race, language, nor religion. German, French, and Italian are spoken. Illiteracy, however, is virtually nonexistent. The Protestants are slightly more numerous than the Catholics. Higher education is cared for by seven universities, that at Zurich dating from 1460. A distinctive type of dwelling is used in Switzerland, known as the chalet. It has a projecting roof under which are placed balconies and staircases.

Bern is the capital and Zurich is the largest city. Geneva was the capital of the League of Nations.

Turkey. The European territory of Turkey consists of the territory north of the Sea of Marmora extending to the borders of Bulgaria and of Greece. It includes Adrianople and Istanbul, formerly Constantinople. Istanbul is treated among the cities of Europe, but the geography of Turkey is dealt with under *Asia*, page 811.

Yugoslavia (*yōō'gō-släv'ĭ-ȧ*). A republic of southern Europe with a southwestern coast line on the Adriatic Sea. On the land side, the country adjoins Italy, Austria, Hungary, Rumania, Bulgaria, Greece, and Albania. Its area is 98,426 square miles. In the peace treaty of 1947, Yugoslavia gained the state of Venezia Giulia plus the enclave of Zara and the islands of Cherso, Lussino, Pelagosa, and Pagosta at the expense of Italy. Trieste was made a free territory under United Nations control.

Much of the coast is rocky and precipitous, rising inland to a mountainous plateau covering the western and southern part of the country. The eastern portion of the country contains a southern spur from the Carpathian mountains. The greater part of the surface is drained toward the east and the north by the Drave, the Save, and the Morava river, which empty into the Danube. The Danube river, traversing the northern part of Yugoslavia and forming part of the country's Rumanian boundary, cuts through the eastern mountain barrier at the Iron Gate. The Iron Gate is a mountain pass through which the river formerly rushed over a plateau of rock 1400 feet wide. This point has been made navigable by extensive blasting at a cost of more than ten million dollars. The river valleys provide most of the country's arable land. Nearly one-half of the surface of Yugoslavia is covered with forest. Lumber leads the exports. The chief minerals are coal, lignite, iron, copper, lead, zinc, gold, salt, chromium, and antimony.

The most important industry is agriculture. The chief crops are wheat, corn, potatoes, barley, oats, sugar beets, tobacco, and temperate zone fruits. Silk culture employs many people. Large numbers of swine are fattened on the beech nuts and the acorns of the wooded land, while cattle and sheep graze on the higher mountain slopes. Flour milling, sugar refining, carpet weaving, tanning, and pottery are the most important industries. One of the largest wood distilling factories of Europe is located at Teslic. State ownership and control characterize the nation's postwar economic and agricultural systems.

The inhabitants of Yugoslavia, numbering 14,500,000, are divided among three chief forms of religion, Greek Catholic, Roman Catholic and Moslem. There are three universities. Belgrade is the capital and largest city.

CITIES AND OTHER POINTS OF TRAVEL INTEREST

The cities of Europe are distinguished by the richness of their historic associations, and, in many cases, by the wealth of their artistic adornment. Some of them, such as Athens and Rome, still preserve the visible evidences of the brilliant civilization which flourished in the southern part of the continent as early as 600 B. C. In others, the remains of outstanding interest are medieval structures—sublime cathedrals, or castles and dungeons of more sinister memories. Cities of southern Spain tell of Mohammedan enterprise; those of Italy remind us of the flowering of art known as the Renaissance; while the industrial cities of northern Europe often afford a curious blending of old interests and of new.

Greater local security and changed methods of warfare are reflected in the crumbling walls which in some cities still remain standing. In others, bulwarks, no longer necessary for defense, have been replaced by boulevards encircling the older parts of the cities.

The scenic beauties of Europe are not only grand in themselves but have the prestige that comes from centuries of description by travelers. The Alps have given us the term alpine, applicable to mountainous scenery of impressive beauty. The natural charm of the pleasure resorts is supplemented by all the attractions that can be suggested by ingenuity aiming to please vast numbers of tourists. The more noteworthy of these resorts are described in the following section, along with the cities and other places of especial interest on the continent.

In many instances, a city is known in English by a name different from that used by the inhabitants of the country in which it is located. In all such cases, the native name is given in bold-face type in parenthesis after the name commonly used by English speaking people.

Alps. An irregular mountain system of south central Europe, occupying most of Switzerland and parts of France, Italy, Austria, and Germany. The system is 600 miles in length and has a width varying from 75 to 150 miles. It covers an area of about 85,000 square miles. The highest point is reached by Mont Blanc, 15,781 feet high. Other notable peaks with their heights are Monte Rosa, 15,217; Mischabel, 14,935; Lyskamm, 14,889; Weisshorn, 14,804; Matterhorn, 14,782; Dent Blanche, 14,318; Grand Combin, 14,164; Finsteraarhorn, 14,026; Aletschhorn, 13,803; and Jungfrau, 13,670.

The glaciers of the Alps number about 1200 and cover an area of 1600 square miles. The largest, called the Aletsch, has an area of 50 square miles. Other well-known Alpine glaciers are the Unteraar, the Gorner, the Viesch, the Mer de Glace, and the Miage, the last two being on Mont Blanc. The glaciers give rise to a number of mountain lakes, several of which have become proverbial for their beauty. The chief ones are Lucerne, Geneva, Como, Garda, and Maggiore. Water is often drawn from the bottoms of Alpine lakes to secure an all-year flow for developing electric power.

The Alps are cut by many passes, of which the more important are the Great Saint Bernard pass; the Brenner pass, through which a railroad has been constructed; and Simplon, Saint Gotthard, and Mont Cenis, at each of which the mountain is pierced by a railroad tunnel.

In addition to these four railroads, which cross the Alps, numerous lines run to scenic points in the mountains. Many of the Alpine automobile roads are marvels of engineering skill. The Swiss Alps and the Tyrol, a picturesque district partly in Austria and partly in Italy, are among the most popular regions. The accessibility of the more beautiful parts of the ranges and the facilities provided for ease and comfort in travel combine to make the Alps the most attractive region of the world for the lover of mountain scenery. See *Switzerland*.

Amiens (F. *ȧ'myăɴ'*; E. *ăm'ĭ-ĕnz*). A cathedral city of northern France, lying about 80 miles north of Paris. The Cathedral of Amiens, for magnificence and for richness of decoration, is not surpassed by any other Gothic building of the world. The city has important textile manufacturing interests and is widely known by tourists for its macaroons. During the World War, Amiens was made the headquarters of the British armies in France. Population, 1946, 84,774.

Amsterdam. The largest city and the statutory capital of the Netherlands, although the actual seat of government is The Hague. Amsterdam occupies a low site at the southwestern extremity of the Ijsselmeer and is connected with tidewater by the North Sea canal. The numerous canals, which divide the city into some 90 islands connected by almost 300 bridges, have given rise to the city's characterization as "the Venice of the North." Amsterdam's defenses consist of dikes, by the opening of which the whole district may be flooded.

The city is named after a dam built in 1240 across the river Amstel. Part of the site originally occupied by this dam is now the central square of the city and is called the Dam. From it the principal streets radiate in a semicircle. Near by stand the New Church and the Royal Palace. In the former, a Gothic structure dating from 1408, the sovereigns of the Netherlands are crowned. The Royal Palace, belonging to the city, is the residence of the country's sovereigns when they are guests of Amsterdam. The Ryks, or State Museum, contains a number of paintings by Rembrandt, who, with the philosopher Spinoza, was among Amsterdam's most famous citizens. The city maintains a municipal abattoir, theater, pawnshop, and museum.

Amsterdam is the chief center of Dutch industry, commerce, and finance. Its diamond cutting factories are the largest in the world. There are also shipbuilding yards, sugar and oil refineries, and factories for making dyes, chemicals, glass, liquor, tobacco and steel products. The city has an extensive trade in the tropical products which come from the Dutch East Indies. The bank of the Netherlands, situated in Amsterdam, is one of the leading financial institutions of Europe. The city is the seat of the University of Amsterdam and is the headquarters of the National Academy of Arts, the Royal Academy of Sciences, and the Royal Dutch Geographic Society. Amsterdam's botanical gardens are among the foremost in Europe. Population, 1947, 798,358.

Antwerp (Antwerpen). A large city of Belgium, situated on the Scheldt river about 50 miles from its mouth in the North Sea. The river, 2200 feet wide at this point, provides Antwerp with one of the best harbors in the world. By means of 28 miles of quays, 3½ miles being granite and equipped with all modern appliances, the port handles merchandise often exceeding an annual total of one billion dollars. Besides its commerce, Antwerp is important for diamond cutting, sugar refining, and the manufacture of liquors, textiles, and cigars. Urban traffic is facilitated by two tunnels under the Scheldt river.

The most conspicuous building in the city is the Cathedral of Notre Dame, the construction of which was begun in the 14th century. It has a tower 400 feet high and contains three celebrated paintings by Rubens, whose tomb is contained in the splendid Church of Saint James. The richly decorated town hall was built in the 16th century. The art gallery contains a priceless collection of masterpieces by Rubens and Van Dyck, the latter having been born in the city. The Steen, part of an old castle dating from the 10th century, was formerly the seat of the Inquisition, but is now used as an archeological museum. Fine boulevards follow the line of the old city walls.

The city has had a stormy history. Founded in the 8th century, it had become, by the 16th century, the financial center of Europe and one of the chief commercial cities of the world. It was destroyed by the Spaniards in 1576. Napoleon revived the city. By improving its harbor, he hoped eventually to make Antwerp a rival of London. In 1914, its fortifications were considered among the strongest in Europe, but the German forces, attacking with heavy artillery, experienced little difficulty in taking the city. Population, 1946 est., 259,622.

Appian (*ăp'ĭ-ăn*) **Way.** A Roman road running from Rome to Brindisi in southern Italy, 446 miles. Begun in 312 B. C. by Appius Claudius as a public work, it is still in use over a considerable portion of its course. For several miles from Rome it is bordered by ancient tombs and the ruins of monumental buildings.

Arcadia. An inland district of the peninsula of Morea in Greece. Its ancient inhabitants long retained their primitive customs, unaffected by the Dorians who invaded the peninsula in the 12th century B. C. A pastoral poetry arose there in the last centuries of the pre-Christian era and gave support to a literary tradition, which represented Arcadia as a land of primitive simplicity and idyllic happiness.

Argonne Forest. A rocky wooded area northwest of Verdun in northeastern France. It was the scene, in September and October 1918, of one of the bloodiest battles ever waged by American troops. The capture of this forest by the Americans threatened the line of retreat of the German army.

ATHENS (Athēnai). The capital and largest city of Greece, situated in the southeastern portion of the country about five miles from the port of Piræus on the eastern shore of the Gulf of Ægina. The city stands in a plain surrounded on three sides by mountains. Athens is a financial, railroad, and commercial city of importance, but its industrial interests center chiefly in Piræus, where there are establishments for manufacturing cotton, flour, leather, chemicals, and rugs. Near Piræus lies Phalerum, the sea resort of Athens. Athens is named after Athena, the ancient Greek goddess of wisdom.

THE MODERN CITY. For several centuries following 500 B. C., Athens was the intellectual and artistic center of the civilized world and, architecturally, was one of the most beautiful cities on the earth. After many centuries of misfortunes, it was finally reduced to a Turkish village. When, in 1832, Greece became independent, Athens was chosen its capital and was rebuilt as a modern city.

The Square of Harmony forms a center from which radiate wide boulevards, two of them ending in Constitution square—the site of the royal palace and gardens. Between the two squares stand the government offices, the buildings of the Academy of Sciences, the National university, the National library, and the archeological colleges. Other notable modern structures include the Parliament buildings, the Palace of Justice, and the National Archeological Museum, the last housing a priceless collection of Greek antiquities. The city contains also the University of Athens, a beautiful library known as the Gennadeion, and the impressive Temple of Youth, headquarters of the Greek Y.M.C.A. There is a large stadium, in which the Olympic games were held in 1896.

The white marble, which is used in most of the public edifices, imparts to the city's architecture a distinctive and impressive brilliancy. The marble used in the ancient buildings has, through age, become tinged with a russet hue.

ANCIENT BUILDINGS. The ancient city centered about a flat-topped hill, called the Acropolis. This hill is surrounded by a wall and contains four beautiful structures: the Propylæa, a building of mixed Doric and Ionic style, which serves as a stately entrance to the enclosure; the Temple of Victory, a small Ionic edifice beside the Propylæa; the Parthenon, which is the classic example of a pure Doric temple and is justly famed as one of the world's most beautiful buildings; and, finally, the Erechtheum, known best for its Porch of the Maidens, in which the columns take the form of Greek maidens, often called Caryatids. These four buildings were all erected in the 5th century B. C., but they still preserve much of their original impressiveness. The Parthenon was partially restored in 1930.

The chief of the ancient buildings outside the Acropolis are the arch of Hadrian, the Theseum, the open-air theater of Dionysus, the Temple of Zeus, the Tower of the Winds, and the monument of Lysicrates, the last being the earliest extant example of the Corinthian style. The Theseum is the best preserved of the ancient Greek structures. Of the 104 Corinthian columns of the Temple of Zeus, each of them 56 feet in height, only 15 remain erect today.

These ruined structures are the original models for the Greek style of architecture as it has been revived in recent times and employed in the erection of many modern buildings. Excavations are going forward continuously, the most stupendous project being that for unearthing the ancient Agora. Population of Athens, 1947 est., 1,000,000.

Athos (*ăth'ŏs*). A mountain of northern Greece, 6350 feet high, occupying the extremity of a peninsula in the northern part of the Ægean Sea. In ancient times it was noted as the scene of the shipwreck of Xerxes' fleet, which sailed to attack Greece in 492 B. C. Since the 9th century A. D., the mountain has been occupied by a group of fortified monasteries, now 20 in number. The control of the mountain was handed over by the Byzantine emperors to the monasteries, which have continued to exercise their rights of self-government to the present day. Under a constitution dated in 1045 A. D., women and female animals are excluded from the holy mountain. The monks, numbering 4800, support themselves by agriculture, fishing, and various handicrafts.

Avignon (*ȧ'vē'nyôɴ'*). A town of southeastern France, situated on the Rhone river about 30 miles from the Mediterranean Sea. Avignon is notable as the former residence of the popes, who made it their seat from 1309 to 1376. The city is built on a wall-girdled height, from the summit of which rise the cathedral and the impressive mass of the old papal palace. Population, 1946, 59,982.

Barcelona. The chief manufacturing center and, with the exception of Madrid, the largest city of Spain, located near the northeastern extremity of the country on the Mediterranean Sea. The city has a fine harbor and ranks as the second seaport in Spain. It is the commercial center of a rich fruit growing district. The chief manufactures are cotton, silk, and woolen goods, lace, leather, machinery, furniture, dyes, soaps, and drugs. Fruit, wine, olive oil, as well as manufactured goods, are among its exports.

The city dates from the 3d century B. C., when it was founded by the Carthaginian Hamilcar Barca, after whom it was called Barcino. From the 2d century A. D., the city has, in spite of varying fortunes, remained one of the chief commercial cities of southern Europe.

The older part of the city was formerly surrounded by walls, which have since been replaced by promenades. This section has, in general, narrow, irregular streets. Its chief thoroughfare, however, the Ramblas, which connects it with the "new town," has a handsome promenade on which are situated many of the principal buildings of the city, including one of the finest theaters in Spain. At the highest point of the Ramblas stands a famous 13th century cathedral in Spanish Gothic style. The "new town" is regularly laid out and has all modern improvements. Among the more recent buildings is the terminal station, one of the finest in Europe. The chief educational institution is the University of Barcelona. Population, 1947, 1,133,345.

Belfast. The capital and metropolis of Northern Ireland, situated on a small inlet in the northeastern part of the island. The city has an excellent harbor and contains immense shipyards, in which most of the White Star liners have been built. In addition to the linen textile industry, the manufacturing interests include the making of rope, liquors, tobacco goods, machine shop products, flour, and chemicals.

Belfast was incorporated as a city in 1888. It is the seat of Queen's university and Campbell college and has several fine churches, an art gallery, and a museum. Population, 1937, 438,086.

Belgrade (*bĕl'grād'*) (**Beograd**). The capital and largest city of Yugoslavia, situated near the center of the country's northeastern boundary at the confluence of the Save and the Danube river. Belgrade is an important railway junction and is the chief trade center of the country. The city is modern in appearance and has several institutions for higher education, including a university, a national library, a museum, and an academy of sciences. There are several fine Greek Catholic churches. Prior to its capture by the Austrians on Oct. 9, 1915, Belgrade was the capital of Serbia. Population, 1946 est., 500,000.

Belleau (*bĕl'ō'*) **Woods.** A forest of northeastern France, 5 miles northwest of Chateau Thierry and about 42 miles east of Paris. It is celebrated for a bitterly contested battle waged there in June 1918, when American marines and regulars dislodged a strongly entrenched German force and captured the village of Bouresches, 2 miles south of the woods. The battle ground was dedicated in 1923 as a permanent memorial to the Americans who fell there. It was named Bois de la Brigade de Marine.

Bergen (*bûr'gĕn*). A seaport and codfish market on the southwestern coast of Norway. Bergen's fish exports are nearly half those of all Norway. The chief manufactures are ships, paper, and ropes. The buildings include a naval academy, an observatory, and a fishery museum. The city maintains a noted marine biological station and is annually the scene of an international fishermen's fair. Bergen was the birthplace of Edvard Grieg, the musician. Population, 1946, 107,957.

BERLIN. The capital of Germany and the largest city of continental Europe both in area and population. It is somewhat northeast of the geographical center of the country, having a central location between the Elbe and the Oder river, with both of which it is connected by canals. The city is 177 miles southeast of Hamburg by rail and is connected with the Baltic port of Stettin by a barge canal. The Spree river flows through the city, which has an area of 340 square miles.

COMMERCE AND INDUSTRY. Berlin has grown, in the past half century, with a rapidity exceeded by few other cities of the world. It is the distributing point for a vast inland trade, being served by 12 trunk railroads and several waterways. The more important industries include cloth printing and the manufacture of locomotives, machinery, and other steel products, of electrical apparatus, dynamos, dyestuffs, porcelain, musical instruments, railroad cars, toys, bronzes, women's clothing, and liquors.

MUNICIPAL IMPROVEMENTS. Berlin maintains an employment agency, a savings bank, and a pawnshop, has free hospitals and public bathing establishments, and owns the gas plant and the water system. Sewage is conveyed by pressure pipes to the country in order to fertilize the soil of farms belonging to the city. Municipal meat markets supply the retail market with meat, which comes, duly inspected, from the municipal stockyards and slaughterhouses.

STREETS, BUILDINGS, AND MONUMENTS. Berlin is essentially a modern city. Streets regularly laid out and flanked by handsome residences combine with numerous squares, parks, playgrounds, monuments, fashionable promenades, and splendid public buildings to render Berlin one of the most imposing cities of the world.

Berlin's most famous boulevard is Unter den Linden, so called from the double rows of lime, or linden, trees with which it is adorned. The street is 196 feet wide and leads from the former imperial palace, with its 600 rooms, to the Brandenburg Gate. The latter is a triumphal arch, built in imitation of the Propylæa at Athens and surmounted by a colossal bronze car of victory. On the boulevard is situated, among many other impressive buildings, the palace of William I, opposite which stands a celebrated equestrian statue of Frederick the Great. The Brandenburg Gate leads into the Tiergarten, a magnificent park of 600 acres, which contains one of the largest zoological gardens in the world. Wilhelmstrasse, a continuation of Unter den Linden, passes the Nazi Chancellery, administrative center of Germany and perhaps the city's most imposing structure. The Lutheran cathedral, der Dom, has a dome rising 380 feet above the street. The Reichstag building, erected in the Italian Renaissance style is surmounted by a huge glass dome. Other noteworthy buildings include the National Gallery and the Royal Theater, both built in the Greek style of architecture.

Educational Institutions. Berlin is the chief intellectual center of Germany. The University of Berlin, founded in 1810, has numbered among its teachers Hegel, Fichte, Grimm, Niebuhr, Lipsius, Mommsen, and Einstein. Besides numerous technical institutions, there are free astronomical observatories, academies of art and of music, public libraries, botanical gardens, and many learned societies. The royal library contains over 1,000,000 volumes. Population, 1946, 3,180,383.

Bern. The capital and fourth largest city of Switzerland. The city is in the northwestern part of the republic and is picturesquely situated on a rocky bluff surrounded on three sides by the river Aar, a tributary of the Rhine. The name Bern is a corruption of the German word for bears, a number of the animals having been slain on the site when Bern was founded in 1191. A den of tame bears is maintained by the city, which has adopted the bear as its emblem.

Bern is noted for its manufacture of toys, engines, scientific instruments, and chocolate. It is the center of the international postal, telegraphic, railroad and copyright associations. The chief edifices are the magnificent Parliament building and a Gothic cathedral begun in 1421 but not completed until 1894. Population, 1941, 130,331.

Bingen (*bĭng'ĕn*). A town on the west bank of the Rhine river in Germany, 17 miles west of Mainz. Like many other towns on the Rhine, it has several picturesque ruins of feudal castles, the most notable of which is the Mouse Tower. This tower stands on a rock in the mid-channel of the river. In it, Archbishop Hatto is said to have been devoured by mice in 969 A. D. The Bingenloch, a famous whirlpool, is found a short distance down the river. Population, 1925, 9146.

Birmingham. The second largest city of England, situated near the geographic center of the country. Being in close proximity to rich coal fields and large iron deposits, it was known for its iron products as early as the 16th century, and it has since become famous for its steel manufactures. Other industrial products include glass, jewelry, chemicals, automobiles, railroad cars, plated articles, pins, and hydraulic presses.

Birmingham has led the cities of England in municipal improvements. There are 17 parks and recreation grounds. An excellent school system provides elementary education, while museums, libraries, art galleries, botanical gardens, technical colleges, and an amply endowed university afford means for higher study. James Watt, John Bright, and Joseph Chamberlain are some of the distinguished names connected with the city. Population, 1947 est., 1,097,900.

Bologna (*bô-lōn'yä*). A city of northern Italy, located in a fertile plain at the foot of the Apennine mountains, almost midway between the Gulf of Genoa and the Gulf of Venice. It is an important railroad junction and has a large trade and extensive manufactures. The products for which the city is especially noted are macaroni, Bologna sausages, liquors, and canned fruit. Other industrial establishments include sugar refineries, rice mills, and railroad shops.

Bologna is believed to have been founded in the 8th century B. C. It figures in the career of Hannibal, Alaric, Charlemagne, and Napoleon. The city uses an aqueduct built by Augustus Cæsar. By a popular vote in 1860, Bologna became a part of the kingdom of Italy.

There are some 130 churches, several dating from the 11th century. One of the most noted is the San Domenico, where lies the body of Saint Dominic, the founder of the Dominican order. Bologna's art treasures include Raphael's portrait of Saint Cecilia. Two leaning towers survive from among 180 which Bologna possessed in the middle ages. One of the two is 163 feet high and inclines 10 feet from the perpendicular. The University of Bologna is the oldest existing university in Europe. Founded in the 11th century, it became famous as a law school and in 1262 had about 10,000 students, among whom were Dante and Petrarch. Galvani, one of the earliest investigators of electricity, was born in Bologna and lectured in the university. Population, 332,989.

Bonn (*bŏn*). A university city of central eastern Germany, beautifully situated on the Rhine river. The river is here spanned by a steel bridge, the central arch of which is 614 feet in length. The University of Bonn, second only to that of Berlin among German universities, occupies the former palace of the electors of Cologne. The city also has a venerable cathedral and a Beethoven museum, the latter containing relics of the famous musician, who was born in the city. The principal manufactures are porcelain, office furniture, and stoneware. Population, 1939, 101,391.

Bordeaux (*bôr'dō'*). A commercial city of southwestern France, situated on the Garonne river at the point where it widens to form the Gironde river. It is connected by canal with the Mediterranean Sea. The chief article of export is wine, besides which hides, sugar, rice, cotton and woolen cloth, salt fish, and fruit are shipped abroad, mainly to South America. The city's industries include shipbuilding, canning, sugar refining, and the manufacture of casks, liquors, chemicals, leather, machinery, and pottery. Bordeaux is an important center for fishing fleets which annually visit the shores of Newfoundland and of Iceland.

The University of Bordeaux was founded in 1441. Among the more notable buildings of the city are the Grand Theater, the Church of Saint Croix, Saint Michael's Church, and the Cathedral of Saint André, the last dating from the 11th century. Montesquieu, Montaigne, and Rosa Bonheur were residents of Bordeaux.

Bordeaux was used as a port of disembarkation by the American forces during the World War. For a short period in 1914, it became the seat of the French government when Paris was menaced. Population, 1946, 253,751.

Boulogne (F. *bōō'lōn'y'*; E. *bōō-lōn'*). A fortified seaport of northern France, situated at the eastern extremity of the English channel. The city is the chief French station of the North Sea fisheries. It consists of a lower town,—the business part close to the harbor,—and an upper town built on a hill, from which, on clear days, the English coast may be seen. As a center for passenger traffic with England, Boulogne rivals Calais. During the World War, many American troopships landed their passengers in Boulogne. Population, 1946, 79,410.

Bradford. A manufacturing city in the north central part of England, the chief center in England for the manufacture of woolen textiles, and the leading wool market of the world. Silks, velvets, and foundry products are also manufactured. Bradford is substantially built, mainly of stone. Among the public buildings are Saint Peter's Church, the Mechanics Institute, the large, covered markets, and the Cartwright Memorial Hall, erected in memory of the inventor of the power loom. Population, 1947 est., 289,280.

Bremen (E. *brĕm'ĕn*; G. *brā'mĕn*). The second largest seaport of Germany. It lies in the northwestern part of the country on both banks of the Weser river. The "old town" on the right bank is the business district, while the "new town" on the left is a well built residential section. Prior to the World War, the bulk of Bremen's commerce was with the United States and the tropics. The chief industrial products include ships, iron castings, machinery, refined sugar, tobacco, and cordage. The city is the headquarters of the North German Lloyd Steamship Company.

Bremen is the capital of a small state of the same name, which retained its rights of self-government when it entered the German Empire. Population, 1946, 390,000.

Breslau (*brĕs'lou*). An important commercial and manufacturing city of Poland, situated on both banks of the Oder river. It has a large trade in raw materials and holds three annual fairs. The chief manufactures are textiles, steel products, railway cars, paper, and furniture. Breslau consists of an old town surrounded by five modern suburbs. One of the most notable buildings is the Protestant church founded in 1250 and dedicated to Saint Elizabeth. It has a steeple 300 feet high. The city is of Polish origin. Population, 1946, 168,466.

Brest. A strongly fortified seaport and one of the chief naval stations of France, located on a wide rock-bound harbor at the northwestern extremity of France. Most of the working population are engaged in industries related to naval maintenance. Between the town and the harbor mouth, the Cours d'Ajot, one of the finest promenades in Europe, skirts the shore. Brest was one of the principal ports used by the American Expeditionary Forces in the World War. A telegraph cable connects the city with Duxbury, Mass. Population, 1946, 74,991.

Brighton. The most celebrated seaside resort in England, situated on the English channel, 51 miles due south of London. A magnificent 4-mile promenade and driveway with two fine piers borders the coast. The most noteworthy building is the Royal Pavilion, in Oriental style, occupied by George IV and succeeding British sovereigns. Population, 1947 est., 154,600.

Bristol. A maritime city of southwestern England, situated seven miles south of the estuary of the Severn, with which it is connected by the navigable river Avon. The city has long been noted for its extensive commerce and for its glassworks, potteries, sugar refineries, soap works, tanneries, tobacco, chocolate, shoe, and chemical factories, and shipyards. In the shipyards of Bristol was built, in 1838, the early steamship *Great Western*.

Bristol is the seat of Bristol university and of two colleges. Besides libraries, museums, and art galleries, the city contains a number of medieval churches, of which the finest architecturally is that of Saint Mary Redcliffe, dating from the 14th century. From Bristol came the first settlers of Newfoundland as well as the island's discoverer, John Cabot. The city was at one time the residence of Southey and of Coleridge. Population, 1947 est., 436,150.

Bruges (E. *broo'jĕz*; F. *brüzh*). A decadent commercial city of western Belgium. Prior to the 16th century, Bruges was a flourishing center of woolen manufacturing. Among the many medieval structures which the city has preserved from its more prosperous days are the Church of Notre Dame and les Halles, the Market Hall, whose tower, 352 feet in height, contains a chime of 48 bells. This tower was celebrated by Longfellow in his poem "The Belfry of Bruges." The port of Bruges is Zeebrugge, 8 miles distant, which was a German submarine base during the World War. The name of the city means bridges and was applied in allusion to the 54 bridges constructed across the numerous canals which intersect the city. Population, 1946, 52,698.

Brünn (*brün*) (**Brno**). An important commercial city of south central Czechoslovakia. Its manufactures include woolen goods, hardware, flour, refined sugar, and machinery. Brünn has several churches of attractive medieval architecture and a beautiful synagogue built in the Saracenic style. The city is a trading center for a thickly populated district. Population, 1946 est., 268,873.

Brussels (**Bruxelles,** or **Brussel**). The capital and largest city of Belgium, situated in the central part of the kingdom. It consists of an upper town,—the new and fashionable quarter,—and the lower, or old, town, devoted to commerce and industry.

Its magnificent boulevards, beautiful squares and parks, and imposing buildings make Brussels one of the most beautiful cities of Europe. The more notable buildings include the Hôtel de Ville, with its open-stonework spire, 374 feet high, and the sumptuous Greco-Roman Palais de Justice. The Church of Sainte Gudule, begun in 1220, is celebrated for its marvelous stained-glass windows. The royal library, the museums, and the art galleries contain many masterpieces of Flemish painters. The University of Brussels is one of the very few European universities which have been founded without the co-operation of church or state. The city has numerous schools and scientific societies.

Brussels suffered severely from the German occupation during the World War. Since that time, however, its industries have resumed their production of Brussels lace, carpets, furniture, steam engines, and other articles manufactured before the war. The city is also the railroad center of the country. Population, 1946 est., 915,604.

Bucharest (*boo'kȧ-rĕst'*; *bū'-*) (**Bucaresti**). The capital and largest city of Rumania, located in the central southern part of the country. Bucharest has an extensive commerce in petroleum, cereals, and timber. The industries include oil refining and the manufacture of flour, liquors, chemicals, and brick.

The city's chief attractions are the splendid public gardens and the bright cupolas of the numerous Greek Catholic churches. Among the more imposing structures are the Royal Palace, the National university, the Palace of Justice, and several fine monuments. The customs of the inhabitants exhibit a blending of Oriental and Western influences. The name Bucharest is a corruption of a Rumanian word meaning city of joy. Population, 1945, 984,619.

Budapest (*boo'dȧ-pĕst'*). The capital and largest city of Hungary, situated in the central northern part of the country on the banks of the Danube river. Budapest comprises the former city of Buda on the right bank and of Pest on the left bank. The two are connected by six bridges, including two suspension bridges which are among the longest in Europe.

Buda, the older section, which was founded by the Romans in the 2d century A. D., is built on two hills and contains the royal castle, the government offices, and the former residences of the aristocracy. The newer town, Pest, founded by the Huns under Attila in the 5th century A. D., is built on a low plain. Pest is the commercial, industrial, and intellectual center of the city. It contains a park 1000 acres in extent with a charming lake. At the park entrance, there is an artesian well 3000 feet deep which yields 260,000 gallons of hot water daily. Pest also contains the new Parliament buildings, the University of Hungary, the National Theater, the Industrial Museum, and numerous other notable buildings.

Budapest is one of the great flour milling centers of the world. It contains some of the largest electrical works of Europe, in which were planned the first successful underground trolley lines. Other manufactures include machinery, textiles, agricultural implements, chemicals, cutlery, glass, leather, and liquors. The city's commercial interests are of even greater importance. Budapest is the railroad center of Hungary and is further served by the Danube, the chief waterway of the country. Population, 1947 est., 1,073,444.

Cadiz (*kā'dĭz*). An Atlantic port on the south coast of Spain. Cadiz is one of the most ancient cities in Europe. Founded by the Phœnicians, 1100 B. C., Cadiz was captured in turn by the Carthaginians, Romans, Goths, Moors, and Spaniards. The town is still protected by walls and fortresses. When Spain was mistress of most of the New World, Cadiz was the emporium of American commerce and was a city of vast wealth and importance. Today its trade is small, the exports being principally salt, wines, olive oil, and fruits. Population, 1947 est., 96,566.

Calais (*kăl'ā*; *kăl'ĭs*). A fortified port of northeastern France, situated on the Strait of Dover near its narrowest part. Calais is the chief point of disembarkation for travelers from England, being only 21 miles from the English coast. It has considerable commercial, manufacturing, and shipbuilding interests and is the chief center in France for the making of lace.

Calais was held by England from 1347 to 1558. During the World War, it was used by England as the principal point of disembarking troops for France. Population, 1946, 50,048.

Cambrai (*kăɴ'brĕ'*). An industrial town of northern France, noted for its manufacture of linen and of cotton textiles. The city has given its name to the fabric known as cambric.

In the vicinity of Cambrai, on Nov. 20, 1917, was fought the battle in which tanks were first used on a large scale. Population, 1931, 28,077.

Canterbury. A cathedral city in the southeast of England, lying south of the Thames and about 56 miles east of London. Christchurch Cathedral is the crowning architectural feature of the city. The Archbishop of Canterbury is, next to the king, the highest official of the Anglican Church. Among the distinguished Catholic archbishops who, prior to the Reformation, presided over the see, were Saint Augustine, Lanfranc, Anselm, and Thomas à Becket, the one last mentioned having been murdered in the cathedral. The building contains, among other tombs, that of Henry IV and of the Black Prince. The city has many interesting ruins, including those of Canterbury castle, a fortress of Norman construction. A public drinking fountain commemorates Marlowe, who was a native of Canterbury. Population, 1947 est., 24,850.

Cantigny (*kăn'tēɴ'y'*). A village of northern France, 18 miles south of Amiens. On May 28, 1918, it was the scene of the first American offensive in the World War.

Capri (*kä'prē*). A beautiful, rocky island at the entrance of the gulf of Naples, Italy, visited annually by more than 60,000 tourists. Its area is nearly 6 square miles, and its highest point is about 2000 feet above the sea. One of its most remarkable features is the Blue grotto, the roof and sides of which are composed mostly of stalactites. The grotto is on the coast and is called blue because the light, refracted in passing through the water at the cave's mouth, causes the interior of the grotto to appear blue.

Capri was anciently famous for the palace there to which the Roman emperor Tiberius retired in order to spend his last years in pleasures. It had also a large Roman lighthouse, the remains of which are still visible. A more recent ruin is that of Barbarossa, a castle named after a pirate who partially destroyed it in 1544. Population, 1931, 4114.

Cardiff. The principal seaport and largest city of Wales, situated at the southeastern extremity of the principality near the northern coast of Bristol channel. The city is the largest coal exporting port in Europe and ranks among the largest ports of England in its total shipping tonnage. Besides coal, its chief exports are iron and steel products, machinery, railroad cars, and vehicles. Its docks cover more than 200 acres, and there are 7 miles of wharves. In Cathays park, at the center of the city, is one of the finest groups of public buildings in Great Britain. Near by is Cardiff castle, which embraces structures dating from Roman and medieval times. Cardiff is also the seat of University College of South Wales. Population, 1947, 234,580.

Carrara (*kär-rä'rä*). A city of northern Italy celebrated for its marble quarries. It is situated 3 miles inland from the eastern extremity of the Gulf of Genoa in a valley surrounded by marble hills. Most of the city's buildings are of marble, and there is a museum containing numerous statues and Roman antiquities discovered in the vicinity. Population, 1931, about 49,600.

Cartagena. A Mediterranean port and strong naval station in the southeastern part of Spain. The chief industries are tunny fishing, shipbuilding, lead smelting, glass blowing, ironworking, and the manufacture of cordage and of other esparto grass products. The city is well built and is still surrounded by walls.

The name Cartagena means daughter of Carthage. The city was founded about 243 B. C. by Hasdrubal, a Carthaginian general, who called the city *Carthago Nova*, "New Carthage." It was captured by the Romans in 210 B. C. and afterward was occupied successively by the Vandals, Moors, Spaniards, English, and French. Population, 1946, 117,075.

Catania (*kä-tä'nyä*). An Italian city on the eastern coast of Sicily, situated at the southeastern base of Mount Etna. The city has broad, well kept streets and many fine public buildings. A large trade in agricultural products is carried on in Catania, and there are important manufactures of linen, cotton, silk goods, and art objects of lava, wood, and marble. The chief attraction is Mount Etna. The city contains the remains of an ancient theater.

Catania was founded by Greeks in 729 B. C. and was held successively by the Carthaginians, Romans, Goths, Saracens, Normans, and the rulers of Aragon, from whom it passed to Italy. Population, 1947, 272,824.

Channel Islands. Three islands,—Jersey, Guernsey, and Sark,—lying in the English channel near the northwestern coast of France. They are dependencies of Great Britain, having belonged originally to the Normans who conquered England in 1066. The islands are rocky but have many beautiful wooded valleys. About one-half their 75 square miles of surface is arable.

The Channel islands are much frequented by tourists. Jersey contains a gorge more than 1000 feet deep in the cliffs at Crabbe. Other features of the islands include a picturesque natural archway of rock on Dixcart bay; a feudal manor house at Samares, dating from the 11th or 12th century; and Mousterian caves which, when explored recently, exhibited the remains of Neanderthal men, of the woolly rhinoceros, the cave hyena, and other animals now extinct. The state of New Jersey was named after the island of Jersey. Population, 93,205.

Chateau Thierry (*shä'tō' tyĕ'rē'*). A town in the northern part of France, on the Marne river 47 miles east and slightly north of Paris. At this point, in June 1918, American troops engaged German forces advancing toward Paris and effectively checked their progress. Several weeks later, a general counter attack swept the Germans back a distance of many miles. The town is named after a castle in the neighborhood, which was built by Charles Martel for the Frankish king Thierry IV. On July 15, 1923, a monument commemorating the American victory was erected in a square of the town, renamed United States place. Population, 1931, 7267.

Chemnitz (*kĕm'nĭts*). The chief industrial city of the German state of Saxony. The city is situated at the base of the Erzgebirge mountains. The principal manufactures include locomotives and engines, textiles, hosiery, carpets, chemicals, and dyestuffs. Founded as a market town in 1143, Chemnitz has a varied but unbroken history as an industrial city extending from the 13th century until the present. Population, 1939, 334,563.

Cherbourg (*shĕr'bōōr'*). A strongly fortified French naval station near the center of the country's northern coast on the English channel. Its ocean railroad station, opened in 1933, is one of the largest buildings in France. It was from this port that the Confederate cruiser, the *Alabama*, was forced by the French authorities to put out to sea before it was sunk by the United States vessel, the *Kearsarge*. Population, 1931, 43,731.

Coblenz (**Koblenz**). A commercial and manufacturing city of western Germany, beautifully situated at the confluence of the Moselle and the Rhine river. It was formerly protected by a system of four forts, including Ehrenbreitstein on the opposite bank. After the World War, however, the fortifications were demolished, and the city was held, until 1923, by the American army of occupation.

Coblenz has an active trade in grain. Its manufactures consist mainly of Moselle wine, ships, hats, machinery, pianos, and lacquered wares. The finest edifice is the government building, in which are centered the administrative activities of the province of Rhenish Prussia. Saint Castor's church, founded in 836, ranks among the oldest in Germany. Population, 1933, 65,257.

Cologne (*kō-lōn'*) (**Köln**). A large commercial and manufacturing city of central western Germany, beautifully located on the left bank of the Rhine river. *Eau de Cologne* is a distinctive product. The chief manufactures are leather goods, chemicals, starch, textiles, rubber goods, machinery, metal wares, beet sugar, tobacco products, and chocolate.

The outstanding feature of Cologne's architecture is the Gothic cathedral, begun in 1248 and completed in 1880. Two of its towers rise to a height of 512 feet. It has a colossal bell, one of the largest in the world. This bell was hung in 1923, replacing a former one, which was destroyed during the World War. The Church of Saint Ursula is reported to contain the bones of 11,000 British virgins who were massacred near Cologne on their way to Rome. In allusion to this tradition, Columbus applied the name Virgin islands to that West Indies group.

Cologne was founded in the 1st century A. D. under the name of Colonia Agrippina, of which its modern name is a corruption. Rubens, the painter, lived in the city, and one of the local churches contains the tomb of John Duns Scotus. Population, 1946, 488,039.

Copenhagen (*kō'pĕn-hā'gĕn*) (**Köbenhaven**). The capital and largest city of Denmark, situated on a deep, safe, and capacious harbor on the northeast shore of the island of Zealand. Across the harbor, on the island of Amager, is the modern suburb of Christianshavn. Copenhagen commands the sea highway from the Baltic to the North Sea and was at one time the chief distributing mart of the Baltic trade. To offset the advantages given by the Kiel canal to Germany's seaports, Copenhagen, in 1894, made part of its harbor a free port. Shipbuilding is the chief industry. Among the manufactures are agricultural machines, porcelains, textiles, sugar, watches, and chemicals.

A characteristic feature of Copenhagen is the large number of spires, which occur on many public buildings as well as on the churches. The Church of Our Redeemer has a winding staircase built outside the spire 295 feet to its top. Copenhagen is the seat of the University of Copenhagen and is the headquarters of many learned societies. The Thorvaldsen Museum contains over 300 works executed by Thorvaldsen, Denmark's greatest sculptor. Hans Christian Andersen was one of the city's most distinguished residents. Population, 1945, 927,404.

Cordoba (*kôr'dô-vä*). An inland city of southern Spain, located on the Guadalquivir river. The city was founded by the Phœnicians and attained to considerable importance under the Romans. It later became the metropolis of the Moors in Spain and, from the 9th to the 12th century, was one of the greatest centers of commerce in the world. The Mosque of Cordoba, now used as a Catholic cathedral, is the most magnificent example of Mohammedan architecture in Europe. The city is now in decline, its manufactures being confined largely to textiles, gold and silver filigree work, and cordovan leather. The last named article obtained its name from Cordoba. Cordoba was the birthplace of the Roman poet Lucan, of the two Senecas, and of the Arab philosopher Averroës. Population, 1947, 177,478.

Cork. A port of central southern Eire, situated on a capacious natural harbor formed by the estuary of the River Lee. It has a lower harbor, Queenstown, located at the river's mouth. A heavy trade in foodstuffs is carried on with England. The city's chief manufactures are leather, liquors, metal wares, gloves, fertilizers, and textiles.

Among the finest buildings are the Anglican and the Catholic cathedral, both dedicated to Saint Finn Barr, who founded the city in 622 A. D. The Church of Saint Anne Shandon has a notable peal of bells. Other features of the city are University college, a school of science and of agriculture, and a public park, 240 acres in extent. Population, 1946, 75,361.

Coventry. An industrial city of central England, noted for its manufacture of automobiles, ribbons, artificial silk, telephone equipment, and electric motors. Coventry is a very old town and was for centuries the scene of an annual pageant commemorating the ride of Lady Godiva. According to tradition, she agreed to ride naked through the streets in order to save the citizens from certain exactions, her husband, Earl Leofric, having demanded this action as a condition of relieving the townspeople. The pageant was last celebrated in 1887. Saint Mary's Hall, built in 1450, is one of the finest examples of ornamental architecture in England. Population, 1947, 248,400.

Dardanelles. A narrow channel, 42 miles long and 1 to 5 miles wide, joining the Sea of Marmora and the Ægean Sea. The territory about the strait, affording an excellent defense of Istanbul from the West, was the scene of a costly offensive against Turkey during the World War. After the war, it was placed under the control of an Allied commission, but Turkey resumed control in 1936.

The ancient name of the Dardanelles was Hellespont, across which, in spite of its strong current, the mythical Leander is said to have swum each evening to visit Hero. Lord Byron swam the Hellespont at the point where Xerxes crossed it in 480 B. C.

Dneproptrovsk. A large and rapidly developing industrial city of the Russian Ukraine located at the junction of the Dnepr and Samara rivers. Its major industries are iron and steel, machine construction, chemicals, and food products. The city shared in the hydroelectric development of the vast Dnepr dam, destroyed in 1941, but since restored. Its population in 1939 was 500,662 almost double that of 1926.

Dortmund (*dôrt'mŏŏnt*). A railway center and manufacturing city of central western Germany in the northern part of the Ruhr district. Located in the midst of rich coal mines, the city has become an important point for the manufacture of steel products, including machinery, wire ropes, rails, mining equipment, and safes. Among other products are flour, lumber, and liquors. Since 1900, its population has more than tripled, standing, according to the 1946 census, at 433,792.

Dover. A heavily fortified port and favorite summer resort of England, situated at the southeastern extremity of the country. White chalk cliffs tower nearly 400 feet above the harbor, and, on clear days, afford a view of the opposite coast of France, 21 miles distant. The chief industrial products are ships, sails, rope, and flour. Population, 1945, 24,320.

Dresden. An industrial city of central Germany and administrative center of the state of Saxony. It is situated on the Elbe river and is an important railway center for Germany and the rest of central Europe. The chief manufactures include pianos, confectionery, silverware, jewelry, chemicals, glassware, and metal goods. Dresden china is made at Meissen, a suburb.

Dresden is one of the most important art centers of Europe. Its art gallery, the Zwinger, contains Raphael's "Sistine Madonna," Correggio's "Holy Night," and many other masterpieces. The city also has two royal theaters, many minor theaters and music halls, and an orchestra famous throughout the world. Sculptural monuments and beautiful fountains adorn the city in great profusion. The Brühl Terrace and the Grosser Garten are famous pleasure grounds. The Royal Palace is the most notable building, its tower rising to a height of 387 feet. Population, 1939, 625,174.

Dublin. The capital and largest city of Eire, situated on an inlet near the center of Ireland's eastern coast. A large part of the country's exported foodstuffs are handled through the port of Dublin. Liquors are made in considerable quantity.

Dublin as a whole, with its fine bay, wide streets, spacious squares, magnificent 2000-acre park, massive public buildings, and beautiful suburbs, is one of the handsomest capitals in Europe. Christ Church, in Early English Gothic style, was begun in 1038 by a Danish king of Dublin. Saint Patrick's Cathedral is about 700 years old. The city has statues of O'Connell, Burke, Goldsmith, and many other famous Irishmen. The University of Dublin is the chief educational institution. Population, 1946, 506,635.

Duisburg-Hamborn (*düs'bŏŏrk-häm'bōrn*). A manufacturing city of central western Germany, in the Ruhr district. Its quays, built along canals and on the Rhine and the Ruhr river, are said to constitute the largest river harbor in the world. The chief commodities handled are coal and the products of the city's industries—iron and steel products, chemicals, liquors, asphalt, varnish, furniture, and tobacco. The former cities of Duisburg and Hamborn were combined in 1929. Population, 1946, 355,487.

Düsseldorf (*düs'ĕl-dôrf*). A manufacturing city of western Germany, situated on the right bank of the Rhine at the influx of the Düssel river. The harbor is spacious and well equipped, and there is a large export trade. The city has great iron and steel industries and textile manufactures. Chemicals, tobacco goods, chocolate, beer, paper, glass, and musical instruments are also made.

Düsseldorf has wide, regularly laid out streets and spacious squares, and is noted for its numerous garden grounds embellished with fountains and statues. The Hofgarten is regarded as the finest public garden in Germany. The city has long possessed importance, also, as an art center, having been the focus of the so-called Düsseldorf school of painting. The Art Academy is an imposing building in the Renaissance style with a façade 520 feet long. Among its paintings is the "Assumption" by Rubens and a Madonna by Bellini. Population, 1946, 419,589.

Edinburgh (*ĕd''n-bŭr-ō*). The second largest city of Scotland. It is built near the south shore of the Firth of Forth, which is here spanned by a bridge 1½ miles in length. Edinburgh is the seat of the supreme court of Scotland and was the seat of government before the country united politically with England. The chief industries include printing and publishing, and the manufacture of liquors, leather, flour, and rubber goods.

Edinburgh consists of an old and a new section. Through the latter runs the magnificent Princes street, one of the finest thoroughfares in Europe. Near it stands the beautiful Scottish American war memorial. Among the city's points of interest are Holyrood Palace; Saint Giles Church, which has a memorial tablet to R. L. Stevenson designed by Saint-Gaudens; a magnificent monument to Sir Walter Scott; a small Greek temple erected to the memory of Robert Burns; and Calton cemetery, which contains a statue of Abraham Lincoln with a freed slave kneeling at his feet. Edinburgh has a handsome library donated by Andrew Carnegie. There are numerous educational institutions, the most famous of which is the University of Edinburgh. The predominance of literary elements in the city's population, combined with its picturesque location, has won for it the name of "modern Athens."

The city was named after Edwin, king of Northumbria, who seized it in the 7th century A. D. and built a fortress on Castle rock, a precipitous height which dominates the city. The Royal Castle now stands on the site of Edwin's fortress. Population, 1947 est., 487,200.

Essen. A steel manufacturing city of western Germany, situated in the Ruhr district and surrounded by rich coal and iron deposits. The recent industrial growth of the city is due mainly to the activities of the Krupp corporation The town, however, traces its origin to 873 A. D., when construction began on the cathedral, which is one of the oldest churches in Germany. Population, 1946, 520,656.

Etna. The largest active volcano in Europe. It is an isolated mountain, 10,758 feet high, in northeastern Sicily near Catania and has a base 90 miles in circumference. On its eastern side is a former crater, now a vast amphitheater with nearly precipitous sides 3000 feet in height.

The first recorded eruption of Etna was in the 8th century B. C. Another, occurring in 477 B. C., is graphically described in Æschylus' *Prometheus Bound*. Later eruptions of a violent character took place in 1169, 1527, 1669, 1693, 1852, 1864, 1879, 1911, 1923, and 1928. In that of 1669 more than 20,000 people were killed. An observatory and a house for the convenience of travelers have been erected near the chief crater. A large part of the world's supply of sulphur came formerly from Mount Etna.

Fingal's Cave. A remarkable cave of basalt formation, on Staffa, a small island off the central western coast of Scotland. The cave extends from the shore a distance of 227 feet within a rocky height and has an arch 66 feet high. Its maximum width is 42 feet. The color effects of the columnar basalt formation are no less striking than the weird sounds produced by the action of wind and wave as they play upon the opening of the huge cave.

Florence (Firenze). A city of north central Italy, lying in a fertile valley near the Apennine mountains. Florence is, next to Rome, the most celebrated Italian city, being noted for its illustrious history and for its art treasures.

The Cathedral of Florence is the city's outstanding structure. Founded in 1296, it occupied about 200 years in construction. Its dome was planned by Brunelleschi. The bell tower of the cathedral was built by Giotto. This tower and the bronze doors of the baptistery, designed by Ghiberti, have enjoyed renown for centuries. The Franciscan church Santa Croce contains the tombs of Galileo, Michelangelo, Machiavelli, and many other distinguished men. The picture galleries contain some of the best works of Titian, Andrea del Sarto, Botticelli, Rubens, Raphael, and other great painters. Among the notable statues are the "Venus de' Medici," "Dancing Faun," and "Knife Grinder."

The city has famous academies of art, a museum of natural history, a university, a botanical garden, a large astronomical observatory, and a number of libraries, chief of which is the Laurentian library founded by Lorenzo de' Medici. Florence was the birthplace of Dante and of Florence Nightingale.

The industries of the city include the manufacture of silks, glassware, porcelain, and objects of art, especially mosaics, wood carvings, majolica chinaware, stained glass, and jewelry. Florence was founded in the 2d century B. C., but the period of its greatest prosperity was in the 13th century A. D., when it was an independent city-state. Population, 1947, 373,544.

Flushing. A strongly fortified Dutch seaport, built on an island at the western extremity of the Netherlands. There is a large passenger traffic between Flushing and English ports. The city was the birthplace of Admiral de Ruyter, one of Holland's greatest naval heroes. Population, 1946 est., 16,154.

Folkestone. An ancient town and seaport of southeastern England, situated on the Strait of Dover. Folkestone has daily steamer communication with Boulogne in France and is also popular as a summer resort. Harvey, the discoverer of the circulation of the blood, was born in this city. Population, 1947 est., 41,810.

Frankfort (Frankfurt). A city of west central Germany, situated on the Main river, an eastern tributary of the Rhine. Frankfort is noted as a financial and mercantile center, and has important literary and historical associations. The chief manufactures are chemicals, electrical goods, machinery, rolling stock, asbestos, rubber, soap, and clothing.

Among the features of the city are the family house of the Rothschilds, the house where Goethe was born, the Goethe Museum, the Saint Bartholemew Cathedral, the Staedel Art Institute, the Municipal Historical Museum, and the large monument to Gutenberg, the inventor of movable type. Frankfort was formerly the electoral city of the Holy Roman Empire, and, after 1816, the German Parliament held its sessions there. Population, 1946, 421,369.

Freiburg (*frī'bōōrk*). A city in the southwestern extremity of Germany, noted for its magnificent Gothic cathedral. This edifice, built of red sandstone, was begun in 1122 and was completed in 1513. It is admired for the delicate symmetry shown in its design as well as for its splendid tower, which is 386 feet high. Population, 1939, 111,860.

Geneva (**Genève**). A beautiful city of western Switzerland, situated at the lower end of Lake Geneva where its waters flow into the Rhone river. The city covers two islands in the river, one of which, called Rousseau's island, is a public pleasure ground commemorating the revolutionary writer, who was a native of the city. The left bank of the river is occupied by the old city and the business section, while, on the right bank, is the quarter called Saint Gervais, mainly residential in character. The latter district contains numerous hotels for the accommodation of the many tourists who enter Switzerland by way of Geneva.

The University of Geneva was originally founded as an academy in 1559 by Calvin, who made Geneva the chief center of Protestantism in the 16th century. Swiss heroes of the Reformation are further commemorated in Geneva by a recently erected monument entitled the "Wall of the Reformers." The manufactures of the city consist principally of clocks, watches, jewelry, enameled ware, and scientific instruments. Geneva is the headquarters of the League of Nations and has been the scene of many international conferences, including the *Alabama* arbitration. The city is predominantly French in language and culture. Population, 1941, 124,431.

Genoa (*jĕn'ō-ȧ*) (**Genova**). A commercial city of northeastern Italy, picturesquely situated at the head of the Gulf of Genoa. The city is strongly fortified against attacks by sea or land. Rail connections render it the sea outlet for much of the foreign trade of northern Italy, Switzerland, and southern Germany. The manufactures include foundry and other metal products, leather, cotton, cement, motor cars, crystallized fruits, and hats, and the city is also noted for its production of works of art in gold, silver, ivory, alabaster, and coral. It has large shipbuilding facilities and the largest dry dock in the Mediterranean Sea.

Among the notable examples of Genoa's many fine edifices are the ducal palaces, the residences of the doges in the days of the city's independence; the Cathedral of San Lorenzo, containing what is said to be the Holy Grail; the Church of Santissima Annunziata; and the Teatro Carlo Felice. The last named edifice was built in 1828 and ranks among the largest theaters in Italy. Genoa has an imposing sculptural group in honor of Columbus. Population, 1947, 664,143.

Ghent (**Gent** or **Gand**). A city of western Belgium, located on the Scheldt river and connected with the North Sea by a ship canal. The city is divided into islands by smaller canals, which are spanned by numerous bridges. The older part of Ghent has narrow, gloomy streets, but the newer part is laid out with wide avenues, flanked by fine houses.

Ghent contains the Cathedral of Saint Bavon, in which is the celebrated "Adoration of the Magi" by Van Eyck. There is also a great walled and moated nunnery, which, since its foundation in the 13th century, has been known for the production of exquisite lace. Ghent's principal manufactures are cotton and linen textiles, leather, and refined sugar, and the city has an active export trade in flowers. The emperor Charles V was born in Ghent, where, also, was signed the treaty which closed the War of 1812. Population, 1946, 162,488.

Giant's Causeway. A line of three perpendicular cliffs on the northeastern coast of Ireland. According to a legend, they were the beginning of a causeway to be built by giants across the channel to Scotland. They are formed of vertical basalt columns, mainly hexagonal in form and fitting closely together. The three cliffs are called the Little Causeway, the Middle Causeway, and the Grand Causeway. The last has a width of 60 to 120 feet and extends about 500 feet into the sea. On the Middle Causeway is the famous "wishing chair." The vicinity abounds in special points of interest, such as an amphitheater of natural formation and ruined castles perched on the top of isolated crags.

Glasgow. The second largest city in Great Britain, situated on the Clyde river somewhat southwest of the geographical center of Scotland. Its harbor has been elaborately improved at the cost of 40 million dollars and has some 8 miles of quays. Glasgow's shipyards are the largest in the world. The industrial development is due partly to the city's location in the midst of extensive deposits of coal and of iron. The chief manufactures, apart from ships, comprise iron and steel products, textiles, coal, paper, chemicals, and whisky.

Glasgow is conspicuous for its successful management of civic operations and improvements, which include the erection of large numbers of modern apartment houses. There are many institutions for technical and higher education, of which the most important is the University of Glasgow. The municipal art gallery contains the finest collection of paintings in Great Britain outside of London, including Whistler's portrait of Carlyle. Saint Mungo's Cathedral, built between 1197 and 1446, is a beautiful example of Early English architecture. It stands on the site of a church erected in the 6th century by Saint Mungo, the patron saint of Glasgow. Population, 1947 est., 1,106,000.

Gorki, formerly **Nizhni Novgorod.** A city of Russia, on the Volga river about 270 miles east of Moscow. From remote antiquity, the city has been famous for its annual fair, one of the greatest of the entire world. Prices of many important commodities throughout Russia depended on those prevailing on this market. Merchandise totaling in some years over 20 million tons changed hands between August 1 and September 15.

The Soviet government chose this city as its chief center for the manufacture of automobiles. About fourteen miles from the old town, an enormous automobile factory, the largest in Europe, was placed in operation in 1931. About it was built a model soviet city designed for 60,000 inhabitants. One-third its area was devoted to parks. Residential units were built to accommodate 200 people per unit, each being equipped for communal meals and provided with facilities for amusement and instruction. The name Nizhni Novgorod was changed in 1932 to Gorki in honor of the famous writer, who was born there in 1868. Population, 1939, 644,116.

Göteborg (*yû'tĕ-bŏr'y'*). The second largest city of Sweden, situated in the southwestern part of the country at the mouth of the Göta river, which discharges into the Kattegat. The town was founded in 1618 by Gustavus Adolphus, but, in consequence of numerous fires, it has been largely rebuilt in recent times. It has numerous fine buildings and broad, well shaded streets, those near the river having canals running through their centers. Favored by an excellent harbor open all the year round, Göteborg conducts much of the country's foreign commerce. The industries comprise shipbuilding, textile weaving, dyeing, iron-working, brewing, and the manufacture of tobacco, furniture, paper, and leather. Population, 1947, 325,563.

Granada. An inland city of southeastern Spain, lying at the base of the Sierra Nevada about 40 miles from the Mediterranean coast. The city, having been formerly one of the chief centers of Moorish civilization in Spain, has a partially Oriental appearance. The residential section of the Moorish nobility is now in ruins and is occupied largely by gypsies. Granada's outstanding edifice is the Alhambra, a magnificent Moorish palace celebrated in America by Washington Irving's book *The Alhambra*. The cathedral, begun in 1529, commemorates the reconquest of Spain by the Christian powers. Granada has a university founded in 1531 by the emperor Charles V.

The city is in a fertile district containing groves of orange, lemon, and fig trees. Its manufactures include textiles, paper, leather, flour, macaroni, chocolate, and soap. Population, 1947, 185,680.

Graz (*gräts*). A commercial and industrial city of southern Germany, situated in a beautiful valley at the eastern extremity of the Alps mountains. The principal architectural attractions include a Gothic cathedral dedicated to Saint Ogidius and noted for its exquisite stained-glass windows, a mausoleum containing the remains of Emperor Ferdinand II, and the parish church, which, built in 1520, is adorned with an altarpiece by Tintoretto. Graz has a university, founded in 1573.

A rich coal district is near the city. The manufactures comprise iron and steel goods, optical instruments, chemicals, paper, and lithographs. Graz is an important railroad and trade center. Population, 1946, 220,100.

Hague, The (**'s Gravenhage**). The capital of the Netherlands, situated in the southwestern part of the kingdom about two miles from the North Sea. The city is chiefly occupied with the business of governing, although there are manufactures of gold and silver lace, jewelry, and articles of iron, brass, and copper.

The Hague has broad, shaded streets, intersected by picturesque canals and lined by many fine edifices. One of the most noted buildings is the Mauritshuis, which contains masterpieces by Rembrandt, Rubens, Van Dyck, and others. The city is the headquarters of the Permanent Court of International Justice and of the International Court of Arbitration. These courts sit in the Carnegie Peace Palace, which was erected in 1913, partly through the generosity of Andrew Carnegie. Other features of the city are the royal library, the various government buildings, Willem's park, and the royal villa Huis-ten-Bosch, "House in the Woods," which stands in the suburbs amid the magnificent forests separating the city from its seaside resort, Scheveningen. Population, 1947, 532,239.

Hamburg. The third largest city of Germany and the third largest seaport in the world. Located in northwestern Germany due south of the Baltic peninsula, it is connected with Cuxhaven on the North Sea, 75 miles distant, by the navigable Elbe river. Hamburg's two harbors are on two small lakes made by damming the Alster, a stream flowing through the city. The docks are 20 miles in length and are among the best equipped in the world. Hamburg is one of the chief coffee markets of the world and handles immense quantities of wool, grain, cotton, ironware, tobacco, coal, and paper. It is also the headquarters of the Hamburg-American steamship line. The chief manufactures include ships, tobacco products, liquors, flour, chocolate, rubber, chemicals, electrical goods, motor cars, and steel products.

Hamburg was one of the principal cities of the Hanseatic League in the 13th century. In 1842, a large part of the city was destroyed by fire and was since rebuilt in a modern fashion. As a memorial of the fire, the Church of Saint Nicholas was erected, with a spire rising 482 feet above the ground. Hagenbeck's private zoological gardens contain one of the largest collections of wild animals in captivity. The city is the capital of the state of Hamburg, some 160 square miles in area, which has self-governing rights within the German republic. It is also the seat of the University of Hamburg. Population of city, 1946, 1,384,106.

Hammerfest. The most northerly incorporated town in the world, situated on an island off the northern coast of Norway 300 miles north of the Arctic circle. The inhabitants support themselves by fishing, raising reindeer, and entertaining tourists, large numbers of whom annually visit the town in order to view the spectacle of the midnight sun. The sun does not set on Hammerfest from May 13 to July 29. Population, 1927, 3470.

Hanover (Hannover). An industrial city of north central Germany, about 150 miles west of Berlin. The leading manufactures are iron and steel products, musical instruments, machinery, rubber, cotton, cork, chocolate, tobacco, furniture, chemicals, and leather. Among the features of Hanover are the city forest, lying in the suburbs and containing a zoological garden; the Grosse Garten, a pleasure ground richly adorned with statuary; Herrenhausen Castle; the Marktkirche, a 14th century church with a tower 300 feet high; and a veterinary school founded by George III of England.

Hanover was formerly the capital of the Kingdom of Hanover, a state which, from 1714 until 1837, had the same rulers as England. Population, 1946, 355,484.

Havre, Le (E. *hă'vẽr*; F. *lẽ àv'r'*). One of the largest seaports of France, situated at the mouth of the Seine river near the center of the country's northern coast. Its exports are mainly silk and cotton goods. The manufactures include chemicals, rope, machinery, flour, dyes, textiles, toys, and refined oil.

The importance of Havre dates from 1517, when the improvement of its harbor was begun. During the World War, the city was temporarily made the seat of the Belgian government. Population, 1936, 164,083.

Heidelberg. A university town of Baden in southwestern Germany. The university was founded in 1385 and numbers among its graduates Melanchthon, Gervinus, Kuno Fischer, and Bunsen. The town has an ancient castle, which contains in its cellar a cask with a capacity of 46,732 gallons. Near Heidelberg, in 1907, the lower jawbone of a prehistoric man was found, and the city has given its name to the racial type which, on the basis of this bone, is believed to have existed many hundreds of thousands of years ago. Population, 1946, 111,766.

Helsingfors (*hĕl'sĭng-fôrs'*) **(Helsinki).** The capital and largest city of Finland, located in the south part of the country on a peninsula projecting into the Gulf of Finland. The city is strongly fortified. It is regularly laid out and has many fine buildings and handsome parks adorned with monuments. The University of Helsingfors was originally founded at Abo in 1640 and was moved to Helsingfors in 1827. Helsingfors is the chief industrial city of Finland, manufacturing tobacco, liquors, and carpets. It has a considerable commerce in timber, paper, and dairy products. Population, 1945, 341,563.

Hull. A large seaport of central eastern England, situated at the mouth of the Hull river in the estuary of the Humber. It is the chief outlet for most of England's exports to Denmark, Norway, and Sweden. Its docks cover 200 acres. The city has extensive fishing interests, and its manufactures comprise iron goods, engines, ships, chemicals, soap, cement, paper, cotton goods, and leather. William Wilberforce was a native of Hull. Population, 1947, 294,730.

Istanbul, formerly **Constantinople.** The largest city of Turkey. It is built on a peninsula on the northern side of the Bosporus strait at its outlet into the Sea of Marmora. Istanbul occupies a key position, commanding a vast commerce between the East and the West. It has an excellent natural harbor in the Golden Horn, a northwestern inlet of Bosporus strait.

Stamboul, or the Turkish section, has a typically Asiatic character, being surrounded by walls, now partly ruined, and having unimproved, crooked streets, picturesque mosques, and extensive, colorful bazaars. There are two suburbs—Galata, the foreign business quarter, built mainly of stone; and Pera, a modern residential section of the foreign inhabitants, which is separated from Stamboul by the Golden Horn. The finest street in the city is the Grande Rue, in Pera, which is lined with fashionable shops and large hotels. Educational institutions include Stamboul university and Roberts college.

The most notable buildings of Istanbul are the mosques. Saint Sophia, originally built by Justinian as a church, and later converted by the Turks into a mosque, is being restored to its original beauty and is to be used as a museum. The Suleymanieh Mosque is the city's outstanding example of genuine Turkish architecture.

Secular buildings of historic interest include the Castle of the Seven Towers, once used as a state prison; the hippodrome, completed by Constantine; and the old seraglio, now transformed into a museum, in which is stored an extremely valuable collection of Greek antiquities. Water for the city's use is conveyed long distances by aqueducts, some of which date from the 3d century A. D., and is held in reservoirs until required. One of these reservoirs is covered with a roof supported by 420 marble columns and is said to be the largest work of its kind in the world.

Large manufacturing establishments in Istanbul are few in number, producing mainly ironwares, leather articles, and tobacco goods. The handmade products, however, are important both in variety and in quantity. The chief exports of the city are carpets and rugs, lambskins and wool, attar of roses, embroidery, and filigree work.

Istanbul was often referred to formerly as the Sublime Porte. This is a French term meaning the lofty gate and referred to an elaborate entrance into the enclosure containing the government buildings. This name was used to designate the city as a political capital.

The city was founded in the 6th century B. C. by Greek colonists, who gave it the name Byzantium. In 330 A. D., Constantine the Great made it the capital of the Roman Empire, changing its name to Constantinople. Taken by the Turks in 1453, the city became the capital of the Ottoman empire and the residence of the head of the Moslem religion. In 1920, however, the Turkish Nationalists revolted, choosing as their capital Ankara, in Asia Minor. The name Constantinople was then changed officially to Istanbul. It is now Turkey's chief link with the Western world. Population, 1945, 845,316.

Jena (*yā'nä*). A university town of central Germany. The university, founded in 1558, has numbered among its professors Humboldt, Hegel, Fichte, Schiller, Haeckel, and Eucken. Goethe resided here at one time. The city is also noted for its production of lenses. Jena was the scene of a disastrous German defeat in the Napoleonic wars. Population, 1933, 58,357.

Karlsbad (G. *kärls'bät*; E. *kärlz'băd*). One of the most celebrated fashionable watering places of Europe, situated in southern Germany. It is famous for its hot mineral springs, the daily flow of which is estimated at 2 million gallons. The name means Charles's Bath, Charles IV of France having bathed there.

The principal buildings of Karlsbad are an iron and glass structure, called the Sprudel colonnade, and an edifice in the Greek style, called the Muhlbrunnen colonnade. The city is noted also for porcelain manufacture. The resort is visited annually by upwards of 65,000 guests. The permanent population of the town is about 19,000.

Kharkov. An industrial city of southern Russia and the administrative center of the Ukraine soviet republic. Being near to the Donetz coal field and to important iron ore deposits, it has become one of the chief Russian centers of heavy industry. The manufactures include iron and steel, machinery, agricultural implements, tractors, elevators, dynamos and electric motors, rope, coal tar products, and airplanes. Kharkov has an Institute of People's Education, an agricultural and economic institute, and museums for the demonstration of improved agricultural methods. Population, 1939, 833,432.

Kiev (*kē'yĕf*). One of the oldest cities in Russia, attractively situated amid wooded hills on the Dnieper river in the southwestern part of the country. The Dnieper is here spanned by a suspension bridge, 3510 feet long. In the upper town is the famous Petchersk monastery. The city has numerous churches, whose gilded cupolas, seen at a distance, impart to it an almost Oriental effect. It suffered severely from civil war and famine in 1917-20, during which period it changed hands six times.

Christianity was first preached in Russia at Kiev, which has long been the chief eastern center of the Greek Catholic religion. There is a large trade in flax, wool, wine, cattle, timber, grain, and fruits. The manufactures include sugar, hardware, tobacco goods, machinery, glass, leather, and yeast. Population, 1939, 846,293.

Königsberg (*kû'nĭks-bĕrk*). A city of East Prussia, Germany, lying on the river Pregel, about 4 miles from its mouth in the Frisches bay, a southern inlet of the Baltic Sea. Prior to the World War the city was a strong naval and military fortress. Its manufactures include locomotives, chemicals, cork, tobacco, sugar, malt liquors, and pianos. Amber articles constitute a distinctive product. The University of Königsberg was founded in 1544. Kant, who was born in Königsberg in 1724, was a member of the university's professorial staff. Population, 1939, 368,433.

Krakow (*krä'kō*). A city of southwestern Poland, situated at the head of navigation on the Vistula river. It was annexed by Germany in 1939. Krakow was the capital of Poland from 1320 to 1609. Favored by its position as a river port and railroad terminal, Krakow has become the trade center of a large territory. The city was founded in 700 A. D. by the Polish duke of Krak. Population, 1946, 299,565.

Lapland. An area of indefinite extent at the northern extremity of Europe. The region has no separate political existence, but includes parts of Norway, Sweden, Finland, and Russia. Reindeer provide sustenance, clothing, and transportation. The people are called Lapps. They belong to an Asiatic race and average about 5 feet in height.

Lausanne (*lō'zän'*). A city of western Switzerland, built on five hills rising from the north shore of Lake Geneva. The city is a railroad and educational center and has a large tourist trade. The manufactures include chocolate, machinery, tobacco goods, and sugar.

The Protestant Cathedral of Notre Dame is the city's most notable church. It dates from the 13th century and was intimately associated with the rise of Protestantism. The University of Lausanne, founded as an academy in 1537, was one of the first schools established for the training of Protestant ministers. The city has been the scene of many important international conferences of statesmen. The language of the citizens is French. Gibbon wrote most of his *Decline and Fall of the Roman Empire* while a resident of Lausanne. Population, 1941, 92,541.

Leeds. A woolen and steel manufacturing city of north central England. The woolen industries especially have been famous for centuries. The chief products of the city, apart from textiles and steel, include machinery, agricultural implements, leather, furniture, artificial silk, and ready-made clothing.

In the midst of the factory district stand the celebrated ruins of Kirkstall Abbey, founded in the 12th century. The city also has a fine university and is noted for a great music festival held every three years. Population, 1947, 498,650.

Leghorn (Livorno). A seaport and commercial city of northwestern Italy, situated on a spacious, improved harbor on the northeastern coast of the Ligurian Sea. The industries include shipbuilding and the manufacture of copper and brass products, coral ornaments, glass, porcelain, chemicals, electrical apparatus, and flour. The city is noted also as a summer resort. The architectural monuments are comparatively few, the most notable being the cathedral, dating from the 17th century. There is a handsome synagogue founded in 1581. Population, 1947, 137,226.

Leicester (*lĕs'tẽr*). A manufacturing city of central England, about 100 miles northwest of London. The chief industrial products are woolen hosiery, boots and shoes, bricks, and dyes. The city lies in a rich coal mining and sheep raising district.

Leicester is a progressive municipality, providing adequately for the health, education, and recreation of its inhabitants. Saint Nicholas church was constructed partly of bricks taken from a Roman wall in the vicinity. The assize court of Leicester is held in a building which was formerly the banquet hall of a Norman castle. Population, 1947, 280,170.

Leiden. A city of the Netherlands about 10 miles east of The Hague and 6 miles inland from the North Sea. It has a famous university founded in 1575 by William of Orange. Leiden is also known as the birthplace of Rembrandt and as the city which received the persecuted English emigrants, some of whom sailed later in the *Mayflower* to Plymouth, Massachusetts. Population, 1946, 83,952.

Leipzig (E. *līp'sĭk;* G. *līp'tsĭĸ*). A city of central Germany, noted as the chief center of the country's publishing industry. There are about 1000 establishments engaged in the business. The city is also a world market for furs, which, along with glass, cloth, and leather, are sold in great quantities at fairs, three of which are held each year.

Leipzig has a famous university, founded in 1409. There are numerous museums, the museum of the book trade being the best of its kind in the world. Other features of the city are the Supreme Court building, the Booksellers' Exchange, the Crystal Palace, the Royal Academy of Plastic Arts, the Conservatory of Music, and Auerbach's cellar, the last having been represented by Goethe as the scene of part of his *Faust*. Near Leipzig, in 1813, was fought the battle in which Napoleon was defeated prior to his banishment to Elba. Population, 1939, 701,606.

Lemberg (Lvov). A city of the Ukraine, almost surrounded by strongly fortified hills. It is the seat of three archbishops and has three cathedrals—a Roman Catholic, an Armenian, and a Greek Catholic. The city has many educational institutions, chief of which is the University of Lemberg, founded in 1784. It was annexed by Russia in 1939.

Lemberg has numerous manufactures, including ironwares, musical instruments, bricks, flour, and spirits, and conducts a large trade in linen, flax, hemp, and wool. The Fair of the Three Kings is held here each January. Population, 1931, 316,177.

Leningrad (E. *lĕn'ĭn-grăd*) (R. *lyĕ'nĭn-grät*). One of the largest cities of Russia, situated at the head of the Gulf of Finland on the delta of the Neva river. The port and fortress of the city is Kronstadt, on a near-by island. Canals connect the city with the White and Black seas.

Leningrad, formerly called Saint Petersburg, and, after 1914, Petrograd, was the creation of Peter the Great of Russia, who built it at enormous cost of labor and of life, in order to obtain communication with Western Europe. He populated it, in part, by compelling his wealthier subjects to spend a portion of each year in the city. Its name was changed to Leningrad in 1924.

From the Admiralty, in the center of Leningrad, radiate three great avenues, one of which—Prospekt of the 25th of October—ranks among the finest streets in Europe. Near the Admiralty stands the Winter Palace. It is connected by a gallery with the Hermitage, which houses an art collection of rare value. Across the Neva river from the palace is situated the prison of Saint Peter and Saint Paul, infamous for the many political prisoners formerly confined within its walls. The city has one of the finest subways in the world.

Leningrad was formerly the capital and the greatest commercial and industrial city of Russia, being the outlet for enormous exports of wheat. The Revolution of 1917 broke out there. In 1918, the national government was removed to Moscow. After a period of industrial paralysis, during which the city's population fell from over 2,300,000 to 722,000 it recovered rapidly as an industrial center. Its chief products are metal and machinery, chemicals, textiles, rubber, leather, tobacco, paper, furniture, matches, and foodstuffs. Population, 1939, 3,191,304.

Liège (*lē-ĕzh'*) or **Luik.** The chief manufacturing city of Belgium, situated amid rich coal mines in the eastern part of the country and built on both banks of the Meuse river. The chief industrial products are guns, steam engines, machinery, motor cars, and textiles. The city has numerous educational institutions, including Liège university, the museum of which contains the skeletons of many prehistoric animals found in the vicinity.

Liège is the center of the Walloon culture, akin to the French. A chapel built in the 6th century furnished the nucleus about which the city began to grow. The German attack on the surrounding fortresses was one of the first battles in World War I. Population, 1946, 150,103.

Lille (*lēl*). An industrial city in northern France, connected by a canal with the North Sea, 30 miles distant. The chief manufactures are linen and cotton textiles, locomotives, structural steel, sugar, chemicals, tobacco, and soap. Lisle thread derives its name from the city.

The city is modern in appearance and well built. Its features include the Church of Saint Maurice, the Palais des Beaux Arts with its extremely valuable collection of paintings, and Lille university, at which Pasteur was a professor. Lille suffered severely during World War I, part of the laboring population having been deported to work in German factories. Population, 1946, 188,871.

Limerick. A port of Eire in southwestern Ireland, at the head of the Shannon estuary. Butter and condensed milk are the most important exports. The industries include flour milling, the curing of bacon, and the manufacture of lace, fishhooks, leather, and clothing. Limerick is an ancient city, known to Greek geographers as Regia. It has given its name to the type of nonsense verse known as a limerick. Population, 1946, 42,987.

Limoges (*lē'mōzh'*). An old city of France, situated somewhat southwest of the geographical center of the country. It is famous for its porcelain industry, Limoges china being known in all parts of the world. Other important industries are printing and the manufacture of liquors, leather goods, hats, and gloves. The city has a museum of ancient pottery. Every seventh year, the Fête d'Ostension is celebrated to commemorate a plague, which, in the 10th century, destroyed 40,000 people. Limoges was the ancient capital of Limousin, a former French province, which gave its name to the limousine. Population, 1946, 107,874.

Lisbon. The capital and largest city of Portugal, beautifully situated at the head of the Tagus estuary about seven miles from its mouth in the Atlantic Ocean. Its harbor has few superiors and facilitates a large commerce. The city has manufactures of cork, textiles, pottery, paper, chemicals, sugar, iron castings, and machine-shop products.

Although founded by the Phœnicians, Lisbon has a modern appearance, having been almost entirely rebuilt after the earthquake and tidal wave which, in 1755, destroyed most of the city and took nearly 40,000 lives. Between the terraced levels of the city, elevators carry people up and down. The Avenue of Liberty, 300 feet wide with a double row of shade trees down the middle, commemorates the freeing of Portugal from Spain in 1640. Other features of the city include the Botanical Garden, the Estrella Garden, the Estrella Church, a university, and numerous other educational and scientific institutions. Camoëns and Vasco da Gama were born in Lisbon. Population, 1940, 709,179.

Liverpool. The third largest city of England, situated near the center of the country's western coast on the northeastern side of the Mersey River estuary. Among British cities, its total commerce is second only to that of London, while its foreign trade exceeds London's by a considerable margin, giving it the distinction of having the largest foreign commerce of any city in the world. The harbor has been elaborately improved. By a system of locks, the water level of the inner harbor is rendered independent of the tides. Docks cover an area of 660 acres, and there are about 40 miles of quays. The storage facilities include a 13-story tobacco warehouse with 36 acres of floor space. There are also installations for storing over 100,000 tons of oil and spirits in bulk.

Liverpool is connected with Birkenhead on the opposite side of the Mersey river by a railway tunnel nearly a mile long and a vehicular tunnel which ranks with the greatest in the world. Beneath the city, also, there are five tunnels used by railroads. Liverpool university is widely known for its school of tropical medicine. One of the most noteworthy of the city's buildings is Saint George's Hall, a structure of the Corinthian order, erected with the proceeds of dock profits. The Anglican cathedral, begun in 1904, is designed to be the largest in England. Also under construction is a Catholic cathedral of Christ the King, to be surmounted by a dome 168 feet in diameter, the largest in the world. Liverpool was the first city in England to provide municipal baths, having maintained such establishments since 1794. Population, 1947, 769,170.

Lodz. The second largest city of Poland, located in the west central part of the country on a site which, in 1800, was covered with impenetrable forest. It has grown with remarkable rapidity, having become, since 1870, largely through the activity of Germans, the chief center of the textile industry in Poland. Other manufactures include chemicals, beer, machinery, and silk. Population, 1946, 496,861.

LONDON. The capital of Great Britain and Northern Ireland, the commercial, financial, artistic, and intellectual center of the kingdom, and the second largest city in the world. It is situated in southeastern England on both banks of the Thames river about 60 miles from its mouth. London consists of three parts: "the City," a space one square mile in area, surrounded by walls; the County of London; and the "Outer Ring," or metropolitan district. The whole constitutes Greater London, which covers an area of 693 square miles lying within a radius of 15 miles from Charing Cross, a central point within "the City."

COMMERCE. London handles one-third of Great Britain's commerce. The docks cover about 650 acres, and the quays have a total length of 28 miles. Each dock is an interior basin accessible by means of a lock. The port officials and their staffs are accommodated in a domed edifice completed in 1922 at a cost of ten million dollars. London's foreign commerce amounts to nearly four billion dollars annually. Products handled by the port come from all parts of the world and exhibit an extraordinary variety. Wool represents the greatest bulk.

INDUSTRY. London easily leads all other cities of Great Britain in the aggregate value of manufactures. The clothing industries engage the greatest number of workers. Other important manufactures are furniture, machinery, silks, and leather products. Printing and bookbinding employ nearly 50,000 persons. The industrial establishments are mainly confined to the eastern and southern parts of the city.

TRANSPORTATION. All the trunk railway lines of England converge in London, which is, also, connected with European points by airplane service. Electric railways operate subways, or "tubes," and cross beneath the river by means of tunnels. The river is spanned by numerous bridges, of which the London bridge, Tower bridge, Blackfriars bridge, and Westminster bridge are among the more noteworthy.

STREETS. The thoroughfares of London are not laid out on straight lines but parallel the winding of the Thames river. The more famous streets include a popular promenade along the Thames embankment; Lombard street, the financial center of the city; Fleet street and Paternoster row, both devoted to printing and bookselling; Whitehall street and Downing street, where the government offices are located; Haymarket, a street of theaters and cafes; the Strand, an avenue of retail stores, hotels, and places of amusement; Regent street, recently reconstructed with handsome shops; Piccadilly, lined with fashionable residences; and Bond street, noted for its jewelry shops.

SQUARES, PARKS, AND MONUMENTS. Charing Cross, standing in the center of Greater London, is named after a memorial cross erected in 1290 by Edward I in the former village of Charing. The cross has disappeared, and its place has, since 1675, been occupied by a statue of Charles I. Popularly, the name is associated with a near-by railroad station, in the courtyard of which stands a modern reproduction of the cross.

Trafalgar square contains a lofty column in memory of Nelson and a statue of Washington, the latter a gift from the state of Virginia in 1922. Hyde park with the adjoining Kensington gardens covers 630 acres and contains a large statue of the duke of Wellington and the national monument to Queen Victoria. Whitehall has a magnificent cenotaph erected "To the Glorious Dead," a memorial to the English soldiers who fell in the World War. In Regent park is located one of the greatest zoological gardens in the world. Other pleasure grounds include Saint James park and Epping forest, the latter being a tract of 5600 acres northeast of London purchased by the city and thrown open to the citizens.

BUILDINGS. The Tower of London, erected by William the Conqueror, stands guard over the eastern entrance of "the City." Formerly used as a prison, it serves now chiefly as a museum and contains the crown jewels of the British sovereigns. The Houses of Parliament, known as Westminster Palace, cover 8 acres on the bank of the Thames river. The building has 1100 rooms and two towers, one with an altitude of 340 feet. The other is 318 feet high and contains a clock which rings "Big Ben," a famous bell weighing 13 tons. Saint Paul's Cathedral, planned by Sir Christopher Wren, is surmounted by a dome which reaches a point 364 feet above the street. Buckingham palace is the residence of the royal family when in London.

Westminster Abbey, dating from 1220, is the coronation church of the British sovereigns. It has a length of 531 feet, a width of 203 feet, and a tower rising 225 feet above the ground. The building is the burial place of many of the country's rulers, and has monuments to famous British warriors and statesmen. The "Poets' Corner," in the south transept, contains the tombs of most of England's great writers from Chaucer to John Ruskin.

Among the other notable buildings and institutions of the city are the British Museum, which contains three million volumes and priceless treasures of ancient art and antiquities; London university, adjoining the British Museum; the Bank of England building, covering four acres of ground; the Greenwich Observatory, from the meridian of which nearly all geographers calculate longitude; the South Kensington Museum, where classes are conducted in art and in industrial sciences; the Temple, a group of buildings long known as the residences of law students; and the People's Palace, used for recreation and for education of the poorer classes. London university comprises upwards of 30 different colleges located in various parts of the city.

London has many reminders of America. A statue of Lincoln faces Westminster Abbey, and within the famous edifice is a bust of Longfellow and a window and tablet to Lowell. John Harvard, the founder of Harvard university, was baptized in Southwark's cathedral. John Quincy Adams was married in All Hallows church, where, too, William Penn was baptized. Theodore Roosevelt's second marriage was solemnized in Saint George's church, Hanover square. In Saint Margaret's church, Americans have installed a beautiful window to the memory of Phillips Brooks, Episcopal bishop of Massachusetts. Pocahontas is commemorated by a window in a small Gravesend church, where she was buried in 1617. Christ church has a Lincoln tower with the Stars and Stripes cut in the stone. In Westminster Abbey, a tablet was erected in 1923 commemorating Walter Hines Page, American ambassador to Great Britain during the years of the World War.

GOVERNMENT. Greater London has no mayor, but, in most matters, is directly under the control of Parliament. "The City," however, is nominally independent even of the sovereign, who may not enter until he receives the key of admission from the lord mayor. London county consists of a large number of boroughs, each having its mayor and alderman.

HISTORY. London is first mentioned in history by the Romans, who built walls about the city. It was later burned by the British queen Boadicea, sacked by the Danes, and later was taken by William the Conqueror, who granted the city its charter. In 1666, the Great Fire destroyed four-fifths of the buildings. In 1851, the first international industrial exhibition took place in London. Population, 1947, 8,244,370.

Lourdes (*lōōrd*). A town of southwestern France, situated at the foot of the Pyrenees mountains and about 80 miles from the head of the Bay of Biscay. It is one of the chief places of Catholic pilgrimage in Europe, being visited annually by upward of 600,000 people.

The fame of Lourdes dates from 1858, when the Virgin appeared to a young girl, Bernadette Soubirous. The grotto near which the apparition took place is now surmounted by the magnificent Church of the Rosary, containing a shrine dedicated to the Virgin, "Our Lady of Lourdes." The church contains numerous crutches, tablets, and gifts, which memorialize cures credited to the Virgin. A near-by spring, which appeared at the time of the apparition, is diverted into several basins, in which the pilgrims bathe. On August 20, each year, a national pilgrimage takes place accompanied with religious ceremonies and a torchlight procession.

The inhabitants of Lourdes are economically dependent on the pilgrims. The chief products are souvenirs. Population, 1931, 7557.

Louvain. A city of central Belgium, formerly the center of a thriving textile industry. In recent times, the city has been chiefly noted for the University of Louvain, founded in 1425-26, and for several fine buildings, a number of which were burned while the city was under German occupation during the World War. A new library building, erected mainly by American generosity, was dedicated in 1928. Population, 1946, 36,417.

Lucerne (Luzern). A city of north central Switzerland, having a location of rare beauty at the northwestern extremity of the Lake of Lucerne. The inhabitants are occupied chiefly in providing accommodation and services for tourists, who throng the city's 70 hotels in numbers exceeding an annual total of 140,000. The most noted memorial of the town is the famous "Lion of Lucerne." It is in a near-by grotto and consists of a colossal figure of a lion transfixed by a spear but still defending the lilies of France. The figure is carved from the solid rock and was executed in memory of the 781 Swiss guards of Louis XVI, who were slain in 1792 during the attack on the Tuileries in Paris. Population, 1941, 206,608.

Lyon. A commercial and manufacturing city of France, situated southeast of the country's geographical center at the junction of the Rhône and the Saône river. The rivers are crossed by 24 bridges, one of which, opened in 1918, is called President Wilson bridge.

Industrially, Lyon is second only to Paris among the cities of France and is the foremost silk manufacturing city of the world. Other important products include rayon and cellophane, chemicals, machinery, macaroni, hats, chocolate, leather, jewelry, and tobacco goods.

Lyon's importance dates from the period of the Roman republic. The ruins of a Roman bath and of a Roman theater still remain. The city's oldest edifice, the Church of Saint Martin d'Ainay, utilizes several columns of a Roman temple which formerly occupied the site. The Cathedral of Saint Jean, begun in 1110, is one of the finest examples of early Gothic in France. Other notable structures are the Hôtel de Ville, the Bourse, and the Palais des Arts. The University of Lyon ranks next to that of Paris among French universities in number of students. The Roman emperors Claudius and Caracalla were born in Lugdunum, as Lyon was called by the Romans. Population, 1946, 460,748.

Madrid. The capital and largest city of Spain, situated 2100 feet above sea level on a plateau near the center of the country. In this city are centered most of Spain's governmental, educational, and artistic activities. Since 1890, manufactures have increased greatly and now include leather, chemicals, pottery and porcelain, matches, cork, paper, glass, foundry products, furniture, and carpet.

Madrid centers about a plaza lined with impressive buildings. The ten most important streets radiate from this plaza. The magnificent Liberty Avenue, traversing the city in a north and south direction and ornamented with four to six rows of trees and with numerous monuments, is one of the finest promenades in the world. The Royal Palace, built of granite and white marble, stands on a hill which overlooks the city from the west. The adjoining armories contain the armor of Columbus and that of Cortés. Other features of the city are the National library, the University of Madrid, the Press Palace of skyscraper-like construction, a magnificent bull ring seating over 13,000 persons, and the National art gallery, the last containing, next to the Louvre, the world's most valuable collection of paintings. Population, 1947, 1,187,142.

Maelstrom (*māl'strŏm*). The literary and former name of Moskenstrom, a celebrated tidal eddy, occurring between two small islands at the western end of the Lofoten group off Norway's northwestern coast. The eddy is caused by the tidewaters passing through a narrow channel between the ocean and Vestfiord. The Maelstrom was memorialized by Schiller in his poem "The Diver." When the current flows fastest and the wind blows directly against it, the sea for miles around becomes so agitated that small vessels cannot survive in it. Ordinarily it may be traversed without danger. The name is often used as a synonym for whirlpool.

Magdeburg (G. *mäg'dē-bōōrk*; E. *măg'dē-bûrg*). A commercial city of north central Germany and the capital of the state of Saxony, situated on the Elbe river 88 miles southwest of Berlin. The chief manufactures include steel products, sugar, chemicals, tobacco goods, gloves, fertilizers, cement, glass, and rubber. The city is strongly fortified. The old royal palace is now used as a museum. Magdeburg was the birthplace of Otto von Guericke, the inventor of the air pump. The city sided with the Protestant powers during the Thirty Years' war and, in 1631, was sacked and burned, 30,000 of the inhabitants being put to the sword. Population, 1939, 334,358.

Malaga (S. *mä'lä-gä*; E. *măl'ȧ-gȧ*). An ancient city of southern Spain, picturesquely located on a fine harbor opening into the Mediterranean Sea. A mountain range surrounds the town on three sides. The principal architectural feature is the vast cathedral dominating the whole view of the city from the sea. Malaga is known for Malaga wine, grapes, and raisins. The site was first settled by Phœnicians. Population, 1947, 277,582.

Malmö (*mälm'û'*). A seaport of southern Sweden, situated on The Sound opposite Copenhagen. Malmö is an important railroad terminal and manufacturing center and has grown rapidly in recent years. Among its industrial products are iron castings, railroad cars, and textiles. The city has a large artificial harbor and exports much farm produce. Population, 1947, 176,659.

Manchester. A manufacturing city and third largest port of England, lying about 200 miles northwest of London and 35 miles inland from the western seaboard. It is connected with the sea by the Manchester ship canal, which was the first ship canal to be built in England.

Manchester is the largest cotton manufacturing city in the world and the center of one of the world's greatest industrial areas. Besides cotton, the manufactures include structural steel, electrical machinery, chemicals, glass, paper, rubber, and silk. The city has 1600 acres devoted to parks. Victoria University of Manchester is the city's leading educational institution.

The more important buildings include the town hall, a Gothic structure costing over five million dollars; the Royal Exchange; The Royal Institution, an art gallery in the Doric style; Free Trade Hall; and Ship Canal House, the tallest commercial building, constructed on American design. Population, 1947, 695,230.

Mannheim (*măn'hīm*). A manufacturing city of southwestern Germany, situated at the confluence of the Rhine and the Neckar river, 43 miles south of Frankfort. Mannheim is said to be the most regularly built city on the continent of Europe. It consists of 136 square sections, the whole surrounded by a semicircular boulevard, known as the Ring Strasse. Outside the semicircle are numerous suburbs. The outstanding building of the city is a palace, which has a front of over 1700 feet.

Mannheim's commerce consists chiefly of grain, coal, petroleum, tobacco, sugar, and ironware. The manufactures include machinery, celluloid, carpets, chemicals, furniture, glass, and leather goods. Population, 1946, 211,614.

Marseille (*mȧr'sâ'y'*). The second largest city of France and the republic's principal seaport, located in the southeastern part of the country on an inlet of the Mediterranean Sea. Southwest of the harbor lies the islet Chateau d'If, celebrated in Dumas's *Count of Monte Cristo*.

Marseille's trade is largely with eastern countries and with the French territory in northern Africa. It consists mainly of woolen goods, ribbons, sugar, and wines. The city has large shipyards and factories for making soap, vegetable oils, and numerous other products.

The national anthem of France, "The Marseillaise," received its name in Paris when a battalion of Marseillais, or citizens of Marseille, sang the song at the storming of the Tuileries. Massilia was the name given to the city by the Romans when the settlement was already many centuries old, having been founded by Phœnicians prior to 600 B. C. It was the home of Pytheas, a Greek explorer who visited Britain in the 4th century B. C. The city's importance in modern times dates from 1848, when the surrounding region was irrigated by a canal from the Durance river about 100 miles distant. Marseille has the finest modern cathedral in France. Population, 1946, 636,264.

Milan (*mĭl'ăn; mĭ-lăn'*) (**Milano**). The second largest city of Italy. It lies in the northwestern part of the country about 40 miles from the border of Switzerland. Milan is the chief financial center of Italy and ranks high as an industrial community and as a seat of art and learning. The more important manufactures include locomotives, automobiles, electrical supplies, and rubber articles. The silk, printing, and furniture making trades of Italy are centered in the city.

The Cathedral of Milan, dating from 1386, is the third largest in Europe. Built of white marble, it is 486 feet long and 356 feet high. It contains 3000 statues, and its stained-glass windows are said to be the largest in the world. The edifice has a capacity for 40,000 people. Other features of the city are the Church of Sant' Ambrogio, dating from the 4th century A. D.; the former convent of Santa Maria delle Grazie, which contains Leonardo da Vinci's "Last Supper"; the Brera Palace, one of the finest picture galleries in Italy; the Teatro della Scala, the second largest opera house in Europe; and a celebrated archeological museum.

Milan was captured from the Gauls by the Romans in 222 B. C. It has frequently been sacked and burned, but its position at the northern entrance to Italy has insured its continued importance as a commercial city. Population, 1947, 1,250,389.

Monte Carlo. A city in the principality of Monaco, beautifully situated on a sheltered bay in the Mediterranean coast. Monte Carlo is best known for its Casino, a palatial building on a promontory in the east of the city. It is the chief fashionable gambling resort of Europe. The principal games played are roulette and *trente et quarante*, "thirty and forty." In the latter game, the minimum stake is 20 francs and the maximum is 12,000, while, for roulette, the stakes may range from 5 francs to 6000. Tickets are obtained free, and playing takes place between 11:30 A. M. and 11:30 P. M. The inhabitants of Monaco are not allowed to participate.

Adjoining the Casino is the *tir aux pigeons*, "pigeon shooting range," where expert marksmen compete in shooting pigeons released for the purpose. A prize of 20,000 francs is offered for a competition held each January. Population, about 10,000.

MOSCOW (*mŏs'kō*) **(Moskva).** The capital and largest city of Russia, situated somewhat north of the geographical center of the country's European territory. Built at the intersection of six important highways, the city has long been an important market for grain, hemp, oil, tea, sugar, hides, wool, timber, metal, drugs, and silk. Its leading manufactures are textiles, chemicals, metal and food products, glass, and leather.

Moscow is a city of striking contrasts, with its old wooden houses of the suburbs, the many-storied apartment buildings for workmen recently erected, the low dwellings of the former aristocracy with their pillared porticoes, huge factories, gilded domes of Oriental-like cathedrals, and magnificent palaces of old Russian or ultra-modern design.

The Kremlin. This is the old citadel of Moscow, and is the city's outstanding feature. It is a triangular enclosure surrounded by walls about 1½ miles in length. Its walls are surmounted by 18 towers and pierced by 5 gates. The main entrance opens on the Red square, and is fronted by the massive mausoleum of Lenin, within which lies his embalmed body in a glass case. Within the Kremlin stand the government offices and a number of palaces and cathedrals. In the Great Kremlin Palace, built of white stone with a gilded cupola, are held the congresses of the Communist, or Third, International.

Other points of interest in the Kremlin are the Tower of Ivan the Great, which is 322 feet high and contains 34 bells with a total weight of 290 tons; several monasteries of considerable antiquity; and the Czar Bell, cast in 1733, which is the largest bell in the world. It weighs 220 tons and measures 22 feet in diameter and 19 feet 3 inches in height. The bell was never hung, having been cracked by a fire before it left the foundry.

Reconstruction. Beginning in 1935, a reconstruction of Moscow was begun, with plans calling for its expansion from 68 to 234 square miles and accommodation for five million inhabitants. Eleven miles of a new subway had already been completed in that year.

Under this plan, the Kremlin, preserved and restored, will remain the central feature of the city. Along one side the magnificent Lenin boulevard will be constructed, flanked by many of the finest new buildings in Russia. At one end is the site of the Palace of the International Soviets, planned to be the world's tallest building. Residential and industrial sections form a circular band about the central portion and the entire city will be ringed with parks and forests. One feature of the city as it is being rebuilt is the manner in which large factories dominate districts, each factory, workers' residences, and facilities for living being planned as a unit. Cultural institutions include the Moscow Art theater, the University of Moscow, and the Lenin institute and library.

History. The earliest reference to Moscow dates from 1147. It was made the capital of Russia, and, in spite of many sieges, conflagrations, and pestilences, it remained the seat of government until 1712, when Saint Petersburg, now called Leningrad, became the capital. In 1812, the Russians burned the city in order to deprive Napoleon of a winter base. In 1918, Moscow was again made the capital of Russia. Population, 1939, 4,137,018.

Munich (*mū'nĭk*) **(München).** One of the largest cities of Germany and the capital of the state of Bavaria, situated near the southern extremity of the country on the Isar river, a tributary of the Danube.

Largely through the effort of King Ludwig I of Bavaria, Munich became, in the 19th century, one of the best built cities of Europe and, architecturally, one of the most beautiful. It is lavishly adorned by numerous squares and pleasure gardens and by buildings constructed in the leading styles. The English Garden, a park of 500 acres adorned with small temples and towers, was designed by Count Rumford, a native of Massachusetts. Other features of the city are the former Royal Palace, the National Theater, the Art Union, numerous museums, and the Old Castle, the last dating from 1253. The art collections in Munich are among the richest on the continent. The University of Munich is one of the leading educational institutions of Germany.

Apart from art and education, the great industry of Munich is the brewing of beer. Other products of the city's workmanship are bronze founding, glass staining, silversmiths' work, wood carving, and lithographing. Railway machinery, wall paper, gloves, and artificial flowers are also made. Population, 1947, 760,929.

Nantes (E. *nănts*; F. *nänt*). A seaport of northwestern France, located at the head of the Loire River estuary and about 50 miles from the sea. The industries include the canning of sardines, sugar refining, shipbuilding, and the manufacture of iron products and of tobacco goods. In history, the city is known for the Edict of Nantes, by which, in 1598, Henry IV granted toleration to the Huguenots. Population, 1946, 200,265.

Naples (Napoli). The third largest city of Italy, situated near the central part of the kingdom on the Bay of Naples, which opens into the Tyrrhenian Sea. On one side of the bay rises Mt. Vesuvius, and on the other side is the picturesque height of Posilipo. The city has a safe and deep harbor. It is an important naval station and commercial emporium and possesses numerous industrial establishments. The manufactures include steel products, textiles, glass, macaroni, and chemicals. The port is a noted embarkation point for emigrants.

Naples is visited yearly by upwards of 30,000 tourists. Its features include the cathedral, built in 1272; the National museum, containing a priceless collection of antiquities, most notably those obtained from the excavated site of Pompeii and of Herculaneum; the San Carlo opera house, one of the largest in Europe; the most complete marine aquarium in the world; and the University of Naples, founded in 1224. Naples was originally a Greek colony, established about 450 B. C. under the name of Neapolis, "New City." Population, 1947, 941,841.

Newcastle. One of the largest coal exporting cities of Great Britain, situated in northeastern England on the Tyne river 8 miles from its mouth in the North Sea. Quays and factories line both banks of the river for a distance of 10 miles. There are also large shipbuilding yards and locomotive, engineering, and ordnance works. Other industrial products include Portland cement, chemicals, grindstones, and refined lead. The city's pre-eminence as a coal exporting center is reflected in the popular expression, "carrying coals to Newcastle," indicating superfluous activity.

Newcastle was the site of a Roman fort built to defend the eastern end of the wall that Hadrian constructed across Britain. The city was named from a castle built here in the 11th century by Robert, the son of William the Conqueror. Population, 1947, 293,570.

Nice. A city and tourist resort of southeastern France on the Mediterranean coast and at the foot of the Alps mountains. Its industries produce perfume, liquors, soap, silk, straw hats, and rubber, metal, and tobacco goods. An 8-acre harbor accommodates an active coastal shipping trade. An equable climate, varying from a winter mean of 49° F. to a summer mean of 72° F., lends Nice an attractiveness which is further enhanced by the meeting of sea and mountain scenery in a subtropical setting. The city is famous for its carnivals, especially the so-called battle of flowers.

Nice is about 2000 years old, having been founded by Greek colonists. The name is Greek for Victory. It was subject at various times to Saracen, German, French, Italian, and Spanish power, but was confirmed in French possession in 1860. Population, 1946, 211,165.

Nottingham. A manufacturing city of central England, 125 miles northwest of London. It is built on the slope and at the foot of a rocky eminence, which is crowned by an ancient castle, now used as a museum. Nottingham college is on a fine 220-acre campus, called Highfields. The chief manufactures include lace, hosiery, clothing, machinery, tobacco, and bicycles. Population, 1947, 296,350.

Nuremberg (Nürnberg). A city of southwestern Germany, noted especially for its manufacture of toys, electrical machinery, and lead pencils. It is the chief German market for hops.

The city retains a medieval appearance, due to its narrow, winding streets and to its houses with projecting upper stories. The old city walls still stand. Nuremberg is the seat of the National Germanic museum, which houses the largest collection of German antiquities in existence. Hans Sachs and the artist Dürer were born in the city. Watches were first made here, being known as "Nuremberg eggs." Air guns and geographical globes are also claimed as Nuremberg inventions. Population, 1947, 322,043.

Oberammergau (*ō'bẽr-äm'ẽr-gou'*). A village in the extreme south of Germany, celebrated for the Passion play, which takes place there once in each ten years, the most recent performance having been given in 1930. The play represents the crucifixion and the ascension of Jesus. It takes place each Sunday during the summer on a large wooden stage open to the sky, and it usually lasts eight hours. The performance was originally undertaken in fulfillment of a vow made in 1633 by the villagers, who thereby expressed their gratitude for the cessation of an epidemic of the plague. Population, 2281.

Odessa. A city of southwestern Russia, situated on the north shore of the Black Sea. Its commodious harbor is divided by moles into six ports. Odessa became great as the point of export for vast quantities of grain, wool, sugar, and lumber. Its industrial products include salt, glass, motion picture apparatus, and canned goods.

Odessa was founded in 1794 by Catherine the Great as a stepping-stone to Constantinople. The city is well built and is adorned by many pleasure grounds and fine buildings. The Victims of the Revolution square contains tombs of the fallen, the city having changed hands eight times in 1917-20. Population, 1939, 604,223.

Olympia. A plain in the western part of the Morea peninsula, Greece. It contains many ruins, including those of a temple of Zeus and of a stadium in which the Olympic games were originally held. In ancient times, the temple of Zeus contained a colossal statue of this god, the work of Phidias. Carved in ivory and embellished with gold, this statue was accounted one of the seven wonders of the ancient world.

Oporto (Porto). A city of northwestern Portugal, beautifully situated on both banks of the Douro river about 3 miles from its mouth in the Atlantic Ocean. The river is spanned by several bridges, one of which, having an arch of 560 feet, is counted among the great bridges of the world. Manufacturing is the most prominent industry. The city's products include leather, woolens, pottery, corks, hats, and tobacco. Prominent among the exports is port wine, which received its name from Oporto. Population, 1940, 262,309.

Oslo. The capital and largest city of Norway, situated at the head of Oslo fiord in the southeastern extremity of the country. The city is the trade center for southern Norway and has large shipyards and important manufactures of woolens, matches, pulp, and nails. Hydroelectric power is abundant and cheap.

Oslo is surrounded on the land side by picturesque hills. The chief edifices are the Parliament buildings, the National Theater, the University of Oslo, the Museum of Art, and a historical museum. Oslo was founded in 1048. Having been destroyed by fire, it was rebuilt in 1624 and named Christiania. The original name was restored in 1925. Population, 1946, 289,000.

Ostend (*ŏst-ĕnd'*) **(Ostende).** A fashionable summer resort of northern Belgium, on the North Sea. The city is also a well-known gateway to continental Europe for travelers from England. During World War I, Germany used Ostend as a naval base. Population, 1946, 48,519.

Oxford. A university city of England, with a population, in 1947, of 104,950. It is situated about 50 miles northwest of London. The city is the seat of Oxford university, which was founded as early as the 12th century. This university is of especial interest to the English-speaking world on account of the Rhodes scholarships tenable at Oxford and open to students from the British dominions and the United States. The Bodleian library, connected with the university, is one of the world's richest collections of early printed books and of ancient manuscripts. Women were first admitted to degrees in the year 1920.

The university consists of a federation of 21 colleges, each with its own government and teaching staff. Degrees are granted, not by the individual colleges, but by the university. The following table gives the name of each of the colleges with its date of incorporation:

College	Date	College	Date
University	1249	New	1379
Merton	1264	Lincoln	1427
Balliol	1266	All Souls'	1437
Exeter	1314 and 1566	St. Mary Magdalen (pron. *Maudlin*)	1474
Oriel	1326	Brazenose	1509
Queen's	1340	Corpus Christi	1516
Christ Church	1525	Wadham	1613
Trinity	1555	Pembroke	1624
St. John's	1555	Worcester	1714
Jesus	1571	Keble	1868
		Hertford	1874

Palermo. An Italian seaport, located on the northwest coast of Sicily. The exports are mainly oranges, lemons, dried fruits, oils, sulphur, and wines. Tunny fishing and shipbuilding are the chief industries. The city ranks third among the seaports of Italy.

Palermo has many architectural monuments dating from the periods when Sicily was held successively by the Saracens, the Normans, and the Spaniards. The city was founded by the Phœnicians and was captured in 254 B. C. by the Romans, who called it Panormus. Population, 1947, 445,132.

PARIS. The capital of France and the third largest city in Europe, situated on both banks of the Seine river about 110 miles from its mouth in the English channel. Paris is the commercial, artistic, and intellectual center of France and is generally acknowledged to be the most beautiful city in the world.

Streets and Boulevards. The streets of Paris do not follow any unified plan. There are, however, several systems of magnificent boulevards. Boulevard is a French word originally meaning bulwark. As the old walls encircling Paris were from time to time torn down to be replaced by others embracing a larger circle, the site of the demolished walls was converted into beautiful driveways, to which the term boulevard was still applied. The boulevards of Paris consist of several concentric systems of roughly circular courses, having their common center in the Ile de la Cité, an island in the Seine river. The longest and most recent of these boulevards owes its origin to the leveling of the 22-mile wall which, until 1919, encircled the city.

Paris is traversed from north to south by an irregular thoroughfare, which, like all the longer streets and boulevards of Paris, is known by different names in different sections of its course. The more important portions of the thoroughfare are called the Boulevard de Sebastople and the Rue Saint Michel. The latter section passes through the so-called Latin quarter, a district south of the Seine inhabited mainly by students and given its name when university lectures were delivered in Latin.

A straighter thoroughfare crosses the city from east to west on the north side of the Seine river. This thoroughfare, which passes many of the most famous squares, gardens, and buildings of Paris, is known, in different sections, under six different names. The more noteworthy sections are the Rue de Rivoli, the Avenue des Champs Elysées, and the Avenue de la Grande Armée. Other famous streets of Paris are Saint Germain, Rue Royal, and Rue du Faubourg Saint Honoré.

Squares, Parks, and Monuments. On the north bank of the Seine, near the center of the city, lie the famous gardens of the Tuileries, a 75-acre park ornamented with numerous statues. It adjoins the Place de la Concorde, which is adorned by sculptured fountains and by a huge obelisk brought by Napoleon from Luxor, Egypt. The adjacent Champs Elysées, "Elysian Fields," contain the Grand Palais built in 1718. Farther to the west lies the Place de l'Etoile, which contains the world's largest triumphal arch. From this square radiate twelve avenues, including the Rue Foch, which leads to the beautiful 2100-acre park in the suburbs called the Bois de Boulogne. A southeastern suburb contains the Bois de Vincennes, an ornamental park with an area of 2300 acres.

Other notable squares and parks of Paris are the Luxembourg gardens, laid out in the 17th century; the Jardin des Plantes, 58 acres in area, where the principal scientific museums of the city are located; the Place de Rivoli with an equestrian statue of Joan of Arc; the Place de la République; the Place d'Iena, containing a large statue of George Washington; the Place de la Bastille, near the site of the historic prison of the same name; the Place de Vendôme, which has a brazen column made by melting 1200 cannon captured by Napoleon; the Square des Innocents, where stands the famous sculptured Fontaine des Innocents; the Place des Etats-Unis, in which stands a bronze monument erected in 1923 to the memory of American volunteers who fought in French armies during the World War; and the Champ de Mars, in which the Eiffel Tower rises to a height of 984 feet. It is named from Alexandre Eiffel, the engineer who constructed it as a feature of the Paris International exposition in 1889. One of France's most beautiful war memorials is a white marble temple in the Parc de Villeneuve-l'Etang, commemorating 67 American aviators who died in French service during the World War.

Buildings. The Ile de la Cité in the Seine contains three remarkable buildings: the Hôtel Dieu, which, founded in 600 A. D., is said to be one of the oldest hospitals in Europe; the Palais de Justice, architecturally one of the finest structures in Paris; and the Cathedral of Notre Dame, the

Photo for 1 from Ewing Galloway; for 2 copyright by Underwood & Underwood; for 3 to 8 inclusive, from Publishers' Photo Service.

SCENES IN EUROPE. I

1 St. Paul's Cathedral, London. 2 Palace of Justice, Brussels. 3 Windsor Castle, England. 4 L'Opera, Paris. 5 Midnight Sun, Norway. 6 Canal and Street, Copenhagen. 7 Lakes of Killarney, Ireland. 8 Muckros Abbey, Ireland.

Photos for Nos. 4, 6, 7, and 8 copyright by Keystone View Co.; other photos from Publishers' Photo Service.

SCENES IN EUROPE. II

1 Aarburg Castle, Switzerland. 2 Matterhorn, Switzerland. 3 Amalfi, Italy. 4 Leaning Tower, Pisa, Italy. 5 Alcazar, Segovia, Spain. 6 Mosque of the Seven Minarets, Istanbul. 7 Rialto Bridge, Venice. 8 Parliament Building, Berlin. 9 Sanct Ulrich, Tyrol.

construction of which was begun in 1163. A few of the other great edifices of Paris are the Louvre, which houses the richest collection of art in the world; the palace of the Luxembourg, which contains the world's greatest collection of contemporary art, the American exhibits ranking second in number after the French; the Grand Opéra, one of the most beautiful theaters in the world; the government buildings, fronting the Seine embankment and known as the Quai d'Orsay; the Palais de l'Elysée, where the president of France resides; the Bibliotheque Nationale, one of the world's greatest libraries; the Panthéon, where many of France's most notable citizens have been buried; the Church of the Madeleine, built by Napoleon in the Greek style as a "temple of glory;" and the Hôtel des Invalides, which contains Napoleon's tomb. The railway car in which the armistice was signed on November 11, 1918, was housed in the Hôtel des Invalides until 1927, when it was transferred to a special shelter in Compeigne woods.

Other Features. Paris has been described by a German writer as the most strongly fortified city in the world. It is protected by a system of modern forts built outside the city limits. No other city of the world makes a feature of its sewers. Those of Paris, 9 to 20 feet in diameter and nearly 700 miles in length, are kept so clean and are so well ventilated that there is a regular tourist route through the system by boat and electric car. The University of Paris, which includes the Sorbonne, is one of the oldest and most famous educational institutions in Europe.

Commerce and Industry. Paris is the largest industrial and commercial center in France, and has a worldwide reputation for the manufacture of articles of taste and elegance, such as gold and silver ornaments, furniture, scientific instruments, toys, and perfumes. These industries, as well as the clothing industry of Paris, which largely sets the standard for the Western world in women's apparel, are carried on mainly in small establishments. The manufacture of machinery, railroad supplies, chemicals, beer, porcelain, and leather is centralized in larger factories.

Paris was one of the first cities of the world to establish large departmental stores, the better known ones being the Louvre and the Bon Marché. The banks of the Seine are lined with docks over which passes a volume of trade exceeding annually one billion dollars in value. There are more than 65 public markets in the city, the largest of which is the Halles Centrales, a steel and glass structure covering 10 acres. The stock exchange of Paris is called the Bourse, a term later applied to the corresponding institutions in other continental capitals.

History. Paris was known to Julius Cæsar, about 50 B. C., as Lutetia. It was then the chief city of the tribe of the Parisii, from whom the city, in the 4th century A. D., adopted the name Paris. In the 10th century, it became the capital of the French monarchy. Paris suffered from an English conquest during the Hundred Years' war and endured several disastrous sieges, the last at the hands of the Germans in 1871. Henry of Navarre, Louis XIV, Napoleon Bonaparte, and Napoleon III contributed most toward the improvement and adornment of the city, thereby making Paris not only a symbol for light-hearted enjoyment, but entitling it also to the claim of being the chief focus of European civilization. Population, 1946, 2,725,374.

Pisa (*pē'sä; pē'zä*). A town of northern Italy, 11 miles northeast of Leghorn. Pisa is noted for a leaning tower, 179 feet in height, which inclines 16½ feet from the perpendicular. The tower is built entirely of white marble with walls 13 feet thick at the base. Its construction was begun in 1174, and it was originally intended as a bell tower for the white marble cathedral near by. Within the past century, the inclination of the tower has increased one foot.

Pisa was formerly notable for the victory which its citizens won over the invading Saracens in the 11th century. In the 13th century, it controlled an extensive territory and had a population of 150,000. In recent centuries it has declined in importance, but its walls and its citadel still stand. The only large industry is the manufacture of cotton textiles. Pisa was the birthplace of Galileo, who used the tower in experiments to determine the velocity of falling bodies. Population, 1936, 72,468.

Plymouth. A naval station and seaport of southwestern England. Situated on a commodious harbor, Plymouth has a large commerce. Apart from naval equipment, the chief manufactures are chemicals. Sir Francis Drake set out from Plymouth for his voyage around the world. The town has a *Mayflower* commemoration stone, which records the fact that Plymouth was the last point touched by the Pilgrim Fathers on their way to America. Facing the waterfront is the Hoe, one of the finest pleasure grounds in Europe. Population, 1947, 185,380.

Portsmouth (*pōrts'mŭth*). A seaport and the chief naval arsenal of Great Britain, situated on Portsea, a small island separated by a creek from the south coast of England. Portsmouth has the most complete fortifications in Britain. Its harbor lies close to Spithead, a capacious naval anchorage in the shelter of the Isle of Wight. The government dockyard covers about 500 acres.

The principal industries of the city are connected with the naval establishment. There is considerable traffic in timber, coal, cattle, and agricultural produce. Portchester castle, a ruined Norman fortress to the north of the harbor, occupies the site of the Roman Portus Magnus, "Great Port." Charles Dickens and George Meredith were natives of the city. Population, 1947, 216,030.

Prague (*präg*) (**Praha**). The capital and largest city of Czechoslovakia, situated on both banks of the Moldau river, a tributary of the Elbe. It belonged to Germany from 1938 to 1945. Its manufacturing establishments, located mostly in the suburbs, produce railway cars, machinery, flour, chemicals, leather goods, sugar, and furniture. Prague is the focus for the rail and river trade of southern Germany.

The most impressive edifice of Prague is the ancient palace of Hradcany, adjoining which is the Cathedral of Saint Vitus, where the Bohemian kings used to be crowned. The University of Prague, founded in 1348, had, as one of its earliest graduates, John Huss, famous as a martyr to Protestantism. Prominent features of the city are the Charles bridge, 546 yards long, spanning the Moldau and ornamented with two medieval towers and with many statues of saints; the 14th century Tyn church; and a famous clock, one of the oldest in Europe, having, for figures, representations of Jesus and his apostles. Population, 1947, 921,416.

Ravenna. An ancient city of northern Italy, lying 45 miles east of Bologna and 6 miles inland from the northwestern extremity of the Adriatic Sea. In the 1st century B. C., Ravenna was a naval base and seaport. Subsequent changes in the coast line, which left Ravenna an inland city, diminished its importance. A canal gives it access to the sea. Wine, silk, sugar, and lace are its chief products.

Reminiscences of Ravenna's former greatness are the Church of Sant' Orso, which, although largely rebuilt since, dates back to Roman times; twelve basilicas used as churches and erected between the 5th and the 8th century; a two-storied mausoleum of Theodoric, the Ostrogothic king who subjected Ravenna to a 3-year siege; and the tomb of Dante. Population, 1936, 81,086.

Reims (E. *rēmz*; F. *răns*). A cathedral city of northeastern France, lying about 80 miles east of Paris. The Cathedral of Reims, in which the French kings used to be crowned, was built between 1212 and 1430 and is considered to be the finest example of Gothic architecture in the world. During the World War, the structure suffered much damage, which has been largely repaired. Reims is also noted for its wines. Population, 1946, 110,794.

Reval. See *Tallinn.*

Reykjavik (*rā'kyȧ-vēk'*). The capital and largest city of Iceland, located on the island's southwest coast. The city has a university and a cathedral; also a museum containing a collection of Icelandic antiquities. Population, 1945, 46,578.

Riga. The capital and largest city of Latvia, situated on the Duna river about 10 miles above its mouth at the head of the Gulf of Riga. By means of canals connecting the Duna with the Volga and with the Dnieper river, Riga has access to the timber-, grain-, and flax-producing regions of Russia. The chief manufactures are paper and wood pulp, matches, paints, textiles, shoes, rubber goods, cement, and tobacco. Saint Peter's church is notable for its lofty spire, which rises 440 feet above the street. Riga was founded in 1201 and became important as a member of the Hanseatic League. Nearly half the inhabitants are German. Population, 1944, 385,000.

Riviera (*rē-vyâ'rä*). A popular name for the narrow but beautiful coast line of Italy and France, mainly about the Gulf of Genoa. Its mild climate, charming subtropical vegetation, and vistas of rare attractiveness make it one of the most popular parts of Europe for winter tourists. The chief resorts along the Riviera are Cannes, Nice, Mentone, Monte Carlo, and San Remo.

ROME (**Roma**). The capital and largest city of Italy, and, historically, the most famous city in the world. Rome is situated on both banks of the Tiber river about 15 miles above its mouth in the Tyrrhenian Sea near the center of Italy's western coast. The traditional date of the founding of Rome is April 21, 753 B. C. April 21 is still celebrated annually in Rome as the anniversary of the city's origin. Rome was successively the head of the Roman Republic, the Roman Empire, and the western branch of the Catholic Church. In 1871, it became the capital of the Kingdom of Italy. This long career of uninterrupted greatness has earned for Rome the title of "the eternal city." In 1929, a tract of 109 acres within the city was granted the status of an independent state under papal rule. It is known as Vatican City. This area is in the northwestern section of Rome and includes the former site of Nero's gardens.

THE MODERN CITY. The Tiber, meandering through the city, divides the more populous eastern part from the western section. The eastern part comprises the Campus Martius, "Field of Mars," and the seven hills of ancient Rome—the Capitoline, Palatine, Aventine, Quirinal, Viminal, Esquiline, and Cælian. The western section consists of the hill anciently known as the Janiculum and of the eminence on which the Vatican is situated. The river is spanned by ten bridges, three being of ancient construction. Rome is 15 miles in circumference and is surrounded by a brick wall 55 feet high, constructed mainly by Aurelian about 275 A. D. The wall is pierced by 12 gates. The Porta del Popolo in the north opens upon a road anciently called the Flaminian way, while the famous Appian way leaves the city through a southern gate.

STREETS AND MONUMENTS. The streets are irregular in plan. From the Plaza del Popolo in the north of the city three important thoroughfares diverge—the Corso, the Ripetta, and the Babuino. The Corso terminates at the Piazza di Venezia at the Capitoline hill, which has a colossal monument to Victor Emmanuel II. The Piazza del Campidoglio is adorned by a large statue of Marcus Aurelius, the Roman emperor who erected the so-called Antonine column, which stands in the Piazza Colonna on the Corso. An obelisk, 104 feet high, brought from Heliopolis, Egypt, has been placed in the Piazza di San Giovanni. Garibaldi, the liberator of modern Italy, is memorialized by a huge equestrian statue on the Janiculum hill. An equestrian statue of Victor Emmanuel II in a magnificent setting towers above the Piazza Venetia. Most conspicuous of all is a 180-foot bronze statue of Mussolini. The Fontana Trevi is among the grandest of the city's many sculptured fountains.

MODERN BUILDINGS. The most famous structures associated with modern Rome are those within Vatican City, notably the Vatican and Saint Peter's Church. The Vatican, or papal residence, consists of a group of palaces, covering 13½ acres and containing about 1100 rooms. It houses a library, museum, and picture gallery, each of inestimable value. The decorations of the Vatican were executed by the best artists of the Renaissance, including Raphael and Michelangelo. Saint Peter's Church is generally admitted to be the world's largest and grandest church. Its construction occupied 126 years. The building is 727 feet in length and is surmounted by a huge dome, which rises to a height of 405 feet above the level of the beautiful colonnaded court before the church's entrance.

Other notable buildings of modern Rome include the Quirinal palace, where the Italian sovereigns reside; the Villa Medici, housing the French Academy of Art; the Santa Pudenziana, the oldest church in Rome; and the palaces called Doria, Ruspoli, Corsini, Orsini, Giustiniani, Altieri, Cicciaporci, Farnese, Berberini, and Colonna. On the Capitoline hill are three palaces appropriated for the assemblies of the magistrates, for the observatory, and for the fine arts collection. There are several palaces, which, being surrounded by extensive gardens, are called villas. The most notable of these is the Villa Borghese, the gardens of which form the most fashionable promenade in the city.

EDUCATIONAL INSTITUTIONS. Rome is the seat of the University of Rome, founded in 1244. In addition to the Vatican library and the 10 public libraries, there are the libraries called Nazionale Centrale, Casanatense, and Angelica, and the libraries of the Barberini and of the Corsini palace. No city of the world has richer collections of Roman antiquities and of Renaissance art. The United States and several European countries maintain archeological schools in the city.

ANCIENT BUILDINGS. The level of the ancient city of Rome is, except where excavated, from 20 to 60 feet below the level of the present city. Within the past century, a considerable portion of the ruins have been uncovered. These ruins include temples, palaces, public halls, theaters, baths, porticoes, and monuments and indicate that, in the first centuries of the Christian era, Rome was a still more impressive city than it is today.

The best preserved ancient building is the Pantheon, now used as a church, which has a dome larger than that of Saint Peter's Church. The Colosseum had a seating capacity of 45,000. The outer wall alone is said to have cost the equivalent of 50 million dollars to construct. The Forum has been despoiled of most of the palatial buildings, the 1200 marble columns, and the 1000 colossal statues which once adorned its 25 acres of surface. Other impressive ruins are the Mausoleum of Hadrian, used for 15 centuries as the fortress of medieval Rome; the triumphal arches of Titus, Severus, and Constantine; and the baths of Caracalla and of Diocletian, those of the latter having originally covered nearly 9 acres. The outlines of the Circus Maximus are still traceable—a building capable of seating 260,000 spectators.

One of the stateliest buildings of ancient Rome was the residence of the emperors on the Palatine hill. It was called the Palatium, a name from which the word palace is derived. The great drains of ancient Rome are still in use today. Dating from early Christian times are the catacombs, underground passages used as places of burial and of refuge by the persecuted Christians. About 75 groups of these have been found, having a total length of about 750 miles.

INDUSTRIES. Manufacturing in Rome is unimportant, being confined mainly to silks, cameos, gloves, mosaics, jewelry, and artificial flowers. There is a considerable commerce, Rome being the chief railroad center of Italy. The population in 1947 was 1,471,971. The city is said to have had almost 2,000,000 inhabitants in the days of the Empire.

Rotterdam. The chief commercial port of the Netherlands, situated in the western part of the country, about 10 miles southeast of The Hague. It is on the Meuse river 15 miles above its mouth in the North Sea. The leading articles of commerce are coffee, tea, tobacco, flour, sugar, spices, coal, oil, and foodstuffs. The most important manufactures are ships, refined sugar, margarine, paint, ropes, and leather.

A labyrinth of tree-bordered canals runs through the city, and most houses are built on piles on account of the city's low site. Rotterdam was the birthplace of Erasmus, a statue of whom constitutes one of the city's chief monuments. Population, 1947, 644,076.

Rouen (*rwän*). A commercial and manufacturing city of northern France on the Seine river, about 70 miles northwest of Paris. Ocean-going ships ascend the river to Rouen. The industrial products include textiles, machinery, and refined oil. The Cathedral of Rouen has a spire 487 feet in altitude, said to be the highest in France. The Place du Vieux Marché is adorned by a statue of Joan of Arc, who, in 1431, was burned there at the stake. Population, 1946, 107,739.

Ruhr (*rōōr*), **The.** An irregularly oval strip of land in northwestern Germany, extending eastward from the Rhine for about 40 miles along both sides of the Ruhr river. It was held by French and Belgian troops from January 1923 to July 1925 as a means of collecting reparations from Germany.

Although this district, having an area of about 400 square miles, covers less than one-fourth of 1 per cent of Germany's total surface, it includes the great industrial centers of Essen, Dortmund, Bochum, Gelsenkirchen, Mülheim, Oberhausen, Duisburg-Hamborn, and Ruhrort. It is the heart of Germany's industrial organization. Containing less than one-thirtieth of Germany's population, it gave employment, before the World War, to about one-fourth of all the factory workers in the country. The reason for this great concentration of industry in the Ruhr is to be found chiefly in the rich coal mines, together with excellent facilities for transportation by rail and by water. From the Ruhr also comes five-sixths of Germany's production of the coal tar. About one-third of Germany's supply of pig iron is made in the Ruhr from ore brought in from other parts of the country and from France.

Saint Gallen (*sånt gäl'ĕn*). A city of northeastern Switzerland, situated 12 miles from the south shore of the Lake of Constance. The city is the highest in Europe, having an elevation of 2196 feet above the sea. Its ancient Benedictine monastery, an architectural masterpiece which is now used for government offices, was founded by the Irish missionary Saint Gall, who settled here in 614. Population, 1941, 62,530.

Saint Mihiel (*săN' mē'yĕl'*). A town of northeastern France, situated on the Meuse river 23 miles southeast of Verdun. The capture of Saint Mihiel and the annihilation of the German salient about the town in September 1918 constituted the first military operation carried out independently by the American army in France during the World War I. Population, 1931, 8126.

Salford. A suburb of Manchester, in west central England. Salford is older than Manchester, however, having been incorporated in 1844, 9 years before Manchester became a city. Several railway viaducts and 16 bridges, built across the small river Irwell, connect Salford with Manchester. Peel park is the finest of the city's four parks, which cover a total area of 83 acres. Population, 1947, 176,600.

Salonika (E. *să'lô-nē'kä*); (**Thessalonikē**). A city of northern Greece, the second largest in the kingdom, situated at the head of Salonika bay, a northern inlet of the Ægean Sea. Salonika, having a capacious, improved harbor, is the sea outlet for Bulgarian and Jugoslavian products. Among the squalid houses which fill most of the city arise lofty spires and minarets, and numerous ruins dating from Greek, Roman, and Byzantine times.

Salonika was founded in 315 B. C. and has been held successively by Macedonia, Rome, the Byzantine Empire, Turkey, and Greece. It was the seat of an early church, to which Saint Paul addressed two epistles. During the World War, Salonika was held as a base by Allied troops. Population, 1947, 236,524.

Sarajevo (*sȧr'ȧ-yȧ-vô*). A city of Yugoslavia, 122 miles southwest of Belgrade. It is partially Oriental in appearance, having an extensive bazaar, but, in recent decades, many modern improvements have been introduced. The chief industries are the manufacture of metal ware, silk weaving, and the making of pottery. At Sarajevo in 1914 occurred the incident which precipitated the World War, and thereby brought independence to Yugoslavia. This was the assassination of Franz Ferdinand, heir to the throne of Austria-Hungary, by F. Princip. A statue of Princip was erected in 1930. Population, 1941, 80,000.

Seville (*sĕv'ĭl; sē-vĭl'*) (**Sevilla**). A city and port of south western Spain, situated on the Guadalquivir river, about 50 miles above its mouth in the Atlantic Ocean. Seville was an important center of the Moorish civilization in Spain. The Alcazar, now partly in ruins, was a Moorish royal palace. The Cathedral of Seville, one of the largest Gothic churches in the world, retained, as a belfry, the Giralda tower, erected by the Moors. Other notable structures include the Moorish Renaissance palace of the duke of Medinaceli; the Museum of Painting, which houses the largest collection of the masterpieces of Murillo, a native of Seville; the buildings of the University of Seville, founded in 1502; a tobacco factory covering 6 acres; and a bull ring with a seating capacity of 12,000.

Seville was a prosperous seaport in Roman times. It had a monopoly of trade with America for a considerable period. The chief articles of trade at the present time are metals, fruits, cork, grain, and glazed tiles, the last being manufactured in a suburb, Triana. Population, 1947, 382,013.

Sheffield. An industrial city of north central England about 30 miles east of Manchester. It is noted for its manufacture of cutlery, armor plate, artillery, scientific instruments, and other steel products. The famous silver Sheffield plate is no longer made, the process being a lost art, but a high quality of silverware is made by a new process. Other industrial products include leather, bicycles, paper, brass goods, brushes, chemicals, and paints. Sheffield university was founded in 1905 by a local steel manufacturer. A new city zoning plan was adopted in 1925. Population, 1947, 514,290.

Sofia (*sô'fē-yȧ; sô-fē'ä*) (**Sofiya**). The capital and largest city of Bulgaria, situated at an altitude of 1800 feet in the western part of the country. Sofia is the commercial and industrial center of Bulgaria and is connected by rail with Vienna, Salonika, and Istanbul. It has an important export trade in agricultural products and attar of roses. The city has been largely rebuilt since 1878. Its principal features include famous baths with hot springs; the ruined Sofia Mosque; and the University of Sofia, founded in 1888. Population, 1946, 436,936.

Southampton. A city and port of southern England, 79 miles southwest of London. It was a royal borough before 1086, its fine natural harbor making it at one time a rival of London. After a decline of trade in the 16th century, it was improved in the 1800's and, in 1914, was the chief port of embarkation for British armies. One of the world's largest dry docks was opened there in 1933. From this port, in 1620, the *Mayflower* began its voyage for America. Population, 1947, 170,360.

Spa (*spä; spô*). A famous watering place and town in central eastern Belgium. Its mineral springs are said to be the oldest in Europe, having been discovered in 1326. The town has been a fashionable resort for centuries. The principal buildings are the Casino and the Pouhon. Population, 1931, 8354.

Stettin (*shtĕ-tēn'*) (**Szezecin**). A seaport and manufacturing city of northwestern Poland, built on both banks of the Oder river, 17 miles from its mouth in an inlet of the Baltic Sea. The largest industries are shipbuilding and the manufacture of clothing. Other products are cement, locomotives, sewing machines, and glass. The chief exports are grain, spirits, lumber, sugar, and cement. Population, 1946, 103,000.

Stockholm. The capital and largest city of Sweden, situated on a group of hilly islands and peninsulas at Lake Mälar's outlet into the Baltic Sea. Surrounding forests advance almost to the city's confines. On account of the varied levels prevailing in different parts of the city, tunnels and elevators are utilized by the citizens in passing from one part to another. Stockholm's capacious harbor facilitates a large commerce. The chief manufactures are ships, iron and steel products, leather, textiles, and pottery.

The features of the city include the Royal Palace; Saint Nicholas Church, where the Swedish sovereigns are crowned; the city hall, one of the finest modern structures in Europe; Skansen, a 70-acre park illustrating the fauna, flora, and peasant customs of various parts of Sweden; an equestrian statue of Gustavus Adolphus; and a colossal bronze figure of Linnæus. Population, 1947, 700,000.

Stoke. A manufacturing city of central England, about 30 miles south of Manchester, noted chiefly for its porcelain and pottery industry. Other industrial products are iron, machinery, electrical and rubber goods, and bricks. The chief public buildings are the town hall, New Market hall and Minton Memorial building. Population, 1947, 273,510.

Stonehenge. The most famous prehistoric monument in Great Britain. It is in Wiltshire county, England, about 32 miles inland from the center of the southern coast. It consisted originally of upright stones in two concentric circles surrounding two elliptical groups. The height above ground of the largest stone is 22 feet. The outer circle is 100.75 feet in diameter and consists of 30 stones, 16 of which are standing. These stones average 26 tons in weight. The river circle, 76.5 feet in diameter, consists of 20 stones, of which 9 are standing. About the group is a deep circular trench 333 feet in diameter.

The people who erected the stones, their purpose, and the quarries from which the stones came remain mysteries. They are believed to date from the later stone age. The land on which they stand was donated to the British government by Sir Cecil Chubb in 1918.

Stratford. A town of south central England on the river Avon, chiefly noted as the birthplace and burial place of William Shakspere. It has a Shakspere Memorial theater, endowed by popular subscription from people in many countries. In the vicinity are the cottages where Mary Arden, Shakspere's mother, and Anne Hathaway, his wife, were born. Population, 1931, 11,616.

Stuttgart. A well built and beautiful city of southwestern Germany. Stuttgart is the capital of the German state of Württemberg. The city's finest structures center about a large square, called the Schlossplatz. There are exceptionally valuable collections of paintings and of antiquities in the city.

Stuttgart is the chief printing and book publishing city of South Germany. The industrial products include furniture, machinery, paper, leather, chemicals, tobacco goods, and textiles. Population, 1946, 414,072.

Tallinn. The capital and largest city of Estonia, situated in the northwest part of the country on a southern inlet of the Gulf of Finland. It has a commodious harbor and exports grain, meats, flax, and timber. The city was founded in the 13th century and became prosperous as a member of the Hanseatic League. It has a guild house containing a valuable collection of Baltic antiquities. The city is often known abroad as Reval. Population, 1944, 147,000.

Turin (*tū'rĭn; tū-rĭn'*) (**Torino**). A commercial and manufacturing city of northwestern Italy, situated on the Po river within view of the Alps. It is about 70 miles inland from the Gulf of Genoa and 40 miles from the French border. Turin is the center of the automobile industry in Italy. Other manufactures are machinery, cotton, silk, rayon, leather, and chemicals. Hydroelectric power for the industries is generated from near-by mountain torrents.

Turin is the only large Italian city having streets laid out on a rectangular plan. Among the features of the city are the Piazza Castello, the chief square of Turin; the palace and park once occupied by the rulers of Piedmont; the Palazzo Carignano, in which the Italian Parliament met from 1860 to 1864; and an imposing monument of Cavour, one of the liberators of Italy. The University of Turin was founded in 1405. Population, 1947, 712,833.

Valencia (*vȧ-lĕn'shĭ-ȧ; -shȧ*). A Mediterranean seaport of Spain near the center of the country's eastern coast. The older part of the city has narrow, winding streets, while the new portion is laid out with wide thoroughfares and well shaded squares. Its features include the cathedral La Seo, with a splendid octagonal tower; the University of Valencia, founded in 1411; the Silk Exchange, a beautiful Gothic structure; the Plaza de Toros, a richly ornamented bull ring, said to be the best in Spain.

The commerce of Valencia consists principally of rice, fruits, silk, wine, and olive oil. The manufactures include tobacco, metal and leather products, glazed tiles, and textiles of silk and of linen. Population, 1947, 562,967.

Venice (**Venezia**). A seaport of northeastern Italy, situated on 120 small islands at the head of the Adriatic Sea. Some 177 canals serve as streets, spanned by 400 bridges. Houses are built on piles. The Grand canal divides the city into two equal parts. A bridge, about 2½ miles long, connects Venice with the mainland and, passing as a viaduct over a portion of the city, slopes downward to a large open square.

Venice's greatest building, the Cathedral of Saint Mark, dating from 1047 A. D., resembles the Church, now the Mosque, of Saint Sophia in Istanbul. It is surmounted by five Oriental domes and contains four gilded, bronze lions, taken originally from Nero's triumphal arch in Rome. The bell tower of the church, standing separate from the main structure, is 322 feet high. Its construction was begun in 874 A. D. The tower collapsed in 1902 but has since been restored. The Doge's Palace, the building of which occupied the two centuries following 1301, is one of the most picturesque buildings in the world.

Among the many other features of this unique and beautiful city are the Royal Palace; a curious clock tower, built in 1496, upon which two colossal bronze figures strike the hours on a large bell; the Bridge of Sighs, connecting the Doge's Palace with a prison; the Rialto, a marble bridge, on which are situated many busy shops; numerous churches and art galleries containing rich collections of paintings by Italian masters, including many by Titian, a native of Venice; and the museum of the city's arsenal, which exhibits a model of the *Bucentaur*. This was the ship from which, each year, the doge of Venice cast a ring into the Adriatic, thereby representing symbolically the marriage of Venice with the sea.

Venice manufactures heavy machinery, clocks, cotton and woolen goods, glassware, lace, brocades, tapestry, wood carvings, and jewelry. The city is a first-class naval station and has an excellent harbor.

Venice is said to have been founded in 452 A. D. by refugees in flight before Attila the Hun. It became prosperous by trading with the East and with the crusaders. The city's importance declined with the fall of Istanbul, but was revived when the Suez canal opened up a Mediterranean route to Asia. Population, 1947, 292,813.

Verdun (*vĕr'dŭɴ'*). A strongly fortified town of northeastern France, about 140 miles east of Paris. It was the objective of desperate German attacks in 1916 and 1917, which, for bitterness and carnage, were unequaled by any other conflict of the World War. The French army retained its hold on the town. Population, 1931, 18,852.

Verona (*vē-rō'nȧ*). A fortified city of northern Italy, lying 71 miles west of Venice. It has an important trade with Switzerland, Austria, and Germany in wines, fruits, rice, and marble. The chief manufactures are cotton, paper, flour, and nails.

Verona was a Gallic town before it passed into the hands of the Romans in 89 B. C. From the Roman period dates the amphitheater, still in use, which the emperor Diocletian built. It is about 500 feet long and 160 feet high with accommodation for 20,000 people. Numerous weather-stained palaces of white marble, mostly built in the period of the Renaissance, give to certain parts of the city an air of sumptuous decay. Population, 1947, 190,828.

Versailles (F. *vĕr'sȧ'y'*; E. *vĕr-sălz'*). A city of north central France, situated about 12 miles southwest of Paris. Versailles is chiefly noted for its palace and park of unparalleled magnificence.

The palace dates mainly from 1661, being mostly the work of Louis XIV. It consists of a central block, surrounding three sides of a large court, and of two immense wings, each enclosing two or more courts. The total length of the building with its dependencies is nearly one-half mile. It houses a picture gallery upon which alone Louis XIV spent 5 million dollars. The play of colored lights in the evening upon the waters of the sculptured fountains within the gardens constitutes a spectacle of rare beauty. An apartment of the palace, called the Hall of Mirrors, was the scene, in 1871, of the coronation of William I as emperor of Germany. In the same hall, in 1919, the representatives of Germany subscribed to the Treaty of Versailles. Population of city, 1946, 70,141.

Vesuvius (Vesuvio). An active volcano of Italy, 4260 feet high, near the Bay of Naples and about 10 miles from the city of that name. Prior to 79 A. D., it was not known that the mountain was volcanic. In that year, however, the top of the mountain blew off and ashes, stones, and mud were ejected, burying the Roman cities of Pompeii and Herculaneum in 20 feet of débris. The elder Pliny perished in this eruption, of which the younger Pliny left a detailed description. Other eruptions occurred in the years 203, 472, 512, 685, 983, 1631, 1822, 1855, 1865, 1872, 1878, 1880, 1895, and 1906.

Vichy (*vē'shē*). French health resort and temporary capital of France is situated 72 miles northwest of Lyon and about 180 miles south of Paris. It owes its location to a group of about 40 springs of warm water having medicinal properties. Heavily charged with sodium bicarbonate and minerals, the water from some of the springs has a temperature as high as 120°F. About 2½ million gallons are bottled and exported annually. The 11 largest springs are state owned and supply public hospitals for treatment of soldiers and of civilians unable to pay for private treatments. The Romans built baths at Vichy, but the modern development, dating from the 17th century, owes much to Napoleon Bonaparte and Napoleon III. When the Germans in 1940 overran France and occupied Paris, the new chief of state, Marshal Pétain, then 84 years old, chose Vichy as the seat of his government. Population, 1931, 22,205.

VIENNA (Wien). The capital and largest city of Austria, built on the south bank of the Danube river. Vienna was the capital of the former empire of Austria-Hungary and, from 1938 to 1945, was a part of Germany. Since the 13th century, Vienna has been the chief artistic and cultural center of east central Europe.

Boulevards and Parks. The most notable driveway of Vienna is the Ringstrasse, which follows the line of old fortifications, demolished in 1858. It separates the old, inner city from the more modern portions. The Prater, a 2000-acre park, is the largest of the many ornamented open spaces which, in the aggregate, cover more than 50 per cent of Vienna's surface.

Buildings. The Cathedral of Saint Stephen is the most famous structure in Austria. It was founded in 1144 and has great catacombs beneath it. The cross on its steeple attains a height of 441 feet. Other great buildings are the Imperial opera house, one of the most superb art temples of Europe; the stately Grecian Houses of Parliament; the lavishly decorated Gothic city hall; the Imperial Palace; and the Votivkirche. Most of the inhabitants live in apartment houses, some of which are built on a magnificent scale, adorned with painting and sculpture.

Institutions of Art and Education. The University of Vienna, founded in 1365, enjoys a world-wide reputation. The most notable of the many public and private museums of Vienna is the Imperial Art-History museum, which contains an extraordinarily rich collection of ancient and medieval antiquities and numerous masterpieces of art, embracing nearly every school in the world.

Industries. The manufactures of Vienna include jewelry, ornaments of gold and silver, musical and optical instruments, leather goods, furniture, machinery, textiles, and chemicals. A large commerce in corn, flour, cattle, wine, and sugar is facilitated by a network of railways centering in the city and by the navigable Danube river.

History. Under the name of Vindobona, Vienna was a city of strategical importance to the Romans. It was taken successively by the Huns, the Avars, and the Franks; attained to prosperity in supplying the needs of the crusaders; and, in 1296, became the residence of the Habsburg emperors. Vienna was besieged by the Turks in 1529 and, again, in 1683, but on neither occasion was the city taken. The treaty of peace following the Napoleonic wars was drawn up in Vienna. Population, 1947, 1,548,137.

Vimy Ridge. An elevated region of northeastern France, 100 miles north of Paris and about 4 miles northeast of Arras. In May 1917, it was the scene of one of the most bitterly contested struggles in which Canadian troops were engaged during World War I. The ridge had been fortified by the Germans but was relinquished as a result of the battle, which is commemorated by an impressive monument erected by the Canadian government in 1936.

Warsaw (Warszawa). The largest city of Poland, situated on the left bank of the Vistula river. It was the capital of Poland prior to its seizure by Germany in 1939. The old part of Warsaw has many dark, narrow, and squalid lanes, but the new section is quite modern, with wide streets flanked by rows of fine buildings. There are numerous squares, parks, and public gardens. The city has over 30 Catholic and 7 Russian churches, the Catholic Cathedral of Saint John being the largest. Iron bridges connect the city with the prosperous suburb of Praga on the opposite bank of the Vistula.

Among the manufactures are textiles, metal wares, tobacco articles, malt liquors, chemicals, and furniture. Small factories and home industries give employment to many thousands. Population, 1946, 476,538.

Windsor. A town of southeastern England, on the Thames river about 21 miles west of London. Its interest lies chiefly in its parks and its castle, which, since before the time of William the Conqueror, have been a favorite retreat of the English monarchs.

Windsor Castle covers 12 acres of ground in the Home park, which is about 4 miles in circumference. A tree-lined avenue connects this park with the Great park, which has a circuit of 18 miles. The castle, consisting of numerous chapels, cloisters, and apartments, is dominated by the Round Tower, built by Edward III. Population, 1931, 20,284.

Ypres (*ē'pr'*). A town of western Belgium about 20 miles from the North Sea. It was the scene of a large number of battles in the World War, being held by the British armies in the face of the most desperate German attacks, made over a period of four years. One of the chief squares contains a monument erected by the Canadian government as a memorial to Canadian soldiers who perished in the sanguinary conflicts near Ypres. The town, almost obliterated as a result of military operations, had a population of 16,720 in 1931.

Zurich (*zōō'rĭk*) (**Zürich**). The largest city of Switzerland, beautifully situated in the northern part of the country on both banks of the Limmat river as it issues from Lake Zurich. In the older quarter, the streets are narrow, but the newer section is very attractively laid out, its main thoroughfare being a broad boulevard lined with shops comparing well with those of Paris. Zurich is the seat of the Swiss National museum, of the University of Zurich, and of several splendid medieval churches and monasteries. The cathedral known as the Grosse Münster, founded in the 11th century, had Zwingli as one of its pastors.

Zurich is the financial center of Switzerland. Its manufactures include silks, cottons, machinery, paper, and musical instruments. Population, 1941, 336,395.

Photos for 1 from Brown Bros.; 2 and 3 copyright by Underwood & Underwood; 4 from Keystone View Co.; 5, 6, 7, 8, and 9 from Publishers' Photo Service.

SCENES IN UNITED STATES DEPENDENCIES

1 Mt. McKinley, Alaska. 2 Reindeer in Alaska. 3 Royal Palms, Samoa. 4 Totem Poles, Alaska. 5 Saint Thomas, Virgin Is. 6 Pali Road, Hawaii. 7 Government Building, Honolulu. 8 Private Residence, Honolulu. 9 Pineapple Fields, Hawaii.

Photo for 2 from Underwood & Underwood; photos for 3 and 5 copyright by Keystone View Co.; others from Publishers' Photo Service.

ASIA

1 Great Wall of China. 2 Taj Mahal, Agra, India. 3 On the Ganges, India. 4 Japanese Garden. 5 Symbolizing the Deaf, Dumb, and Blind God, Japan. 6 Sail Boats on the Yangtze, China. 7 Village Street, Korea. 8 Marble Bridge, Peiping, China. 9 Kiyomizu Temple, Kyoto, Japan.

ASIA

THE largest and the most populous of the continents. It lies entirely in the northern hemisphere and, beginning near the equator, stretches 5270 miles northward to a point within 800 miles of the north pole. Its maximum extent east and west is 6820 miles. Having an area of 17,200,000 square miles, it occupies nearly one-third of the land surface of the globe and is larger than North America and South America combined.

With the exception of Europe on the northwest and of the narrow Isthmus of Suez, Asia is entirely surrounded by water. It has the Arctic Ocean on the north, the Pacific Ocean on the east, and the Indian Ocean on the south. In the southwest, the continent is divided from Africa by a line passing through the Isthmus of Suez, the Red Sea, and the Gulf of Aden. At the northeast extremity, Asia is separated from North America by Bering strait, a neck of water less than 40 miles in width at its narrowest point. The coast line of the continent aggregates about 33,000 miles.

Outline and Islands. The line of demarcation on land between Asia and Europe follows roughly the Ural mountains and the Caucasus mountains. The remainder of the western boundary passes through the Caspian Sea and through the three seas which wash the shores of Asia Minor, the continent's farthest westward extension. These three seas are the Black Sea, the Ægean Sea, and the Mediterranean Sea. The Black Sea and the Ægean Sea are connected by the small Sea of Marmora, which communicates with the Black Sea by the Bosporus strait and with the Ægean Sea by the Dardanelles strait.

The coast line has many irregularities. Those on the north are mainly the enlarged mouths of rivers, the only major inlet being Nordenskjöld Sea. On the south, however, there are three large peninsulas separated by two deep indentations. Between Arabia, the most western peninsula, and India, in the center, lies the Arabian Sea, which has two important inlets, each connected by a strait with an inland sea. The Gulf of Aden in the west is joined to the Red Sea by the strait of Bab-el-Mandeb, and the Gulf of Oman at the north of the Arabian Sea communicates by the strait of Ormuz with the Persian gulf. The third great peninsula is Indo-China with its southern extension known as the Malay peninsula. It is separated from India by the Bay of Bengal.

The eastern coast is notable for a series of deep inlets and for an irregular chain of islands stretching from the north to the south. This configuration results in a number of island-bound seas. Bering Sea at the north is confined by the Aleutian islands, which are geographically a part of Alaska. South of Kamchatka peninsula lies the Sea of Okhotsk. The Sea of Japan is enclosed by Sakhalin island and by the islands of Japan, which stretch southwestward toward the southern end of the peninsula of Chosen. The Yellow Sea and the China Sea extend southward to the Taiwan strait, as the channel is called which lies between the island of Formosa and the mainland. The South China Sea, bounded on the east and south by the Philippine Islands and by Borneo, has two large inlets, the Gulf of Tonkin and the Gulf of Siam.

South and east of the continent lies, in an elongated cluster, the largest group of islands in the world. This group, known as the Malay archipelago, extends as far as Australia. This archipelago, together with the numerous smaller islands which continue to dot the Pacific for more than 2000 miles still farther east, is sometimes embraced under the term Oceania. The only other large island off the southern coast is Ceylon, near the southern tip of India. The New Siberian islands and Wrangell island lie well within the Arctic circle to the north.

Surface. Asia has the greatest mean elevation of any of the continents except Antarctica, its surface being, on the average, more than 3000 feet above the sea. Moreover, the continent contains the highest mountain, the highest plateau, the most extensive lowland, the lowest lake, and the deepest lake, in the world.

About 2000 miles north of the southern tip of India lies the plateau of Pamir, often called the roof of the world. This plateau, 11,000 feet in height, forms a central point from which mountain chains radiate, most of them trending in a general east and west direction.

The highest range is that of the Himalaya mountains, curving from the Pamir plateau to the south and east, where it forms a northern wall of India. Mount Everest, in this range, is the highest peak in the world, having a height of 29,141 feet.

North of the Himalaya mountains lies the world's highest plateau, Tibet, which has an elevation ranging from 9000 to 17,000 feet. The region is volcanic. To the north of the plateau of Tibet lies, at a lower level, the plateau of Mongolia, largely occupied by the Gobi desert, which is believed by some anthropologists to be the original home of the human race. This plateau is separated from Tibet by the Kunlun mountains. The plateau of Mongolia is confined on the northwest side by an irregular group of mountain ranges stretching northeast from the Pamir plateau. Among these mountains lies the deepest body of fresh water in the world, Lake Baikal, in which soundings of 5306 feet have been taken. Both the plateau of Tibet and the plateau of Mongolia widen toward the east and eventually slope downward to the plains of China in the south and, farther north, to the plains of Manchuria.

Westward from the Pamir plateau, a broad mountainous highland stretches to the extreme western part of the continent in Asia Minor. This region contains the lofty Hindu Kush range and, farther west, Mount Ararat, on which Noah's ark is said to have landed. The highland slopes, on the south, down to the plains of Iraq, which drain toward the Persian gulf. South and west of this drainage basin rises the plateau which occupies the greater part of the Arabian peninsula. The northwestern extremity of the plateau falls rapidly to a basin of inland drainage, which constitutes the most remarkable depression on the face of the earth. The lowest point is occupied by the Dead Sea, the surface of which is almost 1300 feet below the level of the sea.

To the north of Asia's great central highland lies the world's vastest plain. Occupying the whole northern part of the continent, it is sometimes called the Great Northern Lowland. Most of it inclines in steppes very gently toward the north, but in the southwest there is an area of inland drainage, part of which slopes toward the Caspian Sea and part toward the Aral Sea.

To the south of the Himalaya mountains lie the plains of India. These plains rise on the southern side to a table-land of moderate height, sometimes called the Deccan. On the east, the plains are confined by a number of mountain ridges, which constitute a southern spur from the plateau of Tibet. These mountains lose themselves in the plains of Indo-China and in the Malay peninsula.

The plateau of Mongolia sends a similar spur to the northeast, known as the Stanovoi mountains, which stretch as far as Bering strait. From this extreme northern point, a partly submerged mountain chain passes south through the ocean, emerging in various places to form the numerous islands off the east coast. Many of these mountains, particularly those in Japan, are actively volcanic.

Drainage. The great central highlands of Asia feed six rivers which exceed 2000 miles in length. Two of them, the Yangtze and the Yenisei, rank among the six longest rivers of the world.

The Ob river, the Yenisei river, and the Lena river are the largest of the streams which take their rise in these highlands and wind slowly through the immense steppes down to broad estuaries at the Arctic Ocean. Their lower courses are icebound eight months in the year. For 100 miles above the mouth of the Lena lies a stretch of frozen silt in which are embedded the remains of numerous mammoths and of other animals which were engulfed in quagmire thousands of years ago.

The three greatest rivers flowing to the east are the Amur, the Hwang, and the Yangtze. Each follows a long, meandering course in the central plateau before descending to the plains and emptying into the waters of the Pacific Ocean. Destructive annual floods frequently follow the melting of the upland snows, particularly in the Hwang river in China, which for that reason is often called "China's sorrow."

The southeastern spur of the plateau of Tibet gives rise to three rivers of southern drainage. Named in order from east to west, they are the Mekong river, the Salwin river, and the Irrawaddy river. The Ganges river and the Brahmaputra river both rise in the Himalaya mountains and mingle their waters in a common delta at the head of the Bay of Bengal. The Brahmaputra river flows eastward along the northern edge of the Himalayas in the plateau of Tibet and, bending southward and westward, passes through a plain which has a heavier rainfall than any other region of the world. The Ganges throughout most of its course flows eastward. The Indus river rises to the north of the Himalaya mountains and, passing around the western end of the range, empties into the Arabian Sea.

The plains of Iraq are drained toward the Persian gulf by the Tigris river, which is joined about 100 miles above its mouth by the celebrated Euphrates river. The Ural river flows into the northern end of the Caspian Sea. The Caspian Sea has no outlet but is itself 86 feet below the level of the ocean. The Aral Sea is the center of another basin of interior drainage. Such basins cover, in Asia, a larger area than in any other continent.

Climate. On account of its range of latitude and of altitude, Asia is subject to a great variety of climate. In the interior of Siberia, temperatures of 92° below zero have been recorded, although in summer on the Arctic coast the thermometer sometimes registers 100°. The hottest part of the continent is in Arabia, where the temperature has reached 120° F. and the average for the year is 93°.

While parts of Assam, in the basin of the Brahmaputra river, have a rainfall of about 500 inches, the rainfall of Asia as a whole is scanty. An arid desert, in which the annual precipitation is less than 10 inches, extends in a broad sweep through the center of the continent from east to west. Beginning with the desert of Gobi in the plateau of Mongolia, it passes through Turkestan, Persia, and Arabia. Siberia also has a light rainfall. Japan, the plains of China and of Indo-China, the Malay peninsula, and eastern and southern India have a copious and, in parts, an excessive precipitation.

Vegetation. Asia is the original source of more of our important economic plants than all other parts of the world combined. From it come wheat, barley, sugar cane, alfalfa, cotton, flax, jute, hemp, tea; such fruits as the apple, cherry, peach, prune, apricot, banana, olive, orange, lemon, grapefruit, date, and pomegranate; and, in the list of vegetables, the radish, cucumber, muskmelon, onion, parsnip, rhubarb, spinach, and eggplant.

Northern Siberia from east to west contains a strip of tundra, or frozen desert, stretching 150 to 500 miles southward from the Arctic Ocean. In this tundra, a permanently frozen subsoil permits the growth of few plants other than mosses and lichens. Coniferous forests and, farther south, forests of deciduous trees cover the steppes. South of the forests lies an immense belt of treeless plains covered with grass. The grass is replaced by a desert flora toward the arid zone of central Asia.

In the regions of copious rainfall, the plant life is extraordinarily rich, India having more species than any other region of equal area in the world. The sacred peepul and the banyan tree, plants producing ginger, members of the pea family, medicinal plants, orchids, gourds, figs, timber trees, gum producing trees, sago palms, bamboos, and teak are representative of the rich flora south of the Himalaya mountains. On these mountains grow magnolias and large rhododendrons; higher up, pines are found, and also the deodar, a species of cedar similar to that growing on Mount Lebanon in southwestern Asia. The better watered parts of Arabia still produce, in limited amounts, the spices and fragrant plants which, in earlier days, won for the peninsula the poetic characterization of "Araby the blest."

Animal Life. Asia is the original home of most of the world's domesticated animals, including the horse, ox, sheep, pig, goat, camel, chicken, and goose. The humped ox, the water buffalo, and the yak are used as draft animals by the inhabitants of the continent. The elephant of Asia, unlike the African elephant, is easily domesticated.

The Himalaya mountains form a barrier north of which the climate is unfavorable to animal life. In the north, however, bears, foxes, and wolves are found, as well as other wild animals which inhabit the corresponding latitudes of Europe. South of the barrier, the fauna is extremely rich. Nearly all the families of tropical birds are represented. India is the home of the tiger. There are several species of the rhinoceros. The deadly cobra takes a yearly toll of many thousands of human lives.

Minerals. The natural resources of Asia have been very inadequately explored. There is reason to believe, however, that the continent is extremely rich in minerals. Coal and iron exist in large quantities in China, and petroleum is obtained in quantity from Persia and Iraq. Most of the world's supply of tin comes from the Malay peninsula and the islands lying near it.

Inhabitants. It is generally acknowledged that Asia is the original home of the human race. Several of the most valuable skeletal remains of the prehistoric ancestors of man have been found in Java and China. The present inhabitants of Asia, including those of Malaysia, are estimated to number 1117 million.

The yellow race comprises about seven-tenths of the total population of the continent. This race, together with the brown race, occupying the peninsula and the archipelago of Malay, is usually considered most distinctive of Asia. About one-tenth of the population, however, consists of Caucasians, people of the white race, living in Siberia, India, and southwest Asia. From these regions, the Caucasians emigrated at an early period, spreading over northern Africa and Europe, whence they came later to America. The aborigines of America are believed to have reached the western hemisphere by way of northeastern Asia. The Negritos of the Philippine Islands and other scattered tribes are the only remaining representatives of the black race in Asia.

Religion. The most widely embraced religions of Asia today are Buddhism, Confucianism, Mohammedanism, Hinduism, Taoism, and Shintoism. Buddhism, Confucianism, and Taoism center principally in China. Shintoism is the chief religion of Japan. In India, Hinduism competes with Mohammedanism, which is the dominant religion of southwestern Asia. Christianity is strongest in northwestern Asia, chiefly Siberia, and in the islands of the Malay archipelago, in many of which it dominates to the virtual exclusion of others. It has also been introduced by missionaries into China, Japan, and India.

POLITICAL DIVISIONS

The independent countries of Asia embrace Japan, China, Turkey, Iran (Persia), Afghanistan, Iraq, Siam, and Saudi Arabia. Russia is in part an Asiatic power, her Asiatic territory being about three times as extensive as European Russia. Recent political developments have immensely affected Asia. Of world wide significance is the loss of colonial possessions many of which changed to independent countries. If this trend is sustained, the beginning of a new era in Asiatic history may well be under way. Owing however to present uncertainties in some of these changes, the following table will catalog the change. On the following pages, most of the political divisions where the status is in question will be discussed under their traditional colonial dependency status, as French Dependencies, Netherland Dependencies, or British Dependencies. Where the dependency has become an unquestionable independent state, as the Philippine Republic, it will be given separate treatment.

Aden and the Protectorate—Special relations with Great Britain.
Bhutan—Nominally independent; special relations with Great Britain.
Burma—Independent, Republic of the Union of Burma.
Ceylon—Dominion status, Great Britain.
Cyprus—Special relations with Great Britain.
Hong Kong—British privileges retained for the present.
Indonesia, Republic of—Promised independence.
Israel—Independent Jewish state. British withdrew in 1948.
Korea—Promised de jure or de facto independence.
Lebanon—Independent, Republic of Lebanon.
Malaya Federation—Organized after World War II into a Malayan Union and later into a Malayan Federation without inclusion of Crown Colony of Singapore.
Manchuria—Reverted to previous status as North Eastern Provinces of China.
Nepal—Independent, recently emerged from isolation, special relations with Great Britain.
Outer Mongolia—Independent as Mongolian People's Republic.
Pakistan—Independent Islamic state (British withdrawal August, 1947).
Palestine—Partitioned into Israel, Jewish state, and an Arab state.
Philippines—Independent, Republic of the Philippines.
Singapore—Crown Colony, Great Britain.
Syria—Independent, Republic of Syria.
Tanna Tuva and Kushka—Have become part of the U.S.S.R.
Tibet—Nearer Tibet includes two Chinese provinces; Farther Tibet, nominally Chinese but in many respects independent.
Transjordan—Independent, Kingdom of Transjordan.
Union of India (Hindustan)—Independent, British withdrawal in August, 1948.
Viet-Nam—Promised independence.

Of outside powers, Great Britain had by far the greatest territorial interests in Asia. Most of her dependencies were grouped under the empire of India, but many others lie in various parts of the continent. The Netherlands and France had important possessions in Asia, while the United States controlled the Philippine Islands and still controls Guam. Papua and part of New Guinea are subject to Australian jurisdiction, and Western Samoa is held as a mandate by New Zealand. Portugal governs a few insignificant possessions in different parts of the continent. While major political control in Asia by foreign nations has apparently been ended, many small holdings are still retained, at least for the present. The status of many of the newly created independent states is not entirely assured.

Afghanistan. An inland country of southern Asia, hemmed in by India, Iran, and Turkestan. Its area is about 250,000 square miles. The surface is, for the most part, a dry, mountainous plateau. It is traversed by the Hindu Kush and by other ranges, which in some places attain a height in excess of 17,000 feet.

The mountain sides are partially clothed by forests of cedar, pine, walnut, and other trees; and the valleys, sometimes with the help of irrigation, support semiannual crops of cereals and a great variety of fruits. Wheat, rice, and mutton are the staple foods. Sheep raising is one of the chief occupations. The flocks include a native sheep with a very large tail. The extraordinary size of the tail is caused by the development of fat upon which the animal may draw for sustenance when fodder is scarce.

The population of Afghanistan is about 12,000,000, some of whom belong to tribes virtually independent of the central government. The capital is Kabul, a city of about 80,000 inhabitants, which is an important center of caravan trade with India and with central Asia. There are no railroads in Afghanistan. Herat, in the northwestern part of the country, contains the ruins of many fine buildings erected by Timur, the great Mogul warrior who overran Asia in the 14th century.

Arabia. The large peninsula in southwestern Asia, having an area of 1,200,000 square miles. It extends southeastward from the borders of Egypt, Palestine, and Iraq, being bounded on the west by the Red Sea and on the east by the Persian Gulf and the Gulf of Oman. The southern shore is washed by the Gulf of Aden and the Indian Ocean.

Most of Arabia is a sandy, arid waste, uninhabitable except by wandering tribes of Bedouins. Camels are the chief form of wealth among the tribesmen, who maintain themselves at oases occurring here and there over the surface of the great desert. Practically the entire peninsula is comprised within the kingdom of Saudi Arabia, although the southeastern littoral enjoys an independent status under the name of Oman. The exports are unimportant and are confined mainly to coffee, hides, and wool. Saudi Arabia contains Mecca and Medina, two cities sacred in the eyes of the Mohammedan world. The kingdom has two capitals,—Mecca and Riyadh. Total population of the peninsula is estimated at 10 million.

British Dependencies. Apart from India, the territories of Asia under British control are the Malay states, the Straits Settlements, Ceylon, Hong Kong, Cyprus, Fiji, and a number of other small dependencies. Palestine had been allotted to Great Britain as a mandate but has been relinquished. The New Hebrides in the Malay archipelago, lying east of Australia, are under the joint administration of Great Britain and France. For the capital, area, and population of each dependency and mandate see the table of *The British Commonwealth of Nations*.

The Malay States, nine in number, occupy the southern half of the Malay Peninsula. All are organized under the present Malay Federation. These are Perak, Selangor, Negri Sembilan, Pahang, Johore, Kedah, Perlis, Kelantan, Trengganu. The Straits Settlements of Penang and Malacca have been added.

The Straits Settlements consist of a number of small islands off the south of the Malay peninsula, together with a small part of the mainland of the peninsula. Rubber, spices, and tapioca are grown, and tin is mined in considerable quantities.

Ceylon is a fertile, well watered island near the southern extremity of India. The surface is mainly an undulating plain, about one-fifth being mountainous and covered with forests. The island is famous for gems, although the exports of rubber and tea exceed in value any other article shipped abroad. Other products are coconuts, cinnamon, cocoa, plumbago, and oil of citronella.

Hong Kong is a small rocky island off the southeastern coast of China near the mouth of the Canton river in the South China Sea. See *Victoria*.

Cyprus is an island in the northeastern part of the Mediterranean Sea. Most of the inhabitants are Christians. Agriculture is the predominant industry. The chief exports are carob beans, wine, and tropical fruits. The island anciently produced copper. Its name was used by the Greeks to designate the metal and is the origin of the English word.

Fiji is a crown colony, consisting of about 250 islands in the south Pacific Ocean some 1500 miles east of Australia. The larger islands are mountainous. The inhabitants support themselves mainly by tropical agriculture, the chief products including sugar, coconuts, rice, rubber, bananas, maize, and beans. The annual exports normally approximate $10,000,000 in value. A large share in the government is conceded to the natives.

The other British dependencies in Asia are as follows: North Borneo, in the Malay archipelago, to which are attached, for administrative purposes, the island of Brunei and of Sarawak; Bahrein islands in the Persian Gulf, noted for their pearl fisheries; and Aden, a small volcanic district of southwest Arabia, to which are attached politically Perim near the coast, the Kuria Muria islands off the coast of southwestern Oman, and Socotra, an island usually regarded as a part of Africa.

China. The immense, roughly triangular country in eastern Asia, lying between Asiatic Russia on the northwest and India and French Indo-China on the southwest. It is about 3000 miles from east to west, and its maximum extent from north to south is 2400 miles. The area of China is 3,913,955 square miles.

As a political region the name of China may refer to either China Proper or Greater China. China Proper is the name generally applied to the original 18 provinces south of the Great Wall, whereas Greater China corresponds roughly to the Old Chinese Empire of the Manchu Dynasty, including China Proper and the four dependencies of Manchuria, Mongolia, Sinkiang, and Tibet. In 1945 China recognized the independence of Outer Mongolia as the Mongolian People's Republic. Another small country called the Tuvinian People's Republic (Tannu Tuva) was incorporated into the Soviet Union. During this same year China recovered the possession of Taiwan (Formosa) and the Pescadores from Japan. France restored Kwangchowan but England and Portugal retain their rights in Hong Kong and Macao respectively. China has only nominal control over such outlying territories as Farther Tibet. While Manchuria has been recovered, the struggle between Communists and Nationalists makes its final political destination scarcely discernible at present.

Three-fifths of the territory of China is inhabited by about 1 per cent of the population. This sparsely settled part, occupied mainly by uncivilized tribes, consists of the lofty, mountainous plateau of Tibet, the desert plateau of Mongolia, and the arid depression of inland drainage known as Sinkiang. The remainder of the country embraces the extremely fertile eastern plains, watered by three great rivers, the Hwang, the Yangtze, and the West river. In China Proper as well as in the outlying territories, the surface of China is mainly mountainous handicapping both transportation and agriculture. While practically all of the level lands are fertile flood plains, they are subject to most disastrous floods causing widespread destruction of property and famine. The great interior basin of Szechwan with its fertile Changtu plain sustained China against the Japanese.

The climate of China Proper, where practically all of the Chinese live, is divided into two main regions, northern and southern. The northern region extends from the crest of the Tsingling and Haiyang mountains to the northern border. It is a temperate region supporting wheat as a major cereal as compared to rice in the southern region. The southern region includes the great Yangtze basin and southward area, with rice as the major climatic adjustment. Northern China is temperate with hot summers, cold winters, and moderate rainfall, while southern China differs by having mild winters and heavy rainfall. China's rainfall is sharply seasonal, falling mainly in summer.

All of China suffers greatly from droughts and floods which are caused by variations in the Monsoon winds which control China's weather. A recent flood of the Yangtze affected 50,000,000 people, directly causing the death of upwards of two million and destroying vast properties. Typhoons, earthquakes, and locusts also plague China.

The deposits of coal, of iron, and of copper in China are among the richest in the world. More than one-half of the world's supply of antimony and tungsten comes from China. The proximity of the coal and the iron deposits in the northeastern district of Shan-si has resulted in a large steel industry. The manufacture of porcelain, centering since 220 A. D. in Ching-teh-chen, a city of about 300,000 inhabitants, is still a distinctive industry of the country. Lacquered ware and textiles of silk and of cotton are other native manufactures for which China has long been noted. Manchuria has vast deposits of oil shale which are being processed. Manchuria also has a large share of China's coal and iron reserves plus considerable industrial development.

The chief occupation of the Chinese, however, is agriculture, which is carried on more intensively than anywhere else in the world. The farms are small and the methods are not the most improved, but, in the arable districts, no land is left uncultivated. The soil is very fertile, and irrigation by canals and by irrigation wheels or even by hand is employed where necessary. Rotation of crops has been practiced for centuries. The chief crops include rice, corn, tobacco, soy beans, tea, cotton, and sugar cane, the last three being grown in the southern part of the country. The mulberry tree is cultivated largely for the silkworms which feed on it and from which silk is obtained. Soy beans and silk are the most valuable articles of export. Other important exports are textiles, tea, coal, and cotton. Chickens and pigs are raised everywhere in China, and pig's bristles have become an important article of export. China's farm problems are complex also because 80 per cent of the people live on farms and must depend on farming for their existence. Farm land per capita is only a fraction of an acre (0.45) or 1485 people for each square mile of agricultural land. While her total production of such important crops as wheat and rice are among the largest in the world, probably totaling upwards of 3 billion bushels, it scarcely suffices to feed her huge population who depend upon cereals for 90 per cent of their diet. Another problem is China's age-old field pattern whereby any one farm is parcelled into scattered plots about the village where the owner lives. This makes economical operation impossible.

By 1947, over 12,000 miles of railroad had been constructed in China. The so-called Grand canal, running from the city of Hangchow a distance of 600 miles north to the Gulf of Chihli, was built 2500 years ago. Parts of it are choked with silt. In 1947, there were more than 75,000 miles of highways. A large part of the country's transportation is provided by the rivers, along which ply numerous "junks" and other boats. Thousands of people live on the rivers in house boats, which are often equipped with gardens made in soil laid on the floors of the boats.

Chinese civilization is ancient and distinctive. For thousands of years, the veneration of parents has been a cardinal principle of Chinese religion, law, and social customs. These cardinal principles of Chinese religion and philosophy were tremendously impressed upon the Chinese people by the zealous teaching of the great philosopher Confucius and his disciple Mencius. This principle encouraged a high birth rate, which, despite recurrent famines, has kept the population of China well above the limits which the country could readily support. As a people, the Chinese have proved capable of adapting themselves both to cold and hot countries, having in recent decades colonized their former northern province of Manchuria and infiltrated as successful traders throughout the various lands of southeastern Asia.

The impact of Western civilization plunged China into social and political chaos. The growth of industrialism, beginning with the manufacture of textiles, flour, and steel, tended to break up the authority of the family, which is further threatened by Western ideas of freedom and the emancipation of women. The political authority of the central government is only nominally effective over much of China. The chief religions are Buddhism, Confucianism, and Taoism. About 4 per cent are Mohammedans, and less than 1 per cent are Christians.

The population of China is estimated at 465,268,019. Nanking is the capital. The largest city is Shanghai, near the center of the coast line. Other cities of importance include Tientsin, Canton, Peiping, Hankow, Wenchow, Chungking, and Changsha. During World War II Chungking was the capital and following the war the internal rift in China caused the Communist government to set up an opposing capital. If China is reunited, Nanking may be retained as the national capital. Kunming is rapidly assuming importance as an air terminal on intercontinental lines. Six cities in China have over 1,000,000 people; Shanghai, Peiping, Tientsin, Hankow, Mukden, Canton, and Hong Kong, while six more are between one-half and one million.

Dutch East Indies (Netherlands Indies or Indonesian Republic). A name applied to the part of the Malay archipelago which belongs to the Netherlands. The larger islands include Java, Sumatra, Madura, and Celebes. Borneo and New Guinea are each in part under the control of the Netherlands. The northern portion of Borneo, however, is a colony of Great Britain, while eastern New Guinea is a mandate of Australia. The total area of the Dutch East Indies is estimated at 733,296 square miles.

The political status of The Netherlands East Indies remained in flux for a long period after the end of World War II. The struggle centered between the Nationalists on Java and Sumatra, who had created the Indonesian Republic, and the Dutch, who were eager to maintain some control over their rich colonial empire in the Far East. In November, 1946, the Linggadjati Agreement was reached providing for the establishment of the United States of Indonesia by January 1, 1949, as an equal partner in the Dutch Crown. The United States of Indonesia as then planned would consist of the following three major divisions: The Indonesian Republic, comprised of Java, Sumatra, and Madura; Dutch Borneo; and the Great East, comprised of Bali, the Moluccas, the Celebes, the Lesser Soenda Islands; and possibly Dutch New Guinea. In 1947, and again in 1948, fighting broke out over a disagreement in interpreting the pact making indefinite the future of the United States of Indonesia in relation to the mother country.

The islands are fertile, warm, and well watered. They show an extraordinary degree of productivity, the exports in some years exceeding 500 million dollars in value. Rice, corn, cassava, tea, sugar, quinine, coffee, rubber, tobacco, indigo, copra, petroleum, and tin are the chief products. Coal is mined also, the annual production exceeding one million tons.

The estimated population in 1941 was 71,534,000, mainly Polynesian in type. Of this number, the island of Java had 41,719,524, one of the three most populous islands of the world. Its beauty and tropical luxuriance have won for it the characterization of the "pearl of the East Indies." Among the more noteworthy forest trees are the teak and the upas. Many of the inhabitants are still organized in uncivilized tribes. The prevailing religion is Mohammedanism. Ruins of magnificent Buddhist temples, however, attest the former prevalence of Buddhism. At Boro Budor in Java stands one of the architectural marvels of the world, the largest and one of the most elaborate Buddhist temples in existence. Java contains Batavia, the capital of the Dutch East Indies.

East of Java lies the island of Bali. Noted for its beauty and its picturesque inhabitants, it is visited annually by many tourists.

French Dependencies. The Asiatic possessions of France on the mainland consist of French Indochina and five small colonies in India: Pondicherry, Karikal, Chandernagore, Mahe, and Yanaon. Among the islands, France rules New Caledonia, Tahiti, and a large number of smaller islands in the Malay archipelago. She also holds a mandate over Syria and Lebanon, shares with Great Britain a protectorate over New Hebrides, and leases Kwangchow Wan, a territory of 190 square miles on the coast of China. Recent political developments point to some marked changes in French holdings in Asia. In March, 1946, the French recognized the Viet-Nam Republic, holding Northern Annam and Tonkin as a free state within the proposed Indo-China Union, and promised a plebiscite to determine whether that state would also include Southern Annam and Cochin China.

The grand plan of the French for Indo-China at first called for an Indo-China Union or Federation consisting of Viet-Nam (Annam, Tonkin, and possibly Cochin China), Cambodia, and Laos, all within the framework of the French Union. Later discussions indicate French Union membership possibly without Federation. Kwangchow Wan has been restored to China, and Syria and Lebanon have been granted independent status.

French Indochina occupies most of the large southeastern peninsula of Asia. Its area is 285,000 square miles. The surface is traversed by mountain ranges in the east but is low in the west, where the rich, copiously watered soil supports a flourishing agriculture. Rice is the chief crop and forms about 70 per cent of the country's exports. Other important exports are rubber, sugar, cotton, and pepper. Coffee and tea are also grown, and teakwood is obtained from the dense tropical forests that cover the mountains. The estimated population in 1943 was 25,369,295, including about 35,000 Europeans. Buddhism is the prevailing religion. The capital is Hanoi, a city of about 135,000 inhabitants. The chief port, Saigon, is a French naval base.

The five colonies in India cover less than 200 square miles and have a population of 323,295. These colonies form the sole remaining portion of a one-time pretentious French empire in India.

New Caledonia, Tahiti, and the other islands of French Oceania cover an estimated area of 10,068 square miles and support a population of 87,678, mainly Polynesians. The smaller islands include the Isle of Pines, the Wallis archipelago, the Loyalty islands, the Huon islands, Moorea, and the Marquezas islands. The capital of New Caledonia is Noumea, which has about 10,000 inhabitants. The New Hebrides have an area of 5700 square miles and a population of about 60,000. The chief products of these island groups are nickel, corn, coconuts, coffee, rubber, vanilla, and preserved meats. There is a penal settlement on New Caledonia, which continued to receive convicts from France until 1896.

India. A large country in south central Asia formerly more or less completely under British rule.

India was divided into two main administrative parts: British India, comprising roughly three-fifths of the country and containing a population of 295,000,000, was annexed to the British Empire and governed directly. The Indian states, with 93,000,000 people and two-fifths of the area, had local autonomy but were under the suzerainty of Britain.

The division of the country into British India and the Indian states did not follow geographical boundaries. Rather, it was the result of historical accident and represented, in general, the political units as they existed at the time Britain assumed control. The two major political areas were not units distinctly set apart, but were fragmented and interspersed throughout the country.

The only differences between the Indian states and British India were political. The political units were not cultural units. Linguistic, religious, and ethnic lines cut across the political boundaries and formed an extremely complex pattern. There are in all about 700 native states, some of which are under the authority of the 15 organized administrative areas, or provinces. There were 562 Indian states outside the British administrative provinces varying in size from Hyderabad, nearly as large as France, to small areas the size of a private estate. The relation of these states with the British Crown were based on individual treaties and agreements and presented a variety of working arrangements. Nepal and Bhutan, situated in the Himalaya Mountain region, although nominally independent, were under the protection of Great Britain. Other semi-independent units included Baluchistan in the west and the tribes of Burma in the east.

In August, 1947, the whole of India was divided into the dominions of Pakistan and Hindustan or the Union of India. Initially within the framework of the British Commonwealth of Nations both dominions were free to leave the commonwealth or to remain within its folds. Most Indian states joined either Pakistan or the Union of India, although Hyderabad remained aloof until overcome by force in 1948.

Pakistan at the end of 1947 had an area of 300,000 square miles, located partially in northwestern and partially in northeastern India. Key areas within Pakistan are eastern Bengal, part of Assam, Baluchistan, western Punjab, Sind, and the northwest Frontier Province. The interim capital of the new state is Karachi.

The population of Pakistan is estimated at about 70,000,000, 72 per cent of which is Moslem. In terms of population Pakistan is now the largest Islamic state on earth. Minority elements are 19,000,000 Hindus and 1,600,000 Sihks.

Pakistan is poor in minerals but rich in agricultural land, with cotton, wheat, rice, sugar cane, tea, and jute leading crops. Karachi, Lahore, and Dacca are the three leading cities.

The constitution will be based on the Moslem law as expressed by the Koran. Ali Jinnah is governor-general. In the fall of 1947 Pakistan was admitted to the United Nations.

Union of India (Hindustan) is over 1,200,000 square miles in area including most of the 562 Indian states and all the great Hindu provinces. The capital is New Delhi, which was the British capital also.

Well over 300,000,000 people live in the Union of India including a large minority of some 38,000,000 Moslems, and another of 3,900,000 Sikhs. Religious strife therefore continues to be serious. It is estimated that 10,000,000 people have crossed boundaries in order to be in the division of their faith.

Hindustan contains the best mineral resources and the leading industrial centers, as Bombay, Madras, Calcutta. A democratic constitution and bill of rights is planned. Jawaharlal Nehru is premier and foreign minister.

Considering India as a whole, the area is 1,581,410 square miles, including the near-by islands with the exception of Ceylon. Three insignificant colonies on the west coast are owned by Portugal, and France has five small dependencies in India.

India has a northern mountain wall, south of which the surface falls to a great plain, arid in the extreme west but copiously watered in the central and eastern regions. Through this plain pass the Indus river and the Ganges river, the latter being joined at its delta by the Brahmaputra river. An upland stretches from the plain to the southern extremity of the peninsula of India. From the head of the Bay of Bengal, a mountain barrier runs north to the Himalaya mountains and divides the rest of India from Burma. Burma is a rich, wild country, being cut, in a north and south direction, by several mountain ridges separated by extraordinarily fertile and well watered valleys.

The central plains of India are the hottest part of the country. The year is divided into three seasons, the hot season, the monsoon rains, and the cold season. The hot season is from late March to early June. In central India temperatures rise daily to over 100° F. in the shade and at times 120° F. Day and night the temperature stands between 95° F. and 115° F. and little outside work can be accomplished during midday.

With the coming of the rainy season, June to mid-September, the temperatures fall appreciably and daily rains prevail. A secondary heat period follows the rainy season, from mid-September to November, when the cold season sets in. This "cold" season is about like summer in northern United States except that no rain falls in India.

Over most of India frost and snow are unknown. Only in the far northwest and in high altitudes do temperatures descend below freezing.

India is a land of great climatic extremes. The droughts caused by failure of the monsoon rains cause terrible famines when literally millions starve to death. Typhoons bring havoc to both coasts of the Deccan. During the rainy season the heaviest rainfall known in the world falls on the windward side of the Khasi Hills. Over 38 feet (457.8 in.) of rain falls here annually between late March and early October. During a particularly wet year 905 inches (75 feet) of rain fell at the station of Cherrapunji and on one day 41 inches, the equal of a year of rainfall in central United States. A great climatic variation is provided by the towering Himalayas which provide important summer resorts, as at Simla. The eastern regions and a strip along the western coast have a heavy rainfall, confined mainly to the rainy season—June to November. The northwestern section is dry, but the land is productive under irrigation. Irrigation works in India dwarf those of any other country in the world. Over 50 million acres of crop land is thus served, mainly by means of canals constructed by the government. Among the largest structures for impounding water for this purpose are the Lloyd dam on the Yelmandi river and the Sukkur barrage on the Indus river.

The vegetable and animal life of India is extremely rich, comprising nearly all the tropical species of the continent. Elephants are still found wild in northern Burma. Venomous snakes are numerous, and every year their human victims are numbered by the thousand. Man-eating tigers have been known to cause whole villages to be deserted. Crocodiles infest the malarial swamps at the mouths of the large rivers. A species of loud-voiced lizard abounds in all the moister regions.

More than two-thirds of the population of India supports itself by agriculture and stock raising. India is the world's chief producer of jute and the second largest cotton producing country. The other chief crops are rice, sugar cane, wheat, and tea. The live stock consists mainly of humped oxen, buffaloes, sheep, and goats. Buffaloes are far more numerous as beasts of burden than are horses, donkeys, or camels. India possesses more cattle than any other country in the world. Owing to their low quality they are not of comparable use.

After agriculture, the most important occupation in India is the manufacture of textiles, which, with other manufacturing industries, affords a living for about 11 per cent of the population. Of the minerals, coal is mined to the greatest value, gold, petroleum, manganese, and salt following in the order named. Salt mining is a government monopoly. The chief exports are jute, cotton, rice, wheat, tea, hides, lac, wool, opium, and metals. The country absorbs enormous amounts of gold and silver for ornaments and hoarded treasure.

The population of India is 388,997,955. Of these, counted on a community basis, Hindus form 65.5 per cent; Mohammedans, 23.6; Christians, 1.6; Sikhs, 1.4; Parsees, .03; and Buddhists, .06. Some 222 different languages are spoken, English being familiar to about 2,500,000 of the inhabitants. About 90 per cent of the population is illiterate. The people are extremely religious and pilgrimages to such great "holy cities" as Benares are the rule. Here bathing in the "sacred waters" of the Ganges river is supposed to remove physical and spiritual ills.

The fabulously wealthy princes of India at times display unusual sentiment, such as the construction of the magnificent Taj Mahal at Agra (1629–1650) by Emperor Shah Jehan as the burial place for his favorite wife Mumtaz Mahal.

The former capital of India was Delhi, and the largest city is Calcutta. Other important cities are Bombay, Madras, Hyderabad, Rangoon, Lahore, Karachi, Benares, Cawnpore, and Lucknow.

Iran (*ē-rän'*). An independent country of southwestern Asia, formerly known as Persia, lying between the Persian gulf on the south and the Caspian Sea on the north and stretching eastward from Iraq to Afghanistan and India. Its surface, covering about 628,000 square miles, is a high plateau rimmed by mountains on every side except the east. Many of the mountains are volcanic, including the country's highest peak, Mount Demavend, which has an altitude of 18,500 feet.

A narrow plain on the southern coast of the Caspian Sea has a heavy rainfall and supports a luxuriant vegetation. Nearly all the remainder of the country is dry and barren. The former name, Persia, gave its name to the peach, the English word being a corruption of the Latin word for Persian. The chief products of the country include petroleum, cotton, tobacco, rice, silk, wool, gums, fruits, opium, cereals, and the famous Persian rugs, the last being made entirely on looms operated by hand. Petroleum accounts for about half the total value of the exports. The development of Iran is handicapped by a serious lack of transportation facilities. There are fifteen regular trade routes, along which goods are carried by caravan.

The estimated population of Iran is 10,000,000. Of this number, about one-third lead a nomadic life. Most of the inhabitants are Mohammedans, although there is a group of about 10,000 Parsis, or Ghebers, adherents of the ancient Persian religion that flourished as early as the 6th century B. C. The main body of the sect was forced by persecution to take refuge in India. Tehran is the capital and largest city of Iran.

Iraq. Formerly known as Mesopotamia, this country stretches northwest from the Persian Gulf to Turkey and Syria. It lies between Iran and Arabia, and comprises the valleys of the Tigris and Euphrates rivers. Its area is 177,148 square miles. The soil is rich, but requires irrigation. Dates, cotton, and wheat are the chief crops; petroleum the principal mineral product. The population of Iraq in 1932 was 2,857,077, mainly Arabs and Kurds. Its capital is Baghdad.

Japan. An ancient empire, consisting of a chain of mountainous islands off the eastern coast of Asia. The largest island is called Honshu. To the north lies Hokkaido, or Yezo; to the south, Shikoku and Kyushu. Chosen, or Korea, the southern half of Sakhalin, and Kwantung were lost by Japan in World War II, as was Taiwan, or Formosa. The area of the empire was reduced from 260,770 to about 148,000 square miles. From 1932 to 1945 Japan also controlled Manchukuo, the Chinese province of Manchuria, 503,013 square miles in area.

The islands of Japan, being the projecting portions of an immense submarine mountain range, have a mountainous surface, traversed from end to end by a high ridge. Numerous spurs from the mountains, descending to the coasts, result in a highly irregular coast line. There is, consequently, an abundance of good harbors, most of which are on the Pacific side.

The highest mountain in Honshu is Huzi, formerly Fuji, 12,395 feet in altitude. This peak is exceeded in height, however, by Mount Morrison in Formosa, which is 14,300 feet high. There is probably no region of its size in the world which has so many active volcanoes and is subject to such violent earthquakes as Japan. The largest active volcanic peak is Asama in central Honshu, which has a crater 600 to 800 feet deep with absolutely perpendicular sides.

The climate of Japan varies from subarctic to subtropical conditions. The cold northwestern winds from Siberia bring heavy snows in winter on the western side of the northern islands. Farther south, and more especially on the eastern side, the ocean exerts a moderating influence on the temperature and provides a copious rainfall. Violent and destructive windstorms, known as typhoons, usually mark the end of the hot, moist summers.

Japan has a very rich flora. The forests contain such trees as bamboos, camphor trees, oaks, maples, walnuts, laurels, and willows. The cultivation of flowering plants is very extensive, the Japanese being noted for their appreciation of floral beauty. Their national emblem is the chrysanthemum.

The animals include bears, monkeys, hares, wild boars, deer, foxes, wildcats, and pheasants. The buffalo is used for food and for plowing. The crane is considered sacred, being regarded as a symbol of longevity. The silkworm and numerous kinds of fish are of great economic importance.

The minerals of Japan produced in the most important quantities are coal and copper. Gold, silver, and petroleum are obtained, and iron is mined on the islands but the main source of the empire's supply was Manchuria.

The chief industries are agriculture, fishing, and manufacturing. Land cultivation is carried on intensively over the small arable portions of the principal islands. The fisheries support nearly one million workers. Rice, fish, wheat, barley, rye, and poultry provide the staple foods of Japan. The product representing the greatest export value is silk, Japan supplying 60 per cent of the United States silk market. Among the manufactures, the textile industry and shipbuilding are the most important. Other manufactures are steel, paper, matches, toys, and lacquered ware. Formosa produces the bulk of the world's camphor obtained from trees.

The population of the Japanese empire in 1940 was 105,226,101; of Japan proper, 73,114,308. There is complete freedom of religion. The chief forms are Shintoism and Buddhism. Elementary education is compulsory. There are 37 universities in the empire. Japan has an ancient and virile civilization, and, alone among the peoples of Asia, has shown herself the equal of the Western nations in energy and enterprise. Illiteracy is less than 1 per cent.

The capital and largest city is Tokyo. Osaka is the principal port. Other important cities are Kobe, Kyoto, Nagoya, Yokohama, and Nagasaki. The government is a constitutional monarchy under an emperor.

Korea. At the end of hostilities in World War II, Korea was separated into two zones by the 38° parallel for the purpose of disarming the Japanese, with the Russians to the north and the United States to the south. Under approval of the General Assembly of May, 1948, elections were held to set up a Korean government. This was approved overwhelmingly. Russia withdrew her troops, but the northern and southern divisions have not as yet formed a United Government.

Korea is a beautiful land of sparkling streams and high mountains. The peninsula composing it extends for 600 miles and covers an area of 85,246 square miles. Latitude is from 33° to 43° north. The northern part has cold winters and short summers, but the southern part has a warm moist rice climate.

The population is 24,326,327 and is of Mongoloid origin. The people are proud and intensely nationalistic, tracing their origin back to the mythical dynasty of Tangun 2333 B.C. Their written history begins in 1123 B.C.

Their economy is based on agriculture, with cereals, especially rice, basic. A considerable variety of minerals abound, as coal, gold, silver, copper, iron, and kaolin. Manufactures have developed, as textiles, cement, paper, pottery, electric bulbs, and chemical fertilizer plants. The capital city is Keijo (Seoul). Fusan is a prominent port.

Manchuria. After fourteen years of control by Japan, Manchuria has reverted to its status as the northeastern Provinces of China. The population is largely Chinese and numbers about 43 million. This area has had recent and rapid development and is now one of the most important economic areas of the Far East. It is a fertile plains area of temperate climate, cold winters and hot summers. Important crops are kaoling, wheat, soybeans, millet, and corn. Minerals are abundant and being rapidly developed —iron, coal, and especially shale oil. Mukden is a city of over one million people. Hsinking and Harbin are large and rapidly growing.

Palestine. A country situated on the southeastern coast of the Mediterranean Sea, having an area of 10,000 square miles bounded north by Syria and south by Hejaz and Egypt. About half of its surface is adapted for agriculture, most of this land being in a plain bordering the sea. The chief exportable product is oranges, grown mainly about the Mediterranean port Jaffa. Salt and potash are obtained from the waters of the Dead Sea, which lies on the eastern part of the country in the so-called Great Rift. Electric power is distributed from Tiberias, Haifa, and Tel Aviv, the last being a city built by Jewish enterprise since 1922, when Palestine was officially declared a national home for Jews. Manufacturing has expanded markedly, and includes the making of bricks, vegetable oil, flour, soap, cement, furniture, and matches. The capital of Palestine is Jerusalem, where a Hebrew university was opened in 1925. The population is chiefly Arab; Jews comprise about 28 per cent. Arabic, Hebrew, and English are the official languages. The Jewish population of Palestine has rapidly increased and at the withdrawal of England the Jewish state of Israel was created in Palestine and was recognized by the United Nations.

Persia. *See* **Iran.**

Philippine Islands. An independent island commonwealth forming the most northern division of the great Malay archipelago. The Philippines lie southeast of China, about 500 miles from its coast, and are bounded on the north and the east by the Pacific Ocean, on the south by the Celebes Sea, and on the west by the South China Sea. The island group is situated north of the equator but entirely within the tropics. It extends north and south for a distance of 1150 miles and east and west for a distance of 650 miles.

There are upwards of 7000 islands and islets, of which only 466 have areas of one square mile or over. Luzon, 40,800 square miles, and Mindanao, about 36,900 square miles, rank among the large islands of the world. These two islands contain about 70 per cent of the total land area of the group.

Besides the two largest islands, there are 9 others of importance. Their names and approximate areas in square miles are as follows: Samar, 5100; Negros, 4900; Palawan, 4500; Panay, 4450; Mindoro, 3800; Leyte, 2800; Cebu, 1700; Bohol, 1550; and Masbate, 1250. The total area of the entire Philippine group is approximately 114,400 square miles. The population of the islands, 18,500,000. Manila, the capital and largest city, had a population of 623,492.

The islands of the Philippine archipelago are largely volcanic. There are 12 volcanoes which have been more or less active in modern times, and slight earthquakes are of frequent occurrence. The islands are traversed by irregular mountain ranges, the main ridges of which extend usually in a north-and-south direction. In Luzon, the mountains rise to heights of from 3500 to 4500 feet. Mount Apo, in southern Mindanao, with an elevation of 9610 feet, is the highest peak in the Philippines. But comparatively little of the surface is level, and much of it lies at considerable elevations above the sea.

In the larger islands, there are extensive drainage systems. The Cagayan river, in Luzon, 220 miles in length, with a drainage basin of some 10,000 square miles, is the largest river in the Philippines. Other important rivers in Luzon are the Agno, the Pampanga, and the Pasig, all of which are navigable to some extent for small vessels. In Mindanao, the Cotobato and the Agusan are the chief rivers. There are numerous small lakes, the largest of which are Laguna de Bay and Bombon in Luzon, and Buluan, Liguasan, and Lanao in Mindanao.

By reason of their location, the Philippine Islands have a warm climate. From about the first of November to the last of June, the northeast trade wind prevails. During this period, the eastern coasts have a heavy rainfall, while the interior parts and the western coasts are dry. From July to October, inclusive, the southwest monsoon prevails. This produces a rainy season throughout the greater part of the islands, though the eastern coasts are comparatively dry.

At Manila, the mean temperature for January is 77°, and for June it is 82°. The mean yearly rainfall varies from 40 inches to 120 inches, according to location. At Manila, it is about 75 inches. As in other eastern tropical regions, violent cyclonic storms of wind and rain, known as typhoons or *baguios*, sometimes cause extensive destruction of life and property.

The islands, though not rich in mineral wealth, contain varied and valuable deposits, most of which await development. For hundreds of years, placer gold has been obtained in small quantities. Since the introduction of American mining methods, the yield of gold has been substantially increased. There are large beds of lignite; and silver, copper, and iron ores are found. Among other minerals which occur in the islands are asbestos, salt, sulphur, gypsum, petroleum, and various building stones.

The plant life of the islands is exceedingly luxuriant and varied. The flora is distinctly tropical in character, and is especially rich in trees. Magnificent primeval forests cover more than half the archipelago. According to the Philippine bureau of forestry, more than 700 species of commercially useful trees have been found in the forests. Dyewoods, wild rubber, and gutta-percha trees, cedars, ebonies, various palms, and many other valuable trees occur.

The most valuable native plant is that which yields the fiber called manila hemp. This is a wild plantain, which, in appearance, closely resembles the edible banana. The valuable coconut palm and the useful bamboo grow in all the islands, as does also the nipa palm, prized as a source of sugar. The banyan is common and attains immense size. Tamarind, mango, and wild orange trees flourish, and, in the southern islands, cinnamon, clove, and pepper occur in the wild state. Various other native trees and shrubs yield rattans, nuts, resins, gums, spices, oils, cabinet woods, and numerous minor forest products. Important cultivated plants successfully grown in the islands include rice, sugar, tobacco, coffee, cacao, Indian corn, and sweet potatoes.

The Philippines are poor in native mammals but rich in birds. The timarau, a ruminant related to the water buffalo, is the largest native mammal. Monkeys, deer, wild hogs, civet cats, and fruit bats are found. There are various smaller mammals, including a pygmy squirrel no larger than a mouse. Humped cattle are reared for their flesh and hides, and the carabao, or water buffalo, is everywhere used as a draft animal and as a beast of burden.

There are about 700 species of birds, about half of which are found only in the Philippines. Parrots, parrakeets, cockatoos, firebirds, fairy bluebirds, sunbirds, and other bright-hued tropical birds abound in the forests. There are also jungle fowl, beautifully colored wild pigeons, snipe, plover, and other game birds. Crocodiles, pythons, and venomous snakes are common. Flying lizards, geckos, iguanas, and turtles are found in all the larger islands.

Interisland commerce is carried on exclusively by Philippine ships. In 1900, the islands had only 120 miles of railway. The railroad mileage has been increased sevenfold. About 11,000 miles of highway have also been constructed. The economic development of the Philippines has been greatly aided by these increased facilities for transportation. Foreign trade is handled almost exclusively by non-Philippine shipping. The principal exports are manila hemp, sugar, coconut oil, tobacco goods, and copra. Among the principal imports are cotton goods, iron and steel wares, and foodstuffs. Manila, Iloilo, Cebu, and Zamboanga are the chief seaports. The rapid growth of Philippine commerce is shown by its rise from 32 million dollars in 1905 to 151 million dollars just previous to World War II.

The soil is exceedingly fertile, but as yet less than half the arable land is under cultivation. Among the chief crops grown are corn, rice, manila hemp, coconuts, sugar, tobacco, and maguey. Rice is the staple food crop, and mangoes and bananas are extensively cultivated. Many millions of coconuts are annually consumed for food and much dried coconut meat, the copra of commerce, is exported.

Tobacco goods and coconut oil are important manufactured products. Household industries are encouraged by the government, and the Filipinos show skill and artistic taste in the making of embroideries, textiles, hats, baskets, and matting. Lumber working is a large industry, a great variety of hard woods, suitable for general construction work, being readily obtainable.

About 90 per cent of the inhabitants are of the Malay race and profess Christianity. The remainder are largely Mohammedans and pagan wild tribes living in the mountains. The original inhabitants were the Negritos, a small, semisavage people, of whom about 25,000 remain in the islands. The Mohammedan Malays, called Moros by the Spaniards, are found in the southern portions of the archipelago. The Igorrotes, formerly fierce headhunters, live in the mountains, where they cover vast slopes with terraces in which they raise rice by irrigation. The official language is Tagalog, although English is taught in the schools and is used for commercial purposes.

Elementary instruction is free, secular, and coeducational. In addition to the state supported University of the Philippines, there are 27 institutions of higher learning. These include the University of Santo Tomas, founded in 1611, which is the oldest university under the American Flag. There are numerous schools for industrial education.

The Philippine Islands were discovered in 1521 by the Portuguese navigator Magellan. In 1542, a Spanish exploring expedition named the group in honor of Prince Philip, later Philip II of Spain. The Spanish began the permanent conquest of the islands in 1565, founding the city of Manila in 1571. The Spanish missionaries extensively Christianized the inhabitants, who constitute the only large body of Asiatic people permanently converted to Christianity in modern times.

The islands remained under Spanish rule until 1898, when, as a result of the Spanish American war, they were ceded to the United States. In 1899, an extensive insurrection of the Filipinos broke out. Aguinaldo, the leader of the rebellion, was captured in 1901, and, in 1902, the insurrection was formally proclaimed at an end. A ten-year period of semi-independence began in 1935, when a constitution was adopted in accordance with an enabling law of the United States Congress in 1933. Under the Tydings-McDuffie Act of 1934, the commonwealth was to enjoy a semi-independent status until 1945 and then to become independent. The islands were given their independence as promised, July 4, 1946, as the Republic of the Philippines.

Portuguese Dependencies. Portugal has five small colonies in Asia—Goa, Daman, Diu island, Macao, and part of Timor island. The first three, lying on the western coast of India, produce salt and manganese. Macao is an island off the southeastern coast of China. Its trade is mainly of a transient nature and is handled by Chinese. The northeastern part of Timor in the Malay archipelago is Portuguese and produces coffee, sandalwood, copra, and wax.

Russia in Asia. Russian territory in Asia covers 5,816,000 square miles, which is nearly three times the area of European Russia. The larger part is comprised in the Russian Socialist Federal Soviet Republic (R.S.F.S.R.), subdivided into the Far Eastern area, the Yakutsk autonomous republic, the Siberian area, and many smaller units. In addition, Asiatic Russia comprises eight states which are federated with the R.S.F.S.R. in the Soviet Union. These are the three Transcaucasian republics of Armenia, Georgia, and Azerbaijan, between the Caspian and Black seas; and the Turkoman, Uzbek, Tajik, Kazakh, and Kirghiz republics, situated north of India, Afghanistan, and Iran (Persia).

Geographically, this huge territory may be divided into three parts—the Great Northern Lowland, over four million square miles in area, which has mainly a northern drainage into the Arctic Ocean; the semi-arid region of Central Asia, some 1,700,000 square miles in area, with an interior drainage into the Caspian and Aral seas; and Transcaucasia, a dry, mountainous, subtropical region of about 75,000 square miles.

The Great Northern Lowland, formerly comprised largely under the name of Siberia, has on the whole a severe winter climate. The northern belt is barren tundra. An intermediate belt of forested land, stretching east and west, is suitable for dairying and flax culture and has enormous lumber resources. The southernmost belt is an immense grassland plain, potentially one of the great wheat areas of the world. The two latter belts, until recently very sparsely inhabited, are in the process of rapid settlement. They are served by the Trans-Siberian railroad. The Ural area, in the west, contains great mineral wealth, including one of the richest iron deposits of the world. For its exploitation one of the world's largest steel plants was erected in 1932 at the city of Magnitogorsk.

The region of Central Asia was from time immemorial the abode of nomadic tribes, with grazing and a primitive type of agriculture carried on in the oases. The Mongolian conqueror Timur had his capital in Samarkand, now an important city of the Uzbek soviet republic. Irrigation on a large scale has been undertaken under the Soviet government and rapidly expanding areas are devoted to the cultivation of cotton in this region.

Transcaucasia has a subtropical climate. Its principal industry is the production and refining of petroleum, which centers about Baku. Oil is piped to the Black Sea port of Batum for export. Tea is grown here and in Central Asia.

The principal cities of Transcaucasia include Baku, Tiflis, and Batum; those of Central Asia, Tashkent, Bukhara, Khiva, and Samarkand; and those of the Great Northern Lowland, Omsk, Sverdlovsk, Novosibersk, Vladivostok, and Irkutsk. See also *Russia*, page 785.

Syria. An independent republic of the Middle East, since 1944, extends along the eastern shore of the Mediterranean Sea. The area is 74,000 square miles and, in 1946, the population was estimated at 3,400,000. Although most of the people are Sunni Moslems, some 500,000 are nomadic Bedouins. Damascus, the capital, with a population of 290,000 is the oldest inhabited city in the world.

Only about half of the area is suitable for farming. Sandy deserts are common. Tobacco, wheat, fruits, cotton, barley, corn, sorghums, hemp, and silk are produced. Besides foodstuffs, manufactures include matches, alcohol, soap, cotton cloth, and cement. There are agricultural, engineering and teachers training colleges as well as a University. Damascus is the capital and largest city.

Thai (*tä'ē*) (**Siam**). An independent kingdom of southeastern Asia, bounded by India on the west and by French Indo-China on the north and east. It has a southern coast line on the Gulf of Siam. The area of the country is 200,148 square miles.

The richest part of Thai is the wet, tropical valley of the Menam river. This river valley lies between a western mountain wall and a central plateau that divides the Menam River basin from the western reaches of the Mekong River system. The valley produces valuable timber and dyewoods. Agriculture is carried on intensively. Rice is the national food and is the staple article of export. The live stock of the country consists mainly of oxen and buffaloes but includes several thousand elephants. The white elephant, really a light ashy gray in color, is considered sacred by the inhabitants. Tin is the chief mineral produced on a commercial scale. Most of the trade is in the hands of foreigners, more especially of Chinese.

The population of Thai in 1947 was 17,256,825. Buddhism is the prevailing religion. Thai has, in recent years, introduced many of the methods of Western civilization, having employed the services of European and American advisers in finance, education, drainage, and many other departments. The capital is Bangkok, through which nearly all the foreign trade passes.

Turkey. An independent country occupying the whole of Asia Minor and extending eastward to Transcaucasia and Iran. It includes also a number of islands off the coast and a small district of Europe, in which the city of Istanbul is situated. Asiatic Turkey is sometimes called Anatolia, "the land of the rising sun."

The estimated area of Turkey is 296,107 square miles, including 9257 square miles in Europe. It consists mainly of a plateau which, except in the mountainous eastern region, sinks on all sides to wooded foothills cut by valleys leading to the sea. The northern coast district is most heavily wooded; the chief region of cultivation is on the west. The interior, particularly the eastern part, is hot and dry.

The principal occupation of the Turks is agriculture. Tobacco, cereals, cotton, figs, grapes, olives, and sugar beets are the chief products of the soil. Rugs, gums, and opium are among the exports. Mineral wealth is considerable but is undeveloped. Meerschaum is a distinctive product. Manufactures are confined mostly to handmade articles, including rugs and copper utensils, although lumber mills, cement works, and an automobile assembly plant have been opened in recent years.

The population according to the 1945 census was 18,860,222. The seat of government is Ankara (Angora). The surrounding region is the native habitat of the Angora goat and the Angora cat, both of which are known for their long, soft hair.

CITIES AND OTHER POINTS OF TRAVEL INTEREST

The following articles describe the principal cities of Asia. Most of these cities present an appearance in which the marks of ancient civilizations contrast strikingly with the changes introduced by a rapidly penetrating industrialization. In addition to cities, a number of other notable features of Asia are described, such as the Dead Sea, the world's lowest and saltiest body of water; Tai Shan, the sacred mountain of Chinese Confucianists; and the Malay archipelago, the largest group of islands in the world.

Agra (*ä'grä*). A walled city of northern central India. The Mogul emperors left in Agra several monuments of striking magnificence, including the Taj Mahal, "Gem of Buildings," a white marble mausoleum, the construction of which is said to have engaged 20,000 workmen for 22 years. The city has a large trade. Its industries include gem setting and inlaid mosaic work. Population, 1941, 284,149.

Amernath. A cave in the Himalaya mountains near the extreme northern border of India. In the cave stands the sacred symbol of the god Siva, which is the object of pilgrimages from all parts of India.

Ankara. The capital of Turkey, officially chosen as such in 1923, replacing Istanbul. It was rapidly transformed from an oriental hamlet in a malarial plain to a modern city with sanitary improvements and well laid out streets. Railroads connecting with other parts of the country were constructed, electric power was provided, and manufacturing industries arose, notably for producing tiles and cotton and linen textiles. A park was laid out, and attractive government buildings were erected. Population, 226,712.

Baghdad. The capital of Iraq, situated on the Tigris river near the geographic center of the country. Like many other Oriental cities, Baghdad has a striking appearance at a distance, but the streets are narrow, unpaved, and dirty. There are many ruined mosques, monuments of the city's former splendor. Baghdad is said at one time to have had two million inhabitants. It was, in the 8th century, the capital of the caliphate of Haroun-al-Raschid, a hero of the *Arabian Nights*. Population, 1945, 550,000.

Bangkok. The capital and chief seaport of Siam, located on the Menam river about 25 miles from its mouth in the Gulf of Siam. Its industrial establishments include large lumber and rice mills. The streets are intersected by small canals, on which many people dwell in house boats. Most residences are built of bamboo. The city is made attractive by numerous beautiful gardens and tall palm trees. Palaces and gorgeously colored temples present a romantic contrast to the up-to-date public utilities, with which the city is equipped. Population, 1947 census, 827,290.

Batavia. The capital of the Netherlands East Indies, situated on the north coast of Java island. It forms the chief outlet for the numerous products of the Netherlands East Indies. The European section, in the higher, more healthful part, contains the Museum of the Batavian Society of Arts and Sciences, a beautiful structure in the Greek style which houses the largest collection of Javanese art in existence. The word Batavia is the Latin name for the region now occupied by the Netherlands. Population, 1930, 435,184.

Benares (*bĕn-ä'rĕz*). A city of north central India on the Ganges river. It is sacred to the Hindus, who come there from all parts of India to wash away their sins in the Ganges, to traverse the 50-mile road encircling the sacred area, or to die on the banks of the river. There are over 1500 Hindu temples in the city, which abounds in beggars living on the alms of wealthy pilgrims. The river banks are lined with stone and have many landing places, often highly ornamented. The city is a busy trading center. Gold brocade, gold and silver thread, embossed brass vessels, and lacquered toys are manufactured. The Benares Hindu university is situated there. Population, 1941, 263,100.

Bethlehem. A town of Palestine about five miles southwest of Jerusalem. Its chief center of interest is the basilica of Constantine, built in the 4th century at the spot where Jesus was believed to have been born. A chapel near by commemorates Jerome, the author of the Vulgate edition of the Bible, who resided and died in Bethlehem. Population, 1946, 9140.

Bombay. The second largest city of India, situated on a small island near the center of the empire's southwest coast. By reason of its industrial development and of its modern improvements, Bombay is the most European in appearance of the cities of India. It has one of the six federal universities of the country. The characteristic Oriental features remain, however, in much of the city, where decorated houses, tea shops, bazaars, and temples bear witness to the more ancient civilization of the Hindus. Bombay was the birthplace of Rudyard Kipling. Population, 1941, 1,489,833.

Calcutta. The largest city and, until 1911, the capital, of India, located about 85 miles from the sea at the west of the enormous delta of the Ganges river. Calcutta is the terminus of many railroads and canals and handles about one-third of the entire foreign trade of India. The European section has numerous splendid buildings. Cotton mills, sugar refineries, sawmills, silk mills, flour mills, and shipbuilding yards are among the more important industrial establishments.

The city is the seat of the University of Calcutta, founded in 1857. Victoria Memorial, one of the finest buildings in Calcutta, contains documents and pictures illustrating Indian history. Thackeray, the novelist, was born in Calcutta. Population 1941, with suburbs, 2,108,891.

Canton. A commercial city of southeastern China, situated about 70 miles northwest of the island of Hong Kong. The city is one of the chief centers of the Chinese silk trade. The industries include the manufacture of paper, lacquered wares, textiles, and glass, and the painting of porcelain.

The city is surrounded by a brick wall and partitioned by a cross wall into the old town and the new town. The latter has many wide, paved streets, Canton being one of the most progressive cities of China. Among the pagodas of Canton is one covering an area of seven acres. There is a Mohammedan mosque dating from the 9th century. Population, 1931, 861,024.

Chinese Wall. The most gigantic defensive work in existence, consisting of a wall more than 1500 miles in length, which was begun by the rulers of China in the 3d century B. C. and received its last addition in the 16th century A. D. A part, now destroyed, began near the Gulf of Liaotung in northeast China. The wall follows a general western direction along the southern border of Mongolia. The average height is about 22 feet. The base is from 15 to 25 feet wide, narrowing to 12 feet at the top. Its course passes through valleys and over mountains irrespective of the difficulties of construction.

Colombo. The capital of Ceylon, situated on the eastern coast of the island. The city was founded by the Portuguese in 1517 and was named in honor of Columbus. The European section is well built and modern in appearance. Population, 1946 census, 353,374.

Damascus. The capital of the republic of Syria. It is one of the few very ancient cities of the Mediterranean region which have survived until the present day. It is situated in a fertile region 53 miles southeast of its port, Beirut, on the Mediterranean coast. At the time of the Crusades, Damascus produced a famous type of ornamented steel, which has given the name damascening to modern steel etching.

The city has been often destroyed and rebuilt. The Ommiad, the largest of the city's 200 mosques, was formerly a church, which had earlier replaced a temple said to have contained the head of John the Baptist. Damascus, on account of its beautiful surroundings, is believed to have been the model for the paradise described in the *Koran*. The city contains the burial place of Fatima, the only child of Mohammed. Population, 1946 est., 290,000.

Dead Sea. A salt-water lake in Palestine. It is 47 miles long and 10 miles wide. Its area is 340 square miles and it has a maximum depth of 1280 feet. Lying 1290 feet below sea level, it is the lowest body of water on the surface of the earth. Its principal affluent is the Jordan river. It has no outlet, its excess water being taken off by evaporation, estimated at about 6,000,000 tons daily. The salinity of the Dead Sea is 23 to 27%, which is about 5 times that of the ocean. The economic value of the various salts in solution is very great, the principal ones being potash and common salt. Their commercial exploitation was begun in 1931.

Delhi (*dĕl'ē*). The capital of India, situated in the north central part of the country. Delhi was formerly the largest city of India. The Mogul emperors made it their capital, and erected many fine buildings, the ruins of which still attest their original grandeur. The Great Mosque, built in 1650, still stands, and is regarded by Mohammedans as one of the wonders of the world. In the vicinity of the city is the Kutb Minar, a tower 238 feet high built of stone, ranging in color from red at the bottom to orange at the top.

The transfer of the seat of government from Calcutta to Delhi in 1911 was the occasion for the building of a new and beautiful division of the city. This centers about Raisina, a hill six miles south of the walls of old Delhi, with which it is connected by broad, tree-lined avenues. Over 150 million dollars was spent on this city building project, which is the most magnificent the Orient has witnessed in modern times. Population, 1941, 521,849.

Hangchow (*hăng'chō'*). A city of China near the center of the country's eastern coast and standing at the head of Hangchow bay, an inlet of the China Sea. The city is near the southern terminus of the Grand canal, which serves as an artery of the commerce centering in the city. The chief manufactures are silk and fans.

Hangchow is one of the best-built cities of China. The city is surrounded by a massive wall, 12 miles in circuit. The western part of this wall is washed by West lake, a beautiful sheet of water 8 miles in circumference dotted with islands on which are built monasteries, memorial halls, and shrines. To the west of the lake are numerous Buddhist temples. Population, 1931, 506,930.

Hankow (*hăn'kō'*). A commercial city of China, standing at the head of ocean navigation on the Yangtze river about 680 miles from its mouth in the China Sea. The city contains large iron and steel works, which utilize the extensive iron and coal deposits in the vicinity. Cotton goods, flour, and leather are also manufactured. The chief exports of the city are black tea, wood oil, and sesamum seed. Population, 1931, 777,993.

Hiroshima. A large city near the southern end of the island of Honshu, Japan. Its population was almost 350,000. It was an important political and commercial center having rail, air, and ocean connections. As a victim of the first atomic bomb, it was almost completely demolished but is being rebuilt.

Hsinking (*shĭn'gĭng'*). The capital of Manchuria, situated in the southeastern part of the country. It is also known as Changchun. The new government buildings are the chief feature of the city. Population, 1945, 787,778.

Irkutsk (*ĭr-kŏŏtsk'*). A commercial city of south central Siberia, situated near the south end of Lake Baikal. It has a large caravan trade from Mongolia and is one of the three important points on the Asiatic section of the Trans-Siberian railroad. The articles of commerce include tea, silk, porcelain, dried fruit, fur, and fossil ivory. Population, 1939, 243,000.

Jerusalem. The capital of Palestine, located at an elevation of 2500 feet between the Mediterranean Sea and the north end of the Dead Sea. In certain medieval maps, Jerusalem is marked as the center of the world. About it has centered the devotion of Christians, Mohammedans, and Jews. A Hebrew university was opened there in 1925.

The city is surrounded by ravines on three sides. The water and drainage facilities have been greatly improved since the city was occupied by the British in 1918. The streets are narrow, crooked, and dirty. The most prominent building of the city is the Mosque of Omar, standing on the site of Solomon's temple. The Church of the Holy Sepulchre and the Via Dolorosa are of interest for their connection with the crucifixion of Jesus. The "wailing wall," said to be a vestige of Solomon's temple, is sacred to Jews as a place for prayer and lamentation. Population, 1946, 164,440.

Kabul. The capital and largest city of Afghanistan. It is near the center of the eastern frontier. Surrounded on three sides by mountains, it commands passes leading to India and Russia. Well built roads connect the city with these countries. The city itself is unattractive but it has a fine palace in a magnificent setting overlooking fruitful plains. It has also a small arms factory. Population, 80,000.

Keijo. The capital and chief port of Korea, situated near the center of the west coast of Chosen, of which it is the chief port and the capital. It is connected with the Trans-Siberian railroad. Silk, tobacco, mats, paper, and fans are made in the city. Keijo is often known as Seoul. Population, 1946, 1,141,766.

Kobe (*kō'bĕ*). A seaport of Japan, situated on the southern coast of Honshu island. It is the chief center of Japan's silk export trade. Prominent among the industrial establishments is an imperial ship-building yard. Population, 1940, 967,234.

Kyoto (*kyō'tō*). An inland commercial and industrial city of Japan, situated near the southern coast of Honshu island. Kyoto was formerly the capital of Japan and bears evidence of the fact in the regularity of its plan and in its magnificent monuments and temples. Its industries include the manufacture of porcelain, brocade, toys, metal products, and silk fabrics. The city is the seat of an imperial university. Population, 1940, 1,089,726.

Lhasa (*läs'ä*). The sacred city of the Lamaists, members of a widespread, ascetic sect of Buddhism. The city is situated in south central Tibet on a plateau having an altitude of 11,830 feet. Being forbidden to the uninitiated, Lhasa was seen by no more than three Europeans before 1904, when the British forced an entrance. Just outside the city stands a most imposing residence of the head of the religious sect. Thousands of people each year make a pilgrimage to a life-sized image of Buddha standing in the chief temple. Monastic institutions house some 16,000 initiates. The remaining inhabitants, about two-thirds women, number approximately 10,000.

Madras. The third largest city of India, situated on the southeastern coast of the country. The industrial output includes textiles, cigars, iron, cement, and dyes. The city contains an ornamental park, many fine buildings and monuments, an observatory, museums, a university, and a number of colleges. Population, 1941, 777,481.

Malay Archipelago. The largest group of islands in the world, lying at the extreme southeastern corner of Asia. The principal islands are Sumatra, Java, Borneo, Celebes, and the Philippine group. Of these, Sumatra, Java, and Borneo are on a continental shelf less than 600 feet deep, which connects with the Philippines by two submarine banks; the others are surrounded by water of great depth. Nearly all the islands present bold profiles and have mountains which are actively volcanic.

The equator passes through the center of the group. A rich soil and the warm, moist climate combine to make these islands extraordinarily fertile. They abound in tropical fruits of many kinds. Among the cultivated crops are rubber, rice, tea, sugar, coffee, kapok, cinchona bark, and coconuts. The mineral wealth of the islands is important, including tin in Banka and other islands near Sumatra, petroleum in Sumatra, coal in Borneo and Sumatra, and lead in all the larger islands. The inhabitants are largely Malaysians, although the Filipinos have a negroid strain. Chinese tradesmen are numerous. The total area of the archipelago is estimated at 1,094,857 square miles, supporting a population of over 60 million. Politically, the greater part is comprised in the Dutch East Indies, but the Philippine Islands are an independent republic and northern Borneo is British territory.

Mandalay. A city of central Burma, India, standing on the Irrawaddy river. There are a number of Buddhistic shrines, the most remarkable of which is the Kuthodaw, a square surrounded by 450 pagodas. Within each pagoda is inscribed a part of the Buddhist scriptures, the aggregate of the inscriptions constituting the whole of the sacred writings. A walled section of the city encloses Fort Dufferin, formerly a royal palace. Population, 1941, 163,537.

Manila. The capital and chief city of the Philippine Islands, on the west coast of the island of Luzon. It is built on both banks of the Pasig river at its entrance to Manila bay. On the south side of the river is the ancient Spanish town, surrounded by a wall, with the cathedral, monastic buildings, and numerous quaint Spanish houses; also the principal residential section, hospitals, and government buildings. On the north side is Binondo, containing the principal shopping and financial district. Manila is important for its foreign and coastwise commerce. It is the world's greatest shipping market for hemp. The Spanish city of Manila was founded in 1571. In 1898, Admiral Dewey destroyed a Spanish fleet in Manila bay. Population, 1939, 623,492.

Marachi. The interim capital of the new Islamic state of Pakistan. It is the fourth most important port of India and ships wheat and raw cotton, and is also the outlet for the Indus basin of northwest India. Population, 359,492.

Mecca. The most sacred city of the Mohammedans, situated in a barren valley in the southern part of the Saudi Arabia, of which kingdom it is one of the two capitals. It is about 50 miles inland from Jidda, its port on the Red Sea. Most of the inhabitants find support from lodging the pilgrims who, in numbers exceeding 100,000 annually, flock here from all parts of the Mohammedan world to visit the Sacred Mosque, which marks the birthplace of Mohammed. Population, about 85,000.

Medina. An inland city of central Hejaz, sacred to the adherents of Mohammedanism. Mohammed's flight there from Mecca in 622 A. D. marks the year in which the Mohammedan calendar begins. The prophet died in Medina, and a large mausoleum, said to contain his undecayed body, attracts numerous pilgrims. Population, about 30,000.

Mukden (*mo͞ok'dĕn'*) (**Shenyang**). The largest city of Manchuria, located about 150 miles north of the Yellow Sea. It is a railroad junction and a point of convergence of several caravan routes. Near the city are the tombs of the Manchu emperors, who, in the 17th century, made Mukden their capital. Huge stone elephants stand on guard over the tombs. In the vicinity of Mukden was fought the decisive battle of the Russo-Japanese war. Population, 1947, 1,175,620.

Nagasaki. An old and large Japanese port of just over 250,000 people. It is important in both trade and industry with steel work and shipbuilding predominant. It is located on the extreme west of the southernmost Japanese island of Kyushi and was the second target of the atomic bomb, from which devastation it is rapidly rebuilding.

Nanking. The capital of China. It is about midway between Peiping in the north and Canton in the south and lies on the south bank of the Yangtze river 235 miles from the sea. The first sovereign of the Ming dynasty chose it as his capital in 1368. From 1403 until 1928, the Chinese government had its seat at Peiping (Peking), but returned in the latter year to Nanking. Most of the magnificent buildings of earlier days were destroyed in the Taiping rebellion in 1853. The Republican government in 1928 proceeded to modernize the city. A boulevard has replaced the ancient city wall. On Purple mountain near by, a magnificent monument was erected to Sun Yat Sen, founder of the Chinese republic. Population, 1947, 1,037,655.

Nagoya. The third largest city of Japan, 235 miles southwest of Tokyo. It is one of the greatest centers of Japanese pottery manufacture. Other industries include cotton and silk mills. Many people are engaged in the embroidering of handkerchiefs. Nagoya has a very fine Buddhist temple and a castle dating back to 1610. Population, 1940, 1,328,084.

Nazareth. A town of northwestern Palestine, about 20 miles from the Mediterranean seacoast. It is memorable among Christians as the early residence of Jesus. A richly decorated basilica, the Church of the Annunciation, stands on what is said to be the site of the residence of Mary, the mother of Jesus, her house having been miraculously transported to Loreto, Italy. The town was captured from the Turks by Australians in 1918. Population, 15,540.

Omsk. A city of southwestern Siberia on the Trans-Siberian railroad. It is a noted trading center for wheat and for dairy products. Manufactures include agricultural machinery, cloth, and sausages. Population, 1939, 281,000.

Osaka (*ō'zä'kä*). The second largest city of Japan, situated on Osaka bay in the southern part of the island of Honshu. Being intersected by the Yodo river and by numerous canals spanned by hundreds of bridges, the city has been styled the Venice of the East. Ironworks, cotton and sugar mills, shipyards, and a large government mint are among the more important industries. The city is regularly laid out and contains many notable temples. Population, 1940, 3,252,340.

Pacific Islands or **Oceania.** Under these terms are included the numerous islands of the Pacific Ocean east of the Malay archipelago and north and east of Australia. On racial grounds they are frequently divided into three groups —Polynesia, Melanesia, and Micronesia. Melanesia lies directly north and east of Australia and west of the international date line. It includes the Solomon, Santa Cruz, New Hebrides, New Caledonia, and Fiji islands. Its inhabitants are generally dark skinned. North of this group lies Micronesia, comprising the Caroline, Marshall, Gilbert, Guam, Nauru, and neighboring islands. In race, the inhabitants are more akin to the Malays. Polynesia includes most other islands of the Pacific Ocean east of the groups described above. Among the more important are the Hawaiian, New Zealand, Friendly (Tonga), Society, Cook, Samoan, Marquesas, Manahiki, and Union islands. The islanders are light colored. They were apparently driven eastward by the Melanesians, traversing the open sea in canoes. Most of the islands are under the authority of Great Britain, United States, and France.

Peiping (*bā'pĭng'*). The most famous of Chinese cities. It is about 80 miles west of the Gulf of Chihli, an inlet of the Yellow Sea. Peiping consists of an old city and a new city, usually called the outer city and the inner city. Each is surrounded by a wall, which, in one section, separates the two cities. The new city is larger and more populous. The old city contains a walled imperial city, within which lies the "purple forbidden city," the former palace and court of the emperor. These divisions are now traversed by a broad thoroughfare which passes through Peiping from north to south. The finest building in the old city is the famous Temple of Heaven. To the west of the city, on the so-called Mountain of Ten Thousand Ancients, stands the emperor's summer palace, near which, upon a lagoon, floats a marble boat, built as a pleasure house. The grounds contain the celebrated camel back bridge, and near by is a pagoda built of porcelain. Peiping was the capital of China, 1403–1928.

Peiping is a great educational center. It is the seat of Yenching university, established by American philanthropy, a number of technical and professional schools, and the oldest observatory in the world. Most of its equipment was removed to Berlin in 1900, but its restoration was stipulated by the Treaty of Versailles. Population, 1947, 1,602,234.

Pichola. A small lake near Udaipur in central west India. Each of two small islands in the lake is enclosed by marble walls, within which is erected a marble palace. These marble palaces were built by rulers of Rajputana and exhibit a grace and elegance which are equaled in very few of the great buildings of the world.

Rangoon. The capital and leading port of Burma, located on the southern coast near the Gulf of Martaban. The chief industrial establishments include lumber, rice, and oil mills, the products of which are exported in large quantities. Rangoon has a Buddhist pagoda, 370 feet high and covered with gold leaf, the foundation of which is said to have been laid in 588 B. C. This pagoda, called the Shoay Dagon, contains objects sacred to Buddhists and is annually visited by thousands of pilgrims. A university is situated in the city. Population, 1931, 400,415.

Samarkand. A historic city of southern Russia, the capital of the Uzbek republic. Its ancient name was Maracanda. It was destroyed by Alexander the Great in 329 B. C. After its capture by the Moslems in 911-12 A.D., it became a brilliant seat of Arabic civilization. Jenghis Khan destroyed it in 1221. Timur made it his capital in 1369. The palace and tomb of Timur are among the finest of the city's buildings. The Rigistan square is surrounded by four ancient structures, formerly Moslem colleges.

The modern part of the city has broad, shaded streets. Its industries are served by electric power. They include cotton ginning and the manufacture of leather, flour, brick, pencils, and liquor. Population, 1939, 134,346.

Shanghai. The largest city, principal port, and chief industrial center of China. It lies at the junction of the Huang river and Soochow creek 12 miles from their mouth in the estuary of the Yangtze river. It is the sea gate for the trade of the richest portion of China and is the spear point of its advancing industrialization. Flour and rice milling, shipbuilding, publishing, and the manufacture of engines, machinery, cotton and silk textiles, paper, cigarettes, leather, and food products are the leading industries.

A portion of the city is modern and well built, having grown up entirely since 1854. In 1932 Japan captured a part of the city and held it for a short time. Population, 1947, 3,853,511.

Singapore. The capital and chief port of the Straits Settlements, situated on the island of Singapore off the southern extremity of the Malay peninsula. The city is the smelting center for the immense amount of tin mined in the surrounding regions. More than half the block tin of the world is shipped from the port. Singapore is a British naval station of the first class and is strongly fortified. Population, 1946 estimate, 769,216.

Smyrna (Izmir). A seaport and commercial city of west central Turkey, standing at the head of the Gulf of Smyrna, an inlet of the Ægean Sea. The rugs for which Smyrna is famous are made, for the most part, in the surrounding towns. Other articles of trade are silks, cottons, opium, olive oil, gums, and figs. Smyrna is one of the oldest continuously inhabited cities in the world. It was assigned to the Greeks as a mandate in 1920. In 1922 the Greeks were driven out, and the city was put to flames. Population, 1940, 184,652.

Srinagar (*srē'nȧ-gŭr'*). The capital of the native kingdom of Kashmir in the northern extremity of India. In the picturesque scenery of the surrounding country was located the "Vale of Cashmere," celebrated in Moore's poem entitled *Lalla Rookh*. Population, 1941, 207,787.

Tai Shan. A sacred mountain about 120 miles southwest of the Gulf of Chihli, an inlet of the Yellow Sea. On its summit are several temples, beneath one of which Confucius is said to have been buried. Each year during February and March as many as 10,000 pilgrims in a single day ascend to the summit, 4700 feet in height. The ascent is facilitated by a six-mile mountain road, paved and provided with steps in the more precipitous stages.

Tashkent. A city of southern Russia, capital of the Uzbek republic. It is situated in a vast surrounding plain of arid land on which cotton is grown with the aid of irrigation. Its industrial interests include cotton ginning and lumber mills and tobacco, leather, machinery, and rayon factories. The city has up-to-date water, electric, and street railway systems. Population, 1939, 585,005.

Tehran (*tĕ-h'rän'*). The capital of Iran, lying on an elevated plain in the north central part of the country about 66 miles south of the Caspian Sea. Manufactures include rugs, silks, cotton goods, and ironware. It has a citadel, called the Ark, within which is the handsome palace of the shah. The principal street is the Boulevard des Ambassadeurs, running through the foreign section. Tehran was founded in the 12th century and became capital of Persia (now Iran) in 1788. Population, 1942, 699,110.

Tel Aviv. The largest city in Palestine. The population, by latest estimate 140,000, has rapidly increased with influx of displaced European Jews. *Sarona*, a suburb, is the capital of the new Jewish state, Israel.

Tientsin. A commercial city and port of northeastern China on the Pei river about 70 miles from its mouth in the Gulf of Chihli. It is 70 miles southeast of Peiping. The waterfront, which is under foreign jurisdiction, has buildings resembling the commercial structures of Western cities. The remainder of the city, which lies on a low plain, has small buildings and narrow, ill-kept streets, although municipal services have been much improved since 1900, when the city walls were destroyed in the Boxer uprising. Tientsin has an immense trade in salt, rice, and tea. Within recent years cotton factories have been established. Population, 1947, 1,679,210.

Tiflis (Tbilisi). The capital and largest city of the Georgian Republic, in the Soviet Union, situated midway between the Black Sea and the Caspian Sea. It is the distributing center for the country and has manufactures of bricks, tobacco, leather, soap, flour, cotton, and furniture. In picturesque contrast to its many wide streets and modern water, electric, and transport services are the Oriental bazaars and markets, where merchants from the East display their silverware, swords, rugs, dried fruits, and silk goods. Tiflis was founded in 379 A. D. Russia obtained it in 1799. Population, 1939, 519,175.

Tokyo. The capital of Japan and largest city in Asia. It stands at the head of Tokyo bay near the center of the eastern coast of Honshu island.

The city was largely destroyed in 1923 by earthquake and fire, which laid waste 25 square miles. This catastrophe provided the opportunity for rebuilding according to modern plans. The streets were widened, at the cost of moving some 200,000 houses; sewers were installed; public school playgrounds were enlarged; and a subway for rapid transit was constructed. Buildings in general are low or made of reinforced concrete to minimize danger of damage from earthquakes. The Hall of the Nameless Dead commemorates 33,000 victims of the great fire of 1923.

The chief of the city's many parks is called Tukiage, which contains the palace of the emperor built in a mixed Japanese and European style of architecture. The University of Tokyo is an institution of higher learning of the most advanced type. The eastern portion of the city contains regions known to visitors for their display of flowers. Here, too, is the temple of E-ko-in, where matches are held in jujutsu, the type of wrestling for which Japan is known.

Industries in Tokyo are carried on largely in the lowlands and suburbs, where there are numerous textile mills of a typically Japanese type. They are operated chiefly by girls, who live in huge dormitories owned by the mills.

The site of the city was a fishing village in the 13th century. It first became important in 1457 as the residence of the feudal lord. The name was changed in 1868 from Yedo to Tokyo, meaning Eastern Capital. Population, 1940, 6,778,084.

Trans-Siberian Railroad. A railroad which traverses Russia in an east-west direction, connecting Leningrad in Europe with Vladivostok on the extreme edge of Asiatic Russia. Over 5,500 miles in length, it occupied 11 years for initial construction, which cost 172 million dollars. It was practically completed by 1902.

At a point east of Lake Baikal the road was divided, one line passing through what is now Manchukuo and the other one going north of Lake Baikal entirely in Russian territory, the two joining near Vladivostok. The former branch, known as the Chinese Eastern railroad and shared in ownership with China, was seized by Manchukuo in 1931 and a small indemnity was paid to Russia.

The railroad is now double tracked. With feeders and connections running to southern Russia, it has been the central factor in one of the greatest migrations of people in history—settlement of the Siberian plains. Strategically, it makes eastern and western Russia a unit.

Victoria. The capital of the British island of Hong Kong by which name it is usually called. Victoria is a free port and the center of British commerce with China and Japan. The British fleet used the island as a naval base in the first Opium war, 1839-42. Then practically uninhabited, it was ceded to Great Britain in 1841.

It rapidly developed into an important commercial center and now harbors numerous industries, including the manufacture of ships, cement, paper, rope, glass, soap, cigars, and knitted goods. Population of Victoria, 1931, 358,351; of Hong Kong island and adjacent leased territory, 1947 est.. 1,750,000.

Vladivostok (*vlȧ'dyĭ-vŏs-tôk'*). The chief Pacific Ocean port of Russia and the eastern terminus of the Trans-Siberian railroad. The city is situated in the extreme southeastern part of Asiatic Russia, in the vicinity of valuable iron deposits. Most of the commerce is in the hands of Chinese. The chief products handled are the numerous derivatives of the soy bean. Vladivostok was settled in 1860, two years after its site was acquired by Russia. Population, 206,000.

Yokohama. A leading seaport of Japan, situated on Tokyo bay near the center of the western coast of Honshu island. The harbor is elaborately improved. The city is of recent growth, having sprung up in the past 60 years as a result of foreign commerce. The chief exports are silk and tea. Yokohama was the first Japanese port open to foreigners and it is still the headquarters for most tourists who visit Japan. The city was almost totally destroyed in 1923 by earthquake and fire. It was reconstructed with wide streets, handsome concrete buildings, and bridges. Population, 1940, 968,091.

AFRICA

THE second largest continent of the world, situated in the eastern hemisphere south of Europe and southwest of Asia, with which it is connected by the Isthmus of Suez. Apart from this isthmus, 75 miles wide at its narrowest part, the continent is entirely surrounded by water. It is separated from Europe by the Mediterranean Sea, an inland body of water which narrows to a width of nine miles at the Strait of Gibraltar. Between Africa and Asia, lie the Red Sea and the Gulf of Aden connected by the Strait of Bab el Mandeb. The Atlantic Ocean on the west and the Indian Ocean on the east meet at the southern point of the continent.

Africa lies farther to the north than South America. In length, the continent is almost equally divided between the northern and the southern hemisphere. On account of its shape, however, about two-thirds of Africa's surface lies north of the equator. Its most northern point is in the latitude of Washington, D. C., and it extends nearly 5000 miles south to the approximate latitude of Buenos Aires. It has an area of about 11,500,000 square miles, being about 1⅓ times as large as North America and second only to Asia in extent.

Outline. As in the case of South America, the maximum width of the continent is in the north. By reason of a huge western extension, Africa attains a width of 4600 miles, just 400 miles less than its length. Between the western extension and the southern portion of the continent, lies the Gulf of Guinea. The only other major indentation is the Gulf of Sidra near the center of the northern coast. On the eastern coast, Somaliland projects as a cape, separating the Gulf of Aden from the Indian Ocean. The coast line is remarkably regular and, consequently, affords very few good harbors.

Africa is notable for its lack of important islands. Most of the smaller ones are of volcanic origin, and Madagascar, the one large island of the continent, does not belong to the same land formation. Madagascar lies about 300 miles off the southeastern coast. The smaller islands include Madeira islands, Canary islands, Cape Verde islands, Ascension island, and Saint Helena island, all of which are off the west coast. To the east of the continent lie Zanzibar, Mauritius island, and Socotra island.

Surface. Africa is, for the most part, a plateau surrounded by a very narrow strip of coastal lowlands. The southern and the eastern parts of the plateau are higher than the western and the northern parts. The latter contain certain sections, in the interior of the Sahara desert, where the elevation is that of the sea level or even less. The continent has no central highland comparable to the region of the Rocky mountains in North America.

In the extreme southern part of the continent, a ridge rims the plateau, rising, on the eastern side, to a height of nearly 9000 feet. The east central part of the continent consists of a wide, irregular highland cut longitudinally by the so-called Great Rift valley, which contains lakes rivaling in size the Great Lakes of North America. Lake Victoria is the largest, being second only to Lake Superior in area. Lake Tanganyika, farther south, is the longest lake in the world, having a length of 400 miles. Lake Nyasa, the most southern of the group, has the extraordinary depth of 2580 feet. In this region are to be found also the highest mountains of the continent, usually rising abruptly from the surface of the plateau. Mount Kibo, situated about 200 miles south of the equator and 200 miles from the east coast, reaches an altitude of 19,710 feet. Mount Kenia and Ruwenzori mountain are other notable peaks of the district. Continuing northward, the highland narrows to form the lofty, mountainous region of Ethiopia. An elevated ridge skirts the Red Sea as far as the Isthmus of Suez.

The mean level of the northern and the western parts of Africa is below 2000 feet. Isolated mountain ridges, however, occur in various parts. The highest is the Atlas range at the extreme northwest, running parallel with the coast and attaining to an altitude of 14,000 feet. A broken range trends in a northwest and southeast direction across part of the north central region of the continent. Other noteworthy elevations are found near the northern coast of the Gulf of Guinea.

Drainage. The absence in Africa of a pronounced continental divide has had the effect of producing two kinds of rivers. Those on the outer slopes of the continental plateau are short and rapid, while those rising in the interior follow a long, winding, inland course. Then, penetrating the mountain rim, they make their way over cataracts and through narrow channels to the sea, where a sand bar is often formed by sediment carried down the stream. Rivers which have not sufficient volume to enable them to cut their way to the sea form basins of inland drainage. In no case is there a large navigable waterway by which easy access may be had to the interior of the continent. It is due especially to this fact and to the scarcity of harbors that the exploration of Africa has been deferred until recent decades.

The four largest rivers of Africa are the Nile, the Congo, the Niger, and the Zambezi. The basins of inland drainage, which occupy more than three million square miles in northern Africa, are usually too arid to give rise to large bodies of water. There is a notable exception, however, in the case of Lake Chad.

The Nile is, next to the Mississippi-Missouri, the longest river of the world. Rising in a stream that flows into Lake Victoria, it wends its way northward, and, after passing over six cataracts and traversing a distance of 4000 miles, it empties through a large delta by seven mouths into the Mediterranean Sea. Its lower course lies through the desert region of Egypt, a strip of which it renders productive by means of its annual flood. The river is navigable about 590 miles above its delta to the foot of the first cataract at Assuan and, with interruptions, for a distance of 1550 miles farther toward the source.

The Congo river is the second river of the world in volume of water discharged and in the area of its basin. By means of numerous tributaries, of which the Ubangi is the largest, the Congo drains a tropical basin of central Africa in a general westward direction and discharges its waters into the Atlantic Ocean through a mouth ten miles in width. Its eastern reaches, affluents of Lake Tanganyika, are within a few miles of the source of the Nile. The river admits of navigation, with some interruptions, for a distance of 2000 miles above its mouth.

The Niger river offers greater facilities for navigation than any other river of Africa. It drains a comparatively low plain in Africa's westward extension. Rising within a few hundred miles of the Atlantic coast, it flows inland toward the northeast, then, bending southeast, it follows a meandering course to an immense delta on the Gulf of Guinea.

The Zambezi river rises on a ridge near the west coast of southern Africa, and flows eastward across the continent to Mozambique channel. Near the middle of its course, it plunges over Victoria falls, the greatest cataract in the world. Here, over a width of a mile, the river drops 343 feet. During the flood season, the volume of water going over the falls is greater than that of the Niagara cataract. Below the falls a dense vapor rises, which has suggested for it a native name meaning thundering smoke.

Southern Africa contains two other rivers of note—the Limpopo river, flowing into the Indian Ocean, and the Orange river, draining westward to the Atlantic Ocean.

Lake Chad, situated about 850 miles northeast of the head of the Gulf of Guinea, has no outlet. During the rainy season, it occupies an area of about 40,000 square miles, but, being very shallow, it diminishes during the dry season to one-sixth of this area. It is said to be drying up, just as other lakes of the Sahara Desert region have done in the past, leaving "salt pans" as evidence of their former existence.

Climate. Africa extends almost equal distances north and south of the equator. It is, therefore, subject to a smaller variation in temperature than any other large division of land. At the extreme north and at the extreme south, there are belts of temperate or subtropical climate. Between these limits the heat is greater, although, on account of the elevation, the highest temperatures are not recorded at the equator but in the lower parts of the great Sahara desert.

The rainfall is greatest in the basin of the Congo. On each side of this equatorial belt of abundant and well distributed rainfall, stretches a zone in which the rainfall is seasonal, a short, wet season being followed by a long, dry one. These two zones pass gradually into the two great desert areas of the continent, Kalahari desert in southern Africa and the Sahara desert in the north. Beyond these arid regions, in the extreme north and in the extreme south of Africa, there are narrow coastal lowlands having a moderate, or even a copious, rainfall.

The Sahara Desert is the largest continuous arid region of the world. Its area, about 3,500,000 square miles, is larger than that of the United States. It occupies all that part of northern Africa from the Atlas mountains on the northwest to the mid-course of the Nile river on the southeast. It is a part of the dry belt stretching across Asia and Africa, the aridity of which is caused mainly by the trade winds. The small amount of rain which does fall occurs in one season only and, as a rule, sinks immediately into the sand to issue here and there as springs. These springs foster islets of vegetation, known as oases, which are estimated to cover one-fortieth of the desert's surface. A considerable portion of the surface exhibits a rocky formation, especially where the desert is partially traversed by a broken range of mountains. The remainder is a shifting, sandy waste, swept by scorching winds. These winds, called simooms, frequently attain to a great violence and carry clouds of sand dense enough to suffocate men or animals caught without shelter. There are several depressions in the Sahara desert which are lower than sea level. They are usually salt marshes or oases rendered productive by springs from the surrounding hills. The deepest of these depressions is estimated to be 440 feet below the level of the sea.

Vegetation. The plant life of Africa varies in a manner determined mainly by the rainfall. The extreme northern section has a flora resembling that of Europe. The forests in this part consist largely of oaks, while the olive, vine, fig, and the cereals of Europe thrive. The extreme southern region, being comparatively isolated, has a characteristic vegetation marked by the prevalence of heaths and of other plants producing brilliant flowers. Forests are scarce, but there is abundant pasturage for sheep.

The deserts have little vegetation. Thorny acacias, however, and stunted plant forms occur, except on the shifting dunes. In the northern part of the Sahara desert, the esparto, or alpha, covers considerable areas. The date palm is found in dense groves at the oases and in the valley of the Nile river. The regions of seasonal rainfall are broad, grassy plains, or savannas, which stretch over most of Africa between the semiarid land bordering the deserts. Here grow the baobab, or monkey-bread tree, a candelabra-like euphorbia, and the watermelon, all characteristically African forms of vegetation. The equatorial belt, except in the eastern highlands, is covered with dense tropical forests. These forests contain an immense variety of trees, including the wine palm, the oil palm, the silk-cotton tree, and the camwood, besides ebony, mahogany, and many other valuable cabinet wood trees.

Forests are found also in parts of the eastern coast and on the sides of mountains where the temperature is equable and the rainfall is well distributed throughout the year. On the mountain sides and extending above the true forests are thickets of bamboos, replaced still higher by tree lobelias and by shrubby senecios.

Among the plants cultivated by the natives are yams, sweet potatoes, bananas, peanuts, and millet. Manioc and Indian corn have been introduced and are used as staple foods by the inhabitants. Along the Gulf of Guinea coast, cacao is cultivated more extensively than anywhere else in the world. Coffee is a native African plant, having received its name from Kaffa, a district in the east central part of the continent.

Animals. Africa is the home of many distinctive types of animals, including a number of large mammals. The giraffe, okapi, hippopotamus, gorilla, and chimpanzee are among the more notable of African mammals which occur nowhere else. Lions, leopards, two-horned rhinoceroses, zebras, antelopes, and African buffaloes are representative of the large animals which attract hunters. The conservation of such animals was, in 1900, made the subject of an international conference, as a result of which game preserve areas were established in British Africa, Somaliland, and other countries. The African elephant is hunted for its ivory tusks, which for centuries have been brought from the interior of Africa by caravans and still constitute one of the characteristic commercial products of the continent. The guinea fowl and several species of hyenas are native to the continent.

The ostrich is found in the drier regions. In South Africa, it is reared on farms for the sake of its feathers. Other birds of note are the honey guide,—so called because of its peculiar habit of leading its pursuers to beehives,—the marabou stork, and the secretary bird, the last named being valued for its practice of feeding on serpents. Our domesticated parrot is a native of Africa, where its flesh is sought as a food by the natives. Crocodiles are found in the large rivers and in the tropical lakes. The insects are numerous. They include the formidable white ant and the deadly tsetse fly. One species of the latter has a bite fatal to cattle, and another species is a carrier of the sleeping sickness, which, for the white race, makes the greater part of equatorial Africa the most unhealthful region of the world.

A European type of fauna characterizes the extreme north, where the bear, the jackal, and the fox are found. The wild ass of east central Africa is said to be the ancestor of the domesticated ass. Camels were introduced very early into the northern desert regions from Asia. In Egypt, the inhabitants anciently regarded as sacred the ibis, the crocodile, and the cat, the last being an ancestor of our domestic cat. Cattle, sheep, and goats are raised where the climate and the vegetation are suitable.

Minerals. Africa produces nearly all of the world's supply of diamonds and more than one-third of the world's yearly output of gold. South Africa is the region most productive of both minerals, although gold is also obtained from the Gulf of Guinea region and elsewhere. Some of the richest copper deposits in the world exist west of the great interior lakes, and iron has from the earliest times been obtained and worked by the natives. Salt is abundant.

Inhabitants. The most northern and the most southern regions of Africa are the only parts inhabited by societies of a civilized type. The remainder contains a variety of races differing in origin, language, appearance, and in means of subsistence.

The Pygmies of the equatorial forests and the Bushmen of the southern arid districts are believed to represent the earliest African races extant. They live by hunting; their dwellings are of the most primitive type. The Hottentots stand, in culture, as in location, between the Bushmen and the Bantus. The Bantus constitute the southern half of a negroid race which inhabits most of Africa from the region of the great lakes northward to the Sahara desert. The Bantus have a greater unity of language than the true Negroes. Both practice a primitive form of agriculture, with which the Bantus combine stock raising where the climate and the insects permit. The Bantus drink milk and live in round huts, while the Negroes have rectangular huts and use bark instead of skins for clothing. The native iron industry is widespread, some authorities even believing the use of iron to have originated from the African races. For some centuries, the Negro races formed the chief source of slaves. They were taken to various Mohammedan countries and, especially, to America, where, after the abolition of slavery, they continued to thrive. The West Indies, in fact, contains, with the exception of Liberia, the only Negro state which is still an independent country, namely, Haiti.

North of the true Negroes, the population has a miscellaneous complexion, consisting of races which are not aboriginal inhabitants of the continent. These races include Europeans, Arabs, Turks, Berbers, Hamites, Semites, and Libyans.

The total population of the continent is estimated at 160 million. The majority live under tribal organizations of a more despotic character than those found among the American Indians. Slavery persists in some sections. Polygamy is widespread. Magic is a powerful influence in the native religions. It is estimated that less than half the population has been affected by religions of foreign origin. Of this proportion by far the most are Mohammedans. The Christian population is believed to be less than 4 per cent of the total, even with the inclusion of the members of the Coptic sect, a heretical form of Christianity which arose in northern Africa in the 4th century.

The white colonization in Africa is important as a potential outlet for European settlement. The Netherlands and Britain have colonized South Africa and the white population there numbers about 2,000,000. France has planted nearly a million settlers in Algeria, Morocco, and Tunisia. Italy has sent some 200,000 colonists to Tunisia, Eritrea, and Ethiopia. There are some 70,000 Europeans in Rhodesia. Large areas of cool, healthful uplands lie in Kenya, Tanganyika, and Angola. But the whites are as yet a small minority. Even in South Africa the natives outnumber the whites four to one.

Discovery. The valley of the Nile river was the seat of what is perhaps the world's earliest civilization. The interior of the continent, however, remained unknown until the 19th century and the work of exploration is still far from completion.

As early as the 7th or 6th century B. C. a Phœnician ship sailed around Africa. The possibility of circumnavigation, however, was forgotten until 1486, when the Cape of Good Hope was rounded by Diaz.

Numerous early attempts were made to penetrate the interior of Africa. Herodotus in the 5th century B. C. and a party sent out by Nero in the 1st century A. D. tried to solve one of the standing riddles of the ancient world by tracing the Nile river to its source. The solution was delayed, however, until the year 1876, when the explorations of Colonel Speke and of many others enabled geographers to fix with certainty the origin of the Nile. The first European to cross Africa from ocean to ocean was David Livingstone, who completed the journey in 1856. More recently, our knowledge of the "dark continent" has been increased by missionaries and by international commissions, the latter being sent in for the purpose of fixing boundary lines between spheres of influence claimed by various European powers.

The Sahara desert, which for centuries constituted an effective barrier to travel into central Africa from the north, is still one of the least-known parts of the world. A new map of this region was published in 1923 by the French government, by whom an expedition had been sent out previously to make a survey of the region. Floyd Gibbons, a correspondent of the *Chicago Tribune*, made a journey through this desert from end to end in 1923.

POLITICAL DIVISIONS

The last quarter of the 19th century witnessed the partition of Africa into protectorates and colonies of various nations of Europe. Great Britain, France, Germany, Italy, Portugal, Spain, and Belgium were the most active in the division. As a result of World War I, the German portions were transferred to other powers. Italy, by two wars of conquest in the 20th century, increased her share of territory and attained to third place in the rank of African colonial powers. Egypt, formerly a British dependency, is officially independent though still by treaty tied to British interests. Liberia is an independent country. The Union of South Africa is an autonomous British dominion.

As a result of World War II, Italy lost all of her African possessions, relinquishing her sovereignty in the peace treaty of 1947 with a form of United Nations trusteeship to replace control by Italy.

Other nations voluntarily sought the protection of the United Nations in their colonial possessions by securing trusteeships as follows:

Tanganyika—United Nations trusteeship under Great Britain, 1946.

Ruanda, Urundi—United Nations trusteeship under Belgium, 1946.

Togoland—United Nations trusteeship under Great Britain, 1946.

Togoland—United Nations trusteeship under France, 1946.

Cameroons—United Nations trusteeship under Great Britain, 1946.

Cameroons—United Nations trusteeship under France, 1946.

Southwest Africa—Technically a mandate as Union of South Africa refuses to accept trusteeship but demands annexation.

Tangier—Restoration of international control, 1945.

Ethiopia—Restored to sovereignty under Haile Selassie as king.

Belgian Congo. Belgium's only African possession, a colony occupying a large part of central Africa and having access to the sea by means of a coast line on the estuary of the Congo river. Its area is 902,082 square miles. The population in 1947 was 10,667,087. The European inhabitants in 1936 numbered 34,786. For administrative purposes the mandated territories of Ruanda and Urundi are attached to Belgian Congo. These districts, once parts of German East Africa, have an area of 20,550 square miles.

The colony occupies the greater part of the Congo River basin and has a moist, tropical climate. Most of its area is covered by dense forests, in which live many of the Pygmy tribes. Rubber, nuts, palm oil, resin, and cocoa are the chief products of the country. Cattle thrive in the eastern highlands, but elsewhere the tsetse fly abounds, the bite of which is fatal to the live stock. Gold, diamonds, and, more especially, copper exist in great abundance. With the completion, in 1931, of a railroad connecting the copper mines with Benguela and the excellent harbor of Lobito Bay, Angola, copper from Belgian Congo became an important factor in the world's metal markets. Practically all the world's radium comes from Belgian Congo. Most of the trade is with Great Britain. The capital and chief port is Leopoldville, on the estuary of the

Photos for Nos. 1, 5, and 8 from Brown Bros.; photos for Nos. 2, 3, 4, 6, and 7 from Publishers' Photo Service.

AFRICA

1 Sahara Desert. 2 The Citadel, Cairo. 3 Pyramids, Egypt. 4 Algiers, City and Harbor. 5 Ivory for Shipment, Belgian Congo. 6 Making Bark Cloth, Uganda. 7 Ostrich Farm, Cape of Good Hope. 8 Town Hall, Durban, Natal.

Photos from Brown Bros.

AUSTRALIA

1 Public Buildings, Adelaide, South Australia. 2 Railway Bridge, Hawkesbury River, near Sydney, N. S. W. 3 Sampling Wool in Warehouse, Sydney, N. S. W. 4 Collins Street, Melbourne, Victoria. 5 Wheat Awaiting Shipment, Melbourne, Victoria. 6 Sydney, N. S. W., from the Harbor.

Congo. This city lies on the transcontinental water and rail route connecting with Dar-es Salaam on the Indian Ocean. In the heart of the colony lies the Albert national park, an 800,000-acre wild life sanctuary of great natural beauty.

British Africa. British colonies in Africa, while not larger, are nevertheless richer than the African possessions of any other nation. If Egypt, over which Great Britain has special rights, and the Union of South Africa are included, British territory extends from the northeastern extremity of Africa throughout the whole length of the continent on the eastern side to the Cape of Good Hope at the extreme south. An all-British railway is planned, which, upon completion, will traverse this territory from Cairo in the north to Cape Town in the south. Various sections of this "Cape to Cairo" railway are already constructed.

The colonies and protectorates within this African belt of British territory are as follows, given in order from north to south: Anglo-Egyptian Sudan, Uganda, Kenya, Tanganyika, Northern Rhodesia, Nyasaland, Southern Rhodesia, Bechuanaland, Swaziland, and Basutoland. For the area, population, and capital of each of the divisions of British Africa see the table of the *British Commonwealth of Nations*.

Great Britain possesses, to the east of the central belt, the Somaliland Protectorate on the Gulf of Aden; Socotra, an island about 180 miles east of the Somaliland peninsula; Zanzibar and Pemba, two fertile coral islands about 20 miles off the center of Tanganyika's coast; the Seychelles, a fertile, well watered group of 90 islands, about 900 miles east of Zanzibar; and Mauritius, a sugar producing island, lying some 500 miles east of Madagascar. The British territory in the west of the continent embraces British Cameroon and Nigeria, at the head of the Gulf of Guinea; British Togoland and Gold Coast, on the northern shore of the Gulf of Guinea; Ashanti and the Northern Territories, lying directly north of Gold Coast; Sierra Leone, lying farther west on the Atlantic coast; Gambia, a narrow British wedge stretching back from an Atlantic seacoast into French West Africa; Ascension island, lying 1600 miles southwest of Nigeria; and Saint Helena, the lonely island where Napoleon spent his last days, 1050 miles off the coast of South West Africa.

The commercial products drawn from these numerous regions exhibit a great diversity. The Anglo-Egyptian Sudan produces most of the world's supply of gum arabic. Live stock products, cotton, cocoa, gold, rubber, palm tree products, ivory, spices, tropical fruits, and coconuts are prominent among the exports. Copper, zinc, and vanadium are produced in large volume in Northern Rhodesia; chromium and asbestos in Southern Rhodesia. The actual production, however, is negligible compared with the value of products which, in time, the territories may be made to yield.

The total area of British Africa is about 3,075,000 square miles, upon which lives a population estimated at about 50,000,000. From these totals are excluded the Union of South Africa and the territory of South West Africa, held by the Union under a mandate.

Egypt. An independent country, situated in the extreme northeast of Africa. Its area is about 386,198 square miles, most of which is arid and unproductive. The population, numbering 19,040,000 in 1947, is almost entirely concentrated in the fertile valley of the Nile river, and is devoted principally to agriculture. The area of the cultivated region is about 13,600 square miles, which includes not only the Nile valley but the delta and oases in the desert. Much of this area has been reclaimed by irrigation works.

The chief crop is cotton. The papyrus plant of Egypt was used in the making of paper more than 4000 years ago. Today, however, Egypt imports practically all her paper.

The productivity of the Nile River valley is due to the annual flooding of the river banks. The area of cultivation has been greatly extended by the construction of irrigation works, consisting of canals, of several barrages, and of the great Assuan and Sennar dams, each over a mile in length.

Southern Egypt has a dry, healthful climate, which makes it desirable as a resort for tourists. A further attraction is found in the pyramids, the sphinx, various tombs, and other remains of the ancient civilization of the Nile. The northeastern extremity of the country has one of the world's two most celebrated ship canals, the Suez, which connects the Mediterranean Sea with the Red Sea.

The native inhabitants are called fellahs. They are mostly Mohammedan in religion. A sect of Christians, called the Copts, traces its ecclesiastical origin back to the 4th century.

Ethiopia. An independent country, formerly the "Land of Cush," "Queen of Sheba," and "Prester John," lies at the base of the peninsular area of northeast Africa roughly 5 to 10 degrees north latitude. Its area is about 350,000 square miles and is the most mountainous country of Africa. Most of the surface is covered by the Highlands of Ethiopia which reached their greatest height in Ras Dashan, 15,160 feet. The country is naturally rich with fertile soil and abundant rainfall. The climate is cool and bracing because of the high elevation. The chief rivers of Ethiopia, the Blue Nile and Atbara are tributary to the Nile and mainly responsible for its floods. The population is 5,300,000 and is a mixed race of Negroids, Semites, and Hamites. Some of the Semites are known as the Falasha or "Black Jews." The ruling group are Hamites. Specific Hamitic groups are the Nubians and Galla, the latter composing nearly half of the population.

The commercial products include hides, cattle, and coffee. Musk from the civet is used in perfumes. Gold is washed in the beds of the Atbara and its tributaries. Addis Ababa is the capital and chief city and Haile Selassie is the present ruler.

French Africa. The French colonial empire in Africa exceeds in area the African possessions of any other country. It occupies a huge block of territory, comprising nearly the whole of Africa's western extension and stretching as far east as the upper reaches of the Nile system and as far south as the Congo river. In addition, France governs the island of Madagascar and French Somaliland, a small territory at the head of the Gulf of Aden. The extensive territory in the west is divisible into three regions. These are the northern Berber states, the southeastern section, called French Equatorial Africa, and the remainder, called French West Africa. France's colonial empire in Africa covers over 4,000,000 square miles and is inhabited by over 45,000,000 people.

The northern section, embracing Tunis, Algeria, and Morocco, is geographically akin to Europe. The chief exports are phosphate, wheat, barley, eggs, hides, dried vegetables, almonds, and palmetto fiber. The native population consists of Arabs and Berbers, and there are several Moslem universities. French, Arabic, Berber, and Spanish are spoken.

French Equatorial Africa, formerly called the French Congo, is drained by the northwestern affluents of a part of the Congo river. To the colony is attached French Cameroon, held as a mandate. Approximately a third of its area, totaling about 1,000,000 square miles, is covered with tropical forests. Ivory is the leading article of export.

French West Africa consists of seven colonies and one mandate, having as a hinterland the great Sahara desert. The names of the colonies are as follows: Mauretania, Senegal, French Guinea, French Sudan, Ivory Coast, Dahomey, and Niger. The mandate is Togoland. These territories occupy most of the basin of the Niger river. Agriculture and cattle raising are the principal industries of the colonies, although some minerals are produced. The chief exports are palm oil, palm nuts, rubber, cacao, cotton, timber, peanuts, hides, gums, and cattle. The total railroad mileage amounts to about 2500. In charge of the whole region is a governor-general, who is represented by a lieutenant-governor in each colony.

France's island possessions in Africa include Madagascar, to which are attached, for administrative purposes, Mayotta, the Cormoro, and other islands. Réunion and a few smaller islands are also under French administration. Agriculture and cattle raising are the principal industries, although gold, silver, iron, and other minerals are produced. The chief exports are gold, cattle, bark, manioc, hides, rice, and rubber. See *French Colonial Dependencies* for area and population of colonies.

Italian Africa. The Italian possessions in Africa were Italian Libya (formerly Tripoli) and Italian East Africa (formerly Eritrea, Somaliland, and Ethiopia). Ethiopia was conquered in 1936 and with it Italy ranked third in colonial possessions in Africa next to France and Great Britain.

Tripoli, formerly Italian Libya, lies directly across the Mediterranean Sea from Italy. It has an area of 684,764 square miles and a population, in 1938, of 850,250. From the coast inland, there are three zones. The first is the Mediterranean zone, in which grow, in oases, the date palm, olive, and orange trees; in a stepped district, cereal crops and pasture; and, in a mountain region, olives, figs, and other fruits. The other zones are classified as sub-desert and desert. Tripoli, under Italian administration, was made a part of the national territory of Italy in 1938. For administrative purposes, it is divided into four provinces, namely, Tripoli, Misurata, Benghasa, and Derne. The principal city and headquarters of the governor is Tripoli, on the northwestern coast, with 98,861 inhabitants.

Eritrea, Somaliland, and Ethiopia were included in the former colony called Italian East Africa.

Eritrea lies on the Red Sea across Yemen. It has an area of 45,754 square miles and a population of 601,000. The most valuable products are sea pearls, salt, and potash. Massawa is an important port and possesses a fine harbor. *Somaliland* (formerly Italian Somaliland) is located on the easternmost extension of Africa ending in Cape Ras Hatun. The area is 194,000 square miles and the population 1,300,000. The natives are not Negroes but Hamitic or dark Caucasians. They are known as the Somalie race, bold, quarrelsome, excitable, and fanatical Muslems. The land is mainly a high arid plateau. Its products are ostrich feathers, hides, salt, and coffee. In ancient times, frankincense and myrrh came from its desert plants.

Liberia. A Negro republic, occupying the southwestern extremity of Africa's western extension. The area is about 43,000 square miles, supporting a population estimated at over one and a half million. The low, unhealthful coast regions are inhabited by the more progressive part of the population, including over 12,000 descendants of freed slaves from the United States; the interior is occupied by uncivilized tribes. There is little systematic cultivation of the soil apart from a large rubber plantation owned by the Firestone Tire and Rubber Company. With the exception of Haiti, in the West Indies, Liberia is the only independent Negro country in the world. The capital is Monrovia.

Portuguese Africa. The continental empire of Portugal in Africa consists of three colonies. Portuguese Guinea is near the extreme western part of the continent. Angola, on the Atlantic coast, and Mozambique, fronting the Indian Ocean, are in South Africa, separated from each other by the British territory of Northern Rhodesia. Rubber and palm oil are exported from Portuguese Guinea and from Angola, the latter producing also coffee and dried fish. Sugar, copra, fresh fruits, and ground nuts are exported from Mozambique. Gold, silver, tin, and zinc are produced, and there are large coal deposits. Parts of Mozambique are governed by commercial companies holding royal charters that give sovereign rights to the holders.

Among the islands of Africa, the Cape Verde group, Saint Thomas, and Prince's island are Portuguese dependencies. The Madeira islands are governed as a province of Portugal. Saint Thomas and Prince's island produce a large proportion of the world's supply of cocoa.

The following table gives the capital, the area, and the population of each of the divisions of Portuguese Africa:

Division	Capital	Area	Population 1940 census
Cape Verde Islands	Praia	1,539	181,286
Portuguese Guinea	Bissâu	13,944	351,089
São Tomé and Principe	São Tomé	373	60,490
Angola	Loanda	478,788	3,740,787
Mozambique	Lourenço Marques	297,731	5,085,630
Total		792,375	9,419,282

South West Africa. The region, about 322,400 square miles in area, lying on the Atlantic coast of Africa north of the Union of South Africa and attached to the Union as a mandate of the League of Nations. It is arid or semiarid, although the eastern belt has sufficient rainfall to support grazing. The chief source of wealth is diamonds, which are found in alluvial deposits along the coast. Copper, lead, vanadium, and tin are also exported. The population in 1944 was estimated at 303,848.

Spanish Africa. The possessions of Spain in Africa consist of two sections of Morocco, called Spanish Morocco and Ifni; the Spanish Sahara (Rio de Oro and its hinterland) on the Atlantic coast to the southwest of Morocco; Spanish Guinea, Rio Muni, on the eastern coast of the Gulf of Guinea; and the Canary islands, which, for administrative purposes, are regarded as a part of Spain. These islands are partly European in flora. They produce three or four crops of grain and fruit annually. The canary bird is a native of the group. The island of Fernando Po, which, politically, forms a part of Rio Muni and contains its capital, is one of the most fertile spots on the west coast of Africa. Spanish Morocco was occupied effectively by Spain in 1927.

The following table gives the capital, the area, and the population of each of the political divisions of Spain's possessions in Africa.

Division	Capital	Area	Population 1944 estimate
Spanish morocco (Including Ifni)	Tetuan	18,454	1,284,000
Western Sahara	Cabo Yubi	116,200	72,000
Spanish Guinea	Santa Isabel	10,900	168,000
Total		136,554	1,524,000

Union of South Africa. A self-governing British dominion at the southern extremity of Africa. Its area is estimated at 472,494 square miles. The territory surrounds the British protectorate of Basutoland and almost surrounds Swaziland. To the northwest lies South West Africa, which has been assigned to the Union as a mandate from the League of Nations. South West Africa had formerly been a German colony. Its conquest by an army from South Africa constituted one of the campaigns of World War I.

The surface is, for the most part, a high plateau, interrupted by isolated flat-topped hills called kopjes. The plateau slopes rapidly down near the coasts. A ridge, low in the west, passes around the southern and eastern parts of the plateau, reaching its highest point in the east central region of the country. This eastern ridge is the divide separating a large number of short rivers, draining toward the east and the south, from the Orange river, which flows westward across the country and empties into the Atlantic Ocean. Farther north, the Limpopo river rises on the interior plateau and makes its way north of the eastern ridge; then, turning southeast, it flows into the Indian Ocean.

The climate of South Africa is warm, and the soil is fertile. The precipitation varies greatly, being nearly 50 inches on the southeastern coast and falling to less than 3 inches farther north on the western coast. In the western part of the country, semiarid conditions prevail, and grazing rather than agriculture is the principal industry. Wool is one of the chief exports, and about half the world's supply of mohair comes from the Union. Corn, wheat, oats, barley, and tobacco are also grown, and such products of subtropical agriculture as cotton, tea, and sugar cane are raised in the lower and moister coastal regions. The operation of ostrich farms constitutes a distinctive industry. Much trade is still carried on by barter with the natives, from whom the white traders obtain ostrich feathers, gold dust, ivory, and hides.

The exports of the greatest value are the products of the mining industry. South Africa is the world's chief source of diamonds and is by far the greatest gold producing region of the world. The output of gold is several times that of Canada, the country which ranks second to South Africa. Other minerals obtained in important quantities include coal, tin, and copper.

The white population in 1946 was 2,335,460, while the native population stood at 7,735,809. The 1946 census listed the total population at 11,391,950. About one-half those of the white race are of Dutch descent. The religion is predominantly Protestant. There are ten universities. Most of the country's 13,284 miles of railway is owned by the government.

South Africa is divided into four provinces. Cape of Good Hope is in the extreme south, and Transvaal, on the eastern side of the country, lies farthest north. Between the two lie the inland province, called Orange Free State, and Natal, which borders on the Indian Ocean. In eastern Transvaal is the Kruger national park, a 5-million acre sanctuary for big game. The center of governmental administration is Pretoria, but the legislature sits at Cape Town, which is the terminus of the partially constructed "Cape to Cairo" railway. The largest city is Johannesburg, situated in the Witwatersrand, among the richest gold mines of the world. Kimberley is the chief diamond mining center.

CITIES AND OTHER POINTS OF TRAVEL INTEREST

Africa has a relatively small number of cities. This fact is due to the primitive economic conditions prevailing throughout most of the continent, nearly all the inhabitants being engaged in agriculture or hunting.

The valley of the lower Nile, however, was the seat of one of the world's earliest civilizations. It still contains the largest cities of Africa and many of the most interesting ruins in the world. The only other cities of any considerable size are in South Africa, where European settlers have built up a civilization of the characteristic Western type.

The following section contains descriptions of the principal cities and of other places in the continent which merit especial attention.

Addis Ababa. This city, the capital of Ethiopia (Abyssinia), is of greater importance politically than industrially or commercially. Since its recapture from the Italians by the British and Ethiopians in 1941, it has been the seat of Emperor Haile Selassie's government. Population, est., 140,000.

Alexandria. The chief seaport of Egypt, situated at the west of the Nile delta. The city has an Arab quarter with Oriental bazaars, a large European quarter, and an industrial district with asphalt works and oil, rice, and paper mills. The chief exports are cotton, grain, rice, and sugar.

Alexandria was founded in 332 B. C. by Alexander the Great and was, for several centuries, the chief commercial city of the world. In ancient times, its harbor was famous for the Lighthouse of Pharos, a huge structure completed in 282 B. C. and regarded as one of the seven wonders of the ancient world. This lighthouse was destroyed by an earthquake in 1303. Alexandria was long a center of Greek culture and contained the most valuable library of Greek books in the world. Near the palace and temple of the emperors stood two obelisks, erected by Julius Cæsar in honor of Cleopatra and known as Cleopatra's needles. One of these obelisks was removed to New York City in 1881, and the other was taken to London three years earlier.

In the 7th century, Alexandria was captured and sacked by the Arabs. Its importance in modern times dates from the construction of the Suez canal. Population, 1947, 900,000.

Algiers. The seaport and largest city of Algeria and the seat of the French administration there. It lies near the center of the country's Mediterranean coast. The lower part has been recently built under French direction. With its modern hotels, spacious squares, and ornamented parks, it presents a marked contrast to the narrow streets and characteristic mosques of the Moorish section. The city has a university of the European type and is a favorite resort of tourists.

Algiers is one of the most important coaling stations on the Mediterranean Sea. It has an important trade, mainly with France. The chief exports are wine, fruits, olive oil, and cork. Population, 1947 est., 519,200.

Cairo (*kī'rō*). The capital of Egypt and the largest city of Africa, situated on the Nile river about 100 miles from its outlet in the Mediterranean Sea. The city is an important center of caravan trade, receiving ivory, ostrich feathers, and hides brought from the interior of Africa.

Cairo's Oriental quarter is poorly built, with crooked, unpaved streets. The modern portion centers about a 20-acre park, called the Place Ezbekieh. This part is well laid out and has many impressive buildings.

Chief of the numerous sacred edifices of Cairo is the Sultan Hassan Mosque, which is regarded as the finest example of the Byzantine-Arabian architecture in existence. The El Azhar university, situated in the city, holds the leading place among the world's institutions for Mohammedan education. Cairo's site covers the remains of many cities that had fallen into ruins before the founding of the present city in 968 A. D. Population, 1947, 2,100,486.

Cape Town. The legislative capital of South Africa, occupying a picturesque site on the southwestern coast of the Union. It stands at the head of Table bay, an inlet of the Atlantic Ocean. The city and several beautiful suburbs extend along a narrow coastal strip between the water and a group of precipitous mountains.

Cape Town is the chief seaport of South Africa, the exports ranking highest in value being diamonds and bar gold. Among the notable features of the city are the Parliament buildings; the public library; a 14-acre botanical garden; the Cape observatory; and the Castle. The last-named edifice was built as a defensive work in 1666, 14 years after the founding of a Dutch colony on the present site of the city. Cape Town passed into the hands of the English in 1806. Population, 1946, 454,052; white population, 1946, 214,201.

Casablanca. The chief city and seaport in Morocco. It has a large airport as well as a fine harbor. Following its capture by American forces in 1942, Casablanca became headquarters for the movement of Allied troops on their way to North Africa and the Mediterranean region. It was also the scene of a historic conference between President Roosevelt and Prime Minister Churchill, which took place in 1943. Population, 257,430.

Dakar. Strategically located on the Cape Verde peninsula in Senegal, Dakar is at the westernmost point on the coast of West Africa, and is therefore closest to South America. As capital of French West Africa, it was held by the Vichi government during the first part of World War II. After passing into Allied hands it became a favorite terminus for transatlantic flights connecting Brazil and West Africa. Population, est., 100,000.

Dar es Salaam. Developed as a capital for German West Africa, the town was carefully laid out by the Germans, with elaborate streets and buildings. It was taken by the British in 1916 and became the capital of Tanganyika. It has a good small harbor and enjoys a flourishing trade in sisal, cotton, coffee, and copra. Population, 74,036.

Freetown. Capital of Sierra Leone province. Freetown has the finest harbor on the west coast of Africa. Previously important as a trading center, it became headquarters for a great deal of war work, causing an increase in its population from approximately 55,000 to an estimated 80,000. Formerly unhealthful because of malaria, it has recently been rendered sanitary and comparatively safe for Europeans.

Giza (*gē'zĕ*). A village of Egypt about three miles from Cairo. It is notable for the pyramids which stand in the vicinity. The largest was erected by Cheops, an Egyptian king who lived about 3000 B. C. According to Herodotus, 100,000 men were employed for 20 years in building it, while 10 years were occupied in transporting the stones. It is about 480 feet in height with a base 764 feet square. The pyramid is believed to have been originally encased with marble. Since 1000 A. D., however, the exterior stones have been removed, leaving visible a structure of rough limestone blocks forming steps with a platform of considerable area at the top. This pyramid was one of the seven wonders of the ancient world and is the only one of the seven still in existence. Two other major pyramids and nearly 40 minor ones are included among the pyramids of Giza. They were intended to serve as tombs for their builders.

The great sphinx is located in the approach to Giza, where it might serve to frighten evil spirits away from the pyramid tombs near by. The sphinx is an image of the head of the god Harmachis attached to the body of a lion. The whole figure is 66 feet high and about 172 feet long and is carved out of the solid rock.

Johannesburg (*yô-hän'ĕs-bûrg*). The largest city and commercial metropolis of South Africa, lying in the south central part of the Transvaal province. The city was founded in 1886 and owes its importance to its location on the Witwatersrand, in the midst of the richest gold field in the world. Johannesburg is regularly laid out and well built, presenting a more completely modern appearance than any other city on the continent of Africa. It contains the University of the Witwatersrand.

Johannesburg was the center of the agitation which resulted in the Boer war. The days of the Boer régime are recalled by a dismantled fortress overlooking the city and by a monument, which stands in a near-by field, commemorating the Boer declaration of independence in 1880. The city was occupied by the British in 1900. Population, 1946, 727,943; white population, 1946, 324,304.

Karnak (*kär'năk*). A village of Egypt on the right bank of the Nile river about 400 miles above Cairo, famed for its ruins of ancient Egyptian temples. The chief one is the temple of the god Amen-Ra. It was erected about 4000 years ago and is the largest temple in the world. There is comfortable standing room for as many as 90 people on the top of many of the columns still erect.

Luxor. A village of Egypt near the Nile river a short distance southwest of Karnak and about 400 miles above Cairo. Luxor is known for the numerous tombs near by, which contain the mummies and treasures of ancient Egyptian monarchs. These treasures, which were intended to serve the spirits of their deceased owners, amount to millions of dollars in value. The tombs are hewn in the rock and usually have, on their walls, elaborate carvings, which have done much toward the unfolding of early Egyptian history. One of the more remarkable of such tombs was that of Tutankhamen, discovered by Lord Carnarvan in 1922. It was especially rich in articles of furniture inlaid with ivory and with precious metals.

In Luxor stand two colossal statues, one of which is said to represent the god Memnon. It is a Roman restoration of a former statue, which, before its destruction by an earthquake, is said to have given forth a sound each morning when struck by the rays of the rising sun. Most of the extant Egyptian temples are grouped about Luxor and the neighboring village of Karnak. See *Karnak*.

Nairobi. Located on the Kenya and Uganda railway, Nairobi adjoins a coffee-raising district and is a clearing point for an extensive trade with the interior. Its altitude of more than 5000 feet and its favorable climate make it a suitable residence for Europeans, but these constitute almost a negligible percentage of its estimated 100,000 population. A great number of the inhabitants are Indians. Nairobi is noted, not only as the capital of Kenya province, but also as the seat of an elaborate Indian bazaar.

Port Said (*pōrt sä-ēd'*). A seaport of Egypt at the Mediterranean end of the Suez canal. It has an export trade in cotton and is an important coaling station. Its features include a large lighthouse, whose light is visible 24 miles out at sea, and a colossal statue of De Lesseps, the French engineer under whose direction the Suez canal was constructed. Population, 1947, 250,000.

Pretoria. The administrative capital of the Union of South Africa. It is an inland city, situated in the northeastern part of the Union in the Transvaal province. Its streets are broad and regularly laid out. The outstanding architectural feature of the city is the large group of government offices. They are in the Renaissance style of architecture and have a central tower surmounted by a statue of Liberty. Pretoria is the seat of Transvaal University college. Population, 1946, 236,367; white population, 1946, 124,542.

Timbuktu (*tĭm-bŭk'tōō*). An inland city of French West Africa near the southern border of the Sahara desert and on the edge of the marshes of the Niger river. The city is the focus of the caravan trade of an immense territory. Commerce is carried on largely by barter, the chief articles of exchange being gold, ivory, wax, salt, hardware, beads, and cloth.

Timbuktu has a large Mohammedan library and several mosques of striking appearance. These buildings date from a period before the 19th century, having been erected when the town was one of the principal centers of Mohammedan influence in Africa. The city was first visited by Europeans in 1826, and it passed into the hands of the French in 1894. Timbuktu's population has declined greatly in recent years, being 6900 in 1946.

PRINCIPAL WORLD PORTS

Showing Ship Entrances with net register tonnage* in 1935
From figures supplied by Bureau of Foreign and Domestic Commerce

Rank	Port and Country	Number of Vessels	Net Register Tons	Rank	Port and Country	Number of Vessels	Net Register Tons
9.	Antwerp, Belgium	11,125	18,730,000	15.	Marseille, France	9,135	16,612,000
6.	Baltimore, U.S.A.	56,067	21,008,000	38.	Melbourne, Australia	3,396	7,613,000
45.	Batavia, Dutch East Indies**	2,183	5,338,000	36.	Montevideo, Uruguay	1,631	8,087,000
41.	Bombay, India	33,731	6,547,000	33.	Montreal, Canada	5,725	8,516,000
17.	Boston, U.S.A.	7,340	14,978,000	29.	Naples, Italy	9,008	10,809,000
20.	Buenos Aires, Argentina	14,826	13,435,000	32.	Newcastle, England	8,532	8,596,000
48.	Calcutta, India	1,296	4,059,000	21.	New Orleans, U.S.A.	16,287	13,319,000
43.	Capetown, South Africa	1,629	5,454,000	1.	New York, U.S.A.†	92,032	68,598,000
50.	Charleston, S.C., U.S.A.	10,668	3,226,000	24.	Norfolk, U.S.A.	7,089	12,222,000
42.	Cherbourg, France	952	6,478,000	8.	Osaka, Japan	18,999	19,600,000
7.	Colombo, Ceylon	2,708	20,425,000	11.	Philadelphia, U.S.A.‡	8,302	17,907,000
39.	Copenhagen, Denmark	25,432	7,452,000	37.	Piraeus, Greece	13,396	7,758,000
49.	Curacao, Dutch West Indies	5,047	3,700,000	40.	Portland, Oregon, U.S.A.	9,548	7,051,000
22.	Duluth, U.S.A.	2,807	12,882,000	27.	Rio de Janeiro, Brazil	3,924	11,226,000
44.	Galveston, U.S.A.	1,762	5,383,000	5.	Rotterdam, Netherlands	110,406	22,415,000
28.	Genoa, Italy	5,421	10,860,000	18.	San Francisco, U.S.A.	17,353	14,974,000
10.	Hamburg, Germany	16,141	18,418,000	47.	Savannah, U.S.A.	1,395	4,075,000
25.	Havre, France	9,018	11,572,000	35.	Seattle, U.S.A.	3,416	8,210,000
16.	Hong Kong, China§	5,947	15,340,000	12.	Shanghai, China	8,488	17,418,000
30.	Houston, U.S.A.	7,275	10,091,000	19.	Singapore, Straits Settlements	5,934	14,800,000
46.	Jacksonville, U.S.A.	1,810	4,523,000	23.	Southampton, England	15,628	12,509,000
3.	Kobe, Japan	26,776	28,334,000	31.	Sydney, Australia	6,855	10,057,000
14.	Liverpool, England	14,614	16,640,000	26.	Vancouver, Canada	16,970	11,488,000
2.	London, England	29,137	29,673,000	4.	Yokohama, Japan	5,757	26,785,000
13.	Los Angeles, U.S.A.	5,369	17,211,000				

*Statistics for United States ports include barges but exclude tugs and ferries. †Upper bay shipping only. ‡On Delaware River, Philadelphia to the sea. §Excluding 9,304 junks. **In Tandjong Prock.

AUSTRALIA

An island continent lying southeast of Asia between the Indian and the Pacific Ocean. The western portion of Australia forms one of the oldest land surfaces of the globe. The continent is about one-fourth less in area than Europe, but is nearly as large as the continental United States and, with the exception of Antarctica, is the only continent lying wholly in the southern hemisphere. Australia is 1800 miles from Asia, 4500 miles from Africa, 6300 miles from South America, 6700 miles from the United States, and 11,000 miles from England. The island lies between 10° 39′ and 39° 11′ south latitude and between 113° 5′ and 153° 16′ east longitude, and from east to west is 2400 miles long and from north to south, 1971 miles. The total area is 2,977,600 square miles, of which 1,149,320 square miles, or about five-thirteenths, are within the Torrid Zone. The population in 1946 was 7,580,800.

Surface. Strong contrast in elevation above sea level is strikingly absent in Australia. The highest point is Mount Kosciusko, which has an elevation of 7328 feet. The greater part of Western Australia consists of a low plateau averaging about 1000 feet in height. This plateau extends eastward into South Australia and Northern Territory. To the eastward of this plateau lie the lowlands of the Lake Eyre and Murray River basins. Along the eastern coast of the continent the land rises to an average elevation of from two to three thousand feet, forming the Great Dividing range. This range extends practically the full length of the eastern coast. At the southern end of the coast, the range turns westward and disappears in western Victoria. The most elevated area, the Australian Alps, is in the southeastern part of the continent, near the border of New South Wales and of Victoria. The low-lying coastal strip is very narrow along eastern Australia, but it widens about the Gulf of Carpentaria in the north and around Western Australia. The main watershed of the continent is formed by the Great Dividing range, from which practically all the rivers of importance rise. The country around Lake Eyre is a basin of internal drainage. The West Australian plateau is an arid region with only a few short streams flowing down the western scarp.

Climate. The climate of northern Australia is tropical, and the mean annual temperature rises in places to 85° F. The range of temperature in the interior is very great. In central Australia, heavy frosts occur at night during the winter, while in summer the temperature in the shade may rise above 130° F. The southern part of Australia lies within the South Temperate Zone and near the south coast the mean annual temperature is about 60° F. In summer, the southern coastal areas are tempered by sea breezes, but are subject to extremely sudden changes of temperature. Hot north winds from the interior may be replaced by cold south winds, the thermometer showing a fall of 20° or more in about 20 minutes. These southerly changes rarely occur in the inland districts, and within 100 miles of the coast the temperature at midday may rise to 100° F. or over for days or even for weeks.

Snow may lie for months on the higher portion of the Australian Alps, but over the greater part of the continent snow is rarely, if ever, seen.

Rainfall. A line running generally from Sharks' bay on the west coast to Sydney on the southeast coast divides the northern area of summer rains from the southern area of winter rains. In the winter months, June to September, areas of low pressure move northward from the antarctic region to a latitude sufficiently low to bring rain to Tasmania and the southern projections of the continent. In the summer, however, these areas do not move so far to the north. As a result, summer rains seldom occur, except on the west coast of Tasmania. In summer, the thermal equator is over northern Australia, and the northwest monsoons bring rain to the northern coast line, January and February being the wettest months. Monsoonal tongues sometimes extend southward as far as northern Victoria and produce extremely useful rains.

The rainfall in the remaining portion of Australia is governed mainly by the southeast trade winds. These winds bring summer and autumn rains to the eastern coast. The greater part of the moisture is deposited on the eastern highlands. The trade winds pass on as dry winds and, becoming heated, absorb moisture rapidly, thereby causing the aridity which characterizes large parts of central and western Australia. Cairns, on the northeast coast, receives over 100 inches per annum, while a large portion of the interior receives less than 10 inches. Wheat may be grown in some areas in the south, which have about 10 inches of rain, because the rain that does fall comes at the right time.

The rains of northern and of southern Australia are fairly reliable, but the central area shows great variation, and disastrous droughts sometimes occur over a large portion of the continent. During such drought periods, there is an immense loss of cattle and sheep, as it is impossible, under present conditions of transportation, to move the vast numbers of stock to the better-watered areas. Artesian wells have improved conditions somewhat by affording a supply of drinking water for the stock; but unfortunately the water is not suitable for irrigation.

Irrigation. Owing to the small rainfall over large portions of Australia, irrigation is impracticable except in limited areas, such as the Murray River basin. In recent years considerable areas in northern Victoria and southwestern New South Wales have been irrigated either by gravity channels or from pumping stations. The Goulburn valley is served from the Waranga basin. Water for the Mildura and Red Cliff fruit growing settlements is pumped from the Murray river.

Rivers. The interior of the continent being dry, there are comparatively few rivers. Australia has no snow fields from which they may be fed. Of the streams flowing into the Pacific, the Burdekin and the Fitzroy are the largest. They drain, each, an area of about 55,000 square miles. The chief river of the north, the Roper, flowing into the Gulf of Carpentaria, is navigable for 75 miles from its mouth. The largest river system is the Murray with its tributaries—the Darling, the Murrumbidgee, and the Lachlan. These rivers drain south Queensland, western New South Wales, and northern Victoria. There are other streams, such as Cooper's creek, which, in time of abnormal rains, carry enormous volumes of water inland to lakes which have no outlet, such as Lake Eyre, Lake Gairdner, and Lake Frome. Generally, however, these streams contain water in their upper courses only, because, by evaporation and soakage, the water is lost, and the remainder of their channels is marked by occasional water holes, which also dry up in time of drought.

On the east, north, and west coasts, short rivers flow from the mountain slopes to the sea. But there are no long navigable waterways penetrating far into the interior, like the Mississippi in North America and the Nile in Africa. Hence the development of the continent has been much retarded.

Minerals. Australia is fairly rich in mineral resources. Gold, discovered here in 1851, has yielded the most valuable returns. In the early days most of the gold was obtained from alluvial deposits or gold placers. Deep leads or deeply buried alluvial deposits also gave splendid returns. When the alluvial areas were worked out, the miners turned their attention to the quartz reefs from which the alluvial gold had been derived, and more costly methods of winning the gold were introduced. Copper, tin, lead, silver, zinc, manganese, antimony, wolfram, and bismuth have been mined, and important deposits of such minerals as gypsum and phosphates are being worked.

Precious stones, including diamond, sapphire, topaz, and opal, are found. Agates are fairly abundant.

Black coal occurs in large areas in eastern Australia and in Tasmania. Western Australia draws its supply largely from the Collie coal field, situated in the state. Thick seams of brown coal occur in southeastern Australia, especially near Morwell in Victoria. Building stones have been quarried in all the states.

MINERAL PRODUCTION OF AUSTRALIA

ITEM	Value 1938	Value 1945
	£	£
Gold	14,026,615	7,031,024
Silver and Lead	4,745,046	4,927,993
Copper	893,080	2,284,805
Tin	711,628	759,370
Coal	7,187,901	11,661,292
Other Minerals	4,898,725	5,773,467
Total	32,462,995	32,437,951

Total mineral production to end of 1945 £1,642,984,854
Total gold production, to end of 1945 . £ 781,970,091
Total gold production, 1945, fine oz. . . 657,213

Vegetation. The continent has over 7000 species of plants found nowhere else in the world. Many of them have fossil representatives in America and in Europe. Characteristically Australian are the gum trees, or eucalyptus, and the acacias. Eucalypts number over 230 species and are found in all places capable of supporting vegetation. Some are only a few feet in height, as the mallee and snow gum; some rival California's giant sequoias. Oil is secreted in the leaves of numerous species, and a gumlike resin exudes from the trees when the bark is injured. Some of the most durable timber known is furnished by various eucalypts, as the jarrah, red gum, and ironbark.

Much sunshine and too little rain compel many Australian trees to hang their leaves vertically, only the edges being turned to the sun. By this means the amount of evaporation from the leaves is diminished. The eucalypts are evergreens, but in many cases they shed their bark. The acacias, or wattles, constitute another important group, the members of which vary, according to their environment, from small shrubs to trees 100 to 150 feet in height. The bark of some varieties is used for tanning. The golden wattle is regarded as Australia's national flower.

Other forms of natural vegetation include the grass tree, resembling a tall stump from which grass sprouts at the top; tree ferns as large as palm trees; the banksia or Australian honeysuckle; and the native cherry, noted for having the stone outside the fruit.

Fodder Plants. Many acacias provide fodder for sheep and cattle. Other shrublike fodder plants, growing in the dry interior, are saltbushes, cotton bushes, and bluebushes. Australia's saltbushes have proved so valuable as sheep foodplants that they have been introduced into the arid regions of the southwestern United States.

Timber. Forest areas occupy 24,500,000 acres, which is about one-twentieth of the surface of Australia. Of this total, 15,895,781 acres are held as timber reserves. Soft woods, such as kauri pine, red cedar, silky oak, and Queensland maple, are found in the tropical forests of Queensland. Murray pine and Huon pine, the latter growing in Tasmania, are other important soft woods. The hard woods include many species of eucalypts, such as ironbark, red gum, gray box, yellow box, blue gum, and stringybark. These grow mainly on the highlands of eastern and southeastern Australia. Jarrah and kauri flourish in southwestern Australia. Blackwood, a species of acacia, is used extensively for furniture.

Grassland. The eastern half of the interior is a vast sheep pasturing country, though the rainfall is light. The soil is rich alluvium, and in good seasons grass is abundant. In time of drought the grass dries and is scattered by the wind, leaving the land perfectly bare. When the drought breaks, the grass springs up and grows with great rapidity. European fodder grasses have been planted over considerable areas. Farther west, plants needing but little water, wattles and saltbushes, mallee and mulga scrub, and the wiry spinifex, or porcupine grass, cover a large part of Australia's semidesert.

Jungles. In the northern part of Australia, a region of tropical heat and of heavy rains, there are found, in all the lowland districts, dense forests containing eucalypts, bamboos, palm trees, beautiful orchids with singular flowers, and gigantic lilies six to eight feet high, bearing dark red blossoms. Such jungle growth is variously known as bush, brush, or scrub. The term "bush" is frequently applied to any area in which the natural trees have not been cleared off to any extent.

Fauna. The fauna of Australia is quite distinct from that of the northern hemisphere. It is most closely related to that of South America. The characteristic mammalian forms are the marsupials, which, with few exceptions, are found elsewhere only in the fossil state. The higher mammals are represented only by the dingo, or native dog, probably introduced by the aborigines, and by a few rodents. The marsupials, or pouched animals, include the kangaroo and the wallaby, which are typically Australian. Other forms are the wombats, bandicoots, opossums, or possums, and the native bear, or koala. The Tasmanian wolf and Tasmanian devil are marsupials now confined to Tasmania. Outside the Australian area the only living pouched animals are the Patagonian opossum-rat and the North American opossum. The Monotremes, which are the lowest order of the mammals, have no living representatives outside Australia. The Australian forms include the duck-billed platypus and the echidna, or anteater. Both are egg laying forms and constitute a link between the mammals of today and the great reptile family from which the birds and mammals have developed.

Among the more remarkable birds are the emu, cassowary, kookaburra (laughing jackass or giant kingfisher), native turkey, black swan, lyre bird, and bower bird. Brilliant plumaged parrots and the yellow-crested cockatoo are abundant.

Two species of crocodiles are found in north Queensland. The largest lizard is called the "iguana" or "goanna" and may reach a length of 5 feet. Snakes, both venomous and nonvenomous, are fairly abundant.

Fish. Excellent food fish of many kinds abound in Australian coastal waters and in most of the rivers. The remarkable ceratodus or lungfish occurs in the Burnett and the Mary river in Queensland. Several species of European fish have been acclimatized. Trout may now be caught in a number of the mountain streams.

Pearling. Pearl fishing is a lucrative occupation off the northern and northwestern coasts of the continent. Some of the nearer pearl-oyster banks, however, have been practically exhausted, owing to persistent gathering of the shellfish and failure to allow the beds time enough to restock.

Sheep Raising. Gold brought Australia into the circle of the nations, but her greatest source of wealth is her merino sheep. Sheep raising is the continent's main industry. Pasturage for sheep is less dependent on rainfall than is pasture for cattle; sheep thrive where cattle would starve. Australian wool is the thickest and finest in the world. Hence wool growing is a profitable industry in the east central part of Australia. Wire fencing is used to enclose the "stations" or "runs" on which sheep are grazed. Merino sheep, improved wonderfully from the old Spanish stock, form the largest flocks. The stations vary greatly in size and in the number of sheep carried. Many of the very large stations have been subdivided, but recently, in the Riverina, there was one station which carried 150,000 sheep. Australia has over 95,000,000 sheep and exceeds in number any other sheep raising area in the world.

Large cattle stations are situated in the northern parts of Australia, especially Queensland. Dairy farms are abundant in the well watered districts of eastern and southern Australia. Horses and pigs are also raised.

Animal Industry of Australia

Item	Season 1938-39	Season 1945-46
Cattle, No.	13,080,180	13,878,006
Horses, No.	1,698,797	1,265,398
Pigs, No.	1,455,341	1,425,709
Sheep, No.	119,305,391	96,396,405
Butter produced, lbs.	455,834,329	300,094,000
Wool produced, lbs.	983,581,974	936,239,000

Agriculture. The area under cultivation in Australia is gradually extending. In the southern coastal regions the rainfall is generally good; and oats, barley, maize, and lucerne are the principal crops. Apples, pears, peaches, and other such fruits are largely grown. Inland, wheat is extensively cultivated, the area under cultivation increasing as means of communication are improved. Apples, oranges, lemons, peaches, apricots, grapes, and currants are readily grown in the irrigation areas. In the coast regions of Queensland, sugar cane, bananas, pineapples, and other tropical fruits are cultivated. Rice, cotton, and tobacco have been grown in various portions of the Commonwealth.

Manufacturing. Manufacturing is rapidly developing. Flour, woolen goods, leather, boots and shoes, furniture, iron and steel goods are among the products made for home consumption; and an export trade in manufactured articles is gradually developing.

Value of Chief Classes of Products

Item	Value 1934	Value 1946
	£	£
Agricultural	70,670,428	100,285,000
Pastoral	84,495,489	86,312,000
Dairying, Poultry and Bee-Farming	36,072,181	65,082,000
Forests and Fisheries	9,637,965	23,415,000
Mining	16,967,589	26,288,000
Manufacturing	129,091,761	354,479,000
Total	346,935,413	655,861,000

Commerce. Imports are principally European manufactures. Most of the trade is with Great Britain. Australia exports more wool than any other country. Among the other exports are wheat, butter, hides, tallow, and dressed meats, comprising chiefly beef, mutton, and rabbit. Summer dairy products, shipped on fast steamers with cold-storage chambers, reach Great Britain in a few weeks when the cows in that country are housed for the winter.

Canada and New Zealand are linked by cable with Australia. Most of the foreign capital invested in Australia is British. The country has about 28,000 miles of railway, nearly all owned by the state governments. The telephone and telegraph are Federal property.

The Federal District. In 1911, the Commonwealth acquired from New South Wales an area of approximately 912 square miles to be used as a Federal district. An additional area of 28 square miles on Jervis bay was obtained in 1917 to be used as a naval station. This Federal district was named Canberra. Building operations began in 1923, and the Australian parliament convened there for the first time in May 1927.

Inhabitants. The estimated population of Australia in 1946 was 7,580,800. Protestants constitute the larger proportion of the inhabitants, but there is an influential Catholic minority. The Federal constitution forbids the establishment of any state-supported religion. In all parts of the Commonwealth, education is free, secular, and obligatory. Illiteracy is virtually unknown. The population is almost entirely of British origin, less than 3 per cent being of any other extraction. These figures do not include the aborigines, or "blackfellows," who are people of the Stone Age grade. They have Negroid features, but their hair is wavy, and ethnologists do not class these savages with any of the African races.

Name. The continent was formerly called New Holland. *Australia*, from the Latin word for southern, was suggested by Captain Matthew Flinders (1774–1814), an English navigator, who had explored the southern part of the island. The name came into use in 1817.

STATES OF THE COMMONWEALTH

The Commonwealth of Australia, a self-governing British dominion, was formed on January 1, 1901. It consists of six states—New South Wales, Queensland, South Australia, Tasmania, Victoria, and Western Australia; one territory—the Northern Territory; and a Federal district. The following section contains a brief description of the states and of the Northern Territory.

New South Wales, a state of southeastern Australia. The Great Dividing range extends along the east side at a distance of 20 to 100 miles inland. On the west is a magnificent pastoral country which gradually changes to arid plains farther inland. The pastoral area is the basis for Australia's great sheep industry. There are 48,000,000 sheep in this area alone. Also this state includes Australia's most important mining, farming, and industrial developments. Coal, gold, silver, lead, tin, antimony, manganese, bismuth, and copper are locally mined and iron ore is nearby and available. Farm crops are wheat, maize, barley, oats, potatoes, lucerne, tobacco, sugar cane, and grapes. Sydney, Broken Hill, Tarnworth, Bathurst, Goulburn, Wagga, and Albury are important urban centers.

Forests cover the western slopes of the mountains and include such trees as the red cedar, eucalyptus, red gum, and murray pine. Acacias and mulga are shrubs of the arid regions. Unusual animal life is found, as kangaroos, duckbills, and echidnas. Rabbits introduced from Europe have multiplied and become a serious menace to sheep grazing since they also are herbivorous.

Queensland lies in the northeast part of the continent. The climate is subtropical to tropical. Along the coast and on the windward eastern side of the Great Dividing range the rainfall is heavy. Across the mountains and inland to the "Never, Never Country" the land is arid, again supporting immense herds of cattle and sheep. Tropical crops, as sugar cane, bananas, and rice, are grown along the coastal plains. Wheat is prominent about Brisbane. Natural forests still abound including such valuable trees as cedar, kauri, pine, silky oak, and maple. Leading cities are Brisbane, Rockhampton, Towns-ville, Maryborough, Gympie, Ipswich, Toowoomba, and Charters Towers.

South Australia lies in south central Australia. The Flinders range, Spencer's Gulf, and a series of shallow, saline lakes divide it into eastern and western sections. The east is well watered and fertile; the west is desert. The Murray river flows through the southeastern corner. Temperatures are extremely high in desert sections in summer but frosts occur in the higher lands in winter. Rainfall annual average at Adelaide is 21.03 inches. Again, as in other states, ranching prevails, with sheep by far the most prominent. Adelaide is the state capital and most important city. Other cities of note are Moonta, Port Pirie, Port Augusta, and Gawler.

Victoria is a comparatively small state on the southeast corner of Australia. The section of the Great Dividing range known as the Australian Alps is in the eastern part. The coastline is 680 miles long on the south and the Murray river forms the north boundary. As in Tasmania, just across the straits, the climate is temperate with moderate temperatures and sufficient rainfall for cropping except in the northwest. Grazing is important with sheep raising first. Farming and manufacturing are rapidly developing. Temperate zone crops are being raised. Melbourne is the capital. Other important cities are Ballarat, Bendigo, and Geelong.

Western Australia comprises all of western Australia to the 129° Meridian east. It is a huge area with greatest dimensions being 1480 miles north-south and 1000 miles east-west. It is largely an arid tableland with a narrow strip of coastal lowland. The southwest corner of the state has moderate temperatures and sufficient rainfall, crops and livestock. The extreme north is tropical with abundant rainfall. Gold is the most valuable in mineral output. About Perth, the capital city, a wide variety of temperate and subtropical crops are grown, such as wheat, oranges, grapes, lemons, and olives. Other important cities are Fremantle, Midland Junction, Albany, Coolgardie, Kalgoorlie, Geraldton, Northam, Collie, and Bunbury. To the north lies the port of Broome.

The Northern Territory is the central northern state including the great Arnhemland peninsula. Its dimensions are 900 miles north-south by 560 miles east-west. The coastline is 1040 miles in length. The area is largely tableland with a low narrow tropical coastal plain in the north. This state is not especially well developed because of heat and aridity. The northern part has tropical rainfall mainly in summer. Darwin is a port.

STATISTICS OF AUSTRALIA

States and Territories	Area Sq. Mi.	Pop.*	Capital
New South Wales	309,433	2,985,464	Sydney
Victoria	87,884	2,055,252	Melbourne
South Australia	308,070	646,216	Adelaide
Queensland	670,500	1,106,269	Brisbane
Tasmania	26,215	257,117	Hobart
Western Australia	975,920	502,731	Perth
Northern Territory	523,620	10,866	
Federal District	939	16,905	

*1947 Census.

PRINCIPAL CITIES

The following section contains a brief description of the chief cities of Australia, including each of the state or territorial capitals. The population of Australia shows a marked tendency to concentrate in the cities, the five largest of which contain almost 50 per cent of the total inhabitants of the country.

Adelaide. The capital of South Australia, situated in the southern part of the state on the Torrens river, about six miles from its mouth in the Gulf of St. Vincent. A dam here forms the river into a lake a mile and a quarter long. The city stands on a wide plain near the base of the Mt. Lofty range and is divided by the Torrens into South Adelaide and North Adelaide.

The manufactures comprise iron wares, leather, woolens, pottery, starch, soap, flour, and malt liquors. Adelaide is the trade emporium of South Australia and has a large commerce. Port Adelaide, the seaport of the city, is about 7 miles distant by rail. It is the seat of considerable manufacturing; is a port of call for vessels from Europe; and is connected by railway with the principal cities of the Commonwealth. Near by is the summer resort of Glenelg.

Adelaide was founded in 1836 and was named in honor of Queen Adelaide, consort of King William IV of England. Population, 1947, 375,000.

Ballarat. A prosperous inland city of Victoria, Australia, the center of a rich gold yielding district. It was the finding of gold nuggets near the present site of Ballarat in 1851 that started the rush of gold seekers into Australia. At Bakery Hill, there was found, in 1858, a nugget that was sold for about $50,000. Population, 1947, 40,214.

Brisbane. The capital of Queensland, Australia, situated in the southeastern part of the state on the Brisbane river, about 25 miles from Moreton bay. Brisbane is the center of commerce and of manufacturing for southern Queensland.

Steamers ascend the river and berth at the wharves. There is a regular steamer communication with other ports in Australia and with the chief ports of Europe, and of the United States. Among the manufacturing establishments are flour mills, tobacco factories, breweries, tanneries, and shoe factories. Coal is mined in the vicinity.

The climate is healthful though the mean yearly temperature is 68.9° F. in the shade. Higher education is afforded by a technical college, the Brisbane grammar school, and a university, established in 1910. Population, 402,172.

Canberra (*kăn'bĕr-ȧ*). The capital of Australia. It is a Federal territory, 912 square miles in area, situated about 150 miles southwest of Sydney and 60 miles inland from the east coast of Australia. The town is built on the Molongola river and is picturesquely surrounded by mountains. It was laid out by W. Burley Griffin, of Chicago, whose plans were adjudged best in a world-wide competition. These plans call for streets in concentric circles with radiating avenues. A port on Jervis bay, 70 miles to the northeast, is reckoned as part of Canberra. Population, 1943 estimate, 15,099.

Darwin. A coast town in and the government seat of the Northern Territory, Australia.

Darwin is the terminus of the overland telegraph and of the cable to Java and Singapore. The town is also the coast terminal of a railroad which, running to Birdum, 316 miles inland, is destined to meet the railroad to be constructed north across the country from Oodnadatta. Population, 1933, 1566.

Hobart. The capital of the Australian island state of Tasmania. The city is situated on the Derwent estuary.

The manufactures include woolens, hats, flour, pottery, leather, and jam.

Most of the exports consist of fruits, hops, grain, wool, and timber. Many Australian visitors are attracted to Hobart by the cool and invigorating climate. The city is the seat of the University of Tasmania.

Hobart was founded in 1804 and was named Hobart Town in honor of Lord Hobart, then secretary of state for the colonies. In 1881 the name was changed to Hobart. Population (with suburbs), 1945, 72,155.

Melbourne. The capital of Victoria, on the Yarra Yarra river about two miles from its mouth in Hobson's bay, an arm of the Port Phillip inlet. The river is navigable by vessels drawing less than 22 feet of water, but large steamers usually anchor in the bay at Port Melbourne.

The University of Melbourne, with its imposing Wilson Hall and its four affiliated colleges—Trinity (Anglican), Queen's (Wesleyan), Ormond (Presbyterian), and Newman (Catholic),—stands in the foremost rank of higher institutions of learning. Ormond college is a remarkably fine structure.

Melbourne has large docks. Served by regular steamer communication with ports in Asia, Europe, and America, the city is a great emporium of foreign commerce. Railroads connect it with all the chief cities in Australia, and its interstate trade is enormous.

From 1901 to 1925 it served as the temporary capital of the Commonwealth. Population, 1947, 1,226,923.

Perth. The capital of Western Australia, occupying a picturesque site in the southwestern part of the state on

Melville water, an expansion of the Swan river. The city is 12 miles by rail from its port, Fremantle, a town at the mouth of the river on the Indian Ocean.

The University of Perth was founded in 1912. Population, 1947, 272,586.

Sydney. The largest and oldest city in Australia and the capital of New South Wales. Sydney is picturesquely situated on Port Jackson, a magnificent expanse of water, which forms a landlocked harbor extending 20 miles inland. The harbor is spanned by a steel arch bridge having a main span of 1650 feet, one of the longest in the world. The water in the harbor is deep enough to permit ocean-going ships to dock at the wharves and quays. Favored by this advantage, the city has become a naval station of the first rank.

Sydney has an enormous commerce. The harbor is crowded with shipping from foreign ports, and the staple Australian products are exported in immense quantities. Favored by the proximity of vast coal deposits, Sydney is also a manufacturing city. Cars, locomotives, hardware, foundry and machine shop products, clothing, boots and shoes, textiles, machinery, and malt and distilled liquors are some of the manufactures. An annual sheep show is an event of great commercial importance.

Sydney has 647 acres of parks within the city boundary and 680,000 acres of reserves and commons in the metropolitan area.

Adjoining Victoria park stands the sumptuous main edifice of the University of Sydney with the Macleay museum of natural history.

The city's mean annual temperature is about 63.1° F., which is nearly the same as the average yearly temperature of Lisbon. Sydney was founded in 1788 by Captain Arthur Phillip, who had been sent by the British government to select a site for a colony. Population, 1947, 1,484,434.

NEW ZEALAND

A British dominion consisting of two large islands to which are attached politically a number of small islands lying at some distance from the main group. The Dominion of New Zealand is situated in the south Pacific Ocean about 1200 miles east of Australia. It lies 7000 miles almost due south from Alaska and is 4000 miles west of the coast of Chile. It is 5400 miles by direct route from San Francisco. The two large islands are called North island and South island and are separated by Cook strait, which has a width varying from 16 to 90 miles. The two islands lie entirely in the South Temperate Zone and form a group stretching about 1000 miles in a general northeast and southwest direction and having a maximum width of 180 miles. The total area of the dominion, including Stewart island and the Chatham islands is 103,722 square miles.

North Island. The northern portion of the dominion has an area of 44,281 square miles. It is 515 miles long, and its greatest breadth is 180 miles. The island may be likened to an inverted shoe the toe of which is a long irregular peninsula extending to the northwest. This peninsula is attached to the rest of the island by a narrow isthmus, consisting of a neck six miles in width separating Hauraki gulf on the east from Manukau harbor on the west. The arch of the shoe is represented by the Bay of Plenty in the north. The only remaining inlet of any considerable size is Hawke bay on the east. North island has the two best ports of New Zealand, Port Nicholson in the south and Waitemata at the isthmus in the northwest.

Most of the surface is gently undulating with low, heavily forested hills. A volcanic area, beginning in the south, passes through the center of the island as far as the Bay of Plenty. Much of this region will not support grasses, but trees cover parts of it. It occupies the southern extension of the island from coast to coast, but, where the width of the island increases, a fertile area spreads out on each side and runs along each coast in a belt averaging about 40 miles in width. These tracts are well adapted for grazing. The northwestern peninsula is in large part covered with a heavy clay, which yields returns only in response to intensive cultivation. The peninsula has areas of rich alluvium, however, in which the mangrove, the orange tree, various palms, and the giant kauri pine flourish. The partially fossilized resin of this pine is excavated and exported in quantity to be used in the manufacture of varnish and of linoleum.

The volcanic area of North island contains many notable features. The highest volcano is Mount Ruapehu, which has an altitude of 9715 feet. It is situated in Tongariro national park, about 20 miles southwest of Lake Taupo, New Zealand's largest inland body of water. Stretching north from the mountain is a region of about 5000 square miles abounding in hot springs, geysers, pools of boiling mud, and colored lakelets. This region formerly contained a famous series of pink and white terraces of volcanic formation. In 1886, however, they were blown up in an eruption which tore a chasm in the earth nine miles in length. Farther south, on Cook strait, stands one of the most beautiful mountains of the island, Mount Egmont, an extinct volcano 8340 feet in height. No country has so large a proportion of its area incorporated in national parks as New Zealand. Covering over 2,500,000 acres, these reserves embrace a variety of scenery unmatched in any other park system of the world.

The rivers of the island are short. The longest is the Waikato river, which drains the waters of Lake Taupo northward to an outlet on the west coast. It is navigable for 70 miles of its course, but it shares with nearly all the other rivers of New Zealand the disadvantage of having at its mouth a bar which obstructs navigation.

South Island. The southern portion of the dominion is slightly larger than the northern, having an area of 58,092 square miles. Off its southern coast, and separated by Foveaux strait, lies Stewart island, which has an area of 670 square miles. About 350 miles to the east lie the Chatham islands, 372 square miles in area. The length of South island is 530 miles. It has a fairly uniform breadth of about 100 miles.

The outstanding feature of the surface is a mountain range called the Southern Alps, which runs from end to end near the western coast of the island. The mountains reach a maximum elevation at Mount Cook, which has an altitude of 12,349 feet. The scenic grandeur of the region is comparable to that of the European Alps. On the western slope, many glaciers flow down to the edge of the coniferous forests which cover a large part of the mountain sides. East of the divide are several long glacial lakes. The largest, Lake Wakatipu, has a depth of more than 1500 feet, and its wild, mountainous surroundings impart to it a beauty rivaling that of Lake Lucerne in Switzerland. The eastern slope descends to a plateau flanked on the east by a ridge of mountains passing through the center of the island. East of this ridge the land inclines toward the sea in grassy terraces, which provide the largest stretch of arable land in New Zealand.

Other Islands. New Zealand controls a number of islands in the south Pacific Ocean. They have a total area of about 500 square miles and a population of approximately 15,000. The more important of these islands are Cook islands, about 1500 miles northeast of North island, and Auckland islands, uninhabited, 200 miles south of the dominion. The Cook islands support about 14,000 inhabitants, mainly of Polynesian race, who export tropical fruits and coffee. New Zealand also holds a mandate over the territory of Western Samoa, a group of fertile islands 1000 miles to the north, supporting a population numbered in 1947 at 71,905. Their area is about 1130 square miles.

Climate. The prevailing winds of New Zealand blow from the west. They carry sufficient moisture to foster everywhere on the islands a vegetation of a uniform greenness that recalls the verdure of Ireland. In South island, where the mountains reach a greater height, much of the moisture is precipitated as rain on the plateau, and the warm, dry winds, descending from the elevated regions into the eastern plains, occasionally cause droughts of sufficient duration to injure the crops. Except in the mountains, the dominion is free from severe frosts, while in North island, where two-thirds of the population is concentrated, the climate is subtropical. Tempering breezes, however, blow incessantly from the ocean; yellow fever is unknown, and there are few mosquitoes or other pests usually found in subtropical regions. As a result, the mortality rate of New Zealand is one of the lowest in the world.

Flora and Fauna. The most characteristic plant of New Zealand is the fern, which flourishes in great variety everywhere. The so-called tree fern often reaches a height of 40 feet. About two-thirds of the indigenous species of vegetation are found nowhere else, and most of the others resemble those of Australia. The eucalyptus and acacia, however, which predominate in Australia, are not found in New Zealand. The nikau palm occurs even on South island, which is the southern limit for true palms. The kauri pine, the beech, and many other hardwood trees formerly covered much of the dominion's surface. Phormium, or New Zealand flax, is the dominion's outstanding contribution to the economic plants of the world. The fiber is used for binder twine and ropes. The cultivation of phormium has been introduced into Ireland, America, and several other regions of the earth. A noticeable feature of New Zealand's flora is the comparative absence of brilliant flowers.

New Zealand has not a single indigenous mammal. The dog and the rat, however, were brought by Polynesian settlers, and wild pigs, rabbits, and many other forms of animal life have been introduced by Europeans. There are no snakes, but there are a few lizards peculiar to the country. The dominion is the sole habitat of many species of birds, including the kiwi, or apteryx, a wingless and tailless bird the size of a hen. The kiwi is related to the moa, a bird which was formerly very numerous in New Zealand but which has been exterminated within the past few centuries.

Stock Raising. The bulk of New Zealand's wealth is derived from sheep and cattle. The wool clip normally amounts to more than 200 million pounds, approximately 20 to 25 per cent of that of Australia. Sheep skins to the value of 10 to 15 million dollars are exported annually. Frozen meat exports are valued at more than 50 million dollars, and 60 to 80 million dollars worth of butter and cheese is shipped. The stock is carried and fattened mainly on cultivated grasses, although in North island most of the pasturage is unplowed.

Agriculture. The greater part of the land sown to field crops is in South island. The produce, absorbed almost entirely by the domestic market, consists principally of wheat, oats, barley, and potatoes. Grain growing is not a specialized occupation, but is carried on along with stock raising. About two-thirds of New Zealand's surface is said to be capable of successful cultivation.

Mining. The four minerals produced in quantity by New Zealand are coal, gold, kauri gum, and silver. Most of the coal is mined in South island, but very little is sent out of the dominion. Gold is found in both islands, and heads the list of mineral exports. Gold mining was an attraction which drew large numbers of settlers in the decade 1861-71.

Manufacturing and Trade. The chief manufactures of New Zealand are connected with stock raising and dairying. After meat packing and the making of dairy products, the most important industries are lumber mill operations, printing, and the manufacture of flour, textiles, leather, and metal products. Industrial disputes in the dominion are settled by compulsory arbitration.

Most of the trade is with Great Britain. The United States, Canada, and Australia rank next in order. The exports normally amount to over 300 million dollars in value, most of which is represented by the products of New Zealand's characteristic industry, the raising of sheep and other live stock. The imports usually approximate the same value as the exports, the chief articles being iron and steel products, textiles, motor cars, oils, clothing, paper, and tobacco products.

Internal Communications. New Zealand has about 3450 miles of railroads, practically the entire mileage being owned and operated by the government. The greater part of the mileage is on South island. The telephone and the telegraph system are also under government ownership.

Inhabitants. The aborigines of New Zealand are called Maoris, a Polynesian people which is believed to have displaced an earlier race some six centuries ago. In their uncivilized state, they were polygamous, and occasionally indulged in cannibal feasts. Among them, it was supposed that the seat of the soul was the left eye. In warlike arts, wood carving, dyeing, and tattooing, they had developed a considerable skill. After a desperate resistance to the British settlers, they accepted the religion and the manner of life of the newcomers. In 1945, the Maoris in the dominion numbered 98,744.

The population of New Zealand in 1945 was 1,790,256, nearly all of whom were of British descent. A little less than two-thirds of the population resides in North island, the rest living in South island and the dependencies. The capital is Wellington and the largest city is Auckland, both of which are in North island.

The dominion has an excellent educational system, at the head of which stands the University of New Zealand with four affiliated colleges. The university is not a teaching body. It has the power of granting degrees and is charged with conducting the examination of students prepared by the colleges. Over one-third the population are members or adherents of the English Church. The Catholics number about 11 per cent of the total.

New Zealand is divided into nine provincial districts, of which four are in North island, five are entirely in South island, and one is partly in South island and partly in other islands. Those in North island are Auckland, Wellington, Hawke's Bay, and Taranaki. Within South island are the provincial districts of Canterbury, Nelson, Westland, Marlborough, and the greater part of Otago. Otago includes also Stewart and other outlying islands.

PRINCIPAL CITIES

Auckland. The largest city of New Zealand, beautifully situated on a cluster of extinct volcanoes at the neck of the northwestern peninsula of North island. The isthmus is six miles in width, thus providing the city with two natural harbors, one on each side of the isthmus. The eastern harbor is protected by a volcanic cone rising to a height of 1000 feet. This harbor has been elaborately improved and is the point of export for kauri gum and a large part of the lumber shipped abroad. The chief industries include shipbuilding, sugar refining, and the manufacture of rope and of machine shop products.

Auckland is the seat of Auckland University College and has an art gallery, a library with a valuable collection of rare manuscripts, and a museum containing many Maori relics. The mountain sides in the vicinity are terraced by former Maori fortifications. The Domain, one of the four parks of the city, contains a fine botanical garden. Auckland was until 1865 the capital of New Zealand. Population, 1947 estimate, 281,900.

Christchurch. The capital of the provincial district of Canterbury and the third largest city of New Zealand, situated near the center of the eastern coast of South island on the Avon river seven miles from its mouth. The city lies on a fertile plain and is the center of the surrounding agricultural and grazing interests. Frozen meats, wool, and lumber are exported. The chief manufactures include agricultural machinery, leather goods, furniture, and clothing.

Christchurch was founded by the "Canterbury pilgrims," a group of churchmen who left England about 1849. Many of the streets are named after English dioceses. Canterbury college is the leading educational institution. The Anglican cathedral with its dominating spire is the finest piece of church architecture in New Zealand. A museum contains numerous remains of the moa, an extinct wingless bird which is peculiar to New Zealand. Population, 1947 estimate, 159,400.

Dunedin. The capital of the provincial district of Otago, situated on Otago harbor, an inlet on the south-eastern coast of South island. The chief exports are wool, frozen meat, and gold. Dunedin is the seat of Otago college, the largest institution for higher education in New Zealand.

Dunedin is connected by rail with Christchurch to the north and with Invercargill to the south. The population in 1947 was estimated at 87,700.

Invercargill (*ĭn'vẽr-kär'gĭl*). A port and city at the southern extremity of South island. Invercargill is the regular starting point for journeys to Lake Wakatipu and other glacial lakes of the Southern Alps. It has several woolen and lumber mills. Population, 1947 est., 29,300.

Wanganui (*wŏ'ngȧ-nōō-ē*). The principal port on the west coast of North island, lying about 120 miles north of Wellington. It is regularly laid out at the foot of low hills, from the summit of which may be seen the snow-clad volcano of Mount Ruapehu. Wanganui is the export center for a pastoral and agricultural region. Population, 1947 estimate, 27,600.

Wellington. The capital and second largest city of New Zealand, situated at the geographical center of the Dominion, on a mountainous site at the southern end of North island. It fronts on Lambton harbor, the most commodious in New Zealand. The port is equipped with modern facilities for handling the city's extensive commerce, which includes a large export trade in wool, meat, hides, skins, butter, cheese, and hemp. Wellington's manufactures embrace chiefly packed meats, woolen goods, soap, matches, rope, and brick. Printing and the assembling of motor vehicles are other important industries.

The government and principal office buildings are substantial, modern structures. The city has a university, two museums, an art gallery, and a Dominion research laboratory. Besides 1613 acres of parks and reserves in the city, Wellington owns a 970-acre belt of grazing land, accessible to the public, and Williams park, a seaside resort on Days bay. The 30-mile drive around the Wellington waterfront is one of the finest scenic routes in Oceania. Population, 1947 estimate, 183,100.

GREAT CITIES OF THE WORLD

City	Country	Population
Ahmedabad	India	591,267
Alexandria	Egypt	928,237
Amsterdam	Netherlands	798,358
Athens	Greece	1,000,000
Baku	USSR	809,347
Baltimore	U. S.	859,100
Bangkok	Siam	827,290
Barcelona	Spain	1,117,000
Berlin	Germany	3,170,000
Birmingham	England	1,090,150
Bombay	Union of India	1,489,883
Boston	U. S.	770,816
Brussels	Belgium	800,000
Bucharest	Rumania	984,619
Budapest	Hungary	1,026,883
Buenos Aires	Argentina	3,000,371
Buffalo	U. S.	575,901
Cairo	Egypt	2,100,486
Calcutta	Union of India	2,108,891
Canton	China	1,276,843
Changsha	China	606,972
Chicago	U. S.	3,396,808
Chungking	China	1,062,000
Cleveland	U. S.	878,336
Copenhagen	Denmark	927,404
Dairen	China	600,000
Detroit	U. S.	1,623,452
Dublin	Eire	506,635
Essen	Germany	520,656
Genoa	Italy	664,143
Glasgow	Scotland	1,075,700
Gorky	USSR	644,116
Hague, The	Netherlands	523,703
Hamburg	Germany	1,384,106
Hangchow	China	506,930
Hankow	China	777,993
Harbin	Manchuria	638,000
Havana	Cuba	673,376
Hyderabad	India	739,481
Istanbul	Turkey	845,316
Kharkow	USSR	833,432
Kiev	USSR	846,293
Kobe	Japan	1,006,100
Kyoto	Japan	1,089,726
Lahore	Pakistan	671,659
Leningrad	USSR	3,191,304
Lima	Peru	522,826
Lisbon	Portugal	709,179
Liverpool	England	751,820
London (Greater)	England	8,244,370
Los Angeles	U. S.	1,504,277
Madras	Union of India	777,481
Madrid	Spain	1,156,000
Manchester	England	684,640
Manila	Philippines	623,362
Marseille	France	636,264
Melbourne	Australia	1,226,923
Mexico City	Mexico	1,749,916
Milan	Italy	1,250,389
Milwaukee	U. S.	587,472
Montevideo	Uruguay	770,000
Montreal	Canada	903,007
Moscow	USSR	4,137,018
Mukden	Manchuria	863,515
Munich	Germany	760,929
Nagoya	Japan	1,328,084
Nanking	China	1,037,655
Naples	Italy	941,841
New York*	U. S.	7,454,995
Odessa	USSR	604,223
Osaka	Japan	3,252,340
Paris	France	2,725,374
Peiping	China	1,602,234
Philadelphia	U. S.	1,931,334
Pittsburgh	U. S.	671,659
Prague	Czechoslovakia	923,946
Rio de Janeiro	Brazil	1,563,787
Rome	Italy	1,471,971
Rosario	Argentina	522,403
Rostov-on-Don	USSR	510,258
Rotterdam	Netherlands	637,165
Saint Louis	U. S.	816,048
San Francisco	U. S.	634,536
Santiago	Chile	1,068,114
Sao Paulo	Brazil	1,269,319
Seoul	Korea	935,464
Shanghai	China	3,853,511
Sheffield	England	508,850
Singapore	British Malaya	769,216
Stockholm	Sweden	700,000
Sydney	Australia	1,484,434
Tashkent	USSR	585,005
Tehran	Iran (Persia)	699,110
Tientsin	China	1,679,210
Tiflis	USSR	519,175
Tokyo	Japan	6,778,804
Toronto	Canada	667,457
Tsingtao	China	514,769
Turin	Italy	712,833
Valencia	Spain	544,039
Vienna	Austria	1,406,509
Washington	U. S.	663,091
Wenchow	China	631,276
Yokahama	Japan	968,091

*1947 estimate of Greater New York about 11,000,000

ANTARCTICA

The continent occupying the greater part of the South Frigid Zone. Its area is about equal to that of Australia. The continent lies 500 miles south of the southern tip of South America. Its distance from Australia is 2000 miles; from New Zealand, 1600 miles; and from South Africa, 2300 miles. The chief interest in the continent has been due to the fact that the south pole is situated near the center of this land mass.

The surface of Antarctica is high and mountainous. The south pole is in a plateau, about 10,000 feet high, around which rise a number of peaks exceeding 15,000 feet in altitude. Nearly all the surface is covered by a sheet of ice, 2000 feet thick in places and split here and there by great chasms. On the side nearest New Zealand, the so-called Great Ice Barrier extends along the coast for about 400 miles. This ice wall rises abruptly from the ocean to a height of from 100 to 400 feet. In winter, the whole continent is surrounded by a wide belt of frozen ocean. During the summer, this breaks up into floating pack ice, which often extends for hundreds of miles from land.

Antarctica is uninhabited. The flora is confined to lichens and mosses which, in the brief summer, may be found attached to the few bits of exposed rock and soil. Penguins, petrels, seals, and sea lions are the principal forms of animal life existing on the continent.

All expeditions in search of the south pole have landed on the side nearest New Zealand, because, on that side, the Ross Sea extends as a deep gulf into the land, thereby considerably shortening the overland distance to the pole. Near this sea is the volcanic Mount Erebus. The land west of Ross Sea is called South Victoria land, and that to the east of the sea is King Edward VII land. A lofty range of mountains rising from the sea on the side nearest South America has been named the Antarctic Andes. Gales of great violence sweep northward over the continent almost continuously from the region of the south pole. Temperatures lower than 70° below zero have been recorded by explorers.

Discovery. The more recent voyages undertaken for discovery and research in Antarctica were a Japanese expedition under Shirase, which set out in 1910; the expedition of Amundsen, which reached the south pole on December 14, 1911; that of Captain Scott, who arrived at the pole on January 18, 1912; an Australian expedition under Mawson, which, in the years 1911-14, collected much valuable information regarding the climatic conditions and the surface of the continent; Shackleton's two parties which set out in 1914 in the *Endurance* and the *Aurora*; and Byrd's famous expedition which set out in 1928 with elaborate equipment for surveying the south polar region.

SEAS AND OTHER BODIES OF SALT WATER

Name	Location	Area Sq. Miles
Adriatic Sea	Southern Europe	60,000
Ægean Sea	Southeastern Europe	70,000
Albemarle Sound	North Carolina	495
Baffin Bay	Canada-Greenland	200,000
Baltic Sea	Northwestern Europe	160,000
Bass Strait	Australia-Tasmania	32,000
Bay of Biscay	France-Spain	160,000
Bay of Fundy	New Brunswick-Nova Scotia	6,300
Bering Sea	Alaska-Siberia	878,000
Black Sea	Southeastern Europe	165,000
Buzzards Bay	Massachusetts	235
Caribbean Sea	Central America-South America-West Indies	750,000
Chesapeake Bay	Maryland-Virginia	6,000
China Sea, East	China-Japan	480,000
Delaware Bay	Delaware-New Jersey	1,000
English Channel	England-France	30,000
Gulf of Aden	Arabia-Somaliland	85,000
Gulf of Bothnia	Sweden-Finland	43,000
Gulf of California	Northwestern Mexico	64,000

SEAS AND OTHER BODIES OF SALT WATER—Con.

Name	Location	Area Sq. Miles
Gulf of Carpentaria	Northern Australia	120,000
Gulf of Finland	Finland-Estonia, Europe	15,000
Gulf of Mexico	United States-Mexico-Cuba	700,000
Gulf of Riga	Estonia-Latvia, Europe	7,000
Gulf of St. Lawrence	Canada-Newfoundland	75,000
Gulf of Siam	French Indo-China-Malay Peninsula	100,000
Gulf of Tonkin	China-French Indo-China	45,000
Hudson Bay	Northeastern Canada	470,000
Irish Sea	Ireland-Great Britain	75,000
Japan Sea	Japan-Korea	400,000
Long Island Sound	Connecticut-Long Island	1,500
Mediterranean Sea	Europe-Asia-Africa	1,145,000
Mozambique Chan.	Mozambique-Madagascar	430,000
Narragansett Bay	Rhode Island	140
North Sea	Great Britain-Continental Europe	220,000
Okhotsk Sea	Eastern Siberia	580,000
Persian Gulf	Iran-Arabia	89,000
Puget Sound	Washington	2,000
Red Sea	S. W. Asia-N. E. Africa	177,000
St. George's Channel	Ireland-Wales	8,000
San Francisco Bay	California	350
Sea of Marmora	European Turkey-Asiatic Turkey	4,500
Skagerrak	Denmark-Norway	12,000
Strait of Magellan	Chile-Tierra del Fuego	2,000
White Sea	Northeastern Russia	45,000
Yellow Sea	China-Chosen-Southern Japan	240,000

NOTED WATERFALLS

Name	Location	Height (feet)
Angel	Venezuela	3,300
Bridal Veil	Yosemite, Cal.	620
Gastein	Austria	480
Gavarnie	Pyrenees	1,385
Grand Falls	Labrador	316
Great Falls	Montana	526
Great Falls	Potomac River	35
Great Umgeni	Natal	364
Harsprang	Sweden	110
Iguassu	Argentina	215
Illilouette	Yosemite, Cal.	370
Juanacatlan	Mexico	70
Kaieteur Fall	British Guiana	741
Kar Kloof	Natal	350
Krimmler	Austria	1,300
Kukenaam	Guiana	2,100
Minnehaha	Minnesota	60
Montmorency	Quebec	265
Multnomah	Oregon	607
Nevada Falls	California	594
Niagara Falls	New York	167
Portage Falls	Portageville, N. Y.	110
Rhine Falls	Schaffhausen	710
Ribbon Falls	Yosemite, Cal.	1,612
Roraima	Guiana	2,000
Ruikanfos	Norway	805
St. Anthony	Minnesota	50
Seculéjo	Pyrenees Mts.	820
Sellesche	Switzerland	128
Seneca Falls	New York	50
Shoshone	Idaho	210
Skykjefos	Norway	660
Snoqualmie	Washington	267
Staubbach	Switzerland	870
Sutherland	New Zealand	1,904
Takakkow	British Columbia	1,400
Taughannock	New York	215
Tequendama	Colombia, S. Am.	475
Terni	Italy	650
Trollhattan	Sweden	108
Twin Falls	British Columbia	400
Vernal Fall	California	320
Victoria	Africa	343
Voringsfos	Norway	520
Widow's Tears	Yosemite, Cal.	1,170
Yellowstone (2 falls)	Wyoming	420
Upper	Wyoming	110
Lower	Wyoming	310
Yosemite (3 falls)	California	2,370
Upper	California	1,430
Middle	California	620
Lower	California	320

NOTED MOUNTAINS AND VOLCANOES

The following list is a selection representative of important mountains. It contains one or more of the higher peaks in various regions of the world, includes some of the greatest volcanic mountains, and embraces also a number of the most active volcanoes. All volcanic mountains, including extinct, quiescent, and active volcanoes, are in italics; some of the more active volcanoes are indicated by an asterisk thus, _Stromboli_*.

Name of Mountain or Peak	Location	Height Feet
Aconcagua	Chile-Argentina	22,834
Adams	Washington	12,307
Altar	Ecuador	17,730
Antisana	Ecuador	19,260
Apo	Philippine Is.	9,610
Ararat	Turkey	17,212
Arequipa (Misti)	Peru	20,013
_Asama_*	Japan	8,280
_Aso-San_*	Japan	5,545
Baker	Washington	10,837
_Bandai-San_*	Japan	6,035
Ben Nevis	Scotland	4,406
Blackburn	Alaska	16,140
Borah Peak	Idaho	12,078
Bruce	Australia	4,024
Cayambi	Ecuador	19,186
Cenis, Mt.	France	11,755
Chimborazo	Ecuador	20,498
Chinati Peak	Texas	7,730
Clingmans Dome	Tennessee	6,644
_Colima_*	Mexico	13,000
Cook	New Zealand	12,349
Coseguina	Nicaragua	3,830
_Cotopaxi_*	Ecuador	19,613
Cradle	Australia	5,069
Crillon	Alaska	15,900
Demavend	Iran	18,500
Dhawalaghiri	Nepal, Asia	26,826
Elbert	Colorado	14,420
Elbruz	Russia	18,465
Elgon	Uganda, Africa	14,140
_Erebus_*	Antarctica	12,370
_Etna_*	Sicily	10,758
Everest	Nepal, Asia	29,141
Fairweather	British Columbia, Can.	15,287
_Fuego_*	Guatemala	12,579
Galdhöppigen	Norway	8,399
Gannett Peak	Wyoming	13,785
Godwin-Austen	Kashmir, India	28,250
Haleakala	Hawaii	10,032
_Hecla_*	Iceland	5,110
Hermon	Palestine	9,050
Holy Cross	Colorado	14,170
Hood	Oregon	11,225
Huascaran	Peru	22,051
Huzi (Fuji)	Japan	12,395
Illimani	Bolivia	21,192
_Izalco_*	Salvador	6,000
Iztaccihuatl	Mexico	16,960
Jorullo	Mexico	4,265
Jungfrau	Switzerland	13,670
Kanchanjanga	Sikkim-Nepal, Asia	28,156
Katahdin	Maine	5,273
_Katmai_*	Alaska	7,500
Kenia	East Africa	17,191
Kibo Peak (Kilimanjaro)	East Africa	19,710
_Kilauea_*	Hawaii	4,000
Kings Peak	Utah	13,498
Korintje	Sumatra	12,480
Kosciusko	Australia	7,323
_Lassen_*	California	10,453
Lebanon	Syria	10,050
Llullaillaco	Chile	20,598
Logan, Mt.	Yukon, Canada	19,850
Loma Tina	Haiti	10,300
Long's Peak	Colorado	14,271
McKinley	Alaska	20,300
Maipu	Chile-Argentina	17,576
Marcy	New York	5,344
Matterhorn	Switzerland	14,782
Mauna Kea	Hawaii	13,823
_Mauna Loa_*	Hawaii	13,675
Mercedario	Argentina	22,300
Miltsin	Morocco	11,400
Mitchell	North Carolina	6,684
Mont Blanc	France	15,781
Monte Rosa	Italy	15,217
Morrison	Formosa, Japan	14,300
Mount of Olives	Palestine	2,723
North Truchas Peak	New Mexico	13,306
Olympus	Greece	9,794
Orizaba	Mexico	18,564
Parnassus	Greece	8,070
Peaks of Otter	Virginia	4,001
_Pelée_*	Martinique, W. I.	4,300
Perdu, Mont.	France	10,994
Perote, Cofre de	Mexico	13,419
Pico, Peak of	Azores	7,613
Pikes Peak	Colorado	14,108
Popocatepetl	Mexico	17,876
Rainier	Washington	14,408
Robson	British Columbia, Can.	12,972
Rogers	Virginia	5,719
Roraima	Venezuela	8,740
Ruapehu	New Zealand	9,715
Ruwenzori	Uganda, Africa	16,800
Sahama	Bolivia	21,047
Saint Bernard	Switzerland	8,110
Saint Elias	Alaska	18,024
Saint Gotthard	Switzerland	10,490
Saint Helens	Washington	9,697
San Francisco	Arizona	12,611
_Sangai_*	Ecuador	17,464
San José	Chile	20,020
_San Miguel_*	Salvador	7,120
Santa Fé (Baldy Peak)	New Mexico	12,623
Shasta	California	14,380
Simplon	Switzerland	11,117
Sinai, Mt.	Arabia	8,593
Sir Sandford	British Columbia, Can.	11,590
Skaptar Jokull (Laki)	Iceland	2,790
Snehaetta	Norway	7,615
Snowdon	Wales	3,560
Sorata	Bolivia	21,500
_Soufrière, La_*	St. Vincent, W. I.	3,700
Spruce Knob	West Virginia	4,860
_Stromboli_*	Lipari Is. N. of Sicily	3,040
Tahiti, Peak of	Friendly Is.	7,349
Teneriffe	Canary Is.	12,190
Terror	Antarctica	10,900
Tolima	Colombia	18,325
Toluca	Mexico	14,950
_Tunguragua_*	Ecuador	16,690
Tupungato	Chile	22,329
Vancouver	Alaska	15,666
_Vesuvius_*	Italy	4,260
Washington	New Hampshire	6,288
Wheeler Peak	Nevada	13,058
Whitney	California	14,496
Wrangell	Alaska	17,500

IMPORTANT MOUNTAIN PASSES

Pass	Location	Altitude (feet)
Alpine	Colorado	13,550
Argentine	Colorado	13,286
Athabaska	Alberta	6,025
Bolan	Baluchistan	5,880
Brenner	Austrian Alps	4,588
Cajon	California	3,820
Chilkat	Yukon	4,950
Chilkoot	Alaska	3,500
Cottonwood	Colorado	13,500
Crowsnest	Alberta	4,830
Fremont	Colorado	11,313
Glorieta	New Mexico	7,421
Kearsage	Sierra Nevada	12,000
Khyber	Afghanistan	3,373
Kicking Horse	Alberta	5,332
Kootenay (North)	Alberta	6,774
Kootenay (South)	Alberta	7,100
Marshall	Colorado	10,841
Raton	New Mexico	7,608
Rogers	British Columbia	4,340
St. Bernard, Great	Swiss Alps	8,100
St. Gotthard	Swiss Alps	6,936
San Gorgonio	California	2,559
Shipka	Bulgaria	4,300
Simplon	Swiss Alps	6,595
Simpson	Alberta	6,650
Siskiyou	Oregon	4,125
Tehachapi	California	3,963
Tennessee	Colorado	10,418
Truckee	California	5,818
Uspallata (Cumbre)	Chile	12,870
Vermilion	Alberta	5,264
White Pass	Alaska	2,600
Yellowhead (Tete Jaune)	Alberta	3,738

PRINCIPAL ISLANDS OF THE WORLD

Name	Location	Dependency, Territory, or part of	Discovery, Conquest, or Settlement: By Whom †	Date	Area Sq. Mi.	Population	Chief City or Town
Aleutian	Bering S.-Pac. O.	Alaska	Russians	1741	6,821	1,298	Unalaska
Azores	Atl. O. W. of Port.	Portugal	Cabral, *P*.	1432	888	286,885	Ponta Delgada
Baffin	Arctic O.	Canada	Baffin, *E*.	1616	201,600	2,052	
Bahama	Atl. O. E. of Fla.	Great Britain	Columbus, *S*.	1492	4,375	71,850	Nassau
Balearic	Mediterranean S.	Spain	Romans.	123‡	1,936	410,000	Palma
Barbados	West Indies	Great Britain	British	1625	166	212,366	Bridgetown
Bermuda	Atl. O. N. of W. Ind.	Great Britain	Bermudez, *S*.	1515	19	34,965	Hamilton
Borneo	East Indies	Gr. Brit. and Neth.	De Gomez, *P*.	1518	289,860	3,000,000	Banjermasin
Bornholm	Baltic Sea	Denmark	Norse.	B.C.?	217	46,542	Rönne
Canary Is.	Atl. O. W. of Afr.	Spain	French	1334	2,894	776,027	Las Palmas
Cape Breton	Atl. O.-G. of St. Lawr.	Nova Scotia	Cabot, *E*.	1497	3,975	150,157	Sydney
Cape Verde	Atl. O. W. of Afr.	Portugal	Cadamosta, *P*.	1456	1,539	181,286	São Vicente
Celebes	East Indies	Netherlands	Portuguese	1512	72,986	4,231,906	Macassar
Ceylon	Ind. O. S. of India	Great Britain	Portuguese	1505	25,332	6,658,999	Colombo
Corsica	Mediterranean S.	France	Phocaeans.	560‡	3,367	322,854	Bastia
Cuba	West Indies	Cuba*	Columbus, *S*.	1492	44,206	4,778,583	Havana
Cyprus	Mediterranean S.	Great Britain	Egyptians	1500‡	3,572	450,114	Nicosia
Elba	Mediterranean S.	Italy	Romans.	B.C.	86	29,851	Porto Ferrajo
Falkland Is.	Atlantic O.	Great Britain	Davis, *E*.	1592	4,618	2,361	Stanley
Faroe	N. Atlantic O.	Denmark	Norwegians	9th c.	540	29,198	Thorshavn
Fernando Po	G. of Guinea, Afr.	Spain	Portuguese	1486	810	20,873	Santa Isabel
Fiji	S. Pacific Ocean	Great Britain	Tasman, *D*.	1643	7,083	259,638	Suva
Formosa	China Sea	China	Portuguese	1590	13,890	5,872,084	Taihoku
Gottland	Baltic Sea	Sweden	Swedes	9th c.	1,220	58,444	Visby
Great Britain	Atl. O.-North Sea.	Great Britain	Romans.	55‡	94,504	48,017,000	London
Greenland	Arctic O.	Denmark	Norwegians	982	840,000	21,384	Sydproven
Guadeloupe	West Indies	France	Columbus, *S*.	1493	688	271,262	Pointe-à-Pitre
Guam	East Indies	United States	Magellan, *P*.	1521	206	24,139	Agana
Haiti	West Indies	Haiti*-S. Domingo*	Columbus, *S*.	1492	29,536	5,651,000	Port au Prince
Hawaiian Is.	Pacific Ocean	United States	Jas. Cook, *E*.	1778	6,435	525,477	Honolulu
Hebrides	Atl. O.-The Minch	Great Britain	Norw. vikings	6th c.	2,812	205,000	Rothesay
Iceland	No. Atlantic O.	Republic—1944*	Norwegians	870	39,709	132,000	Reykjavik
Ireland	Irish S.-Atl. O.	Great Britain	Ancient Celts	B.C.	31,839	4,290,452	Dublin
Isle of Man	Irish Sea	Great Britain	Ancient Celts	B.C.	221	49,338	Douglas
Isle of Wight	English Channel	Great Britain	Romans.	43	147	88,454	Newport
Jamaica	West Indies	Great Britain	Columbus, *S*.	1494	4,450	1,237,063	Kingston
Japan	S. of Japan-Pac. O.	Japan*	Portuguese	1542	147,425	73,110,995	Tokyo
Java	East Indies	Netherlands	Portuguese	1511	51,033	48,416,000	Batavia
Kodiak	Gulf of Alaska	Alaska	Russians	1783	36,000	2,094	Kodiak
Long Island	Long Is. So.-Atl. O.	New York	Hudson, *E*.	1609	1,682	4,103,638	Brooklyn
Madagascar	Ind. O. E. of Afr.	France	Portuguese	1506	241,884	4,189,090	Tananarive
Madeira	Atl. O. W. of Afr.	Portugal	Portuguese	1419	314	250,124	Funchal
Madura	East Indies	Netherlands	Dutch	1747	2,113	1,962,462	Bankalan
Malta	Mediterranean S.	Great Britain	Phœnicians	1000‡	122	279,187	Valletta
Manhattan	Hudson R.-East R.	United States.	Verrazano, *I*.	1524	22	1,904,000	New York§
Marshalls	N. Pacific	U. S. Trustee	British	1788	160	10,434	Jabur
Marthas Vineyard	Vineyard So.-Atlantic O.	Massachusetts	Gosnold, *E*.	1602	100	4,953	Tisbury
Martinique	West Indies	France	Spanish	1493	385	261,595	Fort de France
Mauritius	Ind. O. E. of Afr.	Great Britain	Portuguese	1505	720	428,273	Port Louis
Nantucket	Atlantic O.	Massachusetts	Gosnold, *E*.	1602	51	3,401	Nantucket
New Caledonia	Oceania	France	Jas. Cook, *E*.	1774	8,548	61,250	Noumea
Newfoundland	Atlantic O.	Great Britain	Cabot, *E*.	1497	42,734	320,101	St. John's
New Guinea	East Indies	Neth.-Australia	Portuguese	1526	308,486	1,300,000	Madang
New Zealand	Tasman S.-S. Pac.O.	Great Britain	Tasman, *D*.	1642	103,722	1,702,298	Auckland
Novaya Zemlya	Barents S.-Kava S.	Russia	English	1556	35,000	100	
Orkney	Atlantic Ocean	Scotland	Ancient Picts	B.C.?	376	21,700	Kirkwall
Philippines	East Indies	Republic—1946*	Magellan, *P*.	1521	115,600	18,500,000	Manila
Prince Edward	G. of St. Lawrence	Canada	Cabot, *E*.	1497	2,184	95,047	Charlottetown
Puerto Rico	West Indies	United States	Columbus, *S*.	1493	3,435	1,869,255	San Juan
Queen Charlotte	Hecate St.-Pac. O.	Brit. Columbia	Jas. Cook, *E*.	1778	3,780	2,335	
Réunion	Ind. O. E. of Afr.	France	Portuguese	1513	970	220,955	St. Denis
Saint Helena	S. Atl. O. W. of Afr.	Great Britain	Portuguese	1502	47	4,992	Jamestown
Sakhalin	Okhotsk S.	Russia	Dutch	1650	24,560	439,357	Alexandrovsk
Samoa, Amer.	S. Pacific Ocean	United States	Roggoveen, *D*.	1722	76	16,493	Pagopago
Santa Catalina	G. of St. Catalina.	California	Cabrillo, *P*.	1542	85	1,986	Avalon
Sardinia	Mediterranean S.	Italy	Carthaginians	500‡	9,298	1,034,206	Cagliara
Shetland	Atl. O.-North Sea.	Scotland	Ancient Picts	B.C.?	550	20,200	Lerwick
Sicily	Mediterranean S.	Italy	Phœnicians	1000‡	9,925	4,356,000	Palermo
Spitsbergen	Arctic Ocean	Norway	Barents, *D*.	1596	24,294	2,226	Longyearbyen
Staten	New York Bay	United States.	Verrazano, *I*.	1524	57	174,441	New York§
Sumatra	East Indies	Netherlands	Portuguese	1508	167,480	7,841,175	Medan
Tasmania	Bass St.-Ant. O.	Australia	Tasman, *D*.	1642	26,215	257,117	Hobart
Tierra del Fuego	St. of Magellan-Antarctic O.	Chile-Argentina	Magellan, *P*.	1520	28,000	2,592	Ushuaia
Tobago	West Indies	Great Britain	Columbus, *S*.	1498	114	27,679	Scarborough
Trinidad	West Indies	Great Britain	Columbus, *S*.	1498	1,862	540,940	Port of Spain
Unalaska	Bering S.-Pac. O.	Alaska	Russians	1741	800	226	Unalaska
Vancouver	St.of Georgia-Pac.O.	Brit. Columbia	Vancouver, *E*.	1792	12,408	147,262	Victoria
Victoria	Arctic O.	Canada			80,340	41,878	
Virgin Is.	West Indies	United States	Columbus, *S*.	1493	132	24,889	Charlotte Amalie
Zanzibar	Ind. O. E. of Afr.	Great Britain	Egyptians	B.C.	640	150,000	Zanzibar

* Independent state. † Capital letters in italics, following names, indicate nationality of the discovery, thus *D.* signifies Dutch; *E.*, English; *I.*, Italian; *P.*, Portuguese; *S.*, Spanish. ‡ Before Christ. § Island forms part of New York City.

IMPORTANT RIVERS OF THE WORLD

Name	Location	Length Miles	Drainage Basin Sq. Miles	Outlet	Largest City or Town on Banks
Amazon	South America	3,400	2,500,000	Atlantic Ocean	Pará
Amur	Northeastern Asia	2,700	780,000	Sakhalin Gulf	Blagovieschtchensk
Arkansas	United States	2,000	189,000	Mississippi R.	Tulsa
Assiniboine	Manitoba-Saskatchewan	450	52,600	Red R. of North	Winnipeg
Athabaska	Alberta	765	58,910	Lake Athabasca	Athabaska
Brahmaputra	India-Pakistan	1,800	425,000	Bay of Bengal	Dibrughur
Clyde	Scotland	100	1,480	Irish Sea	Glasgow
Colorado	United States-Mexico	2,000	250,000	G. of Cal.	Yuma
Columbia	Canada-United States	1,400	298,000	Pacific Ocean	Vancouver, Wash.
Congo	W. Equat. Africa	3,000	1,500,000	Atlantic Ocean	Leopoldville
Connecticut	New England	350	11,000	Long Is. Sound	Hartford
Cumberland	S. E. United States	688	18,000	Ohio River	Nashville
Danube	Southeastern Europe	1,750	300,000	Black Sea	Vienna
Darling	Australia	1,160	200,000	Murray River	Bourke
Delaware	E. United States	360	12,012	Delaware Bay	Philadelphia
Dnieper	S. European Russia	1,400	202,000	Black Sea	Kiev
Don	S. E. European Russia	1,300	166,000	Sea of Azov	Rostov
Douro	Spain-Portugal	500	37,500	Atlantic Ocean	Porto
Dvina	Latvia-Russia	1,000	140,000	White Sea	Archangel
Ebro	Spain	470	30,000	Mediterranean Sea	Saragossa
Elbe	Germany	700	55,000	North Sea	Hamburg
Euphrates	Iraq, W. Asia	1,700	260,000	Persian Gulf	Basra
Fraser	British Columbia	750	91,700	Strait of Georgia	New Westminster
Ganges	India	1,500	400,000	Bay of Bengal	Cawnpore
Hudson	New York	300	13,000	New York Bay	New York
Hwang	China	2,600	400,000	Gulf of Pechili	Lanchow
Indus	Pakistan	1,800	372,000	Arabian Sea	Hyderabad
Irrawaddy	Burma	1,250	158,000	Bay of Bengal	Mandalay
Jordan	Palestine, S. W. Asia	200	1,500	Dead Sea	
Kuskokwim	Alaska	700	50,000	Bering Sea	Bethel
Lena	Siberia	2,800	900,000	Arctic Ocean	Yakutsk
Loire	France	650	45,000	Bay of Biscay	Nantes
Mackenzie	N. W. Terr., Canada	2,525	680,000	Arctic Ocean	Ft. Providence
Marne	France	325	4,894	Seine	Chalôns-sur-Marne
Mekong	Indo-China	2,600	280,000	South China Sea	Pnompenh
Meuse	Belgium-France	575	12,740	North Sea	Liège
Mississippi	United States	2,500	725,000	Gulf of Mexico	Saint Louis
Missouri	United States	3,000	525,000	Mississippi R.	Kansas City
Missouri-Mississippi*	United States-Canada	4,200	1,250,000	Gulf of Mexico	Saint Louis
Murray	Australia	1,450	270,000	Indian Ocean	Albury
Nelson*	Canada	1,660	370,000	Hudson Bay	Port Nelson
Niger	Western Africa	2,600	600,000	Gulf of Guinea	Bamako
Nile	Cent. and N. E. Africa	4,000	1,100,000	Mediterranean Sea	Cairo
Ob	N. W. Siberia	2,500	1,125,200	Gulf of Ob	Barnaul
Oder	Germany-Poland	560	43,000	Baltic Sea	Breslau
Ohio	Eastern United States	975	214,000	Mississippi R.	Pittsburgh
Orange	Southwestern Africa	1,300	400,000	Atlantic Ocean	Hopetown
Orinoco	South America	1,500	368,000	Atlantic Ocean	Ciudad Bolivar
Ottawa	Ontario-Quebec	685	86,000	St. Lawrence R.	Ottawa
Peace	British Columbia-Alberta	1,065	117,000	Slave River	Peace River
Plata-Parana*	South America	2,500	1,200,000	Atlantic Ocean	Rosario
Po	Italy	420	27,000	Adriatic Sea	Turin
Potomac	Eastern United States	450	15,000	Chesapeake Bay	Washington
Red	Texas-Arkansas	1,200	90,000	Mississippi R.	Shreveport
Red River of the North	United States-Canada	545	63,400	Lake Winnipeg	Winnipeg
Rhine	N. W. Europe	800	75,000	North Sea	Cologne
Rhone	France	500	38,000	Mediterranean Sea	Lyon
Rio Grande	S. W. United States	2,000	240,000	Gulf of Mexico	El Paso
Sacramento	California	400	27,100	Suisun Bay	Sacramento
Saguenay	Quebec, Canada	405	35,900	St. Lawrence	Chicoutimi
St. Lawrence	United States-Canada	750	500,000	Gulf of St. Law.	Montreal
San Francisco	Eastern Brazil	1,800	200,000	Atlantic Ocean	Penedo
San Joaquin	California	350	30,000	Sacramento R.	Stockton
Seine	France	480	30,000	English Channel	Paris
Shannon	Ireland	250	4,500	Atlantic Ocean	Limerick
Susquehanna	N. E. United States	500	....	Chesapeake Bay	Harrisburg
Tagus	Portugal	565	31,850	Atlantic Ocean	Lisbon
Tennessee	S. E. United States	1,200	44,000	Ohio River	Knoxville
Thames	England	215	6,000	North Sea	London
Tiber	Italy	240	6,840	Mediterranean	Rome
Ural	Russia	1,400	85,000	Caspian Sea	Orenburg
Vistula	Poland-Danzig	650	76,000	Baltic Sea	Warsaw
Volga	Russia	2,300	563,300	Caspian Sea	Saratov
Weser	Germany	300	18,530	North Sea	Bremen
Yangtze	China	3,300	650,000	East China Sea	Nanking
Yenisei	Mongolia-Siberia	3,000	1,000,000	Arctic Ocean	Krasnoyarsk
Yukon	Alaska-Canada	2,300	330,000	Bering Sea	Dawson
Zambezi	South Africa	2,200	600,000	Indian Ocean	Livingstone

* River system.

WORLD TRAVEL DISTANCES

The chief ports of the world are named in alphabetical order across the top and down the sides of the tables. The distance between any two ports will be found at the intersection of the two columns which contain the names of the selected ports. Thus the distance from Baltimore to Bombay is given as 8431, and the small "s" shows that the route is via Suez Canal. Distances are for full-powered steam vessels reckoned in nautical miles.

	Amsterdam	Antwerp	Barbados	Belfast	Bombay	Boston	Bremen	Buenos Aires	Cape Town	Cherbourg	Genoa	Glasgow	Hamburg	Havana
Amsterdam	.....	135	3877	733	s 6336	3164	272	6370	6193	303	2237	818	290	4335
Antwerp	135	.....	3841	697	s 6300	3128	357	6334	6157	267	2201	782	385	4299
Baltimore	3696	3672	1853	3204	s 8431	674	3851	5945	6913	3357	4343	3322	3934	1107
Barbados	3877	3841	.....	3637	s 8199	1880	4090	4169	5284	3596	4100	3719	4108	1472
Belfast	733	697	3637	.....	6245	2730	880	6271	6089	459	2146	113	891	3899
Bermuda	3248	3112	1222	2958	7876	707	3459	5175	6181	2967	3771	2885	3477	1158
Bombay	s 6336	s 6300	s 8199	6245	.....	s 7962	6549	c 8349	4749	6040	4473	6327	6567	s 9000
Boston	3164	3128	1880	2730	s 7962	.....	3377	5804	6776	2883	3863	2777	3395	1422
Bremen	272	357	4090	880	6549	3377	.....	6583	6406	513	2450	922	171	4548
Buenos Aires	6370	6334	4169	6271	c 8349	5804	6583	.....	3778	6074	6130	6350	6601	5669
Cape Town	6193	6157	5284	6089	4604	6776	6406	3778	.....	5897	5972	6168	6424	6716
Charleston	3846	3810	1630	3561	s 8388	845	4059	5790	6828	3565	4459	3498	4077	605
Cherbourg	303	267	3596	459	6040	2883	513	6074	5897	.....	1941	544	531	4029
Colon	4818	4782	1225	4543	s 9283	2173	5031	5318	6410	4537	5184	4625	5049	987
Constantinople	2898	3158	5057	3103	3837	4820	3407	7381	s 6137	2898	1312	3185	3425	5852
Galveston	5031	4995	2240	4595	9696	2118	5244	6378	7470	4725	5591	4641	5262	765
Genoa	2237	2201	4100	2146	4473	3863	2450	6130	5972	1941	.....	2228	2468	4895
Gibraltar	1389	1353	3252	1298	4953	3015	1602	5282	5124	1093	854	1380	1620	4047
Glasgow	818	782	3719	113	6327	2777	922	6350	6168	544	2228	.....	1049	3945
Hamburg	290	385	4108	891	6567	3395	171	6601	6424	531	2468	1049	.....	4566
Havana	4335	4299	1472	3899	s 9000	1422	4548	5669	6716	4029	4895	3945	4566	.....
Havre	267	231	3662	528	6115	2949	480	6151	5966	71	2018	610	498	4120
Hongkong	9764	9728	p 10,589	9673	4090	11,390	9977	c 10,643	6898	s 9468	7901	9755	9995	p 10,351
Honolulu	p 9569	p 9533	p 5976	p 9294	8375	p 6924	p 9782	m 7709	m 10,390	p 9288	p 9935	p 9376	p 9800	p 5738
Jamaica	4314	4278	1040	4039	s 8844	1658	4527	5166	6260	4033	4739	4121	4545	716
Lisbon	1111	1087	3085	1020	5249	2797	1324	5304	5148	815	1150	1102	1342	4174

	Havre	Hongkong	Liverpool	London	Melbourne	New Orleans	New York	Plymouth, Eng.	Rio de Janeiro	San Francisco	Shanghai	Singapore	Southampton	Valparaiso	Yokohama
Amsterdam	267	9764	711	201	11,131	4837	3346	385	5280	p 8135	10,507	s 8324	277	p 7473	11,226
Antwerp	231	9728	675	180	11,095	4801	3310	349	5244	p 8099	10,471	8288	238	p 7437	11,190
Baltimore	3478	p 11,618	3393	3627	p 10,319	1632	410	3319	4844	p 5189	p 10,576	s 10,419	3383	p 4560	p 9725
Barbados	3662	p 10,589	3627	3801	p 9214	2051	1825	3503	3079	p 4542	p 9937	s 10,187	3622	p 3880	p 8967
Belfast	528	9673	137	663	s 11,040	4401	2912	360	5168	p 7860	10,535	8233	488	p 7198	s 11,135
Bermuda	3033	p 11,052	2945	3172	p 9677	1643	699	2851	4094	p 5005	p 10,400	s 9864	2956	p 5343	p 9430
Bombay	6115	4090	6223	6260	6535	9502	8153	5997	c 7824	9780	4633	2452	6090	m 9875	5352
Boston	2949	p 11,390	2854	3088	p 10,162	1924	379	2791	4714	p 5490	p 10,885	s 9950	2909	p 4828	p 9915
Bremen	480	9977	924	409	s 11,344	5050	3559	598	5501	p 8348	s 10,720	8537	479	p 7686	s 11,439
Buenos Aires	6151	c 10,643	6258	6294	9099	6255	5838	6029	1135	m 7536	c 11,386	9376	6124	m 2766	c 12,105
Cape Town	5966	6898	6076	6117	5814	7347	6795	5852	3267	p 9727	7641	5631	5947	5447	8360
Charleston	3631	p 10,930	3548	3770	p 9555	1107	614	3473	4700	p 4883	p 10,278	s 10,546	3591	p 4221	p 9308
Cherbourg	71	s 9468	437	227	s 10,835	4531	3065	108	4984	p 7854	10,211	8028	83	p 7192	s 10,930
Colon	4603	p 9364	4530	4742	p 7989	1380	1972	4445	4228	p 3317	p 8712	s 11,271	4563	p 2655	p 7742
Constantinople	2975	7266	3081	3118	8633	6354	5011	2855	5997	p 9464	8009	5826	2948	9583	8728
Galveston	4816	p 10,864	4719	4955	p 9489	380	1893	4658	5288	p 4817	p 10,212	s 11,678	4776	p 4155	p 9242
Genoa	2018	7901	2124	2161	9268	5397	4054	1898	5040	p 8501	8644	6461	1991	p 7839	s 9363
Gibraltar	1162	s 8381	1276	1313	9748	4549	3206	1050	4192	p 7653	9124	6941	1143	p 6991	s 9843
Glasgow	610	9755	210	745	11,122	4447	2959	442	5158	p 7942	10,498	8315	570	p 7280	s 11,217
Hamburg	498	9995	942	427	11,362	5068	3577	616	5519	p 8366	10,738	8555	497	p 7704	s 11,457
Havana	4120	p 10,351	4023	4259	p 8976	597	1197	3962	4579	p 4304	p 9699	s 10,982	4080	p 3642	p 5022
Havre	.....	9537	503	194	10,904	4622	3131	175	5061	7920	10,280	8097	105	p 7258	11,999
Hongkong	9537	.....	9651	9688	5031	p 10,744	p 11,336	9425	c 10,118	6041	853	1440	s 9518	10,536	1580
Honolulu	p 9354	4858	p 9281	p 9493	4916	p 6131	p 6723	p 9196	m 8587	2089	4333	5925	p 9314	5916	3445
Jamaica	4099	p 9914	4026	4238	p 8539	1115	1457	3941	4076	p 3867	p 9262	s 10,826	4059	p 3205	p 8292
Lisbon	884	8677	998	1035	10,044	4676	3025	770	4214	p 7597	s 9420	7237	865	p 6935	10,139

K, via Kiel Canal. P, via Panama Canal. S, via Suez Canal. C, via Cape Town. M, via Strait of Magellan. H, via Cape Horn. T, via Torres Strait.

WORLD TRAVEL DISTANCES—Continued

The chief ports of the world are named in alphabetical order across the top and down the sides of the tables. The distance between any two ports will be found at the intersection of the two columns which contain the names of the selected ports. Thus the distance from Manila to Havana is given as 10,420, and the small "P" shows that the route is via Panama Canal. Distances are for full-powered steam vessels reckoned in nautical miles.

	Amsterdam	Antwerp	Barbados	Belfast	Bombay	Boston	Bremen	Buenos Aires	Cape Town	Cherbourg	Genoa	Glasgow	Hamburg	Havana	Havre	Hongkong	Liverpool	London	Melbourne	New Orleans	New York	Plymouth, Eng.	Rio de Janeiro	San Francisco	Shanghai	Singapore	Southampton	Valparaiso	Yokohama
Liverpool	711	675	3624	137	6223	2854	924	6258	6076	437	2124	210	942	4023	503	9651	.....	638	S 11,018	4525	3036	345	5158	P 7847	S 10,394	8211	463	P 7185	S 11,113
London	201	180	3801	663	6260	3088	409	6294	6117	227	2161	745	427	4259	194	9688	638	.....	S 11,055	4761	3270	309	5204	P 8059	S 10,437	8248	201	P 7397	S 11,150
Manila	9667	9631	P 10,658	9576	3793	S 11,293	S 9880	C 10,546	6801	9371	7804	9658	9898	P 10,420	9440	640	S 9554	S 9591	T 4511	P 10,813	P 11,405	9328	C 10,021	6238	1130	1435	S 9421	10,406	1768
Melbourne	11,131	11,095	P 9214	S 11,040	6535	P 10,162	S 11,344	9099	5814	S 10,835	9268	11,122	11,362	C 12,512	P 8976	5031	S 11,018	11,055	.....	P 9369	P 9961	S 10,792	8827	6966	5234	3823	S 10,885	6280	4875
Montreal	3317	3281	2715	2645	8141	1222	3530	6421	7108	3036	4042	2693	3548	2475	3102	S 11,569	2760	3241	P 11,132	2977	1451	2944	5331	P 6460	P 11,855	S 10,129	3062	P 5798	P 10,885
New Orleans	4837	4801	2115	4401	9502	1924	5050	6255	7347	4531	5397	4447	5068	597	4622	P 10,744	4525	4761	P 9369	.....	1699	4464	5160	P 4697	P 10,092	S 11,484	4582	P 4035	P 9122
Newport News	3514	3478	1699	3080	8307	550	3727	5774	6789	3233	4208	3126	3745	988	3299	P 11,136	3204	3438	P 9761	1490	286	3141	4590	P 5089	P 10,484	S 10,295	3259	P 4427	P 9514
New York	3346	3310	1825	2912	8153	379	3559	5838	6995	3065	4054	2959	3577	1227	3131	P 11,336	3053	3270	P 9961	1699	.....	2973	4748	P 5289	P 10,684	S 10,141	3091	P 4627	P 9714
Panama	P 4858	P 4822	P 1265	P 4583	P 9323	P 2213	P 5071	M 5280	P 6450	P 4577	P 5224	P 4665	P 5089	P 1027	P 4643	9324	P 4570	P 4782	7949	P 1420	P 2012	P 4485	P 4268	3277	8672	M 13,405	P 4603	2615	7702
Para	4319	4193	1142	4056	S 8262	2943	4442	3235	4330	3933	4163	4138	4460	2577	4010	C 11,204	4043	4153	C 10,120	3136	2915	3883	2145	P 5621	P 11,016	S 10,250	3983	P 4959	P 10,006
Petrograd	1070	K 1165	4888	1606	7353	4052	951	K 7381	7204	1311	3248	1648	860	5346	K 1275	KS 10,755	1716	K 1207	12,142	5848	4234	1396	6299	P 9209	11,518	9335	1277	P 8547	12,237
Philadelphia	3482	3446	1828	3048	8284	517	3694	5870	6861	3201	4185	3094	3712	1158	3267	P 11,302	3172	3406	P 9927	1660	234	3109	4782	P 5255	S 12,455	S 10,272	3227	P 4593	P 9680
Plymouth	385	349	3594	360	5997	2791	598	6029	5852	108	1898	442	616	3962	175	9425	345	309	10,792	4464	2973	.....	4939	P 7762	10,168	S 7985	129	P 7100	10,887
Portland, Me.	3086	3050	1927	2652	7912	98	3299	5849	6787	2805	3807	2698	3317	1470	2871	S 11,334	2776	3010	P 10,210	1972	427	2713	4759	P 5538	S 12,077	S 9894	2831	P 4876	P 9963
Rio de Janeiro	5280	5244	3079	5168	7824	4714	5501	1135	3265	4984	5040	5250	5519	4579	5061	C 11,118	5158	5204	8827	5160	4748	4939	.....	P 7545	C 10,861	C 8851	5034	M 3644	C 11,580
St. Thomas	3846	3810	440	3586	8265	1516	4059	4629	5708	3570	4160	3668	4077	1040	3639	P 10,384	3573	3770	P 9009	1590	1435	3473	3539	P 4337	P 9722	10,247	3591	P 3675	P 8722
San Francisco	P 8135	P 8099	P 4542	P 7860	9780	P 5490	P 8348	7536	P 9727	P 7854	P 8501	P 7942	P 8366	P 4304	P 7920	6041	P 7847	P 8059	6966	P 4697	P 5289	P 7762	P 7545	.....	5491	7330	P 7880	5140	4791
San Juan	3867	3831	502	3600	8307	1480	4080	4694	5773	3583	4202	3681	4098	975	3652	P 10,364	3588	3791	P 8989	1525	1428	3494	3604	P 4317	P 9712	10,289	3612	P 3655	P 8702
Savannah	3916	3880	1648	3443	8640	928	4129	5820	6860	3684	4535	3489	4147	634	3701	P 10,927	3618	3840	12,650	1136	695	3543	4730	P 4880	P 10,275	10,622	3661	P 4218	P 9265
Seattle	P 8914	P 8878	P 5321	P 8639	9515	P 6269	P 9127	M 8315	P 10,506	P 8633	P 9280	P 8721	P 9145	P 5083	P 8699	5779	P 8626	P 8838	7326	P 5476	P 6068	P 8541	P 8324	799	5209	7068	P 8659	5917	4259
Shanghai	10,507	10,471	12,370	10,535	4633	S 12,133	10,720	C 11,380	7641	S 10,211	8644	10,498	S 10,738	S 13,165	10,280	853	S 10,394	10,437	5234	P 10,092	P 10,684	10,168	C 10,861	5491	.....	2183	10,267	10,266	1030
Singapore	8324	8288	10,187	8233	2450	S 9950	8537	9376	5631	8028	6461	8315	8555	10,982	8097	1440	8211	8248	3823	S 11,484	S 10,141	7985	C 8851	7330	2183	.....	8078	M 10,899	2902
Southampton	277	238	3622	488	6090	2909	479	6124	5947	83	1991	570	497	4080	105	S 9518	463	201	S 10,885	4582	3091	129	5034	P 7880	S 10,261	8078	.....	P 7218	10,980
Suez	3376	3340	5239	3285	2960	5002	3589	8154	5259	3080	1513	3367	3607	6034	3157	6388	3263	3300	7755	6536	5193	3037	6179	12,278	7131	4948	3130	9768	7850
Valparaiso	P 7473	P 7437	P 3880	P 7198	M 9875	P 4828	P 7686	M 2766	M 5447	P 7192	P 7839	P 7280	P 7704	P 3642	P 7258	10,536	P 7185	P 7397	6280	P 4035	P 4627	P 7100	M 3644	5138	10,266	M 10,899	P 7218	.....	9339
Yokohama	11,226	11,190	P 8967	11,135	5352	P 9915	11,439	C 12,105	8360	10,930	9363	11,217	11,457	P 9122	10,999	1580	11,113	11,150	4875	P 9122	P 9714	10,887	C 11,580	4791	1030	2902	10,980	9339	.....

K, via Kiel Canal. P, via Panama Canal. S, via Suez Canal. C, via Cape Town. M, via Strait of Magellan. H, via Cape Horn. T, via Torres Strait.

PRINCIPAL FRESH-WATER LAKES OF THE WORLD

Name	Location	Area Sq. Miles	Elevation Above Sea Level	Depth	Discovery or Early Exploration: By Whom	Date
			Feet	Feet		
Albert	Central Africa	1,800	2,100	20	Speke and Grant	1862
Athabasca	Alberta	2,762	697	Shallow	Hearne	1771
Baikal	Eastern Siberia, Asia	13,200	1,500	5,306		
Bangweulu	Central Africa	1,670	3,700	15	Livingstone	1868
Cayuga	New York	75	381	400		
Chad	French Sahara-Nigeria	10,000	850	20	Denham and Clapperton	1823
Champlain	New York	750	93	600	Champlain	1609
Chapala	Mexico	1,400	6,000			
Chautauqua	New York	35	1,300	....	La Salle	1669
Como	Italy	55½	650	1,365	Mentioned by Virgil	30 B. C.
Constance	Switz.-Ger.-Aust.	208	1,309	827	Lake Dwellers	Stone Age
Crater	Oregon	20	6,177	2,001	Hillman	1853
Edward	Central Africa	1,500	3,000	....	Stanley	1876
Erie	United States-Canada	9,968	573	210	Chaumont and Brebeuf	1640
Garda	Italy	189	216	1,916	Described by Virgil	35 B. C.
Gatun	Panama, Cent. Amer.	164	85			
Geneva	Switzerland-France	225	1,230	1,095	Lake Dwellers	Stone Age
George	New York	50	323	400	Friar Jogues	1642
Great Bear	N. W. Terr., Canada	12,200	450	270		
Great Slave	N. W. Terr., Canada	11,170	391	650	Hearne	1771
Huron	United States-Canada	22,978	581	750	Brulé and Le Caron	1615
Itasca	Minnesota	2	1,457	50	Schoolcraft	1832
Ladoga	European Russia	7,000	55	730		
Lake of the Woods	Ontario-Manitoba	1,485	1,058	....	De Noyon	1688
Lucerne	Switzerland	49	1,435	700	Scene of Tell legends	
Maggiore	Italy	82	636	1,220	*L. Verbanus* of Romans	B. C.
Managua	Nicaragua, Cent. Amer.	560	154	Unknown	Cordoba	1522
Michigan	United States	22,336	581	870	Nicolet	1634
Mweru	Belg. Congo-Rhodesia	1,700	3,189	....	Livingstone	1867
Neuchatel	Switzerland	90	1,420	472	Lake Dwellers	Stone Age
Nicaragua	Nicaragua, Cent. Amer.	3,000	106	260	Cordoba	1522
Nipigon	Ontario	1,590	850			
Nipissing	Ontario	330	640	....	Brulé and Le Caron	1615
Nyasa	Equatorial Africa	14,200	1,645	2,580	Livingstone	1859
Okeechobee	Florida	730	16	15	Spaniards—Fontaneda?	1552?
Onega	European Russia	3,764	125	400		
Ontario	United States-Canada	7,243	246	738	Champlain	1615
Rangeley	Maine	80	1,350			
Reindeer	Manitoba-Saskatchewan	1,765	1,150			
Rudolf	Equatorial Africa	3,500	1,250	....	Count Teleki	1888
Seneca	New York	75	445	630		
Simcoe	Ontario	271	130		Champlain	1615
Superior	United States-Canada	32,060	602	1,012	Brulé	1622
Tahoe	California	200	6,275	1,650	John C. Fremont	1844
Tanganyika	Equatorial Africa	12,700	2,600	2,000	Speke and Burton	1858
Tezcuco	Mexico	85	7,300	2	Cortes	1519
Titicaca	Bolivia-Peru	3,200	12,500	900	Ancient Incas	
Victoria	Equatorial Africa	27,000	3,775	270	Speke	1858
Winnepesaukee	New Hampshire	178	475	300	Johnson and Willard	1652
Winnipeg	Manitoba	9,398	710	70	Verendrye	1733
Winnipegosis	Manitoba	2,086	828	40	Verendrye	1739
Yellowstone	Wyoming	140	7,740	300	Colter	1807

PRINCIPAL SALT-WATER LAKES OF THE WORLD

Name	Area Square Miles	Location	Elevation Above Sea Level*	Depth
			Feet	Feet
Aral, Sea of	26,200	Kirghis-Khiva, W. Asiatic Russia	155	220
Balkash	8,600	Russian Central Asia	780	135
Caspian Sea	170,000	S. E. Europe-Western Asia	−86	3,000
Dead Sea	340	Palestine, S. W. Asia	−1,290	1,280
Eyre	3,600	South Australia	−35	Shallow
Great Salt Lake	1,750	Utah, W. United States	4,218	40
Issyk-Kul	2,230	Asiatic Russia	5,400	Unknown
Kuku-nor	2,300	Central China	10,000	Unknown
Maracaibo†	8,000	Venezuela, South America	Sea level	500
Salton Sea	266	S. E. California, North America	−280‡†	Shallow
Urumia	1,795	Azerbaijan, S. W. Asia	4,100	40
Van	1,400	Armenia, S. W. Asia	5,214	Unknown

*** A minus sign indicates below sea level. † Partially fresh. ‡ Approximate level before the inflow from the Colorado river in 1905-06.**

MEANINGS OF PLACE NAMES

Many interesting stories lie hidden in the names of places. These stories are usually concealed from the average reader, by reason of the fact that the original names are from languages that are unknown to him. Balearic, for example, applied to islands in the Mediterranean Sea, is derived from the Greek word *ballein*, meaning hurl, and commemorates the islanders' prowess with the sling. The Latin name Mediterranean, meaning In the Midst of the Earth, recalls the days when the known world was confined to the territory encircling that sea.

Other names contain picturesque descriptions. Such, for instance, is Boise, a river and a city of Idaho. This French word, meaning wooded, describes the forest-clad banks of the stream on which the city is built.

In some cases, the descriptions have ceased to be applicable. Thus Key West, a corruption of Spanish words meaning Bone Reef, referred to bones formerly found on the island and believed to be remains of earlier inhabitants.

The following pages explain the origin and meaning of a large number of such place names, selected from all parts of the world. The majority, however, are names of places in America, where Indian words have been used so extensively to designate places and localities.

But many of the Indian languages are no longer spoken. Moreover, there is no complete dictionary of Indian terms, even for the dialects that are still in use. As a result, the meanings of many Indian names have been lost beyond all hope of recovery. Those that *are* known, however, are seen to be highly descriptive and helpfully informative. When once interpreted, these meanings add a new interest to the places to which these various names have been given.

Meanings of the names of American states will be found on page 382; those of the Canadian provinces, on page 448.

Aalborg (*ôl'bôrk*). Danish for Eel town. A city in northern Denmark on a fiord, where eels may be caught in considerable numbers.

Aberdeen (*ăb'ẽr-dēn'*). A city of Scotland, anciently called Aberdon, from the Celtic *aber*, "river mouth," and Don, the river at whose mouth the city is situated.

Abyssinia (*ăb'ĭ-sĭn'ĭ-ȧ*). Former name of Ethiopia, Italian colony in Africa. The name comes from the Arabic *habish*, "mixed"; hence "country of the mixed races."

Acadia. Name originally given to Nova Scotia, from *akade*, a Micmac Indian word meaning plenty.

Acropolis. The citadel at Athens, Greece, so named from *akron*, "height," and *polis*, "city"; hence "the city on the height." It contains the Parthenon and other beautiful buildings.

Adrianople (*ăd'rĭ-ăn-ō'p'l*; *ā'drĭ-*). City of European Turkey, named from Hadrian, a Roman emperor, and Greek *polis*, "city."

Adriatic (*ā'drē-ăt'ĭk*; *ăd'rĭ-*) **Sea.** Indicates the Sea of Adrian, or Hadrian, a Roman emperor.

Akron. City in Ohio, believed to occupy the highest ground in the northern part of the state. Also other places named for the same reason. The word is Greek, meaning summit.

Alameda (*ăl'ȧ-mā'dȧ*; *-mē'dȧ*). County and city in California and precinct in New Mexico. The word is Spanish for grove of poplar trees.

Alamo (*ä'lä-mō*). A city in Texas and other places named from the historic fort in Texas, so called from a Spanish word meaning poplar.

Alaska. Territory of the United States. An Indian word meaning great country. After purchase by the United States, the names of Walrussia, American Siberia, Zero islands, and Polario were suggested, but Alaska was adopted in accordance with a proposition of Charles Sumner.

Albuquerque (*ăl'bû-kûr'kē*). City of New Mexico. The name is a corruption from Alburquerque, a governor of New Spain.

Alcazar (*ăl-kä'zär*). From the Arabic *al gasr*, "the palace." The palace of the Moorish kings and later of Spanish royalty at Seville, Spain.

Aleutian (*ȧ-lū'shăn*; *ȧ-lōō'-*). Islands in the north Pacific Ocean, named from Russian *aleut*, "bald rock."

Alexandria. An Egyptian city, named after its founder, Alexander the Great.

Algiers (*ăl-jērz'*). City in northern Africa. From the Arabic *al-jaza'ir*, "the islands," referring to islands in the adjacent bay.

Alhambra (*ăl-hăm'brȧ*). From the Arabic *al-hamra*, "red." A great palace at Granada, Spain. It is surrounded by a red brick wall.

Allegan (*ăl'ē-găn*). A town of Michigan at the head of navigation on Kalamazoo river. Its name is derived from the French *allée*, "passage."

Allegheny (*ăl'ē-gā'nĭ*). River and county in Pennsylvania and mountains in eastern United States. An Indian word, most generally believed to be from *oolhikhanna*, "the fairest river."

All Saints Bay. In eastern Brazil. Discovered by Vespucci on the Feast of All Saints in 1503.

Alps. Mountains of central Europe, named from the Celtic *alp*, "high," or, according to others, from the Latin *albus*, "white," in allusion to the snow-capped peaks.

Altai (*äl-tī'*). A mountain range in central Asia. Altai is a Tartaric corruption of the Mongolian *altain ula*, "golden mountain." Gold dust is obtained there.

Altoona. City in Pennsylvania, so named because of its high situation in the Allegheny mountains; also town in Iowa, situated on the highest point between the Des Moines and Mississippi rivers. Altoona is a derivative of the Latin word *altus*, "high."

Amagansett (*ăm'ȧ-găn'sĕt*). Bay in Long Island, N. Y. The name is a Montauk Indian word for fishing place.

America. From Amerigo Vespucci, sometimes spelled Vespucius, who landed on the western continent south of the equator in 1499. His name was first given to the continent by a German geographer, Martin Waldseemüller, who published an account of the four voyages of Vespucci, at Frankfort, Germany, in 1507.

Amiens (F. *ȧ'myăɴ'*; E. *ăm'ĭ-ĕnz*). French city on the Somme river, anciently the capital of the Ambiani, "Dwellers by the Water," from whom the city took its name.

Amiskwi. A peak of the Canadian Rockies. The name is Cree Indian for Beaver.

Andalusia (*ăn'dȧ-lōō'shĭ-ȧ*). Name for southern Spain, which was called by the Moors *Belad-al-Andalus*, "Land of the Andalus, or Vandals," a people formerly dwelling there.

Andes. Mountains of South America. The name is variously derived from the Anti tribe in Peru or from the Peruvian *anta*, "copper," copper ore being abundant in the Peruvian Andes.

Androscoggin (*ăn'drŏs-kŏg'ĭn*). River in Maine and New Hampshire and county in Maine. As a compliment to Sir Edmund Andros, the name was changed from the original Indian form, Ammoscoggin. The earlier name is said to mean a Fishing Place for Alewives or Fish Spearing.

Annapolis. A city in Maryland and seat of U. S. Naval Academy, named for Queen Anne of England and from the Greek word *polis*, "city."

Antarctic (*ănt-ärk'tĭk*) **Ocean.** Denotes the ocean *anti*, "against" or "opposite to," the Arctic Ocean.

Antwerp. A city of Belgium on the Scheldt river, named from Old German *aent werf*, "on the wharf." Some authorities derive it from Dutch *hand-werpen*, "hand throwing," in allusion to the practice of a noted robber, who threw into the Scheldt river hands severed from his prisoners.

Apalachicola (*ăp'ȧ-lăch'ĭ-kō'lȧ*) **River, Fla.** From an Indian town, Apalatichiokoli, "Those on the Other Side."

Appalachian (*ăp'ȧ-lăch'ĭ-ăn*; *-lā'chĭ-ăn*) **Mountains.** In eastern United States. They were so called by De Soto after the Apalachee Indians.

Appomattox (*ăp'ō-măt'ŭks*). River, county, and town in Virginia. An Indian word, meaning a tobacco-plant country. The village was the scene of the surrender that ended the Civil War.

Arabia. A peninsula of southwestern Asia. The name is derived from a Semitic word for desert.

Arctic (*ärk'tĭk*). Derived from the Greek *arctos*, "bear," referring to the constellation of that name in the northern sky.

Areopagus (*ăr'ē-ŏp'ȧ-gŭs*). A hill west of the Acropolis in Athens, Greece. The name is from the Greek *Areios pagos*, "Mars' hill," Ares, or Mars, being the god of war among the Greeks.

Argentina. South American republic, named from Latin *argentum*, "silver."

Arles (*ärlz*; F., *ȧrl*). A city of southern France, anciently known as Arelate, from the Celtic *arlaeth*, "on the marsh." It is on the delta of the Rhone river.

Aroostook (*ȧ-rōōs'tŏŏk*). River and county in Maine. An Indian word, meaning good river.

Ascension Island. Southwest of Africa, discovered by the Portuguese on Ascension Day, 1501.

Asia (*ā'shȧ*; *-zhȧ*). From the Sanskrit *ushas*, signifying land of the dawn.

Atchafalaya (*ăch'ȧ-fȧ-lī'ȧ*) **River, La.** From Choctaw Indian *hucha*, "river," and *falaya*, "long"; hence "Long river."

Athens. The capital of Greece, named in honor of Athene, the goddess of wisdom. Also cities in Georgia and Ohio.

Atlantic Ocean. Named from the mythical island of Atlantis, believed by the Greeks to have lain west of the Strait of Gibraltar and to have been submerged during prehistoric times.

Augusta. A city in Maine, named for the English princess Augusta Charlotte, eldest granddaughter of George II. Also a city in Georgia.

Aurora (*ô-rō'rȧ*). Cities of Illinois, Indiana, Missouri, and Oregon, a town of Ontario, and villages of Nebraska and New York. The word is Latin for dawn.

Austerlitz (*ôs'tẽr-lĭts*). A town in Germany, the scene of a decisive battle in 1805. From German *ost*, "east," and Littawa, the river on which Austerlitz is situated; hence. "the east town on the Littawa."

Austria. Former country of Europe. The English name is a Latin translation of the German, *Osterreich* "Eastern Empire."

Aztec. Village in San Juan county, New Mexico, named for an Indian tribe of Mexico. The word is said to mean place of the heron.

Balearic (*băl'ê-ăr'ĭk*) **Islands.** East of Spain. From Greek *ballein*, "to hurl"; so called because of the islanders' skill in the use of the sling.

Balkan (*bȧl-kăn'*; *bôl'kăn*). Mountainous peninsula of southeastern Europe. From Turkish *balkh*, "high ridge."

Baltic. Sea in northern Europe, named from Swedish *balt*, "a strait"; hence "a sea having many straits." The irregular shape of the sea gives rise to a number of narrow channels.

Baltimore. County and city in Maryland, named for Cecil Calvert, Lord Baltimore, who settled the colony in 1635.

Banbury (*băn'bẽr-ĭ*). A town in England, situated 22 miles north of Oxford. Its Old English name was Berenburig, "Bera's fort."

Bangor (*băn'gôr*). City of Maine, so called from a hymn tune of that name. Previously, the locality was known as Sunbury.

Barbados (*bär-bā'dōz*). West Indian islands, named from the Latin *barba*, "beard," in allusion to the bearded fig trees abounding there.

Barcelona. A city of Spain, called after the Carthaginian, Hamilcar Barca, who founded it.

Batavia. A city in Java and in New York and Illinois. It is the Latin designation for the territory now called the Netherlands.

Baton Rouge (*băt'ŭn rōōzh*). City in Louisiana. The name is French, meaning Red Staff.

Bayeux (*bȧ'yû'*). French town, so called from Bajoccas, a Celtic tribe name, meaning Great Conquerors.

Bellefontaine (*bĕl-fŏn'tān*; *-foun'-*). A city of Ohio, given a French name meaning Beautiful Fountain, in allusion to the beautiful springs in the vicinity.

Belle Isle. French for Beautiful Island. A strait and island northwest of Newfoundland and an island in Detroit river.

Belleville. Cities in Illinois, New Jersey, and Ontario. In French, the name means Beautiful City.

Bering (*bē'rĭng*). Strait north of Alaska, named after the Russian navigator who discovered it in 1728.

Berkshire. County in Massachusetts, named after one in England. The name is from *barruc*, "polled oak," under which public deliberations of the shire were anciently held.

Berlin. Capital of Germany. Berlin is variously explained as from the Wendish *berle*, "uncultivated ground," *barlin*, "a shelter," or *brljina*, "pool," the original site having been marshy.

Bermudas. Islands in the Atlantic Ocean, named for their discoverer, Juan Bermudez.

Bethlehem (*bĕth'lê-hĕm*; *-lê-ĕm*). A village in Palestine. The name is from the Syrian *beit el lehm*, "house of bread," alluding to the productive region about the town.

Biscay (*bĭs'kā*). Bay of western Europe, named from the Basques dwelling on its southern coast.

Boise (*boi'sĭ*). The capital of Idaho on the Boise river, so called from the French *boisé*, "wooded."

Bokhara (*bô-ĸä'rä*). A city of central Asia in the Uzbek Soviet Republic, Russia, named from Mongolian *bukhar*, "church." It has numerous mosques, or Mohammedan churches.

Bolivia. South American country, so called in honor of Bolivar, "the liberator."

Bombay (*bŏm-bā'*). City of India, named for an Indian goddess *Bambai*, but understood by the Portuguese as *Buon bahia*, "Good bay." It has an excellent natural harbor.

Borgne (*bôrn*) **Lake, La.** French, meaning "blind of one eye." The legendary account of the name is that a cyclops was met on its shores, a cyclops being a giant of Greek myth having one eye, which was put out by Ulysses.

Bosporus (*bŏs'pô-rŭs*). A Greek term composed of *bous*, "ox," and *poros*, "ford," alluding to the Greek legend that when Io was transformed into a cow she forded this strait of southeastern Europe.

Boston (*bŏs'tŭn*). Capital of Massachusetts, called after Boston, England, whose name is a corruption of Botolph's town, Saint Botolph having founded an abbey there.

Brahmaputra (*brä'mȧ-pōō'trȧ*). River of India. The name, of Sanskrit origin, means Offspring of Brahma, a Hindu god.

Brandenburg (*brän'dĕn-bŏŏrĸ*). A district of Prussia, Germany, anciently called Branneborch, a name of Slavic origin, meaning Forest fortress.

Brazil. Named for the color of its dyewoods, from Portuguese *braza*, "a live coal."

Brazos (*brä'zōs*) **River, Texas.** Called Brazos de Dios, "Arm of God," by Spaniards. A Spanish mission, which had been established on the river bank, was, in the absence of guards, destroyed by Indians. The guards, returning, found many bodies of their friends floating in the river. Discerning no mark of violence, they attributed the destruction to a miracle performed by the "arm of God."

Bristol. A county and a town of Rhode Island, so called from Bristol, England. The name is derived from Anglo-Saxon *Briegstow*, "Place at the Bridge." The English city is at the junction of two small rivers.

Brooklyn. Borough of the city of New York. It is named from Breuckelen, a village in Holland. The Dutch name signifies broken land.

Bruges (*brōō'jĕz*; F. *brüzh*). City of Belgium, named for its many bridges from Dutch *brugge*, "bridge."

Brussels. Belgian city named from German *bruch*, "marsh," and Latin *sella*, "seat"; hence "the site on the marsh." Part of the city is on low ground.

Budapest (*bōō'dȧ-pĕst'*). The capital of Hungary. The city consists of two parts—Buda, named for Buda, the brother of Attila the Hun, and Pest, so called from the Old Slavic *pesti*, "oven"; a limekiln having stood on the present site of Pest.

Buenos Aires (*bwā'nōs ī'rās*; *bō'nŭs ā'rĭz*). Capital of Argentina. Its name is Spanish for Good Breezes, given on account of the city's favorable location for the enjoyment of the sea air.

Butte (*būt*). City in Montana, named from a bare hill, or butte, overlooking the place. Butte is a naturalized French word, meaning small knoll.

Cadillac. A city in Michigan, named for La Motte Cadillac, who established a fort there in 1701.

Cadiz (*kā'dĭz*). City of southern Spain, named by the Phœnicians Gadir, "Fortress." "G" and "C" were frequently interchanged in the earlier forms of the alphabet. Cadiz is on an easily defensible peninsula.

Cairo (*kī'rō*). The capital of Egypt; also (pron. *kā'rō*) a city of southern Illinois and a town in Greene county, New York. The name is a corruption of Arabic Alkahirah, "Victorious," and was given to Cairo, Egypt, because Kahir (Mars), the planet of victory, was visible on the night when the city was founded.

Calumet (*kăl'ū-mĕt*). River in Illinois and Indiana, and city in Illinois. The word is Indian for pipe of peace.

Canada. Probably derived from the Indian word *kanata*, "a collection of wigwams."

Canandaigua (*kăn'ăn-dā'gwȧ*). Lake and city in New York. The word is Indian, meaning a chosen spot. Others derived the word from *cahnandahgwah*, "sleeping beauty."

Canaveral (*kȧ-năv′ẽr-ăl*) **Cape, Fla.** A Spanish name, meaning the land of the rose tree.

Candia (*kăn′dĭ-ȧ*). An alternative name of the Mediterranean island of Crete. It is from the Arabic *khandae*, "island of trenches," probably in allusion to the isolated valleys of the island's mountainous surface.

Canterbury. Name of an English city and of a district in New Zealand, meaning Kentish men's town from Anglo-Saxon *Cantwar*, "Kentish man," and *burh*, town.

Capri (*kä′prē*). An island in the Mediterranean Sea near Naples. Its name signifies Goat island, from the Latin *caper*, "goat."

Caribbean Sea. So called from the Caribs, a fierce tribe whose name, by corruption, has given us the word cannibal.

Carpathians (*kär-pā′thĭ-ănz*). Mountains in east central Europe. The name is derived from Karpa, the local name of the main chain, which is explained by the Slavonic root *chrb*, signifying ridge.

Carthage. Cities in Missouri and Illinois, and a village in New York, named from an ancient African city. The word is said to have come from Phœnician Kerethhadeshoth, "New City."

Casa Grande (*kä′sä grän′dā*). Prehistoric ruins found in Arizona. The name is Spanish for Great House.

Casco Bay, Me. From an Italian word, meaning crane; hence "Crane Bay."

Catawissa River, Pa. From the Delaware Indian word *gattawissa*, "getting fat."

Catskill. Name of a small river and of mountains in New York. Catskill is Dutch, meaning Cat, or Panther, creek; from *kat*, "cat or panther," and *kill*, "stream." Panthers are said to have abounded formerly in the district.

Cayuga. Lake and county in New York and county in Ontario, called after an Indian tribe, whose native name was Give-w-qweh-o-no, "People of the Mucky Lake."

Cazenovia (*kăz′ê-nō′vĭ-ȧ*). Lake and town in Madison county, New York, named for Cazenove, a general agent of the Holland Land Company.

Ceylon (*sê-lŏn′*). An island of the Indian Ocean. The Hindu form of the name is Silan, derived from *sinha*, "lion"; hence "land of lions." The lion is not now found in the island.

Chattahoochee (*chăt′ȧ-hōō′chê*) **River, Ga.** Translated Painted Stone, from the Indian *chateo*, "stone," *hoche*, "marked."

Chattanooga (*chăt′ȧ-nōō′gȧ*). City in Tennessee and creek in Georgia, named from a Cherokee Indian word, meaning crow's nest or eagle's nest.

Chaudiere (*shō′dyâr′*). A river in Quebec and Maine and a falls in the Ottawa river. The word is French for caldron, referring to the water beneath the semicircular falls.

Chautauqua (*shȧ-tô′kwȧ*). A village and lake in western New York. The name is Indian and is variously interpreted to mean foggy place, bag tied in the middle, place where a child was washed away, where the fish was taken out, and place of easy death.

Cheapside. A thoroughfare of London, so named for its passing a *cheap*, as markets were formerly called in England.

Cheboygan (*shê-boi′găn*). River, county, and city in Michigan. Cheboygan is Indian and is variously interpreted as from *chabwegan*, "a place of ore," or from *che*, "great," and *poygan*, "pipe"; hence "Great Pipe."

Chenango (*shê-năng′gō*) **River, N. Y.** From an Iroquois word, *ochenung*, "bull thistles."

Chesapeake (*chĕs′ȧ-pēk*). Bay in Maryland, which gives its name to several places in the country. The name is Indian, variously explained as meaning salty pond, great waters, mother of waters, and country on a great river.

Chester, Caster, Cester. Name terminations derived from the Latin *castra*, "camp."

Chesuncook (*chê-sŭn′kōōk*) **Lake, Me.** Indian word meaning goose place, from *chesunk*, "a goose," and *auke*, "a place."

Cheyenne (*shī-ĕn′*). City in Wyoming and several small places named for an Indian tribe. The word is probably a corruption of the French *chien*, "dog," applied to the tribe as a translation of a native word.

Chicago (*shĭ-kô′gō*). City and river in Illinois. The name is probably from the Indian word *cheecaqua*, "strong chiefs." Other derivations have connected it with words for wild onion or skunk.

Chickahominy (*chĭk′ȧ-hŏm′ĭ-nĭ*). Name of a river in Virginia, said to be derived from the Indian word *checahaminend*, "land of much grain." Another derivation is from *tschikene-mahoni*, "a lick frequented by turkeys."

Chickamauga (*chĭk′ȧ-mô′gȧ*) **River, Tenn.** From a Cherokee Indian word, meaning river of death.

Chicopee (*chĭk′ô-pē*) **River, Mass.** An Indian word, meaning the birch-bark place.

Chile (*chē′lā*). A South American country, named from Indian *chili*, "cold," in allusion to the climate on the mountains which occupy much of the country.

Chillicothe (*chĭl′ĭ-kŏth′ê*). Cities in Ohio, Illinois, and Missouri and a town in Iowa, so called from an Indian tribe. The word means town.

Chippewa. River in Wisconsin and counties in Michigan, Minnesota, and Wisconsin, named from an Indian tribe. Chippewa is a variant form of *ojibwa*, "puckered moccasins."

Christmas Island. In the Indian Ocean. Discovered Christmas 1777; hence the name.

Cimarron (*sĭm′ȧ-rōn′*) **River, Okla.** A name of Spanish derivation, meaning Wild.

Cincinnati (*sĭn′sĭ-năt′ĭ*). City in Ohio, named in honor of the Roman patriot Cincinnatus.

Circleville. A city of Ohio, named from its original location within a circular Indian mound.

Cleveland, Ohio. Named for General Moses Cleaveland. The first "a" was omitted by example of the town's first newspaper, which adopted the shorter form of the name for typographical convenience.

Cochituate (*kô-chĭt′ū-āt*) **Lake, Mass.** Indian word, meaning land near a waterfall.

Coeur d'Alene (*kûr dȧ-lān′*). Lake and city in Idaho. The expression is French for needle heart and was earlier applied to a tribe of Indians.

Cohasset (*kô-hăs′ĕt*). A town in Massachusetts. Cohasset is Indian, signifying a place of pines.

Cohoes (*kô-hōz′*). A city in New York. The name is a corruption of Iroquois *gahaoose*, "shipwrecked canoe."

Colon (*kô-lōn′*). Seaport at the Atlantic end of Panama canal. Colon is the Italian form of Columbus.

Colorado (*kŏl′ô-rä′dō*) **River.** "Red river." A Spanish name, applied for the color of its waters.

Conemaugh (*kŏn′ê-mô′*) **River, Pa.** An Indian name, meaning otter creek.

Copenhagen (*kō′pĕn-hā′gĕn*). The capital of Denmark, called in Danish Kobenhavn, "Merchants' Haven."

Cornwall. A county of England. Cornwall is a corruption of the Anglo-Saxon Cornweallas, connected with Cornubia, "Horn-shaped land," the Latin name for the district, and the Welch *weallas*, "strangers"; hence "Horn-shaped land of strangers."

Corsica. A Mediterranean island, said to be named from a Phœnician word for wooded.

Coshocton (*kô-shŏk′tŭn*). County and city in Ohio, named from the Indian town of Goshocking. The word is said to mean habitation of owls.

Costa Rica (*kŏs′tȧ rē′kȧ*). Name of a Central American country, meaning, in Spanish, Rich Coast.

Cotswold (*kŏts′wōld*) **Hills.** In England. So called from Anglo-Saxon *cot*, "hut," and *wold*, "meadow"; hence "a village meadow."

Coventry. An English city. Its name is derived from Anglo-Saxon *cofa*, "cove," and *treo*, "tree"; hence "Cove Tree." An erroneous popular explanation gives the name as a corruption of Convent Town.

Cuba. An island of the West Indies. Cuba is said to be a West Indian word for district. The complete Indian designation of the island was Cubanacan, *nacan* meaning central.

Cumberland. A name derived from Early English *combe*, "valley," and applied to an English county, a city of Maryland, and numerous other places. The English county is in the hilliest part of the country.

Cuzco (*kōōs′kō*). A department of Peru. The name is from Indian *quichua*, "navel," since the district was central to the Inca empire, which formerly occupied territory now called Peru.

Dahlonega (*dä-lŏn′ê-gȧ*). A city, of Georgia, so called from the Indian *taulawneca*, "yellow wampum," gold having been discovered here.

Delhi (*dĕl′ê*). Capital of India, said to be named from the Sanskrit, *dahal*, "a quagmire." Others derive it from Old Hindu *dil*, "eminence." The modern city is on two rocky elevations, but the ancient city included a low area along the bank of the river Jumna.

Des Moines (*dē moin′*). A city in Iowa on the Des Moines river. The name is French, meaning Of the Monks and was associated with Trappist monks dwelling near by. The word Moines is said to have been originally Moins, a French corruption of the Indian *mikonang*, "road," the river being called Riviere des Moins, "River of the Roads."

Detroit. A city of Michigan on the Detroit river. Détroit is the French word for strait.

Dnieper (*nē'pẽr*). A European river, formerly called Danapris, a name derived from Slavic *dan*, "river," and *apris*, "northern"; hence "Northern River."

Dniester (*nēs'tẽr*). A European river. Dniester means Southern River, being derived from the Slavic *dan*, "river," and *aster*, "southern."

Dover. The name of an English port on the Strait of Dover, probably derived from the Welch *dwfr*, "water." Also the capital of Delaware and a city in New Hampshire.

Dublin. The capital of the Irish Free State. The Irish form of the name, Dubh-linn, means Black Pool, in allusion to a near-by bog.

Easter Island. In the south Pacific Ocean, so called from its discovery on Easter Sunday, 1722.

Ecuador. Name of a South American country, meaning, in Spanish, Equator. The equator passes through the country.

Egypt. Country of Africa. The modern name is derived from the Hellenic form Aiguptos, which the Greeks fancifully derived from *aia*, "land," and *guptos*, "vulture," hence, "Land of Vultures."

England. The Anglo-Saxon form was Engla-land, "Land of the Angles," a Germanic race which settled in the country in the 8th century.

Erie. One of the Great Lakes. Erie, meaning Wild Cat, formerly designated an Indian tribe, now extinct.

Erzerum (*ĕrz'rōōm*). An Asiatic city, named from Arabic *arazi*, "lands," and *Rum*, "Roman"; hence Roman lands. This district was formerly held by Byzantines, often called Romans.

Espiritu Santo (*ĕs-pē'rē-tōō sän'tōō*). A state of Brazil. Its name is Portuguese, meaning Holy Spirit.

Estremadura (*ĕs'trâ-mä-dōō'rä*). A province of Portugal. The word is Portuguese and Spanish for frontier and was earlier applied to a province of Spain forming the southwestern limit of the kingdom.

Ethiopia. African colony of Italy. The name was applied to Africa south of Egypt by the Greeks, who derived it from *aitho*, "burn," and *ops*, "face," the inhabitants having faces supposedly blackened by the sun.

Etna. Volcanic mountain in Sicily. The name is Greek, derived from *aitho*, "burn."

Euphrates (*ū-frā'tēz*). A large river in Mesopotamia. The name is a Greek adaptation of the Old Persian *Ufratu*, meaning Broad river.

Europe. Originally derived from the Old Assyrian *ereb*, "the sunset, or west." The word Europe is a Greek adaptation.

Euxine (*ŭk'sĭn*). The name formerly applied to the Black Sea, derived from Greek *euxeinos*, "hospitable." The name embodies a hope rather than a description.

Finisterre (*fĭn'ĭs-târ'*). A cape of northwestern Spain. Finisterre means Land's End, from Latin *finis*, "end," and *terræ*, "of the land."

Florence. A city of Italy. The English form is a translation of the Italian name Firenze, "Flourishing."

Fond du Lac (*fŏn' dōō lăk'*). City of Wisconsin at the outlet of Winnebago lake. Fond du Lac is French for Foot of the Lake.

Fontainebleau (*fôn'tĕn'blō'*). A town of France 35 miles southeast of Paris, the site of a beautiful palace and ornamental gardens. The name is a corruption of *fontaine de bel eau*, "fountain of beautiful water."

Formosa. An island east of China. Formosa is Portuguese for beautiful.

Fuji (*fōō'jē*). A famous mountain of Japan. Its name means Peerless.

Galena. Mining cities in Illinois and Kansas, named from the Latin *galena*, "lead ore."

Galilee. A sea and, formerly, the northern portion of Palestine. Galilee is derived from the Hebrew *galil*, "circuit," the Jews being in the habit of passing around the district instead of through it, because it was inhabited partly by Gentiles.

Gallipolis (*găl'ĭ-pô-lēs'*). A city of Ohio, settled by French, who gave it a name derived from the Greek *Gallos*, "a Gaul, or Frenchman," and *polis*, "city." Literally, "French city."

Ganges. A river of India, named from the Sanskrit word *ganga*, "stream."

Gasconade (*găs'kô-nād'*) **River, Mo.** The French word *gasconnade* means a boaster and was probably applied on account of the noisy rapids in the river's upper course.

Geneva. City of Switzerland. The name is probably from Celtic *genava*, "jaws," applied in allusion to the shape of two islands in the city.

Germany. A country of Europe. It is derived from a Celtic word meaning mountaineers, and was applied originally to the inhabitants of the mountainous country of the Ardennes in France.

Gibraltar. A strait south of Spain and a near-by British fortress. Gibraltar is from the Moorish Jebel al Tarik, "Mountain of Tarik," Tarik being the general who led the Moors into Spain in 711 A. D.

Gila (*hē'là*) **River, Ariz.** The name is a corruption of the Spanish *guija*, "gravel," given in allusion to the nature of the river bed.

Glasgow. City of Scotland. Glasgow is variously explained as from Gaelic *clais-dhu*, "black ravine"; *glaise-dhu*, "black brook"; or as a Gaelic name given to Saint Kentigern, the city's patron saint.

Granada. A city of Spain. Granada is the Spanish word for pomegranate. The city was built on four hills and so reminded its founders of a pomegranate, which also shows a division into four parts.

Grand Manan (*mà-năn'*) **Islands, Me.** The name is from French *grand*, "great," and Indian *munnohan*, "island."

Grand Pre (*grăɴ' prā'*). Name of a Nova Scotia village, meaning, in French, Great Meadow.

Greece. A European country. Greece comes from the Latin Græcia, which was applied by the Romans to the inhabitants of Hellas, as the Greeks have always called their country. The Latin word is derived from Graii, the name of an early people living on the west coast of Greece.

Guatemala (*gwä'tà-mä'là*). A country of Central America. The name is said to be a rendering of the Mexican *quahtemali*, "a decayed log" and to have been given by Mexican Indians who, accompanying Alvarado, found a decayed tree near an ancient palace, thought to be the center of the country.

Hackensack. A city of New Jersey on the Hackensack river. The name comes from the Indian *haucquansauk*, "hook mouth," applied to the river in allusion to the meandering of its lower course.

Haiti. A mountainous island and country of the West Indies. Haiti is a Carib Indian word, indicating mountainous country.

Harz (*härts*) **Mountains.** In central Germany. The earlier name was Hart, Old Saxon for Forest. The modern name is popularly connected with the German *harz*, "resin."

Havana. The capital of Cuba and a city in Illinois. The word is Spanish for harbor.

Havre (*hä'vẽr*). A French seaport. Havre is the French word for harbor.

Helgoland (*hĕl'gô-länt'*). A North Sea island. Helgoland is Danish for Holy Land, probably given because Saint Willibrord preached on the island when introducing Christianity into northern Europe.

Henlopen (*hĕn-lō'pĕn*) **Cape, Del.** From Dutch *hinlopen*, "to run in," having reference to the entrance of a bay near by.

Herculaneum. An ancient city of Italy, buried by the eruption of Vesuvius in 79 A. D. The name means City of Hercules.

Himalaya (*hĭ-mä'là-yà*). Mountains in Asia. Himalaya means Abode of Snow, being derived from the Sanskrit *hima*, "snow," and *alaya*, "abode." The higher peaks are always snow-capped.

Holland. Provinces of the Netherlands. The name is derived from the Dutch *holtland*, "woodland," the region having formerly been well wooded.

Honeyville. A town of Utah. Honeyville is a euphonious contraction for Hunsackerville, Hunsacker having been the original settler.

Hongkong. "Fragrant Streams." An island southeast of China near the mouth of the West river.

Hoosac (*hōō'săk*). River in Massachusetts, New York, and Vermont. Hoosac is derived from the Mohican Indian *wudjoo*, "mountain," and *azhubic*, "rock"; hence "Mountain Rock river."

Hopatcong (*hō-păt'kŏng*). Lake in New Jersey. The name is Indian, said to mean stone over water, being given because of a causeway which connected an island with the shore.

Housatonic (*hōō'-sà-tŏn'ĭk*). River of Massachusetts and Connecticut. The word is said to mean proud river flowing through the rocks, being derived from the Indian *wassa*, "proud," *aton*, "stream," and *azhubic* (shortened to *ic*), "rock."

Hungabee. A peak of the Canadian Rockies. Hungabee is Indian for chieftain.

Huron. One of the Great Lakes, called after an Indian tribe. Huron is variously derived from the Indian words *ohkwe honwe*, "true men," or from *irri roron*, "cat tribe."

Indianapolis. The capital of Indiana. The name consists of that of the state with the addition of the Greek *polis*, "city."

Innsbruck (*ĭns'brŏŏk*). Name of an Austrian city, meaning bridge over the river Inn.

Isle of Man. In the Irish Sea. The name is adapted from the Manx word *mannin*, "middle."

Itasca (*ĭ-tăs'kă*). County and lake in Minnesota, named from a portion of the barbarous Latin phrase *veritas caput*, "true head," the lake being near the head of the Mississippi river.

Ithaca. City in New York and village in Michigan named for the native island of Ulysses, as described in the *Odyssey* of Homer.

Jaffa (*yă'fä*; *jăf'ȧ*). A seaport of Palestine. Jaffa is derived from the Semitic *yapho*, "beauty."

Jamaica. A west Indian island and a section of New York City in Long Island. The name is derived from the Indian *haymaca*, "island of fountains," being given because the island is copiously watered.

Japan. A European corruption of the native name Nippon, "Rising Sun." Marco Polo called the country Zipangu, from which the form Japan arose.

Java (*jä'vȧ*). Island of the Malay archipelago, said to be named from the Sanskrit *yava*, "millet."

Jerusalem. City of Palestine. The Babylonian form of its name was Urusalim, "City of Peace."

Jordan. River of Palestine, Utah, and Nova Scotia. The Hebrew name Yarden means Descender.

Juniata (*jōō'nĭ-ăt'ȧ*) **River, Pa.** Named from a tribe of Indians that inhabited its banks. The root of the word is said to mean a stone.

Kaffraria (*kă-frā'rĭ-ȧ*). The region of South Africa inhabited by the Kafirs, natives so called from the Arabic word *kafir*, "unbeliever."

Kalamazoo. A city and river in Michigan. Kalamazoo is Indian and is variously explained as meaning beautiful water or boiling water or as derived from *negikanamazo*, "otter tail."

Katahdin (*kȧ-tä'dĭn*). Name of a mountain in Maine, derived from Indian *katahdu*, "great mountain."

Kearsarge (*kēr'särj*), **Mt., N. H.** A derivative of the Indian *keas*, "high," *auke*, "place." The name was also borne by a famous battleship.

Kennebec (*kĕn'ē-bĕk'*) **River, Me.** From the Indian *quinninippiohke*, "long place of water."

Kenosha (*kē-nō'shȧ*). A city of Wisconsin. The name is from the Algonquin Indian *kenosa*, said to mean long fish, or pike, probably in allusion to the fishing in the adjacent waters of Lake Michigan.

Keokuk (*kē'ō-kŭk*). City in Iowa, named for an Indian chief, the word meaning watchful fox.

Keweenaw (*kē'wē-nô*) **Point, Mich.** So called from the Indian word *kewauenau*, "portage," it being easier for canoeists to effect a portage across the point than to paddle around it.

Key West. City in Florida. Key West is a corruption of *Cayo Hueso*, Spanish for Bone Reef. The reef when discovered contained bones, supposed to be those of the aboriginal inhabitants.

Kiskiminitas (*kĭs-kĭ-mĭn'ĭ-tăs*) **River, Pa.** From the Indian kithanne, "place of the largest stream."

Kitchener. City in Ontario. The former name was Berlin, which was changed during the World War to Kitchener, commemorating Lord Kitchener.

Kittatinny (*kĭt'ȧ-tĭn'ĭ*) **Mountains, Pa.** From the Indian name Kitadini, "Largest Mountain."

Kokomo. A city of Indiana. Kokomo is Indian, meaning Young Grandmother.

Labrador (*lăb'rȧ-dôr'*; *lăb'rȧ-dôr*). Peninsula of Canada. The name is said to be derived from the Portuguese *lavradores*, "laborers," an early navigator having brought 57 natives to Lisbon as laborers.

Lachine (*lȧ-shēn'*). City of Quebec, named from rapids in the Saint Lawrence river. La Chine is French for China and was applied by early explorers, who believed they had reached Asia.

Lackawanna (*lăk'ȧ-wŏn'ȧ*) **Creek, Pa.** Said to be derived from the Delaware Indian words *lechau hanne*, "the stream that forks."

La Crosse (*lȧ krŏs'*). City in Wisconsin, the site of which had been a favorite place with the Indians for playing the game of lacrosse. The game was called *la crosse* by the French.

Ladrones (*lȧ-drōnz'*). Islands in the north Pacific Ocean. Ladrones is the Spanish word for thieves and was given by Magellan when, on landing there in 1520, he was robbed by the natives.

Lamoille (*lȧ-moil'*) **River, Vt.** A corruption of the French *la mouette*, "the gull."

La Paz (*lä päs'*). A city of Bolivia. Translated, this Spanish name signifies Peace.

La Porte. City in Indiana. La Porte is French for The Door and is said to have referred to an opening connecting two prairies otherwise separated by forest.

Las Vegas (*läs vā'gȧs*). A city in New Mexico. The name is Spanish for The Meadows.

Lehigh River, Pa. Corruption of the Delaware Indian word *lechau*, "a fork," the stream being one of the forks of the Delaware river.

Lemberg (*lĕm'bĕrĸ*). A city of Poland, named Leopolis in honor of a Ruthenian prince Leo. Lemberg, the English form, is a corruption of Leonberg, "Leo's city," berg being employed instead of the Greek *polis*, "city." The name Leo means Lion.

Levant (*lē-vănt'*). A term of Latin or French origin meaning sunrise or east and applied to the countries bordering the eastern Mediterranean Sea.

Liberia (*lī-bē'rĭ-ȧ*). Country of Africa, settled by emancipated American slaves. Liberia, derived from Latin *liber*, "free," means Land of the Free.

Lille (*lēl*). City of northern France. Lille is a corruption of the earlier L'Isle, "The Island," alluding to an island in the stream on which the city is situated.

Lisbon. Capital of Portugal. It was formerly called Olispo, said to contain the Phœnician *hippo*, "fortress."

Litchfield. A city of Illinois and a town of Connecticut. The name is borrowed from Lichfield, England, an Old English name, meaning Field of the Dead.

Llano Estacado (*lä'nō ĕs'tä-kä'dō*). Plateau in Texas and New Mexico. The name is Spanish for Staked Plain, being given in allusion to the stakelike boles of the yucca plant growing there.

Lombardy (*lŏm'bȧr-dĭ*; *lŭm'-*). A province of Italy named from the early inhabitants, who were called by the Romans Longobardi, probably "Long Beards."

London. Capital of Great Britain. London is said to be derived from the Old British *lyn*, "lake," and *din*, "town"; hence "Lake Town."

Los Angeles (*lōs ăng'gĕl-ĕs*; *lŏs ăn'jĕl-ĕs*). City of California. Los Angeles is Spanish, meaning The Angels.

Lucerne (*lū-sûrn'*). City of Switzerland, named from Latin *lucerna*, "beacon," one having been formerly placed on a tower in the river Reuss.

Lucknow (*lŭk'nou'*). City of India. Lucknow is a corruption of the native name Lakshmanauti, "Fortunate."

Luxor. An Egyptian village, the scene of magnificent ruins. Luxor is an Anglicized form of the Arabic name El Kasur, "The Palaces."

Lycoming (*lī-kŏm'ĭng*) **River, Pa.** Derived from Indian *legaui hanne*, "sandy stream."

Lynn. A city of Massachusetts, named from Lynn, England. The word is Old British for lake.

Macao (*mȧ-kä'ō*). A Portuguese city in China. Macao is probably a corruption of Amangao, "Gulf of the Goddess Ama," from *gao*, "gulf."

Mackinac (*măk'ĭ-nô*). Name of an island of Michigan in Lake Huron, derived from the Indian *mickilimackinac*, "island of the great turtle," or, in other dialects, "island of the giant fairies."

Madeira (*mȧ-dē'rȧ*). Islands in the Atlantic Ocean and a tributary of the Amazon. Madeira is a Portuguese word meaning forest.

Madrid. Capital of Spain, named from Arabic *madarat*, "town."

Maelstrom (*māl'-strŏm*). The former name of Moskenstrom, a strong current in the Lofoten islands west of Norway. It was reputed to contain a vast whirlpool. Probably Dutch, from *malen*, "grind," and *stroom*, "stream."

Mahoning River, Pa. Derived from the Delaware Indian word *mahonink*, "at the lick," a lick being a spot where wild animals resort to lick up exposed salt.

Malta (*môl'tȧ*). A Mediterranean island. Malta is said to be of Phœnician origin, meaning refuge.

Manayunk (*măn-ȧ-yŭngk'*). A suburb of Philadelphia, named from Indian *meneiunk*, "place for drinking liquor."

Manchuria (*măn-choo̅'rĭ-ȧ*). (now Manchukuo). A region north of the great wall of China, so called from the dynasty of the Manchus, "The Pure Ones."

Mandalay (*măn'dȧ-lā*; *măn'dȧ-lā'*). City of Burma, India, named from the Poli word *mandala*, "flat plain." It is in the broad valley of the Irrawaddy river.

Manhattan. An island in New York. The name is Indian, said by some authorities to mean "little island"; by others, "the people of the whirlpool," referring to Hell Gate; by another, "place of drunkenness," Henry Hudson, as the story goes, having, in 1609, taken some chiefs into his cabin and made them drunk.

Manila. The capital of the Philippines. It is named from the native word *maynila*, designating a shrub formerly common on the site.

Manitou (*măn'ĭ-too̅*). A name applied to a Colorado pleasure resort and other localities. It is an Indian word for spirit.

Mankato (*măn-kā'tō*). A city in Minnesota. The name is Indian for Green Earth.

Marmora (*mär'mô-rȧ*). A sea, southeast of Europe, named from Latin *marmor*, "marble," the sea containing an island with extensive marble quarries.

Marne (*märn*). River in France. The Latin form of its name was Matrona, "Matron."

Matanzas (*mȧ-tăn'zȧs*) **Inlet, Fla.** Spanish for massacre, applied by Menendes to commemorate his destruction of Ribaut's company.

Mauch Chunk (*môk chungk*). A borough and a township in Pennsylvania. The word is Indian, variously interpreted to mean on the mountain or bear's cave.

Mediterranean Sea. Between Europe and Africa and so named from Latin *medius*, "mid" and *terra*, "earth," hence "In the Midst of the Earth," this sea occupying the center of the world as known when the name was given.

Memphis. A city of Tennessee, named after the ancient Memphis, Egypt. The Egyptian name of the city was Mennufer, "City of the Good."

Menasha (*mê-năsh'ȧ*). A city of Wisconsin. The word is Indian for thorn.

Mendota (*mĕn-dō'tȧ*). A city of Illinois, village of Minnesota, and lake of Wisconsin, named after an Indian tribe. The word means mouth, the tribe having formerly lived at the mouth of the Minnesota river.

Menominee (*mê-nŏm'ĭ-nē*) **River, Wis.** From an Indian tribe, the Menominees, a name derived from *monomonic*, "wild rice," which is said to have been cultivated by the tribe.

Merrimack (*mĕr'ĭ-măk*). River, county, and town in New Hampshire. Merrimack has an Indian origin and is said to mean sturgeon or swift water. As used of localities in other states, the word is spelled without the final "k."

Mesa Verde (*mā'sȧ vâr'dā*). A plateau and national park in Colorado. Mesa Verde is Spanish for Green Table-land.

Mesopotamia. A territory of Asia now embraced in Iraq. Mesopotamia means Between the Rivers, having been formerly applied to the region between the Euphrates and the Tigris river. The word is derived from the Greek *mesos*, "middle," and *potamos*, "river."

Mexico. A word derived from Mexitl, a form of the name of the Aztec war god.

Miami (*mī-ăm'ĭ*). Cities in Florida and Oklahoma and a town in Arizona named after the Maumees, an Indian tribe. The word is variously explained to mean mother or pigeon.

Michigan. One of the Great Lakes, named from the Algonquin Indian words *michi*, "great," and *guma*, "water;" hence "Great Water."

Milan (*mĭl'ăn*; *mĭ-lăn'*). City of Italy, called by the Romans Mediolanum, from Latin *medius*, "middle," and from *lanum*, believed equivalent to Latin *planum*, "plain;" hence "In the Midst of the Plain."

Milwaukee. A city and river of Wisconsin, said to be named from the Algonquin *minwaukee*, "rich country."

Minneapolis. Metropolis of Minnesota, named from the Dakota Indian words *minni*, "water," and *ha*, "curling," and from the Greek *polis*, "city." Minneapolis, therefore, means City of the Curling Water and was applied in allusion to Saint Anthony falls in the city.

Minnehaha River, Minn. An Indian name said to mean Falling, or Curling, Water. The river has a cascade with a fall of about 60 feet.

Minnewanka. Lake in Rocky Mountains park, Canada. Minnewanka is an Indian word meaning lake of the water spirit.

Minorca (*mĭ-nôr'kȧ*). A Mediterranean island, having a name derived from Latin *minor*, "smaller." A near-by island is called Majorca, from *major*, "larger."

Mississippi. River and state, so called from the Algonquin Indian *missi sibi*, "great river," sometimes freely translated as "father of waters."

Missouri (*mĭ-soo̅'rĭ*; *mĭ-zoo̅'rĭ*). River and state, named from the Algonquin *mis*, "great," and the Dakota *souri*, "muddy;" hence Great Muddy.

Mobile (*mô-bēl'*). City of Alabama, at the delta of the Mobile river, so called from Maubila, an Indian village formerly on the river.

Mohawk. River in New York. The name is that of an Indian tribe and is said to be derived from the native word *mahaqua*, "bear."

Mohegan (*mō-hē'găn*) **Lake, N. Y.** From a tribe of Indians whose name was from *maingan*, "wolf."

Monadnock (*mô-năd'nŏk*). A mountain in New Hampshire. Monadnock is Indian, variously explained to mean spirit place, difficult, or silver mountain.

Monocacy (*mô-nŏk'ȧ-sĭ*) **River, Md.** From the Indian name Menagassi, "Creek of Many Bends."

Monongahela (*mô-nŏng'gȧ-hē'lȧ*). City and river of Pennsylvania, so called from the Indian word *menawngihella* said to mean falling-in bank.

Mont Blanc (*môɴ' bläɴ'*). Highest peak of the Alps. The name is French for White mountain.

Monte Rosa (*mōn'tā rō'zä*). Name of an Alpine peak, meaning, in Italian, Rosy mountain.

Montreal. City in Quebec. Montreal is a corruption of Mont Royal, the French designation of a hill partly covered by the city.

Moscow (*mŏs'kō*). Capital of Russia. The word comes from Moskva, the name of a river signifying, in Finnic, Place for Washing.

Munich (*mū'nĭk*). A city of Germany. The name means Monk and was given because of a monastery formerly standing on the site.

Muskegon (*mŭs-kē'gŭn*) **River, Mich.** From the Indian name, meaning Plenty of Fish.

Muskingum (*mŭs-kĭng'gŭm*). River and county in Ohio. Muskingum is Indian, meaning Moose-eye river.

Nakimu. Caves in the Canadian Rockies, designated by this Indian word for grumbling. The caves contain noisy waterfalls.

Nanaimo (*nȧ-nī'mō*). A city of British Columbia. Nanaimo is an Indian word for sturgeon.

Nantucket. Island and county in Massachusetts. This name is said to be of Indian origin, meaning Far Away.

Naples. A city of Italy. Naples is a corruption of Neapolis, "New city," from the Greek *nea*, "new," and *polis*, "city."

Narragansett. Summer resort in Rhode Island. An Anglicization of the Indian name of a tribe, Naiagansett, "People of the Point."

Nashua (*năsh'ū-ȧ*). City in New Hampshire on the river Nashua, having an Indian name meaning Between.

Natal (*nȧ-täl'*). Province of South Africa, so called because the region was discovered on the Feast of the Nativity, 1497, *natalis* being the Latin word for birthday.

Natchez (*năch'ĕz*). City in Mississippi, named for an Indian tribe, the word meaning hurrying men.

Naugatuck (*nô'gȧ-tŭk*). A borough and a town in Connecticut. Naugatuck is of Indian origin and is variously explained to mean Point between Rivers or One Tree.

Nauvoo (*nô-voo̅'*). City in Illinois, named in obedience to a revelation reported by Joseph Smith, one of its Mormon founders.

Netherlands. A country of Europe, partly below sea level. The name means Low Lands.

Neversink River. Two small streams in New York and in New Jersey. Neversink is said to be derived from the Indian *newa sink*, "mad river."

Niagara (*nī-ăg'ȧ-rȧ*). Name of a river and a famous cataract, explained by the Indian word *neagara*, "neck," in allusion to the river as a narrow strait connecting Lake Erie and Lake Ontario. Others derive the word from *oniawgarah*, "thunder of waters," referring to the cataract.

Nile. A river of Africa. The English designation is from the Greek *Neilos*, which probably represents the Phœnician name *Nahal*, "Stream."

Niobrara (*nī'ô-brâr'ȧ*) **River, Neb.** "The Broad Water," derived from the Indian *ni*, "water," and *abrara*, "wide."

Normandy. Name applied to part of northern France. An earlier form was Normannia or Northmannia, "Land of the Northmen."

Norwalk. A city in Connecticut, named from the Indian *nayaug*, "middle land."

Nova Zembla. Island group north of Russia. The name means New Land, derived from Latin *nova*, "new," and Russian *zembla*, "land."

Ochlockonee (*ŏk′lŏk′ô-nē*) **River, Fla.** A Seminole Indian name, meaning Yellow Water.

Ocmulgee (*ŏk-mŭl′gē*) **River, Ga.** From the Creek Indian *oko mulgi*, "turbulent stream."

Oconee (*ô-kō′nē*) **River, Ga.** Oconee is a Seminole Indian word, meaning water course.

Okeechobee (*ō′kē-chō′bē*) **Lake, Fla.** "Grassy lake." A Seminole Indian name.

Okefenokee (*ō′kē-fē-nō′kē*) **Swamp, Ga.** From the Choctaw word *okefinocau*, "quivering water."

Oklawaha (*ŏk′lȧ-wô′hô*) **River, Fla.** From the Seminole Indian language, meaning Muddy Place.

Omaha (*ō′mȧ-hô′*). City in Nebraska, named from an Indian word meaning up-stream. The designation formerly applied to an Indian tribe, who were thus referred to as the Up-stream people.

Oneida Lake, N. Y. From the name of an Indian tribe meaning Beacon Stone.

Onondaga (*ŏn′ŏn-dô′gȧ*) **Lake, N. Y.** From an Indian tribe, the name meaning Place of the Hills.

Ontario. "Beautiful lake." One of the Great Lakes; also a province of Canada. The word is Indian.

Opelika (*ŏp′ē-lī′kȧ*). A city in Alabama, named from the Indian *opilualaikata*, "large swamp."

Orkney Islands. North of Scotland. Orkney is from Irish *orc*, "porpoise."

Orleans (*ôr′lā′äɴ′*). A city of France. The name is a corruption of the Latin Aurelianenesis, "Aurelian's City," named after the Roman emperor Aurelian.

Osage River, Mo. An Indian word, interpreted to mean strong.

Oswego. City and river of New York. Oswego is from the Iroquois *oswageh*, "flowing out," alluding to the river

Ottawa. The capital of Canada, on the Ottawa river. The name is derived from the Indian *adawe*, "trade." Also cities in Illinois and Kansas.

Owego. Village and town in New York so called from the Delaware Indian *ahwaga*, "where the valley widens."

Ozark. Low mountains of the central United States. Ozark is said to be a corruption of the French *aux arcs*, "with bows," descriptive of the inhabitants.

Pacific Ocean. The name means Peaceful, being given by Magellan, who first traversed the ocean, probably entering it when it was calm.

Palo Alto (*pä′lō äl′tō; păl′ō ăl′tō*). City in California. Palo Alto is Spanish, meaning High Timber, the site being heavily wooded in earlier days.

Panama (*păn′ȧ-mä′*). Central American country, a gulf, an isthmus, and a famous canal. The word is Indian, being variously explained to mean butterfly or mudfish.

Papua (*pä′pōō-ä; păp′ū-ȧ*). Part of New Guinea, an island north of Australia. The word is derived from Malay *papuwah*, "woolly," and was applied in allusion to the hair of the natives.

Pasadena. City in California. Pasadena is Indian, said to mean Crown of the Valley.

Passaic (*pȧ-sā′ĭk*). City in New Jersey, on the Passaic river. An Indian name, explained either as meaning Peace or as derived from *passajeek*, "valley," in allusion to the river.

Passamaquoddy (*păs′ȧ-mȧ-kwŏd′ĭ*). Bay on the coast of Maine. An Indian word, meaning pollock ground.

Passumpsic (*pȧ-sŭmp′sĭk*) **River, Vt.** This word is Indian, meaning much clear river.

Patagonia. Name given to southern Argentina, said to be derived from the Spanish *patagon*, "large foot" and applied because of the large footprints of the inhabitants. It is also explained as from the Indian *patacuna*, "terraces." The land slopes in terraces eastward from the Andes mountains.

Patapsco (*pȧ-tăps′kō*) **River, Md.** From the Indian name Patapsqui, "Black Water."

Pecos (*pā′kōs*) **River, Tex.** Named by the Spaniards from *pecoso*, "freckled," a local suggestion in the appearance of its waters.

Peiping (*bā′pĭng′*). A Chinese city, formerly the capital and known as Peking. The name Peiping means Northern Peace.

Pembina (*pĕm′bĭ-nȧ; -nô*). Name of a city in North Dakota, contracted from the Ojibway *anepeminam*, a species of cranberry growing there.

Pend Oreille (*pŏnd′ĕ′rā′*) **Lake, Idaho.** French word meaning earring, suggested by the lake's shape.

Penobscot. A bay, river, and county in Maine. The name is from the Indian *penobskeag*, "rocky place."

Pensacola. City and bay in Florida, named from an extinct tribe of Indians, the Panshaoklas, "Hair People."

Peoria (*pē-ō′rĭ-ȧ*). City in Illinois, named from an Indian tribe. The word means place of fat beasts.

Pernambuco (*pĕr′năm-bōō′kō*). City of Brazil. The name means, in Portuguese, Mouth of Hell and was given in allusion to the violent surf near by.

Persepolis (*pēr-sĕp′ô-lĭs*). The Greek designation of a city of ancient Persia, meaning Persian city.

Persia (*pûr′shȧ; pûr′zhȧ*). Country of Asia. Persia is from *parsa*, probably a Semitic term for horsemen.

Philadelphia. A city of Pennsylvania, whose name is derived from two Greek words *philia*, "love," and *adelphos*, "brother"; hence "Brotherly Love." It expresses an ideal of its Quaker founders.

Pinole (*pĭ-nō′lȧ*). A town of California, so named from a Spanish term for parched grain.

Piscataqua (*pĭs-kăt′ȧ-kwȧ*) **River, N. H.** From the Indian *piscataquanke*, "a great deer place."

Plata, Rio de la (*rē′ō dā lä plä′tä*). South American river. "River of Silver," so called by the Spaniards.

Platte (*plăt*). A river in Nebraska, Colorado, and Wyoming. Platte is French, meaning Calm.

Pocomoke (*pō′kô-mōk*) **River, Md.** From its Indian name Pockhammokik, "Broken by Knolls," probably referring to the surrounding country.

Point Pinos (*pē′nōs*), **Cal.** Originally named Punta de Pinos, Spanish for Point of Pines.

Poland. Country of Europe. The name means Land of Plains, from Slavonic *pole*, "plain."

Potomac. River in the United States. The name is Indian and is variously explained as meaning Place of the Burning Pine or as from *potowmak*, "they come by water."

Potsdam. Suburb of Berlin, Germany. Potsdam is a corruption of the Slavonic Poddubami, "Under the Oaks."

Poughkeepsie (*pô-kĭp′sĭ*). A city in New York, named from a near-by waterfall, Peoghkepsingh, which signifies a place where the water breaks through.

Prague. City of Germany and former capital of Czechoslovakia. The Czech form of the name is Praha, meaning threshold, and having reference to a reef of rocks in the bed of the Moldau river, on which the city is located.

Prairie du Chien (*prā′rĭ dōō shēn′*). A city in Wisconsin, having a French name, which means Dog Prairie.

Provence (*prô′väɴs′*). A region of southeastern France. Provence is derived from Latin *provincia*, "province." It was the first Roman province in Gaul, and anciently was called Provincia Romana.

Prussia. A state of Germany, whose inhabitants were formerly called, in Lettish, Pruzzi, "Neighbors."

Pueblo (*pwĕb′lō*). A city in Colorado, named from a Spanish word meaning village. The word was earlier applied to a tribe of Indians who, unlike other tribes, built permanent homes.

Puerto Rico. An island of the West Indies, given a Spanish name, meaning Rich Port.

Punjab (*pŭn-jäb′*). "Five Rivers." A province of India, through which flow five tributaries of the Indus—Jhelam, Chenab, Ravi, Sutlej, and Beas.

Punta Arenas (*pōōn′tä ä-rā′näs*). A seaport of Puerto Rico, appropriately given this Spanish name, meaning Sandy Point.

Quebec. Province, city, and river of Canada. Quebec is variously explained as from Quebesq, a village of Brittany, or from an Algonquin term meaning beware of the rock.

Quinsigamond (*kwĭn-sĭg′ȧ-mŏnd*) **Lake, Mass.** Indian name, meaning Fishing Place for Pickerel.

Rangoon. City of Burma, India. The name is derived from the Burmese *ran kun*, "end of the war" and was given by Alompra, the founder of a native dynasty, after he had conquered a rival established at Pegu.

Rapidan (*răp′ĭ-dăn′*) **River, N. C.** A corruption of Rapid Anne.

Rappahannock River, Va. From Indian *lappihanne*, "river of quick, rising water."

Regina (*rē-jī′nȧ*). Capital of Saskatchewan. *Regina* is the Latin word for queen.

Rhine. A river of Germany. Its name is connected with the root of German *rennen*, "flow."

Rhodes. An island in the Mediterranean Sea, named from the Greek *rhodon*, "rose."

Rideau (*rē'dō'*). A river and canal in Ontario. Rideau is French, meaning Curtain, and alludes to the appearance of a waterfall on the river.

Rio de Janeiro (*rē'ō dā zhȧ-nā'rō*). Capital of Brazil, on the bay of Rio de Janeiro, "River of January," so called by its Portuguese discoverers, who, on January 1, 1502, entered the bay, supposing it to be a river.

Rio Grande (*rē'ō grän'dā*). River between Mexico and the United States. The name is Spanish for Great River.

Riviere du Loup (*rē'vyâr' dōō lōō*). A city and a river of Quebec. A French term, meaning Wolf river.

Roanoke. A city in Virginia, named from the Indian *roenoke*, a word for shell, or wampum.

Rockaway. A section of greater New York, in Long Island, named from the Indian word *ackewek*, "bushy."

Rodeo (*rô-dā'ō*). A precinct of Hidalgo County, New Mexico. The name is Spanish for Round Up, a term signifying the assembling of cattle grazing at large.

Rumania. A country of Europe. Rumania is a corruption of the Latin Romania, "Country of the Romans," the region having been anciently settled by Romans.

Sabine (*sȧ-bēn'*) **River, La.** Said to have been so named in allusion to the Roman story of the rape of the Sabine women, because the early French voyagers there carried off Indian women as wives.

Saco (*sô'kō*). River and city in Maine, named from an Indian word *sauk*, "pouring out."

Sacramento. Capital of California on Sacramento river. The word is Spanish for sacrament.

Sag Harbor. Village in New York. Sag is a shortened form of Sagaponack, an Indian name meaning Place Where Groundnuts Grow.

Saginaw. City in Michigan on Saginaw river. The name is said to be derived from the Indian *sauk sachoon*, "pouring out at the mouth."

Sahara (*sȧ-hä'rȧ*). Desert in Africa. Sahara is an Arabic word for desert.

Salem. City in Massachusetts. The name is a shortened form of Jerusalem, "City of Peace." Salem by itself means Peace.

Sandusky. City in Ohio. Sandusky is variously explained as from the Indian *sanduste*, "large pools of water," or as given for Jonathan Sandousky, a Polish trader.

Sandwich Islands. Former designation of Hawaii. The name commemorates Lord Sandwich, formerly of the British Admiralty.

San Francisco. City of California. The name is Spanish for Saint Francis.

San Salvador (*sän säl'vȧ-dōr'*). Designation applied by Columbus to the first land sighted by him in America. The place is now believed to be Watling island, or Guanahani. San Salvador means Holy Savior.

Santa Cruz. City of California. A Spanish expression, meaning Holy Cross.

Santa Fe. City in New Mexico. The name is Spanish for Holy Faith.

Santiago (*sän'tē-ä'gō*). The capital of Chile. Santiago is a Spanish form for Saint James.

Saragossa (*să'rȧ-gŏs'sȧ*). A city of Spain. Saragossa is a corruption of the city's Roman name, Cæsarea Augusta, "City of Cæsar Augustus," a Roman emperor.

Saranac. A river and group of small lakes in New York so called from an Indian word meaning river that flows under a rock.

Saratoga Springs. Summer resort in New York. The name is said to mean Sparkling Place, from Indian *assarat*, "sparkling," and *oga*, "place."

Sarawak (*sä-rä'wäk*). District in North Borneo, named from Malay *sarakaw*, "cove."

Saskatchewan (*săs-kăch'ē-wŏn*). A river and province in western Canada. Saskatchewan is Indian and is said to mean Swift river.

Saugatuck (*sô'gȧ-tŭk'*). A river in Connecticut. The name is derived from the Indian *sauketuck*, "at the mouth of the tidal stream."

Sault Sainte Marie (*sōō' sânt mä-rē'*). Cities of Michigan and Ontario. Sault is a French word for cascade. Hence "Cascade of Saint Mary."

Savannah. City and river of the southeastern United States. The name is of Indian origin and means grassy plain, alluding to the surrounding country.

Saxony. A state of Germany, named for the Saxons, so called from the *seax*, as they designated the sword which they carried.

Scandinavia. A peninsula of northern Europe. The word is explained as "Land of Darkness," derived from the Teutonic *shadino*, "dark." Northern Scandinavia has, in winter, a night which lasts for several months.

Schoharie (*skô-hăr'ĭ*). A village in New York, on a stream of that name, which is a corruption of the Indian *towosshoher*, "driftwood."

Schroon (*skrōōn*) **Lake, N. Y.** Variously explained as from Scharon, adopted in honor of the duchess of Scharon, favorite of Louis XIV, or from an Indian word meaning "child of the mountain."

Schuylkill (*skōōl'kĭl*) **River, Pa.** From the Dutch *schuylen kill*, "hidden creek."

Scioto (*sī-ō'tō*) **River, Ohio.** Shawnoese Indian word, meaning hairy. Its waters at flood were said to have been filled with hairs, attributed to the herds of deer bathing when shedding their coats.

Scutari (*skōō'tä-rē*). City in Turkey. The name is from the Turkish *uskudar*, "messenger," the city having been a station for couriers. Also a city of Albania.

Seattle. City in Washington, named for the chief of the Duwamish Indians, *See-aa-thl*.

Sebago (*sē-bā'gō*) **Pond, Me.** From an Indian word meaning great water.

Sebastopol. City of southern Russia, named from the Greek *sebastos*, "august," and *polis*, "city"; hence "August City."

Sheboygan (*shē-boi'găn*) **River, Mich.** From the Indian *showbwawaygum*, "a stream that comes from the ground."

Shenandoah. A tributary of the Potomac river. Its name is Indian and is variously explained to mean Sprucy stream, Hillside stream, or Daughter of the Stars.

Shrewsbury River, N. J. From a town of England. Its early name was Scrobbesbuhr, which, in Anglo-Saxon, signifies Underbrush town.

Sierra Nevada. Mountains of Spain and of California. Sierra Nevada is Spanish for Snow mountains. Sierra is a Spanish word meaning saw. It is applied also to a mountain range, the peaks of which show analogy to the teeth of a saw.

Sinai (*sī'nī*; *sī'nā-ī*). A mountain of Asia, named for Sin, the Babylonian moon god.

Singapore (*sĭng'gȧ-pōr'*). A city of southeastern Asia. The earlier form of the name was Simhapura, Sanskrit for Lion city.

Sing Sing. The name of the state prison near the village of Ossining, New York, and, until 1901, the name of the village. It appears to have been named from the Sin Sincks Indians, formerly located near by.

Skagerrack (*sgăg'ĕr-răk*). A strait of northern Europe. Skagerrack means Rocky Cape channel, being derived from the Danish *skagi*, "promontory," and *rack*, "channel."

Skaneateles (*skăn'ē-ăt'lĕs*). A village and a lake in New York. The name is Indian for Long lake, given in allusion to the long and narrow shape of the lake.

Spain. Country of Europe. Spain is derived originally from the Greek Hispania, an alternate form of Hesperia, "Land of the West."

Spitzbergen. Island group north of Norway. The name is Dutch for Sharp-peaked mountains.

Spokane (*spō'kăn'*). City of Washington. Spokane is of Indian origin, meaning Children of the Sun.

Spuyten Duyvil (*spī'tĕn dī'v'l*). "Spitting Devil." A channel in Manhattan island, so called by the Dutch.

Stockholm. The capital of Sweden. The older form of the name, Stakholm, was a compound of the Swedish *stak*, "sound," and *holm*, "island," meaning Island in the Sound. The city is built mainly on islands in a strait.

Sudan (*sōō'dän'*; *sōō-dăn'*). Name of a portion of northeastern Africa, being Arabic for The Blacks.

Suez (*sōō-ĕz'*; *sōō'ĕz*). A town, isthmus, and canal in Egypt. The name comes from Suweis, part of the Arabic designation of a fortified well, some distance from the town.

Sunapee (*sŭn'ȧ-pē*). Lake in New Hampshire, named from the Indian word *shehunknippe*, "wild goose pond."

Superior. One of the Great Lakes. Superior is Latin, meaning Higher.

Susa (*sōō'sȧ*). A city of ancient Persia. The name is from the Persian *shushan*, "lilies."

Susquehanna. A river in Pennsylvania, so called from the Indian *suckahanne*, "water."

Suwannee (*sōō-wô'nē*). Towns and rivers in Florida and in Georgia. The word is Indian, said to be from *sawani*, "echo river."

Syria. A district of western Asia. Syria is derived from Assyria, a lengthened form of Assur, "Water Bank." Assur was situated on the Tigris river.

Tacoma. City in Washington. The name means Big Snow mountain and was borne by an Indian chief, after whom the city was called.

Tagus (*tā'gŭs*). River in Iberian peninsula, Europe. The word goes back to a Phœnician name meaning Fish river.

Tahlequah (*tä'lĕ-kwä'*). City in Oklahoma. Tahlequah is derived from the Cherokee Indian *talikwa*, said to mean place of two large towns.

Tallahassee (*tăl'ȧ-hăs'ē*). Capital of Florida, so called from an Indian word meaning old town.

Tallahatchie (*tăl'ȧ-hăch'ē*). County in Mississippi named from Tallahatchie river. The word is Indian for River of the Rock.

Tallapoosa (*tăl'ȧ-pōō'sȧ*). River in Georgia and Alabama, giving its name to a county in Alabama and to a city in Georgia. Tallapoosa is Indian, variously explained to mean Swift Current or Stranger.

Tarragona (*tär'rä-gō'nä*). City of Spain. The earlier form was Tarraco, from the Phœnician *tarchon*, "citadel."

Tarrytown. Village in New York. The origin of the name is found in the Dutch *terwen*, "wheat."

Tay. River in Scotland. Tay is derived from the Pictish *tau*, "tranquil."

Tennessee. Tributary of the Ohio river in the United States. The name is of Indian origin, said to mean Curved Spoon, probably in allusion to the course of the river.

Terre Haute (*tĕr'ē hōt'*). City in Indiana, built upon a bank 60 feet above the river. Terre Haute is French for High Land.

Texarkana. A city on the line between Texas and Arkansas; hence the name.

Thames (*tĕmz*). A large river in England; also rivers in Ontario and Connecticut. The name is of Celtic origin, meaning Broad river.

Thebes (*thēbz*). Two ancient cities, in Greece and Egypt. The origin of the Greek name is from *teba*, "hill"; the name of the Egyptian city is from *t' ape*, "the capital."

Thermopylæ (*thĕr-mŏp'ĭ-lē*). A mountain pass in Greece. Thermopylæ means Pass of the Hot Springs, from the Greek *thermos*, "hot," and *pylæ*, "pass." The hot springs have disappeared since ancient times.

Tibet (*tĭ-bĕt'*; *tĭb'ĕt*). A district of China. Tibet is said to be a corruption of Thupo, "High Country."

Ticonderoga (*tī-kŏn'dĕr-ō'gȧ*). Village in New York named from the Indian *cheonderaga*, "brawling water," referring to the noise of a near-by cataract.

Tien Shan (*tĭ-ĕn' shän'*). "Celestial mountain." A range on the western border of China.

Tierra del Fuego (*tyĕr'rä dĕl fwā'gō*). South American archipelago. The Spaniards applied this designation, meaning Land of Fire, because the Indian inhabitants used fires at night for signals.

Tigris. A river of Mesopotamia. Tigris is derived from Old Persian *tigra*, "arrow."

Tippecanoe River, Ind. From the Indian name of a fish living in this stream, "the long-lipped pike," or "buffalo fish."

Tokyo (*tō'kē-ō*). The capital of Japan, on the east side of Honshu island. Tokyo means Eastern Capital.

Tombigbee. River in Mississippi and Alabama, named from the Choctaw Indian *itimbibikpi*, "undertaker."

Topeka. Capital of Kansas. Topeka is from the Indian word *topeakae*, "a good place to dig potatoes."

Toronto (*tō-rŏn'tō*). Capital of Ontario. The name is a Huron word for place of meeting.

Tortugas (*tôr-tōō'gȧz*) **Islands, Fla.** A Spanish word meaning tortoise, probably used as a designation because of the number of the animals found there.

Trebizond (*trĕb'ĭ-zŏnd'*). Name of a Turkish city, derived from Greek *trapeza*, "table." The city is on a table-land.

Trinidad. Island of South America. The name is Spanish for Trinity, being given because the first view of it, when discovered, revealed three mountain peaks.

Tucson (*tōō-sŏn'*). City of Arizona. Tucson is from the Indian *stynk son*, "black base," applied in allusion to the color of the lowest rock layer of a near-by mountain.

Tulare (*tōō-lâr'ȧ*) **Lake, Cal.** From *tule*, Spanish for bulrush, that plant being common on its shores.

Turin (*tū'rĭn*; *tū-rĭn'*). A city of Italy. The name in Italian, *Torino*, goes back to a Celtic word *tors*, "hills," and means City of the Hill-dwellers.

Tuscaloosa (*tŭs'kȧ-lōō'sȧ*). City in Alabama, called after an Indian chief, the name meaning Black Warrior.

Tuskegee (*tŭs-kē'gē*). City in Alabama, so designated probably from the Indian *taskialgi*, "warriors."

Tuxedo (*tŭk-sē'dō*). Settlement in New York. The name is said to be derived from the Indian *p'tauk seet tough*, "place of bears."

Ukraine (*ū'krān*). District of Russia, called in Russian Ukraina, "Borderland." It was formerly part of Poland and bordered on Russia.

Umbagog (*ŭm-bā'gŏg*). Lake lying partly in New Hampshire and partly in Maine. Umbagog is Indian and is variously explained to mean Doubled Up, Clear Lake, or Near-by lake.

Urbana (*ûr-băn'ȧ*). Cities in Illinois and Ohio. Urbana is a form of the Latin *urbanus*, "refined."

Uruguay (*ū'rōō-gwā*; *ōō'rōō-gwī'*). South American country and river. The name means Bird's Tail, derived from Guarani Indian *uru*, "bird," and *guay*, "tail," and was applied in allusion to a falls on the river, which spread out like a bird's tail.

Valenciennes (F. *vȧ'läN'syĕn'*; E. *vȧ-lĕn'sĭ-ĕnz'*). City of France, said to have been called after the Roman emperor Valentinian. The name means Powerful.

Volga (*vŏl'gȧ*). The greatest European river, called Volga from the Old Slavonic *wolkoi*, "great."

Wabash. Counties in Indiana and Illinois, river flowing through both states, and city in Indiana. The word is Indian, explained as from *unabache*, "cloud borne by an equinoctial wind," or as meaning white water.

Wales. Part of Great Britain. Wales is derived from Anglo-Saxon *wealas*, "foreigners."

Walla Walla. City in Washington on a river of the same name. Walla Walla is Indian for Many Waters.

Wastach. A river in Rocky Mountains park, Canada. The name is Indian for Beautiful.

Watervliet (*wô'tĕr-vlēt'*). "Flowing Stream." A city in New York, named by the Dutch.

Weehawken (*wē-hô'kĕn*). A township in Hudson county, New Jersey, named from Indian *weachin*, "maize lands."

Wetterhorn (*vĕt'ĕr-hôrn'*). A mountain of Switzerland. Wetterhorn means Storm Peak.

Wheeling. City in West Virginia, named from Indian *weal ink*, "place of a human head," in reference to a white man's head placed on a pole there by the Indians.

Willamette (*wĭ-lăm'ĕt*). River in Oregon, named from Indian *wallamet*, "running water."

Windsor (*wĭn'zĕr*). Cities in England, the United States, and Canada. Windsor is a contraction of the Anglo-Saxon *windlesofra*, probably meaning place by the winding shore.

Winnepesaukee (*wĭn'ē-pē-sô'kē*). Lake in New Hampshire. The name is Indian, meaning Good Water Discharge, or, according to others, Beautiful Highland lake.

Winnipeg. Capital of Manitoba; also a lake in that province. Winnipeg is Algonquin Indian for Muddy Water, referring to the lake.

Winona. City in Minnesota. Indian for First Born Daughter.

Wissahickon (*wĭs-ȧ-hĭk'ŏn*) **Creek, Pa.** From the Indian word *misamekhan*, "catfish stream."

Yangtze (*yäng'tsĕ'*). A large river of China. The name means Son of the Sea.

Yankton. City in South Dakota, named from Indian *eyank ton wah*, "people of the sacred lake."

Yazoo (*yăz'ōō*). City and river in Mississippi. The name means River of Death, being of Indian origin.

Yoho. A valley and national park in the Canadian Rockies. The word is Cree Indian, meaning Wonderful.

Yosemite (*yō-sĕm'ĭ-tē*). A valley and national park in California, named from the Indian *osamit*, "grizzly bear."

Youghiogheny (*yŏk'ô-gā'nĭ*) **River, Pa.** From Indian *yukwiakhanna*, "meandering stream."

Ypsilanti (*ĭp'sĭ-lăn'tĭ*). City in Michigan, named for a Greek prince.

Yukness. A mountain of the Canadian Rockies. Yukness is derived from a Sioux Indian word for sharpened as with a knife.

Zambezi (*zȧm-bā'zē*; *zăm-bē'zĭ*). A large river of Africa. Zambezi is a native word for great river.

Zanzibar (*zăn'zĭ-bär'*; *zăn'zĭ-bär'*). An island of Africa. The name is a Portuguese form of the Persian Zangibar, "Land of the Blacks."

Zuider Zee (*zī'dĕr zē'*). Formerly a southern arm of the North Sea in the Netherlands. The name is Dutch for South Sea. Cut off from the North Sea by a dike in 1932, it was drained leaving a small inland lake, Ijsselmeer.

BIBLIOGRAPHY

The following titles of books have been selected from lists prepared by eminent authorities on geography for the use of students and teachers and for general reference.

GENERAL GEOGRAPHY

Brooks, Charles, with Nelson, John and others—Why the Weather? . . . . . . *Harcourt Brace*
Brunhes, Jean—Human Geography. . . . *Rand*
Campbell, Douglas H.—An Outline of Plant Geography. . . . . *Macmillan*
Case, Earl and Bergsmark, Daniel—College Geography. . . . . *Wiley*
Davis, D. H.—The Earth and Man. . *Macmillan*
Huntington, Ellsworth and Cushing, Sumner W.—Principles of Human Geography. . . . *Wiley*
Jones, Clarence F.—Economic Geography. . *Holt*
Newbigin, Marion I.—Animal Geography. *Oxford*
Packard, L. O., Overton, Bruce, and Wood, Ben D.—Our Air-age World. . . . . . . *Macmillan*
Pearcy, G. E., Fifield, R. H., and Associates—World Political Geography. . . . . *Crowell*
Renner, George and Associates—Global Geography. *Crowell*
Seeman, Albert—Physical Geography. *Prentice-Hall*
Smith, J. Russell and Phillips, N. Ogden—Industrial and Commercial Geography. . . . *Holt*
Tarr, R. S.—College Physiography. . *Macmillan*
Van Loon, H.—Geography. . *Simon and Schuster*

REGIONAL GEOGRAPHY AND TRAVEL

The following titles of books have been chosen chiefly from lists of standard works of travel recommended by librarians for the guidance of general readers.

United States and Dependencies

Brittain, Vera—Thrice a Stranger. . . *Macmillan*
Carmer, Carl—The Hudson. . *Farrar and Rinehart* (See other books in the "Rivers of America" Series.)
Comstock, Sarah—Old Roads from the Heart of New York. . . . . *Putnam*
Cram, Mildred—Old Seaport Towns of the South. *Dodd Mead*
Dulles, Foster R.—America in the Pacific; a Century of Expansion. . . . . . . *Houghton Mifflin*
Fenneman, N. M.—Physiography of Eastern United States. . . . . *McGraw-Hill*
Freer, W. B.—Philippine Experiences of an American Teacher.. . . . . *Scribner*
Greely, A. W.—Handbook of Alaska. . . *Scribner*
Gruening, Ernest H. (Ed.)—These United States. *Boni & Liveright*
Gunther, John—Inside U. S. A. . . . . . *Harper*
Jenkins, Elmer (Ed.)—Guide to America. (In collaboration with the Am. Automobile Assn.) *Public Affairs Press*
Perry, George S.—Cities of America. *McGraw-Hill*
Winn, Mary D.—The Macadam Trail. . . *Knopf*

Canada

Beston, Henry—The St. Lawrence. *Farrar and Rinehart*
Currie, A. W.—Economic Geography of Canada. *Macmillan*
Hamilton, Louis—Canada. . . . . . . *Brentano*
Hutchinson, Bruce—The Unknown Country, Canada and her People. . . . . . *Longmans Green*
Peat, Louisa W.—Canada's New World Power. *McBride*
Quinn, Vernon—Beautiful Canada. . . . . *Stokes*

Mexico, Central America, West Indies

Corwin, Herbert—These are the Mexicans. *Reynal and Hitchcock*
Hancock, Ralph—The Magic Land: Mexico. *Coward-McCann*
—The Rainbow Republics. *Coward-McCann*
Hastings, Elizabeth—Motoring to Mexico. *Pan-American Union, Wash., D. C.*
Mitchell, Carleton—Islands to Windward. *Van Nostrand*
Roberts, W. A.—Lands of the Inner Sea, the West Indies and Bermuda. . . . . . *Coward-McCann*
Strode, Hudson—Now in Mexico. . *Harcourt Brace*

South America

Bates, Nancy Bell—East of the Andes and West of Nowhere. . . . . *Scribner*
De Sherbinin, Betty—The River Platte Republics. *Coward-McCann*
Harding, Bertita—The Southern Empire: Brazil. *Coward-McCann*
Madariaga, Salvador de—The Rise of the Spanish American Empire. . . . . *Macmillan*
Miron, Burgin F.—Handbook of Latin American Countries. . . . . . . *Harvard Univ. Press*
Tavares de Sa, Hernane—The Brazilians, People of Tomorrow. . . . . *J. Day Co.*
Ybarra, T. R.—Lands of the Andes. *Coward-McCann*

Europe

Belloc, Hilaire—Path to Rome. . . . . . *Nelson*
Blanchard, Raoul and Crist, R. E.—A Geography of Europe. . . . . *Holt*
Bogardus, J. F.—Europe; a Geographical Survey. *Harper*
Clark, Vinnie—Europe, a Geographical Reader. *Silver Burdett*
Goodall, George (Ed.)—Soviet Russia in Maps. *G. Phillip & Son, Ltd.*
Hutton, E.—England of My Heart. . . . *Dutton*
Lauterbach, R. E.—These are the Russians. *Harper*
Lyde, Lionel W.—The Continent of Europe. *Macmillan*
Rajchman, Marthe—Europe; an Atlas of Human Geography. . . . . *Morrow*
Van Valkenburgh, S. and Huntington, E.—Europe. *Wiley*
Welles, Samuel G.—Profile of Europe. . . *Harper*
Wright, John K.—The Geographical Basis of European History. . . . . *Holt*

Asia

Bergsmark, Daniel—Economic Geography of Asia. *Prentice-Hall*
Cressey, G. B.—Asia's Lands and Peoples. *McGraw-Hill*
Lauterbach, R. E.—Through Russia's Back Door. *Harper*
Mallory, W. H.—China: Land of Famine. *Macmillan*
Saunders, Kenneth J.—The Heritage of Asia. *Macmillan*
Stamp, L. D.—Asia; a Regional and Economic Geography. . . . . *Dutton*

Africa

Fitzgerald, W.—Africa, a Social, Economic and Political Geography. . . . . *Methuen*
Flandrau, (Mrs.) Grace C.—Then I Saw the Congo. *Harcourt Brace*
Gregory, John W.—Africa; a Geography Reader. *Rand*
Powell, E. A.—The Last Frontier. . . . *Scribner*
Suggate, L. S.—Africa. . . . . . . *Harrup, Ltd.*

Australia and New Zealand

McGuire, Paul—Australia, her Heritage, her Future. *Stokes*
Shann, Edward O. G.—An Economic History of Australia. . . . . . . *Cambridge Univ. Press*
Taylor, Thomas G.—Australia in its Physiographic and Economic Aspects. . . . . *Oxford*
Upton, Sydney—Australia's Empty Spaces. *Allen & Unwin*

Polar Regions

Amundsen, R. E. G.—My Life as an Explorer. *Doubleday Page*
Macmillan, Donald B.—How Peary Reached the Pole. . . . . *Houghton Mifflin*
Stefansson, V.—My Life with the Eskimo. *Macmillan*

TEST QUESTIONS

Give the derivation of the word geography. State the name and the subject matter of each of the principal divisions into which the science of geography is classified 639

Characterize the three chief periods of geographical progress 639

Name one of the founders of the science of geography 639

Give two reasons based on climate for the superior state of civilization in the temperate zones . 639

State four benefits that may be derived from the study of geography 639–640

Who were the earliest navigators known to history? Name a notable discovery made by each of them 657

Mention six Greek geographers and state the chief contributions made by each to the science of geography 657

What conception of the world's shape prevailed in Europe during the middle ages? How was the geographical knowledge possessed by the Greeks transmitted to Western Europe? . . 657

What chief discovery was made by each of the following men: Marco Polo, Vasco da Gama, Captain Cook, Mackenzie, McClure, Nordenskjöld, Peary, and Amundsen? 657–658

What is meant by the poles of the earth? Contrast the character of the earth's surface at the north pole with that at the south pole . 659

Of what use are circles of latitude and of longitude? How does a degree of latitude differ in length from a degree of longitude? 659

What is the cause of the alternation of day and night? of the difference in length of day at different seasons? 659–660

Explain how an observer may tell in what zone he is by observing the noonday position of the sun throughout the year 660

NORTH AMERICA

To what part of the earth is the name America applied? In whose honor was it so named? Explain the use of the term New World . . 661

Give the north-and-south length of America. How near does America approach to the north pole? to the south pole? 661

Compare North America and South America as regards shape and climate. Name prominent features common to both continents 661

What oceans and other bodies of salt water border the shores of North America? Describe the character of the North American coasts. On which coast are the harbors most numerous? 661

What great mountain systems form the chief surface features of the North American continent? Locate these systems and indicate the extent of each. Name the highest mountain peak in North America 661

Describe the Great Basin, the Colorado plateau, the Mexican plateau. What noted valley lies in the Mexican plateau? 661

Give the location and extent of the Medial plains. By what important river systems are these plains drained? 662

In what part of the continent are volcanoes found? Name one or more active volcanoes in Central America, in Mexico, in the United States, in Alaska 662

Describe in general the climate of North America. Characterize the climate of Central America; of Mexico; of the Great Plains. Where, in North America, is the region of greatest rainfall? of least rainfall? 662

State the rank of North America among the continents in respect to mineral wealth. Name 10 important mineral products of this continent. 662

Indicate the extent and the general character of North American forests. In what respect are the trees of the Pacific slope remarkable? 662–663

Compare the bird and animal life of North America with that of Europe and Asia. Name several birds and larger animals characteristic of North America 663

State the chief facts about Hudson bay, mentioning its location, its size, the character of its waters, shores, and tributary rivers. Describe its fisheries and fur trade, and point out its commercial importance 663

Name and describe the Great Lakes, in the order of size, giving outlets and connections. State the commercial importance of the Great Lakes, naming the largest port on each . . 664

THE UNITED STATES

State the location of the United States, naming the countries and the oceans between which it lies. Describe briefly the character of the Atlantic coast; of the coast of the Gulf of Mexico; of the Pacific coast 665

What mountain system extends along the Atlantic side of the United States? along the western side? Where is the Great Basin located? the Columbia River plateau? . . . 665

Name the chief drainage basins of the United States. Into what oceans, seas, or gulfs do their drainage waters flow? How large a part of the United States lies in the Mississippi basin? Estimate the agricultural importance of this region 665

Describe in general the climate of the United States. Where do the greatest extremes of heat and cold occur? Where are the regions of greatest rainfall? 665–666

Discuss the mineral wealth of the United States, naming several important minerals produced. In what parts of the United States are extensive forests found? Name several important forest trees 666–667

Mention some of the larger native animals of the United States. Name six well-known song birds; six highly prized game birds; eight valuable food and game fishes 667

State the rank of the United States in manufactures among the countries of the world. Give reasons for its position 667

Locate the northernmost point in the United States; the easternmost; the southernmost; the westernmost. Where is the geographic center of the country? Indicate the location of the center of population 667

Locate the following national parks and mention a prominent feature of each: Crater Lake, Glacier, Lassen Volcanic, Rocky Mountain, Mount Rainier, and Sequoia . . 668

New England States

Locate the group of New England states and give their names. To what single western state are they nearly equal in total area? Compare them with that state in respect to population 670

Describe the surface, the rivers, and the climate of the New England states 670

What are the chief mineral productions of these states? Which of these states leads in the value of quarry products? 670

Describe briefly the fisheries of New England. Which state stands first in value of sea fish taken? 670

What is the leading occupation of the people of New England? Mention ten important products of New England factories. Give four reasons for the success of New England as a manufacturing region. Compare Massachusetts with other states of the Union with respect to manufactures and commerce . . 670

Describe the commerce of the New England states. Name five leading New England seaports 670

Middle Atlantic States

Name the states usually called the Middle Atlantic states. Which of these are sometimes called the Middle states? 670

What fraction of the total area of the United States do the Middle Atlantic states embrace? what proportion of the total population? of the total manufacturing capital? of the total number of wage-earners? 671

Describe in general the surface of the Middle Atlantic states. Through what part of this group does the Appalachian Mountain system extend? Describe the coastal plain. Name four important tidal rivers found in this group. What large river on the west serves as an interior waterway? 671

State in general the climate of the Middle Atlantic states. To what influence does the fruit belt of western New York owe its favorable climate? 671

In what does the mineral wealth of the Middle Atlantic states consist? Where and when was petroleum first discovered? In what manufactures do these states, by reason of their mineral resources, lead all other states? . . 671

Describe the development of agriculture in the Middle Atlantic states. Name the leading agricultural products. What state pays special attention to dairying? In what state do peanuts and tobacco form an important crop? 672

Name the most valuable single product of the salt-water fisheries of the Middle Atlantic states 672

Give two reasons for the commercial supremacy of the Middle Atlantic states. In what respects does the state of New York rank first among the states of the Union? What important waterway connects the Hudson river with the Great Lakes? 672

Central States

Name the states comprised in the division called the Central states. Describe the character of their surface and the nature of their soil 672

By what river systems are the Central states chiefly drained? Name some important navigable rivers. Describe the climate and rainfall of the Central states 672

Compare this group of states, as regards mineral wealth, with other parts of the United States. In which of these states is coal mined? iron ore? In which are petroleum and salt obtained? 672

State the importance of the Central states as an agricultural region. Name the principal crops produced. What state leads in the production of tobacco? What state leads in production of sugar beets? 672

Name the principal farm animals raised in the Central states. What proportion of the country's wool clip is produced in these states? . 672

In what article of manufacture do the Central states lead the world? Name other important manufactures. In which of the Central states is the manufacture of iron and steel chiefly centered? 672

What proportion of the railway mileage of the country is located in the Central states? Name the rivers and lakes that form important inland waterways 673

Southern States

Give the boundaries, extent, and area of the Southern states. What proportion of the total area of the United States do these states form? 673

Name the states comprised in the eastern section of this group; in the western section. Describe the surface of each section 673

Summarize the chief features of the climate of the Southern states. Which parts receive the heaviest rainfall? the lightest rainfall? . . . 673

Describe the forests of each section of the Southern states. Compare these forests with those of other parts of the United States. . . 673–674

Name the principal mineral deposits found in the eastern section; in the western section. What important minerals are found in Alabama and in Tennessee? in Florida? Indicate the leading state or states in the production of petroleum and natural gas; of sulphur; of rock salt 673–674

State the chief occupation of the people of the Southern states. What is the most valuable crop produced in the Southern states? What fruits does southern Florida produce? Which of the Southern states leads in cotton growing? in sugar production? in cattle raising? in wool production? 673–674

Estimate the importance of stock raising in the eastern section; in the western. Name the chief animal products of each section . 673–674

State the principal manufactures of the eastern section. Name the three states which lead in manufactures. Which states in this group lead in the manufacture of iron and steel? of cotton goods? of tobacco? 673

What are the chief manufactures of the western section? Which of these states leads in manufactures? 674

What are the chief articles of export of the Southern states? Name the principal seaports of each section 673–674

Plateau States

Name the Plateau states. Describe their surface. Which state has the highest elevation above sea level? the lowest? Which contains the highest mountains? 674

By what drainage systems are the states in this division drained? Name four important rivers in each system 674

Describe the climate of the different parts of this region, stating reasons for the great diversity. Which parts are hottest? which are coldest? Why does each of these states contain tracts of desert? Describe these desert areas 674–675

In what locations are the forests in these states found? Of what trees do they chiefly consist? How many national forests are located in these states? State their total area 675

State the chief mineral productions of this region. Name the states which lead in the production of gold; of silver; of copper; of tungsten 675

By what methods is agriculture carried on in the Plateau states? What are the chief crops produced? In what states or sections are apples grown? melons? long staple cotton? . 675

State the importance of stock raising in these states. Name the most important animals reared. What proportion of the total wool clip of the United States do these states produce? 675

Pacific States

Name the states which form this group. Describe in general their surface. Name and locate three important mountain ranges. Mention five important valleys noted for their fertility 675

Name the chief navigable rivers of the Pacific states. Name three important uses of the rivers of the Pacific states 675

Describe the climate of the Pacific states, giving its chief characteristics. What sections receive the greatest rainfall? the least? . . 675–676

Name important mineral products of the Pacific states. Indicate the present rank of California among the states in gold production . 676

For what characteristics are the forests of the Pacific states noted? In which of the states is the most important lumber region located? . 676

State the importance of agriculture in the Pacific states. Mention leading crops. What class of crops outranks all others in value? 676–677

Which of these states leads in fruit production? Of what classes of fruits does this state's production chiefly consist? In what district are citrus fruits extensively grown? Of what three kinds of fruits does this production principally consist? 677

Discuss the value and extent of irrigation in the Pacific states. What is the position of California as regards irrigation? 677

State the value of the fisheries in these states. Where are the principal fishing grounds? Name the most important food fish taken . . 677

Point out factors that have stimulated manufacturing in the Pacific states. Name the chief classes of manufactured products. Describe the commerce of the Pacific states. Indicate the value of the Panama canal to this region 677

UNITED STATES DEPENDENCIES

Name the dependencies of the United States. In what zone do most of them lie? 683

Locate and give the extent of Alaska. Describe the chief surface divisions of the mainland. Describe also the principal river 683

List Alaska's principal volcanoes, glaciers, straits, canals, and other points of scenic interest, including her largest mountain. What special characteristic distinguishes the Muir glacier? What is the "Valley of Ten Thousand Smokes?" 683–684

According to climate, into what principal districts is Alaska divided? What varieties of vegetation and animal life are found in these different regions? 684

Name the chief mineral products of Alaska State the value of its fisheries. What parts of Alaska does the government railway connect? Sketch briefly the history of Alaska . . 685–686

Describe American Samoa. Name its chief seaport. Locate and give important points about Guam 686–687

Briefly describe Hawaii, mentioning location, extent, surface, soil, and climate. Name the capital. What are the chief productions of Hawaii? Outline its history 687–688

Locate Puerto Rico. Briefly describe its surface, climate, vegetation, and soil. Name the principal industry and products of the island. What city is the capital? Name three other important cities. Outline the history of Puerto Rico 689

Briefly describe the Virgin islands. Sketch their history. In what does the chief value of the Virgin islands now consist? 690

AMERICAN CITIES AND POINTS OF TRAVEL INTEREST

What noted features of travel interest are situated near Adamana? Describe them briefly. State the chief industry of Akron, O.; give reasons for the city's growth 691

Describe briefly the city of Albany, mentioning noteworthy features. What widely known educational institution is located at Annapolis? at Ann Arbor? at Athens, Georgia? 692–693

Of what state is Augusta the capital? Austin? Compare these cities with respect to manufactures and commerce. Briefly describe Baltimore. State its rank in population and give reasons for its industrial and commercial prominence 693–694

Locate and describe Ausable Chasm, Black Rock desert, Blue-Grass Region. For whom was Berkeley named? For what is the city noted? State the chief industries of Bayonne; of Beaumont; of Bethlehem; of Binghamton; of Birmingham 693–695

Briefly describe Boston, giving important points regarding its site, parks, monuments, buildings, and educational institutions. State its rank in population, in manufactures, and as a seaport. Mention features of historic and literary interest. Outline the history of the city. 695–696

In what manufacture does Brockton rank high among American cities? What are the chief manufactures of Bridgeport? 696

Give a brief description of Buffalo, covering important features. State its rank in population; in manufactures. What great commercial advantages does the city possess? Near what celebrated point of interest is it located? . . 696

Locate and give points of travel or other interest regarding Carlsbad Cave, Casa Grande, Castle Gate, and Lake Champlain. Of what importance is Cambridge? Locate and describe Charleston, South Carolina . . . 697–698

Describe in brief the city of Chicago, giving chief points regarding its site, area, streets, parks, and buildings. State the rank of the city in population, in manufactures, in commerce, and as a railway center. To what advantages does Chicago largely owe its commanding position? Give six important events in the history of Chicago 698–699

Where is Cincinnati located? Describe its site. Mention fine residence districts, parks, buildings. Name its leading manufactures 700

Locate and describe the city of Cleveland. State its rank in population and in manufactures. Of what does its civic center consist? With what are the city's chief industries concerned? Point out factors which have greatly aided the city's growth 700–701

Name points of interest in the vicinity of Colorado Springs. Describe the Columbia River highway. For what is Concord, Mass., noted? What and where is the Continental Divide? 701–702

Describe the Corn Belt; the Cotton Belt. . . . 702

Briefly describe Detroit. State its rank in population and manufactures. Of what great industry is it the world center? Of what importance is the lake traffic of Duluth? What are the chief manufactures of Elizabeth? of Elgin? 703–704

For what special industry is Fresno noted? Gary? Gloucester? Gloversville? Of what political importance is Frankfort? Harrisburg? Hartford? Where is the Grand Canyon? Describe some of its principal features. For what historic associations is Gettysburg widely known? Harpers Ferry? Hodgenville? 706–709

Describe Honolulu. Of what races and nationalities is its population composed? Where and of what importance is Houston? Locate and describe the Imperial valley. What is the Inland Empire? Briefly describe Indianapolis, giving important points regarding its commerce and industries. Mention factors aiding its development 709–710

Describe and give the commercial importance of Kansas City, Mo., and Kansas City, Kans. Of what great industries do these cities form a leading center? For what is Key West remarkable? 711–712

Trace the route of the Lincoln highway. For what is Lookout mountain noted? Of what political importance is Lincoln, Nebr.? Little Rock? 713

Briefly describe Los Angeles. State its rank in population, in manufactures, in commerce. Mention factors which have contributed to its growth. Name notable features and places of interest in its vicinity. State the commercial importance of Louisville. For what product is the city a leading market? 713–714

Locate and briefly describe Madison. For what is the city mainly important? Of what production is Memphis the chief center in the United States? State the rank of Milwaukee in manufactures. Briefly describe its site, harbor, parks, buildings, manufactures, commerce 715–716

Give a short description of Minneapolis. In the manufacture of what product is it a leader among American cities? Locate and describe the Mohave desert. For what historic associations is Monterey noted? 716–717

Why are Monticello and Mount Vernon, Virginia, places of national interest? Mention important points concerning Moundsville, Mount Clemens, Mount Rubidoux, Mount Tom, Muscle Shoals 717–718

In what manufacture does New Bedford lead? Of what commercial importance is New Orleans? 718–719

In what characteristics of its buildings does New York excel other cities? What are the chief means of transportation within the city? Describe the harbor and its connections by water and by rail. Discuss the rank of New York in commerce, in finance, in manufactures. Give reasons for the city's supremacy. 719–721

Locate and describe briefly Niagara falls. What important industries are located at the city of Niagara Falls? By what means is the power of the cataract transformed into electric power? Name cities to which this electric power is distributed 721

Locate Philadelphia. Describe its site and street plan. Mention important public edifices and commercial buildings. Name and locate the city's most famous historic landmark 723–725

On what rivers is Pittsburgh located? State its chief industries. In what manufactures does it lead? Give reasons for the city's industrial prominence 725–726

For what is Pittsfield noted? Plymouth? Port Arthur? Portland, Maine? Portland, Oregon? 726

Locate and compare three cities named Portsmouth. Name an important educational institution at Poughkeepsie; at Princeton; at Providence 726–727

For what historic associations is Portsmouth, N. H., noted? Quincy, Mass.? Richmond, Va.? 726–728

Briefly describe Saint Louis. Discuss its commercial importance. State its rank as a manufacturing center. Name leading industries. Sketch the city's history 729–730

What is the standing of Saint Paul as a wholesale center? Mention historic associations of Salem, Mass. Describe Salt Lake City . 730–731

Describe the site and harbor of San Francisco. What is the Golden Gate? State the importance of San Francisco in commerce, in finance, in manufactures. Mention features of scenic or historic interest 731–732

State the rank of Seattle in commerce and manufactures. Give reasons for the city's importance. In what lines does Shreveport lead? Sioux City? South Bend? 733–734

Locate and compare briefly four cities named Springfield. For what is Starved Rock noted? Stone mountain? 734–735

Describe Syracuse as a manufacturing center. Mention factors which have aided the city's growth. Locate and name features of interest regarding Lake Tahoe; Mount Tamalpais; Thousand Islands; Ticonderoga . . . 735–736

For what special product is Trenton noted? Troy? Tulsa? Utica? Waltham? Give points of historic interest regarding Trenton, Valley Forge, Vicksburg 736–737

By whom was the city of Washington planned? How were these plans finally carried out? with what result? Name four of the most noted public buildings. Describe the Washington monument; the Lincoln memorial . . 737

Locate and briefly describe Mount Washington; Watkins Glen; Mount Whitney, Mount Wilson 738–739

Of what industry was Wilkes-Barre the birthplace? Locate the Wheat Belt. Of what manufacture is Winston-Salem the leading center? 738–739

Locate Yellowstone park. Name and briefly describe its chief scenic features. Where is Yosemite park? What remarkable scenic attractions does it contain? Describe its waterfalls; its big trees 739–740

Where and what is Zuñi? Compare it with Acoma, Laguna, Walpi. . . . 741, 675, 696, 737

CANADA

Is the area of Canada greater or less than that of the United States? How far does Canada extend east and west? how far north and south? 747

Into what five natural divisions may the surface of Canada be divided? Characterize each briefly 747

How does the climate of the interior plains of Canada differ in temperature and in rainfall from the climate of British Columbia? Describe the climate of the arctic region in Canada 749

What are the four chief drainage basins of Canada? Name the chief rivers belonging to each basin 749

Indicate the approximate extent and location of the different vegetation areas in Canada . . 749

What are the three chief forest areas of Canada? What kind of timber is obtained from each? What steps have been taken by the government to preserve the forests? Where is the principal market for Canadian forest products? 749

Name 20 animals commonly found in Canada; one animal distinctive of the Canadian fauna; the animal which is a national emblem of Canada 749–750

Indicate the location and extent of land in Canada suitable for agriculture. How much of it is under field crops? 750

Name in order the four cities of Canada which rank highest as industrial centers 750

Mention distinctive features of Canada's railroad system; language conditions . . . 750–751

Provinces

Mention a distinctive feature of the climate of Alberta. What recent trend is noticeable in the province's agricultural industry? What minerals are found in Alberta? 751

What are the two chief industries of British Columbia? 752

Describe the conditions of soil and of climate which make Manitoba an important wheat growing region 753

What are the three principal industries of New Brunswick? 753

State the area of Nova Scotia, its population, and the length of its coast line. Name a large island and a productive fruit district of the province. Where are its richest coal mines? 753–754

How does Ontario rank with other Canadian provinces in each of the following respects: population, wealth, mineral production, value of field crops, output of dairy products, lumbering, and manufactures? 754

What is the maximum elevation of Prince Edward Island? What distinctive industry has recently become important there? 754
Give the boundaries of Quebec. Mention an important factor influencing its climate. Name a distinctive mineral obtained in the province. Discuss Quebec's rank among the Canadian provinces in forest products and manufactures. What is the predominant religion and the language of Quebec? . 754–755
Describe the climate of Saskatchewan. What is the most important product? 755
Name the highest mountain in the Yukon. State the approximate value of gold which has been obtained from the territory 755

Cities and Points of Travel Interest

Name three lakes of great scenic beauty in the vicinity of Banff. 756
What are the leading industries of Brantford? of Calgary? of Charlottetown? 756
Where is Churchill? For what reason is it notable? 756
Locate Edmonton, Fort William, and Halifax. For what is Cobalt noted? Dawson? 756
State reasons for Hamilton's growth as a manufacturing city. 756
Discuss Kingston from the point of view of transportation, education, and historical associations 757
Name two respects in which Montreal exceeds in importance any other city of Canada. Specify two notable examples of engineering skill, three squares, and two great buildings of Montreal 757
For what are the following places chiefly noted: Hull, New Westminster, Niagara Falls, Oshawa? 757
How large is Muskoka? What provincial park lies near it? 757
When was Ottawa made the capital of Canada? Mention an outstanding scenic feature near the city. Name six buildings of note. What is the chief industry? 757–758
Describe Quebec under the heads of location, history, industries, great buildings, and educational institutions 758
For what is Sainte Anne de Beaupré noted? . 758
What is the oldest city in Canada? What is the distinctive industry of each of the following places: Sherbrooke, Sudbury, Sydney, Thetford Mines, and Three Rivers? 758
How does Toronto rank among the cities of Canada in each of the following: industry, commerce, and finance? What distinctive annual institution has Toronto? 759
What are the leading industries of Vancouver? Name the principal park of Vancouver; the chief recreation ground of Victoria. 759
What is the most southerly city of Canada? Name the Border cities. What industry is of especial importance in them? 759
Show how Winnipeg's location is favorable to its growth. Mention the city's outstanding edifice, the largest park, and a distinctive feature of the municipal supply service 759
What is the chief industry of Newfoundland? How does it compare with the remaining industries in workers employed and in products exported? 760

MEXICO, CENTRAL AMERICA, AND WEST INDIES

How much of Mexico is in the Torrid Zone? What is the length of the country? its greatest and its least width? 761
What name is applied to the portion of Mexico between 3000 and 8000 feet elevation? to that above 8000 feet? Name the chief mountain ranges and volcanoes. Give 10 products of Mexico's agriculture or forestry 761
State the reasons for saying that Mexico is potentially one of the richest mineral producing countries in the world. What are the chief manufactured products?. 761
Give the names of the two largest cities of Mexico. Describe the situation of Mexico City. For what is its museum famous? What three notable features are there in the vicinity of the city? 762
Describe Central America under the heads of mountains, climate, and inhabitants 762
Who named Costa Rica? What are the staple products of Costa Rica? of Guatemala? 762–763
Name the chief article of domestic consumption in Honduras; a distinctive fact regarding its capital; the largest lake in Central America; and the volcano of Salvador that has risen one mile in height in the past century. What annual payment does Panama receive from the United States in return for granting the use of the Canal Zone? 763
What are the chief exports of Belize? of Managua? Why is the cathedral of Guatemala noteworthy? Give interesting historical facts about San Salvador and Tegucigalpa . 763–764
Explain the meaning of the terms British West Indies, Greater Antilles, Lesser Antilles. What is the origin of the name Antilles? . . 764
What is the prevailing racial strain in the population of each of the following islands or island groups: Bahama, Leeward, Cuba, and Haiti? 764–765
Mention distinctive features of the rivers and of the fauna of Cuba. What is Cuba's outstanding economic interest? What language is spoken in Cuba? in the republic of Haiti? Name five cities of Cuba 765

SOUTH AMERICA

Compare South America with North America in regard to location, area, coast line, and western mountain system 767
Name the three great plains of South America; the three greatest rivers. What is the most southerly point of the continent? 767
Where are the most arid parts of the continent? What part has the greatest rainfall? 767
Give the names of four important economic plants which flourish in South America; ten characteristic species of animals native there. 767
Name three distinctive mineral products of South America. What countries have a population predominately of the white race? of pure-blooded Indians? What is the prevailing religion? the most widespread language? 767
What are the two highest peaks of the Andes mountains? four volcanoes in this range? For what is Lake Titicaca remarkable?. . . 768
Name the chief tributaries of the Amazon river; of the Plata-Parana River system; of the Orinoco river 768
What is the maximum range of temperature recorded in Argentina? For what economic products is the country noted? Mention two respects in which Argentina leads all other South American countries 768
Specify four of the highest mountains of Bolivia. Discuss the mining and transportation difficulties of Bolivia. What are the chief minerals produced? 768-769
State the area, chief products, and population of Brazil. Describe its climate. Name a notable gold mine of Brazil; a famous cataract of British Guiana 769
Give a distinctive mineral product of Chile; of Colombia; two distinctive products of Ecuador. Name and locate the highest active volcano in the world 770
What are the chief exports of Paraguay? three distinctive products of Peru? State the principal industry of Uruguay; the origin of the name Venezuela 770–772

Name the largest city of South America. Describe the city's principal avenue. Mention interesting features of Easter island, Galapagos islands, Juan Fernandez island, Magallanes, and Santos. What city of South America was formerly a residence of the royal court of a European country? . . 772–774

EUROPE

State the boundaries of Europe. Compare the continent's area with that of the United States. What is the most noticeable characteristic of Europe's coast line? How has this feature proved advantageous for settlement? Name the principal islands of Europe . . . 775

Describe two changes of elevation that have occurred in parts of Europe within historical times. Name six mountain ranges of southern Europe; four plains of the continent. What are the chief volcanic regions? 775

Specify the four longest rivers of Europe. Into what body of water does each empty? What are the two largest lakes of Europe? 775

Account for the warm climate on Europe's northern coast; for the absence of deserts in Europe 776

Name 16 cultivated plants and 5 animals the original habitats of which were in Europe . 776

Indicate the chief areas of Europe which produce each of the following minerals: coal, iron, zinc, platinum, and quicksilver 776

What are the principal mammals found on the continent of Europe? Which domesticated animals originated there? 776

How does Europe's industrial output compare with that of other continents? Account for the concentration of her industries in a few areas 776

Mention five products which European countries export in substantial amounts to countries in other continents 776

What basis is there for the saying that Europe is a collection of small, stubbornly independent states? Give some examples of these autonomous countries 776

Bound Austria. What is her latest estimated area and population? On what industries do the inhabitants depend chiefly for support? 776

Countries

What is the density of Belgium's population? Name the chief manufactures; the most celebrated university. Indicate a peculiarity of the racial and linguistic conditions of Belgium 776–777

Give the boundaries of Bulgaria. Name a distinctive product of Bulgaria; the chief waterway; the prevailing religion; the three largest cities 777

Describe the political relation of Denmark to the Faroe islands; to Greenland. Characterize the agricultural industry of Denmark. Specify a change in Denmark's territory occasioned by World War I 777

State the boundaries of France. How does the character of the coast and of the rivers affect the location of French ports? Name the highest mountain of France; the leading minerals produced; the principal manufactures. What is the prevailing religion of France? the most notable university? . . . 778

Give the names of a high mountain in Germany; five rivers; five minerals obtained; the two leading field crops; two products for which German industry has shown special aptitude 779

How high is Gibraltar? Describe a memorable siege which it endured 780

Distinguish between Great Britain as a geographical entity and as a political division. Name the principal coastal indentations of Great Britain. What benefits accrue to Great Britain from the shallowness of the surrounding seas? 780

Name the chief rivers of England; the largest lake; the highest mountain. Discuss the rank of England among European countries in coal exporting, iron production, shipbuilding, and the manufacture of cutlery and of textiles. Name the four largest cities . . 780-781

What is the chief economic interest of Wales?. 781

Into what three parts may Scotland be divided by the nature of its surface? Where is the densest population? What are the chief industries? the leading crop? the established religion? the four largest cities? 781

Specify the largest island of Greece; the ancient and the modern name of the chief peninsula; the largest mountain range; a notable drainage project; and a distinctive product. Describe the climate of Greece 781–782

Give the boundaries of Hungary. Why are the people sometimes called Magyars? 782

Describe and locate Hecla and the Great Geyser 782

How many people emigrated from Ireland since 1850? Approximately what percentage of the inhabitants can speak the Irish language? What is the island's longest river? a district which attracts numerous tourists? Give a reason for Ireland's designation as the "emerald isle" 782

Contrast the Irish Free State with Northern Ireland in regard to economic interests and religion 782

State the boundaries of Italy; two notable rivers of the country; the leading industry; two distinctive artistic products. Compare the northern Italians with the southern Italians in occupation and percentage of illiteracy. Mention a method by which many Italian city dwellers combine city and country life. What two disastrous earthquakes have visited Italy in modern times? 783

Indicate the location of Latvia and of Lithuania. Name the principal river and the chief exports of each country 783

Why is the Netherlands sometimes called Holland? Characterize the surface of the country. Describe the formation and the reclamation of the former Zuider Zee. Indicate the country's canal mileage, three distinctive products, a breed of cattle developed there, a chief source of raw material for the industries, and the seat of government . . . 784

Mention a distinctive attraction for tourists in Norway. What are the chief occupations of the inhabitants? 784

Specify three characteristic products of Portugal. Mention a noteworthy political fact concerning the country 785

State the boundaries of Rumania; the chief exports; the predominant religion 785

How much of the Danube river lies in Rumania? Give the name of one of its large tributaries. 785

Name and locate the highest mountain in Russia. Name the nine constituent republics of the Soviet Union? What is the principal watershed in Russia, and what rivers of southern drainage rise from it? Describe some of the measures taken by the Soviet government to bring about the industrialization of the country. From what is Russian caviar made? Specify the chief minerals produced . . 785-786

Characterize the surface of Spain. Name six rivers of the country. Which ones are navigable? What are the principal economic values of the plateaus in Spain? Where is Andalusia? What does it produce? Name two distinctive products of Spain. Describe the mineral wealth of the country 786

Name four great lakes of Sweden. Characterize the three principal divisions of the country. Specify three important industries; the three principal cities 786–787

Describe the surface and drainage of Switzerland. Name five notable mountains. Discuss avalanches in Switzerland, stating their cause and some precautions taken against loss due to them. Mention a famous tunnel of Switzerland; the chief industries; three distinctive products. What characteristics distinguish a Swiss chalet? 787

Describe the surface of Yugoslavia. What is the Iron Gate? How much of the country's area is forested? What are the three chief religions of the inhabitants? 787

Cities and other Points of Travel Interest

Name five glacial lakes in the Alps mountains. State an important item of interest concerning each of the following places: Amiens, Arcadia, Argonne forest. In what industry does Amsterdam lead the world? How long is the Appian way? 788

Give the names of two important squares in the city of Athens; the four ancient edifices on the Acropolis. Specify an important fact regarding Mount Athos; Avignon; Belleau woods 789

What is the most famous boulevard of Berlin? Mention a great park, six important buildings, and 10 industries of Berlin. . . . 789–790

State the origin of the name Bern. Mention an interesting fact concerning Bingen. What is the chief industry of Birmingham? of Bradford? of Brest? 790

Name a famous ship which was built at Bristol. Specify two important industries of Budapest. When was Cadiz founded? State an important point of interest regarding each of the following: Calais, Cambrai, Canterbury, Cantigny, Capri, Cardiff, Carrara 791

What American state was named after one of the Channel islands? Indicate at least one interesting fact regarding Chateau Thierry; Chemnitz; Cherbourg. Describe briefly Cologne cathedral 792

Name the chief museum of Copenhagen; the founder of Cork; the principal art gallery of Dresden; the finest public garden of Düsseldorf; a thoroughfare of Edinburgh . . . 792-793

Describe Fingal's cave. Discuss Florence as an art center. Mention some of the literary and historical associations of Frankfort and important religious and political associations of Geneva; a sculptural group in Genoa. . 793–794

State at least one outstanding fact regarding Hammerfest. Indicate the chief commercial interest of Hamburg; of Gorki 795

Explain the terms Stamboul, Sublime Porte, Golden Horn, Byzantium, Galata, and Pera. Name the two greatest mosques of Istanbul 795

What great philosopher lived at Königsberg. Name the two chief industries of Leeds; the principal manufacture of Limoges . . . 795–796

Who founded Leningrad? 796

Name the three divisions of Greater London; eight important streets of London; three parks or pleasure grounds; ten famous buildings of the city. For what is Lourdes noted? 797

Describe the "Lion of Lucerne" and the Maelstrom. What is the largest industry of Lyon? of Manchester? What are the chief attractions of Monte Carlo? 798–799

Give a description of the Kremlin in Moscow. Mention a famous opera house of Naples; important facts regarding Nuremberg, Oberammergau, and Olympia 799-800

What is the chief interest in Ostend? in Oxford? Explain the plan followed in the construction of the boulevards of Paris. What is the Latin quarter? the Louvre? the Quai d'Orsay? the Sorbonne? the Bon Marché? the Bourse? 800-801

What is Pisa's most celebrated building? Mention famous persons connected with Portsmouth; Prague; Ravenna 801

Justify Rome's designation as "the eternal city." Name the seven hills of Rome; three important thoroughfares; a fashionable promenade of the city. Describe the Vatican briefly 801–802

Discuss the industrial importance of the Ruhr district to Germany. Name its chief cities. . 802

State interesting facts about the Cathedral of Seville and the Cathedral of Saint Mark in Venice. What is the most famous prehistoric monument in Great Britain? 803

Name the most notable driveway and the largest park of Vienna. For what is Verdun noted? Versailles? Windsor? 804

ASIA

Compare the area of Asia with that of North and South America. Name the three great peninsulas on the south of Asia. What is meant by the term Oceania? 805

Name and locate the world's highest plateau; highest mountain; deepest lake; vastest plain 805

Describe briefly the course of the following rivers: Lena, Hwang, Brahmaputra, Indus. 806

Specify the coldest part of Asia; the hottest part; the area of the greatest rainfall; the desert portion 806

Name 25 cultivated plants and 8 domesticated animals that are believed to have originated in Asia. Indicate the chief minerals known to exist in Asia. What are the principal religions of the continent? 806

Name the independent countries of Asia. What political changes have taken place in Asia since World War II? 807

What country has the greatest territorial interest in Asia? 807

Indicate the chief product of the Malay states; six products of Ceylon 807–808

Describe the mineral wealth of China; Chinese agriculture; transportation; religion; government 808

Name ten products of the Dutch East Indies. What is the prevailing religion of Java? What religion did it supersede? 808

What is France's largest Asiatic colony? What is that colony's chief export? In what part of India is irrigation required? Specify wild animals of India which are a source of danger to the inhabitants. How many languages are spoken there? 809–810

Specify five products of Iran 811

Indicate the two highest mountains of the Japanese empire; the highest active volcano; the chief market for Japanese silk 811

Discuss the origin of the inhabitants of Korea. 811–812

Name the two largest islands and the four most populous cities of the Philippines. Describe the vegetation and the animal life of the islands 812–813

What are the chief crops of the Philippines? Name the principal exports and imports. Describe the people. When did the Philippines attain their independence? 813

Characterize the agricultural resources of Russia's Great Northern Lowland; the agricultural industry of Turkey 813–814

Indicate the nature of the religious interest centering in Amernath; in Bethlehem. Mention a striking historical fact regarding Agra; Ankara; Baghdad; Calcutta 814–815

What is the chief commercial interest of Canton? Hankow? Kobe? Madras? To what religion is each of the following places sacred: Lhasa, Mecca, Jerusalem, Medina? . . 815–816

AFRICA

What is the distinguishing characteristic of Africa's coast line? How does this continent compare in size with North America? What is the Great Rift Valley? Name three lakes in this valley. Locate Africa's highest mountain 818

Name four great rivers of Africa; the greatest cataract in the world. Mention a remarkable fact concerning Lake Chad 818–819

Indicate the two desert areas of Africa and the region of the greatest rainfall. Describe the surface of the Sahara desert. Name five native cultivated plants of Africa; five distinctive species of mammals; a deadly insect; two important mineral products 819

Contrast the Bantus and the true Negroes in Africa. What religion of outside origin has the greatest following in the continent? Give the names of two 19th century explorers in Africa; of two agencies which have more recently added to our knowledge of the continent 820

What are the chief products and the capital of Belgian Congo? the principal exports of British Africa? Where and of what historic importance is the island of Saint Helena? 820–821

What changes in Italy's possessions resulted from World War II? What is Egypt's principal crop? What part of the country is most productive? What is the chief cause of its productivity? 820–821

State the area, population, and leading exports of French Africa. What does Italian Libya produce? 821–822

Name the only two independent Negro countries in the world. For what are Saint Thomas and Prince's islands noted? 822

Specify the leading industry and a distinctive industry of the Union of South Africa; three products of which the country provides a large part of the world's supply 823

Who founded Alexandria? Name a famous building which distinguished the city in ancient times. What is the largest city of Africa? Indicate two notable edifices of Cairo. 823

What are the chief attractions of Giza? of Karnak? of Luxor? 823–824

Of what importance is Casablanca? Dakar? Dar es Salaam? Johannesburg? Freetown? Nairobi? 823–824

AUSTRALIA

Compare the area of Australia with that of the United States; that of Europe. What is the highest mountain in Australia? What regions are arid? 825

Account for the fewness of Australian rivers. Name the largest river system; three lakes of inland drainage systems. What two minerals are obtained in the greatest value? Name six other minerals produced in the continent 825–826

Mention two distinctive families of plants found in Australia. Note an adaptation by many Australian plants to their arid environment. What is Australia's national flower? Give the names of four valuable fodder plants of Australia 826

Indicate four soft woods and six hard woods obtained from Australian forests; two characteristic mammals and five remarkable birds found in the continent 826

What is the main industry of Australia? an export in which Australia leads the world? What is the meaning of the name Australia? What was the continent called before 1817?. 827

Locate New South Wales; describe its surface, rainfall, forests, and chief industry. What is its capital? Describe Queensland 827

Mention a noteworthy fact about the lakes of South Australia. What is the chief industry? 828

Where are the "Australian Alps?" Which state of the Australian Commonwealth has the largest area? The greatest population? . . . 828

What parts of Western Australia have sufficient moisture for agricultural purposes? What are the principal crops? The chief mineral product? 828

Name five manufactures of Adelaide; a prominent summer resort near the city; the chief industrial interest of Ballarat 828

What is the mean annual temperature of Brisbane? State facts of the city's early history. Name a notable square of Hobart 828

What is the population of Melbourne? Name four colleges affiliated with the University of Melbourne 829

Point out an important advantage of location enjoyed by Sydney. Name three outstanding manufactures 829

NEW ZEALAND AND ANTARCTICA

Describe an interesting volcanic region in North island. What is the chief mountain range of South island? the largest lake? the highest peak? 829–830

Name the most characteristic plant of New Zealand; an outstanding contribution to the world's economic plants; a distinctive wingless bird; the chief industry. Mention a noticeable feature of the Dominion's industrial life; of the transportation system 830

What are the aborigines of New Zealand called? Specify the chief exports of Auckland; of Dunedin. Who founded Christchurch? . 830–831

Compare the area of Antarctica with that of Australia. Why have south polar expeditions landed on the side of Antarctica nearest New Zealand? Describe the climate of the continent. Name six recent expeditions which set out to explore Antarctica 832

PLACE NAMES

What picture origin underlies the name of the Balearic islands? From what principal sources have place names been derived, particularly in the United States? 839

Why were the following places so called: Aalborg, Akron, Arabia, Bellefontaine, Boise, Brazil, Brussels? 839-840

What historical personages are recalled in the names of these cities: Augusta? Baltimore? Cadillac? Cincinnati? Cleveland? . . . 840–841

Indicate the meaning of each of the following place names: Candia, Cayuga, Ceylon, Chaudiere. Account for the spelling of Cleveland and for the application of the following names: Circleville, Colon, Colorado, Corsica, Costa Rica, Cuzco, and Des Moines . . . 841

From what language did each of the following names originate: Detroit, Costa Rica, Ethiopia, Formosa, Galena, Gibraltar, Haiti, Harz, Himalaya, Jerusalem, Kaffraria, Kenosha, Lackawanna, Lisbon, Lynn, Maelstrom? 842–843

Explain the origin of each of the following names: Manila, Mendota, Mesopotamia, Minneapolis, Montreal, Nakimu, Natal, Niagara, Ozark, Papua, Pend Oreille, Philadelphia, Provence, Punjab, Rhodes. Why was the Mediterranean Sea so called? Indicate the source of the name Nauvoo. What is the meaning of Mesa Verde? Missouri? Mont Blanc? Munich? Nile? Norwalk? 844–845

Identify place names representing the Spanish for Saint Francis; Holy Cross; saw-tooth mountains; land of fire; place of the tortoise 846–847

State the reason for the application of each of the following place names: Rodeo, Rumania, Sabine, Scioto, Scutari, Stockholm, Tennessee, Texarkana, Thermopylæ, Tierra del Fuego, Trebizond, Ukraine, Uruguay, Zuider Zee 846–847

V

Science

SUBJECT GUIDE

LINCOLN LIBRARY INDEXES

• • •

Dictionaries	***Page 2114***
General	***Page 2115***
Illustrations	***Page 17***
Tabulations	***Page 2114***

THE ATOMIC AGE BEGINS

INTRODUCTORY

In popular speech, science is often used to mean ordered knowledge concerning the things which occur in nature. In other words, science is a short term for "natural science," and it is in that sense that it will be used in this section. It includes such branches of knowledge as astronomy, geology, physiography, physics, chemistry, zoology, and botany.

Nature of Science. Because of its method as well as of its subject matter, science differs from philosophy, which professes to examine the presuppositions of science, that is, the trustworthiness of observation and reasoning. Science differs also from history in that it deals exclusively with observable, material objects, while the subject matter of history must usually be inferred rather than observed. Again, science differs from art, which is essentially action based on knowledge and on practice. As Jevons says: "A science teaches us to *know* and an art to *do*, and all the more perfect sciences lead to the creation of corresponding useful arts." Astronomy, for example, is a science upon which the art of navigation is based.

VALUE OF SCIENCE

The debt which the modern world owes to science is incalculable. Most of the great advances made by Western civilization in the last 500 years were achieved primarily through science. It was enlarged knowledge of astronomy and improvements in the mariner's compass which resulted in the discovery of America and in the circumnavigation of the globe.

Science and Invention. Every notable modern invention has had its origin in a new application of the laws of science. The application of scientific principles to the control of steam resulted in the invention of the steam engine. By this single achievement, industry and transportation were revolutionized throughout the world. The experiments of Faraday in electricity led to the creation of the dynamo and the electromotor. Electric energy, thus utilized, became a powerful competitor of steam, and transformed numerous industries. A half century after Faraday, experiments with explosive inflammable gases made possible the internal combustion engine. The utilization of this new form of motive power added first the automobile and then the airplane to the list of great modern mechanical achievements.

Practical Benefits. Consequently, instead of the oxcart, the stagecoach, and the sailing ship, we now have the railway train, the trolley car, the ocean liner, the automobile, and the airplane, all of which are results of progress made in science. But, striking and important as these mechanical advances have been, they form only a small part of the grand total of achievements to be credited to modern science.

In countless ways, present-day civilization is deeply indebted to each of the sciences. The practical benefits which have grown out of the discoveries made in chemistry and physics, for example, extend to nearly everything connected with daily life. They affect food, water supply, clothing, housing, heating, ventilation, lighting, and the thousand-and-one conveniences with which the modern home is equipped. In some important way they affect also almost every operation in connection with the farm, factory, mine, store, or business office.

Progress in Chemistry. Advances made in chemistry have completely changed many of the world's leading industries. Processes based upon the application of chemical discoveries lie at the foundation of great enterprises, such as iron and steel making. The recovery of gold and other precious metals from their ores and the preparation of many valuable mineral products alike require advanced chemical knowledge. Present-day methods of manufacturing soaps, fertilizers, synthetic dyes, and illuminating gas have been made possible only through chemistry. The processes of refining petroleum so as to make it yield a veritable Pandora's box of useful products depend upon chemical principles. So, likewise, do the elaborate methods required for the preparation of hundreds of foodstuffs. Chemistry makes possible the photographer's art, furnishes the physician with his medicines, and provides the surgeon with anesthetics, such as ether, chloroform, and cocaine.

Progress in Physics. In the domain of physics alone, the discoveries of the last century have been epoch making. The early work on electric cells by Volta and others stimulated Morse to devise the electric telegraph. With later improvements, this became the transoceanic cable telegraph. Experiments in sound and electricity enabled Bell to perfect the telephone. These two great inventions, the telegraph and the telephone, have revolutionized methods of communication in all civilized lands.

Wireless and Radio. But, by wresting further secrets from the unknown, investigators prepared the way for a still more marvelous achievement. In an obscure laboratory in Germany, a high school teacher of physics, Heinrich Hertz, discovered the properties of the electrical waves, now known as Hertzian waves. This discovery enabled Marconi and others to work out practical methods of wireless communication, which soon proved invaluable for the use of ships at sea. These seemingly magical waves are also the basis of the recent great development in "radio" transmission. By means of improved sending and receiving devices, spoken messages and vocal and instrumental music are broadcasted at great distances to millions of listeners.

Had physics, since the 18th century, done nothing more than to revolutionize the world's methods of communication, science, as a whole, could rest proudly upon the laurels thus impressively won. But these achievements represent only a fraction of the contributions made by physics, and physics is only one of several major divisions of science. Some of the other contributions are equally worthy of consideration.

Microscope and Spectroscope. About 100 years ago, certain physicists, studying with especial care the laws governing the efficiency of lenses, made possible the achromatic objective lens and the modern high-power microscope, which was given to the world in 1835. As Pasteur later remarked, this instrument revealed the realm of the infinitely small, just as the telescope revealed the universe of the infinitely great. The use of the improved microscope led to discoveries of the first rank in the plant and in the animal world, and made possible the great modern developments in the science of biology.

Further researches in light led to the invention of the spectroscope. This instrument enables the astronomer to determine the elements composing the sun and stars with the same certainty that the chemist determines the composition of minerals in his laboratory. Later studies in light led to the detection of the X rays and to the finding of radium. These discoveries rank among the foremost scientific achievements, both of which have already proved of great value in various fields.

Progress in Biology. Humanity owes much to modern biology. Beginning with the revelations first made possible by the high-power microscope, there has been a continuous record of discovery concerning all forms of living beings, including man. Like the great advances in chemistry and in physics, the increase in biological knowledge has been of immense practical value.

First came the proof that the cell is the unit of all plant and animal structures, and, therefore, the unit of life. This fact at once placed botany and zoology on a new and firm foundation and radically changed the viewpoints of all related sciences.

Then came the doctrine of evolution, advocated by Darwin and other scientists. In the effort to test the validity of this theory, biological research was stimulated to a degree never before known. This led to many important discoveries. All classes of plants and of animals were studied with exceeding thoroughness and accuracy.

Antitoxins and Serums. In the course of these researches, investigators proved that certain minute forms of life, protozoa and bacteria, were the cause of contagious and infectious diseases. Out of this knowledge grew antiseptic and aseptic surgery, both of priceless value in saving human life. A further outcome was the successful use of antitoxins and serums in combating diphtheria, typhoid fever, and other dangerous maladies. Increased knowledge in this field has resulted in the eradication or control of malaria, yellow fever, and other insect-borne diseases. Modern sanitary science and preventive medicine owe their origin to biological discoveries.

Zoology and Animal Industry. Advances in zoological science have conferred great benefits upon animal industry. Among these have been the improvement of various breeds of domestic animals, the scientific rearing of live stock, and the prevention and control of animal diseases. Valuable improvements have been made also in the preparation, preservation, and marketing of various animal products, especially those of the dairy, poultry yard, and packing house.

In numberless other ways the knowledge contributed by zoology is of great assistance. By means of it, barren waters have been stocked with valuable food fish, noble game animals have been saved from extinction, depleted seal herds have been largely restored, and Alaskan Indian tribes have been preserved from starvation through the introduction of the reindeer.

Botany and Plant Industry. Similarly, the numerous enterprises dependent upon plant industries have been benefited by the great advances made in economic botany. To these may be attributed the remarkable progress in agriculture, horticulture, floriculture, and forestry made during recent years. Improved varieties of grains, grasses, fruits, vegetables, and other important economic plants have been developed more rapidly than ever before in the history of mankind.

Crop plants suitable for special conditions of soil and climate have been developed or obtained from other parts of the world. By means of these better adapted plants, vast areas formerly lying waste have become productive and the older lands have been made to increase their yields. New kinds of crops have been made profitable in many sections. Examples are seen in a quickly ripening wheat for northern regions, alfalfa and Kafir corn in Kansas, the orange and grapefruit in Florida, and the grape, prune, walnut, and various citrous fruits on the Pacific coast.

METHODS OF SCIENCE

The immense success of science is due to the way in which it seeks, finds, and tests knowledge. More valuable than any of its discoveries are its effective methods, which make still greater achievements possible.

The true scientific investigator never jumps at conclusions, never takes anything for granted, never considers his judgment better than his information, and never substitutes opinion or long established belief for fact. No matter how plausible a given statement may be or how logical a proposed explanation of it may seem, it must be treated merely as a supposition until it has been proved true by searching tests. Moreover, these tests must be of such kind that other scientists can repeat them, and of such nature that others repeating them will inevitably come to the same conclusion. Only in this manner can a body of dependable scientific knowledge be built up.

The Working Hypothesis. Where exact observation is impossible, a tentative explanation, adopted temporarily as a *working hypothesis*, has often proved of great service. Such working hypotheses have led to some of the most important discoveries in science. Noted examples are: in astronomy, the nebular hypothesis and the planetesimal hypothesis; in biology, the hypothesis of natural selection; and in chemistry and physics, the hypothesis of the electron, atom, and molecule. Each of these, in its field, has been a fruitful stimulus to scientific research.

Not only the scientific method, but also the scientific attitude, is of incalculable value. The true scientist seeks neither to confirm nor to confute ancient dogma or current speculation, except as his proved facts lead him. He endeavors simply to report the truth as the methods and tests of science show it to be. The true scientist never assumes the rôle of an advocate or special pleader, presenting the strong points on one side while ignoring or belittling like points on the other side.

Science, therefore, is nonpartisan and seeks only to establish the facts regardless of whether their pronouncement will be welcomed or resented. It carries on no propaganda for or against a given view, but trusts the truth to make its own way. For this reason, there is nothing regional, racial, or national about science. It is international and universal, making no exceptions for or against any nationality, race, or creed.

Use of Scientific Methods. Because of their universal effectiveness, the methods, first conspicuously developed in the natural sciences, are being more and more widely extended to other fields of knowledge. Subjects which formerly were not considered primarily as sciences are studied profitably by scientific methods. Indeed, various subjects so treated are now commonly called sciences. Moreover, there seem to be no valid reasons why they should not be so regarded. Among these are such important subjects as economics and sociology.

The most conclusive proof of the value of scientific methods is seen in their successful application to practical affairs. A noteworthy example is the use of scientific methods to increase the output of factories, to facilitate the process of merchandising, and to improve the general conduct of business. This has become known as *Scientific Management*. Salesmanship has likewise been developed by such methods, so that there has come to be a science of salesmanship which has led to great advances in the art of selling. From these and many similar practical developments, it is clear that the tendency of the times is to apply the scientific methods to every important activity of modern life.

PHYSIOGRAPHY

PHYSIOGRAPHY is another name for the science of physical geography, which is closely related to geology, on the one hand, and to geography, on the other. It is concerned with the three primary divisions of the earth: (1) the solid part of the earth, or *lithosphere*, which forms the land; (2) the water of the earth, or *hydrosphere*, which comprises the oceans, lakes, and rivers; (3) the air, or *atmosphere*, which is the outermost part of the earth.

The science or study of physiography considers the conditions and the processes which brought the surface of the earth into its present state. These processes are largely the result of the activities of air and water and of the plant and animal life which they support. Other factors are volcanic action and the slow subsidence and elevation, or warping, of the crustal portion of the earth.

Physiography, therefore, has to do chiefly with the land surface of the earth and with the relations of the air and the water to the land surface. Consequently, physiography does not attempt to treat all phases of earth science exhaustively. The comprehensive science of the atmosphere is *Meteorology*; of the ocean, *Oceanography*; of waters in general, *Hydrography*; of the lithosphere, *Geology* with its several subordinate sciences, such as *Geognosy*, *Petrology*, and *Mineralogy*. Geology is the very broad earth science which includes the history of the lands, of the oceans, and of the air.

In the following pages will be found topical treatment of more than 165 subjects connected with the science of physiography. These are arranged in alphabetical order, with numerous cross references.

Adobe (*ȧ-dō'bĕ*) **Soil.** The name given to certain clay formations or soils which cover thousands of square miles in Colorado, Utah, Nevada, Texas, New Mexico, Arizona, and California. They are composed of particles of clay, quartz, and other minerals, in an extreme condition of fineness. When moist, adobe soils are plastic and readily worked, but when dry, their compactness and coherence make easy tillage impossible. Under irrigation, adobe soils show remarkable fertility, producing for many years undiminished crops of grains and alfalfa.

While their origin has been a matter of perplexity, adobe soils, in some sections, are believed to have been formed by streams which brought down the materials from the mountains or from other highlands. In other sections, adobe soils appear to have been formed by the accumulation of wind-blown materials, in a manner similar to the formation of loess. See *Alluvium*, *Loess*, *Soil*.

Æolian (*ē-ō'lĭ-ăn*) **Deposits.** Accumulations of wind-blown material, consisting chiefly of dust, fine particles of soil, and minute sand grains. These are borne by the wind to sheltered places in much the same way as similar particles are transported and deposited by running water. In arid regions æolian deposits sometimes attain much importance. The most conspicuous and best known of these are the sand dunes. These occupy extensive areas, especially in deserts and along ocean shores. When buried under other deposits, sand dunes sometimes form sandstones.

In certain regions, especially in China and in the Mississippi valley, fine wind-blown dust, called loess, has accumulated in deposits of great thickness. When buried under other strata, loess deposits become shales. In Bermuda, dunes are formed of ground-up fragments of coral blown from the beaches. When consolidated, these dunes form æolian limestones. See *Dune*, *Loess*, *Sedimentary Rocks*, *Wind*.

Air. The transparent medium forming the outermost part of the earth, in which plants, animals, and human beings live and breathe. It is a mixture of several gases, which, though ordinarily invisible, can be weighed, compressed to a liquid, or frozen to a solid. At the sea level, the weight or pressure of the air is somewhat more than a ton to the square foot, but, at high elevations, as on great mountains, the pressure is much less. However, as the tendency of all gases is to expand, every portion of the air presses upward against the weight of the air above it, so that ordinarily the upward pressure counterbalances the downward pressure at the same point. If it were not for this property, it would be impossible for one to lift a sheet of writing paper from a table, as the air above it has a weight or pressure of many hundred pounds.

In a multitude of ways the air assists all living things to exist. Besides providing oxygen for breathing, air conveys both sound and light, absorbs heat during sunshine, enables fires to burn, propels ships, turns windmills, and makes possible the use of air brakes, vacuum cleaners, and many other valuable machines. Air in motion forms winds which modify climate, equalize heat and cold, and distribute the rainfall on the earth. Air plays such an important part in the world that the ancients ranked it with earth, water, and fire, as one of the four chief elements. For chemical constituents and physical properties, see *Atmosphere*; see also *Climate*, *Rainfall*, *Wind*.

Alluvial Fan. A deposit of sand and gravel formed usually at the base of a mountain range where the gradient of the stream bed becomes notably less steep and the stream is forced to deposit. Tiny fans form at the base of small cliffs after a single rain storm. In size, alluvial fans range from these diminutive forms to large areas including many square miles of territory. See *Erosion*.

Alluvium. The soil material produced by the processes of weathering and by the wearing-down action of water, collected by rivers, and deposited along their lower courses. Alluvial deposits consist of sand, clay, gravel, cobblestones, and bowlders. Part of this material is left in the beds of rivers, part along their banks and on their flood plains, and part at their mouths, building up deltas.

The exceedingly fertile lands of many valleys have been formed of alluvium, carried down and deposited by rivers in the course of long periods of time. Large tracts of such land are found in the valleys of the Mississippi, the Nile, the Ganges, and the Hwang. Early civilizations began in the alluvial valley plains of Egypt, Babylonia, India, and China.

Gold found in the sands of stream beds or in the soil of river banks is called *alluvial* gold. It usually consists of very fine grains brought down by streams in wearing away gold-bearing rocks. See *Delta*, *River*, *Soil*, *Valley*.

Anchor Ice. Ice which forms on and encrusts the bottom of a river, lake, or shallow sea; called also *ground ice*. On the bottoms of stony rivers, where the current is swift, ice sometimes freezes around stones in the stream bed. When large amounts of ice are thus formed, even heavy bowlders may be raised from the bottom and floated downstream. In a similar manner, ice forms on the bottom of shallow seas, as in the Baltic Sea and the Gulf of St. Lawrence. When such ice forms about an anchor and lifts it, the ship moored by the anchor may drift away.

The formation of such ice in rivers is believed to be due sometimes to the fact that the stream bed is frozen, so that the water upon coming into contact with it freezes. Again, the temperature of the entire stream may be slightly below 32° F., so that the quieter water below freezes while the swifter motion in the upper parts prevents freezing. The cause of the formation of ground ice in shallow seas is not well understood. Some scientists advance the view that fresh water, issuing from springs in the sea bottom, is frozen by the prevailing low temperature before it becomes mixed with the salt water. See *Ice*.

Anticyclone. The opposite of cyclone. An atmospheric condition prevailing over a large area in which there is high barometric pressure with outblowing winds. At the center of an anticyclone, cool, heavy, dry air descends from the upper regions to the surface of the earth and then moves outward toward areas of warmer and lighter air. In the temperate zones, anticyclones usually appear in the west and move slowly eastward. Cool, pleasant weather generally accompanies their passage. In winter, however, an anticyclone following a storm may result in a cold wave. See *Blizzard, Cold Wave, Cyclone, Storm*.

Aridity. The state of dryness in the atmosphere, which prevails in regions of low rainfall. Aridity characterizes the climate where the annual rainfall does not exceed 10 inches. The notable deserts of the world, such as the Sahara, Arabian, Persian, and Atacama deserts, are extremely arid. Parts of the polar regions and of high mountain slopes, while usually snow-covered, receive scant precipitation, and are essentially arid.

In arid districts, not only the yearly rainfall, but the average humidity, or amount of moisture present in the air, is low. Profitable agriculture usually cannot be carried on without irrigation where the annual rainfall is less than 20 inches, or where the average humidity is less than 60 per cent. In regions of extreme aridity, such as the Atacama desert, the yearly rainfall is almost nothing, and the average humidity is often less than 40 per cent.

Wherever extreme aridity prevails, peculiar types of vegetation are developed, especially adapted to withstand heat and drought. Some of these consist of thick-stemmed, thick-leaved, often very spiny plants, whose entire surface structure is modified to prevent rapid evaporation of the water stored in their fleshy interiors. Striking examples of this kind of adaptation are found in the cactuses, yuccas, and agaves of the southwestern United States.

The types and habits of animals are likewise greatly modified wherever aridity is pronounced. For example, the smaller animals usually live in burrows, to which they retire to escape the extreme heat of the day. During the hottest and driest period of the year, many such animals *æstivate*, that is, they go into a state of summer torpor in their underground retreats. This condition is somewhat similar to the hibernation, or winter sleep, of various animals in cold regions.

Portions of the Atacama desert are so dry that neither plants nor animals can live there. When men visit or go to work in those districts, they must take with them everything they need to eat and drink. See *Climate, Desert, Humidity*.

Atmosphere. The mixture of gases and vapors, called also the air, which surrounds and is a part of the earth, extending to a height estimated at from 100 to 500 miles and upwards. According to the calculations of Humphreys, the constituents of the air at the sea level are: nitrogen 77.08 per cent, oxygen 20.75 per cent, argon 0.95 per cent, carbon dioxide, or carbonic acid gas, 0.003 per cent, hydrogen 0.001 per cent, and water vapor averaging 1.20 per cent, together with exceedingly minute quantities of the rare gases,—helium, krypton, neon, niton, and xenon.

Except water vapor, which is mostly confined near the surface and varies greatly with the temperature and altitude, the constituents of the air remain remarkably uniform to a height of seven miles, above which they exhibit marked changes. At a height of 45 miles, it is calculated that hydrogen composes 50 per cent of the atmosphere, at 60 miles, 96 per cent, and at 87 miles, over 99½ per cent, the chief other component being helium. Assuming that the atmosphere extends upward 200 miles, its volume is about one-sixth that of the rest of the earth.

The density of the air at the earth's surface is about $\frac{1}{800}$ that of water. The normal pressure or weight of the air at the sea level is 14.7 pounds per square inch, corresponding to a barometric height or pressure of 760 millimeters, or 30 inches. The total mass or weight of the air is estimated at about $\frac{1}{270}$ that of the water, or somewhat less than a millionth that of the solid portion of the earth. The density or pressure of the air varies with the elevation. In the lower altitudes it decreases about one inch on the barometer for each 900 feet of rise above the sea level. At 16,000 feet altitude the barometric pressure is about 16 inches; at 7 miles it is 6½ inches, and at 18 miles it is calculated to be only a third of an inch. By weight, one-half of the atmosphere lies below a plane about 3½ miles above sea level; three-fourths, below a plane about 7 miles above the same level; and seven-eighths, below a plane about 10 miles up.

The pressure of the air at any given point on the earth's surface varies greatly from day to day. These changes are associated with the movements of areas of high barometer attending fair weather and with movements of low areas attending storms. Hence, the variations of the barometer are of great value in forecasting the weather. In addition, local air pressure undergoes both diurnal and annual changes.

Like its density, the temperature of the air decreases with the altitude, averaging, near the earth's surface, a fall of 1° F. for each 330 feet of elevation. A mile of ascent in the air means about the same decrease in temperature as a poleward movement of 800 miles. By self-registering thermometers, sent up in balloons to a height of 10 miles, temperatures of −104° F. have been recorded. It is believed, however, that at about 18 miles elevation there is a region of constant temperature, which is computed at about −67° F.

An important property of the air is its power to absorb and radiate heat. The specific heat of the air when kept at a constant pressure is 0.2412, water being unity. The specific heat of the air when kept at constant volume is 0.1721. The ratio between the two is 1.4. This determines the rate at which air will cool when allowed to expand without the addition of heat from the outside. This ratio or property is made use of in cooling air to a liquid or solid state. It is also the principle that controls the cooling of ascending masses of air from which the water vapor therein contained condenses into cloud, rain, snow, or hail.

The amount of heat absorbed from a vertical sunbeam by the air is computed at from 40 to 50 per cent of the sunbeam's original energy. By virtue of this absorbing power, the atmosphere retains a large amount of heat which it can lose only by the slow process of radiation. The air, therefore, acts as a universal moderator, reducing extremes of temperature at all seasons. See *Air*; *Humidity*; *Temperature, Atmospheric*; *Wind*.

Atoll (*ȧ-tŏl'*; *ăt'ŏl*). The Malay name of a type of coral island, consisting of low, circular coral reefs which form a ring of land around a central lagoon. Atolls are numerous in the tropical portions of the Indian and Pacific oceans. Some are nearly 100 miles in circumference, and contain lagoons having a depth of 100 to 350 feet.

In 1835, Darwin advanced the explanation, since widely accepted, that atolls are produced by the growth of coral reefs around the shores of islands which have subsided, but that this subsidence does not proceed faster than the upward building of the coral. As a result, the reef eventually encircles a central body of water covering a sunken island. While this explanation has been proved correct regarding many atolls, it has been found that some are formed in other ways, without subsidence. See *Barrier Reef, Coral, Fringing Reef*.

Aurora Borealis. A luminous appearance in the heavens, called also "northern lights," occurring in high northern latitudes. The center of the zone of greatest frequency passes through the southern part of Hudson bay, through North cape, Norway, to the mouth of the Lena river in Siberia, and thence through Point Barrow, Alaska, to Hudson bay. Observers north of this belt see the aurora more often to the south than to the north. Moreover, the farther north they go, the less frequently it appears. Similarly, observers south of this belt see the aurora less often as they go nearer the equator.

The aurora is now believed to be the result of a discharge of electricity through the very thin atmosphere existing in a region from 50 to 100 miles above the earth. The luminous display takes the form of arcs, bands, rays, wavy curtains, patches, or of a broad corona, varying in color from silvery white to yellow, green, violet, or red. These ever-changing forms move about, sometimes coruscating and sometimes resembling illuminated clouds. There is an intimate connection between the aurora and magnetic disturbances and also between the aurora and sun spots. The similar display which occurs in the southern hemisphere is called *aurora australis*. See *Sun Spots*.

Avalanche. A mass of ice or snow, often mixed more or less with earth, which, having become loosened from a mountain slope or a glacier, dashes downward into the valley, occasionally causing great destruction. In the mountainous regions of the western United States, an avalanche is usually called a "slide." This term is also used to describe the portion of a mountain slope which has been denuded by the passage of an avalanche. See *Glacier, Landslide*.

Bad Lands. The name given in the western United States to certain sterile regions. They are characterized by an almost entire absence of vegetation, and by the labyrinth of fantastic forms into which the soft strata of clays, sands, and gravels have been carved through the action of wind and water. The best examples are found east of the Black Hills in South Dakota, though similar formations occur in Wyoming, Colorado, Arizona, New Mexico, and Texas. See *Erosion*.

Barrier Beach. A ridge of sand and gravel, built up by the work of the winds, the undertow, and shore line currents, that completely closes the mouth of a bay and thus forms a definite barrier. See *Beach*.

Barrier Reef. A coral reef bordering a shore line but separated from the mainland by a lagoon. The Great Barrier Reef of Australia, hundreds of miles in length, is perhaps the best example. It is composed chiefly of the exoskeletons of corals. About the margin of this reef, corals live in immense numbers, and, by their stony deposits, constantly add to its vast extent. See *Coral, Fringing Reef*.

Bayou (*bī'ōō*). A lake occupying the abandoned part of a stream channel. Such lakes, called also oxbow lakes, are formed when a stream cuts off its own loops or meanders. The name is probably derived from the French word, *boyau*, meaning gut, and is used chiefly in Louisiana, Texas, and Arkansas. See *Meanders*.

Beach. That part of the shore of the sea or of a lake which is washed by the waves. More specifically, the beach is the sandy or pebbly part borne up by waves, tides, and shore currents and deposited between the lines of low and high water. The width of the beach depends upon the angle of slope in the shore, and upon the height attained by the tide and by storm waves. Shores of little slope have wide, nearly flat, usually sandy beaches; shores with greater slope have narrow, comparatively steep beaches, formed largely of coarse gravel and pebbles. See *Barrier Beach, Land-tied Island*.

Blizzard. A severe, blinding storm of dry snow, typically with a very sudden onset and accompanied by a freezing wind. It often attends an anticyclone. About 1880 the word became widely employed in connection with severe storms in the Western states. Following the great storm of March 1888, during which snow fell to a depth of 3 feet in the Atlantic states and in New England, and was driven for days by powerful gales into drifts 5 to 20 feet high, the term blizzard came into universal use in America. In the winter of 1919, violent storms of this type swept the eastern United States, paralyzing traffic and causing immense damage.

The most destructive blizzards occur in the plains region from North Dakota to Kansas and eastward to Ohio. The typical blizzard is very similar to the *buran* of southern Russia and the *purga* of Siberia. See *Anticyclone, Storm*.

Bluff. A name, first used in the American colonies, for a hill, cliff, bank, or headland with a broad, steep face. High banks presenting nearly perpendicular faces, especially if on the shore of a lake, river, or sea, are commonly called bluffs, as are also steep rises of ground between bottom lands and higher table-lands. See *Cliff, Escarpment*.

Bogs. Wet, spongy grounds, covered with decayed moss and other vegetable matter, and sometimes underlaid by it to a considerable depth. Bogs are frequently saturated with water and converted into a kind of quagmire, called *quaking bog*. Those which contain accumulations of peat, formed by the decay of sphagnum moss, rushes, and various other aquatic plants, are known as *peat bogs*. See *Fens, Marshes, Moor, Muskeg, Peat Bogs, Swamps*.

Bore. In running up funnel-shaped bays and the estuaries of certain rivers, the tide is so retarded and crowded by the narrowing channel and shallower bottom, that its front may become a wall-like wave. Such a tidal wave is known as a bore and is often dangerous to shipping. In the Bay of Fundy, the range of the tide is from 40 to 70 feet, producing an enormous bore. The most remarkable river bore is that in the Tsientang, in China, the advancing wall of water being sometimes 25 feet high. The noted bore of the Severn in England is produced by a tide which rises 18 feet in an hour and a half. The bore at the mouth of the Amazon is sometimes 12 feet high. Bores occur also in the Wye of England, in the Seine of France, in the Petite Codiac of Canada, and in the Ganges and the Hugli of India. See *Tides*.

Butte (*būt*). The name given to a steep-sided, round-topped hill or mountain. Buttes stand out as more or less solitary and conspicuous hills, or mountains, in arid plateaus that have undergone great erosion. They are the more resistant portions of the land, which have withstood the processes of erosion better than the lands that formerly surrounded them. Elevations of this type are characteristic features in the landscape of many plains in the western United States. They form landmarks which can be seen at great distances, and they often give their names to localities and towns, as Butte, Montana. A formation with similar sides, but with an extensive, flat top, is called a *mesa*. See *Mesa, Monadnock, Mountain, Plateau*.

Caldera (*kăl-dā'rȧ*). A broad, open, and usually flat-bottomed crater of a volcano, like that in the volcano of Kilauea in Hawaii. See *Crater*.

Campos. The term loosely used in Brazil for tropical prairies or savannas. Those which contain numerous trees are called *campos cerrados*. See *Savannas*.

Canyon. A large, deep gorge cut by a river, typical of dry climates in plateau regions where the stream deepens at the bottom faster than the rains and atmospheric action can wear down the sides of the gorge to gentle slopes. The Grand Canyon of the Colorado river in Arizona is the greatest canyon known. It is more than 200 miles long, with nearly vertical walls rising 3000 to 6000 feet, and is often 1 to 15 miles from rim to rim. The Rio Grande and the Yellowstone have similar but much smaller canyons. In the western United States the term canyon is now quite generally applied to any deep and extensive ravine along a water course. See *Erosion, Gorge, Valley.*

Cave. Caves or caverns are hollow places in the earth, produced partly by the dislocation and fracture of rock strata and partly by the solvent and eroding action of ground water. They are most numerous in limestone regions, where rivers sometimes plunge into them through openings known as *sink holes.* Sea caves are made along shores by the wearing power of storm waves.

Among caves celebrated for their immense size or for features of scientific interest are Carlsbad Cave, in New Mexico; Mammoth Cave, in Kentucky; Wyandotte Cave, in southern Indiana; Luray Cavern, in Virginia; the cave of Gailenreuth, in Germany; and the cave of Kirkdale, in Yorkshire, England. The famous picturesque cave of Fingal, in the island of Staffa, Scotland, is formed in basalt.

In many caves of Europe, remains of early human tribes, known as *Cave Dwellers,* have been found associated with those of the mammoth, rhinoceros, hippopotamus, cave hyena, cave lion, and other animals long extinct or absent from Europe. These remains furnish much valuable material for the study of anthropology and archeology. See *Fault, Ground Water.*

Chinook (*chĭ-nōōk′*). A wind which descends from the mountains, becoming warm as the air reaches lower elevation. Such a wind often sweeps far over the neighboring plains, melting snows and causing floods in winter, or burning the vegetation and ruining crops in summer. This wind takes its name from the Chinook Indians, formerly a numerous tribe which inhabited a part of the state of Washington. See *Wind.*

Cirque (*sûrk*). The large, rounded, steep-sided heads of valleys developed by the erosion of valley glaciers are called cirques. In the Uinta, Big Horn, Sierra Nevada, and other ranges of the western United States, cirques are remarkably numerous and well developed. They served as collecting areas for the snows which, when compressed, formed the valley glaciers in these mountains. At the heads of the present alpine or mountain glaciers there are cirques filled with snow and ice. See *Glacier.*

Cliff. A high, steep, precipitous or vertical face of rock. Cliffs may be formed by the erosive action of water, as, for example, those along ocean shores, due to the beating of the waves, and those forming the sides of bluffs, canyons, gorges, and ravines, due to the erosive action of running water in various streams. Cliffs are formed also by the unequal weathering of rock strata of differing hardness, through the action of rain, frost, and the atmosphere. Cliffs are produced, too, by the faulting of rock strata, as when the resulting uplift or subsidence exposes nearly or quite vertical rock faces or scarps. See *Bluff, Canyon, Escarpment, Fault, Gorge.*

Climate. The average weather for a considerable period of time in a locality or a region constitutes its climate. In popular language, climate is described as warm or cold, dry or moist. The chief elements of climate are *temperature, humidity,* and *wind.*

Other important factors influencing climate are ocean currents, the position and height of mountain ranges, and elevation above the sea level. However, the most widespread single cause of variations in climate is the unequal distribution of the sun's heat between the equator and the poles.

With regard to temperature, it is important to notice the average annual and seasonal temperatures, the extremes of temperature, and the temperature of exceptional seasons. A distinction must be made between absolute temperature, as measured by the thermometer, and sensible temperature, as it actually feels. Air of a given temperature seems warmer when at rest than when in motion. If the temperature is high, dry air seems colder than moist air; if the temperature is low, moist air seems colder than dry air.

As regards humidity, the absolute humidity, the relative humidity, the average cloudiness, and the actual precipitation must be taken into account. Further, the average amount of yearly precipitation, the variations of precipitation, from year to year and from season to season, and the proportions which fall as rain and as snow, must be noted. Similarly, the variations in the force, velocity, and direction of the wind must be considered.

Climates are classified as *continental* and *oceanic;* also as *tropical, temperate,* and *polar.* Oceanic or maritime climate is equable, damp, and cloudy. Continental climate is more severe, with great ranges of temperature, much sunshine, and less frequent rainfall. Desert climate is an extreme type of continental climate, with an excessive range of temperature, high winds, calm, cold nights, and very low average rainfall. While fluctuations of climate occur in relatively short periods, there is no evidence that shows any material change of climate in any region of the world within historic times.

In general, the west shores of continents in the temperate zones possess warmer and more equable climates than their eastern shores, as is the case in Europe and in North America. This condition is due to the fact that climate is very largely determined by the character of the prevailing winds. By reason of the earth's rotation on its axis, the prevailing winds throughout the temperate zones are, for the most part, westerly. In consequence, the winter winds which blow on the west coasts of Europe and North America from the surface of the adjoining oceans, are *warmer* than those which blow on the eastern parts of these continents, from their much colder interiors. Similarly, in summer, the winds blowing from the oceans are *cooler* than those blowing from the heated inner portions of the continents. See *Aridity; Climatology; Humidity; Rainfall; Temperature, Atmospheric; Weather.*

Climatology. The study or science of weather conditions. Climatology seeks to express in simple language the technical facts of meteorology, so that they may be used to advantage by farmers, planters, fruit growers, and stock breeders. The study of these facts is important, because crops, industry, and health depend upon climate.

Climatology records temperature, moisture, barometric pressure, winds, and evaporation, and takes into account the regular and irregular variations from the average of these conditions throughout the year. The highest and lowest temperatures, the rainfall, the direction, velocity, and frequency of winds, and the forecasting of any of these conditions are all of much importance to the farmer and the stock grower. Various plant and animal diseases are known to be associated with particular types of weather. The forecasting of fog and wind conditions is of great value to ship captains and is essential to airplane operators. See *Climate, Weather.*

Cloud. A collection of water droplets or ice particles, formed by the condensation of water vapor, and remaining suspended in the air. Ordinarily the heights of clouds vary from a few feet to about five miles, though some of the lighter forms may attain an altitude of twenty miles. Clouds assume many forms,—the most common are the cumulus, the stratus, the nimbus, and the cirrus clouds.

Cumulus clouds are white, thick, and dome-shaped, with irregular, fleecy protuberances and nearly horizontal bases. They commonly form in the afternoon during hot weather, often developing into so-called "thunderheads." The various forms of cumulus are among the most beautiful of clouds, especially when lighted and tinted with the rays of the setting sun. On the average, the top of a cumulus cloud is about 5500 feet and the base is about 4000 feet above the ground.

Stratus clouds are horizontal sheets of lifted fog, sometimes very low, and usually less than 4000 feet high. *Nimbus* or *rain clouds* are also low clouds formed of thick, dark layers, lacking definite shape, from the ragged edges of which rain or snow falls. *Cirrus* clouds, the highest of all, usually at about six miles elevation, though sometimes at ten miles, appear most frequently in dry weather. They are composed of particles of snow and ice and take on a delicate, feathery appearance.

There are also intermediate forms of clouds: the *cirro-stratus*; the *cirro-cumulus*, which produces the "mackerel sky," heralded by sailors as a forecaster of fair weather; the *alto-stratus*; the *cumulo-stratus*; and the *cumulo-nimbus*, or "thunder" cloud. The last has the appearance of heavy, mountainous masses of cumulus clouds, with a layer of nimbus beneath, from the base of which local showers of rain and hail often fall. Taking the earth as a whole, it is estimated that clouds cover, on the average, about one-half of its surface. See *Fog, Humidity, Rain, Snow, Storm, Wind.*

Cloudburst. A name given to an extraordinarily heavy fall of rain, affecting a small area and lasting for only a short time. It is impossible to draw a clear line of distinction between a cloudburst and a heavy rainfall. Usually, however, the term cloudburst is not used unless six or more inches of rain falls at the rate of ten or more inches an hour. Probably the heaviest cloudbursts do not cover more than an acre, nor the lightest, more than a square mile in area. In the United States, cloudbursts occur most frequently in the Rocky mountains and in the Great Basin.

In arid regions, small whirlwinds sometimes take up heated air from the surface with such rapidity, and to so great a height, that the sudden expansion and cooling cause the condensation of even the small amount of moisture contained in the desert air. Sharp, short showers may then occur, and, if heavy, they are known as cloudbursts. In a storm of this nature, during the summer of 1898, sufficient rain fell in a few minutes near Bagdad, in the Mojave desert of California, to cause several washouts along the railroad. A cloudburst at Clifton, S. C., in June 1903, caused the loss of fifty lives and damaged property to the extent of millions of dollars. See *Rain, Rainfall.*

Cold Wave. In 1872 the United States Weather Bureau first applied the term "cold wave" to the areas of cold, clear, dry air (anticyclones) that flow near the ground from Canada southward over the United States, becoming the so-called "northers" in the Gulf states. The rate of progress of the front of a cold wave is so steady and uniform that the Weather Bureau is usually able to forecast its advance with satisfactory accuracy. The hoisting of a cold wave flag by the Weather Bureau indicates that the thermometer will fall at least 20° within 24 hours, and that the temperature will drop below freezing. Cold waves often cause a fall in temperature exceeding 30° in 24 hours. They usually last only two or three days. See *Anticyclone.*

Continent. The continents are the great land areas of the world, in contrast to the oceans, which are the great water areas of the world. Continents differ from islands in their size. Physiographers usually recognize six continents: (1) Eurasia, the natural grand division consisting of Europe and Asia, (2) Africa, (3) North America, (4) South America, (5) Australia, (6) Antarctica. Europe and Asia, however, are commonly called continents.

Each continent stands upon a submerged shelf, called a continental platform. These platforms surround the continents to a considerable width, sloping gently down to a depth of about 600 feet until there is a sudden drop down to about 6000 feet, where the true ocean basin begins. Some 10,000,000 square miles about the shores of continents are thus covered with shallow water. The area of the oceans is nearly three times that of the land, but the area of the ocean basins is only about twice that of the continental platforms with their respective continents.

The major surface or relief features of the land are plains, plateaus, and mountains; the minor relief features include valleys, canyons, hills, buttes, mesas, cliffs, bluffs, and many small basins.

If all the continents were graded to a common level, their height above the sea would be about 2800 feet. If all the sea bottoms were likewise graded to a common level, the water would have a uniform depth of between 12,000 and 13,000 feet. The average height of the land is, therefore, slightly more than half a mile above sea level, while the average depth of the ocean bottom is about 2½ miles below sea level.

The lowest known point, near Puerto Rico in the Atlantic Ocean, is 44,000 feet, or 8.33 miles, below the surface of the sea. The highest point, Mount Everest, is 29,141 feet, or 5½ miles above the same plane. About three-fifths of the land lies less than 500 meters, or 1640 feet, above sea level, and upon this area most of the earth's population lives. See *Ocean.*

Crater. The bowl-shaped depression or cavity marking the orifice through which lava and other materials are or formerly have been ejected from a volcano during eruption. Small volcanoes usually erupt through a single crater at the summit; the larger volcanoes often have numerous subsidiary funnels. The Peak of Teneriffe, for example, has many minor craters both in its sides and in its summit. Craters vary greatly in size, some being very small, while others are a mile or more in diameter. Haleakala, in Hawaii, has a crater twenty miles in circumference. Aniakchok, in Alaska, is said to have a crater whose circumference is 21 miles.

The size of the crater, however, in no way measures the intensity of an eruption. At the time of their most violent paroxysms, Krakatoa, Vesuvius, and Pelée had craters of very moderate size—that of Pelée being about 2500 feet in diameter. In volcanoes of the explosive type, the entire top of the mountain may be blown off, leaving an immense crater. The craters of extinct or of dormant volcanoes are often filled with water, forming crater lakes. In the case of Mount Mazama, in Oregon, the top of the mountain fell in, and in the great hole formed in this way is the famous and beautiful Crater lake. See *Caldera, Lava, Volcano, Vulcanism.*

Crevasse (*krĕ-văs'*). A great fissure or crack which may form in rocks or in the great mountain glaciers.

Cyclone. Cyclones are violent storms, ranging from 100 to 1000 miles in diameter. In these storms high winds rotate somewhat spirally about a calm central area having an atmospheric pressure much lower than that of the adjoining areas. This central area of low pressure (below 30 inches) moves onward, often with a speed of 20 to 30 miles an hour, surrounded by a system of cool winds, which blow inward, and around it, from areas of high barometer, called anticyclones, with a pressure of upwards of 30 inches. Cyclonic storms are attended by rising temperature, moist air, abundant precipitation, and a cloudy sky.

Because of the rotation of the earth, a cyclone in the northern hemisphere blows about its center from right to left, or in a direction opposite to the movement of the hands of a clock. For the same reason, cyclones in the southern hemisphere rotate from left to right. Cyclonic storms move eastward in the middle latitudes and westward in the tropics.

The general term "cyclone" includes the hurricane, typhoon, baguio, and various other severe tropical storms. The name, however, should not be applied to tornadoes, waterspouts, whirlwinds, or "twisters," in which the vertical motion of the storm is far more significant than the horizontal. In various parts of the United States, tornadoes are often incorrectly called cyclones. In middle latitudes, cyclones, or low-area storms, are the most important type of storms. While sometimes developing wind velocities of 40 to 60 miles an hour, they rarely become destructive like the more violent "hurricanes" of the tropics. See *Anticyclone, Hurricane, Storm, Tornado, Typhoon.*

Delta. A tract of land enclosed by the branches of a river's mouth; so named from a general resemblance to the shape of the Greek letter Δ. Deltas are usually somewhat triangular or fan-shaped tracts of low-lying land, formed by deposits of fine silt brought down by river currents.

The delta of the Mississippi embraces an area of about 12,300 square miles, and it is advancing into the Gulf of Mexico at the rate of 260 feet a year. The combined delta of the Ganges and Brahmaputra, one of the great rice-producing districts of the world, contains about 50,000 square miles. The famous delta of the Nile, long known as the granary of Egypt, is 200 miles wide on the sea and 100 miles long. The delta of the Niger covers some 30,000 square miles.

Other noted deltas are those of the Danube, the Po, and the Hwang. The Po delta is advancing into the sea so rapidly that the city of Adria, formerly the seaport from which the Adriatic Sea was named, is now 15 miles inland. Many deltas are cultivated, and some of them, such as that of the Hwang, support dense populations. Deltas, however, are often unhealthful and are subject to disastrous floods. See *Alluvium, Erosion, River.*

Desert. Broadly defined, a desert is any land area which supports but little plant and animal life. In this sense, all barren regions, such as southern Patagonia, the ice-covered interior of Greenland, and other arctic and antarctic lands, are deserts. As ordinarily understood, however, deserts are the continental wastes lying within the tropical and temperate zones, whose sterility is due to scanty rainfall. The most extensive deserts are situated in Africa, Asia, and Australia. Smaller arid regions are found in North and South America. In Europe there are no true deserts.

The Sahara desert of northern Africa is the largest arid region in the world. It is a part of a nearly rainless belt which extends across Africa and continues through Arabia, Persia, Turkestan, and Mongolia, almost to the Pacific shores of Asia. The wide eastern expansion of this area is known as the Desert of Gobi. In southern Africa, the so-called Kalahari desert occupies an area between the Zambesi river and the Orange and Limpopo rivers. The extent of this desert is much less than has been commonly represented on maps. Large portions of the Kalahari district have recently been found to be excellent grasslands. On the west coast of southern Africa there is a narrow strip of country of extreme aridity. The vast deserts of Australia are in the central part of the continent. In North America, the most extensive arid region, sometimes called the "great American desert," lies between the Sierra Nevada and the Rocky mountains. The Atacama desert of Chile is one of the driest places in the world. In this area an entire year may pass without a single drop of rain.

Deserts are caused by (1) the prevalence of dry winds, (2) by separation from the ocean by mountain barriers, and (3) by their great distance from oceans or other areas of evaporation. The climate of deserts is characterized by cloudless skies; by extremely high temperatures during the day, sometimes exceeding 120° F.; by a very pronounced and rapid drop in the temperature at night, even in the tropics; and by a yearly rainfall varying from a few inches to almost none. Violent windstorms occur, frequently accompanied by whirlwinds producing severe sand storms or sand spouts. Whirlwinds sometimes develop so rapidly, and rise so high in the atmosphere, as to cause brief but very heavy local rains called "cloudbursts."

While deserts, except in limited areas, are never entirely barren, their permanent vegetation is scanty and limited to the most hardy and resistant types, such as cactus, sagebrush, and saltbush. However, during brief seasons of rainfall, the vegetation in some desert areas bursts into a profusion of bloom, only to wither quickly and largely disappear when the usual arid condition is resumed. See *Aridity, Climate, Humidity, Rainfall.*

Dew. A formation, after sunset, of water globules upon the leaves of plants and upon other objects on or near the ground. Dew usually occurs as small drops of water which may be seen sparkling in the sunshine until evaporated by the heat of the day. A good illustration of the formation of dew is shown by the moisture which gathers on the outside of a pitcher filled with ice water. The temperature of the surface of the pitcher is lower than the dew point of the surrounding air. In consequence, the moisture in the air nearest to the pitcher condenses in droplets upon the cool surface.

Similarly, if the temperature of grass blades, or other plant surfaces, becomes lower than the dew point of the surrounding air, moisture will be condensed upon them. If the temperature at which the moisture condenses is below the freezing point, *frost* will be formed. For a copious formation of dew, the sky must be clear, the air calm, and the objects on which it is formed must be situated near the ground.

Clouds prevent the formation of dew by reflecting back to the earth much of the heat radiated by its cooling surface, and thereby keeping the temperature above the dew point. Winds also prevent the formation of dew by carrying away the cooler air before the vapor in it has been condensed. While it is common to speak of a heavy "fall" of dew, or the "falling" dew, such expressions are not scientifically accurate. Dew never falls from the sky, as does rain, but merely condenses out of the air upon the object on which it is found.

Dew sometimes forms on the under sides of objects. For example, if a pan be placed on the ground, bottom up, in the morning there will be dew on the inside of it as often as on the outside of it. Similarly, a rubber blanket spread on the ground will often be wet on the under side in the morning, even in a desert. This is explained by the fact that the air in the ground, which contains some moisture, becomes warmed during the day. At night, the air above the surface cools more rapidly than the air in the ground. The heavier cool air from above sinks into the ground, forcing up the warmer air with its contained water vapor. Upon coming into contact with the cool pan or the cool rubber blanket, a part of this moisture is condensed.

In some nearly cloudless regions, such as parts of Arizona, California, Syria, and Arabia, the amount of dew formed is sometimes so great as to become available for the roots of plants, and is an important factor in agriculture. When the air is very dry, however, objects near the surface may not cool below the dew point at night, and, consequently, no dew will be formed. See *Dew Point, Frost, Humidity.*

Dew Point. The temperature at which the water vapor in the atmosphere begins to condense. It is not a fixed temperature but varies according to the amount of vapor present in the air. In case the amount is large, the temperature of the dew point will be relatively high, and only slight cooling will

Photos for 1 and 6 from Publishers' Photo Service; for 4, 5, and 7 from Ewing Galloway.

VOLCANOES

1 Mt. Asama, Japan. 2 Seneco Volcano, Java; *copyright by Keystone View Co.* 3 Lassen Peak, California; *copyright by P. J. Thompson.* 4 Bromo and Smerve Volcanoes, Java. 5 Flowing Lava, Kilauea, Hawaii. 6 Cooled Lava, Kilauea, Hawaii. 7 Poas Volcano, Costa Rica.

NOTED WATERFALLS

1 Victoria Falls, South Africa. 2 Niagara Falls. 3 Minnehaha Falls; *copyright by Detroit Photographic Co.* 4 Multnomah Falls, Oregon. 5 Yosemite Falls, California. 6 Great Falls, Potomac River; *copyright by Harris & Ewing.* 7 Argentine Falls, South America; *copyright by Underwood & Underwood.* 8 Shoshone Falls, Idaho; *copyright by Detroit Photographic Co.* 9 Howick or Great Umgeni Falls, South Africa; *copyright by Keystone View Co.*

be required to cause some condensation. In case the amount of water vapor present is small, the temperature of the dew point will be relatively low, sometimes below the freezing point. When the temperature of condensation is above the freezing point, the vapor condenses in the form of water droplets; when below the freezing point, the water crystallizes into ice particles as it condenses. See *Dew, Frost.*

Dike. A sheet of lava lying in a vertical or nearly vertical fissure in the earth. Such a sheet is formed when molten rock material, rising toward the surface along some line of least resistance, fills the fissure in which it later cools. Dike rocks are sometimes much more resistant to erosion than the surrounding formations. When the softer adjacent rocks have been worn away, the harder dike rocks stand out as great walls or ridges in the landscape. See *Igneous Rocks, Lava, Vulcanism.*

Distributaries. The branches of a stream that form when it divides in its delta or at the base of a mountain slope. They are the converse of the *tributaries* that come together and form one main river. In the delta of the Mississippi, as in all other great deltas of the world, there are numerous distributaries. See *Delta, River.*

Doldrums (*dŏl′drŭms*). A belt or zone of calm within 15° north or south of the equator. This belt is characterized by the highest temperatures and humidities, coupled with the feeblest winds, that occur on the ocean. The surface of the sea is often of a glassy smoothness, frequently bearing a thin layer of oil left by passing vessels. The region of calms, which varies with the seasons in extent and location, was formerly much dreaded by navigators sailing ships across the equator.

Drumlin. A smoothly rounded, oval hill, rarely more than 250 feet high or more than a half mile long, and composed of unstratified glacial drift. Drumlins occur usually in flat lowlands, often in clusters. They are believed to have been formed by the deposition of glacial débris underneath the ice at a period when the onward movement of the great ice sheet was sluggish. The material composing them consists of clay, bowlders, sands, and gravels. Drumlins are always elliptical in form, and their larger axes are always parallel to the direction of the ice movement. They occur north of the terminal moraine of the great continental glaciers of Europe and North America.

In the United States, drumlins are found in eastern Massachusetts, around Boston Harbor; in western New York, just south of Lake Ontario; and in southeastern Wisconsin. At the battle of Bunker Hill (Breed's Hill) the Americans occupied and fortified a drumlin. Beacon Hill, Boston, is also a drumlin. See *Glacier, Pleistocene Period.*

Dune. A mound or ridge of loose sand heaped up by the wind. The name was first applied to the great sand mounds along the seacoasts of northern France, Holland, and Denmark. Dunes occur near large bodies of sand and where the prevailing winds are fairly constant in direction, being found on seashores, on the shores of some inland lakes and large rivers, and also in sandy inland districts having a low rainfall. They have a gentle windward slope and a steep leeward descent. The winds which heap the dunes roll the sand grains up the easy slope, from the crest of which they fall abruptly down the steep leeward face.

Under continuous winds, dunes often move onward at the rate of 60 or 70 feet a year, sometimes engulfing buildings and orchards and destroying fertile fields. The average coastal dunes are from 200 to 300 feet high, but the great crescent-shaped dunes of the Sahara attain a height of 600 feet. In the United States, dunes are abundant on the Atlantic coast south of New York, on the southern and eastern shores of Lake Michigan, on a limited part of the Pacific coast, and over many thousands of square miles of semiarid tracts of the Great Plains, as in western Kansas, western Nebraska, and west central Wyoming.

Large quantities of dune sand have been taken from the south end of Lake Michigan into Chicago and there used in elevated railroad embankments. Dune sands are used also as building material. See *Æolian Deposits, Wind.*

Dust. Atmospheric dust consists of minute particles of matter, both inorganic and organic. These are present in large numbers in the purest air of the country and of high mountains, as well as in vastly greater quantity in the air of cities.

The inorganic particles consist of tiny pieces of mineral matter blown up from dry roads and fields, particles of soot and smoke from chimneys, ashes from volcanoes, and meteoric dust which comes to the earth from outside space when shooting stars are burned up in the atmosphere. Organic dust is composed chiefly of bacteria and the spores and pollen of various plants.

Dust particles play a very important rôle in "scattering" the light of the sun so as to illuminate the entire atmosphere. The blue color of the sky and its varied sunrise and sunset tints are, in a large measure, determined by the presence of dust in the atmosphere. See *Atmosphere, Lava, Meteoric Dust, Volcano, Wind.*

Earthquake. A trembling or shaking of the earth, varying from a slight tremor, perceptible only with the aid of delicate instruments, to a tremendous convulsion which may cause immense destruction of life and property. Great earthquakes may or may not be heralded by preliminary tremors. The principal shock or series of shocks usually continues over a few minutes, during which buildings are demolished and huge fissures appear in the earth. After the main shock, a series of minor disturbances, gradually decreasing in intensity, may continue for a period of many weeks, or even for several years.

Earthquakes are believed to result from a number of causes. Some minor earthquakes are no doubt produced by the falling in of subterranean caverns. Some are evidently caused by the violent explosions accompanying volcanic eruptions. Others are due to landslides, avalanches, and various slumpings on the slopes of deltas and on the outer faces of the continental platforms under the sea. But many of the greatest convulsions are clearly connected with still other types of crustal movements. Faulting, or the slipping of one great body of rock upon another in the earth's crustal or outer portion, seems to be the principal cause of earthquakes. Such faulting is commonly associated with mountain-making movements, and, therefore, earthquakes in a mountain region may safely be interpreted as an indication that the mountains are growing.

The earthquake of April 18, 1906, on the coast of California, injured and practically destroyed many buildings and caused the fire which burned a large part of the city of San Francisco. This earthquake was the most disastrous in North America during historic times. It was caused by a horizontal fault of from 8 to 21 feet displacement, with a vertical movement of from 1 to 3 feet, traced northwest and southeast of San Francisco in a line near the sea for a distance of about 270 miles. On August 31, 1886, the city of Charleston, South Carolina, was very seriously damaged by an earthquake which was felt over a large portion of the United States. From 1811 to 1813, a series of earthquakes, some of which were very violent, occurred in the Mississippi valley near New Madrid, Missouri.

Great earthquakes are most numerous in volcanic regions, and particularly near the mountainous edges of continents, bordering upon the ocean. Minor earthquakes are of very common occurrence. On an average, more than 30 per year occur in California, practically all of which are so slight as to cause no damage. The countries most severely shaken by earthquakes are Italy, Japan, Greece, the western coast of South America, the West Indies, Java, Sicily, and Asia Minor. The lands least disturbed are Africa, Australia, Russia, Siberia, Scandinavia, and Canada.

Even in severe shocks, the vibration of the earth particles usually extends through only a small fraction of an inch. As a rule, buildings with foundations resting upon solid ground do not suffer greatly from such displacements. But, when earthquake vibrations pass through land that has been "made" by filling in, the soft earth is thrown into waves, somewhat like the sea. Frequently, all structures whose foundations rest upon loose soil are completely destroyed. This was noted at Lisbon in 1755, and was very strikingly illustrated at San Francisco and Valparaiso in 1906.

At Valparaiso, the steel frames of brick buildings situated on made land were destroyed, while houses standing on rock foundations were but slightly damaged. At San Francisco, even on made land, the oscillations did not exceed three inches in width. Owing, however, to the frequency of these vibrations, few buildings withstood them. Yet on hard ground, where the vibrations were only about one-fourth of an inch, often the only result was the cracking of plaster. See *Fault, Landslide, Volcano, Vulcanism*; also *Dynamical Geology*, page 888.

Erosion. The process whereby the surface features of the earth—mountains, plateaus, valleys, and coasts, together with all their intermediate forms—are sculptured and worn down. Rainfall, sunshine, frost, wind, and the chemical action of the atmosphere combine to disintegrate and break down the rocks. Surface waters, supplied by rain and melting snow and ice, wash down the particles of disintegrated rock from the mountains and plateaus into the valleys. Thence these fine materials are carried downward by streams and deposited along their channels or finally borne to the sea.

Glaciers, like rivers, serve as denuding and transporting agents. While, in the warmer zones, glaciers are now confined to highly elevated regions, in former ages they covered vast continental areas. The grinding action of these glaciers and ice sheets brought about great changes in the surface features of the areas occupied by them. The sea is another important earth-shaping agent, producing erosion through the action of waves, tides, and currents. Wave action wears down cliffs, and gives a constantly changing form to the coast lines of the continents and islands. Tides bear out to sea the sediment brought down by river currents.

The tendency of erosion is to bring down the continents to a lowland or base plane a little above sea level. This process of degrading the land is counterbalanced by movements of the earth's crustal portion. These elevate the lands and restore, to a large degree, that which has been lost by denudation. See *Butte, Canyon, Fiord, Glacier, Gorge, Mesa, Mountain, Plateau, Pothole, River, Valley, Water Gap.*

Erosion Theory. The theory now universally held by geologists that valleys are produced by the wearing, chiseling, and sculpturing agency of water and ice, the latter chiefly in the form of glaciers. This theory has entirely replaced the earlier view, which regarded valleys as the result of fissures in the earth's crust, produced during upheaval. See *Erosion.*

Escarpment. A high, steep slope, or precipitous face of rock, of considerable length, often marking the line of strike of different strata. An escarpment frequently separates one nearly level expanse of land from another similar expanse situated at a higher elevation. For example, the Niagara escarpment divides the lower lands about Lake Ontario from the higher lands about Lake Erie. In plateaus and mountain regions, escarpments frequently mark the line of outcrop of stratified rocks, produced by unequal weathering or erosion, or by the faulting of strata. Such escarpments usually consist of a succession of steep cliffs. In the plateau regions of Utah and Arizona there are many such escarpments, some of which are 2000 feet in height. See *Cliff, Fault.*

Esker. A low, narrow, winding ridge of gravel and sand, examples of which are found in Scandinavia, North America, and other countries formerly covered by ice sheets. Eskers are from 1 to 20 miles long, and are often from 40 to 80 feet high. It is believed that these deposits were formed by the action of streams underneath the glaciers which existed in the Glacial period. See *Glacier.*

Fault. The name given to any displacement along a fissure, or series of fissures, in any kind of rock. Sedimentary strata that have been faulted may not always retain a horizontal position. They may show that they have been upheaved and displaced since they were first deposited. When seams of coal or other mineral veins are faulted, miners sometimes have great difficulty in locating, underground, the different parts of the coal seams or mineral veins.

Faulted blocks are sometimes tilted, and are frequently of such size and so displaced as to form mountains and basins. Faulting has taken place on an immense scale in the plateau region between the Rocky mountains and the Sierra Nevada, where numerous mountain ranges and lines of cliffs are the result of such movements. Death valley, in California, is a down-faulted basin, as is also the Dead Sea, in Palestine. The Sierra Nevada of California is being carved by erosion out of an uplifted block. The Great Rift valley of Africa is due to faulting. Faulting is probably the principal cause of earthquakes, as the slipping of one vast body of rock upon another causes vibrations which spread far from the center of disturbance. See *Earthquake, Escarpment, Structural Geology.*

Fens. Lowland areas overflowed, or covered entirely or in part, with water. In Great Britain, the term fen is applied to marshy or boggy lands, especially to low-lying districts in Lincolnshire and adjacent counties, called the "Fens." See *Bogs, Marshes, Moor, Swamps.*

Fiord (*fyôrd*). A narrow inlet of the sea, having high, bold cliffs on either hand, and extending far into the land. Fiords occur along mountainous coasts and were formed largely by inland glaciers which gouged out narrow valleys on their way down to the sea. Sinking of the land relative to sea level has also affected the fiorded coasts. This movement has caused the sea water to enter the great canyons in the mountains near the coast, and it has also produced the numerous islands found along such coasts.

The fiords are exceedingly deep and their sides are often lined with waterfalls. Those of Norway are the most notable, Sogne Fiord, one of the largest, being 100 miles long. Fiords are found also in Iceland, Greenland, Alaska, British Columbia, Chile, and New Zealand. See *Canyon, Erosion, Glacier.*

Flood. Floods or inundations are most commonly due to excessive rains or melting snows. These cause rivers to rise and overflow their banks, sometimes resulting in great destruction of property and loss of life. Tidal waves produced by tropical hurricanes and by earthquakes also cause disastrous floods, as do the bursting or sudden overflow of dams and reservoirs. Some rivers have annual floods which are in no sense disastrous; as, for example, the Nile, whose risings and fallings, with their regular yearly deposit of fertile silt in the valley, form the basis of Egyptian agriculture.

In the United States, the valleys of the Mississippi, the Ohio, and the Missouri are liable to springtime floods. In 1913, a flood in the Ohio River valley destroyed large portions of Dayton, Ohio, and various other places, resulting in the loss of 400 lives and of property valued at $100,000,000. The greatest flood that has befallen the United States occurred in

1927, when the lower Mississippi river broke its levees and spread over a total area exceeding 20,000 square miles. The property loss exceeded $270,000,-000. Serious loss of life was avoided by reason of the accuracy with which the flood peak was predicted and the promptness with which warnings were sent out. In 1887, the Hwang river, in China, burst through the huge levees, at some points 70 feet high. The uncontrolled waters flooded an area of 50,000 square miles and drowned 1,000,000 people.

In 1421, great sea waves burst the dikes protecting the Netherlands, destroying 72 villages and about 100,000 human lives. Tidal waves produced by a tropical hurricane caused immense destruction of property and thousands of lives at Galveston, Texas, in 1900. Typhoons in the Pacific produce waves of terrific destructive power. In 1876, 150,000 people were drowned by a typhoon wave which overwhelmed the delta of the Ganges and Brahmaputra in India.

The prodigious tidal waves following the earthquakes at Lisbon in 1755, in the Strait of Sunda in 1883, and on the coast of Japan in 1896, caused the loss of tens of thousands of lives. See *Cloudburst, Earthquake, Rainfall, River.*

Flood Plain. An area of level land, bordering the channel of a stream, and formed during periods of flood by deposits of alluvium. On account of the frequent addition of new material, the soil of flood plains, commonly called "bottom lands," is exceedingly fertile. However, crops grown on these lands are often in danger from recurring floods and, in northern countries, are subject to early frosts. Among the best-known examples of flood plains are those in the valleys of the Nile, the Ganges, the Danube, the Po, and the Mississippi. See *Alluvium, Erosion, River, Valley.*

Fog. Tiny globules or droplets of water condensed from the water vapor or moisture in the lowest layers of the air at a temperature above freezing point. Usually every particle of fog has a minute nucleus of dust in it, but electrons and ions also serve as points of condensation in the forming of fog. Fog, therefore, is a cloud resting upon the surface of the earth.

When cold air flows over warm land or water, the vapor rising from the latter is quickly condensed. Thus fogs are formed over lakes, rivers, and marshes when the warm vapor from these meets the cooler air above them. Whenever cold and warm currents of water lie adjacent to each other on the ocean, air from the warmer and moister water is carried over the colder water, and cools until fog is formed. For example, the intense fogs off the coasts of New England and Newfoundland, one of the foggiest regions of the world, occur when moist easterly or southerly winds blow over the colder waters of the Labrador Current. Fogs often form about icebergs and obscure these great masses of floating ice.

City fogs are more persistent than country fogs, and, usually, more dense, owing to the immense number of dust and soot particles in the air. Largely on account of the blanketing effect of fogs, winter temperatures do not drop so low in cities as in the country. In London as many as 74 fogs have been recorded in a single year. Some of these are so dense as to compel suspension of traffic and the closing of stores. Fogs seriously impede navigation, often occasioning disastrous collisions and shipwrecks. On land also, fogs greatly hinder travel, and are responsible for many railroad and other accidents.

Regularly recurring fogs sometimes partly take the place of rain, and, in various localities, prove of great value to growing crops. For example, in certain coast districts of California, Indian corn and other crops requiring much moisture in midsummer are successfully grown, by reason of the abundant fogs which occur during parts of the rainless season. See *Cloud, Humidity, Rain.*

Fringing Reef. A coral reef which borders a coast line. The reef material is composed chiefly of the exoskeleton of the coral polyp. This stony substance consists mainly of lime, which the coral animal secretes from the sea water, and forms the horny outer framework, which supports and protects the soft parts of the body. In time, fringing reefs may become mantled with soil and clothed with vegetation. See *Atoll, Barrier Reef, Coral.*

Frost. A covering of minute ice crystals which form on the ground, on leaves of plants, or on other objects; called also "hoarfrost," or "white frost." It is the water vapor, or moisture, always found in the air, condensed on the surface of objects whose temperature has fallen below the freezing point. At sunset the earth begins to give up the heat absorbed from the sun's rays during the day. The surface of the ground cools quickly, so that the moisture in the air immediately surrounding it is chilled and condensed. As long as the temperature remains above the freezing point, dew is formed, but, when it falls below 32° F., frost is formed. Frost, therefore, corresponds to snow, and dew, to rain.

The ground cools on clear nights much more rapidly than in cloudy weather. For this reason frosts occur most frequently when the sky is cloudless. Further, if the air is calm, frost may form on the ground when the temperature a few feet above the surface is several degrees above the freezing point. This is owing to the fact that the surface of the ground parts with heat at a much more rapid rate than does the surrounding air. Moreover, cold air is heavier than warm air and tends to settle and remain at the surface. Consequently, if a layer of air next to the ground remains undisturbed, it may be cooled below the freezing point, despite the warmer air above. A wind, however, will mix the layers of cold and warm air and thereby prevent the formation of frost. It thus becomes plain why frosts, like dew, are most plentifully formed on calm, clear nights, and why they are least likely to occur when it is cloudy and windy.

In autumn, frost occurs in valleys and on low grounds earlier and more frequently than on adjacent hills. This is because the colder air naturally drains to the lower levels, and also because narrow, hemmed-in valleys are less disturbed by winds.

Frosts occurring unseasonably late in the spring or early in autumn, often cause severe damage to field crops, vegetables, and fruits. The growing parts of plants are turgid with sap which is composed chiefly of water. Upon freezing, this expands and bursts the delicate cells, thereby killing the plant outright or greatly impairing its growth and productiveness. During high winds or when the air is abnormally dry, freezing of plant tissues may take place without the formation of ice particles on the surfaces of the leaves. This is sometimes called "black frost." See *Dew, Dew Point, Humidity.*

Geyser. An eruptive hot spring, which, from time to time, violently ejects boiling water and steam. The best-known geysers are those in Yellowstone national park, though there are geysers in Iceland and New Zealand. In some geysers, eruptions are frequent; in others, infrequent. In some, eruptions take place at regular intervals; in others, they are of very irregular occurrence. The geyser named "Old Faithful," in Yellowstone park, spouts at nearly regular intervals of about an hour.

A geyser consists of two parts, a basin and a tube. The basin is usually situated at the top of a mound of mineral matter, often of fantastic form, commonly composed of silica deposited by the water. The tube, or opening, leads from the basin down to unknown depths.

Scientists are agreed that steam is the force which explosively ejects the water of a geyser, sometimes to a height of 100 feet or more. It is believed that ground water enters the geyser tube in much the same manner as it flows into a well, but that the walls in some parts of the tube consist of hot rock.

It is believed further that water in the lower portion of the tube, where it is under great pressure, is heated to temperatures above the boiling point, and that the steam thus formed forces out violently the column of water above it. This explanation of geyser eruption is more readily understood when it is remembered that water, when changing into steam, expands to 1700 times its original volume. See *Ground Water, Hot Springs, Vulcanism.*

Glacier. A large mass of ice and snow moving slowly over a land surface. On all high mountains which are subject to moist winds, so that the snowfall is greater than the yearly melting, glaciers are formed. Consequently, they are found in most of the higher mountains of the world, and also on high plateaus in the arctic and antarctic regions.

There are six types or classes of glaciers: (1) *continental glaciers*, or ice sheets; (2) *plateau glaciers*, or local ice caps; (3) *alpine glaciers*, or valley glaciers—the most common form; (4) *piedmont glaciers*, formed when a number of alpine glaciers unite and spread out upon a plain at the foot of the mountains, as in the Malaspina glacier, in Alaska; (5) *hanging glaciers*, perched on shelves on mountain sides; (6) *reconstructed glaciers*, formed of recongealed remnants of other glaciers.

The rate of movement in a glacier varies from an almost imperceptible motion to several feet a day. Most of the well-known valley glaciers flow at the rate of a foot or two a day. The Mer de Glace, the swiftest moving glacier of the Alps, advances about 3 feet a day. The Muir glacier in Alaska has a speed of about 7 feet a day. However, the great Upernivik ice stream in Greenland has been observed to move at the rate of about 100 feet per day.

Glaciers vary greatly in size. Of about 2000 glaciers in the Alps, less than 40 are 5 miles long, and the longest is about 10 miles. A few are a mile wide, and the thickness of the ice is measured in hundreds of feet. Much larger alpine or valley glaciers occur in the Caucasus mountains and in Alaska. The great Seward glacier in Alaska exceeds 50 miles in length and is 3 miles wide at its narrowest part. The glaciers of the western United States are mostly smaller than those of the Alps. The continental glaciers or ice sheets cover vast areas in Greenland and in Antarctica, sometimes measuring thousands of feet in thickness. In Alaska, many large alpine glaciers emerge from the valleys of St. Elias range, and, by uniting on the plain, form the immense Malaspina glacier, 70 miles long and more than 20 miles wide.

Glaciers perform a twofold work; they erode or wear down the rocky surfaces over which they pass, and they carry and finally deposit the materials thus acquired. They thus degrade mountains and hills, deepen and round out valleys, and upbuild plateaus and plains. Glacial action, therefore, is a natural earth-shaping process of great importance. When glaciers flow down to the edge of the sea, their ends are broken off and float away as icebergs.

During the Ice age, which occurred in very recent geological time, great continental glaciers covered much of the northern United States and of Canada. This immense glaciation produced many important effects, one of which was to make possible the Great Lakes route. Supplemented by canals, this waterway provides interior transportation for 2000 miles, a natural advantage possessed by no other continent. Another earth-shaping work of the "great ice" was the deposition of the glacial drift which has become transformed into vast areas of fertile soil. Again, glacial deposits turned many streams from their valleys, producing rapids and cataracts, as, for example, the Falls of St. Anthony, at Minneapolis. Innumerable ponds and small lakes were likewise formed, as in Minnesota, where their number is said to exceed 10,000. The deposits left by glaciers are called moraines. See *Cirque, Crevasse, Drumlin, Erosion, Esker, Fiord, Iceberg, Ice Cap, Kettle Hole, Moraines, Striæ, Terminal Moraines, Valley Train.*

Gorge. A narrow ravine or defile, with steep rocky walls, through which a stream flows. In the western United States, gorges are usually called canyons. Gorges are deepest and most frequent in dry regions where the downward erosion of the stream bed is much more rapid than the weathering of the walls. While the sides of small gorges are often nearly vertical, those of larger gorges or canyons are rarely so. Notable examples of gorges are Ausable Chasm in New York, the Royal Gorge in Colorado, and the Gorge of the Metlac in Mexico. See *Canyon, Erosion.*

Ground Moraine. A mantle of glacial débris left on the retreat or final melting of the ice over the territory which the ice of the Glacial period invaded. This moraine forms the extensive prairie country of Indiana, Illinois, Iowa, and other more northerly states. It has a rolling surface, or topography, in which there may be broad, shallow, saucer-like depressions containing lakes. The material of a ground moraine is a bowlder clay. The stones in it vary in size and kind, and the fine material grades from gravel down to the finest of silts and clays. See *Glacier, Moraines, Till.*

Ground Water. The water which passes into the earth and circulates through the ground, nourishing vegetable life, dissolving out parts of the rock and forming caves, and assisting in the concentration of mineral matter. This water usually saturates a layer of ground beneath the surface. The upper surface of this saturated layer is the *ground-water table.* Into excavations made beneath this, water will flow. Common wells are thus formed and deep excavations become flooded. See *Geyser, Hot Springs, Mineral Springs, Springs, Structural Geology.*

Gulf Stream. The best known and most important ocean current in the North Atlantic. It takes its name from the Gulf of Mexico, from which the larger portion of it issues between the coasts of Florida and Cuba. At its narrowest portion, in the vicinity of the Florida Keys, this so-called Florida current is about 50 miles wide and 2000 feet deep, and moves at a speed of from 2 to 5 or 6 miles an hour. At 30° N., it is joined by the Smaller Antilles current from the eastern side of the West Indies. The Gulf Stream is readily detected by its high temperature (in lat. 34° ranging from 79° F. in winter to 88° F. in summer), by the character of the marine life which it supports, and by its deep blue color.

When the Gulf Stream reaches latitude 32° N., between the Bahamas and South Carolina, it divides into several much slower streams, about 600 feet deep and aggregating 150 miles in width. North of lat. 40°, these become simply a part of the great general drift of warm waters from the southwestern or equatorial Atlantic northeastward toward Europe. Prevailing westerly winds passing over this North Atlantic drift are warmed and, upon reaching western Europe, are laden with moisture. It is in this manner that the Gulf Stream indirectly modifies the climate and causes the greater warmth of western Europe, as compared with eastern North America in the same latitude, See *Japan Current, Labrador Current, Ocean Currents.*

Hail. Compact, round masses of ice that fall from the clouds to the ground, commonly accompanied by rain. When these are more than a fourth of an inch in diameter, they are called *hailstones*; when very small and falling with rain, they are called *sleet.* While ordinarily ranging from about the size of a pea to that of a walnut, hailstones occur in all sizes up to about 3 inches in diameter and sometimes reach a weight of about 2 pounds. Usually only a few hailstones fall at any one place and these commonly at the onset of a thunderstorm. Sometimes, however, they are so numerous as to cover the ground to a depth of several inches, completely destroying growing vegetation.

As a rule the larger hailstones are composed of concentric layers of transparent, solid ice alternating with layers of snowy white, soft ice. Frequently the large stones are formed around a central particle of small gravel, or other foreign substances such as are sometimes borne high in the air by tornadic winds. In some cases the large stones are formed around a central core of snow in which air, or some of the gases composing it, is imprisoned under a pressure estimated at 50 atmospheres.

The method or process by which hail is formed is not well understood. However, it seems to be clearly proved that when warm, moisture-laden air rises and cools, it first condenses into a cloud. Continuing to rise, it reaches a colder region where hail, or hail and rain, is formed. Rising still higher, it reaches a region so cold that only snow is formed. It is believed that ordinary small hailstones or sleet are formed in the first cold region, but that the larger stones are carried up and down many times from the rain region to the snow region until they can no longer be held up by the whirling air currents.

In certain districts, particularly in the Great Plains region, hailstorms cause the yearly destruction of crops and window glass, and even of young live stock. In the United States, hailstorms are most frequent in Ohio, Indiana, Illinois, Iowa, and Missouri. See *Rain, Snow, Tornado.*

Hardpan. A firmly compacted bed of hardened clay which sometimes underlies a thin covering of topsoil. Extensive deposits of hardpan occur in various parts of the United States and other countries. Lands whose subsoil consists of a more or less impermeable layer are often called hardpan lands. Because of their lack of internal drainage, they are inferior for crop growing. See *Soil.*

Heaths. Tracts of open, usually level, waste land, covered with a characteristic vegetation consisting chiefly of heather and other low shrubs of the heath family. Heaths occupy extensive areas in northern Europe. A few small tracts similarly covered with low evergreen shrubs are found in the United States and Canada. See *Prairie, Steppes, Tundras.*

Hot Springs. Springs are called *thermal* when their waters show a temperature exceeding 70° F. Those whose temperatures are between 70° and 98° are called *tepid*, and all those whose temperatures are above 98° are called *hot*. A hot spring which erupts intermittently is called a geyser.

The high temperature of thermal springs may be caused either by the contact of the waters with buried lava or by the circulation of the waters to great depths where the rocks are much warmer than at the surface. The rising hot water usually bears various mineral salts in solution, some of which may be deposited near the spring, forming incrustations and icicle-like masses. Many hot springs possess valuable curative properties, owing to their mineral content and, in some cases, so it is believed, to their radioactivity.

The temperatures of some well-known thermal springs are as follows: Sweet Springs, Va., 74° F.; French Broad River, Tenn., 95°; San Bernardino, Calif., 108°–172°; Washita, Ark., 140°–156°; Las Vegas, New Mexico, 110°–140°; Aix-les-Bains, France, 108°; Carlsbad, Bohemia, 162°. The volume of water discharged by hot springs varies greatly. The noted Hot Springs in Arkansas discharge about 20,000 gallons per hour, while the Warm Sulphur Springs, at Bath, Va., flow at the rate of about 350,000 gallons per hour. See *Geysers, Springs, Vulcanism.*

Humidity. The moisture or water vapor in the atmosphere. Water vapor exists in the air as an invisible gas, and, as regards quantity, it is the most important component after nitrogen and oxygen. When this vapor becomes visible it is called dew, fog, mist, haze, cloud, rain, sleet, hail, snow, frostwork or frost, according to the method and manner in which it condenses.

The actual amount of water vapor which the air contains at a given time is its *absolute humidity*. The percentage of water vapor which the air contains at any temperature, in comparison with what it *might* contain at that temperature, is called its *relative humidity*. When the air is completely saturated with moisture, its humidity is said to be 100 per cent. If it contains only half as much moisture as it might contain, it has a relative humidity of 50 per cent.

Air is called dry when its relative humidity is small, and moist when its relative humidity is high. Over the land surface of the earth the average relative humidity is probably about 60 per cent, and over the sea it is about 85 per cent. Cold and heat are much more easily resisted in regions where the humidity is low than where the air is damp. See *Aridity, Climate, Dew, Frost, Rainfall, Snow.*

Hurricane. A violent tropical storm, or true *cyclone*, called also *typhoon* and *baguio*, generally accompanied by rain, thunder and lightning, and very destructive winds. About two-thirds of the hurricanes occur in the West Indies and in the China Sea during August, September, and October. While reaching the highest force of all horizontal winds, hurricanes do not attain the intense violence of tornadoes, and they rarely exceed a velocity of 100 miles an hour. The general circulation of the air in a hurricane is spirally inward, and, in the northern hemisphere, in a direction opposite to that of the hands of a clock.

Tropical cyclones moving northward often do immense damage along the southern Atlantic coast of the United States, both to shipping and to lowlands near the shore. The storm which caused great devastation at Galveston, Texas, in September 1900, was a tropical hurricane which veered farther northwest than usual. Similar storms of cyclonic origin occurring in the Pacific Ocean are commonly called typhoons. Baguio is the Philippine name for such a storm. See *Cyclone, Storm, Tornado, Typhoon.*

Hydrosphere. The water on the surface of the earth, forming the liquid envelope of the globe, intermediate between the gaseous envelope, or *atmosphere*, and the solid land, or *lithosphere*.

The sea, including the Pacific, Atlantic, Indian, Arctic, and Antarctic oceans, together with various great gulfs and bays, covers about 72 per cent of the earth's surface. The Pacific Ocean comprises more than half of the total water surface of the globe. The average depth of the sea is about 2½ miles, or about 13,000 feet. The greatest depth in the Atlantic Ocean, at a point north of Puerto Rico, is 27,972 feet, or about 5.3 miles. In the Pacific, a sounding of 35,401 feet has been obtained east of Mindanao, one of the Philippine Islands.

The water of the ocean is strongly saline, but less so than that of landlocked seas situated in warm regions, such as the Mediterranean Sea and the Red Sea. The mass or weight of the sea is about 265 times the mass of the air, and about $\frac{1}{4300}$ part of the mass of the solid portion of the earth. As water is much lighter than an equal volume of rock, the mass of the sea is only about five times the mass of the land above the sea.

The temperature of the surface water varies from the freezing point in polar regions to 90° in enclosed tropical seas, such as the Caribbean and Red seas. At medium depths the temperature is constant, and at great depths the temperature in all parts of the ocean is but little above the freezing point.

At great depths the sea water is almost motionless, and, as sunlight penetrates but a few hundred feet, darkness prevails throughout most of the ocean. See *Lake, Ocean, River.*

Ice. Water in the solid state, produced by freezing. Ice is a brittle, colorless substance, which in crystallizing assumes six-sided or six-rayed forms, sometimes of exquisite beauty, as in snow crystals and hoarfrost. Under ordinary conditions, water freezes at 32° F. or 0° C. and, in freezing, expands about one-eleventh of its volume, exerting great force against any surface by which it is confined.

Unlike most substances, water is lighter in the solid than in the liquid state. The specific gravity of ice is 0.918, so that it floats on water with about nine-tenths of its volume submerged. However, under low temperatures and high pressures, physicists have produced special forms of ice which are heavier than liquid water. The specific heat of ice has been found to be about half that of water. In melting, ice absorbs more heat than any other solid.

Since water ordinarily expands upon freezing, it follows that its freezing point will be lowered with any increase of pressure, the rate having been determined at 0.0075° for each additional atmosphere of pressure. By this are explained various properties of ice, particularly that of *regelation*, which is illustrated as follows: If a piece of wire, with a heavy weight attached at each end, is thrown over a block of solid ice, the wire gradually cuts its way through the block, though the latter remains entire. Where the wire presses heavily on the ice the melting point is lowered so that a thin film becomes liquid, permitting the wire to descend through a minute distance. The water immediately above the wire instantly freezes again because it is relieved from pressure. The descent of the wire through the entire block is held to be due to repetitions of this process. The theory is held that the flowing motion of ice under pressure in glaciers is due in part to modifications of the foregoing process.

Freezing is retarded by substances in solution. For example, sea water freezes at 29° F., the ice separating out as pure ice and not as a mixture of ice and salt. The entire Arctic Ocean is practically covered with permanent ice, averaging between six and seven feet in thickness. The vast continent of Antarctica is fringed with a belt of sea ice, several hundred miles wide, which is formed annually. The continent itself, like Greenland, is covered with a permanent ice sheet, from which glaciers extend down to the sea. Portions of these, by breaking off, become icebergs. Permanent ice occurs also in the glaciers on high mountains. See *Anchor Ice, Glacier, Iceberg, Ice Cap.*

Iceberg. A large mass of floating ice broken from a glacier, or from an ice sheet, when its front has reached the sea. Among the various arctic lands, Greenland stands pre-eminent for the number and size of the icebergs which drift from its shores into North Atlantic waters. Some of the Greenland icebergs tower from 100 to 250 feet or more above the ocean. As, usually, only about one-seventh is above water, the total height of such icebergs is from about 700 to about 1600 feet. In the Atlantic Ocean, the southern limit of icebergs extends southwesterly from about lat. 60° N., near Iceland, to lat. 45° N., off the Grand Banks of Newfoundland. In a collision with an iceberg in this region, April 14, 1912, the steamer *Titanic*, then the largest ship in the world, was sunk, with a loss of 1517 lives.

Icebergs, however, are most numerous and attain their greatest size in south polar regions. The shores of Antarctica include more than 10,000 miles of icy coasts. So far as known, there is nowhere 100 consecutive miles of antarctic coast where glaciers are not discharging icebergs into the sea. The antarctic icebergs are usually tabular, that is, flat-topped, with perpendicular sides often 200 or more feet high. Tabular icebergs 30 to 40 miles long, with surface areas estimated at 1000 square miles, have been observed. See *Glacier, Ice Cap.*

Ice Cap. A glacier-like sheet of ice and snow which lies on a plain or plateau, and moves slowly in all directions from its center. Large ice caps, however, may cover both valleys and hills. Exceedingly large ice caps are called continental glaciers, or inland ice sheets. Greenland, the largest known island, embracing an area of some 825,000 square miles, is entirely covered, except along very narrow borders, with a vast ice cap. In the interior this attains an elevation of 8000 or 9000 feet and averages probably thousands of feet in thickness. The south polar lands of Antarctica are likewise covered with an ice cap of immense extent and thickness. See *Glacier.*

Island. A body of land entirely surrounded by water, of small size when compared to a continent. In area, islands range from tiny tracts in rivers and lakes to great land masses in the ocean, tens of thousands of square miles in extent. As a whole, islands may be divided into two main classes, *continental* and *oceanic.*

Continental islands are formed chiefly (1) by the subsidence of a coast below sea level, leaving only the higher portions above water; (2) by the erosive action of the sea, cutting off peninsulas or other portions of the land; (3) by the constructive work of rivers, building up deltas; and (4) by ocean currents, forming sand bars. In structure, continental islands are essentially similar to the mainland, from which they are separated by narrow areas of usually shallow water overlying a portion of the continental platform or shelf.

The small islands near the coasts of Maine, Scotland, and Norway are remnants of hills and mountains whose basal portions and intervening valleys have been submerged in a general subsidence. Japan, Sicily, and the British Isles are regarded as larger masses which, likewise, were once united to the mainland, as indicated by the submarine banks in the intervening seas. The islands at the mouth of the Mississippi and the Nile are good examples of islands formed in deltas by rivers.

Oceanic islands are formed in various ways. When a peak on an elevation in the deep ocean floor rises above the surface, a true oceanic island is produced. Submarine volcanoes raise material above sea level, producing volcanic islands. Earth movements, resulting in the buckling or upfolding of the ocean bed, may elevate portions of it above the surface. Coral islands are formed by the limy secretions of coral polyps. They occur in numerous groups on oceanic plateaus where the waters are warm and shallow, or are found singly, crowning isolated peaks which rise from deep water. Oceanic islands are found in exceedingly large numbers in the Pacific where they constitute the division of the land world called Oceania.

Volcanic islands occur most frequently in the Pacific and the Indian Ocean and include both active and extinct volcanoes. Examples of volcanic islands in the Atlantic are St. Helena, Ascension, and the Azores. Many submarine eruptions, forming volcanic cones above sea level, have occurred in recent times. In 1796 the island of Johanna Bogslava appeared on the coast of Alaska. Within four years it had grown to a height of 3000 feet. In 1831 Graham island, in the Mediterranean, was thrown up. It attained a height of 200 feet and a circumference of 3 miles, but soon afterward disappeared.

Through the action of various agencies, islands undergo changes of form and contour. Wave action, together with tidal and other oceanic currents, may gradually wear them away. At the present time the east coast of England is being rapidly eroded. Helgoland, the famous German fortress in the North Sea, has been steadily eaten away by the sea for many hundreds of years. On the other hand, islands situated near the shores of continents may become joined to them. By the growth of the Hwang delta the peninsula of Shantung, China, formerly an island, has become connected with the mainland. See *Atoll, Land-tied Island.*

Isobars (*ī'sô-bärz*). Lines joining places at which the barometric pressure of the atmosphere is the same, either at a given time or for a certain period; called also *isobarometric lines*. A map showing such lines of equal pressure is called an isobaric map or chart. The daily weather maps issued by the Weather Bureau are isobaric charts. See ***Atmosphere, Climate, Storm.***

Isostasy (ī-sŏs'tȧ-sĭ). A theory regarding the crust of the earth according to which the weight of any one portion of the earth's crust is in equilibrium with the weight of all other portions. Thus a mountain range, with its huge bulk, does not ordinarily overbalance in weight a neighboring portion of the earth's crust of a much lower altitude, since the lowness of plain and sea find compensation in a greater density of the underlying material. Earthquakes are due, by this theory, to an unsettling of this condition of equilibrium largely through the transference, by erosion, of a great weight of material from mountains to plains and ocean beds.

Isothermal Lines. A line drawn on the surface of the earth connecting points having the same average temperature is called an *isotherm.* A line connecting places having the same average temperature for the year is an *annual isotherm.* Similarly, seasonal, monthly, or daily isotherms may be drawn. A map showing the distribution of isotherms by any of these periods is called an *isothermal chart.* See *Climate; Temperature, Atmospheric.*

Japan Current. A warm current in the Pacific Ocean, smaller and cooler than the Gulf Stream in the Atlantic; called also the *Kuro Siwo.* It originates in an equatorial current which turns north near Japan, whence it crosses the Pacific in a northeasterly direction. Upon reaching the northwest coast of North America, it divides, the southern part, called the California Current, following down the coast of California, while the other part, known as the Alaska Current, turns northward. The Japan Current has a certain moderating influence on the climate of the Pacific Coast of North America, although for the most part this condition of climate is due to the prevailing westerly winds blowing over vast areas of temperate oceanic waters. See *Gulf Stream, Labrador Current, Ocean Currents.*

Kettle Hole. An undrained depression, usually only a few hundred feet in diameter but with steep sides, found in glacial moraines. Such a depression may have been formed by the lodgment of a block of ice which melted after the glacier retreated. The place occupied by the block of ice then became a great hole in the land. See *Glacier.*

Labrador Current. An ocean current of the North Atlantic. It flows southward from polar waters through Baffin bay and along the shores of Labrador, to which it imparts a severe climate. Upon passing Newfoundland, the main current continues southward, and, in the region of the Grand Banks, meets the warm waters of the Gulf Stream Drift. Here the icy waters from the north chill the vapor-laden winds from the south, condensing their moisture and producing one of the foggiest regions in the world. The Labrador Current is the chief conveyor of icebergs in the North Atlantic. It brings south, sometimes as far as lat. 40°, immense numbers of floating ice masses broken from glaciers on the west coast of Greenland. Both the fogs and the icebergs are sources of grave danger to navigation.

The Grand Banks, whose shallow waters provide invaluable fishing grounds, are believed to have been built up to some extent by the earthy materials transported in the icebergs brought down by the Labrador Current. South of the Grand Banks the colder and heavier waters from the north sink beneath the warmer and lighter but shallow drift of waters from the tropics. These heavier waters then continue as cold undercurrents as far south as Florida. See *Gulf Stream, Japan Current, Ocean Currents.*

Lake. An inland body of standing water larger than a pool or a pond. Lakes and ponds differ from most inland seas, bays, and lagoons in being completely shut off from tidal connection with the ocean, and in being usually situated with their surfaces considerably above sea level—very rarely below it. In lakes which have a regular outlet, the water is fresh, but in lakes without an outlet the water is usually salt. A few lakes, such as Great Salt lake, contain proportionately much more salt than the ocean itself. Some salt water lakes are called seas, as the Dead Sea and the Caspian Sea.

Lakes are found in nearly all parts of the world, though they are most abundant in high latitudes, where they occupy innumerable natural basins scoured out by former glaciers, or formed by the uneven deposition of debris by the ice. It is estimated that in northern Europe and in North America, there are hundreds of thousands of lakes of glacial origin. In Minnesota alone there are said to be 10,000 lakes of this kind. Lakes also occur in mountain regions, along rivers and coasts, on plateaus and coastal plains, and in the craters of volcanic mountains. Most lakes are of comparatively small size, but the Great Lakes—Lake Superior, Lake Huron, Lake Michigan, Lake Erie, and Lake Ontario—have a total area of about 95,000 square miles. Five of the large lakes of Canada possess a combined area exceeding 32,000 square miles.

Lakes vary greatly in altitude above the sea. Yellowstone lake, the highest lake of any great size in the United States, with an area of about 140 square miles, is 7740 feet above sea level. Lake Titicaca, next to Lake Maracaibo, the largest lake in South America, with an area of 3200 square miles, stands at an altitude of nearly 12,500 feet. A few lakes are below sea level,—the Caspian Sea being 86 feet, the Dead Sea 1290 feet, and the Sea of Tiberias 682 feet.

Most lakes are shallow, the great majority being probably less than 50 feet in depth, but some are exceedingly deep. Lake Superior exceeds 1000 feet in depth; Lake Huron, Lake Michigan, and Lake Ontario each exceed 700 feet; Lake Erie, however, has a maximum depth of only about 200 feet. The deepest lake, so far as known, is Lake Baikal with a reported maximum depth of about 5300 feet. Next deepest is the Caspian Sea, about 3000 feet deep. Other very deep lakes are Crater Lake, Oregon, about 2000 feet; Lake Tahoe, California, 1650 feet; and Lake Chelan, Washington, about 1500 feet. Lakes Maggiore, Como, and di Garda, in Italy, and the Dead Sea, in Palestine, exceed 1000 feet in depth.

The combined volume of water in lakes is insignificant when compared with that of the sea, and if added to the ocean, it is estimated that it would not raise the ocean's surface two feet. The waters of lakes are subject to many movements, including waves, currents, drifts, seiches, and tides, though the latter are very small, the tide in Lake Michigan being only about two inches. Lake water is derived from precipitation, through rain, melting snow and ice, springs, and rivers.

A large body of water exerts a beneficial effect upon the climate of the immediately surrounding land, making both the cold of winter and the heat of summer less extreme. In consequence, conditions of agriculture near the shores of large lakes are materially changed. For example, the great fruit belt of Michigan is a narrow strip about 200 miles in length along the eastern shore of Lake Michigan, where the prevailing winds from the broad expanse of water modify a climate otherwise too rigorous for fruit growing. The grape and peach belt of New York lies along the shores of Lake Erie and Lake Ontario. In southern Ontario, likewise, many fruits are extensively grown where, without the presence of these bodies of water, the climate would be too severe.

Most lakes abound in food and game fishes, and some support extensive commercial fisheries. The annual catch of whitefish, ciscoes, lake trout, and other food fish in the Great Lakes amounts to many millions of pounds.

Large lakes play an important rôle in inland navigation, furnishing convenient waterways for transportation and communication. The world's most striking example of the economic value of lakes is seen in the remarkable commercial and industrial development on the shores of the great chain between the United States and Canada. This embraces manufacturing and trade centers with a total population of many millions, including Toronto, Buffalo, Cleveland, Toledo, Detroit, Duluth, Milwaukee, and Chicago, together with many important smaller cities. See *Hydrosphere, Salt Lakes, Seiche.*

Landslide. When the soil and earthy material on a steep slope become heavily charged with water, their weight is greatly increased. The water also renders the material more liquid and mobile. In consequence, a portion of the earthy mass sometimes slides or slumps downward. A movement of this kind on a large scale is called a landslide.

Landslides occur chiefly in mountainous regions. They most commonly result from the effects of freezing and thawing, or from excessive rains. Extensive cracks in deep layers of earth, resulting from shrinkage during severe drought, occasionally cause landslides. Earthquake tremors sometimes produce them.

On April 29, 1903, at Turtle mountain, Alberta, Canada, a huge mass of material, about a half mile square and some 400 or 500 feet deep, suddenly slid down the mountain slope. The length of the slide was about 2½ miles. This was traversed in less than 2 minutes. When the earth mass came to rest, it covered an area of more than a square mile, completely filling a valley a half mile wide. Many lives were lost and much property destroyed. See *Avalanche.*

Land-tied Island. An island which, by the development of a sand and gravel beach, has been tied to the mainland. In this manner the famous rock of Gibraltar has become a land-tied island. Many of the islands along the coast of New England are joined to the mainland by beaches of sand and gravel. See *Beach.*

Lava (*lä'vȧ*). Rock material in a molten state, within the earth's crust, or, that which has been poured out on the earth's surface in a molten state. Lava is erupted by volcanoes or poured out through fissures on the earth's surface. The temperature of molten lava is estimated at from about 2200° to about 3600° F. At times, the liquidity is so great that the lava appears as fountains rising and playing in the air.

After ejection, the rapidity of a lava flow depends in part upon its volume and its own fluidity, in part upon the slope of the land and the conditions of cooling. During an eruption of Mauna Loa, Hawaii, in 1855, there was a lava stream with an estimated velocity of forty miles an hour. A lava flow with an initial speed exceeding fifty miles an hour at the moment of eruption was observed at Vesuvius in 1805.

Lavas have been divided into many classes according to their chemical composition, such as rhyolites, trachytes, phonolites, andesites, tephrites, and basalts. Silicious lavas flow sluggishly and build up steep volcanic cones. Basaltic lavas are much more fluid and form cones of gentle slope, such as those of Mt. Etna and the Hawaiian volcanoes. Some lavas quickly disintegrate and form soils of remarkable fertility. Others remain practically unchanged for centuries. Obsidian or volcanic glass, much used by primitive peoples for arrowheads, spearheads, and knives, is a form of lava, as is also pumice stone, a porous mineral widely used for polishing.

Lavas from volcanoes have overflowed tracts many square miles in extent, sometimes overwhelming villages and towns, filling lakes, damming rivers, and otherwise altering the configuration of the landscape. All such changes, however, are exceedingly small when compared with those caused by the outpourings from fissure eruptions.

In Oregon, Washington, Idaho, and California, lava from ancient fissure eruptions built up a vast plateau, some 200,000 miles in extent.

In India, a lava plateau of still greater size and age occurs. The rich soils of the Deccan, famous for cotton growing, owe their marvelous fertility to disintegrated lavas. In Iceland, fissure eruptions have occurred in recent times. During such an eruption in 1783, lava, from a fissure about twenty miles long, spread out in sheets which covered wide valleys. See *Crater, Dike, Igneous Rocks, Soil, Volcano, Vulcanism.*

Lightning. A brilliant flash of light in the sky, caused by the discharge of atmospheric electricity from one cloud to another or between a cloud and the ground. Electricity is produced when the air currents are in violent motion and the water vapor in the air is condensing rapidly, creating large differences in electrical potential between different regions. As the current discharges from one region to another through the air, which is a very poor conductor, intense heat is generated which causes the air to glow, thus creating the visible flash. Flashes which take place between low clouds and the earth are comparatively narrow and vivid, and are accompanied by thunder. Flashes which take place in the higher clouds are more diffuse, and usually no thunder is heard. There are three general classes of lightning: (1) *forked, zigzag,* or *chain lightning;* (2) *sheet lightning;* and (3) *globular,* or *ball lightning.*

Forked lightning appears to the eye as a single, narrow, intensely brilliant line of light, which sometimes splits into one or two branches. Photographs, however, show that the line of light is never actually zigzag, but is composed of irregular, sinuous curves. Sheet lightning does not show a definite form, but appears as a rosy or reddish glow, lighting up clouds or haze on the distant horizon. Globular or ball lightning is a rare form which appears as a small globe of brilliant light, moving slowly through the lower air, or rolling along the ground. This ball, which sometimes has been observed to roll into a house through an open door or window, usually breaks up in a mild explosion, which is not very destructive or dangerous.

A flash of lightning represents the release of enormous energy. Scientists in laboratories of the General Electric Company succeeded in producing artificially a flash of only 30 feet with a current of 10 million volts.

The average annual loss of human life from lightning stroke in the United States, about five per million of population, is greater than in most countries. The danger to buildings is about five times greater in the open country than in cities. About 2000 buildings are struck annually.

For exposed buildings, authorities are agreed that good lightning conductors are very desirable. Concerning the various forms of conductors, Sir Oliver Lodge, an eminent authority on the subject, says: "Almost any conductor is probably better than none, but few or no conductors are absolute and complete safeguards." See *Electricity, Storm, Thunder.*

Lithosphere. The solid portion of the earth, as distinguished from the aqueous portion, or *hydrosphere,* and the gaseous portion, or *atmosphere.* About 28 per cent of the surface of the lithosphere is occupied by the exposed solid portion, or land, and the remaining 72 per cent is covered by the oceans, or hydrosphere. The average height of the land above the sea level is about 2300 feet. The average depth of the ocean is about 13,000 feet. It is estimated that the average level of the solid crust of the earth is about 7500 feet below the level of the sea. The density of the lithosphere is slightly more than 5½ times that of water. See under Geology: *Igneous Rocks, Sedimentary Rocks, Metamorphic Rocks.*

Llanos (*lä'nōz*). A name commonly used in Spanish America for plains or prairies. Geographically, the term Llanos is applied to a large treeless tract in Venezuela and Colombia, lying between the Orinoco and the Andes, immediately north of the Amazon forests. This region, which is about equal to California in area, presents for the most part an unbroken expanse of level land. During the wet season, the upper, more undulating portions are grass covered, but in the dry season they become almost barren. The lower portions, mostly more or less subject to floods, produce, during the rainy period, a rank growth of grasses which usually keep green throughout the year. See *Pampas, Prairies, Steppes.*

Loess (*lō'ĕs*). A distinctive loamy deposit, the particles of which are finer than sand grains but coarser than ordinary particles of clay. Loess deposits cover considerable areas in China, in Europe, and in the Mississippi basin. By many geologists these are believed to have been formed during the Pleistocene period, largely by the action of the wind, though some loess deposits are certainly of river origin. They lack, however, the bedded arrangement characteristic of most sedimentary deposits. Moreover, they possess the remarkable property of an almost vertical cleavage. Cliffs or bluffs of soft loess will stand for a long time with almost perpendicular faces.

In parts of China, people have excavated successive tiers of houses along the faces of steep slopes of the loess, which attains a thickness of from 250 to 1000 feet. In the United States, loess deposits are usually from 30 to 50 feet thick. When loess deposits are eroded by great rivers, as, for example, the Mississippi, the Missouri, or the Hwang, nearly vertical cliffs or bluffs are often formed, like those at Kansas City, Missouri.

If properly supplied with moisture, loess forms a fine-grained soil of immense fertility. The famous black soils of southern Russia consist of loess generously mixed with organic matter. The rich but very cohesive adobe soils of the western United States are believed to have originated in a manner somewhat similar to that of loess. See *Adobe Soil, Æolian Deposits, Alluvium, Soil.*

Magnetic Poles. The earth is an immense magnet and, like all other magnets, has two poles called the north magnetic pole and the south magnetic pole. These poles, however, are situated far from the geographic north pole and south pole, and, further, they are not exactly opposite each other on the earth's surface. Moreover, their positions are not fixed, but shift slightly from time to time.

In 1916, the approximate position of the north magnetic pole was lat. 70° N., long. 97° W., and of the south magnetic pole, lat. 72° S., long. 153° E. A straight line connecting these two points would pass 750 miles distant from the earth's center. No satisfactory explanation as to why the earth is so unequally magnetized can be framed on the basis of the observed facts now available.

As the north end of a magnetic needle points in the direction of the north magnetic pole, it follows that the compass does not indicate true north and south except in comparatively few places. In all other localities, correction for its declination east or west of the true north is necessary. See *Magnetism.*

Marshes. Tracts of soft, wet land, usually covered wholly or in part by shallow water, and containing aquatic vegetation. In cool regions, this vegetation may, by a process of slow decay, transform into peat and, in time, fill up the marsh. In warm regions, the rate of decay is too rapid to permit the accumulation of peat. Extensive marshes occur around the margins of many lakes and along low ocean shores. In the United States, large marshes are found along the lower Atlantic and Gulf coasts, the most notable being the *Everglades* of Florida. See *Bogs, Fens, Moor, Muskeg, Slough, Swamps.*

Meanders. The broad, sweeping curves of a river in the old-age stage of development, as, for example, those in the lower Mississippi flood plain. See *Bayou.*

Mesa (*mē'sä; mā'sȧ*). A Spanish word meaning "table," commonly used in the southwestern United States as the name for a high, broad, and flat tableland bounded at least on one side, and sometimes on all sides, by a steep cliff or declivity. In the erosion of plateaus, isolated flat-topped areas of considerable size are sometimes left as the last remnants of the former land level. The top is usually a layer of hard rock which wears away less rapidly than the softer strata beneath it. In consequence, the top of a mesa not infrequently overhangs the walls of the cliffs that encircle it.

Many such table-like formations are found in the arid plains of the West, especially in Colorado, New Mexico, and Arizona. Among the most noted of these is the Mesa Verde, in southwestern Colorado. This is a plateau fifteen miles long and eight miles wide, with precipitous sides of yellow sandstone rising almost perpendicularly from 400 to 800 feet above the surrounding plain. The famous Enchanted Mesa near Acoma, New Mexico, is more properly called a butte.

The name mesa is applied also to a level or somewhat sloping area of high land lying against the side of a mountain. See *Butte, Monadnock, Plateau.*

Meteoric Dust. The so-called shooting stars or meteors come into our atmosphere from interplanetary space. By friction in the air these become heated, and they are often burned to a dust, which falls to the earth. See *Dust, Meteors.*

Mineral Waters. Spring or well waters containing in solution a sufficient amount of various substances to exert a medicinal effect upon the human body are called mineral waters. They are classified as alkaline, alkaline-saline, saline, and acid waters. The curative qualities of the waters of some of the most famous springs have been known since ancient times. The Romans discovered not only the thermal springs of Italy, but also many of the most valuable springs in other parts of Europe, such as those of Aix-la-Chapelle, Baden-Baden, Bath, and Spa.

In the United States, the Saratoga Springs, New York, were known as early as 1767; Berkeley Springs, Va., as early as 1777; and White Sulphur Springs, W. Va., as early as 1778.

It is estimated that there are not less than 10,000 mineral springs in the United States, of which nearly 1000 have produced waters in commercial quantities. The springs having the greatest commercial value are located in the Eastern states, in the Mississippi valley, and on the Pacific coast. Besides those already mentioned, the best-known mineral springs are: Hot Springs, Arkansas; Waukesha Springs, Wisconsin; Las Vegas Hot Springs, New Mexico; and Medical Lake, Washington. Among the most noted foreign mineral waters are those known as Apollinaris, from Ahrweiler, Germany; Friedrichschall, from Hildenburg, Germany; Hunyadi-János, from Budapest, Hungary; Kissingen, from Bavaria; Vichy, from France; and Carlsbad Sprudel, from Bohemia. See *Hot Springs, Springs.*

Mirage (*mê-räzh'*). An optical effect or illusion, occasionally seen at sea or on large lakes, but occurring very frequently on arid plains or deserts, and often in the polar regions. In mirages, various images of distant objects appear, usually in an inverted position, or top side down, while the objects themselves may or may not be in sight. Less frequently, a mirage consists of greatly magnified or heightened images of distant and often invisible objects, appearing as if projected against the sky. Mirages are caused by the extensive refraction and reflection produced when light, in reaching an observer from a distant object, passes through layers of air which are unequally heated, and which, therefore, are of very different densities.

In case the reflecting layer of air is level and lower than the eye of the observer, the mirage usually appears as an isolated sheet of water in which various distant objects are reflected. Sometimes the illusory water appears as if ruffled by the wind. This is the deceptive form of mirage commonly seen in the deserts of Sahara, Persia, Turkestan, the western United States, and other arid regions.

When the reflecting layer in the air is higher than the eye, the illusory image appears as if located in the sky. This is the kind of mirage usually seen on the ocean, or over lakes, in which distant and otherwise invisible ships, icebergs, cliffs, shores, hills, towns, or buildings appear inverted in the clouds. In this case there is a layer of very cool and, therefore, dense air next to the water, with a layer of much warmer and rarer air above it. In the case of the common desert mirage, a layer of heated rare air lies next to the ground, with a layer of cooler and denser air above it.

The *Fata Morgana*, often observed at the Straits of Messina, consists of the apparent heightening of objects on the opposite shore. The famous "Spectre of Brocken," seen in the Harz mountains of Prussia, is a form of mirage called *looming*, in which objects appear greatly magnified horizontally as well as vertically.

Monadnock (*mô-năd'nŏk*). A hill or mountain standing out conspicuously above its surroundings because of its superior resistance to the agencies of weathering and erosion. The typical example from which all such formations take their name is Mt. Monadnock, in southwestern New Hampshire. This is a rocky outlier of the White mountains which rises abruptly from the surrounding plains to an altitude of 3186 feet. Such remnants, when composed of horizontal, stratified rocks, are called *mesas* or *buttes*. See *Butte, Mesa*.

Monsoon (*mŏn-sōōn'*). Any wind which blows regularly at fixed seasons, but particularly the periodic winds which blow over the Indian Ocean from Australia to India. Such winds are due to the unequal heating of the atmosphere over the land and over the water. From April to October, the Indian monsoon winds blow from the southwest, rushing in from the cooler ocean over highly heated land. From October to April, they blow from the northeast, moving down from the cooler land over the warmer ocean. In some parts of India, the summer monsoon begins with violent thunderstorms and torrential rains. In Bengal, the rainy season is ushered in by the winter monsoon. Besides their immense climatic influence in modifying temperature and rainfall, the Indian monsoons were formerly of great commercial importance.

The principle involved in the daily land breezes and sea breezes along coasts is identical with that of the monsoon, but the winds produced are local and usually are not felt far from shore. The influence of the monsoon principle is felt also in local winds in the vicinity of the Great Lakes. In all cases, such winds are caused by a surface movement of cool air rushing in to take the place of ascending warm air. See *Climate, Rainfall, Wind*.

Moor. An extensive tract of infertile, sandy ground, commonly overlaid with peat, and more or less marshy. In popular usage, the term is applied only to the European moors in which heather is frequently the most common plant. Similar areas, however, occur in the United States. Two types of moors are distinguished: those in which sphagnum or peat moss is present, called *high moor*, or *heath*; and those without sphagnum, called *low moor*, and known also as *swamp meadow*, or *fen*. In America, high moors are commonly called *bogs*. See *Bogs, Fens, Marshes, Swamps*.

Moraines. Extensive accumulations of coarse stones, sands, gravels, and clays carried on the surface of mountain glaciers or left in the country which has been invaded by a glacier. In mountain regions, the stones which rattle down and come to rest on the surface of the ice near its margin are called *lateral moraines*, because they are at the sides of the glacier. When two mountain glaciers unite and the two inside lateral moraines come together, a *medial moraine* is formed. At the end of a mountain glacier there is a *terminal moraine*.

In regions where formerly there were huge continental ice sheets, such as northern United States, Canada, and northwestern Europe, there is a mantle of glacial moraine which forms the soil. Throughout New England the moraine soils are very stony, but in New York and in the great prairie states of the Mississippi valley, the stones, though present, are not so numerous. These stones often carry striæ, indicating that they were scratched as they moved forward at the base of the glacier.

The material in a moraine is not arranged in an orderly fashion. It remains where the ice, upon melting, dropped it. Unlike the deposits laid down by water, morainic material is not stratified. It contains large and small stones of various kinds, picked up by the ice in its long route of travel. Along with these coarse constituents, moraines contain some of the finest of silts and clays. See *Glacier, Ground Moraine, Recessional Moraine, Terminal Moraines*.

Mountain. A lofty elevation of land, higher than a hill, with but little surface at the top, rising conspicuously above its surroundings. Where very high mountains abound, many elevations are commonly called hills which, in other regions, would usually be termed mountains. Similarly, in level districts, a hill or escarpment, rising only 100 or 200 feet above the plain, is sometimes styled a "mountain." In general, elevations which rise abruptly 1000 feet or more above the adjacent country are commonly called mountains.

Mountains occur as single peaks and as more or less elongated ridges. A mountain group is made up of several peaks or of short ridges. A mountain chain or mountain system is an elongated mountain group made up of many single mountains, of mountain ridges, or of both forms. In most continents the chief mountain systems are near the borders of the land, but in Europe and Asia there are great mountain systems in the interior.

Mountains are formed by three processes: (1) by *uplift*, effected through the intrusion, folding, or faulting of strata; (2) by *erosion*, called also circumdentation, or land sculpture, effected chiefly by running water; (3) by *volcanic action*, effected by the eruption of igneous rocks.

In height above their actual bases on the land, or on the ocean floor, mountains vary from about 1000 feet to nearly 6 miles. In North America, the highest mountain is Mt. McKinley, in Alaska, with an elevation of 20,300 feet. The highest peak in Canada is Mt. Logan, 19,850 feet. In the United States, the highest mountain is Mt. Whitney, in the Sierra Nevadas, 14,496 feet. In the Rocky mountains of Colorado alone there are 40 peaks exceeding 14,000 feet elevation. Mt. Rainier, in Washington, attains an altitude of 14,408 feet.

The highest mountains of South America exceed an elevation of 23,000 feet; those of Africa, 19,000 feet; and those of Australia, 7000 feet. In Europe, Mont Blanc, in the Alps, rises above 15,000 feet in altitude, and in Asia, Mt. Everest, in the Himalayas, the highest mountain in the world, towers to 29,141 feet. The oceanic mountain Mauna Loa, in Hawaii, rises about 13,675 feet above the sea level, but more than 30,000 feet above the ocean floor upon which it stands.

As the temperature of the air decreases, on the average, 1° F. for every 300 feet of rise, the climate of the highest mountains resembles that of the polar regions. Above a certain level called the *snow line*.

there are fields of perpetual snow and ice, from which glaciers are often formed. The vegetation of mountains becomes less and less abundant with increased elevation and practically disappears when the snow line is reached.

Mountains are of great importance in the economy of nature. They profoundly affect climate, rainfall, and the distribution of water. Although they often stand as barriers to transportation and greatly restrict the diffusion of plants and animals, on the other hand, they contain vast deposits of valuable minerals and metallic ores, bear immense forests, support a considerable agriculture, and furnish the grandest and most inspiring scenery in the world. See *Alpine Plants, Cirque, Erosion, Glacier, Snow Line, Timber Line, Volcanic Mountains.*

Muskeg. A name, derived from the Indian, widely used in Canada for the tussocky peat bogs which cover large areas north of latitude 55°. The vegetation consists of peat moss, rushes, sundews, and various aquatic plants, often interspersed with shrubs and small trees. In summer, the muskeg is, for the most part, impassable, but in winter it remains frozen for many months, during which it is readily traversed by hunters and trappers. See *Peat Bogs.*

Natural Levee. A low ridge of alluvial material built up on the flood plain of a river, immediately adjoining its channel. This land is usually sought first by settlers for farms. Later, roads and settlements become located on the levee, and even large cities may be built upon it. New Orleans is situated on a natural levee. See *Alluvium, River, Valley.*

Ocean. The entire body of salt water, called also the sea, which occupies about 143,000,000 square miles, or about 72 per cent of the earth's surface. Its five larger divisions are called the Pacific, Atlantic, Indian, Southern or Antarctic, and Arctic oceans. The average depth of the ocean is estimated at about 13,000 feet. The greatest known depth, 35,401 feet, is found in the Pacific Ocean, near Mindanao, in the Philippine Islands. The volume of the ocean is about fifteen times that of the land lying above sea level. The mass or weight of the sea is about five times that of the land above the sea, or 265 times the weight of the air, and $\frac{1}{4300}$ of the weight of the solid part of the earth.

Sea water contains, on the average, about 3½ per cent of dissolved mineral matter, over three-fourths of which is common salt. Besides solids, sea water contains many gases in solution, the chief of which are oxygen, nitrogen, and carbon dioxide, or carbonic-acid gas. The color of sea water, though widely variable, is usually blue or green. The deep blue color seems to be intensified by saltiness, the Gulf Stream being much more blue than the less salty Labrador Current. The temperature of the ocean at the surface varies from about 80° F. in the tropics to about 28° F. in the polar regions. Below the surface, except in polar regions, the temperature decreases with depth. At 5000 feet, even in the tropics, the temperature is below 40° F., and in deep sea bottoms it is below 35° F. The average temperature of the sea is below 39° F.

Various movements in the waters of the ocean are produced by unequal temperature, unequal salinity, inequalities of level, winds, the differing attractions of the sun and the moon, and also by earthquakes, volcanic explosions beneath the surface, and landslides on coasts. The chief movements are waves and undertow, shore or littoral currents, ocean currents, tides, drift or slow currents, and creep.

The sea teems with plant and animal life. All of the great groups of animals are represented. An immense variety of plants occurs, but the highest forms are wanting. Life is most abundant in shallow water or on bottoms within 600 feet of the surface. Plants occur more rarely down to 1200 feet, but animals are found at much greater depths. The bottom of the sea, as revealed by dredgings, is composed of gravel, sand, mud, shells, coral, and ooze. In deeper parts, below 13,000 feet, the bottom is covered with red clay.

In the economy of nature the sea plays a great part. The ocean everywhere tempers climates, making them less extreme, and is the chief source of water for rain and snow. Ocean waves modify the outlines of coasts, and water, evaporated from the sea and condensed on the land, irrigates the soil, wears down mountains and plateaus, and builds up plains and deltas. The sea produces an enormous supply of foodstuffs and other economic materials, and serves as a highway for the commerce of the world. See *Hydrosphere, Ocean Currents, Tides, Waves.*

Ocean Currents. Great streams flowing through the ocean, more or less distinctly divided from adjacent waters, and forming a regular system of water circulation. They are classified as *warm* currents and *cold* currents; as *surface* currents and *deep-sea* currents. A current sharply separated from surrounding waters is called a *stream*; a general movement of surface waters without definite bounding lines is called a *drift*. The speed of ocean currents varies from 3 or 4 miles an hour in swift, narrow streams to the very slow, almost imperceptible movement of some great oceanic drifts.

The great ocean currents are caused by the prevailing winds. In the belts north and south of the equator, the trade winds blowing equatorward tend, by friction, to move the waters at the surface of the sea in the direction which they are blowing. As these waters come toward the equator on the two sides, they move westward in each of the great oceans, the Atlantic and the Pacific. When they reach the western margins of these oceans they divide, turning in part northward and in part southward. In the Atlantic Ocean, Cape St. Roque, at the eastern point of Brazil, divides the south equatorial current into the Brazilian Current and a north equatorial current. This north equatorial current goes in part east of the West Indies, and in part through the Caribbean Sea and the Gulf of Mexico, issuing from the gulf around the southern point of Florida. To the northeast, the current from the gulf becomes known as the Gulf Stream.

In the Pacific Ocean, the equatorial currents are divided when they reach the islands north of Australia, the northern branch becoming the Japan Current and the southern branch, the Australian Current. When the waters flow northward or southward beyond the zone of the trade winds, they are guided in large part by the configuration of the land areas, but they are helped forward by the prevailing westerlies.

By making the waters of the equatorial regions cooler and those of the polar regions warmer, ocean currents equalize the temperature of the globe. The great poleward movement of heated surface waters from the tropics warms the prevailing winds, over vast areas of the ocean. These, in turn, profoundly modify the climate of the continents upon which they blow, as is strikingly exemplified in the mild climate of northwestern Europe and western North America. In a similar manner, polar currents impart a cold climate to the shores along which they pass.

Among important ocean currents are the north and the south equatorials of the three great oceans; the Gulf Stream and the Labrador, Canary, Brazilian, and Benguela currents in the Atlantic; the Japan, Alaska, California, Peruvian, and Australian currents in the Pacific; and the Monsoon and Mozambique currents in the Indian Ocean. See *Gulf Stream, Japan Current, Labrador Current.*

Outwash Plain. A land of even surface, composed of sands and gravels that were washed out from beneath a glacier when the margin of the ice remained stationary for a period of time. An outwash plain may often be very rich farming land, or it may be valuable as a source of sand and gravel for building purposes. The southern half of Long Island is an outwash plain, and the city of Plainfield, N. J., is located on such a surface. At many other points in the United States, the waters issuing from the continental glacier during the Ice age developed outwash plains. See *Glacier*.

Pampas. Vast, grassy plains in central Argentina. They occupy an area about equal to that of Texas, merging on the north into the forests of the Gran Chaco and on the south into the steppes of Patagonia. During the rainy season, the pampas are covered with a luxuriant growth of grasses, providing pasturage for immense numbers of cattle and sheep. See *Llanos, Prairie, Steppes*.

Peat Bogs. Swamps or bogs underlaid by accumulations of peat formed by the slow decay of sphagnum moss, rushes, and various other aquatic plants. Peat bogs occur over large areas in cool temperate regions, especially in Ireland, northern Europe, and Canada. They are usually found on the sites of old lakes which have gradually filled up, or of old marshes. While the layer of peat does not often exceed three or four feet in thickness, it sometimes extends to a depth of thirty feet or more. See *Bogs, Marshes, Swamps*.

Plateau. An elevated area of fairly level land, called also table-land. Most plateaus rise conspicuously above their surroundings, at least on one side. Plateaus differ from plains chiefly in being much higher, and they are almost invariably associated with or surrounded by mountains.

The Colorado plateau, which lies between the Rockies and the Sierra Nevada, is from 6000 to 9000 feet high. The lofty plateau of Tibet, flanked by the Himalayas, is from 10,000 to 13,000 feet high. The Columbia and Snake River plateau is a broad, elevated region composed of flows of lava. The Deccan of India is a similar plateau. Plateaus are often very deeply eroded by rivers which cut immense gorges, the most notable example of which is the Grand Canyon of the Colorado river in Arizona.

Plateaus are usually cool because of their elevation above the sea; they are often arid, and sometimes deserts, because surrounded by mountains which capture the moisture of rain-bearing winds. When the process of erosion has left a portion of a plateau with a flat top standing higher than the surrounding country, this remainder, if large, is known, in western America, as a *mesa*; if small, it is called a *butte*. See *Butte, Mesa*.

Pothole. A cylindrical hole in the rock beneath a waterfall or in the rapids of a river course. It is produced by the whirling motion of stones in the bed of the channel. In this way a pothole is bored out, little by little, until it is 50 or 100 feet in depth and varies in diameter from a few inches to 20 or 30 feet. See *Erosion*.

Prairie. The name given to the extensive grass-covered plain which occupies nearly the entire region between the Ohio and the Mississippi-Missouri river. It stretches from western Ohio to eastern Nebraska and includes the southern portions of Michigan, Wisconsin, and Minnesota, together with northern Missouri and the eastern parts of Kansas, Nebraska, and the Dakotas. On the east, it merges imperceptibly into the Allegheny plateau; on the west, into the Great Plains. For the most part, the prairies are characterized by an exceedingly fertile soil, especially suitable for the production of cereals. The great "corn belt" of the United States lies mostly within this area, which produces also immense crops of wheat and oats.

Various explanations have been advanced to account for the treelessness of the prairies. Among the most common of these are: the lack of sufficient rainfall; the excessive transpiration caused by the winds; the grazing of vast herds of animals, such as buffalo and deer; and the destructive action of fires systematically started by the Indians. See *Llanos, Pampas, Steppes*.

Quicksand. A mass of loose sand in which heavy bodies readily sink. It is composed of grains which have very smooth, rounded surfaces. When wet, these do not cling together in compact, solid form as do the rougher, angular particles of common sand. On the contrary, water lubricates the smooth particles, so that moist quicksand behaves like a liquid. Quicksands are frequently found on flat shores and at the mouths of rivers. When dry, quicksands may be firm and safe, but, as they cannot be distinguished from ordinary sands by their appearance, they are exceedingly dangerous when wet. Men, horses, wagons, and even railway trains have been swallowed up in quicksands. See *Sand*.

Rain. Drops of water large enough to fall rapidly by their own weight, formed by the condensation of moisture in the atmosphere. Drops which fall very slowly are called mist, fog, or cloud. The largest raindrops are between one-fourth and one-third of an inch in diameter; the smallest drops which are called rain are about one-twentieth of an inch in diameter.

For every temperature there is a definite amount of water vapor which can be held in the air. As condensation follows cooling, and as precipitation follows condensation, rain may be produced (1) when air is blown up a cold mountain side, (2) when air is blown toward the poles of the earth, (3) when warm air rises from the surface by convection, and (4) when cooler air is brought into contact with warm air.

Rain water would be chemically pure except for the substances which it washes out of the atmosphere. These consist of dust, soot, pollen grains, spores of fungi, and various other solid substances, together with dissolved gases, including oxygen, nitrogen, ammonia, carbon dioxide, and sometimes nitric acid, sulphuric acid, and other impurities in the air of cities. See *Humidity, Rainfall, Storm, Wind*.

Rainbow. An arc of prismatic colors seen at times when the sun shines while it is raining, caused by the reflection and refraction of the rays of sunlight in the drops of rain. Rainbows are always seen in the part of the sky opposite the sun, and they vary with the extent of the rain, appearing either as short arcs or as complete arcs which rest at each end on the earth. The colors are arranged in the order of the spectrum,—violet on the inside, then indigo, blue, green, yellow, orange, and red. Frequently a secondary bow, outside the first, is observed, with fainter colors arranged in an order the reverse of that in the primary bow.

The amount of the bow seen at any time depends upon the height of the sun, being low when the sun is high, and high when the sun is low. On high mountains or from balloons, when the sun is very low, completely circular rainbows are observed. Small rainbows are seen in the sprays of fountains and in the mists arising from cataracts. Lunar rainbows, formed by the light of the moon and appearing as luminous arcs with very faint colors, are occasionally seen.

Rainfall. Water precipitated from the clouds as rain or snow, usually measured by its depth in inches. The rainfall or the snowfall of a region depends principally upon what winds affect it, upon the character of the surface over which the winds have already blown, upon elevation above the sea, distance from the sea, and the relative position of mountain barriers.

The winds most affecting rainfall are the *trade* winds, the prevailing westerly winds, and the *monsoon* winds. Trade winds blow mostly from cool to warm latitudes, and are usually dry winds. The Sahara is a desert because of the dryness of the prevailing trade winds. However, the prevailing westerlies, southwesterly in the northern hemisphere and northwesterly in the southern hemisphere, blow from low to high latitudes, this is, from warm to cool regions, and are *moist* winds. When these warm winds, laden with water vapor produced by the immense evaporation from tropical oceans, pass over cool lands or meet countercurrents of cool air, they give up much of their moisture as rain. Similarly, monsoon or seasonal winds bring rain when they blow from warm regions of high evaporation to cooler areas. Minor winds, such as land breezes or sea breezes, rarely yield much rain, though valley breezes, and even desert whirlwinds, sometimes give rise to local showers.

Other conditions being equal, countries lying near the sea and not far above sea level, have a heavier rainfall than those situated at a great distance from the sea or at high altitudes. Forested regions receive more rainfall than grassy areas, and mountainous or hilly districts receive more than level plains. The seaward slopes of mountains, facing prevailing winds, are commonly wet, while their landward slopes are dry.

In general, tropical regions receive the heaviest rainfall, estimated at an average of about 100 inches yearly. Temperate regions receive about one-third, and polar regions about one-eighth, as much as the tropics. However, there are some very arid regions within the tropics, and some very wet regions in the temperate and the polar zones.

In the temperate zones, the regions of most profitable agriculture are those receiving a yearly rainfall of from 20 to 60 inches. In the United States, the Gulf coast receives about 60 inches of rainfall annually; the Atlantic coast, from 40 to 60 inches; the central Mississippi valley and the Lake region, from 30 to 40 inches; the high plains east of the Rockies, about 20 inches; and the great American desert west of the Rockies, usually less than 10 inches. On the Pacific slope, the yearly precipitation varies from a few inches at Yuma, Arizona, to about 100 inches near Puget sound, and to 130 inches in Alaska.

The greatest annual rainfall in the world is believed to take place in the hill region of Assam, India, southeast of the Himalaya mountains, where an average of 550 inches annually for a period of ten years has been observed. See *Climate, Humidity, Ocean Currents, Snow, Wind.*

Rain Making. Various methods have been employed in attempts to produce rain by artificial means but, without exception, the results have been unsuccessful. A method frequently used is that of causing explosions of various kinds in the higher levels of the air. Even if cloud particles were in abundance, it is probable that the actual amount of rainfall which could result from even the heaviest explosions would be too small to be of consequence. The other methods which have been experimented with, or recommended, appear to be equally futile.

Recessional Moraine. A deposit left at the margin of an ice sheet or glacier at a stage of its retreat when the margin of the ice remained for a time relatively stationary. Such recessional moraines resemble in appearance and material the terminal moraines. They form many of the ridges of hilly country where bowlders are abundant. Recessional moraines occur throughout the New England and the upper Mississippi Valley states. Smaller ridges are found in the lowland plains of Germany, Poland, and northwestern Russia. See *Glacier, Moraines.*

River. A large stream of water flowing through the land in a definite channel. The bottom of a river is called its *bed*, and the sides of the channel are its *banks*. The *right* bank of a river is that on the right hand of an observer when facing downstream; the *left* bank is the opposite side.

Rivers usually empty into the ocean, either directly or by uniting with other rivers which do so, although some flow into landlocked seas or lakes, and, in arid regions, some lose themselves in desert sands. Most rivers are of small size, but a few, such as the Amazon, Nile, Congo, Yangtze, and Mississippi, are very large. Thousands of brooks, creeks, and small rivers, draining a total area of hundreds of thousands of square miles, may unite to form a single great river. Such a stream, with its numerous tributaries, is called a *river system.*

In descending to the sea from their sources in mountain snows, glaciers, lakes, ponds, and springs, rivers perform a double work. By erosion, they carve out and wear down mountains and plateaus along their upper courses. At the same time, they upbuild valleys, plains, and deltas along their lower courses.

The river systems of the earth are estimated to carry to the ocean each year about 6500 cubic miles of water. In this river water about 5 billion tons of dissolved mineral matter are in solution. The mineral matter, together with about 15 billion tons of sediment, is borne to the sea. The amount of sediment a stream can carry depends upon its volume, its velocity, and the amount and kind of sediment available.

The Thames river of England, a relatively small stream, carries to the sea each day, in solution, about 1500 tons of material. It is calculated that the Mississippi river carries into the Gulf of Mexico more than a million tons of sediment every day, and that it would require 1000 trains, each made up of 45 cars of 25 tons capacity, to transport an equal amount of silt and sand. If all the silt brought in one year by the Mississippi river to the Gulf of Mexico were placed on one square mile of land, it would rise to a height of 270 feet.

The speed at which a river flows increases with the slope of its bed and with its volume. In the Volga and in the lower Mississippi, the slope is about three inches a mile. The Missouri river is comparatively swift, having an average descent of 28 inches a mile. In mountainous regions the descent may be very great, though the speed of mountain torrents rarely exceeds 20 miles an hour, or about 29 feet a second. In case of large rivers flowing through nearly level valleys, a speed of a foot a second is common. The volume of rivers varies greatly with the slope of the drainage basin, the character of the soil and vegetation, and the rainfall. Some rivers are raging torrents at one season and have almost dry channels at another.

Rivers are factors of tremendous importance in the general economy of nature. They drain the land of surplus water, returning to the ocean a large part of the water removed from it by evaporation and precipitation. They provide water for irrigation and add rich silts to valley bottoms and deltas which support vast populations. They also furnish water to many cities and towns, and to millions of homes in the country places. Moreover, they generate an immense amount of water power and hydroelectric power and, wherever navigable, greatly facilitate inland commerce. See *Alluvium, Bayou, Delta, Erosion, Flood, Hydrosphere, Meanders, Valley.*

Salt Lakes. Salt lakes are inland bodies of water containing an unusual amount of salt in solution. They are without any regular outlet to the sea, and are found chiefly in arid climates. Their waters, as in Great Salt lake and in the Dead Sea, are sometimes much more saline than sea water.

As a result of changes of climate, a fresh-water lake may become salt or a salt-water lake may become fresh. If the aridity of the climate increases so that the evaporation from the surface of a fresh lake is greater than the inflow of fresh water from precipitation, a fresh lake may gradually become salt. On the other hand, if evaporation becomes less than the inflow of fresh water, the level of the lake will rise, in time an outlet will be found, and the lake will then soon become altogether fresh.

The saline content of the water in Great Salt lake varies from 12 to 23 per cent, according to the level of the lake, which is determined by the seasonal rainfall. At a depth of 1000 feet, the water of the Dead Sea, the saltest lake in the world, contains 27 per cent of solid substances, largely common salt. The salinity of these lakes, therefore, is several times as great as that of the ocean, which contains only about 3.44 per cent of dissolved mineral matter. The great deposits of salt that have been found in various parts of the world are the result of the complete evaporation of ancient salt lakes.

Sargasso Sea. A tract of the north Atlantic Ocean stretching north and east of the West Indies as far as the Azores. Forming an eddy in the midst of ocean currents, its surface carries much floating material, chiefly a floating alga called sargassum. This occurs in patches and shifts with the wind. Scientific observation has not confirmed the reports of earlier explorers to the effect that the floating vegetable matter was sufficiently dense to impede the progress of ships.

Savannas. Open level plains characterized by vegetation intermediate in character between grasslands and forests. Savannas abound in tropical and subtropical regions. In appearance they are parklike, with an undergrowth of drought-resisting grasses intermingled with sparsely scattered trees.

Seasons. Divisions of the year based on changes in climatic conditions. These changes are the joint effect of the earth's revolution around the sun and the inclination of the earth's axis. Except in the tropics, this results in great variation in the length of the day when compared with that of the night, and also in great differences in the angle of the heat-giving rays of the sun. In temperate zones the sun's height above the horizon at noon may vary by 47°. This variation, combined with variations in the length of day, occasions great changes in temperature.

In most latitudes the number of seasons is said to be four—spring, summer, autumn, and winter. In Europe and North America, March, April, and May are arbitrarily called the spring months; June, July, and August, the summer months; September, October, and November, the autumn months; and December, January, and February, the winter months.

However, spring is also defined as the period between the vernal equinox and the summer solstice (March 21–June 21); summer, the period between the summer solstice and the autumnal equinox (June 21–September 22); autumn, the period between the autumnal equinox and the winter solstice (September 22–December 21); and winter, the period between the winter solstice and the vernal equinox (December 21–March 21). In the southern hemisphere the order of the seasons is interchanged, summer in one coinciding with winter in the other, and spring in the one coinciding with autumn in the other.

In the tropics, where no part of the year is much warmer or colder than any other, there are usually no well-defined seasons. However, the period of the year regularly marked by abundant rainfall is commonly called the *wet* season, and that marked by scant rainfall, the *dry* season. In the arctic and antarctic regions, spring and autumn are very brief so that the natural division of the year is into summer and winter. At the poles, the warm season is the *light* season, and the cold season is the *dark* season of the year.

In the northern hemisphere, the coldest season occurs when the earth is nearest to the sun, and the warmest, when it is some millions of miles farther away. This is due to the fact that the northern hemisphere is inclined away from the sun during winter, and toward the sun in summer. See *Climate*; *Days, Lengths of*; *Equinoxes*.

Seiche (*sāsh*). Irregular pulsations or variations in the water level of a lake, set up by changes in the pressure of the air over various portions of its surface, are called seiches. They are highest under areas of low barometer. These movements were first observed in the lakes of Switzerland, where they have been much studied. In Lake Geneva, seiches with a height of six feet have been noted, during which the whole mass of water in the lake for a time swings rhythmically from shore to shore. Seiches have been observed in the lakes of Scotland, in Lake Erie, Lake Michigan, and various other lakes. See *Lake*.

Selvas. Natural forested lands, especially plains in tropical South America; as, for example, the vast, densely forested regions in the valley of the Amazon. See *Taiga*.

Slough (*slo͞o*). A wet, marshy place or reedy pond, but properly a side channel or inlet from a river. In the central and western United States, a small, sluggish creek which becomes wholly or partly dry in summer is called a slough, as is also a long, narrow pond formed in a ravine or other depression in a prairie. See *Marshes*.

Snow. Minute crystals of ice which form when the water vapor in the air condenses at a temperature below the freezing point. These crystals are six-sided and, when magnified under a lens, often show great beauty of form. They usually combine to make snowflakes, sometimes large and woollike, but often small and arranged with remarkable regularity. Snowflakes are not in any sense frozen raindrops; they are formed instead of raindrops when the temperature at which the moisture in the air condenses is less than 32° F. Under usual conditions, about 10 inches of snow will yield one inch of water.

At high latitudes, snow falls during the greater part of the year; in middle latitudes, it falls during the winter; and in low latitudes, except on high mountains, very little falls and this melts quickly. Within the polar circles and on lofty mountains, even in the tropics, snow lies continually on much of the land. Often in such regions the snowfall is much heavier during the cold summer than during the still colder winter. However, on about two-thirds of the earth's surface, snow never falls. In regions near the sea level, snow rarely falls between lat. 30° N. and lat. 30° S. On the Pacific coast of North America, snow falls at the sea level only north of lat. 47°, or about the latitude of Seattle, Washington. On the Atlantic coast of North America, the southern limit of such snowfall is Brownsville, Texas, lat. 26°. In the northern hemisphere, the southernmost point of record where snow falls at the sea level is Canton, China, which is just within the tropics, lat. 23°.

In Maine the annual snowfall sometimes reaches 8 feet; in New York, 7 feet; in the Sierra Nevadas of California it ranges from 10 to 30 feet. Most snow disappears by melting, running off the land in streams; but a considerable amount, especially in arid regions, disappears by evaporation, passing into the air as invisible vapor. Snow shields, like a blanket, the surfaces on which it falls, preventing deep freezing of the soil and protecting the roots of tender vegetation. Snowfalls on high mountains form glaciers and feed streams, maintaining and equalizing their flow during dry seasons, thus greatly benefiting agriculture in the plains below. See *Blizzard, Glacier, Humidity, Snow Line, Storm*.

Snow Line. The line or elevation on a mountain slope above which snow and ice exist perpetually. This elevation varies greatly in different localities and from year to year. It is influenced by the direction of the slope and by the temperature, moisture, and prevailing winds. In the tropical Andes, the average height of the snow line above sea level is about 18,400 feet; in the Himalayas, 19,000 feet; in the Rocky mountains, 11,000 feet; in the Alps, 7500 to 9000 feet; in Patagonia, 6000 feet; and in Iceland, 3000 feet. In Spitsbergen, lat. 78° N., the snow line practically corresponds with the sea level.

Soil. The loose surface material of the earth in which plants grow and animals burrow. Soil is usually composed of broken or disintegrated rock mixed with varying quantities of decaying organic matter. Loose or stony material beneath the top layer of loam is called *subsoil.* When a soil rests upon the parent rock strata from which it was largely formed, it is classed as *residual.* Many such soils show gradual gradations from the solid rock below to the soil at the surface. This class includes also the peaty soils in bogs, swamps, and marshes. A soil composed of materials removed from the place of their formation by glaciers, streams, or winds, is classed as *transported.*

Among the soils brought down by glaciers are the extensive and very productive glacial drift soils of the northern United States, of Canada, and of northwestern Europe. Among the soils brought down by streams are the rich alluvial soils of flood plains and deltas, such as those of the Nile and the Mississippi. Among the soils transported by the wind, or æolian soils, are sand dunes, usually of inferior quality, and ash soils, often exceedingly fertile, composed of ashes ejected from volcanoes. The valuable loess soils of China and of the Mississippi valley are believed to have been formed in part by wind action. Soils formed by the disintegration of volcanic lava, frequently very productive, occur in Idaho and other northwestern states, and in Italy, Mexico, India, and Hawaii. In arid regions, soils are found which contain an excess of soluble salts; they are known as alkali soils.

The productiveness or fertility of soils depends upon their plant food elements and upon their biological and physical constituents. The food elements most essential to plant growth are nitrogen, phosphorus, calcium, sulphur, magnesium, potassium, and iron, in various chemical combinations. Living organisms, including insects, earthworms, the roots of plants, and bacteria, have much to do with soil formation and fertility. Various bacteria possess the power of transforming the nitrogen of the air into plant food. The physical constituents, chiefly silica, which serve as a medium for root growth, make up 90 to 95 per cent of the mass of the soil. See *Adobe Soil, Alluvium, Hardpan, Lava, Loess, Till.*

Springs. Water issuing from the ground through a natural opening, at sufficient speed and volume to make a distinct current, is called a spring. Water issuing from rocks or soil, too slowly to form a current, is called *seepage.* Springs occur where there are natural passageways or channels through which the ground water may emerge on dry land, or in the beds of streams, ponds, and lakes. Cold springs are usually formed by rain or melted snow soaking into the ground and reappearing at the surface on a lower level. Hot springs may be of volcanic origin or may be formed when surface waters become heated underground by contact with uncooled igneous rocks.

Spring water usually contains various mineral substances in solution. Its composition varies with that of the surrounding rocks and soil. The volume of water flowing from a spring usually varies with the season and the amount of rainfall. Some springs, however, have a nearly constant flow, of sufficient volume for domestic or even municipal water supply. Numerous springs, particularly hot springs, are of medicinal value on account of the mineral substances which they contain. The Hot Springs of Arkansas and those at Carlsbad, Bohemia, are noted examples. See *Geyser, Ground Water, Hot Springs, Mineral Waters.*

Stalactites (*stȧ-lăk′tītz*). Crystalline, icicle-like forms that sometimes hang from the roofs of caves. They are composed usually of lime, which is dissolved by waters passing through the ground and is left at the roof of the cave when these waters evaporate. Stalactites grow in length, little by little, as the water comes to their tip ends and evaporates, each drop leaving a tiny additional amount of lime. See *Stalagmites.*

Stalagmites (*stȧ-lăg′mītz*). Crystalline forms that rise as monuments from the floors of certain caves. They are commonly developed directly below stalactites of the same material. When the water, after passing through the ground, reaches the roof of a cave and drops to the floor, it may evaporate there and leave behind what it holds in solution. The precipitated material increases little by little and, in time, forms upright crystalline columns, or stalagmites. See *Stalactites.*

Steppes (*stĕps*). The name given to vast, usually level, tracts of land in European and Asiatic Russia, of which the most characteristic feature is the absence of forests. The steppe region really begins near the border of the Netherlands and extends across northern Germany where such lands are called *Haiden* or heaths; thence it stretches across Russia and Siberia almost to the Pacific Ocean, a total distance of about 4500 miles. See *Heaths, Llanos, Pampas, Prairie, Tundras.*

Storm. A disturbance of the atmosphere, accompanied by wind, rain, snow, hail, sleet, or lightning and thunder. A storm is usually produced whenever currents of air flow from areas of high barometric pressure to areas of low barometric pressure, the latter being called "lows" or storm centers. Storms characterized by destructive winds include windstorms, sandstorms, tornadoes, and typhoons, or hurricanes. Storms in which precipitation is the chief feature include rainstorms, hailstorms, snowstorms, monsoons, cloudbursts, and floods. A storm in which there is much thunder and lightning is called a thunderstorm. A cold, driving wind combined with a fall of dustlike snow is called a blizzard.

Usually, the winds preceding a storm blow around and in toward the areas of low pressure, thereby producing still lower pressures near the center. The air in the center, being lighter and forced to rise, expands and cools. In consequence, it precipitates its surplus moisture, producing, according to the prevailing temperature, rain, snow, or hail. The violence of the winds and the amount of precipitation are somewhat proportional to the difference in pressure between the high and the low areas. Hence, a large and sudden fall of the barometer usually indicates a severe storm. See *Blizzard, Cyclone, Hail, Hurricane, Lightning, Rain, Snow, Thunder, Tornado, Typhoon, Waterspout, Whirlwind, Wind.*

Stratosphere. A layer of the atmosphere having characteristics which make it of great importance for aviation. The stratosphere surrounds the lower atmosphere, or troposphere, and is surrounded by an upper envelope, known as the ionosphere.

The *troposphere,* extending on an average 7.5 miles above the earth's surface, is the only portion of the atmosphere in which clouds normally form. Vertical air currents are usual. Temperature falls in proportion to the distance above the earth.

The *ionosphere* is the region where radio waves are deflected, as by a curved ceiling, thus making possible transmission of signals between distant points on the earth's surface. It begins at a height of about 18½ miles.

The stratosphere, or intermediate envelope, is practically cloud-free. Air movements are horizontal almost exclusively and very even. The temperature increases little with increasing height. Its importance for aviation lies in its freedom from clouds and the low air pressure, which, while requiring greater speed for supporting airplanes, permits such speed with less expenditure of power because of reduced air resistance.

The stratosphere in polar regions begins at the lowest levels—five to six miles—and in the tropics at the highest levels—about ten miles. The temperature generally is lower than −100° F.

The name stratosphere was given by the French meteorologist Teisserenc de Bort (1855-1913).

Stream Piracy. In the history of many river systems, one stream, either because of its greater supply of water or by reason of the greater ease of down-cutting in its course, has worked headward

TEMPERATURE AND RAINFALL OF REPRESENTATIVE CITIES OF THE WORLD

Name of City	Latitude	Height Above Sea Level Feet	Average or Normal Temperature Degrees F.		Extremes of Temperature Degrees F.		Average Annual Rainfall Inches
			Summer	Winter	Lowest	Highest	
Amsterdam	52° 23′ N.	9	62.2	38.5	8	91	27.95
Athens	37° 38′ N.	351	79.1	49.1	20	109	15.48
Berlin	52° 30′ N.	125	63.3	32.2	–13*	99	22.88
Bombay	18° 54′ N.	37	80.4	75.2	56	100	71.88
Brussels	50° 51′ N.	131	61.6	35.4	–4	97	28.85
Budapest	47° 30′ N.	369	68.5	30.1	–5	99	25.20
Buenos Aires	34° 36′ S.	72	72.7	51.2	22	104	37.86
Capetown	33° 56′ S.	30	68.8	55.3	31	104	25.01
Chicago	41° 53′ N.	673	71.6	27.5	–23	105	32.86
Dublin	53° 20′ N.	47	59.4	42.0	13	87	27.37
Geneva	46° 12′ N.	1329	64.9	33.7	2	101	33.81
Glasgow	55° 53′ N.	180	57.0	39.1	7	85	37.18
Honolulu	21° 19′ N.	39	77.2	71.3	56	88	28.60
Istanbul	41° 2′ N.	246	73.0	42.8	13	104	28.86
Leningrad	59° 56′ N.	16	61.2	17.4	–38	97	20.44
Lisbon	48° 43′ N.	312	68.9	50.7	30	103	28.87
London	51° 28′ N.	18	61.2	39.3	4	100	24.47
Madrid	40° 24′ N.	2149	73.0	41.2	10	112	16.48
Marseilles	43° 18′ N.	246	70.3	44.2	12	100	22.59
Melbourne	37° 50′ S.	115	66.4	49.9	27	111	25.58
Mexico	19° 26′ N.	7480	62.8	54.7	24	91	22.84
Montreal	45° 30′ N.	187	67.2	16.0	–29	97	40.65
Moscow	55° 45′ N.	512	63.4	14.7	–44	100	23.49
New York	40° 43′ N.	314	71.9	32.4	–14	102	42.99
Oslo	59° 55′ N.	82	61.0	24.5	–26	95	23.21
Paris	48° 52′ N.	108	64.1	37.6	–14	101	22.62
Peiping	39° 57′ N.	125	77.1	26.7	–4	107	26.10
Quebec	46° 48′ N.	296	64.0	12.5	–34	97	42.25
Rio de Janeiro	22° 54′ S.	197	76.8	68.1	50	102	43.25
Rome	41° 54′ N.	207	74.5	45.5	17	108	35.50
San Francisco	37° 48′ N.	155	58.7	51.1	27	101	22.02
Shanghai	31° 12′ N.	23	78.0	39.6	10	103	44.95
Stockholm	59° 21′ N.	144	59.7	26.9	–22	92	18.64
Tokyo	35° 41′ N.	70	73.9	39.0	15	98	57.84
Vancouver	49° 17′ N.	136	63.2	37.7	2	92	58.60
Vienna	48° 15′ N.	666	65.7	30.7	–15	98	25.37
Washington	38° 54′ N.	112	74.7	35.1	–15	106	42.16
Winnipeg	49° 53′ N.	760	62.8	1.6	–47	108	20.59

* The minus sign (–) is equivalent to "below zero". Data for table supplied by U. S. Weather Bureau.

and stolen the headwaters of a neighboring river system. This is called stream piracy. For example, the headwaters of Beaver Creek, in Virginia, were stolen by the Shenandoah river. See *Erosion*, *River*, *Watershed*.

Striæ (*strī′ē*). Very fine scratches made on the rock surfaces over which, during the Ice age, the great continental glacier moved; also similar scratches on the stones carried by the glacier at its base. These scratches indicate the direction of ice movement. On the coast of Maine their direction is a little east of south; in New York, except in the mountain regions, chiefly south. Farther west, their direction is west of south. In high mountain regions, where there were alpine glaciers, the striæ follow the direction of the canyon. See *Glacier*.

Swamps. Tracts of wet, spongy ground, more or less overgrown with various coarse grasses, shrubs, trees, and other plants adapted to such situations. The character of the vegetation in swamps depends largely upon the extent of drainage. River swamps, being comparatively well drained, often bear a luxuriant growth of aquatics. On the other hand, totally undrained swamps develop a cold, acid soil, very unfavorable for ordinary plant growth. In consequence, they contain an entirely different (*xerophytic*) type of vegetation. See *Bogs*, *Fens*, *Moor*, *Muskeg*, *Peat Bogs*, *Tundras*.

Taiga (*tī′gä*). One of the greatest forest areas in the world. It extends across Siberia immediately south of the subarctic tundra belt but north of the western steppes and the central and eastern highlands. For the most part, the taiga is a vast, cold, sparsely inhabited region, about 4000 miles in length and from 1000 to 2000 miles wide. The immense forests, which consist chiefly of coniferous trees, such as pines, firs, and spruces, are a valuable source of timber. See *Selvas*.

Talus (*tā′lŭs*). An accumulation of rock débris at the base of a cliff. Such accumulations occur chiefly in high mountain regions. By changes of temperature and by the action of frost, angular fragments of rock are broken off from nearly vertical cliff walls. These detached fragments fall to the base of the cliff, where they often form vast heaps with steep outward slopes. Sometimes these heaps take the shape of cones and are called *talus cones*.

Temperature, Atmospheric. The air receives practically all of its heat directly or indirectly from the sun. It is supposed that the temperature of space surrounding the atmosphere is about 459° F. below zero (–273° C.). The difference between this extreme degree of cold and the comparative warmth of the air is due to the amount of solar heat which the air absorbs, directly or indirectly, and retains. The air absorbs some solar heat as the waves from the sun pass through it. However, much of the solar heat that comes to the earth is absorbed by the land and water bodies, and then returned to the air by radiation and convection. It is estimated that the amount of heat so received and held each year would be sufficient to melt a layer of ice 140 feet thick covering the entire globe. The air receives and loses heat by radiation, conduction, and convection.

Each hemisphere receives the same amount of heat each year, but different latitudes receive very different amounts. These differences are due to the inclination of the earth's axis. This inclination causes great variation in the length of the day and in the angle at which the sun's rays strike the

TEMPERATURE, RAINFALL, AND HUMIDITY IN THE UNITED STATES

From U. S. Weather Bureau Reports for Representative Stations

City, Town, or Station	Altitude Feet	Average or Normal Temperature Degrees F.			Extremes of Temperature Degrees F.		Average Annual Rainfall, Inches	Average Annual Humidity, Per Cent.
		Year	Summer†	Winter‡	Lowest Recorded	Highest Recorded		
Abilene, Tex.	1,378	64.0	81.3	45.8	−6*	110	25.17	61
Albany, N. Y.	97	48.4	70.5	25.2	−24	104	34.58	74
Amarillo, Tex.	3,676	56.3	75.1	36.8	−16	106	20.99	62
Atlanta, Ga.	1,173	61.2	77.0	44.2	−8	103	48.27	71
Atlantic City, N. J.	52	52.0	70.0	34.0	−9	104	40.56	79
Bismarck, N. Dak.	1,674	40.5	66.9	10.9	−45	114	16.34	71
Boise, Idaho	2,739	50.9	70.0	32.2	−28	121	13.10	57
Boston, Mass.	125	49.6	69.4	29.7	−18	104	40.14	71
Buffalo, N. Y.	767	47.0	67.6	26.2	−20	97	36.00	76
Charlotte, N. C.	779	60.2	77.0	42.7	−5	103	46.05	71
Chicago, Ill.	673	50.2	71.6	27.5	−23	105	32.86	73
Cleveland, O.	762	49.2	69.5	28.4	−17	100	33.82	72
Denver, Colo.	5,292	50.0	69.7	31.6	−29	105	14.05	53
Des Moines, Iowa	861	49.5	73.0	23.3	−30	110	32.04	72
Dodge City, Kans.	2,509	54.3	76.2	31.6	−26	109	20.51	67
Duluth, Minn.	1,133	38.0	61.2	11.7	−41	106	27.94	78
Eastport, Me.	76	41.7	58.7	22.7	−23	93	39.39	79
El Paso, Tex.	3,778	63.3	80.0	46.3	−5	113	9.16	40
Fresno, Cal.	327	63.0	79.5	47.8	17	115	9.39	56
Galveston, Tex.	54	69.6	82.4	55.5	8	101	44.77	80
Green Bay, Wis.	617	44.0	67.5	18.5	−36	104	31.58	72
Harrisburg, Pa.	374	52.1	72.6	30.6	−14	104	37.94	70
Havre, Mont.	2,505	41.6	65.2	15.6	−57	108	13.90	70
Helena, Mont.	4,110	43.3	63.3	22.5	−42	103	13.63	60
Huron, S. Dak.	1,306	43.6	69.1	14.8	−43	111	20.65	72
Indianapolis, Ind.	822	52.7	73.7	30.6	−25	106	39.90	71
Jacksonville, Fla.	43	69.3	81.2	56.6	10	104	49.74	80
Kansas City, Mo.	963	54.4	76.1	30.6	−22	113	37.11	69
Knoxville, Tenn.	995	58.4	75.8	40.3	−16	104	47.38	73
Lander, Wyo.	5,372	42.5	64.5	20.4	−40	102	12.63	60
Little Rock, Ark.	357	62.0	79.4	43.5	−12	108	48.38	72
Los Angeles, Cal.	338	62.4	69.2	55.6	28	109	15.23	69
Louisville, Ky.	525	57.0	76.8	36.4	−20	107	43.26	68
Lynchburg, Va.	681	57.6	75.9	39.1	−7	106	40.53	72
Montgomery, Ala.	223	65.5	80.7	49.7	−5	107	51.19	72
New Orleans, La.	53	69.3	81.7	55.7	7	102	57.46	78
New York, N. Y.	314	52.3	71.9	32.4	−14	102	42.99	71
Northfield, Vt.	876	41.4	63.5	17.3	−41	98	33.84	79
North Platte, Nebr.	2,821	48.3	70.4	25.4	−35	108	18.39	68
Oklahoma City, Okla.	1,214	59.4	78.8	38.4	−17	113	31.15	69
Omaha, Nebr.	1,105	50.6	74.2	24.6	−32	114	27.77	70
Oswego, N. Y.	335	46.8	67.9	25.6	−23	100	35.21	76
Palestine, Tex.	510	66.0	81.0	49.8	−6	108	40.73	73
Parkersburg, W. Va.	637	54.2	73.6	34.0	−27	106	39.41	75
Philadelphia, Pa.	114	54.0	74.0	34.0	−6	106	40.41	70
Phoenix, Ariz.	1,108	69.7	87.6	52.8	12	119	7.78	43
Port Huron, Mich.	638	46.0	66.9	24.2	−25	104	28.93	77
Portland, Oreg.	153	53.1	65.3	40.9	−2	105	41.62	74
Rapid City, S. Dak.	3,259	46.1	68.2	24.1	−40	106	17.98	59
Red Bluff, Cal.	332	62.2	78.4	47.1	17	115	24.81	56
St. Louis, Mo.	568	55.9	76.9	33.3	−22	110	37.44	69
St. Paul, Minn.	837	44.2	69.5	15.8	−41	104	27.24	72
Salt Lake City, Utah	4,360	51.6	72.5	31.6	−20	105	16.13	52
San Antonio, Tex.	693	68.9	82.8	53.8	4	108	27.18	67
San Francisco, Cal.	155	56.1	58.7	51.1	27	101	22.02	78
Santa Fe, N. Mex.	7,013	48.8	67.1	30.9	−13	97	14.27	51
Sault Ste. Marie, Mich.	614	39.2	61.5	15.5	−37	98	32.33	80
Seattle, Wash.	125	51.0	61.7	40.8	3	98	34.03	77
Shreveport, La.	249	65.8	82.0	49.0	−5	110	43.37	72
Spokane, Wash.	1,929	48.2	66.6	29.8	−30	108	16.62	63
Springfield, Ill.	636	52.7	74.4	29.2	−24	110	36.45	72
Springfield, Mo.	1,324	55.7	75.0	35.0	−29	106	41.78	72
Tampa, Fla.	35	71.8	81.0	61.1	19	98	49.36	79
Vicksburg, Miss.	247	65.6	80.4	50.0	−1	104	51.93	74
Walla Walla, Wash.	991	53.1	71.1	35.1	−17	113	17.01	62
Washington, D. C.	112	55.0	74.7	35.1	−15	106	42.16	71
Williston, N. Dak.	1,878	39.3	65.9	9.4	−49	110	14.80	70
Wilmington, N. C.	78	63.1	77.8	47.8	5	103	46.93	79
Winnemucca, Nev.	4,344	48.4	67.6	30.7	−28	108	8.54	53

* The minus sign (−) indicates "below zero."
† Average for June, July, and August. ‡Average for December, January, and February.

atmosphere. So far as the length of the day is concerned, the poles in summer should receive more heat than any other part of the earth. But, for equal areas, the earth receives more heat where the sun's rays are more nearly vertical. For this reason, a unit area at latitude 40° receives about three-fourths as much heat as a unit area at the equator.

During that half of the year when the sun's rays are nearly vertical north of the equator, the greatest amount of heat is received in latitude 25° N. From about May 6 to August 6, the three months centering around June 21, or the period of the longest days in summer, the zone receiving the greatest amount of heat is in latitude 41° N. Between about June 1 and July 16 the north pole receives more heat than any other part of the earth. But the polar region does not become warm, because much of the heat is used in melting ice and snow. No amount of heat would make the temperature of Greenland like that of the tropics until all the snow and ice was melted.

The unequal heating of the land and the water, as well as the unequal heating of the air in different latitudes, produces wind movements and water currents which tend to equalize the extremes in temperature. It is estimated that without these equalizing influences, the average temperature at the equator, instead of being about 80° F., as at present, would rise to 131° F., and that the average temperature of the poles, instead of being about zero, would fall to about 100° F. below zero.

The greatest extremes in the temperature of the air occur in regions of scant rainfall. For example, at Azizia, 25 miles south of Tripoli, Africa, a temperature of 136.4° F. was recorded on September 13, 1922. This is probably the highest natural air temperature in the world. On the other hand, temperatures of 60° F. below zero in winter occur in Montana and 75° F. below zero in arctic Canada. On Mount McKinley, in Alaska, a thermometer left in 1913 and recovered in 1932 recorded a minimum of over 95° F. below zero—probably the lowest natural temperature on the surface of the globe. See *Climate, Rainfall, Wind.*

Terminal Moraines. Deposits left at the margin of a glacier at its position of maximum advance.

In the United States, the terminal moraine, marking the southern limit of the advance of the great continental glacier, may be traced from the Atlantic coast to the foot of the Rockies. In New England, the terminal moraine lies in the islands just off the coast—in Marthas Vineyard, Nantucket, and Long Island. It crosses New Jersey and, veering northwestward through Pennsylvania, reaches nearly to the southern boundary of New York. It then swings southwestward into Ohio and Indiana, attaining its southernmost point in Illinois. Then, changing direction to the northwest, it follows approximately the line of the Missouri river, until, in the Dakotas, it turns westward into Montana, and continues to the base of the Rocky mountains.

In Europe, the terminal moraine, marking the maximum advance of the European ice sheet, crosses southern England. In the western part of the continent it lies just north of the southern highlands of Germany. Thence it extends eastward along the north base of the Carpathian mountains, and swings northeastward through Poland into Russia.

Terminal moraines are usually hilly belts, and they may have many small, undrained depressions, called *kettle holes,* in which lakes or ponds exist. A terminal moraine is sometimes only a narrow ridge a few hundred feet in width, but more often it is a hilly belt from a quarter of a mile to two miles wide. See *Glacier, Moraines.*

Terraces. Benches or flat lands bordering the main channel of a river. Usually they are covered with alluvial material left on their surfaces at times when the river was much higher. Such terraces form rich agricultural lands. In the valleys of the interior plains of the United States, terraces contain some of the best farms of that region. Some river terraces furnish sands and gravels suitable for concrete construction, and, in the vicinity of large cities, these materials are used for building purposes.

In plateau regions and in some mountain regions, resistant layers of rock sometimes form benches along the sides of a valley. When worn down through such formations, river valleys may have rock terraces. See *Alluvium, Erosion, River.*

Thunder. The loud noise which follows a flash of lightning. It is produced by the sudden disturbance of the air, due to the discharge of electricity. The character of the sound depends upon the intensity and distance of the discharge, the form, number, and distance of the clouds, and the nature of the surrounding country.

In case the observer is about equally distant from the two bodies between which the discharge takes place, the thunder clap will be short and sharp. If the observer is nearly in line with the path of the discharge, but much farther from one body than from the other, the sound is prolonged into a long roll. In hilly or mountainous districts and where there are many clouds, the original sound is echoed and reechoed many times, producing a continuous roar.

Owing to the irregular refraction of sound caused by varying temperature and wind, thunder begins to rise from the ground before it has traveled far. For this reason one often sees flashes of lightning without hearing the thunder, which passes far over-

TEMPERATURE AND RAINFALL IN CANADA

From Dominion Meteorological Service Reports for Representative Stations

City, Town, or Station	Altitude Feet	Average or Normal Temperature Degrees F.			Extremes of Temperature Degrees F.		Average Annual Precipitation Inches		
		Year	Summer*	Winter†	Lowest Recorded	Highest Recorded	Rain	Snow	Total
Anticosti, Que.	30	35.1	54.3	15.2	‡−40	85	28.44	96.0	38.04
Charlottetown, P. E. I.	74	41.9	62.8	21.0	−27	98	29.19	98.5	39.04
Dawson, Yukon	1062	22.5	56.8	−15.4	−68	95	6.77	56.4	12.41
Edmonton, Alberta	2158	36.6	59.4	10.5	−57	98	12.64	44.7	17.11
Fort Chipewyan, Alta.	714	26.4	57.0	− 6.7	−60	93	7.73	44.8	12.21
Fort Vermilion, Alta.	950	27.3	58.9	− 7.8	−78	103	8.95	29.9	11.94
Fredericton, N. B.	164	40.5	63.4	15.5	−35	101	33.02	97.5	42.77
Haileybury, Ont.	707	37.7	64.0	9.1	−48	102	22.65	93.4	31.99
Kamloops, B. C.	1246	47.1	67.5	25.4	−31	104	7.26	29.9	10.25
London, Ont.	808	45.4	67.1	22.7	−27	106	29.37	88.8	38.25
Medicine Hat, Alta.	2365	42.1	66.4	15.8	−51	108	9.55	34.0	12.95
Montreal, Que.	187	42.6	67.2	16.0	−29	97	28.69	119.6	40.65
Parry Sound, Ont.	635	41.4	64.7	16.5	−39	100	26.77	122.1	38.98
Port Arthur, Ont.	644	36.2	60.1	9.7	−51	104	19.39	39.7	23.36
Prince Albert, Sask.	1432	32.7	60.6	0.9	−70	96	11.31	45.6	15.87
Prince Rupert, B. C.	170	45.5	55.5	35.8	− 6	88	93.77	42.7	98.04
Qu'Appelle, Sask.	2147	35.0	61.8	4.9	−55	102	12.81	56.6	18.47
Quebec, Que.	296	39.1	64.0	12.5	−34	97	29.39	128.6	42.25
Toronto, Ont.	379	45.0	66.3	23.8	−26	105	25.88	62.7	32.15
Vancouver, B. C.	45	54.7	63.2	37.7	2	92	51.49	31.1	54.60
Victoria, B. C.	228	49.2	57.6	40.1	− 2	95	27.76	14.3	29.19
Winnipeg, Man.	760	34.7	62.8	1.6	−47	108	15.49	51.0	20.59
Yarmouth, N. S.	101	43.9	59.1	27.9	−12	86	39.02	78.4	46.86

*Average for June, July, and August. †Average for December, January, and February.
‡The minus sign (−) is equivalent to "below zero."

head. Thunder is rarely heard at a distance of 15 or 20 miles, though discharges of cannon may be heard 30, 50, or 100 miles. See *Lightning, Storm.*

Tides. The alternate rising and falling of the water of the ocean, which occurs twice during every 24 hours and 52 minutes, caused by the differential attractions of the sun and moon. The tide rises, *flood tide,* for about 6 hours, when it is said to be *high*; it then falls, *ebb tide,* usually for a slightly longer period, when it is said to be *low.* Frequently the tide comes in as a series of waves which do not recede to the former level of the sea. In other cases the tide rises rapidly without distinct waves.

While not perceptible in the open ocean, as there is nothing to indicate the slight elevation of the water level, tides are easily seen wherever there are shores upon which the rise and fall of the water may be measured. The change in level caused by tides in the open ocean is estimated at between 2 and 3 feet. Along coasts the rise and fall usually amounts to several feet. In case of broad bays with narrow heads, the variation between high and low tides may amount to 20 or 30 feet or more, as in the Bay of Fundy, where it exceeds 50 feet.

Tides often run up broad open rivers such as the Amazon, the St. Lawrence, and many smaller streams. The tide runs up the St. Lawrence to Three Rivers, near Montreal, a distance of 283 miles. In the Hudson, there is a tide exceeding 2 feet at Troy, about 150 miles inland. In some shallow rivers the tide advances as a solid wall of water, called a *bore.* Tides involving the visible movement of large masses of water occur only in oceans and in gulfs, straits, rivers, and other waters immediately connected with the sea. In small lakes, tidal risings and fallings are imperceptible, and even in large lakes or enclosed seas they are very slight.

Tides are produced by the combined attractive forces of the moon and sun, as exerted upon the waters of the earth. The moon is the nearest of the heavenly bodies to the earth, and, by reason of this nearness, its attractive influence, or tide-raising force, is about 2½ times as great as that of the immensely larger but far distant sun. The part of the waters directly under the moon's path in the heavens is pulled out toward the moon. At the same time, the moon attracts the solid part of the earth and, as it were, draws the earth away from the waters on the surface farthest from the moon. In consequence, the waters there are heaped up, although not quite to the same extent as on the side of the earth immediately beneath the moon.

The waters are thus drawn up into ridges at the same time on opposite sides of the earth, and the waters situated between them are, for the same reason, correspondingly lowered. As the earth rotates on its axis the two slight elevations or ridges of water, properly called *tidal waves,* travel steadily across the oceans and seas, the one keeping almost directly under the moon and the other on the side of the earth opposite to it. When these tidal waves reach the edges of the land, they heap themselves upon the shore, producing high tides, and then recede, producing low tides. As a result, two high tides and two low tides occur in each lunar day, or in a period of slightly more than one revolution of the earth on its axis.

The sun's tide-raising force is only about two-fifths that of the moon, and its effect is to increase or diminish the tides produced by the moon's much greater attraction. Whether the sun's influence makes higher or lower tides depends upon the relative positions of the sun and moon with reference to the earth. At new and at full moon, both the sun and the moon attract in nearly the same line, giving rise to tides higher than the average, called *spring* tides. At first and last quarters, the sun and moon are pulling upon the earth at right angles to each other. The moon's force is then partly counteracted by that of the sun, resulting in tides lower than the average, called *neap* tides.

By their erosive action, tides greatly modify coast lines. They also carry immense amounts of débris out to sea, prevent the formation of deltas, and help rivers to build up their lower valleys or flood plains. Tides have an immense influence upon the plant and animal life of the seashore.

Till. Unstratified glacial drift. This material consists of a mixture of clay, bowlders, gravel, and sand. It is frequently called "bowlder clay." Beyond question a part of it was deposited as the great ice sheet was advancing; the greater portion of it, however, undoubtedly was deposited upon the final melting of the ice. When deposition occurs in this way, there is no assorting of material, and therefore the great body of glacial drift is unassorted or unstratified. The rolling prairie lands in the upper Mississippi valley, in portions of Canada, and in the lowland plains bordering the Baltic Sea in northwestern Europe are composed for the most part of glacial till.

In the continent of North America and in Europe the glacial deposits have been so weathered and disintegrated at the surface that the upper two or three feet now constitute excellent soils. Many of the richest farm lands in the northern United States and in Canada, as well as many of those in England and the countries to the south and east of the Baltic Sea, have glacial soils. See *Glacier, Moraine.*

Timber Line. The line of elevation on mountains above which there are no trees. This line is not regular but extends highest on those slopes which afford the most shelter from the winds or the longest exposure to the sun. The height of the timber line varies greatly with the latitude and general climatic conditions, rising above 12,000 feet in the tropics, and descending to the sea level in high latitudes. Wherever there is soil above the timber line and below the snow line, the surface is usually covered with low shrubs and hardy herbaceous plants. These form the alpine flora, noted for the size and beauty of its flowers. See *Alpine Plants, Mountain.*

Tornado. The most violent and destructive of all local storms, often incorrectly called a "cyclone." Tornadoes most commonly form in connection with thunderstorms, usually on warm, sultry afternoons when there is great humidity. The tornado cloud proper is intensely black and funnel-shaped, and points downward from a mass of storm clouds advancing rapidly and in great commotion. Like the little dust whirls seen in summer, this funnel-shaped cloud revolves about its center at tremendous speed, at the same time moving forward at the rate of 30 miles or more an hour.

Nearly all tornadoes travel from the southwest to the northeast, moving in a narrow path, usually from 100 to 300 yards wide, with an average length of from 20 to 30 miles, and they are generally accompanied by thunder, lightning, heavy rain, and hail. By reason of its small diameter and rapid movement, the duration of a tornado at any one point is exceedingly brief. The progress of the whirling funnel-cloud is often very irregular. Sometimes it appears alternately to rise and descend with a sort of bounding motion, leaving parts of its path unscathed while other portions are marked by ruined crops, uprooted trees, demolished buildings, and often by loss of human life.

A tornado may be regarded as a greatly concentrated cyclone or as a much intensified whirlwind. While a cyclone may be more than 1000 miles across, with marginal winds blowing around a center of low pressure, sometimes at the hurricane speed of 100 miles an hour, a tornado may be less than one-eighth mile across, with whirling winds rushing about a vortex or center at a speed estimated as equaling or exceeding that of a rifle bullet. In strong tornadoes the air pressure at the center may be fully one-fourth less than normal. It is to this marked difference in pressure as well as to the extreme velocity of the accompanying wind that tornadoes owe their terrific destructive power.

The normal pressure of the air at sea level is 14.7 pounds per square inch, or more than 2100 pounds per square foot. When this is reduced by one-fourth, or to 11 pounds per square inch, as estimated for the center of a tornado, the pressure is only 1584 pounds per square foot. Consequently, when a strong tornado passes a closed building, the pressure of the outside air is suddenly reduced and the inside air thrusts itself against the walls with force equal to the difference in pressure. As this difference exceeds 500 pounds per square foot, or more than two tons per square yard, the walls, unless unusually strong, will collapse outward toward the storm as if the building had exploded.

Tornadoes may occur in some part of the United States at any time of the year. During winter and early spring they occur in the Gulf states and the South Atlantic states. During June they are most frequent in the Mississippi valley. In the Middle Atlantic states and in New England they occur most often in July and August. Tornadoes are of the greatest frequency in the lower Mississippi valley. West of central North Dakota, Nebraska, and Texas, they are of rare occurrence. See *Cyclone, Storm, Whirlwind.*

Trade Winds. Constant winds which occur on the open sea, and to some extent on land, on both sides of the equator, to a distance of about 30° north and south latitude. On the north of the equator their general direction is from the northeast; on the south of the equator they are from the southeast.

The trade winds are caused by the unequal heating of the air between the tropical and the polar regions; they are influenced also by the rotation of the earth. The great heat of the tropics makes the air of that region lighter. In consequence of this, the air of the tropics ascends into the upper regions of the atmosphere. It is there condensed and flows northward to supply the deficiency caused by the undercurrents blowing toward the equator. These undercurrents coming from the north and the south are, by reason of the earth's rotation, deflected as they approach the equatorial regions, becoming northeast and southeast currents, thus forming the trade winds.

Trade winds are constant only in the open sea, and they reach their greatest strength in the south Indian Ocean. Those of the Atlantic are stronger than those of the Pacific. In some regions, trade winds are periodical, blowing for half the year in one direction and, for the other half, from the opposite quarter, as in case of the Indian monsoons. Before the era of steam, trade winds played an important part in navigation and commerce. See *Ocean Currents, Wind.*

Tundras (*too͝n'dräz*). The Russian name for the level, treeless, and often marshy plains peculiar to extreme northern and arctic regions. Shrubby vegetation reaches its northernmost limit in these areas, which consist chiefly of mucky or peaty soil with a permanently frozen subsoil.

In the nearly continuous sunshine that prevails from late May until early August, the tundras are thawed to a depth of a few inches. During this period they produce a dense growth of mosses and lichens more or less intermingled with dwarf herbs and shrubs, many of which bear large showy flowers. In summer the tundras are visited by various small fur bearing animals and numerous migratory birds. Tundras occupy considerable portions of northern Russia and of the Siberian plain, and also parts of northern Canada and Alaska. See *Heaths, Marshes, Steppes.*

Typhoon. A violent hurricane occurring in the China seas and adjacent regions, principally from July to October inclusive. Typhoons are identical with the West Indian hurricanes which take place in the same latitude in the western hemisphere. They are prolonged cyclonic storms of great intensity, with wind velocities sometimes exceeding 100 miles an hour. See *Hurricane, Storm.*

Valley. A depression in the surface of the land, generally elongate, through which usually a stream of water flows. However, a small depression in which water runs only after heavy showers is not ordinarily termed a valley. When very small, such a depression is usually called a *gully*; when somewhat larger, a *ravine.* Just as rivulets and brooks unite to form creeks and these unite in larger streams called rivers, so gullies lead to ravines and ravines to valleys. Most valleys end at the sea, or at a lake, but, in arid regions, some valleys end on dry land.

In a broad sense the term valley is used to indicate the whole drainage basin of a river system, as the Mississippi valley, or the Amazon valley. Depressions between mountains, whether occupied by streams or not, are also called valleys.

The chief agency in the formation of a valley is *erosion*; first, by the *weathering* of its sides, and second, by the *deepening* of its channel. If the channel wears away faster than the sides, the valley will be narrow and deep; if the sides wear away faster than the channel, the valley will be broad and shallow. When the sides wear away much faster than the channel, a wide, flat *flood plain* is formed from the silt brought down by the current, through which the stream wanders from side to side.

River valleys are natural communications, or highways, and, when extensive, sustain large populations, such as are found in the valleys of the Nile, the Ganges, the Hwang, the Danube, and the Mississippi. See *Alluvium, Erosion, River.*

Valley Train. Deposits of sands and gravels which follow the line of a valley, but which were deposited by waters issuing from a glacier. In the United States, these deposits often form the great alluvial terraces along the rivers which flow southward from the area which, during the Ice age, was occupied by the great continental glacier. See *Glacier.*

Volcanic Mountains. Many mountains are formed by the eruption of igneous rocks through volcanic action, and occur either singly or arranged in lines. While usually built up in the form of cones, the volcanic materials may be so grouped as to form a high upland of considerable extent.

Some of the greatest single mountains of the world are of volcanic origin, including both extinct and active volcanoes. Among these are Mt. Rainier and Mt. Shasta in the United States, Mt. Wrangell in Alaska, Orizaba and Popocatepetl in Mexico, Aconcagua and Chimborazo in South America, Kilimanjaro and Kenia in Africa, Demavend and Fujiyama in Asia, and Elbruz in Europe. See *Volcano, Vulcanism.*

Volcano. A cone-shaped elevation or mountain which, during a period of activity, throws out lava, cinders, ashes, steam, and gases from the interior of the earth. Volcanoes constantly in eruption are called *active*; those which have been quiescent for a long period, though at times emitting small quantities of vapor, are termed *dormant*; while those whose craters are closed and cold, with no evidences of a connection with interior lavas, are said to be *extinct.*

In size, volcanoes vary from small hillocks to giant mountains which include some of the earth's loftiest summits. Orizaba and Popocatepetl in Mexico, Cotopaxi and Aconcagua in the Andes, Demavend and Ararat in western Asia, and Kilimanjaro in east central Africa range between 17,000 and 23,000 feet in altitude. The mass of most volcanoes is composed of the material which they have erupted. However, the size of a volcano is not an index to the force of its activity. Many exceedingly violent and destructive eruptions have occurred in volcanoes only a few thousand feet high, such as Vesuvius in Italy, Krakatoa in the Sunda Strait, La Soufrière in St. Vincent, Pelée in Martinique, Skaptar Jokull in Iceland, and Bandai-San in Japan.

A volcano usually consists of a basal part, or mountain proper, a steeper conical part, or *cone*, and a basin-shaped pit, or *crater*, at the summit.

In some cases, however, the entire mountain may be called the cone, and sometimes eruptions take place through slits or fissures, without the formation of a definite crater. The amount of material ejected depends upon the violence and length of the eruption. During the famous eruption of Vesuvius, 79 A. D., which destroyed Pompeii and Herculaneum, there was no lava, but much of Campania was covered with a layer of cinders and ashes several feet thick. It is estimated that during the violent eruption of Krakatoa, in 1883, material equivalent to more than four cubic miles was thrown out. Scientists computed that the material ejected by Tambora, on the island of Sumbawa, in 1815, was equivalent to 400 cubic miles.

It is believed that on certain days during the eruption of Pelée, in 1902, ashes equal in volume to the total quantity of sediment discharged by the Mississippi river in an entire year, were thrown into the air. Dust particles thrown from Krakatoa, in 1883, are believed to have reached finally a height of 30 miles, and to have remained suspended for more than a year, traveling completely around the earth and causing "red glows" after sunset. The sound of volcanic explosions is occasionally heard at points, several hundreds of miles distant. Destructive earthquakes and tidal waves sometimes accompany volcanic eruptions.

Volcanoes are believed to be situated in areas of weakness in the earth's crust, being found in ocean basins, in the borders of ocean basins, and in mountain ranges which form or border the edges of continents. The belt of greatest volcanic activity is in the chain of mountains and islands which partly encircles the Pacific Ocean. No entirely satisfactory explanation of the cause of volcanic action has been worked out. It is believed, however, that molten lava is slowly formed in the deep interior of the earth by the force of gravity. From time to time some of this liquid is forced to the surface by the enormous pressure of heavier rocks and the terrific expansive force of the steam and gases imprisoned in the lavas. See *Crater*, *Lava*, *Volcanic Mountains*, *Vulcanism*.

Vulcanism. All phenomena associated with the rising of melted rock, from deep in the interior of the earth toward or to the surface, are grouped under the general head of vulcanism. In many cases, lavas formed at great depths in the earth fail to reach the surface. For example, in Yellowstone national park, thousands of feet beneath the earth's surface, there are great masses of hot rock. These supply heat to the waters which issue from various openings as hot springs and geysers.

When lava breaks forth at the earth's surface, a true volcano is usually formed. After a series of explosions, a mountain, with a crater at its summit, may be developed. In 1943, volcanologists had their first opportunity to study such a growth, at Paricutin, Mexico. Starting with a burst of smoke and lava from a crack in a cornfield, it grew to a thousand foot cone in ten weeks. Then from the crater lava poured forth at the rate of 2700 tons a minute, covering the countryside for seven miles, while a blanket of black ash spread for 35 miles around.

Lavas also flow out upon the surface through long, slitlike openings, *fissure eruptions*. When lava is forced up through vertical fissures, *dikes* are formed. Many such formations, composed of dark lavas, appear along the coast of New England, in the White mountains, in the Green mountains, in the Adirondacks, and in various other mountain regions. See *Dike*, *Volcanic Mountains*, *Volcano*.

Water Gap. A narrow place in the valley of a river, where, owing to the unusual resistance of the rocks to erosion, the stream has failed to broaden its valley as much as it has both above and below. A good example is the Delaware Water Gap, near Stroudsburg, Pa. At this point, the Delaware river flows through a narrow gorge in the Kittatinny range of the Appalachian mountains. Other typical instances are the gap at Harpers Ferry, in the valley of the Potomac river; the notch north of Harrisburg, Pa., through which the Susquehanna river flows; and the Royal Gorge of the Arkansas river, in Colorado. See *River*.

Watershed. Properly, the meeting line of diverging slopes is a watershed, water parting, or divide. Such a line marks off the drainage area, basin, or valley of one river from that of neighboring rivers. However, the term watershed is now widely applied to the whole area contributing to the drainage supply of a river or lake, and especially to the higher or steeper portions of such a region. See *River*, *Stream Piracy*.

Waterspout. A local storm similar in origin and form to a tornado, occurring over the surface of the sea or a lake. From a large storm cloud above, a whirling, funnel-shaped mass appears suspended. This seems to grow downward, tapering toward the surface of the water, which becomes violently agitated. When the spout is completely formed, water from the surface appears to be drawn up to join the cloud above. This, however, is an optical illusion, as practically all of the water carried along by the revolving spout is condensed from the air. Even when spouts form over the surface of the sea, the water composing them is found to be fresh.

The actual volume of water contained in a spout is not large. When damage is caused by a waterspout, it is due to the tornadic violence of the accompanying wind. Waterspouts, therefore, should not be confused with cloudbursts. Although by no means confined to low latitudes, waterspouts occur most frequently over warm tropical seas. See *Tornado*, *Whirlwind*.

Waves. The alternate rising and falling of successive ridges of water, produced by the friction between the wind and the surface of seas, lakes, and rivers. In the open ocean, wave motion does not result in an actual forward movement of the water. Each particle of water composing a wave describes a curve and comes back practically to the point from which it started, though the *wave form* moves on as other particles of water similarly rise and fall. The motion of ocean waves, therefore, is somewhat like that of a waving field of grain where the base of each moving stem is attached to the ground, though wave after wave passes across the field.

The top of a wave is called its *crest*. The depression between two crests is called the *trough*. The horizontal distance between two crests is the *length* of the wave, and the vertical distance from the bottom of the trough to the crest is the *height* of the wave. The time required for a crest to travel the length of the wave is called the *period* of the wave.

Under pressure of strong wind, the top of a wave may be blown forward, so that it "breaks," thus producing some motion of the water independent of the true wave motion. Large waves of this kind, striking against the shore, are called *breakers*. The destructiveness of waves depends upon their length as well as upon their height. With a given wave, the shorter its length, the greater its destructive force. Waves raised by a heavy storm often run to great distances from their starting points, forming what is known as the *swell* or *ground swell*.

When a wave comes from the open sea into water so shallow that it "drags" bottom, the velocity and length of the wave are reduced and the height is increased, so that the crest pitches forward as *surf*. The water forced against the shore in the wave runs back toward sea again, and this away-from-shore motion is called *undertow*. Whenever waves strike the shore at an angle, the water moves more or less along shore, producing a *shore current* or *littoral current*.

Storm waves in the open sea are frequently 30 to 40 feet in height, and sometimes even 70 feet. When driven against shores, the surf of broken waves is sometimes thrown to heights of from 100 to 300 feet, with sufficient force to destroy lighthouses and even cliffs of rock. The length of great waves may sometimes reach 1500 feet and the speed may be as high as 60 miles an hour, but such wave lengths and velocities are rare.

The motion of waves is confined to the water near the surface. There is little wave disturbance at a depth of 30 feet, and wave motion becomes imperceptible at a depth of a few hundred feet. Waves possess great erosive power. They greatly modify the coasts of continents and islands. See *Erosion, Flood, Ocean, Tides, Wind.*

Weather. The state of the atmosphere at any time as regards heat or cold, wetness or dryness, clearness or cloudiness, calm or storm, or electrical condition. Hence the expressions, warm, cold, dry, wet, and various other terms applied to weather. Weather differs from climate in that it is simply the condition of the atmosphere at a given place at a given time, while climate is the *general* or *average* condition of the weather. The weather of a place or of a region may change from day to day, yet its climate, or average weather, will remain practically unchanged from year to year. The last half century, however, shows a gradual increase in the warmth of the climate in the northern hemisphere.

If the principal conditions and features of storms are borne in mind, a forecast of the weather, more or less conjectural but frequently exceedingly useful, may be made from observations of the barometer, the winds, and the appearance of the clouds. In the last half century, great progress has been made in this direction by collecting and comparing reports of simultaneous conditions at different points through use of the telegraph. Forecasts are then sent out by teletype machines for aid to shipping, aircraft, agriculture, and the public generally. The United States Weather Bureau began a forecasting service in 1891 under the direction of Cleveland Abbe. See *Climate, Climatology.*

Weathering. The result of all forms of atmospheric action whereby surface rock is disintegrated or decomposed. This action includes both mechanical and chemical processes.

Mechanically, the atmosphere produces changes mainly by means of wind, frost, sudden changes of temperature, and the impact of driving rain. The effect of all mechanical weathering, or *disintegration,* of the rocks is merely to grind them to finer particles of the same material.

Chemically, the atmosphere effects changes chiefly by means of oxidation, carbonation, hydration, and solution. Chemical weathering, or *decomposition,* results in the removal of the soluble substances, mostly lime, magnesia, soda, and potash, leaving behind the insoluble substances as soil-forming elements. The insoluble portion consists mainly of sand, clay, and iron oxide.

All soils were at first formed by the weathering of rocks. The residual sands sometimes consolidate to form sandstone; the clays become bedded into shales; and the gravels, into conglomerates. The soluble lime and magnesia are borne by the rivers to the ocean, where they enter into the formation of limestone. The soluble soda is likewise transported to the ocean, where it becomes part of the salt of sea water. See *Atmosphere, Erosion, Wind.*

Whirlwind. A mass of air rotating rapidly in a nearly vertical position, at the same time moving more or less rapidly forward. Whirlwinds vary immensely in size and intensity. Most whirlwinds are small, harmless eddies which occur in dusty streets, roads, or fields. The larger forms, however, include the blinding sand pillars of tropical deserts, the terrifying waterspouts of tropical seas, and the destructive tornadoes in temperate regions.

Whirlwinds are best observed in arid regions. In the Mohave desert of California, as many as six or eight whirlwinds, some of them conspicuous and imposing, may be seen at one time on a hot summer day. Some part of the surface of the ground becomes more strongly heated than the surrounding parts. The air in contact with it quickly rises in temperature, immediately becomes much less dense, and is forced rapidly upwards by inrushing currents of cooler air. The inequality in the force of these currents gives rise to the whirling motion. While most whirlwinds rarely extend to a height of 1000 feet, and are of short duration, a large whirlwind, even in a most arid desert, may develop into a violent local thunderstorm or cloudburst. See *Tornado.*

Wind. Air naturally in horizontal motion at the earth's surface, coming from any direction with any degree of velocity. All movement of the air is from a region of greater pressure toward a region of less pressure. The air in low latitudes is heated more effectively than the air in higher latitudes. From this arises the constant tendency of the air above the bottom of the atmosphere to move from tropical regions toward the poles. The cooler air at the surface tends to move toward the equator. As a result, there is formed a double trade wind zone, with equatorial calms or doldrums in the center, and two zones of prevailing westerly winds, with tropical calms on the equatorward side of each.

But these larger movements of the air are complicated, first, by the fact that the land and the water are very unequally heated, and, further, by the effect of the rotation of the earth. In consequence, the westerly winds are often overcome by seasonal winds, such as the monsoons of India, and by various local air movements, such as sea breezes, land breezes, valley breezes, and mountain breezes. Winds are classed as *steady,* such as the trade winds; as *periodical,* such as the winter and summer monsoons; and as *variable,* such as those occurring in connection with areas of high or low pressure, or storms.

In the North Temperate Zone, the normal wind is westerly, and all other winds soon veer to that direction. Winds blowing toward and around an area of low barometer, or storm center, are called *cyclonic.* When these are violent they are known as typhoons or hurricanes. Winds whirling around a center, in which the vertical motion greatly exceeds the horizontal, are called *tornadic.* These sometimes cause great local destruction.

The direction of a wind is always stated as that from which it blows. A wind from the east, therefore, is called an east wind. The force of a wind is commonly indicated by its velocity in miles per hour, as measured by the anemometer. A light breeze has a velocity of 13 miles; a strong breeze, 34 miles; a strong gale, 56 miles; a storm, 75 miles; and a hurricane, 90 or more miles per hour. The destructive winds revolving about the funnel-shaped cloud of a tornado attain velocities estimated at from 400 to 1500 miles per hour.

Wind is one of the most important of natural agencies. It is the factor upon which all the processes of the weather finally depend. Prevailing winds profoundly influence climate and rainfall. Even gentle breezes, by keeping the air in circulation, equalize temperatures and prevent the accumulation of impurities. Wind is an active agent in the upbuilding of sand dunes along shores and in deserts, in the weathering and wearing away of rocks in arid regions, in the dissemination of atmospheric dust, and in the formation of various soils. See *Æolian Deposits, Anticyclone, Chinook, Climate, Hurricane, Monsoon, Rainfall, Tornado, Trade Winds, Whirlwind.*

Wind Gap. A former water gap from which the stream has been diverted, usually by stream piracy. See *Stream Piracy.*

GEOLOGY

Geology is the science which considers the earth in all of its aspects,—its origin, its varied features, the composition and the structure of the material which composes it, and the life upon it. It is concerned with all the forces which have acted upon the earth and the effects of those forces. It attempts to reconstruct the history of the earth, particularly as it is recorded in the rocks of the outer crust.

In working out this history, geology makes use of the principles of many other sciences; as, astronomy, physics, chemistry, mineralogy, lithology, zoology, and botany. It is essentially an application of the various sciences to an understanding of the earth. For this reason the science is subdivided into many subjects.

Among these subdivisions are: Dynamical Geology, which treats of the forces at work upon the earth and their effects; Structural Geology, which treats of the architecture of the earth; Historical Geology, which treats of the succession of events, both organic and inorganic, upon the earth; Physiographic Geology, or Physiography, which treats of the sculpture of the surface of the earth by various destructive agents; Glacial Geology, which treats of the origin and effects of the great masses of ice which have periodically covered considerable portions of the earth's surface; Economic Geology, which treats of the origin and occurrences of the various useful natural products as metals, minerals, building stones, soils, clays, oil, gas, and coal; Stratigraphic Geology, which treats of the nature and succession of the various layers of sedimentary rocks which form the greater part of the earth's crust. Many other subdivisions of the subject might be listed.

An especially valuable aid to Stratigraphic Geology is the subject of Paleontology, which treats of the past life upon the earth as revealed by the fossils. The development of life with its succession of characteristic forms enables the stratigrapher to date the various layers and to connect layers of equal age which are exposed at widely separated places.

Geology is one of the most recently developed of the sciences. Its fundamental principles were first announced in 1785 by the British scientist, James Hutton (1726–1797). The division of the geologic record into ages was established on a working basis by the investigations of William Smith (1769–1839), published in 1799. About 1830 geology was placed upon a secure foundation by the teachings of Sir Charles Lyell (1797–1875) who, in his *Principles of Geology*, embodied the work of Hutton and Smith into an orderly system. Lyell won acceptance for the two great principles upon which modern geology rests: (1) that the age of the earth is very great, and (2) that in the processes in operation at the present may be found illustrations of most of the changes of the past.

In America, Lyell's principles were ably confirmed by the pioneer labors of James Hall (1811–1898), by the extensive researches of J. D. Dana (1813–1895), and by the notable contributions of Louis Agassiz (1807–1873), whose defense of the doctrine of a glacial period destroyed the last remnants of scientific opposition to Lyell's teachings. During the last half century the various branches of geological knowledge have been notably advanced by American and Canadian investigators, among whom are: J. D. Whitney, Sir J. W. Dawson, Joseph Leconte, A. Winchell, C. A. White, F. V. Hayden, Joseph Leidy, O. C. Marsh, C. H. Hitchcock, Clarence King, E. D. Cope, N. S. Shaler, S. W. Williston, H. F. Osborn, W. B. Scott, C. D. Wolcott, T. C. Chamberlin, H. M. Ami, and C. R. Van Hise.

MATERIAL OF THE SOLID EARTH

Rocks are the portions of the earth composed of mineral matter. Most rocks are of complex composition, usually, though not always, containing a number of different minerals. While 10 or more kinds of minerals may be present in the same rock, some rocks are composed of but a single mineral, and commonly only two or three constituent minerals are present in large quantity. With regard to their origin, rocks are divided into three great classes: *sedimentary* rocks; *igneous* rocks; and *metamorphic* rocks.

Sedimentary Rocks. These are formed of the material deposited from the air or water, rarely from ice. In most cases they are the result of the breaking down of other rocks and for this reason are sometimes called clastic (broken). Some sediments are deposited as the result of chemical action or of the action of plants and animals; these are called respectively chemical sediments and organic sediments. Among the sediments of clastic origin are sand, gravel, breccia, conglomerate, and shale. Those of chemical origin include certain tuffs, stalactite, travertine, veinstones, gypsum, and limonite. Those of organic origin include chalk, flint and chert (in part), marl, most oolites, peat, coal, shell limestone, lithographic limestone, some compact limestone, and dolomite. When deposited on the ocean bottom, rocks of this class, such as some shales and limestones, are called marine; when deposited along shores, such as conglomerates and sandstones, they are called littoral; when deposited in lakes, lacustrine; when deposited in streams, fluviatile.

Igneous Rocks. These are the result of the cooling of molten masses of material. When the molten material is injected into the crust of the earth and cools in the form of great masses (bathyliths and laccoliths), or in long sheets (dikes or sills), the resultant rocks are known as plutonic (underground) igneous rocks. When the molten material is ejected upon the surface from fissures or the openings of volcanoes and cools in the form of ash beds, lava flows, and the like, the resultant rocks are known as volcanic, or eruptive, igneous rocks. Igneous rocks are characterized by their massive structure. They lack the stratified form of sedimentary rocks and the gneissic or schistose structure of many metamorphic rocks. In texture, igneous rocks are granitic, composed of distinct crystals as in granite; porphyritic, composed of larger crystals embedded in a matrix of smaller crystals or volcanic glass; and vitreous, or glassy, as in obsidian (volcanic glass). When the matrix is composed of crystals visible to the naked eye, the igneous rocks are plutonic in origin; when the matrix is composed of microscopic crystals, or is vitreous, the rocks are volcanic or eruptive in origin.

Igneous rocks are classified as acid or basic, according to the amount of silica (SiO_2) in their composition. The amount of silica present has much to do with the form the rock takes when cooling from the molten state and with the kind of soil which results from its decomposition.

Metamorphic Rocks. Altered from their original form. There are three general classes: (1) metamorphosed sedimentary rocks; (2) metamorphosed igneous rocks; (3) rocks similar to one or both of the foregoing but of indeterminable origin. The agencies producing these changes are chiefly heat, pressure, and migrating waters. Metamorphic rocks may be so far altered that their original condition cannot be made out, as in the case of certain schists which may have been originally either sedimentary or igneous. Other metamorphic rocks have been changed so little that their origin is easily determinable. **All intermediate stages may be found.**

Among metamorphosed sedimentary rocks are marble, crystalline limestone, quartzite, slate, anthracite coal, mica schist, hornblende schist, and various other schists. Examples of metamorphosed igneous rocks are aporhyolite and granitoid gneiss. Examples of the third group of metamorphic rocks are soapstone and serpentine rock.

BRANCHES OF GEOLOGY

The three most important branches are Dynamical Geology, Structural Geology, and Historical Geology.

Dynamical Geology. This branch of the science deals with the forces at work upon the earth and the effects of those forces. It considers the origin and effects of pressure, heat and cold, chemical action, and the various stresses and strains set up within the earth by tidal or other action.

The heat of the earth is either an initial heat, retained from a time when the whole material of the earth was in a gaseous or molten condition, or the heat of a secondary action of compression and friction, caused by the gradual concentration of an originally incoherent mass of relatively cool matter. There are two hypotheses of the origin of the earth: One, called the Laplacian hypothesis, suggests that the earth was originally a mass of incandescent gas revolving in space and that the subsequent history has been one of cooling and concentration. The other, called the planetesimal hypothesis, suggests that the earth was originally a mass of hot or cold particles, similar to the spiral nebulæ of the heavens, and that by the concentration of the particles, called planetesimals (little planets), heat has been secondarily produced. According to this theory, the history of the earth has been one of heating, at least up to a certain stage of its development.

The heat of the earth is confined to the interior of the solid portion, called the lithosphere or the rock sphere, as opposed to the hydrosphere or water sphere, and to the atmosphere or air sphere. It is the internal heat which produces the effects of an igneous character, such as volcanoes, the migrations of molten material within the crust of the earth, the heating of waters which have penetrated to the interior and which reappear at the surface as geysers, hot springs, and the abundant steam which accompanies every volcanic eruption. The heat of the interior increases rapidly with the depth, about 1° Fahrenheit for every 50–60 feet, and at no great distance down is sufficient to soften many of the rocks. It has an important effect in permitting the various stresses within the body of the earth to find relief as folds, faults, and other disturbances of the rocks, which are discussed under the head of Structural Geology.

The stresses which are set up in the earth are very largely pressure stresses, but there may be tensional stresses as well. The pressure is generally considered to be very largely due to the gradual contraction of the earth due to loss of heat. The solid crust, settling down upon the interior, is subjected to enormous lateral pressure which finds relief in the formation of great wrinkles and breaks in the crust. Such movements result in the formation of mountain chains, and the movements of the crust of the earth at such times produce earthquakes. Mountain-making movements are so slow that any growth would not be observed in the duration of many generations. The minor slips, which are a part of the great general movements, are the ones which we appreciate as earthquakes.

In general, there is a balance between the weight of the portions of the crust which lie in the great ocean basins and the portions which form the continents. As the land masses are being continually worn down and the loosened material deposited in the ocean basins, the continents become lighter and the balance is disturbed. At irregular periods, the balance is restored by the re-elevation of the continents until the weight of the two columns is again equal. This accounts for the more or less perfect periodicity of the mountain-making movements.

Chemical action is the result of the infiltering waters coming in contact with various minerals, taking more or less material into solution, and carrying it to other places where there is a reaction between the various chemical elements. This process is aided by the waters becoming warmed or heated as they penetrate into the lower part of the crust. Such chemical action results in a change of composition and in a change in size of the minerals and, at times, produces very profound stresses.

Less well understood, but probably very important, are the stresses set up in the earth by the tidal influence of the moon and other heavenly bodies and the stresses resulting from changes in the position of the polar axis.

Structural Geology. This branch of the science has to do with the form of the rock masses in the earth. It may well be called the architecture of the earth. The rocks which are formed by the cooling of an originally molten mass of material are deposited in great irregular bodies, as flows upon the surface, or as injections into the crust. The sedimentary rocks are deposited from air or water and occupy an originally horizontal position. The great movements of the crust have disturbed the original position of the rocks in various ways.

If the rock is bowed up into a great arch, it is called an anticline; i.e., the rocks slope (technically, dip) away from the center of the fold. If the rock is bowed down, it is called a syncline; i.e., the rocks slope toward the center of the fold. If but one side of the fold is seen, so that the rocks slope, or dip, in a single direction, the structure is called a monocline; i.e., a one-way slope. Such structures are of the utmost importance in determining the possible location of underground water, oil, and gas.

If the movement of the earth's crust is relatively sudden, the rocks may not be able to bend fast enough to relieve the stress but may break and slip. Such a rupture and displacement is called a fault. Sometimes the breaks and slips are of such magnitude that the upraised side of the fault may be mountainous in character; sometimes they are very small. At times the rocks are broken without any movement; the cracks thus formed are called joints.

It is along the cracks, joints, and fault lines that the underground waters most easily find their way through the crust of the earth, and it is in regions where such things have happened that a very considerable amount of the mineral wealth of the earth is found, for the underground waters carry the material to such places and deposit it. A crack which has been enlarged by water and then filled with deposited mineral is called a vein.

Many times in the earth's history mountain ranges have been raised upon the surface and then completely worn down by the action of running water and other destructive agents. Over such worn-down ranges the waters of the sea have flowed again and another series of rocks has been deposited. It is only by the study of the structure that such a history is revealed. When the mountain range was formed, the originally horizontal rocks were tilted up; when the range was worn down and covered anew by horizontal rocks, there was a difference in the position of the older tilted rocks and the younger horizontal rocks. Such a structure is called an unconformity, and its detection is of the utmost importance because of the history it reveals.

The structure of the rocks underlying any country has a great deal to do with the character of the surface. If the rocks are horizontal, the country will be a great level plain or will be sculptured into a land of large, flat-topped blocks, called mesas or buttes. If the rocks have been tilted up on edge, the land will be worn into a country of long ridges or parallel mountain ranges; such a country is always difficult to cross and may constitute an almost impassable barrier to the development of roads or other means of communication. If the structure of the rock is irregular, the surface will be worn into an irregular form, such as occurs in many mountain ranges with high-topped peaks. Only in an extremely old country, where the forces of destruction have been at work for an enormously long time, will the surface of land be worn down to a featureless plain independent of the structure of the rock beneath.

Almost every feature of the landscape is affected by the structure of the rock. The direction of rivers, the character of the shores and cliffs of great lakes and oceans, the shape of the surface of the land—all are more or less directly determined by the structure. It is these things which have determined the migrations of peoples, the settlement of countries, the character of military campaigns, and the development of routes of communication. It can readily be seen how important to man is the structure of the rocks which lie below him.

Historical Geology. The determination of the geological age of the rocks depends upon two important principles: first, that the rock strata are normally found in the order of their deposition, the oldest below, the youngest above; second, that in the evolution of plant and animal life there has been in general an increase in complexity of structure. Consequently, a study of the fossil plants and animals of given strata (layers) makes it possible to determine the stage of life development to which they had attained, and to assign the rock formations in which they occur to a more or less definite age.

The use of the terms era, period, epoch, and age in this connection does not imply any exact number of years. They are simply terms which indicate definite periods of development in the earth's history, characterized by particular assemblages of life forms or by particular activities of an inorganic nature, either constructive or destructive. The terms Paleozoic era, Mesozoic era, and the like, refer to long periods of life development just as the terms Bronze age and Stone age refer to long periods of cultural development in the history of man.

The geological history of any region is recorded in the stratigraphy, or succession of the various sedimentary beds and their structure. The study of the stratigraphy of any region should begin with a consideration of the most ancient rocks, perhaps the Archeozoic, and continue progressively through the various later formations to the uppermost. This study should consider the fossils, their characteristics, variations, and associations, together with a careful examination of the structure, position, composition, and relations of the rocks in which they occur. If the study extends to the paleogeography of the region, it should include also the evolution of life, climatic developments, character of sedimentary deposits, relations of land and sea, geographic conditions, nature and extent of volcanic activity, and the growth and reduction of mountains. In fact, it should embrace everything that would bear upon the conditions of life of the organisms, both plant and animal.

In no place upon the earth can we expect to find a complete succession of the layers from the oldest to the youngest. Each region where there is an exposure of rocks reveals but a portion of the geological column. The partial series must be patched together to form the complete whole. Such a process of patching is called correlation. This is accomplished by identifying equivalent layers in separate regions (1) by the character of the rock, (2) by the mineral content, (3) by the fossils. The last is by far the most important. Local names, usually geographical names, as the Trenton limestone or the Detroit River series, are given to the layers for purposes of identification and description, but all are referred as accurately as possible to the standard geological column. Such a column is necessarily undergoing constant revision.

In the following table is shown the standard geological column, or time scale, in common use in America. The names for the important divisions and subdivisions are arranged chronologically in ascending order, beginning at the bottom with the most ancient. The arrangement corresponds with the position of the rocks in the earth's crust.

DIVISIONS OF GEOLOGIC TIME

Era	Period	Age	Revolutions
Cenozoic (*Modern Life*)	Recent, Pleistocene — Quaternary	Age of Man; Glacial Age	
	Pliocene, Miocene, Oligocene, Eocene — Tertiary	Age of Mammals	Great volcanic activity in the northwestern United States.
			Laramide Revolution
Mesozoic (*Middle Life*)	Cretaceous, Comanchean, Jurassic, Triassic	Age of Reptiles	Sierra Nevada Revolution; Palisade Revolution
			Appalachian Revolution
Paleozoic (*Ancient Life*)	Permian, Pennsylvanian (Coal Measures), Mississippian	Age of Amphibians	Acadian Revolution
	Devonian, Silurian	Age of Fishes	Taconic Revolution
	Ordovician, Cambrian	Age of Trilobites	Epi-Proterozoic interval
Proterozoic (*Primitive Life*)	Keweenawan, Animikean, Huronian		
			Laurentide Revolution
Archeozoic (*Primal Life*)	Laurentian; Keewatin, Couchiching, Grenville; Basement Complex		

In the history of the earth, the long periods of mountain building and subsequent erosion, sometimes called "revolutions," are as important as the periods when the earth was covered by the sea and sedimentary beds were being deposited. The periods of quiet after a mountain-making disturbance, when the land was exposed to the action of destructive agents, were sometimes so long that whole ranges of mountains were removed and many feet of the sedimentary beds as well. The existence of such periods is recorded in the rocks by the presence of an unconformity, described in the section on structural geology.

The uplift and subsequent destruction of one portion of the earth's crust furnishes the material for the sedimentary beds which are being laid down on another portion of the crust. It is, then, obvious that the history of the earth must be made out for individual regions, as both building up and destruction are going on at the same time, but in different regions.

The age of the earth from the beginning of the Paleozoic to the Recent has been variously estimated, from 30 million years to many times that number. A very generally accepted figure, which states approximately the order of the figures in which we must think, is 100 million years.

THE GEOLOGICAL HISTORY OF NORTH AMERICA

Archeozoic Era. This era, called also the Archean, includes all the rocks from the very oldest up to and including the earliest recognizable stratified sediments. The name Archeozoic signifies most ancient, or primal, life, and implies that life in some form existed on the earth when a part, at least, of these rocks were formed. The rocks are dominantly igneous and metamorphic and, because of the high degree of complexity and the extreme metamorphism which has obscured their original nature, they are frequently referred to as the Archean or Basement Complex.

Archeozoic rocks are the product of great plutonic and volcanic activity and the metamorphism of the early sediments. In North America they are classified as a great schist series, the Keewatin and other formations of metamorphosed sediments in the Lake Superior and Adirondack region, and as a great granitoid series, called the Laurentian, which occupies much of eastern Canada and various portions of the United States. The duration of the Archeozoic era is believed to have been exceedingly long, possibly longer than all subsequent geologic time.

Proterozoic Era. This era, called also the Algonkian, includes that portion of geologic time which elapsed between the formation of the Archeozoic rocks and the earliest formations composed largely of unmetamorphosed sediments and carrying abundant fossils, the beginning of the Paleozoic era. The Proterozoic formations include the first great series of stratified rocks which clearly show in their history the geologic processes of weathering, transportation, and sedimentation. Such processes were, in all probability, active during Archeozoic time, but the extreme complexity produced by repeated disturbance and profound metamorphism has obscured the history.

In North America there are three divisions of Proterozoic rocks, the Huronian, the Animikean, and the Keweenawan. They are best known from the region around Lake Superior where the valuable deposits of iron and copper ore have led to their thorough exploration. There is evidence of the elevation of a great mountain range, or a series of mountain ranges in this region, at the end of the Archeozoic, followed by a period of exposure and erosion so long that the land was again reduced almost to the level of the sea, before the deposition of the first Proterozoic sediments. The recognition of this enormous interval of time increases our appreciation of the age of the earth. A period of similar activities and of equal duration intervened between the Proterozoic and the Paleozoic.

Paleozoic Era. This is the earliest era of dominantly unchanged sediments and abundant fossils in the rocks. Beginning with the earliest, it is usually divided into the following periods: (1) The Cambrian, (2) the Ordovician, (3) the Silurian, (4) the Devonian, (5) the Mississippian, (6) the Pennsylvanian, (7) the Permian.

Throughout the Paleozoic era there were no Appalachian mountains. The site of these mountains was occupied by a sinking trough in which accumulated over 25,000 feet of sediments derived from high land to the east. At the close of the Paleozoic a great lateral pressure raised this mass of sediments into the Appalachian mountains; this movement is called the Appalachian revolution. In a similar manner, the Rocky Mountain axis, in the western part of the continent, was an indefinite range of pre-Cambrian rocks around which was accumulating a vast mass of sediments. These were finally raised into the mountains we know, but not until the end of the Mesozoic.

Cambrian Period.—The rocks of this period consist of shales, slates, sandstones, and quartzites, sometimes of great thickness, with a subordinate amount of limestone. In North America they are grouped as Lower Cambrian or Waucoban (Georgian), Middle Cambrian or Acadian, and Upper Cambrian or Croixan (Potsdam). Cambrian rocks occur along the axis of the Appalachian mountains from Newfoundland to Alabama, along the Rocky Mountain axis from the Great Basin northwestward to the Arctic Ocean, and in scattered areas in the Mississippi valley.

These rocks are formed from the débris of great mountain ranges which outlined approximately the North American continent even in the earliest stages of its growth. The débris was deposited in a great interior sea which covered what is now the Mississippi valley, and is called the Mississippian sea. It is the history of this sea, with its alternate growth and retreat, its sediments, and the life that inhabited it, which constitutes much of the geological history of North America during the Paleozoic era.

The known fossils include no vertebrate animals, no insects, and no plants. The most characteristic fossils are trilobites, but remains of many other lower animals, as crustaceans, mollusks, brachiopods, worms, crinoids, sponges, and corals, are known.

Ordovician Period.—The formations of this period, originally called the Lower Silurian, consist chiefly of limestones, dolomites, shales, and sandstones.

During the Cambrian period the great interior sea was slowly advancing over the Mississippi valley. Early in the Ordovician the sea had established itself and the waters stretched uninterruptedly from the site of the Appalachian mountains, on the east, to the old ranges which marked the present site of the Rocky mountains, on the west. About the middle of this period two islands were probably present in the interior sea, one about where Cincinnati is located and one in southern Missouri. These islands persisted, as more or less dominant features of the continent, from that time on, and had the utmost significance in determining the location of the courses of the Ohio and Mississippi rivers and the great coal fields of the Ohio valley, Kansas, Oklahoma, and Texas.

In the rocks of this period are found the marbles and slates of Vermont and New Hampshire; the oil and gas of Ohio and eastern Indiana; the zinc and lead ores of Wisconsin, Iowa, and Illinois; and the phosphate beds of Tennessee. Trilobites reached their greatest variety in this period. Certain indefinite fossils, found in the rocks of Colorado and Wyoming, suggest the first appearance of fishlike vertebrates.

At the close of the Ordovician, a great mountain range was elevated in western New England and as far south as Virginia. It was the heat and pressure developed in this earth movement which metamorphosed the limestones and shales of western New England into marbles and slates. Before the region was again covered by water, the range had been worn down nearly to the level of the sea. This great disturbance is known as the Taconic revolution.

Silurian Period.—The rock formations of this period consist of limestones (dolomites) with interstratified beds of shale and sandstone. In North America three groups or epochs are recognized, the Oswegan, the Niagaran, and the Cayugan. The Niagaran epoch was one of great extension of the interior sea. In its pure waters there was an abundance of corals and other lime-secreting organisms, which furnished the material for the great bed of limestone that occupies much of the north central portion of the United States and extends far north into Canada. Niagaran limestones, or dolomites, are conspicuously developed in the gorge of the Niagara river, where their resistance to erosion has determined the formation of the great cataract at the falls. The saline beds in the Cayugan formations of New York and Ohio contain valuable deposits of salt and gypsum.

Remains of Silurian plant life are scarce. It is probable that there was an abundance of marine plants, but the terrestrial flora was either so scant, or so lacking in hard parts which could be preserved as fossils, that no certain remains have come down to us. It is altogether probable, however, that a terrestrial flora of some kind was in existence. The only vertebrate animals were primitive fishes, but the invertebrates were abundant. Especially was this a time when enormous reefs of coral were built up by such forms as the "wasp-nest coral," *Favosites;* the "chain coral," *Halysites*; and the "organ-pipe coral," *Syringopora*. Scorpions appeared for the first time, one of the first bits of evidence of air-breathing terrestrial life. The largest animals were giant crustaceans, called eurypterids, some of which were over six feet long.

Devonian Period.—This period is often called the "age of fishes" because of the great development of fish life and the abundance of fossil remains that have been preserved. In North America the Lower Devonian formations include the Helderberg limestones and Oriskany sandstones; the Middle Devonian includes the Onondaga limestones and the Marcellus and Hamilton shales; the Upper Devonian is made up of the Tully limestones, the Genesee shales, the Portage sandstones and shales, and the Chemung-Catskill sandstones and shales. Devonian formations occur extensively in the eastern United States and in the Mississippi valley.

In contrast with the Ordovician and Silurian periods, the Devonian was a time of shallow seas and isolated basins. The Mississippian sea was broken up into many parts with constantly shifting boundaries. For this reason the Devonian deposits are dominantly shallow water beds—muds and sands and shore pebbles—which hardened into shales, sandstones, and conglomerates. The deposits of one region are very dissimilar to those of another. It was a period of minor disturbances with such a wealth of different environments that the life was abundant and extremely varied.

The land plants included ferns, lycopods, horsetails, and conifers. In the Devonian a true terrestrial flora is in evidence for the first time, and for the first time the earth was covered with a forest growth. In New York, Pennsylvania, West Virginia, and Ontario the rocks of the Onondaga series yield immense quantities of petroleum and gas.

At the close of the Devonian, a mountain range was elevated in the region of Nova Scotia and New Brunswick, in Canada. In the period of erosion which followed, this range was very nearly destroyed. This is called the Acadian revolution.

Mississippian Period.—Originally this and the two succeeding periods were considered as one, and called the Carboniferous period, because of the large amount of coal contained in its formations. It was later found necessary to divide it into three periods. The old name Carboniferous is sometimes used for the Pennsylvanian. After the Acadian revolution the Mississippian sea again spread over the continent, reaching from the site of the Appalachians on the east to the ranges which marked the axis of the Rockies on the west. On the eastern side of the country the débris of the recently elevated Acadian mountains furnished an enormous mass of coarse material which is now the very heavy bed of fine conglomerate called the Pocono sandstone. In the region of New York there was more of mud and fine material, now called the Mauch Chunk shales.

Over the whole of the Mississippi valley and far to the west there was a clear sea with an abundant life of lime-secreting organisms which furnished the material for the heavy beds of limestone forming the bluffs of the Mississippi river in southern Wisconsin, Iowa, and Illinois, and visible on the slopes of the Rocky mountains. In the clear seas such forms of life as the crinoids, the stone lilies, flourished amazingly, and their remains are found in great numbers. Innumerable sharks inhabited the waters, but of them we have left only the teeth and spines.

The record of the land life is very poor; only a few footprints of amphibians, newt- or salamander-like creatures, occur in the shales which were the soft muds of local pools. That such life must have been present in considerable quantity, and in a fairly advanced stage of development, is proved by the fact that the imprint of an amphibian foot has been found in the shales of the preceding, Devonian, period.

Pennsylvanian Period.—This period is sometimes referred to, in nontechnical writings, as the Carboniferous, or the Coal Measures. With the oncoming of the Pennsylvanian period began the death of the great Mississippian sea which had dominated the center of the continent during the whole of the Paleozoic era. The land began to rise slowly and the great sea gave place to swamps, similar to the Great Dismal Swamp of Virginia and the Everglades of Florida, on the Atlantic coastal plain. In these swamps were laid down a succession of sandstones and shales with beds of coal, and, rarely, some limestones.

The coal beds are the result of a luxuriant growth of vegetation in the swamps; the decaying vegetation was gradually deprived of much of its volatile matter, and the residual carbon was mineralized into bituminous (soft) coal. The portion of bituminous coal formed in eastern Pennsylvania was later metamorphosed by the heat and pressure developed in the elevation of the Appalachian mountains into anthracite (hard) coal. In North America the productive coal deposits of this series occur in various areas ranging from Nova Scotia south to Alabama,—in the Ohio valley, in Iowa, Missouri, Oklahoma, and Texas, and in small amounts elsewhere, covering in all approximately 200,000 square miles. The oil of the mid-continental field (Kansas, Oklahoma, and Texas) is found in rocks of Pennsylvanian age.

The abundant plant and animal life of the period is remarkably well preserved in the shales associated with the coal beds. About 2000 species of Carboniferous plants are known, chiefly calamites (ancient horsetail rushes), lycopods, cycadofilices (seed-bearing fernlike plants), ferns, and conifers. The lycopods, now represented only by small clubmosses, then grew 50 feet high and 5 feet in diameter and in such enormous profusion that they are believed to have furnished much of the vegetable matter for the formation of coal. Animal life, likewise, occurred in great variety and profusion, the highest forms being primitive amphibians, which were the first land vertebrates.

Permian Period.—The gradual uplift of the continent finally drained away the waters from the swamps, and the surface became very largely dry land with only a few swamps and some small inland seas. Although Lower Permian formations occur in Pennsylvania and West Virginia, Permian strata, largely of terrestrial origin, are best known in Oklahoma, Texas, Kansas, and Nebraska, where they cover large areas and attain great thickness. In the Permian strata of Kansas and Oklahoma, valuable deposits of gypsum and rock salt occur. Compared with that of the Pennsylvanian, the plant and animal life of the Permian is greatly impoverished, the number of known species being only a fraction as large. The most notable advance in animal life was the appearance of true reptiles.

Mesozoic Era. At the close of the Permian period, came one of the greatest revolutions of the earth's history. Throughout the Paleozoic era, enormous quantities of material had been accumulated in a sinking trough in the place where the Appalachian mountains now stand; through the same time the gradual shrinking of the earth's crust had caused an accumulation of stresses which were only partially relieved by the Taconic and Acadian revolutions. At the end of the Paleozoic these stresses were relieved by crushing together the relatively weak sediments in the trough and elevating them into a great mountain system of folded rocks. This revolution drove the Mississippian sea from the continent, never to return, and the whole history of North America took on a new character.

The new phases in the development of life and the character of the sediments are the determining features of the Mesozoic era. The era is divided into four periods: (1) The Triassic, (2) the Jurassic, (3) the Comanchean, and (4) the Cretaceous. The Mesozoic is distinguished by the remarkable development and predominance of the *Reptilia* (whence the name "age of reptiles"), the appearance of the modern type of plants, and the first appearance of birds and mammals.

Triassic Period.—The Triassic deposits of North America occur in three areas. On the eastern side of the United States the destruction of the recently elevated Appalachian mountains furnished a large amount of débris, which was washed down the eastern slopes and deposited in the deltas and great flood plains of rivers that flowed into the Atlantic Ocean. The red and brown sandstones of Connecticut and New Jersey, and even those as far south as the Carolinas, are of this age.

The second area of deposition is in the west central portion of the United States on the slopes of the axis of the Rocky mountains; here great thicknesses of red sandstones and clays tell of terrestrial conditions with accumulations in deltas, flood plains, and local pools. The Permian and Triassic deposits form the "red beds" which are such prominent features of the landscape, always noted as one approaches the Rocky mountains from the east.

On the Pacific coast and even in the Great Basin there are great thicknesses of limestone which tell that the Pacific Ocean penetrated far over the western edge of the continent.

At the close of the Triassic occurred the last great earth disturbance on the eastern side of North America. From the Bay of Fundy south to the Carolinas, the region east of the Appalachians was broken in a most intricate manner by series of earthquakes, and through the cracks there were extruded great quantities of lava. One of the largest of these lava sheets forms the Palisades of the Hudson on the western side of the river at New York City. This disturbance is known as the Palisade revolution, though it did not attain the magnitude of some of the other revolutions.

In the Triassic rocks occur the fossils which, because of their nearer approach to modern forms, have given to the era the name Mesozoic. In the plant world the conifers and cycads had replaced, in large measure, the simpler plants of the Paleozoic. The invertebrate animals had taken on new characters and were very much more like the modern forms. Among the vertebrates were the advance legions of the great horde of reptiles which dominated the earth in the Mesozoic and justify the name, "age of reptiles," which has been applied to it. Some of these forms are briefly described in the section on Mesozoic life.

Jurassic Period.—During Jurassic time, the continent of North America was very largely out of water, and the coast line was probably farther out in the oceans than at any other time in the Mesozoic. A few uncertain deposits on the eastern coast of Maryland may be of Jurassic age, and there are marine Jurassic deposits in the Pacific Coast region and in Mexico. Most of the Jurassic of North America is terrestrial; a series of deposits along the slopes of the Rocky Mountain axis is probably Jurassic. These deposits are radically different from the red Triassic beds below them. The Jurassic beds are dark in color, with included remains of an abundant vegetation showing that the extreme aridity of Triassic times had given place to a far more humid climate, very favorable to the development of the life of the Mesozoic, both plant and animal.

For a brief interval of time, an arm of the ocean crept over the Rocky Mountain states from the North Pacific and left a thin layer of marine deposits amidst the mass of terrestrial material.

During the Triassic and Jurassic periods there was a sinking trough on the site of the present Sierra Nevada mountains. In this trough accumulated many thousands of feet of sediments, and at the close of the Jurassic a lateral pressure folded and faulted the sediments up into a mighty mountain range, the original Sierra Nevada range, which was to undergo many changes before it attained its present form. This was the Sierra Nevada revolution, one of the great disturbances in the geologic history of the continent.

Comanchean Period.—In the older textbooks this is referred to as the Lower Cretaceous. The close of the Jurassic period left the continent of North America well out of water, but a series of broad folding movements warped the surface so that the waters of the oceans spread inland for greater or less distances on all the borders of the land. The Atlantic coast, the Gulf coast, and the Pacific coast were all covered by the advancing floods. On the Atlantic and Pacific coasts the waters did not extend inland very far, as they were stopped by the barriers of the Appalachian and Sierra Nevada mountains, but the waters of the western Gulf spread over Mexico and Texas and advanced northward as far as central Oklahoma.

A counter movement raised the land again, a long period of erosion removed much of the Comanchean and older sediments, so that a great structural break (unconformity) marks the line between the Comanchean below and the Cretaceous above. There was no important mountain making at this time.

Cretaceous Period.—The surface of the land was again warped and the seas spread over the continent in much the same areas as in the Comanchean but attained greater mastery over the land. This is especially true of the invasion from the Gulf. The waters covered most of the Plains states and the portion of Canada which lies directly north of them. The great inland sea stretched from the Gulf of Mexico to the Arctic Ocean, the greatest sea that ever lay upon the surface of North America, and the last, for never again did the waters of the ocean cover more than the edges of the land. The sediments of the great Cretaceous inland sea show many phases in its development. The most important phase was the deposition of a thick bed of chalk, similar to that of southeastern England

and western France, which covers western Kansas and parts of the adjacent states.

One of the most important events of the late Cretaceous was the growth of a very luxuriant vegetation. The remains of this vegetation now form the lignite deposits of Montana, North Dakota, and the adjacent parts of Canada.

The Cretaceous period, and with it the Mesozoic era, closed with the elevation of the old ranges previously referred to as the Rocky Mountain axis. In this elevation, both the old pre-Cambrian core and the sedimentary rocks of the Paleozoic and Mesozoic ages were involved and the true Rocky mountains, as we know them, made their first appearance. This disturbance is one of the greatest in the history of the continent. It is known as the Laramide or Rocky Mountain revolution, and marks the line between the Mesozoic and Cenozoic eras, just as the Appalachian revolution marks the line between the Paleozoic and the Mesozoic.

Life of the Mesozoic Era.—With the dawn of the Mesozoic, most of the archaic forms of life which had their development in the Paleozoic, passed away forever, and their place was taken by new forms far more closely related to those now existing. In the Triassic and Jurassic, the vegetation was composed of conifers and cycads, with ferns and some old forms that held over from the previous periods. There were no flowering plants, and the trees had not as yet developed the habit of shedding their leaves in the fall of the year and gaining a new foliage with the coming spring. The forests were dark and somber, with little of grace or beauty in stem and branch. There were no flowers and nothing of the variety that now comes with the changing seasons.

By the early Cretaceous all was changed. The forests were composed of modern types of trees and we would have recognized the willow and the sassafras, the plane tree and the maple, with many other familiar kinds bearing fruits and flowers. The smaller forms of vegetation also had changed. There were fruit- and nut-bearing shrubs, and bushes and the grasses had begun to appear. There is no hint of where this new vegetation was developed. It appears with dramatic suddenness, the fossil leaves fill the sandstone which lies below the great chalk beds, and we are left to speculate upon the time and place of origin of this new flora.

Among the invertebrates the change is nearly as striking. The trilobites were gone, and with them many other archaic groups. In their place were forms much more like the modern inhabitants of the seas and fresh waters. One group is peculiarly characteristic of the era: great cephalopods, like the modern squid and cuttlefish, swarmed in the Mesozoic seas, but most of them lived within shells coiled like those of snails. The shell was divided into chambers and the partitions between the chambers were extremely complicated, so that the mark of the chamber walls on the outer shell is a very irregular line. Such coiled shells are called Ammonites. They are extremely common Mesozoic fossils and are confined entirely to the Mesozoic. If we see such a shell in a museum or in the field, we know that we are viewing a Mesozoic form. Ammonites are among the most definite and characteristic time markers or index fossils known.

Among the vertebrate animals the change was even greater than in the other groups of life. The time of the fish and the amphibian had passed; the time of the reptiles was at hand. Over 20 orders of reptiles have been identified from the fossils found in the rocks. The reptiles spread in enormous numbers and were adapted to all possible modes of life. Certain forms, as the Dinosaurs (terrible lizards), dominated the land. Of these, some were carnivorous forms which first appeared in the Triassic as animals not larger than dogs but reached giant size at the end of the Cretaceous. These animals gradually assumed a kangaroo-like form; the strong hind feet were armed with powerful claws, like the talons of an eagle; the fore feet were relatively small and useless; and the jaws were filled with sharp, conical teeth fitted for tearing the flesh of their prey. Other Dinosaurs were plant eaters; some had a kangaroo-like habit of body; still others went upon all fours and were covered with a bizarre armor. Some of the herbivorous Dinosaurs dwelt in the swamps and pools; these forms reached the largest size attained by any animal that has lived upon the land, 80 feet in length and 50 or more tons in weight.

Other reptiles were crowded from the land into the sea, as the seal and the walrus have been in recent times. Some, the Plesiosaurs, had a long neck and tail with a heavy body and powerful flippers; they have been aptly likened to a turtle strung upon a snake. Still other reptiles, the Icthyosaurs, became purely aquatic in habit and took on fishlike form. They occupied the same place in the Mesozoic seas that the whales and dolphins fill in the oceans of today. Still other forms, the Mosasaurs, were veritable sea serpents, with a long snakelike body, small paddle-shaped limbs, and powerful jaws.

Other reptiles, the Pterosaurs or Pterodactyls, took to the air; the forelimbs were converted into supports for membranous wings and the animals glided or flapped through the air in pursuit of their prey.

There were many other kinds of reptiles, too numerous to mention, but it may be noted that the beginnings of the lizards, the turtles, and the crocodiles were made in the Mesozoic. At the end of the Mesozoic, the great host of reptiles was almost entirely wiped out and only the few and lowly forms that we know today were left.

In the Jurassic appear the beginnings of the birds; the first forms were little more than feathered reptiles, with teeth in their jaws and functional claws on the fore limbs, but they speedily developed into the kinds of birds now existing. The history of the birds is not well known, for relatively few fossil forms have been discovered.

The first of the mammals appeared in the Triassic, but through all the Mesozoic they made little progress, dominated as they were by the innumerable reptiles of that time.

It is probable that the great change which came over the plant world in the Cretaceous period had much to do with the appearance of higher forms of life. The new food supply of nuts, seeds, and grasses made possible the development of new types of vertebrate life, and with the appearance of flowers came the flower visiting insects which had never before brightened the woods and fields with their presence.

Cenozoic Era. This is the era of modern life. By some it is made to include the Tertiary and the Quaternary, while the time since the appearance of man upon the earth is set off as a distinct era, the Psychozoic—the age of the dominance of mind over matter; by others, the Cenozoic is made to include all time since the Mesozoic.

The Tertiary was the age of dominance of the mammals upon the earth and is commonly called the "age of mammals"; the Quaternary was the age of the great climatic disturbance which clothed portions of the earth in sheets of ice, and it is commonly called the "ice age" or the "glacial age."

The Tertiary is divided into the Eocene, the Oligocene, the Miocene, and the Pliocene periods. It was a time of elevation of the land; the seas invaded only the edges of the continent. There are no marine deposits in the central portion but only the deposits of lakes, streams, swamps, wind, and ice. Upon the borders of the Atlantic and Pacific oceans are marine sands and clays with marine fossils. These did not extend far inland as the invading waters were stopped by the barriers of the Appalachian mountains and the mountains of the Pacific coast. The waters of the Gulf of Mexico penetrated much farther inland; in Eocene time they extended as far north as the mouth of the Ohio river, but in later times they did not reach nearly so far. These marine deposits have furnished much of the fertile soil of the Atlantic and Gulf coastal plains.

In the interior of the continent, the Tertiary deposits are found in the Great Plains and in the intermontane basins of the West. The deposits are largely the result of the degradation of the adjacent mountain ranges.

The Rocky mountains, the Sierra Nevada mountains, the Cascade mountains, and the Coast ranges of the Pacific border were never at rest after the beginning of the Tertiary. Uplifts and readjustments occurred between the periods, and these, with the accompanying volcanic activity, furnished abundant material for the scattered sedimentary deposits in which the record is written. We read this history not only in the deposits but in the gorges, the valleys, and the canyons—the results of the erosive agents. The volcanic activity in mid-Tertiary time was extreme; in Washington, Oregon, and the adjacent states there was one of the greatest fields of volcanic activity the world has ever seen. Over 200,000 square miles of territory are covered by the lavas and ash beds. The chain of volcanoes beginning with Mount Lassen, in northern California, and ending with Mount Rainier and Mount Baker, in Washington, was formed at the same time. Intrusions of igneous material into the earth's crust in northwestern Wyoming, occurring at this time, are responsible for the geysers, the hot springs, and the other wonders of the Yellowstone National Park.

At the close of the Pliocene came the final great elevation of the mountain ranges of the West. To this very recent disturbance and the consequent vigorous action of the erosive agents, we owe the grandeur of the scenery displayed in the Yosemite valley of California, the Grand Canyon of Arizona, and the mountains of the Glacier national park and the Canadian Rockies.

Pleistocene Period.—This is commonly referred to as the Quaternary division of the Cenozoic era. It was introduced by a climatic change which lowered the temperature and increased the precipitation in the northern hemisphere until great areas were covered by moving sheets of ice (glaciers), such as now lie upon the surface of Greenland and the Antarctic continent. The ice did not accumulate at the pole and descend as a uniform cap into lower latitudes, but gathered at separate points south of the north pole. In North America there were three such centers: One in Labrador, one just east of Hudson bay, and one to the west of Hudson bay. From these the ice slowly crept out in all directions. In the United States it reached approximately as far south as the present courses of the Ohio and Missouri rivers.

It is known that the advance of the ice was not a single movement but several, with periods of retreat between the advances, when the climate was warmer and vegetation covered for a time the regions that had been covered by the glaciers. The record of the great glaciers is left in the thick mantle of mixed sand, clay, and bowlders, which was dragged beneath the ice or borne upon its surface. Such material forms the surface soil of the glaciated region. In places there are long ridges of mixed material (moraines) which was shoved before the ice or deposited at its front; they mark the farthest advance of the ice in its various stages.

The ice itself and the material which it deposited altered the courses of the streams, changed the contours of lakes, and obscured the rocks and soils of all the invaded country. The ice carried many stones frozen in its bottom, and as these stones were dragged over exposures of rock or were rubbed together, both the solid rock and ice-borne bowlders and pebbles were scratched and scored by lines (glacial striæ). These indicate the direction of the ice movement and give some idea of the amount of work done by the glaciers.

The mixed glacial material has been rehandled and sorted, in many places, by the waters from the melting ice. This is the origin of the gravel hills, the sand plains, and the fertile clay lands of the glaciated region.

It is not certain that the Ice age has passed away. We may now be living in one of the interglacial periods and the ice may again accumulate and spread over the land. The last great ice sheet disappeared from the surface of North America about 25,000 years ago.

Life of the Cenozoic Era.—The life of this era was essentially the same as that of today. Many forms that lived have passed away, but the differences which distinguished them from modern forms are differences of degree only. The plants were modern in all their characters. One of the striking innovations of the time was the development of vast areas of grass land on the growing plains of the western part of North America. This led to the development of herds of grazing animals and the rise of the carnivorous forms which inevitably follow such herds. The increase of seed- and nut-bearing plants led to the development of the rodents and the burrowing mammals. The increase in flowering plants led to the development of the insects in countless profusion, and the growth of the forests and the open lands with their diversity of climate and conditions permitted the birds to increase their numbers.

The inevitable result of all this increase in animal life was a high degree of specialization—just such as had repeatedly occurred in the older years of the earth. The animals developed all sorts of ways to gain a living and survive in the struggle for existence. Some of the mammals took to the sea, as the whale, the dolphin, the seal, and the walrus; others became swift runners, or good climbers, or burrowers in the earth. Some became eaters of flesh, some of fish, some of carrion, some of plant food; some retired to the warmer parts of the land while others found refuge in the ice-clothed North. The same thing occurred in the other groups of animals and to a lesser degree in the plants—all resulting in the wonderful diversity which prevails today.

Each period of the Tertiary has its own peculiar group of animal and plant forms by which the paleontologist can distinguish the age of the beds. These differences are too minor and too technical, particularly in the case of the invertebrates and the plants, to be understandable to the layman. In the case of the vertebrate animals, however, especially the mammals, the differences are more striking.

In the Eocene time the mammals were more simple and primitive than they are today. The earliest forms had within them the possibility of developing into any one of the modern groups. Very soon some developed the characters of the carnivorous forms, others the characters of the hoofed grazers, browsers, and runners, while still others showed the beginnings of the elephant-like forms, and so on through the entire series.

To illustrate by one or two examples: In Eocene time, there was already a group of primitive carnivores which followed the herds and fed upon the sick, the weak, and the aged; they were not yet separated into the cats, the dogs, the bears; they had not yet the agility of body nor the fine and close adjustment of tooth and claw to the peculiar life led by the modern flesh eaters. They were, however, as much superior to plant eaters in activity and cunning as are the lion and tiger of today. From these primitive carnivores developed all the modern forms which depend upon their swiftness, their cunning, and their strength to destroy other animals and feed upon them.

Another excellent example is that of the horse. We know the history of the development of the horse almost from the beginning and through all of its stages to the modern form. It is one of the most perfect bits of paleontological history and one of the best demonstrations of continuous advance and improvement with the passage of geological time. Beginning with a small five-toed form, with nails instead of hoofs, with numerous teeth fitted for eating anything, it gradually developed through the various periods into the horse as we know it today. This was accomplished by the loss of the outer digits and the strengthening of the third, by the development of the nail into a hoof, by the elongation of the limb, and by the change of the teeth into grinding organs fitted for the mastication of hard grains and grasses.

The two-toed grazing and running forms, as the deer, the sheep, the camel—"all such as have a cloven hoof and chew the cud"—went through similar stages. They retained, however, the second and third digits of the fore and hind feet instead of the third digit only.

An enormous number of different forms of mammalian life developed and disappeared because they were unfitted to the changed conditions that came with the passage of geological time. Some of these were fully as weird in form as the reptiles of the Mesozoic. The giant Dinotheres of the Eocene and the Titanotheres of the Oligocene occupied approximately the same place in nature that the elephant does today. The enormous Zeuglodon, the whale-like mammal of the Gulf of Mexico, the giant ancestors of the elephants, of the sloths, and of the armadillos, all lived their appointed time and passed away to make room for higher forms.

The form of the continents in the Tertiary was not fixed. Constant changes, such as the opening and closing of Bering strait or the alternate establishment and breaking down of the isthmus of Panama, permitted frequent migrations of the mammals from one region to another.

It is strange to think of the camel, the rhinoceros, and the elephant as inhabitants of North America, but their remains have been found in great numbers in deposits of Tertiary and even of Quaternary time. South of the ice sheets, in Pleistocene times, the mammoth and mastodon, as well as the bison, reindeer, and muskox, were abundant and characteristic animals. The mammoth occurred in great numbers in the region which is now Mexico and the southern United States, and ranged far northwestward. The mastodon occupied a more northerly area, extending into what is now western Canada, but also to the south. At this period, however, the saber-toothed tiger, tapir, llama, and horse had become nearly extinct. Many forms now unknown in North America originated here and migrated to other lands as conditions changed; other forms which originated in other continents migrated into North America and are now well established.

The Primates, the group to which the monkeys, the apes, and man belong, originated in the Eocene, but man did not appear upon the earth till the earliest Pleistocene. The oldest remains that can be referred to man were found in the island of Java, but primitive implements, fashioned from flint and some of them marked by fire, have been found in the upper Pliocene of England. Other remains a little younger were found in Germany, near Heidelberg, and then, in increasing abundance, the remains of man have been found in the river deposits, and in the caves and shelters of many parts of the world. The history of man from the earliest apelike form to the modern man is as truly a matter of historical geology and paleontology as the history of any other form of the mammals. In Europe, man lived during the great Ice age and his remains are found mingled with those of the Hairy Mammoth, the Woolly Rhinoceros, the reindeer, and other inhabitants of the polar world. It is still uncertain whether man had reached North America before the ice had passed away, but the evidence seems to point to the probability that he was a late migrant into the Western world after a long period of development in Europe and Asia.

PALEONTOLOGY

Paleontology is the science which treats of the forms of life that inhabited the earth during past periods of geological time. There are two natural subdivisions,—Paleobotany, which deals with extinct plants, and Paleozoology, which deals with extinct animals. The science is based upon the comprehensive study of fossils. It is closely interrelated with geology and biology. In a broad sense, it is the history of the evolution and development of plant and animal life from its earliest discoverable beginnings in remote geological epochs to the present time.

While Palissy (1510–1589), the famous potter, and other early observers held that fossils were the remains of organisms that had existed in former ages, paleontology was established as a science about the beginning of the 19th century through the monumental labors of Cuvier (1769–1832) and Lamarck (1744–1829). Their investigations showed that fossils from the lower or earlier rock strata differed from the present forms of plants and animals more than do fossils from the upper or later rock formations. The extensive researches made since Cuvier's day have confirmed scientists in the view that paleontology gives a true though incomplete record of the development of the existing forms of life, and that throughout geological time successive faunas and floras show a rise in the scale of life. This is sometimes called the law of continuous improvement.

In the Cambrian, the most ancient period in which evidences of life are abundant, a group of crustaceans called trilobites were the highest animals. In the Silurian period fishes first appeared; in the Devonian period amphibians appeared; in the Carboniferous period amphibians had their greatest development and reptiles appeared; while in the Triassic period the reptiles began their great development and the first primitive mammals appeared. Wherever the fossil record can be followed, it is found that each group of animals or plants begins with simple types; that gradually more complex and specialized forms appear; and that frequently decadence sets in with great suddenness, resulting in extinction or the reduction of the group to relative unimportance.

For example, the trilobites, which were immensely varied and abundant during the Ordovician period, are not found later than the Permian period. The ammonites were a group of forms related to the modern cuttlefish, but which lived in a coiled shell. Developing from simpler forms, they appeared at the beginning of the Mesozoic, attained great importance during that era, and became extinct at the end of the Cretaceous period. The great scorpion-like eurypterids, so abundant in the Silurian, are unknown later than the Permian. Similarly, most of the orders of reptiles, which ruled the sea and land during the Mesozoic era, became extinct at the end of the Cretaceous period. In various groups the number of known fossil species is much greater than that of the living species.

Certain fossils are so characteristic of the different periods, epochs, or formations of rocks, that they serve as index fossils, enabling the geologist to fix the exact geological age of the rocks from which they come. On this account paleontology is of immense service as a working adjunct to geology, particularly to stratigraphy. As a knowledge of the latter is indispensable in economic geology, particularly in locating the beds which contain precious metals, useful minerals, coal, oil, gas, and artesian waters, it is easily seen that paleontology is of great practical value.

Among eminent pioneer and later paleontologists in America may be mentioned Joseph Leidy, Leo Lesquereux, James Hall, J. W. Dawson, C. A. White, C. D. Walcott, O. C. Marsh, E. D. Cope, W. B. Scott, David White, S. W. Williston, H. F. Osborn, E. O. Ulrich, and Charles Schuchert.

MINERALOGY

Mineralogy is a branch of the great earth science, Geology. It deals with the origin, composition, and properties of inorganic chemical substances existing already formed in the earth's crust, known as *minerals.* An allied branch, *Petrology,* treats of the origin, properties, and relations of the minerals forming the various rock masses.

While Theophrastus and Pliny the Elder among the ancients, Avicenna and Albertus Magnus during the middle ages, and Georg Agricola in the 16th century wrote treatises dealing with minerals and rocks, little real advance was made until near the close of the 18th century, after which the science made rapid progress.

The study of minerals may be divided into six branches: (1) *Crystallography,* which deals with the description, character, and classification of crystals; (2) *Physical Mineralogy,* which deals with the optical, electrical, magnetic, thermal, and other physical properties of minerals; (3) *Chemical Mineralogy,* which deals with the chemical composition and relations of minerals; (4) *Descriptive Mineralogy,* which deals with all phases of the description and classification of mineral species; (5) *Determinative Mineralogy,* which makes use of classified tables of physical and chemical properties as an aid to the identification of a mineral; (6) *Economic Mineralogy,* dealing with the use of minerals by man.

Crystallography. This branch of mineralogy is the science concerned with the form, structure, and properties of crystals. Such knowledge is essential to systematic study and classification of minerals.

Nicolaus Steno, a Danish scientist, discovered in 1669 that, while the faces of quartz crystals vary in size and shape, the angles between corresponding faces are always the same. This relationship applies to all crystals of any one species, and is known as the law of *constancy of angle.* The interfacial angles of a crystal are measured by means of an instrument called a *goniometer.* The science of crystallography became firmly established in the period 1772–83, when Romé de l'Isle and Haüy discovered the *law of symmetry* and the *law of rational indices* in crystals and derived all crystals from six primitive forms. Hessel, in 1830, proved that only 32 types of symmetry are possible in crystals. All crystals are now grouped in 32 classes corresponding to these types, which are usually arranged in six systems.

The commonly accepted systems are: 1. The *isometric* or *cubic system,* having three equal axes at right angles to each other. 2. The *hexagonal system,* including trigonal forms, with four axes, three of which are equal and cross each other in one plane at an angle of 60°, while the fourth may be either longer or shorter and is perpendicular to the others. 3. The *tetragonal system,* with three axes at right angles to each other, two being of equal length and the third either longer or shorter. 4. The *orthorhombic system,* having three axes of unequal length at right angles to each other. 5. The *monoclinic system,* with three unequal axes, two of which intersect at an oblique angle in a plane at right angles to the third. 6. The *triclinic system,* having three unequal axes intersecting at oblique angles.

Examples of crystals in each system are: *isometric* or *cubic,*—diamond, fluorite, galena, garnet, common salt; *hexagonal,*—apatite, emerald, quartz, ruby, sapphire, tourmaline; *tetragonal,*—cassiterite, chalcopyrite, zircon; *orthorhombic,*—barite, sulphur, topaz; *monoclinic,*—borax, gypsum, mica; *triclinic,*—albite, cyanite, rhodonite.

The great majority of minerals fall within seven classes, and all known minerals are probably covered by 22 of the 32 classes which make up the six systems. Of the remaining ten classes of crystals, nine have been prepared in the laboratory and one is still unknown. Aided by chemistry, physics, mathematics, and mineralogy, the science of crystallography has made great progress. Practically every known substance which assumes crystalline form can be identified by means of accurate and proper measurements of its interfacial angles.

A peculiar property of some crystals is indicated in the phenomena known as *dichroism* and *pleochroism* or *polychroism.* These are variations in color when the crystals are viewed in different directions. Crystals possessing polar symmetry axes may develop positive and negative electrical charges at opposite ends. If these charges are induced by changes in temperature, the phenomenon is known as *pyro-electricity.* If the electricity is developed by pressure, it is termed *piezo-electricity.*

Physical Mineralogy. The branch of the science which is concerned with all of the physical properties and characteristics of minerals. Most of these properties, with the exception of those such as taste and odor, are greatly affected by the crystalline or, in some cases, by the noncrystalline form.

An examination of the physical characteristics of a mineral will generally include the following: color, transparency, luster, and hardness; cleavage, or the tendency to separate in certain definite directions; specific gravity; the effects produced by heat, electricity, and magnetism; and especially those properties depending on light,—such as the index of refraction, polarization, and pleochroism, or a change of color when viewed from different directions.

Hardness is determined by the resistance which a mineral offers to being scratched. It is generally expressed according to Mohs's scale, which consists of a series of ten well-known minerals arranged in order of increasing hardness, as follows:

COMPARATIVE SCALE OF HARDNESS

1. Talc	6. Orthoclase
2. Gypsum	7. Quartz
3. Calcite	8. Topaz
4. Fluorite	9. Corundum
5. Apatite	10. Diamond

The degrees of this scale are not of the same value. For example, the difference between diamond and corundum is said to be greater than that between corundum and talc. An unknown specimen which can scratch orthoclase but is itself marked by quartz is said to have a hardness of 6½—written H. = 6½. Minerals of H. = 6 or greater, all scratch window glass; those of H. = 5.5 or less can be scratched with a knife; a finger nail can mark substances up to H. = 2.5; and a copper coin, up to H. = 3.

Chemical Mineralogy. This branch of the science deals with the composition of minerals, with their chemical relationship, and with chemical methods for their identification.

A complete quantitative analysis is necessary to determine the exact composition of a strange mineral. However, qualitative tests of fusibility, color imparted to a flame, and reactions produced when the mineral is heated on charcoal before a blowpipe flame with borax and other fluxes, are often sufficient for chemical identification.

Descriptive Mineralogy. An important branch of the science, which is concerned first with a complete description of each mineral species. This includes not only the form and structure, as well as the chemical and physical properties of a mineral, but also its geological history, its geographical distribution, and its relation to other minerals and rocks.

When the properties of a mineral are known, it may then be classified in various ways. One of the most convenient systems of classification is that outlined by Dana, in which minerals having a similar chemical composition are placed in the same class, which is subdivided according to crystalline form and other physical properties. The principal classes are: (1) native elements; (2) sulphides, arsenides, and similar compounds; (3) sulphosalts, such as the sulpharsenites; (4) haloids; (5) oxides; (6) oxygen salts, including carbonates, silicates, sulphates, and others; (7) salts of organic acids; (8) hydrocarbons.

It has been estimated that there are approximately 1000 different minerals; but fewer than 100 species are common, while fewer than 25 enter universally into the composition of rocks. Of these rocks, more than 90 per cent are composed of the feldspars, quartz, amphiboles, pyroxenes, and micas. A large proportion of the remainder consist of olivine, calcite, and oxides of iron.

The classification of rocks is based on the nature and arrangement of their constituent minerals. In the case of the igneous rocks, the arrangement of the mineral content is subject to great variation induced by the conditions under which the *magma* or mother rock was cooled. In consequence, only a specialist in rocks, a petrologist, can accurately determine any given igneous rock. For this reason, group or family names are used, such as *granite, basalt, obsidian*, and others, there being many different kinds within each group. Similarly, each of the common groups of sedimentary rocks—*sandstone, limestone*, and *shale*—includes widely different types.

Most of the common igneous rocks and all of the sedimentary rocks are useful in commercial enterprises. They are entitled, equally with gems and precious stones, to consideration with the useful minerals. See under Geology: *Igneous Rocks, Metamorphic Rocks, Sedimentary Rocks*.

Determinative Mineralogy. The branch of mineralogy which makes use of complete, classified tables of mineral properties. The more obvious characteristics of an unknown mineral place it first in some large group. Careful consideration of the special properties then assigns it to smaller and more restricted divisions of the table until the mineral is finally identified.

Economic Mineralogy. Minerals of economic importance are considered in two great groups, the metal-bearing and the nonmetallic minerals. The production of metals from the first group—especially gold, silver, iron, copper, lead, zinc, nickel, aluminum, and platinum—is the most important use to which minerals as a whole are put. Gold, copper, and platinum are frequently found as native elements. But most metals occur combined as sulphides, oxides, or carbonates; less commonly, as chlorides, silicates, tellurides, and arsenides. A knowledge of mineralogy and geology is usually necessary for the successful location, identification, and mining of these valuable metallic ores.

Although the nonmetallic minerals are of less importance commercially than the metallic ores, nevertheless, they are collectively of immense value in the various arts. With reference to these uses, the nonmetallic minerals may be classed in 9 groups:

1. *Abrasives*, including some of the hardest known minerals, such as the diamond, quartz, sand, garnet, and emery.
2. *Ceramic Materials*, such as kaolin, clays, shales, and sands used in the manufacture of pottery, porcelain, glass, terra cotta, tile, and brick.
3. *Chemical Materials*, comprising minerals employed in making soda, alum, plaster of Paris, acids, alkalies, and other chemicals.
4. *Fertilizer Materials*, such as phosphates, nitrates, land plaster, potassium salts, and marls.
5. *Fuels*, such as coal, petroleum, and natural gas.
6. *Gem Stones*, including the minerals used for jewelry, for the bearings in watches, and for other similar purposes.
7. *Graphic Materials*, including the minerals used in writing, marking, and printing,—such as graphite, chalk, and lithographic stone.
8. *Pigments*, such as ocher, which are used in making paints.
9. *Refractory Materials*, embracing the minerals employed in making asbestos fabrics, fireproofing, furnace linings, retorts, and crucibles.

ROCKS, MINERALS, GEMS, AND PRECIOUS STONES

Adamant (*ăd′ȧ-mănt*). An imaginary substance, either a metal or a stone, supposed by the ancients to be of impenetrable hardness. By various early writers it was confused with the magnet or lodestone. About the 17th century the word adamant came into use as a synonym for diamond, but it is now rarely so used. The term *adamantine*, as employed in mineralogy, means like a diamond in hardness and luster.

Agate. A variegated form of chalcedony, somewhat harder than steel, and capable of taking a high polish. Agates are believed to have been formed in cavities of rocks by layers of silica deposited from water. They are marked most commonly with delicate, wavy bands of white, gray, brown, yellow, blue, or black. Such forms are called *banded agate*. The colors of *clouded agate* are blended and indistinct; in *moss agate* the internal impurities have a curious mosslike appearance.

Agates are found throughout the world, but the chief supply comes from Uruguay and Brazil. When cut and polished, they are much used for making vases and other ornaments, and in jewelry. Chemists use mortars and pestles of agate with which to crush and grind hard substances. Fine playing marbles are sometimes ground from agate. Agate polishing has long been an important local industry in Scotland, Austria, and Germany.

In the Petrified Forest of Arizona, driftwood is found, sometimes occurring in logs 120 feet long and 8 feet thick, which has been converted into agate. When polished, these silicified woods are used as ornaments and paper weights, and are favorite objects for museum display. See *Chalcedony*.

Alabaster. A soft, usually white, granular, semi-transparent form of gypsum, or calcium sulphate. It is found in various countries, the finest occurring in Tuscany, where it is carved into small pieces of sculpture, vases, clock stands, and other ornamental articles. Excellent alabaster occurs also in Derbyshire, England, and in limited amounts in Nova Scotia. By reason of its softness and slight solubility in water, alabaster, when exposed to the weather, soon becomes rough and opaque.

A compact, crystalline carbonate of lime, deposited from water as travertine, formed the alabaster of the ancients, and is still used for ornamental purposes. It is really a marble and is much harder than the true or gypseous alabaster. The ancient alabaster will effervesce with an acid; the other will not. See *Gypsum, Travertine*.

Alexandrite. See *Chrysoberyl*.

Alumina. Aluminum oxide, the most widely distributed and abundant of the earths. It is found nearly pure as bauxite and as corundum. Mixed with extremely small quantities of metallic oxides, it occurs as ruby, sapphire, oriental amethyst, oriental emerald, and oriental topaz. Mixed with iron oxide, it occurs as emery. Combined with silica, it is found in many rocks and minerals of the feldspar group, which, by decomposition, become the chief constituents of clay. See *Bauxite, Clay, Corundum*.

Amber. A fossil resin of pale yellow, reddish, or brownish color. It is frequently thrown up by the waves on the shore of the Baltic Sea, and is also mined extensively in that region. Amber occurs usually in small grains, drops, or lumps, rarely in pieces weighing several pounds. It is slightly brittle, translucent, and burns with a bright flame, emitting a pleasant odor. The ancients ascribed great, but entirely imaginary, medicinal virtues to amber. It is still in demand in the Orient, where large quantities are burned in Mohammedan worship at Mecca.

Beads and other ornamental articles are made from amber, and it is also used in varnish. Numerous extinct species of insects are found fossilized and perfectly preserved in amber. These form interesting exhibits in many museums. The earliest recorded electrical experiment is said to have been performed about 600 B. C. by Thales of Miletus, who noticed that, when rubbed, amber attracts light particles. See *Electricity*.

Amethyst. A violet or purple variety of crystallized quartz, much used in jewelry. It was valued by the ancient Greeks as a charm against the intoxicating effects of alcoholic beverages. In value it ranks about the same as the garnet. The finest amethysts are found in Scotland, Siberia, India, and Ceylon. Amethysts occur in many localities in the United States, particularly in the Lake Superior region. See *Quartz*.

Amphibole (*ăm′fĭ-bōl*). The name amphibole is used by many mineralogists interchangeably with hornblende. It is given to an important group of rock-forming minerals, which occur abundantly in igneous and metamorphic rocks. Chemically, amphiboles are salts of metasilicic acid, in which hydrogen has been replaced by calcium, magnesium, or ferrous iron, or by mixtures of these. They may also contain sodium, potassium, ferric iron, and other elements. When amphibole is combined in igneous rocks the color is usually black, varying to greenish black; when it occurs in metamorphic rocks the color ranges through various shades of green to black,—less commonly it is pink, yellow, or even whitish. Amphibole is rather hard but may be scratched by quartz. Under proper conditions, amphiboles may become changed into serpentine, chlorite, and carbonates, and, therefore, are important geological minerals.

Ordinary amphiboles are so similar to pyroxenes, both in appearance and in composition, that it is often difficult to distinguish them. However, if distinct crystals can be found, separation is usually possible. Amphibole crystals are long and bladed, and, on cleavage, form prisms whose faces meet at angles of 56° and 124°. Pyroxene differs by forming short crystals which cleave into nearly square prisms, the facial angles of which are 87° and 93°.

From the variety of amphibole called tremolite is derived the valuable long-fibered asbestos of commerce. Among other varieties of amphibole are actinolite, crocidolite, edenite, gedrite, glaucophane, and pegasite. See *Asbestos, Pyroxene.*

Anthracite. A dense, black, hard variety of coal, which has a bright luster and breaks with a shining fracture. It is the form of coal containing the highest percentage of fixed carbon and the smallest percentage of volatile matter. Anthracite ignites with more or less difficulty, burns slowly with very little flame or smoke, and produces intense heat. Average anthracite contains about 87 per cent of fixed carbon, as compared with somewhat less than 60 per cent for bituminous coal.

By imperceptible stages, anthracite grades into bituminous coal, from which it has been formed by the action of intense pressure or heat. While anthracite occurs in extensive deposits, it is found only in comparatively small fields in widely separated localities. In the United States, the principal anthracite field, aggregating about 470 square miles, is in Pennsylvania. The workable seams in this area have a total thickness ranging from 70 to 150 feet. Some portions of the noted "Mammoth" seam are 100 feet thick. Anthracite occurs also in Colorado and New Mexico. In Europe, it is found in Wales, France, and Belgium. The largest anthracite deposits in the world are probably in the province of Shan-si, China.

Anthracite is used almost exclusively as a domestic fuel, for which its cleanliness and freedom from smoke and dust render it especially suitable. Flying dust is often prevented by wetting the pile of coal. Contrary to popular belief, this practice decreases rather than increases the amount of heat obtained from the fire. For steaming, smelting, and various other industrial purposes, bituminous coal is superior to anthracite. See *Coal.*

Apatite (*ăp'ȧ-tīt*). Calcium orthophosphate containing calcium fluoride which may be partially or entirely replaced by calcium chloride. It forms hexagonal crystals, H. = 5, which are sometimes transparent, of pale green to purple color, and used as gem stones. It is also found in large opaque crystals. Apatite has been used for the production of phosphorus and in commercial fertilizers. It is of greatest importance, however, because it is almost universally distributed, though in small amounts, through igneous and metamorphic rocks. As a result of the weathering and decay of these rocks, it eventually reaches the soil, to which it furnishes the phosphates necessary for plant growth. See *Phosphate Rock.*

Aquamarine (*ā'kwȧ-mȧ-rēn'*). A transparent, sea-green variety of beryl, used as a gem. Siberia and Brazil furnish excellent aquamarines. A clear crystal weighing 243 pounds was found in Brazil, and fine gem stones have been mined in South Carolina, Colorado, and other localities in the United States. See *Beryl.*

Aragonite (*ăr'ȧ-gŏn-īt*). A mineral consisting of anhydrous calcium carbonate, identical with calcite in chemical composition, but different in crystal form. Aragonite forms orthorhombic crystals which are usually small, white, and prismatic or needle-shaped, with a glassy luster. It is the principal constituent of the pearly layer of sea shells and of the skeleton of corals. A fine, compact, fibrous variety is known as *satin spar*, although this name is given also to similar forms of calcite and gypsum. Aragonite is slightly heavier than calcite and lacks the latter's perfect rhombohedral cleavage. It was first discovered in the province of Aragon, Spain—whence the name—and is now found in many parts of the world. See *Calcite.*

Argentite (*är'jĕn-tīt*). An important ore of silver, often called silver glance. It is a sulphide of silver, containing, when pure, 87 per cent of the metal. The ore usually occurs massive, but sometimes forms isometric crystals. On a freshly broken surface it has a lead gray color with a metallic luster; usually, however, it appears black and dull. Argentite is about as soft as lead and is very heavy. When argentite is fused on charcoal the sulphur burns away, leaving a bead of metallic silver. See *Silver.*

Asbestos (*ăs-bĕs'tŏs; ăz-*). Any silicate mineral composed of fibers which may be spun and woven into heat-resisting fabrics, or which may be used as light, insulating materials. Asbestos is generally found in rather small veins. The best quality is white, but gray, green, brown, and blue varieties are known and used.

The pieces of mineral, as removed from the open-workings, are crushed without injuring the fiber. This is cleaned and sorted by air blast, and then carded and spun similarly to cotton or wool. From the yarn, fireproof cloth, fireproof curtains for theaters, and fireproof rope are made. Sheet asbestos for protecting hot surfaces, electrical insulation, packing for valves, lining for brake bands, shingles, and wall board, are some of the many forms in which asbestos is used.

The Canadian province of Quebec is one of the most important sources of mineral asbestos. It is mined in large quantities also at Azbest, in the Ural Mountains, Russia. Mineralogists generally define asbestos as a fibrous form of amphibole, but in industrial practice the term is used for any fibrous, heat-resisting mineral. Thus, *chrysotile*, which is the most important commercial asbestos, is not amphibole but serpentine. It is known as Canadian or short-fibered asbestos. The amphibole called *tremolite*, known as long-fibered or Italian asbestos, is second in importance. See *Amphibole.*

Ash, Volcanic. The materials blown into the air by the sudden liberation of gases during a volcanic eruption. These are of four varieties, arranged roughly according to the size of the fragments. The pieces which are about the size of an apple are known as *volcanic bombs*; those the size of a nut, *lapilli*; those the size of a pea, *volcanic ashes*, while the finest material is *volcanic dust.*

The ashes and lapilli are frequently spoken of as *volcanic cinders*, and small mounds or cones made of them are known as *cinder cones.* Since many million tons of dust and ashes are discharged during an eruption, they form immense deposits usually near the volcano. Many times, however, the dust is carried hundreds of miles away and distributed over an immense area. On account of its light, cellular nature, volcanic ash is employed as an abrasive in certain types of scouring soaps. See *Pumice.*

Asphalt (*ăs'fôlt*). A brown or black mineral pitch, or bitumen, occurring both as a viscous liquid and as a solid. A brittle variety, 90 to 98 per cent pure, known as glance pitch or gilsonite, is found in Utah, Cuba, and other regions. It is used chiefly in the preparation of asphalt varnish. Liquid bitumens, known as malthas, occur in California. Asphaltic and bituminous limestones are found in many parts of the world.

The chief sources of native asphalt are the marshy beds of Venezuela and the famous "pitch lake" on the island of Trinidad. From this lake, which has an area of 114 acres, the asphalt is dug out in heavy blocks. The holes thus made fill up from below in a short time. The surface of the lake is sufficiently firm to support a movable railroad track, although the ties gradually sink and require frequent replacement. By far the greatest amount of asphalt used in the United States is a by-product of the refining of petroleum.

Asphalt is employed for making varnish and protective paints and for roofing; most important of all, it is mixed with sand and ground limestone and used as the surface layer of roads. For street paving, asphalt was first used in Paris in 1838. The first asphalt pavement in America was laid in Newark, N. J., in 1870.

Azurite (*ăzh'ů-rīt*). A basic copper carbonate, containing about 55 per cent of the metal, occurring in dark, azure blue crystals, columnar masses, and incrustations. Azurite is a valuable ore of copper, and is found in immense quantities in the mines of Clifton and the Bisbee districts in Arizona. The small crystals, though too soft to wear well, are sometimes used in cheap jewelry. In Russia, azurite from Siberia is cut into thin slabs and used as a veneer for furniture. See *Malachite.*

Barite (*bā'rīt; bâr'īt*). A natural barium sulphate, known also as *barytes* and *heavy spar.* It occurs as transparent tabular crystals and in massive laminated forms, usually white, opaque, or translucent. The principal uses of barite are as a filler in paints, and for the manufacture of lithopone. It is also employed as a filler to give weight to paper, in finishing leather, and in making asbestos cement, rubber goods, and artificial ivory. In the United States, barite is produced chiefly in Missouri and in the Appalachian region. See *Barium.*

Basalt (*bȧ-sôlt'; băs'ôlt*). Any heavy, dark colored, basic rock of volcanic origin, having a structure so fine that the grains cannot be seen, or at least cannot be recognized by the eye. Such rocks, which usually consist of soda-lime feldspar, pyroxene, iron oxide, and olivine, are commonly known as "trap rock" or "trap." Because of its weight and toughness, basalt is valued as a paving material.

When cooling, the lava from which basalt is derived often forms hexagonal prisms or columns, which are occasionally of great size. These basaltic columns, often 150 feet high, produce interesting scenic effects, especially in Fingal's Cave, in the island of Staffa, Scotland; in the famous Giant's Causeway, Ireland; and in the cliffs along the Columbia river in Washington.

Dense lavas, red, purple, brown, gray, or white, and differing from basalt in the arrangement of their constituent minerals, are called *felsite*. See *Diabase, Trap Rock*.

Bauxite (*bō'zīt*). A claylike mineral, the most important ore of aluminum. It consists of from 20 to 40 per cent of the metal and commonly contains some silica and iron. Bauxite occurs in France, Italy, Yugoslavia, Hungary, and British and Dutch Guiana. In the United States, it is found in Alabama and Georgia, but the chief production is in Arkansas. Besides its use as an ore, bauxite is employed in making alum and alundum, and in lining converters and steel furnaces. See *Aluminum, Cryolite*.

Beryl (*bĕr'ĭl*). A silicate of aluminum and beryllium which crystallizes in the hexagonal system. It is commonly associated with granite veins, clay slate, mica schist, or limestone, and frequently forms enormous crystals. A beryl found in New Hampshire weighed 5000 pounds.

The crystals are usually of a dull, cloudy green or yellow, but are sometimes transparent and of various colors. H.=7½. Of these, the rich green *emerald*, colored by a trace of chromium, if without flaws, is valued as highly as the diamond. Crystals of blue-green beryl are called *aquamarine*. The finest specimens are supplied by Siberia and Brazil. Yellow or *golden beryl*, sometimes called *heliodor*, is obtained chiefly from southwest Africa, Maine, Connecticut, and Pennsylvania. Rose beryl, or *morganite*, is found in Madagascar and California. See *Aquamarine, Emerald*.

Bloodstone. A green chalcedony sprinkled with flecks of red jasper, as if with blood. A variety called the heliotrope or St. Stephen's stone, occurs in Siberia, Scotland, and the United States. During the early period of the Christian Church, the bloodstone was used for the engraving of sacred subjects. Several famous carvings representing Jesus Christ have been made in bloodstone so selected that the red spots seem to be drops of blood. This stone has been used in making seals since early Babylonian and Egyptian times. See *Chalcedony*.

Breccia (*brĕch'ȧ*). A conglomerate composed of angular fragments of rock, held together by some natural cement, such as quartz, iron oxide, or claylike material. *Volcanic breccia* results from the natural cementation of coarse particles emitted by a volcano. *Fault breccia* is frequently formed from the pieces broken between the faces of a fault passing through a limestone formation.

Volcanic breccias and fault breccias are sources of rock for road making. Calcareous rocks called *breccia marble* are used as ornamental stones. Sandstone breccias are rarely employed for building purposes. See *Conglomerate*.

Brookite. A mineral, consisting of titanium dioxide, found only in the form of orthorhombic crystals. In color it varies from yellowish to reddish brown or black. It occurs in Wales, Switzerland, and the Tyrol in Europe, and a variety with thick black crystals is found in Arkansas. Together with anastase and rutile, brookite forms the source of the metal titanium. See *Rutile, Titanium*.

Calcite. A mineral composed of anhydrous calcium carbonate, which forms crystals belonging to the rhombohedral class of the hexagonal system. It thus differs from aragonite, which has the same chemical composition but forms orthorhombic crystals. Calcite is very widely distributed, occurring in limestone, marble, and chalk, and, excepting only quartz, is the most abundant of minerals. It forms fine crystals which are usually transparent or white, although almost all colors are known, including blue, green, yellow, red, and even brown and black. Typical varieties are *dogtooth spar* and *nailhead spar*. Pure, transparent crystals, known as *Iceland spar*, exhibit double refraction, and are used for making polarizing prisms.

Calcite enters directly into the production of lime, cement, fertilizers, whiting, whitewash, crayons, and building material. See *Aragonite, Calcium, Chalk, Limestone, Marble*.

Cameo. A gem stone cut in relief, usually an onyx, sardonyx, or agate, composed of different colored layers, so that the portions in relief appear in contrast with the background. The value of a cameo depends upon the artistic merit of the engraved figure.

Cameo cutting reached high perfection among the ancient Greeks and Romans, engaging the attention of their greatest artists. Some examples of their work, such as the Sainte Chapelle agate, 12 by 10½ inches, now in the National Library, Paris, representing the triumphs of Augustus and Tiberius, surpass in size and delicacy of execution the best modern productions.

In the United States, the demand for cameos reached its height between 1870 and 1880, giving employment before its decline to many excellent artists. Among these was Lebrethon, the early instructor of Saint-Gaudens who began life as a cameo cutter. Later Saint-Gaudens became America's foremost sculptor. See *Onyx*.

Carbuncle. An old name for garnet and other red stones, used at present to designate such stones when cut in oval form. Carbuncles were formerly highly prized for their reputed power of giving out light in darkness. See *Garnet*.

Carnelian (*kär-nēl'yăn*). A variety of chalcedony ranging in color from a reddish white to a deep red. It is of medium hardness, takes a good polish, and formerly was much used for seals. Blood red carnelians were highly prized by the ancients, who executed beautiful engravings upon them. The finest carnelians now come from India, though excellent specimens are found in Florida and in Nova Scotia. The playing marbles used by children, popularly called carnelians, are usually made of agate. Since ancient times, a translucent, very deep red variety of carnelian, known as the *sard*, has been greatly esteemed as gem stone.

Cassiterite (*kȧ-sĭt'ĕr-īt*). The most important ore of tin, called also "tinstone." It consists of tin dioxide, and, when pure, contains about 79 per cent of the metal. The mineral generally occurs in yellow, brown, or black compact masses; it sometimes has a fibrous structure, when it is known as *wood tin*; and it frequently forms tetragonal crystals. The world's supply of tin ore comes from Tasmania, New South Wales, Queensland, and other states of Australia; from Bolivia; and from the Malay States. Cassiterite occurs also in Cornwall, England, in Saxony, in Bohemia, and in Mexico. In the United States, limited quantities have been found in Maine, Virginia, South Dakota, and California.

Cat's-eye. See *Chrysoberyl*.

Celestite (*sĕl'ĕs-tīt*; *sē-lĕs'-*). Native strontium sulphate, occurring as white, yellow, or light blue orthorhombic crystals. Fine specimens are found near Bristol, England; in the sulphur mines of Sicily; and on Strontian island, Put-in-Bay, Lake Erie. Celestite is used for tracer bullets and flares. See *Strontium*.

Chalcedony (*kăl-sĕd'ō-nĭ*; *kăl'sē-dō-nĭ*). A beautiful quartz material, occurring in various shades of red, yellow, brown, green, and blue. It is indistinctly crystalline (amorphous), has a waxy luster, and is transparent or translucent, or, in some milk white varieties, opaque. It is believed to have been deposited from solutions of silica and is chiefly found lining or filling cracks and cavities in igneous rocks.

Ordinary chalcedony is white or gray. The bright red variety is known as *carnelian*, and the brown-red as *sard*. The red color due to iron oxide is often produced artificially by heating yellow chalcedony. *Chrysoprase* is a variety of chalcedony, colored apple green by a small amount of hydrated nickel oxide. The natural color fades on exposure to the sun or heat, but can be restored and even improved by treatment with a solution of nickel sulphate. *Plasma* is a leek green chalcedony. When marked by spots of red jasper it is known as *bloodstone* or *heliotrope*. *Agate* is a banded variety of chalcedony. These stones, although hard, fine grained, and very tough, are nevertheless easily worked, so that for centuries they have been used as seals, cameos, and other ornaments.

India and Brazil are the chief sources of chalcedony, although good specimens are found in many other parts of the world. See *Bloodstone, Carnelian, Chrysoprase, Onyx*.

Chalcocite (*kăl'kō-sīt*). An important ore of copper, known also as "copper glance" and *redruthite*. It generally occurs massive, has a conchoidal fracture, a blackish, lead gray color, and a metallic luster. This ore consists of cuprous sulphide, and, when pure, contains 79.8 per cent copper. It is found in large quantities in Montana, Alaska, Nevada, Arizona, and Mexico, usually in the upper, enriched parts of copper veins. See *Azurite, Chalcopyrite, Copper, Malachite*.

Chalcopyrite (*kăl'kō-pī'rīt*; *-pĭr'ĭt*). The most common and important ore of copper, copper-iron sulphide, commonly known as "copper pyrites," or yellow copper ore. It possesses a metallic luster, is brass-yellow or iridescent in color, and is often called "peacock ore." When pure, the mineral contains 34.5 per cent copper and 30.5 per cent iron. It is widely distributed in metallic veins, commonly with iron sulphide, and at times with nickel and cobalt sulphide. Large deposits of chalcopyrite are found in various parts of the Old World. It occurs extensively also in Colorado, Montana, Arizona, Utah, and California, and often bears gold and silver. See *Azurite, Chalcocite, Copper, Malachite*.

Chalk. A soft, fine-grained, white or yellowish rock, with an earthy texture, and somewhat rough to the touch. Under the microscope, some chalk is found to contain minute shells, spicules, and spines of protozoans, sponges, sea urchins, and other marine animals. As these remains consist of calcium carbonate, chalk is one form of limestone. Chalk was formed ages ago on former ocean bottoms, either by chemical precipitation of calcium carbonate or by the accumulation of organic remains. It is still in process of formation in modern oceans.

The Cretaceous system of rocks, while not composed exclusively of chalk, takes its name (Latin *creta*, chalk) from the extensive chalk beds, hundreds of feet thick, which are abundant in this geological period in Europe and America. England received the poetic name "Albion" from the immense white chalk cliffs on the English channel.

While not usually suitable for building stone, chalk may be used in making lime and Portland cement. Ground and washed free from grit, it forms "whiting," used in whitewash, putty, and silver polish. See *Limestone*.

Chlorite (*klō'rīt*). The name given to a group of minerals consisting of hydrous silicates of aluminum with ferrous iron and magnesium. In color, chlorite is green to dark green, and, like mica, has one perfect cleavage. It is tough but not elastic, occurring in scaly masses or in flat, hexagonal tablets. Chlorite is found in many igneous and metamorphic rocks.

Chromite. A native chromate of iron and the chief source of chromium. It occurs in grains, veins, and irregular masses in peridotite and serpentine rocks. Chromite is usually converted to ferrochrome to render it commercially usable. See *Chromium, Ferrochrome*.

Chrysoberyl (*krĭs'ō-bĕr'ĭl*). A crystallized form of beryllium aluminate. It varies from green to yellow in color, is transparent or translucent, and very hard—H. = 8.5. The type most favored as a gem stone is a clear golden yellow. Cat's-eye, or *cymophane*, is a green, cloudy variety characterized by a streak of light that seems to follow the eye as the stone is turned.

Alexandrite is a pleochroic form of chrysoberyl valued almost as highly as the diamond. When properly cut, it appears emerald green, changing to raspberry red when viewed by artificial light or by light passing through the stone. It was named for Czar Alexander II because it was discovered in Siberia on his birthday, and because green and red were the military colors of Russia.

The chief sources of fine specimens of chrysoberyl are Brazil, Ceylon, and the Ural mountains.

Chrysoprase (*krĭs'ō-prāz*). An apple green variety of chalcedony. Its color is due to nickel oxide in its composition. Chrysoprase occurs in Siberia, in Silesia, and in North Carolina, Oregon, and California. It was formerly highly prized as a gem stone, being mentioned by the ancients and in the Bible. However, when kept in a warm place, its color fades; in consequence, it has lost much of its popularity. See *Chalcedony*.

Cinnabar. The most important ore of mercury. It consists of mercuric sulphide and occurs either massive or in hexagonal crystals which are bright red or brown in color. There are productive cinnabar mines at Almaden, Spain; in Idaho, and at New Almaden, California. Cinnabar occurs also in southern Russia, Peru, China, New Zealand, Australia, and South Africa. It was well known to the Romans, and its uses were described by Vitruvius and by Pliny. See *Mercury*.

Clay. Soft, very fine, earthy material which can be molded when wet and which retains its form when dry. Clay is formed chiefly by the decomposition of aluminous silicate rocks, especially the feldspars. It consists of hydrous aluminum silicate usually mixed with small quantities of quartz, mica, feldspar, iron oxide, lime, or other impurities. The plastic or moldable quality of clay, together with its property of hardening under heat, gives to the various kinds a high economic value. Clay is used for a vast number of purposes,—among them, the making of brick, tile, terra cotta, fire brick, retorts, crucibles, pottery, Portland cement, electrical insulators, mineral paint, paper fillers, soap, and ultramarine. Clay is used also for modeling.

Deposits of clay are widely distributed and are found in the formations of many geological ages. The chief varieties are kaolin or china clay, and adobe, alum, ball, brick, fire, flint, gumbo, marly, paper, pipe, pottery, saggar, slip, and terra cotta clays. In the United States, valuable clay deposits occur in a large number of localities and form the basis of important industries. See *Kaolin, Porcelain, Pottery*.

Coal. An important mineral of vegetable origin, the most valuable of all fuels. It occurs as a brown or black rocklike material, usually in layers or beds. These beds are found between strata of shale, clay, sandstone, or sometimes limestone. Coal has been produced chiefly from plant matter deposited in swamps during former geological ages. The immense vegetation of the Carboniferous period formed the world's chief deposits of coal. Extensive beds were laid down also during Triassic, Cretaceous, and Tertiary times.

The change from decaying vegetation to coal has been so gradual that the dividing lines between the various stages are not sharp. Peat, which occurs extensively in northern swamps, represents the first stage in coal making. When the submerged mosses and other vegetation composing peat are subjected to the pressure of accumulating sediments, and also to heat, further changes take place. The fibrous mass becomes more solid and uniform in structure. It loses oxygen and becomes transformed into a series of mineralized products, more and more unlike the original plant material from which it was derived. These changes are marked chiefly by an increase in the proportion of carbon and a decrease in the oxygen contained in the ever hardening mass. Successive steps in this process of carbonization are represented by peat, lignite, bituminous coal, semibituminous coal, semianthracite, and anthracite.

Peat consists of a spongy mass of vegetable matter which has partially decayed under water. Lignite is more compact and uniform in texture, but careful examination usually affords evidence of its vegetable origin. Though inferior to coal in various respects, both peat and lignite are used to a considerable extent for fuel.

Bituminous or soft coal is the most important of all varieties of coal. It is black, compact, and brittle, and frequently shows a cubical cleavage. It burns easily with a smoky flame and is the chief fuel used for making steam. When heated in a retort, it gives off gases and tarry substances, and, in the case of coking coal, the nonvolatile residue cakes together into a mass of coke. Free burning coals do not form coke. *Cannel coal* is a smooth variety with a waxy appearance, which may contain as high as 65 per cent of volatile matter. It burns with a long, smoky flame and is used chiefly for grate fires. It is believed to have been produced largely from the spores of giant fern-like plants.

Semibituminous coal and *semianthracite* represent intermediate steps in the carbonization process which, in the series of coals, ends in anthracite. *Anthracite*, or hard coal, is dense, comparatively hard, and, when broken, shows a lustrous black surface. It has a high content of fixed carbon with a low percentage of volatile material, and burns with an intensely hot, smokeless flame.

The following table represents an average made from analysis of representative types of coal taken from all parts of the United States.

APPROXIMATE COMPOSITION OF COALS

Type of Coal	Fixed Carbon	Volatile Combustibles	Moisture	Ash
Peat	26.5	53.5	10.0	10.0
Lignite	36.0	35.5	17.0	11.5
Bituminous . . .	58.0	34.0	2.5	5.5
Semibituminous .	75.0	16.2	1.3	7.5
Semianthracite .	85.0	7.8	1.0	5.2
Anthracite . . .	87.0	3.7	2.7	6.6

The best-known sizes of domestic anthracite are approximately as follows: broken, 4–2.5 inch; egg, 2.5–1.75 inch; stove, 1.75–1.25 inch; nut, 1.25–.75 inch; pea, .75–.5 inch; buckwheat, .5–.25 inch. In some districts, bituminous coal is washed and screened to the following sizes: lump, over 3 inch; egg, 3–1.5 inch; nut, 1.5–⅜ inch; slack, less than ⅜ inch.

Coal is the most important source of industrial power in the United States, providing in 1930 about 60% of the total. Consumption of coal in the country reached its zenith in 1917, when it amounted to 6.08 tons per capita. In 1930, the per capita use was 4.2 tons.

Liquefaction of Coal. A petroleum-like substance, rich in gasoline content, may be obtained from certain low grades of coal by the so-called Bergius process, devised by Friedrich Bergius near Mannheim, Germany, and patented in 1914. Low-grade coal, of which Germany has large deposits, is pulverized and blended in oil with a 5 per cent mixture of iron oxide. This mixture is heated to a temperature of 450° C. in an atmosphere of hydrogen under 200 atmospheres' pressure. Commercial production of gasoline by this process was begun in Germany about 1927.

Powdered Coal. In order to meet the competition of other fuels, such as oil and gas, and of hydroelectric energy, those interested in the marketing of coal have developed various means of making its use more efficient. One of the most important of these developments is the use of powdered coal. Soft coal is broken to a fineness comparable to that of talcum powder. In this form it is highly inflammable. It is, therefore, stored in tanks and fed into furnaces by air pressure. In this manner, hand stoking is eliminated. Clinkers and ashes are not formed, and a quicker, steadier, and more easily controlled heat is produced. In heat units per dollar, it is said to be superior to unpowdered coal and and to various competing fuels.

COAL PRODUCED IN THE UNITED STATES, 1939

State	Short Tons	Value
Bituminous:		
West Virginia	107,938,000	$189,971,000
Pennsylvania	92,190,000	188,990,000
Illinois	46,450,000	76,178,000
Kentucky	42,805,000	74,481,000
Ohio	19,632,000	32,196,000
Indiana	16,650,000	24,642,000
Virginia	13,230,000	24,608,000
Alabama	11,995,000	27,708,000
Colorado	5,890,000	14,548,000
Wyoming	5,383,000	10,766,000
Tennessee	5,280,000	10,402,000
Utah	3,340,000	7,114,000
Missouri	3,275,000	6,124,000
Iowa	3,050,000	7,503,000
Other States, Alaska	15,957,000	33,003,000
Total Bituminous	393,065,000	$728,234,000
Anthracite:		
Pennsylvania	51,487,377	$187,175,000
Total 1935	444,552,377	$915,409,000
Total 1929	608,816,788	$1,338,423,751

Conglomerate. A sedimentary rock composed of rounded pebbles, or even of bowlders, set in some finer material which acts as a cement. When there is a noticeable difference in size between the pebbles and the binding material, the rock is often called "pudding stone." The cementing material may be quartz, clay, limestone, or iron oxide, and the pebbles may consist of any kind of rock.

Conglomerates form usually in the shallow water along a shore. Beds of this material generally indicate the former presence of oceans, lakes, or, occasionally, large rivers. Conglomerate formations frequently have resulted from the deposition of material by melting glaciers.

Coral. See *Coral* under Zoology.

Corundum. A native oxide of aluminum found granular, in masses, and as hexagonal crystals. H. = 9. It is the hardest of the rock-forming minerals, and is exceeded in hardness only by the diamond and the rare natural carborundum called *moissanite*.

Ordinary corundum is dark colored and nontransparent, and is used as an abrasive. The most important deposits are found in Canada. *Emery* is a black granular corundum containing magnetite as an impurity. Like emery, common corundum is used as an abrasive material.

The clear, crystalline forms of corundum include some of the most valuable of all gem stones. According to their color, these are named: *ruby*, red; *sapphire*, blue; *oriental emerald*, green; *oriental topaz*, yellow; *oriental amethyst*, purple; and *white sapphire*, colorless.

Cryolite. A natural fluoride of sodium and aluminum. It generally occurs as light colored, brown, or even black masses, but also as monoclinic crystals. Formerly, cryolite was the only important ore of aluminum, but, for the production of the metal on a large scale, it has been displaced by the cheaper bauxite. Cryolite is now used chiefly as a flux to dissolve bauxite for the electrolytic production of aluminum, and as the principal ingredient in milk glass and certain kinds of enamel. The chief source of cryolite is near Ivigtut, Greenland. See *Aluminum, Bauxite.*

Crystal. In physical science, a body formed by the solidification of a chemical element, compound, or isomorphous mixture, in accordance with a definite internal structure. A crystal is bounded by flat, usually smooth surfaces, called faces, which are symmetrically disposed about a system of imaginary lines, called axes.

The word crystal was first used by the Greeks as the name for a hard, transparent material which they believed to be a durable form of frozen water or ice. The substance which they thus named is the colorless variety of quartz still known as rock crystal. Its angular form and smooth surfaces were noted by the ancients but were considered merely as "accidents" or as forms "pleasing to the gods." Modern science, however, has shown that all of the apparently intricate forms of crystals occur in accordance with definite laws.

Many thousand kinds of crystals have been studied, described, and named. These include many of the most delicate and strikingly beautiful objects in nature. They embrace not only precious gems and valuable metallic ores but also an immense number of handsome minerals and chemical substances, as well as the wonderful forms exhibited in snowflakes and frost work. See *Crystallography.*

Dendrite. A stone in which there are branching figures, resembling shrubs or trees. These are produced by a foreign mineral, usually by an oxide of manganese, as in the moss agate or mocha stone. Dendrites are often cut and used as gems.

Diabase (*dī'a-bās*). An important igneous rock. It is composed of pyroxene, labradorite feldspar, and iron ore, with a certain textural arrangement of the minerals. It forms the greater part of the great sheets of dark igneous rocks of the lower Connecticut valley and of northern New Jersey. Diabase is an altered form of basalt and is popularly known as "greenstone" and "trap."

Diamond. The diamond is unique among gem stones, because it is the hardest known substance and because it consists of a single element, carbon, crystallized in the cubic system. Native crystals are usually octahedrons with convex faces. When clear, colorless, and free from flaws, diamonds are said to be of the "first water." Crystals of inferior quality are usually more or less tinged with yellow due to traces of iron as an impurity. "Fancy" shades of rich yellow, pink, blue, green, and red are extremely rare and bring enormous prices.

Light passing into or out of a diamond is bent to an unusual degree, and white light passing through a wedge-shaped section of diamond is broken up into a broad rainbow-colored band. The "brilliant" form, in which over 98 per cent of all diamonds are now cut, takes the greatest possible advantage of these properties. It is so designed that most of the light passing into the stone from above does not pass out through the sides, but is reflected upward. A standard brilliant has 58 facets, 33 above and 25 below the girdle, or widest part. These facets are cut by holding the stone against a revolving metal plate covered with diamond dust. About 60 per cent of a rough stone is removed in cutting.

Diamonds were probably unknown in ancient times, and India was the only source of these precious stones until 1728, when they were discovered in Brazil. In 1867 a bright pebble was picked up by children on the banks of the Orange river, South Africa; it proved to be a perfect diamond of 22½ carats. Since then, South Africa has become the chief source of diamonds. Except for the occasional discovery of a single stone, the only source of diamonds in the United States is Pike county, Arkansas, where, since 1906, more than 2000 crystals have been found.

Diamonds are found usually in mud, sand, gravel, or conglomerate, deposited by rivers. The original source of the diamond bearing rock of India and Brazil has never been found, but most of the South African diamonds are dug from volcanic "pipes" or shafts extending down through the surrounding strata to an unknown depth. These pipes are filled with breccia resulting from alteration of the basic, igneous rock, peridotite. This altered material is called "blue ground." Usually, however, it is dark green up to within a short distance of the surface, where exposure to the atmosphere has changed the color to yellow. In this ground more than 80 varieties of minerals have been found.

Diamond mining in South Africa is carried on by natives who live in a guarded compound for periods of three to six months at a time, and who are carefully searched for concealed stones before they are allowed to depart. The blue ground is brought to the surface and exposed to the atmosphere for several months. When sufficiently softened by weathering, it is washed, sifted, and concentrated by machinery. The heavy concentrate is then passed over tables coated with grease which retains the diamonds and allows less valuable minerals to pass.

Rounded forms of imperfectly crystallized diamond are called *bort*. *Carbonado*, a black, opaque diamond without cleavage, is extensively used on the cutting face of diamond drills. Glaziers' diamonds are usually selected so as to present a naturally rounded marking edge. Diamond dies are used for drawing fine, hard wire; and diamond-tipped lathe tools are often the cheapest for use on soft, tough material, because they outwear several tools of hardest steel. Diamonds are also used in rock drilling, while diamond dust, embedded in various matrices, finds many industrial applications. A simple method of identifying genuine diamonds is based on the fact that they are transparent to X-rays, while paste imitations are not.

Diamonds have been produced artificially by heating iron filings and sugar to 3000° C. for a week, then plunging into ice-cold brine, causing enormous pressure on the sugar carbon. Crystals have been produced in this manner about the size of a grain of sugar. This method indicates how diamonds may have been formed within the earth. Diamonds have also been found in meteorites.

The largest diamond ever found was the Cullinan. This was discovered, January 1905, in the yellow ground of the Premier mine, near Pretoria, in South Africa. The crystal weighed 3106 metric carats, or about 1⅓ pounds avoirdupois. It was presented to King Edward VII by the Union of South Africa, and in 1908, at Amsterdam, was divided and cut into 105 brilliants. Of these, the two first in size are called "Star of South Africa" and "Lesser Star of South Africa." They weigh 516½ carats and 309³⁄₁₆ carats, respectively, and are the largest and finest brilliants in the world.

The most famous diamond is the Koh-i-nor. The gem was acquired by the East India Company and given to Queen Victoria. It was recut in London and now weighs 106 1/16 carats. The "Orlov," given by Count Orlov to Catherine II of Russia, weighs 199.73 carats. It is supposed to have been stolen from the eye of a Hindu idol. The Darya-i-nor, among the royal jewels of Persia, weighs 186 carats. The "Regent" or "Pitt," the most famous of the French jewels, weighs 137 7/8 carats, and was purchased by the French Regent, Duke of Orleans, from Thomas Pitt for about $675,000. It is now in the Louvre Museum. The Hope diamond is a blue brilliant of 45.5 carats. A red diamond of 10 carats was among the Russian crown jewels, and a green diamond of 41.1 carats is contained in a collection at Dresden. See *Carbon.*

Diatomaceous (*dī'ȧ-tô-mā'shŭs*) **Earth.** A porous, white or yellow, chalklike earth, composed of silica. This earth was formed chiefly by deposition of the shells of microscopic one-celled plants called diatoms, and is found in beds of various thickness. It is used in scouring-soaps and polishes, as a light, insulating material, as a clarifier and aid to filtration, and for absorbing nitroglycerin to form dynamite.

Diorite. A granular, gray, green, or almost black, igneous rock. It is composed largely of hornblende, with not more than an equal quantity of feldspar, and often contains shiny flakes of black mica. In the classification of igneous rocks, diorite comes between granite and gabbro.

Dolerite (*dŏl'ẽr-īt*). A dark gray-green or black igneous rock. It is composed of ferromagnesian minerals and feldspar, generally with smaller amounts of iron oxides. Dolerite is rather fine grained, and the small crystals so interlock that there is difficulty in distinguishing one from another. Among igneous rocks, dolerite is classified between basalt and gabbro.

Dolomite (*dŏl'ô-mīt*). A native calcium-magnesium carbonate crystallized in the rhombohedral system. Dolomite rock, transformed from limestone by the action of solutions containing magnesium, is widely distributed, and in appearance cannot be distinguished from ordinary limestone. Many types of marble used for statuary are more or less dolomitic, as are also various building stones. The Houses of Parliament, in London, and St. Patrick's cathedral, in New York City, are built of dolomite. It is also used in manufacturing certain kinds of cement, in making refractory linings for furnaces, and for reducing magnesium by means of ferrosilicon. See *Limestone.*

Emerald. The most highly prized variety of beryl, a precious stone of a rich green color, slightly harder than quartz. The magnificent color, which gives unusual qualities to this gem, is due to chromium. Fine emeralds closely approach the diamond in value.

The ancients, who greatly esteemed the emerald, seem to have obtained their supply chiefly from Upper Egypt, whose mines were worked at the time of Alexander the Great and later produced stones for Cleopatra. Many and varied virtues were formerly ascribed to the emerald, among which was protection to the wearer against epilepsy and evil spirits.

The finest emeralds are now obtained from Colombia, where they are found in bituminous limestone. The Colombian mines have been productive since the 16th century. Emeralds occur also in Russia and Australia. In the United States, excellent emeralds have been found sparingly in North Carolina. See *Beryl.*

Emery. A black, granular variety of corundum. Among available natural abrasives, it ranks next to the diamond in hardness, and is much used in cutting and polishing gems, plate glass, and various metals. Most of the emery used in the United States is obtained from Asiatic Turkey, the chief source of supply, but small quantities are found in the United States at Peekskill, New York, and in Virginia. See *Corundum.*

Epidote (*ĕp'ĭ-dōt*). A native orthosilicate of calcium, aluminum, and iron. It occurs in granular masses, in fibrous forms, and as monoclinic crystals. The color may be red, white, or black, but is generally pistachio green. Fine epidote crystals used in jewelry are found in France, Switzerland, Austria, Norway, and many parts of America.

Feldspar. One of the most important of rock-forming minerals. It consists of aluminum silicate, together with a silicate of one or more of the metals potassium, sodium, calcium, or, rarely, barium. Feldspars do not contain magnesium or iron. They occur in igneous, metamorphic, and some sedimentary formations, and are an essential constituent of granite, gneiss, syenite, and various other rocks. They show good cleavage; H.=6 to 6.5; and the color is white, or pale shades of pink, yellow, green, or gray.

The feldspars crystallize in the monoclinic and triclinic systems, and are classified first according to form and secondly according to the metals combined with the aluminum. Thus *orthoclase* is monoclinic, and *microcline* is triclinic, potash feldspar; *albite* is soda feldspar; *anorthite*, lime feldspar; *plagioclase* is soda-lime feldspar; and, when soda displaces part of the potash, the products are soda-orthoclase or soda-microcline. Classification of igneous rocks depends largely on the feldspars which they contain.

Ground feldspars are chiefly used in making porcelain, other pottery, and enamels. Very pure, white feldspar enters into the composition of artificial teeth. No commercially successful process has yet been developed by which the potash in feldspar can be made soluble for use as fertilizer.

Felsite. See *Basalt.*

Flint. A massive, more or less impure form of quartz. It varies in color from gray to brown or nearly black, and breaks with a conchoidal fracture and a sharp edge. Flint is of wide occurrence and is found chiefly in the form of nodules, in beds of chalk and limestone. Under the microscope, flint shows the remains of sponges and diatoms around which, it is believed, silica was deposited from solution. By prehistoric peoples, flint was used for making axes, arrowheads, and knives. In later days, it served, when struck by a piece of steel, to produce sparks for setting fire to tinder. The principal use of flint is in the manufacture of fine pottery and abrasives. See *Quartz.*

Fluorite (*floo͞'ŏr-īt*). A native calcium fluoride, called also *fluorspar* and *fluor.* This beautiful mineral usually crystallizes in cubes having perfect octahedral cleavage. Transparent crystals are found in many handsome colors and, although too soft for general use as gems, are frequently made into ornaments.

Fluorite is found in many European countries, in Canada, and in the United States. It is used chiefly as a flux in metallurgical processes, also as a source of hydrofluoric acid, and in making opalescent glass, enamels, and special types of lenses.

Fusulina (*fū'sû-lī'nȧ*) **Limestone.** A highly prized building stone found in the midwestern United States. It is formed largely of the shells of a foraminiferous protozoan called *Fusulina.* The shells, which are of the size and shape of small grains of wheat, are usually cemented together by calcium carbonate. On weathering, the softer cementing material becomes somewhat eroded, leaving a rough and very pleasing surface composed of the harder shells. The interesting type of protozoan forming such shells has existed since Cambrian times, but its chief rock-building activities took place during the great Coal period. See *Limestone.*

Gabbro (*găb'rō*). The name given to a family of granitoid rocks. They are greenish in color, and formed essentially of crystals of plagioclase and other minerals allied to pyroxene. Gabbros are coarse-grained, heavy, igneous rocks which grade from porphyries on the one hand to diabases and diorites on the other. Only a specialist in petrology can determine the various intermediate grades. All rocks of this type, if uniform in coloring and texture, are useful in fine buildings, monuments, and other structural purposes. However, many of the constituent minerals often oxidize and cause a discoloration.

Galena. An important ore of lead, consisting chiefly of lead sulphide. It occurs in fibrous, granular, or massive forms, or in cubic or octahedral crystals, and is very widely distributed throughout the world. In the United States, it is found chiefly in Illinois, Iowa, Wisconsin, and Missouri. When pure, galena contains more than 86 per cent of lead. Usually, however, it is found mixed with varying amounts of antimony, bismuth, cadmium, zinc, and silver. In the Rocky Mountain states, galena is often worked for the silver that it contains, the lead becoming a by-product. See *Lead.*

Garnet. A mineral orthosilicate which forms various types of isometric crystals. These differ in color and composition but have the same general chemical formula. The hardness is usually greater than that of quartz, and in color precious garnet is usually red.

Almandine, a favorite variety, is an iron-aluminum silicate. Other garnets may have magnesium, calcium, or manganese in place of iron, and chromium or iron in place of aluminum. The ornamental and gem stones known as *cinnamon stone, rose garnet, oriental garnet, Arizona ruby,* and *Cape ruby* are varieties of garnet.

A *carbuncle* is often said to be a garnet, but it is in truth any red stone cut convex—*en cabochon*—without facets.

The name garnet is thought to be from the Latin *granatus*, "grainlike," because the crystals resemble the red seeds of a pomegranate.

About 5500 tons of inferior garnet is mined annually in the United States for use as an abrasive.

Gem Stones. Minerals of any kind, which, because of their beauty, are customarily cut and polished for use in jewelry, as seals, and for similar ornamental purposes. The *precious stones* are the diamond, ruby, sapphire, and emerald. The *semiprecious stones* include opal, garnet, turquoise, spinel, alexandrite, amethyst, cat's-eye, and various others.

The ancient Babylonians, Assyrians, Egyptians, Hebrews, Greeks, and Romans greatly prized many of the gem stones popular at the present day. They developed great skill in cutting, engraving, and polishing them for use in rings, seals, amulets, and other ornaments, large numbers of which are still preserved.

Many healing, protective, and other magical qualities were ascribed to various gems by ancient peoples. Some believed that each month of the year is under the influence of a precious stone. The effect of this belief is still seen in the widespread European fashion of wearing birth stones in preference to other jewels. Again, certain gems were supposed to be under the influence of the planets.

While the ancients rarely cut or engraved diamonds, rubies, or sapphires, they made extensive use of many stones of less hardness, including the carnelian, sard, chalcedony, sardonyx, onyx, agate, jasper, hyacinth or jacinth, beryl, emerald, amethyst, topaz, tourmaline, obsidian, and opal. According to the Mosaic law, the breastplate of a Jewish high priest should contain twelve precious stones, namely:

Sardonyx, Topaz, Emerald
Carbuncle, Sapphire, Jasper
Ligure, Agate, Amethyst
Chrysolite, Onyx, Beryl.

The nature of *ligure* is uncertain, the stone being variously regarded as a jacinth, opal, or tourmaline.

During the middle ages the use of gems and the art of gem cutting declined greatly. About the year 1500 it was revived in Italy, and somewhat later in other countries. At the present time a large and increasing number of stones and minerals are used as gems. Imitation and artificial gems are likewise produced in great variety and excellence.

Glauconite (*glô'kô-nīt*). A hydrous silicate of iron and potassium, which often lends a greenish color to beds of sandstone and chalk. It sometimes forms as much as 90 per cent of the greensand marls of England and New Jersey, where it is extensively mined for use as a potash fertilizer.

Gneiss (*nīs*). The name given to a group of metamorphic rocks, which, in composition, much resemble granite. Gneisses consist of granular masses of feldspar and quartz, together with mica, pyroxene, or hornblende, and sometimes rare metals. These component materials are arranged in alternate parallel bands of light and dark. Because of this banded structure, the gneisses somewhat resemble stratified rocks. Gneiss formations are the most widely distributed of metamorphic rocks. They underlie the earliest sedimentary deposits nearly throughout the world. They furnish important quarry material and are extensively used for structural stones. See *Granite*.

Granite. A group of granulated, crystalline, igneous rocks. They are composed of feldspar and quartz, alone, or more commonly with mica or hornblende—rarely with pyroxene—and with small quantities of other minerals. Granites are now regarded as plutonic rocks that have cooled at immense depths below the surface. They occur as large, irregular masses, which form the heart of many mountain ranges, as rounded exposures in other rocks, and as dykes. In color, granite is usually gray but sometimes varies to pink and red.

Granite is an important building stone because it is hard, offers unusual resistance to crushing and to weathering, and has a pleasing appearance. However, it does not stand fire well. It is much used for monuments and ornamental work, and refuse from granite quarries is often dressed for paving blocks or crushed for road building and railway ballast.

On account of being constructed largely of granite, Aberdeen, Scotland, is known as the "Granite City." Vermont has been styled the "Granite State" because of its extensive deposits and quarries of this valuable building stone. Other states noted for the production of granite are Maine, Massachusetts, and Delaware.

Graphite. A dark, steel-gray, or black mineral; called also plumbago, and, improperly, black lead. Like the diamond, it is nearly pure carbon, but it conducts electricity and is characterized by softness—H. = 1—a black streak, and a greasy feel.

Graphite may occur in layers, massive, or as hexagonal crystals, and may be of either organic or inorganic origin. It is widely distributed throughout the world, but rarely occurs in large beds or masses. The chief commercial souces of native graphite are Madagascar, Ceylon and Mexico. Since 1898, artificial graphite has been extensively made from coke at Niagara Falls, N. Y.

Graphite is universally used in making lead pencils, the name being derived from a Greek word meaning "to write." It is also extensively employed in the manufacture of lubricants, paint, stove blacking, foundry facings, and crucibles.

Gravel. Small, loose fragments of rock, from the size of a pea to approximately that of a walnut, usually rounded by water action and aggregated into beds of loose material, are known as gravel. The individual pieces are called *pebbles*. They are generally composed of quartz. This is largely because the hardness and resistance of this mineral enable it to withstand attrition better than most other rock materials. Gravel is widely distributed and is a very important building material, entering largely into the composition of concrete. When bound together by a natural cement, beds of gravel become *conglomerate*.

Greensand. See *Glauconite*.

Gypsum. Native, hydrous calcium sulphate containing 20.9 per cent of water. It is found massive, fibrous, and as monoclinic crystals, often in connection with beds of rock salt. It can be scratched with the finger nail, varies from transparent to opaque, and is usually white, although it may be red, green, blue, gray, brown, or, when very impure, black. Clear, colorless crystals are known as *selenite*; the massive, fine-grained form is *alabaster*; the fibrous variety is called *satin spar*; and an impure, earthy type is known as *gypsite*.

When heated to about 350° F., gypsum loses three-fourths of its combined water and the resulting product is called *plaster of Paris*. When heated above 400° F., gypsum loses its property of rapidly setting, but if heated to 900° F. and finely ground, it will set slowly, and this form is used for *flooring plaster*. Various materials mixed with plaster of Paris will retard setting, and slow-setting mixtures of this type are known as *cement plasters*. Gypsum is used for a fertilizer on alkaline soils, as a cement retarder and for wallboard and sheathing.

Among the world's producers of gypsum, France is first; the United States, second; and Canada, third. See *Plaster of Paris*.

Hematite (*hĕm'ȧ-tīt*; *hē'mȧ-*). The most important ore of iron, ferric oxide, containing, when pure, 70 per cent of the metal. It occurs as steel-gray rhombohedral crystals, but more commonly massive, fibrous, earthy, or as kidney-shaped nodules. Powdered or earthy forms are red, and hematite is generally the source of red color in soils and rocks. It was named from a Greek word meaning "blood."

Great beds of hematite, believed to have been deposited from solution, are found in many parts of the world. The hematite deposits of the Lake Superior region, which includes the famous Gogebic, Marquette, Menominee, Mesabi, and Vermilion ranges of Minnesota, Michigan, and Wisconsin, constitute the world's most important iron-producing field. See *Iron*, *Limonite*, *Magnetite*, *Siderite*.

Hornblende. See *Amphibole*.

Iceland Spar. See *Calcite*.

Ilmenite. A native oxide of iron and titanium and the chief ore of titanium. It is an essential constituent of many basic igneous rocks. Commercial ore is found in Canada, Australia, Brazil, India, Portugal, and near Tahawus, N. Y. Ilmenite is used chiefly in pigments and alloys. See *Titanium*.

Iolite (*ī'ô-līt*). A silicate of aluminum, iron, and magnesium, used occasionally as a semiprecious stone. The orthorhombic crystals, when clear, are remarkable for dichroism, and are called also *dichroite* and *water sapphire*.

Jade. A very tough, compact stone, creamy white to dark green in color. Since prehistoric times, it has been used for carved utensils, and for jewelry and other ornaments. The term jade includes the minerals *nephrite*, which is a variety of amphibole, and *jadeite*, a silicate of sodium and aluminum. The Chinese, who are particularly fond of jade, apparently do not distinguish between these two varieties. The name nephrite is from a Greek word meaning "kidney," and the ancient Greeks believed, as do the Chinese today, that jade acts as a charm to cure all kidney diseases. In the East, milk white jades are the most highly valued. While jade has a hardness of only about 6.5, it is so tough that it can withstand blows which would pulverize diamond.

Jasper. A compact, opaque, impure variety of quartz. In color it is usually red or yellow, but varies to gray-blue and dark green. It takes a high polish, and was much used by the ancients for seals, carvings, and other ornamental purposes. It was one of the jewels in the breastplate of the Jewish high priest. The Greeks and Romans believed that jasper possessed healing qualities.

Jasper is still employed as a decorative stone. In the United States, well-known jasper quarries are located at Pipestone, Minnesota, at Sioux Falls, South Dakota, and in Colorado.

Jet. A hard, velvet black, fossil substance found in beds of lignite and coal. It is easily cut, takes a high polish, and was formerly much used for beads, toys, buttons, dress trimmings, and mourning jewelry. Since Roman times jet has been found along the seashore or obtained from mines near it in Yorkshire, England, where for many centuries it has been extensively made into ornaments. It is found also in various other European localities and in the United States.

Kaolin (*kā'ô-lĭn; kā'-*). A soft clay, usually of low plasticity, which burns to a pure white color. It takes its name from a hill in China, where it occurs, and is often called china clay. Its chief use is in the manufacture of porcelain, white earthenware, and wall tile. Kaolins which are white *before* burning are used for "filling" paper. While kaolin is mined in several parts of the United States, especially in Georgia and in North Carolina, production is insufficient for domestic purposes and a large amount is imported. This comes mostly from France, Germany, and England. The kaolin producing district of Cornwall, England, is the most important in the world. See *Clay*.

Lazurite (*lăz'ū-rīt*). A beautiful blue mineral, crystallizing in the cubic system, but usually massive and compact. It is essentially sodium-aluminum sulphosilicate and is the natural source of the pigment *ultramarine blue*.

The stone known as *lapis lazuli* and called sapphire by ancient writers is a compact mixture of many minerals, generally colored blue by lazurite. The finest lapis lazuli comes from northeast Afghanistan. It is found also in metamorphic limestone in Siberia and Chile. The stone is used for cameos, vases, and for mosaic and other ornamental work.

Lignite. A mineral substance of vegetable origin; called also "brown coal." To the naked eye, lignite often shows a distinct fibrous or woody structure. It represents the second stage of coal formation, intermediate between peat and bituminous coal. Lignitized tree trunks and fragments of lignitized wood are often found in rock formations of the Cretaceous and later periods.

Lignite is usually characterized by a dull luster, brown or black color, brown streak, and open texture. It ignites readily, burns with a smoky flame, but falls far below bituminous and other higher grades of coal in heating power. By reason of the moisture which it contains, sometimes exceeding 43 per cent, lignite dries out and disintegrates rapidly following exposure to the air. Consequently, it can be neither stored nor transported to a considerable distance without crumbling more or less into powder. Hence, lignite must be consumed as fuel near the mine, converted into briquettes, used in a gas producer, or manufactured into gasoline by the so-called Bergius process.

In 1941, the production of lignite in the United States amounted to 2,775,832 net tons, North Dakota, Texas, South Dakota, and Montana being the chief producers. Lignite is found also in Canada, and extensive beds occur in Russia. See *Coal*.

Limestone. Rock composed chiefly of calcium carbonate is called limestone. If magnesium carbonate also is present, the rock becomes dolomitic limestone. Impurities, such as silica and alumina, are generally found, and iron frequently imparts a yellow or brown color. Limestones were formed chiefly by the accumulation of the shells and other hard parts of marine organisms. They were produced also by precipitation of calcium carbonate due to chemical or bacterial action.

Chalk, coquina, dolomite, lithographic stone, marl, and marble are all forms of limestone. *Travertine* is a limestone that has been deposited from hard water. *Oolitic limestone* is composed of small, round, concentric grains having the appearance of fish eggs. When the concretions are about the size of a pea, or larger, the stone is called *pisolite*. *Nummulitic limestone*, an important Old World type, is made up of coin-shaped shells. *Fusulina limestone* is composed largely of shells having the size and shape of a grain of wheat.

Typical limestone is fine-grained, or compact, gray to yellow-brown, with hardness less than 4, and of sufficient resistance to crushing to be valuable as building stone. It is found in all parts of the world, sometimes in beds more than 100 feet thick. Limestone is very important also for making lime and cement, and in smelting ores.

Ohio, Pennsylvania, Missouri, and West Virginia lead in the production of limestone in the United States. In Canada, much limestone is quarried in the vicinity of the cities of Montreal and Quebec. See *Calcite, Chalk, Dolomite, Fusulina Limestone, Lithographic Stone, Marble, Marl, Nummulitic Limestone, Oolite.*

Limonite (*lī'mô-nīt*). An iron ore of commercial importance; known also as *brown hematite*. Chemically, it is a hydrated ferric oxide containing, when pure, almost 60 per cent of the metal. It occurs massive, often in forms similar to a bunch of grapes, as bog ore, as yellow ocherous deposits, and as a compact brown clay-ironstone. In the United States, the production of limonite is relatively small when compared with that of other iron ores. In Europe, the most important deposits are found in Lorraine and Luxemburg. See *Hematite, Iron, Magnetite, Siderite.*

Lithographic Stone. A smooth, porous, even grained and compact variety of limestone. When a flat surface of such a stone is marked with a design in soapy ink or crayon, moistened, and then passed under an inking roller, the ink from the roller is retained only by the material forming the design. The process of printing from a stone treated in this manner is known as *lithography*.

Lithographic stones of the finest quality are obtained at Solnhofen, Bavaria. In limited quantities, lithographic stone occurs in France, England, and America. In the United States, the most important deposit is at Brandenburg, Kentucky. See *Limestone*.

Magnetite. An important ore of iron, which may be considered as a combination of ferrous and ferric oxides. It generally occurs massive or granular, and also forms black isometric crystals which are usually octahedrons. When pure, it contains 72.4 per cent of iron.

Magnetite is strongly attracted by a magnet but, as a rule, it does not draw small pieces of iron to itself. Certain specimens, however, act as permanent magnets and, when thus possessed of polarity, are known as *lodestones*. Good lodestone is found in Siberia, in the Harz mountains, and at Magnet Cave, Arkansas. Most of the famous iron ores of Sweden consist of magnetite. In North America, valuable deposits of the ore are found in Canada, in the Appalachian region, and in Washington, California, and other states. See *Hematite, Iron, Limonite, Siderite.*

Malachite (*măl'ȧ-kīt*). A mineral consisting of a bright green basic carbonate of copper. It sometimes forms tufts of needle-like, monoclinic crystals, but generally it is earthy or in the form of fibrous concentric nodules, which are often of great size. This compact material is translucent or opaque and has a hardness of 3.5 to 4. Malachite owes its formation to the alteration of other copper minerals, and is therefore often found in the upper parts of copper mines. When present in sufficient quantities, it may become an important ore of copper.

Malachite was mined in the Sinai peninsula by the ancient Egyptians and constituted their chief source of copper. They used the mineral also as a gem stone and for making various ornaments. In ancient times, charms cut from malachite were worn as a protection against lightning, disease, and witchcraft. As malachite takes a high polish, it has been extensively employed, especially in Russia, for ornamental purposes. It is used, for example, in making clock cases, panels, table tops, mosaics, and as a veneer or inlay for costly furniture. The mineral is obtained chiefly from the Ural mountains, Australia, and Arizona. See *Azurite*.

Marble. A granular, crystalline form of limestone that can be highly polished. Marble was metamorphosed, or changed from ordinary limestone, by the action of heat, with or without pressure, within the earth's crust.

Pure marble is white, but most specimens contain impurities which produce the many varieties of colored, streaked, and banded marbles. The fine, white Parian marble used by the ancient Greek sculptors was obtained from the island of Paros, in the Ægean sea. The best marble used by modern artists comes chiefly from the famous quarries of Carrara, Italy. Marble is much superior to granite in resistance to fire and is therefore extensively used for interior decoration of fine buildings.

Vermont and Georgia are the chief producers of marble in the United States, but quarries are worked also in Alabama, Tennessee, Arizona, Colorado, Nevada, California, and Alaska. See *Limestone*.

Marl. A natural earthy deposit of calcium carbonate and clay, containing more or less sand. In color, marl is generally gray but, owing to impurities, may be yellow, red, green, blue, or black. Marl is much used as a fertilizer for soils requiring lime. Besides lime, however, marl usually contains small amounts of potash and phosphates, which greatly increase its fertilizing value. Pure marl is sometimes found containing limestone and clay in such proportions that it can be burned in a kiln to form Portland cement. Extensive marl beds occur in the Atlantic coastal plain from New Jersey to South Carolina.

The term marl is often improperly applied to the greensands and other fertilizing earths containing very little calcium carbonate. See *Limestone*.

Meerschaum (*mēr'shôm; -shŭm*). A soft, porous, white or cream colored mineral, composed of hydrated silicate of magnesium. It is called also *sepiolite*. Meerschaum occurs as wet masses buried in clayey earth. It is mined chiefly in Asia Minor, but is found also in Moravia, Morocco, Spain, and Mexico. When brought to the surface it may be easily cut with a knife; when dried it has a hardness of 2–2.5, and is light enough to float on water. The name meerschaum, in German, means "sea foam," while the term sepiolite was given because of the resemblance of the mineral to cuttlefish bone. Meerschaum is used chiefly for the manufacture of tobacco pipes. These absorb tarry materials and, after continued use, acquire a rich, dark color. Before it is made into pipes, the mineral is soaked in wax, which renders it capable of taking a high polish.

Mica. A group of minerals composed of aluminum silicate together with silicates of other metals which characterize the different varieties. Thus, *muscovite* is a potash mica; *phlogopite*, magnesium mica; and *biotite*, black iron-magnesium mica. Mica is widely distributed as small glittering particles throughout many igneous and metamorphic rocks. It crystallizes in the monoclinic system, but generally appears as six-sided tablets, all of which have very perfect cleavage parallel to the base.

Mica is often found in tablets more than two feet square. Because of the perfect cleavage, these "books" can be divided into leaves or sheets so thin that there may be 500 or more to an inch. Such plates are transparent, tough, and flexible. They are nonconductors of electricity, and are quite resistant to heat. Because of these properties, sheets of mica are valuable as insulators in electrical apparatus, for chimneys on gas burners or lanterns, and for windows on ovens and furnaces. Powdered mica is used to produce a glittering effect on wallpaper and stage costumes; when mixed with an equal weight of nitroglycerin, it forms the high explosive called mica powder.

Common potash mica was at one time so much used for windows in Russia that it became known as "muscovy glass" and later as *muscovite*. Commercial micas are generally muscovite or phlogopite. Of these, India produces about one-half, and Canada and the United States each about one-quarter of the world's supply. The chief Canadian mines are in Quebec and eastern Ontario. In the United States, the richest mica fields are in North Carolina and New Hampshire.

Mispickel (*mĭs'pĭk-ĕl*). The chief ore of arsenic, a compound of iron, arsenic, and sulphur, containing 46 per cent. arsenic, called also *arsenopyrite*. It is found massive and as rhombohedral crystals, usually associated with ores of silver, tin, copper, and lead. The color is silver white to steel gray; the luster, metallic; hardness equals 5.5. Arsenic is obtained as an oxide by roasting the ore in air. Mispickel occurs extensively in England, Germany, Canada, and the United States. See *Arsenic*.

Molybdenite (*mô-lĭb'dē-nīt; mŏl'ĭb-dē'nīt*). Molybdenum disulphide, the chief ore of the metal molybdenum, is a soft, lead gray mineral, very similar to graphite in appearance and feel. It is widely distributed, usually disseminated through granular rocks, and seldom in large quantities. Australia, Canada, and Peru are the principal sources of the ore for the world market. The United States, however, produces enough for the domestic demand. At the time of the World War, it was for a period the largest producer. See *Molybdenum*.

Monazite (*mŏn'ȧ-zīt*). A phosphate of the cerium metals, which usually contains from 3 to 10 per cent. of thorium. Because of supposed scarcity, it was named from a Greek word meaning "to be solitary." It is usually found as brown fragments or yellow, rounded grains, rarely as monoclinic crystals.

Monazite is now known to be widely distributed in pegmatite veins and in gneiss. When the gneiss decomposes, the grains of monazite, which are about five times as heavy as water, become concentrated in alluvial or placer deposits. India and Brazil are the chief producers of monazite. Monazite is the principal ore of the thorium and cerium used for incandescent mantles. It is also a source of helium, which exists as a gas absorbed in the mineral. See *Cerium, Thorium, Pyrophoric Alloys*.

Moonstone. A translucent variety of feldspar, showing pearly or opaline reflections from within, and sometimes displaying a pale tint of blue, red, or green on a gray ground. Moonstones are of wide and rather common occurrence, the best specimens coming from Ceylon. They are usually cut either *en cabochon* or round and are frequently worn as lucky charms. In olden times, many believed that a moonstone held in the mouth would improve the memory and also that the gem was a cure for epilepsy.

Native Metals. Nearly all the ninety-two chemical elements are found in combination in various minerals. However, only a small fraction of them occur free or uncombined with other elements, as native minerals. The ten solid elements which occur native are: the nonmetals,—sulphur and carbon—the latter in the form of graphite and the diamond; the so-called semimetals,—arsenic, antimony, and bismuth; and the metals,—gold, silver, platinum, mercury, and copper.

Natural Gas. A term generally restricted in meaning to inflammable gas obtained from beneath the earth's surface. The existence of such gases has been known since prehistoric times, and flames from natural vents have been kept burning for centuries in the temples of fire worshipers in India.

Natural gas, as a rule, consists largely of methane, together with small amounts of other gases such as ethane, nitrogen, oxides of carbon, hydrogen, hydrogen sulphide, and, occasionally, notable amounts of helium. This mixture is usually about .62 as heavy as air, weighs from 47 to 49 pounds per 1000 cubic feet, and has a heating value of 920 to 1250 British thermal units per cubic foot.

The origin of natural gas is unknown, the principal explanations being (1) that it was produced by decomposition of organic matter or (2) by the action of underground water on iron carbide. Deposits of soft coal and oil are usually accompanied by gas, which suggests that they might have a common source. General conditions most favorable to underground accumulation of gas require: (1) a porous layer of rock, such as sandstone, in which the gas is held; (2) an impervious covering layer, such as slate or shale, which prevents the escape of the gas; (3) a bend or arch in the strata, which permits the gas to gather at the higher points and to separate from the oil and salt water which are often present.

Natural gas has been found in many parts of the world, but probably 98 per cent. of the total production is consumed in the United States. The producing sections of the United States may be divided approximately into six districts: (1) the Appalachian region, consisting of New York, Pennsylvania, southeastern Ohio, West Virginia, Kentucky, and Alabama; (2) the Trenton rock of Ohio-Indiana; (3) the Clinton sands of central Ohio; (4) the Mid-continent or Kansas-Oklahoma field; (5) the Caddo field of northwestern Louisiana; (6) the California field. Notable quantities of gas are found also in various states whose location does not fall within these divisions. Producing sections have been discovered by means of natural vents in the earth, by accident when drilling for oil or salt brine, and by expert geologists who traced out the summits of rock waves.

To obtain the gas, wells are drilled down through the covering layer of rock. The size of the bore varies usually from 2 to 8 inches and the depth from 250 to 3000 feet. At the village of Fredonia, N. Y., where, in 1821, natural gas was first used commercially in America, a supply sufficient for 30 street lamps was obtained from a well 1½ inches across and only 27 feet deep. The Geary well in Pennsylvania reached a depth of 7248 feet. Several producing wells in West Virginia are more than 4000 feet deep. The cost of a well may be figured roughly at six dollars a foot.

When gas-bearing strata are reached, the gas usually rushes out with great force which is thought to be due chiefly to water pressure. All large wells are tubed and capped with a valve so that the flow may be controlled. The shut-in pressure varies usually from 1 to 1500 pounds per square inch, the highest reported being 1700. The open flow of gas may be from 500 to 35 million cubic feet a day. A very good well will produce about one million cubic feet per day, at 300 to 400 pounds pressure.

The greatest yield on record was that of a Pennsylvania well which produced an average of 2,842,700 cubic feet a day for 7½ years, and continued for several years more at the rate of one million cubic feet a day. The supply in any field is not limitless, and new drilling is constantly required. The average yearly production of natural gas in the United States is well above 2000 *billion* cubic feet. Its value is more than five times the total value of the gold and silver produced in the country.

The chief use of natural gas is as fuel for the production of heat, light, and power. Large quantities also have been burned in order to secure a deposit of the fine pigment, *gas black*, extensively used in making printing ink. It has been found that natural gas usually contains vapors of gasoline which may be removed either by condensation or by absorption.

The gas which rises between the tube and the casing of oil wells, collecting in the casing head, is especially rich in gasoline, sometimes yielding as much as 10 gallons from 1000 cubic feet. The name *casinghead gas* is now quite generally applied to gasoline obtained from any natural gas. The total production of gasoline from this source is about 2 billion gallons annually.

Natural gas is the chief source of helium, used for inflating the gas bags of airships. Gas used as fuel is often distributed long distances by pipe lines. One of the longest of such lines supplies Illinois and other states with gas from Texas. Gas is sometimes shipped in liquid form. See *Petroleum*.

Nummulitic (*nŭm'ū-lĭt'ĭk*) **Limestone.** An important constituent of the Eocene strata of Africa, Europe, and Asia. It occurs from 10,000 feet above sea level in the Alps to 15,000 feet in the Himalayas, in beds often thousands of feet in thickness.

The rock, which varies in character from limestone to marble, is useful as a building stone. It is composed mainly of the shells or tests of a large foraminifer called *nummulites*. These shells are usually of the size and shape of a small coin (Latin, *nummulus*), whence the name. The shell, which is without an apparent aperture, has an internal spiral cavity divided into a number of chambers by partitions, through which there are minute openings. In size, the shells vary from ⅛ of an inch to 1½ inches in diameter.

The Great Pyramid in Egypt is built chiefly of nummulitic limestone. See *Limestone*.

Obsidian (*ŏb-sĭd'ĭ-ăn*). A kind of glass produced by volcanoes, chemically identical with pumice, but different from it in structure. It is usually black and opaque though sometimes green, red, or brown, or even striped or spotted. Obsidian takes a high polish and is exceedingly brittle, breaking with a conchoidal fracture, much like flint. It was used by primitive peoples, especially in Mexico, for arrowheads, spearheads, knives, mirrors, and ornamental figures. Various kinds of obsidian are found in volcanic regions, sometimes in immense masses, such as the famous Obsidian Cliff, a mountain of volcanic glass in Yellowstone national park. See *Lava, Pumice.*

Olivine (*ŏl'ĭ-vĭn*; *-vēn*). An orthosilicate of magnesium and ferrous iron. This mineral forms an important constituent of the basic, igneous rocks, such as basalt and peridotite. It is found also in some metamorphic rocks. Rock composed almost entirely of olivine is called *dunite.* Olivine occurs as grains or small granular masses and rarely as well-formed orthorhombic crystals. The color is usually olive green, but it may range from yellow to brown. The terms olivine and chrysolite are generally used interchangeably. The commercial olivine used in refractories is obtained largely from dunite and its alteration products, serpentine and steatite. See *Serpentine.*

Onyx (*ŏn'ĭks*; *ō'nĭks*). A banded chalcedony having even, parallel layers of different colors, usually white and black, white and red, or white and brown. When the layers are white and red-brown, the stone is called *sardonyx.* Onyx and sardonyx are highly valued by makers of cameos, because the straight bands permit the artist to carve white or colored figures on a differently colored base.

Onyx was employed for ornamental purposes in ancient times, and it is still used for table tops, mantels and stairs, clocks, and similar objects. Mexican onyx and onyx marbles, such as those found in Mexico, Algeria, Missouri, Arizona, and California, are composed of calcite deposited from solution. They show onyx-like bands and are used for decorative purposes. See *Chalcedony.*

Oolite (*ō'ō-līt*). Small concretionary grains, resembling fish roe, have been observed in sandstone, in iron ore deposits, as in the Clinton ores of eastern North America, and in large strata of limestone, useful in various localities as a building stone. Rock composed of such formations is called oolite. In some cases it appears probable that the deposition of oolite was influenced by external particles, such as sand grains and bits of organic matter, which acted as nuclei for the concretions.

The well-known building material called Bedford stone, extensively quarried in southern Indiana, consists in part of oolite. In Europe, oolitic rocks are very abundant, especially in the Middle Jurassic formations, which are named Oolite.

Ooze. Fine, soft deposits in the abysmal depths of the oceans. These are of three types,—volcanic, cosmic, and organic. The last, which is by far the most important, is subdivided into calcareous and siliceous, the character depending on the nature of the shells or tests of minute organisms from which the ooze was formed. Oozes cover many million square miles of the ocean floors.

Opal. A variety of hydrated silica which occurs usually in noncrystalline masses. H. = 5.5 to 6.5. In many cases opal may be considered as a silica jelly which has dried up until it contains only from 3 to 10 per cent of water. Opal is found filling cavities in igneous rocks, and also bedded in limestone, sandstone, and clays, and as a deposit around hot springs. Fossil wood and the remains of fossil fishes and reptiles, which have been changed to opal, are occasionally found. Opal may be clear and transparent, but it is usually white, yellow, green, brown, red, or gray, generally pale, and with a characteristic milky appearance.

The play of colors reflected from a piece of *precious opal* is richer and more varied than that from any other gem. The flashes of color are caused by diffraction of light due to physical irregularities within the stone. *Fire opal* varies from hyacinth-red to yellow and shows firelike reflections. *Harlequin opal* has small patches of color. *Black opal,* which is the most highly valued of all varieties, has a dull black background lighted by intense flashes of red, green, blue, orange, and other colors. *Common opal* is generally semitranslucent but lacks fire.

The superstition that opals are unlucky is gradually disappearing. In consequence, fine opals are continually increasing in popular regard. Precious opal is found in Mexico, Honduras, and Nevada, but the finest specimens are obtained from Hungary and New South Wales.

Ore Deposits. Natural concentrations or accumulations of metal-bearing minerals are found in various formations of the earth's crust. Those portions which contain enough metal in the proper combination to be profitably worked are called *ores.* Ores may occur in the form of *veins, chimneys,* or *stocks,* distributed throughout all kinds of rocks—igneous, metamorphic, and sedimentary—and in all geological formations. They may occur also in surface and placer deposits.

Gold and platinum are usually found native; copper, lead, and zinc, as sulphides; iron occurs in the form of oxides; and other metals are found in various combinations. Associated with the true ore minerals, there are often minerals of nonmetallic character, called "barren minerals" or "gangue." Common gangue minerals are quartz, calcite, barite, fluorite, dolomite, hornblende, and feldspar.

In the United States and Canada, ore deposits are of wide distribution, but they are most abundant in the Cordilleran region, the Black Hills, the Appalachians, and the Lake Huron region of Ontario.

Gold and silver ores are in the main confined to fissure veins and placer deposits in the Cordilleran region, though some are known in the Black Hills, in the southern Appalachians, and in Ontario, Alaska, and Yukon. Copper ores occur in vast deposits in Michigan, Arizona, Utah, Montana, and British Columbia. Lead and zinc ores are found in Iowa, Illinois, Wisconsin, Missouri, and New Jersey.

The hematite iron ore deposits of northern Minnesota are the largest known. Iron ores are also worked in the Appalachian region. Nickel is restricted mostly to the rich mines of the Sudbury district in Ontario. The ores of the rarer metals are, for the most part, found in the same parts of the continent as the foregoing.

Orthoclase. See *Feldspar.*

Pearl. See *Pearl* under Zoology.

Peat. Brown or black carbonaceous material formed in swamps and bogs by the partial decomposition of vegetable matter under water. It consists of a loosely compacted mass of partially decayed plant fiber and represents the first stage in coal formation.

One of the chief constituents of peat is the sphagnum moss; but sedges, rushes, water lilies, and various other kinds of aquatic vegetation take part in its formation. Although occurring chiefly in temperate, and sometimes in tropical countries, peat is formed also in arctic and subarctic regions; as, for example, Siberia, Alaska, and Labrador. Peat mosses, growing in peat-forming bogs, cover many thousands of square miles in North America and northern Europe. While most peat formations are not more than 4 feet thick, deposits exceeding 30 feet in thickness are sometimes found.

Peat is extensively quarried for use as fuel. When well dried, it has a higher heating value than wood, though it is inferior to coal. However, peat often contains a jelly-like substance which retains moisture and makes thorough drying difficult. Peat has long been used for fuel in the countries of northern Europe, especially in Ireland, where about one-tenth of the land surface is covered by peat bogs. In England, the peat moors have been a source of fuel since Roman times. See *Coal.*

Peridotite (*pĕr'ĭ-dō-tīt*). A granular, basic, igneous rock. It usually ranges in color from dark green to black, and is composed chiefly of olivine. Peridotite occurs with or without pyroxene, hornblende, magnetite, chromite, or other accessory minerals, and contains little or no feldspar. Peridotitic rocks are found occasionally as independent masses forced in among other rocks, but they are usually associated with gabbro. Peridotite is regarded as the original source from which, by weathering and concentration, platinum and ores of chromium and nickel were produced. Alteration of peridotite rock generally yields serpentine. The blue ground in which diamonds are found is an altered peridotite. See *Olivine.*

Petroleum. A mineral oil which varies in color from yellow to black. It is usually a dark green liquid which may be as thin as kerosene or as thick as molasses. This material was known in the most ancient times of which there is any record. The American Indians, who found it floating on the surface of certain springs, believed that it would make them strong. White men, who came later, also believed that it had medicinal properties, and sold it as a cure for rheumatism.

Petroleum is found in all parts of the world, occurring underground in porous layers of sand or limestone. The porous layer is always covered by a hard layer, such as shale, which prevents the oil from escaping. To obtain the oil, a hole about 8 inches in diameter is drilled down and cased with steel tubing, until it passes through the covering layer. The first well was only 69½ feet deep; some later wells have been sunk to a depth of more than a mile.

If no liquid appears, it is customary to *shoot* the well by exploding, at the bottom of the shaft, a long narrow torpedo containing nitroglycerin. This explosion shatters the oil-bearing layer and leaves a reservoir into which the oil can drain. Often the fluid is under enormous pressure so that great quantities of oil are thrown high into the air and lost before the *gusher* can be controlled by covering the mouth of the well with an iron cap. A famous well in Russia spouted for several days at the enormous rate of 4½ million gallons a day. Not all wells are gushers, and it is often necessary to pump the oil to the surface. In addition to the petroleum obtained from wells, a small but increasing quantity is extracted from oil-bearing shales. This product is called shale oil.

The *crude petroleum*, as it comes from the wells, may be used for making water gas, for oiling roads, and for fuel. For most other purposes it is *refined* by heating in a closed *still*. This is so arranged that the vapors which are given off at different temperatures may be condensed by cold water and collected separately. The various liquids are further purified by treatment first with sulphuric acid and then with alkali. Substances which boil at a low temperature are the first to come from the still. These are followed in turn by materials having higher boiling points.

Kerosene, for lighting purposes, was formerly the product most desired, while gasoline was considered a nuisance and was often thrown away. But, because of the great demand for motor fuel, every effort is now made to obtain all the gasoline possible. To increase the yield of this light product, so-called *cracking* processes have been developed. In these the oil is heated under pressure in such a way that some of the heavier vapors condense and fall back into the hot liquid. This causes them to "crack" or break up, producing a much greater proportion of gasoline.

Other valuable petroleum products are: lubricating oils; paraffin wax, which is used in the manufacture of candles and for covering jellies; and petroleum jelly, used for ointments. The final residues consist of pitch and coke. More than 200 different products are obtained from the crude oil.

Oil refineries are usually located near large cities and are connected with the wells by lines of iron pipe. These pipes are usually about 8 inches in diameter, and through them the crude oil is pumped, often for hundreds of miles. This system of pipe lines is so extensive that, if necessary, oil can be pumped for the entire distance from the Kansas or Oklahoma fields to the Atlantic coast. The amount of pipe used for this purpose is so great that, if connected in one continuous line, it would more than circle the earth at the equator. Tank cars and specially designed tank ships also are used for transporting large quantities of petroleum products.

Concerning the origin of petroleum, there are several theories. The one most generally accepted holds that it was produced by the decomposition of marine organisms, both vegetable and animal, at ordinary temperatures and pressures.

The United States leads the world in the production of petroleum. The first successful well, sunk at Titusville, Pennsylvania, by Colonel E. L. Drake, produced oil August 28, 1859. Since that date extensive petroleum fields have been developed in many countries.

For the year 1940 the chief petroleum producing countries in the order of their production were: United States (contributing nearly two-thirds of the total), Russia, Venezuela, Iran, Netherlands India, Mexico, Rumania, Colombia, Iraq, and Argentina. See *Natural Gas, Shale Oil.*

CRUDE PETROLEUM PRODUCED IN THE UNITED STATES

Rank in 1940	State	Barrels of 42 gallons	
		1929	1940
9	Arkansas . . .	24,917,000	25,583,000
2	California . .	292,534,000	223,881,000
19	Colorado . . .	2,358,000	1,350,000
4	Illinois . . .	6,319,000	146,788,000
14	Indiana. . . .	981,000	4,843,000
6	Kansas . . .	42,813,000	66,270,000
13	Kentucky . .	7,775,000	5,193,000
5	Louisiana . .	20,554,000	103,961,000
10	Michigan . . .	4,528,000	19,764,000
15	Mississippi . .	....	4,380,000
12	Montana . . .	3,980,000	6,768,000
7	New Mexico .	1,830,000	39,001,000
16	New York . .	3,377,000	4,999,000
18	Ohio	6,743,000	3,169,000
3	Oklahoma . .	255,004,000	155,952,000
11	Pennsylvania .	11,820,000	17,353,000
1	Texas	296,876,000	493,126,000
17	West Virginia .	5,574,000	3,444,000
8	Wyoming . .	19,314,000	25,683,000
	Other	26,000*	339,000†
	Total United States . . .	1,007,323,000	1,351,847,000

*Tennessee, Utah, and Alaska.
†Missouri, Nebraska, Tennessee, and Utah.

Phosphate Rock. An amorphous rock, usually gray in color, but occasionally yellow, blue, or black. It contains a large proportion of calcium phosphate, together with limestone, sand, and other impurities. It may be firm or spongy, and occurs either earthy or in rounded lumps.

The question of the source of phosphate rock deposits has caused much discussion. Some deposits, apparently, are formed from the bones and teeth of animals, but most beds of phosphate rock are believed to have been deposited from solutions which had been formed elsewhere. The rock occurs in beds from 3 to 50 feet thick and usually is removed from open pits rather than from sunken shafts. The types of material are hard rock, land pebble, and river pebble. For the preparation of fertilizer, the hard rock is used.

In the United States, Florida and Tennessee are the chief commercial producers of phosphate rock. The deposits which have been discovered in Idaho, Wyoming, Utah, and Montana are the largest known. See *Fertilizers, Chemical.*

Pitchblende (*pĭch′blĕnd′*). A radioactive mineral, more properly called *uraninite*. It consists chiefly of uranium oxides together with oxides of various other elements. While sometimes found as isometric crystals, it occurs usually as gray, green, brown, or black opaque masses, pieces, or grains, which have a pitchlike luster. These occur either in granite rocks or as a secondary mineral associated with sulphide ores of silver, lead, copper, nickel, and other metals. While mined chiefly in Belgian Congo, pitchblende occurs also in Bohemia, Saxony, Hungary, Turkey, the United States, and the Mackenzie district, Canada. Besides radium, it yields uranium, the source of atomic energy. See *Radium, Uranium.*

Porphyry (*pôr′fĭ-rĭ*). An igneous rock in which comparatively large and distinct crystals are held in a groundmass of much finer texture. The large crystals are called *phenocrysts*. According to the nature of the phenocrysts, porphyries may be classified as *Quartz-porphyry, feldspar-porphyry, mica-porphyry*, or *hornblende-porphyry*. Porphyries are intermediate between the true granites and the volcanic glasses or obsidians. Various porphyries are used for building and for ornamental stones. Their value depends upon the nature of the phenocrysts, some of which resist oxidation and weathering better than others. See *Granite, Obsidian.*

Precious Stones. Various minerals which, on account of their beauty, hardness, and rarity, are prized for use in ornamentation, especially in jewelry. Strictly speaking, the diamond, ruby, sapphire, and emerald are the only stones which are entitled to be called precious in this sense. However, the opal, on account of its beauty, is often classed with the precious stones, as is also the pearl, which is really not a true mineral but the secretion of various mollusks.

Very fine specimens of choice varieties of the softer gem stones sometimes have a higher value than average specimens of the standard precious stones. In their natural state, precious stones are often dull or coated with an external layer or crust which obscures their real beauty. Consequently, they are almost invariably cut and polished before they are mounted as gems. See *Gem Stones.*

Pudding Stone. See *Conglomerate.*

Pumice (*pŭm′ĭs*). A light, glassy rock of spongy texture, produced by the cooling of lava which has been puffed up and made porous by innumerable bubbles of expanding steam. Pumice, therefore, is a hardened lava froth, and may be regarded as a variety of obsidian. On account of its roughness and hardness, it is extensively used as an abrasive for polishing. Some of the more porous forms will float upon water. Pumice is obtained mostly from the Lipari islands, Italy, though it occurs also in western United States, Hungary, Mexico, and Iceland. See *Obsidian.*

Pyrite (*pī′rīt; pĭr′ĭt*). A native iron disulphide, a compound of iron and sulphur containing, when pure, 46.6 per cent of the metal. It is usually found massive but occurs also as opaque, isometric crystals. Because of their metallic luster and brass yellow color, pyrite crystals have become known as "fool's gold." Pyrite is widely distributed through almost all kinds of rock and is sometimes mined for copper or gold, with which it is associated. When heated, pyrite readily gives off sulphur dioxide and is therefore roasted as a valuable source of sulphur for making sulphuric acid. Important deposits are found in North America and Europe, notably in Spain. In the United States, Tennessee, Virginia, California, and Wisconsin are important producers of pyrite. See *Iron, Sulphur.*

Pyrolusite (*pī′rô-lū′sīt; pĭr′ô-lū′sīt*). Black oxide of manganese, or manganese dioxide, the most important manganese ore, generally occurring as soft, black masses. It is used for making manganese steel and in the chemical industries for such purposes as the preparation of chlorine and bromine. Pyrolusite is found to a limited extent in Montana, Arkansas, Virginia, New Mexico, and Cuba, but the main supply comes from Russia. See *Manganese.*

Pyroxene (*pī′rŏk-sēn; pĭr′ŏk-*). Any one of a group of important rock-forming, iron-magnesian minerals, very similar to the amphiboles. The crystals are usually short, stout prisms with pointed ends and a cross section having angles of 87 and 93 degrees. Chemically, pyroxenes are metasilicates; *augite*, for example, is aluminum-calcium-iron-magnesium silicate. They often occur in grains and shapeless masses and are typical components of dark green or black igneous rocks. See *Amphibole.*

Quartz. Crystallized silicon dioxide, which, in its various forms, is the most common and widely distributed of minerals. The many varieties of quartz may be divided into (1) those which are obviously crystalline and (2) others which are so fine and compact that by ordinary inspection no crystals can be detected.

A crystal of pure quartz, called *rock crystal*, is remarkably transparent. It occurs usually as a hexagonal prism with pointed ends, has a hardness of 7 and no cleavage planes. Quartz crystals of piezo-electric grade are required for radio oscillators and filters, telephone resonators, and other sound equipment.

Quartz is found in all colors. Its numerous forms include the amethyst, rose, and smoky quartz, cat's-eye, chalcedony, agate, onyx, and flint. It is an essential part of granite and sandstone, and is found almost everywhere as sand. In the western United States, quartz veins are the common source of gold. Fused quartz is used for making chemical apparatus which is resistant to most acids and does not crack when heated. See *Agate, Amethyst, Carnelian, Chalcedony, Flint, Gem Stones, Gravel, Onyx, Sand, Sandstone.*

Quartzite. A metamorphic rock consisting chiefly of quartz. It was produced by the alteration of sandstone to a dense vitreous rock which shows little trace of its original structure. The various forms of quartzite possess great hardness and resistance to weathering, and have a sharp-edged, splintery fracture. Some varieties, such as the Potsdam quartzite, of New York, are widely used for building stone. In some localities quartzite is used as a flux in smelting copper. Ground quartzite is employed in making sandpaper, filters, wood fillers, and ferrosilicon.

Realgar (*rē-ăl'gär*). Arsenic disulphide, a red mineral usually occurring with the yellow arsenic trisulphide or *orpiment*. These are found associated with silver and lead ores in Hungary, Bohemia, and Saxony. The two minerals are also deposited from geyser waters in Yellowstone park. Realgar is mined in Corsica and in the state of Washington. Formerly, it was mixed with saltpeter to form the white Bengal fire used in pyrotechny, but it has been largely displaced for this purpose by the artificial product. The name realgar comes from the Arabic, meaning "powder of the mine." See *Arsenic.*

Rhodonite (*rō'dô-nīt*). Manganese spar, or manganese silicate, combined with some iron, calcium, or zinc. It occurs crystallized and also in masses, and is usually rose-red in color. It is found in northern Europe and in New York, Massachusetts, and Connecticut. Massive varieties are used for table tops and for similar ornamental purposes. Fine crystals are used to a limited extent as gems.

Ruby. One of the most highly valued of precious stones. The true ruby is a red, transparent, crystallized variety of corundum. As such, it is generally said to have a hardness of 9, although it is actually slightly softer than the sapphire. It is sometimes called oriental ruby to distinguish it from other red stones improperly called rubies.

Genuine rubies are of very limited distribution. They occur chiefly in the gem gravels of Burma and Siam, where they became concentrated after the wearing away of the crystallized dolomitic limestone in which they were formed. They are found in smaller numbers in Ceylon, Russia, Australia, North Carolina, and Montana. The dark red variety from Siam, called ox-blood ruby, has about the same value as the diamond. The world famous variety from Burma, called pigeon-blood ruby, is carmine red. A flawless pigeon-blood ruby weighing more than one carat is usually worth several times as much as a diamond of the same size. Rubies exhibit various shades of color when viewed from different directions by transmitted light (dichroism). When heated they lose color but, on cooling, turn green and then regain their original hue.

The so-called "Cape rubies" of South Africa, the "Australian rubies" of South Australia, and the "Arizona rubies" of the western United States are fine forms of garnet. The "Siberian ruby" is red tourmaline or rubellite, and the "balas ruby" is spinel. Ancient writers used the term ruby for almost any red gem.

Artificial rubies that only an expert can distinguish from the finest oriental gems are now an inexpensive commercial product. They are built up by gradually fusing, in an oxyhydrogen flame, a mixture of powdered aluminum oxide with a small amount of chromium oxide which imparts the red color. These built-up or "synthetic" stones have all the physical and chemical properties of a natural ruby and are often superior in color. Under a magnifying glass either type of stone is seen to contain fine bubbles; in a natural ruby these bubbles are angular, while in the synthetic stone they are rounded. If very fine lines also are noticeable, they will have a common center in the synthetic, but not in the natural stone. See *Corundum, Sapphire.*

Rutile (*ro͞o'tĭl; -tēl*). A mineral composed of titanium dioxide, which sometimes forms beautiful, reddish brown, tetragonal crystals. Rutile is found in the more ancient rock formations of Europe and the United States. It is valuable as one of the ores of the metal titanium. The mineral is used also in welding-rod coatings, alloys, ceramics, and in ivory-tinting artificial teeth. Fine specimens of rutile are sometimes cut for gems. Rutile is obtained chiefly in Norway, South Australia, and Virginia. See *Titanium.*

Sand. A loose, finely granular mass of mineral, commonly consisting of small particles of quartz with a slight admixture of feldspar and mica or other resistant materials. Sand is produced by the decomposition of rocks through chemical action, weathering, and abrasion. It is immensely abundant along the courses of rivers, on the shores of lakes and the ocean, and in arid regions. In most soils, sand is an important constituent.

Many varieties of sand are of great practical value in making mortar, cement, glass, pottery, and foundry molds. Sand is used also for polishing and scouring, as a cutting and etching agent in the sand blast, and for numerous other purposes. See *Gravel, Quartz, Soil.*

Sandstone. A stratified rock, commonly composed of small grains of quartz, but sometimes containing other minerals, such as mica, feldspar, pyroxene, and hornblende. All of these components are more or less solidly cemented together with calcium carbonate, iron oxide, or silica. In color, sandstones are white, gray, yellow, brown, or red, and in hardness and texture they likewise vary greatly. Sandstones are widely distributed throughout the world in rocks of all geologic ages. Among the important varieties are *quartzite, arkose, freestone, brownstone, flagstone, bluestone, novaculite,* and *grit.*

Many kinds of sandstones are of high value as building material. In the eastern United States, the brownstones of Connecticut, the Berea sandstone of Ohio, the Medina sandstone and the Potsdam quartzite of New York are the most extensively used. Valuable deposits of sandstone occur in Washington, Michigan, Iowa, and other states. In Canada there are important quarries in Nova Scotia and Alberta. Grindstones and oilstones are made from certain forms of sandstone. Other kinds are much prized for making pottery, glass, and silica brick. See *Quartz.*

Sapphire (*săf'īr*). A beautiful crystalline variety of corundum or aluminum oxide, highly valued as a gem stone. In composition the sapphire is essentially the same as the ruby, differing from it chiefly in color, and slightly exceeding it in hardness and density. Sapphires vary from pale blue to dark indigo, the most esteemed shade being deep bright blue.

Like rubies, sapphires exhibit different colors or shades when viewed from the proper angles by transmitted light (dichroism). When heated, sapphires lose their color and, unlike rubies, do not regain it upon cooling. The action of radium is said to change the blue color of sapphire first to green and then to yellow. By artificial light, some sapphires seem dark or inky, while others appear violet, so that they seem to be transformed into amethyst.

The finest specimens of blue sapphire are about as valuable as the diamond. These are found chiefly in Ceylon and Siam, but gem sapphires occur also in Burma, Kashmir, Madagascar, Australia, and in North Carolina and Montana in the United States. The sapphires of the ancients and of the Bible are believed to have been varieties of lapis lazuli. Synthetic sapphires are made in the same manner as synthetic rubies, titanium oxide being used, alone or with oxide of iron, as the coloring material. See *Corundum, Ruby.*

Scoria (*skō'rĭ-ȧ*). Volcanic rocks, usually dark to black or reddish in color, which form the porous, cindery, or slaglike products of a volcanic eruption. They belong in the basalt class and are formed in the liquid lava through the action of gas bubbles which give the molten rocks a spongy, cellular, or vesicular character. See *Lava, Obsidian, Pumice.*

Selenite (*sĕl'ê-nīt*). A variety of gypsum, hydrous calcium sulphate, which occurs in large, beautiful, clear crystals, sometimes five feet long, and also in foliated transparent plates, occasionally several feet across. Foliated selenite, like mica, may be split into very thin, flexible sheets. These clear sheets were sometimes used by the ancients to serve the purpose of window glass.

Fine crystals of selenite are found in various parts of Europe, also in Utah and Ohio, while the foliated form is abundant in Nova Scotia and in western New York. Selenite is used to some extent in making paints and as a filler for wall paper. It is employed also for polarizing prisms on petrographic microscopes and for microscopic objectives. See *Gypsum.*

Serpentine (*sûr'pĕn-tīn; -tĭn*). A metamorphic mineral, or rock, composed of hydrous magnesium silicate. It has a resinous luster, is usually massive, and may be white, brown, yellow, or red, but is generally green, often with a mottled appearance resembling the skin of a serpent. Fibrous serpentine, *chrysotile,* is the most important variety of asbestos.

Serpentine is formed by alteration of olivine, pyroxene, amphibole, and other magnesium minerals, and, consequently, from rock such as a peridotite. Because of its attractive color, durability, and easy working quality, serpentine is one of the most valuable of ornamental building stones, especially for interior decoration. Many structures in and near Philadelphia are built of a green serpentinous rock quarried at West Chester, Pa. Serpentine is found in commercial quantities in England, in the Transvaal, in Maryland, New Mexico, Washington, and California. See *Amphibole, Asbestos, Olivine, Peridotite, Pyroxene.*

Shale. A stratified rock composed largely of hardened or mineralized clay that has become solid chiefly because of the pressure of overlying strata. As a result, shales show lines of cleavage essentially parallel to the original bedding plane. In this respect they differ sharply from the slates, to which they are closely related.

Upon being ground and mixed with water, many shales become as workable as ordinary clays, and may be made into bricks. Very refractory shales are used for making fire brick. Those containing much iron oxide may enter into the manufacture of mineral paint. Calcareous shales are frequently used in making Portland cement. Shales containing iron pyrites can be used as a source of alum; shales rich in carbonaceous matter are known as bituminous shales. Many of these carbonaceous deposits contain coal, and others are sources of petroleum.

As the most common of the rocks associated with the Coal Measures, shales frequently contain interesting fossils of the plants and animals of the Carboniferous and other periods. See *Clay, Slate.*

Shale Oil. A mineral oil, similar in character to petroleum, obtained by distilling shales which are rich in bituminous matter. All sedimentary rocks of marine origin contain hydrocarbons. In some fossiliferous black shales, oil may form as high as 20 per cent of the total rock mass. In the Carboniferous rocks of Scotland there are large deposits of oil shale, a ton of which yields about 40 gallons of oily distillate. Rich oil-bearing shales occur also in Utah, New Brunswick, and New South Wales. Many oil shales can be worked profitably, even when the percentage of hydrocarbons is low. On account of the greatly increased demand for petroleum, the production of oil from bituminous shales is a growing industry. See *Petroleum, Shale.*

Siderite (*sĭd'ẽr-īt*). Iron carbonate, called also *chalybite* and spathic iron ore. When pure, it contains 48.3 per cent of iron. It forms yellow-brown rhombohedral crystals of a glassy luster, and is also found in massive deposits and irregular nodules. Siderite occurs in various rock formations, often with other metallic ores. It constitutes the chief commercial supply of iron ore in Great Britain, but it furnishes less than one per cent of the iron ores produced in the United States. See *Hematite, Iron, Limonite, Magnetite.*

Slate. Any fine-grained, metamorphic rock characterized by definite cleavage in one plane, so that it may be easily divided into slabs. In color, slate may be blue, green, or red, but it is usually gray or nearly black on account of the carbonaceous plant matter in the original material from which it was derived.

Slate was formed by the action of enormous pressure on fine, sedimentary deposits such as mud, ash, or, usually, clay. Under this pressure each grain tended to flatten out and to turn with its short axis in line with the acting force. The cleavage planes were therefore produced at right angles to the pressure, in the directions assumed by the longer axis of the grains. As the action was generally produced by a thrust from one side, slaty cleavage is frequently perpendicular to the layers in which the sediment was originally deposited. Slates thus differ from shales, whose cleavage is parallel to the original bedding plane.

Thin slabs of slate are extensively used for roofing, and larger pieces for flooring, sinks, blackboards, the beds of billiard tables, for electrical switchboards, flagstones, grave vaults and coverings, and for school slates. Wales and France are the chief European sources of slate. In the United States, slate is quarried in commercial quantities in some 14 states. Pennsylvania, Vermont, Maine, and Virginia usually lead in slate production. See *Metamorphic Rocks, Shale.*

Soapstone. See *Talc.*

Spinel (*spĭn'ĕl; spĭ-nĕl'*). A beautiful mineral, magnasium aluminate, which occurs usually as red octahedrol crystals. It has a hardness of 8, and, in color, varies to green, blue, white, or almost black.

Spinel may be considered as a compound of magnesium oxide and aluminum oxide. Various members of the spinel group are known, in which these oxides are entirely or partially replaced by similar oxides, such as those of iron and chromium. The red variety is the gem stone *ruby spinel.* This is found associated with rubies and is frequently mistaken for the more valuable stone. But true ruby can scratch spinel, and spinel is not dichroic. Rose-red spinel is usually sold as *balas ruby*; yellow-red or orange-red, as *rubicelle*; the blue variety, as *sapphirine*; and violet to purple crystals, as *almandine.* In the last case it should be noted that true almandine is a garnet.

The most valuable varieties of spinel come from Ceylon and Siam, though some are obtained from New York and New Jersey. See *Ruby.*

Spodumene (*spŏd'ū-mēn*). A mineral composed of lithium and aluminum silicate. It occurs as light green, gray, yellow, or purple monoclinic crystals, with a vitreous luster. The emerald green variety, known as *hiddenite,* found in North Carolina, and the beautiful lilac variety, known as *kunzite,* found near San Diego, California, are popular as semiprecious gem stones. Large crystals of the mineral occur in the Black Hills, South Dakota. Spodumene is found in various other localities of the United States, also in the Tyrol, in Switzerland, and in Scotland. It is valuable as a source of the metal lithium and various lithium salts. See *Lithium.*

Stibnite (*stĭb'nīt*). The chief ore of antimony, consisting of antimony trisulphide. When pure, it contains 71.4 per cent of the metal. Stibnite is a steel-gray mineral with a metallic luster and a hardness of 2. It is found usually as needle-like crystals in beds or veins, in quartz, gneiss, or granite, and occurs chiefly in France, Spain, Germany, Italy, Australia, China, and Japan. Practically no stibnite is mined in the United States, the supply of antimony being obtained largely as a by-product of smelting antimonial lead ores. The ancients used stibnite as a dye for coloring the hair. See *Antimony.*

Talc (*tălk*). A very soft, silvery white, gray, or green mineral, with a pearly or semimetallic luster and a soapy feel. Chemically, talc is a magnesium silicate containing a small amount of water. Ordinarily it is mixed with various impurities. It is an exceedingly abundant mineral, sometimes occurring in large deposits.

The granular massive kinds, commonly called *soapstone,* are much used for hearthstones, mantels, sinks, laundry tubs, table tops, electric switchboards, and insulators. Purified powdered talc is used in paper making, in dressing leather, as a pigment, as a lubricator, and in various toilet preparations, such as talcum powders. Fine granular kinds, known as French chalk, are used in marking.

In the United States, Virginia is the chief producer of soapstone. The purer mineral used for making powdered talc is obtained mostly in St. Lawrence county, New York. Other producing states include Vermont and California. The largest European deposits are in southern France.

Topaz (*tō'păz*). A crystalline mineral, generally yellowish and pellucid, but also colorless and of various shades of blue, green, and brown. In composition, topaz is aluminum fluosilicate; it has a hardness of 8, and, when of good quality, is highly prized as a gem. The finest varieties are found in India, Ceylon, Russia, and Brazil. In the United States, fine topaz, suitable for gems, occurs sparingly in Maine, Colorado, Utah, and California.

The favorite color in topaz gems is a rich orange-yellow. Most of the jewels ordinarily sold as topaz are really *citrine* or yellow quartz. When heated, the yellow Brazilian topaz turns pink. This "burnt topaz" is often called "Brazilian ruby." Yellow corundum is sometimes known as "oriental topaz." Among the ancients the yellow gem stone known to them as topaz (probably chrysolite) was the symbol of friendship. When mounted in gold and hung about the neck, it was supposed to dispel enchantment. See *Aluminum, Ruby, Sapphire.*

Tourmaline (*tōōr'mȧ-lĭn*). A beautiful but very complex mineral, consisting of aluminum borosilicate variously combined with chromium, iron, magnesium, and the alkali metals. It crystallizes in the hexagonal system, has a glassy luster, occurs either transparent or opaque, and may be colorless or blue, green, red, brown, or black. Some crystals are green externally and red internally; other crystals are red at one end and black, green, or blue at the other. Tourmaline usually occurs in granite, gneiss, or mica schist, though it is sometimes found in dolomite, in limestone, and in pebbles.

The white tourmalines are known as *achroite*; the black, as *aphrazite*; the blue, as *indicolite* or *Brazilian sapphire*; the red, as *rubellite* or *Siberian ruby*; and the transparent green, as *Brazilian emerald.* When of marked purity and clearness, the colored varieties are highly valued as gem stones. Such tourmalines occur in Ceylon, Russia, and Brazil. Very fine specimens are found also in Maine, California, and other parts of the United States.

Tourmaline displays remarkable physical properties. By heating or friction it becomes highly electrified. The colored varieties are the most dichroic of the gem stones, while transparent tourmaline possesses to a high degree the power of transmitting polarized light.

Trap Rock. A name somewhat loosely used to designate various close-grained igneous rocks of a black or dark green color, commonly with a columnar structure and a somewhat stairlike arrangement. The term trap has almost the same meaning as basalt or diabase but applies equally well to diorites, gabbros, and other related forms. The trap rocks which assume a dark green color are known also as *greenstone.* Trap rock is used for highway construction, road metal, and concrete aggregate. The Giant's Causeway in Ireland, Fingal's Cave in Scotland, North mountain in Nova Scotia, and the Palisades of the Hudson are noted formations of trap rock. See *Diabase, Gabbro.*

Travertine (*trăv'ẽr-tĭn*). A variety of limestone, commonly with an irregularly banded structure, formed by the deposition of calcium carbonate from springs and rivers. The porous varieties are called also calcareous tufa. Extensive quarries near Tivoli, Italy, furnish the travertine from which a great part of the city of Rome is built. The stone is also used for floor tile, steps and wainscoting. Deposits of travertine occur around the Mammoth Hot Springs in Yellowstone national park. See *Limestone.*

Tufa (*to͞o'fȧ*). Porous rock formed by deposits from the waters of mineral springs. Calcareous tufa, known also as travertine and calcareous sinter, is formed by water containing carbonate of lime (calcium carbonate). Siliceous tufa is deposited by water containing silica. Tufas are coarse, cellular rocks frequently containing twigs, leaves, or other remains of plants, around which the deposits are formed.

Tuff (*tŭf*). Rock composed of more or less finely divided particles of mineral matter, originally ejected from volcanoes and partially or completely compacted. The most noted example of tuff is the thick layer of hardened volcanic ash thrown out by Vesuvius in 79 A. D., under which Pompeii remained buried for many centuries. See *Ash, Volcanic*; *Lava.*

Turquoise (*tŭr-koiz'*; *tûr'kwoiz*). A beautiful, semiprecious stone highly prized for its delicate blue or bluish green shades. In composition it is a hydrous aluminum phosphate colored by copper. Turquoise occurs usually as opaque, kidney-shaped masses with a nodular surface, like that of a bunch of grapes, in igneous or volcanic rocks. The finest turquoise comes from Persia but excellent specimens are found in New Mexico, Colorado, Arizona, Nevada, and California.

When used as a gem, turquoise is usually cut in circular or elliptical form with a low, convex surface. Irregular pieces are often utilized in Eastern lands, where turquoise is used not only for personal ornament, but also for decorating dagger handles, horse trappings, and various other articles. The turquoise is commonly held to be a "lucky stone," especially as a protection against falling.

Wolframite (*wo͝ol'frăm-ĭt*; *wŏl'-*). One of the chief ores of tungsten, composed of a tungstate of iron and manganese. It occurs as black, monoclinic crystals, with a hardness of 5.5. This ore is found usually in igneous rocks, associated with tinstone, bismuth, quartz, and other minerals. Wolframite is mined in various localities in the United States and in Europe. See *Tungsten.*

Wulfenite (*wo͝ol'fĕn-īt*). One of the most beautiful minerals known, occurring in square tabular crystals, in various pyramidal forms, and in crystalline masses. It is an ore of molybdenum, consisting of lead molybdate, and in color ranges usually from yellow to red, with a resinous luster. It occurs in veins, with other lead ores, in various parts of Europe and the United States. Wulfenite is worked to a limited extent as a source of molybdenum. See *Molybdenite, Molybdenum.*

Zincite (*zĭngk'īt*). A valuable ore of zinc, commonly known as the red oxide of that metal. It forms hexagonal crystals of dark red color and somewhat dull luster. Zincite occurs with franklinite, willemite, and other zinc-bearing minerals at various mines in New Jersey. See *Zinc.*

Zircon (*zûr'kŏn*). A native silicate of zirconium which occurs as rounded pebbles and as tetrahedral crystals with pointed ends. Zircon has a hardness of 7.5, and is usually brown and opaque, though some is transparent and beautifully colored.

Because of their hardness, double refraction, and rich colors, the transparent varieties of zircon have long been highly prized as gems. In dispersive power, zircon is exceeded only by the diamond. The red zircons are called *hyacinth*; those that are golden yellow, *jacinth*; while those that are colorless, a condition usually produced by heating, are known as *jargon.* Colorless zircon, more than any other gem, closely resembles a diamond. It is easily distinguished, however, because the diamond is not double refracting.

The most valuable zircons are obtained in Ceylon and New South Wales. Excellent crystals are found in Norway, Russia, and Canada. In the United States, zircon is produced most extensively in Florida, but is found also in North Carolina, New York, New Jersey, and Colorado. The ordinary opaque varieties are employed for furnace and crucible linings, and in making the brilliant zircon light, which is similar to the limelight.

MINERAL PRODUCTS OF THE UNITED STATES

The following is a list of the principal minerals mined in America, with the states leading in the production of each, named in the order of their rank in 1939 as stated in the reports of the United States Bureau of Mines.

PRODUCT	States Leading in Production
Aluminum	New York, Tennessee, North Carolina
Arsenious Oxide	Montana, Utah
Asbestos	Vermont, Arizona, Georgia
Asphalt, Native	Texas, Kentucky, Oklahoma, Alabama
Barite (crude)	Missouri, Georgia, Tennessee, California
Bauxite	Arkansas, Alabama, Georgia
Borates	California, Nevada
Bromine	North Carolina, Michigan, California
Calcium-Magnesium Chloride	Michigan, West Virginia, Ohio
Cement	Pennsylvania, California, Michigan, New York
Chromite	California, Oregon
Clay, Raw	Pennsylvania, Georgia, Ohio, Missouri
Clay Products	Ohio, Pennsylvania, California, Illinois
Coal: Bituminous	West Virginia, Pennsylvania, Illinois, Kentucky
Anthracite	Pennsylvania
Coke	Pennsylvania, Ohio, Indiana, New York
Copper	Arizona, Utah, Montana, Nevada
Emery	New York
Feldspar (crude)	N. Carolina, S. Dakota, New Hampshire
Ferro-alloys	Pennsylvania, New York, Ohio, W. Virginia
Fluorspar	Kentucky, Illinois, Colorado, New Mexico
Fuller's Earth	Georgia, Texas, Florida, Illinois
Garnet, Abrasive	New York, N. Carolina, New Hampshire
Gold	California, Alaska, S. Dakota, Colorado
Graphite: Amorphous	Nevada, Georgia
Crystalline	New York
Grindstones and Pulpstones	Ohio, West Virginia, Washington
Gypsum	New York, Michigan, Iowa, Texas
Iron: Ore	Minnesota, Michigan, Alabama
Pig	Pennsylvania, Ohio, Indiana, Illinois
Lead	Missouri, Idaho, Utah, Oklahoma
Lime	Ohio, Pennsylvania, Missouri, West Virginia
Lithium Minerals	South Dakota, California
Magnesite	Washington, California, Nevada, Vermont
Magnesium	Michigan

PRODUCT	States Leading in Production
Manganese Ore	Montana, Tennessee, Arkansas, Georgia
Manganiferous Ore	Minnesota, New Mexico, Colorado
Mercury	California, Oregon, Idaho, Nevada
Mineral Paints, Zinc and Lead Pigments	Pennsylvania, Illinois, Kansas, Indiana
Molybdenum	Colorado, Utah, New Mexico, Arizona
Natural Gas	Texas, California, Louisiana, Oklahoma
Natural Gasoline	Texas, California, Oklahoma, Louisiana
Oilstones	Ohio, Arkansas, New Hampshire, Indiana
Petroleum	Texas, California, Oklahoma, Illinois
Phosphate Rock	Florida, Tennessee, Idaho, Montana
Platinum and Allied Metals	Alaska, California, Oregon
Potassium Salts	New Mexico, California, Utah, Maryland
Pumice	Kansas, California, Nebraska, New Mexico
Pyrites	Tennessee, Virginia, New York, California
Salt	Michigan, New York, Ohio, Louisiana
Sand and Gravel	New York, Washington, Michigan
Sand-lime Brick	New York, New Jersey, Michigan, Minnesota
Silica Sand and Sandstone (finely ground)	Illinois, New Jersey, Ohio, Pennsylvania
Silver	Idaho, Utah, Montana, Colorado
Slate	Pennsylvania, Vermont, Virginia
Sodium Salts (other than common salt) from Natural Sources	California, Texas, Wyoming, Utah
Stone	Pennsylvania, Michigan, Ohio, New York
Sulphur	Texas, Louisiana, California, Utah
Sulphuric Acid from Copper and Zinc Smelters	Pennsylvania, Illinois, Tennessee
Talc and Soapstone	New York, Vermont, North Carolina, California
Tungsten Ore	Nevada, California, Colorado, Idaho
Uranium and Vanadium Ores	Arizona, Colorado, Utah
Zinc	Oklahoma, New Jersey, Kansas, Idaho

GLACIERS AND GLACIAL ACTION

Illecillewaet Glacier, Selkirk Mountains, British Columbia
Mt. Sir Donald and Glacier, Selkirk Mountains

Moraine Lake, Canadian Rockies
Crevasse Formations, Illecillewaet Glacier

ASTRONOMICAL OBSERVATORIES

Dominion Astrophysical Observatory, Victoria, British Columbia—Dome of 72.5-inch reflector

Yerkes Observatory, Williams Bay, Wis.—Dome 40-inch refractor on right

Greenwich Royal Observatory, London, England
By Burton Holmes, From Ewing Galloway, N. Y.

Mount Wilson Observatory near Pasadena, California—Dome of 100-inch Hooker reflector

ASTRONOMY

ASTRONOMY is the science which has for its subject matter the sun, moon, planets, comets, and stars. It is concerned with the distances, dimensions, constitution, motions, origin, and evolution of these bodies.

HISTORY OF ASTRONOMY

Astronomy is the most ancient of the sciences. It seems to have had its origin, long before the earliest recorded history of mankind, in the everyday needs of primitive peoples. They hunted, sowed, reaped, and held their religious ceremonies at times determined by the phases of the moon and the locations of the heavenly bodies. Familiarity with the positions of the stars enabled the semisavage to penetrate vast forests, to cross wide deserts, and to hold sure course upon pathless seas. These conclusions are supported by the fact that the earliest writings now existing abound in references to important facts of astronomy, and reveal an extent of knowledge which could have been accumulated only by centuries of observations.

The present division of the visible stars into star-groups, or constellations, is believed to have been made by the Babylonians about 5000 years ago. The Chaldeans and the Egyptians measured the length of the year and found that it consists of about 365¼ days. Chinese annals relate that, about 2100 B. C., two royal astronomers were executed for failure to observe an eclipse with proper rites. About 1100 B. C., the Chinese determined the amount of the obliquity of the ecliptic. But it remained for the Greeks to advance astronomy to the plane of an exact science.

Thales (about 640–546 B. C.), one of the "seven wise men" of Greece, systematized and extended the learning of the Babylonians and the Egyptians. Pythagoras (about 582–500 B. C.) taught that the earth is a sphere; Eratosthenes (276–196 B. C.) attempted to measure its circumference and obtained results which were approximately correct.

Hipparchus (about 180–110 B. C.) and Ptolemy (about 100–170 A. D.) were the greatest astronomers of the ancient world. Hipparchus taught that the earth is the center of the universe. He determined the length of the sidereal and tropical years, and made a catalogue of 1080 stars, which he divided according to their apparent brightness into six classes, or magnitudes. Completing the notable work of Hipparchus, Ptolemy explained in detail the apparent motions of the sun, moon, and stars by the theory that these bodies revolve about the earth in circles. His celebrated treatise, the *Almagest*, remained the authoritative work on astronomy for 1500 years.

During the middle ages, astronomy was cultivated by the Arabs, who translated the *Almagest*, by the Moors in Spain, and by the Tatars. The Tatar prince, Ulugh Beg, a grandson of Tamerlane, erected about 1420 a splendid observatory at Samarkand.

The teachings of the *Almagest* held undisputed sway until overthrown by Copernicus (1473–1543), who explained the motions of the sun, moon, and stars by the theory that the earth rotates on its own axis and revolves around the sun. The discovery of the laws of planetary motion by Kepler (1571–1630), the construction and use of the telescope by Galileo (1564–1642), and the discovery of the law of gravitation by Newton (1642–1727) completely confirmed the doctrines of Copernicus.

Since the time of Newton, the theories of the motions of the planets and their satellites have been perfected. The chemical constitution and physical condition of the sun and stars have been determined by means of the spectroscope. On the basis of this knowledge, hypotheses of the origin and evolution of the heavenly bodies have been developed.

VALUE OF ASTRONOMY

Astronomy is the most perfect, most beautiful, and noblest of the sciences. There has never been anything low or mean associated with it. It has the merit, moreover, of having been important in many practical matters, and of still being very useful.

First, astronomy has fixed the dates of events in ancient history which happened to occur at the times of eclipses. (See *Eclipses*.) *Second*, astronomy is of supreme importance in navigation, because observations of the heavenly bodies enable mariners to conduct their ships in safety from port to port throughout the world. *Third*, astronomy is of great assistance in surveying, making it possible to construct accurate maps of continents and oceans, and to fix the boundaries between countries and states. *Fourth*, the correct time is determined daily by observations of the stars (in the United States, principally at the Naval Observatory in Washington), and is sent by telegraph or wireless from observatories to all parts of the world. *Fifth*, the laws of motion and the law of gravitation, which are the fundamental basis of mechanics, were discovered through observations of the relatively simple motions of the heavenly bodies. *Sixth*, the greatest value of astronomy is in the intellectual horizons it has opened up, and in the contributions it has made to philosophy and religion.

SCOPE OF ASTRONOMY

The best-known astronomical object is the earth. All facts concerning it that are determined wholly or chiefly by astronomical means are properly regarded as belonging to astronomy, as are similar facts concerning the various celestial bodies.

The celestial body nearest the earth is the moon. By gravitational control, the earth holds the moon in its orbit, and this satellite, in turn, produces tides upon the earth. The earth is one of nine planets which, owing to the gravitational dominance of the sun, revolve around it in nearly circular orbits. All of the planets except three are accompanied by one or more satellites. Besides the large planets, there are more than 800 small planets, or planetoids, and numerous comets which, likewise, circulate around the sun. The seemingly countless stars which fill the heavens on a clear night, are, in reality, suns, many of which greatly exceed our own sun in size and brilliancy.

The sun and its accompanying system of smaller bodies, the millions of remotely distant suns that we call stars, and the numerous cloudlike objects known as nebulæ, together make up the visible universe. The accumulated knowledge concerning it, gained by observation and tested by measurements, constitutes the science of astronomy. In the following pages various important astronomical subjects are treated in alphabetical order.

Aphelion (*ȧ-fēl'yŭn*). The point in the orbit of a planet or a comet where it is farthest from the sun is called aphelion. The earth is in aphelion about July 1 each year. It is then more than 95,000,000 miles distant from the sun. At this point, the earth is nearly 3,000,000 miles farther from the sun than when in perihelion. See *Perihelion*.

Betelgeuse (*bĕt'ĕl-gûz'*). Betelgeuse is the most brilliant star in the constellation Orion, the Warrior. It is situated on one of the shoulders of the imaginary figure of the hero and may be recognized by its red color. With Sirius in the Great Dog (*Canis Major*) and Procyon in the Little Dog (*Canis Minor*), Betelgeuse forms a conspicuous triangle of first-magnitude stars, which are visible in the southern sky during winter evenings.

Betelgeuse is the first star whose size has been determined. The problem of measuring the diameters of the stars is one of very great practical difficulty.

This is because their distances from us are from 300,000 to many million times as far as the distance from the sun to the earth. Betelgeuse is one of the nearer stars, yet its distance is 70 light years, or more than four hundred million millions (400,000,000,000,000) of miles.

Astronomers suspected Betelgeuse to be a very large star. This suspicion was confirmed in 1920 when the star was measured at the Mount Wilson solar observatory by Professor Michelson's interferometer method. It was found that the diameter of Betelgeuse is 300 million miles. An idea of the immense size of this star can be obtained from the fact that its volume is about 30 million times that of the sun, and from the fact that the volume of the sun is more than a million times that of the earth. See *Orion, Stars*.

Big Dipper. The best-known group of stars in the sky is the Big Dipper, in *Ursa Major*. Its seven second-magnitude stars form an almost perfect outline of a dipper, whose bowl is about 7° wide and 5° deep. The two stars in the bowl, opposite to the handle of the dipper, are almost exactly in a line with the Pole Star, and are known as "the pointers." By means of these stars, one can locate the Pole Star on any clear night. First find the Big Dipper. Then follow an imaginary line from the pointer at the bottom of the bowl through the other pointer and continue beyond it for about 5 times the distance between the two pointers. The bright star at the position indicated is the Pole Star.

The star Mizar at the bend in the handle of the dipper is accompanied by a faint one near it, whose name, Alcor, is said to have meant in Arabic "the test." A person who could see it was regarded as having excellent eyesight, but at the present time it is easily seen by anyone whose eyes are normal. Although Alcor and Mizar appear very close together, the distance between them is more than 15,000 times the distance from the earth to the sun.

The telescope shows that Mizar is a double star, the first telescopic double ever discovered. The two components are so close together that, with the unaided eye, they could not be seen as a double star unless their distance apart were 15 times greater than it is. The fact that the two stars appear to be very close together does not mean that they actually are close together, but simply that their distance from us is so great that they appear to be near each other. They are actually great suns, radiating more than 100 times as much light as our own sun; they are, however, so remote that 75 years are required for their light to come to us.

By means of the spectroscope each of the two components of Mizar has been found to be a double. The system, therefore, consists of four suns—two pairs whose component stars are close together, as compared to the distance between the pairs. The stars comprising the better-known of these pairs revolve about their center of gravity in a period of 20.5 days, at a distance from one another of 25 million miles.

The principal stars in the Big Dipper belong to a group of great suns which are moving through space at the same speed in parallel lines. These stars are so remote that, on an average, 60 years are required for their light to come to us, and they radiate from 7 to 400 times as much light as the sun. See *Constellations, Pole Star*.

Calendar. The week, consisting of seven days, is a unit of time dating from prehistoric antiquity. Each of the seven days corresponds to one of the seven moving heavenly bodies then known, and may, indeed, have been set apart for the worship of a corresponding god or goddess. Sunday was the sun's day; Monday, the moon's day; Tuesday, Mars's (Tues in Norse) day; Wednesday, Mercury's (Wodan's) day; Thursday, Jupiter's (Thor's) day; Friday, Venus's (Frigga's) day; and Saturday, Saturn's day.

In very ancient times the calendar was based almost entirely on the moon. The month is the period from full moon to full moon, about 29.5 days, or a little more than four weeks. Consequently, the month was introduced and twelve months were taken to make a year. But, since there are 12.4 months, by the moon, in a year, the year was gradually displaced with respect to the seasons.

The confusion was serious until 45 B. C., when Julius Cæsar decreed that there should henceforth be three years of 365 days each, and then one year of 366 days, in perpetual cycle. Since there are approximately 365¼ days in a year, this arrangement was satisfactory for many years. But there are not exactly 365¼ days in a year, and, in the course of centuries, the error became appreciable. The accumulated error in the Julian calendar was corrected by Pope Gregory XIII, in 1582, by omitting eleven days from that year. At the same time he instituted a leap year rule.

The leap year rule is as follows: Those years whose date numbers are exactly divisible by 4 are leap years, unless they are also exactly divisible by 100. In such cases they are not leap years unless they are exactly divisible by 400. Thus the year 1900 was not a leap year, but the year 2000 will be a leap year.

The fact that January 1 falls on different days of the week and the fact that the months are of different lengths make our calendar far from satisfactory. The source of the difficulty in attempting to make a more systematic calendar is that a year equals about 52 weeks and 1¼ days. Several suggestions for improving the calendar have been made.

The plan open to the fewest serious objections appears to be the so-called world calendar. According to it, the year consists of twelve months, of which the first, fourth, seventh, and tenth have 31 days and each of the others thirty days. At the end of the year, a day is set aside as Year Day. Every fourth year, Leap Day is added at the end of June. These days are not reckoned as parts of the regular months or weeks, and are recommended to be holidays. The year, as well as each quarter, begins on Sunday and ends on Saturday, the additional days mentioned above being regarded as additional Saturdays. Under this system, the corresponding days in the different years always fall on the same day of the week. Each month has 26 week days. The quarter years are of equal length. See *Day, Time, Chronology*.

Comet. Comets circulate around the sun in elongated orbits, and consist of a head and usually of a tail and a nucleus. The head is spherical in shape, from ten thousand to a million miles in diameter, very tenuous, and generally faint. The tail, which always points away from the sun, whether the comet is approaching or receding, is even fainter and more tenuous than the head, and is often millions of miles in length. The nucleus, which, when present, is situated within the head, is small and starlike.

A few great comets have been visible even in the daytime, but most comets are so faint that they cannot be seen with the unaided eye. About 400 comets were recorded before the invention of the telescope in 1608, and since that time a somewhat larger number have been observed. At the present time from three to ten comets are seen each year.

Many comets come from far beyond the orbit of Neptune, pass around the sun, and then recede to the distances from which they came. Possibly some of them never appear a second time. But the orbits of others are much smaller and extend only to the orbits of the larger planets, especially Jupiter. These comets are supposed to have been captured by the planets with which they are associated.

The existence of comets beyond the orbit of Neptune was one of the indications that possibly there were other planets yet to be discovered. This view was confirmed by the discovery of Pluto in 1930. Some astronomers believe that still other planets may be found when more powerful telescopes are available.

Comets have very small masses. This is proved by the fact that when they pass near a planet they are drawn entirely away from the orbits on which they were traveling, yet they do not affect the planet appreciably. Their nuclei probably consist of swarms of small particles, while their heads and tails are largely gaseous. The earth has passed through the tails of various comets, and, in every case, the effects have been inappreciable. For example, on May 18, 1910, the earth passed through the tail of Halley's comet.

If the nucleus of a comet should strike the earth, probably nothing more serious would happen than a fine meteoric shower. Meteors are simply small particles of matter which are made luminous by friction when they encounter the earth's atmosphere. In fact, there are several meteoric showers which are supposed to be due to the scattered remains of former comets. The best-known is that which occurs each year on November 14–16 in the early morning hours. Every 33 years, corresponding to the period of revolution of the comet of which they are the remains, the shower is conspicuous. Meteoric showers occurred in 1833, 1866, and 1899, but one predicted for 1932 did not come up to expectations. These meteors are called the Leonids because they seem to radiate from a point in the constellation Leo.

In many respects, the most celebrated comet in history is Halley's. This comet, which was visible in 1682, was not discovered by Halley; but in 1687 he computed its orbit by the methods which had just been developed by his friend Newton. Halley found that its orbit was very similar to those of comets which had appeared in 1531 and 1607. Since the three dates—1531, 1607, and 1682—are about 75 years apart, Halley concluded that the three comets were three successive appearances of the same object, and that it revolves around the sun in a period of about 75 years.

From his calculations Halley predicted that this comet would reappear in 1759. In spite of the doubts of his contemporaries, their successors found that Halley's predictions were fulfilled. The comet later passed around the sun and near the earth in 1835 and 1910. It is now invisible in the part of its orbit which extends beyond the paths of the remote planets. Astronomers follow it with their calculations, determine the characteristics of its motions, and know that in obedience to the law of gravitation it will return in 1985.

Greater comets than Halley's are observed at intervals averaging from 20 to 50 years. Very great ones appeared in 1811, 1858, 1861, 1880, and 1882. See *Meteors*.

Constellations. A glance at the sky on a clear night shows that the stars are not uniformly scattered over its surface, but, in many cases, are arranged in natural groups. These natural groups, early observed and variously named by the ancients, became known as the constellations. Often these were given very fanciful names, such as the Lion, the Scorpion, the Lyre, and Orion (the Warrior). Originally, certain parts of the sky did not belong to any of the constellations. Modern astronomers, therefore, added new constellations, especially in those far southern parts of the heavens that were not visible to the ancients, and modified the outlines of others so that the entire sky is now covered.

Ptolemy (about 140 A. D.) enumerated, located, and described 48 constellations. Their names are as follows:

(1) The twelve zodiacal constellations, or those through which the sun passes in its apparent annual motion,—the Ram (*Aries*), the Bull (*Taurus*), the Twins (*Gemini*), the Crab (*Cancer*), the Lion (*Leo*), the Virgin (*Virgo*), the Balance (*Libra*), the Scorpion (*Scorpius*), the Archer (*Sagittarius*), the Goat (*Capricornus*), the Water Bearer (*Aquarius*), and the Fishes (*Pisces*).

(2) Twenty-one constellations found in the northern hemisphere,—the Great Bear (*Ursa Major*), the Little Bear (*Ursa Minor*), the Champion (*Perseus*), the Dragon (*Draco*), the Monarch (*Cepheus*), the Woman in a Chair (*Cassiopeia*), the Woman Chained (*Andromeda*), the Winged Horse (*Pegasus*), Horse's Head (*Equuleus*), the Triangle (*Triangulum*), the Charioteer (*Auriga*), the Hunter (*Boötes*), the Northern Crown (*Corona Borealis*), the Serpent Holder (*Ophiuchus*), the Serpent (*Serpens*), the Kneeling Hero (*Hercules*), the Arrow (*Sagitta*), the Lyre (*Lyra*), the Swan (*Cygnus*), the Dolphin (*Delphinus*), and the Eagle (*Aquila*).

(3) Fifteen constellations in the southern hemisphere,—Orion, the Whale (*Cetus*), the Winding River (*Eridanus*), the Hare (*Lepus*), the Great Dog (*Canis Major*), the Little Dog (*Canis Minor*), Hydra, or the Monster (*Hydrus*), the Cup (*Crater*), the Crow (*Corvus*), the Centaur (*Centaurus*), the Wolf (*Lupus*), the Altar (*Ara*), the Southern Fish (*Pisces Australis*), the Ship (*Argo*), the Southern Crown (*Corona Australis*).

Various other groups have been added since 1600, and now 87 constellations are accepted by astronomers.

In most cases the outlines formed by the stars bear no resemblance to the animals or objects after which the groups were named. There are some exceptions, however, such as the Northern Crown, which is a semicircle of stars. The Indians called it the camp circle, and it is not difficult to imagine that the individual stars represent warriors, seated about a camp fire. The principal stars in the Great Bear are those which constitute the Big Dipper. The Indians called the bowl of the dipper a stretcher on which a sick man was being carried; the first star in the handle was the medicine man who follows behind; the next one at the bend of the handle was the medicine man's wife; and the faint one near it was the dog of the medicine man's wife. *Coma Berenices* (Berenice's hair) is a group of small stars bearing some resemblance to flowing hair, while *Cassiopeia*, in outline, is not unlike a reclining porch chair in which one may imagine a woman is sitting. See *Big Dipper*, *Orion*, *Pleiades*.

Cosmogony (*kŏz-mŏg'ô-nĭ*). The science of the origin and development of the physical universe is called cosmogony. Men in all ages have speculated on the beginning of things. Accounts of the creation are found not only in sacred and classic literatures but also in the folklore of primitive peoples. With the development of civilization and science, fanciful ideas and vague specualtions gave way to theories which were based on ascertained facts, and which were elaborated by careful reasoning.

The Ancient Greeks not only made the first great advances in science but were the first to attempt to found theories of cosmogony on observational data. Unfortunately, their data were wholly inadequate for the successful completion of so great an undertaking. Many centuries of observations of celestial phenomena, and the establishment of the laws of mechanics and the law of gravitation, were necessary before their followers attained any considerable measure of success. And, before success came, the peoples of western Europe sank into the intellectual stagnation of the dark ages, during which only faint sparks from the intellectual torches which the Greeks had lighted were kept alive in the monasteries of Europe. During the 14th and 15th centuries, the blackness of the night of the dark ages gradually gave way to the dawn of the Renaissance, and that has been succeeded by the full day of our own time.

In 1750, Thomas Wright, an Englishman, undertook to explain the origin and evolution of the stars on the basis of the laws of motion and the law of gravitation. His success did not equal either the sincerity of his efforts or the soundness of his point of view. His work had little influence except upon Immanuel Kant, a young German philosopher, into whose hands it chanced to fall.

Kant turned his brilliant and versatile mind to cosmogony and, in 1755, published a book on the subject. The theories which he developed are what might be expected from so keen an intellect, though they are not wholly free from defects in the application of mechanical principles. But the work of Kant had very little immediate effect, for the world seems not to have been ripe for such magnificent and revolutionary speculations. Indeed, Kant so thoroughly recognized the fact that his theories were divergent from current ideas that he published his book anonymously. The welcome accorded recent theories furnishes a measure of the advance in the world's point of view in 160 years.

Laplace, a celebrated French astronomer and mathematician, made the next great step when he published, in 1796, what is known as the *Nebular Hypothesis*. This theory undertook to account only for the planets. Laplace advanced the idea that the atmosphere of the sun, in a highly heated state, once extended beyond the orbit of the most remote planet. He supposed that the whole mass was rotating in the direction in which the planets now revolve. His conclusions were: As the nebula lost heat by radiation, it contracted; as it contracted, it rotated more rapidly; it finally rotated so rapidly that a gaseous ring was left behind in the plane of its equator; later other rings were abandoned, one at the distance of each planet. These rings finally condensed into planets which were at first gaseous, then liquid, and later covered with solid crusts.

The nebular hypothesis of Laplace soon obtained wide acceptance among scientific men. This was partly because the world was ready for such ideas, partly because of the great name and prestige of its author, and partly because of the simplicity of the theory and its obvious harmony with many observed facts. It gave the geologists authority for the theory that the interior of the earth is fluid and that its crust may be only a few hundred miles in thickness, and these conceptions profoundly influenced the development of their science. The work of the geologists in turn reacted on the biologists and paved the way for biological evolution as it appeared, in 1859, in Darwin's *Origin of Species*. At the present time, the doctrine of evolution of both the inanimate and the animate world is central in all scientific theories.

For a century the nebular hypothesis was not seriously challenged. Then, in 1900, Chamberlin and Moulton, starting out to examine it and perhaps to justify it on dynamical grounds, found instead irrefutable arguments against its soundness. It has now been almost universally abandoned, although its value for a century in stimulating thought and directing investigations is universally recognized.

The *Planetesimal Theory* of Chamberlin and Moulton has succeeded the theory of Laplace as a working hypothesis. This new theory starts with the fact that there are hundreds of millions of suns in rapid and diverse motions. At long intervals our own sun, for example, will pass near another sun. At such a time a small part of its mass will be ejected from it and left revolving about it in the form of a small spiral nebula. Modern telescopes show that there are hundreds of thousands of spiral nebulæ. The arms of the spirals will have local condensations, or nuclei, which, in the course of time, will sweep up the scattered material and grow into planets, just as our earth is even yet sweeping up meteoric material and increasing in mass.

According to the planetesimal theory, the planets are all of the same age—at least several hundred million years. The smaller ones are solid through and through, as the earth, by the Michelson-Gale tide experiment, is now proved to be. Moreover, the planets will continue approximately in their present state for hundreds of millions of years in the future, unless the light and heat of the sun should fail or the sun should pass near another sun.

When the sun passes again near another sun, the planets will be broken up and destroyed, and their remains will be scattered along the arms of a new spiral nebula, in time possibly becoming parts of a new family of planets. In this connection it is interesting to note that many meteorites bear internal evidence of having been parts of bodies of worldlike dimensions, and it may be that they are fragments of a family of planets antedating our own. See *Comets*, *Meteorites*, *Nebulæ*, *Planetoids*.

Day. Time is measured by the rotation of the earth. The interval between two successive passages of a star across the meridian is called a *sidereal*, or star, day. Since the stars are fixed and the earth rotates uniformly, all sidereal days are of the same length.

The interval between two successive passages of the sun across the meridian is called a *solar*, or sun, day. Since the sun moves eastward among the stars about one degree a day (360 degrees in 365 days), the solar day is nearly four minutes longer than the sidereal day. The apparent eastward motion of the sun among the stars is not quite uniform, and, consequently, the solar days vary slightly in length. The day of ordinary use is the *mean solar* day, the average of all the true solar days in a year.

The astronomical day begins at noon, and its hours are numbered from 1 to 24. The *civil*, or ordinary, day begins at the preceding midnight. The Greeks counted day from sunset, the Romans, from midnight, and the Babylonians, from sunrise. See *Time*.

Days, Lengths of. The lengths of days and nights vary greatly with the season of the year and with the latitude. These variations are due chiefly to the inclination of the earth's axis of rotation to the plane of its orbit, which is about 66½°.

At the equinoxes, March 21 and September 22, the sun is exactly over the earth's equator and day and night are everywhere practically equal. At the summer solstice, June 21, when the sun is far north, the days attain their greatest length in the northern hemisphere and are shortest in the southern hemisphere. At the winter solstice, December 21, the days are shortest in the northern hemisphere and attain their greatest length in the southern hemisphere. From March 21 to September 22, in the northern hemisphere, the days are longer than the nights. From September 22 to March 21, in the northern hemisphere, the days are shorter than the nights. In the southern hemisphere, these conditions are exactly reversed.

At the poles, the sun remains above the horizon continuously for six months, and remains below the horizon continuously for six months. At the equator, it is day for practically twelve hours and night for practically twelve hours throughout the year.

In all latitudes, the actual length of the day, or the duration of sunlight, is increased somewhat by the effects of the earth's atmosphere. When the sun is near the horizon, the earth's atmosphere acts somewhat like a lens and makes the sun appear to be higher than it actually is. When it seems to be setting it is already a little below the western horizon; similarly, it appears to rise while it is still slightly below the eastern horizon. The result is that the lengths of all days are increased, while the lengths of the nights are correspondingly diminished, and the longest days in summer are everywhere somewhat longer than the corresponding longest nights in winter.

The lengths of the longest and the shortest day, which in the northern hemisphere are June 21 and December 21 respectively, are shown for various latitudes up to 65° 55′ in the following table. The day in the table means the interval between the apparent rising and setting of the sun's center. Above latitude 65° 55′ the longest days exceed 24 hours, and they rapidly increase in length toward the poles, where the sun is above the horizon continuously for a little more than half of the year. At the equator, the shortest days (12 hrs. 5 min.) are March 21 and September 22, and the longest (12 hrs. 6 min.) are June 21 and December 21.

LONGEST AND SHORTEST DAYS

Latitude	Longest, June 21		Shortest, Dec. 21	
	Hrs.	Min.	Hrs.	Min.
10°	12	37	11	30
20°	13	16	10	52
30°	14	2	10	10
40°	14	58	9	16
50°	16	18	8	0
60°	18	44	5	44
65° 55′	24	0	2	38

Earth. The globe on which we live is approximately spherical in shape, as is proved by the fact that it has been circumnavigated, that ships disappear below the horizon hulls first and masts last, and that when the ocean is viewed from an elevation the horizon appears to be a circle. But the best proof of the earth's sphericity is that its surface everywhere has nearly the same curvature, a fact that has been established by measurements of arcs and the corresponding changes in the direction of the plumb line with respect to the stars.

As a matter of fact, the rotation of the earth produces a slight bulging at the equator and a flattening at the poles, the difference in the polar and equatorial diameters being about 27 miles. The polar diameter is nearly 7900 miles and the equatorial diameter is about 7926.6 miles, the possible error in the results being less than 1000 feet. The equatorial circumference is 24,902 miles.

The average density of the earth is 5.5 times the density of water, and its total mass is 6,592,000,000,000,000,000,000 (6.592 billion trillion) tons. The interior of the earth is very hot, but the material of which it is composed is not melted because of the great pressure to which it is subjected. At the earth's center the pressure is 22,500 tons per square inch. The tidal experiments of Michelson and Gale have shown that the earth is not only solid but that it is as elastic as steel.

The earth's atmosphere is composed of about 78 per cent nitrogen, 21 per cent oxygen, and small quantities of a few other elements and compounds. The pressure of the atmosphere at the earth's surface is 15 pounds per square inch, and its total mass is about one-millionth that of the entire earth. It extends in appreciable quantities to a height of approximately 100 miles, as is proved by the fact that meteors become visible up to this altitude.

The earth rotates eastward, and the eastward velocity of the surface at the equator is more than 1000 miles an hour, or about 1500 feet per second. The rotation of the earth causes the easterly drifts of the winds in the middle latitudes.

The earth revolves about the sun in an elliptical, or slightly elongated, orbit, in a period of 365 days, 5 hours, 48 minutes, and 46 seconds, at an average speed of 18.5 miles per second. The average distance of the earth from the sun is 92,900,000 miles, the difference between the greatest and least distances being about three million miles. The earth is nearest the sun the last of December. Nevertheless, it is then winter in the northern hemisphere. This is due to the fact that the seasons are caused chiefly by the inclination of the earth's axis, the northern end of which, at that time, is turned away from the sun. See *Moon, Planets, Satellites.*

Eclipse. An eclipse of the sun occurs when the moon passes between the sun and the earth. If the entire disk of the sun is obscured, the eclipse is *total*; if only a part of it is obscured, the eclipse is *partial*. Although the moon is much smaller than the sun, it is so much nearer to the earth that usually it a little more than covers the sun's disk, just as a small coin held at arm's length will more than cover the sun's disk. The moon's apparent diameter, however, exceeds that of the sun by only a small amount. In fact, when the moon in its elongated orbit is farthest from the earth, its apparent diameter is a little less than that of the sun. If an eclipse occurs under these circumstances, a bright ring is left uncovered around the sun, and the eclipse is said to be *annular*. Since, under the most favorable circumstances, the moon but slightly more than covers the sun, an eclipse of the sun is of short duration, never exceeding 7.5 minutes.

An eclipse of the moon occurs when the moon passes into the earth's shadow. If the moon passes entirely into the earth's shadow, the eclipse is *total*; otherwise, it is *partial*. The diameter of the earth's shadow at the distance of the moon is about three times the diameter of the moon; therefore, when the moon passes through the center of the earth's shadow, it is totally eclipsed for nearly two hours.

Eclipses of the sun are somewhat more numerous than those of the moon. However, the infrequency with which solar eclipses are observed, when compared with observations of the lunar, might lead to the opposite conclusion. The reason is that when an eclipse of the moon occurs, it is visible from the whole half of the earth which is toward the moon, while an eclipse of the sun is visible only from the narrow zone on the earth across which the moon's shadow sweeps. The path of totality is usually less than 100 miles in width. From this it follows that only very rarely will any particular place be in the path of totality.

The times and places of eclipses depend upon the motions of the sun and the moon. The motions of these bodies can be predicted so accurately by astronomers that all the circumstances of eclipses for indefinitely long periods can be foretold with great accuracy. Similarly, the times and places at which eclipses have occurred in the past can be calculated with corresponding accuracy. This fact has been of use in establishing several important dates of ancient history. In a number of instances, ancient writers have referred to historical events in connection with total eclipses of the sun. Astronomers, by extending their calculations back across the intervening centuries, have been able to determine, in our system of reckoning time, the dates of these events.

Eclipses are phenomena of considerable scientific interest. They afford the best opportunities for searching for planets interior to the orbit of Mercury, and they enable astronomers to observe comets if any happen to be close to the sun. It is only during total eclipses that the sun's corona can be observed and Einstein's theory of the bending of light rays tested. This test of the theory of relativity was first made in 1919.

Ecliptic. The apparent annual path of the sun among the stars is called the *ecliptic*. It is a great circle in the heavens and is inclined to the celestial equator at an angle of 23° 27′. The two points where the ecliptic and the equator cross are the *equinoxes*.

The twelve zodiacal constellations lie along the ecliptic. The moon and planets move around the sky through these constellations and always remain near the ecliptic. In ancient times, and later wherever astrology flourished, the positions of the sun, moon, and planets among the zodiacal constellations were supposed to have important influences on human affairs. See *Constellations, Equinoxes.*

Equinoxes. The two points where the sun, in its annual motion among the stars, crosses the celestial equator are called the *equinoxes*. These are so named because, when the sun is at either of these points, day and night are equal in length. The celestial equator is a circle on the sky parallel to the earth's equator.

On March 21, at the *vernal equinox*, the sun crosses the equator from south to north; on September 22, at the *autumnal equinox*, it crosses from north to south. In the northern hemisphere, from March 21 to September 22 the days are longer than the nights;

from September 22 to March 21 the days are shorter than the nights. In the southern hemisphere the reverse is true.

Island Universes. Certain spiral nebulæ outside the Milky Way are so far distant from our system of stars that they are regarded as separate, or island, universes. A nebula in the Great Dipper and one in the constellation of Andromeda have been shown to be almost a million light years distant. Light reaching us from the more distant of these universes began its travels before man existed on the earth. Our universe, however, is larger than any other yet known.

Jupiter. The largest planet in the solar system is Jupiter, whose diameter is about 88,000 miles, or more than 11 times that of the earth. Although nearly 400 million miles distant, this planet is brighter than any other except Venus.

Jupiter revolves around the sun at a mean distance of 483 million miles in a period of 11.86 years. Notwithstanding its great size, its average period of rotation is 9 hrs. 54 min. The equator of Jupiter, like those of the sun and Saturn, rotates a little faster than the higher latitudes. Since different parts of the surface rotate at different rates, it follows that the planet must be largely in a liquid, or even gaseous, condition. This might be inferred also from the fact that the planet's average density is only 1.25 times that of water. There are great belts parallel to Jupiter's equator which undergo continual and often radical changes. In 1878 a great red spot, 7000 by 30,000 miles in extent, suddenly appeared and remained conspicuous on the surface of the planet for about 20 years.

Jupiter has 9 satellites, the largest 4 of which were discovered by Galileo in 1610. They were the first celestial objects discovered with a telescope. The largest of these satellites is 3558 miles in diameter, and, were it not buried in the brilliant rays of the great planet, could be seen with the unaided eye. A fifth satellite, about 100 miles in diameter, was discovered in 1892. The last 4 have been discovered by photography. The 2 most remote from the planet revolve in the direction opposite to that in which all the other satellites move. See *Planets, Satellites*.

Light Year. When astronomers found that the distances of the stars were too great to be conveniently expressed in miles, they began to employ a new unit, the *light year*. This is the distance that light travels in a year. Since the velocity of light is 186,000 miles per second, it follows that this great unit is about 63,500 times the distance of the earth from the sun, or nearly six trillion miles.

The nearest known star is more than 4 light years distant, and only a few are less than 50 light years from the earth. Most of the stars visible to the unaided eye are not more than 200 or 300 light years away. The telescope, however, reveals nebulæ as far off as 50 million light years. See *Stars*.

Mars. The next planet beyond the orbit of the earth is ruddy Mars, a world which revolves around the sun at an average distance of 141,500,000 miles in a period of 1.88 years, or nearly 23 months. The earth and Mars are on the same side of the sun every 2 years, 1 month, and 18.7 days, and then their distance from each other, on the average, is only 48,600,000 miles. At such times Mars is favorably located for observations from the earth. The earth and Mars both revolve in somewhat elongated orbits which are so situated that every 17 years these planets pass within about 35 million miles of each other.

Mars has two little satellites, Phobos and Deimos, each about 10 miles in diameter and barely visible through the largest telescopes. Phobos is less than 4000 miles from the planet and revolves eastward more rapidly than the planet rotates. Consequently it rises in the west and sets in the east.

Measurements show that Mars has a diameter of 4339 miles. Its volume, therefore, is only about one-seventh that of the earth. Moreover, its average density is only two-thirds that of our planet. Objects on Mars weigh only 36 per cent as much as the same objects would weigh upon the earth's surface. Hence the size, density, and surface gravity of Mars are intermediate between those of the earth and the moon. The moon does not have enough attraction to hold the swiftly darting particles of which an atmosphere is composed. It would, therefore, be concluded that Mars could not retain so extensive an atmosphere as that which surrounds the earth. For our observations of this planet, it is fortunate that such is found to be the case, as its surface is rarely obscured by clouds.

The surface of Mars bears little resemblance to that of the earth. It has no great water-covered areas like our oceans. Most of the surface is dull brick red in color, though there are large darker regions having a greenish tinge. These dark markings are permanent, and, from observations of them, it has been found that the length of the planet's day is 24 hours and 37 minutes, or only a little longer than that of the earth. Moreover, the inclination of the equator of Mars to the plane of its orbit is 23 or 24 degrees. Consequently, the planet not only has days and nights similar to those of the earth, but also seasons which are similar, except that they are nearly twice as long.

In 1877 an Italian astronomer, Schiaparelli, saw numerous long, narrow, dark-colored streaks, which he called *canali*. Similar ones were later observed in greater numbers by Percival Lowell. On the other hand, many astronomers having larger telescopes than either Schiaparelli or Lowell have been unable to see these streaks, or "canals," as they have come to be called. They cannot be canals in the ordinary sense, for it would be necessary for them to be at least 20 miles wide in order, under the most favorable conditions, to be visible at the distance of 35 or 40 million miles which separates Mars from the earth. According to the descriptions, very remarkable things about the streaks are that they are of uniform width and often two or three thousand miles in length, that they always extend along the arcs of great circles, and that they undergo changes in appearance with the seasons of the planet.

Elaborate theories have been built up, explaining the "canals" as streaks of vegetation growing along the banks of actual canals constructed by beings of a high order of intelligence. At first, such a theory meets a ready response in the minds of most persons. Upon critical examination, however, it is found to be beset with so many serious difficulties that few, if any, astronomers now regard it with favor. This does not mean that astronomers are averse to the hypothesis that many worlds support life, but indicates simply that the evidence for the existence of high forms of life on Mars is weak. Besides, there are good reasons for believing that the conditions on the planet's surface are very unfavorable.

Among the most interesting phenomena observed on Mars are its white polar caps. These make their appearance rather suddenly, late in the planet's autumn. They persist during its long winter, and gradually disappear as its spring advances to midsummer. They have the appearance of snow fields which come and then disappear, just as snow falls and later melts away in the higher latitudes on the earth. The phenomena of the polar caps long supported the belief that the climate of Mars is warmer than that of the earth.

Since Mars is farther from the sun than the earth is, it receives less heat per unit area; in fact, it receives only 43 per cent as much heat per unit area as the earth. The amount of heat Mars receives compares with that received by the earth, almost exactly as the heat received at the earth's pole in a year compares with that received at the earth's equator. Since the temperature of the earth's surface at its poles is much lower than that at its equator, it would be expected that the temperature of Mars is much below that of the earth. Such is undoubtedly the fact.

If the earth were as distant from the sun as Mars is, its average temperature, instead of being 60°, as it is now, would be about 40° below zero. Since the atmosphere of Mars is much thinner than that of the earth, it seems very probable that the average temperature of this planet is colder than 40° below zero. The polar caps of Mars do not disappear by melting, but because the snow, or hoarfrost, of which they are composed, evaporates into the dry, cold air of the planet. They vanish just as do the snows of the western prairies, which often disappear into the dry, frigid winds that blow over them in midwinter. See *Planets*, *Satellites*.

Mercury. Mercury is the planet nearest to the sun, with a mean distance of about 36 million miles and a period of revolution of 88 days. On account of the eccentricity of its orbit, which is greater than that of any other planet, its greatest and least distances from the sun differ by nearly 15 million miles.

Mercury is morning star for a period of about two weeks three times each year, and evening star also for similar periods three times each year. It never rises more than two hours earlier than the sun, nor sets more than two hours later than the sun. For these reasons, Mercury must always be observed either in dawn or twilight. Consequently, it is somewhat difficult to see it with the unaided eye.

Mercury is the smallest planet, being only 3000 miles in diameter. Although so small that it holds no appreciable atmosphere, the planet is so unfavorably situated that few surface markings have been observed. Its period of rotation is uncertain, but observations indicate that Mercury always keeps the same side toward the sun.

Meteorites. Meteorites, known also as aerolites, uranolites, and siderites, are solid masses, weighing from a few pounds to many tons, which plunge down upon the earth from the regions beyond its atmosphere. Two or three per year are seen to fall, but the number striking the earth annually is probably as many as 100. The largest ever known fell in an uninhabited region of Siberia in 1908. It consisted of over 200 pieces, aggregating possibly 40,000 tons. Trees were felled and charred within a radius of 25 miles, and the earthshock was felt at a distance of 500 miles.

The exterior parts of meteorites are fused and glazed and their less refractory parts are burned out by the heat generated in their passage through the earth's atmosphere. Characteristic pits are left in their surfaces, while the rapid heating to which they are subjected produces frequent chipping and fragmentation. Most meteorites are stony in composition, much like our granites, although they sometimes contain particular combinations of elements not found in the earth's rocks. A small fraction of them are almost pure iron, or a mixture of iron and nickel. About 30 of the 90 known elements occur in meteorites. All elements so far found in them occur abundantly in the earth.

The question of the origin of meteorites is one to which the answer is not certainly known. They are probably the remains of the masses circulating around the sun, out of which the planets have grown by processes similar to those which are going on at the present time. They may, indeed, be fragments of a family of planets, antedating our own, which were broken up by the near approach of a passing star. See *Cosmogony*.

Meteors. The swiftly moving points of light which flash out suddenly and dart across the sky are called meteors, or "shooting stars." They are not stars, as they appear to be, but are tiny masses of matter, often the remains of disintegrated comets. These small particles become heated and luminous by friction with our atmosphere when they plunge into it with a speed averaging more than 20 miles per second. Meteors often emit sparks, sometimes they explode, and occasionally they leave behind a luminous trail, which persists for several seconds. If the product of their combustion is gaseous, it is added to the air; if it is solid, it slowly settles to the surface of the earth. In either case the total mass of the earth is increased; but the earth's rate of growth in this way is now exceedingly slow.

The heights at which meteors become luminous can be determined by observing them from two stations a few miles apart. By this means it has been found that meteors usually become visible at an altitude of 70 to 90 miles, and that they disappear at altitudes of 30 to 50 miles. The same observations determine the lengths of their trails, usually 50 to 100 miles, and the velocities with which they move.

Two or three meteors per hour can be observed on almost any clear night. Since only a very small part of the entire atmosphere of the earth is within the range of a single observer, this means that from 10 to 20 million strike the earth daily. Usually they are quite unrelated to one another.

Occasionally meteors occur in great numbers and all seem to radiate from the same point in the sky. These "meteoric showers," as they are called, appear year after year on the same dates, and their radiant points are at the same positions among the stars. The best example of these meteoric showers is that of the Leonids. These radiate from the Sickle in Leo, and appear between midnight and dawn on November 14–16. They are the remains of a comet which was captured by the planet Uranus in 126 A. D. At their nearest approach to the sun they just touch the orbit of the earth. Since their present period of revolution is 33 years, unusually noteworthy showers occur at this interval, the last having been observed in 1932.

Another well-known shower is that of the Andromedes, which are seen in the evening hours on November 24. These meteors appear in unusual numbers at intervals of 13 years, but the greatest showers of Andromedes do not compare in numbers with the thousands of Leonids that were seen in 1833 and 1866. The Perseids may be observed in considerable numbers each year from about the 5th to the 15th of August. There are many other lesser showers. See *Comet*, *Meteorites*.

Milky Way, or **Galaxy.** The Milky Way is a hazy, somewhat irregular band of light, about 20° wide, which completely encircles the heavens. It can be seen on clear, moonless, summer evenings, stretching entirely across the northern sky. In May and early June, at 8 o'clock in the evening, it extends from the eastern horizon to the western horizon, crossing the meridian about 30° north of the zenith. On other dates and at other times of the night, its course across the sky is oblique.

The most conspicuous constellations crossed by the Milky Way are Cassiopeia, Cygnus, Perseus, the eastern part of Auriga, the western parts of Taurus and Orion, Scorpius, and Ophiuchus. Deneb and the red Antares are in its midst, while Capella, Betelgeuse, Procyon, and Sirius are near its borders.

The unaided eye gets the impression that the Milky Way is made up of faint stars. The telescope confirms this impression by showing that the light of the Milky Way is caused by millions of stars. In reality these stars are great suns, and they appear faint only because of their immense distances. Most of them are so remote that several thousand years are required for their light to come to us.

The form of the Galaxy shows that the system of stars to which our sun belongs has the shape of a flattened disk whose diameter is about 10 times its thickness. The dimensions of this system are so vast that thousands of years are required for light to cross it, even in the direction of its smallest diameter. The sun and the planets are far within the interior of the system. Its diameter is so great that they cannot approach its borders for millions of years, although the solar system is now moving with respect to the stars at the rate of 400 million miles a year. See *Stars*.

Moon. The moon is the earth's only satellite, and it revolves around the earth from west to east at an average distance of 238,862 miles in a period of about 27.3 days. Its period from full moon to full moon, or the ordinary month, is about 29.5 days. The moon rotates on its axis in the same direction as that in which it revolves round the earth, and with the same angular velocity. The result is that it always keeps the same face toward the earth.

The moon shines entirely by reflected light, and its phases depend upon its position relative to the earth and the sun. When it is between, or nearly between, the earth and the sun, its dark (unilluminated) side is toward the earth, and then its phase is *new*. It is then seen, if at all, as a very thin crescent, either low in the west in the evening or in the east in the morning. A week after the moon is new, it is in the south when the sun is setting, its western half is illuminated, and its phase is *first quarter*. In another week the *full moon* rises as the sun sets. In still another week its phase is *third quarter* and the moon is in the south as the sun rises, with the eastern side illuminated.

The moon's diameter is 2163 miles, or a little more than one-fourth that of the earth. Its average density is only about 60 per cent that of the earth. As a consequence of its small size and moderate density, its surface gravity is only one-sixth that of the earth. Such a feeble gravity cannot control the rapidly moving molecules in a gas, and, as a result, the moon has no atmosphere.

The surface of the moon is very rough, being largely covered with rugged mountains and steep-walled craters, but there are on it a few comparatively smooth areas several hundred miles in diameter. The smooth areas are relatively dark and cause those markings which appear to some people as "the man in the moon." Some of the mountains are 20,000 feet in height and their sides are often very steep. The craters are circular pits with steep walls, quite unlike the volcanic craters on the earth, and they range in diameter from the smallest that can be seen through the most powerful telescopes to immense cavities more than 100 miles across.

Since the moon has neither water nor an atmosphere, there has been no disintegration and washing away of its rocks and mountains. The moon's surface, therefore, preserves for examination through our telescopes the records of the violent forces by which it has been disturbed. The earth's surface, on the other hand, has been subject to the action of the elements during the immense periods of the geologic ages. The earliest mountains and craters were long ago totally destroyed, and their disintegrated remains were scattered in primitive oceans and valleys.

Since the moon rotates in the same period as that in which it revolves, its day from noon to noon is 29.5 of our days in length. Its surface is subjected alternately to the burning rays of the sun for 14.75 of our days, and to the frigidity of a night of equal length, and neither the heat of the day nor the cold of the night is ever tempered by a passing cloud. It is clear that a body having neither soil nor water and no atmosphere, and with a temperature ranging from 100 degrees below zero to the boiling point, cannot support life. See *Earth, Satellites, Tides*.

Nadir (*nā'dẽr*). The point in the celestial sphere exactly beneath the place where one stands is the nadir. It is directly opposite to the zenith and is called the inferior pole of the horizon. Using the zenith and the nadir as starting points, the horizon may be defined as a great circle of the celestial sphere situated at 90°, or equidistant, from each of them. See *Zenith*.

Nebulæ (*nĕb'ū-lē*). The invention of the telescope was followed by the discovery of numerous very faint clouds of matter which were called nebulæ. Two of these, the Great Orion Nebula and the Great Andromeda Nebula, under favorable conditions are barely visible to the unaided eye; most of the remainder are very faint, and some are at the limits of the most powerful photographic telescopes.

In the days of William Herschel (the latter part of the 18th century) nebulæ were supposed to be immense aggregations of stars which were so remote that their individual members could not be distinguished. The spectroscope showed, however, that in many cases nebulæ are vast masses of gas lying among, and often associated with, the stars. For example, the principal members of the Pleiades group are involved in thin wisps of nebulæ which extend from star to star.

The principal classes of nebulæ are (a) those which are irregular in form, (b) the spirals, (c) those which are ring-shaped, and (d) the planetaries. The irregular nebulæ, of which several thousand are known, are often many degrees in length. Since an object a thousand million miles across, at the distance of even the nearer stars, appears to be less than a second of arc in diameter, the dimensions of these nebulæ are enormous. The diameter of the Orion nebula, for example, is probably much more than 20 million times that of the sun.

The spiral nebulæ usually have two fairly well defined arms winding out on opposite sides from a central nucleus. Knots and local condensations are generally scattered along their branches, and they have little resemblance to gaseous bodies. Their light resembles that received from the stars rather than that received from the irregular nebulæ. Certain spiral nebulæ have recently been proved to be galaxies, several of them having been shown to be at a distance of approximately 1 million light years. The view has also been advanced that some spiral nebulæ are fragments of stars or of star groups diffused as a result of the close passage of two stars or of two star groups.

A number of nebulæ are ring-shaped, the best example of the type being in the constellation Lyra. This nebula is a symmetrical, nearly circular oval, and has a faint star at its center.

The planetary nebulæ consist of circular disks of nebulous matter having a dense, or starlike nucleus, surrounded by one or more zones of more tenuous materials. It is believed that they represent the last stages in the condensation of rare nebulæ into stars. See *Cosmogony, Orion, Pleiades*.

Neptune. The second most remote planet is Neptune, which revolves about the sun at an average distance of 2792 million miles in a period of nearly 165 years. The planet is faint because it is so far from the sun that it is feebly illuminated and because it is so far from the earth that its apparent size is small, although its diameter is nearly 35,000 miles.

The discovery of Neptune like that of Pluto is one of the triumphs of modern science; for its position in the heavens was determined by mathematical processes before it had been observed. The planet Uranus was discovered in 1781 and its orbit was computed. Observers found by 1821, or 40 years after its discovery, that it was not exactly following its predicted path. By 1830 the discrepancy was a little larger; by 1840 it was still more serious. This does not mean that the difference between theory and observation was very great; it was actually too small to be detected with the unaided eye. The importance of this trifling disagreement arose from the fact that it called in question the laws of motion, the law of gravitation, and the processes of mathematics.

The suggestion was made that the unexplained peculiarities in the motion of Uranus might be due to the attraction of an unknown planet. The problem of finding the hypothetical planet from its effects, which were so slight as to be scarcely discernible after they had accumulated for 60 years, was one of such great difficulty that it was supposed to be insoluble. It was attacked, however, and, in 1846, solved independently by Adams, a young English astronomer, and by Leverrier, a young French astronomer. The planet was first seen through a telescope by Galle, a German, who directed his instrument in accordance with Leverrier's instructions. See *Planets, Satellites.*

Orion (*ō-rī'ŏn*). The finest constellation in the heavens is Orion, which may be seen in the southern sky in the evening during the winter months. It contains the bluish white, first-magnitude star Rigel and the ruddy Betelgeuse. Rigel is very remote and radiates several thousand times as much light as our sun. Betelgeuse is a nearer and more enormous sun. Professor Michelson in 1920 measured its diameter with a special instrument of his own invention, and established the fact that its volume is about 30 million times that of the sun.

A little east of the line joining Rigel and Betelgeuse are three second-magnitude stars which constitute the Belt of Orion. They are equally spaced on a line which crosses the celestial equator in a northwest-southeast direction. A few degrees below the belt are three fainter stars on a north-south line. The central one of the three appears slightly fuzzy to the unaided eye. Through a telescope it is found to be a nebula, the Great Orion Nebula. See *Betelgeuse, Nebulæ.*

Perihelion (*pĕr'ĭ-hē'lĭ-ŏn*). When a planet or a comet reaches the point in its orbit where it is nearest the sun, it is said to be in perihelion. The earth reaches this point about January 1 each year. On account of the eccentricity of its orbit, the earth in perihelion is about 3,000,000 miles nearer the sun than on July 1, when it is farthest away, or in aphelion. See *Aphelion.*

Planetoids (*plăn'ĕt-oids*). Between the orbits of Mars and Jupiter there revolve small, planet-like bodies called planetoids. They are known also as asteroids. Those at present known number over 1500 and range in diameter from one-third of a mile to nearly 500 miles. The first one was discovered by Piazzi on the first day of the 19th century.

After two or three of these bodies had been discovered, astronomers thought that they might be the fragments of what was once a large planet which had been broken up by unknown forces. If this were the case, the orbits of all the planetoids would intersect at the point where the disruption occurred, because all of the fragments would move in closed curves. The later discovery of planetoids whose orbits were far removed from the orbits of some of those earlier known completely disproved the shattered-planet hypothesis.

Many more planetoids were discovered during the 19th century. A new epoch was started in 1891 when Wolf found planetoids by means of photography. Since these objects are moving among the stars, their images on plates which have been given long exposures are little streaks instead of points like the images of the stars.

In 1936 a planetoid was discovered whose orbit, at its nearest approach to the sun, comes within 1,376,000 miles of the earth's orbit. It is known as Adonis. The planetoid Apollo may approach within 3,000,000 miles of the earth. Planetoids have been found whose distances from the sun are about the same as that of Jupiter. It is not improbable that there are others beyond; but, because of the distance from the sun and the earth, it would be difficult to see such small bodies.

It is probable that the planetoids are similar to the larger planetesimal masses out of which the planets grew. The great number existing between the orbits of Mars and Jupiter is due to the fact that no dominating planetary nucleus circulated in this region and swept up the smaller masses. See *Cosmogony.*

Planets. The planets are the largest nine bodies revolving about the sun. They travel in elliptical orbits. Their diameters range from 3000 miles, in the case of Mercury, to 88,000 miles, in the case of Jupiter; their periods of revolution range from 88 days, in the case of Mercury, to 165 years, in the case of Neptune, and about 250 years in the case of Pluto, which was discovered in 1930 but is still inadequately studied.

The nine known planets are arranged in the accompanying table in the order of their distance from the sun. Mercury, Venus, Earth, and Mars are dense and solid; they have short periods of revolution and long periods of rotation, as shown in the table. They have only 3 satellites, as against 25 possessed by the other four well-known planets, Jupiter, Saturn, Uranus, and Neptune. These latter are rare and gaseous and have long periods of revolution and short periods of rotation.

All the planets, except Uranus, Neptune, and Pluto, are easily visible to the unaided eye, and have been known since prehistoric times. Uranus is on the limits of visibility without a telescope. Neptune is visible only through a telescope, and Pluto, the most distant, can be detected only by means of photographic plates exposed through telescopes. See articles on individual planets.

TABLE OF PLANETS

PLANET	Mean Diameter (miles)	Density (earth's 1)	Mass (earth's 1)	Mean Distance from sun (millions of miles)	Period of Revolution	Period of Rotation
Mercury	3,000	0.81 (?)	0.045	36.0	88 days	88 days
Venus	7,700	0.88	0.807	67.2	225 days	68 hrs.(?)
Earth	7,918	1.00	1.0	92.9	365 days	1 day
Mars	4,339	0.65	0.106	141.5	687 days	24.6 hrs.
Jupiter.	88,392	0.23	314.5	483.3	11.862 yrs.	9.9 hrs.
Saturn	74,163	0.11	94.1	886.0	29.458 yrs.	10.23 hrs.
Uranus	30,193	0.26	14.4	1,781.9	84.015 yrs.	10.75 hrs.
Neptune	34,823	0.20	16.7	2,791.6	164.788 yrs.	15.8 hrs.
Pluto	4,200 (?)			3,525.0	249.17 yrs.	

Pleiades (*plē'à-dēz; plī'à-*). The Pleiades are a compact group of faint (fourth-magnitude) stars in the constellation Taurus, and they are popularly known as the Little Dipper or the Seven Sisters. These stars are visible in the evening during the winter months. Six of them can be seen easily by persons with normal eyes, while the seventh, which is at the end of the handle of the dipper, is nearer the limits of visibility. Under the most favorable conditions, those who have exceptionally keen sight can make out 10 stars in the group. With a 3-inch telescope, about 100 stars are visible in the cluster, while the powerful photographic telescopes of recent times show that the whole group is involved in immense, tenuous nebulæ extending from star to star.

According to Greek legend, the Pleiades were the seven daughters of Atlas and Pleione who were translated to the sky and transformed into stars. According to the tribal tales of the Pawnee Indians, they were the seven brothers of a famous chief who lost their earthly lives in glorious battles. They were "The Many Little Ones" of the ancient Babylonians, and "The Little Eyes" of the savages of the South Pacific islands. No other stars have been mentioned more often in sacred and classic literature, or occur more frequently in the folklore of primitive peoples. The Aztecs determined the times of religious ceremonies by their time of crossing the meridian, and the primitive Australian tribes held dances in their honor.

According to modern astronomical measurements, the Pleiades are magnificent suns, 200 or 300 times as great in light-giving power as our own sun. They appear faint only because of our great distance from them. When we look at them at night, we see them with light which has been on its way for 300 years; if they should suddenly cease to exist, we should continue to see them for 300 years in the future. See *Constellations*, *Nebulæ*.

Pluto. This is the outermost of the planets. Its orbit, inclined at 17°9′ to that of the earth, is a pronounced ellipse, its distance from the sun varying from 2.75 to 4.3 billion miles. Its mean distance from the sun is estimated at 3,525 million miles, and it requires 249.17 years for one complete revolution. Its size is believed to approximate 4200 miles in diameter. The planet is observable only on the photographic plates of powerful telescopes. Percival Lowell in 1915 predicted the position of Pluto on the basis of previously unexplained deviations of Uranus and Neptune from their expected paths. On January 21, 1930, evidence of its existence was first seen on photographic plates at the Lowell observatory, Flagstaff, Arizona, by an assistant, Clyde W. Tombaugh.

Pole Star. The second-magnitude star which is situated almost at the north pole of the sky is known as the Pole Star, North Star, or *Polaris*. It can be found by means of the pointers of the Big Dipper, which are in a line with it. *Polaris* is not exactly at the north pole, but it describes each day a circle about the pole with a radius a little more than twice the diameter of the moon.

The pole of the heavens is the point where the earth's axis extended would meet the celestial sphere; consequently it depends upon the position of the earth's axis. The attractions of the moon and sun for the equatorial bulge of the earth change the positions of the earth's equator and axis in such a way that the pole of the heavens describes among the stars a circle having a radius of about 23.5°, in a period of 26,000 years. In the days of Hipparchus, 150 B. C., the pole was 12° from *Polaris*. The pole is still approaching the North Star and in 200 years will pass about half a degree from it. In 12,000 years it will have circled in the sky until it will be less than 5° from the brilliant first-magnitude star Vega, which will then be the North Star. This phenomenon is known as the precession of the equinoxes.

The Pole Star is accompanied by a faint companion of the ninth magnitude which can be seen only with telescopic aid. By means of the spectroscope, the Pole Star itself has been found to be a system of three stars, which is at least 40 light years distant. The two closer components revolve around their center of gravity in 4 days, while the third revolves around the first two in a period of 12 years. See *Big Dipper*.

Satellites (*săt′ĕ-lītz*). The secondary bodies which revolve around the planets, as the planets revolve around the sun, are called satellites. With the exception of Mercury and Venus, all of the planets are accompanied by one or more satellites. The earth has one satellite, the moon; Mars has two; Jupiter, nine; Saturn, nine; Uranus, four; and Neptune, one. Four of Jupiter's satellites, two of Saturn's, and the satellite of Neptune are each about as large as the moon. The other satellites are smaller, each of the tiny satellites of Mars being about 10 miles in diameter. See *Moon*, *Planets*.

Saturn. As seen through a telescope, Saturn is the most striking and the most beautiful of the planets because of the system of enormous rings which surrounds it. The diameter of the planet itself is about 75,000 miles; the extreme diameter of the rings which encircle it in the plane of its equator is 173,000 miles. Notwithstanding the great extent of the rings, they are probably not more than 50 miles thick.

The rings of Saturn are three in number. The smallest one, known as the crape ring because it is faint and filmy, begins about 6000 miles from the surface of the planet and has a width of about 11,000 miles. The next ring is very bright, the outer part of it being as brilliant as the planet. It begins where the crape ring terminates and has a width of 18,000 miles. Beyond this bright ring there is a vacant space 2,000 miles wide, known as Cassini's division, after its discoverer. Outside of Cassini's division there is another ring about 11,000 miles wide.

The rings of Saturn are composed of innumerable small bodies similar to meteors, each pursuing its own path about the planet. The particles on the inner edge of the crape ring revolve about the planet in about 5 hours, while those on the outer margin of the largest ring require nearly 14 hours.

Saturn is the rarest planet, having an average density only 63 per cent of that of water. There are no permanent markings on its surface, and its physical condition is far different from that of the earth. Saturn's period of rotation is about 10 hours and 14 minutes, and, as in case of the sun and of Jupiter, the period of rotation of its equatorial zone is shorter than the periods in the higher latitudes. Although Saturn's day is less than half that of the earth, its period of revolution about the sun is 29.5 of our years. Its mean distance from the sun is 886 million miles.

Saturn has nine satellites, five of which are more than 1,000 miles in diameter. The most remote one, discovered by W. H. Pickering in 1899, revolves around Saturn in the direction opposite to that of the rotation of the planet. This direction is opposite also to the motion of the remaining eight satellites and to that of the innumerable particles composing the rings.

Sirius (*sĭr′ĭ-ŭs*). The brightest star in the heavens is Sirius, the Dog Star, in *Canis Major*. It is a brilliant, bluish white sun which can be seen in the southern sky in the early evening from January to spring.

The apparent brightness of Sirius is owing not alone to the fact that it is one of the nearer stars but also to the fact that it is one of the most brilliant stars. Its distance is about 500,000 times the distance from the earth to the sun, or 8.4 light years, and its luminosity is about 50 times that of the sun.

The spectroscope shows that Sirius is approaching the solar system at the rate of about 5.6 miles per second, or 336 miles per minute. If it were coming straight toward us, it would eventually overtake the sun. Sirius has, however, a cross-component of motion which, in time, will take it into parts of space far distant from those which the solar system will traverse. But even if this star were overtaking the sun at the rate of 336 miles per minute, its brightness would not rapidly increase, because its distance from our system is enormous compared with that through which it would travel in a year. In fact, its brightness would not increase ten per cent in 10,000 years.

Sirius is accompanied by a faint companion star which was discovered in 1862. The two components revolve around their center of gravity at a distance from each other of 1800 million miles in a period of 48.8 years. The combined mass of the pair is 3.4 times that of the sun. See *Stars*.

Solstice (*sŏl′stĭs*). The solstices are the points on the ecliptic at which the sun is farthest from the equator, 23½° north or south. The word solstice is from the Latin, and means "the sun stands." The points are called solstices because, when the sun is at either of them, it stands still for a time in its northward and southward motions in the sky.

The sun is at the northern solstice, 23½° north of the equator, on June 21, which is the longest day in the northern hemisphere and the shortest in the southern. The sun is at the southern solstice, 23½° south of the equator, on December 21, when the northern hemisphere has its shortest day and the southern, its longest. See *Day, Length of*.

Southern Cross. A constellation in the southern hemisphere. It consists of four bright stars, which are fancied to show the shape of a Latin (Christian) cross. The two stars forming the summit and foot point approximately toward the south pole.

Standard Time. Standard time is a system of time divisions adopted in 1883 by the principal railways of the United States and Canada, and since then has been widely employed in Europe and various other countries of the world. The time divisions depend upon a series of *standard meridians* differing from the longitude of Greenwich, England, by exact multiples of 15°. A difference of 15° in longitude corresponds to a difference in time of exactly one hour. Consequently, the local times of the different standard meridians differ from the local time of Greenwich by multiples of an hour.

The standard time meridians of the United States and Canada are those whose longitudes west of Greenwich are 60°, 75°, 90°, 105°, and 120°. The times of these standard meridians are 4, 5, 6, 7, and 8 hours, respectively, slower than Greenwich time. The time of meridian 60° is called Atlantic or Colonial Time; that of meridian 75°, Eastern Time; that of meridian 90°, Central Time; that of meridian 105°, Mountain Time; and that of meridian 120°, Pacific Time.

A time belt is associated with each time meridian and extends, on the average, half way to the neighboring time meridians. Under this system, it is noon, Atlantic or Colonial Time, at the same moment at all places within about 7½° east or west of meridian 60°; 11 o'clock Eastern Time in the belt of meridian 75°; 10 o'clock Central Time in the belt of meridian 90°; 9 o'clock Mountain Time in the belt of meridian 105°; and 8 o'clock Pacific Time in the belt of meridian 120°. At the same instant it is 4 P. M. Greenwich time.

The nearer a place is to its time meridian, the less the difference, never more than 30 minutes, between its *standard* and its *local* time. In journeying from one standard time belt into another, it is necessary only to change one's watch by a whole hour, setting it ahead when traveling eastward and setting it back when traveling westward. See *Time*.

Stars. Stars are great suns whose volumes average a million times greater than the volume of the earth.

Those visible to the unaided eye at one time number about 2000, and in all there are only 5000 within range of the human eye. But the telescope reveals enormous numbers of them. Even a 3-inch glass, which would cost only a few hundred dollars, shows more than 200,000 stars.

The best telescopes of the present time penetrate beyond the borders of the great aggregation of stars to which our sun belongs, passing through virtually unoccupied spaces to other universes beyond ours. (See *Island Universes*.) Our sun and all the visible stars constitute a great cosmic unit, flattened in shape somewhat like a watch, and the total number of suns within this cosmic unit is somewhere between one and two thousand million. In the opinion of some astronomers, the center of our universe is about 52,000 light years distant in the general region of Sagittarius. Our sun is believed to be revolving about this center at the rate of 200 to 300 miles a second.

Stars obviously differ in apparent brightness. The differences in brightness are due in part to the differences in their actual luminosities, and in part to their different distances from us. They are divided into groups, or magnitudes, according to their apparent brightness. The group of brightest stars, 20 in number, are of the first magnitude. These stars of the first magnitude are 2.512 times as bright as those of the second magnitude, and those of the second magnitude are 2.512 times as bright as those of the third magnitude. Lesser magnitudes are determined by the same ratio of brightness. The faintest stars visible with the unaided eye are of the sixth magnitude, and the faintest within reach of our largest telescopes are of about the 17th magnitude. Typical first-magnitude stars are Arcturus, Vega, Capella, and Procyon. Sirius is the brightest star. The North Star and the stars in the Big Dipper are of the second magnitude; the Pleiades are of the fourth magnitude.

The intrinsic luminosities of the stars differ greatly. Millions of them are comparable with the sun. Some of them are 100 or 200 times more luminous than the sun, as, for example, the Pleiades and the stars in the Big Dipper. Others are thousands of times as great as the sun in light-giving power, as, for example, Rigel and Canopus. On the other hand, many stars are less luminous than the sun. For example, Sirius is composed of two stars,—one 48 times as luminous as the sun and the other 400 times less luminous than the sun.

There is a direct relation between the intrinsic luminosity of stars and their mass. Since it is possible, by means of the interferometer, to measure the size of stars, a computation of their density may be made. Such computations have revealed certain astonishing results. A star, for instance, measured by Dr. Adrian van Maanen of the Mount Wilson observatory, showed a specific gravity of 400,000. One cubic inch of this star would weigh about seven tons. This is explained by assuming that the constituent atoms break down under the almost inconceivably high temperatures and pressures prevailing in the star.

The stars are all so remote that their distances can be determined only with great difficulty. In fact, it was not until 1840 that the distance of a star, *Alpha Centauri*, was first measured. Although this is the nearest star, its distance is 275,000 times that of the earth from the sun. Perhaps the remoteness of the stars from one another can best be understood from the fact that there is, on the average, only one star to about 4 units of stellar space. The unit of stellar space is a sphere whose radius is 206,000 times as great as the distance from the sun to the earth, or in round numbers 20,000,000,000,000 miles.

The colors of the stars differ greatly, depending upon their temperatures and the constitutions of their atmospheres. The hottest stars, of which Sirius and Vega are examples, are bluish white. Stars of the class to which the sun belongs are yellowish and include such objects as Capella and Pollux. They are somewhat cooler than the blue stars and are about as numerous. The first two types include most of the stars. There are orange stars, such as Arcturus, and red stars, such as Betelgeuse and Antares.

The composition of the stars has been determined, at least in the case of the brighter ones, by means of the spectroscope. It is a remarkable fact that they contain elements which are found in the sun and the earth, and even in ourselves. Notwithstanding the vast extent of the universe in space and the great diversity of its organization, there is a fundamental unity of the materials of which it is composed.

In many cases, what are apparently single stars are found by the telescope to be composed of two stars revolving about their common center of gravity. Sometimes the two components are nearly equal; in other cases they are very unequal. Each of the stars may be accompanied by planets, but there is no direct evidence on the question. At the great distances of the stars, planets would be invisible even if telescopes were thousands of times more powerful than any so far made.

The stars are said to be "fixed" because they are so far away that neither the motions of the earth and the sun, nor those of the stars themselves, have ordinarily appreciable effects upon their apparent positions. They are, however, in rapid motion, their average speed being 20 miles per second, or about 600 million miles per year. Some stars move with much higher velocities, and the apparent positions of the nearer ones change slightly. The Big Dipper and the other constellations, however, appear to the unaided eye almost exactly as they did when they were being marked out and named by prehistoric men in the valleys of the Tigris and the Euphrates.

In the relatively short time during which stellar motions have been studied, the stars observed have moved in approximately straight lines with uniform speed. But, in the course of time, they move about in apparently irregular paths, somewhat like individual bees in a swarm. Moreover, there is no great central sun, or other central mass, around which all the stars revolve.

The origin of stars and the length of their duration are quite unknown, although it is highly probable that they continue to exist as luminous bodies some thousands of millions of years. Our sun is but one of millions of similar objects moving about in an enormous space; worlds similar to our own probably exist to the number of hundreds of millions. Contemplation of these facts and of the notable advances that have been made in the solution of the difficult problems associated with them arouses increased respect for the power of the human mind and greater hope for the future progress of the race. See *Betelgeuse, Constellations, Pole Star, Sirius, Sun.*

Sun. The sun is the dominant member of the solar system. Its mass is 1000 times the combined masses of all the other bodies in the system. It controls their motions by its gravitation, and it warms and lights them with its abundant rays.

The sun appears small—no larger than the moon—only because of the great distance of the earth from it—92,905,000 miles. The diameter of the sun is 866,000 miles, and its volume is, therefore, more than a million times that of the earth. The sun's average density, however, is only one-fourth that of the earth, or 1.4 times that of water. The surface gravity of a body depends both upon its size and upon its density—the influence of great density counterbalancing the effect of small size, and vice versa. In the case of the sun, immense size more than makes up for low density. In consequence, an object which weighs one pound upon the surface of the earth would weigh nearly 28 pounds on the surface of the sun.

It is obvious that nearly all the light and heat received by the earth come from the sun. In the sun originate, directly or indirectly, almost all the active forces operating on the earth. The wind blows because the sun heats different parts of the earth's atmosphere unequally. The rain falls after the sun's rays have caused water in the form of vapor to rise into the regions occupied by the clouds. Wood burns because the sun's energy has been stored in its cells. Coal and petroleum are sources of power because they have preserved the solar energy contained in plants of earlier geological ages. Animals and men are warm-blooded and can move because they feed on plants or on other animals that subsist upon plants, and these plants obtain their energy from the sun. It has been found that a square yard of the earth's surface exposed perpendicularly to the sun's rays receives energy equivalent to 1.5 horse power.

The temperature of the surface of the sun is about 10,000° F., or twice that of an electric furnace, while the heat of the interior is much greater. As might be expected, the sun is the seat of violent storms. Whirling masses of intensely heated matter, in volume many times greater than the earth, often sweep along its surface at the rate of several hundred miles a minute. Occasionally there are eruptions in which streams of glowing gas are thrown up from the sun's surface to a height of several hundred thousand miles, or farther than the distance from the earth to the moon.

Geological evidence shows that the sun has been giving the earth heat and light at approximately the present rate during all the long periods of geological time, probably for much more than one hundred million years. It is difficult to account for energy sufficient to supply radiation for this long interval. The most acceptable theory is that this energy is due to the transformation of hydrogen atoms into helium atoms with carbon acting as a catalyst. At the high temperatures prevailing there, electrons are projected with force sufficient to enter into close association with protons, thereby neutralizing their electric charges. What formerly was mass then exists as energy, which is radiated from the sun. It is calculated that the sun in this manner loses 4 million tons of its mass per second. The mass of the sun is sufficient to sustain this loss for many hundreds of millions of years.

The visible surface of the sun is called the *photosphere*, or light sphere. It is in this surface that sun spots develop. Immediately above the photosphere is a layer of gas about 500 miles deep, called the *reversing layer* because it makes a dark-line spectrum. Outside of the reversing layer is the *chromosphere*, or color sphere, a deep layer of tenuous gas. And outside of the chromosphere is the *corona*, a halo of pearly light which can be seen only at times of total eclipses. The corona extends outward to a distance of a million miles.

The chemical constitution of the sun has been determined by means of the spectroscope, a marvelous instrument that analyzes the light from a radiating gaseous source. About 40 of the 92 terrestrial elements have been found on the sun. Most of these are familiar metals, such as sodium, calcium, iron, nickel, copper, zinc, silver, tin, and lead. It is a remarkable fact that not only the sun but also the distant stars are made up of familiar elements, a considerable number of which are found in the human body. See *Stars.*

Sun Spots. Sun spots are dark spots or patches, generally circular or oval in shape, which appear from time to time on the surface of the sun. They range in diameter from less than 500 to more than 150,000 miles, and last from a few days to several months, the average duration being a month or two. They consist of a central dark nucleus, the *umbra*, surrounded by a lighter ring, the *penumbra*.

Sun spots occur in cycles whose periods vary somewhat, the average being slightly more than 11 years. At times of greatest frequency, from 10 to 20 sun spots may sometimes be seen; at other times no spots are visible. They always occur in two belts, one on each side of the sun's equator, and extending from latitude 6° to latitude 35°.

The cause of sun spots is unknown. They consist of conical tornadoes often towering 20,000 miles high. The particles in these tornadoes rush away from the center of the spot, rise, are drawn toward the center, and then plunge downward. Their motion is almost inconceivably rapid, being upward of 3000 miles an hour. Sun spots are about 1000° cooler than other parts of the sun's surface.

Disturbances of the magnetic needle are most frequent and violent on the earth during periods when sun spots are most numerous. The aurora borealis is caused by the impact, on the earth's magnetic field, of electrical particles released in the formation of sun spots. These particles, or electrons, are drawn toward and spiral around the magnetic pole, ionizing the rarified gas of the upper atmosphere and causing it to glow just as in a neon tube. It has been suggested also that sun spots influence the weather by modifying temperature and rainfall.

Telescope. Two principal types of optical instruments have been produced for the purpose of adding to the power and effectiveness of human eyes. One is the microscope, which magnifies objects much too small to be seen without its aid; the other is the telescope, which shows distant objects as though they were nearer than they are. A large telescope will make a remote object appear as though it were at one-thousandth of its distance.

When a person sees an object, light from it has passed through the pupil of his eye and has made its image on the retina, just as when a photograph of an object is secured, light from it has passed through the lens of the camera and has made its image on the plate. The diameter of the pupil of the eye averages about one-fifth of an inch. Therefore, the amount of light that can enter the eye is limited. The diameter of a telescope may be many inches, and, consequently, a large amount of light may pass through it. For example, a telescope 20 inches in diameter transmits (neglecting small losses by reflection and absorption) 10,000 times as much as passes through the pupil of the eye. The lenses in a telescope are so arranged that the rays are condensed before they enter the eye of the observer, and the brightness of such an object as a star is correspondingly increased. Without telescopic aid only 5000 stars can be seen in the entire sky, even under the most favorable conditions. With the large telescopes of the present time several hundred million stars are visible. These facts are a measure of the importance of telescopes in astronomy.

As a telescope brings an object nearer to the observer, it makes it appear larger in diameter in the same proportion. The so-called magnification depends both upon the large lenses (the objective) at the outer end of the telescope and upon the small lenses (the eyepiece) near the eye of the observer. When the atmospheric conditions are favorable, an eyepiece can be used on the largest telescopes so that the apparent diameter of an object is increased a thousandfold. Under these conditions the apparent area of an object—the moon, for example—is magnified a million times.

Combinations of lenses similar in principle to the telescope were first made by Lippershey, in Holland, about 1600. Galileo constructed actual telescopes about 1608, and was the first man to scan the heavens with optical aid. He studied the markings on the moon, observed spots on the sun, and discovered four of the satellites of Jupiter and the rings of Saturn.

A serious difficulty in the construction of telescopes is that a lens does not bring rays of light of different colors to a focus at the same point. Since all objects radiate light which is a mixture of many colors, some confusion results. For example, when the red rays are in focus, the blue rays form a blurred image. This difficulty has been very largely overcome by making the objectives of telescopes of two kinds of glass having suitably different properties. It has been avoided also by condensing the rays by means of concave mirrors instead of by lenses. The result is that there are two kinds of telescopes: the *refractors*, in which the light passes through, and is condensed by, a lens or combination of lenses; and the *reflectors*, in which the light is reflected from, and is condensed by, a concave mirror. Both types use the same kinds of eyepieces.

A second obstacle to the construction of larger telescopes having glass lenses or mirrors is the distortion of light rays which takes place when temperature changes cause expansion or contraction in the glass. Consequently, a new era in telescope construction was inaugurated by the production of fused quartz, which shows virtually no expansion due to heat. The technique for producing this substance was sufficiently advanced by 1928 so that plans were made in that year for constructing a reflecting telescope with a mirror 200 inches in diameter, just twice the size of the largest then existing.

In a modern telescope, the lens or mirror may weigh up to 30 tons. With its tube and counterweights, also weighing many tons, the telescope must be mounted and controlled with such precision that it can follow the stars in their courses across the sky. Many auxiliary instruments are required for its effective use, since direct observation is now largely superseded by recording devices of great accuracy. Among these are many varieties of photographic plates sensitized to light rays that may be invisible to the human eye. The spectroscope, fed by the telescope, reveals the constituent elements of celestial bodies. By means of the interferometer, the size of distant stars may be measured. Thermocouples enable astronomers to measure the temperature of planets or stars.

LARGE REFRACTORS

Institution or Location	Aperture in Inches	Focal Length in Feet	Date of Erection
Yerkes Observatory, Williams Bay, Wisconsin	40.0	62.0	1897
Lick Observatory, Mt. Hamilton, Cal.	36.0	57.8	1888
Naval Observatory, Nikolaev, Russia	32.0	....	....
Meudon Observatory, near Paris	32.5	53.0	1891
Astrophysical Observatory, Potsdam	31.5	39.4	....
Bischoffsheim Observatory, Nice	30.3	52.6	1889
Allegheny Observatory, Pittsburgh, Pa.	30.0	....	....
Imperial Observatory, Pulkova	30.0	45.0	1885
University of Pittsburgh	30.0	....	....
National Observatory, Paris	28.9	....	....
Royal Observatory, Greenwich	28.0	28.0	1894
Berlin	27.5	....	....
Imperial Observatory, Vienna	27.0	34.0	1882
Royal Observatory, Greenwich	26.0	26.0	1897
Johannesburg, South Africa	26.0	....	....
Naval Observatory, Washington	26.0	32.5	1873
McCormick Observatory, Charlottesville, Va.	26.0	32.5	1882
Cambridge University Observatory	25.0	....	1891
Meudon Observatory, near Paris	24.4	52.2	1891
National Observatory, Cordoba, Argentina	24.0	....	....
National Observatory, Santiago, Chile	24.0	....	....
Detroit Observatory, Ann Arbor, Mich.	24.0	....	....
Cape Observatory, Cape Town, South Africa	24.0	22.6	1897
Radcliffe Observatory, Oxford, Eng.	24.0	....	....
Swarthmore College, Pa.	24.0	36.0	....
Lowell Observatory, Flagstaff, Ariz.	24.0	31.0	1895
National Observatory, Paris	23.6	59.0	1891
Hamburg, Germany	23.6	....	....
Halstead Observatory, Princeton University, N. J.	23.0	32.0	1883
Mount Etna, Sicily	21.8	....	....
Edinburgh, Scotland	21.2	....	....
Lick Observatory, Mt. Hamilton, Cal.	21.0	....	1939
Mt. Porro Observatory, Turin, Italy	20.5	....	....
Chamberlin Observatory, Denver, Col.	20.0	28.0	1891
Manila Observatory, Philippines	20.0	....	1892
Chabot Observatory, Oakland, Cal.	20.0	....	....
Dearborn Observatory, Evanston, Ill.	18.5	....	....
Amherst College Obs'y, Amherst, Mass.	18.0	....	....
Flower Observatory, Philadelphia	18.0	....	....

LARGE REFLECTORS

Institution or Location	Aperture in Inches
Mount Palomar, Cal.	200.0
Mt. Wilson Observatory, Pasadena, Cal.	100.0
McDonald Observatory, Fort Davis, Tex.	82.0
Paris Observatory	76.0
David Dunlap Observatory, University of Toronto	74.0
Radcliffe Observatory (Oxford), Pretoria, S. A.	74.0
Dominion Observatory, Victoria, B. C.	72.5
Perkins Observatory, Ohio Wesleyan Univ.	69.0
National Observatory, Cordoba, Argentina	61.0
Harvard Observatory, Cambridge, Mass.	61.0
Solar Observatory, Mount Wilson, Cal.	60.0
Harvard Observatory, Bloemfontein, S. Africa	60.0
Melbourne, Australia	48.0
National Observatory, Paris	48.0
Ritchey-Chretien Naval Observatory, Washington, D. C.	40.0
Lowell Observatory, Flagstaff, Ariz.	40.0
Simeis, Crimea	40.0
Berlin-Babelsburg Observatory, Germany	40.0
Carre, near Geneva, Switzerland	39.4
Meudon Observatory, near Paris	39.0
Hamburg, Germany	39.0
Detroit Observatory, Ann Arbor, Mich.	37.5
National Observatory, Santiago, Chile	36.6
Cambridge University, England	36.0
Solar Observatory, South Kensington, England	36.0
Lick Observatory, Mt. Hamilton, Cal.	36.0

Time. The fundamental means of measuring time is the rotation of the earth. The ultimate standard by which all clocks are regulated is furnished by observatories from their observations of the stars. The primary unit of time is the *mean solar day*. It is the average of the true solar days, which vary slightly in length. The difference between mean solar time and true solar time is called the *equation of time*, and is given in the *Nautical Almanac*. Mean solar time and true solar time agree four times a year; namely, on April 15, June 14, September 1, and December 24. The maximum difference between them occurs on November 2, when it amounts to 16 minutes and 21 seconds.

Every meridian has its own mean solar time. In order to avoid continual changing of time as one goes east or west, standard time belts are introduced, each being 15 degrees of longitude in width. The difference in time between adjoining belts is one hour.

The *tropical year*, consisting of 365 days, 5 hours, 48 minutes, and 46 seconds of mean solar time, is the standard unit of time for longer intervals. It suffices not only for history but for the long periods of the geological ages as well. Only when the evolution of the stars is under consideration, do the time-intervals mount to such heights that still larger units seem advisable. See *Calendar, Day, Standard Time.*

Uranus (*ū'rȧ-nŭs*). Uranus was discovered in 1781 by Sir William Herschel. This was the first discovery of a planet in historical times. Uranus can barely be seen with the unaided eye and appears as a star of the sixth magnitude. It has a diameter of about 30,000 miles, and its volume is about 53 times greater than that of the earth. Its density is only about one-fourth that of the earth, and its mass is therefore only about 15 times the mass of the earth. The period of its rotation on its axis is believed to be about 10 hours, and its period of revolution around the sun is 84 years. Its average distance from the sun is 1782 million miles.

When viewed through a telescope, Uranus appears as a small, greenish disk, the color being caused by the character of its atmosphere. Uranus has four satellites, ranging from 500 to 1000 miles in diameter. These revolve around the planet from east to west, or in the direction opposite to that of the motion of our moon. Since Uranus is nearly 20 times as far from the sun as the earth is, it receives only $\frac{1}{368}$ as much light and heat per unit area as does the earth. See *Planets, Satellites.*

Venus. Venus is the most brilliant planet in the heavens, and the one most nearly like the earth. The diameter of Venus is about 7700 miles, the planet almost equaling the earth in size. Objects on the surface of Venus weigh about 85 per cent as much as they would weigh on the earth. The atmosphere of Venus, which seems as extensive as that of the earth, appears to be filled with clouds. The length of the planet's year is equal to 225 of our days, but the length of its day is unknown.

The average distance of Venus from the sun is 67,000,000 miles; hence its orbit is interior to that of the earth. As a consequence, the planet has phases similar to those of the moon. When the planet is most brilliant, a telescope shows that it is crescent in form. Venus is at times so bright that it can be seen in full daylight, provided the observer focuses his eyes on a distant object and then looks in exactly the right direction.

Venus is seen, alternately, in the west after sunset and in the east before sunrise. In Greek mythology, Venus, as evening star, was known as Hesperus, and, as morning star, was called Phosphorus, or Lucifer. It is a notable fact that some of the tribes of American Indians knew that Venus as morning and as evening star is the same object, and that it changes from one to the other by passing from one side of the sun to the other. The period of Venus from evening star back to evening star is one year and seven months. See *Planets.*

Year. In general, a year is the time required by the earth to make a complete revolution around the sun. Astronomers have defined three different kinds of years,—(1) the *tropical*, (2) the *sidereal*, and (3) the *anomalistic*. The first is the year in ordinary use; the second and the third are employed only in astronomical calculations.

The tropical year, called also the solar, equinoctial, and astronomical year, is the time included between two successive passages of the sun through the vernal equinox. Its length is 365 days, 5 hours, 48 minutes, 46 seconds. Since the seasons depend upon the sun's place with respect to the equinox, the tropical year is used in the calendar in order that dates shall not shift with respect to the seasons.

The sidereal year is the period of the earth's revolution around the sun, from one apparent position among the stars back to the same apparent position again. On account of the westward motion, or precession, of the equinoxes, the sidereal year is about 20 minutes longer than the tropical year, the length of the sidereal year being 365 days, 6 hours, 9 minutes, 9 seconds.

The anomalistic year is the time between two successive passages of the earth through the perihelion point (point nearest the sun) of its orbit. The attractions of the other planets produce a slow eastward motion of the perihelion of the earth's orbit. Consequently, the anomalistic year is nearly 5 minutes longer than the sidereal year, its length being 365 days, 6 hours, 13 minutes, 53 seconds. See *Calendar.*

Zenith (*zē'nĭth*). The point in the heavens that is exactly overhead is called the zenith. It is the point where the plumb-line, if extended upward, would pierce the celestial sphere. The zenith is called also the upper or superior pole of the horizon, and is directly opposite the nadir, or inferior pole. By using these poles as co-ordinates, the astronomical horizon is defined as a great circle of the celestial sphere, 90° from the zenith. See *Nadir.*

Zodiac (*zō'dĭ-ăk*). A belt in the heavens extending 8° on each side of the sun's annual path is called the Zodiac, or Zone of Animals, as the constellations forming it, with one exception, are figures of animals. This zone was recognized by many ancient peoples independently, because all the anciently known heavenly bodies which had relative motions—the sun, the moon, Mercury, Venus, Mars, Jupiter, and Saturn—make their circuits of the sky in this belt. The division of the zodiac into twelve signs, or constellations, each extending over 30° and serving to mark a division of the year, is believed to have been of Babylonian origin.

Beginning with the vernal equinox, the sun travels through *Aries* (Ram), *Taurus* (Bull), and *Gemini* (Twins) in the spring; *Cancer* (Crab), *Leo* (Lion), and *Virgo* (Virgin) in the summer; *Libra* (Balance), *Scorpius* (Scorpion), and *Sagittarius* (Archer) in the autumn; and *Capricornus* (Goat), *Aquarius* (Water Bearer), and *Pisces* (Fishes) in winter. However, owing to the precession of the equinoxes, the signs of the zodiac do not now correspond to the constellations bearing their names, as they did in the times of Hipparchus (156 B. C.). See *Constellations.*

Zodiacal (*zô-dī'ȧ-kăl*) **Light.** This is a somewhat triangular, faintly luminous area which extends upwards from the horizon along the ecliptic, visible at the end of twilight or at the beginning of dawn. At its base on the horizon, this wedge of light is from 20° to 30° wide. It narrows upwards, and, usually, can be followed 90° from the sun. From about the brightness of the Milky Way, it shades very gradually into the dark sky. In strong moonlight, the zodiacal light is not sufficiently bright to be seen. The spring months are the most favorable for observing it in the evening, and the autumn months, for seeing it in the morning. It is believed to be caused by the reflection of light from an immense number of small particles of matter revolving around the sun in the plane of the earth's orbit.

PHYSICS

PHYSICS is the basic physical science. Its subject matter ranges from the study of the motions and structures of stars to the study of the internal structure of atoms and their nuclei. Physics is fundamental to the sciences of astronomy, chemistry, and geology, and, to an unknown extent, the biological sciences. Physics is an exact science; its laws are the result of accurate quantitative experiments and are expressed as mathematical equations. In this respect it is the most advanced of the sciences.

Although some beginnings were made by the Ancients, physics in its modern sense had its beginning in the 16th and 17th centuries with such men as Galileo, Huygens, Hooke, and Newton. The great development of what is known as classical physics, the subjects of mechanics, heat, sound, light, and electricity and magnetism, came in the 19th century. The end of the 19th century saw the beginnings of developments in physics along new lines, particularly in ideas of the structure of atoms. These developments have been carried on at a continuously accelerated rate throughout the 20th century, and these new ideas and conceptions are frequently referred to as "modern physics."

The breakdown of physics into the classical topics of mechanics, heat, sound, light, and electricity and magnetism is now viewed as largely a matter of convenience. The same guiding principles and many of the same concepts are used in all the branches of physics. In the same way, the division of physical science into astronomy, physics, chemistry, etc., is largely due to historical development. It is becoming increasingly evident that there is no sharp borderline between chemistry and physics, for example. Much of the progress in chemistry in recent years has been a direct result of the investigations in physics of the structure of atoms. In the early stages of science all physical science was known as "natural philosophy." Gradually the sciences of chemistry, geology, and so forth, evolved as separate fields, and natural philosophy came to be known as physics. Thus, both from the viewpoint of history and that of the basicness of subject matter, physics may legitimately be considered the fundamental science.

Our 20th century civilization is largely a product of physics and chemistry. Engineering, for example, is in all its branches a straight application of the principles of physics. It is worth noting, however, that the great achievements of physics have come from pure curiosity of man, with no thought of eventual practical application. The greatest cooperative project ever undertaken by scientists, the development of the atomic bomb, was "practical," but basic principles involved had been developed with no thought of either atomic bombs or atomic energy. Rightly or wrongly, the pure scientist has little cared to what eventual use his work will lead.

MECHANICS

Mechanics is the study of the motions of material bodies and of the forces which cause those motions. It is the fundamental branch of physics in the sense that in all parts of physics mechanical concepts are used and an attempt is made to describe phenomena in mechanical terms. In recent years it has appeared that such things as the internal structure of atoms cannot be understood in ordinary mechanical terms, but nevertheless the laws of mechanics do hold for all the systems of ordinary experience. Mechanics is also the foundation of engineering. A complex mechanism such as an automobile can be broken down into a large number of what are called simple machines, which in turn are straightforward applications of the simple laws of mechanics.

The branch of mechanics which analyzes the forces in a system which is at rest, such as a suspension bridge, is called *statics*. *Kinematics* deals with the description of motion, and *dynamics* deals with the relation between force and motion.

Fundamental Units. Physics is an exact science, which means it deals with precise measurements. No physical law, principle, or theory is accepted as valid until it has been subjected to quantitative test. Quantitative measurement of any quantity implies a unit for that quantity. Three fundamental units are required in mechanics: units of mass, length, and time. Other measuring units can be expressed in terms of these. Because of the basic rôle of mechanics, these same units are fundamental to all physical science.

English and Metric Systems. Most of the civilized world has adopted the metric system of weights and measures, which exploits the advantages of the decimal system in its relations between units. The exceptions, the United States and Great Britain, use the more cumbersome English system in ordinary life, and even there the units are established by law in relation to the metric units. The metric system is used universally in scientific work.

Unit of Length. The unit of length in the metric system is the meter, which is the distance between two lines on a bar of platinum-iridium alloy kept in the vaults of the International Bureau of Weights and Measures near Paris. The meter was intended to be equal to one ten-millionth of the distance from the equator to either pole of the earth, and is nearly that. An accurate replica of the international meter, placed in the vaults of the Bureau of Standards in Washington, is the legal meter of the United States, and the yard is legally defined as 3600/3937 of the meter. The centimeter, more commonly used in scientific work than the meter, is 1/100 of the meter. An inch is equal to 2.54 centimeters.

Should the standard meter be destroyed, it could be replaced, since it has been measured by Michelson in terms of the wave-length of red cadmium light, with a precision as good as the width of the lines on the standard meter itself.

Units of Mass and Weight. The metric unit of mass is the kilogram, the mass of a platinum-iridium cylinder preserved along with the standard meter near Paris. It was originally intended to be the mass of 1000 cubic centimeters (one liter) of water at its maximum density. Because of the relation between mass and weight (See *Weight, Mass,* and *Force*), the standard kilogram also serves as the standard of weight. In the United States the legal pound is, by law, 1/2.204622 parts of a kilogram. The other commonly used units are expressed in terms of the kilogram or the pound, the gram being 1/1000 of the kilogram, for example, and the ounce 1/16 of a pound. One pound is approximately 454 grams.

Unit of Time. The second is universally used as the unit of time, the second being 1/86400 of a mean solar day. The mean solar day means simply the average time of the sun from noon to noon.

The C.G.S. System. In scientific work the centimeter, the gram, and the second are most commonly used although there is a growing tendency to use the meter, the kilogram, and the second. The centimeter-gram-second system is commonly referred to as the c.g.s. system, and the meter-kilogram-second system as the m.k.s. system.

Motion. When a body moves from one position to another, it is said to have suffered a *displacement*. The concept of displacement involves both distance and direction. The rate at which a body moves along its path, that is, the distance traveled per unit time, is called the *speed*. The *velocity* of a body is its displacement per unit time, and hence velocity involves both the speed and the direction of travel. The *acceleration* of a body is the time rate of change of its *velocity*. For a body moving along a straight line path, the acceleration is simply the rate of change of the speed, but this is not true for an object moving along a curved path. A body moving in a circular path with constant speed, for example, has an acceleration since its velocity is changing in direction; this acceleration turns out to be toward the center of its circular path, and from Newton's laws, discussed below, it follows that there must be a force in the same direction. A quantity much used in discussing the effects of force on motion is *momentum*, which is defined as the product of the mass of a body and its velocity. If the momentum of a body changes, it must have an acceleration, since the mass remains constant.

The Acceleration of Gravity. The correct description of the motion of bodies falling freely under the action of gravity was given by Galileo. The Ancients had supposed that heavy bodies fall faster than light bodies. Galileo recognized that, except for the effects of air resistance, all bodies falling freely behave in the same way; namely, they all possess the same constant acceleration. This acceleration has the approximate value of 32 feet per second per second, which means that the downward velocity increases by 32 feet per second every second. For example, a stone which is dropped with no initial velocity will have a velocity of 16 feet per second in 1/2 second, 64 feet per second in 2 seconds, etc.

A simple consequence of the uniformity of the acceleration of gravity is the behavior of a simple pendulum, which consists of a weight at the end of a string. The time for a full swing of a pendulum depends, not upon the weight hung at the end of the string, but only upon the length of the string.

The law of freely falling bodies seems to be contradicted by the behavior of extremely light objects, such as feathers, or objects falling very rapidly, such as raindrops. The effect of air resistance is such that the acceleration of a falling body decreases, the faster the body is falling. Eventually any object will attain what is known as its *terminal velocity*, when the pull of gravity is just equaled by the resistance of the air, after which its speed of fall remains constant. The terminal velocity depends upon the weight, size, and shape of the body. For a feather it is extremely small, but if a penny and a feather are placed in a long tube from which most of the air has been evacuated, they will be found to fall at the same rate. The terminal velocity of an average size raindrop is about 26 feet per second, and that of a man falling out of an airplane without a parachute is about 160 miles an hour.

Newton's Laws of Motion. The general principles of dynamics, the rules which give the relation between the motions of all objects and the forces which produce those motions, were published by Newton in 1687 in his famous *Principia*. Newton's fame is richly deserved; his laws of motion and his law of gravitation remain among the greatest achievements of the human mind, and he made notable contributions in other fields as well, principally in optics. Recognition must be given to Newton's predecessors of the previous century, however. The Ancients had made little progress in science. They had made remarkable advance in mathematics and a few advances in physical science, such as Archimedes' principle in hydrostatics, but many of their conceptions were incorrect. These misconceptions persisted until the 16th century, chiefly due to the "authority" of Aristotle.

Galileo laid the groundwork for Newton in correctly describing the behavior of falling objects and in recognizing that no force is required to maintain the motion of an object but that rather the effect of force is to change motion. Aristotle had taught that the "natural state" of a body was a state of rest, and that if a force did not act to maintain the motion, a moving object would come to rest. Huygens realized that a change in direction of motion involves acceleration just as much as change in speed, and hence requires the action of a force. Copernicus recognized the falsity of the Ptolemaic idea of the earth as the center of the universe, and taught that the earth and other planets revolve about the sun. Kepler, using the remarkable astronomical observations of Tycho Brahe, deduced the laws which describe the motion of the planets about the sun, and it was from those laws that Newton in turn deduced his law of gravitation.

Newton's laws of motion are three, and may be stated as follows:

1. *A body at rest remains at rest and a body in motion remains in uniform motion along a straight line, unless acted upon by an unbalanced force.* This is called the law of inertia, and, as mentioned above, had been recognized by Galileo.

2. *If an unbalanced force acts on a body, the momentum of the body changes, the time rate of change of momentum being proportional to the force and in the same direction as the force.* In case the mass of the body does not change, this law says the rate of change of velocity, or the acceleration, is proportional to the force and in the direction of the force, and the law becomes "force is proportional to mass times acceleration." Ordinarily, the mass of a body does not change; an example of a case where the mass does change is a rolling snowball. According to Einstein's theory of relativity, the mass of an object changes as its speed approaches the speed of light, but such speeds are of little importance in discussing ordinary objects.

3. *To every action (force), there is an equal and opposite reaction.* This law expresses the familiar fact that you cannot exert a force against nothing. The law is frequently misunderstood. The action and reaction mentioned in the law are not two forces exerted on the same object, but forces exerted on two different objects. The law expresses the following: if object A exerts a force on object B, then object B exerts an equal and opposite force on object A. Don't give something a hard blow with your fist without expecting to bruise your fist!

If the second and third laws are applied to a collision between two bodies, an important result is obtained. Each body exerts a force on the other, these forces being equal and opposite at all times. The change in momentum of each body is proportional to the force acting on it and the time during which that force acts, so that the changes in momentum of the two bodies are equal and opposite. Considering the two bodies together as one system, there is no net change in momentum. The two bodies need not actually collide; they may exert gravitational or electrical forces on each other. There may be more than two bodies. In all systems in which the only forces involved are forces between bodies which are part of the system, the net momentum does not change. This result, known as *the law of conservation of momentum*, ranks along with the principle of conservation of energy as one of the great fundamental laws of nature.

Motion Along Curved Paths. Two specific cases of motion under Newton's laws will be discussed, each case a simple but important one. The first is motion under a constant force, hence motion with a constant acceleration. Such motion occurs when bodies near the surface of the earth move under the action of gravity. For bodies falling straight down, the motion is described above under the heading "Acceleration of Gravity." The motion need not be confined to vertical motion, however. A projectile may be thrown so that it has horizontal motion as well. Since there is no horizontal force (neglecting air resistance), the horizontal speed remains constant. The vertical part of the motion is exactly as described for straight line fall, and the resultant motion is a combination of horizontal and vertical motion. It may be shown that the combination of these two motions always leads to the result that the path followed by the projectile is the curve known in mathematics as a parabola. In the case of high speed projectiles such as are fired by long range artillery, air resistance cannot be neglected, and the rotation and the curvature of the earth must be considered as well.

A second example is illustrated by the motion of a particle along a circular path with constant speed, such as the motion of a stone on the end of a string which is being whirled in a circle, and the motion of the moon about the earth. There is an acceleration and hence a force in these cases, because there is a change in velocity due to the change in direction. Since the speed does not change, the force must be at right angles to the motion at all instants. Analysis shows that the force, which is always directed toward the center of the circle, is related to the speed of the body and the radius of its circular path. This force is given the name centripetal force. It is important to notice that this force is directed toward the center of the path; if the force were suddenly removed the body would continue on in a straight line, but this straight line would be tangent to the circle at the point where the force was removed and would not, as commonly supposed, be radially outward. Many misconceptions exist about motion of this type.

The term "centrifugal force" is in common use, and it is frequently supposed that there is some outward force on the body acting away from the center of its path. This is not true. Part of the misconception arises because people have "felt" centrifugal force when going around sharp curves in an automobile. If an automobile curves to the right, the occupants do feel thrown to the left of the automobile, but this is merely an example of inertia. The occupants want to go straight ahead; the car moves to the right, and straight ahead looks like motion to the left to an occupant of the automobile. There is a force which can properly be called centrifugal force; it is the reaction to the centripetal force, and acts on an entirely different object. This can be illustrated by the earth and moon. The earth exerts a force of attraction on the moon, making the moon travel in a circular path. This is the centripetal force. The moon in turn exerts an equal force of attraction on the earth. This may be referred to as centrifugal force if wished, but it does not act on the moon.

The Law of Gravitation. According to the second law of motion, freely falling bodies must be acted upon by forces proportional to their masses, since they all have the same acceleration. This force for each body is called the *weight*, and, according to Newton, is the attraction of the earth for the body. Newton, in his law of gravitation, supposed that all bodies in the universe attract each other, and by assuming that the force of attraction is proportional to the product of the two masses divided by the square of the distance of separation, he was able to deduce Kepler's laws describing the motions of the planets about the sun. Thus the force which pulled Newton's apple to the ground was of the same nature as the force which pulls on the moon, making the moon travel in a circular path around the earth and preventing it from flying out into space, along a straight line.

Weight, Mass, and Force. The law of gravitation explains why the same block of platinum-iridium can be used as a standard of mass and a standard of weight. At any point on the earth's surface, weight and mass are proportional. Weight and mass are frequently confused because of this proportionality. Mass is the measure of the property of inertia, the resistance to change in motion. Weight is simply the name given to a particular force, the attraction of the earth for an object. A pound mass is the same anywhere in the universe, but a pound weight, the pull of the earth on a pound mass, varies from point to point on the earth's surface, and would have little meaning at a point far removed from the earth.

In engineering, the weights of objects are usually important forces in a system, and it makes little difference that a pound weight is not the same at all points on the earth, both because the variation in weight is slight and because the ratio of the weights of two objects is the same everywhere even though the weights themselves are different at different places. Consequently, the pound weight is used as the unit of force. In science, however, definitions must be exact, so force is defined without reference to weight. The *dyne* is defined as the force which will give a mass of one gram an acceleration of one centimeter per second per second. The dyne is an extremely small force. Since the acceleration of gravity is about 980 in centimeters per second per second, the weight of a gram mass is about 980 dynes and the weight of a pound mass is about 980X454, or almost 500,000 dynes.

Work, Energy, and Power. In mechanics, *work* is said to be performed by a force if the body upon which the force acts suffers a displacement in the direction of the force, and the work is measured by the product of the force and the displacement in the direction of the force. This definition may seem a little queer, as it leads to some results which at first seem rather strange. A force is required just to hold a heavy suitcase, for example, but no work is done in the sense of mechanical work, because there is no motion. Further, even if the suitcase is being carried along a level street, no work is done because the force exerted on the suitcase is vertical, and there is no vertical displacement of the suitcase. Anyone who has carried a heavy suitcase will disagree with the statement that he was not doing work. Physiologically speaking, he was doing work; he was not doing work on the suitcase, however. The definition of work is nevertheless useful and has been extremely fruitful in the advance of physics and of all science. The concept of work leads to the concept of energy and finally to the principle of the conservation of energy. In the case of the man carrying the suitcase and doing no work on the suitcase according to the definition, there were many energy changes taking place in his body, and these energy changes are concepts based on the very definition of work to which the man objects.

Energy is defined as the ability to do work, and is measured by the amount of work which can be done. Mechanical energy may be of the form of kinetic energy, the ability to do work in virtue of motion, of potential energy, the ability to do work in virtue or position. The advantage of the concept of energy is that in many systems, all systems in which there is no transformation of energy into heat, etc., the total mechanical energy remains constant. This is an example of the law of conservation of energy. A pound of water near the bottom of Niagara Falls has more kinetic energy (is moving faster) than it had at the top, the increase in kinetic energy being given by the decrease in gravitational potential energy. Energy can be many forms other than mechanical, however, such as heat, electrical energy, and chemical energy, and energy can be transformed from any of these forms into any other. The *law of conservation of energy* says that the total energy of the universe remains constant.This law is apparently one of the most important laws of nature. It can never be proven true, but so far no violation of the law has even been found. It has been necessary to include mass as a form of energy, however.

Power is the time rate of doing work. A strong man and a ten year old boy would perform the same amount of work in carrying two equal piles of stone up a hill, but the man could perform the work in a shorter time. This is described by saying his power is greater. Power is commonly measured in *horse power*, the rate of doing 550 foot pounds of work per second, the *foot pound* being the work done by a force of one pound acting through a distance of one foot. Another unit of power is the *watt*. A watt is ten million ergs per second, the *erg* being the work done by a force of one dyne acting through a distance of one centimeter. A horse power is about 746 watts.

Simple Machines. A machine is a mechanism for doing work, or rather, a mechanism for facilitating the performance of work. A machine can do no more work on another object than is performed on it, and in general it will do less. The ratio of the amount of work done by the machine to the amount of work done on the machine, expressed in per cent, is called the efficiency of the machine. The law of conservation of energy guarantees that the efficiency will not exceed 100%, and the presence of *friction* will always decrease the efficiency, the work done against friction appearing as heat.

Frictional forces may be of two types. When two surfaces slide one over the other, frictional forces oppose the sliding. These forces depend on the nature of the surfaces, and may be decreased by lubrication. When one object rolls on another surface, no sliding occurring, rolling friction appears. Rolling friction is usually considerably smaller than sliding friction, and the introduction of ball bearings to replace sliding parts of a machine increases the efficiency. That frictional forces are always present is probably the reason that the Ancients, and, for that matter, uneducated moderns, thought force necessary to maintain motion. In order to find frictionless motion, one must go to astronomical bodies. Even there, friction plays a slight rôle. Due to friction in the tides, the earth is slowing down in its own rotation.

A machine can be considered as a device for transmitting force. With respect to force the situation is different from that with respect to work. The force exerted by a machine, the *load*, can be, although not necessarily, considerably greater than the *applied force*.

A complicated machine can be analyzed into simple components which are called simple machines, examples being the lever, the pulley, the wheel and axle, the inclined plane, the screw, and the wedge. The *mechanical advantage* of a simple machine is defined as the ratio of the load to the applied force. The theoretical mechanical advantage, which assumes the absence of friction, can in a given case be easily calculated from the principle of the conservation of energy. The load can be greater than the applied force, providing the distance through which the applied force acts is proportionately greater than the distance through which the load moves, the conservation of energy requiring the product of the load and the distance through which it acts to be equal to the product of the theoretically required applied force and the distance through which it acts. The theoretical mechanical advantage calculated in this way is, of course, always greater than the actual mechanical advantage, because of friction.

There are essentially two principles involved in simple machines, that of the lever and that of the inclined plane. The principles of the lever is illustrated by the seesaw of childhood. Two children of different weights can balance the seesaw, providing the lighter child is farther away from the pivot (the fulcrum). If the lighter child's weight were half that of the heavier, then he would have to be twice as far from the fulcrum, so that the work done by him on the seesaw as he moved down a certain distance would be equal to the work done by the other child, who would move up half as far. Other simple examples of the lever action are a crowbar, a pump handle, and the key and hammer mechanism of a piano. The lever principle is the basis for pulleys and for the wheel and axle.

The principle of the inclined plane is as easily understood from the viewpoint of work. A heavy box may be lifted a given height more easily by sliding it up an incline than by lifting it vertically. The force required to slide the box up the incline, in the absence of friction, is less than the weight of the box by the same factor that the distance along the incline is greater than the vertical height. In moving pianos, however, it is best to remember friction and have some rollers around!

The wedge is an example of the inclined plane principle. A blow on the wedge by a sledge hammer may make a wedge exert a considerably greater sideway force, because this sideway force acts through a much smaller distance than the force exerted by the sledge hammer. Screw action also illustrates the inclined plane principle.

Properties of Matter. It is customary to classify all matter into three divisions or states. A *solid* is a portion of matter which has a definite volume and a definite shape. A *liquid* has a definite volume but not a definite shape, assuming the shape of its container. A *gas* has neither a definite shape nor a definite volume, both shape and volume being deter-

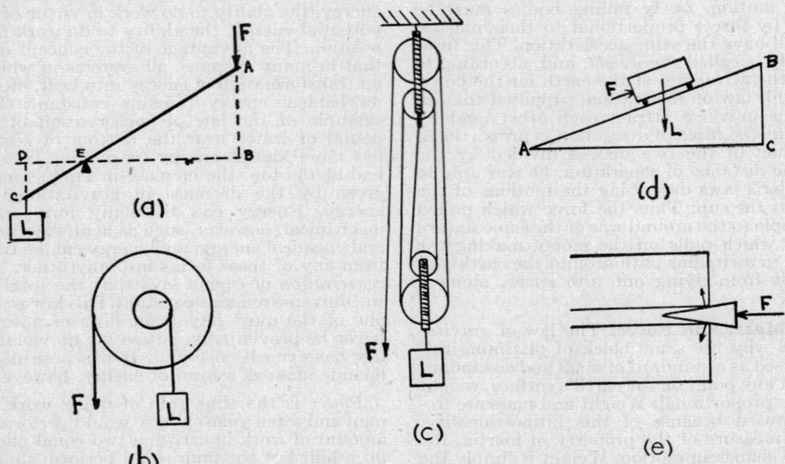

Figure 1. Some simple machines. (a) The lever. The mechanical advantage L/F is given by AB/CD=BE/DE, since the work done by the machine, L×CD, equals the work done on the machine, F×AB. (b) The wheel and axle. The mechanical advantage equals the ratio of the radius of the wheel to the radius of the axle. (c) A block and tackle. The mechanical advantage here is 4, since the force F moves through four times the distance the load is raised. (d) The inclined plane. F/L=AB/BC. (e) The wedge; an application of the inclined plane.

mined by that of the container. Liquids and gases alike are referred to as *fluids*. The borderlines between these states are not always completely sharp, however. All solids possess some degree of plasticity; i.e., they can be deformed. Sometimes large forces are required to produce an appreciable deformation; other times the weight of the solid itself is sufficient, as in the case of a lump of wet clay. The classification into solids, liquids, and gases is nevertheless useful in discussing the properties of matter.

All matter has mass (and, consequently, weight on the surface of the earth). The mass of a given object depends upon its size and the substance of which it is made. This is exemplified by the fact that people are accustomed to thinking of lead as "heavier" than feathers, whereas a pound of lead and a pound of feathers have the same mass and weigh the same. Of course, it takes a larger volume of feathers to make a pound than it does of lead. This is expressed by saying that lead is more dense than feathers. The *density* of a substance is defined as the mass per unit volume. So long as the exact relation of weight to mass is understood, it is often convenient to think of density as weight per unit volume.

The number which measures the density of a substance depends upon the units for mass and volume. The density of water, for example, can be expressed as 1 gram per cubic centimeter or 62.4 pounds per cubic foot. The *specific gravity* of a substance is defined as the ratio of the density of a substance to the density of water. The density of a substance can thus be found in any units providing the density of water is known in those units and the specific gravity of the substance is known. For example, the specific gravity of aluminum is 2.70; hence the density is 2.70×1 or 2.70 grams per cubic centimeter and 2.70×62.4 or 168.5 pounds per cubic foot. A table of specific gravities of some common substances is given below.

SPECIFIC GRAVITY OF COMMON SUBSTANCES

Substance	Specific gravity
Alcohol, ethyl	0.791
Aluminum	2.70
Brass	8.60
Cork	0.22—0.26
Ice	0.917
Iron	7.86
Lead	11.34
Mercury	13.59
Water	1.00
Wood, Balsa	0.11—0.14
Wood, Oak	0.60—0.90

Elasticity. The property of a body of resisting deformation and of returning to its original condition when the deforming force is removed is called elasticity. A rubber band or a steel wire may be stretched by the application of a pulling force, and the band or the wire returns practically to its initial length when the force is removed. Elastic bodies obey a simple law stated by Hooke over two and a half centuries ago and known by his name: "The deformation is proportional to the deforming force."

When a body is deformed, internal resistances to the deformation come into play and these are called the *stress*. The deformation itself is referred to as the *strain*. Hooke's law then can be stated by saying that the stress is proportional to the strain. Hooke's law holds only within limits. If too great a force is applied, the deformation proceeds more rapidly, and the *elastic limit* is said to have been exceeded. In such instances the body does not completely recover when the force is removed. Still greater forces will cause the body to break.

In the case of solids there can be two classes of strain, those corresponding to a change in shape and those corresponding to a change in volume. An example of a change in shape is the change in length of a wire. Another type of strain which is also a change in shape is *shear*. Shear occurs when layers of the body slide one over the other, as when one pushes in opposite directions on the two covers of a book. The twisting of a rod is an example of shear. It is because of this type of elasticity that power can be transmitted by means of a rotating rod or shaft.

The stress producing a change in volume is measured by the pressure, or the force per unit area, on the surface of the body. The corresponding strain is measured by the fractional change in volume. The elasticity of most solids is extremely high, that is, an enormous pressure is required to produce an appreciable change in volume. In order to produce a change in volume of one tenth of one per cent with steel, for example, a pressure of 27,000 pounds per square inch is required.

Another property of solids which is closely related to elasticity is *hardness*. This is a measure of the plasticity, or "giving" under strain. The more nearly an object returns to its original shape when given a blow, the harder the object is said to be. Hardness also indicates how nearly mechanical energy is conserved in a collision, because if there is permanent "give" in a collision, work must be done against a sort of internal friction, this work appearing as heat. For this reason, one method of testing hardness is to drop a steel ball onto a surface and see how close the height of rebound is to the original height of drop. For a steel ball dropped on a steel surface, the height of rebound is 8/10 of the height of drop, which means about 20% of the energy goes into heat.

Volume elasticity is the only kind displayed by a liquid, as a liquid has no definite shape, or in other words, cannot support a shear. The elasticity of most liquids is in general smaller than that of solids, the elasticity of water, for example, being about one hundredth that of steel. That would still mean that a pressure of about 270 pounds per square inch would be required to decrease the volume by one tenth of one per cent or by one part in one thousand. For ordinary purposes, water can certainly be considered incompressible.

Gases also exhibit volume elasticity, and this is discussed below as Boyle's law.

Mechanics of Liquids. The only strain that a liquid can suffer is a change in volume, and accordingly the only stress which can be developed in a liquid is *pressure*. It should be noted that pressure as used in physics means force per unit area, and not merely a "push" as in ordinary speech. A liquid exerts a force against any surface with which it is in contact, the force per unit area measuring the pressure. Pressure does not have direction as force does. One can speak of the pressure at a point as the force per unit area which would be exerted on a surface placed at that point. In this sense, the pressure at a point in a fluid is the same in all directions, and the force exerted by a fluid on a surface is always perpendicular to the surface.

A liquid can exert a pressure due to its own weight. This pressure at any point is determined by the density of the liquid and the depth of the point below the surface. This can be easily understood. If a rectangular vessel of unit cross-sectional area is filled with liquid of density d to a depth h, the weight of the liquid, which is given by the volume multiplied by the density, is hd. Since the pressure at the bottom of the vessel is given by the force per unit area, and the area is unity, the pressure is hd. The pressure, of course, does not depend upon the cross-sectional area, because for any area other than unity, the weight of the fluid and hence the force on the bottom of the vessel would be proportional to the area, but the force per unit area would always be the same. The pressure must be the same at all points at the same depth, as otherwise the liquid would move about. From this it follows that the pressure at a given depth not only does not depend on the size of the vessel, but is also independent of the shape of the vessel.

This leads to a curious result known as the *hydrostatic paradox.* The force on the bottom of a vessel can be greater or less than the weight of the liquid contained in the vessel, depending on the shape of

Figure 2. The hydrostatic paradox.

the vessel. This is illustrated in Figure 2. The liquid level in the communicating vessels must be the same in each vessel, otherwise the pressure would be different at the different ends of the connecting pipes and liquid would flow from one vessel to another. As a consequence, the pressure must be the same at the bottom of each vessel, and, if they have the same area, the force is the same on the bottom of each vessel. Only in the case of the vessel with straight sides is the force on the bottom equal to the weight of fluid contained in the vessel. This diagram also illustrates the common saying, "Water seeks its own level."

If a fluid is confined in a closed vessel, an increase in pressure at any point is transmitted undiminished throughout the fluid. This is known as Pascal's principle, and was established by him in the 17th century. An illustration of Pascal's principle is

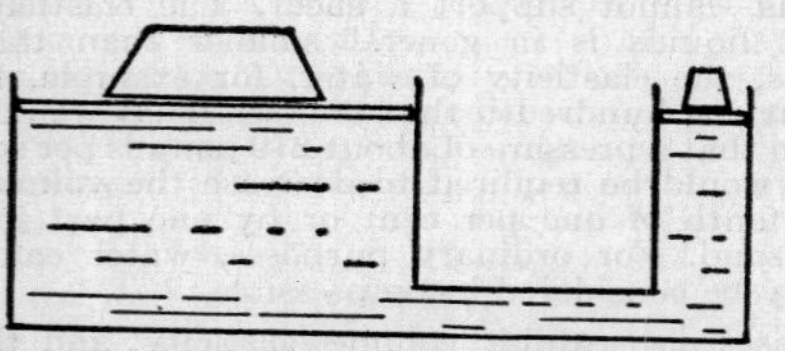

Figure 3. The hydraulic press. The mechanical advantage is given by the ratio of the areas of the pistons.

offered by the hydraulic press (Fig. 3). A small weight placed on the piston in the small chamber creates a pressure which is transmitted undiminished to the larger chamber, whose piston can then support a larger weight. The ratio of the weights (forces) must be equal to the ratio of the areas, since force equals pressure times area. This same result can be established from the principle of conservation of energy in the same manner that the mechanical advantage of a simple machine is determined. If the small weight pushes the small piston down a certain distance, the larger weight is pushed up a proportionately smaller distance. Hydraulic presses are used for compressing cotton into bales, etc., and the same principle is involved in hydraulic brakes for automobiles.

It is a matter of common experience that objects appear to weigh less when submerged in water. This is a consequence of the celebrated *Principle of Archimedes,* which states that a body immersed in a fluid is buoyed up by a force equal to the weight of the fluid displaced. Archimedes discovered the principle, according to the story, in the bath, while pondering the problem of how tc determine if Hiero's crown was pure gold or whether it had been debased by the addition of silver. The buoyant force is a consequence of the variation of hydrostatic pressure with depth. In the case of a body whose density is less than that of the fluid, cork in water, for example, the body floats, sinking just far enough to displace its own weight of fluid. Archimedes' principle is applied by geologists in determining the specific gravity of irregular objects whose volume would be difficult to determine directly. The object is weighed in air and in water, and the volume can be inferred from the apparent loss of weight in water. This was the method Archimedes used to test the crown.

Molecular Forces. It is now commonly accepted that all matter consists of minute particles called molecules. These molecules are constantly in a state of motion. In a solid, the molecules retain their relative positions because of forces between them, and their motion consists essentially of vibrations. In a gas the molecules are sufficiently far apart that they exert little or no force on each other and are completely free to move about. In a liquid the situation is intermediate, the molecules being free to move around but still close enough together to be bound by the forces between molecules. These molecular forces are evidenced by the difficulty encountered in attempting to change the volume of a liquid or solid or to change the length and the shape of a solid. The forces must have a very small range. Considerable difficulty is encountered in breaking a steel rod; once it is broken the pieces can be placed together again and pulled apart with no difficulty. If two pieces of steel are highly polished to very flat surfaces and then are placed in contact, however, again very large forces are needed to separate the pieces because of their close contact. Similar forces of attraction between liquid molecules are shown by the manner in which two drops of water or two drops of mercury will fuse into one drop when they touch. Forces between molecules can be of two kinds: forces between like molecules are called *cohesive* forces, and forces between unlike molecules are called *adhesive* forces.

The cohesive forces between water molecules are responsible for the spherical shape of free drops, such as rain drops, since in the spherical shape the molecules are arranged in such a manner as to make the potential energy due to the forces of attraction a minimum. A system always tries to assume the state of lowest potential energy, as in the case of water "seeking its own level" or a ball rolling down hill. In the case of the water drop, the shape assumed is one in which the surface area is smallest. Increasing the surface area increases the potential energy, as every molecule which is brought to the surface has to be pulled there against the forces of attraction of its neighbor. As a consequence of this the surface of a liquid acts somewhat similarly to a sheet of rubber, in that work is required to increase its area. This effect is described by the name *surface tension.*

The adhesive forces of attraction between glass and water molecules are stronger than the cohesive forces between water molecules. Consequently, if a drop of water is placed on a piece of clean glass, it does not retain its spherical shape but flattens out to increase the area of contact with the glass more than it would due to gravitational effects alone. A striking example of the same effect is *capillary action.* If a hollow glass tube of small internal diameter, a "capillary tube," is dipped into a vessel of water, the water rises in the tube above its outside level. The water no longer seeks its own level, because molecular energy as well as gravitational energy is involved, and, taking into account the energy of attraction of water for glass, there is less total potential energy when the water climbs up in the glass tube. In a tube of smaller diameter the water rises still higher, because the surface area of the inside of the tube, which determines the molecular potential energy, decreases less rapidly with a decrease in diameter than does the volume, which determines the weight of water supported and hence the gravitational energy.

Capillary action plays an important part in nature, as in the passage of water through soil. In the case of mercury and glass, the forces between the glass and the mercury molecules are smaller than the cohesive forces between mercury molecules. As a result, mercury does not "wet" glass. A mercury drop on glass retains a somewhat spherical shape even though gravity alone would cause it to flatten. If a glass capillary tube is dipped in mercury, the mercury level in the tube is depressed, rather than raised. Mercury columns in glass tubes are used in many measuring instruments, as in barometers, and in accurate work the depression due to surface tension must be taken into account.

When two fluids which do not react chemically are placed in the same vessel, it is frequently found that after a time the mixture is uniform throughout. The two fluids have penetrated each other due to their molecular motion. If a drop of ink is placed in a glass of water, for example, the water eventually becomes uniform in color. This process is known as *diffusion*. Sometimes a liquid such as water is able to diffuse through a membrane, while larger, more complex molecules, such as sugar molecules, cannot. If such a membrane separates two vessels, one of which contains pure water and the other a sugar solution, water will diffuse more rapidly into the vessel containing the sugar solution than it does into the other vessel, thus building up a pressure difference between the two sides of the membranes. The reason for this action is that more water molecules strike the membrane on the pure water side, and hence more leave that side. The phenomenon is known as *osmosis*. Osmotic pressures can be very high, and are responsible for the rise of sap in trees and numerous other material processes.

Mechanics of Gases. The most distinguishing feature between liquids and gases is that liquids have a definite volume whereas a gas assumes the volume of its container. For practical purposes, liquids are incompressible, but gases may be relatively easily compressed. Gases do have elasticity of volume, however, the elasticity being measured by the pressure of a gas. The more a gas is compressed, the more difficult it is to compress it further. The behavior of the pressure of a gas is described by *Boyle's Law*, which says that the pressure of a gas is inversely proportional to the volume, at a given temperature. This means, for example, that for air at atmospheric pressure, an increase of pressure just equal to the atmospheric pressure, about 15 pounds per square inch, will halve the volume of a sample of air. This elastic behavior of gases is demonstrated by pneumatic automobile tires. That gases are elastic is shown by the springiness of a tire; that the elasticity depends upon the pressure is shown by the fact that the hardness of a tire increases as the pressure of the enclosed air increases. Boyle's law is not exactly obeyed by all gases, but is obeyed fairly well at ordinary temperatures and pressures.

Gases have weight. Because of this and because gases are fluids, many of the properties of liquids are properties of gases. The weight of the air in the earth's atmosphere is responsible for atmospheric pressure, just as the weight of water produces hydrostatic pressure. Archimedes' principle applies to gases. Effects which depend upon the weight of the fluid, as in Archimedes' principle, are not so readily noticeable with gases, because the density of gases is so low, air under ordinary conditions being about 800 times lighter than water. The buoyancy of a hydrogen or a helium filled balloon is an example of Archimedes' principle applying to a gas, however. The hydrogen and the helium are lighter than air and so a balloon rises, just as a cork placed under water will rise in the water. In extremely accurate weighing, corrections must be made for the buoyant effect of the air on the weights and the object being weighed. That air has weight can be demonstrated directly by providing a glass bottle with a stopper and a valve permitting the air to be pumped out. The bottle weighs less when the air is pumped out.

People are not conscious of the considerable pressure of the earth's atmosphere, about 15 pounds per square inch. Presumably, however, deep sea fish are not conscious of the enormously greater pressure at great depths in the ocean, because they are built to live at such pressures. The pressure of the air was demonstrated in a spectacular fashion in about 1650 by Von Guericke, mayor of Magdeburg. He made two large, closely fitting hemispheres, which he evacuated, and showed that eight horses pulling on each hemisphere were required to pull the spheres apart. The atmospheric pressure had been demonstrated a few years earlier by Torricelli with a much more fundamental experiment.

The principle of Torricelli's experiment is the basis of mercury barometers, which are used to measure atmospheric pressure. If a long glass tube with one end closed is filled with mercury, a finger placed over the open end of the tube and the tube inverted and placed with the open end in a dish of mercury, the mercury column will fall to a definite height above the level of the mercury in the dish when the finger is removed. If care has been taken to exclude even tiny air bubbles, the height of the mercury column will be about 30 inches. That this effect is due to the weight of the air is shown by the fact that at the top of Pike's Peak the mercury column would stand at just about 17 inches. The air pressure can support a water column about 13.6 times as high as a mercury column since the specific gravity of mercury is 13.6. Thus, at sea level, the air can support a water column about 33 feet high. Without the pressure of the atmosphere, an ordinary lift pump would not lift water. As it is, a lift pump cannot lift water over 33 feet. The frequently heard statement that "nature abhors a vacuum" must not be taken too literally. Air rushes through a leak into an evacuated chamber, not because of any particular property of the "vacuum," but simply because it is pushed in by the pressure due to the weight of the earth's atmosphere. The empty space above the mercury column in a carefully made barometer is a fairly good vacuum.

HEAT

Heat is a form of energy into which other types of energy are readily converted, and which can itself, in part, be converted into other forms of energy. When a piece of wood or coal burns, chemical energy is being converted into heat energy. When one rubs his palms together briskly, the energy that he has expended in doing the work of shoving one palm past the other is converted into heat energy and his palms are warmed. When a hammer strikes a nail and drives it into a board, the hammer, the nail, and the board are all heated; the lost kinetic energy of the hammer has been converted into heat. If the hammer comes completely to rest upon striking the nail, i.e., if it does not rebound, then all of its kinetic energy is converted into heat. If two pieces of ice at 32° Fahrenheit are rubbed together, the energy put into the rubbing is converted into heat and some of the ice melts.

Whenever, by any means whatsoever, work is done against frictional forces, the energy required to do that work is converted into heat. In particular, heat is that type of energy whose transfer to or from a body results in a change in *temperature* or *change of state*. (q.v.)

Temperature. Everyone has a *sense* which enables him to distinguish between a "hot" object and a "cold" one. This "temperature" sense is distinct from the sense of touch, for a person can tell that an object is hot without actually touching it. Given two objects, he can, either by coming near or by actually touching them, tell which is the warmer of the two. If he were to place the two objects next to one another, he would find that eventually the warmer one would cool down, and the cooler one warm up, until the distinction "warmer" or "cooler" could no longer be made. Again, given a large number of objects, his temperature sense would enable him to arrange them in order of hotness or coldness.

This sense, however, is a rather unreliable one; it is too subjective to be of scientific use. A room that seems quite hot to one entering it from the outside on a cold day may at the same time seem quite cool to the lady who has been "slaving away over a hot stove."

The temperature of a body is an objective measure of its position on a scale of hotness or coldness. It is that physical property of a body which determines which way heat energy will flow. If bodies of two different temperatures are placed near one another, the direction of energy transfer will always be such that the warmer one is cooled, and the cooler one warmed, until the two finally come to equilibrium at the same temperature. The rate at which this transfer takes place depends upon the difference in temperature of the two objects involved. Before quantitative statements can be made, one must have an instrument for measuring temperature, and must establish a definite temperature scale.

Thermometers. Qualitative experiments show that many physical properties of materials depend on temperature. Perhaps simplest of these are the linear dimensions of an object. Though some few materials exhibit anomalous behavior, most solids increase in linear dimensions (and, therefore, of course, in area and in volume) as their temperatures are increased. Similarly, liquids, and gases kept at constant pressure, exhibit an increase in volume with increasing temperature.

A thermometer is a device for measuring temperature; its operation depends upon some measurable physical property of the "thermometric substance" which changes with temperature but which is relatively uninfluenced by other factors. The most common form consists of a closed length of glass tubing having a bore of very small diameter, terminating at one end in a glass bulb containing a liquid—usually mercury or alcohol. When the temperature of the thermometer is raised, the volume of the bulb and bore increase slightly, but that of the liquid increases by a greater amount (see *Expansion Coefficients*); hence, some of the liquid must move farther up into the bore of the tube. The position of the end of this liquid column is used to indicate the temperature.

Temperature Scales. In general, temperature scales are established in a completely arbitrary way. Two temperatures which are readily duplicated, such as temperatures at which *Change of State* (q.v.) occurs, are used to define two "fixed points" on the thermometer scale, and the interval between the two fixed points is divided into a number of equally spaced divisions, called *degrees* (°). The two most common scales are the so-called "Fahrenheit" and the "Centigrade" scales. Both use the temperatures of melting ice and of boiling water to establish their fixed points. After the liquid has been introduced into the bulb and the upper end of the stem sealed off, the bulb, together with the lower part of the stem, is immersed in water containing melting ice, and the position of the end of the liquid column is marked on the stem. On a Fahrenheit thermometer this point is arbitrarily called 32 degrees (32°); on a Centigrade thermometer it is called 0°. The entire thermometer is then placed in the steam just over the surface of boiling water, and the position of the end of the liquid column marked. For a Fahrenheit thermometer this point is arbitrarily called 212°; for a Centigrade thermometer, 100°. The distance along the stem between the two fixed points is then divided into equal intervals: 180 (i.e. 212 minus 32) on the Fahrenheit scale, 100 on the Centigrade scale. Temperatures outside the range 0-100° Centigrade or 32-212° Fahrenheit are marked by extending these scales, using intervals of the same length as those used in dividing the region between the fixed points. For example, 0° on the Fahrenheit thermometer is located by marking off 32 additional scale marks below the 32° mark, using intervals of the same length as those between 32° and 212°.

One can readily convert a temperature measurement on one scale to the corresponding reading on the other. Suppose, for example, one wanted to find the Centigrade temperature corresponding to normal body temperature, knowing that the latter is a 98.6° on the Fahrenheit scale. Referring to Figure 4, it is seen that this temperature is 66.6 Fahrenheit degrees above the temperature of melting ice. Now 66.6 Fahrenheit degrees correspond to how many Centigrade degrees? One needs only to note that 180 Fahrenheit degrees constitute a temperature difference equivalent to 100 Centigrade degrees, and

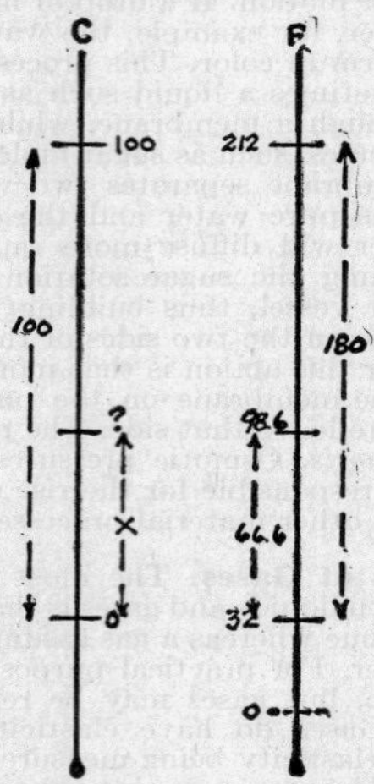

Figure 4. Temperature scales.

that the ratio of any interval measured in Centigrade degrees to the same temperature interval measured in Fahrenheit degrees will be 100/180. So, calling the unknown interval on the Centigrade scale "x", one can write $x/66.6 = 100/180$, from which one obtains $x = 37$. That is, a temperature interval of 66.6 Fahrenheit degrees is equivalent to one of 37 Centigrade degrees. Body temperature, therefore, being 66.6 Fahrenheit degrees above the melting point of ice, must be 37 Centigrade degrees above that temperature, and since, on the Centigrade scale, the melting point of ice is at 0°, body temperature must be at 0+37, or 37° Centigrade. The reader can check his understanding of this method of converting from one scale to the other by showing that both scales will read the same at —40°. (See *Absolute Zero.*)

Coefficients of Thermal Expansion

Linear. If the temperature of a rod of some solid is increased uniformly over the entire length of the rod, every unit of its length becomes somewhat longer. The increase in length of each unit of its length is proportional to the increase in temperature; the increase in length per unit of length per degree temperature rise is called the *coefficient of linear expansion* of the material. Coefficients for several representative materials are listed in the Table of *Coefficients of Linear Expansion.*

COEFFICIENTS OF LINEAR EXPANSION PER ° C

Aluminum	24 $\times 10^{-6}$	Platinum	9 $\times 10^{-6}$
Copper	17 "	Silica	0.5 "
Glass, Soft	8 to 9 "	Silver	19 "
Glass, Pyrex	3 "	Steel	11 "

One can see from the table, for example, that a length of aluminum expands a little over twice as much as the same length of steel for a given temperature change. Soft glass expands about half as much as copper, but at about the same rate as platinum. This means that it is difficult to seal soft glass to copper, for, if the temperature changes, the two parts of the seal will expand at different rates and place the joint under high stresses. On the other hand, a glass to platinum seal will be much more likely to survive a change in temperature.

A material which cannot withstand high internal stress will break when an attempt is made to change its temperature too rapidly. A thick glass tumbler suddenly filled with a hot liquid may shatter because the inside layers of the glass heat up and attempt to expand, while the outside layers of the glass are still cool. The thinner the glass wall, the more uniformly will the glass be heated throughout, and the less will be the tendency to shatter.

Volume. The coefficient of volume expansion is defined as the change in volume per unit volume per degree temperature change. Here, a separate tabulation is not required; for isotropic solids the volume coefficient may be taken as three times the linear coefficient. A cube of copper 2 inches on a side at 0° C has a volume of 8 cubic inches. Since the change in volume is just the initial volume times the volume coefficient times the change in temperature, raising the temperature of this cube to 100° C will increase its volume by $8\times(3\times17\times10^{-6})\times100=0.04$ cubic inches. Similarly, if a measuring container made of copper holds 8 quarts at a temperature of 0° C, it will hold 8.04 quarts at 100° C.

Liquids also increase in volume with increasing temperature, and in general at a greater rate than do solids by a factor of from 10 to 100 or more. Had the copper container been filled to the brim with 8 quarts of glycerine which has a volume expansion coefficient of 53×10^{-5}/° C at 0° C, the 100 degree temperature increase would have resulted in an expansion of the glycerine amounting to $8\times53\times10^{-5}\times100=0.42$ quarts, or about 1/3 quart more than the increased volume of the container.

Water differs from other liquids in one important point as regards expansion. Instead of expanding uniformly as its temperature is raised from 0° Centigrade, it *contracts* as the temperature is raised from 0° to 4°, and then expands as the temperature climbs above 4°. The volume of a given quantity of water at 100° C is about 4 per cent greater than its volume at 0° C—about 10 times the expansion of an equal volume of steel undergoing the same temperature change.

The expansion of gases is remarkable in two ways: (1) it is very large, about nine times that of water, and (2) the rate of expansion is very nearly the same for all gases. The value of the volume coefficient of expansion is very nearly 1/273; i.e., for any gas there is an increase in volume of very nearly 1/273 its volume at 0° C for each degree rise in temperature. Further, it is found that, if the volume of gas is held constant and its temperature increased, the *pressure* of the gas rises for each degree temperature rise, by 1/273 of the pressure at 0° C. One can therefore construct a thermometer using the pressure of a gas kept at constant volume as a temperature indicator. (See *Thermometers, Absolute Zero.*)

Absolute Zero. There is no very obvious reason why the temperature scales described above cannot be extended indefinitely to temperatures above and below the "fixed" points. There is excellent evidence, however, that there is a *lowest* possible temperature.

Assume that a certain mass of gas is inclosed in a container whose volume does not change. At 0° C this gas would exert a certain pressure on the walls of the container. Since the pressure coefficient of the gas is 1/273, a drop in temperature of 1° C would result in a decrease in pressure amounting to 1/273 of the pressure at 0° C. It follows that if the gas continued to behave in this fashion, a drop in temperature of 273° C would result in a pressure drop of 273/273 of the pressure at 0° C; i.e., the pressure which the gas exerts on the walls of its container would become zero if the temperature of the gas were reduced to −273° C. This is considered to be the absolute zero of temperature.

More precise experiments place absolute zero at −273.16° C. On the Absolute (A) Temperature scale, therefore, the melting point of ice is at +273.16° A, and the boiling point of water is at +373.16°A.

It has not been possible in any actual experiment to attain a temperature as low as 0° A. All gases liquify, and in fact solidify, before that temperature is reached. Helium is known to liquify at −268° C, and to solidify at below −272.3° C, or within a degree of absolute zero. (See *Change of State.*)

Quantity of Heat. Everyone is familiar with the fact that the more water a kettle contains, the longer it takes to heat that water. That is, the amount of heat energy required to produce a definite temperature change depends on the mass of material to be heated. Suppose two gas flames to be burning (and therefore to be producing heat) at the same steady rate. Suppose one of them to be surrounded by a mass of copper, initially at 0° C, so that all the heat energy produced goes into the copper, and suppose the other flame to be arranged so that all of the heat it produces goes into an equal mass of water. This energy will, of course, cause the temperature of the water and the copper to rise, but not by the same amount. After a time sufficiently long for the temperature of the copper to have increased to 100° C, the water will be found to have a temperature of only about 9.3° C. Apparently it takes more heat energy to raise the temperature of a given amount of water 1° C than it does to raise the temperature of an equal amount of copper 1° C.

Quantity of heat can therefore be measured in terms of the temperature change produced in a given quantity of some particular material. For the two units of quantity of heat in general use, water is taken as the standard, and the units of heat energy are defined as follows:

The *calorie* is that amount of heat which will raise the temperature of 1 gram of water 1° C.

The *British Thermal Unit* (BTU) is that amount of heat which will raise the temperature of one pound of water 1° F.

Since one pound is equivalent to 453.6 grams, and since a temperature change of 1° F is 5/9 as much as a temperature change of 1° C, it is seen that one British Thermal Unit is equivalent to $5/9\times453.6$, or 252 calories.

Specific Heat. It takes more heat energy to raise the temperature of water a given amount than to produce the same temperature rise in an equal mass of any other material. The ease or difficulty with which the temperature of a given type of material can be raised is described by that property known as its *specific heat.* The specific heat of a material is the number of calories (BTU's) of heat required to raise the temperature of 1 gram (pound) of it 1° C (1° F). For example, the specific heat of lead (See *Table of Specific Heats*) is .030. To raise the temperature of one pound of lead 1° F takes .03 BTU of heat. To raise the temperature of 15 pounds of lead 30° C requires $.03\times15\times30$, or 13.5 BTU's.

TABLE OF SPECIFIC HEATS

Material	Specific heat	Material	Specific heat
Aluminum	0.214	Lead	0.030
Copper	0.092	Magnesium	0.246
Glycerine	0.540	Paraffin	0.694
Ice (around 10° C)	0.530	Water	1.000

Specific Heats of Gases. A bit of care needs to be exercised in talking about the specific heat of a gas. A gas might have any number of specific heats, depending upon the exact conditions under which it is heated, for in general the heating of a gas may be accompanied by changes in both its pressure and its volume. There are two limiting cases, however, that deserve consideration. First, a gas may be heated while confined in a container so that its volume does not change. In this case, as the temperature rises, so does the pressure. All of the heat supplied to the gas, however, goes into raising its temperature. The number of calories of heat energy required to raise the temperature of one gram of the gas 1° C when the volume of the gas is held constant is called its *specific heat at constant volume.*

In the second limiting case, the gas may be heated while confined in a container fitted with a movable wall, the arrangement being such that as the temperature of the gas goes up the pressure remains constant. This necessitates an increase in the volume of the container. Not all of the heat energy added to the gas goes to produce an increase in temperature; some of this energy is used up in doing the work of pushing back the movable wall and so increasing the volume of the container. To produce a temperature rise of 1° C under these conditions, therefore, requires more energy than to heat the same mass of gas at constant volume. The number of calories of heat energy required to raise the temperature of one gram of gas 1° C at constant pressure is called the *specific heat at constant pressure.* The specific heat of a gas at constant pressure is always greater than its specific heat at constant volume. For diatomic gases the ratio is about 1.4. For example, it takes 2.418 calories of heat to raise the temperature of one gram of hydrogen gas 1° C, if the gas is kept in a container whose volume does not change, and, on the other hand, the specific heat of hydrogen at constant pressure is 3.410 calories/gram ° C, just 1.41 times the specific heat at constant volume.

The Kinetic Theory. The kinetic theory is one which attempts to explain the behavior of matter in terms of the motions of the individual particles of which it is composed. Applied to gases, it leads to a simple demonstration of the distinction between heat and temperature. A gas is pictured as being made up of myriads of tiny particles—molecules—continually moving with completely random velocities, and colliding with one another and with the walls of the containing vessel. The pressure which the gas exerts on the walls of the container is conceived as arising from the billions and billions of random impacts of these tiny particles against the walls.

Each of these moving particles has a kinetic energy (q.v.) determined by its mass and its velocity. It was pointed out in the first paragraph of this section on heat that when work is done against frictional forces, the energy which disappears is converted into heat energy. The kinetic theory pictures this process as one of conversion of the mechanical energy which apparently disappears into kinetic energy of motion of the molecules. "Heating" a body, therefore, means increasing the kinetic energy of its molecules. The kinetic theory completely explains the dependence of the pressure of a gas on temperature, providing the *absolute temperature* is taken to be proportional to the *average kinetic energy* of the molecules.

If several different kinds of gas are all at the same temperature, the average kinetic energy of the molecules is the same for all. If their average kinetic energies are equal, it means that the lighter molecules must have an average speed which is greater than that of the heavier molecules. At 0° C, the average speed of hydrogen molecules is about 1700 meters per second, and the average speed of oxygen molecules a bit over 400 meters per second. While molecules travel with these very high speeds, they do not in general go very far, at normal pressures, without colliding with other molecules. For example, an oxygen molecule in the air at normal atmospheric pressure, and again at 0° C, travels an average distance of only about 9×10^{-6} (i.e., nine one-millionths) of a centimeter before it collides with another molecule. On the average, therefore, such a molecule suffers collision with another molecule about once every 2 one-hundred-billionth of a second, or suffers about 50 billion collisions per second.

Change of State. Matter can exist in three different states—as a solid, as a liquid, or as a gas—and it is a matter of common experience that it requires heat energy to convert a solid into a liquid, or a liquid into a gas. It is perhaps not so apparent that the conversion of a gas into a liquid, or a liquid into a solid, requires the removal of heat energy.

If a dish containing ice and water is kept in a room where everything else is at 0° C, the ice will not melt nor the water freeze. Should the room become warmer, the ice will melt, but the temperature of the mixture will remain at 0° C, until all of the ice has disappeared. The heat from the surrounding air flows into the mixture and does the work of melting the ice, but not until all of the ice is melted will the temperature of the liquid begin to rise. On the other hand, should the room become cooler, heat will flow out of the water-ice mixture into the room, the liquid turning to solid as a consequence. Not until all of the liquid has solidified will the temperature of the solid begin to go down.

Freezing and Boiling Points. The temperature at which the liquid and solid states of a given material remain in equilibrium with one another, neither growing at the expense of the other, is called the *melting point* of the solid, or the *freezing point* of the liquid. This is a very definite temperature for a crystalline solid. An amorphous solid, on the other hand, does not have a definite melting point; within a rather wide temperature interval it gradually softens and turns to liquid as the temperature is raised.

MELTING POINTS & BOILING POINTS AT NORMAL PRESSURE

Material		Freezing Pt. °C	Boiling Pt. ° C
Aluminum		659.7	1800.
Bromine		−7.2	58.8
Copper		108.3	2300.
Helium	less than	−272.2	−268.9
Lead		327.	1620.
Mercury		−38.9	356.9
Sodium		97.5	980.
Tungsten		3370.	5900.
Water		0	100.
Alcohol, ethyl		117.3	78.3

Effect of Pressure. Both the freezing point and the boiling point depend on pressure. At normal atmospheric pressure the melting point of ice (freezing point of water) is at 0° C. At a pressure of 2 atmospheres, the melting point of ice is lowered by about 1/100 of a ° C. As a result, ice at 0° C subjected to a pressure of 2 atmospheres is about 1/100th of a degree above its melting point, and therefore will melt. It is a consequence of this fact that glaciers "flow", and that ice skates slide so readily. The skate blade subjects the ice beneath it to high pressure, depressing the melting point, and if the ice itself is at its normal freezing point temperature, it melts under this pressure and the skate slides, not over the ice, but on a thin film of water. As soon as the skate blade passes over a given region the pressure is removed and the liquid water immediately freezes again. This process is known as *regelation.*

For any material which, like water, contracts on melting—or expands on freezing (witness the bursting of a water pipe if the water in it freezes)—increase in pressure lowers the freezing point temperature. For a material which contracts on freezing, or expands on melting, increase in pressure raises the melting point temperature.

Similarly, increase of pressure raises the boiling point of a liquid, or decrease of pressure lowers it. At normal atmospheric pressure water boils at 100° C. If the steam or vapor produced by the boiling is confined above the liquid. so that the pressure increases, the temperature to which the liquid must be heated to make it boil goes up above 100° C. If the pressure is, for example, 2 atmospheres, water must be heated to a little over 120° C to make it boil, or if the pressure is reduced to that at the top of Pike's Peak (about .6 of normal atmospheric pressure) the boiling point is reduced to around 85°C.

Latent Heats. Experiment shows that it requires about 80 calories of heat energy to melt one gram of ice at 0° C. Exactly the same quantity of heat must be removed from one gram of water at 0° C in order to convert it into 1 gram of ice. This quantity of heat, 80 calories per gram, is called the latent heat of melting, or *latent heat of fusion*, of ice.

Even more heat is required to cause water to boil. To convert 1 gram of water, already at 100° C, into 1 gram of steam at the same temperature, requires 539 calories of heat. This is the so-called *latent heat of vaporization* of water. One gram of steam at 100° C, condensing to form one gram of water at the same temperature, gives off to the surroundings exactly the same amount of heat energy. It should be understood, however, that the condensation is not the cause, but the result. Only if the surroundings are at a temperature below 100° C, so that the steam *can* lose heat energy, will the heat be given off and the condensation occur. Heats of fusion and vaporization of several common substances are listed in the table below.

HEATS OF FUSION & VAPORIZATION

Material	Heat of Fusion (cal/gm)	Heat of Vaporization* (cal/gm)
Alcohol	24.9	208
Aluminum	92.4	
Bismuth	13.0	
Water	80.0	539
Mercury	2.8	68
Tin	14.6	

*At normal boiling point.

Transfer of Heat. Heat energy will, of its own accord, flow from one substance to surrounding substances only if the surroundings are at a lower temperature. When this flow of heat does take place, it may be by one or by any combination of the three methods (1) conduction, (2) convection, or (3) radiation.

Conduction. When an iron poker is thrust into a fire, the end held in the hand soon becomes hot. If the poker were made of copper or silver, the effect would be even more noticeable; on the other hand a, wooden stick thrust against glowing coals transmits very little heat to the other end. What actually happens can be pictured in terms of the kinetic theory (q.v.). The glowing coals are "hot" because the molecules of which they are composed have a large amount of kinetic energy. When the poker is thrust against the coals, these molecules collide with the molecules in the poker and transfer kinetic energy to them; therefore, the end of the poker gets "hot." Now that the molecules in the end of the poker have had their kinetic energy increased, they begin to collide more strongly with other "poker" molecules, thus increasing their kinetic energy. By successive collisions such as this, kinetic energy is passed along the length of the poker, from molecule to molecule, until finally even that part of the poker which is held in the hand begins to feel the effect of these collisions, and as a matter of fact, begins to transfer molecular kinetic energy to molecules in the hand.

Materials along which molecular kinetic energy is transferred readily are said to be good *conductors* of heat; those along which it does not take place readily are called *insulators*. Metals are almost all good conductors, silver being the best. Wool, wood, and cork are among the best insulators. Liquids are much poorer conductors of heat than solids, and gases much poorer than liquids. For example, iron conducts heat 100 times as well as water, and water is 25 times as good a conductor as air.

Convection. When heat is supplied to the top of a column of liquid or gas, the temperature at the bottom of the column rises very slowly, because liquids and gases are poor conductors of heat. When heat is supplied at the bottom of the column, the lower layers, upon becoming warmed, expand and are pushed upward by the cooler, more dense, portions of the fluid. These cooler portions are then warmed and rise in turn, setting up a circulation of the fluid, and thus resulting in a warming of the entire column. In this process, known as convection, it is readily seen that heat energy is transferred, not by a passing on of kinetic energy from molecule to molecule as in the conduction process, but by an actual transfer of the molecules themselves.

Most systems of heating and ventilating depend upon convection currents, and these currents, in turn, depend upon the fact that liquids and gases expand when they are warmed. The draft in a stove, furnace, fireplace, or factory chimney is a convection current. Winds and other atmospheric movements are largely caused by, or are themselves, convection currents.

Radiation. When a hot iron is suspended in midair, some object placed under it receives heat energy. This heat energy cannot be transferred by convection, which would cause rising rather than descending currents of heated air, nor can it be transferred by conduction, for gases are poor conductors. The earth receives from the sun some 42,500 million million calories of heat energy every second, though the space between the earth and the sun is almost completely free of molecules and therefore cannot transfer heat by either of the two processes mentioned above. The transfer is accomplished by a third process known as radiation.

When an electric heater is operating, one not only feels warmth from the heater, but he sees light coming from the glowing coils. When the current is first turned on, one can begin to feel "heat" from the unit before the glow is apparent. As the coil warms up, more and more heat is emitted, but not until the temperature of the coil reaches some 600° C does one begin to be aware of a dull red glow, which becomes bright red and then yellowish at around 1000° C, and "white hot" at around 1500° C. Experiment shows that the heat radiation that one feels is exactly the same sort of thing as the light radiation that he sees, the only difference being in the "wave length" of the radiation. The longest wave lengths to which the eye is sensitive are those at the red end of the spectrum; the wave lengths of heat radiation are just longer than these, and therefore heat radiation is often referred to as infra-red radiation. This radiation has its origin in a heated object, and the hotter the source, the more radiation it emits and the shorter is the wave length of the emitted radiation. (See *Electromagnetic Spectrum.*)

Some materials, such as air, permit infra-red radiation to pass through with relatively little absorption, and therefore are only slightly warmed. Others do not transmit the radiation readily, but either absorb it (as does water) becoming warmed in the process, or reflect it (as do polished metals) without themselves taking energy from the radiation.

Glass transmits the shorter of the infra-red rays about as well as it does visible light, but very effectively blocks passage of the longer wave length portion of the infra-red spectrum. This is the origin of the so-called "greenhouse" effect. Light from the sun passes through the glass roof of the greenhouse and is absorbed by the soil. The soil thus warmed emits radiation, but since the soil temperature is relatively low, the emitted radiation is of very long wave length which is not transmitted by glass. The heat energy is therefore "trapped" in the greenhouse; it can get in as short wave length infra-red or as visible radiation, but as long wave length infra-red radiation it cannot get out again.

Of two objects at the same temperature, the one with the blacker, rougher, surface is found to be the best emitter of heat radiation. It is a well established law that objects that are good absorbers of radiation falling on them are good emitters of radiation when they themselves are at high temperature—poor absorbers (i.e., good reflectors) are poor radiators. A sooty, black, surface will emit 20 times more radiation than a highly polished surface at the same temperature. The radiators in a hot water or steam heating system would radiate much more efficiently were they painted a dull black than they do with their usual bright, highly reflecting coating. The practice of giving radiators a gilt or aluminum surface is not as serious as it might seem, however—radiators do very little heating by radiation anyway. Heat from the radiator is transmitted to the adjacent air by conduction, and to the rest of the room by convection.

Heat and Work. It has been stated that when work is done against frictional forces, heat energy is produced. The work done can be measured in ordinary work units (ergs or joules or foot-pounds) and the heat produced, in ordinary heat units (calories or BTU's). Nothing has been said about the relative sizes of the work and heat units, however, nor about the question "How much work must be done to produce a given number of calories of heat energy?"

This question was studied by Joule (1854) using a weight suspended from a cord connected to a paddle wheel immersed in water, all arranged in such a way that the weight, in descending, caused the paddle wheel to rotate. As a result of friction between the paddle wheel and the water, the water was warmed. Joule measured the mechanical (potential) energy lost by the weight in descending, and, from the temperature rise of the water, determined the heat energy produced in the water, and showed that the heat energy produced was always proportional to the mechanical energy that disappeared. He had no way of showing—there is no way of showing—that all of the mechanical energy was converted into heat, but being a believer in the law of conservation of energy, and being unable to find energy appearing in any other form, he assumed (and no experiments performed since that time give any reason to doubt the validity of his assumption) that the heat energy produced was exactly equivalent to the mechanical energy disappearing. He was able to show that to produce one calorie of heat energy required 4.18 joules of mechanical energy. This figure, 4.18 joules per calorie (or the equivalent in the English system, 778 foot-pounds per BTU) is called the mechanical equivalent of heat.

Heat energy can be converted into mechanical energy, and any device which will accomplish this is known as a *heat engine.* In general the heat energy supplied to such an engine warms a gas or vapor which therefore expands and in so doing pushes back a piston. This piston can be linked to some mechanical system which will do work. Since the cylinder in which the piston operates cannot be infinitely long and still be useful, the engine must operate in some sort of *cycle* which will bring it back to the starting point once more. When the return stroke starts the expanded gases will not have lost all their thermal energy—that is, the temperature of the expanded gas will not have been reduced to absolute zero—and all of the heat energy put into the machine will not be recovered as mechanical energy.

It was a French physicist, Carnot (1759–1832) who showed that no heat engine can be more efficient than what he called an ideal engine, that even his ideal engine cannot have an efficiency of 100%, and that the efficiency of such an engine depends on the absolute temperatures of the intake and exhaust gases. If I represents the former and E the latter, he showed that the efficiency of an ideal engine would be (I-E)/I. For example, an ideal engine taking in saturated steam at 165° C (438° A) (this corresponds to a steam pressure of 100 pounds per square inch) and exhausting it at atmospheric pressure, i.e., at a temperature of 100° C (373° A), will have an efficiency of (438-373)/438, or about 14.8%. Less than 15% of the heat energy supplied to the engine could be recovered as mechanical energy. No *real* engine will be this efficient; an actual steam engine is unlikely to be more than 2/3 as efficient as an ideal engine operating between the same temperatures.

WAVE MOTION AND SOUND

Waves. A discussion of sound can well begin with a discussion of the general properties of wave motion which sound possesses in common with other wave motions, such as water waves and light. Like other fundamental concepts, wave motion is more easily illustrated than defined. If a long rope is snapped sideways, a transverse displacement or pulse travels along the length of the rope. If one end of a helical spring is struck, a compression travels the length of the spring. If a stone is thrown into a pond, a set of circular ripples, a disturbance of the surface of the water, travels out. In each of these examples there is a medium through which a disturbance is propagated, the disturbance consisting of a distortion of the medium. In each case there is motion of the medium, but this motion of the medium consists of an oscillation and does not involve the progression of anything material along with the wave. A floating leaf in the path of the water ripples does not move along with the ripples, but moves up and down, and the motion of the leaf is the motion of the water under the leaf.

Two kinds of waves are distinguished. In a *transverse wave,* of which the pulse in the rope is an example, the motion of the medium consists of an oscillation in a direction perpendicular to the direction of propagation of the wave. The compression in the spring is an example of a *longitudinal wave,* in which the oscillations of the medium are in the same direction as the direction of propagation of the wave. Water waves are nearly transverse waves, although there is some to and fro motion of the water along the surface. Sound is a compressional or longitudinal wave in ordinary matter.

Wave Terminology. The speed with which a given part of a wave disturbance, such as the crest of a water wave, is propagated is known as the *wave speed.* The speed of a wave depends in general on two factors, the elasticity of the medium and the density of the medium. The speed is directly proportional to the square root of the elasticity and inversely proportional to the square root of the density.

In the examples given above, the pulse along the rope and the compression in the spring, the wave disturbance was irregular. In most of the interesting cases of wave motion, however, the disturbance is regular, repeating itself periodically. This is true of sound waves to which we can ascribe a definite pitch, for example. In such cases it is useful to speak of the *wave length,* the distance between two successive points in the medium which are undergoing exactly the same disturbance, such as the crests of a water wave. In these cases one also refers to the *frequency* as the number of these periodic disturbances which passes a given point in unit time. A moment's reflection will show that the product of the wave length and the frequency is equal to the speed of the waves.

Superposition of Waves: Interference. If two stones are thrown at neighboring points on the surface of a pond, the two sets of circular waves arising from the two stones are easily distinguished. After passing through each other, each of the circular sets proceeds as if the other were not present. This is an example of the fact that the behavior of a wave passing through a medium is unaffected by the existence of other waves which may be present at the same time. Careful distinction must be made here between the actual disturbance or displacement of the medium, and the waves, the traveling disturbances. Two waves passing a given point simultaneously have no effect on each other's subsequent motion; the actual displacement of the medium at that point is the sum of the displacements it would have due to the individual waves acting alone.

This superposition of waves leads to a whole class of phenomena grouped under the name interference. If the displacements due to each of the two waves are in the same direction at a given point, so that reinforcement occurs, one speaks of *constructive interference.* If the displacements are in opposite directions so that partial or complete cancellation occurs, one then speaks of *destructive interference.* The colors of a thin oil film on a water surface, and the effect known as beats in sound, although very much different, are both interference effects.

Reflection and Refraction. Whenever a wave encounters a boundary separating two media in which the wave has different speeds, part of the wave is in general reflected and part transmitted across the boundary. If the boundary surface is large enough so that diffraction effects (q.v.) are not too pronounced, the reflected wave travels away from the boundary in a direction making the same angle with the boundary as the direction of the incident wave. This is known as the *law of reflection,* and is illustrated in Figure 5.

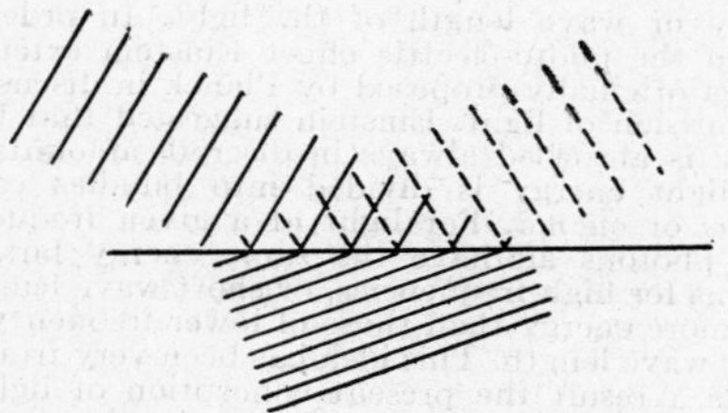

Figure 5. Reflection and refraction of a wave train. The reflected wave (broken line) has the same wave length as the incident wave, but the refracted wave has a shorter wave length as it is traveling more slowly.

In general, the part of the wave which is transmitted travels in a different direction from the incident wave. This change in the direction of the wave is known as *refraction.* In Figure 5, the speed in the second medium is less than that in the first, the wave length is consequently shorter, and the refracted wave travels away from the boundary making a smaller angle with the boundary than the incident wave.

Diffraction. Unless a change in speed is encountered, in which case refraction occurs as discussed above, waves appear to travel in straight lines. If an obstacle is placed in the path of a wave, however, a departure from this straight line motion will be observed. There will be some bending around the obstacle, an effect known as *diffraction.* The magnitude of the effect depends upon the size of the obstacle in comparison with the wave length of the waves. Figure 6a illustrates the diffraction occurring when a wave strikes a small opening, and Figure 6b illustrates the effect when the opening is considerably larger than the wave length. The cause of diffraction is easily understood when one remembers the mechanism of wave propagation. A disturbance at some point in the medium causes a disturbance at neighboring points, because of the elasticity of the medium. The disturbance in the medium just beyond the openings creates disturbance at the sides as well as straight ahead, causing a spreading of the wave.

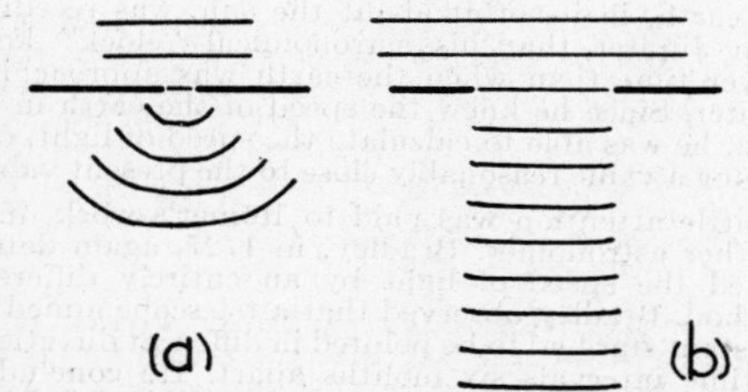

Figure 6. Diffraction of a wave. In (a) the aperture has a diameter about equal to the wave length. In (b) the diameter of the aperture is considerably greater and the diffraction is less noticeable.

The Nature of Sound. Sound is a compressional wave through matter. That a medium is necessary for the transmission of sound is easily demonstrated. If an electric bell such as a doorbell is placed in an airtight chamber connected to a vacuum pump, the sound of the bell can be easily heard so long as there is air in the chamber. If the air is removed by means of the pump, the sound can no longer be heard.

Sound can be transmitted through any form of matter, since gases, liquids, and solids alike, have elasticity of volume, that is, resist changes in volume, although sound waves in gases, particularly in air, are of chief importance from the point of view of sound as that which affects the ear. Sound waves in water have considerable practical importance, however, in such cases as submarine detection and sound ranging, and determination of the depth of the sea by the time of passage of sound waves.

The speed of sound in a gas depends upon the pressure and the density of the gas, being greater for light gases than for heavy gases at the same pressure. The speed of sound in the air, however, does not depend upon the barometric pressure, as might be first supposed, since the pressure and the density of a gas increase proportionately if the temperature does not change. An increase in the temperature of the air, on the other hand, increases the ratio of the pressure and the density, and consequently increases the speed of sound. The speed of sound in dry air is 1130 feet per second at 70° F, and increases by about 1 foot per second for each degree rise in temperature. The speed of sound in liquids and solids is considerably greater than that in gases, because of the much greater elasticity or resistance to changes in volume. The speed of sound in water is about 4800 feet per second.

All sound waves travel with the same speed, regardless of the frequency. The truth of this statement is obvious to anyone who reflects for a moment on what he would hear at a band concert if the statement were not true! (See *Characteristics of Sound* for relation between frequency and pitch.)

Wave Properties of Sound. Sound exhibits all the phenomena which have been described as general properties of waves. The phenomenon of *beats* is an example of *interference.* Two sound waves of nearly equal frequencies exhibit alternately constructive and destructive interference as they get in and then out of step. The familiar and fascinating *echo* is an example of the reflection of sound. *Refraction* of sound is also common, though less obvious. In the evening the air near the surface of the earth is frequently cooler than that higher up, and refraction occurs as indicated in Figure 7. In the daytime the reverse condition frequently holds, and refraction accordingly bends sound waves away from the earth. Sound consequently travels farther along the surface of the earth at night than in the day. *Diffraction* of sound is demonstrated by the fact that a person sitting in a room with an open window

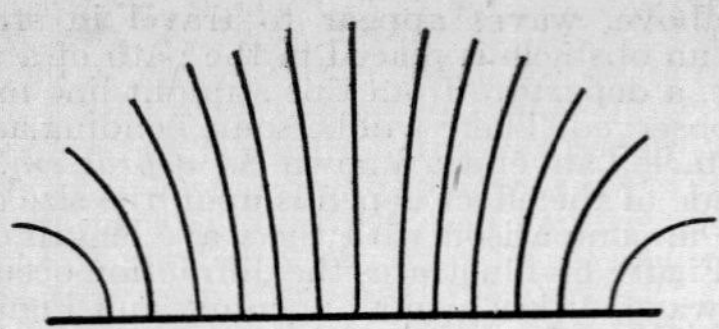

Figure 7. Refraction of a sound wave. In the evening, the air near the surface of the earth may be cooler than that at a higher altitude. The speed of sound is greater at the higher altitude.

has no difficulty hearing sounds from outside whose source is not in line with the window and the listener's ear.

Characteristics of Sound. Sound waves which are regular in the sense that the wave pattern repeats itself are more or less pleasing to the human ear and are called *musical sounds*. Irregular sound waves, on the other hand, are interpreted as *noise*. The *loudness* of a sound is determined by the amplitude of the sound wave. Further characteristics of musical sounds are pitch and quality. The *pitch* of a sound is determined by the frequency, although great changes in loudness apparently create the impression of a change in pitch even when the frequency is unaltered. If one imagines several simultaneous waves of frequencies which are all multiples of the lowest of the frequencies, called the fundamental, the resulting wave form may be complicated, but it repeats itself with the periodicity of that lowest frequency. Consequently it is the fundamental frequency which determines the pitch, the effect of the other frequencies or *overtones* being to determine the quality or timbre of the sound. Overtones which have frequencies which are multiples of the fundamental are also called *harmonics*.

LIGHT

The Nature of Light. The phenomenon of light has interested and puzzled men from earliest times. The ancients were acquainted with the simpler phenomena such as rectilinear propagation, refraction, and, possibly, the principle of some optical instruments. They thought of light as a stream of particles or corpuscles. During the 17th century, the phenomena of interference and diffraction were noted. Huygens offered the explanation that light was a wave motion. Newton, who is most famous for his work in mechanics and the law of gravitation but who also made extensive researches in light, rejected Huygens' wave theory because this did not seem to be compatable with the rectilinear propagation of light, i.e., the fact that light travels in straight lines and casts sharp shadows.

The weight of Newton's authority was so great that for a century little attention was paid to the wave theory of light. It was then shown that the straight line motion of light is only approximately true, the departure in most cases being small because the wave length of light is extremely short, about two one-hundred-thousandths of an inch. The particle theory of light then lost favor, and was discarded completely when the speed of light in water was measured and was found to be less than the speed in air, a result predicated by the wave theory and contrary to the prediction of the particle theory.

Once it was established that light was a wave motion, the problem remained as to what constituted the medium for this wave motion. In order to account for the high speed of light and the fact that light travels in empty space, the ether was invented. The ether was conceived as an intangible elastic medium that pervaded all space. It explained fairly well the way light behaved, as is only natural since the properties which were assigned to it were chosen for exactly that purpose. In the 19th century, Maxwell, in the course of his development of the theory of electricity and magnetism, predicted the existence of electromagnetic waves. His theory included a prediction of the speed of these waves, and the predicted speed was the same as the known speed of light. Hertz then generated electromagnetic waves in the laboratory and showed that his waves possessed all the properties of light waves. Since then the electromagnetic basis of light has never been questioned.

After light was recognized as an electromagnetic wave, the ether was retained as the medium through which these waves travel. Attempts were made to measure the speed of the earth through the ether, and they all met with failure. Various attempts were made to explain the failure, and finally, in 1905, Einstein presented his famous Special Theory of Relativity in which he proposed that there is no such thing as absolute motion such as is implied by talking about the speed of the earth through the ether, but that all motion is completely relative. The Relativity theory has been so successful that the ether, no longer considered necessary, now is no longer postulated. Electromagnetic waves in empty space are no more difficult to conceive than the original ether waves.

At the beginning of the 20th century a phenomenon was observed which the wave theory by itself appears to be unable to explain. When light falls on certain substances such as caesium metal, electrons are ejected, a phenomenon known as the photo-electric effect, and the energy of these electrons is determined, not by the intensity of the light as anticipated from the wave theory, but by the frequency or wave length of the light. In order to explain the photo-electric effect Einstein extended an idea originally proposed by Planck in discussing the emission of light. Einstein suggested that light energy is absorbed always in discrete amounts, or that light energy is divided into bundles called *photons* or *quanta*. For light of a given frequency these photons all have the same energy but the photons for high frequencies, or short wave lengths, have more energy than those of lower frequency, or longer wave length. This idea has been very fruitful, and as a result the present conception of light is that it is dualistic in nature, possessing wave properties in so far as its propagation is concerned, and particle properties in its generation and absorption.

The Speed of Light. The speed of light is so great, about 186,000 miles per second, that for all practical purposes it may be considered instantaneous. Galileo attempted to measure the speed by stationing two men with lanterns on distant hills. One man was to operate a shutter on his lantern, the second man was to flash his lamp when he saw the first lantern, and then the first man was to see how long the time was between sending his signal and his observing the other signal. It is small wonder the attempt was a failure. Not too surprisingly, the first successful attempt was based on astronomical observations. Römer, in 1676, used the periodic eclipsing of one of the moons of Jupiter by the planet itself as a sort of clock; he observed that when the earth, in its orbit about the sun, was receding from Jupiter that his astronomical "clock" kept slower time than when the earth was approaching Jupiter. Since he knew the speed of the earth in its path, he was able to calculate the speed of light, obtaining a value reasonably close to the present value.

Little attention was paid to Römer's work until another astronomer, Bradley, in 1727, again determined the speed of light by an entirely different method. Bradley observed that a telescope aimed at a distant star had to be pointed in different directions at time intervals six months apart. He concluded that a telescope must be tipped slightly in the direction of motion of the earth, due to the motion of the earth about the sun, and, of course, this tipping would have to be in opposite directions at six month intervals because of the reversal of the earth's motion. The effect is similar to that which makes raindrops which are actually falling straight down appear to be falling at an angle to someone moving rapidly. From the angle of tipping and the speed of the earth, Bradley was able to compute the speed of light.

The first non-astronomical measurement of the speed was by Fizeau in 1849. The principle of his method was something like that of Galileo's. He replaced the second man by a mirror, and instead of a manual opening of a shutter he used a rotating toothed wheel to interrupt a beam of light. When his wheel rotated at the correct speed, a tooth moved into the path of the returning light and blocked it out. From the speed of rotation of the wheel and the distance to the distant mirror, he could calculate the speed of light. Fizeau's method is essentially that of accurate modern experiments, notable among which are those of Michelson.

Geometrical Optics. The everyday observations on light, as well as the behavior of optical instruments, can be explained in terms of light *rays*. Light rays are simply lines, which indicate the direction light is traveling; their importance lies in the fact that for practical purposes they obey very simple laws. So long as light is traveling in a uniform medium, the light rays are straight lines. When light is reflected from a smooth surface, the incident and reflected light rays lie in the same plane and make equal angles with the surface. When light crosses a boundary between two different media, the light rays are bent or refracted. Light rays can cross without interfering with their subsequent behavior.

The simplest phenomenon explained by light rays, and one which illustrates the straightness of the rays, is the casting of *shadows*. It is not always recognized just how sharp shadows can be. If the source of light is sufficiently small, the shadow on a wall of a man several feet away will show individual hairs on his head. Ordinarily, shadows are not quite so sharp as this, simply because of the size of the light source. The shadow of a hand in the path of light from an electric lamp is fuzzy because, near the edge of the shadow, light rays from some points on the lamp are intercepted, while those from other points are not.

A further illustration of the straightness of light rays is the pinhole camera. If a light-tight box is equipped with a pinhole in one end and photographic film at the other, excellent photographs may be taken. The disadvantage of such a camera is that long exposure times are required in comparison with an ordinary camera which has a lens to gather more light. The pinhole camera may be duplicated by a pinhole in a drawn window shade with the wall opposite the shade receiving the image. An extremely striking demonstration of the same effect may be noticed on the ground in the shade of a tree during a partial eclipse of the sun. The ground is covered with myriads of tiny crescents, pinhole images of the sun formed by the interstices between the leaves.

The *reflection* of light depends upon the nature of the surface. With a rough surface, the light is reflected in all directions and the reflection is said to be diffuse. With a smooth surface, the law of reflection is obeyed. An ordinary mirror offers an example of the latter, or regular, reflection.

The *refraction* of light is responsible for the bent appearance of a straight stick placed in water. A simple but striking demonstration of refraction can be performed with a coin and a teacup. If a penny is placed in a cup and the eye placed so that the coin is just out of the line of sight, and water is then poured into the cup, the penny comes into view. The effect is as if the penny had been lifted. A further result of refraction is that the sun is seen setting after it has actually gone below the horizon, an effect due to the refraction in the atmosphere.

The study of light based on the properties of light rays is called geometrical optics. Although these properties do not indicate the exact nature of light, they are consistent with the wave theory. In discussing wave motion in general, it was seen that reflection and refraction occur for all wave motions. It will be seen below how the straightness of the light rays can be explained even when light passes an obstacle so that one should expect some spreading, or diffraction, to occur.

Optical Instruments. Perhaps the simplest example of an optical instrument is the ordinary looking glass or plane mirror. All the light rays coming from a point on an object strike the mirror and are reflected so that they behave as if they were coming from a point behind the mirror, which point is called the image of the corresponding point on the object. The image formed by a plane mirror is in back of the mirror, and is the same size as the object. This is not true of curved mirrors. A convex spherical mirror forms an image which is closer to the mirror and smaller than the object, while a concave mirror acts oppositely as a magnifying mirror. With an object a far enough distance in front of a concave mirror, the image will be found to be in front of the mirror. Such an image is called a *real image*, whereas the images behind mirrors are called *virtual images*. In the case of a real image, the light rays actually intersect at the image. The largest astronomical telescopes make use of concave mirrors.

Images can also be produced by means of refraction. A *lens* consists of a piece of glass with curved surfaces so chosen that light rays from an object are bent in passing through the lens so that they either intersect to produce a real image, or behave as if they were coming from a virtual image closer to or farther from the lens than the actual object. The images formed by a camera lens on a photographic plate and those formed on a screen by a motion picture projector are examples of the production of real images by lenses. The magnifying glass produces an enlarged virtual image. In a micro-

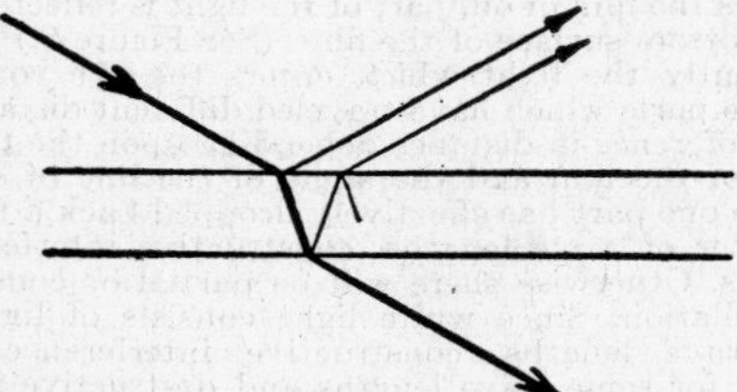

Figure 8. Reflection and refraction of a ray of light at the two surfaces of a slab of glass with plane, parallel faces.

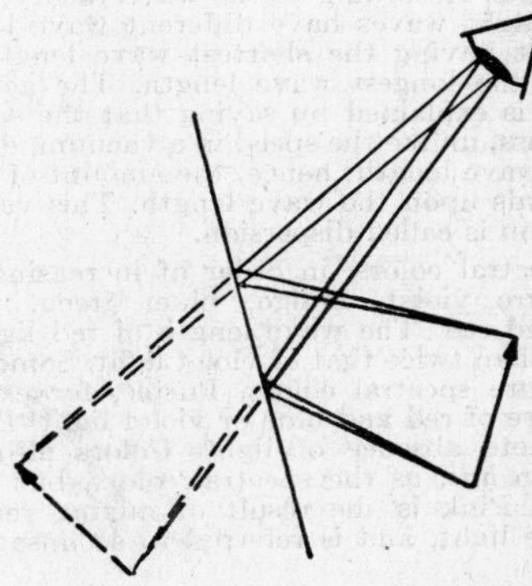

Figure 9. Image formation by a plane mirror. The image is virtual, as the rays behave, after reflection, as if they were coming from behind the mirror.

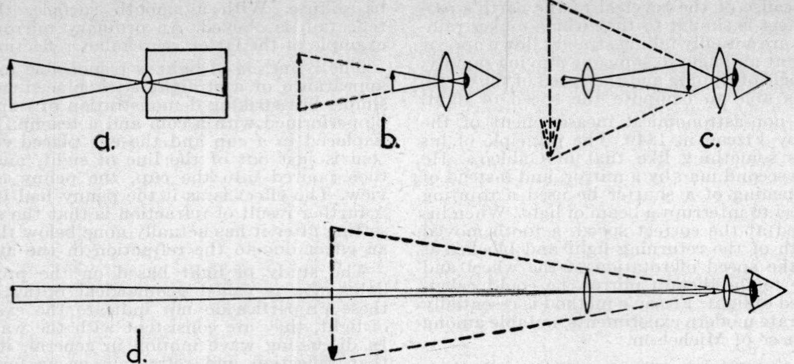

Figure 10. Some optical instruments. (a) illustrates the principle of the camera and of the human eye. In the case of the eye, the brain properly interprets the inverted image. (b) illustrates the principle of a simple magnifier. The lens enables the eye to focus on an object placed closer to the eye than would be possible with the unaided eye. (c) represents the optical system of the compound microscope. (d) represents the optical system of the refracting astronomical telescope.

scope or telescope there are in general two lenses, one of which produces a real image which is examined by using the other lens as a magnifier.

There is considerably more to the analysis of an optical instrument than the size and position of the image as determined by the behavior of light rays. The brightness of and the detail in the image must be considered. The size of the lenses used are involved in both these questions. No visual instrument can make an object with size appear brighter than it does to the naked eye, and if the magnification is too great for the size of the lens used, the brightness may be decreased. A telescope can increase the brightness of a point object such as a star, however. The reason that the size of lenses affects the detail in the images is that light rays give only an approximate description of light. Due to diffraction, the image formed by a lens of a point object is a disk, and the size of this disk depends upon the size of the lens. This is a further example of the fact that the bending or diffraction of a wave depends upon the size of the obstacle or aperture which causes the diffraction. (See Figure 6 under *Wave Motion.*)

Dispersion and Color. If a glass prism is placed in the path of a narrow beam of white light falling on a white card, it is found that the light is not only bent (refraction) but also the light is spread out into colors. Newton showed that if these colors are recombined, such as by passage through a second prism which bends the light in the opposite direction, white light again results. Hence the action of the prism must be to split white light into component parts. According to the wave theory, different color light waves have different wave lengths, violet light having the shortest wave length, and red light, the longest wave length. The action of the prism is explained by saying that the speed of light in glass, unlike the speed in a vacuum, depends upon the wave length; hence, the amount of refraction depends upon the wave length. This variation in refraction is called dispersion.

The spectral colors, in order of increasing wave lengths, are violet, indigo, blue, green, yellow, orange, and red. The wave length of red light is a little less than twice that of violet light. Some colors are not pure spectral colors. Purple, for example, is a mixture of red and blue or violet light. Black is the complete absence of light. Colors also differ not only in *hue*, as the spectral colors, but also in *saturation.* Pink is the result of mixing red light with white light, and is referred to as unsaturated red.

The color of a source of light depends upon the nature of the source. Most sources of light are objects which have been heated to incandescence. In

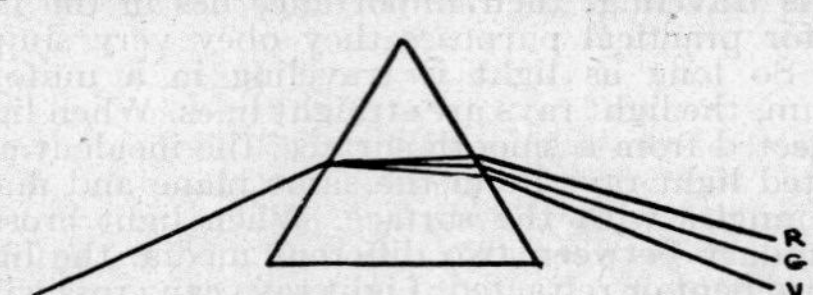

Figure 11. Dispersion of light. The prism analyzes white light into colors. The red, green, and violet rays are indicated.

such cases, all wave lengths are emitted, but the relative intensities of the wave lengths, and hence the color, depends upon the temperature. Light from the sun is considerably richer in blue light than the light from a tungsten lamp, the sun being considerably hotter. Some sources of light, such as heated gases or gases through which an electric arc or spark is passing, emit light of definite wave lengths. Examples of this are the familiar "neon" signs, whose colors depend upon whether the gas used is really neon, or whether it is argon, krypton, mercury, etc. This dependence of the wave length of the light upon the kind of atoms in the source is much used in chemical analysis.

Most objects are seen by reflected light, and the color is due to the fact that some wave lengths are reflected more strongly than others. A piece of red cloth, for example, looks red because the cloth reflects chiefly red light and absorbs the other colors. If the source of light contains no red light, the piece of red cloth looks black. Since electric lamps and sunlight differ in whiteness, a careful shopper carries a piece of cloth to the store window to see "what color it is in daylight."

Interference and Diffraction. Interference and diffraction have been discussed under wave motion, and both are exhibited by light. An example of interference is afforded by the colors exhibited by thin films of oil on water. When light from the sky strikes the film of oil, part of the light is reflected by the bottom surface of the film. (See Figure 8.) Consequently the light which enters the eye consists of two parts which have traveled different distances, the difference in distance depending upon the thickness of the film and the angle of the line of sight. If the one part has effectively dropped back a whole number of wave lengths, constructive interference occurs. Otherwise there will be partial or complete cancellation. Since white light consists of light of all wave lengths, constructive interference will occur for some wave lengths and destructive interference for others, thus producing colored reflected light. This same phenomenon is responsible for many colors in nature, such as the colors of certain butterfly wings.

Diffraction of light can be detected by careful observations on shadows. The light source must possess properties not ordinarily found, however. The light source must be extremely small and must give light of just one wave length, otherwise the effect looked for will be obscured. With the proper light source, however, the shadow of a pencil would be found to contain light and dark lines near the edge of the shadow, parallel to the edge of the shadow, and this is explained by the spreading of the light waves around the pencil. Another reason why diffraction effects are not ordinarily noticed with light, is that besides the failure to have the proper light source, the wave length of light is so short. Placing a pencil in a beam of light is analogous to placing an object a mile wide in the path of a sound wave!

Polarized Light. The advent of Polaroid glasses has made polarized light a phenomenon of general use if not of general understanding. Light is a transverse wave motion, the direction of vibration being at right angles to the direction of travel of the wave. Ordinary light is a mixture of light vibrating, that is, polarized, in all directions. Polaroid has the property, which is also possessed by certain natural crystals, of permitting only that light to be transmitted which is polarized in one direction. When unpolarized light is reflected at an angle from a surface, it is partially polarized. When sunlight strikes a highway, for example, that part of the light which is vibrating horizontally is reflected more than that vibrating vertically. This reflected light constitutes glare, and if the Polaroid glasses have been turned so that they transmit vertical vibrations and cut out horizontal vibrations, the glare is removed.

Certain crystals, notably quartz and calcite (Iceland spar) exhibit a property known as *double refraction.* If a crystal of Iceland spar were placed on this page, the printing as seen through the crystal would appear double.

The reason for this behavior is that unpolarized light entering such crystals is split into two components polarized at right angles to each other. These two components travel with different speeds in the crystal and hence are refracted differently. One of these components is bent as it enters the crystal even if the incident ray is perpendicular to the face of a crystal. This never occurs with ordinary refraction, as in glass, where the speed of light is the same in all directions. Double refraction is a consequence of the fact that the crystals which exhibit it have different electrical properties in different directions. Since light is an electromagnetic wave, these different electrical properties give rise to different speeds in various directions.

ELECTRICITY

Electricity is that field of knowledge which deals with all those phenomena which arise because of that fundamental quantity in nature which is known as electric charge. The study of the behavior of electric charges at rest is known as *electrostatics*. The study of electric charges in motion, and of the effects produced by moving charges, is called *electrodynamics*.

There are in general three sets of units in terms of which electrical quantities are measured. Of these, the so-called electrostatic and electromagnetic systems are the ones which the scientist uses initially in defining his units of measurement, and it is in terms of these units that those of the so-called practical system are defined. It is the practical system which is used most often by the electrical engineer, and whose units and terminology are most familiar to the layman.

Quantity of Charge. Investigation shows that there are two kinds of electric charge; that like kinds repel one another, but that unlike charges attract one another. To distinguish between the two types, one type is called *positive*; the other, *negative.* Since electric charges at rest are found to exert forces on one another which depend on the distance between the charges and on the medium in which the charges lie, the unit of quantity of charge can be defined in terms of these forces. That quantity of electric charge which will exert a force of 1 dyne on an equal charge placed 1 centimeter away from it in a vacuum is defined as the unit quantity of charge in the electrostatic system. This turns out to be a sort of intermediate quantity of charge—much larger than the charge on the electron (q.v.) but much smaller than the quantity of charge one deals with in normal everyday experience. The unit of charge in the practical system, therefore, has been taken as a much larger quantity of charge, equal to about 3×10^9 of the electrostatic units defined above, or very nearly equal to the total charge on 6,300,000,000,000,000,000 electrons. This quantity of charge is called a *coulomb.*

Electric Currents. In some types of materials, some of the electric charges of which matter is composed are relatively free to move around within the body of the material, and by means to be described later, can be made to do so. Metals, in particular, contain large numbers of "free" electrons which can be caused to move through the metal, and for this reason are said to be *conductors* of electricity. *Insulators,* on the other hand, are materials in which the charges are pretty much bound in position, and therefore are not readily transferred. Glass, amber, wood, and rubber, for example, are good insulators—poor conductors.

While it is unsafe to carry the analogy too far, a metal conductor containing free electrons may be thought of as being similar to a sand filled pipe containing water. Just as the water can be caused to circulate through the pipe by a pump which draws water from one end of the pipe and replaces it at the other end, so can the free electrons be caused to drift through the conductor by any device which will remove charge from one end of the conductor and restore an equal quantity of charge to the other end. When this happens—whenever electric charges are caused to drift through a conductor—one says that an *electric current* flows in the conductor. One might imagine that he places a boundary somewhere completely across the conductor and counts the electrons, or measures by other means the total quantity of charge, that cross this boundary in a given time. This would be a measure of the current through the conductor. If charge is moving through the conductor at such a rate that, in one second, one coulomb of charge passes through any imaginary wall across the conductor, a current of one *ampere* is said to be flowing in that conductor. This is the practical unit of current.

Several types of current are distinguished. A *direct* current is one in which the moving charges never reverse direction in going through the conductor. A direct current may be either *pulsating* (the magnitude of the current changing in a regular, periodic way) or *steady* (the magnitude as well as the direction remaining constant). An *alternating* current is one in which the direction of motion of the charges reverses at regular intervals. The charges move first in one direction, then stop and reverse direction, stop and reverse again, and so on. The magnitude of the current therefore varies periodically from zero to a maximum in one direction, back to zero to a maximum in the opposite direction and back to zero again. If the reversal takes place every 1/120th second, so that the charges go through a complete cycle of their motion every 1/60th second, the current is said to be 60-cycle a.c. If the maximum value attained by the current is about the same during every cycle, the current is said to be a *continuous* alternating current. If successive maxima are not equal, but vary in a regular fashion, the current is called an oscillating current. In homes supplied with 60 cycle a.c., the currents through lights and heating devices will in general be continuous alternating currents; the currents flowing in the complex circuits in the radio set will in general be oscillating currents.

Electromotive Force. To make water move through the pipe mentioned above requires some sort of pump which can do work on the water. The pump transfers energy to the water; this energy is then dissipated as a result of frictional forces between the water and the sand in the pipe. The pump does not get water from outside the circuit, nor does it produce water; its function is only to cause the water to circulate. So, too, in the electric circuit, a device is required which can do work on the electric charges. It is not to produce charges; it is merely to cause circulation of the charges already there in the conductor. Whatever this device may be, its ability to produce motion of the charges can be measured by the work it is able to do on, or the energy it can supply to, each coulomb of charge that passes through it. This ability of the device to supply energy is called its *electromotive force* (abbreviated emf). Emf is measured in *volts*. Any device which is able to supply one joule of energy to each coulomb of charge is said to have an emf of one volt. Note that the name electromotive "force" is a misnomer —it is not connected with force, but with energy. (See *Batteries, Generators*.)

Potential Difference. Just as there is a dissipation of energy against friction as the water filters through the sand, so there is a dissipation of energy as the charge passes through the conductor, and in any given time the total energy lost must be equal to that supplied by the source of emf. One can imagine that he isolates some particular section of the conductor, and measures the energy loss within that section. This energy loss per unit quantity of charge is a measure of what is called the "potential drop" across that section, or the "difference of potential" between the ends of that section. Potential difference, therefore, like emf, can be expressed in volts. If, between two points in a conductor, each coulomb of charge dissipates 6 joules of energy, the potential difference between those two points is said to be 6 volts. Since the total energy dissipated must be equal to that supplied by the source, the sum of all potential differences around any closed circuit must be equal to the emf of the source.

Ohm's Law and Resistance. Suppose a conductor to be set up in such a way that the current through it can be varied, and suppose one arranges to measure, for each value of the current, the corresponding value of the difference of potential between the ends of the conductor. If the temperature of the conductor does not change, he finds that this potential difference is directly proportional to the current through the conductor; that is, that the potential difference is equal to some constant times the current. This constant is called the *resistance* of the conductor. It is measured in *ohms*, a conductor being said to have a resistance of one ohm if a potential difference of one volt exists between its ends when a current of one ampere passes through it.

Those materials which are good conductors of electricity (and this means, essentially, the metals) are also good conductors of heat. Nonmetals, liquids, and gases, are, generally speaking, poor conductors. (See *Transfer of Heat*.)

Resistance is affected by temperature. For most materials, the resistance increases as the temperature of the conductor increases, and for many the temperature coefficient—that is, the change in resistance per unit resistance per centigrade degree temperature rise—is between 0.003 and 0.006. One notable exception to the above rule is carbon, whose resistance drops rapidly with increasing temperature. Several alloys have been developed which have extremely small temperature coefficients. For example, constantan, an alloy of copper and nickel, and manganin, containing copper, nickel, and manganese, have temperature coefficients around 0.000001.

Power. The rate at which energy is supplied to a circuit is given by the energy—that is, the product of the emf and the charge transported—divided by the time required to transport that charge. For steady currents, this is just equal to the product of the emf and the current, and when the emf is measured in joules/coulomb (i.e., volts) and the current in coulombs/second (amperes) this product will be in joules/second, or *watts*. Similarly, the power dissipated in any resistance will be the product of the potential drop across that resistance and the current through it, and will likewise be in watts. Electric power is often measured in *kilowatts*, a larger unit equal to 1000 watts.

What the consumer pays for is not power, but energy; power times time. The unit usually employed is the *kilowatt hour*, the cost of which varies from locality to locality, but averages around 3 cents. The cost of operating any electrical appliance can be calculated by taking (wattage rating of the appliance divided by 1000) × (hours of operation) × (cost of energy per kilowatt hour). The wattage rating of an appliance is marked on it by the manufacturer, as is the potential difference at which it should be operated. Only if operated at the rated voltage will the manufacturer's power rating apply.

TABLE OF ELECTRICAL QUANTITIES, SYMBOLS, AND UNITS

Quantity	Symbol	Unit
Quantity of charge	Q	coulomb
Electromotive force	E	volt
Time to transport a given charge, or time current flows	t	second
Electric current	I	ampere
Potential drop across a resistance	V	volt
Resistance of a conductor	R	ohm
Energy supplied by a source, or energy dissipated in a resistance	W	joule
Power supplied or dissipated	P	watt

Equations. All of the relations discussed thus far can be described, using the symbols in the table above, by a few simple equations as follows:

From the definition of current,

$$I = Q/t, \text{ or } Q = It$$

Ohm's Law leads to

$$V = IR, \text{ or } I = V/R, \text{ or } R = V/I$$

The energy input to a circuit is

$$W = EQ = EIt,$$

and the power input is therefore

$$P = W/t = EI.$$

The energy dissipated in a conductor is

$$W = VQ = VIt,$$

and the power dissipated therefore

$$P = W/t = VI.$$

Effects of Electric Currents. There are in general three classes of effects produced by electric currents—(1) heating, (2) electrochemical, and (3) magnetic.

Heating Effects. Whenever a current passes through a conductor, the energy dissipated appears as heat energy in the conductor. The heat energy produced, measured in joules, is therefore just VQ, or VIt. Since V = IR, this can also be written as I^2Rt. The *rate* at which heat energy is produced is simply I^2R, and is very often called the "I-square R" loss. This rate is given, in *calories/second*, by $0.24I^2R$. (See *Heat and Work*.)

The existence of this effect means, of course, that electrical power can be used wherever a heat source is required; often more conveniently and with greater safety than other types of heating. However, the fact that heating *always* occurs in any conductor often leads to undesirable losses. In a line used for cross-country transmission of power, for example, there may be considerable loss of energy, especially if large currents are used.

This heating effect is used to protect circuits against excessively large currents. A "fuse" is a short section of conductor which will melt and thus break the circuit, if the current through it exceeds the value specified on the fuse. Without the fuse, the melting, with its consequent danger of fire, might occur in the circuit itself. Plugging a fuse with a penny is an extremely foolish act.

Electrochemical Effects. If the two terminals of a battery or generator (q.v.)are connected respectively to two pieces of metal (electrodes) which are immersed in a pure liquid, so that the emf of the battery or generator is applied across the liquid, very little current will flow. Liquids are poor conductors—they have high resistance—because there are in them very few "free" charges. However, if the liquid contains some metallic salt, or a small amount of an acid or a base in solution (See *Chemistry.*) the liquid becomes conducting. These materials do not go into solution as neutral molecules, but each molecule splits into two charged fragments, one fragment with an excess of electrons, the other with a deficiency of electrons, and these fragments, called *ions*, will migrate through the liquid, those of one type toward one electrode, those of the opposite sign toward the other. Chemical reactions occur at the electrodes often with the liberation of gas. For example, if the electrodes are immersed in water containing a few drops of acid, hydrogen is liberated at one electrode and oxygen at the other, and in just the proportions in which those two elements are present in pure water. The water is said to be "decomposed" by the current, and the process is called *electrolysis*.

If the electrodes are of copper, and are immersed in a copper sulfate solution, it is found that copper ions move toward one electrode and "plate out" there, i.e., deposit at the surface of that electrode as metallic copper. The sulfate ions move toward the other electrode, and as a result of the reaction there, copper from that electrode goes into solution, in an amount just equal to that plated out at the first electrode. The chemical composition of the solution in the cell (the *electrolyte*) in this case remains unchanged.

Faraday's Laws of Electrolysis. Investigation of these phenomena by Faraday showed that

(1) The mass of material liberated or dissolved at an electrode is proportional to the total charge transported through the cell.

(2) The mass of any given material deposited is proportional to the atomic weight of that material divided by its valence. This quotient is called an *equivalent weight* of the material. (See *Chemistry* section.)

These two laws lead to the conclusion that a definite quantity of charge (about 96,500 coulombs, and this quantity of charge is called a *Faraday*) must be transported through an electrolytic cell to deposit exactly one equivalent weight of any element. The equivalent weight divided by 96,500, therefore, represents the mass deposited per coulomb of charge transported, and is called the *electrochemical equivalent* of the element.

Cells and Batteries. If two dissimilar metals—say copper and zinc—are partly immersed in an electrolyte, and their protruding ends connected by a wire, a current flows through the wire. This arrangement of two dissimilar metals and an electrolyte, called a *cell*, is therefore one of the current-producing devices mentioned previously. As a result of chemical action taking place at the electrodes, chemical energy is transformed into electrical energy. The electromotive force (q.v.) developed by the cell

ELECTROCHEMICAL EQUIVALENTS OF SOME ELEMENTS

Element	Atomic Weight	Valence	ECE
Aluminum	26.97	3	0.000093
Chlorine	35.457	1	0.000367
Copper	63.57	2	0.000329
Hydrogen	1.008	1	0.000010
Lead	207.21	4	0.000537
		2	0.001074
Oxygen	16.000	2	0.000083
Zinc	65.38	2	0.000338

is found to depend on the particular metals employed as electrodes. A copper-zinc cell develops an emf of about 1.1 volts, that is, each coulomb of charge passing through the cell gets about 1.1 joules of energy, the chemical energy of the cell being decreased by that amount. Now some of this energy gets dissipated in the cell itself, for the electrolyte, like any conductor, is heated by the passage of current. Another way of saying this is to say that there is a potential drop across the "internal resistance" of the cell, and the potential difference at the cell terminals, when it is supplying current to some external circuit, is its emf minus this internal potential drop. If the cell is not supplying current then there is no heating in the electrolyte—there is no internal potential drop—and the terminal potential difference is equal to the emf. The internal resistance depends on the size and spacing of the electrodes, and on the concentration of the electrolyte. If the electrodes are large and close together, and the electrolyte contains a sufficient number of ions, the internal resistance will be small.

A simple cell cannot be used to supply large currents for very long times because, in the same chemical reactions that result in the production of electrical energy, gases are liberated. These gases usually collect on the electrodes, reducing the effective area of the electrode and at the same time setting up an opposing emf. This phenomenon is called *polarization*. In some types of cells, the familiar "dry" cell, for example, a material called a *depolarizer* is added. Its function is to react with the gas and thus remove it from the electrode.

Cells may be "simple" cells, in which the electrodes get used up and need to be replaced or the cell discarded, or they may be "storage" cells. When a storage cell is supplying current it is said to be "discharging." When it has been used for some time and its available chemical energy is about used up, it can be "charged" by connecting it to some other source of emf and sending a current through it backwards. In this charging process electrical energy is converted into chemical energy and is stored in the cell in that form to be used later as required. Not all of the energy put into the cell on "charge" can be recovered during "discharge." As much as 30% or 40% may be lost as heat.

When a number of cells are connected into a single unit, in "series" to obtain a higher emf, or in "parallel" to reduce internal resistance, the combination is called a *battery*.

Magnetic Effects. If two straight wires running parallel to one another carry currents in the same direction, it is found that there is a force causing them to move toward one another; if they carry currents in opposite directions, there is a force causing them to move apart. These forces are not just simple electrostatic forces, for the net charge on the current carrying conductors is zero. The forces arise from the fact that charges are *in motion* through the conductors. Similar effects are observed if currents flow through two nearby coils placed with their planes parallel. If the currents flow in the same direction, as in Figure 12 (a), the coils experience an attractive force; if in opposite directions, as in (b), the forces are repulsive.

Further experiments such as are indicated in Figure 13 lead to more information about the interactions of current carrying coils. If a small "test"

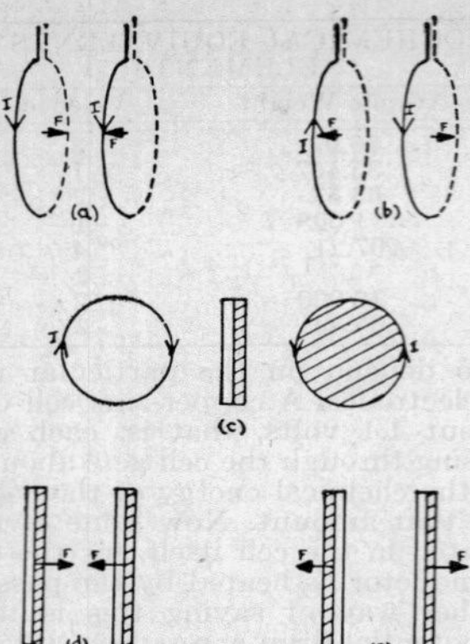

Figure 12. (a) Attractive force between 2 coils carrying currents in the same direction. (b) Repulsive force between two coils carrying currents in opposite directions. (c) indicates scheme used for showing current direction in a coil, the latter being represented by a rectangle rather than as in (a) and (b). That side of the coil toward which one would look to see current flowing in the counter-clockwise direction is indicated by showing that side of the coil shaded. (d) (e) Scheme described in (c) used to show situations illustrated in (a) and (b).

coil B, its plane not parallel to that of A, is mounted near A in such a way that it is free to rotate, there will be a torque causing it to turn until its plane is parallel to that of A. In general, if B is placed with its center at any point near A, it will rotate until it reaches some definite equilibrium orientation; only for points on the axis of A or in the plane of A will these equilibrium positions be such that the planes of the two coils are parallel.

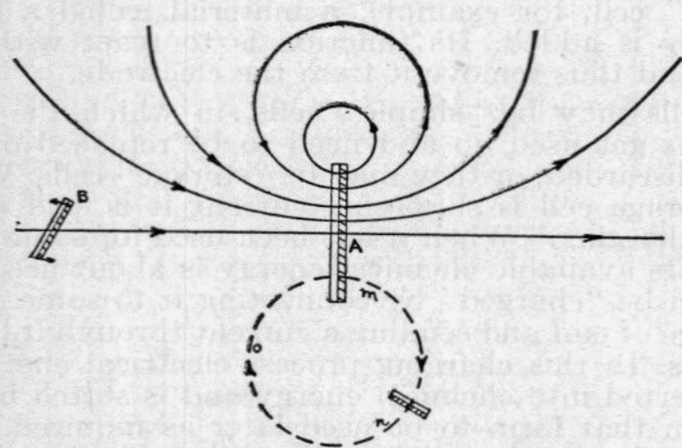

Figure 13. The magnetic field of a coil.

The region around A where a test coil will be affected is called the *magnetic field* of the current in coil A. Throughout the field of the coil it is possible to draw continuous lines such as mno in Figure 13. These lines, called *lines of force,* have this property: a test coil placed with its center at any point X on the line tends to set itself perpendicular to the line. Lines of force also have direction, as indicated by the arrowheads, which indicate the direction toward which the "shaded" side of the coil will face. (See Figure 12.)

Instead of using the single-turn coil A, one can use a *solenoid* (a number of turns of wire wrapped around a cylinder) and, upon investigating the region around the solenoid, one finds a field such as is shown in Figure 14. He also discovers that a short compass needle placed with its center at any point in the field will turn so as to align itself *parallel* to the same lines of force mapped out with the test coil. As a matter of fact, a compass needle turns out to be a more convenient tool than the test coil for plotting magnetic fields. Upon further investigation with either a test coil or a compass needle,

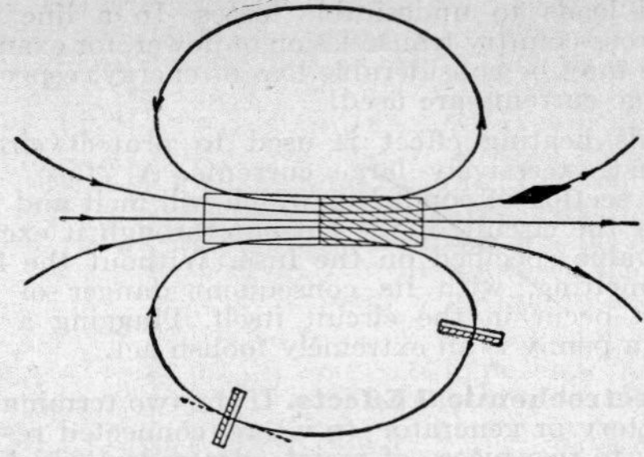

Figure 14. The magnetic field of a solenoid (or a bar magnet).

one discovers that there is, in the region around a so-called "bar magnet," exactly the sort of field found around the solenoid. One therefore immediately asks, "Can the behavior of magnets be explained in terms of electric currents?" But first, how do bar magnets behave?

Bar Magnets. If a bar magnet is suspended by a fine fiber, with no other magnets or current-carrying coils in the neighborhood, it will take up a north-south position. This is the well-known property of a compass needle, which is itself a small bar magnet. The end of the magnet which points toward the north is referred to as the *north pole* of the magnet; that pointing toward the south, the *south pole* of the magnet. Two magnets, their north and south poles having been determined by such means, may now be placed end to end as shown in Figure 15, and they

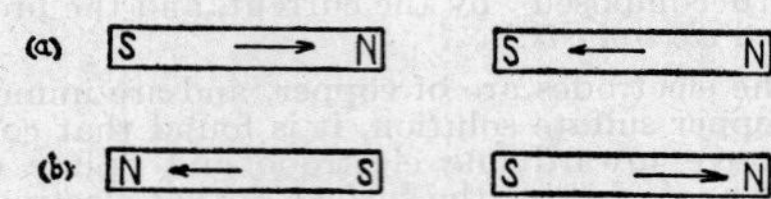

Figure 15. Forces between bar magnets. (a) Unlike poles attract. (b) Like poles repel.

will be found to exert forces on one another; attractive forces if they are oriented as in (a) of the diagram, repulsive forces if they are oriented as in (b). Comparison of these diagrams with those in Figure 12 (d) and (e) indicate the similarity in the behavior of coils and magnets. Once it is observed that it is the *north* pole of the compass needle which points in the direction of the line of force, it is but a simple step to identify the north pole of the magnet with what we called the "shaded side" of the coil.

There are further similarities. If a piece of soft, unmagnetized iron is placed near a current-carrying coil, it is pulled into the coil. If a like piece of iron is placed near a magnet it is attracted toward the magnet. What really happens is that the unmagnetized iron becomes magnetized when it is placed in the magnetic field of the coil or of the other magnet. Magnetism produced by the action of a magnetic field is called *induced* magnetism.

Theory of Magnetism. An atom is pictured as a miniature solar system, made up of a nucleus around which electrons circulate as do planets around the sun. These moving electrons are equivalent to electric currents, and therefore each circulating electron sets up a magnetic field like that of a single current-carrying coil. In most molecules the various electron currents are oriented in such a way that their fields cancel one another out. In iron, however, and in a few other materials such as cobalt, nickel, oxygen, and certain alloys, this does not happen, and each iron atom acts like a tiny current-carrying coil. In a bar of unmagnetized iron the planes in which these atomic currents circulate are oriented in random directions throughout the bar so that no noticeable magnetic field is produced in the region outside the bar. However, if the bar is placed in a magnetic field, each of these circulating currents experiences a torque just like that on the "test" coil in Figure 13, and tends to align itself with its plane perpendicular to the magnetic field in which the bar is placed. A completely magnetized bar is one in which *all* of the circulating currents have been brought into alignment.

If the bar used is of so-called "soft" iron, this alignment is accomplished readily, but is also readily destroyed as soon as the iron is again removed from the magnetizing field. If the iron is of the so-called "hard" variety, the alignment is not so readily attained. It requires strong magnetic fields, and perhaps some jarring of the bar. On the other hand, once the bar is magnetized and the field removed, the alignment remains for some time. All of the circulating currents are in parallel planes, and the net effect is that of a single current such as flows in the solenoid.

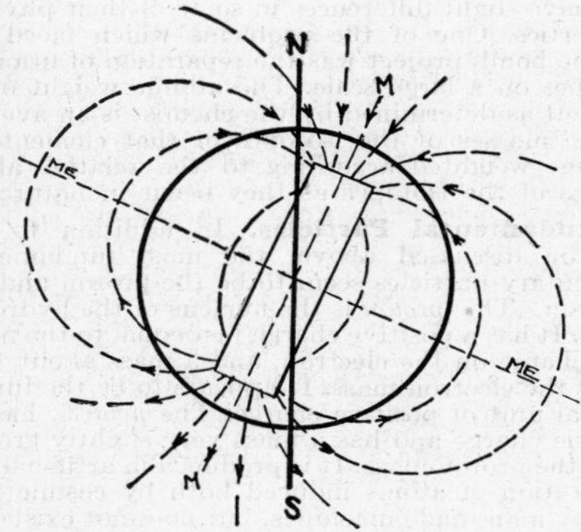

Figure 16. The magnetic field of the earth. NS represents the axis of rotation of the earth, MM the magnetic axis, and ME the magnetic equator.

Magnetic Field of the Earth. The fact that a compass needle assumes a definite orientation with respect to the earth is proof that the earth has a magnetic field of its own. Detailed investigation of the strength and direction of this field reveals that it is the sort one would expect to find if there were a huge magnet within the earth, with the axis of the magnet not quite parallel to the earth's axis of rotation since the magnetic poles are not located exactly at the geographic poles. A compass needle free to turn about both horizontal and vertical axes will, in general, not point parallel to the earth's surface, but will, in the northern hemisphere, point below the horizontal, and in a direction somewhat different from true geographic north. The angle between the needle and the horizontal is called the *angle of dip*; the deviation from true north is the *declination.* At the magnetic equator the angle of dip is zero, at the magnetic north pole it is 90°, and at Washington, D. C., about 70°. The declination at Washington is about 9° W, i.e., the compass needle points some 9° west of true north.

From the direction of the field it can be seen that the north magnetic pole has the characteristic of what was called an S pole; i.e., it is the type of pole which exerts an attractive force on the N pole of a compass needle. It should be emphasized that *there is no bar magnet within the earth*; one merely says that the earth's field is *like* that of such a magnet. The earth's field has been studied very carefully for hundreds of years, but the true story of its origin is as yet unknown. Some other celestial bodies, including the sun, are known to have similar fields associated with them.

Induced Electromotive Force. When a conductor connected into a closed circuit, without a battery or similar source of current, is moved through a magnetic field, a current flows in that conductor. Experiment shows that whenever there is relative motion between a conductor and a magnetic field, if the motion of the conductor is such that it cuts across magnetic lines of force, an electromotive force is *induced* in the conductor, and it is as a result of this induced emf that a current flows in the conductor. The induced emf is proportional to the strength of the magnetic field, the length of the conductor, and the speed with which the conductor moves across the field It is by means of this effect that most of the world's electrical power is developed.

Steam driven or water powered turbines are arranged to rotate huge coils of wire in a strong magnetic field, the coils and field being so disposed that in their rotation the coils cut magnetic lines of force. Such a device is called a *generator*.

MODERN PHYSICS

The physics discussed in the previous sections of this article was largely a development of the 19th century. Near the close of that century, physicists as a rule thought that most of the physical laws of nature had been discovered and that all that remained were a few refinements and more accurate measurements. Then came a series of discoveries—electrons, X-rays, radioactivity—which indicated the way to vast realms of unexplored phenomena. As a result, the 20th century has been a busy one for physics; startling new discoveries have been made every decade. No one today would make the mistake of supposing that the end of knowledge of the physical world is in sight.

Many of the developments of modern physics have been in the realm of very small particles, the atoms and molecules. The notion that matter consists of tiny elements or atoms was advanced by the ancient Greek, Democritus (400 B.C.), but the modern concept of atoms and molecules dates to the early 19th century, with chief credit due to Dalton (1766–1844) and Avogadro (1776–1856).

The hypothesis of an atom as the smallest division of a chemical element and of a molecule (which may be composed of one or more atoms) as the smallest division of a substance, was introduced to give an explanation of the rather simple laws obeyed by the relative amounts of different substances which take part in a chemical reaction. Soon the kinetic theory (q.v.) was developed, explaining the physical behavior of gases in terms of the motions of molecules.

Here is further illustration of the artificiality of the division of physical science into separate branches such as physics and chemistry. The contribution of modern physics has been to show that atoms are not indivisible, and to examine the internal structure of the atoms. Physics borrowed the atoms and the molecules from Chemistry and returned them with an explanation of one of the puzzles of chemistry—just what the nature is of the forces which hold atoms together into molecules. Today the structure of the atom is as thoroughly understood as the structure of the solar system. This does not mean that there is no room for further development. Only a beginning has been made in the understanding of the atomic nucleus, the part of the atom analogous to the sun in the solar system, even though that meager understanding has been sufficient to give the world an atomic (really nuclear) bomb.

It must not be surmised that modern physics has dealt only with the structure of atoms. Extensive progress has been made in the study of the proper ties of matter at high pressure and at low temperatures, in the understanding of such properties of matter as electrical and thermal conductivity and elasticity, in the study of the internal constitution of stars and of the source of energy of stars, and in numerous other fields.

The Electron. The laws of electrolysis first gave an indication that electricity, as well as matter, is atomic in nature. The amount of a substance which is deposited in electrolysis is directly proportional to the charge which has passed through the solution, and the relative amounts of different substances deposited by a given charge are in exactly the same ratio as the weights of those substances which take part in a chemical reaction. Atoms were introduced in chemistry to explain the relative weights that are involved in chemical reactions. Remembering this, the laws of electrolysis are equivalent to saying that the same charge is required to deposit each atom of a particular substance, and that although different charges are required to deposit one atom of different substances, these charges are proportional to the chemical property called valence. To deposit each atom of hydrogen a certain charge is required, and to deposit one atom of oxygen, exactly twice as much charge is required, and so on. No atom requires less charge than the hydrogen atom, and this charge, at least in so far as electrolysis is concerned, must be a fundamental unit. This unit of charge can be measured, since the charge required to deposit one gram of hydrogen is known, as is also the number of atoms in a gram of hydrogen.

Further evidence of the atomicity of electricity was obtained from measurements on "cathode rays," a strange sort of radiation which is produced when a high voltage is applied between two electrodes in a highly evacuated glass tube. J. J. Thomson (1856–1940) showed that these rays could be deflected by electric and magnetic fields, and he guessed that they consisted of high speed particles with negative electric charge. He further showed that these particles all had the same ratio of charge to mass, surmised that they were identical particles, and gave them the name electrons.

Still more evidence that electricity is atomic was given by R. A. Millikan (1868–). He introduced charged oil drops into an electric field, where he was able to balance the pull of gravity by electrical forces, and showed that all charges are multiples of a fundamental charge—exactly the same fundamental charge as obtained from the analysis of electrolysis.

Atomic Structure. The elementary particles which are constituents of atoms appear not to obey the ordinary laws of mechanics; hence there can be no truly mechanical "picture" of the atom. Nevertheless, a mechanical model of an atom is useful, and the one which seems nearest to the truth is that which describes the atom as a miniature solar system. This model is chiefly due to the theoretical work of Bohr (1885–) following the experimental and theoretical work of Rutherford (1871–1940). Rutherford bombarded thin foils of gold and other elements with alpha particles (See *Radioactivity.*) and found that the alpha particles were scattered in different directions. He was able to calculate just what fraction of the alpha particles would be scattered in a given direction on the assumption that the atom had a core which was positively charged and which repelled the positively charged alpha particles. His calculations agreed with his experiments.

The alpha particles were deflected by the core similarly to the way a comet is deflected by the sun, except that the force was one of repulsion instead of attraction. Bohr completed the picture by assuming that the electrons, which, being negatively charged, are attracted by the core, travel in orbits around the core just as the planets travel around the sun. It should be emphasized that this model of the atom is not just something that "sounds good." Bohr calculated the wave lengths of light which the hydrogen atom, as he pictured it, should emit, and got the correct answers.

The positively charged core of the atom is called the *nucleus.* Most of the mass of an atom (all but about 0.05%) is in the nucleus. There is a fundamental unit of positive electricity which is just equal to the fundamental negative unit, and the number of electrons revolving in orbits about the nucleus in a neutral atom is equal to the number of units of charge on the nucleus. Different elements differ in this number, which is called the *atomic number.* Hydrogen, the simplest atom, has atomic number 1; i.e., has one electron revolving about the nucleus in the neutral state. In a neutral uranium atom (atomic number 92), ninety-two electrons revolve about the nucleus. The chemical properties of elements are determined by the atomic number.

In general, the masses of atoms increase along with the atomic number. Hydrogen is the "lightest" atom and uranium the "heaviest" of the naturally occurring atoms. All atoms of a given element do not have the same masses, however. Atoms of a given element which have different masses are called *isotopes.* Isotopes have identical chemical properties but have slight differences in some of their physical properties. One of the problems which faced the atomic bomb project was the separation of uranium isotopes on a large scale. The atomic weight of an element as determined by the chemist is an average of the masses of the isotopes of that element, an average weighted according to the relative abundances of the isotopes as they occur in nature.

Fundamental Particles. In addition to the electron discussed above, the most fundamental elementary particles seem to be the proton and the neutron. The *proton* is the nucleus of the hydrogen atom. It has a positive charge just equal to the negative charge on the electron, and a mass about 1840 times the electron mass. It appears to be the fundamental unit of positive charge. The *neutron* has no electric charge and has a mass very slightly greater than the proton mass. It is produced in artificial disintegration of atoms induced both by cosmic rays and by man-made machines, but does not exist long as a free particle as it is readily absorbed by matter. Protons and neutrons appear to be the constituents of atomic nuclei, the number of protons determining the atomic number and the number of neutrons and protons together determining the atomic weight. Isotopes have the same number of protons in the nucleus, but different numbers of neutrons.

The *positron* is a particle having the same mass as the electron but with the positive charge of the proton. Positrons have been created in the laboratory but do not exist free in nature. Cosmic rays give evidence of particles intermediate in mass between the electron and proton, and having both positive and negative charges. These particles are called *mesotrons,* and their precise rôle in the scheme of elementary particles is not completely understood.

X-rays. When a stream of high speed electrons impinges upon a metallic target, that target becomes the origin of a type of radiation having quite surprising properties. Because the exact nature of these rays was unknown at the time, Roentgen, who discovered them in 1895, chose to call them X-rays.

Subsequent study has shown that X-rays are an electromagnetic radiation of exactly the same type as ordinary visible light, and that the peculiar properties of the radiations can be shown to arise from the fact that their wave lengths are only of the order of 1/1000th to 1/10,000th of those of visible light. Every substance is more or less transparent to X-rays. Some absorbtion of the rays occurs when they pass through matter, and in general the absorbtion is greater the denser the matter. Lead absorbs X-rays more readily than human flesh. A piece of glass does not show reflection and refraction of X-rays as it does visible light but both reflection and refraction X-rays can be produced by various crystals. Important information both about X-rays and about the structure of crystals has been obtained from the passage of X-rays through crystals.

X-rays affect a photographic plate in much the same way light does. Any object which is partially opaque to X-rays, will, if held between an X-ray tube and a photographic plate, cast a shadow upon the plate. Consequently, photographs or *radiographs* may be made with X-rays to aid in locating foreign objects in a human body, and in detecting dislocation or fracture of a bone. The practical use of X-rays in photographing the skeleton, teeth, internal organs, and abnormal growths within the body has been of inestimable value in medicine, surgery, and dentistry. X-rays also have some therapeutic value.

X-rays may be made perceptible to the eye by means of a fluoroscope, a dark box containing a screen coated with material which fluoresces or becomes luminous under the action of X-rays. Shadows may be seen on such screens just as with photographic plates.

The Electromagnetic Spectrum. Visible light and X-rays are just two examples of what is known as electromagnetic radiation. The essential difference between the various types of electromagnetic waves lies in the wave lengths involved. Electromagnetic waves range in wave length from millions of millions times as long as visible light wave lengths, as with radio waves, to a million times as short as ordinary X-ray wave lengths, as with some of the cosmic rays.

Electromagnetic waves consist of oscillating electric fields traveling through space, accompanied by oscillating magnetic fields. All electromagnetic waves travel in empty space with the same speed—the speed of light. In all cases the radiation is caused by the oscillation, or acceleration, of an electric charge. In the case of radio waves, there is an oscillating electric current—and hence, oscillating charges—in the transmitting antenna. In the case of visible light, there are oscillations of electrons in the atom. In the case of X-rays, electrons are suddenly stopped; hence there is acceleration of electric charge. These changes in motion of an electric charge produce changing electric and magnetic fields, and the self-propagation of these changing fields constitutes the waves.

The longest electromagnetic waves are the *radio waves.* These range in wave length from the order of a few hundred feet in the standard broadcast band to a few feet in the short-wave bands. Very similar are the *microwaves* used in *radar.* Here the wave lengths involved are just a few inches. Ordinary radio waves do not travel in very straight lines, due to diffraction (q.v.). They are also reflected by the earth and by the upper layers of the atmosphere. The microwaves, because of their short wave lengths, appear to travel in more nearly straight lines. Their use in radar (radio detection and ranging) is due to the facts that they are readily reflected by objects such as airplanes, that the direction of a beam of waves can be precisely determined, and that the time of passage of a pulse of waves can be measured. Radar was of inestimable value in World War II, and should prove to have great peace time uses.

Heat radiation consists of electromagnetic waves primarily in the region known as *infra-red*—shorter than radio waves but longer than visible light. The waves arise from the oscillations of atoms. Next in the spectrum comes *visible light.* Visible light, ranging in wave lengths from one and one-half to three one-hundred-thousandths of an inch, occupies an extremely minute portion of the entire electromagnetic spectrum. *Ultraviolet* radiation is the name given to those waves, emitted by atoms, which are shorter than visible light. Ultraviolet wave lengths range down to about 10 Angstrom units. The *Angstrom unit* is one-hundred-millionth of a centimeter, and visible light ranges from 4000 to 7500 Angstrom units.

X-rays overlap the ultraviolet, but extend to shorter wave lengths. X-rays range from about 30 Angstrom units to about 1/1000 of an Angstrom unit. The shorter X-rays, in general, are much more penetrating than the longer ones. This is implied by using the terms "hard" (penetrating) and "soft" (less penetrating). The *gamma rays* emitted by both naturally and artificially radioactive substances have roughly the same order of wave lengths as X-rays. Still shorter wave lengths are found as part of the *cosmic rays.*

When a metallic surface is illuminated by electromagnetic radiation, electrons are found to be emitted from the metal. This emission of electrons by light —a sort of inverse of the X-ray process, where the stopping of electrons gives rise to electromagnetic radiation—is called the *photoelectric effect.* The number of electrons emitted per unit time is found to be proportional to the intensity of the light. The energy with which each individual electron is emitted depends on the wave length of the light; the shorter the wave length, the higher the energy. Further, there is for each metallic element a definite limiting wave length or "threshold", and only waves shorter than this limit are capable of ejecting electrons from the metal. These results are not understandable on the basis of a purely wave theory, and have led to important modifications of the conception of the nature of electromagnetic radiation. (See *Nature of Light.*)

Radioactivity. In 1896, shortly after the discovery of X-rays, Becquerel sought to determine if the rays might be connected with phosphorescence, the glow of certain substances after they have been irradiated with light. He found that photographic plates wrapped in black paper were affected not only by phosphorescent compounds of uranium, but also by non-phosphorescent compounds of uranium. Something besides phosphorescence was involved and was given the name radioactivity. A few years later the Curies announced the discovery of an element, which they called radium, which possessed the property of radioactivity to a much greater extent than uranium. Since then, many radioactive elements have been discovered.

The radioactivity of an element such as uranium is unaffected by any chemical reaction in which the element participates. It is a property of the nucleus and represents a spontaneous change of the nucleus into a nucleus of an entirely different chemical element. Three types of radiation are recognized in radioactivity. The *alpha rays* are positively charged particles which have been identified as nuclei of helium atoms. The *beta rays* are negatively charged particles which have been identified as high speed electrons. The *gamma rays* are electromagnetic radiation similar to hard X-rays. When an atom emits an alpha particle, it is converted into an atom having four fewer units of mass and having an atomic number smaller by two—hence it is a new element. When a beta particle is emitted, a neutron in the nucleus is changed into a proton and the atomic number increases by one. Again a new element results, but in this case the atomic weight does not change. The emission of gamma rays, in general, accompanies both alpha emission and beta emission.

Transmutation of the Elements. The dream of the old alchemist was to transmute the baser elements into gold or silver, but the task of changing one element into another was too much for him. His modern prototype has been more successful. The modern physicist, using high speed alpha-particles from naturally radioactive substances, or protons, deuterons (nuclei of a hydrogen isotope of mass 2), or alpha-particles driven to high speeds in a modern machine known as the cyclotron, has been able to transmute almost every known element into some other element lying near it in the periodic table. For example, if nitrogen, atomic weight 14, is bombarded by alpha-particles, weight 4, the alpha-particle is captured by the nitrogen nucleus, producing a new nucleus of weight 18. This nucleus is unstable and splits apart, producing oxygen, atomic weight 17, and hydrogen, atomic weight 1. This example represents the first man-induced transmutation of an element, and was accomplished by Rutherford in 1919. Furthermore, in this example the breakup results in a normal, stable atom; sometimes one of the nuclei produced is still unstable, in which case it goes over, by emission of one of the fundamental particles or of a gamma-ray, into a stable nucleus. These unstable products constitute the artifically radioactive elements.

In the early days of 1934, Irène Curie, daughter of Madame Curie, and her husband Frédéric Joliot exposed samples of aluminum, boron, and magnesium to alpha-particles from polonium. After a short exposure they found to their great surprise that these samples had become radioactive. They behaved just like the natural radioactive elements, except that their radioactive lives were very short. Since that first work by Curie and Joliot, almost every known element has been subjected to bombardment by electrons, protons, neutrons, deuterons, and alpha-particles, and for almost every known element at least one isotope that is radioactive has been produced. Many of them have half-lives, that is, lose half of their activity, of from a fraction of a second to a few days; a few are found to have half-lives measured in years.

These artificially radioactive elements find practical use as "tracers." For example, atoms of an artificially radioactive element, combined with other elements to form a compound that can be assimilated by living tissue and fed to a plant or animal, will enable one to trace the course of that compound to its ultimate destination in the tissue.

Cosmic Rays. The earth is constantly being bombarded with high energy radiation which seems definitely to be coming neither from the sun nor from other stars, but from interstellar space. In its passage through the earth's atmosphere, the radiation seems to have two components, a "soft" component and a more penetrating "hard" one. The soft component consists chiefly of high energy electrons and of electromagnetic radiation similar to high energy X-rays or gamma rays. The hard component has properties unlike those of any other particles known, and is believed to consist of charged particles, called *mesotrons*, of roughly 200 times the mass of an electron.

Both the hard and the soft components are, at least for the most part, created in the earth's atmosphere. The electromagnetic radiation, called gamma rays just as in radioactivity, arises from the slowing down or stopping of electrons just as X-rays arise. The electrons themselves are created from the gamma rays—the gamma rays strike matter and have their energy converted into electrons and positrons in equal number. The mesotrons are the result, presumably, of something like a nuclear disintegration.

The exact nature of the primary radiation, that is, the radiation from space which originally creates the electrons, gamma rays, and mesotrons in the earth's atmosphere, is not known. From measurements performed with equipment carried by balloons to very high altitudes and from the deflections of the incoming radiation by the earth's magnetic field, it is generally agreed now that the primary radiation, at least in large part, consists of positively charged particles—possibly protons.

Einstein's Theory of Relativity. The principle of relativity is as old as mechanics. It is the easiest to state the principle by using the expression "frame of reference." A *frame of reference* is a coordinate system used to locate a particle or system of particles in space. A frame of reference is called an *inertial* frame if Newton's first law of motion is valid in that frame of reference; i.e., if a particle which is not acted upon by a force has no change in velocity as measured with respect to the frame of reference. Since Newton's second law involves only acceleration or change of velocity, and not velocity itself, it follows that if the law holds in one frame of reference, it will hold in a second frame moving with constant velocity with respect to the first. As far as mechanics is concerned, there is no one frame of reference which is better than all others. This is the relativity principle.

As the wave theory of light was being developed, the relativity principle was dropped and absolute motion was assumed to have meaning. Light was assumed to be a wave motion in the ether, and the ether, presumably, defined a primary frame of reference, the frame of reference which determined the absolute velocities. Maxwell's development of the electromagnetic wave theory of light was assumed to support this view, as his theory predicted a speed for light, and this speed had to be measured with respect to something—the ether. There were two possibilities:

1. The relativity principle is invalid.
2. The relativity principle is valid, but either Maxwell's theory or Newtonian mechanics is wrong.

People chose the first alternative. Attempts were made to measure absolute velocities. In every case, the attempt met with failure, but the theory of the ether was always then modified to explain this failure. Finally, in 1881, Michelson and Morley attempted to measure the speed of the earth by a method involving interference of light. The basic idea of the experiment was to detect, by interference means, the difference in different directions of the speed of light with respect to the earth. The speed of light with respect to the earth should depend, the argument went, on whether the light was traveling in the same direction as the earth through the ether, or in some other direction. This experiment also met with failure, even though the precision of the experiment was such that the experimenters expected to detect at least the motion of the earth about the sun. It was too much to assume the earth standing still with the sun revolving around it, so another explanation was sought. Theories were advanced that objects, when moving through the ether, contract just enough to remove the difference in time looked for by Michelson and Morley. Finally, in 1905, Einstein offered an explanation of the failure of this attempt, and, in fact, of all attempts to measure absolute velocity.

Einstein adopted the relativity principle; i.e., he assumed that all motion is relative and that there is no such thing as absolute velocity. He then had to make a choice between Maxwell's theory and Newtonian mechanics, and he chose to consider Maxwell's theory as right and Newtonian mechanics as wrong. He made this choice by assuming that the relativity principle applies to light and that the speed of light is the same in all inertial frames of reference. On the basis of these two assumptions, Einstein reached some conclusions which were startling to physicists of the time. The concepts of space and time had to be modified. No signal can be propagated, and hence no material object can move, with a speed greater than the speed of light. Newtonian mechanics is invalid for large velocities; the masses of objects change as their speeds increase, and velocities cannot be added by the methods of Euclidean geometry. There is an equivalence between mass and energy. Einstein's results have been borne out by experiment, however. The change in mass of protons has to be taken into account in the design of a cyclotron, for example. The conversion of mass into energy and electromagnetic energy into mass has been observed in the laboratory. The enormous energy of the atomic bomb comes from the conversion of a small fraction of the mass of the bomb into energy.

CHEMISTRY

CHEMISTRY is the science which deals with the composition and transformations of matter. It is concerned with and explains changes which take place in materials connected with the practical acts of everyday life as well as in rare or complex substances investigated only by specialists.

Chemical processes and principles are brought into play in building a fire, in making bread, in cooking meat, in breathing air, in digesting food, in the hardening of cement and plaster, in the drying of paint, in making lime, cement, and brick, in preparing fertilizers, in purifying water, in producing soap, vinegar, cheese, charcoal, illuminating gas, aniline dyes, and medicines, as well as in the manufacture of aluminum, copper, iron and steel, and in smelting precious metals. Chemistry, therefore, is a most useful science, and in an immense number of important ways contributes to human welfare.

DIVISIONS OF CHEMISTRY

Chemical science has developed into an extremely complex field with many branches. Although the same basic principles are common to all, the descriptive features and experimental techniques differ considerably. In general the colleges teach the fundamental branches of chemistry while the applications to specific industries are developed by research staffs of the industries and in institutions set up for the purpose.

Inorganic Chemistry. This broad branch of chemistry deals with the mineral kingdom. It includes the chemistry of all elements and their compounds excluding the special large group of compounds of carbon which define the province of *organic chemistry*. The study of inorganic chemistry consists of such topics as the properties of the metals and the non-metals in their elemental states, the stability of the elements toward reaction with each other, and the characteristic properties of the products of such reactions. The refining of iron ore, the preparation of chlorine, silver plating, and the ignition of a magnesium flash bulb are all examples of inorganic chemical processes.

Analytical Chemistry. This branch of chemistry is concerned with the determination of the composition of substances. In *qualitative analysis* only the presence or absence of a constituent is determined; in *quantitative analysis* the relative amounts of the elements or compounds that are present are measured.

Qualitative analysis employs characteristic chemical reactions or tests such as the appearance of a precipitate or a color change upon the addition of a test chemical or reagent. In addition to these, quantitative analysis employs gravimetric methods which involve weighing, volumetric methods which require measuring of volumes of standardized solutions, colorimetric methods based upon the intensity of characteristic colors which are developed, and electrolytic methods involving the decomposition of substances by an electric current. Special instruments such as the spectrograph, polarograph, spectrophotometer, and glass electrode pH meter are now used extensively for quantitative analysis of a wide variety of substances.

The methods of chemical analysis are of great practical value in manufacturing processes where the specifications of the products must conform to particular compositions. The analysis of ingredients that go into the manufacture of medicines, foods, dyes, and all other synthetic materials is common industrial practice.

Chemical Kinetics. This is the study of mechanisms and rates of reactions. Even in seemingly simple chemical reactions there are often several intermediate steps before the end product is reached. By studying these intermediate steps it is possible to find which governs the overall reaction rate and how this rate may be accelerated or depressed.

Organic Chemistry. This branch of chemistry started as the chemistry of the plant and animal kingdoms in contrast to inorganic chemistry which pertains to the mineral kingdom. One characteristic of almost all substances that are formed by living systems or which constitute the building blocks of organisms is the presence of the element carbon. As a result, organic chemistry is now better defined as the chemistry of carbon compounds. Carbon has the peculiar property of combining endlessly with itself, and, by virtue of this property, gives rise to an immense number of derivative compounds, some of which are extremely complex.

It was formerly believed that there is an essential difference between mineral substances and substances produced by living organisms. For many years it was believed impossible to prepare artificially in the laboratory the organic compounds formed in the bodies of plants and animals. But, in 1828, Wöhler, a German chemist, prepared urea artificially by building it up from inorganic compounds. Since that time an immense number of compounds found in plants and animals have been built up from inorganic substances, or from other organic substances, so that it is well established that there is no fundamental difference between organic and inorganic chemistry.

Indeed, an unlimited series of new compounds, unknown in nature are constantly issuing from the laboratories. Among these are dyes, synthetic fibers, synthetic rubber, insect repellants, and hydrocarbon fuels.

Physical Chemistry. The properties of chemical substances that do not involve chemical change or changes which are measured by physical instruments fall into the category of physical chemistry. Included are vaporization processes, electrical properties, and crystal structure studies. Many aspects of thermochemistry, photochemistry, spectroscopy, and electrochemistry are dealt with in physical chemistry.

Thermochemistry. In most cases, chemical combination is accompanied by the development of heat. The quantity of heat thus developed by the formation of a given weight of a particular substance under standard conditions is always the same. Further, the decomposition of any compound requires the expenditure, in the form of heat or otherwise, of exactly the same amount of energy as was liberated by its formation. However, the formation of some compounds is attended by absorption of heat. In such case exactly the same amount of heat is liberated when the compound decomposes. The branch of chemical science that deals especially with the development or absorption of heat which accompanies chemical reactions is termed thermochemistry.

Besides heat changes in chemical reactions other forms of energy may undergo a shift. The study of all forms of energy change is termed *thermodynamics*. The knowledge of thermodynamical properties makes possible predictions as to whether or not a chemical change can take place.

Agricultural Chemistry. This branch of applied chemistry deals with the problems of soil fertility, the nutrition of plants and animals, the chemical composition of plants and animals, and the composition and value of plant and animal products for food or other useful purposes.

Physiological Chemistry. The branch of chemical science which deals with those processes and functions of living organisms, both plant and animal, that can be explained by chemical laws and studied by chemical methods. It examines the chemical changes involved in the two great groups of processes connected with growth; namely, the *building up* and the *breaking down* of various forms of organic matter, in such important functions as digestion, assimilation, metabolism, and excretion.

Chemical Engineering. In order to adapt chemical processes to industrial operation the services of chemical engineers are required. These engineers study various aspects of the problem not necessarily encountered on the laboratory scale, such as *fluid flow, power requirements, corrosion, heat transfer*, and select the types of manufacturing equipment that can be used for the large scale process.

Nuclear Chemistry. This new branch of chemistry deals with reactions of atomic nuclei. In most nuclear reactions a different element is formed and the products are often radioactive. The field is characterized by the extreme sensitivity of analytical procedures since individual atoms can be determined through their radioactivity. Some radioactive species exist in nature almost exclusively among the elements of the heavy end of the periodic table. Radioactivity can be induced in all other elements by the "atom smashers" such as the cyclotron. *Applied nuclear chemistry* makes use of radioactive isotopes for tagging atoms which makes possible the solution of problems in all branches of chemistry. The atomic energy developments are concerned with nuclear reactions and applied nuclear chemistry on an industrial scale.

Specialized Branches of Chemistry. Many industries are built around specialized fields of chemistry in each of which a large body of knowledge exists. A few of these industries may be mentioned: petroleum, rubber, explosives, pharmaceuticals, fertilizers, sulfuric acid, steel.

CHEMICAL LAWS AND CONCEPTS

Like other branches of science, chemistry has grown from many observations and experiments which suggested generalizations and theories which in turn stimulated further research. Some of these generalizations can be stated as laws, others are not so simply stated but can be developed as general theories.

Atomic Theory. This theory, associated with the name of Dalton (1766–1844), conceives of atoms as the building blocks of all chemical substances. A substance which consists of only one type of atom is known as an *element.* Different types of atoms may unite in definite numbers to form molecules. Just as an element contains only one type of atom, so a *compound* is an aggregate of one type of molecule. One of the characteristics of elements is the definite weight associated with each that enters into a given compound. This property is a consequence of the constancy of weight associated with each atom and the laws of combining weights constituted the earliest proof for the existence of atoms.

Because of the minute sizes of atoms, the weight of the individual atom is seldom used. Instead, the standard of atomic weights has been adopted on a relative scale in which that for oxygen has been set at exactly 16. Relative to oxygen, hydrogen has the atomic weight 1.008, iron 55.84, and uranium 238.14. Water is a molecule consisting of two atoms of hydrogen and one atom of oxygen; therefore the *molecular weight* of water is approximately 18.

Avogadro's Hypothesis. The established facts concerning the relation of atomic weights and volumes led Avogadro, a professor of physics in Turin, Italy, to offer, in 1811, as an explanation, his hypothesis, which has proved of great value in the development of modern chemical theory. It is usually stated thus: Under the same conditions of temperature and pressure, equal volumes of gases contain equal numbers of molecules. This hypothesis is known also as "Avogadro's rule," and "Avogadro's law."

Atomic Structure. The atom is itself not the ultimate structural unit although in chemical reactions it is not changed. However, the differences in properties of the different elements are best explained in terms of their atomic structures. Almost the entire weight of the atom is centered in a positively charged nucleus which itself is composed of neutrons and protons. Neutrons and protons are of approximately the same weight and the protons each bear one unit of positive electric charge while the neutrons are neutral. At considerable distance from the nucleus are a number of virtually weightless electrons which each contain one negative electric charge. The charge on the nucleus, or the number of protons, is equal to the number of electrons surrounding the nucleus.

The simplest atom is hydrogen which consists of a single proton in the nucleus surrounded by a single electron. It is the single nuclear charge and single electron that defines the atom as hydrogen. Actually ordinary hydrogen contains a small proportion of atoms that contain a neutron as well as a proton in the nucleus but this hardly alters the chemical properties. (See *Isotopes.*) Other elements contain greater numbers of electrons and each number is characteristic of a different element. The basic definition of an element is therefore its *atomic number.* Elements from atomic numbers 1-96 are now known either through their existence in nature or by artificial production.

As the elements are built up the electrons arrange themselves in definite configurations. Some arrangements result in elements which are very stable and unreactive, others create elements with widely varying properties. In this manner the chemical properties of the elements are explained. (See *Periodic System.*)

Chemical Attraction. Combination between different substances is due to the existence of *chemical attraction* between the atoms of which they are composed. The strongest type of binding is that caused by the interaction of an electron from each of the two atoms in question. The properties of a compound resulting from the combination of two or more different types of atoms bear no relation to those of the component substances. For example, ammonia, a gas, unites with hydrogen chloride, a gas, to give ammonium chloride, a saltlike solid.

Another type of chemical attraction is that due to opposite electrical charges in atoms or groups of atoms. Thus positively charged sodium atoms are held with negatively charged chlorine atoms to make up sodium chloride or common table salt.

Chemical Reactions. Chemical reactions or chemical changes are constantly encountered in the most common daily experiences as well as in the research laboratory. Chemical reactions are involved in the rusting of iron, the burning of wood, the digestion of food, and in the growth and decay of plants. In all cases the original substances seem to lose their identity and substances when different properties appear. One of the characteristics of a chemical reaction is an energy change, usually an evolution or absorption of heat. Chemical changes which produce heat are termed *exothermic*; those which absorb heat, *endothermic.* A very obvious exothermic reaction is the burning of wood; however, with adequate measuring devices the heat change in the rusting of iron can also be measured.

Chemical reactions may be placed in several categories. *Oxidation* is a type of reaction which was once restricted to the uptake of oxygen by a substance, but now it has the much broader definition: the loss of electrons. The uptake of oxygen is now treated as just an example of oxidation reactions. The opposite of oxidation is *reduction*, which in its restricted term means the loss of oxygen, or, more general, the gain of electrons. The rusting of metallic iron to form iron oxide is an example of oxidation; the iron is no longer in the metallic state or zero oxidation state, but is said to be in a higher oxidation state. The conversion of iron ore to the metal involves the *reduction* of iron oxide to the metal. In this reaction coke is used to take the oxygen away from the iron and supply it electrons to place it in the neutral or metallic state.

Chemical Synthesis is a general term usually applied to a variety of reactions of simple organic materials in building up more complex materials. The reaction upon which all life depends is *photosynthesis* carried on by plants in which carbon dioxide from the air is *reduced* and synthesized into organic substances. From some of these primary products, plants and animals build the extremely complex compounds necessary for life processes.

Double Decomposition or **Metathesis** refer to reactions in which compounds change partners in order to arrive at a more stable system. For example, if silver nitrate is dissolved in water and then sodium chloride is added, the two components of each compound exchange; silver chloride *precipitates* or drops out of solution leaving sodium nitrate still in solution. The driving force behind the reaction in this case is the insolubility of silver chloride.

Neutralization is the general term for the reaction between an acid and a base. The products of the reaction are always water and a salt. For example, if sodium hydroxide (caustic soda) and hydrochloric acid (muriatic acid) are mixed there is produced water and sodium chloride (table salt).

Conditions for Chemical Change. There must always be a driving force for chemical reactions to proceed. In thermodynamics this driving force is defined rigorously in terms of the *free energy* change in the reaction. In oxidation reactions the substance which promotes the oxidation is said to have a higher potential than that of the substance which is oxidized. Tables of values for the *potentials* of many substances have been made and from these it is possible to select a substance that will oxidize or reduce other substances. For this and other types of reactions, *free energy* tables have similarly been compiled.

For atoms or molecules to react they must come into intimate contact with each other. Almost always a reaction can be speeded up by heating since this produces more rapid movement of the atoms and molecules allowing them to mix more rapidly. At very high temperatures the substance formed may become unstable and decompose into its constituent parts again. Mercury and oxygen react but very slowly at ordinary temperatures but do so rapidly when heated almost to the boiling point of mercury. If the temperature is further elevated a point will be reached where the compound, mercuric oxide, decomposes into mercury and oxygen again.

Laws of Combining Weights. Since atoms cannot be changed in chemical reactions the combination of atoms into compounds is characterized by the combination of definite weights of the elements. For example 16 parts by weight of oxygen always combine with two parts of hydrogen to form 18 parts of water. Since the atomic weight of hydrogen is 1 and that of oxygen is 16 it is seen that one atom of oxygen combines with two atoms of hydrogen. Hydrogen is said to have a *valence* of one and oxygen a *valence* of two. Another way of stating this is that oxygen has two *chemical equivalents* while hydrogen has one. Carbon has four equivalents so that it will combine with four atoms of hydrogen (methane or marsh gas) or with two atoms of oxygen (carbon dioxide.)

The concept of chemical equivalents applies to all chemical reactions.

It is found that if a piece of iron is placed in a solution of copper sulphate, metallic copper is deposited on the iron, while a portion of the latter is dissolved, and for every 63.4 parts of copper deposited 56 parts of iron are always dissolved. Again, when iron is placed in dilute sulphuric acid, hydrogen gas is given off and the metal is dissolved, and it is found that for every 1 part of hydrogen given off, 28 parts of iron are dissolved. It follows that 56 parts of iron are capable of replacing, or are chemically equivalent to, 63.4 parts of copper or two parts of hydrogen.

The Elements. All matter as it is normally encountered either consists of elements or combinations of elements called compounds. Studies of atomic structure have shown that the elements can be arranged according to *atomic number*, or according to the number of electrons in each atom, starting with hydrogen of atomic number, one, with a single electron. In all, ninety-six elements are now known although not all are found in nature.

The former belief in the immutability of elements has been modified by the discovery of the nature of radioactive changes. That elements retain their identity in all chemical processes is firmly established, however. In nature, radioactive substances are found which spontaneously change to other elements. By artificial means it has been possible to prepare radioactive forms of all elements found in nature and to produce radioactive species of elements that do not occur in nature.

For convenience, the elements are spoken of as comprising two groups, the *metals* and the *nonmetals*, or *metalloids*. There is, however, no sharp line of distinction between them, various metals having some of the properties of nonmetals and various nonmetals possessing some of the characteristics of metals. Among the 60 or more metallic elements are gold, silver, iron, copper, aluminum, tin, zinc, nickel, and lead. Among the nonmetallic elements are oxygen, hydrogen, nitrogen, chlorine, carbon, silicon, sulphur, and phosphorus. All mineral, plant, and animal matter on the earth is composed of the various chemical elements, singly or in combination.

Most substances are made up of a relatively small number of the common elements. For example, about 13 elements compose the great bulk of the mineral matter in the earth's crust. A similarly small number enter into the composition of all plant and animal matter. Most of the elements are not common, and more than half of them are comparatively rare. The inert gases, argon, helium, krypton, neon, niton, and xenon, occur singly. The other elements enter into various combinations with each other, though some are found native or uncombined. Important facts concerning the elements will be found in the accompanying table.

Periodic Law. A principle of classification for the chemical elements, discovered and worked out chiefly by Mendeléev (1834–1907), a Russian chemist, who proved that "a periodic repetition of properties is obtained if all the elements be arranged in the order of their atomic weight." From this he derived the law which he summarized as follows: The properties of the elements are a periodic function of the atomic weight. In accordance with this principle, the elements have been grouped in nine classes possessing similar or recurring properties.

While not perfect, Mendeléev's system, based on the periodic law, has been of great value in predicting the discovery and the properties of new elements. It has led also to the revision and the adjustment of atomic weights, and has been of immense service in developing a systematic study of the elements.

CHEMICAL TERMS

Acids. An important class of chemical substances, possessing the property of neutralizing alkalies and having a sour taste. When acids are dissolved in water they yield hydrogen ions. The degree to which an acid dissociates to give hydrogen ion is a measure of its "strength" as an acid. The acidity of a solution is measured roughly by characteristic colors

TABLE OF CHEMICAL ELEMENTS

Element	Symbol	Atomic Weight 0=16	Atomic Number	Discoverer	Year	Specific Gravity *	Melting Point (Centigrade)
Actinium	Ac	227	89	Debierne, Giesel	1899	......	......
Aluminum	Al	26.87	13	Wöhler	1827	2.69	660
Americium**	Am	241	95	Seaborg, James, Morgan	1945	......	......
Antimony (stibium)	Sb	121.7	51	Valentine	1450	6.69	630.5
Argon	A	39.94	18	Rayleigh and Ramsay	1894	1.59	−185.7
Arsenic	As	74.93	33	Known in 13th century A. D.	....	5.72	850
Astatine	At**		85	Corson, MacKenzie & Segré	1940	......	......
Barium	Ba	136.36	56	Berzelius, Pontin, Davy	1808	3.6	850
Beryllium (glucinum)	Gl	9.02	4	Wöhler	1828	1.84	1280
Bismuth	Bi	209.0	83	Valentine	1450	9.8	271
Boron	B	10.82	5	Davy, Gay-Lussac, Thenard	1808	1.73	2300
Bromine	Br	79.916	35	Balard	1826	3.14†	−7
Cadmium	Cd	112.41	48	Hermann and Stromeyer	1817	8.6	320.9
Calcium	Ca	40.08	20	Davy, Berzelius, Pontin	1808	1.55	810
Carbon	C	12.0	6	Known many centuries B.C.	....	3.52‡	......
Cerium	Ce	140.13	58	Berzelius, Hisinger, Klaproth	1803	6.8	640
Cesium	Cs	132.81	55	Bunsen and Kirchhoff	1860	1.87	26
Chlorine	Cl	35.457	17	Scheele	1774	1.55†	−101.6
Chromium	Cr	52.01	24	Vauquelin	1797	7.1	1600
Cobalt	Co	58.94	27	Brandt	1735	8.8	1480
Columbium (niobium)	Cb	93.1	41	Hatchett	1801	8.4	1950
Copper (cuprum)	Cu	63.57	29	Prehistoric	....	8.93	1083
Curium**	Cm		96	Seaborg, James, Ghiorso	1944	......	......
Dysprosium	Dy	162.46	66	Boisbaudran	1886	......	......
Element 61**		147	61	Glendenin, Marinsky	1945	......	......
Erbium	Er	167.64	68	Mosander	1843	4.77	......
Europium	Eu	152.0	63	Demarcay	1896	......	......
Fluorine	F	19.0	9	Moissan	1886	1.14†	−220
Francium	Fr		87	Perey	1939	......	......
Gadolinium	Gd	157.26	64	Marignac	1880	1.31	......
Gallium	Ga	69.72	31	Boisbaudran	1875	5.9	29.7
Germanium	Ge	72.6	32	Winkler	1886	5.4	958.5
Gold (aurum)	Au	197.2	79	Prehistoric	....	19.3	1063
Hafnium	Ha	178.6	72	Coster, Hevesy	1923	13.3	2200
Helium	He	4.002	2	Ramsay	1895	0.5†	−272
Holmium	Ho	163.5	67	Soret	1878	......	......
Hydrogen	H	1.008	1	Cavendish	1766	0.07†	−259.4
Indium	In	114.8	49	Reich and Richter	1863	7.25	155
Iodine	I	126.92	53	Courtois	1811	4.94	113.5
Iridium	Ir	193.1	77	Tennant	1802	22.4	2350
Iron (ferrum)	Fe	55.84	26	Prehistoric	....	7.86	1530
Krypton	Kr	83.7	36	Ramsay and Travers	1898	2.16†	−160
Lanthanum	La	138.92	57	Mosander	1839	6.15	826
Lead (plumbum)	Pb	207.22	82	Prehistoric	....	11.34	327.5
Lithium	Li	6.94	3	Arfvedson	1817	0.53	186
Lutecium	Lu	175.0	71	Urbain, Welsbach	1907	......	......
Magnesium	Mg	24.32	12	Bussy	1830	1.74	650
Manganese	Mn	54.93	25	Gahn	1774	7.3	1260
Mercury (hydrargyrum)	Hg	200.61	80	Known in 4th century B.C.	....	13.60	−38.9
Molybdenum	Mo	96.0	42	Hjelm	1790	10.2	2620
Neodymium	Nd	144.27	60	Welsbach	1885	7.00	840
Neon	Ne	20.183	10	Ramsay and Travers	1898	.695A	−249
Neptunium**	Np	237	93	McMillan and Abelson	1940	......	......
Nickel	Ni	58.69	28	Cronstedt	1751	8.8	1452
Nitrogen	N	14.008	7	Scheele, Benj. Rutherford	1772	.8†	−210
Osmium	Os	190.8	76	Tennant	1803	22.48	2700
Oxygen	O	16.0	8	Priestley	1774	1.12†	−219
Palladium	Pd	106.7	46	Wollaston	1803	11.5	1555
Phosphorus	P	31.02	15	Brand	1669	1.8	44
Platinum	Pt	195.23	78	Known in 16th century A.D.	....	21.4	1755
Plutonium**	Pu	239	94	Seaborg, McMillan, Kennedy, Wahl	1940	......	......
Polonium	Po	210	84	Curie	1898	......	......
Potassium (kalium)	K	39.10	19	Davy	1807	.86	63
Praseodymium	Pr	140.92	59	Welsbach	1885	6.6	940
Protactinium	Pa	231	91	Hahn & Meitner, Soddy & Cranston	1918	......	......
Radium	Ra	225.97	88	M. and Mme. Curie	1898	5	960
Radon (Niton)	Rn	222.0	86	Dorn (as radium emanation)	1900	7.5A	−113
Rhenium	Re	186.31	75	Noddack, Tacke & Berg	1925	20.53	3167
Rhodium	Rh	102.91	45	Wollaston	1804	12.3	1950
Rubidium	Rb	85.44	37	Bunsen and Kirchhoff	1860	1.52	38
Ruthenium	Ru	101.7	44	Claus	1845	12.28	2450
Samarium	Sm	150.43	62	Boisbaudran	1879	7.7	>1300
Scandium	Sc	45.1	21	Nilson	1879	2.5	1200
Selenium	Se	79.2	34	Berzelius	1817	4.6	220
Silicon	Si	28.06	14	Berzelius	1823	2.33	1420
Silver (argentum)	Ag	107.88	47	Prehistoric	....	10.5	960.5
Sodium (natrium)	Na	22.997	11	Davy	1807	0.97	97.5
Strontium	Sr	87.63	38	Davy	1808	2.6	782
Sulphur	S	32.06	16	Prehistoric	....	2.07	120
Tantalum	Ta	181.4	73	Ekeberg	1802	16.6	3000
Technetium	Tc	99	43	Perrier and Segré	1937	......	......
Tellurium	Te	127.5	52	Klaproth	1788	6.25	453
Terbium	Tb	159.2	65	Mosander	1843	......	......
Thallium	Tl	204.39	81	Crookes	1861	11.85	303.5

*The factors in these columns vary with the form which the element takes (e.g., in carbon the specific gravity varies as diamond, charcoal, or lampblack is taken), but as far as possible the factor of the most typical form is given. **Not definitely found in nature or produced principally by artificial means.
†Of the liquid element. ‡Diamond A—Air=1. >More than.

TABLE OF CHEMICAL ELEMENTS—Con.

ELEMENT	Symbol	Atomic Weight 0=16	Atomic Number	Discoverer	Year	Specfic Gravity*	Melting Point (Centigrade)*
Thorium	Th	232.12	90	Berzelius	1828	11.5	1842
Thulium	Tm	169.4	69	Cleve	1879	......	......
Tin (stannum)	Sn	118.7	50	Prehistoric	....	7.28	231.8
Titanium	Ti	47.9	22	Gregor	1789	4.5	1800
Tungsten	W	184.0	74	d'Elhujar	1783	19.1	3380
Uranium	U	238.14	92	Peligot	1841	18.7	1690
Vanadium	V	50.95	23	Sefstroem	1830	5.7	1710
Xenon	Xe	131.3	54	Ramsay and Travers	1898	3.52†	-112
Ytterbium	Yb	173.5	70	Marignac	1878	....	....
Yttrium	Yt	89.92	39	Gadolin	1794	4.57	1490
Zinc (zincum)	Zn	65.38	30	Known B.C.	....	7.14	419
Zirconium	Zr	91.22	40	Berzelius	1824	6.53	1900

See footnote page 952.

developed in dyes called indicators of which litmus is an example. Acidity is more accurately measured electrically.

The addition of equivalent amounts of an acid and an alkali results in a solution which is neither acidic nor alkaline. The process is termed *neutralization* and always results in the formation of a *salt*. For example, if solutions of hydrochloric (muriatic) acid and sodium hydroxide (caustic soda) are combined the resulting solution will contain merely sodium chloride (table salt). In addition, the solution will become quite warm since neutralization involves the production of much heat.

Although all acids share the property of yielding hydrogen ions in solution, they may vary widely in other properties. Acids of inorganic compounds are termed *mineral acids*. Some of the mineral acids are of greatest commercial importance. Among the most important are hydrochloric acid, nitric acid, and sulfuric acid. Other mineral acids are boric, hydrobromic, chromic, hydrofluoric, iodic, phosphoric, silicic, stannic, and telluric acids.

Acids containing carbon, hydrogen, and oxygen, in various proportions, are called organic acids, for the reason that many of them were first found in animal or plant substances. For example, acetic acid occurs in vinegar; malic acid in gooseberries, currants, and unripe apples; citric acid in oranges and lemons; tartaric acid in grapes; and oxalic acid in various sorrels. Carbolic acid is obtained from coal tar. Other organic acids are benzoic, formic, gallic, lactic, oleic, palmitic, stearic, and tannic. An exceedingly large number of organic acids have been produced by laboratory methods.

Some acids are healthful and are used for food; as, for example, those contained in most fruits. Other acids, such as prussic, oxalic, and carbolic, are among the most violent poisons. Some are harmless to the touch; others are biting and corrosive to the skin. Strong sulphuric acid will char and destroy nearly all animal and vegetable substances. Nitric acid stains the skin yellow and leaves a painful wound. In some respects, hydrochloric acid is the most powerful of all, yet in a diluted state it forms an indispensable part of the digestive fluids of the human stomach. The practical uses of acids in medicine, in the industries, in the arts, and in scientific investigation are exceedingly numerous and valuable.

Bases (alkalies). The hydroxide of any positive element, or, any substance whose aqueous solution contains hydroxyl ions. A base reacts with an *acid* to form a *salt* and, usually, water. The metallic hydroxides are all bases but they differ greatly in activity. Some, such as magnesium hydroxide, are so mild that they may be taken as medicine in fairly large quantities; others, such as the hydroxides of sodium and potassium, are powerful caustics. Many organic substances, such as aniline, also act as bases. The modern method for determining the relative strength of a base is to measure the electrical conductivity of its aqueous solution. Those bases which are so active that, when they are dissolved in water, the solution has a soapy feeling and changes red litmus to blue, are known as alkalies.

The principal alkalies are caustic soda, or sodium hydroxide; caustic potash, or potassium hydroxide; and ammonia, or ammonium hydroxide. The strongest alkalies are caustic soda and caustic potash, commonly known in an impure state as soda lye and potash lye. These are exceedingly caustic, act as powerful corrosive poisons, and react with fats and oils to form soaps. Alkalies are of great value in chemical research, and are extensively used in the industrial arts, especially in soap making and in dyeing. Lime, magnesia, and sodium carbonate are sometimes regarded as alkalies.

Alloys. Mixtures of two or more metallic elements, usually as solid solutions of one metal in the other or as definite compounds of the metals. Alloys are of great practical importance as most of the commercial "metals" are actually alloys of several metallic elements. The alloys have a wide variety of properties not possessed by pure elements and often combine the best features of the component elements or they may even take on properties which none of the components exhibit to any marked extent.

Examples of alloys are steels, stainless steels, solders, coinage alloys, bronze, antifriction metals, duralumin, monel and type metal.

Analysis (assay). Generally, analysis refers to the determination of the chemical composition of a substance. In its broader meaning it includes the splitting of molecules into smaller or simpler constituents in contrast to *synthesis* which refers to the building up of complex molecules from simple ones.

Chemical analysis has developed into an extremely diversified subject with many different types of methods called into play. (See *Analytical Chemistry.*)

Atom. According to the atomic theory advanced by Dalton in 1803 and widely accepted by chemists during the 19th century, an atom is the smallest particle of an element which can exist either alone or in combination with similar particles or atoms of the same element or of a different element. This conception of the structure of matter, based on the atomist theory in philosophy, was confirmed by the work of Avogadro (1776–1856), who made the important distinction between atoms and molecules. Subsequent discoveries, such as the law of atomic heat, isomorphism, substitution, and isomerism, and, more recently, ionization and radioactivity, have greatly advanced scientific theory regarding the nature of the atom.

According to recent researches, the atom is no longer to be regarded as the ultimate, indivisible particle of matter, but as a more or less complex system consisting of a nucleus accompanied by *electrons* in rapid rotation. In the case of radium and other radioactive substances, portions of the nucleus together with some of these electrons are thrown off to unite in new arrangements; that is, to form atoms of another element having a smaller atomic weight. (See *Isotopes, Atomic Theory, Elements, Atomic Structure.*)

Catalysis. The advancing or retarding of a chemical reaction produced by the presence of a substance called a *catalytic agent*, or *catalyzer*, which itself remains apparently unchanged.

Numerous enzymes or ferments produce catalysis, such as pepsin in the digestive fluids, or the zymase of yeast, which causes fermentable sugars to decompose into alcohol and carbon dioxide. Various metals also act as catalyzers. In the manufacture of sulphuric acid on a large scale, sulphur dioxide and oxygen are transformed into the needed sulphur trioxide simply by passing a mixture of these gases over metallic platinum and other metallic substances, the metals remaining unchanged.

Similarly, ammonia is now manufactured in commercial quantities by heating a mixture of nitrogen and hydrogen over metallic iron, in the presence of which these gases unite. Again, many organic substances can be reduced by treating them with hydrogen in the presence of finely divided nickel. By this method, liquid vegetable oils, as, for example, cottonseed oil, are now changed to solid fats and widely used for culinary purposes.

Colloidal Solution. A solution characterized by a certain state of subdivision of the dissolved or suspended component. The dispersed phase, as it is called, may consist either of very large molecules such as proteins or aggregates of smaller molecules of such small dimensions that they remain suspended indefinitely. Some familiar *colloids* are glue, starch, and gelatin, which, when treated with water, give a colloidal solution of characteristic properties.

Colloids remain suspended in the surrounding liquid in contrast to crystalloids, such as salt and sugar, which go into solution. Colloids do not pass through vegetable or animal membranes, neither do they lower the freezing point nor raise the boiling point of the liquids in which they are suspended. Nongelatinous substances, such as gold and silver, can be prepared in colloidal form as extremely fine particles which do not settle out from the water or other liquid. The structure and growth of the protoplasm and cells in the human body are largely dependent on colloids. Many colloids are coagulated by the action of heat or acid, as is shown by cooking the white of an egg or adding vinegar to milk.

Combustion. The operation of fire on any inflammable substance; chemically, the union of such a substance with oxygen or some other supporter of combustion, attended with heat and in most instances with light.

The combination of the carbon in various fuels with the oxygen of the air by combustion is a universal method of obtaining heat, light, and power. However, many substances besides carbon, such as phosphorus, sulphur, magnesium, and other metals, burn in the air and in various other substances, as, for example, chlorine. While the chemical action between these uniting or burning materials is mutual, the more solid substances, such as coal, wood, charcoal, and petroleum, are called *combustibles*, while the reacting gases, such as oxygen and chlorine, are called *supporters of combustion.* A very large number of substances containing carbon, including the numerous kinds of coal, asphaltum, petroleum, and illuminating and natural gas, are combustible.

The slow oxidation of various carbon compounds in the animal body, resulting in the production of animal heat and of the carbonic-acid gas thrown off by the lungs, is also called combustion.

Compounds. When two or more elements unite to form a substance having properties different from those of either component element, the resulting substance is called a chemical compound.

When the gaseous element oxygen unites with the gaseous element hydrogen, the resulting liquid substance, water, is a chemical compound. Similarly, when the gas nitrogen unites with hydrogen, the resulting substance, ammonia, is a chemical compound. Again, when the metallic element sodium unites with the gaseous element chlorine, the resulting substance, common salt, is a chemical compound.

Chemical compounds may be very simple, consisting of a union of single atoms of only two elements, as in case of common salt, or they may be exceedingly complex, consisting of the union of several elements in greatly differing proportions, such as those which exist in albumen and in many other organic substances. As a rule, mineral compounds are comparatively simple and organic compounds very complex.

When two or more elements are brought together but do not form a chemical union, the result is a simple mixture, not a compound. For example, the oxygen, nitrogen, and other gases in air form merely a mixture. Similarly, when copper and tin are melted together to form bronze, the result is a mixture called, like other similar mixtures of metals, an alloy.

Distillation. The process of heating a liquid or solid in a closed vessel, and condensing some or all of the resulting vapors.

When water boils in a teakettle, steam escapes from the spout and disappears. If the spout were connected with a cold pipe, the steam would condense and run from the pipe as distilled water. If the boiling water contains salts in solution, as most water does, the distilled water will nevertheless be pure and free from dissolved substances, because salt is not volatile. This process was used as early as the third century to purify sea water for drinking purposes. The apparatus necessary for distillation includes a still, or retort, in which the material is heated, a condenser to cool the vapors, and a receiver in which to collect the condensed liquids.

Crude petroleum contains many substances which are separated by distillation. When the still is heated, gasoline of low boiling point is first to come from the condenser. The temperature gradually rises and kerosene is given off, followed by heavier oils until only solid coke remains in the still. Each material may be collected separately, so that the crude oil is divided into a number of fractions, and the process is called fractional distillation. Each fraction is still a mixture which may be further purified by the same method.

Distillation of fermented liquids in order to concentrate the alcohol was practiced at least as early as the 10th century. This separation takes place because of the difference in boiling point of pure alcohol and water, and may be carried out until a liquid containing about 96 per cent alcohol is obtained. Greater concentration cannot be obtained, because alcohol of this strength has a boiling point lower than that of water or of pure alcohol.

Water boils at about 100° C., and turpentine boils at 165° C., but a mixture of turpentine and water can be boiled at about 95° C. Aniline oil and many other liquids of high boiling point are often distilled at lower temperatures by passing steam through the still. This process is called steam distillation.

When coal is heated in a retort, it gradually decomposes so that ammonia, illuminating gas, coal tar, benzene, and many other substances are given off, and coke remains in the still. This type of distillation, which involves chemical as well as physical changes, is usually called destructive distillation.

Electron. A particle or corpuscle, carrying a charge of negative electricity and possessing about $\frac{1}{1800}$ the mass of a hydrogen atom; now regarded as a common constituent of the atoms of all chemical elements. According to the theory of electrons, the charge borne by an electron is the natural unit or atom of negative electricity, and, whenever a body is charged with negative electricity, the charge is due to the congregation of electrons upon it.

Electrons have been detected only when they are in rapid motion, and, so far as known, they are all of one kind and always bear the same charge of electricity. They are emitted from the surface of glowing metals, from the electric arc, from flames, and from metal plates exposed to ultra-violet light. In such cases an external force or stimulus is necessary to liberate the electrons. But all radioactive substances, such as radium, thorium, and uranium, continuously and spontaneously emit these same small, negatively charged particles.

Further, it has been found that the charge carried by the electron or gaseous ion is identical with that carried by a monovalent anion in electrolysis. Moreover, the charge carried on a monovalent cathion is equal in quantity but opposite in sign. This constancy in the mass and in the charge of the electron, regardless of its origin, has led scientists to the conclusion that all matter contains this primordial element. See *Electricity*, *Isotopes*.

Formulas, Chemical. The formula of a chemical compound is indicated by grouping together the symbols of the atoms composing a molecule of it. The molecule of common salt is composed of one atom of sodium (Na) and one atom of chlorine (Cl). Hence the chemical formula for common salt is written NaCl. In case a molecule contains more than one atom of the same kind, the number of these atoms is usually written as a subscript to the symbol. For example, the formula for water, a molecule of which contains two atoms of hydrogen and one atom of oxygen, is written H_2O. Similarly, the formula for sulphuric acid is H_2SO_4; of nitric acid, HNO_3; of amonia, NH_3.

The arrangement of the atoms in a compound is often more easily understood when shown by means of a graphic or structural formula. For example: The formula for aniline might be given as C_6H_7N; and for toluene, as C_7H_8, instead of $C_6H_5NH_2$ and $C_6H_5CH_3$ as shown in the table. But the first formulas do not show any relation between these two substances, while the second method shows that both contain the important phenyl group C_6H_5, and are probably made from benzene. If necessary, a graphic formula can illustrate the relationship of each atom to every other one in the molecule.

Chemical Formulas

Inorganic Compounds:

Aluminum acetate	$Al(C_2H_3O_2)_3$
Aluminum oxide	Al_2O_3
Barium sulphate	$BaSO_4$
Bismuth subnitrate	$BiONO_3$
Boric acid	H_3BO_3
Calcium carbonate	$CaCO_3$
Calcium phosphate	$Ca_3(PO_4)_2$
Carbon dioxide	CO_2
Carbon disulphide	CS_2
Carbon monoxide	CO
Carbon tetrachloride	CCl_4
Cobalt chloride	$CoCl_2 6H_2O$
Cyanogen	C_2N_2
Fulminate of mercury	$Hg(ONC)_2$
Gold chloride	$AuCl_3$
Hydrofluoric acid	HF
Hydrogen peroxide	H_2O_2
Hydrogen sulphide	H_2S
Iron hydroxide	$Fe(OH)_3$
Iron oxide, red	Fe_2O_3
Lead nitrate	$Pb(NO_3)_2$
Magnesium carbonate	$MgCO_3$
Mercuric nitrate	$Hg(NO_3)_2.\ 2H_2O$
Nickel ammonium sulphate	$NiSO_4(NH_4)_2SO_4.6H_2O$
Nitrogen pentoxide	N_2O_5
Potassium arsenite	$KAs\ O_2$
Potassium bromide	KBr
Potassium cyanide	KNC
Potassium dichromate	$K_2Cr_2O_7$
Potassium iodide	KI
Potassium permanganate	$KMnO_4$
Radium bromide	$RaBr_2$
Selenium oxychloride	$SeOCl_2$
Silver bromide	AgBr
Silver iodide	AgI
Silver nitrate	$AgNO_3$
Sodium acetate	$NaC_2H_3O_2$
Sodium benzoate	$NaC_7H_5O_2$
Sodium oxalate	$Na_2C_2O_4$
Sodium salicylate	$NaC_7H_5O_3$
Stannous chloride	$SnCl_2$
Sulphur dioxide	SO_2
Sulphur trioxide	SO_3
Zinc sulphide	ZnS

Organic Compounds:

Acetanilid	$CH_3CONH.C_6H_5$
Acetone	CH_3COCH_3
Acetylene	C_2H_2
Alizarin	$C_6H_4(CO)_2C_6H_2(OH)_2$
Amyl acetate	$C_5H_{11}CH_3CO_2$
Amyl alcohol	$C_5H_{11}OH$
Aniline	$C_6H_5NH_2$
Anthracene	$C_6H_4(CH)_2C_6H_4$
Antipyrene	$C_{11}H_{12}N_2O$
Benzene	C_6H_6
Caffeine	$C_8H_{10}N_4O_2.H_2O$
Camphor	$C_{10}H_{16}O$
Chloral	CCl_3CHO
Chloroform	$CHCl_3$
Citric acid	$C_3H_4OH(COOH)_3$
Glycerin	$C_3H_5(OH)_3$
Iodoform	CHI_3
Lactic acid	C_2H_5OCOOH
Menthol	$C_{10}H_{19}OH$
Morphine	$C_{17}H_{19}NO_4.H_2O$
Naphthalene	$C_{10}H_8$
Nicotine	$C_{10}H_{14}N_2$
Oleic acid	$C_{17}H_{33}COOH$
Oxalic acid	$H_2C_2O_4$
Picric acid	$C_6H_2OH(NO_2)_3$
Saccharin	$C_6H_4CO.SO_2.NH$
Salicylic acid	$C_6H_4OH.COOH$
Stearic acid	$C_{17}H_{35}COOH$
Sugar	$C_{12}H_{22}O_{11}$
Tannin	$C_{14}H_{10}O_9$
Tartaric acid	$(COOH)_2.(CHOH)_2$
Toluene	$C_6H_5CH_3$

Ion. An atom or group of atoms (molecule) which has either gained or lost electrons and thus become charged either negatively or positively. Those with negative charge are called *anions*, while those with positive charge are termed *cations*. Most neutral salts, acids, and bases split into positive and negative ions when dissolved in water. The hydrogen ion (positive charge) is responsible for the well-known properties of an acid while hydroxide ion (negative charge) is characteristic of a base.

The presence of ions in solution are responsible for the conduction of electricity through solutions.

Metal. The metals constitute an important division of the chemical elements. In general, metals have a characteristic shiny surface or luster, and are usually hard, heavy, opaque, malleable, ductile, tenacious, and good conductors of heat and electricity. They differ greatly, however, in regard to the foregoing qualities, and no sharp line can be drawn between the metals and the nonmetals.

Sodium and potassium, for example, are as soft as wax, while titanium surpasses quartz in hardness. Gold may be hammered into exceedingly thin sheets, but antimony is very brittle. Most metals are heavier than water—osmium being 22½ times and platinum 21½ times heavier—though sodium, potassium, and lithium float like wood. Under ordinary conditions all metals exclude the light, yet gold in very thin sheets is translucent. In chemical behavior some metals act in part like nonmetals, the oxides of several, such as arsenic, tin, and chromium, uniting with oxygen and hydrogen to form acids.

In ductility, malleability, and tenacity, metals also differ greatly. The most malleable metal is gold, followed in order by silver, copper, platinum, palladium, iron, aluminum, tin, zinc, lead, cadmium, nickel, and cobalt. Gold is also the most ductile metal, and next to it are silver, platinum, iron, nickel, copper, palladium, aluminum, zinc, tin, and lead. In tenacity, nickel stands first, followed by iron, copper, platinum, silver, gold, palladium, and zinc.

Except gold, which is yellow, copper, which is red, and silver and tin, which are nearly pure white, metals are grayish in color, sometimes with a bluish or pinkish tinge. Except mercury, which is a liquid, all metals at ordinary temperatures are solids, and all can be melted or volitalized.

Iron, nickel, and cobalt possess magnetic properties. Silver is the best conductor of electricity, followed by pure copper, pure gold, and aluminum next in order. Those metals which resist oxidation, as do gold, silver, and platinum, have been styled the noble metals. Those which do not possess this quality, such as iron, zinc, and lead, have been called the base metals.

The metals comprise about three-fourths of the elements, and, together with their compounds, embrace an immense number of valuable mineral substances. Of more than 60 metals now known, only seven—gold, silver, mercury, copper, iron, tin, and lead—were known to the ancients. Bismuth, antimony, zinc, and arsenic were added to the list of known metals between 1400 and 1700. Nine metals, including platinum, magnesium, nickel, and cobalt, were discovered between 1700 and 1800, while all the other metals, some 40 or more, have been found since 1800. About half the metals are very scarce, and some are exceedingly rare. A limited number, such as gold, silver, and copper, occur in the native state, but most metals are found combined with oxygen or sulphur in numerous mineral compounds or *ores*, from which they are extracted by various processes of *metallurgy*.

By chemical methods, metals are combined with various nonmetals, forming an immense number of compounds, such as oxides, hydroxides, sulphides, and the salts of various acids. When fused, many metals mix with various other metals, forming, upon being cooled, solid solutions called *alloys*. Most metals ordinarily seen are not pure, but consist of various mixtures or alloys; as, for example, gold and silver coins, cast iron, steel, or bronze. Mercury possesses the power to dissolve many other metals, forming *amalgams*.

Molecular Weight. The molecular weight of a compound is the sum of the weights of its component atoms. As a molecule of oxygen gas contains two atoms, its molecular weight equals 2 x 16, or 32. Thus it follows that the molecular weight is equal to the sum of the atomic weights multiplied by one or more.

Since the gram is the unit of weight, 32 grams is called the gram-molecular-weight of oxygen. Now, one liter of oxygen weighs 1.429 gm., so that 32 gms. would occupy 22.4.1., which is known as the *gram-molecular-volume*. It is a very important value, because from Avogadro's hypothesis it follows that the molecular weight of any *gaseous* substance may be found by determining the weight of an amount of it which would occupy 22.4.1. at 0° C. and 760 mm. pressure.

For convenience, the molecular weight of a solid or a liquid is usually considered to be the simple sum of the atomic weights of its component atoms. Thus the molecular weight of water, H_2O, is usually given as 2+16=18; similarly, for common salt, NaCl, it is 23+35.5 or 58.5, and for cane sugar, $C_{12}H_{22}O_{11}$, it is 144+22+176, or 342.

Molecule. The smallest quantity of a substance which can exist and retain its identity in character with the mass of which it forms a part. As the atom or atoms composing it do not separate during physical change, the molecule is the unit of the mass. A molecule usually consists of a union of two or more atoms of the same or different elements, and some organic molecules contain a very large number of atoms. A molecule of water, H_2O, consists of two atoms of hydrogen and one atom of oxygen, and a molecule of hydrochloric acid, HCl, consists of one atom of hydrogen and one atom of chlorine.

In the case of many elementary gases, as, for example, oxygen, hydrogen, and chlorine, their molecules consist of two atoms each. In the case of ozone, which is an allotropic form of oxygen, the molecule consists of three atoms. On the other hand, the molecule may be identical with the atom, as in the case of mercury and argon.

Salts. Substances formed when metals or bases combine with acids; so named because in appearance many of them resemble common salt. Chemically, a salt is a compound formed by substituting the metal of a base for the hydrogen of an acid. In a sense, all acids may be regarded as salts of hydrogen. When the hydrogen is exchanged for a metal, the resulting compound is a salt of the metal. Or, what amounts to the same thing, a salt is formed by eliminating the elements of water (hydrogen H and hydroxyl OH) between an acid and a base.

The number of salts is exceedingly large and embraces a great variety of very useful substances. Besides common salt, which is sodium chloride, other well-known examples are: *Glauber's salt*, which is sodium sulphate; *Epsom salt*, which is magnesium sulphate; *saltpeter*, which is potassium nitrate; *borax*, or sodium borate; *sal ammoniac* or ammonium chloride; *washing soda*, or sodium carbonate; *baking soda*, or sodium bicarbonate; *common alum*, or aluminum-potassium-sulphate; *copperas*, or *green vitriol*, which is an iron sulphate; and *blue vitriol*, which is copper sulphate.

Many substances, very unlike common salt in appearance, are, chemically, true salts. Among such are chalk, which is calcium carbonate; kaolin, or china clay, which is aluminum silicate; and glass, which is a mixed silicate of sodium, calcium, and other metals.

Solvent. Any substance which may be used to dissolve something. Water is the most generally useful of all solvents, as it dissolves sugar and most salts, as well as many liquids and gases. But water will not dissolve shellac, or camphor, or iodine, for which alcohol is the best solvent. Flavoring extracts cannot be made with water, because it is not a solvent for the essential oils and resins. Neither water nor alcohol will remove a grease spot that quickly disappears when treated with gasoline or ether, both of which are good solvents for fats, oils, and waxes. Acetone, methyl alcohol, amyl acetate or banana oil, and carbon tetrachloride are frequently used organic solvents.

In ordinary solution there seems to be little if any combination between the dissolved substance and the solvent. Sugar can be obtained again by boiling off water from a sirup; but another type of solvent acts by causing a chemical change in the dissolved substance. Thus, when hydrochloric acid dissolves zinc or iron, the free metal cannot be obtained again by evaporating the acid, because it has been changed to a chemical compound. In certain methods of mining, sodium cyanide is employed as a solvent for gold, to separate the yellow metal from quartz and similar impurities. Practically every substance can be dissolved by use of the proper solvent.

Solvent Extraction is the term applied to the process by which one substance is selectively removed from others through the use of a suitable solvent. It is a process widely used industrially.

Symbols, Chemical. The symbol of an element is usually the capitalized initial of its name, as H for hydrogen, O for oxygen, and C for carbon. Where many elements have the same initials, a second, small letter is added, as Ca for calcium, Cd for cadmium, Cl for chlorine, and Co for cobalt. When the name of an element is not the same in all languages, the symbol is frequently taken from the Latin or from the name as known to the alchemists. Thus, Cu is from *cuprum*, copper; Fe from *ferrum*, iron; Hg from *hydrargyrum*, mercury; Na from *natrium*, sodium; and K from *kalium*, potassium.

Such symbols are necessary in order to represent in a simple manner chemical compounds and their changes. Thus sodium chloride or common salt is represented by NaCl, which means 23 parts of sodium combined with 35.5 parts of chlorine. As generally employed, a symbol means a definite proportion of the element it represents, but not a definite quantity.

Synthesis. The general term applied to the formation of a more or less complex chemical compound from simpler substances or elements. Of great industrial importance is the synthesis of ammonia from the elements nitrogen and hydrogen since this substance is the primary material for the further synthesis of many important materials such as nitric acid, explosives, and fertilizers.

Living organisms constantly synthesize a wide variety of complex substances. The synthesis by plants of carbohydrates from carbon dioxide and water through the harnessing of the energy of sunlight is termed *photosynthesis* and is the reaction upon which all life depends.

The organic chemical industry is built up largely of processes involving syntheses of carbon compounds. Plastics, synthetic rubber, drugs are but a few of the examples of tremendous number of substances which are synthesized from simple organic compounds.

Valence. The valence of an element was originally defined as the number of hydrogen atoms with which it may combine, or which it may replace.

Any element which combines with hydrogen, or replaces it in combination, atom for atom, is said to have a valence of one, and is called *univalent.* For example, hydrogen, chlorine, sodium, and silver are univalent. An element which unites with, or replaces, two hydrogen atoms, has a valence of two, and is said to be *divalent.* Oxygen, copper, zinc, and, most common metals are divalent. An element which combines with three atoms of hydrogen has a valence of three and is called *trivalent.* Similarly, an element may have a valence of four, *quadrivalent*; of five, *quinquivalent*; and of six, *sexivalent.*

Valence, or *oxidation-number* as it is often called, is now thought of in terms of the electrons with which it can form compounds with other elements. Thus, carbon, which has four *valence electrons*, can combine with four other atoms. Aluminum is trivalent, silicon is quadrivalent, vanadium is often quinquivalent, and tungsten is sexivalent. Many elements show two or more valences; for example, iron has a valence of two and three; phosphorus, of three and five; sulphur, of two, four, and six; chromium, of two, three, and six; and carbon, of two, three, and four. The inert gases, such as argon and helium, do not unite with hydrogen or any other known element and hence have no valence.

CHEMICAL SUBSTANCES

The Elements

Actinium (atomic number 89). This element was discovered in pitchblende soon after the discovery of polonium and radium. It is a trivalent element exclusively and behaves very similarly to lanthanum, the first element of the rare earth group. All isotopes of actinium are extremely radioactive and it lends its name to the "actinium radioactive series." It is one of the disintegration products of uranium 235.

Aluminum (atomic number 13). A bluish white metal, with a satiny luster, distinct in color from silver, tin, and nickel. Aluminum is the most abundant of the metals, and, excepting oxygen and silicon, there is more aluminum than any other substance in the earth's crust. However, it is not found in a free state, but always in combination with one or more elements, occurring in clay, marl, slate, granite, and scores of other minerals, including such precious stones as the ruby and the sapphire.

Although it is computed that a cubic yard of ordinary clay contains about 900 pounds of aluminum, no cheap method of extracting it was known until 1886, when C. M. Hall invented the electrolytic process which has made aluminum a widely used metal. In 1855 aluminum sold at $55 a pound; in 1888, at $2 a pound; but in 1910 the price had fallen to 20 cents a pound. Nearly all of the commercial aluminum produced in the United States is obtained from bauxite, a very pure ore mined chiefly in Arkansas. In 1885 only 285 pounds of the metal were produced; in 1937 the output was more than 290 million pounds. Under pressure of the war demand, production in 1940 rose above 412 million pounds, valued at over $75,000,000.

Aluminum is only about a third as heavy as iron or steel, is not changed by fresh water or sea water, and does not rust in either moist or dry air. It is not affected by organic acids, such as those contained in fruit juices or in vinegar. Cold nitric and sulphuric acids act upon it very slowly, but hydrochloric acid and the caustic alkalies readily dissolve it. Aluminum is nearly as hard as silver, yet it may be drawn into a wire 1/250 of an inch in diameter,—about half as strong as a copper wire of the same size. In malleability, aluminum ranks high among the metals; it may be rolled into sheets less than 1/500 of an inch thick, and these may be hammered into foil only 1/1000 of an inch thick.

As a conductor of heat and electricity, aluminum exceeds all metals except silver, copper, and gold. Its tensile strength is such that, weight for weight, an aluminum girder will carry a greater load than a steel girder. Weight for weight, aluminum wire will carry a heavier electric current than copper wire. Further, it is nonmagnetic and, hence, very useful in electrical work.

When warm, aluminum may be pressed into molds of any shape, including bars and tubing of any length, fancy architectural moldings and cornices. For a given thickness of plate, one ton of aluminum is equal in area to 2.7 tons of tin, 2.8 tons of iron, 3.3 tons of copper, and 4.2 tons of lead. Compared with copper, aluminum sheets are 66 per cent lighter, usually 25 to 50 per cent cheaper, and, for many purposes, much more serviceable.

With all the common metals, except lead, aluminum readily forms alloys, some of which have proved very useful, such as combinations of aluminum with antimony, bismuth, cadmium, copper, chromium, magnesium, manganese, molybdenum, nickel, and tin—all of which are harder than pure aluminum. The former difficulty of soldering aluminum has been solved by the invention of autogenous welding. Aluminum may be plated with other metals by an electrolytic process.

By reason of its many remarkable qualities, aluminum is now devoted to an immense and increasing number of uses. Some 500 or more articles are made direct from the metal and its alloys. Among the most important of these are airplanes and automobile parts, cooking utensils, dental plates, foil for wrapping foods and confectionery, horseshoes, gas and oil stoves, telephone fixtures, and scientific instruments. Powdered aluminum is used to keep up the heat of molten iron and steel, and is the basis of the valuable "thermit" process of welding. It is also used in making explosives, as, for example, ammonal, and as a basis for bronze powders in the painter's trade. Salts of aluminum are much used as mordants in the dye industry. Cables made of aluminum wires twisted about a strengthening core of steel, are extensively used for electrical transmission lines. See *Bauxite, Duralumin, Magnalium, Thermit.*

Americium (atomic number 95). One of the new synthetic elements discovered by Seaborg, James, and Morgan in 1945 during work on atomic energy problems. All isotopes of americium are intensely radioactive; nevertheless, it has been isolated in very small quantities and its chemical properties determined. Its chemical properties are predominantly those of a trivalent element like the rare earths. Americium has no practical application at present but its properties are of great scientific interest.

Antimony (atomic number 51). A bluish white metal so brittle that it may easily be pounded to a powder. While it is found in the pure state, commercial antimony is obtained mostly from the mineral stibnite, a sulphide of the metal. It is a poor conductor of heat and electricity, and at ordinary temperatures is not acted upon by air or water. Its most important use is in alloys, to which it imparts its peculiar property of expanding when cooling. It is therefore a very valuable component of type metal and it enters into the composition of pewter, britannia metal, Babbitt metal, and shrapnel shot metal. See *Britannia Metal, Type Metal.*

Argon (atomic number 18). A colorless and odorless gas, heavier than air and forming 0.933 per cent of the volume of the atmosphere. It was discovered in 1894 by Sir William Ramsay and Lord Rayleigh, through their efforts to learn why nitrogen produced from air was slightly heavier than the same gas prepared from other sources. Argon is obtained commercially from liquid air. It is used to fill certain types of incandescent electric lamps, because the pressure of the gas prevents evaporation of the filament at high temperature, thus giving a more efficient and satisfactory light. All attempts to combine argon with other elements have failed. The gas forms a liquid which boils at 303° below zero and becomes solid at 306° below zero F.

Arsenic (atomic number 33). A hard, steel-gray, very brittle metal, usually occurring in ores of iron, antimony, lead, silver, cobalt, and nickel, found in large quantities in Siberia and Silesia, and widely distributed in many other countries. The white powder, commonly called arsenic, is the oxide or rust of the metal, and, like all other compounds of arsenic, it is a deadly poison. Arsenic is used in making shot, speculum metal, opal glass, aniline dyes, Paris green, London purple, in taxidermy, in medicine, and for various other purposes.

Astatine (atomic number 85). A radioactive isotope of this element was prepared in the Berkeley cyclotron by Corson, MacKenzie, and Segré in 1940. From its position in the periodic table it is a halogen like iodine but its chemical properties differ considerably from this element. It is a curious fact that animals concentrate this element in the thyroid glands as they do iodine.

Barium (atomic number 56). A silver-white metal, slightly softer than lead, most commonly found in various carbonate (witherite) and sulphate (barite) ores. Various salts of barium, particularly the chloride, hydroxide, and sulphate, are of value in manufacturing glazed or coated paper, in chemical analysis, and as pigments in paints. Barium sulphate is one of the most insoluble salts known. When mixed with zinc sulphide, this compound is sold as lithopone, which is widely used as a substitute for white lead in paint. Barite ore is mined in the United States chiefly in Missouri and Georgia. Average annual production is valued at nearly $2,000,000. The soluble salts of barium are poisonous.

Beryllium (atomic number 4). A steel-colored, malleable metal, only about two thirds as heavy as aluminum, called also glucinum, found in various minerals such as phenacite, chrysoprase, and beryl. The metal imparts valuable properties to various alloys. The principal application of the metal is in beryllium-copper alloys. Beryllium hardens copper and increases its tensile strength without greatly decreasing electrical conductivity. Certain promising beryllium-aluminum alloys have encountered fabricating difficulties that remain to be solved.

Bismuth (atomic number 83). A shining, brittle metal, with a peculiar reddish tinge, usually found mixed with the ores of cobalt, nickel, copper, silver, tin, and lead. While of little value in the pure state, bismuth is widely used in making alloys with various metals. An alloy composed of 3 parts of lead and 2 parts of bismuth has 10 times the hardness and 20 times the toughness of pure lead. Alloys of bismuth with tin, lead, and cadmium have very low melting points, and hence are used in soft solders and in the so-called "fusible metals," several of which, such as Rose's metal and Wood's metal, melt below the boiling point of water.

Bismuth is highly diamagnetic, a piece of the metal being noticeably repelled by a magnet. Various forms of bismuth are used in staining glass, in gilding porcelain, in making cosmetics, and in medicine. In the United States the commercial supply of bismuth is obtained as a by-product in smelting lead, copper, gold, and silver ores. See *Fusible Metals*.

Boron (atomic number 5). A nonmetallic element which occurs chiefly in borax, large deposits of which are found in various parts of the world, notably in California. Pure boron is an odorless, tasteless, greenish brown powder. It combines with nitrogen and hydrogen, and dissolves in nitric and sulphuric acids. It is also soluble in melted aluminum, from which it crystallizes out upon cooling. The resulting crystals, called "boron diamonds" which always contain a small amount of aluminum, are among the hardest substances known, scratching the ruby and also corundum. The most valuable compounds of boron are boric acid, boric oxide, and borax.

Bromine (atomic number 35). A dark, red, volatile, liquid element, one of the halogen group, discovered in 1826 by Balard, a French chemist, in the salts obtained on evaporation of sea water. It is now produced commercially in this way, one specially equipped ship being able to extract the bromine from 7000 gallons of sea water in a minute. Bromine boils at 145° and freezes at 19° F. It is an irritating poison which, during the World War, was extensively used in the preparation of tear gas. Bromine is used in making various dyes, and, in the form of its salts, is used in medicine. The principal compounds of bromine are the *bromides*. One of these, silver bromide, because of its sensitiveness to light, is extensively used in photography.

Carbon (atomic number 6). One of the most important and widely distributed of all elements, occurring free as diamond and graphite, and, in noncrystalline forms, as charcoal, coke, and lampblack. In combination with other elements, carbon is an essential part of all living things and also composes a large group of important minerals. The hardness and brilliancy of diamonds, the soft, lubricating properties of graphite, the power of charcoal to absorb gases, and of hot coke to reduce many ores to metal, are all characteristics of carbon. Carbon does not melt, and, at ordinary temperatures, does not dissolve in any solvent. It is, however, soluble in melted iron and platinum.

Carbon is usually quadrivalent. It forms a greater number of complex compounds than any other elements because the atoms of carbon seem able to combine with themselves to an almost unlimited extent. The chemistry of carbon compounds is called *organic chemistry* because it was originally held that such compounds were formed only by living organisms.

Combined with hydrogen, carbon forms the great group of *hydrocarbons*, although there are only three compounds with oxygen, or oxides of carbon. Carbon dioxide from air or water is necessary for plant life. With sulphur, carbon gives the evil smelling liquid, carbon disulphide; with nitrogen, the poisonous cyanogen gas; with metals, the *carbides*, which are very important industrially. Vast quantities of limestone and numerous ores are *carbonates* or compounds of a metal with carbon and oxygen. All organic compounds contain carbon. These include glucose and the sugars, fats and oils, starch and cellulose, petroleum, alcohol, ether, dyestuffs, and perfumes.

Stated in another way, practically everything we eat and everything we wear contains carbon. Wooden houses are built of carbon compounds, and bricks are held together by the formation of carbonates in the mortar. The house is usually heated by burning coal, oil, or wood, all of which contain carbon. General diffusion of knowledge depends greatly on the art of printing, which would not exist to any extent without carbon ink and paper, a highly purified carbon compound. Carbon is the base of most new synthetic products, some 400,000 of which can be produced from soft coal. See *Carbides, Carbohydrates, Charcoal, Coke, Diamond, Graphite, Hydrocarbons.*

Cadmium (atomic number 48). A bluish white, lustrous metal found in association with zinc ores, chiefly in Silesia. As a metal, cadmium is used in making fusible alloys of low melting point, and an amalgam of cadmium and tin is used in dentistry. *Cadmium yellow*, a valuable pigment of great permanency of color, is cadmium sulphide.

Other compounds are used in making fireworks and in calico printing.

Calcium (atomic number 20). A light yellow metal, slightly softer than gold, very malleable and ductile, and only about half as heavy as aluminum. While very abundant and widely distributed, calcium is never found free but always in combination with other elements, from which it is separated by electrolysis. Calcium forms a part of many common rocks and minerals, such as limestone, marble, chalk, and gypsum. It occurs also in the bones of animals, and in shells and corals. In dry air calcium does not tarnish, but in moist air it rapidly becomes coated with a layer of calcium hydroxide (slaked lime). The metal burns with an orange flame, forming calcium oxide (*quicklime*).

The compounds of calcium are very numerous, and several are of great industrial value. Limestone, used in building and for making quicklime and mortar, is a form of calcium carbonate, as are marble, chalk, and calcite. Gypsum, from which plaster of Paris is made, is calcium sulphate. Calcium chloride is used as a drying agent and calcium hypochlorite is used as bleaching powder. Calcium carbide is the source of commercial acetylene gas. Calcium bisulphite dissolves the resins and separates the fibers in manufacturing wood pulp for paper making.

Cerium (atomic number 58). A soft, steel-gray ductile and malleable metal, not quite as heavy as iron, belonging to the "rare earth" group. It is obtained chiefly from the mineral monazite, found in North Carolina and Brazil. Cerium dissolves violently in dilute acids, forming salts, some of which are used in dyeing and in medicine. Ferrocerium, an alloy, is used in welding, in metallurgy, and in cigarette lighters. The oxide of cerium is now used in polishing optical glass.

Cesium (atomic number 55). A soft, ductile, silvery white metal, much lighter than aluminum, found chiefly in the scarce mineral pollucite, usually associated with the rare element rubidium. In its properties, cesium strongly resembles potassium, oxidizing rapidly in the air, decomposing water, and forming very stable salts. Cesium was the first new element discovered by the aid of the spectroscope, being detected by Bunsen and Kirchhoff in 1860. While displaying interesting properties, the metal and its known compounds are of slight practical importance.

Chlorine (atomic number 17). A greenish-yellow, gaseous element, discovered by Scheele in 1774. It may be compressed to a liquid which boils at −28.5° F., and at lower temperature forms a solid which melts at −152° F. Chlorine is so active chemically that copper foil catches fire when placed in a jar full of the gas. Under the same conditions, a lighted candle will continue to burn, depositing much soot because the chlorine combines with the hydrogen of the candle and sets the carbon free.

Chlorine is never found free in nature, but, combined with metals, especially as sodium chloride or common salt, it exists in enormous quantities. Gaseous chlorine is prepared from salt by means of an electric current or by the action of manganese dioxide on hydrochloric acid. It is used chiefly for bleaching and for preparing bleaching powder; also in making certain dyes, for recovering tin from scrap tin plate, and as a powerful germicide, disinfectant, and deodorant. As a germicide, it is largely used to sterilize drinking water and sewage.

As dry liquid chlorine does not attack iron, it can be stored under pressure in steel cylinders. The gas itself is 2½ times as heavy as air, and is an intensely irritating poison which will cause death if inhaled in quantity. For these reasons, chlorine was the first of various poisonous gases to be used in chemical warfare. See *Bleaching Powder, Hydrochloric Acid.*

Chromium (atomic number 24). A very hard, steel-gray metal, with a melting point between that of iron and platinum. Chromium is so named because of the bright colors of its compounds,—the green of the emerald and the red of the ruby being due to its oxide. It never occurs pure but is usually found in minerals containing lead or iron, such as chromite. The world's supply of chromium comes from Rhodesia and India.

Chromium forms both acids and salts, yielding various useful compounds. *Chrome yellow*, a valuable pigment, is lead chromate. Potassium bichromate, an important oxidizing agent, is used in electric batteries, for bleaching, and in photography. The addition of a small percentage of chromium notably improves the strength, hardness, and elasticity of steel. Besides serving as an alloying element, chromium is used for its refractory properties and for plating, pigments, dyes, and tanning. See *Chrome Steel, Ferrochrome, Stellite.*

Cobalt (atomic number 27). A hard, white metal, showing a trace of pink. It is slightly heavier than iron, strongly magnetic, and usually found associated with nickel, arsenic, and sulphur. Formerly cobalt came chiefly from Europe, but since 1904 northern Ontario and the Belgian Congo have been the chief producers. Owing to brittleness, cobalt has no practical use as a metal, but, when alloyed with chromium, molybdenum, and tungsten, it is admirably adapted for cutting tools. With nickel it forms the alloy konel, used in place of iridium in radio tubes. Various compounds of cobalt are highly valued for making fine colors, such as cobalt blue, Thenard's blue, cob bronze, and Rinman's green or cobalt green. See *Stellite.*

Columbium (niobium) (atomic number 41). A rare metal, called also niobium, which occurs in the minerals columbite, found in Connecticut, and tantalite, found in Sweden. It is a steel-gray powder, slightly lighter than iron, which forms salts called columbates or niobates. Addition of small quantities of columbium to stainless steels improves their weldability and impact strength.

Copper (atomic number 29). A brilliant metal of a peculiar red color, somewhat heavier than iron, known and used since remotely ancient times. Copper is the only metal which occurs widely distributed in nature in the free state. Blocks of nearly pure metallic copper, sometimes weighing hundreds of tons, have been found. For this reason it was the first metal extensively used by man. The copper or bronze age followed the stone age. Copper utensils found in Egypt are believed to be more than 5000 years old. The Indians of North America made use of copper, obtained in the Lake Superior region, long before the discovery of the continent by the white man. In the time of the Romans the island of Cyprus was famous for the production of copper or Cyprian brass, whence the name *cuprum* from which the word copper is derived.

Copper is the most ductile and malleable of the common metals and is exceeded only by gold, silver, and platinum in respect to these properties. In tenacity, copper is surpassed only by iron. Copper is more highly elastic than any metal except steel, and as a conductor of heat and electricity is surpassed only by silver. Copper has a distinct odor and an unpleasant metallic taste. It takes a high polish and is not acted upon by water, but in the air it becomes coated with a thin layer of green carbonate which protects it against further corrosion.

Nearly all acids act upon copper, forming a large number of salts, the most important of which are copper sulphate, commonly known as *blue vitriol*, and basic copper carbonate, sometimes called *blue verditer*. The important ores, malachite and azurite, are basic carbonates of the metal. Copper oxides are used in staining glass.

Copper is universally used as an alloy for silver and gold, imparting hardness and wearing qualities to these metals when used for coins and in jewelry. Various alloys of copper, especially bronze, which consists of tin and copper, and brass, which is made of zinc and copper, have been widely used since ancient times. *German silver* is an alloy of copper, nickel, and tin; aluminum bronze is an alloy of aluminum and copper.

Immense quantities of copper are used for industrial purposes, the most important being for wire and cables for electrical machinery and for the transmission of electric currents in telegraph, telephone, and power lines. For this purpose, metal of practically absolute purity is required. Copper is used also for sheathing ships, covering roofs and domes, for electrotyping, for engraving, and for making numerous utensils and fittings for domestic and scientific purposes, including water heaters, vacuum pans, and kettles. The use of copper in cooking vessels is attended with some danger, as the action of vegetable acids on the metal produces poisonous compounds similar to *verdigris.*

While copper occurs widely distributed in the metallic state, commercial copper is obtained chiefly from various ores, in which it is usually combined with sulphur and iron and often associated with silver and gold. Among the most abundant ores are chalcopyrite, cuprite, and malachite. From these the metal is separated and finally refined to a state of great purity by electrolysis.

The United States leads all other countries in copper production, contributing more than half of the world's yearly output, the chief producing states being Arizona, Montana, Utah, and Michigan. Among foreign countries, Japan, Mexico, Spain and Portugal, Russia, Chile, and Canada are important producers. Immense deposits of copper ore, as yet but little worked, are found in the highlands of central Africa. The largest single copper mine is said to be the Anaconda at Butte, Montana. See *Brass, Bronze, German Silver.*

Curium (atomic number 96). This element of highest atomic number known up to 1947 was discovered by Seaborg, James, and Ghiorso in 1944 as a consequence of the cyclotron bombardment of plutonium. All isotopes now known are intensely radioactive. Its chemical properties are much like those of the trivalent rare earth elements.

Dysprosium (atomic number 66). A rare earth element found in gadolinite. Its salts are yellow or green and dysprosium exhibits the trivalent state in these compounds. The oxide is colorless.

Element 61 (atomic number 61). This element has probably never been seen in nature but has been produced in radioactive form as a result of uranium fission. Its properties, as expected, are those of a rare earth element.

Erbium (atomic number 68). A rare metallic element found in gadolinite and other minerals. The oxide of erbium, a rose-colored powder, has not yet been melted, but, when heated to a high temperature, glows with a brilliant green light.

Europium (atomic number 63). A metallic element found in minute quantities in monazite sand, associated with various other elements of the "rare earth" group. Its oxide is a pinkish powder, and its sulphate forms pale pink crystals.

Fluorine (atomic number 9). An irritating, pale yellow, gaseous member of the halogen group of elements, which occurs chiefly in the minerals fluorite and cryolite. Small quantities of fluorine compounds are found in the blood, in the bones, and in the enamel of the teeth. The element was recognized by Ampère and Davy in 1810, but was not isolated until 1886 when it was first prepared by Moissan.

Fluorine is chemically the most active of the elements, and combines rapidly with all others, excepting only oxygen and the noble gases. Dry gold and platinum are affected least. It decomposes water, attacks glass, and combines so vigorously with such substances as cork, alcohol, and turpentine as to set them afire.

The gas has in recent years assumed commercial value, sodium fluoride is valuable as an antiseptic, insecticide, and preservative, while hydrofluoric acid is used for etching glass. See *Hydrofluoric Acid.*

Francium (atomic number 87). This element has only been found definitely as an extremely unstable radioactive substance. It was found by Mlle. Perey in 1939 as a rare constituent of the actinium series of radioactive isotopes. Chemically, francium is an alkali metal belonging to the same family as cesium, potassium, and sodium.

Gadolinium (atomic number 64). A rare metallic element, known as yet only in the form of its oxide and in various colorless salts formed from the oxide, such as the chloride, sulphate, and nitrate.

Gallium (atomic number 31). A hard, slightly malleable metal, somewhat lighter than iron, found in minute quantities in various zinc ores. It melts to a silvery white fluid at 29.75° C. or 85.5° F.,—or some 13° F. lower than the temperature of the human body. Fluid gallium adheres to glass and does not tarnish in the air. In chemical properties gallium resembles aluminum, but the various compounds of gallium are of little practical importance. The spectrum of gallium shows two brilliant violet lines which afford the chief means of detecting the presence of the metal.

Germanium (atomic number 32). A grayish white, lustrous metal, found in the silver ore called argyrodite. While the metal has but little practical value, its discovery in 1886 was a great triumph of chemical science. Fifteen years earlier, in 1871, Mendelèev, on the basis of the "periodic law," not only prophesied the existence of such an element but also indicated with remarkable accuracy its chemical and physical properties.

Gold (atomic number 79). A heavy yellow metal, with a resplendent luster, found in many parts of the world, well known and highly prized from time immemorial. On account of its beautiful color, the ease with which it may be worked, the fact that it does not become tarnished or corroded in ordinary use, and its universal scarcity, gold is regarded as the most uniformly precious of the metals. For this reason, it has been adopted as the principal standard of value throughout the civilized world.

With the exception of platinum, iridium, and osmium, gold is the heaviest known substance. It is more than nineteen times as heavy as water and nearly twice as heavy as silver or lead. Gold is the most malleable of the metals and may be hammered into sheets less than 1/300000 of an inch in thickness. In such condition it is somewhat transparent and appears green by transmitted light. Gold surpasses all other metals in ductility and may be drawn into a wire less than 1/20000 of an inch in diameter, 900 miles of which would weigh scarcely a pound. Gold is also one of the best conductors of heat and electricity, being surpassed only by silver and copper.

Neither water nor the oxygen of the air acts upon gold in any way. No single acid except selenic has the power to dissolve it, though it dissolves readily in aqua regia, or in any solution in which chlorine, bromine, or iodine are set free. Gold also dissolves in either potassium or sodium cyanide, a property made use of in extracting the metal from its ores. Under certain conditions, gold is attacked by alkalies and nitrates, and yields to the powerful solvent action of selenium oxychloride.

While harder than lead, gold is softer than platinum, silver, copper, nickel, iron, or zinc. In fact, it is much too soft for most practical purposes, although only the purest form of the metal can be used for making gold leaf. To increase its hardness and wearing qualities, it is usually alloyed with copper or silver, or with both. Copper makes gold redder, and silver makes it lighter than its natural color. When alloyed with silver, gold forms the various "white alloys" used by jewelers. With mercury, gold readily forms a white, pasty amalgam. This property of amalgamation is the basis of one of the most effective processes in use for the recovery of fine particles of gold from placer sands or crushed ores.

The proportion of gold entering into the composition of an alloy is expressed either in "carats" or in "degrees of fineness." Pure gold is rated as 24 carats fine, and the carat value of any alloy is expressed in parts of 24. For example, 14-carat gold consists of 14 parts pure gold and 10 parts of some alloy. Fineness is stated in parts per thousand—for example, 925—or in the form of a decimal, 0.925. American, German, and Italian standard gold for coinage contains 9 parts of gold and 1 part of copper, and is therefore 21.6 carat or 900 fine. British standard gold contains 11 parts of gold and 1 part of copper, and hence is 22 carat or 916.6 fine.

Gold is employed for an immense number of useful and ornamental purposes, the most important of which are coinage, jewelry making, gilding, electroplating, and dentistry. The use of gold for rings, ornaments, and coins dates to remote antiquity. Goldbeating and also gilding by the use of extremely thin sheets of gold, as is now done in lettering signs and in stamping titles on books, are likewise very ancient arts. On Egyptian mummy cases, believed to be at least 5000 years old the gold leaf gilding still retains its brilliance and luster.

While gold occurs in minute amounts dissolved in sea water and in small deposits in nearly every country, it is obtained in paying quantities only in comparatively limited districts. South Africa leads the world in gold production, the great mines of the Witwatersrand, in the Transvaal, have sometimes yielded nearly half of the total output. In recent years Russia has attained second place, its production approaching close to that of South Africa. The United States and Canada rank next, with about equal output. Other important gold producing countries are Mexico, Australia, Rhodesia, and India.

From America's discovery in 1492 until 1936, 1190 million ounces of gold were produced, worth at today's valuation nearly 42 billion dollars. Over half this amount was mined since 1900, a result due largely to the discovery of rich fields and improved methods of treating low-grade ores. The gold in monetary stocks amounted in value to about 22 billion dollars in 1937. This gold would make a cube with a side of about 33 feet. The total gold mined since 1492 would make a cube with a side of about 41 feet. Important discoveries of gold include those in California in 1848; Australia, 1851; South Africa, 1868; Juneau, Alaska, 1880; Klondike, Yukon, 1896; Nome, Alaska, 1899; Porcupine, Ontario, 1910; Kirkland Lake, Ontario, 1911.

Gold is usually found in the metallic state, in the form of nuggets or smaller particles, diffused in sand and gravel or distributed through rocks and veins. Nuggets weighing from a few ounces to some hundreds of pounds have been found but most of the metal is obtained in the form of fine flakes called gold dust. Native gold commonly contains some silver. The metal is found also in combination with tellurium as "telluride ore," and often accompanies copper ores and iron pyrites. See *Coinage Alloys.*

Hafnium (atomic number 72). An element with chemical properties closely allied to zirconium and found in small quantities in zirconium ores. Hafnium was discovered in 1924 by Coster and Hevesy and is therefore one of the later elements to be found. Its valence is exclusively 4.

Helium (atomic number 2). A light, colorless, chemically inert gas, which was first detected in 1868 by means of a strange yellow line in the solar spectrum. As this line was not produced by any known terrestrial substance, it was interpreted by Lockyer and Frankland as the sign of an unknown element. This element was first recognized on the earth by Ramsay in 1895, and he showed later that it existed in air to the amount of four parts per million. Efforts to combine the gas with other elements have been without success.

Helium is given off when various minerals are heated, and is also found in the waters of certain springs. It is produced on a commercial scale from natural gas wells of Texas and Colorado by liquefying all other gases except the helium, which is collected separately. It may be prepared also from monazite sand. As helium is not inflammable and is less than one-seventh as heavy as air, it is considered the most valuable of all known gases for filling balloons and airships. When condensed, it forms a liquid about one-eighth as heavy as water, which boils within 4.5° C. of absolute zero, or about −451.5° F.

The most interesting fact concerning helium is that it is *actually created* as a *new* substance during the disintegration process of radioactivity. The *alpha rays,* given off by radium and other radioactive elements, consist of electrically charged atoms of helium moving at enormous velocities. As helium has an atomic weight of four, radon, the substance remaining when helium has been given off, has an atomic weight of four less than radium, the parent element. Helium and radon are the immediate products of the disintegration of radium. See *Radioactivity, Radium.*

Holmium (atomic number 67). One of the rare earth elements found in gadolinite. Its oxide is colorless and its salts are slightly yellow. Holmium, like the other rare earths, is trivalent.

Hydrogen (atomic number 1). A colorless, odorless, and tasteless gas. It was first found to be an element by Cavendish in 1766 although it had been produced but not recognized by Paracelsus in the 16th century. It is the lightest of all substances, being 14½ times lighter than air, and therefore useful for filling balloons. For practical purposes the lifting force of one cubic yard of hydrogen is considered to be about 1⅔ pounds.

Hydrogen is found free in natural gas, in volcanic vapors, in gases from the Stassfurt salt beds, and, in traces, as part of the atmosphere. Combined hydrogen makes up about 11 per cent of the weight of water. It is found in almost every organic substance and is the essential element in all acids.

When a mixture of hydrogen and oxygen is ignited, the two gases combine with explosive violence to form water. The name hydrogen, derived from the Greek, means "water-forming." Although the mixed gases explode, a stream of pure hydrogen burns quietly in air with a flame so intensely hot that it easily melts platinum. Used in combination with electric arcs, it will produce a temperature of over 8000° F. Hydrogen combines with many other elements, the compounds with carbon being especially important as the great group of *hydrocarbons*.

In the laboratory, hydrogen is usually prepared by the action of dilute hydrochloric acid on zinc. Commercially, it is produced by the action of sulphuric acid on scrap iron, and also by passing steam over red-hot iron turnings and filings. In the first case, the iron combines with the radical of the acid, forming a salt, and the hydrogen of the acid is set free. In the second case, the iron combines with the oxygen of the steam, releasing the hydrogen. During the World War, a process used by the army to prepare hydrogen for filling balloons utilized the actions of caustic potash on ferrosilicon. A very important process consists of decomposing slightly acidulated or alkaline water by means of the electric current. Two volumes of hydrogen are given off at the negative pole for every volume of oxygen produced at the positive electrode.

In addition to its use for filling balloons and for obtaining high temperatures, hydrogen is used for deodorizing oils, and for changing liquid fats to solid fats in the presence of finely divided metallic nickel or other substances, used as a catalyzer. It is also required for the synthetic production of ammonia by the Haber process. Artificial sapphires and rubies, almost indistinguishable from the genuine, are made by melting powdered aluminum oxide with a trace of coloring matter in the oxyhydrogen flame.

Under proper conditions, hydrogen may be condensed to a liquid and then to a solid which melts at −434° F. All other gases except helium become solid when passed through a tube surrounded by liquid hydrogen. It is the lightest known liquid, only 0.07 the density of water, and boils at 423° below zero F. See *Acids, Alkalies, Carbohydrates, Hydrocarbons.*

Indium (atomic number 49). A ductile, silver-white, lustrous, easily fusible metal, about as heavy as iron, which occurs in minute quantities in various zinc, lead, and manganese ores. Its most distinguishing property and the characteristic which led to its discovery by Reich and Richter in 1863, is the indigo-blue line displayed by its spectrum. Bearings for aircraft, truck, and marine engines are coated with indium to resist the corrosive action of acids in lubricants.

Iodine (atomic number 53). A soft, gray-black, crystalline solid having a metallic luster. It is one of the *halogen* group of elements, and was discovered in 1811 by Courtois in the ashes of seaweeds. The crystals, which are almost five times as heavy as water, melt at 236° F. and boil at about 380° F. The violet color of the vapor suggested the name iodine, which is taken from the Greek and means "violet-like". Iodine is soluble in about 6000 parts of water. It dissolves readily in chloroform, giving a violet solution, and in alcohol, forming a brown liquid.

Iodine is produced from the ashes of seaweeds and from the "mother liquors" remaining after the purification of Chile saltpeter. In the United States, it is obtained from brine found in oil wells. It forms with nitrogen and hydrogen the so-called *nitrogen iodide*, a violent explosive which is so sensitive when dry that it explodes if touched with a feather. The element is extensively used in medicine as tincture of iodine for treatment of swellings, and as a powerful germicide. Various compounds such as potassium iodide and ammonium iodide are used also in medicine. Large quantities of silver iodide are used in photography, and iodine is necessary for the preparation of certain artificial dyes. With starch, iodine gives a blue color, which is used as a delicate test for either substance. Iodine is present in the thyroid gland of the human body. A deficiency of it causes goiter.

Iridium (atomic number 77). A very hard, brittle, whitish metal, one of the heaviest substances known, found pure, or mixed with platinum and osmium. It is obtained chiefly in Russia, Borneo, and Brazil, and in small quantities in California. Compact iridium resists the action of acids, air, and moisture. It is used chiefly for tips of gold and stylographic pens and in constructing standards of measurement. The standard meter at Paris is a bar of platinum alloyed with 10 per cent of iridium.

Iron (atomic number 26). The most common, useful, and important of metals. While it occurs sparingly in nature in the metallic state, it is usually found in combination with oxygen (iron oxide) or carbon and oxygen (iron carbonate), the most important ores being red hematite, brown hematite, and magnetite, all widely distributed throughout the world, and especially abundant in the United States, England, and Germany. Small masses of nearly pure iron sometimes fall from the sky as meteorites. Iron in some form is a constituent of nearly all rocks, clays, and other earths, to which it usually imparts their red color. Small quantities of iron are found in most waters, in various parts of plants, and in the blood of animals.

When absolutely pure, iron is nearly as white as silver, is softer and more malleable than ordinary wrought iron, and takes a high, lustrous polish. It is the most tenacious of the ductile metals, and may be rolled into sheets so thin that their weight is less than that of sheets of paper of the same size. The finest grades of commercial iron are never entirely pure but contain small quantities of carbon, silicon, manganese, phosphorus, and sulphur. These substances, as well as other impurities, are present in much larger amounts in cast iron as it comes from the smelting furnaces. The numerous varieties of steel are forms of iron which usually contain considerably more carbon than wrought iron but always less carbon than cast iron.

Iron does not change in dry air, but in moist air it soon unites with the oxygen of the air, forming iron oxide, or rust. To prevent the formation of rust, articles made of iron are given a thin coating of tin, lead, nickel, copper, or zinc, or are otherwise protected by some form of waterproof paint or varnish.

Like most metals, iron combines freely with acids, forming a large variety of salts, some of which are very valuable. Among the most important of these are *green vitriol* or *copperas* (ferrous sulphate), used in dyeing and in making *prussian blue* and other pigments; ferric nitrate, used as a mordant in dyeing; ferrous oxalate, used in photography; and ferric chloride, widely used in medicine. Iron combines directly with chlorine, bromine, iodine, fluorine, sulphur, carbon, boron, silicon, phosphorus, and arsenic, producing a great diversity of compounds. Melted iron dissolves carbon, some of the carbon uniting to form iron carbide and some remaining uncombined as graphite. Iron also forms a vast number of invaluable alloys with other metals, particularly the different varieties of steel.

The most remarkable single property of iron is its magnetism, iron being the most powerfully magnetic substance known. Magnetite (lodestone), an ore rich in iron, is a natural magnet. Wrought iron becomes temporarily magnetic and steel is made permanently magnetic when brought into a magnetic field.

Next to bronze, iron ranks as the most anciently used of the common metals. Articles made of iron, found in the pyramids of Egypt, are believed to be more than 5000 years old. Throughout all history iron has played an important part in social and industrial development. At the present time, iron and steel form the foundation of the greatest manufacturing industries of the world. See *Cast Iron, Galvanized Iron, Steel, Wrought Iron.*

Krypton (atomic number 36). One of the inert gases belonging to the group with helium and neon. It occurs in the atmosphere to the extent of about one part per million. No compounds of krypton are known.

Lanthanum (atomic number 57). The first member of the rare earth series and one of the more abundant elements of this group. It is found in cerite, monazite, lanthanite, and gadolinite; the metal is gray in color and quite reactive. Lanthanum shows exclusively the trivalent state. In recent years this element has become important as a component of optical glass.

Lead (atomic number 82). A very heavy bluish gray metal, easily cut by a knife or scratched by the finger nail. It is highly malleable and ductile, being readily rolled into sheets or drawn into a wire, though its tenacity is small. Lead is a poor conductor of heat and electricity. By pressing freshly cut surfaces together, lead may be welded at ordinary temperatures. Under pressure and gentle heat it may be forced through openings and pipes. When exposed to the air, lead soon becomes covered with a thin film of rust or oxide which protects it from further corrosion.

While found sparingly in the metallic state, lead is obtained chiefly from ores, the most important being galena, or lead sulphide, in which it is usually associated with small quantities of silver, arsenic, copper, and various other metals. The United States contributes about a third of the world's output of lead, which comes chiefly from Missouri, Utah, and Idaho. Spain, Germany, Australia, Mexico, and Belgium are also important producers.

As it is but slightly acted upon by air or water and is highly resistant to most acids, except dilute nitric acid, lead is employed for a great variety of purposes, particularly in plumbing, for water pipes, gutters, cisterns, and tanks. Sheet lead is used for roofing, lining tea chests, and wrapping snuff. Lead enters into many valuable alloys. For example, with arsenic it forms *shot metal*; with tin, *pewter* and *solder*; and with antimony, *type metal*.

Many compounds of lead are exceedingly useful. Among these are *white lead* (basic lead carbonate), used in making white paint; *red lead* or *minium* (red lead oxide), used in making red paint and flint glass; *litharge* or *massicot* (lead monoxide), used in making oil varnishes; *sugar of lead* (lead acetate), used in calico printing; and *chrome yellow* (lead bichromate), used in making yellow paints. The carbonate iodide, and oleate of lead are much used in soothing plasters and ointments.

When taken into the human system, even in small quantities, various lead salts in time cause severe and sometimes fatal cases of poisoning, the most common form of which is painter's colic. Consequently, the glazing of cooking vessels with lead, the coloring of candy with lead chromate, or the drinking of water left standing in new lead pipes may result in dangerous illness. In 1926, after much controversy, the use of lead tetraethyl for producing an "antiknock" gasoline was permitted by the United States Public Health Service.

Lithium (atomic number 3). The lightest of the metals, about as heavy as ash or maple wood, widely distributed in nature but always in minute quantities. It occurs most abundantly in spodumene and a few other rare minerals but is present in sea water, various mineral springs, numerous plants, and in blood and milk. Lithium is soft, silvery white, and can be pressed into wire or welded at ordinary temperatures. It is classed with the alkali metals, and, like sodium and potassium, tarnishes quickly in air, decomposes water with great readiness, and dissolves in liquid ammonia. With acids it forms various salts widely used in fireworks on account of the splendid red color which they impart to flame.

Lutecium (atomic number 71). The last element in the rare earth group and sometimes known as cassiopeium. While it exhibits predominantly the trivalent state it is probable that the tetravalent state also exists.

Magnesium (atomic number 12). A soft, lustrous, silver-white metal, which can be hammered into sheets or drawn into a wire. It is one of the lightest of metals, being only two-thirds as heavy as aluminum. While never occurring free, magnesium is exceedingly abundant in nature as a constituent of various limestones and other common rocks. In the form of filings, wire, or ribbon, magnesium takes fire readily when heated and burns with a dazzling bluish white flame. Finely divided particles of the metal form flashlight powders. Increased use of the metal, especially in airplanes, has been assured by the development, since 1940, of a new welding process by which magnesium can be arc-welded in an atmosphere of helium.

When burning in air, magnesium unites with oxygen, producing the oxide, a tasteless white powder, called *magnesia*. This does not melt except at extremely high temperatures, and is extensively employed in making crucibles and fire bricks. Besides the oxide, there are many other valuable compounds of magnesium. Among the most important of these are the *sulphate*, known as *Epsom salts*, used for fertilizer, in dyeing, and in medicine; the carbonate called *magnesia alba*, also used in medicine; the *chloride*, employed in cotton spinning; and the *citrate* widely prescribed as a laxative. See *Magnalium*.

Manganese (atomic number 25). A very hard gray metal, with a gray luster, about as heavy as iron, which it resembles in many of its properties. Unlike iron, however, manganese is neither malleable nor magnetic. While not found free, manganese occurs very widely distributed in pyrolusite and other ores, especially these bearing iron, and, to a lesser extent, those containing silver, lead, or zinc. The chief source is Russia, but it is also produced in India, South Africa, the Gold Coast, Cuba, and Brazil, and in the United States. In the pure metallic state manganese has no uses, but it forms exceedingly valuable alloys with many metals, particularly copper, iron, zinc, tin, aluminum, lead, and magnesium. Iron containing 8 to 20 per cent manganese is the spiegeleisen used in making Bessemer steel. Iron with 20 to 80 per cent manganese is called *ferromanganese*. In the modern manufacture of iron and steel, the strength, toughness, and elasticity of which it greatly increases, manganese is practically indispensable. It is present in varying small percentages in nearly all commercial grades of iron and steel. These industries take much the larger part of the manganese ores, but some is used in making flint glass, in coloring pottery, tiles, and bricks, and in smelting the precious metals.

Manganese combines with various other elements, forming both salts and acids. *Potassium permanganate* is extensively used as an oxidizer, in bleaching, for purifying water, as a disinfectant, and to counteract the venom in the bites of poisonous snakes.

Mercury (atomic number 80). A silver-white liquid metal, nearly twice as heavy as iron, called also quicksilver. It becomes solid or freezes at −39.5° C., or about 39° F. below zero, and boils at 357° C., or 610° F. It occurs in small quantities in the metallic state but chiefly in the sulphide ore, *cinnabar*, containing over 86 per cent of the metal. Mercury was known in ancient times, and during the middle ages was the subject of much study by the alchemists.

Mercury dissolves and perhaps enters into combination with nearly all the metals, forming a group of alloys known as *amalgams*. It combines with oxygen to form two oxides, mercurous and mercuric, and with various acids to form a double series of mercurous and mercuric salts. Among the most important of these are the sulphide, known as cinnabar when native, and as the pigment *vermillion* when artificially prepared; *mercurous chloride*, or *calomel*; and *mercuric chloride* or *corrosive sublimate*. Metallic mercury and most of its salts are highly poisonous.

The numerous uses of mercury include making drugs, thermometers, barometers, and other scientific instruments, fulminate for explosive caps, and in separating gold and silver from their ores. It is used also in making neon lights and as a more efficient substitute for steam in boilers. Production comes chiefly from Italy and, in the United States, from California and Nevada. It is produced also in Spain.

Molybdenum (atomic number 42). A white metal, slightly heavier than iron, with a melting point higher than platinum, but lower than tungsten. It is softer than steel, somewhat malleable, and may be drawn into thin sheets or fine wire. Molybdenum occurs chiefly in the mineral molybdenite, from which the world's commercial supply of the metal is obtained. It is produced chiefly in the United States, Norway, Sweden, Canada, and Australia.

The most important use of molybdenum is in making special alloy steels, commonly in conjunction with manganese, chromium, nickel, cobalt, vanadium, or tungsten. These steels are used for the so-called self-hardening or high-speed machine tools; for propeller shafts, crank shafts, connecting rods, and similar purposes in the motor industry; for boiler plates, armor-piercing projectiles, gun linings, and armor plates.

Molybdenum is also employed in making various electric devices, such as targets in X-ray tubes and supports for incandescent lamp filaments, various reagents, dyes, glazes, and disinfectants. See *High-speed Steels*.

Neodymium (atomic number 60). A pale yellow metal about as heavy as iron, with properties similar to those of cerium. Neodymium occurs only in certain rare minerals, such as cerite and monazite, from which it is finally separated by electrolysis. It rapidly decomposes boiling water, and combines with various acids, forming rose-colored salts, none of which is of practical importance.

Neon (atomic number 10). One of the rare inert gases discovered by Ramsay and Travers in the atmosphere where it occurs to the extent of about 20 parts per million. No compounds of neon are known. Neon is most commonly known as the gas in discharge tubes known as neon lights which emit intense red light and are much used in advertising signs.

Neptunium (atomic number 93). The first of the synthetic transuranium elements, discovered by McMillan and Abelson in 1940. Although neptunium is not found in nature it is prepared as an important by-product in the atomic energy developments and its chemistry has been thoroughly studied. Like uranium and plutonium it has multiple oxidation states and is part of a transition group of elements including uranium and plutonium. The discovery of neptunium served the important function of breaking through the bounds of the classical periodic system making way for the discovery of plutonium, americium, and curium.

Nickel (atomic number 28). A very hard, silvery white, lustrous metal, somewhat heavier than iron, which it resembles in many properties. Nickel is ductile and malleable, possesses great tenacity, and, next to iron and cobalt, is the most magnetic substance known. Unlike iron, however, nickel does not rust or tarnish in ordinary air, a property which makes it one of the most useful of the more common metals.

Metallic nickel occurs in the form of grains in the bed of the Fraser river in British Columbia and is a common constituent of meteorites. Commercial nickel is obtained chiefly from niccolite and garnierite ores found in many countries. The main sources are the mines of the Sudbury district, Ontario, which produce more than three-fourths of the world's output, and the mines of Noumea, New Caledonia, which furnish most of the remainder. Only very small quantities of nickel are produced in the United States.

By far the most important uses of nickel are in electroplating and in making alloys. By reason of the high lustrous polish which it affords against rust, nickel is employed in electroplating an immense variety of useful articles. In alloys with other metals, nickel is used for coins and for innumerable other purposes. German silver, monel metal, invar, and platinite are examples of valuable nickel alloys. With iron it forms the so-called "nickel steel" alloys.

Nickel enters into many compounds, the most important of which commercially is nickel-ammonium sulphate, a bright green crystalline salt used in the process of nickel-plating. An interesting compound is nickel carbonyl, which is formed by placing the finely divided metal in a stream of carbon monoxide gas at a temperature of 85° F. The nickel absorbs the gas, forming a volatile liquid which freezes at 13° below zero and boils at 109°. When the vapor from the boiling liquid is heated to 145°, it explodes violently, depositing pure metallic nickel upon the walls of a tube containing it. This reaction is the basis of the Mond gas process for refining nickel. Pure nickel, finely divided, is used as a catalyzer in hydrogenation of fats. See *German Silver*, *Invar*, *Monel Metal*.

Nitrogen (atomic number 7). A colorless, tasteless elementary gas composing about 78 per cent of dry air, which was discovered by Karl Scheele and Benjamin Rutherford in 1772. As the gas did not support life or combustion it was called *azote*, meaning without life. This name is still used by the French; the English term, nitrogen, was given because the element is found in niter. Nitrogen is ordinarily an inert gas which can be made to combine directly with only a few elements. In 1911, an active modification of nitrogen which unites directly with phosphorus, mercury, and other elements was obtained by J. W. Strutt, Lord Rayleigh, who passed electric sparks through the ordinary gas. The change in condition is accompanied by phosphorescence. Nitrogen may be condensed to a liquid which boils at −321° F. and becomes solid at −346°F.

Compounds of nitrogen are great both in number and in importance. The niter beds of Chile and India furnish valuable fertilizer, as do ammonia and its salts. Nitric acid is necessary for explosives; cyanogen gas is a deadly poison; acetanilid and the alkaloids are of great use in medicine. The beautiful azo colors contain nitrogen, which is also an essential part of the proteins and therefore is found in every living thing. There are five different oxides of nitrogen.

Because of the great industrial need for compounds of nitrogen and the plentiful supply of the free element in air, various processes of *nitrogen fixation* have been developed. One of the earliest employed huge electric arcs, sometimes 20 feet long, to produce oxides of nitrogen, which combined with water to give nitric acid. In the *cyanamid process*, nitrogen is passed over heated calcium carbide, with which it combines. When cyanamid is treated with steam, ammonia is given off, which can be absorbed in sulphuric acid and used for fertilizer. In a somewhat similar manner, free nitrogen is combined with alkali to form cyanides. By the *Haber process*, a moderate temperature and a high pressure together with a catalyzer are employed to combine nitrogen and hydrogen directly into ammonia. *Vapor phase nitration* carries still further the scope of usefulness to which atmospheric nitrogen may be put. See *Nitric Acid*.

Various soil bacteria, especially those which grow in nodules on the roots of leguminous plants, such as clover, vetch, peas, and beans, are able to fix free nitrogen so that it ultimately becomes available as plant food. See *Air*, *Ammonia*, *Atmosphere*, *Cyanamid*, *Explosive*, *Fertilizers*.

Osmium (atomic number 76). A very hard, bluish white metal, with a violet luster, the heaviest substance known, infusible except in the electric arc. It occurs native, commonly alloyed with iridium or with platinum, which it resembles. It forms oxides and the so-called osmic acid, used for technical purposes, such as staining nervous tissue for microscopical examination. Points for gold pens are made of an alloy of osmium and iridium.

Oxygen (atomic number 8). The most abundant of all the elements, which, in its free state, occupies about 21 per cent of the volume of the air. Oxygen is a colorless, tasteless gas, discovered in 1774 by Priestley, who prepared it by heating red oxide of mercury. It may be condensed to a pale blue magnetic liquid which boils at −297° and freezes at 360° below zero F. Oxygen has been given the atomic weight of 16, and, chiefly because of its chemical activity, it is the standard by which the atomic weights of all other elements are compared.

Almost one-half of the earth's crust is oxygen. Water alone contains about eight-ninths of its weight of the element, and the human body more than 60 per cent.

Oxygen is absorbed by all animals in breathing. When passing through the lungs, the blood takes up about six per cent of its volume of oxygen, and gives off about eight per cent of carbon dioxide. It is the heat produced by the chemical action of changing oxygen to carbon dioxide that maintains the normal temperature of the body. When a ton of fuel is burned in a furnace, almost three tons of oxygen are required, and if this oxygen were not available in the air, no heat could be obtained from the coal or wood. Similarly, if a living animal can no longer obtain oxygen, it dies. There are, however, certain forms of bacteria known as anaerobes which develop normally only in the absence of free oxygen. In the presence of sunlight, green plants absorb carbon dioxide and give off free oxygen.

Rusting is due to the slow combination of iron with oxygen, in the presence of moisture and carbon dioxide. If both iron and air are perfectly dry, no rusting will occur. When a thin piece of iron, such as a watch spring, is heated red hot and plunged into a jar full of oxygen, the iron burns with a brilliant shower of sparks. The ash formed is magnetic oxide of iron.

In the laboratory, oxygen is easily prepared by heating a mixture of manganese dioxide with potassium chlorate. Commercially, it is produced simultaneously with hydrogen by electrolysis of water, or by liquefying of air and boiling off the more volatile nitrogen. The oxygen obtained is compressed and transported in heavy steel cylinders.

The principal use of oxygen is for welding and other high temperature operations with the oxyacetylene and oxyhydrogen flames. It is frequently used in medicine for treating certain diseases and cases of asphyxiation, in submarines, in airplanes at high altitudes, and as an aid to complete combustion. See *Acids*, *Air*, *Alkalies*, *Atmosphere*, *Ozone*, *Water*.

Palladium (atomic number 46). A white, lustrous, ductile, and malleable metal, about as heavy as lead. While occuring native, associated with platinum and other precious metals, the chief sources of palladium are the nickel ores of Sudbury, Ontario. It does not tarnish in the air, is resistant to most acids, and has the property of absorbing many times its own volume of hydrogen. Palladium is used in making scientifie instruments, in jewelry, and in dentistry.

Phosphorus (atomic number 15). A nonmetallic element discovered by the merchant alchemist, Brandt, in 1669. It does not occur free in nature, but, usually combined with calcium, is widely distributed in various phosphate minerals and beds of fossil bones. It is generally prepared in an electric furnace from a mixture of sand, coke, and calcium phosphate. Phosphorus distills from the furnace, is collected under water, and purified by filtering through canvas or chamois leather.

The element prepared in this manner is a yellowish white, intensely poisonous, waxlike solid, which is very soluble in carbon disulphide, melts at 111° F., and has a specific gravity of 1.83. It combines readily with oxygen, glows in the dark, and takes fire spontaneously at low temperatures. Under the influence of light or when heated in closed pots to about 500° F., white phosphorus gradually changes to a red allotropic modification having entirely different properties. Red phosphorus is a dull red powder 2.3 times as heavy as water. It does not phosphoresce, is not poisonous, does not dissolve in carbon disulphide, and does not catch fire in air below 460° F., although the common variety burns at about 105° F.

When common or white phosphorus burns, it forms a dense cloud of phosphorus pentoxide. For this reason, large amounts of the element were used in smoke bombs during the World War. A small amount, mixed with lard and flour or corn meal is made into rat poison. Large quantities were formerly employed for tipping matches, but because the poisonous element causes necrosis, or rotting of the jawbones, among the workers, it can no longer be lawfully used for this purpose. The rubbing surface on a box of safety matches usually contains red phosphorus.

Phosphorus forms three different oxides and a great variety of other compounds of which the most important are the phosphates.

Platinum (atomic number 78). A very heavy, steel-gray metal, somewhat harder than copper, very malleable, ductile, and tenacious, which does not rust or change in the air, cannot be melted by ordinary furnace heat, and resists the action of all common acids. By reason of these properties, platinum is exceedingly useful for many important purposes. Retorts, crucibles, stills, and blow-pipe tips for chemists' use are made of the metal, and it is very widely employed in the construction of electrical appliances. Large amounts are used in dentistry and, in recent years, for jewelry, especially in making watch cases, small ornamental pieces, and settings for diamonds and other precious stones.

Platinum is of great value in the manufacture of sulphuric and nitric acids for explosives, and in the construction of airplanes, electrical devices, and other war machinery. During the World War, the price of the metal rose to more than five times that of gold.

Platinum is the heaviest of the commonly known metals, being nearly three times as heavy as iron and about twice as heavy as lead. Like gold, platinum dissolves in a mixture of hydrochloric and nitric acids (aqua regia), and chlorine, bromine, and iodine attack it.

Various salts of platinum are useful in photography. At high temperatures platinum is attacked by sulphur, phosphorus, and arsenic. Finely divided platinum, called platinum black, has the remarkable property of absorbing 800 times its own bulk of oxygen. With gold and several other metals it forms alloys which melt much more easily than the metal itself. However, when alloyed with iridium, platinum gains greatly in hardness.

Platinum is found in the form of little scales, flakes, or grains, in sand or gravel deposits, often in company with gold, and commonly with one or two of the so-called platinum metals. Russia, which publishes no statistics, and Canada, producing 149,000 ounces in 1939, each contribute about 35 per cent of the world's supply; South Africa, 10 per cent; Colombia, where the metal was discovered about 1735, and Alaska, 9 per cent each. Minute quantities occur in many regions. It is estimated that up to 1914, Russia had contributed 95 per cent of the world's total stock of platinum, estimated at about five million ounces.

As compared with gold, the price of platinum has varied enormously. In 1788 Colombian platinum was sold for 14 cents an ounce. While Russia was coining platinum, 1828-45, it was valued at about $7 per ounce. In 1906 the price had advanced to $20 an ounce, and in 1913 to $45 an ounce. In 1918 the United States government established the price of platinum at $105 an ounce.

Plutonium (atomic number 94). This element, the most famous of the transuranium elements, was discovered by Seaborg, McMillan, Kennedy, and Wahl in 1940. It has also been found by Seaborg and M. L. Perlman in very minute quantities in uranium ores. Plutonium has been artificially produced in large quantities in the nuclear chain reactors or piles. It is reputed to be the active component of the atomic bombs used at Nagasaki and in the tests at Alamagordo, N. M., and Bikini. The large plants at Hanford, Washington, are devoted to its production.

The chemical properties of plutonium follow somewhat those of uranium and are characterized by valence states of 3, 4, 5, and 6.

Polonium (atomic number 84). A rare element discovered in the mineral pitchblende by Madame Marie Curie in 1898, and named in honor of Poland, her native land. Polonium is Element No. 84 in the periodic system. Many polonium isotopes are known, all are highly radioactive and would have disappeared long ago were they not constantly replenished by their long-lived uranium and thorium parents. The polonium isotope whose discovery gave its name to the element is a product of the radioactive series of which uranium 238 and radium are members. It is 4000 times more radioactive than radium, over a billion times more radioactive than uranium.

Potassium (atomic number 19). A silvery white, lustrous metal, lighter than water, brittle at 32° F. but wax-like and easily cut with a knife at 60°. It melts at 144°, boils at 1250°, and, with the exception of lithium, is the lightest of the metals.

While never occurring in the free metallic state, potassium in combination with other elements is an essential constituent of many important rocks and minerals, as, for example, feldspar, mica, carnallite, and niter. Potassium salts occur in sea water, in various springs, in the bodies of animals, and in plants. The most familiar source of potassium carbonate is wood ashes (potashes) which are still leached in some districts to obtain "lye" for soap making, whence the names potash and potassium. However, the bulk of the world's supply of potash is obtained from the famous mines in central Germany, notably those at Stassfurt. The metal is separated from its salts by electrolysis.

A freshly cut piece of potassium quickly rusts in the air, becoming immediately covered with a white film of the hydroxide. When thrown upon water, potassium floats upon the surface, where an intense chemical reaction takes place, with a brilliant display of heat and light. The metal decomposes the water, setting hydrogen free. By the great heat evolved, the liberated hydrogen gas is set on fire, burning with the beautiful violet-purple color which potassium salts impart to flame. By reason of its great avidity for oxygen, potassium can be kept only in fluids which contain no oxygen, such as benzol or petroleum.

Potassium belongs to the group of alkali metals. It unites with oxygen and hydrogen, forming a powerful hydroxide or base. Because it destroys the skin or other organic tissue with which it comes in contact, potassium hydroxide, called also potassium hydrate, is commonly known as "caustic potash."

Potassium enters into almost innumerable compounds, many of which are of great economic value. Among these are saltpeter, or niter (potassium nitrate); potash (potassium carbonate); cream of tartar (potassium bitartrate); sal polychrest (potassium sulphate); muriate of potash (potassium chloride), used as a fertilizer; potash alum (potassium-aluminum sulphate); potassium bichromate, used in photography and dye making; and potassium cyanide, a powerful poison, used in metallurgy.

Various potassium salts are useful drugs, such as potassium bromide, potassium iodide, potassium chlorate, potassium permanganate, and potassium hypophosphite. Seidlitz powder contains potassium tartrate, and Rochelle salt is potassium-sodium tartrate. Large crystals of Rochelle salt, which are piezo electric, were used during the World War in the production of so-called "supersound," by means of which submarines were located even when resting quietly on the ocean bottom.

Praseodymium (atomic number 59). Like the other rare earth elements the principal valence state is three, but praseodymium is one of the few rare earth elements that definitely possess one or more higher states. The predominant colors of the salts are green and yellow-green.

Protactinium (atomic number 91). This radioactive element was discovered in 1918 by Hahn and Meitner and is the immediate transformation product of uranium 235 and the parent of actinium. Chemically, protactinium displays a pentavalent oxidation state. It is characterized by its low solubility in aqueous solutions and the readiness with which it adsorbs on solids.

Radium (atomic number 88). The discovery of this remarkable element by Pierre and Marie Curie was one of the outstanding achievements of these pioneers in radioactivity. As a chemical entity radium is a reactive metal belonging to the same family as the non-radioactive elements calcium, strontium, and barium. One of the steps in its separation from the ore is the precipitation of insoluble radium sulfate along with barium sulfate. The radium and barium are then separated by fractional crystallization of certain of their salts.

With respect to its radioactive properties radium has played an important role in the study of radioactivity and in cancer therapy. Radium itself gives off an alpha-particle from its nucleus and thereby is transformed into an element lower by two atomic numbers. This results from the fact that an alpha-particle is actually a helium ion; consequently its emission removes two positive charges from the nucleus which allows the nucleus to hold two less electrons and results in a lower element. The so-called "daughter" of radium is the element radon or niton which belongs to the rare gas family of elements. Radon is more radioactive than radium and in turn decays to another lower element. In all, a series of nine transformations carry radium down until the series stops with the formation of an inactive isotope of lead. Some of the intermediate products do not decay by alpha-particle emission but give off beta-particles which have been shown to be electrons of nuclear origin. Both alpha- and beta-particle emitters, in general, also produce *gamma-rays.* These are penetrating electromagnetic radiation similar to ordinary visible light and X-rays but of shorter wave length and consequently higher energy. It is because these rays can be injurious to living organisms that radium and many other radioactive substances must be kept in thick lead containers.

It is a property of nuclear transformations such as radioactive decay that no means at our disposal can alter the rate of the disintegrations. Radium will continue to produce radon and, in turn, its other descendants no matter what conditions of temperature or pressure are imposed or irrespective of what the chemical state of radium may be. The constant regeneration of these radioactive substances accounts for their presence in nature even though they are short-lived. Radium itself decays with a *half-period* of a little over 1600 years; that is, if one were to start with any given amount of radium only half would be present as radium after 1600 years. After another similar period one-half of the remainder would have been transformed via the decay chain to stable lead. With this half-period radium would have long since disappeared through geological time but it is constantly regenerated through the decay of uranium which has a *half-period* of several billions of years.

The alpha-particles of radium and indeed the emissions of almost all radioactive substances are expelled from the nucleus with great velocity and energy. These high energy particles and rays have the property of ripping electrons off from atoms of any substance which they traverse and these electrons can be collected and measured as an electric current by means of suitable devices. Because of the high energy of a nuclear particle the current set up by a single particle can be measured. A device usually used for counting beta-particles and gamma-rays is the Geiger-Muller counter. One gram of radium gives off 37 billion alpha-particles in one second. Since considerably less than one alpha-particle per second can be readily detected it is obvious that amounts of radium far below that which can be seen are measurable. The ability to measure accurately submicroscopic quantities of radioactive substances causes this type of measurement to be the most sensitive known to the chemist.

Although radiation will injure all living tissue if used indiscriminately, it apparently is most effective on tumorous tissue. The judicious application of radium has been one of the most effective means known for destroying cancer. In practice, not radium but radon is used for this purpose. A radon gas is pumped, when needed, into tiny gold capsules which can be inserted locally into the tumor. Since the radon decays with a half-period of 3.6 days discrete irradiations can be given periodically.

A curious property of an alpha-particle is that a tiny luminous flash is seen when it impinges upon certain substances such as zinc sulphide. The aggregate of many alpha-particles causes a luminescence. Luminous paints of this type are used for a variety of special purposes, the most common of which is to render watch dials visible in the dark.

Radium is found in uranium ores, notably pitchblende. It requires several millions of parts of pitchblende to yield one part of radium. The separation of such small quantities is responsible for the high price of radium. The richest sources of pitchblende are the Great Bear Lake region in Canada and the Belgian Congo. Pitchblende is found in other places, however, and carnotite ores of Utah and Colorado are also moderately rich in uranium and radium. See *Radioactivity, Polonium, Niton, Luminous Paint.*

Radon (atomic number 86). A gaseous element, detected in 1900 by Dorn, who called it radium emanation because it is generated by the element radium. In 1910 its elemental nature was proved by Ramsay and Gray. Under pressure, radon becomes a liquid at ordinary temperatures. When pressed into a glass tube with an exceedingly fine bore, and sufficiently cooled, radon becomes solidified into a microscopical rod of ice-like material. Although this minute rod is too small to be seen with the unaided eye, it produces a brilliant pink light in the tube, whence its former name niton, from the Latin *nitere*, "to shine."

When an atom of radium gives off an atom of helium, the atom of radium is no longer radium but thereby has become an entirely new element, the intensely radioactive gas radon. Like helium and argon, radon is chemically inert, forming no salts or other compounds. Its existence, too, is only temporary. Like radium, radon has a definite "half period" of decay, which, however, is comparatively very brief. In 4 days only half remains, and half has changed into something else. In 8 days a fourth of it remains, in 12 days an eighth, and so on until at the end of a month practically all has disappeared.

To radon is largely due the remarkable heating effect of radium. In comparison with its weight, radon gives off a million times more energy than is released by the most violent chemical reaction. It is computed that a pound of radon, immediately after being separated from radium, would emit energy equivalent to 10,000 horsepower.

Radon is constantly produced by any compound of radium and is readily obtained from any solution of a radium salt. On account of its greater convenience, radon is widely used in medicine instead of radium itself. See *Radioactivity*.

Rhenium (atomic number 75). Rhenium is a rare noble metal which displays some of the properties of its homologue, manganese. The metallic state is the most stable but all valence states from −1 to 7 have been reported. The most common series of compounds of rhenium are the perrhenates. The metal does not melt until 3400° C. and an oxidizing acid, such as nitric acid is required to dissolve it. It has been used as a catalyst in the conversion of alcohols to aldehydes and ketones.

Rhodium (atomic number 45). A very hard, difficultly fusible metal, slightly heavier than lead, found in small quantities in platinum and gold ores. An alloy of platinum containing about 18 per cent rhodium is used in making thermo-electric pyrometers.

Rubidium (atomic number 37). An alkali metal, resembling sodium and potassium, found in minute quantities in certain minerals and mineral springs, in seaweed, tobacco, tea, and sugar beets. It is soft and waxy, silver-white, slightly more than half as heavy as aluminum, and melts at 38.5° C., or 101.3° F. Like potassium, rubidium decomposes water with evolution of hydrogen gas which takes fire on account of the heat evolved. The metal and its compounds show two characteristic dark red lines in the blue portion of the spectrum.

Ruthenium (atomic number 44). A rare, whitish gray metal of the platinum group, about as heavy as lead, found in small quantities in platinum ores. Neither the metal nor any of its compounds is of commercial importance.

Samarium (atomic number 62). One of the rare earth elements which displays a valence state of two as well as three. The salts of samarium are green or pink.

Scandium (atomic number 21). A rare metallic element, found in gadolinite and other minerals, chiefly interesting because its existence and properties were foretold by Mendeleev, on the basis of the periodic law, ten years in advance of its actual discovery in 1879.

Selenium (atomic number 34). A nonmetallic element somewhat similar to sulphur, discovered in the dust found in the flues of sulphuric acid factories. It occurs free in small amounts, usually together with sulphur, and in combination with many metals. It is obtained chiefly as a by-product in the electrolytic refining of copper. The principal forms of selenium are a red amorphous powder and a gray variety obtained by slowly cooling the melted element.

The electrical conductivity of the gray form increases under exposure to light. This property is the basis of *selenium cells*, which are used for various purposes, including the measurement of changes in the light from the stars. Selenic acid is notable because it dissolves gold. Selenium oxychloride has been shown to be a valuable solvent for many substances.

Silicon (atomic number 14). A nonmetallic element which, in its many compounds, makes up about one-fourth of the earth's crust. After oxygen, it is the most plentiful of the elements, but, unlike oxygen, it is found only in combination.

Silicon is usually prepared in the electric furnace by heating pure sand with an amount of coke insufficient to form carborundum. It exists chiefly as a brown amorphous powder and as gray-black crystals which are sometimes used for the detection of signals in wireless telegraphy. The chief use for silicon is in the production of ferrosilicon alloys. Cast-iron apparatus employed in the chemical industries usually contains a large amount of silicon and is almost unaffected by acids which would quickly ruin ordinary iron or steel. Silicon forms compounds with all of the halogens except iodine, and with sulphur, nitrogen, carbon, oxygen, and several other elements.

Silver (atomic number 47). A brilliant white metal, known and used since the dawn of history. Like gold and platinum, it is ranked among the "precious metals." Silver is extremely malleable and ductile, has great tenacity, and is the best conductor of heat and electricity known. At ordinary temperatures it does not rust or oxidize, nor is it affected by any atmospheric agent, except sulphur compounds, which quickly tarnish its surface. Silver is slightly lighter than lead, or a little more than half as heavy as gold. It takes a high polish and is a powerful reflector of light, whence its use among ancient peoples for mirrors.

Silver occurs native, sometimes in masses of several hundred pounds of nearly pure metal, but chiefly in ores, such as argentite, stephanite, and cerargyrite, in combination with sulphur, arsenic, chlorine, antimony, or tellurium, and also in association with copper and lead. While silver occurs in every continent, it is most abundant along the Rocky Mountain-Andes systems of the Americas. The mines of the United States, Canada, Mexico, and Peru are the richest known, yielding about five-sixths of the world's output of silver, those of the United States and Mexico far surpassing the combined production of all other countries.

In the United States, Utah, Montana, Idaho, Nevada, Arizona, and Colorado usually contribute nine-tenths of the total production of the country. Outside of the Americas, Germany, Spain, Japan, and Australia are leading producers of silver. However, the output of any of these countries is small when compared with that of single rich districts in the New World. For example, the mines near Cobalt, Ontario, yield about as much silver as those of Europe, Asia, Africa, and Australia combined.

The uses of silver are exceedingly important and world wide. In most countries a large part of the coinage consists of silver. Industrially, silver is employed in making various kinds of tableware and an immense number of decorative articles. It is used also for silver plating, for silvering mirrors, and in many valuable alloys. The standard United States coin consists of 9 parts of silver to which 1 part of copper is added to give greater hardness. Articles made entirely of silver of about the same fineness as standard coins are called "solid silver."

Many of the compounds of silver are exceedingly valuable. The whole art of photography is based upon the fact that certain salts of silver (the chloride, bromide, and iodide) are sensitive to the action of light. Silver nitrate, commonly called *lunar caustic*, is used in dyeing hair and in making indelible ink. It is used also in medicine, as in argyrol and various other compounds of silver and albumen. See *Coinage Alloys, Sterling Silver.*

Sodium (atomic number 11). A silvery white metal, lighter than water, which is hard at zero Fahrenheit, becomes waxlike at ordinary temperatures, and melts at 207°. While exceedingly abundant in nature, sodium is never found in the metallic state but always in combination with other elements. Upon exposure to the air, sodium unites with oxygen and moisture, forming a white powder, sodium hydroxide.

If a piece of sodium is thrown into water, it will float on the surface, decomposing the water and setting hydrogen gas free. In case the water is hot, the hydrogen will take fire, burning with a yellow flame. Sodium cannot be preserved if permitted to come in contact with air or water, but must be kept in sealed containers. Metallic sodium is prepared by various processes which take away the oxygen from soda, leaving the metal free.

Sodium unites with most acids, forming many salts which are of great importance. Among the most valuable are common salt (*sodium chloride*), Glauber's salt (*sodium sulphate*), washing soda (*sodium carbonate*), baking soda (*sodium bicarbonate*), Chile saltpeter (*sodium nitrate*), "water glass" (*sodium silicate*), borax (*sodium tetraborate*), and "hypo" (*sodium thiosulphate*), used in photography.

Sodium belongs to the group of so-called alkali metals, which unite with oxygen and hydrogen to form hydroxides or bases. Sodium hydroxide, called also sodium hydrate, "caustic soda," or "soda lye," is a powerful alkali, used in large quantities in making soap, in mercerizing cotton, and for many other useful purposes. As a rule, the properties of sodium salts closely resemble those of potassium salts. For many purposes, a salt of either metal may be substituted for the corresponding salt of the other. All the volatile salts of sodium impart a characteristic yellow color to flame, affording an unfailing test for the presence of the metal, even in the minutest quantities. See *Glauber's Salt, Hypo, Salt.*

Strontium (atomic number 38). A malleable, ductile, yellow metal, slightly lighter than aluminum. Strontium oxidizes or rusts quickly in the air, and, when heated, burns with a brilliant red flame. It is found in various minerals, particularly strontianite, celestite, and brewsterite; in mineral springs; and in certain plants. Strontium forms various salts, some of which are of practical value. The oxide is much used in beet-sugar making; the nitrate finds employment in fireworks because of the red color with which it burns.

Sulphur (atomic number 16). A solid, nonmetallic element known since ancient times. It is found free in many places, especially in volcanic regions either active or ancient, where it occurs mixed with pumice, gypsum, and other substances.

It is usually separated from such impurities by heating until the sulphur melts, when it can be drawn off and cooled in round molds, forming ordinary *roll sulphur.* A purer form is obtained by boiling the crude material and cooling the vapors, which condense into a crystalline powder known as flowers of sulphur. The flowers are often remelted and cast as pure roll sulphur.

Ordinary sulphur is a yellow, tasteless, and odorless solid, insoluble in water and alcohol but soluble in carbon disulphide. It forms rhombic crystals, has a specific gravity of 2.06, melts at 235° F., and burns easily, with a blue flame, to form the suffocating gas, sulphur dioxide. It is the odor of the gas which is often referred to as the smell of sulphur. Sulphur is a poor conductor of heat and electricity. As a mineral or stone that burns, it received the common name of *brimstone.* Above 205° F. and below 246°, rhombic sulphur gradually changes to another variety which forms long, almost colorless, monoclinic crystals that melt at 247° F. and are 1.96 times as heavy as water. When either type is heated, it melts to a pale yellow, mobile liquid which, at about 320° F., suddenly becomes dark, and so thick that it will not spill if the container is inverted. With further heating, the gummy mass again becomes liquid and boils at 832°F.

When sulphur is boiled with milk of lime, and acid is added to the resulting solution, a fine, almost white powder called *precipitated sulphur* is deposited. Another form known as *colloidal sulphur* gives a solution, or rather a colloidal suspension, in water. When boiling sulphur is poured into cold water, it assumes a semi-fluid form known as *plastic sulphur*, which becomes hard after a few days. The hardened product then consists of a mixture of the ordinary form with *amorphous sulphur*, which is not soluble in carbon disulphide.

The *sulphides*, or direct compounds of sulphur with a metal, form numerous minerals. Examples are: Cinnabar or mercury sulphide; galena, a sulphide of lead; pyrites or iron sulphide; stibnite or antimony sulphide; realgar and orpiment, sulphides of arsenic; sphalerite or zinc sulphide. Gysum is representative of the large group of sulphates. Many organic compounds, such as the oils of mustard and garlic, hair, wool, and white of egg, contain sulphur. Combined with hydrogen, it forms hydrogen sulphide, a poisonous, evil smelling gas. This gas, which is the chief cause of the odor of rotten eggs, is extensively used in chemical analysis. Four oxides of sulphur are known, the most important being sulphur dioxide, and sulphur trioxide which combines with water to produce sulphuric acid. Sulphur may be found in compounds with almost all of the other elements.

Sicily was for many years the chief source of sulphur, but the United States now produces about 85 per cent of the world's supply, chiefly from mines in Texas, Louisiana, Nevada, and Utah.

The American deposits, which occur in thick beds hundreds of feet below the surface, are mined by a process patented by Herman Frasch in 1890. A series of five pipes, one within the other, the largest about 17 inches, and the smallest one inch, in diameter, are driven to the proper depth. Superheated water is forced down into the sulphur, which melts, collects in pools, and is forced to the surface by compressed air sent down through the smallest pipe. The melted sulphur is run into bins, where it cools, forming huge blocks 50 or more feet high from which the material is removed by blasting. This sulphur is often more than 99.9 per cent pure.

Sulphur is burned in enormous quantities for the preparation of sulphur dioxide, which is used as a disinfectant, as an active bleaching agent, as a preservative of dried fruits, and for manufacturing sulphuric acid. Gunpowder, fireworks, paper manufacturing, and the fertilizer industry also require large amounts of sulphur. It is necessary for vulcanizing rubber and is employed extensively in medicine for skin diseases. Powdered sulphur is a valuable fungicide.

Tantalum (atomic number 73). A rare metal found in tantalite and other minerals, almost invariably in association with columbium. It is obtained chiefly in Australia, though some occurs in the Black Hills of South Dakota. It is a black substance with a metallic luster, soluble in hydrofluoric acid but not acted upon by hydrochloric, sulphuric, or nitric acid, or even by aqua regia, with a remarkable power of absorbing gases; and a one-way electrode. Tantalum is used principally in electronic tubes and carbide tools and as a catalyst in producing butadiene synthetic rubber.

Tellurium (atomic number 52). A silver-white, brittle, semimetallic element. It is nearly as heavy as iron and does not tarnish upon exposure to air. While sometimes occurring free, tellurium is usually found associated with gold, silver, lead, and bismuth, chiefly in Austria and the United States. In many properties tellurium resembles sulphur. Tellurium toughens lead and is now used for chromium in the development of wear-resisting surfaces on gears, wheels, and other cast-iron products. Additions of tellurium and selenium improve the machinability of stainless steels and copper alloys.

Technetium (element 43). This element, not found in nature, bears the distinction of being the first artificial element produced. It was discovered in 1937 by Perrier and Segré by bombarding molybdenum with deuterons. It can now be produced in weighable quantities since it occurs as one of the products of uranium fission. In its chemical properties, technetium most resembles manganese and rhenium.

Terbium (atomic number 65). A rare earth element whose compounds are predominantly colorless. The characteristic valence state is three.

Thallium (atomic number 81). A brilliant, silver-white metal which tarnishes very rapidly in the air and is softer than lead. Thallium occurs in the mineral crooksite and in various natural sulphide ores of iron, copper, zinc, bismuth, and other metals. The spectrum of thallium shows a characteristic green line, and thallium salts impart a green color to a nonluminous flame. Most of the thallium supply is consumed in the form of sulphate, an odorless, tasteless poison used in rodent and ant control.

Thorium (atomic number 90). Occurs along with rare earth elements in the mineral monozite which is found in North Carolina, Norway, Brazil, and India. Thorium is weakly radioactive and is the parent substance of the thorium radioactive series some members of which are highly radioactive. Thorium along with uranium is of importance in the release of atomic energy. Thorium exhibits a valence state of four almost exclusively.

Thullium (atomic number 69). One of the rare earth elements. The valence of thullium in its compounds is three and the predominant colors of the compounds are white and light green.

Tin (atomic number 50). A bluish-white, ductile metal, with a brilliant luster, about as heavy as iron, somewhat harder than lead but softer than gold. Tin is very malleable and may be beaten into sheets only 1/2000 of an inch in thickness. It is very flexible, emitting while bending a peculiar creaking sound called the "cry" of tin. While it may be drawn into wire, its tenacity is much inferior to most common metals. Tin melts at about 460° F., and, if cooled slowly, the metal may be obtained in crystallized form. At a temperature of 54° F. below zero, tin becomes brittle and loses many of its characteristic properties.

On account of its brightness and the fact that it does not tarnish or rust in ordinary air, tin is very extensively employed as a covering or plate for other metals. Its most important industrial use is in coating thin iron plates for tinware. Copper and brass are similarly coated with tin; as, for example, pins, cooking vessels, and bathtubs. Tin is used in making tin foil and in forming many valuable alloys, the chief of which are those made with copper, including various bronzes, and those made with lead, such as britannia metal, type metal, pewter, and solder.

The Phœnicians made utensils of bronze at least as early as 1000 B.C., obtaining much of the tin for its production from the famous mines of Cornwall, England, which were later worked in turn by the Greeks and by the Romans. Commercial tin is obtained from a single kind of ore, called tinstone or cassiterite, found chiefly in the East Indies, Bolivia, Siam, China, Australia, Nigeria, and England. Although mining only insignificant amounts of tin, the United States consumes more than half of the world's output of the metal. See *Bronze, Pewter*.

Titanium (atomic number 22). A steel-like metal, somewhat more than half as heavy as iron, found in various mineral ores, particularly in Scandinavia. When heated in the air, titanium burns to the oxide with great brilliancy. At high temperature in the electric furnace, titanium unites directly with nitrogen, forming a bronze-yellow nitride, which is very nearly if not quite as hard as the diamond. When used as an alloy, titanium imparts hardness and toughness to steel and gives a fine, brilliant luster of silver. Various compounds of titanium are employed in dyeing and making paints for the protection of iron from the air. Electrodes for arc lights, composed of titanium carbide, give twice as much light as those made of carbon.

Tungsten (atomic number 74). A bright, steel-gray metal, which occurs in wolframite, scheelite, and other minerals, usually associated with tin, found in veins and placer deposits in Burma, Portugal, and the western United States, particularly in Nevada, Colorado, and California. Most of the world's supply, however, comes from China. Pure tungsten is nearly as heavy as gold, very resistant to acids, and, although hard enough to scratch glass, is somewhat malleable. It has an exceedingly high melting point, about 3400° C., or 6150° F.

When alloyed with other metals such as iron and aluminum, tungsten greatly increases their hardness and tenacity. Some of the best high-speed tool steels are tungsten alloys. Except the limited use of various carbonized fibers, tungsten wire is now practically the only material employed in making incandescent electric lamp filaments. *Partinium*, a light and tough alloy of tungsten and aluminum, enters extensively into automobile construction.

Uranium (atomic number 92). A hard, nickel-like, malleable metal, almost as heavy as gold, found only in combination with other elements in a few rare minerals. It occurs chiefly in ores from which radium is extracted. Uranium melts at bright red heat, and acts both as an acid-forming and as a base-forming element, yielding numerous compounds. Of these, sodium uranate, known as *uranium yellow*, is used in making fluorescent glass and in decorating porcelain.

Uranium is the element of highest atomic weight found in nature and is naturally radioactive. It is the parent substance of radium which occurs in all uranium ores. It is from one of these ores, pitchblende, that Pierre and Marie Curie extracted the first samples of radium and polonium.

Uranium has recently attained the position of being the most sought after element as it is the basic substance required for atomic energy. One of its isotopes of mass 235 is a direct source of atomic energy while another isotope of mass 238 is the substance transformed by neutrons into plutonium, element 94.

Vanadium (atomic number 23). A white metal, about two-thirds as heavy as iron, found very widely distributed but in small quantities, particularly in iron, copper, and lead ores. In the United States it occurs in mineral deposits in Colorado, Utah, and elsewhere. Peru produces most of the world's supply. Vanadium forms various compounds, the most important of which is vanadic acid. Some vanadium salts are very useful in the manufacture of aniline black, vanadium inks, mordants for dyeing, and photographic developers. The most important use of vanadium is as an alloy with steel. The addition of vanadium to chrome steel and various other steels greatly increases their elasticity and tensile strength, making them especially valuable for automobile construction.

Xenon (atomic number 54). The heaviest of the rare gases aside from the radioactive element, radon. Xenon occurs in the atmosphere in very minute concentration and is over four times as heavy as air. It forms no compounds with other elements.

Ytterbium (atomic number 70). One of the heaviest of the rare earth group of metals. Its salts are trivalent and are either white or green in color.

Yttrium (atomic number 39). A trivalent element which has much the same properties as the rare earth group of elements but is lighter in atomic weight. It is found in the same minerals as the rare earth elements and is separated from them with difficulty. The compounds of yttrium are white or pink in color.

Zinc (atomic number 30). A bluish white metal, with a bright luster, about as heavy as iron, widely found in various ores, such as zincite, franklinite, calamine, and zinc blende. Commercial zinc, commonly known as spelter, is a coarse, flaky metal, rather hard to file, and usually containing impurities, chiefly lead and iron. After being freshly melted, zinc when bent gives forth a peculiar creaking sound similar to the "cry" of tin. At ordinary temperatures zinc is brittle, but, when heated to between 200° and 300° F., it can be rolled into sheets or drawn into wire. In dry air zinc does not tarnish, but in moist air it soon becomes covered with a thin film of grayish rust (zinc carbonate) which effectively protects the metal itself from further corrosion. This peculiar property gives zinc its great value as a protective coating for iron and steel.

As one of the most useful of the common metals, zinc is employed for an immense number of industrial purposes, such as making brass, German silver, Zamak, and numerous other alloys; for galvanizing sheet iron and wire; for electric batteries; and for die-castings. Of the numerous compounds of zinc, some of the most important are *zinc oxide*, known as *zinc white*, widely used in making paint and for increasing the wearing quality of rubber products; *zinc chloride*, used as a preservative and disinfectant; and *zinc sulphate*, or *white vitriol*, used in dyeing, calico printing, and as a dryer in varnishes.

Although the Romans made brass by fusing certain zinc ores with copper, zinc, as a pure metal, was unknown until modern times. During recent years the United States has been the leading producer of zinc, the chief zinc producing mines being in Oklahoma, Kansas, New Jersey, and Montana. Other producing countries are Belgium, Germany, and Canada. See *Brass, Spelter*.

Zirconium (atomic number 40). A metallic element found in combination with silica in zircon and in various rare minerals, chiefly in Brazil. Zirconium is obtained either in the form of a black powder or as a gray, lustrous, crystalline solid. The latter is nearly as heavy as cast iron, which it somewhat resembles. Zirconium is used chiefly in ceramics, as an opacifier. It is also a constituent of refractories, electrical and chemical porcelains, and glasses resistant to heat and chemicals. See *Cooperite*.

EVERYDAY CHEMICALS

Acetates (*ăs'ē-tāts*). The salts and esters of acetic acid. The salts are generally formed by the action of the acid upon metallic carbonates and hydroxides. Iron acetate is usually produced by the direct action of acetic acid on iron filings.

Solutions of *aluminum acetate,* known as *red liquor,* and *iron acetate,* or *black liquor,* are valuable mordants in the dye industries. Lead acetate, called also *sugar of lead,* as well as ammonium and potassium acetates are employed in medicine. Verdigris, a basic acetate of copper, is used to prepare Paris green.

Many of the esters, or combinations of acetic acid with alcohols, have pleasant odors and are extensively employed in perfumery. *Benzyl acetate* imparts the principal odor to jasmine; linalyl acetate is found in the perfume of orange flowers, gardenia, ilang ilang, and lavender. *Amyl acetate,* or *banana oil,* a valuable solvent, is frequently used to dissolve guncotton and *cellulose acetate.* Such solutions form the airplane *dopes* applied to the wings of airplanes as a protective varnish. Cellulose acetate is formed into many substances similar to celluloid but noninflammable.

Acetic Acid. (CH_3COOH) The sour principle of vinegar, an organic acid composed of carbon, hydrogen, and oxygen. Acetic acid occurs sparingly in nature; as, for example, in sweat and in the juices of various plants. It is formed by the acetic fermentation (oxidation) of ordinary alcohol in making vinegar from cider or wine. Crude commercial acetic acid, known as *pyroligneous acid,* is obtained as one of the products from the destructive distillation of hard wood. Any material which may be fermented to alcohol may serve as a source of acetic acid.

The pure anhydrous acid is called *glacial acetic acid* because below 62° F. it is a white crystalline solid. At a higher temperature it is a colorless liquid with a very pungent odor. In concentrated form, acetic acid burns the skin although it is a comparatively weak acid. It is extensively used in making white lead, acetone, and various acetates, among which are sugar of lead and verdigris; in making certain dyes; and in dyeing silk and wool. Acetic acid is especially important for the manufacture of amyl acetate and cellulose acetate, used for making noninflammable picture films and airplane dopes. Diluted acetic acid is often sold as wood vinegar. See *Vinegar.*

Acetone (*ăs' ē-tōn*). (CH_3COCH_3) A colorless, volatile liquid having a peculiar odor and taste. It is used for preparing chloroform and iodoform, and as a solvent for many resins, gums, waxes, and other organic materials; as, for example, in the process of making smokeless powder. Acetone dissolves large volumes of acetylene gas. Portable tanks containing acetylene so dissolved are used in various lighting devices and for the acetylene torch.

Acetylene. (CH_2CH_2) A colorless gas, composed of carbon and hydrogen, widely used as an illuminant, particularly for house lighting and in portable lamps. When ignited in but little air, acetylene burns with a smoky flame, but, when thin sheets of the gas are ignited in an abundance of air in specially designed burners, it forms an intensely brilliant flame, producing a light very similar to sunlight.

For commercial purposes, the gas is made by treating calcium carbide with water,—the resulting products being acetylene and slaked lime. When mixed with air or oxygen, or if kept under a pressure of more than two atmospheres, acetylene becomes dangerously explosive. It is, however, one of the best illuminants, and, provided reasonable precautions are observed, the risk involved in storing and handling it is slight.

In making nonexplosive, portable tanks of acetylene, advantage is taken of the great solubility of the gas in acetone. Such tanks contain acetone absorbed in some porous material. About 100 volumes of the gas will dissolve in the acetone, and, in this form, may be transported without danger. When acetylene is burned with pure oxygen, the resulting blast has one of the highest temperatures of any known flame, the theoretical maximum being 7878° F. It is used industrially to cut through steel beams and plates. Properly applied, the flame divides steel or other hard metals almost as smoothly and quickly as a saw cuts through soft wood. The oxyacetylene torch is also extensively used for *welding* or fusing pieces of metal.

Acetylene may be used as the starting point for the chemical production of alcohol. It combines with iodine to form di-iodoform, an antiseptic similar to iodoform but without its unpleasant odor.

Albumin (*ăl-bū'mĭn*). A group of organic substances of which white of egg is the best-known example. These substances are composed of carbon, hydrogen, oxygen, sulphur, and nitrogen, and, although very complex in structure, are classed as *simple proteins.* In water, the albumins form colloidal solutions which are coagulated by heat above 160° F. They are also coagulated by acids and other substances, such as alcohol and corrosive sublimate.

Albumins are found in plants and in animal tissue, in blood, in milk, and in the humors of the eye. Albumin obtained from blood or from white of egg is frequently used for clarifying liquids, because, when the albumin coagulates, it retains various coloring matters and impurities, which settle or may be removed by filtration. It is for this reason that white of egg is used to clear coffee. See *Protein.*

Alcohol. Common or grain alcohol, known chemically as ethyl alcohol, is a light, colorless liquid, which burns with an intensely hot, nonluminous flame. When pure and free from water, it has a specific gravity of 0.7936 at 60° F., boils at 173° F., and does not freeze until about 200° below zero F. As mercury freezes at about −38°, alcohol is often used for low temperature thermometers.

Alcohol may be produced by chemical means from acetylene, and is produced naturally by the action of yeast in solutions containing fermentable sugars. The stimulating and intoxicating effects of fermented drinks have been known for thousands of years. Alcohol is the active principle of beer, wine, hard cider, brandy, whisky, rum, cordials, and the many other fermented and distilled beverages.

As strong liquors are usually subject to a tax corresponding to the amount of alcohol which they contain, a standard has been fixed which is known as *proof spirit.* English proof spirit contains 49.24 per cent alcohol by weight or 57.06 per cent by volume. The United States standard proof spirit contains 50 per cent alcohol by volume or 42.52 per cent by weight at 60° F.

When alcohol is mixed with water, a contraction of volume takes place, so that when 49.8 parts of water are added to 53.9 parts of pure alcohol, the volume of the mixture is 100 instead of 103.7. According to the United States Pharmacopœia standard, alcohol contains not less than 92.3 per cent by weight of pure ethyl alcohol. Rectified spirit contains about 95 per cent alcohol, while pure alcohol free from water is known as *absolute alcohol.* It can be prepared by distilling rectified spirit over unslaked lime, which absorbs the water.

Alcohol may be produced from sugar solutions, such as molasses, but it is usually prepared from starchy materials, such as potatoes, corn, rice, and barley,—whence the name *grain alcohol.* These are first subjected to the action of diastase or of an acid which changes much of the starch to glucose. The action of yeast then changes the glucose to alcohol, which is obtained by distillation. Synthetic alcohol may be made from ethylene gas derived from petroleum or coke oven gases. The ethylene gas is converted to ethyl alcohol, which is purified by distillation.

In medicine, alcohol is extensively used for making tinctures, and solutions of alkaloids, resins, essential oils, and many other materials. As alcohol coagulates albumins, arrests the development of micro-organisms, and prevents putrefaction, it is employed to preserve specimens of organic material. Highly refined alcohol known as *cologne spirits* is used for making perfumes, while industrial alcohol of various grades is used for heat, power, and, by the aid of the Welsbach mantle, to some extent for light. It is employed also as a solvent for varnishes and dyes and for making many organic chemicals, such as ether, chloral, chloroform, and acetic acid.

Because of the many needs for alcohol in the industries, a tax-free *denatured alcohol* is prepared by adding to the spirits some substance such as ether, iodine, carbolic acid, pyridine, creosote, benzine, or wood alcohol. The added material is selected so that it does not interfere with the intended use of the alcohol but does spoil it for beverage purposes. After water, acids, and petroleum, alcohol is one of the most important industrial liquids. See *Chloroform, Ether, Wood Alcohol.*

Alizarin (*ȧ-lĭz'ȧ-rĭn*). A valuable dye, originally obtained from the madder root, used for ages in dyeing cotton Turkey red. It was the first vegetable color to be prepared artificially, and, since 1869, it has been manufactured on a large scale from *anthracene,* a product of coal tar. Chemically, alizarin is a complex compound of carbon, hydrogen, and oxygen, known as dioxy-anthraquinone. From it a number of beautiful dyes are made, among them *alizarin orange, alizarin blue,* and *alizarin carmine.* The extensive production of alizarin by chemical industry has greatly changed agriculture in the regions where madder was formerly the chief product.

Alkaloids. The name given to a series of substances derived from the vegetable kingdom which, in their chemical action, closely resemble the alkali ammonia. They all contain nitrogen, and, in solution, exert a powerful influence on the ray of polarized light. Like ammonia, they combine directly with acids to form salts. Most alkaloids react powerfully when taken into the animal body. As a rule, they constitute the chief medicinal properties of the plants from which they are extracted.

When administered in proper doses under the direction of a competent physician, the alkaloids are remedial agents of the greatest value. Among the most important of these are atropine, cocaine, codeine, morphine, quinine, and strychnine. Some alkaloids are exceedingly violent poisons. Examples are *conine*, the active principle of the fatal hemlock, which, it is believed, Socrates was sentenced to drink; *curarine*, the destructive agent in curare, the famous South American arrow poison; and *physostigmine*, extracted from the deadly Calabar bean.

Alum. ($K_2Al_2(SO_4)_4.24H_2O$) Common alum is a double salt of aluminum sulphate and potassium sulphate which forms beautiful, colorless, octahedral crystals containing 38.5 per cent of water. Small amounts occur native, but alum is usually prepared by roasting alum shales or by treating clay or bauxite with sulphuric acid and extracting with water the aluminum sulphate thus formed. The proper amount of potassium sulphate is added to these solutions, which are then allowed to crystallize. Alum is used in medicine, as a mordant in dyeing, for tanning leather, for purifying water, in sizing paper, and for fireproofing fabrics. When heated, alum falls to a white powder, known as *burnt alum*, which is sometimes used in medicine as a caustic.

Various other double sulphates and selenates form crystals similar to potash alum and are classed as alums. In place of potassium these may contain sodium, ammonium, or other alkali metal, while iron, chromium, or manganese is sometimes substituted for aluminum.

Ammonia. (NH_3) A colorless, suffocating gas having a characteristic odor. It is composed of nitrogen and hydrogen and is about three-fifths as heavy as air. Ammonia is formed when animal matter decomposes, and was formerly obtained by destructive distillation of hides, feathers, and horns; hence the old name, *spirits of hartshorn*, for its water solution.

This solution is usually known today as *aqua ammonia*, or *ammonia water*, and is widely used as a cleansing agent. At 60° F. one volume of ammonia water can contain 760 volumes of the gas, which is given off when heated. The solution acts chemically as an alkali to neutralize acids, forming *ammonium* salts. Smelling salts, or *sal volatile*, consist chiefly of ammonium carbonate. *Sal ammoniac*, or ammonium chloride, is used in medicine, in soldering, and especially in dry cell electric batteries, such as are used in flashlights. Ammonium nitrate is heated in order to prepare nitrous oxide, or laughing gas.

When ammonia gas is subject to pressure, it becomes *liquid* or *anhydrous ammonia*. This liquid, which is widely used for refrigeration, and ammonium sulphate, the valuable fertilizer, are probably the most extensively used forms of ammonia. Large quantities are also used for the artificial production of nitric acid.

The principal source of ammonia is the gas given off during the destructive distillation of coal for the production of coke and illuminating gas. Increasing amounts of ammonia are being produced by treating cyanamid with steam, and the gas is prepared in large quantities by the Haber process, directly from nitrogen and hydrogen. The destruction of Oppau, Germany, in 1921, was caused by the explosion of immense stores of ammonium nitrosulphate, made from ammonia prepared by the Haber method.

Aniline. ($C_6H_5NH_2$) A colorless, poisonous liquid, with a slight, somewhat unpleasant odor, which boils at 184° C., or about 297° F.; extensively used in the preparation of aniline dyes. It is a coal tar product prepared commercially from nitrobenzene. Aniline was discovered in 1826 by Unverdorben while distilling indigo, and was first found in coal tar by Runge in 1834. Since the discovery of mauve by Perkin in 1856, the manufacture of aniline has been increasingly important. From this colorless, slightly oily substance, many beautiful dyes, embracing a wide range of colors, are made by chemical processes. By reason of their brilliancy, permanence, and cheapness, synthetic dyes, made artificially from aniline and other coal-tar products, have practically replaced the vegetable dyestuffs, formerly obtained from indigo, madder, and other plants.

Aspirin. A trade name for acetylsalicylic acid. It is a white powder used in the treatment of rheumatism, gout, tonsilitis, pleurisy, and sometimes for colds and headaches. Aspirin passes unchanged through the stomach and liberates salicylic acid in the intestine.

Benzene. (C_6H_6) A colorless, volatile, and highly inflammable liquid having a characteristic odor; obtained chiefly from the distillation of coal tar. Benzene is a valuable solvent for gums, resins, and many organic compounds. It is used in paints and varnishes, is added to gas to increase the illuminating power, and is the raw material from which *aniline*, hundreds of *aniline dyes*, and many other chemicals are made.

Benzine. A colorless, volatile, and highly inflammable liquid consisting chiefly of a mixture of paraffin hydrocarbons obtained in the earlier stages of the distillation of petroleum or asphalt oil. It thus differs greatly from *benzene*, which is a definite chemical compound obtained from coal tar. There is very little, if any, difference between *benzine*, *gasoline*, and ordinary *naphtha*.

Benzine is a valuable solvent for fats, oils, and resins, and is used as such in paints and varnishes, and in the preparation of linoleum and oil cloth. It is also much used for dry cleaning. As its vapor, when mixed with air, is explosive, benzine has been the cause of many serious accidents.

Benzol. A term often applied to *benzene*. As an article of commerce, benzol consists chiefly of benzene together with various proportions of similar compounds of higher boiling points. It is used as a solvent and as a substitute for benzene whenever purity is not essential.

Bleaching Powder. A valuable powder made by the action of chlorine gas on slaked lime, extensively used for disinfecting purposes and for bleaching cotton and linen. It is commonly though incorrectly known as *chloride of lime*.

A bleaching solution, called *Javelle water*, is valuable for bleaching the yellow color of old linen and is very effective in the removal of stains. It may be prepared as follows: Dissolve one pound of washing soda in one quart of boiling water and let cool. Dissolve one-half pound of "chloride of lime" in two quarts of cold water; let settle and then pour the clear solution into the soda; let settle. Bottle the clear liquid and keep in a dark place. Apply it directly to stains or mix with an equal volume of water and immerse the garment for not more than half an hour. After this treatment, the fabric must be thoroughly rinsed.

Borax. ($Na_2B_4O_7 \cdot 10H_2O$) An inorganic salt, sodium tetraborate, which occurs native in monoclinic crystals on the shores of various lakes in the Old and the New World. It is also mined in a state of high purity as kernite ore in the Mohave desert, Kern county, California. At Searles lake, California, borax is obtained through evaporation of the brine. Next to the United States, Chile is the largest producer of borax.

Borax is extensively used for household purposes, in soaps, and as an antiseptic. It is employed as a flux in glazing pottery, in making enamels, in assaying ores, as a reagent in chemical analysis, and for softening "hard" water. Borax is also very widely used in soldering and welding, because it dissolves the oxides which form on hot metals and leaves their surfaces clean and free to unite. See *Boric Acid, Boron*.

Bordeaux Mixture. A valuable and probably the best known general fungicide that is sprayed upon growing plants and trees in order to prevent blight, rot, and other growths of destructive fungi.

It is prepared as follows: Five pounds of copper sulphate are dissolved in about five gallons of water; five pounds of good lime are slaked and likewise mixed with five gallons of water. The copper solution is poured into a barrel about three-quarters full of water, and the lime is added slowly with vigorous stirring. This makes about fifty gallons. Smaller amounts may be prepared in the same proportions. The combined solution does not keep well and should be mixed fresh for each application.

Boric (or **Boracic**) **Acid.** (H_3BO_3) A weak mineral acid occurring as thin white plates or flakes which feel soapy. It is somewhat volatile in steam, and large quantities are obtained in Tuscany from the vapors of hot springs. It is also prepared by treating borax, or calcium borate, with sulphuric acid.

A solution of boric acid is often used as an eyewash or for similar purposes when a very mild antiseptic is desired. Together with various essential oils, it forms the basis of many well-known mouth washes and throat sprays. It is also used in the production of fusible glazes, of optical glass, and of many types of hard glass.

Calomel. (Hg_2Cl_2) A heavy, white, tasteless powder, insoluble in water. It is a compound of mercury with chlorine, and is called mercurous chloride—the *subchloride* or mild chloride of mercury—to distinguish it from the poisonous corrosive sublimate—mercuric chloride or the *bichloride of mercury*. Calomel acts medicinally as a purgative. When used with quinine, it is valuable in the treatment of malarial fever, and is most effective when followed by a saline cathartic. Vinegar, lemonade, and similar acid substances are to be avoided when calomel is used. See *Corrosive Sublimate, Mercury*.

Carbides. Various substances composed of carbon combined only with a metal or metalloid, the most important of which are iron carbide and calcium carbide. Under the proper conditions, molten iron combines directly with carbon to form iron carbide, or *cementite*, the presence of which in metallic iron greatly influences its properties. *Steel* may be considered as an alloy of pure iron with cementite, which, when cooled, also contains *pearlite*, a mixture of small particles of iron with its carbide. Iron carbide is consequently immensely important in the manufacture of iron and steel.

Calcium carbide, upon being treated with water, yields acetylene gas and is the chief commercial source of this valuable illuminant. Like calcium carbide, most other carbides, when treated with water or dilute acids, yield various hydrocarbons. For example, aluminum carbide yields marsh gas, or methane. The carbide of silicon, known commercially as *carborundum* and by other trade names, possesses great hardness and is widely used as an abrasive. The carbide of boron is even harder. Carbides are usually produced in the electric furnace.

Carbohydrates. The important group of chemical compounds which includes sugar, starch, cellulose, and related organic substances. These are composed of carbon, hydrogen, and oxygen, of which the last two elements are present in the proportions necessary to form water. Crystalline and soluble carbohydrates are classed as *sugar*; amorphous, insoluble forms, as *starch* or *cellulose*. If treated with dilute acid, the more complex forms are changed to simple sugars or *monosaccharides*.

Cane sugar and milk sugar are known as disaccharides because, when treated with acid, they yield two molecules of simple sugars. Similarly, starch and cellulose, which yield many molecules of sugar, are called polysaccharides. Carbohydrates form the greater part of human food. See *Glucose, Starch, Sugar.*

Carbolic Acid or **Phenol.** (C_6H_5OH) A powerful antiseptic, germicide, and disinfectant, which is used also in making picric acid, many dyestuffs, and pharmaceuticals. With formaldehyde it condenses to a valuable material which may have the properties of hard rubber and the beauty of amber. This material is known as bakelite. Carbolic acid is obtained chiefly from coal tar and is also made from benzene. When pure it consists of colorless crystals. Carbolic acid is the standard by which the germ destroying power of all other disinfectants is measured. It is used in medicine and for disinfecting surgical instruments, walls and floors of sickrooms, and other materials. As carbolic acid is a powerful, caustic poison, great care should be exercised in its use.

Carbon Tetrachloride. ($C\,Cl_4$) A heavy, colorless, volatile liquid, very similar to chloroform. It is an excellent solvent for fat and wax, and its vapor is not inflammable. For these reasons it is valuable for removing grease spots from clothing, and its use in place of benzine for "dry cleaning" is free from the danger of fire. A bottle of carbon tetrachloride, placed where it is quickly available, may be of great use in extinguishing small fires. The fumes are heavy, and act as a blanket which prevents air from reaching the flame.

Carborundum. A trade name of an abrasive material of great hardness. Chemically, it is an artificial carbide of silicon produced by heating together coke, sand, and salt in powerful electric furnaces to a temperature of 4000° F. Like emery and garnet, carborundum is used in making various forms of abrading cloth, and is one of the most valuable abrasives, especially in the form of grinding wheels. It is used also for polishing steel balls and stone surfaces, as a constituent of refractory cements, and for various similar purposes.

Caustic Alkalies. (NaOH, KOH) The hydroxides of the alkali group of metals, of which the best-known are *caustic soda* and *caustic potash*. They do not occur free in nature, but are prepared by passing an electric current through melted or dissolved alkali chlorides or by adding milk of lime to a solution of the carbonates. They are white when pure, and have a strong caustic action upon flesh. Caustic potash is used chiefly in the preparation of soft soap. Caustic soda is used for making hard soap, for refining oils, for mercerizing cotton, and for manufacturing paper pulp, dyestuffs, and many other materials.

Charcoal. The residue of impure carbon remaining after destructive distillation of vegetable or animal substances. The largest proportion of all charcoal is prepared from wood. It is black, porous, and brittle, and retains the form but has only about three-fourths the volume and one-fourth the weight of the original wood.

Charcoal is often prepared by covering a heap of wood with earth and lighting the pile at openings near the bottom. The earthy covering keeps out air so that the wood does not burn to ashes, while the heat of combustion drives off most of the volatile matter, which escapes from small holes at the top. This wasteful process is being supplanted gradually by the retort method whereby the wood is heated in closed vessels from which the escaping gases may be collected and purified. Large amounts of wood alcohol, acetone, acetic acid, creosote, and turpentine are obtained in this manner.

Immense quantities of charcoal are used for fuel, especially in Europe. It burns with a small, hot, colorless flame. Willow charcoal is an important ingredient of gunpowder. *Charbon rouge*, or red coal, is a gunpowder charcoal produced from wood by the action of hot air or superheated steam. Pencils of soft charcoal are extensively used for artistic purposes. Powdered charcoal is used as a pigment and as a polishing material. *Animal charcoal*, prepared from bones, is especially valuable as a decolorizing agent for bleaching oils and solutions such as sugar sirup.

Charcoal has the property of absorbing large amounts of gases. For this reason, it sometimes gives relief during gastric indigestion. It is also extensively used in connection with a mask to protect troops against poisonous gases. One of the most efficient materials used for this purpose, called *activated charcoal*, is prepared by heating coconut shells in retorts and treating the charcoal thus formed with steam at high temperature. See *Carbon, Coke.*

Chloroform. ($CHCl_3$) A heavy, colorless liquid, having a pleasant odor and a sweet, burning taste; usually prepared from alcohol or acetone by the action of "chloride of lime." It is a valuable solvent for many organic substances, is noninflammable, and acts as an antiseptic. Chloroform has several uses in medicine but is best known as one of the most important general anesthetics. Its use for this purpose was first demonstrated in 1847 by Sir James Simpson of Edinburgh. See *Anesthetic.*

Chrome Yellow. A brilliant yellow pigment, chemically known as lead chromate. It is usually made by adding sodium or potassium bichromate to a solution of lead nitrate. Chrome yellow is permanent to light, and, in addition to its use in paint, it is applied to textile fibers as a dyestuff.

Citric Acid. ($C_6H_8O_7 \cdot H_2O$) An organic acid found in many tart fruits, such as gooseberries and currants, but especially abundant in lemons and limes. It can be made by the action of certain micro-organisms on sugar and glycerin, but is produced commercially from the juice of low grade lemons. The white crystals, which have a pleasant sour taste, are used in dyeing and textile printing, for making cooling drinks, and for the preparation of mild laxatives, such as magnesium citrate.

Coal Tar. A thick, black, oily liquid, slightly heavier than water, which is deposited in the condensers of gas works during the process of making coke and illuminating gas from soft coal. This liquid, called also gas tar, is an exceedingly complex mixture of substances. The separation of these into their various constituent parts is a most important division of chemical industry, for they form the only known source of an immense number of very valuable compounds. Among these are solvent naphtha, benzene, toluene, xylene, phenol, naphthalene, cresol, and anthracene.

From these crude coal-tar products are derived such substances as the beautiful coal-tar dyes; pure carbolic acid, with strong antiseptic properties; trinitrotoluene, or TNT, and picric acid, powerful explosives; naphthalene, used in making dyes and moth balls; and creosote oil, used as a preservative—together with other, almost innumerable, compounds of greater or less value, including many drugs, such as antipyrin and acetanilid.

The pitch, remaining after the foregoing have been distilled off, is used in the manufacture of asphalt, varnishes, and tarred paper, and as a binder in making coal briquettes. Many of the most valuable discoveries in the field of organic chemistry have resulted from the study of the coal-tar compounds.

Codeine (*kō-dē'in*). One of the alkaloids found in opium. It is a white, crystalline substance, very similar to morphine. Codeine is used in medicine, chiefly to diminish sensibility to pain when a sedative milder than morphine is desired. See *Morphine.*

Collodion. A thick, colorless, and highly inflammable liquid, consisting of soluble guncotton or pyroxylin dissolved in a mixture of alcohol and ether. When exposed to the air, it dries quickly to a tough, transparent film. It was formerly much used in photography. Collodion is frequently applied as a protection to scratches and cuts, and, when medicated, is used for the removal of corns and callosities, and for blistering the skin.

Corrosive Sublimate. ($HgCl_2$) A salt of mercury, called also bichloride of mercury and mercuric chloride. It is produced commercially by heating mercury in chlorine gas, and forms heavy, colorless crystals soluble in water. Corrosive sublimate is a powerful irritant and an intense poison, for which *white of egg* is given as an antidote. It is used in dilute solution for the treatment of certain skin diseases, and as a powerful antiseptic and preservative. See *Calomel, Mercury.*

Cream of Tartar. A white, sour, crystalline compound of potassium and tartaric acid. It is used chiefly as the acid ingredient of some baking powders, and also in medicine. To the chemist it is known as potassium bitartrate, and is prepared by purifying the *argols* deposited in vats where wine is fermented. See *Tartaric Acid.*

Creosote. An oily liquid having a burning, smoky taste. It is obtained by the distillation and purification of wood tar, especially that obtained from the destructive distillation of beechwood. When fresh it is colorless, but, after standing, it becomes yellow or brown. Creosote means *meat preserver* and it is frequently used for that purpose, as well as in the treatment of tuberculosis and bronchitis, and as a stimulant to digestion. *Creosote oil,* a crude creosote obtained from both wood and coal tar, is widely applied as a sheep dip and wood preservative.

Cyanamid (*sī'ăn-ăm'ĭd*). The trade name of a fertilizer, known also as calcium cyanamid. It is prepared in special electric furnaces by heating powdered calcium carbide to about 1800° F. in the presence of pure nitrogen. The gas combines with the carbide, giving a product that contains about 20 per cent nitrogen. As a fertilizer, calcium cyanamid is rather slow in action. It is usually applied before the seeds are planted, and not to the growing plants.

Equally important with its use as fertilizer is the employment of cyanamid for the preparation of ammonia. When calcium cyanamid is treated with steam, calcium carbonate is formed and ammonia gas is given off. In this way the inert nitrogen of the air is combined into a valuable product. See *Ammonia, Fertilizer.*

Dextrin. A soluble, gummy substance, called also *British gum,* prepared from starch by the action of heat, dilute acids, or ferments. It is employed for gumming postage stamps and envelopes, for making paste, for sizing paper and cloth, and as a substitute for natural gums in many other processes. See *Starch.*

Epsom Salt. ($MgAO_4 \cdot 7H_2O$) White or colorless crystals of hydrated magnesium sulphate, best known because of their use as a purgative. The salt was originally obtained from spring waters in Epsom, England, but is now prepared chiefly from the mineral *kieserite.* Epsom salt is employed in finishing cotton fabrics, and for weighting paper, leather, and silk.

Essential Oils. The group of volatile, oily, odoriferous substances to which is due a large part of the odor of plants. The essential oils are composed of many very different chemical compounds, and as a group they are classified chiefly by their physical characteristics. They are volatile, and are often called volatile oils to differentiate them from the fixed or fatty oils also found in plants; they make a temporary grease spot on paper; they are combustible; and they usually have a characteristic odor.

Essential oils are obtained from plants or plant products in which they occur, by expression, distillation, and extraction. For example: oil of lemon is obtained by subjecting lemon rinds to pressure; turpentine, and many others, such as the oils of cloves, wintergreen, lavender, peppermint, and rose, are obtained by steam distillation; while the delicate odorous substances of such flowers as violet, tuberose, and jasmine are often extracted from the petals by means of ard or vaseline.

The essential oils are used chiefly for making perfumes and flavoring extracts; many are powerful antiseptics and germicides, and turpentine is largely employed in the paint and varnish industries.

Ether. ($C_2H_5OC_2H_5$) A light, colorless, volatile, and extremely inflammable liquid known chemically as *diethyl ether.* Because it is prepared from alcohol by the action of sulphuric acid, it is often called *sulphuric ether.* Ether is used extensively in the manufacture of artificial silk and collodion, but is most highly valued as an anesthetic. It is occasionally used as an intoxicant, with effects similar to those of opium.

Explosive. Any chemical compound or mixture capable of producing suddenly a large volume of gas at a high temperature. When confined in a small space, the hot gas exerts enormous pressure which may be used for throwing projectiles, shattering rock, making trenches or pits in the ground, and similar purposes.

Explosives may be classified as: (1) mixtures of inflammable substances with some oxidizing material; (2) organic nitrates and nitro-substitution products; and (3) detonators similar to mercury fulminate. Black powder is an example of the first type; nitroglycerin and TNT, or trinitrotoluene, of the second. Detonators. because of their extremely violent action, are employed in small quantities for exploding compounds of the second class. Mixtures act more slowly than chemical compounds, and the somewhat longer pressure of blasting powder is, in mining, often more useful than the shattering effect of dynamite. See *Gunpowder, Nitroglycerine.*

Fats. Greasy or oily compounds which yield soap and glycerin when treated with caustic alkalies. Fats are found in all animals and most plants, where they serve as a store of energy- and heat-producing material. They are often classified as fats if solid, and fatty oils if liquid at ordinary temperatures. This arrangement depends largely on climate, for the fat from coconuts, which is usually a solid in North America, is an oil in the countries where it grows.

As all fats are compounds of glycerin with the higher fatty acids, the characteristics of any fat depend largely on the acids of which it is composed. Hard fats, such as beef and mutton tallow, contain much palmitin and stearin. Olive oil consists largely of liquid olein. Linseed oil is very valuable for paint and varnish because it contains certain fatty acids which harden on combining with the oxygen of the air. A *rancid fat* is one which has more or less decomposed, with the formation of evil smelling compounds other than glycerin and fatty acids.

Well-known animal fats are beef and mutton tallow, lard, and butter. Large amounts of fish oil are obtained chiefly from the menhaden, sardines, and salmon. Seal oil and whale oil are widely used, and high-grade cod liver oil is valuable in medicine. Oils extensively employed for finishing leather and for lubrication are obtained from the feet of cattle, horses, and sheep.

Vegetable oils are usually pressed or extracted from crushed seed or fruit. They include cottonseed, peanut, corn, olive, soy bean, linseed, castor, coconut, palm, and palm kernel oils, cocoa butter, and very many others. Sperm oil and wool fat are waxes rather than fats, because they are not glycerin compounds, while Japan wax, so called because of its appearance, is really a fat.

The finest and purest oils are generally used for food. Other grades are made into soap, candles, and glycerin. Large amounts are also used for tanning and dressing leather, for lubrication, and in paints.

Fehling's Solution. A blue liquid formed by mixing an alkaline solution of Rochelle salt with a solution of copper sulphate. It is used as a test for certain sugars which when boiled with it cause the formation of a red precipitate.

Fertilizers, Chemical. Chemical compounds and mixtures added to the soil in order to stimulate plant growth. Such materials may be divided into two classes: those which are a direct source of plant food, and those, such as gypsum and lime, which tend to make available the plant food already in the soil. True fertilizers contain compounds of nitrogen, phosphoric acid, and potash, alone or mixed in various proportions.

Commercial fertilizer is usually marked with a formula similar to 4–8–2 or 3–6–4. This gives the percentage content of nitrogen, phosphoric acid, and potash, in the order stated. A ton of 4–8–2 fertilizer thus contains 80 pounds of nitrogen, 160 pounds of phosphoric acid, and 40 pounds of potash, combined with mineral and organic substances, such as lime, oxygen, carbon, and sulphates, which make up the bulk of the material.

Nitrogen is obtained from various organic materials, including cottonseed meal, tankage, and guano; also from Chile saltpeter, cyanamid, ammonium salts from gas works, and the products of artificial nitrate plants. Phosphoric acid is prepared chiefly from natural deposits of phosphate rock. The principal source of potash has been the Stassfurt deposits of Germany, but during the World War other sources were developed, some of which will probably be of permanent value. Wood ashes are valuable as fertilizer because they contain potash, phosphoric acid, and lime. See *Cyanamid, Phosphates.*

Formaldehyde. (HCHO) A colorless. irritating gas produced by passing the vapor of methyl alcohol mixed with air over heated copper gauze. It dissolves readily in water and is sold in about a forty per cent solution under the name of *formalin.* It is one of the best-known disinfectants, a valuable preservative, and when diluted is used as a fungicide on vegetables and plants. Combined with carbolic acid, it gives products used in varnish and as a substitute for hard rubber and amber. Formaldehyde is a poison which forms leather-like compounds with skin and similar protein matter. It should never be used as a food preservative.

Fowler's Solution. A solution of potassium arsenite made to contain one per cent of arsenic trioxide or white arsenic. It was named for Fowler, an English physician, who first used it in medicine as a convenient form for dispensing definite amounts of soluble arsenic.

Glauber's Salt. Sodium sulphate in the form of white, bitter crystals contining 55.9 per cent of water. This salt was originally prepared by J. R. Glauber, a German chemist. Although found in many natural deposits, it is usually obtained from *salt cake,* a by-product in the manufacture of hydrochloric acid. Glauber's salt is used in glass making, in medicine, especially for veterinary purposes, and as a mordant in dyeing.

Halogens. A name meaning "salt-forming," given to the group of similar chemical elements consisting of fluorine, chlorine, bromine, and iodine.

Hydrocarbons. A large group of chemical compounds composed only of hydrogen and carbon. As a class, they are insoluble in water, combustible, and neither acid nor alkaline. Some are gases, some liquids, and others solids. Methane, acetylene, benzene, the constituents of gasoline, and also the principal constituents of turpentine and India rubber are all hydrocarbons.

Hydrocarbons should not be confused with *carbohydrates,* which are compounds of carbon, hydrogen, and oxygen. See *Acetylene, Benzene, Methane, Naphthalene, Paraffin.*

Hydrochloric Acid. (HCl) A colorless solution of hydrogen chloride gas in water, forming one of the strongest acids. In view of this fact, it is interesting to note that the *perfectly dry gas* is not acid and does not attack metals. The gas is produced by the action of sulphuric acid on common salt, and is then absorbed in water. This yields the commercial product called *muriatic acid,* which is often yellow from impurities. It is used to clean sheet iron before coating with tin, in making chlorides and chlorine, in the production of glue, and for many other purposes. The gastric juices in the human stomach generally contain about one-third of one per cent of free hydrochloric acid.

Hydrofluoric Acid. (HF) A colorless, corrosive liquid having a suffocating odor, prepared by heating calcium fluoride with sulphuric acid and dissolving the resulting gas in water. The acid attacks silicon and all of its compounds; consequently, it decomposes glass and porcelain, and must be kept in bottles of lead or wax. It is used chiefly for etching and marking glass, and in the chemical analysis of materials containing silica or sand. See *Fluorine.*

Hydrogen Peroxide. (H_2O_2) A heavy, colorless liquid, composed, like water, of hydrogen and oxygen, but having twice as much oxygen. It is unstable, and readily breaks down into water and a form of oxygen which is chemically very active. Because of its oxidizing action, hydrogen peroxide is used chiefly as a mild antiseptic and for bleaching hair, feathers, silk, wool, and ivory. It is prepared commercially by treating barium peroxide with dilute sulphuric acid. As the pure substance decomposes easily, it is usually sold as a three per cent solution, preserved by a small amount of acetanilid.

Hypo. ($Na_2S_2O_3$) A white, soluble, crystalline compound, made by boiling a solution of caustic soda or of sodium sulphite with sulphur. Its chemical name is *sodium thiosulphate.* Hypo is extensively used in photography for removing from negatives and prints any silver salts that have not become insoluble through the action of light and the developer. It is used also for removing excess chlorine from bleached fabrics.

Iodoform (*ī-ō'dô-fôrm*). A yellow, crystalline compound containing nearly 97 per cent of iodine. It has been used extensively as an antiseptic in the treatment of sores and wounds. Iodoform has a powerful, unpleasant odor, and has been largely displaced in medicine by more effective and less poisonous substances.

Litharge (*lĭth'ärj*). A heavy, yellowish red powder, obtained by grinding the scaly material produced when lead is roasted in the presence of air. It is used as a drier in paint oils, in the preparation of rubber goods, and for making lead glass, enamels, and many lead compounds. Chemically, it is lead monoxide and has the same composition as *massicot,* which is a lighter powder produced in the same way but at a temperature below its melting point. Massicot is used for making red lead.

Litmus. A vegetable dyestuff obtained from certain fermented lichens. The pure substance is a red organic acid that turns blue in the presence of alkalies. Litmus is used chiefly by chemists, in solution or dried upon porous paper, as an indicator of the acidity or alkalinity of any substance. When a drop of the solution, or a piece of blue *litmus paper* is placed in an acid liquid it immediately becomes red and will again change to blue in an alkaline liquid. A solution is often said to be neutral when it does not change the color of either red or blue litmus.

Lye. A water solution of any alkali, such as caustic potash or washing soda. Lyes are extensively employed in manufacturing soaps, refining oils, making paper, and for many other industrial purposes.

Mercurochrome. A synthetic germicide containing about 23 per cent of mercury in combination with bromine and other elements. It appears as irridescent green scales, which are readily soluble in water, forming a bright red solution. Since its announcement in 1919, it has made rapid progress, due to the fact that, although a powerful disinfectant, it is almost nonirritant.

Methane. A light, odorless, inflammable gas produced by the natural decomposition of organic matter, and in other ways. It is often called *marsh gas* because it rises from the bottom of marshy pools. Miners know it as *fire damp,* which issues from seams in the coal beds and often causes explosions. Methane is the simplest of the hydrocarbons, and is the principal constituent of natural gas.

Morphine. The principal alkaloid of opium, from which it is separated as bitter, white crystals. It is generally used in medicine as the chloride, sulphate or acetate, for relieving pain, producing sleep, or to allay certain nervous disorders. The action of the drug is quickest when injected hypodermically. See *Codeine, Poppy.*

Naphtha. A term often used to describe any volatile, inflammable liquid obtained by distillation of organic material. Thus *wood naphtha* is crude methyl alcohol, obtained by destructive distillation of wood. In some countries naphtha refers to the product called gasoline in America. When refining petroleum, the first products coming from the still are classed as light and heavy naphthas.

Naphthalene. A hydrocarbon obtained in large quantity from coal tar. In a pure state it forms beautiful white crystals, which are insoluble in water and have a characteristic odor. Naphthalene is the starting point for many dyes, including most of the azo colors. It is used also in making celluloid and certain smokeless powders, and as the basis of noninflammable artificial wax. Moth balls are cast from melted naphthalene.

Niter. A term used to include both India saltpeter, or potassium nitrate, and Chile saltpeter, or sodium nitrate. The latter occurs in great beds in the rainless northern provinces of Chile. See *Saltpeter.*

Nitric Acid. (HNO_3) One of the earliest known and most valuable mineral acids; usually prepared by adding sulphuric acid to sodium nitrate and distilling off the nitric acid that forms. It is also produced commercially from ammonia gas; and, where electric power is extremely cheap, by passing air through a powerful flaming electric arc.

Nitric acid is a colorless liquid when pure, but the commercial product is yellow. It is a powerful oxidizing agent as well as an active acid which attacks all metals except gold and platinum. Its salts are called nitrates. It corrodes the skin, leaving a yellow stain. *Fuming nitric acid* contains an oxide of nitrogen (NO_2) in solution. Nitric acid is necessary for the production of almost all explosives, a large proportion of the coal-tar dyes, and celluloid and similar pyroxylin compounds. Thousands of tons of nitrates are used yearly for fertilizers.

The discovery was announced in 1939 that, at one point in the vaporizing of nitric acid, nitrogen from the acid will unite readily with certain other compounds to form nitrate explosives and amino acids. The process, discovered by Prof. Henry B. Haas, Purdue University, is known as vapor phase nitration. See *Explosive, Fertilizers.*

Nitrous Oxide, or **Laughing Gas.** (N_2O) A general anesthetic discovered by Sir Humphry Davy in 1800, and usually believed to have been first used in surgery in 1844 by Dr. H. Wells an American dentist. The gas is produced by heating ammonium nitrate. When the gas is inha ed,the first effects are usually pleasantly exhilarating and may cause singing, laughing, and quick violent motions. This state is soon followed by unconsciousness and insensibility to pain.

Noble Gases. A group of gaseous elements, including argon, helium, krypton, neon, niton, and xenon, so named because they do not enter into combination with any of the other elements.

Ocher (*ō'ker*). A naturally occurring pigment which varies in color but is usually yellow. It consists of clay, colored by an oxide of iron that contains combined water. If ocher is heated until this water is driven off, it becomes orange or red, and is known as *burnt ocher*. The ochers give permanent color, mix well with oil, have good covering power, and are cheap. *Sienna* is similar to ocher but is usually somewhat finer grained. *Burnt sienna* is a reddish orange pigment.

Oxalic Acid. ($H_2C_2O_4$) A poisonous organic acid, occurring as its potassium or calcium salt, in sorrel, rhubarb, many lichens, and other plants. It was formerly prepared by heating sawdust with caustic soda, but is now chiefly produced from sodium formate or carbonate. Oxalic acid forms transparent crystals which are used in the dyeing and printing of fabrics, for purifying glycerin, bleaching straw and leather, and for removing ink stains. Milk of lime is the best antidote for oxalic acid poisoning.

Ozone. A colorless gas with a strong penetrating odor which is often noticeable near sparking electrical machines. It is a modified or allotropic form of oxygen, formed by condensation of three volumes of ordinary oxygen into two volumes of ozone. At very low temperature it forms a deep blue, magnetic liquid. It is a different substance from oxygen and is notable for its extreme chemical activity. Oxygen does not tarnish mercury or silver, but ozone quickly changes them to their oxides.

Ozone is formed in small quantities from oxygen in the upper atmosphere by certain rays of ultra-violet light from the sun. This minute constituent of the atmosphere is believed to cut off that section of the spectrum of the sun which is so powerful that, if admitted to the earth, would destroy human sight by its chemical action. It admits a sufficient amount of ultra-violet rays to produce vitamin D in animals, the lack of which results in rickets.

Ozone may be produced in small amounts by chemical action, by vaporization of water, by incandescent solids, by radioactive elements, by ultra-violet rays, and especially by means of a high tension electrostatic field. It is prepared commercially in various forms of apparatus, called *ozonizers*, in which air or oxygen is passed through an electric field charged by a rapidly alternating current at a pressure of from 5000 to 60,000 volts.

Small ozonizers are frequently used as an aid to ventilation because ozone has the power to destroy many organic odors. However, when used in this manner, the ozone is not sufficiently concentrated to exterminate disease germs. Ozone rapidly decomposes articles made of rubber.

The chief technical application of ozone has been for the sterilization of drinking water. It has also been used to prevent bacterial growth in the cold storage industries, to bleach delicate fabrics, oils, and waxes, and as an oxidizing agent in the preparation of organic chemicals such as vanillin, the flavoring principle of the vanilla bean.

Paraffin. A white, tasteless and odorless, waxlike mixture of hydrocarbons which occurs naturally in the mineral ozocerite. It is also obtained by distillation of coal, shale, and peat. The chief source of paraffin is the tar distillate formed in the process of refining crude petroleum. After the lighter and more volatile oils have been removed, the crude wax is separated by chilling and pressing the residue. It is refined by being heated gradually in a warm room, and the final product bleached white with fuller's earth or bone black. Refined paraffin varies in melting point between 110° and 200° F. It is used for making candles, for preparing waxed paper, and for protecting the surface of jellies and jams from mold and other infections. In medicine, paraffin is used to cover burns so that the wound will heal without a disfiguring scar.

Paris Green. A poisonous green powder consisting of a double salt of copper acetate and copper arsenite. Paris green was formerly used as a pigment, but, because of its poisonous nature, this employment of it has been largely abandoned. It is now very commonly applied to growing plants in order to destroy potato bugs, cotton worms, slugs, and similar harmful insects. Usually it is mixed with water and used as a spray, or mixed with air-slaked lime and dusted upon the plants.

Pepsin. An enzyme or ferment produced by certain glands in the stomachs of the higher animals. When in a weakly acid solution, it acts upon the proteins of the food, changing them to simpler compounds called amino acids, which can pass through the walls of the intestine and be absorbed. Pepsin is produced commercially from the stomachs of pigs and sheep, and is used in medicine as an aid to digestion. It is usually sold in the form of light yellow flakes or scales which should digest at least 3000 times their weight of boiled white of egg. See *Enzymes*.

Permanganates. Salts of permanganic acid, of which the deep purple crystals of *potassium permanganate* are best known. As they have powerful oxidizing properties, solutions of permanganates are used as disinfectants. In order to destroy the poison, crystals of potassium permanganate are often applied directly to a wound caused by the bite of a venomous snake.

Phosphates. Compounds of phosphoric acid, many of which are of great importance because they are necessary for the life and growth of plants and animals. The term phosphate, when used commercially, generally refers to phosphate fertilizer or to beds of calcium phosphate which occur in Tunis, Algeria, Florida, Tennessee, and other parts of the world. Natural phosphate rock is insoluble; it is changed to soluble phosphate, or *superphosphate*, by treatment with sulphuric acid, which renders most of the phosphorus available for plant food. When phosphates are purchased for fertilizer, it is the *available* rather than the *total* phosphoric acid which is most important. Other phosphate fertilizers are steamed bone meal, spent bone black, and Thomas slag, a by-product from the manufacture of steel.

The fluids and soft tissues of the human body contain phosphates, usually as the sodium and potassium salts. The bones contain more than half their weight of normal calcium phosphate, while the enamel of the teeth is composed of 80 to 90 per cent of the same substance. The ash obtained from blood, milk, or the yolk of eggs has a large content of phosphates, thus indicating the importance of these salts in the life processes. The brain and the nerves contain an unusually large proportion of phosphates. See *Fertilizers*.

Plaster of Paris. A white powder made by heating gypsum until three-quarters of the water it contains is given off. When the powder is mixed with water, these constituents again combine and set to a hard mass. Plaster of Paris is used chiefly for plaster and stucco work and for making molds and casts. It expands slightly on setting, and so yields a sharp reproduction of the details of a mold.

Protein (*prō'tē-ĭn*). An important class of exceedingly complex organic compounds which are found in all active plant and animal cells. Proteins always contain carbon, hydrogen, oxygen, and nitrogen. They usually contain sulphur, and occasionally phosphorus, iodine, and other elements. The nitrogenous food of animals, which is absolutely necessary for their life and growth, is essentially protein food. Eighteen per cent of the human body is protein.

Proteins are chemical combinations of simpler substances known as *amino acids*, of which certain ones are necessary for animal growth. Plants have the power to build up these acids and combine them into proteins, while animals usually seem able only to modify and reconstruct those proteins which are received in the food. Consequently, the *amount* and *kind* of protein eaten is of great importance. It acts chiefly to build and to renew muscular tissue but may serve also as a source of energy.

Lean meat consists largely of protein, as do the white of egg and the curd of skim milk. The first known vegetable protein was the gluten of wheat. Peas and beans contain large amounts, and the protein of peanuts is one of the most satisfactory vegetable substitutes for meat.

Prussian Blue. An artificial blue pigment known chemically as a ferrocyanide of iron. It mixes well with oil, but lacks covering power and fades somewhat in light. The color is not affected by acids but is destroyed by alkalies. Prussian blue dissolved in oxalic acid is the basis of much of the liquid *bluing* used in the laundry.

Prussic Acid. The common name of hydrocyanic acid, a colorless liquid with an odor similar to bitter almonds, which boils at about 79° F. It is one of the swiftest and most deadly of known poisons; a single drop, if swallowed, is sufficient to cause almost instant death. Its most important salts are *potassium cyanide* and *sodium cyanide*, which are used in electroplating and, in the *cyanide process*, for recovering gold from pulverized ore.

Quinine. An intensely bitter, crystalline alkaloid extracted from the bark of the cinchona tree. It is produced in Peru and adjoining South American countries and in Java. As the free alkaloid is almost insoluble, it is generally used in medicine as the sulphate, hydrochloride, or salt of some other acid. Quinine finds its greatest use in the treatment of malarial fevers, for which it is regarded as a specific. It is also valuable, when properly used, as a tonic and preventive. The average dose varies from one-half grain to five grains. Excessive amounts depress the heart and cause temporary deafness.

Rochelle Salt. A white, crystalline salt known to the chemist as sodium-potassium tartrate. It has a mild, salty, somewhat bitter taste and is used as a laxative, specially in Seidlitz powders.

Saccharin (*săk'ȧ-rĭn*). A white, crystalline, intensely sweet, coal-tar product discovered in 1879 by Fahlberg and Remsen. Saccharin has definite antiseptic properties, does not ferment in the stomach, is not a food, and when pure, is about 500 times sweeter than sugar. Consequently, it is often employed during treatment of diabetes, obesity, intestinal infections, and other diseases where sugar is to be avoided. The use of saccharin in food and drink for sale is prohibited under the national pure food regulations, and by the laws of many states. This does not prevent its employment in medicinal products which are properly labeled.

Salt (NaCl) Sodium chloride or common salt is one of the most important and widely distributed chemical substances. When pure, it is in the form of white, cubical crystals that often have concave sides. It melts at 1474° F., and is almost as soluble in cold water as in hot. Saturated brine contains 26.4 per cent of salt and is 1.2 times as heavy as pure water.

The chief sources of salt are the water of the sea and of salt lakes, rock salt, and natural brines. Sea water contains only about 2.75 per cent of salt and is utilized when no richer source is available. Large quantities have been produced from Great Salt lake, which contains from 12 to 23 per cent of salt. In 1927, a concession was granted for obtaining salt from the waters of the Dead Sea.

When thick beds of rock salt are near the surface, it is usually mined like coal, and, if sufficiently pure, the mineral is merely ground and sifted to proper size. Impure salt is often dissolved in water and recrystallized. Salt mines are usually less than 1000 feet deep. If the beds are far below the surface, it is customary to drill narrow holes down to the salt. Fresh water is then run in, and, after it becomes saturated, the brine is pumped to the surface. Often wells are sunk until natural brines are reached. At least two wells of this type are more than a mile deep; that drilled to a depth of 6600 feet at Paruschowitz, Upper Silesia, Germany, is the deepest salt well in the world.

The largest and most famous salt mine is that of Wieliczka, Poland, which is tunneled to a depth of 982 feet and forms a subterranean town. There are 77 miles of passage on seven levels. Roads, churches, monuments, and a crystal ballroom are all carved from the solid salt.

In the United States, Michigan leads in total output as well as in the production of brine salt. New York is second. The total production of the entire country is normally about 7.5 million tons.

Brine may be evaporated by exposure to the sun, when large crystals of *solar salt* are produced, and by artificial heat in open tanks or vacuum kettles. It is often evaporated in long, shallow vats called grainers, heated by steam pipes hung about six inches from the bottom so that the crystals that settle may easily be removed.

Many different grades of salt are prepared, such as table, dairy, common, fine, packers, solar, milling, and rock salt. Table salt must be free from magnesium and calcium chlorides, which are impurities that absorb moisture and cause the crystals to cake. Special grades of shaker salt often contain small amounts of magnesium carbonate, which is added to prevent caking and thus to allow the salt to run freely. Rock salt does not dissolve so quickly as finer crystals and is used for feeding cattle, curing meat, and preserving hides. Salt is usually packed in barrels containing 280 pounds net. The principal uses of salt are for food, and for the production of sodium carbonate, caustic soda, chlorine, and all other sodium compounds. It is used also for preserving meat and fish, glazing cheap pottery, and salting out soap.

Salt is a natural constituent of all animal fluids and is therefore necessary for life. What is known as a *normal* or *physiological salt solution* contains 8.5 grams of salt per liter. A man or race living on raw meat requires no extra salt, but a diet of boiled meat and vegetables requires the addition of this important substance.

If all of the waters of the seas were to be evaporated, about 4,500,000 cubic miles of salt would remain. This is about 14½ times the volume of all Europe above sea level, or enough to cover the entire earth with a layer of salt 112 feet thick. See *Chlorine, Sodium.*

Saltpeter. White, crystalline potassium nitrate. It occurs naturally to a limited extent, and is sometimes called India saltpeter, to distinguish it from sodium nitrate, or Chile saltpeter, from which it is usually prepared. It is valuable for making gunpowder and as a fertilizer, and is sometimes used in medicine.

Silica and **Silicates.** The oxide of silicon and compounds of silicic acid are the most abundant of all substances which compose the earth's crust. Clean white sand and quartz or rock crystal are almost pure silica, which is known chemically as silicon dioxide. The porous infusorial earth used in making dynamite is silica, while agate, jasper, onyx, and amethyst are colored forms of the same substance. Opal is silica containing a variable amount of water. Clear crystals of quartz are used for optical purposes; and valuable chemical "glassware" that will not break, even though dipped in water when red hot, is made from fused silica.

The silicates, which are often very complex compounds, are exceedingly numerous. Kaolin or clay is an acid silicate of aluminum; mica, which is so different in form from clay, is very similar chemically but contains also a silicate of potassium; granite is a mixture of silicates. Glass, pottery, porcelain, and water glass are artificial silicates which illustrate the great value of these compounds to mankind. See *Clay, Glass, Kaolin, Porcelain, Pottery, Water Glass.*

Soda. (Na_2CO_3) A term applied to sodium carbonate, or washing soda, but also used in a more general way to include baking soda and caustic soda. Sal soda consists of crystals of sodium carbonate which also contain 63 per cent of combined water. The *Leblanc process* for making soda from salt by means of sulphuric acid, limestone, and coal was introduced in 1791 and existed without competition until 1863, when the Solvay process appeared. Some soda is obtained from natural deposits occurring in Egypt, California, and other places. Sodium carbonate is used in enormous quantities for making glass, soaps, washing powders, dyes, and in preparing explosives. See *Caustic Alkalies.*

Sulphanilimide (Sulfanilimide). A synthetic drug discovered in 1936 which was found to have the effect of arresting the ravages of several types of infections not otherwise controllable. Among the diseases for which it and a derivative, sulphopyradine, were found helpful are gonorrhea and certain types of meningitis and pneumonia. It is believed to act on an enzyme in the body known as catalase, which normally frees from hydrogen peroxide produced by the germs the oxygen needed by them to breathe. Sulphanilimide poisons the enzyme, thus cutting off oxygen from the germs. In their weakened state, the germs fall a prey to the white blood corpuscles.

Sulphuric (Sulfuric) Acid. (H_2SO_4) A heavy, colorless, oily liquid, composed of hydrogen, sulphur, and oxygen; one of the most important of all chemicals. It was known as early as the 8th century, and is commercially called *oil of vitriol* because in the early days the alchemists prepared it by distilling the vitriols, especially green vitriol or iron sulphate.

Sulphuric acid is produced by chemical combination of the fumes of burning sulphur, oxygen of the air, and water. The sulphur fumes are generally obtained by burning sulphur, or a native sulphide of iron called *pyrites*. An increasingly important source of sulphur fumes is the waste gases from smelters where copper and zinc are produced from their sulphide ores.

There are two principal methods for manufacturing the acid, the *chamber process* and the *contact process*, which differ chiefly in the means used to cause the gases to combine. In the chamber process, the gases, mixed with oxides of nitrogen which speed up the reaction, are passed into large lead chambers and then through towers where the combination is completed. The more modern contact process is so called because the gases are caused to combine by contact with a catalyzer, such as finely divided platinum. The chamber process produces a large proportion of the weaker commercial acid; the contact process produces a purer and more concentrated product as well as *oleum*, or fuming sulphuric acid, which is 100 per cent acid containing dissolved sulphur trioxide. The standard commercial grade known as oil of vitriol has a gravity of 66° Bé. and contains 93.2 per cent of sulphuric acid. Dilute acids are usually handled in lead or special iron containers, while the stronger acids can be shipped in steel tanks.

Sulphates, or the salts of sulphuric acid, are of two kinds: acid sulphates in which only half of the hydrogen in the acid is replaced by a metal, and neutral sulphates in which all of the hydrogen has been replaced. Barium sulphate is probably the most generally insoluble of all known salts. When sulphuric acid is mixed with water, a large amount of heat is generated. Consequently, in order to avoid danger, the acid should always be added to the water and water should never be poured into strong acid.

Manufacture of sulphuric acid is one of the greatest chemical industries because the use of this acid is necessary in preparing almost all other chemical products. The largest amount of the acid is used in the preparation of fertilizers. Purification of petroleum, cleaning of iron and steel, production of nitric, hydrochloric, and mixed acids, and the textile industries, all require large amounts of sulphuric acid.

The concentrated acid is a powerful corrosive poison, with such a great attraction for water that it often causes charring of organic tissue. Sulphuric acid burns should immediately be rinsed with large quantities of water and then treated with solution of baking soda or other weak alkali.

Tannin. A substance extracted from nutgalls, oak and hemlock bark, quebracho and chestnut woods, sumac, and many other plants. It has the power to combine with raw skin and change it to leather. The active tanning materials from these different sources are not all the same substance, but all are very similar to *tannic acid.* This tannin is obtained from powdered galls and purified by chemical methods. It is used not only in tanning but also in medicine and as a mordant in dyeing. When a solution of tannic acid is added to a solution of an iron salt, a black substance is formed which is the basis of most writing ink. See *Ink, Leather.*

Tartaric Acid. A white, crystalline, organic acid obtained chiefly from *argol,* the sediment that forms during the fermentation of grape juice. Tartaric acid is used in medicine, dyeing, bleaching, calico printing, and the manufacture of cooling drinks. It is sometimes used as an ingredient of baking and of Seidlitz powders.

Vitriol. A term used by the earlier chemists to include certain glasslike salts, of which the best known are: *white vitriol* or zinc sulphate, *blue vitriol* or copper sulphate, and *green vitriol* or iron sulphate. Sulphuric acid is often called *oil of vitriol* because it was originally prepared from green vitriol.

Wood Alcohol. (CH_3OH) A colorless, volatile liquid, with a peculiar pungent odor, known chemically as *methyl alcohol,* or *methanol,* and called also *wood spirit,* or *pyroxylic spirit.* It is one of the important constituents of the distillates produced when wood is heated in closed retorts, without free access to the air. Like ordinary alcohol, it is highly inflammable and is an excellent solvent for many substances. It is composed of carbon, hydrogen, and oxygen, and is the simplest in molecular structure of all the alcohols. It boils at 65° C., or 149° F., and mixes readily with water, ether, acetone, and other alcohols.

Wood alcohol is employed chiefly for making shellac varnishes, and for denaturing grain or ethyl alcohol so that it may be used tax-free in various industries. It is used also in making formaldehyde and dyestuffs and for many other purposes. When taken into the human stomach, wood alcohol is a violent poison, with the peculiar property that a small dose, insufficient to produce death, may cause total blindness. If inhaled in quantity, the fumes are also dangerous.

CHEMICAL SUBSTANCES, COMMON NAMES OF

Common Name	Chemical Name
Alcohol, grain	Ethyl alcohol. C_2H_5OH.
Alcohol, wood	Methyl alcohol, Methanol. CH_3OH.
Alum, chrome	Potassium-Chromium sulphate. $Cr_2(SO_4)_3K_2SO_4 \cdot 24H_2O$.
Alum, common	Potassium-Aluminum sulphate. $Al_2(SO_4)_3K_2SO_4 \cdot 24H_2O$.
Aqua fortis	Nitric acid. HNO_3.
Aqua regia	Mixed nitric and hydrochloric acids.
Arsenic, white	Arsenous oxide. As_2O_3.
Bauxite	Hydrated alumina. $Al_2O_3 \cdot 2H_2O$.
Bleaching powder	Calcium hypochlorite.
Borax	Sodium tetraborate. $Na_2B_4O_7 \cdot 10H_2O$.
Calomel	Mercurous chloride. $HgCl$.
Carbolic acid	Phenol. C_6H_5OH.
Caustic potash	Potassium hydroxide. KOH.
Caustic soda	Sodium hydroxide. $NaOH$.
Cementite	Iron carbide. Fe_3C.
Chalk	Calcium carbonate. $CaCO_3$.
Chrome yellow	Lead chromate. $PbCrO_4$.
Copperas	Sulphate of iron. $FeSO_4 \cdot 7H_2O$.
Corrosive sublimate	Mercuric chloride. $HgCl_2$.
Cream of tartar	Potassium bitartrate. $KHC_4H_4O_6$.
Epsom salts	Magnesium sulphate. $MgSO_4 \cdot 7H_2O$.
Fire damp	Methane. CH_4.
Fruit sugar	Fructose. $C_6H_{12}O_6$.
Galena	Lead sulphide. PbS.
Glauber's salt	Sodium sulphate. $Na_2SO_4 \cdot 10H_2O$.
Goulard water	Basic acetate of lead. $Pb(OH)(C_2H_3O_2)$.
Grape sugar	Glucose. $C_6H_{12}O_6$.
Gypsum	Calcium sulphate. $CaSO_4 \cdot 2H_2O$.
Hematite	Ferric oxide. Fe_2O_3.
Hypo	Sodium thiosulphate. $Na_2S_2O_3 \cdot 5H_2O$.
Iceland spar	Crystallized calcium carbonate. $CaCO_3$.
Iron pyrites	Iron disulphide. FeS_2.
Jewelers' putty	Tin oxide. SnO_2.
Laughing gas	Nitrous oxide. N_2O.
Lime, quick	Calcium oxide. CaO.
Lime, slaked	Calcium hydroxide. $Ca(OH)_2$.
Limestone	Calcium carbonate. $CaCO_3$.
Litharge	Lead monoxide. PbO.
Lunar caustic	Silver nitrate. $AgNO_3$.
Magnetite	Magnetic oxide of iron. Fe_3O_4.
Marsh gas	Methane. CH_4.
Minium	Red oxide of lead. Pb_3O_4.
Mosaic gold	Tin sulphide, stannic sulphide. SnS_2.
Muriatic acid	Hydrochloric acid. HCl.
Orpiment	Arsenous sulphide. As_2S_3.
Phosgene	Carbonyl chloride. $COCl_2$.
Phosphate rock	Calcium phosphate. $Ca_3(PO_4)_2$.
Prussian blue	Ferric ferrocyanide. $Fe_4[Fe(CN)_6]_3$.
Prussic acid	Hydrocyanic acid. HNC.
Quicksilver	Mercury. Hg.
Realgar	Arsenic sulphide. As_2S_2.
Red lead	Red oxide of lead. Pb_3O_4.
Red oil	Crude oleic acid. $C_{17}H_{33}COOH$.
Rochelle salts	Sodium potassium tartrate. $NaKC_4H_4O_6 \cdot 4H_2O$.
Sal ammoniac	Ammonium chloride. NH_4Cl.
Saleratus	Sodium bicarbonate. $NaHCO_3$.
Sal soda	Sodium carbonate crystals. $Na_2CO_3 \cdot 10H_2O$.
Salt, common	Sodium chloride. $NaCl$.
Saltpeter	Potassium nitrate. KNO_3.
Saltpeter, Chile	Sodium nitrate. $NaNO_3$.
Salts of sorrel	Acid potassium oxalate. KHC_2O_4.
Soda, baking	Sodium bicarbonate. $NaHCO_3$.
Soda, washing	Sodium carbonate. Na_2CO_3.
Spirits of hartshorn	Ammonia, solution of, NH_3.
Spirits of salts	Hydrochloric acid. HCl.
Sugar (cane or beet)	Sucrose. $C_{12}H_{22}O_{11}$.
Sugar of lead	Lead acetate. $Pb(C_2H_3O_2)_2$.
Superphosphate	Monocalcium phosphate. $CaH_4(PO_4)_2 \cdot H_2O$.
Tartar emetic	Potassium antimonyl tartrate. $KSbOC_4H_4O_6 \cdot \frac{1}{2}H_2O$.
TNT	Trinitrotoluene. $C_6H_2 \cdot CH_3(NO_2)_3$.
Verdigris	Basic acetate of copper. $Cu_3(OH)_2(C_2H_3O_2)_4$.
Vermilion	Sulphide of mercury. HgS.
Vitriol, blue	Copper sulphate. $CuSO_4 \cdot 5H_2O$.
Vitriol, green	Ferrous sulphate. $FeSO_4 \cdot 7H_2O$.
Vitriol, oil of	Sulphuric acid. H_2SO_4.
Vitriol, white	Zinc sulphate. $ZnSO_4 \cdot 7H_2O$.
Water glass	Sodium silicate. $Na_2Si_4O_9$.
White lead	Basic lead carbonate. $Pb_3(OH)_2(CO_3)_2$.

METALLIC ALLOYS

Allegheny Metal. A trade name of a chrome-nickel iron alloy. It consists of approximately 18 per cent of chromium, 8 per cent of nickel, and .2 per cent of carbon, the rest being iron. This valuable alloy is hard, non-rusting, and capable of taking a mirror-like polish. It is adapted for exposed metal work on buildings and automobiles, for durable cooking utensils, and for plumbing fixtures and chemical apparatus.

Alnico. An alloy composed of 8 to 12 per cent aluminum, 14 to 28 per cent nickel, and 5 to 24 per cent cobalt, the balance consisting of iron. Alnico is used in the manufacture of strong permanent magnets which are replacing electromagnets in much electrical equipment.

Aluminum Bronze. An alloy of copper containing 2.3 to 10.5 per cent aluminum. It is easily fusible, has a beautiful golden color, and possesses very high chemical and mechanical resistance. As it is unaffected by salt water, this alloy is much used for marine fittings.

Aluminum Gold. A beautiful alloy consisting of gold 78 parts and aluminum 22 parts, remarkable for its rich purple shade. It is used in the manufacture of jewelry.

Aluminum Steel. While aluminum combines with iron in all proportions, only alloys containing minute quantities of aluminum are of practical value. Aluminum steel usually contains only from 2 to 12 ounces of aluminum per ton. This addition gives the metal greater tensile strength and a smoother and closer grain.

Antifriction Metals. Certain alloys employed in the construction of machine bearings to minimize friction. Four metals chiefly are used in these mixtures; namely, tin, lead, antimony, and copper, to which zinc, nickel, or bismuth are sometimes added. The original antifriction metal, called Babbitt metal, after its inventor, has long since been largely supplanted by alloys containing combinations better adapted for use in the various classes or kinds of bearings. For example, entirely different proportions of the component metals are required for light-work bearings and for heavily loaded bearings. The alloy known as "universal bearing metal" consists of tin 6 parts, lead 77.75 parts, antimony 16 parts, and bismuth 0.25 part.

Babbitt Metal. An alloy of copper, tin, and antimony, invented in 1839 by Isaac Babbitt, widely used as an antifriction metal. The original alloy consisted of tin 24 parts, antimony 8 parts, and copper 2 parts. A tough and serviceable variety contains tin 96 parts, antimony 8 parts, copper 4 parts. On account of cheapness, lead is often added, and commercial Babbitt metal often contains a much larger percentage of inexpensive lead than the selling price would indicate.

Bell Metal. A kind of bronze, usually consisting of an alloy of copper and tin in varying proportions. Soft-toned bells contain about 16 per cent tin; cymbals, gongs, and house bells, 18 to 20 per cent tin; school bells, 22 per cent tin; church bells and fire bells, about 24 per cent tin. In some cases larger proportions of tin are used. A very fine bell metal is made of copper 90 parts, tin 5 parts, zinc 5 parts, and manganese 1 part.

Brass. An alloy composed of varying proportions of copper and zinc, usually about 2 parts copper to 1 part zinc. It was known and used in very ancient times, and is employed for a great variety of purposes, including the manufacture of an immense number of useful articles, which have given rise to extensive industries. Varieties of brass well known in trade and industry are red brass, yellow brass, brass foil or Dutch leaf, gilding metal, Mannheim gold, pinchbeck, bath metal, Bristol brass, Munz metal, and spelter solder.

Britannia Metal. A kind of pewter, an alloy composed of tin and antimony, with small additions of zinc and copper. It is much harder than earlier forms of pewter and is nearly as white in color and handsome in luster as silver. Britannia metal is largely used for making coffeepots, teapots, soup tureens, and other dishes and household articles.

Bronze. An alloy of copper and tin, in proportions varying from 5 to 1 to 24 to 1, to which other metals are often added. Bronze was used by prehistoric peoples in Europe and South America, and by the ancient Assyrians and Egyptians. At the present day an immense variety of bronzes are made; as, for example, those used for mathematical instruments, gear wheels, statues, medals, coins, bells, machine bearings, and speculum metal.

The commercial "bronzes" are usually three-metal alloys made by adding other metals,—chiefly lead, zinc, phosphorus, manganese, or aluminum—to the true copper-tin bronze. Many so-called bronzes are only varieties of brass. Titanium-aluminum bronze is the hardest form of all but is very difficult to work. Statuary bronzes are always cast hollow, the standard thickness of the shell filling the mold being from about a quarter to a third of an inch. See *Coin Bronze, Phosphor Bronze*.

Carboloy. A trade name of an extremely hard alloy of tungsten, carbon, and cobalt originated by the Krupp works in Germany about 1927. It is used for the cutting edge of machine tools, being hard enough to shave glass. In Germany it is called widia, from *wie Diamant*, "like diamond."

Cast Iron. A casting of iron, known also as pig iron. It is run directly from the smelting furnace into open sand or metal molds, forming small oblong bars of a weight convenient for handling, called *pigs*. Cast iron is usually very impure, containing various other elements and metals which make it much harder, more brittle, and much more easily fusible than wrought iron. The substances which give to cast iron its peculiar qualities are mainly carbon, manganese, sulphur, phosphorus, and silicon. Sometimes copper, nickel, chromium, or titanium are present. Cast iron commonly contains from 1½ to 4 per cent of carbon. In case the carbon is in the form of carbide, the iron is hard and brittle; if in the form of graphite, the iron is soft and tough. Foundry irons used for ordinary castings may contain not to exceed 3½ per cent of silicon. Such castings will be fairly soft and easily machined.

Pig iron low in phosphorus is used for making steel by the Bessemer process. Such iron is called *Bessemer pig*. When high in phosphorus, cast iron is suitable for making steel by the basic Bessemer and the open-hearth processes, and is called *basic pig* or *Thomas pig*. Owing to its brittleness, cast iron cannot be hammered like wrought iron or soft steel. It may be cast in molds, and, since it resists corrosion, is used extensively for underground pipes. See *Iron, Wrought Iron*.

Chrome Steel. A special steel containing in some high-speed tool steels as high as 7 per cent of chromium. The addition of chromium materially increases the strength, hardness, elasticity, and erosion resistance of steel, giving rise to so-called stainless steel and rustless iron.

Coinage Alloys. As established by acts of Congress, the standard gold coins of the United States contain 9 parts of gold and 1 part of copper. Coinage gold, therefore, is 900 fine. Similarly, all silver coins contain 9 parts of silver and 1 part of copper and are, likewise, 900 fine. The present day five-cent coins, or "nickels," are an alloy of copper 75 per cent and nickel 25 per cent. The copper cent is an alloy of copper 95 parts and zinc and tin 5 parts.

Cooperite. An alloy of nickel and zirconium used in making high-speed tools for metal working. It is lighter and stronger than stellite and various other alloys used for the purpose and is comparatively inexpensive.

Copper Aluminum. An alloy of aluminum containing 7 to 10 per cent copper. This tough metal is especially useful in making automobile and other constructional parts which are subjected to sudden and severe shocks.

Crucible Steel. A fine grade of cast steel made in crucibles and characterized by great hardness due to a high content of carbon. The crucible process was originally used for obtaining homogeneous metal by melting bars of blister steel, which contain more carbon near the surface than at the center.

In the modern process, pure wrought iron is melted with selected materials high in carbon, such as pig iron, scrap steel, or pure charcoal. Small amounts of manganese are generally added, together with chromium, vanadium, or other metals required for special products. After melting is complete, the metal is held liquid for about half an hour at the "killing" temperature. During this time gases are given off, silicon is taken up from the slag or crucible, and the liquid becomes quiet. Slag is then removed from the surface and the steel poured into molds.

In England the crucibles used are made entirely of clay, but in America they generally contain about 50 per cent of Ceylon graphite. A standard graphite crucible holds about 90 pounds of metal and lasts for from 5 to 10 heats.

Crucible steel is used especially where hardness is required —for cutting tools, razors, springs, dies, and similar products. It usually contains from .9 to 1.4 per cent carbon, although extremely hard steels contain larger amounts.

Duralumin. An alloy whose average composition is 95% aluminum, 3½% copper, and the remainder magnesium and manganese. It was patented in 1909 by the German chemist Alfred Wilm. It is comparable with steel in strength and has the additional merit of lightness of weight. Its tensile strength per ton is nearly 3 times as great as that of 40 tons of steel. One of its most important applications is in the construction of aircraft.

Dutch Metal. A variety of brass containing a large percentage of copper; called also Dutch foil or Dutch leaf. It is made by rolling the metal into very thin sheets and then beating it to a foil, often not more than $\frac{1}{50000}$ of an inch in thickness. It is widely used for gilding.

Electrum. A name given to natural alloys of gold and silver, known and used for inlaying and for coins since very ancient times. Pliny states that the term electrum was given to gold containing at least 20 per cent of silver. The electrum found in various mines of California and Nevada bears about 40 per cent of silver.

Ferroboron. A ferro-alloy containing 10 to 20 per cent of boron. The effect of small amounts of boron on steels is to increase their depth of hardness, ultimate strength, and elastic limit.

Ferrochrome. A ferro-alloy containing from about 60 to 70 per cent of chromium; used for making special chromium steels.

Ferromanganese. An alloy of iron and manganese containing 80 per cent of the latter; the name is given also to any ferro-alloy containing over 30 per cent of manganese. It is used chiefly in steel making.

Ferrosilicon. An alloy of iron produced in the blast furnace and containing about 12 per cent of silicon. A high grade containing over 40 per cent of silicon is made in the electric furnace. Ferrosilicon is used in producing steel of a special quality and for generating hydrogen.

Fusible Metals. A name given to a group of alloys characterized by very low melting points, such as D'Arcet's metal, Lipowitz' metal, Rose's metal, and Wood's metal.

All of these contain bismuth mixed with lead, tin, or cadmium in various proportions and have melting points ranging from 140° F. to 201° F.,—all below the boiling point of water.

Galvanized Iron. Sheet iron or steel coated with zinc. This coating is most commonly put on simply by dipping well cleaned sheets or articles in a bath of molten zinc. It is also effected by heating the sheets of iron in a drum filled with zinc dust, and by electroplating them with zinc. As the last method, which is but little used, is the only one employing the galvanic current, zinc-coated iron is a more accurate term than galvanized iron. As this coating prevents rust, galvanized iron (or steel) is very extensively used for roofing, gutters, cisterns, tanks, wire ropes, wire netting, ship fittings, and innumerable minor purposes. In making the so-called galvanized tinware, the sheet iron is first thinly coated with tin and then coated with zinc.

German Silver. An alloy composed of copper, zinc, and nickel, in proportions varying according to the purpose of its use. When intended to replace silver, it contains copper 50 parts, zinc 25 parts, and nickel 25 parts. This alloy is harder than silver and is capable of taking a high polish. It is used as a substitute for silver in making bells, candlesticks, and various utensils, and, more especially, as a foundation metal in the manufacture of silver-plated ware.

High-speed Steels. A large number of alloys of steel, containing tungsten, or molybdenum and manganese, or chromium; known also as self-hardening or air-hardening steels. These special steels are capable of doing from two to four times as much work in machinery or metal lathe work as can be done with tempered carbon steel, now called ordinary tool steel.

High-speed steel tools are most useful in making rapid rough cuts with the lathe or planer. For fine finishing, tempered carbon steel tools are superior. However, a tungsten steel tool will hold a cutting edge at a temperature more than twice as high as any plain carbon steel. The speed of lathes for rough cuts can be raised from two to five times their normal rate when high-speed steel is used instead of ordinary tempered steel for tools. Consequently, a workman can triple his former output in axle turning and similar rough cutting work. This increased efficiency has revolutionized shop practice in both metal and wood lathe and planer work throughout the world.

Invar. An alloy composed of nickel, 36 per cent, and steel. Under the influence of heat and cold, invar shows the least variation of all available metals; it is therefore very valuable for instruments of exact measurement. It is soft, bends easily, and resembles nickel rather than steel. Its tensile strength, while less than that of steel, is sufficient for surveyors' measuring tapes. Invar is used in making bars for standards of length, for comparators, for clock pendulums, and in constructing other instruments of precision.

Konel. An alloy of cobalt, nickel, and ferrotitanium in the proportion of about 18:73:9. It has the rare property of becoming tougher when heated, withstanding a pressure of 60,000 pounds to the square inch at 1100° F. It replaces iridium in the filament of radio tubes and is adapted for use in internal combustion engines. It can be drawn into a wire one-thousandth of an inch thick.

Magnalium. An alloy of aluminum with 2 to 10 per cent of magnesium; lighter than aluminum, but equal in strength and workability to high quality brass.

Magnetic Alloys. A group of interesting alloys discovered by F. Heusler in 1898; called also Heusler alloys. Besides manganese, or manganese copper, these more or less complex mixtures contain one or more of the elements aluminum, antimony, arsenic, bismuth, boron, and tin. Of these, the aluminum-manganese-copper alloys exhibit the greatest magnetism,—about one-third of that of soft iron—though none of the component metals, when taken separately, is magnetic. Manganese tin is magnetic, and continues so when copper is added to the mixture. Manganese copper is nonmagnetic but acquires magnetism when tin is added. See *Alnico*.

Manganese Bronze. An alloy of copper and manganese, with tin or zinc. The red variety, composed of 80 parts copper, 10 parts tin, and 10 parts of a 20 per cent manganese-copper alloy, is used for gear wheels. The yellow variety is composed of 50 parts copper, 44 parts zinc, and 6 parts of a 20 per cent manganese-copper alloy. It is used for automobile castings, gun mechanisms, and especially for motor boat shafts and propeller blades, as it is unaffected by the action of sea water.

Manganese Steel. A form of steel containing from 7 to 15 per cent manganese, which imparts great hardness, toughness, and resistance to abrasion. It is used for pulverizers, rock crushers, and other similar purposes.

Molybdenum Steel. A special steel containing molybdenum and manganese; one of the first to be used in high-speed tool work, but found, for this purpose, inferior to tungsten steel. The addition of molybdenum, however, exerts a beneficial effect upon the magnetic qualities of the metal, and molybdenum steel ranks as one of the best materials known for making permanent magnets. Alloys of steel with molybdenum, nickel, and chromium are employed in making guns, armor plates, steel helmets, and airplane and automobile parts.

Monel Metal. An alloy consisting of about 65 parts of nickel and 30 parts of copper, with smaller amounts of iron, manganese, silicon, and cobalt. This metal, which is manufactured direct from native Canadian nickel ore, possesses great tensile strength and resists, to a remarkable degree, tarnishing by the air. It is particularly suitable for window screens, ship fittings, and various similar purposes.

Nickel Steel. Various alloys of steel and nickel which melt at a lower heat than the corresponding carbon steels. While tough and possessing high tensile strength and elasticity, nickel steel forgings are not difficult to machine. The alloy called invar or invar steel, containing 36 per cent of nickel, is remarkable for its small rate of expansion when heated. As its expansion is only one-twelfth that of pure iron, invar is very valuable for clock pendulums, chronometers, and measuring rods. It also possesses great power to resist corrosion.

Noble Metals. A name given to those metals which do not tarnish or corrode in the air, such as gold, silver, platinum, rhodium, mercury, and palladium. Sometimes, however, the term is applied only to the first three; again, it is made to include copper and other metals which are fairly resistant to oxidation.

Permalloy. An alloy of 39 parts of nickel and 11 parts of iron. It is extremely sensitive to magnetizing and demagnetizing influences. For this reason it is valuable for encasing submarine cables and adds greatly to their capacity. A New York-London cable, laid in 1926 and encased in permalloy, showed a transmitting capacity of 2500 letters a minute. This rate is about four times the previous maximum.

Pewter. An alloy usually composed largely of tin with small parts of antimony, copper, and zinc. It is used in place of silver plate for making many articles of table ware and other utensils. Pewter ware of earlier times contained about 20 per cent of lead, but the modern ware, which is non-tarnishable, usually has no lead and is very similar to Britannia metal. It is, as a rule, harder than the earlier pewter ware.

Phosphor Bronze. An alloy generally composed of about 92 per cent of copper and 8 of tin, with .15 per cent of phosphorus. It possesses unusual toughness and hardness and hence is especially valuable for piston rings, valve covers, cog wheels, and screw propellers.

Platinum Metals. A group of precious metals found associated with platinum and more or less resembling it in various properties. Besides platinum, it includes palladium, osmium, iridium, ruthenium, rhodium, and the natural combination or alloy called osmiridium or iridosmine. Each of these has its special characteristics and usefulness. Of these, iridium and osmium are heavier than platinum, being the heaviest substances known.

Pyrophoric Alloys. A group of alloys so named on account of their peculiar property of emitting hot sparks when rubbed with a rough file. They consist of metals of the cerium group in alloy with cobalt, nickel, iron, or manganese. The pyrophoric alloy used in making automatic gas lighters is composed of 65 per cent of cerium metals and 35 per cent of iron. In gunnery, pyrophoric alloys are set in the shells of projectiles so that the friction caused by their rapid passage through the air ignites the alloy, producing a shower of sparks which mark their path of flight.

"Rare Earth" Metals. The name given to a group of metals whose oxides are known as "rare earths." For a long period these resisted all efforts of chemists and metallurgists to reduce them to the metallic state. Among these metals are cerium, gadolinium, lanthanum, terbium, thorium, samarium, scandium, ytterbium, yttrium, and zirconium.

Rose's Metal. An alloy composed of 1 part lead, 1 part tin, and 2 parts bismuth, which melts at 94° C., or 201° F.,—or below the boiling point of water. It is used in various safety devices in which advantage is taken of its low melting point.

Solder. An alloy or metal used, when melted, to join other metals. Soldering alloys may be classified as *hard* solder if they melt above a red heat, and as *soft solder* when they melt at lower temperatures. These are also called brazing solder and tinning solder. The melting point of a solder should be lower than that of the metal on which it is used.

A well-liked soft solder is that known as half and half, made from equal weights of tin and lead. For electrical work, antimony is usually added so as to impart a low melting point. Forty parts of copper and 60 parts of zinc make a good hard solder for copper and hard brass; a mixture of 60 parts of copper with 40 parts of zinc is often used for soldering iron. Gold is usually soldered with a mixture of gold, silver, and copper. No completely satisfactory solder for aluminum has yet been found.

Soft solders are usually applied by means of a pointed bar of copper, called a soldering iron, while hard soldering is almost always done with a blowpipe. In certain branches of the canning industry the soldering is often performed entirely by machinery. A flux of rosin, sal ammoniac, zinc chloride, borax, or similar substance, is generally applied to the parts to be joined, so as to dissolve any oxides and clean the metallic surfaces.

Spelter. The trade name for ordinary commercial zinc which usually contains various impurities, chiefly lead and iron. As only the purer grades can be used for making ductile brass, the price of spelter depends very largely upon the amount of lead and iron present. Some forms of hard solder are also called spelter.

Stainless Steel. An alloy of iron, chromium, and carbon, combining hardness with a remarkable freedom from corrosion. It was patented in 1916 by the English metallurgist Brearley. Chromium is present in amounts of 9 to 16% with carbon not exceeding .7%. The alloy is heated to a bright red heat and then quenched rapidly, the latter operation being necessary to the noncorrosive property of the alloy. It is used for cutlery and in automobile manufacture.

By employing a lower percentage of carbon, about .1%, a *rustless iron* of high tensile strength may be produced. Heat treatment of the finished forms is unnecessary. Being cheaper and more easily worked, this alloy is suitable for wide industrial application. Among the first uses to which it was put was the manufacture of a rustless wire rope having a tensile strength of about 100 tons per square inch.

Steel. A form of iron possessing many qualities greatly superior to those of ordinary iron for an immense number of purposes. Steel is a compound of iron and carbon intermediate between wrought iron and cast iron, usually containing more carbon than wrought iron, but always less carbon than cast iron, and is sometimes alloyed with small quantities of various other metals. So many varieties of steel are made that no single quality, except excellence or adaptability, can be said to be characteristic of it. In general, steel is stronger, harder, finer, smoother, and more elastic than iron. It takes a higher polish and does not rust so readily. The different forms of steel are grouped in two general classes:

High-carbon steels, containing from 0.8 to 2 per cent carbon, are granular in structure, and may be cast and tempered, but are not easily welded. They are very hard when tempered, form permanent magnets, and are used for cutting-tools, springs, and dies.

Low-carbon and *medium steels*, with from 0.05 to 0.8 per cent carbon, are either granular or fibrous in texture, moderately soft, and may be either cast or welded and, when containing above 0.3 per cent carbon, tempered. To this class belong the varieties of metal used in making sheet steel, structural steel, steel rails, steel wire, and steel nails. The various steels of this group, manufactured in forms adapted to a multitude of uses, constitute the most valuable metallic product of modern times and are indispensable to present-day civilization.

Formerly, practically all steel was made by heating bars of wrought iron covered with charcoal in an air-tight furnace for a week or ten days. In this process some of the carbon of the charcoal enters into the iron, forming what is called *blister steel*. The bars are then hammered into *shear steel* or, after being melted and cast into ingots, are forged and rolled into bars, called *cast steel*. This process, which yields only small quantities, is very slow and expensive, so that before the introduction, about 1870, of cheap methods of steel making, very little steel, as compared with wrought or cast iron, was used.

Cast steel is now made almost entirely by the Bessemer and open-hearth processes, whereby a great variety of steels are produced directly from cast iron. By making possible the manufacture of steel in quantities at low cost, these processes have not only completely revolutionized the iron and steel industries of the world, but also all mechanical and engineering construction. A more recent major advance in efficiency was introduction since 1914 of the cold rolling process, in which the ingot in a few minutes is passed through a continuous series of rollers, coming out in a coiled ribbon of sheet metal. Besides the gain in time and handling this process increases the hardness and tensile strength of the steel.

Besides the many common or carbon steels, there is a large number of special steels, called *alloy steels*. These are alloys of steel with varying, but usually small, proportions of one or more metals, including aluminum, chromium, molybdenum, nickel, tungsten, vanadium, and zirconium. Of these, chrome steel, molybdenum steel, nickel steel, tungsten steel, and vanadium steel are of great value in the construction of modern machinery, especially in making automobiles and airplanes. See *Aluminum Steel, Chrome Steel, Crucible Steel, High-speed Steels, Invar, Molybdenum Steel, Tungsten Steel.*

Stellite. The name given to a group of alloys consisting chiefly of cobalt and chromium, patented in 1913 by Elwood Haynes. When polished, stellite displays a beautiful luster, which does not become tarnished by exposure to the air, water, or household acids. It may be readily forged into knives, forks, spoons and similar articles of superior hardness. With the addition of tungsten or molybdenum its hardness is very greatly increased making it suitable for use as a tool metal.

Stereotype Metal. An alloy composed of lead 67 parts, tin 17 parts, antimony 16 parts; used in the printing trades for casting stereotype plates from which daily newspapers and sometimes books are printed.

Sterling Silver. An alloy consisting of 925 parts of silver and 75 parts of copper, established by law as the standard of fineness of British silver coins, whence the use of the term sterling silver for all articles made from silver of equal purity and wearing qualities.

Tin Plate. Sheet iron or sheet steel covered on both sides with tin. The process of making tin plate is simple. The iron or steel sheets are first thoroughly cleaned with acid, and are then dipped into vats of molten tin and palm oil. When the sheets have become coated to the required thickness, they are taken out of the vats and cleaned. The greater part of the tin now produced is devoted to the manufacture of tin plate.

Tungsten Steel. A special steel containing varying amounts of tungsten, sometimes as high as 12 or even 25 per cent, especially valuable for high-speed metal cutting. Tools made of tungsten do not lose their temper until very high temperatures are reached, and may be worked up to white heat without impairment of cutting power.

Type Metal. An alloy commonly composed of about 10 parts of lead, 4 parts of antimony, and 2 parts of tin. The tin gives toughness; the antimony, hardness and also the property of expansion when solidifying. This combination produces the required sharp casting. A softer type metal, widely used in linotype work, is made by increasing the amount of lead and decreasing that of tin.

White Gold. The name given to various alloys of gold, chiefly silver alloys. To the Greeks it was known as electron. Alloys of palladium or silver with gold, under this name, are frequently used in jewelry in place of platinum. The name is applied also to the mineral sylvanite ($AuAgTe_4$).

Wood's Metal. An alloy composed of bismuth 15 parts, tin 4 parts, and cadmium 3 parts; remarkable for its low melting point, only 60° C., or 140° F.,—the lowest of all the fusible alloys. This and similar bismuth alloys are used for safety plugs in automatic fire-sprinkler systems.

Wrought Iron. One of the purest forms of iron industrially used. It is a soft, grayish white metal with a melting point much higher than that of cast iron and approaching that of platinum. Wrought iron is made from cast iron in specially prepared furnaces by the puddling process, during which most of the carbon, sulphur, phosphorus, silicon, and manganese is removed. By the Aston process, molten refined iron is poured into slag. It presses out dissolved gases and takes in some slag. Settling as a spongy, red ball, it is placed in hydraulic presses and then hot rolled. This process leaves no blisters and permits of mass production.

Wrought iron is very malleable and ductile, and, when heated, may readily be hammered into bars, rolled into plates, or drawn into wire. Further, it can easily be welded at red heat, and is highly resistant to corrosion, properties which make wrought iron the most useful of metals for an immense variety of purposes. It is used for making boiler plates, ship's plates, pipes, anchors, sheet iron, chain cables, wire, wheel tires, horseshoes, nails, spikes, bolts, and the iron parts of innumerable tools and implements. See *Cast Iron, Iron.*

PHYSIOLOGY AND ANATOMY

PHYSIOLOGY, strictly defined, is the science which treats of the *uses* or *functions* of organs in living beings. Anatomy deals with the structure and organization of plants and animals. These subjects as treated here are limited to the physiology and anatomy of man.

Closely allied to these sciences are several others whose subject matter is drawn on slightly in making the following articles as helpful as possible. The chief ones are *histology*, that is, minute or microscopic anatomy; *hygiene*, the study of the ways of living that promote health; *sanitation*, which deals with external conditions conducing to health; *dietetics*, the study of foods and food values, including their use in health and disease; and *pathology*, the study of disease.

Structure of the Body. The human body is composed primarily of solids and liquids. In childhood and youth, fluids are more abundant, giving softness, roundness, and pliancy to the flesh. In advanced age, the fluids are much less abundant, so that the flesh is firmer, and the skin is more wrinkled. In a sense the fluids contain the entire body in a state of solution, that is, they contain the various materials out of which the tissues and organs are built up.

Chemical Constituents.—Seventeen different chemical elements have been found in the human body, as follows: oxygen, carbon, hydrogen, nitrogen, sulphur, phosphorus, chlorine, fluorine, silicon, sodium, potassium, lithium, calcium, magnesium, iron, manganese, and iodine. Of these, oxygen, carbon, hydrogen, and nitrogen comprise nearly the whole bulk of the fluids and softer portions. The others, mostly in a state of combination and in comparatively small quantities, enter into the composition of various tissues. The chemical compounds occurring in the body may be classed as organic and inorganic. The organic compounds contain carbon, oxygen, hydrogen, and some nitrogen, the most important being albumins, fats, and carbohydrates. The chief inorganic compounds are water, common salt, carbonate of lime, and phosphate of lime.

Physical Constituents.—The body consists of various organs and systems of organs, each serving some special use or function in carrying on the various vital activities and processes.

System.—A system is a group of several separate organs spread throughout the body for a definite use, as, for example, the circulatory system or the nervous system.

Organ.—An organ is a group of different tissues of the body capable of performing some special action, as, for example, the liver, the heart, or the lungs.

Tissues.—The substances which make up the organs of the body are called tissues. Of these, the most important are the *epithelial* or *areolar*, *mucous*, *serous*, *fibrous*, *adipose*, *lymphoid*, *cartilaginous*, *bony* or *osseous*, *muscular*, and *nervous* tissues. These various tissues are the primary building materials which enter into the structure of the different parts of the body.

Cells.—Every bodily tissue is made up of cells. The cell is the unit of life, of structure, and of function. A fully developed cell consists of the cell body or *protoplasm*; the *nucleus*, a minute spherical body of denser protoplasm embodied in the contents of the cell; and the *nucleolus*, a small object lying within the nucleus. While differing greatly in shape, cells are usually rounded or flattened, and, in size, rarely exceed a thousandth of an inch in diameter. Some cells, however, are greatly elongated into fibers, attaining a maximum of about a yard. Cells are reproduced by dividing themselves into two parts, each half soon developing into a new cell, exactly similar to the original or parent cell from which it sprang.

Protoplasm.—The main bulk of the bodies of most cells consists of protoplasm, the so-called physical basis of life. It is living matter. In active cells it is a jelly-like, semitransparent, grayish, viscid substance somewhat resembling the raw white of an egg. It possesses all the vital properties by means of which the processes of nutrition, secretion, and growth go forward. The important principles of *contractility* and *irritability* and the fundamental processes of *metabolism* and *reproduction* are exemplified in the protoplasm of a single actively growing cell.

Function.—A function is the normal work performed by a healthy organ, as the function of the stomach in the secretion of gastric juice, or the function of the liver in secreting bile.

Metabolism.—The process by which living cells are nourished by the nutritive material in the blood, or that by which they change their cell protoplasm into other substances, is called metabolism. As this process may both build up and tear down cells and tissues composed of cells, it may be either constructive (*anabolism*) or destructive (*katabolism*).

Abdomen. The portion of the body lying between the thorax and the pelvis, containing the abdominal cavity. This cavity, the largest in the adult body, is separated from the thorax or chest, which lies immediately above it, by a thin muscular wall called the diaphragm or midriff. The abdominal cavity extends from about the lower end of the sternum or breastbone to the pelvis and contains the most important digestive organs, including the stomach, intestines, liver, pancreas, and spleen, and also a part of the urinary system.

The walls of the abdomen consist of various layers of flat muscles, covered on the outside with skin and lined throughout the inside with a thin, smooth, moist serous membrane, called the *peritoneum.* All abdominal organs are covered on the outside with this membrane. On account of this characteristic lining, the abdominal cavity is often called the *peritoneal cavity.* The disease known as peritonitis is an inflammation of the peritoneum. See *Pelvis*, *Thorax*.

Alimentary Canal. The digestive tract; in man a highly developed and differentiated tube or canal in which food is received, digested, and absorbed. It includes the whole passage traversed by substances taken in as food, from their entrance into the mouth to the excretion of the indigestible residue.

In an adult the alimentary canal has a total length of from 25 to 30 feet, and is lined throughout with mucous membrane. Outside this membrane are layers of muscle and other tissue to give strength to the walls of the various organs forming the canal, to help mix the food with the digestive fluids, and to push it along its course.

The principal organs of the canal in the order that the food passes through them are the *mouth pharynx*, *esophagus*, *stomach*, and the *small* and the *large intestine.* The mouth opens into the pharynx or throat. The pharynx opens into the esophagus or gullet, a cylindrical tube about 10 inches in length. Passing back of the windpipe and lungs, the esophagus leads into the stomach through the *cardiac orifice.*

The stomach is a somewhat pear-shaped organ, varying in size with different individuals. Its widely expanded upper portion is called the *cardiac pouch.* The tapering lower or *pyloric* portion communicates with the small intestine through a ring-shaped constriction formed of sphincter muscle, called the *pylorus.*

The small intestine usually occupies a length of about 20 to 25 feet, and, necessarily, is decidedly coiled. The first 10 or more inches is called the *duodenum*; the next 8 or more feet, the *jejunum*, and the remainder, about 11 or 12 feet, the *ileum*. The small intestine finally communicates with the large intestine through a slitlike opening, called the *ileocæcal valve*.

The large intestine is divided into the *cæcum*, the *colon*, and the *rectum*. The first portion is the cæcum, into which the small intestine opens. The cæcum, however, projects below this opening and its lower part forms a blind sac, while the part above the opening continues upward into the colon. A small wormlike appendage of the cæcum, the function of which has not been exactly determined, is called the *vermiform appendix*. The colon is divided into an *ascending*, a *transverse*, and a *descending* portion, which, by their position, form an outer wall almost completely surrounding the small intestine. The colon is held in place by peritoneal ligaments. The rectum, or final portion of the large intestine, is a short, wide, smooth tube. See *Intestines, Mouth, Stomach, Throat*.

Allergy. A condition of supersensitivity of tissues to certain substances, which for this reason act as poisons to persons having such sensitiveness. Ailments so caused include hay fever, caused by pollen of certain flowers, and poisoning of certain people by food harmless to others. Persons so affected are said to be allergic to the causes.

Aorta. The great artery or trunk of the arterial system, proceeding from the left ventricle of the heart, and giving origin to all the arteries except the pulmonary. It first rises toward the top of the breastbone, when it is called the *ascending aorta*. It then makes a great curve, called the *transverse arch* or *great arch* of the aorta, which gives off branches to the head and upper extremities. Thence proceeding downward toward the lower extremities, under the name of the *descending aorta*, it gives off branches to the trunk. Finally, the aorta divides into the two *iliac* arteries, which supply the pelvis and lower extremities.

Arteries. The blood vessels by which the blood is carried out from the heart and distributed to the general system and to the lungs. The arteries which proceed to the general system, or body as a whole, commence in one large vessel, the *aorta*. This divides and subdivides into many branches, until they finally terminate in exceedingly small vessels called *capillaries*. These *systemic arteries* contain pure, oxidized, scarlet blood, known as arterial blood.

On the other hand, the arteries which proceed to the lungs, called the *pulmonary arteries*, are two vessels which have their origin in the right ventricle of the heart, and carry the blood to the right and to the left lung respectively. The pulmonary arteries contain unpurified, dark-colored blood, the same as in the veins and known as venous blood, while the pulmonary veins carry arterial blood.

The principal arteries are the two *carotid arteries*, which supply the head; the two *subclavian arteries*, which proceed to the arms; the two *iliac arteries*, to the legs; the *cœliac axis*, which supplies the liver, spleen, and stomach; the *mesenteric arteries*, which supply the walls of the intestines; and the *renal arteries*, which supply the kidneys. The walls of the arteries are composed of elastic fibers, connective tissue, and muscle cells.

Owing to its rigid walls, an artery, when cut, continues to bleed until death ensues, and the only way to arrest the bleeding permanently is to tie the severed end that is nearest to the heart. From a cut artery the flow of blood is of a jetlike nature, owing to the force with which the blood is propelled from the heart, while from a cut vein the blood merely trickles out. After a cut artery has been tied to prevent bleeding, the circulation of blood through it is re-established by what is called *anastomosis*, in which a network of small branches of the artery carries the blood around the point of injury and again unites with the main trunk.

The inner lining of the arteries is perfectly smooth, and there are no valves as in the veins. The arteries were so named because the ancients supposed that they contained air, being generally found empty after death. See *Aorta, Circulatory System, Heart*.

Assimilation. The changing of nutritive material into the fluid or solid portions of the body. Living tissues possess the power of working up into their own substance various food elements derived from the outside, as from the substances digested in the alimentary canal, absorbed by the lymphatics, and distributed throughout the body by the blood. Assimilation is the final stage in the process of nutrition. It takes place in the tissues side by side with the tearing down process, called dissimilation, which results in the removal of waste matter. See *Digestion, Nutrition*.

Bile. A yellowish brown or greenish, viscid fluid, secreted by the liver. It has a peculiar, musklike odor, a bitter taste, and an alkaline reaction. Of normal bile, various solids in solution form from 9 to 14 per cent. The chief constituents are the bile salts, sodium taurocholate and sodium glycocholate, and the bile pigments, or coloring matters, bilirubin and biliverdin. In addition, bile contains small quantities of mucinoid substances, fats, soaps, cholesterin, lecithin, urea, and mineral salts. The amount of bile secreted in a day by a healthy adult is estimated at from somewhat more than a pint to slightly more than a quart.

In digestion, the principal action of the bile is as an aid to the pancreatic juice, especially in emulsifying fat. Owing to its alkaline character, bile assists in neutralizing the acid chyme received in the intestine from the stomach. The bile seems to act also as an antiseptic, reducing excessive fermentation in the intestines. Moreover, the bile stimulates the muscular movements of the intestinal walls, *peristalsis*, thereby preventing constipation. Waste products, eliminated from the blood by the liver, are carried off by the bile.

Bladder. A membranous sac which serves as the receptacle of the urinary fluid secreted by the kidneys. It is situated in the pelvic cavity, behind the pubic bone, and is held in position by ligaments. When moderately distended, the bladder is about five inches long and three inches across, and ordinarily contains about a pint of urine. The bladder is connected with each kidney by a tube called a *ureter* and discharges its contents through a tube called the *urethra*. The walls of the bladder consist of a thick coat of unstriped (smooth) muscular tissue lined by a mucous membrane.

Blood. The thickish, opaque, red fluid which circulates through the tissues of the body, conveying digested food and oxygen and carrying away waste. Blood has a faint odor, is salty to the taste, and is alkaline in reaction. It consists of a transparent, colorless fluid, the *plasma*, or *liquor sanguinis*, in which float extremely minute solid bodies called *corpuscles* and still smaller bodies known as *platelets*. The plasma is composed of water in which are dissolved fibrin, albumin, common salt, calcium phosphate, and various digested food nutrients and waste materials connected with the upbuilding and the tearing down of tissues. The corpuscles, which are of two kinds, *red* and *white*, occur in enormous numbers,—a single drop of blood containing 25 million red ones.

The *red corpuscles* are very small flattened disks, about $\frac{1}{3200}$ of an inch in diameter, and thicker at the edge than at the center. They contain an important substance, called *hemoglobin*, which has the power of absorbing oxygen from the air in the lungs and of conveying it to the various tissues. The red color of hemoglobin is caused by the iron which it contains.

The *white corpuscles* are larger but far less numerous than the red, existing in healthy blood in the proportion of two or three to 1000. While ordinarily spherical in form, they are seen under the microscope to vary their shape in the same way as does the amœba, and these characteristic movements are called *amœboid*. An important function of the white corpuscles is to protect the body against disease by destroying the various harmful bacteria which find their way into the tissues of the body.

In the systemic circulation, the color of the blood in the arteries is bright scarlet, while in the veins it is dark red or purple. The bright-colored arterial blood contains oxygen and nutrient materials which are given up to the tissues in passing through the capillaries. The much darker-colored venous blood contains carbon dioxide and other waste products accumulated during the passage through the tissues. The oxygen conveyed by the blood is obtained during its circulation through the lungs. The nutrient fat materials absorbed from the intestines by the lacteals reach the blood through the thoracic duct which discharges into the subclavian vein. The materials contributed by the liver pass directly from that organ into the circulatory system by the hepatic vein.

The loss of blood through a wound would constitute the greatest single danger to which the body is liable were it not for the peculiar action of blood known as clotting. When exposed to air, blood soon takes a solid form which effectively dams the further escape of the fluid. Clotting is explained by the presence of *fibrinogen* in the blood, which, when acted upon by an enzyme formed on exposure of blood to the air, becomes fibrin. This appears in rodlike forms which soon close the ruptured blood vessel. The main source of fibrinogen is the liver. The platelets are believed also to have an important part in stopping the flow of blood from a wound. They gather in large numbers at the break and appear to stick to the edges, gluing themselves and near-by red corpuscles into a protective blanket. A vitamin, K, found in alfalfa and spinach and later synthesized from coal tar, speeds up clotting through catalytic action as does also oxalic acid injected into the blood. Failure of the blood to clot normally is a condition known as *hemophilia*, a disease of males inherited only through females.

The amount of blood in the human body is approximately one-twentieth of its weight, or from 8 to 10 pounds,—about four quarts, in a man of average weight.

Blood Pressure. In flowing through the vessels the blood exerts a lateral pressure upon their walls. The amount of this pressure depends on the energy of the heart stroke, the volume of blood in the vessels, the elasticity of their walls, and the resistance offered by the capillaries. The blood pressure may be readily measured by means of an instrument called a *sphygmomanometer*.

Blood pressure varies in different individuals and at different times in the same individual. It is lowest during sleep, is increased by muscular exertion, and varies markedly as a result of emotional excitement. It is influenced by changes in external temperature and by altitude. The average arterial blood pressure of adults in health ranges between 90 and 150 mm. During childhood a pressure of from 90 to 110 mm. may be regarded as normal. After middle life the blood pressure increases so that 145 to 160 mm. may be taken as the range for good health.

In certain kidney and brain diseases, pressures as high as 250 mm. are by no means rare. A high blood pressure is regarded as one of the causes of *arteriosclerosis*, or hardening of the arteries. Prominent among the conditions which lead to high blood pressure are chronic worry, fear, and anger. A well-balanced emotional life is, therefore, one of the chief requirements for a healthy blood pressure and consequently one of the principal means of avoiding heart disease, since an excessive blood pressure puts an undue strain on the heart.

Abnormally low blood pressure is also observed, especially in case of wasting diseases, hemorrhage, collapse, and shock.

Bones, Structure of. In shape, bones are *long*, as in the clavicle or humerus; *short*, as in the wrist and ankle bones; *flat*, as in those of the skull; *irregular*, as in the backbone; and *sesamoid*, as in the kneecap. During life, bones are bluish white in color, and are more or less flexible and elastic. They usually consist of an outer compact layer and an inner spongy portion containing red marrow. The compact portion is porous, but its cavities are much smaller than those in spongy bone. Bones are made up of both mineral and animal matter. The mineral matter, chiefly carbonate and phosphate of lime, gives them hardness and strength. From the animal matter they derive their elasticity.

In the *periosteum*, or tissue which covers the bones, and in the marrow which fills their central cavities, the blood vessels and nerves spread out before entering the bone proper. The periosteum is a necessary part of bones. If it is removed, the bone will die; but, if the bone be removed without destroying the periosteum, the bone will grow again. In the solid portion of bones there are numerous microscopic tubes, called *Haversian canals* which usually run lengthwise of the bone. These are connected by many cross branches, some of which open on the surface beneath the periosteum where blood vessels enter to bring nourishment. From small vessels in the Haversian canals, blood penetrates throughout the bone in extremely fine tubes called *canaliculi*. See *Skeletal System, Skeleton*.

Brain. The great central organ of the nervous system, situated within the cranial cavity of the skull. It is the chief mass of nervous tissue in the body, and consists of three divisions,—a large part called the *cerebrum*, a much smaller part known as the *cerebellum*, or "little brain," beneath which a still smaller part, the *medulla oblongata*, tapers downward into the spinal cord.

The brain is a very complex organ. In it are connected all the nerve fibers from the different parts of the body. By means of these fibers and their connections, all bodily movements and other functions are co-ordinated. Dominating and controlling the whole, the brain has the exceedingly important function of adapting man to his environment, through the thinking or intellectual processes.

In its action and workings, the brain may be likened to a great central telephone switchboard, by means of which all parts of the body are connected and bound together, and the whole body placed in touch with its surroundings. From the entire surface of the body and from the internal organs, nerve fibers pass either directly into the brain or into the spinal cord and then up the spinal cord into the brain. These fibers are the bearers of impressions of all kinds, such as touch, taste, smell, sight, hearing, temperature, and pain. From the brain itself, somewhat similar fibers run outward through openings in the skull or downward through the medulla oblongata into the spinal cord. Thence they pass outward into nerves, and end in some muscle or other organ having a special character or use. These outgoing fibers are the bearers of nervous impulses originating in various centers in the brain. The total number of these fibers is very great. There are millions of incoming and outgoing fibers, with minute interconnecting branches, and an equally vast number of minute nerve cells, in direct association with these fibers. The brain, therefore, may be regarded as a vast collection of *nerve-ganglion cells* together with their associated *nerve fibers*, commonly called nerves.

Cerebrum.—This constitutes by far the greater part of the brain, and is composed of two symmetrical halves, called the *cerebral hemispheres*. Above, these are separated by the great *longitudinal fissure*, but, at the bottom of the fissure, they are held together by a firm band of fibers called the *corpus callosum*. At their bases, the hemispheres are bound together by the *cerebral peduncles*, which unite below to form the *pons varolii* and the *medulla oblongata*. The pons varolii is the bridge by which fibers from one side of the body or brain pass to the cerebral hemisphere of the opposite side.

Each hemisphere is divided by various fissures into four major lobes named after the bones of the skull nearest them. These larger lobes are more or less divided by shallower indentations into still smaller lobes called *lobules*. The further extensive division into *convolutions* increases the outside surface of the hemispheres. This affords room for the vast number of nerve cells forming the *gray matter*, which is located in the outermost layer, or *cortex*, of the convolutions. These nerve cells are connected with each other and with other parts of the brain and body by the nerve fibers which compose the *white matter*. Most of the gray matter occurs in the outer layers of the cerebrum, though some is found in the interior parts of the brain and spinal cord. The white matter makes up the remainder of the brain and spinal cord, and also the nerves.

By means of experiments and the study of injuries and disease, localization of function in the *cortex* of the brain has been well established. Thus the *sensory area* lies just back of the central fissure in the post-central lobule; the *motor area* is in the pre-central lobule, in which the subdivisions represent a man standing on his head, that is, the foot and leg areas are above the arm and trunk areas; the *visual area* lies around the *calcarine fissure* in the occipital lobe; the *auditory area* is in the superior temporal lobule; *taste* and *smell* are deficient in man and their centers lie within the brain, around the *hippocampus*; the *speech area* is in the left frontal lobe in right-handed individuals and in the right frontal lobe in left-handed. *Intellect and reason* are thought to have their centers in the *association areas*, which occur in the frontal, parietal, and occipital lobes. All of these areas and lobules, with their *fiber tracts*, intercommunicate by means of short and long *association fibers* and by *projection fibers* throughout the body.

All of these different localized areas, or centers of specialized activities, are brought into connection, one with another, by immense numbers of fibers. Moreover, the two largely separated hemispheres are connected by millions of fibers in the corpus callosum. So, in the normal adult brain, the various nerve centers of the cortex, or outside layer of gray matter, are placed in close connection with each other and with similar centers in the other half of the cerebrum. Further, all of these centers have very definite connections with the cerebellum and the spinal cord.

Cerebellum.—The cerebellum is situated behind and nearly beneath the cerebrum, to the stem of which it is attached by the cerebral peduncles. The connections of the cerebellum with the cerebral nerve centers and also with those of the spinal cord are very numerous and complex. While possessing characteristic features, the nerve cells of the cerebellum are fundamentally similar to those of the cerebrum. The main function of the cerebellum seems to be to co-ordinate and harmonize the muscular movements of the body, as, for example, those which are necessary to keep it in an upright position when standing, walking, or running. In proportion to the size of the cerebrum, the cerebellum of lower animals is much larger than in man.

Medulla Oblongata.—This relatively small part of the brain is composed chiefly of nerve fibers, and connects the cerebrum and cerebellum with the spinal cord. Nerve cells in the medulla oblongata control the beat of the heart, involuntary respiration, and the work of the alimentary canal.

Size of the Brain.—Compared with the size and weight of the body, the human brain is larger than the brain of any other animal, except possibly some of the smallest mammals and birds. With the exception of the elephant and the larger whales, the human brain is actually larger and heavier than that of any other animal. The brain of man is usually larger than the brain of woman, though at birth and at the age of 14 the female brain is heavier than the male brain. The average weight of the adult male brain is estimated at from 48 to 50 ounces; that of the average female brain, at from 43 to 45 ounces. Tall, heavy persons usually have heavy brains. There is, however, no direct relationship between weight of brain and intelligence. Cuvier's brain weighed 64½ ounces, while Gambetta's weighed only 39 ounces. Similar comparisons may be made in the case of many other persons of great intellectual capacity. See *Nervous System.*

Capillaries. The minute vessels connecting the arteries with the veins. They are the smallest vessels of the body. In width a capillary is from $\frac{1}{3000}$ to $\frac{1}{2000}$ of an inch, while in length it varies from $\frac{1}{1000}$ to $\frac{1}{50}$ of an inch. The capillaries form such a dense network of tubes that a needle cannot be thrust into any part of the body without puncturing several. Each capillary consists of a single layer of epithelial cells, such as those which line the arteries. Through the walls of these tubes an exchange of food and oxygen and waste products occurs in every cell by *osmosis.* Osmosis is the intermingling of two liquids or gases of different densities through a membrane, the greater flow being toward the denser substance. Only the thin membrane of the capillaries separates the blood containing digested food and oxygen from the contents of the cells and their waste products,—carbon dioxide, water, and urea, produced by oxidation.

Chyle. A creamy fluid absorbed by the lacteals of the small intestine during the final stage of digestion. This fluid is slightly alkaline, and, when outside the body, coagulates into fibrin and serum. Chyle differs from ordinary lymph chiefly in containing globules of emulsified fat. To these it owes its milky color. The fat is derived from the food materials in the chyme after they have been acted upon by the bile, the pancreatic juice, and the intestinal juice. Lymphatic vessels take chyle from the lacteals to the thoracic duct, which conveys it to the left subclavian vein. Here the chyle becomes mixed with the blood and is distributed to various cells and tissues of the body. In the process of absorption, chyle serves as the principal medium for the transfer of ingested fats to the blood. See *Assimilation, Bile, Digestion, Intestines, Nutrition, Pancreas.*

Chyme. The semifluid mass of partly digested food passed from the stomach into the small intestine. At this stage of digestion, the food materials have been reduced to finely divided particles. This condition is brought about first, by chewing in the mouth; secondly, by admixture with the saliva and the gastric juice; and, finally, by the churning movements (*peristalsis*) of the stomach. The starchy portions have been largely changed into a form of sugar by the action of the saliva, and the protein components have been mostly turned into peptones (or amino acids) by the action of the gastric juice. Besides these principal changes, various other transformations have taken place. As a result, the nutrient materials contained in the chyme are ready for the completion of the digestive process which takes place in the intestines. See *Digestion, Gastric Juice, Stomach.*

Circulation. The natural motion of the blood in a living animal, by which it proceeds *from* the heart to all parts of the body by the arteries, and returns *to* the heart by the veins. There are in reality two circulations: the *pulmonary*, from the right side of the heart through the lungs to the left side of the heart; the *systemic*, from the left side of the heart through the body back to the right side of the heart.

The blood is returned to the right auricle of the heart by the descending and the ascending vena cava. The right auricle, when distended, contracts and sends it into the right ventricle. It is prevented from returning to the auricle by the tricuspid valve. From the right ventricle it is propelled through the pulmonary artery, to circulate through and undergo a purifying change in the lungs, being prevented from returning into the right ventricle by the closing of the semilunar valves at the mouth of the pulmonary artery.

Having been purified in the lungs, the blood is brought to the left auricle of the heart by the four pulmonary veins, and thence is emptied into the left ventricle. The left ventricle, after having been distended, contracts, and forces the blood through the aorta into the arteries which carry it to every part of the body. The blood is then returned by the veins into the venæ cavæ. The blood is prevented from passing back from the left ventricle into the auricle by a valvular apparatus called the mitral or bicuspid valve. The pulmonary artery and the aorta are also furnished with similar valves, called the semilunar valves. These prevent the blood from returning into the ventricles.

Circulatory System. The organs of the circulatory system comprise the *heart*, the *arteries*, the *capillaries*, the *veins*, and the *lymphatics*. The heart pumps the blood to all parts of the body through the blood vessels. The arteries carry blood from the heart; the capillaries distribute it throughout the cells of the tissues; the veins and the lymphatics return to the heart impure blood filled with waste matter from the tissues. The heart then sends this impure blood to the lungs for purification, after which it comes back to the heart to be again distributed throughout the body. The time required for blood to travel from the right arm through the heart and lungs to the left arm is from 15 to 22 seconds.

The circulatory system plays a very important part in the activities of the body. Without it there could be no distribution of nourishment nor removal of waste matter. See *Arteries, Capillaries, Heart, Veins.*

Diaphragm. The muscular partition separating the cavity of the chest from the cavity of the abdomen, called also the midriff. The diaphragm has a flat, tendinous center, from which striped muscular fibers radiate in all directions, and are attached by their outer ends to the lower ribs, the breastbone, and the vertebral column or backbone. In its middle part the diaphragm rises high in the chest, somewhat in the shape of a vaulted roof, with the heart and lungs above and the stomach and liver beneath. In respiration the strong muscles of the diaphragm play an important part. The spasmodic breathing movement known as *hiccup* is caused by sudden contraction of the diaphragm.

Digestion. The process in the animal body by which foods are so acted upon that the nutritive parts are prepared to pass through the walls of the blood vessels and lacteals of the small intestine and become a part of the blood. The organs effecting this process are called the *digestive organs* and consist of the mouth, the stomach, the small and large intestines, the liver, and the pancreas.

When foods, after being properly prepared and mixed with saliva by chewing in the mouth, reach the stomach, they are then thoroughly mixed with the gastric juice by the motion of the stomach. By this motion the various forms of food are separated into their smallest parts, penetrated by the gastric juice, and transformed into a uniform pulpy or fluid mass. The gastric juice acts upon the protein or albuminous parts of the food, converting them into peptones and finally into amino acids, in which form they can pass through organic membranes and thus enter the blood. This action is also aided by the warmth of the stomach.

The resulting pulpy mass, called *chyme*, proceeds from the stomach, through the pylorus, into the small intestine, where it is mixed with the pancreatic juice, bile, and intestinal juice. The pancreatic juice converts the starch into sugar, changes the remaining albumins into peptones and amino acids, and emulsifies the fats, so that all these kinds of food are rendered capable of absorption. The process is aided by the intestinal juice; the bile also acts upon fats; and thus the food is finally transformed into *chyle*. This nutritious chyle is absorbed into the system by the capillaries and lacteals of the villi situated on the inner walls of the small intestine. The nonnutritious matters pass farther down the intestinal canal and are carried off. See *Assimilation, Bile, Chyle, Chyme, Gastric Juice, Nutrition.*

Ductless Glands. A group of organs of which most are related, in function or development, to the circulatory system. The most important of these are the spleen, the thymus, the thyroid, the parathyroids, the suprarenal glands, or adrenals, the hæmolymph glands, the pituitary body, the pineal gland, the coccygeal gland, and the carotid glands.

The function of a gland that has a duct is comparatively easy to determine. But the use of ductless glands was long a perplexing problem. Recent investigations, however, have shown that most of the ductless glands form a secretion though it is not discharged through a duct. This *internal secretion*, as it is called, is taken away from the gland by the venous blood or by the lymph. In this manner, the internal secretion is distributed and ministers to the needs of the various parts of the body.

In many cases, the internal secretion is absolutely essential to life. The removal, or destruction by disease, of the gland that forms it, results in derangements culminating in death. In other cases, however, the internal secretion is not essential, or its place is taken by that formed by similar glands in other parts of the body. See *Parathyroids, Pineal Body, Pituitary Body, Spleen, Suprarenal Glands, Thymus, Thyroid.*

Ear. The organ of hearing, composed of three parts, namely, the *external ear*, the *tympanic cavity*, or *middle ear*, and the *labyrinth*, or *internal ear*.

The external ear consists of a cartilaginous portion, called the pinna, auricle, or pavilion, and the auditory canal (*meatus auditorius*) about an inch in length, extending inward from the pinna to the drum of the ear. The eardrum, or *membrana tympani*, is a thin, semitransparent membrane about three-eighths of an inch in diameter, placed obliquely across the inner end of the auditory canal.

The middle ear is an irregular bony cavity situated within the temporal bone. It is traversed by a chain of three small bones called the hammer (*malleus*), anvil (*incus*), and stirrup (*stapes*). There are ten openings in the middle ear, five large and five small. These connect it with the mastoid cells in the temporal bone, with the internal ear, and with the throat. Two openings connect the middle ear with the internal ear. They are called the *fenestra ovalis* and the *fenestra rotunda*. Leading from the middle ear to the pharynx or throat is a small canal called the *Eustachian tube*.

The internal ear, or labyrinth, is the essential part of the organ of hearing. It is composed of three chief parts,—*vestibule, semicircular canals*, and *cochlea*. In the central part lies the vestibule, the outer side of which is fitted to the base of the stirrup bone. Behind the vestibule are bony semicircular canals which open into the back of the vestibule at each end. In front of the vestibule is the cochlea, a tube coiled on itself somewhat like a snail's shell. Within these complex organs are various membranous bodies in which are spread out numerous branches of the auditory nerve.

Vibrations striking the eardrum are conveyed through the series of small bones in the middle ear to the nerve endings in the internal ear where the sensation of sound is produced. Thence they are transmitted to the brain.

Excretion. The process whereby waste, useless, or harmful matter of all kinds is separated and carried away from the body. The principal organs of excretion are the large intestine, the lungs, kidneys, bladder, and skin. Among the most important excretions are carbon-dioxide gas from the lungs, perspiration from the skin, and urine from the kidneys. See *Secretion.*

Eye. The organ of sight or vision, of which the essential part is a globular structure, the *eyeball*, contained in a bony cavity in the skull, called the orbit, communicating with the brain by the optic nerve, and moved in the cavity by a set of small muscles. It has three refractive media through which the rays of light pass,—the *aqueous humor* in front, the *crystalline lens* in the middle, and the *vitreous humor* behind. The eyeball is almost a perfect sphere, about an inch in diameter, the front portion bulging slightly forward.

There are three coats, the outer or *sclerotic*, the middle or *choroid*, and the inner, called the *retina*. The sclerotic coat, a hard, fibrous, protective outer covering, is white and opaque, except in the more prominent front part, where it is transparent, forming the *cornea*. The sclerotic coat continues around the back of the eyeball to the optic nerve, which pierces it. The middle coat consists of the *choroid membrane*, the *ciliary processes*, and the *iris*. Of these the choroid membrane, a black vascular layer, extends forward almost to the edges of the cornea; the ciliary processes extend radially around the eyeball at the junction of the sclerotic coat and the cornea, while the iris is a thin, colored curtain behind the aqueous humor in front of the crystalline lens. In the center of the iris is a small circular aperture, the *pupil*, for the transmission of light.

The retina, or inner coat, is a soft, delicate structure lining the back portion of the eyeball. It has two small, round marks upon it,—one in the middle, called the *yellow spot*, which is the point of keenest vision, and the other, somewhat below it, called the *blind spot*, which is the point where the optic nerve enters. In structure the retina is exceedingly complex, consisting of various layers in which are spread out radiating fibers of the optic nerve.

Between the cornea and the crystalline lens is the *aqueous humor*, composed chiefly of water with a very slight solution of salt and albumin. Behind the pupil, and in contact with the iris, is the *crystalline lens*, composed of many thin layers of transparent, ribbon-like fibers. This lens, which is convex on both sides, is held in place by ligaments from the ciliary processes. The *vitreous humor*, which fills the eyeball behind the lens, is a transparent, jelly-like substance.

The accessory organs of the eye are: the four small *rectus* muscles, which rotate the eyeball in its orbit; the *eyelid*, which protects the eye in front; the *conjunctiva*, a thin, transparent membrane which covers the entire outer coat of the eye and lines the eyelid; the *lachrymal gland*, which secretes the tears that moisten both the cornea and the conjunctiva; and the *tear ducts* or small canals by which the surplus fluid is carried into the nose.

As an optical instrument the eye is remarkably perfect and is capable of adjusting itself quickly to an immense range of visual conditions. In the act of seeing, the rays of light from a luminous object strike the cornea and converge from it to pass through the aqueous humor. The outer rays are shut off by the iris, but the central rays pass through the pupil to the crystalline lens, which, owing to its high refractive power, greatly converges them. Passing on through the vitreous humor, the rays are brought to a focus on the sensitive retina, forming an inverted but otherwise exact image of the object. By the stimulation of nerve elements in the retina, an impression of the object is transmitted by the optic nerve to the brain. Thus the sensation of sight is produced.

When the eyeball is too short or too long, the image is formed either in front or behind the retina. If in front, the defect is known as nearsightedness or *myopia*; if behind, farsightedness or *hypermetropia*. The use of concave lenses overcomes myopia, while convex lenses correct farsightedness. Sometimes the cornea or crystalline lens may be more strongly curved in one direction than in another. In such case a part of an object will appear distinct and another part blurred, because of the imperfect focusing of the light rays. This defect of vision, called *astigmatism*, may be remedied by the use of proper glasses.

Fauces. The opening at the back of the mouth, leading to the throat cavity, or pharynx. Above, it is bounded by the soft palate and uvula; below, by the root of the tongue; and, on the sides, by muscular ridges called the *pillars of the fauces*. Each of these pillars divides below, and in the depression between the two divisions lies a tonsil.

Gall Bladder. A pear-shaped membranous sac, about four inches in length, situated on the underside of the liver, beneath its right lobe. The gall bladder serves as a reservoir for the bile secreted by the liver. It constantly discharges its contents into the small intestine (duodenum) through the bile duct when digestion is going on, but accumulates and stores bile during the periods when no food is being digested.

Gastric Juice. The powerful digestive fluid secreted by the glands of the stomach. It is a thin, colorless liquid, with an acid reaction. This is due to hydrochloric acid, of which, during digestion, about 0.3 per cent is present. The gastric juice contains also small amounts of mineral salts, principally the chlorides of sodium, potassium, and calcium. Besides, there are several enzymes, the chief of which is pepsin. It is estimated that the stomach of a healthy adult secretes daily about eight pints of gastric juice.

The great importance of the gastric juice is due to its action upon the protein elements in food. In combination with hydrochloric acid, pepsin converts the proteins in meat, milk, eggs, beans, and other nitrogenous protein-bearing foods into proteoses, forming also smaller quantities of peptones and acid albumins. In these changed forms, the protein food elements are ready for the final stage of digestion. They are finally broken up into their constituent amino acids and, as such, are absorbed by the lacteals of the small intestine.

Gastric juice is an effective antiseptic. The hydrochloric acid present destroys nearly all of the disease germs and other micro-organisms swallowed with the food. Upon starch, gastric juice has no effect, but it changes sucrose into glucose and fructose. Owing to the action of the fat-splitting enzyme, called lipase, the gastric juice transforms a small amount of fat into glycerol and fatty acids. The rennet enzyme, rennin, in gastric juice, curdles milk. In this process, the caseinogen of the milk coagulates, forming casein. The casein thus produced is then digested in the same manner as other proteins. See *Chyme, Digestion, Stomach.*

Hair. An appendage of the skin, distinctive of all animals higher than birds, including man. Hair is produced on almost all parts of the human body, attaining its greatest growth on the scalp. Each hair is a long filament of epidermis which grows continuously from a small, bulbous *root* seated at the bottom of a *hair follicle* in the skin. At the base of each is a *papilla* which forms the hair. If the papilla is destroyed, a new hair will not be formed.

The portion of a hair buried in the skin is called the *root*; this is succeeded by the *shaft* or *stem*, which, in uncut hair, tapers to a *point*. The shaft of a hair is covered by a very thin layer of overlapping scales forming the *hair-cuticle*. Beneath the hair-cuticle is the *cortex*, consisting of greatly elongated cells united into fibers. In the center of the shaft in many hairs there is a *medulla*, made up of rounded cells.

The color of the hair depends mainly upon pigment cells in the cortex, or fibrous layer. All hairs contain some air cavities, particularly in the medulla. In white hairs air cavities are very abundant, causing the whiteness by reflecting all the light. Slender muscle fibers run down from the true skin to the side of the hair follicles, which are usually implanted obliquely, so that most hairs lie down on the body. These muscles are so fixed that, when they contract, they will erect the hair, causing it to bristle, for example, as in an angry cat, or sometimes in case of a greatly terrified man. Connected with each hair follicle are commonly two *sebaceous glands* that secrete an oily substance, or *sebum*, which lubricates both the skin and the hair.

If the hair follicle or root of the hair be destroyed, there is no way of reproducing the hair; but if the hair falls, leaving the root intact, as is the case after certain fevers, the hair grows again. In health each hair lasts only a certain length of time, and is replaced by another, so long as the papilla is not weakened. See *Nails, Skin*.

Heart. The living force pump which propels the blood through the blood vessels and maintains circulation throughout the body. It is a muscular organ, about the size of one's fist, lying somewhat obliquely between the lungs in the center of the chest cavity. In shape it is somewhat pearlike or conelike, with its broad end or base in the direction of the right shoulder and its narrow end or apex pointing downward and to the left. From base to apex the heart of an adult measures approximately 5½ inches, and across its broad basal surface, 3½ inches. In men its weight is usually about 11 ounces; in women, 9 ounces.

The heart is surrounded by a sac called the *pericardium*. This secretes a lubricating fluid which prevents friction. The walls of the heart are formed of thick, muscular tissue composed of interlacing fibers, and are nourished through blood vessels which are termed *coronary*. The heart is divided in the middle by a strong lengthwise partition. Each half is divided by a transverse partition into an upper and a lower cavity. The two cavities in the broad basal portion are the *right* and *left auricles*, and the two in the narrower apex are the *right* and *left ventricles*.

In the right auricle there are four openings, two of the *venæ cavæ*, or great veins, one of the coronary vein, and one an opening into the right ventricle. In the left auricle there are five openings, one into the left ventricle, and four into the pulmonary veins. Each ventricle has two openings, one from the auricle, and another into the outgoing artery. The ventricles are supplied with valves. Those at the arterial openings are called *semilunar*; those between the right auricle and the right ventricle, *tricuspid*; and those between the left auricle and the left ventricle, *mitral* or *bicuspid*.

In reality, the heart is a double organ, pumping two different blood streams and maintaining two separate circulations at the same time,—a lesser one in the lungs, *pulmonary circulation*, and a much greater one in the body, *systemic circulation*. The blood is pumped to the lungs by the right ventricle through the pulmonary artery, and to the body by the left ventricle through the aorta. While all four cavities of the heart have muscular walls, those of the ventricles, which do the hardest work, are much stronger than those of the auricles. Furthermore, the walls of the left ventricle, which pumps blood to the entire body, are about three times as thick as those of the right ventricle, which pumps blood only to the lungs.

Throughout life, the heart works ceaselessly day and night, but less rapidly during sleep. In infancy it beats about 120 times per minute; in adult life, usually between 60 and 75 times, with a normal of about 62 for men and 69 for women. Variation in rate is considerable with varying activities or thoughts. The alternate contraction (*systole*) and dilatation (*diastole*) of the heart are entirely involuntary, depending for control upon nerve centers in the medulla oblongata and the sympathetic nervous system. See *Circulation, Circulatory System*.

Intestines. The bowels, or tubular portion of the alimentary canal, which occupy the greater part of the abdominal cavity, extending from the lower end of the stomach to the anus. In man the intestines are from five to six times the length of the body, and consist of the *small intestine*, about twenty feet long, comprising the *duodenum, jejunum*, and *ileum*, and the *large intestine*, about five feet long, comprising the *cæcum, colon*, and *rectum*. Like the stomach, the walls of the intestine are composed of four coats: a *serous*, a *muscular*, a *submucous*, and a *mucous* coat.

Through most of its length the mucous coat of the small intestine is raised into folds, called *valvæ conniventes*, which greatly increase its absorbing and secreting surface. The mucous coat of the small intestine is everywhere covered by innumerable, minute, finger-like projections from 1⁄50 to ⅛ of an inch in length, called *villi*. These contain blood vessels and lacteals, by which the nutritious digested portion of the food is absorbed. Between the bases of the villi, small glands, called the *crypts of Lieberkühn*, open upon the inner surface. These glands secrete a digestive fluid called the intestinal juice. The muscular coat of the small intestine consists of two layers of muscular tissue, of which the inner is circular, and the outer longitudinal. By their contractions, these muscles mix the food with the digestive fluids and force it to move along the tube. Food remains in the small intestine from five to fifteen hours.

The *large intestine* forms the last portion of the alimentary canal. It is from one and one-half to two and one-half inches in diameter, has two muscular layers, like the small intestine, but the inner mucous coat, while containing numerous glands, has no villi or valvæ conniventes. The small intestine opens into the large intestine by means of the *ileocæcal valve*, which permits matter to pass into the colon but not back into the ileum. The opening of the small intestine into the large intestine is on the side of the colon at some distance from the end. The portion of the colon below the opening is called the *cæcum*, from the end of which projects the *vermiform appendix*.

The small intestine receives food through the *pylorus*, the orifice at the lower end of the stomach About four inches below the pylorus, it receives secretions from the liver and pancreas through the common bile duct. The intestines also receive secretions from glands within their walls. The function of the intestines is to complete the digestion of food begun by the stomach, through the action of the various secretions, so that it can be taken up by the blood vessels and lacteals in the villi of the small intestine and passed on to the blood. The large intestine is also an organ of excretion. See *Alimentary Canal, Digestion*.

Joints. The chief kinds of joints are: *ball and socket*, as in the hips and shoulders, a powerful joint adapted for great ease of motion; *hinge*, as in the knee; *pivot*, as in the upper two vertebræ, permitting the skull to turn to the right or the left; and *gliding*, as in the closely packed bones of the wrists and ankles. Most bones are enlarged at the ends forming the joints, which are held firmly together by strong ligaments. These enlarged ends of bones which move upon each other are covered with rubber-like pads of very smooth cartilage, and the whole is moistened or lubricated with the *synovial fluid*, secreted by the *synovial membrane*, which lines the joints. The mechanism of the various joints is remarkably perfect, and upon it depend all the wonderful powers of movement displayed by the human body. There are also immovable joints, such as the skull *sutures* and the *symphyses* of the pelvic bones and the sacrum.

Kidneys. Two large, glandular bodies situated within the abdomen on either side of the spine, in what is commonly known as "the small of the back." In an adult they are usually from four to five inches long, about two and one-half inches broad, and about one inch thick; and each kidney weighs from four to six ounces. In shape they resemble kidney beans. Each is supplied with blood from the aorta by a *renal* artery. From each kidney issues a membranous tube, or ureter, about the size of a goose quill and eighteen inches long. The ureters run down the back wall of the abdomen behind the peritoneum, and empty the urinary secretion into the bladder, one ureter on either side.

The body of the kidney is composed of two structures, an outer *cortical* portion, and an inner *medullary* portion. The latter is made up of fibrous pyramids or cones with their bases resting upon the cortical layer and their points emptying into the central cavity, which is an expansion of the upper portion of the ureter. The kidneys are the organs of urinary secretion. Their function is to remove urea, uric acid, and other harmful or useless substances from the blood. The serious and often fatal malady, called Bright's disease, is an affection of the kidneys.

Ligaments. Bands of strong tissue connecting and covering the bones forming a joint, or holding any other organ of the body in place. Ligaments are usually composed of parallel or interlacing fibers of flexible, dense, white, fibrous tissue.

Liver. The largest gland in the body, weighing somewhat more than three pounds, situated just beneath the diaphragm under the short ribs, rather more on the right than on the left side.

The liver is dark reddish brown in color and of soft glandular texture. In form it is irregular, being convex and smooth above, where it is in contact with the diaphragm, and irregularly concave below. It is thick behind but ends in a thin edge in front, and is somewhat divided into two upper lobes,—a much larger right lobe and a much smaller left lobe. From each half of the organ a duct passes out and unites to form the *hepatic duct*. On the underside of the right lobe is the *gall bladder*, which serves as a reservoir for the bile, and empties through the common bile duct into the small intestine. The glandular structure of the liver is composed of an immense number of minute lobules, each consisting of *hepatic cells*.

The chief function of the liver is the secretion of bile, which performs important work in digestion. The liver is the chief source of fibrinogen, the main factor in the clotting of blood. It also removes the excess of sugar from the blood and stores it up in the form of *glycogen*, a kind of animal starch. The hepatic cells give out glycogen again as sugar whenever the blood needs it. The hepatic cells also destroy old red corpuscles, probably changing them into urea which is excreted by the kidneys.

The liver is well furnished with blood vessels, including the *hepatic artery*, *hepatic veins*, and the *portal vein*. Two kinds of blood are received by the liver,—arterial, for the nourishment of the gland, and venous, from which bile is chiefly formed. See *Digestion*, *Gall Bladder*.

Lungs. The breathing organs of man and the higher animals. The essential idea of a lung is that of a sac communicating with the atmosphere by means of a tube, the trachea or windpipe, through which air is admitted to the internal parts of its structure, the air serving to supply oxygen to the blood and to remove carbon dioxide.

The lungs are situated one on each side of the heart; the upper part of each fits into the upper corner of the chest, about an inch above the collar bone, while the base of each rests upon the diaphragm. The right lung is shorter and broader than the left, which extends downward farther by the breadth of a rib.

Each lung exhibits a broad division into *two* lobes, an upper and a lower portion, the division being marked by a deep cleft which runs downward obliquely to the front of the organ. In the case of the right lung, however, there is a further partial division at right angles to the main cleft. Hence, while the left lung is always said to have two lobes, the right lung is sometimes said to have *three* lobes. These lobes again are divided into lobules which measure from one-fourth to one-half inch in diameter, and consist of air cells, blood vessels, nerves, lymphatic vessels, and the tissue by which the lobules themselves are bound together.

The trachea, or windpipe, connects the throat cavity with the lungs. At its lower end it divides inside the chest cavity into a right and a left *bronchus*, or *bronchial tube*. Each bronchus enters a lung and there branches into finer and finer tubes, called *bronchioles*, which at last open into minute globular or cup-shaped air sacs. The walls of these sacs consist of thin, elastic connective tissue, through which run small capillary blood vessels connected with the pulmonary arteries and veins. Impure or venous blood is brought into contact with the air through the exceedingly thin walls of the air cells, and is transformed into pure or arterial blood. The total extent of air-absorbing surface presented by the air cells is estimated at upward of 2500 square feet.

In man and the higher animals the lungs are freely suspended in the cavity of the chest, or *thorax*, which is completely separated from the abdominal cavity by the muscular diaphragm, or midriff. Both lungs are covered with a delicate membrane, called the *visceral pleura*. The chest cavity is lined with the *parietal pleura*. The painful disease known as *pleurisy* arises from inflammation of these membranes.

The elasticity of the lungs, by which they expand and take in air and contract and expel air, is due to the highly contractile tissues found in the bronchial tubes and air cells. This elasticity is further aided by the delicate surface tissue or pleura. The lungs are popularly termed "lights," because they are the lightest organs in the body, and, except when diseased, float when placed in water. See *Respiration*.

Lymphatics. The system of vessels, glands, and ducts which absorbs digested fat from the intestines and transfers it to the blood, and also removes various waste or harmful substances from the tissues and the blood.

The *lymphatic vessels* are minute, delicate, transparent structures, found in almost every tissue of the body, being absent only from the brain, spinal cord, eyeball, cartilages, and a few other tissues. The larger lymphatic vessels, which are provided with numerous valves, somewhat resemble the veins in structure.

The *lymphatic glands*, which are about the size of small almonds, are commonly arranged in groups along the trunks of the larger lymphatic vessels. Each gland is composed of a spongy network of fiber filled with cells which are known as *lymphocytes*. These glands are most numerous in certain regions of the body, as, for example, the armpit, the neck, and the groin.

In case poisons, disease germs, or other irritating substances are forced into the system, the lymphatic glands situated between the point of entrance and the vital organs of the body absorb the foreign substance into their cells. These often become greatly inflamed and sometimes even suppurate, thereby expelling the injurious material. The lymphatic glands thus act as guardians of the body. On this account they are peculiarly liable to attack in infectious diseases. The lymphatic glands also help to produce white blood corpuscles.

The lymphatics of the small intestine are usually called *lacteals*. Their function is to convey the digested fat, or chyle absorbed from the intestine, to a central vessel, the *receptaculum chyli*, an elongated pouch which lies along the spinal column. From this receptacle, the lymph elaborated by the lymphatic glands goes upward through the *thoracic duct*. This vessel, which has about the diameter of a goose quill, proceeds along the aorta, finally emptying near the base of the neck into the large subclavian vein.

The *lymph*, produced in the lymphatic glands and vessels, is a colorless or slightly yellowish red fluid, with a salty taste, closely resembling the plasma of the blood. The lymph has two important uses. First, it conveys from the tissues to the venous blood various waste matters to be excreted later by the lungs, skin, and kidneys. Second, the lymph brings to the blood new materials for its upbuilding. Sometimes lymph collects in the lymph spaces faster than it can be removed. This causes the uniform swelling called dropsy. See *Blood, Digestion, Nutrition.*

Mouth. The mouth cavity, the beginning of the alimentary canal, is bounded in front by the lips and cheeks, above by the hard and soft palates and the uvula, and below by the tongue. At the back it opens into the throat through the fauces. The mouth and its accessory organs,—the tongue, lips, teeth, and salivary glands,—perform very important functions in the mastication of food and the articulation of speech. In the tongue are situated the organs of taste. See *Salivary Glands, Teeth, Tongue.*

Muscles. In the human body there are more than 500 muscles, varying in length from a small fraction of an inch to two feet. These cover the skeleton almost entirely and make up nearly all the fleshy parts of the body.

Forms of Muscles.—Muscles are usually rounded in form, but some are flat, particularly those which form the walls of body cavities. Most muscles consist of a soft, red, middle part or belly, tapering toward each end into whitish, fibrous tendons which serve to attach them to the various bones upon which they act. Among the numerous forms of muscles are: *simple*, tapering toward each end; *biceps*, or two-headed, divided at one end; *triceps*, three-headed, as at the back of the upper arm; *digastric*, where a tendon occurs in the middle as well as at each end; and *polygastric*, where there are several portions separated by short tendons, as in some abdominal muscles.

Kinds of Muscles.—There are three distinct kinds of muscles,—striated, nonstriated, and heart muscles. Voluntary muscles act chiefly under the control of the will and are usually called *striated*, from the fine lines or striations on their fibers. Involuntary muscles, or organic muscles, which act independently of the will, such as the muscles of the stomach, are called also *nonstriated* or *smooth*, because their fibers do not show the markings which characterize the striated muscles.

The voluntary muscles are usually attached to the skeleton, and are capable of very rapid action. Involuntary muscles are not directly attached to the skeleton, and are not involved in the ordinary movements of the body. They act with comparative slowness and mostly without our knowledge or consciousness. They occur chiefly in the walls of hollow organs, as the stomach, intestines, and arteries. The muscles of the heart are intermediate between the striated and nonstriated types, so that relatively rapid action is possible.

Structure of Muscles.—Muscles are composed of contractile tissue made up of true muscle cells, connective tissue, and blood and lymph vessels which bring in nourishment and carry off waste material, together with the nerves which control their activities. The striated voluntary muscle cells occur in bundles. These are made up of the fiber-like cells which are about an inch long and $\frac{1}{500}$ of an inch in diameter. The nonstriated involuntary or smooth muscle cells are very much smaller, being usually less than $\frac{1}{100}$ of an inch long and $\frac{1}{4000}$ of an inch in diameter. They are not arranged in bundles but consist of masses of single spindle-shaped cells held together by a cement-like substance and connective tissue. They have no tendons and are controlled by nerve centers not under direct control of the will. Muscles consist of 75 per cent or more of water and salts. The remainder is true organic matter, chiefly of a protein or an albuminous character.

Uses of Muscles.—The primary function of muscles is to produce motion. By their power of contractility, muscles cause the bones to move upon each other at the joints, thus producing bodily movements. The muscles protect various bones and assist in holding them together at the joints. Muscles also enclose various body cavities, as the mouth and abdomen.

The muscles perform work and enable the various organs of the body to carry on their activities. The central portion, or belly, is the working part of a muscle. When stimulated by nerves under the control of the brain or spinal cord, the muscular tissue in the central portion contracts, growing larger in the middle and shorter at the ends. As a result, the muscle transmits a *pull* through its tendons upon the parts to which they are attached.

This contraction, or use of muscular force, is accompanied by a waste or change in the substance of the muscle itself. The minute muscular fibers or the cells composing them make up the loss by taking the proper material or food from the blood. But, when the contractions are too frequent, severe, or prolonged, the waste becomes much greater than the supply. The muscle then grows tired and is said to be *fatigued*.

Extreme fatigue is dangerous because in time it may destroy the power of the muscle cells to repair waste. On the other hand, the disuse of a muscle causes it to become weak and flabby and, in time, to lose the power of repairing itself. When muscles at work under normal strain are allowed short periods of rest, they very quickly recover from fatigue. See *Joints, Tendons.*

Nails. Outgrowths of the cuticle, or outer layer of the skin, specially modified to protect the sensitive ends of the toes and fingers. Each nail is a flattened, horny plate, the base of which, called the *root*, fits behind into a furrow of the dermis, or true skin. The visible part of a nail consists of a *body* fixed to the dermis beneath, and of a *free edge*. Near the root of the nail is a small whiter area called the *lunula*. The portion of the true skin on which the nail is developed is called the *matrix*. By new cells added on at the root, a nail grows in length, and by new cells added to its lower surface, it grows in thickness, so that a nail is thickest at its outer end. If all parts of a nail except the matrix be destroyed, a new nail will grow again. In chemical composition, nails are identical with the cuticle, or outer layer of the skin. See *Hair, Skin.*

Nervous System. The nervous system is concerned with the functions of sensation, motion, and volition, and through it all actions, whether voluntary or involuntary, are controlled. It consists of three parts: *central nervous system*, including the brain and spinal cord; *nerves*, extending from the central system to all parts of the body; and *sympathetic nervous system*, consisting of bunches of cells, chiefly in the body cavity, and their nerves supplying the glands and involuntary muscles.

Brain.—The part of the nervous system located within the skull. It is composed of three principal parts: the *cerebrum* or brain proper; the *cerebellum*, or little brain; and the *medulla oblongata*, the stem or bulb joining the higher parts of the brain to the spinal cord. The cerebrum is composed of two hemispheres connected with each other by nerve fibers. Broadly speaking, the cerebrum is made up of gray matter containing cells in groups forming centers for thought, action, or sensation, and white matter containing nerve strands acting as lines of communication. It is the seat of the mind. The cerebellum regulates and co-ordinates muscular movement. The medulla oblongata is the center which controls the respiratory and circulatory organs. If it is destroyed, death rapidly follows.

Spinal Cord.—That part of the nervous system which is fastened in the canal of the spinal column, composed of white matter outside and gray matter inside. The cells of gray matter send off long processes to help form the nerves of the arms and legs. It is the path of communication between the brain and the nerves of the arms, legs, and trunk. The spinal cord is also the seat of many muscular movements necessary in routine work.

Nerves.—As usually classified, there are twelve pairs of *cranial nerves* springing from the brain, and thirty-one pairs of *spinal nerves* arising from the spinal cord. The branches from these primary nerves reach all parts of the body. In addition to the cranial and spinal nerves, there is the *sympathetic nervous system.*

Each nerve is made up of a bundle of nerve fibers surrounded by sheaths of connective tissue. Each nerve fiber connects a central nerve cell with a peripheral end-organ. The distinguishing characteristic of a nerve cell is its irritability; that of a nerve fiber is its faculty of transmitting nervous energy at the rate of about 100 feet per second. While in many respects this nerve energy resembles electricity, it is far from being identical with that force. Each spinal nerve is from two roots, one containing *motor* and the other *sensory* fibers. The motor nerves dispatch impulses which produce contractions of the muscles. The sensory nerves transmit sensory impressions.

Sympathetic Nervous System.—This consists of a double chain of ganglia, lying on each side of the vertebræ, and nerves connecting these to the internal organs and the central nervous system. It controls the involuntary muscles in all parts of the body; for instance, it governs the heartbeat and the movements of the intestines. See *Brain.*

Nose. An organ connected with the respiratory system, and the seat of the sense of smell. Externally, the prominent part of the nose, which gives character to the features, is composed of several cartilages connected to the nasal bones and to each other by strong fibrous tissue. This is sufficiently firm to preserve the shape of the nose, and yet so elastic and flexible as to permit the expansion and contraction of the nostril during breathing. Internally, the nose consists of two large cavities, or *nostrils*, formed by the nasal cartilages and the bones of the face, and separated from each other by a perpendicular flat partition, known as the *septum.* At the rear the nostrils open into the nasal passages which lead back to the throat.

Various cavities in the bones of the face are connected with the nostrils and nasal passages by small openings, among which are the *frontal sinuses*, the *antrum*, and various *ethmoid* and *sphenoid* cells. The nose not only contains in its upper mucous membranes the sense organs of smell, but serves also to clean, warm, and moisten the air during its passage to the lungs, and has an important influence on the quality and character of the voice.

Nutrition. The process whereby the body takes, changes, and uses the substances necessary to maintain life and growth. In nutrition the final appropriation of food material takes place in the individual cells of the various tissues. The cell has the power, not only of attracting materials from the blood, but also of causing them to assume its own structure and properties. Besides this power of *assimilation*, the cell has the power of discarding the waste matter produced by its own vital activity.

In order that nutrition may proceed properly, the blood must be normal in composition and amount; it must circulate with suitable rapidity; there must be the right nervous stimulation and control; and the tissue or organ to be nourished must be able to use the materials brought to it by the blood. Further, it is necessary that the food supply should consist of the proper elements. In order to maintain normal nutrition, food must contain proteins, fats, carbohydrates, mineral matter, and water in the proper proportions. Further, it must contain the right amount and kind of *vitamines.* In other words, what is known as a *mixed diet* is required. See *Assimilation, Digestion, Vitamines.*

Pancreas. A glandular organ of a pinkish yellow color, in lower animals commonly called *sweetbread*, lying along the great curvature of the stomach. In man the pancreas is of an irregular, elongated form, from six to eight inches long, an inch and a half broad, and from half an inch to an inch thick. In structure it somewhat resembles the salivary glands. It secretes a watery looking fluid called the *pancreatic juice*, of great importance in digestion. In an adult the amount of pancreatic juice secreted daily is from five to seven ounces. It is discharged by a duct emptying into the small intestine through the common bile duct. The pancreatic secretion changes starch into glucose, a form of sugar; dissolves proteins, converting them into peptones, and breaks up and emulsifies fats so that the lacteal vessels in the intestines can absorb them. Diabetes, a disease characterized by sugar in the blood, is caused by a destruction of certain groups of cells in the pancreas.

Parathyroids. Small, ductless, glandular bodies, usually four in number, situated near or embedded in the substance of the thyroid. Although connected with the thyroid anatomically, they have different functions, and may be thought of as acting as a neuromuscular balance wheel, or control. They have also antitoxic functions, and serve to neutralize poisonous substances in the body. If the parathyroids are removed or are destroyed by disease, tetany (muscular spasms) results. See *Ductless Glands, Secretion, Thyroid.*

Parotid Glands. Two soft bodies situated, one on each side, in front of the lower portion of the ear, just above the angle of the jaw. The function of these glands is to secrete *saliva*, which affords the necessary moisture to the mouth, assists in the mastication of food, and digests starch, changing it into maltose, a form of sugar. The saliva is conveyed to the mouth through the *salivary ducts*, which open, one opposite each second molar tooth in the upper jaw. The disease known as mumps (*parotitis*) is an inflammation of the parotid glands. See *Salivary Glands.*

Pelvis. A somewhat basin-shaped bony structure situated at the base of the spinal column so as to transmit the weight of the body to the bones of the legs. It consists of an irregular girdle composed of three bones; namely, the two hip bones, or innominate bones (*ossa innominata*), which form its sides and front, and the sacrum. The coccyx consists of vestigial bones attached to the sacrum.

Each innominate bone is made up of three portions, separate in early life but firmly united in adults, called the *ilium*, the *ischium*, and the *pubis* or pubic bone (*os pubis*). These meet and form the cup-shaped cavity called the *acetabulum*, or socket of the hip joint, in which the head of the thigh bone (*femur*) rests. The ilium is the broad upper expanded portion, in shape somewhat resembling the blade of a screw propeller. This forms the prominence of the hips, and is joined behind to the sacrum. The ischium is the lowest and strongest portion. When the body is in a sitting position, its weight rests principally upon the ischium. From the inner side of each acetabulum a pubic bone runs horizontally inward and then downward and forward to meet the corresponding pubic bone from the opposite side. The union of these bones forms the *pubic arch*, or frontal portion of the bony girdle of the pelvis.

The cavity formed by the pelvic bones is shallow in front, only about 2 inches in depth, and deepest behind, about 5 inches. The *pelvic cavity* is divided into a *true* and a *false* pelvis. The false pelvis comprises the expanded portion bounded on the sides by the flattened hip bones. It lies above a line drawn through the crests of the pubic bones in front to the top of the sacrum behind. This broad, shallow false pelvis serves largely to support the weight of the intestines above it. The true pelvis lies below a line drawn through the crest of the pubic arch and the top of the sacrum. It contains the rectum, the bladder, and other organs. See *Abdomen, Thorax.*

Perspiration. The perspirable fluid, or *sweat*, is excreted from the blood by means of the *sudoriferous* or *sweat glands* of the skin, of which about two and one-half millions are distributed over the body. It is a colorless fluid, consisting of water, over 99 per cent, and small amounts of urea, common salt, and other salts. This excretion exerts a very important influence on the health. A sudden check or prolonged retention of perspiration produces serious derangements. Its principal uses are to moisten the skin, to regulate the temperature of the body, and to remove waste, poisons, or irritating material from the system.

A portion of the fluid evaporates as rapidly as it is secreted. This is called *insensible* perspiration. When a part of the secretion accumulates in drops, it is called *sensible* perspiration. The amount of perspiration normally discharged by a healthy person varies from about 1½ to 5 pints per day, increasing with exercise and high temperature. The evaporation of large quantities of perspiration from the skin during warm weather greatly aids in keeping the body cool. See *Excretion.*

Pineal (*pĭn'ē-ăl*) **Body.** An upward and forward outgrowth of the mid-brain, called also epiphysis, conarium, and pineal gland. It is a small, ovoid, reddish gray organ about one-fourth of an inch long. Its exact function in the human body is not known. Some researches seem to indicate that the pineal body is a gland, or, at least, has an internal secretion which is believed to influence physical and mental growth during early life. In all vertebrate animals possessing a skull the pineal body is present. Comparative anatomists have shown that the pineal body in man corresponds to the third eye possessed by some reptiles, and hence may be regarded as a vestigial organ. The ancients had a grotesque theory that the pineal body was the abiding place of the human soul. This view was shared also by some of the modern Cartesian philosophers. See *Ductless Glands, Secretion.*

Pituitary (*pĭ-tū'ĭ-tā-rĭ*) **Body** or **Gland.** A small, oval body attached to the infundibulum of the brain; called also the hypophysis of the brain. It occupies the sella turcica, a depression in the middle line of the anterior surface of the sphenoid bone. It consists of two distinct lobes, and, in size, averages about one-half inch in length and in width, and one-third of an inch in thickness. It weighs somewhat less than one-half ounce.

The larger, or *anterior* lobe, of a reddish-gray color, partly incloses the smaller, or *posterior* lobe, yellowish-gray in color. Each lobe has an entirely different function. When the anterior lobe is affected, the body is built up into gigantic form, known as giantism. The posterior lobe exerts a powerful influence over the vasomotor nervous system and the regulation of blood pressure. Complete removal of the pituitary body speedily results in cachexia and death.

An extract, *pituitrin*, has been made from the posterior lobe of the pituitary bodies of sheep and is used in obstetric medicine and as a circulatory stimulant.

Respiration. The act of breathing. In its broadest sense, respiration is the taking of oxygen to all cells of the body and the giving off of carbon dioxide. The essential organs are the lungs, but the accessory or helping organs include the nose, throat, trachea, ribs, diaphragm, and various tissues and muscles.

Respiration is both a mechanical and a chemical process. The mechanical process consists of *inspiration* and *expiration*, or the taking in and the forcing out of air. The action of the organs of respiration in forcing air in and out of the lungs is similar to that of a bellows. The muscles of the chest and of the abdomen, by simultaneously elevating the ribs and depressing the diaphragm, enlarge the cavity occupied by the lungs. In consequence, the air, by reason of its own natural pressure, rushes in to fill the extra space, thereby equalizing the air pressure inside and outside of the lungs. This completes the act of inspiration.

In expiration the muscles of the chest and the abdomen reverse their action. By depressing the ribs and elevating the diaphragm, the cavity of the chest is made smaller, and the surplus air is expelled through the passages by which it entered. At all times the lungs, which are composed of highly elastic tissue, completely fill the chest cavity, swelling like a rubber balloon when it enlarges, and diminishing in size when it contracts.

In normal breathing, the air, after being moistened and warmed nearly to the bodily temperature in passing through the nose and throat, enters the lungs through the windpipe or trachea. Thence the air passes into the bronchial tubes, which divide and subdivide until they finally reach the individual air cells, whose walls are enmeshed in a fine network of blood vessels. Here the chemical process of respiration takes place. A part of the oxygen of the incoming air diffuses through the very thin walls of the capillaries and is absorbed by the red corpuscles of the blood. At the same time, carbon dioxide, water vapor, and various impurities in the blood diffuse through the walls of the capillaries into the air cells and are expelled from the body with the exhaled air.

Respiration thus includes both breathing and oxidation. Oxidation is the chemical union of oxygen and any other substance. It occurs in all the cells of the body. When the oxygen in the blood reaches the cells, it combines chemically with the protoplasm, and heat and energy are produced. As a result of this union, carbon dioxide, water, and urea are formed. These eventually enter the blood and are carried by it to the different excretory organs to be given off from the body.

From 20 to 30 cubic inches of air are normally changed with each act of breathing. This amount, however, is always increased by physical exertion. But, at no time, is all of the air in the lungs changed at a single breath. While about 100 cubic inches above the normal 20 or 30 inches may be drawn in or expelled by forced breathing, there remains in any case about 100 cubic inches of *residual* air. Nearly 400 cubic feet of air pass through the lungs of an adult each day, but this quantity can be doubled by prolonged muscular exertion.

In health, respiration is easy, gentle, regular, and without noise. The act of breathing proceeds unconsciously, except when one voluntarily tries to inhale or to expel more or less than the normal or usual quantities of air. The rate of respiration during the first year of infancy is about 35 per minute, during the second year about 25, during adolescence about 20, and in adult life about 18.

The function of respiration is absolutely essential to life. All higher animals, including man, quickly perish if the supply of air to the lungs is cut off. The vigor of the system is soon impaired if the air is contaminated by smoke, noxious gases, or by overcrowding in heated rooms. Abundance of fresh air, good ventilation, and correct habits of breathing are necessary conditions of health for persons of all ages. See *Lungs*.

Salivary Glands. The glands which secrete the saliva, or watery fluid which moistens the food in the mouth and performs an important part in digestion. There are three pairs of salivary glands: the *parotid*, lying in front of each ear behind the lower jaw; the *submaxillary*, lying between the halves of the lower jawbone; and the *sublingual*, lying under the tongue. Each gland is provided with one or more ducts discharging into the mouth cavity. Saliva contains a digestive ferment, called *ptyalin*, which turns starch into sugar. See *Parotid Glands, Secretion*.

Secretion. The process of forming, through the action of certain cells, membranes, and glands, various substances to perform special functions in the body, as, for example, the *gastric juice* secreted by the glands of the stomach to aid in digestion. Among important secretions are: *saliva*, secreted by the salivary glands; *bile*, secreted by the liver; *pancreatic juice*, by the pancreas; *serous fluid*, by the serous membranes; *mucus*, by the mucous membranes; *synovial fluid*, by the synovial membranes; and *sebum*, by the sebaceous or oil glands of the skin. See *Bile, Ductless Glands, Liver, Pancreas, Parotid Glands, Salivary Glands, Thyroid*.

Skeletal System. The human skeleton consists of *bone, cartilage*, and *connective tissue*. There are slightly more than 200 separate bones. The actual number, however, varies at different periods of life. Many bones which are separate in youth grow together in advanced age. The bones make up the framework of the body, provide levers and points of attachment for the muscles, and, by surrounding cavities, furnish protection for delicate organs, such as the brain, spinal cord, heart, and lungs.

Cartilage is found at the ends of bones, forming elastic pads or shock-absorbing cushions for the joints. It sometimes serves in the place of bone, as at the outer ends of the ribs. *Connective tissue* occurs in the form of *ligaments* which serve as stout cords binding bones together, as *tendons* which attach muscles to bones, and as *periosteum* which protects and assists in nourishing bones. *Articulations* are the points where bones meet, or are joined together, in the body. *Joints* are forms of articulations which permit considerable freedom of movement.

Skeleton. The bony skeleton is made up of two chief divisions, the *axial skeleton* and the *appendicular skeleton*. The axial skeleton, which supports the head, neck, and trunk, consists of the skull, the hyoid bone, which attaches the tongue to the skull, the vertebral column, ribs, and sternum, or breastbone. The appendicular skeleton, which supports the legs and arms and attaches them to the trunk, consists of the pectoral girdle, the pelvic girdle, and the bones of the arms and legs.

Axial Skeleton.—The skull is composed of 28 bones as follows: *cranium* or brain box, 8; bones of the face, 14; bones of the inner ear, 6. The *hyoid bone*, to which the tongue is attached, is suspended from the skull by ligaments. The *vertebral column*, or backbone, consists of 24 vertebræ, of which 7 are cervical (neck), 12 dorsal (chest), and 5 lumbar ("small of the back"). Below the separate vertebræ are the *sacrum* and the *coccyx* consisting, in adults, of one bone each, but, in children, of 5 and 4 bones respectively. There are 24 ribs, 12 on each side, of which 7 are joined to the sternum in front, 3 are attached by cartilage, and 2 have free outer ends. The axial skeleton thus consists of 54 bones.

Appendicular Skeleton.—The pectoral arch, or shoulder girdle, consists of two bones, a *clavicle*, or collar bone, and a *scapula*, or shoulder blade, on each side. The two clavicles, or collar bones, lie one on each side of the sternum, their upper and outer ends being attached to the scapulas and their lower and inner ends to the sternum. The two scapulas, or shoulder blades, lie outside of the ribs on the back of the chest. The pelvic arch, or girdle, consists of three bones, namely the two hip bones and the sacrum.

Bones of the Arms.—There are 30 bones in each arm: *humerus*, extending from shoulder to elbow; *radius*, forearm bone, thumb side; *ulna*, the second forearm bone; 8 *carpal* bones, in the wrist; 5 *metacarpal*, in the palm of the hand; and 14 *phalanges*, two for the thumb and three for each finger.

Bones of the Legs.—There are 30 bones in each leg: *femur*, or thigh bone; *tibia*, lower leg, inside; *fibula*, lower leg, outside; *patella*, or kneecap; 7 *tarsal* bones, below the ankle joint; 5 *metatarsal*, in the front part of the sole; and 14 *phalanges*, 2 in the great toe, and 3 in each of the others. See *Pelvis, Skull, Spinal Column, Thorax*.

Skin. The strong, elastic integument which invests and surrounds the body, consisting of two fundamental layers, the *cuticle* or *epidermis*, the outer skin, and the *cutis* or *dermis*, the true skin.

The cuticle, or epidermis, is a thin layer of epithelial cells, varying somewhat in thickness in different parts of the body. It is without blood vessels and nerves and, therefore, is devoid of sensibility. It may be divided into two layers, a *superficial* and a *deep* layer. The superficial one is what is usually termed the epidermis. This is the so-called "dead skin" often rubbed off with the towel after bathing. The inner or deep layer lies on the true skin, and consists of softer, moister, and more rounded cells than the outer layer. This inner portion, sometimes called the *Malpighian* layer, or *rete mucosum*, is the seat of the coloring material or pigment of colored races, such as the Negro. Freckles result from the formation of coloring matter in spots or patches in this layer.

The cutis, or dermis, from about one-sixteenth to one-eighth of an inch in thickness, forms the much more complex lower layer of the skin. It consists of densely-interwoven fibrous tissues, and is abundantly supplied with blood vessels, lymphatics, glands, hair follicles, touch-papillæ, and nerves. This layer contains the *sudoriferous* or *sweat glands*, which pour out the perspiration, and also the *sebaceous glands*, which secrete oily matter, the use of which is to keep the skin and hair soft and flexible. The *papillæ* of the skin consist of small conical processes on the surface of the cutis. The central portion of each papilla contains a group of blood vessels and a nerve, and on the more sensitive parts of the skin minute touch organs are also present. Hair and nails are developed from special structures in the dermis.

The skin is one of the most varied and useful of the bodily structures. It protects the outer parts of the body, serves as an organ of excretion, regulates the bodily temperature by the evaporation of water, and is the seat of the sense of touch. See *Hair*; *Nails*; *Perspiration*; *Touch, Organs of*.

Skull. The skeleton or bony framework of the head in early adult life consists of 28 separate bones, in case the 6 small ossicles of the ear are included. In infancy and youth, however, the number is greater, and in old age it is less. Of these, 8 bones form the cranium, and 14, the face.

The bones of the *cranium* are arranged so as to enclose the brain and to protect the inner parts of the ear. They include the *frontal* bone, extending across the forehead; the *parietal* bones, one on each side, forming the lateral walls of the cranium or brain case; the *temporal* bones, one on each side, forming part of the wall of the cranium and containing the internal ear; and the *occipital*, behind and at the base of which, through a circular opening, called the *foramen magnum*, the spinal cord and the vertebral arteries pass. The base or floor of the cranium, in front of the part formed by the occipital bone, is composed of two very irregularly shaped bones. These are the *sphenoid*, with wings extending upward to the parietal bones on each side, and the *ethmoid*, which occupies a central position between the orbits of the eyes at the root of the nose.

The bones of the *face* include two *nasal*, at the base of the nose: two *superior maxillary*, which form the upper jaw, bound the nasal cavity and the inner margin of the eye socket; two *lachrymal*, small bones taking part in the formation of the orbit; two *malar*, or cheek bones; two *pterygoids*, lying just back of the nasal cavity; the *vomer*, which divides the rear portion of the nasal cavity; two palatal processes of the maxillary, forming the *hard palate*; and the *inferior maxillary*, forming the lower jaw.

Except the inferior maxillary, all the bones of the skull are joined to one another by *sutures*, many of which become completely changed to bone and disappear in adult life. The upper cranial bones of a baby's skull do not normally unite until several months after birth, as is easily observed in the fontanels or "soft spots" on the top of the head. This condition permits the brain to grow rapidly. Imbecile children are often born with the fontanels closed, although the idiocy is not due to the union of the bones.

Smell, Organs of. The sense of smell resides in the mucous membrane that lines the upper parts of the cavity of the nose. From the underside of the *olfactory lobes*, or *bulbs*, lying on the skull floor, *olfactory nerves* arise and pass out through the roof of the nose. These ramify into finely divided branches throughout the olfactory portions of the mucous membrane. The function of the olfactory nerves is to carry to the brain the impulses which cause the sensation of smell.

Only a very minute quantity of a substance is required to affect the sense of smell. For example, a grain of musk will perfume a room for a long period without appreciably losing weight. To appreciate odors, that is to exercise the sense of smell, one must draw the air containing them through the nose, or sniff. If the air remains motionless in the nasal passages, usually but little smell will be noticed. The sense of smell is of great importance in detecting improper food and injurious impurities in the air.

Solar Plexus. An important plexus or center of the sympathetic nervous system, situated in the abdomen, behind the stomach and in front of the aorta. It contains several ganglia which distribute nerve fibers to the stomach, liver, kidneys, and intestines. If this nerve center is severely shocked, as by a heavy blow, temporary suspension of the vital functions, or even death, may ensue. Hence the origin of the expressions "to strike a solar plexus blow," and "to strike in the solar plexus."

Speech, Organs of. The larynx, a somewhat triangular box of cartilage, situated at the top of the windpipe, is the chief organ of the voice. It is composed of nine plates of cartilage, connected together by ligaments and moved by numerous muscles. The *vocal cords*, two narrow bands of dense, fibrous, and highly elastic tissue, are stretched between the thyroid and arytenoid cartilages. They lie in the pharynx so that only a narrow slit, the *glottis*, is left between them.

When air is forced through the glottis, the vocal cords vibrate, giving rise to sounds. The shorter the vocal cords, the higher the pitch of the voice. Children's voices are high-pitched and shrill, because the larynx is small. A woman's voice is usually higher than a man's for the same reason. At the age of sixteen or seventeen years, a boy's larynx grows rapidly and his voice becomes an octave deeper in tone.

Besides the larynx there are several accessory or helping organs for the production of speech, including the tongue, teeth, lips, and resonant cavities of the nose, together with the lungs and the chest muscles which force the air between the vocal cords. See *Nose, Teeth, Throat, Tongue.*

Spinal Column. The series of twenty-four bony structures, or vertebræ, comprising the spinal column, commonly called the *backbone*, is admirably adapted for its many uses. First, the column widens and increases in stability from the neck to the sacrum. Again, the column is bound together with a system of flexible ligaments which give it almost the strength of steel. Moreover, the column has four curves, imparting to it somewhat the shape of an elongated letter S. These add greatly to its springiness and prevent the transmission of shocks. Besides, there are elastic cushions of cartilage between the vertebræ, called *intervertebral disks*. These permit some movement between the vertebræ and aid in protecting the spinal cord.

Each vertebra or separate bone of the column consists of four parts: a *body*, a *neural arch*, a *neural ring*, and *bony processes* projecting from both the body and the arch. The succession of the neural rings forms the *neural tube* or *canal* which contains the spinal cord. Through openings leading into this canal, called *vertebral foramina*, nerves pass out of or into the spinal cord.

The spinal column serves several extremely important uses: it supports the body and the head; gives attachment to the ribs and various muscles of the trunk; encloses and protects the spinal cord; and absorbs shocks which otherwise might injure the brain. At the same time it is so constructed as to combine great strength with remarkable freedom of movement. See *Pelvis, Skull, Thorax.*

Spleen. A long, flat, red organ, which lies on the left side just under the diaphragm, near to the stomach and pancreas. While normally about five inches long and weighing six ounces, the spleen varies greatly in size, enlarging during digestion and shrinking until the next meal. The spleen is now regarded as a kind of blood gland or lymphatic gland, because of its similarity in structure to the lymphatic glands. The blood circulates through it freely. It has no duct, and, whatever its product is, it enters the blood directly. *Lymphocytes*, small, white blood corpuscles, are formed in the spleen. Experiments upon dogs, so conducted as to make observable the expansion and contraction of the spleen, indicate that the spleen serves as a place of storage for the red blood corpuscles. Thence they may be released upon demands, generally connected with an emotional stimulus, from another part of the body, and increase the power of the blood to convey oxygen to the muscles called into action. The spleen contracts on their release.

It is certain that the spleen is not an absolutely essential organ, as it may be removed from man and from lower animals without apparent bad consequences. Among the ancients the spleen was believed to be the seat of melancholy.

Stomach. The human stomach is an elongated, curved pouch, from ten to twelve inches long, and four or five inches in diameter at its widest part, having somewhat the form of a bagpipe. It lies nearly transversely across the upper left portion of the abdomen, immediately beneath the diaphragm at its left end, but overlapped by the liver at its right end. The stomach is very dilatable and contractile, with an average capacity of about two pints. It has two openings, one connected with the esophagus, called the *cardiac orifice*, and one connected with the small intestine, called the *pyloric orifice*.

The wall of the stomach is composed of four coats or membranes: (1) the exterior or *serous* coat.

very tough and strong, and covering every part of this important organ; (2) the muscular coat, composed of three layers of muscle fibers, one arranged longitudinally, the second, circularly, and the third, obliquely; (3) the *submucous* coat made up of lax areolar tissue; and (4) the interior or *mucous* coat, arranged in wrinkles or folds, containing the glands which secrete the *gastric juice*.

Food enters the stomach through the esophagus by the cardiac orifice. Its presence in the stomach excites the gastric glands, which pour forth their secretion. By powerful motions of the stomach muscles, the gastric juice becomes thoroughly mixed with the food, the digestion of which proceeds rapidly. The gastric juice is a clear, yellowish fluid consisting chiefly of water but containing salts, two ferments, pepsin and rennin, and free hydrochloric acid. The principal action of the gastric juice is to change albuminous or protein principles of food into peptones. This is brought about by the hydrochloric acid and pepsin. After having been properly acted upon by the gastric juice, the food thus digested is passed on in a semifluid or pulpy mass, called chyme, through the pyloric orifice into the small intestine. The time required for the stomach to empty itself ranges from two to five hours. See *Alimentary Canal, Digestion, Gastric Juice.*

Suprarenal (*sū'prȧ-rē'năl*) **Glands.** Two small, ductless, glandular bodies, each of which surmounts the upper end of a kidney. They are called also suprarenal bodies, or adrenals. In color they are yellowish, and in shape each somewhat resembles a liberty cap. Their size is variable, but the length rarely exceeds two inches, the width one and one-fourth inches, and the thickness one-fourth inch. Each suprarenal body weighs about a dram.

The internal secretion of the suprarenals is absolutely necessary to life. Removal of the glands from the body, or their complete degeneration in disease, is rapidly followed by death. The function of the suprarenals is to control the pigmentation of the skin, to counteract the effect of various poisons found in the body, and to regulate blood pressure. The most active substance produced in these glands is adrenaline. This is a definite chemical substance (a methyl-amino derivative of catechol), which is extracted in the form of white crystals.

Adrenaline, in small quantities, is continually passing into the blood stream. This stimulates the sympathetic nervous system, increases arterial blood pressure, causes the liver to discharge more sugar into the blood, and increases the efficiency of the heart and other muscles. Adrenaline is so powerful that a solution containing one part in a million will produce physiological effects. In medicine, various preparations of adrenaline are used as a stimulant and as a hæmostatic to control hemorrhages. See *Blood Pressure, Ductless Glands, Secretion.*

Taste, Organs of. The organs of taste are situated in the mucous membrane on the upper surface of the tongue, and, in some persons, on the soft palate and pharynx. On the tongue are a great number of little projections, or *papillæ*, which are of three kinds, *filiform, fungiform*, and *circumvallate*, in which the branches of the gustatory (glosso-pharyngeal) nerve ramify, ending in *taste buds*. The taste buds are minute circular bodies; from one end of each, fine hairs project, while at the other end a nerve filament enters. Besides taste buds, there are believed to be other sense organs of taste, for the sensation of taste can be perceived at other places on the tongue.

In reality, however, many so-called tastes are smells, as the olfactory sense is much more keen than the sense of taste. For example, in case of various people, if the nose be closed, an apple cannot be distinguished from a potato by taste alone. Most persons taste bitter things with the back part of the tongue and sweet things with the tip. Some substances are known which, for some persons, cause a pure sweet taste if placed on the tip of the tongue, and a pure bitter taste if placed on the back of the tongue. See *Tongue.*

Teeth. In adults the teeth are 32 in number, 16 in each jaw, of which 4 are incisors, or cutting teeth, 2 are canines, 4 are bicuspids, and 6 are molars, or grinding teeth. Each tooth is composed of a *crown*, covered with *enamel*, a *neck*, and a *root*, or *fang*, covered with *cement*. The root is surrounded by a thin layer of bone, *crusta petrosa*, embedded in the alveolar process formed by the jawbone. The interior of a tooth is composed of *dentine*, in the center of which is the *pulp cavity* containing blood vessels and nerves.

The temporary teeth of children are 20 in number, of which 10 grow in the upper jaw and 10 in the lower. These temporary, or so-called "milk teeth," usually appear during the first three years of life. The teeth of the lower jaw commonly erupt somewhat in advance of the corresponding teeth of the upper jaw. The following are the most usual times of eruption: lower central incisors, 6 to 9 months; upper incisors, 8 to 10 months; lower lateral incisors and first molars, 15 to 21 months; canines, 16 to 20 months; second molars, 20 to 24 months.

There is, however, much variation in the periods at which the temporary teeth appear. For example, some authorities state that, at the age of one year, a child should have 6 teeth; at one and one-half years, 12 teeth; at two years, 16 teeth, and at two and one-half years, 20 teeth.

The permanent teeth, likewise, vary considerably in the time of their appearance, and, as in case of the temporary teeth, those of the lower jaw slightly precede those of the upper. The permanent teeth erupt in the following order and usually at about the periods stated: first molars, the 6th year; two central incisors, the 7th year; two lateral incisors, the 8th year; first bicuspids, the 9th year; second bicuspids, the 10th year; canines, the 11th to the 12th year; second molars, the 12th to the 13th year; third molars, the 17th to the 25th year.

The layer of enamel covering the crown of a tooth is the hardest substance forming a part of the human body, being composed almost entirely of earthy matter. The enamel enables the teeth to withstand their important work of cutting and grinding food so that it can be acted upon by the saliva and easily swallowed and digested. Great care should be taken not to break the enamel by biting hard substances or by using metal toothpicks, since it is the only substance in the body which nature does not replace.

Tartar, a limy deposit from the saliva, forms on the teeth. To prevent decay, it should be removed by a dentist once or twice a year.

Tendons. White, glistening cords of fibrous tissue, varying in length and thickness, which connect the ends of muscles with bones, cartilages, and ligaments. Tendons are usually round, sometimes flattened, of considerable strength, and only slightly elastic. Examples of tendons are the so-called "leaders," connecting the muscles of the arm with the hand, and the "heel cord" or *tendo Achillis*, connecting the muscles of the lower leg with the foot. See *Joints, Muscles.*

Thorax. The part of the body situated between the neck and the abdomen, commonly called the chest. Externally, it is bounded by the ribs and is somewhat conical in form with the broad lower end closed internally by the diaphragm. The important vital organs contained within the chest are protected by a combination of bones, cartilages, muscles, and tendons. These are arranged so as to permit the expansile movements necessary in breathing and, at the same time, shield from injury the delicate organs within.

The structures which form the walls of the thorax are: (1) the thoracic portion of the backbone or spinal column, comprising twelve dorsal vertebræ; (2) twelve ribs on either side, attached behind to the dorsal vertebræ and ending in front in costal cartilages; (3) the sternum or breastbone, situated in the middle line in front and forming the attachment for the costal cartilages which extend from the ends of the ribs; (4) the diaphragm, a strong muscular partition, convex toward the thorax and concave toward the abdomen; (5) various muscles and tendons connected with the backbone and ribs and concerned with respiration and other movements. These form much of the fleshy part of the chest wall.

The organs contained within the thorax are the heart, lungs, trachea or windpipe, bronchi or branches of the trachea leading to the lungs, the esophagus or gullet, certain important nerve trunks, and the thoracic duct through which chyle and lymph from the lymphatic system are discharged into the blood. As these comprise some of the most essential of the vital organs, a healthy condition of the chest is a matter of the highest importance. Several of the most fatal maladies develop in connection with the organs of the thorax. Among these are bronchitis, pneumonia, and pulmonary tuberculosis, affecting the lungs, and pericarditis, angina pectoris, and other diseases, affecting the heart. See *Heart, Lungs, Respiration.*

Throat. The throat cavity, or *pharynx*, is a portion of the alimentary canal lying between the back of the mouth and the esophagus or gullet. In shape it is a somewhat conical bag, with the broad end upward. The throat cavity has seven openings: the fauces opening into the mouth, the two rear nostrils, the two Eustachian tubes leading to the middle ear, the opening of the larynx, and the opening of the gullet. Except when one is swallowing or speaking, the soft palate hangs as a curtain between the mouth and the pharynx. During the act of swallowing, the soft palate rises to a horizontal position, shutting off the openings of the nostrils. Through the upper part of the pharynx only air passes; through the lower part, both food and air pass—the food when going to the gullet and air when going to the larynx and the windpipe.

Covering the opening to the larynx is a small plate of cartilage called the *epiglottis*. In the act of swallowing, the epiglottis closes over the top of the larynx like a lid. When food sometimes accidentally "goes the wrong way" it enters the windpipe instead of the gullet.

Thymus, The. A ductless gland situated within the chest, between the lungs in front of the heart, and extending upward nearly to the thyroid. The thymus is a temporary organ, attaining its largest size at the age of two or three years, when its weight is about one-half ounce. Thereafter it slowly and steadily shrinks in size. At the age of fifteen it has nearly disappeared, although traces of it may be discovered in old age.

The thymus consists of two nearly symmetrical lobes,—the *right lateral* and the *left lateral*—each completely independent of the other. The lobes are divided into lobules. These, in turn, are divided into nodules or follicles and are surrounded by numerous lymphatics and blood vessels. The functions of the thymus are undetermined, but it is generally believed that the gland exerts a strong influence upon growth and development. See *Ductless Glands, Secretion.*

Thyroid, The. A large ductless gland, situated in the lower part of the front of the neck. It consists of two lobes, one on each side of the trachea and usually connected at their lower parts by a narrow bridge or isthmus. The lobes are broadest below and taper to a point above. Each lobe is about two inches long, one and one-fourth inches wide at its broadest part, and three-fourths of an inch thick. The thyroid is larger in women than in men and, on the average, weighs about one and one-half ounces. The gland, however, is subject to great variations in size, and may become enormously enlarged, as in *goiter*.

In maintaining growth and health, the thyroid, which, doubtless, forms an internal secretion, is an organ of great importance. Its removal, or impairment by disease, is followed by grave disturbances. When the gland is diseased in children, so that its function is destroyed, a species of idiocy, called *cretinism*, is produced. In adults the corresponding condition is called *myxœdema.* Its most marked symptoms are slowness both of body and mind, accompanied by muscular twitchings and other derangements. *Graves's disease*, known also as *exophthalmic goiter*, is due to enlargement and overactivity of the thyroid. See *Ductless Glands, Parathyroids, Secretion.*

Tongue. The chief seat of the sense of taste and an important auxiliary or helper to other organs in articulation or speech, mastication or chewing of food, and deglutition or swallowing. The tongue is a double organ situated in the floor of the mouth. It is composed chiefly of muscular fibers which run in almost every direction, so that it possesses great freedom of motion and can be changed into a variety of shapes. The two sides of the tongue are absolutely distinct, so that sometimes, as in paralysis, one side is useless while the function of the other side continues unimpaired.

The tongue is well supplied with blood vessels, receiving an artery on each side. It is also well furnished with nerves, filaments from the fifth, ninth, and twelfth pairs of cranial nerves entering it. A branch of the fifth, called the *gustatory nerve*, is commonly regarded as the nerve of taste. The surface of the tongue is thickly covered with *papillæ*, or *villi*, which give it a somewhat velvety appearance.

The papillæ are of three kinds,—*circumvallate, fungiform,* and *filiform*. The circumvallate, from 7 to 12 in number, lying near the root of the tongue, are elevations of the mucous membrane, much larger than the other papillæ; these secrete mucus that helps to lubricate the food in swallowing. The fungiform papillæ consist of small, rounded heads supported on short stalks, somewhat resembling a mushroom in shape, and are found over the middle and fore parts of the upper surface. The filiform papillæ, the smallest and most numerous, are scattered over the whole surface except near the base. The *taste buds* occur around the fungiform and circumvallate papillæ and receive fibers from the gustatory nerves. See *Taste, Organs of.*

Tonsil. A soft, rounded body, normally about the size of an almond, lying in a depression of the fauces on either side of the opening into the throat. Small, white blood corpuscles are formed in the tonsils. Goblet cells on the surface secrete mucus. During a cold or other infection, the tonsils sometimes become greatly enlarged, and, by pressure, close the Eustachian tube leading to the middle ear, causing partial deafness. Tonsillitis is an inflammation of the tonsil, and quinsy is due to an abscess around the tonsil. Because of their tendency to become seats of infection, the tonsils are often surgically removed.

Touch, Organs of. The sense of touch, called also the *tactile sense*, enables the mind to become acquainted with some of the properties of bodies,—whether smooth or rough, warm or cold, and, in some degree, too, with their form and weight. The principal seat of the sense of touch is the skin. The hand, with its fineness of skin, great sensibility, and length and flexibility of the fingers, is admirably adapted for exercise of the tactile sense. Nearly all parts of the skin are more or less sensitive to the touch. There are, in the skin, special nerve endings to receive the stimulus of cold, heat, pressure, or pain, respectively. See *Skin.*

Veins. The blood vessels which convey the blood from the capillaries to the heart, gradually joining together to form larger and larger vessels as they near that organ, finally uniting in the ascending and descending *venæ cavæ* which pour the impure venous blood into the right auricle of the heart.

The *pulmonary veins* lead from the lung capillaries to the left auricle of the heart, conveying to it purified or arterial blood, forming the only part of the circulatory system in which veins carry pure blood. The *portal veins* take venous blood from the capillaries of the intestines to the liver, where these vessels in turn break into capillaries. The *hepatic vein* carries the blood from the liver toward the heart.

As in case of the arteries, the walls of veins are composed of three coats, but much thinner and weaker in structure. Many veins, especially those of the legs and arms, contain valves, which permit blood to flow only toward the heart. In some of the large veins, including the venæ cavæ, the pulmonary, and the portal veins, there are no valves. There is no pulsation in veins as there is in the arteries, and the blood is of much darker color.

The circulation of the blood in the veins is indirectly caused by the pulsation of the heart and arteries and the great pressure thereby produced in every part of the system. This, together with the force of capillary attraction and restriction of the flow of blood to only one direction by the valves, is believed to account for the regularity of the venous circulation. To stop bleeding from a severed vein, pressure should be applied on the side of the wound farthest from the heart. See *Circulation, Circulatory System*.

Vermiform Appendix. A small, worm-shaped, blind tube, from two to four inches long and somewhat larger than a goose quill, which arises from the upper end of the large intestine or colon. The appendix is situated in the right iliac region of the abdomen. While it is hollow to the tip and its cavity communicates with that of the large intestine, its function or use in the body is considered unimportant. The vermiform appendix, however, is often the seat of the serious inflammatory disease called *appendicitis*.

Vitamins (*vī'tȧ-mĭnz; vĭt'ȧ-*). This name has been given to certain substances which experiment has shown are necessary for the normal growth, health, and reproduction of men and animals.

For many years it was believed that the human body might be compared to a steam engine. If the human machine received sufficient air and water and plenty of fuel in the form of proteins, fats, carbohydrates, and mineral salts, it was expected to operate steadily and efficiently. It has been proved, however, that, unless vitamins are present along with the other required elements of food, not only will the human engine fail to perform expected work, but its entire mechanism will soon become deranged or wrecked. The action of vitamins is believed analogous to that of catalytic agents, which, with little or no change in themselves, promote the chemical reactions of other substances.

Nine vitamins are of special importance and research is constantly adding to the number of possible substances of this nature. The effects of the more important are given below, followed by a table showing the chief food sources of each vitamin.

Vitamin A. The absence of this vitamin checks growth, causes a general weakening of the body, and promotes infections. Night blindness and abcesses are among the effects of deficiency. Often called the growth-producing vitamin, Vitamin A is fat-soluble and can be stored in the body for a considerable period. It has been isolated and is not appreciably affected by cooking.

Vitamin B. Research on the first-discovered Vitamin B has revealed a complex group, now described as B_2 or G, while the original Vitamin B is designated B_1. B_1, known as thiamin (or aneurin), is a promotor of growth, and stimulates the appetite. The lack of it causes the tropical disease beri-beri, also fatigue, nervousness, heart disorders, and loss of weight and appetite. Being water-soluble, it is not stored in the body in quantity; a supply of it must be constantly renewed. It is more easily destroyed by heat than is Vitamin A. It has been synthesized.

Vitamin C. This vitamin, known as ascorbic acid, is a preventive of scurvy. Lack of it causes soreness and stiffness of the joints, soreness of the gums, loosening of the teeth, a tendency to bleeding, and fragility of the bones. It is water-soluble and is destroyed by cooking.

Vitamin D. Known as caliciferol, this is the so-called antirachitic vitamin, a term indicating that it prevents rickets. It is essential for conversion of calcium and phosphorus into tooth and bone substance. In its absence the bones become soft and the teeth readily decay. It is fat-soluble. It may be produced in the body by the action of light, as explained below under *Ultra-violet Rays*.

Vitamin E. This vitamin, alpha-tocopherol, is necessary for fertility. Its absence produces sterility in both males and females. It is soluble in fat and may therefore be stored in the body. It is not easily destroyed by cooking.

Vitamin-complex G (or *B_2*). This includes riboflavin, nicotinic acid, B_6 or pyridoxin, and perhaps some others. The three named have been isolated and are water-soluble. The absence of riboflavin causes growth failure and lesions of the skin and eyes in humans. It is not formed in the body and must be introduced in the diet. Nicotinic acid, known for some years before its function as a vitamin was understood, is called, because of its effect, the Pellagra-Preventive (P-P) member of the complex, although it is not always sufficient by itself to produce this result. B_6, pyridoxin, may promote growth and apparently co-operates in relieving pellagra.

Vitamin K. Deficiency in this vitamin prevents the blood from clotting. It is fat-soluble and has been synthesized and isolated.

FOODS AND VITAMINS

The mark "x" indicates that the vitamin named at the head of the vertical column is present in the food named at the extreme left.

Foods	Vitamins						
	A	B_1	C	D	E	G	K
Bread (white)[1]	..	..	..	..	..	..	..
Butter	x	..	..	..	..	..	..
Cereals (whole grain)	..	x	..	x	x	x[2]	x[3]
Cheese	x	..	..	..	..	..	..
Eggs	x	x	..	x	x	x[4]	..
Fish	..	..	..	x	..	x[2,5]	..
Fruit	..	x	x[6]	..	..	..	..
Legumes (peas, beans)	..	x	..	..	..	x[2,4]	..
Liver (fish)	x	..	..	x	..	x[5]	..
Liver (animal)	x	x	..	..	..	x[4,5]	..
Meat (lean)	..	x	..	..	..	x	..
Milk	x	x	..	x[7]	..	x[4,5]	..
Vegetables (green)[8]	x[9]	x	x[10]	..	x[11]	x[4,5]	x[12]
Vegetable oils	..	..	..	..	x	x[2]	..
Yeast	..	x	..	x	..	x	..

1. White flour through processing loses much of the vitamin content of wheat, but this may be restored. 2. Contains B^6. 3. Also grasses and alfalfa. 4. Contains riboflavin. 5. Contains nicotinic acid. 6. Esp. citrus fruits. 7. If fortified. 8. If cooked, the water should be saved. 9. Also carrots, sweet potatoes, tomatoes. 10. If fresh; also peppers, tomatoes, potatoes. 11. Esp. lettuce. 12. Esp. spinach, kale, cabbage.

Ultra-violet Rays. In addition to certain foods, these light rays are productive of Vitamin D. A substance in the skin known as ergasterol is activated by the rays and forms chemically this vitamin. Foods containing ergasterol, when similarly irradiated, become richer in Vitamin D.

Ultra-violet rays are radiations similar to those of light, but having a wave length so small as to place them beyond the range of light sensation in the human eye. They cannot be seen as light or color. Sunlight, unimpeded by smoke or ordinary window glass, is rich in ultra-violet rays.

PSYCHOLOGY

The Rise of Modern Psychology. Modern scientific psychology had its inception in the year 1860 with the publication of the *Elements of Psychophysics* by Gustav Fechner. In this important book, Fechner demonstrated that mind could be measured in the same way that matter is measured. Two years later, Wilhelm Wundt, another German scientist, set forth a program for a scientific psychology. He insisted that psychology, like other natural sciences, could be scientific and quantitative. Wundt established the first formal psychological laboratory (1879) at the University of Leipzig to which students from all parts of the civilized world came to learn and to perform experiments. Wundt's first American student, G. Stanley Hall, founded the first pyschological laboratory in the United States at the Johns Hopkins university (1883).

Modern psychology is the offspring of two disciplines, philosophy and physiology. Down through the ages philosophers have been interested in mind and its relation to the body and the external world. Aristotle taught that the world is known through the senses. Descartes believed that mind and body are separate but interact with one another. Locke asserted that the contents of the mind were ideas which were connected with one another by the laws of association. Berkeley put forth the radical doctrine that mind is the only reality; the external world and the body are but images in the mind. These and numerous other speculations concerning the mind had been formulated by philosophers prior to 1860. Physiology with its specialized knowledge concerning the sense organs and the nervous system too made important contributions to the new science.

The Task of Psychology. Wundt's original program provided that the task of psychology was to analyze mind into its constituent elements, to determine the ways in which these elements were connected, and to discover the laws of their connection. The method by which the psychologist was to study mind was that of introspection, a disciplined, analytic, and systematic way of observing the mind. That psychology is the science of the mind remained unquestioned until 1913 when John B. Watson, a prominent American psychologist, launched a movement which came to be known as behaviorism and which constituted a revolt against the tradition established by Wundt. Watson contended that mind could not be studied scientifically and that the introspective method is subjective and therefore unscientific. He defined psychology as the science of behavior, "a purely objective, experimental branch of natural science which needs introspection as little as do the sciences of chemistry and physics." The impact of behaviorism upon American psychology was very great and for many years Watson's definition of psychology was the standard one. Other viewpoints were expressed, notably those of Gestalt psychology (Wertheimer, Kohler, Koffka), psychoanalysis (Freud), purposive behaviorism (Tolman), topological psychology (K. Lewin), and the psychology of personality (G. W. Allport), each of these formulating the province of psychology in a different fashion. Although it is difficult to define the task of psychology in terms acceptable to all psychologists, there is considerable agreement that psychology is the science which treats of the individual and his adjustments to the social and physical environments.

The Fields of Psychology. The most significant development in contemporary psychology is the practical application of the basic laws and principles regarding man which have been discovered by the use of the experimental and other scientific methods. As a result of these applications numerous specialities or fields have come into existence. The *psychology of infancy, childhood, and adolescence* is an important field because it is felt that the child is the measure of the man, that what he is as an adult is conditioned by his experiences during the growing-up period. *Educational psychology* is concerned with the application of psychology in the classroom. The nature of learning, the teaching of tool subjects such as reading, writing, and arithmetic, and the rôle which the school plays in developing intelligence, aptitudes, personality, and character are aspects of educational psychology. *Abnormal psychology* deals with individuals whose behavior and mentality deviates markedly from those of the typical person.

Industrial and business psychology concerns itself with the person at work. The selection, placement, and training of new employees, efficient methods of preventing accidents, and the counseling of poorly adjusted workers are among the topics covered by this field. *Vocational guidance* provides the young person with information about himself and about occupations which he may make use of in choosing a vocation wisely. The most important field of applied psychology is *clinical psychology.* Clinical psychology consists of the diagnosis and treatment of the maladjusted individual. The diagnosis of the problem is made on the basis of psychological tests, interviews, and case history material, and the treatment of the individual is called *psychotherapy.* There are numerous psychotherapeutic methods, e.g., suggestion, hypnotism, psychoanalysis, catharsis, environmental.

Psychological Activities of the Individual. The principal psychological activities engaged in by nearly all men are perceiving, learning, remembering, thinking, and feeling.

Perceiving. Man is aware of the world about him because he is equipped with sense organs which are sensitive to certain forms of energy and which transmit impulses by way of the nerves to that part of the brain, the cerebral cortex, which is the center of conscious awareness. A form of energy, e.g. light, to which a sense organ responds is called a stimulus.

When a person is aware of the external world or of stimuli originating within his body he is perceiving. Customarily, a perception consists of two aspects, figure and ground. The figure is that feature which stands out against the ground. An airplane in the blue sky, a light shining in the darkness, a prominent odor or taste, the cry of a baby at night, the prick of a needle on the skin are examples of figure and ground. Camouflage illustrates how figures can be made to disappear by blending them into the ground.

What a person will perceive at any given moment is determined by his past experience and training, his interests and needs, the condition of his sense organs and nervous system, and the nature of the stimuli. Other things being equal, the stronger the stimulus the greater is the probability that it will be perceived. The loud noise has the advantage over a weak one. Defects of the sense organs influence perception. A few people are totally color blind so that red, green, blue, and the other hues are perceived as different tones of gray. More people are partially color blind (about 5% of the male population). They usually confuse red and green. Deafness for certain tones and insensitivity to certain tastes and odors are not uncommon. Disorders of the central nervous system may distort perception. Finally, perception is controlled by what a person wants to perceive and what he has learned to perceive. The hungry person is food-alerted, the botanist sees many things on his walk through the woods which would go unnoticed by the botanically untrained.

Learning. All animals with a synaptic type of nervous system possess the ability to modify their behavior and thereby adjust themselves to the environment. This is called learning. Man, because he has a highly developed nervous system, is very plastic and learns to make many complicated adjustments. From birth on he is continually adding new habits and skills to his repertoire of behavior.

The simplest form of learning is association formation and may be illustrated by the learning of color names by the child. While the child is looking at a blue object, his mother says "blue." Through repetition, the child learns to connect the verbal response "blue" to a particular color. In addition to repetition, it is necessary to have the two experiences which are to be associated occur close together in time. This is called the principle of contiguity. A third law of association forming is reenforcement, which means that when the correct response is made it is rewarded. Repetition, contiguity, and reenforcement are the primary laws of association.

In the learning of a skill, like knitting or playing the piano, or learning something "by heart" (rote learning) the same principles apply. Practice is essential and the more complex the skill or the longer the selection to be memorized, the more practice is necessary. The rate at which one learns is portrayed by a learning curve. The learning curve shows graphically the improvement of the learner with practice. Improvement is usually most rapid during the early stages of practice and slows down with continued repetition. This is the law of diminishing returns, which states that as the person expends more energy in acquiring a skill the return on his investment of energy decreases.

The smooth running off of a perfected skill is due to the formation of strong connections between the component parts of the skill. In playing a piano selection, for example, each reaction becomes an association with the next reaction by the principle of contiguity so that the muscles of the hand literally guide the pianist through the proper series of movements. Finally, improvement manifests itself more rapidly if the learner is interested in what he is learning and feels rewarded by the doing of it correctly.

A third type of learning situation is problem-solving. Unlike the formation of a simple association or the acquisition of skill and rote memorizing, no model is provided the person in the problem-solving situation. He must find his own solution by the use of trial-and-error and insight. The usual steps in problem-solving are (1) inspection of the conditions of the problem, (2) formation of an hypothesis, (3) trying-out of the hypothesis, (4) discarding it if it does not prove correct, (5) adoption and trial of other hunches until the person gives up or finds the correct answer.

The rate at which one learns is influenced by numerous conditions. If the person has an active interest in what he is learning and feels that it will be of benefit to him, he learns more quickly. Several short practice periods are more efficient than cramming during one long period. Learning a skill as a unit is usually better than to break it down and learn it part by part. Young people learn more rapidly than old people and the more intelligent learn complex tasks faster than the less intelligent. If a person has already learned something which will help him in learning something new, improvement in the new task will proceed more quickly. This is called transfer of training. On the other hand a previously learned skill may interfere with and thereby slow down new learning. This is called habit interference.

How can established habits be broken? The best method is to discover why the habit is satisfying and then learn to gain satisfaction by other means. Drinking alcoholic beverages to excess is rewarding because through intoxication the person forgets his troubles and his feelings of inadequacy and inferiority. By removing the causes of anxiety and inferiority feelings, the need to become intoxicated will disappear. Any habit will be given up as soon as one obtains more satisfaction through some substitute activity.

Remembering. Learning would be fruitless if the individual failed to retain what he had learned. Fortunately retentivity, like modifiability, is a property of the nervous system. Any experience leaves a memory trace in the nervous system, and when this trace is reactivated, remembering occurs. In order for a past experience to be recalled, the trace in the nervous system which represents this experience must be of a certain strength. This strength is called the *threshold of recall*. If the trace is weaker than the threshold value, no recall will occur.

Traces become stronger through practice and weaker through disuse and interference by new learning. As they weaken, forgetting occurs. The rate of forgetting is ordinarily more rapid during the initial period of disuse and slows up as time passes. A good memory depends upon the establishing of strong traces through continual practice and review. This is called the principle of *overlearning*.

Amnesia is an abnormal type of forgetting. The victim of amnesia forgets who he is, where he lives, what he does. He fails to recognize friends and relatives. He loses his personal identity. This condition is produced by physical damage to the brain or by strong emotional shock.

Forgetting may be purposive, that is, the person represses a memory which evokes anxiety. Failure to remember unpleasant appointments, the names of distasteful people, and childhood experiences which were humiliating are examples of purposive forgetting.

Thinking. Several types of thinking may be differentiated. There is the very directed and purposive type which is called *reasoning*. Reasoning occurs when the person is faced by a problem for which he wants to find a solution. The characteristics of reasoning have been discussed under problem-solving learning above.

Closely akin to reasoning is the creative thinking of the inventor, the artist, and the writer. The creative thinker organizes familiar material in such a way as to produce a novel synthesis. For this, he needs imaginative ability. Imagining is a mental process in which the thinking of the person is not dependent primarily upon memory or perception.

A third type has been called the stream of consciousness. There is a flow of ideas, relatively undirected and apparently aimless, although it is well known that there are always meaningful connections between any succession of thought elements. Closely related to this type is day-dreaming, which, like its counterpart during sleep, night-dreaming, is often motivated by a desire to gratify some wish. That kind of thinking in which the individual allows his hopes and desires to dominate his critical judgment is called wishful or *autistic* thinking.

Thinking may make use of images (mental pictures), sub-vocalization (talking to one's self), or abstract concepts.

Feeling. Feeling constitutes the emotional aspect of mental life. The two basic feelings are pleasantness and unpleasantness. In general, man seeks the pleasant and avoids the unpleasant. Even a young baby soon learns to repeat that which is pleasurable and to reject that which is painful. A pleasant feeling is produced by the gratification of a need such as eating when hungry or finding a friend when lonely. An unpleasant feeling is evoked by anything which interferes with the satisfaction of a desire.

Strong feelings, for example, anger, fear, and joy, are called emotions. In emotion, the whole body becomes agitated. The heart beats more rapidly, breathing is deeper and faster, the muscles tense. These and other physiological changes prepare the person to react strenuously in an emergency situation.

Two types of feelings deserve special mention because of their influence on one's mental health. These are anxiety and guilt feelings. Anxiety is characterized by a feeling of mental tension and by apprehension regarding some future threat to one's security and happiness and by fear of something in one's past being discovered. One cause of anxiety is a feeling of guilt. Guilt arises when a person does something or thinks of doing something which his conscience tells him is wrong. Anxiety is not only unpleasant but, because it is accompanied by physiological disturbances, is often a contributing factor to physical disorders and illness.

THE INDIVIDUAL

Modern psychology tries to understand the individual in order that he may be helped and guided to make the most satisfying adjustment. Each individual is unique. He differs from every other human being. The first task of psychology is to describe individuality, the second is to explain it, and the third is to apply this knowledge.

Describing Individuality. The individual has many psychological facets, some of the more important of which are General Intelligence, Special Aptitudes, Personality Traits, Motives, and Attitudes.

Precise and objective description calls for dependable and accurate measurement. One serviceable yardstick is the psychological test.

Tests of Intelligence. The first test of general intelligence was devised in 1905 by the French psychologist, Alfred Binet, for use primarily with children of school age. Lewis Terman, professor of psychology at Stanford university, adapted the Binet test for American school children (1916) and revised it again in 1937. This is the famous Stanford-Binet test. It consists of a series of questions graded by age and reveals the mental age (MA) of the child. If a child can answer all of the questions that the average eight year old can, he is said to have an MA of eight. By dividing his MA by his chronological age (CA), and multiplying the quotient by 100, the well-known intelligence quotient (IQ) is obtained. Thus if a child has an MA of 8 and a CA of 7, his IQ is computed by the following formula:

$$IQ = \frac{MA}{CA} \times 100; \; IQ = \frac{8}{7} \times 100 = 114$$

If the IQ is above 100, the child is advanced for his age; if it is below 100, he is retarded for his age. The following classes of intelligence and the percentage of people in each of the classes is given in the following table.

IQ	*Classification*	*% in Population*
140 and above	very superior	1.5
120–139	superior	11.0
110–119	bright	18.0
90–109	average	48.0
80– 89	backward	14.0
70– 79	very dull	5.0
0– 69	feeble-minded	2.5

Three classes of feeble-minded are recognized,—idiots, imbeciles, and morons. Idiots are the lowest in intellect, having IQ's under 25. They must be cared for in an institution. Imbeciles have IQ's between 25 and 50. They can perform only the simplest routine tasks under supervision. Morons, the highest grade, have IQ's between 50 and 70. They can become useful, self-supporting citizens in a favorable environment.

Two other well-known tests of general intelligence are *Army Alpha* of World War I and the *General Classification Test* of World War II. These tests were used for assigning men to duties which they could be capable of discharging with competence. Intelligence tests have proved to be very useful in educational and vocational guidance.

Tests of Special Aptitudes. An aptitude test yields a measure of a person's potential ability to perform successfully in a given line of work. For example, a clerical aptitude test measures an individual's probable success in a clerical position. There are aptitude tests for motor dexterity, mechanical proficiency, music, art, and medicine.

Personality Traits. Personality is a complex affair. It has been well defined as "The dynamic organization within the individual of those psychophysical systems that determine his unique adjustments to his environment." (G. W. Allport) The fundamental components of the personality are traits, whenever we use such words as assertive, austere, persistent, talkative, introverted, touchy, we are characterizing personality traits. There are scores of traits, few of which as yet have been accurately depicted by scientific measurements. There are tests of introversion-extroversion, ascendance-submission, emotional stability. One promising way of appraising personality is the projective method as exemplified by the Rorschach Ink Blot test. Devised by a Swiss psychiatrist, H. Rorschach, the test material consists of ten symmetrical ink blots, which are shown to a person one at a time. The person is asked to say what he sees in the blot. His responses represent projections of his own unique personality.

Motives. The driving forces of the personality are called motives. There are two general classes of motives, the organic ones which arise from the biological make-up of man and the psychological ones which originate primarily through learning. Examples of the organic motives are hunger, thirst, and sex. The sexual motive which plays such an important rôle in social relations is controlled originally by the secretion of hormones by the gonads. There are countless psychological motives and probably no two individuals possess the same motivational pattern. Important psychological motives are to obtain recognition, to love and be loved, to be with others, to be independent, to be powerful, and to conform. When a highly motivated person cannot attain the desired goal by normal means, he will often resort to bizarre forms of conduct. The accurate measurement of an individual's motives is one of the knottiest problems in contemporary psychology.

Attitudes. An attitude is the way a person feels about himself, another person, or something in his environment. He usually expresses this feeling by acceptance, rejection, or indifference. Public opinion polling illustrates one method by which attitudes may be gauged. Questions regarding some issue are framed in such a way that the person polled may register his opinion regarding the issue. The Gallup and Fortune polls use this technique. By asking a representative cross-section of the nation's population, the percentage of people favoring or opposing a candidate for public office or a controversial topic can be accurately determined.

Attitudes toward one's self are termed ego-feelings. These self-attitudes are often inaccurate since few people possess the ability to evaluate themselves objectively. Inferiority feelings are especially widespread and produce much unhappiness, even though there may be no valid reasons for the existence of such feelings.

The Causes of Individuality. The two principal causes of individuality are heredity and environment. The heredity of the individual consists of the genes, which are microscopic elements grouped together like a chain of beads. A chain of genes is called a chromosome, and there are twenty-four pairs of chromosomes in every cell of the human body. The child obtains his heredity, that is, his genes, from his parents. When the sperm (the father's germ cell) fertilizes the egg (the mother's germ cell) and a new individual is thereby conceived, the sperm contributes half of his heredity or twenty-four chromosomes and the egg likewise contributes half or twenty-four chromosomes. The twenty-four from the father and the twenty-four from the mother make the twenty-four pairs of their offspring. No two individuals have exactly the same heredity with the exception of identical multiple births, for example, identical twins. Identical twins are produced by the splitting of the fertilized egg so that each half makes an individual instead of combining to make a single individual. Identical twins are remarkably similar in looks and behavior. Another type of twin is the fraternal which is produced by the simultaneous fertilization of two eggs by two sperms. They are no more alike in heredity than are children of the same family born at different times. It has been demonstrated by numerous experiments that the genes are partly responsible for differences in intelligence, special aptitudes, personality traits, and motives.

Environment. The environment of the individual consists of all of those conditions and experiences which influence and modify him from conception to death. Environment causes differences between individuals because no two persons ever encounter exactly the same situations. The experiences of infancy and childhood are of great importance in determining the kind of person one will become. That is why family environment, especially that provided by the mother, is so formative. The child who receives care, love, and security will turn out quite differently from one who is mistreated and rejected. Other important environmental influences are to be found in the character of the neighborhood, the kind of educational, social, recreational, and religious facilities available, and the vocational opportunities. Next to the family, the school plays the most important rôle in moulding the individual. Motion pictures, the radio, advertising, newspapers, and other reading material are influential in shaping the young person. Attitudes are susceptible to propaganda, an underworld form of education which makes use of lies, half-truths, glittering generalities, and appeals to prejudices.

The Relative Importance of Heredity and Environment. There are some people who believe that man can be improved by encouraging those with superior genes to reproduce, and discouraging those with inferior genes from reproducing. These are the *eugenicists*. They believe heredity to be more important. Others would improve man by improving his environment. They put their stake on better schools, better housing, better economic standards, a better environment in all ways. These are the *euthenicists*. Which is the more important, heredity as the eugenicists assert or environment as the euthenicists contend? The answer lies somewhere in between.

Without schooling, the intellect would not develop properly, but, lacking a certain level of intelligence, no amount of schooling will make up the deficit. A child who is shy by nature can be made bold through training, yet another child may be bold by nature and remain that way despite the environment. Nature and nurture work together. In this individual, nature may outweigh experience; in that one, nurture may take precedence over the genes. For one, characteristic heredity may be the major determinant; for another, environment may be the crucial factor. As more knowledge and skill is acquired regarding the ways in which human nature can be changed, the importance of heredity will diminish. For the time being it is safe to say that the uniqueness of the individual is the product of his heredity and his environment.

The Application of Knowledge Regarding the Individual. As scientific knowledge of the person accumulates, it is possible to make use of this information in practical ways. Several applications of psychology will be described.

Vocational Guidance. The choice of a vocation need no longer be left to chance. Modern guidance makes use of tests and other methods of appraising the individual for the purpose of helping the young man or woman select a career for which he is best fitted and in which he will find the greatest satisfaction. Hidden talents are discovered, which open up new opportunities to the young person. Every city of any size has a vocational guidance clinic where counsel may be obtained.

Employee Selection. Many companies employ psychologists to help them select new workers. Testing and interviewing are done in order that the right person will be secured for the available position. During both World War I and World War II, aptitude tests were given to the men and women of the armed services so that they might be placed in the type of work for which they had the proper qualifications.

Marriage Counseling. Many times married couples have personal problems which they cannot work out by themselves. By seeking the advice of a trained psychologist it is often possible for them to arrive at a satisfactory solution and thereby avoid the divorce courts.

School Psychology. The school psychologist performs a variety of services. He determines the level of intelligence of the pupil in order to find out what he is capable of learning. The dull child is placed in a special class so that he can be given the proper attention. He discovers weakness in reading, spelling, and arithmetic and remedies them through specialized treatment. He helps children who have emotional disturbances which are interfering with their learning. He finds out why children misbehave and attempts to remove the causes.

Psychology is both a science and a profession. As a science, it uses scientific methods to gain understanding of the individual and his activities. As a profession, it applies this understanding for the benefit of mankind.

Parapsychology. This is a branch of psychology which is concerned with clairvoyance, telepathy, and other "psychic" phenomena. Although many psychologists do not believe that one mind can communicate with another directly, a few believe in extra-sensory perception. Rhine of Duke university is perhaps the leading exponent of parapsychology and claims to have experimental proof for telepathy and clairvoyance. This is still a field in which there is considerable controversy.

Character Analysis. Since ancient times, men have been interested in finding a reliable method for "sizing up" character. Many of these methods make use of physical characteristics. In the 19th century, *phrenology* was popular and was even called a science. By examining the contour of the head, the phrenologist read the character of a person. This method was based upon the erroneous assumption that character traits were determined by different parts of the brain. Thus, for example, if a person was exceptionally honest that part of his brain which was said to control honesty would be large and would cause his skull to bulge. Other physical characteristics which have been used in character analysis are complexion, shape of the face, lines in the palm of the hand (palmistry), and length of the fingers. There is no good evidence that these characteristics are related to character. On the other hand, there is evidence that body shape and personality are related. The three principal body types, thin, rotund, and athletic, seem to be associated with different types of temperament. W. H. Sheldon has devised a system for indexing body types which is called *somatotyping*.

Graphology is the reading of character from handwriting. Extravagant claims for the value of graphology have not been supported by the results of scientific experiments.

Hypnotism. Hypnotism was discovered by Mesmer in the 18th century and is often referred to as "mesmerism." Mesmer erroneously thought that the hypnotic trance was due to the flow of animal magnetism from the body of the hypnotist to that of the patient. Others have held that the trance is similar to sleep. The most recent work on hypnotism indicates that it is a state of increased suggestibility. People who are very suggestible make the best subjects for hypnotism. It is not true that a person who is hypnotized can be forced to commit crimes and other deeds against his will. Hypnotism is used in treating people with mental disorders.

PSYCHIATRY

PSYCHIATRY is that branch of medicine which deals with the cause, the nature, the treatment, and the prevention of mental illnesses and personality disturbances. It is concerned, therefore, in the broadest sense with human behavior and with those factors which motivate it whether they be instinctive, physical, hereditary, emotional, or sociological. Because the field is so extensive many separate specialties have been developed such as child psychiatry, psychoanalysis, industrial psychiatry, criminal psychiatry, mental hygiene, etc. Psychiatry has made valuable contributions to the fields of medicine, education, religion, law, sociology, anthropology, art, and literature, because of its advances in understanding the human mind.

Incidence of Mental Disease. The problem of mental illness represents not only a tremendous medical problem, but a social one as well. There are more hospital beds in the United States for the mentally ill than for all other types of illnesses combined. It has been estimated that one out of every twenty babies who reach maturity will require treatment in a mental hospital sometime during his life and it has also been estimated that approximately 10,000,000 people of the present population are either insane, neurotic, or mentally deficient. This figure does not include the epileptics, the chronic alcoholics, or certain other personality disorders.

History. Mental disease is as old as the recorded history of mankind. An interesting account of Nebuchadnezzar's emotional upset is given in the Old Testament. Epilepsy was known among the ancients as the "sacred disease," and its nature and cause was held to be divine. Insanity, according to some ancient records, was attributed to evil spirits which possessed the body, and in Medieval Europe treatment of these illnesses was left to the priests. It is little wonder that these superstitious beliefs opened the way for unbelievably inhumane treatment of the insane. Not until 1792 did Pinel in France and Tuke in England unlock the chains which literally restrained the mentally ill, and rightly demanded that they be treated as sick patients and be accorded the same consideration given to any patient. It was not until the middle of the 19th century that an extraordinary personality by the name of Dorothea Dix travelled the length and breadth of this country and England inciting public opinion to demand construction of good mental hospitals for the more sympathetic treatment of the mentally ill. From such recent humble beginnings modern psychiatric hospitals and clinics have developed where emphasis is now on the curative side of treatment and not simply on custodial care. Psychiatric departments are now being integrated with general hospitals, prevention is being stressed, and much attention is given to the training of physicians, nurses, and social workers in this field.

Research in psychiatry has followed along two paths which unfortunately have been most divergent on occasions, the organic and the psychological. During the latter part of the 19th century when great strides were being made in the field of organic medicine, many psychiatric investigators followed in the wake of these discoveries and sought for the cause of mental disease in the brain and other organs of the body. Their findings shed light on certain types of insanity such as general paresis (syphilis of the brain) and senile dementia, but their investigations concerning other illnesses such as schizophrenia, manic-depressive psychosis, and the psychoneuroses were oftentimes fruitless. It remained for another group of investigators, Charcot, Freud, Jung, Adler, Bleuler, Meyer, and others to inquire into the mysteries of the mind and to find hidden there the cause of much human suffering. These workers showed that many personality disorders cannot be explained on the basis of organic disease, and they further demonstrated that deep-seated psychological conflict can arise in the earliest years of childhood, and that it is frequently these hidden emotional conflicts that are the cause of certain types of psychological disorders.

Freud (1856–1939) was without doubt a genius in the field of psychiatry and despite the fact that his teachings have caused widespread controversies, he contributed greatly to our understanding of human behavior and personality disorders. It is impossible in this limited space to describe psychoanalysis, which is the school of thought Freud developed, for it is a psychological system which is not only a theory of behavior, but it is a method of research with special techniques and a method of treatment of emotional difficulties. Although the term psychoanalysis is used freely by many people, it is more properly applied to the system of psychology which Freud propounded.

Within comparatively recent times, psychiatry has brought together the contributions of these various schools of thought and now recognizes that it is impossible to separate man into organic or psychological parts if his personality is to be adequately understood. He acts as a unit and his behavior is the result of the intimate interplay and interdependence of physical and psychological factors which do not function in an isolated manner but in relationship to the total personality. Every individual from his own experience knows that severe emotional reactions can actually cause one to feel physically ill; and that a physical illness such as a common cold can cause unpleasant reverberations in his mental life.

CAUSES OF MENTAL DISEASE

In uninformed circles there is still the belief that mental diseases are mysterious, and that the causes are unknown. Although the causes of certain types of mental disease still remain as unsolved problems, the etiological factors responsible for others are well known. Frequently the causes are those encountered elsewhere in the field of medicine and surgery such as arteriosclerosis, syphilis, tumors, drugs, and infectious agents. From this it cannot be assumed that all mental illness is caused by disease of the brain, because probably more mental suffering arises from the emotional conflicts within the individual. In the vast group of psychoneurotic patients no organic basis for their complaints can be demonstrated; but in their emotional lives the psychiatrist can often find the cause of their psychological difficulties. This maladjustment which may have various manifestations represents the end result of many factors which have made it impossible for the individual to work out a satisfactory adjustment to a given life situation. This type of illness is usually one which is rooted in the early life of the patient although it may at times manifest itself later in life.

For the purpose of study it is helpful to consider the various factors which frequently contribute to the production of mental disorders, realizing that no one single factor can, as a rule, explain the whole picture.

Heredity. In the past this was greatly overemphasized as the cause of mental disease. Although there are a few types of mental disease, for example, Huntington's Chorea, which are hereditary, there is no scientific evidence to show that heredity is the primary cause of mental illness.

Age. It is well known that certain illnesses arise in certain periods of life, and for this reason the chronological age of the individual has something to do with his type of illness. For example, involutional melancholia is an illness which is encountered during the climacteric.

Environment. If, as is proper, all of the individual's personal relationships, his educational, social, cultural, and economic background are included under this heading, then environment becomes an extremely important factor in mental disturbances. Certainly environment is of the utmost importance in the development of the personality.

Organic Factors. Under this heading can be placed infections of various types, endoctrine imbalances, vitamin deficiencies, tumor of the brain, drugs, trauma, etc. These factors act by interfering with the normal function of the central nervous system.

Psychological Factors. This heading covers an extremely wide field, because these factors may be present from early childhood to the actual precipitation of the mental illness. As a result of the individual's relationship with his parents, brothers, and sisters, teachers, and friends, the pattern for his personality is quite well developed during the first six years of life. If the individual has not received adequate love and affection, and he has been rejected by his parents, or if on the other hand, he has been spoiled and over-protected so that he has not been able to develop a feeling of security and self-confidence, the ground work has been prepared for possible future unhappiness. During the formative years some individuals also have very painful psychological experiences which may cause a distortion of the personality. Although extremely trying situations in life which are fraught with much worry and anxiety can bring about emotional disorders, it is usually the psychological difficulties of early life which are most important in the production of certain types of emotional illnesses.

CLASSIFICATION OF MENTAL DISEASE

To the untrained it appears that one is sane or not sane, and that all mental disease is of the same type. There are, however, different types of mental illness just as there are various types of physical illness. For the sake of simplicity and clarity, however, Adolf Meyer pointed out that all mental disorders may be considered as a type of reaction on the part of the individual; hence in referring to a mental illness the term reaction-type may be used. This is not the official classification, but it is a very helpful one.

Organic Reaction Types. Under this heading are grouped those mental diseases which are brought about by either localized or diffuse destruction of the brain. The specific causes for such damage are numerous and well-known, such as syphilis, arteriosclerosis, brain tumors, trauma, senile changes in the brain and residuals of encephalitis.

Patients with illnesses of this sort have as a rule histories which reveal insidious changes in the personality. These are usually manifested by carelessness in personal appearance, irritability, forgetfulness, and errors in judgment. As the disease progresses there is gradual deterioration with periods of uncontrollable crying, and unpredictable outbursts of temper. The behavior is foreign to what it had been; sexual indiscretion and disasterous decisions concerning business matters reveal glaring defects in judgment. The intellect becomes dulled, the memory becomes more impaired, orientation becomes poor, and the ability to grasp a situation deteriorates. Hallucinations and delusions may appear. Into this group fall such diseases as general paresis, senile psychosis which is brought about by degenerative changes in the brain with advancing years; psychosis with cerebral arteriosclerosis (hardening of the arteries); traumatic psychosis; psychosis with brain tumor; psychosis with encephalitis, etc.

Delirious Reaction Types. This type of reaction is caused by a toxic agent which acts upon the brain. The toxic substance may be exogenous such as alcohol, barbiturates, morphine, bromides, lead, carbon-monoxide, etc. On the other hand, it may be endogenous and arise in the body as a result of a disease process. Fever, metabolic disturbances, such as those associated with uremia and thyroid disease, and chronic physical illness accompanied by much wasting and malnutrition are examples of endogenous factors.

A patient with a delirious type of reaction shows some degree of restlessness and, at times, he may become acutely disturbed, screaming and shouting. The speech is usually incoherent, and the emotion is as a rule that of fear. Visual and auditory hallucinations are commonly accompanied by fragmenttary delusions. The patient is frequently confused and shows disturbance of orientation for time, place, or person. The memory is impaired, and attention poorly sustained. The illness appears rather suddenly, and with adequate medical and psychiatric treatment, usually disappears in a comparatively short period.

Under this heading are grouped the various types of psychoses due to alcohol such as delirium tremens and Korsakov's psychosis, psychosis due to barbiturate intoxication, psychosis due to uremia, psychosis due to thyrotoxicosis.

Affective Reaction Types. Because the illnesses in this group of disorders are accompanied by such a profound disturbance in the emotional life of the patients, they are referred to as affective disorders. Under this heading fall the manic-depressive psychoses, and the involutional psychoses. There are several types of manic-depressive psychoses, but as the name implies there are two common types, the manic and the depressed.

In the manic phase of the illness the patient is very overactive, frequently being too disturbed to eat or sleep. He talks incessantly and shows a characteristic flight of ideas. The mood is mercurial, euphoria and boastfulness giving way to transient outbursts of anger and at times tears. Grandiose ideas are common, and not infrequently the patient describes nebulous schemes for making fabulous sums of money, and for altering the entire social and political structure of the country over night. The plans are often of a wish fulfilling nature. Fundamentally there is no impairment of orientation or memory although the patient may be too disturbed to permit careful examination of his memory. Occasionally there are hallucinations.

During the depressed phase of the illness the patient shows both psychomotor and mental retardation. Physically the patient has many complaints and lacks pep. His appetite is poor, and his sleep disturbed. Because his thoughts come slowly, it is difficult to formulate the answer to simple questions. His mood is one of severe depression with feelings of utter hopelessness. Death wishes and suicidal ideas are common and not infrequently these patients attempt suicide. Delusions of sin and unworthiness are prominent and the overwhelming belief that God is punishing the individual makes his existence a "living hell" in his own mind.

The exact cause of manic-depressive psychosis is unknown; but broadly stated the illness is the result of powerful emotional conflicts flourishing in the soil of a constitutional predisposition. It is this illness which is frequently seen in the extroverted personality, but this is not always the case.

Involutional melancholia is a mental illness occurring near or during "the change of life." Endocrinological changes together with definite psychological problems underlie this condition. It is characterized by marked restlessness, agitation, and anxiety. Feelings of unreality and hypochondriacal complaints round out the mental trend in which there are delusions of sin, poverty, and punishment. The memory and the other intellectual functions are intact.

Paranoia and Paranoid Reaction Types. Paranoia is a rare illness and seldom seen by psychiatrists. This condition is manifested by a slowly developing, highly organized system of delusions which may be grandiose or persecutory with little obvious disorganization of the personality. The intellectual capacity of these individuals is often above the average and well-preserved. Hallucinations do not occur and, aside from the false beliefs, the patient may appear on the surface to be "normal." The illness develops in sensitive individuals who are of a suspicious nature and who have found it very difficult to accept other points of view throughout life. Their sexual and social adjustments have been most inadequate, and having been thus frustrated they find solace in their false beliefs through projection and overcompensation.

The paranoid conditions which are included under this heading are much more common and show less systematization of the delusional structure than that seen in true paranoia. There is, however, greater disorganization of the personality. This distortion of the personality is not as marked as it is in schizophrenia.

Schizophrenic Reaction Types. Dementia Praecox was the term originally applied to the mental illness which is classified here. The term schizophrenia is a better term and is derived from the Greek meaning "split mind" or "split personality." This is one of the most serious of all human illnesses, because it often results in a veritable mental death but a living body. Unless these patients are treated early and properly, they are doomed to a lifetime of insanity. Schizophrenic patients make up about 20 per cent of all admissions to mental hospitals.

In this illness the ideas, emotions, and actions are not in harmony with each other as in a normal person. Being split off, one from the other, the resulting clinical picture is a most incongruous one, and for that reason, it is difficult for the untrained person to understand it. Although the symptoms vary greatly, these patients usually present a bizarre type of behavior ranging from silliness and impulsiveness to outbursts of wild excitement. The talk may be superficially normal, or rambling and incoherent. The patients are characteristically evasive and at times are mute. The emotions run the gamut from utter apathy to marked suspiciousness and rage. Delusions of persecution, and beliefs that they are being talked about, spied upon, and controlled by sinister outside forces are common. Auditory and visual hallucinations are often present. As a rule the memory and ability to calculate are unimpaired during the early part of the illness.

Although no sharp line of demarcation can be drawn between them, there are four main types of schizophrenia: simple, hebephrenia, catatonic, and paranoid types.

The exact cause represents a scientific challenge; but many contributing factors are known. Psychological difficulties from early childhood resulting in disturbances in interpersonal relationships are known to be important. The illness represents a complete failure on the part of the individual to work out any sort of satisfactory adjustment to life. After a series of repeated unrealistic and unsuccessful attempts to cope with the problems of life, the patient loses touch with reality and builds for himself a world of phantasy into which he retreats.

Psychoneurotic Reaction Types. In terms of human unhappiness and inefficiency, this is by all odds the most important type of emotional disorder; yet the psychoneurotic individual is *not* psychotic. A vast horde of poorly adjusted individuals who are buffeted about by inner conflicts, which they do not understand nor are they able to control, come under this classification. Because of the multiplicity of physical symptoms of which they often complain, they consult physicians and frequent hospital clinics, and unfortunately are often told "nothing is wrong." There is something wrong in the emotional life of these patients, and no lack of vitamins, malfunction of the endocrine glands of the body, nor any other organic factor can explain the condition. The cause is to be found in the psychological conflicts which often result when the instinctive strivings and inner needs of the personality cannot be expressed openly because they are incompatible with the individual's own ideals and the standards of the group. The conflict which underlies all psychoneurotic reactions represents a clash between opposing forces of the personality.

The manifestation of this mental struggle may be physical symptoms such as headaches, choking sensations, palpitation, pain over the heart, weakness, loss of appetite, abdominal discomfort, sleeplessness, and numerous other ones. Or the difficulty may be expressed by marked anxiety, recurring thoughts (obsessions), fears (phobias), or acts (compulsion), which the patient often times says are "silly" but which he is unable to change despite repeated efforts to do so. These symptoms are significant, and they play a useful rôle in terms of the hidden emotional conflict. The condition results in an unharmonious functioning of the personality, and although it does hinder the individual in working out a good adjustment to life, a compromise is reached which enables him to carry on in a limited capacity. The behavior of these individuals as a rule is considered "normal" and much of the very important work of the world is done every day by psychoneurotic people.

There are many types of psychoneurotic reaction. The common ones are anxiety neurosis, hysteria, neurasthenia, obsessive-compulsive states, and hypochrondriasis.

MENTAL MECHANISMS

Before psychiatry had given us a dynamic concept of human behavior in terms of unconscious drives, it was assumed that man was aware or conscious of all his mental processes, that he was "master of his fate" and possessed complete freedom of his will. Although many mental functions go on at a conscious level and with a complete sense of awareness, it is now recognized that many psychological processes go on without the individual even being vaguely aware of them. It has been shown that the unconscious part of the mental life of the individual is much more important than the conscious so far as influencing human behavior is concerned. There is no general agreement as to the structure, the contents, and the operation of the unconscious; but it was first pointed out by Freud that the dynamic core of the unconscious is the instinctive drives. "It is the reservoir of the psychic energy." Also in this unaware, unacknowledged part of the mind are many of the painful experiences of life which one does not want to remember. Exerting a tremendous influence in the unconscious are many of the experiences of childhood which cannot be recalled at will. The unconscious, therefore, molds our thinking and feeling, controls to a large extent our behavior and shapes our goals in life without our being aware of it.

Because many of our basic drives cannot be openly expressed, the personality seeks ways and means of circumventing this difficulty, but if a satisfactory compromise cannot be worked out a mental conflict arises. No one is free from emotional conflict of some sort, for it is too much to expect that the inner needs and basic urges of the personality would always be acceptable to the individual and meet with the approval of society.

Man has developed, however, psychological means by which he attempts to meet these problems of his mental life just as he has evolved many anatomical and physiological mechanisms for maintaining a harmonious relationship between the various parts and functions of his body. By these psychological and physical mechanisms man has greatly increased his capacity for adjusting to his environment. The mind like the body attempts to ward off those things which threaten it and are painful. Just as many of these physiological processes go on without the individual being aware of it, so do many of the mental processes take place. These processes are referred to as mental mechanisms. Some of the more common ones are described below.

Repression. This is an unconscious process by which dangerous thoughts and feelings that are unacceptable to the individual are prevented from reaching consciousness. It is, in a sense, forgetting, because the individual does not want to remember. The person who repeatedly forgets his dental appointments is repressing the thought in an effort to avoid a painful experience. This is to be distinguished from suppression in which ideas and memories are deliberately banished from consciousness.

Rationalization. By this mechanism the individual seeks to justify his behavior on the grounds of "reason" when in reality his actions spring from unconscious motives which he cannot consciously accept. The person attempts to "look good" in his own eyes by the use of "alibis." It is as though he seeks self-protection through self-deception.

Reaction-formation. This is a method whereby conscious desires, ideas, and behavior are made just the opposite to repressed unconscious motives. For example, the mother who rejects her child may profess great love and overprotect it.

Projection. Through this mechanism the individual attempts to avoid criticism of himself by blaming other people or objects for his own faults. "The poor workman always blames his tools," and thus seeks to maintain his own self-respect.

Identification. By identification one unconsciously takes unto himself those qualities and ideals which he admires in other individuals and institutions. Thus he feels that he actually possesses the very qualities he covets and hence makes up for his own weaknesses and inadequacies. This mechanism is seen in "hero worship," and in the individual who assumes a position of great importance after becoming associated with a militant, vociferous political group whose "ideals" are often but an attempt to rationalize its own socially unacceptable avarice.

Conversion. Psychological conflicts are at times changed into organic symptoms by this mechanism. The pain or impairment of function is symbolic of the emotional difficulty and affords the individual some satisfaction even though he may not be aware of it. The patient who suddenly loses his voice or develops a paralysis of an extremity without any organic disease reveals this mechanism.

Displacement. By transferring the emotional values from one object or experience which has been repressed to a substitute which is acceptable, the individual can keep that which is intolerable from consciousness. A student may displace unconscious hate of his father onto his instructor.

Dissociation. In some types of patients, when certain repressed elements are in marked conflict with the rest of the personality, they become split off. When they are thus freed, these dissociated elements act without regard to the rest of the personality, and hence seek the satisfaction which had been denied. This mechanism is seen at work in those individuals who suddenly leave home and "come to" several days later, hundreds of miles away, without any memory of how they got there or what they had been doing. These patients are spoken of as having "dual" or "multiple personalities."

Sublimation. This is a process through which the energies from instinctive drives are diverted from these primitive socially unobtainable goals into constructive activities and socially desirable fields such as art, religion, music, literature. The repressed energies are thus freed and allowed to flow into consciousness and into satisfying channels of behavior. This mechanism is seen in the childless woman who becomes vitally interested in the day nurseries in the slums of a great city.

TREATMENT OF MENTAL DISEASE

There have been numerous approaches to the treatment of mental illness. All of the early ones were directed toward some possible physical disorder of the body, and this is understandable because in early times little was known about the structure of the personality. Unfortunately there are still innumerable patients being treated for some questionable organic condition when in reality the illness stems from the emotional conflicts within his mental life.

Psychotherapy. This is a type of treatment in which an attempt is made to help the patient understand the meaning of his illness and, by emotional re-education to assist him in attaining a sufficient degree of emotional stability so that symptom formation is no longer necessary. In the broadest sense any measure which helps the patient achieve a better adjustment to his environment may be called psychotherapeutic in nature.

Psychoanalysis. This is the most intensive psychotherapeutic procedure and is based entirely on the Freudian school. As a rule from one to four years are required to complete the analysis. The patient sees the doctor for an hour, four to six times each week. While lying relaxed on a couch and with the analyst sitting out of sight of the patient, the patient expresses any thought or feeling which come to mind No restriction is placed on the patient concerning the topics or the persons discussed. In this way conflicts which are buried deep in the unconscious are brought to light, and the patient is able to gain greater understanding of himself and thus work out a better adjustment to life.

Insulin Shock Therapy. In 1933 Sakel working in Vienna first reported the use of insulin in the treatment of mental disease. Since then this has found widespread use principally in the treatment of schizophrenia. By gradually increasing the dose of insulin, a degree of hypoglycemia (low blood sugar) is reached where the patient goes into coma. The coma is terminated after twenty to thirty minutes by the administration of glucose. The treatment is given five or six days a week until twenty-five to fifty comas have been given depending upon the response of the patient.

Electro-Shock Therapy. This form of therapy was first reported by two Italians, Cerletti and Bini, in 1937, and since its introduction, it has very largely replaced metrazol, a drug which when injected into the vein causes a generalized convulsive seizure. The treatment consists of passing an electric current through the brain with a resultant convulsive seizure and coma. The treatment causes little or no discomfort to the patient and he has no memory of it. This treatment is particularly helpful in depressed states such as manic-depressive, depressed psychoses, and involutional melancholia.

Hypnosis. A trancelike state is brought about in the patient by the monotonous repetition of suggestions concerning sleep and relaxation. In this state the patient is very suggestible and responds to the commands of the hypnotist. Repressed material may be recalled which was instrumental in the production of symptoms, and disabling symptoms may be abolished by the suggestions of the therapist. This is not a very satisfactory type of treatment because as a rule the patient does not work through his emotional difficulties, and the symptoms return.

During the war, patients suffering from neuroses arising in combat were given a hypnotic drug such as pentothal or sodium amytal intravenously to alleviate acute anxiety and to permit them to bring to light their repressed memories and conflicts. The patients were then helped by emotional re-education and rehabilitation toward a better adjustment to their life situation. This therapy is called narcosynthesis.

BIOLOGY

Biology treats of living organisms. Broadly stated, it is the science of life. In its most inclusive sense it embraces every form, activity, and function of living beings. From this standpoint, all human knowledge, human history, and human progress, including anthropology, ethnology, psychology, and sociology, as well as all the facts of zoology, botany, and paleontology, may be regarded as part of biological science. As commonly understood, however, biology is the study of the *general principles* concerning the *origin, development, structure, function, reproduction,* and *distribution* of plant and animal life. Among the most important and widely accepted tenets of biology are the cell theory, the doctrine of evolution, and the principle of metabolism or chemical change accompanying all vital processes.

HISTORY OF BIOLOGY

Even the savage is gifted with some powers of observation. He can divide living matter into its two great divisions of plants and animals. He can further divide these into tree, shrub, herb, beast, bird, and fish. In so far as he is able to do this, to that extent he is a biologist. From this it is readily seen that developing powers of observation will produce two kinds of naturalists—those who observe plants, or botanists, and those who observe animals, or zoologists.

Ancient Period. Early in authentic Greek history Hippocrates (460–357 B. C.) began to study the human body and discarded the theory that disease was due to the wrath of the gods. About a century later Aristotle (384–322) began to classify animals. Soon afterward Theophrastus (372–287) described and classified more than 500 kinds of plants as trees, shrubs, and herbs. In the early years of the Christian era Pliny (23–79 A. D.), the Roman naturalist, wrote his voluminous natural history. About the same time Dioscorides, a Greek physician, collected a vast store of information on plants, embodying it in a famous *Materia Medica* which remained an authoritative work for 1500 years. Galen (130–201) described two sets of nerves and proved that the arteries contain blood.

Modern Period. During the middle ages science seems to have become lost in the vagaries of alchemy. But beginning with the 16th century the study of biological science began to subdivide into specialized branches. Vesalius (1514–1564) advanced the study of anatomy. Gesner (1516–1565) formed a botanical garden and a zoological cabinet. Cæsalpinus (1519–1603) originated the first system of classifying plants.

In the 17th century Fabricius (1537–1619) discovered the valves in the veins, and Harvey (1578–1657) discovered the mechanism of the circulation of the blood, opening a new branch of anatomy. Harvey also advanced the study of embryology by his famous assertion *Omne vivum ex ovo*, that is, all animals are produced from an ovum or egg. Rudbeck (1630–1702) discovered the lymphatics. Malpighi (1628–1694) applied the microscope to physiology and anatomy, discovering air cells in the lungs, and, with Grew, revealing the cellular nature of plants. Ray (1628–1705) and Willughby (1635–1672) classified the entire animal and vegetable kingdoms, and laid the foundation for the later work of Linnæus and Cuvier.

In the 18th century Boerhaave (1668–1738) began the science of organic chemistry. Haller (1708–1777), of Gottingen, investigated muscular irritability. John Hunter (1728–1793) advanced the study of comparative anatomy. Bonnet (1720–1793) contributed to plant physiology and originated the term "evolution." Buffon (1707–1788) wrote the first modern natural history and added the geographical distribution of animals to science. Linnæus (1707–1778) revolutionized the study of botany and zoology by inventing the binomial system of classification and by originating the exceedingly valuable divisions of genus, species, order, and class, which led to the present world-wide use of scientific names. Hutton (1726–1797) founded modern geology by teaching that present processes are sufficient to explain the formation of stratified rocks and the formation and preservation of fossils.

The 19th century began with the recognition of the work of Jussieu (1748–1836), who founded the natural system in botany. Cuvier (1769–1832) likewise established an exceedingly valuable natural system for the classification of animals. Bichat (1771–1802) studied the tissues or parts of organs, laying the foundation for the science of histology. Sprengel (1766–1833) studied the fertilization of plants by insects. Robert Brown (1773–1858) developed embryological botany. Lamarck (1744–1829), the true father of the modern doctrine of evolution, advanced the theory of the development of organs by environment, or by the results of use and disuse. Von Baer (1792–1876) placed the study of embryology on a scientific basis. Schleiden (1804–1881), working from the botanical side, and Schwann (1810–1882), working from the zoological side, resolved all living organisms into cells, and, in 1839, established the cell theory which is the foundation of modern biology.

Early in the second half of the 19th century, Charles Darwin (1809–1882) and A. R. Wallace (1823–1913) simultaneously developed the theory of organic evolution beyond all previous attempts by their hypothesis of natural selection, or the survival of the fittest. The controversy which this new doctrine aroused greatly stimulated biological investigation and research, leading to discoveries of immense practical and theoretical value, and finally placed biology in the front rank among modern sciences. The theory of evolution became firmly established in the scientific world largely through the teachings of Huxley, Hooker, Herbert Spencer, Fritz Müller and Asa Gray, supported by numerous other investigators. Following the lead of Darwin, Galton (1822–1911) developed a theory of eugenics. Weismann (1834–1914) showed that heredity has a physical basis and maintained the "all-sufficiency of natural selection."

About the beginning of the 20th century, De Vries advanced the theory of mutations and, in 1900, simultaneously with Correns and Tschermak, discovered and brought to light the long obscured but valuable researches of Gregor Mendel (1822–1884) on heredity. During the first two decades of the 20th century, extensive investigations were carried on in the field of genetics, centered chiefly around the Mendelian principles, and testing the validity of Mendel's laws of heredity, which, on the whole, have been confirmed. Among the leading investigators in this field were Bateson, Morgan, Whitman, Riddle, Castle, Tower, Jennings, and Davenport.

The practical results of biological research since the middle of the 19th century have been of incalculable value,—the advances in curative and preventive medicine alone being greater than during any preceding period. In agriculture, horticulture, stock breeding, animal industry, hygiene, and sanitation, the progress due to the discoveries of modern science has been revolutionary. In addition, the methods and principles of modern biological study have been extended into psychology, sociology, economics, and other important fields.

Organic Evolution. The doctrine of evolution undertakes to explain the origin and development of the various forms of plant and animal life upon the earth, both past and present. Comprehensively considered, it is a theory of descent, or progressive development, from earlier simple, generalized types of life to later complex, highly specialized forms. The theory attempts to account for the origin of the different species of plants and animals, including man, by the operation of natural laws.

This doctrine, which has great philosophical as well as scientific significance, has its foundation in certain unities in nature which are universally existent and demonstrable. Chief among these are:

1. The unity of action of the processes of nature.

2. The unity of structure in plants and in animals,—all being composed of cells.

3. The unity in the mode of reproduction in plants and animals,—all arising from germs, seeds, or eggs.

4. The universal presence of protoplasm as the material basis of life.

5. The contractility of protoplasm as the source of all movements of plants and animals.

In its finished and definite form, the doctrine of evolution is a modern product, and its history shows that the idea itself is the result of a long process of evolution. Empedocles (493–435 B. C.) has been styled "the father of the evolution idea." This Greek philosopher believed in spontaneous generation as the explanation of the origin of life, and held that the different plant and animal forms were not produced simultaneously. Aristotle, the greatest natural philosopher of the ancients, is regarded as the originator of the theory of descent. He believed in a complete gradation in nature and held that man is the culminating point in a long and continuous ascent from the simplest or lowest animals.

During the middle ages and until the 19th century, the doctrine of special creation almost universally prevailed. A few, however, questioned it. In the 4th century, Saint Augustine (354–430 A. D.) spoke of the creation of things by a series of causal factors, and, 900 years later, Thomas Aquinas (1227–1274) supported this teaching. The German philosopher Leibnitz (1646–1716) declared his belief in a universal connection between species, which, he maintained, could be changed by a change in environment. The French naturalist Buffon asserted his belief in the mutability of species. Erasmus Darwin (1731–1802), grandfather of Charles Darwin, more or less clearly defined some of the causes of variation in plants and animals.

The French zoologist Lamarck was the true founder of modern evolution. He taught that all organisms develop from germs; that development is always from the simple to the complex; and that the effects of use and disuse may be inherited. His views were almost totally disregarded until Darwin and Wallace formulated upon a different basis the theory of descent which has since revolutionized scientific teaching. The chief tenet of this new theory was natural selection, later defined by Herbert Spencer as "the survival of the fittest."

Darwin did not claim that natural selection was the only factor in evolution, but emphasized, by a monumental array of scientific facts, that it is an important one. Stimulated by the masterly example of Darwin, later investigators have contributed a vast mass of confirmatory evidence. This has established practically universal acceptance by the scientific world of the general theory of evolution as a cosmic process.

Scientists, however, are not agreed as to the relative importance of the various recognized factors in evolution. For example, the principle of natural selection itself is being subjected to rigorous review. In fact, there is an increasing tendency among zoologists to recognize in the Darwinian theory of selection many difficulties not formerly perceived. This has led to a search for supplementary or possibly replacing theories.

According to Davenport, the most advanced theory used in explaining evolution is essentially anti-Lamarckian and anti-Darwinian, and may be described as orthogenetic and vitalistic. It reverts to the idea of evolution from *within*, by virtue of a perfecting or progressive tendency. This conception, which goes back to Aristotle, includes among its modern advocates such eminent scientists as Nägeli and Huxley and also the philosopher Bergson.

Mendel's Law. A principle governing the inheritance of many characters in animals and plants, discovered through experiments on garden peas by Gregor J. Mendel (1822–1884), an Augustinian abbot, of Brunn, Austria. These researches were made between 1851 and 1868, but the results remained unknown to the scientific world until they were brought to light about 1900 by De Vries and others.

Mendel showed that height, color, and other characters depend upon the presence of determining factors which act as units in heredity. For example, there are tall and dwarf peas which breed true from generation to generation. Such plants, therefore, have a pair of marked and easily recognizable opposite "unit" characters, *tallness* and *shortness*. In Mendel's experiments the tall and the short forms were crossed with one another, and their ripened seeds collected and sown. The new plants resulting from this crossing were found to belong *entirely* to the *tall* variety, which had apparently extinguished the short.

However, when the flowers of this generation were self-fertilized and their seeds sown, the resultant plants were a mixture of tall and short plants. Furthermore, these mixed tall and short plants were found to occur in *definite numerical proportions*. On the average, *three* of the tall forms occurred to every *one* of the short forms. From this it was clear that the quality of shortness or dwarfishness was not extinguished in the second generation, but was merely temporarily obscured, though present potentially.

To the character which alone appears in the first cross was given the name *dominant*. In this particular case tallness is dominant. To the obscured character which remained hidden in the first cross, the name *recessive* was given. In this instance shortness or dwarfishness is recessive. Mendel further found that in case the talls and the shorts of the *third* generation are allowed to be self-fertilized, all of the recessives, or shorts, breed true, and will continue so to breed unless again artificially crossed. On the contrary, the dominants, or talls, after self-fertilization, produce both talls and shorts. A *part* of the talls, like *all* of the shorts, will breed true, and continue to breed true. But the others will produce a mixed progeny of talls and shorts.

From this Mendel found that, out of each 100 descendants of the first cross, 75 on the average will be dominants (talls) and 25 recessives (shorts). Of the 75 talls, 25 will be pure and will continue to produce talls, and 50 will be mixed and their descendants will consist of pure dominants, mixed dominants, and recessives. The mixed will continue to breed indefinitely in the proportion of 25 pure talls, 50 mixed, and 25 pure shorts.

While Mendel's original experiments were confined chiefly to seven pairs of contrasting or unit characters, as exemplified in peas, it has been proved that this same qualitative and numerical relation exists in regard to many different qualities and characters of plants and animals, such as the colors of flowers, of hair or eyes, peculiarities of structure, or power of resisting certain diseases. The task of modern biology is to ascertain what characters or qualities are subject to Mendel's law of inheritance, and to test the results practically in the field of agriculture, horticulture, stock breeding, and eugenics.

Experience has already shown that great improvements can be made by applying Mendelian principles to the breeding of such anciently established crop plants as wheat, oats, and tobacco. From this it follows that many important economic plants which have only recently been placed in cultivation, such as rubber, coconut, jute, and cacao, offer limitless possibilities for scientific improvement.

ZOOLOGY

Zoology is the science that treats of animal life. The study of animals from various points of view gives rise to special divisions of the science. Thus *Anatomy* is concerned with the gross structure of animals; *Histology*, with their minute structure and tissues; *Cytology*, with the structure and development of the cells which compose the tissues; *Physiology*, with the function or use of organs; *Taxonomy*, with classification; *Paleontology*, with extinct or fossil animals; *Ecology*, or *Bionomics*, with the relation of animals to their environment; and *Economic Zoology*, with the relation of animals to man.

The study of certain groups of animals is known by special names, as, for example, the study of mammals is *Mammalogy*; of birds, *Ornithology*; of reptiles, *Herpetology*; of fishes, *Ichthyology*; of insects, *Entomology*; of mollusks, *Malacology* or *Conchology*; of worms, *Helminthology*.

CLASSIFICATION OF ANIMALS

Systematic zoology, called also *Taxonomy*, treats of the orderly arrangement of animals according to their natural relationships. The animal kingdom is divided into primary groups, or subkingdoms, called *Branches* or *Phyla*. These, in turn, are divided into *Classes*. Classes are divided into *Orders*, orders into *Families*, families into *Genera*, genera into *Species*, and species into *Varieties* or *Races* composed of individuals.

The naming of animals and of the groups to which they naturally belong, so as to make clear the character of the animal and its place in nature, comprises what is called *nomenclature*. Scientific nomenclature consists of the technical terms employed uniformly by scientists throughout the world, regardless of their nationality or language.

The *scientific name*, by which an animal or plant is universally known, consists of two Latinized words. The first of these is the name of the *genus* to which the animal or plant belongs. It is called the *generic name* and always begins with a capital letter. The second word of a scientific name denotes the *species* to which the animal or plant belongs. It is called the *specific name*. Usually this word is in the form of a Latin adjective. In zoology, and for the most part in botany, it begins with a small letter.

The difference between a scientific name and a common name is well illustrated in the case of the puma, a large, catlike animal which is found over much of North and of South America. Even in the United States, the puma is known by several other common or local names, such as cougar, catamount, panther, painter, and mountain lion. In Argentina and other South American countries it has various names of Spanish and Indian origin. In consequence much confusion of names arises. But the scientific name by which the puma is instantly recognized by zoologists in the United States, in Argentina, or in any other country in the world, is *Felis concolor*. *Felis* is the Latin name of the cat, which, in zoology, is used as the name of the "cat" genus, while *concolor*, the name of the species, is a Latin adjective meaning "of a uniform color." The adoption of this form of scientific name, consisting of two words indicating at once the genus and the species, was one of the great contributions made to modern science by Linnæus, the famous Swedish naturalist. Its use has revolutionized systematic zoology and botany.

The complete classification of the puma, showing its place in the animal kingdom is as follows:

Subdivision:	*Metazoa*, or Multicellular animals.
Phylum:	*Chordata*, or Chordate animals.
Subphylum:	*Vertebrata*, or Backboned animals.
Class:	*Mammalia*, or Mammals.
Order:	*Carnivora*, or Flesh-eaters.
Family:	*Felidæ*, or Cat Family.
Genus:	*Felis*, or True cats.
Species:	*Concolor*, or uniformly colored.

Most scientific names are derived from Latin and Greek words, but some are Latinized forms of words from other languages. Although some scientific names are long, complex, strange sounding words, many are shorter and simpler than the corresponding common names. In numerous cases the scientific name of an animal or a plant has been adopted as the common name. Examples of this use among animals are alligator, boa constrictor, gorilla, hippopotamus, hyena, ibis, octopus, python, rhinoceros, trogon, and vireo. Similar examples among plants are alyssum, anemone, asparagus, aster, azalea, begonia, cactus, chrysanthemum, clematis, fuchsia, geranium, magnolia, petunia, and sassafras.

According to the widely used classification of Parker and Haswell, the animal kingdom comprises twelve phyla or branches, arranged in two subdivisions, as follows:

ANIMAL KINGDOM

Subdivision Protozoa

(*Unicellular Animals*).

Phylum I. Protozoa, or Protozoans. Animals composed of a single cell; or, if of several cells, these are of the same kind.

- Class 1. *Rhizopoda*. Amœbas.
- Class 2. *Mycetozoa*. Slime molds.
- Class 3. *Mastigophora*. Protozoa without cilia but with flagella.
- Class 4. *Sporozoa*. Internal parasites.
- Class 5. *Infusoria*. Protozoa with cilia or with sucking tentacles.

Subdivision Metazoa

(*Multicellular Animals*).

Phylum II. Porifera, or Sponges. Fixed aquatic animals whose body wall is perforated with incurrent pores.

Phylum III. Cœlenterata, or Polyps. Animals with radial structure and possessing nettling or stinging organs, whose body cavity is a food sac.

- Class 1. *Hydrozoa*. Hydroids.
- Class 2. *Scyphozoa*. Jellyfishes.
- Class 3. *Actinozoa*. Sea anemones and corals.
- Class 4. *Ctenophora*. Ctenophores.

Phylum IV. Platyhelminthes, or Flatworms. Bilaterally symmetrical, soft-bodied animals, without true segmentation of the body.

- Class 1. *Turbellaria*. Planarians.
- Class 2. *Trematoda*. Flukes, parasitic.
- Class 3. *Cestoda*. Tapeworms.
- Class 4. *Nemertinea*. Nemertines, aquatic, carnivorous.

Phylum V. Nemathelminthes, or Roundworms. Bilateral, unsegmented, round-bodied; usually with alimentary tract.

- Class 1. *Nematoda*. Threadworms.
- Class 2. *Acanthocephala*. Parasitic; mouth wanting.
- Class 3. *Chætognatha*. Marine "arrow worms."

Phylum VI. Trochelminthes, or Wheel Animalcules.

- Class 1. *Rotifera*. Microscopic wheel animalcules.
- Class 2. *Dinophilea*. Minute, wormlike, marine forms.
- Class 3. *Gastrotricha*. Minute, spindle-shaped, fresh-water forms.

Phylum VII. Molluscoida, or Sea Mats and Brachiopods.

- Class 1. *Polyzoa*. Bryozoans.
- Class 2. *Phoronida*. Wormlike polyzoans.
- Class 3. *Brachiopoda*. Lamp Shells.

Phylum VIII. Echinodermata, or Echinoderms. Animals with radial structure, with calcareous plates in the skin, and with intestinal wall distinct from body wall.

- Class 1. *Asteroidea*. Starfish.
- Class 2. *Ophiuroidea*. Brittle Stars.
- Class 3. *Echinoidea*. Sea Urchins.
- Class 4. *Holothuroidea*. Trepangs or Sea Cucumbers.
- Class 5. *Crinoidea*. Crinoids or Sea Lilies.
- Class 6. *Cystoidea*. Fossil forms.
- Class 7. *Blastoidea*. Fossil forms.

Phylum IX. Annulata, or Worms. Bilateral, segmented worms without jointed legs.

- Class 1. *Chætopoda*. Annelids.
- Class 2. *Myzostomida*. Parasites of crinoids.
- Class 3. *Gephyrea*. Marine sessile annelids.
- Class 4. *Archi-Annelida*. Minute marine annelids.
- Class 5. *Hirudinea*. Leeches.

Phylum X. Arthropoda, or Arthropods. Symmetrical, segmented animals, with jointed appendages.

- Class 1. *Crustacea.* Crustaceans.
  - Subclass 1. *Entomostraca.* Water Fleas.
  - Subclass 2. *Malacostraca.* Crabs, Crawfish.
- Class 2. *Trilobita.* Extinct (fossil) trilobites.
- Class 3. *Onychophora.* Peripatus.
- Class 4. *Myriapoda.* Centipedes and millipedes.
- Class 5. *Insecta.* Insects.
- Class 6. *Arachnida.* Spiders, scorpions.

Phylum XI. Mollusca, or Mollusks, Animals with unsegmented body, and without jointed appendages, with a muscular organ of locomotion, called the "foot," and usually with a shell.

- Class 1. *Pelecypoda.* Bivalves,—clams, oysters.
- Class 2. *Amphineura.* Chitons.
- Class 3. *Gastropoda.* Gastropods,—snails, whelks, limpets.
- Class 4. *Scaphopoda.* Tusk Shells.
- Class 5. *Cephalopoda.* Cephalopods,—cuttlefish, squids, octopods, nautilus.

Phylum XII. Chordata, or Chordates. Animals having a notochord which may persist from birth and in the adult become replaced by a bony or cartilaginous axis, the spinal or vertebral column.

- Subphylum A. *Adelochorda.* Balanoglossus,—marine, wormlike animals.
- Subphylum B. *Urochorda.* Ascidians,—marine animals having a notochord when larvæ.
- Subphylum C. *Vertebrata.* Vertebrates. Animals having a backbone.
  - Section I. *Acrania.* Animals without a head, includes the lancelets (*Amphioxus*).
  - Section II. *Craniata.* Animals with a head, includes fishes, amphibians, reptiles, birds, mammals.
    - Class 1. *Cyclostomata.* Cyclostomes,—lampreys.
    - Class 2. *Pisces.* Fishes.
    - Class 3. *Amphibia.* Amphibians.
    - Class 4. *Reptilia.* Reptiles.
    - Class 5. *Aves.* Birds.
    - Class 6. *Mammalia.* Mammals.

ANIMALS

Adjutant (*Leptoptilus*). A very large land bird of the stork family, so named for its measured walk, which at times absurdly resembles that of a self-important army officer.

The Indian adjutant (*L. dubius*), of southeast Asia, a huge, untidy looking bird, stands about 5 feet high, with a wing spread of about 10 feet. It has long legs, an enormous bill, a curious pouch hanging from the chest, and the head and neck are bare. In color it is ashy gray above and white below. The tail coverts are composed of beautiful, soft, downy plumes. The adjutant is a true scavenger, feeding largely on carrion, but also capturing living prey, such as fish, tortoises, snakes, and other small animals, and is protected by law in various Indian cities. It nests on rocky cliffs or in high trees, and lays from 2 to 4 chalky white eggs.

The somewhat smaller African adjutant, or Marabou Stork (*L. crumeniferus*), a conspicuous bird throughout tropical Africa, assists the vultures in cleaning up the refuse of towns and cities. The similar Javan adjutant (*L. javanicus*) is widely distributed in the East Indies. From the tail and wing coverts of all three species are obtained the beautiful marabou feathers or plumes of commerce.

Albatross (*Diomedea*). A group of large oceanic birds, with long, narrow wings, webbed feet, and tubular external nostrils. There are about 18 species, found chiefly in warm southern seas.

Albatrosses display truly remarkable powers of flight, sailing in the air for perhaps an hour without the slightest apparent motion of the expanded wings, which are of the type that best fulfills the conditions required by an airplane. Those of a full-grown albatross may have a spread of 11 feet, yet they are not more than 9 inches wide. The weight of the body rarely exceeds 18 pounds. Albatrosses feed upon fish, cuttlefish, jellyfish, and offal thrown overboard from ships. At nesting time they resort in great numbers to isolated islands, where they build moundlike nests of mud and grass, in which a single very large egg is laid.

The wandering albatross (*D. exulans*), widely distributed over southern oceans, with a wing spread of 10 to 11 feet, is the largest and handsomest species. Its white plumage is marked with narrow, black, transverse lines on the back. The similar royal albatross (*D. regia*) occurs in New Zealand waters. The white-winged albatross (*D. chionoptera*) inhabits the Indian Ocean. The black-footed albatross (*D. nigripes*), with dark plumage and a wing spread of only 4 feet, and the short-tailed albatross (*D. albatrus*), with white plumage and a wing spread of about 4½ feet, are found in the Pacific from California to Alaska.

Alewife (*Pomolobus pseudoharengus*). A small, herring-like fish, 8 to 10 inches long. It is very abundant on the Atlantic coast, leaving the ocean to ascend rivers at spawning time. While inferior in quality to salmon and shad, the alewife is taken in such enormous numbers that, in commercial value, it ranks next to them among sea fishes taken in American rivers. See *Herring*.

Alligator. A genus of saurian reptiles, natives of America and China, closely related to the crocodile. They differ from the true crocodiles in having a broader head, blunter nose, and cavities or pits in the upper jaw into which the long canine teeth of the under jaw fit. Alligators also have thicker, heavier bodies than crocodiles, and, when full grown, are dull black, while crocodiles are dull gray. The largest alligators attain a length of 16 feet, but living specimens exceeding 12 feet in length are very rare.

The female alligator lays from 30 to 40 hard white eggs, about the size of those of a goose. These are deposited in a heap of sand, muck, or vegetable matter, where they are hatched by the heat of the sun or by the fermentation of the vegetable mass. The mother watches the nest until the young appear, immediately conducting them to the water. Alligators live chiefly on fish, but they also catch various land animals that venture into the water. According to W. T. Hornaday, they have rarely, if ever, caused the loss of human life.

Unlike crocodiles, alligators rarely leave fresh water. They prefer sluggish creeks and stagnant ponds, along large rivers. In these they lie in wait for their prey, with only the tip of the snout and the eyes protruding from the water. During the hottest part of the day they often bask in the sun on shore, returning to the water at night.

The American alligator (*A. mississippiensis*) was once exceedingly abundant throughout the Gulf states from southeastern North Carolina southward throughout Florida and westward to the Rio Grande river in southern Texas. Alligator hide makes excellent leather for various purposes. Consequently, the alligator, like the buffalo, has been slaughtered by millions, so that it has become comparatively rare. The much smaller but very similar Chinese alligator (*A. sinensis*) is only 6 feet long. It was discovered in the Yangtze river in 1870 by Swinhoe. See *Cayman, Crocodile, Gavial*.

Alpaca (*Lama pacos*). A domesticated form of the guanaco, a ruminant animal smaller than the llama, belonging to the camel family. It is raised in large herds in the high valleys of the Andes for its valuable silky wool. In appearance the alpaca is very sheeplike, except for its slender neck and erectly carried head. It bears a heavy coat of dark brown wool, which sometimes attains a length of two feet. Remains of blankets woven from alpaca wool have been found in the most ancient Incan tombs.

Like the llama, the alpaca feeds on the coarse, scanty grass and mosses of the higher Andes. It seems incapable of existing upon any other food or in any other climate. All attempts to rear the alpaca in other regions of the world have failed. Alpaca wool, long an important article of commerce in Peru and Bolivia, has, since 1836, been extensively exported to the outside world. See *Guanaco, Llama.*

Amœba (*ȧ-mē'bȧ*). A minute protozoan, about $\frac{1}{100}$ of an inch in diameter, one of the simplest forms of animal life. It inhabits fresh water and moist earth. When observed under a microscope, its body is found to consist of a single cell of naked protoplasm. The amœba moves about by thrusting out portions of protoplasm in one direction and drawing them in from the opposite direction. It takes in food by a similar process, is sensitive to light, heat, and the contact of foreign bodies, and reproduces its kind by simple division,—the parent amœba splitting into two smaller similar organisms which, upon attaining maturity, split into new individuals as before. This animalcule is often selected to illustrate the fundamental animal processes of motion, sensation, nutrition, and reproduction, all of which it clearly exemplifies in a single cell. See *Protozoans.*

Amphibians (*Amphibia* or *Batrachia*). This class contains the cold-blooded vertebrates known as frogs, toads, salamanders, newts, proteans, sirens, and their allies. These form an interesting connecting link between the reptiles and the fishes. A typical example of this class hatches from an egg deposited in the water and begins life as a *gill-breathing* water animal, like a fish. Later, it becomes a *lung-breathing* land animal, like a reptile. From this arises the name amphibian, which means literally a "creature of two lives."

The number of existing species of amphibians is estimated at from about 1100 to 2200. In size they range from cricket frogs a half inch long to salamanders three feet in length. None has a poisonous bite though some protect themselves from attack by acrid secretions of the skin. Amphibians feed chiefly on worms, slugs, and insects, and hence are useful to agriculture. While not of much importance economically, practically all are of some value to man.

The class *Amphibia* comprises three living orders: *Anura*, tailless amphibians, including frogs and toads; *Urodela*, tailed amphibians, including salamanders, newts, proteans, and sirens; and *Apoda*, wormlike amphibians, including the cæcilians. See *Frogs, Salamander, Toad, Tree Frogs.*

Anaconda (*Eunectes murinus*). The largest of New World snakes, sometimes exceeding 30 feet in length, and second in size only to the reticulated python. Combining aquatic with arboreal life, the anaconda inhabits swamps and rivers in the dense forests of tropical South America. Its vertical nostrils are provided with valves which can be closed when submerged. Its eyes are elevated so that it can look downward as well as forward. It spends much time in the water, watching for its prey, with only a small part of its head above the surface. While powerful enough to crush a small deer, it feeds chiefly upon small mammals and water birds. Unlike other boas, it is ill-tempered. On land it is sluggish and not feared by the natives who kill it for its skin and use its flesh for food. See *Boa, Python.*

Anchovy (*ăn-chō'vĭ*) (*Engraulis*). A dwarf herring with the snout projecting beyond the wide mouth, frail bones, and oily, tender flesh. The European anchovy (*E. encrasicholus*), about 3 inches long, is caught in immense numbers along the shores of the Mediterranean when it comes in from the Atlantic to spawn. Anchovies are preserved in oil, often with spices, or made into a fish paste and used as a relish. Anchovy sauce is made now just as it was by the ancient Romans, by boiling the fish over a slow fire with melted butter. See *Herring, Sardine.*

Anteater (*Myrmecophaga jubata*). A large edentate mammal, of Central and South America, so named because it feeds entirely upon ants; called also tamanoir. It is an animal of truly remarkable appearance, with an immense bushy tail, narrow head, and small ears. The nose and jaws are prolonged into a sort of tube, with a small, circular, toothless mouth at the end. Through this tubular snout it thrusts out its slender elongated tongue, about 18 inches long, covered with glutinous saliva, with which it gathers its insect food. Its body is about 4 feet in length, its tail 2½ feet, and it measures about 2 feet in height at the shoulder.

While large and strong, the anteater is timid and inoffensive, and is easily overcome by the jaguar and other enemies. It lives upon the ground, hunts its insect food by night, and sleeps in a lair in the tall grass during the day. See *Armadillo, Pangolin, Sloth.*

Antelope (*Antilopinæ*). A large group of hollow-horned ruminants of the ox family (*Bovidæ*). They are intermediate between the ox and the goat, and include some of the swiftest and most graceful of the four-footed animals. There are about 150 species, all except some 15 of which are found in Africa, the others occurring in Europe and Asia, no true antelope being found in America or Australia. The American pronghorn, popularly called an antelope, belongs to a different family.

Most antelopes are slender, deerlike creatures with horns more or less twisted, and generally, though not uniformly, borne by both sexes. In size they vary from pygmy duikerbok gazelles, only a foot tall, to huge oxlike species, such as the eland, which sometimes attain a weight of 1500 pounds. In color they range from black to brown, roan, sandy, purple, orange, dun, bluish, and gray to white, and are often strikingly marked with brilliant spots and stripes. Antelopes are useful and valuable animals, seldom damaging cultivated fields, and are highly prized for their flesh, horns, and hides.

Some of the most noteworthy African antelopes are the addax, bushbuck, eland, gazelle, gemsbok, gnu, hartebeest, koodoo, oryx, rietbok, sable antelope, steenbok, and waterbuck. Among the Asian antelopes are the chousingha, the nilgai, the saiga, and the sasin or blackbuck of India. Many species were once immensely abundant in various portions of Africa, but, like the buffalo in America, they have been so extensively hunted for food that their numbers have become greatly depleted. See *Chousingha, Eland, Gazelle, Gnu, Nilgai, Pronghorn.*

Ants. Insects with four membranous wings; in some cases, wingless. They are related to sawflies, wasps, bees, and other members of the order *Hymenoptera.* These insects are the highest developed representatives of their class, the six-footed creatures of the world. No insects are more familiar than ants, which, in some ways, are the most intelligent and interesting examples of the order, yet even these are often confused with insects that are not ants at all. The so-called white ants resemble the typical ants only in their colonial habits, and the velvet ants are hymenopterous insects allied to the wasp group. True ants may always be told by the *one* or *two scalelike segments* between the thorax and abdomen of the body, a characteristic found in no other group of insects.

All ants live in communities or colonies, and these assemblages are composed of several kinds of individuals. There are winged males and females as well as wingless workers in all typical colonies. In addition, there may also be exceptionally developed workers with tremendously specialized heads and jaws, the so-called soldiers, together with fertile wingless males and females. Eight different kinds or castes of ants are known to science, but not all of these can be found in any one colony, as certain castes peculiar to one species are not developed in another.

It is thought that most colonies are established by a single young fertile queen which, immediately after mating, builds a small nest, lays a few eggs, and at first cares for the issuing brood unaided. The first larvæ are always workers; these develop rapidly and, upon reaching the adult condition, take over the responsibility of the colony.

Ants, like all hymenopterous insects, undergo complete metamorphosis. They pass through an egg, larva, pupa, and adult stage in the course of their life cycle. The larvæ and pupæ are commonly mistaken for eggs by the untrained observer; indeed, when dried they are sold as bird food under that name. The eggs of these insects are very small and rarely seen except by students of entomology. Many ants secrete formic acid and when fighting inject it into wounds made by their jaws. Some species are provided with a well developed sting which resembles that possessed by the queen and the worker of the honeybee.

Colonies of ants often consist of many thousand individuals, the greater number of which are workers. These extend the nests, defend the colony, raid other colonies, care for eggs, larvæ, and pupæ, and feed the fertile males and females. Ants swarm in summer, but only to mate and disseminate their kind. Females allowed to mate are selected and apparently limited in number according to the requirements of the colony. After mating, the winged males die, and the fertilized females, upon taking up domestic duties, bite off their wings and never again leave the colony. A queen may live many years, and large ant mounds often represent colonies that have been established from 10 to 50 years.

A central feature of ant life is trophallaxis, by which is meant their obtaining food from each other's bodies. Food is stored in a sac, distinct from the stomach. From this sac is regurgitated food not only for the young by nursing workers, but for any other ant which desires to partake of it. The act of regurgitation apparently is quite as pleasant for the one ant as the consumption of the food is for the other. This peculiar fact is said to form the physiological basis for the social life of ants. Among the Amazon ants, a class of warrior individuals would perish from hunger unless fed in this way by a class of "slaves." The honey ants of Mexico and southern United States store food for the colony, receiving from workers food which they take into their sacs until their bodies become greatly distended. Useless for other purposes, they then cling to the ceiling of their nests as living receptacles of food. These ants are an article of food in Mexico.

Ants make homes or nests of many kinds. Each species, however, makes the same type of nest. The earth-dwelling kinds construct homes which vary in form from a simple tunnel to large complex mounds containing a labyrinth of passages, galleries, food larders, snug breeding chambers, nurseries, and rest rooms. Some species have several mounds belonging to a single colony. These may be connected by tunnels, roofed passageways, or by hard beaten paths. Of the wood-tunneling species, the large, black carpenter ants make the most elaborate homes. Their nests frequently occupy the greater part of large tree trunks. Tunnels and chambers are cut by the jaws of the workers out of the solid wood. The weaver ants of the tropics weave houses of silk. The larvæ, when ready to spin their cocoons, are carried back and forward in such a way as to leave behind threads of their still viscous silk fibers, which are thus woven into walls.

Ants have been divided into three classes according to their mode of procuring food. There are first the predatory ants, represented by the tropical "drivers," a column of which will consume every animal found in its path. Other ants are pastoral, keeping aphids, or plant lice, as dairy cattle, which they protect, put out to pasture, as it were, and use as a source of honeydew, an excretion highly palatable to the ants. It is obtained by stroking the lice with the antennæ. Some species take corn plant lice to the roots of growing corn, on which the lice feed. The ants protect the lice from insect enemies and often shelter them in sheds constructed of mud. In addition, many ants are agricultural. Some of these collect, husk, and store seeds in granaries and crush them to provide softer food for the smaller individuals. Others cultivate fungi in soils specially prepared in gardens within their nests. Fertilizers are applied, and weeds are destroyed.

Ants often make war on neighboring colonies. Certain species are of such belligerency that they never retreat until they have overcome and enslaved their enemies. Other ants will never fight. Those enslaved by conquerors commonly labor for them and defend them as they would their own kind. The activities of colonies appear to be regulated in the interest of the whole in a way that still presents one of the most baffling mysteries of the animal world.

Economically considered, ants are, for the most part, detrimental to human interests. The large black carpenter ants are extremely destructive to growing trees and wooden houses, which they weaken or destroy by tunneling. See *Aphids*, *Honeybee*, *Wasp*.

Aoudad (*ä'o͞o-dăd*) (*Ovis tragelaphus*). A goatlike wild sheep of northern Africa, often called Barbary sheep. It is somewhat larger than the domestic sheep and is at once distinguished by a long shaggy mane on the breast which covers the forelegs and reaches nearly to the ground. The Arabs use its flesh for food, weave rugs of its wool, and make morocco leather from its skin.

Ape. A name often employed, in common language, as a synonym for monkey. In its more accurate sense, it is applicable only to the anthropoid apes, so called because they most resemble mankind.

The group of manlike apes (*Simiidæ*), found only in the Old World, includes the chimpanzee, the orang-utan, the gorilla, and the gibbons. Most of these approach and some exceed man in size. They differ from baboons and monkeys in having teeth of the same number and form as in man. All are devoid of tails and cheek pouches; the arms are remarkable for their extreme length and the hind limbs for their shortness. Their hands and feet are equally suited for grasping and climbing. The great length of their arms gives them a peculiar advantage in their native forests, enabling them to climb to the topmost branches or to pass from tree to tree with surprising facility.

The skeleton is substantially similar to the human skeleton, but the spinal column lacks the curvatures which enable man to stand erect with ease. The skull is thicker, the brain case is smaller, and the bulk of the brain much less than that of man. See *Chimpanzee*, *Gorilla*, *Monkey*, *Orang-utan*.

Aphids. Minute, greenish, sap-sucking insects of the order *Hemiptera*. They are commonly found infesting house plants and they abound on field and garden crops. They are gregarious and defenseless, and are preyed upon by many carnivorous animals; but they are able to survive by reason of their extraordinary fecundity.

Aphids are remarkable for their manner of life. Many of them regularly shift from one kind of plant to another during the course of the season. This change of hosts is accompanied by a change in reproductive methods: winged forms are reproduced at the time for the migration, though many generations of wingless forms may have been produced on a single plant prior to the time for the change. Females only are present during the greater part of the season; but both males and females are produced at its close, and eggs are then laid, instead of living young, and only these eggs, produced in autumn, survive the winter. See *Ants*.

Aquarium. An artificial container of water for keeping living aquatic plants and animals under control, and made wholly or partly of glass to facilitate observation. Tumblers, fruit jars, and battery jars serve very well for the smallest aquaria; the larger ones are usually specially built for the purpose. Clean sand and gravel are placed in the bottom to give a foothold for plants. When the amount of animal life present is properly proportioned to that of the green plants, so that the animals yield sufficient carbon dioxide for the plants and the

By permission (except No. 3) N. Y. Zoological Society; photos by E. R. Sanborn

HOOFED MAMMALS

1 Arabian Camel or Dromedary. 2 Bactrian Camel. 3 African Buffalo (*Group Mounted by C. E. Akeley, Field Museum*). 4 Alpaca. 5 Grevy's Zebra. 6 Siberian Wild Horse or Steppe Horse (*Equus przewalskii*). 7 Musk Ox.

From painting by Louis Agassiz Fuertes; copyright by The Frontier Press Co.

NORTH AMERICAN SONG BIRDS

1 Bluebird. 2 Baltimore Oriole. 3 American Goldfinch. 4 Rose-breasted Grosbeak. 5 Mockingbird. 6 Brown Thrasher. 7 Cardinal. 8 Wood Thrush.

From painting by Louis Agassiz Fuertes; copyright by The Frontier Press Co.

NORTH AMERICAN GAME BIRDS

1 Bobwhite. 2 Mountain Plumed Quail. 3 Ruffed Grouse. 4 Mallard. 5 Green-winged Teal. 6 Canvasback. 7 Wilson's Snipe. 8 American Woodcock.

By permission (except No. 7) N. Y. Zoological Society; photos by E. R. Sanborn

RARE OR CURIOUS MAMMALS

1 Great Anteater. 2 Five-toed Echidna. 3 Two-toed Sloth. 4 Brazilian Porcupine. 5 Rat-tailed Opossum. 6 Armadillo. 7 Okapi (*photo by American Museum of Natural History*). 8 Kangaroo.

plants yield sufficient oxygen for the animals, the result is a balanced aquarium. This will run itself, just as nature runs the ponds out of doors, with infrequent changes of water. The plants require sunlight and the animals require food; and the bodies of any of either that die require prompt removal. A cage for terrestrial animals, containing both land and water, is sometimes called a *vivarium.*

Armadillo (*Dasypodidæ*). A group of edentate mammals, chiefly South American, intermediate between the sloths and the anteaters. They are so named because of the hard bony armor which protects the body everywhere except the breast and abdomen. When attacked, it rolls itself up into a ball. Short, stout legs and strong claws adapt it for burrowing. The snout is elongated, and the tongue is long. Armadillos are usually small in size, nocturnal and inoffensive in habit, subsisting chiefly upon roots, fruits, worms, ants, and carrion.

The nine-banded armadillo (*Tatusia novemcincta*) is found from southern Texas and Arizona to Paraguay. Inclusive of tail, it is about 2 feet long, being nearly equal in size to an opossum. This species feeds upon worms, snails, small lizards, beetles, grasshoppers, and other insects. Its flesh is well flavored and is generally considered palatable food.

The Peba (*Tatusia peba*), with a body 16 inches long and a tail of 14 inches, burrows in open plains from Texas to Argentina, storing in its underground chambers supplies of carrion upon which it largely subsists. Notwithstanding the character of its food, the peba is much hunted for its flesh, which is said to be wholesome and of excellent flavor. See *Anteater, Pangolin, Sloth.*

Arthropods (*Arthropoda*). A branch of the animal kingdom which includes all invertebrates having segmented bodies and jointed legs or appendages. It embraces the crustaceans, spiders, myriapods, and insects.

In the arthropods the body is composed of segments or rings covered by an outer wall, called the exoskeleton, which serves both as a means of protection for the soft, internal parts and as a place of attachment for muscles. In insects this outside skeleton is composed of a horny substance called chitin. In crabs and crawfishes it is strongly charged with a limy deposit, forming a very hard shell. While closely allied to the higher worms, arthropods differ from them in having jointed appendages consisting of antennæ or sense organs, jaws or mandibles, maxillæ or accessory jaws, palpi or feelers, and legs, *all arranged in pairs.*

The arthropods constitute the largest branch of animals, numbering more than 400,000 known species. By some authorities the unknown and undescribed species are estimated to total several millions.

Ass (*Equus*). An equine mammal distinguished from the horse by its usually smaller size, longer ears, and rougher and more shaggy coat. It differs further from the horse by the absence of warts or callosities on the hind legs, by having the hair of the tail short on the sides and long only at the end, and by having a harsh bray. It differs from the zebra chiefly in the absence of stripes encircling the body. There are two types, the Asiatic and the African.

The Asiatic asses occur throughout the arid interior of Asia, where they have been much hunted since ancient times for their flesh which is ranked in excellence with venison. The Kiang, Koulan, or Dziggetai (*E. hemionus*) inhabits high desert steppes and mountains of Tibet and Mongolia, ranging upward to the snow line. It is one of the largest, most horselike, and swiftest of the wild asses, standing about 4 feet high at the shoulder, dark reddish in color, with black mane and tail and a narrow black stripe along the spine. The Onager, or Ghorkhar (*E. onager*), which occurs on the plains of central Asia, is smaller and silvery white in color, varying to pale sorrel, with a broad back stripe bordered with white. The Syrian wild ass (*E. hemippus*), very similar to the onager, found in Persia and Assyria, is doubtless the wild ass referred to by writers of the Old Testament. It is one of the most agile of four-footed animals.

The African wild ass (*E. africanus*), believed to be the parent species of the donkey, has larger ears, shorter mane, and scanter tail than the Asiatic kinds. In color it is creamy or bluish gray, with a distinct dark stripe along the spine and across the shoulders. It ranges from Somaliland to the Red Sea, and westward in the Sudan. In its native deserts it is a remarkably spirited and active animal, galloping over the rocks and sand with the speed of a horse. The rare Somaliland ass (*E. somalicus*) is grayer in color and the shoulder stripe is wanting. See *Donkey.*

Auk. A maritime diving bird, somewhat intermediate between the loons and the gulls. The great auk (*Plautus impennis*), of the North Atlantic, called also garefowl, became extinct about 1850. In size it was about equal to a goose. It was the only sea bird in the northern hemisphere which could not fly, the rudimentary wings having been used only in swimming. While formerly immensely abundant, the pursuit of this bird for its feathers resulted in its total extinction.

The razor-billed auk (*Alca torda*) is about 18 inches long, sooty black above and white below, with a white line from the beak to the eye. It is abundant on the coasts and islands of the North Atlantic, and in winter migrates southward to Long Island. At nesting time it congregates by thousands on rocky cliffs where the female deposits a single, large, handsome egg on the bare rock. In Greenland this auk provides both food and clothing for the Eskimos.

Axolotl (*ăk'sô-lŏt'l*). A remarkable salamander, native of Mexico and the Rocky mountains. As an axolotl, it is a dark gray, smooth-skinned animal, which lives wholly in the water. It is about 9 inches long, with large, ragged, external gills, four strong legs, and a fin-bordered tail. Although this is the larval stage, yet it breeds successfully without attaining the adult form, producing eggs which develop into similar axolotls. But, if the pond in which it lives dries up, the gills and fins shrink and disappear, and the animal begins to breathe air at the surface of the water. Later it emerges with serviceable lungs, but with no gills or fins, and lives on land as a spotted salamander (*Amblystoma tigrinum*). The axolotl is abundant in central Mexico where it is much used for food. See *Salamander.*

Babiroussa (*băb'ĭ-rōō'sȧ*) (*Babirusa alfurus*). A peculiar wild hog, called also "pig deer," with long slender legs and nearly naked body, native to Celebes and other Malasian islands. The male possesses two pairs of remarkable tusks, both of which grow upward and curve backward. The upper pair, instead of protruding from the mouth, as in the wild boar, grow upward like horns out of long sockets through the skin on the front of the snout, sometimes reaching a length of 10 inches and curving backward nearly to the eyes. The babiroussa feeds chiefly upon aquatic vegetation and fallen fruits instead of rooting in the ground for food like most swine. See *Swine.*

Baboon (*Cynocephalus*). A group of Old World monkeys, ranging below the anthropoid apes, found only in Africa and southern Arabia. They have limbs of nearly equal length, the canine teeth are long, and the large head, with the nostrils situated at its extremity, somewhat resembles that of a wolf. They are large, strong animals, extremely unattractive in appearance, and of great ferocity. More than any other monkeys, they use the fore limbs when on the ground, running upon all fours, like the quadrupeds, with the greatest ease. They travel in troops of ten or more and steal grain and fruit with great skill and boldness. See *Monkey.*

Badger (*Taxidea americana*). A carnivorous, burrowing animal, allied to the bears and to the weasels. It is of clumsy appearance, with short, thick legs, and with long claws on the forefeet. In size it is intermediate between the skunk and the wolverene. The badger is found on dry plains from Manitoba to the Pacific coast, southward to Mexico and northward to Alaska. It feeds largely upon ground squirrels and prairie dogs. Badger fur is used for robes, muffs, tippets, and trimmings.

Banteng (*Bos sondaicus*). An East Indian ox, native to Burma, the Malay peninsula, Java, Borneo, and Bali, sometimes called the Javan ox. The wild banteng lives in the jungle and is exceedingly wary and pugnacious. It is smaller and more slender than the gaur, and the female is of a light dun color. The banteng has long been tamed by the Malays of Java and Bali, who have interbred it with the zebu and other domestic cattle, producing a useful hybrid stock which is reared in large herds. See *Gaur, Gayal, Ox.*

Barnacle. The name of an order (*Cirripedia*) of marine crustacean animals always found as parasites on other marine animals or attached to some foreign object, such as a ship's bottom, rocks, piles, or floating timbers. They have a partially segmented body, surrounded by a mantle which is generally calcified and forms more or less of a shell. They have no heart, gills, or other organs of respiration. They live either as parasites or by feeding on small marine animals, brought within their reach by the water and secured by their tentacula. Some of the larger species are used for food in China, Chile, and elsewhere. According to an old fable, the so-called goose barnacle (*Lepas anatifera*) produced barnacle geese.

Barnacle Goose (*Branta leucopsis*). A small sea goose, closely related to the brant, common in northern Europe and Greenland, but rare in continental North America. It is so named on account of the curious belief which gained much credence from the 11th to the 17th century, when its remote arctic nesting places were as yet unknown, that it was developed from the barnacle, a small crustacean which grows on timbers exposed to salt water. This myth, long since discredited by scientific zoology, was one of the most bizarre in the chronologies of superstition. It gave rise to grave discussion among theologians as to whether geese so born were fish or flesh, and placed on the Church the necessity of deciding whether they could be eaten on Fridays or fast days.

Basilisk (*Basiliscus americanus*). A lizard of tropical America. It is so named on account of a fancied resemblance to the basilisk of ancient fable, whose breath envenomed the air and whose mere glance was fatal. While of grotesque and forbidding appearance, this modern namesake is wholly harmless. It is about 2½ feet long and greenish brown in color. The head, back, and tail have serrated crests. It lives chiefly in trees, feeding on fruits and insects.

Basking Shark (*Cetorhinus maximus*). According to Jordan, this huge, clumsy shark of the northern seas, called also elephant shark and bone shark, is the most massive of all fishes, attaining a length of 36 feet and an enormous weight. It is a dull and sluggish animal, but it is said that a blow from its tail will destroy an ordinary whaleboat. Whalers occasionally take it for its liver. It has been captured most frequently in the North Sea and about Monterey bay, California.

Bass (*Micropterus*). A highly prized game fish, found in cool streams and lakes from New Hampshire to Manitoba and southward. The small-mouthed black bass (*M. dolomieu*), olive green above and lighter below, 12 to 18 inches long, and attaining 5 pounds in weight, is one of the most active and gamest of fishes.

The large-mouthed black bass (*M. salmoides*), found in ponds and sluggish waters from Canada to Florida and Mexico, 1 to 2½ feet long, and weighing 2 to 8 pounds or more, is dark green above and silvery below, the young being spotted and banded. It is called also Oswego bass, green bass, bayou bass, and chub. The rock bass, or Red Eye (*Ambloplites rupestris*), abundant in cool waters from Canada to Texas, sometimes a foot long and weighing ½ to 1½ pounds, is olive green above, brassy on the sides, with rows of dark spots. The large eyes have red irises.

The calico bass (*Pomoxis sparoides*), a handsome fish found from the Great Lakes to Texas, a foot long and weighing 1 to 2 pounds, is silvery olive in color, beautifully mottled with green. The very similar Crappie (*P. annularis*) is more common in the South. See *Sea Bass.*

Bats (*Chiroptera*). A group of wing-handed, flying mammals, having the fore limbs peculiarly modified so as to serve for flying. Bats are animals of the twilight and darkness, common in warm and temperate regions, but most numerous and of largest size in the tropics. About 450 species of bats have been recognized. While not frequently seen, owing to their nocturnal habits, they, nevertheless, occur in enormous numbers.

There are two main divisions of the order: the large sized, fruit-eating species, mainly of the Oriental tropics, including the so-called flying fox or fox bats (*Megachiroptera*), and the much smaller insectivorous or carnivorous bats of temperate and warm regions (*Microchiroptera*). About 5 species of South American bats are known to suck the blood of other mammals, and hence are called "vampire bats," though this name has also been given to various species not guilty of this habit.

In cold climates, bats either migrate southward as winter approaches, somewhat after the manner of birds, or seek shelter in caverns, vaults, ruinous buildings, and similar retreats. In these they cling together in large clusters, hanging, head downward, by the feet, and remain in a torpid condition until the warmth of returning spring recalls them to activity. Bats bring forth one or two young, which, while suckling, remain closely attached to the mother's breast. The parent shows a strong attachment for her offspring, and, when they are captured, will follow them and often submit to captivity herself rather than forsake her charge.

Our common bats measure 3 to 5 inches in length, with a wing spread of 9 to 14 inches. The great fruit-eating bats of the West Indies sometimes attain a length of 15 inches, with a wing spread of nearly 5 feet. See *Flying Fox, Vampire.*

Bear (*Ursus*). A group of large carnivorous mammals of the bear family (*Ursidæ*), nearly all natives of the northern hemisphere. They are distinguished by their heavy, clumsy bodies, very short tails, thick legs, and flat, plantigrade feet, each with 5 toes armed with strong claws. The teeth are 42 in number, the same as in the dog. Their fur is usually long, thick, and shaggy, and brown, black, or yellowish white in color. Bears are omnivorous, eating, besides the flesh of animals, fish, reptiles, birds' eggs, fruits, leaves, roots, and honey. In temperate regions, bears are unable to procure food in winter, and therefore hibernate during that season. Most bears thrive in captivity and are the best known of the large carnivorous animals.

In North America, according to Dr. C. H. Merriam, 22 species of bears occur, including 5 kinds of grizzly bears, 8 kinds of brown bears, 8 kinds of black bears, and the polar bear. The American black bear (*U. americanus*), rarely more than 5 feet long, with black, shining hair, is a very active climber. It is much less dangerous than the grizzly bear or the brown bear, and is much hunted for its fur and flesh. The grizzly bear (*U. horribilis*), of the Rocky mountains, sometimes 9 feet long and weighing 1000 pounds, is an exceedingly ferocious animal. While bulky and unwieldly in form, it is capable of great rapidity of motion and fights with desperate fury when cornered.

The Kodiak bear (*U. middendorffi*), a huge brown species discovered on Kodiak island, Alaska, about 1895, is not only the largest of all living bears, but is also the largest living carnivorous land animal. It stands more than 4 feet high at the shoulder and attains a length of 9½ feet and a weight of 1200 pounds. The glacier bear (*U. emmonsi*), a rare species, first found in 1895 near Mount St. Elias, Alaska, is the smallest American bear. It stands only about 2 feet high at the shoulder.

The European brown bear (*U. arctos*), native of Europe and Asia, sometimes reaches the length of 7 feet. It has been known in captivity since the days of the Roman arena, is the docile companion of wandering bear tamers, and a common inmate of zoological gardens and menageries. Other important species are the Himalayan black bear (*U. torquatus*), Japanese bear (*U. japonicus*), sun bear (*U. malayanus*), sloth bear (*U. labiatus*), and the spectacled bear (*U. ornatus*). See *Polar Bear*.

Beaver (*Castor*). An aquatic rodent mammal. Only two species are known, the European beaver (*C. fiber*), now largely extinct, and the American beaver (*C. canadensis*), once common throughout North America from Mexico to the Arctic circle. Formerly, immense numbers of these animals were killed for their valuable fur.

The American beaver is now restricted to a few northern and mountainous districts, dwelling in communities on the banks of rivers and ponds in forested regions. The beaver is about 3½ feet long, with a thick, heavy body, sometimes weighing over 40 pounds. The skin is covered by two sorts of hair, of which one is long, stiff, glossy, and reddish brown in color; the other is short, thick, soft, and silky. The hind feet are completely webbed, and the tail, 10 or 12 inches long, is flattened horizontally and covered with scales.

In engineering ability and industriousness, the beaver easily ranks first among the mammals. With remarkable skill and indefatigable labor, it constructs wide dams of logs, sticks, and mud, in order to retain streams at an even level. It then builds its houses or lodges of similar materials in the water above them, felling trees sometimes 12 inches in diameter and transporting their boughs for use in these structures.

Bees (*Apoidea*). The bees form a numerous group or superfamily of insects belonging to the order *Hymenoptera*. There are about 1500 species, widely diffused throughout the world but most numerous in the tropics. The true bees (*Apidæ*) and the bumblebees (*Bombidæ*) are social in their habits, living in communities in which each member performs some service for the common welfare of all. The other families of bees are solitary in their habits, each individual living and working alone. Among these are the digger, cuckoo, carpenter, mason, leaf cutter, potter, and burrowing bees. See *Honeybee*.

Beetle. Any insect of the order *Coleoptera*. Beetles are characterized by having a pair of horny wing covers, called elytra, which meet in a straight line down the middle of the back. Beneath the covers is a single pair of membranous wings, the tips of which are folded transversely. The mouth parts are formed for biting. The beetles form a very numerous group, more than 11,000 species being known in the United States and Canada. Among the most important families are the blister, buprestid, carrion, click, featherwinged, ground, leaf, long-horned, rove, scarabeid, tiger, and water beetles, also the fireflies and ladybugs. On the whole, the order is one of the most destructive in the insect class. It includes such pests as potato beetles, apple-tree borers, carpet beetles, wireworms, white grubs, and fruit, grain, and cotton-boll weevils. Among the beneficial forms are the ladybirds, carrion beetles, and tiger beetles. See *Firefly*, *Ladybird*, *Weevils*.

Bighorn (*Ovis*). The popular American name for the wild Rocky Mountain sheep, so called because of their immense semispiral horns. There are about 6 species distributed through the mountains northwestward from Mexico to Alaska and Yukon. The best-known bighorn (*O. canadensis*), found on high mountains from Mexico to northern British Columbia, is gray-brown in color, with a large white patch on the hind quarters. It stands nearly 3½ feet high, is about 5 feet long, and weighs about 300 pounds. Horns measuring 18 inches in circumference and 52 inches in the curve have been taken from large rams. The female has small, flat, erect horns about 6 inches long.

The bighorn lives in bands, sometimes 50 in number, and is very alert, wary, and difficult of approach. It has been incessantly hunted, not only for sport, but also for its excellent flesh and for its horns which make handsome trophies. In consequence, the bighorn has become nearly extinct throughout much of its former range, except where strictly protected by law.

Bird of Paradise. The name for members of a family of birds (*Paradiseidæ*) of splendid plumage, allied to the crows and bower birds, inhabiting New Guinea and the adjacent islands. The family includes about 65 species, some of which are remarkably beautiful, ranging in size from that of a sparrow to that of a crow.

The Great Bird of Paradise (*Paradisea apoda*), about 18 inches long, has thickset feathers like velvet pile, straw-colored above and emerald green below. From under the shoulders spring tufts of orange plumes about two feet in length which the bird can elevate over the back at will. In the tail of most species are two narrow, wirelike feathers sometimes elongated to the length of 30 inches. These splendid ornaments are confined to the male bird; the female has very plain plumage.

Birds (*Aves*). A class of warm-blooded, egg-laying vertebrates whose bodies are clothed with feathers, with the fore limbs forming wings normally capable of flight. They are classified as intermediate between the reptiles, which are ranked below them, and the mammals, which stand above them at the head of the animal kingdom.

Birds vary exceedingly in size, form, and appearance. They are adapted to every kind of climate and food, inhabit all regions of the world, and are of immense economic value to man. They display high mental qualities, are usually beautiful in outline, movement, and color, and many of them possess melodious voices. Since the Mesozoic era, birds have been present on the earth and they now comprise the most numerous class of higher animals.

All existing birds have horny, toothless beaks or jaws, but some extinct fossil forms had teeth in both jaws. Birds have a four-chambered heart, complete double circulation, and very warm blood. Their bodily temperature varies from 100° in the wingless kiwi to 102° in emus and penguins; from 105° to 107° among the ducks, fowls, and game birds; and from 107° to 111° among the sparrows and warblers. In size, birds range from pygmy humming birds about 2 inches long to ostriches which stand about 8 feet high and weigh 300 pounds.

The number of species of living birds is computed at from 10,000 to nearly 20,000, inclusive of varieties. These are usually grouped in about 20 orders. The most numerous order, *Passeres*, which includes the perching and the song birds, embraces more than half of all known species.

According to Parker and Haswell, living birds are classified as follows:

Division *Ratitæ*,—breastbone without a keel; flightless birds, containing 3 orders: *Megistanes*, kiwis, emus, and cassowaries; *Rheæ*, rheas; *Struthiones*, ostriches.

Division *Carinatæ*,—breastbone with a keel; flying birds, containing 18 orders: *Pygopodes*, diving birds, loons, grebes; *Impennes*, wingless birds, penguins; *Tubinares*, tube-nosed swimmers, petrels, albatrosses; *Steganopodes*, totipalmate birds, cormorants, pelicans; *Herodiones*, storklike birds, herons; *Anseres*, gooselike birds; *Accipitres*, falcon-like birds, hawks, eagles; *Crypturi*, tinamous; *Gallinæ*, fowllike birds; *Grallæ*, cranelike birds; *Gaviæ*, gulls, terns, auks; *Limicolæ*, shore birds; *Pterocletes*, sand grouse; *Columbæ*, pigeons; *Psittaci*, parrots; *Striges*, owls; *Picariæ*, cuckoos, humming birds, woodpeckers; *Passeres*, sparrow-like birds.

Bison (*bī'sŭn*). The name applied to two species of ruminants very closely related to the true ox. One of these, the European bison (*B. europæus*), is now found only in a few forests of southern Russia. The other, or American bison (*B. americanus*), commonly but incorrectly termed "buffalo," is likewise nearly extinct. The two forms closely resemble each other, though the American bison is somewhat smaller. They are at once distinguished from all other cattle by their immense fore quarters and small hind quarters.

The American bison is especially remarkable for the great hump or projection over its fore shoulders, at which point the adult male is sometimes almost 6 feet in height. It is also conspicuous for the masses of long, shaggy, rust-colored hair on the head, neck, and fore part of the body. In summer, from the shoulders backward, the skin is covered with a very short, fine hair as smooth and soft as velvet. The short tail is tufted at the end, and the short but massive horns are curved inward. As in case of many other animals, the male bison is much larger and more powerful than the female. While the skeleton of the bison is similar in many points to that of the ox, it differs in having 14 instead of 13 pairs of ribs.

Although easily subjugated when taken young, the bison has not proved docile and is of little practical use as a farm or pasture animal. The crosses frequently produced between the bison and domestic cattle have not displayed qualities that make them desirable for the stock grower.

The bison formerly ranged in vast herds over immense areas in North America, from the Sierra Nevadas eastward to North Carolina and from Great Slave lake southward to central Mexico. The flesh makes excellent beef, scarcely distinguishable from that of cattle, either in appearance or flavor. It was formerly dried and transported in immense quantities. The hide furnished material for clothing, lodges, trappings, robes, and leather. In consequence, the bison was hunted and slaughtered on a wholesale scale. By 1850, it had disappeared east of the Mississippi, and, by 1875, it had vanished from the central plains.

In 1889, when the American bison reached its lowest ebb, there were only 835 wild and 256 captive animals in existence. In 1926, the American Bison Society, organized to reclaim the animal from extinction, took a census of all living bisons as of that year. This census showed a total of 16,417 throughout the world, comprising 4376 in the United States 11,957 in Canada, and 84 in other countries, of which England had 45 animals. The largest single herd consisted of 8300 at Buffalo park, Wainwright, Alberta. See *Buffalo*.

Bittern (*Botaurus*). A group of wading birds closely related to the herons, but with shorter necks and with more mottled plumage. There are several species widely distributed in both hemispheres. The American bittern (*B. lentiginosus*), about 26 inches long, with varied plumage of buff, brown, and slate-blue, occurs throughout temperate North America. It lives in marsh meadows, nests on the ground, laying 4 or 5 greenish brown eggs, and feeds on snails, lizards, frogs, and insects. It is remarkable for its curious, booming cry, which has given rise to the local names "stake driver" and "thunder pumper." The least bittern (*Ardetta exilis*), only about a foot in length, much darker in color, with the top of the head, back, and tail shining black, ranges from Oregon, Manitoba, and Maine, south to Brazil.

Blackbird. A name given in America to several birds of the family *Icteridæ*, closely related to the bobolink, meadowlark, and grackles. About a dozen species are found in the United States and Canada, distinguished from each other by size and color. When in full plumage, the males are more strikingly colored than the females. All are somewhat smaller than the robin, with uniformly dark plumage sometimes brilliantly marked with red, orange, yellow, or white. They live chiefly on injurious insects, grains, and weed seeds.

The red-winged blackbird (*Agelaius phœniceus*), with bright scarlet shoulders varying to light buffy on the wings, nests in swampy places from New Brunswick to Manitoba and southward to the Gulf of Mexico. The tricolor blackbird (*A. tricolor*), with silky blue-black plumage and red shoulder marks bordered with white, inhabits the interior valleys of California and Oregon.

The yellow-headed blackbird (*Xanthocephalus*), with yellow head, throat, and chest, and a white wing spot, ranges from British Columbia and Hudson bay south to Mexico. It builds its nest a foot or two above water in reedy marshes. The rusty blackbird (*Scolecophagus carolinus*), glossy black in summer but rusty brown in winter, is a forest-loving species common east of the Rocky mountains. The Brewer blackbird (*S. cyanocephalus*), with glossy, greenish black plumage, the common dooryard blackbird of the Pacific coast, ranges eastward to Nebraska and Minnesota. The grackles are sometimes called crow blackbirds. The European blackbird, noted for its song, is a species of thrush. See *Bobolink*, *Meadow Lark*.

Blind Fish (*Amblyopsis spelæus*). A peculiar fish, related to the mud minnow and killifish, found in underground streams in Mammoth Cave and in other caves of Kentucky and Indiana. It is from 2 to 5 inches long, entirely white, with no trace of external eyes.

Bluebird (*Sialia sialis*). A small bird of the thrush family, very common in the eastern United States, nesting from the Gulf states to Manitoba and Nova Scotia, and wintering from southern Illinois and southern New York southward. It is about 7 inches long; the upper part of the body is blue, and the throat, breast, and sides are dull red. It makes its nest in the hole of a tree or in the box that is so commonly provided for its use by the friendly farmer, and feeds chiefly upon insects and wild berries. The bluebird is the harbinger of spring, its cheerful song being most frequently heard in March and April.

The exquisite mountain bluebird (*S. arctica*), purplish blue above and greenish blue below, ranges from the Great Plains to the Pacific Ocean, and the western bluebird (*S. mexicana occidentalis*), with chestnut and blue back and purplish blue throat, occurs on the Pacific coast. Their habits are very similar to those of the eastern bluebird.

Bluefish (*Pomatomus saltatrix*). A highly valued, widely distributed food fish, common along the Atlantic coast. It is bluish above, silvery white beneath, with an average weight of 3 to 5 pounds, though often larger. It is exceedingly active and voracious, traveling in large schools and feeding chiefly on menhaden. As a table fish, it is ranked next to shad, and in commercial value is surpassed by but few fishes taken in American waters, such as the salmon, cod, shad, alewife, and mullet.

Boa (*Boidæ*). The boas constitute a family of very large nonvenomous snakes which kill their prey by constriction. It includes boas, pythons, and anacondas. They possess teeth in both jaws and rudimentary hind limbs which are developed into horny spines or hooks. There are more than 50 species, nearly all tropical.

The boa constrictor (*Boa constrictor*), of South America, is typical of the whole family. A full-grown specimen is about 12 feet long. It has a prehensile tail by which it suspends itself, head downward, from a tree while waiting for its prey. It feeds mostly upon birds and small mammals. When one of these comes within reach, the boa seizes it with its jaws by a quick darting movement of the head, and instantly throws about its victim a fold of the upper part of the body, enveloping and crushing it. After the prey is dead, the boa coats it with saliva and swallows it whole, a process which sometimes takes several hours. While digestion is going on, the snake is sluggish and torpid.

The rubber boa (*Charina bottæ*), of the Pacific coast from Washington to Mexico, ranges farther from the equator than any other member of the family. Although only 15 inches long, this chubby little snake kills small mice and birds by constriction in the same fashion as the huge pythons. See *Anaconda, Python*.

Bobolink (*Dolichonyx oryzivorus*). An American song and game bird, closely related to the blackbirds and orioles. It is about 7½ inches long, with handsome buff, black, and white plumage. In summer it nests on the ground in grassy meadows from New Jersey northward to Nova Scotia and westward to Utah and Montana. It migrates southward in early autumn and passes the winter south of the Amazon. When in their sober fall plumage, the young and the adults alike are called reedbirds or ricebirds. During migration, they pause to fatten in the rice swamps and grainfields of the Southern states, where they are shot in immense numbers for the city markets.

Bobwhite (*Colinus virginianus*). A small game bird of the grouse family, commonly called quail in the northern United States and partridge in the South. It is an alert, handsome bird, 10 inches in length, with beautifully barred and mottled brown and white plumage. From Maine to Minnesota southward to Florida and Texas, it is a familiar native bird, and, by naturalization, it has spread westward to California, Oregon, and Washington, thriving wherever food conditions are favorable. The bobwhite receives its name from the spring call of the male,—a clear, ringing, musical "bobwhite!" Wherever found, it is a year-round resident, frequenting clearings and cultivated fields, and feeding upon insects, seeds, and berries. It nests on the ground in grassy places, laying 10 to 18 white eggs. Although largely exterminated in many localities by excessive hunting, it rapidly regains its numbers wherever reasonably protected. See *Partridge, Quail*.

Boll Weevil (*bōl wē'v'l*). The name applied to various insects which attack the cotton plant. The most destructive of these, the Mexican boll weevil (*Anthonomus grandis*), was formerly confined chiefly to Central America and the West Indies. About 1888 it reached Matamoros, Mexico, and soon after appeared across the Rio Grande, near Brownsville, whence it spread throughout the cotton belt of Texas, causing enormous damage.

The adult insect, a long-snouted, grayish weevil, somewhat less than a fourth of an inch in length, punctures the bolls in which it lays its eggs. Upon hatching, the larvæ feed upon the soft tissues of the buds and bolls. The mature larvæ pupate within the bolls. After hibernating, chiefly in old bolls, the adult weevils appear about blossoming time. The most effective protection is afforded by early planting in wide rows to admit the sunshine, by frequent cultivation, and by burning or plowing under affected plants early in autumn. See *Weevils*.

Booby (*Sula leucogastra*). A species of gannet found in most tropical seas. Its name, said to have been given by Portuguese sailors on account of its stupid habit of alighting on ships and allowing itself to be captured, has become an English byword.

Bower Bird. A name given to a family (*Ptilonorhynchidæ*) of Australian birds on account of their remarkable habit of building bowers as places of resort. The bowers are constructed on the ground, usually under overhanging branches in the most retired parts of the forests. They are decorated with variegated feathers, shells, small pebbles, and bones. At each end there is an entrance left open. These bowers do not serve as nests, but seem to be places of amusement, especially during the breeding season. The various kinds of bower birds build rude nests in trees and subsist chiefly on fruits. The best-known species is the satin bower bird.

Bowfin (*Amia calva*). A remarkable fish, called also grindle, dogfish, mudfish, and lawyer, the only living representative of the group *Halecomorphi*. It inhabits lakes and swamps of the Mississippi valley, and the Great Lakes region southward to Virginia, attaining a length of 2½ feet, and sometimes weighing 12 pounds. In structure it stands between the true lungfishes and the garpikes. The air bladder is a well-developed lung, enabling it to breathe out of water, so that it will live in air longer than any other American fish. It is a very voracious, hard-fighting game fish, but its flesh is watery and ill-flavored.

Buffalo (*Bos*). True buffaloes are large, ruminant animals of the Old World, closely related to the domestic ox. They should not be confounded with the American or the European bison, popularly, though wrongly, called buffalo. Although heavily built with strong limbs and a short neck, the buffalo lacks the hump and the mane which at once distinguishes the bison. Buffaloes have long, flattened, angulated horns, and in mature age their dark-colored skin is nearly bare.

The water or Indian buffalo (*B. bubalus*), found wild in India, Ceylon, and the Philippines, sometimes exceeds 5 feet in height at the shoulder. It has very long, flat horns, measuring, along the curve, 8 to 12 feet from tip to tip. It lives in grassy swamps near streams or lagoons and spends much time in the water. Domesticated breeds, highly valued for their flesh, milk, and as beasts of burden, have been reared in India and the Malasian region for at least 2000 years. During the middle ages, the water buffalo spread westward, appearing in Italy about the year 600 and somewhat later in southern France and in Hungary. It is now extensively used in many parts of southern Europe, Asia Minor, and Egypt.

As a labor animal, the water buffalo is particularly well suited for warm, moist climates and marshy regions, such as Java and other parts of the East Indies. The buffalo cow gives more milk than the common cow, but the flesh of the buffalo is inferior to that of the ox. The Cape buffalo (*B. caffer*) is a similar but wild species found in southern and eastern Africa. See *Bison, Ox*.

Bullhead (*Ameiurus nebulosus*). The best-known American catfish, called also bullpout and horned pout. It is common everywhere in slow streams and muddy ponds from Maine to South Dakota and south to Florida and Texas. It has been introduced into California and Oregon, where it has become abundant.

The bullhead differs from the channel catfish in having a plumper body and a rounded instead of a forked tail fin. It is dark brown above and yellowish below, with a smooth, rubber-like skin. It attains a length of from 12 to 18 inches or more, and, at full age, sometimes weighs 5 pounds. Sluggish in habit, the bullhead lives near the bottom, moving slowly about, with its catlike feelers widely spread, in search of food. It is a gluttonous feeder and will take any kind of bait, swallowing it, hook and all, into a capacious stomach. When caught from cool waters, especially in early spring, the bullhead is an excellent food fish. See *Catfish*.

Bull Snake (*Pituophis*). A genus of large, constricting snakes with pointed snouts. They are unique among American serpents in possessing a filament of cartilage in the mouth, so placed that when the breath is expelled violently against it, a very loud, hissing sound is produced. They are among the most useful of reptiles, feeding upon animals injurious to man.

The pine snake, or white gopher snake (*P. melanoleucus*), found in pine woods from New Jersey to Ohio and southward, is one of the largest serpents of the Eastern states. It attains 8 feet in length, has a turtle-shaped head, and the tail ends in a spine. In color it is whitish above, with large black blotches, and marble-white below. It is a bad-tempered reptile, vibrating its tail rapidly when angry, and emitting a hiss audible at a distance of 50 feet. A powerful constrictor, it preys upon rabbits, squirrels, and other rodents.

The bull snake, or yellow gopher (*P. sayii*), ranges from Canada to Mexico between the Mississippi river and the Rocky mountains. It is the largest North American serpent, attaining a length of 9 feet and a circumference of 6 inches, and is often exhibited by showmen. In color it is rich orange-yellow with large, square, dark blotches above and yellow below.

The Pacific bull snake (*P. catenifer*), often called gopher snake, is found west of the Sierra Nevada. It is smaller than the bull snake, usually about 5 feet long, with smaller marking on the back.

Butterfly. The butterflies belong to the order *Lepidoptera* or scaly-winged insects. Unlike the moths, to which they are closely related and which they sometimes resemble, butterflies fly only by day and, when at rest, hold their wings erect above the back. They also differ from moths in the shape of their antennæ, which terminate in club-shaped knobs, while those of moths are pointed and often fringed on the sides.

One of the most remarkable and interesting circumstances connected with these beautiful insects is their series of transformations before reaching a perfect state. The female butterfly lays a large number of eggs, which produce larvæ, commonly called caterpillars. After a shorter or longer period of feeding and growth, these assume a new form, becoming chrysalids or pupæ, which are attached to twigs and other objects in a variety of ways. These chrysalids occur in various forms and are often strikingly marked with brilliant golden or silvered spots. Within the hard outer covering of the chrysalid, the insect still further develops, to emerge at last as an active and brilliant butterfly.

More than 7000 kinds of butterflies have been described, about 1000 of which are found in North America. While various species, particularly many tropical forms, are of surpassing beauty, their larvæ, as in case of the cabbage butterfly, are often exceedingly destructive pests.

Buzzard. Properly, any bird of prey of the genus *Buteo*, including both American and European species, commonly known in the United States as hawks. The Red-tailed Hawk (*B. borealis*), the largest American species, 25 inches long with a wing spread of 4 feet, ranges throughout eastern North America. The Red-shouldered Hawk (*B. lineatus*), slightly smaller, is of similar range. Both are sometimes wrongly called chicken hawks or hen hawks, though they rarely destroy poultry.

The Western Red-tailed Hawk (*B. borealis calurus*) and Swainson's Hawk (*B. swainsoni*) are the most common large hawks from the Mississippi west to the Pacific. Like the eastern species, they prey chiefly upon mice, ground squirrels, and other injurious animals and are of great benefit to agriculture. All of the foregoing may be called buzzards. The so-called turkey buzzard is a vulture. See *Hawk, Vulture.*

Cacomistle (*kăk'ô-mĭs''l*) (*Bassariscus astutus*). A small carnivorous mammal closely related to the raccoon, called also bassarisk, raccoon fox, civet cat, and ring-tailed cat. It is found in Mexico and from Texas to California, northward to Oregon. In size and habits the cacomistle is similar to the raccoon. In color it is brown above, white below, and the long bushy tail has 6 or 8 broad white rings. It is often tamed and is regarded as a pleasing pet. See *Raccoons.*

Caddisfly (*Trichoptera*). A group of aquatic insects found in all sorts of fresh waters in vast numbers, and of great importance as fish food. The adult insects are mothlike in appearance and mostly nocturnal. The larvæ, known as caddisworms, are familiar to every boy who collects from brook or pond, because of the cumbrous cases which they carry about. These cases are cylindric dwelling tubes made of sticks and bits of leaves and pebbles, stuck together with a silklike secretion which also lines the tube, and they are built in a great variety of designs. On approach of danger, the caddisworm retreats into his case, and most fishes that eat caddisworms swallow the case and all. Some caddisworms of streams live in fixed cases and gather their food from the passing current by means of nets spun beside the upstream opening. A few kinds do not build cases but live among sheltering stones.

California Quail (*Lophortyx californicus*). A handsome crested game bird, called also California partridge, found in the mountains from the vicinity of Monterey northward to British Columbia. It is about 9 inches long, with dark brown plumage and a black recurved crest. It feeds upon seeds and insects and nests in sheltered places, laying 12 to 16 white, irregularly spotted eggs.

The valley quail (*L. californicus vallicola*), known also as the valley partridge, very similar but lighter colored, abounds in arid valleys and foothills from Oregon and Nevada to Mexico. It is the most common game bird of southern California. The larger mountain plumed quail (*Oreortyx pictus*), called also plumed partridge, 11 inches long, with olive brown plumage and a blackish crest composed of two slender, drooping plumes, occurs in the mountains from Mexico to Washington.

Camel (*Camelus*). Large, hornless, ungulate mammals of the camel family (*Camelidæ*). They are distinguished from other ruminants by the presence of two incisor teeth in the upper jaw, and by broad padded feet, with two toes, the hoofs of which cover only the upper surfaces, the sole not being divided. The legs and neck are long; the head is small with short ears. The hair is soft, unevenly distributed over the body, and in color usually sandy, though sometimes white, gray, brown, or black.

Although very ungainly and awkward in appearance, and both stupid and vicious in disposition, camels are exceedingly valuable and useful animals. The peculiar structure of the stomach enables them to go some days without water, and the surplus fat stored in the hump provides a reserve of food. These characteristics, together with their padded feet, great strength, and remarkable powers of endurance, fit them especially for living in arid regions.

There are only two species, and these are known only in the domesticated state. The Arabian camel (*C. dromedarius*), found both in Asia and in Africa, has one hump on the back; the Bactrian camel (*C. bactrianus*), of west central Asia, has two humps. Both kinds have been domesticated in southwestern Asia and in northern Africa since exceedingly remote antiquity—so long, indeed, that the parent wild species, from which they have sprung, are no longer known or remembered. For ages they have been invaluable as beasts of burden, as means of travel, and as sources of food and clothing, their flesh, milk, and wool being indispensable to many desert peoples. Camels were known to the ancient Egyptians and are often mentioned in the Bible and in the writings of the ancient Greeks and Romans.

Saddle camels of either species, bred especially for speed and usually called dromedaries, can travel from 8 to 10 miles an hour for 8 to 10 hours a day. Baggage camels carry loads of 450 to 600 pounds, sometimes 1000 pounds, at a pace of about 2½ miles an hour. Caravans or trains of baggage camels often contain 1000 and sometimes as many as 4000 or 5000 camels.

Overland commerce between China and eastern Europe, from the beginning of the Christian era until the present day, has been carried across the Tibetan plateau and over the high passes of the Hindu Kush by caravans of Bactrian camels. The Arabian camel thrives in Spain and has been successfully established in Australia. In 1856 the United States government introduced camels into Texas, New Mexico, and Arizona. They were used for a time in carrying mails, but the experiment finally proved unsuccessful.

Canary (*Serinus canarius*). A highly prized song bird of the finch family, native of the Canary islands. It has been domesticated for over three hundred years and many varieties have been developed. In Great Britain, Belgium, and Germany, the breeding of canaries has attained some commercial importance. Practically all the caged varieties are of a yellow plumage, though in the native state they are of a dull greenish color. The domestic birds are also much larger than those of the parent wild species. The canary is the most popular house bird in the United States and a fine songster frequently commands a price of $100 and upwards.

Cardinal (*Cardinalis cardinalis*). A handsome bird of the southeastern United States, belonging to the finch family. It has fine red plumage, a crest on the head, and a large, conspicuous, reddish beak. In size it is about equal to the oriole. The cardinal has a rich sweet song which makes it very popular in the southern United States, where it is common. It breeds as far north as Iowa and southern New York and resides permanently throughout its range. The cardinal builds a frail nest in a bush or low tree, laying 2 to 4 white, irregularly spotted eggs. Its food consists of insects, berries, seeds, and grain.

Caribou (*Rangifer*). A flat-horned deer closely related to the European reindeer, and much resembling it in appearance and habits. The full-grown animal stands about 4 feet high and weighs about 475 pounds. Its winter coat consists of a thick feltlike covering of fine hair, through which grows the coarser hair of the outer or rain-shedding portion. The legs are stout and muscular, terminating in broad flat hoofs which permit it to walk safely over snow fields or quaking bogs. Nine species have been described, which fall into two groups, of which the woodland caribou (*R. caribou*) and the barren ground caribou (*R. arcticus*) are typical. The woodland caribou inhabits the forests and open country of British America from Manitoba eastward to Newfoundland and Nova Scotia, and the northern part of Maine. It feeds chiefly upon the tender branches of shrubs. The antlers of this group are much palmated and have a somewhat treelike appearance. The barren ground caribou inhabits the treeless and inhospitable region of northern Canada, with a range extending from western Alaska to eastern Greenland. It lives mainly on lichens, moss, and swamp grass. Caribou afford the principal source of food of the Indians and Eskimos inhabiting subarctic regions, and the skins furnish material for wigwams, harness for dogs, and serve other useful purposes. See *Reindeer*.

Carnivores (*Carnivora* or *Ferœ*). An order of mammals embracing the flesh-eating animals or beasts of prey. Most carnivores are predatory, living chiefly upon other animals, but some live partly or almost wholly upon vegetable food. The canine teeth are large and powerful, and the other teeth are adapted for cutting and tearing flesh. Most carnivores have toes armed with strong, sharp claws. The brain is well developed, and the senses of sight and of smell are remarkably keen.

Active habits, high intelligence, and a fierce disposition characterize the animals of this important group. They range in size from the ermine, which one may conceal in his pocket, to bears which may weigh a ton, and are fitted for the chase of nearly every other kind of living creature. There are four well-marked divisions of the order, the catlike, the doglike, the bearlike, and the marine carnivores.

The catlike group contains the true cats (*Felidœ*), the civets (*Viverridœ*), the hyenas (*Hyœnidœ*), and the aard-wolf (*Protelidœ*). The doglike group (*Canidœ*) includes the dogs, wolves, jackals, and foxes. The bearlike group comprises the bears (*Ursidœ*), the raccoons (*Procyonidœ*), and the marten or weasel family (*Mustelidœ*), of small fur bearers. The marine carnivores consists of the sea lions (*Otariidœ*), the seals (*Phocidœ*), and the walruses (*Trichechidœ*). The first three divisions have toes armed with claws and constitute the suborder *Fissipedia*, or fissiped carnivores. The marine species have webbed feet for swimming and form the suborder *Pinnipedia*, or pinniped carnivores.

True carnivora are widely distributed over the world except in the Australian region, where their place is taken by the flesh-eating marsupials. There are more than 300 living species, upwards of 50 of which belong to the cat family, 70 to the civet family, 40 to the dog family, and 80 to the marten family. Some 90 species occur in the United States and Canada, about half of which are small fur bearing animals.

In North America the cats are represented by the puma, the jaguar (in southern Texas), the ocelot, and the lynxes; the dog family by various wolves and foxes; the bear family by the brown, grizzly, black, and polar bears; the raccoon family by the raccoon and cacomistle; and the marten family by the otter, mink, ferret, weasel, skunk, wolverene, and badger. Various species of sea lions, seals, and walruses occur along the shores of the continent.

While some carnivores are destructive to human life and to domestic animals, on the whole they are of economic value as fur bearers. They serve also as a necessary check upon the hordes of rodents and various other animals injurious to agriculture, which otherwise would multiply excessively.

Carp (*Cyprinus carpio*). An important food fish, native of China, where it has been domesticated for about 2000 years. It was introduced in eastern Europe before 600 A. D., has been reared in France and Germany since the 13th century, and is first mentioned in England in 1496 as "German" carp. In 1872 it was introduced into ponds, lakes, and streams in the United States and has since become as thoroughly naturalized as the English sparrow. The flesh of the carp is coarse-grained and inferior in flavor, but, owing to its abundance, ease of propagation, and rapidity of growth, it is extensively used for food, especially in central Europe. It ranges in length from 12 to 20 inches or more and often attains a weight of from 15 to 30 pounds. Many millions of pounds of carp, under a great variety of names other than the true one, are sold annually as food fish in American markets. See *Goldfish, Minnows*.

Carrier Pigeon. A variety of the domestic pigeon, having a slender form and great powers of flight, called also homing pigeon. It is trained to return to its home from great distances and is employed to carry messages in places where no other means of communication is available. In the Orient, carrier pigeons have been used since very ancient times. They were brought to the attention of Europeans during the First Crusade when the Saracens were found to employ them regularly for conveying information to their armies. During the siege of Paris, in 1870, communication with the outside world was regularly maintained by carrier pigeons. Thereafter various European governments established pigeon corps for the use of their armies and navies.

The carrier is of large size, with long wings, and represents the highest type of pigeon development. The young birds are first trained to return home from short distances; these are gradually lengthened until they may be made to return swiftly from points 500 or 600 miles away. Their flight is steady, direct, and strong, and their speed, which is often greatly exaggerated, averages about 30 miles an hour.

Cassowary (*Casuarius*). A large, flightless, ostrich-like bird, with a heavy, massive body, standing more than 5 feet high. The legs are stouter and shorter than those of the ostrich; there are 3 toes on each foot; and the blackish plumage is coarse and hairlike. The top of the head is surmounted by a horny and helmet-like excrescence, the head and neck are bare, and the skin is usually blue-black in color. The wings are mere rudiments, and there is no visible tail.

According to Rothschild, there are about 9 species, natives of Australia and the Papuan islands, all very fleet-footed, forest-loving birds, feeding upon vegetable matter, insects, and various other animals. Unlike ostriches, only one female lays in a nest. The greenish blue eggs, about 7 in number, are 5 to 6 inches long. The hatching and the care of the young are assumed by the male. Cassowaries are easily domesticated and become very tame and docile. See *Emu, Ostrich, Rhea.*

Cat (*Felis domestica*). The domestic cat had a secure place around the family hearthstone when recorded history began. Unquestionably, it was highly cherished by many prehistoric peoples. Numerous mummies of sacred cats, as carefully preserved as the human mummies, are found in the most ancient Egyptian tombs. The cat is mentioned in Sanskrit writings of India dating back to 2000 B. C. While its origin is not certainly known, the domestic cat is believed to be a permanently established mixed strain, originally derived from the Egyptian wild cat (*F. caffra*) crossed with the European wild cat (*F. catus*).

The common house cat belongs to a genus—that which contains the lion and the tiger—better armed than any other for the destruction of animal life. The short, powerful jaws, long, sharp teeth, strong claws, combined with a cunning disposition, nocturnal habits, and much patience in pursuit, give these animals great advantages over their prey. In a degree, the cat partakes of all the attributes of its race. In the state of domestication its food is necessarily various, but always includes flesh or fish if these can be obtained. Though the cat is usually extremely averse to wetting itself, instances of its catching fish are known.

The cat is a very cleanly animal, avoiding any sort of filth, and preserving its fur in a very neat condition. Its fur is easily injured by water because of the want of oil in it. By friction the fur may be rendered highly electric, as is shown by the sparks produced by rubbing a cat's back. The cat usually brings forth from 3 to 6 young at a litter. These remain blind for nine days. The cat is usually regarded as less intelligent than the dog, but this is by no means certain. It is less loyal and less demonstrative than the dog, and shows a remarkable attachment for places. When taken to a distance and covered up while on the way, it has a singular power of finding its way home.

Among the various breeds or races may be mentioned the tailless or Manx cat; the larger Angora and Persian cats, with long, silky fur; the curious Siamese cats; the Abyssinian cats; the orange, brown, gray, and silver tabbies; and various forms of the common short-haired cat.

Catbird (*Galeoscoptes carolinensis*). A well-known American song bird, related to the wrens and mocking birds. Its home is in copses and thickets, often near dwellings. It is about 9 inches in length, deep slate-color above and lighter below, with a black cap and tail. In habit it is lively, familiar, and unsuspicious. Its call note is a taunting, long-drawn "kee," or mew, a most unpleasant cry, but its song is rich, melodious, and often imitative of other birds. It ranges over most of North America, but chiefly east of the Sierra Nevada. During the winter it inhabits the extreme south of the United States, and is found also in Mexico and Central America. It nests in thickets and orchards, laying 3 to 5 bluish green eggs, and feeds on insects and small fruits and berries.

Caterpillar. The active immature stage of moths and butterflies (called also a larva), more or less wormlike in form, and usually covered with bristles or hair. It is during this stage of their existence that moths and butterflies do most of their feeding and attain all of their growth. Therefore it is in this stage that they are of economic importance. Most caterpillars feed upon plants, and very few plants are exempt from the ravages of certain of them. Cut worms, army worms, palmer worms, silk worms, and many other so-called worms, are caterpillars and not true worms. The apple worm is the larva of the codling moth.

All caterpillars, when they have attained their full growth, go into retirement and enter upon a quiescent pupal stage (or chrysalis), usually first spinning about themselves a silken cocoon. This stage is a period of making over of the materials of the body of the larva into the form of the adult insect. The butterfly or moth emerges from the cocoon at the final transformation.

Cat Family (*Felidæ*). An important and well marked group of flesh-eating animals. There are about 50 species, widely distributed throughout the world, embracing the most powerful living beasts of prey, including the lion, tiger, leopard, ounce, jaguar, puma, and cheetah, as well as lynxes, wild cats, and other small carnivores.

As a group, the cats are distinguished by their uniformity of structure, flexibility of spine, looseness of skin, and also by their exceeding suppleness, quickness, and muscular power. They are predatory in habit, procuring their prey by lying quietly in wait, or by a stealthy approach, terminating in a sudden spring, a clutch of their lacerating claws, and a crushing bite. Their entire physical structure embodies agility and strength to a remarkable degree. They are mostly nocturnal in habit, with eyes adapted for seeing in dim light. The pupils of the eyes are vertical, except in case of the lion, which has round pupils. All are clothed in rather long, soft fur, and the male lion is provided with a conspicuous mane.

The cats, great and small, live and hunt alone or in small family parties, never in numerous groups, and all except the lion are monogamous. None are migratory, and few, except the tiger, wander far from their lairs. Most of them live at constant enmity with man, being dangerous and destructive either to him or to his domestic animals. In consequence they have been largely exterminated in all civilized lands. For example, the lion and the tiger inhabited Europe in historic times, but none are now found there. The puma has practically disappeared from the eastern United States and the jaguar has likewise largely vanished north of central Mexico. See *Cheetah, Jaguar, Leopard, Lion, Lynx, Puma, Tiger.*

Catfish (*Nematognathi*). An important group of fishes, characterized by the presence of barbels or feelers on the head, somewhat like the "smellers" of a cat. They have scaleless bodies and are usually armed with a stout spine in the front of the dorsal fin and with one in front of each pectoral fin. These spines, which are capable of inflicting painful wounds, are provided with revolving socket joints, so that they may be elevated and made rigid or depressed and made movable. The most important family is that of the true catfishes (*Siluridæ*), containing about 700 species, most abundant in South America and Africa. About 30 species occur east of the Rocky mountains, but none is native on the Pacific coast.

The Channel Cat (*Ictalurus punctatus*) is found in large streams of the Mississippi valley. It is 2 to 3 feet long, weighs 25 to 30 pounds, and is a fine food fish. The Great Blue Cat (*I. furcatus*), of the Mississippi and southern rivers, is the giant among American catfishes, sometimes exceeding 150 pounds in weight. While ugly in appearance, it is a highly prized steak fish. The Great Lakes Cat (*I. lacustris*), also of very large size, has a more northern range. Many millions of pounds of the foregoing species are annually sold in the markets. The common bullhead or horned pout, of muddy ponds and sluggish streams, belongs to the catfish family. See *Bullhead*.

Cattle. In a broad sense this term refers to any kind of live stock, that is, all four-footed domestic animals which may do labor or serve to provide food or clothing for man. With this meaning the term may include horses, asses, camels, llamas, alpacas, goats, sheep, and even swine, as well as all domesticated bovine animals. This is the general meaning of the word as used in the Scriptures and in various other earlier writings. In the common usage of the day, however, the word cattle is restricted to mean domestic beasts of the cow kind, such as the ox, zebu, yak, water buffalo, gaur, gayal, and banteng.

Cayman (*Caiman*). A large crocodilian which much resembles the alligator, but differs in having bony armor on the lower as well as on the upper part of the body. There are five species peculiar to Central and South America. The great cayman (*C. niger*) of Brazilian rivers, usually 9 to 14 feet long, is reported by Bates to attain a length of 20 feet. The spectacled cayman (*C. sclerops*) of tropical America, sometimes 18 feet long, is so named for the rims of bone which surround the eyes. The rough-backed cayman (*C. trigonatus*) of the Upper Amazon is only 6 feet long.

Cetacea or **Cete.** An order of aquatic mammals, chiefly marine, which includes the whales, the dolphins, and the porpoises. They have no distinct neck, external hind limbs are lacking, the fore limbs are modified into finlike paddles, and the tail ends in a broad horizontal fin or fluke. Although fishlike in form, they are warm-blooded, breathe air, bring forth their young alive and nourish them with milk from their own bodies. Usually, cetaceans swim together in groups called schools. For the most part they feed upon small fish, marine crustaceans, and especially squids and cuttlefish. Most cetaceans are harmless to larger animals, but the orca, or whale-killer, is the most savage and dangerous animal that swims.

The order consists of about 100 species, of which about 25 are whalebone and sperm whales, and over 60 are porpoises and dolphins, widely diffused in all oceans and in a few tropical rivers. Cetaceans range in size from the common porpoise, 5 feet long, to immense sulphur-bottom whales, 95 feet long and weighing about 300,000 pounds, the largest animals, so far as known, that have ever lived upon the earth. See *Dolphin, Killer Whale, Porpoise, Whale*.

Chameleon (*Chamæleontidæ*). The chameleons constitute a family of Old World tree-dwelling lizards. They are distinguished by a wormlike, extensile tongue, and by the structure of the feet, in which the toes are divided into two opposing parts, forming grasping organs. The eyes are prominent, with thick lids, and may be moved independently of each other. Chameleons live on insects captured by means of their viscid tongues, which can be protruded with great rapidity to a distance of 4 to 6 inches.

All chameleons possess the power of rapidly changing the color of their bodies. The prevailing green color may quickly turn to yellowish, blackish, or gray. Their colors are brightest on warm, sunny days, and dullest on dark days or when the animal is frightened or angry. There are more than 60 species, most abundant in Africa and Madagascar.

The American chameleon (*Anolis carolinensis*), a remarkable little creature belonging to the *Iguanidæ*, is not closely related to the true Old World chameleons. It is about 7 inches in length and much resembles a small alligator. It is usually green in color, but it can vary its bodily hue with great rapidity, sometimes changing from brown to leaf green in three minutes. This dainty little lizard, which is found from North Carolina to Texas, makes a pretty and amusing pet.

Chamois (*shăm'ĭ*) (*Rupicapra tragus*). A hoofed mammal intermediate between the goats and the antelopes. Its home is in the high mountains of southern Europe. Its horns, which are about 6 or 7 inches long, are round, almost smooth, perpendicular, and straight until near the tip, where they suddenly terminate in a hook directed backward and downward. Its hair is brown in winter, brown fawn color in summer, and grayish in spring. The head is of a pale yellow color with a black band from the nose to the ears and surrounding the eyes, and the tail is black. Its flesh equals venison in quality, the horns are valuable, and the hide makes fine leather. The agility of the chamois, the nature of its haunts, and its remarkable powers of sight and smell render its pursuit exceedingly difficult and hazardous.

Cheetah (*Cynælurus jubatus*). A large carnivorous mammal of the cat family (*Felidæ*), native of Africa and southwestern Asia, trained since ancient times for hunting game, hence often called hunting leopard. It differs from the true cats in having more slender limbs and short, blunt claws, which are only slightly retractile. In color it is tawny, thickly marked with small black spots. For a short distance its speed is said to be greater than that of any other large animal.

While similar in size to the leopard and the jaguar, the cheetah does not possess their tiger-like ferocity, but is docile and doglike in disposition, being easily tamed and sometimes kept about houses as a pet. Its use in hunting is now confined to Persia and India, where it is trained by wealthy natives for the chase of the antelope and other swift game. Cheetah hunting is depicted on early Assyrian and Egyptian monuments. It flourished extensively in the Mogul Empire, in Asia, and was introduced into Europe by returning crusaders. During the 14th and the 15th century, hunting with cheetahs was regarded a noble sport in Italy and France.

Chewink (*Pipilo erythrophthalmus*). A well-known American bird of the finch family, called also towhee and ground robin. It is about 8 inches long, black above and white below with chestnut sides, breeding from Manitoba to Maine and southward, and wintering in the Southern states. It constructs its nest on or near the ground, laying 3 to 5 finely speckled eggs. Its food consists of insects and seeds. The chewink is a bustling, vigorous bird, inhabiting thickets and bushy undergrowths, greeting all passers with an inquiring "chewink, towhee!" Ernest Thompson Seton well expresses its mating song as "chuck-burr-pil-a-will-a-will-a."

Chicken Hawk (*Accipiter*). A name popularly given to various birds of prey supposed to be destructive to poultry. In North America, three species may rightly be called chicken hawks or hen hawks. Cooper's hawk (*A. cooperi*), 14 to 20 inches long, is found throughout the United States and southern Canada. It is bluish gray above, with the top of the head black, and white below, barred and spotted with reddish brown. The rounded tail has 3 or 4 black bars and a narrow white tip. Throughout the United States it is the most common and destructive chicken hawk.

The much smaller sharp-shinned hawk (*A. velox*), 10 to 14 inches long, uniform bluish gray above, and white below, barred with reddish brown, ranges from the Arctic circle to Guatemala. It feeds chiefly upon small birds and young poultry. The much larger goshawk (*A. atricapillus*), about 24 inches long, occurs throughout the northern United States and Canada. It is dark bluish gray above, becoming black on the head, and whitish below marked with fine gray zigzags and darker streaks. In Canada and Alaska it is exceedingly destructive to poultry and game birds.

The red-tailed hawk and the red-shouldered hawk, which live chiefly on mice, gophers, and other injurious small animals, are often wrongly called chicken hawks. See *Buzzard, Hawk*.

Chigoe (*chĭg'ō*). A species of flea (*Sarcopsylla penetrans*), called also chigger or jigger. It is found in the West Indies and South America, where it is an exceedingly troublesome pest, burrowing in exposed places on the human skin and causing painful and often dangerous sores. In the Southern states the name is applied also to various kinds of minute red mites (*Trombidiidæ*) which fasten upon or penetrate the skin. Their bite, while very annoying, is not fatal to the larger animals but, when numerous, chigoes sometimes cause the death of newly hatched poultry.

Chimæras (*kĭ-mē'ràs*) (*Holocephali*). A group of fishes of curious form, allied to the sharks and the rays, known also as spookfishes, ratfishes, and elephant fishes. The Sea Cat (*Chimæra monstrosa*), of the North Atlantic, inhabits deep waters and is rather infrequently seen. It attains a length of 3 or 4 feet and has a sharklike body with a long, slender, finned tail. The eyes have a greenish pupil, surrounded by a white iris, and shine, especially at night, like cats' eyes. The spotted chimæra, or Elephant Fish (*C. collei*), first discovered at Monterey, California, is the best-known species. It occurs in shallow waters, is brown above, with whitish spots, and reaches a length of 2½ feet. It is harmless, and also useless, except for the oil obtained from the liver.

Chimpanzee (*Pan troglodytes*). The native Guinea name of a large ape of equatorial Africa, belonging to the anthropoid or manlike monkeys and to the same family as the gorilla (*Simiidæ*). There are about ten known species, all forest-dwelling animals.

When full grown, the chimpanzee is sometimes about 5 feet high, with shining black hair, but is not so large and powerful as the gorilla. It has large ears, distinct eyebrows and eyelashes, and whiskers. Like the orang-utan, it has the hair on its forearm turned backward, but differs from it in having an additional dorsal vertebra and a thirteenth pair of ribs. It walks erect, better than most of the apes. It feeds on fruits, often robs the gardens of the natives, and constructs a sort of nest among the branches. No other large ape is so human in its characteristics, appearance, and intelligence. See *Ape, Gorilla, Orang-utan*.

Chinch Bug (*Blissus leucopterus*). A small gregarious insect pest, of the order *Hemiptera*, which attacks grasses and cereal grains. It is about one-eighth of an inch long and of contrasting black and white color. It came originally from Central America, where it lives upon native grasses, but it thrives even better upon our cultivated grain crops, and has spread with them all over the continent, doing most damage to corn and wheat in the Middle West. In the state of Illinois it was estimated to have caused a loss of $73,000,000 in the year 1864 alone. The chinch bug has been the subject of much investigation by agricultural experiment stations, any of which, on application, will furnish information as to means for its control.

Chinchilla. The Spanish name of a small rodent mammal, native to South and Central America, allied to the guinea pig, but outwardly very similar to a ground squirrel. There are several species, all gregarious, living in holes or burrows, and feeding upon roots, bulbs, and bark. All are valued for their fur, particularly the common chinchilla (*C. lanigera*), of the Andes, whose soft, silky, mouse-gray fleece now constitutes an important article of commerce.

Chousingha (*chou'sĭng-hä*) (*Tetraceros quadricornis*). A small East Indian antelope, about 2 feet high, distinguished from all other living ruminants by having two pairs of horns. It lives singly or in pairs in thinly forested or bushy hills, always in the near vicinity of water. The horns, which are small, short, and smooth, are borne only by the males.

Chuckwalla (*Sauromalus ater*). Next to the Gila monster, the largest lizard of the southwestern desert region of the United States. It is 14 inches long, with a broad body, stubby limbs, and a flattened tail. It is herbivorous, quite harmless, and lives among rocks.

Clam. The common name for various bivalve mollusks, especially those which are edible. The soft-shell or long clam (*Mya arenaria*), a common article of food, about 4 inches long and 2½ inches wide, is found in the sand between tide lines from the Arctic Ocean south to Cape Hatteras and San Francisco. The highly prized hard-shell or round clam (*Venus mercenaria*), called quahog in New England, is abundant on the Atlantic coast. The painted clam (*Callista gigantea*), 16 inches long, is a large edible species of the Southern states. The very numerous species of fresh-water mussels are often called clams.

The largest known bivalve is the giant clam (*Tridacna gigas*) of the East Indies. The fleshy portion of this animal, which is highly valued for food, weighs about 20 pounds. The huge, deeply ridged shell, often 2 feet long, sometimes weighs more than 500 pounds. The halves or valves are used in some French churches as fonts for holy water. The painter, Botticelli, in his "Birth of Venus," represents the goddess as standing in one of the valves of this shell.

Climbing Fish (*Anabas scandens*). A small, perchlike, fresh-water fish of the East Indies, which is able to live out of water for a long time in moist situations. It is remarkably active, hitching itself over the ground and even climbing the wet trunks of trees to a height of several feet by means of its spiny fins and gill covers.

Cobra (*Naja*). A genus of about 10 exceedingly venomous snakes of Asia and Africa, which cause a greater destruction of human life than all other poisonous serpents combined. It is estimated that in India 20,000 persons perish annually from their bites. The cobra de capello (*N. tripudians*), 4 to 6 feet long, occurs from the Caspian Sea to South China, but is most numerous in India. When about to strike, it lifts its head and spreads its neck into a broad shell-like hood. The similar Egyptian cobra (*N. haie*), called also the asp, found throughout Africa, is one of the most deadly serpents. The king cobra, or Hamadryad (*N. bungarus*), the longest and most deadly of all venomous snakes, occurs sparingly from Ceylon to the Philippines. It sometimes attains 15 feet in length, lives on other reptiles, and is extremely active and vicious. It will attack man without provocation, and, if abundant, would be the most terribly destructive of all serpents. The Krait (*Bungarus cæruleus*), smaller and less deadly than the cobra de capello, is very abundant in India. The eradication of the cobra in India is made more difficult by the fact that the natives regard it with religious veneration.

Cochineal (*Coccus cacti*). A scale insect feeding upon the nopal cactus (*Opuntia cochinillifera*), anciently grown in Mexico as a dyestuff. Following the Spanish Conquest, it was successfully transplanted into the Canary islands, Algeria, Java, and other warm regions. The dried bodies of the females, some 70,000 of which are required to weigh a pound, are used in making a crimson and a scarlet dye and also in the preparation of carmine and lakes. Cochineal has been largely replaced by aniline dyes; consequently, the formerly extensive cochineal industry has greatly declined.

Cockatoo. The common name of any bird of the family *Cacatuidæ*. They are very closely related to the true parrots, but differ in having a conspicuously crested head and less highly colored plumage. There are about 30 species, natives chiefly of the Australian region where they are hunted for food by the natives. They are large, noisy, active birds, frequenting the tops of high forest trees and feeding upon nuts, seeds, grains, bulbs, and roots, usually nesting in hollow trees or in crevices in rocks. Among the more striking species are the great black, the sulphur-crested, the white-crested, and the rose-crested cockatoos. While readily imitating various animals and birds, none learn to speak many words.

Cockroach. A nocturnal household insect of the order *Orthoptera*, allied to the grasshoppers. It is half an inch or more in length and brown or blackish in color. Several species of the large group of cockroaches have taken up their abode in human habitations, and have followed man to every part of the earth. They like the shelter that his house affords and they like his food. They like warmth and moisture and so are frequently found about kitchens near the water pipes, most commonly in dark recesses. Their flat bodies enable them to enter narrow crevices, and into these they scurry on the approach of light. Cockroaches are best controlled by blowing borax powder into the cracks which they inhabit.

Codfish (*Anacanthini*). The codfishes comprise an important group containing some of the world's most valued food fishes, and forming, like the herring and the salmon, the basis of great industries. Codfishes may be known by the complete absence of spines in all fins, by the jugular position of the ventral fins, and by the usually isocercal tail.

The common codfish (*Gadus callarias*), found everywhere on the shores of the North Atlantic, averages about 10 pounds in weight, but sometimes exceeds 150 pounds. It is exceedingly voracious and prolific, feeding close to the bottom to a depth of 100 fathoms, chiefly on small mollusks, crustaceans, and other fish. Each year a mature codfish produces several million eggs which are spawned in the open ocean. Codfish are caught in immense numbers, especially on the banks of Newfoundland. The codfish industry supports hundreds of vessels in the fishing fleets of Atlantic waters. The very similar Alaska codfish (*G. macrocephalus*), equally abundant as the Atlantic species, abounds from Oregon to the Aleutian islands and Japan.

The Haddock (*Melanogrammus aeglifinus*) closely resembles the cod, from which it may be distinguished by the black lateral line. It occurs on both shores of the Atlantic, usually weighs 3 to 5 pounds, and ranks second to the cod in economic value among codfishes. When smoked it is the finnan haddie of commerce.

The Pollack (*Pollachius carbonarius*), of similar range to the haddock, is darker and more lustrous in color than the cod, and swims at the surface instead of at the bottom. It sometimes attains a length of 3 feet and a weight of 25 pounds. Though it is a favorite food fish in Great Britain, it is generally considered inferior to the cod.

Cœlenterates (*sē-lĕn'tẽr-âts*) (*Cœlenterata*). A branch of the animal kingdom comprising invertebrate animals in which the stomach cavity occupies the whole interior of the body. This digestive cavity is connected with the outside only by means of the mouth through which all food enters and all indigestible portions are thrown out. The cœlenterates include the hydroids, polyps, jellyfishes, sea anemones, and corals, and are ranked as next to the lowest branch of the *Metazoa* or many-celled animals. Over 6000 species are known.

Condor (*Sarcorhamphus gryphus*). A huge South American vulture. It is one of the largest of all flying birds, although the California vulture and the albatross sometimes exceed it in expanse of wing. The condor is found in the Andes from Peru to Patagonia, usually at altitudes of from 9000 to 16,000 feet. It is from 44 to 55 inches in length, with a wing spread of 8½ to 10½ feet. As in other vultures, the head and neck are naked. The plumage is uniformly black with a white ruff on the neck and broad white bars across the wings. It nests on inaccessible ledges of rock, depositing 2 white eggs. The young are unable to fly until about two years old.

Condors feed chiefly on carrion but under stress of hunger successfully attack sheep, goats, calves, and deer. When gorged with food, they cannot rise readily from the ground and are easily captured. In flight, condors are remarkably graceful, wheeling in majestic circles, often at immense heights, and seeming to sail in the air without apparent movements of their wings. See *Vulture*.

Coot (*Fulica*). A wading bird of the rail family, differing from the true rails in having broader-lobed toes and by its more aquatic habits. There are about 12 widely distributed species, all uniformly slaty in color, with a darker head and neck, and usually with white bills and white edges on the wings. They frequent reedy swamps, borders of ponds, and sluggish streams, feeding on water plants, insects, worms, fish, snails, and other small aquatic animals. Coots swim well, with a bobbing motion of the head and neck, and obtain much of their food by diving.

The American coot (*F. americana*), called also mudhen and crowduck, about 15 inches long, is found in ponds and marshes everywhere from Greenland and Alaska south to the West Indies and Central America. It nests among reeds in the water, laying 8 to 15 creamy-white, finely speckled eggs. Usually its flesh is of a rank flavor, but when it fattens by feeding on water celery the coot is said to rival the canvasback duck as a table bird.

Coral. The horny or limy secretions or skeletons of various kinds of polyps, chiefly *Actinozoa*, some of which occur in strikingly beautiful forms. The coral-producing polyps, sometimes wrongly called "coral insects," form colonies which increase mainly by gemmation, or budding. From some portion of the parent polyp, young polyp buds spring. From these, when grown, new generations, similarly produced, appear. In many cases, the colony thus developed assumes a branching or treelike form, as in the sea fan and the staghorn coral. In others, as in the mushroom coral and the brain coral, the colony becomes oval or dome-shaped.

The large stony corals (*Madrepora* and *Mœandra*) build up extensive coral reefs in tropical seas. Since early Paleozoic times, various corals have been important rock-forming agents, and today are actively producing rock material. In warm, shallow parts of the ocean, limestone is often formed by the combined activity of coral polyps and calcium-precipitating bacteria. The rate of growth in corals is not well known, but the reef-building mæandrinas at Key West, Florida, are estimated to make an average growth of half an inch a year. Madrepores, developing upon submerged wrecks, have been observed to maintain, for a half century, a growth averaging 3 inches annually.

The red coral, or precious coral (*Corallium nobile*), of the Mediterranean, grows about a foot in height, with a slender, branching stem. It occurs in many handsome tints and shades and takes a high polish. This valuable coral is much used, especially in India, for jewelry and ornaments. The finest rose-pink varieties command a price of $400 to $600 and upwards an ounce. Ordinary red-colored small pieces are worth about $10 an ounce, while the coral grains or fragments used in children's necklaces cost about $15 a pound.

Cormorant (*Phalacrocorax*). A large group of fishing birds, with completely webbed feet, closely related to the pelicans. Cormorants are chiefly maritime and usually inhabit rocky coasts. They are swimmers rather than fliers and feed exclusively on fish, which they are extremely skillful in catching. They are between 2 and 3 feet in length, with a strong, elongated body, short stout legs, rather lengthy neck, and a hooked bill with sharp cutting edges. The throat is greatly dilatable so that fish of large size may be swallowed. There are more than 30 species, ranging from Greenland and Siberia south to New Zealand, but most numerous in the tropics. Cormorants are sociable birds, often congregating in immense flocks. They breed in communities, building crude nests on cliffs or in trees, in which the female lays from 3 to 5 large greenish eggs.

The common cormorant or shag (*P. carbo*), glossy black above and sprinkled with white on the head and neck, is found in eastern North America, Greenland, Europe, Asia, Africa, and Australia. It possesses a marked degree of intelligence and, if taken when young, may be readily tamed. Since ancient times this species has been trained to catch fish. The young birds have a ring placed around the neck to prevent swallowing, and they soon learn to bring all captures to their masters. A well-trained male cormorant will continue to catch fish for about five years. While usually regarded merely as a sport in Europe, fishing with cormorants is an important industry in China and Japan. Besides the common cormorant, about 9 others are found in North America.

Corn Borer, European (*Pyrausta nubilalis*). A destructive insect pest, one of the most injurious introduced into America. Following its discovery in Massachusetts in 1917, it spread rapidly to New York and other states, causing the department of agriculture to undertake vigorous measures for its control. Like various other pernicious insects, the corn borer inflicts its chief damage when in the larval or caterpillar stage.

The female moth is pale yellow, with a stout body and a wing spread of slightly more than an inch. The outer third of the fore wing is marked by two darker, sawtooth-like lines; the hind wings are unmarked. The male moth is reddish brown, with a long, slender body, and is slightly smaller and much darker than the female. On the fore wings of the male moth there is a pale yellow streak between the two sawtooth-like lines, and, near the middle, there are two small yellowish spots. The hind wings of the male are grayish with a broad band of pale yellow.

The European corn borer produces one or two generations each year. Usually the moths fly from early June until late July. They appear about 9 o'clock in the evening and ordinarily make flights of 20 to 30 feet in length, reaching a height of some 6 feet from the ground. The female moth lays from 300 to 700 eggs in clusters on the underside of corn leaves. Upon hatching, the young caterpillars eat small portions of the leaves. As they grow larger, they attack the unfolded tassel, often causing it to break at the base and fall over, one of the surest signs of the presence of the pest. When full grown, the caterpillars enter the stalk and tunnel through all parts of the plant, except the fibrous roots, greatly weakening its vitality. They also bore into the cob and destroy the growing ear, the damage to a badly infested field ranging from 25 to 50 per cent and upwards.

In growing corn the presence of these insects is easily detected by hanging masses of borings on the stem, and by the sap which exudes from the entrance holes. In winter the presence of borers in dry cornstalks is indicated by the entrance holes, which are about one-eighth inch in diameter, usually with discolored edges and more or less plugged with borings. These holes lead to interior burrows, each of which is inhabited by a yellowish gray caterpillar, about three-fourths of an inch long, with a brown head and with minute brown spots on the body.

Besides devouring field and sweet corn, the European corn borer feeds incidentally upon various vegetables, garden flowers, and weeds, all of which harbor the insect and assist in spreading it from one locality to another. The chief protective measures employed are total destruction of infested cornstalks, vegetable refuse, and weeds, together with rigid quarantine regulations against infested districts. Fermentation of infested corn in silos kills the insect. The possibilities of damage and the problems of control are so great that, wherever the pest is discovered, immediate and complete cooperation with the department of agriculture is necessary.

Cowbird (*Molothrus*). A small group of parasitic birds, closely allied to the blackbirds and orioles, found only in the New World. Like many cuckoos of the Old World, cowbirds are notorious for the practice of laying their eggs in the nests of other birds and leaving them to be hatched and the young to be nourished exclusively by the foster parents.

The American cowbird (*M. ater*), about 7 inches long, glossy black, with head, neck, and chest uniform brown, ranges nearly throughout temperate North America. It is also called cow blackbird, cow bunting, and buffalo bird, from its habit of closely following cattle in pastures or of alighting upon their backs in search of insects. Major Bendire gives a list of more than 90 different birds in whose nests the cowbird has been known to deposit its eggs. Among these are thrushes, woodpeckers, towhees, flycatchers, pewees, orioles, vireos, sparrows, wrens, and warblers.

Crab. The crabs form a large group (*Brachyura*) of invertebrate animals belonging to the class *Crustacea*. There are more than 1000 species, chiefly marine, which vary exceedingly in size, color, and modes of living.

In the main, crabs do not differ essentially in structure from the lobster and the crawfish. The body, however, is usually broader than long, with the very short abdomen and tail hidden under the cephalothorax. The sense of sight is peculiarly acute. The mouth is furnished with strong jaws, in addition to which the stomach has internal projections, or teeth, for grinding. Crabs furnish food for many valuable fishes, serve as useful scavengers, and some are much prized as human food. Like the crawfishes and lobsters, crabs molt or throw off periodically their entire calcareous covering. They are then soft and helpless. In this condition, they are the "soft-shelled" crabs of the markets.

In the United States the blue crab (*Callinectes hastatus*) is the principal food species, though the shore crab (*Cancer irroratus*) of the Atlantic coast and the rock crab (*C. magister*) of the Pacific coast are edible. Crabs range in size from less than an inch in width to the giant crab (*Macrochira kæmpferi*), which sometimes measures 18 feet across the outspread legs. See *Lobster*, *Shrimp*.

Crane (*Grus*). The largest of the wading birds, resembling the heron in appearance but the rails in structure. Cranes have long legs, a long neck, a straight, sharp-pointed bill, and the short hind toe is elevated above the others. A striking peculiarity is the enormous development of the windpipe within the keel of the breastbone, where it is coiled and twisted, sometimes for a length of more than two feet, before emerging into the neck.

Cranes frequent marshes and open plains throughout most temperate regions, migrating southward in winter and returning north in the spring. They fly in large flocks, usually at night, often uttering a trumpet-like cry which can be heard for two miles. All are strictly terrestrial, never perching upon trees, and build their nests on the ground, usually in swamps, laying 2 brownish, dark-spotted eggs. Cranes are omnivorous, feeding upon small animals, insects, roots, and seeds. When sleeping, they stand upon one leg with the other drawn up under the body, and the head and neck are tucked among the feathers of the back. There are about 19 species, nearly all natives of the Old World.

The whooping crane (*G. americana*) is a magnificent bird, standing over 4 feet high, with a wing spread of over 8 feet. Excepting the dark outer wing feathers, the plumage is white throughout. While formerly ranging from Saskatchewan to central Mexico, it has become exceedingly rare. The sandhill crane (*G. mexicana*) is found from the Mississippi valley and Manitoba westward to the Pacific coast, and eastward along the Gulf coast to Florida. It is about 4 feet long and slate-gray or brownish gray in color. It prefers dry prairies, plowed fields, and sandy hills rather than wet situations.

Crawfish (*Astacus* and *Cambarus*). A fresh-water crustacean, called also crayfish, much used for food in Europe and to some extent in the larger American cities. In appearance and structure it much resembles a small lobster.

The body of the crawfish is composed of a front part, the cephalothorax, in which the head and chest are united, and a posterior part consisting of the abdomen and the tail. The cephalothorax, which is incased in a hard shell, called the carapace, has three groups of appendages: first, a group of three pairs of mouth parts, belonging to the head; second, a group of three pairs of foot jaws, belonging to the thorax; and third, a group of five pairs of walking legs. The gills are attached to the bases of the walking legs. The stomach is provided with internal toothlike projections or teeth which serve in grinding the food. Like lobsters and crabs, crawfishes molt or cast off their outer shells periodically, keeping out of sight until the new shell has become hard enough to protect the body.

Crawfishes frequent fresh-water lakes, ponds, rivers, and small streams in most parts of the United States. Some kinds live in banks and moist meadows, burrowing down to the water. They feed on water insects, worms, small frogs and fish, and various plants and roots. See *Lobster*.

Crocodile (*Crocodilus*). The true crocodiles have a somewhat triangular, more or less pointed head, intermediate between the slender-snouted gavials and the broad-snouted alligators. They differ from alligators in that the fourth tooth of the lower jaw fits into a notch in the upper jaw so that it can be seen when the mouth is closed.

Crocodiles lay from 20 to 50 or more eggs, covered with a hard, white shell and about equal in size to those of a goose. They are deposited in some depression, covered with sand, and left to hatch by the warmth of the sun.

The American crocodile (*C. americanus*), first discovered in the United States by W. T. Hornaday in 1876, has a more slender muzzle than most crocodiles. It attains a length of 14 feet and is found in southern Florida, the West Indies, Mexico, and southward to Ecuador. While much more agile and vicious than the alligator, it exhibits no hostility to man.

The Egyptian crocodile (*C. niloticus*), mentioned by Herodotus and described by Aristotle, is plentiful in African rivers. It was held sacred by the ancient Egyptians, who built temples in its honor and placed the bodies of thousands of embalmed crocodiles in their tombs. It attains a length of 20 feet, and is sometimes so bold as to attack people in canoes or boats. See *Alligator*, *Cayman*, *Gavial*.

Crow (*Corvus*). A large perching bird, noted for its intelligence and considered by many scientists as standing at the head of the entire avian class.

The crow family (*Corvidæ*), which includes the common crow, the raven, the rook, the magpie, the jackdaw, and the jays, embraces about 200 species, which are widely found throughout the world, except in New Zealand. Of these, about 25 occur in North America. All inhabit wooded regions, usually residing permanently wherever nesting, and are omnivorous feeders, eating seeds, fruits, insects, small mammals, also birds and their eggs and nestlings.

The common crow (*C. americanus*) of North America, about 19 inches long, is remarkable for its gregarious and predatory habits. Crows pair in March. The nest is built of sticks and is usually placed in a low tree, preferably an evergreen, about 20 feet from the ground. The eggs, usually from 4 to 6 in number, are pale green, clouded and spotted with purplish and brownish markings. Although they feed chiefly on worms and the larvæ of insects, crows also eat grain and seeds, whence they have sometimes been regarded as injurious to the farmer; but they amply repay him for what they take, by destroying immense numbers of grasshoppers, weevils, cutworms, and other noxious insects.

The smaller fish crow (*C. ossifragus*), 16 inches long, with somewhat brighter plumage, frequents the coasts and rivers of the southern United States, ranging northward to Massachusetts. While fond of shellfish and crabs, it feeds also on berries and grain, and is especially destructive to small birds and to their eggs and young. See *Jackdaw*, *Magpie*, *Raven*, *Rook*.

Crustaceans (*Crustacea*). A large class of gill-bearing, aquatic arthropods, containing the lobsters, crabs, crawfish, prawns, shrimps, water fleas, and barnacles. They derive their name from the hard armor, or outer skeleton, in which the body of most of them is incased, which serves not only for protection but also for the attachment of the muscles. Crustaceans differ from insects and from most other arthropods in having gills and two pairs of antennæ or feelers.

Some 16,000 species of crustaceans are known, the vast majority of which live in the sea, though some inhabit fresh waters and a few dwell on land. They are of great importance in the economy of the ocean, as they constitute the chief food of many valuable food fishes and are the natural scavengers of the sea. See *Barnacle*, *Crab*, *Lobster*, *Shrimp*, *Water Flea*.

Cuckoo. The cuckoos constitute a large family of birds (*Cuculidæ*), numbering about 175 species, mostly natives of warm regions, 35 of which are found in the New World. They are of medium size, with a compressed, somewhat arched beak, and feet with two toes in front and two behind. Many cuckoos are birds of shams and pretenses, imitating the habits, plumage, or voices of other birds and seeking to be mistaken for them. In addition, most cuckoos are parasitic, never building nests of their own, but placing their eggs in the nests of other birds and leaving them to be hatched and the young to be fed by the proper owners of the nests.

In North America there are two common species, the yellow-billed cuckoo (*Coccyzus americanus*), found across the continent, and the black-billed cuckoo (*C. erythrophthalmus*), found east of the

Rocky mountains. Both are slender, dovelike, brownish gray birds, about a foot long. Unlike most cuckoos, they usually build their own nests and rear their own young. In the Middle West and the South they are called "rain crows," from the belief that their peculiar notes predict rain.

Cuttlefish (*Sepia officinalis*). A small cephalopod mollusk, about 8 inches long, closely related to the squid and the octopus, found in Old World waters. The limy plate or shell protecting its back is the cuttlefish bone used to feed canary birds. Like the squid, it has an ink sac from which, when pursued, it discharges a blackish fluid, beclouding the water and often enabling it to escape. Since ancient times this fluid has been used in making ink, yielding the sepia used by artists and some kinds of india ink. Dried cuttlefish form an article of food in southern Europe and Asia. See *Octopus*, *Squid*.

Deer. A large group of hoofed mammals of the family *Cervidæ*. Deer are animals of graceful form, combining much compactness and strength with slenderness of limb and fleetness. They have a long neck, a small head, which they carry high, large ears, and large full eyes. Below each eye, in most species, there is a sac or fold of the skin called the tearpit, the use of which is not well known. Deer have no cutting teeth in the upper jaw; the males usually have two short canines in the upper jaw but neither sex has any in the lower jaw. They are distinguished from all other ruminants by their solid branching horns or antlers, which, with few exceptions, are possessed by the male only. The horns fall off annually, and are renewed with increase of size and number of branches, according to the kind, until the animal has reached mature age. In most English-speaking countries, the male deer is commonly called a buck, the female deer, a doe, and the young of either sex, a fawn.

There are more than 50 known species of deer, found in almost all parts of the globe except Australia and South Africa. They range in size from the diminutive pudu of Chile, about the size of a hare, to the so-called American elk or wapiti, as tall as a horse, and to the moose which is still larger. Some of them live amidst the snows of very northerly regions and some in tropical forests. The greater number inhabit the warmer temperate countries and are found chiefly in wide plains and hills of moderate height. The flesh (venison) of most kinds of deer is highly esteemed for the table. Deer have long been regarded as among the noblest objects of the chase. Only one species, the reindeer, can be said to have been fully domesticated and reduced to the service of man.

The most common American species, the white-tailed deer (*Odocoileus virginianus*), called also Virginia deer, with the tail snow-white underneath, was formerly abundant nearly throughout the eastern United States and Canada. In summer its coat is rusty brown above, in autumn, gray-brown, and in winter, dark brown. The under parts are white. While shy and timid, it is strongly attached to its haunts, and will remain around them even when intruded upon by populous settlements. On this account it has been largely exterminated by hunting, except where protected by law. During the day this deer retreats to swamps or thickets, coming out at night for food and drink. It is fond of the water and is an excellent swimmer. In summer it often feeds on water lilies and other aquatic plants, as well as swamp grasses and various tender shrubs. In winter it eats buds, young branches of trees, various berries, leaves, mosses, lichens, and sometimes nuts and acorns, which it paws out of the snow. A smaller form, known as the Florida deer, occurs in the southeastern United States.

The somewhat larger mule deer (*O. hemionus*), so-called from its large ears, is known also as black-tail. It is brownish gray above and whitish gray beneath, with a pale reddish tail tipped with black. It occurs in the Rocky Mountain region from Canada to Mexico. The mule deer prefers a rough, broken country, with small groves of trees. It grazes when grass is in season, browses on tender buds and branches, and also eats various fruits.

The black-tailed deer (*O. columbianus*), the most beautiful American species, is found on the Pacific coast from the Columbia river to Alaska. It is smaller and more graceful than the mule deer, and is brighter colored than the Virginia deer. Its summer coat is reddish brown above and white beneath. In winter its coat becomes grayish. The outer surface of the tail is black above and white below. Its habits are similar to the other deer, roving chiefly at night, and feeding largely upon twigs of wintergreen, huckleberry, and various other shrubs.

The best-known European species are the graceful fallow deer (*Cervus dama*), often kept in herds in parks for ornament, and the large red deer or stag (*C. elaphus*), once abundant in forested mountains and formerly the object of the favorite sport of stag hunting. The full-grown male stag is called a hart and the female a hind. A very handsome Old World species is the spotted axis deer (*C. axis*) of the East Indies. The large, handsome American deer, called wapiti, and popularly, though incorrectly, styled "elk," is closely related to the stag of Europe. See *Musk Deer*, *Wapiti*.

Dodo (*Didus ineptus*). A clumsy, defenseless bird, about the size of a swan, found living on Mauritius when the island was discovered, near the beginning of the 16th century, by the Portuguese. It had a very stout, hooked beak, short, stocky legs, and was covered with downy feathers. Its wings were small and quite incapable of flight. Such a creature could survive only in isolation. Consequently, it speedily succumbed under the changed conditions introduced by the coming of man. Unable to cope either with his weapons or with his domesticated animals, this helpless bird was soon exterminated (1651) and no entire specimens are anywhere preserved. The dodo is known to science mainly from the study of its bones and from some quaint pictures left by Dutch artists.

Dog. The dog family (*Canidæ*) is an important group of carnivores, intermediate between the hyenas and the bears. It includes the various kinds of dogs, wolves, jackals, and foxes. There are about 50 species, with living representatives in every part of the world except Madagascar.

The domestic dog (*Canis familiaris*) was a member of the family circle long before the dawn of recorded history, having been used by Neolithic man. The oldest human monuments in the valleys of the Euphrates, the Indus, and the Nile show that many important breeds of dogs were then already common among the ancient peoples. The parent wild species, from which the many varieties of domestic dogs have sprung, are unknown and apparently indeterminable. Modern scientists, however, believe that they have been derived from numerous species of wolves and jackals, intermingled, diffused, and modified through centuries of breeding.

Ages of domestication have produced adaptations to climate, varying from the hairless dogs of the tropics to woolly Eskimo breeds possessing the heaviest fur of any known animal. In size, dogs vary from tiny lap dogs no larger than kittens to Great Danes which stand 3 feet high at the shoulder. There are some 200 recognized varieties or breeds of dogs. These present far greater differences in size, structure, and appearance than all the wild members of the dog family combined. Most domestic breeds are believed to have arisen from the intercrossing of a few leading types, such as mastiffs, wolflike dogs, greyhounds, spaniels, hounds, and terriers.

The dog is at once the most intelligent, affectionate, and loyal of the domestic animals. It is the devoted companion of man throughout a wider range of climatic conditions than any other animal, greatly surpassing in this regard the cat, the donkey, and the horse. Dogs are employed as draft animals in various countries, and share, with the reindeer, the burden of transportation in arctic regions. Trained sledge dogs made it possible for Peary to cross the frozen ocean to the north pole and for Amundsen to ascend the high antarctic plateaus to the south pole. See *Fox, Jackal, Wolf.*

Dogfish (*Squalus acanthias*). A small, slate-colored shark, 3 feet long, with a strong spine in the dorsal fin. It inhabits both shores of the North Atlantic, southward to Cuba. The flesh is used for food, the liver yields oil, and the very rough skin is dried and used, like sandpaper, for polishing wood. Sometimes as many as 20,000 dogfish have been taken in a single haul of the net.

Dolphin (*Delphinidæ*). The dolphins are marine, fishlike mammals, closely related to the whales, which they somewhat resemble in form, but much smaller and differing from them in usually having teeth in both jaws. The dolphin family contains about 60 species, widely distributed in all seas, and includes the dolphins, the porpoises, the grampuses, the beluga, or white whale, the so-called black fish, and the terrible orca, or killer whale. The names "dolphin" and "porpoise" are frequently used interchangeably, but the true dolphins have the snout prolonged into a slender beak, while the snout of the porpoise is blunt.

The common dolphin (*Delphinus delphis*), 6 to 10 feet in length, with a beak half a foot long, blackish above and satiny white below, is frequent in European but rare in American waters. This is the dolphin of the ancients, sacred to Apollo whose most famous oracle at Delphi bore its name. Dolphins are very active and voracious, feeding chiefly on squids and other small marine animals. They live in herds, which often gather about ships and delight the voyagers with their graceful gambols. Their flesh is palatable and was formerly very highly esteemed.

Domestic Animals. The taming of useful animals ranks, with the cultivation of plants, the making of tools, and the use of fire, among the great achievements of early man. In case of the most important animals, domestication is remotely ancient. Practically all animals of the first rank appear to have been in age-long use when recorded history began, including the dog, ox, humped cattle, sheep, goat, ass, horse, camel, elephant, cat, pigeon, goose, and honeybee. The chicken, peacock, rabbit, and guinea fowl had reached Europe before the beginning of the Christian era. No animal of prime economic importance has been brought into domestication during the last 2000 years.

Of the many thousands of wild species, only about 40 animals are now considered as domesticated, and in case of some of these domestication is only partial. The parent wild species of the camel, sheep, and humped cattle appear to have become extinct during prehistoric times, and the ancestry of the horse and the dog cannot with certainty be assigned to animals now living.

The Old World has contributed about seven-eighths of all domesticated animals, including every species of high economic rank. Of these, Asia is the native home of by far the greater number,—including the humped ox, water buffalo, banteng, gaur, gayal, yak, elephant, Bactrian camel, horse, goat, cheetah, chicken, peacock, cormorant, carp, goldfish, honeybee, and silkworm. The parent wild species of the pig, reindeer, pigeon, duck, and goose are of European as well as of Asian distribution, but their domestication is believed to have first taken place in Asia. Africa has contributed the ass, cat, ostrich, parrot, canary, and possibly the one-humped camel. In the New World, South America has furnished the llama, alpaca, and guinea pig, while North America has contributed only the turkey. Australia and the adjacent islands as yet have added none to the list.

Donkey (*Equus asinus*). The common ass, donkey, or burro, widely used throughout the world as a beast of burden, is a domesticated form of the African wild ass (*E. africanus*), native of Ethiopia, Nubia, and Somaliland.

The donkey was probably first domesticated in the valley of the Nile, where it was known and used for centuries in advance of the horse. It found its way into ancient Greece through Asia Minor, but is mentioned much less frequently than the mule by Homer and other early writers. In Bible times it was the custom of great personages to ride upon white asses, and a preference for breeds of this color still persists in some parts of the Orient.

With the westward spread of vine and olive culture, the ass was introduced into Italy, Spain, and France. In England it was known as early as the time of Ethelred and was re-established during the reign of Elizabeth. It was brought to South America and Mexico by the Spanish during the period of exploration and conquest. The numerous breeds vary greatly in size from pygmy West Indian donkeys, less than two feet high, to large Spanish asses, over five feet high.

While not adapted to cool moist climates, such as that of the eastern United States, asses are invaluable as baggage animals in warm, arid, and mountainous regions. They are extensively employed for transportation in southern France, Spain, Italy, Mexico, and Andean South America. The burro is a small breed much used by miners and prospectors in the western United States. See *Ass.*

Dragonflies (*Odonata*). A group of long-winged, carnivorous insects, also known as "darning needles" and "snake feeders," of which some 250 species are known to occur in North America. All are aquatic in their immature stages, and are eaten extensively by fishes. The adult insects fly by day over ponds and along streams, and feed upon mosquitoes, midges, and other insects which they capture in flight. Many dragonflies are large insects, and some are of brilliant coloration. The slender, low-flying, mostly blue-banded forms that flit about among the sedges by the waterside are often called damselflies.

Duck. The duck family (*Anatidæ*) belongs to a large group of web-footed, swimming birds which includes, besides the true ducks, the mergansers, the geese, and the swans, the whole constituting the important natural order *Anseres*. The true ducks differ from the mergansers in having a broad and flat bill; they differ from the geese and swans in having shorter necks, and, further, the male and female of the true ducks are unlike in color. Ducks are strong, swift fliers, and are noted for their powers of diving and swimming under water. They live largely on animal food, such as insects, snails, frogs, and small fish, though some prefer aquatic plants, such as water celery. Many species are highly prized for food and are much hunted as game birds.

There are two divisions of the true ducks, the river ducks (*Anatinæ*) and the sea ducks (*Fuligulinæ*). The sea ducks have a lobe or web on the hind toe; this is lacking in the river ducks. The river ducks frequent sluggish streams, ponds, lakes, and even ocean shores. They usually feed at night and obtain their food by probing on the bottom in shallow water. The sea ducks inhabit seas, bays, lakes, and inland rivers. They feed by day, securing their food by diving, sometimes descending 150 feet, and spend the night on shore.

There are about 70 species of river ducks, including the mallard, teal, pintail, widgeon, shoveler, gadwall, baldpate, and wood duck. The sea ducks comprise more than 50 species, among which are the canvasback, redhead, scaup, scoter, and eider. Most ducks breed far northward, often within the

Arctic circle, and winter in warm or tropical regions. In the greater part of the United States they are seen only during their migrations.

The various breeds of the domestic duck are believed to have been originated from the mallard (*Anas boschas*), found wild throughout Asia, Europe, and North America. In China the rearing of ducks is a very important industry. Since the introduction of the Peking duck, about 1870, duck raising has been extensively developed in various parts of the United States.

Dugong (*Halicore dugong*). A fish-shaped, aquatic mammal, of the order *Sirenia*, found along the shores of the Indian Ocean. It is from 8 to 12 feet long, with a rounded body, thickest in the middle and tapering toward the tail, which ends in a flattened fin or flukes. The front limbs, which are paddle-like, have no trace of nails or of division into fingers. There are no hind limbs. The upper lip is very fleshy and thick, and both lips are provided with a horny edge, which enables the animal to tear off seaweeds and other marine vegetation growing upon the bottoms of shallow seas in which it feeds. The dugong sometimes enters wide estuaries, but it never ascends rivers or appears on land.

It is supposed by some that the habit of the dugong in suckling its single young, clasped by one flipper, while it paddles with the other, keeping the heads of both out of the water, gave rise to the fable of the mermaid. See *Manatee*.

Eagle. A large bird of prey belonging to the same family as the hawks, kites, and falcons, often called the king of birds. From ancient times the eagle has been universally regarded as the symbol of might and courage.

There are more than 40 species, found in all parts of the globe. Eagles have a strong bill, much arched at the hooked tip, and the toes are armed with sharp, curved claws. The females are larger than the males. Most eagles kill their own prey but nearly all will eat animals found dead. They build huge nests of sticks, usually on inaccessible cliffs or in tall trees, and lay 2 or 3 eggs. They have great powers of flight, soar at immense heights, and possess remarkable keenness of vision.

The bald eagle or white-headed eagle (*Haliœtus leucocephalus*), the national emblem of the United States, is a large, handsome sea eagle, found nearly throughout North America. It is about 3½ feet long with a wing spread exceeding 7 feet. The head, neck, and tail of adult birds are pure white. The bald eagle lives chiefly on fish which it captures alive, finds thrown up on shores, or secures by robbing fish hawks.

The golden eagle (*Aquila chrysaetus*), a magnificent bird inhabiting mountain regions, occurs throughout Europe, northern Asia, and most of North America, though rare east of the Mississippi. It is similar in size to the bald eagle, but with dark brown plumage, and the feet are feathered to the toes. It preys chiefly upon small mammals and birds, including rabbits, lambs, and grouse.

Earthworms. Burrowing annelid worms of the order *Oligochœta*, commonly called angleworms. Numerous species are found in all parts of the world except frozen regions, dry sandy soils, and certain parts of the prairies of North America. They have cylindrical bodies, tapering slightly at each end, and are commonly flesh-red in color, though varying to dull pink and muddy brown. In length they usually range from a few inches to a foot, though several Australian and South African forms are 5 feet long.

In their habits the different kinds of earthworms are very similar. All burrow in damp earth, the more common kinds usually to a depth of about two feet. They come to the surface only to avoid drowning when their burrows are flooded, or at night to throw their castings or sometimes to obtain food. In the morning after a night of heavy rain, great numbers of earthworms are frequently seen on sidewalks and other hard surfaces. This circumstance often gives rise to the erroneous report that they "rained down." The fact is that earthworms, upon emerging from their flooded burrows, crawl about very actively in their endeavor to escape from the water, often climbing up comparatively smooth surfaces. The firm texture of a sidewalk or roadway prevents them from burrowing out of sight when daylight returns, hence they remain exposed to view.

Earthworms feed exclusively upon vegetable matter. For the most part, they swallow soil containing it, digest out the nutritive elements, and reject the remainder as castings from the mouths of their burrows. During the night they sometimes partially leave their burrows to feed upon the stalks of leaves and other plant parts with which, in cold weather, they close their tunnel openings.

As they exist in countless millions, earthworms play an important part in the formation and improvement of soil. They fertilize it with their castings, and keep it stirred up and exposed to the air by incessant tunneling. It is estimated that in some districts earthworms deposit each year a layer of castings one-fifth of an inch in thickness over the entire surface of the land.

Earthworms form the prey of many animals; they comprise the chief food of moles and shrews, and are extensively eaten by numerous birds. As earthworms sometimes go into the water and as immense numbers are borne by floods into streams and ponds, they provide food for many fishes, and are the most popular bait for stillfishing.

Echidna (*ē-kĭd'nȧ*). An egg-laying mammal native to Australian regions, called also porcupine anteater. The five-toed echidna (*Echidna aculeata*), found in Australia, New Guinea, and Tasmania, is 14 to 20 inches long, with a powerful body beset with stiff spines, short legs with strongly clawed feet, and a birdlike head and beak. The forefeet are adapted for digging, and the creature burrows with remarkable rapidity. It lives in dry woodlands, coming forth from its burrow at night, in search of its food, chiefly ants and termites, which it catches with its glutinous tongue. The much larger three-toed echidna (*Zaglossus buijni*), found only in New Guinea, is about 2 feet in length, with a long, somewhat curved snout. See *Monotremata, Platypus*.

Echinoderms (*ē-kī'nō-dûrmz*) (*Echinodermata*). A branch of the animal kingdom, consisting of marine invertebrate animals in which the body, while varying greatly in form, is built on the radiate plan, usually with five diverging parts as in the starfish. All have a tough outer skin or a sort of shell composed of many small plates. They have a well-developed digestive system and organs of locomotion. The latter consist of tubular ambulacral feet, having sucking disks enabling the animal to cling to rocks or to move about on the sea bottom. Echinoderms are carnivorous, eating crustaceans, mollusks, and other marine animals.

There are about 4000 species of echinoderms, divided into 5 classes: the Starfishes, *Asteroidea*; the Brittle Stars, *Ophiuroidea*; the Sea Urchins, *Echinoidea*; the Sea Cucumbers, *Holothuroidea*; and the Sea Lilies or Feather Stars, *Crinoidea*. See *Starfish*.

Edentata (*ē'dĕn-tā'tȧ*) or **Bruta.** An order of mammals, characterized by the absence of incisors or front teeth, and, in a few instances, by the absence of all teeth. It includes the sloths, the anteaters, the armadillos, the pangolins, and the aard-varks. There are about 40 species, mostly natives of South America and Africa. See *Anteater, Armadillo, Pangolin, Sloth*.

Eel (*Anguilla chrysops*). A long-bodied, serpent-shaped fish without ventral fins. It is abundant along the Atlantic coast from Newfoundland to Central America and in all streams and lakes con-

By permission N. Y. Zoological Society; photos by E. R. Sanborn.

BEARS, WOLVES, AND FOXES

1 Alaskan Brown Bear. 2 Bald-faced Grizzly Bear. 3 Polar Bear. 4 Black Bear. 5 Timber Wolf. 6 Prairie Wolf or Coyote. 7 Arctic Fox. 8 Red Fox.

By permission N. Y. Zoological Society; photos by E. R. Sanborn.

DEER

1 American Elk or Wapiti. 2 Red Deer or Stag. 3 Caribou. 4 Fallow Deer. 5 Mule Deer. 6 Virginia Deer. 7 Axis Deer. 8 Florida Deer.

nected with it. In color it is olive brown above and paler below. Its skin is smooth and slippery.

Eels breed in a region of the Atlantic Ocean south of Bermuda. The young are exceedingly numerous, often 10 million eggs being produced by one female. They are transparent for about a year, by which time they reach the coast and assume a more cylindrical, opaque form like the adult, about 2½ inches long. The males remain in the ocean, but the females swim into streams and fresh-water lakes, attaining an average length of 25 to 40 inches in some five to twenty years. They eat any kind of animal food voraciously, especially dead fish, and will attack any living animal, including man. The females eventually, ceasing to eat, return to the sea, where they proceed with the males to the breeding grounds in mid-Ocean. After breeding, they die.

The eel is an excellent food fish, and great quantities are taken annually for the markets.

The European eel (*Anguilla anguilla*) breeds in the same general region south of Bermuda. The young remain transparent three years, corresponding to its longer journey to the European coasts.

Eider (*Somateria*). A large sea duck, native chiefly of arctic regions. It is famous for its fine, elastic, gray down, the valuable eider down of commerce, used in making bedcovers and in trimming ladies' dresses. There are several species, all handsome birds, with strongly marked colors.

The European eider (*S. molissima*) breeds on rocky shores from Spitsbergen to the Faroe islands. As soon as the eggs are laid the female plucks the soft down from her breast with which to hide them and protect them during her absences from the nest. About a sixth of a pound of down is said to be obtained yearly from each nest. In Norway and Iceland many eider folds are kept in which the birds nest and become partially domesticated.

The Greenland eider (*S. molissima borealis*), very similar to the European eider, breeds from Labrador northward, and winters southward to Maine. Its down is gathered in Greenland and in Iceland. Except at nesting time, eiders live in the open sea. They obtain their food, which consists chiefly of mollusks and crustaceans, by diving.

Eland (*Oreas canna*). An oxlike antelope, with twisted horns, native of South Africa, sometimes called the "Cape elk." It is the largest of the antelopes and forms a connecting link between them and the oxen. Its body resembles that of an ox and its head that of a deer. The eland stands 5 to 6 feet high at the withers, and weighs from 800 to 1500 pounds. While formerly exceedingly abundant, living in large herds throughout grassy plains of southern Africa, it is now rare from excessive hunting, except in the interior. The natives cure its excellent flesh by salting, make candles from the fat, and leather from the hide. See *Antelope*.

Electric Eel (*Electrophorus electricus*). A large, eel-like fish, 6 feet long, closely allied to the carp and the sucker, inhabiting the rivers of Brazil and Guiana. It is the most powerful of all electric fishes. The electric organs situated on its tail are capable of producing a shock sufficient to kill other fishes and small mammals. See *Torpedo*.

Elephant (*Elephas*). The largest existing land animal. Elephants are the only living representatives of the *Proboscidea*, or mammals with a proboscis or trunk. They are exclusively confined to the tropical regions of the Old World, in the forests of which they live in herds.

Only two living species are known, the Asiatic elephant and the African elephant. In both species the two upper incisors, or front teeth, are enormously developed, forming long tusks. The nose is prolonged into a cylindrical trunk, movable in every direction, highly sensitive, and terminating in a finger-like, prehensile lobe. This trunk is the elephant's weapon of offense and defense, and by means of it all food is gathered and conveyed to the mouth. The limbs, which are of colossal thickness and strength, are remarkably straight and column-like. The feet are furnished with five toes; the sole of the foot is formed of a thick pad of integument.

The Indian elephant (*E. indicus*), the species which is now caught and domesticated, averages from about 8 to 10 feet in height, and weighs from 2 to 3 tons. As it does not readily breed in captivity, the demand for it is supplied almost entirely by the capture of adult wild individuals. The taming and the use of elephants date back to prehistoric times in India. The Indian elephant is distinguished by its concave forehead and its comparatively small ears.

The somewhat larger African elephant (*E. africanus*), often exceeding 10 feet in height, has a strongly convex forehead and great flapping ears. It is hunted chiefly for its ivory, a pursuit which threatens the complete extinction of these fine animals. While it is presumed that the African elephant was the species domesticated by the Carthaginians and used by Hannibal in his wars against the Romans, none of the Negro peoples seem to have tamed it.

The elephants are vegetable feeders, living almost entirely on the foliage of shrubs and trees, which they strip off by means of the prehensile trunk. As the tusks prevent the animal from drinking in the ordinary manner, the water is sucked up by the trunk, which is then inserted in the mouth, into which it empties its contents. Many species of fossil elephants are known, the most familiar of which are the mastodon and the mammoth. See *Mammoth, Mastodon*.

Emu (*Dromæus*). Next to the ostrich, the largest of living birds. There are only two surviving species, both found in Australia, where, like the kangaroos, they once formed a characteristic part of the landscape. While closely allied to the ostrich, they differ in having three toes on each foot, the neck and body are completely covered with hairlike feathers, and there are no ornamental wing or tail plumes. The common emu (*D. novæ-hollandiæ*), of eastern Australia, which stands more than 5 feet high, has light brown plumage mottled with gray. The more slender spotted emu (*D. irroratus*), of western Australia, has feathers barred with white and gray.

Emus go about in small parties, preferring open or sparsely wooded country. They subsist chiefly upon fruits, seeds, roots, and herbage. The nest is a mere hollow in the earth or a low platform of grass and bark. The eggs, about 9 in number and about 5 inches in length, are of a beautiful green color. The male emu takes full charge of hatching the eggs and rearing the young. Emus are readily domesticated and make interesting pets. Their flesh and eggs are palatable. See *Cassowary, Ostrich, Rhea*.

English Sparrow (*Passer domesticus*). A name popularly given in America to the common house sparrow, native of Europe but now introduced and naturalized in many other regions where it usually becomes a pest, notorious for its fecundity, voracity, and destructiveness. Since ancient times it has fearlessly associated with man, living in towns and cities more than in the country and rarely visiting or nesting in wild regions.

The English sparrow was first introduced into the United States from England, at Brooklyn, N. Y., by Nicholas Pike in 1850. During the ensuing 20 years it was brought to various other American cities, mainly with the view of freeing shade trees of destructive caterpillars. The house sparrow, however, is a grain-eating rather than an insect-eating bird. In some localities it destroys much grain and fruit; in other places it drives away bluebirds, wrens, swallows, and other native insect-eating birds.

Ermine (*Putorius*). Various species of weasel, found in the northern parts of Europe, Asia, and North America, whose fur, except the tip of the tail, turns white in winter. The European ermine (*P. erminea*) is also known as the greater weasel or stoat. In the northern United States and Canada, the common or New York weasel (*P. noveboracensis*), the short-tailed weasel (*P. cicognani*), and the Arctic coast weasel (*P. rixosus*) yield ermine fur during the winter season. White ermine fur is very valuable. It has long been regarded as emblematic of royalty and authority and is extensively used in ornamenting the official robes of kings, nobles, and judges. See *Weasel.*

Finch. The popular name of various small seed-eating birds belonging to the family *Fringillidæ*, some of which possess remarkable powers of song. By many authorities the name finch is applied to this entire group, which constitutes the most numerous family of birds, comprising more than 1000 species. They are found throughout the world except in Australia, over 200 occurring in the United States and Canada. The birds known as finches, buntings, sparrows, grosbeaks, linnets, redpolls, snowbirds, and also the canary, belong to this family. They are closely related to the tanagers, weaver birds, and blackbirds, and, by some ornithologists, are ranked as standing at the head of the entire avian class. See *Canary, Chewink, Goldfinch, Grosbeak, Snowbird, Sparrow.*

Firefly. A nocturnal beetle, called also lightning bug, belonging to the family *Lampyridæ*, found chiefly in the warmer parts of the United States and southern Europe. Fireflies have long, soft bodies, with leathery wing covers, and possess a light-giving organ which produces flashes of greenish white light. Not only are the adult beetles luminous, but in some kinds the pupæ, the larvæ, and even the eggs, emit light. The wingless, somewhat wormlike females of certain species are known as "glowworms."

In Paraguay there is a remarkable form, called the railway beetle, which flashes a red light at the ends of the body and a green light along the sides. In tropical America several species of elater beetles or click beetles (*Pyrophorus*) are styled fireflies. Of these, the best-known is the Cucuyo (*P. noctilucus*), about 2 inches long, with two eyelike spots on the thorax which emit a steady light. The ladies of Cuba and Mexico place these beetles in little lace nets which they fasten as ornaments upon their dresses and hair.

Fishes (*Pisces*). The lowest of the five large classes of vertebrates. A typical fish is cold-blooded, breathes by means of gills throughout life, lays eggs for the production of its young, and lives entirely in the water. It has a bony skeleton which supports an elongated, wedge-shaped body, narrowest at the tail, thin at the sides, and covered with overlapping scales. It has highly developed fins for steering, balancing, and propulsion, eyes which are movable only in a vertical plane, and a swim bladder filled with air. The tail is the chief organ of progression. The swim bladder, it is believed, serves as a balancing organ, enabling the fish to adjust itself constantly to the water pressure and to rise or descend with ease.

There are, however, among fishes, numerous variations from the type. For example, the lungfish has limblike fins and practical, air-breathing lungs; certain sharks and a few other fishes bring forth their young alive; the sturgeon has a cartilaginous skeleton; the catfish has no scales; the climbing perch can climb trees, and the flying fish can rise out of the water for gliding flight.

Fishes were the first true vertebrates to appear in geologic history, and the living forms abound in enormous variety and numbers in oceans, lakes, rivers, and smaller waters throughout the world. The number of existing species at present known is estimated at about 13,000. A large number of these are of great economic value as food fishes. The skin of certain species yields shagreen, and the swim bladder of others yields isinglass.

Fishes are grouped in four subclasses: *Dipnoi*, the lungfishes; *Teleostomi*, the bony fishes; *Holocephali*, the chimæras; and *Elasmobranchii*, the sharks and rays.

Flamingo (*Phœnicopterus*). A genus of large, web-footed, wading birds. They are intermediate between the storks and the ducks, with very long legs and necks, gooselike bodies, webbed feet, and large, peculiarly shaped bills curved downward near the middle. There are about 8 species, all more or less rose-red in color when in full plumage. These inhabit the warmer regions of the world. Flamingos feed upon small mollusks, crustaceans, fishes, worms, insects, and seeds, which they fish up from the water and mud. They breed in companies, sometimes of immense numbers, in mud flats or salt marshes, such as the Marasmus of Spain and the Great Atacama of South America. They raise the mud into a small hillock, made slightly concave at the top, so as to form a rude nest. In this hollow, the female lays 2 eggs and hatches them by sitting on the nest with her legs doubled up beside her.

The North American flamingo (*P. ruber*), deep red in color, stands about 4½ feet high. While formerly common in the southern United States, it is now very rare north of the West Indies and Central America. Small colonies still persist in the Bahama islands. The European flamingo (*P. antiquorum*), of southern Europe, northern Africa, and the warmer parts of Asia, is rose-white in color, with scarlet wing coverts. It was well known to the ancients, being highly esteemed as food by the Romans, who considered its fatty tongue a rare delicacy.

Flea (*Pulex*). A small insect of the order *Siphonaptera*, characterized by its compressed body and by the absence of true wings. The mouth parts are adapted for biting and sucking, the eyes or ocelli are single, and the antennæ are threadlike. The flea is remarkable for its agility, leaping to a surprising distance. About 100 species of fleas are known, some 30 of which occur in North America. The common flea of the Old World (*P. irritans*), which attacks man, poultry, pigeons, and swallows, is rarely seen in America. The so-called house flea of the United States is the cat and dog flea (*P. serraticeps*). The rat flea is regarded as the chief carrier of bubonic plague.

Flies (*Diptera*). A numerous order of insects characterized by usually having only two wings. In place of the hind pair possessed by most insects are two knobbed threads, called *balancers*, which are supposed to assist in maintaining equilibrium while in flight. Flies are exceedingly rapid and prolific breeders, laying great numbers of eggs, and the young upon hatching pass quickly through larval and pupal forms to the mature state. In one group, however, the *Pupipara*, the young are brought forth as full-grown larvæ ready to pupate.

The various flies which disseminate disease are the most dangerous insect enemies of man. Certain mosquitoes transmit malaria, yellow fever, and filariasis; the house fly spreads typhoid fever, Asiatic cholera, and prurient ophthalmia; the tsetse fly transfers sleeping sickness, African fever, and various animal plagues. The Hessian fly, onion maggot, and apple maggot rank high among injurious insects. On the other hand, the dried larvæ of certain species of *Ephydra*, which swarm in myriads around alkaline lakes in California and Mexico, form a nutritious food used by the Indians and the Mexicans.

There are about 50,000 known species, of which 7000 or more are North American. Among these are the house flies, flesh flies (or bluebottles), horseflies (greenheads), flower flies, bee flies, pomace flies, botflies, robber flies, black flies and punkies, midges, gnats, and mosquitoes. See *Fruit Flies, House Fly*.

Flycatcher. A name originally applied to various birds of the thrushlike, insectivorous family, *Muscicapidæ*, which comprises some 700 species found exclusively in the Old World. In America the name is universally given to birds of the so-called "tyrant" flycatcher family (*Tyrannidæ*). This includes over 500 species peculiar to America. They are most abundant in the tropics where their services as insect destroyers are in greatest demand.

Flycatchers are solitary birds, mostly of dull plumage, and have the habit of remaining perched for a long time on a single spot, darting away only to catch passing insects with a swift snap of the bill, and then returning. They vary in size from pygmy South American forms less than 3 inches long to the derby flycatchers of Mexico nearly a foot in length. Of some 35 species which migrate to the United States and Canada, among the best-known are the great-crested, scissor-tailed, Acadian, Traill, and least flycatchers, the familiar phœbe or pewee, and kingbird. See *Kingbird, Phœbe*.

Flying Dragon (*Draco volans*). A small arboreal lizard provided with a parachute-like expansion of the skin, with which it is enabled to fly or glide from tree to tree. It is about 8 inches long, with irregular scales and a very long whiplike tail. This brilliantly colored, entirely harmless creature lives in the forests of the East Indies.

Flying Fish (*Syentognathi*). A group of exceedingly interesting fishes, allied to the pikes on the one hand and to the mullets on the other. There are two chief divisions or families, the flying fishes (*Exocœtidæ*) and the garfishes (*Belonidæ*).

The common flying fish (*Exocœtus volitans*) is widely distributed throughout the world in warm seas. It rises 4 to 6 feet above the water and sustains a flight of 50 to 100 feet by means of its strongly developed pectoral fins which act as wings. While a mid-ocean fish, it occurs in schools near the Barbados, where it is taken in large numbers for food.

The Catalina flying fish (*Cypselurus californicus*), of southern California, sometimes 18 inches long, is perhaps the largest known species. It is one of the strongest fliers of the group, having its ventral as well as its pectoral fins greatly enlarged.

Flying Fox. The name given to various large, fruit-eating bats of the Oriental tropics and Australia, because of their doglike or foxlike heads. There are about 70 species, mostly tailless, with small, pointed ears and large eyes. The Kalong (*Pteropus edulis*), of Java, Sumatra, and adjoining regions, is the largest of the fruit-eating bats,—its body attaining a length of 15 inches, with a wing spread of about 5 feet. It subsists on various kinds of fruits, especially figs and mangoes, and frequently does great damage in orchards. The kalong is much hunted by the Malays for its flesh which is highly esteemed for food. See *Bats*.

Flying Squirrel. A small rodent mammal of the squirrel family (*Sciuridæ*). The expanded skin of the flank, extending between the fore and hind legs, enables this animal to support itself as with a parachute, and to make very long gliding leaps. The American flying squirrel, or Assapan (*Sciuropterus volans*), of eastern North America, is one of the most exquisite of small mammals. The limbs are delicately formed and its fur is as soft as silk. Its body is about 5 inches long and the tail about 4 inches. Owing, however, to its nocturnal habits, it is not often seen. The flying squirrel nests in hollow trees, sleeping in the daytime, and appearing for play about sunset.

Fowl (*Gallus domesticus*). The numerous breeds of domestic fowl—cock and hen, or chicken—are believed to have originated from the red jungle fowl (*G. gallus* or *bankivus*), native of eastern India and Indo-China. In plumage this wild species, which is closely related to the pheasants, strongly resembles the modern black-breasted game fowl. Various circumstances warrant the belief that jungle fowls were first domesticated in Burma or in adjacent countries during prehistoric times.

Apparently the domestic fowl reached eastern Europe about 500 B. C. and, at the time of Julius Cæsar's visit, had already become established in Britain. It is now the most thoroughly domesticated, widely distributed, generally useful, and economically important of birds,—the total value of its eggs and flesh greatly exceeding that of all other domesticated birds combined. Long periods of selective breeding in many lands have developed numerous races, varying in size, form, and color from pygmy bantams to huge brahmas approaching the turkey in weight, and from pure white to pure black strains, with almost innumerable intermediate forms. In Japan a remarkable breed has been produced in which the tail of the cock attains a length of 10 or 15 feet.

Fox (*Vulpes*). A carnivorous animal, closely related to the dog and the wolf. It is characterized by its sharp muzzle and its long bushy tail, and also by its cunning, which has passed into a proverb. The pupil of the eye is elongated, and not circular as in the dog; the ears are triangular in shape, and pointed. A very powerful scent is emitted by the fox from glands placed near the root of the tail.

The fox usually remains concealed in a burrow during the day and ventures stealthily abroad at night in search of food. Birds, mice, rabbits, or hares constitute its usual prey, but, when pressed by necessity, it will have recourse to certain kinds of fruit, such as grapes. To poultry it is terribly destructive. It is to its power of endurance, its great speed, and its cunning that the chase of this animal owes its exciting character. Among its various expedients for escape is that of feigning death.

Numerous species of fox are found in the Old and the New World, of which the most important are the European fox (*V. vulgaris*), celebrated in fox-hunting, the arctic or blue fox (*V. lagopus*), and the American or red fox (*V. fulvus*). The arctic fox abounds in far northern regions, and is remarkable for changing its color with the season, being brown or bluish in summer, and white in winter. The soles of its feet are hairy. The red fox is found throughout North America; it is quite variable in color and marking, and varieties of it are known by different names.

The skins of all species of fox are valuable, and make warm and soft furs, used for muffs and linings. Choice pelts of the so-called silver fox or black fox, which is a northern variety of the American red fox, command the highest prices paid for any kind of fur,—a single silver-black skin fetching $2000 and upwards. Fox-farming, for the commercial rearing of these foxes, became established about 1900 in Prince Edward Island, Canada, where, in 1913, there were 277 ranches, possessing more than 2500 foxes, with an estimated value of $15,000,000.

Frogs (*Ranidæ*). A large family of tailless amphibians. The true frogs have four limbs, the skeleton is without ribs, and there are teeth only in the upper jaw. Their bodies are short and broad, with the hinder legs greatly developed for leaping. The skin is soft, smooth, and often brightly colored. It sometimes secretes a milky fluid, which, in some tropical species, is highly poisonous. This forms the only means of defense possessed by frogs.

In the adult, breathing is carried on by means of lungs, but, as there are no movable ribs, the method is somewhat peculiar. It is, in fact, a process of swallowing air, and it is possible to suffocate a frog simply by holding its mouth open. The moist, delicate skin, however, also performs an important part in respiration. In the frog, as in the toad, the tongue is fixed to the front of the mouth, while it is free behind. Consequently, it can be rapidly protruded at some distance from the mouth, greatly aiding in the capture of insects.

Practically all frogs live in or near the water, to which they go to breed, usually in the spring, when the males make themselves conspicuous by incessant rattling or croaking calls.

In pools and other quiet waters the female frog deposits large masses of tiny eggs. These are velvety black above, creamy white below, and surrounded by a jelly-like secretion. When hatched, the young, commonly called tadpoles or polliwogs, are fishlike in form, with a broad, rounded head, no mouth, and a long, compressed tail. At first there are external gills, but internal gills soon develop and the outer ones disappear. At the time of transformation, the internal gills are replaced by lungs. At the same time, the lower jaw develops and the limbs make their appearance. The tail gradually disappears, and the transformed animal rises to the surface to breathe. Thus, the fishlike tadpole becomes a four-limbed, active frog, quick of sight and hearing, a strong swimmer, and a powerful jumper.

In cold regions frogs hibernate in mud or damp places during the winter. During dry seasons some species burrow deeply underground in search of moisture. Frogs feed chiefly upon worms, slugs, insects, tadpoles, small fish, and other frogs. Nearly all of the true frogs may be used for food. Usually only the large hind legs are eaten, though all of the muscular parts are edible.

There are more than 250 species of true or water frogs. These are widely distributed in moist regions, except in Australia. Some 15 species occur in the United States and Canada, chiefly in the South and the East. Among these are the bullfrog, green frog, leopard frog, and wood frog. The American bullfrog (*Rana catesbiana*), sometimes 8 inches in length, is exceeded in size by only two known species, the larger of which, the goliath frog (*Rana goliath*) of West Africa, reaches 10 inches in length.

Fruit Flies (*Rhagoletis*). A group of dipterous insects which are a serious menace to fruit culture, since the immature stages or larvæ feed upon the pulp of many kinds of valuable fruits, such as apples, oranges, and currants. The adult insects are harmless little flies, about the size of house flies, with the wings beautifully banded in brown. The extensive damage caused by fruit flies is done by the larvæ which burrow through the flesh of the fruit, feeding upon it and causing it to decay. Because of its prolific breeding and the shortness of its life cycle, covering a few days, the fruit fly is the most valuable medium for investigations into the laws of inherited qualities.

Fur Seal (*Callorhinus*). A marine mammal, belonging to the eared seal family (*Otariidæ*), more properly called sea lion or sea bear. The fur seal differs from the true seals in that it has external ears and its flapper-like limbs are adapted to some degree of locomotion on land. There are about 9 species, of which 6 occur in the southern hemisphere and 3 in the northern. Except in a few specially protected localities, the southern fur seals, once abundant, have become practically extinct through ruthless fur hunting. The northern fur seals are confined to islands in Bering Sea and adjacent waters. All are very highly prized for their valuable fur, formerly an article of much commercial importance.

The mature male fur seal attains a length of 6 feet and a weight of 500 pounds. The body fur is dark brown in color with long, yellowish white outer hairs which form a mane on the neck. The female is much smaller, averaging only about 80 pounds in weight. The young are brought forth on rocky beaches in summer, and take to the water at about the age of 6 weeks. At the approach of winter the Alaskan herds migrate to shallow feeding grounds in the ocean as far south as Lower California, while the Siberian herds journey as far as the Sea of Japan, all returning to their northern breeding grounds in May and June.

At the time of its greatest size, the Pribilof herd contained about 2,500,000 animals, but owing to excessive land and open sea sealing, it became reduced to less than 300,000. In 1911, by international agreement, open sea sealing was suspended for a period of 15 years, later extended, and, in 1912, land sealing was similarly restricted. Under continued protection the Pribilof herd had increased in numbers to more than 1,000,000 by 1931. See *Sea Lion.*

Gallflies. A general term loosely covering insects of several orders that attack growing plant tissues, disturbing the growth process and causing the plants to produce the abnormal growths and swellings known as galls. Within the galls live the insects that cause them to be developed, profiting by the increased accumulation of food materials brought to these growths by the plant. The galls furnish both food and shelter. Many galls are so well known as to receive common names, as "oak apples," "bullet galls," "cone gall" of the willow, and the "mossy rose gall" of the sweetbrier.

Gall wasps of the order *Hymenoptera* cause the finest galls, often with three-layered walls,—a spinous or defensive outer layer, and a close-fitting central chamber. These abound on oaks and rosebushes. Sawflies, of the order *Hymenoptera*, and gall midges, of the order *Diptera*, cause fleshy and leafy galls of many sorts on a great variety of plants, especially willows, hickories, and touch-me-nots. Aphids and psyllids of the order *Hemiptera* cause galls of various forms, but always open to the outside, on many kinds of plants; as, for example, witch-hazel, elm, and goldenrod. A few true flies (order *Diptera*) and a few moths (order *Lepidoptera*) cause large stem galls on goldenrods. Many mites (order *Acarina* of the class *Arachnida*) cause very imperfect galls on leaves and twigs of various plants, the galls being often but little more than hollows filled with overgrown and felted plant hairs.

Garter Snake (*Eutænia*). The most common North American snake, called also "striped snake" and "ribbon snake," found almost everywhere in grassy places and along streams. It is usually from 2 to 3 feet in length, with three yellowish stripes on a darker ground. There are 11 species, all inoffensive and harmless, feeding on worms, fishes, frogs, and toads. Upon the approach of winter, these snakes creep as far as possible into some opening in the ground, and become dormant, emerging, however, somewhat earlier in spring than most other serpents.

The common garter snake (*E. sirtalis*), of which there are several varieties, occurs throughout the United States and southern Canada. It brings forth its young alive, sometimes as many as 45 in a single brood.

Gaur (*Bos gaurus*). A handsome wild ox, native of northeastern India, where it is kept in partially domesticated herds for its flesh. It is probably the largest living species of wild cattle. Full-grown males sometimes stand 6 feet high at the shoulder and have horns 3 feet long with a basal diameter of 6 inches. In its native haunts the wild gaur is a very alert, wary, and cunning animal, and exceedingly pugnacious when brought to bay; an old male is said to be a match even for a tiger. The gaur is much hunted by sportsmen, by whom it is often erroneously called "bison." See *Banteng, Gayal, Ox.*

Gavial (*gā′vĭ-ăl*) (*Gavial gangeticus*). In general form, the gavial, found in the rivers of India, resembles the crocodiles. It has, however, a very long, slender snout, and the upper jaw ends in a knob. The snout is one-fifth of the length of the body and gives the animal a peculiar appearance. This huge reptile sometimes attains a length of 25 feet. Gavials feed exclusively upon fish and small animals. They are entirely harmless to man and by some Hindu sects are considered sacred. Fossil remains of the gavial have been found in the Pliocene deposits of India, so it is perhaps the oldest of all living species of air-breathing vertebrates. See *Crocodile*.

Gayal (*gā'ăl*) (*Bos frontalis*). A wild ox found in the forest regions of northeastern India, Assam, and adjacent portions of China. It is domesticated to some extent by the native peoples for its flesh and skins, though it is not employed as a beast of burden and no use is made of its milk. The gayal is smaller than the gaur, and its head, which is very broad and flat above, with a wide space between the horns, contracts abruptly toward the nose. See *Gaur*, *Ox*.

Gazelle (*Gazella*). A group of beautiful antelopes. There are about 20 species, natives of northern Africa and southwestern Asia, of very graceful shape, and usually rather smaller in size than the chamois. The dorcas gazelle (*G. dorcas*), or true gazelle, is fawn or dun on the back, with a reddish brown band on the sides, and with the lips, nose, buttocks, and under parts white. The horns, which are stronger in the male than in the female, are twice bent, in the shape of a lyre, and without sharp edges. The eyes of this animal are beautiful and soft in expression, and its movements are elegant and light. It inhabits the large plains and the Saharan region of northern Africa as well as Arabia and Syria, living in numerous herds. When taken young, the gazelle, though naturally wild and timid, is readily domesticated, and becomes quite tame. See *Antelope*.

Gila Monster (*Heloderma suspectum*). A poisonous lizard, inhabiting deserts of Arizona, New Mexico, and Mexico. It is about 20 inches long, with short, stubby limbs and a stout body, covered with beadlike tubercles, jet-black and yellow in color, arranged as if in a Navajo pattern. When wild, it is active and vicious, but it becomes very docile in captivity. It is the only lizard provided with venomous salivary glands. Its bite is very poisonous to small animals and is sometimes fatal to man.

Giraffe (*Giraffa camelopardalis*). The tallest living animal, attaining a height of 18 feet, measured from its head to the ground. It is native to Africa, and, with the okapi, constitutes a well-marked family of ruminants (*Giraffidæ*).

The giraffe has two straight horns, without branches, about 8 inches long, covered with hair, blunt at the end and tufted. The shoulders are of such great length as to render the fore part of the body much higher than the hind part. The legs are long and slender. The neck is exceedingly long, although, as in case of most mammals, it contains only 7 neck bones. The head is slender and elegantly formed, and the color of the body is dusky white with large rusty spots. The eye is exceptionally large, prominent, and lustrous, and commands a wide field of vision. The sense of smell is highly developed and the nostrils are provided with muscle by which they can be closed against drifting sand.

The giraffe feeds almost entirely upon the leaves of trees, which it plucks with its long tongue. When it grazes, which is but rarely, the giraffe is forced to spread its legs far apart to enable it to bring its head to the ground. In disposition the giraffe is mild and inoffensive and usually seeks safety by immediate flight. It fights by kicking powerfully with the hind legs. While formerly occurring throughout most of Africa, from Nubia to the Cape of Good Hope, the giraffe is now restricted to desert regions of the interior, where it is much hunted for its excellent flesh and valuable skin. See *Okapi*.

Glass Snake (*Ophisaurus ventralis*). A species of lizard, popularly regarded as a snake. It has an elongated, serpent-like body, about 2 feet in length, with no trace of limbs. However, it may be instantly distinguished from a snake by its well-developed eyelids and ear openings. Its long tail, about two-thirds of the length of the body, is very brittle. Like many other lizards, the glass snake may divest itself of its tail in case of emergency, and possesses the power of partially reproducing the lost part. It lives in burrows in dry ground and feeds chiefly on insects. It occurs from North Carolina to Wisconsin and Nebraska and southward.

Globefish (*Tetraodontidæ*). A peculiar family of oceanic fishes. In this group the abdominal walls are capable of great distention, so that, when inflated, the fish appears like a globe with a beak and a tail attached. These fishes have the power to distend their bodies with air to such a size that it is very difficult for any ordinary enemy to swallow them. Some kinds are as large as a football. The common swellfish (*Spheroides maculatus*), of the Atlantic coast, is called also "puffer" or "swelltoad" by coastwise boys who tease it to cause it to inflate itself like a huge bladder. The Mukimuki (*Tetraodon hispidus*), a strikingly colored, highly inflatable swellfish of tropical seas, is regarded in Hawaii as the most poisonous of all fishes. It is said that its gall was formerly used for poisoning arrows.

Gnu (*nōō*) (*Connochætes gnu*). A peculiar South African antelope now nearly extinct, intermediate in appearance between the antelope, the ox, and the horse. Its height is about 4 feet and it attains a length of 9 feet. Both sexes are horned, the horns nearly meeting on the forehead, then bending downward and outward with a final sharp upward turn. The muzzle is broad like that of an ox; the neck short and surmounted by a mane of bristly hair; the withers are high; and the tail is long and hairy like that of a horse. Between the forelegs is a pendulous hairy extension of the dewlap, like that of the buffalo. The feet and the head resemble those of the buffalo, while the mane, tail, and general form are horselike, probably suggesting the name "horned horse" by which it is also known. See *Antelope*.

Goat (*Capra hircus*). A ruminant animal closely related to the sheep. The common goat was derived from the wild bezoar goat of southwestern Asia and, doubtless, was one of the first animals to be subjugated by man. It was domesticated by the ancient Egyptians, by the Lake Dwellers of Switzerland, and is very frequently mentioned in the Bible.

The uses of the goat are numerous. Its flesh is good, particularly that of the young goat, or kid, which, in many countries, is esteemed a delicacy. The milk is very rich and nutritious and is more easily digested than that of the cow. It is often useful for consumptive patients. Some goats yield four quarts of milk per day, but the average quantity is more nearly two. The skin of the goat was early used for clothing, and is now extensively dressed as leather for many purposes, particularly for making gloves, the finer kinds of shoes, and for binding books. The hair, which may be profitably clipped each year, is used for making ropes which are indestructible in water. The horns are made into knife handles and similar articles, and the fat is used for candles.

Most of the world's goats are grown in the dry, warm regions of southern Europe, northern Africa, and southwestern Asia. Centuries of selective breeding have developed many valuable varieties, such as the Angora, Kashmir, Egyptian, Syrian, and Sudan goats. The fleece of the Angora goat is called mohair. Kashmir shawls are woven from the fine underwool of the Kashmir goat. Since 1900, flocks of Angora goats have become established in various parts of the western United States.

Goldfinch (*Carduelis elegans*). A highly prized song bird of the finch family, native of the Old World, with golden-yellow plumage marked with black. It has long been a favorite cage bird in Europe, being very docile and greatly attached to its keepers. In one of Raphael's masterpieces, called the "Madonna of the Goldfinch," the Madonna is represented as offering a tame goldfinch to the Infant Jesus. Since about 1880 the goldfinch has become naturalized in the vicinity of New York and Boston. It builds a neat, carefully concealed nest in the fork of a shrub or low tree, in which it lays 4 or 5 white eggs, somewhat marked with purple.

The American goldfinch (*Astragalinus tristis*), 5 inches long, called also yellowbird and thistle bird, is bright yellow, with black crown, wings, and tail. It ranges throughout eastern North America, where it is well known on account of its characteristic song and undulating flight. It breeds from South Carolina to Labrador, building an elegant nest in a bush or low tree and laying 3 to 6 bluish white eggs. Its food, like that of the European goldfinch, consists chiefly of weed seeds.

Goldfish (*Carassius auratus*). A small, carplike fish, sometimes called golden carp, highly valued for aquariums on account of its handsome golden color and striking variety of form. It is a native of fresh waters in China, where it was domesticated about 450 A. D. By careful selection, many grotesque forms and striking colorations have been developed, a Japanese variety with three large tail fins being a great favorite. With the establishment of maritime trade with the Far East, the goldfish was brought westward, reaching England in 1691, and has since been widely diffused throughout the world. When it escapes from domestication and becomes naturalized, as in the Potomac and other eastern streams, the goldfish reverts to its original dark olive color and attains a length of 6 to 12 inches. Many thousands have been distributed by the bureau of fisheries, so that it is taken in nets and sometimes brought to market. See *Minnows*.

Goose. A large, web-footed, swimming bird, closely related to the duck and the swan.

True geese differ from swans in that the neck is always shorter than the body, and from ducks in that the male and female are alike in color. Geese walk better than ducks, live more on land, and are essentially vegetable feeders. When disturbed they hiss with outstretched necks, like the swans. They usually fly in V-shaped companies and utter a characteristic cry, or honk, when on the wing. In color, geese are usually grayish or white, with darker markings. Nearly all are highly prized for food.

There are about 30 species, most abundant in the northern hemisphere. Many rear their young, called goslings, well within the Arctic circle in summer and range southward over wide areas in winter. In North America some 12 species or varieties are found, several of which migrate throughout the United States. Among the best-known are the Canada goose (*Branta canadensis*), the white-fronted goose (*Anser albifrons gambeli*), and the snow goose (*Chen hyperborea*). Among other wild geese are the brant, barnacle goose, graylag, emperor goose, bean goose, and spur-winged goose.

The domestic goose (*Anser domesticus*), valued for its eggs, quills, feathers, and flesh, is a domesticated form of the wild graylag goose (*A. anser*) of Europe, Asia, and northern Africa. Its domestication dates back to prehistoric times in northern Africa and southern Asia. It is pictured on the oldest Egyptian monuments and was well known to the ancient Greeks and Romans. Goose raising, while never extensive in the United States, is an important industry in various parts of Europe.

Gopher, Pocket. A small burrowing rodent, native only to North and Central America. It has a ratlike body and is peculiar in possessing large cheek pouches, lined with hair, which open on the outside of the mouth.

The common pocket gopher (*Geomys bursarius*), widely distributed in the Mississippi valley, is about 11 inches long, including the tail, reddish brown above and ashy below, with white feet. It is an agricultural pest, enormously destructive in its habits and its appetites, despoiling meadows by throwing up countless hillocks of loose earth, devouring immense quantities of vegetables, small grain, and corn, and destroying young fruit trees by eating their roots.

The northern pocket gopher (*Thomomys talpoides*) is a native of Canada, and is found everywhere west of the Rocky mountains. It is about a foot long, lead color above and white below.

Gorilla. The largest and fiercest of the anthropoid apes, and the one most resembling man in certain structures and in size. The hands and feet are strong and well adapted for living either in trees or on the ground. It is able to walk erect, somewhat like a man. However, its skull, which is of a low type, and its strong canine teeth indicate a savage nature. In height the gorilla equals an average man, and its thick, muscular body sometimes attains a weight of 400 or 500 pounds. Its black skin is covered with grayish black or grizzly hair, about 2 inches long. The home of the gorilla is in the forests of western Africa near the equator. Although of a less adaptable disposition than most apes, the gorilla may be successfully reared in captivity. See *Ape, Chimpanzee, Orang-utan*.

Grasshopper. A popular name for several kinds of leaping insects which produce a strident sound by rubbing their hind legs against their wings. Usually the males only produce this sound. The name is most commonly applied to the short-horned grasshopper of the Acrididæ family. This insect is known also as a locust. Katydids and large green crickets, both having long, thready antennæ, are also called grasshoppers. All have a pair of large, muscular hind legs. Sharp, horny mandibles enable them to eat the green parts of plants, and they are often highly destructive to crops.

The 17-year locust has three weeks of active life. Its eggs are laid in trees. Nymphs hatch, fall to ground, burrow in, and remain for 17 years before emerging as active locusts. Its body is black, banded about the abdomen with orange. It has reddish legs and bright protruding eyes.

Grebes (*Podicipidæ*). A family of diving birds, called also "dabchicks." They are closely related to the loons, but much smaller, ranging from 8 to 20 inches in length. There are 25 to 30 widely distributed species, 6 of which are found in North America. Grebes are distinctly aquatic birds, living chiefly on fish, frogs, and crustaceans, and rarely venturing on land. The wings are short and there is no visible tail. When on land, the grebes assume a somewhat erect position, like the penguins, and walk with much difficulty. The nest, in which about 5 chalky white eggs are laid, is made of coarse-stemmed vegetation, and sometimes practically floats on the water. The handsome chicks take to the water as soon as hatched. Like the loons, grebes are expert divers and swimmers.

The pied-billed grebe (*Podilymbus podiceps*), called also "dabchick," "dildapper," "hell-diver," and "water witch," occurs from Hudson bay southward to Argentina. It is about 15 inches long, dull in color, and the whitish bill is crossed by a black band. Like other grebes, it can swim with only the tip of its bill out of the water; hence its seeming disappearance when pursued by hunters.

Grosbeak. A name given to several medium-sized birds of the finch family, noted for their large, thick beaks, brightly colored plumage, and charming song. The best-known is the pine grosbeak, found in northern coniferous woods of North

America and Europe. It is about 8½ inches long, rosy-red above and ashy below, and is often kept as a cage bird. Other American species are the evening grosbeak, yellowish olive marked with black, and the rose-breasted grosbeak, of the northeastern United States and Canada, the blue grosbeak of the Southern states, and the black-headed grosbeak of the Pacific coast.

Grouse. The grouse family (*Tetraonidæ*) contains about 200 species of gallinaceous birds, and includes the quails, bobwhites, and partridges as well as the true grouse. The true grouse (*Tetraoninæ*), numbering some 25 species, inhabit northern temperate regions. They are nonmigratory, though after the nesting season they usually gather in small coveys or bevies, sometimes uniting in large flocks. Grouse are game birds of the first rank, trusting largely to the concealment afforded by their inconspicuous colors, but flying rapidly when flushed, with a startling whir of their small, stiff-feathered wings.

The ruffed grouse (*Bonasa umbellus*), which ranges across the continent, is the best-known American species. This grouse is called partridge in the North and pheasant in the South. It is 17 inches long, with reddish brown, barred and mottled plumage, and black neck tufts, and is noted for the peculiar habit, exhibited by the male, of drumming with its wings. The ruffed grouse lives in woodlands, feeding upon insects, berries, seeds, buds, and leaves, and nests on the ground, laying from 8 to 14 pale buff eggs. Its flesh is superior to that of any other American grouse.

The pinnated grouse, commonly called Prairie Chicken (*Tympanuchus americanus*), formerly abundant on prairies in the Mississippi valley, is now comparatively rare. It is 18 inches long, with brownish, barred plumage. In addition to erectile neck tufts, the male has an inflatable air sac, as large as an orange and of the same color, on each side of the neck.

The Heath Hen (*Tympanuchus cupido*), similar to the prairie chicken, which formerly lived in woodlands in the Northeastern states, is now extinct, except for perhaps a few survivors on the island of Marthas Vineyard. The sharp-tailed grouse (*Pediœcetes phasianellus*), with no neck tufts and a pointed tail, occurs from New Mexico to Manitoba and eastward to Illinois. The Sage Hen (*Centrocercus urophasianus*), which inhabits the sagebrush plains of western North America, is the largest American grouse, attaining a length of 30 inches and a weight of 6 pounds. The buds of the sagebrush upon which it feeds impart a bitter taint to its otherwise excellent flesh.

The Canada grouse, or Spruce Partridge (*Dendraphus canadensis*), 15 inches long with dark barred plumage, lives in coniferous forests from northern New England and Minnesota northwestward to Alaska. It feeds largely upon the leaves and young shoots of the spruce and the tamarack.

Among Old World species are the famous black grouse, or Blackcock (*Lyurus tetrix*), 23 inches long, and the Capercaillie (*Tetrao urogallus*), sometimes 35 inches long and weighing 12 pounds, which is the largest of all grouse. See *Bobwhite, Partridge, Ptarmigan, Quail.*

Guanaco (*gwä-nä'kō*) (*Lama guanacus*) A South American mammal which, excepting the vicuña, is the only living wild representative of the camel family in the New World. The guanaco is much smaller than the camel and is more alert and intelligent in appearance. It stands 3 to 4 feet high at the shoulder, while the head is carried about 5 feet high. There is no hump on the back, the feet are narrow, divided above into 2 toes, each with a horny hoof above and a thick cushion or pad beneath, for traveling on stones or sandy ground. Near the equator, as in Ecuador, the guanaco is found only in the higher mountains, but in temperate Patagonia it lives on plains at the sea level. The Indians hunt the guanaco for its flesh, which they cure by salting and drying.

Two domesticated forms of the guanaco are of great economic importance in the Andean region—the llama, used as a beast of burden, and the alpaca, valued for its excellent wool. See *Alpaca, Llama.*

Guinea Fowl (*Numidinæ*). A group of game birds closely related to the pheasants. There are about 23 species, all natives of Africa. The common guinea fowl (*Numida meleagris*), native of West Africa, about the size of the domestic fowl, has slate-colored plumage, covered with rounded white spots, and the head is surmounted by a naked, bony helmet. It lives in forests, often in large flocks, feeding upon seeds, fruits, and insects; it nests in thickets, laying 16 to 24 yellow-white, finely speckled eggs.

The guinea fowl was domesticated by the Greeks and Romans but disappeared from Europe during the middle ages. It was re-introduced in the 16th century by the Portuguese and has since become widely diffused throughout the world. While its flesh and eggs are excellent, the guinea fowl is not widely popular, because of its noisy cries and the difficulty of rearing its young in moist regions.

Guinea Pig (*Cavia cutleri*). A small, tailless, rodent mammal, about 6 inches long, native of South America, where it has been domesticated since prehistoric times. Mummies of the guinea pig have been found in the tombs of the Incas. While related to the porcupines, it is also somewhat intermediate between the rabbits and the mice. In color it is usually yellow, white, or black, variously spotted. It is an extremely prolific animal, sometimes beginning to breed at the age of two months and producing five or six broods a year, each litter consisting of from 4 to 12 young.

Guinea pigs are now introduced into many parts of the world as household animals. As they are cleanly, gentle, and never bite, they make pleasing pets for children. They are also in wide use as subjects of experiment in medical and bacteriological research, especially in the study of germ diseases.

The name guinea pig is a double misnomer, for the animal did not come from Guinea and it is not a pig. Its present English name is thought to be a corruption of "Guiana pig," at once referring to its native country, to its somewhat piglike form, and to its habit of grunting.

Gull (*Larus*). A long-winged, web-footed swimming bird, closely related to the terns. There are about 50 species, widely distributed throughout the world. They are especially abundant along ocean shores and occur also about many inland bodies of water. In size they range from the little gull (*L. minutus*), of northern Europe and Asia, only 11 inches long, to the great black-backed gull (*L. marinus*), of the North Atlantic, sometimes 32 inches long. Their usual color is white with a gray mantle varying from pearl gray to blackish.

Gulls feed largely upon fish and serve as useful scavengers in cleaning up the refuse of shores and harbors. They are gregarious at all seasons, but at nesting time they congregate in vast numbers, sometimes almost in millions. Their nests are placed on the ground, on bare ledges of rock, or among tall grasses on swampy shores. The eggs are 2 to 4 in number and irregularly spotted or blotched. The soft feathers of various species are used for stuffing pillows. The flesh of old birds is tough and unfit for food, but that of young gulls is palatable, and the eggs are good eating.

Halibut (*Hippoglossus*). A large flatfish, living on shallow sea bottoms. It is found off both shores of the Atlantic and the Pacific, north of about the latitude of Paris, Boston, Cape Mendocino, and Mutshushima bay in Japan. The halibut exists in great numbers, sometimes attaining a length of 9 feet and a weight of 700 pounds, though usually from 100 to 200 pounds. The flesh is of excellent quality, that of the small forms, called "chicken halibut," being very highly esteemed. The catch in 1912 off the coasts of New England, the Puget Sound region, and Alaska totaled 35 million pounds; the Canadian catch for the same year amounted to 23 million pounds.

The Monterey halibut (*Paralichthys californicus*), a highly valued food fish of the Pacific coast, much resembling the true halibut, sometimes reaches a weight of 60 pounds.

Hammerhead Shark (*Sphyrna zygœna*). A large shark, sometimes 15 feet long, with an oddly formed head, shaped somewhat like a mallet, more than twice as broad as long, and with the eyes on the outer ends. This peculiar species, which is much dreaded for its ferocity, is found in all warm seas, and ranges northward to Cape Cod and to California.

Hare (*Lepus*). A small rodent mammal, with long hind legs, short bushy tail, large eyes, very long ears, and close, almost woolly fur. There are many species, found over all the world except in the Australian region. Hares differ from rabbits in their larger size, longer ears, and longer hind legs. Unlike the rabbits, they do not live in burrows, but in the open or among rocks in thickets, and their color usually or often changes with the season. They feed chiefly on herbage and the bark of shrubs and trees.

The varying hare (*L. americanus*), about twice the size of a cottontail rabbit, found from New England to Ontario and north to Hudson bay, changes from pale cinnamon brown in summer to pure white in winter. The polar hare (*L. arcticus*), of the arctic regions, remains white during the entire year.

The jack hare, commonly called the jack rabbit (*L. texianus*), easily recognized by its slender body, long legs, very large ears, and by a black mark on the tail, occurs from Nebraska to Oregon and southward to Mexico. It is exceedingly abundant in California and Colorado, where great rabbit drives are made to reduce its numbers, resulting in the slaughter of thousands. This hare does not change color with the seasons. The very similar prairie hare (*L. campestris*), with a pure white tail, inhabits the great sagebrush plains from Kansas to Saskatchewan and west to northern California and Oregon. It varies from gray in summer to white in winter. See *Rabbit*.

Hawk. A name indiscriminately applied in the United States to various buzzards, falcons, harriers, and kites, or to any bird of prey that is not an eagle, an owl, or a vulture. More than twenty different raptorial birds are thus popularly known as hawks, including the sharp-shinned hawk, Cooper's hawk, goshawk, red-tailed hawk, red-shouldered hawk, Swainson's hawk, duck hawk, fish hawk, marsh hawk, pigeon hawk, and sparrow hawk.

The first three of the foregoing, wherever found, are terribly destructive to poultry and game birds, and may properly be called chicken hawks or hen hawks. Various other species, particularly the red-tailed hawk and the red-shouldered hawk, often wrongly called chicken hawks, are among the farmer's best friends, destroying immense numbers of mice, rats, gophers, and other injurious small animals, and rarely attacking poultry.

All hawks have strong, hooked beaks, and long, powerful, curved claws, fitted for seizing and holding their prey. They also possess remarkable keenness of vision, and, upon sighting their prey, swoop down upon it with great rapidity. See *Buzzard, Chicken Hawk*.

Headfishes (*Molidœ*). The fishes of this group, called also sunfishes, have the body so shortened behind that the dorsal, anal, and caudal fins seem to be attached to the rear border of the head. The common headfish, or sunfish (*Mola mola*), occurs sparingly in all temperate and tropical seas. It is almost circular in form, and its body is covered with a rough, leathery skin. It is found on both coasts of the United States. Specimens 8 feet long and weighing 1200 pounds have been taken in southern California waters.

Hedgehog (*Erinaceus europœus*). A small Old World mammal, belonging to the order *Insectivora*, so named for its piglike snout and because it is generally found under hedges. It is about 10 inches in length. The upper surface of the plump body is completely armed with sharp prickles or spines intermixed with the hair. These spines are about an inch long, brownish black in color, tipped with white. The legs are short and the five toes are armed with claws adapted for digging.

Hedgehogs are nocturnal in habit, and live chiefly upon insects, snails, worms, eggs, small mammals, and birds, but sometimes upon fruits, roots, and seeds. They hibernate in burrows or hollow trees during the winter season. When frightened, they have the habit of rolling themselves into a ball with only their spines exposed, thus presenting a most effective defense against dogs and foxes, which are their principal enemies. Hedgehogs are easily tamed and are sometimes used to catch mice, cockroaches, and water bugs. In the United States and Canada the porcupine is sometimes wrongly called hedgehog. See *Porcupines*.

Heron (*Ardea*). A genus of storklike wading birds, somewhat resembling the cranes and rails. They have thick, compressed bodies, long legs, long necks, and long and pointed bills. There are about 12 species of true herons, ranging in length from 28 to 56 inches. They frequent swamps and marshes and occasionally the seacoast. Many species are gregarious, feeding and breeding in communities, where they build large bulky nests, often in trees, laying from 3 to 6 bluish white eggs. Herons are noted for their tireless watchfulness and great voracity. They subsist chiefly upon fish, frogs, small mammals, birds, and insects.

The great blue heron (*A. herodias*), called also blue crane, ranges from northern South America northward to the arctic regions, breeding throughout its range and wintering from the Middle states southward. It is from 42 to 50 inches in length, with a wing spread of 6 feet. In color it is uniformly bluish gray above, with black lower parts broadly striped with white. It nests in trees, usually at a height of 50 feet or more.

The great white heron (*A. occidentalis*), of Florida, Cuba, and Jamaica, 45 to 54 inches long, is pure white, with long ornamental neck plumes. The little blue heron (*A. cœrulea*), 22 inches long, occurs from Nova Scotia to Nebraska and southward. The little green heron (*A. virescens*), 17 inches long, is found from Nova Scotia to Oregon and southward.

Herring (*Clupeidœ*). A family of important food fishes, with narrowly oblong bodies and cycloid scales, but lacking the fatty back fin characteristic of salmon and trout. Practically all are marine, though some ascend rivers to spawn. The family contains the herring, sardine, alewife, menhaden, and shad, and other fishes of economic value.

The common herring (*Clupea harengus*), of the North Atlantic, is one of the most important food fishes of the world. It attains a length of 12 inches and a weight of about a pound. It moves in immense schools or shoals, sometimes several square miles in extent, and is taken in enormous numbers by fishing fleets. The largest fisheries are in Norway and Sweden and on the British coasts, employing thousands of boats, with an annual catch of more than four billion fish. The similar Pacific herring (*C. pallasi*) is equally abundant and, with a similar market, would be equally valuable. See *Alewife, Anchovy, Sardine, Shad*.

Hippopotamus. A huge, semiaquatic, thick-skinned mammal, closely allied to the pigs and peccaries, native of African rivers and often called river horse. Only two living species are known. On account of their more or less swinelike structure and habits it would be far more accurate to call these animals river hogs instead of river horses. However, they differ from true swine in having a broad, rounded snout, with the nostrils on the upper surface and with no trace of a terminal rooting disk.

The common hippopotamus (*H. amphibius*) occurs in rivers and lakes in central and southern Africa. It is an enormously bulky and unwieldy animal, attaining a height of 5 feet, a length of 12 feet, and a weight of 4 tons. Next to the elephant, it is the most bulky of land animals. The massive feet terminate in 4 hoofed toes, each toe resting upon the ground. The nearly naked, exceedingly thick and tough skin contains an oily substance, which exudes from the pores. When the animal is excited this flows out very freely, and is somewhat tinctured with blood, producing the so-called bloody sweat for which the hippopotamus is famous. It is most at home in the water, swims well, and is able to dive quickly. By use of sphincter muscles it can close its nostrils and its ears. It is thereby enabled to keep out the water while submerged. Having infolded lips, it is able to browse while under water.

Although subsisting chiefly upon aquatic vegetation, commonly feeding at the bottom of rivers, the hippopotamus often leaves the water by night and makes extensive inroads upon cultivated fields, consuming and injuring growing crops. The natives eat its flesh and fat and make some use of its skin, but by white men it is hunted chiefly for sport.

The pygmy hippopotamus (*H. libericus*), about 6 feet long, 2½ feet high, and weighing 400 to 600 pounds, is an exceedingly rare animal of the Guinea coast. It is more swinelike than the common hippopotamus, seeks its food chiefly in woodlands and swamps, and never gathers in herds.

Hog (*Sus scrofa domestica*). The European breeds of domestic swine are believed to have been originated from the wild boar of Europe (*S. scrofa*) and the Asiatic breeds from the wild boar of India (*S. cristatus*), called also wild pig. In China the domestication of the pig dates back at least 5000 years. The Lake Dwellers of Switzerland and the ancient Greeks and Romans used the flesh of the pig for food. By the Mosaic law the Hebrews were expressly forbidden to eat it. The hog is now reared almost throughout the world, though it does not thrive in high mountain regions.

The hog is remarkable as the only important domestic animal grown primarily for food,—the use of its hide for leather and its bristles for brushes being rarely considered by the breeder. Ages of domestication have greatly changed some of the prominent characteristics of the wild pig. The domestic pig is omnivorous, while the wild pig is practically herbivorous. The wild boar is armed with large tusks with which it fights fiercely; the domestic pig has largely lost its tusks and the disposition to use them.

During the last hundred years many valuable breeds have been developed by careful selection and crossing. The various Yorkshires and Berkshires, the Tamworth, Victoria, Large Black, and Essex swine are among the English breeds thus originated. Among standard breeds developed in America are the Chester White, Poland-China, Duroc-Jersey, and Hampshire. The rapidity with which these improved breeds can be grown and the ease with which their flesh can be cured and marketed, place the modern hog among the world's chief food-producing animals.

Hognose Snake (*Heterodon platyrhinus*). A flat-headed, thick-bodied snake found in the United States east of the Rocky mountains. It is about 2½ to 3 feet long, with an upturned, shovel-like snout. In color it is an indefinite mixture of brown, yellow, and black. While absolutely harmless, it pretends to be very fierce and dangerous, advancing menacingly toward an intruder, dilating its neck like a cobra, and hissing loudly. It strikes viciously but always with its mouth closed. If assumed hostility fails, it will turn on its back and feign death. This species is called also "blowing viper," "spreading adder," and "blow snake."

Honeybee (*Apis mellifica*). A remarkable social insect belonging to the *Hymenoptera*, a highly developed order which includes also the ants and the wasps. Of more than a million known species of insects, many of which are useful to man, only one small group, comprising the various kinds of honeybees, contributes directly to his food supply.

The honeybee has been fostered and studied by man for many centuries. In the course of time a number of races have been bred in several widely separated countries. These numerous races, some of which are known as Egyptians, Caucasians, Cyprians, Holy-land, Italian, Carniolan, and German, indicate the universal interest that has been taken in this valuable insect. The honeybee was introduced into America more than 300 years ago.

The typical colony of bees, as found in modern, scientifically operated apiaries, consists of one queen, or mother, several hundred drones, and about 70,000 workers. The *queen* is a sexually fully developed female, produced from a fertile egg in a specialized cell by a process of feeding that results in the complete development of the ovaries. She normally lays all the eggs, and, consequently, is the mother of the entire colony.

The *workers* are sexually undeveloped females hatched from eggs that under the conditions just described result in queens: indeed the very young larva of any worker is a potential queen if the colony desires to create one. In the economy of the hive the workers play varied and important rôles. They build comb, ventilate the hive, defend the colony, nurse the young, and gather all stores. The field force is made up entirely of workers. These garner nectar, pollen, and propolis, or bee glue, and, while so engaged, perform for man the important office of cross-fertilizing his fruit trees.

The *drones* are males developed from unfertilized eggs. The drone functions only in mating, meeting the virgin on the wing, a fact that accounts for his extraordinary size and remarkable powers of flight.

In their metamorphosis, bees pass through four stages, namely, egg, larva, pupa, and adult. The queen develops in 16 days; the worker, in 21; and the drone, in 25 days. The life history of the worker is worth recounting. The egg hatches in 3 days, and the resulting white, footless larva, fed by the nurse bees, grows rapidly until, between the 9th and the 10th day, it is sealed up in its cell. The insect then rests in the pupal condition until, on the 21st day, it emerges a perfect winged bee.

The life of the adult worker during the active summer season is about six weeks. The fall brood lives throughout the winter. Drones live during the summer at the pleasure of the workers, who dispose of them early in the autumn. Queens may live 6 or 7 years, but usually they are replaced when their ability to lay large numbers of eggs begins to fail. In commercial apiaries queens are commonly replaced at the end of the second year. During the height of the season, a good Italian queen is capable of laying from 2000 to 3000 eggs per day. Queens and workers are provided with stings. These defensive organs are simply modified egg-placers, or ovipositors. Swarming is the natural means of dividing the colony and disseminating the race. If left free to follow their instincts, bees will swarm at least once a year.

The saccharine exudations of flowering plants, known as *nectar*, form the main source of honey. These wholesome juices would be lost were it not for two highly specialized organs that have been developed in the honeybee. These are the *tongue* and the *honey stomach.* By the aid of the delicate tubelike tongue, nectar is sought out and sucked into the mouth. It is retained in the mouth for some time before it is transferred to the honey stomach, which is a storage vessel of astonishing capacity. In it a worker bee can transport nectar equal to its own weight. Returning to the hive with its load, the bee disposes of it by regurgitating the nectar into a cell of the honeycomb. *Nectar is not honey.* Beginning in the honey stomach of the bee, changes take place in the sugary plant juices. These changes continue in the hive until the substance reaches the altered condition known as ripened honey. The process results in an inversion of sugars and in the expulsion of excess water.

Pollen is a necessary food substance for the young, or larvæ, of the honeybee. The way in which the bees gather and carry this food to the hive is a unique performance in the insect world. On the head and thorax of the honeybee are hairs modified to catch and hold the pollen of the plants visited by the insect. Pollen brushes have also been developed on the hind legs of the workers; these are found on the inside of the flattened tarsi. With these special brushes, the pollen is removed from the hairs after which it is conveyed to the mouth, moistened, and finally packed away in the wonderful pollen baskets on the tibiæ of the hind legs. In the form of a pellet, the pollen mass is carried to the hive. Like honey, it is stored in the cells of the comb and is then known as beebread.

Beeswax is secreted by worker bees in the following remarkable manner. Large numbers of young bees, after gorging themselves with honey, hang up in the hive, clinging to one another, thus forming living chains or festoons. While they are in this inactive condition, the honey is transformed by special glands into beeswax. The wax then flows out on the plates under the abdomen, in a liquid condition. In contact with air it hardens in the form of tiny scales. These are removed from the body, manipulated by the jaws and mixed with saliva before being built into comb. It requires from 10 to 15 pounds of honey to produce one pound of beeswax.

The honeybee does not hibernate, but winters in the following interesting manner. When the temperature outside the hive falls below 57° F., the colony forms what is known as the winter nest or cluster. This cluster is really a hollow ball composed of many closely packed bees, which thus construct an insulating shell of their bodies, within which many bees remain active. These consume their stores, and by muscular activity generate the heat necessary to keep the colony alive. The insulating bees and those engaged in heat production often exchange places, though many individuals perish in the course of the winter. It has been found, by measuring the oxygen consumed and the carbon dioxide and water formed, that the energy spent by the working bee while generating heat, is proportionally greater than that exerted by a man engaged in hard manual labor.

The true economic importance of the honeybee is difficult to calculate accurately. In the United States the annual honey crop amounts to over 80 millions pounds. Production in Canada is estimated at about 27 million pounds yearly. Beeswax is also an important article of commerce. However, the value of the honeybee, in cross-fertilizing fruit trees and other fruit-bearing plants, greatly exceeds that of its natural products. See *Bees.*

Honeydew. A sweet, honey-like fluid that is produced by aphids, or plant lice, and by a few other sap-feeding insects. In the alimentary canal of these insects the sugar of the sap is not digested but is passed through the body in such quantity as to give this character to the residue of the food. It is discharged from the anal opening, often by many aphids simultaneously when a tree that is full of them receives a jar, and falls as a shower on whatever lies below. Undershrubs become coated with honeydew, and bees gather it from their leaves; or ants may follow and tend and guard an aphid colony in order to profit by their product.

The ants behave like herdsmen, stroking and patting the aphids with their antennæ to induce them to yield up a drop of honeydew, which the ants then suck up.

Honeydew is sticky, and deposits of it on the leaves of trees in smoky cities gather a coating of black soot and render the trees very unsightly. See *Ants, Aphids.*

Hookworm (*Necator americana*). A small nematode worm, closely related to the trichina and whipworm, slightly less than a half inch long. It infests the small intestine of man and the gorilla, where it moves about, sucking blood, often causing severe anemia, terminating in exhaustion and death. This species is common among the poorer classes in the southern United States. The young worms live in moist earth, and the infection may be caught by drinking infected water, by eating infected food, and sometimes by contact of the feet and hands with infected soil.

The similar Old World hookworm (*Anchylostoma duodenale*) is very abundant throughout a large zone over 4000 miles wide, from 36° N. latitude to 30° S. latitude, some 46 countries, with a population exceeding 900,000,000, being more or less afflicted. In India and southern China about 75 per cent of the population suffer from it. The disease, however, readily yields to medical treatment, and its prevention and control depend almost entirely upon sewage disposal. See *Trichina.*

Hoopoe (*hōō'pōō*) (*Upupa epops*). A peculiar Old World bird, about the size of a blue jay, related to the hornbills, found in Europe, southern Asia, and northern Africa. It has a large crest on the head, a long slender bill, and beautiful white, buff, and black plumage. Hoopoes are tame, familiar birds, usually frequenting open grounds, and feeding upon grubs and insects obtained by probing in the earth with their long bills. In autumn they become very fat and, in some European countries, are highly esteemed for food. They nest in holes in trees or walls, laying four or five greenish blue eggs. Various other hoopoes occur in Asia and Africa, including some 16 species of wood hoopoes.

Horned Lizard (*Phrynosoma*). The so-called "horned toads" are native only to North American deserts. Seventeen species occur in the western United States and in Mexico. They are usually 4 to 6 inches long, with grotesque, flattened, toad-like bodies, covered with spiny scales, and with sharp, conical horns upon the head. They inhabit hot, arid, sandy situations, lying quiet by day and coming out in the evening to search for insects, which they catch with the tongue, somewhat after the manner of true toads. All species are entirely harmless.

Horse (*Equus caballus*). A one-toed ungulate mammal, the best-known representative of the horse family (*Equidæ*). The true horse is characterized by the tail being furnished with long hairs from its base outward; by the long and flowing mane; by the presence of a bare callosity on the inner surface of the hind as well as of the forelegs; and by the head and ears being smaller and the legs longer than those of the ass and other closely related species.

The horse seems to have been first domesticated in central Asia. It was pictured on ancient Assyrian monuments, was early known in Egypt, and is mentioned throughout the Bible and the classic Greek and Roman writings. Horses were probably first used for war in central Asia. Bodies of cavalry and horses drawing war chariots are shown in the oldest sculptures at Nineveh.

According to Ewart, at least four wild species have contributed to the origin of the modern breeds of horses; namely, the woodland horse (*E. robustus*), adapted for forest life, the steppe horse (*E. przewalskii*), adapted for plains life, the desert horse (*E. agilis*), adapted for life in arid regions, and the Sivalik (*E. sivalensis*), which formerly lived in northern India. Of these, only the steppe horse still exists in the wild state.

The horse is the most spirited, trustworthy, and affectionate of the larger working animals, and is held in such intimate regard by man that sentiment practically prohibits the use of its excellent flesh for food. Ages of domestication have produced numerous breeds, ranging in size from a Shetland pony to a Percheron draft horse. In weight, horses vary from a few hundred pounds in the small breeds to 2200 pounds in English shire horses. The average horse normally lives to 18 or 20 years, though a few attain the age of 40 or 50 years. They are, however, rarely serviceable for work or speed after reaching 15 years.

House Fly (*Musca domestica*). A small two-winged insect found around human habitations almost throughout the world. The strongly veined, transparent wings are never folded when at rest, as are those of the grasshopper or beetle, but are always extended flat. In place of hind wings are two small rodlike organs which are believed to aid the insect in balancing and steering when in flight. The greater part of the head is made up of two remarkable eyes, each composed of thousands of facets, enabling the insect to see in nearly all directions. At the top of the head, between the two large compound eyes, are three small, single or simple eyes.

The mouth of the fly is provided with a curious, fleshy, tonguelike organ or sucking proboscis which is bent beneath the head when at rest. Upon alighting on a food substance, the fly unrolls and extends its tongue. The knoblike end opens into two flat muscular, corrugated surfaces. With these the fly laps up plant and animal juices or sugar that it has moistened and dissolved with its own saliva. The inside of the muscular surfaces of the tongue is rough, like a rasp or file, and is used to scrape delicate surfaces, or even to puncture the skin of animals, causing a minute flow of blood.

The feet of the fly are beset with small hairs, each terminating in a disk, which is believed to act as a sucker, enabling the insect to walk on smooth surfaces, as, for example, on a ceiling, with its back downward.

The fly multiplies with extreme rapidity. The few scattering flies which are usually all that survive the winter, are capable of producing countless millions during the summer season. In stable manure, decaying garbage, or other refuse matter, the female lays from 120 to 160 eggs. In 6 or 8 hours these hatch, producing the larvæ or maggots, which become full grown in 4 or 5 days. These then pass into the pupa or transition stage, emerging about 5 days later as fully developed, perfect flies,—or from egg to adult in about 10 days! It is estimated that in six months the progeny of a single pair might exceed 100 quintillion flies.

Flies act as scavengers and consume filth that otherwise would become offensive from decay. But, far outweighing all this benefit is the fact that they carry germs from sores, decomposing animal matter, and cesspools, and deposit them on human food, thereby spreading many dangerous diseases. Among these are typhoid, diphtheria, and tuberculosis. The house fly, therefore, should everywhere be ruthlessly exterminated, and its breeding places removed or thoroughly treated with insecticides. See *Flies*.

Humming Bird. The numerous family (*Trochilidæ*) of humming birds contains the smallest, most active, and most brilliantly colored of all feathered beings. While they differ in a marked degree from all other birds, they are most nearly related to the swifts. They have powerful wings which move so rapidly in flight as to become almost invisible, giving forth the buzzing sound from which the birds take their name. They fly backward as well as forward. The bill, usually long and slender, and sometimes strongly curved, is occasionally very short, and the feet are small and weak.

The plumage fairly glows with flashing, jewel-like combinations of the most resplendent colors, and is fittingly described by Audubon as "glittering fragments of the rainbow." Contrary to widespread belief, humming birds feed chiefly on minute insects found in and among flowers, and rarely upon honey or nectar. Their elegant cup-shaped nests, usually placed on trees, shrubs, or reeds, rank among the marvels of bird architecture. They are made chiefly of plant down and spiders' webs, ornamented on the outside with lichens and mosses. The pure white eggs are almost invariably two in number. As in the case of the swifts, the young are fed by regurgitation. Except for a weak twitter, humming birds possess no voice nor song.

There are more than 500 species of humming birds, all natives of the New World and most abundant in the tropical Andes. About 50 are found in Mexico, and 17 occur in the United States, mostly near the Mexican border, only one ranging east of the Mississippi. The largest known species is the giant hummer of the high Andes, 8½ inches long; the most diminutive is the fairy humming bird of Cuba, only 2¼ inches long, which, so far as known, is the smallest bird in the world. Among many species noted for their handsome plumage are the topaz-throated, fire-tailed, saber-wing, sylph, sun-gem, and coquette humming birds.

The ruby-throated humming bird (*Trochilus colubris*), 3¾ inches long, shining green above, with dusky under parts and a ruby-red throat, nests from Labrador to Nebraska and south to Florida and Texas, and winters in Cuba and Mexico. The rufous humming bird (*Selasphorus rufus*), 3½ inches long, bright reddish brown, with a gorget of fire red, orange, and green, breeds from Arizona and California northward to Alaska, migrating to southern Mexico in winter. The calliope humming bird (*Stellula calliope*), of the Southwest, barely 3 inches long, is the smallest species native to the United States.

Hyena (*Hyæna*). Carnivorous mammals, combining in their structure features characteristic of the cats, the civets, and the dogs. There are three species, found only in Africa and in southern Asia. Hyenas have a repulsive appearance, and are covered with coarse, bristly hair, short over the greater portion of the body, but produced into a mane along the ridge of the neck. The hind legs are shorter than the fore, giving the body a slope from the withers to the haunches. In size they are somewhat larger than a shepherd's dog. The cheek muscles are greatly developed, and the large teeth have great crushing power.

While they sometimes attack cattle, hyenas rarely molest man though they occasionally seize children. Contrary to popular belief, hyenas are capable of being tamed, and have even been used as watchdogs. As carrion feeders they are useful scavengers. All are nocturnal in their habits. The striped hyena (*H. hyæna*) occurs from Ethiopia and Asia Minor eastward to India. The spotted hyena (*H. crocuta*) ranges through nearly all of Africa south of the Sahara. The brown hyena (*H. brunniens*) is confined to southern Africa.

Ichneumon (*ĭk-nū'mŏn*) (*Herpestes ichneumon*). A small carnivorous mammal, native of northern Africa, called also "Egyptian mongoose" and "Pharaoh's rat." In size, the ichneumon is a little larger than a cat. It was held sacred by the ancient Egyptians, who depicted it upon the walls of their temples, because they believed it was sent by their gods to destroy the eggs of the crocodile, of which it is very fond. The ichneumon is readily tamed and becomes greatly attached to persons and places. It has been domesticated since ancient times in Egypt and used, like the cat, to rid houses of rats and other animal pests.

Iguana (*ĭ-gwä'nȧ*). A large lizard of tropical America and the West Indies, sometimes 6 feet long. It is surpassed in size among living lizards only by the monitors of the Old World. The body is much compressed, with powerful limbs, long-toed feet, and an elongated tail, sometimes two-thirds of the total length. There is a continuous crest of flat spines from the nape of the neck to the end of the tail. Under the throat there is a large pendent fold of skin.

The common iguana (*Iguana tuberculata*), 4 to 6 feet long, is green, black, and yellow in color. It has long, slender toes for climbing, and lives chiefly in the tops of trees overhanging streams in Central and South America and the West Indies. When frightened, it has the habit of leaping downward into the water, where it remains for some time before returning. The iguana is said to be fond of music and to enjoy having its body stroked. It lives mainly on the leaves, blossoms, and fruits of various trees. The flesh and eggs of the iguana are palatable, and it is much hunted for food.

Injurious Insects. Of the vast group of insects, more numerous in kinds than all other groups of animals combined, only a few species have been brought into human service, notably the honeybee and the silkworm. Many kinds, however, are capable of doing much injury in a very great variety of ways.

For example, insects may injure health by carrying germs of disease, as do the typhoid or house fly and the mosquito; they may destroy comfort, as do the black flies, lice, bedbugs, and fleas. They may injure domesticated animals, as do horseflies, botflies, screw worm flies, and ticks. They may injure clothing and textiles, as do the clothes moth and the carpet beetle. Some may destroy buildings and wooden implements, as do white ants (termites) and powder-post beetles. Others may destroy foods, as do the flour moth, larder beetle, and the cockroaches. Some may destroy stored grains, as do the weevils and the grain moth. Some kinds, like the timber beetles, the bark beetles, and the carpenter worm, may destroy timber. Other kinds, like the radish fly, tuber moth, and onion maggot, may destroy root crops. Fruits are subject to injury by such pests as the codling moth, the fruit flies, and the curculios; while various borers and miners do much hidden damage to growing crops.

But most numerous of all, and capable of inflicting the most extensive damage, are the insects that feed upon the surface of plants. While the other injurious groups are controlled in a great diversity of ways, these plant-destroying kinds are in the main controlled by spraying, as follows:—

1. Those that chew up the plants are killed by spraying an arsenical poison upon their food.
2. Those that suck up the sap only are killed by spraying their bodies with some insecticide that kills by contact, such as nicotine sulphate. See *Ants, Aphids, Boll Weevil, Caterpillar, Chinch Bug, Corn Borer, Fruit Flies, House Fly, Mosquitoes, San Jose Scale, Scale Insects, Weevils.*

Insectivora (*ĭn'sĕk-tĭv'ô-rȧ*). An order of mammals, so called because they feed chiefly upon insects and other small invertebrates. All are of small size and nearly all are nocturnal, burrowing animals. In external appearance they resemble the rodents, but in structure they are more like the bats. Usually they have five toes, armed with claws for digging, and soft fur, though some, such as the European hedgehog, are covered with spines or bristles. There are about 250 species, widely distributed throughout the world, comprising the various moles, shrews, hedgehogs, desmans, and tenrecs, also the solenodon, potamogale, and colugo. See *Hedgehog, Moles, Shrews.*

Insects (*Insecta* or *Hexapoda*). A class of six-legged arthropods which comprises the most numerous group of animals, embracing a greater number of species than all other groups combined. A true insect may be known by the division of its body into three distinct regions: head, thorax, and abdomen,—the thorax bearing three pairs of legs and usually two pairs of wings, though sometimes only one pair, and sometimes wingless. All insects are air-breathing and chiefly terrestrial, feeding upon vegetable matter, though some are carnivorous and others are parasitic. A few insects bring forth living young, but the vast majority lay eggs, which, after hatching, undergo complete or partial metamorphosis. Complete metamorphosis involves the cycle of *larva*, usually in the form of a worm or caterpillar, *pupa*, a dormant stage in a protective covering, and *imago*, or perfect insect.

Some species, such as the honeybee, silkworm moth, lac insect, and cochineal insect, are of great economic importance. Various insects are carriers of disease, among them the mosquito which transmits malaria, the house fly which conveys typhoid fever and Asiatic cholera, the rat flea which spreads the bubonic plague, and the tsetse fly which infects man with sleeping sickness. Many insects have poisonous stings. See *Injurious Insects.*

Insects are found everywhere throughout the world, flourishing prodigiously in the tropics and abundant even within the Arctic circle. The number of living species is conservatively estimated at 5,000,000. More than 300,000 species have been collected and described. These are usually classified in the following 19 orders: *Thysanura*, springtails; *Ephemerida*, May flies; *Odonata*, dragon flies; *Plecoptera*, stone flies; *Isoptera*, termites; *Corrodentia*, book lice; *Mallophaga*, biting bird lice; *Euplexoptera*, earwigs; *Orthoptera*, cockroaches, grasshoppers; *Hemiptera*, true bugs; *Neuroptera*, ant lions; *Mecoptera*, scorpion flies; *Trichoptera*, caddis flies; *Lepidoptera*, butterflies and moths; *Diptera*, true flies, mosquitoes; *Siphonaptera*, fleas; *Coleoptera*, beetles; *Hymenoptera*, bees, ants, and wasps.

Jackal (*Canis*). A doglike carnivore, smaller and more foxlike than the wolf. There are several species, all natives of the Old World. They are seldom more than 15 inches high, generally buff or tawny in color, with the tip of the tail always dark. Jackals are nocturnal in habit, living in burrows in caves, rocks, or ruins, venturing forth to hunt in packs at night. Like dogs, they are omnivorous feeders, devouring small animals, poultry, carrion, vegetables, sugar cane, and even fruit. Their howlings at night are regarded as peculiarly unpleasant. The formerly prevalent notion that the jackal is the "lion's provider" is an exploded fable of natural history.

Jackals are readily domesticated, and they everywhere interbreed with native dogs. Crossings of jackals with wolf dogs or wolves are supposed to account for the origin of many of the existing varieties of the dog. The Indian jackal (*C. aureus*), found in northern Africa, southeastern Europe, and southern Asia, acts as a scavenger in the Orient, prowling about the streets of large towns. See *Dog.*

Jackdaw (*Corvus monedula*). A European bird of the crow family, somewhat smaller than the common crow, with the entire plumage glossy black, excepting a slaty-gray collar about the neck. The jackdaw frequents ruined buildings, old towers, steeples, and cliffs, and sometimes is found in the midst of populous cities. It builds a large nest of sticks in all sorts of abandoned places, and lays 4 to 6 greenish eggs, spotted with gray and brown. In its habits the jackdaw is very similar to the crow. It is readily tamed, taught various tricks, and sometimes learns to speak a few words. See *Crow.*

Jaguar (*jăg'wär*) (*Felis onca*). The largest, fiercest, and most formidable of the wild cats of the New World. Its massive body is about 4 feet long, the head large and strong, the tail relatively short. The ground color is usually golden yellow. On the back and sides are hollow patches of black enclosing spots of the ground color. On the head, legs, and belly the spots are of solid black.

The jaguar inhabits North and South America, ranging from southern Texas through Mexico, Central America, and Brazil, as far south as Paraguay. Wooded banks of rivers are its favorite haunts, and it is said to frequent the reedy margins of lakes, seeming to have a great predilection for water. It preys chiefly upon weaker mammals, and is said to catch fish; occasionally it kills horses and cattle, and even men. The jaguar is a noisy animal, roaring much at night, especially on the approach of bad weather.

Jays. A numerous group (*Garrulinæ*) of perching birds, closely allied to the crows and the magpies. In general their plumage is brightly colored, usually with a tint of blue predominating, and the tail is always at least three-fourths as long as the wings. They are active, noisy, forest-loving birds, with harsh, discordant voices. About 20 species occur in North America, most numerous in the West and Southwest, usually remaining the year round wherever they breed.

The blue jay (*Cyanocitta cristata*), about a foot long, with black and white markings and a conspicuous crest, is a common resident from Labrador to Nebraska and south to Florida and Texas. It constructs a well built nest of twigs and roots lined with rootlets, usually in a tree either in the woods or in an orchard. In this it lays 4 or 5 brownish olive or ashy green eggs.

The Canada jay (*Perisoreus canadensis*), called also "whisky jack" and "moose bird," inhabits coniferous forests from Nova Scotia, northern New York, and Minnesota northward to the arctic regions. It is about a foot long, gray in color with darker and lighter markings. Less shy than the blue jay, it becomes almost tame if unmolested. It nests early in March, incubating its eggs when the temperature is far below zero.

Among the numerous kinds found in the western United States are the Steller, blue-fronted, long-crested, black-headed, blue-eared, green, woodhouse, Rocky Mountain, Oregon, California, Arizona, and Texan jays. While omnivorous feeders, subsisting largely on insects in summer, and on seeds, particularly acorns and pine seeds, in winter, some species, as the blue jay and the California jay, eat the eggs and also the young of other birds.

Kangaroo (*Macropodidæ*). A family of pouch-bearing mammals. They are the most highly developed of the marsupial animals, and are peculiarly suited for the conditions of life in Australia, Tasmania, New Guinea, and adjacent islands.

The family comprises no fewer than 60 species, and, of these, the gray kangaroo (*Macropus giganteus*) may be taken as a type. This species was formerly plentiful and roamed over all the plains, but it is now fast retiring before the colonist. The fore limbs are small; the hind limbs very large and thick; the head small, with rather long ears, and a long, dusky brown muzzle; the body long, with the fur short but thick, and of a gray-brown tint. Full-grown specimens are about 4 feet high and attain a weight of 200 pounds.

When moving quickly the hind limbs alone are brought into action, and by means of these the animal bounds along in great leaps of from 15 to 20 feet, the body being carried in a nearly horizontal position, and the tail extended to balance it. The fore limbs are chiefly used in handling, and with these the female lifts her young which she carries in a pouch on the underside of the abdomen.

The number of young produced at birth is from 1 to 3. When born they are very small, usually about an inch in length, blind, naked, and helpless. After birth the mother places them in her pouch where they usually remain several months. Into this pouch the milk glands of the udder open, and the young are fed at the will of the mother.

The kangaroos are vegetable feeders, delighting in grasses, leaves, and herbs. The skins of kangaroos are prized for leather used in making shoes.

Killdeer (*Ægialitis vocifera*). A large, ring-necked plover, common throughout temperate North America, so named because of its familiar and persistent cry. The killdeer is about 11 inches long, grayish brown in color, with a white and a black band circling the neck, and with various other black and white markings. It frequents meadows and fields, in the vicinity of water, and lives upon worms, grasshoppers, beetles, snails, and other small forms of animal life. At nesting time it lays 4 buffy white eggs spotted with chocolate brown, in a slight hollow in the ground. When an intruder approaches the nest or young, the parent birds endeavor to lead him in another direction by uttering frantic cries, limping, fluttering, and falling over as if injured. See *Plover*.

Killer Whale (*Orca*). A group of large, powerful, carnivorous dolphins, armed with very strong, sharp teeth. They are the only cetaceans which habitually attack and devour mammals. On account of their habit of destroying more animals than they can eat, they are generally known as killers. A full-grown male attains a length of 20 feet, with a back fin 6 feet high. The surface of the body is smooth and glossy, black in color, and marked with white spots or patches. Killers are found in all oceans and sometimes even ascend rivers to attack their prey, which consists of large fish, dolphins, seals, and even the great whales. The speed, strength, and ferocity of the killers make them veritable tigers of the sea.

About 8 species have been described. The Atlantic killer (*Orca gladiator*) has been longest known, but the habits of the Pacific killer (*Orcinus orca*), which kills and eats the California gray whale, have been more generally observed.

Kingbird (*Tyrannus tyrannus*). An American bird of the flycatcher family, noted for its pugnacity; called also "bee bird" and "bee martin." It is about 8½ inches long, blackish slate-gray above and white below, with a concealed orange-red crest on the head, and a black tail tipped with white. It nests in trees from New Brunswick and Manitoba southward, rarely crossing the Rocky mountains, laying 3 to 5 white, somewhat spotted eggs.

During the nesting period, the male kingbird will fearlessly attack cuckoos, blackbirds, jays, crows, and even hawks and eagles which may come near its home, driving them off with swift darts and peckings. While sometimes eating a few bees, the kingbird on the whole performs very valuable service by destroying injurious insects which form its chief food. The somewhat larger Arkansas kingbird (*T. verticalis*) and Cassin kingbird (*T. vociferans*), with yellow under parts, which range from the Great Plains westward to the Pacific, are similar in habit to the eastern kingbird.

Kingfisher. The kingfishers form a numerous and interesting family of birds (*Alcedinidæ*). They are related to the cuckoos and hornbills, but are distinguished by having a long, straight bill and unequal toes united for about half their length. There are about 200 species, mostly native to the Malay archipelago. Of about 12 American species, all but one are practically confined to the tropics. They are mostly solitary birds of beautiful plumage, living near the water and feeding chiefly upon fish. They nest in holes in banks or in hollow trees, laying several glossy white eggs.

The handsome belted kingfisher (*Cercyle alcyon*), found throughout North America, is about 13 inches long, ashy blue above, white below, with conspicuous white markings and a crested head. It is an alert, active, but rather shy bird, frequenting clear streams and lakes. It has the habit of sitting quietly and then suddenly darting into the water for its prey. The beautiful ringed kingfisher (*C. torquatus*), 17 inches long, and the little Texas kingfisher (*C. americana septentrionalis*), of South and Central America, range northward into southern Texas.

King Snake (*Ophibolus*). A genus which includes some of the most interesting North American serpents. They range from 14 inches to 6 feet in length and are strikingly colored. All are powerful constrictors, feeding largely upon small rodents, but some kill and eat other snakes, including the most venomous. Toward man, however, the king snakes are remarkably mild-tempered and inoffensive. Seven species, with several varieties, occur in the United States.

The king snake, or Chain Snake (*O. getulus*), from 5 to 6 feet long, is black with narrow, chainlike, yellow or white crossbands. In its several varieties it extends throughout the United States. It is highly useful, destroying immense numbers of rats and mice. A bold fighter and entirely immune to snake poison, it frequently kills and eats copperheads and rattlesnakes. It is, however, very easily tamed and is gentle and hardy in captivity.

The common Milk Snake, or House Snake (*O. doliatus*), about 3 feet long, is gray above with large chestnut-brown saddles bordered with black. It occurs from New England to Wisconsin and southward. Owing to its habit of invading barns and dairies, and even houses, in search of mice and rats, it has acquired the reputation of stealing milk, a myth which has no foundation in fact.

Kiwi (*kē′wĭ*) (*Apteryx*). The Maori name of a peculiar New Zealand bird. It is somewhat related to the ostrich, but possesses no visible wings or tail, and the nostrils are placed at the end of a long, slender beak. There are about five very similar species, the largest of which, the South Island kiwi (*A. australis*), attains a length of 27 inches. Kiwis are nocturnal in habit and feed largely upon berries and worms. They nest in holes in which the female lays one or two very large eggs which are incubated by the male. See *Moa*.

Lac Insect (*Carteria*). The name given to several scale insects which secrete the valuable substance known as lac, much used in making varnishes. The Asian lac insect (*C. lacca*) lives chiefly on fig trees. The body becomes coated with a resinous secretion, after which the insect dies. Immense numbers thus live and perish upon the same twig, which becomes enveloped in a coating sometimes a half inch thick. When melted and refined, this resinous material becomes the gum lac or shellac of commerce.

In the southwestern United States a native lac insect (*C. larriæ*) feeds upon the creosote bush (*Larrea mexicana*), an immensely abundant desert shrub. The species secretes lac identical in composition with the Asiatic product, but as yet it has not been commercially utilized. See *Scale Insects*.

Ladybird. A small beetle of the numerous family *Coccinellidæ*, 150 species of which are found in the United States. Ladybirds, called also ladybugs, are uniformly of small size, hemispherical shape, and are usually readily distinguished by their polka dot markings. They are often of a brilliant red or yellow color variously spotted with black, white, red, or yellow. Ladybirds feed almost entirely upon scale insects and plant lice, and, hence, are immensely beneficial to agriculturalists and fruit growers.

The two-spotted ladybird (*Coccinella bipunctata*), found throughout the United States, is one of the most valuable native species. In 1886 the Australian ladybird (*Novius cardinalis*), a red and black species, was brought to California to check the cottony-cushion scale then rapidly destroying the orange and lemon orchards. Within a few years this ladybird had practically exterminated that destructive pest.

Lamprey (*Hyperoartia*). The lampreys form an order of round-mouthed eels (*Cyclostomata*). They resemble the hagfishes in form, but the single nostril ends in a blind sac instead of penetrating the palate. The scaleless skin is not usually slimy, as in case of the common eel. The eyes are well developed, and the mouth is a round disk formed for sucking and armed with rasplike teeth. Their small eggs are usually laid in brooks away from the sea, and, in nearly all cases, the adult lamprey dies after spawning. The lampreys feed upon the blood and flesh of fishes, attacking shad, sturgeon, cod, halibut, and other valuable food species. In Cayuga lake, New York, lampreys destroy great numbers of horned pout.

The sea lamprey (*Petromyzon marinus*), wrongly called lamper eel, common in North Atlantic waters, 2 to 3 feet long, follows the shad up the rivers to spawn. Its flesh is edible and was formerly much used for food.

Lance-head Viper (*Lachesis*). A genus of exceedingly virulent crotaline snakes, differing from rattlesnakes in having keeled scales and in possessing a horny spine at the end of the tail. There are 40 species, found in tropical America and southeastern Asia. The Fer-de-Lance (*L. lanceolatus*), of Central and South America, 4 to 7 feet in length, has a broad head and very long fangs. It will attack without warning and its bite is often fatal.

The Bushmaster (*L. mutus*), of the Amazonian region, is the largest known viperine snake, attaining a length of 12 feet, with a much thicker and stronger body than that of the king cobra. By vibrating its horned tail, it makes a warning noise somewhat like that of the rattlesnake. It has enormous fangs and its bite is most deadly, that of an eight-foot snake having caused death in 10 minutes.

Lark. The larks make up a numerous family of passerine birds (*Alaudidæ*). They are land birds of sober plumage which build their nests upon the ground and feed chiefly upon seeds and insects. There are about 100 species, mostly natives of Europe, Asia, and Africa, only one of which is found in America. Many are noted for their melodious songs.

The most celebrated is the Old World Skylark (*Alauda arvensis*), which rivals the nightingale in sweetness. This famous song bird is now introduced and naturalized in Oregon and on Long Island, New York. It is a favorite cage bird and sings well in captivity. During migrations the skylark is shot in immense numbers for the European markets.

The Horned Lark (*Otocornis alpestris*), called also shore lark, about 8 inches long, has earlike tufts and yellow markings on the head. It breeds in northern Europe, Greenland, and Canada, wintering in eastern America as far south as North Carolina. About a dozen varieties of the horned lark are found in the western United States.

Leopard (*Felis pardus*). One of the largest of the cats (*Felidæ*), being exceeded in size only by the lion and the tiger, with which it ranks in grace, quickness, ferocity, and destructiveness. The leopard is found throughout Africa and in Asia from Palestine to China and Japan, south of the Himalayas, and also in Borneo. The color is usually some shade of buff, sometimes tawny or rufous, irregularly but strongly marked with spots of black. The body of this fierce and rapacious animal is about 4 feet long. From the great flexibility of the limbs and spine, it can take surprising leaps, swim, crawl, and ascend trees. Leopards feed chiefly upon antelopes, deer, monkeys, goats, and dogs. They also capture peafowl and other ground birds.

Occasionally, leopards attack women and children, but they rarely, if ever, molest men. See *Cat Family*.

Lion (*Felis leo*). The most famous of the great cats, distinguished from all other species by its mane and tufted tail. A lion of the largest size stands about 3 feet high, with the body about 6½ feet long and the tail about 3 feet long, and sometimes weighs 500 pounds.

When mature, the lion is of a nearly uniform tawny or yellowish color, though sometimes reddish and occasionally almost black, and always paler on the under parts. The whole frame is extremely muscular, and the fore parts, in particular, are remarkably powerful. The large head, bright, flashing eye, and copious mane give a noble appearance to the animal. This, together with his immense strength, has led to his being called the "king of beasts." The lioness is smaller, has no mane, and is of a lighter color on the under parts.

The lion is found chiefly in Africa, although it occurs in some parts of Arabia, Persia, and India. It is not an inhabitant of deep forests, but rather of open plains in which the shelter of occasional bushes and thickets may be found. When taken young the lion is easily tamed, breeds readily in captivity, but is never trustworthy. See *Cat Family*.

Lizards (Suborder *Lacertilia*). A numerous group of reptiles. Together with the snakes (Suborder *Ophidia*), they constitute the large order *Squamata*, which includes more than nine-tenths of all living reptiles. Most lizards have four well-developed limbs with five-toed feet, and long, slender tails. Some degenerate lizards lack one or both pairs of limbs. In lizards the lower jaws are firmly united by sutures, while in snakes they are connected by an elastic ligament. An ear opening is always present in lizards, and the eyelids are usually movable. The skin is covered with scales or armed with spines. Nearly all are egg-laying, although a few bring forth their young alive.

Except the Gila monster (*Heloderma*), no lizard has a venomous bite. Nearly all lizards are land animals, though a few tropical species are aquatic. Many live in deserts, some among rocks, and others are arboreal. The vast majority are insectivorous or carnivorous. Some herbivorous lizards, as, for example, the iguana, are used for human food. There are about 1800 species widely diffused in warm and temperate regions. These are grouped in some 20 families. Among the more important groups are the geckos, chameleons, iguanas, amphisbænas, true lizards, monitors, and skinks. See *Basilisk, Chameleon, Chuckwalla, Flying Dragon, Gila Monster, Glass Snake, Horned Lizard, Iguana, Moloch, Monitor*.

Llama (*Lama glama*). A South American mammal of the camel family, used as a beast of burden in the Andes mountains. It is a domesticated form of the guanaco (*L. guanacus*), still found wild from Peru to Patagonia. The llama has a height of about 3 feet at the shoulder and resembles a small camel, except that it lacks a hump and carries its head erect. It will carry a load of 100 pounds at the rate of 12 to 15 miles a day, and, being sure-footed, is the principal carrier of burdens on the narrow, mountainous trails of the Peruvian Andes. The long hair or wool is used for making coarse fabrics. At the time of the Spanish conquest, the llama had long been in use by the native Peruvians. See *Alpaca, Guanaco*.

Lobster (*Homarus*). A well-known marine crustacean highly prized for food. It is very similar in form and structure to the common fresh-water crawfish, but of much greater size, and with very large, unequal front claws or pincers. It has blunt teeth situated in the stomach for crushing shells, and swimming legs on the abdomen, though the tail is the chief swimming organ.

The American lobster (*H. americanus*) is found from southern Labrador to North Carolina, usually near rocky shores, at a depth of 10 to 20 fathoms, migrating to deeper waters in winter. It is a bottom feeder, subsisting chiefly upon fish and other animals, both living and dead. Mature lobsters average about 10 inches in length and weigh about 2 pounds. They sometimes attain a length of 24 inches and a weight exceeding 30 pounds. See *Crawfish, Crustaceans*.

Longevity or Age of Animals. According to accredited data collected by Carl W. Neumann, the following may be regarded as normal life spans of some of the more important animals.

Between 200 and 300 years: eider duck, giant tortoise, goose, parrot, raven.

Between 100 and 200 years: elephant, 150–200; falcon, 162; pike, 150; carp, 150; vulture, 118; golden eagle, 104; swan, 102.

Less than 100 years: ant, 10–15; ass, 40–50; bear, 40–50; beaver, 20–25; bee, queen, 4-5; bee, worker, 6 weeks; blackbird, 18; canary, 24; cat, 9-10; chicken, 15–20; crab, fresh-water, 20; crane, 40–50; crocodile, 40; cuckoo, 40; dog, 10–15; dove, 60–70; dromedary, 40–50; earthworm, 10; eel, fresh-water, 10–12; elk, 20; fox, 10; goat, 12–15; guinea pig, 5–7; gull, 44; hare, 7-8; heron, 60; hippopotamus, 40; horse, 40–50; lion, 20–25; magpie, 25; mouse, 3-4; ostrich, 60–70; owl, 68; pearl mussel, 60–70; pig, wild, 20–30; rat, 3; reindeer, 16; rhinoceros, 40–50; roebuck, 15; salamander, 10–12; sheep, 10–15; squirrel, 10–12; stag, 30; tiger, 20; toad, 40; tree frog, 10; wolf, 10–15; woodpecker, 60–70.

Loon (*Gaviidæ*). A family of large diving birds, two or three feet in length, with powerful wings and somewhat webbed or lobed feet. Their legs are placed so far back on the body that they can scarcely walk on land, but in the water they are among the most expert divers and swimmers known. A loon can disappear below the surface so quickly that it is very difficult to shoot it even with a rifle. There are about 5 species, found in northern regions.

The common loon, or Great Northern Diver (*Gavia imber*), occurs throughout northern America, Europe, and Asia. In America it nests, usually in old muskrat houses in ponds or lakes, from the northern United States to within the Arctic circle, migrating in winter as far south as Mexico. Its general color is black above and white below, with the back spotted and the sides streaked with white. It has a loud, weird, startling cry, somewhat like that of a wolf or the scream of a human being.

Lungfish (*Dipneusti*). The lungfishes, or dipnoans, form a subclass of fishes which have, in addition to the regular gills, the air bladder modified so as to serve as a lung. The heart is more highly developed and the paired fins are more leglike than in ordinary fishes. By many zoologists the lungfishes are considered as a connecting link between the fishes and the amphibians. While very abundant in earlier geologic times, only a few living species are known.

Lynx. The lynxes are short-tailed, tree-climbing wildcats found in various parts of the world. In North America two species, very nearly equal in size, are known, the bay lynx, or bob cat (*L. rufus*), and the Canada lynx (*L. canadensis*). The former is of a reddish gray color, sometimes spotted, and varying greatly in the rufous shades. It is found in nearly all wild regions of the United States.

The Canada lynx is found principally in southern and western Canada as far north as the sixtieth parallel. The body is about 32 inches long, the tail 4 or 5 inches, and the height at the shoulder about 18 inches. It may be distinguished from the bay lynx by its lighter gray color, huge hairy paws, and by a slender tuft of stiff hairs on the tip of each ear. The Canada lynx is much hunted and trapped for its fur, highly valued for robes, coats, and collars. Lynxes feed upon small mammals and birds, which they catch after the manner of the cat family. Although reputedly dangerous animals, lynxes lack courage and seldom, if ever, voluntarily attack a man even when he is unarmed and alone. See *Cat Family*.

Lyre Bird (*Menura superba*). A handsome Australian bird, somewhat intermediate in structure between the woodpeckers and the perching birds. It is so named because the remarkable tail feathers of the male, when erected and spread, are arranged somewhat in the form of a lyre. The lyre bird measures about 42 inches in length, of which the tail comprises 25 inches. In color, it is brown above, grayish below, with reddish markings.

Lyre birds live in pairs on the ground, frequenting rocks and bushes and feeding upon beetles, slugs, and snails. They build an oven-like, covered nest of sticks, in which a single purplish brown egg is laid. The tail feathers of the cock are shed at the end of each season and renewed the following year.

Macaw (*Ara*). A genus of large, beautiful birds of the parrot family. They are sometimes 3 feet long, and are distinguished by having their cheeks destitute of feathers, and their tails long and wedge-shaped. There are about 15 species, all natives of tropical South America. The largest and most splendid in regard to color is the great scarlet or red-and-blue macaw. The great green macaw and the blue-and-yellow macaw are somewhat smaller. Unlike the true parrots, the macaws do not readily learn to articulate words. See *Cockatoo, Parrot.*

Mackerel (*Scombridæ*). A family of marine, spiny-rayed fishes, highly valued for food. The common mackerel (*Scomber scombrus*), abundant on both shores of the North Atlantic, supports important fisheries. It is a beautiful fish, brilliant green and blue above, and silvery below, with numerous transverse black streaks. Usually, it is from 12 to 18 inches long and weighs from 1 to 3 pounds. Mackerel appear in immense schools, rarely approach land, and live chiefly on small fish. The similar chub mackerel (*Scomber japonicus*), found in both the North Atlantic and the North Pacific, is common off southern California.

The Spanish mackerel (*Scomberomorus maculatus*), a most excellent food fish, averaging 3 to 4 pounds in weight, is, likewise, found on both coasts of the United States. The Kingfish (*Scomberomorus cavallus*) is a fine southern food fish common on Florida coasts. It usually ranges from 10 to 20 pounds but sometimes attains a weight of 100 pounds. The Sierra (*Scomberomorus regalis*), common off Florida and Cuba, 2½ feet long, silvery with brown spots, is a fine game and food fish.

The Tunny, horse mackerel, or Great Albacore (*Thunnus thynnus*), highly esteemed for food since ancient Phœnician and Roman times, is called Tuna in Mediterranean countries and also in California. While sometimes reaching 10 to 15 feet in length and 1500 pounds in weight, it usually weighs much less than 500 pounds. In southern California the Santa Catalina sportsmen pursue it as a game fish, taking specimens weighing from 50 to 250 pounds with rod and reel.

The Pompano (*Trachinotas carolinus*), of the Florida and Gulf coasts, 18 inches long, bluish and golden in color, is the most prized table fish taken in southern waters.

Maggot. The immature stage (larva) of a dipterous insect or true fly. It is more or less wormlike, soft, whitish, and thin skinned, lacking eyes, legs, and head, and incapable of living except in soft organic substances, such as the flesh of animals, the pulp of fruits, or the softer tissues of plants. The larvæ of blowflies are the maggots that quickly consume carrion. The larvæ of house flies feed by preference in manure piles. Apple, grape, and currant maggots live in fruits. (See *Fruit Flies.*) The larvæ of many other flies are important consumers of soft plant substances.

Magpie (*Pica*). A bird belonging to the crow family. There are several species, two of which belong to America. The European magpie (*P. pica*) is about 19 inches in length; the plumage is black and white, the black glossed with green and purple; the bill is stout, and the tail is very long. The magpies continue in pairs throughout the year, and subsist on a variety of food, chiefly animal. They are determined robbers of other birds' nests, devouring the eggs and young birds. In captivity they are noted for their crafty instincts, their power of imitating words, and their propensity to purloin and secrete glittering articles.

The American magpie (*P. pica hudsonica*) is a beautiful bird, about 20 inches long, purple-black with large patches of white on the breast, rump, and top of the wings. The tail is very long and pointed. Although sometimes preying upon small mammals, birds and their eggs, this magpie feeds chiefly upon insects, including many destructive kinds. It is a resident of the Rocky Mountain region from Arizona to Alaska, east to Nebraska and Hudson bay, and west to the Sierra Nevada. The smaller yellow-billed magpie (*C. nuttallii*) inhabits portions of central California. See *Crow, Jackdaw, Raven, Rook.*

Mallard (*Anas boschas*). The most common and widely distributed wild duck, found nearly throughout the northern hemisphere, wintering as far south as India, Egypt, and Panama. The mallard is usually about 2 feet long and the plumage of the male is handsomely colored. The head and neck are glossy green, with a white border below, and the breast is rich chestnut. The wing has a broad band, or speculum, of brilliant purple, bordered on each side with black and white bands.

In North America the mallard breeds from Indiana and Iowa northward and is most numerous in the interior. It builds a nest of grass and leaves, usually on the ground, in which it lays from 6 to 18 greenish eggs. It feeds chiefly on seeds, roots, worms, snails, and insects. The mallard is the parent wild species from which most varieties of the domestic duck have sprung. See *Duck.*

Mammals (*Mammalia*). The highest group of vertebrates, comprising all animals whose young after birth are fed by the mother with milk from the mammary glands. The class includes man, the apes and monkeys, the quadrupeds, bats, seals, and whales. Mammals are warm-blooded, have a four-chambered heart, breathe by lungs, and, except the duckbills and echidnas, bring forth their young alive. Most mammals are provided with hair, a distinctive skin-covering possessed by no other group of animals. While authorities differ, there are said to be at least 7500 living species of mammals. These are usually classified in from about 10 to 20 orders.

The widely used classification of Parker and Haswell groups the mammals in 11 orders as follows: *Monotremata*, egg-laying mammals—echidna, duckbill; *Marsupialia*, pouched mammals—kangaroos; *Edentata*, edentates—sloths, armadillos; *Cetacea*, cetaceans—whales, porpoises; *Sirenia*, sirenians—manatees, dugongs; *Ungulata*, hoofed mammals—ox, deer, horse; *Carnivora*, flesh-eating mammals, or beasts of prey—lion, tiger, jaguar; *Rodentia*, rodents, or gnawers—rats, squirrels, beavers; *Insectivora*, insectivores—moles, shrews; *Chiroptera*, winged mammals—bats; *Primates*,—lemurs, apes, man.

Mammoth (*Elephas primigenius*). An extinct elephant whose fossil remains are abundant in the northern parts of Europe, Asia, and North America. In size and general appearance the mammoth was very similar to the Indian elephant, but was covered with a heavy coat of long black hair, beneath which was an inner coat of reddish brown woolly hair. The tusks were strongly curved both upward and outward. These great animals lived in the Pleistocene period, and in Europe were contemporaneous with early man. They appear to have become extinct about the same time as the woolly rhinoceros, the cave bear, the cave tiger, and other great animals which, unlike man, did not survive the Ice age.

Many specimens of the mammoth have been found in Siberia frozen in ice, where they have lain, as in cold storage, for unknown thousands of years. In some cases their flesh is so perfectly preserved as to be eaten by bears and dogs. Remains of this animal are so numerous along some Siberian islands and river shores as to support, for many centuries, a considerable trade in its tusks, which yield valuable ivory. For the last 200 years, at least 100 pairs of tusks have been sent out from northern Siberia annually. In North America, remains of the mammoth occur from the vicinity of Washington, D. C., northward and westward to Alaska. A somewhat larger species, called the southern mammoth (*E. columbi*), has been found in the southern United States. See *Elephant, Mastodon.*

Manatee (*Trichecus*). An aquatic mammal of the order *Sirenia,* called also sea cow. Three species are known, one of which is found in West Africa and the others in America. The American manatees frequent rivers from Florida and Cuba to the Amazon, usually choosing the quiet reaches of the streams above tidewater. Their food consists of water grasses and other aquatic plants. They have a long, fishlike body, somewhat resembling that of a whale. Their anterior limbs are flat and not adapted for walking, hence they never come upon land. The hind limbs are wanting, and the broad, horizontally flattened tail is adapted for swimming. They are large, awkward animals, attaining, as a rule, a length of 8 to 10 feet but sometimes growing to 13 feet. The skin is of a grayish color, sparsely covered with hairs. Their flesh is excellent, and they furnish a soft, clear oil which does not become rancid. See *Dugong, Sirenia.*

Marsupialia (*mär-sū'pĭ-ā'lĭ-ȧ*). An order of mammals, standing at the foot of the *Eutheria,* or true mammals. They are so named because they carry their young for some time after birth in a marsupium, or external pouch, in which they are suckled by the mother. Excepting the opossums, which are found only in North and South America, all living marsupials are native to Australia, New Guinea, and adjacent islands. There are about 175 species, divided into two groups,—the vegetable-eating marsupials, including the kangaroos and phalangers, and the flesh-eating marsupials, including the bandicoots, the thylacines, and the opossums. See *Kangaroo, Opossum, Wombat.*

Marten. The marten family (*Mustelidæ*) is a numerous group of small carnivores. It includes many valuable fur bearing animals, as the weasels, ermines, sables, martens, minks, otters, ferrets, skunks, fishers, badgers, and wolverenes. There are upwards of 80 species, found chiefly in the northern hemisphere. The true martens (*Mustela*) also include the sable and the fisher.

The American marten (*M. americana*), often called American pine marten and American sable, is a highly prized fur bearing animal, found from Alaska to Labrador, southward to California, Colorado, and the Adirondacks. It has a slender body 18 inches long, and a bushy tail 8 inches long, and its general color is a rusty brown. This marten is a very active and cunning animal, living in pine woods, and feeding chiefly upon small mammals and birds. It is incessantly trapped for its excellent fur.

Mastodon. An extinct mammal of the elephant family. It much resembled the living kinds of elephants but had a longer head, very different teeth, and possessed, when young, rudimentary tusks in the lower jaw. About 30 species, widely scattered throughout the world, have been discovered. Mastodons originated in the Miocene period, flourished in all continents during the Pliocene period, and became extinct in Pleistocene time.

The American mastodon (*M. americanus*) formerly ranged over the greater portion of the United States. It was slightly less than 10 feet tall and was somewhat more heavily built than elephants of the same height. The strongly curved tusks were 7 to 9 feet long, and a short pair was sometimes present in the lower jaw. Great numbers of mastodon bones have been unearthed in the Mississippi valley.

Upon being dug up in various countries during ancient and medieval times, the huge limb bones of mastodons were often described as those of a former race of human giants. See *Elephant, Mammoth.*

Mayflies (*Ephemerida*). A group of very delicate aquatic insects, remarkable for the extreme brevity of their adult life. The immature stages are not shorter in duration than those of other insects, and are spent in the water feeding upon various plant substances. The adults, however, eat absolutely nothing, feeding and growth having been completed before the final transformation. Their sole business is to reproduce their kind. They have no jaws or other mouth parts, but they possess great powers of flight, and some of the larger species fly in vast swarms about the waterside for a brief period in summer. Some species live only a few hours after leaving the water, and those of longest life live but two days. They lay their eggs in the water and then die. In both the adult and the immature stage, mayflies are excellent food for fishes.

Meadow Lark (*Sturnella magna*). An American bird of the family *Icteridæ,* related to the blackbirds and orioles, found from New Brunswick to Minnesota and southward. It is about the size of a robin, the upper parts being black, brown, or buff, the under parts yellow, the neck with a scarf of jet-black, the sides with black spots arranged in rows, and the outer tail feathers white. They frequent meadows, preferring short thick grass, living much upon the ground. The nest is built in a tuft of grass, and usually contains from four to six whitish eggs spotted with brown.

The western meadow lark (*S. magna neglecta*), similar in plumage but superior in song, ranges from Manitoba to British Columbia and southward to Mexico. Meadow larks live mostly upon injurious insects.

Migration of Animals. Seasonal migrations constitute one of the most remarkable features of animal life. In general, birds fly south for the winter and north for the summer. Among the more remarkable flights are those of the golden plover, which travels some 8000 miles south from the Hudson Bay region, crossing about 2000 miles over the sea from Nova Scotia to the Caribbean countries, and winters in Argentina. It returns to Arctic America by way of Central America and the Mississippi valley. The arctic tern migrates almost from the north pole to the south pole and back again each year. Few North American birds, however, pass the equator, Mexico being the southern limit for many.

Whales, seals, salmon, lemurs, and various other animals migrate. Salmon, for instance, leave the deep sea and ascend rivers to spawn, usually in the same locality which they left in their earlier life.

The causes of migrations and the sense of direction shown by migrating animals remain among the most baffling problems of science.

Mink (*Putorius*). A small carnivore, closely allied to the weasel, native to cool parts of the northern hemisphere. The American mink (*P. vison*) is an animal of semiaquatic habits, living on the borders of ponds and streams. Its body varies in length from 13 to 18 inches, and the tail from 8 to 10 inches. In color it is usually yellowish brown with a dark tail and a white chin. Although it kills and eats fish, it feeds principally upon small mammals and birds, and is very destructive to poultry. It is much trapped for its fine fur, which is becoming increasingly valuable.

Minnows (*Cyprinidæ*). The largest family of fishes, comprising more than 2000 species, of which more than 225 are North American. With few exceptions they are small, feeble fish, of very little economic value, confined almost exclusively to fresh waters of northern temperate and tropical regions. Here is grouped the great assemblage of fishes known as carp, dace, chub, minnows, bleak, bream, and shiner. The majority are from 2 to 7 inches long, though the squawfish, of Pacific Coast rivers, attains a length of 4 or 5 feet. Various minnows are much used for bait. See *Carp, Goldfish.*

Moa. A gigantic bird of New Zealand which became extinct in comparatively recent times. When the first colonists arrived on the islands, the plains were still strewn with the immense bones of moas, and their eggs and feathers have been found preserved in various surface deposits. From these abundant remains, scientists have recognized about 20 different species, ranging in size from that of a turkey to a stature exceeding that of the ostrich. The largest moa (*Dinornis maximus*), of South island, probably stood about 10 feet high. The moas possessed only very rudimentary wings and were, therefore, flightless. Among living birds their nearest relatives appear to be the kiwis. See *Kiwi.*

Moccasin (*Agkistrodon*). The name of a group of highly venomous serpents. They are characterized by large, shieldlike scales on the head, a pit between the eye and the nostril, and a spiny-tipped tail. There are 10 species,—7 Asiatic, 3 North American.

The water moccasin, or Cottonmouth (*A. piscivorous*) is one of the largest and ugliest poisonous snakes found in the United States. While sometimes 4 to 5 feet long and 3 inches in diameter, it is usually smaller. It has a flat head, very distinct from the neck, with large scales projecting somewhat over the eyes. Its skin is muddy brown and very rough. It occurs from North Carolina to Texas, frequenting shore lines of swamps, where it lies partly out of water. It feeds chiefly on fish and frogs.

The Copperhead (*A. contortrix*), a serpent of the woods and rocks, is found from Massachusetts to Illinois and southward. It is smaller, usually about 30 inches long, hazel-brown above with darker crossband, and the head often coppery tinged. If caught at close quarters, it will strike viciously and its venom is nearly as deadly as that of the rattlesnake. Unlike the rattlesnake, the copperhead strikes without warning, and hence has become a symbol of treachery. It feeds upon mice, frogs, and small birds.

Mocking Bird (*Mimus polyglottus*). A famous American song bird, closely related to the wrens and thrushes. It is noted, not only for its unusual powers of song, but also for its remarkable ability to imitate the songs of other birds. In size it is about equal to a robin; in color it is ashy gray above, with darker wings and tail marked with white, and whitish below. It ranges from the Bahamas and Mexico northward to New Jersey and southern Illinois, nesting in trees and thickets, laying 4 to 6 greenish blue eggs, spotted with brown, and feeding chiefly on earthworms, insects, and berries.

The very similar but slightly larger western mocking bird (*M. polyglottus leucopterus*) is found from Oklahoma and Texas to California and southward into Mexico. Throughout its range, the mocking bird is even more active, alert, and familiar than the robin, living in gardens, parks, public squares, and city streets, singing almost continuously, even during the noonday heat and often throughout moonlit nights. While varying greatly in their powers of mimicry, some mocking birds have been known to imitate the songs of more than 30 different birds within a period of 10 minutes. See *Bluebird, Robin, Thrasher, Thrush, Wren.*

Moles (*Talpidæ*). A family of small insectivorous mammals, natives of temperate regions. Moles usually have a thick, clumsy body, clothed in soft fur, a small, pointed head, no external ears, very small eyes, a short tail, and extremely large, spadelike front feet admirably adapted for digging. They live in elaborate burrows, which they dig with marvelous dexterity, rarely coming to the surface. As they feed mainly on an animal diet, chiefly insects and worms caught underground, they are very beneficial to the farmer, though they disfigure lawns and meadows with their galleries, and sometimes eat potatoes and other root crops.

The common mole (*Scalops aquatica*), of the eastern and southern United States, about 6 inches long and 2 inches high, is covered with shining, velvety, gray fur. Though this animal is entirely blind, its senses of smell, hearing, and touch are remarkably acute. The rudimentary eyes are hidden under the hairy skin. See *Insectivora, Shrews.*

Mollusks (*Mollusca*). An important phylum or branch of the animal kingdom, usually distinguished by the presence of a shell which incases the body. The mollusks include the oysters, clams, snails, limpets, chitons, cuttlefish, and octopuses. They are soft-bodied, cold-blooded animals, lacking an internal skeleton, but mostly provided with an external bivalve or univalve shell, which serves in place of bones and affords protection. The body typically consists of four parts: the head, with the mouth, feelers, and eyes; the visceral mass or trunk, containing the internal organs; the so-called "foot," a muscular portion by means of which the animal moves; and the mantle, or outer fold of integument, which secretes the shell.

Mollusks are chiefly aquatic, the great majority living in the sea, though many inhabit moist situations on land. While most mollusks, as, for example, the snails, are vegetable feeders, some, such as the octopus, are powerful predacious animals, and a few are parasites. Next to the arthropods, mollusks comprise the most numerous branch of animals, the number of species being computed at upwards of 60,000. They range in size from minute, almost microscopic forms, to the giant squid, 50 feet long, which is the largest of the invertebrate animals.

The Mollusca are divided into five classes: *Pelecypoda*, bivalves—oysters, clams, scallops, about 11,000 species; *Gastropoda*, univalves—snails, whelks, sea slugs, limpets, about 49,000 species; *Scaphopoda*, tooth shells, 200 species; *Amphineura*, chitons, about 600 species; and *Cephalopoda*, squid, cuttlefish, octopus, about 400 species. Many mollusks, such as oysters, clams, mussels, snails, and scallops, are highly prized for food. A few, such as the shipworm and the octopus, are injurious. See *Clam, Cuttlefish, Mussel, Octopus, Oyster, Scallop, Snail, Squid.*

Moloch (*mō′lŏk*) (*Moloch horridus*). A small Australian lizard, 8 inches long, whose entire body is covered with conical spines and tubercles. While very uncouth and ugly-looking, its armor is only for defense. It feeds chiefly on ants and is entirely harmless.

Mongoose (*Herpestes griseus*). A species of ichneumon, native to India, but introduced into Jamaica and other countries, for the purpose of destroying rats and other animal pests, upon which it largely feeds. The mongoose is reddish gray in color, and in size it is somewhat larger than a rat. Being easily domesticated, it is kept in many houses in Hindustan, to rid them of reptiles, mice, or other vermin. The mongoose kills and devours the most venomous snakes, such as the cobra, whose bite it avoids by its quickness of sight and remarkable agility. Unfortunately, the mongoose also destroys small terrestrial mammals and the eggs of all birds that nest upon the ground. In Puerto Rico it has driven the common rats from the ground and compelled them to take refuge and habitation in trees. See *Ichneumon.*

Monitor (*Varanus*). The largest of living lizards, found in Africa, India, and Australia. It is so named because of its habit of giving warning, by a whistling sound, of the approach of a crocodile. Monitors have a long body, five-toed feet, a long-forked tongue, and a long tail. Some are aquatic, some arboreal, and some live in sandy deserts. All are carnivorous, living on frogs, snakes, small mammals, and birds. All lay white, soft-shelled eggs, which are more highly esteemed than hens' eggs by some Eastern peoples. The Nile monitor (*V. niloticus*), of tropical African rivers, attains a length of 6 feet. It is the chief enemy of the crocodile, destroying immense numbers of its eggs.

Monkey. The name popularly used for any animal of the families *Simiidæ*, anthropoid apes and gibbons; *Cercopithecidæ*, Old World monkeys; *Cebidæ*, American monkeys; and *Callitrichidæ*, marmosets. In its more proper, restricted sense, however, the term monkey is applicable only to the group first named. The Old World monkeys and baboons are widely distributed over Africa and Asia. The American monkeys differ from those of the Old World in having an additional molar tooth, or grinder, in each jaw. Some have a prehensile tail, which is as useful to them as an additional hand. The members of this family are strictly confined to the forest regions of tropical America, from southern Mexico to northern Chile. The marmosets are distributed from southern Mexico to southern Brazil.

Monkeys live chiefly in forests, for which their structure is especially adapted, enabling them to climb trees with ease, and to leap from branch to branch with extraordinary agility. Their food consists chiefly of fruits and other vegetable substances. Of all animals, monkeys are the most intelligent and playful; when captured young they can be taught many interesting ways. They are full of curiosity and of unbounded activity; and in all tropical countries they are prime favorites as pets. See *Ape, Baboon.*

Monotremata (*mŏn′ō-trē′mȧ-tȧ*). An order of egg-laying mammals, intermediate between the higher mammals and the birds. The group includes the platypus, or duckbill, of Australia and Tasmania, and the echidnas of Australia, Tasmania, and New Guinea. While resembling the birds, reptiles, and amphibians in that their young are incubated from eggs laid by the female, the monotremes correspond to mammals in that the young after being hatched are suckled by milk secreted by the mother. See *Echidna, Platypus.*

Moose (*Alces americana*). The tallest North American quadruped, and the largest known representative of the deer family. It is closely related to the European elk and may properly be called the American elk, a name which is often, though incorrectly, applied to the wapiti. The moose stands from 6 to 7 feet high at the shoulder, and sometimes weighs more than 1000 pounds. It has long fore limbs, humped shoulders, and short hind limbs. The head is very large, with a broad, square-ended, overhanging nose. The male bears enormous flattened and palmated antlers, with a spread of 5 to 6 feet.

The moose is a browsing animal, feeding chiefly upon leaves, small branches, and bark. Its range extends from Nova Scotia to the Rocky mountains and northward through Canada and Alaska to the limit of trees. In the United States the moose is now found only in Maine, Minnesota, Montana, Wyoming, and Idaho. Except where specially protected by law, this splendid game animal is being rapidly exterminated. The Alaska moose (*A. gigas*), said to stand as high as 8 feet at the shoulders, with an antler spread of 6 feet, occurs from British Columbia northwestward to the Arctic Ocean.

Mosquitoes. Small two-winged insects, of the family *Culicidæ*, closely related to the midges, black flies, and crane flies. There are more than 350 species, abundant in arctic as well as in temperate and tropical regions. Mosquitoes have a narrow body, a long, slender but firm proboscis, or beak, and narrow wings, more or less fringed with minute scales. In the males the mouth parts are not adapted for piercing. The females, however, have a set of extremely sharp, needle-like organs in the beak. With these they readily puncture the skin of fruits or of animals and then suck their juices or their blood.

Mosquitoes lay their eggs in stagnant water, often in raftlike masses. In from 1 to 4 days the eggs hatch into legless larvæ, called "wigglers." These live in the water but come to the surface to breathe. After a week or more the larvæ molt and transform into pupæ which are also active wigglers. In a short time the pupæ transform into imagoes. These promptly cast off their pupal coverings and emerge from the water as flying mosquitoes. The total period of life in the water varies greatly in different species, but, in case of the common mosquito, it ordinarily ranges from 10 to 15 days.

Among the enemies of the mosquito in the aquatic stages are various fishes, newts, leeches, dragon fly larvæ, and water beetles. In the flying stage, mosquitoes are preyed upon by bats, nighthawks, swallows, swifts, dragon flies, hornets, and various other birds and insects. The natural food of both males and females of some species of mosquitoes, and the only food of the males of nearly all species, consists of plant juices However, the females of various species attack mammals, birds, turtles, frogs, fishes, and sometimes other insects.

Until recently, mosquitoes were looked upon merely as annoying pests. But, following the discovery that various mosquitoes transmit dangerous diseases, their great importance has become recognized. Three very serious human maladies, *malaria*, *yellow fever*, and *elephantiasis*, as well as various diseases of lower animals, are known to be spread by mosquitoes. The common mosquito (*Culex pungens*), of the United States and Canada, is not known to be a bearer of disease. A spotted-winged swamp mosquito (*Anopheles*) is responsible for the spread of malaria. In the South the most dangerous mosquito is the *Aëdes aegypti*, which transmits yellow fever.

Mosquitoes are best combated (1) by draining as thoroughly as possible all swamps, pools, and other stagnant waters, and (2) by pouring small quantities of kerosene upon the water surface of their breeding places.

Moth. The common name for a numerous group of scale-winged insects, which, with the butterflies, form the important order *Lepidoptera.* Moths are distinguished from butterflies by their antennæ, which are filiform or feathered instead of knobbed; by their holding the wings in a horizontal position when at rest; and by their nocturnal habits.

There are some 40 families of moths, embracing more than 40,000 species, about 6000 of which occur in North America. Many of these, such as the cankerworm, cutworm, army worm, codling, brown-tailed, gypsy, grain, and clothes moths, are among the most destructive of injurious insects. The silkworm moth, which has been grown in China for more than 5000 years, and is now extensively reared throughout the world, ranks next to the cotton plant and the sheep among the world's most valuable producers of textile fiber. Many species of moths are strikingly beautiful, such as the cecropia, polyphemus, emperor, luna, and other handsome forms. See *Silkworm.*

Motmot. A group of small birds, forming the subfamily *Momotinæ*, closely related to the kingfishers. They are handsome birds with brilliant green, blue, cinnamon, and black plumage. Usually the central tail feathers are elongated and end in racket-shaped tips. In length motmots range from 6½ to 20 inches. They are solitary birds, living usually in pairs in gloomy forests, feeding upon insects, small reptiles, and fruits, and nesting, so far as known, in holes excavated in banks, usually along watercourses, laying 3 or 4 glossy white eggs. There are about 24 species, native to tropical America, one of which, the blue-headed motmot (*Momotus cœruliceps*), ranges northward nearly to Texas.

Mouflon. See *Sheep*.

Mouse (*Mus*). The common name of the smaller rodent mammals of the family to which the rat belongs, and which includes also the lemmings, voles, and muskrats. Mice much resemble rats but are smaller, more graceful in movement, and more cleanly in habits.

The house mouse (*Mus musculus*), supposed to be a native of Asia, has been unintentionally distributed by man throughout nearly the entire world. The date of its arrival in Europe is unknown, but it is mentioned by Aristotle, Pliny, and other ancient writers. Mice are pretty, gentle, timid little animals, with cunning ways, and dainty in their choice of food. Yet, by reason of their destructive habit of gnawing woodwork, furniture, books, fabrics, and other valuable articles, they are universally regarded as pests to be exterminated.

There are many interesting wild mice, such as the meadow mouse, harvest mouse, white-footed mouse, mole mouse, cotton mouse, and rice-field mouse. Nearly related also are the pocket mouse and jumping mouse.

Mule. A hybrid animal, the progeny of a male ass and a mare, highly valued and widely used as a draft and pack animal. The mule has a large, clumsy head, long, erect ears, a short mane, and a thin tail. In these points, the mule resembles the ass rather than the horse. However, as regards size, height, and strength, the mule approaches more nearly to the horse. In intelligence the mule seems to surpass both the horse and the ass. Its powers of muscular endurance are remarkable, making it highly serviceable in mountainous countries. No other beast of burden is so sure-footed or so capable of enduring fatigue. Further, the mule is more easily kept, can subsist upon a greater variety of food, and endures heat, hunger, and thirst better than the horse. The mule also lives to a greater age and is less susceptible to diseases. In size, strength, and appearance the mule is very greatly superior to the "hinny," which is the offspring of the male horse and the female ass.

Mules were reared more than 3000 years ago in Asia Minor, whence they were taken to Greece at a very early period, being frequently mentioned in Homer. While reference to mules is made in the Bible, the Israelites were forbidden by law to rear them. In ancient Italy they were used for hauling loads on the highways much as in modern times, and the ancient Latin names *mulus* and *hinnus*, mule and hinny, have been adopted in many languages.

The finest mules are bred in Spain and in the United States, but good breeds are extensively reared in France, Italy, Mexico, and northwestern India. The best imported breed is the Catalonian; other leading foreign breeds are the Andalusian, Maltese, Italian, and Majorcan. A mixture of various strains is used as the standard in the United States. Missouri and Texas lead in the rearing of mules, which are extensively used throughout the South, especially in the cotton growing states. In the United States, as a whole, there are about one-fifth as many mules as horses.

Mullet (*Mugil*). A spiny-finned fish of the family *Mugilidæ*. There are about 70 species, widely distributed in warm seas, some of which are of high economic value. The striped mullet (*M. cephalus*), very abundant on Florida coasts, is found also from California to Chile and in Hawaii. It sometimes attains a weight of 6 pounds. The white mullet, or silver mullet (*M. brasiliensis*), of Florida waters, is a big-scaled, round-bodied, trim little fish about 9 inches long, with spotless, silvery sides. Both the foregoing are excellent food fish, many millions of pounds being marketed annually by Florida fishermen. Mullets are eaten fresh, salted, and smoke-dried.

The closely related European mullet (*Mullus barbatus*) is celebrated for its brilliant colors. It was a great favorite with the ancient Romans, who are said to have paid enormous prices, sometimes exceeding $300, for a single fish.

Murre (*mûr*) (*Uria*). A marine diving bird, closely related to the auks and puffins, found only on the shores of northern oceans. The common murre (*U. troile*), 16 inches long, native of northern Europe and America, migrates in winter as far south as New Jersey. At breeding time it congregates in vast colonies on rocky cliffs, where the female lays a single, large, pear-shaped egg on a bare ledge of stone. The eggs, which are used extensively as food, are often gathered in immense quantities.

The similar California murre (*U. troile californica*) is found on Pacific shores from southern California northward. Millions of eggs, obtained from murre rookeries on the Farallon islands, were sold in the San Francisco markets until, in order to save the species from threatened extinction, the traffic was prohibited.

Musk Deer (*Moschus moschiferus*). A kind of deer found chiefly in the elevated table-lands of central Asia, and particularly of Tibet. It stands about 20 inches high at the shoulder, with large ears and a rudimentary tail. Both sexes are hornless, but the upper jaws of the male bear long, saber-like canine teeth which project downward and backward below the chin. The males alone yield musk, which is secreted by an abdominal gland of about the size of a hen's egg. Musk is extensively used by perfumers. Its scent is more penetrating and powerful than that of any other known substance.

Musk Ox (*Ovibos moschatus*). A ruminant animal intermediate between the ox and the sheep, resembling in general appearance a large, goatlike sheep. It stands about 5 feet high at the shoulder. Its body is covered with a coat of tufted hair, brownish in color and of great length. The hair about the neck and shoulders is so thick as to give the animal a "humped" appearance; on the rest of the body it is very long, smooth, and flowing. The horns, broad at the base and covering the forehead and crown, curve downward between the eye and the ear, and then upward and slightly backward. The ears are short, the head large and broad, and the muzzle blunted. The average weight of the musk ox is from 400 to 600 pounds. Its food consists chiefly of grasses and lichens.

The musk ox inhabits the arctic regions of America north of latitude 64°. While its musk-like odor is sometimes perceptible at a distance, the flesh is free from the odor or taste of musk. The beef is excellent and has been an important source of food to arctic explorers.

Muskrat (*Fiber zibethicus*). An aquatic rodent, found throughout North America. It has a ratlike body 15 inches long and a flat tail 10 inches long. In color it is brown above, darker on the back, and gray below. The fine, close, silky fur is intermingled above with long, coarse hairs. The muskrat lives in burrows with the entrances under water. In marshes it sometimes builds mounds of twigs and leaves, 2 to 4 feet high, containing grassy nests large enough for several animals. It is an expert swimmer and an omnivorous feeder, subsisting on roots, fruits, vegetables, grasses, mussels, and sometimes flesh. Immense numbers are trapped for their fur, which is becoming increasingly valuable.

Mussel. A common name applied to two groups of bivalve mollusks. The marine mussels number several hundred species, of which the edible mussel (*Mytilus edulis*) is a familiar example. It is about 3 inches long, half as wide, dark brown with violet margins, and is found on all northern coasts where it attaches itself in enormous masses to tide covered rocks and shallow shores.

The fresh-water mussels comprise the family *Unionidæ*, embracing more than 1000 species, some 500 of which occur in the United States, flourishing in lakes, ponds, rivers, and smaller streams. Some large forms are 8 inches long and 4 inches wide, but they are usually much smaller. While occasionally used for food, their flesh is inferior. The shells of many fresh-water mussels are extensively used in the manufacture of pearl buttons, now an established industry along the Mississippi river. Some of these species also yield valuable pearls, and form the basis of the American fresh-water pearl industry. As high as $25,000 has been paid for a single fresh-water mussel pearl. The most important mussel fisheries are located near Muscatine, Iowa, and the total value of their products amounts to millions of dollars annually. See *Pearl*.

Mythical Animals. Before the days of careful observation in natural history, the world was filled with travelers' tales of strange beasts found in remote lands and seas. These creatures were in some cases wholly imaginary; many, however, were illustrated by figures created in the imagination of the artists of the day. Such are the various sea serpents of world-wide fame, and most sincerely believed in by some even down to the present time. Two of extraordinary interest, familiar throughout the world through their appearance upon the insignia of great nations, are the unicorn, which still has a place upon the seal of Great Britain, and the great dragon, which was until recently conspicuously displayed upon the flag of China.

Nighthawk (*Chordeiles virginianus*). A small insectivorous bird, sometimes called bull bat, closely related to the whippoorwill and goatsucker. The nighthawk is found from Labrador to British Columbia and southward to Argentina. It is about 9 inches long, blackish brown mottled with gray and buff, with a prominent white wing spot, a white bar across the tail, and a white V-shaped mark on the throat.

Nighthawks fly high at evening or in cloudy weather, often in flocks, with their broad mouths wide open to catch insects, and uttering a sharp, rasping cry. Their flight is rapid and irregular, and they sometimes dive almost vertically for a considerable distance. They build no nests, but lay two white eggs blotched with brown, on the ground or in a hollow tree. While occasionally shot because of their somewhat hawklike appearance when on the wing, they are harmless except to small insects, which they devour in immense numbers.

Nightingale (*Luscinia megarhynca*). A famous song bird of western and central Europe, belonging to the warbler family (*Sylviidæ*) and closely related to the English robin redbreast (*Erythacus*). It is a small migratory bird, about 7 inches long, wintering in Africa, and visiting Europe and western Asia in the summer. The plumage of this delightful songster is of a somber hue, being reddish brown above, redder on the head and rump, the tail a lighter tint, and the throat, lower part of the breast, and the abdomen, grayish.

The nightingale is a shy bird, frequenting woods, copses, and hedgerows. Its food consists of insects, soft fruits, and berries. The nest, which is either on the ground or in a low bush, is composed of dry leaves, lined with grass, roots, and hair. The eggs are 4 or 5 in number, and of a uniform olive brown color. Only the male nightingale sings, beginning at mating time in the spring and continuing until the young are hatched. Its song is most pleasing on quiet evenings, and, when the moon is shining, the bird may often be heard until midnight.

Nilgai (*nĭl'gī*) (*Boselaphus tragocamelus*). The largest of the Indian antelopes, somewhat intermediate between the deer and the ox. It is about the size of a mule, bluish gray in color, standing 4½ feet high at the shoulder, with an oxlike head and body, long, slender legs, and small, short horns. The nilgai lives in herds on the plains and hills of India, where it is much hunted for its flesh.

Octopus. A marine cephalopod mollusk, closely related to the cuttlefish and squids, called also "devilfish" or "poulp." It has a short, bag-shaped body from which project eight long arms or tentacles, covered with sucking disks, with which it seizes its prey. There are two large, glaring eyes, one on each side of the head. The mouth, which is provided with powerful, horny, parrot-like jaws, is situated between the encircling arms. The octopus swims rapidly, crawls on the sea bottom, and feeds chiefly on shellfish and other invertebrates.

There are about 50 species, found among rocks along the shores of all oceans. Some, such as the small octopus (*O. bairdii*), found from Cape Cod northward, have arms only a few inches long, but the largest species, which measure from 12 to 15 feet across the outstretched tentacles, are powerful and dangerous animals. The common octopus, or devilfish (*O. vulgaris*), of Mediterranean and West Indian waters, attains an arm expansion of 9 feet and a weight of 60 pounds. The Pacific octopus (*O. punctatus*), which ranges from Alaska to Lower California, sometimes has an arm spread of 14 feet. It lives just below low-water mark, and, in the vicinity of San Francisco, is often caught for food by the Chinese and the Italians.

The huge devilfish described by Victor Hugo in *The Toilers of the Sea* as inhabiting the Channel islands and attacking fishermen, is a creature of the imagination. However, the large species found in Pacific waters may severely injure or even cause the death of pearl divers and shell collectors. See *Cuttlefish, Squid*.

Okapi (*ō-kä'pē*). The native African name for a recently discovered animal of the giraffe family (*Ocapia johnstoni*). The first complete skin sent to Europe was received in England from Sir H. H. Johnston in 1901. The okapi is a native of the Semliki forest between Lake Albert Edward and Lake Albert at the northeastern border of the Congo basin.

In height the okapi stands nearly 5 feet at the withers, and is, therefore, about as large as a good-sized American elk or wapiti. While closely related to the giraffe, which is the only other living representative of the family now known, the okapi differs in having a much shorter neck and forelegs. The male okapi possesses two small, dagger-shaped horns, the tips of which usually protrude through the hairy skin with which they are covered. Unlike the giraffe, the female okapi is hornless.

In coloration the okapi is truly remarkable. The forehead is red, the cheeks are yellowish white, while the neck, shoulders, and body range from jet-black to purplish and wine red. The hind quarters and the hind and fore legs are either snowy white or light cream color, touched with orange and transversely barred with purplish black stripes and blotches.

Little is known concerning the habits of the okapi except that it dwells in dense primeval forests, where it feeds upon an undergrowth of swamp-loving plants. Observers affirm that it would be impossible to distinguish an okapi in its native haunts at a distance greater than 25 paces. This suggests that the peculiar coloration of this animal is of a purely protective type. Indeed, this effective natural "camouflage" may serve, in part, to explain why so large an animal remained so long unknown to the scientific world. See *Giraffe*.

Opossum (*Didelphidæ*). The opossums constitute a family of pouch-bearing mammals, belonging to the order *Marsupialia*. They range throughout the wooded districts of America, from the southern boundary of Texas to the valley of the La Plata, where they are most numerous. One species, however, the Virginia opossum (*Didelphis virginiana*), is found in North America, from Florida to the Hudson river, and west to the Missouri.

The opossums are ratlike in form; the largest species are about equal in size to a cat. The long tail, which is almost destitute of hair, is very useful. From its prehensile nature, it enables the animal not only to hang by it but also to climb and to descend trees. The opossums are sly and intelligent, and live chiefly in trees, hiding in the daytime and roaming abroad at night in search of their food, which consists of fruit, insects, small reptiles, and birds' eggs. Some species have no marsupium, or pouch, or one which is only very slightly developed. In the case of the murine opossum (*Marmosa murina*), a South American species about the size of a chipmunk, the young, on leaving the nipples, are carried on their mother's back, retaining their position by entwining their tails around hers.

When caught, the Virginia opossum feigns death, whence the common expression "playing 'possum."

Orang-utan (*ô-răng′ōō-tăn′*) (*Simia satyrus* or *Pongo pygmæus*). A large, manlike ape, with brick red hair, brown skin, and small ears, native to the swampy forests of Sumatra and Borneo. According to W. T. Hornaday, the largest specimen on record stood 4 feet 6 inches in height from heel to head, measured 42 inches around the chest, and between the finger tips stretched 8 feet. The weight of a full-grown male orang may reach 250 pounds. The legs are very short, the arms disproportionately long, reaching to the ankle when the animal is placed in an erect position. The males have a longish beard, and they sometimes develop warty protuberances, called cheek callosities, on each side of the face. The resemblance to man in appearance is greatest in the females and in young animals.

In its native home, the orang-utan lives in the tree tops and seldom descends to the ground except for water. Instead of leaping from tree to tree like the monkey, it swings from one branch to another with great accuracy. In its wild state the orang makes a nest of leafy branches laid crosswise in a forked tree. It sleeps lying flat on its back on this nest, grasping an overhead branch with both feet and hands for security. In captivity the orang-utan has been taught to wear clothes and to imitate various actions of men. See *Ape, Chimpanzee, Gorilla.*

Orioles (*Icterus*). The American orioles, or "hangnests," comprise a group of perching birds closely allied to the bobolink and the blackbird. There are about 50 species, mostly confined to the tropics, noted for their richly colored plumage, pleasing song, and skill in weaving nests. All are solitary, tree-loving birds, living in pairs, and feeding chiefly on noxious insects, and thus are highly beneficial to the farmer and fruit grower.

Some 8 species of orioles occur in the United States. Of these, the best-known is the handsome Baltimore oriole (*I. galbulus*), called also "firebird," "golden robin," and "hangnest." It is about 7½ inches long, with the head, neck, throat, and upper back black, and with the breast, wing coverts, and lower parts bright reddish orange. It breeds from Saskatchewan to New Brunswick and southward, building a long, skillfully constructed, bag-shaped nest, usually suspended from slender branches 8 to 50 feet from the ground. It lays from 4 to 6 pale brown eggs, variously spotted and lined with dark brown.

Ostrich (*Struthio*). The largest of living birds, standing nearly 8 feet high and weighing about 300 pounds. It belongs to the natural order *Ratitæ*, which includes other large flightless birds, such as the rhea, the emu, and the cassowary. In these birds the breastbone is raft-shaped, and lacks the narrow keel which is present in birds of flight.

The wings of the ostrich are rudimentary, with long, bending, soft plumes. The legs are long and powerful, with the thigh partly bare; the neck is slender and naked; the head is small with a short, broad beak. Ostriches are unique among birds in that they have only two toes on each foot. While formerly covering a much wider area, they now range over the desert countries from Arabia and Syria to South Africa. Some authorities recognize four species; others regard all of these as forms of the northern ostrich (*S. camelus*), mentioned by Aristotle and also in the Bible.

In habit, ostriches are gregarious, going about in small companies. At breeding time they are polygamous, each male accompanying three to five females, all of which deposit their eggs in a single large nest scooped out in the sand. Almost the entire duty of guarding and sitting upon the eggs is performed by the male. Ostriches are omnivorous, feeding upon herbage, seeds, fruits, small mammals, birds, lizards, and snakes. The voice of the ostrich resembles the roar of a lion, though its most common sound is an angry hiss.

The ostrich is perhaps the swiftest of all land animals, covering 25 feet or more at a stride and attaining a speed of 60 miles an hour. Its proverbial foolishness in hiding its head in the sand, and thinking it is thereby concealed, is one of the many myths that have been discredited by modern science. In fact, the ostrich is a very alert and wary bird, and, except for its habit of running in a circle, could rarely be captured.

While the ostrich has been partially domesticated for centuries by native tribes of Central Africa, ostrich farming for the commercial production of plumes was unknown prior to 1860. South Africa is the chief center of this industry. See *Cassowary, Emu, Rhea.*

Otter (*Lutra canadensis*). An aquatic fur bearing animal with webbed feet, closely related to the marten, inhabiting lakes and streams and feeding on fish. It is about 4 feet long with a rather stout body and a strong, flattened tail adapted for swimming. In color it is dark brown above and lighter below. The otter makes burrows in the banks of streams, with the entrance under water. Although an expert swimmer and diver, it is awkward upon land. While formerly widely distributed north of Mexico, it is now most numerous in Canada. Otter fur is highly prized, and, wherever the animal is numerous, forms an important article of commerce.

Ovenbird (*Seiurus aurocapillus*). A small song bird of the warbler family, abundant in woodlands in eastern North America, called also "golden-crowned thrush." The ovenbird is about 6 inches long, olive green above and white below, with buff and black on the head. It is noted for building a bulky, oven-like nest of coarse grasses, which it places on the ground, with the entrance at one side. Several small South American birds of the genus *Furnarius*, which construct huge globular nests of mud, are also called ovenbirds.

Owl. A nocturnal bird of prey, resembling the hawks and eagles in the shape of its bill and feet, but more closely allied to the goatsuckers in structure. The head is extremely large; the eyes huge and directed forward; the bill short and stout; the ears very large; the legs feathered; the toes four in number, the outer one capable of being directed backward. The plumage is full and remarkably soft, the feathers of the face being so arranged as to form two disks around the eyes.

More than 400 species and subspecies of owls are known, forming the distinct group or suborder *Striges*. They range over the whole of the globe from the highest northern latitudes and are found in the remotest oceanic islands. Owls vary in size from the gray owl of polar regions, 28 inches long, to the curious elf owl of Arizona, less than 6 inches long. They feed on small mammals, birds, fishes, and insects, swallowing the hair, bones, feathers, and scales, which they afterward disgorge in the shape of "pellets." Their flight is buoyant and noiseless. They place their nests on the ground, among rocks, in hollow trees, and in buildings, while some resort to the old nests of other birds. They lay from 2 to 5 roundish white eggs.

Of the 18 species which occur in North America, among the best-known are the long-eared owl, short-eared owl, barred owl, great horned owl, snowy owl, screech owl, burrowing owl, elf owl, and barn owl. With the exception of the great horned owl, which is very destructive to poultry, owls are beneficial to agriculture, as they prey upon mice, rats, gophers, English sparrows, and other noxious animals.

Ox (*Bos taurus*). The common ox is believed to be a domesticated form of the wild ox or aurochs (*Bos primigenius*), abundant in historic times in Europe and western Asia.

As a beast of burden and as a draft animal, the ox long preceded the horse, which, among primitive peoples, was chiefly employed for war or the chase. The ox is mentioned early in the Bible, is pictured on ancient Egyptian monuments, and is often referred to by classic Greek and Roman writers. Its introduction into the New World was first made by Columbus, who brought it to the West Indies in 1493. It was taken from Spain to Mexico about 1525; from England to Virginia in 1610, and to Massachusetts in 1624; from Holland to New York in 1627; and from Denmark to New Hampshire in 1631.

The ox is the chief source of wealth in many regions. While the horse now ranks first as a labor animal, the ox ranks first as a food producing animal. The total value of cattle products, including beef, butter, cheese, milk, and hides, immensely exceeds that of the products of any other animal. In intelligence and mental power, the ox is far inferior to many animals of relatively small value to man. Age-long domestication, while it has produced many valuable breeds, has not brought about extreme variations in size and form, as has been the case with the dog, the donkey, the horse, or the zebu. Intensive breeding during the last two centuries has produced such valuable specialized breeds as the Hereford, Alderney, Jersey, and Shorthorn. See *Banteng, Bison, Buffalo, Gaur, Gayal, Ox Family, Yak, Zebu.*

Ox Family (*Bovidæ*). The largest family of hoofed mammals, embracing some 200 known species of hollow-horned ruminants, including the antelope, bison, buffalo, goat, sheep, and the various kinds of cattle. It is distinctly an Old World group, being represented in the New World by only 8 species, all North American. There are no native representatives of the Ox family in Australia or in South America. In the continent of Africa, however, about 140 species occur, or about two-thirds of the entire group. It contains more animals of great economic value to man than any other single family, including the ox, sheep, goat, zebu, water buffalo, gaur, gayal, banteng, and yak.

Oyster (*Ostrea*). A bivalve mollusk, found in nearly all seas, usually near shore, in from about 15 to 35 feet of water. There are upwards of 50 species, of which the common European oyster (*O. edulis*) and the American oyster (*O. virginiana*) are the best-known and most highly prized for food. The Pacific oyster (*O. lurida*) is a small, thin-shelled species, marketed principally on the Pacific coast. The young oyster is at first a free-swimming organism which, after a short time, develops a shell and attaches itself to stones or other hard objects upon the sea bottom. Very commonly it adheres to adult shells, and thus are formed the large masses termed oyster banks. The oyster feeds upon minute plants and animals brought to it by the tide and other water currents.

Oyster culture consists of hatching young, or "seed," oysters, and transplanting them at the proper time to artificially prepared beds where they grow to marketable size. They are then gathered from the beds by means of rakes, tongs, and dredges. Oyster culture is now carried on along various coasts of Europe and very extensively on the Atlantic coast of the United States, particularly in and near Chesapeake bay. See *Pearl.*

Pangolin (*păng-gō′lĭn*) (*Manis*). A small group of burrowing edentate mammals, native to Asia and Africa, often called the scaly anteaters. Like the true anteater, the pangolin has a long, narrow, pointed snout, a toothless mouth, and an extensile tongue. The upper parts of the body and tail are completely protected by large, overlapping, horny scales. The limbs are stout and provided with curved claws suitable for digging. The pangolins are nocturnal, and subsist chiefly upon ants and termites which they capture with their long, glutinous, retractile tongue. When attacked, the pangolin, like the armadillo, rolls itself into a ball completely encircled with horny scales, which defies the attack of most animals. See *Armadillo.*

Panther. In the Old World, a name applied to certain colored varieties of the leopard (*Felis pardus*). In eastern North America, particularly in colonial days, the word panther was commonly used to designate the puma, or cougar, also locally called "painter," "catamount," and "mountain lion." See *Puma.*

Parrot. The name broadly applied to all birds of the order *Psittaci*, which comprises about 600 species, including the parrots proper, the cockatoos, parrakeets, macaws, lories, and nestors.

The true parrots have the upper mandible toothed and longer than it is high, a short and rounded tail, and short, strong feet with two toes before and two behind. These birds combine with the beauty of their plumage a nature of great docility, and have the faculty of imitating the human voice to a degree not possessed by other birds. They are found chiefly in the tropics, and are especially numerous in Africa, the native home of the gray parrot, which is the favorite and best-known species. South America, which is also rich in species, furnishes the well-known green parrot. North America is the home of only two species, the Carolina parrakeet, now rare, and the thick-billed parrot of southern Arizona. The parrots are forest birds, and are adepts at climbing, using for that purpose not only the feet but also the bill. Their food consists of seeds and fruits. They usually nest in hollow trees, and lay from 2 to 5 white eggs.

Parrots were introduced into ancient Europe from Asia through the conquests of Alexander the Great, and are mentioned by Aristotle, Ovid, and other classic writers. In equatorial Africa the gray parrot (*Psittacus erythacus*) has been domesticated for centuries by the native peoples, who rear it as a pet, make use of its flesh for food and of its feathers as insignia of rank. This sober-plumaged bird is the most easily taught of all the parrots, and its powers of speech are sometimes remarkable. See *Cockatoo, Macaw.*

Partridge. A popular name for various gallinaceous birds or other birds resembling them in appearance. The name partridge was first given and rightly belongs to certain small, grouselike birds of the genus *Perdix*, found only in the Old World. In New England the ruffed grouse (*Bonasa umbellus*) is called partridge. In the Southern states the bobwhite, or American quail (*Colinus americanus*), is known as partridge and the ruffed grouse is called pheasant.

The American birds **most** closely resembling the

Old World partridges are Gambel's partridge and the mountain and valley partridges of California, which are also widely known as quails. In India and South Africa the name partridge is given to various francolins, and, in South America, tinamous are called partridges. The common partridge of Europe and central Asia (*Perdix cinerea*) is about a foot long, reddish brown mixed with gray in color, and frequents open grounds, cultivated fields, and heaths. It is a standard game bird throughout its range. See *Bobwhite* and *Grouse*.

Passenger Pigeon (*Ectopistes migratorius*). An American wild pigeon, at one time very abundant in the Mississippi valley and in the states eastward and northward to Hudson bay, but now probably extinct. The passenger pigeon is 16 inches long, with a ruddy breast, blue-gray back, and a pointed tail. In the early days of the United States these pigeons were so numerous that at times the flocks covered the entire view for hours at a time. As late as 1860 they were still so plentiful that, when migrating in the spring or autumn, flocks were visible almost constantly at all hours of the day. When roosting at night their weight broke down large branches and even small trees. Advantage was taken of this gregarious habit to kill them, when sleeping, in great numbers.

The nesting places of the passenger pigeon were often of vast extent. One near Shelbyville, Kentucky, was several miles wide and 40 miles long. The last nesting place in western New York, which was located near Olean, in 1868, extended for 14 miles. In 1876 there was a nesting place in Michigan 28 miles long and 3 or 4 miles wide. In 1911, the passenger pigeon was so nearly extinct that the American Ornithologists' Union made an organized effort to discover and save the remnant then living, and rewards aggregating over $2000 were offered for the discovery of undisturbed nestings. In 1914 what was supposed to be the last survivor died in the zoological gardens at Cincinnati.

Peacock (*Pavo cristatus*). A large bird of the pheasant family, somewhat smaller than a turkey, native of India and Ceylon. It is distinguished by its gorgeous plumage and exceedingly long tail. The upper tail feathers are elongated into a magnificent train, which can be spread out like a fan, beautifully marked at the tip with eyelike or moonlike spots and glowing with iridescent tints of green, gold, bronze, and blue. The wild peacock lives in warm, wooded districts, roosting on high branches, nesting on the ground, and laying a single clutch of from 12 to 18 eggs yearly.

The peacock has been domesticated since very ancient times in India, where it is still reared in immense numbers for its flesh and eggs. From India the peacock spread widely throughout the world. According to the Bible, it was brought in ships from Tarshish to Palestine at the time of Solomon. In classic mythology it became the bird of Juno. Aristophanes mentions the peacock in his plays, and it became well known in Greece after Alexander's expedition to India. By the Romans, peacocks' brains and tongues were served as delicacies at the most sumptuous feasts. During the middle ages, peacocks were often placed on the tables of royalty.

Pearl. A beautiful concretion, usually rounded in form, with a brilliant luster, produced within the shells of pearl oysters, river mussels, and other mollusks. A true pearl takes form in a pearl sac, but, it is believed, a tiny grain of sand or other foreign body must be present as a nucleus about which layers of hard, smooth nacre are secreted. In Japan the growth of pearls in oysters is promoted by skillfully removing the pearl sac, inserting a fragment of fresh water mussel as a nucleus, and transplanting the sac into another oyster, which is planted in a known spot and left for five years. It is then recovered, and the pearl is taken from the oyster.

Pearls occur in many forms, from spherical to irregularly oblong, and their color varies from black to gray, blue, yellow, pink, and white, the finest having a silvery or a satiny luster. When of proper size, shape, color, and luster, pearls are of great value as jewels. The most highly prized are perfectly round or pear-shaped, pure white or nearly translucent, with a delicate iridescent sheen. The choicest pearls are obtained from the Persian gulf and on the coasts of the Philippines, various Polynesian islands, Australia, and Lower California.

Excellent pearls are obtained from various kinds of fresh-water mussels in the Mississippi and the Ohio valley in the United States. Pearl fishing, which often requires the work of expert divers, is an important local industry in many regions.

The most perfect pearl is said to be "La Pellegrina" in the Museum of Zosima in Moscow, a globular Indian pearl of unusual beauty, weighing 28 carats. A somewhat irregularly shaped pearl in the Victoria and Albert Museum, London, is said to be the largest known. It measures 2 inches in length, 4½ inches in circumference, and weighs 3 ounces.

Peccary (*Dicotyles*). An American mammal of the swine family, related to the wild boar of Europe. Peccaries are found from southwestern United States, southward through Mexico and Central and South America. In appearance, the peccary much resembles a small, slender-legged pig, but differs in having only three toes on its hind feet, and no visible tail. Both jaws are fitted with long tusks, and, when enraged, the animal fights with great courage and ferocity. Its food consists chiefly of nuts, seeds, and fruits, but it also eats small animals and carrion. The peccary is provided with a musk gland on its back, which gives the flesh a strong flavor, but, if this gland is removed as soon as the animal is dead, the meat is palatable.

The collared peccary (*D. torquatus*), about 3 feet long and 16 inches high, blackish gray in color with a white band encircling the neck, is found from Arkansas and Texas southward to Patagonia. It lives chiefly in forests, usually in pairs or in small parties. See *Swine*.

Pelican (*Pelecanus*). A group of large fish-eating birds possessing an enormous bill, with an elastic pouch under it, used as a scoop net to catch fish.

Pelicans range from 4 to 6 feet in length, have short legs, completely webbed feet, and very large, strong wings, which often have a spread of nearly 10 feet. There are about 10 species, widely distributed throughout temperate and tropical regions, 3 of which are found in North America. All are birds of very odd form and striking color. They thrive in captivity and are amiable, sociable, and harmless. At breeding time, pelicans nest in communities, usually on islands. The pure white eggs, 3 or 4 in number, are deposited in crude low nests. The young are fed by the regurgitated food of the parents.

The beautiful white pelican (*P. onocrotalus*), 5 to 6 feet long, with a wing spread of about 9 feet, abundant in the Mediterranean region, was well known to the ancients. The American white pelican (*P. erythrorhynchos*), similar in size, is one of the most handsome and dignified of American birds. While formerly ranging throughout North America from Hudson bay southward, it is now rare except in the interior, where it breeds from Minnesota to northern Saskatchewan.

The brown pelican (*P. fuscus*), 4 feet long, nests abundantly in Florida and along the Gulf coast, sometimes straying northward to Illinois and New England. The similar California brown pelican (*P. occidentalis*) ranges from British Columbia to the Galapagos islands.

Penguins (*Impennes*). A remarkable group of flightless birds, found only in antarctic regions. They differ from all other birds in that their wings are modified into swimming paddles, for which they are exclusively used. There are about 20 species, living on the shores of southern oceans, being very abundant in the Falkland islands. In size they range from the blue penguin (*Eudyptula minus*) of Australia, which is 16 inches long, to the great emperor penguin (*Aptemodytes forsteri*) of the antarctic continent, which attains a length of 48 inches and a weight of 60 to 75 pounds.

Penguins are essentially sea birds, feeding chiefly upon fishes and crustaceans. They are excellent swimmers and really fly under water, using their wings as fins. Their bodies are covered with short, stiff, scalelike feathers. Penguins are rarely seen on land except at breeding season, when they congregate in vast rookeries. On land they stand very erect, with drooping wings. They walk clumsily with a peculiar gait. The eggs, usually two in number, are laid on the ground or in holes. Both parents take part in hatching them and attend to the needs of the young with great care.

Perch (*Percidæ*). A large family of fresh-water fishes, found chiefly in northern regions. The yellow perch (*Perca flavescens*) occurs in lakes and ponds from Maine to Minnesota. It is golden yellow or umber brown in color, measures 7 to 12 inches in length, and weighs from ½ to 3 pounds. Along the greater lakes it takes rank as a market fish.

The Yellow Pike-Perch (*Stizostedeon vitreum*), often called "yellow pike" and "wall-eyed pike," is not a pike. The pike-perches have two prominent dorsal fins, while the true pikes, related to the pickerel and muskellunge, have only one. The yellow pike-perch is abundant in many lakes and streams from Lake Champlain to Saskatchewan and southward nearly to the Gulf states. It is usually dark olive above and mottled below, 1 to 3 feet in length, and often weighs from 10 to 20 pounds. It is highly esteemed as a food fish.

Petrel (*Procellariidæ*). A well marked group of strictly oceanic birds, with long narrow wings, webbed front toes, and tubular external nostrils. The petrels take their name from the habit of appearing to walk on the water, as the Apostle Peter is said to have done, the Latin name *petrellus* meaning "little Peter."

There are about 100 species, most numerous in southern oceans, of which more than 30 have been found to occur in North America. All are sooty black or grayish, and more or less marked with white. They literally live on the open sea, never venturing on land except at breeding time. Most petrels nest in holes among rocks or in clumps of grass, though some burrow in the ground, and they lay only one egg. They often follow a ship for days, seemingly without rest. The stormy petrel (*Procellaria pelagica*), called "Mother Carey's chicken," the smallest of web-footed birds, only 5½ inches long, occurs on both sides of the Atlantic from the latitude of Newfoundland northward.

Phainopepla (*fâ-ĭ'nô-pĕp'là*) (*P. nitens*). A handsome crested bird, closely related to the waxwings. It is about 7 inches long, with silky blue-black plumage marked with white wing patches, and is found from western Texas to Utah and California and southward. It builds a compact, saucer-shaped nest in elders, pepper trees, oaks, and blue gums, laying 2 or 3 whitish, thickly spotted eggs, and feeds upon berries and insects. It is a dashing, vivacious bird of fine presence and pleasing song.

Pheasant (*fĕz'ănt*) (*Phasianus*). The true pheasants, of which there are about 30 kinds, all natives of Asia, are among the most gorgeous of the entire feathered tribe. They are of large size, usually from 30 to 70 inches in length, inclusive of the very long tail. In the male, the naked skin on the sides of the head is bright red, and each leg is provided with a pair of spurs.

The common pheasant (*P. colchicus*), widely naturalized in Europe and elsewhere, is now a standard game bird in many countries. In Europe it is reared in enormous numbers in great game preserves for the annual shooting season. About 12 different species have been introduced into North America, including the ring-necked pheasant, the golden and the silver pheasant from China, and the copper and the green pheasant from Japan.

Various hybrids between the common pheasant and the ring-necked pheasant (*P. torquatus*) have been reared in more than half of the States. Some of these have become thoroughly naturalized in Oregon, Washington, western New York, and elsewhere. They live and breed in open woods and thickets, and sometimes mingle with barnyard fowls. They roost in trees like turkeys. Their flesh and eggs are excellent eating.

Pheasants nest on the ground and usually lay 10 or more olive brown eggs in a slight depression among the leaves. Like the domestic fowl, they feed chiefly on seeds, berries, young shoots of plants, worms, and insects.

Phœbe (*Sayornis phœbe*). A familiar North American flycatcher often called "pewee." It nests on beams or rafters and under bridges or banks from North Carolina to Manitoba and Newfoundland, wintering southward to Cuba and Mexico. The phœbe is about 7 inches long, grayish olive brown above, with a dark crown, wings, and tail, and with white outer tail feathers. It builds a nest of mud and moss, lined with grasses and hair, and lays 4 to 6 usually pure white eggs. This confiding bird feeds chiefly on injurious insects. The smaller black phœbe (*S. nigricans*), black above and white below, is a handsome Pacific Coast species.

Phosphorescence. The emission of light by certain animal tissues was so called because it was formerly thought to be due to the presence of phosphorus. Light is produced as an accompaniment of the oxidation of luciferin into oxyluciferin. This process is made possible by the action of a catalytic agent, luciferase. The oxidation of luciferin is reversible, so that the same material, having been reduced from oxyluciferin, may again produce light by being oxidized. The colors of animal light include white, green, blue, red, and lilac.

Among the more noteworthy examples of luminous animals are the firefly, the lantern fishes, and the transparent pelagic animals that float on the surface of the tropical seas. Lantern fishes are usually found at great depths, and frequently bear a light-giving area on their heads, by which their surroundings are illuminated. The production of light is said to serve the purpose of terrifying enemies or attracting mates.

Pigeon. The family of the true pigeons or doves (*Columbidæ*) embraces fully 500 species, widely distributed throughout the world but most numerous in Australia and in tropical islands. They have four toes all on the same level, the rather slender bill is deeply grooved, and the nostrils end in a soft, fleshy membrane. In temperate regions pigeons are plainly colored, but in the tropics their plumage is often gorgeous with striking colorations of green, red, yellow, violet, and blue.

Pigeons are strictly monogamous, and the sexes share alike in the work of nest making, incubating, and caring for the young. The nests are usually placed in trees, and the eggs, almost invariably two in number, are uniformly pure white. The young are hatched naked and are fed with food regurgitated from the stomachs of the parent birds. Pigeons are vegetarian feeders, living chiefly upon grains, seeds, and fruit. Unlike other birds, they keep the bill immersed when drinking. Their soft low notes are well described as cooing. They are usually classed as game birds and are much hunted for their excellent flesh.

About 12 species occur in North America. Of these, 8 are confined to the southern borders of the United States. Those of wider range are the familiar mourning dove, common from Canada to Cuba, the little ground dove of the Southern states, the band-tailed pigeon of western North America, and the rare or perhaps extinct passenger pigeon, formerly enormously abundant from Hudson bay southward.

The domestic pigeon or dove has long been regarded as a direct descendant of the wild blue pigeon, or rock dove (*Columba livia*), of Europe and Asia, but recent investigations seem to indicate a mixed parentage. Its domestication is prehistoric. According to Lepsius the earliest record of the domestic pigeon in Egypt dates to 3000 B. C. Frequent reference is made to it in the Bible, and the early Christians adopted the dove as a symbol of the Holy Spirit. Domestic pigeons are said to have reached Greece by way of Syria about 400 B. C., whence they spread to Rome and other parts of Europe.

Ages of selective breeding have developed more than 250 varieties of the domestic pigeon, including pouters, tumblers, fantails, rough-footed pigeons, and homing or carrier pigeons. While valuable for food, pigeons are now kept chiefly as pets and ornamental birds. See *Carrier Pigeon, Passenger Pigeon.*

Pike (*Esox*). A genus of slender, long-snouted, voracious fishes, widely distributed in the northern hemisphere. The common pike (*E. lucius*), found from the northeastern United States to Alaska, 2½ to 4 feet long, sometimes exceeds 40 pounds in weight.

The Muskellunge (*E. masquinongy*), of the Great Lakes region, is a splendid game fish, attaining a length of 6 feet and a weight of 75 pounds or more. It is a good fighter when hooked and tries the skill of the best anglers. The Chautauqua Muskellunge (*E. ohiensis*), called also salmon pike, of Chautauqua lake and the Ohio valley, sometimes 5 feet long, is a good food fish. It has been successfully propagated by fish hatcheries.

The Chain Pickerel (*E. reticulatus*), common in lakes and ponds east of the Alleghenies, attains a length of 30 inches and is a fair food fish. The Little Pickerel (*E. vermiculatus*), of the Mississippi valley, rarely exceeds a foot in length.

Platypus (*Ornithorhynchus anatinus*). An Australian animal, called also "duckbill," intermediate between mammals and birds. It has webbed feet and a flat bill like a duck; the body is about a foot long and covered with soft brown fur, intermingled with longer hairs; the tail is broad, flat, hairy above and naked below.

The platypus is a nocturnal animal, frequenting quiet pools and streams and therefore not easily found. It digs deep burrows in banks in which it builds a nest and lays two ovoid white eggs, each less than an inch long, with strong, flexible shells. The young, which at first are blind and hairless like young mice, are suckled for some weeks by the mother. The food of the platypus is mostly animal and consists largely of water insects. See *Monotremata.*

Plover. A group of shore birds, closely related to the snipes and sandpipers. They are mostly from 7 to 11 inches long, with a small pigeon-like bill, large, rounded head, short neck, long and pointed wings, moderately long legs, and usually only 3 toes. Plovers frequent marshes, tide flats, sandy, open grounds, and plains, feeding on insects, worms, and other small forms of animal life.

The golden plover (*Charadrius dominicus*) is 10 inches long, with black upper parts spotted and margined with golden yellow. It breeds in the arctic regions, building a crude nest in the sand at the edge of seabeaches, in which it lays about 4 brownish buff eggs splotched with brown. It migrates southward over nearly all North and South America, wintering from Florida to Patagonia. Six species of ringed plover occur in the United States, the largest of which is the familiar killdeer. The so-called crocodile bird is the Egyptian spur-winged plover. Several of the plovers are highly prized table birds.

Polar Bear (*Thalassarctus maritimus*). A tall, powerful arctic species of bear, with thin sides, long legs, and flat, wide, hairy paws. It stands more than 4 feet high and has a length of over 7 feet. Its color is creamy white at all times of the year. The home of the polar bear is the ice packs and the barren islands of the arctic zone, where it wanders at will, living upon fish, seals, walruses, and the scanty vegetable matter of frigid regions. It is a powerful swimmer, and is sometimes seen in the open sea many miles from land. While formerly reputed very ferocious, the polar bear rarely attacks man, unless brought to bay or made fierce by extreme hunger. See *Bear.*

Polecat. A name given to several small animals of the weasel family, but properly applied only to the European marten (*Putorius fœtidus*). The true polecat is dark brown in color and about 17 inches in length. It is a nocturnal animal, sleeping during the day and searching for its prey at night, being especially destructive to poultry, rabbits, and pheasants. It has glands secreting a fetid fluid, somewhat like that of the American skunk, which it ejects when irritated or alarmed. The fur of the polecat, which is exported in large quantities from northern Europe, is known as that of the fitch. Its hairs form a superior kind of artists' brushes. In America the skunk is sometimes called a polecat. See *Skunk.*

Porcupines. Rodent mammals whose bodies are covered, especially on the back, with so-called quills, or dense, solid, spinelike structures, intermixed with bristles and stiff hair. In their usual position the spines lie nearly flat, with their points directed backward. When the animal is excited, the spines are capable of being raised, and form an effective defense against the attack of nearly all animals. The quills, which are barbed at the point, are loosely inserted in the skin. On being violently shaken, they may become detached. Under no circumstances, however, can porcupines actually shoot their quills. The true porcupines of the Old World live in burrows or in caves in the rocks. The American porcupines differ in being largely arboreal in their habits.

The Canada porcupine (*Erethizon dorsatus*), about 2½ feet long, with yellowish white spines, is found in wooded districts from New England to Ohio, north to Hudson bay. It is a slow-moving, dull-witted animal, living either on the ground or in tree tops, and feeding chiefly upon bark, buds, and fruit, often remaining in a tree until it has stripped off all the bark. Porcupines delight to prowl about camps, eating every piece of leather or of greasy or painted wood which they can discover. See *Hedgehog.*

Porgy (*Stenesthes chrysops*). A spiny-finned sea fish, often called "scuppaug" or "scup," found along the eastern shores of the United States. It is a much esteemed food fish, attaining a length of 18 inches and a weight of 4 pounds. The larger but closely related Sheepshead (*Archosargus probatocephalus*), marked with vertical bands of black, weighs from 6 to 20 pounds. It is an excellent table fish, occurring along the Atlantic and Gulf coasts. In California, the surf fish, or white perch (*Damalicthys argyrosomus*), is sometimes called porgy.

Porpoise. A marine, fishlike mammal, belonging to the same family as the dolphin, and to the order *Cetacea.* The common porpoise (*Phocœna communis*), usually 4 to 5 feet in length, is an inhabitant of northern seas. In color it is mostly jet-black above, merging into pink, mottled gray, or white beneath. The porpoise is compelled continually to seek the surface of the water in order to breathe. It is then observed rolling over, as it were, and is heard discharging air from the blowhole on the crown of the head, at the same time taking in a fresh supply at the mouth. From this habit arises the popular expression "to blow like a porpoise."

Prairie Dog (*Cynomys*). A small rodent mammal of the squirrel family, so called because its cry somewhat resembles the bark of a small dog. The common prairie dog, or American marmot (*C. ludovicianus*), was formerly enormously abundant on the plains east of the Rocky mountains from the Canadian border to the Rio Grande. It is about a foot long, with a tail of 4 inches, and in color is reddish brown, variegated with gray. Prairie dogs are very alert and active animals. They live together in societies on the prairies, excavating burrows contiguous to each other, and often forming immense colonies, called prairie dog "towns," sometimes miles or scores of miles in extent. The widely current story that the prairie dog lives in peace and harmony in the same burrow with the rattlesnake and the burrowing owl is a myth.

Primates. The highest order of mammals, including man, the anthropoid apes, monkeys, and lemurs. They are characterized by the presence of well-developed clavicles, two pectoral mammæ, and by eye orbits encircled by bone and directed forward. In at least one pair of limbs the innermost digits of the hands or feet are opposable to each other, and usually they are opposable in both pairs of limbs. The fingers and toes bear flat nails, very rarely claws. Except in the lemurs, the brain is of a high type, with a large, much convoluted cerebrum covering the cerebellum.

Exclusive of man, the primates are chiefly tree-dwellers, and are admirably adapted for such a mode of life. The tail is often long and sometimes prehensile, serving as an additional hand in climbing and in swinging from tree to tree. While mostly small, or of medium size, some of the apes are heavier and stronger than man. As to food, they are omnivorous, but subsist chiefly upon fruits, berries, and other vegetable products.

The primates consist of two distinct suborders, the *Lemuroidea*, with foxlike muzzles and rodent-like teeth, containing the lemurs and their near allies, and the *Anthropoidea*, which includes the marmosets, monkeys, baboons, apes, and man. There are about 260 species, chiefly natives of tropical forest regions. See *Ape, Baboon, Chimpanzee, Gorilla, Monkey, Orang-utan.*

Pronghorn (*Antilocapra americana*). A small, hollow-horned ruminant, intermediate between the antelopes and giraffes, found only in North America, and popularly called antelope. It differs from the true antelopes and from all other bovine animals in having a branch or prong on its horns. Like the deer, it sheds its horns periodically.

The pronghorn stands about 3 feet high at the shoulder, has a slender neck, and carries its head erect. Both sexes possess horns, sometimes a foot long, which rise directly upward above the eyes. In general color the pronghorn is chestnut above and white below. It associates in herds, and, although a shy, timid animal, it never skulks or takes to cover, but trusts for safety to its remarkable speed, which exceeds that of any other North American animal.

While formerly very numerous on the plains and plateaus from Mexico to Saskatchewan and westward to the Pacific, the pronghorn has been practically exterminated except in limited areas. See *Antelope.*

Protective Coloring. Color is one of the most valuable agencies in the survival of many animals. In most instances, it serves to conceal the animal in its natural environment, enabling it to elude the notice of its enemies. This effect is seen, for example, in the white fur of arctic animals, which resembles snow; in fish, whose coloring above resembles the beds of streams and that on the lower part of the body resembles the water surface as it appears from beneath; and in the tiger, okapi, and other tropical animals, whose markings frequently resemble the effect of sunlight shining through rank vegetation. The chameleon and certain fish are able to alter their color rapidly with a change of environment. Many subarctic animals have a darker color in summer than in winter.

Another type of protective coloring is found in the apparent mimicry of one animal by another. Thus certain palatable beetles of the family *Cerambycidæ* resemble very closely in color pattern various wasps and unpalatable beetles, and so are avoided by birds that might otherwise eat them.

Protozoans. The protozoans are minute, microscopic, aquatic animals, each of which consists of a single cell. They constitute the lowest or most primitive forms of animal life. The body, like any other animal cell, is a mass of protoplasm which contains one or more nuclei. While lacking distinct organs, protozoans nevertheless perform all the essential functions of the animal body. They possess the power of motion; engulf and assimilate food; respond to external stimulation, such as that of light and heat; and reproduce their kind.

Protozoans feed upon many forms of organic matter, both plant and animal, living or dead, and a large number are parasitic. Many of the parasitic forms are the cause of disease in man and in animals. For example, the *plasmodium*, when introduced into the human blood by the bites of mosquitoes, produces malaria. Various *trypanosomes*, which are transmitted by certain kinds of flies, produce the deadly sleeping sickness in man and the fatal surra and nagana diseases in horses and cattle. See *Amœba.*

Ptarmigan (*tär'mĭ-găn*) (*Lagopus*). A group of circumpolar grouse. They are remarkable for the seasonal changes of their plumage, which varies from black, brown, buff, and gray in summer, to pure white in winter. There are about **15** species and varieties, most common in arctic America. The white-tailed ptarmigan (*L. leucurus*), 14 inches long, inhabiting alpine summits of the Rocky mountains from Alaska to New Mexico, is the smallest and handsomest species. Other species include the willow ptarmigan (*L. lagopus*) and the rock ptarmigan (*L. rupestris*). The Red Grouse (*L. scoticus*), confined to Great Britain, is the only ptarmigan which does not turn completely white in winter.

Puma (*Felis concolor*). A large animal of the cat family (*Felidæ*), sometimes called cougar, peculiar to America, where it ranks next to the jaguar in importance as a destructive or dangerous creature. It is known also as the American or mountain lion, probably from its resemblance in build and color to the lioness; but it is much smaller in size and lacks the lion's mane. Its length is 7 to 8 feet from nose to tip of tail; its height is about 2 feet.

The geographical range of the puma is very extensive. It is found in the Adirondacks and in Florida, and along the Rocky mountains and the Andes from British Columbia to Patagonia. In North America the principal food of the puma is deer, though it seizes upon other smaller animals. While practically exterminated east of the Missouri river, the puma is still found in the Rocky mountains and on the Pacific coast. In western ranching districts it destroys sheep, calves, and colts. It is of cowardly nature, and is not regarded with fear by hunters. Unlike most of the larger members of the cat family, it is remarkably silent; but sometimes when prowling it screams like a terrified child. While the subject of many thrilling tales of adventure, the puma is nowhere known to attack man, even when he is alone and unarmed.

Python. A genus of very large snakes. Like all other members of the boa family (*Boidæ*), they are powerful constrictors, killing their prey by crushing it within the encircling folds of their muscular bodies. They feed almost entirely upon small mammals and birds, which they swallow whole.

While the boas bring forth their young alive, pythons lay eggs, as do most serpents, but with one remarkable difference. After laying from 50 to 100 roundish, white eggs, about the size of those of a goose, the female gathers them into a somewhat cone-shaped pile. She then coils herself around it so that her head rests in the center at the top of the heap. Here she remains on guard without taking food for about two months, when the shells split open and the little snakes appear.

The largest pythons weigh many hundred pounds and possess tremendous strength. Doubtless they could readily overpower and kill almost any large land animal. But their mouths, though extremely distensible, are probably not large enough to enable them to swallow any creature larger than a sheep or a goat, and this only after the bones have been thoroughly crushed.

Except a single Mexican species, the pythons inhabit tropical parts of Asia, Africa, and Australia. They are chiefly tree-dwellers, preferring the vicinity of water, though some live in broken, rocky places.

The reticulated python (*P. reticulatus*), of Indo-China, Sumatra, and Borneo, sometimes attains a length of nearly 33 feet. It is the largest known snake, although it is very nearly equaled by the anaconda. This species is frequently seen in menageries. The Indian python (*P. molurus*), scarcely smaller, is the rock snake of India and Ceylon. The rock python (*P. sebæ*), of tropical and southern Africa, with a small head, is sometimes 15 feet long. The Diamond Snake, or Carpet Snake (*P. spilotes*), a small python of Australia and New Guinea, 6 or 7 feet long, lives in trees near the water and feeds on small mammals and birds. See *Anaconda, Boa.*

Quail. A name applied to several small game birds of the grouse family. In eastern North America the familiar bobwhite (*Colinus virginianus*) is commonly called quail, though in the Southern states it is known as partridge. In the western and southwestern United States there are several species of handsome, crested quails, which are known also as partridges. Among these are the beautiful California quail (*Lophortyx californicus*), Gambel's quail (*Lophortyx gambeli*), the mountain plumed quail (*Oreortyx pictus*), the blue quail (*Callipepla squamata*), called also scaled partridge, and the Massena quail (*Cyrtonyx montezumæ*).

The American birds known as quails are permanent residents and breed wherever found. After the nesting season they often gather in bevies, sometimes in large flocks, and are much hunted by sportsmen. The true Old World quail (*Coturnix communis*), abundant in the Mediterranean region, is migratory. See *California Quail, Grouse, Partridge.*

Quezal (*kē̇-säl'*) (*Pharomacrus mocinno*). The most beautiful species of trogon and one of the handsomest of all birds. It is a native of Central America, especially of Guatemala, of which country it is the national emblem. In size the quezal is about as large as a dove. The male has a crested head, yellow bill, plumage which is metallic green above and brilliant scarlet below, and white tail plumes 3 feet in length.

Before the Spanish Conquest, the quezal was so highly prized by the natives that no one was allowed to kill it, but only to remove its long plumes, which none but chiefs were permitted to wear. Through the demand for its skin and plumes by European milliners, the quezal has become rare. The quezal, like other trogons, nests in hollow trees, and the greenish blue eggs are believed not to exceed two in number.

Rabbit (*Lepus*). A rodent mammal, very similar to the hare, but smaller, with much shorter legs and ears. Unlike the hare, the rabbit usually lives in burrows, and the color of its fur does not change with the seasons. Rabbits are shy animals and very swift of foot, though less fleet than the hares. They are extremely prolific, sometimes producing in a single year 5 or 6 litters of from 3 to 10 young at a time, which in turn reach maturity in about six months. They feed upon grasses, grains, fruits, vegetables, and the bark of trees, and wherever numerous are destructive to growing crops, pastures, gardens, and orchards.

The gray rabbit, or Cottontail (*L. sylvaticus*), found throughout eastern North America, is easily recognized by its fluffy white tail. This rabbit is about 18 inches long, gray above, varied with black tinged with yellowish brown, and white below. The cottontail is the most abundant small game animal in the Eastern states and is much hunted for food. The sage rabbit (*L. artemisia*), a similar species, inhabits high western sagebrush plains.

The domestic rabbit is believed to have originated from the wild European rabbit (*L. cuniculus*). It was probably first domesticated by the ancient peoples of Spain, whence it was brought to Rome about the time of the Cæsars. Centuries of breeding have developed many varieties, among which are the Belgian, lop-eared, Dutch, Angora, Siberian, and Himalayan rabbits. Of these the Belgian rabbit, often wrongly called Belgian hare, is the best-known. Its flesh is excellent and forms a staple article of food in France, Belgium, and England.

About 1850, three pairs of the domestic rabbit were turned loose in New South Wales, Australia where they multiplied so rapidly is soon to become, a public pest. About 1875, this rabbit gained a foothold in New Zealand, and there also immediately became a menace to agriculture. Millions of these rabbits are now killed each year for food and for fur in these countries, but as yet there is no apparent reduction in their numbers. See *Hare.*

Raccoons. A small family (*Procyonidæ*) of flat-footed, flesh-eating mammals, peculiar to America. They are bearlike in appearance but of small size, and include the raccoon, the cacomistle, and the coati.

The common raccoon (*Procyon lotor*) is a pretty animal, about the size of a cat, but much stouter. It has a long brown or grizzled coat, with black facial markings, a ringed, bushy tail, and a pointed nose. Its legs are short and armed with strong claws, useful for digging or climbing. In its attitudes it is somewhat monkey-like and usually sits upon its haunches when feeding, holding its food in its forepaws. It has a curious habit of washing articles given to it, and of soaking food in water before eating it. It is found in wooded districts from Newfoundland to British Columbia and south to Mexico. Its skin is highly valued as a fur, and its flesh is considered a delicacy. Raccoon hunting, usually with dogs, is a favorite sport, especially in the Southern states. See *Cacomistle.*

Racers (*Zamenis*). A numerous genus of slim, graceful, exceedingly active but harmless snakes, found in both the Old and the New World. The Black Snake (*Z. constrictor*), 5 to 6 feet long, uniform slaty black in color, is found from Canada to Florida and westward to the Mississippi. Despite many romantic folk tales, this agile serpent does not crush its prey by constriction, destroy rattlesnakes, or hypnotize birds. It is rather timid, fights only when cornered, and, whenever possible, seeks escape by its lightning-like speed. A western variety, known as the blue racer (*Z. constrictor*, var. *flaviventris*), is smaller and more slender than the eastern black snake. It is bluish green or olive above and pale yellow below, and occurs from the Mississippi to the Pacific.

The Coachwhip Snake (*Z. flagelliformis*) is found from South Carolina westward to Arizona. It is more slender, longer, and more speedy than the black snake. While only about an inch in diameter, it is sometimes 8 feet long. The arrangement of its large scales gives this snake the appearance of a braided whip.

Rail (*Rallidæ*). A large family of wading birds which includes the rails, gallinules, and coots. They have very narrow, compressed, slender bodies, rather long necks, short wings, and strong legs and feet. All are weak flyers and depend chiefly upon running and hiding in order to escape danger. A few have entirely lost the power of flight. There are about 180 species, found in all temperate regions, inhabiting marshes, ponds, and borders of streams, and feeding upon water plants, worms, snails, tadpoles, insects, and other small forms of animal life. They usually nest in secluded marshes, laying 10 to 12 eggs.

The true rails (*Rallus*) comprise about 21 species, 16 of which occur in the New World. Among these are the clapper rail of the Atlantic coast and the California clapper rail, both of which inhabit salt-water marshes, and also the yellow rail, the king rail, the Virginia rail, and the sora or Carolina rail, which frequent fresh-water marshes of the central and eastern United States and Canada. Most rails are popularly called marsh hens. When fat, many kinds are highly esteemed for the table.

Rat (*Mus*). A well-known rodent of the same subfamily as the mouse, but much larger, uglier, and clumsier.

The brown rat (*M. decumanus*), native of India and Persia, has become distributed throughout the world by the ships of modern commerce. It reached Europe through Russia about 1727, and America about 1775, and is now a common pest. Wherever it gains a foothold, it drives out all other rats and many other small animals. It is enormously prolific, producing in a single year 3 to 5 litters of 10 to 12 young at a time. While scavengers, living mostly in filthy places, rats are usually cleanly in appearance and always have sleek coats. They feed on all kinds of refuse matter and are useful to some extent in the disposal of what otherwise would become injurious to health. On the other hand, rats not only destroy millions of dollars worth of food but they are also bearers of dangerous diseases, especially the bubonic plague. Consequently, a war of extermination is waged against them.

In North America, there are several native wild rats, such as the Florida wood rat (*Neotoma floridana*), common in the South; the gray wood rat (*Neotoma cinerea*), of the Rocky Mountain region, which, like the crow, steals knives and spoons; and the California wood rat (*Neotoma fuscipes*) which builds of sticks a huge nest 4 feet high.

Rattlesnake (*Crotalus*). The most widely known of North American poisonous snakes. It is distinguished by the possession of a series of loosely jointed, horny rings at the end of the tail, the rattle, with which it gives its characteristic warning. About three new rings are added every year, replacing those worn away or broken off.

There are 16 species of true rattlesnakes, of which 12 occur in the United States, 2 in Mexico, 1 in Central America, and 1 in South America. Except in the Southwest, where 10 species are found, most regions in the United States have only one or two species. The rattlesnakes are the most highly developed of venomous snakes. Some are large, powerful, and superbly colored. All are dangerous, and the larger kinds are deadly. But, owing to their habit of giving warning and their disposition not to attack, the fatalities from their bites are very few compared with those caused by other venomous serpents.

The timber rattlesnake (*C. horridus*), 3½ to 4 feet long, extremely variable in color, occurs from Vermont to Iowa and southward to Texas. The diamond-back rattlesnake (*C. adamanteus*), the largest, handsomest, and most deadly of North American snakes, is found in coastal regions from North Carolina to Mississippi. It sometimes exceeds 8 feet in length and 4 inches in diameter. It is strikingly colored with diamond-shaped markings. The western diamond-back rattlesnake (*C. atrox*), ranging from Texas to southern California, sometimes 7 feet long, but averaging much smaller, has a white tail with jet-black rings.

The prairie rattlesnake (*C. confluentus*), abundant on the plains from Saskatchewan to Texas, is usually about 3 feet long. The oft-repeated tale of its fraternal relations with prairie dogs and burrowing owls is a myth. The Pacific rattlesnake (*C. oreganus*), found from British Columbia to southern California, is smaller than the prairie rattlesnake. The horned rattlesnake, or Sidewinder (*C. cerastes*), of Arizona and adjoining desert regions, 18 to 30 inches long, has a hornlike projection above the eyes. When running, it moves at an oblique angle to the direction in which its head is pointing.

Raven (*Corvus*). The largest bird of the crow family, native of both hemispheres. In plumage and appearance the raven much resembles the crow, but is larger, with the feathers of the throat narrow and pointed.

The European raven (*C. corax*), about 26 inches long, lives alone or in pairs, though sometimes gathering in flocks about carrion, which is always its chief food. However, it attacks wounded or dying animals, young rabbits and birds, and sometimes devastates grainfields. The raven nests in high trees or in holes in cliffs. It is intelligent, easily tamed, and in captivity may be taught to speak a few words. In ancient Greece and Italy the raven was sacred to Apollo, and the Roman augurs pretended to be able to forecast the future from its manner of flight.

The similar northern raven (*C. corax principalis*) ranges from Greenland to Alaska and south to British Columbia on the Pacific coast and to North Carolina on the Atlantic coast. In the eastern United States it is a very rare and local bird. The smaller American raven (*C. corax sinuatus*) frequents middle altitudes from the Rocky mountains to the Pacific coast. The white-necked raven (*C. cryptoleucus*), 20 inches long, inhabits deserts from western Texas to southern California. See *Crow, Jackdaw, Magpie, Rook.*

Ray (*Batoidea*). A group of fishes allied to the sharks but differing from them in having the gill-openings always on the underside of the body. It includes the rays, skates, sawfishes, sea devils, and other related forms. The true rays have greatly flattened bodies adapted for life on shallow sea bottoms. For example, the spotted ray of Ceylon, measuring 5 feet across, is only 5 inches thick at the center of the body and tapers to almost vanishing edges. The skates lay large eggs, incased in a leathery covering, but most other rays bring forth their young alive. See *Sawfish, Sea Devil, Skate, Sting Ray, Torpedo.*

Red Snapper (*Lutianus aya*). A beautiful, crimson colored, spiny-finned food fish of the Gulf of Mexico, usually weighing 8 or 9 pounds but sometimes exceeding 25 pounds. Several million pounds of red snappers are marketed annually by Florida fishermen.

Reindeer (*Rangifer tarandus*). An arctic species of deer, native of northern Europe and Siberia. It has been long domesticated in Scandinavia, Lapland, and Russia as a beast of burden, as a means of travel, and as a source of food and clothing. In size and appearance it much resembles the American caribou, which, by some authorities, are regarded as varieties of the reindeer. It differs from ordinary deer in having flat horns which are possessed by both sexes. The domestic reindeer, although smaller than the wild reindeer, possesses remarkable strength and endurance. Its ability to subsist upon stunted shrubs, lichens, and other scanty vegetation makes it invaluable to the far northern peoples.

In 1889, reindeer were introduced into Alaska by the United States government in an attempt to save the Eskimos from starvation, due to the destruction of their walrus fisheries. The original importations of about 1500 animals from Siberia have increased to more than 1,000,000, of which over half are owned by the natives. See *Caribou.*

Remora (*Echeneididæ*). A family of peculiar small fishes of the open seas, called also sucking fish. They are provided with a flat sucking-disk on top of the head, by which they attach themselves to sharks, swordfish, turtles, and even ships. However, remoras do not attack or injure in any way the various animals to which they attach themselves. Like a rider upon a horse, the remora is transported by its host to better feeding grounds, sometimes at great distances. The Shark Sucker, or Mediterranean Remora (*Echeneis naucrates*), well known to the ancients, is about 30 inches long. It is found on our Middle Atlantic coasts. The Swordfish Remora (*Remora brachyptera*), only 12 inches long, usually attaching itself to the swordfish, occurs in our more southern waters.

Reptiles (*rĕp'tĭls*) (*Reptilia*). A class of vertebrate animals which comprises the crocodiles, turtles, lizards, and snakes. They differ from birds and mammals in that they are cold-blooded instead of warm-blooded, and from amphibians and fishes in that they breathe air by means of lungs throughout life instead of temporarily or permanently by gills.

Reptiles are often provided with an exoskeleton, or hardened skin, consisting of horny plates or scales. Ribs are always present. Teeth, which are generally present, are not sunk in distinct sockets, except in crocodiles. The tortoises and turtles, however, are toothless, but their jaws have sharp cutting edges. The young of reptiles are produced from eggs, mostly being hatched after being laid, or oviparously, but in some cases the eggs are hatched within the body, so that the young are brought forth alive, or ovoviviparously.

Upwards of 4000 species of living reptiles are known, comprising over 2000 species of snakes, some 1800 species of lizards, about 300 species of turtles, and less than 25 species of crocodilians. The formerly numerous order of rhynchocephalians now contains only a single living representative. The living reptiles are grouped in the following orders: *Crocodilia*, crocodiles and alligators; *Chelonia*, turtles; *Rhynchocephalia*, tuatara; *Squamata*, lizards and snakes.

Rhea. A large flightless bird, called also the South American ostrich. It differs from the true ostrich in having three toes instead of two on each foot, and these are provided with claws instead of nails. The head and neck are fully feathered, the wings are longer, and there is no tail.

The common rhea (*R. americana*), about half the size of an ostrich, is found in Bolivia, Uruguay, Paraguay, and Argentina. Rheas live in small bands. Several females lay in the same nest, which usually contains 30 to 60 eggs. The sitting and hatching are conducted entirely by the male, who also watches over the young with great care. The speed and endurance of the rhea is so great that it is almost impossible for a hunter to overtake it. When not persecuted, rheas become as tame and familiar as domestic animals. The long-billed rhea (*R. macrorynch*a) occurs only in northeastern Brazil. Darwin's rhea (*R. darwini*), only three feet long, is found in Patagonia. The long wing plumes of rheas are much used in feather dusters. See *Ostrich.*

Rhinoceros. The name of a family of ungulate mammals, natives of tropical Asia and Africa. Next to the elephant, rhinoceroses are the most powerful of land animals. They have large, unwieldy bodies; short, thick legs, terminating in large pads, each with 3 hoof-bearing toes; large elongated heads, with a long horn or horns springing from the snout; small eyes and ears; and short tails. Their hide, while extremely thick, is soft and sensitive, and not bullet-proof, as is popularly supposed. They are wholly herbivorous, some living on grasses, and others on the tender shoots and young twigs of trees.

Two species belong to Africa, both possessing two horns. Of these, the white rhinoceros (*R. simus*) is the larger, attaining a length of over 12 feet and a height of nearly 6 feet; but the smaller black rhinoceros (*R. bicornis*) is the better-known species. The Asiatic species, three in number, are smaller in size; two of the species possess single horns and one a double horn. The Indian rhinoceros (*R. unicornis*), a one-horned species, is the one usually seen in menageries. It leads a tranquil, indolent life, wallowing on the marshy borders of lakes and rivers. Owing to the keenness of its smell and hearing, the rhinoceros cannot be easily attacked; but, when brought to bay, it charges with great fury and impetuosity.

Fossil rhinoceroses are very numerous, especially in the northwestern United States. The woolly rhinoceros (*Atelodus antiquitatis*) is found fossil in England, and complete carcasses of it have been taken from the frozen mud of Siberian tundras.

Robin (*Merula migratoria*). A familiar song bird of the thrush family, found throughout North America east of the Rocky mountains. It nests from Virginia and Kansas northward to Alaska and the arctic coasts and winters chiefly in the Southern states, though a few stragglers remain as far north as southern Canada.

The robin is about 10 inches long, olive gray above with blackish head and tail, and chestnut red below. It nests usually in fruit or shade trees, laying 3 to 5 greenish blue eggs. Its food consists chiefly of worms, insects, small fruits, and berries. By reason of its numbers, friendly disposition, and cheerfulness, the robin has become one of the best-known and most affectionately regarded of American birds. Nehrling says: "The Pilgrim fathers of Massachusetts called this thrush the robin, or robin redbreast, because it reminded them of the beloved robin of their English home, and the love of the latter bird together with its name passed over to the somewhat similarly colored thrush of their new country."

The western robin (*M. migratoria propinqua*), very similar but slightly larger and with a darker head, is found from the Rocky Mountain region westward to the Pacific coast and south to Mexico. It nests in the mountains and in the far north, descending into the valleys or going southward in winter.

The Old World robin, or true robin redbreast (*Erythacus rubecola*), famous in poetry, song, and story, is a much smaller bird, barely 6 inches in length. It belongs to the warbler family (*Sylviidæ*) and is closely related to the nightingale.

Rocky Mountain Goat (*Oreamnus montanus*). An American wild goat, or, more properly, a goat antelope related to the chamois; called also white goat. It occurs at high elevations in the central Rocky mountains and in the Coast ranges from middle California northward to Alaska. In form, though not in color, it somewhat resembles a pygmy American bison. It has high shoulders, low hind quarters, strong legs, a stout body, a shaggy coat, and its head is carried low. A full-grown male stands about 3 feet high at the shoulder, is about 6½ feet long, and its weight is about equal to that of the Virginia deer.

While the white goat is the most expert and daring climber of all American hoofed animals, it is said to be rather stupid and erratic in habit and easily killed by hunters, in case they succeed in reaching the high rocky fastnesses above timber line where it dwells. It feeds upon the lichens, mosses, stunted grasses, and dwarf shrubs composing the vegetation of high altitudes. In 1900 a new species, with somewhat lyrate horns, called Kennedy's mountain goat (*O. kennedyi*), was discovered in the mountains near the Copper river in Alaska. See *Chamois.*

Rodentia (*rô-dĕn'shĭ-å*). Rodents or "gnawers" compose the largest order of mammals, embracing some 20 families and several thousand species, widely distributed throughout the world. They range in size from the mouse, one of the smallest of mammals, to the capybara, somewhat smaller than a hog, although fossil rodents as large as an ox are known.

Rodents differ from all other mammals in the character of the front teeth, the incisors on each jaw being specially developed for gnawing. There are no canine teeth and there is a toothless space between the cutting teeth, *incisors*, and the grinding teeth, *molars*, on each side. The two (rarely four) large incisor teeth in each jaw grow continuously, and, by gnawing on hard substances, are kept at uniform length and given chisel-like edges.

Rodents are chiefly herbivorous, living upon seeds, nuts, roots, and other vegetable products. They are mostly arboreal, though many are burrowers, and some are aquatic. Some, as, for example, the chinchilla, yield valuable fur; others, like the rat, are immensely destructive pests. The brain is small and not highly developed. Most rodents are not distinguished for sagacity, though some, such as the beaver, exhibit truly remarkable instincts. The order includes squirrels, rats, mice, gophers, rabbits, hares, sewellels, beavers, dormice, mole rats, jumping mice, porcupines, chinchillas, agoutis, guinea pigs, and pikas.

Rook (*Corvus frugileus*). A European bird of the crow family, closely resembling the common crow in size, form, and color. It resides permanently in large rookeries which sometimes contain many thousands of nests and birds. The nests are built in the tops of high trees, and are repaired and used over again for many years. While frequenting towns and cities, rooks prefer protected groves, such as those surrounding old mansions, whence they can fly over a large extent of country in search of food. They feed chiefly on insects, worms, grain, seeds, and fruit. Young rooks are often shot for the table. While they possess much cunning, rooks are inferior in intelligence to the crow, raven, and jackdaw. See *Crow*.

Ruminant. Any hoofed mammal that chews the cud. The ruminants comprise a large group or suborder of ungulates, called *Ruminantia* or *Pecora*. They have a complex stomach made up of several compartments. In the largest of these, food is received without being chewed, to be later regurgitated into the mouth, and there chewed at leisure. In the true ruminants, which include all members of the deer, ox, pronghorn, and giraffe families, the stomach has four separate divisions, known as the rumen or paunch, the reticulum, the omasum, and the abomasum. In the camels and llamas the stomach is imperfectly divided and in the chevrotains the omasum is lacking.

Sable (*Mustela zibellina*). A fur bearing mammal, closely related to the weasel, found chiefly in mountainous forests of northern Asia. It has a slender body 18 inches long, and a bushy tail 12 inches long. Its color is a dark lustrous brown, with paler head and neck and black feet. Like the martens, the sables spend most of the day in trees or in holes in their trunks or roots, going forth at night for food. They live chiefly on small animals, such as squirrels and hares, but to some extent upon fruits and fish. The sable is extensively trapped and hunted in Siberia for its excellent fur, which has been very highly valued since ancient times.

Salamander (*Salamandridæ*). Salamanders are small, smooth-skinned, lizard-like amphibians, slow in movement, and incapable of active defense or flight. Some are aquatic, some terrestrial, and others variously intermediate, exhibiting all degrees of adaptation between gill-breathing and lung-breathing. Sixteen species occur in the United States and 18 in Mexico.

The spotted salamander (*Amblystoma punctatum*) is found from Nova Scotia to Nebraska and southward. It is about 6 inches long, dark brown or black above, and marked with about 30 irregular yellow spots. The larva resembles a tadpole but has external gills. This harmless creature, which is fond of dark places and lives largely on worms and insects, is sometimes found in spring houses and cellars. See *Axolotl*.

Salmon, Atlantic (*Salmo salar*). An excellent food and game fish, of northern Europe and America, which ascends northeastern rivers from Maine to Hudson bay. It attains a length of from 3 to 4 feet, and an average weight of from 12 to 30 pounds, but these limits of size and weight are frequently exceeded. It usually continues in the shallows of its native stream for two years after hatching, and during this period it attains a length of 8 inches. In this stage it is called a "parr." When the season of its migration arrives, generally between March and June, the fins have become darker and the fish has assumed a silvery hue. It is now known as a "smolt." The smolts congregate into shoals and proceed leisurely seaward. On reaching the estuary they remain in its brackish water for a short time and then make for the open sea.

Leaving its native river as a fish, weighing perhaps not more than 2 ounces, the smolt, after an absence varying from a few months to two years, returns to fresh water as a "grilse," weighing 4 or 5 pounds. In the grilse stage the fish is capable of depositing eggs. After spawning in the fresh water the grilse again seeks the sea in the autumn, and when its second stay in the ocean is over it returns, after a few months' absence, as the adult salmon, weighing from 8 to 10 pounds. The salmon returns, as a rule, to the river in which it passed its earlier existence.

This salmon is caught by the rod and also by means of nets. It is one of the largest game fishes known to rise to a fly. It is also noted for its remarkable ability to leap up waterfalls, sometimes to a height of 10 to 15 feet.

The Ouananiche (*S. ouananiche*), a landlocked species of Quebec and Labrador, usually weighing 2 to 4 pounds, is likewise a very gamy fish. When hooked it will leap high from the water, often several times in succession. The Sebago salmon (*S. sebago*), another landlocked form, weighing 10 to 15 pounds, but much less active, is found in quiet lakes in Maine. See *Trout*.

Salmon, Pacific (*Oncorhynchus*). A group of exceedingly valuable food fishes, allied to the Atlantic salmon and the trout. There are five kinds,—the quinnat, the blueback, the silver, the chum, and the pink salmon, of which the quinnat, the blueback, and the pink are the most important. They differ somewhat from eastern salmon in form and much more in breeding habits. The young are hatched in cool fresh waters, living in small streams and rivers until they reach a weight of a few ounces. They then descend to the sea where they find suitable feeding grounds, living on small crustaceans, mollusks, and other marine animals.

Upon becoming full grown, in the course of 2 or 4 more years, they leave the sea and ascend to the snow-fed headwaters of rivers to spawn. A remarkable fact concerning these salmon is that none of them take food after leaving salt water. As they proceed up the rivers their stomachs shrivel, and their long fast is broken only by their death, which takes place in the upper waters after spawning time, often more than 1000 miles from the sea. In the gravelly bed of a rapid stream, the male, with tail and snout, digs out a broad shallow nest. In this the female deposits her eggs and the pair cover them with stones and gravel. Both then float down the stream, tail foremost, making no effort to swim, and die usually within a few days. The eggs hatch in from 4 to 6 months.

The Quinnat, Chinook, or king salmon (*O. tschawytscha*), the largest, finest flavored, and most highly prized salmon, has an average weight of 22 pounds, though it sometimes reaches 70 or even 100 pounds. The flesh is usually rich salmon-red in color, becoming paler toward spawning time. It is found near the shore from central California northward, but runs chiefly in streams of large size fed with melting snows. It ascends the Yukon to a distance of 2250 miles. The bulk of the world's pack of this species is obtained in the Columbia river.

The Blueback, Sockeye, or red salmon (*O. nerka*) usually weighs from 5 to 8 pounds. It ranges from the Columbia river to Siberia, being most abundant in Alaska. It is second in quality only to the quinnat salmon and, like it, is taken in enormous quantities for canning. These two species, together with the pink salmon mentioned below, constitute by far the greater portion of the salmon catch.

The silver salmon, or Coho (*O. kisutch*), weighs from 5 to 8 pounds, but the flesh is somewhat paler than that of the king or red, and it is, therefore, frequently marketed as "medium-red salmon." The chum salmon (*O. keta*), called saké in Japan, weighs about 9 pounds. Its light-colored flesh is well flavored but low in oil content. In protein, however, it is equal to the other species. The pink salmon (*O. gorbuscha*) is the smallest of the group, weighing only 3 to 6 pounds. It has pale flesh and a delicate flavor but averages lower in oil content than the king, red, or silver salmon. It forms approximately 45 per cent of the American salmon pack.

Salmon for canning are taken near the mouths of rivers during the spring running, when their flesh is plump and firm. They are caught in enormous quantities in various forms of nets, weirs, and traps. See *Trout*.

Sandpiper. A group of small shore birds of the snipe family, so named from their low notes and a habit of running upon the sand. They are rarely over a foot in length, with sober but pleasing plumage, a very short tail, and a long, slender, curved bill. Sandpipers usually inhabit the seashore, stream banks, and marshes, often in large flocks, probing in the soft earth with their bills in search of worms, aquatic insects, small crustaceans, and mollusks. They breed mostly in arctic regions but migrate extensively in temperate latitudes. There are more than 20 very widely diffused species. The one best known in America is the spotted sandpiper (*Actitis macularia*), 8 inches long, olive gray and white in color, marked with dusky spots and a conspicuous white bar on the wing. It ranges throughout North America, migrating in winter to Brazil and Uruguay. Most sandpipers are considered game birds.

San Jose Scale (*Aspidiotus perniciosus*). A pernicious scale insect, the most destructive found in the United States. It is a native of Japan or China and was introduced at San Jose, California, about 1870, whence it has spread to all fruit-growing districts. It attacks the principal deciduous fruit and ornamental trees and shrubs, causing immense damage, but does not injure the citrous fruits. The individual insects appear as irregularly circular, flattened, waxy scales, the largest about 1/25 of an inch in diameter. When a plant is badly infested, the scales lie close together, often overlapping, and form a grayish scurf over the bark.

While a chalcidid fly and the Chinese ladybird attack the San Jose scale, none of its natural enemies have proved effective. The principal remedies consist of treating the bark with a wash of lime, sulphur, and salt; of spraying the foliage with various soap and oil emulsions and extracts of nicotine, and of fumigating entire trees with hydrocyanic acid gas. See *Scale Insects*.

Sardine (*Sardinella*). Small, herring-like fish, with rich flesh and feeble skeleton, which, when broiled or when preserved in oil, may be eaten, bones and all. All are migratory, inhabiting the deep sea, coming to the shores only in the spawning season. The European sardine or pilchard (*S. pilchardus*), 3 to 4 inches long, greenish blue above and silvery white below, has been highly esteemed since ancient times. The California sardine (*S. cærulea*) closely resembles the European sardine, but is larger, about 12 inches long, and has round black spots on the sides. See *Herring*.

Sawfish (*Pristididæ*). A group of large, sharklike rays which attain a length of from 10 to 20 feet. Like the sawsharks, they have the snout prolonged into a very long, flat blade, with strong, sharp, enameled teeth implanted in sockets along either edge. Sawfish inhabit the mouths of tropical rivers, where they wreak havoc among the schools of sardines and mullets upon which they feed. The sawfish (*Pristis pectinatus*) of the Florida and Gulf coasts, sometimes 15 feet long, has a saw about one-third the length of its body.

Scale Insects. A general name applying to members of the family *Coccidæ*, of hemipterous insects. These, in the female sex, assume a scalelike form and become spot bound upon the bark and leaves of trees and plants. They live by sucking the sap and include some of the worst plant pests, such as the San Jose scale, the oyster-shell scale, and the cottony cushion scale. Among them, however, are two well-known forms that excrete products of value; one, in India, produces the lac of commerce, and another, in Mexico, produces cochineal.

The group is remarkable for the differences between the sexes in size, in form, and in manner of life. The male is much smaller and develops wings for getting about, which the female entirely lacks. Unlike the female, the male passes through a pupal stage before assuming the adult form. See *Cochineal, Lac Insect, San Jose Scale*.

Scallop (*Pecten*). A bivalve mollusk of the family *Pectenidæ*, which has a fan-shaped shell, usually with ribs radiating from the umbo to the margin, and with extended or eared hinges. The common scallop (*P. irradians*), of the Atlantic coast, about 2 inches across, is highly prized for food, the large adductor muscle being regarded as a table delicacy.

Scorpion. The scorpions constitute a distinct order of arthropods, *Scorpionida*, allied to the king crabs and spiders. There are more than 300 species, chiefly tropical, some 25 of which occur in the southwestern and western United States. They are small, jointed animals, somewhat resembling a miniature lobster, with four pairs of legs, a single pair of jaws, a pair of large, crablike pincers, and a long taillike abdomen terminating in a venomous sting. The young are brought forth alive, and, for a time, are carried by the mother. The scorpions are nocturnal in habit and prey chiefly upon spiders and insects, which they seize with their pincers and often kill with their sting. While exceedingly painful, the sting rarely, if ever, proves fatal to man.

Sea Bass (*Serranidæ*). A group of sea fishes, some of which ascend rivers, closely resembling the fresh-water bass. They are represented in North American waters by more than 100 species, some of which attain enormous size. The great Jewfish, or black sea bass (*Stereolepis gigas*), of the southern California coast, is one of the largest of the spiny-finned fishes. The Santa Catalina anglers, with rod and reel, catch black sea bass weighing 300 to 400 pounds. The Black Grouper (*Garrupa nigrita*), found in Atlantic waters from Charleston to Brazil, has a normal weight of 500 pounds.

The striped bass, Rockfish, or Rock (*Roccus lineatus*), a highly valued food and game fish of Atlantic waters, is the finest representative of the family. It is a handsome, silver-white fish with

INDEX

The Lincoln Library has been so built that, in some respects, an index is superfluous. The material in the various departments has been arranged in such a manner that, with a brief period of intelligent use, the reader will be able to turn directly to a required fact without the initial step of consulting the general index.

This advantage is due to the fact that related material is grouped in sections, a large proportion of it taking the form of dictionaries and carefully prepared tables, which are practically self-indexed. In the aggregate, there are some 66 separate dictionaries and 330 tables. A representative selection from these dictionaries and tables will be found alphabetized for quick reference on page 2114.

Advantages of Arrangement. The intelligent user will take advantage of the general plan of this volume by becoming so familiar with the location of the departments, sections, dictionaries, and tables that the mechanical consultation of the index will become less and less imperative. With practice, the driving of an automobile becomes one of the simplest of operations. Likewise, familiarity with the electric switches in a house makes the control of the lighting system easy even for a child. So in the use of this volume, a little practice will insure a surprising mastery over its resources. When the reader has learned, for example, that in the Department of Science there is a comprehensive dictionary of animals on pages 1006–1070, he will go directly to that section in order to learn the difference between a toad and a frog or to settle similar questions regarding animal life. For the geography of Japan, he will consult the Department of Geography and, in particular, the section on Asia, pages 805–814, in which the countries of that continent are treated in alphabetical order.

The extraordinary range of the facts in the text, dictionaries, and tables of this work makes it obviously inadvisable that every individual item should be entered in the general index, which would thereby become much too unwieldy for convenient and quick reference. Thus the populations of many small towns of the United States or Canada appear, not in the general index, but in the tables of populations, to which the reader will be referred under "Population" in the general index. After a brief period of use, however, he will be likely to remember the fact that these tables are on pages 741–746 and 760 respectively, and, on occasion, will turn directly to these pages, where the various entries will be found arranged in alphabetical order. In the same way, he will soon be able, almost on opening the book, to find electrical terms, points in good usage, musical terms, stories of the operas, national flags, historical topics, mythological references, and numerous other types of information, even though the great majority of the items may be located also by means of the general index.

Fullness and Simplicity of Index. Despite this surprising availability of material in a book embracing the essentials of a whole library, a general index has certain supplementary values which make its inclusion necessary in a work that is to give the greatest possible service. The Lincoln Library has, therefore, been provided with a full, simple, systematic key to its contents.

The index which follows is larger than has ever been placed in a single volume of similar scope. It contains more than 22,000 line entries, many of which include two or more page references. The following example will reveal the ease with which a specific fact may be located by means of the index.

If the reader wishes to learn the growth of Chicago's population, he will probably turn first to "Chicago" in the index. He is there referred to the article on Chicago, page 698, in the last paragraph of which, entitled History, the required facts are summarized. The index leads him also directly to the full, authentic figures desired. Under the word "Chicago" in the index, and slightly to the right, will be found the words "Population, Growth of," with a reference to page 677. Turning to this page, the reader will find a table of the 25 largest American cities with their population figures from 1840 to 1940. Chicago appears second in this table. In case the user has thought first of the word population, he will turn to the index, where, subindexed under "Population," he will discover "American Cities" with a reference to page 677. He will thus be led by this route also to the desired information.

Special Values. This index does vastly more, however, than lead the reader to specific passages. It is, in the first place, a guide to the plan of the volume. If one wishes to find a synonym for "Copy" or some other word, a reference to the word "Synonyms" in the index will lead one to the dictionary of synonyms and antonyms on pages 137–171 and to the key to that dictionary on pages 172–178. Similarly, under "Plants," "Agriculture," or other general subjects, the user will be referred to these important divisions.

For gathering many items on a given topic, as for the preparation of a school theme or a club paper, the index will be found indispensable. If, for example, the user wishes to bring together as many facts as possible about the state of California, he will, by turning to "California" in the index, find no less than 24 different references to various informing passages regarding the state. These include, besides area and population, such items as agricultural statistics, birth and death rate, chief manufacturing cities, number of men who served in the World War, number of motor vehicles, petroleum production, and suffrage requirements.

Suggestions. In order to obtain the greatest value from this index, the reader will find it advantageous to keep in mind the following facts:

When a phrase appears in the index, its words are so arranged that the most important, usually a noun, occupies the first place. "Flowering Dogwood," for example, should be sought, not under F, but under D, in the form "Dogwood, Flowering."

In all cases where an indexed item appears in the text as a heading, as the title of a separate article in a dictionary, or as an entry in a table, only the page number is given in the index. If, however, the item cannot so readily be located on its page, a letter is added, which indicates the particular quarter page in which the word or fact occurs. The letters a and b refer respectively to the upper and the lower half of the first column, while c and d refer to the corresponding halves of the second column. Thus 218a means the upper left-hand quarter of page 218; 218d means the lower right-hand quarter of the page.

Where two or more page references appear in one index entry, the most important reference, as a rule, is given first. Under all names of people treated in the Department of Biography, the first page reference is to the biographical article.

When an entry is followed by a second entry in italics, the latter is the title under which the first subject is treated. Thus "Aspen, *Poplar* 1109" means that information regarding Aspen is to be found in the article entitled Poplar, which occurs on page 1109.

DICTIONARIES

TABULATIONS

Letters a, b, c, d following page numbers indicate first, second, third, fourth quarters of page—

a	c
b	d

Letters a, b, c, d following page numbers indicate first, second, third, fourth quarters of page— a c / b d

Letters a, b, c, d following page numbers indicate first, second, third, fourth quarters of page—

a	c
b	d

INDEX

The Lincoln Library has been so built that, in some respects, an index is superfluous. The material in the various departments has been arranged in such a manner that, with a brief period of intelligent use, the reader will be able to turn directly to a required fact without the initial step of consulting the general index.

This advantage is due to the fact that related material is grouped in sections, a large proportion of it taking the form of dictionaries and carefully prepared tables, which are practically self-indexed. In the aggregate, there are some 66 separate dictionaries and 330 tables. A representative selection from these dictionaries and tables will be found alphabetized for quick reference on page 2114.

Advantages of Arrangement. The intelligent user will take advantage of the general plan of this volume by becoming so familiar with the location of the departments, sections, dictionaries, and tables that the mechanical consultation of the index will become less and less imperative. With practice, the driving of an automobile becomes one of the simplest of operations. Likewise, familiarity with the electric switches in a house makes the control of the lighting system easy even for a child. So in the use of this volume, a little practice will insure a surprising mastery over its resources. When the reader has learned, for example, that in the Department of Science there is a comprehensive dictionary of animals on pages 1006–1070, he will go directly to that section in order to learn the difference between a toad and a frog or to settle similar questions regarding animal life. For the geography of Japan, he will consult the Department of Geography and, in particular, the section on Asia, pages 805–814, in which the countries of that continent are treated in alphabetical order.

The extraordinary range of the facts in the text, dictionaries, and tables of this work makes it obviously inadvisable that every individual item should be entered in the general index, which would thereby become much too unwieldy for convenient and quick reference. Thus the populations of many small towns of the United States or Canada appear, not in the general index, but in the tables of populations, to which the reader will be referred under "Population" in the general index. After a brief period of use, however, he will be likely to remember the fact that these tables are on pages 741–746 and 760 respectively, and, on occasion, will turn directly to these pages, where the various entries will be found arranged in alphabetical order. In the same way, he will soon be able, almost on opening the book, to find electrical terms, points in good usage, musical terms, stories of the operas, national flags, historical topics, mythological references, and numerous other types of information, even though the great majority of the items may be located also by means of the general index.

Fullness and Simplicity of Index. Despite this surprising availability of material in a book embracing the essentials of a whole library, a general index has certain supplementary values which make its inclusion necessary in a work that is to give the greatest possible service. The Lincoln Library has, therefore, been provided with a full, simple, systematic key to its contents.

The index which follows is larger than has ever been placed in a single volume of similar scope. It contains more than 22,000 line entries, many of which include two or more page references. The following example will reveal the ease with which a specific fact may be located by means of the index.

If the reader wishes to learn the growth of Chicago's population, he will probably turn first to "Chicago" in the index. He is there referred to the article on Chicago, page 698, in the last paragraph of which, entitled History, the required facts are summarized. The index leads him also directly to the full, authentic figures desired. Under the word "Chicago" in the index, and slightly to the right, will be found the words "Population, Growth of," with a reference to page 677. Turning to this page, the reader will find a table of the 25 largest American cities with their population figures from 1840 to 1940. Chicago appears second in this table. In case the user has thought first of the word population, he will turn to the index, where, subindexed under "Population," he will discover "American Cities" with a reference to page 677. He will thus be led by this route also to the desired information.

Special Values. This index does vastly more, however, than lead the reader to specific passages. It is, in the first place, a guide to the plan of the volume. If one wishes to find a synonym for "Copy" or some other word, a reference to the word "Synonyms" in the index will lead one to the dictionary of synonyms and antonyms on pages 137–171 and to the key to that dictionary on pages 172–178. Similarly, under "Plants," "Agriculture," or other general subjects, the user will be referred to these important divisions.

For gathering many items on a given topic, as for the preparation of a school theme or a club paper, the index will be found indispensable. If, for example, the user wishes to bring together as many facts as possible about the state of California, he will, by turning to "California" in the index, find no less than 24 different references to various informing passages regarding the state. These include, besides area and population, such items as agricultural statistics, birth and death rate, chief manufacturing cities, number of men who served in the World War, number of motor vehicles, petroleum production, and suffrage requirements.

Suggestions. In order to obtain the greatest value from this index, the reader will find it advantageous to keep in mind the following facts:

When a phrase appears in the index, its words are so arranged that the most important, usually a noun, occupies the first place. "Flowering Dogwood," for example, should be sought, not under F, but under D, in the form "Dogwood, Flowering."

In all cases where an indexed item appears in the text as a heading, as the title of a separate article in a dictionary, or as an entry in a table, only the page number is given in the index. If, however, the item cannot so readily be located on its page, a letter is added, which indicates the particular quarter page in which the word or fact occurs. The letters a and b refer respectively to the upper and the lower half of the first column, while c and d refer to the corresponding halves of the second column. Thus 218a means the upper left-hand quarter of page 218; 218d means the lower right-hand quarter of the page.

Where two or more page references appear in one index entry, the most important reference, as a rule, is given first. Under all names of people treated in the Department of Biography, the first page reference is to the biographical article.

When an entry is followed by a second entry in italics, the latter is the title under which the first subject is treated. Thus "Aspen, *Poplar* 1109" means that information regarding Aspen is to be found in the article entitled Poplar, which occurs on page 1109.

Letters a, b, c, d following page numbers indicate first, second, third, fourth quarters of page—

a	c
b	d

Letters a, b, c, d following page numbers indicate first, second, third, fourth quarters of page— a c / b d

General Index

Letters a, b, c, d following page numbers indicate first, second, third, fourth quarters of page—

a	c
b	d

Letters a, b, c, d following page numbers indicate first, second, third, fourth quarters of page—

a	c
b	d

Letters a, b, c, d following page numbers indicate first, second, third, fourth quarters of page—

a	c
b	d

Letters a, b, c, d following page numbers indicate first, second, third, fourth quarters of page—

a	c
b	d

Letters a, b, c, d following page numbers indicate first, second, third, fourth quarters of page—

a	c
b	d

Letters a, b, c, d following page numbers indicate first, second, third, fourth quarters of page—

a	c
b	d

Letters a, b, c, d following page numbers indicate first, second, third, fourth quarters of page—

a	c
b	d

Letters a, b, c, d following page numbers indicate first, second, third, fourth quarters of page— (a c / b d)

Letters a, b, c, d following page numbers indicate first, second, third, fourth quarters of page—

a	c
b	d

Letters a, b, c, d following page numbers indicate first, second, third, fourth quarters of page— a c / b d

* In addition to the 2175 folioed pages, The Lincoln Library contains also 84 full-page plates of illustrations and 12 departmental tables of contents, making a total of 2271 pages.